Civil War EXTRA

A Newspaper History of the Civil War from 1863 to 1865

VOLUME II

From the Collection of Eric C. Caren
Introduction by Brian C. Pohanka

CASTLE BOOKS

ACKNOWLEDGEMENTS

I would like to dedicate *Civil War Extra, Volume 1 & 2,* to Dr. Stephen A. Goldman—friend, partner, and Civil War newspaper guru! Additionally, I extend my gratitude to Dr. Goldman for the use of the following newspapers for this set: Albany Evening Journal (11/7/1860), Jacksonville Republican (1/17/1861), Charleston Mercury Extra (4/13/1861), The White Man (11/21/1861), Richmond Enquirer (6/29/1862), Unconditional US Grant (10/24/1863), Columbia Phoenix (3/21/1865), Richmond Whig + map (4/11/1865).

Eric C. Caren

The following have been reprinted with permission from *The Plain Dealer*: April 15, 1861 © 1861, October 20, 1864 © 1864. All rights reserved.

The New York Times kindly grants the use of the following: April 10, 1865, April 15, 1865, 2 am edition, April 15, 1865, 11:15 am edition. Copyright © 1865 by The New York Times. Reprinted by permission.

We offer special thanks to the *Philadelphia Inquirer* for their permission to the use of the following: May 19, 1860, June 28, 1860, January 26, 1861, April 16, 1861, July 6, 1861, July 13, 1861, July 22, 1861, September 21, 1861, November 2, 1861, November 23, 1861, January 18, 1862, January 28, 1862, February 19, 1862, March 1, 1862, March 10, 1862, March 15, 1862, March 29, 1862, April 11, 1862, April 17, 1862, May 30, 1862, June 2, 1862, August 2, 1862, January 27, 1863, February 15, 1865, February 20, 1865, April 4, 1865, April 8, 1865, April 10, 1865, April 15, 1865, April 17, 1865, April 20, 1865, April 25, 1865, April 26, 1865, April 28, 1865, May 5, 1865, May 10, 1865, May 16, 1865, May 18, 1865, May 19, 1865, May 20, 1865, May 22, 1865, May 31, 1865, June 14, 1865.

Published by Castle Books,
a division of Book Sales, Inc.
114 Northfield Avenue
Edison, NJ 08837, USA

Compiled by Eric C. Caren

ISBN 0-7858-1150-8
Printed in the United States of America

INTRODUCTION

The Civil War—that fiery crucible that forged a nation at a cost of more than 600,000 lives—was a defining watershed in the history of American journalism, as it was for the country as a whole. Editors whose papers had fueled the divisive passions that led to war found themselves caught up in a bloodletting of epic proportions. As contending armies numbering in the hundreds of thousands waged simultaneous campaigns in multiple theaters of operations, the press dispatched scores of reporters to the front. Adventuresome, fiercely competitive and frequently daring in their quest for a scoop, these self-styled "Bohemians" were a link between the soldiers and their families behind the lines.

No more powerfully illustrated was that connection between reporter and reader than in the journals' almost daily publication of casualty lists. Those grim enumerations in columns that bore the stark heading "Wounded and Killed" became painfully commonplace; but, as the editor of the Charlotte, North Carolina *Daily Bulletin* reminded his patrons, "Some eye reads the name to whom it is dear as life, and some heart is struck or broken with the blow made by that name among the list. . . . Every name in that list is a lightning stroke to some heart, and breaks like thunder over some house, and falls like a long black shadow upon some hearthstone."

That poignant observation is but one insight to America's Tragic Era that appears in these fascinating volumes, selected from among the thousands of Civil War newspapers in the Eric C. Caren Collection. Spanning the history of journalism from the sixteenth century to the present day, the Caren Collection comprises the most important assemblage of newspapers in private hands and includes numerous rare and one of a kind editions. Many of the pages reproduced here are not to be found in archival institutions, while others are unique in having survived the ravages of time and the devastation wrought by war. The significant number of Confederate newspapers in the Caren Collection is especially noteworthy, and the samples included here offer a telling view of the plight of the beleaguered Southern states. Reflecting the vast scope of Civil War journalism—from the roots of the conflict to the ultimate reconciliation—*Civil War Extra* provides a veritable window on the past, enabling us to read the news of the day as it was presented to mid-nineteenth century Americans, whose lives were forever altered by those stirring and catastrophic events.

If the folks at home were eager for reports of their loved ones at the front, the soldiers themselves had an insatiable desire for news—not only of their families and communities, but of military actions beyond the limited scope of their own company or regiment. Writing to his hometown paper in Poughkeepsie, New York in December 1861, Sergeant Stephen Bogardus expressed the well-nigh universal complaint of the fighting men when he lamented, "We are as much out of the way of news as if we were confined in a convent." One of the Sergeant's comrades in the 5th New York Infantry Regiment, William McIlvaine grumbled, "For all the war news we hear we might as well be a thousand miles off." Confederate soldiers generally felt even more isolated from the outer world, as lines of supply and communication were increasingly disrupted by marauding Federal armies.

The soldiers coveted journals of any kind, and that craving provided a substantial economic incentive for newspaper vendors to market their wares at the front. In his 1866 memoir, war correspondent George Alfred Townsend recalled one enterprising fourteen-year-old newsboy who regularly purchased several hundred papers for one and a half cents apiece in Washington and sold them in the military camps for ten cents each. The youth's daily earnings were rarely less than thirty-five dollars—nearly three times the monthly salary of a private soldier—and Townsend fully expected the boy to have his own "army express and general agency" by the war's end.

Newspapers were something of a luxury to soldiers in the field, awaited with anticipation and eagerly devoured by private and general alike. The great Confederate commander Thomas J. "Stonewall" Jackson was in the habit of asking one of his staff officers to read the pertinent news aloud. A satirical biography of Jackson that appeared in the New York *Mercury*—one of many Northern papers that fell into Confederate hands during Jackson's victorious Shenandoah Valley campaign—brought a smile to the face of the habitually reserved and serious Southern commander. When regular delivery of papers was possible, it lent an air of domesticity to an otherwise austere and frequently uncomfortable existence. "We have made arrangements with the mail agent to supply us with newspapers so that the *Herald* is in my tent every day when I return from dinner," Union Colonel Charles Wainwright noted in his diary. Wainwright, a New York patrician whose political leanings tended to the Democratic Party, thought the *Herald* "the best paper," even if "half of what it publishes is not true."

Fraternization between the opposing forces was not uncommon in a war that pitted American against American. When the white flags went up signifying a temporary truce, and the burial parties in blue and gray set about the grim task of evacuating the mangled wounded and interring fallen comrades, Union and Confederate officers would meet between the lines with an amicability that belied their deadly business. Often the handshakes and banter were accompanied by an exchange of newspapers—ragged about the edges perhaps, and weeks old, but providing a broader perspective of the contending armies and of the world beyond the battlefield. Though the concept of military intelligence was in its infancy, officers nonetheless recognized that in an era when press censorship was spotty at best, their enemy's hometown papers contained information of potential value to the generals in command. And once the journals made the round of the camp, they generally found their way to headquarters.

Preoccupied with creature comforts, meager though they may be, the typical enlisted man rarely bothered about matters of military security, and was even less concerned with grand strategy. But newspapers did provide temporary relief from the boredom and routine of soldier life, and Yank and Reb regularly included papers with their most popular items of exchange—Northern coffee for Southern tobacco. Officers tended to frown upon this trade unless it occurred during an official truce. But the men in the ranks were not so particular, and when their commanders weren't looking, found all manner of ingenious ways to barter with their counterparts.

The penchant for fraternization became particularly marked during the long winter hiatus from active campaigning, when the armies settled into sprawling encampments of log huts equipped with hearths and chimneys that provided a comfort bordering on the luxurious, by soldiers' standards. During the winter of 1862-1863, when General Joseph Hooker's Army of the Potomac and General Robert E. Lee's Army of Northern Virginia were encamped on opposite sides of the Rappahannock River, the opposing pickets maintained a flourishing trade through the use of miniature boats. Pouches of coffee beans or tobacco were placed in a hollowed-out log, often equipped with a mast constructed of intertwined sticks, with a newspaper like the *New York Herald* or *Richmond Examiner* furnishing the sail.

"The exchange of coffee and tobacco was a comparatively harmless matter," recalled Lieutenant Frederick Hitchcock of the 132nd Pennsylvania, "but the sending of Northern papers into their line, containing news of every movement of our forces, was a thing that must be prohibited. . . . The tobacco our men were allowed to take, but the boat and all rebel newspapers had to be sent to army headquarters." The lieutenant admitted that it was "a traffic very difficult to suppress, for our men wanted the tobacco and were unwilling to take that without sending back the proper *quid pro quo*."

In large volunteer armies comprised of men from all walks of life, it was not uncommon for a given regiment to have in its ranks a number of soldiers whose prewar occupations of type-setter or printer enabled them to produce their own unit newspaper. These volumes include an exceptional sampling of those army journals. *The Vidette*, a broadside "printed and published semi-occasionally" by members of Colonel John Hunt Morgan's swashbuckling Confederate cavalry brigade, disseminated official orders and denounced Yankee "outrages" and "atrocities" against Southern civilians. A Union soldier paper, the *Camp Journal* of the hard-fighting First Division in the Army of the Potomac's Second Corps, reflected similar partisan chauvinism in its motto, "No Peace While Traitors are in Arms."

An extremely rare variation of this unofficial military press appears in the pages of the Berryville, Virginia *Conservator* for March 11 and 12, 1862. Abandoned when Federal troops closed in on the town, the *Conservator's* office was occupied by members of the 1st Minnesota Infantry—a unit whose compliment included some two dozen former newspapermen who styled themselves "The Printer's Fraternity." The Union soldiers displayed their technical and editorial skills by using the captured presses to produce a satirical edition of the Berryville paper, mocking the departed editor and his staff. In July of 1864, publication of the *Lynchburg Virginian* ceased when General David Hunter's Union army launched an attack on the city's defenses. The *Virginian's* editor later apologized to his readers, noting, "Every man connected with the office, including an old man 70 years of age, deaf as a post, and blind in one eye, shouldered arms and went to the field."

While publication of the *Berryville Conservator* and *Lynchburg Virginian* were only temporarily disrupted—in both cases the Yankees soon retreated north down the Shenandoah Valley—many Rebel papers were confiscated, suppressed or taken over as the Federal forces increasingly tightened their hold on Confederate territory. Some papers, like Alabama's *Daily Huntsville Confederate*, literally packed up the presses and moved out with the evacuating Southern troops. But if journals in occupied Southern communities wished to continue publication, they did so under the relentless scrutiny of their Northern garrison, who habitually used the papers to disseminate pronouncements to the conquered citizens.

Such was the case when New Orleans fell under the draconian rule of Union General Benjamin Butler, who compelled *The Daily Delta* to print his notorious General Order of May 5, 1862. The directive stipulated that any woman who should "insult or show contempt" to Union officers or soldiers would be "regarded and held liable to be treated as a woman of the town [i.e. a prostitute] plying her avocation." The *Delta's* editor did "not feel at liberty to decline the publication of said order," but exacted some measure of revenge by publishing a humorous satire titled "The Shunamitish Woman." Couched in Biblical language, it parodied the misadventures of a drunken Yankee officer whose pocket was picked by one of New Orleans' soiled doves.

Editors in Confederate communities that escaped Northern subjugation were confronted with an ever-growing shortage of the ink and paper stock necessary to maintain publication. But Southern publishers met the challenge in a number of ingenious ways, and the Caren Collection includes numerous rare editions of so-called "necessity papers." Heralding an erroneous report that Stonewall Jackson's troops had captured Washington, D.C., the September 20, 1862 edition of *The Confederate States* of New Iberia, Louisiana was printed on wallpaper. Tongue in cheek, the editor confessed that "the existing times have 'driven us to the wall' to procure our supply of paper for printing purposes." Another unusual necessity paper, *The Houston Daily Telegraph* of March 19, 1864, was printed on cornhusks.

That press freedom was severely tried by the hatreds engendered by the Civil War is also evident in the case of Union and Confederate journals whose political stance was not in keeping with the majority opinion of their respective communities. Those editors who dared to publish views that went against the popular grain risked having their offices sacked by angry mobs. Such was the fate of *The Crisis*—a pro-Southern or "Copperhead" paper in Columbus, Ohio—and of the Troy, New York *Weekly Times*, whose attackers disapproved of the draft as a means of prosecuting the Union war effort. One need only consider the disparate views of Abraham Lincoln reflected in this volume to realize that the Nation's divisions were not always clearly defined by the Mason-Dixon Line. It is but one of many fascinating aspects of that epic and terrible conflict that readers will find in the pages of *Civil War Extra*.

Brian C. Pohanka
Alexandria, Virginia

TABLE OF CONTENTS, Volume II

Editor's note to the Table of Contents– Terms used below to describe the issues included in this book :
Broadsheet–A single sheet newspaper with printing on both sides.
Broadside–A single sheet newspaper with printing on one side only and a blank reverse. Commonly used for posting.
Copperhead–Term used for newspapers from Northern cities that were pro-South in sentiment.
Necessity paper–When usual paper supplies ran out (mainly in the South), editors had to resort to using various alternate paper such as wrapping paper, wall paper, and cornhusk. Also, different colored papers were used including blue, yellow, green, brown, and pink.
Occupation paper–When a Southern town fell to Union troops, a new paper would usually be started, turning their point of view from Confederate to Northern.
Troop/Regimental newspaper–Both Union and Confederate forces sometimes carried portable presses into the field and would print up newspapers to inform and entertain the soldiers in camp.
Extra–A special edition outside the normal press sequence (i.e. daily, weekly, etc.). Usually occasioned by late news of importance which was too late for the previous scheduled edition.
Supplement–An addition to the regular edition added at the last moment before going to press.
Publications are presented chronologically except where adjustments have been made to accommodate spreads.

69	June 27, 1863	DAILY CITIZEN (Vicksburg, MS)	Necessity wallpaper edition printed during the siege of Vicksburg.
70	June 29, 1863	N Y HERALD	Front page war map showing, "The Field of Operations in Pennsylvania" just days before the great battle at Gettysburg.
71	June 30, 1863	DAILY CITIZEN (Vicksburg, MS)	Another necessity wallpaper edition printed during the siege of Vicksburg.
72-74	July 1863	EAGLE AND FLAG (Foxboro, MA)	Great patriotic nameplate engraving with eagle, shield, and flag. Note inside, a letter to the editor (a former classmate) from a soldier at "Camp Dale", Carolina City, NC.
75	July 3, 1863	N Y HERALD	The Battle of Gettysburg –First day of battle with accompanying map showing the cavalry fight.
76	July 2, 1863	DAILY CITIZEN (Vicksburg, MS)	Famous last edition printed entirely by Confederates with a piece mocking Grant's intention to take the city of Vicksburg by July 4 (Col. 2, bottom).
77	July 4, 1863	DAILY CITIZEN (Vicksburg, MS	The same paper as above, printed with a note added (last col., bottom) by Union troops getting the last laugh after they took the city, as promised, by July 4. They predicted that this issue, "..will be valuable hereafter as a curiosity".
78	July 4, 1863	SOUTHERN ILLUSTRATED NEWS	A front page look at Lieutenant General Richard S. Ewell.
79-80	July 5, 1863	N Y HERALD	This Sunday extra fills almost an entire column on the front page with stacked headlines reporting the Battle of Gettysburg. (Page 2 is actually Page 4 from the previous day's edition.)
81-82	July 6, 1863	NY TRIBUNE	"The Great Victory–The Rebel Army Totally Defeated"
83-86	July 7, 1863	THE CAVALIER (Yorktown, VA)	Very scarce issue of this Union troop newspaper edited by the Chaplain of the 179th Pennsylvania Infantry. Contains a report on the Battle of Gettysburg.
87	July 7, 1863	NEWBURYPORT HERALD (Newburyport, MA)	Huge type employed to report the Battle of Gettysburg.
88	July 9, 1863	CHRISTIAN OBSERVER (Richmond, VA)	"Great Battle at Gettysburg" and "Call For Chaplains" needed in the Confederate ranks.
89-90	July 9, 1863	LYNCHBURG DAILY VIRGINIAN	"Inauguration of the New State of West Virginia", "The Fall of Vicksburg", and "The Battle of Gettysburg"
91	July 9, 1863	DAILY DISPATCH- EXTRA (Richmond, VA)	Extremely rare Confederate extra broadside on The Battle of Gettysburg with frank coverage headlined, "The Reported Defeat of General Lee".
92-93	July 10, 1863	NEWBURYPORT HERALD (Newburyport, MA)	Front page coverage of "Fall of Vicksburg" and "Battles at Gettysburg" Plus ad, "Men Wanted for the Invalid Corps".
94-95	July 12, 1863	THE ERA (New Orleans, LA)	"Port Hudson–A Complete History of its Investment, Siege, and Capture"
96	July 13, 1863	REPORTER...EXTRA (Lynn, MA)	This extra contains a draft list calling the locals to duty.
97-99	July 14, 1863	NY DAILY NEWS	The New York Draft Riots
100-102	July 15, 1863	SOUTHERN CONFEDERACY (Atlanta, GA-Confederate States of America)	Reports on the Battle of Gettysburg and the Fall of Vicksburg
103	July 16, 1863	N Y DAILY NEWS	The New York Draft Riots
104-105	July 18, 1863	FRANK LESLIE'S ILLUSTRATED NEWSPAPER (New York)	Illustrated scenes of the invasion of Pennsylvania and the Battle of Gettysburg.
106-107	July 20, 1863	CHARLESTON MERCURY (Charleston, SC)	"The Invasion of Pennsylvania–The Battle of Gettysburg–The Retreat to Hagerstown" The back of this single sheet issue contains the first report of the Northern assault on Fort Wagner, which includes details of the charge of black units. This was the basis of the film, "Glory".
108-111	July 22, 1863	FRANKLIN REPOSITORY (Chambersburg, PA)	Large front page map showing "The Seat of War in Pennsylvania and Maryland". Includes the neighboring town of Gettysburg with full page account of the battle. Also covers the NY Draft Riots.
112-116	July 25, 1863	FRANK LESLIE'S ILLUSTRATED NEWSPAPER (New York)	The Battle of Gettysburg The Siege of Vicksburg The New York Draft Riots
117	July 26, 1863	TROY WEEKLY TIMES (Troy, NY)	Article begins, "To Our Subscribers–You are aware that our office was sacked and destroyed by a mob of ruffians on Wednesday of last week," leading this special edition to be printed "at the office of the Albany Morning Express".
118	Aug. 1, 1863	SOUTHERN ILLUSTRATED NEWS (Richmond, VA)	A front page look at Major-General George E. Pickett.
119	Aug. 22, 1863	SOUTHERN SENTINEL (Alexandria, LA)	Rare Confederate necessity wallpaper edition.
120	Aug. 29, 1863	SOUTHERN ILLUSTRATED NEWS (Richmond, VA)	Lieutenant-General T. J. (Stonewall) Jackson, by now deceased, is featured.
121-122	Aug. 29, 1863	ARMY & NAVY JOURNAL (NY)	Vol. 1, #1 issue of this "Gazette of the Regular and Volunteer Forces"
123	Sep. 12, 1863	FRANK LESLIE'S ILLUSTRATED NEWSPAPER (New York)	"The War in Kansas–Fearful Massacre at Lawrence By Quantrell's Guerillas" is depicted in this vividly blunt front page woodcut.
124	Sep. 112, 1863	SOUTHERN FIELD & FIRESIDE (Augusta, GA)	Rare use of illustration in the form of a cartoon of Lincoln greeting a Southern lady as an armed black stands by.
125	Sep. 19, 1963	NY HERALD	War map showing "Important Operations in Gerogia"
126	Sep. 22. 1863	NY HERALD	War map showing "The Battle Field Near Chattanooga"
127-129	Sep. 23, 1863	THE DAILY JOURNAL (Wilmington, NC)	Military Notices (on the front page), "Federal Ride in Natchez," "The Surrender at Cumberland Gap," "What Yankees are Doing for Slaves of the South"
130	Oct. 7, 1863	TRI-WEEKLY TELEGRAPH (Houston, TX)	Confederate necessity single-sheet issue printed on bright green paper.
131	Oct. 14, 1863	NY HERALD	Front page war map showing scenes in Eastern Tennessee and Georgia.
132-133	Oct. 16, 1863	DAILY HUNTSVILLE CONFEDERATE (Marietta, GA)	This paper began in Huntsville, Al (see May 28, 1863 issue) and was subsequently published in several other towns (see Feb. 6, 1864 issue). This issue reports on Alabama troops at Chickamauqua.
134	Oct. 24, 1863	UNCONDITIONAL S. GRANT (New Iberia, LA)	Rare Union occupation newpaper with patriotic title printed on wallpaper.
135-136	Oct. 26, 1863	TRI-WEEKLY TELEGRAPH (Houston, TX)	Single sheet pink necessity paper. Front page offers an official report by General R.E. Lee on "The Pennsylvania Campaign" culminating in the Battle of Gettysburg. Back includes two articles, "By Pony Express".
137	Nov. 12, 1863	TRI-WEEKLY TELEGRAPH (Houston, TX)	Confederate single sheet necessity issue printed on bright yellow paper.
138	Nov. 21, 1863	NATIONAL INTELLIGENCER (Washington, DC)	Lincoln's now immortal Gettysburg Address is relegated to second page (2nd Col) of this District of Columbia newspaper. Edward Everett's long-winded oration upon the occasion is given all of the front page spotlight.
139	Dec. 2, 1863	THE LYNCHBURG VIRGINIAN	"Details of the Late Battle at Chattanooga"
140-141	Dec. 5, 1863	FRANK LESLIE'S ILLUSTRATED NEWSPAPER (New York)	"The Consecration of the Great National Cemetery Near Gettysburg...By Abraham Lincoln..."
142	Dec. 23, 1863	GOLD HILL DAILY NEWS (Gold Hill, Nevada Territory)	The Gettysburg Address is published one month after its occurrence in this daily!
143-144	Dec. 31, 1863	THE LADIES' KNAPSACK (Cincinnati, OH)	Printed and distributed at the "Great Western Sanitary Fair", where funds were raised to be "distributed to Union soldiers".
145	Jan. 1864	THE CHRISTIAN BANNER (Boston, MA)	A paper "For the Soldier and the Sailor". Extremely rare and early use of color illustration in a newspaper.
146	Jan. 1, 1864	N Y HERALD NEWSMEN'S NEW YEAR ADDRESS	Printed as a gift to subscribers to encourage holiday tips for the paper carriers.
147	Jan. 2, 1864	HARPER'S WEEKLY (NY)	"General Baird's Division Capturing the Rebel Guns on the Left of Missionary Ridge"
148	Jan. 7, 1864	DAILY CHRONICLE AND SENTINEL (Augusta, GA)	Note the "Blockade Goods" ad in the last column.
149	Jan. 22, 1864	DER TEXAS DEMOCRAT (Houston, TX)	Confederate wallpaper newspaper printed for the German-speaking residents of Houston, Texas.
150	Feb. 4, 1864	THE PENINSULA (Fernandina, FL)	Rare Union occupation paper with front page anecdote of Lincoln.
151	Feb. 6, 1864	DAILY HUNTSVILLE CONFEDERATE (Dalton, GA)	This well-traveled newspaper started out in Huntsville, AL. (See other issues dated May 28, 1863 and Oct. 16, 1863.
152	Feb. 8, 1864	DAILY SOUTHERN GUARDIAN (Columbia, SC)	Many Southern editors employed patriotic titles in the naming of their newspapers.
153-154	Feb. 9, 1864	STAUNTON SPECTATOR (Staunton, VA)	P. 1, Col. 1–Note the humorous photo gallery advertisement. P. 2–"The Spirit of the Army"
155-158	Feb. 10, 1864	HAMMOND GAZETTE (Point Lookout, MD)	Scarce Union Army hospital newspaper– Page 2 article, "Negro Recruiting Camp" plus, back page, "Official List of Officers and Patients"

159	Feb. 25, 1864	TRI-WEEKLY MERCURY (Charleston, SC)	A report on The Battle of Oluster, Florida in the third column. This was the only major battle fought in Florida.
160-161	Mar. 5, 1864	OPELOUSAS COURIER LE COURIER DES OPELOUSAS (New Orleans, LA)	Bi-lingual (English-French) wallpaper Confederate paper.
162-163	Mar. 19, 1864	HOUSTON DAILY TELEGRAPH (Houston, TX)	Confederate necessity newspaper printed on cornhusk.
164	Mar. 19, 1864	HARPER'S WEEKLY (New York)	A front page look at a dashing young Cavalry officer, "Brigadier-General George A. Custer".
165	Mar. 19, 1864	FRANK LESLIE'S ILLUSTRATED NEWSPAPER (New York)	Custer's 5th regulars charge into "J.E.B. Stuart's Camp Near Charlottesville"
166-169	Mar. 22, 1864	THE CLARENDON BANNER (Manning, SC)	An interesting Confederate newspaper, particularly the touching page 3 article headed, "The Christian Soldier in Death".
170	Mar. 31, 1864	CAROLINA SPARTAN (Spartanburg, SC)	"A Lady in the Yankee Lines"
171-173	April 1864	OUR CAMP JOURNAL (Headquarters, First Division, Second Army Corps, VA)	Extraordinary illustrated Union camp newspaper printed in the field.
174	Apr. 16, 1864	NY HERALD	"Reported Massacre of the White and Black Troops" during the capture of Fort Pillow by the Confederates.
175	Apr. 23, 1864	CHATTANOOGA DAILY GAZETTE (Chattanooga, TN)	Note the unusually large ad for military goods on the back page of this Union occupation newspaper.
176-177	Apr. 23, 1864	SUPPL. TO SOUTH CAROLINIAN (Columbia, SC)	Highly unusual illustrated Confederate broadsheet with a "Grand Demonstration In Honor of Gen. Hampton's Troops" describing a welcoming party by the citizens of Columbia for "returned members of Hampton's Legion".
178-179	April 30, 1864	HARPER'S WEEKLY (New York)	Illustrations by Thomas Nast show the importance of war correspondents in "The Press on the Field".
180	April 30, 1864	SOUTHERN ILLUSTRATED NEWS (Richmond, VA)	Back page cartoon characterizes "Butler, The Beast, at Work"
181	May 9, 1864	DAILY LYNCHBURG VIRGINIAN	"The Battle of the Wilderness Begins"
182	May 10, 1864	DAILY LYNCHBURG VIRGINIAN	"Further Particulars on the Great Fight" plus the arrival of Lieutenant-General Longstreet.
183	May 11, 1864	FLAKE'S BULLETIN (Galveston, TX)	Confederate necessity paper printed on cornhusk.
184	May 13, 1864	DAILY LYNCHBURG VIRGINIAN	"From Gen'l Lee's Army", plus more on the Battle of the Wilderness.
185	May 16, 1864	DAILY LYNCHBURG VIRGINIAN	More on The Battle of the Wilderness.
186	May 26, 1864	THE SWAMP ANGEL (Morris Island, SC)	Union occupation paper with reaction to the Ft. Pillow Massacre. Editor's note states the paper "...will appear semi-occasionally, as circumstances offer themselves."
187	June 1, 1864	WEEKLY STANDARD (Raleigh, NC)	A typical front page of this North Carolina Confederate Newspaper.
188	June 5, 1864	DEMOREST'S ILLUSTRATED NEWS (New York)	A front page look at Major-General Benjamin F. Butler, known not so affectionately in the South as "Beast Butler".
189	June 13, 1864	LYNCHBURG VIRGINIAN	"The Daring Attempt of Kautz's Cavalry to Capture Petersburg..."
190-191	June 21, 1864	LYNCHBURG VIRGINIAN	Local report on the Front– "The Battle of Lynchburg" with an apology from the editor explaining why the paper had not been issued for an entire week. See back page report on the Battle of Petersburg.
192	June 22, 1864	NORTH CAROLINA TIMES (New Berne, NC)	This Union occupation newspaper also had to resort to printing on cornhusk.
193	July 2, 1864	HARPER'S WEEKLY	A full-length look at "The Rebel General Robert E. Lee"
194-197	July 8, 1864	TWENTY-SIXTH (New London, CT)	Almost an entire page of this regimental newspaper is devoted to printing, "Casualties During the Siege of Port Hudson)–26th Connecticut Volunteers.
198-199	July 13, 1864	THE SOUTHERN BANNER (Athens, GA)	Custer and the Cavalry
200	July 16, 1864	DAILY CONSERVATIVE (Leavenworth, KS)	"The Bushwhack Hunt in Missouri–Progress of the Union Raid" in 1st column "The Guerrillas Around Us" in 4th column
201-202	July 20, 1864	DAILY CAROLINA WATCHMAN (Salisbury, NC)	An example of Confederate wishful thinking–Note the headline in the first column of front page, "Death of General Grant?" Back page, "Battle of Kennesaw Mtn.–Yankee Account" and "A Yankee Account of Forrest's Victory".
203	Aug. 1, 1864	CHARLESTON DAILY COURIER (Charleston, SC)	Burnside directs a gigantic mine explosion into the defenses of the town of Petersburg, VA which handily defends itself.
204	Aug. 9, 1864	LYNCHBURG VIRGINIAN	"Important from Mobile"–Report on the battle between Farragut's fleet and Confederate defenders of Mobile, Alabama
205	Aug. 10, 1864	CAMDEN WEEKLY CONFEDERATE (Camden, SC)	Lengthy front page editorial on Hood replacing Johnston as Commander of the Army of Tennessee. Also, "Scenes in Wilson's Raid"
206-207	Aug. 12, 1864	THE SIAM TIMES (Bangkok, Siam)	Even the King of Siam (as portrayed by Yul Brynner in *The King and I*) had news of the Civil War printed in his newspaper; the first newspaper printed in Siam.
208	Aug. 13, 1864	N Y HERALD	Admiral David Farragut leads his famous Federal attack on Mobile Bay, Alabama.
209	Aug. 15, 1864	N Y HERALD	"Farragut– Daring Dash and Brilliant Victory" at Mobile Bay.
210	Aug. 17, 1864	DAILY CONSERVATIVE (Leavenworth, KS)	Very rare recruitment ad for a "Colored Battery" to "Avenge Fort Pillow!" "The Bushwhackers in Missouri" is about "Bloody" Bill Anderson.
211-212	Aug. 18, 1864	PALMETTO HERALD (Port Royal, SC)	"From Morris Island–Destruction of a Blockade Runner"
213	Aug. 27, 1864	FRANK LESLIE'S ILLUSTRATED NEWSPAPER (New York)	Illustration of "The Siege of Petersburg".
214	Sep. 1, 1864	THE MEMPHIS APPEAL–EXTRA (Atlanta, GA)	Special Confederate exile printing of a broadside extra printed the day Hood's forces began to evacuate Georgia.
215	Sep. 3, 1864	THE SUN (New York)	The fall of Atlanta is celebrated with headlines and a woodcut of the Stars & Stripes.
216-217	Sep. 3, 1864	N Y HERALD	"Sherman" and the "Fall of Atlanta"
218	Sep. 8, 1864	LYNCHBURG VIRGINIAN	"The Death of General Morgan"
219	Sep. 20, 1864	THE WORLD-CAMPAIGN EDITION (New York)	This paper issues a special campaign edition supporting McClellan for President against a second term for Lincoln.
220	Sep. 24, 1864	THE SUN (NY)	"Little Phil Sheridan" defeats troops commanded by Jubal Early in the Shenandoah Valley, VA.
221	Oct. 9, 1864	N Y HERALD	Full page war map showing, "The Defenses of Richmond" and made "From a Map Found on the Body of the Rebel General Gherardie".
222	Oct. 11, 1864	DAILY CONSERVATIVE (Leavenworth, KS)	A remarkable edition in that it was printed on the two inside pages only of a four sided folded sheet, leaving the outside pages blank. Perhaps explained in the editor's note, "Do not expect much of us this morning...", describing how the office personnel were all on the skirmish lines during the day, drinking all night, and had hangovers in the morning.
223-224	Oct. 15, 1864	LYNCHBURG VIRGINIAN	Reports on the Morris Island Prison, and Custer and Merritt in the Valley Campaign, plus an article on the value of newspapers in the Confederacy.
225	Oct. 19, 1864	CAZENOVIA REPUBLICAN (Cazenovia, NY)	War map showing the progress of the Union Army and the areas captured.
226	Oct. 20, 1864	CLEVELAND PLAIN DEALER (Cleveland, OH)	Large pro-McClellan, anti-Lincoln front page cartoon used to influence voters in the Presidential race of 1864.
227	Oct. 22, 1864	DAILY CONSTITUTIONAL UNION (Washington)	This paper declares its support of Gen. George B. McClellan for president in the 1864 election.
228	Oct. 24, 1864	WALTON'S MORNING JOURNAL (Montpelier, VT)	This Vermont newspaper has front page coverage of "The St. Albans Raid" , during which Confederate raiders robbed a small Vermont town's bank.
229	Oct. 25, 1864	THE DAILY WANDERER (Amite, LA)	Very unusual edition for the railroad. A soldier's letter from the trenches.
230	Nov. 9, 1864	N Y TRIBUNE	Second election of Abraham Lincoln.
231	Nov. 10, 1864	CITIZEN EXTRA (Canton, MS)	Very rare special narrow strip broadside extra containing a "Synopsis of President Davis' message.
232	Nov. 12, 1864	"NEWS" BULLETIN (Houston, TX)	Scarce single sheet Texas Confederate newspaper.
233-235	Nov. 16, 1864	BROWNLOW'S KNOXVILLE WHIG AND REBEL VENTILATOR (Knoxville, TN)	Parson Brownlow's famous pro-Union Southern Newspaper.
236	Nov. 17, 1864	THE PALMETTO HERALD (Port Royal, SC)	Union occupation newspaper. "Sinking of the Ram Albemarle"

237-238	Nov. 19, 1864	WASHINGTON DEMOCRAT (Olympia, Washington Territory)	This obviously Democratic territorial newspaper bemoans the re-election of Lincoln.
239	Nov. 29, 1864	LYNCHBURG VIRGINIAN	Sherman's march through Georgia and "Burning of Atlanta".
240	Dec. 10, 1864	ATLANTA DAILY INTELLIGENCER (Atlanta, GA)	This rare broadside extra conjures up scenes from "Gone with the Wind" with its description of the destruction wrought by the "God-forsaken, miserable and deluded Yankee crew".
241	Dec. 10, 1864	FORNEY'S WAR PRESS (Philadelphia, PA)	Illustration of Union soldiers bowling at their camp as a momentary distraction from the harsh realities of war.
242	Dec. 20, 1864	LYNCHBURG VIRGINIAN	The condition of Atlanta as described "by the returning exiles".
243-244	Dec. 22, 1864	N Y HERALD	"Sherman's Triumphant March" through Georgia, plus "The Battles Before Nashville".
245	Dec. 26, 1864	NY DAILY NEWS	Front page report on the "Capture of Savannah".
246-247	Dec. 26, 1864	LYNCHBURG VIRGINIAN	"Christmas" at War, "Outrages By Yankee Generals", "High Prices of Negroes" plus, "Evacuation of Savannah"
248-249	Jan 12, 1865	IDAHO TRI WEEKLY STATESMAN (Boise City, Idaho Territory)	An "Overland Stage" brings news of the war to Idaho Territory. (Printed on yellow necessity paper)
250	Feb.1, 1865	THE SUN (NY)	"Slavery Dead" proclaims this Northern newspaper upon news that the House of Representatives had passed the 13th Amendment to the Constitution.
251	Feb. 2, 1865	LYNCHBURG VIRGINIAN	"General Lee Confirmed as Commander-In-Chief"
252	Feb. 7, 1865	CHARLESTON MERCURY (Charleston, SC)	Just ten days before the fall of the city of Charleston, the governor tries to rally the state's citizenry to fight back the Northern invaders.
253-255	Feb. 13, 1865	SOLDIERS LETTER- 2ND COLORADO CAVALRY) (Fort Riley, KS)	Very rare Regimental newspaper printed on lightly ruled composition paper. (Blank back page)
256	Feb. 15, 1865	PHILADELPHIA INQUIRER	Front page map illustrating Sherman's march to the sea.
257	Feb. 20, 1865	PHILADELPHIA INQUIRER	"The Capture of Columbia" (South Carolina) with accompanying map.
258	Feb. 21, 1865	THE DAILY JOURNAL (Wilmington, NC)	Front page article headlined, "Closed Up" describes the dim state of things. "Every store, every shop, every shanty is closed up..." in Wilmington, NC.
259	Feb. 22, 1865	THE SUN (NY)	"Doom of Charleston" is accompanied by a front page map sarcastically headed, "Graveyard of Rebellion"
260	Mar. 6, 1865	N Y DAILY NEWS	This Copperhead newspaper unhappily reports the second inauguration of Lincoln.
261	Mar. 21, 1865	COLUMBIA PHOENIX (Columbia, SC)	"Capture, Sack and Destruction of the City of Columbia"
262	Apr. 3, 1865	NASHVILLE UNION EXTRA (TN)	The fall of Richmond as reported from Union-occupied Nashville in this extra broadside.
263	c. Apr. 3, 1865	POST EXTRA (Buffalo, NY)	Broadside extra on the taking of Richmond. All columns except the fifth are filled with ads.
264-265	April 4, 1865	EVENING WHIG (Richmond, VA)	Publication of this title is resumed under Union authority which report, "Occupation of the City".
266	April 4, 1865	PHILADELPHIA INQUIRER	"Fall of Richmond"
267-268	April 4, 1865	N Y TRIBUNE	The fall of Richmond is celebrated with a giant eagle and shield engraving and a large topographical map of Richmond.
269-270	Apr. 5, 1865	GRANT'S PETERSBURG PROGRESS (Petersburg, VA)	Having taken both Richmond and Petersburg, this Northern-controlled paper proudly proclaim its motto, "Eternal Vigilance is the Price of Liberty (and ten cents a copy for our paper)".
271	Apr. 7, 1865	EVE. EDITION–THE TRIBUNE (NY)	Sheridan's cavalry surrounds Lee's retreating army in Virginia.
272	Apr. 7, 1865	TRI WEEKLY CONSITUTIONALIST (Augusta, GA)	In a front page "Message From the President" dated "Danville, April 5, 1865", Jefferson Davis urges the South to keep on fighting.
273-274	Apr. 8, 1865	SAVANNAH REPUBLICAN (Savannah, GA)	This Union occupation newspaper reports on "Sherman" and his march through Georgia. It uses the term "white trash" to describe Southern refugees who arrived with Sherman's army. Printed on wrapping necessity paper.
275	Apr. 8, 1865	PHILADELPHIA INQUIRER	"Lee's Last Defeat" before Appomattox.
276	Apr. 8, 1865	THE FLORIDA UNION (Jacksonville, FL)	"3000 Rebels Captured", "Heavy Fighting by Gen. Grant in Front of Petersburg"
277	Apr. 10, 1865	THE NEW YORK TIMES	Surrender of General Lee
278-279	Apr. 10, 1865	PHILADELPHIA INQUIRER	"Lee Finds His Waterloo", "Surrender of the Rebel Army"
280-281	Apr. 10, 1865	THE HERALD (NY)	Surrender of Lee
282-283	Apr. 10, 1865	THE SUN (NY)	Surrender of Lee
284-285	Apr. 10, 1865	RICHMOND WHIG (Richmond, VA)	This Union occupation paper details the surrender of Lee's army at Appomattox.
286-287	Apr. 11, 1865	RICHMOND WHIG (Richmond, VA)	Biographical sketches of Rebel generals killed at Petersburg. This issue contains an ad for a special lithograph map of the burnt districts in Richmond offered by the Whig for separate purchase. Our subscriber bought the map as you can see on the following page.
288-289	Apr. 11, 1865	DAILY JOURNAL AND MESSENGER (Macon, GA)	Still in Confederate hands, and apparently still unaware of Lee's surrender, the editor reminds his readers that he takes "none but Confederate not ragged, City of Macon, and State of Georgia money"
290	Apr. 13, 1865	HAMILTON TELEGRAPH (Hamilton, OH)	Small town paper uses big type and graphics to celebrate the surrender of Lee.
291-293	Apr. 14, 1865	CHARLESTON COURIER (Charleston, SC)	Union occupation paper announcing, "The End of the Rebellion"
294	Apr. 15, 1865	HARTFORD DAILY COURANT (Hartford, CT)	"The Assassination of Lincoln" Note the mis-alignment of type in the headline word "Assassination"
295	Apr. 15, 1865	PHILADELPHIA INQUIRER	"Murder of President Lincoln"
296	Apr. 15, 1865	EVENING TELEGRAPH (Philadelphia, PA)	Next day report of the assassination of Lincoln. This was perhaps the only newspaper n the country that pictured Booth, the assassin, on the day after the event.
297-298	Apr. 15, 1865	THE DAILY PROGRESS (Raleigh, NC)	Occupation of Raleigh by Sherman' troops reported in the local paper.
299	Apr. 15, 1865	THE NEW YORK TIMES 2:12 AM EDITION	Note the headline, "The Condition of the President" in the fourth column.
300	Apr. 15, 1865	THE NEW YORK TIMES 11:15 PM EDITION	Note the headline, "Another Account" in the second column.
301	Apr. 15, 1865	NY HERALD 2:00 AM EDITION	The New York Herald put out seven editions the day following the assassination of Lincoln (six issues are represented here). It is also one of the most reproduced papers in American history. Note headline in this edition, "The State Capital" in the fourth column.
302	Apr. 15, 1865	NY HERALD 3:00 AM EDITION	The Assassination of Lincoln Note that "The State Capital" is moved to the last column.
303	Apr. 15, 1865	NY HERALD 8:45 AM EDITION	Extremely rare edition and the first to report, "Death of the President".
304	Apr. 15, 1865	NY HERALD 10:00 AM REWARD EDITION	Note that a reward is offered for Booth in the fifth column.
305	Apr. 15, 1865	NY HERALD 10:00 AM EDITION	Same as above issue but without the reward offer.
306-307	Apr. 15, 1865	NY HERALD 2:00 PM EDITION	Inauguration edition–Note that the front page is the same as the 10:00 edition reward edition. "Extra" on back page with "Inauguration of Andrew Johnson".
308	Apr. 15, 1865	EVENING EDITION–NY TRIBUNE	Extra on the assassination of Lincoln.
309	Apr. 15, 1865	GAZETTE EXTRA (Chattanooga, TN)	Very rare Southern extra broadside announcing the assassination of Lincoln.
310	Apr. 15, 1865	CHARLESTON COURIER (Charleston, SC)	The Union flag is once again raised over Fort Sumter six days after the surrender of Lee.
311	Apr. 16, 1865	N Y HERALD	"Death of Lincoln"
312	Apr. 17, 1865	PHILADELPHIA INQUIRER	Unusual front page portrait of "J. Wilkes Booth, The Assassin", with diagram of "The Scene of the Great Tragedy".
313	Apr. 17, 1865	BUFFALO MORNING EXPRESS (Buffalo, NY)	An entire page as a memorial to Lincoln.
314	Apr. 17, 1865	THE RICHMOND WHIG (Richmond, VA)	The citizens of the former capital of the Confederacy learn of the assassination.
315-316	Apr. 17, 1865	THE MORNING BULLETIN (Memphis, TN)	The South reacts to Lincoln's assassination.
317-318	Apr. 19, 1865	THE DAILY STANDARD (Raleigh, NC)	"General Sherman's Rule in North Carolina", "Daniel Webster on the Union", "Death of Mr. Lincoln" plus, Sec. of War Stanton orders a 200 gun salute at every Army HQ, port arsenal, and at West Point in commemoration of Lee's surrender.
319	Apr. 20, 1865	PHILADELPHIA INQUIRER	Unusual front page graphics show, "The Funeral Car of President Lincoln" and, "The Coffin".
320	Apr. 20, 1865	DAILY MORNING CHRONICLE (D.C.)	"The Obsequies" and a front page memorial portrait of Lincoln.
321-324	Apr. 21, 1865	THE RICHMOND TIMES (Richmond, VA)	Vol 1, # 1 issue of this Union occupation newspaper containing Part 1 of the full story of the fall of Richmond as well as a report on the assassination.

325	Apr. 21, 1865	DAILY TELEGRAPH EXTRA (Houston, TX)	Confederate broadside extra with the surrender of Lee and Proclamation by General Kirby Smith urging the Trans-Mississippi Department to keep fighting.
326	Apr. 22, 1865	THE MONTANA POST (Virginia City, Montana Territory)	Citizens of Montana learn of the surrender of Lee almost two weeks after the fact!
327	Apr. 22, 1865	NATIONAL POLICE GAZETTE (NY)	Pictorial coverage of the assassination of Lincoln and attempted assassination of Seward.
328-329	Apr. 22, 1865	THE RICHMOND TIMES (Richmond, VA)	Second installment of "The Evacuation of Richmond". Also contains Sherman's occupation of Raleigh and the fall of Mobile.
330-332	Apr. 23, 1865	TRI-WEEKLY CONSTITUTIONALIST (Augusta, GA)	This extraordinary newspaper was printed in one of the few Southern towns not occupied at this late date. It mocks the assassination of Lincoln, mistakenly reports the death of Seward, and names "Smith" as the assassin. It also mourns the surrender of Lee.
333	Apr. 25, 1865	PHILADELPHIA INQUIRER	"President Lincoln's Remains in Independence Hall"
334	Apr. 25, 1865	LYNCHBURG VIRGINIAN EXTRA	This broadside contains a "Letter From Gen. Longstreet" in which he says that Lee's surrender at Appomattox Court House was due to the army being surrounded, but that it was "never intended to give up the Confederate Cause," Also, the last column announces, "The Era of Peace...the Closing Up of the War".
335	Apr. 26, 1865	PHILADELPHIA INQUIRER	The Funeral of Lincoln in New York
336	Apr. 28, 1865	PHILADELPHIA INQUIRER	Map showing, "Death Scene of the Assassin".
337	Apr. 29, 1865	FRANK LESLIE'S ILLUSTRATED NEWSPAPER (New York)	Front page illustration of Booth shooting Lincoln in the Presidential box seats at Ford's Theater.
338	Apr. 29, 1865	HARPER'S WEEKLY (NY)	A look at John Wilkes Booth
339	Apr. 29, 1865	THE RICHMOND WHIG (Richmond, VA)	The surrender of Gen. Johnston and the capture of Booth are reported in this occupation paper.
340	Apr. 29, 1865	WASHINGTON WEEKLY CHRONICLE	Rare "extra" edition with dramatic display relating to the killing of "Booth, the Assassin".
341-342	May 1, 1865	THE SIXTH CORPS (Danville, VA)	Troop paper has front page printing of General Order #10 headed, "The Surrender of Johnston's Army". Note, also the "Warning to Marauders".
343	May 5, 1865	PHILADELPHIA INQUIRER	A front page look at "Corbett, the Executioner of Booth".
344	May 6, 1865	FRANK LESLIE'S ILLUSTRATED NEWSPAPER (New York)	Booth leaps from the Presidential box onto the stage at Ford's Theater to make his getaway.
345	May 10, 1865	PHILADELPHIA INQUIRER	"Peace!" and "Hostilities Declared at an End" are the headlines announcing President Andrew Johnson's proclamation stating that the Rebellion is "...virtually at an end."
346-347	May 10, 1865	FEDERAL UNION (Selma, AL)	Fantastic Union occupation broadside printed in blue type announcing "The War is Over" and "Surrender of Gen. Dick Taylor and Com. Farrand". A soldier's letter is written in pencil on blank verso of the sheet.
348	May 14, 1865	LOUISVILLE DAILY JOURNAL (Louisville, KY)	Quantrell, the famous Confederate raider is captured and brought to Louisville.
349	May 16, 1865	PHILADELPHIA INQUIRER	"The Conspiracy!", plus, "Jeff. Davis as "The Stern Statesman (last Act)", a front page cartoon with Davis holding a long knife labeled "Arkansas Toothpick"
350	May 18, 1865	PHILADELPHIA INQUIRER	"Trial of the Conspirators"
351	May 19, 1865	PHILADELPHIA INQUIRER	A look at David C. Harold, one of the conspirators.
352	May 20, 1865	PHILADELPHIA INQUIRER	"Portraits of the Conspirators"–Lewis C. Payne and Samuel C. Arnold
353	May 20, 1865	FRANK LESLIE'S ILLUSTRATED NEWSPAPER (New York)	A front page illustration answers the question of what happened to Booth's body. The publisher supplies an affidavit which vouches for the truth of his illustration but will not reveal his source.
354	May 22, 1865	PHILADELPHIA INQUIRER	"The Trial of the Assassins and Conspirators"–Scene set in the courtroom.
355-356	May 25, 1865	THE DAILY PROGRESS (Raleigh, NC)	"The Last Scene"–Jefferson Davis is apprehended while attempting to escape dressed as a woman. Also, Payne is identified as Seward's attacker.
357	May 31, 1865	PHILADELPHIA INQUIRER	"Infamy! Jeff. Davis Gloats Over Mr. Lincoln's Murder"
358	June 1, 1865	THE FRIEND (Honolulu, Hawaii)	The news of the assassination takes three weeks to reach Hawaii.
359	June 3, 1865	FRANK LESLIE'S ILLUSTRATED NEWSPAPER (New York)	Woodcut illustration of Wilson's troops capturing Jefferson Davis while disguised wearing a dress.
360-361	June 3, 1865	COLUMBIA DAILY PHOENIX (Columbia, SC)	U.S. military general orders fill the columns of this single sheet edition. Note the last one on p. 361 warning of "armed bands of marauders".
362	June 10, 1865	THE REVEILLE (Carver U.S. General Hospital, DC)	Post-war hospital newspaper with front page anecdote of Lincoln.
363	June 14, 1865	PHILADELPHIA INQUIRER	"Reconstruction!" proclaimed as a new pro-Union provisional governor is installed in Mississippi.
364	July 1, 1865	HARPER'S WEEKLY (NY)	A pictorial look at "The Conspirators and the Conspiracy".
365	July 22, 1865	FRANK LESLIE ILLUSTRATED NEWSPAPER (New York)	"Execution of the Conspirators in Washington, DC" is shown in this dramatic woodcut at the gallows.
366-367	Sep. 16, 1865	HARPER'S WEEKLY (NY)	"Andersonville Prison Scenes, Illustrating Capt. Wirz's Trial"
368	Nov. 11, 1865	THE SUN (NY)	In the only execution of a Confederate official carried out by a Federal authority, the commandant of the infamous Andersonville Prison is hung after his conviction by court martial.
369	Dec. 19, 1865	THE SUN (NY)	The 13th Amendment is ratified, making slavery illegal in the United States.
370	Dec. 20, 1865	THE SUN (NY)	"Reconstruction Begins–Georgia Reunited" Also, President Andrew Johnson's message to the Senate.
371	June 1866	THE FREEDMAN (Boston, MA)	This was one of a number of post-war newspapers whose purpose was to help newly emancipated blacks to adjust to their new roles as free citizens. Many, including this publication had religious as well as practical instructions.
372	Oct. 4, 1884	GRAND ARMY SCOUT-SOLDIERS MAIL (Philadelphia, PA)	One of the many Grand Army of the Republic newspapers which would keep stories of the war alive decades after the war had ended.
373	July 2, 1913	GETTYSBURG COMPILER (Gettysburg, PA)	"The Gray and Blue Handshake", printed on the 50th anniversary of the Battle of Gettysburg. The surviving veterans on both sides gathered to honor each other as Americans.

BATTLE OF PRAIRIE GROVE.

Gen. Hindman's Report.

HEADQUARTERS 1st CORPS, TRANS-MISS. ARMY,
Camp near Fort Smith, Dec. 25, 1862.

COLONEL:—

I marched from near Van Buren on the 3d inst., with nine thousand infantry, two thousand cavalry, and twenty-two pieces of artillery. Lack of shoes and arms prevented me from taking my entire force. My intention was to attack Brig. General Blount, on Cane Hill, reported to have between seven and eight thousand men and thirty cannon. I expected, as stated at the time in dispatches to Department Head Quarters, to return immediately after the engagement—having barely ammunition enough for one battle, and not sufficient subsistence and forage for seven days, at half rations.—These meager supplies had been accumulated with extreme difficulty, by hauling in wagons of the general train and regiments eighty miles,—my transportation being very limited, the country around me entirely exhausted, and the river too low for navigation. These facts had made it certain that I must soon retire the greater part of my force towards Little Rock; hence it seemed important, for the security for what was to be left, that Blount should be driven from his position.

Cane Hill is a ridge of perhaps eight miles length and five miles width, in the southwest part of Washington county, Arkansas, just beyond the north base of the Boston Mountains. Three villages are built upon it,—Russellville, Boonsboro, and Newburg,—which almost blend with each other, covering a distance, as the road to Fayetteville runs, of three or four miles. The enemy's main body was about Newburg.

The distance from Van Buren to Newburg is 45 miles. The intermediate country is a rugged and sterile range of mountains. The roads across it are gathered together at Van Buren, on the south side, and at Fayetteville, on the northern. These places are from fifty to sixty-five miles apart, according to the route traveled. There are four principal roads. One bends to the right and east, with the valley of Frog Bayou, crosses the mountain, then follows the west fork of White river, and strikes Fayetteville from a [illegible]east. Another, known as the Telegraph road, proceeds for the most part upon ridges, directly north. The third leaves the Telegraph road twelve miles above Van Buren, runs along the Cherokee line to Evansville, and there branches, through the Cane Hill country, to Fayetteville,—its main trunk going north, by Cincinnati and Maysville, to Fort Scott. The fourth turns to the left, from the Telegraph road, at Oliver's, nineteen miles above Van Buren, follows the valley of Cove Creek to the foot of the mountains, and, after crossing, passes through a succession of defiles, valleys and prairies, reaching Fayetteville from a south-westerly direction.

At Morrow's, fifteen miles above Oliver's, the Cove Creek road sends a branch direct to Newburg, seven miles distant. Eight miles above Morrow's, it is crossed by a road leading from Hog Eye, five miles east on the Telegraph road, to Newburg.—Two miles beyond this, it sends a branch, by Ray's Mill, to Maysville, which crosses the Cane Hill and Fayetteville road at the distance of two miles from the Cove Creek road. This crossing is seven miles and a half from Newburg, and twelve miles and a half from Fayetteville. Two miles and a half above this crossing, the Cove Creek road and the Cane Hill and Fayetteville road unite. There is a road from Newburg, by Ray's Mill, to this junction,—the distance by the latter route being about two miles greater.

The accompanying map may serve to make this description more intelligible.

Marmaduke's cavalry division formed my advance,—moving on the Telegraph road, with detachments on those east and west of it. Col. Watie's Cherokee regiment was ordered to the vicinity of Evansville, instructed, when the firing should commence, to move forward and occupy certain mills in the Cane Hill region, and to attack the enemy's train, if retired towards Cincinnati. The balance of my force moved on the Telegraph road, and bivouacked at Oliver's on the night of the 4th. There I received information that a reinforcement of three or four thousand men had arrived on Cane Hill, making Blount's force fully equal to mine. On the 5th, instead of getting to Morrow's, as I had expected, we went but little further than half way, in consequence of some of those apparently unavoidable delays to which troops so ill-provided as ours are liable. On the 6th we reached Morrow's. In the morning of that day, Marmaduke's advance, under Col. J. O. Shelby, encountered the enemy's cavalry, and drove them back, beyond Morrow's, to within two miles of Newburg.

There, from the crest of the mountain to its base, about sunset, a sharp engagement occurred, in which Col. J. C. Monroe and his brigade of Arkansas cavalry, who had relieved Shelby, greatly distinguished themselves, charging a superior force of the enemy's cavalry with boldness and vigor, breaking his ranks, a[illegible]ly ceasing to pursue when recalled. I had [illegible]viously ordered forward Hunter's regiment of Missouri infantry, of Parson's brigade, Frost's division, to hold the ground which the cavalry might gain. This order was promptly executed. The regiment was in possession of the heights and defiles that might be used for annoying us before the skirmish had ceased. To make sure of this advantage, the remainder of Parson's brigade was thrown forward to the same position.

This being the situation of affairs, the several commanders of divisions were assembled, on the night of the 6th, to receive final instructions, when I learned that a further reinforcement of from four to six thousand infantry, and two thousand cavalry, with thirty cannon, under Brig. Gen. Herron, was at Fayetteville, on the way to Cane Hill, making forced marches.

It had been my intention to throw Marmaduke's cavalry, by the Cove Creek road and its Maysville branch, upon the enemy's left and rear, while I attacked in front, by the road leading from Morrow's to Newburg. It now seemed evident that that plan would simply cause the retirement of Blount upon his reinforcements, without accepting battle till after the junction should be effected.—There was a possibility that I might, by adopting a different plan, destroy the reinforcements, and afterwards fight the main body upon equal terms. [illegible]draw, without fighting at all, would discourage my own troops, and so embolden the enemy as to ensure his following me up. His sudden concentration of troops justified the opinion that a movement against me was intended in any event.

Influenced by these considerations, I determined to risk an engagement.

At twelve p. m., after replenishing his camp fires, Parsons moved back to Morrow's,—Monroe remaining in position on the crest of the mountain, instructed to dismount and skirmish as infantry, at daylight, so as to deceive the enemy and detain him at Newburg as long as possible; and, when he should commence retiring, to press him vigorously. The trains were ordered, by a cross route, to the Telegraph road, and then to Hog Eye, guarded by one hundred cavalry and the disabled men of the infantry, of whom there was, unfortunately, a considerable number. These arrangements left me, for the fight, less than ten thousand men of all arms.

The order was given to march forward at three a. m., on the 7th, on the Cove Creek road and its Maysville branch, to the Cane Hill and Fayetteville road. The command was not in motion till nearly four; and then the route proved so excessively bad, and the detentions so frequent, from the breaking of artillery harness and debility of the battery animals, that the infantry failed to march above two miles an hour.

A little before sunrise Marmaduke discovered the cavalry of Herron's command, moving on the Cane Hill and Fayetteville road towards Newburg. Making his dispositions rapidly, and with excellent judgment, he attacked them in front and flank, routed them completely, killing and wounding many, captured over two hundred, with the train of a regiment, and pursued the fugitives five miles, in the direction of Fayetteville, to the line of battle formed by Herron's infantry.

My infantry was yet far in the rear, but moving up as rapidly as possible. When the head of the column at length reached the Cane Hill and Fayetteville road, Parson's brigade was put in position, facing towards Newburg, to resist any movement of the enemy from that direction,—a regiment of cavalry thrown towards that place to reconnoiter, and the balance of the force ordered forward, with instructions to attack the reinforcements at once;—Marmaduke in advance,—Shoup next,—then Frost. I remained with Parson's brigade, hoping to get some reliable intelligence of the enemy at Newburg. Receiving [illegible], at eleven a. m., I went forward about two miles, and overtook the marching column. It was painful to observe the exhaustion of the men. They had marched nearly fifteen miles. None of them had eaten since the preceding day. The rations of all had been insufficient for over thirty days. Many, overcome with fatigue, were left on the road-side.

Brig. Gen. Shoup met me, and stated that Marmaduke was falling back before the enemy's infantry, which was advancing, and that he had therefore put his division in position to resist attack.

I found the position taken by Gen. Shoup an exceedingly strong one. It was upon the edge of a hill, densely wooded, descending abruptly to Crawford's prairie, half a mile in width, which encircled all its northern half. Five hundred yards in rear was another prairie. Between the two, on the right and left, a skirt of woods connected the timber of the hill with that beyond. The Cane Hill and Fayetteville road cuts the centre of this hill, passing by Prairie Grove church, which is upon its summit. A cross route, from the Cane Hill and Fayetteville to the Cove Creek road, passes also immediately by the church, dividing the south prairie from the growth upon the hill. By the time I had completed my reconnoisance of the ground, a regiment of federal cavalry, with two pieces of artillery, opened fire upon the captured train and prisoners, that had been ordered towards Morrow's, and also upon a hospital established by my Medical Director for the the treatment of the wounded of the federal cavalry. No loss ensued, and this force retired rapidly, upon observing Parson's brigade. Shortly after, dense columns of smoke, in the direction of Ray's Mill, and between there and Newburg, indicated that Blount had retreated hastily, destroying his stores, and was moving to unite with Herron.

I immediately ordered forward Parson's brigade. Blount's advance soon appeared upon the farther side of Crawford's prairie. The interval of time in which I might have attacked Herron was past. Circumstances did not permit me to avail myself of it, for the manifest reason that, at the favorable moment, the rear of my column could not be where the head of it was. Evidently, the combined forces of Blount and Herron would speedily attack me. I made such arrangements as seemed best, to meet that contingency. The line of battle determined on was nearly in the form of a horse shoe, conforming to the shape of the hill.—Only Shoup's division and Shelby's brigade, of Marmaduke's division,—the latter dismounted,—were at first placed upon that line, filling the centre and right, opposite the line taken by Herron, which was upon the farther side of Crawford's prairie, on a bluff that rose up steeply behind a stream flowing into Illinois river. Frost's division,—to which had been added the brigade of Texans, with Clark's Missouri regiment, commanded by Brig. Gen. Roane,—was held in reserve, to await the movements of Blount. McDonald's regiment of Missouri cavalry, and Lane's regiment of Texas cavalry,—the latter commanded by Lieut-Col. R. P. Crump, were held in readiness to meet any attempts upon the flanks.

About twelve, the enemy opened with artillery, to which ours began responding, but this I prohibited. At one p. m., aided by a tremendous artillery fire, the infantry of Herron's command advanced against the position held by Shoup and Marmaduke. It was permitted to approach within sixty yards, and then, as it charged, rushing gallantly past one of our batteries, and having it for a moment in possession, Fagan's Arkansas brigade, part of McRae's brigade, and the Missourians under Shelby, delivered a terrific fire from their shot guns, rifles and muskets, and charged the enemy furiously. Hawthorne's regiment of Arkansians retook the battery. The federals broke and fled. Our men pursued them far into the prairie. The slaughter was great,—the earth in many places strewn with federal wounded and dead.

Very soon, the attack was renewed, a little farther to my right, with great vigor and determination. I ordered Shaver's Arkansas brigade, of Frost's division, to the support of Gen. Shoup. The enemy was again repulsed, with heavy loss, and retired in confusion.

Blount had now formed line of battle, two thousand yards to the front and left of Shoup, and commenced advancing. I ordered Frost's division formed on the left of Marmaduke. The thick undergrowth on that flank rendered it difficult to execute the movement, which was further embarrassed by the well directed and destructive fire of the enemy's batteries. There was, however, no confusion. By the time Frost was in line, the enemy was nearly across the prairie, and our skirmishers engaged his almost as soon as deployed. His attack was directed against Parson's brigade. It was fierce and prolonged, but ended in his being driven back in disorder, with heavy losses. One of Marmaduke's regiments, and one of Roane's,—both Missourian,—shared the honor of this brilliant achievement.

The enemy now brought up all his artillery, many pieces of which were rifled, and endeavored to shake our troops by playing upon our entire line for nearly an hour. Then he attacked with all his infantry, at the same time threatening the extreme left with a heavy cavalry force, and attempting to turn the right. McDonald's Missouri cavalry defeated him in the last manœuvre;—Lane's Texas cavalry and Roane's brigade deterred him from seriously assailing the left;—and Shoup's division, Shelby's brigade, of Marmaduke's division, and Parson's and Shaver's brigades, of Frost's division, gloriously repulsed him in his desperate attack upon their lines. He again fled beyond the prairie, leaving his dead and wounded, and the colors of several of his regiments in our hands, besides a number of prisoners. Some of these were ascertained to be of Totten's division, which had arrived upon the field, still further increasing the disparity of forces.

In the midst of this struggle, information reached me that a considerable body of federal cavalry was approaching Hog Eye, to which place I had ordered my trains. I directed the wagons retired on the Telegraph road, to Oliver's. This was done, without loss.

A furious cannonade was kept up by the enemy till near sunset.

Then a last attack of his infantry was directed against the line held by Frost. This was a most determined effort to retrieve the fortunes of the day. It signally failed, and the enemy paid dearly in killed and wounded for the attempt.

At dark the battle closed, leaving us masters of every foot of the ground on which it was fought.

Our loss, in killed, was one hundred and sixty-four (164);—wounded eight hundred and seventeen (817);—missing three hundred and thirty-six (336.)

The enemy left not less than four hundred (400) dead on the field, and his wounded certainly exceeded fifteen hundred (1500.) The number of prisoners in our hands was two hundred and seventy-five (275) including nine (9) officers. We also [illegible] federal flags, and over five hundred small arms, with twenty-three wagons, containing clothing, and camp and garrison equipage. Invoices of this property have been forwarded.

Of all the troops engaged on our side, Adam's Arkansas regiment alone dishonored itself. It was well armed, ably commanded, and surrounded by good soldiers from the same State, setting it an example of courage and patriotism. But, after delivering a single fire, the greater part of its men broke ranks, threw down their arms and shamefully fled,—many of them even deserting to the enemy. The field and staff officers,—who had been appointed,—rallied about seventy-five around the colors, and these did much to redeem the reputation of the regiment. With but few exceptions, the company officers exerted no influence.

The other troops displayed the greatest courage, constancy and enthusiasm. There was no place of shelter upon any portion of the field. Wounds were given and deaths inflicted by the enemy's artillery in the ranks of the reserves, as well as in the front rank. During five hours, shell, solid shot, grape and canister, and storms of bullets, swept the entire ground. Many gallant officers, and many soldiers, equally brave, fell, dead or wounded. But their comrades stood as firm as iron. Volunteers maintained their reputation;—conscripts rose at once to the same standard, and splendidly refuted the slanders put upon them by men of the class of "exempts."

Gen'ls Frost, Shoup and Marmaduke, commanding divisions,—Gen'ls Roane, Fagan, Parsons and McRae, and Col's Shaver and Shelby, commanding brigades, did their duty nobly. I strongly commend them to the Lieutenant-General Commanding the Department. Gen'ls Shoup and Marmaduke do not appear to have been confirmed as brigadiers. They fully merit the honor. Had the authorities whose consent is requisite been present at Prairie Grove, (or at Shiloh, where these gallant officers equally distinguished themselves,) the act of confirmation could not be delayed.

The reports of the Division Commanders and their subordinates are forwarded herewith. Especial attention is invited to them. They embody many valuable details, and specify instances of courage and good conduct, on the part of field, staff and company officers, and enlisted men, which I will not be expected otherwise to mention here.

I had with me the following staff:

Col. R. C. Newton, Chief of Staff.
Maj. J. P. Wilson, A. A. Gen'l.
Lieut. McK. Hammett, A. A. A. Gen'l.
Lieut. S. B. Reardon, A. D. C.
Lieut. R. W. Lee, A. D. C., Acting Chief of Ordnance.
Col. D. Province, Acting Chief of Artillery.
Col. A. S. Dobbin, Vol. A. D. C.
Maj. E. C. Boudinot, Vol. A. D. C.

All of them were constantly under fire. They displayed great coolness and disregard of danger, in the discharge of their duties. This was the second bloody battle in which Col. Newton and Maj. Wilson served on my staff;—in both, they evinced the same high qualities. The confirmation of their rank has been fairly won, at Shiloh and at Prairie Grove. I present this subject specially to the Department Commander, with the case also of Lieut. Hammett;—and [illegible] of the number of assignments made by me while commanding the Trans-Mississippi District.

Considering the strength of my command, as compared with the enemy's,—considering that my men were destitute of food, their wagons thirty miles in rear, and not to be brought forward without imminent danger of being lost;—that my small supply of ammunition was reduced far below what would be necessary for another day's fighting—and that my battery animals were literally dying of starvation, and could not be foraged in the presence of a superior force of the enemy;—I determined to retire, and gave the necessary orders for that purpose.

Cavalry was extended along both sides of the Cove creek road, distant two or three miles from it, from near Prairie Grove to the mountains.—and scouts were thrown upon all routs leading towards the enemy's position. The prisoners and captured property were removed. At twelve o'clock the rear guard of the infantry had passed out of hearing. I remained, with Marmaduke's cavalry, on the field, occupying the line held at dark, caring for our wounded and dead, and collecting the arms which the enemy had abandoned in his frequent flights before our men.

A federal officer, under flag, brought the following letter;

HEAD QUARTERS FEDERAL FORCES,
IN THE FIELD—Dec. 7th, 1862.

To commanding officer of Confederate forces.

GENERAL—

The bearer, Dr. Parker, visits your lines with flag of truce, for the purpose of caring for my wounded.

Signed JAS. G. BLOUNT,
Brig.-Gen. comd'g.

The bearer of the flag indicated twelve hours, from sunrise next day, as the desired period of truce. To this I acceded, detaining the federal officer, and notifying Gen. Blount, immediately of the fact. Receiving no written reply, and the bearer of my first note not returning, I again gave him the same information. He replied as follows:

HEAD QUARTERS FEDERAL FORCES;
IN THE FIELD, Dec. 8th, 1862, 6 o'clock A. M.

GENERAL:

I have the honor to acknowledge your second note under flag of truce, and express to you my regards for the privilege granted of entering your lines to care for my wounded, which is in accordance with the usage of civilized warfare. Instead of returning a written reply, as I perhaps should have done, I sent an unarmed party with ambulances, accompanied by commissioned officers, to meet Gen. Marmaduke, and to be by him conducted within your lines.

I have the honor to be General,
Your obedient servant,
Signed JAS. G. BLOUNT.
Brig. Gen. comd'g.

Maj.-Gen. T. C. HINDMAN,
Commanding Confederate forces.

Gen. Blount's officer had submitted a proposition, as by authority, that surgeon's, hospital nurses and attendants, sick and wounded, should not, in any case, be regarded as prisoners, but released unconditionally. This was not in such shape as to be conclusive. I therefore requested that Gen. Blount should meet me personally next day. He assented, and we met, about 10, a. m., on the 8th. The result of the conference was the adoption of the proposition before referred to,—with the additional stipulation that ambulances, and hospital trains, medicines, and medical and hospital stores, should be exempt from capture.

About 12 m. I withdrew Marmaduke's command; and overtook the infantry that night, at Morrows. The return to our former camp was attended with no incident worthy to be reported.

After a battle, the mind naturally passes in review all the circumstances connected with it. I hope the expression here of such reflections as now present themselves to me will not be deemed improper.

Undoubtedly, there are serious defects in our military system. Chief among these is the rule of electing to the lowest commissioned officer, and promoting to those above, in companies and regiments. It combines mobocracy and primogeniture in such proportions that it seems almost a miracle that anything of discipline or efficiency survives. As a substitute, I would propose this: That whenever a vacancy occurs, in a company or regiment, an examining board of three capable officers be appointed, by the division or corps commander; That, without regard to rank or restriction to the command all persons desiring the vacant place be invited to appear before the board, within a given time, to be examined as to character and qualifications; and that the board recommend, and the division or corps commander immediately assign to duty, the one found best qualified and most meritorious, conditioned that he shall not draw pay till the assignment be approved by the war department. As auxiliary to this, division or corps commanders should be authorized to order before a similar board any regimental or company officer deemed incapable, neglectful, or otherwise unfit, and on the report of the board against him, to suspend him from duty, and cause the place to be immediately filled, as in the case of any other vacancy; and upon the approval of the proceedings by the war department, the delinquent officer should invariably be put in the ranks as a private soldier. I would apply these provisions to all the staff officers of corps; divisions, brigades and regiments; with the further regulation, that persons assigned to staff duty where bond is required by law, may execute the same before the commander of the division or corps, great delays and detriment to the service result from the existing arrangements as to that matter.

Next in importance is the subject of the pay of the troops. Poor men almost universally make up our armies. Their wives and children, left without protection, are exposed to absolute suffering unless the men are regularly and adequately paid.—No troops that I have known during the war have been paid with anything like promptness. Immense arrearages are now due the men of this corps. Their families are in great suffering. The consequence is that very many desertions have occurred.

If arrearages could be at once discharged, the evil would be checked. If the pay of the soldier was not only promptly given him, but made sufficient in amount to support his family, as it should, desertions would be unknown. This subject involves the fate of the Confederacy. Notions of false economy ought to be discarded in considering it.

The conscript act ought to be revised. Every man between sixteen and sixty, who is able to serve the Confederacy in the army, whether in the ranks, or as an artisan or mechanic, laborer, teamster, cook, hospital attendant, or in any other capacity, ought to be put in service, without regard to avocation, or other plea.

There ought to be no exemptions whatever, except in the case of absolute and permanent physical disability. If by this means more soldiers are raised than necessary, it would be a very just and humane policy to grant furloughs to the old soldiers, and put the young conscripts in their places.

If the men out of the army are the "people," these ideas may fail of popular approval. That however, in no way affects their merits.

Under the same supposition, the last suggestion I have to make will be still more decidedly unpopular. It will be odious in the eyes of speculators, extortioners, refusers of Confederate money, evaders of conscription, deserters, harborers of deserters, spies, marauders, federalists, and that less respectable class who regard these others as the people and pander to them for their votes.

This obnoxious suggestion is. A vigorous and determined system of martial law, covering all the classes of evil doers mentioned above, and compelling them, by stern and swift punishment, either to leave the Confederacy or to bear their due part of the burthens of the war. Without martial law, loyal citizens and the fighting soldiers of the country, their wives and children,—are literally the prey of the basest of the population. The civil laws, State organizations, rights on paper and penalties in statute books, are inert and powerless to help them. A living, active, fearless assertion and enforcement of martial law alone can do it.—If much longer delayed, that remedy itself will come too late.

Respectfully,

T. C. HINDMAN.
Maj.-Gen commanding.

Lt.-Col. S. S. ANDERSON,
A. A. Gen'l. Trans-Miss., Department.

THE NEW YORK HERALD.

WHOLE NO. 9600. | NEW YORK, FRIDAY, DECEMBER 26, 1862. | PRICE THREE CENTS.

THE CAMPAIGN IN MISSISSIPPI.

Movements of Gen. Grant's Army.

THE THEATRE OF OPERATIONS.

Preliminaries to the Great Conflict.

Successful Reconnoissance by Union Troops.

Graphic Descriptions of Recent Military Affairs.

Our Troops Anxious to Move on the Enemy.

Great Battles Expected at Jackson and Vicksburg, Miss.

IMPORTANT FROM THE YAZOO RIVER.

RETURNING LOYALTY IN THE SOUTH.

Our Army and Naval Correspondence.

Destruction of Commerce, Miss., by Union Troops.

REBEL RAID INTO TRENTON, KY.

THE VERY LATEST,

&c., &c., &c.

The storm of war begun at Fredericksburg has not abated. It has only swept by, and will soon be felt in redoubled fury on the Mississippi. To that point everything indicates an impending battle, or series of battles, that will put a new phase on the war. The hostile armies are both moving into position for the coming conflict. Our own army—larger by far than that of Burnside—has already moved into the enemy's territory with some success, the rebels making but feeble resistance and falling back as the Union host advances.

The retrograde movement of the enemy ... Our Commanding General treats it thus. In this view of affairs matters on the Mississippi are looked upon with deep public solicitation. We therefore present to the readers of the HERALD to-day letters from our corps of correspondents accompanying the Mississippi expeditions which cannot fail to be read with deep interest, as the details of them record the preliminary movements and reconnoissances which are the sure auguries of an impending conflict. The letters of our correspondents are illustrated by the accompanying large map, showing the theatre of operations from Memphis to New Orleans, and comprising such portions of the States of Tennessee, Missouri, Arkansas, Mississippi, Alabama and Louisiana as lie within the menaced district. From the map a good idea may be formed of the position of both armies at the time of the date of our letters.

The late operations on the Yazoo river may be considered as a portion of and auxiliary to the Mississippi movement. The avant couriers of the great fleet of Admiral Porter have already felt the enemy's position. The great movement will soon follow.

The latest news from the Mississippi movement—the information coming via Cairo—states that the rebels were threatening General Grant's rear, taking Memphis as his base. It is reported in Memphis that the rebels have gone toward Grand Junction, with the intention of tearing up the road; but nothing is known positively. General Sherman has reached Helena, preparing to move down the river.

It is reported here that Jeff Thompson is moving on New Madrid with two thousand men, from Pocahontas, Ark., and that he was within forty miles of that place on the 22d inst. The rebel force operating in Northwestern Tennessee recently burned Union City and the bridge over the Onion river.

Our Yockena Correspondence.

IN CAMP, NORTH OF THE YOCKENA, Dec. 6, 1862.

THE ENEMY FALLING BACK.

The present pursuit of the enemy's fleeing columns is ended, and the cavalry division of our army has fallen back to the north of the Yockena. We have encountered the enemy, and have been forced to abandon the expedition with a considerable loss of men and material. The enemy had concentrated at Coffeeville an immense force of infantry, cavalry and artillery, which they studiously kept concealed until they had selected the position they desired, when they opened upon us with terrible effect and compelled a hasty retreat to Water Valley.

My last communication was dated in camp near that village, and in it I indicated our plans for the morrow. Col. Misener's Third brigade was ordered to take the advance, Col. Lee's first brigade the centre, and Col. Hatch, Second brigade, the rear. By some mistake in the selection of the route, Col. Misener switched off on the Paris road, and when he reached the Coffeeville road, five miles in advance, his position became the centre, while Col. Lee took the lead, and, in connection with Col. Dickey, who had charge of the expedition, directed our movements. We encamped on the night of the 4th at Water Valley, and two miles south of the Otuckafaffa, across which during the night an excellent bridge was discovered. At noon we were ready to start, and the column moved in the order indicated above.

ENCOUNTER IN WATER VALLEY.

There was no trouble on the route until we reached a point five miles from Water Valley, where we encountered the rebel videttes and a company or two of rebel cavalry. Our advance guard was strengthened and a line of skirmishers thrown out on either side of the road, which succeeded in putting to flight the enemy. They fell back to the hill in the rear, made a stand, were repulsed, and again made a stand on the hill to the rear. Just in front of this latter eminence was an open field and valley through which runs a small stream, each side of the field being skirted with heavy timber, with a dense undergrowth of brush and shrubs. Here Colonel Lee first planted his gun, and fired a dozen rounds of shell and shot, which caused the enemy to abandon the position. A little further on the gun was again planted, and the woods in advance again cleared. At a plantation owned by Wheelis the enemy made another decided stand, from which they were dislodged with considerable difficulty. From here on there was heavy skirmishing for a mile or more, until we reached another open field, where Colonel Lee planted his gun and threw a few shell in advance of our skirmishers. Hardly had the first exploded before the enemy replied with a full battery of heavy artillery, dropping the shell in dangerous proximity to our gun and column. Their shell exploded within ten feet of our cannon. Our small gun could stand no chance with the heavier metal of the enemy, and we were reluctantly compelled to retire with our piece of artillery.

Meanwhile the line of skirmishers and supports were heavily engaged in front and driven back by an overwhelming infantry and cavalry force. The rebel infantry advanced by regiments in solid column, driving everything before them. New lines and supports were formed and again driven back. When we reached the point where our gun was first placed in position we again unlimbered and fired a few rounds of grape and canister at the advancing column. The effect was terrible—men fell before the deadly fire like grain before the reapers' sickle; others, however, stepped forward to fill their places, and the column again moved steadily forward. When they had reached a point four rods from the mouth of the cannon Colonel Lee ordered it to be unlimbered and taken to the rear. Our column was now in full retreat, and companies and detachments were thrown out to the rear, right and left of the road, to protect us against flank movements. By a lane to our left two full regiments were marching upon our flank, and

IMPORTANT OPERATIONS AT THE SOUTHWEST.

Colonel Hatch, with his brigade, consisting of the Second Iowa and Seventh Illinois, were ordered to dismount and repel the attack. This was quickly done, and, concealing his men behind a sharp ridge, he waited patiently the rebel attack. When within twenty yards of our men, as they rose the crest of the hill, the order was given to fire. The order was obeyed with tremendous effect, and the rebels dropped by scores. Five times was the volley repeated, until our revolving rifles were emptied, and we retired to take another position. For two long miles was this attack and retreat continued, during which both officers and men performed prodigies of valor. Then the pursuit began to slacken, and finally ceased altogether. The column was once more in order, and we leisurely took our line of retreat to Water Valley.

The rebel loss we have no means of learning, but it was very much larger than our own, as their columns were solid and presented a better target for our revolving rifles.

Where all did so well it may seem to be invidious to mention particular instances of bravery. I cannot, however, forbear to refer to the distinguished gallantry of Col. Dickey, Col. Lee, Col. Hatch, Col. Misener, Lieut. Col. Prince, of the Seventh Illinois cavalry; Lieut. Col. McCullough, of the Fourth cavalry, and Major Coon, commanding the Second Iowa. There are other cases deserving special mention, but space forbids.

Our Oxford (Miss.) Correspondence.

OXFORD, Miss., Dec. 6, 1862.

The occupation of this point has put an end to our forward movement in force for the present. The supply trains, which have been greatly delayed by bad roads, will have to come up before we are in a condition to advance, though even then I do not anticipate a further movement until the railroad to this point is entirely repaired. The cars are now running regularly to Holly Springs. The railroad from the latter place to this is in a deplorable state, the most severe gap being at the Tallahatchie river, at which point three bridges and a large amount of trestle work has been completely destroyed. The engineers are now working rapidly to repair these breaks, in order to have them in readiness by the time the rest of the road is finished. At least three weeks will be required to complete the reconstruction.

A BOLD VENTURE.

The venture of this army, so distant from its base, constitutes one of the boldest, and promises to be one of the most effective, movements of the war. By it Tennessee has been quieted and apparently restored to the government. Mississippi is invaded, our army, successful and in excellent condition, is already some distance within her borders. It was the boast of the confederacy that our army could never enter this State, except through the ordeal of a most sanguinary conflict. We have entered it upon the heels of a disordered, panic stricken and suffering enemy. Those who spoke most loudly were the first to shirk the defence they conceived would contest our march. Impregnable positions have been evacuated. The country is open to us. It is said Grenada will be held against us. I cannot believe it. The position is not as good as many they have already left. It is true the location is one of vast importance in the operations of our army. This may make it worth a battle. The cause of the enemy is desperate in this section, and daily grows more impotent. If we secure Grenada they are lost—the desirable position is achieved. They will be able to make but a show of resistance before they give up the entire country.

A REBEL AMBUSCADE.

When near Coffeeville, a village about thirty miles south from here, before last, our cavalry came unexpectedly upon an ambuscade of a brigade of infantry and several pieces of artillery. Our men, though surprised, fought nobly, doing the enemy much damage, and subsequently withdrawing in order. Our losses, I have satisfactorily learned, are ten killed, twenty wounded and about thirty five missing or prisoners. Among the number killed is the lamented Lieutenant Colonel of the Fourth Illinois cavalry, Eben McCullough. It was at first reported that an entire company was cut off. Last evening it appeared in our camp, having cut its way out, bringing ten prisoners. This unexpected and uncivilized attack somewhat astonished our boys. They retired about twenty miles and there camped in order to repair what mischief they had suffered. In a few days we will hear of them again in their exploits.

A FLAG OF TRUCE.

Lieutenant D. H. Gile, aid to General McPherson, bearer of a flag of truce, left for the rebel lines yesterday and returned to-day. He proceeded as far as Coffeeville, just inside their pickets, when he was halted, while the papers addressed to General Pemberton were delivered and a reply made. The message was in relation to the exchange of prisoners, of which we have a large number. No satisfactory reply was made. Waiting several hours, Colonel Jackson and staff rode up with the information "that General Pemberton had gone out to ride." He offered to send it to General Van Dorn. The same response was returned. Finally General Lovell opened the papers, but made no satisfactory reply. I deduce from the above that Generals Pemberton and Van Dorn are in Grenada. ... is also at Grenada.

THE HEADQUARTERS OF GENERAL GRANT.

Oxford, where lies the centre of our army, is a beautiful place, both by nature and by art. In buildings it exhibits considerable affluence. In ornamentation it displays rare taste. The place is now nearly deserted by its population. In several instances dinner ... well supplied with the poor fare the people now ... South, were found deserted, though evidently designed for ... of the house, so sudden was our attack. Whither these ... direct their flight I cannot tell.

POSITION OF THE ARMY.

Our army is now in good position and pretty well concentrated. In natural fortification we hold a strong point. No attack from the rebels is anticipated, but it is a good thing to possess such a location. General Grant now has his headquarters here; so also has General McPherson.

A RECONNOISSANCE.

During the late movements our forces have been very successful in the capture of a large number of prisoners. The entire number thus far brought in amount to fourteen commissioned officers, seventy-six sergeants, twenty corporals and six hundred and fifty privates. I add a list of officers. They are as follows:—

CAPTURE OF REBEL OFFICERS.

Major C. Duckworth, First Tennessee cavalry; J. C. Word, Surgeon. Captain W. A. Rogers, Fourth Mississippi cavalry; Captain H. H. Patton, Fifteenth Mississippi infantry; Captain J. H. Shaw, Quartermaster on the staff of General Van Dorn; Lieutenant E. A. Hatchet, Second Arkansas; Lieutenant S. J. Willis, Fourth Mississippi Cavalry; Lieutenant R. B. Patton, Tennessee Reserve artillery; Lieutenant A. J. Williamson, Fiftieth Alabama infantry; Lieutenant J. L. Sandford, Second Arkansas cavalry; Lieutenant J. M. Burkhead, First Arkansas cavalry; Lieutenant J. F. Weister, Ballanstine cavalry; Lieutenant J. McCoy, Ballanstine cavalry; Assistant Surgeon E. H. McClendon.

OXFORD, Miss., Dec. 9, 1862.

OUR CAVALRY OPERATIONS.

The retreat of the rebel forces before the advance of Gen. Grant's army, though mainly owing to the disposition of our infantry, was brilliantly followed up by the cavalry. In fact, all the engagements have been with the cavalry, and the rebel retrograde movement rendered by it painful and disastrous. Our men were incessantly upon their rear, harassing them upon every opportunity. I feel confident they suffered dreadfully in killed and wounded, many of the latter having fallen into our hands. There is no doubt but the dash of our onset in offensive operations has greatly to do with the fear of the enemy to encounter our forces.

The particulars of the cavalry movements since our first engagement of the enemy north of the Tallahatchie will be of interest, and importance. I therefore give them somewhat at length.

It was on the morning of December 2, after a severe running fight on the preceding day, that Col. A. L. Lee, commanding First brigade of the cavalry division, crossed the Tallahatchie river during the night and entered the enemy's works (which were evacuated except by a small party of observation) at the head of the Seventh Kansas, Fourth Illinois, Third Michigan and a battalion of the Second Iowa cavalry. A brief skirmish occurred here, which resulted in the flight of the rebels towards their main body, in march southward. In close pursuit we pushed forward to Abbeville, about six miles on the main road.

At this point Major Moyer, with the Third Michigan cavalry, was sent south on the road west of the railroad, while the rest of the command pursued the main Oxford road. When five miles south of Abbeville our cavalry came up to the rear guard of the enemy's cavalry. We drove it steadily a distance of three miles, without experiencing any strong opposition.

When three miles north of Oxford the enemy's cavalry made another and more determined stand, opening upon our men with two pieces of artillery. A half hour's severe skirmishing sufficed to drive the enemy from his position with considerable loss, among the number being his two gunners, who were killed while serving the guns. Before reaching Oxford they made two more stands, placing their guns in position and firing upon our men. After some severe fighting the enemy was dislodged.

Colonel Jackson, General Pemberton's Chief of Cavalry, had command of the enemy's cavalry, and was in person in the fight.

In the three affairs we took about sixty prisoners. Major Duckworth, commanding the First Tennessee cavalry, is one of the number.

After the third engagement the rebel cavalry retired below Oxford, leaving the Forty-third Mississippi, Second Texas and a regiment of infantry in the town. The Second Texas was posted at the court house, the other regiments a short distance in their rear. Dismounting the larger portion of his command, Colonel Lee deployed them, and, with cavalry supports, entered the town. A sharp street fight ensued, in which the enemy was worsted, driven out, and our forces took possession. Over two hundred prisoners were taken during the day.

Major Moyer, owing to unavoidable circumstances, did not reach Oxford until the following morning. He experienced severe skirmishing the entire distance, and succeeded in capturing fourteen prisoners. His own loss was an officer and three privates wounded.

THE AFFAIR AT COFFEEVILLE.

On the morning of December 3, being ordered to con-

The Oregon Statesman.

VOL. 12---NO. 43. SALEM, OREGON, MONDAY, DEC. 29, 1862. WHOLE NO. 615

Estate of John Fresh, Dec'd.

Probate Court, Marion County, ss.

THIS day, Dec. 1st, 1862, came Benjamin Stanton, executor of the last will and testament of John Fresh, deceased, and presented his petition, asking the court for an order to sell the real estate of decedent. It is therefore ordered that Tuesday, the 6th day of January, A. D., 1863, be set apart for the hearing said petition, at which time all persons interested are notified to appear and show cause why such order should not be granted; and that this notice be published four successive weeks in the Oregon Statesman newspaper. JOHN C. PEEBLES,
4w40 County Judge

Administratrix' Notice.

NOTICE is hereby given that I have been appointed Administratrix of the estate of J. G. Lincoln, late of Linn county, Oregon, deceased. I hereby notify all persons having just claims against said estate to present them to me at my residence in Albany, Linn county, Oregon, with the necessary vouchers, within one year from this date, or forever thereafterwards be barred. ELIZABETH C. LINCOLN,
Dec. 1st, 1862—4w49 Administratrix.

Notice to Absent Defendant.

Anthony Weddle, Pl'ff, *vs.* B. Genoise, Deft. In Co. Court of Polk county, State of Oregon, March Term, A. D., 1863.

TO B. GENOISE, Deft in the above entitled cause—You are hereby notified that an action has been commenced against you by said Anthony Weddle, Pl'ff, above named, in the county court of Polk Co. and State [illegible] the demand of said plaintiff against you in the sum of one hundred and seventy-five dollars ($175) with legal interest thereon from the first day of June, A. D., 1856, said demand arising upon contract entered into by you with said plaintiff before the said 1st day of June, A.D., 1856. Now, unless you appear in the county court of said Polk county, State of Oregon, on the 1st Monday of March, A. D., 1863, and answer the complaint of plaintiff in said cause on file, the same will be taken for confessed, and the prayer thereof will be granted by the court. CATON & CURL,
Att'ys for Pl'ff.
Salem, Dec. 5th, A. D., 1862. 3m40

In Justice's Court.

State of Oregon, county of Marion, ss.

TO H. L. PRESTON—You are hereby notified that a writ of attachment has been issued against you and your property attached to satisfy the demand of Abner Allen, amounting to fifty dollars; now, unless you shall appear before Volney Leonard, a Justice of the Peace in and for said county, at his office in Silver Creek precinct, on the 26th day of January, 1863, at 1 o'clock in the afternoon, judgment will be rendered against you and your property sold to pay the debt.
Dated this 2d day of December, 1862.
4w40paid ABNER ALLEN, Pl'ff.

Notice.

Circuit Court of the State of Oregon for the county of Marion. March Term, 1863. F. X. Matthieu, Pl'ff *vs.* Joseph Hebert and Joseph Matte, Def'ts.

TO JOSEPH HEBERT—You are hereby notified that suit has been commenced against you and Joseph Matte, by said plaintiff, and your property attached to answer the demand of plaintiff in the sum of $2,115 48. Now, unless you appear in said circuit court at Salem, in Marion county, on the 2d Monday in March, 1863, and answer the complaint in this cause filed, the same will be taken as confessed, and the prayer thereof will be granted by the court.
By order of the court at Chambers, Dec. 1862.
CATON & CURL, Att'ys for Pl'ff.
Salem, Ogn., Dec. 5th, 1862. 3m40

Notice.

AS I am about to be absent from the State for several months, Mr. Lucien Heath, of Salem, will attend to business for me in my absence. Persons indebted to me will please settle up with him as my agent. JOSEPH HOLMAN.
Salem, Dec. 31, 1860. 43tf

WHAT GREELEY PREDICTED WHEN HE WAS NOT AN ABOLITIONIST.

There was a time when Horace Greeley was not an abolitionist—that is to say, when, whatever might have been his private notions about negro freedom and negro equality, he did not act with the abolition party. In 1844, Horace Greeley was a Whig, a warm supporter of Henry Clay, and a bitter enemy of political abolitionism. During the presidential canvass of that year, Greeley issued from the *Tribune* office a series of political tracts. In one of these tracts he tried very hard to persuade the Whigs, some of whom had shown decided abolition symptoms, how wrong it would be in them to leave the old Whig party and unite their fortunes with the abolitionists. Then Greeley saw abolitionism as it really was—he was not then its dupe and victim himself. He saw abolitionism then just as Clay, Webster, Cass, Douglas and hosts of other leading intellects of the country saw it, and he exposed its inevitable consequence to the country just as these great statesmen on many memorable occasions had depicted it. In one of the political tracts to which we have referred above, Horace Greeley wrote as follows—and, oh, how true he spoke of the monster iniquity! Who would have supposed that Horace Greely wrote these burning words of denunciation against abolitionism?—

"We are not fond of alarming topics, nor disposed to excite unnecessary anxiety. But the *evils of political abolition, rising up in the north,* must be faced, and THE CONSEQUENCES IT TENDS TO must be considered. However averse the people of the free States may be to slavery, (and we believe they are almost universally so,) yet they cannot but feel that the *remedy of political abolition* is WORSE THAN THE DISEASE; first, because the rudeness and violence of the treatment only aggravate it; and next, because they fear that the medicine, if administered as proposed, *will kill both the patient and the doctor.* A DISSOLUTION OF THE UNION WOULD BE AS CERTAIN as any effect of a moral cause that can be reckoned on. Nor is it likely that *this* would be the end. The political asperities and exasperations that would grow out of such a conflict would themselves naturally be breeders of *other convulsions;* and it would not be strange if SOME CHIEFTAIN or chieftains should rise up in the struggle, *to make slaves of all freemen,* and bind in stronger chains those whom, by such means, it is proposed to set free.

"We are a family of States, bound together by a covenant solemnly ratified, which prescribes THE RIGHTS of each. In this family, concord is beautiful: but *family quarrels* are the worst of all. Civil war is the most terrible and desolating of all wars, and most difficult to be brought to an end. Look to Spain. Will any one say, that *such a movement as the* POLITICAL ABOLITION OF THE NORTH, *does not put in jeopardy the peace of this Union,* AND THE UNION ITSELF? And can any human foresight tell what *scene of strife* it is likely to produce, if it should be encouraged to pass on its way towards the supreme power of the nation, which is now its avowed aim?"

SHINPLASTERS.—The lively New York correspondent of the Sacramento *Union* gives a genial chapter on shinplasters, as follows:

Shinplasters! Lord love you, we paper our houses with our currency, and it doesn't take above five dollars worth to cover the walls of [illegible] Where does it come from? Who makes it? Everywhere and everybody. How do they dodge the law? Just as easy as a pet government tailor gets $18 apiece for $6 uniform coats, or a nephew to a Cabinet Minister's "dear friend" $200 a horse for a lot of twenty-year-old, spavined, ringboned, sweeneyed drove of four-footed abominations, that you can hear wheeze as far off as a locomotive. For instance, there's Rushton who sells soda water and fine tooth combs under the Astor House, issues as much currency, almost, as Uncle Sam. How? Thus: The shinplaster reads "Broadway Bank pay to bearer on demand ten cents. T. Rushton" Any man, you see, can issue a "check;" and such is our desperate condition as to "change" that any one will take it. I actually saw a fellow the other day cut a dollar note into four pieces, and pass each piece for twenty-five cents. Then last week you couldn't even coax any of the city banks to pay out small bills to their best customers. The street beggars hail you with "Please, sir, I hain't had no breakfast, and my mammy's got sixteen small children and twelve at the breast—won't you give us a postage stamp?" Great King! if there ever was a diabolical nuisance it is those stamps. You give a man a five dollar note in a hope to pay for a dollar's worth of anything, and he hands you back four dollars in stamps, ninety-nine out of a hundred of which look as if they had been serving a year among Jeff. Davis' ragamuffins—they're so crumpled, bleared, defaced and filthy dirty.

Let the world slide. Who cares? Army contractors have got money, and their wives are getting diamonds. They are in such a hurry to turn greenbacks into sparklers that Tiffany and Ball & Black can't keep up with the demand. Everything is going up—up in a balloon—in price. Real estate, thank Heaven, is going up with it at last. I've got a little, and if the tide holds may be able to sell out by Spring and get square on what it has cost me to raise soldiers and fight a campaign on the soil of Virginia. Lots about the Central Park begin to touch the ante-war figure, and bricks and mortar smile again above—Bleecker.—Swing out the shinplasters and forward—double quick—with the grand forty million power gas and gammon inflation. That's what's the matter. Hurrah for speculation!

CHING FOO.

SALEM, Dec. 23, 1862.

ED. STATESMAN—I wish to record my protest against that inclination of "tinkering" sciolism, which prompts the "'Oly Brigadier" to remodel the orthography of Willamette.—What "spiritual inclination" induces him to substitute the gutteral, prosaic, cacophonous Wallamet, for the melodious, poetical and common pronunciation, is not evident. If this hypercritic pedant aspires to the rank of a neologist, we hope the good sense of the people will discountenance his innovations, if they are as ill-begotten as this one, and I doubt the proficiency of any cockney to arrogate the tenor of our dialect, or abrogate a time-honored provincialism, if such it be. This "gentleman of aspirations" evidently prides himself of his superficial ken of Indian traditionary lore; but he cannot succeed in palming this Siwash barbarism, on the general attic tendency of the age. In my opinion we al[ready] have too many Indian idioms engraft[ed] on the language; and when it appears to be Pearne's province to propagate the evil, it should be the policy of the enlightened to eradicate it.

Yours respectfully. C.

Pearne's pedantry and cockneyism is also displayed in his affected pronunciation of the words either and neither as ither and nither.

PASTED SHOES.—Some of the regiments attached to the Army of the Potomac had issued to them, while at Harper's Ferry, the requisite number of new shoes to which they were entitled. Some of these same shoes are now without soles. Upon examination, it has been discovered that neither pegs nor thread were used in the manufacture of the same, but that the soles were merely pasted on. The President has made a great mistake in not setting on foot measures, long ago, to have certain army contractors hung.

WHAT IT IS THAT HAS BROUGHT DOWN THE GOVERNMENT CREDIT.

The Philadelphia *Ledger*, an independent paper, of the 18th Nov., in its money article, asks:

"Why is it that the stocks of the government paying a regular interest of six per cent per annum, in specie, equal, at the present rate of gold, to 8¼ per cent in currency, show little or no improvement in price, while other six per cent. stocks, interest payable in currency, equal to about 4½ specie, and liable to double the tax imposed on government stocks, bring a large premium?

There is a matter for serious thought in this question, and those who have charge of the government at Washington, should ponder it well. It is a bad sign when the stocks of the government are thus low in the estimation of our own people. It looks as though they were losing confidence in our rulers. Doubtless, the great amount of dishonesty on the part of men in high places, and on the part of lobbymen, who are known to [hold] great influence in government circles, has had much to do in reducing government stock below other stocks in the market. The known fact that millions of dollars have been plundered from the public treasury, and the probability that this stupendous swindling may not cease for two years to come, have done much to weaken public confidence. The well known fact that such men as John W. Forney exert a great influence in Washington, and aid in shaping the policy of the administration, has been very damaging to the credit of the government, and the facts lately revealed that the agents of the administration in this city have prostituted their authority, has helped to impair public confidence in our managers at Washington. It has become apparent to the public, that, notwithstanding the great distress and danger which the country is in, and notwithstanding the "no party" professions of the administration and its friends, the authorities in the Federal city are conducting affairs on a bigoted, partisan basis. None but abolitionists are appointed to offices of any kind—none but abolitionists are advised with—the policy of the abolitionists has been adopted as the policy of the government, and everything goes to show that the administration is partisan in its character. This fact, as the late election in this State, Ohio, and Indiana shows, is poorly calculated to enlist public confidence in the Administration. Consequently, our government stocks are lower in the market than ordinary stocks, and Treasury notes are from thirty to forty per cent. below the specie standard.

Now that the people have spoken, we trust that the administration will mend its ways, and try to restore itself to public confidence. As a partial means of doing this, Mr. Lincoln should discard all radicals and lunatics from among his advisers, whether inside or outside of his official circle; should pay Forney to stay away from Washington (where he now remains for pay); and close the Treasury doors against all thieves. If he will do this he will do much to raise the price of government stocks, and to revive the confidence of the people.

☞ A correspondent of the Boston *Courier*, an old whig paper, says:

On the boat from New York I had an opportunity of talking with a soldier from Louisiana, taken at Antietam and paroled. He was secesh to the back-bone, said the South was out, that was the uniform opinion in his army. By no means, said he, but the number in favor of of the old Union was daily growing less, and after Northern elections this fall there would not be a vestige left of the Unionists. I asked him what the elections had to do with it.—He said:

"The abolitionists will carry every State, and that will settle the conscience of every old liner in the South."

"But," said I, "suppose the abolitionists are beaten—and there is a chance for it even in egotistical old Massachusetts, and a still better one in New York, and almost a certain one in Pennsylvania.

"Then," said he, "it would be a bad sight for us."

"Why?" said I. "Indeed I don't see it."

"Well," replied he, "every d——d North Carolinian, and half of the rest of them, would then throw down their guns and swear they would not fight another minute. I tell you there is not one thing old Jeff. prays for so much as to have Wadsworth put in Governor of New York. I was in Richmond when the papers with the nominations came, and they all said there could not have been a more lucky nomination for the South, for Wadsworth, having been in Washington, is known, and he will be elected.

"The abolitionists have got control of the North just as we have of the South, and they don't want us any more than we do them, and what persons of both sides don't want they won't have. If Wadsworth should be beaten, and Andrew should be beaten, and the rest of them it would just show that a majority of the North want us back in the old Union, and there are so many now in the South who want the same thing, we should have to come back. But I tell you the abolitionists will have it their own way, and we shall have it all our way, and your Northern old line Unionists and their relations down South will have to cave in."

Much more he said, but enough on this point.

WHERE ARE GREELEY'S NINE HUNDRED THOUSAND?—Where under the sun are Greeley's nine hundred thousand abolitionists?

They certainly have not enlisted; for our armies still need recruits, and Massachusetts, the great abolition State, is obliged to resort to a draft, in spite of her offers of two hundred dollars bounty.

They certainly have not voted; for Pennsylvania and the Northwestern States have given abolitionism the cold shoulder most decidedly, and the State of New York shows a strong disposition to go to the polls and do likewise.

The conservative nine hundred thousand voted at the recent elections, as the results prove. The fact that conservative New Jersey, slaveholding Delaware and anti-negro Illinois have all filled their quotas without drafting is in strange contrast to the case of abolition Massachusetts, and proves that a great many more thousands of conservatives have recently joined our armies.

The emancipation proclamation, therefore, instead of stopping the war and destroying the rebels, has only stopped enlistments and destroyed the abolition party. How do Greeley and Andrew feel now? How are their swarms of recruits and their fabled nine hundred thousand?—*N. Y. Herald.*

"UNION MEN."—The bakers' dozen of abolitionists living in our midst, claim to be the only "Union men left," and denounce all others as "secessionists." Pretty talk this for fellows who for the last ten years have been denouncing the "constitution as a league with hell," and who even now are determined to have an anti slavery Union, or none at all. Such fellows as these were the original secessionists and are not fit to wipe the shoes of the men they denounce.—*Mountaineer.*

☞ The Augusta, Georgia, papers announce the arrival in that city of Morse, formerly editor of the Bridgeport *Farmer*, of Connecticut, which was destroyed and himself hunted by the Lincolnites on account of his advocacy of Southern rights and opposition to the war.

ARE "GREENBACKS" A LEGAL TENDER?

On November 18th, in the Supreme Court of New York State, the question of U. S. paper money being a legal tender arose. The case (an agreed one) was before Judges Ingraham, Leonard and Peckham. Here is a brief statement of the matter:

Lewis H. Meyer *vs.* James J. Roosevelt.—This case came from the Court below, on a statement of facts agreed upon. The plaintiff claims that the defendant should deliver up a certain bond and mortgage to be cancelled and give a certificate of acknowledgment of satisfaction sufficient to discharge the same of record. The defendant remits the claim. In August, 1854, one Bowne gave his bond for $8,000 with interest, payable half-yearly. The bond was to secure a loan made to Bowne of $8,000, for which the defendant gave his check on the Chemical Bank, payable in gold, at the option of Bowne. As a further security, Bowne gave a mortgage on real estate on Staten Island. On the 11th of June, [illegible] $8,170, being the amount of the principal and interest due, in notes of the United States, issued under the act of Congress, approved February 25, 1862, for the redemption and funding of the floating debt of the United States. The defendant refused to receive the same as a legal tender, and claimed that the repayment should be in gold.

It was thereupon agreed to submit the question of legal tender to this Court, and if it should be decided that the said notes were not legal tender, then the plaintiff should pay $326 78 with interest, and the defendant deliver up the bond and mortgage to be cancelled. If the Court decide otherwise then the bond will be delivered up without further payment, thus bringing up the question of whether the notes of the United States Government are or are not a legal tender in this or any other commercial or monetary community.

George Tichnor Curtis, in arguing the case for plaintiff, held these points:

1. The legal tender act, like other statutes expressed in general terms, is to be so construed, independent of any constitutional provisions on the subject, as not to interfere with vested rights or change the effects or impair the obligations of existing contracts. The term "all debts," therefore, used in the act must be taken to mean "all debts hereafter contracted.

2. To give to the act a retrospective operation would be to assume that Congress, in violation of the oath of its members, intended to usurp a power "not delegated to the United States by the Constitution," but on the contrary, either "prohibited by it to the States as well as to the United States or reserved to the States respectively or to the people" (Articles 10 and 5 of the amendments to the Constitution.) The Constitution gives to Congress no power, except in cases of bankruptcy, to pass any act impairing the obligation of such acts; but, on the contrary, declares that "no person shall be deprived of life, liberty, or property without due process of law." An act, therefore, which in effect transfers the property of one citizen to another without the consent, without equivalent, and without judicial proceedings, by the mere will of the Legislature, is unconstitutional and void.

3. Congress had no power, under the Con[illegible] circulation as money, or to coin "money" out of any substance other than metal, or to make anything but metalic coin a compulsory tender in payment of debt.

In the articles of confederation the power was expressly given—in those of the Constitution it was expressly withheld. This is shown by a comparison of the two instruments, and is confirmed by the journal of the convention.

THE NEXT PRESIDENCY.—The Sacramento *Union* suggests, that if the rebellion be suppressed by force of arms, the Presidency will be the reward of the General whose record is most brilliant in the history of the war. At the rate the work of suppressing the rebellion has progressed for the past year and a half, there is little prospect of its being put down before the next Presidential election; but if peace should be restored, it is a matter of little consequence—except to politicians and spoil seekers—who is elected. In times of peace, when there is nothing to do but follow the precedents of office, a man of ordinary capacity will make a respectable ruler. But in troublous times like the present, we need a man for President who has the talent to govern according to circumstances—one who can rule on original principles as well as by following the example of his predecessors. General Butler has shown more of this talent than any one else who has been brought prominently before the public since the war commenced, and so far as the capabilities of men are known, he is the best qualified for President. Gov. Andy Johnson has also shown considerable talent for governing; and if General Banks' expedition is destined for the occupation of Texas, he will have an excellent opportunity to show his incapacity.

The student of history need not be told that men capable of governing on original principles are much more common than great military geniuses. The chances are hardly one in a thousand that a Napoleon or a Cæsar will appear upon the stage of action during the present civil war. But in the absence of such a man, the best the people can do will be to place in the Executive chair the man who has shown the most ability for governing according to circumstances.—*Nevada Democrat.*

GEN. HOOKER.—A correspondent of the N. Y. *Evening Post*, says:

Make way for the center grand division, under Hooker! Let the foe who fronts the men he leads look well to their lines that day. How like a lion he stormed down on their beaten, broken lines at Antietam. When he started that morning, impetuous, resistless, his men, who had caught the fiery impulse of their chief, halted for no obstacle and were stayed by no foe. Over infantry, cavalry, artillery, they fought their way, and, as they went it was clear to see that by midday this resistless advance would roll up the rebel hosts like a scroll, at nine o'clock, Hooker fell, struck by a ball, men who had watched his splendid advance, his magnificent success exclaimed, "Where is the man who will follow up these glorious advantanges, or who will see that they are followed up?" No such man followed Hooker that day. On a distant part of the field, Burnside, stubbornly fighting his way to the bridge, and then across it, did wonders. But no mind equal to maintaining the fruits of Hooker,s grand advance lightened over that part of the field of Antietam.

☞ The Washington correspondent of the Sacramento *Union* says:

Congressman Sargent also made to Secretary Chase some representations in regard to the anomalous condition of things being produced in California by the attempt of the Government to introduce legal tenders—the hardships of Government employes, who had to lose so much percentage of their pay, and the higher price the Government was compelled to pay to cover the margin of discount. Chase expressed an anxiety to do nothing that should embarrass the business of California, or change its currency to its disadvantage. He intended to send no more legal tenders until further advised as to the policy of doing so. He said he had representations of merchants in favor of sending them out, and some adverse to such a course.

PRENTICE-ISMS.

Gen. Beauregard proposes, in a letter to Bragg, to call the Union men abolitionists.—Beauregard is great at calling names. He calls himself by a name that he never got by his father or mother.

A couple of Bowling Green friends ask us to "give John Morgan fits." We will try to give him a nice fit before long. What is the size of your neck John?

Put Gen. Pillow's mind in one scale and an inflated bladder in the other, and the General will have a well-balanced mind.

Our rebel invaders must have had a high opinion of Kentucky. They took a good deal of stock in it.

In a few weeks it will probably be a fair question for secession debating societies whether the rebellion is wound up or run down.

If the people of Charleston wish to burn their city rather than see it fall into Federal hands, let them. We can stand the blaze if they can.

Gov. Wise is still talking about "Old John Brown." [illegible] hasn't got half of old Brown's [illegible] of old Brown's last sensations.

The officers of Bragg's army have reported to the Southern papers that they had a three days' battle with Buell. They evidently mistook a five days' foot-race for a three days' fight.

A paroled rebel writes us a silly letter, telling us that he has "lost one leg in the Confederate cause," and is "ready to lose the other." The fellow evidently has a wooden head, and, if he gets a pair of wooden legs, he will sell pretty well in a hard Winter as fuel.

Gen. Scott's exposition of the treason of Buchanan, whilst President, is terrible. We don't see why anybody should be in Fort Warren or Fort Lafayette while Buchanan is out. And we don't see why the earth should continue to bring forth hemp if Buchanan is to remain unhung.

☞ In Ohio and Pennsylvania the radicals try to make fun of their affliction! The Toledo *Blade* says:

The backbone counties are giving us "fits." They have gone back to their first love, and "liberty lies bleeding." But "Truth crushed to earth will rise again." Hail Columbia!—Nil desperandum! Erin go Unum, E Pluribus Bragh! Go it Butternuts! hemp is plenty.

The Cleveland *Herald*, republican, says:

We feel like the boy who, when his skin was "licked" off his back, asked his father to hold up. Says he, "Dad, let's argur." But the democrats won't "argur," they say time for argument has gone by, and they—laugh all the time.

The same paper "feels" again as follows:

We feel like the grocery keeper when a temperance convention was in session, and everybody was asking for a drink of water. He got out of patience and requested the "water drinkers to go to the pump." So we say to the democrats that have all the morning forced us to shake hands—go to the d—— dispatches.

In Pennsylvania the Ebensburg *Alleghanian* thus laughs off its sorrow.

"Tremenjuous vic-to-ry!—[in a horn!]—Little Cambria heard from! The news by no means cheering! Entire locofoco county ticket elected! 'That's what's the matter!' The 'unterified' on the rampage at the result."

[Here is a cut of a monkey taking a drink].

"Things like these, you know must be

"Well—we have met the enemy another time, and another time are we his—body, breeches and carpet-bag! Once more we have been gloriously routed, cut to pieces, quartered and drawn, decapitated, and otherwise badly used up. Our entire ticket is probably beaten by overwhelming majorities, and our calculations in the main knocked into a very cocked hat. Salt River is just at present the base of operations of our defeated but not dismayed organization.

"So we go! One day we see-saw to the top of the pile; the next we simmer down quietly to a back seat without cushions. Such is life generally, and who can complain?"

ARE LEGAL TENDER NOTES MONEY?—The San Francisco *Herald* has the following notice of a case in this connection:

Not long since the Supreme Court of this State decided that United States Treasury, or legal tender notes, were not payable for local taxes, and now the question arises whether they are legally payable for anything. The important issue is before the Twelfth District Court, in the case of James Lick vs. William Faulkner and others. The defendants are tenants of plaintiff, and lately tendered him "greenbacks" in payment of rent due. He refused to receive them, and now sues for the amount of the bill in coin. H. H. Haight, who argued the case for the plaintiff, contended that legal tender paper was in effect worthless for payment of any debts whatever, as the Constitution gave no authority for the issuance of any but gold and silver coin. H. M. Hastings, who spoke for more than three hours for the defendants, expounded the Constitution, to show that the Government had express power to coin money, and that that "money" might be of any material which might be deemed most fit, as the word "money" did not, of necessity, mean gold or silver or any other metal. The arguments were very able and interesting, and were heard by a large representation of the bar, and many members of the mercantile community also. The case, whatever may be Judge Sawyer's decision, will be appealed to the Supreme Court.

AN OATH OF ALLEGIANCE.—The Frankfort (Ky.) *Commonwealth* has the following:

We give below, verbatim et literatim, et punctuatim, the following orthographical curiosity. It is the copy of an oath of "aleagens" (angeltic allegiance), written out by a guerrilla captain who captured George W. Johnson, of the Fourth Kentucky Infantry, and required him to sign it. We give it as a remarkable specimen of literature, which shows as distinct a rebellion against Webster and Worcester, as against the Government:

Oath or aleagens to the Confedarat Stats Government I solemny swar that I will Not Bar or or take up armes aganse the Confedarat Stats or her army Duering The present War if Shall last ten yeares from this time and that I will Discountenanse Abolitionism let it come from what ever sourse it may for which I am willing to plege my honor and life & property in the Sacred promase of the same—So help me God. GEORGE W. JOHNSON.

That knocks the sand from under Gozef.

PEANUTS IN CALIFORNIA.—The *Bulletin* remarks:

Some 10,000 pounds of peanuts were raised in Yolo and Sacramento counties during the last year; 8,000 pounds of which were purchased by a firm in this city. Had it not been for the flood, there probably would have been over 20,000 pounds produced. The first lot of peanuts raised in this State came into market about three years ago. Their cultivation has been so successful that it is probable the importation of them will entirely cease within the next two years. Dealers purchase them of the producers at twenty cents per pound, and wholesale them at twenty-five cents.

Vice President Hamlin, President of the National Freedmen's Association, appeals to the public for contributions of clothing. There are five hundred destitute blacks in Washington alone.

Eastern News.

Rebel Raid into Poolesville.

WASHINGTON, 15th.

At 8 o'clock last night, 400 rebel cavalry made a dash into Poolesville and captured twenty Federals. They surrendered only after the building in which they were was set on fire. The rebels lost two killed and thirteen wounded.

From the Rappahannock---The Killed and Wounded.

NEW YORK, 16th.

The whole number of killed, wounded and missing of Franklin's division is 5,932. Our army, on Sunday, was mostly engaged in caring for the wounded and burying the dead.—Burnside has been reinforced by General Sigel's corps. General Burnside has, unquestionably, good reasons for delaying another attack.

Southern Accounts of General Foster's Movements.

FORTRESS MONROE, 14th.

Southern papers say that General Foster's North Carolina force is designed to co-operate, either by direct [illegible] or by attempting to seize our railroad communication at Weldon. Richmond papers acknowledge a loss of 225 at the battle of Hartsville, Tennessee.

Rebel View of Federal Preparations and Intentions.

The Richmond *Examiner* says the preparations of the United States, to subjugate the South are now truly gigantic. In the East, West and North, on land and water, everywhere, on all sides, the movement of Federal armies and fleets indicate zeal, hope, fanaticism and desperate avidity that should banish from every Southerner's mind all thought of an early peace, and nerve every Southern hand for battle, in which there will be no quarter.—Northern Virginia is again overrun; Richmond, Petersburg, Weldon, Charleston and Mobile are once more threatened; Texas, undefended, lies bleeding at every pore; the enemy's forces are being concentrated in Missouri and Kansas for the invasion of Arkansas; communication between Richmond and the West is menaced at Chatanooga and Knoxville; the Mississippi and its tributaries are bristling with gunboats, and operations will begin as soon as the floods come. The free labor movement which has been extensively, but quietly organized in Eastern North Carolina, is now understood to be preparatory to an organization of the government of the State on a loyal basis, so that North Carolina may accept President Lincoln's policy of emancipation.

The Federal Army Re-cross the Rappahannock.

HEADQUARTERS ARMY, 16th—1:30 P.M.

During last night, the army of the Potomac evacuated the position of opposite bank of the river. The movement was a perilous one, but it was conducted in safety. The artillery was first across the river. The last of the infantry brought up the rear shortly after daylight.—The enemy never discovered our movement until too late to do us any damage. As soon as the last man got safely over, the pontoon bridges were removed, thus cutting off communication between the two shores. Our wounded are all safe on this side.

Bank's Expedition.

CHICAGO, 16th.

[illegible] papers say a Port Royal letter, da[illegible]tes that it passed there on the 8th [illegible].

Accide[illegible]ses Taylor.

SAN FRANCISCO, 16th.

The opposition steamer *Moses Taylor* returned to port this morning, having broke her centre shaft on the 12th at 9 P. M., during a severe gale. She soon fell into the trough of the sea and lost her foremast. Next morning the port engine was disconnected. The starboard engine was put to work and she got under way for San Francisco. During the night of the gale an unknown passenger jumped overboard. The passengers speak well of the steamer, stating that none but a good steamer, disabled, would have withstood the gale. The *Herman* will probably be chartered to take her place.

The Rappahannock Rising.

WASHINGTON, 16th.

The following dispatch, dated Falmouth, 8:45 this morning, has just been received:—Raining fast; the river is rising rapidly, and all our troops are on this side of the river, and the pontoons up.

Speculations About Changes in the Cabinet.

NEW YORK, 16th.

The Washington correspondent of the *Commercial Advertiser* of the 15th says: If our army is crowned with victory before Fredericksburg, it will insure the appointment of Judge Holt as successor to Secretary Smith, but should any mishap occur, it may lead to a reconstruction of the Cabinet and recall McClellan to the command. Already we have speculations and rumors on the subject, but like everything else, the war news is to decide. In the meanwhile, almost every one is excited with feverish impatience.

Jeff. Davis at Murfreesboro,

A scout from Murfreesboro says that Jeff. Davis in a speech there on Friday, said Tennessee must be held at all hazards. General Polk also made a speech, and said he expected Grant to be defeated at the next battle, and then Nashville is to be assailed. There are about 40,000 rebels between Murfreesboro and Nashville.

Supremacy of the Civil Law Declared in Kentucky.

CAIRO, 16th.

There is nothing new from Oxford.

General Grant has issued an order respecting Kentucky, that as that State has fulfilled the requirements of the Constitution of the United States and the laws of Congress, by choosing Union men to fill State offices and execute the laws, the military authorities are prohibited from any interference. The military is not to be used except to suppress riots and mob resistance to the laws; all civil authority that can be effected at military posts will be permitted.

Report of McClellan's Recall to the Command.

The San Francisco *Herald* of the 17th has the following:

MC CLELLAN AGAIN.—We were assured at a late hour last night, that dispatches had been received announcing the recall of Gen. McClellan to the command of the Potomac.—[Very doubtful].

Money Market.

NEW YORK, 16th.

Exchange, 145¼@146; Gold, 32¾@32¼; Stocks, without change; Demand Notes, 27½.

Burnside's Retreat a Military Necessity.

NEW YORK, 17th.

The morning papers are filled with detailed accounts of Saturday's fighting at Fredericksburg. They contain no reliable news, but comprise mainly incidents relating to the battle. The *Times* says Burnside's retreat across the river was to avoid a battle which would result in nothing but loss of valuable life. Their correspondent adds that Sebastopol was not half so strong as this rebel position. A dispatch to Halleck from Burnside, received last night, says Burnside feeling fully convinced that the position in front could not be carried, it was a military necessity to either attack or retreat, a repulse would have been disastrous.

Rebels Advance their Pickets to the River --Robbing the Dead.

HEADQUARTES ARMY, 17th.

Yesterday morning the enemy seemed astonished to find us on this side of the river.—About 9 o'clock they advanced skirmishers along the entire line, and established pickets on the river bank. We had a large number of dead on what was regarded as neutral ground; the rebels were plainly seen robbing these bodies.

Burying the Dead---The Army Reinforced.

On Monday, General Franklin sent a flag of truce for an exchange of dead, which was done yesterday. Lee sent a flag of truce to Burnside, asking him to detail men to bury his dead, in front of General Sumner's division. Our entire army is now encamped on the ground previously occupied. The army has been considerably reinforced. The opinion of military men is that had we taken the first ridge of the rebel works, their opportunities for slaughtering us would have been greater than before.

The Enemy Increase their Intrenchments.

Last night, the enemy increased their intrenchments on the terrace, in the rear of Fredericksburg, and threw up rifled pits near the river, on the left of the city. Their drills are plainly visible on the plain to-day. No movement of importance takes place by our forces to-day.

Pressure on the President in Favor of Eli Thayer's Colonization Scheme.

WASHINGTON, 17th.

A large delegation of members of both Houses of Congress, with Vice President Hamlin at their head, waited on the President today, with a request signed by the loyal men of Florida, asking the appointment of Eli Thayer military Governor of that State, with authority to raise 20,000 loyal emigrants. They presented a paper signed [illegible]

Breckinridge Threatens to Resign.

NASHVILLE, 15th.

Bragg having issued orders for the conscription of every exiled Kentuckian and Tennessean, Buckner and Breckinridge threatened to resign if this was done. The Murfreesboro *Banner* says Jeff. Davis has gone to Mobile.

Losses at the Battle of Prairie Grove.

ST. LOUIS, 17th.

Official reports place our loss at the battle of Prairie Grove, Arkansas, at 995. Latest accounts increase rebel loss to 2,700 killed and wounded and nearly 6,000 by desertion.—Hindman is on the south side of Arkansas river. Marmaduke is on the north side. Gen. Herren telegraphs to Curtis that the victory at Prairie Grove was more complete than at first reported. Over 2,500 rebels have been buried. Many of the wounded died from want of attention.

Gunboat Cairo Blown up by a Torpedo.

CAIRO, 18th.

The gunboat *Cairo*, when twenty miles below the mouth of Yazoo river, was blown up by a torpedo, no one hurt. The boat and armament a total loss.

Inquiry into the Responsibility of the Fredericksburg Defeat.

WASHINGTON, 16th.

A resolution was offered, that the committee on conduct of the war inquire into the facts relative to the recent battle at Fredericksburg, particularly as to what officers are responsible for the assault, and also for the delay which occurred in preparing to meet the enemy. The resolution was adopted.

No Revenue Stamps----Business to go on Without Penalty.

SAN FRANCISCO, 18th.

The U. S. Assistant Treasurer here received the following dispatch relative to stamps:

"WASHINGTON, 17th.

D. W. Cheeseman, U. S. Assistant Treasurer. No stamps to send—have no power.—Bill pending before Congress to remedy difficulty. Californians need give themselves no trouble about the matter. Business may go on as usual. No penalties.

[illegible]

Com[illegible]ernal Revenue.

The President's Me[illegible]ches it all round. We append a few of the complimentary notices, as they appear in our California exchanges:

This document is most unsatisfactory. It is with deep regret we are compelled to admit so much; we feel humiliated that our criticism is just, and cannot but foresee that the inanity of this State paper will be another powerful weapon in the hands of British and French journalists to sneer at republican institutions. If, however, Mr. Lincoln in the roughness of his honest heart, has placed before the world a message vulnerable to the last degree, he has evinced a warm and disingenuous desire to remove the primary cause of our present dissensions.—*San Francisco Call.*

All men, be they of this or that party, will, upon closely perusing the same, feel the mantle of shame upon their check, that the great Government of the United States of America should at this time be presided over by one whose talents and statesmanship come so far short of the emergency of the times.—*El Dorado Times.*

As a literary production it is worthy of Mr. Lincoln; it sparkles with wit and broad humor; burns with passages of thrilling eloquence and poetic fire; abounds with the most striking and startling metaphors, gives you a full insight into and a complete history of not only the present war but the last one and the next one, and when printed in pamphlet form will come handy to kindle fires with.—*Auburn Advocate.*

The Message was not such a document as was generally expected at this time. There is not that dignity and taste displayed which the American people have been accustomed to look for in the annual messages of the Presidents.—*Calaveras Chronicle.*

Everybody anticipated learning of the policy of the Government in carrying on this war against its rebellious subjects, but, it may be said, the whole matter has been treated as if civil war did not prevail in our midst.—*Napa Reporter.*

For one of the lamest, tamest, and most unsatisfactory documents that ever issued from the White House, we commend our readers to this said message.—*Pacifique Echo,*

MR. SEWARD.—A letter to the New York *Evening Post* (republican) says:

Mr. Buchanan, it is said by persons who are likely to be well informed, asserts positively, for instance, that he consulted Mr. Seward *continually* during the last four months of his administration; and that he did not undertake anything in regard to the rebellious movement during those four months—from the time of Mr. Lincoln's election till his installation that is to say—without previous full consultation with Mr. Seward, and only with the full approval of that gentleman. And that this is not mere gossip, would seem certain from the fact that one of the most respectable citizens of Washington, one who had good opportunities for knowing the fact, assures his friends that he *knows*, and from both the parties—Mr. Buchanan and Mr. Seward—that it is true.

If Mr. Buchanan will not make this fact public, a large part of the odium resting hitherto on him will be carried to Mr. Seward, and justly, too; for it was an honorable act in the out-going President thus to advise with him who was then held the leader of the party then coming into power.

☞ It is charged that General Mitchell's attack on the railroad line at Pocataligo, South Carolina, partly failed on account of certain contrabands conveying information to the enemy. Those negroes had been kept and fed inside of the Union lines. Military rules exclude white civilians from the lines of a military encampment; they should also keep out black civilians. Between the Dough-face dodge of guarding secession property, and the uncalled for petting of runaway negroes, thousands of loyal lives have been lost.

The Oregon Statesman.

Salem, Monday Morning, Dec. 29.

THE NEWS.

The news of Burnside's retreat across the Rappahannock, following so closely upon the high-raised anticipations of the country, has spread the deepest gloom over the heart of the Nation. After so much preparation and long waiting, it was expected that when he moved against the enemy, something better than the too frequent news of disaster, would be telegraphed from the army. The inquiry rises, spontaneously, to whom shall the responsibility be imputed? Heretofore it has been the practise to hold the commanding general responsible for failure, and the President declared, upon the removal of McClellan, that hereafter the success of the general should be the test of his fitness. If this be the rule, Burnside is the man at fault unless he made the movement under the positive orders of a superior. The butchery—for it cannot be called by any other name—of 12,000 men, without a chance of success, must be answered for by somebody.—Common expressions of censure ought not to be the full measure of retribution visited upon the party at fault. Instant removal should be his fate, let the blow fall where it will.

We are disposed to think that Burnside acted under the orders of Halleck. Whether the one or the other is responsible, it is the most criminal blunder of the war. [illegible] barriers, more impregnable than even Sebastopol, [illegible]e and again, only to be shot down like victims of the slaughter house, without the shadow of a chance to carry them. Fighting on the open level plain, they had no cover or screen behind which to approach, fight or retreat.—The rebels fired from screened rifle-pits, and from behind stonewalls, earthworks on the hills, and from behind the hills themselves. Their position being a semi-circle, enabled them to pour in murderous enfilading fires as well as a direct one in front. The result was that our men, though brave as the bravest, were mown down, literally in swaths, at every attempt to storm the rebel works. The battle was more like a wholesale murder than anything that has transpired since the beginning of the rebellion.

The successful extrication of the troops from a position of peril, such as the army was never in before, reflects much credit upon General Burnside, but does not excuse or palliate the criminal blunder which placed them in it.—Had the enemy been aware how badly beaten we were, or had he manifested his usual energy in following up success, our army must have suffered a total and disgraceful rout, if not annihilation. The affair appears in a more culpable view when we remember that the surrender of Fredericksburg within sixteen hours was demanded by General Sumner at a time when only a small force of the rebels occupied the place and that instead of attacking then, a long time was permitted to elapse during which the enemy were suffered to collect the largest army they ever had together, and peaceably construct those works before which our soldiers are now slaughtered, helplessly, by thousands. Is there any possible explanation of these facts which will exonerate everybody from blame?

ARE THEY MONEY?—A suit is pending in the N. Y. Supreme Court which [illegible] the validity of the law declaring the treasury notes to be a lawful tender in payment of debts. A similar case is pending in California. The argument in the New York case will be found on our outside. We presume the case will be carried to the U. S. Supreme Court for final adjudication. We have always been of the opinion that that court would hold that they were *not* a legal tender for debts contracted before the passage of the Act, if, indeed, it did not decide that Congress was without the power to make anything but the precious metals a legal tender. In California, we understand parties usually receive them under protest, and only for their current value, and thus save the right to recover the discount with costs. If Congress has the power to declare irredeemable paper currency a legal tender for existing debts, it is very clear they ought not to have it. It would be a power subject to gross abuse.

HEAVY FRAUD.—A fraud of several millions of dollars has recently come to light, perpetrated by Soloman Kohnstam, of N. Y., connected with the recruiting, subsistence and transportation department in that city. Full fifty and sometimes sixty per cent. of enormous sums expended there have been directed into Kohnstam's pocket, while the government has paid two prices, and sometimes more, for everything, to make up to the contractors what he stole. The *expose* of this last discovered fraud contains the following extract:

Kohnstam became very profuse in his hospitalities. Every official connected with the State and General Governments, including militia and army officers, were favored with invitations to dinner. The latest party of this kind was given by Kohnstam a month ago, in honor of "His friend Simeon Draper," Provost Marshal General. The dinner was prepared at the up-town restaurant of Delmonico, and was got up in the most expensive manner, embracing every luxury of the season, and taxing the utmost resources of even their famous cuisine. At that dinner party were assembled, the host, having on his right the Provost Marshal General, on his left A. Oakley Hall, District Attorney, while around the table were distributed the U. S. District Attorney, U. S. Army officers in the city, several of the Judges, and nearly every prominent republican official in the city. The bill of fare was on satin cards, elaborately decorated, and illuminated with fanciful borderings

The ornaments embraced models of Honesty, Virtue and Sobriety, while the *piece de Resistance* was a miniature temple of Justice.

The wine flowed freely, and the sparkling bon mot and witty repartee was rapid and sparkling; and when the guests separated it was with the consciousness of having spent a delightful evening.

BANKS' EXPEDITION.—The reports as to the destination of this expedition are very contradictory. One has it that a portion of the fleet was seen going into Port Royal, another that several vessels of the expedition had gone into a harbor on the coast of Florida. The most circumstantial account is that Banks landed at Winton, N. C., and had taken command of the forces under Generals Foster, Peck, Auger and Emory, forming a junction with the forces at Suffolk, Va. The various rumors put in circulation evince a design to cover the affair with all the mystery possible. It is not probable the expedition was ever designed to go to Texas or any of the minor seaports on the coast. The more probable supposition is that it has been sent to co-operate with the forces to the south of Richmond, or against Charleston, South Carolina. In either case, his force will be sufficiently large, when added to those in the neighborhood to be formidable, in numbers at least, if not in command.

EMANCIPATION IN PERU.

Our Government may learn something of the practical workings of emancipation by the history of that measure in the State of Peru.—An official statement of the condition of Peru as affected by emancipation, was furnished Congress during last session by the President, in response to a resolution of the House inquiring as to the condition of the Coolie trade.—The information was contained in a document from Dr. William Trevitt, U. S. Consul at Calloa, Peru, dated October 1, 1861, written in reference to the agricultural condition of that country, and its marked deterioration since the emancipation of its negroes. Slavery was abolished in Peru in 1855, and the experiment is, therefore, from its date, worthy of notice in discussing the scheme for ourselves.

Dr. Trevitt says that, with all the advantages of soil, climate, &c., equal, if not superior to any in the world, such as should enable the State to supply itself and export large quantities of the products of the soil, Peru not only falls far short of supplying itself, but is actually obliged to buy of others largely of the commonest products of the country. This results from the want of a well regulated system of labor consequent upon the freeing of a large number of blacks to become vagabonds, thieves, robbers and every variety of outlaws. He represents that they took to all such practises, until it became unsafe to occupy country residences without a strong, armed guard, or to walk in any unfrequented street unattended after nightfall.

Dr. Trevitt adds:

It is perhaps fortunate for the country, however, that this class of population is fast disappearing; through their dissipation, licentiousness and crime, and the penalties attached, at no distant period the liberated negroes of Peru will only be remembered for the crimes they have committed, and regretted for the demoralizing influence their acts have produced upon society.

In Peru, as in the United States, there was a strong feeling against the abstract idea of slavery. The matter was agitated till slavery was voted a curse, and abolished. The freed negroes at once become a nuisance and a greater curse than ever possible before. The inhabitants now look with anxious solicitude to the day when they shall become extinct through licentiousness, dissipation, crime and their penalties. There seems never to have been any attempt at elevating them, or even a thought of its being possible. Extermination is the only remedy in Peru. If twenty-five thousand negroes set free in Peru, are, at once and always, such a curse to society as to preclude all remedies but extermination, the effect of such a scheme where 4,000,000 of blacks are to be turned loose among a white population with stronger prejudices and greater sensitiveness than the Peruvians, cannot be brought within the limits of calculation or prophesy. Will extermination be the remedy with us? If so, how accomplished?

GENERAL McCLELLAN IN NEW YORK.

On the occasion of receiving a serenade in New York, in answer to an opening address from the President of the Young Mens' Democratic Union Association, General McClellan stepping forward on the balcony, said:

I thank you for this spontaneous expression of your regard, and accept it not for myself, but for the Army of the Potomac which I lately commanded, and in which you are so deeply interested. Every battle from Yorktown to Antietam, has added new proofs to the courage and devotion of the citizen soldiers of New York [illegible] gratitude due to them from their country. No portion of the proud Republic has more lavishly spent its treasures and brave men in the cause of their country, than this metropolis.—At the commencement of this struggle no community was more prompt in responding to the call of the country for aid—no community has a greater stake in the success of the cause than this. There is none more closely bound by ties of kindred to the army with which I have been so long associated. I, therefore, and my former comrades with me, will feel deeply honored by the occurrences of this evening, and it is with a heart overflowing with gratitude that I again thank you for your presence here to-night. You know I am still a soldier, and therefore will expect no speech from me. You will, therefore, permit me to now bid you good night.

The following paragraph from the *Express* exhibits the modesty and unassuming demeanor of the General:

General McClellan is dressed in citizen's dress, and a jaunty little fatigue cap is the only piece of uniform denoting the rank of the *great hero and chieftain.* His manner and style of demeanor are characterized by unusually modest, uniform politeness and genuine gentlemanly behavior. He stated that under no circumstances could he accept of any public reception; that while he would appreciate the motives that would actuate the movers, still it would be neither proper nor polite for him to accept of such a demonstration, and besides, he had come to New York to secure quiet, and he desired to remain perfectly retired from all public demonstrations. It is very appropriate that the serenade should take place at the Fifth Avenue Hotel, as it was there that he married. Mrs. McClellan is rather a delicate looking lady, but interesting and attractive. She has a very pretty little infant girl, to whom she is more devoted than to the honors sought to be bestowed upon herself and husband.

WHERE THE TROUBLE HAS BEEN.—A private letter from Washington says:

"A distinguished Englishman who spent 1861 in U. S. says 'the Rebellion has developed great energies and resources in the people of the U. S., and great weakness in the Administration.' It is likewise reported that a distinguished American statesman, not now in public life, has said that 'the people have already furnished muscle and money enough to put down two such rebellions as this, and would furnish twice as much more, could they see that any good was being done with it. But that there had been a woful destitution of *brains* in the administration and management of affairs—that this was unfortunately the weakest administration ever, in possession of the Government, while the world stood appalled at its corruptions. That, if the Union was lost, as he feared there was now danger it would be, impartial history would record that it was the fault, not of the people, but of the pigmies who mismanaged the Government, and trifled with its high destinies."

NARY QUARTER.—The Richmond *Examiner* says the preparations of the Federals for subjugating the South, are of such a character as "should nerve every southern hand for battle in which there will no quarter."

If the rebels go into battle at all, they will need no advice to go in without *ary* quarter in hand. They've got none—nothing but Confederate shin-plasters.

SHORT CROPS IN THE SOUTH.—The Charleston *Mercury*, of Nov. 1st, says the crops of corn and rice have been so far short, this year, of the usual yield as to threaten serious consequences. The corn suffered from drought, and the rice growers of the swamp lands along the coast have abandoned them and fled to the interior.

We hope the *kemp* crop is better.

CONGRESSIONAL PROCEEDINGS.

Mr. McDougall, in the Senate, in the 16th, offered the following resolutions, which were referred to the Committee on Finance:

Resolved, That this Government will maintain its payment in coin of any interest or indebtedness, and consider it a breach of public faith to do otherwise.

Resolved That duties on imports shall continue to be paid in coin and issues of Demand Notes, and when the latter cease to be sufficient for the purpose of such payments, they shall thereafter be paid in coin.

A bill for the relief of persons suffering damages by the late Indian troubles in Minnesota, was offered by Mr. Wilkinson.

The bill to provide for removing the Winnebago and Sioux tribes and the sale of their present reservation for their benefit, was referred. The bill provides for furnishing them a reservation, near the Missouri, sufficient to give eighty acres of good agricultural land to each person. Those who endeavored to prevent the massacre to be allowed to remain where they are and to have 160 acres

The army bill, reported from the Committee of Ways and Means, appropriates $731,000,000 for the year ending June, 1864.

The resolution censuring ex-President Buchanan was debated at length. Saulsbury moved that the old pub. unc. be furnished a copy, and allowed to defend himself. The whole matter was tabled, on motion of Grimes, by a vote of 38 to 3.

On the 18th, Rice, of Minnesota, offered a bill to extend the Walla Walla and Fort Benton road to Fort Abercrombie.

Nesmith introduced a bill for the protection of the overland emigrant road.

The Senate felt itself called upon to inquire into the Fredericksburg saughter and accordingly adopted a resolution providing for such inquiry, and also, to ascerain the reasons for the delay which occurred before the assault was made.

The postal appropriations for the coming year amounts to $12,000,000. A grant of $1,000,000, in addition to the above, was made for the California Central route.

On the 19th, the Committee appointed to inquire into the Fredericksburg affair, left for the Rappahannock.

Same day, in the House, the army appropriation bill was passed by a vote of 107 to 33, after rejecting an amendment offered by Mallory, of Kentucky, that none of the money should be used for the benefit of runaway negroes, or for the colonization of them.

Sargent, of California, introduced a resolution looking to the appointment of an Assistant Commissioner of Internal Revenue, for the Pacific States and Territories. The resolution refers the question of expediency to the Committee of Ways and Means, and was adopted.

A Committee, representing the Border States members, called on the President, to protest against his issuing his 1st of January proclamation, but received no satisfaction. Maynard did not sanction the action of the Committee.

THE LATEST NEWS.—The latest dispatch reports that a Republican Senatorial caucus had been held, at which a resolution inviting Secretary Seward to resign, was adopted, by a vote of 16 to 13; that Seward had resigned, and that pestilent abolitionist and literary abortion, Charles Sumner, of Massachusetts, had been offered the place, by Lincoln. The vote in the caucus was a triumph of the ultras, as Seward was not considered radical enough. A [illegible] tion asking the President to make some changes in his cabinet, was unanimously adopted, the more conservative portion of the caucus thinking it would lead to a complete dispersion of the Cabinet. The Washington *Star* said it was currently reported that Burnside had resigned the command of the Army of the Potomac. When Pope was appointed, the command is said to have been offered to Burnside, and he declined it, telling the President that there was but one officer in the army—McClellan—competent for the post. Pope's experience, and his own terrific disaster at Fredericksburg, have probably confirmed that opinion.

WILBUR, December 17, 1862.

MR. EDITOR: The citizens of Wilbur and vicinity, on Thanksgiving day, contributed for the Sanitary Fund, as follows:

Hon. A. E. McGee, $5; Mrs. A. E. McGee, $5; Mr. Grubbe, $2 50; N. T. Day, $5; J. Bell, $5; A. Nasburg, $5; J. Perdue, $5; Mr. Pinkston, $2 50; C. Barrett, $2 50; G. D. Smith, $1; T. N. Grubbe, $2 50; F. R. Hill, $5; T. F. Royal, $5; Mrs. Royal, $1; P. Harrigan, $1 25; Dr. Ballard, $1; E. A. Lathrop, $3; Geo. Greer, $3.

Children—F. W. Royal, 25 cents; A. Royal, 50 cents; E. Grubbe, 50 cents; E. Fleming, 25 cents; W. W. Royal, 25 cents; S. A. Klinkenbeard, 25 cents. Total, $63 25.

GEORGE GREER, Secretary.

Additional to Sanitary Fund from Jefferson, Marion county:

Jacob Conser, $10; Mrs. Lucy Anderson, $5; Mrs. L. J. Ramsdale, $2; Mrs. E. Baxter, $2; Mrs. Delia Harrison, $2 50; W. A. Johnson, $2 50; James W. Bates, $1; John W. Cox, $1; T. H. Veasy, $5; Mrs. Jane Veasy, $2 50; Ashby West, $2; Dr. J. F. Roe, $5; Miss Kate Harrison, 50 cents. Total, $41.

COMPENSATION.—We are getting to be a devout believer in the doctrine of compensation. Occasionally a subscriber comes along and pays his year's subscription with a "greenback." At such times we have thought of the ten per cent. discount, but on further reflection, have concluded that had it not been for "greenbacks" we should never have got anything and so have been content to receive the depreciated currency.—*Mountaineer.*

We have several thousand dollars on our books for subscription, for which, "greenbacks" at 90 cents on the dollar would be much larger "compensation" than we ever expect to get.

☞ The Boston correspondent of the Springfield (Mass.) *Republican* says of the late elections:

It is no matter of surprise that the republicans are beaten in New York and the West.—The burden of incapacity in cabinet and field, is too grievous to be borne. All rests now with Mr. Lincoln. He has an army and a navy, backed by a people, who will sustain him if he gives them a *victory* to encourage their hearts and reward their sacrifices.

☞ At a Seymour meeting in Syracuse, N. Y., recently, *twenty-two* republicans who voted for Lincoln, acted as Vice Presidents. Like thousands and thousands of others, they are disgusted with the radical yoke, and fall in with the conservatives.

☞ Since the triumph of Sumner, and the success of the disunion abolitionists in Massachusetts, the leading men in the West and North-west are discussing the question of inviting that fanatical State and a few others like it to withdraw from the Union.

☞ The rebels, notwithstanding their professions of hatred to the U. S. Government, think it three times [illegible] than their own. Proof: They readily give three dollars of confederate money for one with the U. S. stamp upon it.

THE LATEST NEWS.

Deserters from the Rebel Army Joining Gen. Herron.

ST. LOUIS, Dec. 19th.

We have a report that Gen. Hindman has crossed the river with dispatches to Marmaduke, while the cavalry remain on the North side. Hundreds from the rebel army are already joining Herron, many of them Missourians, who express the greatest disgust at the rebel campaign, and think its prosecution hopeless.

Jeff. Davis inquires into the hanging of Ten Rebels by Gen. McNeill.

Gen. Curtis, yesterday, received a communication from the rebel Gen. Holmes, forwarded by direction of Jeff. Davis, inquiring into the facts relative to the shooting of ten Confederate citizens by order of Gen. McNeill. Gen. Curtis' reply will probably be published, and it is looked for with much interest.

Republican Senatorial Caucus--Resignation of Secretary Seward.

NEW YORK, Dec. 20th.

Last evening's Washington *Star* states that a caucus of republican Senators was held on the 10th instant, when resolutions were offered, and discussed, requesting Secretary Seward to resign. The vote was, ayes, 16; noes, 13.—The next day another caucus adopted a substitute, recommending the President partially to remodel his Cabinet, which was unanimously accepted, as the conservatives believed it would be regarded as a general invitation to the whole Cabinet to resign. On being informed of the act, the Secretary and Assistant Secretary of State sent in their resignations, requesting their immediate acceptance.

Reported Resignation of Gen. Burnside.

—The same paper says it is also confidently reported that Gen. Burnside has tendered his resignation of command of the army. The *Post's* Washington correspondent says: "It was rumored this afternoon that the entire Cabinet will retire, leaving the President free to construct a new Cabinet. This may be incorrect; but it is not at all improbable that Blair and Bates have already tendered their resignations. I am informed this afternoon that Charles A. Sumner has been tendered the port folio of the Secretary of State."

Capture of the Schooner George.

WASHINGTON, Dec. 20th.

The Navy Department has information of the capture of the schooner *George*, from Nassau, with an assorted cargo of coffee and salt.

News from Santa Fe.

KANSAS CITY, Dec. 20th.

Advices from Santa Fe state that General Carleton has issued an order requiring all persons arriving there to report to the Provost Marshal. Strangers are all to exhibit a written authority, under which they can travel, and give satisfactory evidence of their loyalty. It is rumored that a body of Texans, 6,000 strong, are marching on Santa Fe, via Las Vas and Jazel Pass, under General Bayler. The rumor needs confirmation.

DOMESTIC ITEMS.

....The Duke of Gloucester, who was thought to be as nearly a fool as a royal duke could be, went by the nick-name of "Silly-Billy." His brother, William IV., at one time did a very foolish thing, at which everybody laughed, whereupon the silly duke exclaimed triumphantly, "who is Silly Billy now?" If the *Airgoose* Billy had been at court then, the questioner would have been referred to him without hesitation.

....The following are the officers elected for the ensuing Masonic year by Eugene City Lodge No. 11, A. F. & A. M.: A. A. Smith, W. M.; J. G. Gray, S. W.; C. C. Croner, J. W.; E. F. Skinner, Treasurer; J. B. Underwood, Sec'y; P. J. Lemley, Tyler.

....An exchange anxiously asks: "Where are Greeley's 900,000 abolitionists?" One of them is editing the *Airgoose*, at Oregon City. He occasionally lets go of the crank, however, to draw his salary (in "Greenbacks," of course, he prefers them) for nominally filling the office of Collector. He can't go, for that salary *must* be attended to. Greeley must reduce his figures by one abolitionist.

.... One party at San Francisco has been victimized by countesfeit greenbacks to the amount of $800. California is said to abound in them. We shall soon have them in Oregon doubtless. That is the least of the beauties of shinplaster currency.

....It is reported that Victor Smith has donated $1,632 75 to the United States toward defraying the expenses of the war. Doubtful?

....Billy-goat used to be heavy on the use of Russo-Turkish and Turko-Russian. He will soon bring out in the *Airgoose*, secesho-rebellion and rebello-secession. His picture would be piggopuppish and puppo-piggish, if it be true to the original.

....Jack Walsh, known as "Oregon Jack," has managed to get into limbo at Victoria, on a charge of being a bad character. He formerly figured in Portland.

....Gov. Pickering, in his message to the Legislature, advises the people to "stand by the Constitution and the Union, as the only harbor of national safety." The *Airgoose* will probably now call him a "secessionist."

....A wag, the other night, on the arrival of the Portland mail, manifested a considerable impatience to get the daily papers of that city. On being interrogated as to the cause of his anxiety, he replied, "I want to see how the auction sales and restaurants are getting along."

....We are reliably informed that the Oregon Steam Navigation Company received a check on sub-Treasurer, at San Francisco, in payment of army freight bills; that they drew coin, and bought greenbacks with it at San Francisco, at a discount, to pay employes and others with in Oregon at par. Such conduct is reprehensible in the extreme.

....Billy-goat Adams pretends to have been once a printer's d—l, but his name gives the lie to his pretense Put the letters as they should be, and you have, "I am a saw-mill d—l."

....The Billy-goat chap triumphantly quotes a Mr. Hamilton, of Texas, to prove the necessity and wisdom of making the Union all over, "as it should be." We can't see that Hamilton's residence in Texas, or his coinciding with Silly Billy, concludes the question, for it is possible that a radical fool may live in Texas, as well as in Oregon City or Astoria.

....In the Washington Territory Legislature, a memorial is pending, asking the Secretary of the Interior to order the survey of San Juan, and contiguous Islands. If the survey is ordered, it will bring up the question of title between the United States and England.

....A meeting of the citizens of Oregon City has been held, to take steps for the erection of a woolen factory at that place. No place in the State has better natural advantages for running manufacturing machin[illegible] than Oregon City.

....*Airgoose* Billy says he saw something sticking up in a doggery at Astoria. It was probably a bill he owed for rot-gut. The face of one of the three bruisers, "taking a smile," which are sometimes seen hanging behind bars, bears a striking resemblance to Billy's. It might have been that that he saw.

....The Puppo-pigfaced Billy-goat calls Daniel Webster "a half-breed secesh." Substitute puppy for "secesh," and the term would describe Billy remarkably well.

....The patients at the State Insane Asylum have presented Addison C. Gibbs, Esq., the Governor of this State, with an elegant silver pitcher for the warm interest he has taken in their bodily comfort and spiritual welfare. It was purchased with money earned by themselves, and bears the inscription, engraved by one of their number:—"Patients of the Insane Asylum, to Governor A. C. Gibbs, Portland, Ogn., 1862."—*Oregonian.*

....Some of the ancients held to the belief that at the exact time when one person was born, another died, and that the soul of the latter entered and animated the body of the other. We have made extensive inquiry, and have ascertained that when Silly Billy was born, nothing died but a pig and an infantile "dorg," and there not being a body for each, they both entered Billy's body, and have been each contending for the mastery ever since.

....From a private letter written to a gentleman in this city, from Oro Fino, we learn that Dr. Geo. A. Noble, of Oregon City was robbed of a hundred pounds of gold dust, while on the road from Florence City to Oro Fino. He was attacked by eleven men. The robbery was committed on a thickly timbered section of the road, about six miles from Oro Fino city.—*Times.*

....The *Mountaineer* says an elderly man, known as the "Old Emigrant," was found dead in the river at the foot of Court street, Dalles, on the morning of the 21st inst. It is not known whether his death arose from accident or design.

A *red nigger* has a letter in the *Airgoose*, over the signature of "Honor," to prove that to be *honorable* Mr. Ramsay should have cheated Mr. Williams out of the difference between greenbacks and gold. Silly Billy concurs. That may be honorable among *red niggers*, but certainly not among white men.

....The people of the Dalles paid a large portion of their Federal tax before it was due. In Portland, of the persons required to take out license, over one hundred and fifty had not done so within the time limited by the collector.—Rather than enforce the penalty, the Collector has extended the time. So says the *Oregonian.*

....Silly Billy says an extract from the *Statesman* is posted on a barrel of rot-gut in Astoria. It is billy's barrel, and Billy pasted the extract there. He ought now to paste his own name on the barrel, which, by a little transposition of the letters would read, "I swill a d[ea]l, ma'am."—That would be appropriate and truthful.

The *Sierra Nevada* took down, on her last trip, 6,000 boxes of apples, 500 raw hides, and 100 cases miscellaneous freight.

....The sloop *Leonede* left Bellacoola, British Columbia, Nov. 18th, at which time there had been a heavy fall of snow. Snow has also fallen in nearly all sections of the Oregon and Washington Territory mines.

....Nigger Adams, of the *Airgoose*, with all the malice and meanness of a fifth-rate fiend, asserts that we expect to profit by the depreciation of the U. S. securities and paper currency. The dirty nigger privately chuckles over the fact that it will occasion us heavy loss and *publishes* that we are to be profited by the depreciation, and *expect* to buy up the securities. We will give him a year's salary, barring his stealings, (3000) if he will make up to us our loss by the depreciation occurring during the next year and, in the meantime we will give him two dollars for every one we make thereby. A considerable portion of all we possess is now in United States securities. We have not bought a dollar of them for three months and do not expect in the future to buy one. And during the same time we have omitted no opportunity to sell without heavy loss. There are few if any men in Oregon who have more pecuniary interest, in keeping up the value of securities if interest were to govern, as this scamp meanly asserts, than ourselves.—So much for this dirty slander.

....The Trustees of the Willamette University Salem, voted to pay their teachers in coin, or its equivalent in value in legal tender notes.

USEFUL ARTICLE.—Coal oil kills bed bugs, drives fleas off from dogs, and lice off from calves—but don't put on to much, or it will "drive" the hair off as well. An acquaintance of ours applied it pretty freely to his *cuitan* to "clean out" the ticks, and the result was it took off the *har* clean. The hide only needed skinning off to be ready to be made into shoes by Gen. Pearne.

....Washington Territory has two acting Secretaries, Turney refusing to vacate in favor of Evans, lately appointed, and the latter having assumed the duties of the office.

.... Some time since, Mr. Kendall, of the *Overland Press*, made some remarks in his paper, reflecting on the character of a man named Howe. In retaliation, Howe attacked Kendall on the street at Olympia, on the 20th, with a stick. Kendall, warding off the blows aimed at him, retired, but being pursued, drew a revolver and fired several times at Howe, one of the shots inflicting a serious, if not dangerous, wound.

.... The Governor of Washington Territory and the Legislature consider the office of Public Printer vacant, by the departure of Mr. Poe, from the Territory. The Legislature undertook to elect one, when the Governor anticipating their action, filled the vacancy by appointment. The *Press* says, Mr. Poe is about to return, when another party will be added to the muddle.

.... Gen. Pearne says, in his *Advocate*, that he is in favor of crushing out *the cause* of the rebellion. He had better commence with hanging himself, and invite other meddling abolitionists of his stripe to follow his example.

.... The disgusting vileness of the language used by the Oregon City *Airgoose*, is illustrated by the following extract, which is a fair sample of one-half of Rev. Billy's effusions:

"The difference between the Seymour democrats of New York, and the secession democrats of Oregon, is precisely the same as there is between a *dog* and a *slut.*"

....On the 14th inst., E. H. Meservy, county coroner of Curry county, stabbed Earl A. C. Boyd with a knife—supposed to be fatal—as it is in the region of the heart it is out of the question for him to survive many hours. The cause is supposed to be about a squaw, the wife of said Meservy. So says a correspondent.

....They agree. The *Abolition Airgoose*, at Oregon City, and *Secession Review*, at Eugene City, are disunion papers. The first says we are a secessionist, and the last says we are an abolitionist. The truth lies between the statements of the two liars.

SCHOOL EXERCISES.

There was a school exhibition on Friday evening, December the 26th, in the large school house in Howell Prairie—Messrs. Shaw, Cline, and McCorkle, Directors; Mr. W. F. Jones, teacher. It was a brilliant affair. The stage was beautifully arranged, decorated with flags, evergreens, etc. The exercises, consisting of singing, declamations, compositions, and dialogues, were performed well, and both patrons and the large audience in general, were well pleased and highly entertained. Elder Fisher and his daughters, from Salem, furnished melodeon accompaniment, also assisted in singing. At the close, Elder Fisher made, to the school and audience, a few feeling and appropriate remarks, all of which was well received, and at 11 o'clock the audience dispersed.

DECEMBER, 26, 1862.

ONE PRESENT.

J. W. SULLIVAN.—This enterprising and accommodating news dealer has again laid us under obligations for a liberal file of pictorials and States papers of the latest dates, including Harper's *Weekly*, Frank Leslie's *Illustrated Newspaper*, Baltimore *Weekly Sun*, New Orleans *Delta*, &c., &c.

A GREEN SPOT.—Onager Jacobs, of the *Sentinel*, admires President Lincoln's message, and thinks it just the document for the times. Considering that all the world have arrived at a different conclusion, we think it fair to class the *Sentinel* as a green spot in an arid waste.—*Mountaineer.*

INCONSISTENCY.—The President's proclamation looks to immediate emancipation. In his message, the President declares that "sudden emancipation is on all accounts undesirable, and would be a great evil to its immediate recipients." Will some admirer of Uncle Abe reconcile this inconsistency?—*Mountaineer.*

EASTERN NEWS.

The Late Fighting at Fredericksburg and Withdrawal of Union Troops.

NEW YORK, December 17.

The morning papers are filled with detailed accounts of Saturday's fighting at Fredericksburg, of too extended a nature for telegraphing. They contain no reliable news, but comprise mainly incidents relating to the battle.

The *Times* gives the following account of the withdrawal of our troops from Fredericksburg. It says the movement commenced at dark on Monday night. All the sick and wounded were removed during the day to the hospital tents on this side. Burnside inspected the position of the troops in the afternoon, and the general activity indicated that another battle was imminent. The withdrawal of our forces however, was determined on at a council of all the corps commanders during the day. The undertaking was regarded as perilous, but if successful it would rescue the army from the risk of another battle, which would accomplish but little but the destruction of valuable lives. The troops had received no intimation of the retreat, and had laid down on their arms for the night. When the order was given to fall in, the troops supposed it was for a night assault upon the enemy's works, and were not undeceived until they found themselves on the pontoons. The bridges had been covered with earth to deaden the sound of the artillery. The high wind and the darkness prevented the rebels from hearing or seeing the movement.—Franklin's division moved as soon as it was dark, as did also Hooker's and Sumner's divisions, from under the very guns of the enemy. Very few of the wounded were left on the field.

The *Times'* correspondent thus describes the rebel position which our troops were expected to take: A bare plateau a third of a mile in width, which a storming party would have to cross, during which they would be exposed to the fire of the enemy's sharpshooters posted behind a stone wall running along the base of the ridge, in double rifle pits on the rise of the crest of the hill, and the double, enfilading fire from cannon to the left of the hill. This correspondent adds that Sebastopol was not half so strong as this rebel position.

Dispatch from Burnside to Halleck.

NEW YORK, December 17.

The Philadelphia *Press* publishes a dispatch from Burnside to Halleck, received last night. Burnside says that, feeling fully convinced that the position in front could not be carried, it was a military necessity to either attack or retreat. A repulse would have been disastrous. Under these circumstances the army was withdrawn, without the loss of a man or property.

Foraging Near Fortress Monroe.

FORTRESS MONROE, December 15.

A foraging party, sent from Yorktown last Friday, returned this morning with a large drove of cattle, sheep, etc.

Appointment of Secretary Smith to United States District Judgeship.

WASHINGTON, December 17.

The President has nominated to the Senate Caleb B. Smith, Secretary of the Interior, to be Judge of the District Court of the United States for the District of Indiana.

Steamers Seen Bound South.

NEW YORK, December 17.

The bark *Ann*, from New Orleans, reports that on the 9th, off St. Augustine, Fla., she saw six steamers bound south—probably part of Banks' expedition. Several of his vessels put into Port Royal for coal and then sailed southward.

Jeff. Davis Gone to Mobile.

NASHVILLE, 15th.

The Murfreesboro *Banner* says Jeff. Davis has gone to Mobile, and adds, that while the visit of Davis to the West possesses no military significance, it will have an inspiring influence, upon the people and troops.

Invalid Pension Bill.

WASHINGTON, Dec. 17th.

The Invalid Pension Bill appropriates nearly eight millions for the year ending June, 1863, appropriates a hundred and eight millions [illegible]

Mexican News.

NEW YORK, Dec. 17th.

The latest news from Mexico indicates a disposition on the part of the clergy to co-operate with the French. It is stated that letters have been received from the Archbishops of Guanajuato, Loreda, San Luis, Guadalajara and Mexico, welcoming Forey, and offering him the support of the whole Mexican clergy against Juarez.

Details of the Battle at Fredericksburg.

CHICAGO, Dec. 18th.

The following detailed account of the battle at Fredericksburg on Saturday is interesting:

Franklin on the left moved his column at sunrise, his right resting on the outskirts of the city, his center advanced a mile or so from the river, and his left on the Rappahannock, three miles below. Skirmishing commenced a few minutes after daylight, on the extreme left. A rebel battery opened on our troops, and the fire became so annoying that the Ninth New York Militia was ordered to charge and take it at the point of the bayonet. The order was obeyed with alacrity, but after a fierce struggle the charging party was compelled to fall back. At this critical moment Gen. Tyler perceiving the disorder into which the Ninth were thrown, came to their aid with his brigade. The ninth quickly rallied, and assisted by Tyler's brigade, another attempt was made to storm the rebel batteries, but without success. The fight now became general on the extreme left and another desperate effort was made to capture the rebel battery by Tyler's brigade, but the fire of the rebels was so withering in its effect that our brave fellows were unable to gain any advantage. Each charge thinned their ranks at a fearful rate, and the chances of capturing that much coveted battery appeared no better than at first. By noon the whole of Franklin's corps was engaged with the enemy, and a desperate effort was made to turn the enemy's position on the Massaponax and drive him beyond. General Franklin commanded the movement in person The rebels maintained possession of some small hills with their usual stubbornness, but gradually fell back, as the Union troops evinced a determination to go forward. During the afternoon the rebels came to a stand, and for a time assumed the offensive, but as they advanced on us they were bravely met and repulsed with heavy loss. At this time some three hundred of Hill's command fell into our hands and were conducted to the rear as prisoners. Still the enemy contested every part of the ground, and it was only by dint of the hardest kind of fighting that he could be compelled to change his position. The obstinacy with which the rebels held possession of their ground rendered Franklin's task very difficult. He had to cope with Stonewall Jackson's veterans of Cedar Mountain, Bull Run, and Antietam, troops who understood their busi[illegible]oroughly and were not to be scared by tri[illegible] Hence the turning of the rebels' position on the Massaponax was no ordinary one. Still the Union commander was not discouraged. He had driven the enemy back several rods. Old Stonewall has met his match this time, and notwithstanding his troops fought with their usual bravery, they were gradually pushed southward.

At sundown Franklin had succeeded in driving the enemy nearly a mile, and his troops occupied the field during the remainder of the night. The movement on the left was a complete success. The casualties on both sides were very numerous.

Sumner, commanding the second corps, commenced the action on the right at ten o'clock, and it raged furiously all day. The enemy occupied the woods and hills in the rear of the city, and in point of advantage the odds were decidedly in their favor. The courage of the Union troops was unbounded, however. Every inch of ground was nobly contested. It soon became evident that the first ridge of hills, on which the enemy were posted behind earthworks, could not be carried except at the point of the bayonet. Accordingly, Sumner ordered French's division to charge upon the batteries. General Howard's division acted as support, and the troops sprang forward to obey the order with enthusiasm. By this time the atmosphere was clear, except from the smoke of the artillery, and a good view could be had

LAWS OF OREGON.
BY AUTHORITY.

AN ACT to Organize the Militia.

[CONCLUDED.]

Sec. 29. Within ninety days from the passage of this Act, each and every officer of the volunteer companies now organized, having in his possession any arms, equipments, or military stores, belonging to the State, shall give to the county in which he resides, good and sufficent bonds, to be approved by the county judge, to secure the county from loss, on account of the use or misapplication of the same; and the officer so giving bonds to the county, shall, together with his sureties, be released from his and their liabilities for the same property on any bond heretofore given by him and them to the State, and the same shall be charged to the said county; and after the expiration of said ninety days, no person shall retain or have in his possession at any time, any arms, equipments, or military stores of any kind belonging to the State, unless they have been properly issued to such person in pursuance of law, and he shall be permitted, by proper authority, to retain the same in the discharge of a public duty; and no person shall use any public arms, equipments, or military stores, belonging to the State for his private use under penalty in either of the above cases, of not less than five or over fifty dollars for each offence, to be recovered, in case of a member of the organized militia, or enrolled militia in active service, by sentence of a court-martail, or in case of any other person, by suit, in the name of the State by the district attorney of the county, before any court of competent jurisdiction —and the money so recovered shall be paid into the treasury as a part of the military fund of the State. The commanding general of brigade shall have authority to take possession of such arms and equipments so used, without process of law, and he shall account to the adjutant general for the same.

Sec. 30. Any number of organized volunteer companies, not less than three nor more than eight, may form themselves into a volunteer battalion by giving notice of such intention through their commanding officer to the general of their brigade, who will appoint some suitable officer to hold an election of the officers of such battalion; and the officer so appointed shall fix a time and place for such election, by giving ten days' notice thereof, by publication in some newspaper, or by posting notices in at least three public places in the county. Such election shall be by ballot, by the members of the volunteer companies calling for the organization of the battalion. The officer so appointed to hold the election shall preside over and superintend such election, and as soon as it shall have been determined he shall make out certificates of election of the officers so elected, and a certified account of the proceedings of said meeting, with a certified copy of the notice of said meeting, all of which he shall transmit to the brigadier general of the brigade, who shall transmit them, with a certified copy of the appointment of such officer to hold the election, to the adjutant general of the State, through the ordinary channels of military correspondence.

Sec. 31. A battalion of eight companies shall be deemed a regiment, and shall elect one colonel, one lieutenant colonel, and one major; a battalion of more than four and less than eight companies, shall elect one lieutenant colonel, who shall be the commanding officer, and one major; and a battalion of three or four companies shall elect one major, who shall be the commanding officer.

Sec. 32. It shall be the duty of each and every commanding officer of any volunteer company in this State, on or before the last Monday of July of each year to muster his company, and to make out, in triplicate, muster rolls, setting forth the names and number of the members of his company, the officers, in the order of their rank, and the privates, in alphabetical order, and stating at the foot of such muster roll a list of all arms, accoutrements, ordnance and ordnance stores, and other property belonging to this State in his possession; one of which muster rolls, duly certified, he shall transmit, through his commanding officer, to the adjutant general of the State; he shall file one in the office of the county clerk of his county, and he shall keep the other as a voucher for himself. If such company shall form a part of any organized battalion or regiment, the commanding officer thereof shall transmit the same with a muster roll of the field and staff officers of his regiment or battalion, to the adjutant general of the State, through the proper channels of military correspondence.

Sec. 33. All commissioned officers of the organized volunteer regiments, battalions and companies, shall take rank according to the date assigned them by their commissions; and when two of the same grade be of the same date, their rank shall be determined by length of service in the militia; and if of equal service, then by lot. Officers of organized volunteer regiments, battalions, and companies, shall in all cases be deemed of superior rank to officers of the enrolled militia of the same grade, irrespective of the date of their commissions.

Sec. 34. All commissioned officers of the staff of the commander-in-chief, the major general and brigadier generals, and all the officers of their respective staffs, and all commissioned officers, non-commissioned officers, musicians, artificers and privates, of volunteer regiments, battalions, and companies, whose names are borne upon the muster rolls of their respective regiments, battalions and companies, shall be denominated the organized militia of Oregon, and shall at all times be subject to be called into active service by the commander-in-chief; and when so called into active service, each person shall be called and mustered according to his commission, enrolment, and organization. All other militia in this State shall be denominated the enrolled militia of Oregon.

Sec. 35. In case of war, insurrection, or rebellion, or of resistance to the execution of the laws of this State, or upon the call or requisition of the President of the United States, or upon the call of any officer of the United States army, commanding a division, department, or district, in Oregon, or upon the call of any United States Marshal in Oregon, or of any Mayor of a city, or of any sheriff, the commander-in-chief is authorized to call into active service any portion of the organized or enrolled militia of this State. In case of the absence of the commander-in-chief from the capital, or if it be impossible to immediately communicate with him, the civil or military officer making the requisition for troops may, if he deem the danger imminent and not admitting of delay, serve a copy of such requisition, together with a statement of the Governor's absence, or the impossibility of immediately communicating with him, upon the major general; or, in his absence, upon the general of brigade, who is hereby authorized to exercise, with respect to calling out the troops of his division or brigade, the powers conferred in this section upon the Governor; but if the call shall be disapproved by the Governor, the troops so called into service will be immediately disbanded. Such call for any portion of the organized militia shall be made by an order issued and directed to the commanding officer of the company, battalion, regiment, or brigade which is so called into service, designating in such order the particular troops called, the time and place of rendezvous, and the offices to whom they shall report. If such order be directed to the major general of division, it will be immediately communicated to the brigadier generals, and by them to all the offices of their respective brigades; and any officer receiving such order will rendezvous and report for duty as herein directed; and any officers commanding an organized volunteer company or battalion, on receiving such order, will immediately proceed to notify the same to each individual of his command, by personal notice, or by publication in some newspaper, or by the usual posting in public places of the county or counties from which the call is made, and such officer shall attend in person or by deputing an officer of the organized militia in his place, at the place of rendezvous, and take the names of all volunteers for service under such call; and if the number of volunteers shall be sufficient to form one or more companies or battalions, according to the provisions of this Act, he shall immediately call and superintendent the electon of the officers of such companies or battalions, which elections shall be conducted in the manner prescribed in this Act for the election of officers of volunteer companies and battalions, except as to the publication of notice of such election; a proclamation of the call of such election, made by the officer calling it at the place of rendezvous, being deemed a sufficient notice. But the commander-in-chief shall have authority, if he shall deem it expedient, to direct that a portion of the volunteers so presenting themselves shall be assigned to organized volunteer companies or battalions already in active service, whose numbers are less than the full complement prescribed in this Act, after which, the volunteering shall organize and elect as herein described.

Sec. 36. If the number of volunteers so presenting themselves at the place of rendezvous shall not be sufficient to satisfy the call of the commander-in-chief, the brigadier general of the brigade in which such call is made shall promptly proceed to draft from the enrolled militia of his brigade a sufficient number of men to satisfy said call, and this draft shall be made by putting the names of all the enrolled militia of the county, or counties, from which the order directs the forces to be raised, into a box, and drawing there-from a sufficient number of names to satisfy the call. The persons whose names are so drawn will be summoned by some officer, or officers, appointed for that purpose by the brigadier general, in the manner prescribed by law for the summoning of witnesses in civil cases, the time and place of rendezvous, as ordered by the brigadier general, being stated in the summons. In case of the absence or inability of the brigadier general, the officer next in rank of the brigade, or in default of any officer of that brigade for duty, the major general, or, in his default, the commander-in-chief shall designate some officer to perform the duties prescribed to such brigadier general with respect to making such drafts; and as soon as a sufficient number of such drafted men shall have appeared at the rendezvous to form a company, or companies, they shall proceed to the election of their company officers, in the manner prescribed in this Act.

Sec. 37. Any company, or companies, of the enrolled militia so drafted and organized may, by direction of the commander-in-chief, be enrolled and mustered into any battalion of the organized militia having less than eight companies; and any drafted men of the enrolled militia, not organized into companies, may, at the discretion of the commander in-chief, be enrolled and mustered into any existing company of organized or enrolled militia, not having the full number authorized by law, and which has already been called into active service. If the enrolled militia when drafted into service, shall fail to elect any officer designated in such call for an election in the manner and at the time appointed as provided in this Act, such vacancy or vacancies shall be filled by appointments made by the commander-in-chief.

Sec. 38. Any officer, non-commissioned officer, musician, artificer, or private of the organized militia of this State, who shall neglect or refuse to rendezvous and organize when ordered out by the commander-in-chief, shall be deemed guilty of a disobedience of orders, and shall be tried and punished by a court-martial; and any person of the enrolled militia who shall refuse or neglect to rendezvous and organize when drafted as provided in this Act, shall be subject to a fine of not less than fifty nor more than five hundred dollars, to be recovered by an action to be brought by the district attorney in the name of the State, upon the certificate of the officer appointed to make the draft, before any court of competent jurisdiction in the county from which such person was drafted, and the fine so recovered shall be paid into the treasury, as belonging to the military fund of the State.

Sec. 39. Any private of the organized militia, and any person of the enrolled militia, called, or drafted, into service under the provisions of this Act, may furnish as a substitute, any person fit for military duty, who has not been called or drafted into service.

Sec. 40. The commander-in-chief may order a public parade of all the organized militia of the State ten days of each year; such parades to be held within the limits of the brigade to which such troops respectively belong; and such public parades shall be reviewed by the commander-in-chief, or, in his absence, by the major general, or by the officer of the brigade of the highest rank present. Immediately after all such troops have been reviewed, they shall be inspected by an inspector general and such inspecting officer, after a minute inspecting of dress and military bearing of the field officers and commissioned staff, and the officers of companies, and arms, accoutrements and dress of each soldier, will report the result of such inspection to his commanding officer.

Sec. 41. The rules of discipline and regulations of the army of the United States shall constitute the rules of discipline and regulations of the organized militia of this State; and the rules and articles of war established by Congress for the army of the United States, shall be adopted, so far as they may be applicable for the government of the militia of Oregon in active service.

Sec. 42. Courts-martial appointed shall be organized in like manner, and be subject to the rules and regulations governing courts-martial in the United States army; they shall have the same power to compel the attendance of witnesses, when duly summoned by the judge advocate, to preserve order in and about the court-room during their session, and to punish contempt, as the judges of the district courts have under laws of this State.

Sec. 43. Any commissioned officer of a brigade who shall remove his residence from the limits of his brigade, will be deemed to have resigned his commission; and the major general or any brigadier general, who shall absent himself from the state for more than three months, without the permission of the commander-in-chief, shall be deemed to have resigned his office.

Sec. 44. Whenever any of the militia of this state shall be called into active service for the space of more than one week, they shall receive the same pay and allowances as United States troops serving in Oregon. Any general or field officer being called into active service, such call shall be deemed to include all the officers of their respective staff.

Sec. 45. When the commander-in-chief shall order the return to the state of any arms, equipments, military stores, or other military property, belonging to the state, such arms and military property shall be immediately delivered to the officers authorized in such order to receive it, he receipting for the same, and describing their condition in such receipts; and if the property mentioned in such order shall not be promptly delivered, as directed, the officer named in such order is hereby authorized to take immediate possession of the same, in the name of the state; and any person resisting such officer in the performance of this duty, shall be deemed guilty of a misdemeanor, punishable by imprisonment for not more than six months in the county jail and shall be subject to a fine not exceeding five hundred dollars, to be recovered by an action brought by the district attorney in the name of the state, and be paid into the treasury as a part of the military fund.

Sec. 46. The commander-in-chief, adjutant general and the Secretary of State, shall constitute a state board of military auditors. The commander-in-chief shall be president, and the adjutant general shall be secretary of said board.

Sec. 47. The board of military auditors shall have a seal, an impression of which shall be deposited by the secretary of the board in the office of the Secretary of State, and be attached to all accounts audited by said board.

Sec. 48. It shall be the duty of said board of military auditors to audit all reasonable expenses for ammunition incurred by volunteer companies in the service of this state, and all other claims required under the provisions of this act. It shall be the duty of the Secretary of State to draw his warrants for the amount thus audited, and the Treasurer of State is hereby required to pay the same out of any moneys in the military fund not otherwise appropriated.

Sec. 49. The adjutant general shall, under the direction of the Governor, prepare and keep in his charge all blank military commissions, and such other blanks as may be required for the service.

Sec. 50. The commander-in-chief may from time to time make and publish rules, regulations and orders for the government of the militia of this state in accordance with the spirit and provisions of this act.

Sec. 51. Any volunteer company may on its organization, or thereafter, adopt a distinctive name, but shall be known by a particular letter in the battalion or regiment to which it belongs.

Sec. 52. In the absence of any appropriate cammander, the next in rank in the command of troops, where not otherwise provided in this act, shall succeed to his authority.

Sec. 53. Every senior, in his appropriate command, shall have authority to control the actions of his junior, in accordance with the principles of military subordination, under the laws and usages that govern the United States army.

Sec. 54. Any officer cashiered by sentence of a court martial shall be precluded thereby from holding any commission in the military service of the state, except the sentence be remitted by the commander-in-chief.

Sec. 55. No non-commissioned officer, artificer, musician, or private, expelled from his company or dismissed from service for any disgraceful cause, shall be permitted to again enter any volunteer company, except the offense be pardoned by the commander-in-chief.

Sec. 56. No officer, inferior in grade to a regimental or battalion commander, shall have power to grant discharges to non-commissioned officers, artificers, musicians, or privates, in active service; but commanders of companies of the organized militia, when not in active service, may issue certificates of service and discharges. All discharges shall be in writing and shall set forth fully the cause of the discharge, and shall be signed by the officer granting the same.

Sec. 57. Any officer resigning his commission, shall do so in writing, and transmit the same, through his immediate commanding officer who will make his indorsement thereon, and the resignation shall go into effect when accepted by the commander-in-chief, and not before. Vacancies of commissioned officers of organized companies and battalions (not in active service) caused by resignation, death, dismissal, or removals, or by the expiration of the time fixed by the rules and regulations of such company, or battalion, or by any other cause, shall be filled by election. Such elections of company and field officers shall be presided over by an officer appointed for that purpose, by the brigadier general; and such presiding officer shall report the result of such election to the officer appointing him, which report shall be transmitted to the commander-in-chief, who shall issue commissions in accordance therewith: *Provided*, however, that when the same officer shall be re-elected, no new commission shall be issued; but the officer so re-elected shall continue to hold under his original commission.

Sec. 58. The commission of any staff officer whose term of office depends upon the pleasure of the officer by whom he is appointed, shall, when such officer is not on active service, be considered as vacated upon the qualifiation of his successor, and shall be so noted upon the proper books or rolls kept in the office of the adjutant general of the State.

Sec. 59. The commander-in-chief is authorized at any time by issuing his orders to that effect, to disband any portion of the organized volunteer forces, or of the enrolled militia mustered into service, which may evince a mutinous, disorderly, or disobedient spirit, and to deprive them of arms, a copy of which order shall be transmitted to the clerk of the county court or courts of the county or counties in which such force was raised; after which it shall be a misdemeanor in any person so disbanded to appear with State arms in his possession, or as any portion of the organized volunteer militia, or of the enrolled militia, in active service until again drafted or regularly mustered into service, under the penalty of not less than ten nor more than one hundred dollars for each offence, and such person shall be proceeded against by the district attorney, in the name of the State, before any competent court of the county where such person may happen to be, and all fines so recovered and collected, shall be paid into the treasury as a part of the military fund.

Sec. 60. The systems of instruction in tactics prescribed for the different arms and corps in the United States army shall be followed in the military instruction and practice of the militia of this State, and the use of any other system is forbidden.

Sec. 61. The commanding officer of every organized company, shall, during the months of June and December of each year furnish the county clerk of his county with a list of the names of bonafide members of his company who attend regularly to appropriate duty. He shall also, at the end of each year's service, of any members of his company, who has performed duty in accordance with the regulations and by-laws of such company during the the year, issue to such member a certificate to that effect which certificate shall exempt the holder thereof from the poll tax imposed by this Act. And if such commander of a company shall make a false list of the members of his company who have done duty as aforesaid, or a false certificate of service, he shall, on conviction by a court-martial, be cashiered from service, and shall, moreover, be subject to a fine of not less than fifty nor over five hundred dollars, to be sued for and recovered in the name of the State by the district attorney of the county of his residence in any court of competent jurisdiction, and be paid into the treasury as a part of the military fund of the State.

Sec. 62. When any person drafted for service shall offer at or after the time of rendezvous a suitable substitute of the age of twenty-one years, and such substitute shall consent in writing to subject himself to all the duties, fines, forfeitures and punishments to which his principal would have been subject had he personally served, he shall be accepted by the officer making such draft, and the same rule shall apply to substitutes offered by members of organized volunteer companies called into active service, the commanding officer of such company being the judge of the suitableness of the substitute offered; and the person whose substitute shall be so accepted, shall be exempted from draft during the term of service of his substitute.

Sec. 63. No action shall be maintained against any member of a court-martial or officer, or agent, acting under his authority on account of the imposition of a fine or the execution of a sentence on a person not liable to military duty, if such person shall have been duly summoned and shall have neglected to appear and show his exemption before the court.

Sec. 64. The adjutant general shall have a seal of office to be approved by the commander-in-chief, and all copies of records or papers in his office duly certified and authenticated under the said seal shall be evidence in all cases in like manner as if the originals were produced.

Sec. 65. On the days of military parade the militia so called out and doing military duty shall be considered to be under military discipline from the rising to the setting of the sun, and no officer, non-commissioned officer, musician, artificer or private belonging to the same during the time aforesaid shall be subject to be arrested on any civil process.

Sec. 66. The commanding officer of any parade, review or drill, and the officer in charge of any rendezvous may cause the ground selected for that purpose to be marked or designated in such a manner as not to obstruct the passage of travellers on any public highway, and if any person during the occupation of such grounds for such military purpose shall encroach upon such bounds or enter upon such grounds without the permission of such officer commanding or in charge, he may be put and kept under guard by the order of such commander until the setting of the sun of the same day, and moreover shall be subject to arrest and punishment by any court of competent jurisdiction for a breach of the peace.

Sec. 67. If any person shall intercept, molest or insult by abusive words or behavior, any officer, non-commissioned officer, or soldier, while in the performance of his military duty, he shall be immediately put under guard and kept at the discretion of the commanding officer of the forces engaged in the performance of such military duty until the setting of the sun of the same day on which the offense shall have been committed and moreover shall be subject to arrest and punishment by any court of competent jurisdiction ior a breach of the peace.

Sec. 68. Any officer, non-commissioned officer, or soldier, on military duty, who shall disobey the legal orders of his superiors, use any reproachful or abusive language to his superior, or misbehave or demean himself in an unofficer or unsoldierlike manner shall be immediately arrested, if an officer, and if a non-commissioned officer or soldier, shall be disarmed and put under guard and shall be tried and punished by a court martial according to law and military usage.

Sec. 69. In case of parades, reviews, inspections, or musters of the troops of any brigade, any companies, not organized into a battalion, for the duties of the day, and the battalion so temporarily organized shall be commanded by the officer senior in rank of the companies composing it. It shall be optional with any such unattached companies to attach themselves for the day to any organized battalion or battalions, or to organize a temporary battalion; but no such temporary battalion shall be organized of less than two companies if there be any organized battalion or battalions present on duty, to which they may attach themselves without exceeding the complement fixed by this Act. If such unattached companies shall not attach or organize themselves in accordance with the provisions of this section, the officer commanding the brigade for the day shall order such assignment or organization.

Sec. 70. Horses, arms, equipments, and uniforms, of all officers, non-commissioned officers, and privates, used for military purposes in the organized or enrolled militia of this State shall be exempt from execution.

Sec. 71. The keepers of all ferries allowed to collect tolls, either under the authority of the state, or county, must pass all persons, subject to militia duty, going or returning from muster, with their horses and equipage, free of toll, and if they delay them unnecessarily, shall be subject to a fine of not less than ten dollars for each offence, to be recovered, by any person before a competent tribunal, for the use of the general military fund.

Sec. 72. In case of any conflagration happening in any incorporated town or city, the mayor or chief officer thereof shall have power to demand from the officer commanding the organized militia, of said place, a detachment of men to make patrols, and maintain good order as long as the conflagration may exist, and the commanding officer shall furnish such detachment. The commanding officer of the detachment shall receive from the civil officer, requiring his service, written instructions as to the duty required of him.

Sec. 73. Whenever any change is made in the organization of the militia by Congress, the Governor shall immediately carry such change into effect by general order, and may in the same manner establish such subordinate regulations as the change may render necessary.

Sec. 74. The adjutant general shall also furnish all necessary blanks and blank books, for officers and commanders of companies. Such books and blanks shall be receipted for by the officers receiving the same, to be held and accounted for by him as public property, and no resignation shall be accepted until such books and all other public property, delivered to such officers, shall be delivered to his successor, or to the adjutant or quartermaster general, or satisfactorily accounted for, and double the value of such books or property may be recovered of any such officer, his executors and administrators by proceedings instituted by the district attorney in the name of the state, in any court of competent jurisdiction. All amounts so recovered shall be placed in the general military fund.

Sec. 75. Officers and men of a volunteer corps, who shall serve faithfully for seven years, shall be entitled to a certificate from the adjutant general, that they have faithfully so served for seven years, according to the requirments of law, and shall afterwards be expempt from serving in the milita, unless when called into the service of the United States, or in time of war or insurrection.

Sec. 76. That the military fund created by this act, shall be used exclusively for military purposes, and expended under direction of the board of military auditors: *First*, premiums for the best drilled companies of cavalry, artillery, and infantry, who shall be present at the state agricultural fair. *Second*, in payment of such sums, not to exceed two dollars per day for each man, to each company, which shall produce satisfactory evidence to the board of military auditors that they have gone into camp and drilled for not less than three nor more than ten days in the months of June and September; *Third*, in such manner as may be deemed conducive to advance of military science, and in the purchase of arms and accoutrements for the use of the state, the certificate of the brigadier general or assistant adjutant general shall be evidence of service rendered according to this act.

Sec. 77. That the State printer print three hundred copies of this act, in pamphlet form, and place them in the hands of the adjutant general for distribution to the organized militia;

Sec. 78. That the uniform of the militia of this state shall be similar to that of a like grade in the United States army; with a distinction mark upon the hat or cap to be prescribed by the commander-in chief. This article shall not be construed so as to prohibit any company of the organized militia from having and adopting an additional uniform of any style they may prescribe.

Sec. 79. All fines legally imposed by a court martial, lawfully constituted, after the proceedings and findings of said court in the premises have been approved by proper authority, shall be and the same are made collectable by law, it shall be the duty of the adjutant general to certify a list of fines to the county clerk of the county in which the person who may be fined resides, which list shall be entered by said clerk in a book to be kept by him for that purpose; and an execution issued by him for the collection of the same. All fines so imposed shall have the same lien upon property as if a judgment rendered by a court of record in this state.

Sec. 80. That an Act entitled an Act to organize the militia, passed February 2, 1854; also, an Act entitled an Act to organize the militia, passed January 26, 1856, together with any other Acts or parts of Acts in conflict herewith, be and are hereby repealed.

Sec. 81. Inasmuch as there is no organized militia in this State, this Act shall be in force from and after its approval by the Governor.

Approved October 16, 1862.

DAILY LYNCHBURG VIRGINIAN.

THE RIGHTS OF THE SOUTH AND THE UNION OF THE SOUTH.

BY CHARLES W BUTTON. LYNCHBURG. FRIDAY. JANUARY, 2. 1863 VOLUME 11---NUMBER 130.

SUBSCRIPTION AND ADVERTISING SCHEDULE.

TERMS OF SUBSCRIPTION.

The VIRGINIAN is published Daily, Tri-Weekly and Weekly, at the following rates, INVARIABLY IN ADVANCE.

Daily Virginian, one year,			$8 00
do.	do.	six months,	5 00
do.	do.	three months,	2 50
do.	do.	one month	1 00
Tri-weekly, one year.			$6 00
do.		six months,	4 00
do.		three months,	2 00
do.		one month,	75
Weekly, one year,			$2 50
do.		six months,	1 50

☞ No paper will be sent without the subscription is paid in advance.

RATES OF ADVERTISING.

ADVERTISEMENTS are inserted for 75 cents per square of 10 lines, or less, for the first insertion, and 50 cents for each continuance unless ordered every-other-time and then 75 cents per square will be charged for each insertion. If the number of insertions be not marked on the MSS, they will be published till ordered out and charged accordingly.

THE YEARLY RATES ARE:

For one square daily	$50
For two squares, daily	75
For one square tri-weekly	35
For two squares tri-weekly	59

☞ No advertisement to be considered by the month or year unless specified on the manuscript, or previously agreed upon.

☞ Advertisements not marked on the copy for a specified number of insertions will be continued until ordered out, and payment demanded accordingly.

☞ Advertisements intended for both papers subject to special contract.

☞ REGULAR ADVERTISEMENTS. To avoid any misunderstanding on the part of annual advertisers, we state distinctly, that any advertisements not properly connected with their business will be charged seperately, and also, any excess of matter over the space contracted for.

☞ Transient advertisements payable in advance, all others will be considered due when called for.

☞ Announcements of candidates $5, to be paid in advance

☞ All Obituaries and Tributes of Respect, exceeding eight lines are charged as advertisements.

☞ All notices of private Associations, every notice calling attention to private enterprises, calculated or intended to promote individual interests, can only be inserted with the understanding that the same be paid for.

Daily Virginian.

THE EFFORT TO COVER UP THE DEFEAT AT FREDERICKSBURG

So accustomed have the Yankees grown to claiming a victory in every case, and never confessing a defeat, that they even have desperation to try to disguise their reverse at Fredericksburg, or to mollify it by some ingenious pleading of words. The New York *Herald* says such cruel deception with the people will not do, and denounces it with some very plain words of warning to Mr. Lincoln. Referring to the deception tried to be practised in the case, the *Herald* says—

We have been most grossly deceived.—We have poor Greeley's word for it, that the battle at Fredericksburg was a "gratifying" victory. We have President Lincoln's certifiicate that our apparent repulse was only "an accident." We have the report of the Senatorial War Committee that nobody is to blame and that there is nothing to blame anybody about. We grieve exceedingly to record that the splendid efforts of the Senatorial War Committee to whitewash over that "dammed spot" of bloodshed at Fredericksburg are not as successful as we could wish. We are painfully aware that the people cannot understand that sending a brave army to do an "impossible" thing, and thus subjecting it to a terrible, hellish, enfilading fire, was "not an error," but only "an accident."

None of us poor, ignorant mortals knew that we had won a great victory at Fredericksburg, and had at last found our Napoleon in General Burnside, until we were favored with the certificates to that effect from the President, the Secretary of War, the General-in-Chief, and the radical Senators and journalists. The benighted people understood that the rebels had repulsed our army with very heavy loss, and that, *a la* the celebrated King of France, we had marched across the Rappahannock only to march back again, with ten thousand of our soldiers killed and wounded.

If the administration attempts to go on with its present Micawber policy, skirmishing with a self-satisfied leer over the admirable way in which its has humbugged the country into a little more patience.—We warn President Lincoln to be ware of the disastrous result, or he will lead his administration, as Burnside led our army, to a Fredericksburg—victory?

THE FREDERICKSBURG DISASTER—INCOMPETENT OFFICIALS AT WASHINGTON.

The Nerthern papers devote much space to a discussion of the report of the Congressional Committee on the war, and the officials at Washington get severely lectured on their responsibility for the failure at Fredericksburg. A long editorial in a New York journal concludes as follows:

From General Halleck's ewn testimony it does not appear that he is of any use whatever at Washington. He acts the part of a mere clerk, copying orders, but not seeing that they are carried out. He neither plans campaigns nor gives efficient assistance to the Generals who do plan and fight them. The necessary supplies were withheld from McClellan at Harper's Ferry at the time when the radical Journals were clamoring against him for not moving on, and so it has been in the case of Burnside. General Franklin swears that, notwithstanding the delay of the pontoons, the position of the enemy would have been captured had more men been on the field on the day of the battle. Whose fault is that? Is it not boasted that we have 800,000 men in arms? Is it not the fault of General Halleck and the Secretary of War that we had not enough men at the decisive point? It seems that there is not only no military men at Washington to carry on the war, but not even men of common sense. The only suggestion not to attack too soon, while all his Generals agree that from the imbecility which rules at the capital, his attack was delayed too long, and thus failed.

There is abundant ground in this report for the most determined action of both Houses of Congress, and we trust that immediately after this recess a joint resolution will be adopted, calling upon the president to remove Stanton and Halleck, Meigs, and the whole catch of incompetent officers, whose delays haralyze the best efforts of the Generals in the field.—And, to aid in the same result, we would suggest that a great meeting be called in this city to give expression to public opinion, and send a deputation to Mr. Lincoln. The meeting intended to be held last Saturday was postponed till fuller information could be obtained of the facts. The official report of the Congressional Committee has furnished it on oath from the best sources, and now is the time for the people to act.

RUMOURS FROM RICHMOND.

[Richmond Correspondence of Charleston Mercury.]

I will tell you an anecdote about Lee. At Sharpsburg he hailed one of the many stragglers, and inquired:

"Where are you going, sir?"

"Goin' to the rear."

'What are you going to the rear for?"

"Well, I,ve been stung by a bung, and I'm what they call demoralized."

This was enough. General Lee had not the heart to say more to an innocent who had been "stung by a bung"—meaning perhaps that he had been stung by a bumb.

A Washington paper seems to think that Burnside's army will go into winter quarters near that city. If so, it is conjectured that Jackson will remain near Port Royal and that Longstreet will take position below Petersburg The Examiner is of opinion that Burnside will winter in the strip of country between the Potomac and Rappahannock, were his impotent rage may find employment in pillaging the homes of unaffending citizens.

I took a walk yesterday around the suburbs of the city, and saw fortification after fortification at every turn. When I thought of Burnside sneaking back to Washington these formidable earthworks looked like an absurd waste of labor. Such they are not however. Drury's Bluff, or Darling, as the Yankees insist on calling it also seems absurd. Strange? the enemy has never dared to approch it since his first repulse—isn't it?

The Virginian.

FRIDAY,....................J UARY 2, 1863.

NOTICE.—The cross appended to the names of certain [illegible]bers indicates that the term for which they subscribed will soon expire. They are thus notified in time to renew their subscriptions if they desire.

FIRE.—The stable and workshop of Capt John B. Tilden were consumed by fire yesterday. By dint of exertion, his dwelling was saved It is supposed that the stable was set on fire. His furniture was somewhat damaged. We hope that the loss which this public servant and which he could ill afford, has sustained, will be fully made up to him by the community.

CHRISTMAS DINNER IN BUCHANAN.—Mr. Editor:—It is gratifying to hear of sumptuous dinners having been served up, at various hospitals, for the benefit of the sick and wounded soldiers, and it affords me great pleasure to be able to give publicity to one more, which is not the least, though it may be the last, that will be published. On Christmas day the tables in the hospitals at Buchanan, Botetourt county, Va., were heavily ladened with a great abundance and variety of substantials and delicacies, neatly prepared and beautifully arranged by the unwearied hands of the ever faithful ladies of this community, for the benefit of the invalid soldiers in their midst. The observer could not fail to see the pleasure was mutual, for the soldiers were delighted with "so rich a feast," and much more with the knowledge of the fact that this, with all similar demonstrations upon the part of the ladies was only a faint mark of their high regards for the brave defenders of our land. The ladies, whose happiness consists in making others happy were of course delighted to see that they were capable of making one bright spot in the monotonous path of a soldier. Are they not all ministering angels? Heaven bless and reward the noble and generous ladies of the South, and if for nothing else, for their sake, save this lovely southern land from the grasp of a Northern despot.

ONE WHO LOVES THE LADIES.

THE RICHMOND MARKETS.—We quote below from the Dispatch's report of the 30th:

Groceries and Produce.—The markets at the present time develop nothing new in the course of trade, and there will be nothing of interest to report until after New Year's. The transactions in groceries are small, without any noticeable change in price, and it is useless to repeat quotations. There is nothing doing in Wheat, and the mills will not resume operations until after the close of the holidays. Corn remains at $3 per bushel, wholesale price, and recent auction sales in the neighboring country are reported at $15 per barrel. The trade in Leaf Tobacco is temporarily suspended. It is the opinion of well informed men that business will open with renewed animation early in January. In Manufactured Tobacco there is still considerable activity. We heard of a sale of $5,000 worth yesterday at $1.13 to $1.15. Bacon is unchanged. Butter is selling by the package at $1.25 for inferior, and $1.50 for good article. Potatoes, Flour, and other articles of general consumption, continue at last quotations.

Liquors—We notice a considerable advance in Liquors, under the hands of speculators. A prime article of Apple Brandy now commands $20 per gallon, with an advancing tendency; and Whiskey $25 to $30. It may be interesting to state here that the latest quotations of Whiskey in the Cincinnati market is 35 cents per gallon.

The following prices were obtained at the auction sale of Robinson, Adams & Co:

Three ply Carpeting $6 per yard; Salad Oil $4 50 per bottle; Black Thread $9.12½ per lb; Ladies' Gaiters $14.50 per pair; Bleached Muslin $1.30 to $1 45 per yard; Country Jeans $4.50 to $6.12 per yard; [illegible]ol Cotton $4.87½ per dozen; Brown [illegible] 70 to 82½ cts; Candles 92½ to 95 cts; [illegible]e 26 cts; Soda $3.15; Black Grain [illegible] $2.82½ to $2.85; Brown Sugar 87½ to 93 cts; Golden Syrup $6.10.

RECOGNITION—A Washington correspondent of the New York Herald says: "There are here a number of weak-backed Republicans, who are steadily croaking about the necessity of recognizing the Southern Confederacy. In this list are found a number of Republican members of Congress who openly express despair of the success of the Federal Government under its present military administration, and declare that, under existing circumstances, *no more troops can be raised, even by draft*, in the States which they represent.'

Another writer from Washington says that in diplomatic circles the event next in importance to the Fredericksburg defeat is considered to be the certainty that the Emperor Napoleon will, at his New Year reception, inform Minister Dayton that the sufferings of France will no longer permit him to delay entreating the United States and the Confederate States to terminate the wasteful war."

DINNER TO THE SOLDIERS.—We understand that the soldiers at Claytor's Hospital were served with an excellent dinner yesterday, for which, we have no doubt, they are very grateful to the generous ladies who were instrumental in securing it for them.

SEE advertisement of Matrons wanted at the Liberty Hospital.

MARRIED,

At the Baptist Church in Lynchburg, Va by the Rev. H W Dodge, Dec. 31st, 1862. Mr. GEORGE THOMAS FOX and Miss MARY J DAVIDSON, eldest daughter of Capt. G S Davidson of the Confederate Army.

ATROCITIES OF THE ENEM

The Wilmington Journal says:

During the recent raid of the enemy towards Goldshoro,' their conduct was gratuitously evil and wantonly barbarous. They committed outrages which seemed to have neither sense nor object, and which could have no military reason nor justification. The poor as well as the rich were plundered, and little objects of female attire, and even children's toys were torn up or burned out of mere deviltry.

Many plantations were stripped of servants, horses, pigs, cattle, meat, cloth, meal, and, in fact, of everything that could either be carried off or destroyed. The number of negroes taken off estimated at 500 to 600, and all of them working hands.

Female attire and children's tops, destroyed out of mere deviltry—by christian warriors and gentlemen soldiers!

But here is an excerpt from a Yankee account of what was done at Fredericksburg, before the vengeance of Heaven fell on them from the batteries and muskets of Gen. Lee:

A letter in the Tribune, dated Fredericksburg, Dec. 12th, says:

The old mansion of Douglas Gordon—perhaps the wealthiest citizen in the vicinity—is now used as the headquarters of General Howard, but before he occupied it, every room had been torn with shot, and then all the elegant furniture and works of art broken and smashed by the soldiers, who burst into the house after having driven the rebel sharpshooters from behind it. When I entered it early this morning, before its occupation by Gen. Howard, I found the soldiers of his fine division diverting themselves with the rich dresses found in the wardrobes; some had on bonnets of the fashion of last year, and were surveying themselves before mirrors, which, an hour afterwards, were pitched out of the window and smashed to pieces upon the pavement; others had elegant scarfs bound round their heads in the form of turbans, and shawls around their waists.

We destroyed by fire nearly two whole squares of buildings, chiefly used for business purposes, together with the fine residences of O. McDowell, Dr. Smith, J. H. Kelly, A. S. Cott, William Slaughter, and many other smaller dwellings. Every store, I think, without exception, was pillaged of every valuable article. A fine drug store, which would not have looked badly on Broadway, was literally one mass of broken glass and jars.

Of a former raid by the Yankees in North Carolina, a correspondent of the Boston Traveller wrote. Of Williamston, he said:

This is a small town, having before the war from 500 to 700 inhabitants. We found it almost entirely deserted, one or two white men being all we saw in the place. Our halt there was about three hours, and at the end of that time the town was thoroughly pillaged. Not only were useful and ornamental articles taken from houses, and horses, harness and carriages from barns, but stores were entered and sacked, and with the "apple jack" discovered and the whiskey dealt out by order, not a few were dead drunk, and many more partially frenzied. When we moved a considerable number had to be urged almost at the point of the bayonet, while others were loaded into ambulances and baggage wagons.

Of their arrival near Hamilton, a town of from 300 to 400 souls, he says:

But, instead of marching into the town, we were encamped in a corn-field just outside of it. The order was that two or three men be sent out to forage provisions for each company, and no others allowed in town. But whether by open disobedience, or by the connivance of those who should have enforced the order, the town was soon, in camp language, "cleaned out," even more completely than Williamston.—Not only were houses sacked, and everything portable and desirable carried off, but valuable furniture dashed to pieces, beds dragged into the streets and burned—in one field I myself counted eight or ten—but nearly or quite a dozen houses were needlessly, carelessly, barbariously burned. It is little wonder, if such be the conduct of our forces everywhere, that we should acquire an unenviable reputation.

[From the Sunday Mercury.]

It is fashionable to say that the South, in arming for resistance to Lincoln's election, initiated the revolution. So she did in one sense, and we do not pretend to hold her guiltless. But is the North entirely blameless of any participation in the crimes of a civil war which has been precipitated by events which were foreseen by the prescience of men far wiser than ourselves, and of which we were forewarned with awful emphasis by the Father of his Country, and by a long line of eminent and illustrious statesmen?

If we would desire to know the common source of all our political ills, let us cast our eyes Eastward to New England, that hot bed of isms, schisms, heresies, and fanaticisms. We boldly assert that she has kept the whole North—and may we not say the whole South?—in a state of revolution for years. What were her Slades, her Hales, her Garrisons, her Phillipses, and her Wilsons, but so many teachers of disunion, and her churches but so many magazines to "scatter fire-brands, sorrows, and death" around and through the nation?

When the Kansas-Nebraska bill was passed, and when it was hoped that the question was settled forever, these men and their debauched followers openly proclaimed that sleep should not visit their eyelids until it was repealed. Then commenced an agitation and convulsion scarcely paralleled in history. With Jacobinical zeal and phrenzy, the worst passions were invoked, and faction reared its Medusa's head, shook its snaky locks, and started on its career of madness and of ruin. Then the "Bloody Kansas work" commenced.—Then Massachusetts and other Eastern States were ready for civil war, and Emigrant Aid Societies, fitted out in Boston, were dispatched to the devoted Territory of Kansas, to make her a free State at all hazards, to overawe the peaceable settlers and tillers of the soil and reduce them to servitude, under the domination of blue-light New England Federalism of the Hartford Convention school Then subscriptions were openly taken at a meeting of the Anti-Slavery Abolition Society, held at Buffalo, N. Y., to carry out these nefarious and revolutionary purposes, and to set at defiance the authority of the Federal Government in a Territory she was bound to protect and to sustain in all her legal and constitutional rights.

But these are not a tithe of the wrongs perpetrated by New England, and her allies in other States, against the Constitution of the country, and revolutionary and factious in their character and tendency. The administrations of both Mr. Pierce and Mr. Buchanan were assailed from their beginning to their end, with a bitterness and unrelenting hostility worthy only of men and a party totally lost to every particle of principle and of honor. Their motives were impeached, their integrity questioned, and their policy embarrassed at every step by these ghouls and harpies, who aimed at power through "free speech," "free wool," and "free Kansas," that they might carry out their damnable purposes of dissolving the Union and gorging their rapacious and hungry maws with the spoils and plunder of the Government. And now they have succeeded, and what is the result? Precisely what any sane man would have predicted from the beginning. The John Brown raid—the logical result of the teachings of such men as Garrison and Giddings, who were proven to have been its instigators and co-workers—has culminated in revolution and civil war on Southern soil, and the blood of the thousands of Northern men that has drenched the sodden ground of many a battle-field, and the bones that lie bleaching in the sun, cry aloud for vengeance and retribution on the heads of the guilty authors and abettors of this "gigantic rebellion."

Let us take all these truths home to ourselves. Let us take the beam out of our own eye before we discover and find fault with the mote in that of our neighbor's.—Before God, and in the light of history, we of the North will not be held blameless for the curse of the civil war that is upon us with all its countless evils. We should bow ourselves in deep humiliation, and cover ourselves with 'sackcloth and ashes,' for our transgressions have been many and grievous.

THE ENEMY'S GUNBOATS IN THE CHOWAN.

A gentleman who passed through Raleigh on Sunday last, who had been spending some days on the Chowan river and Albemarle Sound, in Bertie county, N. C., represents that an unusual number of gunboats were in the river and in the Sound near to its mouth. He further states that these gunboats had visited all the saw mills on the waters, and had carried off a large quantity of sawed lumber. This lumber, it is conjectured, is to be used in planking up the sides of their boats, so as to protect the men on them from the fire of our sharpshooters.

FROM FREDERICKSBURG.

[Correspondence of Richmond Enquirer.]

FREDERICKSBURG, Dec. 30.

Matters have been comparatively quiet to-day. One flag of truce passed about 3 o'clock, for the purpose of carrying over Mrs. Lynde, mother-in-law of Major Fitzhugh, on Gen. Stuart's staff. The firing alluded to yesterday proceeded from target firing on the part of the enemy, and not from picket firing, as some supposed.

APPLICATIONS TO GO SOUTH.

The New York Herald says there are at the War Department five hundred applications of persons to go South.

BY TELEGRAPH.

BATTLE RAGING AT MURFREESBORO', TENN.

SAVANNAH, Dec. 31.

A special dispatch to the Savannah Republican, dated Murfreesboro', the 30th, says:

The enemy took position yesterday, P. M, one mile in front of our lines.

We burnt the splendid mansion of Mr. Cowan, on the Nashville Turnpike, four hundred yards in front, together with all the outhouses; also, Mr. Harden's residence on the Wilkinson Turnpike, in order to prevent the enemy from using them for shelter.

This morning is raw and raining.

The inhabitants are rapidly moving beyond our lines.

Heavy skirmishing commenced to-day at nine o'clock.

The force of the enemy is estimated at sixty thousand.

There are indications of a great and terrific engagement; during the afternoon the engagement on our left soon became general, and the battle is now raging heavily.

The greatest confidence prevails amongst our officers and men.

The enemy made a desperate charge upon our lines, but were repulsed with heavy loss.

A brilliant artillery duel is now progressing.

L A T E R.

GREAT BATTLE AT MURFREESBORO'.

Brilliant Confederate Victory.

RICHMOND, Jan. 1, 1863.

The following official dispatch was received this morning:

MURFREESBORO', Dec. 31, 1862.—We assaulted the enemy at 7 o'clock this morning, and after ten hours hard fighting have driven him from every position except his extreme left, where he has successfully repulsed us. With the exception of this point we occupy the whole field. We captured 4,000 prisoners, including two Brigadier Generals; 31 pieces of artillery and some 200 wagons and teams. Our loss is heavy but that of the enemy is much greater.

[Signed] BRAXTON BRAGG,
Gen. Comm'dg.

Another Emilia St. Pierre Affair.

CHARLESTON, S. C., Dec. 31.

Another recapture, similar to the Emilia St. Pierre affair, has taken place.

The schooner Emma Tuttle, Capt. Carver, of Nassau, supposed to be bound for a Confederate Port, was taken by a Yankee cruiser and put in charge of a prize crew. The original officers and crew being left on board as prisoners subsequently recaptured the schooner and carried it back to Nassau with the Yankee prize crew as prisoners.

Later From Vicksburg---The Enemy Again Repulsed.

VICKSBURG, Dec. 30.

A courier has just arrived who states that the enemy attempted to storm our lines again this morning, but after a severe battle were repulsed with heavy loss. No further particulars at present. The loss of the enemy is said to be about 300 in killed and wounded, and 400 prisoners. Our loss about 50 killed and wounded.

FROM THE NORTH.

CAPTURE OF FORT HUDSON.

Retreat of Gen. Hatch Confirmed.

THE ALABAMA AT WORK.

Capture of a California Steamer

LATER FROM EUROPE.

Anticipated Removal of Palmerston and Russell.

RICHMOND, Jan. 1—7:30 P. M.

The Enquirer has Northern dates to the 31st.

The Herald reports that Fort Hudson has been captured.

The retreat of Gen. Hatch across the Tallehatchie is confirmed.

The Etna with four days later news has arrived.

The London Times says that Lincoln's message is a bid for peace. His emancipation plan it denominates a dream.

The London News, organ of Exeter Hall, says it has no faith in Lincoln's emancipation scheme.

Gold was 130 in New York on Monday.

The underwriters in New York have doubled their risks on vessels.

The Washington Chronicle notices important movements of Gen. Stewart's Cavalry and supposes that he is advancing on Frederick City.

The supercedure of Butler by Banks is confirmed.

Banks sent a fleet and strong force to Baton Rouge and recaptured the place.

The Herald says, the Confederate States steamer Florida had succeeded in running out from Mobile unseen by the blockaders.

A Confederate vessel had arrived at Havana with cotton from Mobile.

On the 7th of December the Alabama or 290 captured the California steamer Ariel with the crew 150 strong. Her officers were paroled. Lieut. Law, of the Alabama, boarded the Ariel and took possession of 3,000 treasury notes, and $1,500 in silver. Having destroyed all the sails of the Yankee steamer, and removed all of her steam valves, She was valued at $125,000 and cargo at $135,000 more, the whole to be paid to the Confederate authorities within 30 days after the establishment of the independence of the Confederate States.

The news of this capture produced great sensation in New York and Washington.

Greely has been summoned to Washington.

The Paris correspondent of the Herald says it is rumored in diplomatic circles that Palmerston and Russell will be ousted from the British Cabinet after the opening of Parliament.

Stewart Heard From.

RICHMOND, Jan. 1, 1863.

Ninety-two prisoners, captured at Dumfries, arrived to-day, and two hundred more will arrive to-morrow. They were captured at Occoquan.

The following items from the Washington correspondence of the New York *Herald* dated the 25th inst., will be found interesting:

COL FORNEY AND THE WEAK-BACKED REPUBLICANS.

Col. Forney's organ is busy whipping in weak-backed Republicans who are already croaking about the necessity of recognizing the Southern Republican members of Congress, who openly express despair of the success of the Federal Government under its present military administration, and declare that, under existing circumstances, no more troops can be raised, even by draft, in the States which they represent.

THE PRESIDENT'S FIRST OF JANUARY PROCLAMATION.

There is reason to believe that in the President's 1st of January Proclamation, in reference to negro emancipation, he will except such States and parts of States as have furnished evidences of loyalty, but have been prevented by the presence of a hostile army from complying with the terms of his proclamation of the 22d of September. A strong protest has been presented to him from Tennessee, signed by Governor Johnson and a large number of the most noted loyal Tennesseeans, claiming to be exempt from the emancipation proclamation upon the ground that, if an opportunity were offered to the people of Tennessee to express themselves, unmistakable evidences of the loyalty of a majority of them would be shown; but that the occupation of their soil by contending armies has prevented the holding of elections, as required in the preliminary proclamation, and precluded for the present any other representation of the loyalty of the people than can be furnished by the assurances of men of undoubted patriotism, who are familiar with the people of that State. Similar representations have been made on the part of the people of the 8th Congressional District of Virginia, known as the Harper's Ferry District, composed of the counties of Hampshire, Page, Warren, Clarke, Berkeley, Jefferson, Frederick, Morgan, and Loudoun. Numerous letters have been received here by the Marshal of the District of Columbia, a native of that section, and other prominent residents of Washington, complaining bitterly of the failure of Gov Pierpoint to order an election. There was a time when it might have been held with comparative safety, and the Union sentiment of the district been freely represented.

AFFAIRS IN MISSOURI.

We learn some interesting items from a letter received by a member of Congress from a gentleman in Mississippi, whose wife has recently been banished from the State of Missouri by the Yankees, in order to possess themselves of her property. When the lady referred to left St. Louis, Fremont was holding levees, at which he openly declared his intention of putting a stop to the war by bringing about a secession of the Northwestern States and then uniting them with the South.

When the flag of truce arrived at St. Louis, demanding the surrender of McNeil, it occasioned considerable commotion in the city. The Yankee General in command of the post referred the matter to bogus Governor Gamble, saying the Federal Government would have nothing to do with it. The old army officers were in favor of giving McNeil up. The miserable subterfuge has failed, and Gen. Hindman, it is reported, has executed ten Yankee officers in just retaliation of the McNeil butchery. This, however, we are informed, is only one of numerous cases demanding like retaliatory measures to protect the suffering citizens of that unfortunate State. They are constantly occurring in most aggravated forms, but from various causes do not obtain the prominence given to the Palmyra tragedy. It is hoped that Gen. Hindman's stern lesson will teach the cowardly and bloodthirsty wretches to recognize the rules of civilized warfare.

THE LIBERATOR

—IS PUBLISHED—

EVERY FRIDAY MORNING,

—AT—

221 WASHINGTON STREET, ROOM No. 6.

ROBERT F. WALLCUT, General Agent.

☞ TERMS — Three dollars per annum, in advance.

☞ Four copies will be sent to one address for TEN DOLLARS, if payment is made in advance.

☞ All remittances are to be made, and all letters relating to the pecuniary concerns of the paper are to be directed, (POST PAID,) to the General Agent.

☞ Advertisements of a square and over inserted three times at five cents per line; less than a square, 75 cents for three insertions. Yearly and half yearly advertisements inserted on reasonable terms.

☞ The Agents of the American, Massachusetts, Pennsylvania, Ohio and Michigan Anti-Slavery Societies are authorised to receive subscriptions for THE LIBERATOR.

☞ The following gentlemen constitute the Financial Committee, but are not responsible for any debts of the paper, viz: — WENDELL PHILLIPS, EDMUND QUINCY, EDMUND JACKSON, and WILLIAM L. GARRISON, JR.

"Proclaim Liberty throughout all the land, to all the inhabitants thereof."

"I lay this down as the law of nations. I say that military authority takes, for the time, the place of all municipal institutions, and SLAVERY AMONG THE REST; and that, under that state of things, so far from its being true that the States where slavery exists have the exclusive management of the subject, not only the PRESIDENT OF THE UNITED STATES, but the COMMANDER OF THE ARMY, HAS POWER TO ORDER THE UNIVERSAL EMANCIPATION OF THE SLAVES. . . . From the instant that the slaveholding States become the theatre of a war, CIVIL, servile, or foreign, from that instant the war powers of CONGRESS extend to interference with the institution of slavery, IN EVERY WAY IN WHICH IT CAN BE INTERFERED WITH, from a claim of indemnity for slaves taken or destroyed, to the cession of States, burdened with slavery, to a foreign power. . . . It is a war power. I say it is a war power; and when your country is actually in war, whether it be a war of invasion or a war of insurrection, Congress has power to carry on the war, and MUST CARRY IT ON, ACCORDING TO THE LAWS OF WAR; and by the laws of war, an invaded country has all its laws and municipal institutions swept by the board, and MARTIAL POWER TAKES THE PLACE OF THEM. When two hostile armies are set in martial array, the commanders of both armies have power to emancipate all the slaves in the invaded territory."—J. Q. ADAMS.

WM. LLOYD GARRISON, Editor.

Our Country is the World, our Countrymen are all Mankind.

J. B. YERRINTON & SON, Printers.

VOL. XXXIII. NO. 1. BOSTON, FRIDAY, JANUARY 2, 1863. WHOLE NO. 1665.

Refuge of Oppression.

PRESIDENT LINCOLN'S PROCLAMATION.

That the Constitution gives the President no authority whatever to issue such a decree as the emancipation proclamation, and that the decree, legally regarded, is simply null and void, is a minor consideration, since it must be looked upon as a measure of war, and not of civil policy. But is it, in any point of view, a wise or a warrantable measure? Hardly, we think. It may gain him the more active and cordial coöperation of the New England Abolitionists; but they are not a very numerous though increasing party; and they are for him peculiarly dangerous allies, because their objects and his are altogether distinct, and only casually and not necessarily connected. They would sacrifice the Union to extinguish slavery. He would perpetuate slavery to restore the Union. They can only act steadily or loyally together so long as abolition measures offer, *or are thought to offer*, the best chance of subjugating and reännexing the South. The great majority of people in the North are no friends to emancipation, and no partisans of the negro; they may ultimately consent to go in for abolition, but they will do so only as their last card, and as an evil only less than acknowledging the independence of the South. The proclamation, therefore, at first sight, seems as likely to divide as to reanimate the supporters of the Government. But this time will show.

As to the actual operation of the edict in the South, we ourselves believe that, except in a few districts near towns or ports in the neighborhood of the Federal camps, it will prove a mere *brutum fulmen*; that the slaves dare not rise, do not wish to rise, do not hate their masters, and, except for the sake of idleness, and on special occasions, do not desire freedom. But this cannot have been Mr. Lincoln's conception. He must have believed that it would be the very strongest and most effective measure of hostility which he could adopt towards the Confederate States; that it would terrify some back to their allegiance; that it would weaken the armies of his antagonists by the detachments which it would render necessary to keep down the blacks; in a word, that it would rouse against the slaveholders a formidable host of domestic foes. He must have designed, one would suppose—if he had any definite design at all—and expected—if he had any distinct hopes of benefit from his decree—that his proclamation would raise the black race against the white, would turn [illegible] half-barbarous Africans against their former masters; would, at the very least, disorganize the entire social system in the South, and put a stop to the usual processes of industry and culture, and introduce a fearful state of anarchy and chaos. He must have *hoped* this; he must have *been prepared for* much worse. At the best, he must have *hoped* to create confusion and paralysis: at the worst, he must have *been prepared for* massacre, rapine and devastation. We confess, that in our eyes few crimes can be greater than that, the guilt of which he has *possibly* incurred, voluntarily and with his eyes open. The deed appears to us a step beyond the limits of civilized warfare. As against the slaveholders, it is something very like fighting with poisoned weapons; and as such will certainly be regarded and retaliated by the South. But passing over this view, in which many anti-slavery men will not agree with us, and looking at the decree as regards the negroes only, it is difficult to conceive any proceeding more wickedly selfish and cruel. It is urging an excitable, and ignorant, and helpless population to an outbreak either of violence or of insubordination, where they can neither be aided nor protected. It is exposing them at once to the suspicion of their masters, to further precautionary fetters, possibly to forecasting severities, *in terrorem*; and, if they do rise or strike work, to the harshest and most merciless retribution. It indicates a more utter want of regard for the safety, the welfare, the simplest rights of the negro, than we could have conceived possible. It shows how little in reality those who promulgated and those who advised such a proclamation care for their nominal clients. In order to create a possible diversion in favor of his arms, Mr. Lincoln and his Abolitionist friends have not hesitated to take a step which, if it produces any effect at all—if it produces the effect the hope of which must have been the only motive to it—must result, as its first and necessary consequence, in the most crushing and terrible inflictions on the feebler race whom it is sought to rouse against the stronger. They have not scrupled to bring upon the slaves, whom they profess to pity, and declare to be free, a vengeace which they well know will, if need be, not stop far short of extermination. How any man, or body of men, *dare*, for their own selfish ends, for their own success in war, to lay upon their consciences the sin of goading ignorant and helpless thousands, whom they cannot sustain or save, into insurrection against a class far more powerful, well armed, and in such a case utterly relentless, would be simply inconceivable, if we did not know too well, and had not seen too often, how infuriated passion can obscure the plainest truth, and trample down the most solemn obligation.—*North British Review for November*, 1862.

THE RADICAL CONGRESS.

In the present Congress—to be sure, we mean the majority—there is as much Radicalism as there was in the French Assembly of Robespierre, without the brilliant ability for which that diabolical Senate was distinguished. The shabby disease of "nigger on the brain" afflicts each member of that majority. The malady has taken a fanatic grip of its victims. It will not let them go. They become delirious under its influence. And the ill-colored logic that arises from it is the balm they have for the disasters of the nation. Well may the exclamation of Cicero: "*O, tempora! O, mores! Quam recupublicam habemus!*" be now made. We have indeed a disjointed Republic! Radicalism is the cause, and the cause persists in operation. And the national administration is to be two years longer in the hands of the Radicals! Thus we are in the very centre of evil. There is no remedy but one. The constituents of the Radicals must undo the votes by which they elevated these men by giving opposition to their measures, by nullifying their acts. And if the country is to be made what it was, all that Radicalism has done for years must be subverted. Abolitionism in itself, and in all it has effected, must be expunged from the land, before the land can be what it once was. But will that ever be the case? Alas! the grounds for hope are indistinct. The Abolition radicalism of the North was too great for the South to resist it, and the consequent rebellion of the South, the North, it may be feared, will never completely put down. Still a great effort can save us. Let us hunt Abolitionism from the face of the country. Let us show the Southern States that subjugation is not our aim. Let us return to constitutional principles. What has resulted to us from fighting?—desperate losses. What has resulted to us from "nigger on the brain"?—the destruction of the empire. Well may we go on our knees, and maledict the day Abraham Lincoln's party predominated. Radicalism got then the crown on its temples, and in the excesses of its pride it has disjointed the nation. Are the sages of '76 uncontinued? Has the splendid political wisdom that once marked the UNITED STATES fled forever? Abolition radicalism answers the painful questions.—*Boston (Catholic) Pilot.*

ABOLITIONISM.

The *Evening Post* indulged, a few days since, in the pleasing delusion that those who desire to get rid of the Abolitionists have only to get rid of slavery, and they would accomplish their purpose. "If there were no slavery, there would be no Abolitionists," argues this authority. Mistaken man! have you indeed so little knowledge of the truth? Are you in fact so innocent as to imagine that this mad spirit of radical Abolitionism is the evil evoked from the place of evil spirits, by the existence of slavery in America in the nineteenth century, and that it never before made its appearance among men?

It is undoubtedly true that a great many people do believe that slavery is the sole cause of the existence of Northern radicalism. Hence it is that so many, including Mr. Lincoln, are misled into the idea that if slavery were only removed, we should enter on an American millennium of peace and union.

The error is fatal, and until this error is corrected, the country will not be saved. Remove slavery before this fierce spirit of radicalism, and it will become tenfold more fierce. It grows strong on success. It thrives on the destruction of all that it opposes.

It is no new thing in the world. From the earliest periods the spirit of the Pharisee, which pronounced all other men inferior to him, has animated more or less men. This is part of the spirit of Abolitionism, and another part is the desire to compel other men to submit to its views of right and wrong. The American Union might have existed in peace till the end of time if it contained no radical men; but without slavery, and with radical men, either at the North or South, East or West, it was certain at one time or another to plunge into ferocious sectionalism. If men were content to live and let each other alone, as regards all offensive demonstrations, we should have no quarrels. If men in one State were content to live and let the men of other States alone, we should have no aggressions and no State quarrels. If, when wishes, or opinions, or interests differ and collide, there existed on both sides a willingness and a desire to yield for the sake of harmony, instead of [illegible] sion, we should have eternal peace. Nor can people unite in any form of republican government on any other principle. Peace and prosperity will return to America only when this compromise spirit of our fathers is restored and made permanent. In vain we look elsewhere for union or peace. If Mr. Lincoln by a wave of his hand could remove every slave from America to Africa to-day, he would not add one iota to the permanent character of the American Union, unless he could remove the spirit of radical Abolitionism with it, and restore the spirit of mutual concession and compromise on all points of State or sectional difference. These are truths that radical men do not understand. But it is as solemn truth as the existence of the war itself, that there is no future of peace for America until the Abolitionist spirit is annihilated. It will not cease to exist when slavery disappears. Slavery might have existed in the South till the bondmen and the freemen witness the final catastrophe of the world, and without causing rebellion or war, if the aggressive spirit of Abolitionism had not made the contest.

The simple fact is, that the bad element, the combative element of self-esteem and desire to compel others to submit to our views and opinions, is the spirit of American radicalism, and, whether the radical is a Northerner or a Southerner, the moment he attempts to be a politician, he becomes a disunionist.

In all ages and countries these men have been the inciters of brawls, troubles, revolutions. They were known in old Rome. They were denounced in Greece. They were especially well known among the Hebrews. They were pestilent fellows always and everywhere; nor is it to be doubted that when we come to decipher the Egyptian writings, we shall find that they were executed for sedition and conspiracy in the days of the Pharaohs.

The spirit came down through all the political history of European civilization. It was present in church and state. It was always rampant for the abolition of something; always bent on what it called reform; always using fire and fagot to compel submission. It kindled the flames of the persecutions in the later empire. It burned the Knights of the Temple at the stake in France under Philip. It rejoiced in St. Bartholomew's day. It crossed to England as early as the days of the Saxon kings, and remained there with the Norman line. It was uncompromising in its demands, persecuting in its disposition, cowardly in its action. It drove the Puritans from England. Yet when they departed, it attended them, and triumphed over them when they landed on our shores. For who can doubt that the noble spirit that led the Puritans to New England for "freedom to worship God as we please," soon became perverted into "freedom to worship God as we please, and freedom to make everybody else worship God as we please." It drove Roger Williams out of Boston. It burned witches at the stake, and made hideous spectacles of devout Quakers who became obnoxious to it.

No, no, gentlemen, we shall not have done with radical Abolitionism when we have done with slavery. Satan finds always plenty of work for his servants. When radical Abolitionism has no longer slavery to work at, it will try the vote-yourself-a-farm-ism, or one-religion-ism, or absolute democracy. It will attack the State divisions, as it is now doing, and little Massachusetts will demand that great New York submit, not to equality of representation, but to absolute subjection. For the spirit of Abolitionism is never a spirit of compromise or of arrangement, but always a spirit of domineering, always claims a superior virtue, and demands a humble submission.

There is no exaggeration in the picture we have drawn. We can show the portrait of the modern American Abolitionist, perfectly painted by the old Greek poets, by the Latin satirists—how perfectly by the sacred writers!

This in fact is the grand difficulty in the way of democratic institutions, and we are now trying the experiment, the *experimentum crucis* of the possibility of such institutions being permanent. If radicalism had succeeded in carrying the nation with it this fall in the elections, the doom of the country and the doom of all democratic hopes of self-government would have been decreed. It would have been determined that the intolerance of human passions and pride was so deep seated as to forbid men agreeing in self-government. Now the prospect is better. There is hope yet. But the hope is that this experience will have taught a lesson to America which will prevent radicalism in any part of the land from again obtaining the ascendency for a thousand years.—*New York Journal of Commerce.*

Selections.

THE ABOLITIONISTS.

There is no word more frequently and angrily used and less understood than the word Abolitionists. President Lincoln and Daniel S. Dickinson, Governor Johnson and Governor Andrew, Thurlow Weed and Wendell Phillips, are all called by the same name. Of course, there is but one point upon which all these men agree, and that is a truly vigorous prosecution of the war. But that is not Abolitionism. Emancipation, as a means of war, may be justified by all of them; but that is not Abolitionism. The word Abolitionists designates a party in the country, whose position and influence have never been correctly estimated, because its members have been too much hated to be fairly treated. Nobody has taken the trouble to know what they thought or what they proposed. It has been enough that they were said to be disunionists. What kind of disunionists, or why disunionists, have not been questions thought to be worth asking, especially by the politicians who now call their late companions Abolitionists, because they insist upon the Union at every cost; and who think and call the open, bloody disunionists of the South "erring brethren."

But the history of these times will have to deal differently with the facts, the influences, and the characters which are summarily classed as "Abolitionists." For, merely to call the men known as Abolitionists, a handful of fanatics, incendiaries and agitators, explains them and their cause as much as Sydney Smith's sneering accounts of Methodism and Methodists, or Hume's description of Cromwell and the Independents; but no more. It is certainly not very complimentary to the American people to say that a few bitter fanatics at the North, called Abolitionists, and a few other fanatics at the South, called Secessionists, plunged thirty millions of people into this tremendous civil war. If the individual, James Otis, had held his tongue, would there have been no Revolution? If John Hampden had paid the ship money, would the Stuarts, to-day, be kings of England? James Otis and John Hampden were but men, who spoke for fundamental and decisive principles. When those ideas were in play, those men were inevitable. If fifty Abolitionists and as many Secessionists had been hung, think many, there would have been no trouble. But do you think, if Luther had been hung, there would have been no [illegible] who believed as he did? Unless you could have hung the instinct of popular liberty in England, in 1640, or the same feeling in America, in 1770, you would have struck but one soldier of an army in striking Hampden or Otis. Unless you could kill Protestantism, you might as well spare Luther. And unless you can hang Abolitionism, you will hang Abolitionists in vain.

Correctly speaking, the Abolitionists were, in our history, a body of persons who thought slavery wrong; who held that the Constitution favored it, and that, as the system was sure to corrupt the whites as well as imbrute the blacks, there was no hope for either but in the change of the Constitution, and the dissolution of the Union, of which it was the bond. But they proposed that the change should be effected peacefully and legally, by common consent; and, to that end, they endeavored to show what they considered the ultimate danger and present wrong of the Constitution. This was their "agitation." They opposed violence of every kind. They were, many of them, non-resistants. They did not vote; for to vote was to acknowledge what they thought a wicked Constitution. They did not approve the method, but only the purpose of John Brown; and they said to the rest of us, "You who believe in force have no right to blame him for helping others to do what you praise our fathers for doing in the Revolution." They believed that immediate emancipation was desirable, but they aimed to achieve it solely by influencing public opinion through that perfect freedom of discussion which the Constitution guaranteed. Some among them—but very few—were more vehement, and sometimes attempted to resist the law, as in Boston, at the Burns capture. But the Personal Liberty bills, although the Abolitionists approved and advocated them, were passed by Legislatures in which no Abolitionists sat, because no Abolitionist could swear to support the Constitution and the laws of the United States.

Abolitionism, justly understood, was thus a purely moral power. It sought a moral end solely by moral means. It was fierce, vituperative, and denunciative; but so has every party been. Its leaders deliberately resigned all the prizes of worldly ambition, and accepted contumely, heaped upon them by both the great parties in the country—Republican and Democrat equally eschewed the name or suspicion of Abolitionism. And justly; for the Democrats were in political alliance with slavery, and the Republicans differed fundamentally from the Abolitionists in their interpretation of the Constitution. The latter hold it to be a bond of slavery; the former, of liberty. The Abolitionists thought the only hope of the country was in escaping from the Constitution. The Republicans believed that the slavery question could be settled peacefully for liberty, without change of the Constitution.

They were right. For it was the clear perception of the slave interest that it *would* be so settled—a fact of which Mr. Lincoln's election was the earnest—that drove that interest to arms to destroy the Constitution. Philosophically, the difference between the Republicans and the Abolitionists was one of political method, not of moral conviction. But, in human affairs, a difference of method is radical. The Republicans, therefore, neither decried the Constitution nor the Union. But they deplored the false interpretation of the one, and the prostitution of the other. They believed that the people would yet save both. Consequently, they were, all of them, unswerving Unionists. They did not threaten to rebel, if they were not successful at the polls, and they severely condemned all who assented to such threats. For they had faith in a popular government to right even the worst wrongs. And their faith is justified.

There is no more interesting chapter of our history than that known as Abolitionism, which is an episode in the great movement of liberty upon this continent. To call it fanaticism, and consider that a final and satisfactory explanation, is as ludicrous as to define Washington simply as a rebel, or Luther as a heretic.—*Harper's Weekly.*

TREATMENT OF FEDERAL PRISONERS. Gen. Rosecrans has addressed a letter to Gen. Bragg, complaining that the rebels stole overcoats from the prisoners at Hartsville; also, that the cartel had been violated in returning prisoners by flag of truce to this point instead of to Vicksburg and Aiken's Landing. Traitors are thieves, and never keep their pledges in any thing.

JUSTICE TO SLAVEHOLDERS.

The impression prevails to some extent, more particularly abroad, that the late emancipation triumph in Missouri was a victory over the slaveholders, and that the contest was one partaking largely of the character of the war of classes or interests—one side being represented entirely by slave-owners and their adherents, and the other entirely by non-slaveholders. Such is not the fact; and justice to a large number of earnest, hard-working Emancipationists in Missouri, who are owners of slaves, requires that it should be stated.

Previous to the election, and since, we have been in confidential communication with slaveholders, as well as others, in all sections of the State, and have in consequence the means of judging of their real sentiments upon the subject of emancipation. A disclosure of our entire correspondence would exhibit some singular things—among others, the fact that many of the most liberal-minded men in the State upon the question of free soil are largely interested in slave property. Many of these men were, however, not simply favorable to emancipation at heart, but have been the most zealous and successful workers in its behalf in the late canvass. It is one of the singular, and by no means uninstructive features of the election, that several of the heaviest slaveholding counties in the State have given decided emancipation majorities, while counties, on the other hand, having scarcely a slave in them, have elected pro-slavery representatives to the Legislature.

The great fact established is, that the result of the election is not the product of a prejudice of one class of our people working against another class. It is the result of a general conviction, entertained by men of property and intelligence throughout the State, without reference to the character of their possessions, that slavery in Missouri is a doomed institution, a cumberer of the ground, a dry and worthless trunk, the sooner cut down and cast into the fire the better for the true interests of the State. The triumph of emancipation, although to some extent aided, undoubtedly, by the peculiar condition of public matters in our midst, was not the work of the bayonet, of popular excitement, or anything of a temporary nature, but of the sober second thought of the people, as deliberately executed as it was formed. Outside of St. Louis, where the contest was between two parties of professed Emancipationists, there never was a more quiet and orderly election held in the State, nor one at which loyal sentiments [illegible] acrimonious canvass. It was the deliberate verdict of a people who had calmly weighed all the facts in the case. The result is a revolution which is in no danger of going backward.

We feel a greater anxiety to have the real facts, as we have stated them, correctly understood in the Northern States, on account of the conditions upon which constitutional and legal emancipation in Missouri must take place. If our election had been a triumph over slaveholders and the slaveholding interest purely, we are well aware of the repugnance the people of the North would feel towards contributing out of the national fund for the compensation of the owners of slaves to be set free. There are, of course, a number of slaveholders in Missouri who have bitterly opposed emancipation from the first, and all the time; but these will generally be found to be tainted with disloyalty, and will not, therefore, be likely to derive much benefit from a compensatory system of emancipation, framed, as it will be, with a rigid enforcement of a law of confiscation. Of the loyal slaveholders of Missouri, very many are liberal, high-minded gentlemen, and earnest Emancipationists. To deprive such men of their property for the public good, without some recompense, would be clearly unjust.—*Missouri Democrat.*

HENRY WARD BEECHER ON THE WAR.

We give below the concluding portion of Henry Ward Beecher's Thanksgiving Sermon:—

The political blessings for which we owe thanksgiving are next in order. In surveying these, we must dismiss from our minds the prejudices that have colored the thick coming events of the year, and survey the scene by the light of facts.

First—We find, then, that the nation has passed through the period of the evolution of slavery and its nature. Slavery, here, has had time to develop itself upon a better and wider field than was ever before open to it in the world. In the midst of Christianity, civilization, liberty, and under a Republican system, it has had perfect scope, defended, too, by regulations that gave it all the healthy blood it needed to repair the waste its own workings made.

In the beginning, slavery seemed to be but an accident, and its operation in relation to moral and political government left room for discussion and for doubt. That uncertainty exists no longer. Some pretend to believe that it is good—but they are either men who do not think at all, or who, in their hearts, believe in tyranny. The result is before us, and results cannot be contradicted. The experiment has ended by giving us clear knowledge of its nature.

The effect of slavery upon the slave may be a matter of speculation, or even of sentiment, but its effect upon the master is beyond all controversy. There it is! Its first effect upon the African may be good. I am not prepared to say that the first shipload of poor, wild natives brought to the land was not, at the commencement, benefited by contact with even the low civilization with which it came in contact. But that benefit is only skin deep. The moment it began to sprout in the slave, the master forbade it to grow. The latter germinates the negro, but will not let him put forth into leaf. He is but as grass for the mower.

War has revealed the effect of slavery upon the master. Patriotism could not adhere, public spirit could not exist, where slavery breathes. It was thought that the chivalric South, full of lordly natures, would be more patriotic than the cold, calculating North, but at the first trial its patriotism snapped like a pipe-stem, excepting in a few localities—among the mountains of East Tennessee—and let her name not be forgotten! and one or two other glorious sites, they went down like rotten trees struck by the hurricane. We go forth in the morning after a storm, and we say of the fallen monarchs of the forest, the tempest overthrew them, but look closer and you will see the rot, the carrion at their heart; for twenty years decay had been working at the centre, and the first puff of the blast levelled the hollow shell.

The effect of slavery upon the master is seen in its influence against intelligence and religion—i. e., that the interior policy which slavery renders indispensable, corrupts religion and prevents education. Instruct the slave, and you give him twenty mouths full of hunger that must be fed; the brute man has but one mouth, but the taught man has varied tastes and yearnings. You give him paternal love, not the love of the savage for his young—the love of the bear for its cub, but the love of the spirit, and the spirit's aspirations for the object of its affection. Instruction would make better workmen, but worse slaves—it would break the back of the whole system. But where it is so dark for the slave, it must also be dark for the master—black as charcoal—and the charcoal of that blackness, like its prototype, may be the chief ingredient in the dire explosive that blows up the nation. (Applause.) If there be no books for the million of negro picaninnies, there are none for the million of white picaninnies who run about with them. Hence the dreadful ignorance of the poor whites of the South, and the power of their leaders. After this war, 500,000 men, now soldiers, will return to us with their tongues in their cheeks, and say, "Those Southerners don't know much. They are ignorant fellows."

It cannot be denied that as an element of political economy, the system makes riches. It makes wealthy slaveholders, but poor white men not slaveholders. It builds up a Plutocracy—the very worst form of aristocracy. Prosperous wealth is like the even fall of snow—the poor man's cutter and the rich man's sleigh have a common and untrammeled highway—but this kind of wealth is like the snow-drift that blocks up the road to all but the mighty few. One rich man's hand in Georgia is stronger than the hands of one thousand, aye, than ten thousand in these Free States, and thus it strikes like a hammer at the door of the Capitol, armed with the weight of whole sovereign States. This power would be terrible with us, but there, where men thus armed curse human freedom and the doctrine of human equality, it is appalling. This is the demoniac possession of the South. Dr. Clay has administered the rhubarb of compromise, and Dr. Webster has exhibited his diluents, but all in vain. Now comes the surgeon, War—he with that surgical instrument, the sword, cuts open the body of the patient, and finds him rotten in kidney and heart, in liver and brain.

THAT'S WHAT'S THE MATTER.

(Tremendous applause.) Now cure him, sew him up, and let him go! (Renewed applause.) We shall not any longer be told that these are Abolition lies about slavery. There is the ulcer!—we have seen it, we have probed it, we have cleansed it.

Both North and South have come to one conclusion, viz.: that Slavery and Liberty cannot exist together under one and the same Constitution. The South, laying down this premise, have drawn the inference—Secession. We, too, accepting the premise, [illegible] question is the sword. But, what a stride has been taken — what old prejudices have been quelled! What an opening up of the intelligence of the people! All the prophets would not have been believed two years ago, had they predicted this. John Van Buren, even now, thinks there is some other way—that the patient may be cured, and the demon still left in him; but even he, with returning health, exclaimed in his way of seeing the same truth we have enunciated so feebly: "Wayward sisters, depart in peace." (Laughter and applause.) Our answer to the truth is, that the nationality of this people shall be maintained; and government, liberty and law upheld upon this continent.

Mr. Beecher concluded by referring to the points magnificently proven in this supreme struggle of the Republic, viz.:

1. That it is capable of equipping vast armies on the instant.

2. That it can wage campaigns of unparalleled magnitude, both by sea and land.

3. That its people are capable of taxation, and cheerful submission to the same in the midst of war.

In the trials of the war, this free Government and people have, at every turn, proven their superiority to any monarchy, in all the requisites of grandeur and power.

In the Trent affair, they even conquered pride; and this fierce Democracy, which all Europe thought would revolt at concession, bade pride go down, and acknowledged the act wrong. Mr. Beecher then portrayed the pseudo-conservative action of the recent administration at Washington with the present attitude of Mr. Lincoln. Conservatism had done its best and had derided radicals. Now we were to see what radicals could do to heal the nation. We had closed conservative war with artillery made of sugar plums; we had closed conservative campaigns of mud, and dust, and nothing! (Great applause.) Bad counsellors had wanted to put a snuffer on the President, and say, "Let not your light shine!" but he had said, "Enough of this!" and now men are waging the war who mean war. (Applause.) The faces of the army are turned toward Jerusalem, and, in the language of Christ, we say to the demon in the South, "Come out of him!" He loved the South as he loved his whole country. Error must not obliterate our love for "flesh of our flesh and bone of our bone;" but in this love let us look forward to the hour when the South, regenerated and disenthralled, restored and clothed in its right mind, shall sit at the footstool of Jesus, and, with us, praise God for liberty, virtue, and religion. Let us, then, with one voice, be thankful for the heroic examples of the year, for the perils overcome, for the blessings plentifully gathered, for the transcendent promise of the future dawning in a glorious radiance out of the depths of night.

Mr. Beecher's allusions to the pro-slavery attitude of England at this crisis, notwithstanding all her former professions and exhortations, was a powerful episode of his sermon, and, like many other passages, elicited uncontrollable applause.

In conclusion, he offered, as appropriate, the 104th hymn:—

"My country, 'tis of thee,
Sweet land of liberty,
Of thee I sing;
Land where my fathers died;
Land of the Pilgrim's pride;
From every mountain side
Let freedom ring."

THE NORTH AND THE SOUTH.

Measure the comparative strength of the two parties contending in arms for the dominion of these States, and judge what will be the probable issue of the contest. Between Freedom and Slavery in the abstract, there can be no question on which side lies the greater power. Freedom has the steady nerve, the true aim, and the enduring heart; Slavery the conscious guilt, the boding doubt, the alarming suspicion. Why, then, is the champion of the Philistines allowed to present himself morning and evening for forty days, yea, forty waxing and waning moons, and still utter his taunts of triumph? It is because Rebellion has a vigorous soul; our Government has none! The organism of the rebellion is wholly animated by one purpose; every muscle, nerve and sinew, strained to its utmost tension, obeys the governing will. No antagonistic forces, no palsied limb, no unassimilated elements, are allowed to mar the vital energy of the war for slavery; difference of opinion is punished with death; the unwilling slave himself is made to be the most powerful support of the despotism that crushes him. Trace the history of this war from the beginning. Where has a Confederate officer proved treacherous to his cause? Where has an opportunity for winning an advantage been suffered to pass unimproved? On which side have been the daring raids, the celerity of movement, the ceaseless watching, the wily strategy, the invention and preparation of new engines of destruction, and the prompt use of all possible means and appliances of war?

While such is the spirit that animates the Southern rebellion, what is it that animates our war for its suppression? Is the nation, under the influence of its own mighty soul, Freedom? Are all the organisms, that combine to form the body politic, in strict subordination to that one great principle which gave us national existence? So far from this, the very fact that Liberty is the nation's soul has been ignored, and a new organism attempted, under the name of Union. Is union a source of life? Can mere combination give dead forms vitality? Union is a product of life, not its cause. Liberty creates union, as magnetism gathers atoms around a centre; but union creates nothing, is no life-germ, can give no inspiration. The war has been waged on a false issue. Are we fighting for union? Do we hope to promote union by guns and armies? It is a mere pretence. We are not fighting for simple union; we are fighting for conquest. Our aim is to subdue. We expect no union, unless it be a union of force.

The antagonistic souls are Liberty and Slavery. The one fires the North, so far as it has any fire; the other fires the South. But the Northern soul is bound. It is not allowed to meet its antagonist. It cannot throw its vitalizing energies into every nerve and sinew of the Northern mass, and hurl our army with its full momentum on the foe. The influence of the permeating soul is restrained by the foul ulcers and spreading gangrenes that have appropriated to themselves the substantial forces of the Republic. The grand slave cancer has been suffered to extend its roots down to the very heart. The patient had become reconciled to the disease; wedded to its foul ulcerations, as the drunkard is wedded to the stimulus of his cups. The business of statesmen has been to administer opiates and anodynes. At length, death stares us in the face. We place ourselves in the hand of the physician. The magnitude of the disease appals him. He resolves to run no risks. If he can barely save the life of the patient, he is willing to let the disease run. He dares not withdraw the opiates, and let the full [illegible] normal condition, and drawing sharply the line of separation between health and disease. Was there ever such empiricism? For almost two years, since the ulcer broke, the energies of the nation have been wasting, and, during all that time, the opiates have been administered to its soul and conscience. The connection between liberty and the war has been severed, so far as official action could sever it; and what has been the result? A series of colossal campaigns, fruitless victories, and terrible defeats. Our movements have been without heart, inspiration, or energy; with the right hand we have swung the battle-axe, with the left we have held a shield over the enemy. If a general utters the word Freedom, he is removed; if he fails to gain victories, the same fate awaits him. Repeated failures have made our rulers desperate; in their disappointment, they order impossibilities. Gen. Halleck declares that the army shall march to Richmond, if it goes on crutches; but he forgets to send the pontoon bridges in season; when they arrive, the enemy are massed on impregnable heights; but the order is imperative; the army must advance, and on it marches, under a blind infatuation, and in spite of the judgment of its leaders, to certain defeat and wholesale massacre. The President himself is the most perfect illustration of this national paralysis; not a soul-inspiring sentiment, not a single fresh, warm, hearty appeal to glorious fundamental principles that would touch with glowing fire the sympathies of millions, but vacillation, indecision, and a constant paltering between what is right and what is expedient. We could wish that he had issued his late proclamation in this form: "Whereas, liberty is the inalienable right of all men, and justice demands that this right should be restored to the enslaved and oppressed of our country, therefore I, Abraham Lincoln, declare that all slaves in the rebel States shall, on the first day of January, be thenceforth and forever free; *unless* the rebels shall meanwhile return to their allegiance, in which case the rights aforesaid shall not be restored, but the oppressed and enslaved shall remain as heretofore!" This absurd declaration would have been but a fair exhibit of the opposing principles on which the war has hitherto proceeded, and an honest confession of our political hypocrisy.

Away with the bonds that fetter the nation's soul! Away with the subterfuges and lying pretences that this war is not waged against slavery! Let the real antagonists meet; let them come face to face in the deadly struggle, and we shall then see where Liberty will strike. We know where she will strike; she will put the point of her spear on the source of life, on the very soul of the rebellion, and extinguish it, if possible, at a blow. But has she the power? Can she lay hold of her weapons? Is not the nation too faint and weak to feel the vitalizing current, should it begin again to flow? Through our present government, with the cabinet and army constituted as at present, we fear there is no hope of salvation for the country; but let a FREMONT be placed at the head of military affairs, and with another blast of the Missouri bugle, the flush of life would once more redden the nation's cheek, the flame of Liberty once more fire her heart, and Freedom's soldiers no longer strike in vain.—*American Baptist.*

THE PRESIDENT'S PROPOSED AMENDMENT.

This amendment, which by some is thought to promise so much, is seen, on examination, to promise but little that is of substantial advantage to the cause of freedom, and, especially, it is unworthy of a place in the supreme, organic law of the United States. Its one great defect is, that it does not *require* the emancipation of slaves and the repeal of slave-laws of any State, either now or at any future time. The permission which it proposes to give to such States as may have received compensation for their emancipated slaves, to refund the money and introduce the slaveholding system, shows that there is no intention to enforce its removal. This amendment, if carried, would simply say to the slaveholders, "Very well, gentlemen, keep your slave institutions if you please, and if you do not we will pay you for the slaves; and then if you ever become tired of your bargain, and wish to have slavery again, only just return the money, and suit yourselves entirely. Understand us, gentlemen, we only propose that you should please yourselves." Now, what are the South at this moment fighting for? Is it not that they may the more effectually uphold and guard their slave system? The desire to do this constitutes the vital essence of their struggle. The President's proposal is to yield to them the very point at issue. Such would be the effect, if not the intention.

Moreover, to place such an amendment in the Constitution would remove one of their principal objections to remaining in the Union. Their complaint is that the Constitution does not, with sufficient explicitness, favor slavery. Put this amendment into it, and then that instrument, that has never yet been blotted with the word slave, would, in plain terms, permit the holding of slaves. This would be the "supreme law of the land." The slaveholder would then be secure in what *he* calls his rights. What a burning shame to make this the supreme law, and after all our fighting, suffering and expenditures, to consent, in reality, to rivet upon ourselves the Southern chain more firmly than ever! Freemen, awake! Avert this compromise!

If there is any change made in the Constitution, or any addition to it, let it be one which shall secure equal freedom to every inhabitant of every State, now, and for all time. G. E. O. S.

—*Vermont Chronicle.*

A PROCLAMATION BY THE PRESIDENT OF THE CONFEDERATE STATES.

Whereas, a communication was addressed on the 6th day of July last, 1862, by General Robert E. Lee, acting under the instructions of the Secretary of War of the Confederate States of America, to General H. W. Halleck, Commander-in-Chief of the United States Army, informing the latter that a report had reached this government that Wm. B. Mumford, a citizen of the Confederate States, had been executed by the United States authorities at New Orleans for having pulled down the United States flag in that city before its occupation by the United States forces, and calling for a statement of the facts with a view of retaliation if such an outrage had really been committed under the sanction of the authorities of the United States;

And whereas, (no answer having been received to said letter,) another letter was, on the 2d of August last, (1862,) addressed by General Lee, under my instructions, to General Halleck, renewing the inquiries in relation to the execution of the said Mumford, with the information that in the event of not receiving a reply within fifteen days, it would be assumed that the fact was true, and was sanctioned by the government of the United States;

And whereas, an answer, dated on the 7th of August last, (1862,) was addressed to General Lee by General H. W. Halleck, the said General-in-Chief of the armies of the United States, alleging sufficient causes for failure to make early reply to said letter of the 6th July, asserting that "no authentic information had been received in relation to the execution of Mumford, but measures will be immediately taken to ascertain the facts of the alleged execution," and promising that General Lee should be duly informed thereof;

And whereas, on the 28th of November last, (1862,) another letter was addressed under my instructions, by Robert Ould, Confederate agent for the exchange of prisoners, under the cartel between the two governments, to Lieutenant Colonel W. H. Ludlow, agent of the United States under said cartel, informing him that the explanation promised in the said letter of General Halleck, of 7th of August last, had not yet been received, and that if no answer was sent to the government within fifteen days from the delivery of this last communication, it would be considered that an answer is declined;

And whereas, by a letter dated on the 3d day of the present month of December, the said Lieut. Colonel Ludlow apprised the said Robert Ould that the above recited communication of the 19th of November had been received and forwarded to the Secretary of War of the United States, and whereas this last delay of fifteen days allowed for answer has elapsed, and no answer has been received;

And whereas, in addition to the tacit admission resulting from the above refusal to answer, I have received evidence fully establishing the truth of the fact that the said William B. Mumford, a citizen of the Confederacy, was actually and publicly executed in cold blood by hanging, after the occupation of the city of New Orleans by the forces under General Benjamin F. Butler, when said Mumford was an unresisting and non-combatant captive, and for no offence even alleged to have been committed by him subsequent to the date of the capture of the said city;

And whereas, the silence of the Government of the United States, and its maintaining the said Butler in high office under its authority for many months after his commission of an act that can be viewed in no other light than as a deliberate murder, as well as of numerous other outrages and atrocities hereafter to be mentioned, afford evidence too conclusive that the said government sanctions the conduct of the said Butler, and is determined that he shall remain unpunished for these crimes:

Now, therefore, I, Jefferson Davis, President of the Confederate States of America, and in their name, do pronounce and declare the said Benjamin F. Butler to be a felon, deserving of capital punishment. I do order that he shall no longer be considered or treated simply as a public enemy of the Confederate States of America, but as an outlaw and common enemy of mankind, and that, in the event of his capture, the officer in command of the capturing force do cause him to be immediataly executed by hanging.

And I do further order that no commissioned officer of the United States, taken captive, shall be released on parole, before exchange, until the said Butler shall have met with due punishment for his crime.

And whereas, the hostilities waged against this confederacy by the forces of the United States, under the command of said Benjamin F. Butler, have borne no resemblance to such warfare as is alone permissible by the rules of international law, or the usage of civilization, but have been characterized by repeated atrocities and outrages, among the large number of which the following may be cited as examples:—

Peaceful and aged citizens, unresisting captives and non-combatants, have been confined at hard labor, with chains attached to their limbs, and are still so held in dungeons and fortresses.

Others have been subjected to a like degrading punishment for selling medicines to the sick soldiers of the Confederacy.

The soldiers of the United States have been invited and encouraged in general orders to insult and outrage the wives, the mothers, and the sisters of our citizens.

Helpless women have been torn from their homes and subjected to solitary confinement, some in fortresses and prisons, and one especially on an island of barren sand, under a tropical sun; have been fed with loathsome rations that had been condemned as unfit for soldiers, and have been exposed to the vilest insults.

Prisoners of war, who surrendered to the naval forces of the United States, on agreement that they should be released on parole, have been seized and kept in close confinement.

Repeated pretexts have been sought or invented for plundering the inhabitants of the captured city, by fines levied and collected under threat of imprisoning recusants at hard labor with ball and chain. The entire population of New Orleans have been forced to elect between starvation, by the confiscation of all their property, and taking an oath against conscience to bear allegiance to the invader of their country.

Egress from the city has been refused to those whose fortitude withstood the test, and even to lone and aged women, and to helpless children; and after being ejected from their homes, and robbed of their property, they have been left to starve in the streets or subsist on charity.

The slaves have been driven from the plantations in the neighborhood of New Orleans until their owners would consent to share their crops with the Commanding General, his brother, Andrew J. Butler, and other officers, and when such consent had been extorted, the slaves have been restored to the plantations, and there compelled to work under the bayonets of the guards of the United States soldiers. Where that partnership was refused, armed expeditions have been sent to the plantations to rob them of everything that was susceptible of removal.

And even slaves, too aged or infirm for work, have, in spite of their entreaties, been forced from the homes provided by their owners, and driven to wander helpless on the highway.

By a recent general order, number 21, the entire property in that part of Louisiana west of the Mississippi river has been sequestrated for confiscation, and officers have been assigned to duty with orders to gather up and collect the personal property, and turn over to the proper officers upon their receipts, such of said property as may be required for the use of the United States army; to collect together all the other personal property and bring the same to New Orleans, and cause it to be sold at public auction to highest bidders—an order which, if executed, condemns to punishment, by starvation, at least a quarter of a million of human beings, of all ages, sexes, and conditions, and of which the execution, although forbidden to military officers by the orders of President Lincoln, is in accordance with the Confiscation law of our enemies, which he has affected to be enforced through the agency of civil officials.

And, finally, the African slaves have not only been incited to insurrection by every license and encouragement, but numbers of them have actually been armed for a servile war, a war in its nature far exceeding the horrors and most merciless atrocities of savages.

And whereas, the officers under command of the said Butler have been, in many instances, active and zealous agents in the commission of these crimes, and no instance is known of the refusal of any one of them to participate in the outrages above narrated;

And whereas, the President of the United States has, by public and official declarations, signified not only his approval of the effort to excite servile war within the Confederacy, but his intention to give aid and encouragement thereto, if these independent States shall continue to refuse submission to a foreign power after the first day of January next, and has thus made known that all appeal to the law of nations, the dictates of reason, and the instincts of humanity would be addressed in vain to our enemies, and that they can be deterred from the commission of these crimes only by the terrors of just retribution;

Now, therefore, I, Jefferson Davis, President of the Confederate States of America, and acting by their authority, appealing to the Divine Judge in attestation that their conduct is not guided by the passion of revenge, but that they reluctantly yield to the solemn duty of redressing, by necessary severity, crimes of which their citizens are the victims, do issue this my proclamation, and by virtue of my authority as Commander-in-Chief of the armies of the Confederate States, do order—

First. That all commissioned officers in the command of said Benjamin F. Butler be declared not entitled to be considered as soldiers engaged in honorable warfare, but as robbers and criminals deserving death; and that they, and each of them be, whenever captured, reserved for execution.

Second. That the private soldiers and non-commissioned officers in the army of said Butler be considered as only the instruments used for the commission of crimes perpetrated by his orders, and not as free agents; that they, therefore, be treated when captured as prisoners of war, with kindness and humanity, and be sent home on the usual parole that they will in no manner aid or serve the United States in any capacity during the continuance of this war, unless duly exchanged.

Third. That all negro slaves captured in arms be at once delivered over to the executive authorities of the respective States to which they belong, to be dealt with according to the laws of said States.

Fourth. That the like orders be executed in all cases with respect to all commissioned officers of the United States, when found serving in company with said slaves in insurrection against the authorities of the different States of this Confederacy.

In testimony whereof I have signed these presents, and caused the seal of the Confederate States of America to be affixed thereto, at the city of Richmond, on the 23d day of December, in the year of our Lord one thousand eight hundred and sixty-two.

JEFFERSON DAVIS.

By the President:
J. P. BENJAMIN, *Secretary of State.*

PROCLAMATION OF JEFF. DAVIS.

On the 14th inst., Gen. N. P. Banks arrived at New Orleans, and assumed command there, vice Gen. B. F. Butler, relieved.

On the 15th, Gen. Butler issued his farewell order, announcing his supersedure.

On the 23d—eight days later—Jeff. Davis issued from Richmond his Proclamation herewith given, consigning Gen. Butler and all his commissioned officers to a felon's death—when he shall have caught them.

Mr. Jeff. Davis proposes to kill all "negro slaves" who shall be captured fighting against the Slaveholders' Rebellion, and all white commissioned officers "when found serving *in company with* said slaves"—no matter whether officers of negro regiments or of any other.

Such is the way "the comet" takes "the Pope's bull." Don't he seem to think there's something in it?

Jeff. daintily says "all negro slaves"—but who for one moment imagines that any nice inquiry will be made as to the former *status* of the negro caught in a Federal uniform behind a Federal musket? There will be no time for such inquiry—no thought but to kill as speedily and painfully as possible. Nobody need be told what the punishment of "slaves captured in arms" and engaged in "servile war" is by the laws of Slave States. And our white officers "found serving in company with" them are to be served the same way.

In other words, the Rebel Confederacy proposes to meet the policy of Emancipation by inaugurating a wholesale murder of prisoners.

Is it well for insurgents to thus aggravate the perils and penalties of insurrection?

When Kentucky wanted to hang Gen. Buckner—who was a double-dyed, forsworn traitor according to all laws, human and divine—she was not permitted to do so. On the contrary, Kentuckians and Marylanders serving in the Rebel armies have been paroled and exchanged by us the same as other Confederate prisoners. And yet, there is no serious pretence that Kentucky and Maryland have seceded from the Union; and if we had chosen to treat them specially as traitors, there was ample ground for doing so.

The first battalion of colored men organized for this war was raised in New Orleans, to fight on the side of the Slaveholders' Rebellion, under the authority of Governor Moore of Louisiana. That battalion became the nucleus of Gen. Butler's (now Gen. Banks's) colored force, now amounting to a brigade of three or four thousand men. Is it a law of civilized warfare that slaveholders and rebels alone may arm and use negroes? Let them show their patent!

Jeff. talks largely of "the horrors" and "merciless atrocities" of a "servile war"—but these atrocities are of his own creation purely. The negroes—whether on his side or on ours—have thus far shown no disposition to disregard the most humane rules of civilized warfare. But *he* steps in, and, charging others with exciting to "merciless atrocities," proceeds to inaugurate them himself! Were the negroes to do their worst, they could not surpass the "atrocities" which he, from his snug fireside, orders to be perpetrated, until the whole land shall be drunk with blood.

He will frighten nobody. On the contrary, the whole civilized world will see in this savage manifesto a new proof of the unspeakable brutality and cruelty inseparable from the slaveholding system, and will hail it as a striking proof of Rebel desperation. Murder is the last resort of even the most hardened and reckless felon. And, while it is easy to launch a threat of wholesale execution from the Cabinet, soldiers in the field, who are to be its victims, and who fully comprehend that butchery involves retaliation, will generally do as they see fit about carrying such sanguinary threats into execution.—*New York Tribune.*

☞ The Hanging Proclamation of Jefferson Davis, which appears to concentrate in itself the combined arrogance, wrath and mendacity of all Rebeldom, is evidently intended, principally, if not entirely, as a rejoinder to President Lincoln's Emancipation Proclamation, the time for the operation of which is now near at hand. It would hardly be thought necessary or politic, even by secessionists, to start a proclamation with the falsehood that Wm. B. Mumford had been executed in New Orleans for having pulled down the United States flag in that city before its occupation by the United States forces, and to clinch it with an appeal "to the Divine Judge," merely or principally for the purpose of retaliation for an act committed so long ago. To say nothing of the tiger-like savageness of the whole document, that part of the edict which declares all commissioned officers under Gen. Butler to be robbers and murderers, who are to be reserved for execution, is as diabolical and bloody in its conception and declaration as anything which has been sent forth by any government pretending to civilization since the days of St. Bartholomew, and including even the order for that merciless massacre.—*Boston Transcript.*

The Liberator.

No Union with Slaveholders!

BOSTON, FRIDAY, JANUARY 2, 1863.

CONCERNING THE LIBERATOR.

The war has not only crippled the circulation of the newspaper press generally, but it has produced such a scarcity in the materials for making printing paper,—owing chiefly to the failure of the cotton crop,—that the price per ream is now more than doubled, with a strong probability of a further upward tendency for some time to come. The consequence must be, universally, either a diminution in the size of the sheet or in the quantity of reading matter, or else a proportionate increase in the subscription price. Another alternative is, speedy extinction. In numerous cases, a stern necessity will doubtless compel the acceptance of the last, especially by weekly newspapers, as comparatively few of these have, hitherto, been able to preserve more than a precarious existence. It was the extra ounce that broke the camel's back: in this case, it is a ton's weight, instead of an ounce.

In common with all other publishers, we find ourselves in a very tight place. Our subscription list has been seriously reduced, by various causes, during the last year; and this, alone, is a source of pecuniary embarrassment. To attempt to go on at the same rates, with this loss, with the enormous advance in the price of printing paper, and with no immediate prospect of extending our circulation, would inevitably terminate the publication of the *Liberator* at an early day. On the other hand, to increase the terms to $3.00 per annum,—which, supposing our present list of subscribers should remain firm, would barely cover the additional cost of the white paper,—may cause such a further diminution in the number of our patrons as to hasten the same fatal result. The first course, if pursued, is certain suppression; the second furnishes the only chance of continuance. In these trying circumstances, we cannot hesitate which to adopt. The price of the *Liberator*, therefore, at the commencement of the new year, will be enhanced fifty cents per annum, until the market value of printing paper be restored to its normal condition. Other weekly papers throughout the country have been obliged to make a similar advance in their own case.

ENCOURAGING WORDS AND GENEROUS RESPONSES.

The following letters received (among others) since our announcement of the absolute necessity imposed upon us to advance the subscription terms of the *Liberator*, in consequence of the enormous increase in the price of printing paper, are cheering indications of a hearty and generous spirit of coöperation on the part of our subscribers, and evince an abiding interest in the continuance of the *Liberator*; for which we gratefully tender our heartfelt acknowledgments.

DANVERS PORT, Dec. 24, 1862.

DEAR FRIEND GARRISON,—It was with sorrow of heart that I read your statement in the last *Liberator*, of the financial condition of our beloved sheet; not because of the small advance in price of its subscription, but because of the low state of Anti-Slavery feeling in the community. To think that the pioneer paper in the greatest of moral enterprises this world ever saw should languish for support is really too bad! But it must not be, it shall not be so. Dear friends, you who have the love of God and of the oppressed in your hearts, will you not come to the rescue? Let us put our shoulders to the wheel, and give our old friend such a lift as shall make his new year really a happy one. As mountains are made from atoms, I hereby pledge my atom to the support of the sheet that has done so much for us. So, Mr. Editor, you may put me down for five dollars for the next year. I doubt if you have many subscribers who are not better able to give than is the writer. Let all give in proportion to their means, and thereby enable the publisher to send the *Liberator* to every subscriber at the old price, or less, who signifies to our General Agent that he is unable to pay more. Friends of the slave, will you respond to this call? Or will you leave the only paper that dares to tell the whole truth, (and to let the enemies of truth be freely heard in its columns,) falter and die for support? Talk of severing our connection with the *Liberator*, because of its enhanced expense! Why, we should as soon think of divorcing ourselves from a dear member of our family, because of the increased cost of living!

JOSEPH MERRILL.

—

NEW BEDFORD, 12mo. 24th, 1862.

WM. LLOYD GARRISON:

RESPECTED FRIEND,—I have read with much interest thy honest and characteristic statement of the financial affairs of the *Liberator*, and trust that the subscribers will readily and heartily respond to the necessities of the case; at least, so far as the trifling addition of fifty cents per annum is concerned.

Although the affairs of our nation appear to be more and more complicated, my faith in the ultimate freedom of the slave, as well as the firmer establishment of human rights in our land, has never been shaken from the beginning of the conflict.

I am often reminded of what our friend, and the devoted friend of the slave, CAROLINE WESTON, said to me in conversation some sixteen or more years ago, to this end; that, "when the day should come for the consummation of our great object in the freedom of the slave, others would step in and take the laurels and glory of the victory; and that we, abolitionists, must expect only reproach and self-sacrifice." How truly is this being verified! But this is also true, that the reward of a good conscience cannot be taken away, and that the sacrifices made by the friends of the oppressed and down-trodden slaves of our land will be remembered and appreciated by the good and virtuous in all coming time.

I enclose three dollars as my next year's subscription for the *Liberator*.

With unabated respect and friendly regard for thee and thy family, I remain in the bonds of Christian love, waiting for the grand jubilee of freedom.

Thy affectionate friend,

DANIEL RICKETSON.

—

AUBURN, (N. H.) Dec. 21, 1862.

DEAR FRIEND GARRISON,—Enclosed, please find three dollars to pay my subscription for the *Liberator* for next year. I cannot bear the idea that the old pioneer sheet shall be suspended. I think that the reading of the paper richly repays me for even the advanced price. Notwithstanding all the favorable circumstances and change of public opinion; that nearly all the periodicals, political and religious, are discussing the subject of slavery pro and con—and there is hardly a speech or a lecture delivered but that slavery is the most prominent topic—and even clergymen frequently introduce it into their sermons and prayers; yet something more radical than most of these is needed. A very large proportion of this anti-slavery or emancipation is void of any fixed moral principle. It is mere military necessity or political expediency.

I do not recollect of ever having seen one word from the lips or pen of the President, as acknowledging that the slaves have any claim as an act of justice upon the government or people. Then, colorphobia, the spirit of colonization, pervades all classes, (not all individuals,) from the President to the last Irishman from Cork; and it needs combating more strongly than is done through most other channels.

I hope that most of the patrons of the *Liberator* do not feel quite so indifferent about its continuance as the editor does. I hope that they are willing to make pecuniary sacrifices, to curtail expenses somewhere else, if necessary, to sustain the paper and its editor, until the universal jubilee shall be proclaimed. Then it will be needed to combat the prejudice against the black man, and aid in his education and elevation; and to give publicity to such noble letters as that of Miss Forten.

Yours, with much esteem,

BENJAMIN CHASE.

—

ELKHART, (Indiana,) Dec. 29, 1862.

WM. LLOYD GARRISON:

DEAR SIR,—I am an old subscriber to your paper, and therefore know something of its value. It is a *Liberator* in the fullest sense of the word. It has labored faithfully, manfully and fearlessly to unscale the mental eyes of this people, pouring light and knowledge into their minds, and thereby dissolve the shackles that have so long bound the limbs of the American bondman—not by blood and carnage, but by peaceful and friendly means. It has received the taunts and jeers of politicians, and the anathematised prayers and execrations of the church and clergy. For more than thirty years it has stood the test; and now, as it has reached almost the summit of the mountain, and is about to grasp the prize for which it has so manfully fought, never swerving to the right hand or the left, shall it be allowed to flounder for the want of a little pecuniary aid? No, that will never, never do. It must survive its pioneer achievements, and the downfall of American chattelism. And as prayers are of no avail, unless accompanied by corresponding acts, I hereby enclose eight dollars—three of which please receive as subscription for the *Liberator* for one year; the remainder I donate for the benefit of the paper, for the old pioneer must be kept in the field.

Yours, ever for Truth and Justice,

ISAAC BUCKLEN.

—

CORNVILLE, Me., Dec. 20, 1862.

DEAR MR. GARRISON,—Your notice to the friends of freedom concerning the *Liberator* meets with a hearty response in every fibre of my system. The pioneer paper must be sustained, no matter what the expense. Neither a diminution in the size of the paper, nor its extinction, can be thought of for a moment. The *Liberator* for seventeen years has been to me like water to a thirsty soul. It is a true educator. From it, I have learned more than I can express in words. Where is the man or woman naming the holy name of Abolitionist, who would see it suffer for want of help, though the times in future may demand that the price be quadrupled? It must live until every slave in the land is free.

I get my living by the very hardest kind of labor on a farm, and sometimes it is almost impossible to get the pay for the paper; but it is one of the luxuries that I *will have*. I shall pay the $3 as willingly as the former price.

Yours, for the redemption of man,

SEWARD MITCHELL.

—

WEST BROOKFIELD, (Vt.) Dec. 27, 1862.

BROTHER GARRISON—I see by the last *Liberator* that its price this year, or rather *next* year, is to be three dollars. Slavery is not yet abolished, and, until it is, I think no true Abolitionist can afford to do without the old pioneer sheet; and, above all, he to whom this nation is indebted more than to any other man since the foundation of the American Government, for the vindication of human rights and the defence of universal freedom, should not, at this impending crisis, be deserted or abandoned. No, never! Let us boldly and heroically, like good men and true, stand by him who, under God, is the honored leader and champion in one of the most stupendous moral revolutions this world has ever witnessed; whose earnest words of truth and power have at last, after the indefatigable labors of a third of a century, found a response in the hearts of the American people, causing the very earth to quake beneath its mighty tread, and the dynasties and thrones of Europe to shake and stand tremulous upon their uncertain bases.—"The things that cannot be shaken will remain." The darkness that now overhangs this nation will make the succeeding day all the lighter. Let none who have been instructed by the *Liberator* yield to fear; for from that we all have been taught to have implicit confidence in the omnipotence of right, justice and truth. No, friends, we have nothing to fear, for "the Lord God omnipotent reigneth." There is no strange thing happened. The present state of things is simply the legitimate result of antecedent causes; just what the Abolitionists said would ultimately and inevitably come from the existence and tendency of slavery in our midst. *In the nature of things, it could not have been otherwise.* Let me exhort all the old patrons of the *Liberator* to stand by it now in its time of need. It would be ingratitude indeed to forsake it now. We owe it to its fearless, uncompromising and untiring editor, who has done so much for us and universal humanity. Let us, I say again, stand by the *Liberator* as the foe of tyrants and the friend of man. Let the *Liberator* live, and stand up in all the vigor and freshness of its youth, a terror to evil-doers, until the song of FREEDOM shall have gone up to heaven from the lips of the last slave on the American soil. Then, with good old Simeon it may say, "Now lettest thou thy servant depart in peace, for mine eyes have seen thy salvation." Enclosed are three dollars for the *Liberator*.

JEHIEL CLAFLIN.

[Our friend CLAFLIN belongs to the Abdiels of the pulpit, who, "few and far between," have always been true to the claims of bleeding humanity.]

—

WATERTOWN, (N. Y.) Dec. 29, 1862.

WM. LLOYD GARRISON:

MY DEAR SIR,—I have read with much interest your statement of the financial dilemma in which the *Liberator*, as well as most other papers, is now placed; and most cheerfully do I accept the new terms on which you propose to publish the sheet for the coming year. The *Liberator* has become indispensable to me, and I would much rather pay for two or three copies than have it suspended. You will find enclosed $3 to pay for the *Liberator* for the coming year. Should the enhanced terms fail to meet the necessities of the case, I hope you will frankly make known the fact in time for your friends to aid you.

With the highest respect, I am, dear sir,

Yours, very truly, E. W. REYNOLDS.

[Rev. Mr. Reynolds is the author of that admirable and widely-praised work, entitled "THE BARONS OF THE SOUTH."]

—

SPRINGFIELD, (Vt.) Dec. 30, 1862.

EDITOR LIBERATOR:

DEAR SIR,—I find in your last sheet an appeal to your patrons to sustain the *Liberator*; or, rather, a well-timed and simple statement of the *cause* which has compelled an advance in the price, with more than a hint that it must go down if not sustained. Enclosed, please find five dollars, which place to my credit, with the understanding that, should a further advance become necessary before this is run out, I will take my chance, and share my proportion of the burden, until paper is a dollar a pound, and *Liberators* twenty-five cents apiece; and may God preserve the life and continue the health of its ever-faithful Editor, to witness the last shackle fall from the limbs of the last slave in our land!

JESSE STEDMAN.

—

GORHAM, Me., 8th Dec., 1862.

MR. GARRISON: I herewith renew my subscription for the *Liberator*. I like the *Liberator* better and better for its truthfulness and faithfulness. I am particularly pleased with the "Refuge of Oppression." A great deal of shrewdness is evinced in thus publishing verbatim what enemies say against Abolitionists. It is "holding the mirror up to nature," and often reflects the real character of adversaries far more distinctly than could be done by editorial comment, however graphic the delineation.

Though a member of an Orthodox church, I have generally acquiesced in your rebuke of the Church. With deep mortification and regret, I am compelled to admit that the American Church has been the bulwark of American slavery. I was also a member of the Liberty party and of the Free Soil party, and am now a Republican. Your strictures of these parties have mostly been just. In two of them, there has certainly been more or less of a disposition to compromise with wrong. But the Liberty party was true to its mission. I am not aware that it ever manifested the least desire to compromise. Your objection to it, however, was very natural. The Constitution, which that party avowed its purpose to support, you regarded as *itself* an unwarrantable compromise—indeed, as "a covenant with death, and an agreement with hell." The party, on the contrary, looking at the Preamble, found in the Constitution all that the most ardent and devoted advocate of Freedom could desire. It did not, therefore, feel conscientiously bound by covert intents or erroneous decisions of pro-slavery courts.

But whatever the true construction, the Liberty party and the Abolitionists (I use the latter term in its popular as well as true signification) were alike honest; so that your strictures never disturbed me, since I knew they were made in supposed defence of human rights. And it is a source of gratification that, whether in the church or the political party, in the social circle, or wherever else it has been deemed expedient, I have for the past twenty years or more, to the very best of my ability, defended the *Liberator* and Mr. Garrison against all unreasonable and unreasoning complaints.

The course of the *Liberator* in sustaining the government in its efforts to crush this infernal rebellion has been ground of astonishment to many. They had not expected such support, and think it quite inconsistent with former utterances. But they mistake your position. While the Government was in the interest of slavery, as it had mainly been since its organization, you opposed the Government. But the moment it placed itself on the side of Freedom, then it began to receive your support, in exact accordance with the measure of its faithfulness to that cause.

Very truly, your friend,

C. A. STACKPOLE.

—

☞ The Boston (German) *Pionier*, edited by Karl Heinsen, bestows the following tribute:—

"Among the papers which in these bad times are suffering most, after having striven most for better ones, belongs the Boston *Liberator*. In raising for the new year its subscription price from $2.50 to $3.00, it intimates that only by the faithful adherence of its present friends can it be saved from going under. The tendency of the *Liberator* in various respects, especially in the matter of religion, does not coincide with that of the radical Germans. But in regard to political free-thinking, fearlessness, fidelity to principle, integrity, and lack of prejudice towards 'foreign' enlightenment, it is not surpassed by any American paper. No paper in this country which is edited in English, stands nearer to the Germans than the *Liberator*, which, when it has opportunity, affords its readers specimens of German public opinion on the side of freedom by means of excellent translations. We trust that our readers also know how to value this; and those of them whose means allow them to take an American paper, should not neglect to exhibit their sentiments by subscribing to the *Liberator*."

ANNUAL MEETING OF THE MASSACHUSETTS ANTI-SLAVERY SOCIETY.

The THIRTIETH ANNUAL MEETING of the Massachusetts Anti-Slavery Society will be held in Boston on THURSDAY and FRIDAY, Jan. 29th and 30th, (day and evening,) commencing at 10 o'clock, A. M.

This Society was organized for the utter abolition of slavery throughout the United States. However great has been the change wrought in public sentiment in favor of that godlike object,—and it has been truly marvellous, in view of the mountainous obstacles in the way of success; however effectual may be the President's Emancipation Proclamation in breaking the chains of the bondmen in such rebellious sections of the country as he has just designated,—and Heaven grant it may be as potent in operation as it is comprehensive in its scope; nevertheless, nothing at this hour is settled so surely as the continued enslavement of four millions of the inhabitants of the land; and while any of these remain to wear the yoke, the primary object and specific work of this Society will not have been accomplished. Slavery in the so-called loyal Border States is as inexcusable, as criminal, as revolting, as unendurable, as pregnant with evil and ruin, as in the rebellious Confederate States, and must be as vigorously and uncompromisingly assailed, until liberty is proclaimed "throughout ALL the land, to ALL the inhabitants thereof."

The approaching anniversary promises to be one of surpassing interest; and it is not doubted that the friends of universal emancipation, in the various sections of the Commonwealth, (and, it is hoped, beyond the limits of the State,) will be encouragingly represented on the occasion. As hitherto, an additional attraction will be presented in the holding of the NATIONAL ANTI-SLAVERY SUBSCRIPION ANNIVERSARY on the evening (Wednesday, Jan. 28th) preceding the opening session of the Society.

[Further particulars hereafter.]

By order of the Board of Managers,

EDMUND QUINCY, *President.*

ROBERT F. WALLCUT, *Sec'y.*

IN MEMORIAM.

During the past year, an unusual number of the untiring and ever-faithful friends of the Anti-Slavery cause have seen "the last of earth,"—departing to the Spirit-land at the culminating period of their labors and sacrifices, just within hearing of the songs and shouts of the long desired jubilee. Among these we recall the names, first, of the earliest and most venerable—namely:

(1) DAVID MERRITT, Esq., of Salem, at the ripe old age of 87.

(2) Rev. HENRY GREW, of Philadelphia, aged 80.

(3) ANDREW ROBESON, Esq., of New Bedford, aged 75.

(4) Col. WILLIAM WHITING, of Concord, Mass., aged 73.

(5) DARIUS P. LAWTON, of East Providence, R. I., aged 75.

(6) ZECHARIAH OBER, of Newbury, Ohio, aged 87.

(7) ISAAC STEVENS, Esq., of North Andover, (father of Gen. Isaac I. Stevens, who fell at Fairfax Court House, Va.,) aged 77.

(8) DANIEL ANTHONY, Esq., of Rochester, N. Y., (father of Miss Susan B. Anthony,) aged 69.

Second—the names of those who, though younger in years, were equally steadfast and true—namely:

(1) BENJAMIN S. JONES, of Kennet Square, Pa., for several years the able and uncompromising editor of the Ohio *Anti-Slavery Bugle*, a faithful lecturer in the field, and from his youth warmly interested in the cause.

(2) DANIEL MITCHELL, of Pawtucket, R. I.

(3) JOHN JONES, of Roxbury.

(4) WARNER JUSTICE, of Philadelphia.

Third—the names of those yet younger in years—namely:

(1) GERRIT SMITH HAMBLETON, of Upper Oxford, Pa. Died at Hilton Head, S. C.

(2) ROBERT PURVIS, Jr., of Byberry, Pa.

(3) RANDALL MANN, of Leicester, killed in battle.

(4) WILLIAM FULLER, of Needham, who died of his wounds in the battle of Bull Run.

The Rev. Dr. SAMUEL OSGOOD, of Springfield, (Mass.) who recently departed at the age of 77, deserves to be gratefully remembered for his early adhesion to the cause, which he advocated to his cost and with unflinching courage, though for some years past not appearing on the platform of the American Anti-Slavery Society.

WILLIAM M. CHACE, Esq., formerly of Providence, R. I., who died in the city of New York, was particularly prominent and active in the early period of the struggle, doing efficient service in helping to change the sentiment of Rhode Island in favor of the oppressed.

In this connection, the Rev. JOHN W. LEWIS, for many years a respected minister in the Freewill Baptist denomination, who died in Hayti a few months since, and who was identified in complexion and destiny with the oppressed, is deserving of honorable remembrance for his modest and amiable character, his very respectable talents as a preacher and lecturer, and his unceasing efforts to excite sympathy and obtain deliverance for his fettered countrymen.

Within the past year, also, several estimable and thoroughly devoted women, whose pulsations beat responsive to the throbbings of the slave-mother's heart, have also been translated. Among these we record the names of

(1) The venerable MARIA MARRIOTT, of Hudson, N. Y.

(2) The equally venerable CATHARINE PUTNAM, of Peterboro', N. H.

(3) MARGARET BLYDENBURGH, of Durham, N. H.

(4) LYDIA H. CHASE, of Salem, Mass.

(5) EMMA WILLARD WYMAN, of Worcester, wife of Major John C. Wyman.

(6) HANNAH WEBB, the beloved wife of Richard D. Webb, of Dublin, Ireland.

(7) HANNAH E. STODDARD, of Fall River.

(8) ABBY FENNO MANLEY, wife of John R. Manley, Esq., of Boston.

(9) LOUISA MAY WILLIS, wife of Hamilton Willis, Esq., of Boston.

(10) ANNA P. DONALDSON, of Penmaen, Ohio.

The list on both sides could be considerably extended, but this will suffice to remind the readers of the *Liberator* of the loss sustained during the brief period of twelve months. But the glorious cause to which the departed gave their early or their later years, in the face of popular scorn and often of fiery trials, is immortal, invincible, and we trust ere long to be triumphant throughout the land. Its friends and advocates have never been so numerous, its enemies never so broken and dispirited, as at the present time. Whoever may be called away to another sphere of existence, it bears a charmed life, and no weapon raised against it can prosper. Based upon human nature, demanding simple justice for all men, seeking the welfare of the oppressor and the oppressed alike, divorced from all worldly selfishness, inspired by a divine energy, and upheld by an omnipotent arm, it cannot be vanquished, though all the hosts of hell assail it; and over it death has no power. Others of the early and true are serenely waiting "to be clothed upon" in God's good time, which may not be far off; but, living or dying, they know in whom they have believed, and will remain faithful to the end, ready for every emergency, and through faith overcoming all opposition.

THE NORTH BRITISH REVIEW, for November, is before us, with the following articles:—1. Christian Individuality. 2. The Austrian Empire in 1862. 3. Poems by A. H. Clough. 4. Assimilation of Law. 5. France and Scotland—M. Michel. 6. Popular Prophetical Literature. 7. Syria and the Eastern Question. 8. St. Clement's Eve. 9. The American Conflict. [For an extract from this last article, which is basely pro-slavery, see "Refuge of Oppression."]

Crosby & Nichols, 117 Washington street.

FRATERNITY LECTURE.

The twelfth lecture before the Fraternity was delivered on Tuesday evening, Dec. 23d, by George William Curtis, Esq., of New York. His subject was, "The American Doctrine of Liberty." The Tremont Temple was filled, and the eloquent speaker was frequently applauded.

He represented the motive and mainspring of the gigantic war in which this nation is now engaged to be the maintenance of the great, original, American doctrine of Liberty; the absolute personal and political liberty of every human being, in virtue of his humanity. In spite of colossal efforts, and stupendous sophistry, used by clergymen and political orators to pervert this idea, he felt sure that it was making steady progress among the people—the great body of the nation.

This American doctrine of liberty as an inherent and universal right, is a very different thing from that Athenian liberty, and that Roman liberty, of which scholars talk with so much admiration. Liberty, among the Romans, was only for citizens of Rome. Spartacus, though a man of lofty powers and noble aspirations, being by birth a barbarian and by station a slave, was not a man in Roman eyes, and had no rights which Romans were bound to respect. His rights as a man were ignored and trampled on. But his wild revenge showed his own recognition of those rights, and his scorn of the polished oppressors who would destroy them.

Even British society is only a modified feudalism, a system founded more on class privileges than on human rights.

Our revolutionary fathers took a different ground. They did not argue the principles of the Declaration of Independence, but declared them self-evident. James Otis affirmed—"The colonists are *men*, and *therefore* entitled to freedom." Richard Henry Lee echoed the Declaration. The Bill of Rights of Virginia says it is self-evident that men are created equal. Who shall dare to call this a "glittering generality"?

After a brief reference to the eloquent lawyer of Boston whose sophistry stereotyped itself in the phrase above quoted, Mr. Curtis proceeded to say that the equality which underlies our doctrine of liberty is an equality of rights, and that this is unlimited.

Our fathers were not hypocrites. They expected the quiet disappearance of slavery, and they charged their posterity not to forget the maintenance of liberty. But we did forget it; and now God is rendering us the retribution belonging to neglected duties.

The men opposed to us in this war hate the spirit of liberty as well as all outward manifestations of it. Are our soldiers as zealous for the right as the enemy are for the wrong? If not, recal them, and send men imbued with the intensest love of true liberty. Only such can effectively fight on the Northern side.

After speaking of the power and the undue influence of public opinion in this country, Mr. Curtis said—He best educates the public mind, who, in spite of opposition, persists in teaching the people what they *ought* to desire.

After saying that our present contest is not only for liberty but for civilization, Mr. Curtis spoke of the President, attributing to him the distinguishing merits of Washington and Jefferson, and wishing he had those of Andrew Jackson in addition.

Even we in New England do not hold the full American idea of liberty. Among us, sex and color still disqualify. If a man is born of the wrong color, we assume that he is a rascal. The shameful fact is, that by ill treatment we have done our best to make him such.

Our rights are ours because we are men, not in virtue of any fictitious qualification. Color should no more exclude any one from the rights of citizenship than social position or trade.

Speaking of the prejudice cherished by many Americans against foreigners, Mr. Curtis said he had had the fortune to meet with one logical Know-Nothing. This man wished that every d—d nigger would kill a d—d Paddy, and then be hung for murder.

The course of that ambitious intriguer, Stephen A. Douglas, seemed to have sprung from the belief that a long course of practical indifference to natural rights had depraved the intellect of the American people. His system had for its corner-stone a piece of transparent sophistry. Our American doctrine, he said, is that the majority must govern, and this is obviously just and right. Very well; apply this principle to the great topic of dispute in our country, and it will plainly appear that the majority in any State have a right to decide whether they will hold slaves or not!

This is a doctrine of the sheerest moral indifference, representing liberty and human rights as chimeras. This doctrine overlooks and disregards not only the rights of minorities, (which are never to be left out of sight,) but the yet more sacred rights of humanity—those which inherently belong to the human being.

The truth is, Douglas cared neither for slavery nor liberty. He was a gambler, playing for the Presidency. He was warned that "though the mills of God grind slowly, they grind exceeding small." He disregarded the warning, and the mills of God crushed him.

Those who would lay a firm foundation in politics must remember that not majorities only, but *men*, have rights. Such is the scope of our American doctrine. The question is, Do we believe it? Are we willing to act upon it? The terrible war that is upon us asks this question; and it must be fairly answered.

We are pledged to liberty. We must gain it. But vainly shall we seek it for ourselves and our children unless we also demand it for the unhappy race whom we have hitherto enslaved.

We have been accustomed to take for granted that the rights of this race might be trampled on with impunity. Like Belshazzar, our nation sat peaceful, powerful and prosperous. We disregarded occasional glimpses of the hand, writing our sentence on the wall, and we made foolish excuses for the postponement of repentance and reformation. But, even while we spoke, the slave, like the Afreet emerging from his casket in the Arabian tale, swelled into gigantic proportions, and demanded justice and freedom. An immense and threatening power revealed itself in the very race we had derided as weak; and from the skies a voice repeated the fearful question—Where is Abel, thy Brother?

By the lurid light of this war we see our duty, and we read our doom, corresponding to the fulfilment or the violation of that duty. Our nation may emerge from this contest like the wriggling worm, destined to permanent debasement, or it may soar like the Eagle, shaking off the chains that have hitherto restrained it.

—

Last Tuesday evening, in consequence of the absence of Rev. J. M. MANNING, poetical readings from popular authors, by Miss EMILY SHAW, were substituted for a lecture, and gave very general satisfaction—Miss S. evincing superior elocutionary talent, but lacking in power of voice for so large a hall.

Mr. Slack, the President of the Fraternity, thanked the audience for their attendance, and expressed the satisfaction of the Committee at the full success of this fifth series of lectures. He thought they had accomplished their purpose, of giving to the public of Boston a course fully equal, both in interest and value, to any of those admirable ones which have been given in previous years. And he held out the pleasing hope that, whenever Mr. Manning should return to Boston on furlough, he might be persuaded to throw his experience of camp life into the form of a lecture, in which case the Committee would gladly add that to the course.

It must be admitted that this course has been eminent in excellence and attractiveness. The Fraternity lectures have become one of our permanent institutions. They hold a high place among the educational forces of the city of Boston, giving instruction, intellectual and moral, of a very high order, and also being looked for, from year to year, as among the most attractive of winter entertainments.—C. K. W.

LETTER FROM GEORGE THOMPSON, ESQ.

London, Dec. 12, 1862.

My Dear Garrison:

I have just returned from Staffordshire, where I have been holding meetings at Stanley, Burslem and Newcastle, upon the Emancipation question in America. In every place, I had large and enthusiastic meetings, and although I heard of many persons with Southern sympathies, and though at every meeting I invited opposition, no antagonist appeared. William Andrew Jackson accompanied me, and at every meeting delivered an interesting and telling address. On the preceding Sunday, he was invited to speak at several Sabbath Schools, and addressed, in all, upwards of three thousand children, besides speaking in the evening to the congregation worshipping at the Independent Chapel. He has written a letter to Jefferson Davis, informing him that he (Jackson) cannot be with him on the 25th inst., on which day it will be necessary for the rebel chief to produce him, to discharge a bond for $1,050 which he has given to the owner of his body.

This evening, I attend a meeting in London, called "To express sympathy with the Anti-Slavery party in America." It will be addressed by the Rev. Newman Hall, the Rev. J. H. Ryland, and myself. On the 15th, I speak at a similar meeting in Spa Fields Chapel; on the 16th, at Stratford; on the 17th, at Basingstoke; and on the 19th, at Banbury. After these meetings, I shall have others in the North of England and in Scotland.

I am greatly rejoiced to find that Theodore Weld is again in the field. I have ever deeply regretted the cause of his long silence. His coöperation at this crisis cannot fail to prove very valuable.

I am looking with impatience and nervous anxiety for the appearance of the President's Message. I have been encouraged by what I have seen in the American papers to believe that it will be satisfactory on the slave question; but I want the assurance of the document itself. My disappointment would be great, and the sorrow of the friends of the slave here most poignant, if it should show any infirmity of purpose in reference to emancipation.

Too much praise cannot be awarded to our unemployed and suffering population in the manufacturing districts, for the patience and uncomplaining fortitude with which they have borne their privations consequent on the stoppage of the supply of cotton. Many and evil have been the attempts made to stir them to utter a demand for interference on the part of the Government, with a view to the recognition of the rebel States and the opening of the Southern ports. But they have been proof against all temptation, and have found amongst themselves able spokesmen to answer the arguments of the enemies of the North and of the cause of Freedom.

The meeting of the Confederate States Aid Society held the night before last was a miserable affair. The person they employ as a lecturer will not allow a question to be put to him, nor any remark to be made. A policeman is in readiness to remove any person who may attempt to speak.

If you have not yet seen the reply of Prof. Newman to Mr. Gladstone, you will have much pleasure in reading it in the paper sent with this, and will doubtless print it.

Our Emancipation Society has issued a circular to ministers of all religious denominations, urging them to call attention to the President's Proclamation. I send you a copy, and hope you will approve.

I thank you for printing in the *Liberator* of the 28th ultimo my address at Leigh. You are at all times at liberty to use my communications as you deem expedient. Though I am separated from you by a wide interval, and am a poor correspondent, I am nevertheless continually with you in spirit, and do what I can to second the exertions made by yourself and your coadjutors in the cause of the slave.

Always, most sincerely yours,

GEO. THOMPSON.

THE PRESIDENT'S ABOLITION PROCLAMATION.

The following circular has been issued to the ministers of all religious denominations by the London Emancipation Society:—

London Emancipation Society,
65, Fleet Street, E. C., Dec. 9.

Rev. and Dear Sir,—We beg very respectfully to urge upon you the propriety of giving prominence to the subject of negro emancipation in the religious services, which, in this country at least, always herald the advent of a new year. President Lincoln has appointed the 1st of January, 1863, as the day on which he will, by virtue of the powers vested in him, declare slavery to be abolished in the rebel States. That day will form the commencement of a new era in American history—an era in which the whole power and authority of the Federal Government will be employed, for the first time, to effect the overthrow of a system that embodies in itself every iniquity known to man. It is, therefore, we think, a day eminently worthy of special recognition on the part of the great religious communities of England. Every section of the Christian public cannot fail to rejoice in the prospect of the slave's deliverance, and to pray that Divine Providence may bless the efforts of those who are endeavoring to uproot at once and for all an institution which has sought to degrade to the level of brutes four millions of human beings. We ask then, that, in your New Year's Services, the bondmen of the Southern States may be specially remembered; and that in every church and chapel throughout Great Britain an aspiration for their speedy release from captivity may rise to a just Heaven.

We do not appeal to you from any political motive, or for any mere party object. We ask only that, in this crisis of the negro's fate, you will remember them that are in bonds as bound with them. Many among the slaves and oppressed colored people of America are now looking to England for some token of her goodwill. Let us give it to them at a time when it will excite the deepest gratitude on their part, and exert the greatest influence on the public opinion of the United States, both North and South.

In America, at the present time, the real opinion of this country is grievously misunderstood. There are many in both sections of the republic who imagine that we have departed from the faith of our fathers. The enemies of human freedom, and of the pure religion of Christ, exult in the belief that the spirit of Clarkson, of Wilberforce, and of Fowell Buxton, has become extinct in the breasts of their successors; that the immortal principles which were embodied in the Acts abolishing the slave-trade and West India slavery have ceased to be dear to us as a nation. This should not be. To allow such an impression any longer to exist, to give color to it by a seeming apathy to the cause of the negro and to the traditions of an illustrious past, is to cast dishonor upon the character and the religion of England. To you, then, we make our appeal; to you who are the successors, and even in many instances the colleagues and friends of that noble band of ministers and churches, to whose labors far more than to those of statesmen or political parties the abolition of slavery in the British colonies must be attributed. We beg of you to render now, as far as you may be able, the same service to humanity which you rendered in that great struggle, and, by the expression of your religious feeling in the way we have indicated, to hasten the day when slavery and caste shall cease to pollute the soil of America.

Signed on behalf of the committee,

WILLIAM EVANS, *Chairman.*

F. W. Chesson, *Secretary.*

☞ We copy the following notices from the London *Morning Star*:—

FREEDOM FOR THE SLAVE.—A PUBLIC MEETING, to express sympathy with the anti-slavery party in America, will be held at the LAMBETH BATHS, Westminster-road, THIS EVENING, (Friday,) Dec. 12, 1862. George Thompson, Esq., late M. P. for the Tower Hamlets, and the Rev. J. H. Rylance, A. K. C., will attend as a deputation from the Emancipation Society. The Rev. NEWMAN HALL, LL.D., will take the Chair at Eight o'clock precisely. Working men are especially invited to attend. Admission free.

FREEDOM FOR THE SLAVE.—A PUBLIC MEETING for the purpose of expressing sympathy with the friends of universal liberty in America, in the prospect of the Emancipation of the Slaves of that country, will be held in SPA FIELDS CHAPEL, Exmouth street, Clerkenwell, on MONDAY EVENING, Dec. 15. George Thompson, Esq., Washington Wilks, Esq., and the Rev. J. W. Massie, D.D., LL.D., will attend as a deputation from the London Emancipation Society; the Rev. W. Elliott, superintendent of the Countess of Huntingdon's Mission at Sierra Leone, and other gentlemen, will take part in the meeting. The Rev. T. E. THORESBY will take the chair at half-past seven. Free admission.

TRUMPS THROWN AWAY.

Towards the close of the ever memorable defence of Venice, in 1849, the besiegers had made such progress that their batteries commanded two-thirds of the devoted city, and the inhabitants, crowded into the remaining third, were assailed at once by the Austrian, by pestilence, and by famine. But we read that whenever the enemy slackened fire to repair their damages, the Venitian women wept for fear lest the silence should mean negotiation and armistice.

Compare the situation of Venice and of the North after the 22d of September, and let any one say whether we might not justly have added tears to the thought of the possibilities of the last three months. Two doors stood open for the conspirators of the South, each, as far as human foresight can penetrate, marked, "This way to Victory." There was the opportunity to return, at the eleventh hour, if desired, to a Union and a North more than ever their own. If you doubt it, regard the recent elections, our baffled and wearied army, the entire professions of the President and of the leading Republican presses. Southern pride, or the shrewdness which saw that no victory over conscience could be permanent, and that the conscience of the North was the occasion (not the cause) of the rebellion,—Southern pride or shrewdness and our defeats in battle saved us from the degradation and ruin of a compromise. The South turned her back upon the olive-branch of conciliation, and closed door number one.

The second remained. It was to free the blacks, and secure the rebellion beyond peradventure. The foreigner would have been won over by the common appeal to his humanity and his interests. Unity would have been gained at home. The North, judged by its recorded purpose of restoring the Union as it was, would have appeared as the enslaver of freemen, the oppressor of a people determined to be independent, and morally incapable of subjugation. Amid the threatening murmur of Christendom, we must have had to acknowledge that the Confederacy was the legitimate child of a successful revolution.

Sive Deus an casus? Was it God, or chance, that prompted Jefferson Davis to issue his proclamation of December 22d? The slave not only not freed, but subject to every punishment if caught in the armed service of the North! We breathe again, and bless the arm that withheld our victories in the field, lest the humiliation or despair of the slaveholder might culminate in compromise or emancipation.

Thus has the hugest lie of the rebellion exploded of itself. It is, that the war has nothing to do with slavery. What fool at the North has not marked the lie from the outset? What fool in Europe may not mark it now, though he would not listen to Vice-President Stephens, when, to confirm the South in secession, he declared African slavery to be the "corner-stone" of the new Confederacy,—but hung rather upon the smooth deceptions of Yancey and Slidell? Acts speak louder than words. The Conspirators saw imperilled, through the President's Proclamation, the existence of their State or of their divine institution. "The Confederacy if possible, but Slavery at any rate!" was the voice of the 22d of December. Plymouth Rock will be grateful to its antagonist, because she removed her mask on Forefathers' Day.

—W. P. G.

ANTI-SLAVERY EFFORT STILL NEEDED.

If any body of men and women in this country have a right to look upon the present struggle with serene confidence and hope, it is the Abolitionists. They alone enjoy the consciousness that no drop of fratricidal blood attaches itself to their garments. For more than a quarter of a century, they have toiled and plead and suffered that this nation might be saved from the fiery ordeal of civil war. The people were deaf to their reiterated warnings, stoned the prophets and ridiculed the truth. Now the day of fulfilment is at hand, and the choicest lives are demanded as an atonement.

Abolitionists may well rejoice. Not that they feel less than others the horrors of war, or are wanting in sympathy for the sufferers, but because the justice of God is made manifest to their eyes, and their faith in the ultimate triumph of the right is undoubted.

But the end is not yet, and, until the last black man on the continent is lifted into the sunlight of freedom, it is not time for the Abolitionist to lay aside his armor, or abate a single blow of his battle-axe.

True, the hated heresy of immediate emancipation, starting in that small Boston chamber where

> —— "friendless and unseen,
> Toiled o'er his types one poor, unlearned young man,"

has in the short space of an average life-time conquered obstacles that seemed formidable as the Andes. And in place of "a negro boy," who was the "only visible auxiliary" of Mr. Garrison that Mayor Otis could discover in 1831, behold, in 1863, Abraham Lincoln is substituted, and the despised printer speaks through the President of the United States!

For thus much, gratitude and praise! When the liberation of every bondman in the country is effected, when the present bud of promise has ripened into the golden fruit of performance, the distinctive work of the Abolitionists will have ceased. Then it will be time enough to talk of disbanding anti-slavery societies and stopping anti-slavery papers. In that day, the war-worn veterans of the cause will gladly rest in peace. The problem which has perplexed the pro-slavery press so long, i. e., how to abolish the Abolitionists, will then be solved.

But the jubilee trump has not yet sounded. A partial proclamation of freedom, wrung from unwilling hands by the stern necessities of war, cannot, must not satisfy. Grant that it is to be faithfully executed, it is not enough. Loyalty to the old Union gives Border State men no moral right to hold slaves; and until slaveholders, whether loyal or disloyal, are outlawed by this nation, this nation will be held an outlaw by the civilized world.

Again, what guaranty have we that the present proclamation is given in good faith? Seward, who, since the inauguration of Lincoln, has studied only to betray freedom by a compromise, still leads the Cabinet. Democratic generals with pro-slavery antecedents control our armies. The man who issued Order No. 3 is the appointed officer to execute the military proclamation. Let us not be too sanguine. With no heart in the great work which has fallen to their hands, what can be hoped from Seward and Halleck? Unexecuted, the proclamation is a blow against the North instead of the South. Void of effect, it will be another proof of the impotence of the Republican Administration, and Northern Democracy can ask no better rallying cry than this "abolition failure" to marshal their seditious cohorts and sweep from power the present Government, whose immense resources and available strength are only equalled by its infirmity of purpose and feebleness of execution.

With uncertainties like these hanging over the nation's fate, the mission of the Abolitionists is by no means ended. Before God relieves us from our scourge, the conscience of the people must show more signs of awakening than are visible at present. We give up slavery with the same reluctance that a drowning man relinquishes his grasp of the bag of gold which is dragging him under. A selfish sacrifice solely for preservation is no atonement for a century of injustice. Repentance and reparation must precede forgiveness and peace.

The Abolitionists will therefore increase, not relax their efforts. They urge the necessity of the same assistance which has been tendered in former years. They pray the people not to cherish the delusion that abolition is an accomplished fact. Give liberally of your store to the treasury of the only American Society that never forgets the equal brotherhood of the slave. Circulate with renewed zeal the anti-slavery papers and tracts. So may the "good time coming" be hastened, and the salvation of the nation's heart as well as its form of government be assured.

CREDO.

LETTER FROM HENRY C. WRIGHT.

A Letter from a Soldier touching the Proclamation—The Wants of the Emancipated—Seymour the Representative of the Five Points—The Democratic Party a Representative of "the sum of all villany."

Cooperstown, (N. Y.,) Dec. 4, 1862.

Dear Garrison—I send you an extract from a letter, just received from a nephew in the army, who is Assistant Quartermaster of a division, and has daily and hourly opportunities to know and relieve the wants of the self-emancipated slaves who find protection within our lines in the slave States. He is a noble young man of 23, and enlisted to fight for liberty against slavery. A brother of his was shot, and his body lies in the slavery-cursed soil of Tennessee. As soon as his brother fell, this one took his place. If this one falls, another brother stands ready to fill his place. The noble mother and father said—"Some homes and hearts must be made desolate. They may as well be ours as others." God bless them for their self-abnegation! Some hearts must bleed, some homes must be made desolate, or slavery will rule the nation and continent. But hear the testimony of my brave and noble nephew, touching the Proclamation and its results:—

"I rejoice, with you, in the Proclamation of our Executive. That Proclamation is destined to render Abraham Lincoln's memory of long duration. His name, together with the great philanthropist of Russia, will be immortal.

"But of one thing I am fearful. Indeed, I see it already—i. e., the people of the North are not preparing for the Proclamation. They are not making a commensurate effort to prepare for the freed slaves. Let me tell you, unless some preparation is made ere the first of January for the emancipated slaves, we shall see a reign of starvation worse than Ireland ever saw. I foresee that event thus: In this city, ———, the colored people who escape from slavery to our lines are now dying of starvation! Scores of contrabands daily arrive. They flock within our lines. We protect them; we render their freedom secure; but, alas! freedom cannot supply them food. So, in many instances, they die!

"We have a Contraband Depot here, consisting of one house—quite a large one. The house is filled to overflowing, and the street, for rods, is literally filled with them. I have seen 500 men, women and children at that Depot. Frequently they come into our lines in gangs of over one hundred: when a large number congregate, they are sent away—where I know not. In other places, the freed slaves are starving to death. To sleep together in the streets, by hundreds, as they do, would surely kill white people.

"Now, the North must awake to the great trust of supplying the wants of the poor, despised, long-suffering slaves, or scenes of terrible suffering must ensue. I could tell you many instances that have come under my own observation that have touched me deeply, and would rejoice your heart: one will suffice. As I was riding by the Contraband Depot, not long since, I overtook an old slave and his wife, just as they arrived at the house from their bondage to a traitor. A girl of 15 came out of the door and met them, and instantly recognized in the man and woman her parents. They had been parted five years. You can conceive of the meeting—I cannot describe it."

What, indeed, can the North do to meet the events of the coming year? Millions of chattels will, I trust, be raised to men and women, millions of slaves into free men and free women; and certain it is that no effort will be spared by the kidnappers and traitors, and their Democratic allies in the North, to make the condition of those emancipated slaves as wretched as possible; and then they, and the English allies of slavery and treason, will urge that starvation and suffering as an argument against the policy of emancipation. They will do all they can to hedge up the way of these free men to earn their food and raiment, and then urge the starvation and nakedness that are produced by their own satanic hatred, as a reason against the Administration which freed them. What can the friends of freedom, of Christ, of God and Humanity, in this and in other lands, do to aid those innocent and long-suffering victims of American Democracy and American Religion to earn a comfortable living till the hot wrath of their kidnappers, North and South, shall have had time to exhaust itself?

By the way, the Democrats, since the official report of the election in this State, are glad to keep dark—those of them whose sense of shame and decency is not quite dead. It turns out that Horatio Seymour, as the Governor elect of the Empire State, is simply and solely the representative elect of the 2743 groggeries, the 279 brothels, 170 places of resort for thieves, burglars and ruffians, and 105 gambling hells located in and around the *Five Points* in New Yity! Seymour's majority in the whole State—including New York city—is 10,489. His majority in the twelve wards, embracing the *Five Points* and its precincts and dependencies, is 10,983! Wadsworth having only 1681 votes in all these wards, and Seymour 12,664—being a majority over Wadsworth of 10,983—some 500 more than in all the State, these wards included. Never—in the history of popular elections—in this or in any country—can there be found a fact so significant of the character of a political party and its candidate as this! It is simply a fact, attested by the official returns of the election, and by the police records of the above named wards and election districts in New York, that the Democratic party comes into power in the Empire State, the ally of kidnappers and rebels—simply and solely as the representative of the above enumerated groggeries, brothels, gambling hells, &c., in the *Five Points* of New York city and its dependencies. These brothels, groggeries, hells, and resorts of thieves and burglars were wheeled into the ranks of the Democratic allies of kidnappers and rebels by Isaiah Rynders and Fernando and Ben Wood, who took up their abode in the Five Points, with a view to this end! Why should not the party which, for fifty years, has represented slavery in the nation, now be the representative of the groggeries, brothels, and gambling hells of New York city? It has been nothing else for fifty years but the representative of a huge nation of brothels, in which are confined, without marriage, and in concubinage and prostitution, four millions of men and women. It has been the mere representative of that "sum of all villany" and pollution, American slavery. It is fitting that the same Democratic party should now come into power in New York State as the representative of the Five Points in New York.

Many voted for that party, and the "sum of all villany" and pollution which it represents, as did the Baptist deacon, to whom I alluded in my last—to put down Abolitionism. Many voted for it simply because they were so besotted with their partyism that they were willing to sacrifice their souls, their liberty, their manhood, their God on the altar of their party.

SLAVERY, THE CAUSE—ABOLITION, THE CURE—of rebellion and civil war, and all the evils that come from them to this and to other lands. This is my *one* theme in all my lectures—the Proclamation, its bearing on the Slaves, the Enslavers, the Republic, the Continent, the World.

I have done and am doing what I can to prepare all with whom I come in contact to aid the Administration to give vitality to that Proclamation. Twenty-seven days more must elapse before the set time arrives, but the real day of its power is come—and it came when the slaves learned of its existence. I am engaged to lecture once a day, and sometimes twice and thrice a day, between this and Christmas. Then I shall wend my way to Boston, to reach there, if I can, Wednesday, Dec. 31st. Many have gnashed their teeth, and made all sorts of threats, because I have held up the Empire State as an Abolition Society; and because I have proved to them, to *their own satisfaction*, that, by virtue of their citizenship in this State, they are members of a *radical, rabid, practical* Abolition Society!

Yours, HENRY C. WRIGHT.

Mr. Weld at Plymouth. Our Old Colony readers will see by the notice in the appropriate column, that Mr. Weld is to attend a meeting next Sunday at Plymouth. We learn from Abington that his addresses there on Sunday last, and also on Monday evening, were of the most thrilling interest, and that he was strongly solicited to visit other towns in that neighborhood at his earliest convenience.

ESSEX COUNTY A. S. SOCIETY.

A quarterly meeting of the Essex County Anti-Slavery Society was held in the Town Hall, Danvers, on Sunday, Dec. 21st.

The meeting was called to order by John Cutler, one of the Vice Presidents of the Society.

Joseph Merrill was chosen Secretary *pro tem.*

C. L. Remond, Theodore D. Weld and Parker Pillsbury were chosen a Committee on Business.

Isaac W. Roberts and Lizzie Elwell were chosen a Committee on Finance.

The meeting was addressed by Mr. Pillsbury in his usual argumentative and earnest manner. He thought there was no hope of salvation for us as a nation, unless by genuine repentance and works to accord.

Voted to adjourn to 2 o'clock, P. M.

Met agreeably to adjournment.

Parker Pillsbury presented the following resolutions in behalf of the Business Committee:—

1. Resolved, That a Union made with slaveholders, and continued over the prostrate forms, the outraged rights, the crucified manhood of half a million slaves, with pledges and guarantees under which the inhuman system has fearfully enlarged its territory and multiplied its victims, was a Union accursed of God from the beginning, and sure to be soon overthrown, unless delivered from that element of certain destruction.

2. Resolved, That our present bloody and desolating war is but a fulfilment of the words of the immortal Jefferson, "I tremble for my country when I reflect that God is just, and that his justice cannot sleep forever."

3. Resolved, That while slavery lasts in the land, shielded by the army and approved by the government, the war is but a sacrifice of our young men on an altar more relentless than Juggernaut, and in a cause which invokes in vain the sympathies of mankind, or the aid or approval of the God of the oppressed.

4. Resolved, That with trembling anxiety and hope we wait the approach of the new opening year that is to be, to millions of blacks, "*the year of jubilee*," under Presidential Proclamation, or of blank despair through a failure to execute it: and we hasten to register our hearty approval of that measure, not only as an act of justice, too long delayed, and a sign of contrition and penitence on the part of the government and nation, but also as the only possible escape from utter national destruction, under the just judgments of God.

Mr. Pillsbury sustained the resolutions in a speech of great power. Like Jeremiah of old, he seems to be specially inspired to call the people to repentance.

On motion, it was voted to lay the resolutions on the table.

The meeting was then addressed by that venerable apostle of liberty, Theodore D. Weld, on the hindrances of truth.

To say that the address was able would be tame. It was sublime. Every word was a moral mirror that exhibited our frailties in their true light, but no pen but the author's can do it justice. He was listened to with the greatest attention.

At the close of the address, it was voted to adjourn to 7 o'clock.

Met agreeably to adjournment. Mr. Weld opened the meeting with an address on "*The Lying Pretences of the Rebellion.*" It was listened to by a large audience, in breathless silence, for nearly two hours. It was a masterly argument of iron-linked logic, showing up the iniquitous course of the South in the most scathing manner. He completely demolished that popular humbug, State sovereignty, as defined by the Democratic party. It ought to be delivered in every city, town and parish in the United States.

Mr. Pillsbury then briefly addressed the meeting, showing by facts indisputable that the great mass of the people of the North have not much to boast of over the South, as we continued to fellowship her until she broke from us, and the nation, as such, finds no fault with her to this day, only that she will no longer allow us to participate in her crimes, and we are ready to connive with her again in breaking the hearts of God's poor, if she will cease her attempts to break the Union.

It was voted to adopt the resolutions presented by the Business Committee.

Voted to adjourn three months at the call of the officers of the Society.

JOSEPH MERRILL, *Sec'y pro tem.*

☞ Wendell Phillips gave a highly effective and felicitous discourse at Music Hall, on Sunday last, on the President's plan for colonizing the colored population of this country in some other land—demonstrating its inhumanity, needlessness, and injurious effects upon the interests of the whole country. An immense audience was present. Mr. Phillips will again occupy the desk at Music Hall on Sunday next.

☞ The eloquent discourse, on "The Advent of Justice," delivered by E. H. Heywood, Esq., some time since, before the Twenty-Eighth Congregational Society, at Music Hall, may be found on our last page. Of course, it will repay a careful perusal.

Arrival of Gen. Banks at New Orleans.—General Banks and his expedition arrived safely at New Orleans on the 14th ultimo. He took command of the Department of the South, relieving General Butler, who is ordered to report at Washington. The first movement of General Banks was upon Baton Rouge, which fell into hands on the 17th, without serious opposition. It is stated that Gen. Butler is to be entrusted with an important command elsewhere.

Gen. Butler, prior to leaving New Orleans, gave a reception at City Hall, where hundreds of citizens and officers waited upon him.

Gen. Butler also issued a farewell address to the citizens, in which he says he leaves with proud consciousness of carrying with him the blessings of the humblest loyal man, even in the cabin of the slave, quite content to endure the sneers and curses of the rich. He concludes by saying that months of experience and observation have forced the conviction that the existence of slavery is incompatible with the safety of ourselves and of the Union.

On the 24th Gen. Banks issued an address, to which was appended the President's proclamation of emancipation.

In his address Gen. Banks, after rehearsing the objects and effect of the President's proclamation, calls upon all persons, citizens or slaves, to govern themselves accordingly. All unusual public demonstrations will be for the present suspended, and the Provost Marshals are enjoined to prevent any disturbance of the public peace. Slaves are advised to remain on the plantations until their privileges are definitely established, resting assured that whatever benefit the government intends will be secured them.

Attention is also called to the act of Congress forbidding the return of slaves by the army. The war is not waged for the overthrow of slavery, but to restore the constitutional relations between the United States and each of the States. If slavery is to be preserved, war must cease and the former constitutional relations again be established; for no military man, in the event of the continuance of the war, will counsel the preservation of slavery. The continuance of the war will leave no other permanent track of rebellion, but the emancipation contest, in public as in social life, strengthens and consolidates brotherly affection. It is a baseless nationality that has not tested its strength against domestic enemies. Success of local interests narrows the destiny of a people, and is followed by secession, poverty and degradation. The triumph of national interests widens the scope of human history, and is attended with peace, prosperity and power. It is out of such contests that great nations are born.

Gen. Banks concludes thus: "Let us fulfill the conditions of this last great trial, and become a nation, a grand nation, with sense enough to govern ourselves, and strength enough to stand against the world united."

Public Sentiment in New Orleans. A New Orleans letter in the New York *World* remarks—"It shows something of a change in public sentiment here when the newspapers can publish, as they do, a call for recruits in the 'John Brown Guards.' A bookstore window in Exchange alley displays lithographic portraits of Wendell Phillips and Charles Sumner, and the glass is uncracked."

☞ Claiborne F. Jackson, the fugitive Governor of Missouri, is said to have died at Little Lock, Ark., on the 8th ult.

THE PROCLAMATION.

Three Million of Slaves set Free!

"GLORY, HALLELUJAH!"

Washington, Jan. 1, 1863.

By the President of the United States of America.

A PROCLAMATION.

Whereas, on the 22d day of September, in the year of our Lord 1862, a Proclamation was issued by the President of the United States, containing, among other things, the following, to wit:—

That on the 1st day of January, in the year of our Lord 1863, all persons held as slaves within any State or designated part of a State, the people whereof shall then be in rebellion against the United States, shall be then, thenceforth and forever free; and the Executive Government of the United States, including the military and naval authority thereof, will recognize and maintain the freedom of such persons, and will do no act or acts to repress such persons, or any of them, in any effort they may make for their actual freedom; that the Executive will, on the first day of January aforesaid, by proclamation, designate the States and parts of States, if any, in which the people therein respectively shall then be in rebellion against the United States; and the fact that any State, or the people thereof, shall on that day be in good faith represented in the Congress of the United States, by members—chosen thereto at elections wherein a majority of the qualified voters of such State shall have participated—shall, in the absence of strong countervailing testimony, be deemed conclusive evidence that such State and the people thereof are not then in rebellion against the United States.

Now, therefore, I, Abraham Lincoln, President of the United States, by virtue of the power in me vested, as Commander-in-Chief of the Army and Navy of the United States, in time of actual armed rebellion against the authority and government of the United States, and as a fit and necessary war measure, do, on this first day of January, in the year of our Lord one thousand eight hundred and sixty-three, and in accordance with my purpose so to do, publicly proclaimed for the full period of one hundred days from the day first above mentioned, order and designate as the States and parts of States wherein the people thereof respectively are this day in rebellion against the United States, the following, to wit: Arkansas, Texas, Louisiana, except the parishes of St. Bernard, Placquemines, Jefferson, St. John, St. Charles, St. James, Ascension, Assumption, Terre Bonne, Lafourche, St. Mary, St. Martin and Orleans, including the city of New Orleans; Mississippi, Alabama, Florida, Georgia, South Carolina, North Carolina, and Virginia, except the forty-eight counties designated as West Virginia, and also the counties of Berkley, Accomac, Northampton, Elizabeth City, York, Princess Ann and Norfolk, including the cities of Norfolk and Portsmouth, and which excepted parts are for the present left precisely as if this proclamation were not issued.

And by virtue of the power and for the purpose aforesaid, I do order and declare, that all persons held as slaves, within said designated States and parts of States, are and hereafter shall be free, and that the Executive Government of the United States, including the military and naval authorities thereof, will recognize and maintain the freedom of said persons; and I hereby enjoin upon the people so declared to be free to abstain from all violence, unless in necessary self-defence. And I recommend to them in all cases when allowed, to labor faithfully for reasonable wages; and I further declare and make known, that such persons of suitable condition will be received into the armed service of the United States, to garrison forts, positions, stations and other places, and to man vessels of all sorts in said service. And upon this act, sincerely believed to be an act of justice, warranted by the Constitution upon military necessity, I invoke the considerate judgment of mankind and the gracious favor of Almighty God.

In witness whereof, I have hereunto set my hand, and caused the seal of the United States to be affixed.

Done at the city of Washington, this first day of January, in the year of our Lord one thousand eight hundred and sixty-three, and of the Independence of the United States of America the eighty-seventh.

(Signed,) ABRAHAM LINCOLN.

By the President,

Wm. H. Seward, *Secretary of State.*

PROCLAMATION BY GEN. SAXTON.

A Happy New Year's Greeting to the Colored People in the Department of the South.

In accordance, as I believe, with the will of our Heavenly Father, and by direction of your great and good friend, whose name you are all familiar with, Abraham Lincoln, President of the United States, and Commander-in-Chief of the Army and Navy, on the 1st day of January, 1863, you will be declared "for ever free."

When in the course of human events there comes a day which is destined to be an everlasting beacon-light, marking a joyful era in the progress of a nation and the hopes of a people, it seems to be fitting the occasion that it should not pass unnoticed by those whose hopes it comes to brighten and to bless. Such a day to you is January 1, 1863.

I therefore call upon all the colored people in this Department to assemble on that day at the Head-quarters of the 1st Regiment of South Carolina Volunteers, there to hear the President's Proclamation read, and to indulge in such other manifestations of joy as may be called forth by the occasion. It is your duty to carry this good news to your brethren who are still in slavery. Let all your voices, like merry bells, join loud and clear in the grand chorus of liberty—"We are free," "We are free,"—until, listening, you shall hear its echoes coming back from every cabin in the land—"We are free," "We are free."

R. SAXTON,
Brig. Gen. and Military Governor.

☞ We have delayed putting the *Liberator* to press, this week, in order to place before our readers, at the earliest moment, the Proclamation of President Lincoln, issued January 1st, 1863, carrying out the admonitory one of September 22d, 1862, declaring the immediate emancipation of all the slaves within the limits of Rebeldom—amounting in number to THREE MILLIONS! It will be hailed with joy and thanksgiving by the friends of freedom and human brotherhood throughout the world. It is a great historic event, sublime in its magnitude, momentous and beneficent in its far-reaching consequences, and eminently just and right alike to the oppressor and the oppressed, as well as imperatively called for by the fearfully imperilled state of the country. THE PEOPLE will sustain it—the army will receive fresh inspiration—and all Rebeldom be filled with consternation in view of their inevitable doom. But we have neither space nor time to add anything more.

Emancipation Jubilee. The grand demonstration in this city, yesterday, at the Tremont Temple, was probably the only public celebration of the kind in this section of the country. The Proclamation of freedom was not received at the meeting until just previous to the adjournment last evening, when it was read by Charles W. Slack. The joyous enthusiasm manifested was beyond description. Cheers were proposed for the President and for the Proclamation, the whole audience rising to their feet and shouting at the tops of their voices, throwing up their hats, and indicating in every conceivable manner symptoms of gratification that the hour of deliverance had at length arrived. When the cheers had somewhat abated, the whole audience stood up and joined in singing the jubilee song, "Blow ye the trumpet, blow," and then followed a beautiful prayer of thanksgiving by the Rev. Mr. Waterston, which moved many to tears, and was frequently interrupted by shouts of "Amen!" "Glory to God in the highest!" "Hallelujah!" &c. The whole scene was one remarkably striking and affecting. After the meeting at the Temple, a large number wended their way to the Twelfth Baptist Church, where they joined in prayer and congratulations, and partook of a repast which had been there prepared.—*Boston Journal of Friday morning.*

☞ MEETING AT PLYMOUTH.—There will be a meeting at Plymouth, (in Leyden Hall,) on Sunday next, Jan. 4th, to be addressed by Theodore D. Weld and Parker Pillsbury. Three sessions may be expected: morning, afternoon and evening, at the usual hours.

☞ WENDELL PHILLIPS, Esq., will deliver a discourse before the Twenty-Eighth Congregational Society, at Music Hall, on Sunday next, Jan. 4th.

☞ MERCY B. JACKSON, M. D., has removed on 695 Washington street, 2d door North of Warren. Particular attention paid to Diseases of Women and Children.

References.—Luther Clark, M. D.; David Thayer, M. D. Office hours from 2 to 4, P. M.

☞ Persons disposed to give employment to freed slaves, till occasionally coming among us, both men and women, can apply to Edmund Jackson, 22 Chatham Street, or at the Anti-Slavery Office, 221 Washington Street, Boston.

☞ Members and friends of the Massachusetts Anti-Slavery Society, who are indebted for Pledges made to the Society in January last, or previously to that time, are requested to pay the same as early as practicable, either to the Treasurer, Edmund Jackson, or at the Society's office, 221 Washington Street.

☞ E. H. HEYWOOD'S Post-Office address is Princeton, Mass.

MARRIED—In this city, on Christmas Day, by Rev. John Phillips, George Washburn Smalley, Esq., of New York, and Miss Phebe Garnaut, of Boston.

IN MEMORIAM.

In the obituary notice of the late venerable Zechariah Ober, published in last week's paper, reference was made to his faithful testimony against the Fugitive Slave Law, he being 76 years old at the time of its enactment. That testimony was given in the *Liberator*, April 25, 1851, in the following emphatic manner:—

"How long, I ask, how long shall this nation be cursed with rulers that violate every rule of justice, set their claims above high Heaven's laws, and make this a nation of bloodhounds to catch the poor panting fugitive, and return him to hopeless bondage? Shall we, shall this nation, say—'It is the law of the land—we *must* obey it'? Servile doughfaces will do it; but those who fear God, and are determined to obey his laws, although devils rage and rulers threaten, will not fall down and worship the image which king Darius has set up for the overthrow of freedom in this land.

O, ye Bostonians! Where is the spirit of freedom, that caused you to give Sims into the iron grasp of ferocious tigers! Hell rejoices; Heaven mourns! Shame on them! Shame, as eternal shame must, ere long, be the reward of these modern Judases, who will consign a fellow-man to hopeless bondage. Is the slave law in Boston to be paramount to the higher law, which forbids the returning of him who has escaped from his master to his master again? Will not the hands of the traitors be greatly strengthened by this deed of villany? I would almost say, if such deeds are to be done in Boston, 'Up! get ye from it, lest the Lord destroy it for its wickedness!'"

DEATH OF THEODORE PARKMAN.

Theodore Parkman, the Color Sergeant of the 45th Massachusetts, who was instantly killed at Whitehall, N. C., though belonging by all the affinities of blood and principle to Massachusetts, was not personally known in this community beyond the circle of relatives and immediate friends. How much he was beloved, how sadly and long he will be missed and mourned within that circle, this is not the place to say. The hearts that sympathise the most with bereaved kindred must keep their sorrow sacred from what would be intrusive and distressing publicity.

But we may, even whilst we grieve, proudly tell the simple story of a modest and noble young man, whose early death has come as the result of his intelligent and conscientious convictions of duty.

The eldest child and only son of the Rev. John Parkman, he was born in Paris, and at the time he fell was in the prime of early manhood. He was educated at Columbia College, New York, and a few years since went to Germany, accompanied by his father's family, to finish his studies as a practical chemist. He returned to Boston in the autumn of 1861.

Educated by precept and example to believe in the right of all men to be free, and in devoted attachment to republican institutions, he soon felt the imperative obligation to give himself to the service of his country; though his whole nature and all his tastes were averse to the glories and horrors of war.

He endeavored to fit himself for efficiency as a soldier, and when the nine months' men were called for he enlisted in the 45th. How calmly and steadily he bore the flag in his strong arm, as the regiment marched down State street, many to whom he was a stranger may have noticed. There was an unostentatious determination in his bearing, and a smiling good-bye for the friends who recognized him. In the spirit with which he took his departure he bravely served and nobly fell.

This is all that need be said. Since the conflict began, the land has lost those far more distinguished and far more widely known than Theodore Parkman. Except as his death gives him one, he has no public record. But no purer, more affectionate or more loyal soul than his has taken its flight amidst the tempest of the battle, to the better world of perfect peace.—*Boston Transcript.*

AMUSEMENTS TO-DAY.

NIBLO'S GARDEN, Broadway—Drama, FAUST AND MARGUERITE—8 P. M.
LAURA KEENE'S THEATER, Broadway—BLONDETTE—7½ P. M.
WALLACK'S THEATER, Broadway—Comedy, A BACHELOR OF ARTS—8 P. M.
WOOD'S MINSTREL HALL, 514 Broadway—NEGRO MELODIES, BURLESQUES, DANCES, &c.—7 P. M.
BARNUM'S MUSEUM, Broadway, opposite Astor House—TROPICAL FISH, CURIOSITIES, PERFORMING BEARS, &c.—Drama, THE JEWESS OF FRANKFORT; or, THE VISION OF FATE—3 and 7½ P. M.
GERMAN OPERA HOUSE, 485 Broadway—Comic Opera, JEAN DE PARIS.
BROADWAY MENAGERIE AND ZOOLOGICAL INSTITUTE, Broadway, near Houston street—Wild Animals, ELEPHANTS, LIONS, BIRDS, &c.—10 A. M. to 10 P. M.
GOUPIL GALLERY, 772 Broadway—Mr. CHURCH'S NEW PICTURE, UNDER NIAGARA
IRVING HALL, Irving Place—Concert, HELMSMULLER'S TWENTY SECOND REGIMENT BAND—8 P. M.

The World

MORNING COURIER AND NEW-YORK ENQUIRER.

Vol. III. No. 794. Co. & Enq. 11,972.

NEW-YORK: SATURDAY, JANUARY 3, 1863.

PRICE THREE CENTS.

THE WAR IN TENNESSEE.

Great Battle near Murfreesboro'.

Severe Fighting on Tuesday, Wednesday, and Thursday.

McCook's Corps Driven Back Four Miles the first Day.

Fighting from day-break to 10 p. m. on Wednesday.

MURFREESBORO' TAKEN ON THURSDAY.

IMMENSE LOSS ON BOTH SIDES.

Rebel Gens. Rains and Cheatham Killed.

Rosecrans's Wagon Train Captured.

NASHVILLE, Jan. 2.

The federals encountered the rebels on the 30th ult., near Stewart's Creek. After heavy skirmishing the rebels were driven back. We captured one hundred prisoners, and killed and wounded a large number of rebels. Our loss was seventy killed and wounded

At daybreak on the 31st the fight was renewed with great fury. McCook's corps was opposed to Hardee. After desperate fighting, with heavy loss on both sides, McCook retreated two miles; he soon rallied, and was driven back. At night he was four miles this side of the ground occupied in the morning. The fight continued until 10 o'clock P. M., at which time we had maintained our position.

The federal loss is very heavy.

KILLED.

Brig.-Gen. Gill; Lieut.-Col. Garesche, chief of Gen. Rosecrans's staff; Brig.-Gen. Willick, of Indiana; Col. Kell, Second Ohio; Col. Shaffer, acting brigadier-general; Col. Farmer, Fifteenth Kentucky; Col. Jones, Twenty-fourth Ohio; Lieut.-Col. Cotton, Sixth Kentucky; Lieut.-Col. Jones, Thirty-ninth Indiana; Major Carpenter, Nineteenth Regulars; Major Rosengarten, of Philadelphia; Capt. Garrett, Nineteenth Illinois; Col. Carpenter, Eighteenth Wisconsin, and Lieut.-Col. McKee, Fifteenth Wisconsin.

WOUNDED.

Brig.-Gens. E. M. Kirk, of Illinois; Wood, of Indiana, and Van Cleve, of Minnesota. Col. Cassole, of Ohio; Major-Gen. Rossean, of Kentucky; Lieut.-Col. Berry, Fifth Kentucky; Major Slemmer, Sixteenth Regulars; Major King, Fifteenth Regulars; and many others.

The Twenty-first, Twenty-fifth, and Thirty-fifth Illinois lost two-thirds, and the Fifteenth and Thirty-eighth Ohio one-half their number. The One Hundred and First Ohio lost 125 men; the Thirty-eighth Indiana about the same number.

The total killed and wounded is estimated at 2,500. The rebel loss exceeds ours.

Gen. J. E. Raines was killed. Gen. Cheatham was wounded and taken prisoner.

We have captured 500 prisoners.

The fight was renewed at 3 A. M. on January first. The cannonading was heard at Nashville. At 10 A. M. Wood's and Van Cleve's divisions were in Murfreesboro, driving the enemy, who were in full retreat.

Three hundred prisoners reached Nashville at 6 P. M. on January 1, including the following commissioned officers: Major J. J. Franklin, Thirtieth Arkansas; Capt. W. E. Johnson, Second Arkansas; Capt. J. P. Eagle, Second Arkansas; Capt. S. C. Stone, First Tennessee Cavalry.

Many buildings have been taken for hospital purposes. Great numbers of wounded are being brought in now.

The river has fallen eighteen inches on the shoals.

WASHINGTON, Jan. 2.

The Secretary of War to-day received the following advices:

CLEVELAND, Jan. 2.

The following has just been received by telegraph from Cincinnati, dated Murfreesboro, Jan. 1, 1863:

A terrible battle was fought yesterday. The latest from the field is up to noon. The rebel center had been broken, and things looked favorable. The losses are reported to be enormous. Stanly, Rousseau, and Palmer are wounded, and the rebels Cheatham and Rains are killed.

NEAR MURFREESBORO', Jan. 1.

Our whole line suffered terribly this morning. Four regiments of regulars lost half their men and all their commanding officers.

General Anderson's troops suffered severely.

Maiors Rosengarten and Ward are killed.

2 o'clock P. M.

General Thomas has just broken the rebel center, and driven the enemy a mile.

We are advancing our whole line.

General Rosecrans is personally superintending the movements. One shot killed two of his staff officers.

The Fifteenth Wisconsin Regiment has lost seven captains.

General Negley's artillery is still mowing the rebels in the center.

Gen. Crittenden's left wing has taken the intrenchments at Murfreesboro'.

The rebel Generals Cheatham and Rains are killed.

HEADQUARTERS, LOUISVILLE, Jan. 1.

General Rosecrans captured Murfreesboro' on Tuesday morning, and now occupies it, the rebels retreating to Tullahoma. The rebels made but little resistance, though Rosecrans lost the train of wagons following him, which was captured by the rebels under Col. Morgan, of Tennessee.

The startling reports which reached here about midnight, and caused considerable commotion throughout the city, of the approach of Forrest from the direction of Salt river with a large body of cavalry, are entirely false.

WASHINGTON, Jan. 2.

No intelligence has been received to-night by the government relative to the battle at Murfreesboro.

Details of the Battle.

NASHVILLE, Jan. 1.

I have just arrived from a terrific battle on Stones river, in front of Murfreesboro, west side It has raged with unremitting fury two days, and at last report was not yet decided. It is one of the most furious battles of modern times, sustained by both sides with splendid determination.

Gen. Rosecrans marched from Nashville last Friday with about 45,000 effective men and 100 pieces of artillery, and skirmished all the way to the battle-field, the enemy resisting bitterly.

The whole of Tuesday was spent by our forces reconnoitering.

The enemy was found strongly posted with artillery on the bank of Stone's river, west side, his flanks resting on Murfreesboro, west side. The center also had the advantage on high ground, with a dense growth of cedar masking them completely. Their position gave them the advantage of a cross fire.

Gen. McCook's corps closed in on their left on Wilkisson's Pike; Neyley, of Thomas corps, worked with great difficulty to the front of the rebel centre, Rousseau's division being in reserve. Crittenden's corps was posted in comparatively clear ground on their left; Palmer's and Vancleve's divisions in front; Wood's in reserve.

A battle was expected all day on Tuesday, but the enemy merely skirmished and threw a few shells, one of which killed Orderly McDonald, 4th U. S. Cavalry, not ten feet from Gen. Rosecrans. That afternoon the Anderson Pennsylvania Cavalry on McCook's flanks, was drawn into an ambuscade, and its two majors, Rosegarten and Ward, were killed. Crittenden's corps lost four killed and twenty-one wounded that day, including Adj. Elliot, of the Fifty-seventh Indiana, severely. McCook's loss was about fifty.

On the same day the rebel cavalry made a dash in the rear, on Lavergne, burned a few wagons, and captured thirty-five prisoners.

That night dispositions were made to attack the enemy in the morning. After dark the enemy was reported massing near McCook, obviously to turn our right wing.

This corresponded with the wishes of Gen. Rosecrans, who instructed Gen. McCook to hold him in check stubbornly, while the left wing should be thrown into Murfreesboro' behind the enemy.

At daybreak on the last day of December everything appeared working well. The battle had opened on the right, and our left wing was on hand.

At seven o'clock ominous sounds indicated that a fire was approaching our left. Aids were dispatched for information, and found the forests full of flying negroes and straggling soldiers, who reported whole regiments falling back.

Meantime one of McCook's aids had announced to Gen. Rosecrans that Gen. Johston had permitted the three batteries of his division to be captured by a sudden attack of the enemy, and that it had somewhat demoralized our troops it was obvious.

The brave Gen. Sill, one of our best officers, was killed; Gen. Kirk wounded, and Gen. Willich killed or missing, besides other valuable officers wounded.

Gen. McCook sent word to hold the front and he would help him, that it would all work right.

He now galloped to the front of Crittenden's left with his staff to order the line of battle when the enemy opened a full battery and emptied the saddles of the escort.

Van Cleve's division was sent to the right, and Gen. Beatty's brigade in front.

The fire continued to approach on the right with alarming rapidity, extending to the center, and it was clear that the right was doubling upon the left. The enemy had compelled us to make a complete change of front on that wing, and were pressing the center.

Gen. Rosecrans, with splendid daring, dashed into the furious fire, and sending his staff along the lines, started Beatty's brigade forward. Some six batteries opened, and sustaining a magnificent fire, directly a tremendous shout was raised along the whole line, and the enemy began to fall back rapidly.

The general urged the troops forward. The rebels, terribly punished, were driven back fully a mile. The same splendid bravery was displayed in the lines and advanced, though the enemy made formidable demonstrations on our left, while they prepared for another onslaught on our right.

Meantime, orders had been issued to move our left upon the enemy, but before they had time to execute them they burst upon our center with awful fury, and it began to break. Rosecrans's division was carried into the breach magnificently by their glorious leader.

The enemy again retreated into the dark cedar thickets. Again they essayed our right, and again we were driven back. By this time the number of our stragglers was formidable, and the prospect was discouraging; but there was no panic.

The general, confident of success, continued to visit other parts of the field, and with the aid of Gens. Thomas, McCook, Crittenden, Rousseau, Negley, and Wood, the tide of battle was turned early in the day.

We were suddenly massed against their forces on the left, crossing the river, or moving under cover of bluffs on the right, and for about two hours the fight raged with unremitting fury, to the advantage of the enemy for a considerable length of time, when they were checked by our murderous fire of both musketry and artillery.

President Lincoln's Proclamation in Boston.

BOSTON, Jan. 2.

The President's emancipation proclamation was read in Tremont Temple last night, where a meeting of the Union Progressive Association, composed of colored citizens, was being held. The document was welcomed with unbounded enthusiasm. Previous to the reading of the proclamation the meeting was addressed by the Rev. Dr. Kirk, William Wells Brown, Fred Douglass, Rev James Freeman Clark, and others. The Temple was crowded day and evening. At Music Hall there was also a jubilee commemorative of the proclamation.

Loss of Another Ship of the Banks Expedition.

BALTIMORE, Jan. 2.

The ship before reported ashore near Hog Island, Chesapeake Bay, is the International, one of the vessels of the Banks expedition, with government stores on board. Assistance has been sent from Old Point, but she will probably prove a total loss.

Steamship Caledonia Ashore.

BOSTON, Jan. 2.

The British steamship Caledonia, from Glasgow via Portland for New York, went ashore night of the 31st on Peaked Hill bar, Cape Cod. She is hard and fast.

From Washington Territory.

SAN FRANCISCO, Cal., Jan. 2.

The Legislature of Washington Territory after two weeks spent in an exciting contest over an election for presiding officers and sergeants of the council, which latter is composed of nine members, has commenced the transaction of business.

GENERAL SHERMAN'S EXPEDITION.

A Force Going up the Yazoo River—Severe Engagement with a Rebel Battery—The Benton Struck Six times and Penetrated—69 Cannon Spiked and 10,000 Rounds of Ammunition thrown into the River at Island No. 10.

CAIRO, Jan. 2.

A steamer from below reports that the gunboats accompanying Gen. Sherman's expedition had gone up the Yazoo river. At Drumigol's Bluff, twenty miles above the mouth, a rebel battery was discovered. A severe cannonade followed, during which the gunboat Benton was struck sixteen times, the shots penetrating.

Gen. Sherman's force will debark up the Yazoo, and march to near Vicksburg.

A train with supplies would leave Memphis yesterday for Holly Springs.

When Island No. Ten was evacuated lately, sixty-nine cannon were spiked and 10,000 rounds of ammunition thrown into the river.

Jefferson Davis addressed the Mississippi Legislature at Jackson on the 26th ult.

THE WAR IN KENTUCKY.

Route of the Rebel Guerrilla Morgan—Capture of his Wagons and Ammunition—The Rebel Thrice Beaten—Our Troops in hot Pursuit—Hopes of Capturing him and his Command.

LOUISVILLE, January 1.

The guerrilla Morgan crossed the Cumberland river and cut off Nashville at Gainesboro', and appeared in front of Munfordsville on the 27th of December. Col. Hobson, of the Thirteenth Kentucky, drove part of his force, killing nine and capturing sixteen.

Morgan then crossed Green river above Munfordsville and moved in the direction of Elizabethtown, burning the bridge at Beaver creek and Nolin. He also destroyed the trestle work at Muldraugh's Hill and moved for Rolling Fork. Colonel Harlan, commanding the Tenth Kentucky, overtook him at Rolling Fork and attacked him, killing and wounding a number and capturing a captain and some privates.

The rebel Col. Dull died of his wounds, as also did one of our lieutenants of artillery.

Col. Harlan crossed, pursued, and attacked Morgan at Rolling Fork and the Salt river bridge. This is the first instance, I believe, of infantry attacking and routing cavalry.

Morgan fled before Harlan to Bardstown, and from there attempted to escape between Lebanon and Camp Belleville. Col. Hoskins, of the Twelfth Kentucky, commanding there, attacked him this morning, killing a number and capturing ninety of his men, and capturing his caissons and ammunition wagons. Morgan is flying precipitately.

General Reynolds marched from Glasgow yesterday for Greensburg, and may intercept him.

Col. Hulsey, of the Sixth Kentucky Cavalry, was killed.

Our casualties are not yet reported.

Morgan has paid dearly for what he has done.

Gen. Rosecrans occupies Murfreesboro'.

(Signed) J. T. BOYLE, Brig. Gen.

LOUISVILLE, Jan. 2.

The report that 15,000 rebels crossed the Cumberland last Monday and were moving toward Lonisville is discredited at headquarters.

Another Account.

LOUISVILLE, Ky., Jan. 2.

Colonel Hoskins, of the Twelfth Kentucky Regiment, commanding the federal forces at Lebanon, Ky., attacked the guerrilla Morgan south of the Columbia road yesterday, killing and wounding several and capturing sixty of his force, together with their caissons, ammunition, wagons, and provisions. Colonel Halliday, of the Sixth Kentucky Regiment, Lieut.-Col. Boyle, commanding Ninth Kentucky Cavalry, with the Sixth Kentucky Infantry, are in pursuit of Morgan. The infantry are under command of Col. Hoskins.

Morgan is retreating very rapidly in the direction of Columbia.

GEN. DIX'S DEPARTMENT.

BALTIMORE, Jan. 2.

The *American's* correspondent at Suffolk announces the arrival there of Gen. Corcoran with his entire brigade. He is to take command there.

Gen. Peck's command is moving in another direction.

Skirmishing with the rebels continues to be of daily occurrence, and they have been routed on every occasion.

WASHINGTON, Jan. 2.

GEN. BURNSIDE ANXIOUS TO RESIGN.

Gen. Burnside came to this city Wednesday morning for the avowed purpose of resigning the command of the Army of the Potomac. He cannot agree, it is said, with his general officers, and, on this account, he delayed making a forward movement, which was on the eve of accomplishment. Rumor—and from reliable sources, too—had it that either Gen. Hooker or Gen. Sumner would be his successor, more probably the former. The resignation, however, was not accepted, and Gen. Burnside has gone back to the army as its commander. This, I believe, is the third time that this has occurred, thus falsifying the old saw, "three times and out." If all differences are settled, we may look for lively times on the Rappahannock.

WEST VIRGINIA A STATE.

All speculations as to the President's action upon the bill for the admission of Western Virginia into the Union are now ended, the fact having been ascertained, on inquiry, that he approved and signed the bill on Wednesday night, and it is therefore a law.

MOVEMENTS OF GENERAL M'CLELLAN.

General McClellan arrived here early this morning and testified to-day in the Porter court martial. His presence there attracted an immense crowd, and it was difficult for him to make his way to and from the hotel. Enthusiastic demonstrations meet him on every hand, though he declined all of a public character. His explanation of his dispatch to General Porter, sent at the request of the President, has created a decided sensation, and hurls back in their teeth another of the lies of the radicals on his conduct here during the battles of August fought by General Pope.

THE CABINET.

It is reliably reported that the President will certainly send to the Senate on Monday one if not more nominations for members of his cabinet.

ARRIVAL OF GENERAL BUTLER.

Major-General Butler has arrived at Washington.

SHINPLASTER PROSECUTION.—Prosecution will be commenced at Milwaukee, soon after the 1st of January, against the issuers and circulators of small shinplasters in that city.

THE EMANCIPATION PROCLAMATION

All the Slaves in Rebellious States Declared Free.

Tennessee and Portions of Virginia and Louisiana Excepted.

Slaves to be Received into the Armed Service of the United States.

WASHINGTON, Jan. 1.

BY THE PRESIDENT OF THE UNITED STATES OF AMERICA, A PROCLAMATION.

Whereas, on the twenty-second day of September, in the year of our Lord one thousand eight hundred and sixty-two, a proclamation was issued by the President of the United States, containing, among other things, the following, to wit:

"That on the first day of January, in the year of our Lord one thousand eight hundred and sixty-three, all persons held as slaves within any state or designated part of a state, the people whereof shall then be in rebellion against the United States shall be then, thenceforawrd, and *forever free*, and the executive government of the United States, including the military and naval authority thereof, will recognize and maintain the freedom of such persons, and will do no act or acts to repress such persons or any of them in any effort they may make for their actual freedom. That the executive will, on the first day of January aforesaid, by proclamation, designate the states and parts of states, if any, in which the people therein respectively shall then be in rebellion against the United States; and the fact that any state or people thereof shall on that day in good faith, be represented in the Congress of the United States by members chosen thereto at elections wherein a majority of the qualified voters of such state shall have participated, shall, in the absence of strong countervailing testimony, be deemed conclusive evidence that such state and the people thereof are not then in rebellion against the United States."

Now, therefore, I, Abraham Lincoln, President of the United States, by virtue of the power in me vested as Commander-in-Chief of the Army and Navy of the United States in time of actual armed rebellion against the authority and government of the United States, and as a fit and necessary war measure for suppressing said rebellion, do, on this first day of January, in the year of our Lord one thousand eight hundred and sixty-three, and in accordance with my purpose so to do, publicly proclaimed for the full period of one hundred days, from the day first above-mentioned, order designate, as the states and parts of states wherein the people thereof respectively are this day in rebellion against the United States, to wit:

ARKANSAS,
TEXAS,
LOUISIANA—(Except the parishes of St. Bernard, Plaquemines, Jefferson, St. John, St. Charles, St. James, Ascension, Assumption, Terre Bonne, Lourche, Ste. Marie, St. Martin, and Orleans, including the city of New Orleans,)
MISSISSIPPI,
ALABAMA,
FLORIDA,
GEORGIA,
SOUTH CAROLINA,
NORTH CAROLINA, and
VIRGINIA—(Except the forty-eight counties designated as West Virginia, and also the counties of Berkley, Accomac, Northampton, Elizabeth City, York, Princess Ann, and Norfolk, including the cities of Norfolk and Portsmouth, and which excepted parts are for the present left precisely as if this proclamation were not issued.)

And, by virtue of the power, and for the purpose aforesaid, I do order and declare that all persons held as slaves within said designated states and parts of states are, and henceforward shall be, FREE. And that the executive government of the United States, including the military and naval authorities thereof, will recognize and maintain the freedom of said persons.

And I hereby enjoin upon the people so declared to be free to abstain from all violence, unless in necessary self-defence, and I recommend to them that, in all cases when allowed, they labor faithfully for reasonable wages.

And I further declare and make known that such persons of suitable condition will be received into the armed service of the United States, to garrison forts, positions, stations, and other places, and to man vessels of all sorts in said service.

And upon this, sincerely believed to be an act of justice, warranted by the Constitution, upon military necessity, I invoke the considerate judgment of mankind and the gracious favor of Almighty God.

In witness whereof, I have hereunto set my name and caused the seal of the United States to be affixed.

{SEAL.} Done at the City of Washington this first day of January, in the year of our Lord one thousand eight hundred and sixty-three, and of the Independence of the United States of America the eighty-seventh.

ABRAHAM LINCOLN.

By the President.
WM. H. SEWARD, Secretary of State.

THE ARMY OF THE POTOMAC.

HEADQUARTERS ARMY OF THE POTOMAC, January 2.

General Burnside returned from Washington this forenoon, and has been visited by his grand division commanders.

Several contrabands came into camp to-day, and were received in accordance with the proclamation.

The Recent Raid of the Rebel Stuart.

WASHINGTON, Jan. 2.

The *Star*, of this evening, says:

In the recent raid the rebel Stuart caused the telegraph operator to intercept Union messages at Burke's Station, thus learning more or less concerning the efforts being made to intercept him, and the readiness of our forces at Fairfax Station and Fairfax Court House to give him a warm reception should he venture to visit those points. He also sent various message over the wires, one to Fairfax station, purporing to order from here the instant destruction of a considerable quantity of army stores accumulated there, which however failed of its object. Among the messages found in the office at Burke's Station, having been sent over the wires by his order, is the following:

BURKE'S STATION, Dec. 28—3 P. M.

Quartermaster-General Meigs, Washington:

In future you will please furnish better mules. Those you have furnished recently are very inferior.

J. E. B. STUART, Major-General C. S. A.

GENERAL MCCLELLAN returned to Philadelphia last night.

NEWS FROM NEW ORLEANS.

Arrival of S. R. Spaulding and Geo. Washington with dates to Dec. 25.

Another Proclamation by Gen. Banks.

Gen. Butler's Farewell Address to the People of New Orleans.

Orders of Gen. Butler Revoked by Gen. Banks.

Farragut's Squadron Still at Baton Rouge.

The steamer S. R. Spaulding, from New Orleans Dec. 24, arrived here on Thursday. The steamship Geo. Washington, from the same port Dec. 25, arrived here last evening. We are indebted to the pursers of both vessels for favors in the prompt delivery o our correspondence and exchanges. Among the passengers by the S. R. Spaulding were Gen. Butler and all the members of his staff, except Col. French, provost-marshal, and Capt. Clark, post commissary. Gen. Butler left for Washington yesterday.

LIST OF PASSENGERS.—Major Gen. Butler; Major George C. Strong, A. A. Gen. and Chief of Staff; Col. J. N. Shaffer, Chief Quartermaster; Col. J. N. Turner, Chief Commissary; Surgeon Chas. McCormick, Medical Director; Capt. George A. Russell, Chief of Artillery; Lieutenant Colonel J. B. Rineman, Aid de Camp; Major James M. Bell, Captains P. Haggerty, R. S. Davis, and A. F. Puffer; Lieutenants H. C. Clarke and Fred. Martin, aid-de-camps.

Also the following officers and other passengers: Col. J. W. McMillan, Twenty-first Regiment Indiana Volunteers; Lieut. C. M. Whelden, Thirty-first Regiment Massachusetts Volunteers; Major W. H. Clemence, chief of police, N. O.; Captain H. L. Sturgis, captain of port, N. O.; Captain R. Choate, Second Regiment Massachusetts Volunteers; Lieut. B. Pickman, assistant-surgeon, —— Volunteers; Lieut. J. Cushing, 31st Regiment Mass. Volunteers; W. Harrall, Mrs. B. F. Butler; Mrs. Geo. C. Strong and child, Mrs. W. W. Harrall; W. S. Rossell, W. W. Smith, Wm. Trowbridge, Gelman F. Jones, Quartermaster's department; W. C. Miller, Edw. E. Foster, Eben Kimball, C. F. Whitney, Commissary department; F. C. Taylor, Jas. J. Monroe, H. J. Winsen, P. W. Flynn, Miles O. Reilly, C. C. Malchen, Peter Bruback, Emile H. Bril, H. H. Bennett.

In New Orleans on the 22d, Gen. Butler, attended by his staff, received his friends in the mayor's parlor. Colonel and acting Mayor Dimon received the general and his staff, and introduced them to members of the city government.

The military officers lately under the command of the general called and paid their respects. The citizens also flowed into the parlor for two hours, and such a shaking of hands, says the *Delta*, "we never did see." In the evening the general attended the Varieties, accompanied by his staff. When the general entered his box he was most enthusiastically cheered. The visit of the general to the theater was "inspired" by a threatening letter, that if he appeared in public, he would be assassinated. He was unaccompanied by soldiers, but his staff was heavily armed. Mrs. Butler was attended by Admiral Farrant.

On the 23d rumors received through rebel sources were in circulation in New Orleans to the general effect that the Union army had been defeated in Virginia. The rebels were in the highest glee in consequence of these reports.

FROM THE BANKS EXPEDITION.

[FROM OUR SPECIAL CORRESPONDENT.]

BATON ROUGE, La., Saturday night, Dec. 20.

All quiet at Baton Rouge. More troops arriving daily and going into camp at this place as a basis o operations. The river too low to allow the gunboats to go more than thirty or forty miles above here. Tha is the position of affairs. Reports of gathering thousands at Port Hudson, fortifications building at tha place to resist our land attack, batteries erecting on the bluffs to resist our gunboats—that is what we know of the nearest rebel position. Mounted infantry daily scout the country round, but report little of interest. Bands of rebel guerrillas are occasionally seen skedaddling in the dim distance, and in these thick moss-grown woods it is easy for them to hide. Gen. Grover has established his headquarters at the "Branch of the Louisiana State Bank," in the city. For the first two nights, while there was any anticipated danger of a rebel attack, he camped out with his men, sleeping on the ground by a fire. None of the former inhabitants of the city have returned. The few that remain have opened their stores, and try to keep up the appearanc eof business. The druggists, I observe, are all here, probably as much on account of the difficulty in removing their stock as for any Union sentiments.

THE SIXTH NEW-YORK VOLUNTEERS.

This morning the Sixth New-York Volunteers, Col. William Wilson, familiarly known in New Orleans, where they have recently been staying, as "The Pet Lambs," arrived at Baton Rouge. As soon as the arrival was known the correspondent of THE WORLD, in company with the representatives of two or three other papers, made the regiment and the colonel a short visit. Col. Wilson received us cordially, and inquired with a good deal of interest about affairs political and otherwise in New-York. He is very robust and healthy, and much fleshier than when he left the North, nearly two years ago. His regiment then numbered 900, and has now 680, only about ten recruits having been received. Only one furlough has been given during the whole time of service, and that was to a sick man. On my remarking that the public had been very meagerly informed about them in comparison with other commands one of the regimental officers said that it had been the habit of reporters to treat them with contempt, in which instances they had returned the compliment. Col. Wilson states that his regiment is well trained in all the duties of soldiers, and can act equally well as infantry, cavalry, or artillerymen. They are all good swimmers, as some of them proved by swimming ashore while coming up the river, to vary the monotony of the trip. One of the privates, Andy Aikins, was shot dead by a company officer for robbery and disobedience; it is also said that he struck the officer. Another member of the regiment is reported to have been shot for similar reasons this afternoon. The regiment is to be quartered in the Penitentiary for the present.

PORT HUDSON.

I am quite discouraged in trying to ascertain from "reliable gentlemen" and "reliable contrabands," the strength of the rebel position at Port Hudson. So much seems to be true, that at present the rebels expect to make a stand and risk a fight there if attacked; that they have prepared for the gunboats by placing numerous batteries of one and two guns each on the high river bluffs; that they have at least one 68-pounder there, and probably thirty-five or forty smaller guns, from 12 to 32-pounders; that they have prepared to meet an infantry force marching from here by land by erecting field fortifications breast high, digging rifle pits, loop-holing brick houses for musketry, and using other such means as are generally known for resisting and harassing an approaching enemy; lastly, that there is an infantry force of some thousands at that place. Whatever else may be written is mere speculation. For instance, I conjecture that there are from 8,000 to 14,000 troops there, organized in regiments, which, if full, would represent twice that number of men; that comparatively many are sick; that they are not particularly ill-clad or hungry, but that there is, instead of a healthy *esprit du corps*, such as exists among our own troops, a wavering between desperation and demoralization; that if they are soundly beaten now, they will not have time to make, as it is believed they have not yet made, any other stand, this side of Vicksburg.

NEW ORLEANS—Christmay Day, 1862.

Gen. Banks, so far as I have been able to observe, receives quite as hearty a welcome as any loyal general could expect in this secession city. There ar more people in the streets, more goods in the stores and I believe more money in circulation than tw weeks ago. There is a brightening of public confidence, and, I hope, an increase of loyal feeling.

Gen. Butler left yesterday, with his staff, on the S. R. Spaulding. Gen. Banks and a large number of officers accompanied him till the steamer started away, when some of the military and others gave three cheers for the departing general.

PROBABLE ATTEMPT TO POISON GEN. BUTLER.

Yesterday morning Capt. J. W. McClure, whose efficient labors as assistant quartermaster have recently won him a position on Gen. Banks's staff, was at the headquarters of Gen. Butler. Some person or persons, supposed to be of the female sex, had sent in bouquets of flowers that morning to the general, as he was about departing. Capt. McClure took up a rose to smell its fragrance, and had no sooner inhaled than he fainted away, fe down, and for some minutes seemed nearly or quite dead. Surgeon Alexander made an examination of the rose. It was supposed to have been poisoned very artfully with some subtile powder, but no traces o poison could be definitely discovered except by smelling. Capt. McClure's friends in New-York will be glad to learn that the instantaneous shock that seemed to have been given him was the only effect produced, and from that he soon recovered.

At Baton Rouge everything is still quiet. The postponement of the Texan expedition for a time does not please certain parties. The city is remarkably quiet. No Christmas celebrations, except those in the churches.

SIDNEY.

Gen. Banks to the People of Louisiana.

In promulgating the President's proclamation of emancipation, Gen. Banks issued the following address to the people of Louisiana:

HEADQUARTERS DEPARTMENT OF THE GULF, NEW ORLEANS, Dec. 24.

In order to correct public misapprehension and misrepresentation, for the instruction of the troops of this department, and the information of all parties in interest, official publication is herewith made of the proclamation by the President of the United States relating to the subject of emancipation In the examination of this document it will be observed:

I. That it is the declaration of a purpose only—the full execution of which is contingent upon an official designation by the President, to be made on the first day of January next, of the states and parts of states, if any, which are to be affected by its provisions.

II. That the fact that any state is represented in good faith in the Congress of the United States is conclusive evidence, in the absence of strong countervailing testimony, that such state and the people thereof are not in rebellion against the United States.

III. That the State of Louisiana has not yet been designated by the President as in rebellion, nor any part thereof, and that it has complied with the conditions of the proclamation respecting representation.

IV. That pecuniary aid to states not in rebellion, which may hereafter provide for immediate or gradual emancipation, the colonization of persons of African descent elsewhere, and the compensation of all citizens who have remained loyal, "for all losses by acts of the United States, including slaves," are among the chief recommendations of this important paper

It is manifest that the changes suggested therein, and which may hereafter be established, do not take effect within this state on the 1st of January proximo, nor at any precise period which can now be designated, and I call upon all persons, of whatever estate, condition, or degree, soldiers, citizens, or slaves, to observe this material and important fact, and to govern themselves accordingly. All unusual public demonstration, of whatever character, will be for the present suspended. Provost marshals, officers, and soldiers are enjoined to prevent any disturbance of the public peace. The slaves are advised to remain upon their plantations until their privileges shall have been definitely established. They may rest assured that whatever benefit the government intends will be secured to them, but no man can be allowed, in the present condition of affairs, to take the law into his own hands. If they seek the protection of the government, they should wait its pleasure.

Officers invested with command will be vigilant in the discharge of their duties. Leave of absence from camp will not be permitted, except in cases of great emergency. Soldiers enrolled in the regiments of native guards will not be allowed for the present to visit the localities of their enlistment, nor will visitors be received unnecessarily in their camps. These regulations, enforced with all the troops of the United States in the localities where they are enlisted, are now imperatively necessary. These troops will be confined to the duty specified in general orders, and will not be charged with special authority in making searches, seizures, or arrests. It is my purpose to execute faithfully all the orders of the government, and I assume the responsibility of these instructions as consistent therewith, and require prompt and faithful execution thereof.

Public attention is called to the act of Congress cited in the proclamation, which forbids the return of fugitives by officers of the army. No encouragement will be given to laborers to desert their employers, but no authority exists to compel them to return. It is suggested to planters that some plan be adopted by which an equitable proportion of the proceeds of the crops of the coming year, to be hereafter determined upon the judgment of honorable men justly representing the different interests involved, be set apart and reserved for the support and compensation of labor.

The war is not waged by the government for the overthrow of slavery. The President has declared on the contrary, that it is to restore the "constitutional relations between the United States and each of the states" in which that relation is or may be suspended. The resolutions passed by Congress before the war, with almost unanimous consent, recognized the rights of the states in this regard. Vermont has recently repealed the statutes supposed to be inconsistent therewith. Massachusetts had done so before. Slavery existed by consent and constitutional guaranty; violence and war will inevitably bring it to an end. It is impossible that any military man, in the event of continued war, should counsel the preservation of slave property in the rebel states. If it is to be preserved, war must cease, and the former constitutional relations be again established.

The first gun at Sumter proclaimed emancipation. The continuance of the contest there commenced will consummate that end, and the history of the age will leave no other permanent trace of the rebellion. Its leaders will have accomplished what other men could not have done. The boldest abolitionist is a cipher when compared with the leaders of the rebellion. What mystery pervades the works of Providence! We submit to its decrees, but stand confounded at the awful manifestations of its wisdom and power! The great problem of the age, apparently environed with labyrinthic complications, is likely to be suddenly lifted out of human hands. We may control the incidents of the contest, but we cannot circumvent or defeat the end. It will be left us only to assuage the horrors of internecine conflict, and to procrastinate the process of transition. Local and national interests are, therefore, alike dependent upon the suppression of the rebellion.

No pecuniary sacrifice can be too great an equivalent for peace. But it should be permanent peace, and embrace all subjects of discontent. It is written on the blue arch above us—the distant voices of the future—the waves that beat our coast—the skeletons that sit at our tables, and all the vacant places of desolate and mourning firesides—all cry out that this wa must not be repeated hereafter.

Contest, in public, as in social life, strengthens and consolidates brotherly affection. England, France, Austria, Italy—every land fertile enough to make a history—has had its desolating civil wars. It is a baseless nationality that has not tested its strength against domestic enemies. The success of local interests narrows the destiny of a people, and is followed by secession, poverty, and degradation. A divided country and perpetual war make possession a delusion and life a calamity. The triumph of national interests widens the scope of human history, and is attended with peace, prosperity, and power. It is out of such contests that great nations are born.

What hallowed memories float around us! New Orleans is a shrine as sacred as Bunker Hill! On the Aroostook and the Oregon the names of Washington, Jackson, and Taylor are breathed with as deep a reverence as on the James or the Mississippi. Let us fulfill the conditions of this last great trial and become a nation—a grand nation—with sense enough to govern ourselves, and strength enough to stand against the world united!

N. P. BANKS, Major-General Commanding.

Gen. Butler's Farewell Address.

CITIZENS OF NEW ORLEANS: It may not be inappropriate, as it is not inopportune in occasion, that there should be addressed to you a few words at parting, by one whose name is to be hereafter indissolubly connected with your city.

I shall speak in no bitterness, because I am not conscious of a single personal animosity. Commanding the Army of the Gulf, I found you captured, but not surrendered; conquered, but not orderly; relieved from the presence of an army, but incapable of taking care of yourselves. So far from it, you had called upon a foreign legion to protect you from yourselves. I restored order, punished crime, opened commerce, brought provisions to your starving people, reformed your currency, and gave you quiet protection, such as you had not enjoyed for many years.

While doing this my soldiers were subject to obloquy, reproach, and insult.

And now, speaking to you, who know the truth, I here declare that whoever has quietly remained about his business, affording neither aid nor comfort to the enemies of the United States, has never been interfered with by the soldiers of the United States.

The men who had assumed to govern you and to defend your city in arms have fled; some of your women flouted at the presence of those who came to protect them. By a simple order (No. 28) I called

(*Continued on Eighth Page.*)

THE WORLD.

The DAILY WORLD, published every morning and evening (Sundays excepted), price THREE CENTS; mailed at EIGHT DOLLARS a year; served by carriers, EIGHTEEN CENTS per week.

The SEMI-WEEKLY WORLD, published Tuesday and Fridays, THREE DOLLARS a year; two copies, one address for FIVE DOLLARS.

Any person who will send us a Club of FIVE subscribers may receive an extra copy for himself, or retain Two Dollars and a Half as his commission.

The WEEKLY WORLD Two DOLLARS a year; three copies FIVE DOLLARS; five copies EIGHT DOLLARS. Any person who will send us a Club of TEN subscribers, at $1.50 each, shall receive an extra copy for himself, or may retain One Dollar as his compensation. The Semi-Weekly and Weekly sent to Clergymen at the lowest club rates Specimen numbers forwarded on application

TERMS—Cash invariably in advance.

All letters should be addressed to THE WORLD, 35 PARK ROW, New-York City.

THE NEW YORK HERALD.

WHOLE NO. 9607. NEW YORK, SATURDAY, JANUARY 3, 1863. PRICE THREE CENTS

THE GREAT BATTLE IN TENNESSEE.

Scene of General Rosecrans' Battle Around Murfreesboro on Wednesday, December 31, 1862.

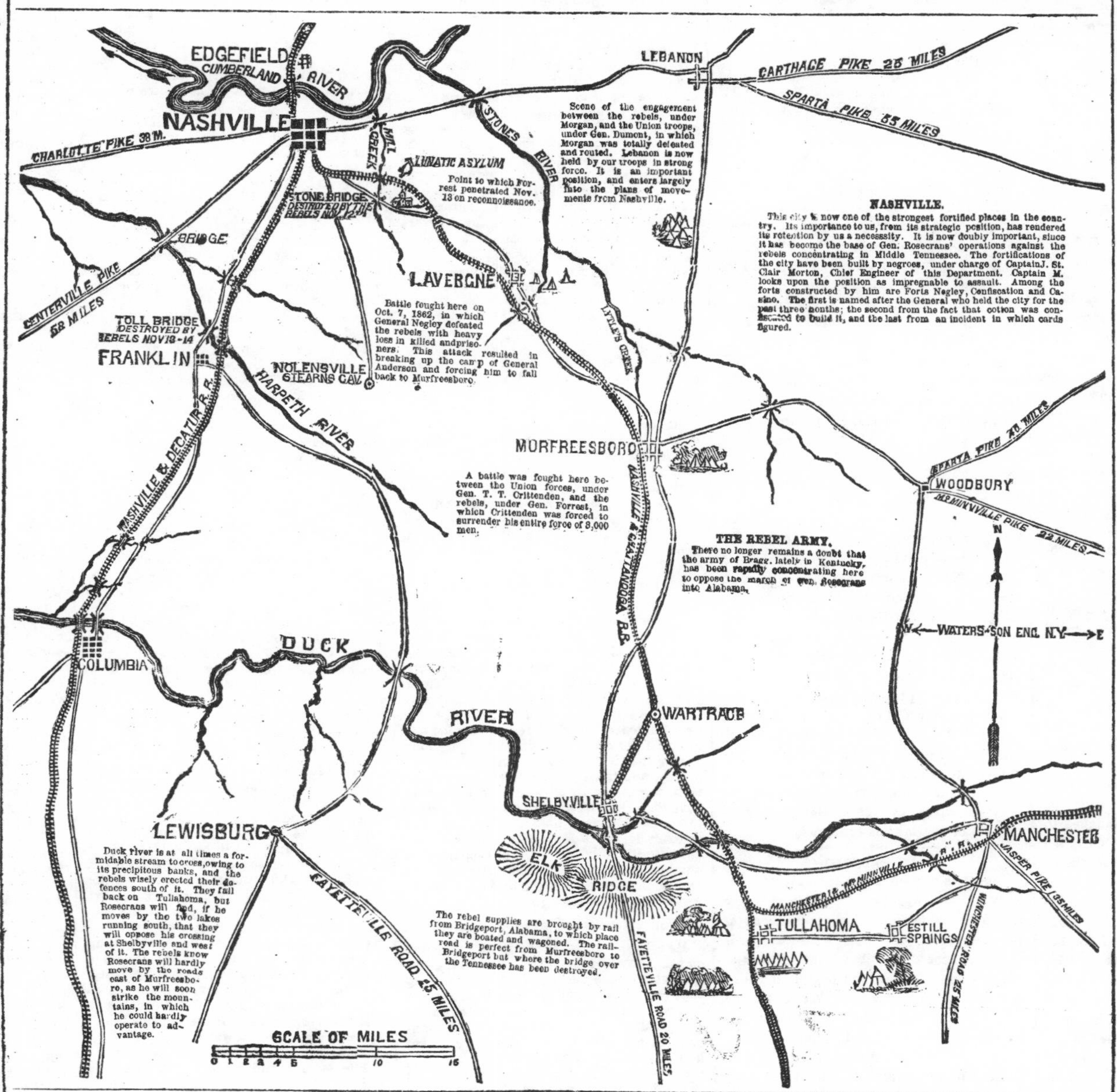

IMPORTANT FROM TENNESSEE.

Terrific Battle Near Murfreesboro.

The Rebel Centre Driven In and Their Intrenchments on Our Left Carried.

TERRIBLE LOSS BY THE UNION FORCES.

Our Troops Occupy Murfreesboro.

NAMES OF THE KILLED AND WOUNDED.

The Union Generals Stanley, Rosseau and Palmer Wounded.

The Rebel General Rains Killed and the Rebel General Cheatham Taken Prisoner.

THE SCENE OF OPERATIONS.

Sketches of the Generals in the Battle, &c., &c., &c.

The news from Tennessee is of the highest importance. A great battle was fought at Murfreesboro on Wednesday last, the 31st ult., between the Union forces under General Rosecrans and the rebels under General Joe Johnston. See the latest telegrams and the accompanying map.

The movement of the Union forces commenced on Christmas Day, and the day following the whole army was in motion. The demonstration against Murfreesboro was made by General Rosecrans for the purpose of possessing sufficient country to feed his army while his communications in the rear were interrupted. It was ascertained that Morgan and Forrest were engaged in raids north and west, and that in consequence of their absence the rebels were badly off for cavalry. It was ascertained also that Murfreesboro was not fortified, and the moment being most favorable for an advance, General Rosecrans determined to take the field in person. The army was divided into three corps under Generals Crittenden, McCook, and Thomas. During the whole of Friday there was considerable skirmishing with the enemy, but the onward movement was not seriously opposed by the rebels. The whole rebel force appeared to fall back slowly, with the intention evidently of concentrating at Murfreesboro or some point in the neighborhood. Communication was kept up with General Thomas' forces on the Nolinsville road, and there the rebels also retired before the Union troops.

On Saturday morning skirmishing became more serious, and the enemy resisted with more than their usual energy. General McCook had a sharp brush with the rebels, one of his regiments—the One hundred and first Ohio—capturing a gun and caisson from a Georgia battery. The loss was trifling, and the troops behaved splendidly. The captured gun was taken from Grant at Shiloh, and belonged to Darden's rebel battery. General Crittenden lost two killed and twenty-seven wounded in his skirmishes. He succeeded, however, in killing and wounding a proportionate number of rebels and capturing thirty-six Alabama cavalry, and the bridges on Stewart's creek. During the day Generals Negley's and Rosecrans' divisions moved to the centre, leaving McCook on the right. On reaching Lytle's creek the enemy was found strongly posted in force, and there the Union troops rested for the night. General Rosecrans had gained his purpose thus far, and was in possession of a country rich in forage. There was considerable speculation during the night as to the probability of a general engagement on the morrow, and all sorts of rumors were afloat as to the number of the rebels and the disposition of their forces. It is estimated that General Rosecrans succeeded thus far in bagging about five hundred prisoners. The rebels wasted considerable ammunition during the skirmishing, while our troops were careful to reserve their fire until it could be made to tell. The weather was damp and the ground heavy, rendering the forward movement exceedingly tiresome; but the troops pushed forward in splendid style.

On Sunday, the 28th, nothing was accomplished. General Rosecrans not deeming it prudent to follow up the pursuit on that day, and the rebels not having the courage to attack him, the troops had a day of rest.

On Monday, the 29th, General Rosecrans ordered the entire army to push forward—General Thomas' corps on the right, General McCook's in the centre on the Nolinsville turnpike, and General Crittenden on the Murfreesboro road. The advance commenced just before daylight, and the troops manifested excellent spirits. General Jeff. C. Davis' division moved upon Murfreesboro in advance on the right, by way of the Bully Jack road, several miles north of Triune, where McCook was engaging Hardee. Generals Negley's and Rousseau's divisions of Thomas' corps occupied the centre, while General Crittenden moved down upon the left. Generals Wood's and Van Cleeve's divisions were right and left respectively, while Palmer's division was held as a reserve. On arriving at Stewart's creek a general engagement was anticipated, but, excepting a duel between Parson's Sixth United States artillery and a rebel battery about nine o'clock A. M., on the right of the Murfreesboro road, crossing the creek, nothing of any magnitude transpired. From ten to one o'clock all was quiet, our army crossing the creek from right to left without opposition.

At one o'clock the Union army was within six miles of Murfreesboro, on the direct pike, the troops pushing on in splendid style; McCook, with Davis', Sheridan's and Johnson's divisions on the right; Thomas, with Negley's and Rousseau's divisions in the centre, and Crittenden's, with Wood's and Van Cleeve's divisions in front, with Palmer on the left, as a reserve. It seemed marvellous that there was no opposition to our crossing at Stewart's creek; for the rebels could not have chosen a better position for bringing on a general engagement. At two o'clock a battle seemed certain; but, with the exception of a stray cannon shot and an occasional skirmish with the infantry, General Rosecrans' entire army got across Stewart's creek in safety. The troops were in excellent spirits, and the commander announced that he would establish his headquarters near Murfreesboro that evening. The rebels slowly retreated to Stone's river, within a short distance of Murfreesboro, where it was expected they would make a final stand. The weather was magnificent, and everything favored the advance.

On Tuesday, the 30th, there was some skirmishing, and as the wind was blowing in the face of the enemy the advantage was in our favor. General Rosecrans was determined to pursue the enemy, even should he evacuate Murfreesboro, anticipating a battle at Shelbyville. General Crittenden reported the enemy drawn up in line of battle on the east side of Stone's river, menacing our army. General Rosencrans ordered him to form in line of battle two divisions in front, one in reserve and cover his flanks, and Generals Negley and Rousseau to close up.

General McCook also reported his corps to be at Wilkinson's creek, seven miles from Murfreesboro, and the enemy to be in line of battle from Murfreesboro to Franklin turnpike. It became evident that a great battle was to be fought, and that the morrow would decide the fate of Murfreesboro. The Union army was in good spirits, the advance being in full sight of the enemy and the village of Murfreesboro.

General Rosecrans was busy all day in making a proper disposition of his forces, and seeing that nothing was left undone to insure a victory to the Union arms on the following day.

The Rebel Army of the Southwest.

General Joseph Eggleston Johnston,
Commander-in-Chief.
DEPARTMENT NO. 2.
DEPARTMENT OF THE MISSISSIPPI.
General Braxton Bragg Commanding.
George William Brent, A. A. G. and Chief of Staff.
George G. Garner, A. A. G.
RIGHT WING.
Located Dec. 3 at Murfreesboro, Tenn.
Lieutenant General Leonidas Polk Commanding.

FIRST DIVISION.
Major General Simon Bolivar Buckner, of Kentucky.
First Brigade.
Brigadier General Chalmers, of Mississippi.
Composed of four regiments, among them one from Georgia and two from Mississippi.
Second Brigade.
Composed of four regiments, among them the Fifth Kentucky, Colonel Thomas H. Hunt.
Third Brigade.

SECOND DIVISION.
Major General Frank Cheatham, of Tennessee.
First Brigade.
Brigadier General George Maney, of Tennessee.
Composed of
First regiment Tennessee Volunteers,
Thirty-eighth regiment Tennessee Volunteers,
and two others.
Second Brigade.
Brigadier General Donnelson, of Tennessee,
Composed of
First regiment Confederate infantry,
Second regiment Confederate infantry,
Fourth regiment Confederate infantry,
and one other Tennessee regiment.
Third Brigade.
Brigadier General Stuart.
Four regiments, one of which is from Florida.

THIRD DIVISION.
Major General John C. Breckenridge, of Kentucky.
First Brigade.
Brigadier General Maxcy, of Georgia.
Second Brigade.
Brigadier General William Preston, of Kentucky.
Third Brigade.
Brigadier General Roger Hanson, of Kentucky.

CENTRE.
Lieutenant General E. Kirby Smith Commanding.
FIRST DIVISION.
Brigadier General Preston Smith.
Composed of three brigades, whose organization is not known.
SECOND DIVISION.
Organization not known—has three brigades.
THIRD DIVISION.
Organization not known—has three brigades.

LEFT WING.
Lieutenant General William J. Hardee Commanding.
FIRST DIVISION.
Major General Withers, of Georgia.
Three brigades, one of which is composed of regulars.
SECOND DIVISION.
Major General R. W. Anderson, of Alabama.
Three brigades.
THIRD DIVISION.
Three brigades.

DETACHMENTS.
Tennessee conscripts.
FIRST DIVISION.
Major General Samuel R. Anderson.
Brigade.
Brigadier General Gideon J. Pillow.

CAVALRY.
First Brigade.
Brigadier General Joseph R. Wheeler.
Third Brigade.
Brigadier General Forrest.
Fourth Brigade.
Brigadier General Stearns.

ESTIMATED FORCE OF THE REBEL ARMY.

RIGHT WING.	
Major General Buckner	5,000
Major General Cheatham	6,000
Major General Breckinridge	4,500
CENTRE.	
Brigadier General Preston Smith	6,000
Second Division	4,500
Third Division	4,500
LEFT WING.	
Major General Withers	5,000
Major General Anderson	6,000
Third Division	4,500
DETACHMENTS.	
First Division Tennessee Conscripts	4,000
First Brigade Tennessee Conscripts, Pillow	3,200
CAVALRY.	
Brigadier General Wheeler	2,000
Brigadier General Forrest	2,500
Brigadier General Stearns	3,300
ARTILLERY.	
Estimated twenty-five batteries	3,750
Total rebel force	62,750

THE LATEST TELEGRAMS.

TELEGRAM TO SECRETARY STANTON.

The Secretary of War yesterday received the following advices:—

CLEVELAND, Jan. 2, 1863.

The following has just been received by telegraph from Cincinnati, dated

MURFREESBORO, January 1, 1863.

A terrible battle was fought yesterday. The latest from the field is up to noon.

The rebel centre had been broken, and things looked favorable.

The losses are reported to be enormous. Stanley, Rousseau and Palmer are wounded, and the rebels Cheatham and Rains are killed.

TELEGRAM TO THE PRESS.

NEAR MURFREESBORO, Dec. 31, 1863.

Our whole line suffered terribly this morning. Four regiments of regulars lost half their men and all their commanding officers.

General Anderson's troops suffered severely.

Majors Rosengarten and Ward are killed.

Generals Stanley, Rousseau and Palmer are wounded.

TWO O'CLOCK P. M.

General Thomas has just broken the rebel centre and *driven the enemy a mile.*

We are advancing our whole line.

Gen. Rosecrans is personally superintending the movements. One shot killed two of his staff officers.

The Fifteenth Wisconsin regiment has lost seven captains.

General Negley's artillery is still mowing the rebels in the centre.

General Crittenden's left wing has taken the intrenchments at Murfreesboro.

The rebel Generals Cheatham and Rains are killed.

LOUISVILLE, Jan. 1, 1863.

Gen. Rosecrans captured Murfreesboro on Tuesday morning, and now occupies it. *The rebels are retreating to Tullahoma.* [There is evidently some error in this announcement. None of the other despatches indicate even a battle on Tuesday.—ED. HERALD.]

The rebels made but little resistance, though Rosecrans lost the train of wagons following him, which was captured by the rebels under Col. Morgan, of Tennessee.

The startling reports which reached here about midnight, and caused considerable commotion throughout the city, of the approach of Forrest from the direction of Salt river, with a large body of cavalry, are entirely false.

TELEGRAM FROM GENERAL BOYLE.

LOUISVILLE, Ky., Jan. 2, 1863.

General Rosecrans occupies Murfreesboro.

J. T. DOYLE,
Brigadier General.

Details of the Battle.

NASHVILLE, Jan. 2, 1863.

The federals encountered the rebels on the 30th ult., near Stewart's creek. After heavy skirmishing, the rebels were driven back. We captured one hundred prisoners, and killed and wounded a large number of rebels. Our loss was seventy killed and wounded.

At daybreak on the 31st the fight was renewed with great fury. Gen. McCook's corps was opposed to Gen. Hardee.

After desperate fighting, with heavy loss on both sides, Gen. McCook retreated two miles. He soon rallied, and was driven back. At night he was four miles this side of the ground occupied in the morning.

The fight continued until ten o'clock P. M., at which time we had maintained our position.

The Union loss is very heavy.

KILLED.

Brigadier General Sill.

Lieutenant Colonel Garesche, Chief of General Rosecrans' staff.

Brigadier General Willick, of Indiana.

Colonel Kell, Second Ohio.

Colonel Shaffer, Acting Brigadier General.

Colonel Farmer, Fifteenth Kentucky.

Colonel Jones, Twenty-fourth Ohio.

Lieutenant Colonel Cotton, Sixth Kentucky.

Lieutenant Colonel Jones, Thirty-ninth Indiana.

Major Carpenter, Nineteenth regulars.

Major Rosengarten, of Philadelphia.

Captain Garrett, Nineteenth Illinois.

Colonel Carpenter, Eighteenth Wisconsin.

Lieut. Colonel McKee, Fifteenth Wisconsin.

WOUNDED.

Brigadier General E. M. Kirk, of Illinois.

Brigadier General Wood, of Indiana.

Brigadier General Van Cleve, of Minnesota.

Colonel Cassole, of Ohio.

Major General Rousseau, of Kentucky.

Lieut. Colonel Berry, Fifth Kentucky.

Major Slemmer, Sixteenth regulars.

Major King, Fifteenth regulars, and many others.

The Twenty-first, Twenty-fifth and Thirty-fifth Illinois lost two-thirds, and the Fifteenth and Thirty-eighth Ohio one half their number. The One Hundred and First Ohio lost one hundred and twenty-five men; the Thirty-eighth Indiana about the same number.

The total killed and wounded is estimated at twenty-five hundred. The rebel loss exceeds ours.

The rebel General J. E. Rains was killed, and the rebel General Cheatham was wounded and taken prisoner.

We have captured five hundred prisoners.

The fight was renewed at three A. M. on January 1.

The cannonading was heard at Nashville.

At ten A. M. General Wood's and General Van Cleve's divisions were in Murfreesboro, *driving the enemy, who were in full retreat.*

Three hundred prisoners reached Nashville at six o'clock P. M. on January 1, including the following commissioned officers:—Major J. J. Franklin, Thirtieth Arkansas; Captains W. E. Johnson and J. P. Eagle, Second Arkansas, and Captain S. C. Stone, 1st Tennessee cavalry.

Many buildings have been taken for hospital purposes. Great numbers of wounded are being brought in now.

The river has fallen eighteen inches on the shoals.

Sketch of Murfreesboro.

Murfreesboro was, previous to the rebellion, a handsome post village; but it has, since 1861, suffered severely from the ravages of war. It is the capital of Rutherford county, Tenn., and is situated on the railroad running from Nashville to Charleston, S. C. It is thirty miles from Nashville, in an air line drawn in a southeasterly direction, and thirty-two miles by railroad. It is situated in a beautiful plain, surrounded by a fertile and healthy country. The Union University at this place was established in 1841 by the Baptists, and was at one time a very flourishing institution; but since the State went out of the Union the University began to decline, and has since failed altogether. There was also a female institute in the place, founded by the same religious body and under their direction, but, like the University, its glory has long since fled. There were five churches in the village and a bank building; and at the beginning of 1860 two newspapers were published in the place, and had a fair circulation. For ten years—viz: from 1817 to 1827—Murfreesboro was the capital of the State, but in the latter year the State House was consumed by fire, and the capital removed to Nashville. The county of Rutherford is situated in the central part of the State, and has an area of six hundred square miles, or three hundred and eighty-four thousand miles. It is intersected by Stone's river, which is an affluent of the Cumberland. The surface of the country is agreeably diversified, the soil highly productive, well watered and extensively cultivated. The country is intersected by the Nashville, Chattanooga and Charleston Railroad, and the population in 1860 was 27,918, of whom 12,984 were slaves. In 1850 the population was 29,122, showing a loss in ten years.

Sketch of General Rosecrans.

Major General William Starke Rosecrans was born in Kingston township, Delaware county, Ohio, on the 6th of December, 1819. His parents were Crandall Rosecrans, whose ancestors were originally from Amsterdam, Holland, and Jemima Hopkins, the former a native of Wyoming Valley, Pa., who emigrated to Ohio in 1808, the latter a daughter of a soldier of the Revolution. The early years of the present General were passed in close application to his studies, so that at the age of eighteen he was well fitted for his appointment as cadet at the Military Academy at West Point, in 1838. He graduated with high honors in 1842, being third in mathematics and fifth in general merit, in a class of fifty six, numbering many distinguished competitors. He entered the corps of engineers as brevet second lieutenant on the 1st of July 1842, and served that year at Fortress Monroe a first assistant, under command of Lieutenant Colonel R. E. De Russey. He was ordered to duty at West Point in 1843, as Assistant Professor of Engineering. About this period he was united in marriage at St John's church, in this city, to Miss E. A. Hegeman, only daughter of Adrian Hegeman, the noted jurist. In 1844 he was detailed as Assistant Professor of Natural and Experimental Philosophy. In 1845-7 he served as Assistant and First Assistant Professor of Engineering, and had charge of the department while Captain Swift served in Mexico, and was also for nine months Post Quartermaster. He was ordered to Newport in 1847, and there took charge of the fortifications and the reconstruction of a large military wharf which had previously been destroyed during a storm. This duty devolved upon him on account of his recognized ability as an engineer, and was then looked upon as a decided compliment. He remained there until 1852. In 1852-3 he was charged with the survey of New Bedford and Providence harbors and Taunton river, and in April, 1854, was ordered to report for duty to the Secretary of the Navy, in the Bureau of Docks and Yards, then assigned as constructing engineer, at Washington Navy Yard until November, 1853, when, on account of ill health, he felt compelled to resign his position and tendered his resignation to the Secretary of War, Jefferson Davis. The resignation was not accepted, from a desire to retain so valuable an officer in the service, and a leave of absence was granted, with the understanding that at its terminus if the resignation was insisted upon, it would be accepted; which was subsequently done in April, 1854. From that date to June, 1855, General Rosecrans occupied an office in Cincinnati, as consulting engineer and architect. In June 1855, he was appointed superintendant of works and president of the Cannel Coal Company, which, with other parties, were engaged in building locks, dams, &c., in Western Virginia, and gave great satisfaction, but relinquished his position to assume control of the Cincinnati Coal Oil Company, then making preparations for an extensive business, in which he was deeply concerned. When General McClellan was appointed, he at once selected General Rosecrans as his aid and acting Chief Engineer with the rank of Major. The Legislature of Ohio then purposely created the office of Chief Engineer of the State, which was intended for General Rosecrans and accepted by him. On the 10th of June, 1861, he was appointed by Governor Dennison Colonel in the 23d regiment Ohio Volunteers, and was sent upon a mission to Washington city to arrange for the maintenance and payment of the Ohio contingent forces. On the 20th of June he was nominated by the President a Brigadier General in the regular army, a promotion universally acknowledged to be as rapid as it was deserved.

When the advance into Western Virginia was made General Rosecrans was entrusted with a brigade, composed of the following regiments—The Eighth and Tenth Indiana, Seventeenth and Nineteenth Ohio, and placed in command at Parkersburg. Here he was particularly noted for his energy of character and competence for command.

He afterwards proceeded to Clarksburg, thence to Buckhannon, and on the 12th of July fought the memorable battle of Rich Mountain, succeeding in achieving a disastrous defeat for the rebels. In this battle he cut a passage nine miles through the woods, and coming upon the enemy's rear, after a desperate fight of an hour and a half, completely routed them, capturing all they had, and taking many officers, as well as privates, prisoners. The rebels numbered about two thousand, under General Pegram, who was soon after obliged to surrender himself a prisoner of war. Subsequently General Rosecrans drove the rebel Generals Wise and Floyd out of Western Virginia, and captured their effects.

McClellan being called to the head of our army of the Potomac the 22d of July, General Rosecrans immediately took his place in command of the Army of Western Virginia, being appointed the 24th of July. On the 1st of August General Rosecrans telegraphed to the War Department at Washington that the Valley of the Kanawha was freed from rebels, and his forces had captured one thousand muskets, a quantity of ammunition, &c. On the 10th of September he routed Floyd, who had sixteen pieces of artillery and five or six thousand men at Carnifex Ferry, and again rid his department of rebels.

When General Fremont took charge of the Mountain Department, General Rosecrans, wishing more active employment, was first placed in command of General Blenker's division of the Army of the Potomac, but was afterwards ordered to the Southwest, and with the rank of Major General of Volunteers, dating from March 21, 1862, placed in command of the Army of the Mississippi, otherwise known as the Third Division of the District of West Tennessee, under General Grant. His headquarters was located at Corinth. On the 19th and 20th of September, 1862, he fought and won the battle of I-u-k-a, Miss., and on the 3d and 4th of October he also fought and won the battles at Corinth. On the 5th he replied to the rebel General Van Dorn's flag of truce, that he made ample provision for the burial of the "Confederate dead." After the battle of Perryville he was ordered to supersede Gen. Buell, and issued his farewell address at Corinth on the 26th of October, 1862. So rapidly did he move that on the 30th of October he assumed command of his new department of the Cumberland at Louisville, Ky., and announced his staff. He at once began organizing and moving his army southward, and on the 4th of November, at Bowling Green, he announced its complete organization into three grand divisions under Generals Thomas, McCook and Crittenden. He issued peremptory orders correcting abuses and summarily punished officers when such occurred—the President having invested him with full power. Finding independent sutlers a nuisance, he, on November 27, dismissed them under heavy penalties if they again appeared within his lines. His reply to Gen. Bragg relative to the robbery of the Hartsville prisoners was sharp and pertinent, and will long be remembered. On the 25th of December, 1862, he took the field and moved his army rapidly upon Murfreesboro, the present result of which movement we now record. Major General Rosecrans is about five feet eight inches high, firmly built, his shape displaying his German origin; his motions are quick, his mind almost intuitive. His age is about forty-two. His face is weather worn, but bears a warm, cordial style, which never leaves it. When conversing he looks you square in the face. There is no air of superiority in his manner; he approaches you as a friend, talks to you as a friend, and bids you good day as a friend. His orders to officers are given with a pleasant recognition of their rights. He cannot but be popular; it is constitutional. He has now a big job on his hands; but it will be done in a soldierly manner.

The Staff of General Rosecrans.

A Adj Gen. and Chief of Staff	Lieut. Col. J. P. Garesche.
Acting Asst. Adjt. General	Major W. C. Goddard.
Act. Asst. Adjutant General	Major W. H. Sidell.
Acting Asst. Insp'r Generals	Lieut. Col. A. C. Ducat. Capt. J. C. Peterson.
Inspector of Cavalry	Lieut. Col. W. P. Hepburn
Inspector of Artillery	Capt. J. H. Gilman.
Chief of Artillery	Col. Jas. Barnett.
Judge Advocate	Major Rolston Skinner.
Chief Engineer	Capt. J. H. C. Morton.
Chief Topograph'l Engineers	Capt. A. Michler.
Acting Chief Commissary	Capt. Samuel Simmons.
Acting Chief Quartermaster	Capt. J. W. Taylor.
Ordnance Officer	Lieut. T. Edson.
Medical Director	Surgeon Robert Murray.
Medical Inspector	Surgeon A. H. Thruston.
Provost Marshal General	Capt. W. M. Wiles.
Chief of Courier Lines	Capt. Elmer Otis.
Aids	Capt. Chas. R. Thompson. Lieut. Byron Kirby.
Volunteer Aid	Capt. R. S. Thoms.

Sketch of General McDowell McCook.

Major General A. McDowell McCook was born in Columbiana county, Ohio, April 22, 1831, was appointed to West Point in 1848, and graduated in 1852. He was appointed brevet second lieutenant in the Third infantry, and ordered to the Department of New Mexico. He took an active part in all the prominent Indian campaigns in that department up to February, 1858, when he was ordered to West Point, where he served as principal assistant instructor in infantry tactics, and also in the art of war, until the fall of Sumter. He then applied for permission to take the field, and was ordered to his native State to muster in volunteers for the three months' service. On his thirtieth birthday he was elected and commissioned colonel of the First Ohio volunteers. He commanded this regiment at the battle of Bull run, where it formed part of Schenck's brigade. He returned to Ohio with the regiment, mustered it out of service, and recruited it again at Dayton, Ohio. He was appointed brigadier general of volunteers September 3, 1861, and ordered to Kentucky. He has four brothers in the army, a fifth having been murdered by guerillas and a sixth killed at the battle of Bull run. Since he has been in this part of the country he participated in the advance through Tennessee, fought

[CONTINUED ON EIGHTH PAGE.]

Lynch'bg Virginian.

WEDNESDAY.........JANUARY, 7, 1863

The Monster.

Lincoln has won an immortality of infamy. Henceforth, Butler the Beast will not stand alone as the synonym of all that is brutal and devilish. His master will be entitled to a place in the same niche that shall be assigned to these twin brothers in crime. Lincoln the Monster, and Butler the Beast, will descend to posterity as the representative men of a debased and half-civilized people. They will stand out in gloomy and revolting isolation; and if the student of history shall seek their parallels, it will be in Alaric the Goth, and Attila the Hern. As common instruments of cruelty, only, will their similitude appear; for the former, whilst evincing the brute ferocity of their prototypes, lack wholly that brute courage which they dare not emulate.

Lincoln and Butler! What names they will have in history. The one as the instigator of servile insurrection, including amongst its victims, (so far as he could effect it,) helpless women and children; the other, as the brute who not only robbed and plundered a defenceless city, but incited the lusts of a debased soldiery to seek gratification on the persons of those whom it should have been his pleasure, as it was his duty, to protect. To what a depth of infamy have these two men plunged their country; and how long, can we imagine, it will be before the civilized world will revolt at their enormities? The day of retribution approaches swiftly; and even England, slow as she has been to recognize the inhumanity of the war that has been waged upon us, will respond in terms that will make the guilty wretch at Washington tremble on his throne. Mark the prediction!

But what shall we do? Why? what, but hurl back scorn and defiance at the incarnate fiend who thinks that he has let loose a new pack of blood hounds upon us. We defy his impotent rage, as we loathe and contemn the miserable creature himself.—Let the proclamation of President Davis, and the laws of the States, be executed upon all this class who shall be induced to act upon the suggestion of Lincoln. We would advise more, and recommend that a fitting response be made by our President to Lincoln's proclamation. He should be declared an out law, an enemy of mankind, and a suitable reward be offered for his head. This would indicate more unmistakably than could be done in any other way, the contempt we feel for the fiat of the negro generalisimo. Not that his head is worth much, should this reward be offered; but because he is not entitled to the immunity which Divine mercy secured to the first murderer, who was only condemned to be a vagabond and a wanderer in the earth. The modern Tamerlane, whose future monument will be the skulls of at least a million of his murdered countrymen, does not deserve to live a day. We sincerely trust that if he ever ventures to set foot on Virginia soil again, there will be found some heroic Jackson, who will not count even his own life dear, to rid the world of such a monster.

Affairs in the West.

The latest news from the Murfreesboro' fight has had the effect to repress the exuberance of that joy with which earlier intelligence was received. The fact that, instead of pressing forward after the enemy, as Gen Bragg declared his purpose to do—our forces are falling back, and the enemy, if not pursuing, at least occupy Murfreesboro'; might suggest to some minds, a serious and unlooked for reverse.

A change in Bragg's programme has evidently taken place; and we suspect that large reinforcements coming up to the enemy, from Nashville, made this necessary. Moreover, in view of the fact that the Memphis and Charleston Railway afforded facilities for the enemy to throw a force in rear of Bragg, it may have been necessary for him to fall back to defeat the execution of such a measure. At any rate, his retreat seems to have been a masterly affair, he bringing off his prisoners, and all the captured arms and stores. The enemy admit that they were terribly handled, whilst gold went up two cents in New York, after their victory! A strange result of victory! Their statement of aggregate loss is evidently false. They admit that four regiments of regulars lost half their men; that three Illinois regiments lost two-thirds; that one Wisconsin regiment lost seven Captains! And yet, the total loss, say they, is about twenty-five hundred! Who can believe such a statement? We venture the assertion that it was more than four times that number. They only claim five hundred prisoners, whilst we took eight times that number from them, and, according to their own admission, captured the wagon train in their rear. We repeat that, whatever may have occasioned the retrograde movement of Gen. Bragg, it is evident that the fruits of victory are in our hands.

Rev. M. D. Hoge, D. D.

It will gratify very many to hear that Dr. Hoge has sailed from our shores upon an important mission of benevolence. It has been found impossible to furnish an adequate supply of Bibles and Testaments from the Confederate Bible Society. To meet this want Dr. H. conceived the idea of going over in person to Great Britain. His plan is to purchase the Word of God, as far as possible, with funds furnished here, and for the rest, to appeal to the Christian people there. What he may obtain is expected to be run through the blockade, and is chiefly for our army.

The above is taken from the Richmond Enquirer of Monday, and, we dare say, will give pain to as many as it will afford pleasure to. We honor the motive that prompted this act—we cannot do otherwise; but England is the last nation on earth that we should go to on such a mission. What! appeal to her people for means with which to purchase the Bible for Southern soldiers! Better ask them to send Missionaries to the Northern barbarians, with bell, book and candle, to exorcise the demoniac spirit that dwells there.

But why should we ask a people for Bibles, to prepare our gallant soldiers for that world where the sound of battle never comes—when they have allowed the work of butchery, which they could have prevented, to go on here for twelve months past? What confidence can we have in their spiritual sympathy, when the horrors of this dreadful strife do not prompt them to that christian effort that would stop the effusion of blood, which cries to Heaven for interposition to stay the hellish work? The Christian people of this country degrade themselves in making such an appeal to England, and we should be glad to know that the Government had instructed our Minister to show no countenance to the mission of Mr. Hoge, so far as his appeals to the charity of the "Christian people" (!) of England is concerned.

Help Cassius!

Lincoln's appeal to contrabands for military aid, betrays the desperate strait to which he is driven. Twenty millions of yankees, with the whole ocean at their command, could not whip eight millions of Southerners without the aid of the four millions of their slaves! What a commentary on Yankee sagacity, that expected seventy-five thousand yankees to finish up the job in three months! The world will take note of this. We wonder if the better thinking people amongst them wont feel ashamed of their government and nation, and wish that they were of that heroic race whom no threats can daunt, and no terrors dismay. What will Maryland and Kentucky think of their government? Alas! for them. The universal Yankee nation has proclaimed its everlasting disgrace in the eyes of the whole world. It will be a hissing and a by-word amongst the nations.

The Monitor.

The far-famed Monitor has gone to Davy Jones' Locker. Peaceful be her slumbers beneath the surging billows of friendly Hatteras; and such be the fate that shall overtake the piratical crews of all Lincoln's sea monsters.

A new species of food for army uses, called the extract of flesh, is highly commended for invalid soldiers and others. A half ounce represents the whole amount of nutriment in a pound of fresh beef The method of preparation is thus described. "The whole process consists in taking lean beef, free of bone and fat, chopping it fine as when used for sausages or mice meat, and mixing it with its own weight of water. It is then slowly heated to boiling and allowed to boil briskly, for a moment or two, when it is strained through cotton cloth to seperate the coagulated albumen and fibrin. The evaperation to dryness of the solution must be conducted at a low temperature by a water bath or a steam heat. The powder is readily soluble in water. When properly dried it will keep for mouths. Enough can be stored in an ordinary watch fob to sustain a soldier a week. An ordinary porcelain lined kettle, holding a gallon, is sufficient for the preperation of the extract. To dry the solution, put the kettle into a larger vessel containing hot water. With but little trouble on the part of their friends, almost every soldier might be provided with some of this valuable nutriment.—*Louisville Journal.*

SPEECH OF PRESIDENT DAVIS.

President Davis addressed the Mississippi Legislature, at Jackson, on the 26th ult. The galleries were filled with ladies, and when the President appeared the whole hall rang with applause. The address was quite a lengthy one. We give the chief points:

The President spoke of his love for the old Union. He alluded to it, however, as a matter of regret, that the best affections of his heart should have been bestowed upon an object so unworthy—that he should have loved so long a Government which was rotten to its very core.

He had predicted from the beginning a fierce war, though it had assumed more gigantic proportions than he had calculated upon. He had predicted war, not because our right to secede was not an undoubted one, and clearly defined in the spirit of that declaration which rests the right to govern upon the consent of the governed, but the wickedness of the North would entail war upon the country. The present war waged against the rights of a free people was unjust, and the fruit of the evil passions of the North. In the progress of the war those evil passions have been brought out and developed; and so far from re-uniting with such a people—a people whose ascendants Cromwell had gathered from the bogs and fens of Ireland and Scotland—a people whose intolerance produced discord and trouble wherever they went—who persecuted Catholics, Episcopalians, and every other sect that did not subscribe to their bigoted and contracted notions—who hung witches, and did a thousand other things calculated to make them forever infamous—the President was emphatic in his declaration that under no circumstances would he consent to reunion.

He drew a glowing picture of the horrors of war, and the ravages of the enemy; and while his tears flowed for those who suffered, yet all those would be endured, cheerfully, before our manhood and our liberties would be surrendered.

THE WAR UPON NORTHERN SOIL.

He alluded briefly to his desire to transfer the war upon Northern soil, but the failure to do this proceeded not from a want of inclination but of power. We were not an old-established nation, with armies and navies at our command. These had to be improvised from the scanty materials to be found within the limits of our own Confederacy. We were blockaded and cut off from other nations, and everybody knows that we had been an agricultural people, and that our facilities for manufacturing materials of war were extremely limited. Notwithstanding this fact, patent to the most casual observer, we had now an army larger than ever before—our arms and munitions of war were increased in number and improved in quality, and we are in a better condition to-day than we were twelve months ago.

CONSCRIPTION AND EXEMPTION LAWS.

He alluded to the conscription and exemption laws of Congress, explaining the necessity of the one and the intention of the other. Was sorry to perceive that there had been a false construction put upon the first of these laws. There was no dishonor in being conscripted. The Government had as much right to make laws requiring the services of its citizens in the army as to compel them to work public roads or to pay taxes. The object of that portion of the exemption law which exempted the owner, agent, or overseer of twenty negroes, was not intended to draw any distinction whatever between classes. No benefit was intended to the rich from it. It was simply to provide a police force which Congress thought necessary, and to facilitate the agricultural productions of the country to supply the wants of both the poor people and the army. Any law intended to bear unfairly upon the poor, even to a feather's weight, would never have received his signature. "The poor *have* fought our battles," says the President, "and so have the rich." The poor in all revolutions are the main stay and props of the country. But while the poor have nobly done their duty, we have no cause to complain of the rich. All have done well, and many of the wealthiest and most distinguished families in the South have sons in the ranks. He instanced Hon Israel Walsh and others, who had fought as privates in the bloodiest engagements of the war. He thought there might be very properly a revision of the exemption law, and trusted there would be no conflict between Confederate and State laws upon the subject of the military. That there should be no war with States; and if any State chose to inflict a blow upon the common cause by enacting conflicting military laws he hoped that Mississippi would be the last to adopt such a suicidal policy.

INDIGENT FAMILIES—RESERVED CORPS.

The President expressed his gratification at the message of Gov. Pettus, and cordially endorsed his views in reference to making provisions for indigent families, and the enrollment of exempts, who could be ready upon an emergency to go forth and occupy the trenches while the disciplined troops and active soldiery could take the field. The calls for such service could be for thirty, sixty, or ninety days, and when the emergency had passed they could return to their pursuits. Raw soldiers, the President contended, could do efficient service in the trenches, and the adoption of such a policy would strengthen our means of defence quite materially.

In his allusion to the vast numbers of the North, the President said that upon any fair field we were willing to fight them two to one; we have often whipped them three to one; at Antiatem Gen. Lee whipped them four to one; but this might not be the case always. As the enemy progressed in discipline, they approached nearer to our own troops in efficiency.—Hence the necessity of providing something like a corresponding force to that which the enemy are bringing against us.

The President denounced in terms of scathing but dignified rebuke the habit of straggling from the army. He invoked public opinion to frown it down, and called upon the women to drive the straggling back to duty.

FILL UP THE RANKS.

He urged the necessity of filling up the thinned ranks of our regiments. Those veterans who had gone through many hard fought battles looked for their kindred at home to supply the places which had been made vacant by the death of their comrades. A brigade which mustered only twelve hundred men, would have to bleed as much as if it had its full quota of 4,000. Their ranks must be filled; humanity demands it. It was a time for patriots to throw off the shackles of private interest, fly to the rescue of those heroes whom the ravages of war had yet spared, and consecrate themselves to the most sacred cause on earth.

THE REAL DANGER.

The President remarked that when he arrived here he thought the enemy were pressing down upon us from the Northern borders of our State, but when he went to Grenada he there learned that nothing could be seen of them but their backs.—They were going back, perhaps, with the intention of reinforcing the heavy column that was now being thrown down the Mississippi river. The real points of attack were at Vicksburg and Port Hudson; and to all who desired to lend a helping hand to the country in her present exigency he would say, "Go to Port Hudson and Vicksburg without delay!"

NECESSITY OF HARMONY—PERMANENT MILITARY SYSTEM.

He spoke of the salutary effects of harmonious action between the several States and the Government at Richmond, and urged upon legislators, both State and Confederate, the necessity of establishing a permanent military system; for even after the present war was ended we might expect trouble from our enemies unless our military establishment was of such character as to give them a wholesome fear of precipitating a war upon us. The true theory was to adopt a military system which would be permanent and operative in times of peace.

THE QUESTION AT ISSUE.

The issue involved in this war was no ordinary one. The question is will you be free, or will you be the slaves of the most depraved and intolerant and tyrannical and hated people upon earth? This was the real question to be decided. Everything else was as dust in the balance. A people who had demonstrated their utter incapacity for self-government, who have destroyed their own liberties in the vain effort to deprive us of ours, seek to be our masters, and inflict upon us such galling chains as have no parallel in the annals of tyranny. Mississippi is the object of their peculiar hatred; upon her is to be visited their refined vengeance. But our cause is just and vengeance belongs to the Lord! We will resist the power of the enemy.—Discard all other considerations but the public defence, and victory will again be ours.

ASPERSIONS OF THE ADMINISTRATION.

The President alluded very briefly to the falsehoods which had been circulated relative to the Administration, which he could not disprove, because such disproval would give the enemy a knowledge of things which the good of the cause required to be concealed from him. That he had committed some errors he did not doubt, tho' they were never the result of improper motives. For a vindication of himself from the aspersions of some of his fellow-citizens he confidently awaited the time when the cause would not suffer from such vindication. He, however, explained the great necessity of public confidence in the officers of the Government, and pointed to that great and good men, Gen. Albert Sidney Johston,, as a shining example of the ill effects of withholding that deserved confidence which the public welfare requires.

DURATION OF THE WAR.

Though the war had somewhat exceeded his expectations, yet he never doubted our final success, and he considered it now as absolutely certain. The duration of the war was a question of time. He thought, however, it was not possible for a war waged upon such a tremendous scale to be long protracted. Be it long or short, however, we could not be the first to cry "hold, enough"

RECOGNITION—FOREIGN NATIONS.

To the question of recognition and intervention, the President devoted only a few words. We had a right to expect recognition long since, but it had not come, and his advice was, "Put not your faith in princes, nor rest your hopes upon foreign nations." It seemed that England still refused to take any steps towards either recognition or mediation. France had made a move that looked friendly to us, and when she extended the hand of friendship we would be ready to grasp it.

NO RETROGRADATION.

The President took a brief retrospective view of the movements of our armies since the fall of New Orleans—an event as unexpected to him as it was to us—and showed that we had not retrograded, but had gathered largely in strength. Armies are not made up in numbers only. We have now an army that we can safely rely on—We have stripped gunboats of their terrors. We have improved in all those things which go to make us invincible. Our prospects are much better than they were 12 months ago.

TWO OBJECTS OF THE ENEMY.

There are two grand objects of the enemy: 1st, to get possession of the river, and thus cut our Confederacy in two; and secondly, to seize the Confederate capital, and hold it up to foreign nations as an evidence that the Confederacy does not exist.

The President dwelt at some length upon the vast importance of thwarting the enemy's designs upon this valley; he considered its defence a necessity not only to the people here, but to the Confederacy itself. Vicksburg and Port Hudson were points that must be defended, and every effort must be strained for this purpose. Vicksburg, he said, would stand, and Port Hudson would stand, if the people were true to themselves. This done, the Northwest would grow restive, and cease to support a war ruinous to them and beneficial only to New England contractors. From the Northwest he looked for the first gleams of peace.

The President expressed his gratification that Gen Pemberton, whom he had sent here believing him eminently suited to this command, had sustained in a signal manner the high character he had given him. He also spoke of Brigadier General Lee, to whom he had entrusted the defences of Vicksburg, in terms of hearty commendation.

THE TRANS-MISSISSIPPI DEPARTMENT.

On the other side of the river our prospects are brighter than ever before, and ere long he hoped that we would be eanbled to proclaim Missouri free. Kentucky, too, was an object of solicitude to him, and he spoke of her gallant people in the kindest and most commendable terms.

OUR CAUSE IN THE ASCENDANT.

The President laid particular stress upon the encouraging fact that we had improved in every respect since the war began. Our armies were superior in number, and improved in quality and appointments. Our manufactories had made rapid progress;—Mississippi alone had clothed and subsisted the whole army upon her soil. Our people had learned to economise. They wear homespun. He felt like taking off his hat to a women dressed in homespun. He had an unfaltering belief in the justice of our cause, and a profound reverence for the decrees of Heaven. He noticed with evident satisfaction, the superior morality of our army to that of the invader. In God and the valor of our troops he trusted.

At the conclusion of his remarks, Gen. Joseph E. Johnston was vociferously called for. The scar-worn hero looked a little nervous, while the house rang with loud swelling and prolonged applause. He arose and said:

Fellow Citizens.—My only regret is that I have done so little to merit such a greeting. I promise you however, that hereafter I shall be watchful, energtic and indefatigable in your defence."

This speech was greeted with tremendous, uproarous and prolonged plaudits.

THE YANKEE ARMY

We find the following in a late United States paper:

MR. SECRETARY STANTON'S FIGURES.

"Mr. Stanton, in his report, says he has 800,000 men under arms. This statement suggests some figuring. Under the three calls of the President there were 1,175,000 men ordered out, 300,000 of whom were to be drafted. These, if all are in the field, added to the regular army, would make a total of, say 1,250,000. But of the 300,000 drafted men there are not probably over 150,000 yet mustered into service.

Dr. Bellows, Superintendent of the Sanitary Commission, states that 150,000 men are sick, and according to the New York Times, 180,000 are stragglers and deserters, making in these three items alone, 480,000 men, which, deducted from the 1,250,000 of the entire levy, would leave 770,000. From this we must further deduct the dead and wounded during the existence of the war, which few readers will be disposed to place at less than 200 to 300 thousand, and many at considerably over these. These are plain facts, and would show that the War Department keeps troops in pay on paper, who have probably never been in service, and dismisses, as it did within a week past, in disgrace, officers and men killed in battle, and dead six months, without its knowledge or record."

Another statement of the Yankee army is suggested by Stanton's figures. He says he has 800,000 men under arms. We presume this means that this is the number now on the muster rolls. Now if 1,100,000 have been mustered into the service, as above stated, since the war commenced, the figures confess that *three hundred thousand* men have been killed, wounded, and permanently disabled on the part of the enemy since the war began. A fearful host of sacrifices, but probably under the true number.

Of the 800,000 now on the rolls and drawing pay, we are told above 150,000 are sick and 180,000 straggling or deserted.—Add 20,000 for our surplus of prisoners, (now considerably increased) and we have a deduction of 350,000 to make in order to get at the efficient strength of the army—So that the enemy would seem to have only 450,000 men actually with arms in their hands.

The Virginian.

WEDNESDAY.........JANUARY, 7, 1863.

NOTICE.—The cross mark appended to the names of certain subscribers indicates that the term for which they subscribed will soon expire. They are thus notified in time to renew their subscriptions if they desire.

TO OUR CITY SUBSCRIBERS.—We would call the attention of our city subscribers to a consideration of their obligations to us. Some of them have not paid their subscriptions for a long time, and having no collector for the city, it is impossible for us to make personal application to them.—They ought not to wait to be thus called on. To avoid the inconvenience of keeping so many accounts, and the loss that is usually occasioned by non-paying subscribers, nearly all the Daily papers have adopted the plan of selling their city list to the carriers. We know not one indeed except the ' Virginian" that has not adopted this policy. We have some objection, however, to transferring our subscribers in this way, and prefer our present plan ; but must request those who know themselves to be indebted to us, to call and pay their bills. This is the proper plan and they need not wait to be called on. Those who neglect this duty need not be surprised if our carrier neglects to serve them with a paper

ANOTHER ATTEMPT AT GARROTING.—Geo Austin, a wounded and discharged soldier, was set upon on Monday night, as follows : He was passing from the corner of Main and Market street to the Orange House when he was interrogated by a man who asked where he was going, and who at the same time, offered to accompany him.—When the two reached the corner of Bridge and Lynch streets and turned into the latter, a man emerged from some dark corner and struck Austin a blow over the head, which owing to a thick wadded cap, did not fell him to the ground. Austin immediately gave the alarm, whilst his companion chided him saying that he "would raise the neighborhood." The Night Watch were not far off, and upon their arrival, the scoundrel who had struck the blow fled. His companion, who was believed to be an accomplice, was immediately taken into custody, brought before Mayor Branch yesterday, and sent on for further trial. He is a Marylander, and his name is Sullivan. Austin was on crutches, but this was not sufficient to protect him from the night marauders and murderers who infest this city.

WE have received sixty-one dollars and twenty cents, the nett proceeds of a sacred drama at Hat Creek, for the benefit of the 11th Va. Regiment. We will pay the same over to any body authorized to receive it.

FORTIFICATIONS OF RICHMOND.—Two Englishmen, direct from Richmond, passed through Fairfax Court-House on Thursday morning, on their way to Washington.—They called at General Sigel's headquarters and gave some valuable information. They stated that the city has within and around it a force of forty thousand, which is fast augmented. On all sides the city is well fortified. An attack is anticipated by its residents. Five superior gunboats have been finished there, and another is in the course of construction. They carry from five to sixteen guns each.—*Cincinnati Enquirer.*

IMPORTANT FROM N. CAROLINA.

The Raleigh *Progress* has been put in possession of very important news, by reliable authority, to the effect that nine steamers and four sailing vessels passed up the Chowan river on Monday night last, and on Tuesday night took on board, at Holly's Wharf, on the Chowan, 5,000 infantry, their destination being for Newbern to reinforce Foster. The *Progress* says :

The fleet left Holly's Wharf on Wednesday morning, and it is the impression of our informant that the design of Foster is to make a raid on the Wilmington Road at or near Rocky Mount, while the main force will make for Goldsboro, and take the W, & W. R. R. to Wilmington By the raid on the W. R. R. at Rocky Mount, reinforcements from Weldon and Petersburg would be cut off. Our informant had a conversation with a Yankee deserter who was in the advance company from Suffolk to Holly's Wharf, and who informed him that 5,000 infantry was destined to take the Wilmington Road at all hazards.

On their march (said the deserter) from Suffolk to Holly's Wharf, one company of artillery and one of cavalry acted as an advance guard, so afraid were they that some of Gen. Pryor's forces would attack them. After the infantry were embarked the artillery and cavalry returned to Suffolk.—The deserter said there were about 6000 men,recruits at Suffolk,(infantry) with four artillery and two cavalry companies. That there were only four fortifications around the town, and only two of them had any guns on them, and they only two pieces each. Our informant saw the steamers and vessel when they went up, and saw them leave with the troops on board.—Therefore the news is perfectly reliable and our authorities ought to act at once.

ADDRESS TO THE ARMY.

We publish this, morning, the beautiful address of Gen Lee to the army, after the battle at Fredericksburg. The Commanding General expresses the sentiment of the whole country.

HDQRS ARMY OF NORTHERN VA,
December 31, 1862.

GENERAL ORDERS,
No 138.

I, The General Commanding takes this occasion to express to the officers and soldiers of the army, his high appreciation of the fortitude, valor and devotion displayed by them, which, under the blessing of Almighty God, have added the victory of Fredericksburg to the long list of their triumphs.

An arduous march, performed with celerity under many disadvantages, exhibited the discipline and spirit of the troops, and their eagerness to confront the foe.

The immense army of the enemy completed its preparations for the attack without interruption, and gave battle in its own time, and on ground of its own selection.

It was encountered by less than twenty thousand of this brave army, and its columns, crushed and broken, hurled back at every point with such fearful slaughter, that escape from entire destruction became the boast of those who had advanced in full confidence of victory.

That this great result was achieved with a loss small in point of numbers only augments the admiration with which the Commanding General regards the prowess of the troops, and increases his gratitude to Him who hath given us the victory.

The war is not yet ended. The enemy is still numerous and strong, and the country demands of the army a renewal of its heroic efforts in her behalf. Nobly has it responded to her call in the past, and she will never appeal in vain to its courage and patriotism.

The signal manifestations of Divine mercy that have distinguished the eventful and glorious campaign of the year just closing, give assurance of hope that under the guidance of the same Almighty hand, the coming year will be no less fruitful of events that will ensure the safety, peace and happiness of our beloved country, and add new lustre to the already imperishable name of the Army of Northern Virginia.

R. E. LEE, General.

The following additional items are furnished from Northern sources respecting the battle at Murfreesboro'. It will be seen that they admit a loss of thirty thousand.

The fight was renewed on the 1st with great fury. There was heavy loss on both sides. Gen McCook fell back two miles before an overwhelming column. He rallied his troops, but was again driven back. At latest accounts he was five miles this side of the ground occupied in the morning. The battle continued until night, at which time the Confederates held their position. The Union loss is very heavy.

The total Federal loss in killed and wounded is estimated at thirty thousand.—The rebel loss is put down as much heavier. The Federals claim to have captured 700 prisoners.

The Herald of the 2d, contains nothing further in reference to the battle.

Gov Seymour was inaugurated on yesterday. He made no address, but spoke a few words, saying he would send in his message to the Legislature.

The Herald's dispatch from Louisville says that Rosencrans still holds his original position. Nothing further had been received from the army up to 3 o'clock on the 2d. General McCook is reported mortally wounded.

Lincoln issued his emancipation proclamation on the 1st. It is ridiculed by the Times. He advises the slaves to make no demonstration of violence except in "self defence."

LINCOLN'S PROCLAMATION.

We omit so much of this balderdash as includes quotations from that of the 22nd September, and subjoin all that is new as follows.

Now therefore, I, Abraham Lincoln, President of the United States, by virtue of the power in me vested as Commander-in Chief of the Army and Navy of the United States in time of actual armed rebellion against the authority and government of the United States, and a fit and necessary war measure for suppressing the said rebellion, do, on this the first day of January, in the year of our Lord one thousand eight hundred and sixty-three, and in accordance with my purpose so to do, publicly proclaim, for the full period of one hundred days from the day first above mentioned, order and designate as the States and parts of States wherein the people thereof respectively are this day in rebellion against the United States, the following, to wit:

Arkansas, Texas, Louisiana (except) the parishes of St Bernard, Plaquemines, Jefferson, St. James, Ascension, Assumption, Terrobone, Lafourche, St. Martin and Orleans, including the city of New Orleans, Mississippi, Alabama, Florida, Georgia; South Carolina, North Carolina and Virginia, (except the forty-eight counties designated as West Virginia, and also the counties of Berkeley, Accomac, Northampton, Elizabeth City, York, Princess Anne and Norfolk and Portsmouth,) which excepted parts are for the present left precisely as if the proclamation were not issued.

And by virtue of the power and for the purpose aforesaid, I do order and declare that all persons held as slaves within the said designated States and parts of said States, are, and henceforward shall be free; and that the Executive Government of the United States, including the military and naval authorities thereof, will recognize and maintain the freedom of said persons.

And I hereby enjoin upon the people so declared to be free to abstain from violence, unless in necessary self-defence, and I recommend to them that in all cases, when allowed, they labor faithfully for reasonable wages. And I further declare and make known that such persons, of suitable condition, will be received into the armed service of the United States, to garrison forts, positions, stations, and other places, and to man vessels of all sorts in the said service. And upon this act, sincerely believed to be an act of justice' warranted by the Constitution, upon military necessity, I invoke the considerate judgment of mankind and the gracious favor of Almighty God.

In witness whereof, I have hereunto set my hand and caused the seal of the United States to be affixed.

[L. S.] Done at the city of Washington, this the first day of January, in the year of our Lord one thousand eight hundred and sixty-three, and of the Independence of the United States of America the eighty-seventh.

ABRAHAM LINCOLN

By the President,
WM. H. SEWARD, Secretary of State.

BY TELEGRAPH.

LOSS OF THE MONITOR!

GOVERNOR SEYMOUR'S INAUGURAL.

Yankee Accounts of the Battle of Murfreesboro'.

A "HEART-RENDING" LOSS OF OFFICERS ADMITTED.

THE CHICAGO TIMES ADMITS THE JUSTICE OF PRESIDENT DAVIS' RECENT PROCLAMATION.

FOREIGN NEWS.

RUMORS OF INTERVENTION STILL RIFE.

PETERSBURG, Jan. 5th.

By flag of truce at City Point, it is ascertained that the Iron-Clad Gunboat, Monitor, foundered off Hatteras a few days since, and was carried down with her thirty souls.

Another account says, all on board perished.

The Galena narrowly escaped, she threw overboard her armament and ammunition. They were supposed to be on their way to Wilmington.

MOBILE, Jan. 4.

A special dispatch to the Advertiser and Register dated Grenada, the 2d, says :

The Arkansas Legislature has enacted that a fine of not less than five thousand, nor more than ten thousand dollars, and imprisonment in the penitentiary from five to ten years, shall be imposed upon parties caught trading with the yankees.

Hindman's scouts bring information of Grant's having sent six thousand troops from Holly Springs to Memphis. It was believed that a large portion of his force would join McClerand's expedition.

Blythe's cavalry drove the Yankees into their trenches at Memphis, and captured and brought off two hundred head of cattle.

Rosencranz wrote that he was about giving Bragg a terrible thrashing.

Our troops are elated at Gen. Bragg's success.

FREDERICKSBURG, Jan. 6.

The New York Herald of the 4th, and the Philadelphia Enquirer of the 5th have been received by flag of truce.

Gov Seymour was inaugurated on the 1st. The following is his inaugural :

I have solemnly sworn to protect the Constitution of the United States, with all its grants, restrictions, and guarantees,and will support it. I have sworn to support the Constitution of the State of New York with all of its powers and rights, and shall uphold it. I have sworn to observe the duties of the office of Governor of the State, and with your aid shall faithfully perform them. The constitution and laws must be for the guidance of my official conduct, and our protection and welfare.—The first law recorded for my observation is that discharging it, it shall be the duty of the Governor to maintain and defend the sovereignty and jurisdiction of the State. The most strict injunction of the constitution is that the Governor shall take care that the laws are faithfully executed, and so help me God they shall be.

I would not dwell on the present occasion on national affairs. Our position as a State has been happily attended to by my predecessor. My views upon the subject will be laid before the Legislature.

While knowing that his position gave him little control over national affairs, he ventured to trust that before the end of his term of service the country would be again great, glorious and united as it once was.

Seymour had ordered the Police Commissioners to appear before him to answer complaints for arbitrary arrests and imprisonment in violation of the Constitution.

The Chicago Times justifies President Davis's retaliatory Proclamation.

The Philadelphia telegraphic dispatches of the 3d say that telegraphic communication with Nashville has been destroyed.

Advices from Murfresboro state that the Federals are advancing, and that the Rebels are falling back across Stone River.—The Rebels were terribly repulsed on the left. The Rebel army at Richmond were furnishing reinforcements to the Rebels at Nashville.

Gen Rosencrans dispatches that the Rebels are whipped decidedly, and that the Federals were at Christianna, nine miles from Murfreesboro'. The dispatch says that the loss of Federal officers is heart-rendering.

On the 2nd, Rosencrans with the 4th U S Cavalry, attacked Wheeler's Cavalry, cut them to pieces and routed them. (What a lie !)

A dispatch from Cairo the 3d says that but one gunboat at Vicksburg, the Benton, engaged the fortifications, and lost the commander and several of the crew.

Banks' forces and Farragut's fleet were expected, but did not arrive.

Grant claims that Forrest and Van Dorn were badly whipped, with a loss of many prisoners and several pieces of artillery.—The rebel Col Napier and Col Deshey were captured.

A dispatch from Fayetteville, Ark, says the rebel papers captured at Van Buren admit the loss at Prarie Grove of 4,000. Gen Hindman's correspondence was captured.

The rebels are concentrating at Arkadelphia.

A correspondent of the Inquirer from the Army of the Potomac, says that on the night of the 2d, two Brigades recrossed the Rappahannock, six miles above Fredericksburg, scoured the country, and returned.

Butler had been received with complimentary demonstrations at Washington and other points.

Lincoln's proclamation was honored with salutes and other demonstrations at Pittsburg, Boston, and other places.

Thirty-eight Sioux Indians were executed on the 26th by Lincoln's instructions.

Banks' issued instructions on the 24th, under Lincoln's proclamation. He advises the slaves to remain on the plantations until their rights are definitely established.—Whatever benefit the government intends shall be secured to them.

In New York the 4th, gold advanced to 134½, and closed at 134¾. . Exchange 147½.

The Asia has arrived with Liverpool dates to the 20th ult.

Vague rumors were afloat that France had sent another note to England and Russia, showing the necessity of peaceful intervention in American affairs.

The London imes believes from the liberality shown towards Lancashire, that a clearer perception of the part displayed by England, during the war prevails in the North.

Schoolfield, M P, in a speech, asserted the right of the South to secede, and advocated recognition.

Bright eulogised the course of the North and predicted the future of the rebellion.—Nearly all of the London journals condemn Bright's speech.

A loan is spoken of in France to relieve the prevailing distress.

The London Times disparages Halleck's official report.

Edgefield Advertiser.

"WE WILL CLING TO THE PILLARS OF THE TEMPLE OF OUR LIBERTIES, AND IF IT MUST FALL, WE WILL PERISH AMIDST THE RUINS."

SIMKINS, DURISOE & CO., Proprietors. EDGEFIELD, S. C., JANUARY 15, 1863. VOLUME XXVIII.---No. 2

The Late Battles in North Carolina.

"Personne," the able and popular correspondent of the Charleston Courier, furnishes that journal with an interesting narrative of the events connected with the war, which have lately occurred in North Carolina. We condense his statement as follows:

His first letter is dated Kinston, N. C., Dec. 20th. He says that the noble deeds of the late campaign redound as much to the honor of the Palmetto State, as any that have yet marked the annals of this war.

The object of Gen. Foster's advance from Newbern was the capture of Goldsboro', and to rebuild the line of railroad between these places, which had been destroyed by General Evans. The information of the advance did not reach us in time, and consequently our forces were divided. The enemy's movements were, therefore, uninterrupted, until Friday, Dec. 17th, when they reached Trenton. Here, Major Nethercutt, of the Partizan Rangers, was reinforced by Col. Baker, with two companies of cavalry; but, owing to some lack of prudence, or knowledge of the country, our troops found themselves suddenly surrounded by the enemy. They cut their way out, however, Colonel Baker being wounded in the ear, in this skirmish; but they were so scattered and disorganized as to be of no further use during the events that followed.

Gen. Evans was, at that time, at Greenville; but he arrived early on Saturday morning. During his absence, the chief command was assumed by Col. Radcliffe, a graduate of the Citadel Academy, of Charleston, S. C.

On Friday night, our first line of defence was formed by Col. Radcliffe, on what is known as the Southwest Creek, and which, after running nearly parallel with the Neuse river, empties into it three miles below Kinston. This line consisted of the 17th, 22d, and 23d South Carolina Regiments, and the 61st North Carolina. The artillery consisted of Bunting's Battery, North Carolina; Starr's Battery, North Carolina; and Bryce's Battery, of South Carolina—the whole force numbering less than 1,700 men, with six pieces of artillery, and not cavalry enough to act as couriers; while the enemy's force numbered 20,000 [illegible] 2,000 cavalry, and 42 pieces of artillery, with all the necessary supplies.

On Saturday morning, the fight was opened—the enemy evidently feeling our strength; a series of heavy skirmishes ensued, the brunt of which was borne by the 17th South Carolina and 61st North Carolina. The pressure of the Abolitionists was so great that our troops had to fall back from Hines' Mill to a position two miles nearer town, and subsequently to a mile and a quarter nearer the town, where we held the enemy in check until dark. The Holcombe Legion, in the meantime, and afterwards Col. Mallet's North Carolina Battalion, 600 strong, had arrived, making our whole force 2,014 bayonets!

It was thought during Saturday night that the enemy were retreating, but Sunday morning found them ready for the fight again, which commenced by about nine o'clock, A. M.

The discovery of the enemy's position here was due to a woman, who signalled our troops by waving a white handkerchief or other object to our troops, and soon after disappeared, and was not seen again.

The battle raged with great fury until 1 o'clock P. M., when it became necessary for our troops to fall back, which was accordingly done between 1 and 2 o'clock P. M.

All the regiments crossed the bridge safely, except the Holcombe Legion, which did not reach it until the flames which had been applied to it burst forth. This created some confusion, and caused the capture of our men as follows: Holcombe Legion, 27; 22d South Carolina, 91; 17th South Carolina, 8; 23d South Carolina, 12; making a total of 138 South Carolinians; and between Mallet's Battalion and the 61st North Carolina, some 252 others were taken prisoners.

These men have been paroled and sent to Raleigh to await an exchange.

General Evans' object was, that, to make the Neuse River his second line of defense; but in this he failed, as the enemy extinguished the flames of the burning bridge, and kept up a sharp fire along the banks of the stream which created some confusion in our ranks, and caused a further retreat. Capt. Bunting lost two of his pieces in the retreat, his horses having been killed in the battle.

Our loss in the brigade here was—killed, 16; wounded, 88; total 104.

Gen. Evans retired about three quarters of a mile from the town of Kinston, where he formed in line of battle, on a slight elevation called Washington Hill, the enemy's line of battle occupying the town.

We here give Personne's account of the demand for the surrender of the town in his own words:

A DEMAND FOR SURRENDER.

About three o'clock, while Gen. Evans was at his headquarters in the large mansion which gives the Hill its name, a body of six hundred horsemen came dashing up the streets as if they intended to carry the place by storm, but suddenly reaching a corner they wheeled, and, as quickly as they had appeared, disappeared from sight leaving behind three individuals on horseback, who now rode slowly forward.

Gen. Evans met them at the foot of the hill, and then ensued that colloquy, the result of which has been so wrongly given to the world in the sententious reply of General Evans, "Go to h—ll!"

The true history of this interview—and I am glad to be the medium of correcting a false impression that has been allowed to emanate most carelessly—is as follows:

The conversation was commenced by one of the officers in the following words:

Officer. "I understand, sir, (bowing) that some of your troops have indicated a wish to surrender, and I have been detached to receive the surrender, by Gen. Foster. I presume, sir, that you are Gen. Evans?

Gen. E. "I am—who are you, sir?"

Officer. (With a supercilious air) "I am Col. Potter, sir, of the 1st North Carolina Volunteers, and attached to the staff of General Foster."

Gen. E. "I am not aware, sir, that any of my troops desire to surrender, nor do I believe there is a South Carolinian under my command who has any intention of doing so. Give my compliments to Gen. Foster, and tell him he knows Gen. Evans too well to suppose that he will ever surrender."

Col. P. "Then you intend to renew the battle."

Gen. E. "Yes, sir—to fight now and here!"

Col. P.—"Do you mean to begin at once, sir, or do you wish time to remove your wounded?"

Gen. E.—"Well, sir, you may say to Gen. Foster that if he will give me an hour and a half to remove the women and children from the town, I shall then be ready for him."

The North Carolina Yankee then made a wave of the hand which he doubtless intended as a polite mode of saying farewell, but which a by stander remarked to me as much resembled the fall of a pump handle as anything else; and, accompanied by his brother officer and courier, turned and rode on. His manner was anything but that of a gentleman, while that of Gen. Evans was all that a proper regard for courtesy could demand.

The most ridiculous part of the affair is that the flag of truce was a pair of white drawers, which flopped about on a bayonet in a decided state of looseness, and excited the risibilities of the spectators to a pitch of re[illegible] Whether the Yankees intended it as an insult, or whether it was an inferential admission that it was a *drawn* game, I have no means of knowing, but one thing is certain, though Gen. Evans has once surrendered to a crinoline skirt, the breeches do not walk the earth or fly the air before which he will bow in homage as a captive.

While the battle was going on around Kinston, Poole's battalion of heavy artillery, stationed at a small fortification on the Neuse river, 3 miles below the town, was engaged with 9 of the enemy's gunboats. We had to abandon the works destroying the pieces. As the gunboats passed down the river, Captain Whitford's Partizan Rangers fired into the rear boats, sweeping their decks, and, it is thought, killing and wounding some 70 or 80.

Discovering the overpowering nature of the enemy's force, General Evans retreated to Falling Creek, 6 miles distant, on the road to Goldsboro', where he arrived at sundown, and was reinforced by the 44th, 47th and 11th North Carolina Regiments.

On Monday, Gen. Evans sent Gen. Robertson, with his 600 dismounted cavalry, Leaventhorpe's 11th North Carolina regiment, and a section of Moore's Battalion of North Carolina Artillery, to contest the enemy's crossing of the Neuse river at Whitehall, while the 44th North Carolina regiment was sent to Thompson's Bridge, seven miles east of Goldsboro', for the same purpose. The fight at Whitehall was conducted generally with artillery, and across the river. Our loss was only 10 killed and 42 wounded. During the skirmish, we burned the bridge at Whitehall and Thompson's, and foiled the enemy, who withdrew from the combat and resumed his march up the river.

When next heard from, the enemy were within six miles of Goldsboro'. Gen. Smith, the Commander-in-Chief, had arrived there, but found everything unprepared for the occasion. Providence, however came to our aid, and the difficulties were surmounted.

At this place, another battle occurred, during which the railroad bridge was burned by some six Abolitionists—five of whom were killed—the sixth—said to be Lieut. Duncan Graham, of Va., a son of Gen. Graham, of the Abolition army, succeeded in making his escape.

The battle lasted until nightfall, both parties holding their positions, when the enemy, under cover of the darkness, retreated to Newbern.

"Personne" thinks that General Foster will renew the attack. He thinks, also, that the credit of the campaign belongs to General Evans; the blame, if any, must rest elsewhere.

The renegades in the neighborhood of the army are known as "Buffaloes."

The occupation of Kinston by the enemy was not marked by any acts of Vandalism, except the burning of three dwelling houses and stores on Main street, for which act, Gen. Foster ordered the incendiary to be arrested and shot.

"The scenes during the fight here are said to have been distressing. The enemy's balls were flying through the town in every direction, piercing the houses and racing through the streets. Cotton was burning in piles, while women and children were wildly flying to the suburbs for their lives.

"In some instances, the sick were taken from their bed *en dishabille*, and tottered along, supported by their relatives. Afterwards, they were found lying by the side of the road so exhausted that they could go no further. One of our officers on the retreat through the town, found just such a group as I have described—a young husband dying with consumption, pale and so feeble he could not stand, and trembling with nervous excitement, a wife of not more than two and twenty years by his side, supporting his head, and a little child. All tears and supplication, the noble woman appealed to the officer for help, and with an oloquence that none but a woman can use, made him dismount, assist her husband to the saddle, and then walking by the side of the horse, supported him in his seat until he reached a place of safety. Such is war. God save us from its repetition."

"Personne" concludes his highly interesting series of letters as follows:

"Though we are scarred with wounds, and then with toil, the South yet stands firm and erect. And "if we have lost the Missi-sippi, that was her girdle, or that splendid city that was the first jewel of the crown she wore on the last feast of the Christian year, we remain undaunted, as then, stronger for our losses, stripped for combat, trained to skill in arms by their employment, and taught by the discipline of three great campaigns, compressed into the brief space of twelve swiftly-passed months. Our adversary, on the contrary, distracted in spirit, pants with distress and streams with blood. Defeated at every point, he staggers unders the blows that have at last reached a vital part, and is now in the throes of an agonized desperation. God only knows what will be the result. Never before has His hand been laid in anger so heavily upon the Northern people, and yet it may be but the precursor of a more bitter end.

"On our part we have every reason to be encouraged. Peaceful influences are becoming stronger in their concentration every day. The Republican element of the North is disintegrated beyond redemption [illegible] enlarged. Their public debt is a nightmare, and the incubus increases at the rate of three millions a day. Private, like public expenses, are on the increase everywhere. Every effort of the Abolitionists has proven a practical failure, distraction is in their councils, and except in the Western country, where they have secured a temporary advantage, the future promises to be as barren of results as the past. They have no sympathy abroad and no help at home. The friends of peace are becoming bolder, and in the defiant attitude we still maintain around our front, there is a lesson of caution being taught that will make Northern leaders ponder well ere they again order their armies to advance.

"Let us hope that in this lull wisdom may take possession of the hearts of our enemies. We may then confidently hope that when the snows of winter have melted away, the green grass and blooming flowers of spring will bring with them the peace for which we pray.

All quiet in front. PERSONNE."

SCENE AT HOTEL.—(Time, midnight) Act 1st. *Room in 3d Story. Dramatis Personnæ.* Parties arriving by train. Belated traveller—just arrived—to luckly traveller snugly ensconced in bed and not anxious for company:

Colloquy.—First Traveller—"Is the bed you're in occupied, stranger?"

Voice from beneath the quilts—"Yes, sir."

First Traveller—"How many in it?"

Second Traveller—"About 15,000 I reckon, from the way they "*crawl*." Exit first traveller with baggage.—Chattanooga Rebel.

At Sharpsburg Gen. Lee hailed one of the many stragglers, and inquired:

"Where are you going, sir?"

"Goin' to the rear."

"What are you going to the rear for?"

"Well, I've been stung by a bung, and I'm what they call demoralized."

This was enough. Gen. Lee had not the heart to say more to an innocent who had been "stung by a bung"—meaning perhaps that he had been stunned by a bomb.—Cor. Charleston Mercury.

The New York Post says there is probably surplus corn enough in the State of Illinois to feed the destitute operatives of Lancashire, England, until the cotton famine is over. As long, however, as the Mississippi river is closed by Confederate batteries, there is little prospect of England's starving millions getting their supplies from that section. Although we pity, we cannot aid—for permanent relief to them would be a great detriment to us. England has taken the position that she will not do what is right in this great struggle until she is forced to—and unless her suffering operatives are provided for in some manner, she cannot sit idly by and permit this war to continue many months longer.

We have heard of a good many substitutes for coffee, and copperas, and such like, but the best substitute for a man who wants to be considered a Southern soldier, but does not want to be hurt—is an office in the Quartermaster's Department.—Chattanooga Rebel.

From the Southern Guardian.

The Late General Gregg.

We publish below two letters which will be read with mournful interest by our people, and the entire people of the South. The first was addressed by Gen. Lee to Gov. Pickens, and the second is from Gov. Pickens to the surviving sisters of Gen. Gregg, covering that of Gen. Lee to him. We have solicited copies for publication, feeling that they but express the universal and just sentiments of the Army and the Confederacy. The language they employ is not mere idle eulogy, uttered as a matter of course. It is well considered and conscientious, and however laudatory, true to the very letter. It is the voice of history, hastening to utter its verdict of approval, to pay its tribute of admiration, and to record its undying sorrow for accomplishments, and virtues, and services so rare and self-sacrificing:

CAMP NEAR FREDERICKSBURG, VA., 18th December, 1862.

To His Excellency, F. W. Pickens, Governor of South Carolina.

SIR; While South Carolina is mourning the loss of her gallant and distinguished son, General Maxcy Gregg, permit me to join in your sorrow for his death.

From my first acquaintance, when you sent him with his gallant regiment to the defence of our frontier in Virginia, I have admired his disinterested patriotism and his unselfish devotion.

He has always been at the post of duty and of danger, and his services in this army have been of inestimable value, and his loss is deeply lamented. In its greatest triumphs and its bloodiest battles, he has borne a distinguished part.

On the Chickahominy, on the plains of Manassas, at Harper's Ferry, Sharpsburg, and Shepherdstown, he led his brigade with distinguished skill and dauntless valor.

On the wooded heights of Fredericksburg he fell in front of his brigade in close conflict with the advancing foe. The death of such a man is a costly sacrifice, for it is to men of his high integrity and commanding intellect that the country must look, to give character to her councils, that she may be respected [illegible] his State will proudly read the history of his deeds, may many be found to imitate his noble example.

I have the honor to be, with great respect, your obedient servant,

R. E. LEE, General.

EDGEWOOD, December 28, 1862.

My Dear Miss Gregg: I deeply regret it was impossible for me to remain in Columbia to attend to your illustrious brother's remains. My house-rent was up, and I had everything packed. I went to the depot on Thursday evening, the 18th, expecting to meet him then, but he did not arrive, and I was obliged to leave in the morning.

I enclose you the within from General Lee, received yesterday. It is a touching tribute to his memory from the first captain of the age. In my opinion, Gen. Lee has not a superior as a general, and as a Christian gentleman, his character is spotless. I therefore think his tribute to your brother's worth, and noble bearing as a hero and a commander, is of the highest value to his friends. I need not say how cordially I join in everything said by General Lee. But all this can never fill the aching void in a sister's heart. When I received the telegram of his death, I felt as though I had indeed lost a brother. True, I never had a brother, but your brother was near and dear to me, and his death went deep into my heart, for I called him to my side, at, perhaps, the most trying period of my life. On the 27th of December, 1860, I had ordered Fort Moultrie and Castle Pinckney taken by force, and there was intense excitement in Charleston. It was then extremely doubtful if Georgia or Alabama would secede. I felt the deepest responsibility, and on the night of [illegible] December, 1860, I sent for your brother, who was then a member of the Convention. [illegible] him it was clear we would have to fight, and I wanted him to command a picked regiment for immediate action, and authorized him to pick his companies in the State, and order them down. I told him that I relied on him to go through with me, no matter how desperate the work. I never shall forget his countenance. It lit up with the joy of battle, and he bowed in his graceful and winning manner, and replied with a smile, which was always so sweet in him, "It shall be done;" "I am ready to obey any order." He was off in a moment, and telegraphed for his companies. With the exception of the city troops I had ordered into the Forts and on the Islands, his regiment was the first in the trenches, and such a regiment no man ever brought into service. It was composed, for the most part, from men in high social position, and intelligence—all eager to defend their State, let the consequences be what they might. They did great service.

You see General Lee alludes to my sending your brother to Virginia at the head of the first regiment that went forth to defend the mother of States. Soon after the capture of Sumter, I telegraphed the Governor of Virginia, and offered to put two thousand men, in forty-eight hours, into Norfolk, and to take the navy yard, but it was declined then. Soon after the navy yard was burnt, and the Governor telegraphed I could send the troops. I immediately started your brother at the head of his regiment, or the largest portion of it, and he was the first man to unfurl the Palmetto banner in front of the capital of Virginia. He gloried in marching to fight over the tomb of Washington. Soon after Colonel Kershaw's regiment was sent on to join him, and they were both stationed under the command of Gen. Bonham up near Alexandria, and occupied for a long time the very front rampart beneath whose battlements the great contests for Southern existence and independence were to be fought. When Alexandria was evacuated and the Northern rabble took possession of the city, I immediately telegraphed Gen. Bonham that no South Carolina troops were to retreat. Your brother, with his command, met the enemy near by at Vienna, and gave them a signal defeat. He has since been in nearly all the bloody battles of Virginia, and at last gallantly fell amid the very front battalions, nearest the enemy, where he had been from the very first days of our struggle. His acts throughout are now known, and I thought it but right and proper to mention the incidents I have, at the commencement of his brilliant career, because, perhaps, I am the only man acquainted fully with the circumstances.

You have lost a pure and affectionate brother, and the country has lost a hero and a statesman. His portrait will stand out on the canvass of history as one of the bravest, truest, and most heroic patriots that ever drew his sword for his country's wrongs, and long will the people of South Carolina plant flowers around his grave, and weave garlands of love to throw over his tomb Let the sublime heroism of his last words sustain and console your sad hearts. He fell where he would have chosen to meet death—in the front rank, pressing hard on the enemy, surrounded by the troops he loved so well, with the shout of victory in his ear.—Peace be to his noble ashes! and may a merciful God deal kindly and tenderly with his sisters, and guide and sustain them through the sorrows of this dark and troubled world.

I have the honor to be, with great regard, yours, very truly, F. W. PICKENS.

An Unparalleled Outrage.

Two depositions which detail circumstances of one of the most infamous acts which our truly diabolical foe has ever perpetrated—have been sent to the War Department in Richmond. They were forwarded by our Generals in North Carolina, where the crime was committed. The deponents are Caswell Woods and Elizabeth his wife, of the county of Craven. Mr. Woods is certified to by General Evans as being a "respectable citizen and loyal to our cause, which seems to be the only causes of the fiendish outrages by the savages." It is also stated that he is a class leader in the Methodist Church. It is due to the civilized world and to outraged humanity, that the facts stated in these depositions should be known, and yet all of them are too obscene to be fully described in a newspaper. The house of these quiet and aged citizens was visited on the night of the 2d of October, by two Yankee troopers armed with pistols and sabres. Mr. Wood had retired to bed. We copy from the Richmond Enquirer a portion of his deposition:

"I came down stairs in my night clothes. The front door had been burst open. One of the men had rode into the house on his horse. The other walked in. The one on the horse, who appeared to be an officer, commenced cussing me, and asked me where I was two days before. When I told him I was home, he said 'You lie, for you shot at me.'" Upon this pretence, they cut the cord from a bed in the room, said they would hang him, but finally tied him, took him out of the house and lashed him to a tree, with the threat of instant death if he made any outcry or attempted to get loose. They returned to the house and locked the door after them, and the old man had the inexpressible agony of listening, for the rest of the night to the screams and doleful lamentations of his wife and daughter.

The statement made by Mrs. Wood in her deposition of what passed inside, is truly heart-rending. The unparalleled villains made the poor helpless women not merely the victims of their brutal lust, but accompanied the outrage, which is worse than death, with circumstances that mark them as the most abandoned of villains. With pistol in hand and with threat of instant death, the deponent was required by one of the beasts to divest herself of every particle of clothing. But this was almost Christian treatment compared with other acts which may not be related. While such were her own sufferings, the shrieks of her daughter in another room told that hers was a similar fate. About sunrise the next morning the human devils departed.

It is with pain that such a sketch as the above is admitted into our columns. But it is due to our own people and to the world that the villainies of our enemies should be known. The Enquirer in some remarks about the depositions says:

"The depositions have been laid before us with the suggestion endorsed thereon by the Adjutant General, "that so much of this account as is not too foul for publication should be given to the public, through the press, in order that the righteous indignation of our people, our Generals and our armies, may, under the Providence of God, visit a just retribution upon an enemy so fiendlike." Concurring in the propriety of the suggestion, we have acted accordingly.

We are happy to say that General Gustavus W. Smith has directed every effort to be made to ascertain the names of the parties, and to "demand their delivery for trial and punishment." We hope copies of the depositions have been forwarded to the authorities of the enemy. Surely there are some, even among them, who would be horrified by such conduct. The vengeance of Heaven must light upon them and their cause!

The Neutrality of the English People as Explained by a Yankee Correspondent.

The London correspondent of the New York Times, under date of November 21st, writes:

The report that Mr. Secretary Seward has written to Mr. Adams, blaming the British Government for its complicity in the fitting out of the Alabama, caused a small flutter and considerable indignation on the Stock Exchange. The English have wished to be perfectly neutral as between the two belligerents. They recognized the Confederates as belligerents in the beginning in their own interests, expressly that they might sell arms, ammunition and ships to both parties, and their only regret is that the blockade has prevented them from carrying out their intentions of neutrality with perfect impartiality. There is a keen regret felt in every Englishman's pocket that they have been compelled to be unfair to the South, and that they have sold ten times as much contraband of war to the North as they could to the Confederates. Their consciences have pricked them to that degree, for this compulsory partiality, that they are now fitting out a fleet of the fastest steamers that ever crossed the ocean, expressly to run the blockade with munitions of war. These are small, sharp steamers, of light draft, made of steel plates, all paddle wheel and funnel, that will run off twenty knots an hour, and that no blockading vessel can think of taking. The success and impunity of the Alabama will also lead to the fitting out and arming of a dozen more, if the war continues; and the answer to any complaint will be, [illegible] Did not President Pierce assert the right of Americans to build ships and sell ammunition to both parties? How, then, can you complain of us for doing what you did and justified?"

"Besides, you have bought artillery, powder, everything you wanted, in England, without hindrance. Why should not the Confederates do the same? You call Capt. Semmes a pirate; but he is no more a pirate than Stonewall Jackson is a brigand; and you treat him according to the rules of war. A Confederate naval officer is entitled to the same consideration as one in the land service. You take Confederate and neutral contraband cargoes wherever you can. Why may not the Confederates do the same?"

This is the answer that will be given to Mr. Adams. If Captain Semmes has had the misfortune to capture a British ship in mistake, his Government will pay for it.

The distress in Lancashire deepens. The bounty of a nation will be exhausted in palliating the suffering. Surat cotton comes, but it cannot be worked to profit. The English are beginning to see that Lancashire is ruined and the cotton trade itself, unless they can get cotton from America. Hence the protest against the war—hence the protest against the Abolition policy of the Government. England is less Abolition than she was a year ago. Never was any measure more universally denounced than that of the proclamation. The freedom of the slaves in America is the ruin of the manufacturing interest in England. Lancashire has built up and extended slavery. Cut off from that it is ruined. Sentiment is a very fine thing, but Englishmen know the beauties of bread, of beef, and beer. They blubbered freely over Uncle Tom's Cabin, but never bought one bale of cotton the less, and are ready to take all they can get. Manchester is the centre, heart, and soul of American slavery. Manchester has grown rich on its profits, and participates in its reverses. Can you expect sympathy from Manchester in an effort to destroy it? If so, you reckon without your host.

THE GEORGIA TROOPS.—A letter from General Early awards great praise to the Georgia troops for their noble conduct in the battle of Fredericksburg. Much of the success of our arms on that stubbornly contested field is due to the valor of Lawton's brigade. The Lynchburg Virginian, also, pays this brigade a high compliment. For some reason or another—probably without any good reason—the command has hitherto been under a cloud, and the present is a favorable opportunity for placing it in a position which it has a right to occupy. Troops that can win the approbation of General Early for coolness and courage on the field of battle, are entitled to it; no officer we have possesses more of these qualities or more heartily despises the lack of them in others; and none are more honest to award praise where it is deserved. All honor to the gallant Georgians.—Richmond Whig.

The very latest Paris fashions state that bonnets will be still worn high in the front, but much less exaggerated. The principal ornaments being feathers for dress bonnets, or a simple trimming of ribbon or lace.

Restricting Cotton.

We have repeatedly and earnestly urged a limitation in Cotton planting during the war, not so much for any political or commercial or international considerations, supposed to be connected with Cotton, as from the evident necessity of large provision crops. To secure this result pending the war, and in view of the large proportion of agricultural producers diverted from the farm to the army, it will be necessary to limit Cotton to a very small planting.

We have doubts whether the desired end can be attained by legislation alone, and it may be doubted whether a besetting sin or error of our day and generation is not undue and excessive reliance on legislation.

The observant reader will find our statute books and our records of legislation in State or City burdened with proper and wholesome laws, which are practically obsolete or virtually abrogated by indifference or neglect in administration. There are many things which patriots and good citizens and even honest men must do or avoid, which cannot be enforced or prevented by law. We look hopefully to the spirit, intelligence and enlightened interest of the planters and farmers for a regulation of the crops, with more confidence than to legislation. Georgia has attempted legislation, as Georgia seems now to believe fully in law as a remedy for every evil.

Under Governor Brown's administration, it seems an accepted fact that law, or even a Governor's act, can stop or seize or arrest or start or promote anything—except the running of interest, the working of yeast, and the course of the Calendar.

For the information of those who desire to see what has been attempted, we present the declaratory clause of the Georgia Act "to prevent and punish the planting and cultivating, in the State of Georgia, over a certain quantity of land in Cotton, during the war with the Abolitionists:"

SECTION I. *The General Assembly do enact,* That it shall not be lawful for any person or persons, whether residing in this State or not, to plant and cultivate in any county in this State, by themselves, their agents or employees, or allow the same to be done, a [illegible] than three (3) acres for each hand owned or employed by them between the ages of fifteen and fifty-five; and when said person and persons may own or employ hands over fifty-five years of age and under sixty five, or over twelve years of age and under fifteen, two of said hands shall be counted as one hand, and therefore said persons or persons may plant and cultivate three acres of land in Cotton, and no more, for every two of said hands so owned and employed by them.

The other Sections prescribe the penalties ($500 for each acre in excess) and the modes of procedure.—Charleston Courier.

The Cincinnati Enquirer talks very plainly about the McNeil massacre in St. Louis. It says that "there is hardly its parallel to be found in the whole annals of military history. It is a foul disgrace upon the American flag and upon the American name. No one who loves his country and desires her to have a favorable record in history, but will not cry for justice upon this wretch who has inflicted such a stain upon her. It should be remembered that this is a civilized war, and it has always been claimed that we in the North are civilized beings; but the future historian who records the cool and deliberate murder of those ten men, and as far as the world has any knowledge, innocent men, will have a big task on his hands to reconcile the deed with the manners and customs of civilization."

SAD RESULT OF A RUNAWAY MARRIAGE.—The New York correspondent of the Philadelphia *Inquirer* writes:

A few years ago the marriage of Miss Boker, a young, beautiful, and accomplished lady, with her father's coachman, John Dean, set all the scandal mongers in Gotham on end. A sad *addendum* to the "strange, eventful history" has now to be added. After the marriage, the couple, notwithstanding their different "bringing up," lived happily enough together, in a small cottage over in Williamsburg. The husband obtained an office in the custom house, and saved money enough to open a public house at the foot of Grand street Williamsburg. But alas! for John Dean, he could not keep a hotel. It said "he was his own best customer," and as a natural result he commenced treating his wife harshly. In a short time all their money was spent, and with poverty coming in at the door, love, as usual, flew out of the window. John beat and abused his wife, but all this she put up with until starvation stared her in the face, when she was compelled to ask admission into the almshouse. The petition was granted, and the fashionable, elegant, and accomplished belle of the Fifth Avenue—a few years ago—is now the associate of beggars and paupers.

LATEST FROM ETHIOPIA.—"Say Pomp, a 'liable darkey tell me just now dat Jeff. Davis 'gwine to taliate 'bout the President's proclamation—he gwine to declare all de niggers in the Norf States slaves.

Pomp—"Bress us all!"

RICH.—A dispatch from North Carolina states that a negro challenged Col. Wickes of a New York regiment to a duel, and sent a a white man as second. The latter, Wickes refused, and resigned in disgust.

The Tri-Weekly Mercury.

CITY PAPER—TEN DOLLARS PER ANNUM, PAYABLE HALF-YEARLY IN ADVANCE.

VINDICE NULLO
SPONTE SUA SINE LEGE FIDES RECTUMQUE COLENTUR.

COUNTRY PAPER—THRICE A WEEK—FIVE DOLLARS PER ANNUM, IN ADVANCE.

VOLUME LXXXII. CHARLESTON, S. C., THURSDAY, JANUARY 15, 1863. NUMBER 11,655

THE BATTLE AT VICKSBURG.

The Vicksburg *Whig* gives some interesting details of the battle of Chickasaw Bayou. We copy the following:

Some of the Abolition prisoners state that the 28th Louisiana Regiment, in the engagement of Sunday, the 28th ult., with Blair's brigade, killed and wounded upwards of four hundred of the enemy. On Monday, Colonel Thomas was placed by General Lee in charge of a brigade on his left, opposite the point where the enemy attempted to throw across a pontoon bridge. Four companies of the 42d Georgia, and two of the 28th Louisiana, posted on a mound commanding the position, served to turn the enemy at this point; the remainder of the 42d Georgia and 28th Louisiana were advanced to the right to meet a force sent to turn General Lee's flank. The enemy, advancing in solid column for this purpose, were repulsed with considerable slaughter, thus contributing greatly to securing a complete victory. We were in error when we stated that the 42d Georgia lost most men—the 28th lost most men, as they were most frequently engaged. The list we published was for Sunday, the 28th ult., only. On that day they lost forty killed, wounded and missing. Colonel Thomas and the regiment were complimented on the field by General Lee, for gallant conduct.

Companies A and B, of Major Ward's Artillery Battalion, took part in the fights, and are deserving of notice. They arrived here on Friday, and were ordered to the battle field immediately. On Sunday afternoon Company A, under the command of Major Ward, took position at the foot of the hill, in front of General Barton's brigade, and opened upon a battery of the enemy. They were under fire for some two hours, and behaved well. No one was hurt but Major Ward, who received a slight wound on the side of the head. They were assisted in silencing the battery by Lieut. Stowers, of Company B, in charge of three siege guns, on the crest of the hill. At night one section of Company A, in charge of Lieut. Tarleton, went up the lines of General Lee, and were all day Monday in the hottest of the fight. A shell exploded one of their caisons, killing Captain Hamilton, of General Lee's staff, a most excellent officer. He had just rode up to deliver an order to Lieutenant Tarleton. They shot away all their ammunition twice during the day.

Gen. S. D. Lee, who was in command, proved himself capable to lead and worthy of our trust in every way. The soldiers had perfect confidence in him, and felt sanguine that under him victory would be theirs. He was always among them, and wherever the iron hail was falling thickest, there was Lee, noting the progress of the contest, and encouraging his men. We thank President Davis for sending him to Vicksburg. Although we have not seen much of him, we are satisfied he will prove himself in every way worthy of the President's flattering eulogium.

WOMAN AND THE WAR.

What a beautiful tribute to the women of the South was that paid by Bishop ELLIOTT, in his recent sermon at Savannah. Said he:

"The attitude of woman is sublime. Bearing all the sacrifices of which I have just spoken, she is moreover called upon to suffer in her affections, to be wounded and smitten where she feels deepest and more enduringly. Man goes to the battlefield, but woman sends him there, even though her heart-strings tremble while she gives the farewell kiss and the farewell blessing. Man is supported by the necessity of movement, by the excitement of action, by the hope of honor, by the glory of conquest. Woman remains at home to suffer, to bear the cruel torture of suspense, to tremble when the battle has been fought and the news of the slaughter is flashing over the electric wire, to know that defeat will cover her with dishonor and her little ones with ruin, to learn that the husband she doated upon, the son whom she cherished in her bosom, and upon whom she never let the wind blow too rudely, the brother with whom she sported through all her happy days of childhood, the lover to whom her early vows were plighted, has died upon some distant battlefield, and lies there a mangled corpse, unknown and uncared for, never to be seen again, even in death. On those fearful lists of the wounded and the dead! How carelessly we pass them over, unless our own loved ones happen to be linked with them in military association, and yet each name in that roll of slaughter, carries a fatal pang to some woman's heart—some noble, devoted woman's heart. But she bears it all, and bows submissively to the stroke. He died for the cause. He perished for his country. I would not have it otherwise, but I should like to have given the dying boy my blessing, the expiring husband my last kiss of affection, the bleeding lover the comfort of knowing that I kneeled beside him."

BUTLER TO COMMAND THE ATTACK ON CHARLESTON.—A correspondent of the New York *Post* writes:

The Secessionists of Washington boast that the Government has already quailed before the threats of the rebel Jeff. Davis. They claim that the supersedure of Butler was caused partially by the demands of the rebel Government, which have been continually urged upon Mr. Lincoln since last summer. Butler, they say, has been occupied to oppose Jeff. Davis, and they point to the fact that Gen. Banks at once stopped proceedings under the Confiscation Act as soon as he arrived in New Orleans, these proceedings being counted by the rebels as the most offensive of any under Butler's administration. Of course, these boasts of the Secessionists are ridiculous. It is much more probable that the change in the command of the Government troops in Louisiana was made because of a vexatious diplomatic quarrel with the French Government.

The complaints of Louis Napoleon have been contentious, and indeed of such an insolent character, that more than one member of the Cabinet is in favor of taking a bold stand upon our rights, refusing any further attempts to pacify a man who seems bent on a quarrel with us. It is rumored here that Gen. Butler will soon have command of an expedition to Charleston, and this is not improbable, for the Government will hardly lay aside so successful a General as he has been. The President is known to be well affected towards the General, and that would hardly be the case if he were to be removed to private life.

The Charleston expedition was alluded to in this correspondence long ago, as if it were about to sail from New York. Such was at that time the intention of the Government, but for sufficient reasons it was postponed. There is little doubt that an attempt will be made to take Charleston within a few weeks, and Gen. Butler will make an excellent commander of the land forces engaged in the expedition, especially as he has the prestige of success in such undertakings. Baltimore and New Orleans are already inscribed on his flag, and if he can add the name of Charleston, it will be enough honor for one man to win in this war.

BRIGADIER GENERAL STEPHEN D. LEE.—This officer, who has been but a short time with us, is winning golden opinions from all who have seen anything of him since his arrival. He appears to be emphatically "the right man in the right place." From what little we have seen of him, we must say we are of the opinion he is an officer of industry and ability—a man who devotes his whole time and energies to the cause and to the health and comfort of his command. We are pleased with his plain, free and easy manner—his unaffectedness and want of that circumlocution which is so frequently found in our army. Gen. Lee is a native of South Carolina, and graduated at the West Point Military Academy in class of 1854. He entered the 4th Artillery of the United States Army as 2d Lieutenant, and was subsequently appointed 1st Lieutenant, and afterwards Regimental Quartermaster of the same regiment. In February, 1861, he bid adieu to the Yankees, and was commissioned a Captain in the South Carolina Army on the 5th of March. At the time of taking Fort Sumter he was on Gen. Beauregard's staff. We next find him commanding a light artillery battery in Hampton's Legion in Virginia. In November he was promoted Major; in June, 1862, Lieut. Colonel; in July, Colonel of Artillery, and in November he was honored with the appointment of Brigadier General for his meritorious conduct. He was in the battle of Seven Pines; the seven days' fight around Richmond; commanded the 4th Virginia Cavalry for six weeks after the battle of Malvern Hill; commanded a battalion of six batteries of light artillery in the second battle of Manassas and the battle of Sharpsburg—and was engaged in sundry skirmishes on the Potomac and Peninsula last fall and winter. Such is the history of General Lee, now stationed here.—*Vicksburg Whig.*

TRI-WEEKLY MERCURY.

THURSDAY, JANUARY 15, 1863.

Matamoras.

If the intelligence is true that the French have taken possession of Matamoras, we have the most important fact which has taken place since the war commenced, so far as foreign nations are concerned. As France is at war with Mexico, it is a conquest by France, and the Emperor of the French has never been known to relinquish any conquests he has made. It is not at all improbable that he will take possession of the whole of Mexico, and make it a dependency on France; but even should he relinquish Central Mexico, he will certainly retain a portion of Mexico as an indemnity for the expenses of the war. The portion of Mexico lying adjacent to the Confederate States will, in all probability, constitute the indemnity. Thus we may have France permanently on the western border of the Confederate States.

But there is a more immediate result arising from the occupation of Matamoras by the French of no little significancy. If the Rio Grande becomes the property of France and the Confederate States, the French can not only navigate that river, but exclude all other nations, excepting the Confederate States, from navigating it. Matamoras becomes a French port, and, if the Confederate States permit it, cotton may be exported, and French goods be imported, without let or molestation from any other power. All munitions of war can freely enter Matamoras, as they now do at Nassau, and the Confederate States can be supplied with all they need. To this extent, if we can transport these articles to our armies, the trade may benefit us. France will have some cotton, and the Confederate States munitions of war.

But without stringent limitations, a still further result may follow such a state of things, militating against our cause. France getting cotton, and relieving thereby her people from the commercial distress which oppresses them—to the extent to which the trade goes, the grand motive for intervention to end the war between the Confederate and United States may measurably cease. France may be satisfied to let matters take their course. She, too, like Great Britain, may suppose it her interest in allowing both parties to exhaust and enfeeble themselves. Such a trade should, therefore, be carefully guarded and confined.

As events move on, the field for statesmanship in the Confederate States enlarges. So far, our statesmanship with foreign nations has not been efficient. We still allow the Consuls of the United States from foreign nations to reside and exercise their functions in our ports, as if we were now, or shortly would be, again portions of the United States. We have made no bold appeal to the interests of foreign nations. So far as we are aware, we offered no such advantageous commercial relations as might have induced them to espouse our cause. Have we not relied simply on the aphorism that "Cotton is King;" and refused, by adequate legislation, to make him so? Have we not allowed him to be dethroned before our eyes? Has not our whole foreign statesmanship been without dignity—without forecast, and without success? Have not all the mighty advantages we had over foreign nations to control their interests been useless in our hands? Perhaps the time is coming when we will do better. We trust so. There is room for statesmanship, and it is needed.

Reaction in Prices.

There are evident signs, says the Atlanta *Confederacy*, of a reaction in prices, not in all articles, but in those that have felt the influence of the law of demand and supply to some extent. The articles of salt and iron are feeling their influence. The high prices of these commodities above the average advance, have stimulated their production. Labor and capital are being rapidly diverted into these from other channels of employment. The class of articles which depend on natural causes for increase of supply—depending on season and the elements—are more gradually augmented in quantity and reduced in price. Grain and provisions are generally, of course, of this category. Another description of commodities of which the supply is received from abroad, requires the renewal of commercial intercourse with foreign countries to increase the supply. But our reliance upon a reduction of prices is a case of more general operation, to wit: the lessening of demand from the contraction of the currency. The enhancement of prices generally arises from that increase of demand produced by too great an abundance of money. If the treasury note currency were reduced one-half there would be a corresponding fall of prices, because there would be a proportionate falling off in the demand for nearly all articles.

The two measures which will most effectually contribute to this result are: 1st. The increase of taxation by the Confederate Government. 2d. The conversion of the greater part of the floating debt (treasury notes) into a funded debt of bonds and stock. The approaching session of Congress will give rise to a plan of internal taxation that will augment the revenue, and give stability to our monetary and funding system. A well digested scheme of direct taxation by the Confederate Government, will enable it to retire a share of its treasury notes while it will further attract investers to its bonds and stocks. Such a plan of revenue will act beneficially on both parts of our fiscal system, our currency and our bond and stock debt, giving steadiness to the former and imparting a higher value to the latter. The late State guarantees to that debt will operate in the same direction, improving the currency and rendering the Confederate securities objects of investment. These ends are in a course of gradual accomplishment without decisive victories; with such victories they would be rapidly achieved.

NEWSPAPERS AND THE WAR.—No class of men seem so indifferent to their own pecuniary interests as newspaper men. Whilst the merchant sells his wares at from five to ten thousand per cent. advance on the old rates; whilst the farmer is raising upon his products in proportion, and whilst everything necessary to sustain life, as well as a newspaper, is selling at ten and twenty prices, publishers are still furnishing daily papers at a very slight advance on the old rates. We believe it may be safely assumed that there are but two classes of men in the Confederacy, not in the army, who are not "speculators" or "high price men," in some way or other. The parson still preaches to his congregation, at a salary which barely keeps soul and body together, while publishers of newspapers are working for the public gratis and boarding themselves.—*Columbus Sun.*

The Federal steamer Blue Wing was recently captured by our forces near Cypress Bend. She had in tow two coal barges, besides a large lot of ammunition for the fleet, together with eighteen bags of mail matter; one mail bag was filled with official correspondence, and was in charge of a special mail agent. All was captured, and the Blue Wing had been sent up the Arkansas river. The Federal transport Gladiator, with Government stores, was also captured.

NEWS FROM THE NORTH.

We make up an interesting summary from Northern papers of the 6th and 7th of January.

PARTICULARS OF THE LOSS OF THE MONITOR.

The Baltimore *American's* correspondent at Fortress Monroe, gives the following account of the loss of the iron-clad steamer *Monitor*, obtained from her officers:

We left Fortress Monroe on Monday, 29th December, in tow of the steamer Rhode Island, with the Passaic in tow of the steamer State of Georgia. Passed Cape Henry on Thursday afternoon, at five o'clock, with smooth sea and light winds. The Passaic was a little way ahead. The weather continued fine until five o'clock on Tuesday morning, when it commenced to blow from the S. W., with a heavy sea running, making a clean sweep over all. At 9 30 Cape Hatteras light bore N. N. W., distance twenty miles, the gale still increasing. The vessel labored very heavily, the hull coming down on every sea with fearful violence. Up to this time the Worthington pump and the bilge injectors were entirely competent to keep the vessel free.

At ten o'clock several heavy seas struck the vessel in succession, when word was sent from the engine room that the water was gaining on the pumps. Orders were then given to start the Adams Centrifugal pump, capable of throwing three thousand gallons of water per minute. For a while the water appeared to be kept under. In a short time, however, word was passed from the engine room that the water was again gaining on the pumps, and was at that time up to the ash pits, stopping, in a great measure, the draft. The water at this time was standing two feet deep upon the ward-room floor. All hands were set to work with every bucket at hand to bail. The water, however, kept gaining upon the pumps, until within a foot of the fire in the furnaces.

A Coster signal was then flashed to call the attention of the Rhode Island to our condition. After much delay, consequent upon the heavy sea running, a boat was lowered from the Rhode Island and sent to our assistance. After several trials she succeeded in getting alongside of us. The Rhode Island, at the same time, in going astern, caught her launch between her own side and our vessel, crushing the boat badly, and bringing her own counter very heavily down upon our side. For a time she could not move, her engine getting on the centre. She finally started ahead, and the launch, smashed as she was, succeeded in carrying safely to the steamer thirty of the crew of the Monitor.

After the departure of the launch, those remaining on board worked at the buckets with a will. The gale at this time was raging furiously, the seas making a clean sweep over the top of the turret. The water at this juncture had succeeded in rising up to the grate bar in the furnace, and was gradually extinguishing the fire. The steam in the boilers consequently run down, and the pumps could not be worked for want of sufficient steam.

At this time three boats were discovered coming towards the vessel. Word was passed that boats were at hand sufficient to take all from the vessel.

The Monitor was now sinking. Every pump was stopped and her deck was under water. Several of the crew, in coming off the turret, were swept by the waves to leeward, and must have perished, as no assistance could be rendered them. The boats were then shoved off from the sinking vessel. Although several times entreated to come down and get into the boats, some of the crew, stupefied with fear, remained standing upon the turret, afraid of being swept from the deck.

The boats succeeded in reaching the Rhode Island in safety, and all in them were put on board. A picked crew, with the gallant officer of the Rhode Island (Mr. Brown), then shoved off in the launch to return to the Monitor. The moon, which up to this time had been throwing some light upon the waves, was shut in by dense masses of black clouds.

At a quarter to one o'clock in the morning the Monitor's light disappeared beneath the waves.

The Rhode Island then started for the spot where the Monitor was seen to go down. Costar's signals were constantly kept burning, and a strict look-out kept up in all parts of the vessel to catch a glimpse, if possible, of the missing boat.

At daylight nothing was seen on the waves, and, with a heavy heart, we ran around the spot, as near as could be judged, where the Monitor had disappeared until late in the afternoon. Several steamers and other vessels were spoken, to learn, if possible, the fate of the missing boat, but none could be had. The survivors reached Fortress Monroe last evening in the Rhode Island. Nothing whatever was saved, except the apparel the officers and crew stood in.

The Rhode Island's boat (first cutter), referred to above, contained Wm. Brown, Master's Mate, and seven of the crew, whose names we have not been able to ascertain.—They have not been heard of up to this time. There is a possibility that they may have succeeded in reaching the Monitor and taken off some more of the crew, and afterwards been picked up by some coasting vessels, as there were a number passing the next morning.

THE POSITION OF GOVERNOR SEYMOUR—HIS PLAN FOR RESTORING THE UNION.

The Northern papers bring us a more full and accurate abstract of the recent Message of Gov. SEYMOUR than that published in our telegraphic column a few days ago. We make some extracts in regard to his plans and hopes of restoring the Union:

The Union, he says, will be restored by the Central and Western States to the free and slave States, who are exempt from the violent passions which control at the extremes. Those of the central slave States which rejected the ordinance of secession, and which were driven off by a contemptuous compromising policy, must be brought back. The restoration of the whole Union will only be the work of time, with such exertion as can be put forth without needlessly sacrificing the life and treasure of the North in a bloody and calamitous contest. We must not wear out the lives of our soldiers, nor exhaust the earning of labor by a war for uncertain ends, or to carry out vague theories of extermination. This means not only destruction of lives and property South, but also a waste of blood and treasure in the North. The execution of armed power must be accompanied by a firm and conciliatory policy; so as to restore our Union with the least possible injury to both sections.

The Governor concludes as follows: "At this moment the fortunes of our country are influenced by the results of battles. Our armies in the field must be supported; all the constitutional demands of our General Government must be promptly responded to. Under no circumstances can a division of the Union be conceded. We will put forth every exertion of power; we will use every policy of conciliation; we will hold out every inducement to the people of the South to return to their allegiance consistent with honor; we will guarantee them every right and every consideration demanded by the Constitution alone, and by that fraternal regard which must prevail in a common country; but we can never voluntarily consent to the breaking up of the Union of these States, or the destruction of the Constitution."

YANKEE COMMENTS ON THE BATTLE OF MURFREESBORO'—A CHANGE OF TUNE.

The New York *Herald*, in commenting upon the battle of Murfreesboro', says:

But these achievements do not relieve the War Office at Washington from the sweeping charge of a blundering mismanagement of the war in the West as well as in the East. With a proper appreciation of the value of Nashville and of the policy and necessities of the Rebels, instead of being required, with less than fifty thousand men, to fight for five days a Rebel force of probably not less than seventy-five thousand to save Nashville, General Rosecrans would have been thrown forward upon the enemy with an army of one hundred and fifty thousand men, although the consolidation of this army might have required the temporary abandonment of a number of secondary positions and combinations. In this way the Rebel army of Bragg might have been destroyed or scattered to the winds. As it is, Bragg, after inflicting upon Rosecrans a loss of ten thousand of his splendid soldiers, several hundred wagons and thirty cannon, retreats more with the air of a conqueror than with the evidences of a serious defeat.

SEMI-OFFICIAL VIEW OF MEDIATION.

The Washington *Republican*, generally recognized as an Administration organ, thus expresses itself concerning mediation:

We are confident that we are on the eve of some developments respecting foreign mediation. There are many straws which indicate how the wind is soon to blow.

The Richmond Dispatch said, some days since, that, after the battle of Antietam, propositions of peace ought to have been made; that both parties could then have made proposals of this nature with perfect propriety.

The New York Tribune has a well considered article upon the subject of foreign mediation, proposing the Swiss Cantons as the mediatory power. It does not object to the French Government making an effort in this direction, but is not so well satisfied with England. Our people might be satisfied with the interference or mediation of the Swiss Cantons, or even of France, or most certainly of Russia, but never with perfidious England, if we can help it.

Other indications are manifest that something in the shape of interference or mediation is soon to take place. All this may be premature and unfounded; still we are doubtless approaching a crisis in our national affairs.

We may not be pleased with the complexion our public affairs are assuming; still we know the utter folly of resisting the inexorable logic of events. If we cannot, or have not, put down the rebellion, we cannot expect nations which suffer much by our quarrel, to look on as disinterested spectators forever.

BEAST BUTLER IN PHILADELPHIA.

Beast BUTLER arrived in Philadelphia on the 7th, *en route* for New York and Boston. During the evening he addressed a party of ladies and gentlemen in the reception room of the Continental Hotel.

In the course of his remarks he said: "You have been pleased to allude to an act of high executive responsibility, which, in the performance of my duty, became a painful necessity—an act which caused more complaints and praises than any other—the execution of William B. Mumford.—[Applause.]

"Owing to the uncourteous terms in which the so called Confederate Government demanded explanation, no report ever could be made. By offensive language that Government shut off all possible communication on our part.—Then it was assumed that some wrong was done, and the proclamation, which you have doubtless all seen, was issued in consequence.

"Whether rightly or wrongly, the act still commends itself to my judgment. [Applause.] Feeling the utter worthlessness of the man that treason had attempted to exalt into a patriot, I was inclined to spare him; but that was not permitted. The thugs, rowdies and gamblers assembled before the execution and resolved that he should not be hung. It became a question whether they ruled New Orleans or the Commanding General of the United States, and from that day there never was any question upon the subject. [Applause.]"

A SPEECH FROM CAPTAIN SEMMES.

A speech from the "terror of the seas" is a curiosity, and we give the following address from Captain SEMMES to the passengers on the *Ariel*, when he boarded her:

"Passengers, you're safe in our hands. You have no occasion to weep or be alarmed. What do you take us for? We are all honorable men; rest assured of that. Did any one harm you as yet?" A voice: "You were near sinking the ship." The pirate continued: "That is only our duty. We make war on the sea, and the Yankees are our enemies." [More crying and general alarm.]

"I repeat, you have no cause to be apprehensive of us. No one of our officers or crew will insult you. We are gentlemen. Do you think we are ruffians who would attack the helpless, or do you imagine we are robbers? Have confidence in us, and we will protect and not injure you. Not an article of your baggage shall be taken from you. You will find we respect private property."

The prize crew applauded the Captain's courteous speech, and the passengers soon became more confident. During the two days in which the Ariel was a prisoner, after this speech was made, the passengers freely fraternized with the prize crew, and some of them even expressed unqualified sympathy with the Southern Confederacy.

THE CASUALTIES IN THE TENTH S. C. V.—The following is a list of the casualties in the 10th Regiment S. C. V., Colonel MANIGAULT, in the battle of Murfreesboro'. The Regiment is attached to the Fourth Brigade, WITHERS' Division. The Brigade was commanded in the battle by Colonel A. M. MANIGAULT:

COMPANY A.

Killed—Sergeant T J Harrison, Privates Thos Williamson and Jas McMulken.

Wounded—Lieut. J L Easterling, slightly; Corporal L A Matthews, severely; Privates W P Clarkson, S D Guild, severely; J P. Gamble, J. W. McCormick, F L McCants, John Wilson, E S Porter, slightly; Privates W H J Lawrimore and J B Cook, taken prisoners.

COMPANY B.

Killed—None.

Wounded—Color Bearer J A Duggan, severely; Privates W Lane, P P Todd, J O Lewis, severely; A L Readman, S B Tolar, W G Hughes, slightly.

COMPANY C.

Killed—Privates A M Hardwick and Pascal Handcock.

Wounded—Sergeants H Johnson, severely, leg amputated; D S Johnson, slightly; Corporal Jas Tompkins, severely, leg amputated; Privates A B Hardwick, J D Spears, J Suggs, E Phipps, R Hardy, severely; W D Hewitt, J B Hux, slightly.

COMPANY D.

Killed—Privates D M Carmicheal and N Drew.

Wounded—Sergeant G B Coleman, slightly; Corporal D H Lambert, mortally; Privates L Baxly and G S Flowers, severely.

COMPANY E.

Killed—Sergeant C W Cockfield and Private J H Cockfield.

Wounded—Privates J B Russ, mortally; H W Blakely, O B Goude, severely; John McNamee, D O Tilton and Thomas Hataway, slightly.

COMPANY F.

Killed—None.

Wounded—Lieutenant J H Belin, slightly; Sergeant J E Collins, severely; Corporal H P Hutchinson, severely; Privates G W Curry, S Turbeville and S H Johnson, slightly.

COMPANY G.

Killed—Private H S Williams.

Wounded—Captain O S Ford, slightly; Sergeant Jesse Boyd, severely; Sergeant H L Doyle, slightly Privates W L Edge, severely, leg amputated; J J Hardee, J W Smith and John Rogers, slightly.

COMPANY H.

Killed—Private Thomas Jordan.

Wounded—Captain J R Kettles, dangerously in three places; Corporals S F R Godwin, severely, leg amputated; G. W. Huggins, severely; Privates R W Kirby, severely, leg amputated; N Gray, D E Coward, H Lee, J W Matthews, A Parker, severely; John McNight, H Matthews, C W Daniels, G R Matthews and W P Scott, slightly.

COMPANY I.

Killed—None.

Wounded—Capt B B McWhite, severely; Sergeant W L Hyman, slightly; Privates W H McWhite, W D Campbell, severely; C T Altman, F L Poston, E J Wiggins, D W Gilsson and E Hanna, slightly.

COMPANY K.

Killed—J W H Bunch, W D Burris and John Missolia.

Wounded—Capt J S Palmer, slightly; Serg't G B Townsend, severely; Carp'l H J Ervin, slightly; Privates S P Harris, D S Owen, severely; J C Singletary, slightly.

COMPANY L.

Killed—Privates Wm Thompson and E J N Amyet.

Wounded—Sergeant McIntyre, slightly; Corp'l Flowers, slightly; Privates A Weaver, severely, leg amputated; G W Johnson, severely, leg amputated; A Page, A Thomas, severely; J Huggins, J McCall, slightly.

COMPANY M.

Killed—None.

Wounded—Serg't J B Rhenark, slightly; Corp'l W S Vareen, severely; Private J J Vareen, slightly.

CASUALTIES IN THE NINETEENTH S. C. V.—The 19th Regiment S. C. V. went into the battle of Murfreesboro' 240 strong, and lost heavily. The following is the official list of casualties:

Colonel A J Lythgoe, wounded in the thigh, since dead; Major J A Crowder, wounded in leg, severely; Lieut J D Waddell, Acting Adjutant, wounded in thigh, slightly; Color Bearer J C Wheeler, flesh wound in arm.

COMPANY A—CAPT. E. W. HORN COMMANDING.

Lieut J Y Norris, leg, flesh; Sergeant J R Padget, side, serious; Sergeant E Leybran, leg, slight; Corporal J V Claxton, slight; Private H. Grice, foot, severe; Private W A Mitchel, severe; Private M Leybran, severe; Private O'Donnell, head, slight; Private Mitchel Clark, slight.

COMPANY B—CAPT. T. W. GETZEN COMMANDING.

Sergeant M Franklin, slight; Private M Hilburn, slight; M Arthurs, thigh, flesh; A Horn, side, flesh.

COMPANY C—CAPT. H. R. DEAN COMMANDING.

Killed—Sergt J B Outz and Private Simon Parkman.

Wounded—Corporal E W Eidson, leg, severe; Private L G Williams, leg, slight; W S Brooks, arm, slight; W S Terry, slight.

COMPANY D—CAPT. W. S. PETERSON COMMANDING.

Killed—Private W N Watson. Wounded—Corporal K H Eidson, slight; Corporal A M Sacher, slight; Private C Little, leg, slight; Private H A Williams, hip, slight; Private J A Nelson, ankle, amputated; Private W Raburn, thigh, amputated; Private W E Reese, mouth, severe; Private Moses New, thigh, severe; Private L C Goff, leg, severe; Private W C Goff, slight; Private G A Shumpert, slight.

COMPANY E—LIEUT. R. Y. M'LEOD COMMANDING.

Corp'l W B Carnes, arm, flesh; Private T Brown, severe; Private J F Richbourg, arm, flesh; Private J B T Moore, arm, flesh; Private E Atkinson, shoulder, flesh; Corp'l J T Holland, slight.

COMPANY F.

Lieut W K Smith, slight; Serg't E M Corder, foot, slight; Corporal B T Walker, hand, slight; Private D Turner, knee, severe.

COMPANY G—CAPT. R. N. CHATHAM COMMANDING.

Killed—Private J T Boyd. Wounded—Lieut J McM Donald, neck, slight; Serg't S A Jordan, side, severe; Serg't S Hunter, hand, slight; Corp'l L D Lee, lungs, severe; Private H Hall, shoulder, slight; J H Johnson, hip, slight; M Bell, head, slight; J B McAlister, head, slight.

COMPANY H—LIEUT. R. H. M'CASTIN COMMANDING.

Killed—Private Rob't Walker. Wounded—Lieut R H McCastin, stunned; Private W H Walker, hip, mortal, since dead; Serg't Y A Watson, leg, amputated; Serg't E J Belot, jaw and thigh, serious; Serg't T M Jay, slight; Corp'l T J Wilson, shoulder, severe; Private J C Dowden, mouth; Private W G M Williams, arm, flesh; J A Hussell, slight.

COMPANY I—CAPTAIN A. CLINKSCALES COMMANDING.

Lieut Madison, slight; Private J T Clamp, leg and abdomen, serious; D W Yon, leg amputated; John Johnson, wrist, slight; W T Young, elbow, flesh; R L Freman, hip, slight; H Mattox, neck, slight; J Robinson, slight; T B Sims, slight.

COMPANY K—SERGEANT M. JONES COMMANDING.

Killed—Jasper Howard. Wounded—Sergeant M Jones, slight; Lieut Holly, stunned; Corporal W T Turner, abdomen, severe; Sergeant J C Holly, head, serious; Private M Parker, slight.

J. H. JENNINGS,
Assistant Surgeon, 19th Regiment, S. C. V.

LARGE ARRIVAL OF LADIES.—Between five and six hundred ladies and children, who arrived at City Point by the last truce boat from the North reached this city on Saturday by the trains from Petersburg. Many of them are from Baltimore, and have long been waiting for Lincoln's permission to join their relatives in the South. They looked travel worn and fatigued, and as they plodded wearily through the mud from the depot to places of temporary refuge, their first impressions of the Confederate capital seemed anything but agreeable. Still, they are now in a place where they can wear the Dixie colors without the fear of a dungeon before their eyes.—*Richmond Whig.*

THE MEMBERS of Company A, 2d Regiment Artillery S. C. V., would, through Lieut MILLER, return their sincere thanks to the Ladies' Soldiers' Relief Association for donations of under-clothing.

WOMAN AND THE WAR.

What a beautiful tribute to the women of the South was that paid by Bishop ELLIOTT, in his recent sermon at Savannah. Said he:

"The attitude of woman is sublime. Bearing all the sacrifices of which I have just spoken, she is moreover called upon to suffer in her affections, to be wounded and smitten where she feels deepest and more enduringly. Man goes to the battlefield, but woman sends him there, even though her heart-strings tremble while she gives the farewell kiss and the farewell blessing. Man is supported by the necessity of movement, by the excitement of action, by the hope of honor, by the glory of conquest. Woman remains at home to suffer, to bear the cruel torture of suspense, to tremble when the battle has been fought and the news of the slaughter is flashing over the electric wire, to know that defeat will cover her with dishonor and her little ones with ruin, to learn that the husband she doated upon, the son whom she cherished in her bosom, and upon whom she never let the wind blow too rudely, the brother with whom she sported through all her happy days of childhood, the lover to whom her early vows were plighted, has died upon some distant battlefield, and lies there a mangled corpse, unknown and uncared for, never to be seen again, even in death. On those fearful lists of the wounded and the dead! How carelessly we pass them over, unless our own loved ones happen to be linked with them in military association, and yet each name in that roll of slaughter, carries a fatal pang to some woman's heart—some noble, devoted woman's heart. But she bears it all, and bows submissively to the stroke. He died for the cause. He perished for his country. I would not have it otherwise, but I should like to have given the dying boy my blessing, the expiring husband my last kiss of affection, the bleeding lover the comfort of knowing that I kneeled beside him."

with an effrontery, purely American, that he does not doubt that it will be recognised as such by "all the good and wise men of all countries!" We are greatly mistaken in Earl Russell if he allows Mr. Seward to continue in that convenient belief, and if he does not express, in strong terms, the reprobation by the British Government of this atrocious attempt to devastate the South by means of a servile war.

In the immediate effects, and so far as regards the position of the President, the proclamation has been a success. The tub has been thrown to the whale. The Northerners can no longer account for their reverses by imputing them to the half measures of the Government. It is extraordinary the amount of ferocity which exists among the population of the Northern States, especially among the Puritans of the New England States. The clergy, who are entirely dependent on their congregations, show themselves on this, of cities, but there would be a widespread scene of horror over the vast expanse of great States, involving alike the loyal and seditious. Such malignity and cowardice would invoke the interfence of civilized Europe. History tells of the fires kindled in the name of religion, of atrocities committed under the pretexts of order or liberty; it is now urged that scenes bloodier than the world has yet witnessed shall be enacted in the name of philanthropy!"

Although the Democratic party—who may be described as opposed to abolition and all extreme measures—has given little sign of existence since the war began, and although, under the regime of martial law which has now been proclaimed for the whole Northern States, it will encounter, perhaps, insuperable obstacles to its action, still it must be borne in mind that, whether nominally belonging to it or not, some of the ablest and most powerful men in

NEWSPAPERS AND THE WAR.—No class of men seem so indifferent to their own pecuniary interests as newspaper men. Whilst the merchant sells his wares at from five to ten thousand per cent. advance on the old rates; whilst the farmer is raising upon his products in proportion, and whilst everything necessary to sustain life, as well as a newspaper, is selling at ten and twenty prices, publishers are still furnishing daily papers at a very slight advance on the old rates. We believe it may be safely assumed that there are but two classes of men in the Confederacy, not in the army, who are not "speculators" or "high price men," in some way or other. The parson still preaches to his congregation, at a salary which barely keeps soul and body together, while publishers of newspapers are working for the public gratis and boarding themselves.—*Columbus Sun.*

that position by the gradual operation of its own acts. First of all, and as at the outset, if separation takes place, New York will cease to be the entrepot of the Southern trade. The "Empire City," which has grown fat on that trade, will [illegible] or actually decline; while Charleston, Mobile and New Orleans [illegible]. That first act of barbarism, the choking up the harbor of Charleston with stone-laden vessels, showed the bitter jealousy of the New Yorkers, and their desire to obliterate the very existence of a rival port in the South. New York must come down from its high place; half of its merchants will be beggars if the South takes its trade in its own keeping. And what is New York, whose fall is thus threatened? It is the very heart of the North; it is the centre of its resources, the seat of nearly all the available wealth and ready money. It is the bankers and merchants of New York who have supplied Mr. Chase [illegible]. And who but they have been foremost in equipping regiments, and offering bounties? Patriots!—they are but worshippers of the "almighty dollar!" They give their money lavishly, in order that they may retain the power from which the money comes. They do not desire emancipation, nor a servile war; for that means the ruin of their customers; but some of them oppose the proclamation, in the hope that it may force the South into submission, and others, because if the South is to go free, and if Southern trade is to seek other channels, they will rather see the South a desert, than other cities rising into rivalry with New York, with the gains which formerly poured into Yankee pockets.

This motive sufficiently explains the vehemence of New York against the project of secession. But there are other reasons, of wider influence, which actuate the North in waging war to the uttermost against the South. Within less than two years the North has taken upon its shoulders an amount of debt nearly equal to half of the gigantic National Debt of Great Britain; and every new expedition or campaign adds to the already enormous amount. If the South gets off free the North will be left to bear the whole burden of the debt which she has contracted. [illegible] that the [illegible] of the burden [illegible] way of establishing its independence, the Northerners become [illegible] to pay the debt? Who is to become responsible in cash for the enormous issues of paper money? The debt arising from this war will of itself suffice to rupture the Union. Not only does it constitute an additional motive for the obstinate resolve of the South to separate, but it cannot fail to produce still further secession from the Union among the Northern States themselves. Repudiation is not an unknown proceeding in America, and he is a sanguine man who believes it will not be had recourse to in regard to this great war debt. Nearly all the capitalists are to be found in New York, Boston and Philadelphia; and almost all the debt is held by a few of the Atlantic States. The great agricultural States of the West have hardly contributed a dollar, for they have no accumulated capital. When this war ends, therefore—as end it must some time—the South free, and the North burdened with a debt still greater—it may be even double what it is now—the difficulties of the position

"All the good and wise men of all countries"—to use Mr. Seward's phrase—far from approving the proclamation of the President as "a just and proper military act," will see in it a new reason for desiring a prompt termination of this deplorable, lavish and fratricidal contest. [illegible] Sir G. C. Lewis' statement of the import of international law to be the most erroneous and ridiculous statement ever hazarded by a Minister of the Crown. [illegible] recognition of a new State [illegible] is either formally or virtually at an end, we find the argument contradicted by the circumstances which have attended every recognition of a new State by this country since the century began. We hastened to recognise the Spanish republics of South America while they were still engaged in a war with the parent State, and it was a band of British legionaries who turned the scale of battle in the action which finally crushed the hopes of Spain. Greece we also recognized while that country was still struggling under the power of the Turks; indeed, we intervened for the express purpose of preventing the Turks re-establishing their power over the rebellious province. Belgium was a still stronger instance; for in that case, but for the military intervention of France and England, the Dutch would very soon have got a good account of the Belgians. And in the recent case of Naples, did we not [illegible] the annexation to Piedmont, while the King and his army still held their ground in his old dominions? So far, therefore, as it is a question of legality, England would be amply justified in recognizing the independence of the Confederate States. As a question of policy, however, the matter is not so easily determined. [illegible] of the South as an independent State, without taking any steps to put an end to the war, would be of very little benefit to the South, [illegible] whatever. At the same time, it would give great offence to the North, thus making an enemy without gaining a friend. But the case would be far otherwise if our Government were to act in this instance in the same manner as they did in the case of Greece and Belgium—that is to say, if they were to resolve not only to recognize the independence of the South, but to support that independence by a demonstration of force. The case has now become most urgent. For not only does international law justify our recognition of the Southern Confederacy, but humanity demands that we should take measures to put an end to so horrible a war. [illegible] it would be a delicate matter, and a matter also of doubtful policy, for England to intervene alone. But intervention of some kind is now urgently demanded. And if the Great Powers of Europe—or at least England, Russia and France—would solve the difficulty which each Power separately feels, [illegible] they would render an important service to civilization, [illegible] and would show a better example of a "Holy Alliance" than any which yet stands recorded in the page of history.

TRI-WEEKLY MERCURY.

BY R. B. RHETT, JR.

OFFICE NO. 4 BROAD-STREET, CHARLESTON.

THE DAILY MERCURY, five cents per copy, $10 per annum.
THE TRI-WEEKLY MERCURY, issued on Tuesdays, Thursdays and Saturdays, five cents per copy. $5 per annum.

THURSDAY, JANUARY 15, 1863.

Governor Seymour's State Rights Doctrines.

We yesterday noticed the concluding portion of Governor SEYMOUR's message, in which he argues that neither in a Northern nor in a Southern Union can the conflict of interests of agriculture, commerce and manufactures be adjusted; hence that the Union is indissoluble, and that "factions North and South must be put down." We endeavored, briefly, to point out that the whole difficulty of adjusting the relative interests of the two peoples, was the difficulty of obtaining justice for Southern interests, notwithstanding the barriers of constitutional law created for their protection. The overthrow of the fundamental compact, on the limited basis of which the fabric of the General Government was erected, and the attempt of the Northern majority to absorb all the powers of government within its control, and to employ them for the aggrandisement and gratification of the North, to the ruin of this section, rendered the dissolution of the Union and the independence of the South measures essential to the safety of the Confederate States.

Governor SEYMOUR's conclusion is a clear *non-sequitur* to his just and proper strictures upon the unconstitutional tyranny of the General Government of the United States. He admits that the cause of the war was "the pervading disregard of the Laws and the Constitution," and that it is necessary to "reform the people and the policy of the Government. The rights of the States must be respected. The consolidation of the Government of this vast country would destroy the essential rights and liberties of the people. The sovereignty of the States cannot be given up."

The political history of the United States for thirty years previous to the dissolution of the Union, was a long but unavailing effort, on the part of the State Rights men of the South, to "reform the people and the policy of the Government." South Carolina was once deeply attached to a Union, for the establishment of which she probably sacrificed more and suffered more, in proportion, during the revolutionary war, than any other of the old Thirteen. Her statesmen for thirty years have argued, and entreated, and warned the North against the destruction of the Constitution. Over and over they predicted the inevitable destruction of the Union as the consequence. They were called theorists, abstractionists, revolutionists. In their conservative efforts to preserve the Constitution and the Union, and to prevent the issue brought upon the country in 1860, with the evils under which we now suffer in a war for independence, they sacrificed their personal ambition and all hopes of office on the altar of their country's safety. As long as possible, they strove manfully. They waged a hopeless battle under a banner whose symbol was equivalent to proscription. Failing to save the Constitution and Union, they have engaged in a struggle for the salvation of the South. In this they have confidence of success.

The people and the policy of the United States could not be reformed. It is too late to save the Union or to reconstruct it. The immedicable wrongs suffered by the people of the Confederate States, at the hands of their *quondam* allies, constitute a wall of separation which cannot be broken down. Their sentiments as men, and the very instincts of our human nature, revolt at the proposition of re-union with those whose hands are dyed with the blood of our fathers and brothers and sons. The utter want of character, as manifested by the unvarying and almost universal falsification of facts at the North, as a matter of self-respect and self-preservation, independent of considerations of interest and security and honor forbid national association with such a people.

But for the sake of the United States themselves, and in the interest of mankind, we should be pleased to see the State Rights reform of Governor SEYMOUR carried into practice. It is the only alternative to anarchy and a military despotism in the end. A lawless majority must be a vulgar tyranny!

FOREIGN NEWS.

The New York papers contain the following news by the last steamer from Europe:

LAYARD, the Under Secretary of State for Foreign Affairs, had made a speech at London. He said that the principle of his country was non-intervention, and that England sympathized with nations struggling for freedom. He also said that the Government was right in the opinion that the proposal of France for mediation was inopportune, and that if the English Government had accepted that offer at an inopportune moment, then when an opportunity arrived, it would have been lost.

The Paris correspondent of the London *Post*, under date of the 22d, says: "It is reported that the Emperor has assured the Cabinet at Washington, through Mr. DAYTON, that France came forward not to favor the North or the South, but in the name of humanity, and for the good of both parties." He says that the Governments of France and England continue to be united in their policy towards America, and that policy, now as of old, was strict neutrality.

The Liverpool *Journal of Commerce*, of the 23d, contains an order to the British agents of the various ports of the West India Islands, that if the Alabama enters their ports, to prohibit her from coaling or taking in provisions; that she be ordered to depart at once; and the order further states that Capt. SEMMES be informed that, after this notice, should he destroy any merchandize consigned to British merchants in neutral ships, her Majesty's Government will take steps to destroy his vessel.

The Paris correspondent of the London *Herald* says it is rumored in official circles that another attempt will be made by the Great Powers to put an end to the strife in America.

The London *Times* advises the American Government not to continue the ridiculous farce of claiming indemnity from England for losses sustained by the operations of the *Alabama*.

The Philadelphia *Inquirer*, of the 9th, has a special despatch that M. MERCIER, the French Minister at Washington, has dismissed the French Consul at New Orleans for alleged complicity with the rebels against the United States.

The *Inquirer's* latest despatch from Vicksburg announces the arrival of PORTER's mortar fleet. BANKS and McCLERNAND were expected every moment, when the combined fleets would make another attempt to overthrow the Gibraltar of the West.

VALLANDIGHAM was serenaded in New York. He made a bold speech, in which he denounced LINCOLN, his Cabinet and Congress, and said if the Constitution was trampled under foot much longer, the guillotine will be used against traitors

Rev. W. T. FARROW thankfully acknowledges the receipt of $5 from Miss FANNY WILKINSON, of Madison Court House, Fla., to aid in supplying our soldiers with religious reading, and six Bibles and six Testaments from Rev. JAMES HEWETSON, of Ireland. These have come when much needed, and others are requested to help us. Many are the actual necessities in our army.

LETTER FROM RICHMOND.

(CORRESPONDENCE OF THE MERCURY.)

RICHMOND, Friday, January 9.

Capture of the Harriet Lane—Chance for Naval Men at Charleston—Letters from Englishmen—Rosecrans' Falsehoods—Lamar Fontaine—High Price for Ice, etc., etc.

We have just been cheered by the news of the capture of the *Harriet Lane*. It has been a long time since our naval arm has made itself felt, except in the sturdy blows of SEMMES. It is to be hoped that other surprises may follow that at Galveston. Very soon, if telegrams are to be trusted, there will be a chance for our naval officers at Charleston and Wilmington to show the "mettle of their pasture." The Examiner of this morning, commenting on the lack of enterprise in the Navy Department, derives consolation from the fact that the Yankees have defeated themselves by the rigidity of their blockade, thereby making us self dependent and self-reliant, and making our paper money available for all the purposes of war while Europe suffers.

The Whig [illegible] up its first editorial column to a letter from an English gentleman of high position, who pays the highest compliment to the spirit displayed by the Confederacy, and assures us of the warm sympathy of the *people* of England, as distinguished from the Palmerston-Russell administration. He confesses, too, that the English are beginning to take more rational views of slavery. There is a letter copied into the Enquirer from the London Illustrated News, written by its correspondent, Mr. Vizitelly, who, as you are aware, follows Lee's army wherever it goes. This letter breathes the same cordial admiration of the virtues of the Southern people as that in the Whig. Such evidences of British good feeling can hardly fail to awaken a response in the warm-hearted people of the sunny South.

Rosecrans tries to produce the impression that the fighting at Murfreesboro' lasted continuously from Tuesday until Friday. He thus lends himself to a deliberate falsehood. The last fight was on Friday evening, and was not a general engagement, but an assault of the enemy's position by Breckinridge's division. I notice, however, that it is the cue of the Yankee papers, now more than ever—for recognition is imminent—to represent the rebels as defeated at every point. Could you see a copy of the Herald, you would find that not only Bragg but Morgan, Forrest and Wheeler have all been literally cut to pieces; not enough of them left to make a respectable grease spot. Rosecrans' Medical Director says there are 1000 killed outright and 5500 wounded in hospitals. Now a great many wounded never go into hospitals, and it is more than probable that many of Rosecrans' badly wounded can't get hospital accomodations. His loss was at first "truly enormous" and "heart-rending;" now it is 500 less than Bragg's.

I am glad to have been the means of bringing to light the name of Lamar Fontaine, the gallant dragoon from Texas, who can't walk, and carries his crutches with him on horseback. He is, by odds, the most wonderful man the war has produced, according to the letter published in the Mobile Register.

Ice is coming into town freely, and has been for weeks past. The Government buys it at eight cents a pound or $4 a bushel. HERMES.

—o—

RICHMOND, Saturday, January 10.

Bad Day—Seymour's Message—False Logic—How Cotton Burning is Regarded in England—Reported Capture of Vicksburg—The Northwest—Cruelty to Confederate Prisoners and Negros, etc.

A miserable, gloomy morning, with a misty drizzle, instead of a good honest snow, as we had every right to expect after so much cold weather.

One of the morning papers gives a very truthful heading to the telegraphic report of SEYMOUR's Message, to wit: "Significant Declarations and Illogical Conclusions." When the Governor of a great State proclaims that the rights of the States must be respected, and declares that "if the Constitution cannot keep the Executive within its restraints, he cannot retain the States in the Union," what folly thence to conclude that the Union is indissoluble, because, forsooth, the Upper and Lower Valleys of the Mississippi are so closely bound together, that when cotton is burned in Louisiana corn is used as fuel in Illinois, and hence further that a desolating war must be carried on! It shows how utterly distorted the Northern mind has become under the wicked influences of a war waged in violation of the sacred compact of the Constitution. It shows, further, how weak the reed is that we lean on when we look for help from any party at the North. The truth seems to be, that all men there are so bewildered that they do not themselves know what they are going to do. Can we rely on those who do not rely on themselves?

I learn from a pretty good source that the resolution passed by Congress authorizing the burning of cotton excited a great deal of bad feeling in England, where it was regarded as a crime not less heinous than the destruction of the necessities of life. It is said that if this law were repealed as soon as Congress meets, there would be no difficulty in selling our cotton to the British, who would take care that the Yankees do not obtain it. Nor would there be much trouble in getting it abroad in British bottoms, if report speaks truly.

Some are disposed this morning to believe that Vicksburg has been taken by the enemy. They say there is an ominous silence on the part of our authorities in that direction—a silence nearly of a week's duration. At the War Department, this morning, there was nothing to confirm Grant's despatch to Halleck. It is worthy of remark that Gen. Banks and Gov. Seymour both dwell with great emphasis on the impossibility of sundering the States that are washed by the Mississippi.—Banks, indeed, expends the whole force of his rhetoric on this theme, as if he expected to accomplish more with the pen than the sword. It should be remarked, too, that the President, in the speech made the other night, when he was serenaded, said he looked for the first gleams of peace to come from the Northwest. We may conclude from all this that the force of the enemy for the next few months will be thrown upon Vicksburg and its approaches; and in case the assaults fail, we may expect the Northwest to lose heart, begin a serious quarrel with New England, and thus inaugurate those political dissensions which must prelude peace.

The cruel treatment of our prisoners on board the Yankee transports has come under the eye of an eminent Englishman, who will make it his business to acquaint the European Governments and peoples therewith. He was also witness to a brutal act of violence upon an inoffensive negro in Norfolk by a member of a New York regiment, and saw the squalor and destitution of the thousands of runaways congregated in and around that city for *protection!* HERMES.

—o—

RICHMOND, Monday, January 22.

Reports from Paris—Our Armies to be Filled Up—Hostilities Predicted at Fredericksburg—"The Doom of Devergoil," etc., etc.

Not much faith is put in the story told by the correspondent of the N. Y. *Tribune* with regard to the resignation of DROUYN DE L'HUYS and the determination of the French Cabinet not to mediate in American affairs, though the report seems to be confirmed by the Paris correspondent of the London Post. We know not what steamer could have arrived in New York on the 7th with Paris dates to the 28th, yet this is what the Tribune would have us believe. Some of our officials are, as usual, sanguine about French intervention, but Mr. Seddon, I am told, places his reliance on the strength of our armies, and to this end is bending all his great energies. A special bureau, with Gen. Rains at its head, is charged with the execution of the Conscript Law, and a friend just from the army at Fredericksburg, tells me the conscripts continue to come in pretty rapidly.—As fast as they arrive they are blended with the veterans of twenty battles, and become at once veterans, or very nearly, themselves.

The Fredericksburg correspondent of the Enquirer predicts the resumption of hostilities in that quarter at an early day. What he bases his predictions upon he does not say. We in Richmond look for fighting to begin in North Carolina sooner than anywhere else. The weather is fine for military operations. As for the Fredericksburg line we have no fears. It was always strong; and now it will not do to tell what it is. Pemberton assures us that Vicksburg is stronger every day, and Rosecrans is too crippled to advance. Hence we look to North Carolina and to Suffolk.

In his message, Governor Letcher consigns Lincoln to a doom worse than that of Devergoil. The *literati* of the city are much exercised to know what the "doom of Devergoil" is or was. The Legislature is completely in the dark as to this fearful sentence, and will, it is expected, appoint a committee to wait on Honest John and demand an explanation. HERMES.

THE STATUTES AT LARGE of the Confederate States of America, passed at the second session of the First Congress, have just been published in handsome style at Richmond.

Eight sacks of Liverpool salt sold in Savannah, on Saturday last, at auction, at fifty dollars per sack.

GENERAL NEWS SUMMARY.

Negros are hired in Ohio at two dollars a month.

The Baltimore and Ohio Railroad has been opened all its length to Wheeling.

Medary's paper, the Crisis, of Columbus, Ohio, says that Curtis has made $70,000 by cotton speculations in Arkansas.

The Northern papers say that the rebels, in their retreat from Murfreesboro', burned the cotton wherever they could get hold of it.

On Thursday of last week two deserters from General Floyd's command, by the names of John Charles and Adam Davis, were shot.

Coast salt was sold at auction in Columbus on the 8th at 28@30 cents per pound, by the sack—a decline of nearly 100 per cent. in three weeks.

When the battle of Murfreesboro' first began, before our advanced guards fell back to the main army, we lost some of the field pieces captured at Perryville.

C. P. Pelham, Esq., of the Columbia (S. C.) Guardian, has secured a site, and is making arrangements to establish a paper mill near that city.

Lieutenant General E. Kirby Smith reached Lynchburg Friday evening by the Western train on his way to Richmond. General Bragg, who was also expected, did not arrive.

The Northern papers say that a brother of Butler has assigned a cargo of merchandize to the mouth of the Rio Grande, which he offers to sell to the rebels "for gold or cotton."

Major General Gustavus W. Smith, commanding the Department of North Carolina, arrived in Raleigh on Wednesday last, and is the guest of his Excellency Governor Vance.

After the battle near Vicksburg the Federals undertook to remove the artillery they had left on the field under a flag of truce, but they were prevented by our sharpshooters.

The residence of Mrs. Mary Newton, near Wilmington, North Carolina, was burned on the 4th inst., and Mrs. Newton, an aged lady, was so badly injured as to cause her death in a few hours.

A diary taken from the body of a Federal Lieutenant, killed at Vicksburg, says that the Federal expedition to come down the river will consist of seventy-nine transports, six gunboats and six rams.

A grand military review took place in Savannah on the 9th. The entire artillery of the coast were in the city for review. The Republican says it was a fine display; the men, horses and guns were all in splendid trim.

They have had heavy rains in the vicinity of Vicksburg within the past few days. This is very favorable for us; for it will be impossible for a Federal land force to operate in the Yazoo bottoms with artillery after long storms.

By occupying the Louisiana side of the river, the Federals have cut off our communication in that channel with the salt mines of Lake Bristeneau, which were supplying about 5000 bushels of salt daily to the Confederacy.

A Cincinnati paper announces the death of Col. Basil Duke, who held a command in Morgan's division, and was mortally wounded in the fight near Lebanon Junction. He was a brother in-law of Gen. Morgan.

The gunboat Pawnee left Philadelphia on Tuesday as convoy to the iron-clad Patapsco, bound to Fortress Monroe. The Hendrik Hudson, six guns, the Rover, seven guns, and the Londona, converted from a prize, left the same port on the same day for the South.

Philadelphia has suffered a severe mortification in the fact that the Anderson Troop, a cavalry regiment raised out of the "wealthiest and most respectable young men of the city," refused to go into the Murfreesboro' fight, alleging that their officers were inexperienced.

In the Yankee Congress, on the 5th, a resolution declaring Grant's order expelling the Jews from his department tyrannical, usurping and unjust, and requesting the President to countermand the same, was introduced by Mr. Powell, and laid over.

Information has been received from Baton Rouge to December 29. The total force of the Federals at that place is about twelve thousand men. All the gunboats and transports, except the Essex and one sloop-of-war, had gone below, it was reported, for the purpose of bringing more troops. The Federals are busy felling timber on the Clinton and Bayou Sara Roads, within a circuit of three miles from Baton Rouge, and are throwing up intrenchments. They have no pickets on the opposite shore. They have burned the beautiful State House at Baton Rouge, and destroyed much other property. It is also reported that they have made a raid into the country and attacked our cavalry pickets, driving them in, and mortally wounding Capt. Stuart.

SAVE YOUR RAGS.

This would perhaps, in ordinary times, be quite an unnecessary piece of advice, but at this moment it is of vital importance. As our readers know, the price of paper has advanced enormously, and as a consequence, publishers have been compelled to make a corresponding advance on their prices. One great reason of this increased tariff on paper is the scarcity of rags with which to manufacture it. The manufacturers inform us that rags are exceedingly difficult to obtain, even when, as is the case, the rates paid are higher, by at least 800 per cent. than formerly.

We write this article solely with the view of calling public attention to the scarcity, that it may, as far as possible, be remedied, and that speedily. The press is one of the most potent auxiliaries of this Government in carrying forward its objects, and subserving its interests. As a medium of communication, in times like these, when every day adds some memorable event to our history, the newspaper is as indispensable as our daily food. And it is essential to our individual intelligence, and as a record of current events. And as we sit down to read the pages of the favorite book or journal, let us not fail to remember that the materials for its manufacture must be obtained, or we shall have no book or newspaper. Until the blockade is removed—a desideratum altogether among the uncertainties—we must rely upon our own resources. Let then every family carefully save up all the rags—all the shreds—all the scraps—either linen, cotton, or woollen, and furnish them to the Paper Mills, and the proprietors of those mills will pay them handsomely therefor. Husbands, tell your wives to see to this—and not only the wives, but let every member of the family, white and black, commence the saving of rags to make paper. The possible contingency of a country like ours deprived of newspapers is shocking to contemplate. And we will not believe but what, as we have thus sounded the note of alarm, every one interested (and who is not?) will do all in his or her power to keep the mills supplied with rags, that the press may thereby continue to dispense intelligence to the people. — *Augusta Chronicle.*

To the Editor of the Mercury:—To prevent any misunderstanding upon the subject, I will restate my proposition published recently in the *Courier*, to wit: "I, therefore, propose that a committee of gentlemen, competent to judge, be chosen by 'Dalton' and myself, and that this committee make a joint report, or separate reports, and offer it or them to different societies of science in America and Europe for final decision." And in my communication in Thursday's MERCURY, January 8, 1862, I stated the following: "And I will offer no objection to those mentioned by *Dalton Secundus*, should *Dalton Primus* feel disposed to select them for himself, according to my proposition in the *Courier* of the 25th inst." Intending, should "Dalton" accept my proposition, to select an equal number with himself, and leave the subject for the committee to prosecute to the end, desiring and expecting that the subject be discussed calmly, dispassionately and scientifically.

I select W. B CARLISLE, JOHN VANDERHORST and P. F. STEVENS, Esquires. I do not know what views these gentlemen may have taken upon the subject, and I am acquainted with only one of them personally, but I am confident that the cause of Truth and Science will receive no detriment at their hands. I am, &c.,

LAWRENCE S. BENSON.

FORAGE FOR OUR CAVALRY AND ARTILLERY.—Owing to the fact that but little was planted last season on our line of coast below the Charleston and Savannah Railroad, the supply of forage for horses is getting very scarce. The period is near at hand when a more thorough system must be organized than has heretofore existed, to secure to the very large force on our coast the necessary supplies for their horses. Corn, hay and blades are to be had in abundance, and our railroads must arrange to transport supplies on a more extensive scale. What is most particularly needed is an energetic officer who would take this matter especially in charge—with authority to organize a thorough system and see that each post is supplied with forage. It will be no child's play to do this, and we know of no one more capable for the work than Major E. WILLIS, late Quartermaster on the staff of General DRAYTON. We do not know where he is now assigned to duty; but if not permanently located, we hope to hear of his being assigned to this important duty. COM.

LOCAL MATTERS.

A NEW NOVEL, BY BULWER.—Messrs. S. H. GOETZEL & Co., the Mobile publishers, have just issued, in very creditable style, a reprint of BULWER LYTTON's last novel, "A Strange Story." The book is a weird and thrilling narrative, full of the mysticism which marks several of the previous works by the same author, and more especially *Zanoni*. It will doubtless be eagerly received by the Southern reading public, now absolutely famishing for want of the literary novelties of old England. The publication of the reprint forms an era in the development of publishing enterprise at the South; and we hope that, after the war, the only reprints of English books circulated amongst our people will be those issued within the borders of the Confederacy.

The "Strange Story" may be had at the book store of SAM. HART, Sr., who will mail it, postage paid, to any one sending an order for it, enclosing $3.

THE COURT OF GENERAL SESSIONS, Judge GLOVER presiding, met Monday. No jury having been drawn, the Judge ordered that a jury be drawn for a special term to be held in February, and also for the regular April term. The Court then adjourned.

IN THE CONFEDERATE COURT on Monday, the Grand and Petit Juries were organized as follows:

GRAND JURY.

C H. West, Foreman; N. Devereaux, R. S. Hanahan, F. Hitch, M. Herbert, H. C. Schroder, J. L Courtney, N. M. Porter, J. C. Martin, Barnarc Murray, Ernest Klein, Francis Police, Anton Hernholm, J. Horlbeck.

PETIT JURY.

Jury No. 1.—George S. Hacker, Foreman; A. Drago, O Tiedman, B. Foley, Jno. H. Heyer, Jno. Kuck, Lewis Buck, M. McMammon, Rev. Jno. Moore, James Kennedy, F. Weinholtz, F. W. Bahtnge.

The Court then adjourned until Thursday morning.

COURT OF APPEALS—JANUARY TERM, 1863.—TUESDAY, January 13, 1863.—The Court met at 10 o'clock. Present, Chief Justice O'NEALL and Associate Justices DUNKIN and WITHERS, and proceeded to a call of the docket.

Mr. Attorney General HAYNE, after a few remarks, submitted to the Court the proceedings of the Charleston Bar on the occasion of the death of Hon. MITCHELL KING, and moved that, as a testimony of respect to his memory, the preamble and resolutions be entered on the minutes of the Court, and that the Court do now adjourn.

The Chief Justice briefly responded, and ordered that the proceedings be entered on the minutes, and that the Court do now adjourn. Adjourned.

CALHOUN INSURANCE COMPANY.—The following gentlemen were on Monday unanimously elected officers of the Calhoun Insurance Company for the ensuing year:

PRESIDENT.
SAMUEL Y. TUPPER.

DIRECTORS.

Hon. CHARLES MACBETH.	FRANCIS J. PORCHER.
WILLIAM KIRKWOOD.	WM. L. TRENHOLM.
R. WAINWRIGHT BACOT.	JOHN S. RIGGS.
WILLIAM WHALEY.	A. R. TAFT.

The statement of affairs of the company shows a very satisfactory result of the business for the past year. After paying dividends in June and December last, at the rate of 12 per cent. per annum, a surplus remains of over $20,000 as net profits of the company. This speaks well for the Directorship, as the stockholders attested by their unanimous re-election.

CHARLESTON INSURANCE AND TRUST COMPANY.—At an election for Directors of this Company, held on Monday, the following gentlemen were elected to serve the ensuing year:

JOHN H. HONOUR.	CHAS. KERRISON.
WM. C. DUKES.	O. J. CHAFEE.
JAS. WELSMAN.	A. O. ANDREWS.
CHAS. M. FURMAN.	W. H. HOUSTON.
JAS. BANCROFT.	RICHARD YEADON.
JOS. PREVOST.	GEO. E. GIBBON.
J. W. CALDWELL.	JAS. K. ROBINSON.

T. D. WAGNER.

THE SALES OF STOCKS AND REAL ESTATE at the Exchange Tuesday were numerously attended, and the securities offered realized very full prices.

Mr. JOHN S. RIGGS sold $7000 City Sixes at $100¾; 129 shares Planters' and Mechanics' Bank at $31¼@31⅜; 170 shares Bank of South Carolina at $45⅝@46¼; 20 half shares South Carolina Railroad Company at $62½; 94 shares Elmore Insurance at $23½@23⅝; 10 shares Gas Stock at $26 50; 113 shares People's Bank at $31⅜@31¼; 8 shares Farmers' and Exchange Bank at $27¼; 1 Greenville and Columbia Railroad Bond of $500 at $101½ per cent; $5000 City of Memphis Bonds, $1000 each, at $98; 90 shares Bank of Fairfield at $25¼; 100 shares Union Bank at $62¾.

Mr. Z. B. OAKES sold 100 shares Insurance and Trust Company at $26¾; 150 shares South Carolina Insurance at $25¼; 110 shares People's Bank at $63¼; 41 shares Planters and Mechanics at $31¼, and 40 shares State Bank at $26⅝.

Mr. T. A. WHITNEY sold the following Real Estate:—A two story Brick Dwelling and Kitchen, No. 143 Market street, on a lot fronting 25 feet by 63½ feet deep, for $3025; a House and Lot, 33 Hasell-street, $11,000; a two story Wooden House, northwest corner of Coming and Montague-sts., lot 43 by 44 feet, $2200; a two story House, No. 75 King-street, lot 17½ by 78¼ feet, $1550; a three story Brick House on Tradd-street and a two story Brick House on Church-street (northwest corner of Tradd and Church) with outbuildings, for $4575.

SOLDIERS' RELIEF ASSOCIATION.—The regular weekly meeting of this Association was held on Monday last, when the various reports were read. During the week the following donations have been received:

Through Mr. Rickard Yeadon, 1 blanket, 1 oil cloth and 5 pair of socks.
From Mrs. Kirkpatrick, 1 bottle pepper vinegar, 2 bottles catsup, 1 mustard, 1 scarf, 2 balls yarn and tracts.
From Miss E. C. Gibbs, of Windsor, 3 pair socks.
From Miss C. P. Walker, 4 caps, 1 havelock.
From Mrs. A. M. Lee, 8 pair socks (for soldiers in the West).
From Mrs. Wickenberg, 1 blanket, 1 cotton shirt, 12 handkerchiefs and old linen.
From Miss Carrie Klinck, 4 curtains, 10 shirts and old linen.
From the Misses Robb, 10 pair socks and 2 scarfs.
From Miss M. Holmes, 1 blanket.
From Mrs. Norman, 2 pair socks.
From Mrs. Gurgappus, 6 pair socks.
From Mrs. R. M. Powell, 1 pair socks.
From Mrs. P. Thomson, 7 caps, 1 scarf and paper cambric.
From J. L. S., 2 blankets.
From H. S. Rhett, 5 carpet blankets.

During the week the following articles have been donated:

To Camp Warren Hospital, 15 shirts, 10 pair drawers, 10 pair socks, 10 towels, 10 handkerchiefs, old linen and 1 sheet.
To individual applications, 8 worsted shirts, 9 pair of drawers, 13 pair socks, 9 cotton shirts, 1 overcoat, 3 handkerchiefs, 2 towels, 3 testaments, 2 comforters.

The following amounts have been received:

From Miss C. A. Stewart, $10.
From Mrs. John Bowie, $10.
Donation, $4.
From Mrs. T. Bennett, through Mrs. Forrest, $20.
From Rev. H. A. Tupper, through Mr. R. Caldwell, $100.
Through Mrs. S., $10.
From Miss S., through Mrs. Forrest, $2.
Given to Soldiers' Relief Hospital, chipped lightwood.
To Roper Hospital, grist and chipped lightwood.
To Citadel Square Hospital, grist and lightwood.

TELEGRAPHIC NEWS.

THE POSITION OF KENTUCKY.

RICHMOND, January 13.—The message of Governor ROBINSON to the Kentucky Legislature, recommends that the State should reject and protest against LINCOLN's Proclamation. It inflicts, he says, upon Kentucky a fatal though indirect blow.

FROM THE MISSISSIPPI.

GRENADA, January 12.—Scouts arrived here from opposite Helena, report that the Yankee transports have not yet passed that place on their way northward. The Yankees had landed at Friar's Point, and burned the Church and principal buildings of the town.

General PRICE's journey southward has given rise to the rumor that he is the bearer of peace propositions from the Northwest. The rumor is, of course, absurd.

VIRGINIA LEGISLATURE.

RICHMOND, January 13.—In the State Legislature to-day the election of a Confederate Senator was postponed until to-morrow. Judge ALLEN, WM. C. RIVES and CHAS. W. RUSSELL were nominated in the House of Delegates.

THE CONFEDERATE CONGRESS.

RICHMOND, January 13.—The Senate to-day having no quorum (only thirteen Senators being present), adjourned until to-morrow.

In the House a quorum appeared. Mr. CURRY, of Alabama, was elected Speaker *pro tem*. Several bills were introduced to modify the exemption law. Mr. PERKINS introduced a resolution approving the conduct of certain citizens of Louisiana within the enemy's lines. Mr. FOOTE offered a series of resolutions declaring that the South will consent to no plan of reconstruction of the former Union, that no armistice is to be entered into until LINCOLN's proclamation shall be revoked, that no propositions to negotiate are to be entertained, except upon the basis of unconditional recognition, and that we will never consent to any alliance, commercial or otherwise, with the New England States, but would be willing to negotiate with the States bordering on the Mississippi River, which may be willing to stipulate and enter into a league, offensive and defensive, when a party at the North shall overthrow the LINCOLN power. The resolutions further offer to guarantee to the Northwestern States the free navigation of the Mississippi, whenever they declare their inclination to withdraw from the war, and present inducements to the States west of the Rocky Mountains to withdraw from the Yankee Union. All these resolutions were appropriately referred.

Resolutions were also introduced demanding an investigation into alleged frauds in flour contracts, etc., pending which the House adjourned.

—o—

THE LATEST.

—o—

THE PRESIDENT'S MESSAGE.

RICHMOND, January 14.—The Message of President DAVIS was read before Congress to-day.

It opens with a brief review of the military position of affairs, which is described as very satisfactory. The fourth great army of invasion, it says, has been defeated in Virginia, and General BURNSIDE has experienced the fate of his three predecessors, McDOWELL, McCLELLAN and POPE. In the West, the fortunes of war have been various; battles have been fought with fearful carnage on both sides, but the hopes entertained by the enemy of any decisive results have been baffled. On the Atlantic coast the enemy are still confined to the protecting cover of their fleets. A review of our history shows that the war has entered its third and last stage. The first effort was to restore the Union, and has been abandoned. The second was to conquer the South and govern it as a dependency. This, too, has proven impossible, and has been abandoned. The third design is to destroy and plunder what they could not subjugate. If we continue the same efforts as in the past, this design will likewise be defeated, and we may confidently expect that this is the closing year of the war. The enemy will possess neither spirit nor resources for continuing it into the fourth year on so exhaustive a scale. We desire peace but will continue the war at any sacrifice, until our right to self-government and the sovereignty and independence of the States are vindicated and established.

Foreign relations are then reviewed. Our right to recognition is shown by reference to the past history of other States, some of which were recognized as independent by Great Britain in the treaty of peace in 1783, and had been previously by the Allies in their war with France. When our Commissioners demanded recognition, they were told that foreign governments could not decide between the conflicting statements made by our Government and that of the United States, in respect to our mutual relations; and that Europe would simply recognize us as belligerents, and preserve a strict neutrality. This apparent refusal to decide was, in reality, a decision against us, because we were thus unjustly deprived of diplomatic intercourse on the same footing as our enemies.

The question of the blockade is discussed at length. Its invalidity is shown, as tested by the principles of the Congress of Paris in 1856. The whole conduct of neutral nations is summed up so as to show that they have enforced all neutral rights that affected us injuriously, and refrained from asserting those that would injure the United States. The correspondence between the Courts of France, Great Britain and Russia is adverted to. The language of the French despatch is construed as a formal admission of our ability to maintain our independence, and justifies the hope of early recognition.

The barbarities committed by Northern troops are referred to, and the action taken in relation to the atrocities committed by Generals McNEIL, BUTLER and MILROY explained. The opinion is expressed that the infamy of their conduct must be approved by their superiors, who have in no one instance punished the perpetrators of these crimes.

In regard to LINCOLN's Proclamation, he says our detestation is tempered by profound contempt for his impotent rage. The action of the Government will be confined to delivering up all commissioned officers hereafter captured in the ten States named in the Proclamation, to be tried by the States, under the laws which punish those that excite servile insurrection. The Proclamation is treated as possessing great significance in a political point of view. It proves what were the designs of the Republican party from the beginning, notwithstanding their efforts to conceal them by false declarations.

The Proclamation is next considered as a guarantee against the possibility of reconstruction. It is also treated as a confession of inability to subjugate the South, which Europe will be bound to consider as justifying our immediate recognition, and as an intimation to the people of the North that they must submit to a final separation of the States.

Adequate taxation is recommended; also the issue of bonds, to be guaranteed by the States.

The Message, which is the longest yet issued by the President, embraces a comprehensive review of the whole internal and external relations of the country. It is confident, and even triumphant, in tone, and closes with a tribute to our women, without whose sublime sacrifices, it declares, that our success would have been impossible.

THE HARRIET LANE.—The *Harriet Lane*, a vessel of six hundred tons burden, was originally built for the Revenue service, but at the beginning of the war with the South she was turned over to the Navy, and at once underwent such alterations as were thought necessary to adapt her to her new service. At the time of her capture she mounted eight guns of heavy calibre, her bow gun being a fifteen inch rifle.

YANKEE FORCE AT NEWBERN.—The Raleigh *State Journal* learns from a perfectly reliable source that there were in the waters of Newbern, on Wednesday last, no fewer than *fifty five* Yankee transports. The forces there include the commands of three Major Generals, usually in the Yankee army 15,000 each, which gives the full force there at some 45,000 to 50,000 at least.

NEW COUNTERFEIT.—The Western papers mention that a new counterfeit fifty, with a green face, dated September 2, 1561, had made its appearance. The only defect mentioned in the counterfeit is a want of water lines in the paper. Look out for it.

OBITUARY.

DIED, in this city, January 10, 1863, Mr. SAMUEL GAILLARD BARKER, in the sixty-fourth year of his age.

DIED, in this city, on the 2d instant, Mrs. SOPHIA LADSON GRIMKE, aged 65 years and 11 months.

VOL. I. RICHMOND, SATURDAY, JANUARY 17, 1863. No. 19.

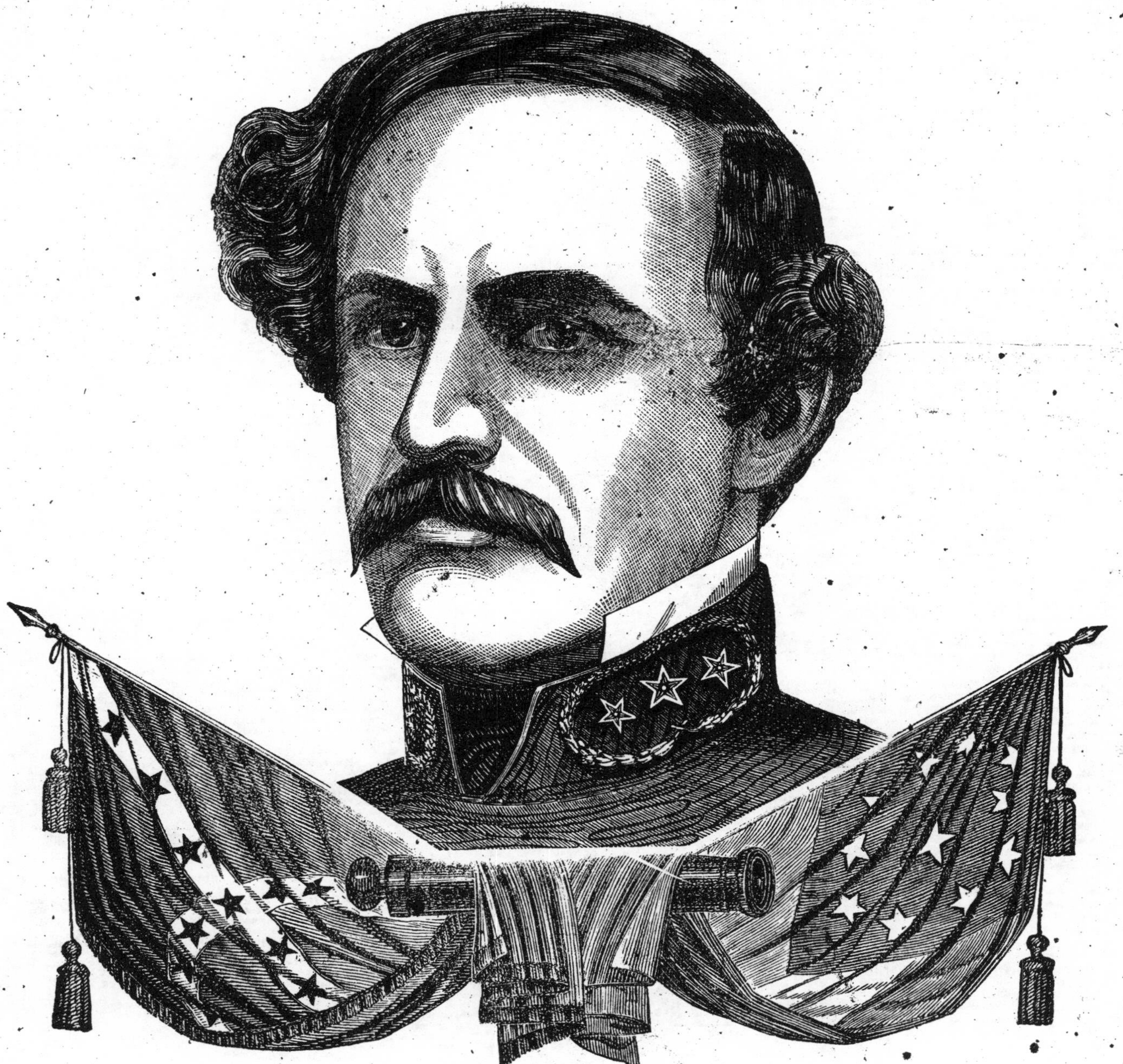

ROBERT EDMUND LEE,

COMMANDER-IN-CHIEF OF THE CONFEDERATE FORCES.

[W. B. CAMPBELL, Engraver.] [FROM A PHOTOGRAPH BY REES, TAKEN TEN YEARS AGO.

VOL. I. THE DAILY MISSISSIPPIAN. JACKSON, MISS., JANUARY 25, 1863. NO. 231.

Daily Mississippian.

F. T. COOPER, Editor.

SUNDAY MORNING.

JACKSON, - - JANUARY 25, 1863

FOREIGN PAPERS.

Our friends would greatly oblige us by sending any Northern, Western, or other Foreign papers they may chance to get in their possession to this office.

☞ The funeral services of Dr. J. GLASS will take place at the Presbyterian Church on Sunday, January 25th, at 4 o'clock. The public are invited to attend.

☞ Rev. Dr. Ford will preach to-morrow morning at the usual hour, at night he will deliver a lecture on the prophecies.

☞ The poet who writes acrostics for our Main street cotemporary, must be an attentive reader of the Mississippian.

MAJ. GEN. STERLING PRICE arrived in the city yesterday evening on his way to Richmond.

☞ Three car loads of sick soldiers, transported from the Vicksburg to Jackson hospitals, arrived here yesterday evening.

☞ Persons wishing to send small packages to Capt. Ridley's battery, may leave them at this office until Monday evening.—They will be taken in charge by Adjutant Power, who returns Tuesday morning.

FROM VICKSBURG.—We learn from our correspondent, who left Vicksburg at one o'clock yesterday, that every thing was quiet up to that hour. The morning being cloudy, nothing could be seen of the enemy's operations. Their transports, however, were still in the vicinity of the canal. As the train left, several guns were fired in rapid succession, apparently from the levee batteries.

The steamer Vicksburg was fired into yesterday by one of the enemy's light batteries, and penetrated her in three or four places.

☞ We publish in another column a short sermon, eminently suitable to the times, entitled "Gog (of) the land of Magog; or, Lincoln, of the United States." It is written by a distinguished divine, whose name is withheld from motives of delicacy. The reader will be much edified and interested in its perusal. We would be glad to publish a short sermon upon subjects adapted to the times from the same author every Sunday morning.

NEWS AGENT.—The well known newspaper Agent, S. A. Wells—who, in days lang syne used to gladden the people on the line of the Mississippi and Tennessee Railroad—is, we are glad to learn, making arrangements to supply the public with the daily papers on the railroads and rivers of Mississippi, Alabama and Tennessee, within our lines. We know him of old, and confidently recommend him as an energetic news agent. He will furnish the MISSISSIPPIAN regularly to all within his circuit of business. Headquarters at Selma, Alabama.

From New Orleans.

We have a copy of the Picayune of the 21st. As usual there is scarcely anything in it but a batch of Northern intelligence about six weeks old. Since the Yankee occupation of the city, the Pic has been sadly behind the times.

We find that orders from the office of the Provost Marshal-General have been issued, giving notice that the list of prisoners of war for exchange will be closed on Wednesday, (the 21st) at 2 o'clock P. M., and that all officers and enlisted men now on parole, who shall fail to report and register by that time, will be considered as having violated their parole, and will be dealt with accordingly.

Notice is furthermore given to the effect that persons who have registered their names since the 12th inst., with a view of crossing the lines to Ponchatoula and Madisonville, are to be at the Lake end of the New Canal on Wednesday, the 21st inst., at 6 o'clock in the morning, to leave with their baggage on the steamer S. W. Brown.

Necessity for More Forces.

In a review of the situation of the country in a military point of view, the Richmond Examiner insists that something must be done, and speedily, too, to fill the shattered ranks of our army in the Southwest. It says exemptions must be diminished. The system of details must be adopted. Young men must not be permitted to evade their duty by slipping into safe places. Complaisant friends must turn a deaf ear to their entreaties. Able-bodied men must not be allowed to stay at home on the pretext of attending to twenty negroes. With the first opening of Spring comes the last tremendous shock of this war. Many of the Yankee troops are nine months men. More are enlisted for two years, their time expiring in May next. Up to that time they will be available, and we may be very sure that all the fighting that can be possibly gotten out of them will be had before they are allowed to go home. They outnumber us two to one. There is a limit to the brave men at Tullahoma, Grenada and Vicksburg. They must be sustained, strengthened, reinforced. If within the next two months we do not add seventy-five or a hundred thousand men to our forces in the Southwest we [illegible] If we do add these, we [illegible] and next summer will witness the final triumph of our arms.

Arrival of Citizens from New Orleans.

Two hundred and fifty citizens of New Orleans, [illegible] of Banks, after [illegible] "Confederates," left New Orleans a few days ago. A goodly number, male and female, are now in this city—some to stay and others bound for various points in Dixie. Those whom we have seen, although they have left almost all they are worth in worldly goods behind, [illegible]

Yankee Commissioned Officers.

Upon the subject of the disposition of the Yankee commissioned officers who are captured in any of the Southern States attempting to carry out Lincoln's proclamation by exciting servile insurrection, the President in his message says: "So far as regards the action of this government on such criminals as may attempt its execution, I confine myself to informing you that I shall, unless in your wisdom you deem some other course more expedient, deliver to the several State authorities all commissioned officers of the United States that may hereafter be captured by our forces in any of the States embraced in the proclamation, that they may be dealt with in accordance with the laws of those States providing for the punishment of criminals engaged in exciting servile insurrections. The enlisted soldiers I shall continue to treat as unwilling instruments in the commission of these crimes, and shall direct their discharge and return to their homes on the proper and usual parole."

This disposition of the Federal commissioned officers has been suggested and endorsed by nearly every paper in the Southern Confederacy, and we have no doubt but it meets fully the views and wishes of the entire Southern people. There can be no question of the justice and propriety of the President's policy in this respect, and we hope that Congress will not hesitate a moment in the adoption of his suggestion.

If it be contended that the rigid enforcement of the State laws will exasperate and render still more vandall the horde who come to despoil our homes, and incite our slaves to insurrection, we have only to say in answer to such an argument that they have and will continue to revel in every species of wanton destruction. We have tried temporizing measures, and steadily refused the resort to harsh ones, in the vain hope that the ravages of our cruel and vengeful foes might be stayed. All such means have proved signally abortive. The very mildness and humanity of our government has invited and stimulated outrages.

We must deal with our case with an eye to the protection of our own people. The time for child's play has passed. Lincoln's proclamation is denounced by a large majority of his own people as the most monstrous and diabolical blot which any government has ever fastened upon its escutcheon. Its object is to call forth the most stupendous horrors ever entailed upon any country—to drench a once happy and prosperous land in the innocent blood of women and children—It is a cool, calculating, hellish plot, which promises not the amelioration of the negroes' condition. Lincoln does not expect it to have that effect, but he hopes by arousing servile insurrection to produce a war between the blacks and the whites which will result in the extermination of both. This is the bloody object of the proclamation.

It would, therefore, be suicidal and outrageous if our government suffered this infamous and wicked policy to be carried out when it has the power to turn its horrors [illegible] the minions who attempt its execution.

The great object of this government has been and is to be just. If then the suggestion of the President in this respect is just, there is no reason why it should not be promptly adopted and sternly enforced.

If the Yankees know not what the State laws are upon this subject, they will have ample opportunity to learn when they fall into our hands. We don't believe, however, that they are ignorant on that subject, and our own opinion is that when they become thoroughly convinced of our unalterable determination to sustain our State laws, a majority of them will be disposed to relinquish their commissions; and those few whose fanaticism is upon the John Brown order, will evince on the battle-field a decided disinclination to be captured—so great will be their aversion to such a hapless fate that we believe the most of them will take to their heels when serious danger threatens them.

But whatever may be its effect upon the Yankee officers we must be entirely satisfied of the propriety of the measure, if, indeed, we do not doubt the justice of our own laws upon such matters. The safety of our women and children, of ourselves, our country and our slaves, absolutely requires the adoption of some such policy as is indicated by the President, and we can think of none so wise, so appropriate, expeditious and effective as the turning over of the commissioned officers to the State authorities. The laws of all the States are clear and well defined, and a Yankee has no more right to trample upon these laws than has the native citizen. Let it be once thoroughly understood that the willing instruments of Lincoln's diabolical policy are to be held amenable to the violated laws of the Southern States, and the fate of John Brown will so haunt their sleeping visions that a general nervous restlessness will be evinced in their waking hours.

We confess that we are highly pleased with this portion of the President's message. It is another evidence that the President fully understands the wishes of the people, and is determined to do right no matter what the hazard. We are firm believers in the salutary effects which the adoption and rigid enforcement of this policy will have upon the cause. By all means let this be the policy of our government.

THE CONSCRIPTION LAW SUSPENDED IN FLORIDA.—The Conscription Law has been temporarily suspended throughout the State of Florida, in order to allow all persons between the ages of eighteen and forty-five years, subject to military duty under said act, a chance to volunteer in companies and regiments of their own choice.

PORT HUDSON COURIER.—The tiniest and the prettiest, and the best printed paper we ever met with is published at Port Hudson, La., by ELLIOTT & CO. Although, for the want of paper, which they expect soon to receive, their sheet—measures not more than 10x12, still there is evidence in it that "somebody who knows something" has it in hand. We are sufficiently experienced to know a "hawk from a handsaw."

☞ During the battle at Murfreesboro [illegible]

For the Mississippian.]

Gog (of) the Land of Magog; or, Lincoln, of the United States.

I propose to show the striking resemblance between Gog (of) the land of Magog and Lincoln of the United States, as it appears in the 38th verse of the 38th chapter of Ezekiel and a part of the 11th chapter of Daniel.

FIRST.—AMERICA IS TO BE THE SCENE OF THIS CONFLICT.

1st. Commentators generally disagree as to the *time, character* and *locality* of this conflict.

2d. Some of the best commentators agree in the opinion that Gog of the Old Testament is different from Gog of the New Testament.

3d. They also teach that Gog, spoken of by Ezekiel, is to make his appearance just before the millennium and another just before the end of time.

4th. The expression "latter years" and "latter days," Ezekiel, 38th chapter, 8th and 16th verses, when compared with other similar expressions, is generally thought to mean the time just before the millennium, and as most writers on the subject predict the millennium to begin between the years 1866 and 1878, we have reason to expect Gog to make his appearance in our day.

5th. This conflict is to be in a land that for a long time was a wilderness, but is now inhabited by those gathered out of many nations—Ezekiel xxxviii: 8. America answers to this land.

6th. The enemy coming out of the "north part" were to come upon the "mountains" (or States) "of Israel," (or of the South.)—Mountains in symbolic language mean States.

From these six arguments, we think it can be fairly inferred that America is to be the scene of the conflict spoken of in these chapters without adducing further proof.

SECOND.—THE CHARACTER OF THE NORTHERN ARMY.

1st. "Clothed with all sorts of armor"—Ezekiel 38th chap. and 4th verse. By this is meant an army well equipped. Have not the Northern army all the implements of war used in this enlightened day?

2d. Five different races of people are spoken of as being in this Northern army—Ezekiel 38th chapter, 5th and 6th verses. Are there not many races of people in the Yankee army?

3d. In the seventh verse they are described as making great preparations. Was not this the case in their repeated "On to Richmond?"

4th. Yet they shall be drawn back as with a hook in their jaws—Ezekiel 38th chapter, 4th verse. Our thanksgiving days appointed by the President are sufficient proof of this.

THIRD.—OBJECT OF THE WAR.

The invasion is made for gain.

1st. They came to a land "at rest," without natural defenses, having neither bars nor gates, "to take a spoil and to take a prey."—Ezekiel 38th chapter, 11th and 12th verses. Are they not a set of thieves and robbers plundering where they can?

2d. In the 13th verse their object is clearly seen. Three personages are represented as asking the Abolition army if they come to take them as their prey. The first that speaks, representing the principal ones they were after, is Sheba and Dedan, the descendants of Ham, (or Africans) who were the "occasion of the war," as Mr. Lincoln says; and the irony that is intended in the question, proves that the most of the slaves will be true to their masters.

The next that speak are the "merchants of Tarshish," which means any kind of merchants. Thus the second occasion of the war is, to get possession of our merchandise in cotton.

Then the "Young Lions" speak. Young Lions, in symbolic language, mean young States, and represent these Southern States, young in this Confederacy, asking if the third "occasion" of the war is to make them slaves for the North.

Is not this three-fold object of the war in which we are engaged a remarkable coincidence—a three-fold cord not easily broken?

FOURTH.—GOD WILL HELP THE SOUTH.

1st. In the 15th verse they are represented as coming with "a mighty army," in the 16th verse as "clouds to cover the land." These prophecies find their fulfillment in the large armies they have brought into the field, and we can say, "If it had not been the Lord who was on our side, when men rose up against us, then they had swallowed us up quick, when their wrath was kindled against us."

2d. Have not our enemies come to destroy our peace? Did they not expect to make an easy prey of our "unwalled villages?" Did they not boast that eight millions of people could not stand before twenty millions?—But God hath said, "when my people dwell safely thou shalt know it"—verse 14; and at the appointed time "my fury shall come into my face"—verses 18th and 19th: that is, his anger will be kindled against them. And when that day comes, there shall be great fear and trembling in these Confederate States, and for a while our enemies will seem to triumph over us. Then will God "call for a sword," that is terrible slaughter among our enemies from "all my mountains," or States of this Confederacy—that is, every man that we can spare will be called into the field, and in this slaughter God will help us as he did the army of Gideon, and in the battle against Tisera: pestilence shall thin their ranks, and the bullets that fall like "rain," and the cannon balls and grape that crush like "hailstones," and the shells that burst and blaze like "fire and brimstone," will thin their ranks, and God will magnify his name upon the earth—verses 19 to 23.

3d. In the 14th verse allusion is made to the "great and crooked serpent," spoken of in Isaiah 27th chapter and 1st verse, or Mr. Lincoln's Anaconda that was to crush out the rebellion in "ninety days." The prophesy in Isaiah 27th ch., 1st verse, evidently refers to Gog of the Old Testament, and there can be no doubt that the 17th verse points to it.—Then how striking the analogy and how sure the punishment that awaits "Levathan," or the Anaconda.

FIFTH.—GOD WILL DESTROY THE NORTH.

1st.—The 39th chapter of Ezekiel treats principally of the destruction of the North. "And I will turn thee back, and leave but the sixth part of thee." * * "And I will smite thy bow (or deceit) out of thy left hand;" that is, he will reveal their deception, both to the people at home and abroad.—"And will cause thine arrows (swift destruction) to fall out of thy right hand," and "thou shalt fall upon the mountains," (or States of the South) and "I will give thee to the ravenous birds of every sort, and to the beasts of the field to be devoured."—2d, 3d and 4th verses.

2d. The 9th and 10th verses speak of the number of arms falling into our hands.

The number of arms falling into our hands within thirty days from the battle of Manassas No. 2, have been estimated at 69,000 small arms and 266 cannon, not to say anything of the number since hostilities began.

3d. In the 11th chapter of Daniel, commencing at the 40th verse, (which the best commentators agree to be parallel with these two chapters in Ezekiel, we are told that the Abolition army shall take our treasures, and that the "Libyans (who are natives of the Southern country; or, in other words, Southern traitors, such as Andy Johnson and others,) and the Ethiopians, shall follow them for protection. But at last "tidings out of the East and out of the North shall trouble Gog," and, leaving us he will go after them and come to his end in a valley at the foot of a mountain or hill noted for its beauty, or sacred in the memory of the land. Here, so many of the enemy will fall that the valley shall be called "Hamongog," (valley of multitude.) I think everything in these chapters have had its fulfillment but the "tidings out of the North and East." God grant that the Peace party at the North and foreign intervention may bring these tidings, and Gog may come to his fearful end with "none to help him."

SUBROSA.

JOSEPH E. JOHNSTON NO GENERAL.—It is painful to have one's confidence in the character or abilities of a distinguished man rudely shaken, or to find one's cherished convictions, delusions though they were, dissipated. But the logic of facts is inexorable, and by that logic we are forced to conclude that the public and ourselves have been deceived in [illegible]

Cavalry Operations in the Rear of Rosencranz' Army.

A correspondent of the Montgomery Advertiser gives the following account of the operations of our cavalry forces in the rear of Rosencranz' army. The letter is dated "Rear Guard, Wheeler's Brigade, near Murfreesboro', January 6:"

Upon Christmas day, the First Alabama cavalry occupying the advance posts near Lavergne, was driven in by an advance brigade of the enemy. So soon as the intentions of the enemy became known, General Wheeler slowly withdrew his cavalry towards Murfreesboro', turning upon him at every convenient point, and delaying his approach by successive gallant skirmishes.—During the severest of these contests our Adjutant, E. T. Ledyard, was seriously wounded while charging among the foremost. After a resistance of three days our cavalry retired behind the infantry lines and took its position upon the right wing. At 11 P. M, the night of the 29th, Gen. Wheeler, with a command composed of his old brigade under Col. W. W. Allen, a regiment of Gen. Pegan's brigade under Col. Carter, and a section of Robert's battery, started upon an expedition from the right wing, the purpose of which was not known or even guessed. Passing around the left of the enemy he pushed forward by a circuitous by-road, and early on the morning of the 30th, intersected the Jefferson pike in the rear of the Federal army. Far away to the southeast we heard distant cannonading which told us that the enemy was feeling the strength of our lines. Before us we saw, moving along the pike, a long train of Federal wagons hurrying to the battle field. Detaching Col. Carter to intercept their advance, General Wheeler fell upon their rear with a charge and a whoop which spread consternation among the guards and teamsters. Quick as thought the traces were cut, linchpins removed, the forewheels cut down, and fire set to at least fifty wagons laden with the baggage of officers, with company stores, ammunition and clothing. Every soldier who wished, provided himself with comfortable clothing, boots, hats, overcoats, overalls, pistols, revolving rifles, saddles, bridles, horses, mules, or what else might suit his fancy or comfort.

"To saddle and away" before the roar of Carter's pieces in the rear should bring up superior forces of the enemy. Over stock and rock, hills, fences and ravines, burning wagons behind us, roaring artillery far to the right of us, hams strung to the saddle bow, mules with tattered traces scouring the country around us. We cavorted with the sport of a Christmas holiday, towards the village of Lavergne. The Yankee pickets had promised to give the First Alabama a Christmas ball. Bragg was giving them the music, while we were dancing to Wheeler's quickstep. Right upon Lavergne we rushed through the wood on all sides—scores of Yankees were seen flying about the streets, while teamsters forsook their wagons and endeavored to escape, but escape was impossible. Five hundred prisoners surrendered; one hundred and fifty richly laden wagons were consigned to the flames; one thousand mules and horses were carried off, or stampeded. Gen. McCook's large tent, containing the wardrobe, &c., of his military family, was sacrificed to the flames. The wagon of the chief paymaster was burned, containing the accounts and vouchers for the army of the West, and one million dollars Federal green backs. The booty was rich, and the men felt as though they had entered the den of the forty thieves. Everybody had a prize—a horse, watch, negro, rifle, sword or flag. Your correspondent had the honor of dining upon Gen. McCook's Christmas turkey, without so much as saying "By your leave, sir." We were [illegible] the main Nashville pike and every moment might bring the enemy upon us.

So again to saddle and away. At a gallop we scoured the hills and fields until approaching night brought us upon the village of Nolansville. Fifty wagons more before us—again a charge, a stampede, a line of flame along the pike, and one hundred prisoners of war. Thus, three times had we struck the main arteries of the enemy. The result of the expedition being 250 wagons heavily laden, 1,500 mules and horses, and 700 prisoners of war. The entire loss of the enemy falling little short of $1,000,000; of course the burnt Treasury notes was only the loss of so much paper.

That night we bivouacked five miles from Nolansville. At early dawn of the 31st, we passed swiftly around the right wing of the enemy to the music of artillery, and threw ourselves on the enemy's flank with an impetuous charge. The enemy was not surprised. He received us with a battery on front and enfilading fire on each flank of the column. General Wheeler quickly wheeled from the flank and threw his brigade against the front of the enemy's right—the first Alabama leading the way. Captain Elmore's squadron gallantly cleared the woods of skirmishers, driving them back upon the line of cavalry. Then Allen charged with his regiment, supported nobly by John T. Morgan, Wade, Hogan and others. The Federal cavalry was thrown into confusion upon the line of infantry. We had accomplished our purpose, had marched against a superior force of the enemy's cavalry and beaten him in an open field. But, eager to win new laurels, we rushed upon the infantry, and were received by a volley which emptied many a saddle. Colonel Allen is severely wounded and forced to leave the field. His regiment under Lieutenant Colonel Hundly, wearied out by a two days' march, nevertheless stands its ground, and pours an answering volley into the enemy. For two hours the battle raged. Lieuts. G. S. Allen and Dever, of Captain Hodgson's squadron, are killed. Many others of the regiment have bitten the dust. The gloom of evening was still brightened by the flash of cannon, and the ceaseless blaze of rifles seemed "like a swarm of fire-flies tangled in a velvet screw." In the midst of it all, General Wheeler, our little corporal as he was called at West Point, dashed about unconcerned for personal safety. Just as night came on he waved his hand and bade us give them a good night. With a last blaze of rifles we closed out the old year, and bivouacked on the field of battle with the dead and dying around us. The great battle of the 31st was over; the enemy driven for miles from the field; five thousand prisoners taken, forty pieces of artillery captured, the battle-ground strewed with dead and dying.

The New Year opened with Wheeler hurrying around the enemy's right towards Lavergne. Performing a circuit of twenty miles, he rushed again upon the enemy's rear, and waving his hat dashed upon the wagon trains which seemed now to be moving towards Nashville. This time the trains were defended by a strong body of cavalry, but it fled before the charge, and left in our hands seventy-five wagons, two hundred prisoners and a battery of artillery. The scenes of the first raid were re-enacted. Moving back around the enemy's right, we rested next day within sound of the furious and unsuccessful cannonade against the enemy's left wing. On the following day we attempted a third raid upon the rear, but fell back in consequence of the enemy's having guarded his trains with a brigade of infantry and cavalry. We drove the cavalry before us, but were unable to displace the infantry, which resisted us behind the shelter of their wagons. In this attack Major Prentice was wounded, and we regret to say Lieutenant J. A. Whiting is among the [illegible]

[illegible] a courier reached General [illegible] his return. We [illegible] hours on the [illegible]

The Battle of Galveston.

We glean from the Texas Telegraph the following particulars of the recent battle:

Among the volunteers on the Neptune was Captain A. Ridley, Adjutant of the Arizona brigade. The captain has a splendid rifle presented to him by General A. S. Johnson, for having safely brought him across the plains. He took three fires with his rifle at close quarters and emptied his revolver. Captain Ridley commanded a company of guides under General Johnson, and was with the General at Shiloh.

Governor J. R. Baylor fired the LAST shot at the Owasco as she sailed off. He fired six shots from a rifled cannon, four of which took effect. Captain Shoalwater, late member of the Legislature in California, assisted the Governor in working the gun.

Captain Shoalwater attempted to escape with a company from California, but was captured at Warner's Ranch, and imprisoned five months, but managed to escape and came by land through Mexico.

Three privates from among those who boarded the Harriet Lane, took possession of a 24 pounder, that had been deserted, trained it on her as she came up towards the Harriet Lane, and the first shot went crashing through her bow, when she immediately backed out and left. It was the only shot left for the gun. Governor Baylor was at Eagle Grove when the fight began, and ran the entire distance, and first took part in the fight by assisting to place a Columbiad in position. He joined his old regiment as a private, went down and joined his old company.

The duty of the Lucy Gwin was to prevent the small boats of the enemy from approaching the railroad bridge, to cut off our land forces, and assist generally, should any of the other boats become disabled and obliged to draw out of the fight. As soon as it was ascertained that the Harriet Lane was captured, the Gwin came to the wharf, and with her crew assisted in disengaging the Bayou City from the Harriet Lane. As she approached the Owasco fired upon her and the Carr.

One of the Texans who boarded the Harriet Lane immediately jumping aboard, grasped a Fed by the collar, exclaiming, "Surrender, or I will blow your brains out!" The other replied: "You'd better look at me first!" Recognition was instantaneous; they were brothers!

An enormous shell from the Harriet Lane entered the cabin of the Neptune, just as the latter was first passing; exploded in the dense crowd of men gathered there, waiting eagerly for the moment to board, and killed eighteen and wounded many more. This terrible disaster, in so narrow a space, did not, however, daunt the spirit of the men for a moment.

Captain Henry Lubbock had a shot gun and two six-shooters ready, beside him, for use when his launch boat should reach the Lane; but they were swept away in an instant by the rush of the "horse marines" behind him, fierce for the fray. He endeavored, but in vain, to keep some of them back, fearing that the Owasco would board them.

James Dowland, clerk of Captain Wharton, A. Q. M., absented himself—plea of sickness—went on the Bayou City, and was the first on the Harriet Lane, and pulled down her pennant.

Lt. Sid. Sherman, of Fontaine's company, was among the first killed. He fell at his gun, and lived about an hour and a half. He was an only son—the idol of his parents—the pride of the heroes who made San Jacinto's field famous. His last words are reported to have been: "Tell my dear mother I die happy—it is for my country!"

Only four men were killed on board the Bayou City. They were killed by the explosion.

Capt. Wm. M. Armstrong went on board the Lane after the battle, and found lying in the blood on deck a bible. He picked it up and remarked, "Now I am going to open this bible this new year's day, and the first passage I read I will take as an omen for the new year." He opened it carelessly and the first passage his eyes fell on was the 1st verse of the 20th chapter of Deuteronomy: "When thou goest out to battle against thine enemies, and seest horses and chariots, and a people more than thou, be not afraid of them; for the Lord thy God is with thee, which brought thee up out of the land of Egypt!" It is a good omen as well as a most startling circumstance.

The guns of the Westfield have all been fished up and found to be in good order.—The enemy will hear from them in due time.

When Gen. Scurry demanded the surrender of the 42d they asked three hours time to consider. Scurry replied, that if they chose to take the fire of his batteries during the time they could have it. They at once gave in.

The prisoners of the 42d Massachusetts are lucky fellows. They enlisted four months since for nine months. They have had to stand fire but once, are well clothed and will be well fed. By the time they can be exchanged their time will be up. They will have spent their winter in the South, and will be back home again in time to enjoy a Northern summer.

Prospects of Galveston.

From the Galveston News.]

For a period of just eighteen months on the 2d instant, Galveston is now without any blockading vessel, and it is gratifying to be able to state that, if the Blockade is again established, it will have to be done by something more than old hulks of mere sail vessels. Although the steamers that captured the Harriet Lane and defeated the Federal fleet, were not by any means fitted up as rams, or cased with iron, for want of time since General Magruder assumed command, yet we believe they will now speedily be rendered far more formidable. Fortunately, we have the material to do it, and we are glad to see that there is now no lack of disposition to put it to a proper use, or of determination to meet the enemy whenever he makes another attempt to enter our harbor. By this victory we have added largely to our future means of defense, for we have now secured many large guns of the very kind we most needed, and also about the best gunboat for our purposes we could have selected from the whole Federal fleet, for while she is strong and of light draft, she is admitted to be the fastest steamer the Federals had. These, with the other acquisitions in arms, munitions and stores of various kinds, under such a commander as General Magruder, and with such able and determined officers and men as has been selected to assist him from among the very best fighting material of Texas, give us assurance that Galveston will never have to submit to the disgrace of another surrender, and that if it is ever taken it will be one of the dearest conquests the enemy have ever made. We have only to name the men who now hold command under General Magruder, to satisfy those who know them that what we say is no idle bravado. In addition to General Magruder's efficient and accomplished staff, we may name some old Texas fighters who have seen some service in former times as well as more recently: Brig. Gen. Scurry, now in command of Galveston; Col. DeBray, Col. James Reiley, Col T. Green, Colonel Bagby, Col. Cook, Col. Pyron, Col. P. Hardeman, Col. Griffin, Governor J. R. Baylor, who assisted in the retaking of Galveston, as a private, and who is still ready to take any position assigned to him—and though last, by no means least, Major Leon Smith, who, we understand, is now appointed by General Magruder to the command of our fleet. We could name many others holding subordinate positions, who have the ability and daring requisite to execute the most hazardous enterprise.

☞ The Atlanta Intelligencer learns "that Mrs. Gilliland, near Tunnel Hill, and her four daughters, have spun and wove seven hundred [illegible]

From Abroad.

The Charleston Courier has a correspondent at Nassau, where he had lately arrived by a fast steamer out of Charleston. His first letter is of the date of this month, and was brought by a steamer just now into Charleston harbor. We make some extracts from his fresh and racy letter:

NASSAU, N. P., January, 1863.

Nassau, for reasons needless to mention, now possesses considerable interest to the people of the Southern States. If there had been no war, its only connection with us would have been, as heretofore, through the fruit traffic. A few months has changed its character to a great depot for goods of all kinds to which London, Paris and New York largely contribute. This business has added heavily to its wealth and importance. A year ago, it was only an obscure colonial town, where, I am told, comparatively few of the comforts of life could be procured. Now, the shops are as well filled and patronized as those of large cities in America and Europe. It is not strange, therefore, even if the inhabitants were unimpressible to feelings of sympathy with a people struggling for liberty against despotism, that they should from motives of interest side with the South. The sentiment appears to be all one way: the natives of the North living here are mostly pro-Southern, or at least in favor of peace; and, more strange than all, the negroes—the victims of British "freedom"—throw up their hats for "Dixie." I have talked with a number of intelligent Northern gentlemen here, and have found them vehemently opposed to Lincoln and his war policy. Among the British, as at home on their own island, there is scarcely a dissentient from the popular current of feeling. A surprising and gratifying illustration of this was afforded upon our arrival at Nassau. As we approached the town, flags on the British vessels in the harbor dipped to the Confederate Stars and Bars, and as we neared a large war vessel lying at anchor, we received the same courtesy. Near the frigate was a tender filled with a portion of its crew, at least fifty in number. As we returned the salute, the gallant man-of-war's-men broke forth with the "Bonnie Blue Flag," which they sang with a loudness and spirit that did credit to their heads and their hearts. As they shouted the last refrian—

"Hurrah! hurrah!
For *Southern Rights* hurrah!
Hurrah! for the 'Bonnie Blue Flag'
That bears the single star."

the thrill that passed through our band of exiles as we stood on the deck of our vessel, involuntarily brought our hands together in applause. I find, upon landing, that the "Bonnie Blue Flag," as well as "Dixie," and "My Maryland," are the only dities used by the piano players and street boys. As I write, a small darkie under my window is giving the world vocal assurance of his determination to "live and die in Dixie."

The white population form a refined and cultivated society. I have had the pleasure of meeting many agreeable gentlemen, among both the natives and resident English. The Fair and a Concert held last evening reveal the fact that Nassau can claim, perhaps a larger share of female beauty than most settlements of its size.

There have been no arrivals from the North or England since my reaching Nassau, furnishing later dates than you have already at hand. The steamer bringing the English and American mails is due here from New York shortly, and I trust that in my next letter I may be able to give you a *resume* of the latest intelligence from the outside world.—The only item of news that has reached us is a report brought by a schooner from Key West, that the ubiquitous "290" has captured a California steamer and lightened it of its specie. Captain Semmes is said to have permitted the steamer to proceed on its voyages in consideration of its many lady passengers. The report of the capture gives great satisfaction, and the hope is everywhere expressed that it may be confirmed.

—oo—oo—

TO FARMERS.—The Athens Watchman gives the following seasonable advice to farmers:

We hope every man, woman and child in the Southern Confederacy who has a single acre of tillable land unoccupied by small grain will plant it in peas, corn, potatoes, or something else suitable for man or beast. To do this it is important it should be put in order early. Do then, go to work at once. Let the land be well prepared. If you have, or can get manure, be sure to apply it. Plow deep and plow often. If your ditches are filled up, clean them out, and do everything you can towards getting ready for the greatest corn crop ever grown in these lands. We will need it, whether the war continues or not. Every grain that can be produced will command a high price.

One word more. If you can procure the seed, sow Spring oats. We know that the Fall crop usually succeeds the best, but sometimes Spring oats do well. According to our prognostications the present year will be a great crop year, and Spring oats will do well. Don't neglect sowing if you can find seed.

Take care of your hogs and sheep, your calves and goats, and everything that will make meat. Raise all the poultry you can. There is a constantly growing demand for everything to eat. Don't be afraid of raising too much.

—oo—

THE CHINESE CANE.—The Southern Cultivator says:

We are glad that the public are at last waking up to the merits of the Sorgho. We found it cultivated very extensively all through North Carolina, and we repeat our first opinion of it, viz: that, considering all the uses to which it may be applied, it is the most valuable plant for the South that we have obtained since the introduction of cotton.

HEADQUARTERS, Jackson, Miss., January 3, 1863.

General Order, No. —.

ALL absentees belonging to the departments of Tennessee, Alabama and Mississippi and Louisiana, who will return to their regiments or companies before the 20th instant, will be pardoned for any unauthorized absence.

By command of Gen. JOHNSTON.
A. P. MASON, Major & A. A. G.
Lieut.-General PEMBERTON, Commanding Department of Mississippi and East Louisiana.
jan1–2w

Military Orders.

ADJUTANT AND INSPECTOR-GENERAL'S OFFICE,
RICHMOND, January 8th, 1863.

General Orders, No. 2.

THE following orders are published for the information and guidance of all concerned:

I.—Recognizing the necessity of officers of railroads having full control of their business, in order to ensure safety and dispatch in transportation, military officers are prohibited from interfering with the engines, cars, running of trains, or with the control and management in any way of railroads.

II.—When transportation of troops or freights by railroad is necessary, a Quartermaster or other authorised officer shall make requisition for the same upon the Superintendent or proper officer of the railroad, furnishing the necessary evidence of transportation, and delivering the troops or freight to be transported.

III.—In the event that more freight is to be transported over any road than the road has the ability to carry promptly, the officer furnishing evidence of transportation will indicate to the railroad officer what shall take precedence. In the absence of any special officer as to what freight shall go first, the railroad officer shall be governed by any general order the Quartermaster General may issue in regard thereto.

IV.—When troops or freight is to be moved out of the usual routine of a railroad, the officer having charge of such movement, will fix with the Superintendent, or other officer of the road, on which the movement is to be made, the day and hour of departure, and when so fixed the troops or freight must be ready at the appointed time.

V.—In the event of any military necessity for an unusual movement at any particular point, the commanding officer at such a post will communicate fully the character and extent of service to the principal officer of the road or roads from which it is required, and ask the personal supervision of the proper railroad officers to the duty.

VI.—Quartermasters and commissaries will exercise discretion in shipping freight not wanted for immediate use, and that may be stored at safe and convenient points, taking care not to block up roads and thereby impede transportation.

VII.—When it is necessary to send a special messenger with freight, such messenger must travel with the freight placed in his charge, and his transportation shall be so specified on its face, in order to prevent him from traveling in any other way.

VIII.—Enrolling officers will permit conscripts, enrolled while in the employment of railroads, to remain at their duties until Colonel Wm. M. Wadley, A. A. G., may decide as to who of them it is necessary should be detained for service on the road.

IX.—Any violation of these orders, or remissness on the part of railroad officers to perform promptly all government transportation, will be reported to Colonel W. M. Wadley, A. A. G., who will indicate from time to time, where his headquarters will be.

By order.
[Signed] S. COOPER,
jan24–1wd Adjutant and Inspector General.

HEADQUARTERS, STATE OF MISSISSIPPI,
ADJUTANT AND INSPECTOR GENERAL'S OFFICE,
Jackson, January 19, 1863.

Special Order, No. 271.

MAJOR-GENERAL T. C. TUPPER:

I.

YOU will issue orders to the several commanders of Companies, Battalions and Regiments to retain in their commands all men under forty years of age, who have been already detailed or volunteered in the service of the State. Special Orders No. 15, issued from Headquarters of Lieut. General Pemberton, under instructions from the Secretary of War, commands that all men under forty years of age now serving in Mississippi State organizations, will not be interfered with by enrolling officers until the disbanding of said organizations.

II.

You will assemble the companies in the several Counties in the State, and draft therefrom a sufficient number of men to fill each Company now ordered into service to the number of seventy, including commissioned officers; and cause all absentees to return immediately to their commands.

III.

You will order all field, company and staff officers, not in active service, and all white males between the ages of eighteen and fifty, who are either permanently or temporarily residing in the State, to be included in the draft, except such as may be liable and have not been discharged from conscription. All those discharged from conscription, and those discharged from State service by reason of Surgeon's certificates, together with those who are exempt from conscription by act of Congress, are to be included in said draft, unless specially exempt by the laws of the State.

By order of JOHN J. PETTUS,
Governor and Commander-in-Chief.
JONES S. HAMILTON, Adjutant and Inspector General, State of Mississippi.
jan22–d1m

CONFEDERATE STATES OF AMERICA,
WAR DEPARTMENT, Richmond, Va. Dec, 16, 1862.

Lieut. General J. C. PEMBERTON, Commanding, &c., Jackson, Mississippi:

General:

YOUR letter of November 1st, regarding the pay of Provost Marshals, has been received. The existing law does not provide for the pay and allowances of Provost Marshals, such as have been appointed in Mississippi, and the Department does not feel authorized to go beyond that law.

The subject will have to be referred to Congress.

Very respectfully,
Your obedient servant,
JAMES A. SEDDON,
Secretary of War.

Headquarters, Department Mississippi and East Louisiana, Jackson, Miss., Jan. 5th, 1863.
(Official) F. M. STAFFORD,
A. A. A. G.
jan5,1863.

OFFICE ASSISTANT QUARTERMASTER,
Jackson, Jan. 7th, 1863.

WANTED IMMEDIATELY, a large number of negro mechanics (blacksmiths, carpenters and wagon makers) for the Government shops at this post, for which the most liberal wages will be paid. Apply at my office, just below the Post Office.
H. L. BOON, Capt. & A. Q. M.
jan 8,1863.

PROVOST MARSHAL'S OFFICE,
JACKSON, MISS., Dec. 19th, '62.

UNLESS charges and specifications are forwarded to this office, prisoners will not be retained. Guards on duty in this city, and at other Military Posts, will be held responsible for the utmost diligence in arresting all officers and soldiers, improperly absent from their commands.
UPTON M. YOUNG,
Captain and Provost Marshal.
dec19 tf

Important to Tanners and Shoemakers.

HEADQUARTERS, SPECIAL DEPARTMENT,
BANKSTON, MISS., Jan. 10, 1863.

HAVING been appointed special agent by Maj. L. Mims, chief Q. M. Mississippi and East Louisiana, for the collection of hides, in the counties north of Jackson, and the distribution of the same, among the several tanneries within said District; and to contract for shoes and leather for the Confederate States,

Therefore, the proprietors of all tan yards and shoe shops, within said district, will report to me at my headquarters, without delay, the number of vats filled, and when they will be ready to work out, as also the vats empty, and the number of hides necessary to fill the same; and how many sides of leather, and pairs of shoes each proprietor can furnish monthly, and the additional amount of mechanical labor necessary to carry on said factories to the extent of their capacity. The above information is necessary to an equal distribution of hides among the several tan yards, and to produce uniform prices throughout the State, and make available at the earliest period, and in the most economical manner, the records thereof.

All tanners and shoemakers not subject to military duty, not now employed in their vocation, will also report to me, if they wish employment.
J. M. WESSON, Special Agent.
jan11–1m
☞ Appeal copy, and send bill to this office.

WASHINGTON ARTILLERY OF NEW ORLEANS.

Recruits Wanted!

OFFICERS of this Battalion are now in the South to enlist such Young Men, citizens of Louisiana as are within conscript ages, who may come forward and offer themselves for service.

By special authority of the Secretary of War, any person liable to conscription may be enlisted, and conscripts enrolled may be assigned to fill up this organization.

A bounty of FIFTY DOLLARS will be paid to all liable to conscription who come properly recommended.

The recruiting stations will be Mobile, Ala., Jackson, Miss., and other points on the N. O. J. & G. N. R. Road, nearer New Orleans.

Captain M. B. MILLER, 3rd Company, will be stationed at Mobile, as Recruiting Officer; and Captain SQUIRES, 1st Company, Captain RICHARDSON, 2d Company, and Lieut. NORCOM, 4th Company, at Jackson, and vicinity, to whom or to the undersigned at Mobile, applications may be addressed.

J. B. WALTON,
Colonel Commanding and Chief of Artillery,
1st Army Corps, Dep't Nor. Va.

I have established my Recruiting Office at Room No. 82 Bowman House, Jackson, Miss.
C. W. SQUIRES,
Captain and Recruiting Officer, Battalion Washington Artillery.
☞ Alexandria La. papers, please copy and send bills in duplicate to this office.
jan22–tf

WANTED,

ONE Drummer and one Fifer, for the 2nd Regiment Mississippi State Troops. Apply to Major D. H. Dickson, at Snyder's Bluff, or by mail.
By order Col. D. H. QUIN.
HAMGIL, Adjutant.
Jackson, Jan. 13, 1863—dtf.

WANTED, [illegible]

Daily Mississippian.

By COOPER & KIMBALL.

TERMS:

THE DAILY MISSISSIPPIAN will be published every morning, (except Monday) between the hours of 7 and 8 o'clock, at $2 50 per month.

ADVERTISING.—One square of ten lines or less, $1 50 for first insertion, and $1 for each subsequent insertion.

MISSISSIPPIAN OFFICE HOURS!

The Mississippian Office Counting Room will be open in future, from 6 o'clock in the morning till after sunset, every day in the week except Sunday. On Sunday morning it will be open for the delivery of papers, from 6 to 9 o'clock in the morning.

WANTED IMMEDIATELY,

ONE milch cow. Apply at this office. jan7

Head Quarters, 4th Military District, Department Mississippi & East La.,
JACKSON, Jan. 12, 1863.

General Orders.

I.—All officers and soldiers arriving within the limits of this Military Post, or in the case of Regiments or detachments, the officer in command of the same will at once report themselves at the office of the Commandant of the Post, a few doors above the Mississippian Office, on Capitol street, show their authority for being within the limits of the Post, and receive written permission to remain. The Commanders of Regiments or detachments of soldiers, *in transitu*, will permit no officer or soldier to visit the City of Jackson, save on strict military business. The permission so granted, must be in writing, and specify the nature of the business, and in no case will any private, or party of privates be permitted to enter the City of Jackson, unless under charge of a reliable-non-commissioned officer, and so long as such Regiment or detachment of soldiers remain within the limits of this Post, the officer commanding will be held responsible for the good conduct of his men, and for any depredations committed by them. All officers and privates assigned to duty at this Post, who have not heretofore reported, will at once report, show by what authority they were thus assigned, register their names and receive a written certificate of this fact.

II.—The Commander of the Camps of Paroled Prisoners, Surgeon in charge of Hospital, and Commanders of Encampments, will never permit more than two of their command to be absent at once, except upon military business, and then always in squads, under charge of a non-commissioned officer. No officer or private soldier will be permitted to sleep without the limits of his encampment, or be permitted to remain within the City of Jackson, after 9 o'clock at night, except in the case of such officer or privates as are connected with the various departments in the city, or have the consent of the Commander of the Post for the same.

III.—Of all persons save soldiers with transportation or orders from the proper military authority, a passport will be required before they will be permitted to leave the limits of the Post. The sale of liquor is forbidden within the limits of this Post, except upon the written consent of the Commander of the Post.

IV.—The officer assigned to duty as officer of the day, will see that the above orders are carefully complied with, and will have arrested and reported to the office of the Commandant of the Post, all officers and privates that have not their orders endorsed, "Reported," and signed by the Commandant of the Post, except however, such General Officers, Members of the Staff and Orderlies or Couriers connected with their Headquarters, at present within the limits of this Post.

V.—No permits for officers or soldiers to visit this city will be recognized without the endorsement of the Division or Brigade Commander.

JOHN ADAMS,
Brigadier-General Commanding 4th Military District.
jan14-2w

Department Mississippi and East Louisiana.

Lieut.-General J. C. Pemberton.
Lieut.-Colonel J. R. Waddy, A. A. G. and Chief of Staff Department.
Major R. W. Memminger, A. A. G. and Chief of Staff, Army of Mississippi.
Major J. Thompson, Adjutant and Inspector General Department.
First Lieut. J. H. Morrison, A. D. C.
" " J. C. Taylor, "
Major G. M. Mayo, Chief of Ordnance Dep't
Major A. B. Cooke, Paymaster "
Captain C. G. Armistead, Paymaster of Post, Jackson.
Major L. Mims, Chief Q. M. of Department.
Major T. Johnston, Chief C. S. " "
Surgeon N. S. Crowell, Medical Director.

MILITARY DIRECTORY.

COMMANDANT WESTERN DEPARTMENT—General Joseph E. Johnston—Headquarters in Mrs. Kerr's house, corner of Capitol and President streets, below the "Mississippian" office.

COMMANDANT DEPARTMENT MISSISSIPPI AND EAST LOUISIANA—Lieutenant-General J. C. Pemberton,—Headquarters Capitol Street, next to the corner of State street, up stairs.

COMMANDANT 1ST MILITARY DISTRICT—Brigadier-General Daniel Ruggles—Headquarters over Morey's Drug Store.

COMMANDANT OF POST.—Lieutenant-Colonel A. M. Foute—Office five doors above "Mississippian" office.

CHIEF QUARTERMASTER OF THE DEPARTMENT—Major L. Mims—one door above the "Mississippi Baptist" office, up stairs.

CHIEF QUARTER MASTER OF THE WESTERN DEPARTMENT.—Major Alfred W. Barbour: office, Dr. Knapp's house, State street, near the Bowman House. Captain W. M. Cary, A. Q. M. and Assistant Chief Quartermaster: office in the same house with Major Barbour.

PROVOST MARSHAL—Captain Upton M. Young, Office south-east corner of State and Pearl streets, up stairs.

POST QUARTERMASTER—Captain W. M Gillaspie,—One door north of the Postoffice.

POST COMMISSARY—Captain T. L. Maxwell, Four doors south of the Postoffice.

POST SURGEON—Dr. A. B. Cabaniss—One door above "Mississippian" office.

PAYMASTER—Captain J. C. Armistead, Corner of State and Pascagoula streets, Graves' Building, up stairs.

TRANSPORTATION AGENT—Captain T. C. McMackin—Three doors below Morey's Drug Store, up stairs.

INSPECTOR GENERAL OF DEPARTMENT—Major Jacob Thompson,—At General Pemberton's Headquarters.

MEDICAL BOARD.—Drs. J. G. Thomas, Will D. Somers, and J. P. Furniss, at the Dickson House.

MEDICAL PURVEYOR—Dr. Richard Potts,—On State street, Graves' Building.

MEDICAL DIRECTOR—Dr. N. S. Crowell—Headquarters over Post Surgeon's office.

A. A. AND INSPECTOR GENERAL—Colonel J. G. Szymanski, —Headquarters exchanged and paroled prisoners, back of Telegraph Office, up stairs.

ENROLLING OFFICER FOR CONSCRIPTS—Captain Wm. McKeever—Next door to Provost Marshal's Office.

COL. COMMANDING ARSENAL—Phil. Stockton—Office in the State House.

Officers of the State of Mississippi.

Commandant Mississippi State Troops, Maj. Gen. T. C. Tupper—Office in the State House, west corner, next to the Senate Chamber.

Adjutant and Inspector General of the State of Mississippi, Colonel Jones S. Hamilton—Office State street, up stairs, opposite J. B. Morey's.

Quartermaster-General, Col. A. M. West—Office on State street, three doors above Angelo's, up stairs.

Chief of Ordnance—U. Bourne, over General West's office.

Another Row in the Garret.

It has been ascertained through official sources that the Yankee Generals Grant and Hurlbut, enacted a pretty little scene a few days since at Memphis: Hurlbut, who has a sepirate command at Memphis, received some order from Grant which he refused to obey. He said he came South to protect, and not to destroy it. Grant intimated that Hurlbut was a traitor, when Hurlbut replied that he would take his men over to the d—d secesh rather than obey Grant.—And here the curtain closed.

GREAT MEN WILL DIFFER.—Gen. Hurlbut, commanding at Memphis, is said to have given his opinion lately that the policy of opening the Mississippi river was a bad one because when it was accomplished all the Western troops would return home and the rebellion would remain in its full strength.

On another recent occasion, Sherman stated that unless the Mississippi be opened soon, all the Northern troops would certainly return home—that they could not be kept together. In either case the Western troops, it seems, will desert.

☞ Cotton cards are being manufactured in Williams county, Texas, and are pronounced by judges to be good.

The Washington Chronicle of the 9th, one of Lincoln's organs, for a copy of which we are indebted to a friend in the army, says the accepted Democratic newspapers and leaders throughout the country are gradually, but not the less boldly and resolutely, taking ground against the war.

They seem to rely, says this journal so confidently upon the continued credulity and prejudice of their followers, that they are now throwing off all disguise, and putting themselves forward as the apologists of treason, and the assailants of the Government of the United States.

There is a good deal of truth in the Chronicle's statement so far as refers to the growing disaffection of the Democrats. That party begins to see that the Lincoln followers are worse enemies to liberty and the government as it was than the rebels, and there is nothing strange in the fact that they are apologits for such "treason" as Southerners have exhibited. Let the ball of contention and discord roll on. Its momenture will be hard to check.

The Chronicle argues that the pretext for this "unblushing disaffection" is the President's Emancipation Proclamation, but labors to show that it is inherent in the party.—These truckly organs of the tyrant are evincing great alarm on account of the Democratic "boldness" and "disaffection," and well they may, for the time is fast approaching when this same "disaffection" will hurl the fanatics from power. Speaking of these malcontents, the Chronicle says:

Now, that they think their country is plunged in gloom, they denounce not merely the President and his constitutional advisers, but are evidently preparing to take the fatal steps of sowing the seeds of demoralization in the army, and if possible, of inducing such of their friends as they can to leave the ranks and return to their homes, in order to assist them in breaking up the Government itself.

Gen. Grant and the Jews.

The order of Gen. Grant expelling the Jews from his department, it now turns out, says the Richmond Dispatch, was not directed alone against pedlers and smugglers, but was a sweeping and arbitrary decree of banishment against a whole people. Such an act of tyranny unheard of at the present day even in Monarchical Europe. It is worthy of the dark ages, and of the darkest and most hypocritical despotism now in existence in the civilized globe. The chosen people of God, under the Old Dispensation, have been forced in their long and checquered history to endure many indignities as well as oppressions; but to be treated as unworthy the companionship of Yankees is the crowning insult of all. If they can surpass the Yankees in avarice and meanness they have found a lower deep of greed and extortion than any other race under the sun. But it is a foul wrong to place them upon the same level in any respect.

Even apart from the illustrious names they have given the world in the days of their national glory, there is no branch of literature or enterprise, either in the commerce or arms, in which some of their people do not take rank with the master spirits of the earth.—The boasted "merchant princes" of New York could all be put into the breeches pockets of the Rothschilds, without adding much to their influence or power. So far as extortion is concerned, it would be a happy thing for mankind if the only extortioners were Jews. And so far as their religious creed is concerned, it is as much better than the infidelity of Yankeedom as light is than darkness. It is all in keeping with the professed religious toleration of Puritans that they should seek to persecute Jews. Who that dared to differ from them on any subject ever escaped their fangs?

From Middle Tennessee.

The Mobile News of the 19th contains an interesting letter from Gen. Bragg's army, from which we learn that our losses at Murfreesboro' will probably reach, in grand total, nine thousand in killed, wounded and missing. We publish extracts:

The following is the return made of the losses in Lieut. General Hardee's corps, which did the hardest fighting during the two day's battle of the 31st December and 2d January, Gen. Hardee is one of our most popular Generals, and has won the highest admiration and respect of his men and officers alike, for his sterling, soldier-like qualities, and who regard him as a most brave, generous and skillful commander.

LIST OF CASUALTIES IN GEN. HARDEE'S CORPS.

	Killed.	Wounded.	Missing
GEN. BRECKINRIDGE'S DIVISION.			
Hanson's Brigade	49	269	84
Pillow's Brigade	46	322	79
Preston's Brigade	56	399	94
Adams' Brigade	113	419	173
Total	264	1439	430
CLEBURNE'S DIVISION.			
Wood's Brigade	52	339	113
B. R. Johnson's Brigade	61	488	57
Lucius Polk's Brigade	30	298	18
Liddell's Brigade	93	492	21
Total	236	1617	209
M'COWN'S DIVISION.			
Ector's Brigade	29	275	39
Rains' Brigade	20	154	15
McNair's Brigade	42	331	42
Total	91	759	166
Grand total			5211

The loss of Jackson's Brigade and Col. Thos. H. Hunt's Regiment is not included in the above.

There is no interesting news from the front. Our pickets occupy the ground six miles from Murfreesboro', which is supposed to be held by but a small force of the enemy. It is now positively ascertained that the enemy commenced his retreat on Saturday afternoon, before we did, and that his rear had reached seven miles beyond Stewart's Creek, which is ten miles from the town, before our forces had left Murfreesboro'. Rosencranz's defeat was a most signal and positive one. The fact that his forces did not return to Murfreesboro' until the Tuesday following, shows that he did not receive the information of our evacuation until the day before, and that he was the first to retire. He therefore can, with but little grace, boast of the capture of Murfreesboro', much less claim a victory on that score. As it has turned out, our evacuation of Murfreesboro' was extremely unfortunate, and had a tendency to mar the perfection of our most brilliant victory; but the exigencies of the then surrounding circumstances made the movement necessary. It is needless to deny the dissatisfaction of the army on this account

I learn from accredited authority that General Bragg has asked to be relieved from his command. This is no doubt a most judicious step. It gives the President unreserved scope of action. He may, therefore, fully sustain Gen. Bragg, and refuse to relieve him; or, while sustaining him in his course, may think that the interests of the service demand that Gen. Bragg should be relieved and assigned to some other point.

The Nashville Union of the 7th contains a miserable appeal, by its "small chips" editor, to the white laboring class against the slaveholder, which is but an abortive imitation of Prentice's perversion and Brownlow's billingsgate. It also has a list of nineteen hospitals in Nashville, and gives the following list of rebel officers taken prisoners now at Nashville: Major Jas. C. Davis, 17th Tennessee; Captain J. A. Cash, 20th Tennessee; Captain H. Drysdale, 3d Florida; Capt. Wm. Clark, 17th Tennessee; Capt. B F. Eddins, 41st Alabama; Capt. G. W. O'Neill, 17th Tennessee; Lieutenants A. Banna, 13th Louisiana; E. R. Haynes, Blythe's Mississippi; J. D. Leland, 41st Alabama; M. W. Black, 17th Tennessee; Thomas B. Connor, 45th Mississippi; W. S. McShaw, N. F. Wolt, Chas. Liddell, S. E. McNulter, same; J. L. West, 1st Florida; Wm. Caruthers, 2d Georgia; J. E. Holly, Douglas's Cavalry; Wm. Street, 45th Mississippi.

The weather is cold and pleasant, and Tullahoma is becoming a lively place. ORA.

☞ It was a maxim of General Jackson's—"Take time to deliberate; but when the hour of action arrives, stop thinking and go in."

Fragments of a Conversation between Mr. Phax and Mr. Figgers.

From the Little Rock Democrat.

* * * MR. FIGGERS. I don't blame the farmers for charging high prices. The merchants began it by advancing their prices on the plea that they could not replace their goods unless they did so. They absorbed all the specie they could, on the pretence that it would take specie to buy goods.

MR. PHAX. I do, remember the old saying that "two wrongs do not make one right." Though your neighbor is an extortioner or a thief, it is no reason you should be one. If A. steals from B., and B., to get even, steals from C., it will run on till the whole alphabet becomes a set of thieves.

F. That is a moral view of the question, but there is another which country people take and which has some show of fairness.—Says one "two years ago I brought a dozen eggs to town and with them bought a yard of calico. Now calico is two dollars a yard, and as a dozen eggs are worth a yard of calico, a dozen eggs are worth two dollars."

P. The argument is a specious one, as you will see by examination. Certain circumstances have enhanced the value of those things we cannot produce. These circumstances are beyond your control or mine. Salt, iron, and other necessaries can be obtained only in limited quantities and with much danger and difficulty. As a natural consequence the prices of these articles increase. So of calico, which is not a necessity. But it costs no more to keep hens now than it did two years ago. Now, suppose there was no war and salt, iron, or calico could be obtained at the old prices. Then suppose that a drought should utterly destroy the crops so that corn would be held at ten dollars a bushel. Let a farmer come to buy a sack of salt and be told that a sack of salt was worth ten bushels of corn, therefore a sack of salt was worth one hundred dollars, and do you think he would admit the argument as a just one? Suppose the rot should destroy potatoes so they were worth five dollars a bushel when the ordinary price is one dollar. When the farmer went in a store to buy calico, the price of which was twenty cents a yard and the shop-keeper should ask him a dollar a yard because potatoes were scarce, he would fail to see any fairness in such a system. These accidents of seasons, or of war, produce burthens which, if all manfully bear their part can be easily borne, but if one refuses to bear his share and then another, and another, it at last falls with a crushing weight on a few who are prostrated.

F. Very true. But these exorbitant prices were first begun by shop-keepers, or as they style themselves, the merchants.

P. Not by all. There were some who sold out their stock of goods at the old prices, and closed their stores.

F. The exceptions you mention are noble ones. Their names should be preserved and honored. But the greater number, doubled, trebled, quadrupled their prices.—They got gold as long as any was to be had, and then amassed large quantities of paper. They hid goods until the market was exhausted, and then produced small quantities which they sold at twenty times their cost. Some, ashamed, if such beings can feel shame, or afraid, sent their goods to auction to be sold, so it might not be known who was the owner. To add to this, these fellows devised and practised all sorts of schemes to keep out of the army. They sought and obtained petty clerkships or stations in civil or military offices. You will find them as commissaries, understrappers in quartermasters departments, or snugly esconced somewhere, and then talk of being in the army. With fine salaries, they enjoy the privilege of buying all the necessaries of life from the government at low prices. Their corn, flour, bacon, sugar, and even coffee, are obtained at cost as *officer's stores*, rations, or such humbug. Now does the evil stop here. Getting their supplies thus cheaply, and having fine salaries, they can afford to buy luxuries at exorbitant prices. Chickens, eggs, butter, calicoes, which they cannot "draw," they can afford to pay prices for, which are beyond the reach of the poor. The result is that they keep up prices.

P. You speak severely, Mr. Figgers.

F. The severity is in its truth Mr. Phax. If this war should close, these fellows will talk of their being in the army, and try to create the impression that they rendered valuable aid in the great struggle for freedom.—They are at it already. You may hear them talk of "our army," "our division" and "department." All this, while the poor man is in the field, trenches or hospital at eleven dollars a month, and if his wife or mother at home, wants to buy a chicken or a dress, she finds the price is beyond her means because this fellow has offered dollars where she only has dimes.

P. When the war closes, public opinion will fasten itself upon these men and they will find that their demerits are noted and condemned.

F. Public opinion is not worth a fig. It has no votes. It is poor. No sir, if peace should be proclaimed to-morrow at noon, before sunset these fellows would be on the way to the North, with their hoarded gold to buy Yankee goods and nearly break their necks to get them here to sell at high prices.

P. But, surely, the people would not buy them.

F. Indeed they would.

P. But when things settle down these thngs will be remembered and the people will refuse to trade with men who have acted so.

F. You judge others by yourself, Mr. Phax, in supposing that they will remember these things. They do a more flourishing business than ever. They have the capital to commence with. A present of a few yards of calico to a farmer's wife; of a pair of boots to some influential man; a hat to some poor devil of an editor, and lo! their sins are all forgotten; the money wrung from the poor, and wet with the tears of the poor soldier's wife or widow when it came to their hands, will make them influential. Their wives and daughters, in silks and satins, will roll by in their carriages and bespatter us poor plebians with mud or dust, will turn up their noses at the honest, toiling poor, and take the first seat at the synagogue or festival.

P. Every vice has its punishment and will not these men be punished?

F. Yes, because there is a God and a hereafter. Doubtless many will find that their ill-gotten riches take wings.

P. But there is a class who are neither storekeepers or farmers—people who have nothing to sell and who buy of both.

F. These are the real sufferers; these are between the upper and the nether millstone. And what is worse than all is that these are the ones who are carrying on the war. Families of absent soldiers who are exposed to Yankee bullets are bled to death at home. Mechanics have some chance to keep even by extorting for their labor, but there are others who have nothing to sell, or whose income would barely suffice in ordinary times.

P. God help them. These are great wrongs and the remedy is somewhere. Let us study the matter and see if some palliative for these ills can not be found; some plan devised to check this spirit of speculation and extortion, and some measure of relief to be proposed. Till then, Mr. Figgers, good bye.

Northern Political Items.

The message of the Governor of Illinois appears in the Northern papers. The Governor closes in a long stump speech on the war, in which he says that slavery must be abolished before peace can be made. He pitches into the South, praises the emancipation proclamation to the skies, and demands of the Legislature a prompt and energetic support of all the measures of the Administration.

Gov. Curtin, in his annual message to the Legislature of Pennsylvania, gives the President's emancipation proclamation a wide berth. He refuses to touch it.

The Governor of New Hampshire has postponed the draft in that State *sine die*.

The Legislature of New York is at a dead lock in the election of Speaker. Eleven ballots had been held without the slightest change in the result—a tie every time.

A collision is threatened between the military and civil authorities at Indianapolis. The Judge of the Supreme Court of Indiana gives the Federal authorities distinctly to understand that he will issue the writ of *habeas corpus*, and try whether the military or civil power is triumphant.

Hon. John B. Henderson, Conservative, has been elected to the United States Senate from Missouri for the short term, which expires the 4th of March. He now occupies by appointment of the Governor ... term, Hon. John S. Phelps ... of Congress, leads in the ...

☞ Three negro ... garrison duty in Fo... and Pike.

[For the Mississippian.]

STANZAS.

BY MILDRED.

Our Southern land is filled with woe, submerged beneath a flood
That madly o'er its bosom sweeps, a dread, dark sea of blood,
A sea of precious human blood, where'er we cast our eyes—
Our brothers' blood, that from the earth for vengeance loudly cries.

Look down upon our land, oh! God, and send thine angel forth,
To strike with terror, to confound the legions of the North
And may that fratricidal power, whose crimes unsheathed the sword,
Cain-like be stricken with a curse inflicted by the Lord.

Our cities now are desolate, our churches are despoiled,
The graves of those we fondly loved, by vandal footsteps soiled,
The mansions of the wealthy sacked and given to the flames,
With deeds of dark depravity that savage warfare shames.

The poor man's cottage, where his love, *his* wealth, was all enshrined,
Has by the vile despoiler, too, to ruin been consigned:
And the whole nation, late so fair, before the eye appears
Reft of her noblest, dearest sons, like Niobe, all tears.

But to the rescue Southrons come—let them not die in vain,
Whose blood has been so freely shed your liberties to gain;
Better to die in Freedom's cause and sleep in heroes' graves,
Than live beneath a tyrant's yoke, despised and abject slaves.

Then come from every vale and glen, where yet a man remains,
And strike for freedom, lest you weep in slavery and in chains:
O, do not still withhold your aid, till Freedom's cause expires—
Arise! and gallantly defend "your altars and your fires."

Can there be those who will not fight for Freedom's glorious prize,
Yet basely would enjoy that boon for which the brave man dies?
For shame! ye craven-hearted ones, ye semblances of men!
Go hide you in some safe retreat, and ne'er be seen again.

Thus will you live—by man despised, of every honor shorn,
Unblest by gentle woman's love, but withered by her scorn;
Before her glance your conscious eyes will fall for very shame,
For in the most supreme contempt she holds the coward's name.

But would you win her smiles, go forth, and firmly, bravely stand
In the defense of Liberty, of home, and native land;
And should you live to see the time when all this strife is done,
How sweet will be the liberty you have so proudly won.

But death! ah! that must sometimes be the gallant soldier's fate;
Pray Heaven that it may lead you to a brighter, happier state,
And they who fall in such a cause, may, in the Maker's sight,
Be worthy of the martyr's crown amid the sons of light.

But soldier, on the battle-field, before the fight begins,
Look up to God, and humbly ask forgiveness for your sins,
And pray in faith, that if it be His will that you should fall
That He will take you up to Him, through Christ who died for all.

Sister and mother, maiden, wife, you pray for those you love,
Invoking blessings on their heads from Him who reigns above;
But pray for *all* who have gone forth your country to defend—
Pray for the patriot soldiers *all*, for each one is your friend.

And pray for our loved President, that God his steps will guide,
And never into error's path permit his feet to slide;
And may he never dim the fame he has already won,
But to our young Republic be a second Washington.

Pray that our nation may arise, bright as the morning star,
And shed its glorious lustre o'er the nations near and far;
Pray that the Lord, whose one command can bid this conflict cease,
Shall now, in His great mercy say: Enough! let there be Peace.

NEAR TANGIPAHO, LA., Jan. 18, 1863.

THE DENTIST'S WIFE.

Self-conceit in its most extravagant form is one of the numerous failings of our old friend Jones. By some mishap it was instilled into his mind from his earliest infancy, and has shown itself oftentimes within our own knowledge of him, too glaringly. It has been the bane of his social existence, and has made him countless enemies who would possibly all have been firm friends.—It has killed him in the estimation of a large circle of female acquaintances, who think of him only as conceited Jones, and has been the cause of many sore and unkind remarks by mothers of marriageable daughters, who have listened to Jones, as he pictured in glowing imagery, the likeness of the girl he would marry, his beau ideal being so far above the qualifications of their offspring, as to leave them not the shadow of a chance.

This very self-conceit is the prime and we doubt not the cause of his present bachelor existence, and will, unless a great reform takes place, leave him in such a position that even old maids will pass him without regret. We have talked to him by the hour, until our very patience was exhausted, in endeavoring to impress him with the idea of his extreme worthlessness, but without effect, for after our lecture is done, he replies with a yawn, pulls up his shirt collar, and adjusts it to a nicety by a miniature looking glass in his hat, lights a fresh cigar, and goes puffing away down street as conceited as ever. A change has recently taken place, and Jones is in love, or at least was so up to yesterday, and whether a slight interruption which occurred, will serve to weaken his attachment, we leave our readers to judge.

We said he was in love, and of course suppose, as all sensible readers would be apt to imagine, that the object of his affection is some blushing girl, just budding into womanhood, with nut-brown curls, and eyes of black, and figure perfect, or some charming widow, who, used to the arts and wiles of the tender passion, has thrown around him those silken meshes that he struggles to get free from; but speculations are far from the mark. Jones is in love; but we blush for him when we state he is in love with a married lady—a dentist's wife.

It appears that every morning, when Jones, attired in his best, walks with dignified slowness from his property in charge up town he is obliged to pass by the window of the residence of a certain dentist, and husband of the lady referred to above, and it has been while thus passing, for the last month, both evening and morning, that Jones had imagined, with his usual conceit, that the lady had fallen in love with him. It must be so, reasoned Jones to himself, or else why should I find her invariably seated at the window when I pass? She, no doubt, keeps an exact note of the time, and places herself there to see me—and giving his moustache an extra twirl, and arranging his beaver to suit his newly combed hair, Jones marches past and imagines she is looking love at him.

Whether the lady was only amused at the manoeuvrings of our friend Jones, and enjoyed the fun at his expense after he had passed—which was more than probable—or whether she really thought him a handsome young man whom she could admire for pastime, we are unable to say; suffice it, that she even went so far as to induce Jones to believe (though he had become so blind he could not be considered a fair judge) that she, on more than one occasion, made eyes at him, and only waited for him to make the first advances. Jones' self-conceit was tickled to death, to think that a married lady, and one to whom as yet he had never spoken, should fall desparately in love with his exterior. It was too much for him; he must proceed; the passive state would not do any longer, even in matters of love. Jones' self-conceit always gets the better of him, and bringing his courage to the sticking point, he determined to call when the husband was out, and took a friend (our informant) along to witness the impression he had made upon the dentist's wife.

A few mornings sin... culars had ... watched ...

"No, sir," she answered politely, "he has just stepped out, but will be in again shortly."

Jones touched his friend, as much as to say, all right; he having previously led him to believe that at that time of the day the dentist was generally absent for several hours.

A running conversation then took place, during which Jones managed to take a leading part, and had so worked his wires as to introduce the subject of love, and was quoting a verse from a popular author, when the door opened, and the dentist a hale, hearty man, stood before them.

Had a twenty-four pounder been touched off under the chairs of the two enterprising young men, it could not have astonished them more. Jones was speechless, and gait stood out upon his face, in large drops of perspiration. His friend fortunately, yet unfortunately, came to the rescue.

"Good morning, sir," said Jones' friend to the dentist, who, unsuspecting, returned the salute politely, and inquired the nature of their business.

The inventive genius of Jones' friend, which he had so often boasted to us about, now showed itself.

'I am sorry to to trouble you, sir," said he to the dentist, "but my friend, Jones, has been suffering greatly from a tooth. I advised him to call, and if necessary to have it out."

Jones, who had regained his self-possession somewhat, looked daggers at his friend, but a wink from the latter greeted him, and he said nothing.

"Ay, yes! I see your friend has been suffering with the toothache. Horrible affliction, sir, horrible!" and the dentist invited Jones to a seat in an arm-chair.

Jones has not a decayed tooth in his whole head, and assented readily, thinking when the dentist saw the fine set of teeth in his mouth, he would immediately pronounce it a neuralgic affection, and dismiss him.—Shortsighted Jones! The dentist, after overhauling Jones, was about addressing himself to Jones' friend in reference to his fine teeth, when he discovered he had left. Upon announcing the fact to Jones, the latter looked pale, and shook like an aspen.

"Not ill, I hope?" said the dentist.

"Oh no," said Jone, "only a slight chill;" but he felt as if he had been deserted when he most needed his friend's services.

The dentist despairing of finding a bad tooth, pitched upon one that had been plugged, which was near where Jones pretended the pain to be, and before the unsuspecting victim was aware, the forceps had been inserted. Jones writhing in agony for an instant, fell back in the chair, at the same instant one of his best molars fell into the basin at his side!

Jones, while spitting out the accumulated blood, caught a sight of the dentist's pretty wife, peeping from behind the folding doors, convulsed with laughter, evidently having seen through the joke. Jones would have rested awhile after the wrenching he had received, but he was afraid possibly that his love might tell tales out of school, rose from the chair taking the amount of damage—a happy expression in this instance—parted with a dollar with some reluctance and left.

We remember seeing him unrolling something from a piece of paper in the evening, and upon our asking to look at it, his placing it hurriedly in his vest pocket. Since we think of it, it must have been the tooth, the very sound tooth, which Jones in his love scrape, had been deprived of. It is unnecessary to state, we suppose, that Jones has cut his deserting friend. We rather think he takes another street when coming down town, for the dentist's wife has lost favor in his eyes.

From Virginia.

MATTERS ON THE BORDER.

The quiet along the lines of our army on the Rappahannock continues undisturbed.

From the Valley country we have reports which represent the operation of the enemy in that section now held by them as more outrageous than ever. They are stripping the country of everything in the way of horses, stock and provisions. They are also putting in execution the emancipation proclamation of Lincoln. The able bodied negro men they impress into service as teamsters, and the woman and children are assured that they are free and at liberty to act for themselves. Under this assurance many have left their comfortable homes to test the hospitality of the North.

THE ENEMY IN GREENBRIER COUNTY.

The enemy have recently made another raid into Greenbrier county, where they committed a number of depredations. Their number amounted to about one hundred and fifty. They ventured within one mile of Lewisburg, where they burned the barn of Jos. Feamster, Jr., containing six horses, provender, etc.—They also fired his dwelling, but the timely arrival of a company of Edgar's battalion saved it from destruction. They, also, burned the dwelling, barn, granary and stable of Austin Hundley, Sheriff of the county, together with his furniture and grain. The snow was several inches deep, and his family were turned out in their night clothes—his wife barefooted. Mr. H. was kept under guard until his house was so far consumed that he was unable to save anything.

THE LEGISLATURE.

In the Senate the claims of the candidates to the Senatorship were urged by their friends, but no ballot was taken. In the House the question of the Senatorship was discussed until neary 3 o'clock, when one vote was taken, resulting as follows: For Hon. Wm. C. Rives, 31; Judge John J. Allen, 28; Hon. John B. Floyd, 22; and Hon. Chas. W. Russell, 22. No choice was made, and the House adjourned.—*Richmond Dispatch.*

Nominations by the Yankee President.

The President sent to the Senate, to-day, the following nominations;

E. C. Banfield, of Massachusetts, as Consul to Algiers.

Henry M. Carfield, of Connecticut, Consul to Athens.

James A. Kennedy to be Consul at Guayakil, vice James L. De Grau, resigned.

John H. Freeman, Surveyor of Customs at Madison, Indiana, vice Robert P. Jones, resigned.

Captain Thomas Turner, to be a Commodore, vice William M. Grandy, whose nomination is withdrawn, and transferred to the list of Captains on the resigned list.

Commander Charles Steedham to be Captain.

Lieutenant-Commander Abner Read to be Commander.

Lieutenant George H. Perkins to be Lieutenant-Commander.

Lieutenants Moeller, Bowens, Whiting, Lynch, and Woodruff to be Commanders in the Navy, on the resigned list.

YANKEE NAVAL OFFICERS.—The Navy Department has ordered Lieutenant Greene and Acting Master's Mate Williams, late of the Monitor, to the steamer Florida, at New York.

Lieutenant Commander Mead has been ordered to Ordnance duty at Washington.

THE PRESIDENT'S MESSAGE AND MR FOOTE'S RESOLUTIONS.—Too much praise can hardly be givin to the message of President Davis, especially to that portion of it in which he reviews our relations with the Governments of Europe. His logic is too cogent to be answered, and his language is, in every respect worthy of his logic. We find but one fault with him, and that is a fault of omission. He should, in our opinion, have concluded his masterly review of our position with a recommendation to withdraw our diplomatic functionaries from all the Courts of Europe. The resolutions of Mr. Foote cover that ground entirely, and they also cover another which is a consequence of it. They propose to ignore the foreign Consuls who are residing here ... exequaturs signed by the Yankee Secre... ...opinion we ought to ... and if

Gen. Grant and the Jews.

The order of Gen. Grant expelling the Jews from his department, it now turns out, says the Richmond Dispatch, was not directed alone against pedlers and smugglers, but was a sweeping and arbitrary decree of banishment against a whole people. Such an act of tyranny unheard of at the present day even in Monarchical Europe. It is worhy of the dark ages, and of the darkest and most hypocritical despotism now in existence in the civilized globe. The chosen people of God, under the Old Dispensation, have been forced in their long and checquered history to endure many indignities as well as oppressions; but to be treated as unworthy the companionship of Yankees is the crowning insult of all. If they can surpass the Yankees in avarice and meanness they have found a lower deep of greed and extortion than any other race under the sun. But it is a foul wrong to place them upon the same level in any respect.

Even apart from the illustrious names they have given the world in the days of their national glory, there is no branch of literature or enterprise, either in the commerce or arms, in which some of their people do not take rank with the master spirits of the earth.—The boasted "merchant princes" of New York could all be put into the breeches pockets of the Rothschilds, without adding much to their influence or power. So far as extortion is concerned, it would be a happy thing for mankind if the only extortioners were Jews. And so far as their religious creed is concerned, it is as much better than the infidelity of Yankeedom as light is than darkness. It is all in keeping with the professed religious toleration of Puritans that they should seek to persecute Jews. Who that dared to differ from them on any subject ever escaped their fangs?

of State troops, including those whose discharges have been revoked by legislative act, who are absentees without leave or deserters, are hereby ordered to report to their respective commands, on or before Monday, the 26th inst. And all militia officers, the acting Sheriff Tax Assessor, President and members of the Board of Police, and other civil officers in each county, are hereby required to arrest and forward to their respective commands, all such absentees and deserters that may be found in their respective counties after the 26th inst. According to an act of the Legislature, which provides that "it shall be the duty of officers in the military service of the State, and all civil officers in each county, to arrest and forward to their respective commands, all absentees without leave and deserters, belonging to the State or Confederate army, on the requisition of the commanding officer; and on failure to perform such duty, such military or civil officer shall be liable to indictment, and on conviction, shall be fined one hundred dollars in each case." Commanders of State troops will immediately, and from time to time, furnish the above officers with the names of such absentees without leave, and deserters from their respective commands; and Quartermasters will furnish transportation on the requisition of such officers.

VI. All volunteer companies of State troops must be speedily filled to the required number of seventy, or be consolidated. But any company of Minute Men or volunteers, may be increased to any number not exceeding one hundred, rank and file, by volunteers without draft; and the drafted men or volunteers, at least to the number specified, must be forwarded to their respective companies within five days after volunteering, or after the draft shall have been made.

VII. The several Brigadier-Generals of the State are charged with the distribution and execution of these orders.

By order of T. C. TUPPER,
Major-General.
E. R. BENNETT, Captain and A. A. A. G.
jan25-d1t, &w1t

GENERAL ORDERS.

EXCHANGE NOTICE No. 4.—The following officers and men have been duly exchanged, and are hereby so declared.

1. All officers and men captured in Kentucky, Tennessee, Alabama, Mississippi, Georgia, Florida, and South Carolina, up to December 10th, 1862.

2. All officers and men captured in Missouri, Kentucky, New Mexico, Arizona, Arkansas and Louisiana, up to January 1st, 1863.

3. The two foregoing sections apply not only to officers and men of the Confederate service, but also to persons captured in arms or hostile array against the United States, whatever may have been the character of the military organization to which they were attached, and whatever may have been the terms of the paroles given by them. If any are in Federal prisons, they are to be immediately released and delivered to the Confederate authorities.

4. All persons who have been captured on the sea or seacoast of the Confederate or United States, up to December 10th, 1862. If any such are in Federal prisons, they are to be immediately released and delivered to the Confederate authorities.

5. All Confederate officers and men who have been delivered at City Point, up to January 6th, 1863.

6. All Confederate officers and men who have been delivered at Vicksburg up to December 23d, 1862, and including said date.

7. All paroled Confederate officers and men receipted for at Vicksburg, up to December 23d, 1862, and including said date.

8. All confederate officers and men captured and paroled at Fredericksburg, Virginia, in December 1862.

9. All Confederate officers and men captured and paroled at Goldsboro', North Carolina, in December, 1862.

10. Other miscellaneous and minor exchanges, of which the appropriate officers will be duly informed.

NOTE.—All Confederate officers and men who have been captured in Virginia or Maryland before the 1st of November, 1862, and all Confederate officers and men who at any time had been delivered at Aiken's Landing, were declared to be exchanged by a former notice, No. 3.

ROBERT OULD, Agent of Exchange.
jan25,1863-1w

☞ Southern papers will please copy, and send ... the War Department.

HEADQUARTERS, DEPARTMENT MISSISSIPPI AND EAST LOUISIANA,
Jackson, January 21, 1863.

General Order, No. 26.

LIEUTENANT H. C. Tupper is hereby announced as Aid-de-camp to Lieut. Gen. J. C. Pemberton, commanding the Department of Mississippi and East Louisiana; he will be obeyed and respected accordingly.

By order of
Lieutenant General J. C. PEMBERTON.
... A. A. G.

The Weekly Courier.

Volume XXXIV. NATCHEZ, MISSISSIPPI, TUESDAY, JANUARY 27, 1863. Number 6.

ARMY SUPPLEMENT.

Official Paper for the City and County.

BOOK, PAMPHLET, AND JOB WORK, OF EVERY DESCRIPTION, Printed on as liberal terms as the war times will admit, At the Natchez Daily Courier Office.

TERMS, &c.

DAILY COURIER,........per week,................25 cts
WEEKLY COURIER,......per year, in advance,....$3 00 "

☞ TERMS OF THE DAILY COURIER—One Dollar per month; or Five Dollars for six months, in advance.

☞ ADVERTISING $1 per square of 10 lines for the first insertion; 50 cents per square for every subsequent insertion, payable in advance.

☞ All letters relating to the Editorial Department of the Daily and Weekly Courier should be addressed "JOHN M. BALDWIN, Natchez, Mississippi."

TO THE PATRONS OF THE COURIER. Mr. R. M. Spurgeon is now Clerk of the Courier Office, and is authorized to collect and receipt for all monies due the establishment, as also, to do all other business pertaining to his department.

Natchez, Mississippi:

Tuesday, January 27, 1863.

☞ In the absence of our regular reports, through the politeness of Mayor Hunter, we are enabled to furnish dispatches this morning later than previously published.

Thanks.

To Major Samuel Bard, formerly editor of the Memphis Avalanche, we are indebted for late Jackson papers. Mr. Bard, since he left Memphis, has been in active service for the Confederacy and always industriously employed.

Mr. H. H. Herron, pilot of the Indian No. 2, will please accept our thanks for late Jackson and Vicksburg papers.

We are indebted to Rev. J. Castleton, of Texas, for late Houston and Shreveport, La., papers.

Affairs on the Mississippi River.

By our information from Vicksburg, since our last publication, indicates the Federals in full land and naval force above that city. A light battery has also been sent across through Madison parish, La., by the enemy, to cut off all steamboat communication with the city. This battery is said to have fired three times into the steamer Vicksburg, on her late trip up.

It is the opinion of the Vicksburg Whig that the enemy is desirous of crossing the river at, or below Warrenton; thus affording themselves an opportunity to tap the Jackson Railroad, and making an upper and lower combined attack on the city. How well they will succeed at this manœuver, a few days time will determine.

Last Thursday, the Federals, in pushing out their cavalry force, came in contact with the Tensas Cavalry on Roundaway Bayou. A short skirmish ensued, in which an Abolition Colonel, (then acting Brigadier General,) was killed, and on his person were found important papers. Others were supposed to be killed and wounded.

For the latest reports from Vicksburg, we refer to our telegraph column.

There is nothing new from Port Hudson.

The water in the Mississippi river is rising rapidly.

ATTENTION! READERS.

We call the particular attention of our readers, both at home and in the army, to the importance of to-morrow's Weekly Courier. It will contain Merrick's Great Speech, in full; President Davis' eloquent and unanswerable Message to Congress, complete; a full account of Gen. Magruder's great Battle of Galveston; all of the telegraphic news of the week, &c. Had we the means to spare, copies of these documents should be sent to our own troops, and through them reach every Federal camp in the land. In so doing, we would consider it worth more than a great victory to our cause. The moral influence of President Davis' Message and Mr. Merrick's Speech, upon both armies would be immense. As it is, however, by hard work we have made public these documents in our Weekly issue, and have printed a few extra copies, which we hope may be at once secured by individuals, and forward to their friends in the army.

☞ We are informed, by good authority, that dispatches were sent to Richmond, more than a week since, from Illinois and Indiana, relating to the stoppage of this war on amicable terms.

YANKEE GENERALS AT FISTICUFFS. According to the Petersburg Express, a rich scene lately occurred on the great Avenue of the Yankee metropolis, between Gens. Halleck and McClellan—the Commander-in-Chief and the Young Napoleon of the Federal armies. The story is that McClellan met Halleck on the street, and accused him of having published a tissue of unblushing falsehoods in his recent report, when the latter pitched into McClellan, who defended himself to decided advantage. It is further stated with reference to the affair, that one of the city papers had a paragraph noticing it, but before half-a-dozen copies were struck off, the police interfered and had the whole matter suppressed.

Later From Galveston.

We are credibly informed that two of the Federal steamers engaged in the battle of Galveston, sunk after they got out to sea. Out of the seven steamers engaged, one was captured and three destroyed, leaving but three that got off. We are also informed that the flag of truce from the Brooklyn last week came to ask if it was true that the survivors on the Harriet Lane were butchered after the battle! It is stated that in the course of Gen. Magruder's communication, he asked the enemy under what flag they proposed to fight. They came into Galveston under a white flag, and left under the same flag. If they intend to continue that flag, he would like to know, etc. We don't vouch for the truth of this, but think it likely, as it is a fact that Galveston was both taken and released by the Federals under a flag of truce! Commodore Renshaw was blown up in the Westfield. It seems the train to her magazine was laid and fired. He left the vessel. The explosion not occurring as soon as he expected, he returned on board with ten men to see what was the matter, and while there the vessel blew up killing all hands.—*Houston Telegraph, Jan. 14.*

Beast Butler's Peculations—a Good Reception.

The New Orleans Delta, when Butler left, published the following paragraph:

We wish to notify the Northern slanderers of Gen. Butler that they may have time to prepare themselves, that there will be a wreck of matter and a crush of worlds when he opens his mouth in New York.

The "wreck of matter" was not very plainly discernable in New York. The morning Butler arrived, the World published two columns of letters written by Northern men in New Orleans, and some in New York, exposing the thieving operations of the General in the former city. The following are extracts from New Orleans letters:

Of the false, prudent, and traitorous operations of this vile son of my native State, volumes might be written. Quartermaster Makey, of Boston, has forwarded to the Chief of the War Department, some months since, sworn evidence as to the peculations of Gen. Butler from the Government of the United States and from loyal citizens, and if the indictments are not quashed by the political juggling of the advisers of the President, there can be no doubt as to the result of *honest investigation.* The Flag, published at Matamoras, says: "A bark has just arrived, consigned by the banker and broker of Gen. Butler (his brother,) to a concern here, which is loaded with superior barrel pork, (bearing the United States marks,) packed for the use of the Federal army, which had been offered to the commissioners of the Confederate States, to be paid for in gold or cotton. Treasury greenbacks refused," &c.; and I learn from reliable sources that the pork was sold to the Confederate commissary and paid for with cotton. Of such ventures, Butler, the Federal General, receives half the gains, while the robbery is covered by consumption in New Orleans to "prevent starvation," or by reported actual issue to troops. This traitor General has, through all his administration, been receiving the lion's share of net proceeds from powder, saltpetre, muskets, and other war material sold to Confederates, surreptitiously sent out from New Orleans by the lakes, &c., covered by permits for provisions—dealing in the very life-blood of his own soldiers. Of such things, the military infamy is composed of the base coward, who betrays all—true to none.

* * * * * *

It would take a small book to describe the scenes that took place between citizens who had been despoiled by Butler, calling on Gen. Banks for restitution. Mr. Buckner, one of our cotton princes and millionaires was robbed by Gen. Butler of $100,000 in bills receivable, sent him from Natchez. Gen. Banks said he could not find them when called on to return them. $5,000 in cash was taken from the same parties; he said he paid this amount over to the Government. Samuel Smith & Co. had $60,000 in specie taken from their vaults by Butler; $50,000 is in suit at Washington; the rest was returned, less $1,800 stolen. Gen. Butler returned this amount in currency, thereby taking advantage of thirty-five per cent. on the gold.

Acrostics and poetry lampooning him were sent to him in such quantities that Gen. Banks had to protect him by an order, No. 114 (see New Orleans papers.) One verse runs thus:

> Farewell I and if in hell there dwells
> A demon such as thou,
> Then, Satan, yield the sceptre up—
> Thy mission's over now.

* * * * * *

Mr. Davis, the President of the Bank of New Orleans, was thrown into jail without a trial, and in one short month was released, after having had his property stolen, and is now a raving maniac. This is the foulest deed Butler has been guilty of. In my next I will give all the news that transpires.

One of the letters from citizens of New York, begs the World to expose the scoundrel fully. The writer says:

Tell the people here how he charged Dr. Campbell $1,700 for a pass to enter the Confederate lines, and while he was gone, ejected his wife from her palatial home, that he might occupy it himself, to all of which hundreds of New Orleans men now here will not fear to testify, since their property is no longer under his control.

Tell the people about his partnership with his brother, and how he charged $12 a hhd. freight for sugar on his boats from the Lafourche to New Orleans, (when $1 used to be the price,) allowing no competition.

And tell too, how he would permit none but New England men to take goods into the interior of the State to sell them.

☞ All of North Mississippi has been evacuated by the Federal army, to reinforce the troops to be brought into action at Vicksburg. The Confederates will again take possession of that section of country, and hold it.

OUR FRIENDS IN CANADA. The following toast was given in Hamilton (C. W.) on the 24th November, 1862, in honor of many Southern refugees, by Hon. R. J. Hamilton:

Jefferson Davis, the President of the Southern Confederacy—The immaculate hero and christian statesman; may the God of Battles bless him and his cause.

This was responded to by M. Winans, Esq., of Baltimore, Md.

Hon. W. McDonnald, M. P., paid a glowing tribute to Stonewall Jackson. He compared him to the late Gen. Havelock, one of England's greatest Generals.

Gen. Wilson said: With leaders like Davis, Lee, Beauregard, Johnston and Jackson, the South must and will succeed; and it is the duty of our Government to recognize the South. They are bone of our bone, and flesh of our flesh. We insist on their recognition.

This was the largest and most brilliant gathering which has taken place in Canada, since the Prince of Wales' visit.

FROM THE BATTLE FIELD. The Atlanta Intelligencer chronicles some important arrivals from the battle field at Murfreesboro'.

On Sunday last 3,000 Yankee prisoners were received. The city was full of Yanks for a time, but they were all sent on to Montgomery; bound, we suppose, for Vicksburg, to be exchanged. The balance of exchanges on our side must now be very heavy.

On Monday evening, eight cars loaded with cannon and small arms, captured at the battle of Murfreesboro', reached Atlanta by way of the W. & A. R. R.

TELEGRAPHIC NEWS.

From the Jackson Appeal, January 24.

Federal Repulse.

RODNEY, Miss., Jan. 22....A courier arrived at St. Joseph, La., at 2 o'clock this evening, from Major Harrison's headquarters, six miles above Carthage, reports that two hundred Yankee cavalry surprised the Tensas cavalry this morning.

The Yankees were repulsed, with the loss of their Colonel, who was mortally wounded and captured by our men before he expired.

He said his command started out with the avowed intention of capturing Major Harrison and his battalion.

No one was hurt on our side.

Major Harrison was sent down for reinforcements, and expects the attack to be renewed.

Our men were taken wholly by surprise, being dismounted, but fought them on foot.

From the Rappahannock.

FREDERICKSBURG, Jan. 21....The Yankees are building an immense warehouse at Acquia Creek, and repairing the railroad, putting batteries in position in front, and giving other evidences of an intention to make this the permanent base of operations for winter quarters.

A large dwelling, formerly belonging to Gen. Bankhead, was burnt yesterday morning. The conflagration caused the explosion of some shell in the building, which produced great excitement, and both armies were drawn up in line of battle.

North Carolina.

WILMINGTON, Jan. 22....Scouts officially report that the enemy has burnt the bridge at Jacksonville, Onslow Court House, and retired toward Newbern. All quiet here.

TULLAHOMA, Jan. 22....Lieut. Col. Hutchinson, with one hundred men of Morgan's cavalry, made a dash yesterday upon the enemy's camp at Murfreesboro' and captured and brought off safely one hundred and fifty prisoners and thirty wagons. Maj. Holeman, of Wheeler's cavalry, since my last report, has captured and destroyed another large transport on the Cumberland, loaded with subsistence.

The enemy has made no show of an advance upon Bragg from Murfreesboro'.

The Intercepted Correspondence.

RICHMOND, Jan. 23....The revelations of the letters to Mason and Slidell published in the Northern papers, strengthen the conviction that our embassadors abroad should be recalled.

It appears that two French consuls in Texas have been intriguing to separate that State from the Confederacy, and induce it to place itself under the protection of France, in consequence of which both were expelled from the country. It is believed, however, that the French Emperor had no part in the plot.

Lord Russell, it seems, scarcely treats Mason with the courtesy due to a private gentleman, and while Slidell is making calls at the Tuilleries, intrigues are set on foot by French subjects to detach one portion of the Confederacy from the other.

It is advised in influential quarters to annul every consular exequator in the Confederate States, and not allow any foreign consuls to remain here, and plot at leisure our destruction.

The Captor of the Hatteras.

RICHMOND, Jan. 23....The Enquirer predicts it will turn out that the Yankee gunboat Hatteras was sunk by the Florida. Captain Maffitt, who being near Galveston, and learning of the probability of the capture of the Harriet Lane, determined to aid her in sailing from Galveston.

THE PROSPECT OF PEACE. The Richmond Examiner, referring to the success of our brave soldiers, truly says "we are now on the high road to peace. The road does not lie by the way of Europe, and no where pursues a course of indirection. We pursue it when, relying upon thorough organization and hard fighting, we march straight upon the enemy; and we lose it whenever we look beyond our own exertions for the means of ending the war.

The North may be vindictive enough to pursue a way of hatred and spite indefinitely; but it is not in human nature, much less in Yankee nature, to resist in the end the logic of the sober, second thought, which teaches that peace is cheap and war expensive, that peace is a mine of wealth, and war the grave of all prosperity."

☞ According to the Alexandria Democrat, Payne, the counterfeiter, escaped from jail as follows:

"On last Thursday night John A. Payne, the counterfeiter, and I. N. Huddleston, charged with driving beeves to New Orleans for the Abolition army, walked out of our Parish Jail, and left for parts unknown. We must be permitted to say, in justice to the public and in deference to their often expressed opinion, that no one is surprised at this—it was looked for, it was expected, it was predicted. The mode pursued to fulfill these public prophesies is told in a few words. The doors, three in number, with five locks, were opened nicely, snugly and quietly, not even disturbing the slumbers of the adjoining inmates, with the keys of the Jail, by some one used to such work, and the kind permission of the obliging performer given to Payne and Huddleston to walk out. *En passant* we will remark, that the keys were taken from under the pillow of the Jailor and very kindly replaced there. There is a diversity of opinion with the public, at this part of the performance; some speaking in glowing terms of such accommodating courtesy, while others speak harshly of such verdancy. We have our opinion on the point, but reserve an expression for the present.

☞ Col. George Walton, a son of one of the signers of the old Declaration of Independence, died in Petersburg, Va., a few days since, aged 76 years. He was formerly Territorial Governor of Florida, and later in life the Mayor of Mobile. He was the father of the amiable and accomplished Madame Octavia Walton Levert, of Mobile.

☞ "Ned, who is that girl I saw you walking with yesterday?" "Miss Hogg." "Hogg—Hogg—well, she's to be pitied for having such a name." "So I think," rejoined Ned; "I pitied her so much that I offered her mine, and she's going to take it soon."

GEN. BUTLER. The Richmond Dispatch says it is rumored in Northern papers that the Beast is to be sent on an expedition against Charleston, and we are glad to hear it for two reasons. In the first place, Charleston will never be surrendered with the example of Butler and New Orleans before her, and, in the next, we shall have some chance of capturing Butler. If the hoary reprobate could one fall into Southern hands he will not have lived altogether in vain.

☞ **President Davis' Message, in full, on next page.**

"THE ALABAMA." The New York World of January 1st, publishes the marine losses for December. It sums up a total of forty-three vessels, valued at four millions and a half.

The "Pirate Semmes" gets credit for capturing and destroying $947,000 of the amount. Semmes' work for December is then within a fraction of a million of dollars.

OBITUARY.

DIED, near Church Hill, Jefferson county, on the 10th inst., MARY SPEER, infant daughter of James M. and Mary D. Reynolds, aged 2 years 5 months and 21 days.

The brightest charms of childhood are reserved to those whose guardianship nature has committed them, and none feel the pang of grief so sensibly as these. To watch the involuntary motion of the features, until the smile begins to play; to witness the growing consciousness of a familiar presence; to see day by day the slow, yet steady and certain promise of mental appreciation and moral sensibility, are all elements of nature which none can know so well or feel so intensely as they who see in them the promise of vigor, purity and usefulness. That these beginnings should terminate, and these promises fail, is the sad lesson the parents of little Mary have painfully learned. To them she was full of interest, and the prayer, a mother's tenderness had already taught her to utter, gives healing to the hearts that are wounded, for "of such is the Kingdom of Heaven." A FRIEND.

Natchez, January 27, 1863.

Free Market.

Donations to the Free Market can be made to either Jas. N. Stockman, Charles M. Benbrook, or George Mallery, the Committee, who have charge of the Market.

To-Day's Notices.

Lost,

ON THE 21st inst., on the road to Dr. Foster's, a handsome grey Plaid Shawl—small check. A liberal reward will be paid if left at this office. Jan24-d3t*

Special Order No. 4.

HEADQUARTERS, CAMP OF INSTRUCTION, Brookhaven, Miss., Jan. 23, 1863.

CAPT. H. F. WADE, late enrolling officer of Adams county, Miss., was not authorized to grant exemptions or discharges from conscription. All exempted or discharged by him will report to these Headquarters, as his exemptions or discharges will not be respected.

M. R. CLARK, Majr. A. A. G., Com'd't Cons. State Miss.

jan27-d3w1

Unrivalled Tobacco.

JUST RECEIVED and for sale, by E. Lewis, 30 boxes Choice "Unrivalled" Chewing Tobacco. 200 lbs. Excelsior Smoking Tobacco, which will be sold for CASH only. E. LEWIS, Auctioneer.

jan27-d1

Salt.

200 BAGS of Salt on consignment, for sale cheap for cash, at T. C. POLLOCK.

jan27-d3*

Notice to Conscripts of Concordia Parish, La.

ALL CONSCRIPTS of Concordia Parish, between the ages of 18 and 35, are ordered to report within ten days, to Major Harrison at Lake Bruen, Tensas Parish. Details of persons over the age of 35, must be made according to the State law, requiring an agent or overseer on every plantation where there are slaves. House servants, mechanics and carriage drivers, where there are no other slaves on the place are not to be considered; they must be actually employed in cultivating a plantation. By making the affidavit that they are over 35, and are engaged as above required, I will forward them a detail.

By order of Brig. Gen. BLANCHARD.

ALEX. CAMPBELL, JR., Enrolling Officer, Concordia Parish.

Flowery Mound, Jan. 27th, 1863—d&w1m*

Headquarters Camps of Instruction, W. La.

MONROE, LA., January 11, 1863.

THE following order has been received and is published for the information and guidance of Enrolling Officers:

HEADQUARTERS, DIST. WESTERN LA., New Iberia, Jan. 4th, 1863.

Special Order No. —.

II. Brig. Gen Blanchard, in accordance with instructions from the War Department, will revoke all details made by him of Conscripts under the Act of April, 1862, as overseers and for other purposes not connected immediately with the military service.

By command of Maj. Gen. TAYLOR.

WILL. M. LEVY, (Signed) A. A. and Inspector Gen'l.

Enrolling officers will be governed accordingly.

By order of Brig. Gen. BLANCHARD.

A. L. BILISOLY. A. A. A. G.

jan27-d:w-1m*

Brighton Grammar School.

THE SUBSCRIBER will resume the duties of his School, on MONDAY the 2d of next MONTH. Instruction will be given in the rudiments of the English and Latin Languages. No BOARDERS will be received. Terms —Fifty dollars per session of five months, payable one-half in advance. JOHN S. MOSBY.

Brighton, Second Creek, Jan. 27, 1863—d5*

For Sale,

ONE SET DOUBLE, Carriage Harness, and Saddle, for sale by W. H. HARRISON.

jan27-3t*

Wanted,

A 4 OR 6 MULE TEAM, to haul a load to Brookhaven, to start on WEDNESDAY morning.

jan27-d2 E. KIBBE.

Lost.

ON the evening of Saturday, 24th inst., on the road between Natchez and Washington, a six inch barrel COLT REVOLVER. The finder will confer a favor on a soldier, by leaving it at this office.

jan27—1*

For Sale.

MY PLACE, 4½ miles from Natchez, on the Washington road, containing 15 acres, with a good house, containing 8 rooms, good cisterns; the outhouses are, Stable, Carriage-house, Corncrib and Quarters. The stock and stock feed will be sold with the place, if desired.

All will be sold cheap. JACOB STERN.

jan27-d&w6w*

NATCHEZ R. A. CHAPTER, NO. 1, Meets Third Saturday of each Month.

E. Craig	H. P.
A. R. Tyler	K.
M. Izod	S.
F. F. Fowler	C. of H.
J. Deutsch	P. S.
C. F. Merrick	R. A. C.
J. M. Baldwin	M. 3rd V.
W. C. Turner	M. 2nd V.
J. Wells	M. 1st V.
H. G. Perry	Secretary.
R. Stewart	Treasurer.
Jno. McDowell	Sentinel.

HARMONY LODGE NO. 1, Meets first Saturday Evening of each Month.

C. F. Merrick	W. M.
J. A. Steele	S. W.
J. M. Baldwin	J. W.
T. S. Sheridan	Secretary.
G. Kennedy	Treasurer.
Jno. McDowell	S. & T.

ANDREW JACKSON LODGE NO. 2, Meets Second Saturday of each Month.

F. F. Fowler	W. M.
A. G. Wilson	S. W.
H. G. Perry	J. W.
S. Wood	Secretary.
W. A. Sawyer	Treasurer.
Jno. McDowell	S. & T.

To-Day's Notices.

Wanted,

A SITUATION as Overseer, on a Quarter place. Apply at this office.

jan24-d3t*

Wanted,

A FEW BARRELS OF HARD COAL, for which a fair price will be paid. Apply at this Office

jan24

Wanted,

A SITUATION by an experienced manager, with a small family. Enquire at this office. A Quarter place preferred. jan24-d3*

"Granite Store."

WE ARE RE-OPENING for a few days, and will sell from our remaining stock of goods, at old prices. Persons will do well to call and look through our "odds and ends." They may find something they want, and many things worth purchasing, if not in immediate want.

jan24-d-tf ALDRICH & SMITH.

$75 Reward.

STOLEN from the plantation of the undersigned, on the night of the 18th inst., a large MARE MULE—color, dark brown; not branded. I will give fifty dollars for the arrest and conviction of the thief, and twenty-five dollars for return of Mule, or such information as will lead to its recovery. Address, Natchez, care Stanton & Stockman.

Jan 24-d3t* T. H. THORNHILL.

A Desirable Plantation for Sale,

SITUATED on the Natchez and Fayette road, eleven and a half miles from Natchez, containing nine hundred acres, six hundred cleared, and between three and four hundred fresh lands. A good dwelling with five rooms; Gin, Mill, Quarters and outhouses for a force of thirty hands. A Good constant running spring, also three cisterns and six large ponds.

About twenty five hundred bushels of corn, a large supply of fodder; about one hundred head of Beef, milch Cows and Stock Cattle; Seventy five or one hundred head of meat and stock hogs; plenty of meat and salt to do the place; about four hundred bushels of peas; five or six hundred bushels of potatoes; a garden with plenty of vegetables; a large supply of cotton seed; and many other things too tedious to mention, will be sold with or without the place. Apply to the undersigned on the place.

dec. 17-tf WILLIAM M. LEE.

Wanted.

5 BUSHELS OF CHOICE SUGAR CANE SEED Apply to D. L. RIVERS.

Jan21-d10t*

Taxes! Taxes!

THE STATE OF MISSISSIPPI, ADAMS COUNTY.

NOTICE is hereby given, that the State and County taxes are now due. Tax payers are requested to call at the Sheriff's office, and pay up.

O. METCALFE, Sheriff.

Sheriffs office, Natchez, Jan. 21, 1863—2m

Notice.

THE MISSISSIPPI LEGISLATURE having passed an Act, requiring the immediate redemption of all individual issues of change Notes; we therefore, hereby notify all the holders of the change Notes or Checks issued by us, to present them for redemption, before the FIRST DAY OF MARCH NEXT; after that date we will not redeem them. W. A. BRITTON & CO.

Natchez, Jan. 8, 1863—d:w-tf

Green House Plants,

SHRUBBERY, GARDENING, ETC.

THE UNDERSIGNED, has opened at his residence on St Catherine street, immediately adjoining the property of the estate of Gen. Quitman,

A Seedsman's and Florists' Establishment,

where he will keep constantly on hand, a full supply of choice

GREEN HOUSE PLANTS;
SHRUBBERY;
ORNAMENTAL TREES;
GARDEN SEEDS AND FLOWERS,

raised by himself, or under his personal care.

On WEDNESDAYS and SATURDAYS he will remain at home all day, to accommodate, in person, visitors and purchasers. On other week days, he will give his personal attention to gardening jobs in the city or vicinity; laying out gardens, and attending to the ornamental and other branches of the horticultural business.

He solicits a share of public patronage.

Feb13 JAS. McCONCHIE

Headquarters Camp of Instruction,

BROOKHAVEN, Miss., Dec. 23d, 1862.

GENERAL ORDER, No. —.

ALL white male residents of the State of Mississippi between the ages of 18 and 40 are ordered to report immediately at the Camps of Instruction. Those from the counties of Tishomingo, Itawamba, Monroe, Lowndes, Noxubee, Lauderdale, Clark, Wayne, Green, Perry, Jones, Jasper, Newton, Neshoba, Winston, Oktibbeha, Chickasaw, Pontotoc and Tippah, will report to the camp located at Enterprise on the Mobile and Ohio Railroad. Those from all other counties will report to the camp located at Brookhaven on the New Orleans and Jackson Railroad.

All persons failing to report within twenty days will be arrested and treated as deserters.

Those claiming exemption under the late "exemption act" are required to report at the camp, prove their claim and receive certificates of exemption.

"All the laws and regulations applicable to deserters shall be applied to such conscripts as fail to repair to the place of rendezvous for enrollment, or who shall desert after enrollment.

All refugees from other States are included in the above order.

By order of Sec'y of War.

M. R. CLARK, Major and A. A. G., Commandant State Mississippi.

dec27-1m

Jackson Mississippian.

DAVID RAY PETER GRANT.

RAY & GRANT,

—DEALERS IN—

Groceries, Western Produce,

LIQUORS, &C.

WILL KEEP CONSTANTLY ON HAND A supply of fresh St. Louis and Ohio Flour; also, a large stock of best Old and Rectified Whisky, &c.

Natchez Landing, May 24

The Philadelphia Inquirer.

CIRCULATION OVER 60,000. | PHILADELPHIA, TUESDAY, JANUARY 27, 1863. | PRICE TWO CENTS.

IMPORTANT WAR NEWS.

FROM THE RAPPAHANNOCK

Gen. Burnside Resigns.

General Hooker Succeeds to the Command of the Army.

GENS. SUMNER AND FRANKLIN RELIEVED.

General Burnside's Farewell Address to the Troops.

NATIONAL GUARD OF 250,000 MEN.

The Pirate "Alabama" Sinks the U. S. Transport "Hatteras."

LATER NEWS FROM THE SOUTH.

Bombardment and Capture of Acapulco by the French.

LATER FROM GENERAL ROSECRANS' ARMY.

IMPORTANT FROM GALVESTON.

The Pirate "Alabama" Sinks the United States Transport "Hatteras."

New York, Jan. 26.—The steamer *Mary A. Boardman* arrived to-night, from New Orleans on the 13th, and Key West on the 20th. She furnishes Galveston advices of the 17th, which were brought to Key West by the steamer *Northern Light*, from New Orleans.

On the 17th, the United States sloop-of-war *Brooklyn*, in company with six other United States steamers, were off Galveston. They saw a steamer in the offing. The steamer *Hatteras* immediately got under way to speak to her, and, when within hailing distance, asked who she was.

The answer was—"Her Majesty's ship of war *Spitfire*."

The commander of the *Hatteras* then told them to wait and he would send a boat to her, and had just lowered the boat with an officer and crew in her, when the steamer opened her broadside and fired it into the *Hatteras*.

The *Brooklyn* immediately got under weigh, and started in pursuit of the stranger, but night coming on, lost sight of her, and was compelled to give up the chase.

On returning she found the steamer *Hatteras* sunk in nine fathoms of war. The officers of the steamer *Mary Boardman* are unable to give further particulars. The steamer that fired was no doubt the pirate *Alabama*.

The steamer *Hatteras* was merely a transport, but carried four guns of light calibre, similar to those on the transport *McClellan*.

FROM THE ARMY OF THE POTOMAC

General Burnside Resigns the Command—General Hooker to Succeed Him—General Burnside's Farewell Address—Generals Sumner and Franklin Relieved.

Head-quarters, Army of the Potomac, Jan. 26.—This forenoon General Burnside turned over the command of the Army of the Potomac to General Hooker, who came to the Head-quarters Camp for that purpose.

As soon as the change became known a considerable number of superior officers called on General Burnside and took their parting leave with many regrets.

The following is General Burnside's address to the army:—

Head-quarters Army of the Potomac, Camp near Falmouth, Jan. 26.—General Orders No. 9.—By direction of the President of the United States, the Commanding General this day transfers the command of this army to Major-General Joseph Hooker. The short time that he has directed your movements has not been fruitful of victory or any considerable advancement of our lines, but it has again demonstrated an amount of courage, patience and endurance that, under more favorable circumstances, would have accomplished great results.

Continue to exercise these virtues; be true in your devotion to your country and the principles you have sworn to maintain; give to the brave and skillful General who has long been identified with your organization, and who is now to command you, your full and cordial support, and you will deserve success.

In taking an affectionate leave of the entire army, from which he separates with so much regret, he may be pardoned if he bids an especial farewell to his long-tried associates of the Ninth Corps.

His prayers are that God may be with you, and grant you continued success until the Rebellion is crushed.

By command of Major-General Burnside.

Lewis Richmond, A. A. G.

It is understood that Generals Sumner and Franklin have also been relieved from their command of the right and left Grand Divisions, but the names of their successors have not been divulged, if appointed.

General Burnside, with most of his late Staff, have been allowed thirty days' leave of absence. They will go to New York.

The weather is warm and pleasant, and the mud is fast drying up.

THE WAR IN MEXICO.

Bombardment of Acapulco by the French—Capture of the Fort.

San Francisco, Jan. 26.—The steamer *Sonora*, which arrived here to-day from Panama, reports that four French war vessels bombarded the town of Acapulco, Mexico, for three days, commencing on the 16th. The fire was returned from the fort, doing some damage to the vessels.

The people abandoned the town. After killing thirteen of the Mexican garrison, the fort was finally silenced, when a hundred sailors landed and spiked the guns. The fleet then left.

The War in North Carolina—A Body of Rebels Driven from Pollocksville.

Boston, Jan. 26.—Private advices from Newbern, N. C., to Tuesday, the 20th, have been received. No mail had then left for the North for two weeks, but one was about leaving for New York.

The main expedition, of which so much has been said, had not yet started, but a land force was sent forward on the 17th, towards the railroad, which encountered a force of 1200 Rebels at Pollocksville. Our troops drove them from the town and took possession of it. Some of the New York cavalry were wounded. The general health of the troops was excellent.

FROM WASHINGTON.

Special Despatch to the Inquirer.

Washington, January 26, 1863.

The Assistant Secretaryships of War.

The law originally provided for but one Assistant Secretary of War. Mr. T. A. Scott was appointed to this office, under Secretary Cameron. When Mr. Stanton was appointed Secretary of War he requested authority from Congress to appoint two more Assistant Secretaries for one year. This authority was granted by Congress, and Mr. Watson and Mr. Tucker were appointed. When Mr. Scott resigned, Mr. Wolcott was appointed to the permanent Assistant Secretaryship thus vacated. The term of office of Mr. Watson and of Mr. Tucker expired, by limitation, on Wednesday last. The Assistant Secretary, Mr. Wolcott, who is in very bad health, has since resigned, and Mr. Watson has been appointed in his place; so that Mr. Watson is now the permanent and only Assistant Secretary.

The fact that Mr. Watson will remain in the War Department will be received with great satisfaction by all the friends of an earnest and honest Administration of the Department. His ability, untiring industry and integrity have won for him the respect of every one who has had intercourse with the War Department, and it is understood that he remained in the Department against his own wishes, but at the earnest request of the President and Secretary of War.

It is proposed to reorganize the Department still further, by creating the post of Solicitor to the War Department, to which Mr. Whiting will be appointed, and that of Special Commissioner, to which Robert Dale Owen will be appointed.

The Selection of Gen. Hooker to the Command of the Army of the Potomac.

The appointment of General Hooker to the command of the army of the Potomac has given the most sincere gratification to the army, and even here, where opinions are so diversified, a contrary sentiment is rarely expressed. It is true, the sympathizers with treason, of whom we have many still remaining in our midst, and, I regret to say, a few of the friends of other past and present commanders, have demurred somewhat at the present selection, but the masses, the majority of whom have long looked forward to and earnestly hoped for the promotion of General Hooker, express unqualified delight and approval. Other changes in the army of the Potomac are rumored, and if the rumors are correct the changes have evidently been based upon a desire of the Administration to secure in the future the most perfect harmony among the commanding officers of the army—a desire which cannot fail to be gratified to the fullest extent under the new arrangement. The objects to be attained can admit of no interference by impolitic personal bickerings and misunderstandings, and with complete accordance on the part of the commanders with the views of Gen. Hooker, the brave men of the respective corps can anticipate again being led on to victory.

Arrival of General Burnside.

A large number of army officers arrived in the city to-day, among whom are Major-Generals Burnside, Sumner and Park, with a host of lesser lights. Franklin is expected to-morrow.

Wendell Phillips was upon the floor of the House to-day, and was introduced by Mr. Conway, of Kansas. He received the attentions of many of the members.

A bill has been introduced, providing for the appointment of an Assistant Collector, to be located at Jersey City.

All Quiet on the Rappahannock.

Apparently all is quiet along the lines.

Miscellaneous Items.

A rumor is current to-day that Fitz-John Porter has been placed under arrest for improper conduct, but it is incorrect, he having been seen this evening on the avenue, in citizen's dress.

The large majority with which the Ways and Means Committee bill passed astonished even its own frinds. There is but little doubt that it will pass the Senate, or should it not at first, the large majority now committed to it in the House will insure its final passage.

National Guard of 250,000 Men.

Senator Wilson, chairman of the Military Committee, introduced a bill to provide for the organization of two hundred and fifty thousand men, to be raised *pro rata* in the several States, from the militia; to be two hundred regiments, of twelve companies each, and one hundred men to each company—the men to be between the ages of twenty-one and thirty-five. This force is to be called the National Guard, and to be subject to all orders from the President.

Deaths of Soldiers.

Deaths of Pennsylvania soldiers in the hospitals in and about Washington, to-day:—George Mauk, Company E, One-hundred-and-twenty-fifth; Alfred McClay, Company E, One-hundred-and-fourteenth; William Kennedy, Company K, Sixty-ninth; Abram Hanna, Company I, One-hundred-and-fiftieth; D. E. Blaksee, Company D, One-hundred-and-thirty-second; Abraham Bagsley, Company G, One-hundred-and-thirty-first.

Officers Without Commands.

A list of "Major and Brigadier-Generals who are not assigned to any actual command, and the length of time since engaged in actual service:"—

Major-General George B. McClellan. Relieved by General Order No. 182, November 5, 1862.

Major-General John C. Fremont. Not since August 12, 1862.

Major-General Irvin McDowell. Not since September 6, 1862.

Major-General D. C. Buell. Not since October 30, 1862. Before military commission.

Major-General Fitz-John Porter. Not since November 10, 1862. Undergoing trial. Since cashiered.

Major-General C. M. Clay. Not since June 17, 1862, when appointed. Assigned to General Butler, but did not report.

Brigadier-General Andrew Porter. Not since May —, 1862. Now on duty, commanding camp at Harrisburg.

Brigadier-General Wm. S. Harney. Not since May 16, 1861.

Brigadier-General Robert Anderson. Not since October 8, 1861.

Brigadier-General C. P. Stone. Not since February 8, 1862.

Brigadier-General Geo. A. McCall. Not since July —, 1862. Now on court-martial.

Brigadier-General Louis Blenker. Not since July 21, 1862.

Brigadier-General Jas. Shields. Not since June 24, 1862.

Brigadier-General R. B. Marcy. Has been Chief of Staff with General McClellan since appointment, September 13th, 1862. Now with General McClellan.

Brigadier-General T. T. Crittenden. Not since July 13th, 1862. Exchanged.

Brigadier-General J. B. Turchin. Not since appointed as Brigadier-General, July 17th, 1862.

Brigadier-General S. W. Crawford. Wounded at Antietam, and in New York since September 17th, 1862.

Brigadier-General L. P. Graham. Relieved as instructor Cavalry Camp Institute, Annapolis, August 18th, 1862. Sick.

Brigadier-General Z. B. Tower. Wounded at Antietam September 17, 1862. Sick in Washington.

Brigadier-General R. J. Oglesby. Wounded at Corinth, October 4, 1862.

Brigadier-General W. B. Campbell. Not since appointed, June 30, 1862.

Brigadier-General F. C. Barlow. Wounded at Antietam September 17, 1862. Not since on duty.

Brigadier-General J. H. H. Ward. Relieved November 1, 1862.

Brigadier-General H. S. Briggs. Not since September 22, 1862. Sick.

The Confiscation of Rebel Property.

In reply to the resolution of inquiry relative to property heretofore seized by the Military Governor of the District of Columbia as the property of Rebels, the Secretary of War encloses a communication from General Martindale detailing the circumstances of the conflict of military and civil authorities with regard to the property of Judge Campbell, which, after its seizure by the military authorities, was subsequently turned over to the Marshal of the District, upon a writ of replevin.

General Martindale suggests further legislation by Congress, to embrace two points:—first, to authorize the seizure of Rebel property by military authority, as though martial law existed, but to be transferred to the civil authorities for condemnation and sale in those districts where the civil courts are in operation, and to courts-martial where Rebellion has interrupted civil courts; secondly, continued absence and general reputation of disloyalty to authorize condemnation and sale, unless the owner of the property seized shall appear and prove loyalty.

MAJOR-GENERAL HOOKER.

MAJOR-GEN. JOSEPH HOOKER,

The New Commanding General of the Army of the Potomac.

Major-General Joseph Hooker, whose selection to the chief command of the Army of the Potomac has given such unbounded satisfaction to the army and the people of the country, is a native of Massachusetts, from which State he was appointed a cadet to West Point Military Academy in 1833. He graduated on the 30th of June, 1837, standing No. 28 in a class of fifty members, among whom were Generals Benham, Arnold, French, Sedgwick and others of the Union army; Braxton Bragg, W. W. Mackall, J. A. Early and other noted Rebel officers. On the 1st of July, 1837, he was promoted to the second lieutenantcy of the First United States Artillery, and on the 1st of November, 1838, was further promoted to a First Lieutenantcy in the same regiment. From July 1st to October 3d, 1841, he was the Adjutant of the Military Academy at West Point, and from 1841 to 1846 was the Adjutant of his regiment. He served with distinction in Mexico, and was Aid-de-camp to Brigadier-General Hamer. He was, in May, 1847, brevetted Captain for gallant conduct in the several conflicts at Monterey, his brevet bearing the date of September 23d, 1846.

He was appointed on the staff as Assistant Adjutant-General, with the brevet rank of Captain, on the 3d of March, 1847, and in March, 1849, was further brevetted Major for gallant and meritorious conduct in the affair at the National Bridge, Mexico, his brevet dating from June 11, 1847. In the same month he received another brevet—viz: Lieutenant-Colonel—for gallant and meritorious conduct in the battle of Chapultepec. This brevet bore date September 13, 1847. On the 29th of October, 1848, he was appointed a Captain of the First Artillery, and on the same day vacated his regimental commission, retaining his position in the Adjutant-General's Department, with brevet of Lieutenant-Colonel. On the 21st of February, 1853, he resigned from the army and went to California, where he retired into private life.

At the breaking out of the Rebellion he considered that the education he had received at the expense of the Government was a sacred trust, and immediately offered his valuable services, which were accepted, and on the 17th of May, 1861, he was commissioned as Brigadier-General of Volunteers, his appointment being accredited to the State of California. He at first acted under instructions from General Dix, but afterwards was appointed to a separate command, under General McClellan. He then proceeded to reorganize the two disturbed counties of Maryland—Prince George and Charles—and succeeded admirably, entirely re-occupying those counties and disarming the Rebel sympathizers, without loss of life. His division at this time took military possession of the northern and eastern shores, or left bank of the Potomac river, and several spirited excursions were made by portions of his command in the neighborhood of Budd's Ferry, Port Tobacco, &c., to the opposite Virginia shore. A portion of these troops afterwards crossed the Potomac, and took possession of the batteries which had blockaded the river for some time previous, and, having effectually removed these obstructions, and advanced a short distance into the interior, were finally withdrawn, and transferred to the immediate command of General McClellan on the Peninsula.

In the contest at Williamsburg his division bravely stood the brunt of the battle. At Fair Oaks the General again displayed his splendid military talents and fighting qualities. In the seven days' battles and in the minor contests he never failed to attract the admiration of his men by his gallantry and courage, and the same noble traits distinguished him when, subsequently, he participated in the battles before Washington, under General Pope. On July 4th, 1862, he was promoted to a Major-Generalship of Volunteers, to date from May 5th, 1862. At South Mountain and Antietam we again find him battling zealously for the cause of his country, and from the battle-field was carried to the rear with a severe wound in the foot.

On the 20th of September, 1862, he was made a Brigadier-General of the Regular army, vice Gen. Mansfield, killed in battle. When he had recovered from his wound sufficiently to take the field on a litter, he did so, and was made commander of the Fifth Army Corps. On the 14th of November, 1862, he was placed in command of the centre grand division of the Army of the Potomac, and in the record of the battle of Fredericksburg we again find his name prominently mentioned.

No man in the service is more popular with the army, and none have attained a more exalted character with the public as a military leader.

Brave, talented and determined, and with but one object in view, the speedy crushing of the Rebellion, he has on every battle-field where his services have been engaged displayed those qualifications which always characterize the able military leader. His past acts of valor are but precursors of those to follow, and from the Army of the Potomac, in the future, may be expected such active, rapid movements as will add lustre to our arms, and insure the glorious termination of this protracted war.

The Proposed National Guard.

Senator Wilson's Volunteer Militia Bill provides for a force to be called the National Guard of the United States, comprising two hundred regiments of twelve companies each, every regiment to be divided into three battalions, commanded by Colonel, Lieutenant-Colonel, three Majors and twelve Captains, to be appointed by the Governors of the States, among which the force is to be distributed *pro rata*. Any portion of the militia may be called by the President of the United States into service during a war of invasion or a rebellion.

The McDowell Court of Inquiry

Sat with closed doors to-day. It is understood that they were awaiting the arrival of General Milroy and Lieutenant-Colonel Locke, formerly of General Porter's Staff, who are the only witnesses yet to be examined.

Free Labor System in South Carolina.

The United States Tax Commissioners for South Carolina have made a preliminary report, in which they say it must be obvious that the system of free labor has not had a fair trial in the part of that State which is under United States control; indeed, scarcely any system has been put to a practical test. Owing to casualties, and the shifting circumstances of military events, no permanent labor policy can be inaugurated.

The great impediment in its progress is the uncertainty which overhangs the future of the colored people. It is a great mistake to suppose them to be unmindful of the uncertainty of their condition. Nevertheless, they are but tenants at will on the grace of the Government, subject to military caprice and necessity, with a strong desire to obtain permanent and free homes where they were born and reared. This class of people, the Commissioners say, are daily thronging their doors, anxiously inquiring about their destiny.

When the lands shall be sold for taxes they feel the necessity of some guiding minds to direct them in a new state of existence the immense magnitude of which they appreciate, but the details of which they are unable to comprehend. The males especially are anxious to return to their former labor, provided they and their families can be assured of their freedom, moderate compensation, good homes and permanent employment.

Nominations and Confirmations.

James McBride, of Oregon, was to-day nominated by the President as Minister Resident to the Hawaian Islands.

The Senate to-day confirmed the following nominations:—

Frederick Eckfeldt, of Pennsylvania, to be Melter and Refiner of the Branch Mint at Denver, Colorado.

Captains Charles Stewart and William B. Shubrick, to be Rear-Admirals in the Navy. Captains Geo. S. Blake, Cadwallader Ringgold, Henry W. Morris, James L. Lardner, Henry R. Hoff, Charles Henry Davis, Henry H. Bell, William Smith, John W. Livingston, Henry R. Thatcher, Wm. D. Porter, John S. Thisson and Robert B. Hitchcock, to be Commanders in the Navy on the active list, and Captain Joseph Langman to be a Commander in the Navy on the retired list.

The Post Office Department.

In the bill passed by the House to-day, twelve millions were appropriated for the Post Office Department for the year ending with the 30th of June, 1864. For the first time during many years no appropriation from the Treasury for a postal deficit was required, there being enough of last year's appropriation unexpended to cover the small deficit of the coming year.

General Burnside.

General Burnside has made arrangements to be in New York early this week. On Saturday morning he, at his own request, was relieved from the command of the Army of the Potomac, when the President immediately conferred the chief command on Major-General Hooker.

The Navy Yard at League Island.

The Secretary of the Navy has sent a communication to Congress asking an appropriation of two hundred thousand dollars for establishing a Navy Yard at League Island.

PENNSYLVANIA LEGISLATIVE PROCEEDINGS.

Harrisburg, Jan. 26, 1863.

SENATE.

The Senate was called to order at 3½ o'clock, P. M., by the SPEAKER.

Mr. NICHOLS, from the Committee on Railroads, reported, with an affirmative recommendation, an act relative to the bridges over the Wissahickon Creek, on the Philadelphia, Germantown and Norristown Railroad, (allowing the company to fill in certain of the spans with earth.)

Bills Introduced.

Mr. CONNELL read a bill relative to the culverts of Philadelphia.

Mr. REILLY, an act extending the charter of the Miners' Bank of Pottsville.

Mr. NICHOLS, a supplement to the act for the arrest of professional thieves in Philadelphia.

Mr. LOWRY, joint resolutions protesting against the enlargement of the canals of New York at the expense of the General Government.

Mr. BOUGHTER, an act extending the charter of the Harrisburg Bank. Also,

An act extending the charter of the Bank of Lebanon.

Exempts from the Draft.

Resolutions were adopted, calling upon the Adjutant-General to furnish the Senate with the number of persons who were exempted from the draft in each county on account of conscientious scruples.

League Island.

A resolution was also adopted authorizing a committee to be appointed, by the Speaker, to proceed to Washington, and urge upon the Government the acceptance of League Island as a Naval Depot.

Mr. CONNELL read a bill making the offices of member of the Legislature and of City Council incompatible. This bill was passed.

The Senate then adjourned.

HOUSE OF REPRESENTATIVES.

The House was called to order at 7½ P. M., by Speaker CESSNA.

Bills Introduced.

Mr. BROWN (Northumberland), an act requiring administrators, trustees and others to file with the County Prothonotary a copy of their respective accounts.

Mr. KERNS, a supplement to the act incorporating the city of Philadelphia.

Mr. BROWN (Mercer), an act relative to the payment of the State Militia.

Committee of the Whole.

The House then went into Committee of the Whole on Senate resolutions providing for the appointment of a committee of three from the Senate and five from the House, to proceed to Washington, accompanied by the Governor, to urge the acceptance of League Island as a proper place for the establishment of a naval depot. The committee reported the resolutions, which was then passed by the House substantially as above.

The House then adjourned.

FROM GEN. ROSECRANS' ARMY.

Murfreesboro', Tennessee, January 26.—Gen. Rosecrans hopes that the newspapers of Cincinnati, Louisville, and other cities will desist from the practice of publishing reports of the shipment of supplies to the department of the Cumberland, such publications being substantially a notification to the Rebels to prepare their forces for the capture of the supplies. It is understood, however, that the newspapers would not make such announcements if the quartermasters and commissaries did not furnish the items.

Wheeler's Rebel Cavalry made a dash at a train of cars, on Sunday, on the railroad between Nashville and Franklin, and succeeded in destroying two cars, but they were frightened away before destroying the balance of the train.

A convalescent Rebel soldier, who was riding in one of the cars, was killed, and a Sergeant of the United States troops was badly wounded.

Brigadier-General D. S. Stanley followed the Rebels sharply, but they had too much a start of him. He rode a distance of fifty-two miles in twenty hours.

The Rebel cavalry, in considerable bodies, are constantly hovering on our flanks, watching our communication. The Government ought to reinforce our cavalry arm of this department, and supply horses to mount the infantry regiments in order that they may be able to pursue the Rebels.

The Rebel General Wheeler has been made a Major-General, and placed in command of the Rebel cavalry in Tennessee.

Captain Elmore Otis, of the Fourth United States Cavalry, who distinguished himself conspicuously in the successful charges on the enemy in the battle of Stone's river, and who now commands a brigade of cavalry, has been recommended by General Rosecrans for a Brigadier-Generalship; also, Colonel Stanley, and all the officers of his brigade, for promotion.

Brig.-General Garfield, who whipped Humphrey Marshall in Eastern Kentucky, and afterwards distinguished himself in command of a brigade at Shiloh, has reported to General Rosecrans for duty. He will, probably, be assigned to command a division of the army of the Cumberland.

Brigadier-General R. W. Johnson, during the absence of General McCook, commands the right wing, and Brigadier-General Granger commands General Rosecrans' old division.

It is reported that the enemy are being reinforced.

An intercepted letter from a member of General Bragg's staff indicates that the feeling against Bragg is so strong that he will be superseded. The writer admits that, notwithstanding the Rebels captured most of the guns, and several thousand prisoners from us, they were badly whipped. He says the slaughter of their officers was awful; and although the fighting of the Rebel army was splendid, they were beaten by superior Generalship and the obstinacy of the Yankees.

The weather continues stormy, and the rivers are swelling.

Dr. E. Swift, United States Army, Medical Director of this Department, whose services are almost invaluable, will be strongly recommended for promotion to rank as Lieutenant-Colonel.

Late Charleston News.

From files of Charleston papers from January 1st to 12th, received at The Inquirer office, we extract the following items:—

BRITISH DEMAND FOR ADMIRAL WILKES.—We learn by a private letter from Nassau that it is stated there upon the best authority that the British Government has formally demanded of the United States the recall of Admiral Wilkes from his present station. Our readers will already have noticed that the English fleet in that quarter has lately been much increased. There can be no doubt that the Yankee Government will back out in this as meanly as it did in the case of the *Trent*.

THE REWARD FOR GENERAL BUTLER'S HEAD.—Ten Thousand Dollars Reward! $10,000!—President Davis having proclaimed Benjamin F. Butler, of Massachusetts, to be a felon, deserving of capital punishment, for the deliberate murder of William B. Mumford, a citizen of the Confederate States, at New Orleans, and having ordered that the said Benjamin F. Butler be considered or treated as an outlaw and common enemy of mankind, and that, in the event of his capture, *the officer in command of the capturing force do cause him* to be immediately executed by hanging, the undersigned hereby offers a reward of ten thousand ($10,000) dollars for the capture and delivery of the said Benjamin F. Butler, dead or alive, to any proper Confederate authority.

Charleston, S. C., Jan. 1. Richard Yeadon.

SOUTHERN ESTIMATION OF THE STARS AND STRIPES.—Friday, 9th instant, was the second anniversary of that memorable event, the arrival of the *Star of the West*, Captain McGowan, off Charleston harbor, and the firing of the opening ball of the war, by the gallant cadets of the Citadel Academy. This was the first overt act of cowardly duplicity and artifice on the part of the Yankees, cunningly devised and designed under cover of peace to provoke and force the South to an act which would give the North a protext for a howl about "the flag." The old rag for which Yankeedom is so indignantly exercised that the off scourings of the cesspools of European turbulence are engaged for its defence, was never dishonored while it was in the keeping of the South.—*Courier, Jan. 12.*

UNKNOWN ENEMIES ABOUT.—We learn, that as the train from Savannah to this city was on its way yesterday, a large log was discovered thrown across the track, near Coosawatchie, with the evident intention of throwing the cars off and periling the lives of those on board. No clue of the villainous perpetrator of this outrage has been arrived at, but a sharp lookout will be kept, and if the guilty wretch is discovered, it may lead to summary punishment.—*Courier, Jan. 6.*

Interesting from North Carolina.

Newbern, N. C., Jan. 17, via Fortress Monroe, Jan. 24.—The President of the Free Labor Association of Craven, Carteret, Hyde and Beaufort counties, has received letters from prominent Northern statesmen, irrespective of party, expressing the warmest commendation of their object and principles. They are also assured of the hearty sympathy of the President of the United States. Notwithstanding Governor Stanley's persistent opposition to the movement, it is rapidly gaining strength. It already includes the entire First North Carolina Regiment. Hon. C. H. Foster, Free Labor champion of North Carolina, was serenaded last night by the band of the Fifth Massachusetts Regiment.

A movement is on foot to ask authority of Congress for the formation of ten loyal regiments in North Carolina, the material for which is abundant. The following resolutions were adopted by the First North Carolina Union Volunteers:—

"*Resolved*, That one Jennings Pigott, now claiming a seat as Representative from this District, who came down to Newbern a few weeks ago from Washington, D. C., where he has been 'Claim Agent' for fifteen years, for the purpose of getting elected to Congress, through Governor Stanley's aid, and by promises to Secessionists to return their slaves and indemnify them for their losses, and by sympathizing with them generally, and denouncing free labor as Abolitionism, while he himself, at his home, in the District of Columbia, professes to be an Abolitionist, has earned the contempt of all decent men, and richly merits a coat of tar and feathers and a free ride on a rail, should he ever revisit North Carolina.

"*Resolved*, That as native citizens of North Carolina, and loyal men who have taken up arms for the Union, we claim the right to have something to say, as to who shall represent this District. And, inasmuch as the majority of our regiment were disfranchised through the trickery of Governor Stanley and his confederates, and, with the exception of some fifty or sixty of our members, no opportunity given us to vote, we protest against the recognition of the election."

Newbern, N. C., 15th inst. via Fortress Monroe, Sunday January 25.—The following is among the resolutions adopted to-day by the Cartere County Free Labor Association:

Resolved, That Edward Stanley's attempted suppression of the freedom of the press by menaces of summary punishments of correspondents, and by threats to arrest and imprison any and all persons whatsoever who shall dare to speak or write in censure of his course, is in derogation of public liberty, and hostile to the fundamental principles of republican government.

Dr. John M. Davies, Assistant Surgeon, Ninth New Jersey Volunteers, has been appointed Post Surgeon here.

New York Legislature.

MR. CALLICOTT ELECTED SPEAKER.

Albany, Jan. 26.—The Assembly has at length succeeded in effecting its organization. According to the agreement made before the adjournment on Saturday evening, the Assembly this morning proceeded to a ballot for Speaker, and Mr. Callicott (Union Democrat), of Brooklyn, the Republican candidate, was selected.

All the Republican nominees for officers of the Assembly were elected.

A resolution was introduced charging Mr. Callicott with bribery, corruption, &c.

After a long debate, the Assembly adjourned without action.

Honors to General Fitz John Porter.

New York, Jan. 26.—The Common Council of this city to-day adopted a resolution, requesting the counsel of General Fitz John Porter to furnish them with the full evidence in the late trial by court-martial, and tendering General Porter the hospitalities of the city, and a reception in the Governor's room.

LETTER FROM CAIRO, ILLINOIS.

Special Correspondence of the Inquirer.

Cairo, Jan. 22, 1863.

Dismissed the Service.

The late calamitous and almost unpardonable exploit of Colonel R. C. Murphy, in surrendering Holly Springs to the Rebels, along with a large supply of stores and other valuable United States property, has been very properly and promptly punished by General Grant, by the dismissal of the delinquent officer from the Government service. This righteous recompense of imbecility and unworthiness should not end here. Men like Murphy and General Davies, who, upon the least pretext, are guilty of most heinous offences against the country, and who cast disgrace upon our noble volunteer soldiery, cannot too quickly be purged from the pay rolls. By the way, I learn that General Asboth, one of General Fremont's foreign appointees, has already taken the seat of the latter General, Davies, who could not recover from the fight which caused him to spike guns and destroy ammunition when there was not the least use of it—and that Davies is under arrest by the Washington authorities. A few more such dismissals and arrests would not hurt the standing of our army in the West—nor in the East, either, for that matter.

The Arkansas Post Prisoners.

The prisoners taken on the occasion of General McClernand's successful movement on Arkansas Post, to the number of four thousand seven hundred and twenty, arrived here yesterday, laden in rather compact masses upon three river steamers, the *Nebraska*, *John J. Roe* and *Sam. Gaty*. They were not as bad a looking set of men as were captured at Fort Donelson last year, and not quite as dirty in their dress and habits. But they were far from being what my fancy had painted the "Southern chivalry" to be. Uncouth, long, lean, lantern-jawed, tobacco-chewing, whisky-soaking fellows, as a general thing, they seemed to have but very little of the traits of manhood left about them. There were exceptions, however. Among these were General Churchill and some of his staff, who were crowded upon the *John J. Roe*, the ladies' cabin of which appeared as though nobody would hereafter venture within its shabby bulkheads.

General Churchill is somewhat of a gentleman, rather tall and thin, but possessing some of the habits and appearances, in his *personnel*, of a person of education and refinement. He was born in Louisville, Kentucky; at an early age became a resident of St. Louis, Missouri, and there remained until the breaking out of the Rebellion, when he quickly identified himself with the Secession element of the State. He raised some troops, entered the service, and fought at Wilson's Creek, and various other points in Missouri, and, latest, at Springfield, where he was Acting Brigadier-General, and where his command was almost entirely cut up. Since that affair, he has been made a Brigadier-General in fact, and placed in charge of Arkansas Post. He defended that place as well as he could against the assailants, and is now going back to St. Louis, his old home, a prisoner of war. He thinks that had the Union assault been delayed one day longer, he would have had a force within the fort which would have defied all our efforts towards its reduction. But, for once, our army moved swiftly, and conquered by moving swiftly. Gen. Churchill says that he does not place his loss, killed and wounded, at less than two hundred. He had nine regiments. We captured 4720. Thus it would seem their regiments had been greatly reduced by death, desertion and capture.

The prisoners appeared to be in fine spirits, and conversed with Union soldiers and officers, standing upon the levee, quite freely. They were semi-comfortably, but shabbily clad, and appeared to have been poorly fed for some months past.

General G. B. McPherson.

Among the Generals at Memphis, the *Bulletin* of the 20th mentions General McPherson in the following flattering terms:—

"We understand that Major-General McPherson and staff arrived in the city last evening, and are quartered at the Gayoso House.

"General McPherson is one of the most distinguished officers in this Department. At Fort Henry and Fort Donelson and Shiloh he was Chief Engineer on the staff of Major-General Grant, and earned distinction in each engagement. He is a young man, not over thirty-two years of age, and is now assigned to the command of one of the army corps in General Grant's Department."

Gen. McArthur's Division

Moved from Memphis southward, by river, on the 19th, and four or five other divisions, including Generals Quimby and McPherson's, are preparing to move, the steamers having been congregated there for the purpose. It is not generally known where this movement is to be directed, but it is generally believed that it will join in the advance of the old expedition upon Vicksburg, which it will reinforce. Gen. Grant has been down the river, held a conference with other Generals, and returned to Memphis. He is now very busy preparing to come and take the command of the expedition, at least so rumor has it, although we have had no official information of the fact that he proposes superseding Gen. McClernand. Gen. McClernand was appointed to the command of the former expedition, but failed to reach the point in time to become responsible for that failure. He *may* continue in charge of the movement now in progress, though, unless some one be especially sent on for the purpose, one would naturally suppose that General Grant would supersede, as he does outrank him.

Cotton in Memphis.

The last news from Memphis reported cotton coming in quite freely from the newly opened Memphis and Charleston Railroad, and the portion of the Memphis and Tennessee road so recently explored by Colonel Lee's cavalry forces. The price, on the 20th, was going up somewhat, and had, indeed, reached the figures above fifty when my informant left. A case was mentioned to me, a day or two since, where a man named Stewart had purchased a lot of three hundred bales, for which he paid an average of *sixty cents* per pound. This may, perhaps, be set down as the highest price yet paid for cotton this season.

General Grant has just issued an order which is to be put in force in his entire district, which, while it will cause some speculators to grumble terribly, will be the means of adding to the comfort of our sick soldiers, and leave quite a surplus to be devoted to the secret service fund, a fund which our General will undoubtedly wield with proper judgment. The order provides that every person engaged in cotton buying in the district shall first take out a permit, for which the sum of one hundred dollars will be charged by the Provost Marshal granting the same. All other rules in regard to permits are rescinded. Traders in auction goods, where the civil authorities do not prescribe the license, and have control over the matter, are also to be charged the same sum for permits. Several persons had already taken out these permits on the 20th, and more seemed willing to do so. Those who were found grumbling, and who refused to take out the permit—especially those engaged in so profitable a business as purchasing cotton—may safely be set down as disloyal persons, to whom no courtesies should be extended. In fact, the order proscribes such, and makes their arrest incumbent upon the officers of the district in which they may be found.

The Election.

I believe that in former letters mention has been made of the Congressional election having been postponed to the 20th of the present month. Governor Johnson has recently been petitioned by loyal citizens of Tennessee to further postpone the election until August next, when a provision of the State statute makes it incumbent upon the people to elect a Governor and other State officials. But some tricksters in Memphis, who thought they had all the plans arranged for their full success, prevailed upon General Veach, the new commandant there, to allow the election to proceed, even pending an expected answer from Governor Johnson to General Grant's telegram. And hence there was a sham of an election on the 20th, but its results, whatever they may be, cannot be called an expression of the loyal citizens of the congressional district and the member elected, whoever he may be, should not—and probably will not—be admitted to a seat at Washington. There is no doubt of his possessing brass enough to make a trial to that end, should any one be elected. For any man who had not sense enough to see that an election, to be an election, should be held by consent of the voters, as well as by order of a General commanding, would certainly not be wanting in impudence enough to carry him to Washington, even though he had no hope of admittance, and merely expected to be sent back for his pains, but with *his mileage!*

One of the candidates for Congressional honors, B. D. Nabers, came out in a manly manner, in a card, refusing to let his name go before the people under such a state of affairs. Another, Mr. Tomeny, published a card, in which he avowed his determination to "run" at all hazards, and setting forth his patriotism and Union principles, which no one doubted before, in as strong a light as possible. A third, a Chicago ex-publisher, and since lumber dealer, says nothing, keeps quiet, pulls the wires, and probably will be the brassy man who will, ere long, be found banging at the doors of Congress.

The Philadelphia Inquirer

PUBLISHED EVERY MORNING (EXCEPT SUNDAYS) BY

WILLIAM W. HARDING,

INQUIRER BUILDING, No. 121 S. THIRD ST.

THE CIRCULATION OF THE INQUIRER AVERAGES

OVER SIXTY THOUSAND COPIES DAILY,

BEING MORE THAN DOUBLE ALL THE SUBSCRIPTION AND TWO-CENT DAILY PAPERS IN THE CITY COMBINED.

THE Daily INQUIRER is served to subscribers in the City for TWELVE CENTS A WEEK, payable to the Carrier—and mailed to the subscribers out of the City at the rate of SIX DOLLARS a year, payable invariably in advance, or

ONE DOLLAR FOR TWO MONTHS.

TUESDAY, JANUARY 27, 1863.

Burnside and Hooker.

The news received yesterday, that General BURNSIDE had resigned the command of the Army of the Potomac, and that Gen. HOOKER had been assigned to that responsible and exalted position, was not altogether unanticipated. More than once had BURNSIDE declined that command when offered him by the President, and more than once, since he has assumed it, has he urgently requested to be relieved. To General BURNSIDE, therefore, there is no discredit in this change; his record is clear, and he stands in as fair a light before the world as he ever did.

In his examination before the joint committee of Congress on the Conduct of the War, he distinctly asserted that he did not consider himself competent to command such a large army as that. This frankness was justly set down to the account of his known modesty, so rare in such a crisis as this; and he was appointed to and continued in the command. Indeed, from the first there has been so much energy, and industry, and self-sacrificing labor evinced by BURNSIDE, that he has always been a great favorite, and to him many have turned as the very man for the arduous task of reducing Richmond and ending the war.

History will be proud, therefore, to give him full credit for what he has done. A graduate of West Point in 1846, and an officer of artillery for some years, he was out of commission when the news came, like an electric shock, that Fort Sumter had fallen. He literally sprang to arms; led a Rhode Island regiment to the defence of Washington, and since the day of Bull Run, on which he distinguished himself, he has been employed constantly in the most responsible positions, and has everywhere shown himself an honest and noble man, a devoted patriot and a skillful General. His campaign in North Carolina was brilliant and decisive, and his valor, skill and alacrity in large commands since, pointed him out for the Chief of the Army of the Potomac when McCLELLAN was relieved. But, after mature deliberation, he has wished to give up this great responsibility, and the Government has acquiesced. General BURNSIDE's farewell order to the army is very manly and full of sensibility, and the General, with his staff, goes on a month's leave to New York, after which, doubtless, there will be new and more congenial work for him to do.

General HOOKER, who relieves him, is also well known, and although the principal incidents of his life have been frequently made public, we may be permitted to repeat them just now, when he rises before the world as the most responsible Commander of any army now in the field. He graduated at West Point in July, 1837, and was appointed Lieutenant of Artillery. In 1841 he was selected as Adjutant of the Military Academy, which post he left to accept the honor of Regimental Adjutant of the First Artillery. During the campaign of the Rio Grande he was Aid-de-camp to General HAMER, and was brevetted Captain for his gallant services. In 1847 he was appointed an Assistant Adjutant-General, with the rank of Captain. He received a brevet of Major for gallant services at the National Bridge, and of Lieutenant-Colonel for his services at Chepultepec. In 1853 he resigned, and was for some time in California. He, too, offered his services as soon as the war broke out, and has had a brilliant record since. His dashing valor was displayed at Williamsburg and in many of the Peninsular battles.

At Antietam he was wounded, and is reported to have said that he would rather have been shot through the head *after* the battle than through the foot while it was in *progress*. That he is brave needs no further illustration; that he is self-reliant is equally demonstrable. He suggested to BURNSIDE, on the 21st, to let him cross his whole force at Richard's Ford, and move rapidly down to Saxton's Station—a brilliant but dangerous movement—which would have rendered Fredericksburg untenable, but which, owing to prudential considerations, connected with an expected rise in the Rappahannock and Rapidan, BURNSIDE would not permit. General HOOKER is said to have great popularity with the army, among whom he is sometimes called "Fighting JOE." His rank as commander of one of the Grand Divisions points to him as one among very few proper to be chosen for such a command. His own self-confidence will infuse itself into the men, and although he has a task of acknowledged difficulty to perform he is eager to attempt it. The duty of the press and of every patriot is evident. It is to support the Government by upholding the General now placed in this important command. In the past he has manifested such high qualities as give earnest of success. All he asks is the chance to do, and that is now given him. A few days of new organization and new plans and General HOOKER's campaign will open. We give it God-speed, hoping for the happiest results.

When DESAIX arrived upon the field of Marengo, the battle was going against the French. "General," said NAPOLEON, "the battle is lost." "We have time enough," said DESAIX, taking out his watch, "to win another; it is only three o'clock." Our recent movements in Virginia have not been successful. We have marched and countermarched; won indecisive victories, or lost equally indecisive battles; but the great gnomon marks yet upon the dial an hour which tells of *enough daylight* for perfect and final success. Should General HOOKER prove himself, as we feel hopeful he will, the new DESAIX of this modern Marengo, he will dictate a history and make himself immortal. The labor may be Titanic, but the glory will be commensurate.

The report that SUMNER and FRANKLIN are to be relieved is doubtless true, as they both probably rank HOOKER, and he may be able to work more agreeably with new men.

Sinking a United States Vessel by the "Alabama."

Again are the advices from Galveston of an exciting and unpleasant character. On the 17th instant, as the sloop-of-war *Brooklyn* and six other United States steamers were off Galveston, a large steamer was discovered in the offing. The transport *Hatteras*, a side-wheel steamer of eleven hundred tons, and carrying four guns, was immediately ordered to get under way and speak her. When within hailing distance, in answer to the usual inquiry, an answer was returned by the commander of the strange ship that it was "Her Majesty's sloop-of-war *Spitfire*, and before the captain of the *Hatteras* had perfected his arrangements to send a boat to her, her guns were uncovered and an entire broadside discharged into the ill-fated transport, sinking her in five fathoms of water.

The *Brooklyn* immediately started in pursuit, but night coming on the author of the calamity was enabled to escape, and the *Brooklyn* returned from the chase. The full particulars of the affair are not yet received, but no doubt is expressed by the officers of the squadron that the vessel was the pirate *Alabama*, which, on the 5th instant, twelve days earlier, was reported to have been at Havana.

The Gulf of Mexico is filled with our cruisers, many of them approximating closely in speed to that of the notorious privateer, and it is to be devoutly hoped that the impudence of her commander in venturing to perpetrate his enormities in those waters will be summarily checked by the sinking or capture of his craft.

The New Finance Bill.

After concurring in the various and numerous amendments made by the Committee of the Whole to Mr. SPAULDING's Finance bill, the House of Representatives yesterday passed that measure finally. As it stands now the bill is much improved, but still by no means what it should be. It authorizes the Secretary of the Treasury to borrow $300,000,000 for the current fiscal year, and $600,000,000 for the next fiscal year, on six per cent. bonds, payable after twenty years, in coin, which bonds the Secretary may dispose of from time to time on such terms as he may deem advisable. Said bonds may be in sums as low as fifty dollars, and can be purchased either for United States notes or Treasury notes, or for certificates of indebtedness of the United States, and they are exempted from State taxation.

The Secretary is likewise empowered to issue, on the credit of the United States, $400,000,000 of three years' Treasury notes, bearing interest at a rate not exceeding six per cent., payable in coin. They are to be issued in sums of not less than ten dollars; they will be receivable by the United States for bonds, and for all dues except duties on imports; and they will be payable to all public creditors willing to receive them. They will also be convertible into legal tender notes at the option of the holder, under such rules as the Secretary of the Treasury shall prescribe. *But this last provision is not to be construed to authorize any additional issue of legal tender notes.* And all the bonds, Treasury notes and United States notes authorized by this act shall not exceed, in the aggregate, $900,000,000.

By the third section of the bill the Secretary is empowered, *"if required by the exigencies "of the public service,"* to issue $300,000,000 of legal tender notes similar to those now in circulation.

Section fourth authorizes the issue of fractional notes in lieu of the present postage currency, but the whole amount of such fractional notes, including the postage currency, shall at no time exceed $50,000,000. These notes are to be engraved and printed at the Treasury Department.

Deposits of gold coin and bullion in the Treasury, and the issue of certificates therefor, are authorized by the fifth section of the bill. Said coin is to be retained in the Treasury, to be paid on demand by the holders of certificates; and certificates representing coin in the Treasury, whether on deposit or received from customs, may be issued to an amount not exceeding twenty per cent. above the aggregate of coin and bullion; and said certificates may be paid for interest on the public debt, and will be receiveable for duties instead of coin.

The Sixth section merely provides for proper authentication of the bonds and Treasury notes. By Section seven it is provided that coupons of the notes or bonds issued by the United States shall, at any period within thirty days before maturity, be receivable for customs the same as coin. The eighth section levies a tax on all banks of circulation to be paid half-yearly after April 1st, 1863. This tax is fixed at one per cent. semi-annually, on the average amount of deposits, and also upon circulation, according to a graduated scale based upon capital.

In the ninth section the Sub-Treasury law is so modified as to allow the deposit of moneys derived from internal revenue, or from loans, in such solvent banks as will deposit an equivalent amount of bonds or Treasury notes in the Treasury of the United States. And the tenth and last section provides against counterfeiting the bonds, notes and currency authorized by the act.

Such is the new financial *project* as it finally passed the House yesterday. Although, as we have already remarked, it is much improved, we cannot but regret that the House did not adopt the much more simple, safe and effective measure of authorizing the Secretary of the Treasury to issue, according to the necessities of the Government, the proposed legal tender notes, bearing interest at the rate of one cent per day for every one hundred dollars. They would have the precious qualities of affording the Treasury a medium to pay debts, and at the same time, being an investment, they would not pass into and swell the circulation.

The redeeming feature about this bill is that the Secretary of the Treasury has the discretion of fixing the rate of the interest-bearing notes, and also of judging of the necessity for issuing any more of the common legal tenders. From his well-known hostility to a further inflation of the paper circulation of the country, it is to be inferred that he would lean strongly against any issue of legal tenders except under pressure from which he could not escape in any other way; and it is also fairly presumable that he would establish the character of the interest-bearing notes as nearly as possible on the basis so frequently described in this journal.

There is a chance for the Senate to still further amend the bill in the direction of public safety.

The Necessity for Rapid Action by our Armies.

Under ordinary circumstances the need for prompt action in war is sufficiently urgent. It is bad economy if a steamer has been chartered at a certain rate per day to make a certain voyage to move so slowly as to require twelve days to reach the port that might have been reached in eight. If no other ill consequence result the cost of the trip is increased one-third. So, if an army has a certain object to attain, it should never be forgotten that he is the most successful leader who, all other things being equal, secures the desired result in the shortest possible time. An army is a costly machine, and should be run as rapidly as possible, consistently with its safety. To keep it six months in accomplishing what might be as well and as safely done in four, argues bad generalship.

But at the present time, apart from the economized advantages of the most speedy action possible, there are other reasons for rapidity in our army movements. A large number of the men now in the army have been enlisted for two years, and their term of service is drawing to a close; and many of those regiments raised last summer and fall were for only nine months' service. To have these men returning to their homes at the very time when the need of their aid in the field is most pressing, would be in the highest degree unwise. We have had more than once, during the progress of the war, occasion to deplore the consequence of such arrangements, that a critical period in the campaign coincided with the expiration of the term of enlistment of a considerable portion of the force in the field. One of our New York correspondents informs us that in four months the term of enlistment of thirty-eight regiments from that State will expire. There should be due respect had to such facts in the conduct of the campaign. Each day is precious; each week should be made to tell upon the grand result, and each month should see us so far advanced toward our object that the necessity for disbanding old and enlisting new troops will cause us less anxiety.

The first day of summer comes rapidly onward, and a great work ought to be done before it dawns upon the world. Every man in the Army and Navy, from the highest to the lowest, should feel that time now is of the utmost importance. NAPOLEON trained his troops to pause at nothing but absolute impossibilities. Brave and determined men, whose heart is set on an object, will often secure it; while the timid and wavering and half-hearted pause ingloriously, because it is "barely possible" to achieve success. We want Richmond, the control of the Mississippi, and other points which we will not name, before the hot June sun shines along our Southern coast.

League Island.

Senator RICE, of Minnesota, has entered a motion in the Senate to reconsider the resolution forbidding the Navy Department from accepting League Island, to which we referred yesterday. We also learn that the Secretary of the Navy has asked for an appropriation of two hundred thousand dollars to enable him to carry out the law of 1862, contemplating the establishment of a great naval depot on that island.

THIRTY-SEVENTH CONGRESS--SECOND SESSION.

WASHINGTON, Jan. 26, 1863.

SENATE.

Thanks from the Laborers of England.

Mr. FOSTER (Conn.) presented a communication from the laborers of England, many of whom reside in the county of Lancashire, expressing gratitude for the magnificent donation of provisions, &c., from the people of the United States, and expressing a wish that some means might be provided for their emigration to this country.

The VICE PRESIDENT stated that it had been the uniform practice not to receive communications from foreigners.

Transportation of Troops and Munitions of War.

Mr. HARLAN (Tenn.) introduced a bill to provide additional facilities to the Government for the transportation of troops and munitions of war, and to furnish additional commercial facilities to the people of the Western States.

Advertising Official Correspondence.

Mr. WILSON (Mass.) offered a resolution, which was adopted, instructing the Committee on Printing to inquire if any department of the Government has had any official correspondence published as an advertisement, and if so, in what paper, and what has been the cost since March 4, 1861.

The Court-martial of Gen. Porter.

Mr. LATHAM (Cal.) offered a resolution requesting the President to transmit to the Senate a copy of the record, and all the proceedings of the Court-martial of Major-General FITZ-JOHN PORTER. Laid over.

Assistant Collector for New York.

Mr. TEN EYCK (N. J.) offered a resolution, which was adopted, instructing the Committee on Commerce to inquire into the expediency of appointing an Assistant Collector of Customs for the District of New York, to reside at Jersey City.

Organization of a National Guard.

Mr. WILSON (Mass.) introduced a bill to organize a volunteer military force, to be called the National Guard of the United States. Referred to the Committee on Military Affairs.

Removal of Indians.

Mr. LANE (Kansas) called up the bill authorizing the President to enter into negotiation for the removal of the Indian tribes from the State of Kansas. The question was discussed till the expiration of the morning hour.

Protection of Overland Emigrants.

Mr. NESMITH (Oregon) called up the bill for the better protection of the overland emigrants to the Pacific coast, which was passed.

To Provide for a National Currency.

Mr. SHERMAN (Ohio) introduced a bill to provide for a National currency secured by pledge of United States stocks, and to provide for the circulation and redemption thereof. Referred to the Committee on Finance.

League Island.

Mr. RICE (Minn.) entered a motion to reconsider the vote passing the resolution relative to League Island.

South Carolina and Georgia Lands.

Mr. SUMNER (Mass.) called up the bill to suspend the sale of lands on the coast of South Carolina and Georgia, in and about Port Royal. The bill was passed.

Canal Enlargement.

Mr. DOOLITTLE (Wis.) introduced a bill to enlarge the canals and to improve the navigation of the Fox and Wisconsin rivers, from the Mississippi river to Lake Michigan. Referred to the Military Committee.

The Interference with General Burnside.

Mr. ANTHONY called up the resolution instructing the Committee on the Conduct of the War to inquire whether any plan of General A. E. BURNSIDE for the movement of the Army of the Potomac had been interfered with by officers writing to or visiting Washington to oppose them, and if such movements had been arrested, and if so by what authority. Passed.

Indemnification of Minnesota.

Mr. WILKINSON (Minn.) called up the bill to abrogate the treaties with the Sioux, and to indemnify the citizens of Minnesota for the losses incurred by the late Indian outrages. The pending question being on the adoption of the substitute reported from the Committee on Indian Affairs, abrogating the treaties and appropriating one hundred thousand dollars for the immediate relief of sufferers, and providing for Commissioners to examine all claims.

Mr. RICE move to amend the substitute by increasing the appropriation to one hundred and fifty thousand dollars. Rejected.

Mr. RICE then moved to increase the appropriation to two hundred thousand. Rejected. Yeas 10, nays 25.

On motion of Mr. DOOLITTLE, the appropriation was increased so as to include two-thirds of the unexpended balance of certain annuities due but not paid over, not to exceed one hundred thousand dollars.

After a discussion at some length the bill was passed.

Consular Orders and Regulations.

A communication was received from the President transmitting the report of the Secretary of State, and regulations and orders of Government to the Consular powers.

After an Executive session the Senate adjourned.

HOUSE OF REPRESENTATIVES.

Sworn In.

Mr. WALTER D. INDOE (Wis.) was sworn in as successor of the late LUTHER HANCHITT.

Nevada Branch Mint.

Mr. STRATTON (N.J.), from the Committee on Ways and Means, reported back with a favorable recommendation, the bill to establish a Branch Mint in the Territory of Nevada.

Arsenal in New York Harbor.

Mr. DUNN (Ind.), from the Committee on Military Affairs, reported a bill to establish an arsenal and ordnance depot in New York harbor.

The African Army.

Mr. STEVENS' (Pa.) bill, authorizing the President to raise and equip 150,000 militia of African descent, for five years' service, coming up, Mr. STEVENS moved to postpone its consideration till to-morrow.

Mr. HOLMAN (Ind.) moved to postpone it till the third of March.

Not agreed to—Yeas, 45; nays, 80.

Mr. STEVENS' motion to postpone till to-morrow was then agreed to.

Troops for Three Years' Service.

On motion of Mr. HARRISON, (Ohio), a resolntion was adopted instructing the Committee on Military Affairs to inquire into the expediency of authorizing the President to accept for three years the services of any companies of infantry, cavalry or artillery without any limitation as to number.

The Eighth Judicial Circuit.

The House passed the Senate bill amendatory of the Judicial system, making Ohio and Michigan the Seventh, and Indiana, Illinois and Wisconsin the Eighth Judicial Circuit.

The Finance Bill.

The House then went into Committee of the Whole on the state of the Union on the Finance bill.

Mr. STEVENS' substitute for the bill as introduced from the Committee on Ways and Means was considered.

Mr. McKNIGHT (Pa.) offered an amendment, namely—the section from the former bill taxing bank circulation, omitting the clause taxing deposits.

Mr. ROSCOE CONKLING (N. Y.) asked the gentleman whether Congress has the power to impose a tax on the issues of banks chartered by a State.

Mr. McKNIGHT had no doubt of this power Congress has control over the currency, as the Constitution provides.

Mr. CONKLING differed from him. Congress could not tax the franchises of the States.

Mr. McKNIGHT's amendment was rejected.

Mr. Stevens' Substitute Rejected.

Mr. STEVENS' substitute was then voted on and rejected—yeas, 18; nays not counted.

Mr. COLFAX (Ind.) offered as a substitute for the original bill, Mr. STEVENS' substitute, with the bank tax section from the former added. This was rejected.

The Amendments to the Bill from the Committee Agreed to.

The Committee then rose and reported the bill as heretofore amended by the Committee of the Whole on the State of the Union, and which has already been published. Nearly all the amendments made to the bill in Committee of the Whole on the State of the Union were agreed to.

Several were reserved for separate votes, including that authorizing the Secretary to dispose of bonds at any time, on such terms as he may deem advisable, instead of restricting him to not less than par. This was agreed to—yeas 83, nays 50.

The House disagreed to Committee's amendment taxing the aggregate of bank deposits.

Mr. STEVENS again offered his substitute as amended by himself, so as to include the bank tax section of the original bill. Rejected—Yeas, 36; nays, 92.

The bill, as amended by the committee, was then ordered to be engrossed for third reading, and passed without a division.

The bill, as passed, was the same as recently published with one or two important amendments.

The House considered, in Committee of the Whole on the state of the Union, and passed, the Post Office Appropriation Bill.

The House passed the Senate resolution legalizing the transfer of convicted criminals from the District of Columbia to the State Prison at Albany.

Mr. DUNN offered a resolution, which was passed, providing pay of bounties and pensions to officers and men in the Western Military Department.

The House then adjourned.

FROM GEN. SIGEL'S CORPS D'ARMEE

Special Correspondence of the Inquirer.

STAFFORD COURT HOUSE, VA., Jan. 25, 1863.

General SLOCUM's Corps, the Twelfth, has arrived. The advance came in late on Friday afternoon, and the rear was brought up before dusk yesterday. The head-quarters of both the Eleventh and Twelfth Corps, together with those of the Reserve Grand Division, are located here.

General STAHL still remains in command of the Eleventh Corps, although it is understood that Gen. SCHURZ has had it assigned to him. Considerable feeling exists between the respective friends of both Generals—each party claiming the right to that position.

Deserters.

Since BURNSIDE first commenced moving, the roads have been literally filled with stragglers and deserters. In many cases, to evade the pickets, the men have taken to the woods. But few have succeeded in making good their escape, as cavalry detailed to pick them up have brought them in.

After being delivered to the Provost they are subjected to a rigid examination, and if found to be deserters they are placed in the guard-house, to be dealt with hereafter. When a man has really lost his regiment, though it be through his carelessness, every exertion is used to have him returned to it.

The pleas made by these fellows are generally very weak, and entirely too much leniency is accorded them.

Some men, who clandestinely left the command to which they belonged, sold or exchanged their clothing and threw away their arms.

In such cases marked examples should be made, and the laws enforced with the utmost stringency.

If this were done, the Government would have not only more effective soldiers, but its property preserved at a time when it is most needed. The articles thrown away in this manner are collected with much avidity by the enemies of the Union, who are not slow to use them.

A great quantity of the arms now in possession of the Rebels have been surreptitiously cast away by men of little principle.

Extensive Hospital Accommodation.

At Windmill Point, which is on the Potomac, three miles below Aquia Creek landing, extensive hospital accommodations have been erected.

Room for five thousand patients has been prepared. Everything conducive to the comfort of the men will not be overlooked.

Instead of small close buildings, spacious and well ventilated tents have been adopted.

An efficient corps of surgeons and nurses are attached to the hospitals.

The Rebel Cavalry.

Latterly we have been but little annoyed by incursions of the Rebel Cavalry. A constant patrol is kept up on the roads from here to Dumfries. Colonel CANBY, of the Sixty-sixth Ohio, is in command at the latter place, and is very vigilant in preventing the Secesh making a demonstration in our front.

Hardly a day passes but what a few of the "grey backs" can be discovered in the distance. They always flee upon our approach. Their object in hovering around us is, most probably, to gain information from the disloyal farmers, who continually evade our pickets by riding around them.

GENERAL ROSECRANS' SOLDIERS ON THE WAR.

Voice of the Indiana Troops—They are Unconditionally for the Union—They Discountenance Animosity at Home—They Want a Vigorous War—Resolutions Adopted by all the Regiments.

MURFREESBORO', January 23.—The resolutions adopted by the officers of the Indiana Regiments, have been heartily approved by all the regiments to which they have been submitted. They are accompanied by a preamble, stating that while they cheerfully acquiesce in the policy which denied them a voice in the late elections, nevertheless they desire participation in preliminary counsels which are to shape the popular ideas of the State and consequently control the actions of its representatives in the General Assembly. They speak as soldiers whose lives are staked upon the issue of the present struggle, and as United States citizens, because at no distant day the survivors are to again share the responsibility of citizenship. The preamble then deprecates divided councils, and dwells upon the advantages of unity in securing victory, saving life and restablishing the Government. The signers present themselves as citizens petitioning, without apology for what they have a right to expect, either as citizens or soldiers, battling for the integrity of the Union.

They say, "We ask that you will give this war a cheerful and hearty support, that you will strengthen and encourage every department of the Government, that you will pour out the treasures of your State as your soldiers have poured out their blood; that you will abstain from heated political discussions and party wrangling, until the authority of the Government is re-established; that you will resist the infernal spirit which would waste victory in humiliating compromise; that you will sacrifice everything except liberty and political equality, to national interests; that you will sustain all officers of the State and General Government in their efforts to subdue this unholy Rebellion; especially that you will sustain our worthy Governor, whose energies have been so entirely devoted to the Government and its supporters. We appeal to you especially to support him, because it is chiefly to his unceasing care and labor that we have to attribute our present proud position among the loyal States of the Union; and for the further reason that he has demonstrated by acts that he is an honest and zealous patriot. We appeal to you to sustain him in the good work of administering to the wants of our unfortunate comrades, stricken in battle or by disease; that you will confer on him all necessary authority, and place in his hands all requisite means to carry out the good work he begun.

Resolved, 1. We are unconditionally and determinedly in favor of the preservation of the Union.

2. We are in favor of the vigorous prosecution of the war.

3. We will sustain our State and Federal authorities with money and supplies in all their efforts to sustain the Union and prosecute the war.

4. We will discountenance every faction and influence tending to create animosities at home, or to afford consolation and hope to our enemies in arms, and that we will co-operate only with those who will stand by the Union and by those who are fighting the battles of the Union.

5. We tender to Governor MORTON the thanks of his grateful friends in the army, for his extraordinary efforts in their behalf, and assure him that neither time, nor the corrupting influence of party spirit, shall ever estrange the soldiers from the soldiers' friend.

LATE NEWS FROM REBELDOM.

Want of Reinforcements—The United States Senators—East Tennesseans at Work—Europe and the Confederacy.

From our Richmond papers we make the following excerpts:—

Re-Enforcements—Enforcement of the Conscript Act.

From the Mobile Register, Jan. 11.

The Charleston *Mercury* concludes an editorial upon military affairs in Tennessee with the following remarks:—

"Before forming a correct judgment, of course we must obtain the facts of the case; but we make these conjectures for the purpose of urging the speedy execution and thorough enforcement of the Conscription act in each and every State. The Confederate States have always been too late in preparation to meet the foe on favorable terms. And desperate efforts, at the cost of thousands of valuable lives, have been required from time to time to make up for deficiencies of delay, and to redeem the cause from dangers not necessary."

The whole Confederacy has had melancholy proof of the truth of the above, and surely the experience of our public authorities has been hard enough to have taught them the value of timely preparation. Upon how many of the battle-fields of this war has victory been won by the skill of our Generals and the incomparable valor of our soldiers, and its fruits (except in glory) entirely lost for the lack of a few thousand fresh troops to gather them? How often have our Generals, after their triumphs, been forced to exclaim, "Oh for five thousand or ten thousand fresh troops!"

But this is not the worst of the evil of fighting our small armies against the heavy masses of the enemy. It is the fearful loss of life entailed upon our brave men by the desperate fighting which becomes necessary to countervail the inequality of numbers. We have for some time believed that the Confederate States are now engaged in meeting the last desperate struggle of their enemy, and that peace or war will turn on the results of the present winter and next spring campaigns. In other words, if LINCOLN is not able to crush the Rebellion with the armies he has now in the field, he never can, and Confederate indedence is *un fait accompli*. In the last and decisive struggle, therefore, we should be prepared to put forth our whole strength, and leave nothing of an issue so tremendous to chance.

Even 50,000 troops, judiciously distributed at threatened points, would make us secure. The Conscript act, vigorously executed, ought to have supplied the cause with four times that number of additional defenders. With 10,000 fresh troops at Sharpsbburg, Gen. LEE could have annihilated McCLELLAN'S army. With 20,000 more men at Murfreesboro, ROSECRANS would have been hopelessly beaten and forced to relinquish Nashville and the State of Tennessee, to say nothing of the results of such a success upon the military operations of the enemy in Mississippi. We trust that the Government at Richmond will lose no time in organizing new troops under the Conscript law, and in sending them to reinforce our armies in front of the enemy. Such a course will shorten the war, save precious life, be economical of treasure, and redound in every respect to the success of the Confederate cause.

The Conscription Law.

There are unmistakable signs that the conscription law will be rigidly executed, and the military strength of the country, as demanded by the action of Congress, be fully brought out. The Government is awake to the exigencies of the country. It is not relying upon intervention, or upon any peace party in the North. It places its dependence in Heaven, and in the tried valor and devotion of the people. The spring, we hope, will find the South one vast camp, and every man a soldier.—*Richmond Dispatch.*

The Command at Port Hudson.

Major-General FRANK GARDNER has been assigned to the command of Port Hudson. The *News* of that place says:—

"Fully impressed with the importance of holding Port Hudson, the President has placed in command of this point a veteran soldier and an able officer. Major-Gen. FRANKLIN GARDNER and staff arrived here Saturday, the 27th ult., and assumed command of this District on the 28th. Gen. BEAL still retains his command of the troops. With the presence now of two efficient officers, our troops will have additional confidence, and feel that nothing will be left undone for the proper defence of this point."

Conservatism in Illinois.

The Richmond *Dispatch* discusses this topic with evident satisfaction and complacency. The election of Mr. RICHARDSON as United States Senator on the anti-war platform previously adopted by the Illinois Legislature, will, it thinks, have the effect of compelling Mr. LINCOLN "to suspend his jokes longer than they have been at any time since he has been in Washington." The *Dispatch* proceeds!—

"Illinois is a powerful State of the great Northwest, whose real interests are just as hostile to Puritan New England as are our own. That she should take this decided stand against the abolitionism, the fanaticism and malignity of New England, is a sign of the times at the North full of significance. It cannot but be regarded as the outgiving of the impatience of the Puritan rule that must ultimately terminate in a more formidable resistance to it and separation from that detestable portion of the Union which has been the source of all the troubles amongst the States, as it has been of all the new schools of philosophy and religion which have so fearfully demoralized society at the North.

It is true that the men who are making this bold movement in Illinois, and Mr. RICHARDSON at their head, studiously persevere in the idea of that impossibility—the restoration of the old Union. They could do nothing less than this. But they propose, with this view, a cessation of hostilities. It can hardly be doubted that the ostensible cessation of the war must be its permanent *denouement*. It cannot be renewed—at least by the present parties to it.

These conservatives can do no less than praise the old Union, and pray for its restoration; but we doubt whether they dream of a renewal of this war, even if the overtures for the restoration of the Union fail. It is a political sequence of the dissolution that has already taken place that there shall be another dissolution—that the Northwest shall split off from the Northeast.

We are satisfied that there has been among Northwestern men a growing hate for New England, and a growing respect, at least, for the Southern States. The generous exhibition of our disposition for a fair and liberal arrangement with the inhabitants of the Upper Mississippi, and for commercial intercourse, deprives them of the only real apprehension of injury from the dissolution of the Union which disturbed them. To fight hopelessly for a restoration of the Union, when they can enjoy all the commercial advantages they ever had without it, is a folly to which their eyes must be gradually opening. On the one hand these benefits are proffered by the South; on the other they behold endless taxation to maintain the wasteful LINCOLN despotism in an unsuccessful war, and the disgusting and arrogant rule of Puritanism, while they remain tributary to the opulence of the maritime power and grandeur of those Eastern States and cities in which they cannot share. Three years of unavailing war, with all its extravagance and terrors, ought to suggest to them this train of reflection, and we shall be disappointed if a brief time does not prove as much. Indeed, we need not look to the Upper Mississippi altogether for the signs to this effect. The PHILLIPSES and the Abolition presses of New England have already become the accusers of the Northwest. Their own minds have led them to apprehend a secession of the Northwest, and they have transformed their own speculations into open accusation of that section, imputing to it such a purpose. Their speculations are just, and so, no doubt, are their accusations.

These signs are agreeable, of course, to the people of the South, but it would be in the last degree unfortunate for us if, relying upon them or any other extraneous indication, we relaxed in the least our own zeal, our own energies, and brave measures of self-protection from the hordes which the beastly and rapacious power of the North is throwing upon the Southern Confederacy. The only means of securing our own independence is the sure one of increasing the discord among our enemies, and rendering certain the breaking up of the Federal Union. This event is necessary to the just completion of that horrid drama now being enacted, by the punishment, the isolation in misery, of that race of men whose villanies have conjured up all the national woes which now fill this continent."

Northern Senators.

The Richmond *Whig* also has its say on this fruitful topic. It remarks:—

"In the Northern States, where the Democrats have succeeded, they seem disposed to elect to the Senate the persons most bitter and inflamed against the LINCOLN party. In Illinois, RICHARDSON has been chosen, who acquired all the distinction he possesses by his long and consistent opposition to Black Republicanism. In New Jersey WALL has been named for the office, because he has been in a Seward prison, and can bear personal testimony to the regard of the LINCOLN Administration for the liberty of the citizen. In Pennsylvania, a Mr. BUCKALEW has been elected. Of his antecedents, we know nothing; but his beating CAMERON is a first-rate letter of recommendation. In New York, FERNANDO WOOD, and in Indiana, JESSE D. BRIGHT, lately expelled from the Senate, are mentioned as those most likely to succeed. With such materials as these, LINCOLN will find some difficulty in running the machine."

"Europe and the Confederate States."

From the Richmond Dispatch, Jan. 20.

The present war has only afforded additional incentives to the solicitude of the British Government for the destruction of both the United and Confederate States. Not only a commercial and manufacturing rival—not only a country on which she was dependent for cotton, is to be removed from her path, but as the war has shown, one of the most formidable military powers of the earth. Taking into view the tremendous armies and desperate valor with which both North and South have conducted this contest, the reflection naturally occurs to England, what would they be united? What would become of Canada, and every other British possession on this continent? What would become of England herself if, in a future contest with France or Russia, such a power as America should side against her? No wonder, then, that she plotted for thirty years the dissolution, through abolition agitation, of the old American Union; and that, this object being accomplished, she intends to preserve just such a neutrality as will give both combatants a fair chance to worry and destroy each other.

If she believed the subjugation of the South possible, she never would have afforded any degree of encouragement to the Southern cause; but she has long ago been satisfied that such a thing was impossible, and has endeavored to ride both sides the sapling, giving aid and comfort through her Government to the North, and through her Press to the South—now cheering one section, and now patting the other on the head—only anxious that each might rend and destroy the other. The only consolation is, that she has now thoroughly lost the confidence of both belligerents, and whilst President DAVIS, in mild and manly terms, sets forth that fact in his message to Congress, the Washington *Republic*, the semi-official organ of LINCOLN, declares that the United States would accept mediation sooner from any other European Power than what it designates, in the language of Frenchmen, "Perfidious Albion."

We hope never to see the slightest importance attached hereafter to any expression of sentiment in Great Britain upon American affairs. The only voice that has been raised officially in Europe in behalf of suffering humanity in this contest, is that of the great Empire of the French. We hope the day is not far distant when the Southern Confederacy, its independence recognized by the world, will be able to show its first and only friend that it is not forgotful nor ungrateful.

Operations in East Tennessee--Humphrey Marshall in Disgrace.

Correspondence of the Lynchburg Republican.

The raid into East Tennessee has proved successful, the bridges have been burnt, our cause has been damaged, and the enemy has escaped unmolested.

About 5 o'clock on the evening of the 2d of January, General HUMPHREY MARSHALL, with a large force of cavalry, attacked the rear guard of the enemy under General CARTER, in the little town of Jonesville, Lee county, Va. Firing continued about five minutes—the enemy retired a mile or two from town, drew up in line of battle, and awaited the approach of the Confederate officer, who, it is said with shame, satisfied with the honor of holding "the city," struck his camps for the night, gave up the chase, and consoled himself by venting his spleen on the patriotic citizens!

Leading from Jonesville to Crank's Gap, through which the enemy passed, are two roads—the enemy took one, the question naturally asked by all is, why did not General MARSHALL take the other, and cut off their retreat? Did he arrive too late? Not so. For to my own knowledge the advance guard of the enemy were not distant two miles from Jonesville as late as six o'clock in the night—an hour after the firing first commenced. But, strange to say, this General, whose mind and body were doubtless wearied from over exhaustion and want of sleep, (I cannot imagine what else could have made him so stupid—for he is a very temperate man,) had not the least information as late as eight o'clock in the night, of the enemy's having drawn up in line of battle beyond the town, and was actually surprised to learn that they had left their position so late. Tired and worn out as they were, having had but little sleep, and not a mouthful to eat for forty-eight hours, thus threw down the gage of battle, and HUMPHREY MARSHALL, indifferent and unconcerned, indeed, ignorant of the fact, lay there in the town as though he were the conqueror of a hundred provinces, and the hero of a hundred battle-fields.

A Confederate General pursuing an enemy at the rate of fourteen miles in nine hours surely entitles him to be classed among those bold and daring officers who have won so many laurels in our service! Both commands at the same distance from Jonesville, and the enemy held in check by small squads of citizens and soldiers, this hero of Pound Gap marches along "in calm contemplation and poetic ease," like one who has just enjoyed the luxury of a good meal, and anticipates a better when he gets to his journey's end. Neither the enthusiasm of his soldiers, nor the entreaties of his officers could induce him to march more rapidly. Slowly and leisurely he plods on at the rate of two miles an hour. Magnificent marching! At this rate, let the enemy calculate how many bridges they could burn, how much of the railroad they could destroy, and how long they could remain in East Tennessee, and make their escape without being molested.

But, for all this, we might forgive General MARSHALL, had he only pursued and fought the enemy when he reached Jonesville. However, he is a very humane and moral man, and dislikes very much to see anybody hurt. How could his generous heart, so full of love and compassion, bear to see his soldiers butcher (horrible word) those who have come among us to violate the sanctity of our homes, and trample under foot our most sacred rights.

All honor to the gallant officers and men under his command—worthy of a better leader—eager to pursue the worn-out enemy, and chastise him for his rashness, and permission to follow; but the "hero of Jonesville" obstinately refuses all appeals—will not fight himself, nor allow his men to fight.

Prisoners.

From the Richmond Dispatch, Jan. 19.

The following arrivals were booked at Castle Thunder on yesterday:—Twenty-five straggling soldiers sent from Camp Holmes, N. C., to be returned to their regiments; J. H. Bailey, Co. D, Forty-sixth Virginia, desertion; W. S. Alexander, First Tennessee, desertion and forgery; Terry Coleman, Eleventh Georgia, drawing money on false paper; Patrick Fagen, Whittington Artillery, desertion; C. D. Lucas and H. M. Sharp, Palmetto Sharp-shooters, desertion. On yesterday, two desperadoes, named Erastus Gullip, Co. F, Second Vermont (Abolition) Regiment, and Wm. J. McMillan, of the Eleventh Ohio, were brought to Richmond and lodged in Castle Thunder for trial by the civil authorities.

These men were recently arrested by the Provost Marshal of Pocahontas county. They belong to a gang of Union men who have been a terror to the people of the lower end of Pocahontas and upper end of Greenbrier counties, and for months past have been committing every kind of outrage on the persons and property of the people residing in that section of the country. One of their more recent exploits was the destruction of the saltpetre cave in Pocahontas county, which was being worked for the Government. The prisoners would have been imprisoned in Pocahontas county but for the fact that their Abolition cronies would thereby have been afforded an opportunity to turn them loose on the community again. Before the war, McMILLAN had been indicted in Pocahontas county for grand larceny, but had escaped.

The East Tennessee Unionists at Work.

From the Richmond Dispatch, Jan. 20.

On Thursday night, 8th instant, a band of tories from the mountains of East Tennessee and Laurel, North Carolina, attacked the village of Marshal, Madison county, North Carolina, taking the citizens prisoners, and robbing the whole town of whatever valuables were moveable. When they left they said their next raid would be upon the armory at Asheville, North Carolina. A force of three hundred men, under Colonel ALLEN, of the Sixty-fourth North Carolina Regiment, has been sent from Knoxville to capture the marauders.

Recognition.

From the Richmond Examiner, Jan. 20.

Both Houses of Congress having gone into secret session about 1 o'clock P. M. yesterday, it was immediately rumored on the streets that France and England had recognized the Southern Confederacy, and that the announcement was to be made to Congress by a communication. The day, however, passed off without anything transpiring to give color to the story.

Commercial and Financial.

From the Richmond Examiner, Jan. 20.

In the last three days gold has jumped from 190 to 220. This is the effect of the rise in gold in New York. Hereafter let us hear no more about smugglers using gold in their traffic.

Miscellaneous Items.

Governor SHORTER, of Alabama, advertises $500,000 six per cent. bonds, having twenty years to run from January 1, 1863. He says:—"These bonds are exempted from taxation, and the coupons are receivable in payment of all public dues to the State. No bid will be accepted at less than five per cent. premium in currency, nor less than $1000, as the bonds will be issued in sums for that amount."

The steamer which reached "a Confederate port" on the 20th, brought 220 kegs of powder, 40 tons iron plating for gun-boats, a lot of rifles, and 500 bags of coffee, with blankets and other valuable merchandise.

Flour is selling at Charleston for $16 per barrel, and Augusta and Atlanta are close upon its heels. In Mobile it is quoted at $60, and in Wilmington at $33.

REVIEWS OF NEW BOOKS.

VERNER'S PRIDE; MRS. HENRY WOOD'S New Novel.

Messrs. T. B. PETERSON & Brothers have just published, in two parts, this most brilliant work among the very striking and acceptable novels of Mrs. WOOD. We cannot undertake to spoil our readers' pleasure in unraveling its mysterious plot, by giving its incidents. Verner's Pride is a mansion built by old STEPHEN VERNER, and designed to dignify a lineage. The characters are excellently conceived; the scenes extremely spirited and interesting; and the *denouement* so ably withheld, according to Mrs. WOOD's custom, that the mind is in one strain of interest from the beginning to the end. To those who were absorbed by *East Lynne*, or enigmatized by *The Mystery*, we commend this novel as superior to both. Rarely has so prolific a writer as Mrs. WOOD evinced so much new and varied originality. She is now so well known and appreciated in America, that anything from her pen will find many readers. *Verner's Pride* will not only have, but deserves them.

Vol. I. RICHMOND, SATURDAY, JANUARY 31, 1863. No. 21.

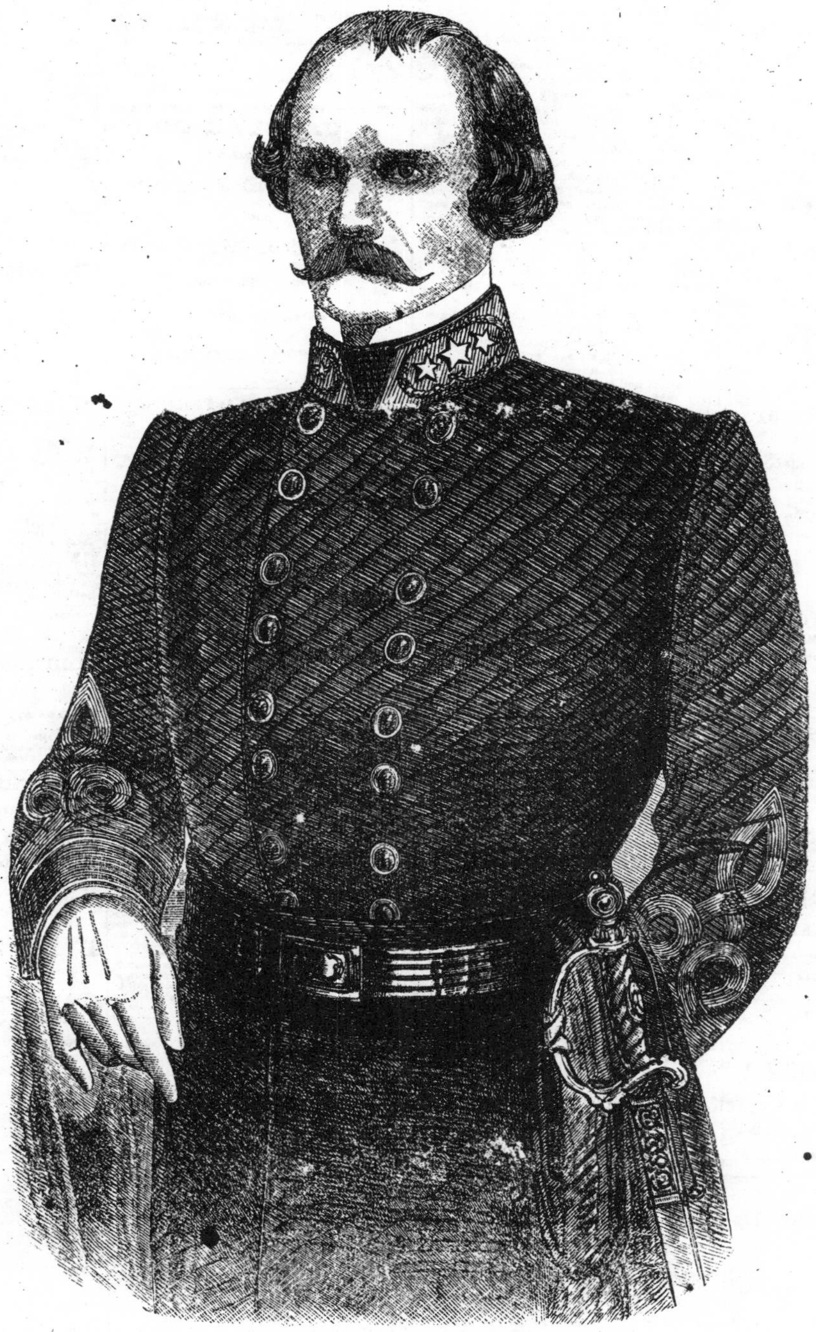

GENERAL ALBERT SIDNEY JOHNSTON.

[W. B. CAMPBELL, *Engraver.*]

Southern  Confederacy.

THE PUBLIC GOOD BEFORE PRIVATE ADVANTAGE.

BY ADAIR & SMITH. ATLANTA, GEORGIA, WEDNESDAY, FEBRUARY 4, 1863. VOLUME II—NO. 300

No. 8.

CRAWFORD, FRAZER & CO.,

GENERAL

Commission Merchants,

AUCTIONEERS

AND

Dealers in Negroes,

NO. 8, WHITEHALL ST,

OPP. INTELLIGENCER OFFICE.

In addition to our AUCTION AND NEGRO HOUSE, No 8, Whitehall street, we have fire proof storage of 3000 barrels capacity, at our warerooms, No 1, Alabama street

Our Negro Yard and Lock Up, at No 8, are both safe a d comfortable. Dealers and other parties will find us prepared to feed and lodge well, and from experience in the business since our boyhood, to handle the negro properly.

Charges reasonable and right. Satisfaction guaranteed in every in tance.

Parties at a distance may know our market by addressing us. CRAWFORD, FRAZER & CO,

jan25-6m No 8, Whitehall street

NO DISCOUNT.

ON EAST ALABAMA INSURANCE COMPANY Change Bills. We give Confederate notes for them AT PAR. CRAWFORD, FRAZER & CO.,

jan25-10t No 8, Whitehall street.

CHANGE BILLS.

WE are buying Alabama Change Bills—payable in in Montgomery or Eufaula, Alabama. CRAWFORD, FRAZER & CO.,

jan25-tf No 8, Whitehall street.

TOBACCO WAREHOUSE

The undersigned are agents for the sale of

TOBACCO,

From the largest and best

MANUFACTURERS

OF

Virginia & N. Carolina,

And will keep constantly on hand a large and well assorted stock of all grades required for the trade of the

Confederate States

AND AT

MANUFACTURER's PRICES.

The attention of

DEALERS

Is invited to this stock before purchasing elsewhere.

WILLIS & YOUNG,

COLLIER'S BLOCK,

WHITEHALL STREET,

ATLANTA, GEORGIA.

N. B.—Lists of all brands with samples and prices, sent by mail or express, when desired. jan18-1m

GROCERIES, &c.

5000 POUNDS TENNESSEE BACON

5000 lbs Carb Soda

4000 lbs Tallow

500 lbs Star Candles

100 lbs Turpentine Soap

300 lbs Copperas

35 lbs Green Tea

30 dozen Brooms

50 lbs Ginger

100 lbs Spice

100 lbs Grain Pepper

For sale at wholesale by S. SOLOMON & BROS., Commission Merchants, at the store lately occupied by Brady & Solomon. dec17-tf

Agency for Va. Tobacco.

A. CONNELL,

Late of Memphis, Tenn.

HAS established in Montgomery, Alabama, a first-class Agency for all kinds of SMOKING AND CHEWING VIRGINIA TOBACCO, to which he would respectfully direct public attention. The store formerly occupied by Messrs. Middleton & Loftin, No, 11 Court street, has been leased for the purpose, where at all times can be found not only the best and most general assortment of Tobacco outside of Virginia; but also a constant supply of the coarsest and finest grades of SUGAR. The facilities for obtaining Sugar cannot be surpassed by any other house in the Confederacy sep30-tf

Notice—Barks Wanted.

MEDICAL PURVEYOR'S OFFICE, ATLANTA, GA., June 20, 1862.

THE best prices will be paid by the undersigned for large quantities of the following BARKS:

Stem, branches and root of Dogwood, (root preferred); branches and roots of White Willow; root, trunk and branches of American Poplar, (called also White-wood, Canoe-wood and tulip-tree,) root preferred.

These barks must be carefully dried and securely packed. They may be brought to this office, or sent to Mr. L. W. Walier, Botanical Agent, Cartersville Ga.; or W. W. Durham, Botanical Agent, Decatur, Ga.

GEORGE S. BLACKIE, Surgeon and Medical Purveyor, C. S. A.

jy1-tf.

$20 REWARD.

A SMALL DARK GREEN TRUNK, marked on the end either Mrs. Sallie E. Hance or Miss Alice Latimer, Manassas, Georgia, was taken from the Passenger Depot, either by mistake or intentionally, on last Friday night, the 28th ultimo. The above reward will be paid for the Trunk and contents to Mr. S. J. Shackelford, under the Post Office, and no questions asked. dec2-tf

S SOLOMON MARTIN SOLOMON A A SOLOMON

NEW FIRM.

S. SOLOMON & BROS.,

HARDWARE

AND

Commission Merchants,

(At the Store lately occupied by Brady & Solomon,)

ATLANTA, GEORGIA,

HAVE IN STORE and are receiving a stock of general Hardware and House Furnishing Goods for wholesale and retail Also receive on storage and sale Produce and Groceries, and every species of Merchandise on liberal terms.

☞ We will give particular attention to consignments, and furnish correspondent with market reports when desired. dec9 3m

MAYER & BERINGER,

Commission Merchants,

AND WHOLESALE DEALERS IN

MERCHANDISE, REAL ESTATE, BONDS AND STOCKS,

Corner Whitehall and Alabama Sts.,

ATLANTA, GEORGIA.

PARTICULAR attention paid to consignments of Merchandise entrusted to us, and prompt remittance made for all Goods sold the day sales are made. nov13-3m

R M PARKS M W HUTCHESON

NEW FIRM.

R. M. PARKS & CO.,

AUCTION

AND

Commission Merchants,

No. 14 Alabama Street, Corner of Pryor,

ATLANTA, - - - - GEORGIA.

RESPECTFULLY solicit a share of patronage and hope by strict attention to business to give entire satisfaction to their patrons. dec5-tf

B B AMOSS D LIGON B H LEEKE

AMOSS, LIGON & CO.,

Wholesale Grocers

AND

COMMISSION MERCHANTS,

Corner of Whitehall and Mitchell Streets,

ATLANTA, GEORGIA,

FOR the sale of Produce, Merchandise, Real Estate, Negroes, &c. dde3-tf

W H INMAN. M COLE. W P INMAN.

INMAN, COLE & CO.,

GENERAL

Commission Merchants,

For the Purchase and Sale of Merchandise, Real Estate, Live Stock, Bonds, Stocks, Negroes, &c.

WE have ample store room, and will give personal attention to all business entrusted to us. Office in Beach & Root's store, Whitehall street. nov1-tf

BONDS, STOCKS, SPECIE,

EXCHANGE,

BANK BILLS OF ALL DESCRIPTIONS,

BOUGHT AND SOLD.

By M. SALOSHIN & CO, Brokers, Alabama street, near Whitehall.

nov26-3m*

GEORGIA

SALT MANUFACTURING CO.,

B. PHILLIPS, AGENT,

MASONIC HALL,

ATLANTA, GEORGIA.

dec10-2m

WANTED,

AT THE

ATLANTA STEAM TANNERY.

FOR CASH,

5,000 CORDS BARK.

R. T. HENDERSON, Agent.

jan17tf

NOTICE.

PRODUCE LOAN SUBSCRIBERS.

SUBSCRIBERS to the Produce Loan are earnestly requested to pay up their subscriptions. The Government desires an early settlement: All persons with funds to invest cannot render a greater service to their country than by taking eight per cent bonds of the $1,000,000 Loan. We are prepared to issue them promptly. All the Bonds ordered by us for subscribers have arrived and are ready for delivery. They will please forward our Receipts, and we will send the bonds as they may direct. We hold them at the risk of the owners. The Cotton of Subscribers will be taken at the market price by the Government in exchange for Bonds.

AGENTS AT

Savannah—R Habersham & Sons.
Columbus—D Adams
Macon—N C Monroe.
Newnan—J. J. Pinson.
LaGrange—Jesse McLendon.
Atlanta—A. P. Dearing.
Griffin—R. King.

PHINIZY & CLAYTON.

jan6-1m General Agents Produce Loan for Ga.

MONEY TO BE MADE.

I HAVE for sale
75 Shares Union Loan and Building Association.
One 1,000-Dollar Confederate Bond.

J. R. WALLACE,

jan18tf At the Store of P. & G. T. Dodd.

Southern Confederacy

GEO. W. ADAIR,.........J. HENLY SMITH,
EDITORS AND PROPRIETORS.

B. C. SMITH, M. D.,......................J. N. CARDOZO,
ASSOCIATE EDITORS.

The War in the West—Confirmation of the Fall of Arkansas Post.

The capture of Arkansas Post, with a large number of prisoners, stores and ammunition, is reiterated in the Northern papers. An unofficial dispatch says that the Federal forces were landed and marched to the rear of the fortifications, and that the iron-clad boats, under the command of Admiral Porter, co-operated in the reduction of the Post Every gun in the fort—eleven in number—was dismounted. The fort was in command of Col. John W. Lunnington, of Kentucky, formerly of the United States Navy. The following official dispatch had been received in Washington:

CAIRO, Wednesday, Jan. 21.

To the Hon. Gideon Welles, Secretary of the Navy:

The gunboat Lexington, Lieut. Commander Shirk, has just arrived, at 11½ a. m., conveying 5,793 rebel prisoners of war from the Post of Arkansas.

A. M. PENNOCK, Fleet Capt.

The Department has received an official account from Commander Parker, relative to the brilliant part performed by his fleet in that action.

A letter from Helena, Ark., dated Jan. 13th, says:

A dispatch boat has just passed here on her way to Memphis, with news of the fall of the Arkansas Post, a strongly fortified position on the Arkansas River, about 20 miles from the mouth. The place was surrendered after after a brief contest. Gen. McClernand is hastening on to Little Rock, and will certainly capture it; for the rebel forces have been drawn off to strengthen Vicksburg and Hindman, and the present movement is both sudden and unexpected, so that for once we shall take the enemy by surprise. We may, therefore, confidently expect the fall of Little Rock in a few days. The forces of Gens. McClernand and Gorman are more than sufficient for this purpose, and for the entire subjugation of the States West of the Mississippi.

The forces of Gen. McClernand have gone up the Arkansas River, and those of Gen. Gorman are proceeding up the White River. The latter left this place quite recently with about six thousand troops, on transports for the latter, and a force of two thousand cavalry have gone across the country to Clarendon.

The army of Gen. McClernand, on his return from Vicksburg, entered immediately on this expedition. The wounded from that battle were sent up the river to the hospitals at St. Louis, and the soldiers of the expedition are in the best possible condition for efficient and active service Stung with disappointment by the reverse at Vicksburg, they are more eager than ever for another chance at the rebel forces, and nothing on the West side of the Mississippi can resist their progress.

From the Paris Monteur, Jan. 8.

Pius the Ninth's New Year's Speech.

HE BLESSES THE FRENCH PEOPLE, THE PRINCE IMPERIAL AND THE ARMY.

The following is the address which the Pope pronounced when receiving on New Year's day the General-in-Chief and Staff of the army of occupation:

"I am deeply touched with the kind wishes expressed by the General in the name of the army which he so worthily commands, and I am happy in having this opportunity of signifying my gratitude for the mission you here perform by the Emperor's order. The French army is as glorious on fields of battle as by its discipline during peace. Allow me, however, to say that its most noble title to glory is to defend the Vicar of Jesus Christ against his enemies, to protect him in his independence and in the possession of the territories which remain to him. You are here to support the rights of the Church and to defend the sacred city sanctified by the death of so many martyrs, and where the Vicar of Jesus Christ has always received the assistance of God (as I, unworthy as I am, do at this moment) in the midst of the attacks of His enemies. What these enemies desire is to destroy the Pope's authority, to overthrow his throne, to make Rome the capitol of I know not what kingdom, and, after having done away with the temporal power, to attack even the spiritual authority.

But you are here, my children, to keep in check the enemies of the Holy See and of religion. When God created the ocean, He told the waves that they might reach the rocks on the shore, but should not go beyond them. You are like those rocks; you are here to say to those bitter enemies who cast trouble over all Italy, "You shall not go further; God has placed our arms as a rampart for His Holy Church, and we will defend the Sovereign Pontiff!" I am happy on this day to give you my paternal benediction. I bless France, your Emperor and the imperial family, *and particularly the young boy who is attached to me by spiritual bonds.* I bless the whole French army. I bless you and your families, all the episcopacy and the French clergy, and all those millions of Catholics who testify so much love for me, and make such generous efforts for the defense of my cause. Why can I not bless my enemies? Let those who strive against me think of the history of the patriarch Jacob, who, after having wrestled all night with an unknown adversary, saw at sunrise that his antagonist was an angel, and, falling on his knees, said, "You are my angel and I will not leave you until you have given me the benediction of God." The revolutionists do not see that they also struggle against an angel, May they one day open their eyes to the truth. I raise my hands and bless you all, my children, to the name of the Father, the Son and the Holy Ghost. Amen.

☞ City subscribers who prefer the evening issue of the Confederacy can get it by having their subscriptions changed from the morning to the evening edition and calling at the office for their papers.—But subscriptions must be confined either to one edition or the other.

A Loyal Negro.

A correspondent informs us that a committee was recently appointed in Portsmouth to urge Robert Butt, a negro of that place, of worthy repute, and who rendered himself famous for his kindness during the prevalence of the yellow fever, to become a candidate for Congress to represent that District. The negro, more loyal than Segar or Cowper, promptly sent the following response, which our correspondent assures us was copied from the original.—*Richmond Enquirer.*

PORTSMOUTH, Dec. 22nd 1862.

To John Council, John O. Lawrence, Nicholas Butler, and others, Committee:

Gents—Accept my grateful acknowledgments for your flattering invitation to become a candidate to represent the District in the 37th Congress of the United States.

There was a day in the history of our once glorious country. when such an invitation would have been received with some consideration, but now things are very different, and to accept such a position when I know, if elected, I cannot represent the voice of the people of this District. In my humble opinion, gentlemen, any individual who would suffer his name to be used in this connection, and under the existing circumstances, would disgrace himself, and show but little respect for his friends of the District who are beyond the lines of the United States Government, fighting for our very existence. I must decline your invitation to become a candidate (to be voted for by ballot) for a seat in a Congress which knows no law, except the higher law, and are every day enacting unconstitutional measures, thereby disgracing the capital of the country. No, gentlemen; I will leave this position to some one who is more anxious to act the traitor, and have his name written high upon the page of infamy, than one who has ever borne within his bosom the true motto of his mother State—"Down with the tyrant."

I am, gentlemen, very respectfully, your obedient, humble servant,

ROBERT BUTT.

A. C. WYLY & CO.,

WHOLESALE

GROCERS

AND

Commission Merchants,

At their Old Stand,

Corner of Peach-Tree and Walton Sts.,

ATLANTA, GEORGIA.

feb1-tf

NOTICE! NOTICE!

UNDER the recent Circular instructions of the Adj and Inspector General of the Army, dated Richmond, January 11th, and approved by the Secretary of War, I have been appointed by Lt Col. H. D. Capers, and under written instructions from Brig. Gen. H. W. Mercer, commanding the Military District of Georgia, will at once proceed to obtain recruits for my Company now in the 12th Ga. Battalion, at Savannah, either as VOLUNTEERS, or *if necessary, by Conscription.* I call upon every man, whether young or old, to rally to the standard of his country in this the crisis of our Revolution. VOLUNTEER, and I will PAY YOU THE BOUNTY allowed by law. If you will not, keep out of my sight—hide behind the Exemption act, or in some obscure place, for I will conscript you, certain.

I will be at the store of Drs. Hamilton & Markley, where any one wishing to Volunteer can receive the BOUNTY MONEY. G. W. JOHNSON, Co. D, 12th Ga. Bat.

jan22 2w

A "GOOD EGG," SURE.

95 ACRES OF WELL-TIMBERED LAND FOR SALE, within seven miles of Atlanta, on the road leading to Turner & Mayson's Ferry, with a comfortable dwelling house and out-buildings; also, a No. 1 Steam Saw Mill in fine running order, with lathe and shingle machines attached, with power sufficient to run them all at the same time. All for the small sum of $5,000. Those wishing to purchase will please apply to J. R. Mayson, Atlanta Female Institute, or J. S. Mayson, on the premises.

dec17-tf

DESIRABLE PROPERTY FOR SALE.

120 ACRES OF LAND, 15 cleared the balance heavily timbered, with a large, completely finished house containing nine rooms with closets and fire places; two framed negro houses, smoke house, carriage house, stable, cow sheds; a fine orchard, a large garden, &c. Said place is situated on the public road, five miles from Marietta and six from Powder Springs—both places of resort in summer. For particulars apply to R. W. Joyner, of the firm of Hamilton, Markley & Joyner, Atlanta, or to J. M. Springer, on the premises. dec18-tf

OFFICE OF ASSISTANT QUARTERMASTER, Columbus, Ga., Sept. 5, 1862.

BY order of Quartermaster General, I have been entrusted with entire command of collecting the hides of the beeves killed for the army, for tanning, and the purchase of Leather for manufacturing. Tanners having Leather on hand and wanting Hides, will do well to address me with proper references. The army must be shod, and it is the duty of all patriotic tanners to assist in so doing. All leather held at unreasonable prices will be impressed F. W. DILLARD, A. Qm.

sep10tf

WANTED.

A LADY qualified to teach all of the English branches, French, and Music on the Piano, with several years' experience in teaching, desires a situation as Governess in some private family. Terms made known. Good reference given.

Address "Inder," Ryland's Depot, Greenville county, Va., or J W Squire, Sr., Gaston, N. C. jan8-1m

THIEVING WOMEN.

SOME *Ladies* this day (Tuesday 27th) about half-past one o'clock, stole from my store, two Ends, or Remnants, of Brown Jeans, one piece of Green Veil Barege, and one piece of Black Veil Lace. These women are *known.* Their movements have been watched for some time, and they have at last been detected. I advise them to send back my goods and steal no more.

jan28tf P. G. BESSENT.

NOTICE.

I WANT to purchase a lot of Sand Paper, and 500 gross Black or White Cotton Tape, ⅝ inches wide, for which a liberal price will be paid,

J. M. HOLBROOK, Atlanta, Georgia.

jan22-2w

FOR SALE,

1,000 LBS WASTE WOOL J. M. HOLBROOL, Atlanta, Georgia.

jan22-2w

VALUABLE CITY LOT FOR SALE.

AN unimproved Lot or Square on Whitehall street, containing two and a-half acres, on which is over one hundred Fruit Trees in full bearing. For terms apply to

sep17-tf J. W. DUNCAN.

CITY RESIDENCE FOR SALE.

A DESIRABLE HOUSE AND LOT for sale, convinient to business and well located. House new, containing five rooms and basement, with good outbuildings, fine garden, and most excellent water. Call on

jan23-1m W. L. EZZARD.

DR. WILLIS F. WESTMORELAND,

OFFICE at his residence on the north side of Marietta street. jy29-1y.

Extract from Orders.

ORDNANCE BUREAU, Richmond, January 3d, 1863.

Maj. W. Richardson Hunt, P. A. C. S. Art'y.

Under the law recently passed by Congress "exemption of certain persons from military service," you will see that I am empowered to authorize an Ordnance officer to exempt all "artisans, mechanics and employees in the establishments of such persons as are or may be engaged, under contract with the Government, in furnishing arms, ordnance and ordnance stores, and other munitions of war, saddles, harness and army supplies." These men must all be enrolled, and then detailed, as provided in section six, General Orders No 82.

You are designated as the Ordnance officer to act, under this law, for all contractors within your jurisdiction.

J. GORGAS, Col. Chief of Ordnance.

In pursuance of the above order, all Iron Masters and other contractors within the States of Alabama, Georgia, South Carolina and Tennessee, will make application to me for the detail of such conscripts as may be indispensible in carrying out their contracts with the Ordnance Department C S A. To prevent frauds, it will be required of each contractor making application for the detail of conscripts, that his requisition shall be accompanied by a certified copy of his contract, on oath that the services of the persons desired to be detailed are indispensable for the fulfillment of his contract and that the laborer cannot be otherwise obtained; and farther, that when the services of the conscripts shall no longer be needed, the affiant will turn the conscript over to the Enroling officer of the district for service in the army; also a certificate of the Enrolling of the district, that the persons named in the requisition have been properly enrolled. Certificates and oaths to be by and before a Justice of the Peace or other magistrate authorized by law to administer oaths.

All communications addressed to me at Selma, Ala., will meet prompt attention.

WM. RICHARDSON HUNT, Maj, &c., on Ordnance Duty.

jan27-4w

CLAYTON HIGH SCHOOL.

Male and Female.

THE exercises of this School will commence January 19th, 1863. Two Sessions of five months each.

TUITION PER SESSION.

Primary Class	$10
2d Class	16
3d Class	20
4th Class	25

Having been engaged in teaching for several years, we feel assured that we will give satisfaction to all who may favor us with their patronage, and give us a fair and candid trial.

Strict faithfulness in the discharge of duties, a cheerful compliance with needful regulations and propriety of demeanor and punctual attendance at all times, will be required of each pupil.

Pupils charged from time of entrance till close of session, except in cases of protracted sickness. For further particulars address THOS. A CRAVEN, or Miss ——, Jonesboro', Ga.

jan17-tf

P. O'CONNOR & CO.,

Commission Merchants,

And General Dealers in

GROCERIES & COUNTRY PRODUCE,

Decatur Street,

ATLANTA, - - - GEORGIA.

☞ Prompt in orders and remittances. jan14-tf

"MEADOWNOOK" FOR SALE.

WE speak advisedly when we say that we have never offered such a rural property for sale, It is situated one and a half miles West of Decatur, on the Fayetteville road, and six miles from Atlanta. The land consists of 250 acres, every acre lying beautifully, and of this number of acres, fully fifty consists of excellent branch bottom. One hundred acres of heavy wooded land, has hardly a stick amiss. The house is not excelled in all its appointments and finish, by one country residence in a thousand, Six rooms, hard finished; closets, pantry, with glass doors—rooms united by folding doors, are some of the advantages. There is a large young orchard, embracing in its catalogue, literally every fruit grown in this latitude. But call and see the place for yourselves. We pronounce it a perfect gem.

jan11-tf S. J. SHACKELFORD, V. M.

T R RIPLEY C F WOOD

RIPLEY & WOOD,

Commission Merchants,

Whitehall Street,

ATLANTA, - - - - - GEORGIA,

WILL attend to buying and selling all kinds of merchandize. All orders for goods must be accompanied with the cash to secure attention. jan11 1y

WHITE & POWERS,

WHOLESALE AND RETAIL

GROCERS,

Marietta Street,

ATLANTA, - - - - GEORGIA.

jan13-1y*

FOR HIRE.

TWO LIKELY NEGRO MEN. Apply to PEASE & DAVIS, Commission Merchants.

FOR SALE.

ONE HOUSE AND LOT, on Peach Tree street, 1¼ miles from the car shed, containing 6 rooms and good outbouildings, by PEASE & DAVIS, Commission Merchants

Atlanta, January 6th, 1863. jan7-1m.

W. H. HANNON & BROTHER,

WHOLESALE

Commission Merchants,

MONTGOMERY, ALABAMA,

dec10 1y

RANAWAY,

FROM BOYLE'S CAMP, on the S. and N. Ala Railroad, two negro men, GEORGE, about 36 years old, weighs 145 or 150 pounds, dark complexion, about 5 feet 8 or 9 inches high, rather quick spoken. NOROE or NORVAN, bright mulatto, 6 feet or over in height, slow spoken, and weighs 160 or 170 pounds, about 30 years old. A suitable reward will be paid if apprehended and delivered to John T. Milner, of Montgomery, or confined in any jail so that I can get him. JAS. H. PRITCHETT, Robinson P. O., N. C.

jan11-1m

[illegible] SCHOOL.

IN the basement of the first Presbyterian Church, the undersigned will open a Female School, on the first Monday in January next. A few boys, under ten years of age, will be received.

Payment, half in advanse.

dec31-tf MRS. M. C. COLE.

WANTED TO PURCHASE.

I WISH TO PURCHASE A GOOD CITY LOT, fine location, either improved or unimproved. Also, a Plantation containing some 500 or 1000 acres, near some of the Railroads. Address or call on N. A. McLENDON, Peach-Tree street.

dec16 tf

HOOP POLES. WANTED,

AT THE EMPIRE DISTILLERY, immediately, 20,000 Hickory Hoop Poles, for whisky barrels. Parties wishing to contract for the above must apply early, either personally or by letter to Wm L High, or the undersigned

jan11-1m* HIGH & LEWIS.

ANDERSON, ADAIR & CO.,

Wholesale Grocers

—AND—

COMMISSION MERCHANTS,

WOODRUFF'S BUILDING,

(Near Georgia Railroad Bank,)

ATLANTA, GEORGIA.

WHISKEY AND BRANDY.

50 BBLS Corn Whiskey.
16 bbls Peach Brandy.
10 bbls Apple Brandy.

On consignment and for sale by ANDERSON, ADAIR & CO., Commission Merchants.

feb1tf

SUGAR.

250 HHDS Sugar.
100 bbls Sugar.
200 Sacks Sugar.

On Consignment and for sale by ANDERSON, ADAIR & CO., Commission Merchants.

feb1tf

SAL SODA.

15 TIERCES SAL SODA on consignment and for sale by ANDERSON, ADAIR & CO., Commission Merchants.

Jan21-tf

NEW RICE.

100 TIERCES NEW RICE, on consignment and for sale by ANDERSON, ADAIR & CO., Commission Merchants.

Jan21-tf

HOSIERY AND BUTTONS.

250 DOZ MEN'S ENGLISH HALF HOSE; 350 great gross Agate Buttons.

On consignment and for sale by ANDERSON, ADAIR & CO., Commission Merchants.

jan11-tf

SALT.

20 BBLS. KANAWHA SALT, on consignment and for sale by ANDERSON, ADAIR & CO., Commission Merchants.

jan9-tf

NEW ORLEANS MOLASSES.

50 BBLS. CHOICE N. O. MOLASSES, on consignment and for sale by ANDERSON, ADAIR & CO., Commission Merchants.

jan9-tf

WANTED.

IN a Rolling Mill at Knoxville, Tenn, a Pudler, to whom good wages will be paid. Apply at ANDERSON, ADAIR & CO'S Store.

jan3-tf

MADEIRA WINE.

ONE BBL. AND A FEW DEMIJONS, "A No. 1" Madeira Wine, on consignment and for sale by ANDERSON, ADAIR & CO.

jan3-tf

CHICORY.

30 BARRELS CHICORY, the only substitute for Coffee, on consignment and for sale by the barrel or sack by ANDERSON, ADAIR & CO., Commission Merchants.

jan2-tf

COFFEE.

FIFTY SACKS PRIME COFFEE, on consignment and for sale by ANDERSON, ADAIR & CO., Commission Merchants.

jan2-tf

LOGWOOD,

10 BOXES EXTRACT LOGWOOD, on consignment and for sale by ANDERSON, ADAIR & CO., Commission Merchants.

jan2-tf

PEA NUTS.

500 BUSHELS PEA NUTS, on consignment and for sale by ANDERSON, ADAIR & CO., Commission Merchants.

dec11-tf

COTTON YARNS.

50 BALES COTTON YARNS, on consignment and for sale by ANDERSON, ADAIR & CO., Commission Merchants.

dec11-tf

QUININE.

200 OUNCES BEST FRENCH QUININE, on consignment and for sale by ANDERSON, ADAIR & CO., Commission Merchants.

nov26-tf

HARNESS.

5 SETS BUGGY HARNESS, on consignment and for sale by ANDERSON, ADAIR & CO., Commission Merchants.

nov21-tf

FLOUR.

150 BBLS. SUPERFINE AND EXTRA FAMILY FLOUR, on consignment and for sale by ANDERSON, ADAIR & CO., Commission Merchants.

nov15-tf

CHAMPAGNE.

20 DOZ. CHAMPAGNE WINE, on consignment and for sale by ANDERSON, ADAIR & CO., Commission Merchants.

nov15-tf

SOAP.

TWO HUNDRED AND FIFTY BOXES YELLOW SOAP. 25 Boxes Toilet Soap, on consignment and for sale by ANDERSON, ADAIR & CO., Commission Merchants.

nov-15tf

4 SEWING MACHINES, on consignment and for sale by ANDERSON, ADAIR & CO., Commission Merchants.

nov15-tf

COUNTRY JEANS.

A LARGE LOT OF COUNTRY JEANS, on consignment and for sale by ANDERSON, ADAIR & CO., Commission Merchants.

nov15-tf

50 BARRELS EXTRA FAMILY FLOUR, for sale by FOSTER, QUEEN & CO.

jan13-tf

75 HOGSHEADS PRIME TO CHOICE BROWN SUGAR for sale by FOSTER, QUEEN & CO.

dec18-tf

50 TIERCES RICE for sale by FOSTER, QUEEN & CO.

dec18-tf

300 SACKS RICE FLOUR for sale by FOSTER, QUEEN & CO.

dec18-tf

200 BARRELS MOLASSES to arrive, for sale by FOSTER, QUEEN & CO.

dec18-tf

10 BARRELS APPLE BRANDY AND CORN WHISKY for sale by FOSTER, QUEEN & CO.

dec18-tf

SMALL LOT FINE SHOES AND FRENCH CALF SKIN Boots for sale by FOSTER, QUEEN & CO.

dec18-tf

FIFTY DOLLARS REWARD.

LOST, on the 9th instant, between Whitehall street and Grant's Hospital, a leather Pocket Book, containing between one hundred and seventy-five and two hundred dollars—Confederate notes—principally in twenties and tens. The finder will receive the above reward by leaving the book and money at this office, or returning it to me at Grant's Hospital.

jan17-tf R. M. FOSTER.

WANTED.

TO HIRE, A DWELLING HOUSE containing five or six rooms, located convenient to the business portion of the city. Apply to ANDERSON ADAIR & CO.

nov25-tf

FORNEY'S WAR PRESS

1861

$2 PER ANNUM. PHILADELPHIA, SATURDAY, FEBRUARY 14, 1863. VOL. 2.—NO. 14

[Original Poetry.]

TO ——— —— ——.

I.

It cannot be a sin that I look back,
  Behind the cloud that dims my wasted years,
And see thee shining o'er its flower-gemmed track,
  The first to flush my blood, the first to wake my
    tears!
It cannot be a sin, however vain,
To worship still a love I ne'er shall know again.

II.

Tho' Time has sprinkled well my locks with white,
  And tho' another, faithful, be my bride;
And thou art wedded, and art happy quite,
  Thy sons and daughters growing by thy side;
It cannot be a sin to linger yet,
To gaze upon a star that ne'er for me will set.

III.

Thou *will* come to me; and I may not strive
  To wave away the vision of a girl
Whose presence palpable is here alive!
  I hear her voice, and see the auburn curl!
I kiss the lips, and press the yielding hand
As tho' the glass of life had lost no grain of sand!

IV.

It cannot be a sin! It lifts my soul
  Above temptation, oft, when I would sin:
It was thy memory caused me dash the bowl,
  The Lethe bowl I longed to revel in!
In gloomy hours dejection flies to thee,
And, as by magic spell, comes back tranquility!

V.

So, thou art in my spirit—and my heart,
  Its wild waves beating, still are swayed by thee.
Yet we are many years and miles apart,
  But all my precious youth is still renewed by thee!
It cannot be a sin, this chastened love,
So with my holiest thoughts and deepest reverence
    wove.

VI.

And that we wed not was no fault of *thine;*
  It might have been! But youthful blood is hot,
And mine was vain and proud. *I missed thy shrine*
  When, in thy soul's soft fane, I found it not.
O, then was madness! But my act had sealed
To me a sweetness never since revealed.

VII.

I have not *worshipped* since, except as erst
  I bowed before thee. So this lesson learn:
Till death, this soul's religion, as at first,
  Upon thy altar, thine alone, must burn.
The love around me were indeed a shade,
But for the light my early love hath made.

VIII.

Is this a consolation? Thou hast made
  No wreck of me because I wear thee not;
I come to thee with what does not upbraid!
  In all life's frosts thou art the summer spot.
In trials sore, in fierce temptation's sway,
The rudder, thou, my passions all obey.

IX.

And sweeter far than all the thought, that thou
  Thus rulest o'er me as th' unconscious star
On whose serenity I gaze e'en now.
  Thou hast forgot me, save with thoughts afar!
And never hath thy gentle spirit known
One jar of discord in its ripe, full tone.

NEW YORK, Nov. 6, 1862.

[Written for The War Press.]

GLOOM AND GLARE.

BY MRS. EMMA EGGLESON.

CHAPTER VIII.

The morning dragged slowly by to Marge, who, with feverish impatience, thought of Tom's promise to talk with her while the rest of the servants were at dinner. The appointed hour came at last, and after satisfying himself that he was not observed, the negro approached the window, and said, in a low, earnest tone:

"I'se come, missis; now tell de errands quick, 'cause de time am short."

Marge leaned her head against the casement, and said eagerly:

"I want to escape from this house to-night if it is possible, Tom. The general's threat was made seriously, and I dare not remain to be sent to Richmond."

"De gen'ral mean what he say, dat true, missis; but it mighty hard to get out ob dis house and 'scape de sentinels," said Tom, thoughtfully.

"I know it will be difficult, but can't you help me, Tom? I have a brother in the army who is tortured with anxiety for me; and my parents do not know where I am, or whether I am living or dead. Oh, if you would aid me to get to them I will bless you with all my heart."

"Dere, dat's enuff," interrupted Tom, speaking nervously. "Only tell dis yer foolish ole nigger 'bout a father and mother, and he's weak as a little chile. Dere's two solgers goin' to guard dis part ob de house to-night—one by de winder, and one on de east side. It's purty likely old Nin got some laudanum in de kitchen; dat catankerous ole nigger allus habs it, and I 'spects I can put it in some coffee, and make de senternels sleepy."

"And what then?" Marge asked breathlessly.

"Den I can steal a horse, and you can climb out de winder, and meet me whar I can guide you to it."

Here the negro paused, and his countenance fell.

"High, now; dere's one ting I'se most forgot," he exclaimed, in a tone of vexation. "De outside pickets will raise de ole boy when dey hears you pass."

"Can't I avoid them?" said Marge.

The negro shook his head decidedly.

"Dere's only one way; if you could 'pear like Mrs. Smiley, and say de secret spy hab business 'mong de planters, dey would let you pass."

"Does Mrs. Smiley go out alone on midnight expeditions?" inquired Marge, in surprise.

"Not 'lone; she takes me 'long for her 'tection. Sometimes, when de gen'ral hab need ob wittals for de quarters, she goes in de night, and makes a bargain wid de settlers dat calls demselves Union men in de day time."

A flash of intelligence crossed Marge's mind. These settlers appeared friendly to the Federal army, and claimed protection from the Government, when all the time they were plotting against it. How much more dangerous they were than its open enemies! Tom spoke again after a moment of silence.

"What do you tink about it, missis?"

"I hardly know what to say," returned Marge. "It is a desperate attempt, but if it fails my situation can be no worse. Would *you* dare to incur the risk?"

"Dunno zactly, missis. Dere's 'siderable danger in tryin', but if I'se *cute* I can trow de blame all on you, and clar myself," said Tom, displaying his teeth, as his thick lips parted in a good-natured smile.

"Then I will go," said Marge, resolutely.

"Berry well, missis; now, keep de wrong side out, for dey's powerful 'spicious, and dere's a heap to do afore night."

"I will be careful, Tom. Is there anything for me to do?" asked Marge.

"Eat all de dinner Nin brings you, and try to sleep some dis arternoon, dat's all;" and the negro turned abruptly away, and stationed himself at a distance from the prisoner's window with a pompous air that was really amusing.

It would be impossible to describe the varied emotions of Marge Wright during the remainder of the day. She could not sleep when her heart was divided with fitful joy and sorrow—impatience, and a dread of the coming events that were to decide her liberty or cement more firmly the bonds her captors had thrown around her.

At dusk her supper was brought, but Marge was surprised to see it borne in the hands of a lady, tall and commanding in form, with bold black eyes, and a handsome, haughty face. It was the first time Mrs. Smiley had visited her room since the commencement of her illness, and as she placed the tray on the table she approached the bed, saying coldly:

"I have brought you your supper, madam, that I might have an opportunity to tell you on how small a thread your fate hangs. If you do not confess that you are a spy, and give to your captor the information he desires, to-morrow, at his request, I shall accompany you, with an armed escort, to Richmond, where you will be lodged in prison as a dangerous enemy; and the Confederate Government will no doubt put an end to your life on the gallows."

"Why am I to be sent to Richmond? It is a needless trouble, since I can as well be hanged here," said Marge, quietly.

"This brigade must join the main army to be ready for action soon, and it will be impossible to superintend female prisoners while on the march," returned Mrs. Smiley, gravely.

"Lady," said Marge, fixing her clear brown eyes on her companion's face, "upon my life, I have nothing more to tell than I have already told to Gen. Smiley. If I am to be hanged for ignorance of our Government's plans, I shall try to endure it bravely. The days of martyrdom are not yet past."

"I cannot waste words with you, Miss Wright. If you persist in stubborn opposition to reason, the fault is your own; but remember when it is too late, that you might have saved yourself;" and with a stately bend of her head the lady withdrew from the prisoner's apartment, bolting the door behind her with firm fingers.

Marge arose and drank a cup of coffee, eating a few mouthfuls of bread, and then, pushing the tray back on the table, she began to walk restlessly up and down the room. A soldier came to the window, closed the blinds, and hooked them securely on the outside; and after a time Nin entered the room to get the supper tray, passing directly out, and fastening the door without speaking. Darkness came on, and soon the room was enveloped in obscurity. Marge was never allowed the luxury of a candle, and so she paced the floor in the thick folds of this gloom, with a thousand strange sensations flushing and chilling her blood. Her first thought had been to proceed at once to Washington, and there take the cars for home, but reflection convinced her that was not possible, for she had no money with which to pay her fare. She must then make her way to some friendly shelter, where she could remain till she had written to Mark, and he would immediately send her the necessary means to convey her back to Harly. Hours passed away, and all about the house grew still. Marge listened to hear the tread of the sentinels outside, but no sound met her ear. She began to watch for the appearance of Tom, and as he did not come, she felt uneasy. What if he had failed her after all? She could hardly repress the tears that were ready to gush forth at the thought. By-and-by she heard a slight grating noise on the lock of the door. It ceased for a moment, and then was resumed, continuing with cautious regularity. She suspended her breath to listen, and after a brief delay, the door swung quietly on its hinges. Some one had picked the lock. Marge did not venture to speak till a hand touched her arm, and then she whispered, "Who is here?"

"It's me, missis," replied Tom, in a cautious breath. "Gib me your hand, and we'll be goin.' De winder aint safe no how, 'cause dat 'streperous ole sojer hab sot down and felled asleep wid his back and head agin de shutters."

Marge extended her hand, and the negro guided her carefully into the narrow passage, where he picked up a dark lantern. and they went on into the kitchen.

"Stop a minnit, missis," said Tom; "dere's Nin's cloak, and one ob de 'latter girls' straw hats—put dem on quicker'n shootin."

Marge obeyed, and he led the way to the outside door that had been left ajar. Through this they passed, and then Marge looked up and saw that they were out in the starlight. Tom paused a moment, and then hurried her across the yard, taking a circuitous path to the stable-door, where a noble horse stood arching his neck and pawing the ground with impatience. The negro assisted Marge to mount. and placed the reins in her hands.

"Dere, missis," said he in a low voice: "take dat yer path, and go straight ahead till it strikes de road, den set de horse in a canter, and ride for de Union lines as if de ole boy hisself war at your heels. When de pickets challenge you, say dat de secret spy is out alone, and dey'll let you pass, 'cause it's de gen'ral's horse, and dey knows it.

"What shall I do with the horse when I get there?" asked Marge.

"Gib him to little Mac, he's for contraban', sure," chuckled Tom.

"Well, good-bye, then," said Marge. "If I never see you again, Tom, I shall always remember your kindness."

"Lord bless you, missis; dribe on, and keep to de norfeast," and giving the horse a gentle pat with his hand Tom started him into a walk.

"I 'spose it's all foolishness," he soliloquized, standing in the stable-door, and watching the dim outlines of Marge's form as she retreated into darkness. "Dat chile neber git more'n fifteen miles afore Massa Smiley cotch her; but den, Lor! how's I gwine to 'fuse my help when she done ask me for it so purty. It's mighty lucky if I gets off wid a whole head, but Massa Smiley neber *did* kill dis yer darkey, and when he does I'll be bound its by'me-by."

He closed the door after delivering these wise remarks, and returning the lantern to its place, ascended to the loft, where he slept when not placed on duty by his master to guard the house. At early morning he was aroused by a stir in the camp near by, and hurried down to be ready for the exciting scenes he knew must follow. He went to the house, and proceeded immediately to the general's apartment, where it was his daily custom to shave his master, black his boots, and brush his uniform.

"Massa Smiley," and the negro put on an indignant air—"I done had all de strouble wid dat horse I'se gwine to. He gnaw de halter and untie it wid his teeth, lifs up de latch an walks out door every night. He's gone dis mornin, and de old Harry hisself knows whar—I don't."

"He is probably tired of lying still, and wants to be marching around; no doubt you'll find him somewhere on the plantation, for he never strays far away," returned the general, who was too much absorbed in the perusal of his paper to pay but little attention to his servant's complaint.

Tom went on with his labors with assiduous care, in momentary expectation of some astounding disclosure before breakfast was ready. It came at last. He was brushing the general's coat, when the door was opened rather unceremoniously, and Nin put her head in with a frightened air, exclaiming:

"Oh, Marse Smiley, dat Union prisoner am gone."

"Gone!" repeated the general, hastily. "You are mistaken. Nin, how could she escape the sentinels? Don't bring such foolish tales to me."

"Humph!" sneered Tom, "'spect 'cause de Yankee gal aint up, dat ole puke tinks she's clar'd out; dere neber was sich a quar ole critter as Nin."

"Shut up," retorted Nin, angrily. "You'se allus stickin in when dere's no sense to it. I say she's gone sure nuff, 'case de door's unlocked, and dere aint a soul in de room."

"Wall, now, dat nigger's crazy an' no mistake," said Tom, staring at her in well-affected wonder. "De door unlocked, eh? P'raps de ghosts did it!"

"Go and see if her words are true, Tom," said the general, sternly.

The negro obeyed with apparent alacrity, and presently returned, wearing an expression of perplexity on his face.

"Oh, Nin got de truf dis time," said he. "De room is empty, and de lock's been picked, dat's clar to any smart pusson."

"Then the prisoner must have had some assistance; call the maids, and we will have the matter thoroughly investigated," said the general, in a deep voice. Tom went out, and soon the servants were all gathered together, while the officer questioned them with regard to Marge's escape; but no one knew anything about it but Tom, and so well did he feign innocence that he escaped suspicion.

"The prisoner must be somewhere on the premises, for it would be impossible for her to pass the guard," said the general, putting on his coat. "I will go down to the camp, and start three or four soldiers after her; and in the meantime, if I find that any of you have aided her escape, I'll tie you up and flog you till the life is out of your bodies." He cast a threatening look on the little group as he went out, but though Tom's heart quailed for a moment, he summoned his courage and determined to brave it out to the last.

It was two hours before General Smiley struck the right clue, and learned, by questioning the soldiers who stood out on picket, that in the disguise of his wife, Marge had passed out of his reach, with his best horse, and was no doubt hastening rapidly on towards the Union army. Almost frantic with rage, he dispatched a half dozen mounted soldiers in pursuit, putting his blood-hounds on the trail of the horse to guide their way. There seemed little hope now that Marge could escape, but Tom fervently prayed that she might leave her pursuers far behind, for he felt his danger would be greater if she was retaken, and he feared for her life in the general's furious state of mind.

And where, meantime, was Marge? She left Tom behind her, and rode on with a feeling of uncertainty and fear, lest, after all their care, she should suddenly be discovered. But gradually she grew more confident, and as she struck the road she urged her horse into a swift gallop. She went on until in the dim light of the new arisen moon she saw two soldiers stationed a few yards apart, with their blankets wrapped around them and their guns by their sides.

She tried to check her horse, feeling that the time of trial had come; but he kept steadily on, and she saw that the soldiers recognized him, for they made no movement to arrest her progress. Just as she passed them, a sudden impulse prompted her to wave her hand, and both the men touched their caps respectfully in reply. The deception was complete. They supposed her to be the wife of their general, and when she had left them far behind Marge bowed her head on the neck of the horse and wept tears of joy. Every mile she passed over was carrying her farther from the foe and nearer to friends who would aid her. Marge felt certain of this, and it was wonderful how the thought buoyed her up.

For more than an hour she allowed the spirited animal to choose his own speed, but she was unaccustomed to such swift riding, and it soon began to fatigue her greatly.

By-and-by she forced him into a walk, and as her excitement began to subside, she felt almost ready to faint with exhaustion. She had not realized how that dreadful fever had taken her strength away till now; her hands trembled so violently she could hardly guide the reins, and a dull pain darted up through her temples, making her feel sick and dizzy. She had traversed the distance of ten or twelve miles, when she saw a faint streak of light in the east, and as she approached a small dilapidated farm-house she saw that the inmates were astir. Drawing rein at the door, she slid from the saddle, and after tying her horse to the rude fence, she went up the steps, and rapped. A woman in a coarse, dark calico dress opened the door, and by the flaring light of a yellow candle, tried to scan the features of her visitor.

"I am very tired and hungry; will you give me something to eat?" said Marge, in a low tone.

"Who are you?" the woman asked, suspiciously.

"I came from the rebel army, and am going on horseback to the Union lines," said Marge.

"Come in;" and as Marge entered the low room, she pushed a chair towards her, and closed the door, saying—

"You're a woman, and if you *are* a rebel, I believe, for the sake of humanity, you will do a kind deed for me. I will give you a meal if in return you will carry some letters for me to the Union army, and mail them to my friends in the North. I don't often get a chance to send communications to them."

"I will do anything I can for you," returned Marge. "I am not a rebel, but have been a prisoner among them, and have just escaped from the headquarters of General Smiley."

"The Lord save you then," cried the woman, growing pale. "Gen. Smiley keeps blood-hounds to hunt down deserters and prisoners."

"Then I am lost!" exclaimed Marge, starting up from her seat. "I must go on without food; there is not a moment to be spent in idleness."

"Sit down," said her companion, calmly. "You can never endure the chase without something to satisfy the demands of nature. I will get you a cup of tea and something to strengthen you, for you look almost gone."

Marge sank back with a groan. In her joy to find herself on the road to freedom, she had not dreamed of being hunted down like a wild beast. She remembered now those hounds she had seen on the veranda with their great starred-[illegible] long silky

[CONTINUED ON THE EIGH[illegible].]

MAJOR GENERAL JOSEPH HOOKER, COMMANDER-IN-CHIEF OF THE ARMY OF THE POTOMAC.

Vol. I. RICHMOND, SATURDAY, FEBRUARY 21, 1863. No. 24.

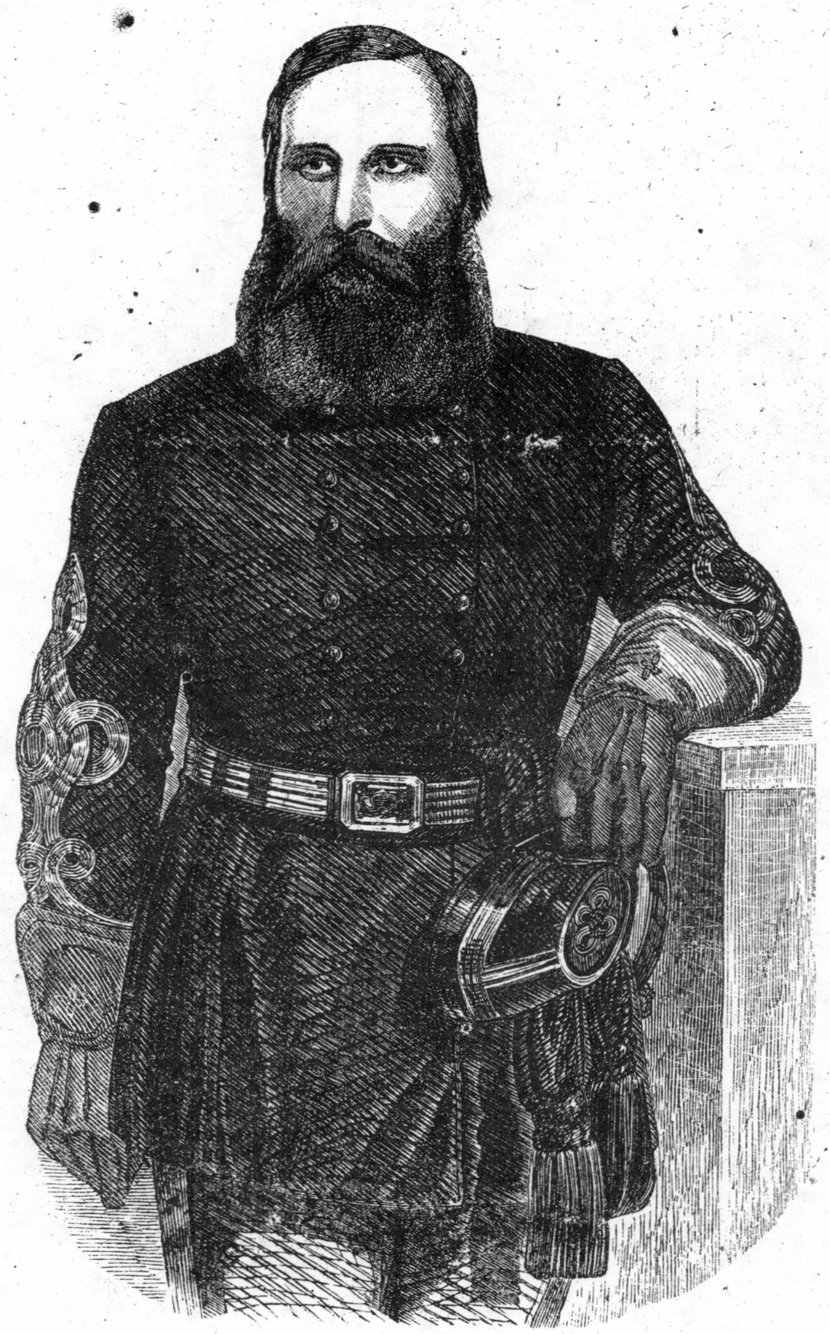

LIEUTENANT-GENERAL JAMES LONGSTREET.

[From a Photograph by Rees.]

HARPER'S WEEKLY.
A JOURNAL OF CIVILIZATION.

VOL. VII.—No. 321.] NEW YORK, SATURDAY, FEBRUARY 21, 1863. [SINGLE COPIES SIX CENTS. $3,00 PER YEAR IN ADVANCE.

MR. AND MRS. CHARLES S. STRATTON (GENERAL TOM THUMB AND WIFE).—PHOTOGRAPHED BY BRADY.—[SEE NEXT PAGE.]

THE CRISIS.

VOL. III. COLUMBUS, OHIO, WEDNESDAY, MARCH 11, 1863. NO. 7.

THE CRISIS.

PUBLISHED AND EDITED BY
S. MEDARY.

TERMS—Two Dollars per year, invariably in advance.

OFFICE—Corner Gay and High Streets

COLUMBUS:

Wednesday, - - - March 11, 1863.

☞ We are not able at present to answer our Fort Row friends whether we shall be able to meet them on the 31st instant or not. See proceedings on inside form.

This issue of our Paper Answers the Query of our Correspondent.

Correspondence of The Crisis.

COLUMBIA, HAMILTON CO., OHIO,
March 7th, 1863.

MR. SAMUL MEDARY:—I notice by a dispatch yesterday morning, that your printing establishment *The Crisis* has been destroyed by a scoundrelly set of military politicians. It appears from this, that they are trying to drive the people of this country into anarchy. What they can't rob and steal from us in the way of taxation, they are determined to mash up. Such seems to be the proclivities of these dastardly scoundrels, but I hope we will work through and pay these rascals back their dues with interest. I want to know of you when you will be able to go to work again. I have never been a subscriber to your paper, but will be, and vouch that I will get up a club for the paper in this vicinity. Write soon and inform me.

Yours respectfully.

Lamentations of a Daughter of Ohio.

For The Crisis.

PORTAGE COUNTY, OHIO,
March 4, 1863.

DEAR CRISIS:—Seeing the columns of your paper open to the female, as well as to those of the sterner sex, I am emboldened to take my pen, although its efforts prove the least among the many contributors to your paper—a paper which is now shedding its light in many a family circle in this vicinity. Every week its advent is hailed with pleasure, because it brings healing to lacerated hearts, and bids us hope for better times come. It unhesitatingly exposes the iniquity of our fallen brethren, pointing out their enormous crimes, warning us look well to our footsteps lest we fall victims to the many pitfalls besetting our pathway. It buoys up the heart of the young Democrat, ably defending his cause, and his aged sire smiles, while he weeps over his country's ruin—yes, even the eye of the Buckeye girl dances with pride as she claims you for her "own native State." O, that we could for a moment shut from our vision the clouds enveloping it—the storms destroying it! True, as yet, the battle cry crosses not the banks of the Ohio, but, in imagination, we behold in our sister States the sight over which strong men turn pale. With your aid we cross the "Father of Waters," and, standing upon the soil of abused Missouri, behold her sons murdered without respect to age or condition; their homes destroyed, and women and children left destitute, seeking protection, they know not where. We see outrages committed which would cause Beelzebub's cheek to blush with shame, and melt the rocks to tears, while from the ground the blood of the slain cry for vengeance upon the crazy fanatics who have been their ruin. Our heart sickens with sympathy, and faints with the thought that, unless some unseen power stays the hand of violence, we may, ere long, be visited with like misfortunes, and, in agony of spirit, in silence, unite our prayer with the few Union, peace-loving men, to the Most High, believing" the Lord's hand is not shortened that it cannot save, neither His ear heavy that it cannot hear." Does Missouri alone suffer? Every State is in commotion. Terror fills every heart, whether a tenant of the richly furnished palace, or the most humble cottage. Shall we go from home to learn of suffering, or find the enemy? He stole into our own little town, finding there those after his own heart; he used them to do the work from which he shrank abashed; they arrested without law, erected hangmens' ropes, and with threats of violence sought in every conceivable way to terrify law-abiding citizens. Our ministers became their servants; fogetting the law of Christ, they no longer exhorted "the wicked to forsake his way, or the unrighteous man his thoughts," but hesitated not to proclaim from the sacred desk the evil doctrine which is bringing destruction upon us.—Many of our young men partook of the excitement, buckling on the armor of war, and went forth to battle. Now in many a household are young widows wringing their hands in untold distress, and Rachels refusing to be comforted. Notwithstanding all that has yet been done, we await in breathless suspense the next news which shall tell of victory or defeat. I would ask how much more blood must be shed to allay the morbid thirst of the unconstitutional party, who have been made mad in order that they may be destroyed.

O had I the eloquence of a Cicero, a throat of iron, and ten thousand tongues, they should all be used, if, happily, they might in the least stanch the wound from which now flows the life current of our wounded country. But because the feeble arm of woman cannot support the torch which shall light her country out of darkness, shall she fold the one talent she may have in a napkin, wrapping herself in nothingness, and with lethargic indifference await destruction? Much has been said of her influence; if it be true, let her now, in this the hour of trial, use the gifts God has given her—proving she has a brain to think and a heart to feel. To encourage those laboring for the welfare of our Government, and cheer you with the truth that in Portage the peace men, and their families, are not dead, or sleeping, is the object of

A DAUGHTER OF OHIO.

Reported Expressly for The Crisis.

OHIO LEGISLATURE.

Summary of the Week's Proceedings.

There is little, or nothing, of interest to report in the doings of the Ohio Legislature this week. It required considerable strategy to secure a quorum in either branch on Monday, and when a quorum did appear, they did not seem to have any particular business there.

SENATE.

DISCUSSION ON FEDERAL RELATIONS.

The discussion upon the subject of Welsh's resolutions denouncing secession North and South, and pledging the support of Ohio to the policy of the Administration in its laudable efforts to suppress the rebellion, of which we made mention last week, continued at intervals during the week. Lieut. Gov. Stanton came down from his chair as President of the Senate, by permission, and made a bitter partisan speech in defense of his record upon the rebellion and in reply to Senators Fink and Kenny, other speeches were made, and when the Senate adjourned on Friday, the question was still pending.

BUSINESS—RESIGNATION OF SENATOR FINCK.

The Senate by a unanimous vote refused to accept the resignation of Senator W. E. Finck, who asked to be excused from attendance on account of his election to the new Congress from the Belmont and Fairfield District.

A bill for the relief of individuals leasing lands in Meigs county, and a bill to authorize the commissioners of Guernsey county to re-imburse Preston Wilson for $200 in money lost in county treasury, were passed; also Senate bill to extend to railroad companies that are constructing roads, the same privilege now allowed to companies closing business, leasing or selling their tracks, &c.

The Judiciary Committee were instructed, if it would be legal to report a bill requiring that spurious and counterfeit currency, offered to bankers as genuine, shall be stamped or marked, with a view to prevent its further circulation.

RESOLUTION FOR ANNUAL SESSIONS.

Mr. Gunckel, from the Committee on the Judiciary, reported back Mr. Perrill's joint resolution in regard to an amendment of the Constitution providing for annual elections and annual sessions of the General Assembly, with one amendment, that, instead of Senators being all elected once in two years, half the numbers should be elected annually, according to the old Constitution.—The amendment was agreed to; and after a very brief discussion, in which there was no opposition the resolution was agreed to. Yeas 25, nays 5—Messrs. Eggleston, Godfrey, Groesbeck, Humphereyville and Miles. It provides for submitting the amendment to the electors of the State at the next election on the Second Tuesday of October.

HOUSE.

CINCINNATI AND COVINGTON BRIDGE.

The question of lowering the altitude of the Cincinnati and Covington Bridge was discussed for several days in the House and its final consideration postponed until Thursday of this week.

BILLS PASSED.

Senate bill to appropriate money for the purchase of additional grounds in Spring Grove Cemetery, for the interment of deceased soldiers. It authorizes the Governor to use for that purpose $3,000 from his contingent fund.

House bill to authorize the city of Cleve land to levy an additional tax of one half mill for the purpose of purchasing steam fire engines.

House bill to reduce the number of Trustees of the Ohio Female College from thirty to five in number.

SALE OF LANDS FORFEITED FOR TAXES.

The Auditor of State made the following report in answer to a resolution of the House:

OFFICE OF THE AUDITOR OF STATE,
COLUMBUS, March 3, 1863.

Hon. James R Hubbell, Speaker of the House of Representatives:

SIR:—In answer to the resolution of the House requesting the Auditor of State to inform the House whether, in his opinion, further legislation is necessary to secure the collection of taxes on lots and lands forfeited to the State Auditor for the non-payment of taxes and assessments, I have the honor to state that no official information has been received by the Auditor, showing that any serious difficulty has been encountered in the sale of lands forfeited to the State for the cause named in the resolution, except in the case of some leased lands in the county of Morgan. These lands are held in trust for the benefit of schools and are occupied under seven years leases. The tax law provides that lands held by lease for a term of exceeding fourteen years, shall be taxed in the name of the lessee, and, hence by clear implication, where the term is for less than fourteen years, the land must be taxed in the name of the owner, who must pay the tax. The title to these lands being in the State, no sale can be made by the County Auditor, because such sale would not divest the State of title, and therefore the lessees escape taxation. The tax law does not authorize a sale of the lease or unexpired term of the tenant.

It seems to me these lands should be placed on the duplicate in the names of the lessees who should pay the taxes thereon. As the law now stands, lessees receive their share of school and other funds raised by taxation, to which they do not contribute, and refuse to contribute. I am told, further, that in some parts of the State sales of forfeited lands cannot because parties inclined to purchase are apprehensive that the courts will rule so strictly in relation to the proceedings preliminary to a sale, as to defeat a title thus acquired, and therefore such parties declined to bid.

If provision were made by law for putting the purchaser in immediate possession of lands purchased at forfeited sales, but saving the right of redemption, the taxes upon such forfeited lands might be secured, I recommend therefore the passage of a law providing that where lands forfeited to the State have been once offered for sale, and remain unsold for want of bidders, the Auditor of the county shall give written notice to the party in possession of the property of the amount of taxes and penalty charged against the same; and if such taxes and penalty are not paid within ten days the Auditor shall upon ten days' notice proceed to sell the property so charged with taxes and penalty, adding thereto the costs of sale. Upon such sale the purchaser should by summary proceedings before a Justice of the Peace, or in the Probate Court, have possession of the land, and retain the same until by the rents and profits, or by voluntary payment, he shall have received the purchase money, with such penalty as may be provided by law, and all taxes paid by him subsequent to the sale. In such proceedings the purchaser should be permitted to make parol proof of the identy of the land sold with that claimed, and the occupant should not be permitted to make any defence except to contest such identity and to prove actual payment of the taxes.

Forfeitures of land have been regarded as penal, and hence courts are inclined to hold purchasers to proof of a strict compliance with the provisions of the law in every particular, even to what in many cases is an impossible description of the land on the duplicate. In the proceedings now proposed, there will be no forfeiture of title acquired by the purchaser, and hence the strictness heretofore required by the courts, will not be necessary to protect the owner in his title. He will only lose the use of the land until the purchaser shall have obtained his dues, from the rents and profits, or until he shall have been paid voluntarily by the owner. I have the honor to be, very respectfully,

R. W. TAYLOR, Auditor.

OTHER BUSINESS.

Four thousand copies of the Auditor's Report were ordered to be printed in German.

The House and Senate got into a snarl upon a question of courtesy, the House having passed a bill to repay local bounty, while a Senate bill on the same subject lay on the table of the House not disposed of. The Senate was indignant, but the House refused to come down. The Senate thereupon threatens to kill the House bill by indefinitely postponing it.

Petitions from eight hundred ladies and voters of Stark county prayed for a law to prohibit the immigration of negroes, were presented and referred to the members from that county.

THE PARTISAN JUBILEE.

Both branches, on Tuseday, did no business in consequence of the visit of Gov Johnson, of Tennessee, and ex-Gov. Wright, of Indiana, who made speeches in the House in defense of the Administration. A vote of thanks to those gentlemen was tendered them.

Both branches adjourned on Friday until Tuesday.

For The Crisis.

GENERAL HOSPITAL NO. 6,
NEW ALBANY, IND., March 5, 1863.

HON SAMUEL MEDARY—*Sir:* I see the name of Hon. G. W. STOKES, of Warren, spoken of for nomination before the Democratic State Convention, to be held at Columbus, Ohio, for the office of *State Treasurer*. This is as it should be, he is an uncompromising Democrat of the true Jackson school, and resides in a county that is, and always has been, largely Republican. He has filled offices of trust with honor, and his nomination to that office would be but justice to the Democrats of Southern Ohio.

W. A. J.

GLORIOUS NEWS FROM NEW YORK.

The Cities and Large Towns all Going Democratic by Decisive Majorities—The Democratic Ball Rolling On—Immense Changes of Public Opinion.

From the Cincinnati Enquirer.

We find the following telegraphic dispatches in the New York *Tribune* of the 4th. They are highly important as indicating the great changes of public opinion now in progress. The fact that five large cities and towns in the interior of New York, cities which usually go against the Democracy, should now go for them, tells a story that all can understand. Oswego, last fall, gave 100 majority against Seymour. Now it is 100 for us. Rochester was 600 against us; it is now 600 for us. Lockport was against us; it is now for us. The majorities in Troy and Utica are greatly increased.

MUNICIPAL ELECTIONS IN NEW YORK.

OSWEGO, March 3.—At the municipal election to-day the Democrats elected their Mayor by 108 majority, and two out of the four Alderman.

TROY, March 3.—At the charter election here to-day, Wm. L. Van Alstyne, Democrat, was elected Mayor by over 1,300 majority. The Common Council stands: Democrats 13, Republicans 9.

ROCHESTER, March 3.—At the Charter election to-day the Democrats elected the Mayor and the entire city ticket by about 600 majority, and eight of the twelve Alderman, and seven of the twelve Supervisors.

LOCKPORT, March 3—The Democrats have elected their whole ticket by a large majority.

UTICA, March 3.—Charles S. Wilson, Democrat, was to-day elected Mayor by 606 majority. The rest of the city ticket is also Democratic. The Common Council is the same as last year.

We predict that the elections run that way through the year. The Abolitionists tell us that since the elections last year the tide has set in their favor. If so, how can they explain these elections? It is owing to *local causes*. Do *local* causes operate uniformly all over the State.

A REBEL PRIVATEER.—The Kingston (Jamaica) correspondent of the New York *Journal of Commerce* says:

"I have but little to add to my notes. The Confederate steamer Antonia (formerly the Herald, a notorious runner between Nassau and Charleston,) arrived here on the 10th instant, in ballast, for repairs. Since the 15th of July last, she has taken out of the port of Charleston 5,500 bales of cotton, mostly Sea Island, sold through the same hands as previously advised, and for like evil purposes, by which the agents have accumulated millions of wealth—solid sterling.

"She has landed in Charleston, in the period above named, very nearly (perfect accuracy I can not pretend to,) 50.000 Enfield rifles, 2,000 barrels gunpowder, 40,000 blankets, 55,000 pairs of shoes—*of neutral English army make*—pistols uncounted, and steel plating to cover a gunboat—one of the iron-clads of the recent water raid in front of Charleston—with many other goods for the general trade."

INDIGNATION AT THE MONSTROUS DOINGS OF CONGRESS.

[From the New York World.]

The Complete Overthrow of the Public Liberties.

This is the darkest hour since the outbreak of the rebellion. Congress, by the act passed yesterday authorizing the President to suspend the writ of *habeas corpus* throughout the whole extent of the country, has consummated its series of measures for laying the country prostrate and helpless at the feet of one man. It was not enough that Mr. Lincoln has been invested with the purse and the sword; that, with an immense power to raise or manufacture money, he has unrestricted command of the services of every able-bodied man of the country, Congress has thought it necessary to give the finishing stroke to its establishment of a military despotism, by removing all checks on the abuse of the enormous monetary and military power with which they have clothed the President. What assurance has the country that we shall ever have another Presidential election? None whatever, except what may be found in the confidence, reasonable or unreasonable, reposed in the rectitude and patriotism of Mr. Lincoln. If any person, in any part of the country, shall think it his duty to resist unconstitutional encroachments on the rights of citizens, Mr. Lincoln is authorized, by what purports to be a law, to snatch up that individual and immure him in one of the government bastiles as long as he shall see fit, and there is no power anywhere in the nation to call him to account. He can send one of his countless provost-marshals into the house of a Governor of a State, or any other citizen, in the dead of night, drag him from his bed, hustle him away under the cover of darkness, plunge him in a distant and unknown dungeon, and allow his friends to know no more of the whereabouts of his body than they would of the habitation of his soul, if, instead of imprisoning, the provost-marshal had murdered him. With this tremendous power over the liberty of every citizen whom he may suspect, or whom he may choose to imprison without suspecting, the President is as absolute a despot as the Sultan of Turkey. All the guarantees of liberty are broken down; we all lie at the feet of one man, dependent on his caprice for every hour's exemption from a bastile. If he wills it, the State Governments may continue in the discharge of their functions; but if he wills it, every one of them that does not become his submissive and subservient tool can be at once suspended by the imprisonment of its officers. Considering the enormous power conferred on the President by the Finance and Conscription Bills, a reasonable jealousy would have erected additional safeguards against its abuse. Instead of that, Congress has thrown down all the old barriers and left us absolutely without shelter in the greatest violence of the tempest.

So far as the detestable act passed yesterday is an act of indemnity to shield the President from the legal consequences of past exertions of arbitrary power, it is a confession that he, his secretaries, provost-marshals, and other minions have been acting in violation of law. It annuls all laws passed by the State Legislatures for the protection of their citizens against kidnapping; it provides for taking all suits for damages out of the State courts and transferring them to the Federal tribunals, and before those tribunals the fact that the injury complained of was done under color of executive authority is declared to be a full and complete defense. It even inflicts penalties on persons coming before the courts for redress of injuries, by declaring that if they are not successful the defendant shall recover double costs. So that the aggrieved party must take the risk of this penalty for venturing to ascertain, in a court of justice, whether his oppressor was or was not acting under the authority of the President. To this alarming pass have matters come, that not only does every citizen hold his liberty at the mercy of one man, but he is liable to be punished for inquiring whether the person arresting him really possessed, or only falsely pretended to possess, that man's authority!

The attempt to disguise the odious character of this detestable act by a sham provision in its second section is an insult to the intelligence of the people. "The Secretary of State and the Secretary of War," so it reads, "are directed, *as soon as may be practicable*," to furnish to the judges of the courts lists of the names of the persons arrested, that they may be presented to a grand jury for indictment. And who is to judge of this *practicability?* Why, the Secretaries themselves, or the President for them. They will furnish such lists whenever it suits their pleasure, and not before. There is not only *no penalty* for neglecting to do this altogether, but the main purpose of the act is to protect these officers, and all persons acting under their directions, against all legal penalties for all arrests wherever made, and all detentions in prison, however long protracted.

The ninety days during which Congress has now been in session are the last ninety days of American freedom. Our liberties had previously been curtailed and abridged by executive encroachments, but the courts remained open for redress of wrongs. But this Congress has rendered their overthrow complete, by first putting the purse and the sword in the hands of the President and then assuring him of complete impunity in all abuses of this enormous, this dangerous, this tremendous power.

Great Democratic Victory in New York—Democratic Gain of 12,000 in Four Months.

A correspondent of the Rome *Sentinel* furnishes that paper with the following analysis of the town meetings held in New York State thus far this year:

	NO. OF TOWNS. Last Fall. Rep.	Dem.	This Spring. Rep.	Dem.	Popular Gains.
Broome	12	3	10	5	700
Chemung	4	6	1	9	645
Chenango	15	6	14	7	500
Cortland	11	1	10	5	500
Delaware	12	6	10	8	200
Franklin	7	9	6	10	800
Fulton	5	5	5	5	100
Hamilton	2	6	1	2	....
Herkimer	15	3	11	7	1,000
Jefferson	18	4	16	6	1,400
Lewis	9	8	5	12	450
Montgomery	5	5	3	7	200
Onondago	16	3	11	8	1,000
Otsego	12	12	10	14	620
St. Lawrence	29	..	25	4	3,000
Schoharie	3	13	3	13	....
Steuben	25	6	17	14	1,000
Tioga	7	2	5	4	300
Schuyler	6	2	5	3	203
Total	213	103	163	148	12,282

This is the way the elections are going this year in all parts of the country.

The Indemnity to the President and his Subordinates for Illegal and Unconstitutional Acts—The Constitution Virtually Suspended.

We invite especial attention to the infamous "Indemnity bill," so-called, of Congress, which seeks to legalize *past illegal* acts of the President and his subordinates; and which virtually suspends or attemps to suspend, the Constitution of the United States in future. Of all the acts passed by Congress it is the most crazy and the most palpably unconstitutional. As a matter of reference, we give the yeas and nays of the passage of the bill:

YEAS—Messrs. Aldrich, Arnold, Ashley, Babbit, Baker, Baxter, Beaman, Bingham, Blair (Va.), Blair (Penn.), Blake, Brown, (Va.), Buffington. Campbell, Casey, Chamberlain, Clark, Colfax, Frederick A. Conkling, Roscoe Conkling, Conway, Cutler, Davis, Dawes, Delano, Dunn, Edgerton, Elliot, Ely, Fenton, Samuel C. Fessenden, Thomas A. D. Fessenden, Flanders, Fisher, Franchot, Frank, Goodwin, Gurley, Hahn, Hale, Harrison, Hooper, Horton, Hutchins, Julian, Kelly, Kellogg, (Mich.), Kellogg, (Ills.), Killinger, Lansing, Leary, Lehman, Loomis, Low, McIndoe, McKean, McKnight, McPherson, Marston, Maynard, Mitchell, Moorehead, Morrill (Maine.), Nixon, Olin, Patton, Phelps, (Cal.), Pike, Pomeroy, Porter, Rice, (Maine), Riddle, Rollins, (N. H,), Sargent, Sedgwick, Segur, Shanks, Sheilabarger, Sherman, Sloan, Spaulding, Stevens, Stratton, Thomas (Md.), Trimble, Trowbridge, Van Horn, Van Valkenburg, Van Wyck, Verree, Walker, Wall, Wallace, Washburne, Wheeler, White, (Ind.), Wilson, Windom, Worcester.

NAYS—Messrs Allen (Ohio), Allen (Ill.), Ancona, Biddle, Calvert, Cravens, Crisfield, Delaplaine, Dunlap, English, Granger, Grider, Hall, Harding, Holman, Johnson, Kerrigan, Knapp, Law, Mallory, May, Menzies Morris, Noble, Norton, Nugent, Pendleton, Perry, Price, Robinson, Shiel, Smith, Steele, (N. Y.), Steele (N. J.), Stiles, Thomas, (Mass.), Vallandigham, Vorhees, Wadsworth, Ward, White (Ohio), Wickliffe, Wood, Woodruff, Yeaman.

The Vote in the House of Congress on the Passage of the Draft or Conscription Bill.

The vote on the Conscription bill was 115 yeas against 49 nays, as follows:

YEAS—Messrs. Aldrich, Arnold, Alley, Ashley, Baubitt, Bailey, Baker, Baxter, Beaman, Bingham, Blair, (Va.), Blair, (Penn.), Blake, Brown, (Va.), Buffington, Calvert, Campbell, Casey, Chamberlain, Clark, Colfax, Frederick A. Conkling, Roscoe Conkling, Covode, Crisfield, Cutler, Davis, Dawes, Delane, Diven, Dunn, Edgerton, Edwards, Elliot, Ely, Fenton, Samuel C. Fessenden, Thos. A. D. Fessenden, Flanders, Fisher, Franchot, Frank, Gooch, Goodwin, Granger, Gurley, Hahn, Haight, Hale, Harrison, Hickman, Hooper, Horton, Hutchins, Julian, Kelley, Kellogg (Michigan), Kellogg (Illinois), Killinger, Lansing, Leary, Loomis, Lovejoy, Low, McIndoe, McKean, McKnight, McPherson, Marston, Maynard, Mitchell, Moorhead, Morrill, (Maine,) Morill (Vermont), Nixon, Olin, Patten, Phelps (California,) Pike, Pomeroy, Porter, Rice (Massachusetts), Rice (Maine), Riddle, Rollins (N. H), Sargent, Sedgwick, Segur, Shanks, Sheffield, Shellabarger, Sherman, Sloan, Spaulding, Stevens, Stratton, Thomas (Massachusetts), Thomas (Maryland), Train, Trimble, Trowbridge, Vandever, Van Horn, Verree, Walker, Wall, Wallace, Walton, Washburne, Webster, Wheeler, White (Indiana), Wilson, Windom, Worcester—115.

NAYS—Messrs. Allen (Ohio), Allen (Illinois,) Ancona, Biddle, Clements, Conway, Corning, Cox, Cravens, Crittenden, Delaplaine, Dunlap, English, Fouke, Grider, Hall, Harding, Holman, Johnson, Kerrigan, Knapp, Law, Lazear, Mallory, May, Menzies, Morris, Noble, Norton, Nugent, Pendleton, Perry, Price, Robinson, Rollins (Missouri), Shiel, Steele (New York), Steele (New Jersey), Stiles, Vallandigham, Voorhes, Wadsworth, Ward, Whaley, White (Ohio,) Wickliffe, Wood, Woodruff, Yeaman—49.

An Elequent Sentiment Applicable to the Present Time.

One of the finest orators and most liberal statesmen Great Britain ever possessed, Chas. James Fox, upon one occasion, in Parliament, when he was opposing the war with France, was startled by doctrines from the British Tories, such as we now hear from the meaner and more despotic American Tories in America. Raising his voice to a high pitch, the great orator said:

"Say at once that a free Constitution is no longer suitable to us; say at once, in a manly manner, that upon an ample review of the state of the world, a free Constitution is not fit for you; conduct yourself at once as the Senators of Denmark; lay down your freedom and acknowledge and accept of despotism. But do not mock the understandings and feelings of mankind, by telling the world that you are free, by telling me that if, for the purpose of expressing my sense of the public administration of this country, of the calamities which this war has occasioned, I state a grievance or make any declaration of my sentiments in a manner that may be thought seditious, I am to be subjected to penalties hitherto unknown to the law."

HOW THE MONEY GOES.—A fine new ship from a port in Maine has been lying idle in Boston harbor for a month past, under charter by the Government, at the rate of $5,000 per month.

THE CRISIS.

Wednesday, - - - March 11, 1863.

The Mob.

We honestly confess, that, could we do so with any propriety, we should very much prefer passing, unnoticed and unheeded, in our columns, the disgraceful and cowardly transactions of last Thursday night, by which some $600 or $800 of our property was destroyed. If we have labored hard to earn the small amount to the eyes of many, we can, if health and freedom from mobs and the still more contemptible Provost Marshals in the West, permit, earn the amount over again, and it need trouble or effect no one but ourself.

But the affair being one of public notoriety and of great public concern to every other man, rich or poor, and more especially to the former, so far as mere property is concerned, we cannot escape the proper notice of the affair, as a part of the history of the times, and the weakness and wickedness of the public authorities, who either do not desire or are wholly incompetent to any longer protect the lives or property of the citizens.

Of all disorders, we despise those among neighbors the most—of all wars, we hold those called civil wars in the greatest abhorrence, and during a life time, we have denounced them—abhorred them as a matter of principle, and as we loved country and the family of men, we have ever shrunk with loathing from the man who, in public or private position, dared so far forget God and humanity, as to advocate either local disorder or national blood letting. And sensitive as we know we are, to personal dishonor or national disgrace, we never saw the day that we would prefer risking for a time, the charge of a proper want of spirit, for the virtue that would come after it, if we supposed we should involve a living soul except ourself in trouble. Mere *personal* risks we always take in our own insurance office and involve no securities.

But let no one mistake the fact that because we so strenuously advocated peace *under the law*, that we are a *submissionist* when laws and constitutions, oaths of office and oaths of morality and religion are thrown aside, and trampled with impunity and contempt in the dirt. Our peace doctrines go no further than the law, and the prompt and reasonable settlement and adjustment of difficulties and dangers originating from a misunderstanding or misconception of the law. When all these fail, and mobs and burglars seize the reins of State and govern as the beasts of prey govern each other in the forests, then submission is meaner and more dastardly, because more dangerous and destructive, than that resistance which God and nature vouchsafed for self-protection.

We desire to be explicit—we use the term "law and order," in no craven, cowardly spirit—not in supplication for self—not even for family or friends, but as a warning to those who should heed it and heed it in time, who cowardly and craven-like rush on to destruction, when, perhaps, least they know it. This is all the meaning there is in *our* use of the term, and we think we can speak truly, also for our friends.

If, however, Governor TOD, who lives and stays in sight of the destruction of our office, with his officials around him, has lost either the *power* or the *will* to administer the law in the spirit of fairness and justice, or at all—if ABRAHAM LINCOLN, the Commander-in-Chief of the Armies, has given over the country to be governed by the brute passions of Provost Marshals, and the country subjected to anarchy and a thousand little despotisms, beyond his control or desire to control, and the whole country living under a mask of "false pretenses" and barbarous pretexts, the great upheaving masses only want to know it, and the original elements of a great, a powerful and intelligent people, pledged to liberty and public order, will re-right the wrongs and in a very short time bring order out of chaos, and public and private preservation out of the ruins of imbecility, rotting about our ears through the timid councils of besotted ambition.

Let no one fear or tremble for the result—after the summer storm the sun shines more brightly, the birds sing more sweetly, the green verdure of a good Providence glistens and glows more cheeringly. 'Tis but the impure and death-drugged elements that the storm has carried away, to give fresh liberty to life and more sweetness to death.

If here and there a tender flower stem should be broken, the little maiden will kiss it a farewell and plant another in its stead, and rear it with a more sedulous care.

But cries one, "will storms not always come?" That depends on you and I and all living. By good and virtuous deeds moral storms are put a long way off—may never come. Courage, firmness, justice, daring to do right and damning the wrong and the doers of wrong, are the principles of God's moral atmosphere, and the only salvation of a free people. The willing slave to power usurped, and the mountebank who holds the rod, have no ears for truths, for truths are as worthless coin to them; be not surprised, therefore, if they can not understand.

We have been appealed to write no exciting articles on the subject of the outrage upon us, for our paper. We know not why this request has been made, especially by those who belong, politically, to the party which committed the outrage upon us, and have urged its doing for a long time in every offensive and annoying way? Will they pledge us as much on their side? Will they guarantee even nothing but *indecent* truths from presses on their side? We will not ask for decency if they will confine themselves to the truth. Will they guarantee that they will instigate no more mobs upon us? Will they guarantee us all those rights and privileges in the protection of life and property, they ask us to guarantee to them? Is it an affair of *equal* benefits? If it is, it was not necessary to ask the dispensation. They know as well as they live that we harm no man, that we would rather not get our own than be guilty of taking unjustly another's. Why, then, ask us to be *moderate?*

We have not touched a printing press of theirs! Can they say as much for themselves? We have not injured one cent's worth of their property! Can they say that they have not injured ours? We have not at the mid hours of the night disturbed, by burglarious rioting, the female portions of their families! Can they say that they have not disturbed ours? When we cause their daughters to rush out in the late and dark hours of the night, with pistol in hand, through snow and mud, to defend their father's property in his absence, as you caused mine, then indeed you might ask moderation in future as a guarantee against repetitions of the same unlawful and riotous acts.

The three thousand bold, brave, daring men who met us at the railroad depot on our return after the disaster, and bore us with shouts which rang to the vaults of Heaven, upon their shoulders, were not, thank God, either rioters or burglars—they were *freemen*—and, knowing their rights, *dared*, in in this beautiful Capital of ours, in the face of Executive scowls and military surroundings, thus give PUBLIC advertisement that they knew how to *defend them*, and that they intended to do it!

They were only desperate men because they were *resolved*. It shall be our glory to defend them, and die with them, if the cold and ruthless foot of despotism comes this way to despoil their households, and wrest from them their LIBERTIES, to furnish riotous livings for unlawful usurpers. If they were "as wise as the serpent," they were as "harmless as the dove" to all men, women and children, to property and law. But there is an end to forbearance—they intended to make that fact prominent—they did it in no sneaking way—they did not "tread lightly on the snow" for fear of being detected. They put their feet down harder than old ABRAHAM ever thought of doing, and not very particular in selecting the place, and sent voices up towards the starry firmament that the angels might have heard. To them, to us all, it was an hour of intense interest—the birth of a new freedom—the resolve that the Rubicon of folly, violence and disorder had been passed, and that they were ready to meet it. It was the more exciting because it was the impromptu movement of but a very brief period, learning that we would be up on that train. Got up without formal leaders, or even the knowledge of those who do things formally, no doubt the impression got out, with some of the guilty destroyers of our property, that it was the rising of a mob, and that the whole town was in danger. Ah! ye timid nervous men, who never will learn! there were deeper and more solemn thoughts crowding round the hearts and swelling the manly bosoms of that fearful (if you please) crowd than the petty thought of stopping printing presses or destroying abolition property.

The holy and unquenched fires of freedom were lit up anew—the high and noble resolve was made that the time had come when it should be tested whether the lawless hand of power was to march on unchecked, unmolested. If it ever was to stop, was there ever a more favorable moment to test the question? If the people had become as pusillanimous as some people would have it believed it was time to test that also. It was time to sift the foul and impure from the stern and resolute—the "just from the unjust," the friends of liberty from those ready and willing to yield base obedience to lawless power riding over constitution, oaths of office, and every guarantee of freedom which had heretofore protected the citizen. The cry of peace, peace and submission, had been busily wafted on every base born tongue until the crash and fall of the government timbers came nearer as they went down. The hungry wolves of power lapped their jaws as they lay under the shade of pusillanimity waiting for the victims as they fell. The Jackalls were in extacy—the cowards crouching and the work went steadily on.

One crash more—another and another, under the very dome and stately pillars of the Capital reared by the sweat of freemen, under the very eye of executive authority, stalked forth the monster, sneaking and crouching like all guilt, not yet quite certain of indemnity from public justice, and struck his blow, and slunk to his cover to await the result.

The *result* it is not necessary to re-iterate—the voice of terrible freedom rushed to the rescue—the cowards quake—outraged justice ceased its blow with a warning for the future, that must not, shall not be unheeded. It will not leave the field nor scatter its labors; but sink or swim, live or die, the infamous sword of inhuman barbarism right here in our beautiful streets, must cease its cravings, its graspings and its calling for new victims. The story is short, the road is plain and brief—mistake it not.

THE CRISIS OFFICE MOBBED.—Sam Medary's editorial rooms in the *Crisis* building were completely "cleaned out" by a mob of soldiers last night amounting to two hundred in number. The destruction of windows, doors, stoves, files, shelves, books, etc, was complete. A violent storm of snow at the time gave a lively coloring to the scene. Medary had gone to Cincinnati on the noon train yesterday. The gang of soldiers crept softly along on the snow till they came to the office, which is situated on the corner of High and Gay streets. They circled around the door with fixed bayonets and declared death on the man that interrupted. The doors were first stove in and then the windows, after which the vile files of corruption and treason were sent by thousands into the streets. The ground for many rods around was loaded with the contents of the office. The crowd was disappointed at not finding any type, not knowing that the composition and press work on the paper were done at the office of the State Printer, Richard Nevins.

When they were informed of this they sallied forth to their work of destruction, and attacked with a heavy timber the back door of the *Statesman* press rooms, where the outside of that sheet was being worked off. The first bolt was not sufficient to give them entrance and before the second was made the police arrived on the spot and remonstrated till they desisted.

Feeling a little relieved, and fearing some trouble, the soldiers now scattered—"every one to his own way." So far as we could see there were but three or four citizens in the crowd.

Gen. James Cooper was informed of the proceedings and arrived on the ground soon after to look into things, but the wreck was complete and the soldiers dispersed.

The reunion and festival of the High Street Methodist Church closed about the time of the commencement of the affair, and many of the ladies were terrified at the sight.

A large police force collected as soon as it was known, and the Captain, Ed. Davis, assured Gen. Cooper if he would take care of the offending soldiers, the police would look after the citizens engaged.

The exitement on the streets became great, and crowds visited the ruins. Among all present, we heard not a word of sympathy for *The Crisis* save from three, one a citizen, one a police officer, and the other, the son of Mr. Medary. At midnight quiet was restored.—*Ohio State Journal, Friday morning.*

THE "CRISIS."—It was with surprise that we learned, on yesterday morning, that a violent demonstration had been made during the night before upon the office of *The Crisis*. We had never heard a single inkling of such an improper proceeding being thought of. Widely as we differ with *The Crisis* in our political views and notions, we nevertheless regret that any such demonstration should have occurred in our city. It is in all cases a bad way of manifesting dislike to any person or to his sentiments. And we cannot refrain, in this instance, as in all like cases, from uttering our condemnation of the spirit of violence and disorder that prompts to such improper and unwarrantable measures. We therefore entirely disclaim any sympathy with a course that we have always heretofore and in all cases condemned.—*Ohio State Journal, Saturday Morning.*

We present, above, two articles from the *Ohio State Journal*, of this city, which it may do well for the reader to compare.—The *first* was published on *Friday* morning, after the destruction; the *second* article appeared on *Saturday* morning, after the demonstration of popular indignation at the foul act, on our return on *Friday night*.—The first appeared in what they call the "local" column, and the last in the editorial column! With this explanation we proceed to analyze article No. 1.

If there was so much ignorance in the *Journal* office how came the local editor of that paper to have been *present* with the mob, from *first* to *last*, from his own statement, made before the good people of Columbus appeared in the streets by thousands to express their indignation at the robber act? and all of which he describes with the gloating of a fiend. He tells us that "*the gang of soldiers crept softly along on the snow till they came to the office.*" This is a very *early* account of the proceedings to come from an office so very ignorant—so very innocent! He next says: "*They circled round the office with fixed bayonets and declared DEATH to the man that interrupted.*"—Poor *ignorant* souls, how *innocent* to know nothing about it!

This *innocent* and *ignorant* daily organ of the Columbus aristocracy and army thieves generally, from whom it sucks its daily milk, in consideration of its lies and slanders, poured out in long columns on each morning upon the heads of unoffending Democrats, who, long suffering and slow to anger, have suffered the vile sheet to proceed, until it produced the intended violence, and gloated like a hungry savage over the destruction of property produced; then proceeds to describe *very minutely* the whole transactions of this vile mob! It even enters into the affrighted feelings of the ladies coming from the High Street Methodist Church.

Till the Church people came forth, he could not see more than "*three or four citizens in the crowd.*" And there were only "three" sympathizers with *The Crisis*, even after the mob had left, "*one a citizen, one a police officer, and the other, the son of Mr. Medary!*"

This fellow, who, in one short twenty-four hours, became a part of the *ignorant* and *innocent* gang of editorial scribblers for the *Journal*, is the same dirty pup, who, after having been twice slapped in the face and his hat mashed over his head, by "the son of Mr. Medary," came out in his paper and plead *conscientious non* combativeness, sickness and being a cripple!!! Was there ever cowardice, meanness, baseness of the lowest degree, that surpasses this. The hired pimp, the daily slanderer, the midnight associate of "burglars," (see Gen. COOPER'S definition,) the gloating hyena on his midnight prey, (see his article above) on his filthy knees pleading innocence, conscientious scruples on the "*resistance* question," and all the other baby acts of a mean, guilty coward, fresh from riot, robbery and threatened "DEATH" to any one who dared "interfere."

If the Republicans of the City are really sincere in the preservation of that "order in the city" for which they ask, let them lock up in some charity asylum or the penitentiary, such idiots and knavish asses as this, instead of employing them to cater for their daily amusement in their political organ. A word to some people ought to be enough, but we claim not to dictate, nor advise, but are prepared to meet the world as it chooses to come.

But if any one sustains the article above, from the *Friday* morning's *Journal*, and then mouths "law and order," he is a bigger fool than has any business to exist in this critical juncture of our affairs.

EXPLANATORY.—We have been informed that some excitement and much denunciation were yesterday indulged in by certain personal friends of Mr. Medary as against the *Ohio State Journal*, in reference to the unfortunate occurrence of Thursday night. And a son of Mr. Medary so far forgot what was due to himself as to attempt to provoke a street brawl with Mr King, the city editor of the *Journal*, who is unfortunately disabled by a a physical infirmity, as well as averse by moral principle, from engaging in pugalistic encounters. We do not propose any comments on this transaction more than to say that, while bullyism can confer no honor upon any human being, moral courage, such as Mr. King displayed, is an enviable characteristic of true manhood.

We can pardon much to Mr. Medary by reason of his undue and perhaps not unnatural excitement. But we feel it, nevertheless, due to ourselves as citizens to say that Mr. Medary's public charge that the *Ohio State Journal*, or any person or persons connected therewith, was concerned in exciting or promoting the mob violence against *The Crisis* is utterly unfounded. Mr. Medary charges that this office not only excited the outbreak but also furnished the riotous party with liquor to stimulate them to this act. This is also absolutely and entirely untrue. The affair was as utterly unknown and unlooked for by those of this office as it could have been to Mr. Medary himself. He has therefore been most erroneously informed in this regard as well as in every other tending to fix the slightest complicity in this affair upon us, or upon any about us.

We make this statement simply to disabuse the public mind of the idea that we could by any means be brought to excite such a demonstration, which in common with all law-abiding citizens, we do not hesitate to deprecate as in the highest degree improper.

After the part the local Editor of the *Journal* took in the mob proceedings, as shown in another article, the above is a most singular affair for *that* paper to put forth. Every one who has read the *Journal* and *Fact* of this city for the past three weeks, could plainly see that their purpose could be no other than the exciting of a mob. We admit we come to the conclusion very reluctantly that Mr. ALLEN, the responsible Editor of the *Journal*, was guilty. The columns of the *Journal* were, however, singularly used by some one, for him not to be apprised of it. As to the local who pleads *conscientious scruples*, there is no doubt about, as he wrote, with his own pen, his complicity in the matter. But there let it rest for the present.

ST. MARYS, March 7th, 1863.

DEAR FRIEND:—We have just heard of the damnable outrage upon you and *The Crisis* by the infernal mob. We have not heard the details, nor do we know the extent of your loss; but we know SAM. MEDARY, and we therefore have good right to believe that it will not be long until *The Crisis* will be again afloat and battling as of old. What do you need of the *people* for your sustenance? Do you want any money? If so, let us know it, and I venture that we will respond our share in that or any other thing that is necessary for the preservation of our rights as freemen. If you have time, answer me.

Your old friend,
WM. SAWYER.

COL. S. MEDARY.

We thank you friend—for a friend in need is a friend indeed—but all we ask, or can conscientiously receive, will be in the legitimate progress of our business. If the Capital City of Ohio, with all its machinery of *law*, cannot protect our property or compensate us for our losses, we cannot conscientiously receive anything from individual citizens. We feel truly grateful to our friends in this somewhat trying occasion, and we take this early opportunity to say that we can only take money in the regular course of our business. The propriety of this will strike every one, we presume. We cannot permit the *suspicion* even to rest upon us that we claimed pecuniary sympathy for any misfortunes that may happen us. We are in too much earnest in the cause of right, justice and a suffering country, to involve our friends in our pecuniary losses. We will go to work with renewed energy, and earn our money over again. So numerous were the articles—books, papers, pens, broken doors and windows, old and new files of volumes bound and unbound—that we are not able yet in the confusion to make any exact estimate of our losses.

We have turned our attention so far almost wholly in getting out this number of our paper; after which we shall look up and arrange the internal affairs of our editorial and packing rooms. We shall then be able to give a full statement of our affairs.

We again thank our friends, one and all, for their expressions and offers of kindness. We feel their force, and shall duly treasure them up to encourage us in the labor we have to perform.

MOB VIOLENCE IN COLUMBUS.

From the Statesman of Friday

Violence in the Capital of Ohio

On Thursday night about 10 o'clock, some fifty to seventy-five men, representing themselves as soldiers from Camp Chase, and armed with swords, and revolvers, forcibly entered the editor's rooms of *The Crisis* and destroyed whatever they could lay their hands on. No person connected with the office was there at the time, and the work was accomplished and the mob left in a few minutes. They also made an effort to gain admittance to the press-room of the *Statesman* office from the alley, in the rear, but officer Davis and some of the employees meeting them there, they retired, doing no damage, beyond forcing open the door.

By some singular coincidence the city police (except one) did not happen to be in the neighborhood of the city in which *The Crisis* office is situated, at the time of the disgraceful transaction. The remark was made among some of the participators in this outrage, that they had no fear of the police, and it was said among them, interrogatively, DID NOT GOV. JOHNSON TELL US TO DO SO?

Our readers will bear us witness that it has been the constant effort of the *Statesman* to impress upon all men obedience to law and order, and it shall be our effort still to impress this duty upon all good citizens; but if the property and lives of citizens cannot be protected by law, then the question is forced upon the people, as to the mode and manner in which this object can be accomplished. If it be expected that the people will tamely submit to such indignities, those who thus delude themselves, whether high or low, in official position or out of it, will find themselves mistaken. We do not say this by way of threat, but it is not for one moment to be expected that such outrages will be quietly submitted to. The opposition to the Democracy in this city have as much interest in maintaining law and order as any other men under the sun, and we hope they will fully appreciate this fact.

A notice will be found in another column of our paper for a meeting at the City Hall on Saturday evening to consider what steps are necessary to protect private property. It will be a large assemblage of the friends of law and order.

From the Ohio Statesman of Saturday.

An Overwhelming Impromtu Demonstration.

GOV. MEDARY was absent from home on Thursday night, when the outrageous assault was made upon his office, having visited Cincinnati that day to be present at a surgical operation to be performed on one of his grand children. Last evening, just before dark, it was ascertained that he would return home in the nine and a half P. M. train. Immediately many Democrats of the city determined to meet him at the depot and escort him to his residence; and for that purpose several hundred, accompanied by Hemmersbach's band, carrying the Fifth Ward banner, departed in that direction about half past eight o'clock. From this indication and no other notice, the news ran, and as it was received, the people took up the line of march, and thus the crowd increased at the depot, until by the time the train arrived, there were thousands on hand.

The Governor was taken from the cars by the people and borne on their shoulders to a carriage in waiting, from which the horses were disengaged, and he was hauled by the populace, preceded by the band and followed by an immense procession up High street to the American, where Judge Thurman welcomed him home in a neat and very appropriate speech. In reference to the occurrence which brought out the demonstration and in treating the subject throughout, Judge Thurman was exceedingly distinct, clear and happy, and all that he said was well received by the vast audience.

Gov. Medary in responding was very much affected and indeed embarrassed, by the unexpected and extraordinary demonstration, and spoke with much feeling. His remarks were well received and were very appropriate. Of all the numerous speeches we have heard Gov. Medary make, his brief speech last evening was the most pertinent and appropriate.

At the close of Gov. Medary's speech, other gentlemen were called, and among them Hon. Milton Sayler, who responded in a very happy manner.

We were not in a position to take notes, and hence are not prepared to give any extended abstract of the several speeches, and indeed our space to-night would not admit of it, were we otherwise prepared.

The mass of men at that meeting was a noble spectacle. It was composed of patriot citizens who were indignant at the outrage, and who came together to bear their testimony against it. It was composed of firm and true men—lovers of the Union and law-abiding citizens, who are not disposed to trample on the rights of others, and are determined to maintain and defend their own.

From the Ohio Statesman of Sunday.

The Great Meeting of Yesterday Afternoon.

There never was a grander or more significant assemblage of freemen in the Capital City of Ohio than was that of Saturday afternoon. Long before the hour appointed for the meeting, the people began to collect at the Court House, and when that time had arrived, the gathering was immense. The fathers and brothers of many of our soldiers were there, to join with their fellow citizens in the solemn resolve, that there shall be no more mob violence in Columbus; that the liberties and the rights of the people shall be maintained and defended; that property shall not again be destroyed, nor life endangered by a mob.

The meeting was organized in the Court Room, when it immediately adjourned to the yard below, which was full to overflowing, as well as the street beyond. We never before witnessed a grander scene. Decision, determination and firmness, were depicted on every countenance. Every man of the thousands who were present appreciated the responsibilities of the hour, and will see to it that the solemn resolves of the occasion are caried out. There were no cowards at the meeting. It was made up of as good men as ever assembled in this city.

The remarks of the President, Hon. Otto Dresel, on taking the chair were singularly happy and appropriate. He stated the object of the meeting in a few well-chosen words, and recited the outrages and wrongs that have been so patiently endured, in terms of indignant eloquence.

Gov. Medary's speech was one of the best of his whole life. We have full notes of it, as well as of all the others that were delivered on the occasion, and regret that we have not room to print even a synopsis of them, this morning. The Governor reviewed sharply and pointedly the arbitrary and unconstitutional acts of the Federal and State Administrations, and the present Abolition war policy of Mr. Lincoln. He alluded in proper terms to the occasion of this meeting, and on behalf of himself and his children and grand children, he thanked the Democracy for the splendid demonstrations of Friday night, and for the demonstration of Saturday.

Col. Manypenny was called out. He contrasted the condition of this country before the war with its condition now; stated the position of the Democratic party in these troubles and perilous times; characterized the mob violence of last Thursday night as every friend of Law and Order must characterize it; condemned the perversion of the war from its original purpose to that of negro emancipation; closed with an eloquent tribute to the Constitution and the Union, and an earnest appeal in behalf of the country; and thanked the noble Democracy for this magnificent demonstration which insures the peace, quiet and safety of the city.

Senator Kenny was next called for. He responded in a capital speech, which was received with great favor. After Mr. K had concluded his eloquent and effective effort, Judge Thurman, from the committee on Resolutions, reported a preamble and a series of resolutions, which are an honor and a credit to the Democratic party. They contain neither too much nor too little, but just enough; and were adopted by such an emphatic and unanimous vote as is seldom given.

The meeting would not let Judge Thurman off without a speech. So he spoke for half an hour in vindication of the Rights and Privileges of American Freemen, as he alone can speak. It was a speech of great force and power.

Judge Rankin was the next speaker. He made some happy hits, and sharp points, and was rapturously applauded.

Auditor Mat. Martin made an effective and telling speech, and was followed by senator Johnston, who closed the speaking with one of the ablest and best speeches of the day.

The speeches were all good, and were all applauded to the echo.

Altogether, this was one of the best meetings we ever attended, and its good results will be felt and appreciated by all our people.

The Great Democratic Meeting on Saturday Afternoon.

Pursuant to a call of the Democratic Central Committee of Franklin county, an immense meeting of the friends of Law and Order was held at the Court House in the city of Columbus, on Saturday afternoon, March 7th, 1863. The meeting was called to order at two o'clock, by William Domigan, Esq., Chairman of the Central Committee—when Hon Otto Dresel was elected President, and John G. Thompson, Secretary.

Mr. Dresel, in most appropriate terms, stated the object of the meeting: It was to maintain Law and Order; to consider ways and means to preserve and protect the Life, Liberty, and Property of our people.

The Court House was crowded, and the yard and street in front of it were full. Hence, an adjournment to out-doors was moved and carried, where the meeting was held Judge A G Thurman, E F. Bingham, A. G. Hibbs, W. M. Savage, and Michael Treanor, were appointed a committee to draft and report resolutions expressive of the sense of the meeting. During the absence of the committee, the following gentlemen were successively called out, and made able and effective speeches, which were rapturously applauded: Gov. Medary, Col. Manypenny, and Senator Kenny.

Judge Thurman, from the committee on resolutions then made the following report, which was adopted by a unanimous vote of that vast assemblage of freemen:

PREAMBLE.

On the night of the 5th instant, a mob of about one hundred persons, composed of soldiers and citizens disguised as soldiers, armed with swords and revolvers, broke into the editor's rooms of *The Crisis* newspaper, and destroyed whatever property they could lay their hands upon, and in various ways injured the building. They afterwards repaired to and attacted the office of the *Ohio Statesman*, and only desisted upon the police and some citizens rallying to its defence. They also, as we are informed, threatened a destruction of the *Westbote*. They, manifestly, intended to suppress, by illegal violence, the entire Democratic press of this city. These acts were planned and executed with such secrecy and dispatch that *The Crisis* rooms were sacked, and the attack upon the *Statesman* office begun, before the existence of the mob was known to any considerable number of our law-abiding citizens; and thus a defense of *The Crisis* rooms was prevented. That these deeds were instigated by persons who dared not take an open hand in their commission, we have good reason to believe; but until we shall have further and accurate information upon this point, we forbear to mention names, lest we should wrong any one who may be unjustly suspected.—These outrages are the natural consequences of that fatal disregard of the Constitution and the laws that has marked the course of our administrations, Federal and State, ever since the war began, and of the false and flagrant assaults upon the patriotism, motives, and purposes of the Democratic party, daily indulged in by the Republican press and Republican politicians. When the public authorities, sworn to support the Constitution, set the example of violating its most sacred provisions; when citizens guilty of no crimes against the law were illegally arrested, transported and imprisoned; when the writ of *habeas corpus* was practically suppressed; when a censorship over speech and the press was assumed and frequently practiced; when the terrible doctrine (utterly destructive of freedom and free institutions,) that the government, in times like these, may do whatever it deems necessary, however, in so doing, it may violate the Constitution, was boldly proclaimed; when rights of property guaranteed by the Constitution were openly invaded and sought to be overthrown by an executive proclamation: when these and like examples of disregard of our laws and constitutions, of our rights and liberties, were set by the officers of government themselves, it is not singular that rash and unthinking men should be found ready to follow such examples. And when in addition to all this, the Republican press and politicians, in violation of truth, decency, policy, and patriotism, and for the merest and basest partisan purposes, were daily charging one-half, if not more, of the Northern people, with treason, or sympathy with treason; when even Governors of States, in public speeches, cast such imputations upon a majority of their own constituents; when every artifice that malice could invent and industry apply was being resorted to, in order to mislead and prejudice the army against the Democratic party; when, for that purpose, Democratic newspapers were excluded from its lines and camps, while Abolition newspapers were freely admitted; when secret, irresponsible, oath-bound, and armed societies were forming to suppress the voice of Democracy, and trample upon the public will; when all the machinery to produce a reign of terror was being prepared and set in motion; it is not wonderful that ignorance, passion, and prejudice should bid defiance to the laws.

We note these things, not to excite wrath, but to warn every man who desires to preserve the peace of society, the liberties and property of the people, the laws and constitutions of the land, that it behooves him to set his face against all aggressions upon either. Constitutions and law make free government, respect for them preserves it, disregard of them brings despotism or anarchy. The Democratic party has ever been, and yet is, a law-abiding party. It asks nothing but its rights under the Constitution and the laws. It resorts to no violation of either; it countenances no violation of either. It has a right to all the guarantees of public and private liberty, and of property contained in our fundamental laws, and it will surrender not one of them. It has the right to discuss public measures, and will discuss them. It has the right to propose and advocate that policy which it deems best for the nation, and it will exercise that right. It has a right to have its policy passed upon by the people at peaceable and untrammelled elections, and will maintain that right. If found in a minority it yields obedience to all lawful rule of the majority: if it be in the majority itself, it claims that its lawful will be respected. Whether in majority or minority, it obeys all laws that are in force. Those that it dislikes, it seeks to over throw, not by violence, but by a legitimate repeal. Those that it proposes, it seeks to carry, not by force, but by legal enactment. And what it does in all these respects, it demands, and has a right to demand, that all others shall do. They owe the same obedience to the Constitution and the laws that Democrats owe. They have the same interest to maintain a free government, to protect liberty, to be secure in their houses, persons and property, that Democrats have. It is neither their interest nor ours that despotism or anarchy should prevail; and if they wish to avert both, let them see to it in time that they give no occasion for either. We will do our duty, let them remember to do theirs.

In view of the circumstances that have brought us together, we hereby resolve:

1. That the will of the people is the foundation of all free government. That to give effect to this will, free thought, free speech, and a free press, are absolutely indispensible. Without free discussion, there is no certainty of sound judgment; without sound judgment, there can be no wise government.

2. That it is an inherent and constitutional right of the people to discuss all measures of their government, and to approve or disapprove as to their best judgment seems right. That they have a like right to propose and advocate that policy which in their judgment is best, and to argue and vote against whatever policy seems to them to violate the Constitution, to impair their liberties, or to be detrimental to their welfare.

3. That these and all other rights, guaranteed to them by their constitutions, are their rights in time of war as well as in time of peace; and of far more value and necessity in war than in peace. For in peace liberty, security and property are seldom endangered; in war, they are ever in peril.

4. That we now say to all whom it may concern, not by way of threat, but calmly and firmly, that we will not surrender these rights, nor submit to their forcible violation. We will obey the laws ourselves, and all others must obey them.

5. That the attempt recited in the preamble to suppress by force the Democratic newspapers of this city, was an outrage that demands the exemplary punishment of the guilty, and the condemnation of all men. And we call upon the civil and military authorities to ferret out the offenders, in order that they may be proceeded against according to law.

6. That thanks are due, and are hereby tendered to Brig. Gen. James Cooper for the part taken by him in supressing the mob, and for his timely, manly and noble General Order, published in this moring's paper of this city.

7. That our thanks are also due and tendered to Captain Albert B. Dod, U. S. A., and to the soldiers under his command, for the part taken by them in preserving the peace on the night of the 5th inst and since.

8. That the city police deserve our thanks for their exertions, on the occasion above referred to, to preserve the peace.

9. That the Secretary transmit to General Cooper a copy of the above resolution No. 6; to Capt. Dod a copy of resolution No. 7. and to the Chief of Police a copy of resolution No. 8.

After the adoption of the foregoing preamble and resolutions, the meeting insisted upon having a speech from Judge Thurman. In compliance with the call, he came forward and spoke most eloquently and ably in vindication of the rights and liberties of the American people. Judge Rankin, Mat. Martin and Senator Johnston, were then successively called out, and made capital and telling speeches.

The meeting then adjourned with three times three cheers for the Union, the Constitution, the enforcement of the Laws, and the observance of Order.

OTTO DRESEL, President.

JOHN G. THOMPSON, Secretary.

From the Cincinnati Enquirer.

A Press Destroyed by a Mob—Its Meaning—Danger to Public Liberty.

The office of Medary's *Crisis*, at Columbus, Ohio, was destroyed by a mob about half-past ten o'clock, on Thursday night last. Colonel Medary was himself absent from Columbus at the time, having left with a portion of his family on the one o'clock noon train, to visit a daughter in this city, who had, within a day or two, arrived here from Kansas, to have a surgical operation performed on her little child. The editor and proprietor of *The Crisis* was, therefore, in this city when the mob destroyed his office; and the first news he had of the cowardly act was when he took up the morning papers. Advantage was taken of his absence to destroy his property. It was his editorial and counting-rooms that were entered. The type and press upon which *The Crisis* is published were not touched, being in another building, on the opposite side of the street, and not so easy of access to the mob His material injury was in the destruction of his books and papers.

This act of lawless violence does its least injury to the editor and proprietor of *The Crisis*; the blow falls upon every freeman, from the Atlantic to the Pacific; for it is a blow at public liberty itself. If the people do not take alarm at this act, and prepare to defend their liberties, it will ere long be too late, and they will wake to find themselves slaves. We do not mean this admonition for Democrats alone, but for every citizen of whatever party, who prefers a free constitutional government to a despotism. *The Crisis* has been one of the people's battlements. It has guarded their rights, and warned them against the encroachments of lawless power. It has been mobbed because it had the ear and reached the hearts of the people. It had too much influence over those who must be crushed, to enable arbitrary power to accomplish its designs of overthrowing constitutional liberty and erecting on its ruins a despotism. Therein is the offense of *The Crisis*. It is that which has provoked the "military politicians," who got up and pushed on the mob.

The leading acts of the recent Congress can not be successful in their main purpose—that of overthrowing public liberty—without a free press is first disposed of. The purse and the sword, and the control of the judiciary, are now in the hands of the Executive of the United States. But the people, through the ballot-boxes—so long as they have those instruments to execute their will—might make an opposition that would render powerless all efforts to enslave them. The ballot-boxes must be rendered harmless, but to do that, a free press must be overthrown. *The Crisis*, and all other papers that warn the people against the encroachments of arbitrary power must be silenced. When they are silenced, the ballot-boxes will be no longer the instruments of the will of freemen, but instruments to declare the will of a usurper of the rights of the people. With a free press silenced, the ballot-boxes converted into mouth-pieces of usurped power, and the purse and the sword in the hands of the Federal Executive, civil liberty will soon be among the things that were. Every one, therefore, who values his freedom, who cherishes a love of constitutional government, and who wishes to transmit to his children the inestimable blessings of civil liberty, must feel that the mob which struck its blow at *The Crisis*, also aimed a blow at their rights and liberties. Any one that does not feel so, should wake up to a realizing sense of the danger he is in of losing his political freedom, and becoming the slave of a despotism.

The stuff that the course of *The Crisis* and such like papers encourage the enemy, and that if they were out of the way, the war would soon be brought to a triumphant close, is the sheerest nonsense, and the most contemptible of party flummery. No man of sense credits it, and none but party knaves, or weak-minded women, assert it. The acts of Congress, and the proclamations of the Executive, have done more to fire the hearts and strengthen the arm of the enemy than all other causes combined. And were *The Crisis* and every other Democratic paper suppressed to-morrow, it would have no more effect upon a successful close of the war than would the sinking of a ship in the Niagara have upon the onward flow of that mighty river. Sensible people should not allow themselves to be deluded by such miserable, paltry party stuff, into the loss of their own liberties. We warn them of the danger that is before them.

From the Dayton Empire.

A Dastardly Outrage.

The telegraph brings the announcement that the editorial rooms of Governor Medary's paper —*The Crisis*—were destroyed last night by a mob. This dastardly and cowardly act was instigated, planned, and carried out by the members of an "oath-bound" secret political society in Columbus. In *The Crisis* of the 4th inst. Goveror Medary published a full and complete expose of this "oath-bound" society, and because of this expose, they organized a mob and destroyed his office. They, planned the movement, and hired a few drunken soldiers who have for months been laying around Columbus at Government expense, to put it in operation. All the leading men of the Republican party in Columbus, from Governor Tod up, or Governor Tod down, as you choose, are members of this infamous "oath-bound" organization, and of course were concerned in the mob, on the *Crisis* office. If they did not assist in person, they were parties to the plans for its destruction, and would be in the eyes of the law—if we had any—equally guilty with the actual perpetrators. But there being no law for punishment of Abolitionists, the men engaged in this outrage, will go unwhipt of justice. Thus it will be evident to every one that the liberty, lives, and property of Demorcats are at the mercy of a corrupt set of unmitigated scoundrels.

We have always stood up for the Constitution, and plead for the liberty of the citizen under the laws of the land. But if there is no protection for Democrats under the Constitution; if the minions and hirelings of the men in power are to have free license to rob, kill, and destroy Democrats and their property, then we are free to say that our only protection—our only hope of liberty—rests in our own brave hearts and strong arms. If we would be free, we must be worthy of freemen. If we have no protection under the Constitution and laws, then we must protect ourselves by every natural power and right vested in us as freemen. We must make the property of our opponents security for the safety of our own. For every Democratic printing office destroyed by a mob, let an Abolition one be destroyed in turn. For every drop of Democratic blood spilled by Abolition mobites, let theirs flow in retaliation. It is, indeed, a most lamentable and sorrowful contemplation to be forced to such conclusions. But we see no other alternative, if we would preserve our lives, our property, and our freedom. If the Abolitionists are determined to force a revolution, let us meet it as becomes men knowing our rights, and knowing *dare* maintain.

If we are brave men—worthy sons of noble sires—we cannot be enslaved. If we are cowards, unworthy the freedom our forefathers wrested from tyrants' hands, then will we meekly wear, and deservedly, too, the chains which Abolition despots are forging for our hands. We are willing, aye, determined, to stand by the Constitution as long as there is a remnant of it left; but if the Administration and its tools determine that it shall be *bullets* instead of *ballots*, then bullets let it be. If we are forced to the stern necessity of wresting our blood-bought liberties from the hands of tyrants, let us emulate the spirit, the endurance, the iron will and indomitable courage of our revolutionary fathers, and go into the struggle determined to *"conquer or die."*

From the Cincinnati Enquirer of the 8th.

The Gazette and Commercirl on Civil Disturbances.

In their issues on Saturday, both the *Gazette* and the *Commercial*, alluding to the injury committed by rioters upon the office of *The Crisis*, at Columbus, take occasion to speak against the practice of mobbing what they are pleased to call disloyal newspapers. We would be glad to record that they had spoken in support of the pirnciple which forbids all violence against words and opinions. Whether it was this act committed against *The Crisis*, or the retaliation threatened upon the *Journal*, that was the strongest motive to impel them to so unusual an effort at freedom of speech, is a question whose answer must, perhaps, remain forever buried in the bosoms of their several conductors. A week ago, we asked them in all respectfulness and sincerity to say something to discountenance the mob spirit which we knew reigned in their party. They did not see fit to do it. Facts have since come to their knowledge going to show that mobbing is a game which more than one can play at; and now what they have done, carries with it the appearance of an act of great merit—upon compulsion. Thus it was in the days of Baalam. Human prophets spoke through an inevitable influence, but it took a real angel with a flaming sword, to bring the animal to his understanding.

Both the *Gazette* and *Commercial* place their advice against the practice of mobbing Democratic newspapers upon substantially the same ground—the importance which the injury will confer upon those who are its victims, through the popular sympathy. The thing is not, in their view, so wrong as it is inexpedient. It is true they utter a few common-places about law-abiding people setting their faces against the practice, coupled, however, with excuses for the mob, in the case of *The Crisis*, on the score of its malignity, and their natural exasperation.

We are glad, however, of one thing—that our cotemporaries have discovered the possibility of a reaction. We beg them to go a little further and see that in order to a reaction there must be materials in a state of greater or less degree of preparation. If the people rise to retaliate an injury committed to a newspaper, it is because they believe the sentiments which that newspaper inculcates. Such events do not make converts, they only develope them. And we hope, in conclusion, that as they have now seen what may happen, they will persevere in their course, and find a better reason for their advice than any they have yet given.

Riot in Detroit.

DETROIT, March 6, 10 P. M.—As a negro who had committed an outrage upon a young girl was being taken from the court room to jail under escort of military this afternoon, an attempt to rescue was made by a gang of rowdies. The crowd was fired upon and one man killed and several wounded. Being foiled in their attempts to get possession of the negro, the mob perpetrated most horrible outrages upon colored people residing in the vibinity of the jail. Houses were gutted and burned, the inmates maltreated and in many instances killed. Ten or fifteen lives have already been lost, and as many houses burned. All available military here, and a regiment in the interior of the State, have been sent for. A vigorous attempt will now be made to quell the riot.

General Cooper's Order.

We publish the excellent order of Gen. COOPER, and make a single remark, that we hope in future these orders will appear before the acts are committed. As there is an organization in Cincinnati "sworn in" to destroy the *Enquirer* office, would it not be well for the commandant there to issue his order in *advance* of the riot? Not that we object to them afterwards, but the old adage is to lock the stable *before* the horse is stolen.

We hope the "*citizens*" of this city will not overlook the rebuke given them in Gen. COOPER'S order!

HEADQUARTERS U. S. FORCES, }
Columbus, O, March 6, 1863. }

General Order No. 16]

Having been informed, and partly witnessed, that the publication office belonging to the "Crisis," and the printing office belonging to the "Ohio Statesman," newspapers published in this city, were last night broken into by a mob of disorderly persons, composed partly of citizens, and partly of soldiers, who unlawfully and wantonly destroyed furniture, papers, books and newspaper files of the former office, and were only prevented from the commission of similar outrages at the Statesman office, by the fear of being detected and arrested, I desire to offer a word of advice to the citizens, and to warn the soldiers of the penalties they incur by such outrageous violations of the law.

To such citizens as can so far forget their obligations to society, and the respect due the laws, which are as much the safeguard of their own persons and property as of the persons and property of their neighbors, the just condemnation and indignant disapproval of their conduct, by the intelligent and law-respecting portion of community, of all parties, convey a wholesome admonition as well as a merited rebuke; but such citizens should recollect that the condemnation and disapproval of their conduct by the wise and good of all parties is not the worst punishment to which they expose themselves. The mob violence which they invoke to-day against their neighbors, may be, by their neighbors, to-morrow, invoked against them.

Retaliation is the law of the lawless.

To the soldiers, who participated in last night's outrages and violence, I have to say, your conduct is strangely inconsistent with your duty and the holy purpose for which your country put arms in your hands. Your mission is to uphold the laws. And it was proudly presumed that, however unreasoning the armies of despots, the American soldiers, who rushed by hundreds of thousands to the field, to uphold the cause of popular government, and the integrity of the Union, imperiled by a foul and wicked rebellion, were intelligent enough to comprehend and appreciate the character of the issue—an issue involving the rights and security of individuals, as well as the integrity of the republic. How little in consonance with the character of the duties you have assumed, and the mission you have taken upon yourselves to fulfill, was your conduct last night, in lending yourselves to the cowardly attack and felonious outrage committed on the property of private individuals. Forgetting your duties as soldiers, you have become rioters and burglars; and instead of being as you ought to be, the protectors of the rights of citizens, you have become their assailants.

But I desire you to recollect that it is not in admonition that the rules and regulations of the service deal with rioters and plunderers. It will be seen by paragraph 787 of the regulations, that the offense of which you have been guilty is, in the language of the Regulations, "of such enormity as to admit of no remission of the awful punishment which the military law awards against offenses of this nature."

Against the perpetration of such offenses in future, I now warn you. The persons and property of the citizens are sacred in the eyes both of civil and military; and any outrage or assault upon them, will be visited by inflicting upon the perpetrators, the moment they are detected, the extremest penalty authorized by the law.

By command of

Brig.-Gen. COOPER.

WM. VON DOEHN, A A. G.

The Feeling in New York City.

The New York *Express*. in noticing the proceeding of a Democratic meeting in New York, where about fifty millions of capital was represented, says:

"At the next meeting, to which Mr. Draper, if he pleases, can send a Provost Marshal—who can be admitted to look on—we think $100,000 000 will be present.

"The fact is, both the rich and poor of this great mercantile city, the millionaire and the beggar, go hand and hand, heart and heart, against the present *Administration* of the Government. The Five Points and the Fifth Avenue, for the first time in our experience, are as one, with one head, against Proclamation Law and all that sort of law. The poor will vote and the rich will print. Such conspirators in this city voted nearly 33 000 majority the last election, but the next election their majority will run up to about 50 000. What does the *Post* propose to do about it?"

We do not know what the *Post* proposes to do, but we know that there are influential Abolition politicians, who propose that, as they can not carry the elections, to abolish them altogether, and establish a military despotism over the land.—*Cincinnati Enquirer.*

Battle of Springville, Tennessee.

NASHVILLE, March 6.—There was fighting all day yesterday between Van Dorn's command and a Federal force of three regiments of infantry, about five hundred cavalry and one battery, at Springville, thirteen miles south of Franklin. Col. Couburn's three regiments of infantry were cut to pieces and captured by the rebel forces. They fought desperately, but their ammunition became exhausted and the Federals, overpowered by superior numbers, were either killed or captured. The cavalry and artillery got off safely.

No reinforcements from Gen. Gilbert at Franklin reached the scene of action. There were seven regiments of Federals at that place.

Van Dorn is reported to have eighteen thousand men under his command.

SECOND DISPATCH.

Further details of the fight at Franklin yesterday have been received. Five regiments of infantry and one battery of the 18th Ohio, with the 9th Pa. and 2d Mich cavalry, all under command of Col. Couburn, of 33d Indiana, advanced on Spring Hill on the 4th inst. Several spirited skirmishes occurred during the day, our troops camping four miles distant.

On the 5th a movement was apparent, and during some disorder on our left they suddenly opened on our men with three batteries from different points at the same time. The enemy also appeared on each flank in greatly superior numbers.

The unequal contest was maintained with great determination, with heavy loss on both sides, and resulted unfortunately to our troops, a large part of the 33d Indiana, 23d Wisconsin and 85th Indiana, with the most of their commissioned officers, being captured. Our artilly and cavalry were successfully withdrawn. The 124th Ohio was out, but returned without loss.

The rebels have fallen back. Their force was infantry and heavier artillery than ours.

Gen. Gilbert's non-action in failing to reinforce Col. Couburn is severely censured by the officers and men.

[Communicated]

OBITUARY.

B. F. NEISWENDER, our respected fellow citizen, whose health has unfortunately been on the decline for the past eighteen months, after a severe struggle and intense suffering for the last four weeks, in enduring the shocks of the last stages of Consumption, calmly fell asleep in the arms of his Redeemer on Saturday evening, the 7th inst.

Mr. NEISWENDER was respected and beloved by all who knew him; he possessed admirable mental faculties and a sound judgment; it was his invariable method to give every subject the most scrutinizing examination before expressing his opinion upon it. His manner of expression was firm and impressive; his thoughts were of a character to shine by their own light. His earlier years had not been wasted in idleness, for he was a close and deep reader as well as a thinker. His amiability, sterling business qualities, and attractive manner of expression, had won for him a large circle of warm friends, which was daily increasing. He entered the Probate Court with Judge ALBERY, and as his Clerk received the unanimous praise of having faithfully and satisfactorily attended to all the duties connected with that position for several years During the time he served as Clerk he took up the study of the law, and on the 2d of April, 1861, after passing a highly satisfactory examination, he received his diploma as counsellor at law, constituting him a member of the Frankiin County Bar; he commenced the practice of the law in the summer of 1862, with good success, but his health failing so rapidly soon compelled him to close his business, and he has not been able to perform any labor since. Mr. NEISWENDER was in his twenty-eighth year when he died; (he was a son of MICHAEL NEISWENDER, Esq., formerly of Jefferson township, in this county, who was one of the first citizens of that township,) he leaves a wife and a large circle of relatives and warm friends who mourn his early departure from this life, to whom we tender our warmest sympathies.

'Tis past, the voyage of life is o'er,
The wanderer hails another clime;
On perils borne to yonder shore,
He views afar the waves of time.

DIED—On the 25th of February, 1863, JOHN GRIM, at his residence in Clinton Township, Franklin County, Ohio, at the age of 63.

MR GRIM was an old and highly respected citizen of Franklin County, having resided here thirty years, and leaves many friends and a widow and a large number of children to mourn his loss.

THE MARKETS.

New York Money Market--March 7.

Sterling Exchange unsettled, the range being 167@172, and closing at 170@171½ for Bankers' Bills. American Gold fluctuating and irregular, opening at 53½ declining to 54, advancing to 57, and closing firm at 54¾@55 per cent. premium.

Cincinnati Market--March 7.

FLOUR—Superfine is offered at $5@5 75, extra at $5 80 to $5 90, and family at $6@6 25.

WHISKY—387 bbls were disposed of at 45@45½c, the latter rate for wagon.

GROCERIES—A dull market for all articles, and purchases could have been made at ½c lower for Sugar and Coffee, though there is no pressure to sell, and in the small way full rates are being realized. Sugar 12½@13½c; Molasses 58@65c, and Coffee 34c to 35c.

WHEAT—The nominal asking figures are $1 20 for prime Red. $1 28@1 30 for prime Indiana or Ohio White, and $1 35 for prime Kentucky White.

CORN—The distillers refuse to pay above 60c for ear or shelled, in bulk, but several car loads of ear were disposed of to the retailers at 61@62½c.

RYE—The market rules dull at 95c for prime samples, on arrival.

BARLEY—We quote Fall at $1 60@1 65; State Spring at $1 50@1 65, and Chicago Spring at $1 30@1 45.

HAY—The market rules firm at $15@16 per tun for Timothy, in bales, on arrival.

CHEESE—We quote selected W. R. at 13c; Hamburg is held at 13½c, and English Dairy at 14c.

BUTTER—Closed at 25@27c for prime to choice roll, the latter rate in small packages.

SEED—Clover was in better request to-day, but the offerings are liberal, and the market continues to rule dull at $6. The sales were about 250 bush., at this price. Timothy is in moderate demand, with sale of 75 bush. at $2 50.

New York Market--March 7.

Cotton rather more steady, with sales at 84@85c. for Middling Uplands.

BREADSTUFFS—Flour heavy and declining with only a limited business doing, with sales at $7@7 25 for extra State, with some inferior reported at $6 95; 7 30@7 50 for choice do.; $7 50@7 65 for shipping brands extra round hoop Ohio, and $7 75@8 00 for trade brands, the market closing heavy.

WHISKY—Unsettled, with sales at 50c.

GRAIN—Wheat still favors buyers, with a moderate business doing, with sales of Winter Red Western at $1 70@1 75. Corn favors buyers, but there is only a moderate business doing, with sales at 93@95c. for sound shipping mixed Western, and 80@81c. for unsound do. Oats dull and lower, with sales at 81@83c.

GROCERIES—Coffee dull. Sugar dull and heavy, with sales at 11@11½c. for New Orleans; 10¼@10½c. for Muscovado, and 11c. for Porto Rico. Molasses quiet.

PROVISIONS—Pork dull and lower, with sales at $14 50@14 62½ for old mess; $16 75 for new mess; $11 50@11 62½ for old and new prime, and 16 20@18 for new prime mess. Dressed hogs scarce and firmer. Bacon sides quiet. Lard quiet.

New York Wool Market-- March 7.

It is the general impression among woolen manufacturers and woolen goods commission merchants that wool must range in the vicinity of a dollar a pound if not higher, throughout the whole of the present year.

PHILADELPHIA.—There has been more activity in the article since our last notice, but the receipts are trifling and the stocks in the hands of the dealers being reduced to a less amount than for many years past prices have again materially advanced. The sales comprise—

75,000 lbs common and fine at.......(all cash)...85@90c.
6,000 lbs mixed fleece.......................80c.
70,000 lbs low fleece.......................85c.
6,000 lbs common.......................82½c.
8,000 lbs mixed lots.......................90c.
10,000 lbs tub washed.......................$1 00
5,000 lbs No 1 pulled.......................80c.
3,000 lbs Merino pulled.......................83@85c.
5 800 lbs common tub.......................87½c.
10,000 lbs Cordova.......................55c.
5,000 lbs washed Turkey.......................65c.
1,000 lbs washed Turkey, lamb's.......................6[illegible]c.

BOSTON—The excitement in domestic Wool continues without abatement and prices are rapidly tending upward. The sales have been quite large, and would have been much larger but considerable of the Wool now held here is not offered except at a further considerable advance. The sales of the week have been 7@800,000 lb fleece and pulled at prices ranging from 80@90c including considerable sales of fine fleeces at 87@90c per lb. The tendency of the market is still upward and fine fleeces will soon sell at $1 per lb Good lots of tub washed would sell now at about $1. Pulled is very firm, with considerable sales of super and extra at 90c, but the best lots of extra are not now offered under 95c per lb.

PROVIDENCE.—Market more active and higher. The sales for the week have been 74,200 lb Fleece at 87a95c; 20,000 do Pulled at 78a93; 5,600 do Foreign at 34c.

Natchez Daily Courier.

Volume XI. NATCHEZ, MISSISSIPPI, SATURDAY, MARCH 14, 1863. Number 120.

The Natchez Daily Courier.

Natchez, Mississippi:

Saturday, March 14, 1863.

☞ Thos. A. B. Payne, will leave for the Ralston Battery—Simsport—and will take all letters which are left at P. H. McGraw's by Wednesday evening next. mar14

☞ We are indebted to Col. Moore, for a late Monroe (La.) Register.

A Thoughtful Captain and a Valuable Cargo.

Our Charleston papers give us an account of the steamer T. D. Wagner, Capt. W. C. Hammer, who arrived there a few days ago from Liverpool, via Nassau, bringing over from England cotton cardings, or cotton rolls all ready to spin, sufficient for all the cotton manufactories in North and South Carolina, Alabama, Georgia and Tennessee to resume their spinning and the manufacture of fabrics. This is a fact which has not before been made known.

Capt. Hammer is a Baltimore boy, a highly accomplished sailor and navigator, and to his noble, fearless character is due the credit of this feat. He sailed some time ago from the port of Wilmington, N. C., for Liverpool, as commander of the Wagner, a fine screw steamer of 640 tons, and was the first Confederate vessel to carry the "bars and stars" flying from his peak into that port. On his late trip he made the round passage from Liverpool, via Nassau, to Charleston, in 28 days, and brought in a cargo valued at two millions! Of such are the men of the Southern Confederacy.

Storm in Middle Tennessee.

A dispatch to the Mobile Register, states that on the 9th a terrible hailstorm and tornado occurred at Chattanooga, Tenn. Outhouses were destroyed, trees blown down, and window glass broken. On Saturday evening the tornado passed over Shelbyville. The depot and telegraph office were blown down, and the operator badly injured. One man was killed. In addition to much other damage done, several cars were blown from the track.

Army Results.

There has been very little doing in any branch of the Confederate army, for some time past, owing to the inclement weather. There is every prospect now, however, of more stirring times in a few days. The results which we have to note, which have not previously been published, are—

Brig. General Fitzhugh Lee, at the head of five hundred Virginia cavalry, surprised and charged a Yankee cavalry encampment of a much superior force, at Harwood church, Stafford county, and discomfitted them. Some fifty of the enemy were killed, and one hundred and thirty-five prisoners were taken and had arrived at Richmond.

In the valley of Virginia, on the same day, Gen. W. E. Jones, made an attack with his brigade on a Yankee force double his number and completely routed them—killing one hundred and capturing three hundred and fifty. The victory was easy—the enemy surrendering at discretion and crying out for quarter.

The Natchez Rifles.

We have before us a private letter from a member of the Rifles, in which the following passage occurs: "We had a general review last Friday, of all the infantry and cavalry in this Division, by Gen. Beauregard. It was a magnificent sight—more troops than I ever saw together. Our battalion had our "Company Flag," and it was generally declared to be the most beautiful one on the ground. There were a great many ladies out, and we could hear them remark, as we passed in review, 'Oh! what a magnificent flag.' We felt very much flattered, and very much obliged to Miss Linton, for presenting us with such beautiful colors."

The Natchez Rifles are in excellent health, and feel hopeful of success in the expected attack on Savannah.

Military Intelligence. We see that Maj. Gen. D. H. Hill has assumed command of the Confederate forces in North Carolina, and established his headquarters at Goldsboro'.

Major General Mansfield Lovell is now staying at the Congaree House, in Columbia, S. C. He is awaiting orders.

Captain Arthur Sinclair. C. S. N., has been assigned to the command of the powerful iron-clad steam ram Atlanta, at Savannah. Capt. Sinclair succeeds the late Captain Wm. McBlair.

Officers Resigned. The Owensboro (Ky.) Monitor says that Colonel Shanks and most of the officers of the 8th Kentucky cavalry have resigned their commissions in the service. No cause is known beyond the general one of dissatisfaction with the abolition programme.

☞ We learn by the telegraph that a number of ambulances have been sent to Nashville from Cincinnati—indicating an advance of Rosecrans. Late encounters with "the rebels" have satisfied the "Feds," that ambulances are as essential as rifles in subjugating the South, and that the march of the subjugator, is the indentical "path of glory," that—

"Leads but to the grave."

[*Chattanooga Rebel.*

☞ The following should have reached us the morning after the naval engagement. There are some incidents in it, however, that may prove of interest:

On Board the Confederate Gunboat "Dr. Batey," February 26th, 1863.

Mr. Editor: Although an utter stranger to you, I shall make no apology for thus intruding upon your columns, for I know the patriotic citizens of Natchez and vicinity, particularly the ladies, will be pleased to see an account of our fight with the Yankee gunboat, captured by our forces on the 24th inst. After leaving your pretty little city on the evening of the 23d, we proceeded up the river without anything happening worthy of notice until we came almost in sight of Grand Gulf, when we discerned the smoke of a boat, supposed of course, to be the one of which we were in pursuit, about 10 miles ahead; but having to take on a supply of wood, the smoke passed almost from sight. However, we crowded on all steam and at 10 minutes past 10 o'clock p. m., on the 24th, the report of a cannon was heard from the Queen of the West, which boat was ahead, followed by the Webb, the Dr. Batey being in the rear, lashed alongside of the tender Grand Era; the signal was given to prepare for action, when in an incredible short space of time, all hands were at their post, waiting for the word *fire*; several shots were now exchanged between the Queen, the Webb and the Yankee boat; our boats not having their signal lights up, we on the Batey were in doubt about firing, as we could not plainly distinguish the Yankee from our boats; but in a few minutes the Webb and Queen drew off, preparing to strike her and sink or cripple her; we now could perceive friend from foe and our artillery opened on them with a will. Our two rams the Queen and Webb, now struck her several terrific blows, and their artillery and sharp-shooters made all the exposed positions too hot for the disciples of *Abe*. The Queen after striking her came around and hailed us, and requested us to board; the Webb also hailed us and told us she had crippled her, also requesting us to board; they were answered by a yell—but the stentorian voice of our noble commander Col. Brand, could be heard far above all "Stand by to board." The Batey was then laid alongside, our sharp-shooters and artillery raking the deck in every direction. The Yankee in command, just then rushed upon deck and cried out, "*I am in a sinking condition!*" he was answered by Col. Brand with, "*why dont you surrender then?*" his reply was, "*I do surrender.*" You should have been there then to have heard the cheers sent up by the brave boys of our fleet. We went on board and took possession, and found that we had captured the Indianola, a new iron-clad boat, armed with two eleven inch Dahlgren guns on her bow, and two nine inch Dahlgren guns in her stern, with a crew of over 100 men. She was built in Cincinnati, she left there the 7th day of January, 1863. She is said by some of her officers to have been the crack boat in their navy on the Mississippi river. She is now in far better hands, and I trust, will be of service in ridding our country of the mercenary's that now infest it.

Fortunately, as I had nothing to do, having no one hurt on the Batey, I had a full opportunity of observing every thing that passed, and I must say that it was the most sublime thing I ever witnessed, seeing those wooden boats rushing up amid a storm of such balls as were thrown by the enemy, bearding as it were, the lion in his den. One of the Lieutenants captured, said if their crew had been as determined as we, they would never have surrendered.

The Dr. Batey being in the rear, and also in ignorance which was the Yankee boat, prevented them at first from participating in the action; but just as soon as they could make out the enemy's position, they went at it with a will. Consequently the boat was surrendered to the Dr. Batey. The officers of the different boats deserve many thanks for the efficient manner in which they handled their boats; as for the officers of the Batey, all I can say is, they were at their posts and did all that men could do or that was required of them. The artillery also deserve praise for the admirable manner in which they handled their guns, which, although far inferior to those of the enemy, told on the iron-clad with a terrible effect. As to the men on the fleet, suffice it to say, they volunteered for what was considered a dangerous service, and their conduct in every respect, was worthy of men fighting in defence of ther homes. Our fleet is but little injured; the Indianola is sunk to her boiler-decks; but we saved the prisoners, which were sent to Grand Gulf. Our loss was two killed and four wounded. Yankee loss, one killed and two wounded. The action lasted just forty-five minutes. We had a message that two gunboats had passed Vicksburg, consequently we had in our somewhat damaged condition, to fall back, but hope ere many days, to teach them that Southern valor will conquer their boasted iron-clads.

Very respectfully,

HENRY HANSLOW;

Surg'n C. S. A.

P. S. I neglected to say, that a detachment of the Signar corps was along, under charge of Serg't Bowman, and did effective service.

Lieut. Col. Brand's Report.

On Board C. S. Gunboat Dr. Batey, Feb. 26, 1863.

Maj. Gen. Gardner—*Sir:* On the morning of the 21st, whilst wooding at Morganzie, I received information that the Federal gunboat, Indianola, had left the mouth of Red River. I proceeded to the mouth of Red River; arrived there at 3 o'clock P. M.; found a picket with whom I established a code of signals for the boats coming up the river; ran up Red River as far as Black River; laid by until the fog cleared up, which was about 8 o'clock, A. M., 22d; went on the river; when within twenty miles of the fortifications, I met Maj. Brent, in command of the rams Queen of the West and the Webb, with the Grand Era as tender. I turned back and proceeded down the river in company with them, to find the enemy and attack him at night, as I knew their immense superiority of metal and power. Proceeded up the Mississippi river, to within 30 miles of Vicksburg, near the little town of Carthage, where we discovered our enemy, close in shore, at about 10 o'clock, P. M., on the 24th. The Queen of the West and the Webb most gallantly charged upon her, the first and second rams of both boats doing but little damage; the third ram of the Webb struck her at the back part of the starboard wheel-house, cutting down below the water into the hull, making also a large hole in her own bow. The Queen of the West made another gallant charge in the face of two nine-inch guns on her stern, for the purpose of crushing in the whole of her stern. Maj. Brent then gave me notice (I being within 300 yards) that she was disabled. I immediately rushed up to board—I grappled her, and on giving the order to board, Lieut. Brown, U. S. N., commanding iron-clad gunboat "Indianola," said "*he was in a sinking condition.*" *I asked if he surrendered.* He replied that he did. I kept back my boarders, jumped on board myself, and received his sword. I then had her pushed into shore, where we found that they had cut all their pipes and blown the water out of her boilers.

I found her to be one of the most formidable iron clads in the navy; protected by heavy timber, and thick iron plates, in every possible manner; mounting two 11-inch, completely casemated, Dahlgren guns forward, from which she had fired eleven shots at us; she had two 9-inch Dahlgren guns at her stern, from which she had fired six solid shot. Lieut. Brown informs me she would have been used as a ram, had he thought we had the boldness to attack her at night.

Too much credit cannot be awarded to Maj. Brent and his command, for the gallant manner in which they behaved. I therefore turned the prize over to him to have been taken up Red River, where she could be repaired and fitted out. After towing her down as far as his Excellency, President Davis's plantation, we found that she made so much water we were compelled to run her ashore, where she now lies in about ten feet of water. I dispatched by the Queen of the West, to Warrenton, a communication to Maj. Gen. Stevenson, of Vicksburg, for assistance in the shape of pumps, &c. I then started off on the Era with the prisoners, numbering about 90 and 7 negroes, and delivered them over to Col. Wirt Adams' command, to be forwarded to Jackson, Miss. On my return to join the squadron, I met the Queen of the West, Webb, and Batey, in full retreat, having learnt that the two gunboats expected by Lieut. Brown, U. S. N., had passed Vicksburg. Our rams leaking so much it was impossible for us to make another attack. My post guard having been cut into by the Queen of the West, by accident, I was obliged in consequence to leave about 70 bales of cotton on shore, near where the Indianola was sunk. The officers and men, one and all, deserve great praise for their coolness and the promptitude with which they executed all my commands, especially when I gave the order to board. I take the pleasure in saying that I never saw men behave better under any circumstances. The West had two killed, and three wounded, by a 11-inch shot striking the upper bulwarks. The Webb and Batey had not a man hurt. The enemy had one killed and one wounded, by our sharp-shooters. So well protected were the enemy by their iron that our 20, 30, and 32-pounder rifled guns made only slight indentations on her plating, at a distance of ten or fifteen yards. Some forty or fifty of my men were detailed to work aboard the Indianola, who are now aboard the Webb, having gotten aboard of her during the stampede; also Surg'n. Weatherly, Lieut. Thomas, (Brown's Battery) and Lieut Frith, (Mile's Legion). Sergt. Maj. King, with 15 men was detailed to carry dispatches up to Warrenton in a boat; he has not returned yet. The detachment of the signal corps, I had with me, rendered efficient service. Also to Capt. Pulley and Pilot D. Thomas, am I indebted for their bravery and efficient services.

Fred B Brand,
Lt. Col. Comd'g.

Destruction of the Nashville.

About half past 7 o'clock on Saturday morning heavy firing was heard in the direction of Genesis Point, and the general belief was that Fort McAlister had again been attacked by the enemy's gunboats. The firing continued, though not rapidly, and with occasional intervals, until about ten o'clock, after which time only a few guns were heard. About this time news reached the city of Savanah (says the Republican) that the Montauk had come up within range and opened fire on the steamer Nashville, which, in attempting to run up, had got aground on Friday in the bend of what is called Seven-Mile Reach, in the Ogeechee, a short distance above the fort, and that the Nashville was on fire. With a friend we drove down to Coffee Bluff, on the Little Ogeechee, some miles from the city. Arriving at the point where the battery formerly occupied by Reed's Flying Artillery, we had a view across the marsh of the fort, the burning Nashville and the enemy's gunboats.

The firing had ceased some two hours before, and the three gunboats, with the iron-clad turret boat, had dropped some three miles below the fort, where they were lying at anchor, while an immense column of smoke rose from the Nashville, where she lay apparently, from our point of view, about a mile above the fort. All was still, and the few spectators at the point who like ourselves, had arrived after the firing had ceased, could give us no information further than the reports they had received from the retiring salt boilers and others whom they had met on their way from the city. Some said the Montauk alone had engaged the fort and also fired on the Nashville, which being unable to escape had been fired by her crew.

Others were of opinion that the Nashville had been set on fire by the shells from the Montauk. There appeared to be some movement about one o'clock, among the gunboats which were lying at a distance of five or six miles from our position, and, as the tide was nearly full, we thought it probable that the enemy might contemplate another attack on the fort. We waited till about half past one, when we observed one of the gunboats leave her companions and steam off down the river, taking a course in the direction of Tybee, doubtless to communicate their operations to headquarters. When she was out of sight we returned to the city.

It was not until yesterday morning that we learned anything of the particulars of the destruction of the Nashville. It appears that the steamer, having got aground in the Reach on Friday, was observed by the enemy and a few shots were fired at her by the Montauk on Friday evening. The Nashville being unable to get off, and the crew being forced to abandon her, the Montauk, favored by a curve in the river, took a position which brought her in easy range and opened fire on her again on Saturday morning, hitting her some eight or ten times, when she took fire from the shells and was entirely consumed, with her valuable cargo of cotton and all her stores. After the Nashville had been on fire some time, a quantity of powder on board, some two hundred pounds, exploded, blowing out the stern of the steamer. Her guns and shells that were loaded also exploded with a terrific report, which was heard in the city.

Thus terminated the career of the Rattlesnake, which we fondly hoped was soon to be converted into a sea-serpent to plague the Yankees on the ocean. Her owners sustained a heavy loss in the vessel and her machinery, while private parties lose some nine hundred bales of cotton which had been shipped on board of her. The loss being divided among many, will not be serious to any, and we have no doubt that the owners of her cargo would have cheerfully submitted to a much greater sacrifice to have secured her escape to sea.

The Gunboat Indianola, which run past Vicksburg, did not receive a single shot. She had 1700 bushels of coal, besides ammunition and provisions. The Indianola had gone to Red River, where the Rebels received supplies from Texas. Brillant results are expected.

The last boats up report no difficulty from the batteries on the river banks.—*Nashville Union.*

The "brilliant results" were not exactly of the kind the Abolition papers bargained for.

Provisions the Present Year.

By far the most important problem which remains to be solved during the present year, says the Montgomery (Alabama) Advertiser, is that in regard to provisions. Thus far the country and the army have been sustained with great difficulty, thanks to the prudent foresight and patriotism of the producing classes; but, this year, owing to the fact that a considerable portion of country, from which last year's supplies were drawn, is now in the hands of the enemy, and that a still larger extent of country has been desolated and laid waste by the contending armies, greater exertions are necessary, or the people will suffer and the cause perish. Last year, it will be remembered, so great a breadth of land was devoted to wheat, corn and other cereals and vegetables, that many supposed the supply of articles of food would be superabundant, and remarkably cheap. It was thought the price of provisions would not pay the cost of production and hundreds who devoted the larger portions of their lands to breadstuffs, did so more from a sense of duty than any belief that they would reap a pecuniary reward for their labors. Some, without patriotism or foresight enough to guide them, planted largely in cotton in the hope that the ports would be opened in time for them to realize a fortune from their crops, but in this they have been disappointed.

As is well known, the last wheat crop of the country, from various causes, proved almost a complete failure, while the extraordinary drought of the summer greatly diminished all other crops, and the consequence was that there has been no surplus in the markets, and provisions of all kinds have been sold at unprecedentedly high prices. Wheat flour has gone beyond the reach of men of moderate means, and corn commands a price almost appalling to those who have not independent fortunes. This condition of things ought to be a strong inducement to our planters to endeavor to raise large crops of corn, oats, potatoes, peas, carrots, parsnips, beets, turnips, and every sort of vegetable capable of being used as food. There is no danger of overstocking the market; scarcity is the only thing to be feared. Profit and patriotism both urge the policy of planting for provisions. They are certain to command a good price, and will make a better return for labor than could be hoped for under the most favorable circumstances from the same breadth of land devoted to cotton.

The people at home and the armies in the field must be fed. The soldiers cannot fight our battles unless their craving for food is satisfied. The enemy may not be able to conquer us, but starvation certainly will, unless the planters of the Confederacy resolve to do their duty, and plant nothing but articles of food. Let no one be deceived with the cry of peace. It is delusive, and will lure the country to destruction if listened to. If it comes within the year, well; our surplus breadstuffs will find a ready market, and if it does not, we shall be all the better prepared for war, if our granaries and store houses are full. The surest way to obtain peace is to make vigorous preparations for war, and in no way can the country be so well prepared to meet the shock of battle as by attention to the matter of food. The planters of the Confederacy are appealed to by every consideration which can induce men to labor, to spare no effort to increase the supply of provisions. If they do their duty faithfully, they may expect to receive the blessings of heaven, the gratitude of their fellow men, and enjoy the proud consciousness of having contributed in no insignificant manner toward the independence and happiness of their country.

Peace Sentiment Announced.

In an article criticising the temper of Gen. Rosecrans' letter to the Ohio Legislature, and replying to the Gazette, the Cincinnati Enquirer is bold in announcing its opinion as to what it believes to be the sentiment of the people of Ohio. Gen. R. said in his letter that "he who is in favor of peace on any terms is fit only to be a slave, and he who gives utterance to a peace sentiment is a traitor to his country;" to which the Enquirer responds:

"There is not one man in ten in Ohio who is not in favor of peace upon some terms. A large majority of the people are in favor of peace either upon terms of compromise or division. If a vote of the people were taken to-day upon the question, "peace or no peace," without respect to terms of settlement, the peace party would be two to one of the other. * * * The peace party is in a majority in Ohio, and will not much regard the interpretation which General Rosecrans puts upon their views, nor will they be greatly troubled at the Gazette's exclamation point: "Rebellion a party question!" Whether or not "a party against war is as legitimate as a party for war," a party having the majority is a pretty legitimate party at any rate; and if its members are all traitors, they will be able to keep each other in countenance."

British Ships in the Gulf. There are now (says the Charleston Mercury) no less than forty British ships of war in or near the Gulf, from a line of battle ship to the smallest despatch boat, including eleven heavy first class frigates, all carrying the Armstrong gun, which will send a ball through a target nearly six miles. The whole of the force is arranged so as to be concentrated, it necessary, at any point in the Gulf within twelve or fourteen days.

Trouble in Louisville. A gentleman who was at Louisville at the time of the departure of some ten or fifteen thousand Yankee troops for Vicksburg, informs the editor of the Knoxville Register that they had with them some two hundred slaves they had picked up in Kentucky, and intended to take along with them. That the people rose up and apprehended nearly all of the negroes, and in so doing came in collision with the Yankee soldiers. Several heads and ribs were broken with sticks and rocks, but no fire-arms were used. Many of the strongest Union men have become violent Secessionists, and that a Union party will soon cease to exist in that State.

☞ Telegraphic News failed yesterday.

Funeral of the Late Major Wm. H. Lilly.

The mortal remains of that gallant and beautiful young officer (recently brought from the scene of the Railroad breaking of the bridge at Chunkey River,) were followed to the grave in the City Cemetry, by a large company of friends, relatives and acquaintances, day before yesterday evening.

The Episcopal "Order for the Burial of the Dead" was performed by the regular clergy of the Parish, the Rev. Dr. Perry, preceding the procession to Trinity Church, where the body was met by the Rev. H. G. Perry, with the Scripture Sentences.

After the proper office, followed the Rev. Dr's discourse, in which he impressively dwelt upon the principal facts relative to the mournful occasion of thus putting away from us, one of more than ordinary talent, present usefulness, and future promise.

The deceased was truly of that able, energetic, persevering character, that is ever successfully striving. Turning at once from the legal profession to that of arms, as another has said, "One year of faithful and assiduous attention to the duties of a private, sufficed to mark him out to his fellow-comrades," by whose suffrages, William Henry Lilly, only some 24 or 25 years of age, became Major. Ever brave and daring, so he continued constant at work. None can tell, had he lived, to what degree of honorable eminence he might have attained in his country's service.

But wonderful are the ways of Divine Providence, and past Man's finding out. How true, that "In the midst of life, we are in death." And this one, who, though once severely wounded, so oft the sword had spared, and bullets escaped, closed his bright career in the crowded car, by the deep river. Whirling over the iron-track, (just parted from a loving sister's embrace, and travelling on to other kin and welcome,) in the darksome awfulness of night, the treacherous structure yields—a quick plunge into the wild waters beneath—the gurgle, the gash, the death grasp, one last gasp, and hurled from time into Eternity, one by one, the late living are lost to earth, and called to await the resurrectionary mandate of Almighty God, the Judge of quick and dead.

Heaven spare us the horror of another such hearing of sudden death and painful disaster.

Beautifully contrasted the voice of parting Prayer, and sentiments of the closing Hymn before Benediction.

"There is a Land of pure delight,"
* * * * * * *
Eternal day excludes the night,"
* * * * * * *
Death *like a narrow sea* divides
This Heavenly Land from ours."

P.

Funeral Notice.

☞ The friends and acquaintances of E. F. Stewart, are respectfully invited to attend the funeral of his late Wife, CALISTA A. STEWART, to proceed from the residence of her Father, E. R. Cory, corner of Jefferson and Rankin streets, at 10 o'clock, This (Saturday) Morning.

Natchez, Saturday, March 14, 1863.

DIED:

In this city, on the 12th inst., THOMAS PERCY, oldest son of Robert T. Rose.

And. Jackson Lodge,

No. 2, F. & A. M.—A regular meeting will be held SATURDAY EVENING, March 14, 1863, at 7 o'clock. By order of

F. F. FOWLER, W. M.

Henry G. Perry, Secretary. mar14-d1

Louisiana Election.

☞ Hon. EDWIN T. MERRICK, is a candidate for re-election to the office of Chief Justice of the Supreme Court of Louisiana.

Election the first Monday in April. mar12-d:wtd*

The Natchez Daily Courier.

Official Paper for the City and County.

BOOK, PAMPHLET, AND JOB WORK,
OF EVERY DESCRIPTION,
Printed on as liberal terms as the war times will admit,
At the Natchez Daily Courier Office.

TERMS, &c.

DAILY COURIER,......per week,.............. 25 cts.
WEEKLY COURIER,....per year, in advance,...$3 00 "

☞ TERMS OF THE DAILY COURIER—One Dollar per month; or Five Dollars for six months, in advance.

☞ ADVERTISING $1 per square of 10 lines for the first insertion; 50 cents per square for every subsequent insertion, payable in advance.

☞ All letters relating to the Editorial Department of the Daily and Weekly Courier should be addressed "JOHN M. BALDWIN, Natchez, Mississippi."

TO THE PATRONS OF THE COURIER.
Mr. R. M. Spurgeon is now Clerk of the Courier Office, and is authorized to collect and receipt for all monies due the establishment, as also, to do all other business pertaining to his department.

The Experience of a Radical on a Trip to Washington.

What He Saw and Heard.

Under the head of "Spirit of the German Press," the St. Louis Republican translates and publishes the following article from the Neue Zeit, a leading German paper of that city. It is of the date of the 6th ult. The Neue Zeit is one of the radical abolition presses:

THE SITUATION IN THE EAST.

A trip to Washington compensates. One learns much, and gets rid of manifold illusions. The latter may not always be connected with the most pleasant sensations, but such a riddance produces certainly a deeper view into the true situation of the country, which for many years may be of practical value. I have never been very sanguine with relation to the prerequisites of a sure progress of our cause in the East; I have never estimated the patriotism and energy of our representatives in Congress, the penetration of our leading statesmen, the bravery and love of our country of our army very highly; but to return so bare of all hope, I had not expected. In the annexed communication I will endeavor to place before your readers the result of my observations.

The people of the East are completely weary of the war, and desire peace, though this peace be connected with conditions ever so shameful. The conviction is deeply rooted that we cannot beat the Southern army, that, on the contrary, our troops cannot make a stand against those of the Confederates; that it is useless to continue still further the waste of blood; that the Republican party, after a prolongation of probation, has proven itself incapable to administer the affairs of the country, and that the Democratic party understands how to hold the reins; that Lincoln is a weak old woman, and renders our Government ridiculous; that we can end the war only by compromise, and that hence salvation and redemption are only to be hoped for from the Democratic party. The hatred against the negro is greater than ever before; the prejudice against the black race grows day by day; the message of the President excites general disapprobation. The country is exhausted in men and money; the woful condition of our finances is a more heavy affliction than all others, because it is felt at every hour of the day; and but one wish hovers on all lips: Peace! Peace!

The army of the East is still more corrupt than the people. The army is rotten and tresonable from head to toe. The Western troops, as soon as arrived at the East, become equally corrupted. Upon the whole trip I have not met a single soldier who did not curse the Abolitionists, damn the niggers to hell, and declare that he would rather fight for the South than to make a stand for the liberation of the slaves. Of battle courage and victory-assurance, there is none to be found in the Eastern army. The soldiers do not believe that they can beat the enemy, and therefore consider an advance impossible. They seem to be so spiritless that it is doubtful whether they are capable of *hoping* for victory. Of Hooker hardly anything more is expected than of Burnside. The desertions increase with every day. The President's Proclamation is publicly cursed, and the conduct of soldiers in the cars and in the cities is vulgar and brutal beyond description. Of patriotism, you find as little in the Eastern army as among the people of the Eastern States. This people seem to have no longer an idea of patriotism; not a man speaks of sacrifices; from love of the cause, hardly ten men would remain in the regiment. It is a real treat, after having conversed with the soldiers of the Rappahannock, to converse with soldiers from Rosencranz and Grant's armies.

The statesmen in Washington, in their turn, are again more corrupt than army and people. For them there is but one watch word: "Let us steal while it is time." Every one prefers to snatch a portion of the booty out of the strong box of the Secretary of the Treasury, though as if the sin-flood was already rolling against the gates of Washington. Does any one accidentally think of the dreary situation of the country, he has to go and drown his sorrow in a brandy shop. There is not one of all our celebrated men, who ventures soberly and coolly to reflect on the lay of the land, to look into the future, and to take in time the measures of precaution. One only hears words like these: "We do not know what will come out of it." "We will see." "What can be done?"

In Congress time and energy are frittered away with puny measures: and for the main question no one cares. The Cabinet members place the crown upon the whole swindle. Seward has long since gone over to the copperheads; so Blair; Stanton always was a democrat; so the always drunken Halleck; Chase plays a high game for the Presidential candidacy, and Abe Lincoln is the rueful counterfeit of a man whom one need only to look at in order to beat his hands over his head.

Fremont's name is no more heard in Washington. It is totally blown away. He, too, has suffered the favorable opportunity to pass by, and it would be useless now to try to seize it again. The people of the East have become so faithless that it is no more to be saved. Once the radical party had the power within its grasp; then they did not venture openly to oppose the President, but they even labored for the administration, although it was inimical to them. It broke with the best portion of the Democracy, which likewise, by the obtuseness of Lincoln's Administration, was driven into the opposition. Now it is too late. Possible it is, nevertheless, that the last days of Congress may yet bring important and decisive things. Still possible is a change of a Cabinet, although every member grasps with cramped hands to be a money-paying officer. This possibility is, however, very distant, and becomes daily more improbable. The radicals are now in a great minority—the Democracy has the power. He who knows the tough and regardless character of the Democratic leaders, knows what that means.

In Washington they talk only of peace. Then a separation into four empires would become most probable. In Virginia, Ohio, Pennsylvania, Indiana, everywhere, even of loyal people, one hears the same wish: Peace. And the boldest among the copperheads speak already of the annexation to the Southern Confederacy under the regime of Jefferson Davis.

In conclusion, I would venture the question whether an organization of the radical party would not now be in time? The Democracy in every State of the Union is firmly and closely organized. Circumstances may render for it measures necessary, which we would have to war against at any price. Therefore, radicals, organize yourselves, else all is lost. A. E. K.

(From the St. Joseph, (La.) Gazette.

Kingdum aint Kummin.

The Yanks have a "nigger song" called "Kingdum kummin," a copy of which has reached even our little out-and-out "secesh" town; thus showing that it must be immensely popular with the Yanks. Otherwise, it would not spread so. The air is a good lively one, the words are too strong for Southern stomachs. So, to please our young folks, our *devil* has written the following words to the Yankee tune:

Don't you see dem gunboats coming wid de black smoke like a cloud,
Dey's loaded down wid 'freedom-shriekers' and wid cannon big and loud.
Dey's gwine to steal us ev'ry one, our marster's houses burn,
But 'tis a long lane has no turning and de times will take a turn.
CHORUS.—Den marster stay a-ha!
Don't go away, O! no,
Dey can't fool us wid de kingdom cummin or de year of jubele.

Ole Marster Lincum he did tell us all dat on de New Year's day,
We should be free, no man should sell us all and we'd have our own way.
I know jus what dat freedom means, to starve to def;
Den marster Lincum you can't fool us all, so you can save your bref.
CHORUS.—

Oh! darkies I've jus cum from marster and I heerd him read de news,
I b'lieve if he had got no paper he'd a'most died wid de blues.
Our men has got de Western Queen, de Indianola too,
You see our folks is gettin spunky and de gunboats will not do.
CHORUS.—

De Yankees dey sent down a non-descript, our men scared out dere wits,
Dey took and blowed de boat to pieces and de cannon all to bits.
It was a flat-boat scared 'em so,—it really makes me mad
To t'ink dat wat began so promising should all turn out so bad.
CHORUS.—

ST. JOSEPH, LA., March 6, 1863.

☞ Is it true that the commander of the Indianola is perambulating about our streets? We have heard such a report, but are loth to credit it. We hope it is not so. We want no abolitionists walking our streets at present, nor indeed at any time. We want all prisoners treated just as our men are treated in the North. Lieut. Brown may have been a "very nice man" before the war, but he is now in the service of a government whose object is our total annihilation, and when he was captured, the vessel he commanded was on a mission of destruction. What right have such men to any clemency when the government they are acting under keeps our prisoners, officers and privates, closely confined, with orders to shoot them if they attempt to move to a position where they can breathe the fresh air of heaven? Have Camps Douglas, Morton and Sandusky been forgotten? Have the noble sons of the South who were wilfully murdered at those bastiles no longer a place "in memory's casket?"—*Vicksburg Whig.*

THE GALLANT DEFENDERS OF FORT MCALLISTER. The following is the general order of Gen. Beauregard, in compliment to our brave troops who repelled the attack of the Yankee iron-clads on our battery at Genesis Point:

The Commanding General announces to the forces with satisfaction and pride, the results of the recent encounter of our battery at Genesis Point, Georgia, with an iron-clad of the Monitor class, results only alloyed by the life blood of the gallant commander, the late Major John B. Gallie.

For hours, the most formidable vessel of her class hurled missiles of the heaviest calibre ever used in modern warfare, at the weak parapet of the battery, which was almost demolished, but standing at their guns, as became men fighting for their homes, for honor, and for independence, the garrison replied with such effect as to cripple and beat back their adversary, clad though in impenetrable armor, and armed with 15 and 11-inch guns, supported by monitor boats whose practice was of uncommon precision.

The thanks of the country are due to this intrepid garrison, who have thus shown what brave men may withstand and accomplish despite apparent odds.

"Fort McAllister" will be inscribed on the flags of all troops engaged in the defense of the battery.

SOLD. The Hartford (Conn.) Courant, recently published a half a column of highly original poetry, in which there were sprinkled several lines in italics. These lines, read backward, were as follows:

"Oh bless our brave Confederates, Lord!
Scourge with Thy wrath the Yankee horde!
Help Lee, Bragg, Jackson, Johnston Joe,
To give them fits in Dixie, O!
Bring Nincompoop the First down flat,
And all his crew, old Nat Banks too,
And every low-born Yankee rat!"

The Courant, it is stated, gracefully "owned up" by saying it all came from being unaccustomed to the ways of the wicked. The document in question was mailed at New Orleans, accompanied by a letter in the same hand, and was signed Emily H. Washington. It bore every mark of being genuine.

GEN. PEMBERTON BEAT. A good dodge was recently played off on Gen. Pemberton and his officers. They refuse to let produce of any description come down the Mobile and Ohio Railroad, when there is plenty of it lying in the warehouses rotting. The story is as follows: A gentleman wanting meat, purchased it up the road; but knowing that it would be confiscated, if found, he procured a common pine box about six feet long, made to resemble a coffin, such as are commonly used to transport the dead. He filled this box with good sound bacon, which he found at reasonable prices in Mississippi, and then marked his dead body thus:

"John *Shoat*,
32d Ala. Regiment,
Mobile, Ala."

The shoat or shoats came to hand without trouble, and in good order.—*Mobile Tribune.*

GO IT WHILE YOU'RE YOUNG. Two juveniles named Jerome Saunders and Lucy Walsh, the former aged 16 and the latter 14, were married in Davis county, Kentucky, on 9th. ult.

☞ Congress has just paid a deserved compliment to Gen. John H. Morgan. The most substantial compliment they could offer this celebrated chieftain, would be his full *complement* of men, and a Kentucky campaign of his own managing.

NATCHEZ R. A. CHAPTER, NO. 1,
Meets Third Saturday of each Month.

E. Craig,..........H. P.
A. R. Tyler,..........K.
M. Izod,..........S.
F. F. Fowler,..........C. of H.
J. Deutsch,..........P. S.
C. F. Merrick,..........R. A. C.
J. M. Baldwin,..........M. 3rd V.
W. C. Turner,..........M. 2nd V.
J. Wells,..........M. 1st V.
H. G. Perry,..........Secretary.
R. Stewart,..........Treasurer.
Jno McDowell,..........Sentinel.

HARMONY LODGE NO. 1,
Meets first Saturday Evening of each Month.

C. F. Merrick,..........W. M.
J. A. Steele,..........S. W.
J. M. Baldwin,..........J. W.
T. S. Sheridan,..........Secretary.
G. Kennedy,..........Treasurer.
Jno. McDowell,..........S. & T.

ANDREW JACKSON LODGE NO. 2,
Meets Second Saturday of each Month.

F. F. Fowler,..........W. M.
A. G. Wilson,..........S. W.
H. G. Perry,..........J W.
R. S. Wood,..........Secretary
W. A. Sawyer,..........Treasurer.
Jno. McDowell,..........S. & T.

Bishop Green's Appointments.

Yazoo City,..........March 14th and 15th.
Epiphany Parish and Port Gibson, Mar. 21, to 25.
Christ's Church,..........March 28th and 29th.
Washington,..........March 31st.
Natchez,..........April 2d to 7th.
St. Mary's Chapel,..........April 8th.
Woodville,..........April, 10th, 11th, 12th.
Vicksburg,..........April 18th 19th.
Canton,..........April 21st.
Diocesan Council at Jackson,..........April 23d.
Jackson, Feb. 21, 1863. W. M. GREEN.

CONFEDERATE GOVERNMENT.

PRESIDENT,
JEFFERSON DAVIS,
OF MISSISSIPPI.

VICE PRESIDENT,
ALEX. H. STEPHENS,
OF GEORGIA.

CABINET OF THE CONFEDERATE STATES.

J. P. Benjamin, of La., Secretary of State.
G. W. Randolph, of Va., Secretary of War.
C. G. Memminger, of S. C., Sec'y of Treasury.
S. R. Mallory, of Fla. Secretary of Navy.
Thos. H. Watts, of Ala., Attorney-General.
J. H. Reagan, of Texas, Postmaster-General.

CONFEDRATE CONGRESS.

The following is a list of the members of the Congress of the Permanent Government of the Confederate States.

Those marked with an asterisk (*) were members of the Provisional Congress.

Senate.

ALABAMA.	MISSOURI.
Wm. L. Yancey,	John B. Clarke,
C. C. Clay, Jr.,	R. L. E. Peyton.
ARKANSAS.	NORTH CAROLIAA.
Robert W. Johnson,*	George Davis,*
C. B. Mitchell.	William T. Dortch.
FLORIDA.	SOUTH CAROLINA.
James M. Baker,	Robert W. Barnwell,*
A. E. Maxwell.	James L. Orr.*
GEORGIA.	TENNESSEE.
B. H. Hill,*	Gustavus A. Henry,
Robert Toombs.*	Landon C. Haynes.
KENTUCKY.	TEXAS.
Henry C. Burnett,	Lewis T. Wigfall,*
Wm. E. Simms.	W. S. Oldham.*
LOUISIANA.	VIRGINIA.
Edward Sparrow,*	R. M. T. Hunter,
T. J. Semmes.	Wm. C. Rives.
MISSISSIPPI.	
A. G. Brown,	
James Phelan.	

House of Representatives.

Dist.	ALABAMA.	Dist.	NORTH CAROLINA.
1.	T. J. Foster,	1.	W. N. H. Smith,*
2.	W. R. Smith,	2.	R. R. Bridges,
3.	J. P. Rails,	3.	O. R. Kenan,
4.	J. L. M. Curry,*	4.	T. D. McDowell,
5.	F. S. Lyon,	5.	A. H. Arrington,
6.	W. P. Chilton,*	6.	J. R. McLean,
7.	D. Clopton,	7.	— — Ashe,
8.	J. S. Pugh,	8.	William Lander,
9.	E. S. Daegan.	9.	B. S. Gaither,
	ARKANSAS.	10.	A. T. Davidson.
1.	A. J. Garland,		SOUTH CAROLINA.
2.	Jas. M. Patterson.	1.	John McQueen,
	(Incomplete.)	2.	W. Porcher Miles,*
	FLORIDA.	3.	L. M. Ayer,
1.	Jas. B. Dawkins,	4.	M. L. Bonham,
2.	R. B. Hilton.	5.	James Farrow,
	GEORGIA.	6.	W. W. Boyce.*
1.*	Sulian Hartridge,		TENEESSEE.
2.	C. C. Munnerlyn,	1.	Jos. B. Heiskell,
3.	Hines Holt,	2.	W. G. Swann,
4.	Aug. H. Kenan,	3.	— — Tibbs,
5.	David W. Lewis,	4.	J. B. Gardenshire,
6.	W. W. Clark,	5.	Henry S. Foote,
7.	Robt. P. Trippe,	6.	Meredith P. Gentry,
8.	Lucius J. Gartrell,	7.	George W. Jones.
9.	Hardy Strickland,	8.	— — Menses,
10.	Aug. R. Wright.	9.	J. D. C. Adkins,*
	KENTUCKY.	10.	John V. Wright,
	(Not yet elected.)	11.	D. M. Currin.*
	LOUISIANA.		TEXAS.
1.	Chas. J. Villere,	1.	John A. Wilcox,
2.	Chas. M. Conrad,*	2.	C. C. Herbert,
3.	D. F. Kenner,*	3.	P. W. Gray,
4.	Lucien J. Dupree,	4.	F. B. Sexton,
5.	John L. Lewis,	5.	M. D. Graham,
6.	John Perkins, Jr.	6.	B. P. Epperson.
	MISSISSIPPI.		VIRGINIA.
1.	J. W. Clapp,	1.	M. R. H. Garnett,
2.	Reuben Davis,	2.	John B. Chambliss,
3.	Israel Welch,	3.	———
4.	H. C. Chambers,	4.	Roger A. Pryor,*
5.	O. R. Singleton,	5.	Thos. S. Bocock,*
6.	E. Barksdale,	6.	John Goode, Jr.,
7.	John J. McRae.	7.	Jas. P. Holcombe,
	MISSOURI.	8.	D. C. DeJarnette,
1.	W. M. Cook,	9.	Wm. Smith,
2.	T. C. Harris,	10.	Alex. R. Boteler,
3.	Casper W. Bell,	11.	John B. Baldwin,
4.	Adam H. Condon,	12.	Walter R. Staples,*
5.	G. G. West,	13.	Walter Preston,*
6.	L. W. Freeman,	14.	Albert G. Jenkins,
7.	— — Hyer.	15.	Robert Johnston,*
		16.	Chas. W. Russell.*

Taxes! Taxes!

THE STATE OF MISSISSIPPI, }
ADAMS COUNTY.

NOTICE is hereby given, that the State and County taxes are now due. Tax payers are requested to call at the Sheriff's office, and pay up.
O. METCALFE, Sheriff.
Sheriffs office, Natchez, Jan. 21, 1863—2m

County Government.

HIRAM CASSIDY, Judge of Circuit Court.
JAMES A. STEELE, Clerk
REUBEN BULLOCK, Judge of Probate.
RO. S. WOOD, Clerk
OREN METCALFE, Sheriff of Adams co'y.
A. D. PICKENS, County Assessor.
JOHN B. DICKS, County Treasurer.
WM. G. FOULKS, Surveyor.
FORD HOLMES, Overseer of Roads.
JAS. C. BRANDON, County Physician.
H. LAZARUS, Overseer of the Poor.
F. A. NEWCOMB, Ranger.
JOHN McDOWELL, Jailor.

Board of Police.

WILLIAM CANNON, President.
MEMBERS.
FOUNTAIN W. FORD, | GEORGE W. BAYNARD,
WM. HALL, | THOS. C. POLLOCK.
RO. S. WOOD, Clerk.

Natchez City Government.

JOHN HUNTER, MAYOR,
JAS. N. STOCKMAN, } Selectm'n { J. P. WALWORTH,
WM. H. FORBES, } { H. M. BALDWIN,
ROBERT WALKER, } { WM. DIX.
RICH'D [illegible], Assessor and Collector.
SAM'L A. PATTERSON, Treasurer.
J. HEWETT, Solicitor.
CHAS. F. MERRICK, City Clerk.
HUGH LYLE, Health Officer.
JOHN M. BALDWIN, City Printer.
C. M. BENBROOK, Clerk of the Market.
JOS. D. BAKER, City Marshal.
ROB'T H. STEWART, Sexton.
WM. EUSTIS, City Surveyor.
Messrs. BALDWIN, DIX and FORBES, Commissioners of Health.

Standing Committees for 1863:

On Roads.—Messrs. Baldwin, Walker and Dix.
On Finance.—Messrs. Walworth, Stockman and Baldwin
On Accounts.—Messrs. Forbes, Stockman and Walworth.
On Gas.—Messrs. Stockman, Forbes and Walker.
On Public Property.—Messrs. Walker, Dix and Baldwin
On Propositions and Grievances.—Messrs. Dix, Walker and Forbes.
On Safety.—Messrs. Forbes, Stockman and Walworth.
On Landing.—Messrs. Stockman, Forbes and Dix.
On Enrolled Bills.—Messrs. Walworth, Dix and Baldwin

An Ordinance.

To provide a revenue for the City of Natchez, for the year Eighteen hundred and Sixty-three.

SECTION 1. *Be it ordained by the Mayor and Selectmen of the City of Natchez, in Council convened.* That to defray the ordinary and contingent expenses of the city, for the year Eighteen hundred and Sixty-three, there shall be levied assessed and collected by the Assessor and Collector of said city, the following taxes—namely:

An ad valorem tax of *one half of one per centum* on all REAL PROPERTY within the city, not exempt from taxation by law: and of *four tenths of one per centum* on all SLAVES over the age of *five years:* and *one half of one per centum* on all PLEASURE CARRIAGES, and SADDLE and CARRIAGE HORSES, kept for use, and RACE HORSES, and *horses kept for hire;* and on all CLOCKS and WATCHES *kept for use.*

A tax of *three tenths of one per centum*, upon the AMOUNT of goods, wares and merchandise, purchased and brought into the city *for sale*, during the year preceding the first day of February, Eighteen hundred and Sixty-three, by any regular merchant, factor or commission merchant.

A tax of *one half of one per centum* upon the AMOUNT of *sales* of merchandise by AUCTIONEERS, either at *public or private sale.*

A tax of *one per centum* upon the AMOUNT of *all sales* of merchandise, *by or for* transient merchants or vendors.

A tax of *one per centum* on all produce, goods, wares, merchandise and other property *sold* on any steam-boat, flat-boat, keel-boat, barge or other water-craft lying and trading at the Landing in front of the City of Natchez.

A *specific* tax of *One Hundred Dollars*, upon each BANKER and BROKER.

SECTION 2. *And be it further ordained,* That for the support of the NATCHEZ INSTITUTE, during the year aforesaid, there shall be levied, assessed and collected by the Assessor and Collector,—an *ad valorem* tax of *three tenths of one per centum*, upon ALL REAL PROPERTY, not exempt from taxation by law, and *one tenth of one per centum* upon all SLAVES over the age of *five years.*

A tax of *two tenths of one per centum* upon the *amount* of goods, wares and merchandise purchased and brought into the City for *sale* during the year preceding the first day of February, Eighteen hundred and Sixty-three, by any regular merchant, factor or commission merchant.

A *specific* tax of *Seventy-five Dollars* upon each BANKER and BROKER; and upon all other subjects of taxation mentioned in the preceding section, the same taxes, that in said section are ordained for ordinary and contingent expenses of the city.

SECTION 3. *And be it further ordained,* That there shall also be levied, assessed and collected, to be appropriated according to law the same tax, *in lieu* of labor on the streets as is prescribed in the first section of an ordinance entitled "An Ordinance to amend an Ordinance concerning road tax, streets and highways" passed 25th Feb., 1819.

SECTION 4. *And be it further ordained,* That it shall be the duty of the Collector to call upon each transient vendor of merchandise, as soon as he shall arrive and exhibit his goods and wares for sale, and upon each owner of a flat-boat, keel-boat, barge or other water-craft which shall arrive at the Landing, and demand a bond with security for the payment of such taxes as may become due from his or their sales under this ordinance, which bond shall be made payable to the "City of Natchez," and in sufficient penalty for the security of said taxes; or if such transient vendor or owner of a flat-boat, keel-boat, or other water-craft, so lying at the Landing, shall prefer, he or they may make a cash deposit with the Collector of an amount sufficient to pay such taxes, any surplus thereof, shall be returned to said vendor or owner, on closing their sales.

SECTION 5. *And be it further ordained,* That the Assessor and Collector shall have power to administer all oaths which he may deem necessary, for the discovery of property, and subjects of taxation, to the party taxable, or other person having knowledge or information in the premises.

SECTION 6. *And be it further ordained,* That nothing in this ordinance contained shall be construed as a repeal of an ordinance imposing and prescribing the mode of assessment and collection of taxes upon sales of Horses and Mules, in the City of Natchez, passed August 23d, 1854.

Ordained and published this fourth day of February, A. D., Eighteen hundred and Sixty-three.

Attest: JOHN HUNTER, Mayor.
C. F. MERRICK, City Clerk.
Natchez, February 7, 1863—d3

THE DRAMA.

Every human institution has its rise, its culmination, its decline. The art of the stage, improperly called a "profession," is no exception to the rule. In that grand, old Elizabethan era, when Shakespeare wrote, and men, or youths, performed the characters assigned by the author to women, we find the drama struggling up from infancy to manhood. Then came Ellerton, and Macklin, and Quin, the Kembles, and Cooke, and Kean, the elder. Time was when Goldsmith, who according to loquacious old Dr. Johnson, "hung around him an inspired idiot," and "who wrote like an angel, but talked like poor poll," dedicated a portion of his splendid abilities to the stage; when the burly doctor himself waited behind the scenes to witness the representation of his own play, and wept over the woes of his heroine; when gentlemanly Joseph Addison cared more about the prologue to "Cato" than the rent in his ruffled sleeves; when Pope and Bolingbroke awaited impatiently the return of Macklin to his room after his wonderful personation of Shylock; when Lord Essex bored Kean with his congratulations, and Mrs. Siddons and John Philip Kemble wined and dined with the British aristocracy as equals; when Sheridan, orator, and dramatist and wit, the intellectual phenomenon of his times, regarded the stage as a literary institution of extraordinary power; when silver lipped Leigh Hunt delighted to gossip about the great actors of his time; when Lord Byron was thrown into a "convulsion fit" on seeing Kean in one of his great characters, and Monk Lewis saw the actors depict madness with such power that the play was withdrawn because it threw two auditors into convulsions, while two others were carried out in a fainting fit. Golden were the days of this manhood of the drama when Lords Derby, Thurlow, Craven, and Harrington, took wives from the stage, and the Prince of Wales married privately the beautiful and unfortunate Mrs. Jordan. These were the days which Campbell celebrated in his lines at the farewell dinner given to John Philip Kemble, when he wrote:

> "For, by the mighty actor brought,
> Illusion's perfect triumph's come;
> Verse ceases to be airy thought
> And Sculpture to be dumb."

But the glory has departed from the dramatic Israel. Not all the efforts of Macready, nor of Brooke, nor of Forrest, could by any system of transfusion put red blood into the veins of decrepitude. The legitimate drama has, at length, thrown away its last crutch, and is breathing, even in England, its last breath On the boards of Drury Lane the very altar at which the brilliantest of its votaries worshipped, is now seen the antics of raree-showmen. The old men who walked through the snow-drifts to see Kean make his *debut* in Shylock, now can see a comedy in which George Jordan figures, followed by the muscular exercises of agile tight-rope dancers and attitudinizers.

In Yankeeland the illegitimate and spectacular drama has long ago supplanted the legitimate, and in the Confederate States the "profession" is even in a worse condition, for we laugh at the tragedies and are disposed to weep over comedies and farces. With an exception here and there, Falstaff would not have marched through Coventry with such a set as was locked up within our lines, unless, indeed, he wanted them "well peppered." And like Falstaff's famous company, there was scarcely a whole shirt among them at the beginning of the Revolution, yet unless the critic acknowledges them as the aristocrats of the drama, the utmost indignation is exhibited! If the stage is a literary institution, then the actor should be an educated man, so as to appreciate and interpret the meaning of such authors as Shakespeare, and Otway, Massinger, Knowles, and Sir Bulwer Lytton. If acting is an art which should so resemble nature as to cover art, then the actor should be trained to all those little proprieties of the stage which give perfect ease, by an apprenticeship of years. The ladder must be climbed round by round, and in no other way can the top be reached and the histrion sustain himself. In Richmond, and in other Southern cities, the leap from obscurity to position in the programme was so sudden that it has even come to pass that nearly every actor is ambitious of managership.

If fortunately at the new theatre we happen to look for something respectable in the shape of personation, it is usually spoiled by an unfortunate trick of gagging, or rant or the striking of an attitude, and a wait to bring a hand of applause, just as Leon Javelli, when he turned a dozen summersaults, would boldly ask the audience in his silent way: What do you think of that! Not long since, we dropped in to witness that beautiful sentimentalism, the Lady of Lyons. At the close of the celebrated scene of the fourth act, Claude ranted himself hoarse at least five minutes before Pauline fell, and during this undue excitement, the father and mother, Colonel Damas and the rest, sat indifferent spectators. Here was a picture! Sir Bulwer Lytton would have rushed from the auditorium in dismay when it rung with shouts over such misinterpretation and misrepresentation. A few nights since the Hypocrite was performed, and although Mawworm was in good hands, a strange absurdity was presented in the shape of a downright Confederate sermon full of local hits and local names, and that in an old British play, replete with British phrases, saws, customs, characters, costuming! To the critic the illusion was gone for the night. So frequent, however, are the violations of dramatic propriety now-a-days, that we have almost ceased to look for anything save as Pope has it, "leather and prunella." And one generally gets exactly what one looks for at the new theatre, for but little else than high mediocrity could be found with a search warrant.

Par parenthese. "Hard Times" or "Love *vs.* Wealth," is the title of a new one act play, performed Monday night at the Broad Street Theatre, and written by our townsman, Dr. Bricken. It is of the neat order of the "Morning Call," with a simple but well-worked-up plot, in which three characters are presented. The author has so managed plot and speech as to enable even two of them to fill the stage for some time, an exceedingly difficult task. The scene of the imaginary dinner can be made highly entertaining. This *petite* comedy went off well, and would have delighted all had there been less noise and confusion in the rear of the auditorium. We predict for it success in the future, as it can be easily cast, and its adaptability to war or peace times is strikingly apparent.

The production of this *morceau* was something of a relief from the stale Charles de Moors, the Ingomars, the Paulines and Parthenias of that gorgeous mausoleum of the drama recently trumpeted forth as the theatre *par excellence*, in which Hamlet's advice to the players is nightly disregarded, and managerial skill wofully lacking. Selah!

DEATH OF MRS. EDWIN BOOTH.

The N. Y. "Herald" announces the death of Mrs. Edwin Booth. She expired on the 21st ult., at her husband's residence, at Dorchester, near Boston.

ONE GOOD TURN DESERVES ANOTHER.

Old Abe: "WHY I DU DECLARE IT'S MY DEAR OLD FRIEND SAMBO! COURSE YOU'LL FIGHT FOR US, SAMBO. LEND US A HAND, OLD HOSS, DU!"—*London Punch.*

Written for the Illustrated News.

ANSWER TO ENIGMA No. 20.

The Mills of the Gods grind slowly.

MISCELLANEOUS ENIGMA, No. 21.

I am composed of 16 letters.

My 1, 5, 16, is the name of a species of *bipeds.*
My 4, 8, 9, 12, 6, an ancient bard.
My 10, 3, 6, 13, is a celebrated volcano.
My 6, 8, 1, 15, is a city of great fame.
My 1, 3, 14, 5, 6, 16, 2, 16, will ever be regarded sacred by every Southerner.
My 7, 12, 13, 6, 3, 11, may be found in every dwelling

My whole is three words—the most beautiful in the English language.

Answer next week. I. E. W.

Answer to Charades published Last Week.

1st Charade—**Stuart.** 2d Charade—**Millroy.**

Vol. I.} THE "TEXAS ALMANAC"--EXTRA. {No. 68

PUBLISHED TRI-WEEKLY] AUSTIN, TUESDAY, MARCH 17, 1863. [IN ADVANCE OF THE MAIL.

Texas Almanac Extra.

Published on Tuesdays, Thursdays & Saturdays
BY D. RICHARDSON.

TERMS:—for 1 month, $1 00; for 3 months, $2 50. Single copies, 25 cents.

Advertisements inserted at 50 cents per line for each insertion. No advertisement inserted for less than $2 00 for each insertion.

Announcements of candidates will be charged the same as other advertisements, viz: $2 per each insertion, and no announcement will, *under any circumstances*, be published without being paid for in advance.

All correspondence recommending candidates, and all circulars of candidates for office, will be charged at the rate of 50 cents a line, and published only on the same terms.

BY OUR OWN EXPRESS!

☞ Our Express arrived this morning at 6 o'clock, bringing the "News" of yesterday—the "Telegraph" having agai failed to reach us. We, however, received a dispatch from the editor of the Telegraph, in which he says, the Pony Express failed to get through, causing much disappointment, as six days later news was anticipated. We look, therefore, for interesting news by our next Express, on Thursday morning.

We copy from the "News" all the items of interest, received by the Central train and other sources.

HOUSTON, March 14—2 P. M.

The Central Train arrived promptly on time to-day, bringing the mail as late as due, by which we have Alexandria dates of the 9th, and Richmond the 3d, and Washington City 2d inst., which will be found interesting:

RICHMOND, March 3.—Northern dates of the 21st say: "Long live Abraham 1st; President Lincoln temporary dictator!" Under this head the Herald declares that the measure lately passed Congress, and others that will become laws, will partially invest Lincoln with all the powers of Dictator, but there is not the slightest danger of abuse of power by Lincoln; for ambiguous purposes, they accepted the plea of imperious necessity and were cheerfully content to the transformation of the President into a Temporary Dictator.

By an arrival from Port Royal, the Herald has further information respecting the difficulty between Hunter and Foster. Hunter peremptorily ordered the staff of Foster to leave his department and put Gen. Stevenson under arrest for disparaging negro troops.

Chas. C. Hicks, late second officer on the privateer Retribution, ... the old capitol, to be tried as a spy.

The negro soldier bill has not passed the Senate

Charleston, the 27th, ... the British ship Desperate, says the officers of the Yankee iron clad Ironsides, admit that three Federal vessels ... Ingraham's attack, have been missing, also one Federal prop...

The Mobile Tribune learns from a pilot who took the Florida out of this port, that there were nine blockaders outside; two immediately pursued, and by aid of their powerful fresnel lights, signalized the Florida for 40 miles. The chase continued 19 hours, but the Florida ran out of view, and on her way destroyed ... first voyage, laden with sugar, molasses, and rum; value of the vessel and cargo, $140,000.

The speed of the Florida is fifteen miles per hour.

MOBILE, March 2.—A special dispatch to the Advertiser and Register, dated Columbia, Tenn., Feb. 25th, says positive information has been received that Gen. Siegel's army corps, 20,000 strong, from Virginia, recently came up the Cumberland in forty five transports, and is now between Nashville and this point, en route to join Rosencranz.

CHARLESTON, March 2.—Nassau advices report the arrival there of the Confederate privateer Retribution. She had taken and burnt the bark Mary Wright, of Portland, and the brig Erie, of Camden, Maine. She encountered an unknown whaler in the Carribean sea, which showed fight, killing one of the Retribution's crew, when the whaler was sunk with all on board, by the fire of the Retribution.—She also captured and sent to Confederate ports, the brig Elliott, of Bucksport, Maine, and schooner Hanover, of Massachusetts. The Elliott was subsequently recaptured by the Yankees at St. Thomas.—The Retribution also captured and ran ashore on the Bahamas, the brig Emily Fisher, taking the crew prisoners to Nassau. The crew of the Retribution are all well, and would soon finish repairs and continue their cruise.

RICHMOND, March 2.—In the British Parliament, Earl Derby criticised the Queen's speech, and said he regretted that the government had not felt justified in joining the attempt in which they were invited by France, to intervene, not to put an end to the American war, but to obtain by their good offices, if possible, such an armistice and cessation of hostilities, as would lead the two parties themselves to reflect on the miseries and hopelessness of the war in which they were engaged. He differed from the opinion expressed by many of his political friends, that the time had not arrived for the recognition of the Southern States. His conviction was that come what may, a reconstruction of the Union was impossible, but on the whole he approved the course the Government had taken. (Cheers.)

Earl Russel, in reply, justified the policy which the Government had pursued, and expressed an opinion that it would be impossible for a union of the North and South to be again established.

Earl Malmsbury expressed his regret that Eng and had not joined France in the proposed mediation.

Earl Grey took the contrary view.

In the House of Commons, D'Israeli reviewed the ministerial programme, imputing vacillation and inconsistency to the government.

The Foreign Secretary said that the North was fighting for empire; the South for independence.

The President of the Board of Trade alledged that the curse of slavery was at the bottom of the war.

The Chancellor of the Exchequer was warmly in favor of the South, but was followed by the Secretary of War, who ...ed his opinions diametrically opposed the...

Lastly, the ... Secretary for Ireland, declared as his conviction that the Lord of Hosts was fighting for the Confederates.

Bentick said he believed if a proposal for the recognition of the South was brought forward, it would be supported by Parliament.

RICHMOND, March 2.—Northern dates of the 26th have been received. The bill to enroll and call out the militia, passed the House with an amendment—yeas 55, nays 43. Also, the Senate passed a bill authorizing the President to suspend the writ of Habeas Corpus—yeas 24, nays 13.

The N. Y. World says gold was furious on the 24th. It touched 75 premium, mostly heavy sales and generally from foreigners.

The steamer Jura, from Liverpool with dates of the 12th has arrived.

At the Lord Mayor's late banquet, Mr. Mason said he anticipated a speedy establishment of friendly relations between the British and Confederate Governments, and the declaration was received with much applause.

The Times says Mr. Mason is much too fast and misrepretents; the proceedings mean nothing.

The Confederate steamer Sumpter had escaped from Gibraltar, and the Tuscarora had sailed for Cadiz.

It was stated that the new steamer 290 was in the Mersey on the 5th, and expected to sail in a few days for the rebel rendezvous.

Cotton sales at Liverpool for the week 25,000 closing at a decline of a half penny. Breadstuffs dull.

RICHMOND, March 2—Gold advanced here to-day forty per cent., closing at three hundred premium as the market price.

In Senate, Mr. Oldham of Texas, from Committee of Commerce, reported back the joint resolution relative to the free navigation of the Mississippi river, with a substitute and preamble, which declares that it is a settled recognized rule of internation law, that the right of navigation for commercial purposes, a river, which flows from one State through the territory of another State into the sea, is common to all nations inhabiting the parts of its banks, &c.

SAVANNAH, March 3.—The enemy attacking Fort McAlister, commenced at 8:30 A. M., this morning, with three iron clads and two morters boats playing, on the Fort. Our eight-inch Columbiad was dismounted; two men slightly wounded. The firing contiues very heavy.

SAVANNAH, March 3—5:30 P. M.—A dispatch from Fort McAlister, dated 3:45 says one iron-clad has withdraw; two iron-clads and one mortar boat are still playing on the Fort. The Fort is uninjured. None hurt on our side, except the two slightly wounded early this morning. The garrison is in good spirits. Firing still continues at this time, 5:50 P. M.

RICHMOND, March 3—In the Senate, Mr. Semmes, of La. introduced a resolution of instruction to the Committee on Foreign Affairs to enquire into the expediency of repealing so much of the certain resolutions touching Martial Law, defining the position of the Confederate States in respect thereto, as declares that a neutral flag covers the enemy's goods with exceptions contraband of war—adopted.

MOBILE, March 3.—The Evening News has the following dated McMinnville, March 2d: Major Austin, of Morgan's Brigade, with 150 men, passed around Murfreesboro, destroying the Murfreeboro and Nashville railroad, tearing up the track and running a train of soldiers over the embankment.

The Louisville Journal reports Longstreet, Marshall and Forrest approaching Lexington.

KENTUCKY.—We fear the late news of a revolutionary movement in Kentucky in our favor may prove fallacious. A distinguished Kentuckian lately said to the editor of the Appeal.

"The Kentucky Legislature will fight ... proclamation with resolutions, and the Southern Confederacy with balls and bayonets."

And a recent letter from Kentucky says: ... aggerated. There are but few ... signs. Among the Union leaders, I see none of a revolution sentment. The Legislature will only feebly protest. The 20,000 troops said to be ordered out to resist Lincoln's proclamation, are under a last act of the Federal Congress. It is a bribe to officeholders and contractors. The action reported so far is by Democrats entirely, and they are wofully in a minority in the Legislature. The people are mainly right, but subjugated—enslave."

From our Coast.

The "News" says:

"We learn second handed that a schooner from a foreign port run into Sabine Pass, a night or two since, and got aground on the bar, when the blockaders sent out some launches to capture her, but our Magruder fleet was too quick for them, and not only saved the schooner, but drove the blockaders out of sight. The schooner is said to belong to Ennis & Co. of this city.

The following short letter gives our latest intelligence from Galveston. We regret to hear of another of our small vessels being captured.

"GALVESTON, March 14, 1863.

The sloop Miranda, which ran out of San Luis a day or two ago, with 54 bales of cotton on board, has been captured by one of the enemies gunboats and is now lying with the blockaders outside the bar."

Our Galveston correspondent sends us a letter dated yesterday, informing us that a flag of truce boat was sent to the blockaders yesterday with letters from Federal prisoners, and returned with N. Y. papers as late as the 5th ult., with which he was favored. The N. Y. Herald of the 15th contains the official report of the capture of the U. S. steamer Hatteras off Galveston.

GALVESTON, March 12, 1863.

EDS. NEWS:—The quiet monotony of this place was slightly disturbed this morning.

Four, some say five, shots were fired from the Brooklyn at a party of negroes at work on a new fortification a little to the north of Fort Scurry, which, I am told, will be named Fort Bankhead. None of them took effect, but one fell so near as to cause the negroes to throw away their spades and take to their heels for safety.

We did not reply, as the enemy kept out of the range of our guns.

FROM WASHINGTON.—The Cincinnati Enquirer says: "In the Federal Congress, Mr. Conway, an able Republican member from Kansas, in the course of a speech in favor of a cessation of hostilities, suggested the adoption of the following resolutions:

"*Resolved, by the Senate and House of Representatives, &c,*" That the Executive be, and he is hereby requested to issue a general order to all commanders of force the several military Departments of the U. S., to discontinue offensive operations against the enemy, and to act for the future entirely on the defensive.

Resolved, That the Executive be, and he is further requested to enter into negotiations with the authorities of the Confederate States with reference to a cessation of hostilities, based on the following propositions: 1st. Recognition of the independence of the Confederate States. 2d. A uniform system of duties upon imports. 3d. Free trade between the two States. 4th. Free navigation of the Mississippi River. 5th. Mutual adoption of the Monroe doctrine.

AUSTIN, March 13th, 1863.

HON. H. C. COOK—Sir—In reply to your note of the 7th inst., I would say that I am not a candidate for the office of Governor of this State and do not expect to be. Yet as I recognize the right of the public, or any portion of them, to call for the opinions of any citizen, I shall briefly give mine in regard to the questions which are involved in the approaching canvass.

I am utterly opposed to violations of the Constitution and the laws, and the usurpation of power by any officer, civil or military, State or Confederate. It is the duty of all good citizens to resist, without delay, encroachments upon their liberties, and not to permit those who invade and trample upon their rights to do so with impunity, and to plead a passive endurance of wrongs as a precedent to justify the further exercise of arbitrary power, and more flagrant infractions of the supreme law of the land.

All power is inherent in the people—they are supreme. They alone can establish and ordain constitutions, or forms of government. The powers of government are delegated by the people, and are held in trust for the people. Officers are only agents of the people, and derive the authority to exercise certain powers from the constitution and the laws made in pursuance thereof. Any officer who may transcend his authority and presume to exercise power not delegated, is, to the extent of his usurpation, a tyrant. He has betrayed his trust, violated his oath of office and of allegiance to the sovereign power—the people.—He can not offer in extenuation of the crime, that his motives were patriotic; that, in his opinion, the public good, and necessity, required his assumption of powers not vested by the constitution. These are the pleas of despots. They have been made to mislead almost every people who have lost their liberties.

The constitution is competent for all the purposes for which it was established and ordained. It is adequate to secure the people in the exercise and enjoyment of all their rights. Under its broad shield we have been, and will be, protected from all dangers which have assailed us, or may threaten us in the future. If this be not true, our government is a failure, and we are fighting for we know not what.

If the public good, and necessity, are the limitations of power, and the officers who exercise it are to be the judges of its extent, a constitution and laws would be useless. The will of officers would be the law.

The men who advocate these dangerous principles place themselves upon the platform of Seward and Lincoln. They tacitly admit the higher-law doctrine as true, and they justify the Black Republicans in all their inroads upon the constitution, and their outrages of every character, be ... have perpetrated all these enormities as measures dictated by necessity and vindicated by the public good.

We have proclaimed to the world that we are struggling for liberty, against violations of the constitution, and against usurpations of power. But, if this doctrine of necessity, of public good, that the end justifies the means, be correct, and we permit it to supersede and over-ride the constitution ... we are wrong. We must recall our ... fought are wholesale murders. ... right—ask his pardon, and submit to his rule."

The public good, in the ... never did require a violation of the constitution, and it never will.

It is never expedient to violate principle. Principle and expediency go hand in hand. It is a mistake to suppose they can be separated without the commission of error or crime.

Mr Calhoun has well said, there can be no liberty without a constitution. That instrument is the ark of freedom. It is the duty of every patriot to defend it against attacks from any quarter. But in protecting it from encroachments by our own officers the means of defense and redress must not be mistaken. They consist in holding the aggressor to a strict accountability in arraigning him before the tribunals of the country, in holding him up for the execration of an indignant people, and the various remedies known to those accustomed ... the workings of a democratic representative government.

There is no doubt but, that those who have withheld their services, and refused their support to the Confederate Government in the dark hours of peril would be pleased to institute other measures of pretended redress. To open wide the flood-gates of disorder, confusion, and violence, and to introduce anarchy would be to them a labor of love. Against the machinations and the insidious suggestions of these people we cannot be too watchful.

The Government at Richmond has given us no just cause of complaint. The infractions of the Constitution, the disregard of law, and the evils they have created and may inflict upon us, have had their origin from other sources. They have not weakened our confidence in our Government, nor our devotion to our cause. The man whose blood is so cold as not to appreciate the bond of love which unites us to our sister States, who from disapproval of the acts of subordinate officers, from disappointed ambition, or from any selfish motive, could counsel his countrymen to withdraw Texas from the Confederacy, or to prepare for a separation from a brotherhood endeared by so many glorious recollections, and common dangers, has no claims to patriotism which deserve the recognition of a generous and gallant people.

The defense of our frontier is entitled to a prominent place in the public mind. I have long believed, and acted on the belief when I could, that an aggressive policy is the only one which will force the Indians to sue for peace. They should be made to feel the iron hand of war upon their hunting-grounds, and within their lodges. Whip them and then talk of treaties. Cost what it may the pioneer settlers must be protected. It is the imperative duty of the State to do so. It matters not what motive carried them to the frontier. They had a right to go, and they are entitled to the fostering care of the Government.

I am, with great respect your ob'dt serv't,

JOHN S. FORD.

TAXES FOR 1862.—The Act postponing the collection of taxes, by levy and sale, until the 1st of August has been repealed; and the Assessors and Collectors may at any time after the 1st of March (inst) proceed to collect by levy and sale. There is no specie required in payment of taxes for the year 1862. And all the taxes collected during the present year, will be immediately applied to the support of Soldiers families. Hence the necessity of speedy collection. Let each and every one be prompt in paying their taxes forthwith; that the money may be distributed among or to the families of our brave citizens, who have left their homes, and are standing as a wall between us and our merciless invaders.

Special Correspondence of Texas Almanac Extra.

SAN ANTONIO, March 12th, 1863.

The application of the cotton portion of General Order 28 has created so much excitement here, that all other subjects are of secondary importance. The Government *sole agent to supply all the wants of the Department* has been buying goods and making payment in cotton, with the understanding that permits would be furnished for its exportation. But on the application of the vendors, to the officer in command here, they were referred to General Order 28, and informed that permits would not be issued on goods imported prior to the date of that order, and that previous orders, granting permits, were cancelled, therefore the importers of goods previous to the 22d of Feb, who had not taken out cotton *in accordance with the understood contract or permission* of our military rulers were now prohibited from doing so. The gentlemen on receiving this information appealed to the Government agent, who then, in person, applied for the permits, as promised by him in good faith, but he was told that he was not entitled to any more privileges than other individuals. So these gentlemen must duplicate their invoices before they will be permitted to export their cotton.

If a private individual, or company, had thus acted, our Grand Jury would have found a true bill for *obtaining goods under false pretences*, but as the offence is a "military necessity order," of course it is perfectly justifiable, and serves the merchants right for being such fools as to import goods *before this order was issued.*

Order No 28 authorises every person to take cotton to the Texas bank of the Rio Grande, there to remain until they import a sufficiency of merchandise, when permits for its exportation will be granted them, and if so fortunate as to get it across the river before a new *necessity order* be issued they may bless their stars, but if not they are fools, *for not foreseeing some new order and awaiting its issue.* But there is no great danger of many being thus caught. The alarm has become general, and a thorough want of confidence in "military necessity orders" is the result. A gentleman from Mexico, who has a large train of goods on the way to Texas, has despatched an express ordering it to turn back; and has also notified the Quartermaster that a lot of cloth, which he has sold to him under the provisions of the old order, and which has now arrived, he will not deliver. Letters from all parts of Mexico teem with denunciations of such a vacillating and faithless policy. And our own merchants, who, if permitted to act in good faith, untrammelled by the imbecile policy of "military necessity orders," would have filled the markets of Texas with goods, and met the wants of both civil and military, are aghast at such a stretch of military power, and it will be long before confidence is restored to that body of our citizens.

It would be superfluous for me to expatiate on the law governing commerce. That subject has been thoroughly discussed, and is pretty well understood by most readers, and if not by our military authorities it is the fault of the obtuseness of their brains. We have an able General commanding the Department of Texas, but unfortunately a greater than he rules in Arkansas, from whom emanates the wise mandates, a specimen of which ... we are already reaping ...

What is to be the result? Can any ... plain what object the Military D... this lawless course? Is it a want of common sense, or do they really suppose that such a course will lead to beneficial results? Or is it for the personal aggrandizement of a few? Under this order trade with Mexico, the only foreign market open to us, ceases, and what is much worse, though the order be cancelled, it will be long before confidence can be restored. We have a fair prospect for making bread this year, but we cannot clothe ... The Legislature endeavored, though unsuccessfully, to restrict them in the culture of cotton, but the result of order No. 28 will be to prohibit its export, and it is certainly a more thorough blockade than ever old Abe has yet effected.

PRIMO.

SAN ANTONIO, March 13th, 1863.

ED. TEXAS ALMANAC:—As we leave to-morrow for Corpus Christi, I will drop you the only *on dits* current here to-day—probably the last you will hear from me in San Antonio for a time—perhaps forever.

It is currently reported that Gen. Magruder has concluded to "*change his base*" and make San Antonio his general Headquarters. If the report is true, the manœuvre, of course, has a bearing on the illumining war-speck in the Western horizon, to which I alluded in my last. It is also rumored that a military expedition will shortly be organized in Texas for Arizona.

Tairty-five Mexicans belonging to a company quartered here, deserted on Monday last. Several horses belonging to citizens here turned up missing next morning. One would suppose our military authorities had long since had a display of the patriotism of this class of people sufficient to satisfy them. But comment is unnecessary.

Another attempt was made at lynching at the San Rose Mission last week, but was put a stop to by some citizens here.

Several persons here who took the alien oath to avoid conscription have been indited by the Grand Jury, but I understand that Judge Stribling has quashed the indictments without an exception, and bound the parties over to answer new indictments at the next term.

The spring is opening with fair agricultural prospects, notwithstanding the late cold weather.

CAISSON.

☞ We learn from Gen. Pearce, who has just arrived here, that Fox Hart, (nephew of Martin D. Hart, who was hung at Ft. Smith,) with 30 of his men, have been captured near Greenville, Hunt county. The refugees were found in the Journigan Thicket, from whence they had sent out some negroes, which they had stolen in Arkansas, on a foraging expedition, and were captured; and after the negroes were whipped, they gave information of the hiding place of Hart and party. Two boxes of Enfield rifles were also captured, and a large quantity of ammunition. Fox Hart was shot, and the remainder of this notorious party were sent to Little Rock, where we hope they will receive that j... due deserters and traitors to their coun...

☞ We are indebted to the Hon. W. S. Oldham for several late public documents from Richmond.

☞ A private letter from San Antonio, dated the 9th, says "there is great excitement here about the last cotton order. Parties refuse to sell, as they cannot export their cotton, and have ordered all goods stopped on the way that have not already crossed the river."

Here is Prentice's last joke: "A ram is an animal whose but is on the wrong end of him."

INDIANS.—A letter from Cora, Comanche county, dated Feb. 28th, and signed Aaron Cunningham, says "father, myself and two brothers, with some neighbors, discovered, pursued and overtook a party of Indians, going off with a small herd of horses. We killed one Indian, and took 13 head of horses. Two Indians escaped on horseback. Since then, several other parties of Indians have been in this county stealing horses, and scalps too, when they can get a chance."

☞ The editor of the "News" growls considerably at Cushing, of the "Telegraph," for not issuing his paper sooner, in order to give him the benefit of his Express enterprise, and intimates that he will give due credit for the privilege.

We presume Cushing is opposed to the *credit* system, and has, very justly, concluded to reap the benefit of his own enterprise, without regard to the wailings of his *cute* neighbor. Can't you arrange to let the old man in for two-and-a-half?

☞ Capt. Darnell, who arrived here on Sunday says he was informed by Mr. Carter, direct from Arkadelphia, that the Federals had again captured Arkansas Post. Mr. Carter says this news was consederes reliable at Arkadelphia when he left.

☞ Gen. Magruder is hourly expected in Austin.

☞ We are authorized to announce Gen. T. J. CHAMBERS as a candidate for the office of Governor of Texas.

AN ORDINANCE,

To suspend an Ordinance regulating the sale of Fresh Meats.

Be it ordained by the City Council of the City of Austin, That all ordinances or parts of ordinances prohibiting the sale or retail of fresh meats within the corporate limits of the city without license, be and the same are hereby suspended. That this ordinance take effect and be in force from and after its passage. Approved March 16, 1863.

S. G. HAYNIE, Mayor.

Attention! Tom Green Rifles!!

THE undersigned having been ordered to Texas, for the purpose of collecting and returning to duty such members of my company and regiment as may be fit for active service, all such are hereby ordered to report to me in Austin on or before the 1st April, prepared for an immediate return to their respective commands.

Those unfit for duty will report by Surgeon's certificate of disability. All failing to report in person or by such certificate *will be regarded and published as deserters.*

I am also authorized to receive and forward recruits for my own or any company in the Texas Brigade. All who may wish to join are earnestly requested to report to me at once, and they will be furnished with transportation.

T. W. MASTERSON,
mar17-1t* 2d Lt. Co. B., 4th Texas Inf't.

The Daily Bulletin.

VOL. VII.--NO. 1201.] CHARLOTTE, N. C., FRIDAY, MARCH 20, 1863. [$6 PER ANNUM.

THE BULLETIN:

BY EDWARD H. BRITTON.

SECOND EDITION.

BY TELEGRAPH.

Friday Morning, March 20, '63.

[TELEGRAPHED FOR THE ASSOCIATED PRESS.]

From Charleston, S. C.

CHARLESTON, March 19.

No signs of an attack this morning.

The weather is rough and threatening.

The Iron Screw Steamer *Georgian*, from Nassau, with a valuable cargo, including four Blakely guns, was chased ashore by the blockaders on Long Island beach, this morning, before day light and badly riddled by Yankee shot. The crew took to their boats and have reached the city.

The *Georgian* was owned by English parties.

Another Steamer In.

WILMINGTON, March 19.

An English Iron steamer arrived at a Confederate port this morning. She left Nassau on Sunday last at 3 p. m. All the steamers from this port had arrived out except the Denbo. She said she was captured by the Quaker City.

From the West.

MOBILE, March 19.

The Appeal of the 17th says reports of this morning from Port Hudson represent a serious outbreak in the Federal army, which, if correct probably accounts for the retrograde movement. Banks' army scouts report that several Yankee regiments had laid down their arms and were sent back. Another rumor says it was two regiments.

Gen. Rust's command had driven back a greatly superior force of the enemy.

The Tribune has the following dated, Panola the 18th:

The Federal marauders at Hernando, had destroyed the county records at that place; also, made a general jail delivery and had taken all the horses, mules and negroes in reach. They were attacked and routed by Blythe's battalion with a loss of several killed and wounded. Our loss one man wounded.

SECOND DISPATCH.

MOBILE, March 19.

The Appeal of the 17th says everything was quiet yesterday. No enemy in sight of Fort Pemberton.

The schooner Alino, Capt. Mitchell, arrived at a Confederate port to-day, bringing Havana dates of the 12th inst. The news is unimportant. The steamer Alice and schooner Relief had arrived at Havana.

Skirmish in Franklin.

We learn from an intelligent officer just from Weldon, (says the Raleigh *Progress* of the 19th inst.,) that a brisk skirmish took place at Franklin, on Friday, in which the Yankees were worsted. The enemy lost 4 killed, 9 wounded and 12 prisoners. Our loss was only 2 slightly wounded. A regiment of our troops ambushed the enemy and were upon them before they knew it. Our informant was not able to procure further particulars.

WOUNDED AND KILLED.—It takes but space in the columns of the daily papers; but, O! what long household stories and biographies are every one of those strange names that we read over and forget!

"Wounded and killed!" Some eye reads the name to whom it is dear as life, and some heart is struck or broken with the blow made by that name among the list.

It's *our* Henry, it's *our* John, or *our* James, or *our* Thomas, that lies with his poor broken limbs at the hospital, or worse still, with ghastly face on the battlefield.—Alas! for the eyes that read! alas! for the hearts that feel!

"He was my pretty boy, that I've sung to sleep on many times in my arms!" says the poor mother, bowing her head in anguish that cannot be uttered. "He was my brave, noble husband, the father of my little orphan children!" sobs the stricken wife. "He was my darling brother, that I loved so, that I was so proud of," murmurs the sister, amid her tears; and so the terrible stroke falls on homes throughout the land.

"Killed and wounded!" Every name in that list is a lightning stroke to some heart, and breaks like thunder over some house, and falls like a long black shadow upon some hearthstone.

A Queer Statement.

A private letter from Port Royal makes the following curious statement: "General Foster took a Captain and thirty men from the Tenth Connecticut, just before he went North, and made a reconnoisance. They entered Bull's Bay, North of Charleston harbor, and landing there marched through the enemy's pickets to within full sight of Charleston, and even to within view of Fort Sumter, at about a mile and three-quarters distant—so near that the officers from the parpet of the fort could see them. They returned unharmed, and think there is every reason to believe a successful attack can be made upon the Babylon of rebeldom from a quarter deemed inaccessible."

A GOOD WOMAN.—I account a pure, intelligent and well bred woman the most attractive of vision and contemplation in the world. As mother, sister, and wife, such a woman is an angel of grace and goodness, and makes heaven of the home which is sanctified and glorified by her presence. As an element of society she invites into finest demonstrations all that is good in the heart, and shames into secrecy and silence all that is unbecoming and despicable. There may be more of greatness and of glory in the higher developments of manhood; but, surely, in womanhood God most delights to show the beauty of holiness, and the sweetness of the love of which He is the infinite source. It is for this reason a silly young woman, or a vicious one, makes me sigh or shoulder. It is for this reason that I pray that I may write worthily to young woman.—*Timothy Titcomb.*

Reports from Baton Rouge represent that there are numerous indications of an immediate movement, and that great activity prevails in the army.

The gunboat Itasca had arrived at New Orleans. She reports that the Harriet Lane was lying up near Galveston, and was being converted into an iron clad.

Gold in New York, on the 3d, closed at 171; exchange 188 to 189.

The New York Herald says the comments of the London press on the Charleston blockade will teach the rebels what British sympathy is worth.

The Herald hears gratifying reports of the improved condition of the army of the Potomac, and says it will soon move forward.

A Washington correspondent, in noting the last hours of Congress, says money was voted with prodigality and everybody seemed jolly.

"HOW PONTOON BRIDGES ARE MADE.—Pontoon boats are flat-bottomed, thirty feet long, two and a half feet wide at the bow, and five feet wide at the stern, swelling out at the sides to the width of six feet. Each fits on a running gear of four wheels, and is used as a baggage wagon for the pontooners, carrying its proportion of string pieces of plank. On reaching a river the boats are unloaded, floated across by a cable made fast up the stream, then the string pieces are laid across from one boat to the next, and on these are placed the planks, each twenty-one feet long, which form the gangway of that width.

ATTEMPT TO DESTROY ORDNANCE STORES BY FIRE. ONE HUNDRED HORSES, INCLUDING THOSE OF GEN. VAN DORN AND STAFF WERE BURNED.—COLUMBIA, TENN., March 15.—Last night a livery stable adjoining the ordnance stores was set on fire by an incendiary, it is supposed with the intention of destroying our ordnance. About one hundred horses, including those of Gen. Van Dorn and his staff, were burned. Three dwelling houses adjoining the stable were destroyed. The enemy have retired to Franklin.—*Special to the Savannah Republican.*

BEECH TREE LEAVES.—The leaves of the beech tree, collected at autum, in dry weather, form an admirable article for filling beds. The smell is grateful and wholesome, they do not harbor vermin, are very elastic, and may be replenished annually without cost.

☞ Gen. Beauregard, as previously announced, reviewed the Citadel Cadet corps, in Charleston, on Saturday, at the Green. He afterwards examined the quarters of the corps, and expressed himself highly pleased with all he saw.

☞ "Whose pigs are those, my lad?" "Whoy, they belong to that there big sow." "Now, I mean, who is their master?" "Whoy," again answered the lad, "that little 'un—he's a rare 'un to fight!"

A CHASE AFTER THE ALABAMA.—The steamer *Rhode Island*, one of the fastest vessels in Yankee service, reports that she chased, on the 2d ult., about 300 miles North of Abaco, a strange craft, supposed to be the English priate *Alabama*. The Department thinks most likely that she was the *Oreto*.

SCHOOL BOOKS.—We have just received a large lot of School Books at this office, and can now supply orders for the Child's Primer, Spelling Book, 1st, 2d and 3d Readers, and for the Primary Grammar.

[*Salisbury Watchman.*

☞ A youngster from the country was walking along, and upon seeing a lawyer's office, walked in and inquired, "What do you keep to sell here?" "Blockheads," replied the lawyer. "Pretty good business," said the chap, "I see you have got only one left."

SIGNIFICANT.—The Tammany Hall Democracy have invited the members of the Frankfort Convention to meet in New York and hold their Convention there, pledging protection to the Convention during its deliberations.

☞ When we are chastened by God, we should do as children and servants do when they are whipped—run up close.—He can't hurt us much then.

☞ A crusty old bachelor says, the talk of women is usually about the men. Even their laugh is but "he! he!"

☞ Planters, look to your hog-pens. A distinguished author says "the pen is mightier than the sword."

SAM'L J. LOWRIE
Attorney at Law
CHARLOTTE, N. C.

☞ Office in Brawley Building, opposite Kerrs Hotel.
Feb. 18, 1863 ly*

MERCHANT TAILORING.

THE undersigned having located two doors South of the MANSION HOUSE, Charlotte, N. C., is prepared to fill all orders in his line of business, such as Military and Citizens Clothing, Oars, Laces, Buttons, &c., &c.

A liberal share of the patronage of the public is respectfully solicited, as I also desire trusted to my care will be promptly and faithfully filled. I have competent workmen, and can compete with any other establishment in giving a "good fit," and I warrant my work to give entire satisfaction.

Mr. R. M. ROBINSON, an experienced cutter, is engaged in this establishment, and he will be pleased to wait upon his friends.

J. A. CALDWELL.
March 18, 1863—d

BREAKFAST AND SUPPER HOUSE,
CHARLOTTE, N. C.
(OPPOSITE RAIL ROAD SHED.)
RIGHT HAND SIDE GOING NORTH,
LEFT HAND SIDE GOING SOUTH.

☞ Passengers taking meals at this House will travel in Omnibus free.
H. P. ACKERMAN, Proprietor.
March 19, 1863—d1m

NORTH CAROLINA POWDER MANUFACTURING COMPANY.

The Mills of this Company, located 12 miles West of Charlotte upon the Catawba River, are now in full operation with a good supply of material. All orders from any section of the Southern Confederacy for fine rifle and sporting Powder, as also orders from Rail Road Contractors, Miners and others for Blasting Powder will be promptly filled.

Address Charlotte, N. C.,
S. W. DAVIS, Prest.
March 10, 1863—dtf

☞ The following papers will please copy the above advertisement for one month and send bills to this office:

Fayetteville Observer, Greensboro' Patriot, Asheville News, Petersburg Express, Lynchburg Republican, Knoxville Register, Chattanooga Rebel, Augusta Constitutionist, Montgomery Mail, Mobile Advertiser & Register, Daily Southern Crisis, Columbia Carolinian, Charleston Courier.

NOTICE.

HEAD QUARTERS, 48TH N. C. REGT., Pocotaligo, S. C., March 4th, 1863.

Relatives of Soldiers deceased, in this Regiment, are notified that the necessary papers have been adjusted and forwarded to W. H. S. Taylor, Second Auditor C. S. Treasury, Richmond, Va., who will forward the amount due by mail to the claimant who will forward to him by mail the proper papers to prove in each case that the claimant is the legal representative of the deceased.

By command of Col. R. C. Hill,
J R. WINCHESTER,
1st Lt. and Act'g Adj't.
March 7, 1863—d10t

☞ The Iredell Express and Raleigh Standard copy 10 times and forward bills to Capt. L. C. Hanes, A. Q. M., 48th N. C Regt.

J. S. PHILLIPS,
Merchant Tailor.

HAVING located in Charlotte respectfully solicits a share of public patronage.

A complete assortment of Cloths, Cassimers and Vestings always on hand, which will be made to order at the shortest notice, after the latest fashion.

Shop three doors South of the Mansion House.
sept. 19 tf

PROSPECTUS
OF THE
RALEIGH STATE JOURNAL.

ON and after the 1st day of November next, the STATE JOURNAL will be published DAILY, TRI-WEEKLY AND WEEKLY.

The DAILY STATE JOURNAL will contain all the news received up to the latest hour before mailing, and will consist of TWO EDITIONS DAILY. The MORNING EDITION will contain the news by the evening mail, and all TELEGRAPHIC NEWS up to 12 o'clock the previous night, and will be supplied to city subscribers and sent by the mails North and East; the EVENING EDITION will be printed at 3 o'clock, p. m., and will contain the additional news by Telegraph up to 3 o'clock, p. m., and will be sent to subscribers by the trains West and by the Fayetteville mail. Thus subscribers, no matter in what direction they may live, will have the news up to the departure of the mails.

Arrangements have been made to procure TELEGRAPH NEWS FROM ALL PARTS OF THE CONFEDERACY, expressly for the State Journal. GENERAL NEWS BY MAIL will be promptly published. The MARKETS will be fully reported. RELIABLE CORRESPONDENTS will be secured in the Army and elsewhere. The LEGISLATIVE PROCEEDINGS will be reported daily by competent Reporters. The STATE JOURNAL will be essentially a NEWSPAPER.

TERMS:

For the DAILY—12 months, $6; 6 months, $3.50; 3 months, $2; 1 month, $1.

For the TRI-WEEKLY—12 months, $4; 6 months, $2.50; 3 months, $1.50.

For the WEEKLY—12 months, $2; 6 months $1.50.

ADVERTISING RATES.

1 square,	1 day,...$0.50	1 square,	5 days,..$1.50		
1 do	2 days,...0.75	1 square,	1 week,...1.75		
1 do	3 days,...1.00	1 do	2 weeks,..3.00		
1 do	4 days,...1.25	1 do	1 month...5.00		

Ten lines make a square.

☞ Advertisements for the Daily will be inserted in the Tri-Weekly FREE OF CHARGE. This is an inducement which cannot fail to attract the attention of Advertisers.

The above rates apply only to the daily paper. Advertisements will be inserted in the Weekly paper at the usual regular rates, viz: One dollar per square for the first insertion, and twenty-five cents for each subsequent insertion.

Address, JNO. SPELLMAN,
Editor and Proprietor,
Oct 17, 1862—tf Raleigh, N

TO THE LADIES.
NEW PARIS STYLES!!—NEW PARIS STYLES!!!

WE would call the particular attention of the Ladies to our MILLINERY DEPARTMENT, which is presenting a great variety of attractive styles. Our Bonnet Frames are of the latest and most approved Paris styles, *Our Own Importation*. Our stock of Materials is the largest and best assorted and selected in the Confederacy.

The whole department is under the immediate supervision of our Head Milliner, Miss Kerr, late of Charleston, a lady of acknowledged refined taste; the press of business in the line has compelled us to make an addition to our force of Milliners and we have been most fortunate in the selection of Miss Hogan—also of Charleston. Having now, such a fine stock and so large a force to work it up we will be enabled to fill any order with dispatch.

KAHNWEILER & BRO.
Charlotte, Nov. 25 '62—tf

MILLINERY GOODS.

Received per Steamer—from—
Ladies English STRAW BONNETS.
Donstable and Split Straw Hats.
Misses and Ladies Nymph Hats.
Misses and Ladies Isabella Hats.
Misses and Ladies Catharine Hats.
Misses and Ladies Sylph Hats.
Misses and Ladies Westend riding Hats.
Misses and Ladies Jockey and Zouave Hats.
Boys English Straw Hats.
Just received and for sale at the fashionable Bazaar of
KAHNWEILER & BROS.
August 23, '62—tf

Family Flour for Sale.

AT the Charlotte Flouring Mills can be had Family, Superfine and fine FLOUR, SECONDS, SHORTS and BRAN. [illegible] MEAL and GRIST.
JOHN WILKES.

Removal.

THE subscriber begs to inform the public that he has removed to No. 1 GRANITE ROW, where he is prepared with a fell stock of
GOODS FOR MENS WEAR,
To supply all who may favor him with a call. Having secured the services of one of the best Cutters in the South, he feels satisfied that he can please the most fastidious.
Dec. 9—tf [illegible]

Information for Jewellers.

A practical Jeweller and Watchmaker, from Geneva, Switzerland, established since two years, but now short of material, and wishing to go further South, would enter into some arrangements with a person in need of an experienced and reliable partner. References offered.

Address ED. F., (Jeweller,) Henderson, Granville county, N. C.
March 7, 1863—6*

CORN! CORN!
FLAX SEED! FLAX SEED!

We will exchange CORN for FLAX SEED—will give two bushels of Corn for one bushel of Flax Seed, in any quantity, both to be delivered at Statesville. Or, we will pay the highest market price for Flax Seed, in money. Bring on your Flax Seed and get corn or money for them. Persons having large parcels to sell, will let us know.

E B. DRAKE & SON,
Feb 27—d&w2m* Statesville, N. C

TO STOCK RAISERS.
BLACK HAWK MORGAN.

Any person wishing to raise fine stock will find this HORSE, during the Spring season, at the stable of A. B. Davidson, Esq., Mondays, Tuesdays and Wednesdays, and the remainder of the week at the stable of the subscriber, in Gaston Co. Season commencing 9th March.

PRICE—$15 a leap; $20 per season. Insurance $40.

Mares will be kept at 50c per day.

All care will be taken to prevent accidents, but the subscriber will not be responsible for them.

All persons parting with mares will be held responsible for the insurance.

J. S. DAVIDSON.
Mch. 12, '63-tf
☞ Democrat please copy.

ATLANTIC, TENN. & OHIO RAIL ROAD.

THE TRAINS on this Road will, on and after Monday next, leave 3rd Creek, (head of Road,) at 5:30, A. M., and return to that Station 15 minutes later than at present.

E. HURLBERT, Gen'l Supt.
Oct. 8, 1862—tf

FARM HANDS WANTED.

Two able bodied NEGRO MEN, accustomed to farming, are wanted for the balance of the year. Apply at this office.
March 10—6t.*

NOTICE.

GUINEA STATION, Va., Feb. 14, 1863.

SICK and Wounded members of Company "I," 14th Regiment N. C. T., will bear in mind that no one save Army Surgeons have a right to extend furloughs.

By order of THOS B. BEALL,
Feb 23—18t [illegible]

JAMES G. BAILIE & BRO.

OFFER FOR SALE AT THEIR
CARPET AND OIL CLOTH
WARE ROOMS
205 BROAD STREET
AUGUSTA, GA.,

A full assortment of the following Goods:

ENGLISH, VELVET & MEDALLIAN CARPETINGS,
ENGLISH BRUSSELS AND TAPESTRY CARPETINGS,
ENGLISH VENICIAN CARPETINGS,
HEARTH RUGS,
DOOR MATS,
CARPET BINDINGS,
CARPET TACKS,
STAIR CARPETINGS AND STAIR RODS,
COCOA MATTINGS AND HASSOCKS
WHITE & RED CHECK'D INDIA MATTINGS,
WINDOW SHADES, in all sizes, and TRIMMINGS,
FLOOR OIL CLOTHS, from 3 to 18 feet wide.
CURTAIN DAMASKS and SATIN DELAINES,
LACE AND MUSLIN CURTAINS AND BANDS, WINDOW CORNICES, LOOPS, TASSELS, GIMP, &C.,
WALL PAPER, BORDERS, FIRE SCREENS, a Full Supply of CORN BROOMS AND WATER BUCKETS.

☞ Fourteen Fine Pianos in Chickering, Hasseltin's, Gilbert's, Gales', Fisher's, Nuns & Clark's, and other good Makers.

FOR SALE BY
JAMES G. BAILIE & BRO.,
Dec. 9 '62—3m* Augusta, Ga.

CONCORD CLASSICAL
AND
SCIENTIFIC SCHOOL,
CONCORD, N. C.
S. FRONTIS, JR., PRINCIPAL.

THIS SCHOOL will be open for the reception of pupils on Monday, 9th of March, 1863.

RATES OF TUITION PER TERM OF 21 WEEKS:

English course with 1st, 2nd and 3rd Arithmetics,	$16 00
Scientific course with Algebra and French,	20 00
Classical couse with higher mathematics,	25 00
Incidental Tax, (each pupil,)	2 00

For further particulars address the Principal, Concord, N. C.
March 2, 1863—6t*

A. W. ALEXANDER,
DENTIST.

Offers his professional services to the public. He is prepared to execute all operations belonging to Dentistry.

Office opposite Kerr's Hotel, in Brawly Building, 2d floor, North corner room.

I take pleasure in recommending Dr. Alexander, to my patrons. Having confidence in his skill, I have authorized him to operate on the teeth of my own Family.

Feb. 26-dtf. E. H. ANDREWS.

MORE NEW GOODS.

50 dozen Linen Cambric HANKERCHIEFS just received and for sale at
KAHNWEILER & BRO.
Feb 27, 1863—tf

BLACK ALPACCA.

A splendid article, just to hand at
KAHNWEILER & BRO.
Feb 27, 1863—tf

NEW GOODS.

The undersigned have just received and opened a new and beautiful assortment of

Spring and Summer Prints

of the latest styles. Also

BLACK AND WHITE CALICOES
AND
Mourning Mouslin.

Also a few dozens

Pure Olive Oil.

Call and purchase at
KAHNWEILER & BROS.
Feb 23, 1863—tf

COMMERCIAL.

The trading community will find with us all the articles in the GROCERY business now in the market.

We are also manufacturing by the case SHOES of superior quality and workmanship, and being in the regular Commission Business all matters entrusted to us shall be promptly attended to.

WILLIAMS & GRAY.
Charlotte, Feb 18, 1863—tf

WANTED.

Immediate employment will be given to eight or ten good, sober and industrious hands to work in the North Carolina Powder Mills.

S. W. DAVIS, Pres.
Feb 26, '63 tf

APPEAL TO THE CHARITABLE.

The funds for the support of the Charlotte Wayside Hospital are exhausted. The Institution has been sustained during the past year under the supervision of the Board of Commissioners of the Town by donations from our citizens. During this time many sick and wounded soldiers have been taken care of and it is the desire of the Board still to offer aid to our suffering soldiers if our community will aid.

Contributions for the Hospital will be received at the Branch Bank.

THOS. W. DEWEY,
Jan 1, 1863—tf Town Treas.

BLACK ALPACCA.

Just received a superior lot of the above desirable Goods for ladies dresses, which will be sold at a very small advance on cost.

J. S. PHILLIPS.
Feb 16, '63—d1m

NEW GOODS.

JUST RECEIVED AND WILL BE
MADE TO ORDER
OR
SOLD BY THE YARD

Super. West of England Black Cloths,
Satin Finished Black Doeskin Cassimeres,
English Grey Cloths, a fine Article for Confederate
UNIFORMS.
ALSO,
Confederate Staff Buttons.

BY J. S. PHILLIPS.
Feb 14, 1863—d1w2&w4t

L. T. LEVIN,
Commission Merchant,
SELLS ALL KINDS OF COUNTRY PRODUCE.
COLUMBIA, S. C.
March 14, 1862 1y

The Daily Evening Gazette.
PROSPECTUS.

ON MONDAY, the second day of March, the undersigned will commence the above named paper, to be issued every afternoon, (Sundays excepted,) at 5 o'clock. It will contain four pages of reading matter and advertisements. The reading will contain the Army Correspondence, Telegraphic Communications, Summary of War News, City Items and Literary Contributions, &c., &c.

Our object in thus adding another daily is to supply the great demand, so long felt, for a medium of news for the evening.

Advertisements per square	$1 00
Each subsequent insertion	50
Subscriptions, per annum	10 00
" six months	6 00
" three months	4 00
" one month	1 50

Dealers supplied at a reasonable discount.

All communications addressed to M. A. MALSBY, Richmond, Va.

☞ Office corner of Main and 14th streets, over E. A. Myers' Jewelry store.

☞ All papers desiring to exchange will please forward their address to the proprietor of the Gazette. Feb 26—tf

ELEGANT SHOES FOR SALE.

Very neat French Calf BOOTEES for Ladies.
Pegged Calf Bootees, (light) for Ladies.
Pegged Goat Skin Bootees for Ladies.
Gent's High Cut Scotch, neatly made.
Elegant pegged and sewed BROGANS, double sole.
A fresh arrival of Shoe PEGS, to sell by the quart, sizes 4 8, 5 8, 6-8 and 7-8.
Also, a lot of SHOE KNIVES.

JNO. F. BUTT.
Mint Street, Charlotte, N. C.
Feb 13, 1863—dtf

CHARLOTTE & S. C. RAILROAD

WANTED to hire, FIVE SLAVES for the Charlotte & S. C. Railroad Company.

A. H. MARTIN, Agent.
Feb. 18, 1863—tf

IMPERIAL TEA.

A small quantity of this most delicious Green Tea for sale by the single pound at
Jan 17-dtf. THE BOOK STORE.

Atlantic, Tenn. & O. R. R.

Prepayment must be made on all Freights going up this Road at this point, when not paid south of this.

JAS. DANIEL, Agent.
Feb 18, 1863—tf

NOTICE.

All persons indebted to Fullings & Springs, by note or account, are hereby notified to call upon Wm. M. Grier, Ex-Sheriff, and make immediate settlement.

J. M. SPRINGS.
Jan 29, 1863—tf

AT PRIVATE SALE.

Two large Store-rooms and one Dwelling House with five rooms, all located near the centre of the town.

Apply at the Branch Bank of North Carolina Sept. 23, 62—dtf.

STENHOUSE & MACAULAY,
Commission Merchants,
At their Old Stand, Trade Street.

Keep constantly on hand a well selected Stock of Family Groceries.

All orders for Flour, Corn, Bacon, &c., promptly and carefully filled.

Factories supplied with Cotton, on commission of 50 cents per bale.

J. E. STENHOUSE,
ALLEN MACAULAY.
Charlotte, N. C., May 3, 1862—1y

TO RENT.

That handsomely fitted up Store, known as China Hall, one of the best locations in Charlotte may be rented the ensuing year. For terms, &c., apply to Dr. HAYS.
Dec. 25, '62—tf.

FLOUR MILL
FOR SALE.

The subscriber having entered into a contract for building the Rail-Road from Danville to Greensboro, is desirous of devoting his whole time to that work, and offers his STEAM MILL for sale. The property is situated in the town of Charlotte, on the North Carolina Rail Road has six run of Mill Stones and the Flour manufactured has a high reputation throughout the Southern Confederacy.

It has also a Barrel Factory, with improved Machinery, and Cooper shops attached, which will be sold with the Mill or separately.

JOHN WILKES.
August 23, '62—tf.

Wheat and Corn Wanted.

THE planting community will take notice that their Wheat and Corn Crops will be purchased at the Charlotte Steam Flouring Mill, at market prices. Those having Wheat and Corn for sale may find it to their advantage to call at the Mill before closing a sale.

JOHN WILKES & CO
Charlotte Flour Mill
aug 1, 1860-1y

WANTED

[illegible] lbs. good soft SOAP, for which the cash will be paid, either in Charlotte or at the Factory.
[illegible] T. & TATE.

COTTON SCREW.

An person competent to Erect a Cotton Screw can get immediate employment by calling on

WILLIAMS, OATES & Co.
March 3, '63 [illegible]
☞ Democrat and *Whig* copy 3 times.

NOTICE.

All Freight charges not advanced within the last two months, will be increased 25 per centum on the Charlotte & South Carolina and Atlantic, Tennessee & Ohio R. R. on and after the 6th instant. An agents will act accordingly.

WM. JOHNSTON, Pres't.
Oct. 8, 1862—tf

TOWN LOTS FOR SALE.

FOUR LOTS on Church street. Two of them improved. Terms reasonable.—They bring good rent and are convenient to business. Apply soon to

SAML. P. SMITH.
Feb 24, 1863—1m*

WILLIAMS & OATES

have this day associated with them in the *Merchantile and Commission business,*
LEWIS W. SANDERS.

The style of the firm will hereafter be
WILLIAMS OATES & Co.

All persons indebted to the late firm of Williams & Oates will please call and settle up, as we wish to close our old business.

WILLIAMS & OATES.
Dec. 2-tf.

WANTED.

Wanted, at the Medical Purveyor's Office, Charlotte, a large quantity of BOTTLES and VIALS, for which the highest prices will be paid.

JAS. T. JOHNSON,
Jan 24—tf Surg. & Med. Pur.

SUPERIOR SEWING SILK.

The subscriber has just received an invoice of the very best ITALIAN SEWING SILK, which he offers to the public at 12½ cents per skein.

J. S. PHILLIPS.
Feb 14, 1863—dtf

WANTED,

At the North Carolina Powder Mills, 10,000 White Oak and Chesnut STAVES of the following dimentions: 4½ inches wide by 2 inches thick and 36 inches long.

S. W. DAVIS, Pres.
Charlotte, N. C., Nov 17, 1862—tf

BONDS FOR SALE.

North Carolina 6 per cent. and Confederate 8 per cent. Bonds for sale at the Bank of Charlotte.
Feb, 7, 1863—dtf

PAINTERS' INK MANUFACTURED
BY
B. A. RANDALL & CO.,
MARIETTA, GEORGIA.

BOOK, NEWS AND COLORED INKS.

Of an excellent quality, and warranted equal to the best Northern make.

BOOK INK at 50 cents to $4 per lb., in cans of 1 to 10 pounds.

NEWS INK, (fine) at 30 cents per lb. for all orders of 100 pounds and upwards.

NEWS INK, (very fine) at 40 cents per lb., in kegs of 25 and 50 pounds.

COLORED INKS at $1 to $8 per lb., in half pound and pound cans.

☞ Every paper inserting this advertisement for one month and sending us a copy of their paper, will receive pay for the same upon purchasing three times the amount of their bill from us.

mch 22 '62—1m A. B. R. & CO.

WANTED TO HIRE.

Five hands to work on Statesville Railroad and ten for the C. & S. C. Rail Road for three months or longer.

WM. JOHNSTON, Pres't.
Sept. 15, 1862—tf.

CHARLOTTE DRUG STORE.
E. NYE HUTCHISON & Co.

RETAIL DEALERS IN FOREIGN AND DOMESTIC DRUGS, Medicines, Chemicals Perfumery, Fancy Articles, Oils, Paints, Varnishes, Window Glass, Putty, Dye Stuffs, Turpentine Burning Fluid, Alcohol, Pure Liquors, Garden Seeds, Field and Garden Seeds, &c., &c.

Having closed our books, we intend to sell hereafter for cash. [May 4, 1861-tf

ATLANTIC, TENN. & OHIO RAIL ROAD.

At a meeting of the Directors of the Atlantic, Tennessee & Ohio Rail Road Company on the 15th instant, the following resolutions were adopted:

Resolved, That all subscriptions of Stock heretofore made to the Atlantic, Tennessee & Ohio Rail Road Company, on which three or more installments have been paid, and on which default has been made to pay the balance due, are hereby declared forfeited to the use and benefit of the Company, including all payments made on the same, according to the provisions of the Charter, provided all arrearages on said Stock are not paid by the 15th of October next.

Resolved, That suit be instituted against all other solvent and delinquent Stockholders failing to make payment by the 1st of October next.

Resolved, That the reduced rates for passengers returning same day are hereby abolished.

M. L. WRISTON, Treasurer.
Sept. 15, 1862—tf

Charlotte Foundry
And Machine Shop.

HAVING purchased from J. A. Fox the above establishment, the undersigned begs leave to call the attention of the public to the fact that he is now ready to fill every order for making Steam Engines, Cotton and Tobacco Presses, and every description of Machinery. All kinds of Castings in Iron, Brass and other metals made at short notice and reduced prices. Particular attention given to the making and repairing of Threshing Machines, Horse Powers, Cotton Gins, Mill Works and Agricultural Work of all kinds. Blacksmithing, Job, Wagon Work, and Horse-Shoeing done with dispatch. Old Iron, Brass and Copper Castings bought at the Foundry or taken in exchange for job work. All kinds of Wood Turning also done.

dec [illegible] JOHN M. HOWIE

NOTICE.
OFFICE OF N. C. R. R. CO.,
COMPANY SHOPS, Sept. 24, 1862.

Notice is hereby given to shippers and others interested that the tariff of freight rates on this Road will be raised twenty-five per cent, and the rates on passengers to five cents per mile, on and after the first day of October.

T. J. SUMNER, Eng'r & Supt.
Sept 26, 1862—tf

PALMETTO
IRON WORKS.
COLUMBIA, S. C.
WILLIAM GLAZE, Proprietor.
GEORGE A. SHIELDS, Foreman.

MANUFACTURES STEAM ENGINES of any power desired, for Mills and Plantation purposes, at short notice, having at all times on hand some finished, or in a forward state. In connection with our Mill and Engine Work, we have secured the services of Mr. JOHN CRABTREE, who is one of the best Millwrights in the South, to superintend the putting up of Mills and Engines.

CORN MILLS.

I am agent for one of the best PORTIBLE MILLS now in use, and can furnish any size wanted. Persons wishing the Mills are invited to call at the Works, and witness the operation of the one now in use. The Mill-rack, which is the very best, is procured from Edgefield, S. C., and the Mills are built complete at our Establishment.

BRASS AND IRON CASTINGS.

All descriptions of BRASS and IRON CASTINGS executed in the very best manner, and at short notice, as we cast every day in the week. Our stock of patterns is very large, having recently purchased all those formerly owned by G. W. Wright, which being added to those made at my Establishment for the past five years, makes the assortment more full than any other like establishment in the State.

CIRCULAR SAWS.

I am agent for R. Hoe & Co's celebrated CIRCULAR SAWS, and also for a manufacturer of the same article in Richmond, Va. A full supply of these SAWS, of all sizes, always on hand. Persons wishing them, will do well to call on me, as I make no charge for fitting them to the mandrels.

OLD SAWS RE-TOOTHED.

I have a GUMMING MACHINE on hand, and am prepared to re-tooth old saws, making them as good as new.

Wire Railing.

I am agent for one of the largest Wire Railing Companies at the North, and will furnish WINDOW GUARDS, GALLERIES, VERANDAHS, BEDSTEADS, or any description of Wire Work, at the book prices of the manufacturer, which can be seen at my office.

dec 11, 1860—tf WILLIAM GLAZE.

PROSPECTUS
OF THE
STATE JOURNAL.

HAVING become the proprietor of the *Democratic Press*, I have merged that paper into the STATE JOURNAL, which will be published Semi-Weekly and Weekly.

The STATE JOURNAL will advocate Democratic principles in the broadest sense, and will support and defend Democratic measures and their advocates as they are presented, and as occasion may require. In other essentials it will be my aim to make the paper, what its name denotes, a State Journal—eschewing all sectional considerations and working for the entire State and her common interests.

As soon as arrangements can be made, the whole paper shall be re-modeled and printed with new type, on good paper, and in a superior manner.

The Editorial department will be properly attended to in its various branches, and will speak for itself. Neither labor nor expense will be spared in the management of the paper.

The *terms* of the State Journal will be as follows:

Semi-Weekly, per annum....................$400
Weekly....................200

These terms will be insisted upon *invariably in advance*. No name will be put upon the list without the money, and all papers will be discontinued at the expiration of the time for which they have been paid, unless the subscription be renewed. I am satisfied, from years of experience, that upon no other footing can any newspaper hope to succeed.

Advertisements of a proper character will be inserted at the following rates:

One square, first insertion....................$100
Each subsequent insertion....................25 cents.

A liberal deduction on these rates for yearly advertisers in the Semi-Weekly. In the Weekly edition the full rates will be charged.

JOHN SPELMAN,
Nov. 27, 1860. Editor and Proprietor.

THE WEEKLY CONFEDERATE NEWS.

VOL. XII. JEFFERSON, TEXAS: SATURDAY, MARCH 28, 1863. NO. 1

Albert Pike's Letter addressed to Major General Holmes.

LITTLE ROCK, ARKANSAS,
December 30, 1862.

SIR:—My letters, in respectful terms, addressed to yonr Adjutant General, when I re-assumed command of the Indian Country, late in October, have not been fortunate enough to be honored with a reply. This will reach you through another medium, and so that others besides yourself shall know its contents. I am no longer an officer under you, but a private citizen, and FREE, so far as any citizen of Arkansas can call himself free while he lives in this State; and I will see whether you are as impervious to all other considerations, as you are to all sense of courtesy and justice.

You were sent out to Arkansas with certain positive orders, which you were immediately to enforce. You knew that "Gen. Hindman never was the commanding General of the Trans. Mississippi Department," and was not sent there by the War Department; and that, therefore and of course, all his orders were illegal, for want of power. You knew that he never had any right to interfere with my command in the Department of Indian Territory, to take away my troops and ordinance, or to send me any orders whatever; and that therefore I was wholly in the right, in all my controversy with him. You knew, also, that in stripping the Indian Country of troops, artillery, arms and ammunition, he had been guilty of multiplied outrages, contrary to the will and policy of the President, forbidden by the Secretary of War for the future, and hostile to the interests of the Confederacy.

I had been advised by the Secretary of War, on the 14th of July, before you were unfortunately thought of in connection with the Trans. Mississippi Department, that Gen. Magruder was assigned to the command of it; and that although I would be under his command, it was not doubted that my relations with him would be pleasant and harmonious, and that I would have such latitude in command of the Indian country, as might be necessary for me to act to the best advantage in its defence. And by the same letter I was advised, that it was regretted I had met with so many embarrassments in procuring supplies; and that an order had been issued from the Adjutant and Inspector General's Office, to prevent the pursuing of such courses as I had complained of, in the seizure of what I had procured; and the Secretary said it was to be hoped that neither I nor any other officer would hereafter have cause to complain of supplies being diverted from their legitimate destination. And that Gen. Magruder might fully understand my position, &c., a copy of my letter of 8th June, to General Hindman, stating in detail the plundering process to which the Indian Service had before then been subjected, was furnished to the former officer. Three several copies of this letter were sent me, that it might be certain to reach me.

I do not repeat the substance of that letter, for your benefit. You have known it, no doubt, ever since you left Richmond. You told me in August, that the War Department was fully informed in regard to the matters between myself and Generals Van Dorn and Hindman. You spoke it in the way of a taunt, and as if the Department justified them and condemmed me. You meant me so to understand it. You are a very ingenuous person; inasmuch as you knew the exact contrary to be true. When I afterwards received the Secretary's letter, I remembered your remark, and did not doubt, and do not doubt, that when you were substituted for Gen. Magruder, you received the same instructions that had been given him, and were yourself furnished with a copy of the same letter, for the same purpose.

At all events, you were sent out to put an end to his outrages, and to avert, if you could, the mischiefs about to spring from them. But when you reached Little Rock, you found him there, and you found that the troops, artillery, ammunition and stores that had reached and were on their way there from the Indian Country, under his unrighteous orders, and which it was your duty to restore to me, were too valuable to be parted with, if that could be in any way avoided.—Probably you foresaw that you might, by and by need to seize money and supplies procured by me. Twenty-six pieces of artillery, a supply of fixed ammunition and other trifles, on hand, with $1,350,000 in money; and over 6,000 suits of clothing in prospect, were the bait Hindmand had to tempt you withal; and for it you sold him your soul, as Faust sold his to Mephistopheles. Your Lieutenant became your master; you found it convenient to believe his version of every thing, and to justify him in every thing, and you ended in making all his devilments your own, and adopting the whole infernal spawn and brood, with additions of your own to the family.

You told me, in August, that you had been prepared to judge me favorably, until you read my address to the Indians on resigning my command, but after that, you could not judge me fairly. I did not in the least doubt the fact; but I did not believe the reason. What, moreover, had you to judge in regard to me? You were not sent out to judge me. If you were sent to judge any body, Hindman was the criminal you were to operate upon.

And, if you were sent, or had otherwise any right, to judge me, you administered the sort of justice that is in vogue in hell. Before you saw me, you heard him. You adopted all his views, and never asked me a question in regard to our controversy, or as to my own action, or the condition of things in the Indian Country. I had been infamously and assiduously slandered, from the moment when I began to resist his illegal, impolitic and outrageous attempts to deprive the Indian Department of every thing, to make it a mere appanage of, and appendix to, North-Western Arkansas, to take the Indians again out of their own country, and to compel me to unite in that insane and miserable "expedition into Missouri," which was projected and planned by Folly, mis-managed and misconducted by Imbecility, and ended, as I knew it would, in disaster and disgrace. Lies of all varieties were ingeniously and laboriously invented at and about Head Quarters, and despatched by special and fit agents, to be industriously circulated throughout the Indian Country and Texas, as well as Arkansas. The Indians were told that I had carried away into Texas the gold and silver belonging to them; while the Texans were made to believe that I was paying their moneys to the Indians. It was reported, in Bonham, Texas, by officers sent from Hindman's Head Quarters, that I was defaulter to the amount of $125,000 and at last there crawled out from the sewer under the throne, and sneaked about the Indian country and Texas, the damnable lie, that an Indian had been taken, bearing letters from me to the Northern Indians, or, to the enemy in Kansas; or, as another verson had it, from Gen. James H. Lane to me; and three months ago it was whispered about that I was a member of the secret disloyal organization in Northern Texas. Such lies could have been counted by scores. Most of them are dead and rotten; but some still live, by means of assiduous nursing. And all these lies, and more either you or Hindman sent to the President at Richmond.

I say, sir, you never inquired into any thing. You never wished to hear any thing, whatever from me You disobeyed the orders with which you were sent as a public curse and calamity into Arkansas, as if the State we[illegible]ot already sufficiently infested by H[illegible]an. Is it true that he has lately, u[illegible]is single order, and without the ceremony of even a mock trial, caused three men 'suspected of disloyalty' to be shot; and that, two of them being proven to him to be true Southern men, he sent a reprieve, which, either setting out too late, or lagging on the way, reached the scene of the murder after their blood had bathed the desecrated soil of Arkansas. It has como to me so, from officers direct from Fort Smith. At any rate, he has put to death nine or ten persons, without any legal trial. Who is he, that he should do these things in this nineteenth centery? And who are you, sir, that you should suffer, and by suffering approve and adopt them? How many more murders will suffice to awaken public vengeance?

Was the Star Chamber any worse than Hindman's Military Commissions, that are ordered to perserve no records?—Were the Lettres de Cachet of Louis XV, any greater outrage on the personal liberty of French subjects, than Hindman's arrests and committal to the Penitentiary of suspected persons? Was Tristan l'Hermite any more the minister of tyranny, than his Provost Marshals? or Caligula, Cæsar Boreis or Colonel Kirke any more cruel and remorseless than he, that you have sustained all his acts, and made all his atrocities your own? Take care, sir! You are not so high, that you may not be reached by the arm of justice.—The President is above you both, and God is above him, and sometimes interferes in human affairs.

Unless the late Secretary of War, through the President, sent an official falsehood to the Congress of the Confederate States, you were sent to Arkansas with positive and unconditional instructions, that, if Gen. Hindman had declared Martial Law in Arkansas, and adopted oppressive police regulations under it, you should 'recind the declarations of Martial Law, and the Regulations adopted to carry it into effect.' You have not done so. You have not only not recinded any thing; but you have, by a General Order, long ago, continued in force all orders of General Hindman, not specially revoked by you. That order could have no retroactive effect, to make his orders to have been valid in the past. It could only put them in force for the future; and you thereby made them your orders, as fully as if you had re-issued them.—In so doing, you become the enemy of your country, if not of the Human race, and outlawed yourself.

You have yourself established a tariff of prices, exclusively or articles produced by the farmers, including the sweet potatoes raised by old women and superanuated negroes. You leave the Jews and extortioners, some of the former of whom go about in uniforms, claiming to be officers and your agents, to charge these same venders of produce, whatever infamous prices they please for the wares they need to purchase with the pittances received according to your scale of prices, for the vegetables that supply your and other tables.

You pretend, I learn, that the President gave you discretionary power, in regard to Martial Law and the Regulations in question. I do not believe it: for, if he did, then he and the Secretary intentionally deceived Congress by the equivalent of a lie. Do you pretend that the President paltered with Congress in a double sense? I put you and him face to face. Is it your act, in defiance of orders, that continues Martial Law in force in Arkansas, stifles freedom of speech, muzzles the Press, tramples on all the rights at once of the People of that State, and makes the State itself only a congregation of Helots, incompetent to be represented in Congress? Is it merely a contest between you and Phelps, which of the two shall be Military Governor? If it is your act, then justice ought at once to be done upon you, lest the President, winking at the outrage, and not stripping from your back your uniform of Lientenant General, should deserve to be impeached, as your accomplice.

Or, do you dare assert that it is his act, because he gave you discretionary power on the subject, after informing Congress that Hindman never was Commanding General of the Department, and that you had been ordered to rescind his declaration of Martial Law—nay, after publicly proclaiming that no General had any power to declare Martial Law? All the Confederacy thanked and applanded him for so striking at the root of an immense outrage and abuse and an unexpected public curse: but if he has authorized or sanctions your course, he is unworthy longer to be President. If he has not, you have defied his orders and justified men in judging yourself authorized and him guilty; and so you are unworthy longer to be General.

When I saw you in August, you were greatly exercised on the subject of my printed address to the Indians, publication of which in Little Rock you had suppressed, as if it could do any harm in Arkansas. You suppressed it, because it exposed those whose acts were losing the Indian Country. You wanted to keep what had been taken from me, and to escape damnation for the proable consequences of the acts, the profit of which you were reluctant to part with. I do not wonder the letter troubled you; for it told the truth, and condemned and denounced in advance the more unjustifiable course of conduct that you were about to pursue.

You pretended that it had produced a great "ferment" among the Indians; and that even many of the Chickasaws had in consequence of it, left the service. It had preduced no ferment, and none of the Chickasaws had left us. On the contrary, the Indians were quieted by it, the Creeks re-organized, in numbers, two regiments, and the Chickasaws five companies. That was its purpose, and such was its effect.

But to you, its enormity consisted in its exposure of the conduct of two Major Generals. I told the Indians plainly, that it was not my fault or the fault of the Government, but of these two Generals, that moneys, clothing, arms and ammunition, procured for them, had not reached them; that troops raised for service among them had never entered their conntry; and that, finally, troops, artillery and ammunition were carried out of it. This censure of my superiors, in vindication of the President and Government, shocked your tender sensibilities. You were reacy to follow in their footsteps, and already had the plunder: and you told me that "the act of the officer was the act of the Government." Did you really mean that the Indians should have been led or left to suppose that these acts were the acts of the Government? That would have been almost as great an infamy, as it was to take the supplies, and so give them canse and reason to believe the robbery the act of the Government, and thus excite them to revolt. Moreover, when I told you that the act of the officer was not, in the case in question, the act of the Government; that, if I had permitted the Indians to suppose so, they would long before have left us; and that, to quiet them, I had been compelled, for three months and more than a hundred times, to explain to them what had become of their supplies, and how and by whom they had been seized, you admitted that "that was right for local explanation." As there could be no objection to telling all, what I had often told part, that they might tell the rest; and as it was no more a crime to print than to say it; I have the right to believe, and I do believe that your real objection to its publication was that it exposed to our own people the actual conduct of other Generals, and the intended conduct of yourself. Have you left the Indians to believe that the late seizure and appropriations by yourself, of their clothing and money, is the act of the Government? If you have, you ought to be shot as a Traitor, for provoking them to revolt, and for giving aid and comfort to the enemy.

But you told me, that when you first read my letter, you held up your hands, and exclaimed, 'What! is the man a Traitor?' And you said that not one of my friends in Little Rock, and I had, you said, a great many, pretended to justify the letter. You have never found a friend of mine, or an indifferent person, silly enough to think, like you, that it savored of treason. It is only rarely one meets a man so scantily furnished with sense as to misunderstand and pervert what is written in plain English. I was vindicating myself, and still more the Government, and persnading the Indians to remain loyal, notwithstanding the wrongs they had endured.

I too, was an officer; and my acts had been the acts of the Government. My promises to them were its promises.—The procuring of their supplies by me, was its acts; and when, reaching or not reaching the frontier, the supplies were like the unlucky traveler, who journeyed from Jerusalem to Jericho, then the Government ceased to act, and unlicensed outrage took its place. And, further, my act was the act of the Government, when I told the Indians why they had not received their supplies and money, and vindicated that Government at the expense of those who were guilty of the act; and who, having done it, and reaped the profit, should not be heard to object that all the world should know what they did, nor be allowed to escape the responsibility of all the consequences.

If to tell the Indians that other Generals had wrongfully stopped their supplies, in any degree resembled Treason, that could only be so, because it was treason to do the act. It cannot be wrong to make known what it was right and proper to do. The truth is, that the acts done were outrages, which it was desirable for the doers to conceal from the Indians. I refused to become a party to those outrages, by concealing them. I would not agree in advance to be silent, when you should repeat and improve on those outrages, and consummate what had been so felicitously begun.

I do not doubt that there are assassins wearing uniforms, who are knaves enough to pretend to read my letter as you do, and to see in it the desire of a disappointed man to be revenged, even by the ruin of his country. Power always has its pimps and catamites. These would no doubt gladly have made my letter the means of murdering by that devilish engine of Military despotism, a Military commission, that is ordered to preserve no records. You, I think really look upon it with harm. It is, no doubt, very disirable to you, that the blame of losing the Indian country, which, if not already a fact accomplished, is a fact inevitable, should be made to fall on me. You, as the pliant and useful implement of Gen. Hindman, are the cause of this loss: and you know I can prove it. You have left nothing undone, that could be done, to lose it. And you may rest assured, that whether I live or die, you shall not escape one jot or tittle of the damnation to which you are most richly entitled for causing a loss so irretrievable, so astounding, so unnecessary and so fatal, and one which it will be impossible to excuse as owing to ignorance and stupidity. No degree of these misfortunes can be pleaded in bar of judgment. You will have forced the Indians to go to the North for protection. You will have given away their country to the enemy. You will have turned their arms against us. You will have done this by disobeying the orders of your Government, continuing the courses it condemned, and to put an end to which it sent you out here; by falsifying its pledges and promises, taking for other uses the moneys which it sent out to pay the Indians, robbing them of the clothing sent by it to cover their nakedness, and thus thrusting aside all the considerations of common honesty, of justice, of humanity, and even of policy, expediency and common sense.

When Mr. C. B. Johnson agreed, in September, to loan your Quartermaster at Little Rock, $350,000 of the money he was conveying to Major Quesenbury, the Quartermaster of the Department of Indian Territory, you promised him that it should be repaid to Major Quesenbury as soon as you should receive funds, and before he would have disposed of the remaining million. You got the money by means of that promise; and you did not keep the promise. On the contrary, by an order that reached Fort Smith three hours before Mr. Johnson did, you compelled Major Quesenbury, the moment he received the money, to turn every dollar of it over to a Commissary at Fort Smith; and it was used to supply the needs of Gen. Hindman's troops: when the Seminoles, fourteen months in the service, have never been paid a dollar; and the Chickasaw and Choctaw Batalions, and Chilly McIntosh's Creeks, each corps a year or more in the service, have received only $45,000 each, and no clothing. Was this violating of your promise, the act of the Government?

To replace the clothing I had procured for the Indians in December 1861, and which, with near 1,000 tents, fell into the hands of the troops of Gen. Price and Van Dorn, I sent an agent, in June, to Richmond, who went thence to Georgia, and there procured some 6,500 suits, with about 3,000 shirts and 3,00 pairs of drawers, and some two or three hundred tents. These supplies were in Monroe early in September; and the Indians were informed they and the moneys had been procured and were on the way. The good news went all over the country, as if on the wings of the wind; and universal content and rejoicing were the consequences.

The clothing reached Fort Smith; and its issue to Gen. Hindman's people commenced immediately. I sent a Quartermaster for it, and he was retained there. If any of it has ever reached the Indians, it has only recently, and but a small portion of it.

You pretended to believe that the Indians were in a "ferment" and discontented: and you took this very opportune occasion to stop all the moneys due their troops and for debts in their country, and to take and appropriate to the uses of other troops the clothing promised to and procured for them. The clothing and the money were theirs: and you were in possession of an order from the War Department, forbidding you to divert supplies from their legitimate destination; an order which was issued, as you know, in consequence of my complaints, and to prevent moneys and supplies for the Indians being stopped:—and yet you stopped all.

You borrow part of the money, and then seize the rest, like a genteel highwayman, who first barrows all he can of a traveler, on promise of punctual repayment; and then claps a pistol to his head and orders him to "stand and deliver" the rest. And you did even more than this.

For you promised the Acting Commissioner of Indian affairs, when he was at Little Rock, about the 1st of October, on his way to the Indian Country, to give the Indians assurances of the good faith of the Government,—you promised him, I say, that the clothing in question should go to the Indians. He told the Chickasaws and Seminoles, at least, of this promise. You broke it. You did not send them the clothing. You placed the commissioner and the Government in an admirable attitude before the Indians: and the consequence has been, I understand, the disbanding of the Chickasaws, and the failure of the Seminole troops to re-organize. The consequence will be far more serious yet. Indians cannot be deceived, and promises made them shamelessly broken, with impunity.

While you were thus stopping their clothing, and robbing the half naked Indians to clothe other troops, the Federals were sending home the Choctaws whom they had taken prisoners, after clothing them comfortably and putting money in their pockets. No one need be astonished, when all the Indians shall have turned their arms against us.

Why did you and Gen. Hindman not procure by your own exertions what you needed for your troops? He reached Little Rock on the 31st of May. You came here in August. I sent my agents to Richmond, for money and clothing, in June and July. I never asked either of you for anything. I could procure for my command all I wanted. You and he were Major Generals; I, only a Brigadier; and Brigadiers are plenty as blackberries in in their season. It is to be supposed that if I could procure money, clothing and supplies for the Indians, you and he could do so for white troops. Both of you come blundering out to Arkansas with nothing, and supply yourselves with what I procure. Some officers would be ashamed so to supply deficiencies caused by their own want of foresight, energy or sense.

You do not even know you need an Engineer, until one of mine comes by, with $20,000 in his hands for Engineer Service in the Indian Territory, some of which belongs to me for advances made, and with stationery and instruments, procured by me, for my department, in Richmond, a year ago; and then you find out that there are such things as Engineers, and that you need one; and you seize on Engineer, money; and stationery. You even take, notwithstanding Paragraph VI, of General Orders No. 50, the stationery procured by me for the Adjutant General's Office of my Department, by purchase in Richmond in December 1861; for the want of which I had been compelled to permit my own private stock to be used for months.

I no longer wonder that you do these things. When you told me that you could not judge me fairly, because I told the Indians that others had done them injustice, you confessed much more than you intended. It was pregnant sentence you uttered. By it you judged and convicted yourself, and you pronounced your own sentence when you uttered it.

The Federal authorities were proposing to the Indians, at the very time when you stopped their clothing and money, that if they would ruturn to the old Union, they should not be asked to take up arms, their annuities should be paid them in money, the negroes taken from them be restored, all losses and damage sustained by them be paid for, and they be allowed to retain, as so much clear profit, what had been paid them by the Confederate States. It was a liberal offer and a great temptation, to come at the moment when you and Hindman were felicitously completing your operations, and when there were no breadstuffs in their country, and they and their women and children were starving and half-naked. You chose an admirable opportunity to rob, to disappoint, to outrage and exasperate them, and make your own government fraudulent and contemptible in their eyes. If any human action can deserve it, the hounds of hell ought to hunt your soul and Hindman's for it through all eternity.

Instead of co-operating with the Federal authorities, and doing all that he and you could do to induce the Indians to listen to and accept their propositions, he had better have expelled the enemy from Arkansas or "perish in the attempt;" and you had better have marched on Helena, before its fortifications were finished, and purged the eastern part of the State of the enemy's presence. If you had succeeded as admirably in that, as you have in losing the Indian Country, you would have merited the eternal gratitude of Arkansas, instead of its execrations; and the laurel, instead of a halter. I said that you and your Lieutenant had left nothing undone. I repeat it. Take another small example. Until I left the command, at the end of July, the Indian troops had regularly had their half ration of coffee. As soon as I was get rid of, an order from General Hindman took all the remaining coffee, some 3,000 lbs., to Fort Smith. Even in this small matter, he could not forego an opportunity of injuring and disappointing them.

You asked me, in August, what was the need of any white troops at all, in the Indian Country; and you said that the few mounted troops, I had, if kept in the Northern part of the Cherokee country, would have been enough to repel any Federal force that ever would have entered it. As you and Hindman never allowed any ammunition procured by me, to reach the Indian country, if you could prevent, whether I obtained it at Richmond or Corinth, or in Texas, and as you approve of his course in taking out of that country all that was to be found in it, I am entitled to suppose that you regarded ammunition for the Indians as little necessary, as troops to protect them in conformity to the pledge of honor of the Government. One thing, however, is to be said to the credit of your next in command. When he has ordered anything to be seized, he has never denied having done so, or tried to cast the responsibility on an inferior. After you had written to me that you had ordered Col. Darnell to seize, at Dallas, in Texas, ammunition furnished by me, you denied to him, I understand, that you had given the order. Is it so? and did he refuse to trust the order in your hands, or even to let you see it, but would show it to Gen. McCulloch?

Probably you know by this time, if you are capable of learning any thing, wether any white troops are needed in the Indian country. The brilliant result of Gen. Hindman's profound calculations and masterly strategy, and of his long-contemplated invasion of Missouri, is before the country: and the disgraceful rout at Fort Wayne with the manœuvres and results on the Arkansas, are pregnant commentaries on the abuse lavished on me, for not taking "the line of the Arkansas," or making Head Quarters on Spring river, with a force too small to effect anything any where.

I have not spoken of your Martial Law and Provost Marshals in the Indian country, and your seizure of salt works there, or, in detail, of your seizure of ammunition procured by me in Texas, and on its way to the Indian troops, of the withdrawal of all white troops and artillery from their country, of the retention for other troops of the mountain howitzers procured by me for Col. Waite, and the ammunition sent me, for them and for small arms, from Richmond. This letter is but a part of the indictment I will prefer bye and bye, when the laws are no longer silent, and the constitution and even public opinion no longer lie paralyzed under the brutal heel of Military Power; and when the results of your impolicy and mismanagement shall have been fully developed.

But I have a word or two to say as to myself. From the time when I entered the Indian country, in May, 1861, to make Treaties, until the beginning of June, 1862, when Gen. Hindman, in the plentitude of his self-conceit and folly, assumed absolute control of the military and other affairs of the Department of Indian Territory, and commenced plundering it of troops, artillery and ammunition, dictating Military operations, and making the Indian country an appanage of North-western Arkansas, there was profound peace throughout its whole extent. Even with the wild Camanches and Kiowas, I had secured friendly relations. An unarmed man could travel in safety and alone, from Kansas to Red River, and from the Arkansas line to the Wichita Mountains. The Texan frontier had not been as perfectly undisturbed for years. We had fifty-five hundred Indians in service, under arms, and they were as loyal as our own people, little as had been done by any one save myself to keep them so, and much as had been done by others to alienate them. They referred all their difficulties to me for decision, and looked to me alone to see justice done them and the faith of Treaties preserved.

Most of the time without moneys, (those sent out for that Department generally failing to reach it,) I had managed to keep the white and Indian troops better fed than any other portion of the troops of the Confederacy any where. I had 26 peices of artillery, two of the batteries as perfectly equipped and well manned as any, any where. I had on hand and on the way, an ample supply of ammunition, after being once plundered. While in command, I had actually procured, first and last, 36,000 pounds of rifle and cannon powder. If you would like to know, sir, how I effected this, in the face all manner of discouragements and difficulties, it is no secret. My disbursing officers can tell you who supplied them with funds for many weeks, and whose means purchased horses for the artillery. Ask the Chickasaws and Seminoles who purchased the only shoes they have ever received—four hundred pairs, at five dollars each, procured and paid for by me, in Bonham, and which I sent up to them after I was taken "in personal custody" in November.

You dare pretend, sir, that I might be disloyal, or even in thought, called the word Treason with my name! What peculiar merit is it in you to serve on our side in this war? You were bred a soldier, and your only chance for distinction lay in obtaining promotion in the army, and in the army of the Confederacy. You were a Major, or something of the sort, in the old army, and you are a Lieutenant General. Your reward I think, for what you have done or not done, is sufficient.

I was a private citizen, over fifty years of age, and neither needing or desiring military rank or civil honors. I accepted the office of Commissioner, at the President's solicitation, I took that of a Brigadier General, with all the odium that I knew would follow it, and fall on me as the Leader of a force of Indians, knowing there would be little glory to be reaped, and wanting no promotion, simply and solely to see my pledges to the Indians carried out, to keep them loyal to us, to save their country to the Confederacy, and to preserve the Western frontier of Arkansas and Northern frontier of Texas from devastation and desolation.

What has been my reward? All efforts have been rendered nugatory, and my attempts even to collect and form an army frustrated, by the continual plundering of my supplies and means by other Generals, and your and their deliberate efforts to disgust and alienate the Indians. Once before this, an armed force was sent to arrest me. You all disobey the President's orders, and treat me as a criminal for endeavoring to have them carried out. The whole country swarms with with slanders against me; and at last, because I felt constrained reluctantly to re-assume command, after learning that the President would not accept my resignation, I am taken from Tishomingo to Washington, a prisoner under an armed guard, it having deemed necessary, for the sake of effect, to send two hundred and fifty men into the Indian country, to arrese me. The Senatorial election was at hand.

I had, unaided and alone, secured to the Confederacy a magnificent country, equal in extent, fertility, beauty and resources to any one of our States,—nay, superior to any. I had secured the means, in men arms, of keeping it. I knew how only it could be defended. I asked no aid of any of you. I only asked to be let alone. Verily, I have my reward also, as Hastings had his, for winning India for the British Empire.

It is your day now. You sit above the laws and domineer over the constitution. "Order reigns in Warsaw." But bye and bye, there will be a just jury empannelled who will hear all the testimony and decide impartially,—no less a jury than the people of the Confederate States; and for their verdict as to myself, I and my children will be content to wait; as also for the sure and stern sentence and universal malediction, that will fall like a great wave of God's just anger on you and the murderous miscreant by whose malign promptings you are making yourself accursed.

Whether I am respectfully yours, you will be able to determine from the contents of this letter.

ALBERT PIKE,
Citizen of Arkansas.

THEOPHILUS H. HOLMES,
Major General, &c.

An Old Maid after Conrad.

Let the following letter published in the Mississippian, go the rounds of the press to be preserved for future reference:

Mr. Editor:—You tender to us your columns in reply to Mr. Conrad's speech in Congress, and in justice due to that much abused class of my sex, I deem a response necessary. I have long waited for something on the subject, from spinisters more capable of meeting out to the offender, his merited remarks; but it appears that they have concluded to pass by in silence, or have sufficiently recovered from their anger to be in a mood for writing.

This Louisiana "sensation" congressman advocates the conscription of the Editors on the plea that "they are doing more harm than good." I think Mr. Conrad would be the last man in the South, who would wish to send Editors to the war. Why, the newspapers have immortaliged him. Had they been silenced by conscription, this famous speech of his would have never been heard beyond the halls of Congress; as it is, it has been published by every paper, read by every preacher, and scowled at by every old maid in the Confederacy.

I fear Mr. Conrad is something like Erasratus, who wishing to render his name immortal, set fire to the magnificent temple of Diana, at Ephesus, and burned it to the ground. Thus with our venerable Congressman. He was not content to quietly pursue the "even tenor of his way" in the discharge of his duty—the consciousness of being a living Congressman, did not flatter his self-complacency, sufficiently; he must do something to particularly distinguish himself from the common class of individuals, and forthwith set his inventive genius to work to devise a pathway to fame. At last it fell upon an expedient. That speech was to lead him to glory and renown.

Some one has said, "call a woman ill-tempered, stuped anything but ugly, and you need not despair of forgiveness." Now I differ with the gentleman, and say a woman can forgive any offense easier than being treating with utter contempt. Mr. Conrad has done this; he says, "preachers can be better employed, than preaching to empty meeting houses, old maids and grannies." Now if this be true, I wish to offer an amendment, which is, if preachers are not needed at home, there is no use in Congressmen being allowed to stay, to make laws for "old maids and grannies."

George Lan says, "Woman's ire pardons not." Then I forbear further comment, knowing there are yet others to be heard from. I beg however, in conclusion, any one agreeing with Mr. Conrad, will recall to mind the horrors of the French Revolution, and see how fatal to a government it is to interfere with a people's religion. If our government wishes to be subjugated, then Mr. Conrad has shown the way. Close up the churches—suppress the influence of religion—stop the voice of prayer, and subjugation is certain. A pure literature is the palladium of a nation's greatness. Then if our press is silenced, where is our public safeguard? See the soldiers far from home, weary and sad hearted; with brightening eye he seizes the welcome paper, and beguiles the lone dreary hours. Truly it is the soldiers friend—it speaks to his very heart; it tells of home and kindred dead, of his country, her glories and her wrongs; it whispers courage in the hour of despondency, and hope amid the darkest gloom. Then away with such ideas as Mr. Conrad's; let our country's religion be undisturbed, and let her press forever be free and untrammeled.

AN "OLD MAID."

THE UNION VIDETTE.

VOL. 1. PUBLISHED EVERY NOW AND THEN, AT LEBANON, KY. NO. 1.

THE UNION VIDETTE.

PRINTED AND PUBLISHED BY
C. R. GALPIN & CO., 2d. MICH. V.

SALUTATORY.

TO ALL WHOM IT MAY CONCERN: The Union Vidette has blacked his shoes, brightened his brasses, and now stands before you and makes his bow.

Although he has been nearly two years in the service, ... his attentions to *Carolina, Virginia*, and my *Maryland*, that he never before has found time to pass in review before the public. He is somewhat embarassed, and hardly knows what to say or how to begin on this momentous occasion. In fact he was so excited when he learned that he was expected to say something smart on his first appearance, that he forgot for a time his duties as vidette, and leaning his gun against a tree, sat down at its foot. Here he began to cogitate, ruminate, and meditate. He decided at once to say something big or nothing at all; something gay, gaudy, gorgeous—something which would astonish the natives. The fact of the matter was he meant to fire a big gun—get eloquent—soar into the etherial atmospheric air—to *debut*—*E pluribus unum*—*et eetera*—&c.

The next thing was how to do it. What were the principal points to touch upon? Should his dissertation be his orical, metaphorical and political, or syntaxical, geographical and geological? Ought he to compare, to simile, to climax, to hyperbole, or what? This was a query; and while in this deep study he fell into a dreamy reverie. He fancied that somehow he met with unexpected success. He thought he accomplished the greatest possible things in the shortest possible time, with the least possible amount of labor—that the soldiers cheered, the ladies smiled, and the people in general thought he was some. In other words, he concluded he had roused the sleeping lion in his bosom, and had made an impression. But just here some one touched his shoulder and he awoke to find that he hadn't made a speech—hadn't gained glory, honor, fame, "or any other man;" but, on the contrary, he had most assuredly been dozing, and the people were expecting to hear from him. He bestired himself, and here is what he has to say.

Ladies and gentlemen, kind patrons and all ye gude folk; the *Union Vidette* welcomes you to a soldiers' fare, and trusts that his acquaintance with you may partake of a soldier's cheer. In the plebian tongue of the ancients, we "now take our pen in hand to inform you that we are well, and hope these few lines will find you enjoying the same blessing." There, that is old and quoted, but it's just the key we wanted to start the tune on, so we used it. And now for our creed and articles of faith. We believe war is a "big thing on ice," and we shall endeavor to be on the lookout continually for all encroachments of the enemy. We intend to note all great changes on the great programme of this great war for the great Union of the United States of North America, Western Hemisphere, Earth No. 1. We shall watch and chronicle all changes produced by promotion and *anti-grey backs* can see how much cheaper ... than they; state the value of convalescent mules and plaster paris, so the men can form some idea of the probable amount of "salt junk" and "hard tack" to be masticated; with eagle eye note the least fluctuation in the premium on that dead shot fluid known as "Commissary whiskey" so that any one can determine with the utmost precision the cost and length of time required to place himself *hors de combat*. We are down on any of your pesky rattlesnakes rolled up in palmetto trees; go in for good morals, strict discipline, and a great deal less of inebriation and the "flowing bowl," among officers first, and enlisted men second. We shall vote for the Union, sustain the Administration, the Flag of our Country and the screaming Eagle—every time.

We are "heavy" on the Union, and believe in prosecuting the war till the banner of Washington shall again float from the masts of our earth-encircling commerce, and "wave o'er the land of the free and the home of the brave."

The spirits of the great and good, who have gone to their reward, beckon us on and bid us fight for the heritage of our sires. Let us beware lest the bow of early habits, which was once strung in the wild glens of the forest, be too much relaxed, and we prove by our indolence and love of ease and luxury, that we are unworthy of our high ancestry. Let us go forth manfully to the work, and *dare* and *do*, while whistling balls and rolling thunders shake the air above, and bathe the blazing fields in gore, but never surrender our birth-right to traitorous hands. We will

> "Strike till the last armed foe expires;
> Strike for our altars and our fires;
> Strike for the green graves of our sires,
> GOD, and our native land."

Then will our country be saved, and she will rise in beauty and grandeur like the morning sun; but if we act base, ignoble, and cowardly, our prosperity will be like that of the silk worm who encases herself in her golden cocoon, which shall ere long become her own grave.

Friends, we say Adieu! If you feel any better acquainted with us or like us any better than when we made our bow, and shall endeavor to so conduct ourselves as to merit your esteem. Be assured we intend to pursue no course except a straightforward one, and we shall strive to do the fair thing at all times, whether acting as the soldier's friend, or engaged in the more arduous duties of the UNION VIDETTE.

General Poe's Brigade.

Among the troops stationed within this district POE's Brigade is not unworthy of notice. In the Brigade are some of the oldest Regiments organized to assist in ... rebellion. The Brigade belongs to the First Division of the Ninth Army Corps, than which no other Corps in the service bears a higher or worthier reputation for distinguished service in the field. Of the First Division the late General SUMNER said, on the occasion of a review, some months ago, "This Division is one of the best in the United States Army—truly a *grand* division."

Of old Regiments there are in the Brigade the 79th New York (Highlanders,) and the 2d and 8th Michigan, and of comparatively new organizations the 17th and 20th Michigan. The 17th Michigan displayed the best soldierly qualities in the battles of South Mountain and Antietam, and the 20th is full of promise.

The services of the respective Regiments comprising POE's Brigade may be treated of separately. It may not be uninteresting to our readers, in this place, to give a brief sketch of Brig. Gen. POE, and make enumeration of his Staff.

Brig. Gen. POE entered at West Point the 1st of September, 1852, from Coshocton, Ohio, and graduated June 16, 1856; was appointed Second Lieutenant of Topographical Engineers, July 1, 1856; First Lieutenant of Topographical Engineers, July 1, '60; and Capt. of Engineers, March 1863.

Gen. Poe was instructor of Cavalry and Artillery at West Point, in 1856, under the (now) rebel General Hardee. He was afterwards employed from December '56 to April 1861, in the survey of the north and north west lakes. During this period Lieut. Poe was first in charge of the main Triangulation, and afterwards of the Department of Astronomy.

Lieut. Poe was appointed Colonel of the 2d Michigan Volunteers on the 16th of September 1861. This appointment was a very happy one, and the 2d Michigan, which had previously gained a high reputation, attained a distinction for drill, discipline and fighting qualities which has not been surpassed by any other regiments in the field.

Col. Poe was appointed Brigadier General of Volunteers ... state that from April 20th until Sept. 16, 1861, he was Chief Engineer on the staff of Maj. Gen. McClellan.

Knowing that any elaborate commendation of General Poe's character would be unpleasant to him, we shall only state in regard to him what the whole Brigade will endorse with a shout. Physically of fine proportions, he is known after first sight. Sparing of speech, he is gentlemanly in his demeanor, but emphatic in style, and makes himself understood at once. He demands obedience in his bearing, but makes service pleasant. He possesses in short, the true qualities of a gentleman and a soldier and is "obeyed and respected accordingly."

The following are the acting officers of Gen. POE's Staff: Lieut. JAMES REID, Acting Assistant Inspector General, 79th N. Y. Lieut. H. H. DANIELS, Act. Ass't Adj't Gen'l, 2d Mich. Lieut. GEO. D. MARTIN, A. A. Q. M., 79th N. Y. Lieut. W. WINEGAR, A. C. S., 17th Mich. Dr. S. S. French, A. D. S., 20th Mich. Lieut. BEN. H. BERRY, A. A. D. C., 20th Mich.

The majority of the officers of General POE's Staff are well acquainted with active service in the ... promoted from the ranks. We shall merely say further, that on the march from Louisville to this point, the good conduct of the Brigade has been a subject of remark by all citizens. No man has been defrauded of a cents' worth of property and it is our earnest hope that the good character which the Brigade has acquired in Kentucky, may be preserved in all further movements.

"HAIL HOLY FLAG."

WRITTEN FOR THE VIDETTE BY B. M. C.

> Hail holy Flag! Hail, once again;
> Thy starry folds still sweep the skies;
> Oh! let it float o'er hill and plain
> While Freedom lives—till Treason dies.
> Hail banner bright! thy starry light
> Shall guide us through our darkest night.
>
> By thee we stand, firm as the rock
> When surging billows round it close;
> With thee we'll brave each battle shock,
> And hurl it back against our foes.
> Hail banner bright! thy starry light
> Shall guide us through our darkest night.
>
> Hail holy Flag! thy brightly dawns;
> Our night is past—the clouds are riven;
> Thy rainbow hues arch the storm,
> Thy burning stars ... the heaven.
> Hail banner bright! thy starry light
> Shall guide us through our darkest night.

☞ The 25th Michigan, who have been sojourning in this vicinity for several days, took their departure Sunday, for a new field of action, which we forbear mentioning at present. They are fine, soldierly-looking body of men, and we have no doubt they will show true "Wolves" grit, whenever a favorable opportunity occurs.

☞ We are under obligations to Mr. W. P. MILLS, of the Michigan 2d, for coming to our relief at a critical period of our career, and also for the *quality* of the article furnished. Such favors are always duly appreciated by the fraternity.

Address to the People of Michigan.

At a meeting of the Line Officers of the Second Michigan Volunteers, held at Newport News, Virginia, March 17th, 1863, the following address to the people of Michigan was adopted:

Believing that the most perfect understanding should at this time exist between the people and the army, we take this means of communicating ... at home. We believe and desire that the war should be prosecuted till our victory shall be final and complete, and till the enemy shall be reduced to unconditional submission. We will give our cordial and united support to any and all measures adopted by the Government of the State, or of the United States, for the vigorous prosecution of the war. We have been, and still are, cheered and encouraged by the loyalty and patriotism of the body of the people. Our labors are lightened by your sympathy, and our hearts moved by your unceasing efforts in behalf of the sick and wounded. There is, however, a class among you, whose conduct is alike a disgrace to themselves, and the communities where they are allowed to exist. While partaking of all the blessings which the kindest Government can bestow, they strive, with the vicious activity of cowardice and treason, to ruin it by depreciating its currency; harboring deserters; preventing enlistments; by circulating false reports of the demoralization of its army, and by urging a peace more ruinous than defeat itself. In our estimation, such men deserve the bayonet, the halter, and the universal contempt of mankind. We are now about entering on our third year of service. Our torn flag, and thinned ranks, testify that we have experienced ... "prosecute the war," we well know what those words mean, and who will be the first to fall. Nevertheless, give us your support, and we will, with ten-fold ardor and enthusiasm, again, as enjoined by KEARNEY, the bravest of the brave, "bear our colors proudly and defiantly against the enemy." Our success has not always been equal to your expectations. We know of no remedy except to try again. Conscious of our own defects, we are doing our utmost to correct the errors of inexperience, and to perfect organization and discipline. Animated by the same feelings as when we left the State, we are ready to give all we have for the cause. Let the North but give a twentieth part as much, even, and ere another year the Star Spangled Banner will float victorious from the lakes to the gulf. Refuse, and we shall soon have to look back to the day when it was honorable to be called an American. Brand the coward; drive the traitor and deserter with the bayonet, if need be, from your midst; put your hands to the work as you promised to do when we left the State, and as for a time you did; let our former companions, if there be any pride or patriotism in them, show it by coming forth at once, without the delay and expense of the draft. The enemy dictated the war—let us dictate the peace and its terms will probably be satisfactory.

It is hard for us to conceive how any one who is not a traitor at heart, can hesitate. Is not the cause as sacred as when the first gun was fired at Sumpter? Go read the annals of the Revolution, and though you may blush at modern degeneracy, you cannot be so devoid of those qualities which make manhood respectable, as not to profit by their teachings. We are ready to lead the advance. It is our business and privilege. You have a right to expect it of us. Support us as you ought, and, with the blessing of God, you at least may enjoy homes, a country, and a history worthy of yourselves and your ancestors.

CAPT. C. B. HAYDEN, Pres't.
CAPT. C. H. HODSKIN, Sec'y.

THE UNION VIDETTE.

PRINTED AND PUBLISHED BY
C. R. GALPIN & CO., 2d. MICH. V.

"PEACE,"

A few days more will complete the period of two years since the guns of an infuriated and demented mob thundered upon Fort Sumpter, and the national flag was first beaten down by *American* hands. Those two years have been dark and bloody. Thousands upon thousands, who, *personally*, never had an unkind wish or thought towards each other, have fallen in mutual slaughter; and thousands more have dug themselvos nameless graves in the swamps of the Chickahominy, by the bayous of the west, and on the shores of the Gulf, Other thousands, crippled and ruined ... and existence ... have been to them, a sun-lit world. Hundreds of millions of dollars have been expended, and hundreds of millions worth of property have been destroyed. And still the stern, bloody work goes on. And men grow heart-sick, and strain their longing eyes to pierce the dim darkness, and scan the far horizon to catch the faint streakings of coming dawn. And others turn their waiting ear to the dumb walls of night, to hear the first rushing of the pinions of the coming Angel of PEACE. Sorrow sits leaden-eyed at a thousand hearthstones, and stricken ones sigh for peace. And there are those who do not hesitate to clamor for peace at *any* price—even of dishonor. These are they who worship at the shrine of their own comfort; but such, thank heaven, is not the voice of the nation. And yet we all know, we all acknowledge, that peace is a thing to be desired—to be earnestly sought for. If this be so—and who can doubt it—the *prospects and the conditions of peace* become a subject of primary interest. In order to determine how we may have peace, we must first consider how we came to be at war. To know how we may be *united*, we must first know why we are *divided*.

In the first place, then, this unhappy strife is not of our seeking; nor has it been brought about by any wish, act or aggression of ours. All that could be done without positive dishonor and ruin, *was* done to avert it. The loyal people and the Government of these United States forbore, *long* after forbearance ceased to be a virtue, to punish the traitors and demagogues who were seeking the life of the Republic.

They denounced the Government, and we forbore. They passed their treasonable ordinances of Secession, and we forbore. They collected and equipped armies, with the avowed purpose of resisting the Government, and we forbore. They seized our custom houses, post offices, revenue vessels, arsenals, navy yards, mints and fortresses, *"vi et armis,"* and still we withheld the blow that might have crushed them. At last they opened their murderous batteries upon an unarmed vessel, bearing at its peak the national flag, conveying food to a starving but loyal garrison—an insult that this great Republic would have borne from no nation that sits on God's green earth, and yet because we deemed them infatuated brethren, we *still* bore it.

But when amid the sulphurous smoke and fire and thunder of Sumpter, the old flag went down, a nation on whom insult upon insult, and wrong upon wrong had been heaped; a mighty nation filled with righteous, indignant wrath rose up, as the monarch of the desert rises and shakes the dew of sleep from his mane, and with one mighty bound sprang at the throat of this vilest of rebellions. But it was with no vindictive feeling that the great, loyal masses rose. They came but to defend the Government which Washington, and Adams, Jefferson, and Madison, and Monroe, Hamilton, and their illustrious compatriots had made; which Jackson, and Clay, and Webster and their colleagues had *preserved*.—Holding in one hand the *sword*, they held and still hold in the other the *olive*. Aggrieved, as they thought, by a minority party of the north, the rebels retaliated upon the UNION, which had conferred upon them nothing but blessings. Seeking to strengthen and perpetuate their "peculiar institution" they committed the supreme blunder of attacking the very Government which had stood, from time immemorial, like a barrier of rock, between that institution and its enemies.

Led on by demented but ambitious demagogues they perpetrated the foolish and fatal crime of attacking the *Union*, which had never inflicted upon them a wrong or deprived them of a right; that Union which our fathers gave us and which has raised us to power and honor among the nations. It is for the defense of that Union, for the perpetuity of our nationality, the integrity of our country, that we have rallied and that we now bear arms, and not to war upon any institution or class of men. We did not commence a war against slavery or any other institution, and if it has been dragged into the arena, it has been done by other hands than ours. Most scrupulously did the government endeavor to avoid the issue. Fremont touched it; he was superseded. Hunter meddled; he was suspended. Phelps promulgated his decree and he was removed. But still its friends insisted upon dragging it into the struggle, and if it be trodden to death beneath the feet of serried hosts or ground to powder in our "thunder mill," or be crushed beneath the Juggernaut of our civilization, ... the fault or virtue. But this we announce as the deliberate, well considered determination of this great, free Republic: that cost what it may in blood and treasure, let pet institutions survive or perish, the country our fathers gave us we will transmit unbroken to our children and woe to that man or that institution that sets itself up between the people and their heritage.

We did not begin the war, but with God's help we intend to end it. We did not break the peace, but we hope to re-establish it. We desire peace, and the terms are easy and simple. The price is submission. Submission not to us, not to the North, not to the Lincoln Administration, but to the Government as our fathers made it. Let them undo what they have violently done. Let them surrender the forts, arsenals and ships they have seized; give up the mints and customs they have stolen. Let them submit the questions in dispute to the decision of the ballot box rather than of the cartridge box, and there may be peace. Till then, *never!* We are fighting for our heritage, and we would be cowards and slaves to surrender it like cowards. Our sires fought seven years for the *hope* of a country; shall we not fight as least as long for that country established, cemented and glorified? Europe fought thirty years for religious freedom, and we will fight if need be twice thirty years for our national existence.

> "Freedom's battle once begun,
> Bequeathed from bleeding sire to son,
> Though baffled oft, is ever won."

In the language of the patriot soldiers of Ohio, "While grass grows or water runs; while the earth produces fibres or industry forms them to fabrics, so long we will stand by the old flag, though a cripple hold the staff and a corporal's guard do the fighting."

DIRGE TO A SOLDIER.

MEMORY OF BRIGADIER GEN. PHILIP KEARNEY.

BY GEORGE S. BOKER.

Close his eyes—his work is done;
What to him is friend or foeman,
Rise of moon or set of sun,
Hand of man or kiss of woman?
Lay him low, lay him low,
In the clover or the snow—
What care he? he cannot know.
Lay him low.

As man may, he fought his fights:
Proved his truth by his endeavor;
Let him sleep in solemn night,
Sleep forever and forever.
Lay him low, lay him low, &c.

Fold him in his Countrys's stars,
Roll the drum, and fire the volley;
What to him are all our wars?
What, but death bemocking folly?
Lay him low, lay him low, &c.

Leave him to God's watching eye,
Trust him to the hand that made him;
Mortal love weeps idly by,
...
Lay him low, lay him low, &c.

☞ The State election in Kentucky takes place on the first Monday in August next, and the candidates for the several State offices are already busily engaged in canvassing the State preparatory to that event. Monday being court day, an excellent opportunity was thus afforded these gentlemen for meeting their friends from the "rural districts." Speeches were made by Ex-Gov. Wickliffe, Capt. W. J. Heady, candidate for Member of Congress from this district, and Col. Jacobs, of the 9th Kentucky Cavalry and J. P. Barber.

TO PUBLISHERS.—To newspapers wishing to exchange with us, we will only say, that our exchange list is already so extensive we cannot afford to add to it. But to all newspapers who will publish our prospectus in three successive issues, and send us a marked copy containing each notice, and giving us an editorial notice occasionally, we will send a copy of the Union Vidette one year. Hoping the above *liberal* terms will meet with your hearty approval, we shall await patiently the receipt of your papers.

☞ Wo understand that the pupils of Braddock's Institute, intend giving an exhibition of Tableaux, at Shuck's Hall, at an early date, for the benefit of the Lebanon Sabbath School. The elegant and intelligent Mrs Smith, who has had the labor of selecting Tableaux and perfecting and practicing the pupils in their several parts, will certainly make a display of those engaged in the Tableaux both complimentary to their good sense and her admirable taste. We bespeak for the Tableaux a crowded house of the ELITE of the town and the army.

☞ Reports, by way of Washington and New York have been received, to the effect that Charleston, S. C. has surrendered to our land and naval forces. Such reports are always received with caution, owing in great measure to the frequency of *canards*. Should it prove true—and an attack on a formidable scale was certainly imminent—the resources of the rebels will be severely crippled. The numerous chances for running the blockade at that port have hitherto allowed many vessels to escape, notwithstanding the exercise of the utmost vigilance.

☞ The office "boys" return thanks to the gentlemanly proprietor of the ALHAMBRA, for a sample of his Cigars and Ale, the finest we have seen in the State. ... anything in his line will do well to give him a call.

☞ We invite the attention of our readers to the large stock of Military Furnishing Goods, for sale by Phillips & Blandford, on the corner, opposite the Harris House, Lebanon, Kentucky.

☞ We are under obligations to the officers and men of the Brigade, who so kindly furnished us "copy" for this number. Many valuable communications were, however, left out for the want of room.

☞ We would return our thanks to Messrs. Ames & Son for their kindness in permitting us to occupy their office, and use their material to issue our paper.

The New York 79th, (Highlanders.)

Independent Companies, clad in "the garb of old Gaul," have long existed, and made periodical promenades in the principal cities and towns of the United States. Such a company, called the "Highland Guard," was attached to the 2d Regiment N. Y. S. M. An order required, some time previous to the outbreak of the rebellion, that the State uniform should be adopted by all military organizations thus to ensure uniformity, and to do away with "piebald" Regiments. The Scots of New York city speedily took measures to have the Highland Guard mustered out of service, and to have a Scotch Regiment raised. A fine Regiment, equipped, and dressed in the tartan, was speedily offered for service, and was accepted by the Governor.

The 79th soon gained a high reputation, a reputation, let us say, which has only been added to since the regiment came into active service. The men of the 79th have never disgraced the tartan; and although the "bill of dress" has been suspended, both friends and foes know full well the shape and step of the Highlanders.

The 79th was one of the first regiments to volunteer its services to defend the National Capital, on the outbreak of the rebellion. Its services were declined until the month of May, 1861, when the whole regiment gallantly volunteered for the war. In a brief sketch we cannot do justice to the eminent service which this regiment has rendered the country. At the first Bull Run it was the last regiment engaged, and sustained a los of nearly 200 men, killed, wounded, and prisoners.—The great majority of the prisoners were also wounded. Among the killed was the brave old Colonel Cameron.

After Bull Run the regiment mutinied.—The cause of the mutiny we shall state in few words. It was announced on dress parade by authority of the officer in command, (an officer, let us say, who never smelt powder,) that the regiment was ordered home to recruit. Expectations built on this announcement were speedily dissipated, and a portion of the men rebelled. Some innocent men suffered in the punishment which was awarded, the commanding officer resigned, and a humane but firm and resolute officer took command of the Regiment. The new commander was Colonel, afterwards General Stevens, a hero in word and in deed—a patriot and a soldier ... "man of mould." Gen. Stevens was killed at Chantilly, with the colors of the 79th in his hand—after six color bearers had been shot down.

Under Stevens the 79th was perpetually in the front in Virginia, doing excellent service and maintaining a high name. Gen. Stevens, being ordered to join Gen. Sherman in the expedition to South Carolina, the "Tak' us wi' ye!" with which he was then hailed (Oct., 1661,) will be fresh in the memories of all.—He took the 79th with him, and most creditably did the regiment behave in all operations down South. In the battle of James Island, the fiercest of the war the enemy say, there were lost in killed and wounded of the 79th one-fourth its entire strength, while the 8th Mich., a companion regiment on many a well-fought field, suffered still more severely.

Called back to Virginia in July, 1852, after the repulse of McClellan, the 79th Regiment was actively engaged on the Rappahannock until the second Bull Run, and with little pause was sent into Maryland, and took a distinguished part in the battles of South Mountain and Antietam. The 79th was also at Fredericksburg, and it has been the good or evil fortune of the regiment to be booked for a fight wherever it goes.

There are but few old members left in the 79th, but the fame which the regiment has earned. We are compelled to omit the names of many brave officers who have served and bled, but the names of Morrison, Farnsworth and Stevens, have been rendered historical in connection with the regiment.

A history of the 79th is impracticable here, and appreciating well the circumstance that a dry string of facts is uninteresting unless accompanied by incident, the writer of this brief sketch may well beg pardon for the little he has said, and the larger amount which he has left unsaid with regard to a regiment known and admired "all the world over."

☞ We are under lasting obligations to the gentlemanly clerks of the Harris House, for the many courtesies extended towards us while we were a guest of the house.

Kanawha Republican.

[illegible] W. NEWTON, Editor and Proprietor, CHARLESTON, WEST VIRGINIA, APRIL 4, 1863. VOL. XXI.—New Series, No. 1.

The Kanawha Republican.

Terms of Subscription. [illegible] $2 00. After the expiration of six months [illegible] $2 50.

Rates of Advertising. [illegible]

[illegible] ded, is now upon the people. We hope the people in every county will view the coming election as no ordinary one. Upon the practical good sense, the pure character and sound judgment of the men elected, depend not only the peace, security or prosperity of the new State at home but the pure name and honor of West Virginia abroad among her sister States of the Union. The people should prepare to throw aside all former party affinities and associations, frown down all demagogue tricks and influences and in good earnest and untiring perseverance hunt out the best men to put the State government into operation.

In view of the importance of the first election under the Constitution, the representatives in Wheeling last winter, very properly, met and passed the following resolution:

Resolved, That this meeting recommend to the people of each of the forty-eight counties composing the new State of West Virginia that as soon as practicable after the adoption of the amended Constitution they appoint delegates to meet in Convention at Parkersburg on the first Wednesday after the expiration of ten days from the date of the proclamation of the President declaring West Virginia a State in the Union, to appoint unconditional Union candidates for State officers at the first election under the new State Constitution.

The State officers to be elected are, a Governor, Attorney General, Secretary of the State, Treasurer, Auditor, three Judges of the Supreme Court of Appeals, a Judge of each Circuit: and of the County offices a Clerk of the Circuit Court, Sheriff, Prosecuting Attorney, Surveyor of Lands and a Recorder. Members of the House of Delegates and of the Senate are to be elected.—The people of the several Counties will therefore see the importance of holding meetings and appointing delegates to the Parkersburg Convention. We would say to our friends in Kanawha, see that Old Kanawha is well represented in that Convention.

Curious Items of Patriots.—Thomas Jefferson and John Adams both died on the 4th of July, 1826. John Adams died in his 91st year, and was eight years older than Thomas Jefferson. Thomas Jefferson was eight years older than James Madison; James Madison was eight years older than James Monroe; James Monroe was eight years older than John Quincy Adams. The first five of our Presidents, all Revolutionary men, ended their terms of service in the 66th year of their age. Washington, born February 22, 1732; inaugurated 1789; term of service expired in the 66th year of his age. John Adams, born October 19th, 1735; inaugurated 1797; term of service expired on the 66th year of his age. Thomas Jefferson, born April 21st, 1743; inaugerated, 1801; term of service expired in the 66th year of his age. James Monroe, born April 2d, 1759; inaugurated in 1817; term of service expired in the 66th year of his age.

Feeling in the Army.

Enthusiastic expressions of the true American patriotism continue to come up from our brave soldiers in the field, every where. The Copper-heads get no sympathy from them. Here is what one of the boys writes to the Baltimore *American*.

"I see, as yet, no lack of enthusiasm which was manifested—I mean among the troops—at the breaking out of the war. I would hail with joy the day that we can return to our peaceful avocations with honor. But rather than we should behold a peace such as some of our Northern friends would dictate, *I would be a soldier during life*; for the moment that we accept terms of peace other than the laying down of arms of all in rebellion, we lose our nationality and become the laughing-stock for the powers of Europe. But let croakers croak. We enlisted to put down this rebellion, and, with the help of God, we are going to do it.—We are here in front of a city, where we once met with a severe repulse, where hundreds of our comrades are already buried, and these are our feelings: and we despise those who claim to be the soldier's friend, and who are still trying by every possible means to bring disgrace upon our country by clinging to traitors in arms."

The Wheeling Intelligencer says:

We have reliable information from Richmond, to the effect that John Letcher's tax gatherers have disposed of several hundred thousand dollars worth of Wheeling property for taxes claimed to be due to the Letcher government. Among other property thus disposed of, is the Belmont Rolling Mills and the property of James W. Paxton. The purchasers of the Wheeling property thus put under the hammer are generally those who went from this city to fight for their rights. We suppose they think it's a big thing.

Girls get ripe much earlier than boys.—The moment the former get beyond fifteen, they are "young ladies," while boys of that age are only thought fit to lug water and shovel away snow storms. A girl at eighteen knows more than a boy at twenty-one; after that age, however, corduroy not only overtakes calico, but passes her.

Pompey said he once worked for a man who raised his wages so high, that he could reach them only once in two years.

From the Cin. Gazette.

How the Soldiers in the Valley of Virginia Talk.

Eds. Gazette:—I beg leave to occupy a small space in your columns with an extract from a letter which I received from a soldier in Gen. Milroy's division, showing the state of feeling of those gallant freemen who are in the field fighting to maintain that hallowed boon bequeathed us by the sterling patriots of '76, "*Liberty and free Government*," the principle for which they poured out the heart's best blood. In this letter I can perceive none of the manifestations of discontent as portrayed by rebel newspapers in general, and *our own rebellious sheets in particular*, as existing in our army. Nay, [illegible] tend to *vile, infamous* traitors at home, such as Vallandigham, Carlile & Co.

But the letter is short and to the point, and will speak for itself as soldiers always do.

Winchester, West Virginia.
March 8, 1863.

Dear Sir: I received your paper sent some time ago, and in reading it noticed the noble course of the people of the Buckeye State, expressed at the meeting at the Opera House. Would to God all were like the people of Ohio. The soldiers of Milroy's division are getting along finely. The health of the soldiers is good. Ohio has her soldiers here too. I will give you my views as well as the views of *all* the soldiers in this division with regard to the war. To save our country we need that every power in the whole range of moral and political influence be given a contribution and made to work to *one common end*. Whites and blacks, fire and sword, cannon and devastation flood *must all* be used *if needs* be to defeat a desperate and powerful foe.

The memories of many battlefields drenched with the blood of our noble slain, the sufferings and hardships of those who survive, ready in defense of our beloved country, ready to obey the soldier's summons to the deadly strife, all plead trumpet-tongued against the deep damnation of Northern traitors. Our army has claims upon the moral support of *every* man, and that support should be vigorously exacted.

If not given willingly *now*, we lift a warning voice against the dreadful retribution that awaits all recreants when our triumphant hosts shall return to their homes.—"Whoso soweth to the wind shall reap the whirlwind."

The above are the feelings of every soldier and officer in this division. We have had meetings and I have not seen a man yet but what is down on these infamous Copperheads.

Yours with respect,
Lieut. T. W. Bradley,
Co. I, 1st Reg't West Va. Vol. Inf.

The Richmond Whig, of the 18th has an article on the "South-west," in which it admits as possibly true an assertion that "the people of the South-west are more inclined to peace, especially with the North-west, than the Atlantic States of the Confederacy." The Whig attributes this inclination to the reverses of the rebel arms in the West. The Whig says:

"The Yankees now hold Nashville more firmly than before, threaten seriously the occupation of East Tennessee, are not dislouged from Northern Mississippi, have again entered Florence, and make a promise—not altogether idle—of entering Georgia.

"This is the painful history of our arms in Tennessee and Kentucky. If we cross the Mississippi, and enquire the results of our efforts in Arkansas and Missouri, the record is too humiliating to be read at length. No man cares to hear the story of the Confederate cause after the fall of McCulloch and the joining of Price's forces to those of Beauregard. The chronicle is not more sad than it is shameful. It may be summed up by the disheartening announcement made in our latest exchanges that the *armies of Holmes and Hindman have dwindled from thirty five thousand down to a mere brigade*. In Texas and in the Indian Territory the story is much the same—large armies raised and nothing accomplished. Concerning Arizonia and New Mexico, we have ceased to have anything whatever. Perhaps they are no longer considered a part of the Confederacy.

"When the fortunes of war have been so uniformly adverse, it is not surprising that a people who see in its prolongation not subjugation, but the further ravaging of their fields, the loss of their slaves and the burning of their houses, should desire its cessation at the earliest moment, and perhaps be willing to make concessions which others more fortunate would reject. It is not believed that the South-west lack faith in the ultimate success of the cause, or is it unwilling to make as great sacrifices as the people in the valley and in tide-water Virginia have done; but when they perceive month after month pass by without any headway being made by our armies, and with only a partial resistance to the enemy's advance, they naturally enough distrust the arbitrament of the sword and incline to the expedients of diplomacy."

If the South-west would come back into the Union, the door is open. If they wish to be relieved from the Jeff. Davis despotism, the thing can be done decently and in order.

Famine Prices in the South.—From a recent number of a Richmond paper we learn the following, which the editor pronounces to be "stern facts:" Gold rose on Saturday to $2 60 premium—that is, the price of a gold dollar was $3 60 in paper. Butter was scarce and in demand at $2 75 per lb. Beef, none of it first rate, commanded $1 to $1 25 per lb. Corn Meal $5 per bushel. Let us talk no more of depreciation of Northern currency and of inflated prices after reading such accounts as these. Other articles in the Richmond journals are headed, "Blockade Prices," and "Do our Farmers plant Corn." It discovered at last that cotton is not king, but that corn is in the ascendent, and that his rule will be most despotic. These "stern facts" speak volumes. They show more forcibly than the most eloquent language the miserable condition to which the rebellion has reduced the people of the South.—[Her.

A true philanthropist and a well trained horse, always stop at the word *wo*.

The Sufferings of the Southern people.

The people of the north who are making a pitiful mouth about the war, as a general rule know very little about it, and those who are flippantly talking of resisting the enforcement of the laws—that is to say, of inaugurating civil war among ourselves—ought to visit the scenes of active hostilities in the South to take lessons in the horrors of war.

The desolation of those portions of Virginia, Mississippi, and Tennessee that have been fought over is fright[illegible] indescrib[illegible] was as fertile, as highly cultivated, and richly adorned as any portion of America, is one wide scene of ruin. If Tennessee had been true to the Union she would not be desolate and in mourning to-day. If she had been firm in the good cause, the war would have been passed beyond her borders without blighting a blade of her grass. Let her fate be a warning.

The sufferings of the people of the South have been almost without a parallel. Dragged into war by a baleful aristocracy and a ravenous mob, they have been subjected to the exactions of a relentless military despotism. Now the gaunt spectre of famine adds to the terrors of the South, and the alarm is sounded from press to press all over the Confederacy, "plant corn or we perish."—The miserable folly of State rights is bearing its legitimate fruit in the dire calamities of war, joined to the formation of a central power imperious and comprehensive as that of the Empire of Russia.

In a recent debate in the Virginia Legislature, Mr. Anderson, of Rockbridge county, dealt with Confederate tyranny after the following manner:

"We are now living," he said, "under a tyranny as complete as that which was exercised by the Lincoln Government, and it was owing solely to the noble patriotism of our people that they have submitted as they have. What right, he would ask, has a Confederate functionary to seize his property without law, and to allow one-half its value for its compentation? There was no law that authorized the Confederate Government to take property, and so far as it withell compensation, it was robbery and oppression; and he, for one, was not willing to submit to it. If we were to have tyranny it mattered not whether we have it from one Government or from another; but no free people would submit to tyranny from any source."

The Atlanta (Georgia) Intelligencer, in an article on Southern monarchy, says:

"The unscrupulous manner in which property—in the shape of anything to eat and wear—is seized and appropriated by the Government, and that, too, without any reference to the pecuniary interests of the parties owning such property, and when such seizures tend to destroy all trade, and cause the people to lose Confidence and all interest in the Government—such a course, they claim, is very strong proof that a monarchy is the thing aimed at. The recklessness which the Government, through its various agents, conducts trade outside the seizures it makes, tending as it does to place every necessary out of the reach of the poor, looks, they argue, to the same end."

The Richmond Enquirer urges the people of Virginia to plant corn and not tobacco. It says:

"If the country cannot supply the army with provisions this summer, *the army can't remain in Virginia. If it leaves Virginia, it must be given up to the Yankees*, who will appropriate not only tobacco, contraband of war, but seize every thing we have, and reduse the country to a wilderness. If the Legislature adjourns without prohibiting the culture of tobacco, and requring the officers of the law to destroy every leaf which they find growing for twelve months to come, the chance of this State is indeed poor."

The Baltimore American, noticing this beautiful condition of public liberty in Virginia, says:

"When the Richmond papers which contain these injunctions publish, at the same time, the correspondence of Governor Letcher with the proprietors of the Gallego Mills there—refusing to protect them against the wholesale and open robbery of their flour—who need suppose that the people of Virginia are going to raise grain to be in like manner seized for the support of the horde of locusts who infest and devour their substance? And thus it is that, betwixt the *fears* that the Northern troops may seize upon their tobacco, and the *certainty* that the Confederate chiefs will rob them of their corn and wheat, Virginia is sure not to be cultivated to any great extent this year, even if the able-bodied men were left there to do it; and the prospect, therefore, is, as a matter of course, that the rebel troops will be starved out, even if they are not meanwhile whipped out.

"But what a prospect for old Virginia! What a prospect for any State South, when the tyrants at Richmond take upon themselves to prescribe what shall be planted by the farmers, and then assume the right to rob them of it without color of law or right! Governor Letcher, when appealed to, declares his inability to protect the most prominent and enterprising citizens of the State, turning them over for any redress to the law officers, when the iron-heel of the military despotism tramples all law into the dirt.

Our sympathizers with secession ought to have a few week's experience of the real thing to cure them of their distemper.—*Cincinnati Commercial*.

"Matchless misery," has beeen defined to be having a cigar and nothing to light it with.

Anger your friend, and you will be surprised to find what a villain you are, even in his estimation.

Society has come to the belief that marriage vows are but masks to conceal infidelity and hypocrisy.

The Cavalry Fight on the Rappahannock.

Splendid Conduct of Our Troops.

The New York Tribune's Potomac army correspondence of the 19th instant, furnishes the following additional details of the recent spirited and successful cavalry dash under Gen. Averill:

Your correspondent with the late cavalry expedition under Gen. Averill, sent you a full account by telegraph last night, but the success of the affair renders it necessary to enlarge further [illegible] incidents of the [illegible] pride on the part of Gen. Averill, in the success of the expedition. It seems that soon after the last attempt on our lines near Hartwood church, Fitzhugh Lee sent over a flag of truce for the bodies of two of his officers, who were killed on that occation. At this time Lee left a bantering letter with the pickets for Gen. Averill, who was his classmate at West Point, indirectly challenging him to come over and fight him. Lee had not long to wait. It being found necessary to clear one flank in the direction of Warrenton of prowling rebels, and to positively verify some reports of our scouts, General Averill was ordered to make a dash in that direction, cross the river, find Lee, and fight him. All of which was handsomely done.

The expedition left on Monday morning, and arrived near Kelley's Ford late in the day. The force detailed to move toward Warrenton did so early the next (Tuesday) morning; and though advancing to the railroad at Bealeton Station, found nothing but scouts of the enemy, although the citizens reported a brigade of them in that vicinity, and information had come that Stuart was at Warrenton on Monday, but whether with or without force it was impossible to say.

The crossing of the ford was accomplished soon after daylight by Gen. Averill's main force, and for brilliant bravery fully equals the report of Fredericksburg, although no artillery was used on either side. It was certainly one of the most remarkable exhibitions of dash and daring which has yet occurred in the war.

The ford was narrow, the roads on either side barricaded by trees, and the approaches and operations had all to be conducted in the face of a scathing fire from rebel sharpshooters, who were well concealed in and behind houses and ditches on their side. But our men effected the passage with a loss surprisingly small, and executed the movement so suddenly that only a portion of the dismounted rebels managed to escape. The rest were captured to the number of fifty, and they reported that the guard at the ford was about one hundred, it having been increased that morning by a detachment from Rappahannock Ford, four miles above.

The fight at the ford, which delayed our crossing for an hour and a half, served to put Lee on his guard, and Gen. Averill very rightly supposed he would turn out his brigade, and ride down to see what was the matter. He had verified his supposition of Lee's whereabouts from the statement of the prisoners, who said his camp was two miles and a half this side of Culpepper Court House, and that his whole brigade of five regiments was there. He therefore rested his command for an hour or two with pickets well thrown out. About 12½ the advance was ordered, and in fifteen minutes the enemy was discovered.

The largest and most brilliant cavalry contest of the war followed, lasting with slight intermissions, until 5 o'clock, in which Lee was repulsed at every point, driven two miles with heavy loss, the conflict being mainly with the sabre and pistol, though the carbine was frequently used with excellent effect. Our men making several gallant charges, the enemy retreating in every instance, generally not waiting until the flashing sabres of our men got within striking distance, but rushing for the friendly cover of the woods. Your correspondent has seen in this war several brilliant cavalry charges, but he never saw anything so handsome and exciting as the daring charge made in the beginning of the fight on the left of our line, by Col. Duffie, commanding on that part of the field.

Our cavalry was composed partly of new and partly of tried regiments, and I must say that they nearly all behaved with great credit. The affair is of great benefit to our cavalry force, who have thus been taught that they are fully equal, if not superior, to the enemy. Lee was soundly thrashed in every contest he sought, and our forces retired when they got ready, without interruption.

Cultivating Flax.—Several persons have requested us to call the attention of the agricultural readers to the importance of the cultivation of flax. We are assured that the ground in this vicinity is well suited to the growing of flax, and that its cultivation may be profitably engaged in. Cotton which sold in 1860 for twelve cents a pound now commands 90 cents. Could an abundance of flax be obtained, the rise of cotton would in a great measure cease, as an article for manufacturing purposes. As there are no prospects at present of an edequate supply of cotton being furnished for several years, our farmers should at once commence the raising of flax, as one of their crops.

It is stated that from the flax raised on one acre of ground about fourteen bushels of seed can be obtained, and for the seed alone the crop is not unremunerative. Six hundred pounds of fibre can be raised upon one acre of ground. At thirty cents per pound (one-third that of cotton at present prices) the value of an acre's product would be less than one hundred and eighty dollars. Never before has such an inviting prospect for the cultivation of flax been presented.

(Wheel. Intel.)

The statistics of Canada show that the number of skeddadlers from the United States, who became frightened at the prospect of a draft, numbered 1,942. These persons took with them an averag of $1,000 each in American silver, making an aggregate of $2,000,000.

John Minor Botts is said to be still a staunch friend of the Union, and hopes for a speedy restoration of its authority all over the land.

Rebel Cruelties in Texas.

Among the prisoners exchanged and just arrived at New Orleans, were 270 of the 8th United States infantry, who have been held ever since the treachery of Gen. Twiggs, in Texas. They give exciting accounts of the indignities to which they have been subjected. They were alternately coaxed and abused to induce them to enlist in the rebel service, but only fifteen of the men yielded to the pressure. A New Orleans correspondent of the *Times* reports some of their statements:

"They were finally on parole, given the liberty of Bexar county; they were then sent to Camp Verde, where the men suffered all sort of privations. They were then removed to the Indian frontier, and most of the men got the scurvy. Dr. Payne, Confederate surgeon, refused them medical attendance, and said if he had his way he would shoot them like dogs. On New Year's day, 1862, they were drawn up in line and informed by Captain Ashby, of McCulloch's regiment, that if they held any conversation with the citizens or the negroes, they would be hung like dogs to certain trees, which were pointed out in the vicinity; and further, if they passed beyound a certain line of bushes which were pointed out, they would be fired on by the guard. The authorities finally becoming incensed at their determination not to enlist in the rebel service, they were imprisoned at Fort Mason, and kept under close guard.—On the 28th of June, 1862, they were started again for San Antonio, where they arrived in the latter part of July. On the march they were pointed out a tree, near a town called Fredericksburg, upon which seventy-five Union men had been hung.

"Among the heroes of the Confederate rule in Texas is a Capt. Duff, who was at one time a soldier in the 2nd United States infantry, but was for misconduct sentenced to receive fifty lashes and be branded with the letter D on his back and dismissed from the service. This man has, and still is, distinguishing himself for his unheard-of cruelties to Union people. At Fredericksburg, after Gen. Hamilton's escape, he shot the Union men in presence of their wives and children, and then gave the latter up to the wildest abuse of his soldiers. He tied some of these unfortunate Union men to trees and amused himself with shooting at them with his pistol, for a mark. He burned several houses and fired the German church with his own hands. At Austin, these soldiers found that the greatest excitement prevailed against Gen. Hamilton, and nothing so far has saved his children from destruction except their youth. When our men passed his house, the little fellows ran out and clapped their hands, and showed every sign of pleasure and sympathy. The conscription is carried on throughout Texas with the greatest severity—a party of Germans in the southern part of Travis county, who resisted this oppression, were coolly massacred, as an evidence of what might be the fate of others who resisted the authorities. Our men found that North-western Texas was thoroughly loyal, and this fact was impressed upon our soldiers whenever they got an opportunity of speaking unobserved. The people hoped and prayed that the national government would speedily do something to rescue them from the more than Algerine bondage."

The Best Bed.—Of the eight pounds which a man eats and drinks in a day, it is thought that not less than five pounds leave his body through the skin. And of these five pounds a considerable percentage escapes during the night, while he is in bed. The larger part of this is water; but, in addition, there is much effete and poisonous matter. This being in great part gaseous in form, permeates every part of the bed. Thus, all parts of the bed, mattress, blankets, as well as sheets, soon become foul and need purification. The mattress needs this renovation quite as much as the sheets. To allow the sheets to be used without washing or changing, three or six months, would be regarded as very bad housekeeping; but I insist, if a thin sheet can absorb enough of the poisonous excretions of the body to make it unfit for use in a few days, a thick mattress which can absorb and retain a thousand times as much of these poisonous excrations, needs to be purified as often, certainly, as once in three months. A sheet can be washed; a mattress can not be renovated in this way. Indeed there is no other way of cleaning a mattress but by steaming it, or picking it to pieces, and thus in fragments exposing it to the direct rays of the sun. As these processes are scarcely practicable, with any of the ordinary mattresses, I am decidedly of the opinion that the good old fashioned straw bed, which can every three months be changed for fresh straw, and the tick be washed, is the sweetest and healthiest of beds. If, in the winter season, the porousness of the straw bed makes it a little uncomfortable, spread over a comforter or two woolen blankets, which should be washed as often as every two weeks. With this arrangement, if you wash all the bed covering as often as once in two or three weeks, you will have a delightful, healthy bed. Now, if you leave the bed to air, with open windows during the day, and not make it up for the night before evening, you will have added greatly to the sweetness of your rest, and, in consequence, to the tone of your health.

Served Him Right.—The Superintendent of Common Schools for Benton county, Iowa, after due and public investigation, on the 7th inst., revoked the certificate of a teacher of Harrison township, in that county, named Allen, for uttering and inculcating disloyal and traitorous sentiments among his pupils, and generally elsewhere. The charge was fully proved, and the Superintendent held that it was his duty to withdraw the certificate which authorized the employment of the defendant as a teacher in the public schools of the county. We don't know whether or not that decision is "constitutional;" but we are certain that it was sensible and patriotic. The disloyal should not only be spurned from our public schools but from every other public employment. If they want office let them go down to Dixie among the other traitors.—(Burlington Hawkeye.

"Why don't you ask your sweetheart to marry you?"
"I have asked her."
"What did she say?"
"O, I've the *refusal* of her."

To the People of the Congressional District of West Virginia, composed of the counties of Kanawha, Jackson Mason, Cabell, Clay, Wayne, Logan, Boone, Braxton, Nicholas, McDowell, Wyoming, Raleigh, Fayette, Mercer, Monroe, and Greenbrier:

Fellow Citizens:

The time is near when at the polls you will make known your preference of the man to represent you in the next Congress of the United States. In the exercise of the right we all enjoy, I bow before your sovereign power, and present myself as a candidate for your suffrages and that high honor.

The People have the right, and should avail themselves of the privilege, to demand of those who offer to represent and serve them, to inform them of their political opinions and the course they would take if elected to be their representative, and it is proper that this demand should be complied with, and the candidate should also inform them of his political proclivities and acts in relation to the questions and measures, which affect the people, and no honest candidate for their suffrages will try to conceal them.

I am a West Virginian by birth and of choice. My property is in West Virginia, consequently, if you as members of the State enjoy prosperity or suffer adversity, I will with you be affected by either condition.

I consider the Constitution of the Federal Government as the very best and most perfect system of primary or fundamental law that has ever been conceived in the mind or come from the hands of men. If any defect can be found in it, or addition to it or alteration be desired, to change or amend it, if found by experience, it has within itself provisions for all these to be made, as the will of the people of the United States may demand at the polls.

While the Constitution was made to give equal protection to all, it was intended by it to restrain the impulsive, impolitic and hasty legislation, which men influenced by passion, excitement or prejudice, or intoxicated by the accidental possession of power, are liable and disposed to indulge in. But most especially was it made to protect the rights of the minority.

All political power was (before the establishment of the General Government) in the possession of the people of the States. But when they gave existence to the General Government, they yielded and relinquished a certain portion prescribed of their powers to that Government. And that Government in its legislation must restrict itself to the powers ceded to it by the people. It has no constitutional power to interfere with the reserved rights of the people or States, their property or institutions, while they remain loyal to the Federal Union, its Constitution and General Government.

No other people had a better government than we of the United States. Never has any other people so rapidly increased in population, and prospered as we have. None were more happy and contented. Yet notwithstanding we were in the happy enjoyment of all these blessings and advantages of a free government, elected by the people, the best qualified to secure equal rights to all, and greatest amount of liberty, we have allowed political gamblers, demagogues, knaves, prejudiced fanatics, bigots and fools, to involve us in the most suicidal and abominable war that any people has had the misfortune to be scourged with. They have at the instigation of the Devil sown among us the winds of jealousy, contention, hate and bad feelings, and we are now overwhelmed in the whirlwind, which their united concentration has brought about, which no one can control. Too many of our politicians are in the condition of the Scotchman, who selfishly prayed after this fashion: "O Lord I beseech thee to turn the world upside down with great confusion, by some mighty revolution, for well thou knowest by no change or misfortune can my condition be made worse, but possibly something may turn up, by which it may be improved."

I am in favor of doing all that possibly can be done to preserve our great and glorious Federal Union, and for the suppression of the rebellion.

Secession is inexpedient and suicidal in its tendency, as it has within itself the elements of delapidation and dissolution. It concedes the right to subdivide the nation or State. Savages, who know no law but that of force, by acting on it become divided into tribe, bands or clans, who without restraint indulge in envy, ambition, robbery, murder and war to the annoyance and destruction of their neighbors, and render themselves unable to make defence against nations better organized, whose people act together mutually to assist each other.

While the States remain in the Union, we can resist the hostile assaults of all other nations combined, but if they seperate, they will have war among themselves, and the strongest of them, from comparitive weakness, will be liable to be insulted and opposed by foreign nations, who may choose to meddle with their commerce &c.

"Be at peace, and good shall come unto you." I will do all I can to obey this command, because I have faith in the promise of the "good that will come unto us". And I will try to have "the fatted calf got ready to feast returning brethern, who may repent of their sins," and I will "*hasten and run to meet and embrace them*". There should be no strife between us, for we be brethren, and the land is in its length and breadth ample to bear us, our servants and cattle, and the water is sufficient for them all to drink." "We have all gone estray like lost sheep." "O that the Lord the gift would give us to see ourselves as others see us, it would from many a fault relieve us, and foolish notion."

Had I been your representative in the last Congress, I would have opposed the pragmatical imposition and dictation in reference to our slave emancipation in West Virginia. Had I been a member of your State Convention and last Legislature, I would have voted to make West Virginia a free state, as I will as a citizen to ratify the acts of that Convention and Legislature for the object of making West Virginia a free state.

I am an order loving man. If any law is objectionable to me, I will try to have it repealed or amended; but will quietly submit to it while it remains.

Our war of 1812 with England is regarded as our second for our independance. I served a tour in the army in that war, and was severely wounded in the battle of Crany Island, and I am now willing to aid all I can in the present and third war for our independence.

I am for resisting all attempts of foreign nations, that may be made to establish colonies on this continent, or to meddle with the free governments on it. In North and South America the system of republican institutions should be sustained and protected against the assaults of despotic governments. In Europe a monarchical system of Government prevails, with which it is not proper for us to interfere.

In the hope that you will take my proposition to represent you into favorable consideration, be assured that I properly appreciate the honor, which [illegible] confer, and to which I aspire

Yours respectfully,
J. F. CALDWELL, [illegible]
of Lewisburg, Greenbrier Co., West Virginia.

Home Traitors To Be Punished.—The following order was issued by Gen. Wright. This order is published as a warning to all who are in any way corresponding or giving intelligence to the rebels at home or abroad, or furnishing them with arms or amunition:

Headquarters Dep't of the Ohio,
Cincinnati, O., March 29, 1863.

General Order No. 24.

The following articles of war are published for the information of all concerned; and all officers in the military service of the United States, in the Department of the Ohio, are enjoined to arrest all persons guilty of their violation, without regard to age, sex or condition, and submit proper charges against such offenders, that they may be brought before a court martial for trial:

Art. 56. "Whosoever shall relieve the enemy with money, victuals, or amunition, or shall knowingly harbor or protect an enemy, shall suffer death, or such other punishment as shall be ordered by the sentence of a court martial."

Art. 57. "Whosoever shall be convicted of holding correspondence with, or giving intelligence to, the enemy, either directly or indirectly, shall suffer death, or such other punishment as shall be ordered by the sentence of a court martial."

By command of Maj. Gen. Wright,
N. H. McLean,
Ass't Adj't-Gen., Chief of Staff.
Official: C. W. Foster, Ass't Adj't-Gen.

Substitutes for the Rebel Army—Exhaustion of the Military Population.

In a Richmond paper of the 17th inst. we find sixteen advertisements for substitutes, with the condition generally attached that he must be over forty-five years of age, which shows that the population of the regular military age, between eighteen and forty-five, must be exhausted, and that the rebellion is on its last legs, when it must resort to old men to fight its battles.

To show the pressure that exists, we may state that in nearly all the advertisements "a liberal price" is offered, while in one the specific sum of $1,000 is held out, with the remark that "a bugler is preferred," and the man must be of "sober and industrious habits." In another advertisement the sum of $400 is offered as a reward for the arrest of a substitute who deserted after getting his pay. We are told he is "a Canadian by birth." All these are indications of the terrible straits to which the chiefs of the Southern insurrection are now reduced. Their men are exhausted. Their money has become almost worthless, being four or five hundred per cent below the par standard of gold. One vigorous effort now, and the rebellion is forever laid low.

Burning Stubble.—The *Massachusetts Ploughman* says:

Would it not be a good plan to burn the straw, and all the stubble on the wheat ground, after the harvest is over. The ashes on some kind of land would be equal to the straw as manure. It was customary with our farmers before the Revolution, to let the fire over the stubble ground before ploughing it in the fall or spring, calculating on the benefit of the ash manure. We doubt whether the burning of the stubble and of the straw also, may not be the most effectual way of killing Hessian flies, midges, and smut on grain. Has any farmer tried it?

Embalming the Dead—A Process Practicable to All.—The modern process by which the bodies of officers and soldiers of the army have been embalmed and restored to their friends is not the least of the blessings which science has bestowed upon the world since the beginning of the war. The expense of this process, in most cases, places its advantages beyond the reach of people of moderate means. A matter of so great general utility and importance should not be monopolized or turned wholly to individual emolument. The following is a simple receipt by which any physician or surgeon of ordinary capacity can embalm the dead, and preserve them from decomposition for a length of time to answer all practical requirements.

"The liquid chlorid of zinc injected into the carotid or femoral artery, will preserve bodies from decomposition or putrefaction for a great length of time.

"The mode of obtaining this liquid is to take (say) a quart of hydrochloric acid in an earthen vessel, and add small pieces of zinc until reaction ceases.

"This liquid may be diluted in the proportion of one part to four of water. From one quart to three pints of this diluted chlorid of zinc will be sufficient to effect the purpose desired."

Last Lines of Uhland.—Rev. C. T. Brooks sends to the Boston Transcript a translation of the last lines the great German poet Uhland ever wrote. They were on the death of an infant, and, as Mr. Brooks truly remarks, "are in perfect keeping with the simplicity of the poet's walk and character, and form a fitting swan-song for his own true and pure and peaceful life." Does not the little quatrain deserve to be remembered side by side with that Persian one of the new-born child given by Sir William Jones?

We saw thee come—we saw thee go—
Brief guest in this our earthly land—
Wherefrom? Whereto? We only know—
From God's own hand to God's own hand.

Daily Evening Traveller.

VOL. XIX.......NO. 4. BOSTON, MONDAY, APRIL 6, 1863. PRICE THREE CENTS.

Daily Evening Traveller.

MONDAY, APRIL 6, 1863.

WENDELL PHILLIPS, Esq.,

—ON—

A METROPOLITAN POLICE.

[PHONOGRAPHICALLY REPORTED FOR THE TRAVELLER BY J. M. W. YERRINTON.]

WENDELL PHILLIPS, ESQ., spoke at the Melodeon yesterday forenoon, before the Twenty-Eighth Congregational Society, advocating the establishment of a Metropolitan Police. Notwithstanding the dismal weather, the hall was crowded. After the usual preliminary Sunday services, Mr. Phillips said:

I have been requested to speak to you to-day on the subject of a Metropolitan Police. That plan has been already presented, two or three years ago, to this community, and of late, very elaborately and eloquently argued before a committee of the Legislature, by Edward L. Peirce, Esq., and still more comprehensively and in detail, by Chas. M. Ellis, Esq.; but it is one of vital importance to the welfare and progress of our city, and until the object be achieved, it can never be too frequently considered and urged. Other cities have led the way in this path, years ago. The capital of the civilized world, London, many years ago found herself utterly unable to contend with the evils of accumulated population—found municipal machinery utterly inadequate for the security of life or property in her streets; and the national government, by the hand of Sir Robert Peel, assumed the police regulation of that cluster of towns which we call London.

New York, on our continent, about six years ago, followed the example; Baltimore and Cincinnati have done likewise to a greater or less extent, and so also have some of the other Western cities. The experience of all great accumulations of property and population reads us a lesson that the execution of the laws therein demand extra consideration and peculiar machinery. Hitherto, the police regulations in the city of Boston have been modelled on those of a small town; that is, the inhabitants themselves have called into existence a body of constables, in fact, to execute the laws of the State and the by-laws of the city. Our text in presenting this subject to you, is this: in Boston, as everywhere else where large numbers are massed together and great masses of property are found, a police force appointed by the voters of the place cannot be relied on to execute the laws; and in order to secure their full and impartial execution it has been found necessary elsewhere, and I shall attempt to show you that it is necessary here, to put the control of the police force into other hands than those of the voters of the peninsula. That is our claim—that the men of the peninsula, like those of other great cities, are not to be trusted with the execution of the State laws, but that executive power must be based on broader foundations.

Such a course is no uncommon machinery in Democratic institutions. We put the interpretation of the laws—the Judiciary—not into the hands of any local municipal body, but the interpretation of the laws is in the hands of persons appointed by the whole State. I invoke the same principle for their execution—following old Republican precedents, as I shall shortly show.

In order to sustain this claim before you, I ought to show three or four things. First, that in important particulars—*important* particulars—the law has failed of execution; that good and vitally important laws have failed of execution. Secondly, I ought to show you that this failure is due to the machinery which the city puts in motion for the execution of the laws. Thirdly, that a better machinery may be found. And, fourthly, that it is important for the welfare of the State that the attempt to find a better machinery should be made.

My first point is to show you that in important particulars, where great and grave interests are involved, the laws have failed of execution. You perceive that this involves in fact an indictment against the city government. It is in reality arraigning the government of the city for failure to do its duty. Before I pass to it, therefore, let me make one protest.

I do not come here to find fault with individual policemen. I think our body of police is as good, on the average, as that of any great city I know. I think upon all trying occasions they have done their duty, as far as they have been permitted, and have always shown full capacity to do their whole duty. Neither do I come here to arraign the individuals of the city government; not, however, I deem it unnecessary. They are mere puppets, fluttering before us for a little while; they are only victims of a great system which they did not originate and cannot control. Looking over the last dozen years, considering that our city government during those years has been, in the aggregate, only a standing committee appointed by the grog shops of the peninsula, it has been no honor, but a shame, to hold one of its offices. No man with a full measure of self-respect could accept such an office. All politics necessitates questionable compliances. But this serfdom touches a base depth. But it is not necessary, and certainly not within my purview to-day to arraign individuals.

I am merely criticising a system which throws up into unfitting places and undue importance men who have no real right to the power which they are wholly unable or unwilling to use. To return now to my first point, I am to tell you then that in many important particulars the laws have failed of execution. I shall take, in the first place, Temperance. Some men look upon the temperance cause as whining bigotry, narrow asceticism or a vulgar sentimentality, fit for little minds—weak women and weaker men. On the contrary, I regard it as second only to one or two others of the primary reforms of this age, and for this reason: Every race has its peculiar temptation; every clime has its specific sin. The tropics and tropical races are tempted to one form of sensuality; the colder and temperate regions, and our Saxon blood find their peculiar temptation in the stimulus of drink and food. In old times our Heaven was a drunken revel. We relieve ourselves from the over-weariness of constant and exhausting toil by intoxication. Science has brought a cheap means of drunkenness within the reach of every individual; and national prosperity and institutions have put into the hands of almost every workman the means of being drunk for a week on the labor of two or three hours.

With that blood and that temptation we have adopted Democratic institutions, where the law has no sanction but the purpose and virtue of the masses. The statute book rests not on the bayonets of Europe, but on the hearts of the people. A drunken people can never be the basis of a free government. It is the corner-stone neither of virtue, prosperity nor progress. To us, therefore, the title deeds of whose estates and the safety of whose lives depend upon the tranquility of the streets, upon the virtue of the masses, the presence of any vice that brutalizes the average mass of mankind, tends to make it more readily the tool of intriguing and corrupt leaders, is necessarily a stab at the very life of the nation. Against such a vice is marshalled the Temperance Reformation. That my sketch is no mere fancy picture, every one of you know. Every one of you can glance back over your own path, and count many and many a one among those who started from the goal at your side, with equal energy and perhaps greater promise, who has found a drunkard's grave long before this.

The brightness of the bar, the ornament of the pulpit, the hope and blessing and stay of many a family—you know, every one of you who has reached middle life, how often on your path you set up the warning—"Fallen before the temptations of the streets!" Hardly one house in this city, whether it be full and warm with all the luxury of wealth or whether it find hard, cold maintenance by the most earnest economy, no matter which—hardly a house that does not count among sons or nephews, some victim of this vice. The skeleton of this warning sits at every board. The whole world is kindred in this suffering. The country mother launches her boy with trembling upon the temptations of city life; the father trusts his daughter anxiously to the young man she has chosen, knowing what a wreck intoxication may make of the house-tree they set up. Alas! how often are their worst forebodings more than fulfilled. I have known a case—and probably many of you can recall some almost equal to it—where one worthy woman could count father, brother, husband, and son-in-law all drunkards—no man among her near kindred, except her son, who was not a victim of this vice.

Like all other appetites, this finds resolution weak when set against the constant presence of temptation. This is the evil. How are the laws relating to it executed in this city? Let me tell you:

First, there has been great discussion of this evil—wide, earnest, patient discussion, for thirty-five years. The whole community has been stirred by the discussion of this question. Finally, after various experiments, the majority of the State decided that the method to stay this evil was to stop the open sale of intoxicating drink. They left moral suasion still to address the individual, and set themselves as a community to close the doors of temptation. Every man acquainted with his own nature or with society, knows that weak virtue, walking through our streets and meeting at every tenth door (for that is the average) the temptation to drink, must fall; that one must be a moral Hercules to pass unstained. To prevent the open sale of intoxicating liquor has been the method selected by the State to help its citizens to be virtuous; in other words, the State has enacted what is called the Maine Liquor Law. You may drink in your own parlors, you may make what amount of indulgence you please your daily rule, the State does not touch you there; there you injure only yourself, and those you directly influence; that the State cannot reach.

But when you open a door and say to your fellow-citizens, "Come and indulge," the State has a right to ask, "In what do you invite them to indulge? Is it in something that helps or something that harms the community?"

I will try to show you in a moment on what grounds the State decided that these numberless open doors harmed the community, and that the method to be adopted was to shut them up. The majority, after full argument in district schoolhouses, the streets, and the State House, from pulpits, lyceum platforms, and everywhere else, decided that prohibition of the traffic was the only effective method. The law was put upon the statute book. A reluctant minority went to the Legislature and endeavored to repeal or amend it, alleging that this was not a good law, and they were voted down. Again they went—were voted down. A third time they went—were voted down. They then appealed to the Courts, and said, "This is not a constitutional law." The Courts said, "It is." If anything ever had the decided, unmistakable sanction of a majority of the people of this Commonwealth, the Maine Liquor Law has it.

After a quarter of a century of discussion, it was enacted; three times assailed, it was maintained; subjected to the crucible of the Court, it came out pure gold. We have a right to say that is the matured, settled purpose of the majority of the Commonwealth; if the majority have a right to govern, that law is to govern. Have we not? If not, let the minority assail again the Gibraltar of the statute. But meanwhile it is, like all other laws, not immoral, to be obeyed. I have not therefore to argue to-day whether the law is good or not, whether it is wise or not. That is settled. It is good and wise in the opinion of the Commonwealth. The era of *public opinion* is finished, that of *law* has commenced. This is the history of all legislation. Do not find fault with us for enacting, in due time, public opinion into a statute. Where did all statutes come from? Hundreds of years ago men argued the question, "shall one man own a separate piece of land?" They argued it and settled that he should. That became a statute. They then began to argue the question, "shall he transmit to his children by will?" They argued that for centuries, then said, "Yes," and enacted it. Nobody now goes behind those statutes. Hundreds of years ago our race argued the question, "Shall a man have one wife or three?" We settled that he should have but one; it is the law of the Commonwealth.

The era of discussion and opinion is over; the era of legislation has come; the time when the minority sits down and obeys. With all great questions, covering important interests, there is a time when public opinion stereotypes itself into statutes.

Land, wheat, marriage, the rules against burglary and theft, settled themselves years ago. If I raise a harvest, it is mine; that is the law of the land. There was a time when it was a question; it is not a question now. So with temperance and the Maine liquor law. Time was when the question whether a man had a right to sell liquor openly, unlicensed, was discussed; we have passed that point, and reached the time when the majority, in other words, the State, decrees that these shops shall be shut.

Now, let me show you, in a few words, *why* it should decree that. Let me show it by an instance. Take our city. Our city met that statute thus. It said, "You may decree it if you please, we won't execute it. You say we shall not license anybody, but we will effect the same thing, for we will let everybody sell except just those whom we should not have licensed." These are the exact words of the order to the police some years ago. The Chief of Police replied to a question from the Massachusetts Temperance Society, "We have directions never to prosecute a liquor seller, unless he be one who would not have received a license under the old license act."

In other words, the State says, "On mature consideration, I prohibit the sale." The city says, "I shall allow it—help yourself!" Those whom it would not have licensed are "nuisances," as it calls them—houses vulgar, noisy, disorderly; kept, as the Dogberry of the Board of Aldermen told us at the State House, by "imbecile old men and ancient women,"—as the constable of Shakspeare's play arrested all "vagrom men." That is the position of the city. The law is intentionally and avowedly set aside. The City Government announces that it does not intend to obey it; makes no effort and never has to enforce it. What is the result? The result is that there are at least 3000 places in the city where liquor is publicly and continually sold. These consist partly of dram shops, partly of gambling saloons, partly of houses of prostitution. They number in all more than 3000; I am giving an under estimate of an average for two or three years. What are the results of these 3000 places of sale? Six million dollars worth of liquor is sold to the retailers of this city annually; and three million dollars' worth is annually retailed on the peninsula. With what result? With this. They produce poverty and crime to this extent. We arrest for drunkenness alone, on an average for the last three years, about 17,000 persons annually; that is a little less than one-tenth of the population.

There are between twenty-five and thirty thousand persons relieved for poverty by overseers of the poor and by the Provident Association—poverty caused by intemperance. That is, every seventh man in the city is a pauper, helped by the community; every tenth man in the city is a criminal, arrested by the police. Let us look at that a [illegible] wholesome poverty, is no [illegible]. Poverty, motive power that throws a man up to guide and control the community; it is the spur that often wins the race; it is the trial that calls out, like fire, all the deep, great qualities of a man's nature.—That poverty is no evil, at least, it is no unmixed evil; but poverty that is caused by drunkenness—for I am only taking, in these 25,000 persons, the poverty that is traceable to intemperance—the poverty that is caused by drunkenness has what history? The father is a drunkard; the mother often imitates him; the self-respect of the family is lost; the home is gone; it is a scene of quarrel and degradation; the children are thrown neglected on the streets, with no food, no education, no moral sense developed,—the frightful and fruitful source of every vice known to the civil code.

That feeds the gallows, fills the street with impurity, makes thieves and burglars. Out of these houses flows a constant supply for all forms of crime. Without the open and continued sale of drink, almost every hell of the gambler would be closed; he would have few victims. He would find few men in the mood to be victimized. Without open places for the sale of liquor, the houses of prostitution could not be maintained; that is the testimony of all experience in every city. To that shameless pit woman seldom sinks except when betrayed by drink—and even when once ruined, could not bear such a life unless nature was daily stupefied by intoxication. One-tenth of those sent to the House of Industry are common drunkards. Intemperance is the most productive of all causes of insanity. "Truancy" finds its "cause of causes" in intemperance.

Said the Chief of Police three or four years ago, "Intemperance is the direct origin of more poverty, more crime, and consequent suffering, than all other causes combined. Twenty-five thousand men reduced to poverty in a year, or at least every year relieved by the public.

Now let me go to the schools. Twenty-five thousand is an average estimate of the children who attend our public schools. The city pours out a quarter of a million a year to mould those young souls, step by step, to virtue, to make them good citizens. Twenty-five thousand with one hand it lifts up; with the other hand it forces down 25,000 into pollution and crime. It spends $477,000 a year to do it; for that is the cost of our police force, of our own overseers of the poor, of our lunatic asylums, (a large portion of whose inmates are rendered insane by intemperance,) our house of correction and house of industry. You might as well take a third of a million of dollars and toss it off the end of Long wharf—we should be richer at the end of the year. Leave all the children idle in the streets, shut up the grog shops, shut up the schools, throw a third of a million into the water, and the city would be better off on the 31st day of December than she is now.

That is the cost of intemperance. One-half the criminals of the State are found in the city of Boston. We have one-sixth the population, and yet we have more than one-half the criminals. We have one-sixth of the population, but we pay about one-half of all the criminal expenses of the State of Massachusetts—just three times our proper proportion.

What does it come from? I am not to charge it on any particular corporation; I am to charge it to a system. It is the massing up of one-third of the capital of the State and one-sixth the population on this peninsula. That makes a new order of things, one calling for a new machinery to check crime; a hot-bed, where all the tendencies to crime become doubled and trebled, where the dangerous classes of the community get undue power. It is because of that peculiarity that we need a different system from what the country does. Up to a certain point, our city government has always acknowledged this. For instance, in a small country town of a few thousand inhabitants they have two or three constables. Nobody knows who they are. You might visit half a dozen houses and they could not tell you. Only once or twice in a year, on some festive or other occasion, a town meeting, a pic nic, or something of the kind, is he ever seen or needed. He may execute a writ once in a while. If there is any disorder in the town a citizen takes notice of it, reports it to a justice of the peace, and the difficulty is cured. That is a sufficient machinery for a small town.

But, when you have a large and dense population, great wealth invested in certain dangerous and tempting forms, you cannot trust the execution of the laws to the volunteer efforts of the citizens; you must have a large body of police, constantly in the streets, ever on the alert, with grave powers, with extraordinary functions to watch criminals and follow them up. That has been found necessary. Now, the question is whether something further is not necessary also. The returns for ten years show that 42 per cent. of the average population of this county was arrested for crime, while, in other counties, the number arrested was only one, two, or three per cent. Why this difference? Because a city necessarily induces greater temptations, greater dangers, and more frequent crimes. It needs, therefore, a more stringent machinery to execute the laws. Instead of that, in regard to this temperance law, the city government defy it. They, themselves, pay—or did pay until within a year or two, I will not speak of the present year, for I have not consulted the reports—about a thousand dollars a month out of the city treasury for the indulgencies of the Board of Aldermen and Common Councilmen at an illegal liquor shop, which no one of them had a right to see without presenting it to the courts within twenty-four hours.

In that disgraceful Anthony Burns and Sims experience of the city, upon which I am shortly to speak, one of the melancholy features of city sin that day was that the men illegally called out to defy the State laws contracted a bill, within sight of the Supreme Court, within sight of City Hall, of between one and two thousand dollars, for liquor and food furnished them at an illegal grog shop, by order of the city.

Let me pause a moment on this question and turn to another—Free Speech. Free speech is so vital an element of civil life, so important a privilege, that the framers of our government were not willing to leave it to the law—they enshrined it in the Constitution. It was so fundamental that it could not be left to annual legislation; it was grouted and dovetailed into the very first stratum of the foundation of the State. Now, the class of men who have had the ordering of city affairs have never, for the last twenty years, attempted to protect free speech on this peninsula.

Let me tell you what I mean. If a man like the editor of the Boston *Post*, like the Honorable Edward Everett, like Mr. Sumner, any popular person in the community, wished to hold a meeting on this peninsula, he could always do it; but if any set of men who are unpopular wanted to hold a meeting here, it depended entirely upon the mood of the mob that month whether they could hold it or not. These very walls could testify, if they had voice, how many dozen times they have seen their occupants, paying an honest price for a day's use of them, disturbed hour after hour, and finally, perhaps, in some instances, the meeting broken up, by a crowd of boys that the right hand of one policeman could have quelled; and when individu-

leader." But men say at the State House, in reply to the eloquent argument of Mr. Ellis—Mr. Healy, Alderman Amory—said, "We cannot execute an unpopular law." Indeed! Indeed! I can remember when Marshal Tukey put a chain round your Court House to execute a law that was hated by the Commonwealth of Massachusetts full as bitterly as Beacon street hates the Maine Liquor Law; and I can remember when he went up to a legislative committee appointed to examine into his conduct, and inquire why a policeman of the city of Boston was acting in that illegal manner, against the statute of the State, and answered Mr. Keyes, "Sir, I know it is illegal, but I mean to do it. Help yourself!"

In 1843, Latimer was arrested by a policeman, with a lie in his mouth. In 1851, Sims was surrendered by policemen acting illegally, and avowing their defiance. In 1854, Burns was sent back, and his claimants were aided by the police, contrary to the statute. Unpopular laws! The city can execute anything it wants to, unpopular or popular. The city executes every one of its own by-laws perfectly. No man steals with impunity; no man violates Sunday with impunity; no man sets up a nuisance with impunity. As the Grand Jury said, several years ago, "The municipal authorities can remove this nuisance, or at least abate it whenever they will. It is as much in their power as the offal in the sewers or the dirt in the streets."

The Report Credited at Washington.

NEW YORK, April 6.—The *Herald's* Washington despatch says a report has reached here by way of Fredericksburg, derived from rebel sources, that Charleston was bombarded by our fleet and attacked by our land forces last Thursday, and is now in possession of the Federals under General Hunter and Admiral Dupont.

The report is fully credited by prominent officers of the Government, who were in possession of facts in reference to the contemplated attack upon Charleston, which it is not yet prudent to divulge.

It is certain, however, that those who possess this information, are confident that our soldiers and sailors will celebrate the second anniversary of the fall of Fort Sumter in the captured city of Charleston.

The restrictions upon the publication in the Southern papers of any adverse news are so stringent, that it is not expected to find much in them in reference to the capture of Charleston until the disaster can be no longer concealed, but the reports which have arrived are definite and positive, and are believed by those who have the best right to know what foundation there is for them.

The *Times'* Washington despatch says the city is nervous to-night over the news derived from rebel sources, that Charleston has fallen; that an attack commenced on Friday, and was overwhelmingly successful.

A flag of truce came to Falmouth this morning The newspapers smuggled under it made no mention of the fall of Charleston or of its salvation.

5000. About 15,000 voters on this peninsula usually go to the polls, sometimes 22,000, though very rarely. Now, 5000 votes could always hold the balance in such a constituency—Republican, Democrat, Catholic, Protestant. With all varieties of opinion and purpose, three thousand men, bound together by one idea, one interest, with one purpose in view, and demanding one thing, and nothing more, can always hold the balance. There never was a city election which that number of votes massed together could not control. What is the result? The result is, that it is as much a bargain as if it were recorded in the Registry of Deeds, that the prominent aspirants for city office shall not execute the laws against the liquor shops. Is it at all remarkable?

A great many men want office—it is an American failing. Here are the men who can bestow it. They say, "This is the condition: shut your eyes upon us!" The consequence is, that both parties, all parties, are obliged to bow their necks to that yoke, and with rare exceptions there cannot be an Alderman nor a Mayor of the city elected, who is not understood to be willing to shut his eyes to that crime, and leave the law of the State unexecuted. It has been so; it always must be so, while these elements of civic strength exist, and are thus tempted to exert themselves.

The reason why the law is not executed in favor of free speech is germane and sister to this; it is, that the men who are interested in these drinking shops, and the men whose votes they can command, are of the class that hates progress, and and freedom—is naturally antagonistic to them; and any designing leader can stir up such a mass and fling it at virtue, and order, and liberty. Hence these consequences. Their agents, of their own natural bias, run greedily to do such agreeable work.

For the last ten or thirteen years this has been the machinery of the city government. They have said to the State, "We will not execute your law."

Now, law consists of four things—a statute, a policeman to arrest the offender, a jury to try him, and a judge to sentence him. The Constitution says, we shall have judges "as impartial as the lot of humanity admits." We have them. Chosen, how? By the State. The other end of the telegraph is a man to bring the offender before the judge. What is the use of a judge? He cannot move of himself, he is powerless if you do not bring the criminals before him? But the city government of Boston, chosen by this machinery I have spoken of, says to its police officers, "Don't you furnish that judge with any criminals; shut your eyes upon them!" Then, again, if one is arrested, by any accident, what more? Why, this: the statute says, that our jurymen shall be drawn from a box, in which the names of citizens of good moral character and sound judgment, free from all legal exceptions, are put. The city weeds out the jury box on another plan. In all trials that had anti-slavery or temperance in them, you might be certain of one thing—you would never see an abolitionist nor a temperance man on the jury. If he got there, it was an accident, and there was always enough to neutralize it.

It is just like the black element. We have several thousand black men in our community; you have never seen a black man on a jury but once, and that was an accident, and he was not allowed to sit, though he had been regularly drawn. Many of them are of good moral character, but their names never get into the box; or, if they get in, never come out. So of a man known, distinctively, as an abolitionist; if his name goes in, it never comes out. So of a man known as a temperance man; rarely does his name come out. But liquor dealers have always been abundant; no jury was trusted alone without them. If the State furnishes good judges, and the city, at the other end, furnishes no criminals, or, when one is by chance caught, fortifies him with a jury that will disagree on his side, how is the law to be executed? As long as the City Government is chosen by men whose interest is on that side, how can it be otherwise? How is the law to be executed when you have entrusted its execution to men who don't wish or mean to execute it; who were elected expressly not to execute it and have the strongest motive not to do so? No matter how good individual policemen are while such men rule them. You know when Baillie Nicol Jarvie, in Scott's immortal novel, let Rob Roy out of jail—he was an Alderman, a Baillie, and let him out—he said to Rob, "If you continue to be such a thief, you ought to have a doorkeeper in every jail, in Scotland." "Oh, no, Baillie," replied Rob, "it is just as well to have a *Baillie* in every borough." It answers the same purpose to have a servile and complacent mayor and aldermen as to have fettered policemen, because they settle the juries, and they settle the functions of the police. The consequence has been that there has been no effort to execute the law. The defence put in is, "We cannot execute the law." The Mayor said of the riots of 1860–'61, "We can't put them down." The reply of his own policemen was, "Thirty of us will put them down if you will allow us." The reply of the abolitionist was, "When did you ever make an effort to put them down? The only time you ever stood on Tremont Temple platform and issued an order, it was obeyed; the mob recognized you as their

been gone a week, and she came down to the city to hunt him up. She traced him from spot to spot, and finally found that the grog shops had gotten hold of him, made him drunk, taken his money, kept him drunk three days, so that a constable came at last and complain of him as a common drunkard, and he had gone to the House of Correction for three months. Has that town no interest in the streets of Boston? Let me tell you again a story that I have told you once or twice before, for it holds a deep moral. A few years ago, one spring afternoon, when I left the city to deliver a lecture, I alighted from the railroad car at the foot of a hill, whose swelling side was crowned with the most magnificent of country dwellings. Architecture and Horticulture had exhausted their art. It was so unlike any thing about it, I was led to ask how it came there. The man who was driving me said it was built by a village boy, who wanted to show how much money he had made in Boston in fifteen years. "He left here without a cent," said the young man—"went to Boston—became a distiller—returned with two hundred thousand dollars—that is his residence." Do you suppose there was a Yankee boy within sight of that hill-side who was not tempted to repeat that Boston experience, of rapid and easy wealth? I rode on fourteen miles, and was set down opposite one of those village homes which Dr. Holmes describes—a square house of the Revolutionary period,—old elms hung over the lawn before it,—the same driver said, "In that front room lies dying the grandson of the man who built that house. Grandfather and father died drunkards—lay about the streets of the village drunk. That boy and I started together in life. He went with me to Lowell. We went through the mills and a mechanic trade. Never did one drop of intoxicating liquor pass his lips. Social frolic, increase of means, friendly entreaty, gay hours never tempted him. Until thirty, he stood untouched, guarded by an iron resolution. Having gathered a few thousands, he was tempted to Boston for a wider trade. He went there—stayed six years; came home penniless and a drunkard, to lie in the very streets where his father and grandfather had lain before. He could stand up against every temptation, except Boston streets. There he lies dying, as his grandfather and father before him." Do you say that the people of these country towns have no interest in the streets of Boston? You tempt the virtue, melt the resolution and corrupt the morals of the Commonwealth, as far as your influence extends.

No interest! Let me go a little ways off, and be less invidious. New York has one-fifth of the population of the State on Manhattan Island. Recently, in a great national convulsion, the city stirred herself to checkmate the State. For Wadsworth, the candidate of order of liberty of government, the country counties flung twenty thousand majority. The demons of discord stirred up the purlieus of the city and flung thirty thousand against him. Ten thousand, the ultimate majority, carried their candidate to Albany. What was his first blow? Seymour's first act, when he assumed the Governorship, what was it? He fulfilled his bargain. He hurled his defiance at the Metropolitan Police that kept him and his allies, conspirators, from carrying the Empire State into the hands of the Confederacy. Those are the times when, as Macaulay says, "the vermin, burrowing in garrets and cellars, show themselves of terrible importance." Who knows that such times may not come upon us?

I have seen the day, in that city of New York, when Rynders dictated law to the Chief of Police, and Matsell obeyed him. For twenty years, I have seen, in your city, the mob rule when they pleased. I have seen your Mayor order his police, in Faneuil Hall, to take off their badges and join the mob that crowded out free speech from that consecrated hall. You saw, two years ago, the State government reeling before the victims of the Tremont House and the Parker House. The Governor complained then, as I am told he does now, that in the whole county, he had not one single officer whom he could command to execute the law. Who shall say that the security of this great centre of wealth and population is not for the interest, for the peace, for the absolute prosperity of the State? We, too, may have a Fernando Wood—who knows? Our sixth part of the population of the State may attempt, in the interest of liquor and despotism, to defy the Commonwealth. It is too important a machinery to be left in the hands of the dangerous classes. We want to take it out of the hands of the dangerous classes, and put it into the hands of the Commonwealth—nothing else. One of two things is necessary. The law is bad—repeal it; or the law is good—keep it. No other county would be allowed to defy the law, why this?

The Mayor says he cannot execute it. Take him at his word. Undoubtedly HE cannot, for he was chosen not to; but the question is, can it be executed? What do the temperance majority of the Commonwealth claim? One trial—nothing more. We have funded twenty-five years of discussion, any amount of toil and labor, in that statute. It never has had one trial yet on this peninsula. May we not ask simply one trial? The locomotive has never *attempted* to go beyond Groton. Why take up the rails yet? If Berkshire should say, "We can't execute your law against polygamy," what should we do? Why, appoint fresh sheriffs, not repeal the law. So in this case, let not Massachusetts get down and say, "I, too, am a slave to the grog shops of the peninsula."

We do not claim that drunkenness can be wholly rooted out. But we do claim that this law can be executed as perfectly as other laws are, if its execution be intrusted to competent and faithful hands. No crime is wholly prevented. Our crowded prisons prove that. No law is perfectly executed. But there is nothing in the Maine Liquor Law that distinguishes it from other statutes.

No man claims that the *use* of intoxicating drink can be wholly stopped. But it is idle and ridiculous to say that the *public sale* of it cannot be stopped as much as the indiscriminate keeping of gunpowder or the opening of shops on Sunday, or the firing of muskets in crowded streets, whenever magistrates shall really wish and mean to do their duty.

A metropolitan police has been necessary in London, and now its streets are the safest in the world. In New York it has saved the city from convulsion and bloodshed. One of its prominent citizens said to me, a short time ago, "You do not know how near we have been to an outbreak in this very street. But for our police the attempt would have been made to surrender us to Southern dictation." That same civil disorder may impend over us. What is the remedy? Let the State hold her hand on the vices of the peninsula—claim her old democratic right to execute the laws she has made—to execute them if the city cannot, or if, by her constitution of government, she will not try to execute them faithfully.

Our plan is to have Commissioners—three or five—appointed by the Governor or by the Legislature, whichever seems best. Let them hold their offices for three or five years; they appoint, rule, and remove the members of the police force. Such a Commission would be removed, as far as any thing in our civil system is or ought to be, from the control of party politics, and would be largely independent of the "dangerous classes." This peninsula needs it immediately—the neighboring towns and cities will need it soon. The members of such a police force should hold their places during good behavior, and be removed only on charges stated in writing, to which they may have chance of replying.

Now, every fall, the liquor dealer or other criminal, whom an honest policeman has troubled, holds up his warning finger to the Alderman of that Ward—"Remove that policeman or don't expect my vote." What officer can be expected to do his duty in such circumstances?

The moment the liquor interest of the city see that their mixing in city elections will not secure a police force in their interest, they will probably leave the election of Mayor and Aldermen to the natural action of ordinary politics, and then we shall have as good officers as our system will secure, with the present level of education.

Such Mayors and Aldermen will probably, no longer prostitute the jury box to defend Rum and shield mobs. They will have no interest to do so. But if they do, we must press forward and find a remedy for that. I have full faith in democratic institutions. Work on and we shall yet lift them up to much higher perfection. The future is sure. Honest men rule in the end. Only show them their interest and duty and, in due time, they will rally to do it.

Ten years ago I made an anti-slavery speech, painting Southern despotism and demanding that the North should rouse herself against her tyrants. The next day, meeting the oldest statesman of the Commonwealth, he said to me, "Your speech is all true. I knew it thirty years ago. But what can you do about it. They won't listen." I answered—"I mean to protest—claim my rights and denounce those who assail them, whether they listen or not." The policy has been somewhat successful. Agitate—and we shall yet see the laws of Massachusetts rule even Boston.

BY TELEGRAPH.

FROM VICKSBURG.

ST. LOUIS, April 4.—The *Democrat* of this city has a special dispatch from Cairo which says advices from Young's Point on Tuesday night state that the rebels have withdrawn a large part of their force from the front to the rear of Vicksburg, anticipating that the Federals will attack them via Yazoo Pass or Haines's Bluff. Yazoo City and Greenwood have also been strengthened by the rebels, who have moved their heavy guns from the river front to the rear of Vicksburg, and substituted "Quakers" in their place.

During a very high wind on Monday night the rebel gunboat Vicksburg broke from her moorings, floated down the stream, and was captured by Farragut's vessel.

NASHVILLE, Tenn., April 4.—Surgeon Charles Johnson, of the 1st Middle Tennessee Infantry, son of Gov. Johnson, was thrown from his horse to-day and almost instantly killed.

A Union man named Harper, who tried to evade the rebel conscription, was murdered by guerillas on Tuesday night, ten miles from this city, and his house and buildings were burned.

MURFREESBORO', Tenn., April 4.—Gen. Palmer had another skirmish with the rebels to-day at Woodbury, driving them off.

Twenty of the Anderson cavalry were lately condemned to death for mutiny by court martial. Gen. Rosecrans disapproved of the sentence, and the men are ordered to return to duty. The pardon is conditional on their future good behavior.

NEWS FROM THE SOUTH.

A Peace Movement.

NEW YORK, April 5.—Among some Southern items is the following important news:

The peace party of the South, headed by Henry S. Foote, Alexander Mosly, editor of the Richmond *Whig*, and others, are about to introduce a resolution on the subject, which will probably pass the lower House of Congress before the adjournment. It is said that the course of the Richmond *Enquirer* is disapproved of by many of the leading members of the Confederate Congress.

The Chattanooga *Rebel* says that a blow will be struck before June next which will unfetter long manacled Kentucky.

FROM CALIFORNIA.

SAN FRANCISCO, April 4.—Markets quiet. There is a little activity in refined sugars at 13½. There is a slightly increased demand for groceries.

Three brigs have cleared for the mouth of the Amoor, carrying liquors, sugars, dry goods and groceries.

English underwriters charge 1½ premium war risk on California grain laden ships.

The Legislature has extended the session to the 20th of April.

Arrival of the Northern Light.

NEW YORK, April 4.—The steamer Northern Light, from Aspinwall has arrived. She brings $237,000 in treasure from California and $13,000 from Aspinwall.

The Purser reports that the Government of Nicaragua has seized all the property belonging to the Transit Company, including the steamers on the lake. The Government declares that the Company have violated their contract, and in accordance with its terms the property is forfeited. Nothing has been heard at Aspinwall of the steamers America or Moses Taylor when the Northern Light left Aspinwall, 26th ult. It is doubtful whether the passengers will be allowed to cross Nicaragua.

The above news is somewhat doubtful.

Accident on the Baltimore and Washington Railroad.

PHILADELPHIA, April 5.—The *Enquirer* of 3 o'clock Saturday afternoon, says the train from Washington to Baltimore ran off the track in consequence of the sleet. The 5 o'clock train, not seeing the signals, ran into the rear cars, smashing two or three of them, killing one passenger instantly, mortally injuring another, and wounding a dozen more. The train did not reach here until this afternoon.

Miscellaneous Dispatches.

PHILADELPHIA, April 4.—A special dispatch to the *Bulletin*, from Cincinnati, dated to-day, says the attack on Fort Pemberton was recommenced on the 27th ult., by the gunboats Baron de Kalb and Chillicothe. The result is not known.

PORTLAND, Me., April 4.—The steamship Nova Scotian, from Liverpool March 19, and Queenstown 20th, arrived this afternoon.

HEADQUARTERS ARMY OF THE POTOMAC, April 4—9 P.M.—One of the most severe wind storms ever known has been raging here all day. At this hour the storm is still raging and snow falling.

PHILADELPHIA, April 5.—The U. S. Subscription Agent announces the conversion of eight million dollars legal tenders into five-twenties for the week.

NEW YORK, April 5.—The *Herald's* special says it is understood that no further efforts to raise negro regiments in the free States will be made.

PREPARATIONS FOR THE DRAFT.—The following order has been issued by Gen. Wool:

HEADQUARTERS, DEP'T. OF THE EAST, New York City, April 2.

General Orders, No. 29:

The following orders have been received from the Secretary of War, by telegram, on the 1st of April:

There will be made on the 10th April, or as soon thereafter as practicable, a general muster of all troops in the service of the United States, wherever they may be. The muster rolls will be immediately sent to the Adjutant-General of the army for the use of the Provost-Marshal General in making drafts to fill up regiments and batteries to their full complement.

In obedience to these orders a general muster will be made on the 10th instant, or as soon thereafter as practicable, of all troops within this Department, in the service of the United States, including all staff officers, hospitals, whether general or otherwise, &c. The muster rolls will be transmitted to the Adjutant General's office, as directed above, and prompt attention to, and execution of, these orders, are required in every particular.

By command of MAJ. GEN. WOOL.
C. T. CHRISTENSEN, Major and Aid-de-Camp, Act'g Ass't Adj. General.
[Official.] L. KIP, Major and Aid-de-Camp.

PROVOST MARSHAL.—Geo. A. Shaw is to be the Provost Marshal of the Third Congressional District. He is a member of the State Senate.

TRAVELLER EXTRA

ELEVEN O'CLOCK.

BY TELEGRAPH.

IMPORTANT.

REPORTED CAPTURE OF CHARLESTON

—ON—

THURSDAY LAST.

The Report Credited at Washington.

NEW YORK, April 6.—The *Herald's* Washington despatch says a report has reached here by way of Fredericksburg, derived from rebel sources, that Charleston was bombarded by our fleet and attacked by our land forces last Thursday, and is now in possession of the Federals under General Hunter and Admiral Dupont.

The report is fully credited by prominent officers of the Government, who were in possession of facts in reference to the contemplated attack upon Charleston, which it is not yet prudent to divulge.

It is certain, however, that those who possess this information, are confident that our soldiers and sailors will celebrate the second anniversary of the fall of Fort Sumter in the captured city of Charleston.

The restrictions upon the publication in the Southern papers of any adverse news are so stringent, that it is not expected to find much in them in reference to the capture of Charleston until the disaster can be no longer concealed, but the reports which have arrived are definite and positive, and are believed by those who have the best right to know what foundation there is for them.

The *Times'* Washington despatch says the city is nervous to-night over the news derived from rebel sources, that Charleston has fallen; that an attack commenced on Friday, and was overwhelmingly successful.

A flag of truce came to Falmouth this morning The newspapers smuggled under it made no mention of the fall of Charleston or of its salvation.

Rebel Accounts of the Destruction of Pensacola.

News from the South Carolina Coast.

Federal Landing at Seabrook, S. C.

Rebel Pickets Driven In.

Women and Children Ordered Off.

FORTRESS MONROE, April 4.—Yesterday's Richmond *Despatch* says Pensacola was fired by the Union soldiers about the 28d ult., and most of the town destroyed. The soldiers are going to reinforce Gen. [illegible] transports are lying on the island. Skirmishing has already taken place between our and the enemy's pickets. Our pickets are driven in and the enemy is advancing. Gen. Hapgood has ordered all the women, children and non-combatants to be removed from Adam's Run, which is 20 miles from Seabrook's Island.

Federal Victories.

Official despatches from Gen. Curtis, dated St. Louis, April 3d, furnish the following information:

Col. Harriman, commanding at Fayetteville, telegraphs that Capt. J. J. Worthington, with two companies of the 1st Arkansas cavalry, returned to-day from a scout in Carroll county, Arkansas. After four skirmishes with the rebels we killed 22, and took 7 prisoners. Captains Smith and McFarland were killed, and Captain Walker is a prisoner. Our loss was one man wounded, not dangerously.

A band of guerillas took the steamers Sam Gaty and Murdock, and several soldiers and nine contrabands. Gen. Sloam telegraphs that Col. King is in pursuit, and had two fights yesterday with the guerillas, totally routing them, and mortally wounding their chief.

Gen. Schenck telegraphs to Gen. Halleck, from Baltimore, April 4th:

I have now, through Brig. Gen. Scammon, Capt. Carter's account of the Point Pleasant affair. Capt. Carter had sixty-three men. He reports two killed, three wounded, and six taken prisoners, making our total loss eleven.

The rebels lost in killed, wounded and prisoners seventy-two. And so their raid with their largely superior numbers was handsomely repulsed.

Point Pleasant is at the mouth of the Rappahannock in Western Virginia.

Dispatches from Murfreesboro' give an account of a brilliant skirmish on the 1st inst. An expedition under Brig. Gen. Hazen and Col. Edwards started for Woodbury to attempt to capture the rebel force at that point. One hundred men of the 4th Ohio Cavalry accompanied it. The infantry surrounded the rebel camp, but the cavalry dashed in so vigorously that the rebels were dispersed and fled over the hills. A number were killed and wounded, and thirty captured, together with fifty horses, a number of mules, four wagons and the rebel camp. We had only one wounded. The rebels were 600 strong, and were commanded by Col. Smith. The expedition would have been a complete success if the cavalry had not been too eager.

New England Annual Conference of the Methodist Episcopal Church.

SATURDAY MORNING—FOURTH DAY.

The morning session of the Annual Conference, at the High street Church, Charlestown, was opened with religious services by Rev. Isaac Jennison of Natick.

Reports were received from the Biblical Institute. In this connection it was stated that in 1864 or 1865 will occur the centennial anniversary of the Methodist Church in America, and it is intended to erect buildings in commemoration of the event, and as a token of gratitude to heaven. The subject of endowing the above Institute with the sum of $100,000, was therefore referred to Messrs. G. Haven, A. F. Bailey, Z. D. Barrows, Z. A. Mudge, W. Gordon, J. Noon, and L. R. Thayer.

Local Deacons Confirmed—Watson M. Ayres, Edwin Ray, Jacob W. H. Ames, Guilford D. Ames, and C. Henry Newell.

The reports on the different ministers by the presiding elders were concluded. The reports of the churches show that some of them have been affected by the war. The Methodist Church in Southampton furnished no less than 40 of its regular attendants to the army, out of 60 who enlisted in that town.

At his own request, Rev. George Bowler, formerly Colonel of the 46th regiment, was allowed to withdraw from the ministry, and have his name removed from the rolls.

Various other business was transacted, and addresses were made by Rev. Dr. Porter, the New York Book Agent, Rev. Mr. Butler, of the American Bible Society, and others.

Adjourned to 8 o'clock Monday morning.

Military Matters.

Fifty-three soldiers have reported to the office of Col. Day in this city, under the President's proclamation of March 10, requiring all soldiers absent from their regiments to report before the 1st of April, under penalty of being arrested as deserters and punished as the law provides.

Capt. Henry L. Abbott, 20th, is now at home in this city, on a short furlough.

Capt. C. H. Merritt, of Lynn, of the 19th, has just been appointed Quartermaster on Gen. Martindale's staff.

Lieut. C. Washburn, 38th, of Kingston, has arrived at home, having received his discharge on account of disability.

The proposed battalion of the Second Cavalry, to be raised in the western part of the State, has been abandoned.

Saturday's return from Camp Meigs, at Readville, shows an aggregate of 439 men for the 54th Regiment and 62 for the 2d Cavalry. About 50 men enlisted in Buffalo, Cincinnati and Detroit for the 54th have just arrived in camp under command of Sergt. Thos. H Stewart.

Below is a copy of the order relieving General Cowdin from his late command. In private letters, Generals Heintzelman and Abercrombie compliment Gen. Cowdin highly:

HEADQUARTERS ABERCROMBIE'S DIVISION, Arlington House, Va., March 30, 1863.

I. Brigadier General Robert Cowdin is hereby relieved from the command of the Second Brigade of this Division. Col. Burr Porter, Fortieth Massachusetts Volunteers, will assume command.

II. In parting with Brig. Gen. Cowdin, the General Commanding the Division desires to compliment him on the efficiency to which, under his command, the troops of his Brigade have arrived. He feels assured that soldiers so well managed in camp would have been equally well led in the field, where he regrets that he must be deprived of Gen. Cowdin's valuable services.

By order of Brig. Gen. ABERCROMBIE.

The Charleston Mercury.

DAILY PAPER—TEN DOLLARS PER ANNUM, PAYABLE HALF-YEARLY IN ADVANCE.

VINDICE NULLO
SPONTE SUA SINE LEGE FIDES RECTUMQUE COLENTUR.

COUNTRY PAPER—THRICE A WEEK—FIVE DOLLARS PER ANNUM, IN ADVANCE.

VOLUME LXXXII. CHARLESTON, S. C., WEDNESDAY, APRIL 8, 1863. NUMBER 11,723

TELEGRAPHIC NEWS.

LATEST FROM THE WEST.

CHATTANOOGA, April 6.—MORGAN was attacked by the enemy at Liberty, on Friday, and driven back to Snow Hill, where he held his position, and the enemy retired. Our troops, under Colonel SMITH, were repulsed at Woodbury on Saturday, and fell back to within twelve miles of McMinnville, with the loss of one killed and eight made prisoners.

KNOXVILLE, April 6.—Parties from Kentucky report that PEGRAM'S command was attacked two miles beyond Somerset on Monday, March 24, by an overwhelming force of the enemy's infantry and cavalry. After a desperate hand to hand fight, PEGRAM fell back six miles, the enemy making no pursuit. The loss was heavy on both sides. The Confederate Government agents brought out with them a large lot of cattle.

OKALONA, April 6 —The Yankees at Corinth are preparing for some movement—either a raid or an evacuation. Their suttlers are selling out their entire stock to Southern men, and are then leaving.

JACKSON, MISS., April 6.—General CHALMERS on Friday drove the enemy's pickets within five miles of Memphis, killing two and capturing one.

We have intelligence from Fort Pemberton to the 5th, to the following effect: The enemy began to embark last night, and this morning he is in rapid retreat. We shelled their camps and transports, and succeeded in disabling a boat laden with troops. We also made a reconnoissance in force from our left flank, creating great alarm amongst the Yankees.

We have reports from New Orleans that BANKS, with 10,000 men, had crossed to Donaldsonville, and had gone thence down the Bayou Plaquemine, with a view to reinforce WEITZEL, and enable him to attack the Teche country.

COLUMBIA, TENN, April 6.—The following despatch has just been received:

"*To Gen. Bragg:* A report received from Col. WOODWARD says: 'With a section of KING'S Missouri Battery we sunk one gunboat and one transport and disabled others, on the night of the 23 instant, near Palmyra, on the Cumberland river.'

"(Signed) "EARL VAN DORN, "Major General."

On the 4th, in a skirmish near Franklin, we captured seven Yankees.

LATEST FROM THE UNITED STATES.

RICHMOND, April 7.—We have Northern dates of the 21 instant.

The Philadelphia *Ledger* says that the Administration confidently anticipates news of an important success of the Federal fleet in the rear of Charleston, arrangements having been perfected for the commencement of the attack on the 27th. If the batteries on the Stono can be taken, it is believed that the Federal troops can be landed and the city reached without assaulting Sumter and Moultrie.

The *Ledger* says that it is now no longer a secret that BURNSIDE has gone to Western Virginia, and that a large portion of his old corps, ere this, has reached the region west of the Alleghanies. The Boston *Herald* says that BURNSIDE, with his command, has been assigned to the Department of Kentucky, to support ROSECRANS, under the idea that a formidable invasion of Kentucky is at hand.

A despatch dated Cairo, April 1, says that SHERMAN'S expedition to the Upper Yazoo had returned without accomplishing its object. A despatch from Somerset, Ky., says: "Gen. GILMER'S forces attacked the rebels under PEGRAM, in a strong position near Somerset yesterday, fought them five or six hours, and whipped them badly. Our loss does not exceed 30. That of the rebels is unknown. The Republican Unionists have elected their candidate for Governor in Rhode Island by 2800 majority. They have a large majority in the Legislature.

Gold advanced in New York on the 2d to 58⅝ premium. Cotton advanced nearly 20 cents per pound. Sales at 74, with upward tendency.

CONGRESSIONAL NEWS.

RICHMOND, April 6.—The Senate to-day was in secret session on the Tax Bill. In the House, no business of importance was transacted. Mr. SWANN, of Tennessee, moved a suspension of the rules, to enable him to offer a joint resolution looking to the withdrawal of our Commissioners from Great Britain; but two-thirds not voting for the suspension, the motion was lost.

LETTER FROM RICHMOND.

(CORRESPONDENCE OF THE MERCURY.)

RICHMOND, Saturday, April 4.

Roads Drying—Conjectured Army Movements—Stonewall Jackson—Tochman's Case—Gen. G. W. Smith—Chances for Governor—Outlying the Yankees, etc.

The cold March wind blowing this morning is fast drying the roads and paving the way to army operations, which the light April showers will hardly put a stop to. HOOKER'S army must be demoralized, if the half we hear from private sources be true. An attack on his part is not expected. Some sentences in a late order of Gen. Lee have been construed to mean offensive intentions on our side, but that cautious General will see to it that neither Yankees or Confederates get any clue to his designs.

Stonewall Jackson still grows in favor with the army. Lee inspires confidence, Jackson enthusiasm; and many who have been bitterly prejudiced against the latter, are now his most ardent admirers. A friend who called on Stonewall not long ago found him playing with two little girls, and learned that he sends some miles for them every evening to come and cheer him with their artless gaiety.

General Tochman's case is still unsettled. In the course of its investigation before the Special Committee appointed for that purpose, some rather odd incidents have transpired, which induce the opinion that the powers that be are given to devious ways.

It is stated here that General G. W. Smith has received the appointment of State Geologist in Georgia. Another report is, that he will take charge of important iron works.

Opinions differ as to the chances of the various candidates for Governor of this State. Some of the old Whigs think Flournoy will be elected, but the general conviction is in favor of ex-Governor Smith.

Army stories have been coming in to me slowly of late. Here is the last. After the battle of Fredericksburg, a little Yankee officer was talking with one of our Alabama Majors, who stood in that part of the field where we had suffered most severely—dead men and horses, broken cannon and blown up caissons, being all around him: "You hurt us powerful bad yesterday," said the Yankee. "Yes," replied the Major drily. "Guess we hurt you some too," rejoined the Yankee, looking at the wrecks of humanity strewn about. "Did'nt kill a man or a horse," said the Major. The little Yankee looked up at the tall Confederate for a moment, then at the dead men and horses on every side, and then wheeled suddenly around and walked rapidly away, utterly astounded at the cool manner in which the Alabamian had out-Yankeed the Yankees in deliberate lying.

HERMES.

THE MERCURY.

WEDNESDAY, APRIL 8, 1863.

The Attack on Charleston Opened.

At last, the long period of doubt and delay is at an end; and this goodly city, girdled with the fiery circle of its batteries, stands confronted with the most formidable Armada that the hands of man have ever put afloat.

The first scene in the novel drama of the war, which, we trust, is to add new lustre to the fame of Charleston, has closed. Let us render thanks to the Lord of Hosts that the result, thus far, has been one of proud triumph to our country. As yet, however, we have but entered upon the ordeal. It will be for the next few days to tell the tale of our sad disaster, or complete success.

In view of the reticence which (for reasons of military policy) has heretofore marked our allusions to the presence of the iron clad fleet, a brief review of the events of the week will not be out of place. About noon on Sunday last the first intelligence was flashed to the city from Fort Sumter, that the turrets of the far-famed Monitor gunboats were looming up against the southeastern horizon. During the afternoon the entire fleet hove in sight. Eight Monitors, besides the frigate *Ironsides* and twenty-seven wooden war vessels, took up their position just beyond the bar. As the news became bruited about the city, very many of our noncombatant population (previously incredulous of danger) made hasty preparations to depart; and every train that has left the city since has gone heavily laden with the eleventh-hour refugees and their effects.

Sunday night passed quietly by. Monday morning brought us reports of the movements of transports up the Stono River, and the debarkation of a considerable force of Yankee troops on Cole's Island. But throughout Monday and Monday night, the armored fleet held its position beyond the bar. On Tuesday morning it was observed that another Monitor had arrived, making a force of no less than ten iron-clad vessels, including the *Ironsides*.

At two o'clock on Tuesday afternoon a despatch from Fort Sumter announced that these ten vessels had crossed the bar, and were cautiously steaming inward—the foremost one having at that time reached a point about three thousand yards from the Fort. The next news was brought to us, an hour later, by the dull detonation of the first gun from Fort Moultrie, which was immediately answered by a heavy report and a cloud of white smoke from the turret of one of the Monitors. At ten minutes after three, the enemy having come within range, Fort Sumter opened her batteries, and, almost simultaneously, the white smoke could be seen puffing from the low sand hills of Morris and Sullivan's Islands, indicating that the Beauregard Battery on the left, and Battery Wagner on the extreme right, had become engaged. Five of the iron-clads, forming in line of battle in front of Fort Sumter, maintained a very rapid return fire, occasionally hurling their 15-inch shot and shell against Fort Moultrie and the minor batteries, but all directing their chief efforts against the east face of Fort Sumter. Gradually, but visibly, the distance between the attacking vessels and the Fort was lessened, and as the enemy drew nearer the firing became hot and almost continuous.

About half-past four o'clock the battle became fierce and general. The scene at that hour, as viewed from the Battery promenade, was truly grand. Battery Bee had now mingled the hoarse thunder of its guns in the universal din, and the whole expanse of the harbor entrance, from Sullivan's Island to Cumming's Point, became enveloped in the smoke and constant flashes of the conflict. The iron-clads kept constantly shifting their position, but, whichever way they went, their ports, always turned towards the battlements of Sumter, poured forth their terrible projectiles against the walls of that famous stronghold. Ever and anon, as the huge shot went ricochetting towards the mark, the water was dashed up in vast sheets of spray, towering far above the parapet of the Fort, while the wreaths of smoke constantly ascending from the barbette guns showed how actively the artillerymen of the post were discharging their duties. In the foreground, our own staunch little iron-clads, the *Palmetto State* and *Chicora*, could be seen steaming energetically up and down their chosen fighting position, evidently impatient to participate in the fray.

Up to this time the frigate *Ironsides* had born a very conspicuous part in the fight. Her long hull lay at the distance, apparently, of a mile from our batteries, and her tremendous broadsides were more than once fitly answered by broadsides from the Fort. It soon became apparent that she was unable to stand the severe fire directed against her. Steaming rapidly southward, she gave Fort Sumter a few parting shots and withdrew from the action. The *Keokuk*, a double turretted Monitor, soon after followed her example; and before five o'clock the firing had evidently begun to slacken. The remaining Monitors, however, still kept up the bombardment and our forts and batteries replied with undiminished alacrity. At quarter after five, p. m., the Monitors began to retire, and at half past five the enemy fired the last shot of the engagement.

Gratifying as were the general results of the fight, the late hour at which it closed precluded the possibility of our receiving the full details from the Forts. A despatch from Fort Sumter informs us that the *Ironsides* and *Keokuk* were both very roughly handled, and retired seriously injured. The *Keokuk* had her flag shot down, her boat shot away, three holes in her smoke stack and a portion of her bow shot off. The practice of our gunners was most creditable. Nearly every shot struck some one of the iron clads, but with what effect is not known. Fort Sumter was struck thirty-four times. One of our guns was dismounted, but otherwise the Fort is in good condition. Fort Moultrie was uninjured. The casualties at Fort Sumter were a drummer boy, named AHRENS, mortally wounded; two men severely wounded, and three others slightly injured. At Fort Moultrie, one man was accidentally hurt by a fall from the flagstaff, on which he was replacing our flag, which had been shot away. We learn that he afterwards died. Two small houses on the back beach of Sullivan's Island were demolished by the enemy's fire.

After their withdrawal from the action, the enemy's iron-clads anchored off Morris Island where they now lie. Many think that the fight will be renewed at daybreak this morning; but up to the time at which we write (3 a. m.) all is quiet. The reports we get from the Stono River say that the enemy's transports still remain in the stream. Doubtless the Yankee Generals intend, before venturing upon a land attack, to await the issue of the struggle between their ships and our batteries.

THE WAR IN THE WEST.

RETREAT OF THE HARTFORD AND ALBATROSS—A PARTING SALUTE FROM THE VICKSBURG SHARPSHOOTERS—TERRIBLE EXECUTION.

The Jackson *Mississippian*, of the 21 instant, says:

We learn from a gentlemen from Vicksburg yesterday, that the two Yankee men of war, the Hartford and Albatross, which passed Port Hudson during the late battle at that place, weighed anchor on Monday, and left their moorings, for (it is believed) a final departure downwards. There being no hope of succor from Porter's upper fleet, after the disastrous fate of the two vessels sent down last Wednesday, Farragut, no doubt, determined to run the gauntlet of Warrenton, Grand Gulf, and Port Hudson, rather that stay where he was, with the probability of being forced to destroy his own vessels or eventually surrender them. As the two vessels turned out into the stream the crews of each displayed themselves on deck, and on the barges attached, to take probably a farewell view of Vicksburg—or, it may be, to show a specimen of Yankee bravado. This occurred above Warrenton. It seems that a considerable body of our sharpshooters has been stationed and screened at a point on the bank of the river where the current swept in close to shore. When the two vessels reached this locality, such a fatal fire as was poured into the unprotected crews has not been probably delivered during this war. The masses of men on the decks and barges seemed literally to wilt down before the dreadful shower of leaden rain. They must have suffered dreadfully. We opine there will not be much left either of the vessels or their crews by the time they pass Port Hudson. As the Hartford passed the Warrenton batteries she was sixteen times penetrated by rifled cannon shot—a fair foretaste of what she will catch below.

THE FIGHT AT PORT HUDSON.

A correspondent of the Jackson *Appeal*, writing from Port Hudson, La., under date of March 15, gives the annexed account of the Yankee attack on that place:

The long expected contest between the Yankee fleet took place before daylight this morning, the first shot being fired at ten minutes past twelve o'clock, and the last one at twenty minutes past two. It was short, sharp and decisive.

Six vessels were to complete the expedition, divided into two divisions. The vanguard was to consist of the flag ship Hartford, a first class steam sloop-of-war, carrying twenty-six 8 and 9 inch Paixhan guns, leading, followed by the Monongahela, a second class steam sloop, mounting sixteen heavy guns, and the Richmond, a first class steam sloop-of-war, of twenty-six guns, principally 8 and 9 inch Columbiads. The rear guard was composed of the first class steam sloop Mississippi, twenty-two guns, 8 and 9 inch, and the gunboats Kinnes and Genesee, each carrying three Columbiads and two rifled 32 pounders. The Mississippi was a side wheel steamer. All the others were screw propellers. The vanguard was commanded by Admiral Farragut in person, on board the Hartford. The rear guard was under the command of Captain Melancthon Smith, flying his pennant from the Mississippi. They were to proceed up stream in single file, the prow of one following close upon the stern of another, and keeping their fires and lights well concealed, until they should be discovered by our batteries, when they were to get by the best way they could, fighting their passage, and once above, they believed they would have the rebel stronghold on both sides—their guns covering every part of the encampment. Besides this, the Essex and mortar boats anchored at the Point, and supposed to have already acquired our range, were expected to play no mean part in the affair.

Shortly before midnight the boats having formed the line of battle as described, their decks cleared for action, and the men at their quarters, the Hartford led the way, and the others promptly followed her direction. At the moment of their discovery a rocket was to be sent up from the Admiral's flag-ship, as the signal for the Essex and her accompanying mortar boats to commence work. So dark was the night, and so slightly had the armed craft nosed their way up, that the flag-ship had passed some of our guns, and all the fleet were within easy range before their approach was known. Almost at the same time a rocket from our Signal Corps, and a discharge of musketry by an infantry picket, aroused our line. Quick as a flash, while the falling fire of our alarm rocket was yet unextinguished, there shot up into the sky, from the Hartford's deck, another. Then came one grand, long, deafening roar that rent the atmosphere with its mighty thunder, shaking both land and water, and causing the high battery-crowned cliffs to tremble. Every gun on the fleet and every mortar at the Point joined in one simultaneous discharge. Relying greatly upon the suddenness and vigor of their attack to disconcert and confuse the defenders of our cliffs, the roar of their first discharge had not died away upon the ear before it recommenced, and when the quick and irregular but unceasing volleys and broadsides showed that the crews of each Yankee ship were vieing with each other in celerity. The sheets of flame that poured from the sides of the sloops at each discharge lit up nearly the whole stretch of river, placing each craft in strong relief against the black sky. The noise was stunning to the ear, but they knew not yet the position of our batteries, and the shot and shell, fired at random, had no material effect.

Now commenced the battle in all its terrible earnestness. Outnumbered in guns and outweighted in metal, our volleys were as quickly repeated, and the majority of them unerring in their aim. As soon as the enemy thus discovered our batteries, they opened on them with grape and canister, which was more accurately thrown than their shells, and threw clouds of dirt upon the guns and gunners; the shell went over them in every conceivable direction except the right one. The Hartford, a very fast ship, now made straight for up the river, making her best time, and trying to divert the aim of our gunners by her incessant and deafening broadsides. She soon outstripped the balance of the fleet. Shot after shot struck her, riddling her through and through, but still she kept on her way. Every craft now looking out for itself, and bound to make its very best time to get by, the fleet lost its orderly line of battle, and got so mixed up it was difficult, and sometimes impossible, to distinguish one from another. It was speedily apparent to the enemy that the fire was a great deal hotter and more destructive than had been expected, and all the ships except the Hartford undertook to put about and return the way they came. For this purpose the Richmond sheered close in to the left bank, under the batteries, and then circled round, her course reaching nearly up to the opposite point. In executing this manœuvre she gave our batteries successively a raking position, and they took excellent advantage of it, ripping her from stern to stem. From the crashing of timbers plainly heard during every brief interval of the din, and from the view had of shots that struck her, it was plain that her doom was sealed. It was reported among a crowd of observers on the bluff that a voice from her deck had called out: "We surrender! we surrender!" If this was said, it was not probably spoken by her commander, who, however, appealed to our batteries to cease firing upon her, as the ship was sinking. As she was evidently drifting down in an unmanageable condition, and apparently settling, the batteries let her alone, and turned their attention to other craft. Whether or not she sank I do not as yet know.

The Mississippi undertook to execute the same manœuvre of turning round and making her escape back to the point she started from. She had rounded and just turned down stream, when one of our shots tore off her rudder, and another went crashing through her machinery. Immediately after came the rushing sound of steam escaping from some broken pipe, and the now unmanageable vessel drifted aground directly opposite our crescent line of batteries. Her range was quickly gained, and she was being rapidly torn to pieces by our missiles, when the commander gave the order for all hands to save themselves the best way they could. At the same time fire broke out in two places. At this time her decks were strewn with dead and wounded, according to one of her crew, with whom I have conversed, who thought that one-half her complement of men were included in the list of casualties.

The three larger vessels had occupied most of the attention of the batteries, but the other craft had not by any means been overlooked. Two had turned round and started down stream. One of them apparently escaped without serious disability, but the other, which was probably the Kinnes, floated down past the batteries in an unmanageable condition, receiving our volleys without being able to return them; and from the confusion of voices, and the mingling of oaths, execrations and orders heard from her deck, it was evident that great slaughter must have been made among her crew, else that the boat herself was in a critical predicament. A vessel, which was either the Tennessee or Monongahela—most probably the former—slipped by in the confusion, and joined the Hartford up the river. Some fifty-five or sixty persons saved themselves by jumping overboard and swimming or wading from the Mississippi to the shore. Of these, the Major and Captain of Marines and Assistant Engineer, with forty five sailors and marines, have been arrested by our cavalry, and brought across during the day. Some few others are reported to be hiding themselves in the swamps. The dead and wounded were left upon the Mississippi, which soon floated off and started down with the current.

When the burning Mississippi reached the point where the mortar boats and other craft lay, she created a perfect panic among them. At five minutes past 5 o'clock, when the Mississippi was probably within five miles of Baton Rouge, a sudden glare lit up the whole sky. The cause was well known to be the explosion of the magazine. After a considerable interval of time, a long rumbling sound brought the final proof that the Mississippi, one of the finest vessels of the United States navy, which had earned an historic fame before the commencement of the present war as the flag ship of the Japan Expedition, was a thing of the past.

Such are the particulars of this morning's fight at Port Hudson. For the time it lasted it was one of the most desperately contested engagements of the war. Our success is to be attributed to the coolness, gallantry and skill of the officers and men engaged. If the country is not satisfied with the Port Hudson fight, then it must, indeed, be unreasonable. Under all the circumstances, the result has been as surprising as it has been gratifying. The relative loss of life is one of the most significant features of the affair. The loss on board the enemy's vessels must amount to at least 250 killed and wounded. On the Mississippi, alone, the loss was over 150. The loss in our batteries was one Lieutenant, of the 1st Alabama, slightly wounded, and one man, of the 1st Tennessee battalion, severely wounded.

HIGH TAXES.

Congress is understood to have under consideration a bill imposing direct taxes for the support of the Government. The amount of taxes to be raised by the bill, it is estimated, will not fall below one hundred millions, and may reach one hundred and fifty or two hundred millions. The passion for high taxes is become a perfect rage. It is said that the people are begging and entreating their Representatives to pile up the taxes mountain high—the higher the better! We do not know who these people are. We are quite certain they are not the people who will have to pay the taxes. The outcry on the subject may mislead Congress; and it would be a great national misfortune if, acting under an erroneous impression, it should impose burdens too heavy to be borne. Wise statesmen should never go off half cocked and under the impulse of the moment; they may do more mischief in one day than can be repaired in years.

No doubt the great mass of the people are willing to pay taxes to their utmost capacity; but because they are patriotic and liberal, that is no reason they should be crushed at one blow.

The taxes to be imposed by this bill will have to be paid by a portion of the ten States. The narrow strip of country, between the mountains and the head of tide water, stretching from the Rappahannock to the Mississippi, will have the chief burden to bear. Louisiana and Arkansas can pay but little—and Texas not much more. Kentucky, Tennessee and Missouri cannot be expected to contribute anything; and this fact should suggest to the Representatives from those States the propriety of abstaining from a vote on a question in which their circumstances are not affected. This leaves only seven of the Atlantic and Gulf States to bear the brunt. And they are subject to curtailment. Large portions of their territory—mountain and tide-water—have been overrun by the enemy and desolated. Those districts, of course, can pay nothing. Thus leaving the narrow belt first adverted to to pay all, and at the same time to feed the army. With Major Ruffin's, or the War Department's scale of prices of agricultural products, the thing will be simply impossible—except at such a sacrifice of property by the farmers for the benefit of speculators and extortioners, as will be intolerable.

The Congressional tax bill, besides special taxes, imposes a tax of ten per cent. on every hundred dollars worth of property, personal and real. In addition, the State levies a tax of one per cent.—and each county's tax will be as much more—thus making at least four per cent. This levied on an assessment in depreciated currency, and paid by the sale of products at the Commissary's prices, will bring ruin on the farming interest of the country.

The bill contemplates an army of Confederate officers, in the shape of Collectors; vastly expensive, infinitely annoying, and a serious drawback on the army in the field. This, which, in better times, would constitute an insuperable objection, may, we fear, be one of the chief recommendations with many gentlemen, in the existing state of things. There is an awful proneness among too many of our politicians to the Yankee model at Washington. As the willow to the water, so do their hearts incline to that corrupt system.

With a view to avoid the waste and corruption of this system, we publish the suggestion of a correspondent, proposing that the States assume their respective portions of the tax, by exchanging their own bonds for Confederate Treasury notes. We hope the suggestion may receive such consideration as it merits.—*Richmond Whig.*

A CARD.

To the Editor of the Mercury: I have read the correspondence between Governor Pickens and General Simons in your paper of March 20th, and find in it several passages apt to mislead the reader on a collateral point. I will quote the passages.

In his note of the 12th December, 1861, General Simons says: "Your official position forbids me at this time from taking other notice of the endorsement which you made on the report of the Board of Ordnance."

In his letter of the 18th December, 1862, he says: "Your endorsement on the report of the Board of Ordnance on my report on the harbor defences, contains the following words: 'The conclusions of that report I consider would be to order troops from Fort Moultrie and Sullivan's Island, and to abandon the attempt to keep out reinforcements, and in fact to yield without a struggle every point, and thus break down the spirit of our people, and cover our cause with imbecility and probably ruin.'"

In his note of the 5th January, 1863, he says: "The words cited in yours of the 29th ult., to wit: 'I shall do or agree to no such thing,' as part of your endorsement on the report of the Board of Ordnance," &c.

Gov. Pickens, on the 18th of December, 1862, in his answer to Gen. Simons, says:

"The endorsement was made on the report from the members of the Board of Ordnance more than on your letter to me."

On the 19th December, 1862, he says:

"You had resigned when my endorsement was made upon the report from the members of the Ordnance Board, to whom it had been officially referred." And again: "The quotation you have made from my endorsement was only my strong inference as to what might be the results of the recommendations from the members of the Ordnance Board, if I adopted it."

The Governor speaks of the "report from the members of the Ordnance Board," but takes no exception to General Simons' phrase, "the report of the Board of Ordnance."

Now, Mr. Editor, may not the reader of this correspondence fairly conclude that General Simons' report had been referred to the Board of Ordnance?—that the Board had endorsed its recommendations, and advised measures tantamount to abandoning the attempt to defend the harbor?

Yet I am convinced that this would be a false inference, springing only from a misapplication of terms, or a misconception of facts, by the correspondents. If I may trust a pretty good memory, General Simons' report never was referred to the Board of Ordnance. The Board never expressed any such opinion or gave any such advice as is here supposed. On the contrary, it would have been utterly inconsistent with what that department had been before, and were then doing and advising. There was at least one member of the Board who never heard of General Simons' report on the harbor defences until the meeting of the Legislature—nearly a year after—when it appeared that the Governor had referred it to Gen. Jones and Col. Drayton—who were, indeed, members of that Board—but, not being a committee from, or a majority of, it, were not acting in an official capacity. I am satisfied, although I have not examined them, that the minutes of the proceedings of the Board contain no notice of a reference of General Simons' report, or any action on it.

To some persons it may seem that I have troubled you, Mr. Editor, with a communication on a very small matter. Both the Governor and Gen. Simons, however, speak of this report and the endorsement on it as a part of the State Archives. These are the materials of future history. If these gentlemen are mistaken, and the whole matter is of little importance, I beg leave to suggest that accuracy is always important.

G. MANIGAULT.

RELATIONS OF ENGLAND AND THE SOUTH.

DIPLOMATIC CORRESPONDENCE OF MR. COMMISSIONER MASON WITH EARL RUSSELL.

The full correspondence, official or unofficial, as our readers may choose to call it, between Mr. MASON, our Commissioner in London, and the Head of the British Foreign Office, has recently been laid before Parliament. That our readers may have some idea of the manner in which our Representatives are snubbed by the English Government, we make some extracts from the voluminous correspondence which has reached us, choosing more especially the letters bearing upon the question of recognition:

MR. MASON TO EARL RUSSELL.

No. 54 DEVONSHIRE ST., PORTLAND PLACE, London, July 24, 1862.

MY LORD: In the interview I had the honor to have with your lordship in February last, I laid before your lordship, under instructions from the Government of the Confederate States, the views entertained by that Government, leading to the belief that it was, of right, entitled to be recognized as a separate and independent Power, and to be received as an equal in the great family of nations.

I then represented to your lordship that the dissolution of the Union of the States of North America, by the withdrawal therefrom of certain of the confederates, was not to be considered as a revolution in the ordinary acceptation of that term; far less was it to be considered as an act of insurrection or rebellion; that it was, both in form and in fact, but the termination of a Confederacy which, during a long course of years, had violated the terms of the Federal compact by the exercise of unwarranted powers, oppressive and degrading to the minority section. That the seceding parties had so withdrawn as organized political communities, and had formed a new Confederacy, comprising then, as now, thirteen separate and sovereign States, embracing an area of 870,610 square miles, and with a population of 12,000,000. This new Confederacy has now been in complete and successful operation, as a Government, for a period of nearly eighteen months; has proved itself capable of successful defence against every attempt to subdue or destroy it; and in a war, conducted by its late confederates on a scale to tax their utmost power, has presented everywhere a united people, determined at every cost to maintain the independence they had affirmed.

Since that interview more than five months have elapsed, and during that period events have but the more fully confirmed the views I then had the honor to present to your lordship. The resources, strength and power in the Confederate States developed by these events, I think, authorise me to assume, as the judgment and intelligence of all Europe, that the separation of the States of North America is final; that under no possible circumstances can the late Federal Union be restored; that the new Confederacy has evinced both the capacity and the determination to maintain its independence, and, therefore, with other powers the question of recognising that independence is simply a question of time.

The Confederate States ask no aid from nor intervention by foreign powers. They are entirely content that the strict neutrality which has been proclaimed between the belligerents shall be adhered to, however unequally it may operate, because of fortuitous circumstances, upon them.

But if the principles and the morals of the public law be, when a nation has established before the world both its capacity and ability to maintain the Government it has ordained, that a duty devolves on other nations to recognise such fact, then I submit that the Government of the Confederate States of America, having sustained itself unimpaired through trials greater than most nations have been called to endure, and far greater than any it has yet to meet, has furnished to the world sufficient proof of stability, strength and resources to entitle it to a place among the independent nations of the earth. I have, &c., J. M. MASON.

MR. MASON TO EARL RUSSELL.

No. 54 DEVONSHIRE STREET, PORTLAND PLACE, July 24, 1862.

Mr. Mason presents his compliments to Earl Russell, and, if agreeable to his lordship, Mr. Mason would be obliged if Earl Russell would allow him the honor of an interview, at such time as may be convenient to his lordship.

Mr. Mason desires to submit to Earl Russell some views connected with the subject of the letter he has the honor to transmit herewith, which he thinks may be better imparted in a brief conversation.

EARL RUSSELL TO MR. MASON.

FOREIGN OFFICE, July 31, 1862.

Lord Russell presents his compliments to Mr. Mason. He begs to assure Mr. Mason that it is from no want of respect to him that Lord Russell has delayed sending an answer to his letter of the 24th inst.

Lord Russell has postponed sending that answer in order that he might submit a draft of it to the Cabinet on Saturday next. It will be forwarded on Monday to Mr. Mason.

Lord Russell does not think any advantage would arise from the personal interview which Mr. Mason proposes, and must, therefore, decline it.

MR. MASON TO EARL RUSSELL.

No. 54 DEVONSHIRE STREET, PORTLAND PLACE, August 1, 1862.

MY LORD: In the interview I had the honor to propose in my late note I had intended briefly to submit the following views, which I thought might not be without weight in the consideration to be given by her Majesty's Government to the request for recognition of the Confederate States, submitted in my letter of the 24th July ultimo. I ask leave now to present them as supplemental to that letter:

If it be true, *as there assumed*, that, in the settled judgment of England, the separation of the States is final, then the failure of so great a Power to recognize the fact in a formal manner imparts an opposite belief, and must operate as an incentive to the United States to protract the contest.

In a war, such as that pending in America, where a party in possession of the Government is striving to subdue those who, for reasons sufficient to themselves, have withdrawn from it, the contest will be carried on in the heat of blood and of popular excitement long after its object has become hopeless in the eyes of disinterested parties.

The Government itself may feel that its power is inadequate to bring back the recusant States, and yet be unable at once to control the fierce elements which surround it whilst the war rages. Such it is confidently believed is the actual condition of affairs in America.

It is impossible, in the experience of eighteen months of no ordinary trial, in the small results attained, and in the manifest exhaustion of its resources, that any hope remains with the Government of the United States either of bringing about a restoration of the dissevered Union or of subjugating those who have renounced it. And yet, the failure of foreign Powers formally to recognize this actual condition of things disables those in authority from conceding that fact at home.

Again, it is known that there is a large and increasing sentiment in the United States in accordance with these views—a sentiment which has its origin in the hard teachings of the war as it has progressed.

It was believed (or so confidently affirmed) that there was a large party in the Southern States devoted to the Union, whose presence and power would be manifested there as soon as the public force of the United States was present to sustain it. I need not say how fully the experience of the war has dispelled this delusion.

Again, it was believed, and confidently relied on, that in the social structure of the Southern States, they would find the large majority of the dominant race indifferent, if not hostile, to the basis on which that social structure rests, in which they were not interested, and who would be found the allies of those whose mission was supposed to be in some way to break it up; but the same experience had shown that the whole population of the South is united, as one people, in arms to resist the invader.

Nothing remains, then, on which to rest any hope of conquest but reliance on the superior numbers and the supposed greater resources of the Northern States. I think the results of the last (or pending) campaign have proved how idle such expectations were, against the advantages of a people fighting at home, and bringing into a common stock of resistance as a free will offering all that they possess, whether of blood or treasure—a spectacle now historically before the world.

It is in human experience that there must be those in the United States who cannot shut their eyes to such facts, and yet, in the despotic power now assumed there by the Government, to give expression to any doubt would be to court the hospitalities of the dungeon.

One word from the Government of her Majesty would encourage those people to speak, and the civilized world would respond to the truths they would utter, "that for whatever purpose the war was begun, it was continued now only in a vindictive and unreasoning spirit, shocking alike to humanity and civilization." That potent word would simply be to announce a fact which a frenzied mind could only dispute, that the Southern States, now in a separate Confederacy, had established before the world its competency to maintain the government of its adoption, and its determination to abide by it.

To withhold it would not only seem in derogation of truth, but would be to encourage the continuance of a war, hopeless in its object, ruinous alike to the parties engaged in it, and to the prosperity and welfare of Europe.

J. M. MASON.

EARL RUSSELL TO MR. MASON.

FOREIGN OFFICE, August 2, 1862.

SIR: I have had the honor to receive your letters of the 24th of July and 1st instant, in which you repeat the considerations which, in the opinion of the government of the so-called Confederate States, entitled that government to be recognized of right as a separate and independent power, and to be received as an equal in the great family of nations.

In again urging these views you represent, as before, that the withdrawal of certain of the confederates from the Union of the States of North America is not to be considered as a revolution, in the ordinary acceptation of that term, far less an act of insurrection or rebellion, but as the termination of a Confederacy which had, during a long course of years, violated the terms of the Federal compact.

I beg leave to say, in the outset, that upon this question of a right of withdrawal, as upon that of the previous conduct of the United States, her Majesty's Government have never presumed to form a judgment. The interpretation of the Constitution of the United States, and the character of the proceedings of the President and Congress of the United States under that Constitution, must be determined, in the opinion of her Majesty's Government, by the States and people in North America, who inherited, and have till recently upheld that Constitution. Her Majesty's Government decline altogether the responsibility of assuming to be judges in such a controversy.

You state that the Confederacy has a population of twelve million; that it has proved itself capable for eighteen months of successful defence against every attempt to subdue or destroy it; that in the judgment of the intelligence of all Europe the separation is final, and that, under no possible circumstances, can the late Federal Union be restored.

On the other hand, the Secretary of State of the United States has affirmed, in an official despatch, that a large portion of the once disaffected population has been restored to the Union, and now evinces its loyalty and firm adherence to the Government; that the white population now in insurrection is under five millions, and that the Southern Confederacy owes its main strength to hope of assistance from Europe.

In the face of the fluctuating events of the war; the alternations of victory and defeat; the capture of New Orleans; the advance of the Federals to Corinth, to Memphis, and the banks of the Mississippi, as far as Vicksburg; contrasted, on the other hand, with the failure of the attack on Charleston, and the retreat from before Richmond—placed, too, between allegations so contradictory on the part of the contending Powers—her Majesty's Government are still determined to wait.

In order to be entitled to a place among the independent nations of the earth, a State ought to have not only strength and resources for a time, but afford promise of stability and permanence. Should the Confederate States of America win that place among nations, it might be right for other nations justly to acknowledge an independence achieved by victory, and maintained by a successful resistance to all attempts to overthrow it. That time, however, has not, in the judgment of her Majesty's Government, yet arrived. Her Majesty's Government, therefore, can only hope that a peaceful termination of the present bloody and destructive contest may not be distant. I am, &c.,

RUSSELL.

LEGISLATURE OF SOUTH CAROLINA—EXTRA SESSION.

COLUMBIA, Monday, April 6.

SENATE.—The Senate met at 12 m. Prayer by Rev. Mr. Martin.

Mr. Hope introduced a bill to prevent and punish monopolizing and speculating in the articles of prime necessity and for other purposes; which received the first reading, and was referred.

Mr. Moses, from the Committee on the Judiciary, to which had been referred so much of the Message of his Excellency the Governor as relates to the prohibition of the exportation of grain from this State, submitted a report, which was ordered for consideration to-morrow, and to be printed. Also, a bill to prohibit, for a stated period, the exportation of provisions. The bill received the first reading, and was ordered for a second reading to-morrow, and to be printed. Also, on prohibitions in relation to Treasury Notes, and the necessity for legislation in relation thereto; which was ordered for consideration to morrow.

The following Message from his Excellency the Governor was received, and was referred to the Committee on Committee on Confederate Relations:

STATE OF SOUTH CAROLINA,
EXECUTIVE DEPARTMENT, COLUMBIA, April 6, 1863.

Gentlemen of the Senate and House of Representatives:

I transmit herewith copies of resolution of the Legislature of Texas, just received, in relation to the indebtedness of the Confederate States, to which I invite your attention.

M. L. BONHAM.

JOINT RESOLUTION IN RELATION TO THE INDEBTEDNESS OF THE CONFEDERATE STATES.

Whereas, the Legislature of the State of Texas considers the faith of the Confederate States fully and sacredly pledged to the payment of all indebtedness which has been, or may be, incurred by the Confederate States during the war between said Confederacy and the United States of America, and that should any State, comprising said Confederacy, withdraw therefrom, from any cause, before the payment of such indebtedness shall have been fully completed, such withdrawing State will be bound to the payment of her *pro rata* portion of such remaining indebtedness. Therefore,

SECTION 1. Be it resolved by the Legislature of the State of Texas, That, should the State of Texas, from any cause, withdraw from the association as a member of the Confederate States before the indebtedness of said Confederate States is fully paid, the faith of the State is hereby pledged to the payment of her *pro rata* portion of such remaining indebtedness to whoever the same may be due.

SEC. 2. That the Governor of the State transmit to the President of the Confederate States, and to the Governor of each of said States, a certified copy of this resolution.

C. W. BUCKLEY,
Speaker of the House of Representatives.
JOHN M. CROCKETT,
President of the Senate.

Approved February 27, 1863.
F. R. LUBBOCK.

Mr. Wilson introduced a bill to repeal an Act entitled "An Act to prohibit extortion and punish extortioners." The bill received the first reading, and was referred.

The special order of the day for 1 p. m.—a bill to amend an Act entitled "An Act to prevent and punish the planting and cultivating, in this State, over a certain quantity of cotton during the present year," was up for consideration. Numerous amendments were proposed, and finally the bill was sent to the House.

Mr. Palmer, from the Committee on Agriculture and Internal Improvements, reported a bill to suppress the distillation of spirituous liquors in this State, which was read the first time and ordered for a second reading to-morrow.

The Senate then adjourned.

HOUSE OF REPRESENTATIVES.—At the hour to which the House was adjourned, the Clerk called the roll, when the Speaker took the Chair, and the deliberations were opened with prayer by Rev. Mr. Hammond.

The following resolution was received from the Senate, which was ordered for consideration to morrow:

Resolved, That it is inexpedient to introduce and consider, during the present session, any subjects of legislation beyond those embraced in the Governor's Message and the repeal of an Act, passed at the recent session, entitled "An Act to provide for the collection and payment of the Confederate War Tax."

Mr. B. F. Perry, from the Committee on the Judiciary, reported a bill to regulate in future the sale of goods, wares and merchandise by public auction. Also, a bill to regulate and limit the price of the prime necessities of life in South Carolina; which were read the first time, and ordered for a second reading to-morrow. Also made a report on a resolution on the subject of the currency; which was ordered for consideration to-morrow.

Mr. Whetstone gave notice that to-morrow he will ask leave to introduce a bill to amend an Act entitled "An Act to incorporate the Edisto and Ashley Canal Company," ratified 6th day of February, 1863.

Mr. Thomson introduced the following resolution, which was agreed to:

Resolved, That the Comptroller General be, and he is hereby, instructed and required to report to this House whether any of the banks of the Lower Division have returned and paid taxes, for the year 1862, on less capital than for previous years, and to report the amount of any decrease of taxes upon the bank capital of any of said banks, and whether any sum is now due in arrear of such tax, and from what bank or banks.

Mr J. Harleston Read introduced the following resolution, which was agreed to:

Resolved, That it be referred to the Committee on Engrossed Acts, to inquire and report into the apparent discrepancy between the bill entitled "a bill to supply negro labor for coast defences," as passed by the General Assembly at its last session, and the bill as ratified, and that if such discrepancy really exists, they be instructed to report a bill to supply any omission or change.

Mr. S. R. Jones introduced the following resolution, which was agreed to:

Resolved, That it be referred to the Committee on Engrossed Acts, to inquire whether the Act to organize the militia, ratified at the close of the last session, be the same as the Act passed by this House, and if not, to report a bill by which the same may be corrected.

Mr. McCants presented the petition of citizens of Fairfield District, asking that the number of hands employed in the manufacture of turpentine in this State be reduced.

Mr. Broyles, from the Committee on Agriculture, made a report, and reported a bill to suppress the distillation of spirituous liquors in this State; which was read the first time, and was ordered for a second reading to morrow.

On motion of Mr. B. F. Perry, the House proceeded to the consideration of a bill to authorize the Governor to seize and dispose of provisions and articles of food, in certain cases, which had been made the special order of the day for this day, at 12 o'clock, m. The bill was read the second time; and, on motion of Mr. Mullins, the same was made the special order for to-morrow at 1 o'clock, p. m.

Mr. Mullins introduced the following resolution, which was unanimously agreed to:

Resolved, That this House has heard with profound regret the announcement of the death of Captain John C. McClenaghan, late member from Marion.

Resolved, That from an earnest desire to mark their respect for his memory, the members of this House will wear the usual badge of mourning upon the left arm for the remainder of this session.

Resolved, That a copy of these resolutions be sent by the Clerk of this House to the family of the deceased.

On motion of Mr. Graham, as a further mark of respect, the House was adjourned, at five minutes past three o'clock p. m.

EASTER ELECTIONS.

Church of the Holy Communion.

VESTRYMEN.

H. L. TOOMER.	GEORGE A. TRENHOLM.
B. G. WILKINS.	T. D. WAGNER.
J. D. ALEXANDER.	B. G. PINCKNEY.

WARDENS.

R. H. McDOWELL.	JOHN HANCKEL.

DELEGATES TO CONVENTION.

B. G. WILKINS.	H. L. TOOMER.
JOHN HANCKEL.	T. D. WAGNER.

Parish of St. Thomas and St. Dennis.

VESTRYMEN.

JAMES ROSE.	W. L. VENNING.
ALFRED HUGER.	ALEX. ROBERTSON.
JOHN L. NOWELL.	JAMES RAVENEL.

Dr. G. E. MANIGAULT.

WARDENS.

Dr. E. RAVENEL.	Dr. D. C. PRICE.

The Charleston Mercury.

DAILY PAPER—TEN DOLLARS PER ANNUM, PAYABLE HALF-YEARLY IN ADVANCE.

VINDICE NULLO — SPONTE SUA SINE LEGE FIDES RECTUMQUE COLENTUR.

COUNTRY PAPER—THRICE A WEEK—FIVE DOLLARS PER ANNUM, IN ADVANCE.

VOLUME LXXXII. CHARLESTON, S. C., SATURDAY, APRIL 11, 1863. NUMBER 11,726

TELEGRAPHIC NEWS.

LATEST FROM VICKSBURG.

VICKSBURG, April 8.—Everything quiet here. Two more transports left this afternoon, bound up the river. A number of transports are still in sight.

LATEST FROM PORT HUDSON.

PORT HUDSON, April 9.—All quiet here. The enemy's fleets, above and below, have disappeared. The former is above Bayou Sara. Forty exchanged and paroled prisoners from New Orleans arrived here yesterday. Our troops at this point are in excellent spirits, and are vigilantly watching the Yankee vessels.

We have trustworthy information from St. Joseph's, La., to the effect that HARRISON'S pickets are skirmishing with the enemy. Three flats, loaded with Yankees, came down the Tensas a few days ago.

THE LATEST FROM TENNESSEE.

CHATTANOOGA, April 9.—The enemy occupies Lebanon with a division, under Gen. REYNOLDS. The Yankees are also in force at Carthage. The news we get from Kentucky is cheering. The Louisville *Democrat* spurns the tyranny of the Union Democratic Convention and its platform. All is quiet at Columbia. Twenty more prisoners reached here yesterday. We have advices from Memphis that the enemy is preparing more empty boats as "cotton clad," for the purpose of landing troops at Vicksburg. The Yankee boats had returned from Steele's Bayou, badly damaged. More families have been exiled from Memphis on account of "rebel" raids on the railroad.

VAN DORN'S Cavalry has succeeded in capturing one gunboat and two transports on the Cumberland River, near Palmyra, which were burned. A grand review took place yesterday at Tullahoma.

THE FOOD QUESTION AND THE SPECULATORS.

RICHMOND, April 10.—The President will issue his Proclamation to-morrow morning, urging the people to direct their agricultural labor mainly to the production of food crops. He takes an encouraging view of the present position of affairs, and urges the raising of food for man and beast, as the means of averting the only danger that the Government regards with apprehension. He administers a rebuke to the speculators.

CONGRESSIONAL NEWS.

RICHMOND April 10.—In the Senate the report of the Committee on Conference recommending the Senate to agree to the House amendments to the bill exempting contractors from military service, was concurred in. The Senate also concurred in the House bill, amending the Copyright Act and the Senate bill abolishing all ports of delivery in the Confederate States except such as are also ports of entry. The Senate then went into secret session.

The House postponed the Supreme Court and Court of Claims bills to next session It also passed a bill to reorganize the Medical Department. The House concurred in the report of the Committee of Conference relative to the exemption of Mail Contractors.

FATAL RAILROAD ACCIDENT.

LYNCHBURG, April 10.—The train which left here this morning on the Virginia and Tennessee Railroad, with 400 exchanged Confederate prisoners on board, ran off the track near Lowry's Crossing, wounding 11 soldiers—5 seriously.

REPULSE OF THE ENEMY IN FLORIDA.

PALATKA, FLA., March 31.—On Friday, the 27th inst., the large transport steamer *Ben DeFord* landed at this place for the purpose of occupying the town. A fine cavalry corps stationed here, under command of Capt. J. J. DICKISON, met them very handsomely. We fired upon them with Enfield rifles, at a distance of about one hundred yards, killing and wounding a great many, the notorious Colonel MONTGOMERY, the Kansas "jayhawker" and outlaw, among the number. They immediately fled to their boat, and did not return the fire until they were out in the stream It is almost a miracle that we had only one man wounded from the amount of shell and grape thrown. They retreated across the river, and took on board two companies of negros whom they had there engaged plundering and stealing. They then steamed off down the river, and we have not heard from them since. We have just received a despatch which states that they have burnt Jacksonville and left the river.—*Savannah News.*

LATER FROM EUROPE.

We have advices from Europe three days later, by the arrival at Halifax of the steamship *Canada* She left Liverpool on the 21st and Queenstown on the 22d ult.

Intelligence of still further depredations by the Alabama reaches us by this arrival. The ship Washington, from Callao for Antwerp, had arrived at Southampton and reported having been captured by the pirate on the 20th of February, but released on giving bonds in $50,000. She had on board the crews of three vessels which had been captured and burnt—the Golden Eagle, the Olive Jane and the Palmetto.

The rebel cotton loan had caused considerable excitement in the English and French money markets. The bidding was expected to close on the afternoon of the 21st, much more having been offered than needed, particularly in London and Paris. In Liverpool the offers were not very heavy. The London Times says that very little political feeling was manifested in the matter, it being regarded simply as a cotton speculation. The Star and Daily News denounce the loan in most decided terms, as aiding and abetting the Slave Power.

Mr. Seymour Fitzgerald had given notice in the House of Commons of his intention to ask whether the British Government had accepted, or intended to accept, a proposition made by President Lincoln as to measures to inquire into any just complaints of the violations of neutral rights.

There was not much change in the aspect of Polish affairs. The debate in the French Senate was concluded on the 19th. It was decided to send all petitions to the Minister of Foreign Affairs—leaving the whole matter virtually in the hands of the Emperor. A popular demonstration in favor of Poland had taken place in Paris. The latest news from Poland is regarded as showing that the revolution is becoming general. With regard to the success of Langoewicz, dispatches are contradictory. He is said in one to have defeated the Russians, and in another to have been himself defeated.

SOMETHING IN A NAME.—Quilp, who has mounted a hat, has inscribed, instead of his name, the number "290." He assigns as a reason for his eccentric behavior that he has lost a good many hats by felonious capture, and he thinks that the above figure will save the felt—having made up his mind that, under our present navy management, "290" can't be taken.—*Boston Post.*

A FORTUNE MADE IN TWO HOURS.—A gold speculator at New York, who jumped in and out, at the right time, during the day when the "yellow fever" raged most fiercely, and there were the greatest fluctuations in gold, made a nett profit of $100,000 in about two hours.

THE MERCURY.

SATURDAY, APRIL 11, 1863.

Notes of the Fight of the 7th at Fort Sumter.

At two o'clock p. m., just as the officers had seated themselves for dinner, the first advance of the iron-clad fleet was announced to the commandant of the post. Their anchorage had been within the bar of Ship Channel, off the southern end of Morris Island, some four miles from Sumter. Upon inspection, it was judged that good time would be allowed for the conclusion of the meal, and, after communicating the movement by telegraph to Headquarters in Charleston, dinner was comfortably dispatched. At half past two o'clock, after examination of the approaching armament from the terreplein, the order for the "long roll" was issued. The whole garrison knew that the hour of trial was at hand, and the greatest enthusiasm and alacrity prevailed. The men rushed to their guns with shouting and yells of exultation. The regimental band was ordered to the rampart. The garrison flag (the Confederate States) was already flying defiantly from the staff at the northern apex of the pentagonal fortress. The blue and white banner of the Palmetto State was given to the wind on the southwest corner of the work, and the elegant black and white color, of the First Regiment South Carolina Artillery (Regulars), was run up at the southeast angle, in the face of the coming foe. A salute of thirteen unshotted guns was fired, and the band broke forth with the stirring strains of "Dixie."

It was determined to permit the fleet to come well within range before opening fire. Lieutenant Colonel JOSEPH A. YATES, who that morning reported for duty, was assigned to the special command of the barbette batteries. Major ORMSBY BLANDING was assigned the special command of the casemate batteries. They were both at their posts, with officers, men and guns ready, and awaiting the order to begin the engagement. Colonel ALFRED RHETT, the commandant of the post, stood on the parapet watching the progress of the doughty iron-clad dogs of war. Every heart beat high. Every face was flushed with calm excitement, properly incident to such a moment. On they came, steaming slowly north-eastward—seven Monitors, their hulls sunk down to the water level, showing only a black line on the surface and a projecting turret and smoke stack each—the *Ironsides*, looming up from the sea a formidable looking monster, and the *Keokuk*, her hull more distinctly visible than the Monitors, and with two turrets, the most dreaded of all the nine.

In front, a Monitor, supposed to be the *Passaic*, commanded by DRAYTON, pushed forward a long raft, forked and fitting her bow, intended to catch, by suspended grappling irons, any entanglements, or to explode any torpedoes, which might lie in the path of their hostile advance. Next followed, in approximate *echelon*, another Monitor, bearing a pennon, and conjectured to be the flag ship of the commanding officer of the fleet. This was succeeded, in the same order, by two others of similar kind, only distinguishable by slight differences in the adornments of red or white paint upon their generally black turrets and smoke stacks. These constituted the first line or division. After an interval of space came the *Ironsides* of much larger proportions, her sleek and glistening black sides rising high and frowning above the water. She occupied a central position, and was followed, at some distance, by the three remaining Monitors and the *Keokuk* in the rear. These four formed the other line or division of battle.

At three o'clock, when the leading gunboat had got east-southeast of Sumter, at a distance of about fourteen hundred yards, Fort Moultrie fired the first gun. The band was hushed at Sumter, the musicians were dispatched to their pieces, and the order was issued to open fire, carefully and by battery.

At 3 03 min. the guns belched forth their fierce thunders upon the foremost monster. Within two minutes there was a response. His shots were directed against Sumter, and the strife was inaugurated. The east and northeast batteries, *en barbette* and in casemate, were those only engaged, together with a mortar battery on one of the ramparts, which fired for a short time. It may be improper to publish, at this [illegible], the garrison of the fort, but we may mention that the east barbette battery was officered, as we understand, by Captain D. FLEMMING, Lieut. F. D. BLAKE, Lieut. JONES, and Lieut. JULIUS RHETT (a volunteer, absent from PRESTON'S Battery Light Artillery on sick leave). The northeast barbette battery was officered by Capt. HARLESTON, Lieut. McM. KING and Lieut. W. S. SIMKINS. The mortar battery was for a time manned and was officered by Capt. MACBETH and Lieut. JULIUS ALSTON, who were subsequently transferred to one of the casemate batteries engaged. The other, the largest casemate battery engaged, was commanded by Capt. W. H. PERONNEAU and Lieut. FICKLING, while a third small battery was in charge of Lieut. GRIMBALL.

For thirty minutes the guns of Fort Sumter were concentrated on the leading vessel, irrespective of the answering cannon of the others. The garrison fought with eagerness and impetuosity. They had to be restrained, and after trial, firing by battery, it was found that, from the small size of the object at a distance of 1100 to 1400 yards, and its constant and alternate moving and stopping, it was difficult to keep the guns trained to shoot simultaneously with accuracy. The method was changed, with apparent advantage, during the course of the engagement. The gunboats fired deliberately, at intervals. The smokestack of the pioneer boat was riddled with balls. The turret was repeatedly struck and impressions distinctly visible. At 3.25 a flat headed bolt of chilled iron, projected from a Brooke gun (rifled and banded 7 inch), struck with manifest damage. A volume of steam was seen to issue from the creature, and it turned off on a curve toward the east and south-east, steaming out of range and out of the fight. Meantime, the three other Monitors of the first line had bestowed their attentions upon the fort with impunity. They now, after the retirement of the supposed *Passaic*, received each, for a brief season, sundry acknowledgments. That bearing the pennon, at 3 37 had its emblem of command cut down by a well directed shot. Its turret and hull were indented. Several shot were visible, driven and sticking in the iron. The smoke stack was repeatedly pierced through. And at 3 45 this invulnerable man of war also drew off, followed by the two that had accompanied it.

The *Ironsides* seemed shy of the contest. She fired a few shots at a distance of not less than 1400 yards, and perhaps as much as 1800. Three balls were seen to strike her in return. She soon headed off out of range, and was counted out.

The Monitors of the second line were under a concentrated fire, each a few minutes. All were hit, but apparently with no special injury. The longer the fight continued, the more accurate the firing proved with the gunners of that gallant and admirably trained corps.

The *Keokuk* now boldly advanced, bow on, to 850 yards of the east side of Fort Sumter. This was the shortest distance attained by any of the fleet, no other venturing so near. Colonel RHETT now requested Lieutenant-Colonel YATES to take charge of a Brooke gun for a few shots, and to sight it carefully himself. The first shot entered the open port hole of the foremost turret, apparently silencing the boat. The next ball was a centre shot upon the turret. The third penetrated the bow, some ten feet from the stem, making a large opening at the water line; and a fourth also struck the hull. During this time a concentric fire was poured into the monster from all the guns that could be brought to bear. The fire of the fort had been reduced by order to one gun from each battery every five minutes, and was exceedingly precise and effective. For many minutes the boat drifted lifelessly with the tide, under a terrific hail, being torn in different places, and having shot plainly imbedded in the iron armor. It was strongly hoped that it would be so disabled as to surrender, falling into our hands by capture. But, after being under punishment forty minutes, it managed to crawl feebly off and escape, giving a parting salute as it was getting out of range to show that the will was there to fight. The following morning it settled down some five hundred yards to sea from the beach towards the south part of Morris Island.

This was the end of the fight. After a short engagement of two hours and twenty-five minutes, an unprotected brick fort, by the use of its cannon, assisted by Fort Moultrie and the guns of one or two sand batteries, employing few guns, repulsed a fleet of nine of the boasted iron-clad gunboats. The *Keokuk* was sunk. The *Passaic* has disappeared from view, probably sent or towed to Port Royal for repairs. And the flag-boat has been undergoing the mending process in plain sight. The prestige of their invulnerability is gone. The question is reduced to the relative powers of destruction of the fort and the assailing fleet. It is a question of pluck and survivorship in a square stand-up-fight for victory. Iron-clad fleets can be destroyed as well as forts. Fort Sumter, although somewhat pitted, to-day is, we believe, as strong as it was when this fight begun. We deem that, if the attack is renewed as before (and there is good reason to believe it will be), the six Monitors left and the *Ironsides* will come out the defeated party, with worse results than those obtained in their first attempt. *Nous verrons.*

The enemy fired about eighty shots—mostly 15 inch and steel pointed shells—at Fort Sumter. This estimate was made from Sullivan's Island. Forty only struck the work. One 10-inch gun was temporarily disabled by a shot. One Columbiad of old pattern burst. One 7 inch rifled gun dismounted by recoil, and one gun was disabled for a few moments by fracture of the elevating screw through recoil.

Not a person was killed in Fort Sumter from any cause. Sergeant FAULKNER, and Privates CHAPLIN, MINNIX and PENN, Company B, were injured by a shower of bricks thrown from a traverse on the rampart by a large shot of the enemy. A drummer boy, AHRENS, was struck on the head by the explosion of a shell over the parade. A negro laborer was also wounded. All, we learn are doing well, and there is no danger of losing a life or a limb. The wounded were dressed by Surgeon MOORE, of the post, and sent out of the way to a hospital in the city, where they now remain.

The regimental ensign was pierced near the centre by a ball. The Confederate flag was also perforated.

THE BATTERIES OF SULLIVAN'S ISLAND.

FORT MOULTRIE opened the engagement. At three o'clock, the head of the grim procession of Monitors having come within reasonable range, the word was given, and the first shot of the battle went whizzing at the iron fleet. In a very few minutes the batteries of Sumter, with the earth works of Morris and Sullivan's Islands, were mingling their deep voices in the chorus of the fray. During the entire fight the batteries of Fort Moultrie, maintained a well directed fire against the Monitor that happened to be nearest, and the frequency with which the Yankees turned from their main effort against Fort Sumter to give a spiteful shot to Fort Moultrie showed how effectively and accurately the men at the latter post were hurling their metal on the foe.

There was but one casualty at Fort Moultrie. A shot from one of the Monitors cut away the flag staff, a few feet above the parapet, and the staff fell upon Private LUSBY, Company F, 1st S. C. (regular) Infantry, inflicting injuries, from the effects of which he soon died.

The garrison of Fort Moultrie it would not be proper to enumerate. It consists of the First South Carolina (regular) Infantry. The commandant of the post is Colonel WM. BUTLER, of the same regiment, and the companies during the action were severally commanded by Captain T. A. HUGUENIN, Captain B. S. BURNET, Capt. CONSTANTINE RIVERS, First Lieut. E. A. ERWIN and Captain R. PRESTON SMITH—the last named officer having special charge of the mortar battery. The closest range into which the enemy ventured was estimated by the officers of the fort at about 1200 yards. The flagstaff has been replaced, and as no other portion of the fort sustained any damage whatever during the engagement, the post is in excellent condition to join in another trial of strength with the turreted armada.

BATTERY BEE, on Sullivan's Island, just opposite Fort Sumter, was commanded by Lieutenant Col. SIMKINS, of the 1st S. C. (regular) Infantry, and manned by companies of that Regiment. The Captains commanding the companies at this post engaged, were Captains ROBERT DETREVILLE, WARREN ADAMS, and W. T. TATUM. The battery was the recipient of occasional shots from the enemy, but was not in any way injured, nor were there any casualties amongst the men. During the fight Gen. RIPLEY was present at Battery Bee. Whenever the enemy may choose to renew the attack, if his object should be to dash into the harbor, Battery Bee will have a far more important part to play.

The BEAUREGARD BATTERY, with three of its guns, also took part in the general melee of heavy artillery, and twice received a broadside from the enemy. This battery, commanded by Captain J. A. SITGREAVES, 1st Regiment S. C. (regular) Artillery, is situated on the Sullivan's Island beach, northeast of Fort Moultrie, a little beyond the Moultrie House, and is manned from the 1st Regiment S. C. (regular) Artillery, 1st Lieutenant ERWIN commanding, and Co. B, 1st Regiment S. C. (regular) Infantry, Captain WARLEY commanding. The battery was in no respect damaged, although many of the Yankee round-shot fell upon the sand in the immediate neighborhood.

The forces on Sullivan's Island (which is a portion of the subdivision commanded by Brigadier-General TRAPIER) were under the immediate command of Colonel L. M. KEITT, of the 20th Regiment S. C. V. Both General TRAPIER and Colonel KEITT were on the Island at the time of the action, and during the firing were moving from battery to battery.

THE CITY ON CHARLESTON—THE SPIRIT OF HER PEOPLE AND DEFENDERS.

[*From the Richmond Dispatch.*]

The Yankee scribes speak with the same certainty of taking Charleston as they were wont to do of taking Richmond. It is entertaining to read their mysterious hints about the unknown and awful agencies which lie undisclosed in the bottom of their Monitors, but which, at the appointed time (a time which has already been deferred oftener than the Ascension Day of the Millerites), are to be let loose in irresistible power upon the devoted city. Such a generation of braggarts never before occupied the earth. How different the incessant clamoring of the multitudinous frogs outside the harbor and the stern silence which reigns within! The invading hordes will never occupy Charleston. If it ever falls into their hands it will be only as a heap of smoking ruins, the very site of which will be uninhabitable after the heat of summer has set in. But we don't believe that even that much consolation awaits them. We can easily understand their impatience to defile Charleston more foully than New Orleans. They are already squatting down in imagination in those majestic old churches; stationing whole regiments of their foreign braves in that spacious and famous Orphan Asylum, which has sheltered and reared so many poor children of every nationality, and taking for their officers' quarters the stately old mansions of the Huguenot and Cavalier aristocracy. All and more than they have done in New Orleans do they expect to perpetrate in Charleston. But, if ever there was a possibility that Charleston could fall unmutilated into their hands, it has been annihilated by their fiendish and beastly conduct in New Orleans. Every citizen of Charleston would apply the torch to his own house sooner than see his beloved city reduced to such degradation. Not one house will be left standing for the Butlers to revel and riot in, even if their Monitors could force their way to the wharves of the city. Not one roof would be left standing to shelter the heads of the invaders from the blazing sun that would soon render life insupportable to the unacclimated, while our numerous and well appointed army would fall back, leaving the foe a few barren acres on a sickly coast as a grave yard for their soldiers and sailors.

But Charleston, we feel a strong persuasion, is to meet no such fate. We believe that its means of defence are sufficient to set the foe at defiance, and that the God of Battles will defend a city which, without disparagement to any other, may be said to have had no superior, if an equal, in the domestic virtues of its people, in its catholic spirit and noble charities, in its humane provisions for the poor, the orphan, and the aged and infirm. We have abiding confidence in the devoted courage with which it will be defended, and in the great General who, we trust, is destined to immortalize his name, not only by the successful defence of the city, but the annihilation of the invaders.

[*From the Richmond Examiner.*]

It cannot be improper for us to say that we get the most satisfactory reports of affairs at Charleston. The military authorities are alive to the crisis, and the movements there have been directed with great activity and vigor. Until the proper time the people must not know what preparations have been going on for the enemy, and must be satisfied to know that all is well and everything as favorable as could be desired. The spirit and enthusiasm of our troops are said to be splendid. So with the citizens. Under the fate threatening Charleston, we are told that everything is perfectly quiet, and that the people go on as unconcernedly as if nothing were before them. If a stranger could look in upon the streets he would hardly think that the city was threatened by one of the most formidable fleets ever known in history. All is quiet, but yet you can see, our informant tells us, that firm and determined look upon every face—that expression of unbending courage—to fight until death!—to see the city one mass of smouldering ruins, rather than it shall be polluted by the enemy. In the face of all dangers, we are assured the confidence of the people of Charleston remains unshaken to the last. There is a universal conviction that the place cannot be carried, and not a heart quails. Everything goes on in its usual routine without the least manifestation of fear or excitement. Everything awaits the coming of the Yankees, and our batteries reserve their fire, ready to respond in an instant to the first gun of the enemy.

We can say to our readers that we believe that they may cherish their best hopes of the result at Charleston, and that they may look for exciting news from that quarter at any moment.

[*From the Jackson (Miss.) Crisis.*]

It was in this far-famed, cultivated, hospitable city that the people of South Carolina, through their representatives in Convention, declared their separation from the negro worshipping, infidel incendiaries of the North. It was for the possession and defence of this city that the Federal flag was brought down at Fort Sumter. It was this locality which was, in former generations, consecrated to liberty. From before Fort Moultrie the British fleet was driven, though Sir Peter Parker fought like a Briton. This ancient metropolis witnessed the execution of Hayne, as a rebel against the Crown and Government of the Third George. It witnessed, too, the erection of the statue of William Pitt, the statesman, who dared to defend before the British Parliament the principle of English liberty in behalf of the colonies. In the soil of that city were interred the mortal remains of Calhoun. The honored names of great patriots—Moultrie, Rutledge, Pinckney, Turnbull, Middleton, Laurens, Hayne, and many others—cluster together on the page of her history, and bequeath to that old, gallant, liberty-loving city a wealth of greatness. Her glorious past cannot fail to inspire sentiments of sublime devotion to freedom.

And now the minions of despotism—the foul brood of fanaticism—prompted by fiendish hate, envy and malice, mass themselves to crush out the sons of the brave and the free. Let them try! The vulture and raven will be invited to the feast! Let them beard the lion in his den! They will be welcomed to the shock. Let them storm Charleston, and they will descend "to the harvest of death!" Let them take Charleston by any effort—by any combination of numbers and appliances—and they will take a Golgotha of ashes, cinders and human bones!

There she stands, as calm as a summer's evening. "We know how to defend our soil," is the proud language of Carolina's sons, "or we know how to perish!" "We'll hold the graves of our ancestors, or sleep with the illustrious dead!" O, brave mother State! We love and honor your name. The blood of our house has mingled with the fallen brave, and we have an inheritance in the valor and glory of your sons!

[*From the Richmond Whig*]

At last the hour of trial has come for Charleston—the hour of deliverance or destruction; for no one believes the other alternative, surrender, possible. The heart of the whole country yearns toward the beleaguered city with intense solicitude—and yet with hope amounting to confidence. Charleston knows what is expected of her, and what is due to her fame, and to the relation she sustains to the cause. The devoted, the heroic, the great-hearted Beauregard is there, and he, too, knows what is expected of him, and will not disappoint that expectation. We predict a Saragossa defence, and that if Charleston is taken it will be only as a heap of ruins.

[*From the Jackson Mississippian.*]

The shock will be terrible! But we are more than hopeful of the result. The ignominy of New Orleans will not be repeated at Charleston! *Defend the city, or perish*, is the unfaltering determination of the brave men stationed there. It is needless now to speculate upon a subject which the tests of experiment, and the logic of facts, must so soon decide. God bless the old Palmetto State, and defend her ancient metropolis!

FROM THE UNITED STATES.

YANKEE GOSSIP AND SPECULATION IN REGARD TO THE ATTACK ON CHARLESTON.

We have Northern dates to the 4th instant, inclusively. The New York papers teem with statements and speculations in regard to the attack on Charleston. Carleton, the correspondent of the Boston *Journal*, writing from Hilton Head, under date of March 23, shows the difficulties the Yankee forces, especially the naval portion of them, will have to contend against in the siege of Charleston, which the same correspondent says is now about to commence. He writes:

"In former letters I have pointed out some of the obstacles to be surmounted before we come in possession of Charleston. Further intelligence does not lessen the difficulties. The fact that the Monitor received the broadside of the Merrimac so near that the rammers of the cannoniers almost touched as they ran them from the port holes, has been taken as conclusive that our iron-clads can run past Sumter, Moultrie, the batteries of Sullivan and Morris Islands, past the floating batteries, paying no heed to the tornado of shot and shell belched from the one thousand cannon reported to be in position, and make a straight course for the city of Charleston. It is possible to do that, but a thing not probable.

"There are three ways of steering vessels—by sight, by lead, by compass. In a great naval engagement the immense volumes of smoke will be likely to shut out prominent objects from sight, and render steering by that method ineffectual. To stand on the slushed deck of the Nahant or Passaic and throw the lead under such a fire as the rebels will concentrate upon our little fleet, will require a coolness which few men possess; besides, it will be a hazard which Admiral Dupont will not require unless absolutely necessary. To steer by compass in a narrow channel is not practicable. The steering must be done mainly by sight. Fortunately we have accurate surveys of the harbor, and pilots who are intimately acquainted with the channels. If the attack is made at high water the light draft of the iron-clads will enable them to take position to suit their own convenience.

"We have supposed that because the Monitor resisted the shot of the Merrimac, and at the same time accomplished so much with her eleven inch guns, that the fifteen inch guns would knock everything in the shape of masonry or earth-worth defences to pieces; but it has become apparent that our Ordnance Department has not kept pace with progress in marine architecture. All of our large guns are of cast iron. As we increase the calibre, we are compelled to decrease the quantity or quality of powder—or, in other words, reduce the velocity given to the shot. The powder used must be slow burning—grains as large as filberts. Rifle powder, which ignites with the quickness of lightning almost, would send the gun and its carriage head over heels from its position, or split the gun into fragments. By increasing the weight of the ball we increase its crushing power; but a rifled hundred pound Parrot gun, for penetrating or boring purposes, throwing a shot at high speed, will probably be found to be superior to the fifteen inch four hundred pound shot, hurled, as they must be, with comparative slow velocity. Fifteen inch guns are as yet untried. The Ordnance Department is all at sea in regard to them. They may fulfil the most sanguine expectations, and they may be found less efficient even than the eleven inch guns. The experiment is to be tried. You remember that great results were predicted of the Lancaster gun in the Crimea. It was to send the shot completely through Todtleben's fortifications, but it proved to be a failure. Till they have been put to the test, we cannot unqualifiedly and unreservedly expect that these monsters will completely destroy the defences which Beauregard has erected. They cannot be served with the rapidity of lighter ordnance It requires hard lifting to handle shot weighing four hundred pounds. In all, we shall have but eight turretted vessels and the New Ironsides—thirty-two guns. The wooden gunboats undoubtedly will take a part, but it will of necessity be at long range. Thirty two guns against one thousand as reported. Beauregard boasts that ten minutes' exposure of one of our iron clads at close range under his converging fires will use them up. The rebel fire will be hot. It will be a continued roar of thunder, a continual battering of shot upon the iron mail. They have Whitworth guns which throw steel pointed shot. Fortunately we came in possession of several thousand shot intended for them when we captured the Ocean Wave. I have faith in the power of the iron-clads to withstand their hottest fire, but it is yet to be determined whether, with our necessarily slow manipulations, we can silence the batteries opposed.

"The labor will be exhaustive. A crew will hardly handle those heavy guns day after day and week after week without exhaustion. Cessation of fire will enable the rebels to repair damages. You remember how the Malakoff held out and the Redan—knocked all to pieces by day, but made as good as ever by night—how at last they were carried by a terrible assault and the slaughter of thousands of men. The rebel batteries are not like those Crimean strongholds, but they are, nevertheless, formidable works.

"As to sailing straight in, unmindful of shot and shell, we are not to forget that there are rebel rams. We are not to forget that the rebels have given out hints that we shall find ourselves confronted by something new and unheard of.

"In view of all this it is possible that the expectations which we may have had of taking Charleston in a day may not be realized. It may be the work of days, weeks, months. We may be defeated. Storms may compel us to withdraw. Our fleet may be sent to the bottom or driven on shore. These are possible contingencies which are to be taken into the calculations of our chances of success.

"But though there may be delay and failure at first, let there be no despondency on the part of the people of the North, for sooner or later Charleston, Sumter and Moultrie will be "repossessed" by the United States. I have written thus, not from apprehension of failure, but because I am near the expected scene of action and have information of what the rebels are doing.

"The defensive powers of our iron-clads are satisfactorily ascertained, but not so their offensive powers. It is wisdom in everything to take ability into account—to take all contingencies into consideration and then make up the estimate, and obtain a basis for reasonable expectation."

THE YANKEE TERROR OF TORPEDOES—DESCRIPTION OF THE ARRANGEMENTS FOR REMOVING THEM.

The Hilton Head correspondent of the Philadelphia *Press* writes, on March 23, as follows:

When this letter reaches you the attack, by our entire fleet, upon the hot bed of the rebellion, will have fairly commenced. There can be no harm now in giving you some account of the great preparations for the attack and investment and the cause of the various delays.

The prime cause of the delay of the attack on Charleston has not been with the army, as many suppose—for it has been said from the highest authority that the troops have been waiting the word from the Admiral; nor has the delay been caused by the weather alone, but the presence in Charleston harbor of the torpedoes with which, it has been proved, Monitors, unassisted, are unable to cope.

It will be granted by even the most sanguine of our "on to Charlestoners" that, with the experience of the Montauk staring Admiral Dupont in the face, it would have been criminal folly to send Monitors unprepared to meet what these arrangements are devised to overcome. The Monitors engaged in this attack are as follows: The Passaic, Captain Drayton; the Patapsco, Capt Ammon; the Weehawken, Captain Deans; the Nahant, Captain John Rodgers; the Cattskill, Captain Fairfax, of Trent memory; the Nantucket, Captain George Rodgers; and the Montauk, Captain Worden, the hero of iron-clad warfare. It is but fair to remark that Captain Worden, though it has been his lot to see rough experience with Monitors, is enthusiastic in his belief of their efficiency. The Keokuk is also booked for the affair. In addition to these is the iron frigate New Ironsides, Commodore Turner, which has been the flag-ship of the Charleston blockading fleet for a month past. Her armament consists of fourteen 11-inch guns and two 200-pound rifles. From riding out one or two gales of wind, it has been sufficiently proved that the doubts of her seaworthiness were unfounded. The Wabash, with her large crew, 780 men, and heavy armament, unfortunately draws too much water (23 feet) to cross the bar, as also the Powhatan, formerly commanded by Commodore Godon, and the Pawnee (called the blockade devil last year by Secesh), and will, therefore, remain to receive the ram expected to attempt the recapture of Port Royal during the absence of our iron-clad fleet.

The same correspondent, alluding to the delay in the attack upon Charleston, through apprehension of torpedoes in the harbor, says:

But Captain Ericsson, of New York, has devised a plan by which this difficulty is obviated, and has already sent down four of these machines, three of which were lost in a gale of wind, while the remaining one, with difficulty, the steamer Ericsson has safely towed into Port Royal harbor. It may be of interest to describe the principle on which these are constructed. An iron frame, floated to the water's edge by iron sponsons, is pushed ahead of the Monitor as she runs in. Its length, from the bow of the Monitor, is from 20 to 30 feet. An aperture is made next to the vessel of the shape of her bows, intended to receive it. The breadth of the "Obstruction Remover," as it is called, is 12 feet. From each side of the extremity a strong iron bar or shaft runs down also 2 feet; the Monitor drawing but from 8 to 10 feet water, thus rendering it impossible for any torpedoes over which this "Obstruction Remover" passes to injure the vessel.

A number of iron bars are used, not only to form a network so as to either push forward or explode every torpedo less than twelve feet under water, but also to strengthen and steady the masts. At the bottom a heavy tie bar unites these two vertical rods, upon which rests the percussion torpedo, containing seven hundred pounds of powder. Above this is a hammer which catches in a spring so stiff as to require two men to set it, but constructed so that the lever, which protrudes in front, forming the handle or other end of the hammer, will cause the spring to give with little pressure. This is to remove "piles." The experiments made upon this machine in the North have demonstrated the fact that it is a complete success, and an amount of powder greater than has ever been proposed for any torpedo before caused no injury to the vessel, and indeed did not disturb any of the ties of the "Obstruction Remover." It will be readily seen that under no circumstances can any strain be given to the Monitor, so supposing the apparatus to be destroyed, as it floats independently of the Monitor, supporting itself, the worst that can happen is its loss.

THE IRON-CLAD KAATSKILL.

Prominent amongst the vessels engaged in the recent attack upon Fort Sumter was the Monitor Battery *Kaatskill.* A Northern paper gives the following description of her build:

This vessel, which was contracted for in April, immediately after the success of the Monitor against the Merrimac, has, like the Passaic and Montauk, been built by Mr. T. F. Rowland, at the Continental Works, Greenpoint. Though in every essential point the counterpart of the other vessels, she has several peculiarities, which will make a full description not uninteresting. Her shape is nearly that of the Monitor, only her lines are sharper, thereby securing more buoyancy and speed. The vessel has the following dimensions: Length over all, 199 feet ten inches; beam, 45 feet on deck; breadth of the vessel proper, 37 feet; depth of hold, 11 feet from deck; draft of water when armed, 9 feet 6 inches; draught of water when launched, 7 feet 8 inches.

The vessel proper is built of the best seasoned oak beams—12 by 12 inches amidships and 10 by 12 inches on either side—placed two feet apart. The deck, which is flush, is planked with heavy oak planks. The hatches are heavy iron frames, sunk flush in the deck, which, like the dead lights, are covered, when in action, by wrought iron covers. The anchor hangs in a well five feet in diameter, so as to afford no target to the enemy. The armor of the vessel consists of five one-inch plates, securely bolted and riveted so as to overlap each other. The armor in the fore part of the vessel is nine inches thick, obtained by iron stringers four inches wide being inserted under the plating for a distance of some fifty feet. The plating on deck, consisting of two one inch plates, renders it bomb proof.

The turret is twenty-one feet in diameter and nine feet high. It is constructed of eleven one inch plates. The two portholes are seventeen inches wide by twenty four inches deep, and sufficiently apart to allow the two guns to be placed parallel with each other. These portholes are closed immediately after the piece has been fired by heavy shutters. On the top of the turret iron rafters are placed, which are covered with heavy perforated iron plates, so as to admit fresh air and allow the smoke to escape. The pilot house is placed on top of the turret, and so constructed that no shot can touch the man inside of it. It is six feet high, six feet in diameter, and constructed of eight-inch plates. The view of the horizon is obtained by means of eight loop holes, so arranged as to cover about 45 degrees of the horizon.

The engines of the Kaatskill are now nearly ready at the Delamater Iron Works, foot of 13th street, N. R. They are direct acting engines of 45 inch cylinder, 22 inch stroke. The propeller is a four bladed one, of 12 feet diameter and 16 feet pitch. The rudder of the Kaatskill hangs on its iron centre instead of the stern post, as is usually the case, thereby securing a double action and a greater security against shot and shell. Captain R. Rodgers will take command of this ship.

The Kaatskill is the fifth Ericsson Battery launched at this port, and the fourth built by Mr. T. F. Rowland. They were launched as follows:

Monitor, of 776 tons, launched at Greenpoint January 3.
Passaic, of 844 tons, launched at Greenpoint August 30.
Montauk, of 870 tons, launched at Greenpoint October 10.
Kaatskill, of 844 tons, launched at Greenpoint Dec. 4.
Weehawken, of 844 tons, launched at Jersey City Nov. 5.

THE LAND FORCES MOVING FROM PORT ROYAL TOWARDS CHARLESTON—RECALL OF THE YANKEE TROOPS IN FLORIDA.

We find in the Boston *Traveller* the following letter, dated St. Helena Island, S. C., March 27:

Stevenson's brigade, consisting of the 10th Connecticut 24th Massachusetts, and two New York Regiments, received orders yesterday to be ready to leave in forty-eight hours.

There are various rumors as to the point at which we are to land, and Cole's, Stono and James' Islands are each spoken of as likely places for us to bring up at. One or two regiments left here day before yesterday, but I have been unable to learn of any other brigade having received orders to get ready for a start. All the troops on this island, sixteen regiments, were reviewed yesterday by General Hunter, and everything passed off in a manner satisfactory to all parties, I believe. The men are in good spirits and well pleased at the prospect of getting out of close confinement.

As the mail is about closing, I learn that General Hunter has issued an order recalling the Florida expedition. The whole of the troops in that State, with perhaps, the exception of a small force to do garrison duty at Key West and Fernandina, are to return here immediately. Judging from this fact, and other circumstances that have transpired here within a few days, I think the Charleston expedition will start within two days.

MISCELLANEOUS.

John Anthon, a noted lawyer of New York, died on the 11th ult.

The Peterhoff is to be released, though she had a rebel Colonel and a rebel mail aboard.

Mrs. Blandina Dudley, who erected and endowed the Dudley Observatory, at Albany, N. Y., is dead.

Postage stamps have come into use in Turkey. They bear a fac simile of the Sultan's autograph.

The ship Star of Peace, announced in our Bermuda news as having been recently destroyed by the Florida, had a cargo valued at half a million. She was an A 1 ship, belonging to Boston.

According to the Washington correspondent of the Philadelphia Ledger, official advices from Port Royal, received at Washington, represent that the contemplated attack upon the works at Stono had been postponed.

It is stated that despatches have been received to the effect that the Richmond was severely cut up in the late engagement with the batteries at Port Hudson, and it is doubtful whether she can be made available for service for a long time to come. This is not, however, in accordance with advices received from on board the Richmond. Intelligence from Vicksburg, by way of Cincinnati, is to the effect that Steele's Bayou Expedition had got back to Young's Point, and the troops had been disembarked. The work on the cut-off opposite the city is said to have been abandoned, the rebel batteries commanding two-thirds of its length, and rendering labor upon it impracticable.

A general muster of the troops composing the Army of the Potomac will take place on the 10th inst., in accordance with instructions from the War Department. The muster rolls, it is said, will then be immediately sent to the Adjutant General of the army, to be used in making drafts to fill up the regiments now in the field. The drafted men (about 200 000) will be sent at once to the regiments.

A despatch from Cincinnati says that on Monday, 30th ult., Jenkins' rebel cavalry dashed into Point Pleasant, Va., at the mouth of the Kanawha, gained possession of the Court House, fired seven houses, plundered others and burned several thousand bushels of Government corn—Volunteer aid arrived from Gallipolis, Ohio, and the rebels were driven off, with the loss of five killed and thirteen prisoners, who were refused parole and taken to Gallipolis.

EASTER ELECTION.

St. Thaddeus, Aiken, C. S.

VESTRYMEN.

AMORY COFFIN.	WM. GREGG.
ALEXANDER MAZYCK.	B. T. ROGERS.

L. H. ANDERSON.

WARDENS.

H. W. RAVENEL.	O. J. CHAFEE.

NEWS FROM BERMUDA.—A New York paper of the 3d instant says: Advices from Bermuda report the ship *Star of Peace*, of Boston, from Calcutta with a cargo of saltpetre, was burned by the pirate *Florida*. The schooner *Aldebaran* was also captured and a prize crew put aboard, when the *Florida* went in chase of another large American ship. A Havana letter contains a report that the pirate steamer *Alabama* has been lost, which is very doubtful. The rebel steamers *Cornubia*, from Wilmington, with 300 bales, and the *Beauregard*, from Charleston, with 1100 bales of cotton, have arrived at Bermuda recently.

Pilkington Brothers, of London and Liverpool, American merchants and ship brokers, have suspended. Liabilities £40,000, and the liquidation will depend upon remittances from America.

The monthly returns of the Bank of France show an increase in cash on hand of over fifty-four millions of francs; and a decrease in bills discounted of over sixty one millions.

The latest weekly returns of the Bank of England show a decrease in bullion of £176,339.

Great damage has been caused at Troy, N. Y., and other places, by a freshet on the Hudson river.

Nicholas Lehman, an Old Defender of Baltimore, died on the 29th ult.

AGRICULTURE.—Governor VANCE, in an address just issued to the people of North Carolina, speaks to the point as follows:

The bright sunshine again warms and dries the earth. We must use it to our salvation or neglect it to our destruction. Plant, sow, dig and plow, corn, oats, potatos—anything and everything which will support life. Let everybody take to the fields, where the plow, not the maddening wheels of artillery, furrow the generous soil. These will prove the real fields of victory and independence. Hundreds of able-bodied young men in our towns and villages—non-producers—who, having procured substitutes or exemptions, now idle their time about empty stores or other unprofitable places, should be growing something, and adding to, instead of diminishing the general fund. Let none be idle. And above all, my countrymen, let none plant cotton or tobacco. Though the prices are high and the temptation great, your profits would be made from the blood of brave men and the suffering of helpless women and children. Your children and your children's children would reap an abundant and enduring harvest of scorn, and the remembrance of the manner in which your wealth was gained, would burn into your conscience to the hour of death.

Vol. 11. # The Opelousas Courier. No. 22.

Louisiana

MORNING EDITION.

OPELOUSAS: *La.*

WEDNESDAY, : : : : APRIL 22, 1863.

☞ We print this paper just as the form was left for us when the Confederate troops abandoned the town, merely adding for the benefit of the community such later items of news as have reached us through Southern sources. The picture they represent, though not cheerful, is of course the most fa... ble for their side.

Loss of the Queen of the West.

On Monday last, April 13th, the Queen of the West, under the command of Capt. Malloy, and having on board Commodore Fuller, left Bute a la Rose for Grand Lake, Commodore Fuller leaving orders for the Grand Duke and Mary T., both lately converted into powerful gunboats, to follow him immediately. Accompanied by the tender Nina Simmes, the Queen reached Chicot Pass, connecting Chicot Lake and Grand Lake, the same evening, and waited for the Duke and Mary T. until twelve o'clock at night. These boats not arriving, Com. Fuller passed on with the Nina Simmes into Grand Lake, ordering the Simmes to make for Indian Bend or Charenton, where he expected to find three hundred men who were to act as sharpshooters on the gunboats. On reaching this place, which she did about three o'clock Tuesday morning, the Nina Simmes was informed that the expected reinforcement had been driven off the day before, and that the Federal gunboats, three in number, were then in easy gun shot. Pushing off speedily in the direction of the Queen, as day began to appear, the tender soon discovered her, and at the same time the hostile gunboats, which at once opened fire upon both boats. Running down to the Queen the Simmes was ordered to return towards Bute a la Rose and bring on the Duke and Mary T., the Yankee gunboats still keeping a heavy fire on the Queen, when about a mile from the latter, the Simmes saw a shell strike her about the pilot house, and a few moments afterwards she appeared to be on fire all over, and the light of the continued flames was seen for some time after.

The Queen was at this time two and a half or three miles from shore, the wind blowing a furious gale—so that the only chance for those on board, was that the enemy came up in time to save them from destruction by the flames or the waves. Thus ends once more the short lived career of another of our naval successes. Who was to blame will perhaps appear hereafter.—*The Southern Sentinel, April 18th.*

RIVER MOVEMENTS.—It is hard to determine by their movements on the river what the Federals intend to undertake. They have tried the taking of Vicksburg and Port Hudson, and have so far signally failed.

The enemy are now evacuating Baton Rouge and there is now no probability of them coming this way again soon. Report say that Banks is sending a considerable force to Donaldsonville, with a view to gain the rear of Sibley's force, it being impossible for him to advance direct on Livonia as the country is overflowed. It is reported that the greater part of Banks' army is being sent to Texas, but of this there is no certainty. What he will do with his reinforcements from Pensacola, remains to be seen.

We have now three months of provisions on hand, and the supply is constantly increasing by boats from Red river, and as the recent presence of Banks' army has made the planting community about here desirous to sell, the army is being supplied from this country, and the supply on hand is not being diminished.

As we may again hear of an engagement at Ponchatoula or probably at Tangipaho, and as all of your readers may not be acquainted with the location of these and other places, I will conclude this letter by a mention of their distances from New Orleans: Ponchatoula is forty-seven miles above New Orleans on the N. O. & J. R. R. Tangipaho is thirty-one miles from Ponchatoula, or seventy-eight miles from New Orleans and Osyka, Miss., ten miles from Tangipaho, both on the same railroad. Clinton is twenty-five miles by road or twenty miles by railroad from Port Hudson. Jackson, La., is fifteen miles from Port Hudson, and twelve miles from Clinton.—*The Natchez Courier, April 9th.*

The Battle at Camp Bisland.

The enemy advanced in force, about 12,000 strong, towards our entrenchments at Camp Bisland, on the 12th inst. Skirmishing with the outposts continued all day. On the 13th he commenced the attack in earnest, at the same time landing a strong corps at Hutchins Point, in Grand Lake and on our flanks and rear. A furious cannonade was opened on our lines early in the morning, which was kept up during the whole day with an interval of an hour and a half about noon, at which time he advanced in strong force upon our right, for the purpose of assaulting. He was entirely foiled in this attempt, and driven back. In the afternoon he pressed upon the left with equal vigor, but was again repulsed. The Gunboat Diana, lying in the Teche, was disabled early in the engagement by the fire of the enemy's Parrott guns, having her machinery broken and rendered useless. A force was detached, to keep in check the enemy on our flank and rear, which was successfully done against greatly superior numbers. The situation of our army was now most critical, and the troops worn out with fatigue and exhaustion—retreat was absolutely necessary in order to save the army. To effect this the enemy must be dislodged in our rear. Early on the morning of the 14th, our troops, led by Maj. Gen. Taylor in person, made a determined and irresistible attack upon this body of the enemy, and drove him before them several miles beyond Franklin, thus enabling the wagon trains, stores, artillery, etc., etc., to effect their retreat by the only road open to them. The army reached New Ibéria in safety, with the loss of a few heavy guns, which could not be removed from the fortifications and the destruction of the Diana.

The Queen of the West, commanded by Com. Fuller, entered Grand Lake during the night of the 13th, the other Gunboats not getting down in time for some unexplained cause. The Queen of the West was attacked on the morning of the 14th and destroyed.

Our little army is still at New Iberia, in good spirits and condition. Loss, considering the fierceness of the engagements, small; particulars not yet known. Col. Reilly, senior Colonel of Sibley's Brigade, was mortally wounded on the 13th, and died soon after the battle. On the same day Maj. Brownrigg, of Gen. Sibley's staff, was killed, and also Capt. Blair, 2d La. Cavalry. Col. Vincent, same Regiment, severely but not dangerously wounded in the neck.—*The Southern Sentinel, April 18th.*

☞ To the politeness of MAJOR SURGET we are indebted for the information relative to the disastrous reverses which have occurred to our forces at Camp Bisland, and to Capt. Boardman, of the Nina Simmes, for the particulars of the destruction of the Queen of the West, as far as is known. Why the Grand Duke and Mary T., now powerful gunboats, did not follow immediately the Queen, as ordered by Com. Fuller, remains yet to be explained.—*Southern Sentinel.*

EXTRA ON TUESDAY.

We shall on Tuesday morning next issue an Extra containing the latest news received up to that time, and hope to include in it full accounts of the fight at Camp Bisland, and the loss of our gunboats.—*Southern Sentinel.*

☞ THE SOUTHERN SENTINEL, though not an official paper being published at the Headquarters of the commanding Generals of the Department and District and of the Governor of the State, where the latest intelligence is received every day, will always be able to give its readers reliable information of all the interesting and important events transpiring throughout the Confederacy, as well as the most recent Northern and foreign news.—*Southern Sentinel.*

NOTICE.

ALL persons having claims against the Succession of the late Louisa Lodoiska Raulin, deceased widow of the late F. C. DeCourson, are requested to file the same duly authenticated to Mr. Marcel Daire, at Ville Plate, agent of the Administrator, in the shortest delay possible.

A. DARDEAU, *Administrator.*

Ville Plate, April 11, 1863. 19—5t

State of Louisiana.

District Court.—Parish of St. Landry.—No. 9412.

ANASTASIE SAVOIE, of the Parish of St. Landry, Administratrix of the Estate of John H. Maggee, deceased, late of the Parish of St. Landry, having filed a final Tableau of the affairs of said Estate, accompanied by a petition praying that the same may be homologated;—And whereas the prayer of said petition has been granted by an order of Court, dated April 10, 1863.

Therefore, notice is hereby given to all interested to make opposition, if any they have, in writing at my office, within thirty days from the date of the present notice, why said Tableau should not be homologated, the Administratrix discharged from all further liabilities and her bond cancelled.

A. GARRIGUES, Clerk.

Opelousas, April 11, 1863.

Cotton for the Government.

THE undersigned, an agent for the purchase of cotton in the Parishes of St. Landry, Avoyelles and Lafayette, is now authorized to buy cotton put up securely with boards and hoops, as well as that put up in bagging and rope. His office is at Washington, and persons who have cotton to dispose of are requested to inform him of it, and to sell to the government in preference to other buyers. The full market rates will be paid.

THOS. D. MILLER.

Washington, March 28, 1863.

☞ Echo of Lafayette please copy four times and send bill to this office.

TAKEN UP AS AN ESTRAY

BY the undersigned, in Pine Prairie, a dark dun mare mule, branded on the hip J B, and appraised by B. Mayo and T. R. Howard at 45 dollars. The owner will come forward, prove property, pay charges and take her away within thirty days; otherwise she will be disposed of according to law.

E. MIXER.

Pine Prairie, St. Landry, April 18 1863

Public Sale,

Estate of Jacob Anselm.

BY virtue of an order from the Hon. the District Court in and for the Parish of St. Landry, the public are hereby informed that there will be sold at public sale, to the last and highest bidder, by a duly commissioned Auctioneer, at the Coffee House, near the Court House of Opelousas, on

Tuesday, the 19th May next, 1863,

the following described property, belonging to the succession of said Jacob Anselm, deceased, to wit:

A CERTAIN LOT OF GROUND,

situated in the town of Opelousas, bounded North by property of Benj. R. Gantt, South by South street, East by Court street and West by property belonging to J. M. Milsted, together with all and singular the buildings and improvements thereon erected.

THE UNDIVIDED HALF OF A CER-

tain portion of a lot of ground, situated in the town of Opelousas, at the corner of Court and Bellevue streets, bounded North by Bellevue street, South by N. Quatrevaux, formerly J. M. Porter, East by J. P. Satterwhite, and West by Court street, together with all the buildings and improvements thereon. This lot numbers fifty feet six inches on Bellevue street, and ninety-five feet six inches on Court street.

A frame building situated on the public square, in the town of Opelousas.

The undivided half of a BILLIARD TABLE

and other Coffee House fixtures.

A Stallion;
A branding iron;
A lot of household furniture;
Kitchen utensils.

A negro man named JAMES, aged about 42 years.

Terms and Conditions:—All sums of twenty dollars and under, payable cash, and all sums upwards of twenty dollars, payable in one, two and three years credit, from the day of sale. Purchasers furnishing their notes with security in solido, to the satisfaction of the Administrator. Said notes made payable to the order of said Administrator. And all sums not punctually paid at maturity, bearing interest at 8 per cent. per annum from time due until paid. And moreover, the land and slave remaining hypothecated unto said Estate until full and entire payment of capital and the interest which may accrue thereon.

CLEOPHAS COMEAU, *Administrator.*

Opelousas, April 18, 1863

FOR SALE.

THE undersigned informs the public that he has 11 pairs of fine work oxen for sale, for cash.

Apply to F. Feray or J. W. Scott, at Bois Mallet, in my absence.

JOSEPH CHENIER.

Bois Mallet, April 18, 1863.—2t.

PUBLIC SALE.

Estate of Abram Harman Sr. deceased.

BY virtue of an order from the Hon. the District Court in and for the Parish of St. Landry, and to me directed, I, or some other auctioneer, will offer for sale, at public sale, to the last and highest bidder, at the residence of Joseph Harman in Plaquemine Brulée, in the Parish of St. Landry, distant about 18 miles from the town of Opelousas, on

On Tuesday 5th May next 1863,

the following described property, belonging to the Estate of the said Abram Harman deceased, to wit:

About 70 head of
HORSE CREATURES;
Nine Stock Horses.

Terms and Conditions.—One half of the purchase price payable on the first of April 1864, and the remaining half on the first of April next following, 1865; the purchasers furnishing their notes, with good and solvent security *in solido*, to the satisfaction of the Administrator of the Estate, said notes made payable to the order and at a domicil which will be made known on the day of sale, and bearing eight per cent per annum interests from maturity until paid; and moreover, the property remaining specially mortgaged unto said Estate, until full and entire payment of the capital and interests which may accrue thereon.

R. BENGUEREL, *Auctioneer.*

Opelousas, April 4th 1863.

Deserter.—$30 Reward!

THE legal reward of thirty dollars will be paid for the apprehension and delivery to these Head Quarters, or to the jailor of St. Landry Parish, of Louis Vidrine, a deserter from Company A, 2nd La. Cavalry.

Said private Vidrine is 6 feet 2 inches high, fair complexion, hazel eyes, brown hair, is about 33 years of age, and was born in the Parish of Saint Landry.

By order of W. G. VINCENT,
Col. Com'dg. 2nd La. Cavalry.

J. ALPHONSE PRUD'HOMME,
Adjutant. 1m.

Public Sale,

By the undersigned Auctioneer, in and for the Parish of St. Landry.

BY virtue of an authorization from the Hon. the District Court in and for the Parish of St. Landry and to me directed, the public are hereby informed that there will be sold at public sale, to the last and highest bidder, on the Plantation of the deceased, in Prairie Ville Plate, distant about 12 miles from the Town of Opelousas, on

Tuesday, the 12th May next, 1863,

the following described property, belonging to the succession of the late Louisa Lodoiska Raulin, deceased widow of F. Chs. DeCourson, to wit:

A SMALL PLANTATION,

situated in Ville Plate Prairie, in the Parish of St. Landry, measuring about two hundred superficial arpents, together with all the buildings and improvements thereon, bounded on the North by Nicolas Lahaye, on the South by Dr. L. Debaillon, West by the same an... East by Bayou Grand Louis.

A mulatto woman named POUPONNE, aged 18 years.

A negro woman named MARIE, aged 17 years.

3 horses;
4 cows and their calves;
A branding iron figured thus: T
2 sows;
1 spinning wheel;
2 pair cotton cards;
2 tables;
One clock,
One dining table;
10 chairs;
4 mattrasses;
1 feather bed;
Kitchen utensils;
One wagon;
2 ploughs;
One lot of corn, and many other articles

Terms and Conditions:—All sums of twenty dollars and under payable cash, and all sums upwards of twenty dollars, payable in one, two and three years credit, from the day of sale. Purchasers furnishing their notes with two good and solvent securities *in solido*, to the satisfaction of the Administrator, resident of the Parish of St. Landry, and given on the day of sale; said notes payable to the order of said Administrator, at the domicil of Marcel Daire, at Ville Plate and moreover, the land and slaves remaining specially mortgaged unto said Estate until full and entire payment of capital and the interests which may accrue thereon, at the rate of 8 per cent. per annum from time due until paid.

PAUL L. E. GUILLAUMIN, *Auctioneer.*

Ville Plate, April 11, 1863.

PUBLIC SALE.

THE undersigned hereby informs the public that he will offer for sale at auction, through the ministry of Onézime A. Guidry, a Public Auctioneer, at the residence of the undersigned, on Bois Mallet,

On Saturday the 18th April inst 1863,

at 10 o'clock in the morning, the following described property, to-wit:

A SMALL PLANTATION

situated in Bois Mallet, in the Parish of St. Landry, bounded on one side by S. M. Young, measuring 106 superficial arpents of land, 16½ of which are timbered land (a further description will be given at the sale)

2 Cows and their calves;
One horse and one horse cart;
One armoire.

☞ The conditions will be made known on the day of sale. However, cash will be accepted for the whole purchase price

ANT. RIVIERE.

Bois Mallet April 11th 1863.

A RARE CHANCE FOR VOLUNTEERING.

BY authority of the Secretary of War, the undersigned proposes to raise a BATTALION OF SHARPSHOOTERS;

The inducements offered are rare indeed All men liable to conscription are offered the opportunity to volunteer, with all the rights of a volunteer, viz: bounty, clothing, the right to elect all the officers except the Captain and field officers The undersigned has associated with him four officers detailed from the 1st La. Brigade now in Virginia. They have had an experience of two years, and will consequently be better enabled to provide for the wants of the soldier.

Special order No. 71, dated Headquarters District Western Louisiana, March 17 1863, signed by order of Gen. Taylor, empowers the officers of this detail to

PROMISE A FULL PARDON

for all past offences committed by those owing military service to the Con. States

It will be observed therefore that all those who have been conscripted and encamped at the general Camp of Instruction, and who have left said Camp without proper authority, have now an opportunity of returning to the service without fear of punishment. In addition, they will avoid in future all Camps of Instruction, and will be returned on the Muster Roll as Volunteers regularly mustered in the Confederate States' service.

P. F. KEARY,
Capt. & Senior Officer.

Proclamation by Thomas O. Moore, Governor of the State of Louisiana.

WHEREAS the Constitution of the State of Louisiana authorizes the Executive to convene the General Assembly thereof on extraordinary occasion;

AND, WHEREAS, I am officially informed that an error has occurred in the enrollment of an Act of the General Assembly passed at the recent Special Session at Opelousas, entitled: "An Act changing the Annual Meeting of the Legislature of the State of Louisiana," by which error the next annual meeting is appointed for the first Monday in October, instead of the first Monday in May as provided in the bill actually passed;

NOW, THEREFORE, in order that the evident purpose and intention of the General Assembly may be carried out, I do hereby convene the General Assembly of the State of Louisiana in Special and Extra Session at Shreveport the present seat of Government, on

MONDAY THE FOURTH DAY OF MAY NEXT at 12 O'CLOCK, M.

Given under my hand and the Seal of the State of Louisiana this Second day of March A. D. 1863.

THO. O. MOORE,
march7. Governor of the State of Louisiana.

Ranaway

FROM the Plantation of Mr. John B. Keller, at Bayou Chicot, about three months ago, a negro woman of a griff color, aged about 28 years, was formerly the property of Dr. Gober, of Ville Plate. She is supposed to be lurking about Ville Plate.

Any person harboring said girl will be rigorously prosecuted to the full extent of the law.

A liberal reward will be paid for her apprehension and delivery to the undersigned, at Washington, or if lodged in one of the Jails of this State, so that I can get her back.

F. TRAINOR.

Washington, February 14, 1863.

Estrayed,

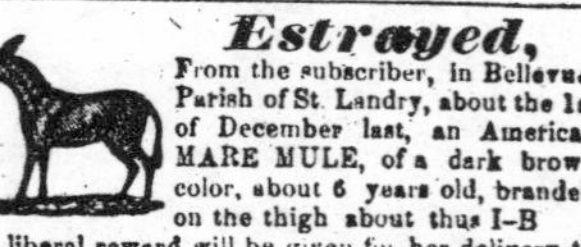

From the subscriber, in Bellevue, Parish of St. Landry, about the 1st of December last, an American MARE MULE, of a dark brown color, about 6 years old, branded on the thigh about thus I-B

A liberal reward will be given for her delivery to B. S. HAW.

Bellevue, St. Landry, Jan'y. 31, 1863. 9—3m

FOR SALE,

A tract of land of 600 arpents, adjoining the farm of John Posey, about a mile and half from Opelousas. Price, $12,000, payable on long terms of credit.

HENRY L. GARLAND.

October 18, 1862.—46.

Taken up as an Estray,

BY the undersigned, at Plaquemine Brulée, on the 16th March, inst., a small american or creole bai horse, white face, and four feet white, aged 9 or 10 years, not branded, but having some saddle and harness marks.—Has been in the neighborhood since about a year.

The owner is requested to come forward, prove property, pay charges and take him away, otherwise he will be disposed of according to law.

F. J. BRUNER.

St. Landry, March 21, 1863.—5t.

STRAYED OR STOLEN

FROM my premises, in Big Cane, on the 4th of last February, a dapple gray stallion, about 5 years old next spring, 14 hands high, heavy mane and tail, heavy built and fat, no mark or brand visible, right fore foot hoof just grown off with foot evil. A liberal reward will be paid for his delivery to the undersigned, or for such information as may lead to his recovery.

E. B. CARTER.

Big Cane, St. Landry, March 7 1863—14—2t

The Opelousas Courier.

PUBLISHED ON SATURDAY BY JOEL H. SANDOZ.

CONDITIONS.

Subscription, for one year, payable in advance, three dollars; if paid at the end of the year, four dollars. No subscription will be received for a period less than one year. A subscriber wishing to discontinue, must give a *written notice* to that effect, and settle up all arrearages.

Advertising:—Advertisements will be inserted at 75 cents per line for each and every publication. A liberal discount will be made for yearly and standing advertisements.

All the advertisements will be inserted in french and english until the editor shall judge it convenient to discontinue the publication.

No advertisement or subscription will be stopped until all the arrearages are paid, unless at the option of the publisher.

No election tickets or other jobs printed without the money, or the person ordering them to be printed is a responsible person.

Ten dollars in advance will invariably be required for the announcement of candidates for office.

This paper was struck off by some of the Soldiers of our victorious Army under Maj Genl Banks. The Rebels fled from the town which was occupied by our troops We found the type already set for issuing this paper and printed a few copies for our own edification.

For particulars of our march from New Orleans through the Teche Country See page 14 } See General Order No 28 on page 16

Daily Republican.

By Glass & Hardwicke.

LYNCHBURG, WEDNESDAY, MAY 6, 1863.

TERMS.

DAILY REPUBLICAN.—One year, $12 00; Six months, 7 00; Three months, 4 00; One month, 1 50.

TRI-WEEKLY REPUBLICAN.—One year, $8 00; Six months, 5 00; Three months, 3 00.

ADVERTISING TERMS.—Advertisements inserted at the rate of *one dollar per square for eight lines or less.* Longer advertisements in exact proportion.

RAGS WANTED.

We will pay the highest cash price for all clean linen or cotton rags deliverod at this office.

JACKSON'S WOUND.

The painful intelligence that General Jackson has suffered the loss of his left arm in the late battle near Fredericksburg, will occasion deep and universal sorrow in every heart in our land, and dims no little our otherwise brilliant victory. We have cause, however, to be grateful to an Allwise Providence that the life of the glorious old hero has been spared us, and that, in all probability, he will be again in his ssddle and in the face of the foe, before many weeks have elapsed.

We are yet without any of the particulars of our late victory on the Rapidan, owing to the rupture of all the means of communication between Richmond and our army. We know not who of our people were engaged, or who has been killed or wounded. We hope to have some intelligence by to-morrow.

The news from the West this morning is rather conflicting. We think it probable that after a long and bloody contest, against vastly superior numbers, we have been compelled to give up Grand Gulf and retire to the interior. The result of it, however, will not be serious, we presume, as Vicksburg and Port Hudson still defy the enemy.

The brilliant operations of Gen Forest in Georgia fully compensates us for our mishap on the Mississippi, while the great and crowning victory of Lee swallows up everything else, and makes our heavens a breeze of glory.

HON. WM. L. GOGGIN.

The Danville Appeal pays the following compliment to the Hon William L Goggin, of Bedford:

On our first page we publish a most able letter from Hon Wm L Goggin, in which he declares his willingness to yield to the solicitations of many friends in various portions of the State, who have requested him to allow his name to be used in connection with the Gubernatorial canvass.

Mr Goggin's fame as a public man, an able publicist, and above all, as an unflinching, earnest and honest defender of the doctrine of States' Rights, as taught by the founders of the old Republic in its halcyon days, is too well known to need anything said in his favor on that behalf. The people of Virginia could not do a more graceful thing now in view of Mr Goggin's position as the defeated champion of one party in the last election, than to elect him as the successor of his competitor. All old party lines have been destroyed, or if they have not, they should be, and we would be glad to see Mr Goggin in the field without any opposition at all. His election would give the entire people general satisfaction.

At the same time that we hold these views in regard to Mr Goggin, we do not wish to be understood as adopting him, or any one else, as our candidate. We have still a faint hope that some measure may be devised and adopted whereby the bitter cup of a general scramble may be removed from the lips of Virginia. We are earnest, if not sanguine in this hope.

EXEMPTION ACT.

This act, amending the former exemption act, has passed both Houses of Congress, as follows:

An act to repeal certain clauses of an act entitled "an act to exempt certain persons from military service, etc., approved 11th October, 1862:

I. The Congress of the Confederate States of America do enact, That so much of the act approved October 11th, 1862, as exempts from military service "one person, either as agent, owner, or overseer, on each plantation on which one white person is required to be kept by the laws or ordinances of any State, and on which there is no white male adult not liable to military service, and in States having no such law, one person, as agent, owner, or overseer, on each plantation of twenty negroes, and on which there is no white male adult not liable to military service," and also the following clause of said act, to wit: "and, furthermore, for additional police for every twenty negroes, on two, or more plantations, within five miles of each other, and each having less than twenty negroes, and on which there is no white male adult not liable to military duty, one person, being the oldest of the owners or overseers on such plantations", be and are hereby repealed.

2 For the police and management of slaves, there shall be exempted one person on each farm or plantation, the sole property of a minor, or person of unsound mind, a *femme sole*, or a person absent from home in the military or naval service of the Confederacy, on which there are twenty or more slaves; provided the person so exempted was employed and acting as an overseer previous to the 16th April, 1862, and there is no white male adult on said farm or plantation, who is not liable to military duty, which fact shall be verified by the affidavits of said person and two respectable citizens, and shall be filed with the enrolling officer; and provided, the owner of such farm or plantation, his agent or legal representative, shall make affidavit and deliver the same to the enrolling officer that after diligent effort no overseer can be procured for such farm or plantation not liable to military duty; provided further, that this clause shall not extend to any farm or plantation on which the negroes have been placed by division from any other farm or plantation, since the 11th day of October, 1862; provided further, that for every person exempted as aforesaid, and during the period of such exemption, there shall be paid annually into the public treasury by the owners of such slaves, the sum of five hundred dollars.

3. Such other persons shall be exempted as the President shall be satisfied ought to be exempted, in districts of country deprived of white or slave labor indispensable to the production of grain or provisions necessary for the support of the population remaining at home, and also, on account of justice, equity and necessity.

4. In addition to the State officers exempted by the act of October 11th, 1862, there shall, also, be exempted all State officers whom the Governor of any State may claim to have exempted for the due administration of the Government and laws thereof; but this exemption shall not continue in any State after the adjournment of the next regular session of its Legislature, unless such Legislature shall, by law, exempt them from military duty in the Provisional army of the Confederate States.

LETTER FROM CHARLOTTESVILLE.

CHARLOTTESVILLE, May 5, 1863.

Editors Republican:—We have no official accounts of the Yankee raid at Columbia, to destroy the water works at that place. Mr Christopher Gilmer, who volunteered to go to Columbia and obtain information, has returned this morning. From him I learn that about 200 (another gentleman estimates the number at 300.) Yankees came on foot to Columbia, with powder and tools to destroy the reservoir, and remained all day on Tuesday, and that while they were engaged in their preparations, one of the citizens, Dr Miller, informed them that Gen W F Lee was near at hand in pursuit of them, and then all these Yankees left without damaging the reservoir. The main body of the Yankee forces was stationed 14 miles from Columbia.

The Yankees burned the barn of Mrs Allen containing a large quantity of grain, broke open the stores, and invited all the slaves present, 300 in number, to help themselves, to which they readily assented. All the farm bridges and gates on the canal for miles were destroyed.

Straggling parties of the Yankees were seen in the neighborhood after the 300 had left Columbia. Fears were entertained that the enemy might return in force last night and destroy the water works.

None of the citizens seemed to know where the Yankee forces had gone, or where Gen Lee was. It seems that Gen Lee had come up with them at Hadin's Cross Roads, in Goochland, and had engagement, which resulted in our killing three, capturing 32 prisoners and 35 horses.

The Commissary and Quartermaster stores have all been ordered back to their former places. Bank officers have returned, and the Banks of this place resumed business to-day. Fruit trees and flowers are in full bloom—balmy zephers float over us—all nature looks cheerful, and we should lift up our hearts with gratitude to God for all His mercies, and especially for crowning our arms with another "great victory."

MONTICELLO.

At a meeting of Co C, 60th Va Reg't, held at Narrows, New River, the object being to select a suitable person to represent the counties of Fayette and Raleigh in the next Legislature of Virginia, Capt S S Dews was called to the chair, and 1st Lieut E H Early appointed Secretary. The following preamble and resolutions were offered and unanimously adopted:

Whereas, it is of the utmost importance that good and true men, men of sound judgment and tried patriotism be selected as representatives in times like these. Be it, therefore,

1. Resolved, That we find in the person of Lt Col B H Linkous, of 36th Va Regiment, one who possesses all the qualifications necessary to make an efficient representative.

2. Resolved, That we call upon the people of Fayette and Raleigh to unite with us in electing Col Linkous to the position which he is so eminently qualified to fill with credit to himself and benefit to his constituents.

On motion, the meeting adjourned.

Capt S S DEWS, Ch'm.

E H EARLY, Sec'y.

may 6 1t*

DUDLEY HALL.

MISSES ELIZABETH AND ANNIE SLOMAN

Harpists, Pianists, Vocalists; and

MR SLOMAN,

The celebrated Comic Dramatic Singer, respectfully inform the ladies and gentlemen of Lynchburg, that they will give one of their

VOCAL AND INSTRUMENTAL CONCERTS

Wednesday evening, May 6th, 1863,

When will be introduced a new musical Instrument, the

ALEXANDRIA ORGAN!!

PROGRAMME.

PART FIRST.

1. Organ and Harp,—"Casta Diva." *Norma.* Misses SLOMAN.
2. Comic Song, *Shakspeare's Seven Ages,* Mr SLOMAN.
3. Kathleen Mavourneen, Miss E SLOMAN.
4. Organ, *Souvenir de L'Opera.* Miss A SLOMAN.
5. Alonzo the Brave and the Fair Imogine, Mr SLOMAN.

PART SECOND.

1. Harp Fantasia on Confederate airs—"Let me Kiss Him for his Mother," "God Save the South," and "Dixie." Arranged and performed by Miss E SLOMAN.
2. Song—"The Musical Traveller" through Italy, Germany, Spain, France, Scotland, Ireland, England and America. Mr SLOMAN.
3. Italian Vocal Duet—"Cara per te," [*Armida.* Misses SLOMAN.
4. Song, *Professional Dinners,* Mr SLOMAN.
5. Piano and Organ—Selections from Trovatore, "The Anvil Chorus," and "Miserere," Misses SLOMAN.

PART THIRD.

A MONOLOGUE!

In which Mr Sloman will sing several Songs, delineating characteristic traits of Individuals, called London Newspapers, or the Evening Party.

☞ Admission $1 00.

☞ Concert to commence at 8 o'clock.

☞ Tickets can be procured at the Music and Book Stores. ☜

may5 2t

FIFTY DOLLARS REWARD.—The above reward will be paid for the arrest and confinement in jail so that I can get him, of WM CORRELL, who deserted from company D, 1st N C Cavalry, on the night of the 4th inst. It is supposed he has gone to Iredell county, N C.—He is about 40 years of age, about 5 feet 10 inches in height, black hair and eyes, heavy built, and weighs about 175 pounds.

J C BLAIR, Capt
Co D, 1st N C Cavalry.

may 6 1w°

NOTICE.—The Stable owned by the Quartermaster General of Virginia, near Langhorne's Brick Factory, but recently built, will be sold at auction on Thursday, the 7th inst, by HARGROVE & CO.

Sale to commence at 4 o'clock, p.m.

may6 2t

BY TELEGRAPH.

SPECIAL DISPATCHES TO THE DAILY REPUBLICAN.

FROM FREDERICKSBURG.

OUR VICTORY COMPLETE.

Gen Jackson's Left Arm Amputated.

RICHMOND, May 5.—No official dispatches were received last night or this morning from Gen Lee's headquarters, but private telegrams represent that our victory was complete.

Gen Jackson's left arm was successfully amputated below the shoulder by Dr McGuire, of Winchester. The Gen was removed to a country house about fifteen miles distant from the battle field, and is doing well.

Direct railroad communication with our army has not yet been re-established.

THE YANKEE RAIDERS—CAPTURE OF THEIR GUIDE.

RICHMOND, May 5.—The guide of the Yankee raiders was captured yesterday at Tunstall's station, on the York River railroad, where a skirmish occurred between the Yankees and a few companies of Confederate infantry.

ANOTHER BRILLIANT EXPLOIT OF GEN FORREST.

CAPTURE OF SIXTEEN HUNDRED YANKEES.

[Special to the Chattanooga Rebel]

ROME, GA, May 4, VIA DALTON, GA.—Gen Forrest accomplished the most brilliant feat of the war yesterday, capturing Col Straith's entire command, consisting of sixteen hundred infantry. He pursued them from Courtland, Ala, and captured them twenty two miles from the Georgia Line and twenty miles from Rome, Georgia, fighting incessantly for five days and nights.

Gen Forrest's loss was ten kiled and forty wounded.

His reception in Rome yesterday was a triumphant ovation. A salute of twenty guns was fired and the ladies welcomed him with smiles of joy and tears of gratitude.

ATLANTA, May 4.—Passengers by the State Road, report that a body of the enemy, sixteen hundred strong, and four thousand contrabands were captured at Cassville.

The Federal loss, fifty killed. Our loss ten killed.

A special from Col Lee, at Etowah, confirms the above.

[These two dispatches evidently refer to the same affair, as Cassville and Rome are both in Georgia, only about twenty five miles apart and on or near what is known as the State Road EDS REP]

FROM TENNESSEE.

CHATTANOOGA, May 4—The federal cavalry which penetrated Georgia were met by armed citizens near Rome and held in check. Forrest is in their rear and will capture all.

All quiet in front.

It is reported that Burnside is hurrying to Nashville.

There was a heavy hail storm here last night.

A heavy force of Federals crossed the Cumberland river at Celina, near the Kentucky line, under cover of artillery and attacked Col Hamilton's forces, who being in inferior numbers and without artillery fell back to Hill's, where he made a stand and after several hours hard fighting repulsed the enemy killing ten and wounding nineteen.

Our loss was two killed and three wounded.

The Yankees while retreating through Celina burned the place.

Col Hamilton pursued them to Hopkinsville, Kentucky, and destroyed the most of that town.

FROM MISSISSIPPI.

OUR FORCES FALLEN BACK FROM GRAND GULF.

JACKSON, May 4.—The Mississippian Extra, says General Bowen fell back from his position at Grand Gulf, being attacked by overwhelming numbers and outflanked.

The 31st Louisiana regiment was captured fighting desperately.

The loss is very heavy on both sides.

General Bowen occupies a position east of Grand Gulf and South of Bayou Pierre, with Port Gibson between him and the enemy.

The enemy are reported at Pontotoc seven thousand strong, intending to march on Meridian via Columbus.

[2D DISPATCH.]

JACKSON, May 4.—Gov Pettus says we sustained no serious disaster at Grand Gulf, and he wishes the people to have confidence in the result. He has come to the rational, deliberate conclusion that the whole State will be held. Our town and the river will probably be taken temporarily, but measures will be taken to meet the enemy at every point, driving him back. He thinks affairs not half so gloomy as they were three days ago.

Wirt Adams ambuscaded Grierson at Amite bridge. He opened fire upon them, killing and wounding several. Col Prince ordered his men to charge, but they refused to obey. Prince charged at the head of some men and was mortally wounded. His body is in our possession. Three companies escaped to Baton Rouge. The remainder are hemmed in and will probably be captured.

FROM NEW ORLEANS.

JACKSON, May 4—The New Orleans True Delta of the 28th has been received. The editor predicts that the North is on the eve of a war with Great Britain and France.

FROM VICKSBURG.

VICKSBURG, May 4.—A Yankee craft with two barges in tow, loaded with medical stores and rations for the army below, attempted to run our batteries last night and was set on fire by our guns, and all burnt to the water's edge.

The crews were taken off by our skiffs and brought here.

☞ KANAWHA.—JAMES M LAIDLEY and J FRAZER HANSFORD will be voted for at the coming election, to represent Kanawha county in the next House of Delegates.

VOLUNTEERS AND REFUGEES.

may 6 5t°

☞ STATE TICKET.—The response from every part of the State to the nomination of Col GEO WYTHE MUNFORD for the office of GOVERNOR having been in the highest degree satisfactory and encouraging, it is now finally presented by his friends, with the confident expectation that it will be sustained by a majority of the voters on the day of election.

may6 tde

AUCTION SALES.

THIS DAY.

BY B AKERS & SON, Auct'rs,

167 MAIN ST, FEW DOORS ABOVE NORVELL HOUSE.

LARGE AUCTION SALE!—We will sell on Wednesday, 6th May, at 167 Main st, a large and varied assortment of GOODS, consisting in part of Dry Goods, Domestics, Bleach Cottons, Spool Thread, Buttons, Hardware and Groceries, together with 8 Barrels of Superior Parraffine Lubricating Coal Oil!

☞ Persons wishing to consign goods to us for this sale, will please have them in store on or before Tuesday evening next.

☞ Sale to commence at 9 o'clock, Wednesday morning.

B AKERS & SON,
Auctioneers.

may 2 4t*

BY J B HARGROVE & CO., Auct'rs.

NOTICE—NEGROES FOR SALE.—We will sell at our Auction Room, this Wednesday morning, twenty likely Negroes. Among the number will be found several extra house

JACKSON'S WOUND.

The painful intelligence that General Jackson has suffered the loss of his left arm in the late battle near Fredericksburg, will occasion deep and universal sorrow in every heart in our land, and dims no little our otherwise brilliant victory. We have cause, however, to be grateful to an Allwise Providence that the life of the glorious old hero has been spared us, and that, in all probability, he will be again in his ssddle and in the face of the foe, before many weeks have elapsed.

The undersigned, a committee appointed to examine the books of the Farmers' and Merchants' Savings Institution, having performed that duty, and respectfully submit the foregoing statement of its condition on the 1st day of May, 1863, which they have compared with the books, and find to be correct, they take pleasure in stating that the books are neatly and accurately kept, and written up in such manner, that the affairs of the Institution are easily examined and understood.

GEO W ROCKE,
MARTIN HOLLINS,
JNO CLARK,
Committee.

may6 1t

DIVIDEND.—The Board of Directors of the Farmers' and Merchants' Savings Institution of Lynchburg, have this day declared a dividend of ten per cent. out of the profits of the last six months, payable to the Stockholders or their legal representatives on application.

M W DAVENPORT,
Treasurer.

may 6 3t

STOCKHOLDERS' MEETING.—An Annual Meeting of the Stockholders of the Farmers' and Merchants' Savings Institution, will be held at their Banking Room, on Thursday, the 7th day of May inst, at 4 o'clock, P M.

M W DAVENPORT,
Treasurer.

may 6 2t

SUNDRIES.—
3 bbls Vinegar.
Linen Sheets.
" Pillow Slips.
Irish Linen.
Tallow Candles.
Calf Skins.
Shoe Thread.

For sale at JONES & MILLER,
102 Main street.

may 6 10t

COYNER'S WHITE AND BLACK SULPHUR SPRINGS.—This well known watering place will be opened for the reception of visitors on the FIRST DAY OF JUNE. It is beautifully situated on the Va & Tenn Railroad, about half a mile from Bonsack's Depot, from which point an omnibus will convey visitors to the Springs.

The virtues of the water of these Springs for the cure of Dyspepsia, affections of the Liver, &c, are too well known to be repeated.

The accommodations are equal to any to be found in the mountains of Virginia, the table and attendance of the most satisfactory character, with good music and every attraction usually found at first class watering places.

PRICE OF BOARD.

Per day,	$ 6 00
Per week,	35 00
Per month of four weeks.	125 00

J A HEFELFINGER,
Proprietor

may1 2m

SPECIAL NOTICE.—We have for hire several good Cooks, Chamber Maids and Boys, suitable for factory hands—belonging to a refugee. These servants will be hired on reasonable terms to parties who will return them when the owner may call for them.

J B HARGROVE & CO,
Auctioneers.

may 5 3t

J P KNIGHT,
COMMISSION MERCHANT.

J P Knight will continue the Commission business at the old stand, No 2, Iron Building, Sycamore street, Petersburg, Va. He will give strict attention to the sale of all produce sent him on consignment. He also solicits consignments of Leaf, Manufactured and Smoking Tobacco. Reference is given to the merchants and manufacturers of Lynchburg and Petersburg generally

J P KNIGHT,
No 2, Iron Building, Sycamore st, Petersburg.

may 5 1m

WANTED.—A situation as TEACHER, either as Governess or Assistant in a Public School, by a lady of Rockbridge, who is competent to teach all the English branches, French, and Latin. Best of references given. Address, immediately, "MISS AMELIA A,"

Lexington, Va.

may2 c2t

J M WILLIS. W EUCLID YOUNG.

WILLIS & YOUNG,
WHOLESALE COMMISSION AND PRODUCE MERCHANTS,
COLLIER'S BLOCK, WHITEHALL STREET,
ATLANTA, GEO.

☞ Refer to Banks of Atlanta. Cash advances made on consignments. apr 24 1m*

NOTICE.—The Enrolling Office has been removed to tee corner of 12th and Church street opposite Dr Walker's office.

Office hours from 9 a. m., to 12 m. and from 2p. m. to 4 p. m.

C D HAMNER
Lt and Enrolling Officer for Lyncburg and co.

may 1 10t

next, a large lot of Stage and Carriage Harness, in very good condition, much of it as good as new.

Terms of sale—Cash, or negotiable notes well endorsed, at six months, with interest added.

By order of the Stockholders,

C R MASON,
Gen'l Supt

apl 16 tds

HEADQUARTERS DEPARTMENT WESTERN VA,
OFFICE CHIEF C S,
Dublin, Va, April 28th,

I CALL the earnest attention of the citizens of Smythe, Wythe, Grayson, Carroll, Floyd, Bland, Russell, Tazewell, Pulaski, Giles, Montgomery, Mercer, Monroe, Roanoke, Craig, Botetourt, Alleghany, Greenbrier, Nicholas and Pocahontas counties to the following plan suggested by the Hon Secretary of War, to obtain supplies for our troops in the Department, and invite their prompt co-operation in carrying out the laudable and necessary object proposed.

The Committees, appointed by their fellow-citizens, are requested as soon as practicable to inform the nearest Commissary of the amount of subsistence obtained and the Depot at which the stores will be deposited, in all cases securing, if possible, a location on or near the line of Railroad.

It is well known that ample supplies are yet within the Department, and the determination of all that our men in the field shall not want, will secure to them the provisions now so much needed.

By command of

MAJ GEN SAM'L JONES.

H W KING, Maj & Chief C S.

PLAN SUGGESTED BY SECRETARY OF WAR.

I. Let the people in each county, parish, or ward, select at public meeting, as early as convenient, a committee of three or more discreet citizens, charged with the duties hereinafter mentioned.

II. Let it be the duty of this committee to ascertain from each citizen in the county or parish what amount of surplus meat; whether bacon, pork or beef, he can spare for the use of the army; after reserving a supply for his family and those dependant upon him for food.

Let this committee fix a price which is deemed by them a just compensation for the articles furnished, and inform the citizens what this price is, so that each may know, before the delivery what price is to be paid for the articles furnished.

Let this committee make arrangements for the transportation of the supplies to some convenient depot after consultation with the officer who is to receive them.

Let the committee make delivery of the supplies on recieving payment of the price, and assume the duty of paying it over to the citizens who have furnished the supplies.

III. Where the duty of the committee is performed in any town or city at which there may be a Quartermaster or Commissary, no further duty need be required of them than to deliver to the officer a list of the names of the citizens and the supplies which each is ready to furnish with the price fixed; whereupon the officer himself will gather the supplies and make payment.

IV. Where the supplies are furnished in the country the cost of transportation to the depot will be paid by the Government, in addition to the price fixed by the committee.

V. As this appeal is made to the people for the benefit of our brave defenders now in the army, the Department relies with confidence on the patriotism of the people that no more than just compensation will be fixed by the committees, nor accepted by those whose chief motive will be to aid their country, and not to make undue gains out of the needs of our noble soldiers.

JAMES A. SEDDON,
Secretary of War.

ap 30 d3t & c3t

FOR SALE.—Two HOUSES and LOTS on Harrison Street, between 3rd and 4th Sts; also three HOUSES and LOTS on Federal street, between 3rd and 4th Streets.

JNO F SLAUGHTER.

may 5 ts

NOTICE. TO REFUGEES OR ANY ONE WANTING A NICE LITTLE HOMESTEAD. Owing to the extraordinary high price of living, I will sell my House and Garden. The lot contains nearly half an acre. It is one of the best garden spots about Lynchburg, is situated on Franklin Hill, within fifteen minutes' walk of the Market House. Address, through the Post Office, "Hard Up," and state where an interview can be had.

may5 3t

FOR SALE—In Lynchburg, on Tuesday morning, the 5th day of May, by Hargrove & Co, five MULES, one WAGGON and GEAR.

ROBERT O GRAYSON.

ap 27 c4t

Daily Republican.

By Glass & Hardwicke.

LYNCHBURG, THURSDAY, MAY 7, 1863

TERMS.

DAILY REPUBLICAN.—One year, $12 00; Six months, 7 00; Three months, 4 00; One month, 1 50.

TRI-WEEKLY REPUBLICAN.—One year, $8 00; Six months, 5 00; Three months, 3 00.

ADVERTISING TERMS.—Advertisements inserted at the rate of *one dollar per square for eight lines or less.* Longer advertisements in exact proportion.

ANOTHER GLORIOUS VICTORY.

The official dispatch of General Lee announces another glorious victory in front of Fredericksburg. It appears that while the battle was raging at Chancellorsville on Sunday a large force of the enemy attempted a movement in our rear by the way of Fredericksburg. This was promptly met by McLaws' division, which held the enemy in check until Gen Lee came up with Anderson's and Early's divisions. On Monday, when the Yankees were badly whipped across the Rappahannock and from its vicinity. This completes our triumph in Northern Virginia. Hooker's great army is beaten and demoralized, and perhaps expelled from our soil. Wonder what route the Yankees will next take for Richmond? Their effort to capture that city has cost them infinite disgrace, millions of money and not less than two hundred thousand men who have died from disease and killed in battle. They have tried every route laid down upon the map—by the Valley, Gordonsville, Fredericksburg, Yorktown, James river and Suffolk, and have been defeated in all of them. McClellan, Pope, Burnside and Hooker have each become famous and infamous in this futile attempt to take the rebel city. Who will be the next victim? We would suggest that as land and water routes have proven hard roads to travel, the next attempt be made exclusively in balloons.

THE RAID UPON COLUMBIA.

The packet which left here Monday evening for Richmond returned yesterday morning being unable to pass lock No. 14, two miles below Columbia, which was destroyed by the Yankees in their raid on the place last Sunday. The passengers were transferred to the boat from Richmond at the lock. We have some particulars of the raid from Capt Bowles of the Packet which may be of interest. The Yankees dashed into the town about sunrise Sunday and forthwith commenced their preparations to destroy the aqueduct by placing underneath it five kegs of powder in a flour barrel which they set fire to, but which fortunately did not ignite, and no other means of destruction being at hand the structure was saved. While this was being done by one party, others were proceeding in other works of destruction. The bridge at the aqueduct was destroyed, two above the town and four more between there and lock No. 14, a few miles below, making nine in all. They also burned the bridge at Elk Island across James River, and burnt a boat at lock 14, loaded with hay, &c. They destroyed the lock by tearing off the gates. At Columbia they burned a boat upon which Mr Snoddy had placed all his furniture and family for the purpose of escaping. A Lieutenant of the party set fire to it with his own hand. They took four horses belonging to Ellsom's packet line. The boat Sallie, of Lexington, loaded with bacon and corn, was saved by the fidelity of a negro hand on the boat who claimed it, and the property on it as his own, representing himself as a free man. They burnt the barn of Mr John Allen, his stables and corn house and all his hay and straw and fodder ricks, and carried off all his horses, and also 27 of his negroes. They took 7 negroes from Mr Galt and several horses, and carried off also seven slaves belonging to Mr B H Agee. Several other persons in the county had their negroes and horses carried off. In Columbia a large number of negroes were gathered, and they broke open the stores in the town and stole the tobacco contained in them, and then told the negroes to take what they wanted, which they did. They broke into the house of Mrs Allen near the town, destroyed all her furniture, and left the place a complete wreck. Many other citizens whose names we did not hear were sufferers, and other depredations too numerous to record were committed by these marauders.—They stated their intention to be to destroy the South Side Road. There were about four hundred in number who visited the town, and it is stated the whole number would reach one thousand or twelve hundred, who remained some distance in the county. They staid until 4 o'clock Sunday evening when they left, expressing an intention to return speedily and complete the destruction of the aqueduct. Several of the citizens were arrested, but all were released when they took their departure.

These are as many of the particulars of this audacious raid as we can make room for, though we might fill our whole paper with the details. The citizens we understand, at four o'clock Tuesday felt apprehensions that they would return, but we are confident they are groundless, as Gen Fitzhugh Lee telegraphed here yesterday evening that they were in full retreat towards Raccoon Ford on the Rapidan, and he was harassing their rear. Hopes are entertained that the whole party will yet be bagged.

The repairs to the canal we understand from the best authority would be completed by yesterday evening and navigation be uninterrupted.

LETTER FROM FREDERICKSBURG.

[Special correspondence of the Republican.]

BATTLE FIELD NEAR FREDERICKSBURG, Sunday, May 3d, 1863.

Dear Republican: We had a severe fight with the enemy yesterday, and repulsed him with heavy loss, with but few casualties on our side. We drove them several miles from the field, and our division (Early's) started up the Rappahannock to reinforce our main army under Lee and old Stonewall, who were engaged near Chancellorsville with the main body of the abolition force. We left a small force on the heights above Fredericksburg to hold the enemy in check and double quicked it up the river until darkness overtook us when we bivouacked on the field.

Shortly after dark we learned that the enemy had been heavily reinforced on our right wing, and had again advanced and taken possession of the field from which we had just beaten them. We immediately countermarched and arrived at the place about one o'clock Sunday morning and set about making preparations for the conflict which daylight would inaugurate.

At 5 o'clock the fight commenced with very heavy cannonading from the Yankee artillery, which was replied to with great effect by Dement's, Raine's and Carpenter's batteries.—Others soon joined in, and the roar of the cannon was the most terrific I have ever heard. At 8 o'clock news came that Lee had gained a glorious victory at Chancellorsville fifteen miles above us the day before, that old Stonewall had gotten in the rear of the enemy, taken all his fords on the river, and captured thousands of prisoners. But alas! mingled with these glorious tidings was the sad and mournful tale that the old Hero, the noblest Roman of them all, was severely, perhaps mortally wounded. Tears coursed down the cheeks of many a gallant fellow, and all felt as though he had lost a father. But we had no time to yield long to sorrow. We must do the work before us; and nobly did our gallant little band do its duty. Cheer after cheer rent the air along our entire line. Our batteries redoubled their fire and drove the Yankee artillery from the ground, and our skirmishers pitched into their infantry, engaging a whole brigade, before our main line advanced, whom they repulsed with loss, forcing them to fly in disorder. They were reinforced and rallied and a desperate conflict is now going on as I write at 10½ o'clock A M, Sunday when I am compelled to close in order to get this off by the mail which is about to leave. Our victory on this part of the line yesterday was a glorious one, and to-day we will make it decisive, and drive the vandals to the other side of the Rappahannock.

I can give you no account of casualties yet, but will write to-night and send all particulars obtainable, as well as a more detailed report of the battle, if I can find any way to get it through. Yours,

B.

[General Lee's dispatch in another column gives the result of the battle of which our correspondent writes, and assures us that our victory was glorious, and that there is not a Yankee south of the Rappahannock.—EDS REP.]

FROM KINSTON.

We learn from the Kinston correspondence of the Raleigh State Journal, that the raid of the Yankees in that direction on the 28th of April was not as formidable an expedition as it was at first supposed to be. The number of the enemy did not exceed five regiments. But as small an expedition as it was, they were permitted to come within eight miles of Kinston before they met with any formidable resistance, and then only by about 200 men of the 56th regiment, who fought them desperately for three and a half hours, they being all that we had on picket duty on the Dover road. The Confederate loss in killed, wounded and missing, is only 20 men.

General S B Buckner has been transferred to Knoxville, Tennessee, and will assume the command of that department.

LADIES RELIEF HOSPITAL, May 6, 1863.

Editors Republican.—Will you do us the favor to publish the accompanying beautiful tribute to our sick soldiers, which speaks for itself. We had the privilege of dispensing the "Nick Nacks" to them, and wish they could have witnessed, as we did, the smiles of appreciation on each face, expressive of their gratitude to their "Little Friends at Coyner's Springs." Many thanks from the soldiers and ourselves.

May that "May Day Party" live to enjoy many happy and plentiful returns of May Day!

MRS LUCY W OTEY, Pres't,
MRS C P SPEED, Treas'r.

COYNER'S SPRINGS, May 4th, 1863.

To the Sick Soldiers.—Enjoying the pleasures of a May day party, we thought of our noble soldiers who have left their happy homes and loved little ones, to fight and suffer, if need be, for us. and we, in heartfelt gratitude, would offer our little mite to aid in comfort to our brave protectors.

Praying God to bless and preserve you, and hoping you will enjoy the accompanying trifle, we are very sincerely

Your little friends,
THE CHILDREN OF COYNER'S SPRINGS.

SOLDIERS' LIBRARY.

Editors Republican.—Please acknowledge for me the following contributions to the Soldiers' Library, received during the month of April:

Two Ladies of Halesford, Va,	10 00
Mrs Fortune, of Campbell,	1 00
Mrs E Fortune	1 00
Miss Martha East, of Lynchburg,	1 00
Mrs Eliza Greer, "	75
Mrs M E Hutchison, "	One book
Mrs Martha Clark and daughter,	Three "
Lt A M Tubman, of Alexandria,	One "
Mr J Newton Gordon of Lynchburg,	Seven "
Rev A E Dickinson, of Richmond,	189 "

JNO L JOHNSON.

NEGRO TROOPS AT FORTRESS MONROE.—The Boston Transcript states that Governor Andrew commissioned John Wilder to go to Fortress Monroe to recruit a company of negroes for the Fifty fourth Massachusetts regiment. When the men were recruited Secretary Stanton sent an order to muster them into the United States service, with Lieut Wilder as Captain, and to retain them at the fortress.

It is stated that a house is being prepared in Vera Cruz for the reception of Gen Don Antonio Lopez de Santa Anna. From this announcement, we suppose he is about to turn up again, wooden leg and all. It was the French, we believe, who deprived him of his leg when they were at war with Mexico on a former occasion.

THE STRENGTH OF THE ENEMY ON THE RAPPAHANNOCK.

The New York World of April 29th gives the following clue to the strength of the army just routed by Gen Lee in Spotsylvania:

"If the enemy are not posted as to the strength of all the armies in the field, it is not the fault of Secretaries Stanton and Chase. The former has given the precise figures of the Army of the Potomac by telling the number of the sick and what proportion they bear to the well soldiers, while the latter completes the exposure by giving in detail the amount of money paid to the soldiers in every military department of the Government. The ciphering in this case is very easy. If Gen Hooker's 150,000 men require $13,000,000 to pay them, how many men has Gen Grant, if $10,000,000 will pay their obligations, and so as to the rest of the armies?

THE FLORIDA AND THE ALABAMA.

A late Baltimore paper brings the following interesting intelligence of the operations of the Florida and Alabama, received from St. Thomas:

The Florida had captured the bark Lapwing, formerly of this port, but now owned in New York, and put on board of her two guns and eighteen men. The bark M J Colcord, of New York, had also been captured by the Florida. The Alabama had chased two vessels ashore on Turks Island, one of which had gone to pieces. The Austrian bark Constantine reports having been boarded off the Western Islands by the privateer Florida, and receiving from her the steward of the schooner Aldebaran and two seamen of the ship Star of Peace.

THE NEW PROGRAMME AT VICKSBURG

The Baltimore American of May 1st, says:

A naval officer from Vicksburg states that no attack on Vicksburg is expected to be made, the programme being to submerge the country on either side of the Mississippi from Helena down, by cutting levees, so that no crops can be raised, and the entire country shall be barren and untenable, which will compel the Confederate forces to leave for more congenial quarters, which, my informant is confident they are doing. The same informant expresses the belief that the river will be clear by May 1st.

FIVE HUNDRED MILES IN ONE AND A HALF HOURS.

Some of the most distinguished engineers in France are said to have approved a plan for a railway from Paris to Marseilles by which the journey, which now consumes eighteen hours, may be made in one hour and a half. The distance is five hundred and ten miles. The plan, being the hydraulic system, in which sliding is substituted for running on wheels, has been submitted to the Emperor for his approbation.

The Vicksburg Whig, of the 23d April says the Yankees seem to be gaining a decided advantage over us in Lower Louisiana, if the Yankee accounts are correct. We fear, adds the Whig, that the sugar region is lost to us.

The Treasury notes funded in eight per cents. at Montgomery, Ala., reached nearly $8.000 000, and at Columbia, S. C., $5,000,000.

BY TELEGRAPH.

SPECIAL DISPATCHES TO THE DAILY REPUBLICAN.

OFFICIAL DISPATCH FROM GEN LEE.

THE ENEMY DRIVEN ACROSS THE RAPPAHANNOCK.

RICHMOND May 5.—The following dispatch was received this evening from Guinea's, near Fredericksburg, dated May 5th:

To his Excellency President Davis:

At the close of the battle of Chancellorsville Sunday, the enemy was reported advancing from Fredericksburg in our rear. Gen McLaws was sent back to arrest his progress and repulsed him that afternoon.

Learning that this force consisted of the corps under Gen Sedgwick, I determined to attack it and march back yesterday with General Anderson and uniting with McLaws and Early, in the afternoon succeeded, by the blessing of Heaven, in driving Gen Sedgwick over the river.

We have reoccupied Fredericksburg, and no enemy remains south of the Rappahannock or in its vicinity.

(Signed) R E LEE, Gen'l.

THE DAMAGE BY THE YANKEE RAID.

DIRECT COMMUNICATION WITH THE ARMY RE-ESTABLISHED.

RICHMOND, May 6.—The packet boat arrived this morning from Lynchburg.

Passengers report very little damage done the canal by the Yankees.

Several farm bridges over the canal were destroyed and one lock gate damaged.

Two trains with wounded arrived this forenoon on the Fredericksburg Railroad, direct communication with the army having been re-established.

Some reliable details of the battle will probably be received during the day from correspondents of the press.

DETAILS OF THE BATTLE OF CHANCELLORSVILLE.

RICHMOND, May 6.—The Dispatch issued an extra this afternoon, giving the first details of the battles of Chancellorsville yet received.

Its correspondent says that the fight, in many respects, was one of the bloodiest of the war.

Our loss was heavy both in officers and men.

The enemy had thrown up entrenchments and constructed an abattis which, after severe fighting, was carried by our troops.

Among the prisoners is Brig Gen Hays, who commanded a brigade in Couch's corps.

Prisoners report that there were some forty regiments engaged mostly foreigners.

On the lower end of the line, where Gen Early commanded, there was some hard fighting Sunday morning.

In the afternoon Marye's Heights were carried by the enemy, and a number of Mississippians captured. Six pieces of the Washington Artillery were taken at the same time.

Monday morning the fight was renewed, the Heights retaken and the pieces recaptured, with a number of others.

Five Yankee batteries were reported captured on the upper line.

From another source I learn that about six thousand prisoners in all have been captured.

Gen A P Hill has resumed his command.

Gen Heath is not much hurt, and is still in command.

Gen McCown was slightly wounded.

The 18th Mississippi killed more than their own number.

Col Stafford, of the 14th La, was killed, also Col Walker, of the 10th Va, and Col Mallory, of the 55th Va.

FROM THE WEST.

JACKSON, May 5.—A special to the Appeal says twelve houses were burned at Bahalia.

The Yankees camped last night at Gwinn Mills seven miles from Bahalia, and established a permanent camp there.

They made a raid on Holly Springs, Sunday. Capt Mitchell ambushed them as they went out with five men, killing Col Jenkins, capturing his horse and papers.

The Chicago Times of the 1st received at Wilkins Bend, says that on the 24th Grants whole army was ordered to move with six days rations.

Four out of six transports attempting to pass Vicksburg was sunk by the rebels.

In the New York papers it is stated that the editor of the Atlanta Confederacy was arrested at Port Royal.

FROM VICKSBURG.

RICHMOND, May 6.—The official account of the destruction of two barges and a tug at Vicksburg on 3d inst., says 24 prisoners were taken, including one correspondent of the New York World, two of the N Y Tribune and one of the Cincinnati Times.

THE CAPTURE OF YANKEES BY FORREST.

TULLAHOMA, May 5.—An official dispatch received at headquarters says that Forrest, after five days hard marching, without provisions or forage, captured, on the 3d, a body of the enemy, sixteen hundred strong, near Rome, Ga, with the same number of Enfield rifles, horses and side arms.

FROM THE WEST.

JACKSON, May 5.—The enemy were reported yesterday at Ankinson's Ferry on the Big Black river, after four hours hard fighting.

[2D DISPATCH.]

JACKSON, May 5—The enemy are reported in force near Edward's Depot, four miles this side of the Big Black.

They captured one hundred of our pickets.

CAPTURE OF YANKEES IN GEORGIA.

TULLAHOMA, May 5.—An official dispatch confirms the report of the capture by Forrest, after five days hard marching, without provisions or forage, on the 3rd inst., of sixteen hundred Yankees near Rome, Ga., with the same number of Enfield Rifles, horses and side arms.

DAILY REPUBLICAN.

VOL. 6. LYNCHBURG, VA., TUESDAY MORNING, MAY 12, 1863. NO. 121.

Daily Republican.

THE GREAT BATTLES.

FULL PARTICULARS OF THE BATTLES AT CHANCELLORSVILLE AND FREDERICKSBURG—A GLORIOUS VICTORY TO THE CONFEDERATE CAUSE.

The following from the columns of Friday's Richmond Enquirer, will be found of more than ordinary interest:

FREDERICKSBURG, Va., May 6, 1863.

The battle seems to be over, and from all I can gather a glorious victory has crowned the Confederate arms. Not having seen a Richmond paper for three days past, I am at a loss to know whether my daily despatches have reached you, and for that reason I propose to give you a history of the whole fight, beginning with the crossing below town on Wednesday morning last and bringing it down to the brilliant charge of Monday evening, when the enemy were driven in confusion across the river, their midnight cry being 'retreat to Banks' Ford.'

The first movement of the enemy, i. e. the crossing below town, can hardly be said to have been a feint. It would be perhaps more proper to speak of it as a movement designed to co-operate with the main attack at Chancellorsville, or it is possible that this force was left in front of Fredericksburg to prevent a rear movement on our part, which, if successful, and the river once crossed by our troops, at a point near town, their access to the railway could have been cut off and their base of supplies rendered useless to them. To guard his rear and protect his base, the force, which afterwards operated offensively, was at first intended to act defensively, in all probability.

Chancellorsville having been the real point of battle it will be most fitting to treat of it first.

On Thursday evening Gen Anderson, who was holding a position in front of the United States Mine Ford, twelve miles above Fredericksburg, ascertained that the Yankees, numbering five army corps, with at least eighty thousand men, crossed the Rapidan at Kelly's and Germanna Fords, having previously crossed the North Fork of the Rappahannock at Ely's Ford in Culpeper county, and were advancing down the plank road. Gen Anderson, however, having too small a force to hold the enemy at this point, fell back to a position some four miles below Chancellorsville and fronting the old mine road. Friday morning Gen Anderson was reinforced on the right by Gen McLaws, and on the left by Gen A P Hill. At this period Gen Jackson took command, and ordered an advance, himself leading it, and succeeded during the day in driving the enemy back, they making but slight resistance. On Friday night our forces rested fully two miles beyond the ground occupied by the Yankee forces on the previous evening. The forces principally engaged thus far in this quarter belonged to Sommes' brigade, of McLaws' division, and Mahone's brigade, of Anderson's division.

Saturday morning wore away without important results. There was some artillery firing and a little skirmishing, but the engagement did not become general until about five o'clock in the afternoon, from which hour the fight raged furiously until about eight o'clock. Jackson, at this time, had thrown a force on their upper flank, and was driving them fiercely down upon our lower line, which, in turn, was hurling them back, and rendering futile all their efforts to break through our lower lines, and making it necessary for them to give back towards the river.

There was an intermission in the firing from eight o'clock until about nine. But from nine until long past midnight the sound of artillery and small arms was well nigh deafening. The explanation was ready. Jackson was pressing them with a night fight. Our boys drove the Yankees, who stoutly held their ground until near day; and at early dawn of the holy of holies, the fight began on both ends of the line, and by eleven o'clock the firing had ceased. On the upper end of the line, near Chancellorsville, the Yankees were badly whipped, and were in full retreat towards the river. On the lower line, near Fredericksburg, however, they had succeeded in carrying Marye's Heights, and were rioting in the wild excess of joy. They had stormed, they said, the Gibraltar of America, and their route to Richmond was plain and easy, little remembering that they had hurled a column of fully ten thousand upon one regiment in front, and thus gained the rear of the rest of Barksdale's brigade.

But "the best laid schemes of men and mice gang aft awiel," and whilst the Yankees were felicitating themselves on their splendid success, and imagining themselves to be in the rear of our army, Gen Lee was so manœuvreing as to meet the enemy, who were now throwing themselves forward from the town on the Plank road. About four o'clock on Sunday evening, McLaws' division, including Wilcox's brigade of Anderson's division, met the advance column of the Yankees, under Gen Sedgwick, at Salem Church, four miles beyond Fredericksburg, on the Plank road, and our line of battle was formed at right angles with the Plank road. The battle here raged for about two hours, but the Yankees were repulsed with considerable loss, including from five to six hundred prisoners. Our line on the Telegraph road, meantime, had been formed at Smock's, about three and a half miles out from town.

Early on Monday morning Lawton's old Brigade, now Gen Gordon's, supported by Gen Smith's and Gen Hayes, all of Early's Division advanced towards Mayre's Heights and charged them without firing a gun, driving the enemy from a position from which less than 24 hours before he had dislodged Barksdale's gallant Mississippians, after a most heroic resistance, in which the enemy's loss was quite considerable. In this condition matters remained until about five o'clock in the evening, when a general advance was ordered. At the firing of a signal gun, Gen Early moved upon the enemy from the right, and Gen's Anderson and McLaw from the left. The enemy, who held a position on the Plank Road, extending up and down, were quickly dislodged and driven with great loss from the field. Their resistance was slight. The charge was grand. Early's men, and especially the Louisianians, under Hayes, walked over the enemy as giants over pigmies, while from above, the men of Anderson and McLaws who had been constantly marching and fighting for five days, showed no signs of relaxation, but marched boldly and fearlessly up to their appointed work.—The enemy was driven in confusion towards Banks' Ford, across which he succeeded in making his way during the night—not, however, without serious loss in killed, wounded and prisoners. Gen Hoke, of the North Carolina Brigade, in Early's Division, was wounded in a charge. Whilst this was going on, Barksdale's men were holding the stone wall, Marye's hill and the heights commanding the Plank Road, so as to prevent a movement on our rear out from Fredericksburg. But this was hardly necessary. Yankee desire for a general advance had been satisfied, and by nightfall the Yankees had begun to prepare for the third and last time to evacuate Fredericksburg—and by daybreak our pickets were in the town, which is once again in the hands of Barksdale's men.

Though the enemy at Chancellorsville did not recross the river at the United States Ford until to-day, there has been no general engagement since Sunday—only some occasional skirmishing and feints of attack to cover up their retreat across the river. Hooker, though having the choice of position, did not act effectually after crossing, but fortified and threw himself on the defensive, thus forcing our men to contend against him in this fight against very superior numbers, aided by breastworks fortifications and obstructions of all sorts. But they were of little avail. Jackson turned their flank and fell upon their rear. And Jackson's boys did their work with all their might and main.—They charged faster over the battle field than they marched to it, and their cheering as they drove the enemy before them broke upon the air with fine, inspiriting effect, and told too plainly that our men were terribly in earnest, and were fighting for home, for woman, manhood and independence. In such a cause it were worse than base not to strike heavy blows for freedom and the right.

Hooker expected success. He had planned well; but Gen Lee has proved himself more than a match for him, and his splendid army now lies a part dead on the south side of the Rappahannock, a part wounded on its north bank and some here, too, and a large part of the advance is already near your city. Hooker had drawn every man from the fortifications, and came prepared with eight days' rations—i. e, eight days hard tack; three days' cooked meat and eight days cattle in a herd and eight days' coffee. Hooker made his men a speech, telling them he had advantage of position and was bound to go forward; all that he asked of them was to fight. He had summoned every man from the fortifications, and had uncovered Washington, and must have put into the fight from first to last not a man under one hundred and fifty thousand.

The bravery, fortitude and endurance of our men in all of these engagements cannot be too highly praised or too gratefully remembered by the country. It would seem invidious to make special allusions where all fought so well, but it is due to candor and truth to say that the troops of McLaws and Anderson were oftener engaged than any other troops, they being engaged in fighting and marching almost without intermission for rest or refreshment, from Thursday night until Tuesday morning, a period of four days and nights. While to D H Hill's old division, commanded by General Rhodes, and Trimble's division, led by General Colston, Early's division, led by Early himself, and A P Hill's men, under their favorite leader, the country is indebted.

The cavalry, too, claim a share of this glorious work, for while the infantry were thus being engaged one brigade under Fitzhugh Lee met the enemy near Spotsylvania Court House and succeeded in whipping and driving back to Chancellorsville, certainly two brigades of cavalry, and, perhaps four, killing the Colonel of the sixth New York Cavalry and two Captains, and taking some sixty prisoners.

It is with sincere regret that I am unable to speak to the praise of all the artillery engaged, but I hear the First Company of Richmond Howitzers and Maney's Battery highly commended for their effective and steady firing. All that I can do is to pay tribute to them all by stating that Col Crutchfield's Battalion and Col Alexander's, in Jackson's Corps, and Major Richardson's, in Anderson's Corps, and Col Cabell's, in McLaw's Division, all acquitted themselves with a skill and bravery that reflects the highest credit upon this arm of the service.

The battle field, which reaches from Fredericksburg to a point above Wilderness, some twelve miles up from town, and out to the river, with the exception of about two miles between Salem and Zoar Churches, attests the skillful aiming and deadly destruction of our artillery. The Yankee dead and wounded are strewn over the entire country. Yet had it not have been one of the most thickly wooded sections of land in Virginia the Yankee loss would have been far greater.

Over the same field of battle are scattered, in immense quantities, blankets, overcoats, canteens, knapsacks, haversacks, cartridge boxes, and any quantity of rifles muskets and various other equipments of the soldier. Our boys, however, found but little to eat. The Yankees had well nigh devoted the commissariat, still a good quantity of hard tack, with some [illegible] cooked meats and coffee were found in the Yankee haversacks. We also captured some fresh slaughtered meats and some corn and oats, all of which are quite valuable, and just the articles we needed.

Fredericksburg, on this occasion, did not suffer severely as she did before, though the Yankees managed to steal a good deal. Private houses, I believe, were in no instance entered, where the families were present, and the town was not shelled, nor were any citizens arrested or carried off in the town. A few were arrested outside, but in every instance I believe they were rescued by our own soldiery.

Hooker commanded in person at the Chancellorsville fight, and occupied a position near that place during the fight. Hooker has made a good fight. He has manœuvred well, and done better than any other Yankee general; but Hooker is not the equal of our commander-in chief. Gen Lee, during the fight, has displayed the highest qualities of an able and successful commander. To him the country is indebted for the most wonderful qualities of the soldier and [illegible] [illegible] has so [illegible] combined as to surround the Yankees twice, and drove them back to the river, which they supposed, on both occasions that they had gotten into his rear and were about to surprise him; whilst Gen Jackson has outdone himself, and exhibited the highest characteristics of a strategist and a skillful general, fully confirming all his past renown and adding new laurels to the many already won in the service of his country.

Our losses are fully 5,000, while those of the Yankees are confessed to be fully 25,000, and about thirty pieces of artillery. We have captured very near 8,000 prisoners, and have lost, I suppose, about 1,000 prisoners. These results of the fight point most conclusively to a most brilliant Confederate victory. We have captured one Brigadier General and any quantity of field and staff officers.

Among the killed on our side are Gen Paxton, of the Stonewall brigade; Gen Nichols was wounded in the leg, having previously lost an arm in Winchester; General McGowan was wounded slightly; General Hoke was wounded in [illegible]. Gens Slocumb, Howard and O'Neil, of the Yankee army, are reported killed. "Fighting Joe" said to be slightly wounded. There are also many other good and true officers and men who have fallen—but our report would be too lengthy to enable us to make mention of all, so, presuming that my report is long enough, I will close.

X

Brig Gen E D Tracy, of Huntsville, Ala., has been killed in the Southwest. He was a native of Macon.

MELANCHOLY INCIDENT OF THE LATE BATTLE.

The army correspondent of the Petersburg Express records the burning of the large brick tavern at Chancellorsville, which had been converted into a hospital, and horrible to relate, one hundred and fifty wounded soldiers were burned alive, it being impossible to rescue the sufferers. One hundred of them were Federals and fifty Confederates. This is one of the most melancholy incidents of the battle. The building was fired by a shell thrown by one of the enemy's guns, but whether accidentally or intentionally, is not stated.

In view of the dangers now threatening Louisiana, Gov Moore has issued a stirring proclamation calling upon the State army and volunteers to rally in defense of their homes.

Col Seymour, the Democratic candidate for Governor of Connecticut, is about to marry the lady of Sam Colt—a very charming lady, richly blessed in basket and store.

A gentleman reports to the Greenville Patriot, that a few stalks of the Elder placed in a barrel of Rice, Wheat or other Grain, will effectively drive off and keep off the insects that usually attack such things.

Gen Marmaduke (Confederate,) with 8000 men and six pieces of artillery, has been operating with success in Missouri, and carried off one hundred and fifty wagons loaded with plunder.

The Republican.

By Glass & Hardwicke.

LYNCHBURG, TUESDAY, MAY 12, 1863.

TERMS.

DAILY REPUBLICAN.—One year, $12 00; Six months, 7 00; Three months, 4 00; One month, 1 50.

TRI-WEEKLY REPUBLICAN.—One year, $8 00; Six months, 5 00; Three months, 3 00.

ADVERTISING TERMS.—Advertisements inserted at the rate of *one dollar per square for eight lines or less*. Longer advertisements in exact proportion.

JACKSON'S DEAD!

This paper will bear to the reading public to-day, by far the saddest piece of intelligence which its pages have chronicled since the commencement of this wicked war. The invincible, ever glorious and immortal STONEWALL JACKSON is dead! A nation mourns his death even as Troy mourned when Hector fell and left the Trojans well nigh bereft of hope. The brilliant and dashing Jackson is a victim to the chances of war. He lives not to see the end of the struggle in which he was so prominent an actor. Who can write his praise? Who can tell the worth of this imperturbable chieftain, and the depth of thought that kept his eyes from sleeping when his men lay wrapt in slumber on the eve of the mighty battle?

'Tis not in the power of the present generation to do aught more than embalm his memory for time to come when cycles have mellowed passion and prejudices, and he will stand on the pages of history as simply a hero whose example will inspire the yet unborn to perhaps seek a place in their country's history akin to his. "Jackson is dead," will be glad tidings to the vandal foe; they will breathe easier. They feared Jackson, and his name was a terror to their Generals But woe to the enemy when next they meet our arms. Swords then will instinctively be drawn and guns pointed when the hour arrives to avenge his death, and his name will be a battle cry that will carry devastation and horror to the homes of the Yankee foe. A good man has fallen, and nerved be every arm to punish the enemy when next they are met in battle array. The history of his deeds and his services are not now called for; they live in the breast of every man, woman and child in our country; for Stonewall Jackson is a household word with all. When the last trump shall sound, the Christian warrior shall rise clad in the panoply of the blest, to take his place among those of whom it will be said—"well done thou good and faithful servant, enter thou into the joys of the Lord."

If we were competent to the task of writing a suitable eulogy to the illustrious character and distinguished and invaluable public services of this great and good man and warrior, our spirits are far too much depressed this morning at the sad news of his death to permit us to indulge such a melancholy task. His best and most glorious and lasting tribute is already written in the hearts of his countrymen in language which will be immortal, and as the lightnings shall flash his sad demise to the ends of the Confederacy, and the press shall speed it upon the wings of the wind, millions of tears will gush unbidden to the eyes of those who, amidst the clash of war, have long been strangers to the tender emotions, and not a heart in all this land but will mourn the event as the saddest in our infant though memorable history. His loss to our cause is perhaps irreparable. No one can fill his place in all its proportions. He was in himself an army with banners, and more terrible to the enemy than frowning breastworks or thundering artillery. His name was magic among his own troops, and made them invincible in the hour of battle and uncomplaining in the march and in the camp. But no more shall his clarion voice be heard amid embattled hosts cheering his gallant soldiers on to victory—no more shall his manly form be seen in the thickest of the fight, striking terror to the hearts and unnerving the arms of the foes of Liberty. That voice is hushed in death—that form lies cold and inanimate and ne'er again shall a Nation's gratitude break upon his ears or a Nation's praises cause that now pulseless heart to throb with emotions of pride.—Nothing can disturb him now—the rattle of musketry, the roar of artillery and the fierce clashing of glittering sa[illegible] alike fall unheeded upon the dull, cold ear of the honored dead.

The wild winds may roar and the loud thunders rattle.
He heeds not, he hears not, he's free from all pain;
He sleeps his last sleep, he has fought his last battle,
No sound can awake him to glory again!

NEWS FROM THE NORTH.

The news from the North this morning is unusually interesting. It is conceded that Hooker has been terribly defeated in the late battles, as well as out generaled and out fought. Though the loss of the enemy is not stated, it is evidently heavy from the tone of the press. The alarm at the North is not a little. Lincoln calls lustily for another heavy draft of troops, and large reinforcements are being hurried down to the support of the vanquished army. The valliant and boastful Hooker, who was going to make Lee come out and fight him or fly to Richmond, is represented as being considerably depressed after a few days' taste of Southern steel and smell of Jackson's gunpowder.

We are told that active operations are soon again to commence. But we doubt it very much. We wish Hooker would come over and give Lee another chance to punish him. But we predict he will do no such thing, at least not for some time. We rather hope that Lee may find it prudent to go over after him and whip him from his entrenched positions behind the Rappahannock.

PROMOTED.

We are pleased to learn that the able and intrepid young Brigadier Robert E Rodes, of Alabama, has been promoted to Major General, for gallantry and good conduct in the battle of Chancellorsville, and in recognition of his uniform skill and courage on every field. The promotion was worthily bestowed, because well merited.

HORRIBLE MURDER IN AMHERST.

The distressing intelligence that General TERISHA W DILLARD was brutally murdered by two of his own slaves on Saturday evening last, reached us yesterday. No particulars of this foul deed have been received, other than the fact that one of the murderers had been arrested and confessed his crime, and the other had made his escape. General Dillard was a lawyer of prominence and a gentleman of fine talents and popular manners, and the announcement of his untimely and cruel death will fall with crushing force upon his numerous family connexions and a large number of friends.

TOBACCO MARKET.

The late "tumble" in the price of "the weed" had the effect to elongate the faces of some of our tobacconists as well as those who, under the excitement of the speculation, had been "dabbling" in the weed.—But the recent rise in prices has produced a more cheerful state of countenance among the "speculators" and holders are only anxious to "hold." Some few transactions, however, have taken place at figures quite as high as those which obtained before the recent decline.—*Danville Appeal.*

LADIES' RELIEF HOSPITAL.—We are in need of bandages and rags for the wounded soldiers. Will our friends send us what they have to spare? We have had an abundance, but we sent it to distant Hospitals when called for, and now we are admitting daily sick and wounded from the late battles, and will be thankful for all that our friends can send us. We also need very much some slippery elm bark for the sick soldiers. Mrs LUCY W OTEY, Pres't. Mrs J M SPEED. Treasurer.

ATTENTION CAVALRY.—The gentlemen who enrolled themselves with Major Langhorne, are requested to meet for the purpose of organizing this evening, at six o'clock. at the store of Messrs Cobbs, Miller & Price. The following is a list of the same:

John S Bass,	M Coffee,
Sam A Boyd,	Thos H Love, Jr,
A W Scott,	F B Deane,
T W Garret,	G Offterdinger,
Frank Thornton,	C H Lynch,
H A Burroughs,	J E Owen,
R M Seabury,	E Whitehead,
E C Seabury,	Wm M Shoemaker,
J L Goff,	Rice Scott,
Sam McAlden,	H A Alexander,
C D Langhorne,	Ed Alexander,
J B Shaner,	Holcombe Adams,
P C Cabell,	Ferdinand Hutter,
Sam Tyree,	C S Fisher,
S M McCorkle,	C S Langhorne,
John A Lee,	Ro W Crenshaw,
Geo W Langhorne,	Nat Guggenheimer,
Dennis Sullivan,	J W Anderson,
Geo W Burch,	R S Payne,
Geo W Lee.	J P Scott.

may 12 1t

NOTICE.—We will sell on Wednesday, the 13th inst. at our auction Rooms, FIFTEEN LIKELY NEGROES. consisting of men, women, boys and girls. Among the number may be found a No 1 Seamstress, several good Cooks, Nurses and Farm Hands.
may 12 2t HARGROVE & CO.

WANTED.—To hire, twenty able bodied MEN to cut wood at the Salt Works.
HARGROVE & CO,
Liggatt's Building, Bridge Street.

FROM THE RAPPAHANNOCK.

[Special correspondence of the Republican.]

HAMILTON'S CROSSING, May 6th, 1863.

In my letter of yesterday, I gave full particulars relative to the fights of Sunday and Monday. To-day all is quiet in front, the Yankees near this point having all crossed the river to their fastness, save those left upon the field to enrich the sandhills of Spotsylvania, and the prisoners taken by our gallant band under the command of "Old Jubal" and McLaws, which amount to upwards of 2,500, among whom are many prominent officers.

I conversed with one of their Brigadiers this morning, who told me that "he did not consider the victory achieved by us to amount to anything, and that Hooker was bound to succeed, for his plan for flanking us out of our position was one of the grandest movements ever conceived by any General of the present or past age." I asked him if he had ever heard of one Bob Lee, who had outflanked Hooker's flank. He smilingly replied. "I think I have."

I also conversed with Capt D C Kendall, who commanded the 21st N J Regiment. He was wounded in the foot, and had to have it amputated this morning. He appeared to be quite talkative, and said that he was an old personal friend and acquaintance of Hooker's, consequently he knew him well, and remarked that Joe would cross over the river if *ordered* to do so with one regiment, and fight the devil and his cohorts, but he had now come and met the so-called *'ragged rebels'*, who he found to be too hard for him." He further said that he thought these battles would demolish "Fighting Joe" and put an end to the war.

Gen Sedgwick, who commanded the Yankees whom we had to contend with at this point, had, I am told, two corps under him in the fight.—The one which he immediately commands numbers 23,000 men, the term of enlistment of 18,000 of which will expire on the 28th of the month, and the prisoners say most of them will retire, and that not one in ten will re enlist.

The loss on Monday evening above Fredericksburg was very heavy on both sides, but it is impossible to give you any estimate as to numbers. Thousands of the enemy must have been slain when they recrossed on the pontoons, and are now in the bottom of the Rappahannock, as our guns poured shower after shower of shell and grape upon them while on the bridge. So great was their excitement that they pulled up the pontoon bridge before a brigade of the rear guard had passed, 1,400 of whom were taken prisoners and many others shot in the stream while attempting to ford.

Last evening we had the heaviest fall of rain that I have seen since the day after the battle of Sharpsburg. It appeared that the very windows of Heaven were opened, and that we were about to have a second deluge. It is still raining with but little prospect of stopping. This is very trying to the poor devil of a soldier who has been on an active battle field seven days, with nothing to protect his weary limbs from the pelting storm. We all look like drowned rats anxious to creep into our holes, but knowing that duty calls and it is ours to obey, we do not grumble.

I have heard nothing since my last relative to Gen Lee's army above us, save that he is driving the scoundrels before him down the river, and that he has captured a large number of cannon and prisoners.

I can learn nothing of the casualties in the companies from Lynchburg, save the "Lee Battery," which is the only one on the right wing, Private Wade N Owen, who was wounded on Sunday, has since died. Privates Norvell and Eades who were slightly wounded Sunday, have both reported for duty, and were at their posts on the field Monday.

I took a hurried trip down to Guinea Station this morning to look after ammunition. Here I found about six acres covered with live Yankees, who had been taken prisoners. There must be between 5,000 and 6,000 of the blue birds in this mighty flock, who will be off for Richmond so soon as all the wounded are carried down. W W H.

WE are authorized to announce Col H A EDMUNDSON, as a candidate for Congress in the Twelfth District.
may 12 tde

TO THE VOTERS OF FRANKLIN COUNTY.—I respectfully announce myself a candidate at the ensuing election, for the office of Commissioner of the Revenue to fill the vacancy occasioned by the death of Richard C Bennett.
THOMAS J HOLLAND.
GLADE HILL, May 9, 1863.

P S—From a long acquaintance with Mr Holland, I state that he is a man of high moral character, and well qualified for the office for which he is a candidate, being a good penman and accountant, and of prompt business habits. WM PANNILL.
GLADE HILL, May 9th, 1863.
may 12 tde

FIFTY DOLLARS REWARD.—Ranaway from the subscriber, on Saturday night, the 2nd inst, my negro man, GEORGE, who is supposed to be making his way to the Yankee lines. George is about 22 or 23 years old, copper color, talks slightly through his nose, rather inclined to be cock eyed, and is above six feet high, and can write a tolerable good hand. I am of the opinion that he has forged a pass or free papers to enable him to pass either as a servant or free negro.

I have good reason to believe that he has another negro man from his neighborhood in company with him.

I will pay the above reward of fifty dollars for his apprehension and detention in any jail so that I get him again, or if delivered to me at my house, if taken out of Pittsylvania county, or twenty dollars if taken in said county, and delivered as aforesaid
JOHN B JOHNSON,
Chalk Level, Pittsylvania county, Va.
may 12 2m

WANTED,—A SUBSTITUTE to go to Co A, 57th Va Reg't, which is stationed at Drewry's Bluff, near Richmond. One over 45 years of age can get a liberal price by calling on John G Hurt, Room No 22, Piedmont Hotel, to-day, before the train leaves for Richmond.

DUDLEY HALL.

FOURTH CONCERT OF
MR AND MISSES SLOMAN,
This Evening, (Tuesday, May 12th.)
A splendid selection of
MUSIC AND NUMEROUS
COMIC SONGS.
See Programme for full particulars.
may12 1t

FOR THE HOUSE OF DELEGATES—CAMPBELL COUNTY—WM A. POORE, Esq.—*Messrs Editors*; In a late issue of your paper we observed the name of Mr Wm A Poore, Esq, mentioned as a suitable person to represent, in part, the city of Lynchburg and County of Campbell in the next House of Delegates, and believing that none more competent or worthy could be selected for so important a position in this great crisis of the affairs of our country, we call upon him to announce himself at once as a candidate. We believe it is conceded by all who know him, that Mr Poore is a gentleman of fine intelligence, eminently practical in his views upon all subjects. and has, perhaps, as full and correct information of the situation of our country as any man in his county. This, in addition to his genial disposition, bland manners, and courteous demeanor towards every body, peculiarly fits him for a representative. He has an interest in the community which will always induce a safe and intelligent vote upon all questions affecting the rights of his constituents; and besides, his fortunate condition in life as a man of easy circumstances and but small white family, will enable him to spare the time from home which few can afford to do at this particular juncture. It is hardly necessary to say that Mr Poore favors a vigorous and untiring prosecution of the atrocious war now waging against us by the abolition vandals of the North, until our national independence is secured. Then, let the watchword be Deane and Poore, and the county of Campbell will present a ticket which all can support with entire confidence that their interests will be in safe hands.
SEVERAL VOTERS.
may12 1td&c†

J B HARGROVE. E P AISTROP. N A MITCHELL.

HARGROVE & CO,
AUCTIONEERS FOR THE SALE OF NEGROES,
(No 3 Liggatt's Building, Bridge Street.)
Daily sales publicly and privately.

Our porter will be in attendance at the different trains and the boats upon their arrival to receive and carry negroes, consigned to us, to safe apartments.
LIBERAL ADVANCES MADE
on Negroes in hand when desired.
Particular attention paid to hiring.
may12ts

WANTED—at my Spoke Factory, on the canal, near Tye river, a study and industrious man to turn spokes, or one who will soon learn. A comfortable house and large garden and a rich lot that will bring ten to fifteen barrels corn free of rent.
Early application desired.
W G CLARKE,
Tye River Warehouse, Nelson co, Va.
may12 2td2c

A DESIRABLE FARM.—We will sell at auction on the premises, Wednesday, May 27th, 1863, our FARM, lying in the county of Botetourt, eight miles from Bonsacks Depot, on the turnpike leading to Fincastle and near Amsterdam, containing 154 acres, with every necessary improvement in buildings, orchard, &c. The soil is good; the conveniences of the farm with reference to churches, stores, mills, &c, are rarely surpassed. The place is well watered. Fifty acres are heavily timbered. Further description is unnecessary, as persons wishing to purchase will examine for themselves. Terms, cash, in current funds. Any person desiring special information, will address us at Clover Dale, Botetourt county, Va.
Refer to Staples & Dillard, Lynchburg, Va.
J C & D C MOOMAW.
may2 tma27

A RARE CHANCE TO INVEST MONEY OR CONFEDERATE BONDS.—A splendid Merchant Mill (Bunker Hill) with 2 pair Burrs, Corn, Plaster and Saw Mill, two Dwelling Houses and 60 acres Land, on Buffalo Creek, half mile from N R Canal, Rockbridge county. will be sold publicly next Tuesday. the 19th of May.
JAS R SANDERS,
may 11 6t* Sanders' Store.

NEW AUCTION AND COMMISSION HOUSE.
BRISTOL-GOODSON, VA. AND TENN.
(Auction Sale Every Week,)
on Wednesdays and Thursdays.

The subscribers have this day associated themselves together under the firm and style of
WILBAR & JOHNSTON,
for the purpose of conducting a GENERAL AUCTION AND COMMISSION BUSINESS.

We are prepared to receive and sell, either at auction or private sale, all Goods, Wares, Merchandize or Produce of every description that may be consigned to us; and we respectfully ask for a share of public patronage.

Liberal advancements will be made on Merchandize and Produce in hand.

Our first sale will be held on Wednesday and Thursday, May 20th and 21st, at 10 o'clock, a m, and will be continued every Wednesday and Thursday till this advertisement is withdrawn.

Parties wishing to send in goods for the sale, will please have them delivered to us on the Tuesday preceding the sale.

Prompt attention will be paid to shipping goods when sold.

Accounts of sales, with net proceeds, rendered promptly.

Correspondents will please be explicit in their instructions when making consignments.

Sutlers are respectfully invited to attend our sales.

Our store is open at all times till 10 o'clock, p m, and parties can have ample time to make purchases upon their arrival from Virginia on the 8:30 mail, and be ready to return on the 12 o'clock train.

We intend to keep always on hand a select assortment of Goods of all kinds. All orders will be promptly attended to.

Our terms to dealers are, Cash on Delivery.

References—Joseph L King, Knoxville; Rucker & Lee, Lynchburg; J E Burress & Co, Richmond.
H T WILBAR,
A P JOHNSTON,
Bristol, Tenn, and Goodson, Va.
may11 3m

Ordnance Office, C S A
Lynchburg, Va, Dec 1, 1862.

NOTICE.—I am prepared to Exchange Powder and Shot for Lead, in the following proportions, viz: One pound of Powder for ten pounds of Lead, (1 for 10) and one pound of Shot for five pounds of Lead, (1 for 5).
G T GETTY,
dec2ts Capt C S A Comd'g

KEROSINE OIL.—15 bbls "Luminating" for sale by
may 9 McDANIEL & IRBY.

SUGAR AND MOLASSES.—Sugar in hhds bbls and sacks, part very choice, 20 bbls Molasses, for sale by
[illegible]

AUCTION SALES.

FUTURE DAYS.

BY J P SCOTT & CO, Auct'rs.

LARGE AND ATTRACTIVE SALE FRESH DRY GOODS AND GROC[ERIES]—On THURSDAY, MAY 7th, 1862, commen[cing] at 9 o'clock, we will sell—
277 ps English Prints,
262 ps English Bleach Shirtings,
50 ps 40 inch Pillow Case do
400 doz Spool Cotton—Clark's and Coats',
1000 yds best Brown Denims,
1500 yds Alamand Plaids,
21 ps Irish Linen.
100 doz Cotton Handkerchiefs,
72 doz Linen Cambric Handkerchiefs,
10 doz Gents
200 doz Fine Combs,
15 ps Black Alpaca.
5 ps Domestic Flannel,
10 ps Heavy Twilled do
290 packs Pins,
20,000 assorted Needles,
24 fine Hoop Skirts,
5 pieces Plaid Linsey,
5 bales Oznaburgs,
35 bales Raw Cotton,
80 bbls Brown Sugar,
100 sacks do
15 kegs Soda,
3 chests Fine Green Tea,
200 kegs Old Dominion Nails,
1000 lbs Copperas,
600 lbs Extract Logwood,
12 boxes Sperm Candles,
15 " Tallow "
20 tierces Rice,
22 bbls Apple Brandy,
5 bales 4-4 Brown Shirtings, to arrive,
Many other goods to arrive.
JAS P SCOTT & CO,
ap 30tds Auct'rs.

The above sale will be postponed until Thursday, 14th inst. J P SCOTT & CO.

STOCKS FOR SALE.—Will be sold, at auction, at the Office of the Lynchburg Fire, Life and Marine Insurance Company, (next door to the Exchange Bank.) at 12 o'clock, on Wednesday, the 13th instant, 295 shares of the Stock of said Insurance Company. Terms cash. BENJ. H. NOWLIN, Pres't.
may 11 tds

AMHERST LAND FOR SALE.—The subscriber wishes to sell his tract of land in Amherst, lately owned by Wm Tucker and on which said Tucker now resides. The tract contains 563 acres, is well watered and has an abundance of timber, is good grain and grass land, and well adapted to the culture of fruit. It adjoins the land of S L Burford, Col Shelton and others. There are two good saw and grist mills in ½ of a mile of the place. There is a good dwelling house and all necessary out houses on the land. It is within ½ a mile of Burfords Summit on O & A R R and 4½ of the city of Lynchburg. The land will be shown any one wishing to purchase, by A D Robertson or S L Burford, who reside near the place. Mr Robertson is also authorized to contract for the sale of the place, and to whom I refer any one wishing further information. His address is Salt Creek P O, Amherst co, Va.

If not sold privately before Thursday, the 4th of June, 1863, it will be offered at public auction, in front of the Market House in Lynchburg, on that day.
WM M PEYTON,
Rockfish Depot,
may 4 tds O & A R R.

NOTICE.—We will sell to the highest bidder on the premises, one mile north of Buchanan, Botetourt county, on the 16th May, 1863 two good STILLS—one supposed to hold 180 gals, the other 100 gals, one good cast iron Apple Mill, a good lot of Still Tubs, together with many other articles.

Terms cash, or negotiable note at 60 days satisfactorily endorsed.
may 4 tds STRICKLAND & COUCH.

VALUABLE PROPERTY FOR SALE.—Will be offered to the highest bidder, on Wednesday, the 13th day of May, 1863, on the premises, that valuable property, known as the ROANOKE RED SULPHUR SPRINGS, ten miles from Salem, and thirty-four miles from the Sweet Springs; there being a good turnpike road between the two places. The improvements are handsome and comfortable, sufficient for the accommodation of two hundred persons. These Springs have established for themselves a high reputation as a watering place, and offer inducements as such; or the character and extent of the improvements would make it an admirable situation for an extensive male or female school.

Terms cash or on time, interest added.
GEORGE W SHANKS,
Salem, apl 16 dtds For Proprietors.

IN PURSUANCE OF A DECREE of the Circuit Court pronounced on the 25th of March, 1863, in the Chancery case of Robertson vs Wilson, the undersigned Com's will sell at Amherst Court House, on the 18th of May, 1863, to the highest bidder, at public auction, a valuable tract of mountain Land in said county, lying on Pedlar river near Oronoko, containing about 400 acres, with small dwelling house and other houses upon it.

TERMS.—Cash, or on a credit of one, two and three years, bearing interest from day of sale, reserving in the latter case, cash enough to defray the expenses of sale, bonds with good personal security for the deferred payment, and title retained till all the purchase money is paid. Immediate possession will be given.
ROBT M BROWN,
JAS P COLEMAN,
apl 20 tw tds Commissioners.

BACON HAMS.—We have just received on consignment 2,000 lbs Bacon Hams, which we are offering low to close.
ap 17 A J CAMP & CO.

800 BALES COTTON YARN.—I am receiving to-day 800 Bales Cotton Yarn, from 8 to 12. A B RUCKER.
ap 20

NOTICE.—Parties wanting WOOD can find our Mr J W LANKFORD, at Virginia and Tennessee R R Depot, when not at the office at the Coal Yard. I H ADAMS & CO.
jan 10 ts

FLAXSEED WANTED—We will pay the highest market price, in cash, for any quantity of Flax Seed.
ap 14 W A STROTHER & CO.

BLACK PEPPER, for sale by
ap 4 W A STROTHER & CO.

SHEETING FOR SALE.—7 bales 4-4 Augusta Sheeting, ma 9 A B RUCKER.

STRAYED OR STOLEN from my farm near Trinity Church, 6 miles west of Lynchburg, on the old Lexington Turnpike, a fine large BAY MARE, rather thin, thirteen years old, blind in her right eye, a hurt above the right nostril, breathes rather hard, a sore and scar on her left hind knee. When put up, dog trots and a natural pacer. Any information given to me will be thankfully received, or a liberal reward will be paid if desired.
may 7 d1w* BUCKNER G ASHBY.

FOR SALE.—One Stationary Engine, complete, 22 Horse power for sale by
may 9 McDANIEL & IRBY.

BY TELEGRAPH.

SPECIAL DISPATCHES TO THE DAILY REPUBLICAN.

CATH OF GEN THOS J JACKSON.

RICHMOND, May 10.—Gov Letcher ceived a dispatch this afternoon, an uncing the death of Gen Thomas J ckson, at Guinea's Depot, at 3:15 P M. died from the combined effects of his und and an attack of pneumonia. His dy will be brought to this city to-mor w, (Monday) by a special train.

RRIVAL OF GENERAL JACKSON'S BODY IN RICHMOND.

RICHMOND, May 11.—Business was sus nded here to-day after 10 A M.

A special train, with Gen Jackson's dy, arrived at half past three.

There was an immense concourse on road street and on Capitol Square awai g the arrival of the train.

The body was removed to the Gover or's Mansion under charge of a large ilitary escort, where it will remain in ate until to-morrow morning, when it ill be removed to Lexington.

UNERAL HONORS TO GENERAL JACKSON.

RICHMOND, May 11.—It has been de rmined to retain the body of General ackson here until Wednesday.

There will be a funeral procession to orrow forenoon to escort his remains om the Governor's Mansion to the Capi ol, where they will lie in state during the day.

GENERAL LEE'S ADDRESS TO THE ARMY ANNOUNCING THE DEATH OF GEN JACKSON.

RICHMOND, May 11—The following ad dress to the army announcing the death of Gen Jackson has been issued by Gen Lee :

HEADQUARTERS ARMY OF NORTHERN VA } May 11, 1863. }

With deep grief the commanding Gene ral announces to the army the death of Lieutenant General THOMAS J. JACKSON, who expired on the 10th inst. at 3½ o'clock, P M.

The daring, skill and energy of this great and good soldier by the decree of an all-wise Providence are now lost to us, but while we mourn his death we feel that his spirit still lives and will inspire the whole army with his indomitable courage and unshaken confidence in God as our hope and strength.

Let his name be a watchword to his corps who have followed him to victory on so many fields. Let officers and soldiers emulate his invincible determination to do everything in defence of his beloved country.

Signed R. E. LEE, General.

PARTICULARS OF THE ARREST OF MR VALLANDIGHAM.

GREAT EXCITEMENT IN DAYTON, OHIO

JACKSON, May 11.—(Special to the Appeal).—The Chicago Times of the 6th has a dispatch from Cincinnati, May 5th, which states that Mr Vallandigham was arrested by a company of soldiers on the charge of violating Burnside's death or der.

Vallandigham has taken high ground, declaring that he will not answer the military. He will be tried immedi ately.

Parties have gone to Cleveland to get out a writ of habeas corpus in the North ern District court of Ohio.

Mr Vallandigham has been sent to the barracks. His arrest created great ex citement in Montgomery county.

Wagon loads of people flocked to Day ton on hearing of the news.

Burnside sent cannon and troops into Dayton, where some pistols were fired, the Journal office and other buildings burned, the telegraph wires cut, and the bridge on the Columbus and Xenia Rail road burned. The residences of Col Harrel, the Provost General, and others, were threatened.

Later intelligence says the Phillips house was burning.

REPORTED DEFEAT OF BANKS BY GEN SMITH.

JACKSON, May 11—The Natchez Cou rier has information from a person at Port Hudson, that Gen Kirby Smith, with ten thousand raw troops, has badly whip ped Banks, and was driving him to Wash ton, La.

The New York World predicts a Dem ocratic majority in the State of Ohio in the coming fall election of 25,000 to 30,000.

FROM THE NORTH.

JACKSON, May 9.—(Special to the Ap peal.)—The Chicago Times of the 5th says intelligence from New York represents the result of the great battles on the Rap pahannock as undecided.

UNITED STATES FORD, May 6, 8 A M— All the trains have been ordered back, and there is nothing on the other side of the river except infantry and artillery. The rain is deluging the roads, tearing up the corduroys, sweeping the bridges and threatening the destruction of the pon toons. The river has so much risen that the upper pontoons have been taken to lengthen the lower ones, and after several hours' hard work the river is again passa ble. The pontoons are covered with boughs to prevent the rebels from hear ing the crossing. At midnight the troops commenced the retreat, and it is under stood they will be over by noon. It is hoped the high water will prevent the enemy from crossing. Great numbers of our wounded are in the enemy's hands. In Sunday's battle the dead were left un buried and the wounded unattended. Hooker is much depressed, and after con sultation a hasty return to our camp was decided upon. It is now raining heavily and the river is rising rapidly.

FALMOUTH, May 6th, 10 A M—Three bridges have been destroyed between here and Aquia Creek. The river has risen ten feet. It is rumored that the enemy's cavalry have crossed above and are ad vancing cautiously.

NEW YORK, May 7.—Nothing concern ing war matters has been telegraphed from Washington. The World says we learn by a special messenger that a great battle was fought on Tuesday, and Hook er with his army driven back across the Rappahannock. He is being heavily re inforced. The last battle exceeds in slaughter those of the previous days Nothing heard from Stoneman, but it is impossible to doubt that his force will be captured.

PETERSBURG, May 10.—The Express has the New York World of the 7th.

It acknowledges the defeat of Hooker and his retreat to the north bank of the Rappahannock. It says that Lee being heavily reinforced is again a victor.

Sedgwick's retreat began at midnight, but was discovered by the rebels, who played terrible havoc on the pontoons, killing and wounding a large number.

The World says its worst fears of the result of Hooker's efforts are more than confirmed. He has been out-generaled and out-fought.

Nothing had been heard from Stoneman on Wednesday night. It was generally believed that his whole force would be captured.

The World says that Heintzleman is on his way to Hooker with 30,000 fresh troops, and that 18,000 are coming from another quarter. (Suffolk, of course.—*Reporter*.) It hopes that these reinforce ments will enable the Federals to retrieve the disasters at Fredericksburg.

The town of Fredericksburg has been recaptured by Jackson. The fighting was desperate. All of Longstreet's for ces rushed from Suffolk and arrived in time.

A partial list of the killed and wounded is given. Among the former are the names of Brig Gen Mott, Brig Gen Barry, of Maine, Gen Schewinleifent, of the 11th corps, and seventeen Colonels. Lieut Col onels and Majors, and twenty eight Cap tains and Lieutenants.

The wounded are Brig Gen Whipple, Gen Divine, of Maine, severely; thirty-one Colonels, Lieut Colonels and Majors, and fifty-two Captains and Lieutenants. Ma ny are mortally wounded.

Hon Mr Vallandigham is at the Bur nett House, in Cincinnati, under a strong guard.

Over 4,000 rebel prisoners reached Washington up to Wednesday night, who were captured in the recent battles. Ten guns of the celebrated New Orleans Ar tillery were captured.

CAIRO, May 6.—The latest intelligence from Young's Point, says the Union gun boats were repulsed at Haines' Bluff.— The iron clad Choctaw was badly dama ged. Her turret was penetrated by a 64- pounder. The Union loss was eighty.

THE LATEST.

RICHMOND, May 10.—The Whig has Northern dates of the 9th.

Lincoln has issued a proclamation call ing on the militia to suppress the rebel lion. All able bodied male citizens and foreigners who have declared their in tention to become citizens, between the ages of 20 and 45, constitute the national forces.

An official order from Stanton says the President and General-in Chief have just returned from the Army of the Potomac. There was no serious disaster to the organ ization or efficiency of the army, and not more than one third of Hooker's force was engaged. Stoneman's operations was a brilliant success. A part of his command advanced to within two miles of Rich mond. The army will speedily resume offensive operations.

The trial of Mr Vallandigham was con cluded by court martial on the 7th. The decision is unknown.

The correspondents of the New York papers are grandiloquent in their accounts of the battles, disguising the fact, of a de feat, as far as possible, by the multiplica tion of words.

Hooker was stunned and thrown to the ground by a shell, which shattered the pillar of a porch against which he was leaning in Chancellorsville.

THE VERY LATEST FROM THE NORTH.

RICHMOND, May 11.—Northern dates of the 10th have been received.

The charges against Vallandigham are, that about the 1st of May he addressed a large meeting at Mount Vernon, Ohio, declaring the war unnecessary and cruel, and not waged for the preservation of the Union, but for the purpose of abolishing liberty and establishing despotism; that he denounced Burnside's order, No 38, as a base usurpation of arbitrary authority, and that the sooner the people informed the minions of usurped power that they would not submit to such restrictions, the better.

An arrival from Wilmington bay re ports the iron clads off Charleston ready for another attack.

There was much excitement at Havana, caused by a Yankee schooner overhauling suspicious vessels. A Spanish steamer had been sent to investigate the matter.

No further news is published in the Washington papers relative to Hooker's defeat.

FROM EUROPE.

The steamer Australasian, with Liver pool dates to the 26th of April, has arri ved.

A spirited debate has taken place in both Houses of Parliament regarding the seizure of British vessels by American cruisers.

Mr Roebuck made a strong war speech, in which he asked Lord Palmerston if the government had come to any deter mination in the matter, and if it had, whether he can tell Parliament what that determination is. Mr Roebuck knew the consequences of that action. Lord Pal merston may take it that it will lead to war, and I, speaking for the English peo ple, am prepared for war. [Loud cheers.] Justice must be done to the honor of Eng land, and the commerce of the country must no longer be subject to the sneering insolence of an upstart race. [Cheers.]

FROM VICKSBURG.

VICKSBURG, May 9.—Nothing new from the front.

The enemy have been landing troops to-day below Young's Point. It is sup posed they are destined to reinforce Grant.

The Whig office was destroyed by fire this afternoon. Origin of fire unknown.

BY THE GOVERNOR OF VIRGINIA.

A PROCLAMATION.

THE Senate of Virginia having declared va cant the 46th Senatorial District, composed of the counties of Ritchie, Doddridge, Harrison, Pleasants and Woods, and the 50th Senatorial District, composed of the counties of Brooke, Hancock and Ohio, and these districts being in the occupation of the public enemy; and the ordinance of the Convention having authorized the qualified voters of said districts, who may be in the military service of the State or of the Confederate States on the day of any general or special election for the General Assembly, to vote in said elections at such place or places within their encampment, as the commander at such encampment shall designate, whether the said encampment shall be within the limits of this State or not; and also authorized the citizens of any county or corporation absent therefrom because of the presence of the pub lic enemy, who would be qualified to vote for members of the General Assembly in such county or corporation during the continuance of the present war, to vote at any general or spe cial election for members of the General As sembly in their counties or corporations at the court house of any county or corporation in the State where they may happen to be on the day of the election. Therefore, I, JNO LETCH ER, Governor of the Commonwealth of Virgin ia, by virtue of authority vested in the Execu tive by law, do hereby proclaim that, to supply said vacancies, elections will be held on the 4th THURSDAY of May next, being the 28th day of the month, in conformity to law and the ordi nance of the Convention passed on the 6th day of December, 1861. Officers in military camps and posts and corporations in the State will conform themselves to the provisions herein cited, and receive such qualified voters as may offer their votes for the said Senatorial Districts.

[L. S.] Given under my hand as Governor, and under the less seal of the Common wealth, of Virginia, this 13th day of April, 1863, in the eighty seventh year of the Commonwealth. JOHN LETCHER.

Teste—

GEO W MUNFORD,

Secretary of the Commonwealth.

apr23 tde

The Natchez Weekly Courier.

VOL. XXXIV. NATCHEZ, MISSISSIPPI, WEDNESDAY MORNING, MAY 13, 1863. NO. 21.

Weekly Courier

Wednesday, May 6th, 1863.

☞ To Capt. F. L. Hale, from Houston, Texas, we are indebted for late Houston and Shreveport papers. Capt. H. gives a gratifying account of affairs in Gen. Magruder's Department.

Rumors.

We again caution our people about entertaining and circulating sensation rumors. Let us pursue our daily avocations with cheerfulness, relying upon the bravery of our defenders. In every instance give them encouragement, and reinforcements when convenient. Nothing shall be left undone on our part, to disseminate early and reliable news, and we again ask our friends to wait patiently for the "Pony Express." We miss the services of our energetic friends at the telegraph office, but while they are cut off we shall endeavor to furnish *them* news, though it may not be as prompt as they have been heretofore to us.

What do they Intend Doing?

It is natural for all mankind to judge an individual, more especially a stranger, by his acts. This is the only mode of arriving at anything definite in regard to the movements of the enemy. We are told, that since they landed in the vicinity of Rodney and Grand Gulf, there has been a general seizure of horses, mules and wagons in that section of this State and the Louisiana parishes, opposite. These facilities for transportation, it is also said, they are concentrating within their lines.

The question is asked, what they intend doing? To us it appears plain the Federals are preparing to march, (those below Vicksburg,) either on the Jackson and Vicksburg or Brookhaven and Jackson railroads. This is doubtless their plan to attempt a reduction of Vicksburg by General Starvation—the only military chieftain they appear to have who has any chance of gaining a victory, and his chances are exceedingly slim.

We know nothing of the movements of Gen. Pemberton, but we feel assured that he will not long allow the enemy to prepare for a journey to either of the railroads.

☞ A man named Schaclett has been tried and convicted on a charge of treason, at Louisville, Kentucky. This is the first case of treason that has been adjudicated by a U.S. court, since the "rebellion" broke out.

From Corinth and North Alabama.

We have reliable information, received through Lieut. J. H. Morrison, aid to Gen. Pemberton, who has just returned from a scout in the Northern part of the State, to the effect that on the 25th instant, there were at Corinth only one battalion and one battery. On the 26th this force was strengthened by one division and one brigade.

We also learn from Lieut. Morrison that from seven to ten thousand troops have crossed the Tennessee river supposed to reinforce Rosecrans. On the 19th inst., there were eleven regiments of infantry, averaging three hundred each, twenty-two hundred mounted men, thirty-six pieces of artillery, six of which were Parrot guns, two hundred and seventy-five wagons laden with pontoon bridges, and from three to four hundred pack mules, laden with hard bread, on big Bear creek in North Alabama.

On Monday evening, the 20th inst., they were at Dixon's lane, on Buzzard Roost creek. Col. Roddy, with four regiments of cavalry were in their front, fighting them. He had checked their progress to such an extent that they had made only twelve miles in four days.—*Appeal, April 30.*

[Correspondence of the Chicago Times.

FROM WASHINGTON.

Duplicity of the Administration—It claimed a Victory at Charleston—Terrible Revulsion of Feeling at Washington when the Truth was known—Demonstration of the Impregnability of Charleston—The Administration Abandoned the Siege as Hopeless—Results of the Failure to Take Charleston—Effects of the Failure in Europe.

During the last four days the Administration has been striving with its utmost power to keep from the people a knowledge of the great disaster that has befallen the national arms in Charleston harbor. On Sunday it was given out under the express sanction of the Administration, that the bombardment of Charleston had commenced, and that the government was in receipt of intelligence which rendered it certain that by that time that nest of treason was in our possession. The same telegram stated that many government officials bet heavy sums that Charleston was taken, or would be taken by the 14th inst., and that those bets found no takers. No such bets were ever made. On Monday the Administration authorized the statement to be made that the affair of the 7th was only a reconnoissance, that proved successful, and that Com. Dupont having ascertained what he wished to know about the defenses of the place, would begin the regular bombardment about the 10th; also, that the affair of the 7th was without loss on our side. Yesterday, the falsehood of the official reports of the previous two days was exposed, and Lincoln and his minions here were obliged to admit that our loss had been severe; that one of the finest iron-clad vessels was destroyed and sunk, and five others so disabled and shattered as to be useless until repaired. But the Administration, with blushing effrontery, caused the statement to be made that the damage could all be repaired by the 18th; that by that time our naval force there would be reinforced by three other iron-clad vessels; and that on that day the bombardment of Charleston would really begin. Mr. Lincoln himself says emphatically that the affair of the 7th was not a repulse, but only a check, and that Commodore Dupont would be ready to begin operations there in earnest on the 15th.

The day for the people to be fooled and bamboozled, however, is over. To-day, neither Mr. Lincoln, nor any member of his weak and wicked Administration, has a single word to say about Charleston. The facts are not known to the world. The people now know that the affair in Charleston harbor of the 7th was no reconnoissance, but that it was the long talked of and much boasted attack on Charleston, which was to demolish Fort Sumter and grind it to powder, and to reduce Charleston to a heap of smouldering ruins. They know that this attack was made deliberately, after months of preparation, and with the utmost power of our naval force. They know that it has proven a total, complete, and confessed failure. They know that some of our iron-clad vessels are entirely destroyed, and others so much strained, bent, and battered, that they can never be made serviceable again. They know that the impregnability of Charleston has been demonstrated and that no further attempt will be made to take that city; in a word, that the campaign against Charleston is over.

The members of the Administration, too, know these facts. They gnash their teeth over this and swear awfully, (you know they are all dreadfully profane swearers, from Abraham down to the tail end of the Cabinet, except Mr. Usher, the new Secretary of the Interior, who, although in bad company, is every inch a gentleman and don't swear); yes, they all swear awfully about it, and are trying to throw the blame of the defeat on Commodore Dupont, Gen. Hunter, and the brave captains of the iron-clad vessels. They say Dupont is incompetent, and almost call him a coward, (they dare not do *that*), and talk of superceding him by Farragut; and they say that if the captains of the iron-clad vessels were men of the Paul Jones stamp, they would have renewed the action on the 8th, and would have taken Charleston or perished in the attempt. They point to the small loss of life on our side as an evidence that our brave sailors did not do *all* they might have done.

I need not tell your readers how unjust all this is; but nothing better can be expected from the men who compose this Administration. As ignorant as children of all that appertains to war, they are attempting to carry on the most stupendous war the world ever say. Commodore Dupont is by far the ablest naval officer in the service. If he were here, no man would dare to call in question his courage or his devotion to his country. When he says the capture of Charleston is impracticable, it is so. As regards Gen. Hunter, I explained, in my letters of February 27 and March 14, the reason that would render his force useless. In those letters I stated the instructions which Gen. Hunter had received from the Administration, and said that, in consequence of them, "The expedition against Charleston will have to be abandoned. What Gen. Hunter is doing will cause the failure of the whole expedition, and he is doing it in obedience to express and imperative orders from the Administration. The demoralization of Hunter's army is such that no results can be expected from it." These statements have now been verified.

The cruel slanders that the Administration is heaping on the heads of the brave captains of the iron-clad vessels will recoil on the heads of the base originaters. The accounts of the battle that have been published proved that never did naval officers fight more bravely, or conduct themselves with greater gallantry. It is a shame that their services are not properly acknowledged.

With the results of the battle your readers are of course well acquainted. Charleston stands to-day where she stood a month ago, and where she will stand till the end of the war—impregnable and uninjured. She has been made so by the scientific skill of General Beauregard. The great battle of the 7th of April, will long live in history. It demonstrated that Charleston is absolutely safe from a subsequent attack; that the Confederates have plenty of English Whitworth guns, carrying steel pointed projectiles; that the strongest and thickest iron-clad vessels can be perforated with these projectiles; and the stone fortresses, mounted with guns such as those possessed by the Confederates, cannot be reduced by the heaviest artillery from on board of vessels. I knew all of these facts, except the last, many weeks ago; and, knowing them, I said in my letter of February 15th, "The expedition will fail."

The result of this expedition, around which many hopes clustered, is another proof of the utter imbecility and inefficiency of the Administration, and furnishes the only demonstration that was needed of their incompetency to conduct the war to a successful termination. How much longer will the people permit them to continue the fratricidal strife. Charleston is no stronger than Savannah and Mobile. We can no more take Richmond or Vicksburg than we can Charleston. These are facts, known to all men whose reason is not clouded by hatred towards the South. And, sooner or later, the Administration will be compelled to acknowledge them, and make peace.

The news of this great disaster, following close on the heels of the news of the failures of the four expeditions to open the Mississippi, which have a most damaging effect upon the Union cause in Europe. The Confederate loan, already a favorite stock in the Paris and London money markets, will go up, up, up; and new loans, to any amount, can be negotiated in those cities with ease. The turning point of the war has been reached. If the South has been in any want of money hitherto, it will not be so in future. The finances of the Confederacy are now established on a firm and secure basis; and you may now look for a declaration from the courts of France and England that the South, having demonstrated her ability to maintain her independence, is recognized as an independent nation. Thus a disruption of the Union will be perfected. Conciliation would have won back the "wayward sisters." But the Administration resolved a "coercion," and behold the result, a dissevered Union. And these men arrogate to themselves the name of *Union men!*

TELEGRAPHIC.

General Forrest After the Enemy in North Alabama.

TULLAHOMA, May 1....Forrest met the enemy near Moulton (which is west by south from Decatur, where the Memphis and Charleston Railroad crosses the Tennessee river,) yesterday, and repulsed him in a hand to hand fight. The enemy is in full retreat and Forrest in full pursuit. All quiet in front.

CHATTANOOGA, May 1....All quiet in front. The enemy is within his intrenchments on Stone river.

A special to the Rebel, dated Huntsville, May 1st, says that Forrest repulsed the enemy with considerable loss yesterday at Danville, fifteen miles from Decatur, and still in pursuit. Our loss, 50. Our pickets are beyond Courtland.

Congressional.

RICHMOND, May 1....The Senate has passed the House bill, placing in military service, after the first of July next, all citizens of the United States, and refugees from Maryland, residing or coming hereafter into the Confederate States.

The House amendment to the bill establishing a flag, was concurred in.

In the House nothing of interest occurred except the amendment to the Senate bill, establishing a flag. The design agreed upon by both houses, is a battle flag for the Union, with white field without bars.

The House took a recess until 8 o'clock.

RICHMOND, May 1....The enemy crossed at several points fifteen or twenty miles above Fredericksburg and made an advance down the river by the plank road from Chancellor, ten miles above Fredericksburg. At this point they were attacked by Mahone's brigade, and after a brief fight, were repulsed with considerable loss. Our loss was slight.

The Yankees who crossed below Fredericksburg, are entrenching.

Yesterday the enemy's batteries below town opened fire on our position, near Hamilton's crossing, the present railroad terminus. Our batteries replied, and a duel continued incessantly until dusk.

There are reports heard of fighting in the vicinity of Richmond.

A letter dated 12 M., near Fredericksburg, says there is no fighting or skirmishing to-day. Both sides are preparing for a battle.

No demonstration has been made by the enemy in front of Fredericksburg. The town will probably receive a shelling. The inhabitants have again evacuated the place.

Latest from the North.

[Special to the Memphis Appeal.]

SENATOBIA, May 2....The Chicago Times of the 28th ult. has been received. At Indianapolis Gen. Haskell, who has superseded Carrington, has issued an order to the effect that newspapers and speakers, endeavoring to bring the war policy of the Government into disrepute, violate Burnside's death order, and will be treated accordingly.

Six hundred infantry and one hundred cavalry had departed for Brown county, Indiana, to make arrests.

A Cincinnati naval officer, from below, says that Vicksburg will not be attacked from the front. The levees have been cut, and other mischiefs perpetrated, with the view of rendering the country south of Helena untenable.

A Cairo dispatch states that Jeff. Thompson, with twenty-five hundred men, attacked Cape Girardeau. He withdrew leaving fifty killed. The Federal loss is small. McNeil is commanding at Cape Girardeau.

The mouths of the Arkansas and White rivers have been connected by a canal, thus cutting off a distance of ten miles.

General Curtis has proclaimed Burnside's death order and put it in force in Missouri.

Grant's headquarters are at New Carthage. Important movements are said to be on foot. At Nashville over three thousand males and females have been forced to take the oath and bonded.

A number of Kentuckians have been court-martialed at Cincinnati, to-wit: Sampson D. Talbott, of Paris, for harboring and shielding from arrest. He was fined one thousand dollars and sentenced to imprisonment for three months. T. Sullivan, Talbott's accessary, was sentenced to sixty day imprisonment. Thos. M. Campbell, a Confederate soldier, found within the Federal lines, was sentenced to death, which was approved by Burnside, and the sentence was to be put in execution on the first of May.

[Special to the Mississippian.]

Cannonading at Snyder's Bluff Yesterday.

VICKSBURG, May 2....Dispatches from Snyder's Bluff, dated to-day, state the enemy maintained a steady fire yesterday on our works on Graveyard Hill, temporarily disabling one gun.

A deserter, who came dashing into our lines yesterday evening, reports that Sherman is in command on the flag-ship DeKalb; that he has only ten regiments, averaging 500, and the present demonstration is only a feint; no real attack is intended.

At the Bluff batteries, on Thursday, private Frank Haggerty, of Company D, 21st Louisiana regiment, was seriously wounded in the right side. Private Daniel Thurston, of Company C, had his right leg broken and amputated.

The deserter reports that Lieut. Cottingham, 3d La., (missing since skirmish of Saturday,) was wounded in four places and taken prisoner. He also reports two killed on the turreted gunboat Choctaw, and that she was struck over forty times by our batteries. Look for nothing but good reports from this quarter. J. L. POWER.

Great Britain and the United States.

The Fitting Out of Confederate Privateers in British Ports.

SPEECH OF LORD PALMERSTON.

In the House of Commons, on the 27th ult., Mr. W. E. Foster made a speech calling the attention of the Government to its relations with the United States arising from the rebel privateers that had been fitted out in English ports. Lord Palmerston spoke on the subject as follows:

Now, sir, turning to the question raised by my honorable friend, the member for Bradford, I cannot but express my regret at the tone of his remarks, and still more at the tone of the honorable member for Birmingham. (Hear, hear.) There is no concealing the fact, and there is no use in disguising it, that whenever any political party, whether in or out of office, in the United States, finds itself in difficulties, it raises a cry against England, (hear, hear.) as a means of creating what in American language is called "political capital." That is a practice, of course, which we must deplore. As long as it is confined to their internal affairs, we can only hope that, being rather a dangerous game, it will not be carried further than is intended. When a Government or a large party excite the passions of one nation against another, especially if there is no just cause, it is manifest that such a course has a great tendency to endanger friendly relations between two countries. We understand, however, the object of these proceedings in the present instance, and therefore we do not feel that irritation which might otherwise be excited. But, if this cry is raised for the purpose of driving her Majesty's government to do something which may be contrary to the laws of the country, or which may be derogatory to the dignity of the country, in the way of altering our laws for the purpose of pleasing another government, then all I can say is that such a course is not likely to accomplish its purpose. I very much regret, therefore, that the speech of my honorable friend, the member for Bradford, and more particularly that of the honorable member for Birmingham, are calculated to encourage those complaints which I think are totally unfounded on the part of the American Government. (Hear, hear.) I should have hoped that gentlemen, bringing this question before the house, would rather have tried to allay the irritation instead of making out, as they endeavor to do, that the Americans have reason to blame England, and the English Government. (Hear, hear.) My honorable and learned friend, the Solicitor General, in that admirable speech which we all listened to with the greatest delight (hear, hear,) has demonstrated indisputably that the Americans have no cause of complaint against us. He has shown that the British Government have done on the report of the American minister here, everything which the laws of the country enabled them to do.

I can easily understand that in the United States, where the civil war has produced so much agitation, and where the course of practice has been to set aside the law, men have been led to forget, in a great degree, the obligations of the law, and are not disposed to give that weight which is due to our argument—that we cannot go beyond what the law prescribes and authorizes. Yet I think that the house at least will see that the statement of my honorable and learned friend proves that we have, in enforcing the foreign enlistment act, done all that the law enabled or permitted us to do. [Hear, hear.]

Honorable members have argued as if the seizure of a vessel were equivalent to its condemnation. They ask, "Why did you not seize the Alabama when you were told that it was known and believed that it was intended for warlike purposes on the part of the Confederates." Now, in the first place you cannot seize a vessel under the proposal to alter the law. [Hear, hear, and a laugh.] I have had some experience of what any attempt of that sort may be expected to lead to [laughter,]—and I think there are several gentlemen sitting on this bench who would not be disposed, if I was so inclined myself, to concur in any such proposition. [Cheers.]

Volunteer Organizations for Home Defense.

It will be seen from a section of the law of the Confederate States to provide for the formation of companies for local defense, that such companies will not be regarded as bush-fighters, but as regular soldiers of the provisional army; and entitled to all the rights of soldiers as prisoners of war, if captured by the enemy. Now let companies be formed all over the State. It will strengthen immensely the arm for the public defense. The following is the clause alluded to:

"That for the purpose of local defense in any portion of the Confederate States, any number of persons (not less than twenty) who are over the age of forty-five years, or otherwise not liable to military duty, may associate themselves as a military company, elect their own officers and establish rules and regulations for their own government, and shall be considered as belonging to the Provisional Army of the Confederate States, serving without pay or allowances, and entitled, when captured by the enemy, to all the privileges of *prisoners of war.*"

A PROTEST. The Federal district attorney in Florida, T. J. Boynton, Esq., has written a letter to Colonel Joseph S. Morgan, commanding at Key West, protesting against Gen. Hunter's orders to transport the families of all white persons residing within the limits of his command who have husbands, brothers or sons "in rebel employment" to the rebel lines, which order that officer construes as meaning all those who have such relatives "residing" within the rebel territory and control. He also says such an act is "illegal upon every principle of constitutional right; it is illegal upon every principle of the law of conquest of territory; it is illegal upon every principle of personal rights, founded on natural law; it is violative of every principle of law, justice or humanity." Mr. Boynton will soon feel the keen edge of the decapitating axe of his abolition masters, we predict.

☞ The Richmond Dispatch, giving details of the enormities perpetrated by the Yankees in Gloucester, says:

The Yankees in Gloucester, we are told, have sworn destruction on everything, and have warned the farmers that it will be worse than idle for them to attempt to raise any crops. They declare their purpose to burn and destroy everything that is planted, and have told the people that their fields shall be laid waste as soon as they dare attempt to raise any crop. They say boastfully, that they have one general that can "whip the rebels," and that is General Starvation, and that they intend to lay waste with fire and sword until "we are starved out." This is the policy the cowardly miscreants have proclaimed as their system of warfare upon the defenseless and unprotected people of the South.

☞ 'Kin you tell me, Sambo, de key to de prosperity of de Souf?'

'Key to prosperity of de Souf? Big words, Juno; guess you must hab been eating massa's dickshunary. Golly, I ain't learned nuff to answer dat.

'Well, chile 'tis de dar-key.'

SPRING TO THE SADDLE!

There should be no need of coaxing or even asking our people to take to the saddle in the present crisis before them. The enemy is near them, with the new military tactics of Gen. Starvation Thomas. We have all read his speech and know his programme. If there is yet a "doubting Jonathan" among us, let him read the plan of this valiant Gen. Thomas for plantation stealing and occupation, which we publish this morning. What other course have our people, than to fly to the saddle and strengthen our cavalry now in the field. There is no use of half-way doing things. If we do not mount our horses, the enemy will. He has already done, and is now doing it. For this purpose his pickets are thrown out ahead of the main army for miles. He gathers up the stock and mounts his men. Do we hesitate for a moment what course to pursue?

Spring to the saddle, and help your struggling countrymen, and not wait to "lock the stable door when the horse is gone." To-day there is a meeting called of our citizens for an organization of a force to join Col. Adams. Don't say you have no outfit. Report yourself, first; and then report what you *have* got. One man with a horse, another with saddle and bridle, and another with a gun, would soon mount a rider.

When the invading fiends commence destroying our means of subsistence, it is high time for us to go to them, and not wait for them to come to us. Do we need arousing on this subject, let us read the late news from Arkansas, in to-day's paper! Like our brethren in Missouri, who have toiled early and late to secure Gen. McNeill, the murderer, we should act promptly and energetically to secure him who would rob us of our homes and our life-sustenance.

We have twenty-four counties, including Warren, Lauderdale, &c., below the capital, and it seems passing strange if a force of 100 from each county cannot be obtained. Let us all try!

One hundred men from each of the twenty-four river counties, would furnish 2400 additional cavalry. The late raid has admonished us that all the Southern tier of counties are exposed to the enemy alike. Then attend the meeting this morning, and do your duty—your whole duty.

Dr.---Adams County Semi-Annual Account from Oct., 1862, to April, 1863, In Account with John B. Dicks, Treasurer. Cr.

To Disbursements as pr. Vouchers No. 1, to 138 inclusive:	
For Roads and Bridges,	$ 9,077 00
" Merchandize and other expenses, Poor House,	1,530 03
" Mrs. Ann Carr, maintainance as a pauper.	50 60
" R. Walker's bill of articles for Court House,	37 00
" Services Dr. J. C. Brandon, physician to poor,	70 00
" " Members Board of Police,	167 55
" " Clerk of Board of Police,	147 33
" " Judge of Probates, 6 mo. to Jan. 7, '63,	1,000 00
" " of Jurors in Circuit Court,	97 80
" " of Constables in State cases,	42 00
" " of Magistrates in State Cases,	58 65
" " of Coroner and others in inquests,	57 50
" " of Officers of Courts,	150 45
" " of County Treasurer to date,	802 58
Expenses moving Records of county,	29 00
C. B. Churchill & Co., work done for county,	252 00
Courier Office, printing for the county,	46 00
For support of soldiers' families, 6 months,	15,545 00
" Donation to Volunteer Aid Association,	8,000 00
" Commiss., collect'g money from State Treas.	50 77
" Stationery for the Courts,	85 95
" Expenses soldiers to the army,	10 00
" Canceled currency, Warrants of county,	16 00
To Balance in Treasury,	2,406 40
E. & O. E.	
	$39,729 01

1863.	By receipts into the Treasury, viz:	
Oct. 29.	By balance per report this day	$ 9,006 69
Dec. 31.	372 Cur. Warrants $10 each, $3,720 00; 385 " " $5 " 1,925 00	—5,645 00
" 31, 1863.	By Military Relief fund from State Treas. per act of the Legislature, approved, Dec. 16, 1861.	1,753 79
Feb. 21.	By cash from O. Metcalfe, sheriff, partial payment of Taxes of 1862,	10,000 00
Mch. 25.	" from O. Metcalfe, sheriff, partial payment of Taxes of 1862,	10,000 00
Apr. 15.	By Cash Military Relief fund from State Treas., per act of Legislature, approved, Jan. 3, 1863,	3,323 53
		$39,729 01
April 27, 1863.	By bal. in Treas. brought down,	$2,406 01

In addition to his Semi-Annual report the Treasurer appends the following:

Outstanding unpaid Warrants of the county due and not due and on General account, to date,		$23,139 25
Currency Warrants, denomination, $1, $2, $3, $5 and $10, issued by Board of Police, amounting to,	$40,208 00	
Less Cancelled,	149 00	—$40,059 00
Total Warrants unredeemed,		$63,198 25
The County has expended for military purposes, from April, 1861, to date, viz:		
Donations to military companies,		$11,950 00
Paid for the support of soldiers families,		42,785 00
Volunteer Aid Association, Adams County,		27,000 00
Total expended for military purposes,		$81,735 00

All of which is respectfully submitted for examination and approval by the Board of Police, of the county

JOHN B. DICKS, Treasurer of Adams County.

*Natchez, April 29th, 1863 my7-d1w1

The Day After the Fight at Charleston.

We copy the following from the New York Times' account of the recent engagement at Charleston:

CHARLESTON BAR, April 8, 1863.

When the Nantucket arrived off Charleston bar this morning, from her snug anchorage at Stone inlet, the vessels of the blockading fleet were rolling uneasily at their anchors, and the entire line of bar, for thirteen miles, was a wide streak of angry foam. The fleet of iron-clads remained in the position they had taken at the close of yesterday's contest, near the upper end of Morris' island, still within range of the guns of Fort Sumter and the Cummings' point batteries, while the navy tug Daffodil was busily communicating, first with one vessel and then another, as if conveying instructions from Admiral Dupont respecting further operations. Neither the fleet nor the forts seemed willing to renew the fight, and all day long silence was preserved, excepting by a battery at the lower end of Morris' island, that sent an occasional shell in the direction of a spreading cloud of smoke that rose from the woods of Folly island, where our soldiers were encamped.

As soon as the sea moderated sufficiently for a small boat to be lowered, I started upon a tour of inquiry and observation, from which I ascertained the following facts:

The Keokuk sunk a few minutes after eight o'clock A. M. All night her crew worked faithfully to keep her afloat, and succeeded pretty well until about daylight. The wind at that time rose, causing a heavy swell, and as the vessel wallowed, the water streamed in at the many shot-holes in her hull, first through those on one side, and then through those on the other, gradually gaining over the ability of the pumps to discharge it. As the vessel settled, the water found additional and still increasing means of entrance by the total submergence of other shot-holes, and finally it poured in with such a volume as to preclude all hopes of keeping the vessel afloat. Surgeon Geo. D. Slocum, who had been unremitting in his attention to the wounded as they lay on the berth deck, was first to discover the imminent peril of the vessel, and hastily ordering the removal of his charge, informed Captain Rhind, who was suffering from a severe wound in the knee that confined him to his cabin, of the condition of affairs. A very slight inspection was sufficient for Captain Rhind to understand that there was not a moment to spare, and he told the crew to look out for their personal safety. Fortunately the tug Daffodil was within hail, and coming closer, the work of trans-shipment commenced in small boats. First the wounded were removed, Surgeon Slocum himself carrying the insensible body of poor Mackintosh, an acting ensign, whose skull had been fractured by a fragment of iron, and in fifteen minutes, the last man having barely time to step from her deck, the ill-fated Keokuk gave a few lurches and disappeared.

Very little in the way of personal effects was saved by either officers or men; and it was providential, considering the hurried manner in which the vessel was abandoned, that no lives were lost. At low tide the top of the turrets, the flag staff and rim of the smoke stack may be seen, just rising out of the water, and we are confident, that the rebels are aware of the disaster. Already they are busy in what appears to us to be the construction of a battery on the Morris island shore, within two miles of the spot where the vessel went down, intending, most likely, to annoy us, if an effort should be made to raise her or destroy her with a torpedo.

THE CASUALTIES OF THE FIGHT.

There were only fourteen persons wounded, and not one but might have escaped injury had ordinary precautions been adopted to prevent the flying of bolt heads. The sufferers were attached to the Keokuk and Nahant, and these were the only vessels, I am told, that had not been provided on the inside of the turrets and pilot-houses with a screen of boiler iron, standing a few inches from the walls, and having the intervening space filled with compressed hemp or some other elastic substance.

INJURIES TO THE VESSELS.

Inqiring among the iron-clads, I learned that each of them were struck on an average thirty times. To a great extent the rebels used projectiles of British manufacture, many of them being the steel bolts, polished like knife-blades, that are thrown from Whitworth guns. [The Richmond Whig says the Keokuk was sunk by guns of Confederate manufacture.—ED. COURIER.] These wicked tokens of the manner in which the English nation sticks to its professions of neutrality, as seen buried in the turrets of the Keokuk, were productive of anything but an increase of good will and respect toward a Government that has proved false to honor, and recreant to humanity, by its attitude in the pending struggle. Wherever a shot struck, it left upon the armor of the vessel a well defined scar, in the shape of a long groove upon the deck, or a deep indentation in the turret or hull. But these are glorious disfigurements, that militate very little against the strength of the vessel. The Nahant, the Passaic and the Nantucket are the only monitors disabled, but the damage will be made good within a few days. Chief Engineer Stimers, of the navy, is here with a corps of mechanics, and the proper tools and material to enter at once upon the repairs.

But though the monitors might go again to-morrow into the fight, I am just informed that the attack will not be renewed.

There is no question that Sumter was badly battered from the effects of our fire. It is thought that three of the casements on the north-east face were knocked into one, and on the south-east face the masonry, for a large space on the outer side, is very much altered in appearance from what it was before the engagement. We think that these light-hued blotches are significant of the commencement of a breach.

RETURN OF THE LAND FORCE.

STONO RIVER, S. C., April 11....The military portion of the expedition against Charleston, under Major-General Hunter, after experiencing a disappointment which you can well imagine, is now under orders to return to Hilton Head, and as these troops have been eagerly waiting to perform the secondary part of taking possession of such batteries as the navy might reduce, it would be unjust to close the record of the unsuccessful movement without giving them a word of commendation. That they have done nothing independent of the navy, is neither the fault of their leader nor of themselves. Contemptibly few in number—so few that it would be difficult to convince the rebels of the real weakness of the force, and yet comprising every available man that could be withdrawn from other points in the department—it would have been sheer madness in Gen. Hunter to attempt independently even the most insignificant work in this direction. The division of General Ferry, was, however, placed on shore, and for the last week has occupied Cole's and Folly islands. Extended reconnoissances have been made, that show the enemy has left nothing undone to strengthen his defenses against the approach of a land force, having this point as its base. On James island, where disaster overtook us last summer, there are now three strong parallels of earthworks commanding the entire length of Morris island, and precluding the possibility of landing a force there. John's island, also, on the southern bank of the Stono, bristles with the bayonets of at least ten thousand men, and the approach by way of Waphoo creek is also strongly fortified.

The Arago is to stop off the bar for dispatches at one o'clock. I send this by her. To-morrow our troops will be at Hilton Head, and we shall await anxiously the next move, whatever it may be.

The iron-clads are still in the position they took after Tuesday's fight. The Ironsides cannot get across the bar until the next season of high tides, and the monitors until then, will keep her company. About next Thursday, probably, they will return to Port Royal from the scene of their discomfiture.

News has just come to us from Port Royal that the army gunboat George Washington, was destroyed by the rebels on Tuesday morning last, near Port Royal ferry. The steamer was under command of Lieut. Blanding, of the 3d Rhode Island regiment, who had been sent by Gen. Saxton to reconnoiter along the Coosa river, which seperates Port Royal Island from the main land. At a point opposite Brickyard creek the rebels opened a heavy fire upon the gunboat from a number of field batteries, and their second shot entered her magazine, which exploded destroying the after part of the vessel, wounding three men and killing outright privates Wm. Greenholsh and John Fallon. A white flag was hoisted, but the rebels continued firing, and the remaining soldiers and crew were forced to jump overboard. Most of them managed to escape to Port Royal Island by floundering a mile through a marsh, but two were killed and several wounded as they made the attempt. The names of the sufferers I could not learn. There were eight taken to the hospital at Hilton Head. The boat burned to the waters edge. H. J. W.

REPULSED AGAIN.

Three of the enemy's gunboats, attempted to make their way to Alexandria, La., on Tuesday last, but were badly repulsed at Gordon's Bluff. The red river fleet, at that point, gave them battle. All three of their boats were badly used; but the Albatross was completely riddled.

Two of the enemy's pilots were killed, and several men killed and wounded in the action. No loss on the Confederate side. Our boats were not injured.

The enemy "skedaddled" down stream, to the Mississippi river, again. This we learn by telegraph, from a substantial source at Bayou Sara.

ROW BETWEEN YANKEE OFFICERS.

Killing of Lieut. Col. Kimball by General Corcoran.

The homicide of Lieut. Col. Kimball, by Gen. Corcoran, at Suffolk, has occasioned much feeling, and demands are made for a rigid investigation. Corcoran has found it necessary to publish a letter of which the following is a copy:

H'DQR'S 1ST DIVISION, 7TH ARMY CORPS, Suffolk, Va., April 17, 1863.

To Col. Hawkins, Commanding Ninth Regiment, N. Y. V., (Hawkins Zouaves,)

Colonel—To prevent any misapprehension, I send you a brief statement in relation to the sad affair of Sunday morning, which resulted, I regret to say, in the death of Lieut. Col. Kimball.

At about 2¾ o'clock, A. M., I left my headquarters, and proceeded along the main road towards the front lines, for the purpose of having the troops under arms at 3 o'clock, in obedience to an order from the Major General Commanding. When I arrived opposite the hospital of my brigade, an officer, whose rank I could not recognize (the night being very dark) and whom I judged to be such only from the fact of his having a sword, rushed out in front of me, and ordered a halt. Halting, I asked if it was Doctor Heath, (one of the Surgeons of the Irish Legion,) and was answered by another order to halt, with the additional remark, "it is none of your —— business; I want the countersign." Perceiving it was not the Doctor, I requested to know the object of his halting me, and his name, rank and authority, but could not obtain any other reply than that it was none of —— —— business. I repeated the question several times, and received similar answers, with the exception that the countersign was not demanded more than once, and he added, "You cannot pass here." I expostulated with him upon such conduct, and told him to remember that he was not on duty, and had no right to be there and stop me from proceeding, and that he must let me pass. I asked him if he knew whom he was talking to, and then gave him my name and rank, telling him also that I was going to the front under orders, and even my business there; but it was of no avail; he answered, "I do not care a —— —— who you are." I again told him that I should pass, and warned him several times to get out of my way, and attempted to proceed.

He thereupon put himself in a determined attitude to prevent my progress, and brandishing his sword in one hand, and having his other on his pistol, (as I then supposed,) made a movement toward me with the evident design of using them, and at the same time stated, "I will be —— —— if I shall." It was at this point that I used my weapon. It seemed that the more I endeavored to persuade, the more obstinate he became. Nothing but the consideration that my life was in danger, which I had every reason to fear, and the duty that was incumbent upon me at that particular time, when an attack upon our lines was apprhended, would have justified me in my own mind in taking the measure I then did. As a soldier of long service, I am convinced that you will recognize the necessity and lawfulness of the act, however much you may regret that it was caused by one of your number, and none does more than myself, for although I had never before seen Colonel Kimball, that I am aware of, I had learned to respect him for his gallantry in several engagements of the present war. It was not until after the occurrence that I learned who it was; but had he been my best friend, I cannot see how it could have resulted otherwise, from the part he acted on that occasion. With no authority to demand the countersign, I would have been derelict in my duty had I yielded to his demand. His refusal to give me his name, or rank, or any information about him, or upon what authority (if any) he assumed to act—the fact being, as you are well aware, that he had none—especially as his request was couched in the terms I have stated, and the enemy was immediately in our front, called upon me to act with more than ordinary precaution in revealing the countersign, and not unless to one entitled to it.

But, besides this, the personal violence I had just cause to fear gave me an undoubted right to protect myself against it.

I intended to have sent this statement before, but my duties for the past few days have prevented it, and I have now been obliged to make it hurriedly, hoping thereby to correct any erroneous impressions that may have been made, and to prevent them in the future.

I will only be too glad to have an official investigation of the matter at any time.

I am, Colonel, your obedient servant,

MICHAEL CORCORAN, Brig. General.

PORK AND BEEF PACKING IN CHICAGO. The packing of Beef shows a decline, but in Pork she is distancing all competitors, and shows an increase over the figures of last season which is really greater than the whole of the business transacted in Cincinnati a year ago, and nearly equal to the latest annual returns of that city. The whole number of Hogs packed in Chicago the past season is *nine hundred and seventy thousand two hundred and sixty-four.*

MISCELLANEOUS ITEMS.

[From the "Chicago Times."]

☞ An Ohio editor recently had a fight. In the scrimmage the combatants had even chances, but in telling the story the editor had the advantage. Here is his description:

"He soon found himself in the wrong pew. We cleaned him out most effectually—fearfully establishing our ability and willingness to chastise insolence and ruffianism whenever and wherever offered. The poor, idiotic creature bellowed like a dying calf as we administered to his *backbone* some well-applied strokes. As soon as he could extricate himself from our grasp, he made a grand rush for the door—out of it he went like a 'streak of greased lightning,' locking it behind him to avoid pursuit, and leaving his hat on the field."

☞ A Detroit paper says: "A gentleman, with a young lady under his charge, was coming East on the afternoon train on the Detroit and Milwaukee Railroad yesterday, when the conductor called for the tickets. The ticket for the young lady was examined, by the careful official, and the dimensions of the girl deliberately surveyed. He shook his head, and expressed the conviction that she was altogether too large to pass on a half-fare ticket. As the train had been detained along the road, from several accidents, and was some hours behind time, the gentleman dryly replied that the girl had grown considerably during the long period she had been on the cars, and he had better say nothing more about the matter. The joke was appreciated, and no further questions were asked."

☞ Extempore praying is a queer thing sometimes. It allows the supplicant very wide license of speech, which occasionally produces whimsical consequences. For example, the Rev. Mr. Shine, Chaplain of the House of Representatives in the Iowa Legislature, on the opening of a session prayed thus: "Bless Thou the young and growing State of Iowa, her Senators and Representatives, the Governor and State officers! Give us a sound currency, pure water, and undefiled religion!—for Christ's sake! Amen!"

☞ The Atlantic telegraph project is prospering. The New York papers say that over one hundred of the leading mercantile and banking firms of the city have subscribed various sums ranging from £100 to $1,000 sterling, amounting in the aggregate to over two hundred thousand dollars. The utmost confidence in the success of this great undertaking is expressed by our merchants, who are rapidly swelling the subscription list.

☞ The California overland telegraph has paid its original cost back to the stockholders, within the first year, and now makes money so fast that the proprietors are troubled what to do with it.

ROTTEN EGGING. Thaddeus Stevens, while making a speech at Lancaster, Pa., on the 12th inst., had several rotten eggs thrown at him. The parties who committed the deed were not discovered.

Sherrard Clemens was pelted with rotten eggs, recently, while speaking at a meeting in Middlebourne, Tyler county, Va., against the formation of the new State government.

GOING TO AUSTRALIA. Mr. and Mrs. Charles Kean are going to Australia professionally.

☞ It is stated a house is being prepared in Very Cruz for the reception of Gen. Don Antonio Lopez de Santa Anna. From this announcement, we suppose he is about to turn up again, wooden leg and all. It was the French, we believe, who deprived him of his leg when they were at war with Mexico on a former occasion.

☞ The Richmond Examiner speaks of the "steel punch of the Brook gun"—a new Confederate invention,—as having done good execution in the recent fight at Charleston. The sunken Keokuk bears testimony to the efficiency of this projectile.

☞ A rich sporting gent of London has presented Jem Mace, the prize-fighter, with a gold vase worth $2,500 as a token of admiration of his pluck.

Grierson at Enterprise, Miss.—A Yankee Trick.

The Mobile News says: We have learned from a reliable source, a gentleman on the spot, of the circumstances of the appearance and retreat of the Yankees from the vicinity of Enterprise.

The number of the enemy was variously estimated by citizens who fell into their hands from 800 to 1500. They were all mounted. They had evidently one or more experienced guides, and these were believed to be traitors who had been expelled from Enterprise. The Confederate forces had gone up the road to meet the invaders, and when scouts first brought the news that they were making for Enterprise, there were only some 70 soldiers (conscripts) in the place. The commandant of the post, a young man whose name we have not learned, was entreated to send above for reinforcements. He declined, and continued to refuse positively either to telegraph for aid or to allow any one else to telegraph. The citizens held a meeting on the subject, and were about to adopt very strong resolutions to hold the officer to an account if the town was sacked through his obstinacy, when Col. Fleming, superintendent of the Mobile and Ohio Railroad, who was in the place, received a dispatch from Meridian stating that troops under General Loring had started down. The Yankees then had six miles to ride and the troops fourteen miles to travel by railroad. It was a hard race, which the Confederates won by fifteen minutes.

The latter had formed line behind some cotton bags, and had their guns leveled on the Yankees as they swept toward the village within short range and were just about to draw trigger when a flag of truce appeared. The flag came forward and demanded a surrender of the town, and during the parley the Yankees withdrew out of range. A cute Yankee trick or fraud which saved many a saddle from becoming emptied. They received the reply of Gen. Loring two and a half miles from the town. The General at once put himself at the head of his men and started in pursuit of the enemy at double quick. Our informant says that the troops made the six miles of pursuit as fast as the same number of horsemen could have done it. The headquarters and camp of the invaders was at Garlandsville, west of Enterprise. After their retreat from the latter place they broke up their camp and took a westerly course, evidently aiming for the Mississippi river or the Mississippi Gulf coast in the vicinity of Biloxi. When last heard from they had crossed one of the branches of Leaf river and burned the bridge behind them.

From all we can learn, their motions have been too rapid to commit very extensive depredation. Wherever they could mount negroes they carried them off. Many escaped and returned to their homes. The Yankees said they did not expect to do much more fighting, their policy being to make raids and starve us out—in other words to pluder and steal.

'SUFFER LITTLE CHILDREN AND FORBID THEM NOT.' 'There was a little cherub-faced boy, of four years old, who attended a Sabbath school, and was taught a text of Scripture—that was the method used with those little ones at that time.

His mother was a widow; and, as she sat with her children at table one day, this little fellow said,

'Ma, ma, why don't you pray?'

His mother tried to turn him off, and bid him eat his dinner. Again he asked, 'Ma, ma, why don't you pray?' At length she replied, 'I can't.' 'Well, I can,' he said. His mother answered, 'Then pray.' The dear little one put together his hands, shut his eyes, and said:

'I thank thee, O Father, Lord of heaven and earth, that thou hast hid these things from the wise and prudent, and hast revealed them unto babes, even so, Father, for so it seemed good in thy sight.'

The mother's heart was touched by the Holy Spirit, through the utterance of her child, while his little all he presented to his heavenly Father. She was soon after converted, and led her child in prayer and pleasant religious duties.

Episcopal Recorder.

A SERENADE MISAPPROPRIATED. An amusing incident occurred at one of the large hotels in Washington the other evening. Certain officers of the Signal Corps, hugely smitten with the charms of Miss Julia Mortimer, a *danseuse* at Canterbury Hall, went to give vent to their pentup feelings through the martial strains of the "Signal Corps Band." Unfortunately mistaking the window of the fair one's apartment, they happened to come under that of Senator Lane, of Indiana, who naturally enough, taking the compliment to himself, appeared before the assembled crowd and responded in such a speech as he is capable of. The discovery of the mistake discomfited the parties exceedingly.

SEXTON'S REPORT.

Deaths within the City of Natchez, for the week ending **May 5, 1863.**

NONE! NONE!!

A true copy from Sexton's report.

C. F. MERRICK, City Clerk.

Friday, May 8th, 1863.

☞ At the special election in Natchez, to fill the unexpired term of the late Mayor Hunter, WM. DIX, Esq., was elected to the Mayorality, and to fill vacancy in the Council, E. CRAIG, Esq., was chosen as a Selectman.

Gen. McNeil Taken.

It will be recollected that this brute, in Missouri, last summer, ordered shot, *ten* Confederate soldiers, because *one* man was missing in the town—and he was afterwards found to be away on business, and returned after the execution. The brute was repudiated by honorable Federal officers for the act, but was bolstered up and kept in power by Lincoln. He was a good subject for the Government to work with in Missouri, and his acts were approved and countenanced by the partisans of the Administration. We are now glad to learn from undoubted authority, that he has been overtaken by Quentrall and his cavalry, and ere this has met with his reward.

A Portrait of the Croaker.

The Monroe (La.) Register, of the 5th, gives the following very accurate portrait of a Croaker, which will reflect the character of the same "animal" in all parts of the world:

"Let not our people be moved by the idle reports and rumors of the croakers. When reverses happen to us, they leave their holes and seem jubilant, but let victories be announced and they are either silent or doubt everything."

From Missouri.

Our intelligence to-day, by private sources, is direct from Missouri and of a cheering nature. In addition to the taking of McNeill, by Quantrell the Confederate partizan, we also learn that Pilot Knob has been taken by the Missouri Confederates, and that our troops are having affairs pretty much their own way in that State.

A Confederate officer, who has been out as a scout in Missouri during this Spring, also informs us that the Union families have all left that State for other settlements, either in Oregon or in the East. The State is now in the hands of the Confederates, with the exception of points garrisoned by Lincoln soldiers and St. Louis.

He thinks matters are in good trim for a speedy reduction of all the few Lincoln strongholds and a redemption of the whole State. The spirit of the people, on the line of the Missouri river, has met with a great change and they are more hopeful of Confederate success.

SPRING TO THE SADDLE!

There should be no need of coaxing or even asking our people to take to the saddle in the present crisis before them. The enemy is near them, with the new military tactics of Gen. Starvation Thomas. We have all read his speech and know his programme. If there is yet a "doubting Jonathan" among us, let him read the plan of this valiant Gen. Thomas for plantation stealing and occupation, which we publish this morning. What other course have our people, than to fly to the saddle and strengthen our cavalry now in the field. There is no use of half-way doing things. If we do not mount our horses, the enemy will. He has already done, and is now doing it. For this purpose his pickets are thrown out ahead of the main army for miles. He gathers up the stock and mounts his men. Do we hesitate for a moment what course to pursue?

Spring to the saddle, and help your struggling countrymen, and not wait to "lock the stable door when the horse is gone." To-day there is a meeting called of our citizens for an organization of a force to join Col. Adams. Don't say you have no outfit. Report yourself, first; and then report what you *have* got. One man with a horse, another with saddle and bridle, and another with a gun, would soon mount a rider.

When the invading fiends commence destroying our means of subsistence, it is high time for us to go to them, and not wait for them to come to us. Do we need arousing on this subject, let us read the late news from Arkansas, in to-day's paper! Like our brethren in Missouri, who have toiled early and late to secure Gen. McNeill, the murderer, we should act promptly and energetically to secure him who would rob us of our homes and our life-sustenance.

We have twenty-four counties, including Warren, Lauderdale, &c., below the capital, and it seems passing strange if a force of 100 from each county cannot be obtained. Let us all try!

One hundred men from each of the twenty-four river counties, would furnish 2400 additional cavalry. The late raid has admonished us that all the Southern tier of counties are exposed to the enemy alike. Then attend the meeting this morning, and do your duty—your whole duty.

☞ Julius Aroni, Esq., editor of the St. Joseph Gazette, was taken prisoner by the Federals last Sunday, and we learn he is now in their camp on this side of the river.

TELEGRAPHIC.

Glorious News from Red River.

Kirby Smith Whips Banks.

The following information was brought by our prisoners from New Orleans, who were exchanged yesterday at Port Hudson. It is also confirmed by men from the opposite side of the Mississippi river:

Kirby Smith, with 10,000 raw troops, has whipped Banks badly and drove him to Washington, La.

Port Hudson through a Yankee Telescope.

[Correspondence of the Brooklyn Eagle.]

IN CAMP NEAR BATON ROUGE, March 30.

On our arrival at Baton Rouge on the 17th of December last, with some 15,000 troops there was a better prospect of reducing Port Hudson than there is to-day with 60,000. The Confederates were completely surprised at the time of our landing, and we were then only 18 miles from Port Hudson, and with all their available force the enemy could not have mustered 6,000 men, with their defenses not by any means formidable. But from the moment we went into camp his energies were increased in every department of the army. Several thousand fresh laborers were set to work upon the batteries and trenches at Port Hudson, while reinforcements, ammunition, and supplies of provisions commenced pouring into the Confederate camp, so that by the middle of February the place was completely shut up and surrounded by treble breastworks and a trench eight feet deep, which can be filled from the rivers in three hours, their batteries on the river mounted the heaviest and best guns in the country, not forgetting quite a number of 100-pound rifled cannon. Their army increased to at least 80,000 men in and about Port Hudson, commanded by some of the best officers in the Confederate army, with as much to eat as we have, and as good a stomach to fight; and during all this time the enemy has kept some three or four thousand troops in the vicinity of our army at Baton Rouge, to draw our attention from what he deems of most importance—and I must say that thus far he has been quite successful. Besides, his spies are walking through our camps daily, gathering up what information they choose. Our means of knowing the defenses at Port Hudson is derived from the most reliable sources, from deserted Union men who have been pressed into the Confederate army, contrabands and from personal observation, so far as supplies and reinforcements are concerned. In point of strength Port Hudson is second to none on the river, not excepting Vicksburg, and, to hold it, the Confederates are prepared to make any sacrifice.

DEATH OF TWO PRINTERS. We learn that A. O. Russell, of Cincinnati, (well known to Memphis printers as Pick Russell,) and George Ridenower, who also worked in the printing offices of Memphis before the war, were both killed at Murfreesboro'. They were unfortunately on the wrong side.—*Mississippian.*

Weekly Courier

BY PONY EXPRESS.

Reported Expressly for the Courier.

Federals at Louisa Court House.

RICHMOND, May 2.... About one thousand Yankees entered Louisa Court House, at 3 o'clock this A. M., and have since that time, torn up the Central railroad track to the distance of four miles in this direction. Trains all safe, also all army stores, the latter having been removed some days. This raid will prove fruitless to the enemy, except injuring the tract, which can be repaired in a short time.

One letter from Hamilton's Crossing states that a conflict occurred yesterday, P. M., in the vicinity of Chancellorville, between a brigade of Gen. Lee's army and an advance column of Yankees, and resulting in driving back the latter several miles, with serious loss. Confederate loss estimated at about one hundred. Nothing definite relative to operations. All accounts from above are of a cheering character as to the spirit of our army and position of our main forces.

Railroad Collision.

WILMINGTON, N. C., May 2.... A collision of trains occurred at Halifax station, on the Wilmington and Weldon railroad, this morning killing one soldier and wounding three or four.

Good News from Gen. Forrest.

CHATTANOOGA, May 2.... A special dispatch to the Rebel, dated Decatur, May 2d, says Forrest is doing glorious work. He has been fighting since Thursday last. In a fight thirty miles from here, he captured a large number of prisoners. He has seventeen hundred Yankees cut off in the mountain south of here, and it is thought they will be captured.

Starnes', Biffle's and Edmonston's regiments, engaged and retook our cannon from the enemy.

The Yankees have evacuated Tuscumbia. Our loss is seven killed and nineteen wounded.

Adjournment of Congress.

RICHMOND, May 2..... Congress adjourned, *sine die* last night, passing the act relative to congressional election in Tennessee.

All bills, the passage of which have heretofore been reported by telegraph, have been approved and signed by the President, except the acts relative to staff officers, and the conscription of Marylanders, which was not signed.

There is nothing definite from Fredericksburg this morning. The weather is fine.

Latest from Virginia, the North and England.

RICHMOND, May 3.... No trains has arrived from above to-day. Nothing definite has yet been received with regard to to-day's operations in Spotsylvania. We have further news, but the Secretary of War is too closely engaged, and no other person authorized to approve dispatches is accessible.

RICHMOND, May 3,... Northern dates to the 1st are received. A rebel force has appeared at Morgantown, Va., near the Pennsylvania line, creating a general scare all along the border from Harper's Ferry to Wheeling.

A rumor was current in Nashville that Breckinridge had killed Bragg, on account of the latter advising the execution of Kentucky soldiers.

General Curtis telegraphs that the rebels routed at Cape Girardeau, on the 26th, were pressed by McNeal and Van Dover.

The steamship Anglo-Saxon, which left Liverpool on the 16th, with three hundred and sixty passengers and a crew of eighty-four men, was wrecked near Cape Race, on the 27th, in a dense fog. Only seventy-three passengers escaped.

The Baltimore and Ohio railroad has been torn up twelve miles west of Oakland, at which place the bridge is burned.

RICHMOND, May 3... The Yankee cavalry which made the raid on the Central railroad proceeded to Fredericksburg railroad to-day, and took up the track at Ashland. It is also reported that an ambulance train on the way to Richmond, was captured by the Yankees. No train has arrived from above to-day. No late accounts received of operations in Spotsylvania. The latest reports indicate that the Yankee cavalry have crossed the Central railroad in the vicinity of Hanover court house, North-east of Ashland.

The Wheeling papers of Thursday state that both Uniontown and Falmouth were in the possession of the rebels.

The specie in the Wheeling banks has been sent to Pittsburg.

Col. Ellett has destroyed every grist mill and distillery along the Tennessee river. The towns of Hamburg and Eastport were also destroyed.

The Europa, from Liverpool the 18th, arrived at Halifax. The London Times is very bitter on the letter of Adams to Admiral Dupont, exempting certain ships for Mexico, from England, carrying supplies and arms for Mexico.

The Daily News says there can be no doubt but that the irritation between England and the United States is gradually increasing.

Sir G. C. Lewis, British Secretary of War, is dead.

The Liverpool cotton market is buoyant, prices one fourth to one half pence better. Stock 359,000 bales, including 47,000 American.

FROM VIRGINIA!

FIGHTING AT FREDERICKSBURG!!

FIVE THOUSAND PRISONERS TAKEN!

RICHMOND, May 4.... Some excitement was occasioned this morning by a report brought by couriers that the Yankee cavalry who were at Ashland yesterday, are at Hungary station this morning, eight miles from the city. Their force is estimated at from two thousand to three thousand. It is expected they will be dispersed or captured.

A dispatch from Gordonsville, received at the War Department, says that Dr. Woodfolk, who left Chancellorsville at three o'clock, P. M., yesterday, reports that the fight is still going on at Fredericksburg. General Jackson occupied all the fords, except Ellis' and has taken five thousand prisoners, and more were coming in. Our men are in fine condition.

There is none of the enemy at Culpeper.

FROM VICKSBURG.

A YANKEE BOAT and two TUGS BURNED

VICKSBURG, May 4.... A Yankee craft with two barges in tow, laden with medical stores and rations for the army below, attempted to run our batteries last night. It was set on fire by our shells, and the three burned to the water's edge. The crew was taken off by our skiffs and brought here.

The Tax Law.

The following is a summary of the leading provisions of the tax law:

A tax of 8 per cent. upon the value of all naval stores, salts, wines and spirituous liquors, tobacco, manufactured or unmanufactured, cotton, wool, flour, sugar, molasses, syrup, rice and other agricultural products, held or owned on the 1st of July next, and not necessary for family consumption, for the unexpired portion of the year 1863.

A tax of one per cent. upon all money, bank notes or other currency on hand or on deposit on the 1st of July next, and on the value of all credits on which the interest has not been paid.

On trade and business the taxes are as follows:

Bankers five hundred dollars.

Auctioneers fifty dollars, and two and a half per cent. on the gross amount of sales.

Wholesale dealers in liquors two hundred dollars, and five per cent. on the gross amount of sales.

Retail dealers in liquors one hundred dollars, and ten per cent. on gross amount of sales.

Retail dealers in merchandize fifty dollars, and two and a half per cent.

Pawnbrokers two hundred dollars.

Distillers two hundred dollars and twenty per cent.

Brewers one hundred dollars, and two and a half per cent.

Hotels, inns, taverns and eating houses, first class, five hundred dollars; second class, three hundred dollars; third class, two hundred dollars; fourth class, one hundred dollars; fifth class, thirty dollars. Every place where food or refreshments are sold, and every boarding house where there are six boarders or more, is deemed an eating house under this act.

Money and exchange brokers, two hund[illegible] dollars.

Commercial brokers or commission merchants, two hundred dollars and two and a half per cent.

Tobacconists, fifty dollars, and two and a half per cent.

Theatres, five hundred dollars; each circus, one hundred dollars, and a tax of ten dollars for each exhibition; jugglers and other shows, fifty dollars.

Bowling alleys and billiard rooms, forty dollars for each alley or billiard table.

Livery stable keepers, fifty dollars.

Cattle brokers, fifty dollars, and two and a half per cent.

Butchers and bakers, fifty dollars, and one per cent.

Peddlars, fifty dollars, and two and a half per. cent.

Apothecaries, fifty dollars, and two and a half per cent.

Photographers the same.

Lawyers, physicians, surgeons and dentists, fifty dollars.

Confectioners, fifty dollars, and two and a half per cent.

Every person is required to return a list of the gross amount of sales from the passage of the act to the 30th of June, 1863, and every three months thereafter.

On salaries, a tax of one per cent. when not exceeding fifteen hundred dollars, and two per cent. upon an excess over that amount.

On all incomes over five hundred and not exceeding fifteen hundred dollars, a tax of five per cent.; over fifteen hundred and less than three thousand dollars, five per cent for the first fifteen hundred dollars, and ten per cent on the excess; over three thousand and less than five thousand dollars, ten per cent.; over five thousand and less than ten thousand dollars, twelve and a half per cent.; over ten thousand dollars, fifteen per cent.; subject to deductions for repairs to buildings, cost of labor, raw material, on incomes for rent, for mining and manufacturing, &c.

All joint stock companies and corporations shall pay one-tenth of the dividend and reserved fund authority. If the annual earnings shall give a profit of more than ten and less than twenty per cent. on capital stock, one-eighth to be paid; if more than twenty per cent. one-sixth. The tax to be collected on the 1st of January next and of each year thereafter.

A tax of ten per cent. on all profits in 1863, by the purchase and sale of flour, corn, bacon, pork, oats, hay, rice, salt, iron, or the manufactures of iron, sugar, molasses made of cane, butter, woolen cloths, shoes, boots, blankets and cotton cloths.

Each farmer, after reserving for his own use 50 bushels sweet and 50 bushels Irish potatoes, 100 bushels corn or 50 bushels wheat produced this year, shall pay and deliver to the Confederate Government one-tenth of the grain, potatoes, forage, sugar, molasses, cotton, wool and tobacco produced. After reserving 20 bushels peas or beans he shall deliver one-tenth thereof.

Every farmer, planter or grazier, one-tenth of the hogs slaughtered by him, in cured bacon, at the rate of 60 pounds of bacon to 100 pounds of pork; one per cent. upon the value of all neat cattle, hosses, mules, not used in cultivation, and asses, to be paid by the owners of the same; beeves sold, to be taxed as income.

Income and moneys of hospitals, churches, asylums, schools and colleges, are exempt from tax.

[From the Columbus Times.]

Dupont's Report.

The Keokuk (confound the luck)
Has sunk! yet fate is civil—
And strange to tell, while we caught h—l,
The rebels caught the *Devil!*

Saturday, May 9th, 1863.

Affairs on the River.

To persons fond of sensation reports and terrible stories, affairs on the Mississippi river, in the neighborhood of Port Gibson, do not appear in the least satisfactory. For all such, we have very little to cheer the morbid appetite.

For a man who has kept his eye singly on final results—who has been willing to calmly and patiently await the issue—we know of much that is encouraging. Movements of troops and combinations of our forces in this Department, we cannot publish; but we have every evidence to show that they are such as must eventually crown our efforts with a glorious victory. It is one thing to defend, and another thing to attack. The enemy is now disclosing some of his plans of attack, and we feel certain that our Generals will not only repulse him, but do as the brave army in Virginia has done, whip him to his heart's content. It may be said of us that we are over-sanguine of success—it cannot be helped. The occasion and the work before them, will bring forth the best energies of the Confederates. They have their homes to fight for, while the enemy are only in the field for revenge and plunder. Does any one doubt who must finally prove victorious? The God of the just is with our brethren on the Rappahannock; surely he will not forsake their kinsmen beside the deep water of the old Mississippi!

Remember the old adage, that "the darkest hour is just before day." Our brothers in Virginia have nobly raised the dark curtain in the East; the morning light broke upon our Forrest, in Georgia; and its genial rays will soon spread itself along the hills and valleys of the South-West. Here, in this Mississippi Valley, let us take courage from the light already broken, and resolve that the work shall be finished. But say we *will do it*, and the day is ours! The heaven above us will look bright again. Home—injured and despoiled by the enemy—will again be made happy!

Does any one doubt of our success on the Mississippi river? We remind them of the words of Cardinal d'Richelieu to his Page—"NEVER SAY FAIL."

Go to work and do all you can.

☞ We return our thanks to Major W. L. Chalmers, for full files of late papers, from Richmond, April 29th, and from all the cities in his line of travel. "May his shadow never become less," and a mint of happiness accompany him after war's troubles are over.

☞ With the exception of an excellent letter from our correspondent "VENTER," we have surrendered our columns to the news of the day and the hour of going to press. There is much of interest and importance.

☞ A rumor was afloat in Jackson last Tuesday, that Gen. Beauregard had been ordered to the Vicksburg fortification. If the rumor has any foundation, it will give Gen. Pemberton a chance in the field.

☞ We cordially thank our friends, Messrs. L'Hommidieu and Baker, for their promptness in furnishing a synopsis of the late Virginia news. Although we had previously received the news in full, we felt the no less grateful for their kind remembrance. It is to be hoped that their telegraphic operations will not be long cut off.

☞ We are glad to state that the free market, for soldiers' families, will be opened again next Tuesday. It does our heart good to make the announcement. See the card elsewhere.

From the Texas Coast.

A friend has furnished us with the following items. The first is from the New Orleans Era of the 24th of April:

"An attempted reconnoissance of Sabine Pass was made on the 18th of April, by two Federal gunboats, the New London and Cayuga. Capt. McDermit, of the Cayuga, was killed and his boat taken. The other boat was riddled by balls and miraculously escaped."

The Delta concludes an editorial notice of the funeral as follows:

"The Union fleet on the Texas coast since the 18th of January, has suffered severely in ships and officers, and to any nation less persevering than ours, the reverses and disasters in that quarter, would induce discouragement."

At Brownsville, Texas, molasses is selling at fifty cents per gallon. Shoes, of good make, at eighteen dollars per dozen. Hats at the same price. Domestics, twenty cents per yard. Two hundred barrels of flour sold at auction at ten dollars and fifty cents per barrel.

Fighting "Joe Hooker," &c.

The last seen and heard of "fighting Joe Hooker," he was making tall strides across his pontoons, on the Rappahannock.

The Appeal says of affairs in this department: "The destruction at Vicksburg night before last, of a boat and two barges, loaded with commissary and medical stores for Grant's army, will to some extent probably retard his movements. He will find it very difficult to provision a large army in his present position.

"We learn from good authority that the advance of Grant's forces yesterday, were at Willow Springs, some ten miles this side of Port Gibson, and two miles north of bayou Pere. Their movement is in the direction of the Vicksburg road, at Edwards' depot. Our generals are prepared to meet them.

"A wounded soldier, of Bowen's army, who was in the engagement last Friday, represents it as one of the severest and most hotly contested of the war. He passed through the battle of Shiloh, but says that it did not near equal in fierceness the engagement at Grand Gulf.

"Grant fought twenty thousand troops and had six thousand in reserve, while Gen. Bowen did not fight more than six thousand. This soldier thinks the Federal loss was at least from four to five times as great as ours. As to the exact number of losses on either side he was not informed."

We have nothing new from the Northeastern part of the State.

A CARD.

It gives me pleasure, in behalf of the managers of the Natchez Orphan Asylum, to acknowledge the receipt, through Lieut. Wilkins of the English Battery, of the sum of one hundred and eighty-eight dollars, contributed by that company, for the support of the orphans under their care. For the liberal contribution we would return our thanks and pray that Heaven's richest blessings rest upon them and that the God of the orphan may protect them in the hour of danger.

MARY CARRADINE,
Sec. N. O. A.

May 9th, 1863.

Associated Press Dispatches.

BY PONY EXPRESS.

Signal Triumph in Virginia!

GEN. PAXTON KILLED.

Jackson, Heath, and Hill, Wounded.

Brilliant Success of Forrest

His Enthusiastic Reception at Rome, Ga.

RICHMOND, May 4.... The following dispatch has been received, dated Milford, May 3d:

PRESIDENT DAVIS—Yesterday, Gen. Jackson penetrated to the rear of the enemy, and drove him from all his positions, from the wilderness to within one mile of Chancellorville. He was engaged at the same time in front by two of Longstreet's divisions. This morning the battle was resumed. He was dislodged from all his positions around Chancellorville, and driven back toward the Rappahannock, over which he is now retreating. Many prisoners were taken, and the enemy's loss in killed and wounded is large.

We have again to thank Almighty God for a great victory.

I regret to state that Gen. Paxton is killed, General Jackson severely, Gens. Heath and A. P. Hill, slightly wounded.

(Signed.) R. E. LEE, Commancing.

CHATTANOOGA, May 4.... The Federal cavalry that penetrated Georgia, was met by armed citizens near Rome, and held in check. Forrest is in their rear, and will probably capture all of them. All is quiet from the front. It is reported that Burnside is hurrying to Nashville. A heavy hail storm here last night.

CHATTANOOGA, May 4.... A heavy force of Federals crossed the Cumberland at Celina, near the Kentucky line, under cover of artillery, and attacked Col. Hamilton's force, which being inferior in numbers, and without artillery, fell back to the hills where they made a stand, and after several hours of hard fighting repulsed the enemy, killing ten and wounding nineteen. Our loss, two killed and three wounded. The Yankees in retreating through Celina, burned it. Col. Hamilton pursued them to Tompkinsville, Ky., and destroyed most of that town.

CHATTANOOGA, May 4.... A special to the Rebel, dated Rome, Georgia, May 4, via Dalton, says: Gen. Forrest accomplished the most brilliant feat of the war yesterday. He captured Colonel Straits' entire command, consisting of sixteen hundred infantry. He pursued them from Courtland, Alabama, and captured them two miles from the Georgia line, and 20 miles from Rome, fighting incessantly for five days and nights.

Gen. Forrest's loss is ten men killed and forty wounded.

His reception in Rome, yesterday, was a triumphant ovation. A salute of twenty guns was fired, and thousands of ladies welcomed him with smiles and tears of gratitude.

ATLANTA, May 4.... Passengers by the State road report that the enemy, sixteen hundred in number, and four hundred contrabands, were captured at Cassville, Georgia. The Federal loss is fifty killed, and our loss ten killed.

A special from Colonel Lee at Etowah, confirms the above.

ATLANTA, May 4.... Reporters and correspondents desiring to extend the connections of the press association, and gentlemen having experience as reporters or correspondents for newspapers, may contribute to their own and the general advantage, by sending me by mail information of their previous experience, recent residence, customs, terms for business, and whether short-hand writers or not.

J. S. THRASHER, Superintendent.

[Special to the Memphis Appeal.]

Latest from the North.

MOVEMENT ON THE COAST.

French Success in Mexico.

SENATOBIA, May 5.... The Cincinnati Commercial of the 29th says, the reported raid throughout Virginia, had reached Washington, Pennsylvania, and a deputation from Uniontown had arrived at Pittsburg, soliciting arms.

A dispatch from New York says, the editor of the Atlanta Confederacy had been arrested at Port Royal.

Advices have been received that troops are being conveyed to Folly Inlet, and Cole and Kianah Islands. North Edisto is being strongly occupied. They were also entrenching on Folly Inlet. Five monitors were at Edisto and two at Port Royal filled with shot and shell. The utmost activity prevails. The troops were suffering in health from the warm weather.

Allen A. Hall, of Nashville, has been appointed minster to Bolivia.

The French occupy one-third of Puebla. Forts Guadaloupe and Loretta, commanding the town, were held by the Mexicans. The French lost five hundred killed, but their ultimate success is undoubted.

The Anglo-Saxon has been wrecked, and two hundred and thirty-seven lives lost.

[Special to the Memphis Appeal.]

Additional from the North.

SENATOBIA, May 5.... The Federals have burned twelve houses at Byhalia, Miss. They camped last night at Quinn's Mills, seven miles from Byhalia, and there are signs of their establishing a permanent camp there.

They made a raid on Holly Springs, on Sunday last. Capt. Mitchell, with five men, ambushed them when they went out, and killed Col. Jenkins, capturing his horse and papers.

The Times of the 1st has a letter from Millikens' Bend, of the 24th. It states that Grants' whole army had been ordered to move with six days rations. Also, that four out of six transports that attempted to pass the batteries at Vicksburg, were sunk. The rebel firing was reported terrific.

A dispatch from Cairo, dated the 30th ult., states that the Marine Brigade had returned to Fort McHenry. Major White's Texans attacked the brigade, killing two, when the men disembarked and followed White. The latter is reported to have been killed.

Ellet destroyed Eastport, Hamburg, and every mill on the Tennessee river.

The Paris *Moniteur* says the growing hostility in the United States towards England, is exciting uneasiness in London, and that the last Washington dispatches were tending to increase the irritation.

A Washington dispatch dated the 30th says: Four *corps de arme* crossed the Rappahannock by ten o'clock, yesterday.

Associated Press Dispatches.

From Vicksburg.

VICKSBURG, May 5.... The enemy and all his transports have disappeared above. Two rams made a reconnoissance as far as the canal, this evening. No further demonstrations are reported on the Big Black. All other news contraband.

Latest from Virginia—Gen. Jackson loses an Arm.

RICHMOND, May 5.... No official dispatches were received last night or this morning from Gen. Lee's headquarters, but private telegrams represent our victory complete.

Gen. Jackson's left arm was skillfully amputated below the shoulder, by Dr. McGuin, of Winchester. The General was removed to his country house about fifteen miles distant from the battle-field, and is doing well.

Direct railroad communication with our army is not yet established. The guide of the raiders was captured yesterday, at Thurstall's station, on the York river railroad, when a skirmish occurred between the Yankees and a few Confederate infantry.

Yankee Raiders Arrested.

TULLAHOMA, May 4.... Forrest, after five days hard marching, without provisions or forage, captured on the 3d the enemy—sixteen hundred strong—near Rome, Georgia, with the same number of Enfield rifles, horses and side arms.

☞ The return of Mr. Spurgeon to his post, as clerk of this office, will enable us to be more prompt in collections. It is only by this method of doing business, that we are enabled to pay extravagant prices for paper, and keep pace with the current daily news. Our patrons will therefore see the importance of fully complying with our terms.

"Letter from "Venter."

Military Speculation—Agriculture—Transportation, &c., &c.

CLINTON, LA., April 28, 1863.

MR. J. M. BALDWIN:

Dear Sir:—Being at a loss for someting to do, after having "finished" my last "Courier" for the third time, I have determined to write you a letter, but times are so very dull, that I do not expect to see it in the columns of your paper.

I know you will be surprised when you receive my letter from this place, but the only explanation I can give for the fact, is, that I am here,—not with a twenty days furlough in my hand, to proudly show it to the guards who are on every corner, (I wish I had,) nor a peculiarly folded sheet of paper in two envelopes, to shake at the guard, and say, "I am on most important private Government business. Where's the officer of the Guard?" which embarrasses the good natured sentry, who has not lived in a school house all his life;—but in the discharge of the regular duties of the Department to which I am attached, with a small piece of inferior "French" paper in my most convenient pocket, bearing a few lines which enable me to pass the guards, when I wish to; and as my duties have called me at times a few miles in the country, I will endeavor to inform you of the prospect for crops; and having employed my spare time in looking around, will also attempt to acquaint you with what I have seen.

In military affairs we have nothing fresh; and even rumor has exhausted itself. There is still a considerable Yankee force at Baton Rouge, and a few vessels of the lower fleet in sight at Port Hudson. Our pickets are stationed in sight of Baton Rouge, and the Yanks do not venture outside of the city, unless to desert, which a great many are doing. I have been on duty here, since the first of the present month, and have seen twenty-three deserters in that time, independent of a considerable number who were brought by railroad from Port Hudson. One party numbered seventeen. Several members of the Port Hudson Signal Corps, who were captured and taken to New Orleans, a few weeks ago, have been paroled, and are now here. They represent most articles very cheap in that city, and purchased fine boots at twelve dollars, shoes at six dollars, and hats at five dollars, paying for all articles in Confederate money at fifty per cent. discount.

On yesterday, Lieut. Wilkins with a guard of twelve of the "English Battery" left here for Jackson, Miss., in charge of nineteen Yanks,—fifteen prisoners and four deserters. The prisoners were nine months' men from Maine; they are very bitter against the South, and think the rebellion will be crushed by the expiration of their term. Two of them having attempted to escape, it was thought prudent to introduce them to the "bracelets." Another of the prisoners is a sailor who was on the "Mississippi," and had his foot and ankle so badly mutilated by a splinter, that it had to be amputated. His statement is, that the Mississippi was fired by hot shot from one of our batteries; that her crew numbered over three hundred, not more than fifty or sixty of whom escaped. He was wounded after getting on shore, and after his foot was amputated, was left on the levee. Among the deserters is a young Kentuckian, seventeen years of age, who was at college in Connecticut, and was drafted.

As said before, military affairs are uninteresting, and was it not for the continual sight of gold lace and wounded soldiers hobbling around on crutches, one would almost forget that a war exists. Every man child, and negro is a speculator, and there is sale for any article from a peck of "goobers" to a condemned mule, for, as everybody says, "*prices are sure to advance*;" and even the commissioned officers of the Government are mixed in, though the "regulations" forbid it, and claim the time of such persons as belonging to the Government, they engage in speculation, can wait on the customer, whether he be a soldier wanting tobacco, or an officer desiring to purchase "Habana," and many of them, I presume, are better posted in the prices of sugar, tobacco, molasses, &c., &c., than they are in regard to movements in Middle Tennessee or Louisiana. Here anything is cheap that can be bought for less than ten dollars, whether it be a palmetto hat or a half pint of shoe pegs, and to inform you of what chance a soldier has to "live and let live," I will add the following, which are the prices asked for the articles mentioned: Molasses, $100 per bbl.; sugar at wholesale, 50 cts. per lb.; tobacco $5 per lb.; corn meal, $3 per bush.; sweet potatoes, $4 per bush.; Butter, $1 50 per lb.; and "goobers" 50 cts. per glass.

On the roads from Port Hudson to Clinton, I notice a few places entirely deserted, but on most plantations large crops of corn, potatoes, &c., &c., are planted, and there is a good prospect of an abundant yield. Very little cotton has been planted, while many planters have every foot of land in corn, &c. More land is in cultivation this year in this parish than any previous year. On the roads to camp Moore, Osyka and Tangipaho, the crops, particularly corn, look extremely well. The weather has been extremely warm lately, with frequent rains.

A few days ago, a wagon train consisting of about thirty teams, arrived here all loaded with rice for the army.

Considerable speculation has been carried on in soldiers' transportation tickets, buyers expecting to receive five or six dollars from the government, but the officer detailed on duty to pay off these tickets, is only allowed to pay the Government mileage, which is ten cents per mile, and which reduces their value to three dollars and thirty cents. I presume the effect of this will be that the soldier will have to pay two or three dollars more than heretofore.

In these hard times of fast surgeons, fast boarding houses and fast everything, 'tis pleasant to meet up with something that will remind one of the good old times when fifty cents was half a dollar, and when extortion was not the "ruling passion." "Venter" was reminded of this during a few hours ride on the C. & P. H. Railroad, and mentally declared that *that* road was more in keeping with the times referred to, than anything he had met with since the war commenced. Of that

Latest from Virginia—Gen. Jackson loses an Arm.

RICHMOND, May 5.... No official dispatches were received last night or this morning from Gen. Lee's headquarters, but private telegrams represent our victory complete.

Gen. Jackson's left arm was skillfully amputated below the shoulder, by Dr. McGuin, of Winchester. The General was removed to his country house about fifteen miles distant from the battle-field, and is doing well.

Direct railroad communication with our army is not yet established. The guide of the raiders was captured yesterday, at Thurstall's station, on the York river railroad, when a skirmish occurred between the Yankees and a few Confederate infantry.

The Appeal's informant had heard nothing of the capture of the 31st Louisiana regiment, as has been announced.

Our forces were all crossing the Big Black, and the enemy were also crossing. It was thought an engagement could not be postponed longer than to-day—(the 7th)—or to-morrow.

OH! THE VIDDERS. The Georgia Legislature has passed a bill relieving Mrs. M. A. F. Sneed, of Floyd county, from the pains of bigamy. Her husband deserted from Capt. Hargrove's company while at Jackson, Miss., about four months ago, and she was informed that he was dead, which has proved since to be incorrect. In the meantime she married another man.

☞ The Cincinnati Commercial quotes the following paragraph as having appeared in Medary's Crisis, of April 1st:

"If we white citizens of the North cannot maintain our Government, let it go to h—ll before we call on the slaves of our country to maintain us."

as your Chief Magistrate to appeal to your patriotism for united effort in expelling our enemies from the soil of Mississippi. It can and must be done. Let no man capable of bearing arms withhold from his State his services in repelling the invasion. Duty, interest, our common safety demand every sacrifice, necessary for the protection of our homes, our honor, liberty itself.

The exalted position, won in her name upon every battle-field where Mississippi's sons have unfurled her proud banner, and hurled defiance in the face of overwhelming numbers, forbids that her honor, the chivalry of her people, the glory of her daring deeds on foreign fields should be tarnished and her streaming battle flag dragged to the dust by barbarian hordes on her own soil.

Awake, then—arouse, Mississippians—young and old—from your fertile plains, your beautiful towns and cities, your once quiet and happy but now desecrated homes, come and join your brothers in arms, your sons and neighbors who are now bearing their bosoms to the storm of battle at your very doors and in defense of all you hold dear.

Meet in every county with your arms; organize companies of not less than twenty, (under the late act of Congress,) forward your muster rolls to this office, and you will be received into the service with all the protection and rights belonging to other soldiers in the field.

Ammunition will be furnished you, and every aid in my power extended to you for your security and efficiency.

Fathers, brothers—Mississippians! while your sons and kindred are bravely fighting your battles on other fields and shedding new luster on your name, the burning disgrace of successful invasion of their homes, of insult and injury to their wives, mothers and sisters, of rapine and ruin, with God's help and by your assistance shall never be written while a Mississippian lives to feel in his proud heart the scorching degradation.

Every moment's inaction and delay but strengthens your enemy and weakens your brothers in arms. Let every man, then, make it his business, laying all else aside, to assist in organizing as many companies as can be raised in each county and report immediately to this office for orders. By this course you will enable our arms in a short time to repel the invader, secure the safety of your homes, and shed imperishable honor on your cause. You will not be without assistances. Let no man forego the proud distinction of being one of his country's defenders, or hereafter wear the disgraceful badge of the dastardly traitor who refused to defend his home and his country.

JOHN J. PETTUS,
Governor of Mississippi.

FROM TENNESSEE. The Winchester Bulletin of the 28th says: The affair at McMinnville presents details of some interest. Gen. John H. Morgan, was in town when the enemy entered, and was halted by a Yankee, but instead of halting, he shot the invader and then escaped. A report is prevalent that the Yankees captured Mrs. General Morgan. Such is not true. They got her wardrobe, however, which consisted of a large supply of valuable apparel.

Major Dick McCann, was captured and severely wounded, the Yankees having sabered him in several places, and left him as a dead man. But the Major came too, and made his escape. The Yankees did not know McCann.

OUR REVISED TERMS.

DAILY COURIER.

FOR THE YEAR,.......(in advance).........	$15,00	Cents.
" SIX MONTHS,.........do..............	8,00	"
" ONE MONTH,.........do...............	1,50	"
EXTRA DAILY PAPERS, at the Clerk's counter or to News Venders, (in advance,)	10	"
TELEGRAPHIC EXTRAS, (except to News Venders,)..................	10	"

WEEKLY COURIER.

WEEKLY COURIER,....(in advance,)...... $5,00 Cents.

ADVERTISING.

PER SQUARE,..(10 lines or less—one time,)..$2,00 Cents.
CONTINUANCE,..(one square, each day,).... 1,00 "

☞ ALL PAPERS NOT PAID FOR IN ADVANCE, will be stopped the day their time expires. The non-receipt of money, will, in all cases, be considered a refusal to continue the subscription.

☞ No other contracts than the above will be made. ☜ All previous contracts will be faithfully complied with, as far as paid for, both in regard to Subscriptions and Advertising.

Business Management.

☞ All letters relating to the Editorial Department of the Natchez Daily and Weekly Courier, should be addressed to "JOHN M. BALDWIN, NATCHEZ, Miss."

☞ R. M. SPURGEON is Clerk of the Courier Office, and is authorized to collect and receipt for all monies due the establishment, as also, to do all other business pertaining to his department.

BOOK, PAMPHLET, AND JOB WORK,
OF EVERY DESCRIPTION,
Printed on as liberal terms as the war times will admit,
At the Natchez Daily Courier Office.
NATCHEZ, Miss., April 27, 1863.

Tuesday, May 12th, 1863.

☞ Lieut. R. W. Williams, Jr., of Florida, will please accept our thanks for a Jackson Appeal of the 8th. Peter Grant, Esq., of our own city, is also remembered for a similar favor. Both are duly appreciated.

☞ Our patrons are asked to read our terms carefully. The pressure of expenses upon our office, forces a strict adherence to the rules there set forth. Punctuality is the life of all business; more especially newspaper publishing at the present time.

☞ The force, according to Northern official accounts, which Gen. Lee has just whipped, numbered 159,238. Lincoln, Mrs. Lincoln, Prince Bob, and Fighting Joe Hooker, reviewed it, and they and the N. Y. Herald declared it the best appointed army in the world! What can these dignitaries say of it now, since it has been completely routed by Gen. Lee's small army? A review of these same forces since the battle, might at least afford food for reflection to all of the ruling genius' about Washington City. The Herald gave a sarcastic account of the review before the battle; will it favor its readers with a review since the fight? It would prove interesting.

☞ We were pleased to meet in our city, last Saturday, Col. O'Bannan, Chief Q. M. of Trans-Mississippi Department, and Major Samuel Bard, of the same Department, both making their way to the headquarters of Gen. Kirby Smith.

☞ The Mississippi river has fallen full seven feet at this point, and is still receding fast. The banks, on the opposite shore, are showing themselves very plainly—much to our gratification, and doubtless sorely displeasing to the enemy.

☞ The Concert of the Relief Minstrels, last Friday night, was largely attended, and the performances gave general satisfaction. Where our people expected but little, they were happily disappointed, and received much that gave them a rare evening's entertainment. While the war has been progressing, our young men who are maturing for the active duties of the camp, have not been idle with their intellectual and musical attainments. The harvest for the poor of the city, on Friday evening, was also rich. Another Concert, at some future day, would prove acceptable and advantageous.

☞ You that have not already, and can do so, should join the cavalry company at once. Our State wants her full force in the field this very moment. A day's delay may prove our ruin.

☞ A steam-tug is said to have passed Natchez Sunday night. We did not see the craft, but hear it so reported. It was apparently in a desperate hurry. What screw is there loose above?

☞ The Mississippi river, at this city, still continues to float on its surface, many articles that are valuable, and some that are of no possible account. Pork, flour and whiskey, by the barrel, and cotton by the bale, were secured on Saturday by our fleet of naval skiffs. A dead Yankee floated past on Sunday morning, but the naval fishermen looked upon it as worthless, and did not bring it to. We differ with our naval officers in this affair. In our estimation, while the Yankees invade our State, one dead one is worth a dozen alive, with arms in their hands.

☞ The reports we have received since Saturday, and publish elsewhere, are encouraging from every point except Alexandria, La. Even from that section of country, there is nothing to make us despond or give up hope. A few days occupation of that town, by gunboats, will not pay the Federals any great per centage as Red river recedes. Gen. Smith will yet have the gunboats in an uncomfortable trap, or we are no prophet.

☞ The professions and practises of the Federalists with their troops, are truly disgusting to any one with a spark of honor remaining. They enlisted three hundred thousand nine-months soldiers, with the express understanding with every one of them, that they were to bring up the rear of the army and do garrison duty, only. What is the result of this pledge? Why, at the late battles on the Rappahannock, these short-termed soldiers were forced to lead the front! This the prisoners all say. It matters very little to us who done the hard fighting, when they all received a severe whipping; but we cannot refrain from contrasting their professions with their practises. We'll wager any amount, that "Fighting Joe Hooker" don't get *nary man of them to reenlist*. Mark that! A Yankee, like everybody else, deceived the first time, it is the fault of others; but if cheated a second time in the same snap, it is his own fault, and he ought to bear the brunt of battle. Human nature is the same this world over, and "Fighting Joe" will soon find it out to a moral certainty.

☞ A Yankee paper says that Gen. Grant's daily expenses for the single item of chartering steamboats are $40,000 a day.

The Battle at Port Gibson.

[From the Vicksburg Whig.]

In our issue of Saturday we had but a limited account of the previous day's fight on Bayou Pierre in front of Port Gibson. Since then we have been able to gather some additional particulars of the engagement in which Gen. Bowen and command acted so gallantly. Our force in the fight was composed of Tracey's, Green's Baldwin's, and the old brigade of Gen. Bowen. At about twelve o'clock on Thursday night the skirmishing commenced several miles from Port Gibson. Gen. Green conducting it on our side, with his Missourians. Early on Friday morning the enemy appeared in force, when the other brigades, (except Baldwin's) moved up and took part in the fray. After several hours fighting the enemy fell back a short distance, when they were heavily reinforced and came at us again, sending torrents of iron ball and lead into our ranks. Our men maintained their position for hours, perfectly mowing down the Yankee columns, but were finally forced to fall back on account of the greatly superior force brought against them, and the scarcity of ammunition. The trains, wounded soldiers who could walk, and everything connected with the government, was ordered across Bayou Pierre bridge, preparatory to evacuating Port Gibson. Late in the afternoon everything was across when the railroad and suspension bridges between Grand Gulf and Port Gibson, the wire suspension and wooden bridges on the Port Gibson and Vicksburg road, spanning big and little Bayou Pierres, and the two bridges on the Rocky Spring road, one near and the other at Grindstone Ford, nine miles from Port Gibson, were burned by our troops. The enemy immediately moved forward and advanced into Port Gibson, when the most of our troops moved around to the Grand Gulf road.

All day Saturday there was some little skirmishing going on, but the Yankees seemed to be making preparations for crossing where the bridges were burned. Saturday night they commenced landing troops above Bayou Pierre, some few miles below Grand Gulf, when it soon became evident that that place, too, must be abandoned. At 11 o'clock Saturday night an order to this effect was issued by Gen. Bowen, and at 2 o'clock on Sunday morning the guns, five in number, were spiked, the shell placed in the magazines and then blown up, tearing the gun-carriages to atoms and dismounting the guns. The troops moved up the road on Sunday towards Big Black where they still remain, and in which vicinity the Yankees will find an army, when they advance, that will render their campaign in Mississippi as disastrous as that of McClellan in front of Richmond.

We have not been able to ascertain the probable loss on Friday. It was heavy on both sides, and quite a number of our men were taken prisoners. Nearly one whole company (the Yazoo Pickets,) of the 46th Mississippi, were surrounded while skirmishing, and taken. Baldwin's brigade, which arrived in the forenoon, having double-quicked it for miles, suffered considerably. Very few of the wounded, except those who could walk, escaped to Port Gibson. The Virginia battery lost four guns, two disabled and two surrounded and cut off, three caisons, five men killed, eleven wounded and nineteen Missing. The 17th La., Col. Richardson, lost twenty-five men in killed and wounded. Lieut. Parsons, an excellent officer, was killed. Adjutant A. L. McFee, of the 31st Louisiana, is missing. The loss in the regiment is small. Some of the Alabama regiments suffered severely, but we could not learn the loss or names. Col. Garret, of the 20th Alabama, is reported badly wounded, Maj. Pickerman killed, and Col. Hunley severely wounded in the thigh.

Bombardment of Port Hudson.

PORT HUDSON, May 9.... The enemy's lower fleet commenced a bombardment yesterday at 2 P. M., and continued it to 3 P. M., without effect; throwing fifty-four shells. The bombardment was renewed at 11 P. M. The enemy fired slowly and obtained most accurate range, throwing many shells within the lines. He fired one hundred and thirty-four shells and ceased firing at 12 P. M.

Our batteries did not reply.

One man was wounded by a splinter from a rail.

Our batteries and works are uninjured.

The enemy had in the engagement, five mortar boats, sloop-of-war Pensacola and gunboat Essex.

All quiet this morning.]

It is rumored that the enemy is evacuating Baton Rouge, but not reliable.

Associated Press Dispatches.

General Lee's Great Battle!

FURTHER PARTICULARS.

RICHMOND, May 6.... The Dispatch issued an extra this evening, which gives the first details of the battle at Chancellorsville. It's correspondent says, the fight in many respects was one of the bloodiest battles of the war. Our loss was heavy, both in officers and men.

The enemy had thrown up intrenchments and constructed abattis, which after severe fighting was carried by our troops.

Among the prisoners is Brig. Gen. Hays, who commanded a brigade in Couches' corps.

Prisoners represent that there were some forty regiments, mostly foreigners, on the lower end of the line where Gen. Eastby commanded.

There was some hard fighting on Sunday. In the afternoon, Mary's Heights were carried by the enemy and a number of Mississippians captured. Six pieces of the Washington Artillery were taken at the same time.

On Monday morning the fight was renewed, the Heights retaken and the pieces recaptured, with a number of others. Five Yankee batteries are reported to have been captured.

On the up per line, from another source, I learn that about 6000 prisoners, in all, have been captured.

Gen. A. P. Hill has resumed command.

army had moved to Shelbyville, and that Breckinridge's forces were close at hand.

[illegible] from San Francisco report that the French had been driven from Puebla, a distance of seven miles, where they were fortifying.

Burnside repudiates the laws of Kentucky regarding incoming and vagabond negroes.

From the Rappahannock the Times reports that the 11th, 12th, and 15th army corps had crossed at Kelly's ford, and were moving toward Chancellorville, and the 1st, 3d and [illegible] army corps, crossed four miles below Fredericksburg. The wagon train was packed at Bank's ford, and the second division was in the rear of the train, with full facilities for crossing. Hooker's headquarters were in the saddle! But little resistance was offered to the crossing.

A dispatch from New York dated the 1st inst., says: The steamer Ericsson will leave to-day with two of Ericsson's "devils." B.

From Alexandria, La.

Our information this morning, May 11th, from Alexandria, La., is direct and positive. Seven of the enemy's gunboats had compelled the surrender of that town. As our informant was leaving, Federal marines were going ashore to garrison the [illegible]. There was great activity in the Confederate army, and reinforcements arriving. Banks was still reported at Opelousas, if anything making a retrograde movement below.

Jackson News of Saturday Evening, 9th.

The Promised Reinforcements.

We presume it will not be considered contraband to announce, as we do with infinite satisfaction, that the reinforcements promised Gen. Pemberton from Charleston and other points, have commenced arriving, and will continue to arrive from day to day, as fast as the trains can bring them over the roads. This will be cheering news to the country everywhere, and, we trust, will have a tendency to strengthen the nerves, and stimulate the energies of our people.

Let, the efforts of the Confederate Government be speedily and promptly seconded and aided by the State authorities, and our invaders will make but a shabby show toward penetrating the country.

All history proves that undisciplined militia, if endued with a spirit of patriotism, is just as efficient behind breastworks and fortifications as the most veteran troops. Let these, therefore, in full force, be brought out at once to be placed in the rifle pits, while the regular troops take the field. The governor is now bending all his energies to put our city in a successful state of defense, and we earnestly hope the people will not be tardy in coming forward to his assistance. The skies are brightening, and our hearts are lightened as the troops pour in from the east, and we exhort the people from all the counties to rally to the defenses of the capital of their State.—*Appeal, Saturday Evening, May 9.*

Federals Driven From Tupelo.

We learn that Governor Pettus has received a dispatch stating that the Federals had been engaged and driven from Tupelo, by the State and Confederate forces under General Gholson and Colonel Barteau, and that the place was held by our troops. We hope the punishment inflicted upon the enemy has been severe enough to entirely check the advance of the forces reported to be moving South from Corinth.—*Appeal of Saturday Evening, May 9.*

Appalling Marine Disaster.

[From the New York World, April 29.]

The Anglo-Saxon was a fine iron-vessel of 1,764 tons burden, with two decks and five water-tight bulkheads. She was built at Dunbarton, Scotland, in 1855, and was owned by the Canadian Steam Company. This company has been peculiarly unfortunate in the loss of its steamers, the Anglo-Saxon being the fifth which has foundered or been wrecked at sea since its organization.

LOSS OF THE ANGLO-SAXON.

ST. JOHNS, NEWFOUNDLAND, April 29.—The Anglo-Saxon sailed from Liverpool on the 16th, with three hundred and sixty passengers and a ship's crew of eighty-four men. She was wrecked four miles east of Cape Race at noon today, 27th inst., during a dense fog.

Seventy-three persons escaped from the wreck by ropes and spars, and twenty-four more in No. 2 life boat, making a total saved of ninety seven.

Number 4 and 6 boats have not arrived off Cape Race in consequence of the density of the fog, and seven more persons who embarked on a raft are also missing. There is still a heavy sea and dense fog.

The commander is supposed to be among the drowned.

The purser and first and second engineers and doctor are saved, and one cabin passenger, Lieutenant Sampson, of the royal artillery.

Hon. John Young and family are supposed to be in one of the missing boats.

The deck broke up one hour after the ship struck.

Nothing but the mizzen mast is standing.

Several persons clung to the fore rigging till the foremast fell, but no assistance could be rendered them.

PICTOU, N. S., April 23.... The steam tug Dauntless picked up two boats' crews of the Anglo-Saxon, between Cape Ballard and Cape Race, and is returning to this port without landing at Cape Race.

The steamer Bloodhound has gone to Cape Race.

ST. JOHNS, N. F., April 28.... The steamer Dauntless, at 9 A. M. on Tuesday, picked up the boats containing ninety persons. The following is a list of the passengers reported on the Dauntless:

Hon. John Young, lady, seven children and servant; Miss Hopp, Miss Bertram, Mrs. Capt. Stoddart, Mr. Green, mail officer; Mr. Loweiz, Rev. Mr. Eaton, Captain Cassidy, Mrs. Jackson and child, Mrs. Wright, John Martin, James Kirkwood and sister, Mrs. Eliza James, Catharine Cameron, Mary Ann Thomas, Mary Ann Adams, Edward Manus, Thomas Caldwell, Mr. Hart, first officer, Mr. Scott, fourth officer, James Henderson, fourth engineer, Charles Carron, fifth engineer.

The steamer Bloodhound has gone to Cape Race for the people there.

☞ A letter to the Richmond Sentinel from Northwestern Virginia, says that the Yankees expect to lose possession of that portion of the State during the present summer. It seems that the Yankees, in conjunction with the Pierpont dynasty, are buying all the corn, wheat and cattle, leaving only a sufficient supply for the families. The writer thinks they are preparing to evacuate the country, and leave nothing for our army to subsist on.

☞ The steamer Giraffe, now called the R. E. Lee, arrived at Washington last week, with a valuable cargo, on Confederate account.

From New Orleans.

Banks has published an official order in New Orleans, (says the Mississippian) dated 1st May, that all persons in that city, male or female, who have taken out the "enemy certificate," must either take the oath of allegiance to the U. S., or be prepared to go beyond the lines by the 15th inst.

The negroes in New Orleans are much dissatisfied with Yankee freedom. Wherever found without papers, they are arrested and shipped off to the plantations, where they are set to work at two dollars a month, and are shot down at the least show of insubordination. They say they are perfectly willing to be whipped or otherwise corporeally punished, but can't stand being shot at. They would co-operate with any Confederate force which might enter New Orleans so great is their disgust for their Abolition friends.

There are barely 3,500 troops in and about New Orleans. The passess on Lake Ponchartrain are guarded by only 150 men. The oath required to be taken by citizens has been amended so as to be much more stringent. It binds those taking it to submit to any regulations or enactments which may be hereafter adopted by Yankee authorities, doubtless with a view to include the Federal conscription act.

News from up the Road.

About the time that our regular edition went to press, there was some excitement on the streets, which grew to a rumor, that our troops had encountered the enemy at Tupelo and been badly worsted. Judge Brown has politely furnished us with the substance of a dispatch of to-day's date from Okolona, sent in answer to inquiries.

It states that there is no danger at that point; that the enemy at last accounts were at Harrisburg, in Pontotoc county, four miles northwest of Verona. It would seem that Col. Barteau has had a brush with them, as the dispatch says the prisoners that Barteau took, arrived at Okalona last night. This does not look as if he was worsted. It is true he was falling back yesterday, which, however, does not necessarily imply defeat.

Gen. Ruggles left Okalona last night with a Kentucky and an Alabama battalion, and three guns, to support Barteau, and if he does not give a good account of them it will because they prefer running to fighting.

The Yankee prisoners represented their force as being 1200, with pieces of artillery.—*Mobile Evening Telegraph, May 6.*

Latest from Vicksburg.

The Lebanon No 2 left Young's Point on Sunday, and, conquently the latest boat up. On Saturday night two tug boats, each with two barges of hay on either side run the blockade without any damage. In fact not a single gun was fired at them. The rebels have come to the sage conclusion it does not pay to shoot at targets without being able to hit them.—*Memphis Bulletin, April 29.*

The pretty story of the Bulletin is a whole sale manufacture. The adventurers who attempted the passage of our batteries on Sunday night last, will tell a different tale, if they are alive. One thousand bales, at least, of the hay, passed floating in the river at Natchez.

From Europe.

NEW YORK, April 28.—The steamship New York, from Southampton the 18th, has arrived.

ENGLAND. The Virginia, which was launched from Clyde for the Confederates, is reported in the British Channel near the French coast, where she took in her armament, warlike stores, etc., sailing westward immediately. She is described as of great strength, very fast, armed with ten heavy guns and two Whitworth 68 pivot guns.

[Special to the Mississippian.]

RICHMOND, May 8.... We have just received partial details of the fight.

Barkdale's brigade was left at Fredericksburg without support. It was attacked in front by three heavy columns, and whilst fighting desperately was attacked in the rear and flanked by tremendous odds.

The 13th, 17th and 21st, made their escape. The most of the 18th were taken prisoners.

General Posey's brigade made itself famous. I cannot get the names of killed and wounded. I will send further dispatches to-morrow.

DIVINE.

HOME DEFENSE. Several military companies are in course of organization in this city, both of cavalry and infantry. The Governor will arm them as fast as they are reported. Similar organizations are in progress in various parts of the State, as we learn through our exchanges.

In Canton the citizens formed a company the other day, and among the signers was the venerable Judge Thos. B. Monroe, of Kentucky, a fugitive from oppression and injustice, and a temporary resident of Canton, who, at the age of seventy-two years, is still prepared to do or die for his country. Upon his announcement to the meeting that it was his intention to join the company, there was the most enthusiastic applause. Let the work go on. Now's the day and now's the hour.—*Jackson Mississippian, May 9.*

To the Treasurer of the Relief Minstrel Club:

SIR:—The proceeds of your concert, amounting to $480 45 to be appropriated to the relief of the poor of our city, was duly received; in behalf of whom, I tender my grateful acknowledgements.

Z. R. METCALFE,
Treas. Committee of Eight.

May 11, 1863.

To-Day's Notices.

Notice to Planters.

THE GOVERNMENT is prepared to compensate the owners of negroes for labor performed on the fortifications at Port Hudson. Payment is made at Jackson, Louisiana, and those who wish the amount collected, will find a power of attorney for their signature at the office of R. S. Wood, Clerk Probate Court.

The amounts when collected will be left with Messrs. W. A. Britton & Co. A. H. FARRAR, Provost Marshal.
my12-d4:w1

Dr. Holcombe

HAS REMOVED HIS RESIDENCE and office to the house lately occupied by Mr. Geo. K. Smith, next door to Mr. Aldrich's, on Monroe street, near its juncture with Commerce. my1-d3t:w2*

Executor's Notice.

WHEREAS, Letters Testamentary of the last will and Testament of MARY ROWAN, deceased, were granted to the undersigned, at the February Term of the Probate Court of Adams County, Mississippi: Now, all persons having claims against the estate of said testator, are requested to exhibit the same, and have them registered in the manner and within the time prescribed by law, or they will be forever barred.

ALFRED W. ROWAN,
JAMES H. ROWAN,
Executors.

Natchez, April 7, 1863—w6

Administratrix' Notice.

WHEREAS, letters of administration on the estate of ROBERT BRADLEY, deceased, were granted to the undersigned, at the April Term, A. D., 1863, of the Probate Court of Adams county, State of Mississippi. Now, all persons, having claims against the estate of her said intestate, are hereby requested to exhibit the same, and have them registered in the manner, and within the time prescribed by law, or they will be forever barred.

MARY C. BRADLEY,
Admx.

Natchez, May 5, 1863-w6

Sheriff's Sale of Runaway Slave.

IN PERSUANCE of Article 20th, Section 5th, of Revised Code of Mississippi, I will, on MONDAY, the 18th day of May next, proceed to sell a certain runaway slave named HENRY; black color, is about sixty years of age, teeth out in front, about five feet, six inches high, and weighs about one hundred and fifty pounds.

Said slave says he belongs to Mrs. Catherine McGinnis, of Leake County, Miss.; said slave has been confined in jail for the space of six months, and under the article and section mentioned, he will be sold as above stated to the highest bidder for cash.

D. McCORMICK,
Sheriff and Jailor of Jefferson Co., Miss.

April10-wts

SOLDIER'S NEWS-LETTER.

VOL. I.] BRASHEAR CITY, LA., MAY 16, 1863. [NO. 10.

THE SOLDIER'S NEWS-LETTER,

IS PRINTED & PUBLISHED,

At the Office of the Southern Steam-ship Company,

(Up Stairs, near the R. R. Depot,)

By A. W. Eastman, Editor and Proprietor,

AT FIVE CENTS PER SINGLE NUMBER.

LINES IN MEMORY OF

CAPT. JOHN S. CLARK, Co. K, 8TH VT. VOLS.

(EDITORIAL.)

The call of our Country resounded—"To Arms!—
Ye lovers of Freedom, in homes of the brave;
Your Rights are endangered by Treason's alarms—
Then gird ye, O Freemen, your country to save!"

In his Green Mountain home, mid the wind-driven snow,
Brave CLARK heard the call, and was fain to obey;
With patriot zeal his soul was aglow,
As to the far South-land he sped him away.

He well lov'd the scenes that his infancy knew—
The wife and sweet babes that he left in their bow'r,
But he smiled thro' his tears as he bade them adieu,
For Duty's cords drew him with still stronger pow'r.

In the sly ambuscade, while the bullets flew by,
And his garments were torn like corn leaves by the hail,—
GOD shielded his life, and kept him on high
Above the base fear which makes cowards to quail.

A martyr-soul'd hero—though not on the field
Did he yeild up the life that his Maker first gave;
Tho' not with the slain in the battle, concealed,
Yet his corse lies entombed in a patriot's grave.

Fare thee well, brother, thy warfare is ended,—
The hoarse Trump of War shall arouse thee no more;
Where victor-throngs reign, by angels attended,
Thy free soul doth dwell on the gold-stranded shore.

Aye, fare thee well, spirit, now fetterless, free,—
Thou hast gone the blest way that the patriarchs trod;
Though we meet thee not here till the Last Reveille,
We will meet thee up there at the Roll-call of GOD.

Brashear City, La, May 5th, 1863.

THE MISSION OF CIVIL GOVERNMENT.

Mr. Editor: Had I not recognized God as the Appointer of government, I should have accepted the theory which would have excluded me from the army;—But God having appointed human government, and the avenging sword of justice, I accept the citizen's duty, and am here a soldier. To us as soldiers and as citizens, the enquiry what is the mission of civil government, has an importance, which rises in magnitude, as we contemplate the duties devolving on us, in the relations we sustain.

It may not be wise, to controvert the declaration of the Revolutionary fathers, that "governments derive their just powers from the consent of the governed" Yet there may be consent to wrong, even in republics, which even that consent cannot justify. I am of those that hold that the eternal laws cannot be annul'd or set aside for a moment by human enactments. When there is conflict between the two, the human must stand aside. The great law of love (Thou shalt love thy neighbor as thyself), must govern; hence it is evident, the province of the governor is to administer justice, to protect the weak from the oppressions of the strong. Many things will require legislation as long as sin lifts its aggressive head; but it will not be required that legislators shall fuddle their heads about what shall make nations rich primarily. Yet wise legislation, protecting persons and corporations in their persons, properties, and employments, may aid in the accumulation of wealth. Still industry and economy must be relied on to mass whatever store of wealth may be deemed desirable. S.

WHAT ARE THE CONFEDERATES GOING TO DO? With a strong girdle thrown around the principal and central portion of their territory by our armies,—their supplies from Texas, Attakapas, &c., cut off,—Vicksburg and Port Hudson at our mercy,—their internal supplies rapidly becoming exhausted, and already commanding fabulous prices, Gaunt Famine threatening them on the one hand, and powerful armies and fleets on the other,—what can they do? Is not their doom as certain as fate? Is it not vain for them longer to fight against God's decree and the Nation's "manifest destiny"? Why then should they wait until utterly destroyed before they acknowledge the rebellion a failure, themselves wrong, and vanquished, the insulted majesty of the American People vindicated, and that Liberty, Free labor, and Human Rights, are henceforth and forever to be the governing principles in our national policy. Have they not yet learned so much wisdom from the things they have suffered? If not, will they ever learn it?

☞ COL. HENRY WALKER, of the 4th Mass. Regt. who has the appearance of being every inch a gentleman, and, we judge, an able and an efficient officer, is at present in command of this Post.

ally supplied by Uncle Sam, than by the rebel pro- (how are you 'rebel pro'?) ducers themselves.

REMOVAL.—Between the printing of our outside and inside forms, we were under the necessity of removing from our old quarters in the office of the Southern Steam-ship Co.,—to make room on the Dock for the swarming employees of Capt. Dennett in the Quartermaster's department. We can now be found in the (late) Hospital building, above the R. R. Depot, just below the Camp of the 4th Mass., on the Bay shore.

☞ The 'City' here begins to wear quite a brisk, business-like appearance. We have several stores, sutlers' tents, a Post office, three 'Bakeries, one or two Daguerrean saloons, one Tin, and two Barber shops, a Hotel, (renowned in the writings of MACPHERSON as the Great Temple of Wisdom,) a Printing office, and a 'Church-house' with a very high and glorious dome—higher than St. Peter's or St. Paul's, or any other man—and having an audience room as large as "all out of doors"; besides numerous and sundry other 'institutions,' including horses, cattle, sheep, goats, mules, cotton and Contrabands.

NAVAL:—By count yesterday morning, we ascertained that there were twelve steamers, one schooner, two launches, and twenty rafts, in our Port, including one just leaving, and one across the Bay.

☞ THE QUESTION 'What shall be done with the Contrabands?' is losing its knottiness, as the nation loses its naughtiness and as it is more clearly seen what they can do and are doing for us. They are now bringing millions of dollars worth of cotton & sugar, which their own labor has produced, from the swamps, and sly corners where the treacherous rebels had hid them, within reach of our transport steamers, and so of the markets. And shall we act on the 'penny-wise and pound-foolish' plan of neglecting, starving, and abusing these persons, rather than treat them as we should other unfortunate fellow citizens in the same circumstances? God forbid.

THE EDITOR IN LUCK.—About the 8th of January last, while at Gretna, the Editor had the good luck to receive a *very late* foreign exchange paper, as all will bear witness, when we give the date and name of the paper— "THE BAHAMA GAZETTE,"— "NASSAU, N. P., Feb. 17, 1811."— As it was printed some 19 years before we were born, all will percieve that it has been *quite late* in getting around to our office. We propose to print a few extracts from its columns, in our next number, both prose and poetical; and one item which may aid the memory of Ex-President Buchanan, in particular, besides other matters of more or less importance. The most important thing, however, in our estimation, as being *appropos* to the subject of *Negro Conscription*, is an order contained therein, from the British Adjt. of the Post, for all persons liable to military duty, as well slaves as white persons, and free persons of color, to enroll themselves in the new Providence Militia, at once, under the pains and penalties provided by law, in case of refusal. We shall endeavor to give this in our next, in connection with Gen. Banks' order No. 40.

We give notice beforehand of our intention to publish these things, that those who wish for copies of the paper, containing them, may order immediately, and so that we may provide accordingly.

GLORIOUS NEWS!

The late news through rebel sources, of the defeat and capture of the rebel forces under Stonewall Jackson, near Fredericksburg, Va., by the Federal forces under Gen. Hooker, is almost too good to be true, yet we think it admits of but little doubt that Jackson lost an arm—and 18:000, out of 20.000 men, with which he went into the fight, in killed, wounded and prisoners. A few more such blows as Banks and Hooker have dealt the Rebellion lately,—and down it must come with a crash.

P. S. We are glad to learn from the yesterday's Era, that northern dates to the 7th inst. per steamer Creole, mainly confirm the above account, although our loss is said to be very heavy, and at last accounts the decisive battle was still to be fought.

☞ THE Government is making soldiers of the able-bodied Contrabands here and taking measures to employ the 'un-soldierly' men, with the women and children, on Plantations, under the care and oversight of officers detailed for the purpose of seeing that they are properly provided for—so at least we are told.

☞ Incipient measures are being taken here, for the formation of a State "Home Colonization Society" among the colored population, with white persons to assist them in establishing schools, churches, press, &c.,—having the object of securing sufficient land, either by grant or purchase, from the Government to sustain the colony, with such supplies as may be necessary to the full and fair trial of the Free labor system, on a plan which recognizes the Manhood of the black, and his right to the proceeds of his own labor, in his native land, and also to more than an "equal right with a rebel" to enjoy under the protection of the American flag the rights of an American citizen.

Several hundred more Contrabands arrived last evening from 'the upper coasts,' bringing the report that they were fired upon by people all along their line of march, and that some twenty of their number were thus wantonly killed on the way.

Do these murderous and cowardly villains consider that they are whetting the sword of vengeance by such deeds of sheer diabolism?

VOL. 1. NEW ORLEANS, TUESDAY MORNING, MAY 19, 1863. NO. 79.

THE ERA

THE LATEST SOUTHERN NEWS.

Death of Stonewall Jackson CONFIRMED.

CAPTURE OF JACKSON, MISS.

IMPORTANT FROM TENNESSEE.

REPORT OF A GREAT BATTLE

Rosecrans again Driving Bragg.

Lieut. Sullivan, of Co. K, 9th Connecticut, just returned from Pascagoula, where he went in charge of registered enemies, brings some most important and exciting news from the rebel lines. The dogs of war have been let loose all through the South-west, and every report rings with encouragement to the cause of the Union.

The Mobile *Tribune*, of the 15th, a copy of which Lieut. Sullivan read at Pascagoula, announces that Stonewall Jackson, the great rebel leader, died from the effects of amputation of the arm, and has been buried with military honors. The date of his death is not positively remembered, but is thought to have been on the 7th or 8th.

The death of Gen. Jackson has cast a depressing gloom over the hopes of the rebels. The Richmond *Examiner* says his loss could not be replaced by an accession of 50,000 veterans. He was killed (accidentally) by his own men, as described in a dispatch, which we published in our Extra, from Fort Pike.

CAPTURE OF JACKSON, MISSISSIPPI.

Jackson was attacked on the 11th by our forces, and the rebels evacuated the place without firing a gun. It has been reported that it was taken by General Grant, but private letters say that it is occupied by General Sherman with 30,000 men. If the intelligence in these letters is correct, it would indicate that Generals Grant and Sherman are within supporting distance of each other, as the former, at last accounts, was at Raymond, with a portion of his command, marching in the direction of Jackson.

FROM TENNESSEE.

There is every reason to believe that there has been another great fight between Rosecrans and Bragg. The rebels say that Bragg was falling back into North Alabama, with Rosecrans following.

Johnston, it was known, had left the vicinity of Tullahoma, and was marching to attack Gen. Grant. Bragg was left in command, and it is probable that Gen. Rosecrans took advantage of the weakening of the enemy to make a forward movement.

The particulars of the movements in Tennessee are confirmed by dispatches from Mobile.

We hope to be able to obtain a copy of a late Mobile paper in the course of the day, when we shall give the intelligence more in detail.

FORT PIKE, May 17, 1863.

Extracts from the Mobile Register and Advertiser, May 14

The special correspondent of the Richmond *Enquirer*, writing from Fredericksburg, on Wednesday, the 6th, says:

"The battle seems to be over, and from all I can learn a victory has crowned our arms. Our losses are fully 5000, while those of the Yankees are confessed to be fully 25,000, and 30 pieces of artillery.

"We have captured very nearly 8000 prisoners, and have lost about 1000.

[Over 4000 rebel prisoners had arrived in Washington from this battle-field before the Creole sailed.—ED. ERA.]

"We have captured one Brigadier General, and any number of field and staff officers.

"Among the killed on our side is Gen. Paxton, of the Stonewall Brigade. Gen. Nichols was wounded in the leg. Gen. McGowan was wounded slightly. Gen. Hope was wounded in the arm.

"Another correspondent of the same paper says that the number of small arms that will be gathered from the field will not be less than 30,000, while many blankets, overcoats, &c., were also picked up.

"During a pause in the fight, Gen. Jackson and staff, accompanied by Gen. Hill, rode to the front by a narrow and crooked path. His whole force was there, while the enemy were retiring at a gallop. Our men, supposing them to be Yankees, fired, wounding Stonewall Jackson in the left arm, breaking the bones below and above the elbow. A shot also passed through his right hand. He then threw up his hand, signalizing them to stop, as he did not then desire to have the attack recommenced, but the men did not perceive his signal in time.

"One of his couriers and a Captain of his staff were killed at the same time Jackson received his wound.

"His wounds are by no means serious, and he will doubtless be ready again for duty in the course of a month or two.

On the margin of the paper is written "Stonewall Jackson was killed by our own men."

The death of Van Dorn is confirmed.

BY TELEGRAPH FROM JACKSON.

JACKSON, May 15th.

The enemy yesterday advanced a column of 10,000 men upon Raymond, the county-seat of Hinds county, about 15 miles from Jackson and six miles from the Southern Railroad, where Gregg had 45,000 (4500 ?) infantry, a few cavalry and no artillery.

Skirmishing began at 9 o'clock in the morning. The enemy was continually reinforced until 1 o'clock P. M., when he opened battle heavily with artillery and musketry.

Gregg fought two hours with musketry alone, when hearing that the enemy had been reinforced, and that his reinforcements were ready to engage, he retreated slowly and in good order through Raymond.

He made a stand at Mississippi Springs, where he has been reinforced with artillery and infantry.

A very heavy and continuous firing has been heard to-day at Jackson.

In the engagement yesterday, Col. McGaveny, of the Tenth Tennessee, was killed.

Report of Capt. Sumner, Aid-de-Camp of Gen. Stoneman.

Headquarters of the Army of the Potomac, May 7, 1863.—Major General Stoneman's aid-de-camp, Capt. Sumner, is just in. He left his chief this morning, having disarranged all the enemy's railroad communication between this and Richmond, and one party having extended their operations to James river, destroying the canal, etc. Three regiments of his command left to destroy the railroad bridges across the Chickahominy, with instructions to go into Yorktown.

ANOTHER CAVALRY RAID.

Col. Davis Destroying Bridges, etc., on the Jackson Railroad.

CAPTURE OF PRISONERS

Burning of the Bridge over Tangipaho River.

The great Tannery and Shoe Factory Destroyed.

Victory after victory, won by the gallant 19th Army Corps, follows each other so rapidly that the city is kept in a continual ferment. We have to record another daring raid and glorious triumph, that equals in results the late achievement of the Illinois heroes.

On the 12th inst., Gen. Nickerson dispatched the 1st Texas Cavalry, Col. Davis, from their position on the Amite river in the direction of the Jackson Railroad. Striking the railroad near Tickfaw Station, they proceeded, supported by a force of infantry under Cols. Clark and Cowles, who were stationed at Pass Manchac, as far up the road as Camp Moore.

A short distance from Tickfaw they came upon a body of rebels, and a brisk skirmish followed, but the impetuosity of our men was not to be withstood, and the enemy rapidly retreated.

Their loss in this fight was ten men killed, among them Capt. Cochran; and twenty-one privates, twenty horses and sixty muskets captured.

Our loss was but one man killed and three wounded.

Having driven all the enemy from the vicinity, Col. Davis commenced a work of destruction more damaging to the rebels than the capture of all the troops in the State, as they depended on the shoe and other factories for supplying the Vicksburg and Bragg's armies.

Every bridge on the road, as far up as Camp Moore, including the splendid structure that spanned the Tangipaho river, has been burned. Every railroad station, and the car factory near Independence, are in ashes. The latter contained a large number of unfinished gun carriages, a battery wagon and eight cars, which were also destroyed.

Colonel Davis then proceeded to the Confederate shoe factory, tannery, and saw and grist mills, a short distance from Tickfaw, and burned them.

Besides this immense destruction of property, there were captured, during the entire raid, one rebel lieutenant and forty-three enlisted men, who are all out of harm's way in this city.

The inhabitants of the Amite country are rapidly taking the oath of allegiance to the United States, and it seems to be a settled conviction with them that the grand rebellion is "gone up."

These important achievements are the fruits of the expedition recently ordered by Gen. Sherman, commanding the defenses of New Orleans, and in their effects upon the complexion of military affairs in this Department are second to none that have taken place on the east side of the Mississippi river.

Stoneman's Raid.

Washington, May 8.—The following was received at the headquarters of the army this morning:

To Major Gen. Halleck:

Yorktown, Va., May 7.—Col. Kilpatrick, with his regiment, the Harris Light Cavalry, and the rest of the Twelfth Illinois, have just arrived at Gloucester Point, opposite this fort.

They burned the bridges over the Chickahominy, destroyed three large trains of provisions in the rear of Lee's army, drove in the rebel pickets to within two miles of Richmond, and have lost only one lieutenant and thirty men, having captured and paroled over 300 prisoners.

Among the prisoners was an aid of Gen. Winder who was captured with his escort far within the intrenchments outside of Richmond.

This cavalry have marched nearly 200 miles since the 3d of May. They were inside of the fortifications of Richmond on the 4th, burned all the stores at Aylett's Station on the Mattapony on the 5th, destroyed all the ferries over the Pamunky and Mattapony, and a large deport of commissary stores near and above the Rappahannock, and came in here in good condition.

They deserve great credit for what they have done. It is one of the finest feats of the war.

RUFUS KING,
Brigadier General commanding this post.

From Port Royal.

Arrival of the U. S. Steamer Circassian—Nothing of Importance from Charleston.

The U. S. steamer Circassian, W. B. Eaton, commanding, arrived at this port this morning. Since leaving New York she has visited every station in the Gulf Squadron. At Sabine Pass received on board Commodore Foster, C. S. N., commanding the rebel gunboats there, that captured the U. S. ship Morning Light. He was captured by the U. S. steamer New London.

No news of importance from Charleston. The iron-clads were all ready for another attack so their Commanders said.

The following are the officers of the Circassian:

Commander, W. B. Eaton; Executive Officer, Geo. Ferris; Chief Engineer, S. N. Hartwell; Surgeon, S. R. Young; Paymaster, Geo. Snowden.

At Apalachicola, received on board a lot of prisoners captured from C. S. steamship Chattahoochie, by our expedition from Somerset and Port Royal.

State Convention.

Wheeling, Va., May 8.—The Convention met at Parkersburg on the 5th to nominate officers for the new State of West Virginia, and adjourned yesterday, having made the following nominations:

For Governor, A. J. Boreman, of Parkersburg; Secretary of State, J. E. Bower, of Middletown; Treasurer, Campbell Tarr, of Brooke county; Auditor, Samuel Crane, of Wheeling; Judges, R. L. Berkshire, of Morgantown; William A. Harrison, of Clarksburg, and James H. Brown, of Kanawha; Attorney General, A. B. Caldwell, of Wheeling.

Defeat of the Canadian Ministry.

Montreal, Friday, May 8, 1863.—The Ministry were defeated last night on a vote of want of confidence, by a majority of five. The dissolution of Parliament and a general election, it is expected, will be ordered.

The Losses of the Enemy at Chancellorsville.

Washington, May 8, 1863.—It is stated that General Dix telegraphs from Fortress Monroe that on an extra of the Richmond *Dispatch*, of the 6th inst., found on a prisoner, was a pencil note, endorsed by a rebel surgeon in one of the hospitals to his wife, stating that the rebel loss was 18,000 in the late battles.

TWO DAYS LATER FROM THE NORTH.

More Details of the Great Battle

THE REBEL LOSS [illegible]

Success of Gen. Stoneman's Cavalry Expedition.

Preparations to Renew the Battle.

By the arrival of the steamship George Cromwell this morning, we have received New York papers of the 8th and 9th, two days later than brought by the Creole. The following, from the Situation articles in the *Herald*, will give the reader a fair idea of the present condition of affairs in the Army of the Potomac and at other points, being compiled from the latest correspondence, dispatches, etc., from the *Herald* of the 8th:

The news of Gen. Hooker's retrograde movement to the north side of the Rappahannock, after sustaining a loss of ten thousand men or more, during a contest of three days, created an intense excitement in the city yesterday. Our latest news reports the army safe at Falmouth. The artillery, ammunition and trains were brought over without loss. The river had risen ten feet, rendering a pursuit by Gen. Lee next to impossible. The failure of Gen Sedgwick to support General Hooker, owing to the overwhelming force brought against him by the rebels at Fredericksburg—the absence of Gen. Stoneman's splendid cavalry force, which was employed on an expedition that now proves to have been quite successful, and the reinforcement of Lee by Longstreet, and the delay in bringing up Heintzelman's reserves, all combined to render Gen. Hooker's position on the other side of the Rappahannock no longer tenable, and his withdrawal became a painful necessity. He crossed by the United States and Banks's Fords in a terrific rain storm, the sudden rising of the waters rendering the use of the pontoon bridges exceedingly precarious.

The success of General Stoneman's expedition is admitted by the rebels themselves. His forces were divided into three squadrons—one commanded by himself and the others by Generals Averill and Buford. All performed their work gallantly by cutting the railroad communications between Lee's army and Richmond and destroying all the bridges to within five miles of the rebel capital.

One party of the cavalry went to Louisa Courthouse, cutting up the railroad there. Another pushed on to Columbia and Goochland, on the James river, breaking the canal at the former point and capturing rebel stores at the latter. A portion of the force are said to have actually got to within a mile and a quarter of Richmond. General Stoneman then pushed on for the Peninsula, and it was reported in Washington yesterday that he had got as far as Williamsburg.

The loss of the enemy in the three days' fights is estimated at fully twenty thousand men, so that their loss is double that of our side.

The heavy rain storm which visited Gen. Hooker's army on its retreat, extended not only to Washington, where it was very severe, but all along the railroad line from here to the capital. The streams and rivers are swollen and overflowing their banks; the country is flooded, and the track of the New Jersey Railroad, at Trenton, is covered to the depth of two feet for over a hundred yards. The trains yesterday passed safely through however.

We learn from the Wheeling *Intelligencer*, of Wednesday, that the rebels are still at Weston, in West Virginia, and that they are seven thousand strong, the forces of Jones and Imboden having united. There is another rebel column under Gen. Wilder, numbering about four thousand, hovering in the vicinity of Summerville, along the New river. This latter force is acting in conjunction with Jenkins, and threatens Charlestown.

By dispatches from Cairo yesterday, we ascertain that our troops positively captured Grand Gulf, taking 500 prisoners, and all the guns, ammunition and stores. Guerrilla forces, at Greenville, Miss., destroyed the transport Minnesota on Sunday; but the gunboats scattered the enemy soon after. Our gunboats, at Grand Gulf stood fire for eight hours, and then passed safely on, with transports and troops.

Our news from Arkansas is interesting. Colonel Phillips encountered and defeated the rebels at Weber Falls on the 24th ult., capturing all their camp equipage.

From the Herald of the 9th.

The official report of Admiral Porter, recording his great success in the capture of Grand Gulf, Miss., was received at the Navy Department yesterday, and created much excitement in Washington. The possession of this point places the formidable rebel strongholds at Vicksburg and Port Hudson at our mercy. Admiral Porter says that he now holds the door to Vicksburg. The fight lasted five hours and a half. The forts were literally torn to pieces by the fire of our vessels, but all the guns captured by our forces were in good condition. The works at Grand Gulf were the most formidable ones the rebels possessed in the vicinity of Vicksburg. Admiral Porter and Gen. Grant now hold them, and are remounting the guns. General Grant is reported by dispatches from Cairo to have reached Port Gibson. Many of the rebels who fled from Grand Gulf were captured by our pursuing forces.

We have the authority of the Secretary of War, in his dispatch to Governor Curtin, of Pennsylvania, yesterday, that the Army of the Potomac will speedily resume offensive operations; that, although the principal operations of General Hooker failed, there has been no serious disaster to the organization and efficiency of the army, and that not more than one-third of General Hooker's force was engaged.

The movements of General Stoneman's cavalry force formed the most brilliant episode in the nine days' fight of Hooker's army.

News reports Col. Kilpatrick as having reached Gloucester Point, through Tunstal's Station, near Yorktown, where he joined Gen. King. Of the brilliant movement of Col Kilpatrick's command, Gen. King says in his official notice of his arrival at Gloucester Point:

"They burned the bridges over the Chickahominy, destroyed three large trains of provisions in the rear of Lee's army, drove in the rebel pickets to within two miles of Richmond, and have lost only one lieutenant and thirty men, having captured and paroled upwards of three hundred prisoners. They have marched nearly two hundred miles since the 3d of May. They were inside of the fortifications at Richmond on the 4th, burned all the stores at Aylett's Station on the Mattapony on the 5th, destroyed all the ferries over the Pamunkey and Mattapony, and a large depot of commissary stores near and above the Rappahannock, and came in here in good condition." A splendid record this for any officer.

The rebels admit the loss of eighteen thousand men in the late battles. This brings the returns very close to the figures estimated in the statements made on our side, which put the loss of the enemy at about twenty thousand.

The President has issued a Proclamation preliminary to the enforcement of the Conscription act, defining the position and obligations of inchoate citizens under that law. Persons of foreign birth who have declared their intentions to become citizens, are, by this proclamation, pronounced liable to be drafted, if after the expiration of sixty-five days from the date thereof they still remain within the territory of the United States.

Arrival of Colonel Kilpatrick's Cavalry at Gloucester Point.

Yorktown, Va, May 7, 1863.—Colonel Kilpatrick, with the Harris Light Cavalry, 12th Illinois Cavalry, &c., have just arrived at Gloucester Point, having accomplished the object of their mission fully, and most gallantly they approached to within three miles of Richmond and destroyed a large amount of property and bridges.

Latest from the Army.

THE REBELS VERY QUIET.

The latest reports from the Rappahannock [illegible] the rebels are undemonstrative, and are evidently completely bewildered at our recent movements. [illegible] the 7th, (Thursday,) small bodies of rebel cavalry [illegible] south bank, reconnoitering and placing [illegible]

From the Philadelphia Inquirer of today

A RUMOR IS AFLOAT

[illegible] in Washington, that Gen. [illegible] the Rappahannock. A large [illegible] bringing in and [illegible] probably [illegible] foundation of the report.

SECOND REPORT.

Washington, May 8th, P. M.—As I close my letter, the rumor that Gen. Hooker is again crossing the Rappahannock, is being vigorously circulated, and it is believed to be true by some persons holding positions in the War Department, but I think it probable that only a few regiments of troops have recrossed the river for the purpose of covering our surgeons and assistants from attack while performing their merciful duties. No advance can possibly be made for a day or two, by the whole army.

FIRE IN THE WOODS, AND WOUNDED MEN BURNT UP.

Sunday a fire broke out in the dense woods, known as the "Wilderness," in which a few of our own wounded and dead men and a large number of wounded rebels were lying. These are supposed to have been destroyed by the devouring element. The rebels report that the loss of life by this accident was very heavy.

ANOTHER RUMOR.

It is reported that the rebels have retreated from our front, a large body of infantry with cavalry going towards Gordonsville. I cannot trace this report to any reliable source.

THE WAR OFFICE DISPATCH.

The dispatch from Secretary Stanton to Gov. Curtin is substantially correct. This is no blind for the Northern people. Gen. Hooker's army is in good condition, and will be moving against the enemy in less than a fortnight, if we have fair weather.

GEN. STONEMAN'S WORK.

All the rebel raids in the history of the rebellion "pale in their brilliancy" before this, as the play bills have it.

FROM THE FRONT.

An officer from Gen. Stahl's headquarters says there are no rebels in force south of Gordonsville, and most of the wandering bands of guerrillas have left the mountains.

CARE OF THE WOUNDED.

Delegations of eminent citizens and surgeons, from the Northern States have arrived here to assist in the care of the wounded at Aquia, whither they proceed as fast as passes and transportation are obtained. Gov. Curtin is here for this purpose from our own State, accompanied by Clement B. Barclay, Esq., and Geo. B. Cenarroe, Esq., of Philadelphia.

[illegible] OVER THE WOUNDED.

Our troops are still engaged to-day in bringing our wounded soldiers across the Rappahannock, and conveying them to the different hospitals. In this city they are unmolested by the rebels. It is thought that all will be over the river by noon.

RETURN OF THE PRESIDENT.

The President intimated to a friend this morning that Gen Hooker did just what he was sent to do, but circumstances beyond our control contracted his operations to their known limits.

NO LEAVES OF ABSENCE GRANTED.

Gen. Hooker will grant no leaves of absence to officers at present, who are able to perform military duty, and [illegible] offensive operations will be resumed at an early day.

THE RAILROAD WASHED AWAY.

The railroad from Aquia Creek to Falmouth has been washed away in several places by the freshets where embankments were built, but it will be immediately repaired, and will not cause any serious delay in the transportation. The army has ample supplies for all needs for weeks.

OUR WOUNDED DOING WELL.

An eminent surgeon from Falmouth, this morning, informs me that our wounded are doing well. The greater portion have received but slight injuries.

CONDITION OF OUR ARMY.

The army is being recuperated and reorganized, and will be ready to operate offensively once more as soon as the weather is settled. The men cannot be induced to believe that the Commander-in-Chief has been defeated, because they have seen him carry out his plans and promises, and retreat across a swollen and boisterous river in safety. This army is stronger than is generally supposed.

From Fortress Monroe.

Fortress Monroe, May 7.—Major Gen. Dix and staff left Fortress Monroe this forenoon for York river.

The propeller Dudley Buck, Capt. Smith, arrived this morning from Newbern day before yesterday. All was quiet in that department. Gen. Foster was at Newbern. One of his aids came on the Dudley Buck, with dispatches for Washington. When outside the blockade they spoke the propeller Gen Banks, from Hilton Head, bound to Newbern. The General Banks reported no news.

Late southern papers announce the death of the rebel Gen. D S. Donelson.

Governor Brown, of Georgia, has vetoed the State Guard or new Militia bill.

The Shreveport (La) *Gazette* recently published a card, signed by one hundred foreigners, who, fearing the draft, took this course to notify the people that they were French subjects, and owned no allegiance to the State of Louisiana. A Mr. Courtade, one of the signers of the card, was taken out of his bed, and tarred and cottoned the same night, and the "Rogue's March" was played before the business houses of the balance.

A line of couriers has been established by the Government for the transmission of official documents and late dispatches from Shreveport to Nevasota, there to connect with the railroad to Houston, Texas. The telegraph line is being rapidly built from Camden, Ark., to Shreveport, for military purposes.

Dispatch from Secretary Stanton.

Harrisburg, Pa, May 8.—The following dispatch from the Secretary of War has just been received by Governor Curtin:

To the Governor of Pennsylvania:

Washington, May 8, 1863.—The President and the General-in-Chief have just returned from the Army of the Potomac.

The principal operations of Gen. Hooker failed, but there has been no serious disaster to the organization and efficiency of the army.

It is now occupying its former position on the Rappahannock, having recrossed the river without any loss in the movement.

Not more than one-third of Gen. Hooker's force was engaged.

Gen. Stoneman's operations have been a brilliant success. Part of his force advanced to within two miles of Richmond, and the enemy's communications have been cut in every direction.

The Army of the Potomac will speedily resume offensive operations.

EDWIN M. STANTON, Secretary of War.

From Tennessee.

Order in Relation to Ladies Visiting the South—Morgan and Wheeler's Rebel Cavalry at Lehigh.

Murfreesboro', May 8.—The following order is important to ladies proposing to visit this department, and Gen. Rosecrans desires it thoroughly ventilated in the Northern papers:

Headquarters of the Cumberland, Office Provost Marshal, Murfreesboro', May 8.—This being the season for active military operations, the presence of ladies, however desirable under certain circumstances, is not so now. The general commanding directs that no passes be issued to ladies to pass from Louisville to Nashville, Murfreesboro', or within the lines of this department until further orders; those residing in the North are warned to avoid the trouble and expense of traveling to Louisville, as they will not be admitted within the lines of the department, except in the most urgent cases, and then under passes issued from the department headquarters.

M. WILES,
Major and Provost Marshal.

LOCAL NEWS.

From our Evening Edition of Yesterday

JACKSON SQUARE.—An hour spent among the flowers in Jackson Square cannot be called time lost. Everything, including Gen. Jackson and his brass horse, looks so fresh and gladdening to the eye, that we cannot help thanking the foresight of former city authorities in providing such pleasant little oases as these public squares, wherein the weary traveler through the great Zahara of the crowded city may pause and breathe awhile. Jackson Square, under the management of Mr. D. Downing, of the Street Commissioner's Department, was never in better condition, or better taken care of than at present. The showers that we have recently had have revived the drooping plants, and shrubs, and flowers, and yesterday all was fresh and beautiful. The many-colored verbena, the blushing roses, the beautiful lillies, and the thousand other flowers—some majestic and grand—others modest and lovely—present a picture of rare beauty to the eye of the admirer of nature and her wondrous works. The care and industry bestowed upon the square by Mr. Downing and his intelligent assistant, Jimmy Garry, are worthy of all praise, and this magnificent square has never been under better management.

LIVE OAK SCHOOL.—On last Friday evening the pupils of the above institution presented to Miss Stuart, Principal, and her assistants, a beautiful American flag. The schoolhouse was filled to its utmost capacity, and everything passed off in the pleasantest manner imaginable. The little girls did remarkably well, Miss Stuart having bestowed on them the most careful training. The band of the 47th Massachusetts Regiment was present, and added greatly to the pleasure experienced by all fortunate enough to be in attendance. We shall notice this affair again when the pressure of news matter subsides.

SEIZURE OF REBEL MUSIC.—One day last week, the 13th inst., Officer Fitzpatrick, by virtue of a warrant issued by Col. Hopkins, Chief of Police, searched the premises No. 74 Camp street, occupied by Blackmar & Co. as a music store. Of course no opposition was made to the overhauling made by the officer, although the proprietor of said music store seemed to think his presence could be comfortably dispensed with. After a thorough upsetting of piles of music, and a slight disarrangement of the usual order of things, the officer brought to light quite a large quantity of "Bonnie Blue Flags," "Beauregard Quicksteps," etc., which he confiscated, and turned over to the Chief of Police.

ARREST OF DR. KNAPP.—This gentleman was arrested on Friday by order of Governor Shepley, but was immediately released on bail, on a charge of having kidnapped a negro. We understand that he is accused of having hired two officers to arrest a contraband by force, and carry him in a cab down to a plantation he has charge of below the city. The trial of the case will come on in a few days, when we shall be able to give all the particulars, which it is thought advisable not to make public yet.

FIRE.—The alarm of fire on Saturday night at a late hour, was caused by a fire breaking out accidentally in the Customhouse, at the corner of Old Levee and Canal streets. It was extinguished before any damage was done. The last time we had a fire in the Customhouse, Gen. Beauregard was both smoked out and burnt out, as his quarters and numerous other small buildings were destroyed in the southeast corner of the third story.

ARMS FOUND.—Sergeant Sinclair, of the Second District, reports that in searching the house No. 25 Hospital street, for property stolen from John McIntyre, he found the following arms, which he seized as contraband: one rifle, one double-barreled pistol, a bowie knife, and dilapidated old sword cane, which he brought to the Police Station.

The Era Court Reports.

PROVOST COURT—H. DeB. Hughes, Judge.

SUNDAY MORNING.

Jacob Zimmer was arraigned on the charge of breaking into the house of Mr. Newberg, in the Third District, on the 14th inst., and robbing it of $2000 in gold. Lieut. White stated that he had arrested the accused on the information of a woman, who said she had seen him come away from the house at the time of the robbery. The Lieutenant and Mr Newberg both testified that they had known Mr. Zimmer a long time, but knew of nothing detrimental to his reputation. The woman, who lived next door to Mr Newberg, testified that she saw Mr. Zimmer coming from the back door of Mr. Newberg's house, at 7 o'clock on the morning of the robbery. She was first attracted by hearing some person walking in her neighbor's yard, and looking over the fence she saw the accused. She had known him for many years, but had never spoken to him. A brown felt hat found at the house of the accused was sworn to by the witness as the same which was worn by the accused when she saw him that morning. The accused, in his defense, stated that he had witnesses to prove that he was in his barber's shop both before and after the time spoken of by the prosecuting witness; and his counsel, Mr. Abel, urged that the well known character of the accused was sufficient to offset the very minute ground of suspicion that might be raised by the statement of the prosecuting witness, who certainly must have been mistaken. The charge thus fell to the ground, and the accused was discharged.

Mrs. Harvey was called to answer a charge of seditious language and disturbance of the peace. Mr. Abel, counsel of the accused, asked for a continuance of the case, on the ground that Mrs. Harvey had been locked up all night and was not prepared with her witnesses. The continuance was opposed by Mr. Day who contended that there had been ample time to provide witnesses. The question involved the Court and counsel in considerable discussion, which finally resulted in a denial of the motion for continuance.

Mrs. Mann, the next door neighbor of the accused, was the prosecutrix; and the substance of her complaint was, that she had been on several occasions annoyed and insulted by Mrs. Harvey and her relatives with contemptuous conduct and seditious language, commencing in October last; that, on remonstrating, nothing had occurred till Monday last, when Mrs. Harvey abused and insulted her particularly, calling her a Yankee spy, etc. The prosecutrix, during her statement, reluctantly testified, in answer to questions from Mr. Day, that she knew of several instances of sedition on the part of the accused. Since December last the two ladies have not been on friendly terms. No other witnesses being called on either side, the counsel (Mr. Day and Mr. Abel) agreed to submit the case to the Court, after a brief statement by Mrs. Harvey as to the transaction last Monday, which seemed to be a tongue quarrel between the two neighbors, in which not very complimentary opinions were interchanged. Mr. Crane, however, stepped forward and made a speech in favor of the prosecution.

Mr. Abel, in reply, argued that there was nothing in the case but a common neighborly quarrel—personal and not political. In the course of his remarks he said he had not particularly referred to Mr. Crane, (as that gentleman had inferred) in his remarks, about ten days ago, relating to many who used to be radical Confederates and are now as radical on the opposite side.

Mr. Day urged, in conclusion, that in this case the punishment should be visited on Mrs. Harvey personally, and not on her husband.

The Court accordingly sentenced Mrs. Harvey to the Parish Prison for thirty days, with bonds to keep the peace in the sum of $1000. Mrs. Mann and Mrs. Harvey reside on Felicity road, next door to each other.

Mrs. Ferguson, the sister of Mrs. Harvey, who wore white, red and white roses, was then brought before the Court, charged with being a participant in the offenses of Mrs. Harvey. Mr. Abel succeeded in having the trial postponed to prepare a defense. The accused gave bail in $250 to answer next Sunday.

Mrs. Bensadon, an elderly lady in spectacles, with white, red and white flowers in her bonnet, was then put on trial for exhibiting and expressing secession proclivities, to the annoyance of good Union people. Evidence was introduced that she sneered at the United States flag, and wished to throw lamp oil on it; that she called her neighbors stinking Yankees, and said the Confederates would shoot them. A witness, with red, white and blue, stated that accused expressed a wish it would be sickly, to bring the citizens back. Drawings of the Confederate flag and Confederate tracts were found in her house, where the Bonnie Blue Flag and shouts for Jeff Davis and Beauregard are often heard. Accused stated that she is an unprotected widow, with four children to support, and never acted as charged since she took the oath.

Mr Day asked for the imprisonment of the lady, to give a proper impression.

Mr. Abel opposed such oppressive punishment, as not calculated to effect the object.

The sentence was thirty days' imprisonment.

J. Nugent was charged with beating police officer Gruber, who wanted to arrest him for not assisting when called upon in arresting three [illegible]. Prisoner had admitted that he beat Gruber, and would not be arrested by him if the gallows were [illegible]. He was sentenced six months to the Parish Prison.

A baker was up for beating young boys with a horse whip, for disturbing his sleep with [illegible]. The boys were proved to be very annoying. Fined $5.

Wm. Brown (colored)—by Harriet Randolph accused: That he had come to her house and struck her with a stick after abusing her. Evidence showed that she was always following him and forcing her caresses on him; at least his wife asserted [illegible] had seen it. Fined $30.

Mrs. Mannel Graves [illegible] and inveterate drunkard, was sent for sixty [illegible] Workhouse.

Two abandoned females [illegible] by officer Foster with keeping a [illegible] den, and assisting sailors to desert, by [illegible] citizen's clothes. Sixty days to the [illegible].

Mrs. Connors charged her [illegible] with beating her with a brick [illegible] up for ten days. A low-classed [illegible] the character the police officer gave [illegible] parties. One of the witnesses, [illegible] Mrs. Connors had been calling [illegible] charge [illegible].

Mrs. Kelly was accused of drinking very hard, furnishing soldiers with liquor and disturbing the peace. A long string of females testified against her. She defended herself by stating that some of her martial relations visited her, but they received no liquor and drank none, and that the witnesses had abused her, and called her Yankee. Thirty days to the Workhouse was her sentence.

A blind man and his wife made their third appearance for being drunk and disturbing the peace at night after they return from their begging excursions. Fined $10 each or twenty days.

Mary Ann Gertels was drunk on Saturday night, cried for Jeff Davis, etc. She was sent for sixty days to the Workhouse to get sober.

John Casner was tried on the charge of selling liquor to soldiers. A soldier testified that he obtained liquor from accused upon the representation that he was now discharged from service. He admitted selling beer and cider. Fined $75, liquors to be confiscated.

PROVOST COURT—Judge Peabody.

MONDAY.

The dock this morning was pretty full of all sorts of people, of all sorts of ages, all sorts of sizes and all sorts of complexions—from among whom Macpherson might have found recruits for every corps in his mammoth army—and plenty of conscripts between the ages of ten and one hundred.

Ex-Lieut. Lynch was charged with disturbing the peace. His resignation as first Lieutenant from the 1st Louisiana Regiment was read. He had been arrested on the levee on a charge of insulting people and resisting the officers. The Court fined him $25.

Two or three lads were accused of stealing spoons from a coffee stand in the Magazine market. The evidence showed they did not steal the spoons, but were only on a mischievous lark, for which they were fined three dollars each.

Joseph Match was charged with selling rotten potatoes. The potatoes were so loud that they could be smelt at a distance of two squares. He sold these potatoes to a gentleman, and refused to take them back. As there is an ordinance against keeping or selling rotten produce, the Court fined him $15.

Henry Campeyer and four other boys were arrested by Lieutenant Duane, for singing a seditious song. The Lieutenant said he heard them singing a song, but could not tell what song it was, except that it closed with the words, "we'll fight for J. Davis till we die." He had asked them at the time what they were singing, but as they refused to give him a satisfactory answer, he arrested them. Had they answered him properly, he would not have made the arrest. The boys said it was a song they were in the habit of singing about the engine house. As the Lieutenant said he thought they had been sufficiently punished by being locked up for the night, the Court discharged the boys.

Louis Steiker and L. Myers were sent to the Parish Prison for thirty days, for stealing about twenty pounds of cotton.

Mary Ann Clark, a little orphan girl, who had been very badly treated by different parties who had charge of her, was brought before the Court by officer Ford as an act of charity, and was sent to the House of Refuge.

Benjamin Gill, accused of having passed himself off as a special officer, and visiting a house with the intention of robbing it, was up for trial. He said he was searching the house for Confederate soldiers and contraband articles. He was fined $25.

FOURTH DISTRICT COURT—Judge Hiestand.

The case of Marie Hyob vs. Joseph Bourdette, her husband, was tried before this court and as it presents some points of interest, we make the following synopsis of reasons for judgment:

Plaintiff, in 1856, obtained a separation in property from her husband, and in accordance with the terms of a settlement of the community of acquits and gains, they continued to live together some time afterwards, but in not a very harmonious manner, as the husband was subject to certain fits of madness, which led him to seek the company of other females, and to which insane conduct the wife raised serious objections. He finally took up his abode entirely with another woman. In her present petition the plaintiff sets forth that when the affairs of the community were settled, the defendant was the owner of $20,000 of stock in the Bank of Louisiana—a fact which he wholly concealed from her, and she asked that the husband be condemned to pay her $690 for house rent, an amount which she was compelled to expend after he left the common domicile; that he be required to account to her for half of the $20,000 of bank stocks; that he be condemned to provide her with a suitable dwelling, and a sum sufficient to support her respectably, at the rate of $150 per month. This petition was filed in 1860—and on the 25th of February last she filed a supplemental petition, in which her pretensions were greatly increased, and she asked for $2100 additional to be refunded, which she had been obliged to expend for house rent, and averring that her husband was much better off than she supposed him to be at the time the suit was commenced, she asked that he be required to contribute $500 per month to her support; which she thought a very reasonable allowance in view of the fact that, according to her statement he annually expended over $6000 in the support of a concubine. Furthermore, she wanted $720 more per annum as house rent for herself, and $27,000 more to offset her expenses since 1858, together with half of the bank stock claimed in her original petition, and in case he should fail to furnish her a house suitable to her condition, he should be required to provide for her maintenance during the term of her natural life, at the rate of $500 per month.

The plaintiff admitted in his answer a judgment of separation of property, and sets up the terms and agreement of the same in bar of plaintiff's demand. He further averred that plaintiff was possessed of ample means of support, and that her temper is so violent as to render living with her impossible, and on the issues thus made the parties proceeded to trial.

It was proved that defendant was possessed of promissory notes and bills of exchange amounting to $50,000, four slaves, real estate valued at $4000, but for which he paid $7000, merchandise valued at $4000, and an interest of $300 in Insurance scrip. But the Court held that in consideration of the existing rebellion and the prostration of commercial interests, this fortune of $50,000 may be looked upon as only nominal, the only thing really tangible being the real estate and merchandise. In this connection the Court remarked: "I do not include the slaves because I am of opinion that henceforth a man's poverty, instead of his wealth, will be increased just in proportion to the number he possesses." "The commercial paper may hereafter prove of some value, but at the present time its value must be regarded as extremely hypothetical." Confederate notes to the amount of $7000 were also regarded as worthless.

It was fully shown by the testimony that, at the time of the division of the community property, defendant was worth $18,000, of which an equal division was made. Since then the plaintiff has followed the business of loaning money at very exorbitant rates of interest, and has thus increased her capital to over $30,000. It was also in evidence that she has no children—a fact which the Court looked upon as fortunate; for, had children resulted from the marriage of the parties, they would be scandalized by the existing state of affairs.

In law it was held that when a husband abandons the common domicile, the wife, *when in need of it*, has an undoubted right to sue for a support.

Art. 2409 of the Civil Code says: "The wife who has obtained the separation of property must contribute in proportion to her fortune, and to that of her husband, both to the household expenses and to those of the education of her children. She is bound to support these expenses alone, if there remains nothing to the husband.

The Court concludes as follows: "The [illegible] making it clear that the plaintiff in this case—the wife who has obtained separation of property—is possessed of a handsome fortune for a woman who has [illegible] That the fortune of her husband—erring [illegible] —is, under the unfortunate circumstance[illegible] try, and the derangements consequent the[illegible] ferior, in my opinion, to her own. T[illegible] think that the plaintiff is in a situ[illegible] her to sue him for her mainten[illegible]

"Let there be judgment [illegible]

THE BATTLES AT CHANCELLORSVILLE—COUCH'S CORPS FORMING LINE OF BATTLE TO COVER THE RETREAT OF THE 11TH CORPS, 2D MAY, 1863.—FROM A SKETCH BY MR. A. R. WAUD.—[SEE PAGE 331.]

Julia, thus pressed, sang one of those songs that come and go every season. She spoke the words clearly, and with such variety and intelligence, that Sampson recanted, and broke in upon the—"very pretty"—"how sweet"—and "who is it by?" of the others, by shouting, "Very weak trash very cleanly sung. Now give us something worth the wear and tear of your orgins. Immortal vairse widded t' immortal sounds; that is what I understand b' a song."

Alfred whispered, "No, no, dearest, sing something suitable to you and me."

"Out of the question. Then go farther away, dear; I shall have more courage."

He obeyed, and she turned over two or three music books; and finally sang from memory. She cultivated musical memory, having observed the contempt with which men of sense visit the sorry pretenders to music who are tuneless and songless among the nightingales, and any where else away from their books. How will they manage to sing in heaven? Answer me that!

The song Julia Dodd sang on this happy occasion, to meet the humble but heterogeneous views of Messrs. Sampson and Hardie, was a simple eloquent Irish song called Aileen aroon. Whose history, by-the-by, was a curious one. Early in this century it occurred to somebody to hymn a son of George the Third for his double merit in having been born, and going to a ball. People who thus apply the fine arts in modern days are seldom artists; accordingly this parasite could not invent a melody; so he coolly stole Aileen aroon, soiled it by inserting sordid and incongruous jerks into the refrain, and called the stolen and adulterated article Robin Adair. An artisan of the same kidney was soon found to write words down to the degraded ditty: and, so strong is Flunkyism, and so weak is Criticism in these islands, that the polluted tune actually superseded the clean melody, and this sort of thing, "Who was in uniform at the ball? Silly Billy!" smothered the immortal lines.

But Mrs. Dodd's severe taste in music rejected those ignoble jerks, and her enthusiastic daughter having the option to hymn immortal Constancy, or mortal Fact, decided thus:

When like the early rose
Aileen aroon,
Beauty in childhood glows,
Aileen aroon,
When like a diadem,
Buds blush around the stem,
Which is the fairest gem?
Aileen aroon.

Is it the laughing eye?
Aileen aroon,
Is it the timid sigh?
Aileen aroon,
Is it the tender tone,
Soft as the stringed harp's moan?
No; it is Truth alone,
Aileen aroon.

I know a valley fair,
Aileen aroon,
I know a cottage there,
Aileen aroon.
Far in that valley's shade,
I know a gentle maid,
Flower of the hazel glade,
Aileen aroon.

Who in the song so sweet?
Aileen aroon.
Who in the dance so fleet?
Aileen aroon
Dear are her charms to me,
Dearer her laughter free,
Dearest her constancy,
Aileen aroon.

Youth must with time decay,
Aileen aroon,
Beauty must fade away,
Aileen aroon.
Castles are sacked in war,
Chieftains are scattered far,
Truth is a fixed star,
Aileen aroon.

The way the earnest singer sang these lines is beyond the conception of ordinary singers, public or private. Here one of nature's orators spoke poetry to music with an eloquence as fervid and delicate as ever rung in the forum. She gave each verse with the same just variety, as if she had been reciting, and when she came to the last, where the thought rises abruptly, and is truly noble, she sang it with the sudden pathos, the weight, and the swelling majesty, of a truthful soul hymning truth with all its powers.

All the hearers, even Sampson, were thrilled, astonished, spell-bound: so can one wave of immortal music and immortal verse (alas! how seldom they meet!) heave the inner man when genius interprets. Judge, then, what it was to Alfred, to whom, with these great words and thrilling tones of her rich, swelling, ringing voice, the darling of his own heart vowed constancy, while her inspired face beamed on him like an angel's.

Even Mrs. Dodd, though acquainted with the song, and with her daughter's rare powers, gazed at her now with some surprise, as well as admiration, and kept a note Sarah had brought her, open, but unread, in her hand, unable to take her eyes from the inspired songstress. However, just before the song ended, she did just glance down, and saw it was signed Richard Hardie. On this her eye devoured it; and in one moment she saw that the writer declined, politely but peremptorily, the proposed alliance between his son and her daughter.

The mother looked up from this paper at that living radiance and incarnate melody in a sort of stupor: it seemed hardly possible to her that a provincial banker could refuse an alliance with a creature so peerless as that. But so it was; and despite her habitual self-government, Mrs. Dodd's white hand clenched the note till her nails dented it; and she reddened to the brow with anger and mortification.

Julia, whom she had trained never to monopolize attention in society, now left the piano in spite of remonstrance, and soon noticed her mother's face; for from red it had become paler than usual. "Are you unwell, dear?" said she, sotto voce.

"No, love."

"Is there any thing the matter, then?"

"Hush! We have guests: our first duty is to them." With this Mrs. Dodd rose, and, endeavoring not to look at her daughter at all, went round and drew each of her guests out in turn. It was the very heroism of courtesy; for their presence was torture to her. At last, to her infinite relief, they went, and she was left alone with her children. She sent the servants to bed, saying she would undress Miss Dodd: and accompanied her to her room. There the first thing she did was to lock the door; and the next was to turn round and look at her full.

"I always thought you the most lovable child I ever saw; but I never admired you as I have to-night; my noble, my beautiful daughter, who would grace the highest family in England!" With this Mrs. Dodd began to choke, and kissed Julia eagerly with the tears in her eyes, and drew her with tender defiance to her bosom.

"My own mamma," said Julia, softly, "what has happened?"

"My darling," said Mrs. Dodd, trembling a little, "have you pride? have you spirit?"

"I think I have."

"I hope so: for you will need them both. Read that!" And she offered Mr. Hardie's letter with averted head.

THE ARMY OF THE POTOMAC.

We devote the bulk of our space this week to illustrations of the recent campaign of the Army of the Potomac. On page 324 we give the Capture of the Heights of Fredericksburg by General Sedgwick—a drawing by Thomas Nast. The following, from the *Times* correspondence, describes the transaction:

It was now eleven o'clock; continuous fighting had been going on for full six hours, and the rebels still held their works. General Sedgwick now determined on having the "Light Brigade" charge the heights. Colonel Burnham, commanding, moved his forces along under the protection of abandoned earth-works, and the hill-side formed by the sloping down of the plain near the city, until he had arrived directly in front of the most formidable position, known as the "Slaughter Pen." Knapsacks and any article of clothing which might impede their rapid movement were cast aside by the men, and they were deployed out in the following order: one half of the Fifth Wisconsin, Colonel Allen, as skirmish line; Thirty-first New York, Colonel Jones, on the left; Sixth Maine, Lieutenant-Colonel Harris commanding, and the remaining portion of the Fifth, in the rear of and supporting the Thirty-first at the same time. At the same time a force consisting of the Forty-third New York and Sixty-first Pennsylvania, and one or two other regiments, were sent up the road at the right of the stone-wall. Going on to the regiments of the Light Brigade, prepared for a charge, were the Thirty-sixth New York and Seventh Massachusetts, and still further on other regiments. At twenty minutes past eleven the lion-hearted men rose from their feet. Every one of the thousand spectators on the hills in the rear held their breath in terrible suspense, expecting to see them all the next moment prostrate in the dust. "Forward!" cried the General, and they dashed forward on the open plain, when instantly there was poured upon them a most terrific discharge of grape and canister. Many lay dead, but not one faltered. Full 400 yards must be passed over before gaining the stone-wall. As they press forward, delivering the battle-cheer, which is heard above the roar of artillery, the rebel guns further to the left are turned upon them. But they falter not. A moment more they have reached the stone-wall, scaled its sides, are clambering the green bank of the bluff, and precisely as the city clock struck they rush over the embrasure of the rebel guns, and the Heights are ours. The enemy, with the exception of the cannoniers, fled in wild confusion, secreting themselves in the houses, woods, and wherever a place of concealment was afforded. The guns captured proved to be the Washington Artillery, the battery so highly complimented by General Lee in his report of the last battle of Fredericksburg, and which has figured more or less since the outbreak of the rebellion. "What men are these?" was the interrogatory of one of the astonished and terrified members, as our brave boys appeared over the ramparts. "We are Yankees, —— —— you; do you think we will fight now?" was the response from one of our men. "Boys," remarked the commander of the battery, "you have captured the best battery in the Confederate service." The Sixth Maine were the first regiment to reach the scene. Lieutenant-Colonel Harris, with unparalleled bravery, rushed right up to the mouth of one as it was belching away, and through the mist and smoke his form could just be discerned as he cheered his men forward. He, together with Captain Furlong, were the first to lay hold of the rebel pieces.

On pages 328 and 329 we illustrate the Fight at Chancellorsville, on May 1, from a sketch by Mr. A. R. Waud. This affair is thus described in the *Herald* correspondence:

About two o'clock on Friday afternoon the enemy were discovered advancing in force down both the old turnpike and the plank road, thus approaching our position nearly from the east. Although these two roads enter Chancellorsville at right angles—one from the east direct, and the other from the south—they join and make a single road near Tabernacle Church. When the discovery was made of the approach of the enemy, General Hooker immediately returned to his head-quarters at Chancellorsville and made his dispositions to meet them. It was yet uncertain whether the attack would come from the east or south, and it was therefore necessary to be in readiness at both points. With this purpose the Fifth Corps, Major-General Meade, was formed on the front facing the east, Sykes's division of regulars occupying a line north of the old turnpike road, and the other two divisions taking the line of the Banks Ford road, on the left of Sykes. The Second Corps, Major-General Couch, was held in reserve to support the right wing of this line, and the Second Division, Major-General Berry, of the Third Corps, Major-General Sickles, to support the left.

On our south front two corps—the Eleventh, Major-General Howard, and the Twelfth, Major-General Slocum—were deployed, the latter in double line of battle, with its left resting on the plank road, and the former on the right of the Twelfth. The two remaining divisions of Sickles's corps—the First, Brigadier-General Birney, and the Third, Brigadier-General Whipple—were ordered up as supports for this line.

Sykes's division was formed in the open field, directly on the slope southeast of and scarcely a quarter of a mile distant from General Hooker's head-quarters. Immediately behind them, on the extreme elevation of the plain, three batteries of field artillery were planted. General Sykes's skirmishers advanced down the field and into the woods, where they waited the approach of the enemy. Soon the brisk cracking of rifles and muskets announced the rebel proximity, and our skirmishers, in compliance with orders, gradually fell back upon the main line of battle. This manœuvre drew the enemy outside of the woods, from which they emerged close after our retreating skirmishers, yelling and shouting like a tribe of wild Indians. The sight was both exciting and amusing at first, and all movement on our part was momentarily suspended, while our brave men gratified their curiosity in scrutinizing their gray-backed adversaries. But the charge of the rebels was not a trifling matter, and as column upon column of them, and line after line came dashing out of the woods, it seemed as though that one little division stationed there to check them would be swallowed up. It was one of those skillful manœuvres for which General Lee is particularly distinguished—the hurling of an immense body upon a small force of his antagonist. The rebel force, as it charged out of the woods, was certainly three times as large as that of General Sykes; yet the latter showed no disposition to quail; but, after giving a moment's glance to satisfy their curiosity, every soldier brought his musket to his shoulder, and five thousand bullets were sent into the rebel line. Such steadiness appalled them. They were unprepared for it. Their front rank quailed before it. The sudden thinning of their numbers amazed and frightened them. They discharged their pieces recklessly and broke in confusion. But there was no flight for them. The heavy bodies behind them, to whom the front rank had been a bulwark, protecting them from the murderous volley of the Union Regulars, were steady and determined. They absorbed the front rank in the second, and still moved forward—firm, unshaken, confident. Meantime our men had reloaded their pieces, and simultaneously a volley was fired from both sides, and then from the brow above our artillery opened with canister and grape, throwing over the heads of our own men and dealing destruction and confusion to the enemy. And as the loud cannon continued its work with fearful rapidity the order was given to our men to "fire at will"—an order that was copied by the enemy—and the continuous roar of musketry that followed almost deadened the reports of the artillery. It was the first fight of the great battle, and for nearly twenty minutes both parties stood firm, as though nothing should lead them to give the prestige of a first success to the other. But, although outnumbered, we had an advantage in the support of artillery, which, while our infantry held the rebels in check, made huge gaps in their ranks. Still they yelled and shouted defiance, and attempted charges and continued their firing, rank after rank of them being broken and thrown back in confusion, while their officers shouted, and ordered and stormed, and cursed, in the vain effort to rally them to a persistent, determined charge. They fought well. They fought as none but Americans dare fight. But with musketry alone they could not contend against both artillery and musketry. It was simply murder on the part of their officers to attempt to hold them to it, and their officers began to appreciate the fact when nearly half their column had been placed *hors de combat*; and then the order was given to retire.

And then came our turn to shout. The rebels were retreating. Our force was sadly thinned and broken; but there were enough left to send up a shout after the retreating rebels that made the woods ring with the echo. Even the wounded joined in the glad cheer, many of them staggering into an upright position and throwing up their hats in their excess of gladness at the victory. The charge had been right gallantly met, and the host of the enemy finely repulsed. It was the first achievement of the great struggle—an augury of success in the end. Our men had stood like veterans, and they had a right to cheer.

The Commencement of the Battle on Saturday, 2d, also from a sketch by Mr. Waud, is illustrated on the same pages. Of this we take the following description from the *Times* correspondence:

In the morning, as we stood on the balcony of Chancellor's house, the attention was aroused by a sharp rattle of musketry coming from a column of rebels coming up by the main Fredericksburg plank road, directly in front of us. Knapp's Battery, however, which was planted directly in front of the position, opened upon them, and after a few rounds caused them to retire.

Immediately afterward a battery opened from the height which I have mentioned as having been gained by Sykes yesterday, and then abandoned by us. The position was rather upward of a mile distant from the cleared space, and its object was to damage our ammunition train which was visible to the rebels from the tops of trees on the height. One of our batteries was, however, immediately opened in reply. The third shot blew up one of the caissons and a subsequent shot blew up another, and this settled their account.

Subsequently a reconnoissance was sent, on our part, consisting of the Twenty-sixth Pennsylvania Volunteers (Carr's brigade, Berry's division, Sickles's corps), on the same road by which the rebels had approached in the morning, for the purpose of feeling their strength. They went out on the plank road, deployed on both sides in the form of a letter V, chased the rebel skirmishers a couple of miles, till they came to a heavy double line of battle, with artillery in position, when they retired, bringing us *that* piece of intelligence.

Another reconnoissance was next sent out on our right, consisting of Berdan's sharp-shooters. They met the enemy's pickets, drove them handsomely, and at 4 o'clock returned with fifty prisoners of the Twenty-third Georgia.

At 4 the rebels are moving down in force on the plank road, where we had a little before made the reconnoissance. Geary's division of Slocum's corps is sent in on the double-quick into the woods—their bayonets flashing in the sunlight. A sharp contest ensues, and in a few minutes they come back in disorder. A portion of Kane's brigade, composed of raw troops, had broken and thrown the column into confusion.

An aid from Slocum comes to ask General Hooker if he can have reinforcements. "No! he *must* hold his own. Howard will, of course, support him from the right. Let Geary's division, however, be thrown to the right of the road, so that the artillery may be able to sweep the enemy on the left." This treatment presently repaired the damage, and checked the hope of the rebels being able to pierce our centre.

Finally, on page 325 we illustrate the terrible Panic which Overtook the Eleventh Corps on the afternoon of the same day. This also is from a sketch by Mr. Waud. The following graphic account of the affair is from the *Herald* letter:

The Eleventh corps had been ordered to advance on the right of Birney, and moved forward to take the position assigned to them on Birney's flank. One brigade succeeded in getting up the hill, and reported, by its commander (whose name I have unfortunately lost), to Generals Sickles and Birney. The rest of the corps met the enemy in force when about two-thirds of the distance up. Here they had a short engagement, in which it does not appear that they had even so large a force to contend against as that which Williams, with his single division, had fought so bravely. Headed by their commander, the gallant Howard, the German corps charged boldly up to the rebel lines. Here they were met, as the rebels always meet their foe, with shouts of defiance and derision, a determined front, and a heavy fire of musketry. The German regiments returned the fire for a short time with spirit, manifesting a disposition to fight valiantly. But at the time when all encouragement to the men was needed that could be given, then some officer of the division (one, at least, as I am informed) fell back to the rear, leaving his men to fight alone. At the same time General Devens, commanding the First division, was unhorsed and badly wounded in his foot by a musket-ball. Thus losing at a ciritical moment the inspiriting influence of the immediate presence of their commanders, the men began to falter, then to fall back, and finally broke in a complete route. General Howard boldly threw himself into the breach and attempted to rally the shattered columns; but his efforts were perfectly futile. The men were panic-stricken, and no power on earth could rally them in the face of the enemy. Information of the catastrophe was promptly communicated to General Sickles, who thus had a moment given him to prepare for the shock he instantly apprehended his column would suffer. The high land of the little farm that formed the base of his operations was parked full of artillery and cavalry, nearly all the artillery of theThird corps, together with Pleasanton's cavalry, being crowded into that little fifty-acre inclosure. But Sickles was not to be thrown off his guard by a trifle, and any thing short of a complete defeat seemed to be considered by him in the light of a trifle. With the coolness and skillfulness of a veteran of a hundred campaigns he set to work making his dispositions. He had not a single regiment within his reach to support his artillery; Whipple was falling back, and must meet the approaching stampede with his own force in retreat; Birney was far out in the advance, in imminent danger of being completely surrounded and annihilated; the rebel forces were pressing hard upon the flying Germans, who could only escape by rushing across his lines, with every prospect of communicating the panic to them. It was a critical moment indeed, and one that might well stagger even the bravest-hearted. But it did not stagger the citizen soldier. Calling to one after another of his staff, he sent them all off, one after the other, lest any should fail of getting through, to warn Birney of his danger, and order him to fall back. Then, turning to General Pleasanton, he directed him to take charge of the artillery, and train it all upon the woods encircling the field, and support it with his cavalry, to hold the rebels in check should they come on him, and himself dashed off to meet Whipple, then just emerging from the woods in the bottom land. He had scarcely turned his horse about when the flying Germans came dashing over the field in crowds, meeting the head of Whipple's column and stampeding through his lines, running as only men do run when convinced that sure destruction is awaiting them. At the same moment large masses of the rebel infantry came dashing through the woods on the north and west close up to the field, and opened a tremendous fire of musketry into the confused mass of men and animals. To add to the confusion and terror of the occasion night was rapidly approaching, and darkness was already beginning to obscure all things.

I must frankly confess that I have no ability to do justice to the scene that followed. It was my lot to be in the centre of that field when the panic burst upon us. May I never be a witness to another such scene! On one hand was a solid column of infantry retreating at double-quick from the face of the enemy, who were already crowding their rear; on the other was a dense mass of beings who had lost their reasoning faculties, and were flying from a thousand fancied dangers as well as from the real danger that crowded so close upon them, aggravating the fearfulness of their situation by the very precipitancy with which they were seeking to escape from it. On the hill were ten thousand of the enemy, pouring their murderous volleys in upon us, yelling and hooting, to increase the alarm and confusion; hundreds of cavalry horses, left riderless at the first discharge from the rebels, were dashing frantically about in all directions; a score of batteries of artillery were thrown into disorder, some properly manned, seeking to gain positions for effective duty, and others flying from the field; battery wagons, ambulances, horses, men, cannon, caissons, all jumbled and tumbled together in an apparently inextricable mass, and that murderous fire still pouring in upon them. To add to the terror of the occasion there was but one means of escape from the field, and that through a little narrow neck or ravine washed out by Scott's Creek. Toward this the confused mass plunged headlong. For a moment it seemed as if no power could avert the frightful calamity that threatened the entire army. That neck passed, and this panic-stricken, disordered body of men and animals permitted to pass down through the other corps of the army, our destruction was sure. But in the midst of that wildest alarm there was a cool head. That calamity was averted by the determined self-possession of Major-General Daniel E. Sickles.

Let me here finish with the Eleventh corps. They did not all fly across Sickles's line. They dispersed and ran in all directions, regardless of the order of their going. They all seemed possessed with an instinctive idea of the shortest and most direct line from the point whence they started to the United States ford, and the majority of them did not stop until they had reached the ford.

Other illustrations of the Army of the Potomac are given on pages 332 and 333. The descriptive matter referring to them will be found in the following brief description by the artist Mr. A. R. Waud:

SYKES'S ADVANCE ON OUR LEFT.

This sketch represents the brilliant advance of Sykes's division of Meade's corps. Watson's battery is partly seen hurling shells over the heads of our advancing lines at the rebel position on the top of the hill. In three lines, the gallant Second Brigade leading the attack, with that steadiness which the regiments of the regular army have always shown, they moved up the hill, the line of battle being formed across the road. The fire was to a great extent reserved till the crest of the hill was reached, and the enemy driven in confusion. In this affair the old Fifth Corps well maintained its old reputation; and after, when it was drawn back to take its place in the line of battle then forming, it repulsed with slaughter the attack which the enemy in their turn made upon them.

THE BATTLE IN FRONT OF CHANCELLOR'S HOUSE ON FRIDAY AFTERNOON.

After the attack upon Meade the enemy continued the battle by a vigorous effort to storm our position on the cross-roads at Chancellor's. This was a magnificent scene. The house occupies the right of the picture; about it the orderlies, servants, and pack-mules belonging to head-quarters were grouped—General Hooker and his staff, with Captain Starr's company of the Lancers, forming a brilliant party at the side of the house. Slocum's line of battle is seen formed in front, supporting the batteries in position about the burned chimney, which was surrounded by cherry-trees in blossom. In front are the lines of men moving up to take part in the struggle, which for a short time was very violently contested at this point.

HOWARD'S POSITION ON THE RIGHT.

Dowdall's tavern, head-quarters Eleventh Corps, is seen in the centre of this view. The rifle-pits across the field rendered this place impregnable in the hands of good soldiers. It was expected all day that the enemy would attack this wing in force, and there was plenty of time for preparation. The German troops, however, were not equal to the occasion. Some of them fought well, but the majority fled in panic without firing a shot, throwing into confusion those troops that were preparing to resist the enemy's advance. In the midst of the skedaddle a noble buck and two does left the woods and fled through the fugitives.

COUCH'S MEN FORMING ACROSS THE PLANK ROAD.

While Sickles was returning with his fine corps on the left, Couch's men on the double-quick tock up position across the road to try and stem the course of the runaways and Jackson's rapid advance. The batteries, massed in front of this line, poured into the woods a savage fire over the soldiers in front, while a confused mass of pack trains, wagons, ambulances, guns, caissons, cattle, and broken troops, with all the crowd of army followers, rushed down the road in panic, the enemy pounding at their rear and capturing what they could. This part of the battle was truly terrible. The sun had set, and threatening clouds threatened rain, and some lightning added to the gloomy horror of the scene; but the Second and Third Corps stood nobly to their work, and the rebels were hurled back. They captured cattle and supplies, ammunition, etc., and spent the rest of the evening in plundering our wounded.

GENERAL COUCH'S HEAD-QUARTERS ON THE CENTRE.

On Sunday the rebels made the most determined efforts to capture this position, held by Sickles and Meade, but they had no Eleventh Corps to deal with. Savagely they were repulsed, and Jackson's celebrated column of 40,000 men was decimated and defeated.

SKETCH OF THE CENTRE.—ANOTHER VIEW.

In this picture the men of Humphrey's division are represented pouring a deadly fire upon the advancing hosts, whose intention was to capture the rifle-pits and batteries represented in the picture. About this time Humphrey made one of his celebrated charges upon the enemy, driving them with such loss that they never dared to attack in force again.

HOOKER'S HEAD-QUARTERS IN THE WOODS.

After the burning of the Chancellor house, and withdrawal of our line from that point, the General bivouacked in the woods near the front, so near that the rebel shells and even the fire of the sharp-shooters came into the camp. Captain Starr's horse was shot quite close to where the General was consulting with his officers.

OLD MILL.

This was a picturesque spot near the front, used as a hospital for Slocum's corps, and as a rendezvous of skedaddlers.

THE DAILY HUNTSVILLE CONFEDERATE.

VOL. 1. HUNTSVILLE, ALA., THURSDAY MORNING, MAY 28, 1863. NO. 9.

The Affair at Jackson.

A gentleman of Columbus, Georgia, just returned from Jackson, gives to the *Times* some interesting particulars relative to the late capture of that city by the Yankees:

It seems that on Tuesday, the 12th instant, a sharp contest was had with the advance of Grant's army at Raymond, six or eight miles southwest of Jackson. The enemy outnumbers us at least five to one. Our forces were compelled to fall back upon Jackson, which they did in good order late at night. On Wednesday evening just at dark the train on which General Johnston and staff had taken passage for Vicksburg arrived in Jackson, and the General remained over, superintending the movements of the troops. On Thursday morning at about 9 o'clock the enemy appeared in force a few miles south of Jackson, and attacked and drove in our pickets. Our force did not exceed 8,000, and so rapid had been the movements of the enemy that several of our regiments had not yet been arranged for action. The force of the enemy was estimated at 30,000. It seemed to be the purpose of Gen. Johnston merely to delay the enemy's arrival in the city as long as possible, in order to allow our forces time to withdraw our commissary and quartermaster's stores. Our imformant left Jackson at 3 o'clock p. m., Thursday. He states some three or four buildings had been burned before he left, set on fire by shells of the enemy.

The train which left Jackson on Thursday evening, came near being overtaken and captured by a battalion of Yankee cavalry. A few miles west of Brandon the cavalry were seen a short distance from the road, but the speed of the locomotive having been increased to nearly thirty miles an hour, the train escaped. We have since learned that Brandon is in the possession of the enemy, and that the road between that place and Jackson has been destroyed.

The people of Jackson and vicinity—including the military as well as the civilians—are greatly incensed at Pemberton, and openly accuse him of bad faith. Our informant states that this feeling is strongest among the Commissaries and Quartermasters, who state that they might have saved everything had Pemberton given them orders to move a few hours sooner.

There appears to have been no fighting but with artillery, and this was at very "long taw." The majority of the public stores were removed. Still, a great quantity was destroyed by our men to prevent them from falling into the hands of the enemy. All the railroad rolling stock, &c., was removed.

THE RETREAT OF GEN. JOHNSTON.

The retreat of Gen. Joseph E. Johnston, when overwhelmed by superior numbers from Jackson to Canton, was certainly a master stroke of policy. Canton is twenty-four miles North of Jackson, being the point of junction of the New Orleans, Jackson and Great Northern and the Mississippi Central Railroads, the latter connecting with the Memphis and Charleston Railroad at Grand Junction. This was the only railroad communication available to the Yankee army at Jackson; and had Gen. Johnston abandoned it, by going either Eastwardly or to Vicksburg, they could no doubt at once have proceeded to possess and run the railroads, via Canton, to Memphis. They doubtless had no idea of his falling back to Canton, and were unexpectedly disconcerted by the movement.

Had they attempted to establish their line of communication with the Mississippi by the route by which they marched to Jackson, and endeavored to procure their supplies by an immense wagon train through the Mississippi and Big Black bottoms, they would either have been cut off by our cavalry and ambuscaders, or would have had to guard the route of fifty miles by an army as large as that at Jackson. Indeed, we do not believe that it would have been practicable to feed an army of forty or fifty thousand men at Jackson by means of a wagon communication of fifty or sixty miles, even if it had been un molested.

We are not, therefore, surprised at the dispatch which informs us that the Yankees have evacuated Jackson, and we shall not be surprised to hear, next, that Gen. Johnston is back at Jackson, or has sought the enemy still nearer Vicksburg, and that the "critical" position in that quarter is the one occupied by the army of Gen. Grant.—*Columbus Enquirer.*

The "Valuable Assistance" of the Negro.

The Washington *Chronicle*, alluding to the aid and comfort given by the negroes to Stoneman's cavalry in their raid, remarks:

It does not look as though the negro slaves were any more devoted to the cause of secession than those in South Carolina and Mississippi. The time will come when we shall appreciate the valuable assistance—valuable beyond that of any other class of people in the South—that we can derive from the negro slaves of those masters who have inaugurated this wicked rebellion.

FINANCIAL.

The *Herald* of the 16th says:

Gold is still dull and neglected at about 150. Speculation in the staple has so entirely died out that no one now cares to inquire what the price is. The gold jobbers are all busily engaged in making money in stocks. Exchange was not active to-day; bankers would not draw under 165; but it was not easy to effect large sales at that figure.

At the pow-wow the Boston Abolitionists made, on Wednesday evening, in their Exeter Hall, in Tremont street, over the negro runaway, Sims, Wendell Phillips and Lloyd Garrison, were on hand, as a matter of course. The former had the grace to say, in the course of a speech on the occasion, that Boston, for sending back Sims to his master, under the Fugitive Slave Law, has been atoning her crime with the blood of some of her best citizens, and that the atonement is not yet complete! A nice man, this Wendell! Garrison, in his elocution, commented in his usual style upon the fact that the Fugitive Slave Law is not yet repealed, and intimated that he was by no means satisfied that Boston would not do again with a fugitive just as she did in the case of Sims, in 1851.

The Washington *Chronicle* of the 9th says that the preparations for the enforcement of the enrollment bill are nearly complete.

The John Brown Raid---An Important Disclosure.

Mr. Sumner was re-elected to the United States Senate, the other day, by the Legislature of Massachusetts. Mr. Swan, a member of the Senate of that State, although a Republican, would not, it seems, vote for Mr. Sumner, and gave the following reasons for so refusing:

"I come now, Mr. President, to what is known in history as the John Brown raid.—This expedition was planned and fitted out in Boston, and its expense defrayed by subscription. The day he started for Harper's Ferry, on his deed of murder, he dined in room No. 4, Parker House, in company with some of the most ardent and zealous supporters of Mr. Sumner, and for this reason I allude to it. The Republican party now disown the act; they call him a monomaniac, an insane man! but when the telegraphic wires, with lightning speed, brought the news of his death to New England, so depraved at that time was the public sentiment here, that the village church bells tolled out his funeral knell, and the ministers of God, with a few honorable exceptions, prayed in their pulpits that the spirit of the "departed saint" might rest in peace. This act, Mr. President, was the death-blow to the peace of the Union. Without it, Virginia would not have seceded, and God grant that we may yet recover from it. I know the names of the persons who were engaged in this transaction, and shall leave a record of them for history.

"Another deed of murder, Mr. President, and I will not detain you longer. When Anthony Burns, the fugitive slave, was confined in the Court House in this city, a meeting was held at Faneuil Hall, to consider the subject. Theodore Parker and the Rev. Thomas W. Higginson were there. Mr. Parker, in concluding an eloquent speech, alluded to the fact that a slave was confined in the Court House, and exclaimed in substance, "Why stand we here idle? To the rescue!" A rush was made for the Court House, and at the door stood a poor laboring man, a Mr. Batchelor, a night watch. His wife and two children were sleeping at home, possibly dreaming of him as he was toiling for their daily bread. The crowd demanded admittance, he refused, and was immediately *assassinated on the spot.* Who killed him, the world never knew. These men, Mr. President, were the confidential friends and supporters of Mr. Sumner, and for this reason I have alluded to the subject.

Latest News from the North.

FREDERICKSBURG, May 19.—New York dates of the 16th inst., have been received here, and afford the following intelligence from the United States:

The New York *Times* has a special telegram from Washington respecting the conscription law, which the United States Government plainly perceives will be practically defeated by the proviso, admitting the payment of $300, to be a discharge from military service.

"WASHINGTON, May 15.—The 18th section of the conscription law has to-day received an interpretation and substantially a warlike adjudication. On the representation of influential citizens of Illinois, that the acceptance of $300 from drafted men, in lieu of service throughout the West, would degenerate the enrollment measure, and defeat the intent to raise an army. Secretary Stanton is understood to have decided that the section is permissive, and not mandatory; that it is optional with him whether to receive the money or reject it; that he is not a national treasurer; that he gives no bond for the safe keeping of money; has no financial officers under him; has no means of enforcing security for the immense sums his subordinates would receive on this commutation of military service, and has no time to go into the business of hunting up substitutes. Solicitor Whiting, of the War Department, concurs in these views. The President also concurs in their legality and policy. The clause of the act selling exemptions at $300, therefore, will be practically ignored. Conscripts will either be left to hunt up substitutes at their own price, or an equal number of volunteers will be called for, at the time the draft is ordered, to be accepted as substitutes for drafted men, and to receive a Government bounty of $100, and the conscripts exemption price at the same time. Any way, the enrollment law will not be a revenue measure, but a war measure."

The subject of another telegram to the same paper is the statement of J. B. Gilfeather, a deserter from the 3d Alabama regiment, Rodes's brigade, who states that the divisions of Hood and Pickett have arrived from the Blackwater since the recent battles, and are now on the Rappahannock line, near Raccoon Ford.

From Washington.

The *Star* says that late information reduces the loss of the army of the Potomac, in the recent battles, to 11,000.

The same paper states that Burnside was in Washington on Thursday, consulting with Lincoln respecting the disposition to be made of Vallandigham.

Fourteen ladies are also announced in its columns as having been released from confinement in the old capitol, among the number, Miss Ford, of Fairfax, "whose behaviour while a prisoner was so entirely modest and correct as to make friends for her of all whose duties were about the prison."

The leading editorial of the *Times* seeks to palliate the sorrow of the public mind over the "unfortunate sequel" of Hooker's late movement on Richmond, by calling attention to the brilliant prospects of success at Vicksburg.

Richmond can scarcely be called a strategic point; its importance is chiefly factitious as the temporary seat of an itinerant Government, and the fall of Richmond would have been but the fall of a city. But the fall of Vicksburg will be the fall of one half of the Confederacy The speedy capture of Vicksburg, therefore, ought to be the prime object of public concern.

THE PURCHASE OF ARMS PROHIBITED IN CHICAGO.—The purchase of arms in Chicago has been prohibited by the acting Provost Marshal, on the plea that agents of the Confederacy were in the habit of purchasing arms and sending them South, and that to put a stop to so damaging a practice, it was necessary to lay an embargo on the entire trade. This may be the true reason, and it may not.

Two hundred and seven of the condemned Sioux Indians have been taken from Mankota, Minnessota, to Rock Island, Illinois.

Army Correspondence.

CAMP, NEAR CHAPEL HILL, TENN.
May 24th, 1863.

MR. EDITOR:—A comparitive lull in military operations seems to pervade our entire front from Sparta to Columbia. For the first time in many long months, our regiment is, quietly, lounging in camp, enjoying the soft, soothing South winds of these glorious Spring days.—The soldiers gather in groups in the deep shade of the tall oak or beech, talking over the events of the past Winter's campaign, marked by the achievements of none but the brave, but saddened by the recollections of a lamented comrade, whom they have left upon the red field of conflict, or distant from home, the victim of disease. The innumerable miles we have marched, the cold, cold terrible nights of Winter we have passed, exposed to the elements, the bloody fields of strife we have withstood, all rise before our minds in vivid distinctness, calling to remembrance the sacrifices we have borne, the devotion we have yielded to the struggling cause of our infant land of liberty.

When involved in a fierce campaign, in dealing blow after blow, in hurried succession, upon the rear of the retiring foe, or repelling with stubborn determination the strokes of the enemy in return, we have but little time to consider the luxurius ease, the sweet hours of genial quietude, we have voluntarily surrendered in leaving our homes, or to calculate the hallowed blessing that would result from a conclusion of this desolating war. But, when idly passing away our time in camp, when no enemy is pressing upon us or picket gun is heard on the outpest, foretelling an approaching conflict, our thoughts naturally turn from the sad contemplation of the thousand horrors of this cruel war, to the endearing memories clustering about our homes, far beyond our overstrained vision, among the silvered vallies of the South. We all want the war to close; we all desire to return to the peaceful walks, the quiet avocations, of our former lives, free from the crash of artillery, the lightning roar of musketry, the din of charging cavalry, but above all, the perishing cries of the unfortunate fallen.

But no thought of yielding ever was in our minds, until the fair flag of the Sunny South floats in triumph from the shores of the Potomac to the buffalo trails through the mountains of the West, or until the thieving foe ceases to tread our soil.

But I regretted, exceedingly, to see the tried patriotism of our soldiers so dampened, their noble efforts so little encouraged, as our Limestone boys were, when they heard of the defeat of Captain J. B. McClellan for Probate Judge. He had stood with them upon the field of Shiloh, he had struggled with them upon the distant plains of Perryville, he had fought with them upon the memorable banks of Stone River, had twice been disabled, once losing his right arm, but the people of his county preferred another. The result has taught some of our soldiers to believe that they need expect no sympathy or support from their countrymen at home, should they lose a limb, or otherwise disabled for life, in performance of their duty to our noble cause on the battlefield or in the sickly camp. But, in spite of this ungrateful reception of a gallant soldier, who has returned with mangled limbs from the scene of battle to ask the suffrages of those in whose defense he had received his lasting misfortunes, we will struggle on, as we have ever done, until established, looking or listening alone to our own consciences, for approval or support. It is true, many of us may sink down to fill a war-worn, despised soldier's grave before our independence is won, leaving none behind to bedew, with a solitary tear, our lonely resting-places, but we will believe, to the latest moment, that men never expired, a sacrifice, in a holier or better cause.

You know, perhaps, Mr. Editor, of the consolidation of our old battalion with another battalion from North Alabama, making it a regiment. It is now the "Seventh Alabama Cavalry," under the daring leadership of our old Lt. Col. James C. Malone, whose gallant name has accumulated celebrity, not only with the Commanding Generals, but with the entire Army of Tennessee. Under the new name of a regiment, we go forth to win fresh laurels in battle against the hated foe whose infamous conduct in North Alabama is remembered by us in every encounter.

All is quiet on the left wing. No fight is expected, unless brought on by us.

John Bell Brownlow has a brigade of cavalry immediately in our front, but no temptations can induce him to leave, even for a mile, the infantry at Triune, back to which his pickets fly at every appearance of our men. I am satisfied that the people of North Alabama need fear no invasion, again, from Tennessee; for the enemy seems to have an uncontrollable horror of ever advancing another foot on Southern soil, for the — thousand cavalry that are now in this State, are but waiting for them to leave their fortifications at Murfreesboro', to sweep away their communications, capture their detachments, and destroy their army in detail.

PETE.

HOOKER'S LOSS.—A citizen of Virginia, who was captured at Fredericksburg and carried to Washington after the battle, gives it as his opinion that Hooker lost, first and last, in killed, wounded, prisoners and deserters, not less than *seventy-five thousand men!*

For the Daily Confederate.

Chapters from my Experience with the Yankees.

BY J. G. WILSON, President of Huntsvilo Female College.

CHAPTER III.

During the period of time embraced in the preceding chapters, there occurred two interesting incidents of the war in this region.—The first was Mitchel's hasty evacuation of Tuscumbia, and the other, the expulsion of the Yankees from Athens, with their subsequent return; and the sacking of that unfortunate town. Mitchel had crossed at Decatur and gone to Tuscumbia, with a considerable force. While he was there, Col. Scott, with about two hundred men, of his Louisiana Cavalry Regiment, being in the vicinity, got possession of a free negro, who had been very intimate with the Yankees, and wrought upon his fears by making arrangements for hanging him instantly.

They, finally, agreed to let him go, on giving a solemn pledge not to inform the Yankees that Price, with 15,000 men, was just behind them.

He went, post-haste to Tuscumbia and informed the Yankees, that the woods and fields were full of Price's men.

Tuscumbia, was hastily, evacuated, and an attack being made upon their train, by two of Scott's companies, a hasty retreat across the river took place, and the Decatur bridge was burned, to prevent *Price's army* from continuing their pursuit. Gen. Mitchel, on reaching Huntsville, rode up to the Bank and informed some our citizens that the R. R bridge at Decatur had been burned by his orders. "The Union army," said he "is not in the habit of burning bridges, but this was a *military necessity.*"

This was at the time that Bishop Lay and myself were in solitary confinement, and hearing some of my guard talking about Price's army, and their own retreat from Tuscumbia, I asked one of them, if he was there: He said, he was. Said I: "Did you see any of Price's men yourself?" On his replying in the affirmative, I inquired, "How many do you suppose you saw?" "About eight thousand," said he, So frequently and persistently did they make such statements, that we, at the time, believed them, and listened, eagerly, for the music of Price's cannon, but; alas! the only cannon we could then hear, were those of Loomis's Yankee battery, firing, every now and then, *a feu de joie* over reported Yankee victories.

On the other occasion, about two hundred of Scott's cavalry stampeded an Ohio regiment out of Athens. Mitchel, himself, like the lame Captain, started first on a R. R. train, and dashed furiously over a bridge, that had been set on fire, but, unfortunately, had not burnt sufficiently to let him through. Through the blazing bridge he dashed, deserving by this feat, if by no other, the name generally given him by Yankee papers, of the 'dashing Mitchel.' For this conduct, he was afterwards, denounced in Huntsville by an Ohio Colonel, Harris, in his true character, as an arrant poltroon.

The people of Athens were, of course, overjoyed at their deliverance, and testified their delight in the most enthusiastic manner.—Amongst the most enthusiastic in her demonstrations, was Miss R., a lovely Alabama girl, and one of my pupils. Their joy was of short duration. Soon, a heavy reinforcement of the the enemy arrived, and, in retaliation for these demonstrations, the town was given up to pillage and rapine.

One of the Yankee soldiers, meeting Miss R., said to her: "Yes, you are the young lady that waved the Secesh flag, all day; Wilson taught you that." He did me no more than justice, for, amongst other good lessons; I tried to teach my pupils, I enforced, earnestly, that of patriotism, and devotion to the South. I endeavored to inspire in them the patriotic ambition, as Southern girls, to make of themselves such ladies as would reflect honor upon the South, and more than maintain the already marked superiority in refinement of soul and manner, of Southern ladies over Yankee women.

To these exhortations I, also, frequently, added the charge, that, when they became young ladies in society, they must never suffer themselves to receive the addresses of any young man, who withheld his services from his country in this hour of her peril. I am sure that no Southern ladies can be found better or truer patriots, than the noble and lovely daughters of Huntsville Female College, and it is with delight, that, since the evacuation of our place, I have received from many of them, in their distant homes, assurances of the indignation with which they learned, from the papers, of the treatment I had received, and of the prayers that had been offered by them in my behalf.

P. S. In printing Chapter II, in your last issue, the printer makes me say, "the Yankee traitors," when it should have been "Yankee Teachers."

There is in Lynchburg, Virginia, on the premises of F. B. Dean, Esq., a willow grown from a slip that was brought from the tomb of Napoleon, at St. Helena; and from this willow made a wreath and adorned it with flowers to lay on the bier of the lamented Jackson when borne through that city.

Places in Mississippi.

Editors Charleston Courier:—Herewith, should you choose to publish, you will find some facts regarding points and places among which a momentous struggle is to take place. These statements are, I believe, mainly correct, and may be of interest to your readers.

A description of Vicksburg would be repeating a tale already thrice told. Suffice it to say the natural defences in its rear are fully equal to those in its front, which look so sternly victorious upon the river.

The Southern Railroad running from Vicksburg to Meridian, a distance of 140 miles, is conducted by gentlemen of energy and ability, who have made every effort to furnish transportation for troops and supplies, and keep the road and rolling stock in the best possible condition. Going East the first station is Mount Albon, seven miles from Vicksburg—a place of twelve or fifteen scattered houses. Next Bovina, ten miles from Vicksburg, three or four houses, two stores, but is the depot for the neighborhood within fifteen miles. Two miles from Bovina and twelve miles from Vicksburg, is Big Black Bridge, crossing that stream some fifteen miles from where it empties into the Mississippi river. The stream is about one hundred yards wide, and was formerly navigable for small vessels as high up as where the railroad crosses, but the stream has become obstructed by trees and the caving in of embankments, so that its navigation would be difficult, if not impossible.

The topography of the country through which the river runs, below the railroad, is generally swampy; above, it gradually arises into undulating and heavily wooded land. As may be supposed, the stream is fordable, but, owing to the nature of its banks, the passage of artillery and wagons is difficult, and confined to few fords. The bridge which crosses the river here is about a half mile long and eighty feet high. The part of it which is immediately over the river is supported by strong columns of stone and brick; the rest is of strong wooden timbers. Of course the destruction of this bridge, or the possession of it by the enemy, would isolate Vicksburg from communication with other parts of the Confederacy. Six miles from the bridge, eighteen miles from Vicksburg, and twenty-eight miles from Jackson, is Edward's Depot. A few houses, few stores, a blacksmith and carriage shop, make up the place. In the season between eighteen and twenty-five thousand bales of cotton are shipped from here. The wagon road to Jackson runs by here—as, in fact, it does all along the railroad. There seems to be no reason, from its position, that it should be considered a strategic point, other than to protect the railroad bridge and to prevent the enemy crossing the Big Black. But, at the same time, the possession of this point, or, in fact, a point either side of it, would open to them the Yazoo country.

Next through an undulating, wooded country, we come to Bolton's Depot, eight miles from Edward's Depot, twenty-six miles from Vicksburg and twenty miles from Jackson. This place is like the last in point of size and importance. A railroad extends from Bolton's to Raymond, a distance of some eight miles, but it is not now in operation. Ten miles on is Clinton, of 1000 or 1500 population—seat of an excellent College and was once one of the most flourishing cities in the State. Another ten miles and you reach Jackson, the junction of N. O. J. & G. N. Railroad with Southern Railroad, forty-six miles from Vicksburg, ninety-nine from Meridian and something over two hundred miles above New Orleans. It is a city of 5000 or 6000 inhabitants, pleasantly situated and contains handsome State buildings. The Southern Railroad crosses Pearl river here. This stream is navigable for small craft to Jackson, but such is the risk of navigation that it is never attempted but as an experiment. This stream runs South and empties into or near Mississippi Bay.—Canton, where the Mississippi Central Railroad and N. O. J. & G. N. Railroads connect, lies twenty-three miles North of Jackson. Brandon, a place of 1500 inhabitants, and quite an enterprising town, is twelve miles from Jackson. Going onward we pass Pelahatchie, Mortan Lake, Forest, Newton, Hickory, and so on to Meridian, where the Southern Railroad connects with three different roads running North, South and East. Meridian, in the hands of the enemy, would give him command of our railroad transportation between Mississippi and all other parts of the Confederacy. Meridian is a low, sandy place, consisting of railroad buildings, two or three "hotels" and a half-dozen houses. The stations between Brandon and Meridian are simply depots and not likely to be the scene of a struggle.

W. H. J.

☞ I cannot refrain from sending you, for publication, a copy of the ballad on Sumter's last fight, written during the recent outward passage of the "Antonica," by one of our own home poets, the sailor-soldier, Capt. E. O. Murden. It is on the lips of all the Charleston boys in Nassau and will do well to go down to posterity in company with the popular "Twas on the 12th of April," of the first fight. Here it is:—*Nassau Cor. Chas. Courier.*

THE LAST BALL AT FORT SUMTER.

AIR—"A WET SHEET AND A FLOWING SEA."

Come all ye jolly mariners,
And bold soldier boys
Who were not killed by iron-clads,
Not frightened by their noise;
Let's sing a song of victory,
And pass around the joke,
For the Yankee Iron bubble's burst,
And ended all in smoke.

CHORUS.—Then blow your horn, old Abraham,
But pray for better luck,
For we battered all your Ironsides
And sunk the "Keokuk"

With your patent cheese-box Monitors,
You came in grand array,
To batter down old Sumter's walls,
And anchor in our bay;
But Beauregard and Ripley
Had our Southern boys and guns,
And the way they ripped into you,
Put a damper on your fun.
Chorus, &c.

In boastful pride and arrogance,
Our calibre you tried,
And with your grand "reconnoissance,"
We hope you're satisfied.
Dupont, your Lord High Admiral,
Was glad to crawl away,
And we'll wager if the truth were known,
His head aches to this day.
Chorus, &c.

With your iron, wooden Devils,
Full of hooks and chains and grabs,
You raked up all the oyster beds,
And frightened all the crabs.
We caught one precious Monster,
And we've got it on the shore,
But such a Yankee Sea Devil
Was never seen before.
Chorus, &c.

'T is true we caught the Devil--Abe,
But not the one you meant,
For we recognized the cloven foot,
And knew your kind intent.
We're thankful for the iron--Abe,
But you'd better save your pains,
For the Devil cannot scare us
Unto Yankee rule and chains.
Chorus, &c.

☞ A private letter from Sparta, Tenn., contains a dispatch from Gen. Morgan, dated Monticello, Ky., May 12, 8 A. M., in which he says:

"I have met the enemy 10,000 strong—the cavalry under Woolford, the infantry under Gen. Carter—and have, repulsed them with heavy loss. They retreated cross the Cumberland, leaving their baggage, camp equipage, &c., in my hands. They lost 300 drowned crossing the river. I am on the field burying dead Yankees. My loss is light, considering two days' engagement."—*Knox. Reg.*

Bad Luck is simply a man with his hands in his pocket and his pipe in his mouth, looking on to see how it comes out. Good Luck is a man of pluck, with his sleeves rolled up, and working to make it come out right.

VOL. I. RICHMOND, SATURDAY, MAY 30, 1863. No. 38.

COMMODORE FRENCH FORREST.

We present to our readers in this number of the Illustrated News, a portrait of Commodore French Forrest, a gallant officer of the Confederate Navy, whose conspicuous and valuable services to his country, both before and since the formation of the new Government, form an important chapter in the history of the age. A brief and rapid *resumé* of these services may not inappropriately accompany the portrait.

Commodore Forrest is the third son of the late Major J. Forrest of Washington City. His mother was the daughter of Benjamin Tasker Dulany of Shuter's Hill. In 1811, he entered the Navy of the United States, being then in the 14th year of his age, as midshipman, and remained for some months in the Naval School under Professor Hunter, but the war with England breaking out, he was ordered to join Commodore Hull in the frigate *Constitution*, then undergoing repairs in the Washington Navy Yard, from which ship he was very soon transferred to the *Hornet*, Commander J. Lawrence. He served on board the *Hornet* during the whole of that celebrated cruise in which she captured the *Peacock*, and returned with her to New York, then blockaded by the English fleet, making a perilous but successful entry through the ships of the enemy.

Throughout the whole of the war with Great Britain, young Forrest shared the dangers and the glory of the naval service, honored with the confidence of Decatur, Jones, Biddle, Lawrence, Downes, Hull and the rest of those brave spirits who humbled the pride of England and disputed with her the sovereignty of the seas. When the British army under General Ross entered Washington City, he was entrusted with the duty of destroying the new sloop *Argus*, which he accomplished under circumstances of great difficulty and danger, and then took command of a battery at the White House on the Potomac, which he worked efficiently until its abandonment became compulsory, and then did not desert until every gun had been silenced or dismounted by the superior armament of the enemy. After the proclamation of Peace, he made a cruise in the Mediterranean in the *Epervier*, of which vessel he would have been a Lieutenant, but for his youth, being just 17, and participated in the naval war with the Algerine pirates, so well known to the readers of American history. The subsequent operations of the American navy, though illustrated by no brilliant achievements, were not without some exciting episodes, such as conflicts with West Indian pirates, and escapes upon the deep from the war of elements more terrific even than that of man, in which he bore his part, until the war with Mexico, when having risen to the first position on the Quarter deck, he was placed in command of the *Raritan*, and contributed to as full an extent as any other naval Captain to the success of American arms in that memorable struggle. Subsequently to the treaty of Guadaloupe Hidalgo, Commodore Forrest commanded the Washington Navy Yard, from which post he was transferred to the chief command of the Brazilian Squadron, and it may be said that the United States never had a more efficient nor a more popular representative on that station. Although watchful of the vast commerce interested with Brazil, intrusted to his care, he was always a welcome visitor at the Court and in the cultivated society of Rio de Janeiro. The polished urbanity of his manners and the charm of his varied conversation will long be remembered in the diplomatic and court circles of the Brazilian capital.

COMMODORE FRENCH FORREST,

C. S. NAVY.

Little remains to be said of Commodore Forrest since the commencement of the existing war, but that little is a shining record. Had the Confederate States owned a navy, and thus given him the opportunity of striking for their cause upon the seas, there can be little doubt that he would have brightened the story of the past two years, by deeds of heroism worthy to be compared with the highest achievements of naval warfare. Upon the secession of Virginia he was among the first to resign his commission in the U. S. Navy and to offer his services to the State. Appointed by Governor Letcher Flag Officer of the Navy of Virginia, he quickly repaired to Norfolk and upon the very night of his arrival there, witnessed the partial destruction by fire of the largest naval depot in America. One incident of that night deserves to be particularly noted. Desirous of saving as much of the public property as was possible, Commodore Forrest, accompanied by Lieut. Harrison, was crossing the river in an open boat, when he was met by Lieut. Rodgers, a Yankee prisoner in our hands, who begged him to turn back. "You know I have always loved you," said he, "and I implore you Commodore, for God's sake, do not enter that yard—*it is mined.*" "Sir," replied Forrest, "my country calls, and I *will* go at every hazard," and go he did, and, with the assistance of the gallant officers comprising the "Norfolk Navy," as it was called and Col. Hodges, with his regiment of volunteers, succeeded in saving millions of dollars in munitions of war, whose real value to the Confederacy cannot be computed.

With unsurpassed energy he there applied himself to the task of reorganizing the vast establishment which had been rescued from the flames. It was found that through the agency of Providence, much had been saved of inestimable value. In fact, the great machine, building shops and foundry had been rescued from the destruction which the Yankees had meditated.—With these agencies at his command, Commodore Forrest soon evoked order out of chaos and made the desolate looking Navy Yard again resonant with the sounds of labor. A complete system was at once established. The operatives were paid off and the energy of his own purpose infused into the whole establishment. In short, a well conducted Dock-yard was the result of his labors. At this Cherbourg of America the Merrimac was fitted for her famous cruise, upon which memorable occasion, Commodore Forrest, with a large staff on board the Harmony, accompanied the squadron on the 8th and 9th of March in Hampton Roads, where he managed with a talent peculiarly his own to keep, during the first day's fighting constantly under the enemy's fire. Shortly after this he was ordered to report for duty with the Secretary of the Navy in Richmond, and more lately he has been assigned to command the James River Squadron.

Many years ago Commodore Forrest married a daughter of the late John D. Simms, for many years Chief Clerk of the Navy Department of the United States. In person he is the very type of the sailor; his expression is frank and pleasing, and the mingled firmness and amenity of his character renders him at once fitted for any circle, the deck and the drawing room, the council chamber and the theatre of combat.

TIME.—The angel of Time, like Milton's cherubim, has six wings: two cover its coming, and two its going, and with two it flies.

FORNEY'S WAR PRESS

$2 PER ANNUM. PHILADELPHIA, SATURDAY, JUNE 6, 1863. VOL. 2.—NO. 30

QUATRAINS.

Gardener.

True Brahmin, in the morning meadows wet,
Expound the Vedas of the violet,
Or, hid in vines, peeping through many a loop,
See the plum redden and the beurre stoop.

Northman.

The gale that wrecked you on the sand,
It helped my rowers to row;
The storm is my best galley hand,
And drives me where I go.

From Alcuin.

The sea is the road of the bold,
Frontier of the wheat-sown plains,
The pit wherein the streams are rolled,
And fountain of the rains.

Nature.

Boon Nature yields each day a brag which we now first behold,
And trains us on to see the new as if it were the old;
But blest is he, who playing deep, yet happy asks not why,
Too busy with the crowded hour to fear to live or die.

Natura in minimis.

As sings the pine tree in the wind,
So sings in the wind a sprig of the pine,
Her strength and soul has laughing France
Shed in each drop of wine.

Orator.

He who has no hands,
Perforce must use his tongue;
Foxes are so cunning
Because they are not strong.

Poet.

To clothe fiery thought
In simple word succeeds;
For still the craft of genius is
To mask a king in weeds.

Artist.

Quit the hut, frequent the palace—
Reck not what the people say;
For still where'er the trees grow biggest
Huntsmen find the easiest way.

Forester.

He took the color of his vest
From rabbit's coat or grouse's breast,
For, as the wood kinds lurk and hide,
So walks the woodman unespied.

Climacteric.

I am not wiser for my age,
Nor skilful by my grief;
Life loiters at the book's first page—
Ah! could we turn the leaf.

[*R. W. Emerson.*

Original Novelette.

[Written for The War Press.]

FLORENCE LISTON.

A STORY OF THE HEART.

BY FERDINAND L. SARMIENTO.

CHAPTER III.

THE TEMPEST OF THE HEART.

It may be expected that I looked anxiously for my friend, and attended regularly at the depot to receive and welcome him the minute he might arrive. But all to no purpose.

Two weeks passed—three weeks—a month—and still no Carl; nor did I, during this time, receive one line of explanation. But at last, one morning, just as I had given up all idea of ever hearing from or ever seeing my new friend, in he bounced, much as a great Newfoundland dog might have done—warm, hearty, and affectionate.

"Dear Edmund," he cried, "I fear that you have lost all patience with me; but really I couldn't help it. I have been beguiling myself in Berlin, that delightful French-Teutonic town, where, too, I met a most charming woman—a friend of the captain."

"The captain?" I exclaimed. "What the mischief was that man with you for?"

"Hush! he is here with me!" interrupted my friend, cautiously.

"You mean in town, here?"

"No, I mean in this house, and at this very moment. He is now closeted with Mr. Liston, who is, I believe, an old friend."

"But this charming creature—this divinity that you discovered at Berlin—was she so fascinating?"

"Fascinating! I never have met a woman so charming. She is intellectual and beautiful with all; and although she is the leader of the beaux monde of the capital, she is as unsophisticated and childlike as a village maiden. It is this that gives such a particular charm."

I laughed—"I see, by these raptures that some German cupid has already had the honor to bring you down. Oh Carl! and that at the first fire! Three weeks in the country, and in love already!"

"Not in *love*—only infatuated, my dear friend, which is a distinction with a difference," answered my friend, good humoredly.

"But what is this engaging lady's name?"

"Constance—Countess de Käroly."

"So, so; high born and titled as well!"

"And as high in mind and purity as in station."

"Well, well, all circumstances taken into consideration, I suppose I shall have to forgive your delay. Friendship never yet withstood the temptation of a pretty woman, and it is vain to expect it. But you must know the Listons. Miss Florence and you, I foresee, will wage a war to the death, what with your high and titled flame and her stern democratic nations; and as this is her mother's grand reception day, you will have an opportunity to commence at once—so *descendous*."

I laughed to myself—"Won't Florence quiz this new-fledged republican about his blind worship of rank? It will be as good as a play."

We were descending the stairway, in whose heavy shadows my fancy so loved to linger, when a merry voice rang out above our heads. "We are *doomed*, I believe, to meet on the stairs!" it exclaimed; and looking up, I saw the sweet object of my thoughts peering down at us. Then barely acknowledging the profound bow of my friend as I introduced him, she continued, in her usual wayward manner—

"I'm in *such* a humor; I don't know when I have been in such a humor!"

"A most charming one, I should say, Miss Liston," I replied, smiling at her impetuosity.

"No, indeed; quite the contrary. I'm in a most dreadful humor. There's ma insists upon having me in the drawing-room, just because that horrid Lord Summerby is there. I declare I'll take as long as I can to dress, and when I do come down, I will do all I can to annoy him—that is, if he has sense enough to be annoyed, which I very much doubt. Bye-bye, until we meet, as ma would say, 'under more genteel auspices'—for, as I take it, you are on your way to the 'blue room,' or 'heavenly apartment,' as I call it, for I am never there two minutes at a time without wishing that I was in heaven, or some other place. Oh, I forgot to tell you that your *friend*, Captain Rocheford, is with ma—at least so my maid tells me, and has flattered her ideas of gentility so that he is already an established favorite."

"How strange that man is," exclaimed I to Carl, as bowing in answer to her graceful wave of the hand, we continued our descent.

"And what an odd creature your little friend is," he answered in a tone of raillery. "Ah, you sly dog; you have been bantering me about love at first sight, and all the time have been luxuriating in it! Now, is that quite fair, I ask?"

"*I* in love! Oh Carl, why that's simply ridiculous," I answered, not relishing this "turning of the tables."

"Well, I'll put it to any one. Here is a young lady—large flashing eyes, magnificent complexion, and a mouth like Cupid's bow—not a German Cupid's, Edmund—not a *German* Cupid's, my friend—and who is as friendly after a three weeks' acquaintance as a sister would be!"

"Oh, nonsense, Carl," I interrupted; "and as for her familiarity—that is her manner."

"And then, here is a young gentleman, sentimental, and all that!"

"Miss Liston is but a child," I exclaimed, now really annoyed.

"A child! Miss Liston must be at least seventeen, and believe me she is no child. At that age a female's life is like a rose-bud whose almost bursting leaves are still held by the gummy dew that loads it petals. Love, its sun, comes, and in a moment it is no longer the bud, but a full-blown rose, fragrant and beautiful."

"Alas!" I answered, sighing, "Carl, if she loved me she would be quieter. One does not talk so much to one who is beloved."

But the only reply my friend vouchsafed was a hearty laugh, which was so full of sarcasm that I said not another word until we reached the drawing-room door.

I will not attempt to describe the impressive state of the Hon. Mrs. Liston upon this occasion; suffice it to say that it was greater than ever.

At the large folding-door stood a tall footman, *en grande tense*, whose duty it was to usher in the expected guests, while in the corridor, outside, another stood, with a silver salver to receive their cards. Mrs. Liston's reception of my friend was of the most flattering character; for wealth was a consideration with the honorable lady, and I made no doubt but that the captain had informed her officially upon this point, viz: that he was the son of a millionaire.

Although early, there were already several guests assembled; among others, Lord Summerby, who was recovering apparently from the irretrievable loss of his favorite pointer, so touchingly dwelt upon in my first interview by the sympathizing lady of my *chef*. His lordship was relating the particulars of this most lamentable affair to the captain, when he was interrupted by Mrs. Liston, presenting Carl and myself; for this was the first time that I had met him.

"My lord," simpered the lady, "allow me to introduce to your lordship Mr. Olmstead, from New York; also Mr. Lawrence, of the Embassy."

"Aw-h, most happy," answered his lordship, having taken a full minute to consider the matter, and endeavoring in vain to screw an eye-glass into his eye, so as to retain it there even for the space of a moment.

"Awh, most happy; I was relating to captain, awh, awh, Rocheford—awh, yes, Rocheford—the circumstances connected with the loss of a favorite dawg. I offered a reward of fifty pounds, do you know—fifty pounds, 'pon honor—but received no tidings whatever, you know. Poor dawg! At last, I determined to set out myself in serach of it, you know, so I told my fellaw, who is a German, and the greatest ass, to bring me a conveyance.

"A conveyance?" says he.

"Yes, any kind of a trap," says I.

"Now, what do you think the stupid ass brought me? A mouse-trap; yes, 'pon honor, a mouse trap, and this fellaw pretended to understand English! Devilish stupid, must say."

The laugh which this anecdote elicited, and in which his lordship joined, though I doubt if it was from the same motive, was interrupted by the entrance of Miss Liston, who, in a charming demi-toilet, looked as fascinating as though instead of being indifferent to admiration, which I really believe, she was now bent upon captivating half the world.

"Oh, Florence, you have missed *such* a treat!" cried the mother. "His lordship has just been relating such an amusing anecdote, and so charmingly, too, that I have laughed until the tears have come into my eyes. You must persuade his lordship to tell it you. Most amusing, I declare."

"Is it the story of the mouse-trap, ma? If so, I must protest against ever hearing it again, for it invariably puts me into a wretched humor."

"Awh," interposed his lordship, "I am sorry that my little anecdote meets with Miss Liston's disapprobation. May I ask, is it my indifferent manner of relating it that strikes her unpleasantly?"

"Oh, not at all, my lord. But it is so annoying, you know, to hear that there are people in this world so stupid as not to understand your lordship!" answered she, regardless of her mother's appealing dumb motions to desist.

"Awh, that's what annoyed me, you know; and I declare, I was upon the point of discharging the fellaw at once; but then, you know, not speaking this horrible language here, I could not do without him. The, awh, the fellaw knew this, and evidently took advantage of it, you know."

"It is plain that the fellow has the advantage of you," replied the mischievous girl, while his lordship, perfectly unconscious of her sarcasm, bowed delightedly at her seeming concurrence with his views.

"What a delightful Darby and Joan you and my lord would make," I whispered to Miss Liston, laughingly.

MAJOR GENERAL OLIVER O. HOWARD,
COMMANDER OF ELEVENTH ARMY CORPS, ARMY OF THE POTOMAC.

"Would we not! Methinks I can realize it, all spread out like a picture before me. He on one side of the fire-place; I on the other. Wouldn't we be happy? Marriages are made in heaven, they say; now wouldn't this be one with a vengeance?"

"You ungrateful girl!" exclaimed the mother, aside, having overheard this last remark. "After all my pains—why are you not more complacent to his lordship? I declare, you are not one bit like I was at your age. Mr. Lawrence, can't you do something with her?"

"My advice would have little weight," I replied. "Beside, I doubt if I should be found arrayed on your side. But, is your aversion to Lord Summerby so very great?" I asked, addressing myself to Miss Liston.

"Can you ask? What feeling can a *woman*—for I am a woman in thought, if not in age—entertain for such an insignificant, brainless iota of a man? I ask you."

"He is what the world calls an excellent match, and I believe wealthy and good-natured."

"He may be all these. But, believe me, a woman needs for a husband some one whom she can look up to—her superior in mind, in strength, and in energy. She has been likened to a vine twining its tendrils about some sturdy oak; but the oak must be stout, and not some puny plant, that, bending to the first blast of adversity, is prostrated by it. It must prove first that it is staunch, and capable of supporting the vine, else it were, indeed, a silly flower that would trust to it its future."

"Miss Liston, I imagine, will find it difficult to find one to her liking," interposed Carl.

Although we had all been engaged in conversation, this was the first time that Carl had addressed himself directly to the fair girl, and I was curious to note the answer. But there was none, unless a constrained bow could be so construed.

Why? I asked myself, was her manner different with Carl from what it had been at OUR first meeting? Why this constraint. this almost timidity, when addressed by him? Was it because he was a stranger? No! I, too, had been a stranger to her, and yet at our first meeting she had bandied words, given saucy rejoinders, and acted altogether differently. I determined to ask her, though indirectly.

"What do you think of my friend?" I asked. "I have spoken so much to you about him, that I am anxious to know your opinion."

"Your friend is, I believe, noble and amiable. He is less handsome than I had expected from your glowing description, but he has an intelligent light about his countenance that is superior to mere beauty; indeed, I dislike beauty in a man."

"Then you are favorably impressed with him?"

"Very much so. But why do you ask?"

"Oh, nothing! without it was that I was wondering that you were less distant with others than with him."

"With whom, for instance?"

"With almost every one. But to be particular, I will designate two present—Lord Summerby and myself."

"Am I? But you must remember that Lord Summerby I consider a mere nobody; and with yourself, doomed as we were to be thrown together almost like brother and sister, constraint would be ridiculous; at least, so I thought, and so I have acted."

But was this flattering? It might be, and it might not; and alas! I was not sufficiently well versed in woman nature to solve the enigma. But there was a little voice that spoke to me, that welled up from my heart, bringing with it bloody tears. Was it jealousy, or was it but the echo of a lover's fears? I knew not. But bidding Carl, who had accompanied me to my room door, good-bye, I locked and doubly locked it, and buried my face in my hands, the most wretched of beings.

"Is her manner the sign of love, or is it mere indifference? Does she, does she really like me, or is her affection that only of a sister?" I asked.

Curses, curses upon platonic love, I say, for hate may be transformed to love, but indifference never. I was startled by a knock at my room door. It was Carl returned.

"I say, Edmund," he whispered, "I forgot to tell you not to say anything to your little friend about the countess."

"Why not?" I asked, half aloud, half in thought; but he had disappeared down the long corridor, and echo alone answered my question. That echo was from my heart.

CHAPTER IV.

THE PHANTOM KNIGHT.

It was a grand festival day. From early dawn, the numerous church bells had been summoning the faithful to commence the day with prayer, and multitudes of veiled females, with now and then a male, might have been seen moving in the direction of the grand old cathedral, or one of the lesser churches, in obedience to the call. Then one could hear the low, rich tones of the organ in some of the neighboring places of worship, and later the swelling bursts of harmony that told that mass was over. Then the people came hurrying along, as though in haste for the warm breakfasts awaiting them at home. Boys came out, hooting and hallooing, glad that church was over for that day, and that their fun was about to commence.

Long files of soldiers, too, marched through the city, all verging to one point, and betrayed alone by their measured tramp; for no beat of the drum or martial tone dare sound till noon shall have drawn the line between the religious and the worldly "fest"—between man's duty and his pleasure.

But after twelve o'clock, all the town is on the move. One sees no longer pious women gliding silently along, with their prayer books in their hand, or old, venerable-looking priests with their rosaries dangling at their sides; but comfortable, smiling wives, all decked out in their best, have taken their places, with happy, boisterous urchins tugging at their dresses; while papa, that respectable old "burgher," and who has been taking a long holiday morning nap while his wife was at prayer, comes jogging along after, expostulating in vain at the rapid gait of the younger portion of the family. Music resounds from every side. The shutters are taken down from the windows of the cafés, crowds of officers collect about them blocking up the sidewalks and ogling the pretty girls that pass; and all is commotion and joy, for there is to be a grand review, at which the Court and some foreign princes are to assist.

Time glides on, slowly for the little folks, but too fast for the hurried housewives, whose husbands are "too mean" to order luncheon from some restaurant, and who are forced, in consequence, to stand "already dressed" over the fire, to prepare that most provoking of all things, an early dinner.

But at last the fumes of hot meats and savory soups die out; the forgiving *fraus*—foolishly good-natured, like all women—smooth their rumpled dresses and their brows, and follow their more fortunate sisters, who have been helping their husbands spend their money at the neighboring "Gasthaus."

Now loud and rich strains of military music thrill the air, making the children kick up their heels anew, and large bodies of troops march through the city gates to form on the glacis outside; while every available place on the overlooking bastions is already occupied. Then the various commanders bellow and grow red in the face; splendidly-appointed aides-de-camp gallop from one point to another, backing their horses into the affrighted crowd, making men swear and children scream, and throwing everything into confusion; during which the troops are drawn up into line, when the multitude quiet down in expectancy.

Then there is a loud flourish of trumpets, and banners wave, lances glisten, and the artillery pours forth its stunning salute; drums beat, the troops present arms, the folks-hymn swells upon the air, and, punctual to the minute, the royal host and princely visitors dash along the front.

It is a sight not to be forgotten—a glittering, confusing memory, that, like the flash of a jewel, is something to be seen, but impossible to describe.

On this particular occasion there were to be at least sixty thousand troops in line, twenty thousand of which were to be cavalry, and, of course, there was a general desire to see such an army together, especially in review.

At the hotel of the Hon. Mr. Liston all had been in commotion from an early period. "Monsieur le Ministre et Madame sa femme" had received cards, and were to be shut up in a kind of pavilion, the peculiar privilege of the elect; while Florence, accompanied by Carl and myself, was to go mounted, and mingle with the less aristocratic but infinitely more pleasant crowd, collected in the open air space reserved for titled or "distinguished strangers."

Two months had rolled over since that memorable reception-day, and Carl had been an almost daily visitor at the Listons. As a natural consequence, Florence and he had been much together; and oh, with what jealous pangs did I not mark their intercourse! Her manner, though more trusting towards him, had lost none of its timidity; while with me she was as off-hand and willful as ever. With him she was the woman; with me, the child. Yet, was this food for hope or not? This was the question that consumed my heart, gnawing at it night and day.

Carl had never spoken to me of his love for Florence. It had been, as it were, intuitively understood that neither was to broach that subject; so in all our association not one word of Florence escaped our lips. But, oh, we both saw the love hidden deep in the other's heart! We knew that we were rivals!

As for Florence, life seemed with her one long glorious day; and never had I seen her spirits so elastic and joyous as now. She was a fearless rider, and in her dark purple riding-habit, looked the beau-ideal of a beautiful Amazon. So thought Carl, and so thought I, as mounted on fiery steeds we both sought inspiration from her eyes. It was a bitter rivalship that day, I acknowledge, between us, for I felt that I loved her, and I *knew* that he did so—had done so, from the first moment he beheld her. Alas! had I had any doubts of this before, they must have instantly been dispelled now. That loving glance, that earnest gaze, that almost wonderful anticipation of her every wish—there was no mistaking it. Or, was it my jealousy merely, that, like a gnome, created horrid visions whereon to feed?

Alas! the flower of love is a thorny one, and he who would pluck it comes seldom, if ever, bloodlessly away.

The review had already commenced when we arrived on the ground. The loud artillery had belched forth its noisy welcome. The rattle of arms had subsided, and the air now resounded with stirring marches and merry polkas, as the troops, in glittering columns, defiled before the royal party.

"Awh, I have the honor, Miss Liston, your servant," exclaimed Lord Summerby, bowing and advancing as we neared the barrier erected to confine the pressing crowd. "Awh, most provoking, must say; make room there, fellaw; don't, awh, don't you see the lady coming? Stupid, devilish stupid, must say!"

"You are late, Miss Florence. Their Royal Highnesses have already arrived!" exclaimed, Mr. Jackson, whom we had not observed before, and who, like ourselves, had preferred the open air.

"In plenty time," answered the beautiful Amazon, bending over regardless of the pageant, to pat her horse's neck. "You know that I am no worshipper of Royal Highnesses. Neither history nor experience teach me to believe that they are a whit superior to the common herd. As for the review, I have seen so many that the novelty has quite worn off."

"But do you not think, Miss Florence, with all your just indifference to mere rank, that it is interesting to see the characters that are destined to play important *rôles* in that grand melo-drama yclept history?"

"Certainly. Are there any such here?"

"There are those whose birth would entitle them to play parts that might astonish the world."

"But do they do it? Are there any here, I ask, famous for any virtue under heaven, wisdom extraordinary, or fit, indeed, but to act the part of 'supes' in that great stage—the world? Look at that fat, bloated old fellow."

"Awh, Miss Liston, I say, it isn't possible you mean the King of Prussia?" cried his lordship, terrified at these rank heresies to his aristocratic faith.

"Yes," she continued, "that old fellow is the King of Prussia, but is he famed for anything but his love for champagne, and the ballet? Mark that tall, youthful form; his dominions stretch for boundless leagues, comprising as many nationalities, almost, as there are nations on the globe. What a sublime *rôle* might that man not fill, to be applauded and blessed by all ages to come! But what is he, really? A drill-master—a drill-master, nothing but that! Pshaw! Note, too, that crowd of petty North-German Princes surrounding him! Do you think they are aught else but choristers—to croak as he croaks, and to sing as he sings? Then there is that beautiful woman there, who sits her horse so majestically. It is the Queen of Greece. For what is she famous but her base intrigues? Yet she is the *real* man of the party, and had I any curiosity on the subject, I would rather see her than any of the rest of the party. Ah, believe me, my friend, and you, my lord, he is the truly great man, one whom I would even run after to see, who has done some good for the world—whatever his birth, whatever his rank!"

"Well spoken!" cried Carl, almost involuntarily, while pride and love beamed in every feature. "By Jove, that annihilates you, gentlemen!"

"Have I been too earnest, Mr. Olmstead?" she asked, blushingly, and almost timidly. The answer was lost in a sudden shout of the crowd; but a deeper hue mantled her cheek, and her eyes sunk softly to the ground; while the old tears welled up from my heart, almost choking me.

The hoarse shouts of the multitude had been in honor of the now departing royal party, and as though this had been a given signal, the carriages and foot passengers all began to stream homewards. Affectionate fathers who had been holding their little ones in their arms, thrt they might see the better, now gladly set them down again on terra firma, where the ungrateful little creatures, seeing that there was to be no more fun, and believing doubtlessly that there was no use in being good any longer, immediately set up a squall in consequence. Mothers, aunts, and grandmothers took the shortest road home. Tired out, and dragging their breathless and struggling charges after them by one arm as one would a toy cart, supposing a cart could kick up in that way: while every now and then they would stop to bestow a cuff—the aunts especially—by way of a safety valve to their discomfiture. Occasionally you meet a good little fellow, who was only quiet because he had his mouth stuffed with candy; nature fortunately having only made him with one mouth. Or again, you would meet a puny, sickly-looking child that was naturally too good to cry. Alas! I don't believe that such children live long. But, as a general rule, all was confusion and discontent with great and small. As long as the music lasted, all went very well, but as soon as the royal party had left, the musicians put up their pieces, the drummers slung their drums, and the different regiments moved in companies or squads towards their relative barracks, as fagged out, almost, as the spectators—then all was dismal.

In the confusion, we had lost my lord and Mr. Jackson; so fortunately our small party was alone again.

"Come, let us make a little excursion," exclaimed Florence, turning her horse's head away from the city. "Papa and mamma are to dine at the palace, so there is no one home but the servants. This, then, is a splendid chance to carry out a pet project, in the accomplishment of which I call upon one of you gentlemen to assist me. You must know that I have had an intense desire to visit that old castle yonder. It is said that, although a ruin now, part of it is still pretty well preserved, and very interesting. Besides, there is, as with all these relics of a feudal age, a curious old legend attached to it. It is a glorious afternoon—one just made for a 'land-partie;' so which of you two gentlemen will sacrifice dinner to me?"

I have said that upon this day Carl and I were rivals. We both, then, sprang forward gladly to obey the summons, each judging it for himself.

"Nay!" interposed the sweet girl, conscious of her mistake; "I said but *one*, because I was fearful of exacting too much, but since you are both so ready to lend yourselves to my foolish whim, I thank and accept of both."

Overjoyed, and not stopping to note the burning glance that Carl bestowed upon me, I placed myself at her side, while he, owing to the narrowness of the road, was forced to fall behind.

It was a lovely summer day, and exhilarated by the balmy air, and the bright presence of my love, my heart was bursting with happiness. There is an intoxication, too, in being well mounted that only a horseman can understand. The spirits soar and soar, while every fresh bound of the horse sends new life through the veins. It was a merry ride, then, to the foot of the mountain, upon whose summit was perched the object of our visit.

The ascent being too steep and dangerous for horses, we found at a little chalet a man with mules, which he kept for the purpose of letting out to visitors to the old castle overhead. But Florence rejected them indignantly, and it was decided to proceed on foot. "To think of jogging on a mule to a place of romance!" exclaimed the merry girl. "There must be a short cut by which we can reach the summit on foot, is there not?" she asked in German of the old peasant.

"Ia wohl; Gnädiger Frätlein. But it is scarce such a road as a charming young lady like yourself would select," answered he, bowing with the innate gallantry of his race.

"Oh, as to that, I am not a young lady; I am only a little child to-day. Beside, I am an excellent climber, and have I not here two gentlemen to assist me if needs be? Gentlemen, we will take the short cut," she continued, springing lightly forward in the direction indicated by the old mule-driver.

Steep and rough as was the path, Florence gayly tripped from height to height, until her light form seemed as that of some mountain spirit."

"How jolly!" she cried, as, attaining a projecting rock, she stopped to rest for a brief moment, her eyes overflowing with fun and excitement, while her cheeks glowed with the unwonted exercise. "I haven't had such a nice romp for many's the day, and I really believe that the chief part of the pleasure is derived from the thoughts of my lady-mother's genteel horror when she hears of it. What lectures! What 'wise saws and modern instances!' Ha, ha, ha! I shall never hear the end of it. Do look.

Vicksburg.

All eyes are now turned eagerly towards Vicksburg. Tremendous firing has been heard there for the last two days, and intelligence as to the result of it is looked for with intense anxiety. Our people, however, evince the most perfect confidence in the valor and endurance of our brave garrison. When all the circumstances of the various sieges and bombardments of Vicksburg are weighed, it will be conceded that the annals of war scarcely furnish a parallel to the stubborn resistance and unflinching heroism which she has displayed. Let her hold out yet and her fame will be more enviable than Gibraltar's or Sevastopol's. Let her still hold out and those who have participated in her defense will deserve and receive the proudest laurels which adorn the Southern hero's chaplet. The gratitude of a nation will be theirs. And she will hold out. We are confident that she is invincible. A few more repulses of the enemy—the loss of a few more of his tens of thousadds, and Vicksburg will rise from the ordeal nobly defiant and wreathe perennial glory.—[Mississippian.

raised against him, but in no tangible shape; this necessarily begets distrust and uneasiness in the country and it is reflected on the army as a matter of course and great injury follows! Before I speak further of Gen. P., allow me to say that I think I have great cause of complaint against him; by an act of his I lost $20,000 worth of property, but it was no act of treason, but one of over-vigilance, on his part. Am I to bring up my personal grievances and decry our general, try and condemn him without a hearing—create distrust and even doubt his fidelity, before the country—the army and even in hearing of our enemy! Forbid it my country!

Gen. Pemberton is not equal to our Lee, for he is without a peer! but he is a soldier by profession and education, is well and favorably known to our President. All admit his untiring vigilance in the cause. No man labors harder. No one toils as he has toiled, since he came amongst us. His defense of the Tallahatchie and the upper Yazoo by the gallant Loring, in the time he had to prepare his defenses, is without a parallel in the war.

He has successfully defended Vicksburg and Port Hudson up to this time and if properly supported by the officers and soldiers under his command, as I have an abiding trust he will be, such a thrashing as Grant and his mercenaries will get, will only be equalled by one of Lee's victories in Virginia.

The President and Gen. Johnston both visited Gen. P. in December last. They approved of his plans of defense then—I think they do now! It is all idle for the people to give credence to and circulate the stories they hear about our commanding generals. Grierson, the robber, denounced Pemberton in his raid in Mississippi as a traitor to our cause—that they had bought him up—paid the money, &c. We have some weak-minded people among us who give currency to such slanders, coming from a highway robber, as they do, I am sorry to say it. Soldiers in the army, don't let such carping and fault-finding get a lodgment in your breast. Act as the crisis demands of you, like men—sustain your officers and frown down every attempt to create a breach between you and them! I am satisfied that General Pemberton is doing everything he can to defend our State and river and they must be defended at every hazard! He has as game officers under him to lead you, as ever drew a sword! Stand by each other, nerve your arms for the conflict and you will yet fill the measure of your country's glory. Victory will perch on your standard and we will be free.

An Old Citizen.

England and the Confederacy.—The late European arrival (says the Dispatch) brought, among other matters, an account of a meeting of fanatics and addresses from them to Mr. Adams, United States Minister, in which was, of course the usual exhibition of phariseeism. The London Post, regarded as the Government organ, referring to these movements, remarks that "no amount of Union meetings in England will detach the masses of the British people from the support of the cause of the rebel Confederate States."

Look at This.—The following intelligence, from an Illinois paper, will serve to show what kind of philanthropy actuates a free-soil or abolition State: "The Whiteside Illinois Sentinel publishes an official notice under date of February, 1863, signed by C. M. Child, J. P., to the effect that, whereas certain negroes named were, on the 5th and 6th ult., tried on a charge of high misdemeanor, having come into this State and county, and remaining therein, for ten days and more, with the evident intention of residing in this State, and were found guilty by a jury, and were each severally fined, in the sum of $50; and whereas, the fine and costs of suit not having been paid, the said negroes will be sold at auction, on the 19th day of February, 1863, at the Courthouse of Carthage, for the payment of said fine and costs.'"

Banishment.—The decree of banishment of loyal Southern men from the enemy's lines, says the Mobile News, is adding strong fighting material to the Confederate ranks. The young men arriving as refugees from New Orleans are rapidly enrolling and rushing to arms. They have a stern account of oppression and cruelty to settle with the invaders. We wonder that the Yankee authorities have overlooked this fact. But the love of plunder outweighs policy, for the homes and property of the exiles are occupied the moment they are left.

ing, 212 paroled Confederate prisoners, who were sent up to Petersburg the same day. They are all Western men, captured from time to time at various places. The truce boat brought no late Northern papers, or, if there were any on board, they were not allowed to come ashore; from which the Petersburg Express deduces that something unfavorable to the Federal cause has been heard at the North which they desire to keep from us.

Vicksburg.

All eyes are now turned eagerly towards Vicksburg. Tremendous firing has been heard there for the last two days, and intelligence as to the result of it is looked for with intense anxiety. Our people, however, evince the most perfect confidence in the valor and endurance of our brave garrison. When all the circumstances of the various sieges and bombardments of Vicksburg are weighed, it will be conceded that the annals of war scarcely furnish a parallel to the stubborn resistance and unflinching heroism which she has displayed. Let her hold out yet and her fame will be more enviable than Gibraltar's or Sevastopol's. Let her still hold out and those who have participated in her defense will deserve and receive the proudest laurels which adorn the Southern hero's chaplet. The gratitude of a nation will be theirs. And she will hold out. We are confident that she is invincible. A few more repulses of the enemy—the loss of a few more of his tens of thousadds, and Vicksburg will rise from the ordeal nobly defiant and wreathe perennial glory.—[Mississippian.

☞ The stupid custom, so common now-a-days, of spelling *negro* in the plural *negros*, instead of negroes, has given rise to the following: "A reliable gentleman from the coast says that the Yankee *heros* are employing the *negros* in the cultivation of *potatos* and *tomatos*.—It is thought that several *cargos* will be shipped to Yankeedom."

Federal Foraging Party Captured.—Our cavalry yesterday, brought into Jackson, a small party of Yankee cavalry which was captured near Edwards' Depot. The party had collected 20 head of cattle and many other articles, and were piloted by a negro who had volunteered for that service. Two other negroes that were pressed into service, were brought to this city, but the guide expressing reluctance at coming to Jackson, was hung.

Resolved,

That we the "Soldiers Christian Association" of the 52d Ga. Regt., set apart all or a portion of the hour between sundown and dark, of each day to supplicate Almighty God, that He will pardon our sins, receive us graciously and deliver us from the hands of our cruel enemies, and that we solicit all Christians and soldiers throughout this beleaguered army to unite with us in prayer at that hour.

GEO. T. QUILLIAN,
President.

W. A. Parks, Sec'y.

THE DAILY CITIZEN.

TUESDAY, JUNE 16, 1863.

☞ We will issue a slip from this office on Thursday morning, at 8 o'clock, when we will be enabled to supply the great demand which we have heretofore been unable to do. Having had the assurance of the use of late Northern and other papers, we will present our readers with a condensed summary of news from the outside world in an acceptable shape.

The Army at Vicksburg.

Great encomiums have been passed upon the Confederate armies in Virginia and Tennessee, and truly do those veteran troops deserve a full measure of credit for the trials and hardships they have gone through. But in point of patriotic determination, bravery, endurance of fatigue, hunger, the heat of the sun, the pelting rain, and an abiding faith in their prowess, there is no army in the Confederacy to compare to that which now interposes its living breastworks in defence of Vicksburg. Such heroism, such determination and such stoical indifference, mingled with a patience and fortitude as is exhibited by these troops, is truly wonderful.

No army composed of such material has ever been whipped, and never can be. The handful of Spartans who have held an overwhelming force at bay for thirty days, without a murmur, presents a spectacle worthy of the palmiest days of Greece and Rome. A continual and incessant fire of shot and shell has been raining upon these veterans since the 19th day of May, and still they occupy their position undismayed, and more determined than ever.

The army at Vicksburg now stands among the veteran troops of the world, and it is but just that full credit should be given it by the Government and by every portion of the Confederacy. No other army has been placed in such a critical position in this war, and those who are compelled to endure the privations and hardships of a protracted siege against such immense odds should be remembered by a grateful country, and their merits fully and liberally rewarded.

Victory at Port Hudson!

By a number of the Memphis Bulletin of the 11th, we learn that the Federals, under Gen. Banks made an attack on Port Hudson on the 28th ult., which resulted in a disastrous repulse. The Federal account reports their loss as very heavy. The defeat puts a damper on their operations in that quarter for some time to come. It is also stated that the fleet made an attack on the front at the same time, and was equally unsuccessful, being driven off with great damage to their boats. Our friends in the Confederacy may rest assured that the next important news will be that the Yankees are driven off from Vicksburg.

☞ The Yankees have destroyed the Mississippian office, at Jackson, and the Hinds County Gazette, at Raymond. They have no good will toward the Confederate Press, and wherever one falls into their hands destruction is sure to follow. Our friends of the Appeal are too quick on the wing to be caught, and always manage to escape to safe quarters.

☞ By a private letter which has run the blockade, we learn the Yankees are making a perfect devastation of the country through which their army is marching. Negro and other property is being taken and carried off, and the country left an entire desolation.

☞ The great victory in Virginia, obtained by Gen. Lee's army over Hooker, at Chancellorsville, foots up in its results as follows:

15,000 Yankees killed;
8,000 prisoners;
60,000 stand of arms, and a great quantity of cannon, &c., taken.

Since the death of Stonewall Jackson, Gen. Ewell has been placed in command of his old division.

☞ We have again entire command of Jackson, Clinton and Raymond, and the country beyond the Big Black is entirely clear of all Yankees.

☞ A private letter from outside our lines has reached us, which says:

"The Yankees have torn this county entirely up. They have robbed and plundered every house in the county. Nearly all the negroes have left their masters and gone to the Yankees. Warrenton is the depot for the negroes of the lower end of the county."

☞ A leading editorial of the New York Times seeks to palliate the sorrow of the public mind over the "unfortunate sequel" of Hooker's late movement on Richmond, by calling attention to the brilliant prospect of success at Vicksburg:

"Richmond can scarcely be called a strategic point; its importance is chiefly factitious as the temporary seat of an itinerant government, and the fall of Richmond would have been but the fall of a city. But the fall of Vicksburg would be the fall of *one-half of the Confederacy*. The speedy capture of Vicksburg, therefore, ought to be the prime object of public concern.

Kirby Smith.—This General's headquarters are at Shreveport, and his army increasing to a powerful force.

Special to the Mississippian.

Panola, June 6.—The Yankees and Unionists are holding a great jubilee to-day, being the anniversary of its occupation by the Federals.

Tagg, of Jones & Tagg, of Memphis, and Tommeny, of railroad memory, were marshals at the Federal occupation jubilee.

Rumor says Grant has applied to Hurlburt, at Memphis, for 50,000 more men, who says he don't know where they are to come from, without the evacuation of Corinth and the Charleston Railroad. Troops are going down daily. Hurlburt has orders to fix the Memphis hospitals for 30,000 wounded; 8000 had arrived up to Saturday.

The Memphis Bulletin, of the 3d, says: Capt. Sol. Street's company, from Okalona, of eighteen or twenty men, were all killed or captured near Middleton. Street and four others escaped. They were surrounded and surprised in Dr. Neely's house.

The St. Louis Democrat, of the first instant, says thirty five rebel sympathizers were to be sent South on that day, some from the interior of the State.

The Governor of Illinois has sent extra steamers to bring home the wounded from Vicksburg.

The Memphis Bulletin, with other lies, gives doleful accounts of the situation and a mutiny in Vicksburg. It says that the rebels are clamorous for a surrender.

The Bulletin says 1600 persons had taken the oath in Memphis under the last order.

The French have taken Puebla, taking 18,000 prisoners, with twenty-four generals.

Panola, June 6—A telegram from Senatobia this morning, says:

The Chicago Times, of the 2d, states that Grant admits a repulse, with heavy slaughter, and has fallen back to the Big Black, awaiting reinforcements from Banks, who is hurrying to him. The same telegram states: I am satisfied from information received from Memphis that the Memphis and Charleston road is about stripped of troops.

Capt. Mott fired on some transports on Wednesday, near Friar's Point. The firing from the gunboats was distinctly heard at Panola.

Grenada, June 6.—A gentleman just down from Panola, on the cars, informs us that last Sunday our cavalry made a dash into LaGrange Tenn., killing a number of Yankees and tearing up the railroad track.

Two cars loaded with the wounded were sent to Memphis.

Bolivar and other places in West Tennessee are next to be evacuated; enough left to move off the stores.

Grant is depleting the robber army in that region, to be bled to death at Vicksburg.

Richmond, June 4.—Porter's official dispatch states that the expedition sent up the Yazoo destroyed and captured property valued at two millions, including three powerful rams, and one monitor three hundred and ten feet long, unfinished. Loss, one killed and seven wounded!!!

Burnside has communicated to Bragg his determination to hang all rebel officers in his hands in case of retaliation for two spies tried and executed according to usages of war.

News from Europe, to the 29th, says: In the House of Lords, Marquis Clanricade denounced the seizure of British vessels by the United States cruizers as a violation of the laws of nations. Russell defended the course of the American Government, and said all their communications showed that they fully respected international law. Law officers of the Crown report no national grounds of objection to the decision of the President of the Courts.

Derby fully concurred with Russell, though every allowance ought to be made for provocation.

Richmond, June 5.—The latest returns indicate the election of Gen. W. Smith for Governor, and Samuel Price for Lieutenant-Governor, Four members of the last Congress, nominated for re-election, have been defeated, viz: Garrett, Lyon, Boteler and Preston. The returns also indicate the defeat of Staples.

Vallandigham, in an address to the Democrats from his military prison in Cincinnati, on May 23d, declared that he shall recognize allegiance to his own State and Government, wherever he may be, as binding in all things, just the same as if he were upon the soil.

Items from the Brandon Republican.

The residence of F. H. Lombard, Esq., was again fired by a negro girl last Tuesday. The time for hanging has come; and unless it is resorted to speedily, we expect to see the whole town laid in ashes before long.

We learn from good authority that our old countryman, R. V. Montague, is doing an extensive business in Louisiana inside the Yankee lines. He is working nine plantations with 1300 hands, and says he will make a million dollars this year. Our cavalry captured forty of his own negroes a few days since, and carried them to Monroe, where they will be confiscated. We think it quite likely the old reprobate will receive the reward due a traitor to his country before long.

Sixteen hundred Yankees advanced on Vernon, in Madison county, on Tuesday last, but were driven back by Col. Wirt Adams' cavalry.

From Port Hudson.—We learn from Mr. T. H. Hogg, sutler of the 39th Mississippi regiment, who left Port Hudson at daylight last Thursday, that there were fifteen gunboats in line of battle below the fort when he left, and that he heard the most terrific cannonading from 7 A. M. to 3 P. M. of that day. He heard nothing of the result, but was confident that we repulsed them. The health of the 39th was very good.

Bold and Successful.—Capt. Wm. M. Jayne left Vicksburg last Tuesday morning with 300 army mules, passed the Yankee pickets, swam Big Black river, and reached this county in safety. Almost every mule had a man on his back, and the Yankee pickets supposing it to be cavalry, took to their heels.

A gentleman who recently passed the Federal lines says the democratic ladies of New York have gotten up a magnificent sword, at a cost of twelve hundred dollars, intended as a present to Gen. Lee. It will be sent to Richmond by some underground railroad.

Com. Porter gives an account of the attack on Grand Gulf, and says that he accomplished all he wanted except *silencing all the batteries*, which he says "were fought with a determination I never before witnessed."

Flour tumbled from $90 to $50 in Columbus in two days. Cause, harvesting wheat.

Vol. I. RICHMOND, SATURDAY, JUNE 20, 1863. No. 41.

GEN. P. G. T. BEAUREGARD.

DAILY MISSISSIPPIAN

COOPER & KIMBALL,
PROPRIETORS.

JACKSON, ...JUNE 20, 1863.

TERMS:

The DAILY MISSISSIPPIAN will be issued hereafter every morning (except Monday) at $5 per month.

No subscription will be taken for a longer period than two months.

ADVERTISING.—Advertisements will be inserted at $3 per square for the first, and $2 for each subsequent insertion

Agents Ordering Papers.

Agents or individuals ordering daily Mississippians, will bear in mind that it is important the order should be telegraphed, so that it will reach us the night previous.—This will enable us to work off an edition large enough to supply the demand. dtf

NOTICE TO ADVERTISERS.—Persons wishing to advertise in the Mississippian, in order to secure insertion will please hand them in by 5 o'clock P. M.

☞ Until we receive paper for the regular size of the Mississippian, the price per copy will be 10 cents to news-venders, and 15 cents at the counter.

☞ We are informed that news-venders of the Mississippian at a distance are sometimes in the habit of selling the papers at 50 cents—in some cases as much as $1 is asked for a single copy. These are clear cases of extortion. News dealers are supplied at 10 cents per copy at the office.

LOST.—Special attention is advertisement in to-day's issue.

Another Yankee Outrage.

The Charleston Courier copies the following from the Nassau Guardian of the 3d inst.:

We have to record this evening, says the Nassau Guardian, another unjustifiable outrage committed by a Federal gunboat, within the prescribed limits of our shores.

On Saturday last the steamer Margaret and Jessie, Capt. Wilson, from Charleston for this port, was fallen in with by the Federal steamer Rhode Island, off Abaco, and chased until she arrived close to the shore at James Point, Eleuthera.

There would have been no legal cause of complaint had the pursuit and firing ceased as soon as the Margaret and Jessie approached within the distance of three miles from the land; but as she neared the coast, and was but two hundred and fifty yards off, that is between the reef and the land, the gunboat, which was not more than a quarter of a mile distant, commenced pouring in broadside after broadside—varying the performance with shot, grape and shell—not only to the imminent danger of all on board (and there were ladies among the passengers,) but to the serious alarm of inhabitants of the Island, who suddenly found themselves subjected to a sharp and decisive bombardment.

The missiles fired from the Rhode Island plowed up the earth in various directions, and came in close proximity to, if not actually passing through dwellings, and driving persons to seek refuge behind the rocks and projections. This was kept up for miles, and at length the Margaret and Jessie received a shot through her boiler and another through her bow, which forced her to take the beach, then only fifty yards distant. We understand that one of the fireman was injured, and if a fatal result should ensue, it will assuredly be an aggravated murder.

Such are the plain facts of this ferocious outrage. No amount of prevarication and shuffling will enable the officers of the Rhode Island to prove that the offense was committed beyond the territorial limits of this colony.—There are too many distinguished witnesses to the transaction, whose testimony will outweigh any combination to pervert the truth. When the same vessel fired into the steamer Sirius a few weeks ago there were no spectators on shore to determine the distance, and the assertion of the commander that he was five miles off was received as conclusive. But the captain of the Sirius, whose character for veracity cannot be impeached, emphatically stated that he was fired at within two miles of the land.

It is high time indeed that the Home Government should act energetically with respect to these aggressions. Certainly the circumstances connected with the attack on the Margaret and Jessie on Eleuthera are so flagrant that they cannot well be overlooked; and whilst no doubt reparation will be expected and made, yet the intimation should be conveyed also that a repetition of such outrages will not be tolerated. It will require in future not the exercise of forbearance but firmness, to prevent a rupture of peaceful relations.

Since penning the above, we have been informed that two men engaged in fishing off Eleuthera were struck by the missiles fired from the gunboat.

The steamer Raccoon was specially dispatched to Eleuthera on Monday by the agents of the Margaret and Jessie, Messrs H. Adderly & Co., in order to render assistance, but the latter had got off the beach, and arrived here yesterday.

The Belt of Desolation.

Day by day the track of the destroyer becomes broader. Two-thirds of Virginia, two-thirds of Tennessee, the coasts of North and South Carolina, parts of Georgia, nearly all of Florida, Northern Mississippi, Western and Southern Louisiana, a great part of Arkansas and Missouri, have already been laid waste, and every hour brings tidings of fresh destruction. Telegrams of Saturday inform us that the enemy had destroyed a million of dollars worth of property on the Combahee and stolen a thousand negroes; it was but a few days ago that they ravaged the county of Mathew in this State, and even while we write tidings come to us that they are burning private houses and destroying every grain of corn they can lay hands on in the county of King and Queen.

Enough has been said of the barbarism of this mode of warfare, and too much has been confessed of the entire impunity with which it is carried on. Our outcries and our admissions of the weakness or the imbecility of our forces in the field but add to the hellish joy of the foe. without stimulating troops, government or people to the pitch of retriburative vengeance. The belt of desolation widens hourly, nor is there much prospect of an abatement of the evil. Citizens complain of the government, which in turn complain of the citizens. Meantime common inquiry is made as to the existence and present whereabouts of the organized forces of the Confederacy.

We may be sure this state of things will continue so long as the war is waged exclusively on Confederate soil. Every day the enemy remains in our territory will add to the width of the belt of desolation, and they who now fancy themselves out of danger will soon discover their mistake. If a thousand Yankee cavalry can ride entirely through the State of Mississippi, without molestation, what is to hinder a like number from going through Virginia, North and South Carolina to Port Royal? Certainly unarmed and unorganized citizens will not hinder them.

The belt of desolation serves many purposes of the Yankee nation. It opens a way to free labor and Northern settlers; it diminishes production and concentrates Southern population within limits inadequate to their support, it prepares a place for Yankee emigration if peace on the basis of separation is declared. But this is not all. It answers the purpose of war as well as peace, by interposing a country destitute of supplies between our own and the Yankee border. Thus it is a safeguard against invasion. If Lee should advance, he must move through a desert, dragging immense trains of food behind him: The case is the same with Bragg, with Johnson, with Price. Indeed we hear that Price will on this account find it difficult, if not impossible, to enter Missouri. In front of all our large armies lie a waste, where there is food for neither man nor beast. Girded by a belt of desolation, the North is safe from invasion; the broader the belt the greater its security. As the months wane and the years roll on, the South, unless something be done, will become in the language of Scripture, "the abomination of desolation." We believe that something will be done—the necessity of the case demands it imperitively; would that we could be sure that it will be done speedily. This can be returned to the lips of the North drugged with ten-fold bitterness. Mercy to ourselves demands this act of retributive justice to them.—*Richmond Whig.*

The New York Times is so complimentary as to say for the benefit of Gen. Fremont, that a man may "cherish the noblest sentiments, and yet be a great blockhead."

Tearfs was born in 1843, is 20 years old, but Smith, who was born in '41, two years earlier, is only twenty, too. How is it?

News Items.

Th Yankee gunboat Alert, while lying at the Norfolk navyyard, caught fire last Sunday, and the flames soon reached her magazine and exploded a shell, which went through her bottom, and she sunk immediately. No one was injured.

An acidulous old bachelor of our acquaintance says that he never hears a place called "Rose Cottage," without thinking of the lots of thorns that there must be inside.

Nine of the eleven cotton mills and the three print work at Fall River, Mass., have stopped running.

Randolph Rogers, the sculptor, has left Cincinnati for Italy taking with him orders for work to the amount of $22,00.

COTTON ORDERS REVOKED.—By a general order at Brownsville, Texas, April 23d, Maj. Gen. Magruder has revoked all the orders restricting exportation of cotton of whatever nature. The five dollar exchange is also abolished. Trade with Mexico is left perfectly free. This, it is understood, has been done under order from Richmond.

At the sacking of Miechow, a Polish town, the Russian soldiers, in their frenzy for liquor, attacked an apothecary's shop and drank everything liquid they could lay their hands on. Twenty died the next day.

A REMINISCENCE OF SHARPSBURG.—The following is a fact: During the bloody engagement at Sharpsburg, Sergeant W. H. Williamson, of Company D, 61st Georgia, captured two Federal prisoners, who stuck hard and fast by him for the remainder of the engagement, loading muskets as fast as he could discharge them at the enemy, and occasionally calling out to "Give the rascals h—ll."

☞ Gen. Kirby, who recently died in Washington, of wounds received in the battle of Chancellorsville, was formerly a Lieutenant of Artillery, and commanded the famous Rocket Battery in the Army of the Potomac.

The fashionable dance of Paris now is the "*Marche Cocasse.*" It is danced backwards, each gentleman holding the lady before him by clasping her round the waist. When well practiced, it is said to be highly entertaining, and the Empress is said to have a peculiar talent for its execution.

Henry Winter Davis has been nominated in Baltimore, for the Federal Congress. He made a speech endorsing Lincoln's emancipation proclamation, and urging a vigorous prosecution of the war.

A subscription has been started in Toronto, C. W., in aid of the funds now raising for the proposed monument to the memory of "Stonewall" Jackson. The editor of the Toronto Leader is the treasurer.

Two new paper mills are getting ready for operation—one in Virginia and the other in Georgia.

There is to be a grand trial of steam fire engines from all parts of the world in London, July 1st, under the patronage of the Duke of Sutherland. The best engine is to receive $1200, and the second $500.

Among the exiles who have arrived at Charleston from St. Augustine, Fla., is the mother of Gen. Kirby Smith. She is seventy-six years of age.

The New York Tribune says of Lee's army: Their motives are difficult to penetrate. Spies, if we have any, can learn little that is definite, and deserters, like private soldiers in our own army, know nothing beyond what occurs in their own immediate vicinity.

There is a report from Cincinnati that Gen. Joe Johnston is advancing on Memphis.

The Medical College at Lexington, Ky., used for a U. S. hospital, was completely destroyed by fire on the 22d of May. Loss $90,000.

Nine persons were arrested in New York on May 30th for using treasonable language.

The gunboat Naumkeag, Capt. John Rodgers, has arrived at Wheeling, from Charleston, on the Kanawha.—Previous to leaving, the most valuable part of the machinery in the salt works was removed, so that should the Confederacy get possession of them they will find them useless. Capt. Rodgers also caused to be removed from the works a large quantity of salt that had accumulated, which could not be got to market.

The Vice-President of the United States has received a draft on London for a sum which amounts to over six hundred dollars, given as an offering to the cause of emancipation by the colored women of the British colony of Victoria, to be applied to the benefit of contrabands at and about Beaufort, S. C. The donors had previously sent one hundred and seventy dollars to Philadelphia for a like purpose. They had much better given their money to their starving white and negro operatives in England.

The prize schooner Maria Bishop, captured by the Yankees last month, went ashore while on her way North, and could not be got off. The prize master set her on fire, and destroyed her.

The gunboat Penobscot, while chasing an English steamer off Wilmington, N. C., came close in shore and was fired upon by the Confederate batteries, by which her assistant surgeon was killed and the steward wounded.

The Fight in Culpeper County.

The reports of the late fight in Culpeper county, brought down by passengers on the Central train yesterday evening, are hardly more satisfactory than those which had previously reached us. That our forces were surprised there seems no longer any reason to doubt, and that they fought gallantly after they recovered from the confusion into which they were at first thrown is also certain. It is equally certain that the battle terminated with the repulse of the enemy and the advantage on our side, the enemy's loss in killed and wounded; and in the number of prisoners captured, being considerably greater than that sustained by our forces.

The greater portion of our wounded has been sent back to Gordonsville, where about 125 had been received up to 12 o'clock yesterday. The whole number of wounded in the engagement, it is believed, will amount to from 150 to 200. The number of killed it is thought will not exceed 50. The number of officers slain is greatly out of proportion to the number of men, which is accounted for by their exposing themselves in efforts to rally their commands after the first onset of the enemy. Our whole loss, including prisoners, is put down at between 300 and 400. A passenger who came down on the train says that we had five Colonels killed, but could not recollect any names in addition to those given by us yesterday morning. Among the wounded was Col. A. W. Harman, of the 12th Virginia cavalry, who was shot in the neck. The 10th Virginia cavalry, Col. J. Lucius Davis, bore a prominent part in the fight, and suffered pretty heavily, as did also the 2d North Carolina, Col. Williams.

One of the enemy's officers, who came over with a flag of truce on Wednesday, says their loss in officers amounted to twenty-five.—*Richmond Dispatch.*

AN EXHUMED CITY.—A most singular discovery has been made on the French coast, near the mouth of the Garonne. A town has been discovered in the sand, and a church has already been extracted from the sand. Its original plan shows it to have been built towards the close of the Roman Empire, but changes made in it had given it the appearance of an edifice of mixed style, in which the gothic architecture had usurped the place of the Roman. The original paintings, its admirably sculptured choir, and Roman capitals, are adorned with profuse ornaments, which are attracting numbers of visitors. This temple is all that remains of Pliny and Strabo. The Gulf of Gascony abounds in ruins of these ancient cities. It has been 1,500 years since Novigamus, the old capital of Medea, which was a very celebrated city when the Romans were masters of Gaul, was buried under the ocean. Of all that tract of territory the Roche du Cordonon alone is visible. The remains of Roman roads, the site of Jupiter's temple, the vestiges of the Spanish Moors, and the roads to Eleanor de Guyenne, have been rescued from the sands in the neighborhood of the long buried city of Soula. Nowhere have the erasions of the oceans been greater than on the coast of Gascony.

THE TYCOON'S GIFT TO LINCOLN.—We announced some time since that the Tycoon of Japan had sent a gift to the President of the United States, consisting of a coat of mail. The following is a description of it:

An umbrella-like helmet, of fabricated sheets of steel and copper, shields the head, while a vandyke of interwoven silk cord and lacquered net-work falls gracefully upon the shoulders. The outside of the helmet is profusely ornamented with chrissantheums of gold, in beautiful open-work, upon black lacquer, with now and then a trimming of purest silver. The visor is of copper, lacquered in scarlet and brown. The armlets are of the finest copper chain-work. The breastplate is of copper, intersected with parallel strips of lacquer, and woven together with delicate wire and golden cord. A sort of kilt accompanies the armor, and, with lacquerated leggings, grotesquely formed, complete the set.

THE EXILE.

From the Register and Advertiser.]

Far, far away in the land of the stranger
The exile now wanders all weary and lone;
Thoughtfully treads he the broad path of danger
That winds thro' the mazes of regions unknown.
He fixes his gaze on the brow of the mountain
That shelters the cottage down on the sea-shore;
The tear-drops that come gushing from memory's full fountain
In sorrow for pleasures that greet him no more.

Thick visions of childhood come gathering around him—
The plaint of his young wife rings loud in his ears,
He grieves o'er the wreck of the ties that once bound him
In the quiet of home to his sweet little dears.
At the lonely hour of midnight the winter wind sighing,
Brings boding of evil from o'er the deep
'Tis the voice of the exile in distant lands dying,
Inviting his cherubs to kiss him to sleep!

As Jackson's battalions dash onward to glory,
Rolling back the fell tide of the Puritan flood,
The exile's tall figure falls lifeless and gory,
On fields deeply dyed with a nation's best blood!
Thus nobly a son of Hibernia had perished
In Liberty's name at the cannon's red mouth;
O! long be the name of the good stranger cherished
Who died to defend the young flag of the South!

A MISNOMER.—We observe with no little surprise that nearly the entire press of the Confederacy, in alluding to the exploits of the Alabama and Florida, or other Confederate vessels, term them privateers. The term privateer implies that these vessels are property, sailing under letters of marque, when, the truth is, we have not an armed vessel afloat save regular vessels of war. The term privateer, while it is by no means a reproach to any gallant seaman who chooses to sail as such, is really a term yf reproach when applied to our national vessels. It detracts from the dignity of our flag, and the naval repute of our struggling country. The exploits of armed vessels are carrying dismay to the commercial circles of the enemy, and are fast filling the world with praises of the gallantry of our little navy. Let us dignify it with a proper and legitimate name, and let the term privateer apply only to those who seek it.—*Augusta Constitutionalist.*

☞ Confederate soldiers should become excellent philosophers. They are all familiar with Bacon.

Testimonial to Col. Auguste Reichard.

ADAMS' LOUISIANA BRIGADE,
Camp near Jackson, Miss., June 18th, 1863.

On this day a meeting of the officers of General D. W. Adams' Louisiana Brigade was held at the Headquarters of the 16th and 25th Louisiana Regiments, for the purpose of giving an expression of regret upon the resignation of Col. Auguste Reichard, of the 18th and 20th Louisiana Regiments.

Upon motion, Col. D. Gober, of the 16th and 25th Louisiana Regiments was called to the chair, and Major Loudon Butler of the 19th Louisiana Regiment, was requested to act as Secretary.

Upon motion, a committee of five was appointed to draft resolutions expressive of the sense of the meeting: whereupon the following officers were appointed: Colonel W. P. Winans and Lieut. Col. R. W. Turner, of the 19th Louisiana; Lt. Col. R. H. Lindsay, of the 16th and 25th Louisiana; Lt. Col. Harry Daury of the 32d Alabama, and Captain Jas. Lingan, of Austin's Louisiana Battalion of Sharpshooters.

The committee retired, and upon reassembling reported through their Chairman Col. W. P. Winans, of the 19th Louisiana, the following preamble and resolutions, as follows, which were unanimously adopted:

WHEREAS, the resignation of Col. Auguste Reichard is about to sunder the pleasant association that has so long existed between him and us, and to deprive the country of his valuable services, we, his companions in arms, desire to give him assurances of the high esteem in which he is held by us: Therefore,

1st. *Resolved*, That it is with unfeigned regret we lose from our association and from the service of our country, one who has shown himself so estimable a gentleman and so excellent an officer: that we cannot forget, nor will the historian of this Revolution forget to record upon his brightest page the name of the "Prussian Consul," who, sacrificing princely wealth, and the comforts of a luxurious home, was among the first to tender his sword to the cause of Southern freedom. We cannot forget, nor will a grateful country forget, the zeal, the ability, the tireless labor with which Col. Reichard has for nearly two years borne the hardships and privations and dangers of three compaigns.

2d. *Resolved*, That we, the officers of this Brigade tender to Col. Reichard our grateful acknowledgments for the amiable courtesy that always marked his intercourse with us while in command of the Brigade; we take this occasion to bear testimony to his ability, zeal and labor which so distinguished the period of his command.

3d. *Resolved*, That our best wishes and prayers for the future welfare and success in life of our brother in arms, follow Col. Reichard wherever he may go. We hope that his disinterested sacrifices and efficient services in the cause of the Confederate States, will yet receive their proper acknowledgment; and we hope, at no distant day, again to greet him, our fellow-citizen, in his home, our loved Louisiana, redeemed and disenthralled from Yankee vassalage.

4th. *Resolved*, That a copy of these resolutions be tendered Col. Reichard, and that the Jackson Mississippian, Mobile Register and Advertiser, Mobile Tribune, and the Chattanooga Rebel be requested to publish the same.

Upon motion, a committee of one officer from each command composing the Brigade, was appointed by the chair to wait upon Col. Reichards, and present him with a copy of the resolutions.

Whereupon the following gentlemen were appointed: Major J. E. Austin, of the Louisiana Battalion Sharpshooters; Captain Dubroca and Captain Kerhwald, of the 12th and 20th Louisiana; Capt. Handly, of the 19th Louisiana; Capt. Watson, of the 16th and 25th Louisiana; Capt. Thompson, of the 32d Alabama, and Capt. Airey, of Gen. Adams' Staff.

Upon motion, the meeting adjourned.

D. GOBER, Colonel 16th & 25th La., Chairman.
LOUDON BUTLER, Major 19th La., Secretary.

MARRIED,

On the evening of the 21st of May, at the residence of Mrs. L. F. Cooper, near Benton, Miss., by Rev. Mr. Price, Mr. S. BARR, of Louisiana, to Miss SALLIE VIRGINIA C. COOPER, of Yazoo county, Miss.

MARRIED, near Clinton, La., on the evening of the 24th May, by Rev. W. F. Camp, Surgeon G. W. BROACH, of the C. S. A., and Miss LIZZIE BRYANT, of Caddo Parish, La.

MARRIED, on the evening of the 24th May, near Clinton, La., by Chaplain H. T. Lewis, Surgeon A. A. ROWLAND, of the C. S. A., and Miss MAGGIE PERKINS, of East Feliciana Parish, La.

TRIBUTE OF RESPECT.

At the third quarterly meeting of Raymond and Spring Ridge Circuit, which was held at Forest Hill Chapel, the following resolutions were passed as a tribute of respect, in memory of Rev. ABSOLOM OWENL, who departed this life in the town of Raymond, May 5, at 3 o'clock, A. M., 1863.

1. *Resolved*, That in the death of Brother Owens, the church has sustained a heavy loss. He was a faithful local preacher. He never sought promotion. He was plain in his appearance, unassuming in his manners, ardent in his temperament, zealous for the cause of God, indefatigable in his labors, and withal original in his compositions. For some months before his death he was disabled by disease to perform his ministerial duties. He was brought down to his grave by scarlet fever; but our loss is his eternal gain.

2. *Resolved*, That we do heartily "weep with those who weep," on account of his death; but we weep not as those who have no hope, for we are confident that he died "in the Lord," and is now at home, where he will forever rest in the bosom of God.

DIED,

At Quitman, Miss., June 12, 1863, FANNIE, daughter of Capt. W. L. McConnico, 10th Tenn. Regiment, C. S. A. Tennessee papers will please copy.

In Jackson, Miss., June 5th, 1863, of a wound received at the battle of Champion Hill EDWARD B. FAGAN, of Company D, 1st Mo. Infantry.
Mobile and St. Louis papers please copy.

In Jackson, Miss., June 18th, 1863, of a wound received at the battle of Champion Hill, PETER L. FITZWILLIAM, of Company D, 1st Mo. Infantry.
St. Louis papers please copy.

NEW ADVERTISEMENTS.

JUST RECEIVED—on consignment, 400 bushels Alabama SALT, which will be sold for cash, or exchanged for bacon. S. P. BALEY.
Jackson, June 20, 1863-7td*

NOTICE.—Any person in want of a substitute, can find one by applying to G. A. RAMSAY, opposite the City Hall, Jackson, at Mogridge's store.
je20-2td*

STRAY HORSES.—A ROAN HORSE, and a SMALL BAY MARE, left the camp yesterday evening, and were last seen on the Brandon road a mile east of the Railroad Bridge.
A liberal reward will be paid for the return of said horses, to Col. W. P. WINANS, 19th La. Reg't.
je20-2td*

$50 REWARD.—LOST, on the night of the 18th of June, between Claridy's Corner and the Post Office in Jackson, a RED MOROCCO MEMORANDUM BOOK with two hundred dollars in it. One $100 interest bearing bill, and five $20 bills: also a note given by the undersigned to A. & C. A. McIntosh, of Crystal Springs, for $22 25.
A reward of $50 will be paid for the delivery of the above at the Mississippian office.
J. W. ABRAHAM.
June 20, '63-2td*

WANTED IMMEDIATELY.—A Furnished House, by a gentleman and lady without children. Any one leaving the city who desire to leave their property in careful hands, can find an occupant by addressing G. B., at this office. je20-2td*

LOST.—In this city, on the 19th instant, a BLACK LEATHER POCKET BOOK, containing $3,025—2,000 of which were in greenback Confederate one hundred dollar notes, one $50 greenback Confederate, and the balance in 5's, 10's and 20's. Transportation tickets were also contained in the Pocket Book
A liberal reward will be paid to any one finding and leaving it with Capt. Robertson, at his office, next door to Captain Gillaspie, Post Quartermaster.
je20-2td JOHN WEBB, Captain & A. Q. M.

NOTICE TO DEBTORS.—All indebted to the estate of C. A. Moore, deceased, will please call on the undersigned, and settle forthwith and save costs.
je19-7td L. S. EVANS, J. P.

LOST.—On the 13th of May, (the day of the battle at Jackson) a medium sized Green LEATHER TRUNK, with brass tacks. The name of the owner M. E. McLAURIN, was written with ink on one of the straps across the top of the trunk. There was also a card on the top, marked "J. F. Foute, Jackson, Miss." The trunk was left on the Brandon Platform, at Jackson, and was there at 12 o'clock noon on the 13th.
Any one who will return the trunk, or its contents, or give me any information concerning it, at this office, will be suitably rewarded. M. E. McLAURIN,
je19-7td* Jackson, Miss.

AUCTION SALE.—Will be sold on Saturday, the 20th instant, at 11 o'clock, A. M., in front of the Capitol, articles saved from the fire, BEDSTEADS, MATTRESSES, WARDROBES, BUREAUS, WASHSTANDS, &c., &c.
je19-2td J. H. BOYD, Auc'r.

ARMY BLANKS.

THE following Quartermasters' and Commissary Blanks are on hand and for sale, by

JONES, WISELY & CO.,

At the "SOUTHWESTERN CONFEDERATE PRINTING HOUSE," corner of President and Pearl streets, Jackson, Mississippi.

QUARTERMASTERS' BLANKS.

No. 2.—Report of Persons and Articles, &c.
" 4.— " Stores received for Transportation.
" 5.—Monthly Return of Public Animals.
" 6.— " Report of Forage.
" 7.— " Report of Officers stationed at, &c.
" 10.—Account Current.
" 12.—Purchase Voucher.
" 15—Receipt Roll.
" 16.—Account for Mileage.
" 17.—Voucher to Abstract B.
" 18.— " "
" 19.— " "
" 20.—Postage Account.
" 21.—Commutation of Quarters and Fuel.
" 22.—Account for Services Rendered.
" 29.—Requisition for Fuel. (Company.)
" 33.— " Forage. (Private Horses.)
" 38.— " Stationery.
" 44.—Account of Auction Sales.
" 47.—Account Current, Expenditures, &c
" 49 & 50.—Requisition for and Bill of Medicines
" 51.—Quarterly Return of Clothing, Camp and Garrison Equipage.
—Abstracts E and D.

BLANKS USED IN PAY DEPARTMENT.

No. 58 & 59.—Final Statement.
" 56.—Receipts for Remittances, &c.
" 57.—Officers Pay Accounts.
" 63.—Statement of Money Received and Expended.
—Descriptive Pay Accounts.
—Descriptive List of Pay and Clothing.

BLANKS FOR THE ADJUTANT GENERAL'S OFFICE.

Field Returns. (Division.)
Regimental Morning Reports.
Company Morning "
Certificates of Disability for Discharge, &c.
Form of Application for Money due Deceased Soldiers.

COMMISSARY BLANKS.

No. 1.—Return of Provisions, &c.
" 2.—Abstract of Provisions Issued, &c.
" 3.— " " to Hospitals.
" 6.—Monthly Summary of Funds received, &c.
" 7.—Account Current.
" 9.—Abstract of Disbursements, &c.
" 10.—Consolidated Abstract of Provisions sold to Officers.
" 12.—Return of Commissary Property received.
" 13.—Provision Return for Company.
" 19.—Bill of Purchase.
" 22—Invoice of Subsistence Stores.
" 24.—Receipt for "
" 20.—Report of Persons and Articles, &c.
" 21.—Receipt Roll.
" 23.—Invoice of Commissary Property, &c.
" 25.—Descriptive List of Persons and Articles.
—Sales to Officers.

☞ Blanks not above enumerated will be printed at short notice. We have on hand a large supply of fine English Paper, and are prepared to do work promptly and in a very superior manner, all ruled complete. Orders from abroad respectfully solicited.
je19-1wd

OFFICE OF QUARTERMASTER,
DEPARTMENT OF MISSISSIPPI AND EAST LA.,
Jackson, June 17, 1863.

NOTICE.—All appointments of Agents for this Department, of date prior to the 1st of June, are hereby revoked. Only such as have authority subsequent, will be recognized. L. MIMS,
je18-1m Department Mississippi & East La.

WANTED.—A Furnished Room, or Board in a private family. Address Col. H. B. KELLY, through the Post Office, or at the Military Court Room in the Capitol,
je18-3td*

STRAYED OR STOLEN from the subscriber, encamped near Jackson, Miss., a DARK BROWN MARE, eight years old, blazed face, 15 hands high, and had when she left a sore back and withers. Any one returning her to me will be liberally rewarded.
S M. HIGH,
Herren's Squadron, First Mississippi Cavalry.
June 18th, 1863-3td*

STRAYED OR STOLEN—from the subscriber, living in Jackson, 2 two-year old COLTS—one a dark gray, the other a bay; the bay a natural pacer.
A liberal reward will be paid to any one taking them up and returning them to me in Jackson, or giving me information so that I can get them. S. P. BALEY.
Jackson, June 11-2wd*

ANY person knowing the whereabouts of a negro boy WILLIAM, belonging to G. M. Baker, who was accidentally shot at the Confederate House about four weeks ago, can get fifty dollars' reward by leaving said boy with A. PATRICK, at the Restaurant.
Jackson, June 16, '63.

A VALUABLE HOUSE AND LOT FOR SALE.

SITUATED on State street, in the City of Jackson.—The House contains ten good rooms, and also a good business room. There are on the lots a good cistern of water, a good garden, a stable, carriage house, &c. &c.—The House is suitable for a Boarding House. The Furniture will be sold with the House, if desired.
Apply to J. W. MORRIS, or to E. JOUVENAT, at the Southern Express office. [je14-6td*

JOB PRINTING.

HAVING purchased a complete NEWS AND JOB OFFICE, to replace the one destroyed by the vandal foe, we are again prepared to do all kinds of

JOB WORK

With promptness and dispatch—from a business card to a mammoth poster.

ARMY BLANKS

Of every description:

GENERAL ORDERS, PAMPHLETS,

And in fact every variety of Job Work done in the best style and without delay.

☞ Give us a call, and we will endeavor to fill your orders to your satisfaction.
june12-tf

MORGAN AND HIS MEN!

I BEG leave to announce to the public, that I have just finished the publication of the first

GREAT NOVEL,

Of this Second War of Independence, entitled

RAIDS AND ROMANCE
Of Morgan and his Men!

BY SALLY ROCHESTER FORD, of Louisville, Kentucky, author of "Grace Truman," "Mary Bunyan," "Romance of Free Masonry," &c. &c.

Complete in One Volume at $3 50.

The reader will be gratified to enjoy all the exciting interest of a first-class standard romance, and all the information of a correct history. The historian will find it a valuable reference book at present, as well as for times to come.

Considering it as a work of art, it happens so, that this is so far, the FIRST ORIGINAL LITERARY WORK of note, that this war has produced, and this Confederacy issued.

On account of the scarcity of materials, we were compelled to reduce this edition to a very limited number, and it is very uncertain, for the same reason, when we might be able to publish a second; hence all those who wish to secure a copy of that historical Novel, will do well to call in time.

S. H. GOETZEL,
je16-d1m Mobile, Ala.

NOTICE!—The following CERTIFICATES, issued by A. J. GUIROT, Esq., Treasurer Confederate States, to W. D. WINTER, under the act of February 20th, 1863, entitled "An Act to authorize the issue of Bonds for funding Treasury Notes," were forcibly taken from the Bank of J. & T. GREEN, Jackson, Miss., by J. W. Jefferson, Lieutenant-Colonel and Provost Marshal U. S. Army, to-wit:

Certificate	No. 137, for	$7,100
"	No. 138, for	1,200
"	No. 139, for	9,100
"	No. 140, for	7,000
"	No. 141, for	3,000
"	No. 142, for	50,200
"	No. 159, for	57,300
In all		$135,000

The public is, therefore, notified not to receive, discount, purchase, or in any manner trade for, the above described certificates, as the illegal seizure of the same has been brought to the knowledge of the proper officer, and no one, except the undersigned, is authorized to claim and receive the Coupon Bonds or Registered Stock called for by said certificates. je5 15t W. D. WINTER.

To Agents of the Produce Loan for Mississippi, &c.

THE office of the General Agent will remain until further advised at Uniontown, Ala., which is only a few hours distance on the railroad from Meridian.

You are authorized to continue the purchasing of cotton, which will be paid for in treasury notes and seven ℔ cent. bonds, until July next, and after that in treasury notes.

The Government expects that you will enter actively into the business and obtain the cotton on the most favorable terms, not purchasing however in close proximity to the enemy.

J. D. B. DEBOW, General Agent.
FRANCIS POE, General Purchasing Agent.
Uniontown, Ala., June 3, 1863—ju10

MILITARY ORDERS.

HEAD-Q'RS, FORCES AROUND VICKSBURG,
JACKSON, Miss., June 8th, 1863.

General Orders, No. 2.

ALL officers and soldiers in the town of Jackson, and vicinity, who have been cut off from their commands, or whose leaves of absence have expired, will report forthwith, to the Commandant of the Post.
By command Major-General BRECKENRIDGE.
JOHN A. BUCKNER, A. A. Gen.
ju9 tBg

HEAD-QUARTERS OF POST,
JACKSON, June 4th, '63.

Special Orders, No. ——.

SURGEON WALKER CURRY, Asst. Surgeon J. R. Furness, and Asst. Surgeon Wm. D. Somers, are hereby appointed members of, and will constitute an examining Board to determine on applications for leave of absence and furloughs, as required by general orders.
By order of JOHN M SMYLIE,
Major commanding Post.
LANDY A. LINDSEY, A. A.
Office on corner of Main and Pearl streets, up stairs, one door below Moore's Drug store.
OFFICE HOURS—From 10 to 12 A. M., except Sundays.
june9

HEADQ'RS DEPARTMENT OF THE WEST,
JACKSON, Miss., June 13, 1863;

Special Orders No. 13.

IX. ALL Quartermasters absent from this command will report immediately to Major Barbour, Chief Quartermaster.
By command of GEN. JOHNSTON.
(Signed) BENJ. S. EWELL,
A. A. Gen'l.
je 14d7t

OFFICE OF POST QUARTERMASTER,
Jackson, Miss., June 11, 1863.

20,000 POUNDS WOOL wanted immediately.—Call on the undersigned, who will pay the highest market price.
W. M. GILLASPIE, Capt. & A. Q. M.
ju10

FOR SALE.—I wish to sell my RESIDENCE and 37 ACRES OF LAND attached thereto. Come and look, any one wishing to invest. JESSE MABRY.
Jackson, June 18, 1863-7td*

FOR SALE.—A desirable House and Lot. The house contains 6 rooms, 2 store rooms, cook room, 4 servants' rooms, smoke-house, corn crib, hen house, cow house, stable, cistern, and a garden in a fine state of cultivation.
The place is in good repair, and will be sold very low. The furniture will be sold with the house, if desired.
je16-tf J. N. DANIEL.

LOOK HERE.—MRS. GEORGE FOLSOM, lately exiled from New Orleans, is anxious to hear from her husband. Address, Mrs. GEORGE FOLSOM, care of Judge Stephen Brown, Columbus, Mississippi.
☞ Monroe (La.) Democrat, please copy three times, and forward account.
je17-5td*

JUST RECEIVED—At Mann's shop, opposite Stevens' old foundry, a small lot of DRY GOODS, LADIES' SHOES, &c., wholesale or retail— BY T. J. MANN.
je17-7td*

OFFICE OF POST QUARTERMASTER,
JACKSON, Miss., June 15, 1863.

WANTED.—A number of MOULDERS AND PATTERN MAKERS immediately. Apply to
WM. M. GILLASPIE, Capt. & A. Q. M.
je16-7td

FOUND.—Within my inclosure a BAY HORSE, 16 hands high, 8 years old, right hind foot white—has a small wound in the breast, has the appearance of a shot or bayonet wound; has no shoes on; he paces well.
The owner is requested to prove property, pay charges and take him away.
L. F. MONTGOMERY.
Madison Station, Madison County, Miss.
je17-7td*

WANTED TO BUY Beds, Bedding, Bedsteads, and all kinds of Household and Kitchen Furniture.
Persons contemplating the sale of such articles, will do well to give us a call. R. W. T. DANIEL & CO.
Jackson, June 17-1w

THE NEW YORK HERALD.

WHOLE NO. 9782. | NEW YORK, SATURDAY, JUNE 27, 1863.—TRIPLE SHEET. | PRICE THREE CENTS

THE TURF.

A SADDLE RACE.
TROTTING.
FASHION PLEASURE GROUNDS.
WEDNESDAY, July 1, at 3 P. M.,
SIXTH RACE BETWEEN PATCHEN AND BUTLER.
Match for $5,000.
Two mile heats, under the saddle.
D. Tallman names b. g. George M. Patchen.
D. Mace names blk. g. General Butler.
The boat which leaves James slip at 2 o'clock connects with the train which leaves Hunter's Point at 2½ P. M.
Boats on the Thirty-fourth street ferry leave New York every ten minutes. JOSEPH CROCHERON, Manager.

HORSES, CARRIAGES, &C.

BLACK MARE FOR SALE.—KIND IN ALL HARNESS; nice for a lady to drive. Also an Express Wagon, with top, and Harness. Apply at 227 West Fifteenth street, between Seventh and Eighth avenues.

CARRIAGES AND HORSES FOR SALE.—TWO HUNdred Carriages and fifty Horses, Rockaways, Buggies and Business Wagons; Family, Road and Trotting Horses; one double team, can trot in 2:50. No. 10 Nevins street, Brooklyn.

FOR SALE—A FAMILY COACH; WILL BE SOLD cheap. Apply at the corner of Grand and Chrystie streets, in the office.

FOR SALE—A FIRST RATE SADDLE OR WAGON pony, about fifteen hands high; also a Business Wagon and Harness. Inquire at 700 Greenwich street. W. TAYLOR.

FOR SALE—TWO LARGE HORSES, SIXTEEN HANDS or over; a gray and bay; perfectly kind in all harness and well calculated for a coupe or carriage. Can be seen at 80 West Thirtieth street.

FOR SALE—THREE VERY FINE HORSES, SUITED for driving or riding; are hardy, and stylish in action; suited for either ladies or gentlemen. Can be seen for three days at 1,550 Broadway, between Fifty-sixth and Fifty-seventh streets.

FOR SALE—HORSES, AND A VARIETY OF ROCKAways, top and no top Wagons, (Jaggers and Doctors' Wagons; also a very fine Gig, Harness, Sheets, Nets, &c., at 1,401 Broadway.

FOR SALE—A BAY HORSE AND SET OF WAGON Harness; horse 7 years old, 16 hands high, will be sold cheap if applied for this week, at coal yard corner of Rivington and Suffolk, streets, N. Y.

FOR SALE—AN IMPORTED TWO YEARS OLD AYRshire Bull, thoroughbred and very handsome. Inquire of E. NYE, 17 South street, New York.

FOR SALE—A FIRST CLASS NEW MILCH COW; gives twenty-four quarts a day: will be sold cheap if applied for this week. Inquire for JOHN GIRLING, Patten House, New Dorp, Staten Island.

FOR SALE—A GOOD WORK HORSE, 15¾ HANDS high, sound and stylish, weighs 1,250 lbs. Can be seen at 172 Monroe street.

FOR SALE—A HANDSOME TWO SEAT ROCKAWAY, with pole and shafts, glass doors, &c., in complete order, built by Miner & Stevens. Apply at at FLANDREW'S Carriage Factory, 138 Elizabeth street.

FOR SALE—A BAY MARE, SEVEN YEARS OLD, 15 hands high, warranted to trot a mile in 2:40, double or single. Apply at Union Hall, 155 First avenue, near Tenth street.

FOR SALE—TEN VALUABLE HORSES, JUST ARrived from Maine, among them are two matched pairs. To be seen at T. C. Butler's stable, 402 and 404 Atlantic street, Brooklyn.

FOR SALE—HORSE, CARRIAGE AND HARNESS, all complete; a superior establishment for a gentleman's family; warranted in every respect; will be sold low. Apply at 147 Perry street.

FOR SALE—A LADY'S SADDLE HORSE; VERY STYlish, perfectly sound, kind and gentle in every respect. Inquire at 160 Fulton street, room No. 6, from 10 A. M. to 2 P. M.

FOR SALE—A FINE PAIR OF BAY CARRIAGE Horses, 15¾ hands high, 8 years old, sound and kind. Also a fine saddle Pony, for children. To be seen at Pelton's stables, corner of Twenty-seventh street and Broadway.

FOR SALE—A BAY MARE, 6 YEARS OLD, 15¼ HANDS high, a splendid animal, perfectly sound and kind in every particular; can trot in 50, just off a farm, has never been trained. Apply to JOHN BLANY, horse shoer, Forty seventh street, between Eighth avenue and Broadway.

FOR SALE—AN ENTIRE ESTABLISHMENT, CONsisting of a four seat Phaeton (made by one of the best makers in town), a pair of Horses, double Harness, Saddle, Bridle, Blankets, &c., &c.; will be sold at a bargain, as the owner is about leaving the city. Apply at Wilson's stable, 87 and 89 Tenth street, near Fifth avenue.

FOR SALE—A BAY HORSE, 16 HANDS HIGH, SOUND and kind in single and double harness; would make a fine coupe horse. Apply at 836 Broadway.

FOR SALE—A VERY HANDSOME PONY, 12 TO 13 hands high, young and sound, well adapted for a boy's use, either under saddle, or in harness. Can be seen at Thomas Morris' stable, 118 Clinton place.

FOR SALE AT A BARGAIN—A FINE PAIR OF JET black Pony Horses, 6 years old, nearly 15 hands high, very stylish and speedy. They are very fine ladies' saddle horses. Also a Phaeton Coach and Harness. They will be sold together or separate at a great sacrifice. Inquire at Cunningham's stable, 115 Barrow street, near Greenwich.

FOR SALE CHEAP—TWO SECOND HAND COACHES. Apply at McMahon's stables, 50 Monroe street.

SADDLE HORSE FOR SALE.—THE THOROUGHbred stallion, raised in Maryland from imported Priam, dam Imp Rebecca, 6 years old, sound, kind and gentle. Was presented to the owner as one of the finest bred Horses in the South; is a splendid animal, both in color and form. Price $600. Can be seen at Excelsior stable, corner Sixth avenue and Thirtieth street.

WANTED—THREE OR FOUR WATER CARTS, FOR sprinkling roads, to purchase or hire for four months. Address box 1,958 Post office.

MUSICAL.

A MAGNIFICENT SEVEN OCTAVE PIANOFORTE, made to order two months ago; cost $500; for sale at a very low price. Call at 859 Broadway, second floor, between 10 and 12 A. M., or after 7 P. M.

A MAGNIFICENT SEVEN OCTAVE ROSEWOOD Pianoforte for sale at a sacrifice—Carved legs and case, overstrung bass, full iron plate, French action, all modern improvements; made to order for subscriber; has been in use but eight months; cost $600, for $275, including Stool and cover. Also rosewood Drawing Room Suits and rosewood Chamber Furniture at sacrifice. Inquire at 113 West Twenty-third street, near Sixth avenue. M. MIDDLETON.

MUSIC TO SUIT THE TIMES.—INSTRUCTIONS given on the Piano, on the most reasonable terms, either at the residence of the pupil or the teacher. Apply at 32 Henry street after 3 o'clock P. M. M. L. DAVIS.

NEW MUSIC.
Just published, a beautiful Song and Chorus, "They Pray for Us at Home."
On Sunday, the day after the battle of Cedar Mountain, as our wounded soldiers were lying in a church at Culpepper, which had been taken for a hospital, one of the mortally wounded whispered to a dying companion, "I wish there was some one here to pray for us;" to which his companion replied, "They are praying for us at home!"
Words by Ednor Rossiter.
Music by B. Frank Walters.
Price, twenty-five cents.
Published by LEE & WALKER,
722 Chestnut street, Philadelphia.
For sale at all the music stores.

PIANOS, MELODEONS AND HARMONIUMS.—THE largest assortment in the city can be found at WATERS', 481 Broadway, at great bargains. 100 new and second hand Pianos, Melodeons and Harmoniums to let; rent allowed if purchased as per agreement; monthly payments received for the same. Cash paid for second hand Pianos and Melodeons, or taken in exchange for new. Instruments tuned and repaired.

CONTRALTO.—WANTED, A GOOD CONTRALTO singer in an Episcopal church up town; must be familiar with the service. Address W. A. B., Herald office, stating where last engaged.

INSTRUCTIONS.

A CARD.—SPECIAL NOTICE TO YOUNG MEN.—TEN full scholarships, including double entry bookkeeping, mercantile arithmetic and penmanship, will be sold this month, at $25 each, to fill vacancies for the summer term. Regular price $40. Time unlimited. Private instruction daily to adults, ladies or gentlemen. OLIVER B. GOLDSMITH, 756 Broadway, corner Eighth street.

BARLOW'S COMMERCIAL AND ART ACADEMY, 923 Broadway.—Drawing, Penmanship and Bookkeeping expeditiously and effectively taught, day or evening. No classes. Ornamental penmanship, diplomas, firemen's and all other certificates designed and filled to order. Terms reasonable.

LANGUAGES.—GERMAN, FRENCH, SPANISH AND Latin taught in a short time, according to an entirely new method, by A. HAIN, formerly Professor of Modern Languages in Queen's College, London. Families attended at their residences. Apply at 147 West Twenty-second st.

STAMFORD, CONN.—MISS TUCKER RECEIVES twenty young ladies to educate, assisted by German and French resident governesses, and by eminent professors from New York. Pupils are received at any period. References—Right Rev. John Williams, D. D., Assistant Bishop of Connecticut, Middletown, Conn.; the Rev. W. Mitchell, rector, Stamford, Conn., &c. For circulars, &c., apply to the Principal.

WATCHES, JEWELRY, &C.

A SECRET.—HOW DOES THE ORIGINAL JACOBS, 407 Broadway, manage to sell Watches, Diamonds and Jewelry so cheap as to defy competition? I will tell you. He buys and sells for cash only.

CALIFORNIA DIAMONDS—EQUAL IN BRILLIANCY to the real; set in solid 18 carat gold. Rings, $2 50 to $25; Breastpins, $2 50 to $25; Studs, $3 to $10; Earrings, $3 to $25. Sent by express or mail on receipt of the cash. Original L. JACOBS, 407 Broadway.

DIAMONDS, DIAMONDS, DIAMONDS.—I AM GIVING the highest cash prices for Diamonds, Watches, Jewelry and Silver Plate, or cash advanced on the same. Old Gold and Silver bought or exchanged. Original L. JACOBS, 407 Broadway.

GOLD PLATED AND COMPOSITION WATCHES, $10 to $25 each; warranted timekeepers. I have just received a superb lot of Gold Plated and Composition Chains, price from $2 to $5; they wear equal to gold. Original L. JACOBS, 407 Broadway.

ORIGINAL L. JACOBS, ORIGINAL L. JACOBS—L. Jacobs, L. Jacobs—Original L., Original L., L. L. L. L., Original, Original, Original Jacobs, Jacobs, Jacobs Jacobs, 407 Broadway.

WATCHES.—JUST RECEIVED, A LARGE LOT OF Gold and Silver new and second hand Watches, which I am selling for legal tender notes at gold prices. Silver Watches from $3 to $30; Gold Watches from $10 to $150. Original L. JACOBS, 407 Broadway.

THE SIEGE OF VICKSBURG.

The Rebel Defences and the Union Parallels at Our Latest Advices.

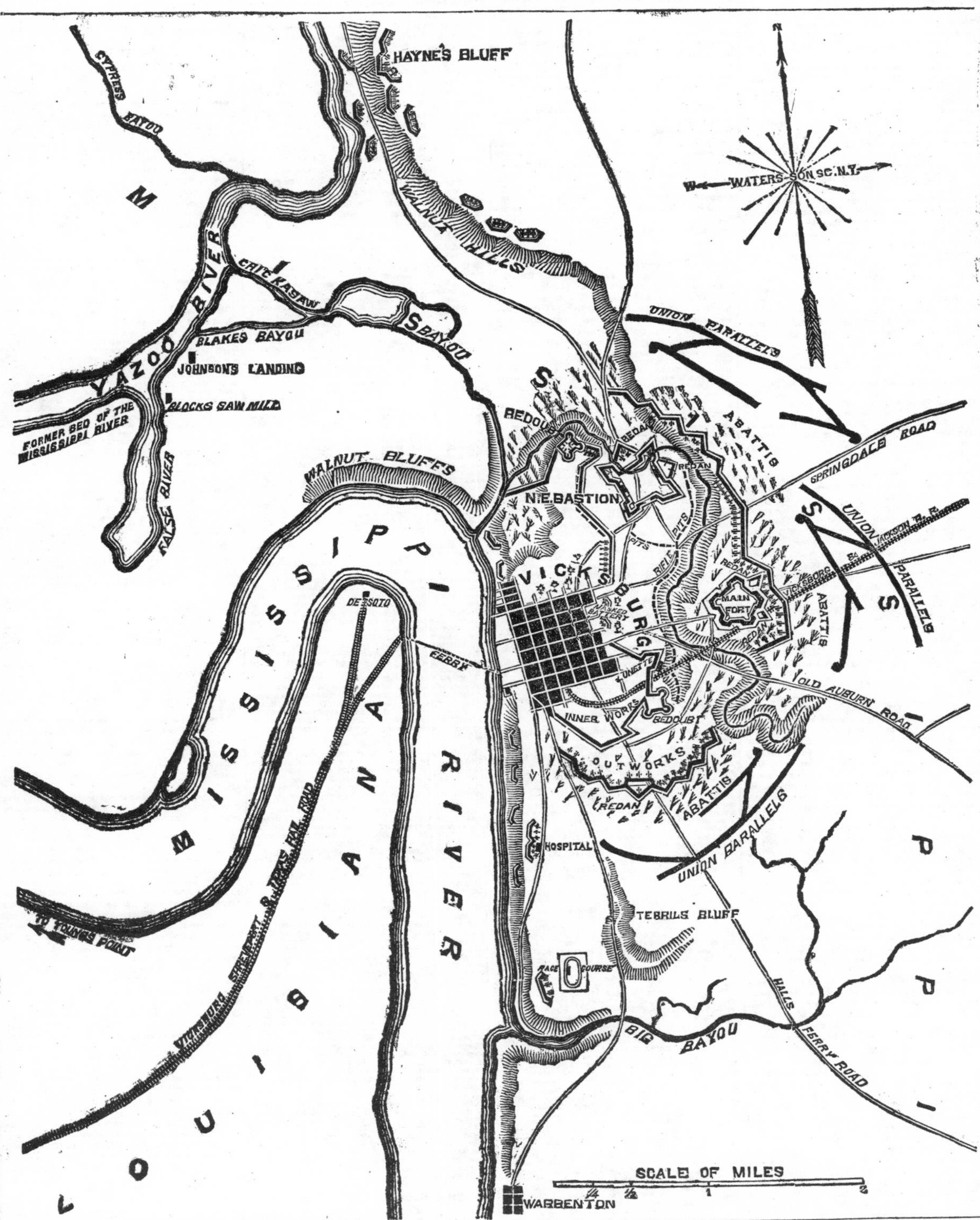

SITUATIONS WANTED—FEMALES.

A NUMBER OF WELL RECOMMENDED GERMAN girls want situations as cooks, chambermaids, laundresses, nurses, girls for general housework, &c., at Mrs. LOWE'S German Institute, No. 17 Stanton street, near the Bowery.

AN ELDERLY WOMAN (A CANADIAN) WANTS A situation as housekeeper, to a gentleman. Address Mrs. James, Stamford, Conn.

A WIDOW LADY OF RESPECTABILITY WISHES A situation as lady's companion, or as stewardess on board a first class steamer running to and from Europe. Best references given. Address J. C., box 126 Herald office.

AN EXPERIENCED COOK WISHES A SITUATION IN a private family to cook, wash and iron. Has three years' city reference. Apply at 172 Atlantic st., Brooklyn.

EUROPE.—WANTED, BY A RESPECTABLE AND well educated young English girl, a situation as child's nurse, lady's maid, or companion; is unaffected by the sea air. Best of reference given, and would go for the passage. Address J. R., station F, New York Post office.

WANTED—AN INFANT TO WET NURSE, BY A REspectable married woman who has lost her child. Inquire of Mrs. Lawler, 212 Front street, Brooklyn.

WANTED—BY AN INTELLIGENT AMERICAN LADY, a situation as housekeeper in a family where there are not many children. Best of references given and required. Call on or address Mrs. Rogers, 23 Norfolk st.

SITUATIONS WANTED—MALES.

A MAN WHO HAS A PERFECT KNOWLEDGE OF distilling Kentucky Bourbon whiskey wishes employment. Address Anthony, Herald office.

A SITUATION WANTED—AS CLERK OR MANAGER, in a respectable mercantile business or manufacturing establishment, by a German, 35 years of age, who has been in business in Chile for a number of years; speaks the four principal languages and understands bookkeeping and mercantile correspondence. Address box 288 Post office.

A YOUNG MAN, AGED 19: IS A PROTESTANT; WILL be disengaged in a few days, would like to meet with a gentleman wanting a valet to travel with him; will be highly recommended by his present employer. Can be seen for three days at 101 Waverley place.

AS TRAVELING SALESMAN.—A GENTLEMAN OF several years' experience in the jobbing shoe business, and who has traveled in the West selling goods, would like to make an engagement with some reliable house as traveling salesman. Satisfactory reference given. Address Salesman, box 180 Herald office.

GROOM'S SITUATION WANTED—BY A YOUNG MAN 22 years of age, just arrived from Ireland, where he has lived in first class families. Understands the care and management of horses thoroughly; can ride, drive, train, and is a first rate farrier. Is very polite, civil and obliging, and is willing to make himself generally useful in a first class private family. Call on or address James Weldon, No. 8 Broadway, corner of Beaver st.

SITUATION WANTED—BY A YOUNG MAN, TWENTY-eight years of age, lately arrived from England, in an office or store; has had seven years' experience in a London office; is willing to make himself generally useful. Can be seen at or address W. F. Collins, 16 Leroy place, Bleecker st.

WANTED—BY A RESPECTABLE AND STEADY young man, a situation as coachman, either in city or country. The best of city reference given. Apply at 208 Columbia st., Brooklyn.

HELP WANTED—MALES.

DRY GOODS SALESMEN WANTED.—CITY REFErence required. Apply to John E. Lenard, 168 Grand st., Williamsburg.

TO CARMEN.—WANTED, A CARMAN, TO TAKE charge of a cart and horse; one who can get about six loads per day for a licensed cart; one having a connection with houses in the neighborhood of Barclay and Greenwich sts. preferred; must be able to give references as to honesty and steady habits. Apply to G. Elsom, 231 Greenwich st., between 9 and 12 o'clock.

WANTED—A STOUT, ACTIVE BOY, 17 OR 18 YEARS old, a little familiar with horses and vegetable gardening, at Wiggins' Hotel, Greenfield Coney Island road, L. I. One used to the country preferred. Coney Island cars bring you to the door.

WANTED—MEN TO ENGAGE IN BUSINESS. CAPItal $100 to $3,00; profit $500 to $1,000 per month; great invention, freely shown, at 609 Broadway, room No. 3. The most skeptical convinced. A. W. GOODELL.

WANTED—BY AN IMPORTING HOUSE, A PERSON having some acquaintance with the branches of the crockery trade, for general and office work, including bookkeeping. First rate references will be required. Address in own own hand B. H., box 185 Herald office.

WANTED—AN ACTIVE, INDUSTRIOUS, CAPABLE young man, to take charge of the soft hat department in a jobbing house. Address, with references, box 3,856 Post office.

WANTED—A SMART ACTIVE BOY IN A DRY GOODS store; one having some knowledge of the business preferred. Apply to E. J. Meehan, No. 25 7th ave.

WANTED—AN OFFICE BOY; ONE RESIDING WITH his parents preferred. Address in own handwriting box 1,082 Post office.

WANTED—SEVERAL FIRST CLASS WAITERS; Germans who are able to speak English preferred, to wait in a restaurant. Good wages will be given. Apply to John Ittner, 106 and 108 Grand street.

WANTED—IN A RETAIL DRY GOODS STORE, A young man, from 16 to 20 years of age; must be acquainted with the business. Apply at 599 8th av. Ring at the private door.

WANTED—A BOY, TO ATTEND A GROCERY STORE, between the ages of 16 and 18 years; must understand the business and of steady habits; must bring good reference. Apply at 542 Myrtle ave., from 8 A. M. until 2 P. M., Brooklyn.

WANTED—FOR FIRST CLASS HOTEL, WASHINGton, D. C., a bookkeeper and two clerks; must be intelligent and energetic. (Address immediately, Neville & Co., box 2,051 Philadelphia Post office, with 25c. for advertisement and postage.

WANTED—IN THE OFFICE OF A WEEKLY NEWSpaper, a boy, from 16 to 18 years of age, who has had some experience in mailing papers. Address, in handwriting of applicant, box 1,647 N. Y. Post office.

$100.—PARTIES DESIRING TO INVEST A SMALL capital in a sure paying, independent business, that can be located in any place, can learn of such by sending their address and stamp to C. Ransom, box 160 Herald office.

For other wants see ninth page.

THE MILITARY.

ATTENTION, COMPANY B, FIFTEENTH N. Y. V. E.—All members of Company B, Fifteenth regiment N. Y. Volunteer Engineers, will meet at 374 Greenwich street, on Saturday, June 27, at 9½ A. M., for the purpose of being mustered out of service. By order of JOSEPH WOOD, Jr., Captain.

ATTENTION, COMPANY A, THIRTY-EIGHTH REGIment.—You are requested to be at the corner of Bleecker street and Broadway this day, at eleven o'clock, to receive your pay. JACOB LEONARD.

COMPANY K, SIXTH NEW YORK VOLUNTEERS.—This company will assemble at the Park Barracks at 10 o'clock A. M., on Saturday, the 27th inst., to be mustered out of the service of the United States.
HENRY L. HOELZLE,
Captain Sixth N. Y. V., commanding Company K.

COMPANY C, SIXTH NEW YORK VOLUNTEERS.—This company will assemble at the Park Barracks, at 10 o'clock A. M., on Saturday, the 27th inst., to be mustered out of the service of the United States.
R. H. HAZELTINE,
Captain Sixth N. Y. V., commanding Company C.

ENFIELD RIFLES FOR SALE—FIVE CASES NAVAL Enfield Rifles with Sabre Bayonets, and four cases Long Enfield Rifles for sale cheap, in bond. Samples may be seen at 54 South street.

FIFTEENTH REGIMENT NEW YORK VOLUNTEER Engineers.—The members of Company D, Fifteenth Regiment New York Volunteer Engineers, will assemble at the State Arsenal, corner of Seventh avenue and Thirty-fifth street, for the purpose of being mustered out of the service, on Saturday, June 27, 1863, at 10 o'clock A. M. The men will parade in heavy marching order, including knapsacks, haversacks and canteens. By order of JULIUS C. HICKS, Captain Commanding.

FIFTEENTH REGIMENT NEW YORK VOLUNTEER Engineers.—Members of Company G will assemble at the arsenal, corner of Seventh avenue and Thirty-fifth street, in heavy marching order, on Monday, 29th inst., at 8 A. M., to be mustered out. By order of
FELIX LARKIN, Captain,
Commanding Company G.

NOTICE.—SOLDIERS OF ALL THE FIRST THIRTY-eight regiments New York Volunteers who have been discharged and not paid their $100 bounty, can have the same collected and cashed by applying to J. NELSON LUCKEY, Nos. 8 and 10 Pine street, room 29.

REORGANIZATION OF THE THIRTY-EIGHTH NEW York Volunteers or Second Scott Life Guard, under the command of Colonel Augustus Funk, late Major. Recruits now received and full bounties given. This old and popular regiment will be commanded by old and experienced officers, men who have served their full term of service, and now in their country's hour of need are prepared to return. Headquarters at Lafayette Hall, 597 Broadway. J. McE. HYDE, Adjutant.

17 REGIMENT NEW YORK VOLUNTEERS.—THIS fine regiment is now being reorganized by Col. Wm. J. C. Grower, late Major, and is fast filling up under the auspices of many of our most prominent citizens. Good clothing, quarters and rations furnished at once to those enlisting in this popular organization. N. B.—The highest bounties paid. Quartermaster's Sergeant wanted. Apply immediately at headquarters, 300 Broadway.

EXPRESSES.

A. BURNHAM'S FURNITURE EXPRESS AND PACKing Establishment, 115 West Eleventh street, between Fifth and Sixth avenues.—Household Furniture boxed and shipped to all parts of the world; covered wagons for removing furniture to and from the country and furniture stored.

PERSONAL.

ADOPTION.—A LOVELY BOY, TEN MONTHS OLD to adopt out to a good home. Call at No. 6 Amity place.

GEORGE W.—I ACKNOWLEDGED THE RECEIPT of your very important communication in last Saturday's Herald. Westchester I am anxious to see you. A personal interview is particularly requested by your musical friend, Lizzie V. W——s, 143 E——h s——t, between Broadway and Fourth avenue.

H. W. J.—ALL WELL.

INFORMATION WANTED—OF JANE BERRELL OR J. Hinas: was in this city in 1856. Any information of her whereabouts will be thankfully received by her son, Robert, 127 Cedar street.

INFORMATION WANTED—OF MARY ANNE LANE, who left the city of Cork 8 months ago. She will oblige her brother, Bartholomew Lane, by calling at 218 East Seventeenth street.

INFORMATION WANTED—OF GEORGE ROBINSON, who left Berley Hill, near Carrick Fergus, in the latter part of February, 1863. Address Mr. Ross, station A, New York city.

INFORMATION WANTED—OF ANDREW BURNET Tait.—If Andrew B. Tait, who left Scotland in the year 1853, and was last heard of at Callao in the year 1854, is still alive, he will be entitled to a share of certain Trust funds and estate on giving satisfactory proof of identity. The factor thereon, and said Andrew Burnet Tait's brother will give a suitable reward to any one affording information regarding him subsequent to the above mentioned dates; and especially, if he is deceased, to any one furnishing evidence of his death. Apply to Robert M'William, S. S. C., No. 23 London street, Edinburg, or to William Wood, accountant, No. 5 Nelson street, Edinburg.

IF MRS. ELIZABETH PIERSON, FORMERLY OF Dubuque, Iowa, will address a note to the subscriber, she will hear of a dear friend, now visiting this city. Address Mrs. Maria Cushing, Herald office.

MR. HUGH TYLER MAY HEAR OF SOMETHING TO his interest by addressing a line immediately to M. M., from W., box 157 New York Herald office.

MISS EUGENIA THOMPSON, LATE OF CINCINNATI, Ohio, now residing in New York, will please address W. D. Doane, 512 Broadway.

RUDOLF KUNZ, BORN IN BASLE, SWITZERLAND, September 1, 1805, is requested to apply to the Civil Court in Basle, for an inheritance at his disposal, or to the undersigned. W. SCHALL & CO.
NEW YORK, June 16, 1863.

WILL THE LADY WHO WAS DISAPPOINTED IN A boarding place by sickness, and called twice about two weeks ago, please call at the same place, where she will hear of something to her advantage.

FINE ARTS.

NEW YORK PICTURE GALLERY,
455 BROADWAY.
ALBUM PICTURES.
CARD PHOTOGRAPHS.
STEEL ENGRAVED CARDS.
CRAYON PORTRAITS.
PARLOR GEMS.
COLLECTIONS OF BIRDS.
LANGUAGE OF FLOWERS.
WHITE MOUNTAIN VIEWS.
RAPHAEL'S MADONNAS.
NATIONAL AMUSEMENT CARDS.
A splendid assortment of Prints, both plain and colored. All at popular prices. Free exhibition. Send for catalogue.
Address B. W. HITCHCOCK.

THE REBEL INVASION.

Proclamation Calling for Fifty Thousand Militia for the Defence of Pennsylvania.

The Occupation of McConnellsburg by the Rebels.

EVACUATION OF CARLISLE.

Telegraphic Communication Cut Off and a Battle Shortly Expected.

General Wm. F. Smith Assigned to the Defences of the Susquehanna.

General Milroy Said to be Relieved of His Command.

General Dana to Command the Defences of Philadelphia.

GREAT EXCITEMENT AT PITTSBURG.

The Position at Maryland Heights Strengthened.

Development of the Rebel Gen. Lee's Plans of Invasion.

Why the Rebels were Not Found in Force by Gen. Pleasanton.

Details of the Excitement in Pennsylvania.

Proclamation of the Rebel General Ewell.

THE LATEST NEWS, &c., &c., &c.

Our Baltimore Correspondence.

BALTIMORE, June 25, 1863.

Development of General Lee's Plans—Detailed Account of the Progress of His March from Warrenton to the Potomac—The Whole Rebel Army Now Crossing the Potomac and Advancing on Frederick—Position of the Opposing Armies—Theatre of the Operations of the Next Few Days, &c., &c.

The light breaks at last. The news which I have received this morning, and which I send you below, dispels the last remaining doubt in regard to General Lee's intentions, and affords, as you will see, a clear prognosis of what that wily and astute general proposes to himself, and the route which he has marked out for the progress of his army towards Washington. Now that this development has become clear, it is impossible not to admire the adroitness with which, up to this time, the rebel general has concealed his real line of march.

On reaching Warrenton, with the head of his army, about ten days ago, General Lee found that Gen. Ewell, in obedience to his instructions, had not only defeated Milroy and General Tyler, and captured Winchester and Martinsburg, with the immense quantity of military stores and all the artillery at the former place, but that he had also, with the aid of the guerillas, under Imboden, Jenkins and Jones, made an extensive reconnoitring expedition into Maryland and Pennsylvania, and had ascertained the exact position of affairs in those two States as far north as Carlisle, and as far east as Point of Rocks and Frederick City. Since that time all of General Lee's manœuvres have been directed to the object of making Hooker believe that he designed to move on Washington through Thoroughfare Gap, and by way of Centreville and Fairfax or Gum Spring and Drannesville. Hence the various skirmishes, even amounting to battles, or at least to engagements of considerable magnitude, at Centreville, between Aquia creek and Occoquan, and at other points between Vienna and Aldie, rumors of which have been circulating for more than a week past. The fact that any such engagements have taken place has been sought to be concealed. But I have positive evidence that they did take place.

In the meantime General Lee was steadily moving his whole army from Warrenton, along the Western slope of the Bull run and Kittoctan Mountains, past Thoroughfare Gap, or rather through the valley that lies between those mountains and the Blue Ridge, directing the march of his columns towards Upperville and Ashby's Gap. While this movement was in progress Hooker was expecting every day to see the rebel army debouching through Thoroughfare Gap. That gap, and the gap near Aldie also, was at that time held by a strong rebel force, posted there in order to prevent any of Hooker's troops from coming west of those gaps, and to mask the important movement of Lee's army, which was then going on. When the rebel army, however, had all got through Ashby's Gap, in the Blue Ridge, and were moving on Winchester, these rear guards were withdrawn and were posted on the west side of the Blue Ridge, holding Ashby's Gap, Snicker's Gap and Upperville. Then it was that Hooker, on sending a strong cavalry force to Aldie and Thoroughfare Gap, found no enemy there at all, except a few scouts, who quickly retired at his approach. Then it was, too, that Hooker occupied Leesburg, Aldie and Thoroughfare Gap, and that the announcment was made by the War Department that there are now no rebel forces east of the Blue Ridge. That announcement was correct. General Lee, with his whole army, was rapidly advancing from Winchester towards Martinsburg, Williamsport and Shepherdstown (and this was only a few days ago), over the route cleared and opened for him by General Ewell. This was on Sunday, the 21st inst., at which time Hooker had sent General Pleasanton's cavalry to reconnoitre towards the Blue Ridge, and it was on that day that the great cavalry fight at Upperville took place. After that fight the rebel cavalry engaged in it crossed the Shenandoah and proceeded to Winchester, covering the rear of General Lee's army, which was then just leaving that place.

Yesterday, as I learned this morning, the whole of General Lee's army was engaged in crossing the Potomac into Maryland, at Williamsport, Falling Waters and Shepherdstown. They had occupied Boonsboro and South Mountain yesterday afternoon, and to day are reported to be in strong force at Frederick City, where we have no troops at all. From that point General Lee will advance on Washington.

When the map is examined in connection with this remarkable movement of Gen. Lee, it will seem strange that he should have made such a wide circuit in order to reach Frederick City, when he might have done so by marching up the shorter road in the valley west of the Kittoctan Mountains, and crossing at Point of Rocks. The explanation of this will be seen in the further progress of the campaign. It deserves to be noticed, however, that the movement of the advance of the rebel army under Gen. Ewell, and the present occupation of the territory between Frederick City, Hagerstown, Chambersburg and Cumberland, enables Gen. Lee to draw from the rich farms of Southern Pennsylvania all the supplies of whatever kind he may need for a long campaign.

There are only two roads by which Gen. Lee can move from Frederick City to Washington. The one is by the great national road, an old turnpike, which would lead, by way of Rockville, directly to Washington, or to a point rection of Leesburg, in the vicinity of which the right wing of General Hooker's army and the left wing of General Lee's was understood to be posted. This firing continued until after ten o'clock, when it ceased until twelve o'clock, when it was again renewed and ceased at four o'clock.

A Rebel Telegraph Operator in Communication with Pittsburg.

[From the Pittsburg Chronicle.]

Last night about ten o'clock a message was received in the telegraph office here from McConnellsburg, which left no doubt that the line at that point was in possession of the rebels. The rebel operator does not seem to have been gifted with any great degree of sharpness, as he made himself known the moment he attached his instrument, so that the different offices along the line had prompt notice of his presence, and were enabled to prevent him obtaining any information whatever as to what was passing over the line. After a few boastful messages, relative to what the rebels had done and intended doing had been received, it was determined to ascertain where the fellow was, and the following conversation between the operater at Bedford and the rebel took place:—

BEDFORD OFFICE—Where are you?

REBEL—At the foot of Cove Mountain. Where are you?

BEDFORD—At the base of Laurel Hill Mountain.

REBEL—Where the hell and damnation is that?

BEDFORD—Would you like to know?

REBEL—Yes, where the hell is it?

BEDFORD—Then ask Jenkins. He'll tell you. He used to steal horses around here.

REBEL—Jenkins will thrash hell out of you damned Yankees yet.

BEDFORD—What force have you got there?

REBEL—Two hundred thousand, more or less.

BEDFORD—Where are you bound for?

REBEL—We're going North, and will take charge of the offices along the line in a few days.

BEDFORD—You'll let us know when you take them, won't you?

After some more language of this kind, the rebel began to lose his temper, and became very abusive, using language which will not bear reporting. In a subsequent conversation with one of the operators here he stated that his name was Scanlan, and that the rebels would be on here very soon. He was very cautious about giving information of any kind, however, and we may say for our boys that he got even less than he gave. After about twenty minutes' stay he stated that he was going to "cut off," as he had been ordered to leave for the North, and that was the last heard from him.

The Herald Guard at Harrisburg.

[From the Harrisburg Patriot, June 25.]

The idea of the *Telegraph* reading the NEW YORK HERALD out of all loyal company and out of all Christian society is refrigerating. Consider for a moment the fact that there is now in Camp Curtin a full company known as the "New York Herald Guard"—Company E, New York Fourth artillery—which was officered and recruited exclusively from the employes of that establishment, and which stands ready to protect whatever remnant of property Mr. Bergner may leave behind in case of a rebel attack—consider these facts, and then tell us if you think it lies in the mouth of the Flying Dutchman to call down the lightnings of Heaven upon the old Scotch editor just at this particular time? Couldn't Hesse Darmstadt's favorite son take the HERALD's little joke, without working himself into a fit of the vapers, and cursing it with all the curses contained in the "Index Expurgatorious?" Disloyal, quotha! Has the Deacon done half as well? Were our nature poisoned with the infernal Jacobinical virus which fills his every vein we would counsel these HERALD men to revenge themselves upon him, just as he besought the mob to destroy us on some pitiful pretext on more than one occasion; but all we can advise Company E to do is to take the buzzing bottle fly up in their fingers, and say to him, in the language of Uncle Toby, "Go, poor devil, go; there's room enough in the world for us and thee!"

THE LATEST NEWS.

Carlisle Not in Possession of the Enemy.

Gettysburg Occupied by the Rebels in Force.

All the Passes of South Mountain Held by Rebel Troops.

Sixty Thousand Pennsylvanians Called Out by Governor Curtin.

General Hooker's Right Wing Reported in the Vicinity of Hagerstown.

Continuous Rain and Rise in the Susquehanna,

&c., &c., &c.

The Harrisburg Telegrams.

HARRISBURG, June 26, 1863.

The rebel advance in this direction still continues at a stand still in the vicinity of Carlisle. Telegraphic communication is open with the town up to the present.

General Knipe, deeming his forces not strong enough to meet the enemy, evacuated Carlisle last night

General Knipe reports that the rebels are advancing ten thousand strong.

A skirmish is reported near Bloody run, between the column under General Milroy and the enemy.

In the skirmish at Bloody run to-day Milroy lost no men. It was a dash upon the enemy.

The citizens were aroused from their slumbers this morning by another scare that the Philistines were then approaching. Matters are becoming more quiet.

General W. F. Smith commands the forces concentrated on the south bank of the Susquehanna in this vicinity.

Work on the fortifications still progresses. The citizens are nearly all organized and ready to turn out with the military for the defence of the city when the opportunity arrives. Several meetings are called for to night to perfect local organizations.

The citizens of this city are busily organizing into companies, to serve in the rifle pits and intrenchments.

Among the military arrivals to-day were about one hundred and fifty men for the Twenty-third regiment New York State Militia.

A battery of four companies of heavy artillery, of one hundred and twenty men each, arrived here from Rochester, N. Y., last evening. They have enlisted for three years or the war.

Colonel Pierce has been assigned to the command of the troops at Bloody run, General Milroy having been relieved.

General Dana has been assigned to the command of the defences of Philadelphia.

It is just reported that Hooker's right wing is in the vicinity of Hagerstown.

It has rained for the last eighteen hours incessantly, and the friendly showers are still steadily falling. The Susquehanna has already risen twenty inches, and is expected soon to be an impassible barrier to the advance of an army. Large droves of cattle forded the river yesterday.

No communication is passing between this point and Pittsburg. But one wire is working, and that is by way of Philadelphia, and consequently the West is deprived of all information from this point.

I learn by the evening train that the excitement at Pittsburg continues unabated, and troops are being rapidly organized all over the Department of the Monongahela for the defence of the State.

A report went over the wires last night reflecting upon Colonel Coppee. This gentleman has assumed an arduous position, and it is his endeavor to deal out intelligence that will not benefit the enemy. So far as the HERALD corps is concerned, with Colonel Coppee's action they have nothing to complain of.

The city is very quiet under the present extraordinary circumstances, and the constant rain gives it a gloomy aspect.

The drinking houses were all closed this morning, in obedience to the Mayor's proclamation.

Many of the dry goods stores are also closed.

Large numbers of refugees continue to arrive from the valley.

Hon. Thomas A. Scott arrived here to-day. His business was altogether of a private nature in New York.

Dr. W. Frank Swalm, of the Sanitary Commission, has provided all possible means to extend aid to the needy in event of an action.

The propriety of proclaiming martial law is seriously considered, but the matter has not yet been definitely decided.

HARRISBURG, Pa., June 26—9 P. M.

Hundreds of horses are being driven over the bridges of the Susquehanna, followed by men, women and children, the defenceless inhabitants of Cumberland valley.

Governor Curtin has received information that the rebels occupied Gettysburg to day with ten regiments of infantry, and with cavalry and artillery.

The operator at Gettysburg, while sending the despatch to General Couch, was forced to leave before finishing it, to avoid capture.

It is believed that this force intends to strike the Northern Central Railroad, either at Hanover Junction or York, which is distant about thirty miles.

The Governor has also received information that the rebels hold all the passes of South Mountain.

HARRISBURG, Pa., June 26—11 P. M.

It has rained all day, and the river is rising.

The rebel force which occupied Gettysburg to-day was the division of General Early, belonging to Longstreet's corps.

This makes two corps which are supposed to have crossed the Potomac.

The troops of Longstreet are supposed to have crossed at Shepherdstown Ford.

When Gen. Rhodes' division of Ewell's corps arrived at Chambersburg, the operator was unable to escape. He remained until Wednesday, when he made his escape by the way of Loudon to the Pennsylvania Railroad and arrived here to-day.

They numbered about twelve thousand, and had five batteries, with a long train of wagons and ambulances. All the officers wore new uniforms which had no doubt been sent to Hagerstown by rebel sympathizers in anticipation of their arrival.

When he left General Johnson's division, belonging to the same corps, was within six miles of the town. The soldiers believed they were going to Harrisburg, and were very anxious to know how far off it was.

The enemy have made no effort to occupy Carlisle to-day, although they were encamped within four miles of the town.

At headquarters to-night they inform me that the rebels appear to be concentrating in the mountain passes of the Blue Ridge and its spurs. They seem to fear advancing with Hooker in their rear; but are living on the country which they now occupy.

Proper precautions have been taken to secure the railroad bridges from a sudden descent from the enemy.

Two rebel cavalry, taken yesterday, near Chambersburg, report the rebels advancing, under General Ewell, into Pennsylvania with twenty-eight regiments of infantry, five thousand cavalry and twenty pieces of artillery, chiefly heavy guns, and that they send out small parties to bring in live stock. A column, six thousand strong, was sent to Mercersburg, with eight pieces of cannon. Half of them have marched to McConnellsburg. Some of the border men are reported sympathetic.

Proclamation of the Governor of Pennsylvania.

SIXTY THOUSAND MEN CALLED OUT TO REPEL THE REBEL INVASION.

HARRISBURG, Pa., June 26, 1863.

In the name and by the authority of the Commonwealth of Pennsylvanja, Andrew Curtin, Governor of said Commonwealth.

A PROCLAMATION.

Pennsylvanians—The enemy is advancing in force into Pennsylvania. He has a strong column within twenty-three miles of Harrisburg, and other columns are moving by Fulton and Adams counties, and it can no longer be doubted that a formidable invasion of our State is in actual progress. The calls already made for volunteer militia in the exigency have not been met as fully as the crisis requires. I therefore now issue this my proclamation, calling for sixty thousand men to come promptly forward to defend the State. They will be mustered into the service of the State for a period of ninety days, but will be required to serve only so much of the period of muster as the safety of our people and honor of our State may require. They will rendezvous at points to be designated in the general order to be issued this day by the Adjutant General of Pennsylvania, which order will also set forth the details of the arrangements for organization, clothing, subsistence, equipments and supplies.

I will not insult you by inflammatory appeals. A people who want the heart to defend their soil, their families and their firesides, are not worthy to be accounted men. Heed not the councils of evil disposed persons, if such there be in your midst. Show yourselves what you are—a free, loyal, spirited, brave vigorous race. Do not undergo the disgrace of leaving your defence mainly to the citizens of other States. In defending the soil of Pennsylvania we are contributing to the support of our national government, and vindicating our fidelity to the national cause. Pennsylvania has always heretofore responded promptly to all the calls made by the federal government, and I appeal to you now not to be unmindful that the foe that strikes at our State strikes through our desolation at the life of the republic, and our people are plundered and driven from their homes solely because of their loyalty and fidelity to our free institutions.

People of Pennsylvania! I owe to you all my faculties, my labors, my life. You owe to your country your prompt and zealous services and efforts. The time has now come when we must all stand or fall together in defence of our State and in support of our government. Let us so discharge our duty that posterity shall not blush for us. Come heartily and cheerfully to the rescue of our noble Commonwealth. Maintain now your honor and freedom!

Given under my hand and the great seal of the State, at Harrisburg, this twenty-sixth day of June, in the year of our Lord one thousand eight hundred and sixty-three, and of the Commonwealth the eighty-seventh.

A. G. CURTIN.

By the Governor: ELI SLIFER, Secretary of the Commonwealth.

The Carlisle Telegrams.

CARLISLE, Pa., June 26—6:45 P. M.

From the number, variety and manner in which rumors are constantly reaching here, it is hard to determine in which direction or on what road the enemy actually has his main force. It is evident, however, that the enemy is doing all he can to mystify us as to his designs, and in such a way as to attempt to prevent us from concentrating forces on any one road or in any particular direction. To this end he has detachments of cavalry more or less strong thrown out in different directions, and their forces scouting here and there are continually coming in contact with our cavalry on the different roads.

It has been raining all day, and the enemy has been unusually quiet. At this time there are eight hundred of the enemy encamped at Mount Rock, and there is no positive indication that the rebels will move on Carlisle to-night.

This town has been remarkably quiet all day.

The telegraph operators saw signal lights last night from the direction of Pike over towards South Mountain. This would indicate a rebel force at the latter place.

The enemy's scouts visited Plainfield and Greason's stations last night.

We carry on our telegraphic operations almost in the face of the enemy making efforts to capture railroad trains. We have had no railroad communication from this point with Harrisburg to-day.

The proprietors of some of the hotels here have taken down their signs. The gaslights were left burning here till a late hour this morning.

Our cavalry got on the flank of the enemy and went to Newville to-day, under command of Captain Boyd.

The enemy has all the mills within his reach grinding corn, &c., for him.

General Ewell's Proclamation.

GENERAL ORDERS.

HEADQUARTERS, SECOND CORPS, ARMY NORTHERN VA., CHAMBERSBURG, Pa., June 22, 1863.

First.—The sale of intoxicating liquors to his command, without written permission from a major general, is strictly prohibited.

Second.—Persons having liquor in their possession are required to report the fact to the Provost Marshal, or nearest general officer, stating the amount and kind, that a guard may be placed over it, and the men prevented from getting it.

Third.—Any violation of paragraph one of this order, or failure to comply with paragraph two, will be punished by the immediate confiscation of all liquors in the possession of the offending parties, besides rendering their other property liable to seizure.

Fourth.—Citizens of the country through which the army may pass, who are not in the military service, are admonished to abstain from all acts of hostility, upon the penalty of being dealt with in a summary manner. A ready acquiescence in the demands of the military authorities will serve greatly to lessen the rigors of war.

By command of

Lieutenant General R. S. EWELL.

A. S. PENDLETON, A. A. General.

The Frederick Telegrams.

FREDERICK, Md., June 26—9 P. M.

I have just returned from the vicinity of the South Mountain battle field, thirteen miles distant from here.

From persons who left Boonsboro this afternoon, I learn that the rebels have all left that place. Anderson's division of Longstreet's corps, which arrived there on Wednesday night and encamped, left on yesterday morning, taking the Waynesboro road toward Chambersburg. The force is estimated at from seven thousand to ten thousand—infantry, cavalry and artillery—accompanied by a large wagon train.

The whole of Longstreet's corps had crossed the Potomac, and is advancing in different directions into Pennsylvania.

There were but few rebel troops at Hagerstown yesterday—all gone to Pennsylvania.

General Lee and staff are on this side of the river.

Capture of a Rebel Spy.

BLOOMSBURG, Pa., June 26, 1863.

A rebel spy was captured at Catawissa, and will be lodged in jail in this place this afternoon.

Our Harrisburg Correspondence.

HARRISBURG, June 25, 1863.

I regret to say that General Couch has been compelled to issue orders restricting the privileges of correspondents. He feels aggrieved, and, though desirous of affording every means of information to the representatives of the various papers, is certain that some advantage has been taken of the liberties afforded them whereby the enemy has been benefited. The

HERALD CORRESPONDENTS

are not blamed; but, while they will be afforded their usual facilities, they are debarred from visiting rooms that were heretofore open to their inspection. This is generally lamented by the various officials here and the several correspondents; but it is a matter of small moment to the HERALD force, who have unusual facilities in the securing of every important item that may transpire, from the fact that the HERALD never gives "aid and comfort" to the enemy by publishing any other information than what is strictly legitimate. You have very rightly suppressed news that I sent you, for which General Couch has expressed his thanks; and, while it was unimportant as to details, it was calculated to give our foes information which it is desirable they should not be made acquainted with. The various.

HEADS OF DEPARTMENTS

here are in excellent hands, that of the State particularly so, and Governor Curtin may be congratulated upon the able assistants he has drawn around him. His Adjutant General, A. L. Russell, is a splendid looking man, standing some six feet in height, and is as quick in his movements as the most alert schoolboy you ever saw. He transacts a great deal of business of the most arduous description daily, answers the begging importunities of scores of needy applicants for commands, organizes squads, companies and regiments, and yet preserves an equability of temper that is really delightful to witness. I of course am thrown a great deal in contact with these officers, and I feel that men who are so poorly repaid for their time and attention deserve some public notice, and there is no way to so thoroughly accomplish this as through the HERALD. The Chief of Transportation and Telegraphic Communication here is

MAJOR O. M. SEES,

an accomplished, able officer, who is never at a loss for something to do. How he finds time to accomplish so much is a mystery; but the graceful courtesy with which he receives visitors and dispenses his various duties surprises me more.

GREY RESERVES OF PHILADELPHIA.

I was in the Executive Chamber this morning when Colonel Smith, of the Reserves; Captain J. D. Keyser, Captain Starr, Major Nicholson and Quartermaster Sergeant R. Rundle Smith came in to see the Governor—I do not know what number of times this makes—about what was to be done for the "Reserves." The Governor received them politely and asked them to be seated. I could see by his manner that he desired "no more private" interviews. Consequently I remained. The Colonel inquired if anything definite had been come to in regard to their regiment.

The Governor said, "I explained fully to you, gentlemen, that I have no power to accept you other than as ordered, and place you upon the same footing with other regiments. What is the disposition of your regiment?"

This the committee could not answer until they held another consultation with them.

The Colonel asked "if it would be possible to muster them in for sixty days?"

"Would you accept it absolutely and without reserve?" inquired the Executive.

"The difficulty then would be," said spokesman Sergeant Smith, "that each man is yet to be asked."

The Governor smilingly replied, "I cannot see the difference between sixty days and the emergency."

Colonel Smith spoke "about definite periods, and their having none when they left home."

"I will muster you in, then, for ninety days," replied Governor Curtin.

"Is it your order?" quoth Colonel or Major.

"No order about it."

"I came to tender the regiment, Governor," remarked the Colonel.

In the meantime a messenger despatched to General Couch returned with an answer from the General that he could only accept them in the regular way; that he had no authority to receive them in any other. While the messenger was absent I thought I detected a shadow of sorrow or pain, or perhaps it was fear, that glimmered over their otherwise handsome, intelligent countenances. There were sundry questions put to his Excellency in regard to their not being supplied with suitable arms and needing sundry other trifles too numerous to mention. The Executive said they should all be furnished, and while the Governor, his aids and a score or two of anxious citizens were congratulating themselves that Philadelphia and the State would not be disgraced, then it was that the messenger returned with the above reply.

Colonel Smith at once arose and said, "We have arrived at the point for which we came; we have nothing further to say as yet."

Governor Curtin advised them in a friendly way upon what he would be glad they would do.

Quartermaster Sergeant Rundle Smith wanted to know if they would be counted in the muster from the day they started from Philadelphia; whether they would be provided with hospital stores, &c; whether they could by any means be mustered into Hooker's army.

To these questions the Governor answered separately in the affirmative and negative, and further told them in these words, with a very distinct emphasis, "You are not, and will not go, out of the Department of the Susquehanna."

The party departed to enjoy their clam chowder, cold cut, boiled lamb or spring chicken, at their elegant retreat a mile or two north of the city. I rode out to see them in the afternoon, and called upon the

BLUE RESERVES,

a regiment fully their equals in wealth, respectability and station. They, too, were from the City of Brotherly Love, and were getting ready to march. Their Colonel (Taylor) was an old friend, and I took the liberty of calling upon him to make a few inquiries. He said his men were eager to go. They felt the city from which they came was being disgraced by the action of the other regiment. It would be their aim and duty to wipe out that stain by renewed energy and devotion upon their part, and all the bravery they possessed would be called into action on their part. This gallant organization left to-night, to take their place alongside of the gallant sons of the Empire State, in the very front, where danger and trial are to meet them, but where honor and glory will surely follow them. I have written thus fully in order to give the thousands of the HERALD readers an opportunity of getting at the facts. Every honorable person amongst the many who will read this will probably blush at the shame this action has caused; but they will rejoice at knowing that there is no quibble, no screen to cover public opinion, and but one sentiment will follow this course; and what that judgment is I forbear to mention.

CAMP CURTIN—CONTRABANDS.

Camp Curtin looks deserted; but few troops are there, and those to come will probably be encamped upon the other side of the river, amid scenes more warlike than the surroundings here.

Vast numbers of ebony colored children are daily arriving in the city—some destitute, others again more fortunate. Their rendezvous is in a section of the city denominated "Smoky Hollow." I have not visited it, and therefore can give you no idea of the scenes being enacted there.

GENERALS ANDREW PORTER AND FRANKLIN

are both here, and will be ready, in case of emergency, to unsheath their swords in defence of their State and country. The crowd of position hunters is thinning out. The Governor has nothing to offer or give them, and they are gradually falling away, making room for fresh comers and their friends to try their abilities as urgent coaxers and bores.

EXTORTIONISTS.

Through the *expose* made in the columns of various papers, the class of people who have robbed the gallant soldier—who was hastening to their protection—of his dollars, have hauled in their horns considerably. When the city was in danger they offered their goods and wares at any sacrifice—were willing to take whatever was offered. But with the feeling of security came that of sordid huckstering, and never have traders, some at least, exerted their callings upon more truly Shylock principles.

News from the Pacific.

SAN FRANCISCO, June 25, 1863.

A large mass meeting to ratify the nominations of the Union State Convention was held here last night. Speeches were made by most of the candidates for States offices. There seems to be no doubt that the Union State ticket will be elected by an immense majority. It is probable, however, that but one opposition ticket will be in the field, viz:—That to be nominated on the 8th of July by the two wings of the democratic party at their Fusion Convention.

Sandwich Island dates have been received to June 6. The Sugar Refinery Company had become embarrassed, and been forced to make assignment.

Missionaries from all the islands were holding their regular annual meeting at Honolulu. Rev D. Andrusan, representing the churches of the United States, was in attendance.

Gen. Franklin Ordered to New Orleans.

PHILADELPHIA. June 26, 1863.

General Franklin has been ordered to a command in Louisiana, under Banks. He is now here, and will leave for New Orleans by the first steamer.

The Missouri State Convention.

JEFFERSON CITY, June, 26, 1863.

Mr. Breckinridge's substitute for the report of the Committee on Emancipation was rejected in the Convention to-day by a vote of 7 ayes to 76 noes. The question then recurred on the adoption of the original ordinance. Colonel Wolfolk moved to amend by substituting the ordinance to the people on the State election of 1864, which was carried by a vote of 56 yeas to 29 nays.

HOOKER'S ARMY.

Mr. George H. Hart's Letter.

HEADQUARTERS, CAVALRY, June 24, 1863.

My despatches embrace all the points of general interest or importance relating to the reconnoissance to the front by a portion of the Union cavalry; but a more detailed account may not be unacceptable.

AT NEW BALTIMORE,

a pretty little village of about fifteen houses and a population in ordinary times of about one hundred, we halted and refreshed man and beast. We found at this place—and, in fact, such was the case all along the route travelled—that the male population consisted only of decrepit old men and small boys under the age of sixteen.

The female portion of the community practised no dissimulation to conceal their political sentiments, but, on the contrary, vauntingly displayed their secession proclivities, forcibly reminding me of Alexander the Great's visit to the Amazons. As a general rule the people are reduced in the way of provisions to the simplest necessaries of life, possessing no luxuries, not even the luxury of a lucifer match.

THE VALUE OF A LUCIFER MATCH.

I was much surprised when, on asking for a light for my segar, I was informed "that they had neither a fire nor means of obtaining one," and learned that the method pursued in this town for creating fire, not having matches, was for each family to keep a fire burning all the time, and when, by accident or neglect, a fire was extinguished, application was made to a neighbor. On learning this fact I took a few matches from my haversack and formally presented them to the venerable matron of the house, who eagerly accepted them, and I left, satisfied in my own mind, that although the mines of Golconda were rich in wealth and a prize to the possessor, yet a mine that yielded lucifer matches would be more valued in the village of New Baltimore.

ON TO WARRENTON.

From New Baltimore, as already previously stated, we proceeded to Warrenton, at which town we arrived precisely at ten minutes past eleven o'clock in the morning by the Court House clock. I had seen much of Virginia, and had visited a large number of its towns prior to visiting Warrenton; I have been in the Shenandoah valley in midsummer, when Nature wore her comeliest garb, and I then thought as I gazed around me that surely the garden of Eden was not a fiction, and in my mind located its site in the Shenandoah valley; but I was not prepared, by the character of the scenery along the route or the appearance of the towns, to find Warrenton, as it is, one of the most charming, neat, chaste and picturesquely situated little towns I have ever seen or expect to see. It is surrounded on all sides by a continuous chain of gracefully clustering hills, whose tops and sides are beautifully bedecked with mantles of fragrant green grass, interspersed and adorned by occasional groups of symmetrical trees, as perfect and precise as if directed by an artist's superior taste. This chain of hills forms collectively a circular ridge. In the hollow and centre can be seen the town of Warrenton, producing a *coup d'œil* like a magical enchantment.

THE POPULATION OF WARRENTON

before the war was in the neighborhood of one thousand five hundred; and this town, being the county seat of Fauquier, has an expensive and elegant Court House, fine hotels and elegantly paved streets. The springs, which are about seven miles distant, used to form a centre of attraction to the fashionable people residing within fifty miles around, and as a summer resort made Warrenton a very lively and aristocratic place. I was struck on entering at the sullen stillness that pervaded the place: every store was closed; the inhabitants, with an exceptionable bewildered darkey staring at the passing troops, remained concealed in their houses; not even a horse or a dog broke the monotonous and impressive silence that almost struck with awe, and I can only compare my feelings to those described by the travellers who visited an old Aztec town in Central America. Just as we entered the clock chimed eleven. Oh! how solemn—how strangely suggestive of a funeral—the mourning for the slain and the tears and moans of the bereaved survivors. But an hour's stay changed the whole aspect of affairs, and in place of monotonous and irksome quiet all was life; in place of the angry but subdued scowls and lowering countenances of a few isolated men, the windows of the houses were thrown open, and pretty faces—if not smiling graciously, it was excellently counterfeited by the young ladies of Warrenton—who we soon found were the principal and most distinguished portion of the inhabitants.

Shortly a lively air was struck on a piano, pressed on the keys by the hands of a charming little secesh; then another, and as if to exemplify the truth of the old adage, "that example is powerfully productive of imitation," every house in town lent its assistance to swell the volume of harmonious concert of sweet sounds that saluted the ears of the surprised yet grateful audience of "hateful Yanks."

THE PRINCIPAL HOTEL.

The Warren Green is not at present prepared to receive guests, for the reason that they have nothing to give them to eat—not, however, a serious objection or impediment to the Virginia hosts generally to keeping a hotel. We were refreshed here by the host with some very welcome deliciously cool ice water, and as a dessert some bouncing ripe black cherries.

We dined at the Warrenton House, and when I sat down to the table a waiter, decorated in a white apron, politely came forward and inquired whether I would take soup. Certainly, I replied, and allowed my fancy to roam, and thought, well, this looks natural. Next will come the fish, according to the recognized *regime* dictated by the *etiquette de table*: but was startled by the darkey confidently remarking:—"Sah, will hab some ham, or"—I heard the balance of the sentence very indistinctly; but if my recollection serves me it was or "der is noting else?"

OUR RETURN.

We remained at Warrenton over night, and at nine the next morning took our departure, on our return repassing New Baltimore, at which place a government (rebel) tannery and outbuildings were burned by order of our general, and we could see the smoke curling in spiral columns through the air when miles away from the smoking ruins. Our cavalry attracted universal comment, and complimentary encomiums could not be withheld on the condition and appearance of the troops as they filed by.

A CAPTURE.

We made a capture in the shape of the editor of the Warrenton *Whig*, Colonel of the Eighty-fifth Virginia, commanding all the State militia of Fauquier county. This gentleman is one of the leading men of the State, and I had an interesting conversation with him, hoping to obtain an insight into the internal arrangements of the confederacy. I found him, of course, a secessionist, but modified and qualified so that with a little careful training we might make a Union man of him: and I understand there are many more such as he, made secessionists by the fanaticism and imbecility of the abolitionists of the North.

OUR RETURN ROUTE

laid through the classic grounds of Bull run; and a suggestion was here made that might afford a capital speculation to some Yankee. It is to purchase the ground, say for $25,000, put up a hotel for $25,000 more, and then make a fortune by exhibiting it to visitors. Certainly a bright idea. Without any occurrence of interest arising beyond Major Van Voorhies, Brovost Marshal, chasing and capturing an attache of the ambulance corps for a rebel, we arrived here, and soon again expect to be ordered away on some other expedition.

THE BLOCKADE RUNNERS.

Capture of a Rebel Blockade Runner, Burning of Another, and Escape of a Third.

PROVIDENCE, R. I., June 26, 1863.

A naval officer, just arrived from off Wilmington, reports that the rebel schooner Hattie was captured last Saturday by the United States gunboat Florida. She was running out with turpentine, cotton and rosin.

The Hattie reported that the Banshee, the fastest blockade runner afloat, was burned in Cape Fear river, when just ready to sail with a cargo of cotton and turpentine.

The Eugenie ran out on the night of the 19th.

The Navy.

MERCEDITA.—The United States gunboat Mercedita arrived at Gonaives June 13, from a cruise, all well.

HONDURAS.—The Honduras, chartered gunboat, sailed yesterday in search of the privateer Tacony. Acting Volunteer Lieutenant H. B. Gregory, late of the gunboat United States, is in command, and will no doubt be active, and we trust successful.

UNITED STATES.—The gunboat United States, Lieutenant Commander R. W. Meade, Jr., will sail to-day in search of the privateers.

ERICSSON.—The Ericsson goes out in command of Lieut. Commander Miller.

AMERICA.—The yacht America, Lieutenant Kane commanding, has returned from a cruise in search of the Tacony.

THE SUPPLY STEAMER.—The United State steamer Massachusetts, recently arrived at this port from the Southern blockading squadron, in consequence of undergoing repairs, will not sail on Saturday next, as advertised. Her officers (Volunteer Acting Lieutenant Wm. H. West commanding) and crew have been transferred to the steamer Tonawanda, chartered by the government to take the place of the Massachusetts, and will sail on Monday next, 29th inst., from Philadelphia, for the Southern squadrons, and will take letters and papers for all on those stations.

The Africa Outward Bound.

HALIFAX, June 26, 1863.

The steamship Africa, from Boston, arrived here at three o'clock this morning, and sailed again for Liverpool at six.

The latest news and commercial intelligence were placed on board of her.

The Legal Tender Note Argument.

ALBANY, June 26, 1863.

In the Court of Appeals to-day Messrs. Doty & Curtis were heard for the Bank Superintendent, against the legality of legal tender notes, and Lyman Tremain replied. The argument on behalf of the banks will be continued to-morrow by Messrs. Noyes and Porter.

NEWS FROM THE SOUTHWEST.

Progress of the Siege of Vicksburg.

Destruction of Four Rebel Vessels Near Yazoo City.

IMPORTANT CAVALRY EXPEDITION.

IMMENSE DESTRUCTION OF REBEL SUPPLIES.

The Rebels West of the Mississippi and Their Operations,

&c., &c., &c.

MEMPHIS, June 23, 1863.

Official intelligence from General Grant's army to the 20th instant is received. Johnston is said to have withdrawn his troops from across the Big Black, moving towards Clinton.

About one thousand Texans attacked Lake Providence on the 10th, but were repulsed with loss by the negro troops, who fought bravely.

Colonel Phillips, with eight hundred cavalry, was attacked by two hundred rebel infantry and one thousand cavalry, under Rockerford, on the Tallahatchie. The fight was very severe. Colonel Phillips lost seven killed and ninety wounded. He cut his way out and came in yesterday.

The rebels are in force at Booneville. Generals Roddy, Ruggles, Chalmers and Biffles threaten our lines, and troops are reported to be moving north from Okalona.

Stirring news may be expected from this section.

WASHINGTON, June 26, 1863.

The Richmond *Dispatch* of the 23d inst. has the following editorial paragraph:—

For the past few days public attention has been withdrawn in a measure from the operations around Vicksburg, by the brilliant achievements of our army under General Lee, on the northern border of Virginia and in Pennsylvania and Maryland. It is gratifying to know, however, that our successes on the Mississippi rival those of our arms on the Potomac. A despatch was yesterday received by President Davis from General Johnston, stating that General Kirby Smith, with his corps, had taken possession of Milliken's Bend, above Vicksburg, cutting off the supplies and communication of the enemy. This is, in effect, raising the seige of Vicksburg, and in a few days we may expect the most cheerful tidings from that important and beleaguered point.

The Richmond *Sentinel* extra of the 20th instant contains the following:—

OSYKA, June 16, Via Mobile, June 19, 1863.

Officers from Port Hudson report that all is safe, and the garrison in good spirits, with provisions for three months. Our loss is three hundred.

JACKSON, June 17, Via Mobile, June 19, 1863.

Numerous couriers have arrived from Vicksburg within the past few days. Their reports are stereotyped. Beyond the fact that Grant's sappers and miners are at work to blow up our works there is nothing new.

A courier from Port Hudson, with despatches to General Johnston, arrived last night. He reports that the garrison is in fine condition and spirits. Banks' force is estimated at twenty thousand. It is also reported that he has abandoned the idea of storming the place, and gone to ditching.

Official despatches from Milliken's Bend state that our attack upon that place was a failure. The enemy had three lines of works. He was driven out of two, but made a desperate stand at the third, and, with the assistance of his gunboats, repelled our forces. Nothing is known outside of official circles of Kirby Smith's movements.

JACKSON, June 18, 1863.

For the first time in four days heavy firing was heard at Vicksburg this morning. The last accounts represent that Grant is busy fortifying and cutting down trees beyond the Big Black to impede Johnston's movements. They also represent that great distress prevails among the citizens inside of the enemy's lines.

These despatches and editorials are purely buncombe. We have advices here directly from Vicksburg up to the 22d instant when the siege was progressing steadily, and with certainty of ultimate success; and the navigation of the Mississippi, from the mouth of Chickasaw Bayou, near Vicksburg, up to Memphis, was unobstructed by the rebels.

It is probable that the report in the *Sentinel*, dated Jackson, June 17, contains a true account of the condition of affairs at Milliken's Bend.

Important Cavalry Expedition.

MEMPHIS, June 24, 1863.

Col. Misener has just returned from an extensive cavalry expedition south from Lagrange. He reports having broken up the command under George at Panoli, destroyed the railroad bridge at Jackaway, the tressle work just beyond, and a portion of the road from these works; he then crossed the Tallahatchie, and pursued Chalmers beyond the Coldwater on the Helena road. Chalmers endeavored to cross the Tallahatchie at the mouth of the Coldwater, when Misener killed fifteen or twenty of his men and took forty prisoners. He paroled all the sick at Panoli, brought away or destroyed all army supplies, workshops, mills, tanneries, depots, &c. He passed within three miles of Austin and Commerce, destroying an immense amount of forage and subsistence, took from six hundred to eight hundred horses and mules, five hundred head of cattle, sent detachments north and east from Helena, to destroy or bring away all subsistence, forage, horses, mules, &c., passed through five counties, travelled two hundred miles and crossed three rivers.

Chalmers had with him Stokes', Stemmer's and Blythe's men, nine hundred strong, with three pieces of artillery. The remainder of his force, nine hundred, fled South, via Charleston.

Phillips destroyed all the ferries at Panola and Coldwater, and lost one man killed and five wounded. His fight at Tallahatchie was very severe. The enemy's loss was over one hundred. A large number of companies raised in Northern Mississippi joined Faulkner, Chalmers, Ruggles and Roddy, who had arranged a movement on our lines, which was broken up by this raid.

Gen. Gorpleson had made a speech at Oxford, Miss., threatening to force into service every man in the county if companies were not organized to reinforce Johnston.

There has been no news from Gen. Grant's army since yesterday.

Heavy rains have fallen here and at Corinth.

The Progress of the Siege.

[From the Chicago Tribune.]

CHICKASAW BAYOU, Miss., June 18, via CAIRO, June 24, 1863.

General Herron, on the extreme left, is working his way up with great rapidity, and getting his batteries in position at short range. He has appoached from one to two hundred yards nearer within a day or two.

A series of rumors are constantly reaching here concerning disasters above and below, such as attack on Memphis, fall of Helena, taking of Haines' Bluff, and trouble in the front of Banks. But it is surprising how little lodgement such rumors, however industriously circulated, obtain among soldiers.

Strangers arriving here constantly remark the wonderful spirit and confidence of our troops.

General Washburn has arrived at and assumed command of Haines' Bluff. Lieut. E. F. Hill, of McAllister's battery, was shot last evening from an embrasure in the front battery, in the very place where Capt. Rogers was killed a short time since. He was watching the effect of the shot from one of his guns, when a ball from a rebel sharpshooter went through his head sidewise, passing under and back of his eyes. He was alive at midnight, but probably cannot live many hours.

Provost Marshal Gillette this morning got possession of a rebel, Major M. W. Boyd, surgeon in the First Mississippi light artillery, who was left in charge of the rebel wounded in one of our hospitals, who was on his parole. It is understood that the Major was trying to get back into the rebel lines with information valuable to Pemberton which he had picked up in our camp.

Yesterday two rebel spies were caught within a mile of McPherson's headquarters. They were from Bragg's army, and had concealed about their persons plans of our fortifications and specifications of numbers and position of our troops.

Spies find it impossible now to penetrate our lines.

CHICKASAW BAYOU, June 18, via CAIRO, June 24, 1863.

On the 16th the rebel General Anderson, with a division belonging to the command of Major General Dick Taylor, marched from Richmond towards Lake Providence, where General Reed was stationed with a small federal force, consisting of the First Kansas and Sixteenth Wisconsin regiments, with some negro troops, less than one thousand five hundred in all.

Richmond is eight miles back from Young's Point, where the Shreveport road crosses the Tennessee river, about twelve miles from Milliken's Bend and thirty from Lake Providence, and important. It is an important point from the fact that from it those places are easily accessible by good roads, and for the enemy it would be an exceedingly offensive position towards us.

General Reed went out to meet him and destroyed a bridge over the Tennessee river, a short distance from the head.

At Lake Providence the rebels opened on him with a six-pounder, damaging him at first considerably; but he succeeded in silencing the gun and preventing the rebels from crossing, also pouring in a terrible fire of musketry upon them as they pressed up to the river. Thinking our force larger than theirs the enemy retreated with a heavy loss.

On the same day, Gen. Mower marched on Richmond from Sherman's Landing, with his brigade of infantry and Taylors old Chicago battery, under the command of Capt. Barrett. On reaching the Tensas, he met the rebel pickets and drove them in. The rebels burnt the bridge and undertook to make a stand. Capt. Barrett opened fire, and was well supported by the infantry. Such was the combined shower of shell and bullets, that, though fighting well, the rebels were obliged to fall back.

With what cavalry force he had Gen. Mower then pursued the flying enemy, succeeding in capturing forty-two prisoners.

The affair was perfected with signal vigor and promptness by our troops, their impetuosity and daring overcoming the disparity in numbers on the part of the enemy.

It is likely from indications that the entire force of Gen. Dick Taylor—who, by the way, is a son of Old Zack—has skedadled to the Red River country.

There was an extensive fire in Vicksburg last night, illuminating the whole country for miles around. It is not known what burned.

Our Cairo Correspondence.

CAIRO, June 21, 1863.

AT HOME.

As far as the city of Cairo itself is concerned I have nothing of surpassing interest to relate. In fact, I may say that Cairo, a little warmer than the lowest depths of Tartarus at the present writing, is about as Cairo was a twelve months since. A few more new buildings, one more church and a few more rum holes, perhaps; but in reality not greatly changed—not changed at all for the better, very certainly. The news from the East has caused a slight ripple of excitement in its passage over the river in every hamlet, city and village, and of course has had its effect here. But those who for a year have lived among such scenes as are now enacting in Pennsylvania, Maryland and New York, are inclined to smile at the consternation the appearance of Ewell's rebel force occasions at different cities in the land of sober habits among the descendents of Penn and the Pilgrim Fathers. We smile, not because we think it a smiling matter, but because we know that in a very short space of time the Eastern people will get used to the sight of rebels—become accustomed to the gray backs, and learn themselves to smile upon rather than fear the followers of the late Stonewall Jackson. The raid, though rather important in its bearing, cannot last always, and will result in ultimate good to the Union cause. Ewell will soon go back to his lines, either as a prisoner, without his men, or fleeing before the aroused and revengeful Pennsylvanians and Marylanders. The longer he stays and the farther he penetrates, however, the better for our side and the worse for his. So let him raid. Who cares? As I said before, the news from Cairo proper is rather of the quiescent character, but, from a reliable source. I have several items of interest from below, by the way of Memphis, which I proceed to detail for you.

THE NEWS FROM BELOW.

Several boats have arrived from below at Memphis. They bring Vicksburg news to Saturday last, which is later than from any other source, if I except that published in Northern papers from rebel sources, giving the fall of General Grant, the death of General Sherman, and half a dozen other items which are as entirely false and baseless as they are irrational. That a battle will soon take place in the rear of Vicksburg we have none of us the least doubt. But that it has already taken place, as the Jackson despatch has it we have every reason in the world to doubt. In fact it, was on Saturday known to be untrue. No battle had been fought up to that day worthy the name since Friday, the 22d of May, unless the rebels intended to report the affair at Milliken's Bend. General Grant is watchful and cautious, and will not advance too fast—will not fight the men he has in his power until he is fully prepared to do so.

THE REBELS

will leave no stone unturned, no labor unperformed, to rescue their men cooped up in the garrison at Vicksburg. They must make an effort. Something must be done, and that quickly, too, for the salvation of their sinking cause. Grierson's raid has done more to awaken the leaders and the people to a just and proper realization of their danger than any event of the war. They see now, and see very plainly, how weak and defenceless they are as soon as the outer circle that now protects them may be once fairly broken and the Northern hordes find an entrance into their immense territory of deserted and unprotected plantations, towns and cities. And they tremble, as well they may. And they strain every nerve to create a diversion that will result in driving us from our positions or cause us to weaken some of our lines so much as to render it an easy matter to drive us off and reoccupy them.

ON THE WESTERN BANK OF THE MISSISSIPPI.

Passengers to Memphis upon the steamer Belle Memphis, who arrived in Cairo last evening at a late hour, report that the rebels in considerable force had been of late observed on the western banks of the Mississippi, leading to the belief that they constituted something more than the usual marauding and not over dangerous bands of guerillas. It was even reported that these rebels had occupied De Soto and taken possession of the terminus of the Vicksburg and Shreveport Railroad, to Monroe, on the Wachita river. This may be the case. If so the rebels within the walls of Vicksburg are in this manner receiving supplies of which they already stand in need. The transportation used is an immense fleet of dugouts, or canoes. Their force is represented as about fifteen thousand. The report alluded to is contradictory in its statements, and as a whole seems to need confirmation, though some of its points may contain a modicum of truthfulness.

HAINES' BLUFF

has been reported, through rebel newspapers, as in the hands of the rebel army, and it is added that General Sherman has been killed. This was no more nor less than a lie out of full cloth, manufactured for the Southern market, to raise the drooping spirits and stimulate the failing energies of Southern troops. The facts are, that up to the 13th—four days ago—Gen. Sherman occupied Haines' Bluff himself, as he has done for weeks, and had not so much as beheld an enemy in any kind of force for weeks. There were not upon that day the remotest probabilities of a rebel sortie upon his works. And had there been he has so improved and fortified the place that he defies any army of three times the strength of his to move upon it with success. Haines' Bluff is no longer a rebel but a Union stronghold, and a strong and secure place it is, too. The rebel papers simply lie—that is all that deserves to be said about their absurd stories.

REINFORCEMENTS

are arriving at Grant's army every day. Were it not that it might convey information to the enemy I might say exactly how many thousand men have reported in the rear of Vicksburg within the past two weeks, but I will not do it at present. But it may be said that enough have been added to make it an utter impossibility for Joe Johnston, had he all the rebel troops inside of the rebel works and which he now boasts in his own command, he would have to hunt up even more yet before he could come at General Grant's army with the least confidence that success would after a battle perch upon his banners.

WHERE THE REBELS ARE.

Joe Johnson, at latest dates, as brought in by spies and scouts sent out for the purpose of obtaining the information, is in the vicinity of Satartia, occupying the banks of the Yazoo river in that neighborhood. A portion of his force is also said to be upon the Big Black. This department is reported to have been heavily reinforced from some direction within the past few days.

What Johnson is going to do is a matter open for debate. It is somewhat doubtful whether he knows himself. If he does he has not made a sign that can be recognized as yet. That he will attempt the rescue of Pemberton from the clutches of General Grant is more than likely. That he will fail is equally patent to those who have examined the preparations made by the latter to meet the shock whenever it may come.

WHAT REBEL PRISONERS SAY.

Several prisoners, lately captured at or near Vicksburg, are now confined in Dining prison. They give very contradictory statements in regard to the state of affairs within Vicksburg, some asserting, with great appearance of candor, that Pemberton has troops enough, food enough for his troops, and can easily hold out until Joe Johnston gathers a grand army of patriots to take Grant's. Others say, with equal appearance of truthfulness, that the rebels cannot possibly hold out much longer, and that, if they wait, expecting to receive aid from Johnston, they have a long time before them to wait—their food and forage is scant—and that the probabilities are they will be compelled ere long to succumb.

NEWS FROM WASHINGTON.

WASHINGTON, June 26, 1863.

GENERAL M'CLELLAN.

The report that General McClellan was here is untrue. His numberless admirers have in vain sought to-day to discover his hotel, on the strength of the groundless rumor in the morning papers.

THE ENROLMENT COMMENCED.

The enrolment under the Conscription law was commenced yesterday.

ARMING FOR THE DEFENCE OF THE CAPITAL.

The employes in the government blacksmith shop are ordered to meet to-night, at seven o'clock, when arms will be given them, to be used in the defence of the capital, should such an emergency arise. These employes seem perfectly willing to put their strong arms to the work of defending their capital and government against a threatened rebel invasion.

ARRIVAL OF GENERAL BUTLER.

Major General Butler and a portion of his family arrived at Willard's this evening. His visit is entirely of a domestic character, to take home a daughter who has been at school at Georgetown, whose vacation is about to commence.

THE CASE OF VALLANDIGHAM.

Hon. George H. Pendleton, chairman, and the other members of the delegation appointed by the Democratic Convention of Ohio to wait upon the President with reference to the return of Vallandigham, have had two interviews with the President, and stated to him in writing their object and purpose. A response will not probably be made before Monday.

NAVAL ORDERS.

Commander John Calhoun has been ordered to the command of the receiving ship at Philadelphia, vice Lieut. Pray, detached.

Commander Henry A. Wise has been appointed Acting Chief of the Bureau of Ordnance.

Sale of Government Bonds.

PHILADELPHIA, June, 26, 1863.

The sale of bonds to-day amounted to $1,270,000 at the various agencies. Deliveries of bonds are now made to June 2.

The New-York Copperhead.

Vol. I.—No. 7. NEW YORK, SATURDAY, JUNE 27, 1863. PRICE—Three Cents.

A New Version of "John Brown's Body."

The "boys," when we were in the field, used to sing very earnestly about "John Brown's body lies a mouldering in the grave." A Jersey paper gives a new version of this song to the old tune. We subjoin it, with a recommendation to our readers that they learn and sing it :—

McCLELLAN'S MARCH.

TUNE—JOHN BROWN.

Old Joe Hooker stands a wondering what he'll do,
Old Joe Hooker stands a wondering what he'll do,
Old Joe Hooker stands a wondering what he'll do,
As the rebs go marching along.

Say, McClellan, won't you show him,
Say, McClellan, won't you show him,
Say, McClellan, won't you show him,
The road through Maryland ?

There's our army waiting for a chief,
There's our army waiting for a chief,
There's our army waiting for a chief,
While the rebs go marching along.

Say, McClellan, won't you lead them,
Say, McClellan, won't you lead them,
Say, McClellan, won't you lead them,
On to victory ?.

There's Father Abraham shaking in his boots,
There's Father Abraham shaking in his boots,
There's Father Abraham shaking in his boots,
As the rebs come marching along.

Say, McClellan, won't you save him,
Say, McClellan, won't you save him,
Say, McClellan, won't you save him,
To split the rails out west ?

There's old Stanton ordering around,
There's old Stanton ordering around,
There's old Stanton ordering around,
And interfering still.

Say, McClellan, don't you heed him,
Say, McClellan, don't you heed him,
Say, McClellan, don't you heed him,
His mind is in a maze.

There's Mr. Seward a writing a dispatch,
There's Mr. Seward a writing a dispatch,
There's Mr. Seward a writing a dispatch,
To China's Great Ty—
... you tell him.
Say, McClellan, will you tell him,
To tend to things at home ?

Grandmother Welles has been disturbed in her sleep,
Grandmother Welles has been disturbed in her sleep,
Grandmother Welles has been disturbed in her sleep,
By the guns of a privateer.

Say, McClellan, won't you shake her,
Say, McClellan, won't you shake her,
Say, McClellan, won't you shake her,
And thereby keep her awake ?

Secretary Chase has bought a paper mill,
Secretary Chase has bought a paper mill,
Secretary Chase has bought a paper mill,
It's no use in gold going up.

Say, McClellan, won't you watch him,
Say, McClellan, won't you watch him,
Say, McClellan, won't you watch him,
For he's a sly old coon ?

There's our banner trodden in the dust,
There's our banner trodden in the dust,
There's our banner trodden in the dust,
By party's [illegible]

Say, McClellan, will you take it,
Say, McClellan, will you take it
Say, McClellan, will you take it,
And lift it to the skies ?

Jacobo.

DR. M. A. RICHTER,

OF BROOKLYN,

ON THE PRESENT STATE OF PARTIES.

THE WAR STORM.

Dr. Richter says, with reference to the present state of parties in this distracted country: The passive lookers-on who wait until the war storm is over, before they act, if they act at all, may be against the war, and, consequently, in favor of peace, but they form no party, and, therefore, cannot come in account here. All the rest are for the abolition war, and form one party—many of them without being aware of it,—represented by the government, flag, press, diplomacy, army, navy, and the whole civil patronage of the government. This is the only real party in the North. Distinctions between democrats (soft and hard), republicans, (black and white), abolitionists (white and black), are—at present—useless, because they are all melted into one great party,—the *abolition war party.* The reaction of it is in the South the *anti-abolition party*, similarly represented by the government. These two great parties, like day and night, are eternal antagonists. If their *pros* and *contras* shall be decided by the sword—an utter impossibility—they will and must fight until entirely prostrated and exhausted. History has an example of such a war full of warning, namely, the Thirty Years' War in Germany, between the Catholics and Anti-Catholics, or Heretics, Protestants, of which the Fourty-Four Years' Religious War of the Netherlands is a sequel. They formed there two parties, represented by the governments, and entirely separated by opposite opinions, as they remain at the present day. Catholics and Anti-Catholics *will* exist forever in such a condition, until *truth*, nothing else, produces re-union and sweeps away the causes of the schism, viz., fanatical superstition, arrogance, and intolerance on both sides. This Thirty Years' War came to its end by the total exhaustion of Germany and the fighting powers. Many villages disappeared from the maps, many cities never recovered from the terrible effects of this war. Fanaticism, arrogance, and intolerance are the main sources of our civil war. Not the sword, but only truth can bring help. The truth is in our Constitution. It has been suspended to make room for fanatic, arrogant, intolerant abolitionism. The terrible effects of this war will be like those recorded by the historians of the Thirty Years's War. I have wandered over the "Marken" where stood populous villages before this war broke out. In such a war are but defeats. Every true citizen must deplore the Bull Run fight, as much as the Donelson fight. The atrociously-duped good people are plundered by the designing men of all parties.

The government of the Confederate States has acted entirely on the defensive, and reiteratedly declared that all the people wish, is to be left alone. Will not the sectional and entirely abolitionized North be so kind and courteous as to grant this very reasonable prayer?

I have humbly tried to prevent this catastrophe. Having failed in it, I humbly try now to mitigate the horrors of this fratricidal war, by examining its real causes and exposing its certain effects. It is a duty I perform which every good citizen owes to his country. Do not misunderstand me. I am no milk and water peace man. I have, a mere stripling, fought for the deliverance of Germany from the grasp of Napoleon I. ; I am ready to fight twice seven years for independence, like Washington and his compatriots, but not one minute against those who wish to live alone in peace, under their own government, as the Confederate States.

ANCIENT AND MODERN

ATTEMPTS

To Hamper the Minds of the People.

In my former article having given the constitutional guarantees in general, we design treating in a few numbers specially of the great right of utterance given by God to man, and its absolute necessity to a Republican government. The Constitution declares that "*Congress shall make no law abridging the freedom of speech, or of the press,*" and entire freedom is the birthright of every citizen, however much the lawful exercise may be hampered, or interferred with by the satraps or shoulder straps of temporary power. That the right exists cannot be denied—that the citizen should exercise such freedom, I will endeavor to prove. Preliminary to doing so, however, I will give a resume of past history and the efforts to suppress free discussion in former ages and in other countries in order that the people may, from having more light on the subject, come to a better understanding of all its bearings.

In the monarchical and despotic governments of former times and in the Old World, the free exercise of the tongue and of the pen was denied to their *subjects*. Men were in such thraldom, that it cost them their property and their lives, to speak or write even the truth concerning the kings, potentates, princes or powers, that were established over them, or to comment in any manner other than in terms of fulsome adulation and praise upon their management of public affairs.

Tyrants and despots have always dreaded free discussion—and have ever been the enemies of freedom of speech and freedom of the press. There is nothing truer than that a bad cause will not bear argument. Whenever the people are forbidden to discuss measures it may be safely set down that the rulers are afraid to have their conduct scrutinized lest honest men should condemn them. Recent events clearly evidence that "there is something rotten in Denmark!"

In the days of Augustus Cæsar every Roman's life and fortune could be destroyed by the [illegible] breath of a pimp and spy. Under his iron rule in texts he imposed upon the penalties of treason regard to [illegible] attached. So that a distinguished writer says, "this law established his tyranny ; and, for one mischief which it prevented, ten thousand evils horrible and afflicting, sprung up in its place." Then as now, informers noted down words and disjointed sentences. The construction of words being arbitrary, and left to the decision of the judges, no man could write or open his mouth without being in danger of forfeiting his head. The process of marking men, sometimes called "*spotting*" was carried to almost as great an extent as now. Spies followed at the heels of distinguished men and in disguise, pretended friendship often while drinking the wine and sharing the hospitality of themselves and their friends.

An able author was put to death for praising Brutus in his history ; another for speaking nobly of Cassius. The reigns of Caligula and Nero were notable for the suppression of public sentiment, and silencing all who were disposed to criticise their iniquitous acts. Every man of ability who was inclined to be independent and outspoken was watched and dogged by dirty whelps who were paid out of the "secret service fund" to play the part of informers.

The brightest poets and ablest writers in Roman and Grecian history wrote under constant dread [illegible] Sweden, Norway, Spain, France, Germany, as well as Turkey, China and Japan—in all such governments as have abounded in modern history—freedom of speech and of the press have been ignored. Even in the boasted Mother country—England, these great privileges were entirely extirpated—and it has been of but recent date that a partial exercise of them has been tolerated. How many, many noble spirited men have fallen victims to the Star Chamber despots ! What manifold acts of tyranny were perpetrated by the minions of the Seventh and Eighth Henry, the bloody Queen Mary, James the First, the First and Second Charles and other Monarchs of Great Britain ! !

At times the subjects became unruly and sudden tumults and insurrections would break out in the kingdom, for it has been well remarked, that "when the tongues of the people are restrained, they commonly discharge their resentments by a more dangerous organ, and break out into open acts of violence." But for centuries terroism prevailed and the tongues of the subjects cleaved to the roof of the mouth and the greatest thinkers submitted in silence rather than undergo the boring of their ears on the pillory, having their cheeks branded with red hot iron and suffering perpetual imprisonment. The cheeks of freemen ever will tingle with shame when they think of the way in which men of talent, virtue, genius and worth have been exposed on scaffolds, mutilated, gibbited, pilloried and crucified for the free expression of opinions in regard to those who have been clothed with power and exercised it tyranically.

Throughout many long years of persecution for utterance of opinion in opposition to the political or religious dogmas of the head that wore the crown, or the hell-hounds of the Star Chambers, who executed their proscriptive laws, Queen Elizabeth was the only one who seemed disposed to have the penalty of fine and imprisonment reduced—for the historian relates of her that "she was often lead to applaud that rescript of Theodosius—"*Si quis Imperatori matediceret, non statim injuria censetur et eo nomine punitur ; sed distinguiter, an ex levitate processerit, et sic contemnitur, an ex insania, et miseratione digna censetur, an ex injuria, et sic remittenda declaratur.*" (If any person speak ill of the Emperor, through a foolish rashness and inadvertency, it is to be despised : if out of madness, it deserves pity, if from malice and aversion, it calls for mercy.) And yet Millar in his History of the English Government 2 p 454, Bigland 2 p 130, Hume, and other historians, are compelled to admit, 'In politics as well as in religion her maxims of government were arbitrary ; and she frequently intimidated parliament by imprisoning the members.'

The students of English history will find much in the reign of King James the First, and of Charles the First, analagous to the high handed operations of certain authorities in a government heretofore classed as Republican, attempting to suppress "Freedom of speech and Freedom of the Press." In the onward progress of intolerance it should be remembered, that when the last named Monarch planned the dispensing with parliaments and the subverting of the popular part of the English Constitution, he issued his royal edict, sealed with the great seal, commanding his subjects not to prescribe to him any time for holding parliaments. Lord Clarendon in his writings remarks, "that all men took themselves to be prohibited under the penalty of censure (the censure of the Star-Chamber, which few men cared to incur,) so much as to speak of parliaments, or so much as to mention, that parliaments were again to be called."

Parliaments when convened acted *per fas et nefus* under threats of arrest and imprisonment. Three of the ablest leaders of the people in the House of Commons were, in 1628, for expressing their opinions in favor of popular rights prosecuted and condemned as disturbers of the State. They were sentenced to pay thousands of pounds and to perpetual imprisonment. The most learned men in the kingdom in the professions of divinity, law and physic were for giving free utterance to their opinions subjected to contumely and scorn. It was nothing unusual then for the speaker and the writer to be torn from the bosom of his family—snatched from the embrace of wife and children—dragged to the tower, incarcerated in the dungeon—and led to the scaffold. Some of the noblest champions of popular rights in English history lost their property, others their limbs ;—some their homes, others their lives ; some were furnished by the tyrants passports to another, if not a better world—while others were banished the realm. Nevertheless the rights of the democracy steadily gained upon the powers of the aristocracy and the monarchy. The graves of those who have fallen in the encounter with crowned heads have been watered by the tears of millions and their memories will be cherished through all time, while general execration follows their oppressors. The pages of English history—the records of all nations verify the statement, that he who asserts the inalienable rights of the citizen and contends for "freedom of speech and of the press" makes to himself a fame as enduring as the name of his country.

Various efforts to trammel and fetter the speaker and writer have been resorted to—In the days of Charles the Second a licencer was appointed for the stage and the press. Sir Roger L'Estrange was the petty tyrant chosen to administer upon the witness and to execute the behests of the great despots. Every monarch has been able to find a willing tool. Slavish spirits worship at the shrine of power and servilely

> "Crook the pregnant hinges of the knee,
> That thrift may follow fawning."

The man of true nobility of soul scorns and despices all such degraded lackeys, or cringing hangers on to power and place.

Whenever an administration, a monarch, or his minister attempts to abridge, or limit the expression of thought—endeavors to suppress free discussion—establishes a rule that the citizen shall not exercise his rights in this respect, it may be set down as a certain evidence that the measures or acts of that power would suffer from ventilation. Yea, the authorities or power that pursue such a course, themselves by their very acts admit their own innate corruption. Yea, verily "[illegible] love the darkness because their [illegible] are evil!"

Vice is hideous, monstrous, revolting ; it cannot bear exposure to the bright sunlight of heaven. Truth, is beautiful ! above all things it is pure and holy. Bright and radiant it comes forth from every combat with error. Falsehood fears to encounter reason and argument ; it seeks to marshal a host of auxiliaries, it cries ever for help, help, and seeks the aid of adventitious circumstances, or perchance shrinks under the mantle of power. Truth is of God, it emanates from Him, and its duration is eternal—Its messengers may be buffeted, scourged, crucified. In our Saviour it was beaten and bruised—but it revived, and in its irradiation, has disseminated blessings and benefits throughout the nations—

> "Truth crushed to earth will rise again,
> The Eternal years of God are hers ;
> But error wounded writhes in pain,
> And dies amid its worshippers."

Monarchs, kings, despots, tyrants, autocrats, aristocrats and all the domineering lords of earth, have steadfastly opposed the rights of the people. The Democracy, have but to be true to themselves, and they will triumph over all *secret leagues* and *unlawful combinations* for even now the deadliest foe to constitutional rights—abolition "error wounded writhes in pain, and dies amid its worshippers," who have declared the cause of our Union, the Constitution, is "a covenant with death and a league with hell."

TO BE

STUCK OUT

OF THE

PORT HOLES

OF

FORT LAFAYETTE ?

A Rejoinder to General Nye's Speech at the Meagher Banquet.

Messrs. Editors of the Copperhead :—I am a timid man ; constitutionally timid—Knowing that fire will burn, I never intentionally put my fingers in the fire. Neither, while I am powerless to protect myself would I provoke the vengeance of a Party which, in the reckless pursuit of its own fanatical desires, does not hesitate to distort and suppress the truth, and violate all laws, Divine and human, in its mad endeavors to make a holocaust of our liberties—a burnt offering on the Altar of Abolition, round which its leaders dance and yell—as the Indians were wont to dance and yell around the victim at the stake. Does not Gen. Nye talk of putting us in Fort Lafayette, leaving our legs and arms sticking out of the windows ?

During the Millennium—or to speak more correctly, at the apparent beginning of the Millennium of Abolitionism in this City, when Fouquier Truville—I beg pardon, I have been studying the French Revolution lately—and confound names—When Superintendent Kennedy was earning the admiration of the *Times*, *Post* and *Tribune*—and something else from Posterity, by incarcerating unfortunate wretches in cell number Four, and exposing helpless women in Station Houses to the delicate attention of his fellow Jac——I mean Patriots, I held my tongue lest General Nye should do as he now proposes—namely, put my body in Fort Lafayette with my legs and arms sticking out of the window. I am not proud of my legs and arms. If they were plump and handsome I might not be ashamed of having them so exposed, but I am afraid that they would at present make a sorry show. I should be sorry to have them displayed there too for Nye's own sake—as Foreigners on entering the Port and seeing them would exclaim, "Look at those shanks ! they are starving their prisoners."

Like the Irishman's owl, "I kept up a devil of a thinking," but I never said that the sanctioning of such deeds was a disgrace to the government. Neither when the *Times* patriotically urges the total subversion of the Constitution and the building up of a worse than Russian despotism on its ruins, do I venture to exclaim "Did our Fathers fight and die for this?"—No ! I was silent, but my wife—who is—if I may be allowed to use the expression—a heroine in hoops and calico ; my wife will talk in spite of all my efforts to prevent her. She continually asserts that the real traitors to the Country are those in power, who being too imbecile to over come the rebellion—have turned to destroy the liberties of the loyal States—and perpetuate a power already tottering to its fall through their own illegal acts, to say nothing of the threats of sticking our legs and arms out of the windows of Fort Lafayette.

If I attempt to stop her she grows more outrageous, even going to the length of asserting that when President Lincoln declares that he will not do a thing you may depend upon his doing it—as was the case when he pronounced the Abolition Proclamation, the Pope's Bull against the Comet—and issued it immediately afterwards.

As such freedom of speech is only an Abolition prerogative, I have always been afraid that my wife's legs and arms might be stuck out of the windows of Fort Lafayette as General Nye proposes—they are not so bad looking as mine, but I should not like to see them there—and in consequence try to keep her quiet. I thought that there was safety in silence.

Alas! how terribly am I mistaken ! The President in his last letter informs us that the man who is silent will be dangerous if not hindered. In Jane Shore, Richard Duke of Gloster calls Hastings a Traitor for using the word "If" so that our President has a precedent for proclaiming "If," "and," and "but," traitorous words—but to denounce silence as dangerous !—Oh ! Lord ! oh Lord ! if we may neither speak nor be silent—how shall we keep our arms and legs from being stuck out of the windows of Fort Lafayette as General Nye proposes?

Freedom of Speech and Freedom of the Press.

HISTORICAL RESUME.

The First Victim to Tyrannical Interference in America.

THE PRINTER, STATESMAN AND PATRIOT, FRANKLIN.

PURITAN MASSACHUSETTS BEFORE THE REVOLUTION, AS SINCE,

Opposed to Free Speech and Freedom of the Press.

THE INTOLERANT SPIRIT OF THE CODFISH ARISTOCRACY OF THE CAPE COD COUNTRY EVER INIMICAL TO DEMOCRARY.

Intolerance and bigotry have ever had a home in New England—Fanaticism may count upon that section as her own. From the first landing of the grim and hoary pilgrims at Plymouth rock to the present time, that "chosen people of the Lord" as Cotton Mather styled them, while vaunting of their love of liberty and their religion, has been the most intolerant and hypocritical. While claiming that they sought the new country as an asylum for the oppressed—a place of refuge where they might worship God according to the dictates of conscience and enjoy freedom—they at the same time established the most arbitrary, tyranical and intolerant rules ever adopted by any people claiming civilization, christianity and intelligence. Those who have been accustomed to hear the self laudation of their descendants—to read the discourses of their writers abounding in panegyric and adulation—might be inclined to consider the foregoing expressions harsh. But, if they will review the past history of that people, and trace the course of their descendants down to the present time, they will be forced to admit that our judgment is just and righteous. In the words of the Declaration of Independence, "let facts be submitted to a candid world."

Examine the records—and when the evidences of their outrageous proceedings come up in solid array before you, there stand—not singly but in battallions—an army of freemen, who have been persecuted for asserting their own right to worship God, to hold religious and political views, to think, speak and act as they were entitled to do. From the days of the persecution of Catholics, Quakers and independent thinkers in Rhode Island and Providence Plantations [illegible] devils of Mary Magdalene. The Blue Laws of Connecticut, the Salem witchcraft trials, the whole civil and ecclesiastical proceedings of that people, manifest a depth of meanness, a lower strata of intolerance, bigotry and degradation, than can be found among any other people professing to be guided by the precepts of christianity.

From the days of the great law-giver, Moses, to the present time, there never has been such a cauting, whining, psalm-singing, nasal-twanged body of hypocrites upon God's green foot-stool !

There was peculiar fitness in that section, being the first in America, where efforts were made to destroy "freedom of speech and freedom of the press." The Saviour had said, "Let him that is without guilt throw the first stone," and these pharisaical creatures, arrogating to themselves all the virtue, religion and decency of the world, have ever considered that it was their mission on earth to regulate the affairs of all others, and to require all to conform to the standard they might themselves set up.

The second newspaper published in America was that of James Franklin, the brother of Benjamin, the distinguished printer, statesman and philosopher whose fame has extended throughout the world. In 1721, these brothers were working together in a little printing office in Boston, Massachusetts. The elder Franklin styled his paper, first, the *Boston Gazette*, and subsequently the *New England Cowrant*. It was a very small paper, principally filled with original articles on politics and matters of general interest. But small as it was, it was nevertheless a great annoyance to the constituted authorities, because it freely canvassed whatever appeared worthy of discussion in the transactions of that day. One of its articles on some political topic bore down too heavily upon the Assembly, and brought the strong arm of its power down on the paper. James was taken up, censured and imprisoned for a month. Benjamin says, in his autobiography, "I too was taken up and examined before the Council : but though I did not give them any satisfaction, they contented themselves with admonishing me, and dismissed me perhaps as an apprentice, who was bound to keep his master's secrets. During my brother's confinement, which I resented a good deal, notwithstanding our private differences, I had the management of the paper ; and I made bold to give our rulers some rubs in it, which my brother took very kindly, while others began to consider me in an unfavorable light, as a youth that had a turn for libelling and satire.

"My brother's discharge was accompanied with an order, and a very odd one, that '*James Franklin* should no longer print the newspaper called the *The New England Courant.*' On a consultation held in our printing office amongst his friends, what he should do in this conjuncture, it was proposed to elude the order by changing the name of the paper. But my brother, seeing inconveniences in this, came to a conclusion, as a better way, to let the paper in future be printed in the name of *Benjamin Franklin ;* and in order to avoid the censure of the Assembly, that might fall on him, as still printing it by his apprentice, he contrived and consented that my old indenture should be returned to me with a discharge on the back of it, to show in case of necessity ; and in order to secure to him the benefit of my service, I should sign new indentures for the remainder of my time, which were to be kept private. A very flimsy scheme it was ; however, it was immediately executed, and the paper was printed accordingly, under my name, for several months."

Here we see the first editor and publisher imprisoned in America on the general charge of having published passages "boldly *reflecting* on his Majesty's government, and *on the administration* in this province, the ministry, churches and college ; and that tend to fill the reader's mind with *vanity*, to the dishonor of God and the disservice of good men." He was sentenced, *as other men have been*, without any specification of these offensive passages, *or any trial before a* COURT OF JUSTICE !

The able, impartial and faithful historian, Mr. Jared Sparks, speaking of this, the first transaction in the American colonies relating to the freedom of the press, truly says, "the paper contains nothing which in later times would have been deemed reprehensible." The course pursued is to be considered not less remarkable for the assumption of power on the part of the legislature than for their disregard of *the first principles and established forms of law*. The men in power at that day, as in former, and *even in later times*, cared not a fig for the rights of the citizen as recognized by the principles and forms of law. Those who minister at the altar of tyranny assume power with all the *sang froid* that the hypocrite ascends the pulpit and puts on the sacerdotal robes that he may make a pick lock of his piety to steal away the liberties of mankind. The course of arbitrary power is ever relentless, vindictive, persecuting. In selecting its victim, it usually takes a "shining mark," and it follows with the keenness of scent of the blood hound the object of its prey. Arbitrary power is insane. Like other insanity it has to run its course. During the height of the deliruim it snaps, bites, breaks, destroys as far as its ability extends, every object in its way. In its fury and flame it is dreaded and feared ; but by the intensity of its own fire it is eventually consumed.

The molten lava of destruction may to-day rain throughout all this land—desolation and ruin mark its course—many noble objects may be stricken down by it—but thought will yet remain and bringing with it reflection—the "sober second thought"—on to-morrow will find expression, and when the madness of the hour shall have spent its force, will assert its rights—*make itself heard and felt.*

The case of Franklin, is analogous to others, that I might name. Let us pursue its history further and somewhat in detail—that it may be unnecessary to dilate upon others of like character—"*ex uno disce omnes.*"

He comes out of prison, and the *Courant* goes on, but not noiselessly. Almost every issue causes a rumbling and stirs up the dry bones of straight laced officials. In January, 1723, he was again arraigned, and other rigorous measures were taken, in which the editors and publishers of the present day may behold the prototype of 1863.

The hand of the clergy appears in this instance ; then as now, there were pimps and panderers to power among those who should preach "Christ and him crucified," and make their mission on earth one of peace and good will to men. They discovered a mote in an essay on *Hypocrisy* which was in general terms, but still of such specific character, that they felt themselves hurt, and as the "galled jade" of abolition to-day "winces," they showed how hard it hurt them by inciting a prosecution. The most objectionable passages in that essay are the following :

"Religion is indeed the principal thing, but too much of it is worse that none at all. The world abounds with knaves and villains ; but, of all knaves, the religious knave is the worst, and villainies acted under the cloak of religion the most execrable. Moral honesty, though it will not itself carry a man to heaven, yet I am sure there is no going thither without it."

"But are there such men as these in thee, O New England? Heaven forbid there should be any ; but, alas, it is to be feared the number is not small. '*Give me an honest man,*' say some; '*for all a religious man ;*' a distinction which I confess I never heard of before. The whole country suffers from the villainies of knaves and hypocrites for their sakes."

For these expressions of opinion, Franklin was again censured, *without being tried by a judicial tribunal, and forbidden to publish any paper or pamphlet, the contents of which had not been previously examined and approved by the Secretary of the province.*

Such was the intolerance and bigotry of Massachusetts—the fountain head of Abolitionism, and every other diabolism of the present day—such was the conduct of the prototypes of the *three thousand and fifty* clergymen of New England, who arrogated to speak for God on a political question, and from this very same Boston, Massachusetts, on the first of March, 1854, "*in the name* of Almighty God, and in his presence" against congressional action. The vicegerents of God on earth in 1723 dropped their mantles on willing shoulders !

"The Secretary of the province" whose "*ipse dixit*" was indispensable to any publication in 1723—finds his character sustained by the secretary of a military Governor, or Commission, or some other knight of the shoulder strap or garter holding staff position under some satrap in Nashville, New Orleans, Cincinnati, Keokuk, Leavenworth, or other place where it is deemed best to curtail freedom of speech and freedom of the press !

To such a sad and humiliating condition have the liberties of the citizen been reduced, that the most sacred rights of freemen are sought to be wrested from them.

There is in the case of Franklin and in the remarks of a contemporary, the Philadelphia *Mercury*, of February 26th, 1723, much that is worthy of reflection at this time, and I embody the sentiments thereof in this number—"My Lord Coke observes, that, *to punish first*, and *then inquire, the law abhors ;* but here, Mr. Franklin has a severe sentence passed upon him, even to the taking away part of his livelihood, without being called to make an answer. An indifferent person would judge by this vote against the *Courant*, that the Assembly of the province of Massachusetts Bay are made up of oppressors and bigots, who make religion the only engine of destruction to the people ; and the rather, because the first letter in the *Courant*, of the 14th of January, which the Assembly censures, so naturally represents and exposes the hypocritical pretenders to religion. Indeed, the most infamous politicians of that government (as the infamous Governor D—y and his family) have ever been remarkable for hypocrisy. And it is the general opinion, that some of their rulers are raised up and continued as a scourge in the hands of the Almighty for the sins of the people. This much we could not forbear saying, out of confession to the distressed people of the province, who must now resign all pretences to sense and reason, and submit to the tyranny of priestcraft and hypocrisy.

"P. S.—By private letter from Boston we are informed, that the bakers were under great apprehensions of being forbid baking any more bread, unless they will submit it to the Secretary, as supervisor-general and weigher of the dough, before it is baked into bread and offered to sell."

The continued oppression of the *administration* compelled James Franklin during the remainder of his residence in Massachusetts to carry on his business under the name of another, and finally, under the disadvantages which he labored, it became necessary for him to remove out of that province. In his paper of February 11th, 1723, he said, "The late publisher of this paper, finding so many inconveniences would arise by his *carrying the manuscripts and the public news to be supervised by the Secretary*, as to render his carrying it on unprofitable, has entirely dropped the undertaking." The way in which he entirely "dropped" it, is somewhat amusing to look back upon. It was published in the name of *Benjamin Franklin* until it ended in 1727—Benjamin, in October, 1723, removed from Boston to Philadelphia, and thus for about *four years* it bore the name of a publisher who did not superintend it, and was in no manner interested in its publication. James removed to Newport and established the Rhode Island *Gazette* in September, 1732. There he died in 1735, highly esteemed as a citizen. The Franklins were men of better character and of more genuine worth than their oppressors—while the names of those who "strutted upon the stagee" in all their pomp of arbitrary power, and attempted to deprive the citizen of his rights of expression, have been lost sight of, or are only mentioned to be execrated—Franklin's will endure forever.

Let editors and publishers be ever mindful of their rights—and fearlessly do their duty. Let freedom of speech and freedom of the press be asserted—even though the strong arm of power may be stretched over the speaker or writer. The censorship of the press may be attempted, the editor or orator may be arbitrarily arrested. Here a "puss in boots," or conceited Secretary, with more brass than brains and more title than honor may interdict. There a "Bombastes Furioso," brimful of wrath and thunder, may threaten or perhaps arrest, but while the ways of Providence are inscrutable, and He "moves in a mysterious way, His wonders to perform," it is certain as that the sun will rise to-morrow, that the people will think and keep thinking over the usurpations and oppressions of the present until the long pent up thoughts will force their way, and the future foot-fall of the people will be heard as with the convulsion of an earthquake shaking the oppressors from place.

The volcano of popular rights will yet burst out and sweep all barriers before it. Historical facts leads us to express this conviction, and in conclusion of this paper we can not but strive to impress upon the minds of the people the result of the reflection of Benjamin Franklin upon efforts to restrain freedom of speech and the liberty of the press—viz. : "THAT WHOEVER ATTEMPTS TO SUPPRESS EITHER OF THESE OUR NATURAL RIGHTS, OUGHT TO BE REGARDED AS AN ENEMY TO LIBERTY AND THE CONSTITUTION."

Hidel.

Shall we Have Another Convention for Peace?

A FOREIGNER

ON THE VALUE OF A

QUIET RECONSTRUCTION

OF THE

UNION.

Editors of The New York Copperhead :—

Your correspondence, signed W. C., in your paper of June 20, is a "settler." To his assertion—"*Peace* and a repudiation of the coercive policy, is the only ground upon which our political difficulties can be settled,"—the following may be added : How shall we get *Peace?* People are divided into two parties at present—viz. : the War Party, including Abolitionists, Black Republicans, War Democrats, niggers, and their influential papers ; numerous priests, etc., and the *Peace Party*, consisting of all good Christian men and women, of all creeds and parties, and their very few papers, and still fewer priests. As naturally the war party's principle, policy, and purpose, is war, it would be absurd to expect from her peace, or anything but war ; as, on the other hand, it would be foolish to expect from the peace party war instead of peace. To wait until the war party makes peace, is tantamount to wait till single man is coming forth to fight for her, and a single greenback is left to pay him for it. Whether those fighters or party men and editors and priests agree with the leaders of this war party in Washington about the war in all particulars or not, makes not the least difference, if they only come forward to fight, and paper can be got to print the price upon for which they do the fighting.

It is entirely different in a monarchy. There the king or prince is the only man interested in the fighting business. The army is his arm, his hand, by which he fights. As soon as he sees that the game does not succeed so well as he expected, his throne, crown or dynastic interests force him to make peace. This is the reason why wars between two monarchs are of a very short duration. A few blows are sufficient to convince one of them that war will not do, and peace is the consequence. This facility of getting a peace is in a certain regard in favor of monarchy ; but, on the other hand, it is also the cause that monarchs are running easily into a war, because each of the combatants must think in the outset—"Let me try ; if not lucky, I make a peace as good as I can, and all is over;" i. e., in regard to the monarch, who does not care of the burdens saddled by the war on his subjects. Entirely different is the war or peace question in a civil war like ours. There every man takes an interest in the feud on his own account ; party makes a handsome business out of it, and naturally carries it on as long as she can. The peace party is therefore a mere phenomenon, or sentiment, if she cannot contrive to deprive the war party of the war—food ; i. e., *fighters* and *money*, and extricate herself from the responsibility for the war. As matters are in our political system, the peace party can only stay this infernal war by making the right use of our State machinery. W. C. says—"*It is true that the Government* (meaning the Federal branch) *under which we now live is no longer the Government of the United States.*" If this is true,—and who will deny it?—why there is not the least obligation in one of our State Governments to support that Government, which has taken the place of the United States, with a single man or dollar ; for if that is true, there is no United States citizenship more, and Congress, if it should convene is nothing but a meeting of private gentlemen and Mr. Lincoln an autocrat or something else, but not the President of the United States.

Would it now be prudent and good statesmanship to support this upstart or bastard Government with the sinews of war, and burden our States and their people with the responsibility for it? Or should the good people of this State not rather insist on being heard in the matter, and that our Governor should act independently and convoke, without delay, a Convention, to take the sense of the people, and assertain their wish and sovereign pleasure? Then ALL would have a fair and legitimate chance of taking care o their rights and interest, while at present all is wild partizan feud, destructive to the rights and interests of all. To allow, tacitly, that our great and leading State drifts along with a Government outside of consitiution and laws, except what it lays down as such in proclamations and general orders, is, to say the least, imprudent, hazardous, and in violation of our duties as citizens of this State. There is good American statesmanship in request to make a right use of the State-check.

Will your Correspondent, W. C., have the goodness to give his opinion on this subject? If the (thought of) Convention should decide that the State of New York refuses to support the arbitrary Government in Washington, peace would be the consequence, for without this support, war and, of course, coercing, would be impossible. There is an immense responsibility in the course which this State pursues. Its duty to terminate this war seems to be clear and paramount.

A. P. M.

Newspaper Suppressed.

The Harrisburg (Pennsylvania) *Telegraph* has been suppressed by military authority (!). It was of the Abolition stripe, and its fate excites surprise as well as *black looks.*

The New York Copperhead

IS PUBLISHED

EVERY SATURDAY

FOR THE

PROPRIETORS,

FROM

No. 66 COURTLANDT STREET,

(CORNER OF WASHINGTON.)

PRICE—THREE CENTS PER COPY.

Liberty of Thought and Discussion.

The time it is to be hoped, is gone by, when any defence would be necessary of the "liberty of the press" as one of the securities against corrupt or tyrannical government. No argument, we may suppose, can now be needed, against permitting a legislature or an executive, not identified in interest with the people, to prescribe opinions to them, and determine what doctrines or what arguments they shall be allowed to hear. This aspect of the question, besides, has been so often, and so triumphantly enforced by preceding writers, that it needs not be specially insisted on in this place. Though the law of England, on the subject of the press, is as servile to this day as it was in the time of the Tudors, there is little danger of its being actually put in force against political discussion, except during some temporary panic, when fear of insurrection drives ministers and judges from their propriety; and speaking generally, it is not, in constitutional countries, to be apprehended, that the government, whether completely responsible to the people or not, will often attempt to control the expression of opinion, except when in doing so it makes itself the organ of the general intolerance of the public. Let us suppose, therefore, that the government is entirely at one with the people, and never thinks of exerting any power of coercion unless in agreement with what it conceives to be their voice. But I deny the right of the people to exercise such coercion, either themselves or by their government. The power itself is illegitimate. The best government has no more title to it than the worst. It is as noxious, or more noxious, when exerted in accordance with public opinion, than when in opposition to it. If all mankind, minus one, were of one opinion, and only one person were of the contrary opinion, mankind would be no more justified in silencing that one person, than he, if he had the power, would be justified in silencing mankind. Were an opinion a personal possession of no value except to the owner; if to be obstructed in the enjoyment of it were simply a private injury, it would make some difference whether the injury was inflicted only on a few persons or on many. But the peculiar evil of silencing the expression of an opinion is, that it is robbing the human race; posterity as well as the existing generation; those who dissent from the opinion, still more than those who hold it. If the opinion is right, they are deprived of the opportunity of exchanging error for truth; if wrong, they lose, what is almost as great a benefit, the clearer perception and livelier impression of truth, produced by its collision with error.
—*John Stuart Mill, "On Liberty."*

NEW YORK:
SATURDAY, JUNE 27, 1863.

WESTCHESTER COUNTY.—All the business of Westchester County, connected with this paper (the COPPERHEAD) may be transacted with Daniel Odell. The address is "Daniel Odell, Tuckaho, Westchester Co. N. Y."

NOTICE.—H. P. Mabee is our authorised Agent to collect Advertisements and Subscriptions for THE NEW YORK COPPERHEAD in Onondagua and adjoining Counties. His address is Syracuse, Onondagua Co., New York.

An Appeal to Freemen—Does Anybody Love White Men?

All readers of THE COPPERHEAD, who believe that the principles it enunciates are essential to the support and extension of pure Democratic Freedom, are informed that we are not subsidized or controlled by any committees or cliques, and that our only reliance for support is *upon the individual members of the patriotic public.* When, therefore, you have read this paper, and have approved its contents, go to work, at once in the best way you can, to extend its influence. This you may do by procuring us subscriptions and advertisements, for these form the life-blood of all newspaper enterprises. If, however, after reading what we have to say, you think that "niggers" are better than "poor white trash," give your support forthwith to the *Tribune* and will aid us with their *mite*, (no matter how little) will lay up glory for themselves here upon earth, and treasure in the future Heaven of unalloyed Freedom, which will surely and shortly dawn upon us.

SPECIAL NOTICE TO PEACE DEMOCRATS.

This paper, THE COPPERHEAD, is now in the seventh week of its existence. Through the persistent and unwearying efforts of its editors and proprietors, (who are experienced members of the New York Press,) it has reached a point of success which has never before been achieved by any paper of a similar age. But as we commenced our enterprise without that abundance of means which has characterised the start of certain Black Republican, or War, Journals—and as we have no bankers to draw upon, excepting the Democratic public, every little bit of solid aid that reaches us is a comfort, and enables us to enlarge and extend the sphere of our usefulness. Those living in any part of the country, therefore, who think that our sphere *is* useful, and who desire the *general* and free dissemination of true Democratic Doctrine, will, at once, send us the names of any sound Democrats, who, they think, will be willing to receive and circulate the paper. The country can never be extricated, from its present danger, unless genuine Democratic Doctrine is freely distributed through it. Get us up clubs of subscribers, or send us such names, (with full directions,) of such persons as you think will be willing to benefit the glorious cause of Peace and Democracy.

One Peace Democrat on the Copperhead.

NEW YORK, June 18, 1863.

Editors New York Copperhead:—

Gentlemen,—I recently had the pleasure of perusing your interesting journal, and I can assure you, that you are aiding, most magnificently, the great work of establishing the *reunion* of the North and South, by peaceful means.

I give you great praise for your boldness and firmness in advocating true and honest Democratic sentiments, and I sincerely hope that you may succeed in maintaining your valuable paper, and, in time, may have the good wishes of a grateful people.

Yours, respectfully,
EDWARD H. BRACKETTE,
No. 480 Pacific St., Brooklyn.

Mr. Brackette's proposition, (which we do not publish,) is accepted.

TO NEWS VENDERS!—THE COPPERHEAD can always be procured, every Friday night, from the following established general News Agents:—

SINCLAIR TOUSEY,
FEEKS & BANCKER,
LONG & CO.,
JAMES JONES,
SAMUEL YATES.

TO ALL GOOD COPPERHEADS WHEREVER LOCATED.—Send us all the good news, in detail, that you know.

WANTS.—New York, a thorough Peace man for Mayor, and not one who "runs with the hare and holds with the hounds."

SAM YATES, the News Agent, takes the COPPERHEAD. The only agents now out of the ring, are the firm of Hamilton, Johnson & Farrely, and the old fashioned Dexters. It appears that Yates did not take the paper because of a mistake in his office, for which he was not responsible.

A PORTRAIT MONTHLY.—The Proprietors of the New York Illustrated News have commenced the publication of a Monthly Portrait Sheet. The first number contains twenty-six portraits of the chief celebrities of the war, with abundant letter press. The price is only ten cents a copy.

THE COPPERHEAD gratefully acknowledges the receipt of one of Wilson & Trow's City Directories for the year 1863. It is a perfect work in all its departments.

WE HAVE MATTHEW KERVAN'S matter in type, but have no room for it. It will appear next week.

The New York Tribune on the Stump—Is the Democratic Party Opposed to Free Speech and Freedom of the Press?

With its usual falsehood and persistent dishonesty, the *Tribune* undertakes to give the history of the Abolition party, and to make out that it always received more kicks than coppers from Democrats before it came into power.

When the Abolitionists first commenced blowing their penny trumpet, it was believed by most people that the effect would be disastrous to the country. We need not stop to inquire whether the latter were mistaken or not in their anticipations: the dreadful result is before us. As Henry Clay and others foretold, we have ruined cities, devastated fields, and desolated homes—*the South swimming in blood and the North struggling in fetters!* All this is the work of Abolitionism.

The very men who are now the loudest in their professions of loyalty to the Administration, which the depraved miscreant of the *Tribune* terms the "Government," in defiance of his better knowledge—the very men who now get contracts and urge the imprisonment of all who oppose the "war measures" of Sumner and Wilson—were foremost in decrying and mobbing the primitive Abolitionists, while Horace Greeley himself was very careful not to peril the subscription list of the *Tribune* by advocating Abolition in its columns, and avoided all allusions to William Lloyd Garrison as if his name had been "a spell to conjure up the wild devil, withal."

At a comparatively recent date, there was a correspondence, published in the *Tribune*, between William Goodell and Greeley, in which the latter turned and twisted himself into every shape to find excuses for not advocating "the cause of the slave" in his paper.

At length, however, the time came when it was safe to advocate Abolitionism, and then Greeley hastened to run over the backs of the tried and weather-beaten veterans, and place himself, if possible, at the head, making the loudest outcry of any, that people might believe that *he* was one of those who had borne the heat and burden of the day; while, in fact, he had been careful to do nothing for the cause only in so far as it jumped with his own interests, and the pecuniary interests of the *Tribune*. He had stood by to catch the bird, while others beat the bush—to enjoy the benefit of other men's labors.

It was for this cause that he meanly avoided all mention of Wm. Lloyd Garrison, to whom the whole honor of *originating* this damnable crusade against the South belongs.

It is true that there was "a little band of despised fanatics," in the first instance, who formed the cynosure of the Black Republican party, but Horace Greeley took very good care not to be one of that little band of fanatics: for there was very little to be made by it in those days, unless you were the editor of a flourishing Abolition paper, or a popular lecturer. The papers were already in the field, and there was scarcely room for the *Liberator* itself; others scarcely lived. As for the lecturers, they were always liable to be hissed and hooted at, and were sometimes pelted, but very seldom injured. Large Abolition meetings were held in Boston, and elsewhere, and transacted their business without interference. Even when mobs arose, they were very generally harmless.

The principal mobs took place during the first visit of *George Thompson* to these shores. The Abolition ladies sent to England a request that Thompson would come here and lecture against slavery.

The people of this country had thought it bad enough that natives should breed a quarrel between the North and South, but the advent of a British emissary, who came here to add his offering to the hurly burly pot, excited men's minds to such a degree that they sometimes mobbed the meetings at which he held forth. But nobody was hurt.

At length, it was given out that Thompson would speak at an Anti-Slavery meeting to be held at 46 Washington street, Boston, in the building where the *Liberator* was published. A large mob collected—*not* of Democrats, *not* of mechanics and labors, but of "gentleman of property and standing from every part of the city."

Everybody knows that this was a mob of Whigs, of the party now styling itself "Republicans." With very few exceptions, the wealthy classes of Boston belonged to the Whig or Federal party. Boston was an Anti-Democratic city, and here it was that the great mob took place.

The mob had been gathered by a meeting in Faneuil Hall, at which Harrison Gray Otis, (a member of the Hartford Convention,) and Mr. Sprague, a Whig member of Congress, delivered addresses, denouncing the Abolitionists, and George Thompson in particular.

Soon after this meeting, a handbill, supposed to have been printed at the Whig office of the *Commercial Advertiser*, was posted about the streets, offering a reward to the man "who should first bring Thompson to the tar kettle."

The meeting was held, but the Anti-Slavery ladies would not permit Thompson to be present. Therefore, Garrison was seized in his stead by the Boston Federalists, and dragged through the streets. He was rescued by one or two *workingmen*, supposed to be Democrats, who bore him through the mob and placed him in the City Hall out of danger. Subsequently Garrison was taken to Leverett street prison, and escaped all harm to his person, though his broadcloth suffered some.

On the next day, all the Whig papers came out against the Abolitionists, and rejoiced in their (supposed) discomfiture. But the *Advocate*, conducted by Benjamin F. Hallett, a thorough Democrat, breasted the torrent of intolerance, and defended the rights of the Abolitionists, free speech, and free discussion, with such determined zeal and energy, that many persons mistook that Democratic journal for an Abolition paper. The *Morning Post*—now called the Boston *Post*—disapproved of mobs, and recommended ridicule as the best medicine for Abolitionism.

There was another Democratic paper called the *Artisan*, which took strong ground in favor of free speech and the freedom of the press, severely denouncing the persecutors of the Abolitionists.

The Abolitionists were nearly all Federalists, of the old Hartford Convention school, and so were their persecutors.

But how is it with the *Tribune* at the present day? Like other Black Republicans, he is in favor of putting down free speech just as far as it can be done with safety to himself and the party.

In this very article to which we are replying, the *Tribune* contends that the *Caucasian*, the *News*, and the *World* ought to be suppresed. These are his words:—

"There are exigencies which make their own laws and which overrule individual rights at the stern demand of the public safety. We do not believe even Seymour would contend that a journal and a club openly, avowedly, devoted to the cause of the Slaveholders' Rebellion would have a right to exist here at this crisis; yet the *Caucasian* makes no disguise of its entire sympathy with that Rebellion, and supports Seymour distinctly on its platform. And if you say that a journal *avowedly* in the Rebel interest has no right to exist here in such an exigency, you will find it very difficult logically to justify the publication of one like the *News* or the *World*."

Is the editor of the *Tribune* an idiot as well as a knave, to exhibit the cloven foot of persecution, at the very moment that he is charging the Democracy with being inimical to free speech and freedom of the press?

Even before Lincoln was inaugurated, he threatened to suppress freedom of speech. Somebody had insinuated that Vice-President Hamlin was a mulatto, when, in his exultation at the election of a Black Republican President, Greeley said in the *Tribune*—"We shall not hear so much of this talk pretty soon: at any rate, Hamlin won't allow it in the Senate."

But we need not refer to the course of the *Tribune* up to the election of Governor Seymour. The November election showed him that his raging intolerence must be partially disguised lest the conservative sentiment should sweep the Abolition party into absolute nothingness.

To conclude. Let no Democrat or conservative be so great a fool as to trust, for one moment, any professions of toleration that shall hereafter be made by Black Republicans. *We know them thoroughly now.*

The Fourth of July Patriots Who Have Invited the President to Philadelphia.

A rabid Royalist Abolition sheet called the Brooklyn *Times*, says:—

In New York the bells rang at midnight and men took up arms. In Cincinnati the stores were closed and business suspended. In Pittsburgh the people are fortifying the city. In Harrisburg thousands of men are throwing up works. What are they doing in Philadelphia? Proving themselves the unsexed sons of *Quakers!*

Again, the same journal says:—

PHILADELPHIA PLUCK.—Stalwart young men standing on the street corners with their hands in their pockets, wondering how far the Rebels have progressed, and why the New Yorkers don't hurry on to stop them. Bah!

So much for the Copperhead City of New York, and the Royal League City of Philadelphia. We wish the President joy of his associates!

New York and New Jersey were up and doing and hurried up troops to drive off the enemy, without a moments delay, while several New Jersey regiments, whose time had expired, volunteered to remain and march to Harrisburgh. So much for Copperhead States and Copperhead Governors. Where are the Abolitionits and Royal Leaguers?

A New Name for an Old Rock!—Calling Things by their Right Names.

We see by the down East papers that they have a rock among them called "Dungeon Rock." It is probably Plymouth Rock with a one of Fort Warren, [illegible] reminds No. Four.

Tod.

Copperheads forgot their partisanship to rush to the defence of Pennsylvania; but Gov. Tod of Ohio must needs insult the Democracy of his State while imploring them to take up arms. The Abolition mind is *peculiar*. Tod says—"In the name and in behalf of the *best Government on earth*, let me implore you to lay aside all other duties and obligations," etc.

When a Democrat speaks of the Government, he means the Constitution and Laws, but a Black Republican means Abe Lincoln and his Abolition friends.

We are not sure about the pronunciation of Tod's name, but think the *O* should be pronounced long. We understand that when addressed affectionately by his friends, he is called *Toddy*.

Too Strong for the Stomach.

We see that Adjutant-General Thomas, late drill-sergeant for negro soldiers, is sick. He deserves credit for standing it as long as he did. The effluvia from niggers is not good for white men.

Rude Journalism—The Post Throwing Mud!

The Evening *Post* is trying the *Tribune* tactics, and charges the *World* with telling a *lie*. When will such men as Bryant and Godwin learn that blackguardism, and the calling of names add nothing to the strength of an argument, and do not aid the cause in behalf of which they are used. We are sorry to see editors resorting to such weapons.

A Strange Production!—Our Rulers Make us the Laughing-Stock of the World!

Mr. Lincoln says, in his Albany letter, that people who *remain silent* when "war measures" are discussed, should be arrested as traitors. Modest diffidence and distrust of one's own judgment is a sin against the State! Several immigrants to this country had taken a great interest in parrots, as they could repeat words which had been spoken in their hearing. One of these sons of Erin made a slight mistake and purchased *an owl* instead of a parrot. His companions found much fault with his "parrot," and complained that he did not talk.

"He don't spake," said Pat, "but you can see that he keeps a d——d good thinking."

It is not to be doubted that Lincoln takes it for granted that when men don't speak treason, they "keep a d——d good thinking," and, like Pat, he places them both on the same ground.

Lookers on in Vienna!—They Don't Come up to the Scratch!

Many of our cotemporaries continue to denounce the Peace Democrats, but they make no attempts to answer our arguments. It appears that they dare not attack us. Even the *World*, which does not fear to pitch into the President himself, fights shy when the COPPERHEAD heaves in sight.

We commend their prudence; it is a tribute paid to our prowess which we affectionately appreciate. Their silence is a tacit acknowledgement that we are invincible.

Black Republican Atrocity—The Evening Post on the War.

Because we have blockaded the ports of the Confederate States, in order, as the *Tribune* expresses it, that the men and women of the South may see their children famishing, and be unable to give them the food which they demand—because, on this account, the naval powers of that country must either destroy the prizes which they capture or let them go, the Abolition demons of the Evening *Post* recommend that the Southern towns and villages be given to the flames by way of of retaliation. This is another of the many evidences that this war is carried on by the party in power, not for the Union, but for revenge and the gratification of their own hellish instincts.

The Murmuring Brooks and Steadfast Woods.

An Abolition paper says that the Brooks and Woods are silent on the subject of Peace, since the invasion of Pennsylvania. If those *Brooks* ever went for peace, they *dried up* long since, though they still *murmur* at illegal arrests. As for the other gentlemen mentioned, don't crow till you are out of the *Woods*, and that won't happen yet a while. The Scripture says:—"From babes and sucklings thou hast ordained praise,"—doubtless is meant "the babes in the *Wood*."

Feminines in the Majority—Splendid Courting in Prospective.

It is said that one object of the Coercionists in keeping up this useless and murderous war is to kill off males enough to have a large majority of women, so that when the ladies go to the polls, there will be she-votes enough to carry every measure that the Woman's Rights party approves. It won't make much difference: the country can't be ruled worse than it is ruled now.

Very Small Business—Let us Have no More of It.

The people of Ohio petition a certain little petifogger, burglar and kidnapper, now living in Washington, and facetiously terming himself the "President of the United States," to recall Vallandigham from exile. We are sorry to see "Democrats" disgracing themselves in that manner.

Spiritual Humbug—The Spirits Choose Darkness Rather than Light!

An Abolition paper published in Boston, misnamed the "Banner of *Light*," since the spirits always prefer darkness, and will do nothing till the "light" is put out, tells us of "a class of manifestations well calculated to convince any honest (!!!) sceptic of their truth."

Musical instruments were played upon—the guitar floated over their heads—some in the circle were presented with a glass of water—the spirits extracted the perfume from flowers, and wafted it in the faces of the company—and, at the close, the medium and the chair in which she was seated, were lifted upon the table.

Now, all this is very nice, very convincing—but wait a moment. Read the next paragraph—"So gently was this done, that those sitting [illegible] not aware of her [illegible] *until lights were called for.*"

Nothing is said about removing the lights till the conclusion. Then we are informed that all these wonders were performed in the dark. Is there any one of these performances that could not easily have been gone through with while the uninitiated were quietly seated with "all their hands joined on the table," so that they were prevented from *feeling*, as well as *seeing*, the "spirits" who did these wonders, and who, doubtless, absconded before the lights were brought in?

Thoughts are Treason in Washington—The Albany Letter Dictated by Spirits!

I'll know thy thoughts!—OTHELLO.

It is evident that Mr. Lincoln could never have discovered that men who speak no traitorous words, have treasonable thoughts, if he had not been aided by the spirits. Other Presidents could judge of men only by their words and actions, but the country is now blessed with a potentate who reads the unspoken words as they pass through the brain. Doubtless, Spiritualism will hereafter be a great agency in the Federal cabinet, and a troop of the invisible inhabitants of the spirit world being kept in the employ of the Administration to act as spies and informers, must prove a most valuable acquisition, as they will require neither pay nor rations.

Epistolary Correspondence With Great Men—The Albany Letter.

It is not creditable to the people of a republic that they should have a rage for addressing persons in authority. That the subjects of a monarchy should have an itching for the distinctions conferred by an interview with the King, or a presentation to the Queen, is in keeping with that "loyalty" which forms the staple of their patriotism. One man, who boasted that he had been addressed personally by the King, when questioned as to the occasion, said—"I was standing on the road when the King came riding up, and he told me to *get out of his way*."

But such aspirations in the people of a republic, who elect a man to do the public business four years, and dismiss him from office at the end of his term if he don't behave himself, are not favorable to the permanency of free institutions.

Still more, when the big-bug thus courted, is an acknowledged transgressor, a felon who has rendered himself liable to prosecution for false imprisonment, for burglary, and kidnapping, it is inconsistent with one's self-respect to address him as a superior and to appeal to a sense of honor and justice which he has abundantly proven that he does not possess.

We once saw the celebrated negro pugilist, "Big Dick," in the streets of Boston. He was followed by a crowd, two or three of whom purposely got in his way, and addressed insulting language to him, in order that he might have an excuse for slapping them in the face. They could then boast that they had been struck by Big Dick—that they had felt the weight of the lion's paw.

It would seem as if the Albany gentlemen, who recently addressed Abraham Lincoln, were emulous of receiving a slap in the face from so great a man—anything from the President of the United States, if it was only a kick *a posteriori*.

They must have known that Lincoln would defend his course; did they expect to make a rejoinder? If not, why place themselves in a position to be answered by plausible arguments, which his own party would applaud and the unstable would wrest to their own destruction, while they could furnish no antidote in the shape of a reply to Lincoln's sophistry?

Nor is that all. With what propriety could the Albany letter-writers subscribe themselves—"*Yours, with great regard?*"

It puts us in mind of the man whose house was entered in the night by robbers, and meeting them in the hall, the polite gentleman cried—"Are you the thieves—I beg pardon—are you the honorable gentlemen who are robbing our house?"

If the Albany gentlemen, who have had the honor to be slapped in the face by Abraham Lincoln, entertain so high a regard for that gentleman as their language implies, and can express that regard even at the moment that his exiled victim is languishing in an enemy's country, they are certainly entitled to a high seat among the Loyal Leaguers.

It is of no use to talk of the respect which is due to the President of the United States. Lincoln has lost all claim to be regarded as the ruler of a free people.

But it is said that *the office* of President is honorable.

Very well; if they have a "great regard" for the office, why did they not say so? It is very credible that the Albany gentlemen have a "great regard" for the office of President, and for every other office.

In future, we hope that Democrats will let the President alone. It is not from him, nor from his advisers, that any good is to be expected, and every letter or petition addressed to such usurpers, felons, and tyrants, as Lincoln & Co., is but an oriental prostration at their shrine, and an invitation to them to place their heels upon your necks.

But what can be expected from men who uphold the war—who defend the exercise of tyranny against the Southern States—who maintain the doctrine of Coercion?

That such [illegible] persons should be also servile—that they should [illegible] kneel down in the presence of power is to be expected. [illegible] the men in authority be the worst criminals in the country, it makes no difference; for are they not "great men?"

We hope there is now an end to letters and petitions from professed Democrats to Abolition tyrants, and that whatever "great regard" they have to spare, will be reserved for honest men, who really merit it.

WHY is a certain Southern general like Broadway?
Ans.—Because he is a *Long Street.*

A Wise Commander!—All Honor to General Skunk!

We cannot too highly praise the course of General Skunk in stopping those violent war papers in his dominions, the *World* and the *Express*. Skunk must perceive that they are the most persevering advocates of Coercion, and as such are calculated to prolong the war which we all wish to see brought to an end. Go it, Skunk! We shall hereafter [illegible] Skunk, of Maryland, as a Peace Democrat, for he suppresses the war journsls, while he has made an exception in our favor. It will be observed that he has not included the COPPERHEAD in his list of proscribed journals.

The Last News from the Spirit Land!

Andrew Jackson Davis, eldest son (we are informed) of Jefferson Davis, says that Stonewall Jackson has become an Abolitionist since his death, and has joined John Brown's phalanx of philanthropists. The spiritualists also say that John C. Calhoun became an Abolitionist soon after his death.

As all the "rebels" turn Abolitionists after death, it accounts for the fact that Wendell Phillips wants to hang them. It is the newest style of making converts.

More Retreats.

Lincoln and wife have gone to their Summer retreat. All right; we don't see why Lincoln should not have the privilege of *retreating* as well as his generals.

The Faithful Among the Faithless Found.

While so many Northern clergymen are yelling for human blood, and clothing themselves with curses as with a garment, that illustrious prelate, Archbishop Hughes, stands up in his place and vindicates the sacred principle of "Peace on earth and good will to man."

WHAT American poet resembles Abe Lincoln?
Ans.—Longfellow. [A long fellow.]

The Materia Medica in Modern Use.

The Northern *Ensign* mentions a singular case

Black Republican Impudence!—The Pot Reproveth the Kettle for its Complexion!

The Evening *Post* edifies its Abolition readers with the following characteristic paragraph:—

AN INCIDENT.—Colonel Frank Hampton (son of the late Wade Hampton, of South Carolina), who was killed in a recent battle, seems to have been overtaken by a just retribution. About six or seven years since he married a young lady of this city, and the day previous to the wedding, being called upon at a dinner party at the house of the bride's father to give a toast, totally regardless of the rights of hospitality and the proprieties of the occasion, he proposed "The downfall of the American Union."

If the said Hampton deserved to be killed for giving, for a toast, "The downfall of the Union," what do the Abolitionists deserve, who have been bellowing for a dissolution of the Union for the last thirty years—who have burned the Constitution, and pronounced it a league with hell, and who are now drenching the country in blood, for the purpose of breaking up the Union, and rendering its reconstruction impossible?

Really, these blind Pharisees and abominable hypocrites of the *Post* would do well to cast the beam out of their own eye before they pronounce sentence against people whose offences are but as a molehill to a mountain when compared with their own.

Right!

The *World* says—"Would that New Yorkers could be as proud of the Government of their country as they are of that of their State."

The time may come. The distance is not insurmountable between the executive mansion at Albany and the White House.

"Where Liberty Dwells, There is my Country."

If Lincoln's letter contains—as we presume it does—his real views on Government, we advise all men who are able to leave the United States, to do so, in case of his re-election, and seek a refuge in some country which can, at least, boast of a *limited* monarchy.

What is Democracy?

Judge Whitley, of Hoboken, N. J., in his paper called "The Circuit Judge," very properly defines democracy to be of two kinds, "professional and real," and then endeavors to show that true Democracy is ingrained Aquarianism, which must be at a low ebb in [illegible] Democracy is always real, but if [illegible] paragraph of the Judge's be true: [illegible] following

Aneas, finding works of art on the coast of Africa where his ship had been stranded, dismissed his fears. Civilization greeted him with her trophies. In Hoboken the evidences of civilization are a filthy, contracted, mean public school-house, with its open *cloacineas*, under the noses of the pupils—a reeking pound adjoining the Mayor's office—a Common Council schooling the people on Bishop Elder's Gospel in a back room. Great City!

Well, Hoboken *is* a great city, in the estimation of certain War Democrats who will endeavor to make money out of this administration by building batteries, &c., until "this cruel war is over;" but if it is as nasty a place as the Judge says it is, we may all cordially thank God! that we don't live there, and that War Democrats, who are worse than nigger worshippers, do.

Never too Late to Mend—The Voice of Wisdom!

The *Post* says:—

"Wisdom crieth in the wilderness, and no man regardeth."

Wisdom cried in that way a considerable time before she was regarded; but the late great Peace Meeting in this city demonstrates that her patience and perseverance in "crying in the wilderness" are beginning to be heard at last.

What is War doing for Us?

War, says the Daily N. Y. *News*, is the incubus under which the Republic now lies panting; It is a War that drains its life blood. It is War that empties its treasuries and oppresses it with inordinate taxation. It is War that takes tyranny by the hand, and invites it to companionship in this carnival of horrors. It is War that the Democracy has to deal with; and no other earthly issue can be dreamed of out of which to make even the phantom of an opposition. If the Democracy enter the campaign *upon* the War platform, and not *against* it, where will it find a political foe to strike at? If it is to be simply a struggle for the spoils or for supremacy, then let it be a steeple chase, and the best political hack will win the goal. But, if there is a principle to be contended for, what is it if not Peace?

Then let there be no timid shifting of position as the tide of war runs hitherward or thitherward. The Democracy is too mighty to descend to a mere squabble upon unimportant questions. It must have a principle to fight for worthy of its own proportions. It must strike at a giant, not at a pigmy.

The Black Republicans cannot do otherwise than uphold the war. It is their only hope. The Democracy must oppose the war and Black Republicanism, for that opposition is the only hope of the country. The issue is already made. New York, Ohio, Illinois and Wisconsin have said it, and the true Democracy of the North will say Amen.

Black Republican Atrocity—The Evening Post on the War.

Because we have blockaded the ports of the Confederate States, in order, as the *Tribune* expresses it, that the men and women of the South may see their children famishing, and be unable to give them the food which they demand—because, on this account, the naval powers of that country must either destroy the prizes which they capture or let them go, the Abolition demons of the Evening *Post* recommend that the Southern towns and villages be given to the flames by way of of retaliation. This is another of the many evidences that this war is carried on by the party in power, not for the Union, but for revenge and the gratification of their own hellish instincts.

THE DAILY CITIZEN.

J. M. SWORDS,......Proprietor

VICKSBURG, MISS.

SATURDAY, JUNE 27, 1863.

GOOD NEWS.—We devote a large portion of our space this morning to the news regarding our Virginia army. It is enough to cause every heart to swell with pride, and send a thrill of joy through every vein; yet we are satisfied "the half is not told." Let all read it attentively.

Northern dispatches say our troops have evacuated Monticello and are on their way to Knoxville, and that we admit we were whipped in the late fight with Kontz. Unfortunately, other of their journals have told a very different tale.

A Parrot shell, from the field, entered the house of a lady in our city early one morning last week, destroying a young lady's Sunday bonnet and some articles of clothing in her trunk. A wag hearing of the young lady's misfortune, remarked—"he thought the enemy were treating her with a great deal of *iron*-y and that she certainly had good grounds for demanding *re-dress*."

The Chicago Tribune has a dispatch from New Orleans via New York, 16th, which says Sherman was in a critical condition, having had his leg amputated. Also, that the hospitals at Baton Rouge are filled to overflowing with sick and wounded soldiers from Port Hudson, and it was feared the extreme heat may prove fatal to many. All the troops excepting three regiments have been withdrawn from the Teche country and sent to Port Hudson.

THE GRAND FEAUX PAS.—It has been generally known by our citizens and soldiers that for some time past Grant has had his poor dolts at work undermining the works on our left. On Thursday afternoon, having carried their operations to a sufficient extent and mined the works, the train was fired. The result was that our works were blown up, leaving a small gap, at which the enemy made a charge, but were gallantly repulsed with heavy loss. With the explosion of this mine a simultaneous attack was made on nearly the whole line, which was nobly repulsed, to the slaughter of scores of the Yanks. By this time the enemy should be satisfied that our works are not to be captured by their utmost efforts.

Some five hundred Copperheads held a meeting in Montgomery county, Indiana, on the 13th, and passed a resolution declaring that no enrollment of the militia of that county should take place. They appointed a committee, who waited upon the Commissioner, read him the resolution, and notified him in person that in attempting to make the enrollment he must do so at his peril.

A dispatch from Indianapolis, dated the 16th, says some fifty armed Copperheads attacked the house of James Sill, an enrolling officer, near Fillmore, and attempted to get possession of his books and papers, but failed. This does not appear to be very encouraging to old Abe.

Porter, it appears, still labors under the erroneous impression that he will succeed in destroying our city and killing all within our defenses, judging from the quantity of shells he hurls over. On Thursday he kept his men busily engaged all day in loading and firing his mortars, and most of the night we were favored with a display of fire-works gratuitously. Yesterday he seemed to rest from the exertion of the previous day, and only afforded his men a little practice. The parrots seemed to be governed by the firing of the mortars, but were occasionally made to skedaddle by a shell from our guns. A party of riflemen have for the past two days been firing across the river, with a view to assist in exterminating the nest of rebels esconsed in the "Gibraltar of the South," but we can only inform him of one accident ensuing from such *sharpshooting*. We would be infinitely delighted to see a copy of the gallant Commodore's official dispatches to old Abe, that we might learn with what soft sodder that personage is gulled.

The Chicago Tribune, of the 17th, has the following dispatch:

An officer who has just arrived here from Libby Prison, at Richmond, says it is understood there that Col. Straight and his officers are to be handed over to the Governor of Georgia, to be tried for stealing. The Governor has called the attention of the Secretary of War to this matter, and no more rebel officers will be exchanged until these officers are released.

EUROPEAN NEWS.—The new steamship America, from Bremen the 24th, via Southampton the 27th, arrived this morning.

The Confederate loan fluctuated greatly on the news of Stonewall Jackson's death. Reports of a probable armistice, and of the prospect of European offers of mediation between the North and South are again revived in London. The Times says of Hooker's address:

"If this document were received without authentication, it might pass for a hoax, ridiculing the Federal commander, and his style."

A great meeting had been held at Sheffield for the recognition of the South, at which 10,000 persons were present. A resolution was passed to memorialize the Government.

The Times says Mason left London Tuesday for Paris. Increased strength was imparted to the rumors of the probability of French mediation. The Confederate loan advanced to par.

NEW PHASE OF THE WAR!

The Great Rebel Offensive Movement—Rumored Battle at Bull Run—A Very Alarming Prospect—The Raid into Pennsylvania—The Rebels Nearing Harrisburg—What is Doing at Philadelphia—Extensive Measure to Repel Invasion—General Items of the Situation!

From the Chicago Tribune, of the 17th.]

JOHNSTOWN, PA., June 16, 1863.

The excitement all along the lines of the Pennsylvania Railroad is increasing. The Governor has issued a proclamation calling out the State militia, and ordering the posting of copies of the proclamation at all the postoffices and public places. The call is responded to with much enthusiasm—the country for miles all along the track appears deserted, except by women and children, most of the men having responded to the call.

According to the latest accounts received, it appears that Harrisburg has not yet fallen into the hands of the rebels, notwithstanding the report to the contrary; neither is it confirmed that the railroad track in that vicinity has been torn up.

Pittsburg was in a state of the most intense excitement, business being suspended, and the citizens join in the preparations for defense. It was reported in that city that Harrisburg was burning, having been fired by the rebels, but this also likes confirmation.

The three o'clock train from Philadelphia was delayed some hours by the breaking down of a freight train.

HARRISBURG, June 16—1 P. M.

The operator at London, Franklin county, reports that our pickets captured a rebel, who says the enemy are in full force at Cumberland Valley.

The Bedford operator reports 6000 rebel cavalry in Cumberland. There was no Union troops there. The citizens are flying.

NEW YORK, June 16.

A Baltimore dispatch to the Philadelphia Inquirer states: All is safe at Harper's Ferry, and Milroy has reached there. The place will be held.

The Baltimore correspondent of the Inquirer, dated 5 P. M., 15th, says: I learn from high authority that a battle has been progressing today on the old Bull Run battle ground, between Lee and Hooker, the latter doing good service.

The train from Baltimore, on Monday, went only to Ellicott Mills. The rebels are also reported in force at Point of Rocks.

The Harrisburg banks have removed all their specie and valuable papers to Philadelphia.

The Democratic Convention will not assemble here to-morrow. A number of Western delegates refused to come further than Altoona, and returned home. Hundreds of persons have arrived from the south side of the river, bring in all their horses, cattle and other valuables. Working parties are engaged in preparing the works and defenses on the opposite side of the river. A good resistance could be made, if troops were here to man the guns. Government officials expect the arrival of the rebels to-night or to-morrow.

If they reach here so soon, there will be little prospect of a successful defense, but if delayed, thousands will reach here within twenty-four hours, as the country is thoroughly aroused.

At a meeting last evening, Gen. Cameron blamed the Government for not sending men to aid in the defense of the Capital, when Pennsylvania had so liberally contributed men and money for carrying on the war. He said that while he had every confidence in the President and the commander of the department. Such men as McClellan or Franklin, whose leadership the people had every confidence in, would rally to their standard every loyal man. He called upon the Government to send for Gen. McClellan to take charge of the militia of the State. Every train from the East is packed with refugees and goods belonging to merchants.

HARRISBURG, PA., June 16—1 A. M.

Everything is gloomy here. The indications are that the rebels will be in sight of here by to-morrow. In the absence of troops to stop the advance of the rebels, the destruction of all the bridges on the Susquehannah is inevitable.

As fast as troops reach here they are sent to the different fords on the river, where works are being constructed.

The attempt to get troops from Washington has failed, and all the energies of the State must be directed toward arresting the progress of the rebels. There is no hope of saving the country south of the Susquehannah.

PHILADELPHIA, June 15.

The business of this city is mostly suspended. Reports from Harrisburg state that the rebels are at Carlisle, only eighteen miles from Harrisburg,

The mayor has issued a proclamation, in view of the urgent necessity of instant action, to protect the Capital, urging the closing of stores, and citizens to connect themselves with existing military organizations for the defense of the city.

The rebels are said to have appeared in full force at Point of Rocks.

A Harrisburg dispatch, dated 2 o'clock this morning, states that all the important documents at the Capital are being removed to a place of safety, in case evacuation is necessary.

HARRISBURG, June 16.

The Pennsylvania Railroad Company received a dispatch stating that the rebels were within nine miles of Carlisle at noon to-day. The station house bell of this city will be rung this evening to call the people to arms. The public are awakening to a sense of the crisis.

ALBANY, June 16.

Gen. McClellan is in Albany, for the purpose of aiding Gov. Seymour in organizing and sending forward troops for the defense of Pennsylvania. About 14,000 are already secured, and they are beginning to go forward. The following additional regiments are under orders to move: 8th, 22d, 56th, 30th and 34th. The volunteer regiments who are here to be mustered out offer their services.

NEW YORK, June 16.

A special Harrisburg dispatch to the World says Hooker is threatened at Warrenton by the main rebel army, supposed to be 60,000 strong, under Lee, in person.

The forces in Maryland and Pennsylvania is estated by Gen. Schenck at 40,000.

At a meeting held yesterday, Gen. Cameron pledged his whole fortune in defense of Pennsylvania, and called upon the Governor to appoint Gen. McClellan or Gen. Franklin commander-in-chief of the Pennsylvania forces.

At Pittsburg all the factories have stopped, and all hands are engaged in throwing up entrenchments.

All the archieves of the State and the speci of the Harrisburg banks have been removed for safety. The inhabitants are preparing in great numbers to leave.

PHILADELPHIA, June 16.

A letter from Harrisburg, dated 1 o'clock, P. M., says a train of one hundred wagons, which left Martinsburg on Saturday, arrived safe.

The rebel advance this morning was five miles east of Chambersburg.

Col. Smith, commanding at Hoganstown, had a fight of an hour and a half, yesterday, when he was surrounded and compelled to surrender.

WASHINGTON, June 16.

It is officially known here that up to this hour the rebels have made no attack on Harper's Ferry. The enemy are in considerable force at Charlestown, eight miles from Harper's Ferry.

A Suffolk, Va., correspondent states that Gen. Corcoran, with 12,000 men, left there on the 13th, in the direction of Blackwater. The rebel Gen. Jenkins is at Franklin, with quite a force, and it is surmised that our troops are destined thither.

All our militia regiments are getting under arms at the city armories. The bells were rung at midnight in Brooklin, calling out minute men, and the regiments of that city assembled at 8 o'clock this morning.

The Baltimore American, of this morning, says: The most reliable information we have been able to obtain is to the following effect: An attack was made on Sunday morning on a small force of our men, at Berryville, Va., under Gen. McReynolds, of which the 1st Maryland battery formed a part. They fell back before superior numbers, and joined Gen. Milroy at Winchester, after a sharp engagement, of which the results are unknown. At the same time Winchester was attacked in front from the South, by a force reported to be under the command of Ewell, the successor of Stone wall Jackson. The troops that made the attack at Berryville are reported to be under the command of Gen. Trimble. A third force, after this encounter, are said to have captured a detachment of our men at Bunker Hill. At 4 o'clock yesterday they demanded the surrender of Martinsburg, giving forty minunes for the women and children to leave town. Gen. Tyler, who commanded at Martinsburg, refused to surrender, and an artillery fight ensued. At 7 o'clock last night the wires were broke between Harper's Ferry and Martinsburg, and what occurred after that is not known.

A battle was also in progress at Winchester yesterday. Result unknown.

Gen. Milroy repulsed Ewell on Saturday, and said he could hold out until reinforcements reached him. If unable to sustain his position he would fall back on the line to Romny, as the Harper's Ferry and Martinsburg roads are held by the enemy.

The estimates of the rebel force in the Valley are so wide apart that they form no reliable data for any conclusion.

No damage was done to the Baltimore and Ohio railroad as far as known. No cars on locomotives on the lines are exposed to capture. Orders were sent to exposed fronts yesterday, and no less than seventy locomotives and 1200 cars were brought to Baltimore in safety. As a precautionary measure, no trains will run beyond Harper's Ferry for the present,

NEW YORK, June 16.

It is understood that Gen Hooker left the station near Falmouth on the morning of the 14th, and proceeded toward Dumphries, where they were to rest for the night. Early on Monday morning they proceeded on the road to Fairfax Station, where they probably arrived on Monday night. Previous to the departure of Gen. Hooker, the 6th army corps, which lay on both sides of the river, below Fredericksburg, proceeded northward and reached the vicinity of Dumphries on Sunday night. Bell Plains and Aquia Creek were evacuated, and all public property shipped or otherwise secured. The effects destroyed were such as were not worth removal.

Up to Monday morning our army held the line of the Rappahannock from Bank's to Kelly's fords, the river being protected by sufficient troops to hold the enemy at bay, should they attempt to cross the river below.

On Sunday evening cannonading was heard in the direction of Thoroughfare Gap. It was thought to be an effort of the rebels to cross in force.

It is ascertained that the main portion of the army of the Potomac have retired from the lines of the Rappahannock—a movement rendered necessary by that of the enemy. All the wounded and sick—a large number—have been brought away and transported to hospitals in the vicinity of Washington.

The exact whereabouts of Gen. Lee is supposed to be near or at Thoroughfare Gap.

ALBANY, N. Y., June 16.

The 7th, 11th, 13th, 28th, 37th, 47th, 65th, 67th, 68th, 69th, 71st and 74th regiments are under marching orders. The 91st and 74th leave to-night.

Marching orders have also been issued to 1500 volunteers at New York, 800 at Rochester and 500 at Pittsburg.

BALTIMORE, June 16.

There is much excitement here, and there is many rumors of rebel cavalry being seen at various points within twenty or thirty miles of this city. Several of the old military organizations of Baltimore will be revived immediately and their ranks filled up by volunteers. There are many military movements in progress and rumors of others, but they cannot be mentioned.

Gov. Bradford has issued a proclamation calling upon the citizens of Baltimore and people of Maryland to rally to the defend their homes from invasion. As there is no organized militia force in the State, he announces that he will fall back upon the recent enrollment for a draft, but he hopes there is patriotism sufficient among our people to raise the forces needed, from voluntary enlistment. The Governor urges immediate action.

There is no later news from the upper Potomac. The city council were convened last night at 12 o'clock, and met this morning, to devise ways and means to co-operate with the Governor of the State and commanding General of the department, to raise the city's portion of the 10,000 men called for to repel the invasion.

NEW YORK, June 16.

The Express prints the following as a letter from Washington: Gen. Hooker retreated from Falmouth to Warrenton Station to intercept Lee, who was advancing on Washington. Lee passed down through Thoroughfare Gap, flanking Hooker, and cut off an entire army corps, (name not given,) which is supposed to be captured. Lee is driving Hooker—the latter retreating to Alexandria. Hooker burned a large portion of his tents, provisions, &c., at almost. A large part of Milroy's division captured, including the whole of his regiments at Berryville, with an entire battery. Milroy lost all his cannon, wagons, &c. The remnant of his forces reached Harper's Ferry in safety.

The Post prints Washington specials as follows: Persons from the front this morning report all quiet. No signs of the rebels this side of Culpepper. Our army is in a new position, thoroughly re organized and full of confidence. No signs of the enemy on the Potomac between here and Harper's Ferry.

WASHINGTON, June 16.

The following official dispatch from Gen. Milroy has been received, dated Harper's Ferry, 16th:

I am in with the greater part of my command. The fortifications at Winchester were invested by about 15,000 rebels and twenty pieces of artillery. They carried my outer works by storm, at 3 o'clock on Sunday morning.

I spiked all my guns on Sunday evening, and left with the whole of my command at 1 oclock on Monday morning, bringing all the horses of my artillery and wagons, but was intercepted by an overwhelming rebel force with artillery, four miles this side of Winchester, on the Winchester road, and after a desperate fight of two hours I got through.

We were pursued by a large cavalry force, which picked up a large number of my weary boys.

I think my loss will not exceed 2,000 in killed, wounded and missing.

News Summary.

Gen. Jackson's war horse has been sent to Charlotte, N. C.

They have commenced cutting wheat in Alabama. The yield is abundant, and free from rust.

Preparations are being made to put a nail and tack factory into operation at Columbus, Ga. This is an enterprise that should meet with the most liberal encouragement from capitalists.

A young "rebel," named Compton, arrested as a spy, was to be hanged at Fort McHenry on the 22d ult. Lincoln, however, pardoned him.

Pork is selling in Macon at from 50 to 60 cents per pound; beef at the same rate; butter at $1.25; lard at $1; flour at $50 per barrel.

We are glad to learn that the damage to the paper mill of J. W. Grady & Co., near Greensville, S. C., is not as serious as at first supposed, and the mill will be in running order again in sixty days.

A gentleman writing from Sheltonville, Ga., says that the wheat crop is fine in that section. Everything premises a very large crop. A great breadth of land has been sown. Harvesting will commence in a few weeks.

A dispatch to Samuel G. Jones, Superintendent of the Alabama and Florida Railroad, states that no lives were lost by the precipitation of the cars into the Perdido river on Sunday. The telegraph operator at Tensas had a leg broken, and several negroes were quite severely bruised, but beyond this there were no further casualties.

The latest edict of fashion in Paris declares that all elegant dames ought to wear the hair in the form of a *cortogan* descending to the waist, bound in the middle with pink, blue and green ribbons, and curled at the extremity in five of those long curls which are called "cork-screws."

There is no doubt of the total failure of the Yankee iron-clad frigate, Roanoke, which was built especially for the protection of New York harbor. A New York letter says that "until she is again remoddled and rebuilt it is a question with the mechanics and engineers, whether she is in a condition to protect herself, much less the harbor."

Last Tuesday there was a large meeting of Louisianians at the Richmond capitol for the purpose of devising means for the relief of the New Orleans exiles. The committee appointed to receive contributions is as follows: Messrs. C. M. Conrad, Wyndham Robertson, T. J. Semmes, S. J. Harrison, John Freeland, T. L. Payne, E. A. Palfrey and Duncan F. Kenner.

The storm in which the steamer Soler was wrecked prevailed with great fury all along the Florida coast. It commenced on the 26th ult., but was felt most on the 28th. At Newport and St. Marks the river rose to a great hight. In the streets the water water was four feet deep. The saltmakers on the coast had to fly. All the furnaces, tents, boilers, &c., were blown away. Forty thousand bushels of salt were destroyed. Six whites and seven negroes lost their lives. Among the salt-makers thirty-five mules and eight oxen were drowned.

Chimneys, roofs, and everything assailable by wind and water suffered terribly.

The Columbus Times very justly complains of the regular commercial intercourse that has been carried on overland with the enemy during the war, and insists that the participants on this side of the line be visited with the public indignation. It is impolitic for the citizens of the two countries to commingle in private intercourse, and we may add, it is impossible without some concussion on the part of traders that involves their fidelity to their government. We have no doubt these itinerant gentry are as good Yankees on the other side of the line as they are Southerners on this side. Else, how can it be explained that they are allowed to pass unmolested over the borders of the enemy?

HOOKER'S DEFEAT IN FRANCE AND ENGLAND. The secesh sympathizers in London and Paris, when the last mail left, were very jubilant over the news of Hooker's retreat. But for that retreat we have an assurance, from loyal Americans, residents in London, that the pro-rebel demonstration at Sheffield would never have taken place. A letter from an eminent American in Liverpool, now before me, closes in this wise: "Do not be deceived by the present apparent indisposition on the part of England and France to interfere in the war for the Union; that indisposition will be superseded by positive action, unless success crowns our arms, and unless the people of the loyal States maintain a solid front in favor of pushing the war with unintermitted vigor. There are ugly rumors revived again respecting the intentions of the French Emperor. Certain it is Mason left London day before yesterday, in a very great hurry, for Paris, and as the rebel clique here affect to be very jubilant over something, the supposition is that Slidell has been communicating to them some good news. In a day or two more we shall probably know what it is."—*Northern paper.*

THE NEW YORK HERALD.

WHOLE NO. 9784. NEW YORK, MONDAY, JUNE 29, 1863. PRICE THREE CENT

THE IMPENDING BATTLE.

Active Movements of the Rebels.

IMPORTANT MILITARY CHANGE.

General Hooker Relieved of the Command of the Army of the Potomac.

General Meade Appointed His Successor.

Addresses of Generals Hooker and Meade.

SKETCH OF THE NEW COMMANDER.

The Whole of Lee's Rebel Army in Pennsylvania.

SKIRMISHING ALL ALONG THE LINES.

The Rebels in York and Mechanicsburg.

The Splendid Bridge Over the Susquehanna at Columbia in Flames.

Wrightsville Shelled by the Rebels.

The Great Battle Expected To-day.

THE INSECURITY OF RICHMOND.

The Citizens Leaving for Staunton, Virginia, &c., &c., &c.

THE FIELD OF OPERATIONS IN PENNSYLVANIA.

Scene of the Impending Battle Near Harrisburg---The Railroad Lines and Strategical Points.

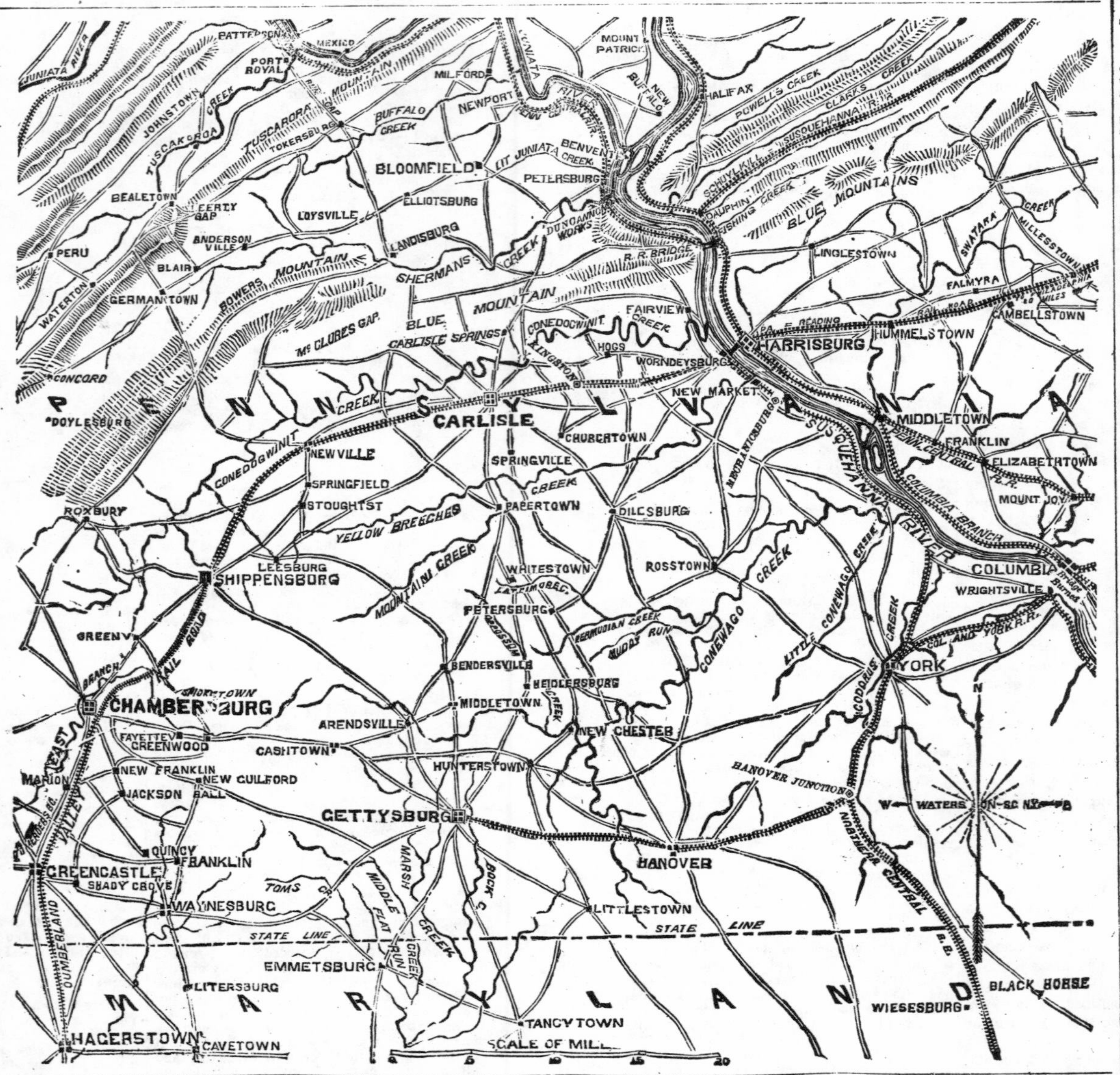

IMPORTANT MILITARY CHANGE.

General Hooker Relieved and General Meade Appointed to the Command of the Army of the Potomac.

WASHINGTON, June 28—10:20 P. M.

The following is from your special correspondent, dated Frederick, June 28:—

General Hooker was this morning relieved of the command of the Army of the Potomac. General Meade succeeds him. General Hooker is relieved at his own request.

General Hooker leaves this afternoon for Baltimore.

It is reported that the rebels are in occupation of York and Hanover Junction, on the Northern Central Railroad. Lee's headquarters were yesterday at Hagerstown. Longstreet's corps crossed yesterday at Williamsport.

Everything is working well with us.

HEADQUARTERS, ARMY OF THE POTOMAC, June 28, 1863.

This morning Colonel Hardie arrived here by special train from Washington, as a bearer of despatches, relieving General Hooker from the command of the Army of the Potomac, and appointing Major General Meade, commanding the Fifth corps, his successor. Soon after the reception of the orders at headquarters, General Hooker issued the following address:—

FAREWELL ADDRESS OF GENERAL HOOKER.

GENERAL ORDER—NO. 65.

HEADQUARTERS, ARMY OF THE POTOMAC, FREDERICK, Md., June 28, 1863.

In conformity with the orders of the War Department, dated June 27, 1863, I relinquish the command of the Army of the Potomac. It is transferred to Major General George G. Meade, a brave and accomplished officer, who has nobly earned the confidence and esteem of the army on many a well fought field. Impressed with the belief that my usefulness as the commander of the Army of the Potomac is impaired, I part from it, yet not without the deepest emotion. The sorrow of parting with the comrades of so many battles is relieved by the conviction that the courage and devotion of this army will never cease nor fail; that it will yield to my successor, as it has to me, a willing and hearty support. With the earnest prayer that the triumph of its arms may bring successes worthy of it and the nation, I bid it farewell.

JOSEPH HOOKER, Major General.

S. F. BARSTOW, Acting Adjutant General.

ADDRESS OF GENERAL MEADE ON TAKING COMMAND OF THE ARMY OF THE POTOMAC.

This order was followed by the subjoined address from General Meade:—

GENERAL ORDER—NO. 66.

HEADQUARTERS, ARMY OF THE POTOMAC, June 28, 1863.

By direction of the President of the United States, I hereby assume command of the Army of the Potomac. As a soldier, in obeying this order, an order totally unexpected and unsolicited, I have no promises or pledges to make. The country looks to this army to relieve it from the devastation and disgrace of a hostile invasion. Whatever fatigues and sacrifices we may be called upon to undergo, let us have in view constantly the magnitude of the interests involved, and let each man determine to do his duty, leaving to an all controlling Providence the decision of the contest. It is with just diffidence that I relieve in the command of this army an eminent and accomplished soldier, whose name must ever appear conspicuous in the history of its achievements; but I rely upon the hearty support of my companions in arms to assist me in the discharge of the duties of the important trust which has been confided to me.

GEORGE G. MEADE, Major General Commanding.

S. F. BARSTOW, Assistant Adjutant General.

Nothing could have exceeded the surprise occasioned by this announcement. The first rumors of the change were scarcely credited, and it was not until the appearance of the farewell address of General Hooker that the report was generally believed.

The reasons for the change of commanders are yet unknown; it is believed, and indeed indicated in the brief remarks of General Hooker to his staff, that he had applied to General Halleck to be relieved from the command of the Army of the Potomac. We are yet in the dark, however, so far as the knowledge of General Hooker's reasons for making such an application are concerned, and can only await the development of events from headquarters.

The report of the change soon extended to the several corps, and their commanders hastened to bid farewell to the General. By three o'clock a large number of officers had assembled, and soon after General Hooker appeared in the avenue before his tent. Some time was spent in social intercourse, and to the last all formalities were dispensed with. The parting was painful to every one, particularly to those who had become endeared to the General by old associations; and not a few felt their eyes moisten as they took the parting hand.

General Hooker was deeply grieved. He had been identified with the Army of the Potomac, he said, since its organization, and had hoped to continue with it to the end. It was the best atmy of the country, worthy of the confidence of the nation, and could not fail of success in the approaching struggle. He spoke of his successor as a glorous soldier, and urged all to give him their earnest support.

At the conclusion of the lave taking the more prominent officers lingered at the general's tent, and spent the evening in reviewing the pleasant reminisences of the past, and the plans for the future campaign.

General Hooker leaves to morrow for Baltimore, to which place he has been ordered to report. His personal staff, including General Butterfield, will accompany him. The officers of the several Departments at Headquarters, will doubtless remain,

General Meade was totally surprised by the order appointing him Commander of the Army of the Potomac, and deeply felt the weight of responsibility resting upon him. His appointment gives universal satisfaction, and all express a determination to extend their heartiest cooperation.

Affairs on the Upper Potomac are reported quiet. The enemy has but a small force south of Hagerstown, and our forces remain in the undisturbed possession of South mountain.

A rebel cavalry force is reported to have crossed the Potomac below Edwards' Ferry, and captured a train of one hundred and fifty wagons. Captain Harry Page, assistant quartermaster at head quarters, had charge of the train, and is probably a prisoner. The mail wagon, with mails from head quarters, had left for Washington, but received timely information of the raid and returned.

This morning one of the wagons in the ammunition train blew up, but fortunately without doing any damage to the rest of the train.

General Pleasanton has been appointed major general, and placed in command of the cavalry forces.

General Stahel is ordered to report for duty with another command in Pennsylvania.

All quiet.

THE NEW COMMANDER.

MAJOR GENERAL GEORGE G. MEADE, THE NEW COMMANDER OF THE ARMY OF THE POTOMAC.

Major General George G. Meade, the new commander of the Army of the Potomac, was born in Spain, about the year 1815, of American parents. His father was at the time of his birth a very wealthy man, and was residing in Barcelona, Spain, where Captain Meade, now commanding the North Carolina, and the subject of our sketch, were born. The two boys were brought to this country; one was educated for the navy, which he entered in 1826, and the other for the army.

HIS ENTRANCE INTO WEST POINT, AND GRADUATES.

George G. Meade entered West Point Military Academy as an appointee from the State of Pennsylvania during September, 1831, and graduated on the 30th of June, 1835, standing number nineteen in his class, which has produced such men as Generals Morell, Naglee, Haupt, Patrick, Martindale, Roberts, and others, as well as Postmaster General Montgomery Blair, &c.

HE ENTERED THE ARMY AND RESIGNED.

He was appointed to the army from the District of Columbia and entered the service as brevet second lieutenant of the Third artillery on the first of July, 1835. He did not receive his full commission until December 31, 1835, when he was made a full second lieutenant. On the 26th of October, 1836, he resigned his connection with the United States Army and was engaged in private pursuits until 1842.

HE IS REAPPOINTED—MEXICO.

On the nineteenth day of May, 1842, he was reappointed to the United States military service as a second lieutenant of Topographical Engineers. In this capacity he joined the troops engaged in the Mexican war. At this time we find the names of his companions in the Topographical Engineer corps were Major Turnbull, Captains Wm. G. Williams, killed at Monterey; Geo. H. Hughes, John McClellan, Thos. B. Luinard, and Joseph E. Johnston (now a rebel General); First Lieutenants Wm. H. Emory (now General), Jacob E. Blake (killed in Mexico), L. Sitgreaves, W. H. Warner (killed by Indians), E. P. Scammon (now General), and C. N. Hager; Second Lieutenants John C. Fremont, J. D. Webster, Geo. Thorn, Martin L. Smith, John Pope (now General), Wm. B. Franklin (now General), and Wm. J. Peek.

HIS CONDUCT IN MEXICO—PROMOTION.

His conduct in Mexico was marked by determination and bravery, and at the battle of Palo Alto he was particularly distinguished, and so mentioned in the official reports. During the several conflicts of Montery, 21st, 22d and 23d days of September, 1846, he again became distinguished, and for his bravery was brevetted a first lieutenant to date, from September 23, 1846. This brevet was awarded in May, 1847.

During the month of August, 1851, he was promoted to a first lieutenancy of his corps, and on the 19th of May 1856, was further promoted to a captaincy, which rank he held at the breaking out of the rebellion.

THE REBELLION—BRIGADIER GENERAL.

When the rebellion broke out, and President Lincoln called for three hundred thousand volunteers, the Pennsylvania reserve corps was raised and placed under the charge of General McCall, as divison commander, and Generals Reynolds, Meade and Ord as brigade commanders. Each of these Brigade Commanders have nobly distinguished themselves during the present war, having all risen to a rank equal with a Marshal of France. General Meade was appointed a brigadier general of volunteers, with a commission to date from August 31, 1861. He was then placed in charge of the Second brigade of that division, and proceeded to organize it at Tennallytown, near the waters of the Potomac, and in this vicinity wintered during 1861-2.

THE ADVANCE OF THE ARMY.

When the Army of the Potomac began to move upon Manassas, during March, 1862, the division in which Gen. Meade served was attached to the First corps, then under General McDowell. With him they remained north of the Rappahannock until after the battle of Hanover Station, when they were added to the Army of the Potomac, occupying part of the right wing, with division headquarters in the vicinity of Mechanicsville.

MAJOR OF ENGINEERS—MECHANICSVILLE.

About this time—viz: June 18, 1862—he was promoted to a majority in the Engineer corps, which rank he still holds in the newly organized Engineer corps of the regular army.

On the 26th of June, 1862, he took part in the famous battle of Mechanicsville, where Gen. Stonewall Jackson made such a terrific dash upon Gen. McClellan's right wing, and Gens. McCall, Reynolds and others were taken prisoners. His noble conduct and bravery on this occasion were particularly noticed.

GAINES' MILL—BREVET.

The next day he was engaged under Gen. Fitz John Porter in the battle of Gaines' Mill, and was so distinguished that he was nominated for a brevet of lieutenant colonel for distinguished services during that battle. He also took part in some of the subsequent engagements of the seven days' fight.

NEW MARKET CROSS ROADS—WOUNDED.

At the battle of New Market Cross Roads he was severely wounded, but, under skilful treatment, he recovered, and almost immediately returned to the army, where he took command of the division until the return of Gens. McCall and Reynolds from captivity in Richmond.

THE MARYLAND CAMPAIGN.

When the rebels invaded Maryland and Pennsylvania, after the defeats of Gen. Pope's army, Gen. Reynolds, who had commanded the division, was then detached to organize the Pennsylvania militia, and Gen. Meade was placed in command of the division of Pennsylvania reserves. He led these troops during the eventful battles of South Mountain and Antietam, and when, at the latter battle, Gen. Hooker was wounded and had to leave the field, Gen. Meade for a short time had charge of the Ninth army corps, formerly under Gen. Reno.

FREDERICKSBURG.

After General Burnside had been placed in charge of the Army of the Potomac, General Reynolds, who formerly commanded the Pennsylvania reserves, after the retirement of General McCall, was ordered to command the whole of the First army corps, and General Meade was formally placed in command of the division of Pennsylvania reserves. At the battle of Fredericksburg, December 13, 1862, he greatly distinguished himself, and his division lost very heavily, the brigade commanders and several field officers being placed *hors du combat* during the attack on the rebel right. The whole loss of the division was 1,624, being the greatest division loss during the whole of that disastrous fight.

COMMANDER OF FIFTH ARMY CORPS.

On the 15th of December, 1862, two days after this eventful battle, he was ordered to command the Fifth army corps, formerly under General Fitz John Porter, and more recently under General Butterfield. To enable him properly to hold that position he was appointed by the President a

MAJOR GENERAL OF VOLUNTEERS,

and was regularly nominated to the United States Senate during January, 1863. The Senate making certain objections to the lists of appointees, it was revised, and General Meade's name again sent in by the President. During March, 1863, the Senate, in executive session, confirmed the appointment, and General Meade took his rank and commission as major general of United States Volunteers, from November 29, 1862, and assumed the command of the Fifth army corps.

UNDER GENERAL HOOKER.

When General Hooker assumed command of the Army of the Potomac, and reorganized the same, he still continued to retain General Meade as the commander of the Fifth army corps, General Butterfield having obtained a position on the staff of the commanding officer. In general orders, dated February 5, 1863, General Meade's name and command is specified accordingly.

THE ADVANCE UPON CHANCELLORSVILLE.

During the advance upon Chancellorsville General Meade's corps formed part of the right wing of Hooker's army. The corps started on its march on the 26th day of April, 1863, and arrived at Kelly's Ford on the 28th. The next day it crossed the Rappahannock by that ford and the Rapidan by Ely's Ford. It then pushed on to Chancellorsville, where it arrived on the 30th and engaged the skirmishers of the rebels, taking their rifle pits and temporary works.

CHANCELLORSVILLE.

During the fearful contests of May 2, 3 and 4 General Meade's corps played its part in the same noble manner that had characterized the troops under his special command since the commencement of the war. It bore its part manfully, and in the end covered the retreat of the whole of Hooker's army.

THE RECENT FORCED MARCH.

During the recent heavy forced march General Meade's troops bore up under the heated rays of nearly a tropical sun, and although other corps straggled and hung back, Meade's corps held its own.

THE FIGHT NEAR UPPERVILLE.

On Sunday, June 21, 1863, in the fight under General Pleasanton's orders, one of the brigades of Gen. Meade's corps took an active part and earned an undying fame. This brigade was commanded by Colonel Vincent, and belonged to the First division.

THE REGULARS.

Among other troops recently under General Meade's command were the regulars under General Sykes. The bravery and endurance with which these men have always acted has told well for the discipline and *esprit du corps* of the men under the command of General Meade.

PROMOTION TO COMMANDER OF THE ARMY OF THE POTOMAC.

Within the last few days General Meade has been placed at the head of "the finest army on the planet," and it is to be hoped that he will be more successful with the troops than was either General Burnside or General Hooker. The material that composes this army is perhaps the best in the whole world, and will do almost anything if properly led; and, judging by General Meade's antecedents, there is but little doubt they now will be.

THE IMPENDING BATTLE.

HARRISBURG, June 28, 1863.

The enemy is within four miles of our works, advancing.

The firing of the artillery is distinctly heard.

The troops are all in position awaiting the attack.

The authorities feel confident of their ability to repulse the rebels.

A battle will probably take place to-day.

The Pennsylvania railroad, so far, is safe.

HARRISBURG, June 28—1 P. M.

A conflict is now going on in this vicinity, and the cannonading can be heard here.

HARRISBURG, June 28, 1863.

Guns are heard. The enemy is at hand.

General Cameron has information that the rebels are twenty thousand strong at Carlisle, and have forty-eight pieces of artillery.

HARRISBURG, June 28.—6 P. M.

The rebels are within three miles, and are throwing shells.

Our troops are within the intrenchments, and will make a bold stand.

HARRISBURG, Pa., June 28, 1863.

We want men. Please give this despatch all publicity. Our fortifications only need good, able and experienced soldiers. Will they come forward? Pennsylvania is now responding largely. The citizens are generally recruiting and exhibiting a far better spirit as the danger seems to increase. The HERALD's influence is solicited in sending men forward. For God's sake, do it.

Transportation will be provided me to our front, and you will have all the late telegrams until my return.

Gen. W. F. Smith is in command west of the Susquehanna, under Gen. Couch. Gen. Knipe will aid him.

General Knipe will put our forces in the fortifications opposite here.

Colonel McClure informs me that General Johnson's division followed General Rhode's division into Chambersburg on Wednesday. He remained there until Friday morning, when they moved towards Shippensburg. They made a formal demand, specifying what they wanted, and were particularly desirous to have a supply of leather. On Friday they moved towards Shippensburg.

Colonel Kennedy estimates their numbers at eight thousand and ten thousand in each division.

The rebels have not crossed Sterrett's Gap as yet.

Michael Dowling was taken prisoner by a party of seven or eight hundred strong, two or three miles outside of Gettysburg, on the Chambersburg pike, and was paroled on Friday afternoon. The rebels said they were going to Baltimore and Harrisburg.

Two others on the outer picket saw rebel cavalry in the distance. The women waved their handkerchiefs, and the "rebs" came and took them. The rebels said they had two thousand cavalry and twelve to fifteen thousand infantry.

The rebels respect private property at York, if not resisted, in accordance with their proclamation.

HARRISBURG, Pa., June 28, 1863.

Nearly every citizen has enrolled himself for immediate duty, at the county Court House, to assemble at the bell signal. Some are leaving with their families and relatives.

Although the anxiety is intense for the result of the present crisis, our people evince great good feeling, and are determined to make the best defence possible.

The enrolment of colored men in the county is vigorously going on. A good force will be raised in a few hours.

The rolling stock of various railroads have been s n East from this place for safety.

At different times during the day, when firing was heard, the people collected on Capitol and Prospect hills for the purpose of viewing the engagement, should it become general.

A gentleman belonging to this city rode out over the river this afternoon to visit some friends at Mechanicsburg, in a vehicle drawn by two splendid horses. He was arrested at that place by rebels, had his horses and buggy seized, and he was paroled and sent back to this city.

The Gray Reserves of Philadelphia have been sworn in, and are determined to do their best.

The best of order is preserved here. Lieutenant Patton, of the Philadelphia police force, has excellent arrangements. He has detailed officers to attend every depot, and his men, though eager to go to the front, are doing everything in their power to allay excitement and preserve order, and when the enemy comes to meet him.

It looks to me as if the bridge burning now was the Codorus bridge on the Northern Central Railroad.

HARRISBURG, June 28, 1863.

The enemy have destroyed two bridges near York Haven, on the Northern Central Railroad.

From Charles C. Williams, a private of Colonel Jennings' Twenty-sixth Pennsylvania regiment, who was captured near Gettysburg, I get the following information:—

After the enemy took us prisoners we were conveyed to Gettysburg. 2,500 rebels passed through Gettysburg on Friday afternoon, and encamped on the road to York. Generals Gordon and Early were with these troops. The former made a speech, in the woods, to his men. After we were paroled and were on our way to Harrisburg, saw reinforcements going to the aforesaid, twenty-five hundred. They must have been a small division. They had a train of one hundred and fifty wagons with them, and behind the train were nearly one thousand stragglers.

HARRISBURG, June 28, 1863.

Our forces have slowly retired, and are now in and around the fortifications of Harrisburg. The enemy is advancing slowly, and in all probability will soon commence an attack. General Smith has made proper disposition of his troops.

Throughout the day men have been coming to the defence of the city, in response to the Governor's proclamation. Among the number are a great many contrabands They were all furnished with guns and ammunition and sent across the Susquehanna.

Captain Brisbane, Chief of Cavalry, who was on a reconnoissance this afternoon, reports the rebel scouts to have been within three miles of our pickets.

The reports from the direction of York are very conflicting. An extra train was run to Philadelphia at twelve o'clock, noon.

The enemy fired several shots rom a position west of Oyster Point this afternoon.

HARRISBURG, June 28, 1863.

When our troops fell back from Carlisle they left in the barracks equipments for one company of cavalry and one regiment of infantry, and twenty thousand rations, which have fallen into the hands of the enemy. There is a report that the barracks have been burned, but this needs confirmation.

The report of the capture of York last night was rather premature. In the afternoon, the Chief Burgess of the town, in company with some prominent citizens, hearing the rebels were coming, started out to meet them, to surrender the town.

They had to go seven miles before they met the advance. In the mean time the operator, believing the Chief Burgess had been captured, telegraphed that the rebels were coming into the town, and then left.

The Governor has information that the rebels are at Bainbridge, twelve miles above Columbia, with a pontoon train sufficiently large to construct a bridge.

The rebels, who drove our men from Sterrett's Gap yesterday, and then moved towards Duncannon, have returned to the gap.

No demonstration has been made on the Pennsylvania Railroad in that direction to-day, so far as is known.

Col. Wynkoop has been appointed by Gen. Couch, chief of cavalry in this department, Capt. Brisbin having been ordered to his regiment.

Troops under the new call are rapidly arriving. Two companies of colored troops, composed of citizens of this place, were armed to-day, and sent across the river

Colonel Jennings' regiment, which had the skirmish at Gettysburg, arrived here to-day. He lost about three hundred men in prisoners and stragglers. The officers were sent to Richmond and the men paroled. Some of the latter have arrived here.

HARRISBURG, June 28—Midnight.

It rests with the enemy when the fight shall open. Our forces in and out of Fort Washington are ready and in good spirits. At six o'clock P. M. Ewell's pickets were discovered only two or three miles off. General Couch and the Governor, with their assistants, have been busied night and day in perfecting arrangements for defence, and the prospect of success to our arms, in the event of a spirited engagement, is better this evening than any time before. The fight promises to be steadily contested by our volunteers. All of Knipe's command is now withdrawn to this neighborhood.

The inhabitants of Harrisburg are not disheartened. No panic as yet, nor prospect of any.

We cannot yet estimate accurately Ewell's strength.

The New York Seventy-first has seen great hardships, but is in good condition, having not lost a man nor a particle of equipage of any sort.

A great many ladies are determined to stay through all the trouble, no matter what may come. But little valuable property can fall into rebel hands should our troops be overpowered by superior numbers.

HARRISBURG, June 28—Midnight.

The artillery firing heard to-day was a skirmish between the enemy's advance and our outposts. No damage is known to have been done on either side. It occurred about five miles from here.

Our troops then fell back, and up to the present time the rebel advance is four miles from here.

The authorities expect an attack to-morrow.

The Governor has received notice of 25,000 men who have enlisted under the last call.

THE COLUMBIA BRIDGE OVER THE SUSQUEHANNA BURNED.

HARRISBURG, June 28.—8 P. M.

The bridge over the Susquehanna at Columbia is in flames.

OUR LANCASTER TELEGRAMS.

LANCASTER, Pa., June 28, 1863.

The great bridge over the Susquehanna near Columbia is at this moment in flames. The firmament is illuminated by it even at this distance. It was fired by our own people to prevent the enemy from crossing.

Two rebel companies of cavalry attacked four companies of the Twentieth Pennsylvania regiment last night below York, but were driven off, badly whipped. Our loss was insignificant.

There is no fighting at Harrisburg yet.

A skirmish occurred in Wrightsville, opposite Columbia, three hours ago. Colonel Frick's men fought the enemy in their rifle pits gallantly till surrounded

(CONTINUED ON FIFTH PAGE.)

THE DAILY CITIZEN.

J. M. SWORDS,......Proprietor

VICKSBURG, MISS.

TUESDAY, JUNE 30, 1863.

☞ Mike Donovan, an old and respected citizen of this place, had his arm frightfully lacerated by a shell which exploded in front of the Catholic Church on Sunday morning, while the early service of the day was progressing. A shell also entered and exploded in the sacred edifice, but miraculously injured no one.

☞ We are pained to announce the death of Brigadier-General Green, of Missouri, who was killed at the trenches on Saturday morning. Gen. Green had a dash of daring bravery, combined with cool courage and a generous heart, which made him almost an idol in the eyes of the of his command, and his death will be another item to the long account the Missouri boys have to settle with their foe.

☞ We regret to announce that last week the following ladies of our city were wounded, viz: Mrs. Major T. B. Reed, Mrs. C. W. Peters, Mrs. W. S. Hazzard, Mrs. W. H. Clements, Miss Lucy Rawlings and Miss Ellen Ganovan. Most of the ladies were severely though not dangerously injured, and it affords us pleasure to state that they are doing well. The wounds were all from fragments of shell and splinters, with the exception of Miss Rawlings, who was struck with a Minie ball.

☞ Grant's forces on Saturday made a considerable fuss, and for some time the opinion was entertained that a serious demonstration would be made on our lines; but the little good judgment they possess prevailed, and further than wasting considerable ammunition nothing was done. Sunday was a day of rest with them, and was quieter than any Sabbath since our city has been invested by the enemy. Yesterday was also extremely quiet, and we are led to the belief they are sick of their undertaking.

☞ We have good cause for believing that Porter was busily engaged on Saterday calculating the number of shell, and the expense it would cause his master, Abe, to make us succumb. Sunday he doubtless devoted to rendering orisons to his patron saint, the devil, for assistance in his laudible undertaking of slaughtering the rebels. We have not learned the result of his figuring or his appeals, but inasmuch as he only had time to pay us limited attention on both days, we naturally deduce that his task was exceedingly onerous. Yesterday we received but few missiles from the mortars, and even the parrot batteries threw few [illegible] at the city.

☞ Gen. Pemberton, in an address said to have been made to the soldiers within our lines, is reported to have stated that he would not surrender our city so long as there was a mule or dog left whereon the men could subsist. The *possibility* being that such animals will ultimately be brought into requisition as food, induced some of our officers, the other day, to try mule meat, and accordingly a couple of these animals were slaughtered, dressed and properly cooked, whereof a large company bountifully partook. We learn the flesh is not only very palatable, but decidedly preferable to the poor beef which has been dealt out to the soldiers for months past, and that a willingness was expressed among those who tried the meat to receive it as regular rations. We have not as yet learned of any one experimenting with the flesh of the canine species. The proprietor of the "Citizen" insinuates that the above officers omitted to extend the customary courtesy to the Press, and broadly asserts that mule meat would not "go bad."

☞ The Mobile Tribune is in receipt of the Mississippian of the 14th, from which it extracted the following news:

We learn from a gentleman direct from Natches that the Yankee gunboat Arizona is aground hard and fast at the head of Natchez Island, about five miles below the city. Communication with Natchez is interrupted.

Kirby Smith's Texas troops, under General Walker, dashed upon the enemy's wagon train opposite Vicksburg, on last Monday, and captured three hundred wagons, with their full complement of wagoners, provisions, &c.

Information was received here yesterday that General Jackson had captured the Big Black bridge, driving the Yankees away from it.

PANOLA, June 12.—Not an item in the Memphis Bulletin of the 12th. A gentlemen this moment from Memphis, informs me that Gen. Burnside had arrived at Memphis with two divisions.

The Provine Block is being filled. There is no more hospital room in Memphis for the wounded from Vicksburg.

There is no doubt of Marmaduke's defeating the Feds near Helena. His taking steamers is doubtful. Boats are continually passing to Vicksburg laden with troops. Reinforcements up to date are estimated by officers stationed on the river at twenty-two thousand.

McCullough destroyed three miles of the Memphis and Charleston railroad, between Germantown and Collierville, and demolished four miles of telegraph. A Yankee and a negro regiment still occupy LaGrange. Hurlburt has given ten days' grace on oath order in Memphis.

The catalogue of the University of North Carolina, shows that there are but seventy-one students in attendance the present session.

The Copperheads in Council.

THE GREAT SPRINGFIELD MEETING

[Special dispatch to the Chicago Tribune.]

SPRINGFIELD, June 16.

The Copperheads are arriving from all quarters, but not yet in such numbers as was anticipated. The leaders attribute this to the hot weather, and are preparing in advance, for a failure, as regards numbers. I believe, however, it has been determined to set the figures at 100,000. There has been quite a contest as to Chairman. The names of Judge Constable, Dick Richardson, John Moore, Gen. Singleton, Sam Marshall, O'Melveny, and Mayor Sherman, of Chicago, have been severally pressed by their friends. Constable was finally agreed upon, but it turned out he would not be here, and he was withdrawn. The friends of Marshall and O'Melveny demand one or the other, as a representative of the untiring Democracy of Egypt, but I learn that, on account of the rivalry, all will be set aside and a man selected, according to the ancient usages of the party.

The resolutions agreed upon, so far, contain but three points, viz: Freedom of speech, freedom of the press, and freedom of the ballot box. The influential leaders desire to pass only these, but it is feared by them that the masses will demand armistice and peace resolutions. The rank and file are ahead of the leaders on this subject. They fear the conscription and the taxes.

All day to-day the leaders are engaged in endeavoring to restrain the masses. They may be seen manipulating the heads of the masses in all directions. The leaders also fear that the rank and file will come in to-morrow with secession flags. Indeed, it is stated that they will place secession flags upon the State House and Governor's Mansion. The leaders want to avoid any display which would give their meeting a disloyal aspect.

The invasion of Pennsylvania and Lee's advance on Washington, are having a bad effect upon the tone of the meeting. It does appear out of character to see a meeting of dastardly peace and concession Copperheads held in the Capital of one of the great States, while that of another is probably being sacked by the public enemy, who is also menacing the Capital of the country. Oh, Democracy, blush for thy degenerated sons.

Gov. Seymour has sent on for the reporter of the New York World to take down his speech, but he cannot now come. He would be here were it not for the alarming state of things at the East. Dick Merrick is here. He is opposed to giving a man or a dollar more for the war, and says the only thing we can now do is to look to the Northwest.

He and Gen. Singleton had a discussion in the street to-day, the General taking ground in favor of the prosecution of the war. I have heard Democrats argue in favor of withdrawing the troops to the free States and not allowing Lincoln another soldier, except to defend the border. Look out for a contest to-morrow between the immediate peace and the war Democrats; but the leaders are working hard to calm the troubled waters.

The Register of this morning contains a very violent article against the administration.

There are from 1000 to 1500 strangers in and about the place already—not more. All the crowds so far are reported. There are trains of wagons from various counties reported, but I have yet to see the first make its appearance. Some Democrats have got up the story that Gov. Yates has left town, but this is not so. He is the last man to leave.

OBITUARY.

COL. EUGENE ERWIN.

Another brave and noble spirit has fallen. On Thursday evening, June 25th, Col. EUGENE ERWIN, of the 6th Regiment Missouri Vols., was killed while mounted upon the works with a view to leading a charge against the enemy. He was struck with a minnie ball, which passed through his body, killing him instantly.

For several weeks previous to his death his health had been delicate, and at times compelled his absence from the field. During the siege of this place he had more than once been driven to his bed; and on the day of his death he was out contrary to the advice and urgency of his friends, feeling, as he said, that it was his duty, so long as he could stand, to stand at his post. No one felt more than he did the importance of every man's discharging his duty—no one did more to discharge it.

Col. ERWIN, at the first outbreak of the war, left his home and family and offered himself a willing sacrifice upon the altar of his country's liberty. He has borne the privations and hardships of the army throughout the campaigns of Gen. Price in Missouri, Arkansas and Mississippi, and that without a murmur. He has ever shown himself an excellent soldier and a gallant officer. More than a half dozen battlefields—Elk Horn, Corinth and Port Gibson included—bear testimony to his coolness and daring bravery. He was strict in discipline, yet generous, kind and true, possessing the confidence and esteem of all his men and officers. He esteemed religion highly, and did all in his power to promote its interests. Those who knew him best loved him most; for the more intimate the acquaintance, the brighter shone the excellencies of his character.

But he has fallen—fallen at his post, defending the cause of justice and truth. At midnight's hour, amid the roar of cannon and the whistling of the enemy's balls, we bore him gently and laid him in the soldier's humble grave, where he shall rest in peace till he is called forth to his reward in the resurrection morn.

He by his example speaks—

"'Twere sweet to live, yet I can die,
And in the grave forgotten lie,
To know I have my duty done,
And nobly life's last triumph won.
Know ye my comrades in the field,
I die a freeman's death;
Cease not to wield the battle shield
With life's last lingering breath—
The banner which we bore on high,
Still bid it all their hosts defy—
For where the war tide wild shall wave,
So fit to be a soldier's grave."

He leaves a wife and three sweet little girls to mourn his loss. May our Heavenly Father sustain and comfort them in their sad bereavement, and grant them all a happy reunion in the Heavenly world, where sorrows and separations, wars and death are known no more.

W. M. PATTERSON,
Chaplain 6th Mo. Infantry.

VICKSBURG, MISS., June 26th, 1863.

GLORIOUS INTELLIGENCE!

Interesting News from Port Hudson—The Enemy Twenty-Five Times Repulsed—Late News from Grant's Lines—Former Advices Confirmed—Discontent of his Officers—Important from Port Hudson—Successful Sortie of the Garrison—The Enemy's Siege Guns Spiked—Despondency of the Enemy at New Orleans—Boat Loads of Wounded Arriving—Dash upon Jackson, La.—Prisoners, Horses, Arms, &c., Captured, &c., &c.

[Special dispatches to the Mobile News.]

JACKSON, June 17.—An escaped citizen-prisoner from Vicksburg by Memphis, confirms the reports of immense slaughter of the Federals. He says many officers wish to resign but can not.

The siege of Vicksburg and Port Hudson are in full blast.

OSYKA, June 16.—A desperate fight took place at Port Hudson on the 12th.

The Confederates left their entrenchments to charge the enemy, drove him from his fortifications and spiked his siege guns.

A citizen, a prisoner of Grierson, from New Orleans on Saturday evening, reports many regiments arriving from Baton Rouge. The Federals are despondent, believing they cannot take Port Hudson by assault.

Provisions are high and rising in New Orleans.

The river is very low. There is other cheering but contraband news.

The St. Charles hotel is filled with wounded from Port Hudson, brought by boatloads at night.

SUMMIT, June 17.—A courier from Logan states that Logan dashed into Jackson, La., on Monday, and captured a hundred Yankees of the 14th New York cavalry, twenty negroes with wagons and arms, and one hundred and twenty horses. A major and other officers are among the prisoners.

CHARLESTON, June 16.—The steamer Margaret and Jessie, from Nassau, arrived here this morning with an assorted cargo.

Fears are entertained of the capture of the steamer Calapso, which left Nassau for Charleston ten days ago.

The peace movement at the North begins to assume important proportions.

Fernando Wood's speech at the Peace Convention was the boldest yet. He declared the Union forever gone; denounced a further prosecution of the war as an impious resistance to the manifest will of Heaven; eulogized Vallandigham, and dared and defied the Administration to assign Burnside to the command of New York.

He announced his readiness to die resisting the Lincoln tyranny, and called on the people to avenge him if he fell.

The convention, numbered 30,000, was unified and determined in spirit, and adopted an address and resolutions of a similar defiant [illegible].

CULPEPPER, June 16.—Gen. Ewell, at the head of Stonewall Jackson's old command, took Winchester on Sunday, capturing many supplies and some prisoners.

PANOLA, June 16.—Burnside in person is not at Memphis. He sends Grant 20,000 troops, of which 5000 left Memphis Friday, the rest are at Cairo awaiting transportation.

The soldiers express an unwillingness to go to Vicksburg.

The Memphis Bulletin says 7000 persons have taken the oath of fealty, and 301 the foreign oath: six have taken the oath as enemies.

A Washington dispatch says the rebel Government have stopped exchanging prisoners in consequence of a violation of the cartel.

Eight transports have passed down for Vicksburg with troops and horses. Some of the troops are reported to be from Virginia.

Correspondents say Banks lost 4000 men. He says 1000, and that the negroes fought better than the whites.

RICHMOND, June 16.—There is no news of interest. The Governor of Ill., upon the pretext that the Legislature could not agree upon the time of adjournment, issued his proclamation adjourning them, and the Republican members had left. The Democrats, not having a quorum, were unable to transact any business, which caused intense excitement.

The Supreme Court of Indiana has decided that the interest on the State debt cannot be paid, as the Legislature has not made any appropriation to meet the same.

Gen. Curtis, late commanding the Department of Missouri, has gone to Iowa with Assistant Quartermaster Larkin.

The railroad companies of Pennsylvania are erecting defensive works to protect their bridges.

Farmers residing near posts where Quartermasters are now stationed, are required to deliver the Government portions of the crops of small grain, hay and clipped wool, for the present year, and take receipts for the quantity delivered in advance of the assessments.

RICHMOND, June 16.—A dispatch to the President from Gen. Lee, of the 15th, says: "God has again crowned the valor of our troops with success. Early's division stormed the enemy's entrenchments at Winchester, capturing their artillery, etc."

The New York Herald, of the 15th, is received. The Herald predicts that Lee will make a descent upon Winchester and Harper's Ferry, with an overwhelming force, and then move Stuart's whole column across Maryland into Pennsylvania upon a mission of plunder and destruction by way of retaliation.

The resolutions adopted by the Democratic Convention declared, among other things, that they will hail with delight a desire of the seceded States to return to their allegiance, and will co-operate with the citizens of those States to restore peace.

A New Orleans letter of the 5th says Sherman is much better. The probabilities are that not only his life but his leg will be saved.

The Siege of Vicksburg.

[Special dispatch to the Chicago Tribune.]

The United States hospital steamer D. A. January, and steamer L. M. Kennett, arrived to-day, direct from Young's Point. The news generally was anticipated. Upon two boats there were about nine hundred sick and wounded soldiers from Gen. Grant's army, mostly from Indiana, Illinois, Kentucky and Missouri. Twenty-one died on the way up from Memphis within the space of forty-eight hours. The bodies of these men were taken off here by Quartermaster Woolfolk, and interred in the soldiers' grave-yard. From commendable attentiveness, the employees in his office have each grave properly designated, and relatives coming for their remains can easily claim them.

MEMPHIS 14, via CAIRO, June 16, 1863.

Arrivals from below this morning bring official dispatches from Gen. Grant up to noon of June 11th. Reinforcements were arriving and taking up the positions assigned to them.

The movement of Kirby Smith's forces on the Louisiana side of the river are attracting attention. He will be closely watched. It is doubtful about his having the means of crossing the Mississippi, but the numerous bayous may possibly enable him to obtain means to make the attempt.

It is pretty well ascertained that the garrison at Vicksburg is on quarter rations of [illegible] and pea flour, and the supply of this is [illegible] very limited. Their fresh beef is all gone.

Gen. Walker is at Yazoo City, and Jackson with a division of cavalry, is said to have arrived from Bragg's army.

Gen. Grant is confident and hopeful. About 200 prisoners arrived in this city from Vicksburg this morning.

The steamer Belle Memphis will leave for St. Louis on Monday evening.

CAIRO, June 16.—News from Vicksburg to the evening of the 12th. No change in progress of the siege. Gen. Dennis, in command at Milliken's Bend, and been largely reinforced, and had started on an expedition to Richmond, La., to attack McCullough, who is reported to have nearly 6,000 troops.

Two hospital steamers arrived here to-day, having on board 550 sick soldiers, mostly from Indiana, Illinois and Iowa. They proceeded to Jefferson barracks. Thirty-seven died on the way up. Five were buried at Helena, nine at Memphis, and twenty-three at Cairo.

Over 600 condemned horses and mules arrived from below on two steamers.

HEADQUARTERS FOUR MILES IN THE REAR OF }
VICKSBURG, June 10, 1863. }

The siege is still prosecuted with more firing during the past two days. Several of their guns have been silenced by our batteries and sharpshooters.

Deserters say that the garrison is upon the point of mutiny, being desirous of fighting its way out to Johnston, to which the chief officers will not consent. All the previous reports of destitution are confirmed. The rebels occupy Sartartia and Yazoo City.

The rebels are communicating from the city to De Soto Point with their Louisiana allies.

Navigation on the Mississippi is becoming more hazardous.

No trouble has been experienced from Gen. Johnston. Predictions are [illegible] of Vicksburg.

CAIRO, June 16.—By the arrival of a steamer, we have news from Vicksburg to Friday afternoon. There is no change in the progress of the siege. Our scouts have been forty miles out in the country from the army, but found no rebels except small squads of cavalry. The country is entirely devastated for fifty miles, and judges say it is impossible for Johnston to move an army, with the transportation he could get, over the hills, and then carry supplies to them. The impression is, that he will not attempt it, and that Pemberton is abandoned to his fate.

Official figures of the battle at Milliken's Bend are as follows: Killed and wounded white men, 65; negroes, 180. Gen. Dennis, in command, has been reinforced, and was preparing to attack McCullough at Richmond, La. One hundred and thirty-seven rebel dead were left on the field, and their wounded fill the court-house at Richmond.

☞ From a perusal of the subjoined correspondence, the reader will perceive that some party or parties have been maligning our old friend and fellow-citizen, A. Genella. The charges are proved to be as base as the heart of the author of the calumny is cowardly and contemptible, and was doubtless concocted to cover the guilt of those engaged in the offence attributed to Mr. Genella:

VICKSBURG, June 29th, 1863.

General Taylor—Sir: As it is currently rumored and credited by soldiers and citizens that the commander of the post seized over two hundred (200) barrels of flour, concealed and held over by me, for speculation on the necessities of the people, I take the liberty to appeal to your office for a specific refutation of the charge.

By so doing you will enable me to refute a calumny, and preserve a reputation, I hope as yet unstained by any [illegible] which ought to [illegible] a good citizen, or a believing Christian.

Respectfully, your much obliged,
A. GENELLA.

HEADQUARTERS POST, }
VICKSBURG, June 29th, 1863 }

No flour has been seized from Mr. Genella, nor has Mr. Genella ever been suspicioned by the commander of the post of having concealed either flour or anything else. Neither has any flour been seized from any other citizen. By order of

Brig. Gen. TAYLOR.

C. MCRAE SELPH, A. A. G.

Mr. Editor: I desire simply to express to the public, through the medium of your paper, the grateful feelings of my heart toward that accomplished gentleman and skilful practitioner of medicine and surgery, Dr. P. B. Minor, for his assiduous attentions and urbane and obliging manners to myself and fellow-sufferers, sick and wounded, under his charge, as chief officer at Hospital No. 1, now removed to the Marine Hospital, which was vacated for him on account of the terrible shelling at No. 1 by the Yankee mortar boats. CONVALESCENT.

Vicksburg, June 29, 1863.

DENTISTRY.

DR. J. D. MILES is prepared to perform all operations pertaining to his profession. Office at his residence, near the old Grave Yard hill. [illegible]

T. E. GROVER, } Editors.
E. M. BACON. }

FOXBORO', MASS. JULY, 1863.

} Volume 1
} Number 7

For the Eagle and Flag.

COUSIN ADOLPHUS.

BY ONE WHO KNOWS HIM.

Cousin Adolphus was born and brought up in the city, and so was his wife, and so was I. Now, I do not speak of this as a marvel, for many people have been born and brought up there before, and probably will be again. I only mention it the better to illustrate the truth which our friend, the "Country Parson," endeavors to teach; namely, that there are different ways of "putting things." Cousin Adolphus, and his wife, and I, all put things differently, and these ways of *putting* have been shown more clearly since they removed to the country. Cousin Adolphus bought a small farm several summers ago, at first intending it only as a summer residence, but the trouble of moving caused him to change his mind before he was hardly settled, and they have since made it a permanent home. I spend much of the summer with them, and sometimes make a visit in the winter, if sleighing is good. I often call Cousin Dolph—Dolph is our family nickname for Adolphus—Mr. Sparrowgrass, though I own the comparison will not bear analysis. Mr. Sparrowgrass, poor man, did have misfortunes, but with Cousin Adolphus most things prosper, if he could only think so, but that is not his way of *putting* them.—His land is good, and generally yields well—remarkably so, I think, considering he is not a native born *countryman*. He is sometimes quite proud of his vegetables and fruits, but his enjoyment of them is spoiled by thinking how much time, labor and wages he has spent in raising them, and he always concludes he would rather have bought them in market. He keeps a cow aud two horses, but bewails his fate in being the proprietor of such troublesome property. He proves mathematically that bought milk and butter, and a hired hack daily, would save a small fortune in one year. Indeed, he seems to have a perfect spite against milk, but sometimes takes a glass on principle, and for economy he says, though to judge by his contortions of countenance he might be imbibing a dose of medicine of the vilest old school mixture. These same principles and economy, which induce him to drink milk, also compel him to partake of every thing he raises, however repugnant to his taste, so that he is truly a martyr to country life. He never would have bought a cow, but his wife had a present of a lovely calf, and out of courtesy to the giver, he consented to raise it. Many times he would fain have sold her but for his wife's entreaties. She "puts things" in a very different way, and as his family government is somewhat like that of the man who boasted of his obedient dog, they generally have their own way unless they *choose* to yield it. The dog-owner above referred to, to show the animal's ready obedience before some guests, ordered him to go out of doors; his repeated commands were only heeded by a deliberate rising and walking under the table. "Well, I meant, go under the table."—Now, I do not mean that Cousin Dolph's wife and daughter willfully disobey him, but then they know they can go under the table instead of outdoors if they choose.—This was the way about the cow, and the horses his wife convinced him they *could not* do without. He frequently threatens the substitution of a hired carriage and horses for their own, but the difficulty of communicating with the nearest livery-stable is not easily overcome. He lives about two miles from the city of B——, and as he *must* have the morning's mail, his little girl must go to school and home again, and "last but not least," Mrs. Dolph *must* do her more than daily shopping, he submits with the best grace he can. As I said, his wife "puts things" differently. To her no horses and carriages are like their own—no cow gives such milk—no milk makes such butter—no fruit nor vegetables are equal to theirs—no house is so convenient—no air so pure as that of Millville.

Though most things prosper with Cousin Dolph, truth forces me to admit he has some troubles; still their weight is chiefly owing to his way of putting things. His servants will trouble him at times. He had one man who would feed the horses till they could scarcely walk, and that when oats were at their highest; while some will not pick his green peas until they are yellow, and sweet corn until it is fit to mill. Still these things rarely happen, but when they do he sets them down as the staples of country life. There are circumstances that he cannot control; chickens will crow—birds will sing and cows will low.—Cousin Dolph does not love to rise with the lark, and one of his greatest troubles is being awakened at dawn by the "infernal robins" and "diabolical roosters."—He prides himself upon not being a profane man, but if it is not profanation to cast such epithets upon the feathered gentry I do not know what is. I did feel sorry for him one morn; he had calculated upon the extra half-hour's sleep in which he indulges once a week. But, alas! his hopes were early doomed to disappointment, for he was awakened at dawn by a noisy concourse beneath his window, and I by the creaking of boots on the stairs. (Dolph wears creaking boots from principle, because he lives in the country.) Being awakened, I heard a commotion outside, and after waiting for what appeared like an hour without its ceasing, curiosity drew me from bed, and to the window. There was Cousin Dolph, in what I suppose might be called *nocturnal dishabille*, by turns coaxing, driving and maneuvering to get the inhabitants of his poultry-yard back to their precincts. His new man had forgotten to shut them up at night, and the whole company, which is not a small one—for Cousin Dolph has been very successful with both chickens and turkeys—was on an early foraging expedition. I went back to bed, and was lulled to sleep by the same noises which so disturbed Cousin Dolph, and to which Mrs. Dolph was utterly oblivious. He returned to rest a few moments before the ringing of the first bell. Poor man!

Cousin Adolphus is fond of flowers, and so is Mrs. A.—to look at, but he spends much labor upon them, and *it is* trying to have the bantams scratch up your choicest seeds, or the dogs make a bed upon some rare plants. Both of these things sometimes happen, for the dogs cannot always be chained, and the bantams will occasionally get through the fence. It may not be evident why any one, even in the country, need keep more than one dog. Cousin grieves over the plurality of his, but knows not how to lessen their number. He thinks he must have one to guard the house, and one the barn, and the surplus number, which rarely overruns six, belong to Uncle Stephen.

I have said my story was designed merely to show our various ways of "putting things," but with a very commendable diffidence, have left myself till the last.

My way of putting things is quite different from either Cousin Dolph's or his wife's. I love the country, but do not feel so much interested in the "back garden where the cabbages grow," as in the flower-beds and the birds. I am nearly related to the old woman who so well exemplified the maxim of, "Every one to his notion." Her notion was to kiss her cow. Cousin Dolph ridi-

THE EAGLE AND FLAG.

Editors' Sanctum Sanctorum.

PETTY TRIBULATIONS.

It is a trite saying that the minor miseries of life are harder to be borne than its great calamities. Religion and philosophy arm us against the latter, but the former find us defenceless. Many a merchant endures the destruction of a warehouse, full of goods, by fire much better than he sustains an attack of the toothache. The sudden sting of a wasp on the calf of a warrior's leg starts from his propriety the man who could stand against "the world in arms."

Confess, if you are a bachelor, that you may be driven wild by a mistake in directing a couple of letters, through which you write to your laundress, "Nothing would be wanting to my happiness, dear Matilda, if you loved me as I love you; waves of glory and gold would flow at our feet; I should be richer, prouder, happier than a king." And to the woman you are courting; "Send me without fail my three false dickies and my two shirts for Sunday, as I am entirely out of clean linen." Confess, dear bachelor, that such a double barreled blunder, as soon as you had found out that you had committed it, would make you feel much more like hanging yourself than if you had lost a fast horse, and would be willing to subscribe to the immoral axiom of Talleyrand, "a blunder is worse than a crime."

OUR ARMY CORRESPONDENCE.

"*Camp Dale,*" *Carolina City, N. C.*
May 24, 1863.

MESSRS. EDITORS:

I have just been looking over your first five copies of the *Eagle & Flag* in which I found much to interest me. I have been carried back to the good old times which we have spent together in the old "English and Classical School." Great changes no doubt have taken place since then. I find by your paper that many of my old schoolmates are either married, buried or "gone to the wars." I think I should be a stranger in the school, if I should enter it at the present time. Before receiving your interesting little paper, I had heard that a "Roll of Honor" was published in the February number, but on looking at the "Roll" as published, I was very much disappointed in not finding the name of every one who had belonged to the school and was now in the Union army. I find only five names; my name (much to the displeasure of Asst. Surg. S. of the 26th M. V.) at the head of the "Roll." I would correct it.—At the time the paper was issued I was 2d Lieut. of Co. G., 23d Regt., Mass. Vols.—never was in Co. F. The old 23d, to which I have the honor of belonging, is not a M. V. M. Regt. but a *Massachusetts Volunteer Regiment;* much difference in them. The M. V. M's are out for nine months, the M. V's *are in for the war.* The Town did not have to drain her treasury to send the M. V's into the field. I would not lead you to think that the nine months troops are not good fighters, for the most of them are; we have seen much of them in this Department and in almost every case they have done *nobly*.

We had quite a lively time in Camp yesterday afternoon; thirty-five non. com. officers and privates left for their homes on a furlough of twenty-four days; they were happy boys I can assure you; who would not be, having been from home and friends for over eighteen months? They can tell much of what they have passed through and seen; as soon as they return, another "squad" will go. Corp. Hiram D. Skinner and private M. R. Hartshorn are to go to Foxboro'.

Our Regiment is now very pleasantly situated on the left bank of Bogue Sound, in full sight of Fort Macon and the broad ocean. We have a company doing picket duty directly opposite our camp, on what is called the "Spit;" we also have a picket boat in the center of the sound to stop all boats from passing up or down. I had a very pleasant sail on the sound yesterday.

A rattlesnake was brought into camp day before yesterday, which was *fifteen years old*, was four feet long, and his body was almost as large around as my arm; he was just upon the point of springing upon a grey rabbit when he was killed. Either a moccasin, copperhead (not such as you have in the North), whip snake, or some other kind of a snake is brought into camp every day; how would you like to live in such a country? Corp. Chadwick is all right, a better soldier is hard to be found.

As I have much to attend to, I will bring these few uninteresting lines to a close.—Go on and prosper my brothers in your useful work. From your old school-mate and most obedient servant,

J. L. SHERMAN,
Lt. & Act. Adjt., 23d M. V.

For the Eagle and Flag.

Look Out! He's Close-fisted.

Thats' what they say of a man who is more mindful of his money and the ways and means of making his property accumulate than of is good name. This world is full of such men who run against them at every turn of the road.

"He is a pretty good meaning man only he is close-fisted;" then look out for him, run away from him, give him a wide road, unless you wish to learn the art of close-fistedness.

Your close-fisted man will talk about the cruel war, how much valuable property it is sweeping away, and how poor it is making him, while if you look into his affairs you will find that the mighty hand of war has missed him—he has successfully "dodged the draft" upon his money purse.

He will moan at the rain because it will spoil his hay and he may not realize the sum that he had set his heart on receiving for it. He will grumble at the dry weather because it may spoil his crops and he lose a little cash by them; not giving one thought to the fact that it is the Father who causeth the rain to fall and the sun to shine and who doeth all things well. Not realizing that God can deprive him in an instant of all the wealth that he worships and of the life which he desires to prolong so as to enjoy his money. Enjoy! Is such a man happy? Is such a man light-hearted and cheerful, who is continually on the worry for fear that he cannot account for a single missing postage stamp? No! better to be desired is the life of the daily laborer than that of a miserly man.

Oh, I hate a close-fisted man! Let you and I steer clear of every and all such men, in our race in life, and let men never have the opportunity to say of us, as they point with the finger of scorn and contempt—"there goes a close-fisted man."

For the Eagle and Flag.

THE BOWER OF LOVE.

BY LEILA.

There's a fount and a tree where the wild bird in glee
Warbles his innocent lay;
There's a moss-covered seat in that wood-land retreat
Begemmed with the flowers of May.
The soft evening star shineth gently afar,
The pale moon looks down from above;
There the ever-green twines, and amorous vines
Encircle that bower of love.

I have sailed o'er the deep when the winds were asleep,
Have trodden the Alps 'neath my feet—
Beneath me the clouds with their silver-lined shrouds,
Above me the proud eagle's seat.
I have ravished the smiles of a thousand bright isles,
Yet oft, like a murmuring dove,
My spirit still sighs for the dark hazel eyes
That shone in the bower of love.

There's a fount and a tree where the spirit is free,
Where the vine wreaths fade never-more;
There earth's rovers may meet and in happiness sweet
Recount all their wanderings o'er.
There no traitor's foul breath, nor the chill blast of death
E'er sweeps through that peace-glade above,—
O grief comes no more to that ever-green shore,
That Elysian Bower of Love.

A young aspirant for fame, having a desire to see his name in print, sent his verses to a paper for publication. In the "pome" the following line occurred;—

A fragrant rose found near the pendant corn.

The compositor in whose hands the manuscript was placed was pretty well "set up," and evidently "set up" the line also, judging from the following, which greeted the astonished author the next morning;

A vagrant's nose sounds like the pedlar's horn.

MORAL.—Do not send carelessly written manuscript even to a *sober* printing office. Compositors have no time to guess at words or correct punctuation.

SATISFACTORY. Some think gold will sink to a very low value. Perhaps so; we may live to see gold eagles twenty-five cents a dozen.

THE PEASANT'S REPLY.

A man of subtle reasoning, asked
A peasant if he knew
Where was the internal evidence
That proved the Bible true?
The terms of disputative art
Had never reached his ear;
He laid his hand upon his heart,
And only answered, "Here!"

LOCAL.

Fatal Accident. A fatal accident occurred in this town on the 11th of June last, which resulted in the death of Minnie Kerr, daughter of Nathan G. and Elizabeth K. Brown of Brooklyn, N. Y. The little girl, who was about six years of age, was playing in the yard with other children who were lighting a bonfire. By some means the ignited shavings came in contact with the child's dress, and before the flames could be extinguished she was so seriously burned as to cause her death. Minnie survived the accident about five hours. The patient resignation with which she bore her sufferings, as well as the previous character and disposition of the child, suggested the following lines which a friend has handed us for publication.

"OF SUCH IS THE KINGDOM OF HEAVEN."

Another sweet spirit has fled from us
Unto God by whom it was given;
Oh, let us remember who said to us,
"Of such is the Kingdom of Heaven."

Chorus—
We could not forbid her to go,
Though with anguish our hearts were riven;
Rejoicing we weep, for we know,
"Of such is the Kingdom of Heaven."

Her life here was like that of the flowers
That blossom above her to-night,
And though clouded with sorrow is ours,
Her life evermore will be bright.
Chorus.

Although stricken hearts feel that they need her,
And long for her presence again,
Now we know the Good Shepherd will lead her
Away from all suffering and pain.
Chorus.

Unto each of us God has now spoken
"Be ready to go or to stay;"
Earthly ties though so tender are broken,
And we all are passing away.
Chorus.

Obituary.—Died, in Foxboro,' 5th ult. of Diptheria, Mr. John N. Carpenter, aged 31. He was a young man of irreproachable character; evincing in his business habits a strict integrity, and influenced in all the relations of life by principles the most pure and elevated. With a heart alive to generous and noble impulses, he was the friend of the sufferer, a guide to the erring, and the patron of human progress in all that is adapted to elevate the race. Without an enemy, he enjoyed the confidence and respect of all classes of our citizens, and died universally lamented.

S.

☞The term of enlistment of the 4th Regiment, in which Co. F of Foxboro' belong, expired on the 26th of June. We learn however that the gallant boys will not be home at present, having volunteered to remain with General Banks until Port Hudson is taken. Hurrah for the 4th and the Foxboro' boys!

WOMAN vs. FEMALE.

Bah! A dose of rhubarb is trying; one of Epsom salts is repulsive; and one of castor oil is utterly abominable; but any one is cream and sugar to us compared with the disgust we feel when we hear a woman called a *female*. Man! who is meant when you use the word? A mare is a female; a cow is a female; a sow is a female—so is a goose, and a duck as well, and thousands of other animals and birds. Which is meant? Do you dare to employ it as a proper specific name for woman? Out on you! Is lady too delicate a term for you to apply to the gentle sex? Then use the good old, euphonious, Bible word *woman*—the name bestowed by a better man than you, even Father Adam. You ask, Why single you out for censure, when multitudes employ the term—even editors in the newspaper and clergymen in the pulpit? We answer you, The greater shame is theirs, for they disgrace their vocation, and of all men they ought to know better and do better, or resign their calling as guides and instructors of the people. If they cannot elevate the tone of public taste and delicacy, let them not degrade it.

The laws of Nature are just, but terrible. There is no weak mercy in them.—Cause and consequence are inseparable and inevitable. The elements have no forbearance. The fire burns, the water drowns, the air consumes, the earth buries. And perhaps it would be well for our race if the punishment of crimes against the laws of man were as inevitable as the punishment of crimes against the laws of Nature—were man as unerring in his judgements as Nature.—*Longfellow.*

There was a stage driver in Connecticut by the name of Jo Crackjaw, who wore such large boots that he had to use the fork of the roads for a boot-jack.

Grumbling. A western editor says he was taught when a boy, to refrain from grumbling at two things; the one is, that which he cannot help; and the other, that which he can help.

Who teaches the bird to build its nest?
Who covers with feathers so soft its breast?
Who strengthens its tiny wing to soar,
And warble its praises at Heaven's own door?
When winter comes, with its ice and snow,
And the bitter north wind doth fiercely blow,
Who leads the bird through the pathless air,
To a warmer clime, and a sky more fair?

Excellency of Christ.

He is a path, if any be misled;
He is a robe, if any naked be;
If any chance to hunger, he is bread;
If any be a bondman, he is free;
If any be but weak, how strong is he!
To dead men life he is, to sick men health;
To blind men sight, and to the needy wealth;
A pleasure without loss, a treasure without stealth.
Giles Fletcher.

When too idle and worthless to succeed in any other occupation, our American patriots turn their attention, as a last resort, to politics, confident that laziness and unworthiness will constitute no bar to their success as office seekers. These worthies are the old class of courtiers, under changed circumstances, and a new name.

Simonides being asked of Hiero, what he thought of God, asked a week's time to consider of it; at the week's end, he asked a fortnight's time; at the fortnight's, a month. At which Hiero marvelling, Simonides answered, "that the longer he thought upon the matter the more difficult he found it.

Kid Gloves. How many of our fair readers, as they draw on their "French kid" gloves are aware that those same gloves are made of rat-skin? The catching of rats for this purpose, is a regular trade in Paris, at which hundreds of men find employment.

☞Interesting. To dream all night of finding heaps of gold, and wonder on waking how you'll pay for a breakfast.

Worth makes the man. Robert Burns, on his way to Leith, one morning, met a country farmer, shook him earnestly by the hand, and stopped to converse a while. A young Edinburgh blood took the poet to task for this defect of taste.—"Why you fantastic gomeril," said Burns, "it was not the great coat, the scone bonnet, and the saundacr-boot hose, I spoke to, but the man that was in them; and the man, sir, for true worth, would weigh down you and me, and ten more such any day."

☞Never hire another person to do the work which you can well do yourself, unless you are suitably employed in some other occupation.

DEATHS.

In Foxboro', June 5, Mr. John N. Carpenter, 31.
June 11, Minnie Kerr Brown, 6 years.

THE EAGLE AND FLAG,

PUBLISHED BY

T. ELWOOD GROVER and EDWIN M. BACON,

AT FOXBORO', MASS.

Terms, 50 cts. per year invariably in advance

All communications, as well as letters of business should be addressed to the Publishers.

Rates of advertising made known on application to the Publishers.

PRINTED BY WILLIAM H. THOMAS, FOXBORO'

THE NEW YORK HERALD.

WHOLE NO. 9788. | NEW YORK, FRIDAY, JULY 3, 1863. | PRICE THREE CENTS

THE INVASION.

Desperate Battle at Gettysburg, Pa., on Wednesday.

The First and Eleventh Corps Engaged with Longstreet and Hill.

Capture of General Archer and Staff and Six Thousand Rebels.

Death of General Reynolds, Commander of the First Corps.

Heavy Losses of the Eleventh Army Corps.

Reports of a Fierce Battle and Union Victory Yesterday.

Occupation of Carlisle by Our Troops.

The Town Shelled by the Rebels, Who Are Compelled to Retreat.

Interesting Accounts of the Recent Cavalry Battles.

The Defences of Baltimore Manned by Ten Thousand Armed Citizens,

&c., &c., &c.

THE BATTLE OF GETTYSBURG.

DESPATCH OF MR. G. W. HOSMER.

BIVOUAC ON THE FIELD, WEST OF GETTYSBURG, July 1—10 P. M.

General Buford's cavalry had previously driven the rebels to the west of the town, beyond the seminary, and between nine and ten o'clock A. M. the rebels gave his pickets a pretty sharp brush and drove them in. General Reynolds, with the First corps, was on the road from Emmettsburg to Gettysburg, *en route* to the latter place, which the road approaches through the very scene of the conflict.

General Reynolds at once threw forward the First division, under General Wadsworth, which began to drive the enemy from the start. Very soon after the Second division of the same corps went on the right of the First division, the Third division on the left of the First, and the whole line began to advance. Nearly west of the town, just in the outskirts, near the seminary, of which I have spoken, is a large brick edifice. Southward from this runs a piece of woods, and the seminary stands on a ridge which slopes to the west into a little open valley of ploughed fields and meadows, rich with grass and grain. Beyond the valley is a ridge of higher land, thickly wooded. The valley runs in a southwesterly direction, and at its lower extremity is a large farmhouse, near which the Eighth Illinois cavalry was drawn up in the field, and formed our extreme left. Several farmhouses dotted this same rich little valley. Across this valley General Reynolds' line advanced somewhat hastily, almost before it was well formed, and in that condition did not go far until against it a heavy force of the rebel infantry was immediately thrown, and General Reynolds was in turn driven. But his troops retired step by step, and in excellent order. Forward with the utmost enthusiasm pressed the rebel line, eager now to turn Reynolds' retirement into a rout. Some of the rebels had too much energy and got too far; for, while they pressed too closely on the right of the centre division, the left of the same division was suddenly swept around, and then enclosed in the handsomest manner an entire rebel brigade under General Archer.

General Archer and his whole staff were taken. About fifteen hundred of the enemy's men thus fell into our hands, and went to the rear. Small regiments were the order in this brigade; and when an Alabama colonel was asked where the rest of his regiment was, he responded laconically, "Gone to Hell, sir."

One of these prisoners said to another, with some astonishment, "Hehl Jakey's, wer'e fighting the Army of the Potomac now." They seem to have thought they had hold of the militia. The regiments which made this capture were the Sixth Wisconsin, the Brooklyn Fourteenth and the Ninety-fifth New York.

Though the First corps still continued to retire, the rebel advance was broken soon after this, and General Reynolds now prepared to go forward in earnest. Apparently forgetful that he had at first only gone in to support cavalry, he was very like to bring on a general engagement with only one corps. Formed as before, his line went forward and drove the enemy across the valley and over the ridge at the further side; but it was at great expense to us, as the fire with which they received our fellows was terribly severe. From the hill the line of skirmishers was thrown out some distance, and General Reynolds went out to the line to reconnoitre, when he was hit by a musket ball in the back of the neck, and killed instantly.

In rather less than an hour after the fight began the Eleventh corps came up the same road by which the First had approached, and General Howard at once assumed command of the whole field, while General Schurz assumed command of the Eleventh corps. General Doubleday had already assumed command of the First corps. Across the north side of the town runs a creek, on which shortly after noon it was reported the rebels were massing troops, apparently to take the First corps on its rear. To guard against an advance from that direction, General Howard sent forward the First and Third divisions of the Eleventh corps, which moved across the rear of the First corps and through the town, and took up position with the First division on the right. General Steinwehr's division—the Second—was held as a reserve.

Meantime two or three of our batteries held a sharp parley with the rebel batteries posted on the hills that encircle the town, and their balls overshot our batteries somewhat and threw several shot in among the solid people of Gettysburg. Whether it frightened them or not I can hardly say. I doubt if they could experience an emotion so lively as that of fear; but they began to get out of the way, not the women and children particularly, but stalwart, able bodied wretches in men's garments were what I principally saw on the road to the rear.

At about half-past two o'clock, while the batteries exchanged a heavy fire and some sharp musketry woke up the echoes on the right, the rebels advanced in heavy force against the First corps, which slowly retreated from the hills beyond the valley to high ground near the seminary, where it prepared to make all the resistance it was capable of. It was reinforced there by some dismounted dragoons, and fought in the open field; for, though some rail fences were thrown down across the front of our line, they afforded no cover. From the woods beyond the farmhouses, and across the open space, a rebel force of perhaps three large brigades advanced handsomely in line of battle, while the rebel batteries near the general centre shelled our position hotly to cover the advance.

On came the line, right up within short range of our position, when it was opened upon with a fire so sharp and well served as to stagger and then completely repulse it. Backward went the line that came forward in such good order, a mere mass of stragglers, each of whom made the best of his way across the plain.

While the musketry was very hot in front of General Doubleday, a party of about one hundred rebels stole through the woods well up on Doubleday's left flank, and fired a large barn, one of those immense magazines of breadstuffs that in Pennsylvania so overpeer the comparatively small farmhouses. An immense black column of smoke soon began to [illegible] a white, sulphurous cloud, and then into a fierce red blaze. Under cover of this fire the rebel skirmishers exchanged numerous shots with a line of skirmishers from the cavalry on our extreme left. Repulsed, but not vanquished, the rebel line was reformed and reinforced; and now, for a second time, came on a force nearly twice as great as at first. Once more, also, the batteries threw shells, answered by our batteries on the left, and also by batteries of ours on the extreme right, which at this time threw shell at the position on the enemy's centre. Once more the packed, rapid rattle of our file fire broke out, and once more the rebel line was broken and went to the right about in rout.

There is a mysterious fatality connected with the third line; and so, after a lull and period of comparative quiet of twenty minutes, onward for a third time came the rebels, quite as orderly as before, their line of skirmishers firing as they came on. In so great force was this line that it completely overlapped the line of the First corps on both flanks. Two brigades on the right were quite out of ammunition, and the order was given to retreat on the town; and our boys accordingly retreated in good order, while the rebels rushed forward with yells to our position. On came the enemy's fourth line, further to the right of the third, in good order, skirmishers ahead, until the position at the Seminary was reached, when they came forward with a rush, and occupied a hill we had deemed it worth while not to hold after the other was taken. On also came another line in support behind this, and our cavalry on the extreme left began to retire.

At this moment the field presented a true war picture. Across the fields to the right came the rebel line, with colors which fluttered in the pleasant breeze; in the centre were two farmhouses, outhouses and barns in flames, and on the left the column of cavalry in retreat, while beyond all the rays of the sun beat down through the showery clouds and gilded every object with a peculiarly golden light, and over the heavens to the eastward stretched a magnificent rainbow.

The new position of the Third corps was at a line of stone wall southwest of the town, along the slope of a hill on which is a cemetery. When the First corps retired to the town the left of the Eleventh was uncovered, and a heavy advance completely on its right flank at the same time compelled it to retire. It affords me pleasure to say that this corps is reported to have fought well and lost many men. As I was on our extreme left I did not see the fight of the Eleventh corps, and leave all particulars in relation to it to the gentleman who was with it.

After our retirement on the town the rebel advance was not pressed further. And so ended a battle that was brought on in the most rash manner, yet which was well fought against a largely superior force, and gotten out of at last much better than we could have expected to get out.

The rebel force fought by us was the corps of General Ewell and that of A. P. Hill. South of the town is a high hill, on which is a cemetery, and this became the headquarters. Its slope to the west was held by the First corps, and a continuation of hills from it toward the east was held by the Eleventh, while the Twelfth corps was placed so as to hold both flanks, the First division, under General Williams, being on the extreme right, and the Second division, under General Geary, on the extreme left. The Third corps, which came on the field just at nightfall, was massed in the centre, ready to be used whenever occasion might require. General Slocum, of the Twelfth corps, had assumed the command upon his arrival.

DESPATCH OF MR. J. H. VOSBURG.

GETTYSBURG, Pa., July 1, 1863.

The First corps of General Reynolds had been engaged with the enemy probably about two hours when the Eleventh arrived on the ground, hurrying up to meet the noise of battle towards us. So far the First corps had appeared to have the advantage; but about the time of our arrival the rebels had partially succeeded in turning their right flank.

Arriving on the ground, General Howard assumed command and immediately made his dispositions for the battle. The First corps was at this time on a wooded ridge near the Lutheran Theological Seminary; to the right was another range of hills, the right being wooded and crossed by the Harrisburg road. General Howard directed that two divisions of the Eleventh corps be placed on this range of hills, the First division on the right and the Third on the left of the Harrisburg road, a stream being on our extreme right. The Second division was held as a general reserve.

General Schurz, being in command of the Eleventh corps, endeavored to take the position indicated; but owing to the flank of the rebels on the right of the First corps we were not able to reach the favorable point desired. The rebel corps of Gen. A. P. Hill had, so far, engaged the First corps. But at this time General Ewell's corps of twenty-five thousand men arrived by the Rock road. It was this overwhelming force which was to be met by seven thousand men. Before they had reached an advantageous defensive position, the rebels had batteries so posted that our columns moving up on an air line afterwards were exposed to a destructive cross fire. General Barlow, on the right, with the First division, made a most desperate effort to take and hold the position assigned him. The brave General, it is said, while riding along in front of his line encouraging his men, while the skirmishers were firing, was hit by a musket ball and severely wounded in the thigh or groin. The division fought bravely, and lost heavily, the brigade of Colonel Von Gilsa holding its position firmly, and that of General Ames doing well. The Third division, General Schimmelpfennig, was meanwhile striving nobly to hold the position it was directed to hold immediately on the right of the First corps and on the cleared part of the hill between the Seminary and the position of General Barlow.

The losses in this division show how well it fought. The brigades were commanded by Colonels Krzyzanowski and Von Amesberg. Colonel Von Amesberg had two horses shot under him, but escaped uninjured. Colonel Krzyzanowski was hurt, but not disabled, by his horse falling with him. Colonel McGroarty, of the Sixty-first Ohio, behaved with his usual distinguished gallantry, but escaped injury as if by a miracle. Colonel Brown, of the One Hundred and Fifty-seventh New York, held an isolated position of particular peril. The regiment lost eighteen of twenty-six officers and three-fourths of its men. Lieutenant Colonel Arrowsmith, a noble officer of this regiment, was killed. Every regimental commander of Krzyzanowski's brigade was killed or wounded. The Eighty-second Ohio, Colonel Robinson, lost eighteen officers. The Twenty-sixth Wisconsin lost all but one of its officers. This regiment last fall joined General Sigel at Fairfax, with nearly the maximum number, and then appeared splendid. It has been in two fights—Chancellorsville and Gettysburg—and came out with less men than are required to form a company. The Seventy-fourth Pennsylvania brought off sixteen men. Captain Dilger's battery did splendid execution—constantly changing position as circumstances required. At one time he dismounted an entire rebel battery; at another, rushed up to two pieces in front of our line to assist Col. McGroarty, who had daringly advanced his regiment to the front.

Our right flank was completely turned and our left at the same time, so superior was the enemy's force. The First corps was giving way, and the Eleventh found it impossible to maintain its position. The First division retired in good order, and the Third fell back nearly at the same time.

Gen. Schimmelpfennig's two aids, Captains Schelten and Klenker, had their horses shot under them. Gen. Schimmelpfennig's horse was shot under him on the retreat, and he was captured. It is presumed that he was wounded, possibly killed, before being taken.

The two divisions fell back slowly, pausing occasionally, and endeavoring to stem the rebel advance. At this juncture the First brigade of Gen. Steinwehr's division was ordered up. This brigade was commanded by Col. Coster, and the force engaged consisted of three small regiments. The brigade formed on the right of Pennsylvania College, a little below the foot of Washington street. The brigade was too late to more than check the rebel advance for a few moments. They were scarcely formed when they were attacked by three rebel columns and completely enveloped on the right. Col. Coster and his men did all that brave men could do; but it was so late when they were called out that it was scarcely worth while for them to be slaughtered by the artillery and infantry force to which they were exposed.

The rebels had two batteries playing upon our right flank and rear almost from the time the Eleventh corps first arrived on the field. The ubiquitous Dilger, with his battery, was on Colonel Coster's left, in the road, on an eminence. It did terrible execution with grape and canister on the advancing rebels. The Eighty-second Ohio was supporting this battery, and it was here that Colonel Robinson was wounded and taken prisoner.

Our men retreated slowly through Washington street, the rebels closely pursuing, and being in advance of many of our troops on the east side of the town. Captain Dilger's battery unlimbered at the foot of the street and gave the rebels a parting charge of grape.

It is a wonder that the rebels did not press us more closely. While passing slowly and densely packed, artillery, infantry and ambulances, along this street up the hill, a battery planted where Captain Dilger's was last stationed would have enfiladed this street completely.

Captain Schiermen's battery, which did excellent service during the day, was especially efficient, while planted on the hill above two batteries of reserve artillery, in protecting this retreat.

As we passed through town, shot, shell and bullets were whistling musically around us, sometimes striking the houses. A shot ricochetted over a regiment in front of me and pierced the wall of an inhabited house. A bullet grazed the ear of Captain Newcomb, with whom I was riding, and struck a house near us.

The ladies of Gettysburg deserve especially honorable mention. While we were retreating they came out upon the sidewalks, with composed though anxious faces, and offered our soldiers everything needful in the way of refreshments. The shot were whistling meanwhile; but they appeared elevated by noble impulses above the sentiment of fear. They took the most tender care of our wounded, as well as those of the rebels who were captured during the day. How we grieved to leave this interesting town in the possession of rebel soldiers.

We fell back to a position south of the town cemetery, which General Howard had first selected as the only good position that we could secure. The rebels did not seem to think it best to attempt to dislodge us. The enemy occupied the town on our retirement, and their sharpshooters were stationed on the houses near us.

The battle of to-day was well fought. We had 22,000 against 50,000.

General Howard distinguished himself for bravery and composure while directing the details of battle. The Eleventh corps did more than all others. It lost 3,000 men, and double the loss of the First corps, which fought bravely.

DESPACTH OF MR. F. G. CHAPMAN.

BALTIMORE, July 2—6 P. M.

About half-past nine o'clock yesterday morning, as the First army corps passed through Gettysburg, on its way northward, its advance encountered the enemy's skirmishers, posted in by-streets and out of the way places. These were quickly dislodged by our skirmishers, and the column proceeded. When our advance reached a point about half a mile north of the town it came upon the enemy under General Buhll, commanding the right of General A. P. Hill's corps.

General Reynolds was immediately notified, and he rode to the front, where he found the advance of the two armies engaging each other, principally upon the right of the road. The fight at first was almost entirely an infantry engagement, as the nature of the ground was such as to preclude the use of artillery upon either side. General Reynolds, seeing that he could not use his artillery to advantage, rode out to an eminence a short distance from the road to find a place to plant a battery, when he received a volley from some sharpshooters posted in a thicket close at hand. His horse became unmanageable, wheeled and reared, and at the same time a ball struck the General in the back of the neck, passing downward, severing the spinal column, and killing him instantly.

His forces fought on and succeeded in driving the enemy before them a short distance, until the rebels reached the cover of their main body. Here the full force of the enemy was discovered, and our men fell back to the line of their first encounter, and word was sent back to the Second, Third and Eleventh corps to come up.

Upon the fall of General Reynolds, Gen. Doubleday assumed command of the First corps and directed affairs until the arrival of Gen. Howard, of the Eleventh, who relieved him. The Eleventh corps was the first to arrive, then the Second and Third corps in order.

When the reinforcements had arrived and arrangements had been perfected, the whole column moved forward, and soon were hotly engaged.

Our forces succeeded in dislodging the enemy and remained masters of the field, but did not essay any further advance.

Skirmishing was kept up all day, and until after ten o'clock in the evening.

General Reynolds' body arrived here at ten o'clock this morning, and was embalmed by James E. Weaver, at whose place I viewed it this afternoon. The left side of the face and neck are much disfigured by his fall after being shot. His remains were taken to the residence of his sister, Mrs. Gildersleeve, and will be conveyed to Philadelphia for interment to-night.

It is also reported that Brigadier General Paul was killed yesterday.

We took a large number of prisoners and lost but few. Our losses in killed and wounded are not heavy.

The secessionists here are jubilant over the affair, and claim it as a victory.

THE BATTLE OF GETTYSBURG.

Scene of the Battle of Wednesday, July 1—The Cavalry Fight.

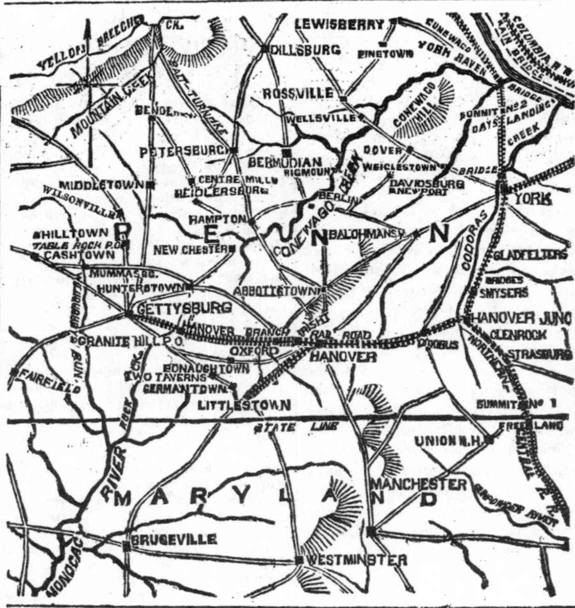

OUR OCCUPATION OF CARLISLE, PA.

The Barracks and Gas Works Burned by the Rebels.

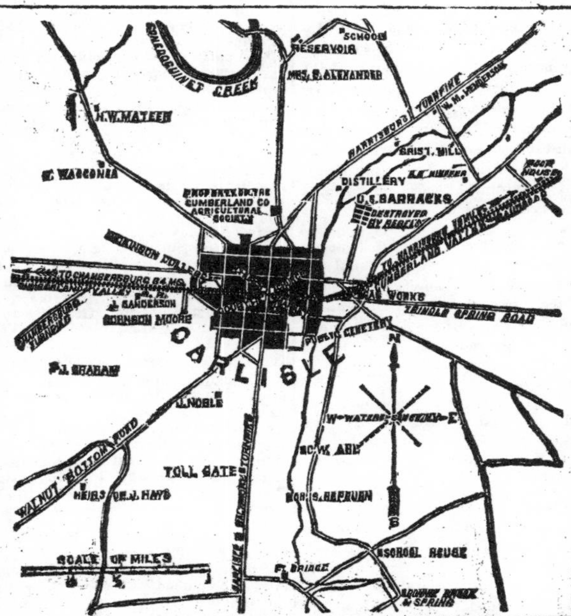

THE CASUALTIES.

BALTIMORE, July 2, 1863.

The following is a complete list of the casualties among the officers yesterday at Gettysburg:—

KILLED WOUNDED AND MISSING OF THE ELEVENTH CORPS.

Brigadier General Francis Barlow, commanding First division, wounded and a prisoner.
Brigadier General Alexander Schemmelfennig, commanding Third division, taken prisoner; probably wounded.
Captain Stoedt, Adjutant General.
Colonel Wladimir Kryzyanowski, missing.
Lieutenant Burneghausen, Aid to Colonel Kryzyanowski, wounded.

FIFTY-FOURTH NEW YORK.

Major George F. Kampe, missing.
Surgeon Carl W. Hagen, missing.
Lieutenant Rosenberg, wounded and missing.
Adjutant Aldstadt, missing.
Lieutenant Veltwort, wounded.

FIFTY-EIGHTH NEW YORK.

Lost four men killed and six wounded. Only one company engaged.

ONE HUNDRED AND NINETEENTH NEW YORK.

Colonel John J. Lockman, wounded.
Adjutant Theodore Dodge, wounded.
Captain August Volkhausen, killed.
Lieutenant A. B. Von Clocdt, wounded.
Lieutenant Otto Trumpleman, wounded.
Lieutenant Frost, wounded.
Lieutenant Edward Bruninghausen, wounded.
Lieutenant Raymond, wounded.
Loss, one hundred and thirty men.

ONE HUNDRED AND THIRTY-FOURTH NEW YORK.

Lieutenant Colonel Jackson, missing.
Captain Elliott, killed.

ONE HUNDRED AND FIFTY-SEVENTH NEW YORK.

Captain Frank, wounded and prisoner.
Adjutant Henry, wounded and prisoner.
Captain Fry, missing.
Lieutenant Bisy, wounded.
Lieutenant Schreder, wounded.
Lieutenant Hepp, missing.
Regimental loss one hundred and thirty-four.

ONE HUNDRED AND FIFTY-SEVENTH NEW YORK.

Captain Harrison Frank, wounded and prisoner.
Adjutant Heny, wounded and prisoner.
Captain J. H. Backus, wounded.
Captain J. R. Stone, missing.
Captain G. A. Adams, wounded.
Captain L. F. Briggs, wounded and missing.
Lieutenant Gates, wounded.
Lieutenant J. A. Coffin, wounded and missing.
Lieutenant Fitch, wounded.
Lieutenant Atwater, wounded.
Lieutenant Waters, wounded.
Lieutenant Bowen, missing.
Lieutenant Durr, wounded and missing.
Lieutenant Pearce, missing.
Of three hundred and twenty-five men of the One Hundred and Fifty-seventh who went into the fight forty had returned last evening.

SEVENTY-FOURTH PENNSYLVANIA.

Colonel A. Von Hartang, wounded.
Lieutenant Colonel Alex. Mitzel, missing.
Captain Myer, wounded.
Lieutenant Newmyer, wounded.
Lieutenant Roth, wounded.
Lieutenant Goldschmidt, missing.
Lieutenant Knoeble, missing.
Lieutenant Schroeders, missing.

TWENTY-SEVENTH PENNSYLVANIA.

Surgeon Heckel, wounded.
Lieutenant Voselback, missing.
Lieutenant Gumple, missing.
Lieutenant White, missing.

SEVENTY-FIFTH PENNSYLVANIA.

Colonel Francis Mahler, wounded.
Captain Feltens, wounded.
Captain Saalman, wounded.
Lieutenant Manry, wounded and missing.
Lieutenant Hauscheldt, killed.
Lieutenant Sill, wounded.
Lieutenant Brandt, wounded.
Loss—One hundred and thirty-seven men.

FIRST OHIO.

Lieutenant Brent, wounded.
Lieutenant O'Sullivan, wounded.

EIGHTY-SECOND OHIO.

Colonel James S Robinson, wounded and captured.
Major James S. Crail, missing.
Captain James B. McConnell, wounded.
Captain Mitchell, wounded.
Captain John Costen, mortally wounded.
Captain A. E. Lee, mortally wounded.
Captain Wm. J. Dickson, wounded.
Lieutenant Fry, wounded.
Lieutenant Blankburn, wounded.
Lieutenant Jacobs, wounded and a prisoner.
Lieutenant Crickett, missing.
Lieutenant Megarse, missing.
Lieutenant Ballankensen, missing.
Lieutenant Meredith, wounded.
Lieutenant Cheswell, wounded.
Lieutenant Marsh, wounded.
Loss, one hundred and forty men.

ONE HUNDRED AND FIFTY-THIRD PENNSYLVANIA.

Captain Howell, wounded.
Captain Young, killed.
Captain Ricker, wounded.
Captain Myers, wounded.
Lieutenant Jager, wounded.
Lieutenant Arther, wounded.
Lieutenant Schaann, missing.
Lieutenant Beaver, wounded.
Lieutenant Dalton, wounded.

EIGHTY-SECOND ILLINOIS.

Captain Fry, missing.
Lieutenant Bisy, wounded.
Lieutenant Schreder, wounded.
Lieutenant Hepp, missing.

TWENTY SIXTH WISCONSIN.

Lieutenant Colonel H. Boebel, wounded.
Major H. Baetz, wounded.
Of this regiment the only officer left is Capt. Fuchs, wounded, but still in command.

KILLED, WOUNDED AND MISSING—FIRST CORPS.

Colonel R. T. Cummings, 142d Pennsylvania, wounded.
Colonel Roy Stone, commanding 2d brigade, 2d division, 1st corps, wounded.
Captain Grimm, 142d Pennsylvania.
W. L. Wilson, Lieutenant and Adjutant, 3d division, 1st Volunteers.
Lieutenant Hoffman, 142d Pennsylvania, shoulder.
Colonel George H. Biddle, 95th New York, wounded.
Brigadier General Gabriel R. Paul, in command 1st division, 1st corps, wounded.
Colonel Fairchild, all the field officers of 2d Wisconsin, wounded.
Major Andrew J. Grover, 76th New York, killed.
Lieutenant Colonel Wm. W. Dudley, 19th Indiana, wounded.
Colonel Adrian L. Root, 94th New York, wounded.
Colonel Henry A. Morrows, 24th Michigan, wounded.
Captain Bloodgood (Aid-de-Camp to General Cutler), wounded in hand.

SKETCH OF GENERAL REYNOLDS.

Major General John Fulton Reynolds, who has met with his death during the recent engagement at Gettysburg, was born in Pennsylvania about the year 1821, and was therefore in his prime when he was killed.

HIS ENTRANCE INTO WEST POINT, GRADUATION AND CLASSMATES.

He entered the West Point Military Academy during the year 1837, and graduated on June 30, 1841, standing No. 26 in his class, in which were the following officers of the present war, to whose names we have attached their individual West Point grades:—General Horatio Gates Wright, second; General Albion P. Howe, eighth; General Nathaniel Lyon (killed in Missouri, August 10, 1861), eleventh; General Joseph B. Plummer (died in camp), twenty-second; General John M. Brannan (now serving in Tennessee), twenty-third; General Schuyler Hamilton (of the Army of the Southwest), twenty-fourth; General James Totten (now serving in Missouri), twenty-fifth; General Don Carlos Buell (formerly commander of the Army of the Ohio), thirty-second; General Alfred Sully (of the Army of the Potomac), thirty-fourth: Gen. Israel B. Richardson, (who died November 3, 1862, of wounds received at Antietam, September 17, 1862), thirty-eighth; General Wm. T. H. Brooks (now commanding at Pittsburg), forty-sixth; Colonel Garesche (killed at Murfreesboro), sixteenth; and other noble Union officers, besides the following rebels:—General Samuel S. Anderson, of Virginia; General Samuel Jones, also of Virginia; Colonel Garnett, of Virginia, killed at St. George, Western Virginia; and others.

HE JOINS THE ARMY.

On the 1st day of July, 1841, the subject of our sketch entered the regular army of the United States as a brevet second lieutenant of the Third artillery; but he did not receive his commission until October 23 of the same year. On the 18th of June, 1846, he was promoted to the rank of first lieutenant, and with that position served in the Mexican war.

MEXICO—REGIMENTAL COMPANIONS.

The regiment was ordered to the seat of war in Mexico, and at this time the following officers of the present war were regimental companions of the deceased hero:—General Robert Anderson, then captain; General Thomas W. Sherman (recently wounded at Port Hudson), then captain; General Braxton Bragg (now full general of the rebel army), then captain; General Edward O. C. Ord (now commander of the Thirteenth army corps), then first lieutenant; General Wm. Tecumseh Sherman (now commander of the Fifteenth army corps), then first lieutenant; General Stewart Van Vliet (Chief Quartermaster of the Army of the Potomac), then first lieutenant and regimental quartermaster; General George H. Thomas (now commander of the Fourteenth army corps), then first lieutenant; General Richard W. Johnston (now serving with General Rosecrans, in Tennessee), then first lieutenant; General Ambrose E. Burnside (now commander of the Department of the Ohio, and recently commander of the Army of the Potomac), then second lieutenant, and others.

CONDUCT DURING THE MEXICAN WAR—BREVETS.

During that portion of the Mexican war in which he was engaged he acted with great bravery and gained a rare amount of distinction among his fellow officers. For his noble conduct at Monterey he was brevetted captain, to date from September 23, 1846, the brevet being worded "for gallant and meritorious conduct in the battle of Monterey, Mexico." This bevet was awarded in August, 1848. He also greatly distinguished himself at Buena Vista, and was awarded, during August, 1848, the brevet of major, to date from February 23, 1847. This brevet was also worded that it was "for gallant and meritorious conduct" in battle.

AID TO GENERAL WOOL—CAPTAIN.

During February, 1852, he was appointed aid to General John E. Wool, then in command of one of the geographical departments of the United States Army. On the 3d of March, 1855, he was promoted to a captaincy of the Third artillery, which rank he held at the breaking out of the rebellion. He was then in command of company K of his regiment, and stood No. 34 on the lineal roll of artillery captains.

THE REBELLION—LIEUTENANT COLONEL.

When the rebellion broke out he warmly espoused the cause of the Union, determined to stand by his country, her flag and government. He rendered the State of Pennsylvania and her Governor, Andrew G. Curtin, very great assistance in organizing the State forces, and more especially the forces known as "the reserves."

The new regular regiments having been ordered, Brevet Major Reynolds was appointed the lieutenant colonel of the Fourteenth regiment of regular infantry, with rank and commission to date from May 14, 1861.

THE PENNSYLVANIA RESERVES.

After the three months regiments of Pennsylvania Volunteers had left the State, the military authorities began to organize a force of reserves, to be used as circumstances might require. This force consisted of fifteen regiments, of which twelve were infantry, one rifle, one cavalry and one artillery. The call for these troops was made by the President in May, 1861; and on May 15 the Pennsylvania Legislature passed an act for organizing the "Reserve Volunteer Corps of the Commonwealth" These regiments were organized into a division under General McCall, and placed for military instruction in camps at Easton, Westchester, Pittsburg and Harrisburg.

THE RESERVES LEAVE THE STATE.

The value of this organization was soon understood; for the day after the battle of Bull run, July 22, 1861, a requisition was made on the State by the general government for the services of more men. Within a few days eleven thousand of these men, fully armed and equipped, were sent into the national capital; and shortly after the whole force of nearly sixteen thousand men were mustered into the service of the United States.

DIVIDED IN BRIGADES—GENERAL REYNOLDS COMMISSIONED AND PLACED IN COMMAND.

The reserves were next sent to Tenallytown, north of the national capital, and there placed in camp. As the force was too large to be commanded properly in the field by only one general, General McClellan at once saw the advantage of having the command subdivided into brigades. These brigades were therefore formed, and the following officers were commissioned on the dates specified to their names and placed in command:—

No. of Brigade.	*Commander.*	*Date of Commission.*
First brigade......	Gen. J. F. Reynolds..	August 20, 1861.
Second brigade....	Gen. Geo. G. Meade..	August 31, 1861.
Third brigade.....	Gen. E. O. C. Ord....	Sept. 14, 1861.

It will thus be seen that at the outbreak of the war General Reynolds outranked his two brigade companions.

TENALLYTOWN—FORT PENNSYLVANIA.

While the command was in camp at Tenallytown they were employed in the construction of one of those many beautiful defensive works which surround the national capital. During the fall and early winter of 1861 a fine earthwork was constructed near the Potomac river at Tenallytown, and was named in general order by General McClellan "Fort Pennsylvania." After this work was completed the division crossed into Virginia and occupied the extreme right or most northern position of the army. In this vicinity it wintered 1861–2, and was thoroughly organized.

GEN. REYNOLDS' BRIGADE—PRESENTATION.

Gen. Reynolds' brigade consisted of the First, Second, Fifth and Eighth regiments of the reserve corps, or those officially known in the State of Pennsylvania as the Thirtieth, Thirty-first, Thirty-fourth and Thirty-seventh regiments Pennsylvania Volunteers. For the services rendered the State of Pennsylvania in the organization of her troops, the General was presented by the State with a very valuable sword at the time he took command of his brigade.

FIRST MOVEMENTS OF THE ARMY OF THE POTOMAC—THE RAPPAHANNOCK.

The Army of the Potomac began its advance during the early part of March, 1862, and Gen. Reynolds' brigade formed part of the Second division of the First army corps, then under Gen. McDowell. When the Army of the Potomac was divided, and Gen. McDowell placed in command of the Department of the Rappahannock, the forces with which Gen. Reynolds acted still remained in the First corps, and guarded the shores of the Rappahannock.

ORDERED TO THE PENINSULA.

When Gen. McClellan discovered, after the battle of Fair Oaks, that his forces were not sufficient to compete with the heavy forces of rebels that were collecting at Richmond, he sent to Washington for reinforcements. After some little delay Gen. McCall's division was detached from the First army corps and added to the army on the peninsula. With this division Gen. Reynolds' brigade entered on a new campaign, and was placed on the extreme right of the line of the Army of the Potomac, occupying Mechanicsville and the vicinity.

MECHANICSVILLE AND GAINES' MILLS.

On the 26th of June, 1862, the seven days' fight commenced by a vigorous attack, made by the rebels, under Stonewall Jackson, upon the extreme right at Mechanicsville. The next morning, the forces having joined with Gen. Porter, they took part in the battle of Gaines' Mills.

CHICKAHOMINY—CHARLES CITY—PRISONER.

The forces then pushed over the bridges of the Chickahominy river, at which point another fight ensued. They next participated in some of the other contests of the seven days, and during the battle of Charles City Cross Roads, Monday, June 30, General McCall was seen to fall from his horse and was taken prisoner. General Reynolds then assumed command of the division. Shortly after he was also taken prisoner, and sent to Richmond.

BREVETS.

For his conduct during these eventful struggles he was nominated for the following brevets:—

To be colonel by brevet, to date from June 26, 1862, for distinguished services at the battle of Mechanicsville.

To be brigadier general by brevet, to date from June 27, 1862, for distinguished services at the battles of Chickahominy and Charles City.

These brevets will doubtless, with others, be confirmed at the next session of Congress.

THE MARYLAND CAMPAIGN—PENNSYLVANIA MILITIA.

Shortly after General Reynolds had returned from his imprisonment at Richmond he found the rebels far advanced on the north side of the Potomac, and the soil of his native State threatened. He found the militia of Pennsylvania had arisen to defend their native State, and he desired to aid in the same good object. He was therefore allowed temporarily to resign the command of his division, and to take full charge of the forces assembled for the defence of the State of Pennsylvania, and assumed command—as he stated in his General Order, No. 1, "in pursuance of orders from the War Department and his Excellency Governor Curtin"—on the 14th of September, 1862.

"Fortunately," to use General McClellan's own words, in his letter of thanks to Governor Curtin, "circumstances rendered it impossible for the enemy to set foot upon the soil of Pennsylvania; but the moral support tendered to the army" engaged, by the action of the Pennsylvania forces, "was none the less mighty. The manner in which the people of Pennsylvania responded to the call, and hastened to the defence of their frontier, no doubt exercised a great influence upon the enemy."

GOVERNOR CURTIN'S THANKS TO GENERAL REYNOLDS.

After the danger to the State was over General Reynolds was relieved from the command of the Pennsylvania militia, the Governor at the same time tendering his thanks and those of the State in the following neatly worded document:—

PENNSYLVANIA EXECUTIVE CHAMBER, HARRISBURG, Pa., Sept. 26, 1862.

GENERAL—Having relieved you from duty as commander of the Pennsylvania Volunteer Militia recently called for the defence of the State, I deem it proper to express my strong sense of the gratitude which Pennsylvania owes for the zeal, spirit and ability which you brought to her service at a period when her honor and safety were threatened. That for her security you left the command of your brave division, the Pennsylvania reserves, thus losing the opportunity of leading this gallant corps at South Mountain and the Antietam, is a just

CONTINUED ON EIGHTH PAGE.

THE DAILY CITIZEN.

J. M. SWORDS,......Proprietor

VICKSBURG, MISS.

THURSDAY, JULY 2, 1863.

☞ Mrs. Cisco was instantly killed on Monday, on Jackson road. Mrs. Cisco's husband is now in Virginia, a member of Moody's artillery, and the death of such a loving, affectionate and dutiful wife will be a loss to him irreparable.

☞ We are indebted to Major Gillespie for a steak of Confederate beef *alias* meat. We have tried it, and can assure our friends that if it is rendered necessary, they need have no scruples at eating the meat. It is sweet, savory and tender, and so long as we have a mule left we are satisfied our soldiers will be content to subsist on it.

☞ Jerre Askew, one of our most esteemed merchant-citizens, was wounded at the works in the rear of our city a few days since, and breathed his last on Monday. Mr. Askew was a young man of strict integrity, great industry and an honor to his family and friends. He was a member of Cowan's artillery, and by the strict discharge of his duties and his obliging disposition, won the confidence and esteem of his entire command. May the blow his family have sustained be mitigated by Him who doeth all things well.

☞ Grant's forces did a little firing on Tuesday afternoon, but the balance of that day was comparatively quiet. Yesterday morning they were very still, and continued so until early in the afternoon, when they sprung a mine on the left of our centre, and opened fire along the line for some distance. We have not been able to ascertain anything definitely as to our loss, but as our officers were on the lookout for this move of the enemy, the expectations of the Yankees were not realized by a great deal.

☞ Among many good deeds we hear spoken of with pride by our citizens, we cannot refrain from mentioning the case of Mr. F. Kiser. This gentleman, having more corn than he thought was necessary to last him during the siege of this place, portioned off what would do him for the brief interval that will ensue before the arrival of succor to our garrison, and since that time has relieved the wants of many families *free of charge!* May he live long and prosper, and his name be handed down to posterity when the siege of Vicksburg is written, as one in whose breast the "milk of human kindness" had not dried up.

☞ Porter is enjoying a season of rest, and his men are doubtless obliged to him for his kind consideration for their welfare. On Tuesday he fired a few shells from his parrots, and kept his men tolerably busy sharpshooting across the river, with no other result than might be expected. The mortars have not been used for nearly forty-eight hours. Poor fool, he might as well give up the vain aspiration he entertains of capturing our city or extermination our people, and return to his master to receive the reward such a gasconading dolt will meet at the hands of the unappreciating Government at Washington.

DEATH OF LIEUT.-COL. GRIFFIN.—General Smith's impetuous division seems singularly unfortunate. He has lost many gallant men whose valor and worth the siege has fully developed, and whose death is a great public calamity. Lieut.-Col. Griffin, commanding the 31st Louisiana regiment, was killed on Saturday. He was a popular and efficient officer. Gifted by nature with undaunted courage, indomitable resolution and energy, he was also possessed of quick determination, keen glance and coolness in danger, which are the most essential qualities of an officer, while by his mingled firmness and clemency of his conduct, he won the confidence and good will of his men. May the soft south winds murmur sweet requiems o'er his manes, and the twilight dews fall gently like an angel's tear-drop and moisten his turfy bed.

☞ If aught would appeal to the heart of stone of the extortioner with success, the present necessities of our citizens would do so. It is needless to attempt to disguise from the enemy or our own people that our wants are great but still we can conscientiously assert our belief that there is plenty within our lines, by an exercise of prudence, to last until long after succor reaches us. We are satisfied there are numerous persons within our city who have breadstuffs secreted, and are doling it out, at the most exhorbitant figures, to those who had not the foresight or means at their command to provide for the exigency now upon us. A rumor has reached us that parties in our city have been, and are now, selling flour at five dollars per pound! molasses at ten dollars per gallon! and corn at ten dollars per bushel! We have not as yet proved the fact upon the parties accused, but this allusion to the subject may induce some of our citizens to ascertain whether such prices have been paid, and to whom; and if so, let a brand not only be placed upon their brow, but let it be seared into their very brain, that humanity may scorn and shun them as they would the portals of hell itself.

GOOD NEWS.—In devoting a large portion of our space this morning to Federal intelligence, copied from the Memphis Bulletin of the 25th, it should be remembered that the news, in the original truth, is whitewashed by the Federal Provost Marshal, who desires to hood wink the poor Northern white slaves. The former editors of the Bulletin being rather pro-southern men, were arrested for speaking the truth when truth was unwelcome to Yankeedom, and placed in the chain-gang working at Warrenton, where they now are. This paper at present is in duress, and edited by a pink-nosed, slab-sided, toad-eating Yankee, who is a lineal descendant of Judas Iscariot and a brother germain of the greatest Puritanical, sycophantic, howling scoundrel unhung—Parson Brownlow. Yet with such a character, this paper cannot cloak the fact that Gen. Rob't E. Lee has given Hooker, Milroy & Co. one of the best and soundest whippings on record, and that the "galorious Union" is now exceedingly weak in the knees.

Gen. Rob't E. Lee Again.

Again we have reliable news from the gallant corps of Gen. Lee in Virginia. Elated with success, encouraged by a series of brilliant victories, marching to and crossing the Rappahannock, defeating Hooker's right wing and thence through the Shenandoah Valley, driving Milroy from Winchester and capturing 6000 of his men and a large amount of valuable stores of all descriptions, re-entering Maryland, holding Hagerstown, threatening Washington City, and within a few miles of Baltimore—onward and upward their war cry—our brave men under Lee are striking terror to the heart of all Yankeedom. Like the Scottish chieftain's braves, Lee's men are springing up from moor and brake, crag and dale, with flashing steel and sturdy arm, ready to do or die in the great cause of national independence, right and honor. To-day the mongrel administration of Lincoln, like Japhet, are in search of a father—for their old Abe has departed for parts unknown. Terror reigns in their halls. Lee is to the left of them, the right of them, in front of them, and all around them; and daily do we expect to hear of his being down on them. Never were the French in Algeria more put out by the mobile raids of Ab Del Kader than are the Federals of Maryland, Washington City, Pennsylvania and Ohio by the mercureal movements of Lee's cavalry. Like Paddy's flea are they to the Federals—now they have got them and now they haven't. The omnipresence of our troops and their throwing dust in the eyes, or rather on the heels of the panic-stricken Federals in Maryland and Pennsylvania, clearly prove that Lee just now is the right man in the right place.

We lay before our readers in this issue an account of Lee's brilliant and successful onslaught upon the abolition hordes, and show e'en from their own record, how our gallant boys of the cavalry have fleshed their swords to the hilt with their vaunting foes, and how each musket of our infantry has told its fatal leaden tale.

To-day Maryland is ours, to-morrow Pennsylvania will be, and the next day Ohio—now midway, like Mahommed's coffin—will fall.

Success and glory to our arms! God and right are with us.

☞ We have heretofore refrained from alluding to a matter which has been a source of extreme annoyance and loss to our citizens. We refer to the lax discipline of some of our company officers in allowing their men to prowl around, day and night, and purloin fruit, vegetables, chickens, etc., from our denizens, and, in the majority of cases, from those whose chief subsistence is derived therefrom. This charge is not confined solely to those at the works, but is equally, if not mainly, attributable to the wagoners and others in charge of animals. Several cases have come to our knowledge wherein the offenders have, in open daylight, entered premises, seized cattle and other things, and defied the owners to their teeth. We are pained to learn that an esteemed citizen of our Vicksburg, Wm. Porterfield, was under the necessity, in protecting his property, to wound one or two soldiers and deprive another of his life. We fully appreciate the fatigue, hardships and privation to which our men are subjected; but upon inquiry it may be ascertained that our city is second to none in contributing to the welfare of those gallant spirits who risk their life and limb for the achievement of an end which will make us one of the most honored people of the earth, and such conduct of which we complain is but base ingratitude. A soldier has his honor as much at stake as when a civilian; then let him preserve his good name and reputation with the same jealous care as before he entered his country's ranks. But so long as this end is lost sight of, so long may we expect to chronicle scenes of bloodshed among those of our own people. We make this public exposure, mortifying as it to us, with the hope that a salutary improvement in matters will be made by our military authorities.

ON DIT.—That the great Ulysses—the Yankee Generalissimo, surnamed Grant—has expressed his intention of dining in Vicksburg on Saturday next, and celebrating the 4th of July by a grand dinner and so forth. When asked if he would invite Gen. Jo. Johnston to join he said, "No! for fear there will be a row at the table." Ulysses must get into the city before he dines in it. The way to cook a rabbit is "first catch the rabbit," &c.

ON DIT.—That the great Ulysses—the Yankee Generalissimo, surnamed Grant—has expressed his intention of dining in Vicksburg on Saturday next, and celebrating the 4th of July by a grand dinner and so forth. When asked if he would invite Gen. Jo. Johnston to join he said, "No! for fear there will be a row at the table." Ulysses must get into the city before he dines in it. The way to cook a rabbit is "first catch the rabbit," &c.

Pennsylvania regiment, (mounted) captured a squad of rebels who were marauding on this side of the river.

We hold Chambersburg and the citizens are arming and fortifying the city. Gen. Couch had ordered that the place be held.

The Fortifications opposite this city are finished, and are considered impregnable.

The rebels are known to be 8000 strong at Hagerstown and Williamsport.

The rebels hold the north bank of the Potomac river, from Cumberland to Harper's Ferry. Gen. Kelly drove them out of Cumberland, and when they left they threatened to return and furnish themselves with horses and forage. The rebels have done an immense amount of damage.

It is thought Gen. Rhodes is opposite Williamsport with 20,000 men. The rebel Gen. Imboden is reported as advancing, but this is considered doubtful.

FREDERICK, MD., June 20.—The enemy's cavalry left Boonsboro last evening, after capturing a number of horses, and returned to Hagerstown yesterday.

Six thousand infantry are reported to have crossed at Williamsport. It is not believed that they will visit Frederick.

The enemy has nearly 6000 infantry this side of the Potomac, under General Rhodes. Two regiments of infantry and a squad of cavalry are at Sharpsburg, and the remainder are encamped between Williamsport and Hagerstown. No artillery has been sent over, nor have any troops crossed since yesterday morning.

Gen. Ewell has left Williamsport and gone to the main body of his command, stationed at Charlestown. Lee's army is not known to be within supporting distance of Ewell, and it is very probable that the force now in Maryland will not penetrate further north. The cavalry force numbers about twelve hundred, under Jenkins.

The party which first advanced upon Greencastle and Chambersburg numbered only six hundred and fifty.

WASHINGTON, June 22.—The Richmond Dispatch of the 21st contains the following: "Dispatches received yesterday from Savannah announce the capture by the enemy of the Confederate ironclad steamer Fingal, commanded by Captain Webb, of Atlanta. Another steamer outside the harbor was attacked and captured after an action of thirty minutes, by two Federal ironclads."

Richmond papers of the 20th say the city of Darien, Georgia, was burned by the Federals on the 11th inst., and is now one plain of ashes and blackened chimneys. Seven Federal ironclads were at Brunswick, Georgia, and large forces had landed from transports. Vallandigham has run the blockade from Wilmington. He is going to Nassau and thence to Canada.

WASHINGTON, June 21.—A Harrisburg, Penn. dispatch to the Herald states that Jenkins passed through Greencastle last evening with 700 mounted infantry, in the direction of Waynesboro. The rebels are reported to have sixteen pieces of artillery with their large force. They occupy the south bank of the Potomac, between Cumberland and Harper's Ferry. Rhodes has 20,000 men at Williamsport.

The opinion in official circles at Harrisburg is, that the rebels have serious designs on Baltimore! Their movements indicate this, and fears are entertained for the safety of that city. Three hundred rebel cavalry fired Mercersburg in several places.

A Chambersburg dispatch says the rebels are scouring the country for horses, and have got about 2000 head of cattle and 2000 horses. They are reported near Waynesboro and Gettysburg. Jenkins left Greencastle to-night with eight days rations, on a foraging expedition.

HARRISBURG, June 21.—A dispatch received here late this evening states that a rebel cavalry force is within eight miles of Gettysburg, and had crossed South Mountain, evidently advancing to the Northern Central Railroad. An ample force is prepared to resist the attack.

NEW YORK, June 21.—A Harrisburg dispatch to-night, contains the following: The rebels are reported 40,000 strong at Hagerstown, and fortifying. Milroy's headquarters are still at Bloody Run. Troops here are expecting marching orders immediately. It is feared Ewell is in Williamsport, but opinion here is that he is not at that point unless Lee is about to cross below. Heavy rains may have raised the Potomac and hurried him off.

Gov. Curtin to-night received a dispatch from Chambersburg, stating that Jenkins had arrived at Waynesboro and had thrown out pickets five miles this side, but withdrew them this morning. There is no information at Waynesboro of rebel infantry at Hagerstown. Jenkins has been plundering horses in the mountains. General Couch received a dispatch to-night confirming the report of rebel cavalry at Gettysburg.

BALTIMORE, June 21, 8 P. M.—Latest advices from Plain No 4, say that heavy firing has been heard there at intervals throughout the day.

BALTIMORE, June 21.—The rebels made their appearance at Frederick yesterday evening, and about 7 o'clock a body of cavalry reached Monocacy bridge, four miles this side of Frederick. The rebels paroled all the sick in the hospital and every Government employe. They searched the stables for horses, seizing all marked U. S. A very large force of rebel infantry, cavalry and artillery crossed at Antietam during yesterday. Refugees say they number from 40,000 to 50,000, but pickets report them at 25,000. Earthworks are being erected around the west and north sides of Baltimore, thus completing the chain of fortifications. Barricades are being erected within the city, extending from the high ground on the east to the southwestern extremity.

Secession flags were displayed at the Central Hotel, and some citizens collected there to welcome the rebels. A majority of the population evinced no pleasure at the visit. The ladies were exceedingly expressive in their demonstrations of disgust, and showered words of sympathy upon our prisoners as they passed through the town. The party, which entered the city did not number over twenty, and many of these seemed to be intoxicated, as they reeled in their saddles. Pickets were stationed on the outside of town. No one was allowed to leave until about midnight, when the cavalry all left, going toward Middletown. This morning they entered the city again, and established pickets in the outskirts. The telegraph poles were cut down and the wires destroyed. There was supposed to be about thirty rebels in the city this P. M. The enemy has no force between Frederick and Boonesboro except a small cavalry camp at Middletown. No attempt had been made to destroy the bridge over the Monocacy river, although the enemy came down last night within a few rods of the junction.

The rebels are reported to be fortifying South Mountain. They have in the vicinity of Williamsport about 6000 infantry, 1000 cavalry, and a few pieces of artillery. A squadron of cavalry could undoubtedly capture the entire force this side of South Mountain.

The rebels appear very uneasy, and will probably vacate town to-night. All is quiet.

AN IMMENSE TRAIN OF NEGROES.—The New Orleans Era, of the 30th ultimo has the following:

It has been known to many persons in this city that an immense train, consisting of about 500 wagons, 3000 mules and horses, 1500 head of cattle, and 6000 negroes, has just been brought from the Teche country to a safe point within our lines. The train was fully eight miles in length, and was under a guard of several regiments of volunteer troops, the whole under command of Col. Joseph S. Morgan, of the 90th New York.

The caravan started from Barre's Landing on the 21st of May, at which place the wagons numbered about 400, which was gradually increased on the march down. These wagons were filled with contrabands of all ages and both sexes, there being an average of about ten in each vehicle. The advance was held by Col. Chickering, of the 41st Massachusetts. The artillery and infantry were provisionally brigaded, and upon the Colonel commanding rested the safe convoy of the train. The first day's march was twenty-five miles, and the second fifteen.

Soon after bivouacking on the second day, a courier brought intelligence to Col. Morgan that a private of the 19th New York, named Loomis, had been shot by the proprietor of a plantation some three miles to the rear, whose name is Wilcoxson. Loomis was engaged in loading sugar into the carts for the use of the 13th New York, when he was shot down by this Wilcoxson, who immediately made his escape across the Teche. A guard was sent back to arrest whoever was upon the place, and found numerous firearms, among which was a revolver found upon the person of Mrs. Wilcoxson, wife of the man who shot Loomis. She was brought to this city, where she is detained as a hostage until her husband shall give himself up.

Reliable intelligence was here received that the train would probably meet with trouble near St. Martinsville bridge, as the guerrilla, Col. Fornet, was reported to be lying in wait to attack it at that place. Every precaution was taken to give Fornet and his guerrillas the proper reception, but upon arrival at the bridge it was learned that he had passed the evening previous, and was secreted in a swamp about four miles farther south. That evening the train encamped at Spanish Lake, near the old rebel Camp Pratt.

On the 23d the whole train passed through Franklin, with colors flying—the band of the 90th and the field music of the infantry playing the national airs. St. Martinsville was passed in the same manner, and the professed loyal ladies of both places affected great disgust at such proceedings. The whole train, including every wagon, negro, horse, mule, &c., came safely through, and are now in a place of security.

The Bowman House.

In yesterday's edition we stopped the press to announce the destruction of this, the only hotel in Jackson. The alarm of fire was given at twenty minutes past 3 o'clock, Wednesday morning, and so rapid was the progress of the flames that in fifteen minutes from its discovery the entire roof on both wings fell in, and ten minutes later the upper story was in flames. The fire originated in the top of the house, under the roof, as there was no fire in the upper story when discovered by the sentinel.

Rumors have been circulated that one or two persons perished in the flames, but it is contradicted by the officers of the house. It was been conjectured to be the work of an incendiary, but we are inclined to attribute it to accident.

The loss of this hotel is a great public calamity, especially as it is impossible to rebuild for the present.

The building was insured for $25,000 and the furniture for $10,000. All the furniture and other preparations of the establishment were lost. We understand that the loss of Messrs. Daniels & Co., the proprietors, in this respect was $20,000.—Mississippian, 11th

A gentleman who recently passed the Federal lines says the democratic ladies of New York have gotten up a magnificent sword, at a cost of twelve hundred dollars, intended as a present to Gen. Lee. It will be sent to Richmond by some underground railroad.

[illegible]E DAILY CITIZEN.

[illegible] SWORDS,......Proprietor

VICKSBURG, MISS.

[illegible]URSDAY, JULY 2, 1863.

[illegible]Mrs. Cisco was instantly killed on Mon[illegible] on Jackson road. Mrs. Cisco's husband is [illegible] in Virginia, a member of Moody's artille[illegible], and the death of such a loving, affectionate [an]d dutiful wife will be a loss to him irrepara[ble].

☞ We are indebted to Major Gillespie for [a] steak of Confederate beef *alias* meat. We [h]ave tried it, and can assure our friends that if [it] is rendered necessary, they need have no [s]cruples at eating the meat. It is sweet, savory and tender, and so long as we have a mule [l]eft we are satisfied our soldiers will be content [t]o subsist on it.

☞ Jerre Askew, one of our most esteemed [m]erchant-citizens, was wounded at the works [in] the rear of our city a few days since, and [br]eathed his last on Monday. Mr. Askew was [a] young man of strict integrity, great industry [an]d an honor to his family and friends. He [wa]s a member of Cowan's artillery, and by the [str]ict discharge of his duties and his obliging [dis]position, won the confidence and esteem of [the] entire command. May the blow his family [hav]e sustained be mitigated by Him who doeth [all] things well.

☞ Grant's forces did a little firing on [Tu]esday afternoon, but the balance of that [da]y was comparatively quiet. Yesterday morn[in]g they were very still, and continued so until [e]arly in the afternoon, when they sprung a [m]ine on the left of our centre, and opened fire [a]long the line for some distance. We have not [b]een able to ascertain anything definitely as [to] our loss, but as our officers were on the [lo]okout for this move of the enemy, the expec[ta]tions of the Yankees were not realized by a [g]reat deal.

☞ Among many good deeds we hear spoken [of] with pride by our citizens, we cannot refrain [fro]m mentioning the case of Mr. F. Kiser. This [gen]tleman, having more corn than he thought [w]as necessary to last him during the siege of [th]is place, portioned off what would do him for [th]e brief interval that will ensue before the [ar]rival of succor to our garrison, and since [tha]t time has relieved the wants of many fami[lies] *free of charge!* May he live long and prosper, [and] his name be handed down to posterity when [th]e siege of Vicksburg is written, as one in [wh]ose breast the "milk of human kindness" had [not] dried up.

☞ Porter is enjoying a season of rest, and [his] men are doubtless obliged to him for his [kin]d consideration for their welfare. On Tues[day] he fired a few shells from his parrots, and [ke]pt his men tolerably busy sharpshooting [a]cross the river, with no other result than [m]ight be expected. The mortars have not [b]een used for nearly forty-eight hours. Poor [f]ool, he might as well give up the vain aspira[tion] he entertains of capturing our city or ex[ter]mination our people, and return to his mas[ter] to receive the reward such a gasconading [ex]ploit will meet at the hands of the unappreci[at]ing Government at Washington.

[D]EATH OF LIEUT.-COL. GRIFFIN.—General [Sm]ith's impetuous division seems singularly [unf]ortunate. He has lost many gallant men [wh]ose valor and worth the siege has fully de[vel]oped, and whose death is a great public [cal]amity. Lieut.-Col. Griffin, commanding the [1]st Louisiana regiment, was killed on Satur[da]y. He was a popular and efficient officer. [G]ifted by nature with undaunted courage, in[d]omitable resolution and energy, he was also [po]ssessed of quick determination, keen glance [an]d coolness in danger, which are the most [e]ssential qualities of an officer, while by his [m]ingled firmness and clemency of his conduct, [h]e won the confidence and good will of his [m]en. May the soft south winds murmur sweet requiems o'er his manes, and the twilight dews fall gently like an angel's tear-drop and moist[e]n his turfy bed.

☞ If aught would appeal to the heart of [st]one of the extortioner with success, the pres[e]nt necessities of our citizens would do so. It [i]s needless to attempt to disguise from the ene[m]y or our own people that our wants are great, [b]ut still we can conscientiously assert our be[l]ief that there is plenty within our lines, by [a]n exercise of prudence, to last until long after [s]uccor reaches us. We are satisfied there are [n]umerous persons within our city who have [b]readstuffs secreted, and are doling it out, at the most exhorbitant figures, to those who had not the foresight or means at their command to provide for the exigency now upon us. A rumor has reached us that parties in our city have been, and are now, selling flour at five dollars per pound! molasses at ten dollars per gallon! and corn at ten dollars per bushel! We have not as yet proved the fact upon the parties accused, but this allusion to the subject may induce some of our citizens to ascertain whether such prices have been paid, and to whom; and if so, let a brand not only be placed upon their brow, but let it be seared into their very brain, that humanity may scorn and shun [th]em as they would the portals of hell itself.

GOOD NEWS.—In devoting a large portion of our space this morning to Federal intelligence, copied from the Memphis Bulletin of the 25th, it should be remembered that the news, in the original truth, is whitewashed by the Federal Provost Marshal, who desires to hood-wink the poor Northern white slaves. The former editors of the Bulletin being rather pro-southern men, were arrested for speaking the truth when truth was unwelcome to Yankeedom, and placed in the chain-gang working at Warrenton, where they now are. This paper at present is in duress, and edited by a pink-nosed, slab-sided, toad-eating Yankee, who is a lineal descendant of Judas Iscariot and a brother germain of the greatest Puritanical, sycophantic, howling scoundrel unhung—Parson Brownlow. Yet with such a character, this paper cannot cloak the fact that Gen. Rob't E. Lee has given Hooker, Milroy & Co. one of the best and soundest whippings on record, and that the "galorious Union" is now exceedingly weak in the knees.

Gen. Rob't E. Lee Again.

Again we have reliable news from the gallant corps of Gen. Lee in Virginia. Elated with success, encouraged by a series of brilliant victories, marching to and crossing the Rappahannock, defeating Hooker's right wing and thence through the Shenandoah Valley, driving Milroy from Winchester and capturing 6000 of his men and a large amount of valuable stores of all descriptions, re-entering Maryland, holding Hagerstown, threatening Washington City, and within a few miles of Baltimore—onward and upward their war cry—our brave men under Lee are striking terror to the heart of all Yankeedom. Like the Scottish chieftain's braves, Lee's men are springing up from moor and brake, crag and dale, with flashing steel and sturdy arm, ready to do or die in the great cause of national independence, right and honor. To day the mongrel administration of Lincoln, like Japhet, are in search of a father—for their old Abe has departed for parts unknown. Terror reigns in their halls. Lee is to the left of them, the right of them, in front of them, and all around them; and daily do we expect to hear of his being down on them. Never were the French in Algeria more put out by the mobile raids of Ab Del Kader than are the Federals of Maryland, Washington City, Pennsylvania and Ohio by the mercureal movements of Lee's cavalry. Like Paddy's flea are they to the Federals—now they have got them and now they haven't. The omnipresence of our troops and their throwing dust in the eyes, or rather on the heels of the panic-stricken Federals in Maryland and Pennsylvania, clearly prove that Lee just now is the right man in the right place.

We lay before our readers in this issue an account of Lee's brilliant and successful onslaught upon the abolition hordes, and show, e'en from their own record, how our gallant boys of the cavalry have fleshed their swords to the hilt with their vaunting foes, and how each musket of our infantry has told its fatal leaden tale.

To-day Maryland is ours, to-morrow Pennsylvania will be, and the next day Ohio—now midway, like Mahommed's coffin—will fall.

Succe's and glory to our arms! God and right are with us.

☞ We have heretofore refrained from alluding to a matter which has been a source of extreme annoyance and loss to our citizens. We refer to the lax discipline of some of our company officers in allowing their men to prowl around, day and night, and purloin fruit, vegetables, chickens, etc., from our denizens, and, in the majority of cases, from those whose chief subsistence is derived therefrom. This charge is not confined solely to those at the works, but is equally, if not mainly, attributable to the wagoners and others in charge of animals. Several cases have come to our knowledge wherein the offenders have, in open daylight, entered premises, seized cattle and other things, and defied the owners to their teeth. We are pained to learn that an esteemed citizen of our Vicksburg, Wm. Porterfield, was under the necessity, in protecting his property, to wound one or two soldiers and deprive another of his life. We fully appreciate the fatigue, hardships and privation to which our men are subjected; but upon inquiry it may be ascertained that our city is second to none in contributing to the welfare of those gallant spirits who risk their life and limb for the achievement of an end which will make us one of the most honored people of the earth, and such conduct of which we complain is but base ingratitude. A soldier has his honor at much at stake as when a civilian; then let him preserve his good name and reputation with the same jealous care as before he entered his country's ranks. But so long as this end is lost sight of, so long may we expect to chronicle scenes of bloodshed among those of our own people. We make this public exposure, mortifying as it to us, with the hope that a salutary improvement in matters will be made by our military authorities.

ON DIT.—That the great Ulysses—the Yankee Generalissimo, surnamed Grant—has expressed his intention of dining in Vicksburg on Saturday next, and celebrating the 4th of July by a grand dinner and so forth. When asked if he would invite Gen. Jo. Johnston to join he said, "No! for fear there will be a row at the table." Ulysses must get into the city before he dines in it. The way to cook a rabbit is "first catch the rabbit." &c

NOTE.

JULY 4th, 1863.

Two days bring about great changes, The banner of the Union floats over Vicksburg. Gen. Grant has "caught the rabbit;" he has dined in Vicksburg, and he did bring his dinner with him. The "Citizen" lives to see it. For the last time it appears on "Wall-paper." No more will it eulogize the luxury of mule-meat and fricassed kitten—urge Southern warriors to such diet never-more. This is the last wall-paper edition, and is, excepting this note, from the types as we found them. It will be valuable hereafter as a curiosity.

land, and when they left they threatened to return and furnish themselves with horses and forage. The rebels have done an immense amount of damage.

It is thought Gen. Rhodes is opposite Williamsport with 20,000 men. The rebel Gen. Imboden is reported as advancing, but this is considered doubtful.

FREDERICK, MD., June 20.—The enemy's cavalry left Boonsboro last evening, after capturing a number of horses, and returned to Hagerstown yesterday.

Six thousand infantry are reported to have crossed at Williamsport. It is not believed that they will visit Frederick.

The enemy has nearly 6000 infantry this side of the Potomac, under General Rhodes. Two regiments of infantry and a squad of cavalry are at Sharpsburg, and the remainder are encamped between Williamsport and Hagerstown. No artillery has been sent over, nor have any troops crossed since yesterday morning.

Gen. Ewell has left Williamsport and gone to the main body of his command, stationed at Charlestown. Lee's army is not known to be within supporting distance of Ewell, and it is very probable that the force now in Maryland will not penetrate further north. The cavalry force numbers about twelve hundred, under Jenkins.

The party which first advanced upon Greencastle and Chambersburg numbered only six hundred and fifty.

WASHINGTON, June 22.—The Richmond Dispatch of the 21st contains the following: "Dispatches received yesterday from Savannah announce the capture by the enemy of the Confederate ironclad steamer Fingal, commanded by Captain Webb, of Atlanta. Another steamer outside the harbor was attacked and captured after an action of thirty minutes, by two Federal ironclads."

Richmond papers of the 20th say the city of Darien, Georgia, was burned by the Federals on the 11th inst., and is now one plain of ashes and blackened chimneys. Seven Federal ironclads were at Brunswick, Georgia, and large forces had landed from transports. Vallandigham has run the blockade from Wilmington. He is going to Nassau and thence to Canada.

WASHINGTON, June 21.—A Harrisburg, Penn. dispatch to the Herald states that Jenkins passed through Greencastle last evening with 700 mounted infantry, in the direction of Waynesboro. The rebels are reported to have sixteen pieces of artillery with their large force. They occupy the south bank of the Potomac, between Cumberland and Harper's Ferry. Rhodes has 20,000 men at Williamsport.

The opinion in official circles at Harrisburg is, that the rebels have serious designs on Baltimore. Their movements indicate this, and fears are entertained for the safety of that city. Three hundred rebel cavalry fired Mercersburg in several places.

A Chambersburg dispatch says the rebels are scouring the country for horses, and have got about 2000 head of cattle and 2000 horses. They are reported near Waynesboro and Gettysburg. Jenkins left Greencastle to night with eight days rations, on a foraging expedition.

HARRISBURG, June 21.—A dispatch received here late this evening states that a rebel cavalry force is within eight miles of Gettysburg, and had crossed South Mountain, evidently advancing to the Northern Central Railroad. An ample force is prepared to resist the attack.

NEW YORK, June 21.—A Harrisburg dispatch to-night, contains the following: The rebels are reported 40,000 strong at Hagerstown, and fortifying. Milroy's headquarters are still at Bloody Run. Troops here are expecting marching orders immediately. It is feared Ewell is in Williamsport, but opinion here is that he is not at that point unless Lee is about to cross below. Heavy rains may have raised the Potomac and hurrried him off.

Gov. Curtin to-night received a dispatch from Chambersburg, stating that Jenkins had arrived at Waynesboro and had thrown out pickets five miles this side, but withdrew them this morning. There is no information at Waynesboro of rebel infantry at Hagerstown. Jenkins has been plundering horses in the mountains. General Couch received a dispatch to-night confirming the report of rebel cavalry at Gettysburg.

BALTIMORE, June 21, 8 P. M.—Latest advices from Plain No 4, say that heavy firing has been heard there at intervals throughout the day.

BALTIMORE, June 21.—The rebels made their appearance at Frederick yesterday evening, and about 7 o'clock a body of cavalry reached Monocacy bridge, four miles this side of Frederick. The rebels paroled all the sick in the hospital and every Government employe. They searched the stables for horses, seizing all marked U. S. A very lage force of rebel infantry, cavalry and artillery crossed at Antietam during yesterday. Refugees say they number from 40,000 to 50,000, but pickets report them at 25,000. Earthworks are being erected around the west and north sides of Baltimore, thus completing the chain of fortifications. Barricades are being erected within the city, extending from the high ground on the east to the southwestern ex-

the cavalry all left, going toward Middletown. This morning they entered the city again, and established pickets in the outskirts. The telegraph poles were cut down and the wires destroyed. There was supposed to be about thirty rebels in the city this P. M. The enemy has no force between Frederick and Boonesboro except a small cavalry camp at Middletown. No attempt had been made to destroy the bridge over the Monocacy river, although the enemy came down last night within a few rods of the junction.

The rebels are reported to be fortifying South Mountain. They have in the vicinity of Williamsport about 6000 infantry, 1000 cavalry, and a few pieces of artillery. A squadron of cavalry could undoubtedly capture the entire force this side of South Mountain.

Mid the din and clash of arms, the screech of shells and whisttle of bullets, which are a continual feature in the status of our beleaguered city, incidents of happiness often arise to vary in a cheery way the Phases of so stern a scene. On the evening of the 20th ult., with gaiety, myrth and good feeling, at a prominent Hospital of this city, through the ministerial offices of a chaplain of a gallant regiment, Charles Royall, Prince Imperial of Ethiopia, of the Barberigo family, espoused the lovely and accomplished Rosa Glass, Arch Duchess of Senegambia, one of the most celebrated Princes of the Laundressina Regime. The affair was conducted with great magnificence, though as is usual in troublesome times the sabler element was predominant.

The foe may hurl their deathly bolts,
And think we are affrightened,
Well may we scorn them, silly dolts,—
Our Blacks are now united.

VICTIMIZED.—We learned of an instance wherein a "knight of the quill" and a "disciple of the black art," with malice in their hearts and vengeance in their eyes, ruthlessly put a period to the existence of a venerable feline that has for time, not within the recollection of the "oldest inhabitant," faithfully discharged the duties to be expected of him to the terror of sundry vermin in his neighborhood. Poor, defunct Thomas was then prepared, not for the grave, but the pot, and several friends invited to partake of a nice rabbit. As a matter of course, no one would wound the feelings of another, especially in these times, by refusing a cordial invitation to dinner, and the guests assisted in consuming the poor animal with a relish that did honor to their epicurean taste. The "sold" assure us the meat was delicious, and that pussy must look out for her safety.

☞ The Federal General McClernand until recently outside the rear of our city has been superceded. He and Grant could not run in the same harness. He was for splurging and Grant for gassing, both got the loggerheads. So poor Mac. had to leave, and Grant has all his own way.

☞ The Yanks outside our city are considerably on the sick list. Fever, dysentry and disgust are their companions, and Grant is their master. The boys are deserting daily and are crossing the river in the region of Warrenton, cussing Grant and abolitionists generally. The boys are down upon the earth delving, the burrowing, the bad water, and the hot weather.

GONE OUT.—The National Intelligencer of Washington has closed its long career in a suspension and a sale of its effects at auction.—It has been highly respectable and very mischievous in its day and generation. An old union prop falls with it. If we had the writing of its epitath we should say, "Old Grimes is 'dead'

NOTE.

JULY 4th, 1863.

Two days bring about great changes, The banner of the Union floats over Vicksburg. Gen. Grant has "caught the rabbit;" he has dined in Vicksburg, and he did bring his dinner with him. The "Citizen" lives to see it. For the last time it appears on "Wall-paper." No more will it eulogize the luxury of mule-meat and fricassed kitten—urge Southern warriors to such diet never-more. This is the last wall-paper edition, and is, excepting this note, from the types as we found them. It will be valuable hereafter as a curiosity.

Vol. II. RICHMOND, SATURDAY, JULY 4, 1863. No. 1.

LIEUT. GEN. RICHARD S. EWELL.

This great officer is, at the present moment, the theme of every tongue, the cynosure of all eyes in the Confederate States. To the Yankees he is an object of unbounded terror. His magnificent exploit at Winchester, and the rapidity with which he followed it to its remotest consequences, prove him to be the worthy successor of the lamented Jackson, to whose successes he so largely contributed, and by whom he was so properly estimated. In the words of a cotemporary, he is the true Elisha of that military Elijah. His mantle has fallen upon him, and along with his mantle a double portion of the spirit which, in the darkest hours of the Confederacy, shone forth to cheer and to illuminate, like the light of Saint Elmo amid the storm.

General Ewell is a native of Prince William county in this State. We have not been able to ascertain the year of his birth; but as he entered the Military Academy of West Point in 1836, and graduated in 1840, we presume he is somewhat turned of forty. He is, therefore, in the very prime of life, with at least twenty campaigns still in him. He was appointed second lieutenant of cavalry by brevet on the 1st July, 1840, and full second lieutenant the November following. On the 18th September, 1845, he was made first lieutenant, and, with that rank, went into the Mexican war. He won his promotion to captain in the field, having received it "for gallant and meritorious conduct" in the battles of Contreras and Cherubusco.

Captain Ewell was among the first to cast his fortune with the South when his native State seceded. His first appearance was at Fairfax Court House, when a party of cavalry were surprised by the enemy, and Governor Smith succeeded in rallying them. Ewell, we believe, had no command; but, when the alarm took place, he rushed into the street, in the very midst of the danger, and by his energetic remonstrances and fearless exposure of his person, contributed greatly to prevent a catastrophe. With the rank of colonel, we next find him in command of the Camp of Instruction for Cavalry at Ashland. His services here were invaluable, and their effect has been felt throughout the war. His discipline was stern and rigid, but humane, and, out of raw mounted militia, he soon formed a most efficient body of troops. At the first battle of Manassas, Ewell, now a brigadier, was stationed with his cavalry on the right. In that position, he was detained all day, without participating in the dangers and glory of the fight. An order was sent to him to advance to Centreville, and fall upon the flank and rear of the enemy. That order never reached him. Had it arrived in time, the consequence would have been the capture of 20,000 men, the utter destruction of the Yankee army, and, in all probability, the capture of Washington. Soon after this battle, Ewell was made a major-general, and placed in command of a division.

Upon Jackson's retreat after the battle of Kernstown, Ewell was sent to reinforce him. The two great soldiers seemed formed to act together. The utmost cordiality always existed between them. Each was too noble, too generous, too brave, to feel the slightest jealousy of the other. Upon all occasions, Jackson bore testimony to the invaluable services of Ewell, and Ewell, in return, always expressed the highest admiration for Jackson. In nearly all of Jackson's battles in the Valley, Ewell was a participant, and the part he bore was always prominent. At Port Republic, Ewell was pitted against Fremont. He routed him completely, and clapped an extinguisher upon his pretensions to be considered a soldier. Since that time, he has been continually sinking in the estimation of the Yankees, and has now at last found his level, as the chief of an army of negroes.

LIEUT. GEN. RICHARD S. EWELL.

General Ewell was in all the battles around Richmond in which Jackson's corps was engaged. When the latter was ordered to the Piedmont country to chastise the miscreant Pope, Ewell was his right-hand man. He distinguished himself greatly in the battle of Cedar mountain, and was the life and soul of the march to Manassas. In the second battle of that name, he was so severely wounded in the leg, that amputation was rendered necessary. He bore the operation with great fortitude and even cheerfulness. As soon as he had sufficiently recovered, he was removed to this city, where, in the house of his friend, Dr. Hancock, who had been his surgeon on a former occasion, he lay several months, occasionally suffering great pain. Having finally recovered, he was, but a short time since, made a lieutenant-general and placed in command of one-half of Jackson's old corps, out of which two had been formed, Gen. A. P. Hill commanding the other. It is said that Jackson, on his death-bed, expressed his earnest desire that Ewell might be his successor. That he was correct in his estimate of Ewell's capacity for command has been rendered sufficiently evident. The capture of Winchester was one of the most magnificent achievements of the war, and places its author, at once, in the foremost ranks of our generals. It is remarkable that Dr. Hancock sent to a cork-leg maker in Philadelphia, to whom, before the war, he had frequently sent orders, for a leg for General Ewell, adding that he need not send it on, for that the general would come for it himself very shortly. It seems, from present appearances, as though it might be so.

Boys, if you don't want to fall in love, keep away from muslin. You can no more play with those girls without losing your heart, than you can play with gamblers without losing your money. The heart-strings of a woman, like the tendrils of a vine, are always reaching out for something to cling to. The consequence is, that before you are 'going' you are 'gone,' like a lot at auction.

When flatterers meet, the Devil goes to dinner.

THE NEW YORK HERALD.

WHOLE NO. 9789. NEW YORK, SUNDAY, JULY 5, 1863 PRICE FOUR CENTS.

IMPORTANT FROM BERMUDA.

Arrival of Mr. Vallandigham, En Route for Canada.

MOVEMENTS OF THE BLOCKADE RUNNERS

The Dismissal of British Consul Moore by the Rebel Authorities.

Letter from Mr. Benjamin to Mr. Mason on the Subject,

&c., &c., &c.

We have the Bermuda *Royal Gazette* of June 23.

The rebel steamer Lady Davis arrived at St. Georges on the 22d from Wilmington. She is reported to belong to the rebel government, and to have brought important despatches from that government to the British government.

There were twelve blockade runners at Wilmington on the 16th. Two of them left in company with the Lady Davis, which passed close to the blockading squadron on her way out of Wilmington. The Lady Davis was formerly the Cornubia.

The steamer Harriet Pinckney had arrived from England, and the Lord Clyde had cleared for Nassau.

The steamer Marion, from Nassau, bound to England had called for coal, but not being able to get supplied she proceeded to Halifax.

A line of steamers is about to be established between Bermuda and Liverpool.

Arrived at Hamilton, Bermuda, June 18, schooner E. A. Willard, Conly, Bangor.

Arrival of Mr. Vallandigham.

[From the Bermuda Gazette.]

This gentleman, who has caused so much excitement in the Northern States, and who was banished to the Southern States for a stated period, arrived here in the Confederate steamer Lady Davis, from Wilmington, on Saturday last. It is reported that Mr. V. is on his way to Canada, and there to await coming events.

Dismissal of a British Consul by the Rebel Authorities.

[From the Wilmington Daily Journal, June 16.]

We give below, from the Richmond *Sentinel*, a despatch of the Secretary of State of the Confederate States to Mr. Mason, our Commissioner in England. It makes known the causes of the late revocation of the exequatur of the British Consul at this port, and in doing so takes occasion to explain the general grounds of the President's action and the views which govern the policy which he is pursuing.—

[No. 24.] CONFEDERATE STATES OF AMERICA, DEPARTMENT OF STATE, RICHMOND, June 6, 1863.

SIR—Herewith you will receive copies of the following papers:—

A.—Letter of George Moore, Esq., Her Brittanic Majesty's Consul in Richmond to this department, dated February 16, 1863.

B.—Letter from the Secretary of State to Consul Moore, February 20, 1863.

C.—Letters patent by the President, revoking the exequatur of Consul Moore, June 5, 1863.

D.—Letter enclosing to Consul Moore a copy of the letters patent revoking his exequatur.

It is deemed proper to inform you that this action of the President was influenced in no small degree by the communication to him of an unofficial letter of Consul Moore, to which I shall presently refer.

It appears that two persons, named Molony and Farrell, who were enrolled as conscripts in our service, claimed exemption on the ground that they were British subjects, and Consul Moore, in order to avoid the difficulty which prevented his corresponding with this department as set forth in the paper B, addressed himself directly to the Secretary of War, who was ignorant of the request made by this department for the production of the Consul's commission. The Secretary of War ordered an investigation of the facts, when it became apparent that the two men had exercised the right of suffrage in this State, thus debarring themselves of all pretext for denying their citizenship; that both had resided here for eight years, and had settled on and were cultivating farms owned by themselves. You will find annexed the report of Lieut. Col. Edgar, marked E, and it is difficult to conceive a case presenting stronger proofs of the renunciation of native allegiance, and of the acquisition of *de facto* citizenship, than are found in that report. It is in relation to such a case that it has seemed proper to Consul Moore to denounce the government of the Confederate States to one of its own citizens as being indifferent "to cases of the most atrocious cruelty." A copy of his letter to the counsel of the two men is annexed, marked F.

The earnest desire of this government is to entertain amicable relations with all nations, and with none do its interests invite the formation of closer ties than with Great Britain. Although feeling aggrieved that the government of her Majesty has pursued a policy which, according to the confessions of Earl Russell himself, has increased the disparity of strength which he considers to exist between the belligerents, and has conferred signal advantage on our enemies in a war in which Great Britain announces herself to be really and not nominally neutral, the President has not deemed it necessary to interpose any obstacle to the continued residence of British consuls within the confederacy by virtue of exequaturs granted by the former government. His course has been consistently guided by the principles which underlie the whole structure of our government. The State of Virginia having delegated to the government of the United States, by the constitution of 1787, the power of controlling its foreign relations, became bound by the action of that government in its grant of an exequatur to Consul Moore. When Virginia seceded, withdrew the power delegated to the government of the United States, and conferred them on this government, the exequatur granted to Consul Moore was not thereby invalidated. An act done by an agent while duly authorized continues to bind the principal after the revocation of the agent's authority. On these grounds the President has hitherto steadily resisted all influences which have been exerted to induce him to exact of foreign consuls that they should ask for an exequatur from this government as a condition of the continued exercise of their functions. It was not deemed compatible with the dignity of the government to extort, by enforcing the withdrawal of national protection from neutral residents, such inferential recognition of its independence as might be supposed to be implied in the request of an exequatur. The consuls of foreign nations, therefore, established within the confederacy, who were in possession of an exequatur issued by the government of the United States prior to the formation of the confederacy, have been maintained and respected in the exercise of their legitimate functions, and the same protection and respect will be accorded to them in future, so long as they confine themselves to the sphere of their duties, and seek neither to evade or defy the legitimate authority of this government within its own jurisdiction.

There has grown up an abuse, however, the result of this tolerance on the part of the President, which is too serious to be longer allowed. Great Britain has deemed it for her interest to refuse acknowledging the patent fact of the existence of this confederacy as an independent nation. It can scarcely be expected that we should, by our own conduct, imply assent to the justice or propriety of that refusal, now that the British Minister accredited to the government of our enemies assumes the power to issue instructions and exercise authority over the consuls of Great Britain residing within this country; nay, even of appointing agents to supervise British interest in the Confederate States. This course of conduct plainly ignores the existence of this government, and implies the continuance of the relations between that Minister and the consuls of her Majesty resident within the confederacy which existed prior to the withdrawal of these States from the Union. It is further the assertion of a right on the part of Lord Lyons, by virtue of his credentials as her Majesty's Minister at Washington, to exercise the power and authority of a minister accredited to Richmond, and officially received as such by the President. Under these circumstances, and because of similar action by other ministers, the President has felt it his duty to order that no direct communication be permitted between the consuls of neutral nations in the confederacy and the functionaries of those nations residing within the enemy's country. All communication, therefore, between her Majesty's consuls or consular agents in the confederacy and foreign countries, whether neutral or hostile, will hereafter be restricted to vessels arriving from or despatched for neutral points. The President has the less reluctance in imposing this restriction because of the ample facilities for correspondence which are now afforded by the fleets of Confederate and neutral steamships engaged in regular trade between neutral countries and the Confederate ports. This trade is daily increasing, in spite of the paper blockade, which is upheld by her Majesty's government in disregard, as the President conceives, of the rights of this confederacy, of the dictates of public law, and of the duties of impartial neutrality.

You are instructed by the President to furnish a copy of this despatch, with a copy of the papers appended, to her Majesty's Secretary of State for Foreign Affairs.

I am, very respectfully, your obedient servant,

J. P. BENJAMIN, Secretary of State.

Hon. JAMES M. MASON, Commissioner, &c., &c., London.

New Bedford Fortified.

The New Bedford *Mercury* says:—"The demonstrations of the privateer Tacony on our immediate coast have caused the work on the fortifications at Clark's Point to be pushed to the utmost. Captain Allen had three ten-inch columbiads mounted yesterday afternoon, and another nearly ready in position. A number of shells were also filled, and three were fired to ascertain the range. The guns mounted point in the direction of Round Hills, and the shells exploded at about two miles from the fort. As the elevation was low, the trial was considered a success."

EXTRA.

SUNDAY AFTERNOON, Half-past One O'clock.

VERY IMPORTANT.

GLORIOUS NEWS.

A GREAT VICTORY!

Terrific and Unparalleled Conflict.

The Rebels Utterly Routed.

They Retreat and Are Pursued by the Union Forces.

The Terrible Battle on Friday.

Official Despatch from General Meade.

The Rebels Repulsed in Every Attack.

General Doubleday Mortally Wounded.

GENERAL SICKLES' LEG AMPUTATED.

Splendid Conduct of the Army of the Potomac.

Generals Hancock and Gibbon Wounded.

The Rebel Generals Longstreet, Hill and Armistead Captured.

Three Thousand More Rebels Taken Prisoners.

The President Congratulates the Country,

&c., &c., &c.

THE GREAT BATTLE.

GETTYSBURG, July 4, 1863.

Glorious Fourth. The greatest and most glorious battle of the war.

The rebels completely routed. Longstreet and Hill wounded and in our hands.

The fighting yesterday was beyond all parallel.

The enemy attempted to turn both right and left flanks in turn, and afterwards attacked the centre; but was repulsed on all hands. He then made a general attack along the whole line; but was defeated terribly.

THE VICTORY OF THE UNION ARMY IS COMPLETE.

The enemy is in full retreat, and is pursued by the Union troops.

THE FRIGHT OF JEFF. DAVIS IN RICHMOND.

BALTIMORE, July 4, 1863.

News from the front was very favorable up to noon day. General Meade had captured seven thousand prisoners, who are on their way here.

General Hancock, badly wounded, has arrived here.

General Sickles has lost his leg, and is at Westminster, doing well.

No passes are granted to civilians to go to the front to-day, on account of medical officers complaining.

The day has been universally celebrated here. Secessionists have almost without exception hung out Union colors. The city is entirely free from drunkenness, and the best of order prevails.

Union men are jubilant and exultant, and secesh are despondent over the news from Meade.

News of the messenger from Jeff. Davis to General Lee with orders to come to the relief of Richmond is confirmed.

Gen. Doubleday was mortally wounded yesterday. Our losses have been heavy, and prisoners say the rebel losses have been terrible.

The battles have been the most terrific and fatal of any ever fought for the numbers engaged.

The wounded are expected here to-night.

Gen. E. B. Tyler has been assigned to the command here. General Daniel Tyler goes elsewhere.

GENERALS SICKLES AND GIBBON.

Arrival of Our Wounded Soldiers in Baltimore.

BALTIMORE, July 4, 1863.

A train with fifteen hundred wounded soldiers is just coming in. Generals Sickles and Gibben are on board.

National salutes were fired from forts McHenry Federal Hill, and the men-of-war in the harbor to-day at noon, Captain Dove, of the Albany, war steamer, leading off with twenty-one sixty-four pounders.

Many supposed the firing was between our own and rebel armies, and for a while there was much commotion in thhe city.

The day has passed off very quietly.

GENERAL MEADE'S DESPATCH.

WASHINGTON, July 4—10:10 A. M.

The following has just been received:—

HEADQUARTERS, ARMY OF THE POTOMAC, NEAR GETTYSBURG, July 3—8:30 P. M.

Major General HALLECK, General-in-Chief:—

The enemy opened at one o'clock P. M. from about one hundred and fifty guns, concentrated upon my left centre, continuing without intermission for about three hours, at the expiration of which time he assaulted my left centre twice, being upon both occasions handsomely repulsed with severe loss to him, leaving in our hands nearly three thousand prisoners.

Among the prisoners is Brigadier General Armisted and many colonels and officers of lesser rank.

The enemy left many dead upon the field and a large number of wounded in our hands.

The loss upon our side has been considerable. Major General Hancock and Brigadier General Gibbon were wounded.

After the repelling of the assault, indications leading to the belief that the enemy might be withdrawing, an armed reconnoissance was pushed forward from the left and the enemy found to be in force.

At the present hour all is quiet.

My cavalry have been engaged all day on bote flanks of tee enemy, harrassing and vigorously attacking him with great success, notwithstanding the encountered superior numbers, both of infantry and cavalry.

The army is in fine spirits.

GEORGE G. MEADE,
Major General Commanding.

THE PRESIDENT TO THE COUNTRY.

WASHINGTON, D. C., July 4—10.30 A. M.

The President announces to the country that news from the Army of the Potomac up to ten P. M. of the 3d, is such as to cover that army with the highest honor; to promise a great success to the cause of the Union, and to claim the condolence of all for the many gallant fallen, and that for this, he especially desires that on this day, He, whose will, not ours, should ever be done, be everywhere remembered and reverenced with the profoundest gratitude.

ABRAHAM LINCOLN.

THE HANOVER TELEGRAMS.

PHILADELPHIA, July 4—3 A. M.

The following is a special to the *Press*:—

HANOVER, Pa., July 3, 1863.

The severe skirmishing on Wednesday between General Pleasanton's cavalry and the enemy's forces under Appel, was followed up by a general battle, which opened yesterday at four o'clock P. M., and raged furiously without intermission till ten o'clock last night.

At the beginning of the engagement our forces were stationed one mile south of Gettysburg, on Seminary Ridge, and occupied the road leading from Emmittsburg to Janeystown and Littletown. The enemy's line stretched upon the opposite town, where the Seminary Hill, crossing the Chambersburg turnpike, and south towards the Millstown road. Pleasanton's cavalry and the First and Eleventh corps were posted on the extreme right.

The battle was opened by the First and Eleventh corps, supported by artillery. The enemy made a feint on the right, then came down on the left, and attacked Sickles' corps. This attack was bravely resisted for several hours, when General Sickles arrived from the rear with reinforcements.

In this engagement General Sickles lost his right leg, which was struck by a shell, and afterwards amputated.

Captain Randall of the artillery of this corp, was seriously wounded.

During the day our forces retired to Rock Ridge, a more eligible position about one mile south of their original post, They, however, afterwards recovered the front they had lost, and subsequently occupied the town of Gettysburg.

THE VERY LATEST.

The Brilliant Battle on Friday.

Some of the Results of the Great Victory.

Lee's Army Hors du Combat,

&c., &c., &c.

MR. T. M. COOK'S DESPATCH TO THE NEW YORK HERALD.

HEADQUARTERS, THIRD ARMY CORPS, NEAR GETTYSBURG, July 4, 1863.

The battle of Friday was the most desperate, most fierce and decisive of the war. It was commenced at early daybreak on our extreme left by a determined attack by the enemy with musketry and artillery. The attack was met by the Sixth corps, and portions of the First and the Fifth, the Third lying close at hand in reserve. The battle raged fiercely at this point for nearly three hours, when the enemy fell back, yielding to us *the whole of the battle field of that morning as well as of the previous day.*

Nearly simultaneously with the opening of the attack on the left, movements were discovered on the right, indicating that an effort was made to flank our position in that direction; our artillery on Cemetry Hill at once opened, throwing heavy vollies of shell over and to the north and east of the town. At this point we had eight or ten batteries in position, covered by earthworks. The enemy responded briskly to our cannonading, but with poor effect, and were evidently much annoyed by our fire. They, however, pressed their columns on to the right and very soon our infantry poured on that flank and were earnestly engaged. The contest here was even more earnest and continuous than on the left. The Twelfth and portions of the Eleventh corps withstood the shock, giving never an inch of ground to their assailants.

The fight raged here on the face of a lofty mountain, densely wooded, from the summit of which batteries could command our position on Cemetery hill. It was evidently with a view of gaining this position that the enemy made the assault for this purpose. Hill's corps that had fought on the left on the previous day was brought around to the right to reinforce Early, and as the scheme was developed, it appeared that the early attack on the left was intended merely as a diversion to cover the movement.

From a distance the progress of the fight could be observed by the curling smoke rising above the woods, marking the line of the fierce contest.

In this struggle our reserved artillery was brought into play and did most excellent service from impromptu positions on the elevated points back of cemetery hill, shelling the face of the mountain where the enemy were supposed to be. This reserve fire of shell, added to the steady and unflinching ardor of the glorious Twelfth corps, ultimately checked the vastly superior force of the enemy, who for an hour or two been gradually advancing. At the critical juncture, about eleven o'clock in the forenoon, one or two brigades of New York troops, supposed to be Pennsylvania militia, arrived, and were immediately thrown into position to reinforce the right wing, which was being so badly pressed. This assistance determined the fate of the day. The enemy quailed before it, and soon the curling smoke that marked the line of the contest began to recede, surely indicating that the enemy were falling back, but if they gave away at all it was but slowly, fighting at every step, and thus the battle raged for hours and until afternoon when the enemy abandoned the field in that direction. But they did not yet yield the day. For a brief period hostilities seemed to be suspended, but the suspension was verry brief.

The rebel columns seemed to be moved as if by magic, and within an hour their whole force was massed directly in our front, and once more the fierce and deadly contest opened. This time it was an assault along the entire line, a last resort, the forlorn hope of the enemy. They were weakened in numbers and dispirited and utterly demoralized; yet Lee had a reputation to save and a name to make, and at any sacrifice of life he seemed bound to win the day; but he strove in vain. The Union troops were fighting at home and among their own people. They fought like heroes, and inspired by success they had no thought of defeat. They could have withstood three times the force the enemy hurled against them. It was mere play for them to drive back the columns of the rebels, and so they did drive them back, and at five o'clock, after more than twelve hours constant fighting, the contest terminated, the national troops victorious at every point, and having nearly the entire battle field in their possession.

Time fails me to dwell upon the details of this brilliant and glorious battle. It would be interesting to state how we took thousands on thousands of prisoners, how the enemy were slaughtered, *how our own men fell by thousands heroically defending their national emblem; but let all this be deferred the day is ours, the victory is won, the country is saved.*

At the close of the action General Lee had the impudence to send in a flag of truce asking a suspension of hostilities, to give him time for the burial of the dead and an exchange of prisoners. General Meade replied that *he intended to recapture all the prisoners the enemy had taken and that he would bury their dead for them.* Failing in this attempt to gain time, and badly worsted at all hands, the rebels had no other recourse but to avail themselves of the fast approaching night to fall back to the mountains. So precipitate was their retreat last night, that their guards and sentinels in town were not relieved, and were captured.

This morning upwards of eleven hundred stragglers were taken in Gettysburg, besides our wounded who had fallen into the enemy's hands on Wednesday, at early day-break. General Pleasonton was started in pursuit of the rebels with his artillery, and at last accounts was pressing them hard.

The summary of this battle it would be difficult to give at this time. Both sides have lost heavily. The country about Gettysburg is crowded with wounded men. Every house and barn is an hospital. Probably in the aggregate of both armies at least 50,0000 men have been placed *hors du combat.* The apportionment of this loss would probably be twenty thousand Union and thirty thousand rebels. In additition to this *we have captured from twelve to twenty thousand prisoners, which is more than quadruple what they have taken from us, including the wounded and recaptured in Gettysburg this morning.*

It is exceedingly doubtful if we have taken either Longstreet or Hill, as reported, though the report is based upon statements of rebel prisoners. Other reports say that Longstreet is badly wounded, and some say that he is dead.

THE BATTLE OF GETTYSBURG.

WESTMINSTER, Md., July 3, 1863.

From the many reports brought here by parties from the battle field, we make the following narrative of the battle of Thursday.

Line of battle was formed about four o'clock P. M., our centre occupying the heights on this side of Gettysburg, at and near the Cemetery. The Second and Third corps, General Sickles, formed the left wing; the First and Eleventh were on the right. Skirmishers were immediately thrown forward along the whole line, in order to feel the enemy's position. Our batteries also shelled the heights and woods, in order, if possible, to develop the place where the enemy intended to mass his forces. We could elicit no reply from the rebel batteries.

Their skirmishers were active and very often reinforced. The strength of the enemy was ominous. Shortly after a terrific cannonade was opened on our centre and left from the rebel batteries, which had been quietly placed in position, having been masked by woods and grain fields. Our rifled guns replied with awful power and telling effect. For two hours the air seemed literally filled with screaming messengers of death.

Old soldiers, who had heard the roar of cannon at Gaines' Mill, Malvern Hill, Fredericksburg and Chancellorsville, declared the cannonading to be equal, if not greater, than that of those engagements.

Suddenly a wild, demoniac yell arose from thousands of rebel throats near the extreme left of our line to where the enemy where to make their great attack.

Sickles' corps sustained the first terrific onset of the rebel forces, which had been massed on our right. The rattle of musketry now became incessant.

As soon as the designs of the rebels became evident a large number of the pieces of the reserve artillery were massed in a splendid position to oppose the rebel infantry.

At this time the centre and left centre advanced, with loud cheers, pushing the rebels from point to point, through the valley and up the heights beyond.

The enemy was secreted behind trees, rocks and ledges, and in many cases they were bayonetted by our troops or taken prisoners.

A space of several hundred yards existing between the left of the Second Corps, First division, and the right of the next corps on the left, the rebels threw forward heavy columns of infantry, overpowering the skirmishers and filling the gap, delivering at the same time a deadly flank fire upon our forces.

It was here that the gallant Col. Edward E. Cross, of the Fifth New Hampshire Volunteers, commanding the Frst brigade, First division, Second corps (Hancock's), fell mortally wounded; also Gen. Zook, of New York, commanding the Second brigade. Our forces at this point were compelled to retire: but only for a short distance, as they were soon relieved by fresh troops.

Meanwhile the rebels were slowly gaining ground on the left, advancing in line of battle by brigades, delivering volley after volley. At that moment it seemed that our decimated and dispirited ranks would be forced back, when suddenly the Fifth corps came pouring forward on the Baltimore turnpike and threw themselves into the breach with a power and energy that nothing could withstand. The volleys of musketry which heretofore had been distinct and detached, now became one constant crash.

Our artillery worked with an energy and desperation almost superhuman, throwing in grape, cannister and case shot. Four several times the rebels charged upon that part of our artillery across the open plain, and four times were they repulsed with terrible slaughter.

The promptness with which this great flank movement of Lee was met and checkmated reflects the highest credit upon the General commanding. Indeed, the troops were handled with consummate ability during the entire day, General Meade being in the field, often under a very heavy fire, holding everything under his own eye and supervision, in which he was aided and accompanied by his chief of staff, the gallant General Gouverneur K. Warren.

Night came at last, and with her sable closed the scene. The result of the day's work may be summed up briefly as follows:—Lee had been attacked on his chosen grounds and our centre had driven the rebel lines more than a mile. The Army of the Potomac fought with a gallantry never before equalled during the war. Our left was pushed back, but very slightly. The great strategic movement had been foiled.

Not more than two-thirds of our forces were engaged during the day.

Although having suffered severely, especially in officers, we may safely set down the enemy's loss as greater than ours. The army had been brought under a new commander, and with necessarily but an imperfect knowledge of the army, with all its appointments.

At the close all the advantages of the day were in our favor, while our troops were inspired with success, and a heavy force which had not previously been engaged, stood ready to renew the attack on the morrow.

The infantry firing ceased at dark, but the cannonading did not stop until near nine o'clock at night, having been kept up with great vigor from our batteries, and mostly replied to by our batteries.

Too much praise cannot be awarded to the rank and file of our noble veteran Army of the Potomac, who have made one of the greatest marches on record, of nearly two hundred miles, part of the time during the most intense heat, making twenty and thirty miles per day, with knapsacks, gun, rations and eighty rounds of ammunition. Large numbers of those who were unable to keep up with their commands during the day, would march the entire night, reaching the encampment in the morning, only to perform another day's work more fatiguing than that of the preceding.

It will be gratifying to the friends of Brigadier General G. K. Warren, formerly of the New York Fifth Zouaves, now chief of Gen. Meade's staff, to know that he performed his duties in a most gallant and heroic manner, riding with the utmost coolness over fields swept by the enemy's fire, seemingly everywhere present, directing, aiding and cheering the troops.

Our artillery again opened fire upon the enemy on Friday morning at daylight, and when our informant left the scene of battle the firing was incessant and rapid.

Major General Sickles lost a leg in the engagement of yesterday. It was reported he was at Hanover to-day, on his way to Baltimore, his leg having been amputated above the knee.

BALTIMORE, July 4, 1863.

Reports deemed reliable, from the battle field, down to six o'clock last evening, represent that the rebels were repeatedly repulsed with fearful slaughter.

The battle lasted all day.

Seven thousand prisoners were taken.

The Union men of this city are highly jubilant and excitedly joyous over the favorable news from our victorious army.

FREDERICK TELEGRAM.

FREDERICK, July 4, 1863.

THE NATIONAL CELEBRATION.

The day has been appropriately observed by the citizens, most of whom closed their places of business, and displayed the national flag from their dwellings.

REJOICING AT GOOD NEWS.

The news from Gettysburg caused considerable excitement and occasioned no little rejoicing.

A REBEL CAVALRY RAID.

About noon a report reached the city that the rebel cavalry were approaching, and soon after a squad drove in our pickets on the Harper's Ferry road and entered the southern portion of the city. Their stay was very short, however, and after seizing a few horses the party precipitately fled. Two of their number boldly dashed through the place, and escaped by the Baltimore turnpike.

Our cavalry was instantly sent out, and succeeded in capturing three of the horse stealers.

Two companies of the Fiftieth New York Engineers under Captain Personius, formed in the streets, and a number of citizens rushed out with shot guns, but the disturbance was soon quieted, and the crowds dispersed.

UNION FLAGS PULLED DOWN.

A few of the citizens were pusilanimous enough to pull down their flags. One individual attempted to do so, but the taunts of the inhabitants and threats of the soldiers, caused him to desist. At the first opportunity, however, he pulled in the flag, and secreted io. Such exhibitions of cowardice merit the contempt of honest men.

A SUCCESSFUL EXPEDITION.

The expedition, composed of detachments from the Sixth Michigan and the Fourteenth Pennsylvania cavalry under Major Fuller, has been eminently successful. They destroyed a pontoon bridge at Falling Waters, five miles below Williamsport. They also destroyed an ammunition train, and a number of wagons loaded with supplies.

In a skirmish with the rebels we killed a number of their cavalry and captured sixteen prisoners.

The enemy has a trestle bridge at Williamsport and a pontoon bridge. The ford at that point is the best one on the Potomac, and is seldom impassable.

THE REPORTS FROM GETTYSBURG.

No definite intelligence has been received from Gettysburg to-day, expect reports confirmatory of success.

It is currently believed that Generals Longstreet and Hill are both killed.

IMPORTANT FROM TENNESSEE.

Occupation of Tullahoma by General Rosecrans,

&c., &c., &c.

TULLAHOMA, July 1, 1863.

The Second Kentucky cavalry, in the advance of General Brannan's division, and the Thirty-ninth Indiana mounted infantry, in the advance of General Mendar's division, entered Tullahoma at noon to-day.

Wheeler's rebel cavalry, the rear guard of the enemy, left as they entered. The town was entirely evacuated. Only one soldier and about two dozen caissons remained.

Gen. Bragg left there last night. His main force retreated on the Winchester road.

The Evacuation of Tullahoma by the Rebels.

MURFREESBORO, July 4—8 P. M.

A despatch just in from headquarters front says that Bragg evacuated Tullahoma this afternoon, dismounting and spiking all his heavy guns. The rebels are in full retreat to Chattanooga.

General Gordon Granger returned from Shelbyville and took command of all the forces of the Department of the Cumberland, except those actively engaged in front. Shelbyville and Guys Gap are held by a strong force.

NEW YORK HERALD.

JAMES GORDON BENNETT, EDITOR AND PROPRIETOR.

OFFICE N. W. CORNER OF FULTON AND NASSAU STS.

Volume XXVIII .... No. 184

New York, Saturday, July 4, 1863.

THE HERALD AND THE FOURTH.

The Herald will not be published on Sunday morning. Our employes have two out of the three hundred and sixty-five days as holidays. We always celebrate the Fourth of July and observe in a becoming manner the First of January. But, as important events may transpire between now and Sunday morning, we shall be prepared for them. We shall therefore issue an Extra Herald early on that morning, with the latest news from the seat of war. We shall hope to hear of the defeat of the rebel General Lee by General Meade, the surrender of Port Hudson to General Banks, the fall of Vicksburg, and a splendid victory by General Rosecrans. What a day for the realization of these hopes!

The New City Postal Rates.

On the 1st instant the new postal law went into effect. All city letters must hereafter be prepaid two cents for the single rate of half an ounce. *Double postage will be charged on all unpaid letters.* All letters prepaid only one cent will be charged two cents additional on delivery. Those who answer advertisements in the Herald will, therefore, have their answers *prepaid in full*, in order to insure their delivery to the advertisers.

THE SITUATION.

The intelligence from the Army of the Potomac is cheering enough to welcome in the Fourth of July with appropriate rejoicing. All doubts as to the proceedings of the two hostile armies in Pennsylvania are now dispelled by the information which we are enabled to give in our columns to-day. The latest news we have from Gettysburg is a despatch from General Meade to General Schenck at Baltimore at one o'clock yesterday, stating that the victory of the Union army was complete. He had then driven the rebels four miles north and west from their position of the day before, and was then following them up. Fifteen hundred more prisoners were taken and sent on to Baltimore.

Previous official despatches of General Meade forwarded to Washington, dated at eleven o'clock on Thursday and eight o'clock yesterday morning, reported that the enemy had attacked him with great fierceness at four o'clock on the afternoon of Thursday and was repulsed at all points, but with severe loss on our side. Among the wounded he reports Generals Sickles, Barlow, Graham and Warren. Generals Paul and Zook were killed. The rebel General Barksdale, of Mississippi, was killed, and his body remains within our lines. It was reported that General Longstreet was also killed, and despatches received late last night partially confirm it. The fight was renewed at daylight yesterday morning, and resulted as above stated in General Meade's account of to-day's proceedings transmitted to General Schenck, in the defeat of the enemy before one o'clock in the afternoon.

General Couch was made aware of the rebel defeat, and would no doubt be ready to act with vigor to complete the disaster of the enemy.

The particulars of Thursday's battle are given to-day in our correspondents' letters, and show that the fight was a most terrific one. Our loss in officers was considerable. The Third corps, under General Sickles, did some splendid fighting. The Fifth corps of General Hancock stood a fearful shock from a charge of the rebels; they were driven up the side of a hill and down part of the way into the valley on the other side, where they rallied, made a magnificent dash at the enemy, and drove them back over the ground they had gained, completely broken and repulsed.

All the rebel generals appear to have concentrated their forces in the neighborhood in Gettysburg. Stuart's cavalry and Imboden's forces had moved up there. Seventy-nine pieces of artillery and over one hundred wagons had gone there from Chambersburg, and all the troops at Greencastle, except a small guard, had also moved up to reinforce Lee. These facts make General Meade's success all the more complete if he has driven this vast army before him.

Rumors were in circulation yesterday that Richmond was closely invested and probably captured by the forces of General Dix; but we have positive assurance that there is no truth whatever in the reports.

The full details of General Rosecrans' splendid movement on Tullahoma and the battles which preceded his occupation of that place are given to-day in the letters of our correspondents in the field. A map accompanies the account, showing the various localities through which our victorious army passed.

Official despatches from General Grant's army to the 28th ult. have been received at Memphis, from which it appears that the rebels are making a desperate resistance to the progress of the siege of Vicksburg, with the hope that relief will soon reach them. Additional reinforcements are said to be on the way from General Bragg to General Johnston, and the latter is perfecting arrangements to attack General Grant's rear. Generals Price, Marmaduke and Kirby Smith are combining to get some point on the banks of the Mississippi, and will probably make an attempt to take Milliken's Bend and stop navigation.

A despatch from Chickasaw Bayou on the 29th ult., by way of Cairo, represents that our firing on the rebel works was better directed than ever before. The enemy still disputed our possession of Fort Hill. General Johnston was then said to be only a few miles from our outer pickets, but our troops were fully prepared for any attack.

By the arrival of the Morning Star yesterday from New Orleans, we are in possession of all the details of the late affair at Port Hudson, the capture of Brashear City by the rebels, and other important intelligence, which will be found in another column. The state of things in Louisiana does not appear very favorable to the Union arms at last reports. The position of General Banks is, to say the least of it, somewhat critical.

MISCELLANEOUS NEWS.

The steamship City of Cork will call at Cape Race on Monday morning, and the City of Manchester on Wednesday morning, where they will receive despatches to be landed at Queenstown, which can be sent through the agency of George Stoker, 145 Broadway.

The British brig Napier, which arrived yesterday from Arecibo, P. R., is the vessel that has been flying the rebel flag in several of the West India ports.

The usual barbecue and hullabaloo of deep dyed abolitionists will take place to-day at Framingham, Massachusetts. The affair will be under the direction of Garrison, Phillips and Burleigh.

John Brough has accepted the republican nomination for Governor of Ohio, in opposition to Mr. Vallandigham.

Eight changes have been made in the command of the Army of the Potomac since its organization. The rebel army of Northern Virginia has had only two commanders since the commencement of the war.

The question between the Mayor and Comptroller as to the construction of the act respecting the city advertising was argued yesterday in the Supreme Court, by Mr. D. D. Field for the Mayor and Mr. James T. Brady for the Comptroller. Decision is reserved. The matter of the new Court House building was also argued; but the General Term declined to take up, at the verge of the summer holidays, the case of the police against the Police Commissioners, for the proper distribution of the money left for them by our distinguished Japanese visitors some three years ago.

Capt. Geo. W. Cunningham has been held to bail by the United States District Court in the sum of \$20,000 on a capital charge of having scuttled and sunk the packet ship Senator, which was on a voyage from New York to Liverpool last August with a cargo of wheat for the benefit of the distressed Irish people. There were insurances to the amount of \$65,000 effected on the vessel and cargo, and after nine weeks being devoted to the matter by United States Deputy Marshal Horton he succeeded in gaining evidence enough to procure the arrest of the captain and first mate. The latter has, however, been used by the government as a witness.

Horace Greeley was yesterday served by Deputy Marshal Borst with a capias to answer in the sum of \$30,000 the complaint of George D. Allan, of Florida, who alleges that he has been grossly and maliciously libelled in the *Tribune*.

The stock market was better yesterday, and operators for a rise were in better spirits and moved with more courage. Gold was dull. The market was at one time agitated by a rumor of the fall of Richmond; but as soon as it was known to come from a Philadelphia newspaper no further attention was paid to it. Exchange was 157½ a 158. Money was easy—call loans 6 per cent.

Transactions in cotton on Friday were quite limited, and rates very irregular, ranging from 68c. a 70c. for middlings. The demand for breadstuffs was fair, at firmer prices for flour, but about previous rates for other articles. There was increased activity in provisions. Pork and lard were higher. Whiskey was steady, with moderate sales. Groceries, oils, metals, hemp, fruit, seeds, spices and naval stores were very quiet. A moderate inquiry existed for hops, tobacco, fish and lime. Hay and wool were in fair demand. There was less animation in the freight line.

Responding to the rapid rise in the price of the raw material early in the week, domestic cotton goods advanced 5 a 20 per cent, according to style and make, and were in lively demand at the improved rates; but the inquiry during the past two or three days has been decidedly less active, owing in part to the extreme firmness of holders, and partly to the decline in raw cotton, which closed yesterday 3c. a 4c. per pound lower than on Tuesday last. The business in domestic woollens has been more animated, and the tendency of the market strongly upwards, in view of the rise in the prices of the new clip of wool. The principal transactions in foreign dry goods have been in desirable styles of dress goods, the supply of which has been quite moderate, and prices of which have favored sellers decidedly. The total imports of foreign dry goods during the week were to the value of \$796,626, and the total amount of the same goods actually marketed was only \$552,729.

Our Home Defences—Enrolment of the Militia.—The work of the organization of the thirty regiments for the defence of the State is proceeding rapidly. The plan adopted is to enroll one or more regiments of exempt militiamen for each city, and from these will be taken the officers for the new regiments. This will insure the proper officering of the whole force, and will in a few weeks place it in a condition to take the field. The example thus set should be followed by the rest of the loyal States, so that they may be prepared for every emergency, whether it threatens them from within or without. The country is now in a pass from which nothing but the firm self-reliance and energy of its citizens can enable it to issue with any promise of security for the future. Every loyally disposed man should bear steadily in mind the fact that upon his co-operation, either in person or purse, at the present moment, depend the safety and integrity of the republic.

The anniversary which we celebrate to-day will furnish an occasion to the Governors of the loyal States to declare their sentiments and intentions in regard to the crisis. From their speeches the people will see how far they are sincere in their professions of a desire to put down this rebellion, and how far they are to be counted upon in the adoption of the measures necessary to repel invasion. The stereotyped eloquence of the usual Fourth of July orations will be out of place on this occasion. Those that indulge in it will properly be accused of a desire to shirk the questions which just now preoccupy men's minds. We trust that this great anniversary, if it does not serve to celebrate the present as well as the past triumphs of the republic, will at least bring substantial assurance to us of the determination of the loyal States and their rulers to persevere in the war until the great object for which we are struggling is attained.

The Victory Undoubtedly Ours.

Our national anniversary, we think, may be celebrated in anticipation to-day as in honor of the nation's greatest deliverance. From the official despatches of General Meade and other accounts of the second and the third days' battles near Gettysburg, we can hardly resist the conclusion that the tide of victory has turned so decidedly against the rebel army of General Lee that the end of this campaign will be the end of the rebellion.

The latest reports from the field come from General Meade at one o'clock yesterday afternoon, and he states that the enemy had attacked him at daylight in large force, but that up to that time he had driven them four miles from the position they occupied on the day previous towards the north and west, and was then pursuing them. He claims the victory as complete, after three days' severe fighting. Our late despatches from Harrisburg state that General Couch was fully aware of the rebel disaster last evening.

In the official despatch of General Meade of July 2 he says that he was attacked at four o'clock in the afternoon of that day, and that, "after one of the severest contests of the war," the enemy were "repulsed at all points;" that we "have suffered considerably in killed and wounded," but that "we have taken a large number of prisoners." Lee appears again to have practised the system of operations which he adopted at Chancellorsville; for here, as there, his first desperate assault to break the lines of our army was made in the afternoon. But, while the experiment in the first instance was a success, it was in the second a complete failure. He seems, however, to have adhered to his tactics of Chancellorsville, in renewing the battle again very early the next morning; but in the despatch of General Meade, dated at eight o'clock A. M. yesterday, the battle still progressing, he says that "the enemy thus far have made no impression upon my position," and that "prisoners report that Longstreet's and A. P. Hill's forces were much injured" in the battle of the preceding day. Rumors from the field down to twelve o'clock (noon) yesterday received at Baltimore, involved the death of General Longstreet; and, from the demeanor of the secessionists of the city, they not only believed this rumor, but seemed to know that it was true.

We are satisfied that General Lee's army, with all the forces which he can rake and scrape together in Pennsylvania, is considerably inferior in strength—in cavalry, artillery and infantry—to ours; and we have no doubt that General Meade's reserves are within hailing distance.

Our anticipations of further and more complete successes are based entirely upon the capabilities of the Army of the Potomac under its new commander; but we cannot imagine that, in the crisis of this desperate struggle of the rebellion between life and death, so good a soldier as General Couch will remain inactive on the line of the Susquehanna, with his auxiliary army of thirty or forty thousand militia, including fifteen or twenty New York regiments, as good, or only wanting the trial by fire of a battle or two to make them as good, as regulars. We expect that General Couch has been following up the rebel rear guard in its retreat from the Susquehanna, and has not failed to give a powerful helping hand at the proper moment to his old associates of the Army of the Potomac.

We conjecture that the relative positions of the two armies were such yesterday morning that it was a necessity with Lee to dislodge his adversary, in order to secure a safe retreat, if nothing else; for, in failing to gain the most convenient roads to the Potomac held by General Meade, Lee would be in danger of being cut off altogether. From the facts connected with the first of these three days' battles—that in which the intrepid General Reynolds lost his life—we think it evident that Lee was not seeking, but endeavoring to avoid, our advancing army, in order to cover the removal beyond the Potomac of the immense stores of his Pennsylvania plunder. We believe that he has been compelled to fight at some disadvantage, but that, as fighting was his only alternative, he has met the emergency with the courage, resolution and terrible energy of despair. He has thus, however, been compelled to meet our Army of the Potomac, not in a snare to our commanding general of a wilderness of woods, underbrush and ravines, in which only a third of his troops could be brought into action, but in a fair field, where all our forces may be called into play.

From the brilliant operations of our cavalry four days ago, down to the despatch of the progress of the battle yesterday afternoon from General Meade, the solid advantages of all these late engagements with Lee's forces, in captured artillery, prisoners, &c., are with us. Accordingly, although we know not what a day may bring forth, we judge from what has been done that the game is in the hands of General Meade, and that he is leading the Army of the Potomac to the crowning victories of the war. Our last Fourth of July was darkened by serious apprehensions of the destruction of our army on the Richmond peninsula; but even then General McClellan, in the terrible slaughter of the enemy at Malvern Hill, had saved the army and the national capital. Now, with the same army, heavily reinforced and successfully advancing against the enemy, we may reasonably anticipate the most glorious results.

Our Armies on This Day.—May the armies of the Potomac, of the Mississippi, of the Cumberland and of the Gulf be impressed this day with the necessity of saving, by their gallant efforts, our glorious Union. The grand roll of 1776, now reduced to thirty or forty names, must be swelled to hundreds of thousands by the achievements of the heroes of 1863.

The Fourth of July—1776 and 1863.

This is the eighty-seventh anniversary of one of the greatest events in the annals of mankind—an event which gave birth to new nations in America, created new nations in Europe, and regenerated the old. The event is the immortal Declaration of Independence, whose principles lie at the foundation of human liberty and are the basis of the constitution and government of the United States.

The thirteen British colonies threw off the yoke of a king on the Fourth of July, 1776. By a seven years bloody struggle they made good their claim, and Great Britain was compelled to acknowledge their independence. A democratic confederacy of States was thus established. The influence of the great achievement was felt throughout all Europe. It resulted in the French Revolution, and in the triumph of the idea that the people are the source of all legitimate power. It was a staggering blow to the alleged "divine right of kings," from which it has never recovered. It was a new era in the world—a new starting point for human freedom.

All went on happily till about thirty years ago, when the principle of fraternal amity and compromise was assailed, and abolition fanatics at the North, led by abolition knaves in the secret service of the country whose yoke we broke, sowed the seeds of national discord, which ambitious and restless politicians at the South watered and carefully cultivated, till at length, in 1861, the bitter fruit was produced in a terrible civil war, which has raged for over two years without result. But it is hoped that before the setting of this day's sun that will be no longer true, and that Union victories all along our lines will render the eighty-seventh anniversary of the Declaration of Independence as important as the birthday of the nation. If Meade should overwhelm Lee, and if Dix and Gillmore and Banks and Grant and Rosecrans shall have done their duty to their country; and if, above all, the military authorities at Washington shall have acquitted themselves like men alive to the awful responsibility which rests upon them, the Fourth of July, 1863, will be a new epoch in the history of America and of the world; and the Union of the States, from the Rio Grande to the St. Lawrence, will be so firmly re-established that no power can divide them for ages to come.

The hopes of humanity in two worlds are centred upon the result which this day trembles in the balance. May God defend the right!

The Fourth of July in 1776.—The Fourth of July, 1776, is a memorable date in the history of our republic. Should it become known to-day that Vicksburg has fallen into the hands of our brave troops; that the Army of the Potomac has gained a victory over Lee, and that Rosecrans has triumphed over Bragg, the Fourth of July, 1863, will rank in our history as an equally eventful date.

This Day One Year Ago.—Last year at this date the country was in a painful state of agitation and doubt. All was gloomy and uncertain. General McClellan, by his able strategy, saved the country from ruin. To-day our prospects are brighter. We have favorable accounts from all parts, and may reasonably hope that General Meade will, like McClellan, ward off all danger and save the country from disgrace.

NEWS FROM VICKSBURG.

Progress of the Siege to the 29th Ultimo.

GEN. JOHNSTON'S FORCES ADVANCING, &c., &c., &c.

Memphis, Tenn., July 1, 1863.

Official advices from the army of General Grant to the 28th of June furnish the following particulars:—

The rebel garrison at Vicksburg is very active.

The rebels are making a desperate resistance to the progress of the siege, with the hope that relief will soon reach them.

Additional rebel reinforcements are said to be on the way from General Bragg to General Johnston, and the latter is perfecting arrangements to attack General Grant's rear.

Generals Price, Marmaduke and Kirby Smith are combining to get some point on the banks of the Mississippi, and will probably make an attempt to take Milliken's Bend and stop navigation.

Chickasaw Bayou, June 29, 1863.

A gentleman from the front reports everything in *statu quo*. Operations continue against the rebel works; but the firing is better than that two days ago. The rebels still dispute our hold on Fort Hill.

Colonel Melancthon Smith died of his wounds yesterday. Colonel Hanesible was mortally wounded by a grenade while entering the fort.

General Johnston's advance is said to be a few miles from our outer pickets; but only a show of force is expected. Nothing can be more desirable than a real attack, as everything is prepared.

Washington, July 3, 1863.

The *Republican* of this afternoon says the government has a despatch, dated Vicksburg, June 27, stating that the siege was progressing finely. No mention is made of rebels in Grant's rear.

Memphis, July 1, 1863.

Everything is quiet in this section.

General Hurlbut is watching the movements of the rebels in the country adjacent to and south of his lines.

The weather is extremely hot.

THE NAVY.

Arrival of the United States Steamer James Adger.

The United States steamer James Adger, Thomas H. Patterson commander, from a cruise off Nantucket Shoals for privateers, arrived at this port last evening. The following is a list of her officers:—

Commander—Thomas H. Patterson.
Lieutenant—Charles Lowe Franklin.
Acting Master—Robert O. Patterson.
Acting Assistant Paymaster—Wm. W. T. Greenway.
Acting Assistant Surgeon—Robert N. Atwood.
Acting Ensigns—Charles F. Keith and Charles Moore.
Engineers—Edward N. Whipple, Acting Chief; John Curren, Acting Second Assistant; Andrew McTurl, Wm. Moran, William R. Nutz, Third Assistants.
Gunner—John H. Pennington.
Master's Mates—Wallace W. Reed, George Couch and Silas A Taber.
Captain's Clerk—Henry M. Patterson.
Paymaster's Clerk—Edward F. Miller.
Surgeon's Steward—John Atkinson.

Arrival of the Steamship Uncas.—The United States steamer Uncas, William Watson, Acting Master, commanding, arrived at this port yesterday, in six days from St. John, Fla. She has been on blockading duty for the last eighteen months, and returns to this port for repairs. The following is the list of officers:—

Acting Master Commanding—Wm. Watson.
Acting Assistant Paymaster—C. E. Taylor.
Acting Assistant Surgeon—G. H. Van Deusen.
Acting Second Assistant Engineer—C. Dandreau; Acting Third Assistant Engineer, P. Dandreau.
Acting Master's Mates—George Newlin, George M. Smith and Thos. F. Tracy.
Paymaster's Clerk—F. O. Thomas.
Surgeon's Steward—C. S. Van Deusen.
Yeoman—James Caldwell.

NEWS FROM WASHINGTON.

WAR GAZETTE.

OFFICIAL.

Circular Regarding the Exchange of Prisoners of War.

GENERAL ORDERS—NO. 209.

War Department, Adjutant General's Office, Washington, July 3, 1863.

I. The attention of all persons in the military service of the United States is called to article 7 of the cartel agreed upon July 22, 1862, and published in General Orders No. 142, September 25, 1862. According to the terms of this cartel all captures must be reduced to actual possession, and all prisoners of war must be delivered at the places designated, there to be exchanged, or paroled until exchange can be effected. The only exception allowed is in the case of commanders of two opposing armies, who were authorized to exchange prisoners, or to release them on parole at other points mutually agreed upon by said commanders.

II. It is understood that captured officers and men have been paroled and released in the field by others than commanders of opposing armies, and that the sick and wounded in hospitals have been so paroled and released in order to avoid guarding and removing them, which in many cases would have been impossible. Such paroles are in violation of general orders and the stipulations of the cartel, and are null and void. They are not regarded by the enemy, and will not be respected by the armies of the United States. Any officer or soldier who gives such parole will be returned to duty without exchange, and, moreover, will be punished for disobedience of orders. It is the duty of the captor to guard his prisoners, and if, through necessity or choice, he fails to do this, it is the duty of the prisoner to return to the service of his government. He cannot avoid this duty by giving an unauthorized military parole.

III. A military parole not to serve till exchanged must not be confounded with a parole of honor to do or not to do a particular thing not inconsistent with the duty of a soldier; thus a prisoner of war actually held by the enemy may, in order to obtain exemption from a close guard or confinement, pledge his parole of honor that he will make no attempt to escape. Such pledges are binding upon the individuals giving them; but they should seldom be given or received, for it is the duty of a prisoner to escape, if able to do so. Any pledge or parole of honor extorted from a prisoner by ill usage or cruelty is not binding.

IV. The obligations imposed by the general laws and usages of war upon the combatant inhabitants of a section of country passed over by an invading army closes when the military occupation ceases, and any pledge or parole given by such persons in regard to future service, is null and of no effect.

By order of THE SECRETARY OF WAR.
E. D. Townsend, Assistant Adjutant General.

GENERAL NEWS.

Washington, July 3, 1863.

CAUSE OF THE REPORTED PRESENCE OF REBEL CAVALRY NEAR WASHINGTON.

The scare of yesterday in reference to the presence of rebel cavalry in the vicinity of Rockville has been traced to its source. General French had sent down from Harper's Ferry a number of laden canal boats, under a heavy infantry escort, which marched down the canal. The country people along the way, seeing this force, were alarmed. Preacher Henning, of Rockville, who had munificently entertained the rebel officers when there, was on a visit to Seneca Mills, and was informed by some wags that the rebels were approaching in large force. He hurried back to Rockville and gave the alarm. The fleeing citizens met this side of the town a small detachment of our cavalry as a butcher's escort. They assured the officer in command that a large rebel force was approaching Rockville. The cavalry were then sent in every direction to warn the people of the neighborhood, and a general stampede took place. Captain Cook, of the First Maryland regiment, a very resolute officer, started out upon a reconnoissance as far as Poolsville on the river road, and returned by way of Rodsville, getting back at four o'clock this morning, and found no traces of armed rebels anywhere on his route.

ADVENTURES OF UNION SUTLERS WITH THE REBEL CAVALRY.

Two sutlers arrived here yesterday from Dover, Pennsylvania, at which point they were released on a parole not to give information as to the number or probable destinations of the forces of General J. E. B. Stuart. They were captured while on their way to Westminster, Maryland. The force of rebels who captured them was undoubtedly the same that made the raid to Rockville and vicinity last Sunday, as they report that they had about the number of men with them as was said to have been captured at that time. The prisoners were treated in the kindest manner by the rebel officers and men, and no severe restraint was imposed upon them. When one of these sutlers, well known in Washington and New York, weighing some five hundred pounds, more or less, was brought before the rebel General Stuart by the Provost Marshal, with a number of prisoners, after the number had been announced as one hundred and ninety-eight men and two commissioned officers, our fat friend immediately said, "And one fat man," which so tickled the rebel commander that he heartily shook him by the hand, being near him at the time. The friendship of General Stuart, however, did not insure him return of a valuable horse and light wagon he had just purchased from a frightened denizen of the county, valued at six hundred dollars. They represent the skedaddle of the rebels before General Fitzpatrick's troopers as universal. Officers, with pistols in their hands, pointed at the soldiers' heads, in vain endeavored to stop the retreat. The attack at Hanover Junction by our cavalry took them perfectly by surprise.

COLONEL WYNDHAM'S NEW CAVALRY BRIGADE.

A large crowd congregated in front of the Herald rooms about noon to-day, to witness the march through our streets of Colonel Wyndham's newly organized cavalry brigade. As many as fifty-seven different regiments are represented in this command, collected within three days from hospitals in this vicinity. He has organized this force with wonderful celerity. It would be improper to state the number of his command; but it is as efficient a body of cavalry as there is in the service.

EXAMINATION OF MIDSHIPMEN.

Admiral Goldsborough has been appointed President of a Board for the final examination of the class of Midshipmen who entered the Naval Academy in 1859.

IMPORTANT TO DESERTERS.

The opinion of the Solicitor of the War Department in relation to the arrest of deserters is published. It is to the effect that the Provost Marshal is to decline to produce a deserter to subject him to the process of the court on writ of habeas corpus, for the reason it would be inconsistent with and in violation of the duty of the respondent, and that it is his legal duty to deliver the deserter to the nearest military commander or military post.

Some of the militia mustered to-day in obedience to the order of the President calling out the eight regiments already organizing will be uniformed cavalry and infantry companies. They are to serve the United States sixty days.

MOSBY'S GUERILLAS AT WORK.

It is stated that about one hundred of Mosby's guerillas were last night about two miles this side of Vienna and Fairfax Court House, Va. He makes Fairfax Court House his headquarters. A gang of rebels, supposed to be a portion of the same band, are now holding Aldie, in London county. They have of late been hovering in front of the fortifications on the other side of the Potomac.

Sad Accident to Mrs. Lincoln.

[From the Washington Chronicle, July 3.]

We regret to learn that a painful accident occurred to Mrs. Lincoln yesterday morning, about ten o'clock, near the Mount Pleasant Hospital. It appears that Mrs. L. was passing across the lot near the hospital, in her carriage, when the driver's seat became detached from the carriage in some way, precipitating the driver to the ground. At this the spirited horses became frightened, and dashed off at the top of their speed.

Mrs. L. was alone in the carriage at the time, but, observing the great danger she was in, quietly and quickly sprang from the carriage, her presence of mind and courage not deserting her for a single instant. Although the horses were running at full speed at the time, Mrs. L. fortunately received no more serious injuries from the fall than several severe bruises, which stunned her for a moment. The most severe of these wounds is upon the back part of her head; but we are glad to learn it is not at all dangerous.

Several surgeons from the Carver Hospital were soon upon the spot, and Mrs. L. was taken to the hospital, where the wounds were dressed by Dr. Judson, the efficient surgeon in charge. It was soon ascertained that no bones were broken, and it was thought that she could be conveyed to the White House without too much risk. Dr. Judson quickly had his carriage in waiting, and Mrs. Lincoln was placed in it and driven home. The escape of the lady was almost miraculous, considering the circumstances, and we learn that she has entirely recovered from her fright. The injuries are not of a serious character, and we hope to see Mrs. Lincoln about in a few days.

The Constitutionality of Legal Tender Notes.

Albany, July 3, 1863.

There is the highest authority for saying that the Court of Appeals will not render a decision on the constitutionality of legal tender notes until the September term of the court.

YACHTING.

Departure of the Yacht Gypsy for England.

The Third American Yacht to Cross the Ocean

Early History of American Yachts in British Waters.

THE AMERICA AND HER ADVENTURES, &c., &c., &c.

The American yacht Gypsy left our waters yesterday for the purpose of crossing the Atlantic Ocean and entering the lists of competitors for prizes offered by the Royal Yacht Club of England.

It was the intention of her owner to have sailed some days earlier; but some over zealous custom house officials threw obstacles in the way, so that she has been delayed up to a period barely sufficient to enable her to cross the ocean and arrive in time to be present at the regatta, which comes off near the close of the present month. Should she meet with calms or heavy head weather it will be impossible for her to reach her destination in time to participate in the grand sailing matches of the season, and we may thank the officials for despoiling the world of a record of another victory for American yachts. With such thoughts as these upon their minds, we cannot imagine how these self-glorified custom house officers can rest well at night. But we cannot expect much better of men who do not know their duty, if the seizure of the Gypsy is a fair sample of their intelligence.

The Gypsy is the third vessel belonging to the New York Yacht Club which is to wave its flag and distinguishing pennant across the blue ocean to the rock bound coast of England. Of the two which have preceded her, the America was the first, and the Sylvie (sloop rigged) the second. The victory of the America was the signal for a great change in the building and sailing of English yachts, and since her famous race at Cowes John Bull has been a trifle troubled about the speed of our craft, and has not sounded his big horn in the way of a challenge to our yachtsmen. Some three years after the advent of the America into British waters the Sylvie crossed over to sail the Britishers; but not one could be found to make up a match with the Yankee boat, and she was obliged to return prizeless; but she brought home the silent acknowledgment of Englishmen that the American yachts were the fastest in the world.

In this connection we deem it of sufficient interest to give our readers a brief summary of the history of the celebrated yacht America, now the property of the United States Navy.

The America was built in this city by George Steers, who was lost early in life, and in the budding of a bright promise to become the greatest shipbuilder of the age. She was constructed for Commodore Stevens, of Jersey City, and was intended to be the fastest vessel afloat. In a few trials on the waters of our Bay it was discovered that, although she was remarkably fast, some of our pilotboats could keep up with her, and at times, it is said, they led her.

The peculiarity of her model and the stepping of her masts were novel, and more than predicted for her a speedy transformation into a fruiter; but her builder and owner had faith in the principles which had guided him in her construction, and they decided that on the other side of the Atlantic there was nothing that carried canvass that could outsail her; and accordingly, without pomp or display, she was fitted out and despatched across the ocean.

Upon her arrival in England she attracted the attention of the people to such an extent that nought but "the America" was considered worth talking about; but, John Bull-like, they felt certain that any one of their clumsy looking craft could sail around her with ease. The America's crew did not give them any cause to suppose that they felt certain of taking off the prize, nor did they boast or bluster over the merits of their vessel.

The 22d day of August, 1851, will be long remembered by every English yachtman, and in fact all over the world; for it was on that day a Yankee yacht carried off the prize, there being no less than eighteen competitors for the Royal Yacht Squadron cup, valued at £100.

The course lay around the Isle of Wight, and the vessels were to sail at ten precisely. They lay in the following order:—

Yachts.	Tons.	Owners.
1—Beatrice, schooner	161	Sir W. P. Carew, Bart.
2—Volante, cutter	48	J. L. Craige, Esq.
3—Arrow, cutter	84	J. Chamberlyne, Esq.
4—Wyvern, schooner	205	Duke of Marlborough.
5—Ione, schooner	75	Alman Hill, Esq.
6—Constance, schooner	218	Marquis of Conyngham.
7—Titania, schooner	100	R. Stephenson, M. P.
8—Gipsy Queen, schooner	160	Sir H. B. Hoghton, Bart.
9—Alarm, cutter	193	Joseph Weld, Esq.
10—Mona, cutter	82	Lord Alfred Paget.
11—America, schooner	170	Commodore Stevens.
12—Brilliant, 3 mast schr.	392	G. H. Ackers, Esq.
13—Bacchante, cutter	80	B. H. Jones, Esq.
14—Freak, cutter	60	W. Curling, Esq.
15—Stella, cutter	65	R. Frankland.
16—Eclipse, cutter	50	H. S. Fearon, Esq.
17—Fernande schooner	127	Major M. Martyn.
18—Aurora, cutter	47	L. M. Thomas, Esq.

The wind was light from W. S. W., and the America was the last to get underweigh; but she had not fairly started before the immense superiority of the Yankee became visible.

The Queen was present at the race in the royal steam yacht, and followed the victorious yacht almost to her anchorage.

At the Nab the America shot ahead of the seventeen Englishmen, and by the time she reached the Needles she was at least eight miles ahead of the leading yacht. On luffing up to the wind she carried away her jibboom, and was obliged to sail the remainder of the race without a jib; but nevertheless she arrived at the stake boat at thirty-five minutes past eight P. M., and the Aurora, a cutter, arrived just twenty minutes after her.

Every one acknowledged her sailing qualities, and again she was the topic of conversation. John Bull owned up frankly that he was beaten in his own waters, and to this particular day he has never forgotten it, nor will he.

The Queen and the entire royal family visited the America after her return from the race, and remained on board of her some time, and subsequently she sent a present of five guineas to each of the yacht's crew.

The wonderful speed of the American yacht, in connection with her beauty and elegant accommodations, induced several noblemen to offer large sums of money for her, and finally her owner disposed of her to a nobleman not a member of the Royal Yacht Club.

She was then fitted out and made a cruise up the Mediterranean; but the new owner and his sailing master knew nothing about sailing a vessel of her class, and upon her return to England she was altered somewhat in her hull, and in the stepping of her masts, the ballast was shifted, and between all the changes she was in a trim to sail badly. Her owner became disgusted with her, and sold the America to a gentleman who kept her for the exclusive use of a maiden sister.

This English brother, sympathizing with the South, either made her a present to the rebels, or, only asking a trifling sum, she was transformed into a blockade runner, performing several voyages and taking to the rebels large cargoes of valuable stores.

Upon the capture of Fernandina, Florida, she was taken up one of the numerous creeks and scuttled; but our sailors and soldiers raised her and brought her to Port Royal, where she was fitted out as a picket boat and sent to the blockade station off Charleston. Here she performed excellent service, and after several months of arduous duty she was ordered North to be fitted for a practice vessel for the midshipmen at the Naval Academy.

She has made one cruise in search of the privateer Tacony, and is at the present time lying at the Brooklyn Navy Yard.

The history of the Sylvie is not fraught with so much interest. It is true she sailed in one race; but the Englishmen would not sail with her again, fearing that she was held back for the purpose of misleading them.

The Gypsy left her anchorage off Castleton on Thursday noon, and dropped down the Kills under easy sail, receiving the parting salutes of the residents along the shore of Staten Island, and in return firing salutes with her own little brass six-pounders.

She is owned by Mr. Anthony V. Morse, of 24 William street, who goes out accompanied by his lady. The yacht may be gone four months, during which time she will visit Queenstown, Cowes and some of the Channel ports, and thence to the Mediterranean. Her movements will be looked forward to with much interest. She sailed from the Lower Bay on Friday, and by night was far out to sea.

A Blockade Runner Checked at Halifax.

Portland, Me., July 3, 1863.

A private letter from Halifax states that the steamer General Banks tried to run out, but was obliged to put back by meeting a federal gunboat which was watching her.

New-York Tribune.

VOL. XXIII....No. 6,943. NEW-YORK, MONDAY, JULY 6, 1863. PRICE THREE CENTS.

THE GREAT VICTORY.

The Rebel Army Totally Defeated.

ITS REMAINS DRIVEN INTO THE MOUNTAINS.

It is There Surrounded and Hemmed in.

Its Retreat Across the Potomac River Cut Off.

TWENTY THOUSAND PRISONERS CAPTURED

One Hundred and Eighteen Guns Taken.

The Rebel General Longstreet Killed

DETAILS OF THE THREE DAYS' FIGHTING.

The Most Terrific Combat on Record

Desperate Charges by the Rebel Troops Massed.

OUR TROOPS STAND FIRM AS A ROCK.

The Rebel Assaults Repeatedly Repulsed.

Their Solid Ranks Dashed into Fragments.

STILL THE UNION ARMY STAND FIRM.

The Rebels Pause—Waver—Break and Scatter.

A great and Glorious Victory for the Potomac Army.

Official Dispatches.

FIRST DISPATCH

WASHINGTON, July 5, 1863—4 p. m.

The latest official dispatch received here up to this hour from Gen. Meade is dated at Headquarters Army of Potomac, 7 a. m., July 4, which merely states that the enemy had withdrawn from his positions occupied for attack on Friday. The information in the possession of Gen. Meade at that hour did not develop the character of the enemy's movement, whether it was a retreat or a maneuver for other purposes.

Trustworthy information received here to-day asserts that Gen. Lee's headquarters were at Cashtown yesterday afternoon, and further represents that the Rebels were fortifying at Newman's Cut, in the South Mountains, apparently to cover a retreat. Later official dispatches are expected this evening.

SECOND DISPATCH.

HEADQUARTERS ARMY OF POTOMAC, July 4—noon.

To Major-Gen. HALLECK: The position of affairs is not materially changed since my last dispatch of 7 a. m. We now hold Gettysburg.

The enemy has abandoned large numbers of his killed and wounded on the field.

I shall probably be able to give you a return of our captures and losses before night, and a return of the enemy's killed and wounded in our hands.

GEO. G. MEADE, Major-General.

THIRD DISPATCH.

HEADQUARTERS ARMY POTOMAC, July 4, 10 p. m.

To Major-Gen. HALLECK.—No change of affairs since my dispatch of noon.

GEO. G. MEADE, Major-General.

The Retreat of the Enemy.

Special Dispatch to The N. Y. Tribune.

BALTIMORE, July 5, 1863.

News has been received from Meade's army up to 12 o'clock to-day. The late victory gets brighter and brighter. The enemy were in full retreat toward Chambersburg and Greencastle. It is thought that Lee will strain every nerve to reach Hagerstown; and it is thought that his aim is to reach Williamsport, and thence escape into Virginia. Intercepted dispatches give the information that Beauregard is in Richmond, and perhaps on his way to Culpepper. Meade is harassing Lee with cavalry, and following close in pursuit. M. D. L.

Destruction of their Pontoon Bridge at Williamsport.

Special Dispatch to The N. Y. Tribune.

WASHINGTON, July 5, 1863.

The report that Gen. French has captured a pontoon bridge from the enemy at Williamsport is confirmed officially. Up to 11 o'clock this (Sunday) morning nothing additional to the dispatches asserting that Gen. Lee was retiring has been received from Gen. Meade.

Highly Important—Rebel Pontoon Bridge Destroyed.

WASHINGTON, July 5, 1863.

The following has just been received:

"FREDERICK, Saturday, July 4, 1863—8 p. m.

"To GEN. HALLECK: An expedition by me last night has just returned, having *entirely destroyed the enemy's pontoon bridge over the Potomac at Williamsport*.

"We captured the guard—a Lieutenant and 13 men. W. H. FRENCH, Major-General."

From Gen. Meade—Rebel Army Withdrawn from Our Front.

WASHINGTON, July 5, 1863.

Dispatches from Gen. Meade, dated yesterday morning (4th), state that the Rebel army had withdrawn from his front, but whether for a retreat, or as a maneuver, was not then known.

Nothing has been received here up to this time (Sunday noon), so far as can be ascertained, conflicting with this intelligence.

The importance of the dispatches from Jeff. Davis and the Rebel Adjt.-Gen. Cooper to Gen. Lee cannot be overrated. They reveal the objects of Lee's campaign and the cause of its failure, and also the present views of the Rebel Government.

Gen. Sickles arrived here to day. His left leg has been amputated, but it is thought that he will recover.

The reports concerning the death or captures of Longstreet and A. P. Hill, are still conflicting.

The Potomac is very high.

The Rebels in Full Retreat.

BALTIMORE, July 5, 1863.

The American has just put upon its bulletin the important announcement that the Rebel army is in full retreat, which was commenced on Friday night. Many thousand prisoners and a large number of cannon are captured.

Thousands of Prisoners en route to Baltimore.

BALTIMORE, July 5, 1863.

Eight hundred and fifty Rebel prisoners, largely composed of Alabama troops, captured from Longstreet's corps in Wednesday's fight, arrived here this morning. More prisoners are announced at the depot, and accounts from up the road say there are large trains at various points, on their way down, while there are said to be acres of them awaiting transportation.

The Enemy Completely Hemmed In.

Our correspondent Beta, at Hanover, Pa., telegraphs us last evening:

"We have the enemy hedged on all sides. We apparently cannot fail to crush them."

Official Dispatch from Gen. Meade.

WASHINGTON, Saturday, July 4—10:10 o'clock, a. m.

The following has just been received:

HEADQUARTERS ARMY OF THE POTOMAC, July 3, 1863—8:30 p. m., Near Gettysburg.

Major-General HALLECK. *General-in-Chief:*

The enemy opened at 1 p. m., from about one hundred and fifty guns, concentrated upon my left center, continuing without intermission for about three hours, at the expiration of which time he assaulted my left center twice, being upon both occasions handsomely repulsed, with severe loss to him, leaving in our hands NEARLY THREE THOUSAND PRISONERS.

Among the prisoners is Brig.-Gen. Armistead, and many Colonels and officers of lesser rank.

The enemy left many dead upon the field and a large number of wounded in our hands.

The loss upon our side has been considerable. Maj.-Gen. Hancock and Brig.-Gen. Gibbon were wounded.

After the repelling of the assault, indication leading to the belief that the enemy might be withdrawing, an armed reconnoissance was pushed forward from the left, and the enemy found to be in force.

At the present hour all is quiet.

My cavalry have been engaged all day on both flanks of the enemy, barrassing and vigorously attacking him with great success, notwithstanding they encountered superior numbers, both of cavalry and infantry. The Army is in fine spirits.

GEO. G. MEADE, Maj.-Gen. Commanding.

The President to the Country!

WASHINGTON, Saturday, July 4—10:30 a. m.

The President announces to the country that news from the Army of the Potomac up to 10 p. m. of the 3d is such as to cover that army with the highest honor—to promise a great success to the cause of the Union, and to claim the condolence of all for the many gallant fallen, and that for this, he especially desires that on this day, He whose will, not ours, should ever be done, be everywhere remembered and reverenced with the profoundest gratitude.

ABRAHAM LINCOLN.

The Great Victory on Friday.

Special Dispatch to The N. Y. Tribune.

WESTMINSTER, Md., via Baltimore, Saturday, July 4, 1863.

Yesterday, the third day's struggle of the Army of the Potomac, brought another triumph to our army, and last night another sun set over a victorious but bloody-fought battle-field. The flower of the Southern army threw itself in one gigantic death-struggle upon our army, its Generals swearing to pierce our center or go down before the valor of our troops. The onset was fierce and bloody, and cost us many brave men, but the repulse of the invaders was complete, and thousands of slaughtered Rebels lay strewn along the ground, while thousands fell into our hands as prisoners. Many battle-flags have been taken. Four thousand Rebels captured yesterday are on their way to Baltimore, and several thousand are in camp guarded by our men.

Gen. Meade has now the admiration of the whole army. His daring acts and military strategy in placing in position his victorious army increase confidence in his generalship. He has fought as no one ever fought the Potomac army before.

Among our wounded yesterday were Gen. Gibbon and Gen. Webb.

The Rebel Gen. Arnold was killed.

Gen. Cauldwell, Gen. Hancock, and Gen. Doubleday, were seriously wounded, beside other officers in great numbers. Several members of General Meade's staff were wounded, so close was the encounter.

Many Rebel Generals have also fallen.

Gen. Hancock estimates the number of Rebel prisoners taken at 12,000.

The following details of the battle were taken by your correspondent from Gen. Hancock, who commanded the Second Corps during the fight till evening, when a Rebel bullet compelled him to fall to the rear.

As the firing ceased on Thursday night and our army, flushed, with victory, covered the enemy's ground, it held command of the bloody battle field of the day.

The Rebel flag of truce was denied, and Friday morning found our army re-enforced by the reserves of the Sixth Corps, Gen. Sedgwick, and Twelfth Corps, Gen. Slocum. Holding the field, our army was in line of battle along the Emmettsburg Turnpike and along the Taneytown Road. Several rifle pits on the extreme right were left in possession of the enemy on Thursday night.

On Friday morning the ball was opened by Gen. Geary, who moved upon the enemy to retake these rifle pits. Firing now became general, and continued without damage to us until eleven o'clock, the rifle-pits falling into our possession. From 11 till 1 o'clock the firing slackened, but as 1 o'clock arrived, there were indications of another clash of arms more bloody than the historian of the war has yet recorded. The Rebels under Gen. Ewell now made a concentration of all their artillery, and opened a terrible artillery fire on our left center. Battery after battery roared, shaking the surrounding hills, and shot and shell rained death and destruction upon our lines.

The Second Corps occupied the center, and the position which withstood the last convulsive attack of the Rebels was commanded by Gen. Hayes. The enemy followed their artillery with a tremendous infantry assault under the Rebel Gen. Anderson, coming up in masses, sometimes in close column by division. Our men stood like serried hosts, and on came the enemy, crowding, shouting, and rushing toward our guns like infuriated demons. There was no waver in our lines. On came the Rebels, while the canister from batteries told fearfully among their dying ranks. Now they are within twenty yards of our guns, and volley after volley of shot and shell and whizzing bullets go crashing down among them, dealing death and scattering the motley ranks to die or surrender.

The slaughter was fearful, and there were a few men of the enemy who did not find even a grave near our guns. The Third and Fifth Corps now joined in the fight. Gen. Hill's division alone took ten battle flags as this last move of the enemy burst upon our center. A panic seemed to seize them. Men laid down on the ground to escape our fire and lying there they supplicatingly held up white pieces of paper in token of surrender. In this repulse we took several thousand prisoners, and crowds of Rebel stragglers came into our lines giving themselves up in despair.

Gen. Hancock's corps now flanked the field, when crowds of disorganized Rebels threw up their arms and surrendered, while the field strewn with Rebel wounded, battle flags and arms fell into our possession.

The result amounted to a rout. Cavalry has been sent out to harvest the straggles. Gen. Hayes is said to have covered himself with glory. General Doubleday fell fighting gallantly, saying, as a ball pierced his head, "I'm killed! I'm killed!" Gen. Hancock thinks he is not killed, but seriously wounded. And thus night has drawn her mantle over another bloody day, but a day so bright with deeds of heroism and grand results, with patriotic devotion and sublime death, that the page of History shall glitter with that light.

Special Dispatch to The N. Y. Tribune.

GEN. MEADE'S HEADQUARTERS, July 4—7 a. m.

The wagon trains of the enemy are seen retreating toward Chambersburg, and about forty pieces of flying artillery have started to cut them off. The 16th Vermont (new troops) have just come in with two captured flags of the 2d Florida Regiment. The left wing have captured five Rebel stand of colors. Last night the Pennsylvania Reserves drove the enemy several miles on the left. The Rebels formed and re-formed, but a battery of artillery being brought to bear, they were literally slaughtered, and retreated. At headquarters, the day before yesterday, of staff officers' horses sixteen were killed out of thirty-two in a few minutes by the enemy's shells. The firing was fearful, and very accurate.

This is universally allowed to have been the most desperate battle of the war. The 20th Massachusetts went into action with two hundred and fifty and came out with NINETY-FIVE. They lost the following officers: Col. Revere, killed; Capt. Patten, wounded in the leg; Lieut. Marcy lost a hand; Capt. Mason, wounded; Lieut. Conegill, wounded; Lieut. Paine, killed; Lieut. Ropes, killed.

The enemy have been slaughtered wholesale. The field is covered with their dead.

The number captured is immense.

A whole brigade of the enemy surrendered yesterday.

Gen. Barksdale of Mississippi is among the enemy's killed. He is buried near headquarters. B.

Special Dispatch to The N. Y. Tribune.

WESTMINSTER, Md., Saturday, July 4, 1863.

Great battle fought yesterday. Rebels driven back from all directions. Gen. Mead held the field as night came on. Victory complete. Generals Hancock, Gibbon, Webb, and Cauldwell were wounded. Things look bright. Nothing from the fight to-day.

The following officers and men were wounded and killed in the attack on Gen. Meade on Friday: Gen. Doubleday, seriously wounded; Major-Gen. Hancock, Gen. Gibbon, Gen. Webb, Gen. Cauldwell, the Rebel Gen. Arnold, Col. Smith, 1st Delaware, Lieut.-Col. Dickinson, Meade's Staff; Maj. Massey, 20th Mass., hand shot off; the Major of the 19th Massachusetts Regiment wounded; Capt. Rarty, of Pettit's Battery.

Special Dispatch to The N. Y. Tribune.

BATTLE-FIELD, NEAR GETTYSBURG, July 3—1 p. m.
Via BALTIMORE, Saturday, July 4, 1863.

The enemy attacked our center and right this morning; and, after a most obstinate fight, were completely repulsed. Our men fought with heroic bravery: nothing could exceed it. It would seem that the Rebel General had determined to break our center line and flank us on the right. He did neither, thanks to the Army of the Potomac.

The battle is still raging, and full details will follow as speedily as possible.

We took a great many prisoners, and twelve stand of colors.

The Rebel Gen. Armisted is a prisoner in our hands.

Gen. Barksdale, who was Commandant at Fredericksburg all the Winter, was killed on Thursday.

Our loss is heavy, but that of the enemy is much greater.

I send a list of casualties as far as I could ascertain them up to the time of my leaving the field.

R. D. FRANCIS.

Special Dispatch to The N. Y. Tribune.

WASHINGTON, Saturday, July 4, 1863.

Dispatches received here state that the Rebel Gen. Longstreet is our prisoner, and that Gen. A. P. Hill has been killed. There is no official confirmation of it however.

To the Associated Press.

BALTIMORE, Saturday, July 4, 1863.

Reports deemed trustworthy from the battle-field down to 6 o'clock last evening represent that the Rebels were repeatedly repulsed with fearful slaughter.

The battle lasted all day.

Seven thousand prisoners were taken.

The Union men of this city are highly jubilant and excitedly joyous over the favorable news from our victorious army.

PHILADELPHIA, Saturday, July [illegible], 1863.

Col. Forney of *The Press* received the following highly important dispatch to-night from the Army of the Potomac:

Special Dispatch to The Philadelphia Press.

HANOVER, Pa., Saturday, July 4—5 p. m.

There has been no fighting up to this time to-day. Last evening we drove the enemy back to Gettysburg. Our lines this morning extend eight miles around Gettysburg, our batteries being on all the hills looking on the town from the south. We occupy Roundtop Ridge, commanding the Chambersburg turnpike, and have cut off all the lines of retreat. Our forces occupy the strongest possible position; a flank movement on our left is impossible.

At about 8 o'clock last night the Florida brigade of General Longstreet's division, with a Brigadier-General in command, advanced within our lines, and gave themselves up with their colors.

A bearer of dispatches from Jefferson Davis to Gen. Lee has been captured. The dispatches order Gen. Lee peremptorily to return to Richmond, and state that the movement into Pennsylvania was wholly against his wishes.

The following were among the officers killed in yesterday's engagement:

Col. Taylor, of the Bucktail Regiment, a brother of Bayard Taylor.

Lieut.-Col. Miles, of the same Regiment.

Lieut. Manton, of Philadelphia, was wounded.

Major Kerney, of the Eleventh New-Jersey, was wounded in the knee.

We have captured about eight thousand prisoners

Reports from Harrisburg.

HARRISBURG, Pa., Saturday, July 4, 1863.

Best informed parties at headquarters are in excellent spirits at the news from Gen. Meade. The battle is probably still in progress.

A gentleman who left Bridge No. 84 on the Northern Central Railroad at 3 o'clock this morning, heard heavy firing. It was also heard in Harrisburg for about half an hour.

All is quiet in our immediate front. The Rebels are supposed to have left this immediate neighborhood entirely.

The Sanitary Committee of Pittsburg have forwarded a lot of supplies to this point.

Our wounded have been all brought from Carlisle to Harrisburg, and are doing well.

Eighteen thousand men are in motion on the flank of the Rebels.

Telegraphic communication is kept up with Gen. Smith wherever he is.

A large number of men are at work on the Cumberland Valley Railroad, and trains run to Carlisle.

HARRISBURG, July 5—1 o'clock a. m.

Most favorable news has been received here from the army of General Meade, but the details, which are mostly of a general character, cannot be obtained, as the censor is silent and the governor has nothing.

The trains on the Pennsylvania Railroad will commence to run regularly on Monday morning. Not a bar of the road has been touched by the Rebels.

No further danger is apprehended to the Northern Central Railroad, the repairs to which are nearly completed.

A gentleman who left the battle-field at Gettysburg last night arrived here at noon. He came by way of York.

He says that the Rebel pickets were posted five miles this side of Gettysburg, and that the country between here and Gettysburg may be safely traversed.

Our troops are in excellent spirits. They say, universally, that this battle is the most desperate the Army of the Potomac ever fought.

From the latest intelligence received here, it is fully believed that Gen. Lee's army has been completely defeated.

There has been no fighting to-day, and the Rebel army is endeavoring to retreat through South Mountain Pass and Boonsboro.

It is certain that Lee's retreat is already seriously interfered with, and his escape from our army will be a matter of great difficulty.

A large force is concentrated here, and ready for offensive operations at any moment.

Nearly the full quota of Pennsylvania is already raised, and organized either in regiments or companies at Reading.

Col. Dougherty, volunteer aid on Gen. Smith's staff, arrived here to-day, having been paroled by the Rebels.

The Captured Dispatches to Lee—The Object of the Invasion—Jeff Davis Opposed to it—Gen. Sickles's Wound and the Services of his Corps.

Special Dispatch to The N. Y. Tribune.

WASHINGTON, July 5, 1863.

The intercepted dispatches from Jeff. Davis and his renegade Adjutant-General, to Gen. Lee, are a more important acquisition than the brief paragraphs that profess to give the substance of their contents would indicate. They reveal the plan of Lee's campaign, wherein and wherefore it was not carried out, the points to which the Rebel Government is sending re-enforcements, and the precarious condition in which it considers its capital to be. According to these dispatches, as we learn through trustworthy channels, Gen. Lee invaded Pennsylvania without the knowledge of Jeff. Davis, who, it would appear, did not altogether approve of the movement. The object of the campaign was the capture of Washington, which was to be effected in this wise: Lee was to draw Hooker into Pennsylvania sufficiently for to uncover Washington, which Beauregard, with 30,000 men, to be concentrated at Culpepper Court-House, was then to attack and take. But, as further appears from these dispatches, Jeff. Davis felt unable to spare Beauregard 30,000 men, or any number of men, to co-operate with Lee. The Rebel President said that he considered the need of Johnston, who was constantly calling for reinforcements to make his army sufficiently strong to relieve Vicksburg, "the vital point," as Jeff. Davis calls it, decidedly more imperative than that of Gen. Lee, and had, therefore, sent him all the men that could be spared by Beauregard or Bragg. Nor could reinforcements be sent from Virginia; Richmond, as Gen. Lee is officially assured, is seriously threatened, and so small is its garrison that the citizens are organizing for its defense. The Rebel Adjutant-General Cooper gives the number of troops in Richmond, at Petersburg, and on the Blackwater, and undertakes to state the strength of the National army, by which he conceives the Rebel capital to be threatened.

The pontoon bridge captured from the Rebels at Williamsport was defended by a small guard, whom Gen. French easily overpowered.

Gen. Daniel E. Sickles, who had his right leg shot off about half-past 6 o'clock on Thursday evening, was brought here this morning by his attending surgeon, Dr. Sim. He was struck by a solid ball midway between his foot and knee, which so shattered the bone as to render an amputation above his knee necessary. This was performed on the field. Dr. Sim says that Gen. Sickles is doing very well indeed, and that there is no doubt at all as to his speedy recovery. The wound is already fast healing up, so successfully was the operation performed.

Officers who have since arrived here direct from the field say that had the enemy succeeded in making the flank movement, which Gen. Sickles successfully prevented, it might have been frightfully disastrous to our army, and might have turned the tables against Gen. Meade. Gen. Sickles's corps lost very heavily in this action.

Friday's Battle—Semi-Official Report.

HEADQUARTERS, ARMY OF THE POTOMAC, FRIDAY, July 3, 1863.

The decisive battle has been fought to-day, and the enemy have been repulsed with terrific loss. At daylight, Lee's right wing batteries opened upon our left, and shortly after those of his center followed. After half an hour's cannonading, doing but little damage to us, the fire slabkened, and only occasional shots were exchanged. Shortly afterward the enemy's left, composed entirely of infantry and sharpshooters, made an attack on our right wing. So sudden and impetuously was it accomplished, that our skirmishers and front line were driven back from their intrenchments, but by the aid of the batteries in the rear, and the indomitable bravery of the 11th corps, we regained the first position, capturing a considerable number of prisoners.

Several hours of ominous silence followed this repulse. At one o'clock the enemy fired two shots, apparently as signals for the grandest artillery fight ever witnessed on this continent. Before a moment had elapsed it is estimated that at least 80 guns opened upon us. Our batteries returned the compliment with interest. The air seemed literally thick with iron, and for more than an hour it seemed impossible that man or beast could live through it. Strange to say, the enemy's accuracy of range, as exhibited on the two previous days, was wanting on this occasion. Most of their shells exploded far in the rear of our front, and generally missing our batteries. Under cover of this *feu d'enfer*, Lee advanced his columns of infantry for the covers, and made several desperate attempts to carry the lines by assault; but each successive attempt was repulsed with terrific havoc to their ranks. After an hour's incessant cannonading the fire grew less intense for a short time, but was again renewed for a little while with great spirit. During this period, some of our batteries, whose ammunition being expended and the men exhausted, ceased to fire, and on the approach of the reserve batteries withdrew to the rear. The enemy only seeing the batteries withdrawing, and mistaking this for a retreat, made a rapid infantry charge up the hill and obtained a position in our line, cutting to pieces and almost annihilating the small infantry supports; but before they had time to rejoice at their imaginary success, the fresh batteries poured in a deadly fire of canister and case shot. The infantry reserves joined on either flank of the gap, chraged them added greatly to their destruction. They were completely surprised, and hundreds threw down their arms, and asked for quarter. Nearly the entire brigade of Gen. Dick Garnett surrendered, and Garnett, himself wounded, barely made his escape.

Longstreet was mortally wounded and captured. He is reportrd to have died in an hour afterword.

About 4:30 p. m. the artillery of the enemy slackened, and had entirely ceased at 5, the last shots which they fired being far beyond the signified position, and the infantry columns had withdrawn to their covers.

We took upwards 3,000 prisoners. The enemy captured but few, if any, of our men. The Rebel prisoners report that Gen. A. P. Hill was kill outright upon the field, and that their officers suffered far greater casualities than in any previous engagement. So terrific was the enemy's fire that the small house where Gen. Meade and staff were quartered, was perforated by several shots. Many of the staff horses were killeda round the house.

Gen. Butterfield was struck in the breast, and it is feared internally injured, by a piece of shell which exploded in the building. Lieut.-Col. Joseph Dickinson of the staff had his left arm perforated by a flying fragment of shell, and it seemed a meracle that no greater damage was done to life or limb. Several of our general officers were wounded in the engagement. Gen. Hancock was wounded in the leg. Gens. Gibbon, Warren, and Hunt, were wounded. In consequence of the excitement and difficulty in ascertaining thesr locations, the names of many prominent officers reported as killed or wounded, cannot be ascertained to-night.

Too much credit cannot be given to our batteries, who for hours stood to their guns under a broiling sun and surrounded by the missiles of death, retiring only to give their positions to others, when their caissons and limbers were exhausted of ammunition. The infantry engaged also nobly did their duty, and the enemy to-day at their hands have received the greatest disaster ever administered by the Union forces. All officers award the highest honors to Gen. Meade, for the able generalship he has displayed since he assumed command, and particularly for his coolness, decision, and energy on this memorable 3d of July. Last night, believing it to be his duty to the cause, and to learn how far he would be supported in the approaching conflict, he summoned his corps and division commanders for consultation.

Occupation of Gettysburg.

BALTIMORE, July 5, 1863.

The messenger who brought the account of Friday's battle, says:

We advanced and occupied Gettysburg during Friday night without opposition. Firing was heard early Saturday morning toward Gettysburg, supposed to be our forces pursuing Lee.

Gen. Neal is under treatment.

The 27th Maine Volunteers.

THEY ARE TO HAVE MEDALS OF HONOR—GEN. FRENCH'S OPERATIONS—GEN. SICKLES IMPROVING.

WASHINGTON, July 5, 1863.

About 300 members of the 27th Maine Regiment, Col. Wentworth, who volunteered to remain beyond their time while Washington was threatened, have been relieved by the war Department, and left for home yesterday (Saturday) evening. Medals of honor are to be awarded them.

Major-Gen. French yesterday succeeded in reaching Williamsport by a forced march from Frederick with considerable force, and has destroyed the pontoon bridge and train of Lee, which the latter left in position there to serve for emergencies.

Major-Gen. Sickles reached here by rail this morning. Though suffering from the loss of his leg, his physical condition is thought to be improving.

The Campaign in Pennsylvania—The March of the Army—The First Shock near Gettysburg—Death of Gen. Reynolds—The Subsequent Battles—The Victory.

From Our Special Correspondent.

HEADQUARTERS ARMY OF THE POTOMAC, GETTYSBURG, Saturday, 7 p. m., July 4, 1863.

At 7 o'clock in the evening of June, Major-General George B. Meade became commander of the Army of the Potomac. That same night he issued orders to the several corps to move, and on the following morning the army moved as if unconscious of the change of commanders. The army was encamped about Frederick, Maryland. The main portion was ordered to move into Pennsylvania, through Emmettsburg, where the First, Third and Eleventh Corps encamped Tuesday. The Sixth was ordered to Carlisle. The Second and Twelfth were also near Emmettsburg. Early on Wednesday morning the First Corps, commanded by Major-General Reynolds, and the Eleventh, commanded by Major-General Howard, were ordered to Gettysburg, where it was reported the enemy had taken position.

The detachment was commanded by General Reynolds.

The troops were pushed forward rapidly, and arrived at Gettysburg, on the Baltimore pike, at half-past ten o'clock in the forenoon.

The First Corps was in the advance. The enemy's outposts were encountered in a wood west of the town, near the Seminary. Gen. Wadsworth, who commanded the 1st division, immediately engaged the enemy in his front, and fought him for the wood.

DEATH OF GEN. REYNOLDS.

Gen. Reynolds rode forward to inspect the ground and select a position for his line of battle. The enemy distinguishing him as well from his soldiery bearing as from his uniform to be an officer of high rank, opened upon him with heavy volleys of infantry fire. He was struck by several balls and died instantly without uttering a word. His acting Adjutant-General, Capt. Bond, was at his side and caught him in his arms to prevent his falling from his horse.

This gallant officer, well and favorably known to the army and the country, never fought battles through orderlies and aids, but always in person. Like Sumner, in battle he was at the head of his column to direct—and by his own example of personal courage sustain his command when death reigned fearfully all around.

That he was too rash will be alleged by many; that he was a superior soldier and a brave man, is the testimony of every one whok new him.

He fell fighting nobly for his country. Still more, he died in the defense of his native State. No treason-breeding soil drank up his blood, but all of him that was mortal is buried in the bosom of his own native State.

Major-Gen. Doubleday succeeded to the command of the First Corps, and vigorously continued the operations commenced by Reynolds, Wadsworth being already engaged near the Seminary west of the town. Robinson's Division formed on the right and Doubleday's Division on the left of Wadsworth, and the whole line advanced through the woods, driving back the enemy. Soon, however, solid masses of Rebel troops were seen coming up and taking position on the right and left flanks, and it was evident that hot work was on hand.

Gen. Doubleday so distributed his forces as to hold a neck of woods on an eminence which was the key to the position. He continued with desperate fighting to hold his ground until the Eleventh Corps arrived and came to his relief. Maj.-Gen. Howard then assumed command of the forces. One brigade from Steinwehr's division, was sent into the town to hold it. Gen. Howard, seeing the vital importance of seizing upon and holding the commanding positions, directed Gen. Steinwehr to take his remaining brigade and the reserve artillery, place it on the Cemetery hill, and to defend the hights.

The divisions commanded by Schurz and Barlow were sent up to the immediate support of the First Corps. The troops were led forward with the memory of Chancellorsville before them, and with a determination to retrieve their lost honor. The two divisions moved through the town and took a position on the right of the First Corps, and fought desperately against Ewell's corps, which outnumbered them three to one. The first and second charges were stoutly resisted by the Eleventh Corps on the right, but on came a third charge with four regular lines for overlapping the little force on both flanks. The men still undaunted fought until both flanks were turned near half a mile.

The force now opposed to the 1st and 11th comprised the corps of A. P. Hill and Ewell, numbering over 60,000 men. Yet against this fearful odds the gallant band fought for hours, inflicting great slaughter on the enemy.

Reynolds and Zook were dead, and Paul and Barlow wounded, and Schimmelfennig a prisoner. Many field and line officers had been lost and nearly half the men before the order was given to retire to the hights held by Steinwehr.

Gen. Howard had carefully examined the topography of the surrounding country. He knew that a very strong force of the enemy lay in the valley; he felt, therefore, that the holding of Cemetery Hill, which commanded the whole surrounding country, was of the most vital importance. Accordingly he took the responsibility of falling back south-east of the town, to the commanding hights on both sides of the Baltimore pike.

The troops retired in the face of an overwhelming foe with a commendable steadiness. At times there was a little wavering, but nothing even approaching a panic. The corps by their conduct on Wednesday and later in the battle are entitled to great commendation, and the Chancellorsville disgrace is swallowed up by the achievements at Gettysburg.

Gen. Slocum with the 12th, and Sickles with the 3d Corps, came up and took position to the right and left of Howard, on the hills.

During the battle in the afternoon, when his troops were outnumbered and sorely pressed, Gen. Howard sent to Slocum, who was within five miles, to come to his relief. He sent a second time, but received no reply. Gen. Howard then sent his brother, Maj. Howard, to urge upon Gen. Slocum to come up in person if he would not send troops. Slocum replied that he did not wish to take the responsibility of the fight.

In the mean time, however, he moved up his corps to be ready to aid in defense of the hights if necessary.

Gen. Sickles on receiving Howard's request, at once moved up rapidly, but owing to the great distance he was in the rear his corps did not arrive until the second position had been taken.

The enemy was not disposed to attempt the carrying of the hights and here the battle ended.

Two advantages were gained. The enemy was obliged to exhibit his strength and to commit himself to a position; and the commanding positions were seized and held by the National troops.

During the night Gen. Meade and staff came up to the front. The Commanding-General carefully examined the surrounding country, and after considering the locations and positions in all their strategical and tactical bearing, he approved of the position taken

See Twelfth Page.

THE GREAT VICTORY.

Continued from First Page.

by Gen. Howard, and so disposed his forces on the several hills or "round tops" and ridges, as to construct a battle line in the form of a crescent, with the center to the southward fro the cemetry.

The hills present outcrops of sandstone rocks in ledges having a dip of from 20 to 90 degrees; these ledges in many cases are full 20 feet high, and afford admirable shelter for troops. The slope of the hills at places is moderate and regular, in some instances abrupt, and even sometimes presents vertical rocky faces.

The enemy was in a valley or on hills at a distance too great to be of use for shelter. The roads on which the enemy would desire to march were commanded by Meade's guns, and hence Lee must fight with the hills against him. For once, then, in the history of the Army of the Potomac, the enemy has been compelled to give battle at a disadvantage.

On Wednesday night all the troops but the Sixth Corps, commanded by General Sedgwick, arrived on the field. The veteran division, known as the Pennsylvania Reserve Corps, was attached to the Fifth Corps. The Second Vermont Brigade, nine months' men, were assigned to the First Corps. On Thursday morning the line was formed as follows: Slocum's Corps on the right, Howard joining on the left; Hancock's (Couch's), Newton's (Reynolds's) and Sickles's Corps in the centre; and Sykes's (Meade's) on the left. Numerically, commencing with the right, the line was formed of the 12th, 11th, 2d, 1st, 3d, and 5th Corps.

This was essentially the position during Thursday and Friday, though Gen. Meade did not fight his army by corps. As the battle raged more fiercely here or there detachments of divisions or brigades were sent to support, and would remain till wanted elsewhere.

So admirably were the several resistances and onslaughts managed that whenever and wherever supporting columns were needed then and there they would be found in sufficient force to accomplish the object desired.

All the hights, and every advantageous position along the entire line where artillery could be massed or battery planted, frowned down on the enemy through brows of brass and iron.

There was no conceivable advance of approach that could not be raked and crossed with the artillery. The reserve artillery and all the essentials to insure victory were in position at the right time. The immense cavalry force, too, for once, was present, covering both flanks of the army and continually harassing the enemy. This was a new and an encouraging feature that gave confidence to the men and security to the trains.

There were no ghosts of stampeding corps or other scapegoats with *horns* fast in the bushes ready to bear away what every censure might befall one too weak to bear the burden of his own folly. These the cavalry prancing along the flanks frightened away to the swamps of the Chickahominy, the banks of the Rappahannock, or to Antietam's bloody fields, where erst they were wont to congregate.

Early on Thursday morning the enemy commenced feeling the lines of Gen. Meade's army. Skirmishing continued more or less severe until 4 o'clock in the afternoon. Suddenly, at about this hour, the enemy opened a terrific fire on the Cemetery Hill held by the 11th Corps on the right—center held by the 2d Corps. The artillery in front of the enemy's fire replied vigorously, and for two hours the roar and thunder and flame and smoke of artillery, and the screech of shells, so completely filled the heavens that all else seemed forgotten.

One form, however, with mind intent on high purposes, stood on an eminence leaning slightly forward, and with eagle eye pierced the vail of smoke, and saw and felt and knew that an hour more terrible by far than the present was coming rapidly—was even present. It was evident the wily commander of the Rebel forces had determined on some desperate charge, but when and in what manner it would be made was unknown to the man who stood calmly yet with deep solicitude regarding every pulsation of the battle.

On the left, through the woods, black masses were seen moving—larger, more frequent and nearer! Skirmishing in that part of the field becomes sharper. Gen. Sickles is ordered forward to develop the enemy's intentions. The black columns come out of the wood and suddenly the thunder of artillery ceased, and, with cheers and yells, the roar of musketry and flash of bayonet, full 50,000 men from Longstreet's and Hill's corps, came rushing against our lines. The Third Corps stood firm for a while, but afterward gave way beneath the weight of the attacking column; and on they came ten-fold more furious than before.

Sickles fell severely wounded in the leg, and his corps was literally cut to pieces. The Second Corps was thrown in the breach from the right and the Fifth from the left. The Second suffered fearfully. Hancock received a painful flesh wound in the thigh, but refused to be led from the field while the engagement continued. Here, too, Gen. Gibbon was wounded in the shoulder. The terrible charge and fierce battle raged with unabated fury. The Fifth Corps, including the Regulars and the Pennsylvania Reserves, struggled in the herculean labor with the determination of men born to conquer in battle.

The aid of the 12th Corps, from the extreme right, was called for, and a division was ordered up, and about the same time Sedgwick came up with the 6th Corps, after a march of 36 consecutive hours. The men were footsore, many without shoes on their feet, hungry and weary, ready to drop on the road from exhaustion. When, however, the situation flashed into the minds of these weary soldiers, the fire and zeal for which this Corps is so justly celebrated, was kindled anew in their hearts. They awaited but the order, and that impatiently to be led against the enemy. The order was given, and, like men fresh from camp, they went down upon the haughty foe like an avalanche. The Rebel column staggered and reeled, and then fell back in confusion, leaving their dead lying against and across each other in this field of slaughter.

The sun went down. Suddenly as the western hills eclipsed his rays the battle carnage ceased on the left.

Equally sudden, a fierce charge dashed against the weakened lines of the right wing. The suddenness of the attack and the weight of Ewell's column gave some advantage to the enemy. Re-enforcements, however, were promptly up and the enemy checked in his advance.

The Rebel general was determined to break through the right and gain control of the valley roads. The failure to turn the left, and the snatching the victory from their clutches, hurling their broken columns back defeated and confused on the left, made their case more desperate, and the attack on Slocum was furious even to madness. The 1st and 6th Corps came up promptly to the support of the 12th Corps. From dark until 9½ o'clock the battle raged with unabated fury. The lines moved to and fro, each in turn advancing and falling back. At this hour of the night the enemy made his final charge on the left of the right wing, held by Gen. Geary's division. He was repulsed with terrible slaughter, and refused to renew the attack. At 10 o'clock the battle ceased, and during the night all was quiet.

Ewell had been largely re-enforced, and held a position of some advantage. Gen. Meade determined that he should be dislodged from the place, and as a matter of personal honor, assigned the task to Gen. Slocum, who had previously occupied the same position, but was compelled to abandon it because of the re-enforcements sent to the support of the left wing, overwhelmed by Longstreet's and A. P. Hill's Divisions.

Gen. Slocum accordingly made preparations for the work assigned. His own Corps was in strong position, and determined to regain the ground lost the night before.

A Division from the Sixth Corps was posted on the right of the Twelfth, thus forming the extreme outpost of the right wing. The Fifth Corps was sent over as a reserve, and Gen. Wadsworth's Division of the First Corps, took position to strengthen Howard's right where it joined Slocum's left.

These were the preliminaries. The men well knew what sort of work they would be called upon to do in the morning, and nerved their hearts and cheered each other against the hour of trial by fire.

On Friday morning, at 4 o'clock, Slocum's line opened a terrific fire on Ewell's men. The enemy responded in a most furious charge, for which mode of fighting they are justly celebrated. The fighting on Thursday on the left, where Longstreet and Hill fought with most terrible desperation for three hours, and the subsequent battle on the right by Ewell, were regarded by the oldest officers in the army as the most obstinate and deadly contest of the war. Officers and men lay dead in fearful numbers. But the enemy's charge in response to Slocum's fire seemed ten times more furious.

With fiendish yell and such contempt of death during six full hours, they hurled their solid masses against the well-defended lines. The National troops stood like a wall of fire, whose flaming tongues enwrapped in death whatever came near, whose foundation were firm as if one with the primal rock on which it rested.

Nothing during the war has equalled this six hours of carnage. In front of Grang's position were more Rebel dead than the number of the entire list of casualties in the 12th corps. The dead were lying literally in heaps, many hit in all manner of degrees, from a clean shot through the head to bodies torn to pieces by exploding shells.

At 10 o'clock Slocum had repulsed and driven back the enemy at every point, and reoccupied his original position. The battle ceased at 11 o'clock, and there was a pause like to the stillness of death rested for three hours on the living and dead.

No matter how long pressed by the enemy the Union troops felt even in the front rifle pits that the Commanding General was conversant with their situatton, and would not suffer them to be overwhelmed. The officers would say to the men, and the men to each other, "Meade will send you help—just hold on a little longer."

Nor were they disappointed. If the General in command was possessed with a degree of calm deliberation truly wonderful, and seemed intuitively to know what was necessary to be done and to be endowed with a superior genius in the distribution and handling of his forces.

At 2 o'clock on Friday afternoon Lee opened a line of artillery fire from about one hundred guns, concentrated against Cemetery Hill and the position along the center held by the Second and a part of the First Corps.

The firing was responded to by all the batteries on the hill, and then ensued three hours of cannonading unsurpassed in incessant fierceness by any artillery battle on this continent. The sight and sound were awfully sublime. The hills trembled beneath the percussion. The sound filled the heavens, and Nature, as it were, stood still to contemplate the scene.

Horses were shot down by scores, gun-carriages were demolished, pieces dismounted, caissons exploded, whole batteries were swept away, and cannoniers and officers killed and wounded in numbers almost incredible. No less than fifteen caissons were exploded on the hights, and two regular batteries on the right of the cemetery were completely demolished.

Much of the enemy's firing was wild, and scattered near and far over the field. Gen. Meade's headquarters were forced to take refuge behind the rocks near Gen. Slocum's headquarters. The non-combatants were especially alarmed, but the fighting members thought it a good joke to see their associates flee the wrath to come, pent up in Rebel shells.

Gen. Howard's headquarters were in the Cemetery, and were raked in a fearful manner; men fell all round him, but himself and staff escaped.

The silent abode of the dead was made the theater of deadly conflict. Tombstones and beautiful monuments were demolished; great holes were torn in the earth by the explosion of shells, and the surface checkered with furrows.

The artillery fire continued till 4 o'clock, when the solid columns of Rebel infantry were again seen moving in the wood in front of the center, held by the 1st and 2d corps.

During the fierce cannonading the men and officers were ordered to shelter themselves behind the hills and rocks. When, however, the Rebel infantry was seen in the woods, several officers came to Gen. Doubleday, volunteering to carry messages to Meade and ask that the center be strengthened.

Doubleday replied to the officers that they might trust to Gen. Meade; that he would keep his eye on movements of the enemy and have his forces ready to meet his attacks. Out they came, and rushed rapidly over the fields in solid mass, but evidently with less fury than before.

The head of the column was directed against a position held by Gen. Webb, commanding 2d Brigade, 2d Division, 2d Corps. His troops were old, and steadily and bravely withstood the charge. The steady fire of the National troops staggered the enemy, and the Rebel Gen. Armistead, who lead the charge, wishing to steady his column, halted it for a moment at a fence.

Gen. Webb seeing, called out to his brigade, "Charge! the enemy is ours." And true enough he was. The commanding Gen. Annistead and 3,500 men were captured by the closing in of the Second Corps on the right and the First on the left.

The enemy was driven back over the fields with great slaughter. The enemy then withdrew from the field, and the battle ended.

During the battles of Friday, Gen. Hancock, though severely wounded, lay under a tree and gave orders, fighting until the battle was ended.

On Friday night, the cavaly, which during the several days of battle had rendered valuable service and kept the Rebel cavalry close within the infantry lines, reported the enemy retreating on the Cooktown road. Large cavaly forces were sent out to watch his movements.

Early on Saturday morning Gen. Slocum was ordered to make a reconnoissance beyond Gettysburg, and in order to feel the enemy's position. He was found intrenching himself in front of the Gap. This was supposed to be a feint, and also a defense to cover his retreat.

In the morning, also, a brigade from Steimwehr's division, 11th Corps, occupied Gettysburg, driving out the Rebel sharpshooters.

The streets were barricaded and the place put in defensive condition. Gen. Lee sent a message under flag of truce, to the effect that if the National troops were not withdrawn from the town it would be shelled. Gen. Meade replied that he would dispose his troops as best suited his purpose; of course, the troops were not withdrawn, nor was the army.

The Rebel army is hedged in and will hardly escape with an organization.

The slaughter on both sides has been terrible. 15,000 will scarcely cover the casualties in killed and wounded in the National army. The Rebels must have suffered a loss of 25,000 in killed, wounded and prisoners.

Rebel prisoners report Lonstreet a prisoner. Gen. Gibbon announced to his troops that they had captured Longstreet; and a member of Kilpatrick's staff says he saw Longstreet a prisoner, mortally wounded, lying in a barn. One of your correspondents the same day saw the dead body of a Major-General in the Rebel uniform in the barn alluded to. Ewell is reported wounded. Gen. Barksdale is dead, and buried in our lines.

The citizens of Gettysburg affirm that Lee is certainly wounded.

Gen. Barlow, who was wounded and taken prisoner, is in Gettysburg, not paroled; the enemy was pressed for time.

General Schimmelfenig was not prisoner, but disguised as a private, he lay concealed in the town shelled.

No movements were made on Saturday, save by the cavalry and the reconnoisance by Slocum. The enemy abandoned the field with his dead and wounded in the hands of the victors. The victory is complete. Meade is master of the position. No matter what Lee may design, General Meade's head is always clear and his heart earnest in the cause.

Officers and men are in good spirits. The only thing talked of is the capture or destruction of Lee's entire army until our forces arrived. He is with his command.

Gen. Meade has greatly distinguished himself in the masterly management of this most terrible of battles. The Army of the Potomac was fought as an army, and has won a victory with fruits commensurate with its labors.

All things are in readiness, and Meade and his army are always in a *condition to fight*, and because of rain will not *retreat*, but rather advance. With the swelling Potomac in his front, Couch and French on his flanks, and Meade's victorious army in his rear, Lee has the alternative of having his army annihilated as an army, or of surrendering to the National forces. Meade will give him but little time to deliberate.

J. R. SYPHER.

The Battle of Wednesday—Desperate Effort of the Enemy to Crush our Left Wing—A Disastrous Repulse—Heroism of the Left Wing—Capture and Death of Longstreet.

Special Dispatch to The N. Y. Tribune.

ON THE BATTLE-FIELD NEAR GETTYSBURG, PA., Friday Night, July 3, 1863.

One of the most desperate and furious contests of the war was fought yesterday near Gettysburg, resulting in a decisive victory for the Union forces. All unite in asserting that in no former battle of the war has so much valorous impetuosity and soldier-like discipline been exhibited as was shown by every regiment of our troops engaged in this terrible encounter. On Thursday Lee attacked our lines, bestowing particular attention on our left wing, at which point he seemed anxious to flank our army. Here he met with a bloody repulse; and, having found it impossible to turn our flank on the left, he next turned his attention to our right, occupying elevated and strong positions just south-east of the town, which he attacked early yesterday morning. Here he was not successful, our batteries making great havoc in his lines, which were steadily driven back beyond their former positions. Rebel prisoners stated that Ewell, who commanded the Rebel force assaulting our right, was determined to break our line, saying that he would lose every man before he would desist from his purpose.

Col. Geary, commanding a division of the 12th Corps, sent word to Gen. Meade that he could and would drive Ewell over the hills, which promise he signally fulfilled. The fight in the morning commenced quite early, and continued until 10 o'clock, when the Rebel batteries were silenced, and Ewell was foiled.

Occasional shelling occupied the time from ten in the morning until one in the afternoon, but skirmishing was carried on briskly as on the preceding day, our skirmishers occupying a position a quarter of a mile in advance of our front line. At 1 o'clock in the afternoon the ball was abruptly opened by the Rebels in our front, nearly south of the town, and from that time until 4 o'clock the cannonading on both sides was fearfully incessant.

Gen. Meade's headquarters, which were just below our rear line, and opposite its center, received during the battle flying visits from thousands of monster shells, round shot, and rifle balls; but although almost every shell exploded all along the road on which the small frame building occupied by him was situated, neither himself nor any of his staff were injured. Men and horses passing along the road were torn to fragments by shells, but Gen. Meade seemed regardless of his personal safety, and was riding along the lines, attended by two orderlies, and guiding and directing every movement. Demoralized officers and men, of whom there were on this occasion but very few, were halted and sent to the front by him, and ordered to remain until the termination of the fight. The day previous his horse was killed under him, the canister shot grazing his pants and passing through the flap of the saddle. He seemed perfectly sanguine of success, and his appearance denoted that should he fail in driving the enemy, he intended to hold his position at all hazards.

The fighting in the center, between one and four o'clock, was terrific, the missiles from the Rebel lines rushing through the air with an abandon which seemed quite refreshing to our veterans. Charging across the open plain, the Rebels advanced toward the crest of the ridge of hills occupied by our troops, who counter-charged down the slope, every time driving the enemy nearly back to his former position on the high ground to the westward of Gettysburg, and inflicting the most severe slaughter upon him. In one of the charges two companies surrounded a house and barn in the valley, capturing in the sortie seventy Rebels, who had used these buildings as breastworks.

Our batteries, meanwhile, kept up a continuous roar, sending shot and shell into the Rebel masses in the valley, and frequently scattering them in the wildest confusion. They were reformed, however, but only to be again shattered and broken by the desperate and irresistible charges of our infantry, aided by our artillery. Our men were nerved to the highest pitch of enthusiasm during the fight, and cheer after cheer was heard above the din of battle as our brave fellows rolled back at each assault the ragged legions of the enemy. Men with severe wounds, when being carried from the field to the hospitals, were heard cheering as the intelligence that we were driving the enemy was communicated to them. One with a ghastly wound in the face, forgetting for the moment his sufferings, swung his cap when our men were cheering, and, giving a heartfelt "Hurrah!" said, "I'll be with you again to-morrow, boys! I'll be with you to-morrow!"

At 4 o'clock the storm of battle had ceased, and only occasional shells and minie balls gave evidence of the existence of the enemy. We had driven them from their battle ground, which was literally covered with their dead and wounded; had captured three thousand prisoners, among whom was the Rebel Gen. Longstreet; had killed Gen. Marshall, and, it is reported, Gen. Lowe; and had taken fully twenty stand of Rebel colors.

The gallant and dashing Gen. Hancock was wounded by a musket ball in the thigh. His wound is severe but not dangerous. A large nail was extracted with the ball from his wound, and must have been driven by the ball from the fence in front. It is to be hoped that his wound will not long incapacitate him from active duty, as his services in the army are invaluable.

Brig. Gen. Gibbon received a serious wound in the shoulder from a rifle ball. He has long been in command of the 2d Division of the Second Army Corps, and is an experienced and able officer.

Two Rebel colors were taken by the 1st Delaware Regiment, two by the 8th Ohio, three by the 19th Massachusetts, and four by the 14th Connecticut. Our men never fought so well as to-day. In fact their discipline and bravery are everywhere mentioned with admiration. Major-Gen. Butterfield was slightly wounded by the fragment of a shell during the engagement.

The fighting was mainly in the center, and there was no firing on the right and but little on the left. Gen. Longstreet died soon after being captured, at Gen. Meade's headquarters. Rebel prisoners admit a great defeat to-day, but assert that they achieved a victory over our forces yesterday.

The fight will probably be renewed to-morrow, and the 4th of July celebrated by the more signal defeat and perhaps annihilation of Lee's whole army. The troops are greatly exhilarated by their success, and desire to strike another and a more stunning blow to the enemy.

Saturday, July 4, 11:30 *a. m.*—Heavy cannonading was heard this morning by persons who left early, and it is supposed the battle of yesterday was renewed to-day. Our lines advanced during last night over the battle-field, and Gettysburg was occupied without opposition. It is believed that Lee is endeavoring to retreat by way of South Mountain Pass. The enemy can escape only by a miracle.

T. C. G.

The Battle of the First of July—The First and Eleventh Corps Engaged—Death of Gen. Reynolds—Gen. Doubleday Succeeds Him—Capture of a Rebel Brigade—Gradual Retirement of our Troops—Loss of the Rebels terrible—Some of our Wounded Captured.

From Our Special Correspondent.

HEADQUARTERS ARMY OF THE POTOMAC, near Gettysburg, Pa., Thursday, July 2d, 1863.

Yesterday witnessed another scene of carnage in the drama of the Great Rebellion, and yet, with all its terrible slaughter, it was but the prelude to a still bloodier struggle yet to take place, provided Lee deems it prudent to venture a general engagement. The sharp and continuous crack of the rifles of the sharpshooters of the opposing armies this morning tells of another and a fiercer combat and of the deafening thunder of battle which is to awake harsh echoes before unheard by the inhabitants of the peaceful old commonwealth of Pennsylvania. Yesterday's fight, although it eventuated in our falling back a short distance, is still evidence of the irrepressible valor of our troops in the cause for which they have so long and so nobly battled.

The First and Eleventh Army Corps, assisted by General Buford's cavalry division, fought yesterday's battle, having no support from the remainder of the Army of the Potomac. The First, as usual, sustained its well-earned reputation, and the Eleventh redeemed its character, tarnished by the rout at Chancellorsville. General Reynolds, in command of the First Corps, was killed almost immediately after its arrival on the field. He had come up with the First Division on the advance from Emmettsburg, and was forming his line for attack when struck by the fatal bullet. He was shot through the forehead and lived but half an hour afterward. It is needless to say that his death has cast a gloom upon the army, softened only by the thought that his death was avenged by the slaughter of thousands of the enemy. The loss on our side is variously estimated at from two to four thousand, but this is, of course, exaggerated. First statements of casualties are always untrustworthy, from the fact that they are invariably over-estimated, but when the confusion incident to a battle has subsided, a more definite idea of our true loss can be gained.

A portion of our forces were on the march from Emmettsburg, when the report that Gen. Buford was skirmishing with the enemy reached them. Haste was made, and by 12 o'clock yesterday the First Division of the First Army Corps was beyond and south of Gettysburg engaging the enemy. Other corps d'armée, on the march for the same point by way of the Gettysburg road, were hastened forward on receiving intelligence of the fight above, and, although no artillery could be heard, there was evidence of another nature that a fight was in progress. A long line of smoke could be seen arising from the direction of Gettysburg, and orderlies were hurrying below toward General Headquarters as if their lives depended on their celerity. Major-Gen. Hancock, of the Second Corps, was relieved from duty with that corps, and ordered forward to take the position of Corps Commander of the First, which had been made vacant by the death of Major-Gen. Reynolds.

The First Division of the First Corps having reached the field, found sharp skirmishing going on between our cavalry and the Rebel forces. They immediately advanced up the road to the left and south of the town, steadily driving the Rebels before them until brought to a halt by an unequal force of the enemy. For three-quarters of an hour, opposed and hard pressed by superior numbers, they maintained their ground and fought with a coolness and bravery never before surpassed, capturing nearly a whole brigade of Rebel infantry with most of its commissioned officers, including its commander, Brig.-Gen. Archer, who, in charging with his brigade, was outflanked and taken prisoner. Capt. James Hall, of the Second Maine Battery, was for a time the only artillerist on the field, and deserves especial mention for the efficiency of his battery. Two of his guns were captured, but without the aid of infantry he almost immediately drove the Rebels from the guns with his remaining artillery, and re-took the pieces. This is the second time he has performed a similar feat, and general officers unite in giving him particular credit for skill and gallantry.

Shortly after the arrival of the Eleventh and the remainder of the First Corps, the enemy received strong re-enforcements and recommenced the attack with renewed fury. For two hours our troops, the Eleventh Corps occupying the right of the line, extending to the north and south, west of the town, withstood every assault of the enemy, until overpowered by superior numbers, and outflanked on either side, they slowly fell back, contesting hotly as they did so every foot of ground, to the eastern outskirts of the town, where they repelled every assault of the Rebels until about 4 p. m., when the fighting ceased, our forces holding the high ground south of the village.

Major-Gen. Abner Doubleday commanded the First Corps after the fall of Gen. Reynolds, as Gen. Hancock was unable to reach the scene of action in time to participate in the engagement. The whole of Ewell's and Hill's corps (it is believed from reports of prisoners) were opposed to our troops. It is somewhat singular that two army corps, unaided, should have been precipitated into a fight with an unknown number of the enemy, but probably some reason existed which rendered it necessary. A pretty definite idea of Lee's strength was ascertained by yesterday's battle which is indispensable to our method of procedure in attacking him.

The provost guard of the 3d Division, 1st Corps, deserve mention for gallantry. Thirty men of the 150th Pennsylvania were stationed at a point beyond Gettysburg, with orders to cover as much as possible the retreat of our forces, and to hold the road, if possible. In compliance with orders, they fought against ten times their numbers for half an hour, thus saving a portion of our force from great injury.

The Rebels fought with their usual desperation, charging with their peculiar yell frequently, but without effect. The loss inflicted upon them, judging from all accounts, must have been very great, as every discharge of our artillery apparently did terrible execution. Those engaged speak of this battle as one of the most desperate of the war, when the numbers engaged are considered. I send inclosed a list of killed, wounded and missing, so far as obtainable at present.

A great battle seems imminent, if Lee remains in the vicinity of Gettysburg. Sharp skirmishing has been going on all day, the two lines lying within short musket range; and at one time toward noon a general engagement was anticipated. At 11½ o'clock the Rebels showed signs of extraordinary activity on the left, and columns of troops could be discerned moving down the valley south-westward. Proper dispositions have been made of our troops to prevent their being outflanked, and the attack on Lee will not be delayed should he remain. But his tarry in Pennsylvania is doubtless but temporary, and should he see any way of escaping he will doubtless seize the opportunity of doing so. With the remembrance of Antietam he must certainly shrink from another contest under somewhat similar circumstances.

Gen. Meade's headquarters are close to our first line of battle, and in a small white building on the road to Gettysburg.

Fifteen or twenty of our skirmishers have been killed and wounded to-day. Several have been shot from the houses in town, which are used as coverts by Rebel sharpshooters. One poor fellow had just returned from the skirmish line unscathed, and was cleaning his piece, when struck and killed by a stray Rebel bullet. Most of our wounded were left in the hospitals at Gettysburg, and were of course captured by the enemy; the remainder were taken down in ambulances last night toward Emmettsburg.

T. C. G.

The Battles of July 2 and 3—Our Line of Battle—Attempt to Flank our Left Defeated—Prisoners and Guns Taken from the Enemy—Gen. Sickles Loses a Leg—Couch Expected from Harrisburg.

From Our Special Correspondent.

ARMY OF THE POTOMAC, FRIDAY MORNING, July 3, 1863.

The great battle commenced yesterday afternoon at four o'clock, and, closing at nine o'clock last night, is again in progress this morning. I have no time to give details, but can only state that our original lines have with but few exceptions been maintained. Our line of battle is of horse-shoe form, the convex portion occupying the crest of the hill just west of Gettysburg.

The enemy did not respond to our random shelling yesterday, until our guns, at four o'clock, were directed to the left of our line, when it was ascertained that the main body of Lee's forces occupied that position. Heavy cannonading then commenced and continued for an hour all along the line, when the infantry became engaged. The main infantry and artillery battle was on the left, the Rebels nearly succeeding in flanking us at that point. The Third Army Corps held the left and, re-enforced by the First and Second Divisions of the Second, and a portion of other corps, maintained their position, and at night drove the enemy some distance. During the battle on the left the enemy, in large force, fell upon our center creating momentary disorder. They were finally driven back, and our old line maintained. About 200 prisoners and several guns were taken by our troops.

Gen. Sickles had his right leg blown away by a shell while fighting on the left. Gen. Zook, of the First Division, Second Corps, was killed.

The fight, considering the time occupied, was one of the most furious of the war, although our casualties are not so large as on Wednesday.

The ball opened this morning by our shelling the enemy, and at half-past six the right is hotly engaged with musketry and artillery. At the center cannonading is going on, and very heavy picket skirmishing.

Gen. Meade seems confident of, at least, holding his position, if he does not succeed in annihilating Lee. Reports of the approach of Gen. Couch from Harrisburg have been in circulation, and it is to be hoped they may prove correct.

I send you the names of a few of our killed and wounded in yesterday's fight.

T. C. G.

Friday, July 3, 10 *o'clock a. m.*—Heavy fighting is still going on at the right. Our troops had been steadily driving the enemy all the morning up to 9 o'clock, when the Rebels received re-enforcements, and pushed us back a short distance. One division of Sedgwick's (Sixth) Corps was immediately sent up, and the cannonading is still going on, with occasional heavy musketry firing. Our right rests just south of the town, and our position is a good one, being on high wooded ground. There has been no infantry fighting as yet on our center and left.

The Rebel Gen. Barksdale, formerly Member of Congress from Mississippi, was killed yesterday, and Longstreet is also reported killed. A rumor says that we have captured Lee's private papers, and that among other things a dispatch from Jeff. Davis was found telling Lee that he could send him no re-enforcements; that he had always opposed an invasion of Pennsylvania, and that he must make his way out as best he could.

I inclose an additional list of killed and wounded in the skirmish yesterday morning:

Lieut.-Col. Merwin, 27th Conn., killed.
Col. Venute, 82d N. Y., killed.
Major Baird, A. Asst. Inspector-General, on staff of Gen. Gibbons, commanding 2d Division 2d Corps, wounded in foot.
Capt. John Teed, 16th Pa., missing.
Capt. Maroney, 69th N. Y., wounded.
Lieut.-Col. Bently, 69th N. Y., wounded.
Capt. Burke, 88th N. Y., wounded.
Capt. McKee, 155th Pa., wounded.
Lieut. Geo. Hulpin, 116th Pa., missing.

Firing now is only occasional.

T. C. G.

From The Battle-field To-day.

PHILADELPHIA, July 5, 1863.

A gentleman who lives on the road to Fayetteville, fifteen miles from Gettysburg, and who arrived to-day, says that at 4 o'clock yesterday afternoon he heard heavy firing, which continued until after dark. This morning in again commenced at an early hour, and continued till 7 o'clock, but not nearly so heavy as the night before. He left at 9 o'clock, and the firing had not been renewed. The sound was in the direction of Gettysburg.

Rebel Prisoners at Baltimore.

BALTIMORE, July 5, 1863.

Twenty-three hundred prisoners have just passed along Baltimore street from the Northern Central depot, and 1,900 more are shortly expected, which will make 5,050 for to-day. This is but a small installment, it is said, of all who are to come. While passing through the streets some parties had the bad taste to raise cheers of triumph, which induced the Rebels to give their peculiar yell and cheer for Jeff. and the Southern Confederacy. In addition to the 5,000, 830 passed through here on Friday night, which will make the entire number so far nearly 6,000.

Our Captures—Prisoners Taken by the Rebels Recaptured.

PHILADELPHIA, July 5, 1863.

The Journal publishes the following in an extra:

"BALTIMORE, July 5, 1863—11:30 a. m.

"The war correspondent of *The Journal* has just arrived from yesterday's battle-field. He states that the rout of Gen. Lee was thorough and complete. Gen. Meade has not only captured 20,000 Rebels, but recaptured all our own troops who were previously in the hands of the enemy.

"3 *p. m.*—It is really true that Lee has been totally routed, and is seeking to escape. Pleasanton cut off his retreat in the Gap leading to Chambersburg.

"We took 118 pieces of artillery and from 15,000 to 20,000 prisoners, and all they took of us in the first day's fight. We hold the town of Gettysburg and all the hospitals. It is a complete victory."

The Potomac Impassable.

WASHINGTON, July 5, 1863.

The recent rains have swlled the Potomac and has rendered the river unfordable, an important fact in view of military operations. The water in some places in the Upper Potomac is said to be eight or nine feet deep.

The city is jubilant to-night over the latest war intelligence from Pennsylvania.

Sensation Reports.

PHILADELPHIA, July 5, 1863—p. m.

A sensation report is current here that 20,000 Rebels and 118 guns have been captured, and that Lee asked an armistice of 48 hours to bury his dead and take charge of his wounded, to which Gen. Meade replied that an unconditional surrender could only be entertained. No confirmation of these reports has been received.

The Second New-Jersey Brigade Again in Battle—They are Terribly Cut Up—Names of Several of the Officers Wounded—Statement of Capt. Healey.

Capt. Healey, Company B, 5th New-Jersey Volunteers, Acting Major, who was wounded by a musket ball through the left thigh, and had the second finger of his right hand shot off, in the battle near Gettysburg, on Thursday last, returned to his home in Jersey City on Saturday.

From him we have obtained the following facts of what occurred under his own observation:

The Second New-Jersey Brigade (Sickles corps), consisting of the Fifth, Sixth, Seventh, and Eighth New-Jersey Volunteers, under command of Col. Burling, located at the left of the line, were posted two miles to the left of Gettysburg. During Thursday everything remained in comparative quiet until about 4 p. m., when it was ascertained that the enemy were concentrating in great force directly in front with a view apparently of breaking our line; our batteries opened upon them vigorously, to which the enemy replied with a single battery, which was soon silenced by Clark's battery. Our artillery then advanced some distance when the enemy opened with artillery from the center to the extreme left, and the action becoming general, he opened battery after battery, and shot and shell rained down like hail, dealing destruction all around. Their infantry then advanced in force, but were met with determination by our men, and were finally repulsed on the left center. Rallying again, the enemy advanced up the Emmettsburg road, and the only force confronting them, Collis's Pennsylvania Zouaves and another regiment were compelled to fall back; but the Rebels showed no disposition to follow up their advantage. Shortly afterward, it then being near dark, re-enforcements came up, and the enemy were driven back into the woods. Seeley's Battery, Co. K, regulars, were brought up on the road, and were supported by the 5th New-Jersey regiment, who were lying on the side of the road directly in front. The enemy brought a battery to bear, and raked the road; at the same time the infantry opened with steady fire. The 5th New-Jersey were then ordered to charge, and while advancing at double quick, our informant received his wounds, and immediately after retired to the rear. Capt. Healy was in most of the battles of the Peninsula, including that at Williamsburg, where he was wounded, also at Chancellorsville, and describes this as the most terrible and destructive that he has ever witnessed. When the battle closed, soon after dark, the enemy had been repulsed at every point, and the advantage was decidedly in our favor. Their great aim appeared to be a determination to turn our left wing, in order to gain possession of the Baltimore road. The Captain left the next morning, and arrived in Jersey City on Saturday. He reports the following officers and men wounded:

Col. Sewell, 5th N. J. V., wounded in the thigh; returned to Philadelphia.
Col. John Ramsay, 8th N. J. V., wounded and reported dead.
Col. Francine, 7th N. J. V., badly wounded.
Lieut.-Col. Price, 7th N. J. V., not dangerously.
Capt. Thos. Kelly, Co. I, 5th N. J., wounded and missing.
Capt. Woolsey, Co. C., 5th N. J., wounded.
Capt. Rodgers, Co. K., 5th N. J., wounded in the leg by a piece of a shell; returned to Newark.
Capt. Berry, Co. E., 6th N. J., acting Adjutant, wounded in the leg by a musket ball.
James Bell, Co. B., 5th N. J., wounded.
Michael Fox, Co. B., 5th N. J., slightly in the cheek by a piece of a shell.
Lieut. Clark, Co. A., 5th N. J., killed.

The Captain reports that at the close of the battle on Thursday the soldiers were in the best of spirits, and felt confident of success.

Provide for the Wounded Soldiers.

Our city is filled with the friends of the gallant men who participated in the late battles in Pennsylvania. Many of them hope to meet their relatives and acquaintances near the seat of war, not knowing the almost insurmountable obstacles in their way, others intend to remain here to meet the wounded on their arrival in this city.

New-York is the great distributing depot of the sick and wounded soldiers. Soon as they arrive here they are taken to the various hospitals in the different States to which they belong—Portsmouth Grove, New-Haven, Brattleboro, Albany, Newark, and the Island Hospitals in our harbor. During the transit of these men to the points where they are to be tenderly nursed and cared for, they need nourishing drinks and delicacies, such as the Government does not furnish—fruit, wines, jellies, sauces, eggs, &c. Now is the time to provide these indispensible articles. Not a moment should be lost. Let all persons who appreciate the services of these brave men contribute something. The delicacies will be administered under the direction of the Medical Superintendent of this port, so that no fears need be entertained of a misapplication of the contributions. Among other depots for the reception of these gifts we may name the office of the Government Agent, No. 61 Barclay street, and the hospital steamer Thomas P. Way, at the foot of Castle Garden. Again we urge the friends of the soldier to remember him in this his time of need. The Government supplies an abundance of common rations suitable for men who are well, but no sufficient provision is made to supply delicacies to the sick and wounded who have no appetite for ham and hard-tack. Here is a fine opportunity to indulge in the luxury of doing good to our best friends.

See Seventh Page.

THE CAVALIER.

PATRIOTISM, VALOR, INTELLIGENCE, RELIGION---PILLARS OF LIBERTY.

VOL. I. YORKTOWN, VA., TUESDAY, JULY 7, 1863. FIRST SERIES, No. XXXI. SECOND SERIES, No. XXIII.

THE CAVALIER

Is issued every Tuesday morning, on the following terms:

SUBSCRIPTIONS.

One copy, one year, in advance,	$2.00
" " six months,	1.00
" " three months,	50
Single copy,	05
Six copies of one issue,	25

ADVERTISEMENTS.

Ten lines or less, first insertion,	$1.00
For each subsequent insertion,	30
Other advertisements as per agreement.	

PUBLISHERS:
S. C. HOUGH & T. C. FELL.

Original Poetry.

TO THE SIXTH NEW YORK CAVALRY.

Oh, dear! it's shameful, I declare,
To make the Sixth all go,
And leave so many sweethearts here
Without a single beau.
We like to see them brave, 'tis true,
And would not urge them stay;
But what are we poor girls to do
When they are far away?

We told them we could spare them here,
Before they had to go;
But, bless their hearts, we did not think
That we should miss them so.
We miss them all in many ways—
But truth will ever out—
The greatest thing we miss them for
Is seeing us about.

On Sunday, when we go abroad,
We look in vain for some
To meet us, smiling, at the door,
And ask to see us home.
And then we can't enjoy a walk
Since all the Sixth have gone,
For what's the good, to use plain talk,
If we must trudge alone?

But what's the use of talking thus?
We'll try to be content;
And if they cannot come to us,
A message may be sent;
And that's one comfort, any way,
For though we are apart,
There is no reason why we may
Not open heart to heart.

We trust this cruel war may come
Soon to a final test;
We want to see our happy homes
Secured in peaceful rest;
But if the blood of those we love,
In freedom's cause must flow,
With fervent trust in God above,
We bid them onward go.

And we will watch them as they go,
And cheer them on their way;
Our arms shall be their resting place
When wounded sore they lay.
Oh, if the sons of freedom's soil,
For freedom's cause must die,
The ladies ask no dearer boon
Than by their side to lie.

VIRGINIA.

Select Story.

THE VISIONARY.

BY WILLIAM MEAGHAN.

No Frenchman will ever forget the detestable name of Blucher, the Prussian Field Marshal, who, owing to an obstinate error of Napoleon, was the means of gaining for the English the bloody battle of Waterloo.

Blucher, discontented with everything and everybody, despised by the French, and even by the allies themselves, left France during the same year he had entered Paris.

Angered by having been reduced to inactivity, he retired to one of his numerous country seats, where he soon became a prey to a profound melancholy, the cause of which no one seemed to know. He was also subject to attacks of dropsy, and afflicted with inflammation of the lungs, the danger of which he considered more imminent than it really was.

He could not bear to remain in obscurity, and solitude he regarded as bodily torment, and so great was the inquietude which his state of health gave rise to, that the King of Prussia departed for Krieblowitz immediately after hearing that the old General had often expressed a desire to see his sovereign before his death.

At the dead of night the prince arrived at the castle, and was at once conducted to the apartments occupied by Blucher, who was then seventy-four years old. The royal visitor found himself in a large, dark room, the old fashioned furniture of which added greatly to the melancholy aspect of the place. Divers arms and trophies of the chase were hanging upon the walls. The old General, enveloped in a large bearskin, was seated in an oaken arm-chair, and the only light by which his wan features could be discerned, was that of the fire which burned on the hearth.

On perceiving the king he made an effort to rise to receive him, but the prince told him to remain seated, and, taking his hand in his own, he sat down by his side. Blucher made a sign to his attendants that he desired to be alone with the new comer, and every one retired. Then, raising himself up, with evident pain, from his half-reclining posture, he broke the silence by saying to the king:

"Sire, I besought you to undertake the journey you have made to Krieblowitz, knowing that you were near by, assisting at the annual review of the troops; but had you been at Berlin, or even at the farthest extremity of Europe, rather than not see you—dying and all as I am—I would have set out to find you, for I have a terrible secret to reveal. But before I tell it, look at me well. Scrutinize the expression of my countenance, the features of my face, listen to the tone of my voice; and pay attention to the order of my ideas. Assure yourself that I am in full possession of my reason, and that I have not become a fool. For, at times, I ask myself if I am not an idiot, who mistakes the dreams of a night for the events of years gone by. But, no," added he, as he drew from his breast a gold bracelet; "no—all is true, all is real, and I can doubt nothing. Listen to me, sire. When the seven years war broke out in 1756, my father, who dwelt in his mansion at Gross-Renzow, sent me and one of my brothers to a relation of ours, the Prince Craswisk, who lived in the Island of Rugen.

"I was then fourteen years old, and, after having passed some time in the old fortress without hearing any news from my family, as Gross-Renzow and its neighboring countries had become the seat of war, I joined a regiment of Hussars in the Swedish service. I was taken prisoner at the battle of Luckow, and the Prussian Government urged me to enter its army. During a whole year I resisted all persuasions to that effect, and at last I obtained my liberty by enlisting as a bugler in the black hussars. I, however, managed to procure a few months' furlough, for sixteen years had passed away since I last heard from my family, and my mind was constantly harassed with fearful thoughts as to what had become of my brothers and sisters. I at last started for Gross-Renzow, and on my way found all the country near Mecklenburg in a dreadfully ravaged state. As the carriage I was in moved but slowly and with great difficulty over the rocky road leading to my ancestor's domains, I abandoned it, and continued my route on horseback, accompanied by a servant man. This happened fifty-nine years ago to-day, on the twelfth of August, and just about the same hour as the hand of that clock you see there is now making—half past eleven. A tremendous storm had commenced, the thunder rolled and crashed with reports like the firing of a park of artillery, the lightning flashed, and the rain fell in torrents. After having wandered for a long time in the forest, I arrived at the door of the castle, and it was only then that I perceived that I was alone, and that my servant had not followed me; the tempest and darkness of the night had probably caused him to stray away.

"Without dismounting, I knocked with the handle of my whip at the iron-bound door, bristling with large rivets. No one answering my call, I knocked again three different times, with the same success. At last, becoming impatient, I dismounted. The door opened of its own accord. I saw no one who could have been the means of giving me admittance. Without paying any attention to this singular incident, I left my horse standing at the door, and, after having crossed the yard, I ascended the stairs and entered into the interior of the mansion. There was not a particle of light in the whole place, not a sound fell on my ears. I must confess my heart seemed to cease its beating, and a cold chill ran over my whole body. What folly, thought I to myself. The castle is uninhabited. My family left it when I did, and have not returned. No matter, as I am here, in this deserted place, I will try to pass the night as comfortable as possible.

"Thus speaking to myself, I passed through several apartments, and arrived at my father's bed-room. A nearly extinguished fire was slumbering amid the ashes on the hearth. With the assistance of its flickering light I recognized my father, my mother, and my four sisters, seated in a demi-circle before it. They all stood up on seeing me. I was on the point of throwing myself into my father's arms, when I was stopped by a solemn gesture he made to prevent me from coming near him. I held out my arms to my mother, but she receded from me with a melancholy look. I called each of my sisters by their name, and the only answer I received was that they took hold of each other's hands without pronouncing a word, and then all sat down.

"'Do you know me?' I exclaimed.—'Is that the way a family should receive a son and a brother after so many years of separation? Have you, then, already learnt that I have entered the Prussian service? But I could not do otherwise; my liberty, the happiness of seeing you, were its rewards. Just think, that in sixteen years I have heard nothing of you. Separated from you by interminable wars, in the Swedish service, prisoner of war, no news ever reached me to calm my anxiety and my doubts. You see yourselves that the first use I made of my liberty was to come and see you here—here where I thought I would not find you alive, but where, at least, I thought I might learn something to set me on the right road to find you. What, father, you do not answer me? Mother, you are silent?—Have you, sisters, forgotten the tenderness and the plays of our childhood? those plays of which this room has been often the spectator!'

"These last words seemed to move my sisters. They began to speak in lower tones to each other, made me a sign to approach, and one of them knelt down before my mother, hiding her head in her lap as if she were desirous of playing 'hot-hands.' Surprised at this singular action, in such a solemn moment, I did not touch the hand of my sister very lightly with my whip. Some mysterious power impelled me to do it. Now it came my turn to kneel down before my mother and hide my head in her lap. O horror! I felt under the silk garments cold and hard substances; I heard a dry noise, like the jumbling of bones together, and when a hand was placed in mine that hand remained there. It was a skeleton's. I arose, breaking forth into a cry of terror. All had vanished and nothing remained of that terrible vision but a few human bones. Wild with terror, and half crazy, I rushed out of the abominable habitation; found my horse, and throwing myself into the saddle, I departed at a break-neck gallop, unconscious of where I was going, letting the horse take his own route.

"About daylight my horse fell dead under me, and my followers, anxious and troubled about my disappearance, after a long search found me with a large wound in my head, lying insensible beside my horse, at the foot of a tree. I was for a long time on the point of death, and it was only after three weeks of a raging fever, of agony and delirium, that I was again in possession of my reason. I then heard from the people of the town that my whole family had perished, victims of the cruel war that had devastated Luxembourg, and that the castle of Gross-Renzow had been pillaged and ravaged several times.

"Scarcely convalescent, I went a second time to the castle to have the remains of my family placed in the family vault, when to my great surprise, and notwithstanding the scrupulous search I made, not a particle of those sacred remains could be found. A hand alone, a woman's hand, round which was this gold bracelet, lay on the floor of the room wherein the fatal vision had appeared to me. I took the bracelet; it was the one I now have in my hand, and the human bones were placed in the oratory of the castle. Since that time, many, many a year has rolled past. About two months ago, as I was sleeping in the very chair I am now seated in, I was awoke by a slight noise. On opening my eyes, I beheld my father, my mother, and my four sisters, before me, and, as they had done in the castle of Gross-Renzow, my sisters joined their hands together, as if to play 'hot-hands,' and beckoned me to approach.

"'No,' I exclaimed; 'no, never.'

"Then all the phantoms, taking each other by the hand, began to turn in a circle round my chair.

"'Justice,' said my father, while passing before me.

"'Penance,' murmured my mother, as she bent her head toward me.

"'Prayer,' said my youngest sister.

"'Sword,' sighed the other.

"Afterward I heard the other one say:

"'THE TWELFTH OF AUGUST.'

"And the last one repeated:

"'THE TWELFTH OF AUGUST, AT MIDNIGHT.'

"Again they commenced to walk around my chair, repeating the same words. After acting thus for some time they joined their sepulchral voices in saying, 'Till we meet again; till we meet again.' I understood, then, that my destiny was about to be accomplished, and that I had nothing more to do than to recommend my soul to God and my family to your majesty."

"My dear Marshal," said the king, "what you have related is certainly very strange! Do you not think that your fever and delirium have had something to do with those two visions? Come, come, take courage, combat and overcome these hallucinations and hope for the best; you will be soon well, and you will live to enjoy life for years to come. Is it not so? Do you not believe me? Come, give me your hand."

As Blucher did not answer, the King of Prussia took hold of the old man's hand. That hand was cold as ice, and the old clock was just striking midnight.

Field-Marshal Gerhard Lebretch Blucher was dead.

A COPPERHEAD REBUKED.—A gentleman informs us that he was present at an interview between Gen. Jenkins and some prominent Union men at Chambersburg, Pa., during the time the rebels occupied that town. After discussing matters connected with the war for some time, a prominent office-holder in Franklin county stepped up and introduced himself to the rebel general. The latter said that he ought to refuse shaking him by the hand. The office-holder desired to know the reason of such treatment. Gen. Jenkins asked the question, "Are you the District Attorney from this county?" "Yes," was the reply. "Then you are a regular Copperhead." "That is what they call me," replied the office-holder. "Well," said the general, "Lincoln ought to have hung you and the rest of the Copperheads long ago. We would not tolerate any such men in the Southern Confederacy. We respect those who are against us in the North much more than we do the Copperheads."—*Harrisburg Telegraph.*

"I'LL bet a sheep," said old Meredith to his other half, "that our boy Otho is going crazy, for he is grinning at the plough, and he is grinning at the barn, and he is grinning at the table, and he is grinning to himself wherever he goes." "Poh!" replied the old woman, "don't you know he got a love-letter this morning?"

THE best way to humble a proud man is not to take any notice of him.

The Cavalier.

EDITOR:
J. HIRAM CHAMPION, A. M.,
Chaplain 179th Pennsylvania Infantry.

TUESDAY, JULY 7, 1863.

WE would call the special attention of our readers to the advertisements, in another portion of our paper, of Mr. B. F. Voorhees, whose extensive assortment of goods, of almost every variety, is just such as will meet the wants of the soldiers and citizens of Yorktown.

OUR HOPES OF SUCCESS.

There is nothing better calculated to strengthen the hearts of our soldiers in the field, and to nerve their arms for action, than to see the war, as at present, being actively pushed forward, under Generals whose deeds prove their ability to lead our forces on to victory.

The energy displayed by Major General Meade in getting the army of the Potomac under way so soon after his appointment to that command—with no waste of precious time in "reorganization"—and the promptness with which he brought his eager and confiding troops to face the invading foe, foiling, at every point, in the well-fought battles of Wednesday and Thursday, the extravagant hopes of Lee and his traitorous underlings to gain a firm footing in Pennsylvania, point him out as the man the Government has long been seeking to lead that gallant army of patriot soldiers. We have the fullest confidence that with Gen. Meade in command, and with the hearty co-operation of the militia, which is showing such alacrity in coming forward in defence of our homes, victory after victory will follow those already gained, until Lee's army (or those of it who do not find their graves on the soil they so much covet) shall be driven, straggling, demoralized and powerless, back to their doomed "Confederacy." From every other department of our army we have cheering news; and as, day by day, the fall of Vicksburg becomes more certain, and the feebleness of Bragg's forces to cope with Rosecrans more apparant, who can doubt that the day is near at hand when the Union and peace shall be restored, and the Stars and Stripes shall again be held sacred in every part of our loved country?

THE ENGLISH BLOCKADE-RUNNERS.

In a recent debate in the British House of Lords upon the siezure of English ships by our cruisers, the Marquis of Clanricarde made a futile effort to induce his Government to reinforce its North American Squadron sufficiently to prevent our further interference with English blockade runners, in which he cut the following rather awkward figure:

"In the House of Lords on the 15th, the Marquis of Clanricarde moved for copies of any reports that may have been received from the Admiral commanding Her Majesty's squadron on the North American and West Indian station concerning the protection from seizure or visitation afforded by the Ariadne and other of Her Majesty's ships or gunboats, by convoy or otherwise; and asked what had been the result of the remonstrances made to the United States Government by Her Majesty's Minister at Washington against the siezure of British vessels engaged in legitimate commerce. The noble Marquis recapitulated the complaints which had been made a few weeks ago in reference to the proceedings of the American cruisers, contending that they were in contravention of international law, and that it was the duty of Her Majesty's Government to reinforce the North American squadron so as to afford adequate protection to our merchantmen. He also urged that the constant seizures which were being made by the Federal fleet were not for the purpose of maintaining the blockade, but of destroying, if possible, a large and legitimate trade w hichhad sprung up with Nassau and Matamoras. He altogether denied the efficiency of the blockade of the Southern ports, and said it ought not to be recognized by Her Majesty's Government. He read a letter from a Lancashire manufacturer, giving details in reference to four steam merchant vessels which had successively run the blockade of Charleston seventeen times in the course of one month, conveying £120,000 worth of British goods into Charleston, and taking out £200,000 worth of cotton. The noble Lord, in conclusion, complained that the Ariadne and other of Her Majesty's ships had been employed, in contravention to international law, in convoying certain vessels engaged in commerce, while they had altogether omitted to afford protection to others.

"Earl Russell said the statements of the noble Marquis were inconsistent, inasmuch as he declared that the vessels he desired to protect were engaged in an innocent trade, while in the same breath he admitted that numerous British vessels were carrying on a profitable trade in running the blockade. The attention of the Government had been drawn to one or two recent cases of seizure, and he had written to Lord Lyons upon the subject, directing him to inform the American Government that it was evident that some of the ships which had been seized were trading with neutral ports, and that a strong impression prevailed in this country that they had been seized in a reckless manner. The answer of the American Government was that there were sufficient grounds to justify the siezure, and that those grounds would be proved before the proper tribunal, namely, an American Prize Court. He had no objection to produce a copy of the correspondence which had taken place upon the subject. The noble Earl added, that in the opinion of the Home Government, the blockade maintained by the American fleet was sufficiently efficient to entitle it to be observed, and he thought every allowance ought to be made for any hasty act on the part of the blockading force. He believed there was every desire on the part of the American Government to prevent injustice being done.

"The Duke of Somerset said it would be inconvenient to produce the reports which had been received by the Admiralty, from the Admiral commanding the squadron on the North American and West Indian station.

"The motion was then withdrawn."

THE CAVALRY BATTLES.

A despatch published in the Northern papers, dated Columbia, Pa., July 1st, says:

The 5th New York, the 1st Vermont, the 1st Virginia and the 18th Pennsylvania cavalry regiments left Frederick on Saturday and moved forward to Hanover.

They arrived there on Tuesday morning, when they were charged upon in the rear by the rebel cavalry of Stuart.

The national forces numbered about 1,800 and the rebel force was nearly or quite 6,000.

The battle commenced at 9 o'clock in the morning, and continued until 7 o'clock in the evening.

The contest was a succession of charges, recharges, advances and repulses.

Our troops fought with desperate gallantry and daring, and gained a brilliant triumph.

We captured all the 1st South Carolina regiment except thirteen. The rebels in return took but sixty prisoners.

A piece of artillery belonging to the 1st South Carolina is among our trophies.

The rebels lost, besides, one field piece and one breach-loading steel rifled piece.

Our cavalry had no artillery.

Mr. W. Young telegraphed to the New York *Herald* from the Cavalry of the Susquehanna, June 30th, as follows:

Gen. Killpatrick, having recently been promoted from a colonelcy, has more recently been placed in command of Staehl's division of cavalry, comprising Ingall's under Brigadier General Farnsworth, and Brigadier General Custer's, both of whom have served on General Pleasanton's staff, and other brigades, besides artillery from the regulars. The cavalry has been steadily winning fame since it has been demonstrated that it is worthy a good name, and that division of it under General Killpatrick will keep its laurels always green.

On our advance into the Keystone State, at a late hour last evening, the boys were almost frantic with joy, and they made the welkin ring with cheers as soon as the State line was crossed.

The head of the column reached Littletown, Pennsylvania, at 11 o'clock, being the first of the Union troops that had marched from Virginia to protect the Keystone of the arch from being broken by rebel hands. The hotels, stores and private dwellings were brilliant with flashing lights, and cheers were given for the "deliverers of Pennsylvania," more than three times three.

The ladies of the village baked bread for the soldiers during the whole night, not once closing their eyes in sleep, and the excitement of seeing for the first time even the advance column of an army kept them awake in the morning.

Gen. Kilpatrick and his staff, as they rode through Hanover on the way to Abbottstown, were most enthusiastically welcomed by the ladies particularly and the citizens generally. The ladies showered bouquets upon the division commander and his staff officers, and gray haired men manifested unbounded enthusiasm. The boys of the cavalry and artillery were bountifully supplied with bread, pies and milk, and the weary ambulance patients were revived by homemade wines and sanitary supplies.

When near Abbottstown, where Gen. Washington encamped his army in 1781, a caisson of battery M, Second United States artillery, exploded, tearing off a leg of the driver, named Mariah, killing two horses and alarming the people, who had before heard no sound of war. Little children, fearing the rebels were coming, wept piteously, and older people apprehended that the town would be "bombshelled."

Hardly had three rebels captured at Berlin, belonging to the 8th Louisiana infantry, who straggled from Gen. Ewell's command, been disposed of, when intelligence came, at 10 A. M., that Stuart's cavalry were at work on our rear. Where they were this morning is not precisely known; but the following note, written by Fitzhugh Lee, undoubtedly to Gen. Stuart, explains why they began to operate so early on the advancing column of Union cavalry:

ON MARCH, 9 A. M.

GENERAL:—A citizen direct from Littletown informs me that Gen. Killpatrick, with four regiments—of which the 1st Virginia, 5th Vermont, and 5th New York are three, and six pieces of artillery—left that place this morning for Hanover. The road that I am on strikes the Littletown and Hanover road at McSherryville road, one and a half mile from Hanover. Very respectfully, your obedient servant,

FITZHUGH LEE,
Brigadier General Commanding.

The attack was made near the intersection of those roads, and in the vicinity of Plum creek, on the road entering Hanover, upon the right flank of our rear, the rebels capturing a few prisoners and two or three ambulances. A charge was made on the three brigades of rebel cavalry—Fitzhugh Lee's, Hampton's and Robinson's—led by the 1st Virginia. The ambulances were recaptured, and the 5th New York captured the battle flag of the 42d North Carolina. Lieut Col. Payne, of the 4th Virginia cavalry, and a rebel lieutenant were also captured, together with some thirty-five prisoners. Capt. Jas. Dickerson, (formerly of Baltimore,) of the 10th Virginia cavalry, and several other rebels were killed.

A rebel battery; stationed in the outskirts of the town, opened on our cavalry, and skirmishing was kept up in the town, the rebel battery playing into the streets, without, however, doing much damage.

Hastily moving the remainder of his command and his batteries from Abbottstown to Hanover, Gen. Kilpatrick directed Ewell's regular battery to open upon the rebels from the north side of the town, they then holding the road to Littletown and Westminster, and forming in line of battle in the skirts of densely wooded forests on the south and southeast. The enemy failed to reply to our artillery, and seemed unwilling to give battle to our cavalry.

Gen. Kilpatrick then ordered two regiments of cavalry to open communication with Littletown, and drove the rebel cavalry back to our infantry approaching from the latter place, piercing their centre and compelling them to move one brigade to the right on the Gettysburg road, and the remaining two brigades to the left on the York road.

There was some skirmishing between both commands with slight loss to either.

BATTLE OF GETTYSBURG.

From the New York *Herald* of the 3d inst. we copy the following details of last Wednesday's battle at Gettysburg:

"General Buford's cavalry had previously driven the rebels to the west of the town, beyond the seminary, and between nine and ten o'clock A. M. the rebels gave his pickets a pretty sharp brush and drove them in. General Reynolds, with the First corps, was on the road from Emmettsburg to Gettysburg, *en route* to the latter place, which the road approaches through the very scene of the conflict.

"General Reynolds at once threw forward the First division, under General Wadsworth, which began to drive the enemy from the start. Very soon after the Second division of the same corps went on the right of the First division, the Third division on the left of the First, and the whole line began to advance. Nearly west of the town, just in the outskirts, near the seminary, of which I have spoken, is a large brick edifice. Southward from this is a piece of woods, and the seminary stands on a ridge which slopes to the west into a little open vally of ploughed fields and meadows, rich with grass and grain. Beyond the valley is a ridge of higher land, thickly wooded. The valley runs in a southwesterly direction, and at its lower extremity is a large farmhouse, near which the Eighth Illinois cavalry was drawn up in the field, and formed our extreme left. Several farmhouses dotted this same rich little valley. Across this valley General Reynolds' line advanced somewhat hastily, almost before it was well formed, and in that condition did not go far until against it a heavy force of the rebel infantry was immediately thrown, and General Reynolds was in turn driven. But his troops retired step by step, and in excellent order. Forward with the utmost enthusiasm pressed the rebel line, eager now to turn Reynolds' retirement into a rout. Some of the rebels had too much energy and got too far; for, while they pressed too closely on the right of the centre division, the left of the same division was suddenly swept around, and then enclosed in the handsomest manner an entire rebel brigade under Gen. Archer.

"Gen. Archer and his whole staff were taken. About sixteen hundred of the enemy's men thus fell into our hands, and went to the rear.

"Though the First corps still continued to retire, the rebel advance was broken soon after this, and General Reynolds now prepared to go forward in earnest. Apparently forgetful that he had at first only gone to the support of cavalry, he was very like to bring on a general engagement with only one corps. Formed as before, his line went forward and drove the enemy across the valley and over the ridge at the further side; but it was at great expense to us, as the fire with which they received our fellows was terribly severe. From the hill the line of skirmishers was thrown out some distance, and General Reynolds went out to the line to reconnoitre, when he was hit by a musket ball in the back of the neck and killed instantly.

In rather less than an hour after the fight began the Eleventh corps came up the same road by which the First had approached, and General Howard at once assumed command of the whole field, while General Schurz assumed command of the Eleventh corps. Gen. Doubleday had already assumed command of the First corps. Across the north side of the town runs a creek, on which shortly after noon it was reported the rebels were massing troops, apparently to take the First corps on its rear. To guard against an advance from that direction, General Howard sent forward the First and Third divisions of the Eleventh corps, which moved across the rear of the First corps and through the town, and took up position with the First division on the right. General Steinweihr's division—the Second—was held as a reserve.

"At about half-past two o'clock, while the batteries exchanged a heavy fire and some sharp musketry woke up the echoes on the right, the rebels advanced in heavy force on the First corps, which slowly retreated from the hills beyond the valley to high ground near the seminary, where it prepared to make all the resistance it was capable of. It was reinforced there by some dismounted dragoons, and fought in the open field; for, though some rail fences were thrown down across the front of our line, they afforded no cover. From the woods beyond the farmhouses, and across the open space, a rebel force of perhaps three large brigades advanced handsomely in line of battle, while the rebel batteries near the general centre shelled our position hotly to cover the advance.

On came the line, right up within short range of our position, when it was opened upon with a fire so sharp and well served as to stagger and then completely repulse it. Backward went the line that came forward in such good order, a mere mass of stragglers, each of whom made the best of his way across the plain.

There is a mysterious fatality connected with the third line: and so, after a lull and period of comparative quiet of twenty minutes, onward for a third time came the rebels, quite as orderly as before, their line of skirmishers firing as they came on. In so great force was this line that it completely overwrapped the line of the First corps on both flanks. Two brigades on the right were quite out of ammunition, and the order was given to retreat on the town; and our boys accordingly retreated in good order, while the rebels rushed forward with yells to our position. On came the enemy's fourth line, further to the right of the third, in good order, skirmishers ahead, until the position of the Seminary was reached, when they came forward with a rush, and occupied a hill we had deemed it worth while not to hold after the other was taken. On also came another line in support behind this, and our cavalry on the extreme left began to retire.

The new position of the Third corps was at a line of stone wall southwest of the town, along the slope of a hill on which is a cemetery. When the First corps retired to the town the left of the Eleventh was uncovered, and a heavy advance completely on its right flank at the same time compelled it to retire.

After our retirement on the town the rebel advance was not pressed further. The rebel force fought by us was the corps of Ewell and that of A. P. Hill.

[COMMUNICATED.]

YORKTOWN, VA., June 28, '63.

Dear Editor:—I know that you are a man of strong sense, and are willing to overlook the error which I am committing in writing an article for your paper on the Sabbath day. But, kind sir, when a young man, far away from home, friends and the object that some day he expects to grace his home, is located in a town so lonely to a stranger, so desolated to an old citizen, so unhomelike to us all, is wandering around through the ancient and modern buildings that are so prominently located, I ask is there any harm in his giving vent to his thoughts even though it be Sunday. Can we help but let our hearts echo the words of the song, "When this cruel war is over?" Then will our hearts lift up in grateful praise to God, and those of us who are yet alive, will return to our homes where our friends, with open arms, will stand to welcome us back to the lovely spot, where they have anxiously watched our progress by the messenger bird, the *press*.

Mr. Editor, as I walk through these streets, my mind revolts, and impresses deeply on my heart the many sad changes that are daily occurring in the history of our country and in the lives of each individual that makes our country what it is. I pass from the wharves where all is bustle and activity, and where pressing forward to scenes of action are our fellow men. I come along up the banks, and there, looking out between the bars, are those who have borne arms against us, and who now pitifully watch those whose liberty they envy. A little further along, and I pass the sutler stores where the soldiers and contrabands partake of those luxuries which are essential for the body, and which almost instantaneously reach their hands upon the presentation to the sutler of a "green back." Well may the sutler exclaim:

My country, 'tis of thee I think,
And the soldier, who, upon the brink,
Wildly to the sutler's takes the right track,
To satisfy the inner-man and spend his
"greenback."

After surveying the inner portions of the sutler's establishment, and watching the heavenly smiles that the soldier casts upon the sutler, I passed along up and into the hospital. 'Twas here that my heart failed me. Sick and wounded boys, men after our own hearts, men who live and breathe, who have friends near and dear to them at home, who lay upon their beds in all stages of diseases, who cast their eyes in pitiful glances from one to the other, who patiently and cheerfully receive the kind attentions of the nurses; who welcome the oft-repeated visits of the kind and noble doctor, and the *Sun of Cheerfulness* that graces the hospital, and whose presence to the sick is like quinine to the nerves. Need I mention who that Sun is? All the soldiers know her, and the memory of her acts will not leave their minds until death shall relieve them of the sorrows of this world.

R———D.

Select Poetry.

THE COPPERHEAD.

There is peace in the swamp where the Copperhead sleeps,
Where the waters are stagnant, the white vapor creeps,
Where the sweet of Magnolia hangs thick in the air,
And the Lillies' phylacteries broaden in prayer;
There is peace in the swamp—though the quiet is death—
Though the mist is miasma—the Upas tree's breath—
Though no echo awakes the soft cooing of doves—
There is peace—yes, the peace that the Copperhead loves.

Go seek him—he coils in the ooze and the drip,
Like a thong idly flung from the slave-driver's whip;
Beware the false footstep—the stumble that brings
A deadlier lash than the overseer swings—
Never arrow so true—never bullet so dread
As the straight steady stroke of that hammer-shaped head.
Whether slave or proud planter who braves that dull crest,
Woe to him who shall trouble the Copperhead's rest!

Then why waste your labors, brave hearts and strong men,
In tracking a trail to the Copperhead's den!
Lay your axe to the Cypress—hew open the shade
To the free sky and sunshine Jehovah has made;
Let the breeze of the North sweep the vapors away,
Till the stagnant lake ripples—the freed waters play—
And then to your heel may you righteously doom
The Copperhead born of its shadow and gloom!

THE SUNNY SIDE.

When darkest hours of sadness
Come stealing o'er the heart;
When false ones dare deceive thee,
And from thy side depart;
Bear up beneath the anguish,
And breast the sinking tide,
For o'er the vale of shadows,
Oh, there's a sunny side.

Let early ties be broken,
Whichever thou held'st dear;
It matters but a little,
The trial how severe;
For there are many others
In whom thou canst confide,
Where'er thy sad heart pineth—
Yes, there's a sunny side.

Our lifetime here is fleeting,
It passeth soon away,
Like fancy's dreamy visions,
And autumn's wan decay.
Then take thou hold in earnest,
Before though thou hast tried;
Life is made up of struggles,
There's yet a sunny side.

This wide world may look dreary,
The tempest louder roar,
While every golden moment
Thy life-boat wafts to shore.
Delay not in thy efforts
Against the wind and tide,
To do what thou wouldst have to do
Upon the sunny side.

THE REBEL RAM ATLANTA.

Annexed will be found an extract from a letter written by an officer on board the iron-clad Weehawken, to some friends in this city, detailing the late capture of the Rebel ram Atlanta. It will be found interesting, as it gives details not heretofore published:

MONITOR BATTERY WEEHAWKEN, }
WARSAW SOUND, GA., June 18. }

* * * * Well, the Weehawken has her name up again, and I suppose will figure largely in the northern papers. We have captured the Rebel ram Atlanta, after about one hour's fighting, killed two of her men and wounded several others. About eighteen months ago she ran the blockade at Savannah, with a valuable cargo of merchandise. Encouraged by this success, the Rebels loaded her with cotton and made a like attempt again, intending to take her to Nassau; but Uncle Sam's cruisers were a little too watchful.

She returned to Savannah, was purchased by the ladies of that city, who contributed a sufficient sum towards converting her into a ram. The iron plates were rolled in Richmond and sent South, and last November saw the pride of the Confederacy launched and ready for immediate service. About two weeks ago word was sent up to the Admiral, at Port Royal, that the Atlanta was about to come out at Warsaw Sound and destroy the blockading vessels. Dupont no sooner heard of it than he ordered the Weehawken to proceed here immediately, and the Nahant, at North Edisto, to follow us. Well, we both arrived here in season, every morning about daylight expecting to see our looked-for friend, and every morning were disappointed. Yesterday, at four o'clock, A. M., I went on watch, and while walking along the deck towards the engine-room, the officer of the deck asked me to take the spy-glass and make out some black object coming directly towards us.

It was not difficult for both of us to arrive at the same conclusion, that our visitor was no other than the Confedrate Atlanta. I went down into the engine room to see everything was ready in case we should be obliged to get under way, and returning on deck found the Captain, First Lieutenant and Pilot watching the movements of the Rebel. She was evidently bearing directly upon us, and no time was to be lost. The First Lieutenant beat to quarters; I went into the engine-room, secured the battle plates, the bell struck, I started the engines ahead, and away we went towards the sea. Soon we turned and faced the enemy, who fired the first gun, but the shot did not come within a mile of us. Onward goes the Weehawken, and "pop" goes her gun. Bang! comes a broadside from the Atlanta, and boombang! go our two "pill drivers" at her again.

After about an hour of this kind of work, all became silent, when suddenly crash, comes something into the Weehawken. I thought sure the ram had come at us, and kept my eyes on the bilge. During this time no guns were fired, and a man who came down into the engine room told me the Atlanta had a white flag up. I did not believe it until summoned by the chief engineer on deck, and there was our prize with a big hole in her side armor, and one of her port shutters knocked off. She was as beautiful an iron-clad as ever I saw. Her officers were all on deck, looking at us, and wondering, I suppose, how this little thing could fight so. We took one hundred and fifty-two prisoners and two hundred small arms. The engineer told us that her captain, in a speech to the crew, said that he was going to tow these two Monitors up to Savannah that night, and then go to Port Royal and destroy the fleet there.

Poor fellow! how miserable he looked when he came on board here. Captain Rogers invited him to breakfast in his cabin, and we had all the other officers in the ward room. They expressed their surprise that we should treat them so well. The Captain of the Atlanta said that she cost the Confederate Government one million dollars, and was the finest iron-clad in the Rebel navy. During the fight the beach, about three miles, was crowded with people from Savannah, who came down in steamers to see the Atlanta *tow us up*. They went back when they saw the white flag. The new flag of the "confederacy" was used in the fight, instead of the "stars and bars."

PRISONERS taken by the rebels at Port Hudson were deliberately murdered and piled upon the earthworks in sight of the negro skirmishers. Others were literally crucified—nailed alive to trees and slowly tormented to death. They could be distinctly seen by the black skirmishers. At night the rebels came down from their earthworks and stripped the slaughtered negroes of their clothing and valuables, and offered indignities to the inanimate bodies During the flag of truce on the following day the negroes were not allowed to take advantage of it, and the next day their bodies were seen stripped and stark, lying close under the guns of the enemy.

Advertisements.

JOS. EAGER. H. CLAY ELLIOT.

EAGER & CO.

Have just received, Ex. schooner Lucy Baker, a select assortment of

DESIRABLE GOODS

from New York markets, and offer them,

WHOLESALE AND RETAIL,

at low figures. The cargo consists, in part, of the following articles, viz:

Dried Apples,
Dried Beef,
Beef Tongues,
Choice Hams,
Syrup in barrels,
Syrup in bottles,
Butter in Cans,
Butter in firkins,
Butter in tubs,
Cheese,
Pickles in half bbls.,
Pickles in glass jars,
Oranges and Lemons,
Almonds,
Walnuts,
Peanuts,
Raisins,
Figs,
Assorted Candies,
Jellies,
Fine French Claret,
Scotch Ale in bottles,
Navy Tobacco,
Tin Foil Tobacco,
Smoking Tobacco,
Kinnekinick Smoking Tobacco,
Various brands of Cigars,
Coffee, Sugar, Spices,
Flour, Corn Meal,
Condensed Milk,
Mackerel,
Brooms, Wooden Buckets,
Hats, Caps, Neckties,
Dry Goods,
French Calf and
Cavalry Boots,
Stoga Boots,
Men's Shoes,
Balmorals, Oxford and Stoga,
Women's Shoes,
Men's Summer Clothing,
Blue Flannel Clothing,
Fine Wool Shirts,
Large assortment Yankee Notions,
Tinware, Matches,
Hosiery, Stationery,
Canned Fruits,
Crackers, Oysters, Soda,
Boston Tea and
Sugar Cakes,
Ginger Cakes,
Cutlery,
&c., &c.

je16-4t

MILITARY CLOTHING!

The undersigned would respectfully call the attention of

THE OFFICERS AND SOLDIERS OF YORKTOWN AND VICINITY,

TO THEIR

FINE ASSORTMENT OF

MILITARY AND FURNISHING GOODS.

which in quality and prices will compare favorably with the best markets in the country.

J. C. JONES & Co.,
Yorktown, Va.

ICE!

ICE!!

ICE!!!

The subscriber has received a cargo of

EXCELLENT ICE,

which he is selling at the building near his Restaurant, formerly occupied by Roberts as a restaurant. All calls promptly attended to.

je16-4t VOLENTINE BAKER.

O. L. LAWSON HAS PROCURED the services of H. N. LANGLEY, Watchmaker, who has had twelve years' experience in Northern cities. All work done with despatch and in the best style. He will always be found at his post, ready to accommodate citizens and soldiers, at the corner of McClellan avenue and Ellsworth streets, Yorktown, Va. je30-tf

LAWSON'S COLUMN.

O. L. LAWSON

Invites the attention of soldiers and others to a new and extensive assortment of

ARMY AND NAVY GOODS,

just received, and for sale

AT FAIR PRICES,

AT HIS

NEW MAMMOTH STORE,

ON THE

S. E. CORNER OF McCLELLAN AND ELLSWORTH STREETS,

where he will always be found ready to wait on those who may favor him with their patronage.

He would call especial attention to his assortment of

OFFICERS' FURNISHING GOODS.

SUCH AS

HATS, COATS, VESTS,

PANTS AND SHIRTS,

of all descriptions. A fine assortment of

SHOULDER STRAPS.

He has, also,

TWENTY CASES OF BOOTS,

McClellan, Grained, Calf and Stogies.

STATIONERY.

In this article especially he defies competition in this part of the world. Official, and all other sizes and patterns of ENVELOPES, and PAPER of every size and style.

BUTTER.

3 tons Orange County, Goshen, and other brands.

CHEESE.

2 tons New York Dairy, Large Cheese.

CANNED MEATS.

Turkey, Chicken, Mutton. Also, Sawyer's Soup in Cans.

CANNED FRUITS.

Strawberries, Blackberries, Pine Apple, Tomatoes, and other kinds too numerous to mention here.

TEAS.

Green and Black.

COFFEE.

Java and Maraicabo.

SUGARS.

Crushed, Coffee and Muscovado.

SPICES.

Nutmegs, Alspice, Pepper, Ginger and Mustard.

CAKES.

Ginger Cakes, Tea Cakes, Boston Biscuit, Soda and Butter Crackers.

APPLES,

Of the choicest varieties, in barrels or smaller quantity.

BLOOD BEETS.

POTATOES.

Irish and Sweet.

TIN WARE, CUTLERY, BRUSHES, LOOKING GLASSES, AND—

If his *column* was longer he'd tell you of more,
But as that is completed, just enter the store;
Though to please you, you may have thought matter of doubt,
You'll then see in a trice he can rig you all out.

SOMETHING NEW.

The subscriber would respectfully inform the citizens of Yorktown and vicinity that he has opened a

PUBLIC HOUSE,

in his new and commodious building, on the corner of

KEYES SQUARE and McCLELLAN AVENUE,

for the accommodation of the Officers and Soldiers of the Fourth Army Corps and their friends and the public generally, and he respectfully solicits their patronage.

Connected with his establishment is a

DINING SALOON,

where meals are served at all hours of the day, and an

ARMY STORE,

where Confectionery, Fruit, Nuts, Tobacco, Segars and a general assortment of such articles will be sold

AT REASONABLE RATES.

Also, an extensive

BAKERY,

from which Pies, Cakes and all other Pastry will be supplied continually.

N. B.—All orders for

FAMILIES AND OFFICERS' MESS ROOMS

will be served at the shortest notice.

VOLENTINE BAKER,
my5-1m Proprietor.

B. F. VOORHEES.

WHOLESALE AND RETAIL

DEALER IN

ARMY AND NAVY STORES,

YORKTOWN, VA.

CLARK FAIRBANK, Agent.

A large assortment of

FRESH AND DESIRABLE GOODS,

Constantly on hand,

AT REASONABLE PRICES.

mh10-tf

JOHN H. GOTSHALL, SUTLER OF the 172d Pennsylvania Regiment, at the sign of "Army and Navy Supplies," on the South side of McClellan street, first door west of the Quartermaster's Storehouse, keeps an extensive assortment of Groceries and Provisions, among which you will find Teas, Coffee, Sugar and Spices, Canned Fruits and Meats, Cheese, Fresh Roll Butter and Fresh Eggs, Fresh Pennsylvania sausages and Bologna, Tea Cakes, Ginger Snaps, Boston Biscuit, Soda and Butter Crackers, Figs, Raisins, Nuts and Candies of all kinds, Luzerne County Buckwheat Flour, Wheat Flour and Corn Meal, Apples, Potatoes, Onions, &c.

Also, Smoking and Chewing Tobacco and Segars, of all varieties.

Stationery of excellent quality and every style.

Boots and Shoes, Shirts, Collars and Neck-ties.

Kerosene Lamps, Chimneys, Wick and Oil.

An assortment of Tin Ware, Knives and Forks, Spoons, and all goods found in first class army stores, which he will sell at reasonable prices, for cash. Call and examine his stock, and you will be satisfied he can't be beat. His motto is, "a quick sixpence is better than a slow shilling." fe10-1m

---

NEWS DEPOT, ON McCLELLAN Street, first door East of F. B. Patterson's Barber Shop, and opposite the Nelson Hospital.

SAMUEL A. BENT keeps the very latest New York, Philadelphia, Baltimore and Washington Daily and Weekly Papers, together with all the leading Pictorials and Magazines.

He will also procure to order, on short notice, any book that you may desire. fe3-1m

---

BARBER SHOP, ON McCLELLAN Street, two doors East of Ellsworth street. Shaving, Hair-dressing, Shampooing, &c., executed in the latest style, and with all possible despatch, by
fe3 1m F. B. PATTERSON.

JOHN WILLIAMS, DEALER IN ARMY AND NAVY GOODS; N. E. cor. McClellan and Ellsworth sts., has a large and choice assortment of everything in this line, which he will sell as cheap as the same can be purchased anywhere in this country.

McNEAL, THE SUTLER OF THE 178th, keeps a good assortment of everything usually found at such establishments, in the Mammoth Tent, northeast corner of the Parade Ground. my 26-1m

---

LAWSON has just received the finest lot of Ladies' and Children's Shoes that has been brought to Yorktown in some years. mh10-tf

[COMMUNICATED.]

The "Peace Men" and the Rebels.

Mr. Editor:—While a portion of Lee's vast army is ravaging the State of Pennsylvania, plundering its towns, destroying its railroads and threatening its capital, there are a few miserable, heartless demagogues, under the specious name of democrats, who, with the cry of "Peace," are laboring to cool the patriotic ardor of those who should hurl back the polluters of their soil and the desecraters of their firesides. And did we not know that the loyal heart of the old Keystone would respond with a will to the call for troops to defend her soil against the invader, we should blush with shame for the want of patriotism in her citizens.

But the spirit of '76 is not dead—the people see their danger, and will rush to the post of duty, knowing it to be the post of safety and honor.

We should like to ask the leaders of the "Peace Convention" of Pike and Monroe counties, which assembled on the 27th inst. at Dingman's Ferry, if *that* is the way they would repel invasion? Is that the way to end the war, by turning over our fair fields and pleasant villages to indiscriminate plunder? "Get you hence," vile traitors, for your "dear Southern brethren" would feel themselves disgraced by owning you as second cousins.

We trust that Gen. Lee will find that he made a fatal mistake in crossing the Potomac a second time. If the sturdy yeomanry of New York, Pennsylvania and Maryland only greet him with a hearty welcome of shells, grape and Minnie balls, and hurl him back on the advancing and avenging columns of Meade, the rebellion will give up the ghost. Then those driveling traitors of the North will find that their *craft* is gone; that they can no longer gather the spoils of office by crying "great is the mud-sill of Southern society." Then there will be no longer a hostile foe to endanger the nation, or molest our persons and property.

We will not listen to the cry of "peace" while rebels are knocking at the door of our capital: but we will imbibe the living loyal sentiment of "Liberty and Union, now and forever, one and inseparable," which will animate and unite every heart to deeds of patriotic devotion that shall tell on the future prosperity of our glorious country, again united, peaceful and happy.

Ah! Freedom's birthright who would sell?
Peace democrats perhaps can tell:
Though rebels taunt their love of ease,
And spurn their "*olive branch of peace.*"
* * * *
Then, freedom's sons arouse, awake!
Your stand against Rebellion take;
Swell the authem loud and long,
Let Freedom, Union, be your song.
Disunion is their battle cry;
To arms! to arms! let freemen fly;
Our Constitution let us save,
Or slumber in a patriot's grave.

A VOLUNTEER.

Yorktown, Va., June 29, 1863.

Peninsular Affairs.

FROM WHITE HOUSE.

WHITE HOUSE LANDING, VA.,
July 4th, 1863.

DEAR CAVALIER:—On Wednesday morning, the 1st inst., at 5 o'clock, the Advance Brigade started from this place in the direction of Bottom's Bridge. At Baltimore Store, about six miles from here, we found a small picket force of rebels, that fled precipitately on our approach. We moved cautiously forward, and about three miles farther on found indications of the enemy being in force. Here our forces halted and carefully reconnoitered to the front and on both flanks.

About 5 o'clock the 5th Pennsylvania Cavalry succeeded in drawing out the enemy's skirmishers in front, and captured several prisoners. Lieut. Robinson and a private dashed in among the rebels, and captured and brought off a corporal. The rebels were very bold, dashing out of the woods and taking deliberate aim at our men and then running back. They shot Sergeant Bennett, of Co. C, through the head, killing him instantly. There were no other casualties on our side. Captain Mink opened upon the rebels from his battery, and they quickly drew back into the dense forest. During the night everything was quiet, and continued so until 6 o'clock on Thursday, when the 5th Pennsylvania Cavalry and 139th Regiment N. Y. Vols. advanced, and the enemy opened upon them from a masked battery and infantry in the woods. In the fight that ensued, the 139th lost two or three killed, two or three wounded and seven or eight prisoners. As the enemy opened from five pieces of artillery, and it is said brought out eight, it was deemed prudent to fall back. The enemy followed very cautiously. We passed our reserves at Baltimore Store, who advanced a short distance, but night soon coming on they returned. During the night the enemy attempted to turn our left flank, but the movement was promptly met by Gen. Keyes, and our forces killed and wounded quite a number and took twenty-five prisoners, without sustaining any damage. The enemy retired in great disorder.

Since Thursday no engagements have taken place, but reconnoitering is going forward in every direction. In regard to the force of the enemy on the Peninsula, we personally have not the means of knowing, but presume our Generals have ascertained pretty nearly.

On Thursday night Lieut. Col. Yost, of the 179th P. M., while making his round as field officer of the day, was slightly wounded by a careless picket. The ball struck his pistol, shattering it all to pieces, and was turned from its course so that it only grazed his side. He was somewhat bruised by splinters from the pistol.

To-day a full national salute was fired here at 12 o'clock. All the vessels displayed their colors, and the various bands played the national airs. At the front, at the camp of the 178th P. M., Chaplain Hunt delivered a very able and appropriate oration. Major General Keyes and other distinguished officers were present.

We have passed three times to and from the extreme front, and have seen no bushwackers, notwithstanding a Brigade Quartermaster was picked up on Wednesday, almost in sight of our rear guard.

About two miles from here we passed St. Peter's Church, the ancient place of worship of the Lees and other "F. F. V.'s" of this region. It is a venerable brick structure, of the English style. On the top of the tower is a pair of huge keyes, the emblem of its patron saint, to whom so many believe was given the custody of Heaven's gate. We were glad to see but few marks of desecration about it. There are traditions of Washington's having been married in a dozen different churches in Virginia, and we were never satisfied about the matter till now. *This is the place.* In a cabin on the White House plantation is a negro 102 years old. He has a son living with him who is 80 years old. No one who sees them doubts that they have seen all these years. The old man remembers all about the wedding, and describes the procession that went to the church and the dinner at the White House afterward. It is worth a trip to this place to see these patriarchs. We had a long conversation with the old man to-day. He is bed-ridden, but his intellect is clear, and he appreciates what is going on around him. Not a particle of sympathy is expressed by the blacks for their master, who was last Sunday borne to Fortress Monroe, a prisoner. The Lee family kept 100 slaves here, 100 at West Point and 100 at Arlington Heights. This plantation extended from the house two miles down the river, between two and three miles up the river, and over ten miles back towards the Chickahominy. It produced from twelve to fifteen thousand bushels of wheat and about the same number of barrels of corn annually. The negroes say it is "a right smart good farm." Last year we saw splendid wheat crops upon it. It is now almost entirely uncultivated, but covered with a most luxuriant growth of clover.

The troops here are in good health and spirits, and present a glowing contrast to the condition of the army last year. All seem anxious to get at the rebels, but our Generals, with characteristic wisdom, are careful how they suffer any to fall unnecessarily. There is a great deal of interesting news that it would not be prudent to publish. We can only add, that everything, so far as developed, goes well.

THE FOURTH OF JULY.—Quite extensive preparations had been made by some of the regiments stationed here to celebrate in a becoming manner the 87th anniversary of our National Independence; but the fortunes of war interfered in most cases to dispel the visions of beer and fireworks in which the soldiers had been indulging, and the time-honored Fourth found them on the front, and beyond the reach of these enjoyments. Those remaining, however, did the thing in a patriotic manner, and various were the festivities of the day.

At 12 o'clock the bell on the church was rung, and a salute of thirty-five guns was fired opposite Gen. King's Head-quarters by Battery F, 1st Pennsylvania Artillery, Capt. Wilson, which was echoed at Gloucester Point by the 8th Independent N. Y. Battery, and in the evening there was a fine display of rockets sent up from both sides of the river.

No other public demonstrations were made in Yorktown, but small social gatherings seemed to be the order of the day, where army rations gave place to roast pig and Scotch ale, and where many a sentiment spoken testified to the patriotism of the men.

The day passed off quietly, and no disturbances occurred, which speaks well for the good discipline of the soldiers here.

At Williamsburg the day was celebrated in something more of the old-time style. A large flag was thrown to the breeze over the Insane Asylum, the Declaration of Independence read, an able oration delivered, and the voices of the citizens mingled with those of the soldiers in loud huzzas for the "Star Spangled Banner," "President Lincoln," "Our Army and Navy," &c.

Major Chamberlain, the Provost Marshal of Yorktown, had the honor of hoisting the colors. Many of the prominent mem here were present at this ovation, which is said to have passed off in fine style. The good news from all quarters received here on that day added not a little to the jubilant spirits of the soldiers.

BUSHWACKERS.—Some ten days since, whilst a portion of the crew of the Crusader were ashore near the mouth of East river, in search of contraband goods supposed to have been stored there by a party of blockade-runners, they were fired upon by bushwackers, and two of the men were wounded. Captain Andrews, in retaliation for this cowardly act, took a sufficient force of his men ashore and ordered them to burn the dwellings of the offenders, which was promptly done, to the number of ten or twelve buildings. A few such examples of retributive justice would be beneficial between Williamsburg and White House, where the woods are infested with citizens who carry on this sort of warfare. A week ago last Saturday, Private Samuel Kemble, of Company H, 5th Pennsylvania Cavalry, left Fort Magruder for White House with the mail. He stopped at Barnsville over night, leaving that place early on Sunday morning, and has not been heard from since. It is greatly feared by his companions that he has fallen into the hands of these merciless brigands, though it is possible that he may have been captured by some straggling party of rebel soldiers.

DEATHS IN NELSON HOSPITAL.—During the past week the following deaths have occurred in Nelson General Hospital: Corporal Henry J. Lent, Company K, 143d N. Y.; Wm. Metcalfe, Company B, 9th Vermont Vols.; Geo. Wescott, Company A. 118th N. Y.; John Millen, Company L, 2d New York Cavalry; T. Conrad, Company H, 167th P. M.

During the past week 50 men have been admitted, and 38 men sent to Hampton Hospital.

THE SECOND MASSACHUSETTS CAVALRY.—In the recent skirmish at North Ann Station, mentioned in our last issue, the 2d Massachusetts Cavalry bore a prominent part with the 11th Pennsylvania, and displayed throughout the greatest coolness and valor. The "California Hundred," which composes part of this command, is particularly well spoken of. The 2d Massachusetts lost one killed and two wounded.

CLOTHING AND FURNISHING GOODS.—The establishment recently opened by Mr. J. C. Jones, on Keyes' Square, supplies a want that has long been felt in this community. Persons desiring clothing or officers' furnishing goods will do well to call and examine his stock.

Personal.

Our readers will be happy to learn that Lieut. Col. C. C. Suydam, Assistant Adjutant General of the 4th Corps, whose ill health compelled him, some weeks since, to retire to his home, has returned to the army, so far recovered as to be able to resume his duties.

Capt. Oswald Jackson, of Gen. Keyes' Staff, has been promoted to the rank of Major and First Aid-de-Camp. Major Jackson, in the temporary absence of Col. Suydam, has been serving as Acting Assistant Adjutant General. It is needless to say that the arduous duties of the position were faithfully performed.

LATE NEWS BY THE MAILS.

ROSECRANS' ARMY.—From the Army of the Cumberland Valley we have dates to June 30th, as follows:

Head-quarters remain at Manchester up to the present time. Gen. H. Thomas' corps has moved to the front, and is in position about four miles from Tullahoma. The dreadful condition of the roads, which embarrass troops and trains, has greatly retarded our forward movement.

General Stanley, Chief of Cavalry, and General Mitchell and his division of horse, have just arrived here from their brigade expedition to Shelbyville, the capture of which place I telegraphed here on Sunday. Our force advanced by the Shelbyville pike, driving the enemy from Guy's Gap, and riding down fifty of them. Col. Mentz's brigade then followed them up and drove them into their fortifications at Shelbyville. Mitchell's whole division then charged through and pushed rapidly into town.

The rebels took position in the public square with artillery, and a charge was then made by the 7th and 9th Pennsylvania Cavalry into the teeth of their guns, which were captured. At the same time the 4th regulars and the 3d Indiana galloped into their flank, near the upper bridge of Duck river. The enemy was completely routed and driven into the river, where a hundred of them were drowned. The rebel General Wheeler escaped on foot. Sixty or seventy officers and seven hundred prisoners were taken. Our loss was six killed and thirty or forty wounded. Lieut. Rhodes, of the Seventh Pennsylvania, was killed.

Col. Wilder's cavalry expedition to the rear of Bragg's army at Tullahoma has also just returned, bringing reports of equally successful work. With his brigade of mounted infantry he started on Sunday, the 28th inst., went to Hillsboro, thence to Decherd, swam Elk river and crossed with his howitzers on a raft, making fifty miles the same day. He tore up the track, burned the cars and the depot full of stores, and destroyed the trestle work. At daylight on Monday he started up to the Southern University, where he divided his force.

One portion was sent to strike the railroad at Tantalon, while Wilder went to strike it at Anderson. There he found Buckner's whole division and a train of cars going up from Knoxville to Tullahoma, and fell back, in the meanwhile tearing up the railroad from Cowan to Jersey City. The rebels, meanwhile, having sent a powerful force to intercept him, he struck through the mountain and returned to Manchester, which he reached to-day. He took and paroled a number of prisoners and captured a lot of mules. The damage done to the railroad is very serious, but would have been more so if the rivers had not been so high.

The expedition made one hundred and twenty-six miles in two days and a half.

THE REBEL PRIVATEERS.—The Baltimore correspondent of the New York *Herald*, writing July 1st, says:

From Capt. McCullum, of the New York ship Gildersleeve, a brief statement of the capture of which I sent to you yesterday, I have derived a graphic account of the affair, as follows:

At 11 A. M., May 25th, in latitude 12 10 longitude 34 55, the rebel steamer Alabama hove in sight. Capt. McC. supposed her to be an American gunboat, as she showed American colors. He dipped his colors in salute, and the Alabama dipped hers, returning the salute with prompt courtesy. Capt. McCullum was then about to proceed on his voyage, when the Alabama fired a gun across his bows and made the signal, "I want to speak to you." The ship was then hove to, and a boat put off from the Alabama, then two hundred yards distant. As the boat approached, Capt. McC. asked, "What steamer is that?" The boat returned no answer; but as her crew ascended the ship's side the United States flag was hauled down and the rebel flag was run up on the Alabama. The boarding officer advanced to Capt. McC. and said, "You are a prize to the Confederate steamer Alabama. Prepare to go on board with me." Captain McC. complied. On reaching the Alabama he endeavored to secure the safety of his vessel by showing that his cargo was coal, on English account. But Captain Semmes said, "Sir, your vessel is worth over sixty thousand dollars. Your coal is not worth twenty thousand dollars. I will burn your vessel." The captain was not allowed to return again to the ship. A boat was sent, which brought away the crew. Capt. Semmes took possession of all the chronometers, nautical instruments, &c., on board, Capt. McCullum thus losing all he had in the vessel. The ship was then fired, and it burned to the water's edge.

Telegraphic News.

THE FIGHT IN PENNSYLVANIA.

Official Despatches from General Meade.

WASHINGTON, July 3.—An official despatch was received here this afternoon from Major General Meade, dated:—

HEAD-QUARTERS OF THE ARMY OF THE POTOMAC, July 2, 11 o'clock, P. M.—The enemy attacked me about four o'clock this afternoon, and after one of the severest conflicts of the war, was repulsed at all points.

We have suffered considerably in killed and wounded.

Among the killed are Brigadier Generals Paul and Zook, and among the wounded, Generals Sickles, Barton, Graham and Warren, slightly.

We have taken a large number of prisoners.

(SECOND DESPATCH.)

WASHINGTON, July 3.—A later despatch has been received from Major General Meade, dated at eight o'clock this morning, which says:—

"The action commenced again at early daylight upon various parts of the field. The enemy thus far have made no impression upon my position.

All accounts agree in placing the entire Rebel army in position in our front. The prisoners we have taken report that Longstreet's and A. P. Hill's forces were much injured yesterday, and many General officers were killed. The dead body of Gen. Barksdale, of Mississippi, is within our lines.

"We have thus far about sixteen hundred prisoners, and a small number are yet to be started."

[This number of prisoners, sixteen hundred, is as stated in General Meade's official despatch. He may possibly mean that they were captured in the fight of Thursday night and Friday morning, or the previous statements of correspondets may have been exaggerated.]

LATEST FROM PENNSYLVANIA.

Despatch to Gen. King.

[A despatch received at Yorktown yesterday, by General King, is embodied in the following Special Order:]

HEAD-QUARTERS 1ST DIVISION 4TH CORPS,
FORT YORKTOWN VA., July 6, 1863.

SPECIAL ORDERS NO. 26.

The Commanding General takes pleasure in communicating to the troops at Yorktown and Gloucester Point the following gratifying intelligence, received by telegraph from Fortress Monroe:

"General French destroyed the pontoon bridge at Williamsport. Enemy's loss 25,000 to 30,000. We have taken from 12,000 to 15,000 prisoners. The Secretary of War telegraphed last night that Gen. Lee's army was in full retreat towards the Pennsylvania Mountains. The victory seems complete and decisive."

In honor of this signal victory a national salute will be fired at 6 o'clock this P. M., and thirteen (13) rockets set off at 9 o'clock in the evening.

By command of Brig. Gen. KING, Commanding Post.

WM. A. LA MOTTE, A. D. C. and A. A. A. G.

MARRIED.

On the 14th of June, 1863, by Rev. John B. Lowrey, Mr. DANIEL HICKMAN, of Chester county, Pa., to Miss ELIZABETH OWEN, of Gloucester county, Va.

New Advertisements.

THE HERALD.

Tuesday Morning, July 7, 1863.

THE ANNIVERSARY OF THE ISSUING OF THE DECLARATION OF INDEPENDENCE has once more come to us, and, as last year, it finds us in the midst of war—civil war, which is the worst of all wars, for a perpetual struggle with all the rest of the world would be better than this, though it may prove temporary in its effects. To-day one more star—for Western Virginia—goes upon our flag, making thirty-five; but we mournfully think that some of them shine dimly for us, and give an uncertain light. What will be the end of the contest no one knows; we can hope for the best; but the issue is with God, and all must be as He disposeth, and not according to our wills. Leaving that to the future, it is well for us all to inquire on this day, what our present duties may be. These are not doubtful. The principles of the Declaration of our fathers are founded on truth and justice. They favor the equal rights and the equal liberty of all men. Liberty, justice, protection, the pursuit of happiness, to each, not from any accident that attaches to him, but because these are his inalienable rights, given by God, his Maker, and which can not be separated from humanity. There is no question of the duty of every man to sustain the principles of the Declaration of American Independence.

Further than this: at the time of that Declaration there were many who doubted its propriety; they were not prepared for all its consequences; but after a government was established it became an axiom with the American people—that government, emanating from the popular will, should be supported by all. Our fathers held to no slavish subserviency. They criticised the acts of their officers, high or low; and called them, as their servants, to an account; but the duty of standing by the government itself was a fixed fact. That also should be settled as much now as ever. Nor should we stop to make the distinction too nice between the government and the administrators of the laws. They are separate in fact; but until officers have proved false to an extent to endanger the country, the only true way to support the government is to support the administration. It does not matter that you did not make it; that you do not approve of all its acts. We can not expect perfection anywhere, and more than ever are we bound to overcome our prejudices, when traitor hands would pull down our flag, and rebel swords are pointed at the nation's breast.

But in this case there is not only the general duty that should lead us to sustain the government, but there are the particular virtues in the administration that demand it. It is not questioned that Mr. Lincoln is a sincere, true, honest and patriotic President. That he don't do everything we desire, is possibly because he cannot do it; that he does differently in some instances, is because he sees and thinks differently. But in his main purpose to uphold the Constitution and restore the unity of the States, and transmit the government to his successor legally chosen, unimpaired, no one can doubt. Let those who most oppose him calmly consider what would be the condition of things if he should die, or be deposed, and not one of them who ever prays for anything, will fail to pray that he may be continued and supported.

The men who are under him are deserving praise for the ability they have shown. Mr. Secretary Chase has had no predecessor from Hamilton, who could have done better in the Treasury department. The restoration of the treasury from the bankrupt condition in which he found it, was almost a new creation. Mr. Seward, though he has not come to what we anticipated, has still done well in keeping the nation from foreign war. The State department has been difficult of management in these stormy times. So the Navy department, that has been most complained of, has been managed with signal ability. The facts are in favor of Mr. Welles. He has had a navy to create; and that from the mere skeleton of one, we now number 530 vessels, 50 of them iron-clad, is sufficient. He has kept all the navy-yards busy; he has employed all the machine shops; and the only reason that the navy is not larger to-day, is that vessels can not be built faster. He has a hundred contracts to give out now, if he could find persons to take them; but the great trouble is iron work—machinery, that can not be had fast enough.

Now we do not say that our form of government is faultless; that the administration in any of its departments is without mistakes; but all should remember the difficulties of our position; that we are in the most terrible civil war of modern times; and all should determine to stand by every official who does his duty; and to aid in perpetuating the best government the world has ever seen.

VICKSBURG. The news from that point is somewhat contradictory, the federal claiming steady progress and looking for ultimate, though not immediate success; and the rebels claiming for it great strength, but speaking despondingly of the future. The mining operations were on both sides, our leads running under the rebel forts, and theirs under our batteries, and both threatening some time to give an awful exhibition of the power of gun powder. On the 25th June one mine was exploded, which gave an entrance to one of the forts, into which a half dozen Illinois regiments rushed in fierce conflict, and the flag of the Union was hung upon the ramparts. Then it was reported that the rebels had an inner line of works, and it might take two weeks longer to reduce the place.

The losses of the rebels had been great; and so of the federals. Men had been "gobbled up" here and there; and the rebels on the night of the 24th, had attempted to break through our line, but were driven back, much slaughter ensuing. There was continued skirmishing on the rear. But on the back of all this and before we expected such news, it is announced, by the Philadelphia Enquirer, at 10 o'clock, July 3, that Vicksburg has surrendered. We hope this is true not only for itself, but because it would give immediate relief to Gen. Banks at Port Hudson, who sorely needs it; but we fear that it is in anticipation of the fact. No better news could come to us for the 4th of July than the fall of Vicksburg.

AN EXCURSION TO THE NORTH. Mr. John W. Dodge will this year make his tenth excursion to the Labrador, in the schooner Nelly Baker, an excellent vessel, in which he has made preparations for passengers of both sexes. The trip will embrace all points of interest on the coast:—The extensive breeding grounds of the ducks and divers; the whale, cod, salmon and trout fisheries; the rude settlements of the half breed hunters; the camps of the Nescopees and Esquimaux; the mission station at Caribou Island, and the trading post of the Hudson Bay Company.

There can not be a more pleasant summer excursion. To the healthy it abounds in unusual attractions; and to invalids, whose energies have been exhausted, it is life-giving. The scenery, the pure air, the game on shore or from the deep, all are inviting.

When the Atlantic telegraph cable is laid we shall have an unbroken line of communication from Victoria, in British Columbia, which will be connected next year with San Francisco, thence 4000 miles to the Atlantic shore, and thence to Ireland and across to England, and under the straits of Dover to the continent, and on eastward to the frontier of China. In three years more it is hoped the line will extend across the Pacific, completing the circuit of the globe.

THIS IS GOOD. The Haverhill Publisher says—"The Constitution as it is, and the Union as it was, and let the accursed institution of slavery share whatever fate the fortunes of war and the moral revolution of the age may settle upon it, is the only true patriotic and safe doctrine."

NEW POTATOES, of very good size, have been received by us, from the garden of Mrs. C. A. Dickson, on Auburn street.

The Battle in Pennsylvania.

The fight opened at Gettysburg on Wednesday, at 10 o'clock, just north of the town, where Gens. Longstreet and Hill with their rebel hordes attacked Gen. Reynolds, inferior in numbers. Gen. Reynolds was mortally wounded early in the battle, when he was placing his men. To conceal the casualty he rode off the field some distance before he dismounted, when a surgeon was called, but he soon died. Gradually our troops fell back from one position to another, fighting desperately. How many of the rebels fell we know not, but the ground was strewn with corpses, while Gen. Archer with 70 officers and 6000 men was made prisoner. This was not accomplished at a light cost. General Howard with the 11th army corps was in the van. At first they faltered, but when he cried—"remember Chancellorsville," they went in like wild demons. They lost 3000 men. The first corps lost half as many more. The 6th Wisconsin Regiment lost every officer but one; the 74th Pennsylvania Regiment brought off but 16 men; the 159th New York lost 19 out of 26 officers, and three-fourths of the men. Brigadier Gen. Paul was killed, and General Barlow was wounded and taken prisoner. Among other statements we take the following, which shows that some Massachusetts Regiments were in the fight.

The 12th Mass. lost 2 officers and 3 privates killed. Col. Bates, the Adjutant of the Regiment, 4 officers and 38 privates wounded, and 49 privates missing.

13th Mass—Col. Leonard, Capt. Palmer and Lieut. Alley wounded. Lieuts. Wiston, Carey and Tower missing.

16th Maine—Capts. Atwood, Bennett, Weldon and Lowell, Lieuts. Learatt and Plumer wounded. Col. Tilden. Capt. Bilcher, Lieuts. Wardsworth, Bisbee, No. 2, Derring, Thompson, Childs and Lord, missing.

New York, July 3. The Philadelphia Enquirer adds the following to the list of casualties in New England regiments:

16th Maine—Capt. Whiteside killed. Among the prominent officers killed is Gen Paul; Gen Wadsworth severely wounded. Gen Robinson had three horses shot under him. Among the officers of less rank more or less wounded are Col. Fairchild, 2d Wis., Col. Root, 94th New York, Capt. Robert Williams, Co. D, 12th Mass, Lieut. Thomas, aid to Gen Baxter, Capt Charles Hovey, 12th Mass., a valuable and efficient aid to Gen Robinson, occupying upon the staff the position of Inspector General. Adjt Weaver, 9th New York. Col Bates, 12th Mass., is wounded badly, but retains command of his regiment.

During Wednesday night Gen Meade came up with 75,000 men; and 25,000 others were within supporting distance.

Of the fighting on Thursday our report is very meagre. We give the despatches below. The battle was not renewed till late in the afternoon:

Wrightsville, Pa., July 2, 12 o'clock, Midnight.—Our forces are known to have gained upon the enemy until 4 o'clock in the afternoon. The rebel force is concentrating on Smith Mountain toward Carlisle, six miles north of Gettysburg.

Gen. Sedgwick corps passed York in the direction of Dover at 4 o'clock this afternoon. It is in the rear of the enemy. The 2d army corps moved up from Hanover at 8 o'clock this morning.

New York July 3. The Herald prints the following as the latest despatch;

Gettysburg, Pa., July 2—6 A. M. Major Gen. Newton of the 3d division of the 6th corps, has been assigned to the command of the 1st corps, made vacant by the death of Major General Reynolds. This is an excellent appointment.

Gettysburg, Pa., July 3 A. M. The enemy still hold the town, and their sharpshooters annoy us somewhat from the houses.

A heavy column is moving toward our right flank, but it will be suitably met. Our batteries are firing upon them, but from a considerable distance.

New York, July 3. A special despatch to the Times from the battle field near Gettysburg, dated Thursday, 4 30 P. M. via Baltimore, Friday, A. M., says:

The day has been quiet up to the present moment. The enemy are now massing a heavy force on our left and have just begun the attack with artillery. The, probabilities are that a severe battle will be fought before dark.

The rebel sharpshooters have been annoying our batteries and men all day from the steeples of the churches in Gettysburg. We hold the Emmettsburg and Baltimore road.

SALISBURY. The Salisbury Villager gives the valuation of property in the town of Salisbury, in 1863, as follows:

On residents' estates	$1,155,073
On non residents' estates, including the Salisbury Mills	319,120
Total	$1,474,193

The town raises the following sums:

For State Tax	$4,368 00
County Tax	1,817 27
Schools	3,000 00
Poor	1,000 00
Miscellaneous expenses	2,000 00
Paying Town Debt	1,000 00
" Interest on Town Debt	1,200 00
Repairs on Powow River Bridge	3,000 00
Overlayings	670 97
Total	$15,356 24

Whole number of Polls, 828. Tax on each Poll, $2. The tax on $100 is 93 cents.

The following is a list of persons and corporations in the town paying a tax of $20 and upwards:

Name	Tax	Name	Tax
Wm Allen	$33 16	Roby Morrill	151 73
Jonathan Allen	55 01	Geo. Morrill	64 78
Edward Allen	44 31	Ezra Morrill	36 04
J. W. Buswell	33 48	True Morrill	26 88
Leonard Brown	45 01	Edmund Morrill	71 82
Francis Brown	46 31	A. Morrill's heirs	140 66
Charles Brown	22 83	B F. Morrill	32 08
Enoch Bartlett	20 97	Benj. Morrill, jr.,	53 20
Moody Barnard	36 84	Eunice Morrill	20 00
H. Bartlett	79 62	Israel Morrill	27 34
Moses Bartlett	74 08	Archelus Morrill	37 44
D. L. Bartlett	25 85	Archelus Morrill, jr.	26 41
Newell Boyd	28 51	Aaron Morrill	32 00
Charles Blake	28 51	Richard Morrill, jr.	30 13
Kingsbury & Brown	51 15	J. Morrill's heirs	60 92
Powow River Bank	74 90	Joseph Merrill	22 65
Thomas Currier	40 23	Mrs. T. P. Morrill	55 80
E. Collins' heirs	25 54	Daniel Merrill	56 17
Ephraim Collins	20 83	S. F. Merrill	20 56
Elias P. Collins	22 56	Abel Merrill	47 16
Enoch Collins' heirs	36 18	Wm. Moody	37 71
David F. Collins	28 79	T. P. Morrill	20 60
Abraham Colby	69 98	Richard Morrill	33 25
John M. Coffin	28 23	J. W. Morrill	20 60
Wm. B. Coffin	29 81	T. P. Osgood	39 57
Jonathan Cammett	20 66	Timothy Osgood	25 02
S. Clark's heirs	26 97	Stephen Osgood	42 92
Seth Clark	238 22	A. B. Osgood	48 27
Thomas J. Clark	187 54	R. Osgood's heirs	26 51
Joseph N. Clark	152 2[illegible]	[illegible] Osgood	36 85
Robert Dow	23 35	T. H. Phillips	20 97
N. Dole's heirs	21 61	S. F. Pike	36 78
Israel Dow	21 12	James Pike	24 92
Edward G. Dole	26 19	Henry Pike	38 27
David M. Deal	27 35	Charles Pike	22 04
H Duckworth's heirs	23 25	Caleb Pike	52 32
Commoners	37 20	Otis Pike	34 55
Jonathan Eaton	20 56	Caleb Pike	29 55
John F. Eaton	22 56	N. T. Pike	55 48
James Eaton	22 14	Alfred Pike	25 72
Joshua F. Eaton	49 68	W. M. Pettengill	49 11
Wyman Eaton	27 58	True Pike	23 30
Dudley Evans	40 22	Wm. Pike	23 72
R. Evans, trustee,	65 10	Geo. Pierce	26 88
Benj. Evans	39 20	Amos Pettengill	51 06
J. Fullerton's heirs	85 05	Abraham Pray	26 88
Moses Fitts	29 90	P. Rowell's heirs	42 13
Dolly Foster	37 20	Jacob Rowell	42 78
Benj. French, Jr.,	28 65	Edward Rowell	56 69
Jos. Flanders' heirs	39 99	T. S. Robinson	40 36
James Fowler	31 76	Samuel Smith	27 35
Capt. J. Fowler	36 87	M. J. Sawyer	26 88
Elbridge Felch	26 18	B. Stevens	25 11
Robert Fowler	58 74	Samuel Stevens	29 53
E. Fowler's heirs	31 78	David Sanborn	22 23
Benaiah Gerrish	26 99	Jethro Swett	28 14
Josiah Gerrish	28 77	Tappan Sargent	36 88
David Gerrish	25 70	J. F. Sawyer	21 35
J. B. Gale	29 44	Frank Tuxbury	25 01
Lewis Greenleaf	21 25	Geo. Turner	55 01
Benj. Godsoe	39 20	Lydia True	23 25
Ebenezer Hills	58 08	S. True, jr.,	368 75
Geo. Hills	32 69	S. True's heirs	32 69
A. S. Hilton	32 05	Samuel True, 3d,	25 81
Merrimace Hat Co.	93 00	Dudley True	26 69
Wm. Hook	37 39	Jabez True	58 96
W. N. Hunkins	38 60	Moses True, jr.	30 60
E. M. Jackman	34 25	Moses True	64 18
Geo. Keniston	24 32	Cyrus True	27 34
F. Keniston	32 23	Benj. Tucker	34 97
J. Keniston	29 90	Jemima Tilton	26 28
W. Knight	24 79	John True	39 94
H. Kingsbury	108 96	A.O.Webster's heirs	40 46
John Kimball	85 70	Dan.Webster's heirs	37 90
Nelson Kimball	22 46	E. F. Webster	41 06
Hiram Lowell	54 55	Daniel Webster	45 95
Lowell Locke	26 27	J. B. Wadleigh	22 46
J. S. Lamprey	36 88	S. Woodman	103 14
W. L. Long	28 04	Robert Wilson	25 72
Moses Morrill	35 95	M. G. Wilson	53 16
John Morrill, jr.	78 26	S. Webster	32 69
Salisbury Mills	2273 50	Joseph Young	29 90

GLORIOUS NEWS FROM THE ARMY OF THE POTOMAC.

As we announced on Saturday that we should issue no paper on Monday, but would furnish our readers with any intelligence of special interest, we print an Extra, which will be read with joy by all. The entrance of Lee's army into Maryland and Pennsylvania was the occasion of sad forebodings to many, they feeling that he would fight with desperation—that it would be the last cast of the die, and on it everything would depend. In this respect they will not find themselves disappointed, though they will be disappointed in the result.

The telegraphic information found in other columns, is cheering in the highest degree; and as the President says in his congratulatory address, should be remembered with profound gratitude to God. The rebel forces have been compelled to abandon the positions taken by them, and from which they expected to deal death to our noble soldiers, and at last accounts were in full retreat, Gen. Meade following them, fully confident that victory awaited him.

The rebel army is evidently demoralized, and having nearly exhausted its ammunition, must surrender or be annihilated. Gens. Longstreet and Hill are prisoners within our lines, with thousands of those who have fought under them, and we cannot but feel that the day of reckoning has come and that justice will now be meted out.

The Battles of Gettysburg.

NEW YORK, July 3. A despatch dated Headquarters Army of the Potomac, 2d, says the contest on Wednesday was desperate and unremitting terminating at sundown. Longstreet was in command, and his force was said to comprise Hill's corps. During the early part of the day our forces failed to make an impression on the rebels, when Gen. Sickles arrived with reinforcements and turned the tide of battle. The result may be stated thus: We advanced rapidly, met the enemy in force, attacked him with the 1st Corps found him too strong, fell back until joined by the 11th Corps, renewed the attacked and regained our ground. Gens Wadsworth, Barlow and Doubleday are reported wounded. Ged. Baxter is reported killed, and Gen. Steinwehr wounded. Our wounded are at Gettysburg, well taken care of. Our forces at Gettysburg were largely reinforced Wednesday night.

Gen. Meade is in front superintending operations.

New York, July 3. The Times' despatch dated on the battle field near Gettysburg, 3 A. M., 3d says:

"At the close of my last despatch, 4 P. M., last night, the enemy had opened a heavy attack by artillery on our left and centre.

The tactics were soon apparent—a massing of their main strength on our left flank, which covered the Frederick road, with a determination to crush it. So intent were they on this purpose every other part of the lines was left alone. The fighting was most desperate on both sides. Our gallant men fought as they never fought before.

Many of our gallant officers have fallen. General Sickles's right leg was shot off. amputation has been performed, and he is doing well. Late in the evening Gen. Meade called a council of the corps commanders, and i was resolved to continue the fight as long as there was any one left to fight.

GETTYSBURG, July 3. The third day's battle begun at 4 o'clock this morning. It is now 7 o'clock and a circuit of fire of musketry and artillery on the south side of the town is discribing the field of contest. The musketry fighting is wholly within the woods. The artillery occupies the hills. The attack was commenced by the rebels on the right. The fight there has been unceasing. Our men are in the best of spirits and the General officers feel confident of the result. The battle has been planned and fought by Gen. Meade. The sky threatens rains and the fog already obscures the outer edge of the field of battle.

7.45 A. M Gen. Barksdale, of Mississippi, is lying dead within our lines. The death of Longstreet is confirmed by prisoners taken this A. M. Longstreet's and Hill's corps are said to be fighting on our right.

10 A. M. Sixteen hundred prisoners have thus far been sent to the rear, and more are here. What the result may b- to-day cannot be predicted.

Philadelphia, July 3. A despatch to Forney's Press dated Hanover, 1 P. M., via Washington 3d, says at 10 this A. M. our forces opened on about 5000 rebels. who advanced on the field at daybreak for the purpose of pillaging our dead. The rebels hastily retreated—The fighting thus far has been the most terrific of the war. The loss on both sides was heavy.

A desperate battle rages.

NEW YORK, July 4. (Herald's despatches from the field of battle up to 2 P. M., 3d)—

The news is of the most favorable character. Meade had driven Lee 4 miles north of his position of Thursday, and when our reporter left was still driving him. The death of Longstreet and Barksdale is confirmed.

IMPORTANT FROM PENNSYLVANIA

THE MOST Terrific Battle of the War.

Tremendous Loss on Both Sides,

NEW YORK, July 4.—A special despatch to the Tribune, dated Hanover, July 3d, says:—The most terrific fight of the war has taken place. Our men never stood up so heroically. To-day was the most awful of all.

The loss on both sides has been tremendous.

We have Longstreet a prisonser sure.

I left the field of battle at 6 1 2 o'clock, and reached here by a relay of horses.

We had the best of the fight to-day, and the General says if Couch arrives to-night the victory is ours beyond a chance.

The Herald has the following, which is the latest;

BALTIMORE, July 3.—News from the front up to noon to-day is of the most favorable character, and great hopes are entertained at headquarters that the rebels have succumbed.

BALTIMORE, July 3, 10 P. M.—A special messenger from Gen. Meade to Gen. Schenck brings news from Gettysburg up to one o'clock this afternoon. Gen. Meade had then driven the rebels four miles North and West from the position of yesterday, and was still following. We have taken 1500 prisoners, who are on their way to this city. The victory is undoubtedly ours.

Official Despatch from Gen. Meade.

TERRIBLE BATTLE FRIDAY.

Rebels Repulsed in Every Attack.

Washington, July 4.—10 A. M. The following has just been received:

HEADQUARTERS ARMY POTOMAC,
Near Gettysburg, July 3—8.30 P. M.

Major General Halleck, Commander-in-Chief:

The enemy opened at 1 P. M. from about 150 guns, concentrated upon my left centre, continuing without intermission for about three hours, at the expiration of which time he assaulted my left centre twice, being upon both occasions handsomely repulsed, with severe loss to him, leaving in our hands nearly 3000 prisoners.

Among the prisoners is Brig. Gen. Armistead and many colonels and officers of lesser rank. The enemy left many dead upon the field and a large number of wounded in our hands.

The loss on our side has been considerable. Maj. Gen. Hancock and Brig. Gen. Gibbons were wounded. After repelling the assault, indications leading to the belief that the enemy might be withdrawing, an army reconnoisance was pushed forward from the left and the enemy found to be in force. At the present hour all is quiet.

My cavalry have been engaged all day on both flanks of the enemy, harrassing and vigorously attacking him with great success, notwithstanding they encounter superior numbers, both of cavalry and infantry. The army is in fine spirits.

(Signed) GEO. F. MEADE.,
Major-General Commanding.

Congratulatory Address of Pres. Lincoln to the People of the United States.

The President to the Country.

WASHINGTON, D. C., July 4, 1863,
10.30 A. M.

The President announces to the country that news from the Army of the Potomac up to 10 P. M. of the 3d, is such as to cover the army with the highest honor, to promise a great success to the cause of the Union, and to claim the condolence of all for the many gallant fallen; and for this, he especially desires that on this day He whose will, not ours, should ever be done, be everywhere remembered and reverenced with profoundest gratitude.

(Signed) ABRAHAM LINCOLN.

From Our Extra Edition of Sunday.

NEWBURYPORT

HERALD EXTRA

Telegraphic Despatches to the Herald.

Glorious News FROM PENNSYLVANIA!

THE REBELS In Full Retreat!

GEN. MEADE — IN — HOT PURSUIT

The Enemy Much Demoralized!

—AND—

SUFFERING FOR WANT OF AMMUNITION!

GEN. LONGSTREET, —AND— GEN. A. P. HILL

Both Wounded and Prisoners Within Our Lines!

Washington, July 4. The victories won by the Army of the Potomac at Gettysburg yesterday is a decisive one. Intelligence received here to-night from the army states that the rebel forces have abandoned the position taken by them yesterday to the rear of the battle field and are in full retreat.

Gen. Meade is in hot pursuit of the enemy. The enemy is much demoralized, and has lost heavily besides suffering for the want of ammunition.

Gens. Longstreet and Hill are both wounded and are now prisoners within our lines.

A special despatch from the army to-night states the above facts. The capture of the entire rebel army is the only thing remaining.

THE REBELS REPULSED!

WITH FEARFUL SLAUGHTER!!

7000 PRISONERS TAKEN!

Baltimore, July 4. Reports deemed reliable from the battle field down to 6 o'clock last evening, represent that the rebels were repeatedly repulsed with fearful slaughter. The battle lasted all day: seven thousand prisoners were taken. The Union men of this city are highly jubilant and excitedly joyous over the favorable news from our victorious army.

Headquarters Army of the Potomac,
Friday, July 3—6 A. M.

The enemy's guns opened on our left wing at daylight, apparently to feel our position. They found us at home and soon suspended operations. They also endeavored to push forward their front on our right, but were driven back with loss.

9.40 A. M.—An hour ago the enemy made a strong infantry attack on our right and endeavored to break our line. The 12th Corps, which formed our right, steadily drove them back for half an hour, when the enemy were reinforced, and a portion of the 6th Corps was sent to its support, but failing in this, the enemy opened a cannonade all along the line. The attack on the right is believed to have been a feint to cover a more formidable flank movement on the left. The cannonading is now heavy in that direction and appears to be extending. The 3d Corps suffered greatly yesterday. The number of wounded is heavy with a large number of officers. No estimate can be formed at this writing. Heavy musketry has opened now on our right again and cannonading on our left is slackening. The enemy are fighting with the greatest desperation. Nothing can surpass the vigor and precision of our artillery. Yesterday the rebels took two of our guns for want of horses and infantry support, but the division (Humphrey's, I think) rallied and recaptured them. We took one from them. Comparatively few prisoners have been taken on either side up to this hour.

10 A. M.—The cannonading has slackened. Rebel prisoners say that when their infantry charged our left wing batteries yesterday, the massacre was beyond parallel. Some of the guns were masked and did not open until the enemy were within canister range.

The Enemy Driven a Mile and a half.

DESPERATE FIGHTING.

1500 More Prisoners Taken.

REBEL LOSS ESTIMATED AT 40,000.

Philadelphia, July 4. The Inquirer has a special despatch from the Army of the Potomac, dated 2 o'clk this morning. It says Gen. Hancock was shot through the groin. Gen. Gibbons was badly wounded. We drove the enemy yesterday a mile and a half and captured 1500 more prisoners. The world never saw such fighting. The rebel loss is estimated at FORTY THOUSAND.

Everything looks encouraging.

No Fighting on the Fourth.

The Enemy Driven Back to GETTYSBURG!

ALL LINES OF RETREAT CUT OFF!

Surrender of the Florida Brigade!

8000 PRISONERS TAKEN!

Lee Ordered to Richmond.

PHILADELPHIA, July 5.—Col. Forney has received the following highly important dispatch last night from the Army of the Potomac:

Headquarters Army of the Potomac,
July 4, 5 o'clock, P. M.

There has been no fighting to-day up to this time. Last evening we drove the enemy back to Gettysburg. Our lines this morning extend 8 miles around Gettysburg, our batteries being on all the hills looking on the town from the South. We occupy the road to Pea Ridge commanding the Chambersburg turnpike, and have cut off all lines of retreat. Our forcess occupy the strongest possible positions. A flank movement on our left is impossible.

At about 8 o'clock last night the Florida brigade of Gen. Longstreet's division, a Brig. General in command, advanced to within our lines and gave themselves up with their arms.

A despatch from Jefferson Davis to Gen. Lee has been captured. This despatch orders Gen. Lee peremptorily to return to Richmond, and states that the movement into Pennsylvania was wholly against his wishes. We have captured 8000 prisoners.

18,000 Men in Motion on the Flank of the Rebels!

LEE'S RETREAT SERIOUSLY INTERFERED WITH!

Our Troops in Excellent Spirits

Harrisburg, July 4th. Best informed parties at headquarters are in excellent spirits over the news from Gen. Meade. The battle probaly is still in progress. A gentleman who left Bridge No. 84 on the Northern Central Railroad arrived at 3 o'clock this morning, heard heavy firing. It was also heard in Harrisburg for about half an hour.

All is quiet in our immediate front. The rebels are supposed to have left this immediate neighborhood entirely. Our wounded have all been brought from Carlisle to Harrisburg and are doing well.

18,000 men are in motion on the flank of the rebels. Telegraphic communication is kept up with Gen. Smith, wherever he is.

A large number of men are at work on the Cumberland Valley Railroad track running to Carlisle.

HARRISBURG, July 5th, 3 A. M.—Most favorable news has been received here from the army of Gen. Meade, but the details being of a general character cannot be obtained, as the Censor is silent and the Governor has nothing.

The trains on the Pennsylvania Railroad will commence to run regularly on Monday morning. Not a bar of the road has been touched by the rebels. No further danger is apprehended to the Northern Central Railroad, the damages to which are mostly completed.

A gentleman who left the battle field at Gettysburg last night has arrived here. He came by way of York. He says that the rebel pickets were posted five miles this side of Gettysburg, and that the country between here and Gettysburg may be safely travelled. Our troops are in excellent spirits. They say, universally, that this battle is the most desperate the army of the Potomac ever fought.

From the latest intelligence received here, it is believed fully that Gen. Lee's army has been completely defeated.

There was no fighting yesterday, (Saturday,) and the rebel army is endeavoring to retreat rapidly through South Mountain Pass and Boonsboro'. It is certain that Lee's retreat is already seriously interfered with, and his escape from our army will be a matter of great difficulty. A large force is concentrated here and ready for offensive operations at any moment. Nearly the full quota of Pennsylvania is already raised and organized either into regiments or companies at Reading.

Col. Dougherty, volunteer on Gen. Smith's staff arrived here to-day, having been paroled by the rebels.

Latest from Vicksburg.

Memphis, July 2d via Cairo 3d. Advices from Vicksburg to the 29th ult are received. Although no positive advantages resulted from the spinging of Gen. McPherson's minie, yet that officer is vigorously pressing the rebels. The rebels sprang a counter mine in Gen. Sherman's front, but the only damage done was to destroy the head of his approaches which one days work will clear up. Col Wood is raising the guns of the gunboat Cincinnati and three of them are now in position on the Bluff.

The rebels keep up a constant firing, but our casualties are not numerous. The weather is extremely warm, but the nights are cool and refreshing. Gen. Johnston is in the vicinity of Canton, preparing for a forward movement.

Vicksburg, June 29th, evening. Our forces were withdrawn to-day from the outer side of the contested fort to the front of Gen. Logan, in consequence of some advantage of position which enabled the enemy to throw shells into our position, thus endangering the lives of our men without present benefit. The withdrawal, however, is temporary. A sharp musketry fire is still maintained. The total casualties in this last struggle are not known, but it is believed they will not exceed 200.

From New Orleans.

CAPTURE OF BRASHEAR CITY BY THE REBELS, WITH ALL OUR TROOPS AND ARTILLERY — OUR LOSS 1000 MEN.

New York, July 3.—The Herald has a New Orleans letter of the 26th. Brashear City was captured by the rebels on the 26th, with all the troops, artillery, &c., there. Our loss is 1000 men, including a camp of 600 convalescents, and 18 or 20 pieces of artillery of heavy calibre.

Our outposts have fallen back to Buck Station, 20 miles from New Orleans. A party of workmen are preparing the railroad bridge over the Pass Manchac, captured by the rebuls.

The correspondent says:—As far as New Orleans is concerned, the city is secure. The guns of the fleet command the city, and General Emery has disposed of his command so that he can effectually defend every point.

From Port Hudson there is nothing new. The bombardment continues; another assault was expected on the 27th.

THE VERY LATEST.

Reported Capture of 20,000 Prisoners.

Recapture of all our Men taken Prisoners.

118 Pieces Rebel Artillery Captured.

Philadelphia, July 5. The Journal publishes the following in an extra:

Baltimore, July 5—1:30 A. M. The Journal's correspondent has just arrived from yesterday's battlefield. He states that the route of Lee was complete. Gen Meade has not only captured 20,000 rebels, but recaptured all our troops who were taken prisoners.

3 P. M. It is really true that Lee has been totally routed and is trying to escape.

Pleasanton has cut off his retreat in the Gap, leading to Chambersburg. We took 118 pieces of artillery and some 15,000 to 20,000 prisoners. We hold the town of Gettysburg.

LATER. A train with 1,500 wounded has just arrived. Gens. Sickles and Gibbons are on board.

Washington, July 5. The following has just been received:

Frederick, July 4—8 P. M. *To Gen. Halleck*: An expedition sent by me last night has returned, having entirely destroyed the enemy's pontoon bridge over the Potomac at Williamsport. We captured their guard, consisting of a lieutenant and 13 men.

W. H. FRENCH, Maj. Gen.

☞ The following persons have been appointed by the President for the

Fifth Congressional District of Massachusetts,

as the

BOARD OF ENROLLMENT.

DANIEL H. JOHNSON, JR., President; Residence, Salem.

HENRY W. MOULTON, Commissioner; Residence, Newburyport.

DANIEL PERLEY, Surgeon; Residence, Lynn.

The Board meet at Headquarters

54 Washington Street, Salem,

DAILY, at 9 o'clock, for the transaction of business.

DAN'L H. JOHNSON, JR., Captain,

Jy2 PROVOST MARSHAL.

Putnam Free School.

Youth over 13 years of age "wherever they may belong," who are desirous of entering this School, may present themselves for examination at the School-house, on WEDNESDAY, July 15th, at 9 o'clock A. M. This will be the only examination for any residing in this city for the year.

Jy2 H. C. PERKINS, Sec'y.

NOTICE.

An Adjourned Meeting of the Society of the Sons of Dummer Academy, will be held at Academy Hall, Byfield, on the 8th of July, inst. A general attendance is requested.

Jy3 A. CHUTE, Secretary.

MEN WANTED FOR THE INVALID CORPS.

Provost Marshal's Office,

FIFTH CONGRESSIONAL DISTRICT,

54 Washington Street.

SALEM, June 18th, 1863.

Only those faithful soldiers, who from wounds or the hardships of war, are no longer fit for active field duty will be received in this Corps of Honor. Enlistments will be for three years unless sooner discharged. Pay and allowances same as for officers and men of the United States Infantry; except that no premiums or bounty for enlistment will be allowed. This will not invalidate any pensions or bounties which may be due for previous services.

The following uniform has been adopted for officers and men of the Invalid Corps:

FOR OFFICERS—Frock Coat—of sky blue cloth, with dark-blue velvet collar and cuffs; in all other respects, according to the present pattern for officers of Infantry.

Shoulder Straps—According to present regulations, but worked on dark-blue velvet.

Pantaloons—Of sky-blue cloth, with double stripe of dark-blue cloth down the outer seam, each stripe one-half inch wide, with space between of three-eighths of an inch.

Forage Cap—Present regulation.

FOR ENLISTED MEN,—Jacket—Of sky-blue kersey, with dark-blue trimmings, cut like the cavalry jacket, to come well down on the abdomen

Trowsers—Present regulation sky-blue.

Forage Cap—Present regulation.

For the convenience of service, the men will be selected for three grades of duty. Those who are most efficient and able-bodied, and capable of performing guard duty, etc., etc, will be armed with muskets, and assigned to companies of the First Battalion. Those of the next degree of efficiency, including those who have lost a hand or an arm; and the least effective including those who have lost a foot or leg, to the companies of the Second or Third Battalions: they will be armed with swords.

The duties will be chiefly to act as provost guards and garrisons for cities; guards for hospitals and other public buildings; and as clerks, orderlies etc. If found necessary they may be assigned to forts, etc.

For enlistment or further information apply to the Board of Enrollment at this office.

Capt. DANIEL H. JOHNSON, JR.,

je18 PROVOST MARSHAL.

Christian Observer.

RICHMOND, JULY 9, 1863.

GOOD RESULTS FROM WAR.

While we deplore the bereavements, the privations and the great losses, experienced by thousands as the fruits of the present war, we should recognise the benignity of Providence in educing good from the evil. We speak not now of its *material* benefits—in rousing the enterprise and energy of the people and directing their attention to various mechanical arts and pursuits essential to our independence—but of its *moral* results. The severe discipline which it imposes has led many to acknowledge, as they never did before, their dependence on God, and to think, as they never before thought, of their relations to Him as their God and Saviour. Thousands, probably, who entered the service of their country without thought or concern on the most important question, have been led to consider the great end of the present life, the highest purpose for which men can live and act.—Isolated from business pursuits and from the cares of ordinary life, they have had leisure for reading portions of the Scriptures, and for thought and reflection on questions of undying interest, to which their attention has been earnestly called by their chaplains and other christian men in our armies.

The severe trials of war are in many cases a salutary discipline. They are a test of character. They *try* the patience, the fortitude, the self-denial and the energy of men. The discipline thus imposed will draw out their good or evil principles. Their virtues will be improved by it and more fully developed than they could be amid the blessings of a life of ease and prosperity. As Archbishop Whately remarks—"*every* kind of trial, if well endured, tends to fortify the good principle. There are, indeed, many things which are more likely to hurt than to improve the moral character; and to such trials we should be unjustifiable in exposing ourselves or others unnecessarily." But if one goes through them well, they will fortify as well as prove his good principles. War, then, though a great evil in itself, is not without comforts and hopes and salutary influences.

To the soldier and every other reader, we would say in the words of the author just cited—that if the trial of war or any other adversity "does not leave you the better, it will leave you the worse. Let no one flatter himself that anything external will *make* him wise or virtuous, without his taking pains to *learn* wisdom or virtue from it. If any one says of his affliction—'no doubt it is sent for my good'—he should be reminded to ask himself whether he is *seeking to get* any good out of it."—"Sweet are the *uses* of adversity;" but there is no sweetness in adversity except to those who take care to extract sweetness by making a good use of it.

It does not become us, in times like the present, to increase the trials or afflictions of life by entertaining dark forebodings of future ills. The Saviour has given us a precept on this point, which should not be forgotten, "Sufficient unto the day is the evil thereof." "Take no thought for the morrow;" that is no anxious corroding thought. (Such was the popular meaning of the word '*thought*' at the time when our translation of the Scriptures was made.) Those who are ever fearing and predicting calamities—poison the enjoyment of the blessings of to-day by their foreboding of evils which they imagine are coming to-morrow. They seem to make an ungrateful return for the goodness of God which has ever sustained them in the past, and to distrust the providence of God and His promises of support in the evil day, and to overlook His infinite condescension in exhorting them, as He does repeatedly, in His Word—"*Fear not*"—in view of threatened judgments.

CALL FOR CHAPLAINS.

The Rev. O. B. Caldwell, who has been making vigorous efforts to supply one Division of our army in Middle Tennessee with the Scriptures, repeats the call for more watchmen among the soldiers. Under date of June 15th, enclosing funds for the "Observer," he says:

"I write to make a plain and simple statement of facts as they exist here. In this whole division of cavalry there are but three chaplains; of course their labors are confined entirely to their own regiments. Then, there are hundreds of men here that have no one to look after their spiritual interests. None to stand as watchmen on the walls of Zion, while they are standing as watchmen on the outposts, of their country to defend her honor and safety.

Now are there none who will volunteer their services and come up to the help of the Lord, to the help of the Lord against the mighty?" Is there no Presbytery within the bounds of the United Synod that can send a missionary to this division of the army? If one should come, let him come prepared to undergo all the hardships of a soldier's life. Let him come clad in the whole armour of God, for he will *need it all*. This is a time and place that will try men's souls, as well as their *stomachs*."

RELIGIOUS SPIRIT OF ABOLITIONISTS

By the favor of the Rev. Dr. Boyd, of Winchester, we have received several numbers of the "Lutheran," published in Philadelphia, also eight numbers of the "New York Evangelist," containing many notices of the war which may be matter of interest to our readers.—The Evangelist in its politics is a thoroughgoing radical abolition paper, and gives its hearty support to the Lincoln tyranny. The first article we notice appears under the head of

"A Noble Sacrifice."

It is an *editorial* record of the death of the Rev. Francis E. Butler, chaplain of a New Jersey regiment, who fell in the battle of Suffolk on the 3d of May last.—The Evangelist says that he "shared the perils of the battle," and was mortally wounded by one of our sharpshooters, and died the next day. His remains were carried to New York and his funeral attended in the 5th Avenue Presbyterian Church, (Rev. Dr. N. L. Rice's,) on the 11th of May, by a large audience. Mr. Butler, it says, "was a man of fine talents and blameless life." "Seldom has the war claimed a nobler sacrifice." Thousands, probably, have been encouraged to sacrifice their lives to Moloch by the Editors of the Evangelist, who are, no doubt, very careful to keep their own *precious* heads out of harm's way.

"A Fallen 'World.'"

This is an editorial lecture to the N. Y. "World" for the enormity of publishing an account of a Prize Fight which came off in Maryland. In this article the Evangelist occupies the position of those who "strain at a gnat and swallow a camel."—Its tender conscience is terribly wounded by the barbarities of a prize fight while it advocates and sustains a war against christian brethren, carried on by the minions of its party in the robbery and murder of unarmed citizens, and even of women. A prize fight is but mere recreation compared with the fiendish barbarities perpetrated by these pusillanimous miscreants under the pretence of a war for union!

Do the Northern People feel the War?

It has been inferred from the sanguinary speeches of a large portion of the Northern ministry, who are fierce for the war, that they are perfectly reckless of the waste of life, worse than thrown away in the wicked and barbarous crusade to subjugate the South. However callous these war-preachers may be, there are, no doubt, many thousands at the North who feel and deplore the heart-rending evils of war. The Evangelist of May 14th says in one article that "sorrow and sadness fill the land because of the death of many of our brave and noble sons and fathers:" and in another, that "thousands of families were weeping over their dead; and others were binding up the wounds of those maimed and mangled in the bloody strife."

W. T. Hamilton Restored to the Ministry!!

In 1854, Rev. W. T. Hamilton, D. D., was deposed from the ministry and suspended from the communion of the Church by the Presbytery of South Alabama, for licentiousness in its grossest forms. He was subsequently restored to the communion of the Church by the same Presbytery. The "Evangelist" states that Mr. Hamilton recently applied to Erie Presbytery (in Pennsylvania) to remove the sentence of deposition from the sacred office. His request was granted—and the Presbytery restored him to the ministry! Did the members of Presbytery know, that the Apostolic order requires that a candidate for the ministry "MUST HAVE A GOOD REPORT among them which are without, lest he fall into reproach and the snare of the devil?" Can the act of Presbytery save him from that snare?

Tabor Church.

This is the name of a new Church recently organized in Philadelphia from persons who had been gathered into the Calvary Church in one of the outskirts of the city by the missionary labors of Rev. G. Van Deurs, who is the Pastor of the new church.

The "Evangelist" records the death of Rev. J. A. Avery, at Syracuse, N. Y., on the 28th of April, aged 68; and Rev. R. Van Brunt, of Waterford, N. Y.

Death of Rev. Dr. Green.

The Rev. Lewis W. Green, D. D., President of Centre College, Danville, Ky., died at that place, May 26th, after a severe illness of a few days. His age was about 56 years.

The Rev. Dr. Joel Parker was installed Pastor of the Park Church in Newark, N. J., on the 6th of May last. Sermon by Rev. H. Crosby, of New York.

Rev. Wm. McKaig was installed Pastor of the 3d Presbyterian Church, Cincinnati, on the 3d of May.

Dr. Anderson, one of the Secretaries of the American Board, arrived in Honolulu, Sandwich Islands, about the 1st of March with his wife and daughter.

Answer to Bishop Colenso.

Rev. Dr. Scott, formerly of New Orleans, and more recently of San Francisco, is now supplying a Church in Birmingham, England. He has recently published a new book, entitled, "Moses and the Pentateuch Vindicated, an Answer to Bishop Colenso."

A New Map.

The "Lutheran" states that Rev. Lyman Coleman and Rev. H. S. Osborn have prepared a new geographical and historical map of the Holy Land and Syria.

N. S. General Assembly.

In two numbers of the "Evangelist" we have a report of the proceedings of the last N. S. Assembly, of which a brief account will be given in our next.

The News from our Armies,

noticed in subsequent columns, will be read with interest by those who do not see the daily papers.

General Intelligence.

NEWS OF THE WEEK.

PROGRESS—EXCITEMENT—GREAT ALARM!

Last week, we had an abundance of news—good news—from all quarters. The ball was in motion. Our men were doing up their summer work. May they have a rich harvest.

The movements of Gen. Lee's army have created great alarm in Washington—in Philadelphia—among the Germans throughout Pennsylvania, and in New York.—Ten days ago, the farmers, in their terrible fright, were driving their cattle, horses and sheep to Harrisburg, at the same time, our troops took possession of York, without resistance, where they "have sugar with their coffee and coffee with their sugar."—Philadelphia was enrolling names by the thousand to defend the city—and New York was saying that Pennsylvania must take care of herself.

FROM THE WEST, the news is equally cheering—Vicksburg stands like the rock of Gibraltar, after a furious bombardment of twenty-eight days.—Our forces at Port Hudson have defeated Bank's army, and taken two regiments prisoners.—At Berwick Bay, La., the Confederates under Gen. Richard Taylor have carried the enemy's position at the point of the bayonet, and captured a thousand prisoners, ten heavy guns, and large stores. At La Fourche's Crossing they have achieved another victory.

We also have cheering news from the North.—The papers state that in portions of Ohio and Indiana, the Yankees are arming themselves to resist Lincoln's draft.

WHERE IS GENERAL LEE?

WHAT ARE HIS DESIGNS?

These questions have sorely puzzled the Northern Editors and soothsayers. They can't "guess" WHERE the General is—or WHERE he is going—or WHAT are his purposes.

A dispatch from Frederick, on the 24th, says: Generals Lee and Longstreet were both at Winchester on Friday last with 100,000 men. They intend to cross the Potomac in two days.

A letter from Washington, of the same date says: "Gen. Lee has his whole army, (125,000,) in the immediate vicinity of the Potomac. Bragg is to take care of Richmond, while Lee takes care of Washington. Richmond was reinforced on the 19th inst."

A Washington writer reports a gentleman from Hagerstown, who saw Ewell's Division marching North, from 20,000 to 25,000 strong. The troops did very little damage besides seizing all the horses they could find.

STARTLING RUMOR AT WASHINGTON.

WASHINGTON, June 25—8 P. M.—There are strong indications to-night that Lee is actually within a short distance of Washington, having moved a considerable force from Shepherdstown and Antietam fords down the tow-path of the canal, or else along the inner roads from Poolsboro'. From these points he has direct access to the rear of Washington, and can destroy the railroad between the capital and Annapolis Junction.

THE PANIC AT HARRISBURG.

HARRISBURG, PA., June 25—2:30 P. M.—During the whole of last night long trains of wagons, laden with goods and household furniture have entered the city. The farmers are flocking in with their horses, also any number of contrabands, of all ages and sexes.

There are about 500 contrabands between here and Carlisle on the way.

Strong, able-bodied men are arriving here hourly from the border. They do not care about enlisting to defend their homes, but make quite a loud talk about what the authorities and government ought to do.

Large droves of horses are arriving from the border. Some of them would make excellent cavalry horses.

A dispatch received here this morning states that Gen. Jenkins' force was crossing Cave Mountain and entering McConnellsburg. The operator had left, but he heard distinctly the voices of the rebel officers giving their orders.

THE MILLS AT WORK.

A dispatch from Carlisle states that the rebels have all the mills within their reach grinding corn, etc., for them.

The rebels had occupied Chambersburg, Gettysburg, York, and had visited many other places in Pennsylvania.

DESTRUCTION OF FREIGHT TRAINS.

On Friday, the 26th ult., the Confederates entered Gettysburg. The Yankee troops left at the same time. The bridge and a train of thirteen freight cars, with supplies for the Yankees, were destroyed by the rebels. Three members of the Philadelphia City Troop, and the same number of infantry are reported captured.

CARLISLE TAKEN.

A dispatch from Harrisburg states that Carlisle was occupied on the 27th ult. by the rebels. At 12 o'clock they were three miles this side, and still advancing. The Yankee cavalry force retired.

The rebels have a line of pickets extending from Carlisle to Gettysburg.

A SKIRMISH.

A dispatch from Harrisburg (on the 27th) says: At 3 o'clock to-day a skirmish took place at Sterritt's Gap. We had four men killed in the skirmish. Sterritt's Gap is 18 miles from Harrisburg.

The excitement here is most intense. The streets are crowded with citizens and strangers, who are turning out by thousands to defend the city.

HARRISBURG, June 27.—Midnight.—The Confederate force which was at Sterritt's Gap at 4 o'clock has arrived in front of Duncannon, the junction of the Susquehanna and Juniata rivers. In that event the Pennsylvania Central will be cut.

STILL LATER.

HARRISBURG, June 28—5 P. M.—The rebel column under Gen. Early, which was at Gettysburg yesterday, reached the Northern Central Railroad a few minutes after 12 o'clock to-day, at a point between York and Hanover Junction. The wires were cut, and no further news of their movements is known up to the present time.

A dispatch from York states that the rebels are in force at Abbottstown, a village fourteen miles from there.

"ON TO RICHMOND" AGAIN.

For two or three days, last week, we had all sorts of rumors about the approach of the enemy, who, it was said, were making their ninth essay to take Richmond.

Gen. Jenkins' brigade met them on Crump's farm in New Kent county, where they were strongly posted. Our men, eager to test the mettle of the foe, hastened forward, and let fly a volley amongst them. The enemy faintly returned the fire, and then fled. General Jenkins pushed on after them, the men roaring with shouts of laughter, but the Yankees were too far ahead to be taken. After a chase of nearly four miles, our forces retired over a part of the ground. Eleven prisoners were taken, and the bodies of ten Yankees were found on the field.—It is not known how many were wounded, as they were carried off the field. Our loss was one killed and one wounded. The prisoners arrived last evening, and from their accounts Dix has not more than four or five thousand men at the White House. They seem dissatisfied, and some of them say that the most of the troops under Dix are tired of the war, and weary of the folly of "taking Richmond."

The same day the enemy appeared in large force in King William county, and were met by the Home Guard, who being overpowered by numbers, were taken. Late in the day they appeared at South Anna bridge, (what is left of it,) on the Central Railroad, which they destroyed a week ago. It is probable that the destruction of the bridge over the South Anna on the Fredericksburg Railroad is the real design of the enemy. We understand that our forces in that section are ample to meet and repel an attack.

THE ENEMY REPULSED AGAIN.

A cavalry force of the enemy was met and repulsed by our Confederate troops, at South Anna bridge, last Sunday morning.

GREAT BATTLE AT GETTYSBURG.

THE CONFEDERATES HOLD THE FIELD.

FEDERAL LOSSES VERY HEAVY.

There was a severe engagement at Gettysburg, Pa., on Wednesday, the 1st inst., between a part of Lee's army and the Yankee army of the Potomac. The attack was made by the Federals, who entered the town on the east side, marched through it, and assailed the Confederates. Gen. Reynolds and Gen. Paul were killed, and Cols. Wistar and Stone were wounded and taken prisoners. The only accounts of the battle that have reached us are from the enemy and these are contradictory. The reports of it in the Baltimore "American" fill several columns.

The Federal army was about eighty thousand strong, under the new Gen. Meade. Gen. Lee's army was strewn up the valley as far as Carlisle. The position of the Confederates was on a hill west of the town. Our artillery commanded the streets and the slopes of the hill. The enemy was allowed to pass through Gettysburg without interruption. He then massed his troops and assaulted the Confederate line, but was repulsed.—He returned to the charge several times; was always "unsuccessful;" and acknowledges a heavy loss. The slaughter indeed must have been great, for the position furnished a play for artillery like that of Marye's Hill. Meanwhile a wing of the Confederate army was swinging round on his flank. A retreat was ordered to avoid the effect of this movement. But it had its effect, which was the retreat of the enemy, and carried his line back a mile to the rear of his first position. His columns were shelled in passing through the town; his hospitals and wounded fell into our hands, where, of course, the possession of the whole field remained. It was not disputed on Thursday. The "Thursday's fighting" of the newspaper accounts was evidently nothing more than a skirmish. Both parties are said to have been concentrating their troops when last heard from; but Lee will gain more than Meade by that operation.

Such are the principal facts of the battle which the "Examiner" has gathered from the confused accounts of it reported in Northern papers.

The Yankees claim almost a victory of course; yet they admit that "no other alternative was left us (them) but to retire to the east of the town;" and that at the end of the action the Confederate cavalry dashed into the town, capturing and cutting them off from their hospitals. "Our approach to many hospitals being cut off," they say, "it is impossible to obtain a correct list of casualties."

The only officer quoted in the accounts admits that the fight "was rather unfavorable to our (Yankee) arms, and states that the enemy (Confederates) held the field at the close of the day, our (Yankee) forces having fallen back." The Governor of Pennsylvania sends a Macedonian cry to the Governor of New York for help—"send all the troops you can raise, without delay, as the need for them is pressing." This, and the confession that their losses are "enormously heavy," is pretty good evidence of something like a defeat.

Gen. Archer's brigade, numbering 800, (the remnants of three Tennessee regiments,) were taken prisoners in an effort to capture a train of wagons containing large supplies. In this effort the brigade was separated from the main army. In reporting this success, one account says that the Yankees took 6,000 prisoners; another 5,000; and another, an "entire brigade." The entire brigade, it appears, was less than a full regiment.

HIGHLY IMPORTANT.

GENERAL LEE VICTORIOUS.

GEN. MEADE RETREATING.

The following dispatch from Martinsburg was received here last Monday:

MARTINSBURG, July 5th.—Gen. Lee defeated the enemy in the battle of Friday last. We took twelve thousand prisoners. We lost four thousand prisoners. The Yankee army is retreating towards Baltimore. Gen. Lee is pursuing.

Generals Barksdale, of Mississippi, and Kemper and Garnett, of Virginia, were killed. Gen. Hood, of Texas, was wounded.

Another dispatch states that the decisive battle was on Sunday. It is dated

MARTINSBURG, July 6th.—Reports to-day all concur that there was a heavy fight yesterday, in which we defeated the enemy and drove him three miles. A vast number of prisoners are reported taken by Gen. Lee. The prisoners refused to be paroled, and are on the way to Richmond by this place. This has been the bloodiest battle of the war. Our loss very great—the enemy's immense.

STILL LATER.

A telegram was received from Martinsburg, at 1 o'clock on Tuesday morning, stating that our forces under Gen. Lee have routed the Federal army and taken forty thousand prisoners.

Thanks be unto God who giveth us the victory.

GREAT NEWS FROM THE WEST.

The Baltimore "Sun," of the 2d, says that Grant has been defeated by Johnston, and his army cut to pieces. Banks has arrived at New Orleans with only 5,000 men.

MOVEMENTS AT THE NORTH.

The Philadelphia papers report a great panic in that city; that citizens were called out to erect fortifications; that stocks had fallen 5 per cent; that several companies had been captured by the rebels at Columbia bridge; that a levy had been made on York for $100,000 in U. S. Treasury notes, 150 barrels of flour, 40,000 pounds of beef, 50 bags of coffee, and large quantities of sugar and groceries; that large supplies had been demanded of Carlisle; and that the rebel cavalry had taken many horses and cattle around Washington. In Philadelphia all the stores were closed, and the men employed in them forwarded for the defence of the city and State. The clergymen of the city offered their services to the Mayor to work on the fortifications.

KILLED AND WOUNDED.

The Federals report among the killed the names of Gen. Reynolds and Gen. Paul. Gen. Wadsworth is severely wounded. Among the names of officers of less rank who are wounded, are Col. Bates, of the 12th Massachusetts; Col. Leonard, of the 13th Massachusetts; Col. Fairchild, of the 2d Wisconsin; Col. Root, of the 94th New York; Capt. Robt. Williams, of the 12th Massachusetts; Lt. Thomas, Acting Aid to Gen. Baxter; Capt. Chas. Hovey, of the 12th Massachusetts, Aid to Gen. Robinson, and Adjutant Weaver, 9th Pennsylvania.

"Among those captured are the names of Dr. Nordgnist, Medical Director of Robinson's division and Capt. Fred. Gerker, of Philadelphia, of the same division. Our losses are enormously heavy, especially among field and line officers. Neither are we warranted in guessing how seriously the rebels have suffered."

INDIANA DEFAULTING.

The State of Indiana has failed to pay the interest on its debt due on the 1st of July, 1863.

ATTEMPT TO ASSASSINATE GOV. YATES.

Gov. Yates, of Illinois, was shot at through his window, while washing in his office, at his residence in Springfield, at a late hour on the 1st of July.

FROM THE SOUTHWEST.

THE ENEMY DEFEATED.

The same dispatches which report the success of our arms in the capture of more than a thousand Yankees at Berwick's Bay also state that the enemy's position at Thibodeaux has been carried.

These achievements give us the command of the Mississippi river above New Orleans, and will thereby enable us to cut off Banks' supplies.

Berwick's Bay is about eighty miles southwest of New Orleans. Thibodeaux, on the Lafourche river, is not more than 15 miles from the Mississippi, midway between New Orleans and Baton Rouge.

[SECOND DISPATCH.]

SUMMIT, June 29.—The New Orleans Daily "True Delta," of the 24th instant, reports a fight at Lafourche Crossing on the 23d. The Confederates captured a Federal battery, with a reported loss of fifty-three killed, including Colonel Walker, of the Second Texas Regiment.

A gentleman who has just arrived from Pascagoula reports the capture of the 19th Connecticut Regiment and two batteries, near New Orleans. Our pickets, he says, are near Algiers, on the opposite side of the river.

A FIGHT AT MILLIKEN'S BEND.

The Natchez "Courier," of the 16th, publishes a letter from Milliken's Bend, dated June 3d, in which the writer says:

"Gen. Walker's brigade fought all day yesterday at Milliken's Bend, completely routing the enemy, and driving them to their boats with great loss. Our loss was, I suppose, about 100 killed and wounded.

The Yankees fled to their boat, but commanded their negroe allies to fight it out, who, seeing themselves deserted, fought desperately. The slaughter among the negroes was terrible. The ground was literally covered with them. We have captured a great many. Unfortunately, their officers (Yankees) all managed to escape.

The Texas cavalry captured a company of negroes on Lake St. Joseph, who were commanded by a Yankee captain. The captain was caught.

IMPORTANT FROM LOUISIANA.

A dispatch from Jackson reports that Generals Magruder and Dick Taylor had crossed the Mississippi at Kenna, ten miles above New Orleans, and were marching on that city, which was garrisoned by about 1,500 Federals.

Another telegram states that Gen. Taylor has captured seven thousand of the enemy near New Orleans, and is marching on that city.

GEN. TAYLOR'S OPERATIONS IN LOUISIANA.

NATCHEZ, July 2.—The Louisiana "Democrat" says the last official advices state that Generals Taylor, Morton and Green surprised the Federal fortifications at Brashear City on the 27th June, and captured 1,800 prisoners, including 33 officers, and a very large amount of commissary stores, ordnance and small arms, 2,000 horses and mules, 7,000 negroes, and all the baggage belonging to Bank's army.

A second dispatch on the 4th says: It is considered certain that Morgan has played havoc with Rosencran's rear. An important movement ment is taking place in Gen. Bragg's army, but it is not prudent to mention particulars.

[illegible], July 2.—Bragg's headquarters are at Bridgeport. The Tennessee river will be the future line of defence.

FROM VICKSBURG.

The Federal troops attempted to blow up an angle of our works on the night of the 21st ult., but it was a complete failure, killing a number of their own men.

The Vicksburg "Citizen" says that for twenty-eight days incessant showers of shell have rained upon the city, and but three casualties occurred. The streets are daily filled with people, including women and children, who go about free from danger.

While the "Citizen" was working off its edition, a 13-inch shell passed through its office, scattering the cases of type, but injuring no one.

One of the enemy's gunboats is fast aground below the city.

The enemy has been firing incendiary shells for three days, but no damage was inflicted.

All now feel that Johnston will arrive in time.

Gen. Parsons' battery at Cypress Creek fired on five transports loaded with troops on Tuesday, crippling them badly. The troops landed and attempted to storm our battery, but were driven back, with a loss of three hundred.

VICKSBURG HOLDING OUT.

The "Enquirer" states that an officer arrived in this city direct from Vicksburg, says that the garrison is in splendid condition. Full rations are issued to our men of flour, meal, rice, sugar, molasses, &c. Our men are unanimous in the declaration that Vicksburg can never be taken.

FROM TENNESSEE.

THE EAST TENNESSEE RAIDERS.

The Knoxville "Register," of the 27th ult., thus notices the capture of a number of the marauding party, who made a recent raid in the vicinity of Lenoir.

It is stated that several hundred of their horses, were captured by our forces. Besides leaving their Parrot guns, they left a great many Enfield rifles, knapsacks, &c.

FIGHT AT UNIONVILLE, TENN.

The Huntsville (Ala.) "Confederate" has the following account of a skirmish at Unionville, Tennessee:

There was a sharp and heavy skirmish at Unionville on Tuesday, the 23d ult., and a still heavier one on Wednesday, near Hoover's Gap, in which our troops fell back for ammunition.—The Confederate troops engaged were Liddell's and Bates' brigades.

In the Unionville fight we lost one killed and one wounded. The Abolitionists fell back, and did not renew the fight Wednesday morning.—The Wednesday's fight was between Hoover's Gap and Shelbyville, and 8 or 9 miles northwest of Wartrace.

Major Fred. Claybrook, of Williamson county, was killed. He belonged to Bates' brigade, in which the reported casualties were 15 to 20.—Liddell's brigade lost about 40 in killed and wounded.

Heavy firing was heard in the same direction Thursday morning.

ANOTHER RAID.

ATLANTA, July 2.—The Yankees are making a raid in East Tennessee. A strong force was at Sequatchie Valley yesterday. To-day there has been no communication with Knoxville, or Loudon bridge. It is believed that important movements of Bragg's and Rosencran's armies are in progress.

OBITUARY.

Died, at Sharon, Bland co., Va., on the 18th of May, 1863, Miss ELIZABETH M. HUDSON, daughter of the late George Hudson, dec'd.

She had long since made her peace with God, and has gone to join Christ, her "elder brother," as joint heir of that inheritance which is incorruptible, undefiled, and that fadeth not away.—She was an exemplary and consistent member of the Presbyterian Church for more than twelve years—an ornament to the Church—an affectionate daughter—a lovely sister, and a kind friend. A beloved father and mother have lately gone before her to that happy land of whom it may be truly said that there was an imposing splendor in their religious character. Two sisters older than herself have departed in the triumphs of faith and gone to join the everlasting song of the redeemed in Heaven. A brother also, we trust, walks in the ever green pastures, watered by streams that never dry. Friends, have we not ties in heaven, and shall not we meet them there? Oh! let our watchword be, make sure of Heaven.

Sharon, Va. H. I. J.

LIEUT. J. L. SNODDY.

Departed this life in Vicksburg, Miss., March 22d, 1863, Lieut. J. L. SNODDY, of Jefferson co., Tenn., of Typhoid Fever, in the 31st year of his age.

In recording the death of this amiable young man, we unite with his venerable parents, several brothers and sisters, and a large circle of friends and acquaintances, in mourning the loss of one who has been an ornament to society in every position which he has ever filled. His parents took great pains in training their children in the doctrines and duties of christianity as laid down in the formulas of the Presbyterian Church. And in no case have they had to mourn a departure from their precepts and example in any of their numerous families. The subject of this notice gave evidence of piety from an early period of his life, but from his modesty and fear that he might not honor his profession, he remained out of the pale of the church until about five years before his death. While engaged in an extensive mercantile business in Dandridge, in the county in which he was born, the Lord poured out His Spirit in a most remarkable manner; and this young man united himself with the church, and from that day, until his death, gave undoubted evidence of the genuineness of his profession.—He entered the army with two or three of his brothers, in the service of his country, to defend it against the ruthless hand of an invading foe.

His companions in arms universally loved him, and had confidence in him as a brave and christian man. The writer of this notice was very familiarly intimate with him from his youth, received him as a member of the church, and can say that truly a good man has fallen; but it is the Lord, let Him do as seemeth Him good.—The large circle of his christian associates can but feel that their loss is his eternal gain. His remains were sent home to his parents, and were interred in the church burying ground where his parents lived. A very large concourse of friends attended his funeral. N. H.

CHRISTIAN OBSERVER,

PUBLISHED EVERY THURSDAY,

OFFICE IN THE LAW BUILDING,

(FRANKLIN STREET, ABOVE GOVERNOR,)

RICHMOND, VA.

TERMS.—THREE DOLLARS per annum in advance; or THREE DOLLARS AND FIFTY CENTS, if not paid before the expiration of the year. Payments may be made to our local agents, and where they are not readily accessible, may be forwarded by mail at our risk.

No Paper to be discontinued until an explicit order to that effect is received at the office of publication and arrearages paid.

POSTAGE.—The postage on the CHRISTIAN OBSERVER is TEN CENTS per quarter—payable in advance by the subscriber at the office where it is received.

SOLDIERS PAPERS.—Papers will be sent to soldiers in service at the rate of THREE DOLLARS year. They will be supplied, for GRATUITOUS distribution in the army, at SIX DOLLARS a hundred copies. Contributions for this purpose are solicited.

ADVERTISEMENTS.—Fifteen Cents a line for the First Insertion, and Ten Cents for each subsequent insertion.

OBITUARIES over ten lines in length will be charged Ten Cents a line—payment in advance.

All communications for the Paper, and letters on business, should be addressed to Rev A CONVERSE, RICHMOND, VA.

Lynchburg Daily Virginian.

"THE RIGHTS OF THE SOUTH, AND THE UNION OF THE SOUTH."

BY CHARLES W. BUTTON. LYNCHBURG, THURSDAY, JULY 9, 1863. VOLUME 11---NUMBER 289

VIRGINIAN.

TERMS OF SUBSCRIPTION.

The VIRGINIAN is published Daily, Tri-Weekly, and Weekly, at the following rates,

INVARIABLY IN ADVANCE.

Daily Virginian, one year,	$12 00
Do. do. six months,	7 00
Do. do. three months,	4 00
Do. do one month	1 50
Tri-Weekly, one year	$9 00
Do. six months,	5 00
Do. three months,	3 00
Do. one month,	1
Weekly, one year,	$3 00
Do. six months,	2 00

No paper will be sent without the subscription is paid in advance.

RATES OF ADVERTISING.

ADVERTISEMENTS are inserted for $1,00 per square of 8 lines, or less, for each insertion. —All yearly advertisements subject to special contract.

MEDICINES &C.

300 LBS MADDER,
2000 lbs Copperas,
400 " Ext Logwood,
500 " [illegible]
Cinnamon, Cloves, Spice, Ginger, Mace, Soda, Coffee and fine Green Tea, Honey and other Toilet Soaps, for sale by
je6 J H THOMPSON.

20 GALLONS CASTOR OIL
For sale by
ap30 W A STROTHER & CO.

AYERS PILLS,
McLane's Liver Pills,
Sellers' Vermifuge, Seidlitz Powders,
Toilet Soaps, Soda Powders,
Comds, Flavoring Extracts,
Tartaric Acids,
For sale by
ap2 W. A. STROTHER & CO.

SOAP.—
200 doz fine Transparent Soap,
100 " brown Windsor Soap,
200 lbs family Soap, for sale by
je18 J H THOMPSON.

LEAD PENCILS.—100 doz Lead Pencils just received and for sale by
je18 J H THOMPSON.

TO THE LADIES.—Soap for washing Lawns, Muslins and fine dress goods for sale by
jy2 J H THOMPSON.

DRUGS.—
5 lbs Glycerine,
15 " Iodide of Potass,
10 " Pure pow'd Opium,
20 " Gum Opium,
50 " Squill Root,
100 " Cream Tartar,
Calomel, Blue Mass, &c &c, for sale by
je2 J H THOMPSON.

WANTED—2,000 bushels of Flaxseed to be received, either in small or large lots.—Persons consigning Flaxseed to us, will be paid the market price, free of commission.
YOUNGER & CO.,
ja 141, Main street.

WANTED to rent or buy a small neat dwelling house in a good neighborhood.
Apply to GRAY & ANDERSON.

CONCENTRATED LYE.—300 boxes Concentrated Lye, for sale by
je18 J H THOMPSON.

LADIES BALMORAL BOOTS.
I have a very large and beautiful supply just opened of Ladies Balmoral and other styles of Ladies Boots, and a few pairs of children and misses shoes.
feb24ts P SEABURY.

LYNCHBURG FIRE, LIFE AND Marine Insurance Company.

OFFICE NO. 84, NEXT DOOR TO EXCHANGE BANK, MAIN ST.

Capital.............. $100,000
Surplus Earnings........ 15,000

Ben. H Nowlin, President,
D W Burton, Vice-President,

DIRECTORS,

Samuel McCorkle, firm of McCorkle Son & Co
Henry O Schoolfield, of H O Schoolfield & Co.
John F Slaughter, firm of Garland, Slaughter & Co.
Jno H Flood, firm of Flood & Crumpton.
A B Rucker, Grocer.
Chas W Price, Bank Officer.

Insures buildings and merchandise in town or country.

Applications received at the office or through any Director.

T H IVEY,
apr8 1y Sec'y.

COYNER'S WHITE AND BLACK SULPHUR SPRINGS.—This well known watering place will be opened for the reception of visitors on the FIRST DAY OF JUNE. It is beautifully situated on the Va & Tenn Railroad, about half a mile from Bonsack's Depot, from which point an omnibus will convey visitors to the Springs.

The virtue of the water of these Springs for the cure of Dyspepsia, affections of the Liver &c, are too well known to be repeated.

The accommodations are equal to any to be found in the mountains of Virginia, the table and attendance of the most satisfactory character, with good music and every attraction usually found at first class watering places.

PRICE OF BOARD.

Per day,	$6 00
Per week,	35 00
Per month of four weeks,	125 00

J A HEFFELFINGER,
my12m Proprietor.

SERVANT WOMEN'S SHOES.—One hundred pair women servants Shoes, coarse but of good quality. Price $12 at
my28 SEABURY'S.

SCOTCH SNUFF AND SMOKING TOBACCO.

The undersigned manufacturer of the celebrated brands of Smoking Tobacco, (Billy Bowlegs, G and Turkish, Winnebago, and Elephant,) has enlarged his capacity for manufacturing, and added to his business the manufacture of a very superior quality of SCOTCH SNUFF, which he is now prepared to furnish to his cusomers and the trade generally at wholesale prices at his Factory, corner of 5th and Jackson streets, Lynchburg, va.
oct 251y S. B. FERGUSON.

NEW BOOKS.

Just received by
D B Payne, No. 91 Main st.—
Strange Story by Bulwar,
Mahans Permanent Work and Plates, Price $20,
War Poems,
Vade Mecum,
Irvine's Practice of War,
New Ordnance Manuel,
Cavalry Drill,
War and Neutrality,
Diary of the War,
Campaigns from Texas to Maryland, &c., &c

Office of the Lynchburg Fire Life and Insurance Company. 7th March, 1863.

THE Board of Directors have declared a Dividend of 20 per cent on the cash Capital, payable to the Stockholders or their legal representatives on the 15th inst.

The Stockholders at their annual meeting authorized an increase in the Capital Stock of this Company to two hundred thousand dollars. The books are now open for subscription at the office of the Company.
T H IVEY,
m9ts Sec'y.

Waggons and Carriages.

THE subscriber returns his grateful acknowledgements for past favors in the waggon and carriage business, and asks a continuance of the same. He is manufacturing work with increased facilities, and selling at moderate prices. All repairing done with neatness and dispatch

Cash in all cases before the work leaves the shop.
JNO. H. BAILEY,
jan22 Agent.

NEW AUCTION AND COMMISSION HOUSE No. 102 Main Street, Lynchburg, Va.

The undersigned have associated themselves together under the style and firm of JAMES P. SCOTT & CO., for the purpose of conducting a general AUCTION AND COMMISSION BUSINESS, they have rented that large and elegant building, No. 102 Main Street, Lynchburg, lately occupied by Jno. T. Davis & Co.,; and on the first of December next will be ready to receive MERCHANDISE of all kinds for private and auction sales.

They solicit consignments of Manufactured and Smoking Tobacco, Sugars, Molasses, Coffee, and other Groceries; Bale Cotton and Cotton Fabrics of all grades; Woolen Goods; Boots Shoes, Leather, and all other goods usually offered for sale.

Their first auction will take place at an early day in December next, of which due notice, with catalogue, will be published.

They respectfully refer to the merchants and business men of Richmond, Petersburg, Danville, and other Southern cities, whose aid and co-operation will be duly appreciated.

JAMES P. SCOTT,
of the late firm of Jno. T. Davis & Co
HENRY E. BOCOCK,
WM. H. PARRISH,
members of the firm of Bocock & Parish.

The concern of Bocock & Parish No. 6, Bridge street, will continue at the old stand as usual.
Nov20 9m B. & P.

NAILS.—100 kegs Nails, assorted sizes, on consignment and for sale by
MOORE, BAYNE & CO.
my20tf 147 Main St.

MISCELLANEOUS.

WE HAVE IN STORE, and at wholesale or retail for sale,
10 bbls. N. O. Molasses, a prime article,
20 bales Raw Cotton,
A small lot of excellent Sole Leather,
500 pounds washed and unwashed Wool,
50 boxes Tallow Candles,
5 hhds. Sugar,
200 boxes Manufactured Tobacco,
500 yards Country Jeans, some very nice,
Together with Cotton Yarns, Brown Sheeting and Shirtings, Rio Coffee, &c., to which we invite the attention of merchants.
BONDURANT & MATTHIAS,
nov1 No. 80 Main street.

LATEST—One case fine & substantial Military Caps,
10 Bales Oznaburgs,
2 do ¾ Domestics,
5 do ⅞ do
15 do 4-4 do
50 Pieces Extra Fine Unbleached Shirting,
200 Yards Jeans, &c., for winter,
1000 Bales Cotton Yarn,
25 Barrels Brown Sugar,
12 do Choice New Orleans Molasses,
1 Chest Black Tea,
1 do Choice Green Tea,
60 to 100 Bales Raw Cotton,
100 Bushels Dried Apples,
200 do Unpealed Dried Peaches,
[illegible] Tobacco, on consignment,
250 Kegs Nails, assorted sizes,
And many other articles, in store and for sale by
JONES & MILLER,
oct20 107 Main street, Lynchburg, Va.

FOR SALE ON CONSIGNMENT.—
200 bbls and sacks of sugar, some very superior.
SPENCE & SLAUGHTER,
ap11 122 Bank Square.

WE have just received a nice lot of fresh Corn Meal, Bacon &c. On consignment and for sale by
ap23 MOSS & DAY.

SODA—Ten kegs SODA for sale wholesale and retail by
S. A. BOYD,
feb 19ts No. 115 Main street.

FOR SALE ON CONSIGNMENT.—
200 kegs box & lining nails.
SPENCE & SLAUGHTER,
ap11 122 Bank Square.

NOTICE.—THE undersigned wishes to inform his friends and customers in the city and country that he has been carrying on his business at No. 167 Main street, near the Norvell House, ever since his old stand was burned out. He has a good and well assorted stock of ready made clothing on hand as usual, and will be pleased to have a share of the public patronage as heretofore bestowed on him. Prices reasonable, notwithstanding the times.
m8ts MAX GUGGENHEIMER.

FOR THE TEETH.—Charcoal in bottles, Snell's Tooth Powder, Tincture of Myrrh.
For sale by
my13 J H THOMPSON.

FOR SALE AT RETAIL.—
Clipped Herring (new,)
Apple Vinegar, (good)
New Orleans Molasses,
Extract Coffee,
Sugar Cane Seed,
Pepper, Soda, Indigo Blue, Tea, Nails, Tar &c &c.
R ROSS,
my25ts

SUGAR AND MOLASSES.—Sugar in hhds, bbls and sacks, part very choice; 20 bbls Molasses
For sale by
my9 McDANIEL & IRBY

SUMMER HATS.—A good supply "for the times," of men and boys Straw and Leghorn Hats at SEABURY'S.
my23

LEATHER.—Sole Leather; upper do; horse do. Sheep skins for sale by
my9 McDANIEL & IRBY

Confederate Insurance Company

CHARLOTTESVILLE, VA.

Capital—$200,000.

THIS Company recently organized with all its capital paid *in cash*, will take fire risks on Buildings and Merchandise of all descriptions.

Losses promptly and satisfactorily adjusted.
E R WATSON, Pres't.
A P ABELL, Sec'y,
J H IVEY, Agent at Lynchurg.
my28 d1m

FRANCIS B. DEANE, JR., AND SON., LYNCHBURG, VA., Manufacturers of Chilled Railroad Car Wheels.

They are prepared to execute, promptly, orders to any extent for their WHEELS, made *exclusively of the best Virginia Coal Blast Charcoal Pig.*

THEY REFER TO

JOHN R. McDANIEL, Esq., President Virginia & Tennessee Railroad Co.
EDW. H. GILL, Esq., Superintendent Virginia & Tennessee Railroad Co
THOS. DODAMEAD, Esq., Superintendent Virginia Central Railroad Co.
Mr. SAMUEL PETERS, Master Machinist Virginia and Tennessee Railroad Co.
Mr. ARCHIBALD POE, Master Machinist Virginia Central Railroad Co.
JOSEPH R. ANDERSON, Esq., Richmond, Virginia
Messrs. MORRIS, TANNER & Co., do.
FRANCIS MALLORY, Esq., President Norfolk and Petersburg Railroad Co.
WM. MAHONE, Esq., Chief Engineer Norfolk and Petersburg Railroad Co.
ADAM DENMEAD, Esq., Baltimore, Md.
S. WYATT & Co., Charleston, S. C.
WM. I. ANDERSON, Esq., Mobile, Ala.
WM. G. SWAN, Esq., Knoxville, Tenn.
GENERAL JACKSON MORTON, Pensacola, Florida

The business at the LANGHORNE FOUNDRY will hereafter be conducted by the subscribers under the firm of F. B. DEANE, JR., & SON.
ap 15-c2tawts.

New Commission House.

THE undersigned have formed a partnership under the firm of
SPENCE & SLAUGHTER.

With the view of conducting a GENERAL COMMISSION BUSINESS, at No 122 main street, Bank square.

Consignments of all kinds will meet with prompt attention,
DAVID E SPENCE,
JNO F SLAUGHTER.
ap11 1y

Stock, Exchange and Banking House.

R. H. MAURY & CO.,
OFFICE CORNER OF MAIN AND 11TH ST.
RICHMOND, VA.

CONFEDERATE State Bonds of various issues.

State and Railroad Bonds of all kinds bought and sold on commission.

STERLING EXCHANGE,
GOLD AND SILVER.

And Bank Notes, bought and sold at market rates.

All orders promptly attended to.
R H MAURY & CO.
Richmond, Va.

Refer to Cashiers of the Several Banks in Virginia.
m201y

LARD OIL.—We have again commenced making Lard Oil, and can furnish a good article in any quantities. Orders left with Jas P Scott will be attended to promptly.
my28ts R J WADE & CO.

Blockade Raised.

THROUGH the energy of blockade running Steamers, I have been enabled to lay in, in spite of of our enemy's efforts to the contrary, a large and well selected stock of Dry Goods and Fancy Goods, now in store and daily arriving. I would respectfully call the attention of my old customers to below named articles, and it will be to the interest of merchants in the country to give me a call.

My stock consists in part of
150 ps dark and light English Prints,
50 " blk and white do,
100 ps 4-4 English Cambrics, beautiful styles,
50 " blk and white Lawns,
20 " superfine Organdies, elegant patterns,
40 " fancy and extra Scotch Ginghams,
20 " 4-4 superfine blk Lustre,
2 cases 4 4 extra English Shirting,
2 " 7-8 " do,
20 ps of extra fine white Cambric and Jaconett,
20 " heavy white Linen Drilling for summer suits,
10 ps heavy brown do,
1000 best Clark's white and col'd Cotton,
100 doz of extra cold Gents Cambric Hank'fs,
with a large assortment of fancy Dry Goods, Pocket Books, Combs of all kinds, Pins, Hoop Skirts, Paper, Envelopes, Irish Linen and other articles too numerous to mention.

Give me a call.
NATH'L GUGGENHEIMER,
my1 144 Main Street.
Republican copy.

To Tobacco Purchasers.

WE have in store and for sale upon as reasonable terms as can be had elsewhere about 3,500 boxes of Manufactured Tobacco, grades from common to very fine. Persons wishing to purchase would consult their interest by examining our stock before purchasing as we are offering very rare inducements.

We are also agents for the justly celebrated Killickinick and Garibaldi Smoking Tobaccoes, which we furnish at Manufacturers prices.
MOORE, BAYNE & CO.
1n6ts 147 Main st.

GENTS PEARL HATS.—Two cases Gents Pearl high crown stiff Hats just received at
my23 SEABURY'S.

BUSINESS CARDS.

General Advertising Agency.

THE SUBSCRIBER having established a General Newspaper Advertising Agency, is prepared to receive and forward without delay, advertisements and subscriptions to papers in any part of the Confederate States.

Advertisers by contracting with me, avoid the expense of postage and correspondence, and the uncertainty of remitting money through the mails.

ADVERTISEMENTS FORWARDED PROMPTLY.
NEWSPAPER ACCOUNTS COLLECTED IN THE CITY.
All orders addressed to the undersigned WILL receive prompt attention.
ROBERT P. BUTTON,
DAILY VIRGINIAN OFFICE
dec2 tf Lynchburg Va.

J. M. COBBS. WM. D. MILLER. C. W. PRICE

GENERL COMMISSION —AND— DRY GOODS HOUSE, LYNCHBURG, VA.

COBBS, MILLER & PRICE

HAVING associated themselves in business, and opened at the old stand of James M. Cobbs, No. [illegible] Main street, will receive on consignment, and give their personal attention to the sale of Manufactured Tobacco, Leaf Tobacco, Cotton, Rice, Wheat, Flour, Meal, Sugar, Bacon, Lard, Butter, Salt, and all kinds of produce consigned to them, and will make liberal cash advancements on produce when in hand. We also expect to keep a general assortment of Dry Goods, and sell them at prices as low as the exorbitant prices for which we have to pay for Goods will admit.
COBBS, MILLER & PRICE.
ap 20 d6mo

SHERMAN & BIGGS
No. 76 Main street
(up stairs) next door
below Merchant Bank

HAVE now on hand a fine Stock of Ladies CALF SKIN BOOTS and SHOES, and will continue to manufacture to order all kinds of Ladies and Childrens SHOES, at the shortest notice.
H H SHERMAN,
feb24d6m N H BIGGS,

NEW FIRM.

R. M. PARKS. M. W. HUTCHESON

R. M. PARKS &, CO.,
AUCTION AND
COMMISSION MERCHANTS
No. 14, Alabama Street, corner Pryor,
ATLANTA, GA.

Respectfully solicit a share of patronage, and hope, by a strict attention to business, to give entire satisfaction to their patrons.
dec28d8m.

Lynchburg Savings Bank.

OFFICE 141 MAIN ST., AT THE STORE OF MESSRS SMITH & ADAMS.

THIS Institution holds its meetings for discounting paper every Friday evening, at 4 o'clock, P. M.

Depositors are paid 6 per cent. on all sums remaining 12 months or more.

Deposits paid on presentation of certificates, without notice.

Henry D Flood, President.
C W Price, Treasurer,

DIRECTORS,

John S Bass,	Wm A Miller,
John A Tanner,	J C Shearer,
Thos H Allen,	W H Langhorne,
W A Strother	J T Murrell.

m6ts

New Commission House.

THE subscribers having taken the house occupied by H A Burroughs, No 104 *Main St*, have associated themselves together, under the style and firm of
BURROUGHS, HOLT & CO.

For the purpose of conducting a GENERAL COMMISSION BUSINESS. Consignments of all kinds of produce respectfully solicited.
H A BURROUGHS,
JAS R HOLT,
Lynchburg, ap96m ROBT W HORNER.

VIRGINIAN BOOK AND JOB Printing Office.

THE OFFICE OF THE LYNCHBURG VIRGINIAN is still prepared to do all manner of Book, Job, Plain and Fancy Printing.

The facilities of this OFFICE ARE SURPASSED by few others in the State, and the character of its work well known.

Orders respectfully solicited.
C. W. BUTTON, *Proprietor.*

New Auction and Commission House.

LYNCHBURG, VA.

THE subscribers having taken the Store House, No. 59 Main street, recently occupied by Geo. M. Rucker as a dry Goods store, have associated themselves together under the style and firm of
RUCKER & LEE.
for the purpose of conducting a GENERAL AUCTION AND COMMISSION HOUSE, and offer their services to their friends and the public generally in the sale of Dry Goods, Groceries, Manufactured Tobacco, Country Produce and Real and Personal Estate of all kind, whether at auction or at private sale.

They will make liberal advances on Merchandise and Produce in hand.

Mr. Rucker having had the experience of twenty five years in the Dry Good trade, and A S Lee an experience of about the same length of time in the Grocery and Commission business, they feel well satisfied that the interest of all who favor them with consignments will be well protected.

Account of sales with net proceeds returned promptly.
GEO. M. RUCKER,
of Lynchburg.
A. S. LEE
dec2dt of Richmond.

New Firm.

THE undersigned have this day formed a copartnership, under the style and firm of
MOORE, BAYNE & CO.,
for the purpose of conducting a General Grocery and Commission business in this city, and have taken the store house recently occupied by McKinney & Co., No 1.7 Main st.

We shall keep constantly on hand and for sale Groceries of all kinds, Manufactured and Smoking Tobacco, &c. We are agents for the sale of the justly celebrated and world renowned Killikinick and Garibaldi Smoking Tobacco, which we will furnish at Manufacturers prices

Consignments of Wheat, Corn, Rye, Flour, Bacon, Lard and all kinds of country produce solicited.

Quick sales and prompt returns made.

We will make liberal advances on consigments in hand when required, and will furnish bags at the usual rent to parties desiring to consign grain to us. Give us a trial.
M MOORE,
of Lynchburg
R BAYNE,
late of Alexandria.
G B HOOD,
jan15ts late of Culpeper.

L. A HORTON,
WITH
GARRETT & BETTERTON,
No 137 MAIN STREET,
Commission Merchants,

FOR the sale of Tobacco, Flour, Wheat, Bacon and country produce generally.

They will make liberal advances on produce in hand.

Mr Horton having had the experience of 22 years as inspector at Friends and Liberty Warehouses, they feel well satisfied that the interest of all who favor them with consignments will be protected.

Accounts of sales with nett proceeds returned promptly.
L A HORTON with
my18d5m GARRETT & BETTERTON.

LATEST ARRIVAL.—
8 cases supr Imported prints,
10 " " fancy "
2 " black and white cambrics,
3 " supr bleached cloths,
2 " white cambrics,
15 pieces check pol de chaver,
10 " figured do,
20 " alamance plaids.
40 bales ¾ oznaburgs;
2 pieces blue cloth.
1 " supr black do,
30 " swiss muslins,
25 " emb'd "
15 " curtain "
10 doz drawers,
5 " cassimer shirts.
ap9 H J ABRAHAM & BROS.

ICE, ICE, ICE.—The subscribers can furnish customers with good Ice for the season. Orders can be left at stall No 6, Market House, or Jno B Shaner's Store Main St.
my292tawts J PHILLIP SHANER & CO.

MISCELLANEOUS.

NOTICE.

ON and after Monday next, May 4th, the Passenger train on the Orange and Alexandria Railroad will leave Lynchburg 5.45 A. M., for Charlottesville.

Leave Lynchburg 5.45 A. M., arrive 6.45 P M.
my13t

Office of South Side Railroad Company, Lynchburg, Sept 29th '62.

Change of Hours of Starting.

ON and after the 2d of October, the mail and Passenger train for Richmond and Petersburg will commence starting from Lynchburg at 4.45 P M. and on Saturday morning the train from Richmond will arrive at 8.30 A M.

The trains will continue to run this way until further notice.
W B GREGG, Agt.
sept30 S S R R Co.

Notice.

FREIGHT will not be received at the Orange & Alexandria Railroad Depot after 4 o'clock P M.
J T LATHAM,
Agent Transportation,
au28ts O & A R.

OFFICE VA & TENN R R Co, Lynchburg, June 13th, 1863.

THE Board of Directors of this Company have declared a dividend of six per cent upon the stock of the company, payable to the Stockholders or their legal representatives at their office in the city of Lynchburg, on and after the first day of August next.

The transfer books will be closed on the 15th July and stand closed til the 1st August; therefore those persons owning stock, who have not had the transfers made to them, will have it done before the 15th July, as the dividend will be placed to the credit of the party in whose name the stock stands on that day.

By order of the Board,
F G MORRISON,
je18 2awt1aug Treas'r.

FARM FOR SALE.—I will sell privately my farm in Bedford co., adjoining the land of Capt Jno F Hawkins, eight miles from Lynchburg and two miles of Forest Depot containing 365 acres, more or less, about 30 Bushels of wheat sown the present season. Any one wishing to purchase a farm of this size will find it to their interest to examine this before purchasing elsewhere. For further information apply to me in Lynchburg.

Possession given immediately.
jan15ts J MATHIAS.

NEW CONCERN—THE subscriber will continue with increased facilities the General Commission and forwarding business, at the old stand of Staples & Anderson, No. 81, Bridge st. next door below A J Camp & Co., and solicits consignments of every discription of Produce, Goods, and Groceries. If the highest prices for their produce, personal attention to weights and delivery, with accounts sales, and cash remitted at once, merits patronage, we shall continue to receive that liberal share extended to us in other connections for years past. Liberal advances on produce in hand. We shall hereafter keep a supply of goods and groceries, &c., as far as can be obtained, purchased for cash. We shall be satisfied with such profits as will enable us to supply our customers cheaper in this way. Those ordering through us will, generally save more than their expenses, an important item these times. During the continuance of the War, we will supply needy soldiers in active service or their families with the prime necessaries of life, at cost and charges. We have no margin to cover expenses of time and books, our sales will be for cash only. Peter H. Dillard, our experienced Tobacco Salesman and Commission Merchant will have charge of Tobacco sales and requests his friends to consign to this house in future.
W. A. STAPLES,
P. H. DILLARD.
dec22tf.

WOOL Carding.—Having secured the service of a first rate Carder, we are ready to receive wool at our mill or store. Have the wool well washed, picked and greased. It should be perfectly dry before greasing, or it will not make good rolls. Send sheets to put the rolls in.
NOWLIN & MURRELL,
No 61 Main Street,
my25 Lynchburg, Va.

HENRY DUNNINGTON & WM S MYLER AUCTIONEERS FOR THE SALE OF NEGROES.

The subscribers having opened an AUCTION HOUSE ON MARKET STREET, NO 56, for the sale of Negroes, beg leave to call the attention of their friends and the public generally, and solicit consignments.

We pledge ourselves to use our best efforts for the interest of all who may patronize us.

We will have our porter at the trains daily, also at the packet boat.

We have a good place to take care of all negroes sent us.
HENRY DUNNINGTON,
je171m WM S MYLER.

ON CONSIGNMENT.—800 packages Manufactured Tobacco, part of which is very fine and old.

We have also in store the following favorite brands Smoking Tobacco:
Elephant,
Grand Turkish,
Winnebago Chief,
Billy Bowlegs,
Beauregard,
Reglico &c.
Lone Jack, a superior article put up in ½ and 5 pound backages.

The attention of sutlers and retail dealers is respectfully called to our stock of Tobaccos.
GRAY & ANDERSON,
je163w 140 Main Street.

DRUGS &C.—2000 lbs Bi Carb Soda, 1 caks Epsom Salts, 150 lbs Balsam Copavia, 150 lbs Castele Soap, Sweet Oil, Spirits Nitre, Arrow Root, Pulv Rhubarb, Arsenic, Tooth Brushes, Oil Anis, Black Pepper, 4 chests Fine Green Tea.
Just received by
je26d1m STABLER & JONES.

VERDIGRIS IN OIL.—50 lbs pure Verdigris in Oil, for sale by
je27 J H THOMPSON.

PERCUSSION CAPS.—250,000 Percussion Caps at wholesale or retail.
je24d1w S M SIMPSON.

SUPERIOR GUN POWDER—Just to hand, at retail or by the quantity.
je24d1w S M SINPSON.

SHOT, SHOT.—1,500 lbs shot, assorted sizes just to hand.
je24d1w S M SIMPSON.

$200 REWARD.—For the apprehension of a Negro Man, named Randall, about 45 years of age, dark complexion, stout made, ordinary heigh, four of his front teeth out, nose flat between his eyes, and rather bad countenance.—He worked at Rebecca Furnace, in Rockbridge during the past winter and spring, called himself "Jim Coons" and had a paper, purporting to be from his master, permitting him to hire himself and collect his wages. He left there the last of April, was arrested by two cavalrymen west of Lexington, who turned him over to a citizen on the road, from whom he made his escape. He is doubtless lurking about some of the Furnaces in that section. I will give the above reward for his arrest and safe keeping until I get him.
je24d6t J B L WILLIAMS.

FOR HIRE—A No 1 Nurse can be had by early application to
GRAY & ANDERSON,
je251w No 140 Main Street.

NEGROES FOR SALE.—Will be sold on Friday, the 10 of July, at the late residence of Drury Tucker, dec'd, in the county of Amherst five likely young Negroes (1 woman, 3 boys and 1 girl) all nearly grown. Also a lot of household and kitchen furniture one horse, farming utensils &c.

Terms cash or notes payable in six months, interest added.
HENRY LOVING,
Ex'r of Drury Tucker, dec'd.
je17d1aw&c1awt10jy

FOR SALE.—A pleasant Residence with all necessary out buildings, and two good gardens attached. Possession given immediately.

Enquire at this office. je281w.

GRAIN SCYTHES.—5 doz. Grain Scythes for sale by
je19ts MOORE, BAYE & CO

ON CONSIGNMENT.—I have in store, some 20 or 30,000 lbs of the old Lynchburg Cotton Factory Machinery, which I will sell on reasonable terms. This is the largest porton of the whole machinery. Persons wishing to purchase would dowell to call on me soon.
25d1m R H STATON.

CONCENTRATED LYE.—300 boxes Concentrated Lye, for sale by
je27 J H THOMPSON.

Wanted.

5,000,000 Rabbit, Raccoon, and Muskrat Skins, for which the highest market price will be paid.
m14ts JOHN DOOLEY.

SUBSTITUTE WANTED.—A liberla price will be paid for a Substitute. Apply immediately.
Address C M.
je11ts Virginian Office.

20 HANDS WANTED.—I wish to hire by the month or day ten carpenters or wheelwrights, and as many common laborers, to be employed in the manufacture of wooden bottom shoes.
Apply to S L BURFORD,
Burfords Summit,
je18 3taw2w Amherst county.

MISCELLANEOUS.

150 DOZ IRON HOOPED WATER BUCKETS just received and for sale on consignment, by
je306t W H ROSE.

$15 REWARD.—Strayed away from the subscriber at Lynchburg, on the 20th inst, a medium sized red cow without horns, motley face red and white. I will give $15 for the return to me at Lynchburg.
1860, W F LUCADO.

$5 REWARD.—Stolen from me on the 28th inst, a small black Tanned Pup, when stolen had on a brass color. I will give $5 for his recovery.
je30ts W F LUCADO.

NOTICE.—By virtue of a deed of trust executed to the Washington Building Fund Association, bearing date on the 27th day of September, 1860, we, the undersigned, trustees, will sell in front of the Market House on Saturday, the 11th day of July next, at 11 o'clock, a. m., a house and lot, containing one acre of ground, and lying on the Lynchburg and Campbell Courthouse Turnpike, it being the property of F. D. Milstead, and sold by his consent. Terms cash.

The title is believed to be good, but acting as trustees, will only give such as is vested in us.
WM. H. MURRELL,
T. H. WALKER,
J. V. MUSGROVE,
Trustees.

N. B. Should the weather not admit of sale on Saturday, we will sell on the next Monday or the next fair day.
je30tds

$50 REWARD.—LOST between Charlottesville and North Garden, on the 17th inst, my Pocket Book, containing two one hundred dollar notes, several fives of the latest issue, the balance in ten, and twenty dollar notes, all amounting to about three hundred dollars. Also my discharge from the 2nd Virginia Cavalry, and several other papers of value. The above reward will be paid upon the delivery of said book to A B Rucker, Lynchburg or to J R Abell, Charlottesville, Va. Address,
Pedlar Mills P O, Amherst co, Va.
je284t WM A RUCKER.

C S ORDNANCE DEPOT, Lynchburg, Va, June 22d, 1863.

I WISH to purchase, in large or small quantities Old Rope, waste Cordage, Old Hemp, Bagging, Junk and other similar materials. A fair price per pound, will be paid for the above articles delivered at this depot.
G A GETTY,
Capt C S A.
je23d2w Ordnance Officer.

JUST RECEIVED—
79 Marseilles Quilts,
188 Linen Sheets,
24 Damask Table Cloths,
48 Pillow Slips,
10 doz Towels,
4 pieces Pink net,
je23 WILLS COLHOUN & CO.

WANTED—ROOTS, HERBS, BARKS, &c.—I wish to purchase for the use of the Confederate Army, the following articles. Each article must be well dried IN THE SHADE and kept to itself, and ready for use when delivered. I will pay the prices here affixed. Further information can be obtained by calling on me at my office.
R. KIDDER TAYLOR,
Surgeon and Medical Purveyor, Lynchburg, Va.

Wild Ginger, dried root, per lb,	$0 30
Red Pepper, dried pods, per lb.	25
Hemlock, dried leaves, per lb,	15
Do. dried seed, per lb,	30
Dogwood—inner bark, freed from wood and coarse outer bark, and well dry, per lb,	10
Columbo, dried root, per lb,	30
Calamus, dried root, per lb,	20
Boneset, leaves and flowers, per lb,	5
Ipecacuanhae Spurge, dried root, per lb,	50
American Gentian, dried root, per lb,	25
Indian Physic, dried root, per lb.	30
Yellow Jasmine Root, per lb	10
Henbane, leaves, per lb,	25
Do. seed, do,	30
Hops, dried flowers per lb,	1 00
Butternut, Dried Bark and Root, per lb	10
Slippery Elm—dried bark, freed from outer coarse bark, per lb,	5
Arnica, dried flowers, per lb,	75
Bene Seed, per lb,	20
Sumach, leaves, bark and root, per lb,	
Marsh Mallow Root, per lb,	
Tulip or Poplar Tree—dried inner bark, freed from wood, coarse bark, per lb,	8
Lavender, dried flowers, per lb,	50
Georgia bark, inner bark dried, per lb	20
Wild Cherry, dried bark, per lb,	5
May Apple, dried root, per lb,	30
Ginseng, dried root, per lb,	30
Blackberry, dried root, per lb,	5
Seneka Snakeroot, dried root, per lb,	75
Puccoon Root, dried root, per lb,	30
Hardhack, plant, per lb,	5
Marsh Rosemary, leaves, per lb,	20
Mustard Seed, per lb,	30
Snakeroot, dried root, per lb,	75
Sarsaparilla, dried root, per lb,	30
Fever Root, dried root, per lb,	20
Dried Apples, per bushel,	2 00
Dried Peaches, per bushel,	3 50
Dried Pumpkin,	1 00
Dried Okra,	5 00
Potato Fly, per lb,	2 00
Castor Oil Beans (hulled) per bushel,	7 00
" " " (not hulled)	3 00

je22d1m

To Farmers and Quartermasters.

ASS'T QUARTERMASTER GENERAL'S OFFICE. Richmond, Va. 18th June, 1863.

TAX IN KIND.

The following is the system adopted for the collection of the tax in kind:

An officer of the Quartermaster General's Department is assigned to the special charge of the subject. A controlling Quartermaster, with the rank of Major, is assigned to each State, and a Post Quartermaster, with the rank of Captain, to each Congressional District, where it is practicable to collect the tenth.

Each Congressional District will be subdivided by the Post Quartermaster in charge of it into sections, for the convenient delivery by the taxpayers of his quota of produce, and agents will be appointed by that officer to take charge of the depots to be established in each section.

Before these depots can be established, or the assessments required under the law be made, the crops of small grain, hay and the clip of wool for the present year will have been secured.

To relieve farmers from the risk and inconvenience of storing the Government portion, as well as to obtain immediate supplies for the use of the army, the Department authorizes and requests farmers, residing near posts where Quartermasters are now stationed to deliver the governments tenth or any part of it, to that Quartermaster.

Under the law, farmers are required to deliver their tenth at depots not more than eight miles from the place of production. If they will deliver under this request, the government will pay for the transportation in excess of eight miles. The Quartermaster receiving produce under this rule will give receipts to the producer as evidence that so much of his tax is paid. And as the Post Quartermaster of the Congressional District is responsible for the tenth, after the assessor has established and made known to him, the Quartermaster to whom the produce is delivered will also receipt for it to the Post Quartermaster of the District, who will endorse a copy of the receipt upon the assessor's estimate before transferring it to the agents at the receiving depot.
LARKIN SMITH,
je191m A Quartermaster Gen'l in charge.

LAND SALES.

VALUATLE REAL ESTATE FOR SALE.—Wishing to purchase a No 1 farm, we have determined to offer at private sale for cash, that most desirable and beautiful Market Garden, purchased of F Morrison, lying in the edge of the city containing 25¼ acres, now in a high state of cultivation, with a great variety of fruit trees, fine grapes and small fruit of every variety, the finest collection of roses and flowers about the city.—Also several houses and lots, containing from ¼ to 4 acres of ground attached, lying in and near the city, all valuable; we will also sell a lot of wood land, about 6 miles from the city, containing 370 acres, well timbered, about 30 acres cleared and in cultivation, with a good dwelling, out houses &c. This land is valuable to any person living in the city for fire wood. Any one wishing to purchase will call on either of us for further information.
JOHN OYLER,
je30d1m S B FERGUSON.

EXECUTOR'S NOTICE.—All persons having legal claims against the estate of the late Edward Price, will bring them forward for immediate settlement, and all debts due the estate must be settled, as I wish to close the accounts and settle up the estate as early as the law will allow.
JOHN OYLER,
je30d1m Ex'r of Ed Price, dec'd.

AQUATIC!
500 fish caught in one hour with the "CHINESE SECRET ART."

This method of taking fish does not injure the flesh, and hundreds may be taken in a few hours without any expense and very little trouble.

I will send this "SECRET" to any person who will inclose to my address 50 cts in specie or $1 in paper currency. We will refund the money if you are not satisfied with the "Secret." A breast-plate gratis to the first lady ordering the Art.
Address,
F. E G LINDSEY,
Raven's Nest, Va.

Entire Southern Press copy, and send bill to the advertiser. jy4w6t

SUGAR &C.—
50 bbls Sugar, (part choice,)
6 doz Grain Scythes,
15 gross Matches,
for sale by
MOORE, BAYNE & CO.,
je301w 147 Main St.

Daily Virginian.

INAUGURATION OF THE NEW STATE OF WEST VIRGINIA.

On Saturday last the State of West Virginia took her place among the Commonwealths of the Federal Union. The ceremonies at Wheeling were imposing. At 9 o'clock the 4th and 5th regiments of militia assembled at the Courthouse, and at the McLure House received the General Assembly and State officers. A column was then formed, and proceeded to the Linsley Institute. Here a commodious platform had been erected, on which 35 little girls, tastefully attired, were seated. On the arrival of Governor Boreman they arose, and greeted him, singing the "*Star Spangled Banner.*"

Senator Hubbard called the assemblage to order, and prayer was offered by the Rev. J. T. McLure. *Gov.* Pierpont addressed the multitude, announcing that West Virginia was one of the United States of America, and that his official relations with them had closed. He reminded them that their career had commenced not in peace, but in the midst of a rebellion; and while he went to Virginia to do what he could to suppress it, he would urge them not to forsake the national flag.

At the conclusion he led Gov Boreman forward, and presented him as "Arthur J Boreman, the elected Governor of the State of West Virginia, who was in their cause as true as steel."

Governor Boreman began by the remark that West Virginia long ago should have had a separate State existence. The rest of Virginia had regarded her as a Territory in pupilage, and every page of the statute book manifested unfairness and inequality of legislation. Heavy taxes had been collected there and expanded for railroads and canals in the Eastern side of the State, while every improvement had been refused to them. They were treated as strangers. The two peoples were distinct. While those East of the mountains adopted the doctrine of *S*ecession, the men of West Virginia spurned and rejected it.

This State is the child of the rebellion; yet its peace and prosperity depended on the permanence of the American Union. It would be his duty, as soon as these ceremonies were over, to proceed to aid the Federal authorities. Theirs was the contested ground of the rebellion, and what course should loyal men of West Virginia pursue? We want no compromise; we want no peace except upon the terms that those in rebellion will lay down their arms and submit to the regularly constituted authority of the United States. As Governor, he should co-operate with the Federal authorities in those measures deemed necessary for the suppression of this rebellion, and do what he could to advance the agricultural, mining and manufacturing interests of the State. If he should discharge the duties of his office as well as his predecessor, he would expect the approbation of a generous people.

Senator Willey was next called forward by the multitude, and congratulated them that West Virginia had become a fixed fact. He had been in the habit of talking sometimes against our armies and Generals in the field, and against our national Administration. He quit doing so about two weeks ago, and did not intend to renew it until the war should be over. We cannot get along if we are to quarrel among ourselves. *G*od bless our old *G*overnor, God bless our new Governor, God bless the State of West Virginia.

Three cheers, at Governor Boreman's suggestion, were then given for West Virginia, and three more for three more States of America.

The General Assembly had assembled in their respective chambers for organization.

Eighteen out of twenty Senators appeared and were sworn. After which, upon the third ballot, John M. Phelps was elected President of the Senate; Ellery R. Hall was chosen Clerk, and other officers were also elected.

The House of Delegates made choice of Dr. Spicer Patrick, of Kanawha, for Speaker, without opposition. Forty three counties were represented, six delegates not yet having arrived. The House being organized, the fact, was communicated to the Senate, and that body then immediately entered the hall. Governor Boreman appeared and took the oath of office the Speaker's desk, Mr. Hildreth, notary public, administering it. Both Houses then adjuurmed.

THE "SLAVE TRADE."

We have now, in New York papers of 27th, a report of what passed in Parliament, when Mr. Coningham proposed negotiations for putting an end to the "Slave Trade," that is the buying and selling of slaves within the Confederate States:

Mr. Conningham asked the First Lord of the Treasury whether the efforts which have been made hitherto by the British nation for the suppression of the African slave trade might not with advantage be extended to the continent of America; and whether the time had not at length arrived when it became the duty of her majesty's Goverament to enter into a friendly negotiation with the Federal Government of the United States, for the purpose of concerting measures for the gradual but total suppression of the Slave Trade in the Confederate States,

"Lord Palmerston said his honorable friend was aware that the Federal Government of America had concluded a treaty with Her Majesty, giving a mutual right of search for the purpose of suppressing the Slave-trade. With regard to the Confederate States, they had passed a law which rendered the Slave-trade highly penal; but his honorable friend must be aware that the Federal government had no relations with the Confederate States, except the relations of war [laughter,] and of course, could not hold intercourse with them with a view to such arrangements. As Her Majestiy's government had not yet acknowled the independence of the Confederate States—that independence not being established in a manner to justify such acknowledgement—no communication could take place between Her Majesty's government and the Confederate States. But in course of time, if things should alter they should, hope, if the Confederate States should, succeed in establishing independedce, they would would make arrangements similar to those which the Federal government had made.

"Mr Coningham said the question he asked the noble lord, was whether, the government could not enter into communication with the Federal States for the suppression of the Slave trade on the continent of America.

"Lord Palmerston thought he had already answered the question. As he had stated, the Federal Government had no relations with the Confederate States, except the relations of war; and that, of course, did not admit of any action of their's, with the view of carrying out the arrangements the honorable member referred to."

NEW ADVERTISEMENTS.

SEWING MACHINES REPAIRED!! Persons having Sewing Machines out of order, can have them Repaired by an EXPERIENCED MECHANIC, by leaving their orders with Mr. A. S. ENGLEDOVE, No. 30 Main St. Terms moderate
jy42w

Dissolution of Copartnership.

THE copartnership heretofore existing under the style of W. A. Strother & Co., was dissolved on the 1st July, by mutual consent. Those having claims against the concern will please present them for payment. and those indebted to us will please make payment as speedily as possible.
W. A. STROTHER,
S. B. CHRISTIAN.

The subscriber will continue the Drug Business at the old stand of W. A. Strother & Co., where he will be pleased to see his friends and the public generally. As he has no time to make off and collect accounts, he trusts his friends will appreciate the necessity of his doing a STRICTLY CASH BUSINESS.
jy7ts W. A. STROTHER.

Valuable Furnace Property at Public Auction.

THE subscriber will offer at public sale, at Goshen Depot, on the Virginia Central Railroad, on Thursday, July 23, 1863, that valuable property, formerly owned by William Weaver, dec'd, known as the

BTAH FURNACE ESTATE,

situated on the waters of the Big Calf Pasture River and its tributaries in the County of Rockbridge.

It consists of several TRACTS OF LAND, containing altogether between

6,000 and 7,000 acres,

including FURNACE STACK, &c.; and valuable beds of IRON ORE; one of which is the ore for Cannon metal in the Confederate States, and also a splended site for a forge.

The Water Power is equal to any in the country. There is an abundance of timber in the immediate neighborhood.

Mr. Leech, at Cold Sulphur Springs, or Mr. Wm. L. Ayres, adjoining the property, will show it to any one wishing to examine it.

Possession given at once.

The subscriber will sell the property with special warranty, of such title as is vested in him.

TERMS—Cash or credit, at the option of the purchaser, and further terms on day of sale.
DANIEL C E. BRADY.
Saunders' Store, Rockbridge Co., Va.
jy3 d3taw121

$400 REWARD.—Ranaway from the subscriber on, the 15th May last, living in the city of Lynchburg, my negro man named HENRY, about 35 or 40 years of age, brown complexion, teeth little bad, about 5 feet 10 or 11 inches high; and when he left had on a drab colored frock coat, and pants of same color, and black hat.

He was purcuased by W S Rogers from W T Peterson, at Richmond. His wife is owned by John Garland Jeffries, who resides within 2 miles of Amelia C H, in which neighborhood he may be. The gentleman sold him with the understanding that he was not to return to the neighborhood

The above reward will be paid for his delivery to the undersigned at the Orange House, or to Ro Lumpkins at Richmond.
jy3 A O ROBARDS.

NOTICE.—The office of the Lynchburg Savings Bank has been removed to No 84, next door to the Exchange Bank, where deposites will be received and 5 per cent interest paid for any length of time. The Board of Directors will meet every Friday evening at 4 o'clock, for the purpose of discounting paper. Notes offered for discount must be handed in by 12 o'clock on discount days.
jy8 1w T H IVEY, Treas'r.

FOR SALE—A FINE YOUNG HORSE.—Apply to (jy83t) W. F. LUCADO.

Disolution.

THE firm of Gray & Anderson, has this day been disolved by mutual consent. Those indebted to the concern will please come forward and settle as it is important that the business should be closed up as speedily as possible.
GRAY & ANDERSON.

AS I shall probably leave Lynchburg shortly, I would be glad if those indebted to the firm of Gray & Anderson would come forward promptly and settle. Thankful for the liberal patronage heretofore extended to the firm, I would bespeak a continuance of the same to *Mr* J N Anderson, to whom I have sold out.
jy1d1m ASHER W GRAY.

New Concern.

THE subscriber truly thankful for the very liberal patronage bestowed on the late concern of Gray & Anderson, will continue the COMMISSION BUSINESS at the old stand, No 140 Main Street, and hopes by strict personal attention to business, to give satisfaction to those who may favor him with their patronage.
jy1 d1m J N ANDERSON.

1,000 BALES RAW COTTON for sale. Apply to
jy1 ts BURROUGHS, HOLT & CO.

A BEAUTIFUL lot of Cloth Balmorals just received at
jy1 SEABURY'S.

A LARGE lot of Heel Kid Buskins just opened at
jy1 SEABURY'S.

LADIE'S Congress and side lace Gaiters, heel and no heel Slipsat
jy1 SEABURY'S.

ON CONSIGNMENT AND FOR SALE.—
A superior article Coperas, Flax and Tow Linen, Tallow and Wax Candles, Smoking and Manufactured Tobacco, White wove English Letter Paper, Corn Meal, Salt &c &c.
jy1 ts BURROUGHS, HOLT & CO.

LADIE'S Kid and Morocco Boots just opened at
jy1 SEABURY'S.

ON CONSIGNMENT.—
75 Sleys, from 4 to 800,
12 bbls Kanawha Salt,
100 sacks Washington Co do, in dry order.
J N ANDERSON,
jy2 2w 140 Main St.

OFFICE LYNCHBURG GAS LIGHT Co, Lynchburg, July 1st, 1863.

IN consequence of the enormous increase in the cost of coal, lime, labor and repairs of the works, the Board of Directors are compelled to advance the price of Gas to *eighteen dollars* per thousand feet, on and after this day.
T H IVEY,
jy2 Treas'r.

ICE, ICE, ICE.—We have this morning and will continue to have a nice lot of Ice. All in want call and supply yourselve. For sale at
jy2 1w MOSS & DAY.

GENT'S SHOES.—An assortment of Gent's Congress and low quarter Shoes just received at
jy1 SEABURY'S.

MISSES' BOOTS.—Misses' Morocco Boots just opened at
jy1 SEABURY'S.

PHŒNIX FOUNDRY,

LYNCHBURG, VA.

The subscribers, successors to A. G. Dabney & Son, have associated themselves together under the firm and style of DABNEY & SOMERS, for the purpose of conducting the Foundry and *Machine* business in all its various branches. The business will be conducted under our personal superintendance, and we promise the former reputation of the establishment shall be fully sustained.

Orders for Iron and Brass Castings, Wrought Iron work and Machinery generally, will receive prompt attention.
[illegible] DABNEY,
April 1, 1863. D. M. SOMERS.

$[illegible] REWARD.—One of my [illegible] Horses was stolen from [illegible], near Lynchburg, on the night of the 30th of June. He is a large bay horse, 15 hands high with full mane, and some 10 or 12 years old. He walks and trots well in harness, and walks, paces, and trots well under the saddle. No particular marks remembered.

I will give $50 for his return and $50 for the detection of the thief.
jy3d2t&c2t WM. D [illegible]EL, Jr.

[illegible] GO Corn [illegible], Pepper, Mace, Cloves, Gum Arabic Spice, Starch, Ext Logwood, Cinnamon, for sale by
jy2 J H THOMPSON.

The Virginian

FRIDAY MORNING, JULY 9, 1863.

The Fall of Vicksburg.

After a siege that will redound to the lasting honor of all who endured it, this gallant city has fallen. It is a misfortune to us, but not an irreparable disaster. Port Hudson still stands; and even if that stronghold should be abandoned or captured, the navigation of the Mississippi will still be interdicted to Yankee commerce. A river running through fifteen hundred miles of our territory cannot be open to free navigation and the pursuits of commerce, when an enemy can appear upon its banks at a thousand points, and sink the hapless barks that would venture with their rich freight upon its waters. This though the enemy hold Vicksburg and Port Hudson, would be altogether too precarious a business to invite enterprise. Commerce cannot live and thrive on those waters while this war lasts.

It will be a query with thousands; why General Johnston never attempted to relieve the garrison at Vicksburg? Many will be ready to blame the war-worn veteran; and criticisms, without number, will be invoked. Men in this age are naturally censorious; and we may not profit by the experience of the past, which would teach us to withhold criticism until we know all the facts in the case. Whether or not, it would be compatible with the public interests to disclose these at present, is a matter for the decision of our authorities. Meanwhile, let us remember the case of the illustrious Albert Sidney Johnston, and be temperate in our expressions for the present.

The fall of Vicksburg—though it must and will be lamented by every body in the South, except the human vultures who prey upon their fellow-man, and who may expect that the stock of sugar on hand will "go up"—should not paralyze our energies in the slightest degree. All is not lost yet, by a great deal; and there is no calamity that overtakes us that might not be worse.

The New York Herald grows desperate on the subject of the ravages of the "rebel sea devils," as it terms the representatives of the Confederate Government on the high seas. In its issue of July 3d, which lies before us, it makes the following startling expose touching the effects on the maritime interests of the North, produced by the operations of our armed vessels:

"Since the breaking out of the rebellion three hundred and eighty five vessels, with an aggregate tonnage of more than one hundred and sixty-six thousand tons, have been transferred to foreigners at this port alone, most of which are now sailing under the flag of Great Britain, our most prominent commercial rival, and ally of the South. At other ports the same practise has prevailed, and it would be fair to estimate the loss of American tonnage under it during the past two years at three hundred thousand tons. This loss to us, as a matter of course, involves a consequent increase of the tonnage and power of our rivals.

It [illegible] to show the effect on our carrying trade, let us glance at the commerce of New York during the first six months of the year 1860, as compared with a like period in the present year. During the former period the number of vessels cleared at this port for foreign ports was seventeen hundred and ninety five, of which eleven hundred and thirty three were American and six hundred and sixty two [illegible]—a difference of nearly one hundred [illegible] in favor of American vessels; while, during the same period of the present year, there [illegible] twenty one hundred and ninety seven clearances, of which fourteen hundred and fifty were foreign and only seven hundred and forty seven American—showing an increase in the number of foreign vessels and a difference in their favor, as compared with the first named period, of about two hundred per cent.

"By this system we not only decrease our tonnage and lessen our power as a commercial nation, but we suffer financially by its operation." The hundreds of vessels which now sail under a foreign flag formerly paid into the Treasury, at every entry at a custom house in the United States, twenty cents per month for every person employed on board, for the use of the United States Hospital. This is now lost to us, and, if paid now, inures to the benefit of the government under whose flag they sail."

NORTHERN ACCOUNTS OF THE Great Battles in Pennsylvania.

The Baltimore American has the following account of the first day's battle:

It appears that at 9 o'clock on Wednesday morning, the 1st inst., the 1st and 11th Corps of the Army of the Potomac reached Gettysburg, entering from the east side of the town, and marched directly through to the west side, the cavalry force of the enemy falling back as we advanced. On passing out of the west end of the town the enemy was observed advancing rapidly from the Chambersburg pike, in line of battle, towards the town, evidently endeavoring to hold an advantageous position commanding the town. The 1st corps, under Gen Reynolds, was in the advance, and pushed forward at double quick to secure the advantageous position. The enemy under Longstreet and Hill advanced steadily, and in a few minutes a heavy fire, both of artillery and musketry, was opened along the whole Federal lines. The 11th Army Corps under Gen Howard was also soon in position, and for a time a heavy battle raged. Several charges were made by the enemy to dislodge our forces, all of which were unsuccessful.

At 3 o'clock the enemy massed his entire forces and endeavored to turn our right wing. Gen Reynolds advanced to meet them, and a heavy infantry fight ensued, in which both parties suffered severely, volley after volley of musketry being poured into the opposing columns with deadly effect. In the charge Major General Reynolds fell mortally wounded, and died soon after he was conveyed to Gettysburg. He was, as usual, leading his corps, and in the thickest of the fight. Gen Paul, commanding the 3d brigade of the 1st army corps, was also killed on the field, and Colonels Wistar and Stone fell severely wounded, and were taken prisoners by the enemy. The field between the contending armies was strewn with the dead and wounded, and it is said that the enemy suffered fully as heavily as we did, though it is not known what was their loss in officers.

The effort to flank our right wing wholly failed, and we held the prominent and commanding position for which the struggle was made, at the close of the fight, which ceased for the day about 4 o'clock in the afternoon. At this time two more corps of Gen Meade's army reached the field, and during the night the main body of our army was in position to meet any demonstration that the enemy might make in the morning, or to advance on him, as the Commanding General might decide. The 1st army corps nobly maintained its position against the effort to flank its right, and scarcely faltered for a moment when its gallant commander fell under the murderous fire of the enemy. A great and decisive battle was considered imminent, and, notwithstanding our severe loss in officers, the advantages of the day were regarded as decidedly with our forces.

The army was in fine condition, full of enthusiasm for the coming battle, and confident of success. Gen Meade had also, it was thought, concentrated his forces to a greater extent than the enemy, a large portion of whose army was still scattered up through the Cumberland Valley.

Col Wistar commanded the Pennsylvania 'Bucktails,' and Col Stone also commanded a Pennsylvania regiment, and both were in the 2d brigade of the 1st army corps. Col. S, at the time of receiving his wound, was acting as brigadier general of the brigade. Gen Newton took command of the 1st army corps on the fall of Reynolds.

Gen Paul commanded the 3d brigade of the same corps, and was a most efficient officer.

Some gentlemen connected with the press who arrived here on last Thursday evening from Gettysburg, having left before daylight in the morning, represent the condition of affairs at the close of the fight on Wednesday evening to have been still more promising of a successful issue than the previous information we had received.—They state that the rebels had held Gettysburg for some time previous to the approach of our army, and had not only occupied, but had commenced fortifying the hills on the west of the town, where they proposed to check our advance towards Chambersburg and the mouth of the Cumberland Valley.

The movement of Gen Reynolds and the rapidity with which he advanced after entering the east end of the town took them somewhat by surprise, and he soon obtained the prominent position which the rebels were fortifying. The fighting through the balance of the day was a futile attempt on their part to regain this important position, from which they were frequently repulsed.

Early in the afternoon both Longstreet and Hill combined their forces for a grand effort to turn our right flank, when Gen'l Howard's 11th corps, (the Dutch corps,) which broke and ran at Chancellorsville, dashed into the fight to regain their lost laurels, and most nobly did they repulse these two veteran corps of the rebel army. The repulse was so complete that no further attempt was made by the enemy during the balance of the day, and night closed in with our holding the position chosen by the enemy to give us battle from. The 3d and 12th army corps also came on the field after the last repulse of the enemy, but owing to the fall of Gen Reynolds, and the lateness of the hour, as well as the exhaustion of the men, and the desire to take care of the wounded, it was determined not to push the enemy for a renewal of the conflict.

When our informant left the field Thursday morning, Gen Meade had arrived, and the main body of our army was in position, ready to push the enemy so soon as day should dawn.

Gettysburg is just 25 miles east of Chambersburg, over a fine rolling country most of the way, which will doubtless be the scene of the great battle of the rebel invasion.

From one of the officers who came down in charge of prisoners, who arrived last night, who left Gettysburg on Wednesday afternoon, we have accounts not so favorable as those given by other parties. He describes the fight of that day as rather unfavorable to our arms, and states that the enemy held the field at the close of the day, our forces having fallen back after the fall of Gen Reynolds; that the attack of the enemy was so sudden and unexpected that both the corps of Hill and Longstreet were for a time engaged with Reynolds' corps, and that the 11th corps took but little part in the battle.

ANOTHER ACCOUNT.

A correspondent of the New York Herald gives the following account of the fighting:

GETTYSBURG, Pa., July 1, 1863.

The First corps of General Reynolds had been engaged with the enemy probably about two hours when the Eleventh arrived on the ground, hurrying up to meet the noise of battle towards us. So far the First corps had appeared to have the advantage; but about the time of our arrival the rebels had partially succeeded in turning their right flank.

Arriving on the ground, Gen. Howard assumed command and immediately made his dispositions for the battle. The First corps was at this time on a wooded ridge near the Lutheran Theological Seminary; to the right was another range of hills, the right being wooded and crossed by the Harrisburg road.—Gen Howard directed that two divisions of the Eleventh corps be placed on this range of hills, the First division on the right and the Third on the left of the Harrisburg road, a stream being on our extreme right. The Second division was held as a general reserve.

General Schurz, being in command of the Eleventh corps, endeavored to take the position indicated; but owing to the flank of the rebels on the right of the First corps we were not able to reach the favorable point desired. The rebel corps of Gen A P Hill had, so far, engaged the First corps. But at this time General Ewell's corps of twenty-five thousand men arrived by the Rock road. It was this overwhelming force which was to be met by seven thousand men.—Before they had reached an advantageous defensive position, the rebels had batteries so posted that our columns moving up on an air line afterwards were exposed to a destructive cross fire. Gen Barlow, on the right, with the First division, made a most desperate effort to take and hold the position assigned him. The brave Gen[illegible], while riding along in front of his line encouraging his men, while the skirmishers were firing, was hit by a musket ball and severely wounded in the thigh or groin.—The division fought bravely, and lost heavily, the brigade of Colonel Von Gilsa holding its position firmly, and that of Gen Ames doing well. The Third division, Gen Schimmelpfennig, was meanwhile striving nobly to hold the position it was directed to hold immediately on the right of the First corps and on the cleared part of the hill between the Seminary and the position of Gen Barlow.

The losses in this division show how well it fought. The brigades were commanded by Colonels Krzyzanowski and Von Amesberg. Colonel Von Amesberg had two horses shot under him, but escaped uninjured. Colonel Krzyzanowski was hurt, but not disabled, by his horse falling with him. Colonel McGroarty, of the Sixty-first Ohio, behaved with his usual distinguished gallantry, but escaped uninjured as if by a miracle. Col Brown, of the One Hundred and Fifty-seventh New York, held an isolated position of particular peril. The regiment lost eighteen of twenty-six officers and three-fourths of its men. Lieutenant Col. Arrowsmith, a noble officer of this regiment, was killed. Every regimental commander of Krzyzanowski's brigade was killed or wounded. The Eighty second Ohio, Col Robinson, lost eighteen officers. The Twenty-sixth Wisconsin lost all but one of its officers. This regiment last fall joined Gen Sigel at Fairfax, with nearly the maximum number, and then appeared splendid. It has been in two fights—Chancellorsville and Gettysburg—and came out with less men than are required to form a company.—The Seventy-fourth Pennsylvania brought off sixteen men.

Our right flank was completely turned and our left at the same time, so superior was the enemy's force. The First corps was giving way, and the Eleventh found it impossible to maintain its position. The First division retired in good order, and the Third fell back nearly at the same time.

General Schimmelpfennig's two aids, Captains Schelten and Klenker, had their horses shot under them. General Schimmelpfennig's horse was shot under him on the retreat, and he was captured. It is presumed that he was wounded, possibly killed, before being taken.

The two divisions fell back slowly, pausing occasionally, and endeavoring to stem the rebel advance. At this juncture the First brigade of Gen Steinwehr's division was ordered up. This brigade was commanded by Col Coster, and the force engaged consisted of three small regiments. The brigade formed on the right of Pennsylvania College, a little below the foot of Washington street.—The brigade was too late to more than check the rebel advance for a few moments. They were scarcely formed when they were attacked by three rebel columns and completely enveloped on the right. Col Coster and his men did all that brave men could do; but it was so late when they were called out that it was scarcely worth while for them to be slaughtered by the artillery and infantry force to which they were opposed.

The rebels had two batteries playing upon our right flank and rear, almost from the time the 11th corps first arrived on the field. The ubiquitous Dilger, with his battery, was on Colonel Coster's left, in the road, on an eminence. It did terrible execution with grape and canister on the advancing rebels. The Eighty-second Ohio was supporting this battery, and it was here that Col Robinson was wounded and taken prisoner.

Our men retreated slowly through Washington street, the rebels closely pursuing, and being in advance of many of our troops on the east side of the town. Captain Dilger's battery unlimbered at the foot of the street and gave the rebels a parting charge of grape.

It is a wonder that the rebels did not press us more closely. While passing slowly and densely packed, artillery, infantry and ambulances, along this street up the hill, a battery planted where Capt Dilger's was last stationed would have enfiladed this street completely.

Captain Schiermen's battery, which did excellent service during the day, was especially efficient, while planted on the hill above two batteries of reserve artillery, in protecting this retreat.

As we passed through town, shot, shell and bullets were whistling musically around us, sometimes striking the houses. A shot ricochetted over a regiment in front of me and pierced the wall of an inhabited house. A bullet grazed the ear of Captain Newcomb, with whom I was riding, and struck a house near us.

The ladies of Gettysburg deserve especially honorable mention. While we were retreating they came out upon the sidewalks, with composed though anxious faces, and offered our soldiers everything needful in the way of refreshments. The shot were whistling meanwhile; but they appeared elevated by noble impulses above the sentiment of fear. They took the most tender care of our wounded, as well as those of the rebels who were captured during the day. How we grieved to leave this interesting town in the possession of rebel soldiers.

We fall back to a position south of the town cemetery, which Gen Howard had first selected as the only good position that we could secure. The rebels did not seem to think it best to attempt to dislodge us. The enemy occupied the town on our retirement, and their sharpshooters were stationed on the houses near us.

The battle of to-day was well fought. We had 22,000 against 50,000.

From the Baltimore Sun, July 3d.

BATTLE NEAR GETTYSBURG

The expected battle between the forces of Gen. Lee and Gen. Meade commenced Wednesday morning, and at last accounts was progressing in the vicinity of Gettsburg.—In regard to this battle we have received at yet no official account.

Yesterday morning the train from Westminster brought to this city the body of Maj. Gen. John F. Reynolds, who was killed in the early part of the engagement on Wednesday morning. The following officers of Gen. Reynolds' staff accompanied the remains.—Maj. Biddle, Capt, Weed, Capt. Mitchell and Lieut. Rosengarter. The remains were in charge of Ordnance Serg't R. B. Clevenger Company F, 88th Pennsylvania. From Serg't Clevenger we learn that the fight at Gettysburg commenced about 9 o'clock in the morning, and that about 10 o'clock Gen. Reynold's was shot while cheering on his men. He was on the left wing of his forces, and the ground where he fell, lies somewhat to the left of the Convent.

We also learn from officers from Gettysburg that Gen. Paul was killed in the same fight, and that Col. Stone and Col. Wistar were wounded and taken prisoners. Gen. Paul commanded the third brigade of the first army corps. Col. Wistar commanded a Pennsylvania regiment—the Bucktails—and Col. Stone also commanded a Pennsylvania regiment in the second brigade of the first army corps, and was acting Brigadier of the second brigade.

Last night 700 Confederate prisoners were brought from Westminster to Baltimore over the Western Maryland Railroad. These men were captured during the battles going on at or near Gettysburg. Twenty-eight hundred Confederates have been taken prisoners since the fighting began The seven hundred who have arrived in Baltimore are on their way to Fort Lafayette.

The latest received in Baltimore, on the night of July 3d: Just before going to press we learned from the military authorities that no official information had been received of the fight at Gettysburg, on Wednesday or yesterday; that it was not positively known whether a fight was really in progress yesterday, and that the information about the number of prisoners taken on Wednesday was not official, but was deemed perfectly reliable.

We also learned from the same source that scouts report that two full brigades of Confederates crossed the upper Potomac at Williamsport yesterday, on double-quick time, going in the direction of Chambersburg.

In rear of the position so taken up, and to the right, the division of Gen. Wadsworth was drawn up in line of battle, with the division of General Robinson holding the second line. At the moment that these formations were completed the rebels, emboldened by their partial success in driving from position the batteries, attempted another charge, with the object of seizing the pieces, when the brigade of the 2d division, with fixed bayonets, made a charge upon them, and such as were not killed were taken prisoners. Two entire regiments—a Tennessee and Mississippi regiment—were then bagged.

Immediately after the arrival and going into position of the first corps, the eleventh under the amiable and brave Gen Howard, who had been in the rear and marching on the same road as the first made there appearance, marched directly through the town and at once formed a line of battle on the right of the Chambersburg road and some half a mile west of the college, which is located at the extreme end of the town! After some three hours of artillery dueling the rebels commenced to retire. There were massed two infantry corps, and in this formation a pursuit of their retreating column was commenced. After driving them back towards the mountain, something over a mile, soon after four o'clock it was discovered that with an extensive force of infantry and cavalry, they were endeavoring to turn our left flank, with a view probably to get between us and our supply trains. Before this being noticed, and it being evident that our reinforcements, the 3d and 12th corps, who had been anxiously inquired after during the entire day, were not yet up, no other alternative was offered us than to retire to the East of the town, and take up a better position upon the top of a hill and along the line of road leading to Emmettsburg. This was done, but in admirable order, no unusual haste being apparent, while at the same time all ammunition and supply wagons as were up to the front were sent to the rear.

A little after 4 o'clock the 3d corps, under command of General Sickles, came upon the field, and went into position upon the left of that held early in the morning by the 1st Corps. The Twelfth, under General Slocumb, as well, arrived about the same time, and were stationed upon the right of the 11th Corps. After those two corps, as well as those who had borne the heat and burthen of the day, were formed in battle array, they made an advance, and with but little resistance succeeded in driving the rebels from the town, and back into the position they first occupied early in the morning. In this manner, and in these locations, both armies are resting for the night.

The 2d, 5th and 6th Corps, are moving this way, and by morning will be ready to do battle with us.

While the latter mentioned movement was being made, the enemy kept up a continual rain of shot and shell upon the town, and, when, ceasing, their cavalry dashed through the town, capturing all stray parties there congregated, together with the wounded, who were occupants of, and the surgeons and nurses who were in attendance in, the many hastily organized hospitals there located. While the firing was in progress some few buildings were set on fire, but the town not being compactly built only such buildings as were struck by the shells were consumed.

LATEST FROM THE BATTLE FIELD.

ON BATTLE FIELD OF GETTYSBURG, Thursday 8. A. M.

Correspondence of the Philadelphia Enquirer.

To-day, and on Pennsylvania soil, has been fought one of the most desperate and bloody battles of this accursed rebellion.

This morning early the first and eleventh corps, which had been during the night encamped near Emmettsburg, advanced, the first corps marching in the following order: 1st division under Gen. Wadsworth; 3d division under Gen. Doubleday; these followed by five full batteries under Col. Wainswrigt; bringing up the really splendid division of Gen. Robinson—this corps having been in the advance during the whole time of our march from Falmouth, were the first force of infantry to reach Gettysburg and to come up with and fight the enemy.

During the day this corps had been under the direction of Gen. Reynolds being in command of the right wing, comprising the 1st, 3d, 11th and 12th corps.

When some three miles from town, and while quietly marching along, the sound of heavy and rapid firing was heard in the direction beyond Gettysburg. Almost at the same instant Capt. Mitchell, a gallant aid upon General Reynolds' staff, came dashing down the road with orders to the various division commanders to push forward their division as rapidly as possible.—The order was given to double quick march, which was instantly obeyed, and kept up until the intervening space where our battery's were engaged was passed over. These batteries, two in number, were a part of the artillery belonging to Buford's division, and were stationed some half a mile to the South of Gettysburg Theological Seminary while the opposing force were stationed and snugly entrenched upon the East side of Marsh Creek, and about the same distance from the seminary as were our own forces. The latter was first to open fire, and were for a time compelling our batteries to retire from their posistion. This they were quietly doing and in good order, when the division of General Wadsworth came to their support, the two able regiment, the 2d Wisconsin and 24th Michigan, rushing up and driving from in front of them the infantry force who were making desperate efforts to capture these peices.—When these supports arrived the batteries again took up a commanding position, which they were enabled to hold during the day.

MARRIED,

At St. Paul's Church, on Tuesday evening, the 7th instant by the Rev. W. H. Kinckle, WM. OTWAY OWEN, M. D., to ALICE LYNDE, of this city.

The Lynchburg Virginian.

NOTICE.—The cross mark appended to the names of certain subscribers indicates that the term for which they subscribed will soon expire. They are thus notified in time to renew their subscription if they desire.

WANTED.—A Printer, who is a good pressman, to whom liberal wages and constant employment will be given, at this office.

SUICIDE.—A German named Geo. Herter, a cigar maker, committed suicide Tuesday night by cutting his throat with a razor.—The act is supposed to have been the result of delirium, produced by intoxication He lived in the shop of Mr. Kunz, Main Street.

ATTENTION ARTILLERY.—A few more names will be received on the roll of Capt. Latham's Artillery Company. Nearly as many members have signed the list as are desired, and the remaining vacancies are fast being filled up. Those who may wish to enter this desirable branch of service, for home defence, and keep out of the militia, had better come forward at once. The roll is at the office of Col. Langhorne.

A NEWSPAPER THIEF.—William Thomas Updike, a negro boy, who has been stealing copies of the "Virginian," from the door of C. V. Winfree, was detected in the act yesterday morning and ordered to be lashed by the Mayor.

We intend to have the law enforced against black and white, who may be detected in such "petty larceny." Our subscribers in various parts of the city are suffering from such depredations.

FAILURE OF INDIANA TO PAY INTEREST ON ITS DEBT.—The State of Indiana has made default in the payment of interest on its debt, due on the first of July, 1863. This is the first instance of default since its compromise with its creditors, sixteen years ago.

A GOOD EXAMPLE.—Capt. Getty, ordnance officer at this place, requests us to return thanks to the wardens of St Paul's Episcopal Church for the contribution of the lead on the railing around the building for the use of the government—Amounting to three hundred pounds. If the other Churches and the owners of private residences here and all over the Confederacy would follow this patriotic example, an immense amount of lead, now doing no good, would be turned over to the government. Every pound that can possibly be raised is needed.

CARLISLE BARRACKS.—These barracks which have recently been destroyed by the Confederates have a historic memory attached to them. They were built in 1777, chiefly by a number of Hessians, made prisoners at Trenton. Major Andre was for some time held there as a prisoner of war, and Washington had his headquarters there in 1794, during the Whiskey Insurrection.—Nothing but the walls of the old structure are now left standing. The Dickenson Methodist College, founded in 1783, is one of the features of the place also; but, with the exception of a few shells from Lee's guns, which fell in the grounds, it was not molested.

FROM BRAGG'S ARMY.—The most satisfactory news we have, at this writing, from our army in Middle Tennesse, is contained in the "situation" article of Saturday's Chattanooga Rebel. It says:

Passengers report the evacuation of Tullahoma by our troops. Whilst we are not positively advised of this, beyond the rumor of the hour, we have no doubt of its correctness. If it be true the movement is a good one, and will meet the sanction of the rank and file of the army, and of all who know anything about the nature of that region of country.

Our first and last duty is, to whip Rosecrans. That the mind of General Bragg has this intent, no more, seems clear; and whether the thrashing comes at Tullahoma or some other point involving a better position, is a question to be determined by those Generals who compose the military family of the Commander-in-Chief.

(From the New York Herald, July 3.)

THE WORK OF THE ALABAMA.

Details of the Destruction of the Ship Gildersleeve.

STATEMENT OF CAPT. MCCULLUM, &c., &c.

[Our Baltimore Correspondence.]

BALTIMORE, July 1, 1863.

From Capt. McCullum, of the New York ship Gildersleeve, a brief statement of the capture of which I sent to you yesterday, I have derived a graphic account of the affair, as follows:

At 11 A. M., May 25, in latitude 12 10, longitude 34 55, the rebel steamer Alabama hove in sight. Capt McC. supposed her to be an American gunboat, as she showed American colors. He dipped his colors in salute, and the Alabama dipped hers, returning the salute with prompt courtesy. Capt McCullum was then about to proceed on his voyage, when the Alabama fired a gun across his bows and made the signal, 'I want to speak to you.' The ship was then hove to, and a boat put off from the Alabama, then two hundred yards distant. As the boat approached, Capt McC asked, 'what steamer is that?' The boat returned no answer; but as her crew ascended the ship's side, the U. States flag was hauled down and the rebel flag was run up on the Alabama. The boarding officer advanced to Capt McC, and said, 'You are a prize to the Confederate steamer Alabama. Prepare to go on board with me.' Capt McC complied. On reaching the Alabama, he endeavored to secure the safety of his vessel by showing that his cargo was coal, on English account. But Captain Semmes said, 'Sir, your vessel is worth over sixty thousand dollars. Your coal is not worth twenty thousand dollars. I will burn your vessel.' The Captain was not allowed to return again to the ship. A boat was sent, which brought away the crew. Capt. Semmes took possession of all the chronometers, nautical instruments, &c. on board, and Captain McCullum thus lost all he had in the vessel. The ship was then fired and it burned to the water's edge. Two hours afterwards the Baltimore vessel Justina hove in sight and was captured, but ransomed on giving a bond for seven thousand dollars. Captain McCullum and his crew were put on board of her, and arrived here yesterday. He describes the discipline on board of the Alabama as of the worst description—as bad as none at all. The men are a hard looking set—of all nationalities. Captain Semmes is a small man, with a red nose covered with pimples. His first officer is a big, burly man, with ample beard, wearing old cowhide shoes with the toes out, dirty linen, &c. The sailing master, an Englishman, is the most decent looking man in the lot.

LATEST BY TELEGRAPH

The Fall of Vicksburg!

RICHMOND, July 8th.

The following official despatch has been received:

JACKSON, July 7th.

Hon. J. A. Seddon, Sec'y of War:

Vicksburg capitulated on the 4th inst.

The garrison was paroled, and are to be returned to our lines; the officers retaining their side arms and personal baggage.

This intelligence was brought by an officer who left the place Sunday, the 5th.

[Signed] J. E. JOHNSTON, Gen. Com'd.

[Approved] J. A. SEDDON, Sec'y War.

Later from Gettysburg.

RICHMOND, July 8th.

A special despatch to the Enquirer, from Winchester the 7th, says there have been four days fighting, commencing on the 1st and ending the night of the 4th, our men capturing immense fortifications of the enemy.

Our loss is estimated at ten thousand.

Between three and four thousand of our wounded are arriving here to-night.

Gen's Scales and Pender, wounded, have arrived.

The hills around Gettysburg are covered with the dead and wounded of the army of the Potomac.

No official confirmation of the news from Martinsburg.

Another Confederate Victory at Port Hudson.

BANKS ROUTED, &C.

JACKSON, July 7th.

Gen. Loring attacked Osterhaus yesterday near Edward's Depot, and after three hours hard fighting drove him across the river.

Our loss is reported heavy.

The enemy's loss not given.

An official from the vicinity of Port Hudson says Dick Taylor crossed under cover of our guns last Saturday, and he and Gardner attacked Banks and routed him with heavy loss.

They are moving to reinforce Johnston.

Nothing farther in regard to the fall of Vicksburg.

Militia Called out in North Carolina.

RALLEIGH, July 7th.

The Legislature passed the militia bill to-day.

It calls out all men from 18 to 50 for home defence for the term of 3 months.

The Yankee Raid in N. Carolina.

GOLDSBORO', July 7th.

The Yankee raiders got home safe.

A large force of Yankees, estimated at five thousand, came out as far as Trenton to secure or cover their retreat.

Gen. Martin sent a force to intercept them at Free Bridge where they found the Yankees posted in force.

They drove in the Yankee pickets, but, finding the raiders coming up in the rear, fell back after an animated artillery skirmish.

The men behaved gallantly.

No casualties reported.

Free Bridge is over Trenton river, ten miles South-west of Trenton and twelve miles South-east of Kinston.

FROM RICHMOND.

RICHMOND, 8th.

No press telegrams from Martinsburg since Monday—no official advices have been received.

The news of the capitulation of Vicksburg is generally discredited, but the closest observers believe the city has fallen.

Another flag of truce boat has arrived at City Point to-day, no papers were received by it.

Sugar advanced fifty cents per pound to-day.

Heavy rains have fallen here to-day.

It is reported that there is a freshet in the Potomac, rendering communication difficult.

The James is reported rising.

Further from the Battle at Gettysburg.

OUR FORCES REPORTED AT HAGERSTOWN. MD.

BATTLE PROGRESSING AT HAGERSTOWN.

&C, &C., &C.

RICHMOND, July 8th.

An unofficial despatch from the telegraph operator to the Secretary of War, dated Martinsburg, 8th, says, from reports, we gained a decided and telling advantage over the enemy at Gettysburg on Wednesday and Thursday. On Friday we charged his works and took them, but were unable to hold them, and, fell back towards Hagerstown.

But little fighting since then, so far the victory is on our side.

We can now hear cannonading, the report is that the fight is now going on near Hagerstown.

Everything is so indefinite that it is impossible to form any correct idea of the fight.

Four thousand prisoners are now at Williamsport on their way to Richmond, many slightly wounded were paroled to-day.

DAILY DISPATCH---Extra.

RICHMOND, THURSDAY, JULY 9, 1863.

LATEST FROM THE NORTH.

THE REPORTED DEFEAT OF GEN. LEE.

The Baltimore *American*, of Monday evening, July 6th, has the following intelligence from Meade's army. It is proper to state that the *American* is the most unreliable of all the Northern papers, and its statements must be taken with a greater degree of caution than even the generality of Yankee lies is received:

THE RETREAT OF LEE.

We publish this afternoon a number of important dispatches from the Army of the Potomac in relation to the rebel retreat. It seems that Gen. Lee, after the terrible repulse of his army on Friday, found the army of Gen. Couch and the late forces of Gen. Milroy in his rear, disputing not only his passage to the fords at Williamsport, but also to the upper fords in the vicinity of Hancock.—He consequently was compelled to retreat on the roads through Emmittsburg and Creagerstown, probably towards the South Mountain. He will there find to dispute his further progress to-day, Gen. French's force, a portion of Gen. Heinzelman's troops, and considerable reinforcements from Schenck's department.—Gen. Meade is also in close pursuit, and will reach Frederick this afternoon. The water in the Potomac is too high to ford with cannon or wagons, and it is more than probable that such portion of his army as escapes will be little more than a disorganized rabble.

POSTSCRIPT.

Just as we go to press we learn that the rebel retreat is towards Williamsport through Hagerstown, by several roads, and that Frederick and the South Mountain are held by a large Federal force. There is a probability of another battle at or near Antietam.

THE LATEST.

The following was obtained Monday morning from the Headquarters in Baltimore:

Advices from the army up to 2 P. M. on Sunday, July 5, state that Gen. Meade's headquarters would be at Creagerstown last night, and were to be in Frederick to-day.

Gen. Meade has telegraphed that Lee's army is retreating in wild confusion. Every available man in Baltimore and Washington is being hurried to Frederick to intercept Lee's flying and demoralized troops. A great battle will probably come off to-morrow, which will doubtless be a finality, as Gen. Meade's forces, reinforced by Generals Couch, Schenck, and Heintzelman, will be nearly double Lee's army.

Headquarters Army of the Potomac, July 6. The rebel General [illegible] was wounded, Gens. Johnston and Kemper are killed. General Farnsworth, of our cavalry, is killed. The rebel losses are estimated at 20,000. Our troops in excellent spirits.

Gen. Butterfield's wound is more severe than supposed, but not serious.

The rebels abandoned their wounded and killed.

[Lincoln has issued a congratulatory address to the country, and the *American* is jubilant at the narrow escape which Baltimore has made from the hands of the rebels]

LATEST FROM THE BATTLE-FIELD.

From parties who left the battle-field at 12 o'clock on Saturday morning, we gather the following particulars of the flight of the enemy:

The enemy is in full retreat, demoralized and almost disorganized, leaving in our hands his many thousands of killed and wounded.

The battle of Friday was the most terrible to the enemy of the three days' conflict, and his repulse so complete and disastrous that Gen. Meade and the leading officers pronounced it to be final and decisive.

Never was there a more vigorous and deadly assault than that made on our centre by Longstreet. It was a deadly struggle on the part of the enemy to break our lines, repeated and renewed a half dozen times during the afternoon, in which they were so often repulsed and driven back with a loss of life unparalleled by any previous battle in which they had come in conflict with the grand old Army of the Potomac.

Officers who have been taken prisoners admit that the loss of the enemy of those in high command is fully equal if not greater than we have sustained, but refuse to give the names of those who have fallen.

The men all felt that they had whipped the enemy, and the joy was great. The shouts of victory could be heard for many miles when the enemy retreated, and was kept up to a late hour of the night. A shout in one division was re-echoed from the next, and so went the rounds of the field, and was renewed as fresh evidence of victory reached them.

During the evening a flag of truce arrived from Gen. Lee, proposing, in his hypocritical manner, a truce of forty-eight hours, as a measure of humanity, to afford time to bury the dead and attend to the wounded.

It was evident that the enemy must at once retreat, and the proposition was regarded by Gen. Meade as a mere ruse to obtain time to push forward his trains towards the river and secure a line of escape. The proposition was promptly rejected, and an advance immediately ordered on the town of Gettysburg.

The enemy slowly retreated before our cavalry and infantry, and by midnight we were in full possession of the town and the battle-field without opposition. During the night scouts arrived reporting that the enemy was rapidly retreating by the Greencastle road towards Hagerstown, and preparations were at once made for a pursuit at daylight. Cavalry were also sent out to harass the enemy, and at daylight a vigorous attack was made on the enemy's rear guard, which in vain attempted to check the pursuit of the fleeing army.

The distance from Gettysburg to the Potomac is fully forty miles, and with the assistance of Gen. French and the old garrison at Harper's Ferry, numbering about 15,000 men, including most of the Maryland regiments, who are understood to be properly posted to check his flight, we have strong hopes of being able to so operate on the fleeing rebel columns as to send it across the Potomac a demoralized and disorganized mob.

Major-General Hancock is considered as the great hero of Friday's battle. His corps met the terrible assaults of the enemy without flinching, and though they lost heavily it fought nobly. When he fell severely wounded, the effect on his men was to give them renewed determination to conquer, and when they learned that their wounded commander was still watching them and directing their movements, they fought like demons and drove back the enemy, when he renewed the assault with the vigor of fresh troops, sending him back to his lines in such a crippled condition that all attempts to rally them again was futile.

Up to 12 o'clock on Saturday night the sound of cannon could be heard in the distance, as our pursuing columns attacked the enemy's rear, and thousands of prisoners and straggling rebels are coming towards Gettysburg, with captured wagons and cannon. In short, there was every evidence that our victory was as decisive as it was glorious—that the enemy was in disorganized flight, getting back to Virginia as rapidly as his worn-out limbs and shattered horse flesh would carry him. Whether he will make another stand on the road is yet to be ascertained.

The advance of Gen. Couch from Harrisburg was expected to be at Chambersburg on Saturday, close enough to join in punishing the well whipped rebels on their way to the river.

In the town of Gettysburg, when we drove the enemy out of it on Friday night, we recaptured a large number of Federal prisoners, reported by some as high as fifteen hundred, many of whom were wounded. There were also several thousand wounded rebels, every house being filled with them.

CITY OF MEXICO OCCUPIED BY GEN. FOREY.

New York, July 5.—The steamer Roanoke from Havana has arrived. Vera Cruz advices to the 16th ult. state that the French army occupied the city of Mexico on the 3d ultimo, and General Forey took possession on the 10th.

Juarez had retired to San Luis Potosi, and a French Division had been sent against that place. Forey was received with great enthusiasm. A French Marquis, who was wounded at Puebla, goes to Paris with the keys of the City of Mexico. Thirteen hundred prisoners, mostly Mexican officers, are about to be sent to France.

Commodore Wilkes arrived per Roanoke.

Com. Lardner has arrived at St. Thomas

The West India squadron is reported in a crippled condition, owing to defective boilers, etc.

The steamers Charleston, Sirus, Banshee, Lizzie, and Fannie, had arrived at Nassau from Wilmington.

The Flora, Calypso, and Ruby are reported captured.

The steamers Danube and Hebe are at Nassau, bound to a Southern port.

FROM VICKSBURG.

The *American* has Vicksburg advices to July 2d. The condition of affairs was unchanged, but Gen. Johnston was reported to be seriously threatening the enemy's rear.

THE FALL OF VICKSBURG.

FURTHER PARTICULARS.

JACKSON, July 7.—Vicksburg has fallen. It was surrendered on the morning of the 4th, the men being in a starving condition, and completely worn out with excessive fatigue.

The terms of capitulation were that the officers should be allowed their side-arms, horses, and all their private property. They and the men were paroled, and immediately allowed to march out with all their colors.

Immediately after the surrender Gen. Grant sent a boat load of supplies to the famished garrison. Some of the officers have arrived here.

[SECOND DISPATCH.]

JACKSON, July 7.—But little more is known of the fall of Vicksburg. Officers who have come out say that had Gen. Johnston reached there twelve days sooner he could not have relieved the garrison, as they could not muster over 7,000 men for duty. Many of the citizens were leaving with their families, negroes, stock, &c. The proprietors of the *Mississippian* are packing up their effects, type, &c., preparatory to leaving.

[THIRD DISPATCH.]

JACKSON, July 8.—Col. Montgomery, Aid to Gen. Pemberton, with 200 mounted men, arrived here to-day.

Gen. Green and Col. Irving, of Missouri, were killed by the enemy's sharpshooters.

Gen. Grant sent ten thousand men back, and about the same number to attack General Price.

Grant's force was near 100,000. He commands in person the forces which are marching on Jackson.

[FOURTH DISPATCH.]

JACKSON, July 8.—Everything here is in the wildest state of excitement. Citizens are flying in every direction, and the streets are filled with stock, negroes, &c. Families are leaving in ox-carts and every other species of conveyance.

There was a terrible storm here last night, with very heavy rains.

Citizens leaving beyond Clinton report that the enemy are burning every dwelling they pass.

A fight is hourly expected here.

[FIFTH DISPATCH.]

JACKSON, July 8.—Dispatches from Panola, the 7th, state that General Holmes attacked Helena on the 4th and captured three batteries. Reinforcements for the enemy arrived and five gunboats drove our forces back. Our loss was five hundred. Heavy firing was heard next day.

[SIXTH DISPATCH.]

NATCHEZ, July 6.—A transport, towing two barges loaded with coal, passed down this morning.

An officer on General Smith's staff reports that Gen. Price was ordered on Sunday, the 5th, to take Helena, Arkansas. He moved immediately.

Nothing from Port Hudson. All quiet

Brave and Able Defender of States' Rights in New York

A gentleman who has recently arrived from the North brings us, among other things, a number of a new monthly journal entitled "The Old Guard; a monthly journal, devoted to the principles of 1776 and 1787." It contains several able papers; among them, "How to Treat Unconstitutional Acts of Congress;" "The Administration as a Gold Gambler;" "Seward on Federal Usurpations and Despotism;" "Strength of Armies;" &c. In the article on "How to Treat Unconstitutional Acts of Congress," it counsels RESISTANCE. It declares that "when a free people submit to oppressive acts, passed in violation of their Constitution, for a single day, they have thrown down the palladium of their liberty; submit to despotism for an hour, and you concede the principle. John Adams said, in 1775, 'Nip the shoots of arbitrary power in the bud.' It is the only thing a people determined to be free can do. * * * It was the cowardice and treachery of the Senate of Rome that allowed the usurper to gain power, inch by inch, to overthrow the Repub-

The history of the downfall of Republics the same in all ages. The first inch that is yielded to despotism—the first blow dealt at Constitution, that is not resisted—is the beginning of the end of the nation's ruin." It advises appeal first to the Courts—the *State* Courts—against unconstitutional acts of Congress; but should they be struck down or suspended, "then *muscle* becomes the supreme law of the land. Then every man's own right [illegible] is not [illegible] the Government [illegible] *jure divino*."

The "Old Guard" is full of the true spirit of '76. It hesitates not to tell the Government and the people what the war has done for the North, as the following article, copied from it, shows:

HOW WE ARE REVENGING SUMTER.

The following are the reported casualties of this war from its beginning to January 1st, 1863:

Federals killed	43,874
" wounded	97,029
" died of disease and wounds	250,000
" made prisoners	68,218
Total	459,374
Confederates killed	20,893
" wounded	59,915
" died from disease and wounds	120,000
" made prisoners	22,169
Total	222,677

They have killed twenty-two thousand eight hundred and seventy four more of our men than we have of theirs.

They have wounded, not mortally, thirty-nine thousand four hundred and fourteen more of our men then we have of theirs.

One hundred and fifty thousand more of our men have died of disease and wounds than of theirs.

They have made prisoners of forty-six thousand more of our men than we have of theirs.

Our total casualties are two hundred and thirty-seven thousand two hundred and ninety seven more than theirs—that is, our casualties have been fourteen thousand more than as much again as theirs.

This is the way we have "revenged the firing on Fort Sumter."

But this is not all. We have spent almost *two thousand million* more of money than they have spent.

We have made two hundred thousand of our women widows.

We have made one million of children fatherless.

We have destroyed the Constitution of our country.

We have brought the ferocious savagery of war into every corner of society.

We have demoralized our pulpits, so that our very religion is a source of immorality and blood.

Instead of being servants of Christ, our ministers are servants of Satan.

The land is full of contractors, thieves, provost-marshals, and a thousand other tools of illegal and despotic power, as Egypt was of vermin in the days of the Pharoahs.

We are rapidly degenerating in everything that exalts a nation.

Our civilization is perishing.

We are swiftly drifting into inevitable civil war here in the North.

We are turning our homes into charnel houses.

There is a corpse in every family.

The angel of death sits in every door.

The devil has removed from Tartarus to Washington.

We pretend that we are punishing the rebels, but they are punishing us.

We pretend that we are restoring the Union, but we are destroying it.

We pretend that we are enforcing the laws, but we are only catching negroes.

That is the way we are "revenging Sumter."

Selling our souls to the devil and taking Lincoln & Co.'s *promise to pay* We have it in greenbacks and blood.

That is the way we are "revenging Sumter."

Palmerston, Russell, and Intervention.

Every arrival from Europe brings us a reiteration, in one form or another, from Palmerston, or Russell, or some less prominent member of the British Government, that they have no sort of intention of interfering between North and South, or in any way compromising their much cherished neutrality.—We really think they might spare their valuable breath. Who expects them to intervene? What living man in the South remains to be disabused of the delusion, once universal, that England would throw her weight in the scale of her own interests and of humanity. Our Commissioners abroad would do a valuable service if they would induce Palmerston & Co. to understand that the South needs no farther information of the intentions of Great Britain. We are no longer looking to that quarter for anything but covert hostility and practical co-operation with the North. Our attention is now directed to other nations, not with the expectation of immediate recognition, but of honest sympathy and of future amicable and advantageous relations in trade and commerce. If France could have freed herself from the trammels of British policy, she would long ago have recognized our independence. Spain is thoroughly with us in sympathy and domestic institution. Spain has the island of Cuba. France will soon have Mexico, in which, in all probability, she will one day find it to her interest to establish domestic slavery. There will then be three formidable empires—three neighborly, friendly and powerful nations—occupying the richest part of the continent of America, and bound to each other by the strongest ties of commercial interest, and of those lofty and chivalric sentiments which are the peculiar characteristics of each. A triple alliance, which will be able to take care of itself. The British Cabinet may spare themselves the trouble of defining afresh their position of neutrality with every steamer that comes to America. We concede the fact; we do not expect their assistance; with the aid of Heaven we can work out our own salvation, and when that is accomplished, and our brilliant prospects of nationhood, greatness and glory have burst into full splendor, we shall remember who it was that gave us the cold shoulder, and would neither herself recognize us nor permit other nations to do it.

A SCENE AT THE TUILERIES.—A correspondent of an English journal describes a scandalous scene which recently occurred during a ball at the Tuileries. A young nobleman, the Emperors leader of the cotillon, selected a young lady who had been the leading star of the ball to share with him the honors of his sovereignty, to the great mortification and vexation of another lady present, who in her day had been a beauty, had led the cotillon, and been proclaimed the star of fashion. It so happened that the seat occupied by this woman was absolutely necessary for the figure about to be danced, and her successful rival requested permission to occupy it. A curt refusal was the reply vouchsafed. "Then we must lessen the circle," replied Mademoiselle calmly, and her partner, procuring a chair, placed it directly before the female, who colored with rage and indignation, and the moment that Mademoiselle had seated herself began kicking her on the shins and pushing the chair with her knees, and, although requested to desist, only repeated the offensive treatment with more energy. The insulted belle appealed to M'lle Murat, who volunteered to exchange places, and was proceeding to occupy the obnoxious chair when it was kicked over the floor right into the middle of the cotillon! Of course the dance ceased at once, the Empress was informed of the circumstances, the offender's husband was sent for, and the irritated ex-beauty was escorted from the hall by her liege lord, bestowing as she went a most scornful glance upon her triumphant rival The next day the offending lady received her *disinvitation* for the Tuileries in due form, and, as it is the first time such a ceremony has been gone through, of course it has created no small sensation.

THE OCCUPATION OF THE CITY OF MEXICO BY THE FRENCH.—President Juarez and Cabinet moved from the City of Mexico to San Louis de Potosi, and the troops were withdrawn from the capital, on the 31st of May.—On the 5th of June the French occupied it:

The force that garrisoned the City of Mexico, said to number twenty thousand men, was withdrawn to the Cuernavaca plaza and to intermediate points around the city, for the purpose of carrying on guerilla warfare.

The whole French army was expected to occupy the capital on the 8th of June.

Three newspapers had been established favoring the policy of the French. One of these papers states that the occupation of the city of Mexico settles with absolute certainty that it is necessary to extirpate by the root the democratic element, and no longer need there be even a dream of popular sovereignty.

Gen. Forey has issued a decree confiscating the property of all parties who have been or are in arms against the French.

Gen. W. H. F. Lee, recently captured by the 11th Pennsylvania cavalry, has been removed to the McClellan Hospital at Hampton.

The Newburyport Herald.

VOL. LXVIII. NEWBURYPORT, (MASSACHUSETTS), FRIDAY MORNING, JULY 10, 1863. NO. 38

The Newburyport Herald,

PUBLISHED BY

WILLIAM H. HUSE & CO.,

OFFICE—No. 42 STATE STREET, NEWBURYPORT.

GEO. J. L. COLBY, EDITOR.

TERMS.

DAILY HERALD, - -	$5,00 per year
" " in advance, -	$4,50 per year
SEMI-WEEKLY HERALD, -	$3,50 per year

Advertisements not exceeding four lines, are inserted three times for 75 cents; six lines and upwards $1; (per square, 12 lines,) $1,50. Probate Notices, agreeably to the customary prices.

THE HERALD.

Wednesday Morning, July 8, 1863

Fall of Vicksburg!

The Most Important Victory of the War!

THE APPROACHING END OF THE REVOLUTION!

THE RESTORATION OF THE UNITED REPUBLIC

Now within the Power of Mr. Lincoln.

ENTHUSIASM IN NEWBURYPORT.

On Tuesday, when we had not yet done rejoicing over the victory in Pennsylvania, and were waiting each hour to hear what the telegraph should announce from the seat of war, we were surprised with the sudden announcement of the surrender of Vicksburg—the event having taken place on the glorious 4th of July, when also our army in the North were just resting with the laurels of Gettysburg on their banners. We say we were surprised; not that we doubted the fall of Vicksburg more than we do death for any mortal man, but we had waited for it so long, and it held out so strenuously—bravely we may add, and then do no more than justice to the enemy—that we had ceased calculating when it would yield. Suddenly also the news came to all the people; for no sooner did the telegraph operator announce it, than the town was wild with delight; every flag was raised; the crowd cheered in the streets; the bells were all rung six hours; India crackers and small arms were exploded more than on the last Independence day; the schools were at once dismissed that the youth might take part in the rejoicing; the artillery pieces, eight pounders, were hauled out, and from their brazen throats thundered the glad news, till the woods and hills back of us reverberated with their voices, and the echoes ran along the river banks and died away over the distant waves of the ocean; and in the evening the Herald office and other buildings were illuminated; while the rockets went shooting into the heavens, as if on the distant blue etherial space, that no mortal ever reached, they would write in burning letters, VICTORY, UNION, FREEDOM—words that in connection with America have thrilled the hearts of patriots over the world for three quarters of a century. And that we might have an idea of the military, and nothing might be wanted to make the occasion truly thrilling, soon were seen the Veteran Artillary and the City Cadets, with music, who, with an electrified multitude—some on horseback, many in vehicles, and more on foot—marched through the principal streets of the city, cheered by the huzzas of men, women and children, and the waving of handkerchiefs, banners and flags. Now let us stop to enquire, as yet the horses go prancing through the streets decorated with miniature flags; as yet the report of guns and the sound of drums, and the blowing of horns, and the voices of men grown hoarse with cheering, are in our ears, why it is that the surrender of Vicksburg causes all this; and that we declare it the great event of the war, and the harbinger of peace! Let us look! Let us reason!

Vicksburg is the heart of the Confederacy; it is there that the life-artery, the Mississippi, pours its tide; and so long as the rebels could hold Vicksburg, they could not be beaten. We might cut off Richmond and Virginia—those were but fingers; we might take Tennessee and drive them out of Kentucky, Missouri and Arkansas—those were but limbs; we might capture Charleston and Savannah and Mobile—those were but toes; Vicksburg was the great central pivot—the key of the Mississippi, the heart of the Confederacy. It was not alone important in location; but it was strong. Nature had fortified it; and military science had been exhausted to strengthen it. It is upon an upheaved bluff, that was surrounded with trenches, where one fortification overlooks another, like the seats of an amphitheatre; and the whole was shot proof and bomb proof, and bristled with guns and bayonets that stood brisk as feathers upon a porcupine. Jeff. Davis was not blind to its value, and had declared that it should be held to the last and defended by all the resources of rebeldom. He knew that while he held that the Northwest, cut off from its natural highway to the sea, must suffer, and could be kept in a state of semi-rebellion. He knew that while Vicksburg stood, cotton and [illegible] for success, was within his control. The fate of Vicksburg was made, in his mind, a type of the fate of the rebellion. So we see the foreign nations regarded it, and the Confederate loan was up or down as the prospect of holding or yielding the place varied.

Its military importance was a hundred fold greater than its commercial value. On the land the rebels have shown great strength, as on the waters they have displayed much weakness. In the field they approached an equality with us; but where our navy could go we have beaten them back and held their territory beyond recovery. The Mississippi will give our ships a short run through the confederacy, and it is equally adapted to military and naval uses. It divides the confederacy in two—cutting its backbone, and actually killing it in all those parts west of the river, while it allows us to surround and girdle the remaining portion. If there was no Mississippi, or they could hold it, the war might be continued indefinitely. They could fall back from State to State away down into Texas, the Indian districts, and Mexico; but now one half is paralyzed and dead, and our anaconda is around its living part, stopping the circulation necessary to its existence, leaving it as a tree girdled by the woodman's axe in the forest; and we may well believe the report that Jeff. Davis has sent messengers to Washington to negotiate for peace.

Let us repeat, that this is not alone an important victory commercially, as opening the storehouse of the Northwest and Southwest—not important simply because Vicksburg has strategic value, as Richmond or Washington have: it is a question of empire. Look on the map! When we have the Mississippi river, we have cut off from Jeff Davis as much territory as he has left east of the river. Louisiana, Texas, and Arkansas contain 332,000 square miles of territory. This is more than France, Great Britain and Ireland together; equal to Austria and Prussia. Texas is bigger than France; Arkansas is bigger than Naples; and Louisiana is bigger than Denmark and Belgium combined. If then we obtained only what is west of the river, it would be an empire in area; but it settles the whole thing, since it makes the future certain.

Now we have beaten the rebels out of Tennessee, out of Arkansas, out of Florida, out of the greater part of Virginia; out of half of North Carolina, and portions of South Carolina and Georgia and Louisiana, and killed the rebellion in Texas, which is isolated and alone, and what more remains to be done? We have scattered their army in the Southwest, beaten it in the Centre, routed and demoralized it in the East—what else remains to peace? One thing—only one thing—that we should follow up and capture Richmond, their capital, which they now hold weakly.—Then we shall be prepared to say to them—"Wayward sisters," return to the Constitution, and we will negotiate and honorably settle the whole trouble. When we were in defeat or without victory we could do no such thing. Now, if Mr. President Lincoln is up to the occasion, he will take the reins into his own hands, and by such a settlement of our difficulties as will be just and honorable, restore the nation; make himself the great man of the age, the friend of humanity and freedom in a practical sense, and force posterity to applaud him to the latest day of time. Now, if we have good management we may have unity and peace and returning prosperity before the snows of another winter come to us.

THE VICTORY IN PENNSYLVANIA is complete. We have not the official report, which will probably be given this day, and the telegraphic figures are very unreliable; but it is enough for us to know that the rebels are not only defeated but routed—thoroughly whipped. We have settled that the army of the Potomac was organized for defeat alone, though so often disaster has overtaken it, that Lee moved into the loyal States as carelessly and unconcernedly as though we had not a regiment or a gun. He has been awakened to his mistake. The war can not be transferred to the loyal States. That is the first thing settled; and no attempt will ever be made to that end again. Then we have shown our ability to drive them—we are driving them, scattering them, destroying them. All that remains is to follow up—for Meade's men to keep on their backs; the 30,000 about Washington to turn upon their flank, and Gen. Dix, if he can not take Richmond, and be in their front as they come down, to strike them above. There is no reason why that army should ever escape to Dixie; and we are now able to capture Richmond within thirty days. That is all we want for peace. Vicksburg will be ours; Tennessee is cleared of rebels; and North Carolina is not with them, so that they will be shoved into the Cotton States east of the Mississippi, and then we may offer them terms that will be gladly accepted, and the Union restored. This is a glorious day to that end; and if Gen. Meade proves to have Napoleonic qualities other glorious days are before us. Let the country rejoice in this hour of victory; and let the banners wave high over the ground already gained; and on the prospect before us.

MEETINGS ON THE 4TH. The Democrats had a great gathering at Concord, N. H., in favor of peace, or the restoration of the Union by means of peace. The "freemen in council" were estimated at 30,000; but we must allow something in this calculation for its being the 4th of July. Ex-President Pierce, Hon. Daniel W. Voorhees of Indiana, Hon. Amasa Parker of New York, Hon. John H. George of New Hampshire, and R. S. Spofford, Esq., of this city, were the speakers. The addresses were reported at length, but in the excitement over the news from the battle field, we have had no time to read them.

In Framingham, in this State, the Anti-Slavery Society had a gathering, Mr. Garrison presiding. He renewed his opposition to Mr. Conway's proposals to the rebel Mason, in London, and said he was for the government against slavery. The principal speech of the day was by Wendell Phillips, who was very severe on the administration—more so than was Frank Pierce or any of the copperheads at Concord. He said Mr. Lincoln, deluded by his own ambition and misled by artful counsellors, had made the government at Washington a national committee, to manage the next Presidency, and to carry on the war subordinate to the chances of a certain party to the Presidency. Mr. Postmaster Blair had approached Mr. Senator Wilson, weeks ago, and asked if it was not time to put Mr. Lincoln in nomination. He denounced Mr. Blair's speech, recently made at Concord, which he called Lincoln's bid for the Presidency. He said Blair was the boldest liar on the continent; Washington was the greatest obstacle to the success of the Union; and the drunkenness of Hooker was nothing compared with Lincoln. Next, Mr. Garrison introduced an Englishman, Mr. Evans, whose remarks were criticised by Charles L. Remond, whose speech Garrison denounced as mean and contemptible; upon which Mr. Remond did not grow pale but roared in rage. Stephen S. Foster made a speech in opposition to the war. He had no choice between the government of Jeff Davis and Abraham Lincoln; they were both fighting for slavery. He had discouraged enlistments, and should do so. He hoped Gen. Lee would succeed in Pennsylvania, and take New York and Boston, and the North be brought to starvation till universal emancipation was proclaimed. War is of the devil, and if followed up will lead to hell.

[illegible] display of rowdyism and reckless outrages. Persons who should know better, or be punished till they learn, went about destroying property and endangering lives. Into a sleeping room in the house of John G. Pearson, Bromfield street, they fired a charge of shot; Edmund Jaques, in Purchase street, had a door fired into; Capt Bogardus' door was served the same way; Enoch Jaques had widow stove by discharge of gun; in the store of J. A. Cooke, a window was served in like manner; in house of George Fitz, Merrimack street, glass was broken and door stove in; Stephen Caldwell, on High street, had glass broken; in store of Joseph Moulton & Henry Frothingham, 30 or 40 panes were smashed by cannon firing. Many other buildings were no better treated; gates were unhung; blinds broken; and fences njured.

A BALLOON ASCENSION was made from Boston, July 4th by Mr. J. B. Stears, (Superintendent of the Fire) Alarm, went up alone and came down on the evening in the woods near South Andover. The balloon was nearly exhausted of gas, and on approaching *terra firma*, he threw out his grapnel, which caught in the top of a tree. He then descended the rope and was making his way down the tree, when he found that the balloon lightened by the loss of weight, was in danger of being blown away by the wind. He accordingly fastened the rope as he thought securely, to the tree but was disconcerted and surprised soon after to find the balloon breaking from its fastenings and making off. The balloon finally came down in a good state of preservation in East Salisbury, about three miles from here.

FEDERAL LOSSES in the late battle were very heavy The Tribune correspondent gives the total of the 11th corps at 4060; of the 1st corps 5000; and of the 12th corps 1215.

The Battles at Gettysburg,

The Battle of Thursday.

The following brief but comprehensive report of the battle at Gettysburg, Pa., on Thursday last, is from the special dispatches sent to the New York Times from the field of battle:

"This (Thursday) morning there were strong premonitions of an early engagement with the enemy in force, but the day wore away and no positive exhibition was made by the enemy. We began to think that perhaps there would be no immediate battle after all. We were hardly in a condition to give battle, as all our dispositions to give battle had not been made, Gen. Meade not having arrived on the ground until 2 o'clock in the morning. The position of our forces after the fight of Wednesday was to the eastward and southward of Gettysburg, covering the Baltimore pike, the Tanneytown and Emmetsburg roads, and still being nearly parallel with the latter. The formation of the ground on the right and left was excellent for defensive purposes. On our extreme left the ground sloped off until the position was no higher than that of the enemy's. The ground in front of our line was a level open country, interspersed here and there with an orchard or a very small tract of timber, generally oak, with the underbrush cut away. During the day a portion of the troops threw up temporary breastworks and an abattis: Gen. Meade's headquarters were at an old house on the Tanneytown road, immediately in rear of the centre.

Our line was not regular in shape. Indeed the centre protruded out towards the enemy so as to form almost two sides of a triangle. Before sundown Gen. Meade's headquarters proved to be the hottest place on the battle field, so far as careless shelling was concerned.

Gen. Howard occupied with his corps a beautiful cemetery on a hill to the south of Gettysburg. Cannons thundered, horses pranced, men carelessly trampled over the remains of the dead. From this hill a beautiful view could be obtained of the valley, and also of a goodly portion of the enemy's line of battle.

Our forces had all been concentrated on Tuesday night save the Fifth and Sixth corps. The former arrived during the morning, and the latter soon afternoon. They were all massed immediately behind our centre.

Whether or not it was Gen. Meade's intention to attack I cannot say, but he was hardly ready for it before the afternoon of yesterday. The day had become almost dull. Skirmishing was now and then brisk, and the sharpshooters in the steeples and belfreys of the churches blazed away at officers and artillery horses. It was by a sharpshooter in a barn just opposite Wadsworth Division yesterday that Captain Stevens of the Fifth Maine Battery got hit. A bullet passed through both legs below the knee, inflicting a severe but not dangerous wound.

At 3 1 2 o'clock Gen. Meade had received sufficient assurances to justify him in the belief that the rebels were concentrating their forces on our left flank, which all felt to be secure under the protection of the invincible Third Corps. Our line was immediately strengthened on that flank. Gen. Sickles corps being sent to its support, and several batteries from the reserve being brought out and placed in position.

At about 4 1-2 o'clock P. M. the enemy sent his first compliments by a salvo of artillery, his first shells falling uncomfortably near Gen. Meade's headquarters.—From this hour forth to 8 1-2 o'clock, occurred by all odds one of the most sanguinary engagements yet chronicled in the annals of the war, considering its short duration. The artillery attack, which was made by the enemy on the left and centre, was rapidly followed by the advance of his infantry The third corps received the attack with great coolness. The rebels at once made for our flank, and kept moving heavy columns in that direction. This necessitated support, which was quickly given by the fifth corps, the division of Gen. Barnes being sent to the right, and that of Gen. Ayres, regulars, to the left, with Gen. Crawford in reserve.

The battle now became perfectly fearful. The armies engaged each other at very short range, and for three long hours the war of musketry was incessant. I have heard more noise and louder crashes in other battles, but I never saw or heard of such desperate, tenacious fighting as took place on this flank. The enemy would often bring up suddenly a heavy column of men, and force our line back, only to be in turn forced back by our own line of glittering steel. Our gallant columns covered themselves with glory over and over again. They fought a superior force in numbers. The dispositions of the enemy were very rapid, for look where you would on that field a body of rebels would be advancing. Our dispositions were equally rapid, and the enemy found more than their equal in such gallant veterans as Sickles, Birney and Humphreys. At half past 5 o'clock Gen. Sickles was struck in the right leg by a piece of shell and borne from the field. The injury was so great that amputation became necessary, and it was performed successfully, the limb being taken off below the knee.

The struggle grew hotter and hotter. The Second corps was called on for aid, and though its own position was strongly threatened, yet the First division, formerly Gen. Hancock's, flung themselves into the fight with desperation, and after a long and obstinate conflict the enemy slowly and sullenly gave way. In this last charge the brigade of Gen. Caldwell, Second corps, and that of Col. Switzer from the Fifth corps, won great honors. The charges made by our men deserve special mention. The rebels made frequent attempts to capture our artillery, and at one time had Watson's battery in their possession, but it was retaken in a furious charge by Birney's division.

The battle lasted till fully 8 1-2 o'clock, when the enemy fell back to his old position, and left our veterans the ensanguined victors of the field. Our pickets were thrown out, and our lines covered most of the field, including a great number of the enemy's dead and wounded.

I visited some portions of the line by moonlight and can bear personal witness to the terrible ferocity of the battle. In front of some of our bridges, who had good protection from stone walls or fences, the rebel dead laid piled in lines like winrows of hay. In front of Gen. Webb's—the Philadelphia—brigade, they lay so thick as to literally cover the ground. Not far from here was found the body of Gen. Barksdale, that once haughty and violent rebel, who craved as a dying boon a cup of water and a stretcher from an ambulance boy. He is literally cut to pieces with wounds, and must die.

A great and magnificent feature of this fight was the splendid use of artillery. Though our line of battle was only a mile and a half long, yet almost every battery belonging to the Army of the Potomac was more [illegible] numerous. The enemy also used artillery largely, but not so near so great an extent as we did. From this they suffered immensely, and specially on the left, where canister was largely used. I believe we lost no artillery, unless it was two or three disabled pieces, though it was very wonderful we did not."

The Battle of Friday.

Headquarters Army of the Potomac, July 3. The decisive battle has been fought to-day and the enemy have been repulsed with terrific loss.

At daylight Lee's right wing batteries opened upon our left, and shortly after those of his centre followed. After half an hour's cannonading, doing but little damage to us, the fire slackened and only occasionally shots were exchanged. Shortly afterward the enemy's left, composed entirely of infantry and sharpshooters, made an attack on the right wing. So sudden and impetuously was it accomplished that our skirmishers and front line were driven back from their intrenchments, but by the aid of the batteries in the rear and the indomitable bravery of the 12th corps, we regained the first position, capturing a considerable number of prisoners. Several hours of ominous silence followed this repulse.

At one o'clock the enemy fired two shots, apparently as signals for the grandest artillery fight ever witnessed on this continent. Before a moment had elapsed it is estimated that at least 80 guns opened upon us. Our batteries returned the compliment with interest. The air seemed literally filled with iron, and for more than an hour it seemed impossible that man or beast could live through it. Strange to say, the enemy's accuracy of range, as exhibited on the two previous days, was wanting on this occasion, most of their shells exploding far in the rear of our batteries. Under cover of this, Lee advanced his columns of infantry and made several desperate attempts to carry the lines by assault, but each successive attempt was repulsed with terrible havoc to the rebel ranks. After an hour's incessant cannonading the fire grew less intense for a short time, but was again renewed for a little while with great slaughter.

During this period some of our batteries, whose ammunition being expended and the men exhausted, ceased to fire, and, on the approach of the reserve batteries, withdrew to the rear. The enemy only seeing the batteries withdrawing, and mistaking this for a retreat, made a rapid infantry charge up the hill, and obtained a position in our line, cutting to pieces and annihilating the small infantry supports; but before they had time to rejoice at their imaginary success the batteries poured in a deadly fire of canister and case shot. The infantry reserves joined on either flank of the gap, charged them and added greatly to their destruction. They were completely surprised, and hundred's threw down their arms and asked for quarter. Nearly the entire brigade of Gen. Garnett surrendered, and Garnett himself was badly wounded and barely escaped.

About 4:30 P. M., the artillery of the enemy slackened and had entirely ceased at 5 o'clock, the last shots they fired being far beyond their original position, and the infantry columns had withdrawn to their covers.

So terrific was the enemy's fire, that the small house where Gen. Meade and staff were quartered was perforated by several shots. Many of the staff horses were killed around the house.

Too much credit cannot be given to our batteries, who for hours stood at their guns under a boiling sun, and surrounded by the missiles of death, retiring only to give their positions to others, when their caissons and limbers were out of ammunition.

The infantry engaged also nobly did their duty, and the enemy to-day at their hands have received the greatest disaster ever administered by the Union forces. All the officers award the highest honors to General Meade for the able generalship he displayed since he assumed command, and particularly for his coolness' decision and energy of this memorable 3d of July.

Later and Better.

12,000 WOUNDED REBELS IN OUR HANDS—IMMENSE NUMBER OF DESERTERS COMING IN.

New York, July 6.—A Bridgeport, Pa., despatch says: We have the most favorable reports as to the movements of Meade's army, and the command which has gone out to gobble up the enemy.

A Harrisburg despatch to the Herald, dated 5th, says: The Surgeon General here has information of 12,000 rebel wounded in our hands.

Gen. Smith has captured 400 stragglers. 1300 paroled prisoners passed through here to day, among whom were many wounded officers. Troops continue to arrive, and Pennsylvania has 60,000 men in the field.

HEADQUARTERS Army of the Potomac, July 5.

The rebel Gen. Pender is wounded. Gens. Kuiper and Johnson, rebels, are killed. Gen. Farnsworth of our cavalry is killed. The rebel losses are estimated at 20,000. Our troops are in the highest spirits. Gen. Butterfield's wound is more severe than was expected, but not serious. The rebels abandoned their killed and wounded.

The New York Times has the following special despatch, dated Harrisburg, July 5: The city to-day has been jubilant over the news received from the Army of the Potomac.

This afternoon Gov. Curtin received a despatch from Philadelphia, confirming the report that Meade had captured 25,000 prisoners and 118 pieces of artillery, and a pontoon bridge at Williamsport.

One thousand paroled Union prisoners came in from Gettysburg to-day, and were sent to Philadelphia.

Deserters from the rebel army are coming in from all quarters.

The New York Times says the contents of Jeff. Davis' despatches to Lee, captured Thursday, are in substance a peremptory order to withdraw from Pennsylvania, an order for his transportations to fall back to Hagerstown forthwith, assigning as a reason that Lee's position is too hazardous, and the condition of Richmond too defenceless to warrant remaining any longer. That the advantages to be gained were not sufficiently great to compensate for the risk run, &c. Also refuses Lee's request to allow Beauregard to reinforce him, and orders him south of the Potomac forthwith.

Gen. Hancock, whose corps defended our centre, was thanked by Gen. Meade in the name of the army and country.

At 7 o'clock Friday morning, the 3d and 6th corps attacked the enemy's right, gaining a good deal of ground. Our cavalry to-day, 4th, is playing savagely on the rebel flank and rear.

The Times' correspondent says, Gibbon's division captured fourteen stand of colors. The 2d corps captured twenty-eight stand of colors.

Col. Ward, 25th Mass., is killed. Prisoners state that the rebel General Hood is killed. In front of Gen. Gibbon's division not less than one thousand dead and wounded lay in the space of less than four acres.

At daylight, Saturday morning, excepting a small force of sharpshooters, the rebel infantry was wholly out of sight.

Lieut. Ropes, 20th Mass and Col. Devereaux, 15th Mass., are among the killed. Major Marcy, 25th Mass., hand shot off.

A Littletown despatch dated 5th says the enemy are moving South, our army was also moving in the same direction. Much firing was heard in the direction of Hagerstown, and it was thought our flying artillery had attacked the rebel wagon train.

NEAR GETTYSBURG, July 5.

The rebels have retreated towards the Potomac.—Their skirmishers were driven in last night and a small cavalry force, probably their rear guard, passed through Emmetsburg about daylight this morning.—Our troops have been engaged all day in burying the dead, relieving the wounded and collecting small arms, many thousands of which belonged to the rebels.

The rebel pontoon bridge at Dam No. 4, has been destroyed by our cavalry almost unopposed, and our cavalry had at last advices, gone up to Williamsport to destroy two bridges there.

Other preparations are in progress to intercept Lee's passage of the Potomac, and our army is already in motion. So much time, however, has elapsed since Gen. Lee commenced to withdraw his forces from our front, his advance may have reached Williamsport before we can prevent it Gen. Lee yesterday paroled about 2000 Federal prisoners.

The enemy kept up a constant fire, more severely than before as they have a better range of the town.

CAVALRY FIGHT.

Hanover, Pa., July 5. There was a cavalry fight to-day, four miles south of Gettysburg, between our forces and the rear of Lee's army, which is now supposed to be on the retreat to Hagerstown.

Our cavalry continued to bring in large numbers of rebel prisoners.

GENERAL ORDER OF THE COMMANDING GENERAL.

HEADQUARTERS ARMY OF THE POTOMAC,

General Order No. 68. The Commanding General in behalf of the country, thanks the Army of the Potomac for the glorious results of the recent operations Our enemy, superor in numbers and flushed with the pride of successful invasion, attempted to overcome or destroy this army. Baffled and defeated, he has now withdrawn from the contest. The privations and fatigue the army have endured, and the heroic courage and gallantry it displayed, will be matters of history to be ever remembered.

Our task is not yet accomplished, and the Commanding General looks to the army for greater efforts to drive from our soil every vestige of the presence of the invader.

It is right and proper that we should, on suitable occasions, return our grateful thanks to the Almighty Dispenser of Events, that in the goodness of His providence He has thought fit to give victory to the cause of the just.

By command of
Major General MEADE.

S. WILLIAMS, A. A. G.

INDIAN TROUBLES IN THE NORTHWEST.

New York, July 5. The Mercury has a special despatch, dated Des Moines, Iowa, July 4th, which says the Indians on the border are aroused to terrible action, and the excitement is momentarily increasing. I have direct and reliable information from the border that no less than 30,000 red skins, principally Sioux, have attacked the Pawnee agency on the Platte river. They are said to have fought like devils. I am unable to give the result, although I understand that many of our men who defended the place were killed and a number wounded Lieut. Col. Pollock of the 6th Iowa regiment, with the second batallion of that regiment, started from Fort Randolph a few days since for Devil's Lake, where the Indians are said to be congregated in considerable numbers. A fight is also anticipated there, and warm times are expected. The Indians are bent on rapine, and thoroughly organized.

CAPTURE OF REBEL STEAMERS.

Washington, July 5. Capt. Marchand, of the U. S. steamer Lackawana, reports to the Navy Department, under date of June 14th, that at daylight the previous morning, while at anchor off Mobile, a black smoke was seen from a steamer, and by a signal from the senior officer, gave chase, gaining gradually upon the vessel. She was kept in sight until 2 o'clock on the morning of the 14th, when it became quite dark and sight of her was lost. At daylight she was again discovered, eight miles distant, and notwithstanding the exertions she made to escape, by frequently changing her course, burning oily substances in her furnace, throwing overboard her cargo, &c., the Lackawana gained upon and nearing she hoisted the British ensign and did not stop her engines until several shots were fired. She was a fast vessel and the Lackawana had to run 109 miles before she was captured, which took place lat. 25 42, lon. 85 32 W. She was found to be the iron paddle wheel steamer Neptune of Glasgow, bound from Havana to Mobile. During the chase most of her cargo was thrown overboard as well as the mail and the principal part of the ship's papers.

Another report from Capt. Marchland, dated at sea June 5th says at 9 o'clock this morning, on the return of the ship towards Mobile, in company with the steamer Neptune, the black smoke of a steamer was seen ahead, for which this ship gave chase. She was not brought to until a shot struck her, which did not injure her, and she was captured after a chase of 26 miles. She was the rebel steamer Planter, of Mobile of 313 tons, and left Mobile Bay on the 13th for Havana, with a cargo of 625 bales of cotton and 125 barrels of rosin. During the chase between 60 and 80 bales of cotton were thrown overboard, and several barrels of rosin were burned.

Lieut. Commanding Baton, of the U. S. steamer Circassian, reports to the Navy Department, dating off New Orleans, June 23d, the capture of the rebel sloop John Wesley, which had evaded the blockade of St. Marks, Fla., on the 13th ult., and was bound to Havana laden with cotton. She was sent to Key West for abjudication.

Twice the bells of Newburyport have been ringing for Federal victories during the war—once when Donelson fell, and news of the capture of Vicksburg. In both instances Gen. Grant was the hero.

BY TELEGRAPH.

FROM GEN. ROSECRAN'S ARMY.

Tullahoma, July 4. The telegraph wires have been extended to this place. The following is a summary of the movements of the last three days: Further developments proved that the rebel retreat from this place had not been so clear as my first dispatches indicated. Haste to record the event induced me to give but a superficial examination. The works are much stronger than I supposed. The real weakness of Bragg was in not holding Manchester. As soon as General Rosecrans took Manchester and advanced towards Winchester, he flanked an equal or inferior force at Tullahoma. As soon as the head of the column got south of Tullahoma, Bragg evacuated. Instead of one we have four siege guns, a large amount of meal and other provisions.

After finding on the 1st inst. that Tullahoma was evacuated, Gen Rosecrans threw foward his force in rapid pursuit, Gen. Thomas taking the Manchester road from Manchester, and Mc Cook on the road from Tullahoma. Gen. Thomas moved rapidly in hope of striking the enemy, moving nearly east to get on the military road built by Bragg. This General Thomas waited to do until the enemy was well beyond the angle, and when he was crossing the Elk river. The division of Gen. Negley encountered the rear of Hardee at a point about four miles north of Elk river, and skirmished with it all day, losing four or five killed and wounded. Among the prisoners was Lieut. Platt of the 11th Michigan.

The rebels rear guard under Wheden made a stubborn resistance delaying Gen. Negley so that the rebel trains got beyond the river during the raid of the 1st. This same process on the part of Gen. Buckner enabled Bragg without reserve artillery, twenty-six pieces, to cross Elk river, and to reach the mountains. The enemy burnt the bridges and took up their pontoon bridges, so as to delay our advance. To aid them in this very heavy rains came up and the river rose very high.

The situation on the night of the 1st is—McCook at Eastern Springs, with Buckner opposite the floods: Thomas and point two miles up the river, with the enemy on the opposite bank.

The main body of the rebels was in the vicinity of Winchester and Dechard, ready to move into the mountains.

Gen. Crittenden, with a full corps, was sent by a rapid march to take possession of the road, leading from Dechard via Tracy City to Chatanooga. This was successful, and forced the enemy to take roads across the mountains.

On the morning of the 2d, McCook crossed the river below the enemy's position in front on our right and thus flanked the enemy, who withdrew to the mountains. At the upper bridges where Negley was posted a similar move was made with little success.—Rosseau and Brannan were sent to the upper crossing to come down on the rear of the enemy, whom Negley was to detain not drive. It was thought that Rosseau could cross by ten A. M., but the swollen stream prevented, and only a few troops got across in time. In the meantime acavalry brigade came in upon the right flank of the enemy. The firing was mistaken for that of Rosseau's and Gen. Negley poored with two batteries on the enemy, dismounting one gun and killing several rebel gunners.

They were taken completely by surprise and made but few replies, retreating precipitately. In the mean time Turchin had engaged the rebel right, and after a fight of two hours drove the entire rebel force from the field, killing 35 of them. The fight only ended at 2 P. M. The troops were unable to cross until the morning of the 3d. They moved only a short distance. Negley encamping on the battlefield, and Rosseau and Brannan on the river bank. McCook in the meantime advanced to occupy Winchester, Dechad and Cowan.

This morning, the whole force marched to the foot of the mountain at Cowan, to find the enemy gone.—We lost not over 1100 men by casualties of all kinds. The troops suffered much by heat and rain. We have from 1500 to 2000 prisoners, many of them deserters. The enemy is entirely out of Tennessee, and our communications are intact. The railroad will be running to this point to-morrow.

THE VICE PRESIDENT OF THE REBEL COFFEDERACY DESIRES AN INTERVIEW WITH PRESIDENT LINCOLN.

New York, July 7. The Herald publishes the following from its Washington correspondent:—

News of a most important character has reached us [illegible] ment, Alexander H. Stevens, and Mr. Commissioner Ould came down the James river on board of the rebel gunboat Dragon on Saturday, under a flag of truce, and requested permission of Admiral Lee to proceed to Washington in order to present in person an important communication from Jeff. Davis to President Lincoln. Admiral Lee at once despatched to Washington for instructions.

A Cabinet Council was accordingly held yesterday morning, and it was decided that permission should not be granted to these gentlemen to fulfil their mission, whatever it was, to Washington. Admiral Lee was instructed to inform them that the ordinary channels of communication would suffice for the transmission of any message they might have to send to Mr. Lincoln.

FROM NEW ORLEANS.

Fortress Monroe, July 6. The steamer Cahawba, Capt. Barker, arrived this A. M. from New Orleans, July 1, freighted with cotton and sugar for New York. She also brought 480 rebel prisoners, which she landed here. She reports the bombardment of Port Hudson when she left.

Our steamers are running up the river regularly with Gen Banks' suppplies. There is no truth in the report of his sapplies being cut off.

Great confidence is expressed that Port Hudson will soon fall. Deserters are daily coming into Gen. Banks' lines from the army.

The steamer John A. Warner arrived from City Point to-day.

LOUISVILLE, KY., AGAIN THREATENED.

Louisville, July 7. The alarm bells are now ringing, calling the citizens together for the defence of the city. Rumors were prevalent of the approach of Gorman's forces. They were reported at Bardstown yesterday morning, and at Shepperdsville yesterday afternoon. His force is estimated at fron 2 to 4000.

Last evening at 5 o'clock the Nashville train due at 6, was thrown off the track by guerrillas. A guard of 50 repulsed the assailants. It is impossible, during the present excitement, to get further news till morning.

THE SURRENDER of VICKSBURG.

Washington, July 7—1 P. M. The following despatch has been received:—

U. S. Squadron, Flag-Ship Black Hawk,
July 4th, 1863.

To Hon. Gideon Welles: Sir—I have the honor to inform you that Vicksburg has surrendered to the United States forces on this Fourth of July.

Very respectfully your obedient servant,
(Signed) D. D. PORTER,
Acting Rear Admiral.

PARTICULARS OF THE SURRENDER.

Cairo, July 7. The despatch boat has just arrived from Vicksburg.

She left at 10 o'clock on Sunday morning.

The passengers announce that Gen. Pemberton sent a flag of truce on the morning of the 4th, and offered to surrender if his men were allowed to march out.

Gen. Grant is reported to have replied that no man should leave except as prisoners of war.

Gen. Pemberton then after consultation with his officers unconditionally surrendered.

This news is perfectly reliable.

MOVEMENTS OF THE REBEL ARMY. ALL QUIET AT GETTYSBURG. THE BATTLE-FIELD CROWDED WITH VISITORS. BATTLE BETWEEN GEN. BUFORD AND GENERAL STUART.

New York, July 7. The Herald's Baltimore despatch, says that Gen. Ewell died yesterday from wounds.

A special despatch to the Herald, dated Bedford, July 6, states that Gen. Fitzhugh Lee, with three brigades of cavalry, comprising the first division of Gen. Stuart's cavalry corps, was at Greencastle at one P. M. to-day. The force numbers about 2000 men.—A regiment or brigade left this afternoon, in the direction of Mercersburg, and another portion proceeded towards Hagerstown, where Gen. Pierce, of the 12th Pennsylvania cavalry, is ready for them. The rebels are seeking for a ford on the Potomac, but they will find themselves checkmated at every point. The firing heard to-day indicates a running fight, and it is believed that Pleasanton is operating successfully on the rebel left wing. The enemy is evidently anxious to escape, but as the roads are in a very bad condition it is quite probable that we can pursue with effect with our cavalry at least from several points.

There was a battle near Mercersburg this afternoon between the rebels under Fitzhugh Lee and General Pierce's forces. Firing continued up to 9 o'clock to-night.

South Mountain, south of Carlisle, July 6. Last night and this morning there was fighting in the vicinity of Cashtown.

Everything was quiet in Gettysburg at 10 to-day. At that time our forces were there. The place was crowded with visitors to the battle-field.

Our forces are passing from many different points to cut off Lee's retreat, and co-operating with General Meade. The victory is not only glorious—it will be decisive. The Potomac is swelling rapidly.

Gen. Stoneman has been ordered immediately to join the army of the Potomac, to take a cavalry command.

Frederick, Md., July 6. Gen. Buford had a fight with Stewart in the vicinity of Boonsboro', whipping him badly. Our loss is very slight, and that of the rebels heavy.

Rebel deserters represent them as dispirited and out of ammunition. It is believed they will endeavor to cross at Williamsport and Shepperdstown.

Gettysburg, July 5.—2 P. M. A despatch from the advance says the rebels are rapidly retreating. We are moving all our sick and wounded into town.

4 P. M.—The 12th Corps is moving in haste toward Williamsport, to cut off the retreat of the rebels. Our left wing has just received marching orders. Part of Pleasanton's cavalry and artillery is in motion toward Frederick.

Chambersburg, July 6. It was Gen. Longworthy and not Longstreet that was killed.

Our scouts report that Gen. Lee is straining every nerve to gain a strong position in the South Mountain Gap. He is on the country roads, which are almost impassable, and his men and animals are much exhausted. Another battle is imminent.

The iron bridge at Harper's Ferry is so far destroyed as to be impassable for the retreating rebels.

ADDITIONAL PARTICULARS OF THE RETREAT OF GEN. LEE.

Geitisburg, July 6. A special despatch to the New York Times. Reports from the front are very cheering. Our cavalry supported by infantry are close upon the heels of the enemy, and important results are likely to occur before night.

A despatch from Gen. Gregg, this morning, reports the rebels instead of going to Chambersburg, are pushing to Greencastle.

Maj. Gen. Trimble is a prisoner in our lines, his left foot gone.

Brig. Gen. Kemper is a prisoner, and in a dying condition.

The enemy are known to have gained the trestle bridge just built across the Potomac above Williamsport; if so, I fear, their main force may escape.

THE NINETEENTH REGIMENT, that never fails to do its part in any fight, has taken four stands of colors at Gettysburg. The following are some of the casualities in the 19th Mass:

Lieut. Col. A. D. Wass, Major E. Rice wounded.

Co. A—Sergeant S. S. Robinson, killed; Sergeant G. Griffin, killed; Corporal C. L. Noyes, wounded, slight; M. Scammell, slight; D. Shaiwood, slight; W. Edwards, severe.

Co. B—Corp. P. Scammell, killed; A. Goodwin, wounded severe; C. H. Porter, missing.

Co. C—Lieut. J. Donash killed; Sergeant. J. H. Harvey, killed; Capt. W. L. Palmer, wounded, slight; Sergt. S. Armitage, slight; A. Rogers, slight; G. E Bird, slight; J. H. Worthend, missing.

By an act of our last State Legislature, every town in the Commonwealth is to provide for it, from the State Department, a printed blank book, in which is to be recorded the name of every recruit furnished by the town to serve in the war of the Rebellion of 1861—his age; place of birth; time of enlistment; time of service; regiment; company, trade; condition in life; rank in his company; promotion, if any; wounds; date of death, if killed—in short, a complete sketch, in carefully digested tabular form, of every man or boy, serving on land or sea, furnished by the State.—These books, some three hundred in number, of various sizes, according to the size of the town, are now completed, and about to be distributed to the several towns. When properly filled out and deposited in the town archives, what a valuable and interesting [illegible] 63 and— It is easy to conceive of the eagerness and pride with which men will trace back their descent from some humble corporal in the great army of the second war of independence. [Salem Gazette.

A letter from Port Hudson, in the Journal, contains the following paragraph relative to a Salem woman, the daughter of an old sea captain, and now the wife of Charles Martin of Newburyport:—

OUR FLORENCE NIGHTINGALE. Mrs. Charles Martin, wife of the Hospital Steward of the Fourth Mass. Battery, has enshrined her memory in the hearts of hosts of our wounded boys by her untiring efforts in the care of the wounded of Augur's division, from the commencement of the assault till the last wounded man was removed to the general hospital at Baton Rouge. No voice is so soothing, no touch so magnetic as that of woman to the sick or wounded soldier. God bless this noble woman. May happiness and joy ever follow her, even as do the prayers of hundreds of soldiers whom she cared for with a mother's devotion and a sister's tenderness.

FIFTY THOUSAND NEW MADE FREEMEN. By a decree of the government of Holland, fifty thousand slaves in Dutch Guiana are made freemen to-day.—What a contrast to the terrible scenes now enacting in this country, where one-third of the people are drenching the land in blood for the purpose of riveting more securely the shackles on four millions of slaves!

The barracks which were burnt at Carlisle, Pa, by the rebels, have a historic memory attached to them. They were built in 1777, chiefly by a number of Hessians, made prisoners at Trenton. Major Andre was for some time held there as a prisoner of war, and Washington had his headquarters there, 1794, during the whiskey insurrection. Nothing but the walls of the old structure are now left standing.

An exchange says that somebody was kicked out of an editorial room the other day for impudently stating "that he had seen in Germany a fiddle so large that it required two horses to draw the bow across the strings, which would continue to sound six weeks."

HAIR DYE. HAIR DYE.

BATCHELOR'S Celebrated Hair Dye

IS THE BEST IN THE WORLD!

The only Harmless, True and Reliable Dye known.

This splendid Hair Dye is Perfect—changes Red, Rusty or Grey Hair, instantly to a Glossy Black or Natural Brown, without Injuring the Hair or Staining the Skin leaving the Hair Soft and Beautiful; imparts fresh vitality frequently restoring its pristine color, and rectifies the ill effects of Bad Dyes. The Genuine is signed WILLIAM A. BATCHELOR, all others are mere imitations, and should be avoided. Sold by all Druggists, &c. FACTORY—81 BARCLAY-ST., N. Y.

Batchelor's New Toilet Cream for Dressing the Hair.

Je24 d&sw—1

MEN WANTED FOR THE INVALID CORPS.

Provost Marshal's Office,

FIFTH CONGRESSIONAL DISTRICT,

54 Washington Street.

SALEM, June 18th, 1863.

Only those faithful soldiers, who from wounds or the hardships of war, are no longer fit for active field duty will be received in this Corps of Honor. Enlistments will be for three years unless sooner discharged. Pay and allowances same as for officers and men of the United States Infantry; except that no premiums or bounty for enlistment will be allowed. This will not invalidate any pensions or bounties which may be due for previous services

The following uniform has been adopted for officers and men of the Invalid Corps:

FOR OFFICERS—Frock Coat—of sky blue cloth, with dark-blue velvet collar and cuffs; in all other respects, according to the present pattern for officers of Infantry.

Shoulder Straps—According to present regulations, but worked on dark-blue velvet.

Pantaloons—Of sky-blue cloth, with double stripe of dark-blue cloth down the outer seam, each stripe one-half inch wide, with space between of three-eighths of an inch.

Forage Cap—Present regulation.

FOR ENLISTED MEN,—Jacket—Of sky-blue kersey, with dark-blue trimmings, cut like the cavalry jacket, to come well down on the abdomen.

Trowsers—Present regulation, sky-blue.

Forage Cap—Present regulation.

For the convenience of service, the men will be selected for three grades of duty. Those who are most efficient and able-bodied, and capable of performing guard duty, etc., etc., will be armed with muskets, and assigned to companies of the First Battalion. Those of the next degree of efficiency, including those who have lost a hand or an arm; and the least effective, including those who have lost a foot or leg, to the companies of the Second or Third Battalions: they will be armed with swords.

The duties will be chiefly to act as provost guards and garrisons for cities; guards for hospitals and other public buildings; and as clerks, orderlies, etc. If found necessary they may be assigned to forts, etc.

For enlistment or further information apply to the Board of Enrollment at this office.

Capt. DANIEL H. JOHNSON, JR.,

je18 PROVOST MARSHAL.

MERCHANT & CARMAN,

Shipping & Commission Merchants

NO. 88 WALL STREET.

NEW YORK.

VESSELS BOUGHT AND SOLD.

FREIGHTS AND CHARTERS PROCURED.

Agents for the Pacific Mail Steamship Company for Coal Charters to Aspinwall, and the ports of Panama, Acapulco and San Francisco.

REFERENCES:

Allan McLane, Esq., President Pacific Mail Steamship Company, New York.
Francis Skiddy, Esq., New York.
David Hoadley, Esq., President Panama Railroad Company, New York.
Messrs. A. & A. Lawrence & Co., Boston.
Messrs. Forbes & Babcock, San Francisco.

—d16

NOTICE.

The Members of the West Newbury Mutual Fire Insurance Company, are hereby notified that an assessment of 3 per cent, has been ordered on all the premium notes of said Company, dated prior to August 23d, 1862, and 1 per cent. on all notes between August 22d, 1862 and March 1st 1863, payable on or before the 28th day of July next. For the accommodation of the members in Newburyport and vicinity, MR. HENRY MERRILL will receive the assessments and give receipts; for West Amesbury and the Mills Village, WM. NICHOLS, Esq.; for Rowley, Georgetown, Byfield, Groveland, &c., Mr. OTIS LITTLE. All others will pay to the Treasurer, in West Newbury.

J. C. CARR, Treasurer.

West Newbury, June 11th, 1863. je12—3w

Truth Stranger than Fiction.

Rev H. V. DEGEN. Boston, Mass, writes—"To Mrs S. A. Allen's World's Hair Restorer and Zylobalsamum promote the growth of the hair where baldness has commenced, I have the evidence of my own eyes."

Sold by Druggists everywhere. Depot, 198 Greenwich street, New York

Dr. Hall's Balsam.

This highly efficacious and popular medicine astonishes, by its good effects, every CONSUMPTIVE sufferer who makes use of it; and those who have tried a thousand remedies in vain, will never regret its trial. A few doses will give proof of its superiority over all other remedies known. Jy1—1w

The Confessions and Experience of an Invalid.

Published for the benefit and as a warning and a caution to young men who suffer from nervous debility, premature decay of manhood, etc, supplying at the same time the means of self cure. By one who cured himself after being put to great expense and injury through medical humbug and quackery.

By enclosing a post paid addressed Envelope, single copies may be had of the author,

NATHANIEL MAYFAIR, Esq.,

my19—d&sw 1y Bedford, Kings County, N. Y.

Seven Hundred Volunteers Sick in Camp.

Young men, be warned in time, supply yourselves with HOLLOWAY'S PILLS AND OINTMENT. They are guaranteed to cure the worst cases of sores, ulcers, scurvy, fevers and bowels complaints. Only 25 cents per box or pot 218

DR. JOHN C. MOTT,

PHYSICIAN AND SURGEON,

☞ 86 COURT STREET, corner of Howard, Boston, is consulted daily from 10 until 2, and from 6 to 8 in the evening, on all diseases of the urinary and genital organs, scrofulous affections, humors of all kinds, sores, ulcers and eruptions, female complaints, &c. An experience of over 20 years' extensive practice enables Dr M. to cure all of the most difficult cases. Medicines entirely vegetable. ADVICE FREE.

Mrs. M., who is thoroughly versed in the afflictive maladies of the sex, can be consulted by ladies.

Patients furnished with board and experienced nurses Boston, April 8, 1863 apl1—1y3taw

High Approval.

REV. PROF. GEO. SHEPARD, Theological Seminary, Bangor, Me., writes—"I find friends, who, on my recommendation, are disposed to make trial of Mrs S. A. Allen's World's Hair Restorer and Zylobalsamum, and there will have to be agent in this place, the demand so increases as it becomes known."

Sold by Druggists everywhere. Depot, 198 Greenwich New-York.

POOR RICHARD'S

EYE AND EAR WATER.

☞ This is the BEST Eye and Ear Water in the world, it opens at once the 8000 tubes and glands around the eyes thus permitting the saltish teary fountain to pass onward to every nook of the flesh. 'Tis from this moisture the system must derive life. Keep the sewers of your head open by bathing your eyes and ears with POOR RICHARD'S EYE AND EAR WATER, you will restore the sight, clear the vision, and strengthen the eye. Also remove every blood streak from the eye ball. Ask the Druggist for a tube (it will cost 6 cents) to drop it into the ear. Bathe the eye with your finger unsparingly. Be sure the water gets inside the eye and ear. This will prevent the loss of hair, cure deafness, headache, catarrh, with all kindred diseases, simply by opening the sewers of the head. Read the following certificate from Rev. P. S. Henson, Baptist Minister:

Philadelphia, Oct. 17, 1862.

From injuries received in my right eye when a boy, a chronic inflammation had been produced, in consequence of which I suffered constant martyrdom. Every moment of my waking life was embittered, and I was frequently unable to sleep a night. A variety of remedies had been resorted to without success, and I entertained the purpose, as a last resort, of having the ball taken out of the socket, in the hope of finding relief. In the meanwhile, most providentially, I noticed one day in a shop window a bottle of "Poor Richard's Eye Water." I had never heard of it before, but determined to try it, and DID, with the most delightful results. In a very few days the painful irritation was removed. I could bear the strongest light and went forth as it were to the enjoyment of a new life. I now keep a bottle of it always in the house, and if my eye seems at all disposed to annoy me, I give it a dose, and that is an end of it. I would not be without it for any amount of money. I take occasion to say further that my wife used to suffer severely at times from protracted pain in and over her eyes, and she has found "Poor Richard's Eye Water" a sovereign specific in her case, giving her almost instant relief. Grateful to God for the benefit that I have personally received, I cannot but commend the preparation most cordially to all who have been sufferers like myself.

P. S. HENSON,
Pastor of Broad street Baptist Church.
Residence 1430 Poplar street, Philadelphia.

For sale by S. A. SMITH, No. 1 State street, Newburyport; Weeks & Potter, Boston; and by druggists generally. Price 25 cents per bottle.

MRS. M. G. BROWN, Proprietor, 410 Arch st. Philadelphia n8—3taw d 2aw sw—1y

"Buy Me, and I'll Do You Good."

HEALTH AND STRENGTH SECURED BY THE USE OF THE

Great Spring and Summer Medicine,

DR. LANGLEY'S

ROOT AND HERB BITTERS,

Composed of Sarsaparilla, Wild Cherry, Yellow Dock Prickly Ash, Thoroughwort, Rhubarb, Mandrake, Dandelion, &c., all of which are so compounded as to act in concert, and assist Nature in eradicating Disease.

This medicine has been before the public for ever fourteen years, with constantly increasing success, and is now THE STANDARD MEDICINE OF THE AGE!

Its effect upon the system is most wonderful—acting directly upon the seat of disease, cleansing the bowels, removing all obstructions from the internal organs, stimulating them into healthy action, purifying the blood, divesting it of all humors, building up the weakened system, and restoring the invalid to health and usefulness. They cure and eradicate from the system, Liver Complaint, that main-wheel of so many diseases; Jaundice in its worst forms, all Billious Diseases and Foul Stomach, Dyspepsia, Costiveness, all kinds of Humors, Indigestion, Headache, Dizziness, Piles, Heartburn, Weakness, Pains in the Side and Bowels, Flatulency, Loss of Appetite, and a Torbid or Diseased Liver, a Disordered Stomach, or Bad Blood, to which all are more or less subjected in Spring and Summer.

It is highly recommended by Physicians everywhere.—Try it, and you will never regret it. No medicine can be like it in its salutary effect, therefore inquire of LANGLEY'S BITTERS, and take no other.

Only 37 and 50 cents per bottle. Sold by Dealers in Medicine everywhere. Orders addressed to

GEO. C. GOODWIN & CO., 38 Hanover St., Boston.

mh26—6msw

Here's Health for the Million.

DR. CLARK'S

SHERRY WINE BITTERS,

PALATABLE AND HEALTHY,

Prepared from Rock Rose, Sarsaparilla, Dock Root, Dandelion, and a very great variety of ROOTS AND HERBS,

PRESERVED IN THE BEST SHERRY WINE AND WHISKEY

Will immediately cure Loss of Appetite, General Debility, Dyspepsia, Sour Stomach, Palpitation of the Heart, Asthma, Coughs, Colds, Boils, Pimples on the Face, and Humors of all kinds.

They are safe for the young, effectual and agreeable for the old, and indispensable for the ladies, as they enrich the blood and invigorate and restore the system

OUR SYSTEM Keep up the quality of the Bitters and make the price in proportion

Price only 38 cents for the pint bottle, 62 cents for 1 quart, $1,00 for 2 quarts and $1.50 for 4 qts. or world's size.

Sold by Druggists, Grocers, Hotels and dealers generally. Also, sale by H. P. TOPPAN, C. FRENCH & Co., and I. C. CLEMENT.

Manufactured by E. R. CLARKE, Sharon, Mass.

STANDARD ARTICLE.

CLARKE'S

Superior Quality Corn Starch,

ORIGINAL BRAND

The Best in the World!

PREPARED FROM SOUND CORN,

And produces the most delicious and healthy dishes in the form of Puddings, Apple Fritters, Corn Cakes, Cream Cakes, Blanc Mange, Custards, Thickening for Gravies, Gruels, Soups, Griddle Cakes, &c.

Manufactured by E. R. CLARKE, Sharon, Mass., and sold at wholesale by grocers, druggists and dealers everywhere.

☞ H. P. TOPPAN, C. FRENCH & Co., and MOSES B. WHEELER, JR., Agents. mr31—3taw3m

NEW DISCOVERY.

CAPILANIA,

—FOR—

Restoring the Hair and Whiskers,

However gray, to their original color, and imparting to the hair any shade required, from a delicate BROWN TO A DEEP BLACK. This compound is offered as the best thing known for the above purposes. It is easy of application, consisting of only one preparation; does not stain, crock or smut, and leaves the hair of a most beautiful ly soft and glossy, and of a most permanent and natural color. In the use of this article all the usual soaping, washing and sponging of the hair is dispensed with, and its application is perfectly simple. Price $1 per bottle.

Sold by M. S. Burr & Co. 26 Tremont street; George C. Goodwin & Co., 38 Hanover street; Weeks & Potter, 170 Washington street; John Wilson, Jr, & Co, 138 Washington street; Carter, Rust & Co., 43 Hanover street; S M Colcord & Co., 86 Hanover street, General Agents, Boston, Mass., and by druggists generally. my25—1aw3m

MARRIAGES.

In this city, July 4th, by Rev John Pearson, Mr Daniel D. W. Jones to Mrs Rowena A. Collyer, both of Newburyport.

DEATHS.

In this city, 8th, Louisa J., wife of Edwin Adams. Funeral this (Thursday) at 5 1-2 P. M. from No. 12 Congress street.

TRADE AND COMMERCE.

CAMBRIDGE CATTLE MARKET.

Thursday, July 8.

Whole number of Cattle at market 2?5; about 250 Beeves; and — Stores, consisting of Working Oxen, Milch Cows, and one, two and three year old.

Prices of Market Beef—Extra 8,50a8,75; first quality 8,00 a—; second quality $7.00a7,25; —; third quality $47,5.

Working Oxen—pr pair—$100a175.

Cows and Calves—$30, 37a60.

Yearlings—none.

Two year old—none.

Three year old—none.

Sheep and Lambs—1350 at market; prices in lots $2,00a 2,50 each; extra $3,00a4 00.

Spring Lambs—$3,50a4,25

Hides 8a8½c per lb.

Tallow—8a8¾c per lb.

Pelts—$50c a 75c each.

Calf Skins 12a14c per lb

Veal Calves $6a$5,50.

Remarks—There was not a large supply of stock at market; quality poor; but few extra; prices lower than at the opening of the market last week, but about the same as at the close. But few old Sheep, and they sold low, as there is not much call for them. Spring Lambs in good supply, and sales quick at an average of $4 per head.

SHIPPING JOURNAL.

PORT OF NEWBURYPORT

SATURDAY, July 4.

ARRIVED—Sch Superior, Robinson, Rondout.
Sch Chieftain, Farnsworth, Annapolis.
Sch Martha May, Cheney, Boston.
Br sch Chieftain, —, Nova Scotia.

SUNDAY, July 5.

ARRIVED—Sch Cornelia, Currier, Bangor.
Sch John & Frank, Bickford, Bangor.

MONDAY, July 6.

ARRIVED—Sch Iowa, —, Bangor.
SAILED—Sch Halo, Newman, Philadelphia.
Sch D. P., Thompson, Philadelphia.
Sch Kossuth, Lee, New York.
Sch Majestic, —, Hampden.

TUESDAY, July 7.

ARRIVED—Br sch Rover, Lunt, Annapolis.
Br sch Mariner, De Von, Nova Scotia.
Sch Amanda Powers, —, Elizabethport.
Sch Kossuth, Granslow, Elizabethport.
SAILED—Sch Martha May, Cheney, Boston.

WEDNESDAY, July 8.

ARRIVED—Sch Gold Hunter, Ware, York.
SAILED—Br sch Rover, Lunt, Digby.
Sch Iowa, —, Bangor.

NOTICE TO MARINERS.

☞ No vessel other than steamers and packets known to be engaged on regular lines, or in the employ of the army or navy, will be allowed to leave port between sunset and sunrise, until further orders. E. G. CURRIER, Collector.

Newburyport, July 5th, 1863.

Memoranda.

Ship Sarah Newman, Cobb, from Hong Kong, arr at San Francisco 1st inst.

Barque Star King, Smith, from Philadelphia 12th Feb for Cape Town, C. G. H., was spoken, no date, &c.

Sch Otranto, Hammond, cld at New York 3d for this port.

Sch Grand Island, Read, was at Mayaguez 21st ult for this port, to sail 27th.

Sch Amelia, Bayley, hence, arr at Mayaguez 21st ult.

THE ANGLO-REBEL PIRACY. A letter received in this city from a merchant in Barbadoes, dated June 30th, has the following:—

"A barque was signalled to windward this morning on fire; and about two hours since the master and crew arrived in their boat, and report as follows:—That the barque was one taken by the Florida some weeks since, with a cargo of coal; a prize master and crew were put on board, and she was to meet the Florida and Alabama at different points and supply them with coal; but somehow he has missed of them, and being short of provisions and water, they sighted Barbadoes and set fire to her."

Ship Rose Standish, Hutchins, from Cardiff for Calcutta, was spoken April 15, lat 9 N, lon 24 W.

Ship Sonora, Brown, from New York 28th for Australia, was spoken May 6th, lat 14 S, lon 35 W.

Barque S H Waterman, Elliott, cld at Gibraltar 16th June for New York.

Fayal, June 6—The American ship Athens, Shields, from Cardenas for Cork for orders, put in May 28, leaking, and is discharging in Quarantine.

Steamer W H Foss, Comstock, from Buffalo, NY, via Pictou for New York, which arrived at Gloucester on the 3d inst, with machinery damaged, and was detained for examination, put into Pictou on the 19th ult, for repairs, after which she took in a cargo of 250 tons coal for Dr T P Shepard, and sailed for Providence.

The sch H Walcott, Dare, from Baltimore for Matamoras, previously reported sunk June 23 off Smith's Point, Chesapeake Bay, after collision, was picked up, and arr at Georgetown, DC, 2d inst, with a breach in her starboard side.

MARINE DISASTERS. The summary of disasters occurring last month to vessels engaged in the trade of Boston, prepared for the Board of Trade, shows the following statistics:

Missing—One ship, of Boston.
Abandoned—One schooner, of Boston.
Arrived at Destination with Damage—One ship and one schooner, of Boston.
Stranded—Two ships and two schooners, of which two schooners were of Boston.
In Collision—Two schooners, not of Boston.
Put in Leaky or otherwise Disabled—One schooner, not of Boston.
Burnt—Two ships, two barques, and two brigs, all of Boston.

Disasters.

Ship Mary Ogden, Hathaway, at San Francisco from New York, reports—Dec 13, lat 33 38, lon 52 04, experienced a heavy gale from SE to ESE; lost long boat and spars off the forward house; was 79 days to Cape Horn: 20 days off the Cape, with strong westerly winds; in 50 S in the Pacific had a heavy gale.

Ship Asterion, at San Francisco from New York, reports—On the 9th of March, off the North entrance to the Straits of LeMaire, Robinson P Gardner (boy) of Newport, RI, fell from the foretopsail yard overboard, and was lost.

Clipper ship Midnight, which arrived at San Francisco 12th June from Boston, encountered Feb 3 at 10 P M. a terrific hurricane. It struck her in lat 48 50 N, lon 58 W. The wind blew from NE to SE. Every sail was swept away; also booby-hatch, binnacle, sky-lights, boats, water casks, coal casks, lumber, &c. During the storm, Alphonso Jackson, an ordinary seaman, of Wiscasset, Me, was washed overboard and drowned. The vessel laid to over twelve hours, with the dead-eyes under water, awaiting the abatement of the storm.

The James Marshal, from Hong Kong, put back, the crew (Chinese) having mutinied and tried to take possession of the vessel, but failing, took possession of a boat and departed. The captain was seriously injured.

The Good Return, from Calcutta for Boston, put back leaking, having been ashore.

The Lepanto, from Calcutta for London, ran ashore in the Hoogley, but got off and proceeded.

The East Indian received damage at Calcutta by going ashore.

Sch Jamestown, at Boston from Georgetown, DC, reports—June 28, picked up the crew of U S steamer Sumter, who were in four boats. The Sumter had been run into by stmr Gen Meigs, from New York for Port Royal, SC.

A fore and aft sch of about 150 tons was seen on Wednesday afternoon ashore on the west end of Fisher's Island Supposed to have gone on during a thick fog that morning.

Stmr W H Foss, Comstock, from Buffalo, via Pictou, for New York, arr at Gloucester 3d. She reports machinery damaged, and has been in the Bay of Fundy disabled for the past ten days. U S sch I G Curtis, Capt Pierce, has determined to detain her for examination. The steamer has 250 tons coal on board. Some of her crew were seen in town a few days ago

We notice sales of the A schr Tranquil, 75 tons, 12 years old, at $800: A2 schr Ann S Salter, 133 tons, built at Chatham, Conn, in 1853, $4000 cash; and A2d brig J M Sawyer, 254 tons, built at Damariscotta in 1854, on private terms.

Several large ships have been detained at San Francisco about a fortnight, awaiting crews. There is a great scarcity of seamen.

LAUNCHED—At East Boston, on Friday, 3d, by Messrs Dolliver & Skeeper, a fine barque of 500 tons, called the Conqueror.

At Machias, July 2d, by Joseph O'Brien and others, a fine double-decked barque of about 600 tons, built by John Shaw of Machias.

At Mystic, July 1, from the yard of Messrs George Greenman & Co, a fine screw steamer, of about 850 tons, called the Weybosset, built expressly for Messrs Corliss & Nightingale, Providence.

At Freeport, 2d inst, from the yard of C H Soule, a ship of about 1000 tons.

THE YACHT PRIORESS,

CAPT B. F. THURLO,

Will leave Ferry Wharf, Newburyport, on **Saturday. July 4th,** and daily during the following week, at 8 o'clk A. M., for the

Isles of Shoals,

Returning in the afternoon.

Fare One Dollar. Chowder Included.

For passage enquire of the Master on board, or of

B. DAVIS, JR., & CO.

Jy3 No. 4 Ferry wharf.

JOHN McCUSKER,

—DEALER IN—

Newspapers, Magazines,

CHEAP PUBLICATIONS,

FRUIT AND CONFECTIONERY.

Jy8—tf **No. 20 Merrimac Street.**

Coal.

150 Tons White Ash and 140 tons Red Ash Coal, stove size, cargo of sch Charles H. Rogers, for sale by SAM'L HALE & CO., 123 Water st.

Jy7

Gold Pencil Lost.

ON Monday afternoon, between the Public Library and Charles st., a gold pencil, with a red stone in the end and a pen attached. The finder will be suitably rewarded by leaving the same at this office. jy8

NEW STORE.

The subscriber having opened the store

No. 31 Pleasant Street,

(directly opposite the Bartlet Mills Counting Room,)

OFFERS FOR SALE

Fancy Goods and Patent Medicines

As Cheap as the Cheapest.

Call and examine my goods whether you wish to purchase or not. Goods freely shown.

Je27 **GEORGE GORWAIZ.**

S. E. BASSETT

Has Just Received a few styles of

Thin Dress Goods,

☞ To sell at Very Low Prices.

Cor. Monroe and Warren streets.

je26 is 6t

SIBLEY'S SCYTHES.

E. T. SIBLEY'S Superior Cast Steel Scythes, of the same excellent quality that I have sold for the last four years, giving entire satisfaction in nearly every case.

D. C. NOYES,

Jy1—tf **31 Market Sq.**

LONDON PORTER.

JUST received one cask Bottled London Porter, extra quality, for sale low by

PARKER ROBERTS,

je17 23 Market Square.

Essex Street Dental Depot,

—FOR—

MOUNTING ARTIFICIAL TEETH

on any desired base, *imiter le naturel.*

LIST OF PRICES:

Upper Sets on Silver, from	$10 to $25.
Upper Sets on Hard Rubber, very much admired by all who have used the , and the very best there is made, from	$15 to $25.
Upper Sets on Fine Gold, good as can be made in this State or any other, from	$40 to $75.

☞ UNDER SETS equally as low. We shall put up Teeth at these prices until further notice, and being permanently located in this city, will warrant them.

Please call and examine specimens of our work. Advice gratis.

W. H. NOYES,

mr26—is ed tf PRACTICAL DENTIST.

BOOTS AND SHOES.

THIS DAY RECEIVED AT

No. 13 Pleasant Street, No. 13,

A good assortment of all kinds of

BOOTS AND SHOES,

generally found in the market.

All kinds of Measure Work made to order at short notice.

REPAIRING neatly executed.

CHARLES PEABODY,

je12 13 Pleasant street.

Large Size Sun Umbrellas,

PRICE only $1,50, at MRS. ALTER'S

PROPOSALS

For Furnishing Fuel for the City of Newburyport.

SEALED PROPOSALS to furnish the following named quantity and quality of Fuel for the Schools and Fire Departments, and for the Public Buildings of the City of Newburyport, agreeably to an Ordinance, will be received by the Committee on Fuel, until WEDNESDAY, July 22, at 2 o'clock P. M., to be endorsed "Proposals for Fuel for the City of Newburyport," said Proposals to be left at the office of the City Clerk, or with either of the Committee, on or before the day above named, the Committee reserving the right to reject any or all of said Proposals. The Proposals to embrace the delivery of said Fuel at such places in the city as shall be designated by said Committee. The Coal for the Schools and Fire Departments and Public Buildings, to be put in the proper receptacles for the same, viz:

100 tons Red Ash (Phoenix vein) Coal, stove size, per ton, of 2200 pounds.

100 tons White Ash, Johns' vein or Locust Mountain, coal size, per ton of 2200 pounds.

50 tons White Ash, same as above, broken size.

1800 bushels Pine Limb Coal, per bushel.

Said Fuel to be delivered previous to October 1st, 1863.

SAMUEL PETTINGELL,
WILLIAM H. HUSE,
NICHOLAS VARINA,
MOSES PETTINGELL, JR.,
GREENLEAF BOARDMAN,
} Committee.

Newburyport, July 2d, 1863.

MRS. A. M. POOLE,

PHYSICIAN,

183 Water Street, Newburyport.

Jel7 3m

To Let,

A nice cottage house and large garden containing a great variety of fruit trees in good bearing condition, situated within ten minutes' walk of the Post Office. Enquire at this office, or of

fe10—¶ W. H. LOVETT, 9 Coffin's Court.

To Let,

The pleasantly situated Mansion House, No. 258 High street. Enquire at the next door.

Jy7 1m—¶

Pensions, Bounties, Prize Money,

—AND—

All Claims Against the United States,

promptly secured at the

LOWEST CHARGES.

☞ ADVICE GRATIS.

Jy9—6m ed is **S. W. MARSTON.**

MISS BRYANT

WISHES to inform the public that she will attend to the

Fitting and Making of Dresses,

at her place of residence, No. 52 High street, or at the residence of her patrons.

Also, nice TATTING, either in Collars, Trimming or Inserting.

Machine work, very reasonable. Jy9

BOOT MAKERS WANTED.

50 Boot Makers can find employment at Chicopee, Mass, at liberal wages. The pegging is done by machinery, and lasts and findings furnished. The stock all cut by dies Pay once a week—Steady employment given.

Jy9 1m C. McCLELLAN & SON.

WANTED,

100 CIDER AND VINEGAR BARRELS. Apply to

Jy9 W. S. COFFIN, 49 Water street.

WANTED,

A Good, steady American girl, to do the work of a family. Enquire at this office. jy9

GREAT REDUCTION.

Still Lower Prices in our Stock of

Thin Summer Goods,

SHAWLS AND SUN UMBRELLAS,

Hosiery and Gloves.

G. I. WILLIAMS & CO.

Hymn Books.

SABBATH HYMN BOOK; Watt's and Select Hymns, new and second-hand; Nettleton's Village Hymn; at Jy9 WOODMAN'S, near Eastern Depot.

Sabbath School Question Books

AT WOODMAN'S,

Jy9 near Eastern Railroad Depot.

Fine Ripe Blueberries,

JUST received; also, a few boxes superior STRAWBERRIES, received every afternoon fresh from the vines, for sale at 32 Washington street.

Jy9 J. STEVENS.

Men's Silk Handkerchiefs.

AT the low price of 25 cents apiece, just received by

Jy9 R. COOK & CO., 18 State street.

Parasols.

160 Parasols at $1 apiece, worth $2, can be found at

Jy9 R. COOK & CO'S, 18 State street.

Sure Death to Flies.

10 0 Papers FLY POISON, only 1 cent a paper, or 8 cents per dozen—cheaper if you wish. For sale by Jy9 JOHN GORWAIZ.

Watch Spring Skirts and Sun Umbrellas.

LADIES, we are now opening the largest assortment of nice Watch Spring Skirts ever offered in this city; also, 100 nice Sun Umbrellas, all sizes, for sale at a very low price. Please call and examine.

Jy9 JOHN GORWAIZ, 11 Pleasant street.

Lackawanna Coal—To Arrive.

188 Tons Old Company Lackawanna Coal, stove and egg size, daily expected per sch Otronto, for sale by S. LITTLEFIELD, 1st whf south RR Bridge.

English Wood.

50 Cords first quality English Wood, now landing per sch Chieftain, for sale by

Jy9 S. LITTLEFIELD, 1st whf south RR Bridge.

FOLLY

TO wear Thick Hose this season of the year when you can buy a first-rate article of COTTON HOSE so cheap at TOPPAN & CO.'S We have just received 500 dozen, of all sizes and colors, from 12½ to 50 cents. Call and get a lot. Jy9

DID YOU EVER SEE

SUCH an extensive assortment of CLOTHING as TOPPAN & CO. keep? Well, I never did; and how low they sell! And what good articles they always have! Such was the conversation overheard by gentlemen standing on the corner of State and Middle streets Those in want must drop in and satisfy themselves of the truth of the above. Jy9

Commonwealth of Massachusetts.

ESSEX, ss.

To the Heirs-at-Law and others interested in the Estate of PHEBE R. SAUNDERS late of Rowley in said County, widow, deceased, intestate—GREETING:

WHEREAS David Sanders administrator of the estate, of said deceased has presented for allowance the first account of his administration upon the estate of said deceased: You are hereby cited to appear at a Probate Court to be holden at Newburyport in said County, on the third Tuesday of July inst., at nine o'clock in the forenoon, to show cause, if any you have, why the same should not be allowed.

And the said administrator is ordered to serve this Citation by publishing the same once a week, in the Daily Herald a newspaper printed at Newburyport, three weeks successively, the last publication to be two days at least before said Tuesday.

Witness, GEORGE F. CHOATE, Esquire, Judge of said Court, this second day of July in the year eighteen hundred and sixty-three. A. C. GOODELL, Register.

NOTICE IS HEREBY GIVEN, That the subscriber has been duly appointed administrator of the estate of JOHN M. SMITH, late of Newburyport, in the county of Essex, yeoman, deceased, and has taken upon himself that trust, by giving bonds as the law directs: All persons having demands upon the estate of said deceased are required to exhibit the same; and all persons indebted to said estate are called upon to make payment to DAVID SMITH.

Newburyport, July 7th, 1863. jy8

NOTICE IS HEREBY GIVEN that the subscriber has been duly appointed administratrix of the estate of AMOS E. SHORT, late of West Newbury, in the county of Essex yeoman, deceased, and has taken upon herself that trust by giving bonds as the law directs: All persons having demands upon the estate of said deceased, are required to exhibit the same; and all persons indebted to said estate are called upon to make payment to ABIGAIL K. SHORT.

West Newbury, July 7th, 1863. jy8

NOTICE IS HEREBY GIVEN, That the subscriber has been duly appointed administrator of the estate of PHINEAS ELLIOTT, late of Amesbury, in the county of Essex, yeoman, deceased and has taken upon himself that trust, by giving bonds as the law directs. All persons having demands upon the estate of said deceased are required to exhibit the same: and all persons indebted to said estate are called upon to make payment to

CHARLES C. ELLIOTT,

or to JOHN S MORSE, his Attorney.

Amesbury, July 7th, 1863. Jy8

Commonwealth of Massachusetts.

ESSEX, ss. PROBATE COURT.

To the Heirs-at-Law, and all others interested in the estate of NATHANIEL PILLSBURY, late of Newburyport, in said county, farmer, deceased,—GREETING:

WHEREAS, George Emery, administrator of the estate of said deceased, has presented to said Court his petition for license to sell so much of the real estate of said deceased as will raise the sum of four hundred sixty-five dollars and eighty-five cents, for the payment of debts and charges of administration:

You are hereby cited to appear at a Probate Court to be holden at Salem, in said county, on the first Tuesday of August next, at nine o'clock in the forenoon, to show cause, if any you have, against the same;

And said administrator is ordered to serve this Citation by publishing the same once a week, three weeks successively, in the Newburyport Herald, a newspaper printed at Newburyport, the last publication to be two days at least before said Court.

Witness, GEORGE F. CHOATE, Esquire, Judge of said Court, this 7th day of July, in the year one thousand eight hundred and sixty-three.

jy9 A. C. GOODELL Register.

NEW ROUTE TO

LAKE WINNIPISSEOGEE AND THE WHITE MOUNTAINS.

EASTERN RAILROAD.

ON and after July 6, 1863, a Train will leave the Eastern Railroad Station, in Boston, at 12.15 and Newburyport at 1.55 P. M., for Alton Bay, via Portsmouth and Great Falls, connecting at Alton Bay with the steamer DOVER for Wolfborough and Centre Harbor, and at these places with stages for Conway, North Conway and the White Mountains.

Through Tickets may be obtained at the Eastern Railroad Station on Causeway street. No change of cars or baggage between Boston and the Lake. Baggage checked to Wolfborough and Centre Harbor.

Jy4—tf J. PRESCOTT, Sup't.

NEW GOODS.

LADIES' MOHAIR MITTS,

Ladies' Mohair Mitts,
Ladies' Mohair Mitts,
Ladies' Mohair Mitts.

Gloves, Hosiery,
Gloves, Hosiery,
Gloves, Hosiery,
Gloves, Hosiery,

Ladies' Mohair Mitts,
Ladies' Mohair Mitts,
Ladies' Mohair Mitts,
Ladies' Mohair Mitts.

In Mitts, Hosiery and Gloves we have a large stock, and shall sell them at the lowest possible prices for good goods.

Black Lace Veils,
Black Lace Veils,
Black Lace Veils,

Bosoms, Bosoms,
Bosoms, Bosoms,
Bosoms, Bosoms,

Black Lace Veils,
Black Lace Veils,
Black Lace Veils.

In Black Lace Veils we have just received a new stock in all the desirable styles and at some decided Bargains.

Watch Spring Skirts,
Watch Spring Skirts,
Watch Spring Skirts.

Note Paper, Envelopes,
Note Paper, Envelopes,
Note Paper, Envelopes.

Watch Spring Skirts,
Watch Spring Skirts,
Watch Spring Skirts.

Bargains. Bargains. Bargains.

CHARLES W. PEABODY,

No. 3 Pleasant Street.

Ballou's Magazine,

FOR August, now ready at the Periodical and Variety Store, 55 State street. A. J. HAYNES.

Farm and Land for Sale.

The subscriber offers for sale the Homestead Farm of Col. Jonathan Smith, late of Salisbury, deceased, situated at the Plains, about one mile from Amesbury and Salisbury Mills Village, two miles from Newburyport, and three-fourths of a mile from Railroad Depot, containing about forty acres of excellent land, suitably divided into mowing, orchard, tillage, and pasture. On the premises are a large house; two barns, with out-buildings, three wells, and in the pasture never-failing springs of water.

Also, about thirty-six acres of Pasture Land, bounded northerly by a highway, easterly by land lately of Dr. Edward Dearborn, southerly by land of Edmund Morrill, and westerly by land of Benjamin Tucker.

Also, about three acres of Mowing and Orchard Land, bounded easterly and southerly by a highway, westerly by land of Joshua Dow, and northerly by land of the late Aaron Clough.

Also, about two and a half acres of Woodland adjoining the highway and land of the heirs of Sarah Colby James L. Morrill and others.

Also, about three acres of Salt Marsh, bounded northerly by marsh of Lowell Brown, easterly by marsh of Mr. Goodwin, southerly by Eaton's Cove, and westerly by land of the late Samuel Eaton.

All the above parcels of land remaining unsold on the first day of March next, will be sold at Public Auction, on MONDAY, the 16th day of March, at 11 o'clock A. M., on the premises, where conditions will be made known.

For particulars, &c., enquire of T. S. ROBINSON, at Rocky Hill, Salisbury, or of the subscriber.

AARON MORRILL.

Salisbury, Mass., January 29th, 1863. f9—sw 6m

Cure Your Cough for Thirteen Cent

The BEST and CHEAPEST Household REMEDY in the World.

MADAM ZADOC PORTER'S

Great Cough Remedy,

MADAME ZODOC PORTER'S CURATIVE BALSAM is warranted if used according to directions, to cure in all cases Coughs, Colds, Whooping Coughs, Asthma, and all affections of the Throat and Lungs.

MAD'E ZADOC PORTER'S BALSAM is prepared with all the requisite care and skill, from a combination of the best remedies the vegetable kingdom affords. Its remedial qualities are based on its power to assist the healthy and vigorous circulation of the blood, through the lungs. It is not a violent remedy, but emolient, warming, searching and effective; can be taken by the oldest person or the youngest child.

MADAME ZADOC PORTER'S BALSAM has been in use by the public for over 18 years, and has acquired its present sale simply by being recommended by those who have used it to their afflicted friends and others.

MOST IMPORTANT—Mad'e ZADOC PORTER'S Curative Balsam is sold at a price, which brings it in the reach of every one to keep it convenient for use. The timely use of a single bottle will prove to be worth 100 times its cost

NOTICE.—SAVE YOUR MONEY! Do not be persuaded to purchase articles at 4s to $1, which do not contain the virtues of a 13 ct Bottle of Madame Porter's Curative Balsam, the cost of manufacturing which is as great as that of almost any other medicine; and the very low price at which it is sold, makes the profit to the seller apparently small, and unprincipled dealers will sometimes recommend other medicines on which their profits are larger, unless the customers insist upon having Madame Porter's, and none other. Ask for Madame Porter's Curative Balsam, price 13 cts., and in large bottles at 25 cts., and take no other. If you can not get it at one store you can get it at another.

Sold by all Druggists at 13 cts., and in larger bottles at 25 cts. HALL & RUCKEL, Proprietors, N. York.

S. A. SMITH, No. 1 State Street, Agent for Newburyport.

GEO. C. GOODWIN & CO., Boston.
General Agents for New England.

1 a w S. W. inside, 1 year.

A JUST TRIBUTE TO MERIT.

At International Exhibition, London, July 12th, 1862

DURYEA'S MAIZENA

Was the only 'preparation for food from Indian Corn" that received a medal and honorable mention from the Royal Commissioners, the competition of all prominent manufacturers of "Corn Starch" and 'Prepared Corn Flour" of this and other countries notwithstanding.

MAIZENA,

The food and luxury of the age, without a single fault. One trial will convince the most skeptical. Makes Puddings, Cakes, Custards, Blanc mange, &c, without isinglass, with few or no eggs, at a cost astonishing the most economical. A slight addition to ordinary wheat flour greatly improves bread and cake. It is also excellent for sweetening sweet sauces, gravies for fish and meat, soups, &c. For ice cream nothing can compare with it. A little boiled in milk will produce rich cream for coffee, chocolate, tea, &c.

Put up in one pound packages with directions.

A most delicious article of food for children and invalids of all ages. For sale by Grocers and Druggists everywhere

MANUFACTURED AT GLEN COVE, LONG ISLAND,

Wholesale Depot, 166 Fulton street,

WILLIAM DURYEA, General Agent.

d22 2awSW1y

MANHOOD,

HOW LOST; HOW RESTORED;

Just published, in a sealed envelope. Price Six Cents.

LECTURE on the Nature, Treatment, and Radical Cure of spermatorrhoea or Seminal Weakness, Involuntary Emissions, Sexual Debility, and Impediments to Marriage generally, Nervous Consumption, Epilepsy and Fits; Mental and Physical Incapacity, resulting from self-abuse, &c. By ROBT. J. CULVERWELL, M. D, Author of the Green Book, &c.

"A Boon to Thousands of Sufferers," sent under seal, in a plain envelope, to any address, post-paid, on receipt of six cents, or two postage stamps, by Dr. CH. J. C KLINE 127 Bowery, New York, P O Box 4586. mr 1—3md & is

PACIFIC GUANO.

AGENCY FOR THE AMMONIATED PACIFIC GUANO.

WE are receiving a constant supply of this superior Guano, which will be found one of the cheapest and best Fertilizers in the market. It is adapted to all soils, and all the various crops,—Grass, Grain, Corn, Potatoes, Root Crops, Tobacco, &c., &c., as will be seen by the numerous letters and testimonials received the last season. A pamphlet, containing testimonials, &c, will be furnished on application.

Also,—continue the Agencies in Fertilizers, Seeds, &c; Coe's Super-Phosphate of Lime; Fish Guano; Ground Bone Meal; Poudrette; Pulverized Charcoal; Grass Seed, &c. At the Lowest Market Prices.

GEO. DAVENPORT & CO.,

mr26—1aw3m 145 Milk Street, Boston.

VARNISHES.

Benzene Coach Varnishes.
Benzene Furniture do.
Benzene Enamelled Top do.
Benzene Japan,

IN ALL THEIR VARIETIES.

BENZENE VARNISHES have been tried for two years and are now acknowledged to be equal, while many think them far better, than Varnishes made with turpentine. I have a good assortment of the above goods, and warrant every gallon I sell. By giving my whole attention to the manufacture of Varnishes, I am enabled to make it an object, in the way of prices, for buyers to give me their trade. All orders for goods promptly filled. Any information in regard to prices may be obtained by addressing

W. C. HUNNEMAN, JR.,

Manufacturer of Varnishes,

j—19—1aw1m 149 Milk street, Boston.

PENSIONS AND BOUNTY MONEY,

—FOR—

Discharged and Wounded Soldiers.

Pensions and Bounty Money for Widows,
Pensions and Bounty Money for Children,
Pensions and Bounty Money for Mothers,
Pensions and Bounty Money for Orphan Sisters,
Pensions and Prize Money for Sailors, or their widows and children,

promptly and faithfully collected by the undersigned, who has had a large experience in the business.

Terms low, and no pay required until the claims are obtained.

Office No. 9 State street, with GERRISH and RAND who will attend to all callers.

Z. K. HARMON.

Newburyport, March 24th, 1863. mr24—tf

Ladies' Cotton Hose.

60 Dozen Ribbed and Plain Hose, just received and for sale cheap, by R. COOK & CO

Ladies' and Misses' Skirts

for sale cheap, by

GEORGE GORWAIZ, 31 Pleasant Street.

STRAWBERRIES,

NEW EVERY MORNING AND FRESH EVERY EVENING,

At the Variety Store, 55 State Street.

A. J. HAYNES.

To Let,

One half of brick house corner of Lime and Atwood streets, containing parlor, sitting-room, kitchen and five chambers. Apply to

je27—tf GEO. W. HALE.

Hugh Miller's New Book—Tales and Sketches,

EDITED with a preface by Mrs. Miller; The Story of My Career, &c., translated by Rev. W. L Gage; Woman and her Savior, by Miss Fidelia Fiske, (well known in this city.) For sale at WOODMAN'S,

je9 near Eastern Depot, Washington st.

AUCTION SALES.

BY GEORGE GREENLEAF.

Office, No. 82 Market Square.

☞ Regular Sales Days, at Office, WEDNESDAYS and SATURDAYS of each week, at 9 o'clock A. M. Liberal advances made on Furniture and other goods left for sale.

☞ Particular attention given to sales of Real Estate, Household Furniture, and other out-door Sales.

Also, a large variety of Goods, of various kinds, at low prices at private sale.

Sale of Furniture.

On SATURDAY at 9 o'clock, at office.

The furniture of a Family, breaking up house-keeping.—comprising tables, chairs, bureaus, carpets, feather beds, under beds, book cases, books, crockery and glass ware, with a great variety of other articles, among the lot are several antique articles, and old books.

CASTILE SOAP—At private sale, 10 bxs Castile Soap.

Sale of Real Estate.

On WEDNESDAY, July 15th, at 12 o'clock, on the premises,

The two story dwelling house and about twenty rods of land, situated on Charles street. The house was built in a thorough manner by the present owner, and for his own occupancy, and is now in good order. It has two large parlors, with sliding doors, kitchen, sink room, bed room, five sleeping rooms and a small kitchen on the second floor; also, a wood house.

Sale positive, as the owner has removed from the city.

Jy4 Jy4

BY EDMUND SMITH.

Salt Grass.

SATURDAY, 11th inst., at 2 o'clock P. M., near the house of Moses Goodwin, (late J. M. Plumer's) in Newbury,—

THE Grass standing on forty acres of marsh, in five acre lots. Jy2

Administrator's Sale.

Will be sold at Public Auction on MONDAY, July 13th, at 9 o'clock A. M., at the residence of the late John M. Smith, in Newburyport,—

ONE yoke of Oxen, 3 Cows, 1 Horse, 3 Pigs, 6 tons old English Hay, 2½ tons Salt and Fresh Hay, and the Grass standing on about 20 acres English mowing land.

DAVID SMITH.

Newburyport, July 8th, 1863. Jy9

JAMES W. CHENEY,

DEPUTY SHERIFF,

Office with JOHN COOK, Esq., Market Square

Residence, No. 163 High street. mr4—1y

GEORGE JANVRIN,

CITY MARSHAL

OFFICE—West end of the Market Hall.

RESIDENCE—No. 11 Spring Street. F14

J. T. BROWN,

Notary Public & Justice of the Peace,

TELEGRAPH OFFICE—ESSEX HALL BUILDING!

☞ All business promptly attended to. d1

EDWARD W RAND

NOTARY PUBLIC

OFFICE,—No. 9 State, cor. of Middle st

☞ Will attend to Notarial business generally.

DR. G. W. KENNISON,

DENTIST,

NO. 17 PLEASANT STREET

M. M. MUMFORD, SURGEON DENTIST—Office, Prince House, State street, opposite Temple street.

New Stock of Goods.

The subscriber having taken the store

No. 177 Water Street,

(formerly occupied by Mr. C. W. Hale,)

Would inform his friends and the public that he is now prepared to furnish them with

FAMILY GOODS AND GROCERIES,

at a small advance from the cost.

Hoping by attention to my business and the wants of customers to merit a share of public patronage.

Jel9—tf **WM. THURLOW.**

To Let.

House No. 1 Titcomb's Court, near head of State st, Apply to THOS. H. COTTER,

je23 No. 44 Merrimac st.

WANTED,

Vessels to take heavy freight to Baltimore.—Apply to SUMNER, SWASEY & CURRIER.

WANTED,

A Man to work at light employment—wages liberal. Enquire at DR. INGALLS,

je25 9 Temple street.

Salt Grass for Sale.

50 Acres of Salt Grass for sale. Enquire of T. K. BARTLETT,

Jy1 Wesley street, Newburyport

Wanted Immediately,

CUCUMBERS IN SALT. Apply to

je27 W. S. COFFIN, 49 Water street.

SAPONIFIER

—OR—

CONCENTRATED LYE

A Ready Family Soap-Maker,

☞ *Of Three Times the Strength of common Potash*

THE public are cautioned against the SPURIOUS articles of LYE for making SOAP &c, now offered for sale. The only GENUINE and PATENTED Lye is that made by the

Pennsylvania Salt Manufacturing Company,

their trade mark for it being "SAPONIFIER; or, CONCENTRATED LYE." The great SUCCESS of this article has led unprincipled parties to endeavor to IMITATE it, in violation of the Company's PATENTS.

All Manufacturers, Buyers or Sellers of these SPURIOUS Lyes, are hereby notified that the Company have employed as their Attorneys,

GEORGE HARDING, Esq, of Philadelphia, and WILLIAM BAKEWELL, Esq, of Pittsburg.

And that all Manufacturers, Users, or Sellers of Lye, in violation of the rights of the Company, will be PROSECUTED at once.

THE SAPONIFIER,

—OR—

CONCENTRATED LYE

Is for sale in Newburyport by

JOHN H. BALCH and E. M. READ.

In West Newbury, ANSON W. NOYES.

Take Notice.

The United States Circuit Court, Western District of Pennsylvania, No. 1 of May Term in 1862 in suit of the PENNSYLVANIA SALT MANUFACTURING CO. vs. THOS. G. CHASE, decreed to the Company on November 15, 1862, the

EXCLUSIVE

right granted by a patent owned by them for the Saponifier Patent dated October 21, 1856.

Perpetual Injunction Awarded

THE PENNSYLVANIA

Salt Manufacturing Company.

OFFICE—127 WALNUT STREET, PHILADELPHIA,
" PITT STREET & DUQUESNE WAY, PITTSBURG.

my14 eD&eois3m

Goods for Boys' Wear.

CASHMARETTS, Tweeds, Fancy Doeskins, Cotton Goods, &c.,—a full line just received at

jy1 R. COOK & CO.'S, 18 State street.

Don't Buy any Silk Bonnets,

BEFORE examining those new styles, at LEVY'S, 34 State street.

Don't Buy any Ribbons,

UNTIL you have enquired the prices at LEVY'S, 34 State street.

CHARLES P. HARDING,

(For the past fifteen years at Barrett's Dye House,)

HAS REMOVED TO

208 Washington Street. Boston,

Where he will be happy to attend to any orders in his line of business.

Gents. coats, pants, vests, and military garments, dyed or cleansed whole.

Felt Hats dyed black or brown, and returned all pressed and trimmed.

Ladies' dresses, cloaks and water-proofs, dyed and cleansed, either whole or ripped.

Crape, stella and merino shawls dyed or cleansed.

Plumes cleaned and dressed Feathers dyed all colors, and curled.

Kid gloves dyed or cleansed without odor.

Goods returned promptly, and satisfaction guaranteed.

CHARLES P. HARDING,

SILK AND WOOL DYER,

OFFICE, NO. 208 WASHINGTON STREET,

Between Franklin and Summer Streets,

BOSTON.

AGENT for receiving goods which will be forwarded free of expense—MRS. J. ALTER, State street, Newburyport. Je25—1m

For Sale,

A two-story dwelling house containing six rooms, convenient for two families, with forty rods of land, situated near the foot of Jefferson street, (at Merrill's yard formerly so-called) and near the Hat Factory and ship-yards. Enquire at 330 High street.

Jy8—8w WM. C. MERRILL.

VOL. 1. NEW ORLEANS, SUNDAY MORNING, JULY 12, 1863. NO. 125.

THE ERA

PORT HUDSON.

A COMPLETE HISTORY

OF ITS

Investment, Siege and Capture.

THE RIGHT WING.

4th to 9th June, inclusive.

THE SITUATION.

Nothing to indicate the presence of an enemy, within a couple of hundred yards, has occurred on the right wing, during this period, except an occasional shot from a picket or a shell from a battery. Even the little firing there was done might easily have been mistaken by the listener for drill practice, had he not been aware of the actual state of affairs.

Still, these occasional shots are productive of injury to the enemy, keeping them on the *qui vive* continually, and preventing their obtaining the rest of which they stand so much in need. Every moment of delay in attacking is regarded as a life saved, and the meanest soldier in the army is too valuable at the present crisis to be needlessly risked.

The Generals commanding the right wing express the belief that Port Hudson could be taken at any moment by assault; but the loss inevitable in assaulting so strong a position, with the works in good order and unbreached, would be too great for the exigencies of the case. When the enemy are reduced by privation and unceasing watching in the trenches, by loss of sleep and desertion, and by the fire of our sharpshooters and big guns, then the assault will be made—and will succeed.

THE WORK COMPLETED.

The mere statement of the fact that the army has been busy, during the suspension of active fighting, in constructing batteries, digging rifle pits and trenches, and in getting into position the siege guns, conveys no adequate idea of the labor performed. The mortars, Dahlgrens, etc., had to be brought to the field from Baton Rouge and the city, as did also the implements necessary to place them in position; cotton had to be hauled from plantations in wagons, to be used in defending them, and the labor on the works themselves had to be done, principally, under cover of darkness. Then the immense quantity of ammunition necessary to batter down the opposing works had to be brought in wagons from Springfield Landing to the battlefield, a distance of fourteen or fifteen miles. This labor of itself is sufficient reason for not attacking, did not the principal one—the daily weakening of the enemy by delay—not exist.

EXPEDITION TO CLINTON—THE CAUSE.

It has been known to the Commanding General for several days that a small rebel force had congregated at Clinton, and squads had in one or two instances made their appearance on the roads in our rear. Rumor of course placed the number of the force at Clinton at several thousand, and as a body of rebels of that size might cause serious annoyance if allowed to remain in the neighborhood of our army undisturbed, an expedition was sent on the 5th instant to either disperse or capture them.

THE TROOPS.

The regiments selected to perform the work of dispersion were taken from the right wing, and consisted of part of Col. Gooding's brigade, the 31st, 38th and 53d Massachusetts regiments, commanded by Col. G., the 8th New Hampshire and 4th Wisconsin, also of Gen. Paine's division, under Col. Fearing, and the 150th New York and 52d Massachusetts, under Col. Van Zandt. One section of the 1st Maine Battery under command of Lieut. Morton, two sections of Daryea's Battery, under Lieuts. Norris and Garvin, Capt. Yeaton's company of 1st Louisiana Cavalry, and the Illinois Cavalry, all under Col. Grierson, also formed part of the expedition. Gen. Paine was in command of the whole.

THE MARCH.

The trip to Clinton and back was the most severe marching that has yet been done in this department. The heat had been almost intolerable in the woods for several days previous to the start, and to march on the open roads, four or five inches deep in dust, and under a burning sun, was trying men to their utmost. The expedition left here on the morning of Friday, the 5th instant, and after proceeding about seven miles they halted and nooned. In the afternoon, they again started, marched three miles, and were compelled to stop, the men being unable to proceed. During this time, forty-eight men fell from sunstroke and exhaustion, and Gen. Paine decided not to advance again during the heat of the day. A short distance was made on Friday night and Saturday morning, when a halt was ordered until midnight. At daybreak on Sunday morning the troops arrived in front of Clinton, and camped around the town.

WHAT THEY FOUND.

None but the Illinois Cavalry entered the town, and they took immediate possession of everything that could be considered public property. The depot, warehouse, and one other building, together with the contents, were burned. The contents were of little value, the principal items being a small lot of corn, and some five hundred barrels Louisiana rum. Some of the Illinois boys took the opportunity of getting quite merry at the expense of the Southern Confederacy, but we should think from the rueful countenances they make up when mention of Louisiana rum is made, that the experiment was not at all merry.

Most of the citizens have deserted or been conscripted out of Clinton, and the once pretty town has now a lonely, neglected look. We found some few of the Illinois Cavalry, wounded and prisoners, in a house, and they speak very highly of the treatment they received from the ladies of the place. They were made prisoners in a skirmish several days ago. About twenty wounded rebels were also taken, and they seem quite willing to remain.

The men returned from the trip on last Monday, and are now in the woods recruiting. They were exhausted more by this march than all their previous trials, and the reports of the different regiments show a large proportion of each unfit for duty. They will doubtless be all right again before the next fight takes place.

June 10th.

SIEGE GUNS OPENED.

At 11 o'clock this morning the siege guns opened slowly, and the splendid manner in which the pieces were handled and the accuracy of their fire were the subject of general comment and praise. In this connection, it is but justice to remark that the artillery is well served in all parts of the field. An old Potomac soldier said, while watching the firing, that this Department had the finest guns and the best artillerists in the world, and he is capable of judging. Each gun is fired about every fifteen minutes, the Generals not being ready for the combined attack.

BUILDINGS BURNED.

This evening several fires broke out inside the enemy's works, caused by our incendiary shells. One large building, used as a warehouse for commissary stores and containing provisions, sugar and molasses, was burned to the ground.

June 11th.

FEELING THE ENEMY.

At 1 o'clock this morning our skirmishers were advanced along the entire lines, and fire opened upon the rebels. The object of the movement was to draw the enemy's fire, and thereby learn at what portions of the line they expected an attack, and had posted men and guns in the greatest numbers. The firing was very heavy, and the enemy manned the works in full force, but would not open with his artillery. As a knowledge of the location of this was the main object of the attack, Gen. Weitzel, who was with the batteries, ordered nine guns to open, hoping to create the impression that a general attack was about to be made. For half an hour the boom of cannon and exploding shells was continuous and incessant, and the enemy must have lost heavily, as they advanced quite a number of men under the fire to the breastworks, but they either designed our object or were holding their fire back for the assaulting party. Only six shots responded to our guns, and they did no damage.

On our side, the 12th Connecticut suffered most. They did not, probably, understand the nature of the movement, and pressed on out of cover and up to the breastworks. Two companies succeeded in mounting them, but were repulsed, with a loss in all of six killed and twenty-nine wounded.

While our men were in this position—close at the foot of the works—a heavy thunderstorm came on completely drenching the men, and rendering the clay soil on the hill side so slippery that they could not retain their footing. They were ordered to return to their old position. By daybreak everything was water-soaked, but the sun came out, and in a few hours set everything right again.

DESERTERS.

Four deserters escaped to our lines, and tell the same story of discontent and dissatisfaction among the rebels within that all previous ones have told. Every day now adds to the list of deserters to some part of our line. Yesterday four deserted to the Native Guards, and were taken by the negro pickets to their commanding officer. This speaks well for the humanity of the colored troops, when it is known by them that every one captured will be murdered.

ANOTHER STORM.

This afternoon a very severe rain and thunder storm prevailed for nearly two hours, and has slightly weakened our newly made batteries and earthworks. We have the satisfaction of knowing, however, that it rains as hard, and that the works are made of the same material, inside of Port Hudson as out.

THE WISCONSIN BOY AGAIN.

We have before mentioned that a Corporal Earl, of the 4th Wisconsin, had been upon the enemy's works endeavoring to kill a rebel colonel, for the purpose of "getting even" with them for shooting Col. Bean, of his regiment, on the 27th. Since then he has mounted the parapet several times, and shot two or three rebels on the inside, without in any instance receiving a scratch. The man certainly bears a charmed life, as it is almost certain death for any one else to merely show his head.

June 12th.

THE SIEGE GUNS AT WORK.

About 11 o'clock this morning the mortars and heavy guns commenced a slow but destructive fire upon the enemy's works. It was not intended as a regular bombardment, but as a trial of the pieces, and to obtain proper range. A battery of four 10 inch Dahlgrens, under command of Lieut. Terry, manned by sailors from the Richmond, and planted on the left of the right wing, does some excellent shooting, and the tars seem to enjoy the shore fight hugely.

DISPATCH BEARERS CAUGHT.

It was thought impossible for any one to escape from Port Hudson and get safely through our lines, notwithstanding their length. But it seems there is a loop hole somewhere. As one of our cavalrymen was riding along the road leading to Bayou Sara, to-day, he suddenly came upon two men in rebel uniform. He at once called on them to surrender, which they did, thinking, as they afterward said, he had a number of others close at hand. He brought them into our lines, (he caught them nearly three miles outside,) and upon one of them was found a cypher dispatch from Gen. Gardiner to Gen. Joe Johnston. Another man was caught during the day with a copy of the same dispatch, and he says that forty messengers have been sent with it to Johnston. The story is not believed, but if it is true, Johnston will soon be in possession of a copy. No one as yet has been able to decypher it, and some express the opinion that it is all "bosh," gotten up to scare some one. One of the men is undoubtedly an officer, but claims to be only Gen. Gardiner's orderly. He possesses a superior education, and is a person of great natural intelligence for such a position.

STILL THEY COME.

Seventeen privates and non-commissioned officers came over and gave themselves up to the Yankees to-day. They had been on duty as an outpost, under command of a commissioned officer, and thinking a better opportunity to regain their freedom might never occur, they killed their officer, and deserted. On all parts of our line the number of deserters picked up yesterday was forty—so many less muskets to be used against our men on the assault.

June 13th.

THE BOMBARDMENT.

At 11 o'clock this morning, in accordance with orders from Gen. Banks, the bombardment commenced from nearly all our batteries, and continued for one hour with unremitting intensity and vigor. We spent the greater part of the hour with the sailors and their battery, and it was amusing to watch their motions. They evidently thought it a good joke. The fire of the other batteries was as well sustained.

At the conclusion of the hour's firing, a flag of truce was sent in to Gen. Gardiner, demanding the surrender of Port Hudson, but, as was anticipated, he refused, saying "his duty required him to defend the place." Shortly after the fire again opened slowly, and was kept up the remainder of the day.

Back from the batteries indications of another assault near at hand were visible. Hand grenades for the stormers were being filled, and bags were being stuffed full of cotton, to be thrown into the ditch, in addition to the usual preparations on the eve of a fight.

Several more deserters came in to-day.

June 14th.

THE ATTACK.

All night long the finishing touches were being put to the preparations for the fight that all knew would take place at daylight. The attack on the right, under Gen. Grover, was to be made in two columns, one commanded by Gen. Weitzel and the other by Gen. Paine, and two better men could not have been selected for the work on hand—both possessing the confidence and respect of their soldiers in the highest degree.

The men had breakfast at one o'clock, and soon after everything was in readiness for the movement.

GEN. PAINE'S COLUMN—ITS FORMATION.

The attacking party, under Gen. Paine, formed on the Port Hudson and Clinton road, in the following order: First came the 8th New Hampshire and 4th Wisconsin regiments, deployed as skirmishers, followed by five companies of the 4th Massachusetts and 110th New York, with the hand grenades. A company of the 38th Massachusetts also took grenades. Behind them and in advance of the column was the 31st Massachusetts regiment, of Col. Gooding's brigade, with cotton bags. Their duty was to fill the ditch to enable the main column to move over rapidly. Next the 3d, 2d and 1st brigades, a pioneer company, to level parapets so that artillery could go over, and last the artillery itself, Nims's battery in advance.

The grenade and cotton bag carriers also took their muskets, strapped to their backs, and were to join the skirmishers as soon as they had disposed of their burdens. The whole were to move at quick time.

THE FIGHT.

At half-past 3 o'clock the column advanced up the road, the 8th New Hampshire and 4th Wisconsin leading, and deployed as skirmishers. Upon reaching the open ground, firing was immediately commenced, and they pressed rapidly forward. The enemy was not an instant behind, and the fire was returned with interest. In fact, they returned it so strongly that it was found necessary to reinforce the skirmish line with the 53d and 38th Massachusetts regiments, and they were deployed as a second line in the direction of what had been a sallyport, but is now built up.

No point along the whole line of works presents less protection to an attacking party than the one selected for the assault of this column. At all the other points, hills and ravines, covered with brushwood and stumps, afford a covering to skirmishers, but here there is nothing of the kind. The ground in places is slightly rolling, but every hollow found that would admit of a man's lying down and being hid, is enfiladed.

Under these circumstances, the sooner the hand-to-hand work could begin the better for our men, and the skirmishers pushed on with cheers in the direction of the parapets. General Paine had gone out with the skirmishers himself, and urged them on to do their utmost. At some points the men of the 8th New Hampshire and 4th Wisconsin had reached and climbed on the parapets, and a number of the grenade men had succeeded in throwing their missiles inside, but nothing human could withstand the devastating fire poured into them by the rebels, and they were forced back.

The brigade of Col. Gooding, that was, according to the plan of battle, to head the column, was now all in action with the exception of the 156th New York, Col. Sharp, which, however, was only part of a regiment. The column was during the fight of the skirmishers moved up the road as close as practicable until the cotton bag men should perform their duty, which, of course, they had found impossible so far.

General Paine now determined with one bold and steady push to reach the works with his skirmishers, and hold them until the 31st could deposit the bags and enable them to cross. He rallied them, cheered them, and ordered a charge; but hardly had he given the command when he fell, his leg broken below the knee. The men, however, again pushed on, followed by the 31st and their bags, and another desperate effort was made to scale the works. Some few succeeded, but were either immediately shot down or taken in by the rebels.

Previous to his fall General Paine had sent to Colonel Gooding for the 156th to advance up the road leading to Port Hudson, and the regiment took position as directed. Owing to the fall of General Paine, the regiment was left in the road under a heavy fire of both artillery and musketry, without orders, or the possibility of injuring the enemy, for nearly half an hour. The artillery was soon silenced by our big guns, however, and the regiment got permission to retire to a better protected position a few yards down the road. It was some time, too, before the fall of General Paine became known, but when it was communicated to General Grover, who was at a point where a cross road led over to General Weitzel's column, and where he had easy access to both, he dispatched Colonel Birge to take command of the division. Colonel Birge had command of two reserve brigades when the order reached him, and he of course knew nothing of the plans or intentions of General Paine. This caused a delay of half an hour, but as soon as he became acquainted with the position of affairs, he ordered three [illegible] made. The order was sent by Colonel Birge to Colonel Gooding, but as his own men were all engaged, he ordered Colonel Ferris, of the 28th Connecticut, who commands the First Brigade, to send the three regiments nearest the point to attack forward at once.

It is impossible to tell whether in the charge which followed the advance of these regiments, all took part or not. Our right overlapped the left of General Weitzel, and the regiments were then somewhat confused. But one thing is certain, Colonel Curry, of the 133d New York, showed that he possessed soldierly qualities of no ordinary stamp. He led his regiment forward to the foot of the works, waving his sword and calling on them to follow him, and had mounted half way up the parapet with fifteen or twenty of his men, when he fell, shot through both arms. He was immediately carried from the field, and his wounds properly attended to, but whether the country will lose him or not it is impossible to say.

The charge was unsuccessful. No men could withstand the murderous fire of the rebel sharpshooters, and when it is left almost optional with men whether they will go in or not, they will seldom come up to the mark. This must necessarily be the case when men are ordered to charge as skirmishers, as each chooses his time and place. It takes a great deal of excitement and enthusiasm to make up for the loss of confidence imparted by numbers and the touch of a comrade's elbow. Had the men been charging in mass, it is the general opinion they would have captured Port Hudson at this time.

The fire was continuous and well sustained, especially on the part of the rebels, during the balance of the day; but our losses were before 10 A. M. All day our men were compelled to hug the ground for shelter, and fire very slowly. The rebels in tree tops inside the works had fine range on them, and could fire with very little danger to themselves; but our boys stuck to their advanced position with a tenacity unparalleled, and would not be driven back.

As darkness fell upon the scene, our main force was withdrawn from the field. The skirmishers maintained their position, but were soon relieved by the brigade of Col. Dudley, which had been in reserve all day. A strong hospital corps was also sent out to bring in the wounded and bury the dead, but the firing of the rebels drove them back. Quite a number of our wounded remained on the field nearly all night.

GEN. WEITZEL'S COLUMN.

ITS FORMATION.

The arrangement of the column of attack of Gen. Weitzel was similar to Gen. Paine's in every particular. His force at the outset comprised but two brigades, the 2d Brigade, 1st Division, and the 2d Brigade, 4th Division. The 75th New York and 12th Connecticut Regiments, under Col. Babcock, deployed as skirmishers, led the way, followed by the 91st New York, with the hand grenades. Behind the grenade men came the 24th Conn., with the cotton bags to fill the ditch, and they were succeeded by the assaulting column. This was composed of the 8th Vermont, 114th New York, and part of the 160th New York, commanded by Col. Smith, of the 114th, and they were supported by Col. Kimball, with the 12th Maine and 52d Mass.

THE ADVANCE.

The point selected for this column to assault the enemy's works, was a short distance to the right of the one Gen. Paine attempted to carry. The face of the country, however, in this short distance, completely changes, and instead of the open plain over which he advanced, and on which he suffered so much, the ground is covered with hills, and cut up with ravines.

OPENING OF THE FIGHT.

One of these ravines offered a cover and protection to our advancing troops to within probably one hundred yards of the outer works of the enemy, and through this they were led. The skirmishers opened the attack almost simultaneously with the other column, and pushed on rapidly as the ground permitted, followed by the hand grenades. So close were the lines of assault of these two columns, that the skirmishers of one overlapped the flank of the skirmishers of the other, and they became mixed up, and fought so all day. This caused no inconvenience or confusion to this column, as the purposes of all pointed in the same direction—the scaling of the parapets, and holding them until the column could cross.

Nothing but what has been told of the other skirmishers is to be said of these. Unflinching bravery and a heroic desire to overcome all obstacles that stood between them and success, marked the conduct and shone in the countenance of every one of them; but they, alas! were doomed to a bitter disappointment. Five times their number would have quailed and fell back before the terribly well directed volleys of the rebels, or sank, like too many of them did, martyrs to their patriotism and love of country.

AN IMPEDIMENT.

The advance of the main body had been delayed for about half an hour, while the skirmishers were fighting by the cotton-bag carriers. As before stated, the way led through a narrow ravine, just wide enough to admit of a regiment's marching by the flank. The regiment with the bags, which immediately preceded Col. Smith's command, had halted in the ravine, and from some unaccountable cause would neither advance nor get out of the way.

THE REBEL FIRING.

This difficulty being got over, the troops proceeded on up the ravine, at the end of which was a hill, on which they were to form for the assault. The 8th Vermont Regiment held the advance, and attempted to ascend the hill by companies. Some idea may now be formed of the deadliness of the enemy's fire. The first company, (Co. B,) on reaching the brow of the hill, were met by a volley of musketry, and 23 men fell, killed or wounded. A slight hesitation took place on the part of the next company at seeing this, and company E moved out of its place, and started over the hill. Hardly had they shown themselves, when another discharge from the enemy's rifles took place, and 14 men were *hors du combat*. Company C had recovered from its momentary but very natural halt, and now dashed boldly on to the crest of the hill, but only to meet a similar reception. A leaden shower whistled among and around them, and 21 brave heroes followed their comrades, who, a moment before, had gone where they were in all the pride of strength and manhood. In less than five minutes 58 men, out of three already decimated companies, were lost to the country—most of them forever.

FALL OF COL. SMITH.

It was plain to every one that the men could not form on the hill and charge across the ravine, up the next hill, and into the works, as was originally intended, and a change had to be adopted. It was determined to form under the brow of the hill, and charge from there. Col. Smith dispatched Capt. Barstow, his Assistant Adjutant General, to place the 8th Vermont, and he himself undertook to point out to the 114th and 160th New York their position. In doing this he exposed himself to the fire of the enemy for an instant, and he was mortally wounded.

VAN PATTEN IN COMMAND—A SPLENDID CHARGE.

By the fall of Col. Smith the command devolved upon Col. Van Patten, of the 160th New York, and this gallant officer led the brigade in one of the most desperate charges of the day. Over the hill and [illegible]ly, some of them crossing the ditch and climbing partly up the breastworks, but only to die or be driven back. The unbreached works were held by men as determined as themselves, and with such advantages on their side, victory for the Union arms was almost an impossibility.

USING THE BAGS.

A ridge that runs parallel with the works, and only about forty feet from them, was held by our men, and Col. Van Patten sent back for and obtained some of the cotton bags to use as a protection to his men. These were placed on the ridge, but did very little good, they being so near that the rebels were enabled to set them on fire.

REINFORCEMENTS—COL. HOLCOMB KILLED.

Gen. Weitzel had at this time sent for reinforcements to Gen. Grover, and Col. Morgan, of the 90th New York, with two brigades, was dispatched to his aid. By the time they reached him, it was determined to risk no more men in attempting to carry the works by assault, but to render Col. Van Patten as secure in his position as possible; Col. Holcomb, of the 1st Louisiana, with a sufficient force, was sent to his support. The men reached the spot where Col. Smith fell, and Col. Holcomb ordered them to charge over the hill. He started forward to lead them on, waving his sword over his head, when a ball entered his forehead and dashed his brains in all directions.

OUR TROOPS WITHDRAWN.

Until the shades of night hid them from each other, our men continued the unequal contest with the enemy, suffering greatly, but still inflicting serious injury on the foe. When it could be done without too much exposure, the troops were withdrawn from the field, a strong line of skirmishers being left to hold the ground so dearly bought and so desperately held.

DIGGING RIFLE PITS.

Orders were issued for the throwing up of rifle pits under cover of the darkness, so that we can hold the ground, and as a cover to any other assault our Generals may see fit to order. Should they direct another attack on these works, cover to so short a distance from the parapets will render success almost certain.

OUR LOSSES.

The losses of the right wing in this day's fight are very heavy, considering the number engaged. The Third Division (Paine's) lost 800 men, and but a few of the regiments were engaged. One regiment lost as high as thirty men and two officers, and never fired a gun; several others losing nearly as many. This was not the fault of the commanders, as there was no place of safety the troops could be removed to, without taking them from the field.

The killed, wounded and missing of Gen. Weitzel's old brigade sum up:

	Killed.	Wounded.	Missing.	Total.
8th Vermont	12	69	9	90
12th Connecticut	1	18	5	24
75th New York	7	54	12	73
114th N. Y. (half reg.)	8	75	30	113
160th N. Y. (half reg.)	1	34	3	38
	29	250	59	338

No doubt is entertained but that quite a number of those reported missing are killed, but so close to the enemy's works that their bodies can not be discovered. Some are prisoners, and the balance will turn up in time, being now with other regiments in the woods.

The 8th New Hampshire, of Paine's Division, out of 208 lost 123 men, and the 4th Wisconsin about the same. The total loss of the right wing will not fall short of 1500, when the returns from both columns and the skirmishers can be obtained.

NARROW ESCAPES.

Hardly a man on the field but can recount several hair breadth escapes as happening him, and perhaps no one oftener touched death and escaped without injury than Col. G. P. Gooding, commanding the Third Brigade of Paine's Division. He was on the field from the opening of the fight until dark, and wherever he went, bullets, unpleasantly well directed, followed him. Fortunately for the service, he escaped scot free.

GEN. PAINE AND STAFF.

Before 7 o'clock in the morning, Gen. Paine and both his aide-de-camps were wounded. Gen. P. was wounded in the leg, Lieut. G. C. Pierce in the leg, and Lieut. Stringer in the same place. Lieut. Pierce was wounded in the arm on the 27th and returned to the field as soon as the wound was dressed, although Gen. Paine ordered him to the rear. He was wounded the last time by a piece of one of our own shells.

NOBLE ACTIONS.

When it became known that Gen. Paine was lying wounded on the field, and that the enemy's sharpshooters commanded the spot where he lay, a number of soldiers volunteered to go to him and either bring him off or carry stimulants to him, but every one that approached near enough to communicate with him was either killed or wounded. Among these brave men were two who had attracted especial attention by their efforts in relieving the wounded. They belonged to the 31st Massachusetts, and had been detailed from that regiment for the ambulance corps. Their names were J. P. Woods, Company E., and John Williams, Company D. Woods, on hearing of Paine's fall, started to his relief with a bottle of cordial, but being unable to reach the place, he threw him the bottle (unfortunately out of the General's reach) and returned. He then procured a couple of lemons and a canteen of water, and endeavored to crawl to the desired spot, and had reached within about five feet of the General, when he was observed to roll over on his side and never move again. Williams had also obtained lemons and water and gone out, but he never returned.

During the hottest of the fight a 4th Wisconsin man was observed to fall in an exposed place, and a rebel sharpshooter fire at him once or twice afterwards, by a private of Company A, 12th Connecticut regiment, named Chas. Constantine. The latter immediately took off his equipments, crawled to him, took him on his back, and carried him safely to a place where he could be reached by the stretcher bearers.

OUR MISSING.

Our losses in prisoners during the day probably amount to 65 or 70. They were all captured on or at the foot of the parapets, and most of them are wounded. They belong principally to the 8th New Hampshire and 4th Wisconsin regiments. Had they not surrendered themselves, they would every one have fallen before the fire of the sharpshooters. It will be a source of pride to them hereafter to say they were captured at Port Hudson, on Sunday, the 14th of June; as none but brave men got near enough to be captured.

CORPORAL EARL GONE.

Our readers have not forgotten Corporal Earl. He charged with his regiment, the 4th Wisconsin, gained the top of the parapet, fired over, and then fell headlong inside, doubtless killed or wounded. He was a brave man and good soldier, and we hope he may yet come out all right.

REBEL ATROCITIES.

We had thought the time when robbing and mutilating dead bodies was countenanced among the rebels had gone by, and no more would such outrages be recorded against them. But we were mistaken. Towards evening, the rebel soldiers that lined the parapet could be plainly seen jumping over into the ditch, and stripping the dead and wounded of their shoes and clothing. A surgeon told us that he saw several corpses with fingers cut off, evidently to obtain rings. A large [illegible] were sent on the field, both black and white, but they were shot down or compelled to retire. A large number had to be left where they fell, near the parapets.

RESULTS.

How much this fight will aid in the final reduction of Port Hudson, it is not easy at first glance to perceive. We have lost in killed and wounded much heavier than the enemy, and have not visibly weakened their works, but we have cleared out and advanced our lines over some important points heretofore virtually held by them, and over which we should have had to advance and lost these men when the final assault did take place. And we have also thoroughly reconnoitered their position; something heretofore impossible, and discovered weaknesses that will prove an immense help in the future. We think the next attack, in view of these facts, will not be long delayed, and must prove successful.

J. W. F.

[TO BE CONTINUED]

From the Boston Transcript.

PRAYER FOR ****

For him I bow at morn and eve,
His name, on wings of prayer,
I send up with this earnest cry
Lord have him in Thy care!

Two children, by the winter hearth,
And wife, blue-eyed and fair,
With loving lips repeat his name,
O, have him in Thy care!

Father and friend! be thou his shield
From every tempting snare:
To foes within ne'er let him yield,
O, have him in Thy care!

In camp, or march, in duty's way,
From suffering, sorrow, spare;
Strength give him equal to his day—
Lord have him in Thy care!

When death on battle-field shall fall
To reaping, everywhere,
Bid the grim angel pass him by,
O, have him in Thy care!

But Father, if it be Thy will
His sun of life set there;
Be to him love, and light, and life.
Still have him in Thy care;

Alas! how many an aching heart,
With burden hard to bear!
Prays thus for soldier—husband, son—
Lord have them in Thy care!

FRANCES.

Miss Dr. Walker.—Among the unmarshaled host of camp-followers of the army, writes a correspondent from the Army of the Potomac, not the least noteworthy personage is Miss Mary E. Walker, or "Dr. Walker," as she is usually styled, a legitimate daughter of Esculapius, and apparently a lady of commendable philanthropy. She is a native of New York, has received a regular medical education, and believes her sex ought not to disqualify her for the performance of deeds of mercy to the suffering heroes of the Republic. Dressed in male habiliments, with the exception of a girlish-looking straw hat, decked off with an ostrich feather, with a petite figure and feminine features, the *tout ensemble* is quite engaging. Her reputation is unsullied, and she carries herself amid the camp with a jaunty air of dignity well calculated to receive the sincere respect of the soldiers. She has been with the army on several critical occasions—was with it at Burnside's defeat, and more recently at Sedgwick's crossing of the Rappahannock below Fredericksburg, where she was very active in her attention to our wounded. She can amputate a limb with the skill of an old surgeon, and administer medicine equally as well.

The Capture of Port Hudson.

ADDITIONAL PARTICULARS.

MANNER OF THE SURRENDER.

THE NEWS FROM VICKSBURG, AND ITS EFFECT UPON THE REBELS.

From a number of naval officers who were at Port Hudson at the time of its surrender to Maj. Gen. Banks, and who have since returned to New Orleans, we have obtained the following particulars in regard to the immediate causes which led to its capitulation, and the manner in which they were brought about. The number and standing of the gentlemen with whom we have conversed on the subject, is convincing that the statement is correct:

On the morning of the 7th inst., as stated in the dispatch of our correspondent at Port Hudson, a salute was fired from both the upper and lower fleets immediately on the receipt of the news from Vicksburg, and the bands of the different regiments struck up national and patriotic airs. The wildest enthusiasm prevailed among our soldiers all day, and the proximity of the contending forces enabled the rebels in Port Hudson to hear the cheering without enlightening them as to the cause.

At several points on the lines, the rebels and our troops were so near together that conversations could be held, and were carried on, without danger to either party.

Towards evening, on the 7th, the curiosity of the rebels to learn what was going on became so great that one of their officers called out to a Union officer, asking: "What are you making all that noise about?" The answer was: "We have taken Vicksburg!"

The rebel officer said he did not believe it, and on being asked what would convince him of its truth, he replied, "Nothing but a copy of the dispatch, or some reliable authority."

The Union officer then told him he would procure a copy of General Grant's official dispatch, and pass it over the parapet to him. The rebel said if he would do so, and vouch for its genuineness on his honor as a gentleman and a soldier, he would be convinced.

The Union officer at once procured a copy of the dispatch, and taking it to the enemy's breastworks, gave it to the officer with whom he had been conversing, and at the same time assured him, on the honor of a soldier, that the dispatch was genuine, and that he had copied it with his own hand. The rebel, having read it, said he was satisfied of its truthfulness, and that he thought it useless for Port Hudson longer to attempt to hold out.

Things remained in the same position as previous to the interview, until 2 o'clock the next morning, when a parley was sounded from the rebel works, which was answered, and an officer came out with a dispatch from General Gardiner asking on what terms a surrender would be accepted.

As soon as the message could be conveyed to Gen. Banks, an answer was returned, in effect that only an unconditional surrender would be accepted.

Gen. Gardiner accepted the terms, and asked a few hours to make the necessary arrangements. He was given twenty-four hours, but did not take that length of time. At 12 M., on the 8th of July, our forces entered Port Hudson, and became the masters of that stronghold.

The rebels were all drawn up in line of battle, with arms stacked in front of them, and the hungry soldiers of Gen. Gardiner were promptly fed from the commissariat of our army.

THE TURF.

Yesterday, the fifth match between the celebrated trotters, Geo. N. Patchen and General Butler, for $5000, mile heats, best three in five, under saddle, came off on the Fashion Course. The attendance was large, in consequence of the general anticipation that extraordinarily fast time would be made, it being well known that both horses preferred this mode of going than any other. Nor were the spectators disappointed in this respect, as in the second heat the fastest time to saddle ever yet shown on the trotting record was made by the winner, Geo. Butler. The track was in admirable condition.

In the first heat Butler was the favorite, $100 to $80 being freely offered, while odds were reduced to $100 to $60, before the word "go" was given by the judges. The stallion had the pole, and led to the quarter in 37 seconds, Butler breaking on the back stretch and losing a full length in consequence. He, however, settled to his work, and closing the gap in a splendid burst of speed, carried the stallion off his feet, and passed the half-mile pole two lengths first in 1.14½. Breaking on the lower turn, he surrendered the lead to Patchen, who, following the example set him, also went up, but catching quickly, he made a magnificent effort to reach the black horse, but failing to do so, was beaten by two lengths in 2.28.

In the second heat the betting was $100 to $28 on Butler. The stallion led to the quarter in 35½ seconds, but was passed by Butler on the second quarter—time, 1 19½. From this point the gallant black had the race safe, as Patchen broke on the turn into the home-stretch, and Butler came home a clever winner by four lengths in 2 21; the fastest time ever recorded under the saddle.

The third heat, like the last, afforded the spectators one of the most magnificent contests ever witnessed on the trotting park. Round the first turn they were side by side, and from here Butler began to draw ahead, doing the quarter in 35 seconds. On the second quarter, the stallion breaking, gave Butler a couple of lengths ahead; but, trotting splendidly, he got almost on even terms at the half mile pole, in 1:11. The black horse, admirably ridden by Dan Mace, now showed his quality, for, letting out a link or two of his wonderful speed, he came home a winner by three lengths of the heat and the race, in 2:23¼.

The rider of the winner received a perfect ovation of applause from the excited assemblage for his splendid riding of the gallant Butler. Patchen was also ridden in admirable style by young Doble. [N. Y. paper, 24th June.

The British Pirate Japan, alias Georgia, is described by one who has been on board as a common iron screw propeller of about 800 tons, brig rigged, painted black, and armed with four guns. She was only half-manned in April. Captain Ducher, of the bark Nye, says she is not half as formidable as the "290," alias Alabama.

THE ERA

SUNDAY MORNING, JULY 12, 1863.

The capture of Port Hudson and Vicksburg gives us the assurance that Louisiana will soon be clear of the traitors who attempted to link her fortunes with those of the Southern Confederacy. The bands of guerrillas and robbers that infest some portions of the State, will, we make no doubt, be speedily disposed of, and the Stars and Stripes will wave over every inch of our soil.

We never have doubted that such would be the issue of this campaign. The fertile imagination of some of our citizens peopled the woods and fields of Port Hudson with such perils that no human power could withstand them. Now we were told that Kirby Smith was about to swoop down upon our devoted army with overpowering force; now it was Johnston, or Breckinridge, or Taylor, or somebody else, who was surely ready to strike a blow that should compel the Commanding General to raise the siege, if, indeed, he should have the rare good fortune to escape capture. Then, Magruder was coming with legions of Texans, and he was to celebrate the 4th of July in New Orleans; and so on through an endless catalogue of horrible things that were to happen surely and speedily. But all these perils, real or imaginary, did not distract attention from the one great and grand pupose, the capture of Port Hudson, and the opening of the Mississippi River. Were the enemy's fortifications and his well-directed line of fire too strong and destructive to be overcome by assault? Then the Union army could wait; it could erect batteries, dig approaches, undermine the citadel, and with sleepless vigilance guard every point, so that none could escape and none enter. The hold of the Union army upon the place was like the gripe of fate; the downfall of Port Hudson we have from the first regarded as certain, for we believed that this was the one great work to be done—the crowning triumph of a campaign characterized by extra ordinary rapidity and success. This was the great prize—a stronghold fortified with elaborate care and scientific skill, difficult of ap proach and possessing most striking natural advantages. To reduce this position, so important not only to the interests of the Southwest, but to the whole country, was an undertaking not to be laid aside; and now that it is accomplished; now that the river is open to our gunboats throughout its entire length, every one feels that the achievement is more than worthy of all the life and labor, the patient waiting and unsurpassed perseverance it has cost.

It will not be long before we shall begin to realize the solid results of the victory. It cannot be expected that we shall have free commerce or even uninterrupted navigation at once. But the immediate advantages, nevertheless, will be very great. We want the produce of the West in our market, and we shall get it. It may be that a convoy of gunboats will be necessary; it may be that here and there a band of guerrillas will attack an unarmed vessel; but, nevertheless, the great work is accomplished; the river belongs to the Union henceforth and forever, and binds the Southwest to the Northwest with the strong bond of commerce.

Faith Without Knowledge.

There is something marvelous and passing strange, in the faith of that portion of our community who sympathize with the rebel cause. There is no story, if it favor their side, that is too wild for their eager credulity, or sufficiently absurd to stagger their imaginations. On the other hand, anything how well soever it may be authenticated, that favors the Union cause, finds these same persons utterly incredulous!

A remarkable illustration of this singular frame of mind, has just been furnished by the reception of the news from Port Hudson and Vicksburg. There is, of course, no more doubt of the capture of both of these places than there is of the direction of sunrise. As for Vicksburg, the information was official; it came from Gen. Grant directly, and was by him sent both to Gen. Banks and to Admiral Farragut. A salute was fired by the army and the fleet, and the air rang with the glad shouts of our happy soldiers. A copy of that dispatch was sent to Gen. Emory, on the official authority of the Commanding General; by him it was made public; and, in short, the fall of Vicksburg is so perfectly certain that it seems as though no one not doomed to hopeless idiotcy could entertain a doubt on the subject.

In regard t Port Hudson, a doubt appears to be too absurd to warrant consideration. And yet, there are many men in this same New Orleans, who say they do not believe that either Vicksburg or Port Hudson has fallen!

With such persons, reasoning is vain; their blind faith in rebel valor and an equally blind disbelief in the possibility of Union success, makes one hesitate whether to regard them with more of pity or contempt.

General Gardiner.

General Gardiner, the rebel commander who surrendered Port Hudson, is a deserter from the United States Army. He held a commission, and did not wait to resign before he entered the service of the traitors.

Our Port Hudson Correspondence.—We continue, to-day, the account of the operations of the right wing of our army in the siege of Port Hudson. It embraces the second assault on the enemy's works, on the 14th of June, and is a record of heroic deeds. Among those who fell on that day, were Col. Holcomb, of the 1st Louisiana, and Col. Smith, of the 114th New York.

Charles Gee has his attention called to an advertisement in another column.

FROM ABOVE PORT HUDSON.

ARRIVAL OF THE HARTFORD & ALBATROSS

The Estrella in Front of the City

ALL QUIET ON THE RIVER.

THE ARIZONA GONE TO VICKSBURG.

SECESH INCREDULOUS.

A scene of the greatest excitement was created on and near the levee yesterday evening, by the announcement that the Hartford and Albatross had arrived from above Port Hudson and were anchored in front of the city.

Cheers for the two noble vessels and their gallant crews were raised by the majority of those present, and it was easy to distinguish a Union man from a rebel by the look of exultation or the malignant scowl at this confirmation of the recent glorious news from above.

Quite a number professed to believe that a deception was being practiced, and that it was the Richmond that was gliding so gracefully through the waters of the Mississippi when the Hartford came in, but there was no mistaking the Albatross, as she swung round and anchored in the stream. The Estrella coming down and dropping an anchor a short distance off, convinced most of them that it was these vessels, but not that Port Hudson was taken. The Jackson *Mississippian* alone can do that.

But the Hartford and Albatross are here, after four months hard and dangerous service between the rebel strongholds, that have for so long blocked navigation on the Father of Waters.

Immediately on the hoisting of the Stars and Stripes over the rebel works at Port Hudson, the Hartford dropped down and fired a national salute in honor of the event. Shortly after, accompanied by the Albatross and Estrella, she steamed slowly down the river, receiving the cheers and congratulations of both the army and navy as she passed along.

While lying opposite Port Hudson, these vessels were visited by Major General Banks, and the officers and crews received the thanks of the Commanding General for the efficient aid they had rendered him in the recent eventful campaigns.

From Baton Rouge down they came along slowly, carefully examining every point where rebel batteries were reported stationed, and firing wherever it was probable rebel guns might be concealed, but they could discover nothing, nor get an answering shot. They arrived here at a quarter past six o'clock last evening.

The Arizona was dispatched to Vicksburg with dispatches from Major General Banks, soon after the surrender was completed, and by this time the glorious news has circulated all over the North, and gladdened the hearts of all true patriots.

We give the names of the Hartford's officers:

James S. Palmer, Commodore.
L. A. Kimbily, Lieut. Commander.
J. C. Watson Lieutenant.
H. B. Tyson, Lieutenant.
W. T. Meredith, Paymaster.
Wm. M. King, Surgeon.
J. H. Higbee, 1st Lieutenant Marines.
J. Hugg, Assistant Surgeon.
J. J. Reed, J. H. Reed, Chas. Jones, Edward Hazletine, D. Wemple, Ensigns.
E. B. Latch, F. A. Wilson, 2d Assistant Engineers in charge.
Isaac de Graff, Chas. M. Burchard, Albert K. Fulton, Hugh L. Pilkington, James E. Speight, 3d Assistant Engineers.
James Walker, Boatswain.
Oliver Stimson, Carpenter.
John Holbrook, Sailmaker.
Mr. Staples, Gunner.
N. P. S. Thomas, Commodore's Clerk.
J. W. Sands, Paymaster's Clerk.

The following is a list of the officers of the Albatross:

Theodore B. DuBois, Vol. Lieut. Commanding.
George Mundy, Acting Master.
Charles P. Washburn, Acting Master.
George R. Martin, Acting Assistant Paymaster.
Wm. J. Burge, Acting Assistant Surgeon.
William Harcourt, Acting Ensign.
James W. Smyth, Acting 3d Assistant Engineer.
Louis J. M. Boyd, Acting 3d Assistant Engineer.
Charles H. Slack, Acting 3d Assistant Engineer.
Thomas H. Elfred, Captain's Clerk.
James C. Graves, Paymaster's Clerk.

METEOROLOGICAL TABLE,

Showing the temperature at 9 A. M., 12 M. and 3 P. M., and also the mean temperature and greatest heat of the weather in New Orleans for the week ending Saturday, July 11th, 1863:

[COPY OF REGISTER KEPT AT CITY HALL.]

DATE.	9 A M	12 M.	3 P. M	MEAN.	GREATEST HEAT.
July 5......	84	92	94	90 33	94
" 6......	84	92	96	90 66	96
" 7......	84	90	93	89.00	95
" 8......	85	89	94	89.33	94
" 9......	82	86	92	86 66	92
" 10......	84	88	88	86.66	88
" 11......	83	83	78	81 33	83

REMARKS.

July 5. Clear and pleasant, and a light breeze from westward.
6. Clear; wind westerly.
7. Clear and pleasant throughout.
8. Clear and pleasant; breeze from southwest; in evening showery, with thunder and high wind.
9 and 10. Clear and pleasant; breeze from southwest.
11. Clear in the morning, noon cloudy and afternoon rainy.

The St. Louis Democrat says that Gov. Yates, of Illinois, has offered the Secretary of War 10,000 men to repel invasion.

VICKSBURG!

ITS CAPTURE FULLY CONFIRMED.

GEN. GRANT AFTER JOHNSTON.

The navy officers who arrived last night, bring the fullest confirmation of the surrender of Vicksburg to Gen. Grant on the 4th inst.

Gen. Grant states that he might have taken the place any day during the last three weeks, but that he delayed for two reasons: 1st, he knew it would have to surrender if he waited, and he would thus save many lives.

2d. He hoped to coax Gen. Johnston to come up and attack him, as he had the fullest preparations made, and would have destroyed his army. He withdrew his forces on the Big Black, to let Johnston cross, but the rebel General would not engage him.

Johnston moved off and divided his force into two columns, expecting to conceal the fact, so that Gen. Grant would pursue but one column, and thus assure the escape of the other. But Gen. Grant was fully informed of his designs, and made his dispositions accordingly.

A gentleman who has been with Gen. Grant's army, speaks in the highest terms of its condition and spirit, and says the capture of Vicksburg infused the wildest enthusiasm through the ranks.

SURRENDER OF PORT HUDSON.

TERRIBLE SICKNESS IN THE GARRISON.

DESTRUCTIVE FIRE OF OUR BATTERIES.

Large Number of Prisoners, &c.

We have some additional details in regard to the surrender of Port Hudson.

The surrender was tendered on the 8th, and Gen. Banks marched in and took possession on the 9th.

The number of rebel soldiers drawn up in line, when the surrender took place, was about four thousand.

In addition to this number there were about fifteen hundred sick and wounded; the wounded numbered about five hundred. The wounds are generally very severe, in the head, and by the bullets of sharpshooters.

Our batteries had done a great deal of damage, having destroyed an immense amount of stores.

The United States flag was run up at nine o'clock on Thursday morning, the 9th instant, and was saluted by the *Hartford* as she passed.

There had been terrible sickness in the gar- [illegible] They suffered terribly from this cause.

There was a good supply of ammunition, all of which fell into our hands.

At the time the *Hartford* left Port Hudson, Gen. Banks had not *paroled* any of the rebel prisoners.

MISCELLANEOUS ITEMS.

Two tons and a half of oysters were stripped from the bottom of the French iron-clad frigate La Gloire not long since.

Vermont farmers have broken out in a new place. Some of them at Salisbury have had sent them a herd of ten buffaloes—eight yearlings and two two-year olds.

Heaven sends us ten thousand truths, but because our doors and windows are shut to them, they sit and sing awhile upon the roof, and then fly away.

The new organ for the Music Hall, Boston, is 47 feet wide, 18 deep and 70 high; contains 6500 pipes, 86 through stops, and has four manuals; it weighs between 65 and 70 tons, and will cost complete about $50,000.

The St. John *Telegraph* says that the American Telegraph Company have determined on building a new telegraph line through that Province, from the Maine to the Nova Scotia borders—St. Stephen to Sackville.

The Charleston *Courier* recommends the people to "develop their resources," by catching skarks, porpoises and alligators for the sake of the oil, which is worth $8 or $10 a gallon. Shark steaks, it says, would find a ready sale.

A contumacious copperhead of a merchant tailor in St. Albans, Vermont, is being overhauled for non-compliance to the Federal excise law. The penalties for his foolishness already amount to $1500, to which $500 will be added for every month he holds out.

The Connecticut House of Representatives is composed of 109 farmers, 15 merchants, 15 manufacturers, 13 lawyers, 9 mechanics, 3 clergymen, 3 physicians; teachers, editors, lumber-dealers, clerks, tobacconists, hotel-keepers, 2 each; shipmasters, printers, mariners, surveyors, glass blowers, 1 each.

Miss Georgiana Letitia McDavish, a Toronto heiress, having eloped from a fancy dress ball in that city with a married British captain, has been making some stir in Rochester, N. Y., whither she was hunted by the police detective. The erring girl seems the least discomposed of any about the affair.

A new oil well, opened at Oil Creek, Pa., the other day, spouted up a stream of oil to a height of fifty feet, with a roar like a hurricane, and escaping at the rate of two thousand barrels per day. A stop-cock was got on after much trouble, and the flow can now be regulated to suit the demand.

The Scene of Jo. Smith's Inspiration.—The Syracuse (N. Y.) *Standard* says that when the train carrying eight hundred Mormons arrived at Palmyra, on Thursday morning, one of their Elders was informed by conductor Chapman that they were then upon the spot where Joseph Smith, the first prophet of their faith, was inspired—where he found by special direction the bible which they now receive as the word of God, and whence he took his departure to preach his newly-found gospel to the world. Their faithful Elder was incredulous, but nevertheless conferred with others of his sort on the subject, and in the end they searched their scripture. There they found that Palmyra, Wayne county, New York, was indeed the scene of their prophet's awakening. Thereupon their whole company was notified of the fact, and in a few moments all of them were out of the cars, gazing in open-mouthed wonder and awe, the leaders increasing the effect by explanations and exhortations. They were with difficulty got again on board the cars, each one taking a stick, a leaf, or a pebble as a memento of the place.

OUR VICTORIES!

Rejoicings Over Port Hudson and Vicksburg

GRAND TORCHLIGHT PROCESSION.

Immense Enthusiasm of the People.

NEW ORLEANS OUT OF DOORS.

HOUSES ILLUMINATED, ETC.

In response to the call of a number of Union citizens, there was a great outpouring of the people and a grand torchlight procession last night in honor of the success of our arms at Port Hudson and Vicksburg.

Hon. Thos. J. Durant addressed a great meeting on Canal street, in his usual eloquent and felicitous manner; another large meeting was also held on Canal street near the Iron House, where patriotic addresses were delivered by several distinguished speakers.

At the conclusion of these proceedings, an immense torchlight procession formed, with the right resting on Canal street, under the direction of Z. Getchell, Esq., Chief Marshal.

It proceeded up St. Charles street to Poydras, down Poydras to Carondelet, up Carondelet to Julia, up Julia to Camp, up Camp to Prytania, up Prytania to Terpsichore, down Terpsichore to Coliseum, up Coliseum, stopping at the residence of Rear Admiral Farragut, to Felicity, down Felicity to Magazine, down Magazine to Julia, up Julia to Camp, down Camp, stopping at The Era office, thence to Canal street, where the procession was dismissed.

A large number of residences were brilliantly illuminated. Among them we noticed the business house of North & Co., No. 48 Chartres street, and the store of Stapleton & Co., No. 95 Canal street. Both these firms had flung to the breeze immense United States flags during the day, and kept open house, with a bountiful supply of the good things of the world.

The rooms of the Sanitary Commission, No. 23 Carondelet street, were also brilliantly lighted up, and a full supply of creature comforts were offered by these gentlemen to the friends of the Union.

The procession halted in front of the residence of Admiral Farragut, and on the appearance of that veteran in response to the call of the crowd, he was hailed with tremendous applause.

The crowd that followed the procession throughout the entire length of the route, was larger than the procession itself, filling the streets from banquette to banquette. Cheers were given for the Union, for Gen. Banks, for President Lincoln, and for Gen. Grant.

The Era, not satisfied with firing off its cannon in honor of the victory, illuminated its office, and the procession did it the honor to halt in front of the establishment, and included it among the subjects of their cheering.

Lieut. Col. Hills was called for, and briefly responded.

The band played the National airs, and after a few appropriate remarks by Mr. Getchell, the great assembly dispersed.

The utmost order prevailed throughout the evening, and we have heard of no accidents or unpleasant incidents to mar the harmony of the occasion.

Parson Brownlow Once More.—A rebel prisoner wrote a letter to Parson Brownlow a few days ago, soliciting money on the score of old business relations. The Parson declined to give money, but gave instead some wholesome advice. In the course of his letter the Parson says:

All I had accumulated in thirty years was taken from me, because I refused to turn traitor, war upon my Government, and act with a band of the most infamous scoundrels, South, that ever God permitted to breathe the vital air. This is not all; my wife and seven children were driven out of the country after me, and refused the privilege of bringing anything with them but their wearing apparel. My two sons are in the Federal service, fighting the corrupt government, and the still more infamous authorities that forced them from their native soil. My wife, and her helpless girl-children, are boarding at a private house in Covington, opposite to Cincinnati.

The Secretary of the Treasury was kind and considerate enough, without any solicitation or my part, to appoint me one of the special agents of the Treasury Department, on the 18th of December last, and my pay meets the board of myself and family, at Covington, and no more. This is my condition in life, at the age of 57. I repeat, no Southern rebel or rebel sympathizer, has any claims upon me. I want no fellowship with such men, and I shall be found opposing them to the end of my earthly career. When they lose their negroes, their lands, houses and homes, and even their lives, I can but thank God, and take courage!

I am for the vigorous prosecution of this war until the old flag, the banner of beauty and glory, shall wave in triumph over every foot of soil, between the cod fisheries of Maine and the Gulf of Mexico. In other words, I am for using every means that God has placed in the power of the Federal Government to crush out this rebellion, if, in doing so, every rebel in the Southern Confederacy has to be exterminated, and every Northern traitor hung! Live or die, sink or swim, survive or perish, I am for the Union—the Union, one and indivisible.

The Crops.—The National Agricultural Department has just issued an abstract of the returns of the amount and condition of the crops in twenty-one States and in Nebraska, in May last. The returns—which have been taken by first averaging those from each county and then from these striking the average of the State—show that there is ten per cent above the average surface of land under winter wheat; about an average of spring wheat; a little over the average of rye; about the usual average of corn; five per cent increase of potatoes, and about thirty-seven and a half per cent of land in sorghum. Cotton culture has far outrun everything else in proportion to the average of last year, nearly four times more having been planted. The appearance of the various crops, with the exception of winter wheat, corn and oats, indicated a better return per acre than last year. The crops excepted—according to the estimate—will apparently only fall a fraction below the average of a good crop.

The Bishop of Havana has ordered the destruction of all the copies of "Les Miserables" that may have found their way into his diocese. The pastoral upon the subject directs the faithful to give up the objectionable work to the parish priests or curates of their respective districts, that they may be burned.

From the Boston Transcript.

E. B.—I Memoriam.

"Shot through the lungs," how he lay, how he lay
At Antietam, all that fearful day,
Slowly bleeding his life away!

And there comes to us now from the scenes of strife,
Soiled with the camp-dust, with memories rife,
All we have left of the soldier's life.

Only a book with, "This for my friend
When I am done with it," thoughtfully penned,
Long ere the battle Is this the end?

Is this the end for the voice of song—
For the hand so skilful, and yet so strong—
For the earnest will that bore him along?

I mind me now of his school boy ways;
"Brave and gentle," the fitting phrase,
And the patient toil of the after days.

Courteous as knight of the times of old,
With a heart as pure and withal as bold—
And his manhood's story all untold.

Yet why our life but to spend it free
As the snow that falls on the angry lea,
For the Right, for the Truth, for Liberty?

And the brave heart knows, with a quiet content,
When treason and murder their shafts have sent,
That the time is at hand for which it was lent.

But oh! Fatherland that we love so well,
Shall the future's annals shuddering tell
It was all in vain that our heroes fell?

We give them up at thy bitter cry,
We say no word when they go to die—
Is it Freedom's dawn that reddens the sky?

Ah, comrade, sleep well in thy soldier's bed
At Antietam, in the field of our dead,
Who know who watcheth overhead?

A. E.

SOLDIERS' CLAIMS.

Scenes similar to the following are often witnessed at the office of the American War Claim Association, No. 35 Chambers street, where the dues of soldiers and sailors are collected under the authorization of the Government, free of charge:

A tall, masculine-looking woman from down East came stumbling into the office, and walking up to the railing peered through an opening at the clerk engaged in writing. After scanning the furniture of the establishment, and looking wonderingly around her, she at length broke the silence by observing in a shrill voice:

"Waal, neow! Is this 'ere the place?"

Clerk—What place?

Woman—Whar I kin git my old man's money without payin' a red cent.

Clerk—Who was the man? Was he a soldier?

Woman—Well, I reckon! He was a soger. He fit in the 4th New Hampshire, and arter he was dead I got all these things about him. (Showing a dozen lithographed and written letters—sent by as many different claim agents—offering to get her old man's back pay, and procure a pension for her, if she would agree to give them sums varying from $5, up to one half the dues to the deceased soldier.)

Clerk—[astonished at the contents of the papers]—Where did all these come from?

Woman—The Postmaster in aour town giv em to me! The fust one that kim told me my old man was killed, and that's the fust I knowed he was dead. Some on em kim from Washington, another from Bostown, two came way from Chi-ca-go. Three on em come from New York, and a feller in Baltimore sent me that ere last one, that looks so stylish, and I spose I might have got lots more ef I hed staid tu hum. But ye see aour folks told me never to mind them ar letters, but jist go right straight to "honest old Abe," and get the money of my old man right from him. They do say he's a kind-hearted creeteer, and won't let the sogers' widders go without what belongs to em. So I started off and on the cars—

Clerk—[stopping the long story he knew by experience was coming]—So you got as far on your way as New York city and have now come here to get your money, which you want us to get for you. Is it not so?

Woman—Well! I declare that's just it. You see, when I got to Cousin Ann's, who lives in 27th street. I hadn't seen her for more'n six years. She told me she had seen all about such things in the *Sun*, and that there was a place right in this city whar I could get the money without paying for it, or spending any more to go to Washington to see Mr. Lincoln.

Clerk—So you can, and this is the place.

Woman—Don't you take any pay, mister, for doin' the business, and tellin' me all about it.

Clerk—It won't cost you a penny for anything we do for you; and you need not stay in the city, but can go home, after the papers are made out, and we will let you know when the money comes and send it to you by mail.

Woman—Well naow! That's cheerin'! I say, mister, you kin take them papers. I like your honest-looking faces about here. Saay, is that ar young man thar with only one arm, a soger boy hurt in this ere war. Sam Sherman, of aour place, lost his arm, too.

The preliminaries being arranged, the loquacious woman was invited to be seated; and when her turn came, Mr. Greenfield, the Secretary, doubtless obtained from the woman all the particulars of her "old man's" enlistment and death, as well as all the other necessary information concerning her marriage, place of residence, etc., from which he will make up the claim, and forward the same to the authorities at Washington. If it turns out that her "old man" did have any money "comin" to him, the woman is in a fair way of getting it without troubling those rapacious persons who began a correspondence with her, almost before the smoke of the battle in which her husband died had blown away from the field.

THE WIELOPOLSKI DUEL.

From the London Morning Star, June 9.

A grand sensation drama, the performance of which has been heralded by flaming announcements advertised all over Europe, has just been played out. Announced as a terrible tragedy, it has ended as a comedy—if not, indeed, a broad farce or a burlesque. We refer to the great Wielopolski duel, which two combatants departed from two ends of the continent to fight. One left Warsaw, the other started from Paris. They met in Belgium; they fought, and they are now returning in comfort, with whole skins and satisfied consciences, to their respective habitations.

Count Sigismund Wielopolski, the principal actor, is a son of the Marquis Wielopolski, whose grand, "thorough" scheme of Russianizing Poland, and whose pet measure, the conscription, have met with such slender gratitude from his Polish countrymen. The Marquis Wielopolski is not, as our readers are aware, a very popular person in Warsaw, or, indeed, an individual much admired throughout Europe. Some months back a speech on the Polish insurrection was delivered in the French Senate, by Prince Napoleon. The imperial orator, who has generally rather a direct and frank way of expressing his sentiments, classed the Marquis Wielopolski with Marshal Haynau and Sir Hudson Lowe. When the report of the speech got to Warsaw the younger Wielopolski, himself not a great favorite in the Polish capital, resolved to resent the attack. He dispatched a challenge to Prince Napoleon, and took the extraordinary step of publishing his cartel in the newspapers. Even the London journals were supplied with copies. The document was printed as a piece of odd news, although its grossly and even ludicrously abusive style seemed at first to throw a doubt upon its genuineness. Nobody who read this fantastic document can have forgotten its contents. We do not profess to be critics of what is called the code of honor, but we should think even the most inveterate duellist might have declined a rencontre with the concoctor of a challenge so coarse and outrageous in its language that it looked like some piece of mad buffoonery. Prince Napoleon took no notice of this Bombastes-Furioso style of thing. He declined to be "staged to the show" with such a sworder. But there were many of Prince Napoleon's friends less discreet. Count Wielopolski, in his letter, had alluded to certain personages who were in the habit of enjoying the hospitality of the Prince in the Palais Royal—alluding to them, it is needless to say, in the coarse and vulgar style of abuse which characterized his epistle. A Polish friend of Prince Napoleon's, Count Branicki, accepted the allusion as a personal offense. Accordingly he challenged the doughty Wielopolski. Following the example set him, he published his challenge in all the newspapers.

Weeks and weeks passed away, and every day's Continental journals had some new announcement about the impending duel. One day it was asserted that Count Wielopolski had positively left Warsaw, en route to be shot at; next day it was discovered that he was still biding his time at home. At last the final moment, the *inaluctabile tempus*, came, and it was officially announced that Count Wielopolski had left Warsaw to repair to the field of Warsaw. Paris, Brussels, Vienna and Warsaw were supposed to be on the tiptoe of expectation. Both the combatants had disappeared from public sight. On what fatal ground would they reappear, and what terrible deed of blood would mark the spot?

They did at last emerge. The once animated, now rather decaying town of Spa, was the rendezvous. The foes were planted, looking like the Corsican brothers in the melo-drama, no doubt. But the affair had not a melo-dramatic ending. First, they fired, and they could not hit each other. Next, they fired, and they could not hit each other. Then the police came in, and took them to the station house. There they were required to pledge their word of honor that they would fight no more duels upon Belgian soil, and they accepted the condition, and the last we heard of them was that Count Wielopolski had gone, safe and sound, back to Warsaw again. So we draw a long breath; the battle is over.

The Richmond Enquirer on Emancipation.—The Richmond *Enquirer*, the recognized organ of the Jeff. Davis Government, in its issues of Friday and Saturday, devotes its leading articles to Mr. Spence, the Liverpool agent of the Confederate States, whom it berates soundly for his intimation that, under some circumstances, the South might be willing to adopt a plan of gradual emancipation The *Enquirer* denounces and spits upon all such methods of recommending the South to the favor of foreign powers, and abuses without stint Mr. Spence and all other preachers of such doctrines. It calls vehemently for the removal of Spence, and wants to know why Mr. Mason has not dismissed him at once, without waiting for orders from home.

Gen. Stoughton has been reappointed Brigadier General on the recommendation of Gen. Heintzelman, who was his commanding General at the time he was taken prisoner.

LOCAL NEWS.

He Left.—A penitentiary individual, known as George Jones, but now flourishing as J. P. Hall, was brought out of the Workhouse last evening as a witness [illegible] made preparations for paying a burglarious visit to the St. Charles Loan Office. The examination of the case was to have been resumed at 5 P. M. last evening in the Provost Court, but in consequence of the absence of the Judge, it was necessarily continued. While waiting for the opening of the court, Jones alias Hall, concluded to escape, and he did so without encountering any difficulty. Last night his bed in the Workhouse was vacant, and he was in the enjoyment of the largest liberty.

A Map.—Mr. Wilder yesterday showed us a map of the Parish of Orleans and those adjoining, which we think is a *chef d'œvre*. It is the most beautiful thing we have ever laid eyes upon, and is without doubt the most truthful. In it you can see every man's name that owns a foot of ground in the State of Louisiana. It is a map that was made to order by Mr. Wm. H. Wilder, topographical engineer, as well as civil, for Mr. Thomas H. May, a planter of Louisiana, who owns several plantations and any number of chattels, called negroes. Speaking of the map as an artistic job, it is well done. It has cost the present proprietor seven hundred dollars—rather more than we would pay for Louisiana, much less for a map of it.

Drowned Boy.—The name of the little boy who was drowned at Post 21, First District, as previously noticed, was Thomas Manon. He was but nine years of age, and fell accidentally into the river.

Died,

July 10, at half-past 8 o'clock P. M., Mrs. AMELIA BUEB, wife of Joseph Schwartz, aged 29 years 2½ months.

REPORTER...EXTRA.

LYNN, MONDAY, JULY 13, 1863.

Drafting to fill the quota of Lynn commenced at Mechanic Hall, Salem, at nine o'clock this morning, under the direction of Capt. JOHNSON, Provost Marshal of the Fifth District. The attendance of spectators was not very large, a large portion of those present being residents of Lynn, who were on the "anxious seats." The machine used for drafting was an octagon-shaped tin arrangement, aboui two feet in diameter and eighteen inches long. It was suspended by the centre, upon a frame work, and turned with a crank.

Dist. No. 27—Wards 1, 2 & 7—50 Names.

The first name drawn was—

WILLIAM H. PECKHAM.

James W. Furbush.
John H. Miles.
Francis F. Barker.
George Vickary.
Daniel Mansfield.
Charles H. Vickary.
James B. Paul.
Geo. W. Rhodes.
Edwin D. Marble.
Francis Furbish.
James R. King.
Thos. C. Murphy.
Lucius E. Newhall.
Daniel Berry.
Francis E. Jeffrey.
Lorenzo D. Evans.
Geo. W. Lowe,
Geo. E. Prescott.
Lyman Choate.
Eben'r Tarbox.
Nahum H. Newhall.
Addison Gage.
Wm. H. Patch.
Geo. H. Berry.
John Falls.
Henry O. Parrott.
Nath'l Adams.
Henry A. Williams.
David Harwood.
Levi I. Whitney.
Duxbury Moon.
Nelson N. Kent.
Josiah Q. Morris.
Loring H. Heath.
Nath'l S. Vickary.
Andrew J. Pope.
James O. Brown.
John Vickary.
Edwin Bacheller.
Alfred M. Fairfield.
Horace F. Lewis.
Hiram M. Newhall.
Willard P. Dailey.
Melville Furbush.
Luther J. Blood.
Henry C. Bisbee.
John F. Brown.
Jacob P. Parrott.
Oliver F. Childs.

Dist. No. 28—Ward 3—99 Names.

William H. Bailey.
James Mahoney.
Michael Elwood.
Joseph W. Richards.
Lucius A. Watts.
William F. Story.
Philip M. Smith.
Samuel I. Graves.
William S. King.
Michael Miley.
Joseph Belt.
James Schouler.
John M. Newhall.
William Brown.
Joseph H. Croscupp.
Daniel L. Estes.
Hezekiah Shaw.
Joseph W. Nichols.
Eben M. Swan.
Horatio S. Galeucia.
Henry T. Farrar.
Horatio G. Castell.
Joseph Lord.
Joseph E. Hildreth.
Simon Clough.
George Bacheller.
Edwin L. Sargent.
Charles S. Sweetser.
Leonard P. Brickett.
James M. Sargent, Jr.
Elwin C. Collins.
John W. Barnicoat.
Moses Andrews.
Benjamin F. Howard.
J. Harding Plumstead.
Charles R. M. Hammond
Charles L. Flint.
Tennison P. Collins.
Asa N. Breed.
John W. Marston.
Samuel A. Widger.
John Mudge.
Wilbnr F. Breed.
John B. Osborn.
Martin V. B. Mower.
Henry B. Bacheller.
Charles M. Dupar.
Isaiah S. Coles.
William Atkins.
George W. Seeley.
John Nichols.
Luther Graves.
William Still.
William O. Newhall.
William R. Clark.
Lucius Ingalls.
Andrew Mace.
Nestor O. Brown.
William N. Parrott.
William R. Swan.
William C. Low.
Benjamin F. Dupar.
George C. Mason.
George W. Benson.
Melville Durrell.
Edward Barnes.
James S. Russell.
Jesse M. Rhodes.
Edward H. Knight.
Hosea Carr.
Owen A. Hammond.
John F. Lamper.
Joseph B. Johnson.
James M. Burrill.
George H. Capen.
John F. Law.
Franklin F. Newhall.
Henry Richards.
Joel W. Norcross.
Philip Chase.
Eugene B. Attwill.
James F. Lamphier.
John Perkins.
Timothy A. Collins.
John B. Patten.
Jonas B. Goodwin.
John Barrett.
Henry C. Thayer.
George H. Marston.
Charles P. Gilman.
Robert G. Steward.
Martın V. B. Folsom.
Joseph W. Eaton.
William L. Silsbee.
Austin Gray.
Edward Y. Austin.
Nicholas Brown.
Joseph S. Pike.
Joseph H. Sanborn.

Dist. No. 29—Ward 4—149 Names.

Joshua H. Coburn.
William H. Jeffers.
Stephen H. Sawtell.
Dudley P. Meader.
William G. Brown.
Frank M. Haskell.
Daniel Emerson.
George E. Kelty.
Charles Downes.
George E. Wentworth.
Charles H. Chaffee.
Jacob Welsh.
John F. Twombly.
Edward L. Hiller.
John Thomas.
Benjamin G. Hosmer.
Linville S. Newhall.
Warren L. Tower.
Marcus M. Cleverly.
Hiram Jenkins.
Nicholas Ford.
Albert Sanborn.
Samuel E. Dwyer.
Joseph W. Hazeltine.
Eben S. Whitney.
James M. Taylor.
George Reed.
Charles H. Totman.
William Ellis Howard.
Sumner Richardson.
Orrin Stocker.
John H. Warren.
Harrison P. Stocker.
James E. Peasley.
Nelson H. Fogg.
William H. Bishop.
William A. Richardson,
Thomas H. Moore.
Franklin Huse.
Morton D. Barrell.
Edward Hill. "Here."
James H. Winslow.
Simon F. Downs.
Samuel W. Wallace.
Augustus Bowtell.
William H. Newhall.
William Pettengill.
Charles H. Partridge.
Edward M. Farnsworth.
Daniel Goodwin.
Josiah T. Seavey.
Abram Whitney.
Melbourne Noyes.
George Stedman.
Alexander M. Collins.
Thomas Green.
George Senter.
Andrew W. Clapp.
William W. Hawkes.
Adolphus W. Emerson.
Daniel E. Nourse.
James W. Goodwin.
Alvah Sawyer.
James Clement.
Christopher A. Johnson.
Daniel Russell.
Nelson Noyes.
Willis L. Snow.
Calvin M. Parlin.
Andrews Sanborn.
Pyam L. Johnson.
Lyman M. Frederick.
George W. Herrick.
Edward D. Flynn.
William Brown.
Stephen Pevear.
Reuben D. Neal.
James S. Lakin.
James W. Low.
Edward C. Smith.
Timothy Stevens.
John H. Gilman.
John D. A. Watson.
Enoch T. Brown.
John Herlihy.
Samuel N. Clements.
Edwin H. Harmon.
True E. Rich.
William H. Reynolds.
James H. Ximines.
Tyler Parrott.
Quincy A. Towne.
Samuel P. Oliver.
James E. Mower.
Benjamin F. Osborne.
Otis Upham.
George F. Massey.
George B. Holland.
William H. Alley.
Allen P. Aldrich.
Charles J. Butler.
Joseph W. Goodwin.
Samuel R. Bushby.
Joseph Johnson.
James E. Oliver.
Winfield S. Partridge.
Jonas Carkin.
Charles H. Healey.
Thomas Fallon.
Thomas McAlvey.
Jonathan W. Keith.
Albert F. Reed. "Here."
Edward Stone.
George T. Clark.
Isaac Brothers.
James N. Pillsbury.
James W. Starkey.
Edwin T. Butman.
George H. Williams.
B. Frank Beal.
George Howe.
Henry H. Wilmot.
Joseph A. Ploof.
George Knight.
Daniel E. Newhall.
Albert W. Hatch.
George F. Clifford.
Charles O. Lewis.
Lucius C. Sargent.
Sidney Haskell.
Napoleon Wood.
John A. Roberts.
James W. Holder.
Orrin Weeman.
James A. Blondell.
Charles B. Clough.
Frederick W. Pope.
Asa E. Mullen.
Warren S. Harvey.
John Owens.
David Brooks, Jr.
William G. S. Keene.
Charles B. Tibbets.
Adell Greenwood.
John A. Porter.
George S. Oliver.
John W. Roundy.
Charles W. Biddle.

Dist. No. 30—Ward 5—128 Names.

Ovando B. Clough.
James Ray.
Augustus N. Preble.
Nathaniel S. Freeman.
Isaac Hastings.
Charles P. Cressey.
Livingston S. Hall.
Benjamin F. Seymour.
George W. Timson.
William A. Bacheller.
John B. Phillip's.
John H. B. Grover.
Henry A. Walton.
Cyrus K. Stanley.
John V. Spalding.
Martin V. B. Allen.
Josiah Fitz, 3d.
Horace B. Stone.
Charles A. Boyd.
Charles S. Hilton.
William. Goodwin.
Preston P. Taplry.
Charles I. Betton.
Charles H. Lewis.
Adam N. Searle.
Benjamin F. Farnham.
Charles L. Adams.
Daniel L. Johnson.
Horace A. Walton.
George F. Estes.
David Knox.
Enoch I. Mudge.
John W. Blaney.
Henry H. Breed.
Harris Pollard.
George F. Drew.
John E. Stone.
Francis Wilson.
Isaac W. Hussey.
John F. Higgins.
Sylvester Butler.
John F. Mansfield.
Castillo Finney.
Charles C. Martin.
Henry O. Burrill.
Joseph Otis Marshall.
Joseph Faulkner.
Hiram J. Hill.
Joseph E. Jacobs.
James F. Laborda.
Joseph E. Estes.
James B. Bancroft.
William J. Neagles.
Edward S. Keene.
Melville C. Harrington.
Foster Andrews.
Charles O. Floyd.
Charles H. Chandler.
William S. Orr.
Laban F. Davis.
Benaiah C. Dustin.
John C. Spring.
William H. Adams.
Sylvester Penock.
Fairfield McIntire.
Melvin F. Clough.
Edwin W. Davis.
Patrick Mealey.
Adams Stevens.
John Roberts.
George Lambert.
William E. Parker.
Nathan B. M. Ingalls.
Thomas M. Bucknam.
Stephen W. Dearborn.
John A. Means.
James B. Fry.
William Lyons.
Nathan W. Lord.
William H. Kimball.
William E. Hammond.
Lyman G. Bigelow.
Charles A. Taber.
Jeremiah O. Marshall.
Thomas S. Pearson.
Andrew B. Maine.
James C. A. Mills.
George T. Dunham.
William J. Larrabee.
Charles E. Hallowell.
James C. Bond.
Horace P. Branscombe.
Daniel F. DeWolfe.
Hiram Huston.
Rufus Finnsy.
Benjamifi F. Bean.
Eben H. Downing.
Francis H. Bacheller.
William Buck.
William W. Doughty.
Timothy Hanley.
John B. Berry.
Jerome Kelty.
Peter D. Bickford.
Joseph A. Dow.
John A. Bradley.
Henry A. Cross.
Ezlin Comstock.
John Booker.
Justin E. Tenney.
James Furbush.
Edward Rowe.
Conant Gale.
Ira E. Woodward.
David E. Whidden.
Henry H. Downing.
William Heffernan.
Henry M. Smith.
Benjamin W. Cutler.
William H. Ingalls.
George H. Rich.
William G. White.
James F. Hartshorn.
Josiah H. Preble.
George Welch.
William C. Holder.
Philip A. Chase.
Samuel H. Bacheller.

Dist. No. 31—Ward 6—105 Names.

Henry Fitz.
Jeremiah Libbey.
William E. Kimball.
Noah True.
Luther D. Grover.
Robert B. Morse,
Eliphalet R. Lovett.
William R. Murray.
Perley B. Mansfield.
William Kennison.
Francis E. Besse.
Oraman Quimby.
Joseph W. Driver.
Perley B. Lake.
John R. Swain.
Andrew J. Harlow.
S. Edwin Ireson.
Sumner B. Heald.
Eldridge G. Allen.
J. Munroe Gibbons.
Arno A. Holt.
James Sullivan.
Joseph S. Carder.
George M. Connor.
William D. Poole.
Edward P. Merrill.
Isaac Perry.
James Murphy.
Bartlett Skinner.
Philip A. Newhall.
Augustus T. Robinson.
Wallace Osborne.
Augustus S. Battles, Jr.
Nathaniel Lindsay.
Daniel F. Webster.
Nehemiah Foster.
Charles R. Smith.
Henry G. Daniels.
Blaney Hawkes.
Edward Steward,
Walter B. Dow.
Elias A. Upton.
Aaron Ames.
Frank O. Taylor.
Jacob Ames.
Edward A. Hulen.
Charles Moulton.
Joshua P. Barrett.
Henry C. Brown.
Samuel B. Valpey.
James Kelley.
Richard Williams.
Wiley P. Davis.
Sylvester B. Breed.
Micajah N. Goodridge.
George W. Newhall.
Charles O. Breed.
John D. Murray.
Otis S. Heald.
John Sheridan.
Washington E. Keene.
Lewis P. Thomas.
Charles H. Haddock.
George H. Mansfield.
Patrick Shanahan.
George B. Tubbs.
Horace Cahill.
Joseph J. Ireson.
Andrew J. Mace.
George O. Tarbox.
Frederick Breed.
Edward L. Legrow.
Benjamin L. Johnson.
Barney Crudden.
Samuel Moulton.
John Lindsay.
George B. Wood.
Richard Fittz.
J. Warren Newhall.
Alfred P. Flint.
John M. Lewis.
Osmus Phillips.
Ignatius P. Ingalls.
Ezra A. Peabody.
Alfred Fall.
John M. Thompson.
Robert Holt.
Ezra Bates.
William C. Ingalls.
Moses A. Lapham.
Charles W. Courier.
Charles H. Spinney.
Henry J. Perry.
William Wadlin.
Ezra M. Emerton.
Willirm H. Hutchinson.
Isaac Bell.
Charles L. Wyman.
Francis Babb.
Charles Willey.
Edward A. Berry.
Martin C. Heald.
John Wales.
Samuel L. Harris.
William Strong.

NEW YORK DAILY NEWS.

VOL. VII......NO. 180. NEW YORK, TUESDAY, JULY 14, 1863. PRICE TWO CENTS.

THE CONSCRIPTION RESISTED

Terrible Scenes Throughout the City.

THE TELEGRAPH WIRES CUT.

The Second and Third Avenue Railroads Torn Up.

THE CARS USED FOR BARRICADES.

Conscription Wheels and Premises Destroyed.

Several Public Buildings Demolished.

AN ARMORY BURNED.

Burning of the Eighth District Draft Station.

The Police and Marines Beaten with Stones and Clubs.

Burning of the Ninth District Draft Station.

The Provost Guard Fire Upon the Citizens.

THE GUARD BEATEN AND DISARMED

Superintendent Kennedy Seriously Injured.

The Colored Orphan Asylum Cleared and Burned.

A NEGRO HUNG AND BURNED.

Seven Private Dwellings Destroyed.

Over Three Hundred Killed, Wounded and Missing.

Regular Troops Called Out for To-Day.

THE DRAFT IN BROOKLYN.

Yesterday was the most exciting, the saddest and most terrible day New York City has ever seen. The feeling of the people against the draft, and particularly against the manner in which it was inaugurated and carried on, was of the most intense character, as we had given assurance that it was before the lamentable occurrences we are about to chronicle had taken place. A peculiar feature of yesterday's disasters, is the fact that that the commonest saying among the citizens who took an active part in the scenes of violence, was, that while there was a general belief that the conscription act is unconstitutional, and a violation of the rights of the State; while they believed Governor Seymour was of that opinion, there had been no movement to stay the draft until its legality could be tested; and, therefore, all that remained to them was to protect themselves. This, right or wrong, was the belief of the men actively engaged, as stated to our reporters, and on it, after having become frenzied by consideration of the position in which they believed they were placed, they proceeded to the perpetration of the deeds of violence described below.

During the earlier portion of the day there did not appear to have been any determination to interfere with any persons or property other than was connected with the Conscription; but a later hour, when the continued excite- had rendered them mad, they be- n attacks upon negroes, upon the Asylum, nd committed other deeds of terrible and apparently unpremeditated violence. The destruction of the draft stations of the Eighth and Ninth Districts met with an opposition which caused the spilling of blood, and from that time the attack seems to have become general against everything and everybody their excited fancies conjured into causes of their dreaded wrongs. Our reports furnish a ghastly variety of those acts which make the blood chill, and which are fortunately seldom committed, except when a maddened populace suddenly take the righting of their real or imagined wrong into their own hands.

What may be done to-day it is impossible to say. There are, as will be seen, considerable additions to the military force in the city ready for service, but whether they are called into active duty or not, it is to be hoped that something may be done by the proper authorities to assure the people that their rights will be protected and thus save further bloodshed.

The Outbreak in the Ninth District.

The continuance of the conscription in the Ninth District took place yesterday morning at the office of the Provost Marshal, No. 677 Third Avenue. It was announced that the drawing would begin at nine o'clock A. M., but as information had been received of preparation by the citizens to institute a stay of proceedings, it was not deemed prudent by the officials in charge to commence until ten o'clock. At this time a crowd of three or four thousand persons were collected in the Avenue and in Forty-sixth street, in the vicinity of the Provost Marshal's office, but all was quiet. Some jests were to be heard about the draft, but few seemed to know of any organized opposition to it. It was known, however, that the employees in Brown's iron factory in Sixty-first Street, Taylor's in Forty-first street, Crimmins, street opening contractor, and of each of the city railroads, more especially those on the west side of town' had quit work, and in bodies of hundreds were gathering from all quarters toward this spot.

In the hour which elapsed ere the drawing began, after that appointed, Provost Marshal Jenkins might have been seen casting many anxious glances at his watch and down the avenue, in expectation of armed protection for which he had sent. Three platoons of police from the several wards forming the district, the Nineteenth, Twenty-first and Twenty-second, at length arrived; the captain deemed his force sufficient, and at once the drawing commenced. The drawing was conducted in the same manner as that of Saturday, with the only exception that a little more haste seemed to be evinced, and the crowd rather more jovial over it.

NAMES OF THOSE CONSCRIPTED.

The following are the names drawn in the Ninth District:

Thos Sprague, 717 8th av
A Hearn, 10th av bet 59th and 60th sts
A Van Hearn, 202 W 53d
C E Colman, 300 W 43d
G Wheeler, 6th av & 58th
G Hatch, 335 W 49th
R Livingston, 340 9th av
F Moore, 10th av, 46 & 47
J Fitzgerald, 453 W 52d
J Carroll, 264 W 56th
R Means, Broadway Hotel, 42d and 8th av
V Lisck, 46 Broadway
H Gray, 4th st & 6th av
A Sherman (colored)
A Bavendaller, 64th st & 10th av
J Helbig, 47th & 11th av
J Van Hinch, 211 W 43d
J Dortman, 348 W 46th
J Larcage, 1413 Broadw'y
Z Kaffer, 65th, 9th&10th av
Hugh Prinnan, 54th st, bet 8th and 9th av
M Balmer, 248 W 42d st
A Pikekey, 611 3d ave
J Mills, 686 9th ave
J Deuar, 662 3d ave
Jas Allenaro
Julius Armispater
J O'Connor, 287 W 40th
E A Winslow 160 W 49th
Jas Coyle, 556 W 44th st
Thos Smiley, 556 W 44th
E Milton, 317 8th ave
C Clark, Broadway & 59th
A Smith, 8th ave n 83d st
J Adams, 146 W 40th st
M Cormick, 56th bet6&7av
Jas Carolin, 10th av & 42d
F Raymond, 717 8th ave
J M Sextror, 1334 Broad'y
Jno Robertson, B'way & 75th st.
H Stinnstocker, 149W 40st
F McArdle, 64 W 41st st
F Englishier, 246 W 45 st
F Meyer, 602 5th av
Geo McIndue, 691 9th av
John McGedney, 49th st
D Carman, 612 8th av
H Riimber, 344 W 45th st
Alex Seeley, 137 W 43 st
Alf Calker, 211 W 43d st
H Peterson, 7th av 60th st
F Glimp, 510 9th av
H A Minche, 7 av 55th st
Wm Stone, 161 W 48th st
Geo Robinson, Broadway 73d and 74th sts
Geo Fielding, 134 E 41st
W Carman, 56th, bet 6th and 7th av
S Shumbte, 242 W 49th
F Vreedel, 63d, 8th and 9th av
T Jack, 281 W 46th
R Stewart, 141 W 45th
Geo Wilsey, 604 8th av
W Douglas, 346 W 47th st
O Ellinjue, 698 8th av
W Kelly, 404 W 47th
J Nichols, 68 W 49th
W Primrose, 491 11th av
H Robert, 114 W 47th
H C Myer, 104 W 49th
H Young, 308 W 46th
F Costello, 519 8th av
W S Crane, 43d st and 6th av
D Casey, 591 9th av
J Baumann, 63d st, 9th & 10th av
John Brown
P Burns, 345 W 43d st
G Greenleaf, 529 10th ave
H Jones, 144 W 44th st
G W Jones, 71 W 43d st
G Laymon, 72 9th ave
J Segel, 861 8th ave
Jos Michaei, 761 6th ave
Dan Mahoney, 460 W 42d
G McCarey, 59 6th ave
J McGuire, 592 W 47th st
Miller Molltiech, 347 49th
C H Arice, 54 Broad'y&8th
J Quisby, 767 8th ave
C Rayton, 71 9th ave
Dan Schuck, 678 8th ave
John Sweeney, 726 8th ave
Geo Spraul, 296 46th st
John Schuck, 348 W 46 st
Z Shay, 633 W 42d st
G Ward, 295 W 43d st
Rev Wood, 598 6th av
Ed Fortenvee, 248 W 45 st
M Feeling. 750 8th av
Thos Potts, 696 8th av
Thos Carwan, 10 Lanita P
Wm H Ming, ——
Jacob Leary, 969 9th av
F O'Neil, 115 W 53d s
Wm Riffle, 140 W 43d st
Wm Legion, 201 W 40th st
Theo C Harding, 141 W 40 st
Eugene Bartholomew, ——

From the rapidity with which these names were read, and in the midst of the confusion which prevailed, it was excessively difficult to catch correctly the names and residences as they were read off, but at the point to which our reporter has carried the list, a rather more serious obstacle presented itself. For some minutes loud and continuous cheering had been heard outside, and occasionally policemen came in, reporting that the avenue was black with people, that women were inciting them to burn the building and break up the draft, &c., &c. Suddenly a half brick came through the window, passing unpleasantly near to the reporters' table, an avant courier of a very storm of bricks, stones, sticks, and other weapons.

Of course an indiscriminate skedaddle was the immediate consequence, everybody getting out into the street or back yard as a mode of exit most conveniently presented itself. The police present, of no more use than a straw to resist a wave, only bent its energies to keeping out of harm's way and looking as innocent as possible. The crowd divided itself into three parts, one rushed into the office of the Provost Marshal, destroyed all the furniture, wheel, chairs, tables, desks, etc., and then emptying a jug of turpentine on the floor, fired it; another part tore up the track of the Third Avenue Railroad, and the third tore down and cut all the telegraph wires in Third, Lexington, Fourth and adjacent avenues.

The flames spread with great rapidity, and it was with great difficulty that the people living in the house could save even a portion of their personal effects by throwing them from the windows. Lieut. Vanderpoel, Deputy Provost Marshal, regardless of the fact that his uniform might provoke his death, came back at this juncture, from a place of safety, to beg the crowd to save the women and children in the upper stories of the building. He was set upon and beaten by the crowd. Police Officer John Cook, while endeavoring to save him, was also badly beaten. Several Engine and Hose Companies were on the gound, but the crowd would not permit them to work.

In such a scene as this the police were of little or no use. They did all they could to help the inmates of the house, but were powerless.

The house, fine brick, four stories high, belonging to Messrs. Grand & Co., lumber merchants, was destroyed. Mr. Jeremiah Duane, an inmate, lost over $6,000. R. Blake also lost heavily. One poor woman, whose husband is in the war, was turned from a sick bed, homeless, houseless and penniless.

Altogether six families were turned out of their homes. The flames quickly communicated to R. Pettigrew's blacksmith and wheelwright shop on the opposite side of the avenue, and totally destroyed it, together with a large and valuable stock which it contained. Mr. Pettigrew, while attempting to save his property, was struck by a stone on the head, and very seriously injured.

A lager bier shop, next to the office of the Provost Marshal, was completely gutted, the crowd using up the liquor from it in a few seconds.

The following policemen were injured: Officers Swainser, Twenty-ninth Precinct, struck in the head and badly cut; Holmes, Twenty-ninth, cut in the head, severely; Morrison, Twenty-ninth, dangerously wounded; Charles R. Law, Eighth, seriously; Nolan McCarty, Twenty-ninth, not expected to live; Nolan Walsh, Eighth, badly cut; Sutherland, Fifteenth, seriously cut and bruised.

About twenty or thirty policemen are more or less injured, nearly all of whom were taken into private houses, where the inmates attended to their wants.

The crowd learning that a number of the officers were in the dwellings threatened to sack every house in which they ascertained a policeman had been secreted.

Burning of Private Residences in Lexington Avenue.

The great number of those taken away with Mr. Andrews, were scarcely missed, as the crowd closed in again, and it was evident that the force was too large to use to advantage in one place, so the crowd now diverted its attention from the ruins in Third avenue to the destruction of two buildings in Lexington avenue, between Forty-fourth and Forty-fifth streets. The motives assigned for their ruin, varied widely; some saying, that Horace Greeley lived there; others, that it was the residence of Provost Marshal Jenkins or of Colonel Nugent, Assistant Provost Marshal General, while the story nearest the truth seemed to be that a police officer, beaten almost to death, had been sheltered by the female inmates of one of the houses. At all events, they were handsome brown stone fronted residences, three stories in hight, evidently well fitted up, and therefore full of plunder. One belonged to Mr. John J. Dowdy, clothing dealer, doing business at the corner of Grand and Columbia streets; the other to Mr. W. Turner, coach manufacturer brother-in-law of Stevenson, the coach builder. The families in both houses were forced to take refuge in flight, but it was rumored in the crowd that a wounded officer, whether police or of the Provost Marshal's force no one seemed to know, was burned alive in one of the houses. The doors were forced, and in a few seconds every room was filled by the crowd. Costly pianos were smashed to atoms with bludgeons and pickaxes, stones were hurled through mirrors, elegant pictures were torn from the walls, and after having been cut and destroyed, hurled into the street; furniture was tossed from the windows, which were broken out, sashes and all; stereoscopes were cast out into the crowd; all the elegant appliances of homes of comfort were ruthlessly, wantonly destroyed. In the street, scores of men, women and children, busied themselves collecting the furniture thrown from the windows and carrying it off. One fellow appeared at a window with a picture of the President, spat on it, split it over his knee and hurled it into the street, where it was quickly trampled into atoms. Then, in half a dozen places at once, the flames burst forth. So rapidly did they spread that some of the plunderers in the house had to escape from the windows by means of ladders. The fire engines were promptly on the ground, but were not permitted to be used until all hope of saving the buildings was long passed; in half an hour the walls fell, and a smoking heap of ruins alone remained to mark the spot.

Assistant Engineer Lamb was badly injured by being struck by a stone. A military officer, in undress uniform, was seized simply because he wore a uniform, and unmercifully beaten. A wounded soldier, in citizen's dress, who ventured a word in his behalf, was knocked down and brutally beaten with bludgeons and stones, again and again, although he exhibited a ghastly wound, showing his incompetency to fight even with one man. A hundred succeeded in nearly murdering him, and it was only by the most desperate exertions of some gifted with a spark of humanity that his life was spared.

Burning of the Bull's Head Hotel.

The crowd next moved to Allerton's, Bull's Head Hotel, where it was known a large quantity of liquors could be taken. The house was burst open, men and boys entering at all the doors and windows. The bar room was sacked in a few moments, liquors in decanters and barrels being taken forth and freely distributed. Two barrels of liquor were rolled into the street, the heads knocked in, and from tins, pans, kettles, buckets and other utensils, the crowd drank down the maddening liquid. The upper rooms were pillaged, furniture thrown from the windows and in a few moments the house was in flames. Being old, very dry, and much woodwork in it, the edifice was quickly enwrapped in flames. The intense heat destroyed even the green trees in the yard and spread to the fences and sheds of the cattle yards, where, however, it soon went out. The engines were again on hand and again prevented working. A body of some three thousand persons made their appearance, coming up Lexington avenue, past the houses pillaged and burnt there, and round to the burning hotel, bearing shovels, boards and signs, showing the words rudely scrawled on each, "no draft," and brandishing clubs, stakes, iron bludgeons, and missiles of varied kinds. Picket fences were torn to pieces to furnish clubs for all, and then the crowd moved on—several citizens for merely looking as if they disapproved of the course of action were brutally beaten—indeed scarcely a minute passed that in some direction a crowd could not be seen beating some unfortunate wretch or chasing a fugitive with yells of "kill the ——" and hurling stones and sticks after him. If once he fell—woe to him. A hundred rumors were now circulating in the crowd. Some avowed their intention to burn the City Hall in the evening, others to pillage and burn two buildings in Fiftieth street. Many favored the destruction of The Tribune, Times, and Post newspaper offices, and the residences of the proprietors if they could be discovered, and a general howl of "kill the nagurs," "burn the nagurs nest," (the Colored Orphan Asylum) "kill every Black Republican," was raised. The crowd then moved on to the Colored Orphan Asylum on Fifth avenue, between Forty-third and Forty-fourth streets, merely stopping by the way to pillage and burn a liquor shop near the corner of Fifth avenue and Forty-fourth street, "because it belonged to a d——d Black Republican." Who he was, our reporter did not learn. Here another liberal stock of liquor was laid in.

Pillage and Burning of the Colored Orphan Asylum.

Before this institution the crowd, now numbering some five thousand, halted. The inmates had received timely notice of the coming storm, and made their escape through the back entrance. A cry was raised of "burn it—burn it," and for this purpose a rush was made through the gates and up to the door. Chief Engineer John Decker, with heroic courage, barred their way, and appealed to the crowd not to cast such a blot of shame upon the city as the wilful destruction of a charitable institution. Heedless of his words, the living mass poured on, and it was only by dint of the desperate exertions of some brave firemen, he managed to escape from being trodden under foot. Again he returned to the effort of calling them to reason. Already a great fire had been kindled in the parlor. Dropping words for action, Mr. Decker and a few gallant firemen rushed in and threw out the burning heap of furniture, thus checking the fire. Again and again was this repeated in different places. The crowd hurried through the building entering every room, "gutting" them as they went. The clothing, school books, beds and benches were showered from the windows, and either torn to pieces or appropriated by the crowd below. In the garden crowds of men, women and children, clutched the articles as they fell, stowed them in bundles and carried them off. Women were foremost in the work of plunder, and incited the men to constant new excesses. Many were injured by the falling of boxes, furniture, etc., from the windows. Several citizens suspected of being in some way connected with the Asylum were cruelly beaten and senseless, covered with blood and wounds thrown from the gates. Riot and rapine ran mad in every part of the fated building. Men smashed pianos, tore up and carried off carpets, maps and furniture, broke the Asylum bell, and fired the building in a dozen places. No efforts of the firemen could check the flames, and at 6 o'clock the edifice was a mass of fire. A barrel of liquor was procured and set open for the crowd at the corner of Fifth avenue and Forty-fourth streets. An express wagon belonging to the firm of J. Dungan & Son, laden with wines and liquors was seized, emptied of its contents and partially wrecked. At 7 o'clock the walls of the Asylum fell in.

From time to time, rumors of the approach of a military force would send half the crowd "skedaddling" away, but when the alarm was found to be false, revenge for the sell would be taken, by battering almost to death some person on whom the chance would fall, without any particular reason.

The Disturbance in the Nineteenth Ward.

[FROM ANOTHER REPORTER.]

From the building on the corner of Third avenue and Forty-sixth street in which the fire originated, the flames spread rapidly to the next house, No. 679, from the windows of which, first dense volumes of smoke and then masses of flame rolled forth. The lower story was occupied by a lagerbier saloon, which was completely "gutted." The second story was occupied by Henry Frank, as a residence. His loss will be about $3,000. A. Domerona, living in the third floor, lost $1,000. H. Digelew and A. Wokatosch, residents in the fourth floor, lost about $1,500 each. The citizens then invaded the next two houses, Nos. 681 and 683, throwing mirror, furniture, crockery, etc., out of the windows, smashing windows, tearing off shutters and finally building a fire in the third floor of No. 681. Meantime the crowd below amused themselves by hurling bricks and stones through the windows and at the shutters of the lower floors.

Superintendent Kennedy, of the Metropolitan force, with a small escort of police, at this time appeared on the ground. Until his appearance the crowd had merely cheered and hooted the police, and no affray had occurred between them; but now an attack was made upon the Superintendent and those with him. All the police were quickly put to flight, with the exception of Sergt. Brackett, of the Twenty-first Precinct, who strove to defend him. Kennedy was, however, quickly knocked down, and terribly beaten; and Brackett was driven against a fence. Coolly folding his arms, he told them "he didn't think that he could whip them all; and if they were not ashamed of so cowardly an action, they might go ahead and 'stone him' and 'kill him,' as they were vociferating." His coolness made him friends, and he was allowed to go unharmed. It is reported, however, that Supt. Kennedy was killed. He is at all events very seriously injured.

A detachment of twenty-five marines, under the command of a Lieutenant, came up the avenue and the crowd commenced hooting and cheering. The Lieutenant, probably, became excited and ordered his men to fire. As disciplined troops, they obeyed, but the act was madness, in view of the presence of over two thousand excited rioters, armed with clubs and stones, and scarcely had the volley been discharged when one mad rush was made and the marines were forced to seek safety in flight. Their muskets and cartridges were seized and themselves badly beaten. One gray-headed man was among the marines. He was first struck on the head by a large stone, but his silver locks saved his life, the mob contenting themselves with stripping him of his uniform and destroying it. Armed with the muskets captured from the marines and flushed with their success, the rioters returned to the scene of their first excesses. The flames were now raging violently in Nos. 679 and 681.

At this juncture Chief Engineer John Decker of the Fire Department, appeared on the ground, and mounting an engine addressed the mob, appealing to them to allow the firemen to save the property of innocent and poor men. They had succeeded in destroying the obnoxious building, and he now begged them to allow the remaining buildings in the block to be saved. His few sentences were loudly cheered, and many were heard saying "That's right," "let them save the property."

ALDERMAN MASTERSON'S ADDRESS.

Alderman Masterson, of the Twenty-second Ward, next addressed the meeting. He said:

GENTLEMEN: I am opposed to this draft as much as any man in this crowd. [Cheers.] I am in favor of burning down that building that was burned down [cheers], but I am opposed to having these poor people's homes burned down. It will do no good to you or to anybody else. [Cheers.] I therefore ask you to stand back, and let us save the building. It is the property of a poor man, who cannot get a cent of the insurance on it if it is destroyed.

At this moment a lot of policemen made an insane charge into the crowd with the clubs. For a moment the human wave rolled back, and then it came on again with overwhelming force, completely engulfing the police who were knocked down and beaten almost to death with their own clubs. Whenever a wearer of the uniform appeared on the west side of the avenue, he was beaten unmercifully. Nos. 1,255 and 1,658 (police) were very severely injured. Some of the police ran down the avenue, and it was reported that one of them was shot dead by a musket in the hands of one of the rioters.

Nothing could, under the circumstances, have been more foolish or useless than the charge upon the crowd by such a small force, armed only with clubs, not well enough disciplined to keep together, and at a time when the crowd were disposed to let the firemen do their duty in extinguishing the flames. Chief Engineer Decker was severely hurt by a club in the hands of a policeman.

Soon after this skirmish, the engines got to work and beyond a small demonstration on Engine Co. No. 46, forcing them to stop for a few moments until explanations were made to the crowd, their work was uninterrupted and the last house of the block, No. 683, the property of Mr. Brady was saved.

No. 681 belonged to Mr. R. Pettigrew, who loses by the burning of this house his blacksmith and wheelwright shop and a large stock in trade, over $30,000.

At a little after two o'clock, a lull occurred, and the crowd was comparatively quiet, when a Mr. Andrews mounted a small frame building at the corner of Third avenue and Forty-sixth street, and addressed the people. He told them that they were fighting for their rights, and he hoped to see them wipe out this Abolition Black Republican party. They should not touch the persons or property of private individuals, but all connected with this infernal draft should swing as high as Haman. He had always opposed this party, and he wished to see it crushed now. He finally offered himself as the leader of the multitude, advising them to form into files of twenty front, and march en masse down to the Eighth District, and wherever this accursed draft was being enforced to wreak their vengeance. He would lead them to death if necessary.

He was constantly cheered, and it was with difficulty that his speech could be heard. At the conclusion he got down off the little building and was taken on the shoulders of the mob, which then moved *en masse* down the Third avenue.

Rumor says that two policemen and a woman, who was struck by a stone, have died from the injuries received.

Destruction of the Colored Orphan Asylum.

Having fired Mr. Turner's dwelling in Lexington avenue, which continued to burn unchecked up to a late hour in the evening, the furious and excited leaders proceeded to the Fifth avenue, and directed their steps to the Colored Orphan Asylum, where they immediately commenced operations. Notice having been given for the removal of the inmates to a place of safety, they were removed, and soon the doors were battered in and windows smashed in a twinkling. The men next entered the building, literally empting its contents through the windows and carrying them out through the doors.

The next proceeding was to fire the house. A quantity of wood having been ignited in the yard, the burning wood was conveyed within the building, and, soon after, the structure gave evidence of its being in flames, amid the excited and maddened shouts of the people.

CONTINUED ON EIGHTH PAGE.

Resistance to the Draft.

Fearful Scenes in Third Avenue

TERRIBLE ASSAULT ON THE POLICE.

A Large Number of them Fatally Wounded.

THE FIREMEN PERMITTED TO WORK.

The Whole Block of Tenement Houses in Ruins.

[Reports from yesterday's Evening Editions.]

The excitement, from an early hour this morning, in the Ninth and Eighth Congressional Districts, was very great. All the corners in the Eighteenth, Nineteenth and Twenty-second Wards were thronged with crowds of working people, all of whom showed considerable interest in the draft going on in their district.

Provost Marshal Jenkins, of the Ninth District, yesterday received information that an armed multitude of workmen from the Sixth, Seventh, and Second avenues intended to seize the wheel with the names and destroy it.

This morning men employed on the Second Avenue railroad refused to go to work, while those on the Sixth avenue railroad asked leave of absence from their work, and in case of refusal, threatened to take summary measures.

All the blacksmiths in the employ of the Third Avenue Railroad Company ceased work, as did also the men employed in Brown's Iron factory, those employed by Mr. Crimmins, the contrator, in Taylor's Foundry in Forty-first street and Eighth avenue, and hundreds of others employed on buildings, street improvements, &c. These crowds paraded through the streets, and forced their fellows to leave work and join them.

In short, the excitement through the Nineteenth and Twenty-second Wards is most intense and increasing every minute, ready to break out into open hostility on the first occasion.

Pending this state of affairs, Captain Jenkins communicated with Col. Nugent, while Captain Porter of the Nineteenth Ward asked Superintendent Kennedy for instructions.

At ten o'clock two platoons of police from the Twenty-first, Seventeenth, Twenty-second and other Wards, amounting to some two hundred men, arrived near the office of the Provost Marshal, thereby increasing the excitement around the building.

LATER.

We have just received a report that the building on Third avenue, where the drafting is taking place for the Ninth district, has been burnt down, and that all the papers have been thrown into the street.

A car full of soldiers, fully armed and equipped, has just gone up the Third avenue.

The firemen are reported to have appeared on the ground, and refused to perform their duties.

At latest accounts the crowd, about seven thousand strong, marched down to Capt. Manierre's headquarters.

Orders have been sent to all military stations in the harbor to forward all military forces to this city.

11½ A. M.—The building is all in flames; No. 679 has caught fire, and threats are being made to burn No. 681.

The ground around is covered with the debris of the drafting books and papers.

Some 12,000 highly excited men are round the building, with a thick sprinkling of women. Many women are on the house-tops waving their shawls and handkerchiefs to the rioters.

The telegraph poles are cut down, and the wires cut.

The cars are stopped. About thirty are now waiting to pass.

It is stated that other offices will be attacked to-day or to-morrow.

A warning, it is stated, was sent, several days ago, to the people inhabiting the upper part of No. 677 that this attack would be made.

Gen. Wool and Staff were at Police Headquarters at 12 o'clock, in consultation with the Police Commissioners.

The Provost Marshal's Guard (the Invalid Corps), while going up the Bowery, near the Hay Market, in a Third avenue car, were insulted and sneered at by a large crowd congregated there. Stones were thrown at the cars repeatedly.

General Sandford has just issued the following:

HEADQUARTERS FIRST DIVISION, N. Y. N. G.,
NEW YORK, July 13, 1863.

The ex-officers of this Division and of the United States Volunteers now in this city, who are disposed to assist in preserving the peace of this city are requested to meet at the Seventh Regiment Drill Rooms, over Tompkins Market, this evening at 8 o'clock. CHAS. W. SANDFORD, Major-Gen.

The Sixth avenue cars have stopped running down town, their men being taken off by the crowd.

SUPERINTENDENT KENNEDY BADLY BEATEN.

During the conflagration, Superintendent Kennedy appeared outside, when the crowd attacked him in such a manner that he received very severe injuries.

THE DRAFT SUSPENDED IN THIS CITY TO-DAY.

We have the names of hundreds of conscripts drawn this morning in the Eighth District. When Capt. Manierre heard of the trouble in the Ninth, he immediately suspended all further operations, with a view, it is understood, to allow the strong police force on duty at his office to proceed to the scene of disturbance.

ANOTHER ACCOUNT.

The armed guard which came on the ground at one o'clock, were set upon by the crowd, who, in less time than it takes to write this, disarmed the soldiers, taking their cartridge boxes and bayonets.

On the corner of Forty-second street and Third avenue, a police officer, in endeavoring to fire into the crowd, shot a horse, which was standing there, and killed a woman, who resides somewhere in Forty-second street, on the Rocks.

The crowd on seeing this, rushed in and taking hold of an officer who was near, struck him with paving stones, iron bars and everything else within their reach. The poor fellow ran across the street, pursued by the mob, when a ball was fired at him, striking him in the back of the head. The man finally got into a brickyard, where a number of females beset him and abused him until he dropped down exhausted, and could only be rescued by the united efforts of several gentlemen, who took him to St. Luke's Hospital.

The greatest excitement prevailed at this time, and the most fierce of all were the women, who with crowbars, clubs, shovels, and other implements of destruction, were running about calling on the men to die at home. Some person here advised the crowds to go round Lexington avenue and look for the police there. But only a few went up, who on the corner of Forty-second street and Lexington avenue, came across a police officer, whose head was beaten to a jelly, but he got off and escaped.

About this time it was stated that a marine had escaped into the house on the southwest corner of Third avenue and Forty-second street. The crowd at once rushed in and, bursting open the hall doors ran up stairs into the apartments of Mr. George W. Yeomans, whose lady had just been confined. On seeing this, and being assured by the gentleman that no soldier was concealed in his rooms, the crowd retired, but some men ran up stairs and breaking into the rooms took a coat, several dresses, and some ten dollars in money, but as the object of their search could not be found, the crowd withdrew.

A comparative quiet ensued for about an hour, during which many procured bars of iron, &c. At about 2 o'clock, crowds began to arrive from the lower Wards, and, as groups arrived, they were loudly cheered by the populace. Some of the men who had now just arrived brought heavy firearms with them, but nearly every one had a pistol or revolver.

At two o'clock Mr. Howard, a gentleman connected with the city press for many years, was standing on the corner of Forty-sixth street and Third avenue, looking at the scene, when the cry was raised, "Here is a d——d abolitionist; let's hang him!" &c., &c.

He was immediately surrounded by a mob, to whom he made known his vocation. A voice here cried out, "He is a Tribune man; hang the ——!"

Mr. Howard was seized by the hair, and taken to an awning post, but fortunately something else diverting the attention of the crowd, he had a chance to escape up Third avenue—but only for a short time, for a blow with a paving stone on the back of the head and another one in the face stunned him so, that he lost all consciousness, and while in this state he lost his gold watch and chain, diamond breastpin and $33 in money.

Four gentlemen—Messrs. W. W. Ryan, F. McGinnis, A. Hunt and E. J. Dunn—here came up, and taking charge of the wounded man, conveyed him to the truck house of Hook and Ladder Co. No. 16, on the corner of Lexington avenue and Fiftieth street, followed all the time by the excited crowd, who wanted nothing less than to hang him, but he was finally got in and the doors closed. The crowd in the mean time kept hammering at the doors, but they had to give up, as the doors resisted, and Mr. Howard was finally got away without further trouble.

At about three o'clock a procession of about five thousand people came up First Avenue, all armed with bars, pistols, &c., threatening vengeance on all persons connected with the draft. They halted in front of the Eighteenth Ward Station House in Twenty-second street, and sent up yells which were anything but human.

Casualties among the Police.

Two of these officers were left lying on the pavement at the corner of Forty-second street for some time, before the crowd would allow them to be removed.

Several of the policemen were so fortunate as to procure disguises, and thus made their escape unnoticed by the crowd. Sergeant Wade was struck in the breast with a stone, but sustained no serious injury. Sergeant McCredie has not been heard from.

Phillip Rubason, a member of the First Battalion Invalid Corps, was attacked by the mob, his musket, bayonet, and equipments, taken from him, and he was beaten in a terrible manner about the head with his own musket. He was finally rescued by some humane firemen when almost exhausted from the treatment he had received. He was conveyed to the Twenty-first Precinct Station House, and there attended by Dr. Ranney. He will probably survive.

The Fire.

At about one o'clock, Chief Engineer Decker arrived at the scene of the fire, and seeing how matters stood, ordered the firemen to go to work to extinguish the flames. The crowd by this time had gone down the Third avenue, and the firemen were not molested. Steamers Nos. 33 and 46, with several hand engines, threw streams of water on the fire, but it was all in vain, as the flames had got such headway that the entire block was eventually destroyed. The further progress of the flames in that direction has, however, been checked.

All is at present quiet in and around the Arsenal in Seventh avenue. Crowds of men are assembled on the street corners and in the grog shops in the neighborhood, talking excitedly, but there is no symptom of disturbance.

The Arsenal is garrisoned by a detachment of Tenth New York Volunteers, under Captain Babcock and a strong force of police.

The Crowd Addressed by Mr. Andrews, of Virginia.

The firemen continued playing on the large burning pile until about 3 o'clock, which, however, did not succeed in checking the progress of the flames; and as our reporter left, nothing remained but a shell of the last house on the block. Meantime, the angry crowd ebbed to and fro, women freely mixing in the debates and denunciations against the $300 clause.

About this period Mr. Andrews, of Virginia, ascended a shanty which stood opposite the burning ruins, where thousands were assembled. Behind this was an open space of untilled ground occupied by dense masses, whom Mr. Andrews proceeded to address:

"He wished he had the lungs of a Stentor, and that there was a reporter present to take down his words. He said he had lately addressed them at a meeting at the Cooper Institute, where he told them Mr. Lincoln wanted to tear the hard working man from his wife and family and send him to the war. He denounced Mr. Lincoln for his conscription bill, which was in favor of the rich and against the poor man. He called him a Nero and a Caligula for such a measure. Had the country not given to this war plenty of men? Were they more liberal in supplying men and money in the time of their Revolutionary Fathers, or in their war with England in 1812, than in the present unhappy struggle? Certainly not. He then advised the people to organize to resist the draft and appoint their leader, and if necessary he would be their leader." (Uproarious cheering.)

[From the distance at which the reporter stood he could but indistinctly hear much of Mr. Andrews address, and any attempt to take a note might bring on the unfortunate reporter an assault from some one in the crowd acting under the impression that the reporter belonged in some way to the Provost Marshal's office. He has however indicated the chief points of Mr. Andrews' address.]

Immediately after this the leaders of the assaulting party, proceeded to a large and beautiful dwelling on the corner of Forty-seventh street and Lexington avenue, followed by an excited crowd, and immediately proceeded to attack this building, which was said to be by some the residence of Major General Sandford, and by others, that of Mr. Dowe, a tailor, who belonged to the Provost Marshal's department—others thought it was Horace Greeley's.

They smashed in the doors, which they tore from the hinges, smashed every pane of glass both front and rear, and then commenced to fling out of the windows everything upon which they could lay their hands. Pictures, with gilt frames, elegant pier glasses, sofas, chairs, clocks, furniture of every kind, wearing apparel, bed clothes, &c., &c., a whole library was scattered in showers through the windows, and they wound up by setting fire to the building, amid the wild cheers, yells and hooting of those who surrounded the house. Whether one liked or disliked the Conscription act, and not a single person had a word to say in favor of the $300 clause, it was condemned by all—this fearful and useless destruction of private property was a most melancholy exhibition of popular fury.

We have referred to the rumors as to the ownership of this house, and briefly indicated the causes which led to its destruction. Other rumors prevailed that it was in consequence of secreting policemen, who had fled and ultimately eluded the mob. Others that the owner was in some way mixed up with the draft; but whatever was real or fancied, the scene was terrible to behold.

The Draft in the Eighth District.

Immediately after Captain Manierre, Provost Marshal of the Eighth District, adjourned the drawing of the names in that district, the wheels containing the ballots, all the lists and papers belonging to the officer were conveyed to the Twenty-ninth Precinct Station House for safe keeping, as an attack on the officers was anticipated. This expectation no doubt caused the drawing of the names to be postponed.

FROM THE ARSENAL.

Regulars Sent for from Governor's Island—They Report to Col. Nugent—The State Arsenal Filled with Troops.

At three o'clock yesterday afternoon, a detachment of Regulars, from Governor's Island, was to report to Col. Robert Nugent, the Acting Assistant Provost Marshal General of this city. The troops were under command of Capt. Watkins, and numbered about one hundred men. It was currently reported that the great throng which had burnt up the Marshal's quarters in Third avenue had taken possession of the arsenal. The rumor, however, was unfounded.

In some streets through which the regulars passed, the spectators seemed to anticipate that they came to enforce the draft. Small groups of women and men, in Wooster and other streets on their line of march, hooted and cursed at them, while some exclaimed: "You can't take our husbands."

The movement of the regulars were kept secret by officers and men. The guide, Dr. White, U. S. A., and Capt. Wilkins, refused to reveal their destination.

At a quarter-past four o'clock a crowd of about three thousand persons, who were being rapidly re-enforced from almost every direction, marched down Fifth avenue, and then crossed over East Thirty-first street toward the Seventh avenue.

They were armed with bars of iron, staves and other implements. They gave continually vociferous groans for the Conscription, and one of them bore a banner, formed of a large panel of wood, on which was inscribed the words: "NO DRAFT."

Scene at the Arsenal.

At a quarter past four o'clock in the afternoon the arsenal at the corner of Thirty-fifth street and Seventh avenue presented a scene of the most intense excitement—large crowds having gathered about the building, and denouncing the acts of the Administration and the draft in the most bitter terms. No attempt, however, was made by them to take possession of the building. A detachment of regulars from Governor's Island and other places were inside, well armed and ready to resist any attempt to take the building. The crowd frequently hooted the soldiers, whenever they made their appearance at the windows.

The excitement for blocks around was very great. Every entrance about the Arsenal was closely guarded and the doors and gates were securely bolted and barred. Shortly after four o'clock two companies of the 1st Cavalry, under command of Captain Knoble, arrived and took a position in the front of the Arsenal. The crowd were terribly excited. A detachment of the Third Cavalry, Col. Pcstley, was also on the ground.

BALTIMORE POLICE COMMISSIONERS.

Sheriff Campbell Fails to Execute the Writ of Attachment—Application for His Removal from Office—Governor Seymour Promises Immediate Action in the Matter.

Another step has been taken by the counsel in the matter of the Baltimore Police Commissioners. The Sheriff of Kings County having certified that he was unable to serve the writ of attachment issued by the County Judge against Colonel Burke (for disobedience to a writ of habeas corpus), the counsel for the political prisoners have now appealed to Governor Seymour to remove the Sheriff. They take the ground, it is understood, that the Sheriff can have sufficient military force, if he chooses to call for it, to capture Fort Lafayette and enforce the State laws; and that the law itself contemplates no such contingency as a successful resistance to its authority.

The charges against the Sheriff, duly verified, were presented to Governor Seymour at the St. Nicholas Hotel, in this city, on Friday, 10th inst. The Governor took them, and promised an early action upon them. It is confidently believed by the complainants that the Kings County Sheriff will be removed, and a new one appointed, who will call to his aid all the military power of the State in the effort to enforce its laws. The following are the charges against Sheriff Campbell, now in the hands of the Governor for action:

NEW YORK CITY, July 10, 1863.

TO HIS EXCELLENCY THE GOVERNOR OF THE STATE YORK:

The undersigned, a citizen of the City and State of New York, presents charges against Anthony F. Campbell, Sheriff of the County of Kings, and shows to your Excellency,

FIRST. That by the law of the State of New York it is expressly directed that "every sheriff to whom any process shall be delivered, shall execute the same according to the command thereof, and shall make due return of his proceedings thereon." (R. Stat., 5th ed., vol. iii, p. 739, sec. 98.)

SECOND. That a certain writ of attachment, in the following words and figures, was allowed, signed and sealed by the Hon. Samuel Garrison, County Judge of the County of Kings, and by J. N. Stearns, County Clerk of said county, and sealed with the seal of said county, and delivered to the said sheriff on the 7th day of July instant, to wit: "The People of the State of New York to the Sheriff of the County of Kings.

We command you, as we before commanded you, forthwith to apprehend and attach Colonel Martin Burke, of Fort Hamilton, in the said County of Kings, and to bring him immediately before our County Judge of the said county, at the chambers of the Kings County Court, in the City Hall, in the City of Brooklyn, to answer for his contempt in not obeying a certain writ of habeas corpus to him directed, and on him duly served, on the relation of Algernon R. Wood, and have you then there this writ of attachment.

Witness the Honorable Samuel Garrison, County Judge of our said county of Kings, at the City Hall, in the said city of Brooklyn, this seventh day of July, 1863.

SAMUEL GARRISON, Kings County Junge.
J. N. STEARNS, Clerk.

JOHN. C. VAN LOON, Attorney for Relator.

Endorsed—Within writ allowed by me July 7, 1864, at Brooklyn. SAMUEL GARRISON, Kings County Judge.

THIRD—That the said place named Fort Hamilton, in the county of Kings, where the said Martin Burke was and is, is a fort situated upon a tract of land, the jurisdiction over which was ceded to the United States of America, by an act of the Legislature of the State of New York, for the erection of fortifications on the said tract, and in and by such act of cession it was expressly provided that "the jurisdiction so ceded should not prevent the execution on said tract of any process, civil or criminal, under the authority of this State, except so far forth as any such process may effect the real and personal property of the United States within the said tract." (R. S, 5th ed., vol, 1 p. 97 and 98, § 21, 24.)

FOURTH—That the said Sheriff did not obey, execute or serve, or attempt to serve the said writ of attachment upon Martin Burke therein named, nor apprehend or attach the said Burke, nor bring him before said County Judge, nor make due return of his proceedings thereon; but instead thereof, made and indorsed upon the said writ the following, which he caused to be filed with the said County Judge of Kings County, to wit: I return to the within writ of attachment that I am unable to arrest the within named Col. Martin Burke as within commanded, the said Col. Burke being commandant of Fort Lafayette and Fort Hamilton, and in Fort Hamilton. I have endeavored to obtain entrance and access to Fort Hamilton, which is held and garrisoned by armed troops of the United States, well armed and provisioned, and cannot be taken or an entrance effected without the aid of a large force of troops with artillery. I further return that I have been formally notified by the officer of the day in command of Fort Hamilton, that they were prepared to resist any attack on the fort, or any attempt upon my part to arrest the body of Col. Burke, within named, who is commandant of the forts. And I further return that the whole militia force of Kings county (except the Seventieth Regiment) is now in the service of the United States in the State of Pennsylvania, and out of the county of Kings, and that the said Seventieth Regiment, as I am informed by Col. Cropsey, in command of the same, is now under marching orders, and not subject to my control, and I have no force or arms within or under my control sufficient for the purpose of executing the within writ. ANTHONY F. CAMPBELL, Sheriff of Kings County.

BROOKLYN, July 9, 1863.

FIFTH.—That the said sheriff did not act under the following provisions of the Revised Statutes, as it was his duty to have done:—"Whenever a sheriff or other public officer authorized to execute any process delivered to him, shall find or have reason to apprehend that resistance will be made to the execution of such process, he shall be authorized to command every male inhabitant of his county, or as many as he shall think proper, and with such arms as he shall direct, and any military company or companies in said county, armed and equipped, to assist him in overcoming such resistance, and, if necessary, in seizing, arresting, and confining the resisters, their aiders and abettors, to be dealt with according to law." (R. S., 5th ed., vol 3, p. 140, sec. 101.) Nor did he make application to the Governor under the following provision:—"On the application of the sheriff, under sheriff, or district attorney of any county of this State, with the assent of a majority of the judges of the county courts of said county, the Governor may, if in his opinion it shall be necessary and proper, authorize such sheriff, under sheriff, district attorney, or some deputy sheriff, to contract with and organize a guard for the protection of any jail or prison in said county, or to arrest, detain, or have in safe keeping any person or persons, or to enforce any process, judgment, or decree of any court."—R. S., 5th ed., vol. 1, p. 748, sec. 72. Nor did he call for aid under the following provisions of law:—"In case of any breach of the peace, tumult, riot, or resistance to process of this State, or apprehension of imminent danger of the same, it shall be lawful for the sheriff of any county, or the mayor of any city, to call for aid from any division, brigade, regiment, battalion, or company; and it shall be the duty of the commanding officers of such division, brigade, regiment, battalion, or company, when such order is given, to order out in aid of the civil authorities the military force, or any part thereof under his command."—Laws of 1862, sec. 291, p. 940.

Wherefore the undersigned prays that the Governor will exercise the power of removal of the Sheriff given him by the Constitution of this State, viz.: "The Governor may remove any officer in this section mentioned, including Sheriffs, within the term for which he shall have been elected, giving to such officer a copy of the charges against him, and an opportunity of being heard in his defense. (Constitution of the State of New York, Article 10, section 1.) And he asks that Anthony F. Campbell, Sheriff of the County of Kings, may be removed from office as such Sheriff, and that some fit person, who was eligible to that office, be appointed to fill the vacancy and execute the duties of such office until it shall be supplied by an election." (R. S. 5th ed., vol. 1, sec. 56, p. 415.) All of which is respectfully submitted. J. C VAN LOON.

CITY AND COUNTY OF NEW YORK, ss.—John C. Van Loon, the complainant above named, being duly sworn, deposes and says that he has read the foregoing charges against the Sheriff of Kings County, and that the same are true of his knowledge, except as to those matters which are therein stated to be upon information and belief, and that as to those matters he believes them to be true. J. C. VAN LOON.

Sworn to before me this tenth day of July, 1863.
W. D. PARSONS, Notary Public.

Abuse of Prisoners.

DELAWARE CITY, July 10, 1863.

The man or men who would take advantage of unarmed, helpless prisoners, to abuse or treat them cruelly is a coward, a natural inate coward. I remember when, during the war of 1812, the press teemd with the cruelties of the Dartmouth Prison, there was one universal cry of detestation from one end of this country to the other; but sir, Dartmouth was a palace to some of the bastiles of this country now. The cruelties of Lafayette have been graphically penned by more than one sufferer from the persecutions of that prison; but, Fort Delaware bids fair to rival it. They, the prisoners, are dying by scores—and no wonder. Their food is cooked and served in such a manner that a gentleman's dog would spurn it. The water they drink would kill the devil, let alone a human being. They are huddled together by the thousands without the proper care or comforts, due a well kept pig. But, if what one of the guards said be true. This is the place to get rid of them. When the guard returned from Fort Delaware, after delivering a load of prisoners, several of them went to a confectionary store at Delaware City, and they were asked why so many were brought here—he replied, "Oh, it will save the expense or trouble of taking them back, as I understand the water is killing them all." The Medical Department demands at the hands of Surgeon General Hammond a full and thorough investigation—not of those who are there as their keepers, but let prisoners themselves be the witnesses—and my word for it, he will learn things that will make his kind heart ache. Let some human, not beast, investigate the conduct to these prisoners—let it be fair and full, and it will produce an impression in this country that will make the satraps there tremble, and be spurned by any honest Christian. If there is not a change, a full history shall be given, and let the people judge for themselves. Let the upstart who sat upon the coffin of a deceased Confederate Major—and said, "Now, damn you, I have got you where I wanted you," beware, and learn that no soldier or gentleman would offer an indignity to a fallen foe. Let us have the investigation—the subject will be continued. BRUTUS.

The Grand Opportunity for Peace and Reunion—Shall it be Improved?

[From The New Haven Register.]

The signal victories of the Federal arms, which have thrilled the heart of the country, within the few days past, may well excite a feeling of exultation, and elicit the heartiest congratulation, if they are to be made the basis of that statesman-like action the condition of the Republic demands. But if they are to be permitted to pass into history, as simply the dates on which a fearful slaughter was enacted, or a mere triumph of brute force achieved, then we can discover no place for anything but sadness at the destruction of human life, and the wide spread misery by which they were accompanied. An opportunity is now presented, such as has not appeared for a twelve month, for a statesman to step forward and rescue his country from the evils of utter exhaustion and military despotism, or a final dissolution of the Union. The great objection to the way of a peaceful adjustment of our differences, has at last been removed. While the South was the acknowledged victor on many well fought fields, we can understand why the advocates of the war should object to any overtures, on the part of the North, for a settlement of the controversy outside the field of blood. But now, the case is different. There is no longer the stigma of defeat upon the arms of the North.

The crowning victory on the Mississippi has filled the scroll of the Great West, while the bloody field of Gettysburg has tested and proved the courage of the North and East, as no humane man will desire to see it tested again. The South has, for two years, withstood and repelled the invasion of Virginia; the North has, a second time, hurled back the legions of the South, which sought to overrun her soil. The courage and manhood of both sections have been demonstrated before the world. The South has learned that the North has not only wealth and numerical strength, but the courage and fortitude of a great people; while the North has learned to respect the South for her marvelous energy and endurance in maintaining a contest against such fearful odds. What is there to deter the two sections of a once united and happy country, from now striking hands and settling their unfortunate differences, upon terms alike honorable to both? Why should the victorious North hesitate to proffer their brethren of the South a magnanimous appeal for a restoration of the Union founded by our common ancestry? The hearts of the people yearn for peace, and the announcement that this bloody strife had ceased, would carry unutterable joy to thousands and tens of thousands of households, hourly trembling with the fear of impending disaster.

How much better for the future peace and prosperity of the country, that this fearful controversy should be terminated with neither section the boaster over the other—with neither disgraced by ultimate defeat, on the one hand, or subjugation on the other. If Mr. Lincoln would save his country from a further infliction of the horrors of war, make this once more a united and invincible republic, and earn the everlasting gratitude of his countrymen, now is the time for him to cast aside every influence of party or sectional prejudice, and make an effort to save his country. He might live a hundred years, and never meet with such an opportunity to write his name so high among those who deserve well of their country. He has the chance to cause his name to be inscribed beside that of Washington, as the saviour of his country. We have not been an admirer of Mr. Lincoln. We have condemned, in what seemed to us fitting terms, the many unwise acts of his Administration. But such is our devotion to the Union, that if he would but use the means which Providence has placed in his hands, for the salvation of the Republic, we would gladly unite with his most ardent admirers in according him the honor to which such an act would justly entitle him.

Let us not deceive ourselves by the seemingly fair prospect of the speedy crushing of the Rebellion. The fortunes of war are fickle in the extreme, and the most trifling accident may turn the scale of the greatest battle. Had not Meade's re-enforcements come up at the precise time, and at the precise spot they did, the history of the Gettysburg struggle might have been very different. Now is the golden opportunity. It may be long before we shall see another. We should remember that our army is growing weaker every day. The places of trained men cannot be filled in a day, and there can be no estimate of the power of a people driven to the wall. The veriest coward will fight in a corner. Let us not take the risks, and, above all, let us not prolong the horrid feats of war while the hope remains of its honorable termination.

The attempt may fail. The South may scornfully reject our overtures. Then upon their head must rest the fearful responsibility of all that follows! The experiment is worth the trial, and we cannot afford to let the occasion pass unimproved.

Peace Now More than Ever.

[From The Metropolitan Record.]

We have noticed of late days a significant change in the tactics of the rampant war party. Formerly they inveighed against peace as disgraceful in itself, derogatory to the dignity of the nation and the manhood of the people, as an eternal disruption of the Union, &c. Now they let the principle alone and attack its advocates, impugn their character and motives, and throw suspicion on their aims and purposes. They gave up argument for invective, and flinging truth and reason to the wind, fall back upon slander and abuse. Every derisive epithet is hurled at their devoted heads as if it were a weapon of offense; and if billingsgate could annihilate, they would have been used up long ago.

There is something in man's nature that makes him shrink from the charge of cowardice as if it were a crime. Knowing this, these men ring the changes on skulk, sneak, coward, hoping by such means to shut the mouths if they cannot chrnge the minds of the Peace party. Let it be borne in mind that, as a general thing, the men who apply these opprobrious epithets never saw a battle; they have not volunteered; and if drafted they would not fight. Their "voice is all for war"—"war, war to the bitter end" is their cry; but war is a game they are too wise to play at. It answers better to slander peace-men; and then it is so easy to obtain a character for courage by calling men who are opposed to the war sneaks and cowards. But why are not these furious war-men in the field? What keeps them from fighting? They approve of the war, and of the manner in which it has been carried on—why, then, in the name of all that is consistent, are they here? With what face can they object to other men doing as they do? How can these men presume to brand as sneaks and cowards men who have been as near to the enemy as they have been? If peace men are cowards, what are they?

Now, whether these verbal insults be intended for slurs or goads, we know not, probably for both; but in either case they tell against the men that have recourse to them. For be it remarked, as we said before, that it is not those who have smelled powder who denounce the peace men so bitterly, but the laggards, the stay-at-homes, the practical peace men.

We ask our readers, is there anything so contemptible as a man, holding back from a mortal struggle from fear, insulting another who holds back from principle? Men who live in glass houses should not throw stones; men who have shrunk from fighting should be chary of applying such terms as skulk or coward to any one. We wonder that the blush of shame does not crimson the very temples of the man who, while clinging to his own door-sill with the tenacity of desperation, would drive by taunts or jeers, by force or finesse, his neighbor from his.

The men who are in favor of a cause are the men who fight for it heartily. Then let the Government conscript all those who are in favor of this war, let every man who urges another to enlist be pressed at once, let every man who calls or has called another coward for not volunteering be mustered into the service, and it will have enough to keep it going for another campaign at least. This will be the right thing to do, this will be the fair thing to do, this will give the new general of the army of the Potomac a chance.

Peace men, say those furious warriors who are willing to drain the last drop of their (proxy's) blood before they would listen to terms, peace men would sacrifice the honor of the country to their own material interest; sooner than have business prostrated and commerce destroyed, they would ignobly sue for peace on any terms. This is a slander on the Peace party, and these men know it. Rather than liberty should suffer wrong, rather than the Constitution should be violated, rather than republican institutions should be endangered and self-government brought into contempt, the Peace party would make peace, not sue for it, as any time, not on any terms.

If the partisans of the Administration had any sense of shame they would shrink from insinuating mercenary motives in connection with the Peace party, for if that party looked only to the loaves and the fishes they would go for the war; if in their eyes country was not above contracts they would go for the war; if national was to be made subsidiary to individual interest, they would go for the war; if they were willing to barter principle for miserable truckling expediency, they would go for the war. Let us hear no more of these slanders upon peace men; their policy is the only one that gives a chance for saving the country, for preserving its integrity. and for bequeathing it whole and intact to our successors.

Lee's invasion of the North, say these men, will squelch out the Peace party forever. They are grossly mistaken. It is but another argument for peace. We can judge from it what a scourge invasions conducted like ours have been. We can imagine what Virginia and Louisiana must have suffered. It has been brought home to our own doors; let us see how we like it. The poisoned chalice that the South has drained has been commended to our lips, and having once tasted of its bitterness, shall we force it upon her again? A thousand times no! We are for peace now as ever; we were against this war while the South was the theater on which it was enacted, we are none the less against it now. Shall we be told that it was all right to be for peace a month ago but all wrong now—all right when Hooker was in Virginia but all wrong when Lee was in Pennsylvania? All we can say is that our principles do not depend upon the movements of our armies. Whether Grant takes Vicksburg or Lee Harper's Ferry, whether Richmond falls or Washington is captured, we are for peace—for peace now and forever—for peace as our only chance for the present and only hope for the future.

A Mysterious Case in Philadelphia.

On Monday, a German, giving his name as E. P. Singer, was arrested at Philadelphia. Under his clothing a leather bag was found containing, among other things, some Prussian bonds, and German money valued at $8,000. A lady's watch was in a small pocket-book, also a receipt for $300, signed by J. Shultz & Woller, of Bremen, dated June 5, 1862, in favor of Traugott Muller. Wrapped in this receipt was a lock of hair, evidently that of a woman. When the officers were examining this hair, Singer seized the receipt, and made an unsuccessful effort to throw it away.

The stories which he told to different parties varied considerably. To one he said he was a doctor. To the German Consul he said that the Prussian bonds had been bought from emigrants whom he had met, and that some of the articles belonged to a man who had been his partner, and who was now in the army. Other parties he told that he collected herbs in Ohio and sent them to Germany.

Two suspicious circumstances were particularly noted. On Monday afternoon Singer met a German and asked him to go to the post office to get out a letter for him (Singer) which was advertised. This was done, and the letter, which was found on his person, was discovered to be from a broker in Pittsburg, and to have reference to the negotiation of Prussian bonds.

When arrested, the officer threatened to send him back to Germany, Singer, evidently frightened offered a bribe of $100 if the officer would release him. There is every reason to believe, that all the valuables belong to Traugott Muller, whoever he may be, and that they are in the unlawful possession of Singer, although how he acquired their possession, whether by the murder of Muller in Germany or on the passage over the ocean, no one can tell.

HIGHLY IMPORTANT FROM THE WEST.

The Rebel Invasion under Gen. Morgan.

MARTIAL LAW DECLARED IN CINCINNATI.

ALL BUSINESS SUSPENDED.

CINCINNATI, July 13, 1863.

General Burnside has declared martial law in Cincinnati, Covington, Ky., and Newport, Ky.

All business is suspended until further orders, and all citizens are required to organize in accordance with the direction of the State and municipal authorities.

There is nothing definite as to Morgan's whereabouts this morning; but it is supposed that he will endeavor to move around the city (Cincinnati) and cross the river between here and Maysville.

The militia is concentrating in obedience to the order of Governor Tod.

FROM THE ARMIES IN MARYLAND.

REPORTS VIA HARRISBURG.

Statement of a Gentleman from Waynesboro.

The Enemy Falling Back from Antietam.

GEN. EWELL REOCCUPIES HAGERSTOWN.

STORY OF AN ESCAPED CAPTAIN.

Thunder Storm in the Antietam Valley.

HARRISBURG, Pa., July 13, 1863.

A gentlemen who left Waynesboro' on Sunday at noon furnishes the following:

It is understood that the Rebels, in falling back from the line of the Conocheague River from Antietam, encountered the forces of Gen. Mulligan, and after several skirmishes in the vicinity of Clear Spring, retired to the eastward. This accounts, no doubt, for the reoccupation of Hagerstown by Gen. Ewell.

The position of the Rebels is now reduced to a space of six miles by nine in which to maneuver.

The Rebels have no naturally strong defensive points left them, and it is believed by persons in official position they cannot possibly escape capture or annihilation.

The report that a large number of Rebels had crossed the Potomac with a wagon train is believed to be entirely false, as there is nothing to cross the river with except a rope ferry.

Two hundred Federal prisoners who refused to take their parole from the Rebels were crossed on this ferry on Thursday evening.

Capt. Norris, who succeeded in making his escape, brought information that as far as he observed, there was no considerable Rebel force on the south bank of the Potomac.

The Grey Reserves and Blue Reserves, of Philadelphia, went on a reconnoissance in force, on Saturday, toward Hagerstown, and succeeded in opening communication with the army of the Potomac and captured several prisoners.

A gentleman who has just arrived from the Antietam Valley, reports that a heavy thunder storm visited that region on Saturday and Sunday evenings. The rain fell in torrents for hours, and the mountain streams are again much swollen.

From the Army of the Potomac.

HEADQUARTERS ARMY OF THE POTOMAC, July 13.—8.30 A. M.

A messenger from Governor Curtin arrived this morning and states that Gen. Couch has formed a junction with our right which rests to the Northeast of Hagerstown. That point is secure against attack by Lee.

There are also reports that Lee has a bridge, composed of thirteen boats, across the center of the river, continued thence to both shores by trestlework, supporting long timbers.

Our siege and heavy guns have gone to the front and left, where it is believed positions can be obtained commanding the bridge.

Suspicious Vessels Seen at Sea.

BALTIMORE, July 13, 1863.

The ship Maggie V. Hugg, at this port from Havre, in forty-six days passage, reports on the night of July 1, in lat. 41, long. 63.50, was boarded by a boat from the United States bark Ethan Allen, she being then in chase of a bark which she deemed of a suspicious character; at about 2 o'clock in the morning saw the flash of some half a dozen guns in the direction of the chase.

The Maggie V. Hugg also reports July 6, in lat. 38 50 north, lon. 71 west, was chased by a bark with her decks full of men, but finding we had outsailed her considerably, she after dark hauled off, and started in the direction of a vessel to leeward that had squared away before the wind some time previously.

Bakers' Protective Union No. 2.

The first meeting of the German Bakers, under the agreement of separation from the parent society was held on Saturday evening at No. 42 Avenue A, Fred. Wolf President, and Wm. Speidel Secretary. A large number of new members were admitted, thus swelling the list to about one hundred and fifty members, who now are working in their native tongue.

Regatta at Troy, N. Y.

Upon the occasion of the annual State Fair at Troy, N. Y., in September next, the managers have determined to arrange a splendid rowing regatta upon the Hudson River, and will endeavor to make it an attractive feature of the fair. The programme is not yet prepared for publication, but we understand that the prizes will be sufficiently liberal to attract the best crews and boats in the United States to compete for them.

Duryee's Zouaves.

The above corps is now organizing for three years or the war. Large bounties are offered and every inducement given to men who enlist. The name which Duryee's Zouaves earned for themselves in the actions in which they took part will be certain to fill up this regiment upon its reorganization.

CONTINUED FROM EIGHTH PAGE.

that some decisive action in the matter should be taken promptly. The Mayor finally concluded to issue a proclamation, calling upon all law-and-order citizens, to enroll themselves for the purpose of aiding in terminating the disturbance.

For some time it was a matter of debate with the military authorities whether martial law should be declared or not. It was finally concluded to wait until this morning before taking any decisive steps in the matter.

Police Headquarters were packed full of policemen early in the evening—about 1,500 men, nearly the whole active force of the city, being present, ready to be sent out on duty at any moment. Squads of these were continually leaving and returning, and the most intense excitement prevailed. A number of omnibuses were in the street to convey the men up town, f their services were required in that quarter.

Owing to the great amount of official business which was transactod in the telegraph office, it was utterly unable to ascertain the exact number of persons killed and wounded. It was estimated that a dozen policemen had died from injuries received, and that thirty or forty otherers of the department were more or less injured. A number of the officers of the Twenty-ninth Precinct were very badly wounded—some of them shot and others badly cut.

Casualties.

Sergeant Smith, of the Ninth Precinct, seriously injured by stones, kicks, etc.

Officer Blackwood, of the Ninth, three ribs broken. Taken to his residence.

Officer Crooker, of the Ninth, injured in the head.

Officer John Walsh, of the Ninth, badly bruised about the head. Taken to City Hospital.

Officer McDonald, of the Ninth, two or three teeth knocked out by a blow from a club.

Officer Cholwell, of the Ninth, injured in the back.

Officer Larkin, of the Ninth, badly cut in the head.

Sergeant Mangin, of the Ninth, seriously injured in the bowels.

Officer John Russell, of the Ninth, injured in the ankle by a brick.

A sergeant and four men were missing all day, but in the evening two of the men returned, but could give no information of the others. They stated that they had succeeded in secreting themselves in a house in the vicinity of Forty-sixth street. The citizens came into the house and searched the upper rooms by a lighted paper, but fortunately did not ascertain their whereabouts. They were obliged to obtain citizens' clothes in order to return to the Station House.

As they were about leaving their place of concealment, they discovered the dead body of Alexander Wood, of the Nineteenth Precinct. The body lay in a privy near the house.

One of the men stated that he saw two men shot dead. One of these is the above named Wood, but the name of the other could not be ascertained.

Several citizens were seriously injured at the fire of the Colored Asylum.

One little girl, whose name could not be ascertained, was killed by a trunk falling upon her. She was taken to the residence of her parents, in Fifty-first street.

It was rumored that a fireman was run over by one of the machines and had his neck and both legs broken, but as no reliable information in regard to the matter could be arrived at it probably is nothing more than a rumor.

The following are some of the names of the police officers who were injured and are missing:

Captain Albert M. Palmer, Twenty-first Precinct, last seen on the corner of Forty-second street and Third avenue at noon, since which time he has not been seen or heard from.

Sergeant S. B. Smith, badly cut and bruised in the head, escaped with difficulty in a Harlem freight car to the Twelfth Precinct Station where his wounds were dressed.

Officer Charles R. Law, Eighth Precinct, seriously cut in the head.

John Walsh, Ninth Precinct, severely cut in the head; lying at the point of death at Bellevue Hospital.

Another officer, name unknown, residing in Franklin street, taken to St. Luke's Hospital; head crushed in and shot in the back of the head.

Officer Morrison, Twenty-ninth, severely wounded in the head and body.

Officer Fleming, Twenty-ninth, skull fractured: taken to Bellevue Hospital.

Officer Holmes, Twenty-ninth, badly cut in the head and about the body.

Officer Henderson, Twenty-ninth, seriously injured; taken to Bellevue Hospital.

Officer McIntyre, Twenty-ninth, badly cut and bruised; taken to his residence on Third avenue.

Officer Walsh, Twenty-ninth, skull fractured.

Officer Leaycraft, Twenty-ninth, frontal bone broken; lying in a dying condition at Bellevue Hospital.

Officer McCarty, Twenty-ninth, cut and bruised about the head; taken to his residence.

Officer Wm. H. Welling, First Precinct, shot in the shoulder during the attack on The Tribune office; supposed to have been shot by a policeman.

Officers Lwainsen and Zair, slightly injured.

It is reported that Capt. Walling, Twentieth Ward, shot a man while the crowd was attacking the Armory in Second avenue.

A large number of other policemen were badly injured, but they were not reported at a late hour.

In the Evening.

Toward evening, about 6 o'clock, thousands of those who participated in the destruction might be seen returning down town through the several avenues, many of them bearing large bludgeons, pieces of wood torn from property destroyed, or pieces of iron, all of which had done execution in the course of the day. Many walked on peaceably, others brandished their weapons in a menacing manner and gesticulated as they went along, giving indications that they had not yet finished their labors.

At Midnight.

The excitement had all subsided, and the streets were completely deserted. A heavy rain was falling which had the effect of preventing the renewal of the scenes which took place during the day.

The principal acts committed during the day were perpetrated by half grown boys, who followed the crowd fully prepared to commit any act of atrocity. All the goods carried away from fire in Breadway were taken by boys, of from 12 to 18 years, whose only object seemed to be plunder. The men who participated in the acts of burning, &c., seemed to be actuated by no other motive than hostility to the draft.

BROOKLYN.

The Riot in New York.

THE BROOKLYN POLICE—THE NAVY YARD—THE FIRE DEPARTMENT—THE PROVOST MARSHAL'S OFFICE IN THE THIRD DISTRICT, &C., &C.

The riot in New York created an intense excitement in Brooklyn, and large numbers of persons crossed the river to see what was going on.

Capt. S. B. Gregory, Provost Marshal of the Third Congressional District, on hearing of the proceeding in New York, packed up all his papers and transported them to a place of safety. There is nothing now in the building of the least importance to any one.

The draft, which was fixed for Wednesday morning, has been suspended for the present Further notice will be given when the drawing will take place.

The number of persons enrolled in the different wards comprising the district, and the number to be drafted is as follows, all of the first class:

	No. Enrolled.	No. to be Drafted.
1st Ward	707	180
2d "	944	257
3d "	1,057	340
4th "	1,367	369
5th "	1,960	551
7th "	1,374	373
11th "	3,378	1050
13th "	1,869	528
15th "	866	235
19th "	686	169

Of the second class about 11,000 persons are enrolled, making in all of both classes nearly 30,000.

Chief Engineer Cunningham, in view of the preseni exigency, ordered, last night, that, in case of fire, the bells shall ring three rounds, designating the district, and then the general alarm. This is for the purpose of assembling all the firemen, so as to extinguish every fire that may occur. These orders will be in force until further directions.

The colored people have a hard time of it. They are attacked everywhere and beaten. They crowded about the Police Stations, last night, asking for protection, being prevented from going to their homes or even walking the streets.

The police to the number of 100, went to New York in charge of Inspector Folk.

There was great commotion in the Navy Yard. The walls were manned and mounted with guns. Thirteen eighteen pounders are mounted on the Flushing avenue side so as to sweep everything. Two three hundred and twenty pounders command the main entrance, and all the vessels have been hauled into the stream, the guns shotted and everything ready for any emergency.

Several companies of marines with sixty rounds of eartrides and twelve boat howitzers, rifled cannon, with ammunition, boxes loaded with percussion caps, shells, schrapnel, canister and grape shot, were sent to New York toward evening. The marines were accompanied by three hundred sailors, armed with cutlasses and revolvers.

Some guns were taken from the State Arsenal in Portland Avenue on Sunday night, which gave rise to the rumor that it had been attacked. The facts are that two companies of artillery belonging to the Seventieth Regiment militia had been ordered to Fort Hamilton, and the guns were taken for their use. They were placed on vessels at the foot of Little Street, and transported to the fort. There are no arms in the building at present.

See Second Page for Further Details.

NAVAL MOVEMENTS.

Effect of the Draft on the Regular Army and Navy.

No sooner had it become certain that the draft would take place in this city and State, than recruiting for the regular army and navy sprang up as if by magic. The regular army, which, if full, should consist of over 40,000 men, had nearly dwindled away; and even the Marine Corps, and the Navy proper, were feeling severely the dullness of enlistments. Since Friday, however, men have been flocking to the military and naval offices to join the service. All the double battalion regiments recently added to the army are taking advantage of the excitement, and have sent out independent recruiting parties. Commissions are given to outsiders who bring in men. The Marine Corps now consists of 3,000 rank and file, 1,000 having recently been added to the usual force. There are some 35,000 men of all grades and ranks attached to our ships of war, but many more are needed in consequence of the number daily receiving their discharges. All the necessary hands can now be easily obtained, and the fighting force of the ships put up to its proper level. The mounted part of the regular army, it is proper to remark, is daily receiving as many men as could be expected were there no volunteer organizations to compete with it.

Brisk Local Movements.

Yesterday, the Provost Marshal General notified Admiral Paulding, of the Navy Yard, and Col. Loomis, of Governor's Island, that the resistance of a mob to the progress of the draft rendered it necessary that all the available United States forces at the disposal of those officers would be required in the city. In compliance with the request of the Provost Marshal General, all the Marines at the barracks and some troops from the Island were dispatched to New York, where they were distributed in proper order. It is said that dispatches were sent to Fort Trumbull, Conn., Fort Preble, Me., and Fort Independence, Mass., directing the commandants of those forts to send on to Governor's Island, at once, as many men as they can conveniently spare. All the recruits congregated at Buffalo, Rochester, and other recruiting stations, are also said to be under orders to report at Fort Columbus.

Reorganization of Hawkins' Zouaves.

This Regiment, which served with so much distinction during the first two years of the war, at Hatteras, Roanoke, Camden, Antietam, Fredericksburg, and many other places, is reforming under the colonelship of E. Jardine, its former major, an officer who served in the Mexican war. It receives a large number of recruits daily, who are immediately supplied with the Zouave uniform of the United States. The headquarters are at No. 510 Broadway.

Swiss Shooting Festival at Jones' Wood.

In September next a shooting festival will take place in Jones' Wood, the proceeds to be donated to the widows and orphans of Swiss soldiers killed during the war. Further particulars will be published previous to that time. Donations are asked for and may be sent to A. Hungerbuhler, No. 691 Broadway.

OUT DOOR SPORTS.

BASE BALL.

Matches to be Played.

July 15—Empire of New York vs. Eureka of N. J. Second nines upon the grounds of the Empire, at Hoboken.

July 17—Union of Brooklyn vs. Resolute, upon the Union Base ground in Williamsburgh. Game called at one, half-past 2 o'clock P. M.

July 23—Mutual of New York vs. Eckford of Brooklyn; the first game of a home and home match. Upon Mutual grounds at Hoboken.

Mutual vs. Gotham.

The first game of a home and home match, between these well known New York Clubs, was played at the Elysian Fields, Hoboken, yesterday afternoon, resulting in a victory for the Mutuals, who scored twenty-one runs to the Gotham's fifteen runs. The contest attracted a large number of spectators, among whom we were pleased to observe a fair portion of ladies. Both Clubs were short of several of their first nine players; the absentees being Van Cott, McGrath, and one or two others for the Gothams, and McKever, Zella, and McCulloch for the Mutuals. The game opened very favorably for the Gothams, who treated the Mutuals to the round 0, for four innings in succession, while they credited themselves with six runs. The change made by the Mutuals in the sixth innings, in placing Wansley, as pitcher, and McMahon, as catcher, was of great advantage to them. We append the score:

MUTUAL.	H. L.	RUNS.	GOTHAM.	H. L.	RUNS.
Brown, 2 b	5	1	Thorn, p	4	2
Goldie, 1 b	3	2	Squires, s. s	1	3
Beard, s. s	3	3	Vincillette, 1 b	3	2
Wansley, c	2	4	Cohen, c	5	0
Green, c. f	4	2	Welling, 2 b	5	1
McMahon, 3 b	2	4	Southworth, 3 b	2	3
Kelly, e. f	2	3	Stokem, c. f	3	2
Mott, a. f	2	1	Connell, e. f	3	1
Harris, p	4	1	Shaffer, w. f	1	1
Total	27	21	Total	27	15

RUNS MADE IN EACH INNINGS.

	1st.	2d.	3d.	4th.	5th.	6th.	7th.	8th.	9th.
Mutual	0	0	0	0	2	5	6	0	8
Gotham	3	0	0	3	6	0	2	1	0

Scorer for Gotham—James B. Mingay.
Scorer for Mutual—James McConnell.
Umpire—F. C. Sebring, of the Empire Club.

AQUATIC.

Empire City Regatta Club.

This fine aquatic organization intend we understand to arrange something very superior in the way of their annual regatta upon the Harlem River. The event is always a treat to every New Yorker who is at all partial to boating matters, and as it has been continued for some eight or nine years, the lovers of aquatic pastime in this vicinity naturally look forward to the announcement of the Empire Club's gala day with considerable interest. The programme will probaby consist of four races: A single scull race—a double scull race—a four oared race—and an amateur six oared race. The course will be the usual distance of five miles, measured by three turns; with liberal prizes for the first and second boats in each race. Boats from Boston, Newburgh, Poughkeepsie, will contend with our city oarsmen for the honors of the day.

LOCAL INTELLIGENCE.

NEW YORK.

Obsequies of Gen. S. K. Zook.

THE FUNERAL LARGELY ATTENDED.

The funeral of the late Gen. Samuel K. Zook took place yesterday at the City Hall, at three, P. M. The body, which has lain in state at the Governor's Room, was visited by the relatives and a large circle of friends of the General. The body was contained in a most costly rosewood coffin, secured with diamond-shaped silver nails, and otherwise elegantly decorated with flowers, flags, &c. On the lid of the coffin were the sword, sash, belt and cap of the deceased General, besides a beautiful wreath of flowers encircling a silver plate bearing the following inscription:

BRIGADIER GENERAL
SAMUEL K. ZOOK,
Killed in action, at Gettysburg, July 2, 1863,
Aged 41 Years.

At 3 o'clock, P. M., the funeral procession departed from the City Hall. The order of the procession was as follows:

First Regiment New York Cavalry, under command of Col. Price.
Third Regiment New York Cavalry, under command of Col. Postly.
Officers of Regular Army.
Officers of Volunteer Army.
Officers of the First Division New York State Militia.
Guard of Honor.
Hearse.

PALL BEARERS:

Hon. Edward Haight,	Brig. Gen. C. A. Arthur,
Big. Gen. T. F. Meagher,	Brig. Gen. C. C. Spicer,
Col. H. P. Martin,	Col. Robt. Nugent,
Col. Lewis A. Sayre,	Col. R. C. Hawkins,
Col. W. W. Price,	Col. M. M. Van Buren,
Maj. E. T. Chamalcuser.	Maj. M. G. Rathburn.

Officiating Clergymen.
The Mayor and Common Council in Carriages, preceded by the Sergeant at Arms.
Citizens Generally.

The procession, under the direction of Major Alexander Hamilton, passed through the east gate of the Park, through Chatham street and the Bowery to Bond street, to Broadway, and down Broadway to South Ferry, from thence to Greenwood, the place of interment. The flags were displayed at half mast from the City Hall, and public and private buildings and residences in the city. The owners and masters of vessels in the harbor also displayed their flags at half mast during the day.

ST. JAMES' CHURCH FESTIVAL.—Owing to the recent lamentable disturbances, the contemplated festival on behalf of St. James' Church has been postponed till further notice.

SALES OF REAL ESTATE.—The following sales of Real Estate were made at the Exchange Salesroom, No. 111 Broadway:

BY J. M. MILLER.

Building and 4 lots n s 54th st, between 2d and 3d ave, lots 25x½ block, $17,000.

BROOKLYN.

BROOKLYN COMMON COUNCIL.—The Board held a regular session last evening.

A communication from the Committee on War and Military Affairs was submitted, on the petition of Col. Murphy, of the Kings County Volunteers, for aid to enable him to complete the organization of his regiment, with a resolution denying the prayer of the petitioner.

Ald. Ternan thought that from events transpiring in New York we were treading on a volcano, which in a moment might belch forth its fires, and advocated the giving of a bounty to all enlisted men.

Ald. Taylor was of the opinion that the money was required by the Colonel only, and not for bounties to the men, and therefore opposed it.

Ald. Strong was prepared to act as a lawful citizen, and frown down all attempts at violations of law. He had witnessed several riots in New York, and the result had always been, that the law was supreme, and the guilty parties eventually punished. This affair would pass away, and be a shame to all who had not raised their voice against it. The American people had always maintained law, and ever would.

The resolution was referred back to the same committee for further report.

The Mayor vetoed a resolution appropriating $200 for a flag for the Fifty-sixth Regiment, the reason being that there was no money in the treasury for that purpose. He expressed gratification, however, that a stand of colors had been furnished by the citizens.

Ald. Belknap offered a resolution directing the Comptroller to make no further payment to any contractor for cleaning streets and removing ashes and garbage unless upon the certificate of the President of the Board of Contracts, certifying that the work has been done in conformity with the terms of the contract and to the satisfaction of the Board of Contracts. The resolution was adopted, and the meeting soon after adjourned.

MARRIAGES.

ACKERSON—ZABRISKIE—On Thursday, July 9, by Rev. A. H. Warner, at the residence of the bride's father, at New Bridge, N. J., Garrett Ackerson, Jr., of Hackensack, N. J., and Annie E., daughter of John A. Zabriskie, Esq. No cards.

RICHARDS—WENTWORTH—On Thursday, July 9, at the residence of the bride's father, by Rev. Moses Ballou, Daniel W. Richards and Sarah C. Wentworth. No cards.

DEATHS.

BROWN—In Brooklyn, on Sunday, July 12, Margaret Jane Brown, wife of James Brown, aged 42 years.

The friends of the family are respectfully invited to attend the funeral, at her late residence No. 49 Douglas street, at 3 o'clock, P. M., on Tuesday, July 14.

Boston papers please copy.

BRIDGE—On Friday, July 10, Lewis K. Bridge, son of the late Lewis K. Bridge, in the 32d year of his age.

The friends of the family are respectfully invited to attend his funeral, from the Church of the Messiah, (Dr. Osgood's,) Broadway, on Tuesday afternoon, July 14, at 4½ o'clock, without further invitation.

JOHNSON—In Newton, Sussex County, N. J., on Saturday, July 11, of diptheria, Helen E., youngest daughter of the late Samuel Johnson, in the 26th year of her age.

SCHENCK—On Friday, July 10, Seth Crowell Schenck, of Morristown, N. J., in the 70th year of his age.

Notice of funeral to-morrow.

TOWNSEND—In Yonkers, on Sunday, July 12, Hon. John Townsend, formerly Judge of Westchester County Court, aged 74 years.

His relatives and friends are invited to attend his funeral, on Tuesday, July 14, at 5½ o'clock, P. M., at St. John's Church, at Yonkers. Hudson River Railroad trains leave Chambers street at 4:10, and return from Yonkers at 6:54.

UNDERHILL—Suddenly, on Sunday, July 12, Miss Albertina S., daughter of Hannah and the late Peter Underhill, in the 49th year of her age.

The friends of the family are invited to attend the funeral on Tuesday, July 14, at the Church of the Holy Apostles, corner Ninth avenue and Twenty-ninth street, at 10 o'clock, A. M. The remains will be taken to Manhasset, L. I., for interment.

SPECIAL NOTICES.

The Festival for the Benefit of St. James's Church is postponed, on account of the disturbances caused by the draft. Due notice will be given when it shall take place.

TRADE NOTICES.

Gilders.—A Regular Monthly Meeting of Journeymen Gilders will be held at Military Hall, No. 193 Bowery, on WEDNESDAY EVENING, July 15th instant. Come one and all, as business of importance will be transacted.

By order W. H. GRIFFITHS, Pres.
JOHN LAWLER, Sec.

Southern  Confederacy.

THE PUBLIC GOOD BEFORE PRIVATE ADVANTAGE.

By Adair & Smith. Atlanta, Georgia, Confederate States of America, July 15, 1863. Vol. III—No. 21.

WEDNESDAY, JULY 8, 1863.

Lee's Order Respecting Private Property.

The Historian who chronicles the events of this war, will point to General Lee's Order to respect Private Property, extended to the forces und r his command in Maryland and Pennsylvania, as worthy of commemora tion with the victories which have addo! lustre to his name. It stands in proud contrast to the military conduct of the enemy. Respecting the sanctities that soften the harshness of civil war and elevate the humanity of the age, it at once places, in the view of the world, the composition of the respective armies at an immeasurable distance. The fiat goes forth from the Chief in command of our forces, that the usages of civilized warfare shall be respected. General acquiescence is the result. It is obeyed through every division, brigade, regiment and company of that mighty host.

Has any similar Order emanated from a Yankee Commander-in-Chief? Would any such be obeyed?—Is it the consciousness that, if issued, it would be disregarded? or is it the sympathetic instinct of commanders with men, that explains the difference? With some few and rare exceptions, it is both.

The armies opposed are constituted, in such large proportion, of foreign materials, as to impart a similar complexion to the whole—it is the lump that leavens the entire mass. Men who in Europe know no principle of action save sordid impulses—who are engaged to kill, when enlisted, for the sake of plunder—whose brutal passions find their congenial element in waste and personal outrage—the refuse of over crowded cities and pauperized provinces—would perhaps, obey no law but that of their own debased natures, if the prizes of licentious war had not been held out to them as incentives; but is there any, the smallest, evidence that Yankee commanders have even attempted to place these passions under restraint of any kind? Has any proof been afforded that they have evinced a purpose of conforming those they command to those rules of discipline that govern European armies? There is no such proof. So that the contrast extends itself not only to the *composition* of the respective armies—the rank and file and subalterns—but to the Chiefs of the one as compared with the other. It is not merely that the Southern commanders feel that they are following the dictates of their purer nature, in restraining excesses, but they are conscious that the Southern soldier has an instinctive abhorrence for acts of vindictive cruelty and sordid meanness. The restraints are intended to reach the few, found in all armies, who might be tempted to violate the usages of civilized hostilities.

We are aware that these views are not in agreement with those expressed in many of the Southern papers, whose doctrine is measure for measure—who advocate an unlimited *lex talionis*. As regards public property of every kind, we express no dissent in exacting a full measure of retaliation, nor as relates to *persons*. Here, eye for eye, tooth for tooth, not in the spirit of vengeance, but to deter the enemy from doing wrong to such of our people as may fall into their hands. C

Our Correspondence from Cobb's Legion Cavalry.

KILLED AND WOUNDED IN THE BATTLE OF MIDDLEBURG.

HEADQUARTERS CAVALRY, GA LEGION,
Near Middleburg, Va, June 23d, '63.

On Sunday, 21st, about 8 o'clock a. m., while our regiment was on picket on the turnpike, the enemy approached from Middleburg, on the pike leading to Ashby's Gap, in strong force—cavalry, infantry and artillery—with the view of [illegible]

Yankee Accounts of the Exploits of the Tacony.

DESTRUCTION OF YANKEE SHIPPIN

A PRIVATEER DESTROYING VESSELS OFF CAPE SABLE.

PORTLAND, ME, June 26.—Fishing vessels arrived here report a large rebel steamer, bark and a three masted schooner off Cape Sable, Novia Scotia, burning our fishing vessels. They spoke the ship Augnil, of Boston, which had been captured and bonded for $10,000, and was bound for New York with the crews of three burned fishing vessels.

MORE PRIVATEERS AT WORK.

PORTLAND, ME June 26—The schooner Julia Ellens, from the Bay of Fundy, arrived to-day and reports a large steamer, a bark and a three masted schooner at the mouth of the Bay, destroying vessels. They have burned the schooner Archer, of Southport, and bonded a bark, name unknown.

BURNING OF THE SCHOONER WANDERER.

GLOUCESTER, Mass, June 26—The fishing schooner Vanguard has arrived here from the banks, and makes the following report:

On Tuesday, saw the schooner Wanderer, of Gloucester, on fire on the west end of Georges At the same time thirty fishermen were in sight Saw nothing of the pirates.

BURNING OF A SIDEWHEEL STEAMER.

BOSTON, June 26—The schooner Vision at Wellfleet, reports that on Tuesday last, at 3 p m., twelve miles South, Southwest of the South Shoal Light, saw a sidewheel steamer of about seven hundred tons, on fire. Remained by her until she sunk. Could not ascertain her name.

MORE OF THE REBEL PRIVATEERS.

YARMOUTH, N. S., June 26—The packet schooner Monitor, from Boston, reports as follows:

At 12 o'clock last night, thirty miles west by south of Yarmouth, fell in with a large ship, burned to the water's edge—name unknown—She was still burnig, and in tow of two Westport schooners. At four o'clock this morning saw a steamer standing southward, partially change her course and speed two or three times Saw a similar looking stermer on Wednesday, seventy miles east of Cape Ann, standing south east.

HEAVY FIRING

GLOUCESTER, Cape Ann, June 26—The schooner Crusader has just arrived from the fishing banks, and reports that on Thursday at 11 o'clock a. m., twenty-five miles southwest from Chatham, heard heavy firing supposed to be from a U S gunboat which passed here the evening previous.

$10,000 FOR THE TACONY

BOSTON, June 26—The underwriters and merchants, at a meeting held to day, decided to offer a bounty of $10,000 for the capture of Florida No. 2, and will dispatch an armed vessel in pursuit tomorrow or next day.

DESCRIPTION OF THE TACONY.

Captain Berry of the brig Umpire, whose vessel was burned by the Tacony, alias Florida, No. 2, says she is far from being a formidable vessel. On the water she appears about 400 tons, although her register is less. Outside she is black; her copper when on an even keel is below the line of flotation, and

The Forest City had only 12-pounders, I understand, and the Chesepeake only 6-pounders; but their intention was to run the cutter down at once, as they had no match for her and her 32 pounders. The Chesapeake was manned by 27 men of the 7th Maine regiment, under Col. Mason, together with company A, State Guards, and city company B, all of which were ready with full ranks in half an hour, and also by as many armed citizens as could be conveniently taken, who volunteered with enthusiasm. Captain Lighter, the Government inspector overseeing and building gunboats here, took charge of the Chesapeake battery. Captain Willets commanded her and Captain Liscom the Forest City. Collector Jewett and Mayor McLellan attended to the arming and dispatching of both steamers which were done with great expedition.

Jackson Correspondence of the Mobile Tribune.

JACKSON, July 1st, 1863.

Mr Editor: The long agony is over, in part. Jackson this morning presents the appearance of a deserted village. No troops, no camp, in sight—all have vanished. But where have they gone? is a question asked by many. Well, I don't know; and if I did I would not tell "for a few days;" but all are in hopes that the devoted garrison at Vicksburg will see many familiar faces which they have not seen for months. To illustrate to you how Gen. Johnston keeps his secrets, I will tell you a little joke I heard yesterday. It is said that Gov. Pettus called on Gen. Johnston a few days since and enquired of the General as to his plans, &c., in relation to the defense of this State, and asked him what was his last order, &c. The General looked all around to see whether any one was listening, and then in a kind of a stage whisper replied, "the last order I gave was for a good vegetable dinner." After hearing this I concluded that Gen. Johnston was very fond of verdant things. As I did not like to be classed in that line particularly I was not "green" enough to ask the General anything about his last order, but concluded that "coming events cast their shadows before." As I have seen a great big shadow, in fact many shadows this morning, I will await coming events. But, to be serious, no one knows anything about when, where or at what time Gen Johnston will strike his blow. That he is on the move we all know.

Some who would like to be thought a little wiser than others name Vicksburg direct; others only a change of camp, his left resting on or near Clinton. Others, again, would not be surprised to hear from him somewhere in the direction of Memphis. My own opinion, and you can take it for what it is worth, is that he will confine Mr Grant in a little smaller space for a short time and give him time to see the shadows and await "coming events," which will be "On to Vicksburg," and then Porkdom and Buckeyes had better stand from under. If the first part of my programme is not carried out, I will always think "he ought to." A few days however will tell the tale.

The Mississippian this morning has an article on the subject of "Bushwhackers," &c., which I think every paper in the South should take up in the same manner, and if possible, force our Government to demand and do justice to them who simply protect their homes and are called "Bushwhackers." A few Yankee thieves can go through the country, rob, steal, plunder and outrage; in short, do every and anything they choose, and they are called "Raiders."—When I think of these things and know that our Government tolerates it, I become under the [illegible]

BY TELEGRAPH

BOLTON STATION, July 5—Yesterday about 12 o'clock the Yankee cavalry crossed Big creek at Birdsong's Ferry and advanced into Blaiuterior, but were promptly met by Whiteford's Brigade and driven back across the river.

JACKSON, July 6.—The mail carrier has just arrived and states positively that Vicksburg has fallen. This same news has been received this morning from different sources, but not by any one here officially.

A courier just from Edward's Depot says Gen. Osterhaus' entire command crossed near there last night. If so, they will have warm work to day. Grant is evidently very uneasy in regard to transportation in his rear. But little firing at Vicksburg yesterday.

Great Confederate Victory!

BLOODIEST BATTLE OF THE WAR!!

40,000 PRISONERS CAPTURED.

RICHMOND, July 7th.—Another telegram, dated Martinsburg, the 6th, says: The latest which seems reliable is that the fight of Sunday was the bloodiest of the war. A P Hill fell back in the centre, which caused the enemy to believe he was retreating. The enemy advanced, and the right and left wings of Lee's army surrounded them and took the heights for which we have been contending, capturing 40,000 prisoners, who refused parole. General Pickett's division is now guarding them to Martinsburg.

SECOND DISPATCH.

The latest dispatches from Martinsburg report the enemy routed and 40,000 prisoners taken on Sunday. We will send fuller dispatches this forenoon.

LATEST.—We have the following from Martinsburg: At six o'clock Saturday morning Lee had changed his front, occupied the ground the enemy had been driven from, and stationed his whole army, in splendid spirits, complete masters of the situation. Gens Pender and Pickett were wounded, and Col. Avery of N. C., was killed.

All reports concur that the enemy was defeated yesterday and driven three miles, and a vast number of prisoners are reported taken by Lee. The prisoners refused to be paroled and are on their way to Richmond. This is the bloodiest battle. Our loss was very great, and that of the enemy immense.

LATEST.

July 6th, (from Martinsburg)—On Saturday our centre fell back, drawing the enemy from their works. Ewell and Longstreet then flanked the enemy and then gained the heights. A general fight ensued, resulting in the rout of the Yanks. Lee captured 40,000 prisoners, according to all accounts.

There has been fighting at Williamsport between Imboden's cavalry and several regiments of infantry and a division of Yankee cavalry under Pleasanton.

NATCHEZ, July 4—Col. Smith of General Grant's staff, accompanied by —— Allen on the gunboat Arizona came down last evening, anchored off Natchez and communicated with the Mayor, threatening to burn the town because Government stores and cattle crossed the river.

The Mayor replied that he had no control over government transportation. Smith replied that he came to declare the terms and [illegible]

THURSDAY, JULY 9, 1863.

Oaths of Allegiance.

The perversion of the phrase, Oath of Allegiance, from its true purpose and signification, is one of the political sins of a deep dye by the administrators, both of high and low degree, of a Government that claimed to be the most free on the face of the earth. In its original significance the Oath of Allegiance was the expression of a feudal relation. An Oath of Obedience to the Law and Constitution is the true expression of fidelity to the State in a Commonwealth. The word Allegiance is not found in the Federal or Confederate Constitution. It is found in the works of European jurists, because it is expressive of the relation that was primitively feudal, and subsequently applied to that which bound the *Subject* to the Monarchy or Oligarchy that succeeded the overthrow of Feudal obligations. *Allegiance* and *Subject* stand in correlation in Europe, as *Obedience* and *Citizen* do in the United States.

There can be no mistake through misapplication when the term Allegiance is held to be due from the foreigner to the Federal or Confederate Governments, for the term is, or should be, familiar to him, and only substitutes Government for King. But where the powers of Government, are susceptible of abuse or usurpation, and the true theory and basis of political authority is the *consent of the governed*, the word Allegiance, as expressive of perpetual obligation to kingly rule, should have no place. This is more especially true in a Confederation where the source of authority is in the members separately, and not in the people collectively.

The Yankees have applied this phrase, Oath of Allegiance, more abusively than any in the vocabulary of politics. They have not only disregarded the fundamental truth, that the origin of the Federal Constitution was the States in the exercise of their primitive sovereignty, but they have contemned the basis of all Republican Government, the *consent of the governed* The consequence has been the utmost violence, not merely of conscientious scruples, but to the indisputable convictions of conscience, and although the penalty of refusal has not been that men were committed to the flames as on refusing to surrender their religious convictions, the next thing in atrocity has been committed—they have been imprisoned, driven from their homes, and divested of their possessions.

We have noticed that an imitation of the Yankee practice has been recommended on the capture of their territory, which of course involves the capture of persons as well as property. We trust that nothing of that kind will be imitated, even in the Border States. Let us adhere rigidly to the principle, the benefit of which we claim for ourselves. The rule and practice, accordingly, ought to be this—if those who inhabit territory we have conquered, voluntarily offer to obey the Confederate Government and its laws, our military authorities may make it a question of expediency, whether such tender of obedience should be accepted, as it may involve the reciprocal duty of protection to large numbers.

As regards the Border States, the question presents itself in a different aspect. Where Secession has been recognized practically, the consent, even there, of the governed, if in a minority, should be the rule, without exception. To a citizen of Maryland, should our arms rescue that State from the dominion of the Yankees, in the counties bordering on Pennsylvania, or a citizen of Eastern Tennessee, it may be a lesser evil to take an oath to obey the Confederacy than to emigrate. If his presence is dangerous, the alternative might be preferred to take the oath, rather than emigrate, but in no case should violence be done to a conscientious conviction, and to the cardinal principle of voluntary consent. C

Short Dresses.

To-day we publish a communication from a fair correspondent taking us to task for some comments we [illegible]

Rome to be Defended.

The people of Rome are making active preparations to defend their city against Yankee raids from the right wing of Rosecrans' army. The *Courier* of yesterday has a call upon the people to furnish hands at once to erect strong fortifications. The natural advantages for defense are very good and can speedily be made very effectual against any attack of raiders. This work is not commenced any too soon.

The Yankees are now close enough to dash into our country almost before it is known.—We ought to have pickets out on every road from here to Huntsville.

Severe Penalties Recommended.

The Richmond *Examiner* suggests that dealing in gold ought to be made a penal offense—the penalty, confiscation and hanging. The following sentence is in the Draconian spirit:

The Confederate Congress has it in its power to restore the currency by one vigorous measure, just as effectually as confidence in the public credit was restored by the New York Legislature and by the French Convention. That measure would be a law closing every bank in the Confederacy and making it a hanging offense, accompanied by the confiscation of all property to carry on the business of brokerage.

It is to be hoped that the Confederate Congress will not stain legislation by any such measure as would be the parallel to similar acts by a French Jacobin Assembly. It is assumed in the above sentence that the New York Legislature and the French Convention restored public credit by a fiat of legislation. The extract from Thiers, the French historian, by the *Examiner*, describes a frightful state of general morals. Thiers is made to assign, as the cause of the restoration of the French currency to par, the law that prohibited the traffic in gold and silver, the selling for different prices, &c The simple fact was, that contemporaneously, or nearly so, with the last acts of the French Assembly imposing the punishment of the guillotine for such illegal practices, the currency began to improve from the large reduction in the quantity of assignats. By this means the standard was nearly being recovered, and by no other. The error of the logic that attributes the cessation of private crime in this regard, to severe legislation, is assigning for a *cause* what was a *collateral circumstance*.

The New York example was a simple prohibition of making gold and silver a subject of speculation on the Stock exchange. It had, perhaps, as little to do with the fall of gold in the New York market, as the French law had with the improvement of the French currency.

As no mere act of legislation can be repressive of such practices as grow out of the abusive exercise of the privilege of issuing paper money, so no remedy short of removing the cause, can abate these practices. There can, therefore, be no conceivable mode of restoring the currency to its normal condition, except by a reduction of its amount. As the cause is the excessive issue of paper money, it points unerringly to the remedy. Legislation aggravates the mischief. All the evil consequences that flow from a departure from the standard of value—the stimulus given to the passion of avarice—the little regard paid to the value of money—various market prices, extortion, monopoly, etc., are traceable to this master mischief—this fountain of social disorder. C

Short Dresses.

Editors Atlanta Confederacy:

I hope the vital importance of the subject will excuse my troubling you. I know the sorrows of women meet with but little sympathy. I don't know, whether it is Eve or [illegible]

BY TELEGRAPH.

JACKSON, July 7.—Gen Loring attacked Osterhaus yesterday near Edwards' Depot, and after three hours' hard fighting drove him across the river. Our loss reported heavy—theirs not known.

An officer from the vicinity of Port Hudson says Dick Taylor crossed the river under cover of our guns on last Saturday. He and Gardner attacked Banks and routed him with heavy loss. They are moving to reinforce Johnston.

We have nothing further in regard to the fall of Vicksburg.

AUGUSTA, GA., July 7.—A special dispatch was received here dated at Wilmington to-day. The damage to the Wilmington & Weldon Railroad is trifling and will be repaired to-night, and the trains will run through to-morrow. The Federals have retreated to Newbern.

WILMINGTON, July 7.—A letter from a reliable source dated Kinston last night, says a courier has just arrived who reports an engagement now progressing between the retreating enemy (retreating from Warsaw) and our forces near Free bridge. Supposed the enemy has been cut off.

PETERSBURG, July 7.—The flag of truce boat arrived at City Point this morning. No papers were allowed to come ashore, and the Yankee officers on board looked dejected.

Captain Milford states that Sickles is dead.

Paroled prisoners overheard one of the Federals say, at Fortress Monroe, that the loss in Gen. Meade's army could not be less than 60,000 killed, wounded and missing.

RICHMOND, July 7. The Baltimore Sun of the 1st, says that Gen. Stuart captured 1200 mules and 400 prisoners in Montgomery co, Maryland.

On Monday 29th June, at Westminister, Carroll county, Md, he captured the Delaware cavalry.

The wildest alarm prevails at Baltimore, and steps are taken to barricade the city.—The Secessionists in the city are threatening.

New York papers of the 4th have been received; The latest dispatches refer to the fight of Friday the 3rd.

A Washington telegram of the 3rd says, "the latest intelligence here is up to 11 o'clock to-day," but the purport is not given

Dix's troops are believed to be evacuating Virginia, en route to Maryland.

Rail road and telegraphic communication with the valley of Virginia is resumed.

The Tribune of the 4th contains many details of the battle of Wednesday, the first.—Brig. Gen. Barlow is mentioned, as twice wounded, and a prisoner. Brig. Gen. Schimmelferin is a prisoner. Gen Merideth is wounded.

A telegram from Hanover, York county, Pa, the 3rd says: "The fight was most terrific and the loss on both sides tremendous. We have Gen'l Longstreet a prisoner sure. If Couch arrives to-night, the victory is ours beyond a chance."

A despatch from Philadelphia the 3d, at 11 a. m., says: "We have stirring rumors in town—the report is current that Longstreet is killed. The siege of Vicksburg is said to be progressing satisfactorily, but the rebels are regarded as very obstinate.

New Orleans dates to the 27th have been [illegible]

About Vicksburg.

[Dispatches to the Mobile Register of the 7th inst]

BIG BLACK, July 4 10 P. M.—via Jackson 6—Firing at Vicksburg is less frequent to-day than usual; few guns are fired, and at long intervals.

Jackson's cavalry division is skirmishing [illegible] to-day, and there has [illegible] loss on both sides. Ten prisoners have been captured by us.

LATER.

July 5.—The enemy's movements are becoming important; their pickets are advanced to-day to Big Black at the different fords north of the bridge

The pickets are largely increased at Messenger's, Birdsong's and Bush's ferries, and there are additional patrols all along the river.

There has been slight skirmishing all day, and this evening they advanced a large force to Birdsong's ferry, with intention, as is supposed, to fortify it.

Heavy firing is going on, and the battle may take place any day.

JACKSON, July 6.—The Mississippian extra of to-day says:

We are pained to learn, on good authority, that the garrison of Vicksburg capitulated last Saturday morning.

There was no assault. The enemy sprung mines, rendering further resistance useless.

The terms of capitulation are that the garrison, numbering 17,500, shall be allowed an acceptable point on Big Black to await exchange. Officers are allowed to retain their side arms.

The Mississippian says Grant's programme is to leave a heavy garrison at Vicksburg, and take the main body of his army North, which will enable Johnston to successfully defend Mississippi.

Osterhaus is said to have crossed the Big Black.

Johnston is falling back to Jackson.

S.

Copy of a dispatch received this evening by Gen. Maury:

JACKSON, July 6, 1863.

Maj Gen. D. H Maury, Mobile:

I have no official information of the fall of Vicksburg. The report originated among civilians and couriers.

T. B. LAMAR,
Lieut-Col. and A. A. G

Bragg's Late Movement.

[Dispatch to the Mobile Advertiser]

MONTGOMERY, July 4.—I arrived this evening from Gen. Bragg's army, which I left on the evening of the 3d, and I send you trustworthy intelligence to that date.

The surprise and capture of the Gaps forced Bragg to retreat from Shelbyville, when he fell back to Tullahoma, where it was expected Rosecrans would attack him, but the latter passed round our right flank, compelling an abandonment of the position and a still further retreat to Alisonia, and afterwards to Corydon, a strong position at the foot of the range of mountains, where it was expected he would be attacked. But the flanking process again compelled a retreat further South.

A large mounted force of Rosecrans' army [illegible]

or two instances lying across each other.

Our dismounted men secreted themselves behind stone fences, and would open on them as they came in good range. I could not judge of their loss in men, (as they were removed,) except by the large number of dead horses. We took 80 or 90 prisoners while making charges on us, and lost about 50, who were captured while acting as sharp-shooters.

When we reached Upperville, we sheltered ourselves in a small peice of woods and waited for the Yankees. When they came up we charged them and drove them back in great disorder, till they came up under the protection of their infantry. In this charge our regiment captured a Major after wounding him pretty severely, and ten other prisoners without the loss of a single man. This was about 4 o'clock p. m. After this they followed us but little further. They retired during the night to Middleburg and Aldie. Yesterday we returned to the position we held previous to the fight.

The following are the casualties in the Legion. Killed: J M Sheffield, co D, by a shell. Wounded: G P Winchester co D, right hand lost by a piece of shell; G T Galloway, co D, in elbow by a grape shot—arm amputated; W H Adams, co D, in the right shoulder by a ball; T F Williams, co B, (Fulton Dragoons) severe flesh wound in thigh by a piece of shell; W Graham, co B, flesh wound in arm; J M Clayton, co B, flesh wound in arm; Ezekiel Mason, co B, shot in the neck and left shoulder; corp'l Harris, co B, slightly injured by the falling of his horse which was killed by a shell; George Williams, co I, color bearer, wounded by a sabre; Pat Wallace co A, shot in the breast; J R Barrett co C, flesh wound; Henry Smith co G, flesh wound; Lieut Basset co A, flesh wound in the arm.

The number of horses killed in the Legion was 14.

Rev Mr Johnson, Episcopal minister of Atlanta, now chaplain of the 1st S C regiment cavalry, had a son killed in this battle. The old parson's horse was shot twice under him in the fight at Brandy Station. He generally goes where the bullets fly the thickest.

This was a more severe fight than that of Brandy Station or Fleetwood, as it is sometimes called.

Z. A. R.

Farewell Address of Gen. Hooker.

The following is Gen. Hooker's farewell address to the Army of the Potomac:

HEADQ'RS ARMY OF THE POTOMAC,
Frederick, Md., June 28, 1863.

General Orders,
No. 65.

In conformity with the orders from the War Department, dated June 27, 1863, I relinquish the command of the army of the Potomac.—It is transferred to Maj Gen. Geo. G Meade, a brave and accomplished officer, who has nobly earned the confidence and esteem of the army on many a well-fought field. Impressed with the belief that my usefulness as the commander of the army of the Potomac is impaired, I part from it, yet not without the deepest emotion. The sorrow of parting with the comrades of so many battles is relieved by the conviction that the courage and devotion of this army will never cease nor fail; that it will yield to my successor, as it has to me, a willing and hearty support. With the earnest prayer that the triumph of its arms may bring success worthy of it and the nation, I bid it farewell.

JOSEPH HOOKER,
Major General.

☞ The Meridian *Clarion* of Thursday last says: "An employee of the Southern express company abstracted about $43,000 from the office in that place on Saturday last, but was detected in the attempt to send it up the Mobile and Ohio railroad, and all the funds recovered. He was placed under arrest.

☞ M. F. Conway, member of Congress from Kansas, and an Abolitionist of the strongest persuasion, has become so enamored of peace that he is in favor of it unconditionally. He says in a letter written at Lawrence, Kansas, on the 6th:

"I can see no possible object to be gained by the war, which will begin to compensate for the sacrifices it involves. I am, therefore, for peace—unconditional and immediate peace—peace on the basis of existing facts, whatever they may be; and I will willingly trust the rest to the steady and irresistible agencies of reason, justice and humanity.

Her mast is quite deep, and she is only a single deck vessel. She is armed with a single brass twelve pounder smooth bore gun, and is manned by twenty British beach combers and two rebel officers. Her commander's name is William Reed, formerly of the U S Navy. Her entire armament is mounted on the poop, as the most conspicuous place, to act as a scare crow.

PORTLAND, June 27.—The United States cutter Caleb Cushing went to sea last night without orders or officers.

SECOND DISPATCH.

The cutter Cushing left here last night before Lieut. Merriman arrived, who was sent to take charge of her. He immediately started in one of the steamers sent in pursuit of her, which steamers are now engaging the Cushing, she having fired six guns at the steamers Chesapeake and Forest City. The engagement is still going on, as the guns are distinctly heard.

THIRD DISPATCH.

2 o'clock.—A tremendous explosion has been heard, and smoke just seen where the cutter was, and she has disappeared. It is thought that she has blown up.

FOURTH DISPATCH.

The cutter has blown up, sure. The steamers sent after her have returned, and report that the boats put off from the cutter before she blew up, and the Forest City was chasing them.

FIFTH DISPATCH.

6 40 o'clock.—The party which cut out the Cushing were of the Tacony, which vessel they burned on the 25th. Lieut Reed and party having been captured, and now under guard at Portland City.

THE PRIVATEER TACONY BURNED.

The Crew Transferred to another Vessel and Subsequently Captured—They are Now Prisoners in Fort Preble.

FORT PREBLE, ME.,
June 27, 6 40 P. M.

Hon. E M Stanton, Secretary of War:

In the private note book of Lieut. C A Reed, of the Confederate States Navy, I find as follows:

"The latest news from Yankeedom tells us that there are twenty gunboats in search of us. They have the description of the Tacony, and overhaul every vessel that resembles her. During the night we transferred all our crew on board the schooner Archer, and at 2 A. M. set fire to the Tacony and steered West. The schooner Archer is a fishing vessel of 90 tons, sails well, and is easily handled. No Yankee gunboat would ever dream of suspecting us. I, therefore, think that we will dodge our pursuers for a short time. It is my intention to go along the coast, with the view of burning the shipping in some exposed harbor, and of cutting out a steamer."

The above appears to have been written since the night of June 24th. The schooner taken to-day is the Archer, of Southport.

GEO. L ANDERS,
Maj 17th Infantry, comd'g post.

SECOND DISPATCH

WASHINGTON, June 27.—The following dispatch was received by the Treasury Department to night:

PORTLAND, June 27, 9 P. M.—*Hon S P. Chase, Secretary of the Treasury:*—The party which cut out the cutter Cushing were part of the barque Tacony, which vessel, as appears by her log book in my possession, they burned on the 25th inst., and transferred her armament to the schooner Archer, which we have captured and stripped. They intended to burn the two gunboats here, transfer the anchors and armament to the cutter, and burn and destroy on the coast of Maine. The men are in Port Preble under guard—Lieut. C. W. Reed, of the Confederate Navy, was in command and is a prisoner.

J. W. JEWETT, Collector.

LATER.

PORTLAND, June 27.—The crew of the cutter seemed to have escaped before she was blown up, in the boats, probably, to a schooner near by, as the Forest City chased one down towards Green Island, caught her, and is towing her in.

The Two Invasions—A Contrast.

The New York *World* thus draws the contrast between the Yankee invasion of the South and the Confederate invasion of the North.

The organs of the administration are begining to discover that the miserable scoundrels who devote themselves to burning defenseless towns and robbing non-combatants at the South, are cursing the cause which they are paid to serve. The man must be blind, indeed, who does not see that the contrast which these villianies establish between our own invasion of the South and the rebel invasion of the North, is one of the most effective blows that has yet been struck by the administration at the hopes of the Union. It is childish to attempt to parry this blow by appealing to the destruction of our ships at sea by the rebel privateers. The laws and usages of civilized war, which utterly forbid the seizure of private property on land, permit private property to be seized at sea. A ship belonging to private citizens is the lawful prize of a belligerent commodore; but a belligerent Majo. General who takes possession of the silver spoons of a private citizen is simply a thief. The vessels which are burned at sea by the Alabama or the Tacony, those "chartered libertines," whom Mr. Welles makes free of the Atlantic, are the property, by the laws of war, of those who burn them, and would be so adjudged to be by the courts if carried into a neutral port. But it would be hard to find any court which would confirm the right of a cavalry colonel to chop up silver salvers with an axe in order to cram them into his holsters, or which would convey to a negro corporal the fee-simple of the houses which he burns over the heads of women and children by the order of his white-faced but black-hearted commander.

When we find Gen. Lee retaliating upon the farmers of Pennsylvania all that Hunter has inflicted upon the planters of Georgia and Carolina; when rapine and arson set up in the captured towns of the North, the same infernal carnival to which they have been invited in the South; then, and not till then, we may call upon the world to witness that the officers and soldiers of the slaveholder's rebellion are really as reckless of humanity and of decency as the officers and soldiers of liberty and the Union! In the meantime it is the solemn duty of every man who respects himself and his country, its present honor and its future fame, to protest with all the power that God has given him against a course of policy which saps the foundation of our hopes, and makes our very name a "hissing and reproach" among the nations.

The Administration on Johnston.

The Richmond *Sentinel*, the organ of the Administration, says:

From Vicksburg the news is calculated to increase our solicitude. Grant has not retired as we had hoped he would; nor has General Johnston struck his blow yet. We cannot for a moment think of Vicksburg's falling without an effort on the part of Johnston to relieve it. The enemy says he has less than twenty thousand men—for with that force he would strike. We are sure he has many more than twenty thousand men, and we believe he will strike. Doubtless he is surrounded with many disadvantages. But this has been the fate of all Generals in every great battle of the war. If we had declined battle whenever the odds were against us, we would never have fought a battle. Johnston must at least *try* and show that the fault was not his; that victory was not in reach of an effort. If Vicksburg falls without a blow from him, his reputation, were it ten times what it is, would not survive it. It would be impossible to imagine Jackson, were he alive, sitting by inactive while his gallant brethren were being assailed by night and by day, and starved into capitulation; and Jackson's example and his great success have taught our people to attach great value to daring and activity, and to place large calculation on such qualities. On the other hand, the sleeping fox catches no poultry. Let Johnston bestir himself.

A NEW WAY TO BLOW UP A TRAIN.—The Chattanooga Rebel of Sunday says:

A few days since a party of our guerillas went round in the rear of Murfreesboro and blew up two locomotives and trains, with torpedoes, one on the Nashville and Chattanooga, and the other on the Franklin and Nashville road. The torpedoes were placed underneath the track, with a screw percussion cap, or friction primer attached, which was so placed on the iron rail that the wheel of the car passing over it, caused the fulminating powder to explode and ignite the magazine. We did not learn the extent of the damage.

fighting at Port Hudson on Saturday and Sunday last. Deserters say the fight was more desperate than ever before.

On the morning of the 2d inst. Logan's cavalry attacked the Federals, six miles below Port Hudson, on the Mississippi, and burned a large amount of Commissary and Quartermaster's stores, wounding 150 and capturing 40 prisoners, among them a colonel, major, captain and quartermaster. He also destroyed 150,000 rations and half a million of dollars in greenbacks, burned 75 wagons and shot 300 mules.

A JUSTICE OF THE PEACE FLINGS UP.—The subjoined is a true copy of the resignation of a justice of the peace in Natchitoches, Louisiana. We hope it may strike the reader as it first struck us. We "had to laugh:"

"State of Louisiana,
Parish of Natchitoches }

"To the Goviner of Louisiana:

"Know all men by this presents, that I, L—— ——, 'squire, do hereby *thro up* for reasins best known to myself.

"L—— ——, *Justice of Peace.*

Not Acquainted With Mr. Bull.

There was a *habea corpus* case the other day before Judge Lochrane, in which his Honor took ground which we think may probably be law, but is certainly common sense.—The case arose upon the arrest of an alleged deserter, and one of the points presented by the defense was a letter from the British Consul at Savannah, showing that the prisoner was a native of Canada West and a British subject. The Judge, in his decision, stated that he had little respect for Consular papers at best, in behalf of men claiming the protection of this government. The benefit of protection carried with it the reciprocal duty of defending the government. But before such consular papers could be respected, the Court must have access to official information of the existence of such functionaries and the States they represent. No officer in the Confederate States knew anything about Great Britain or her Consuls, and they could not go to the newspapers for information. It was the duty of that Government, if she wished to exercise consular jurisdiction in the Confederate States to set forth the fact in official form, and in no other way could the courts become legitimately cognizant of the fact. As a citizen he might understand and believe that there was such a government as that of Great Britain, and certain men in the Confederacy claiming to be Consuls, but he had no proper official knowledge of either fact.—*Macon Telegraph of yesterday.*

BRITISH SUBJECTS.—Lieutenant Sydney H. Davies, Lieutenant H B. M's 16th regiment, and Lieutenant T. I. Braxton, of the Royal Volunteer Rifles, have issued an address to the British subjects in Richmond, in which they say: "If you desire to keep your homes and the homes of your friends from the touch of the ruthless and barbaric invader; if you believe, as we do, in the justice of the Southern cause, and desire its success; if you have interests here to defend, then it is manifestly your duty, as brave and chivalric men, to take up arms at this crisis. The history of the past precludes the possibility of our being cowards; let us here, and now, in this righteous struggle for Constitutional law and liberty, add another laurel to our ancestral glory. Those of you who are willing to offer your services, for either temporary or permanent duty, should apply at once to the undersigned."

Surely an appeal such as this ought not to go unheeded by those to whom it is addressed—It is earnest, eloquent and touching. We hope to hear that a numerous corps has been organized under the command of the above named officers.

☞ Items from the Richmond Enquirer 6th July.

The Confederate steamer Lady Davis arrived at St. Georges on the 22d, from Wilmington, N. C. She is reported to belong to the Confederate Government, and brought important despatches from there to the British Consul. Mr. Vallandigham was a passenger. The Royal "Gazette" says he is on his way to Canada, there to await coming events.

ATTEMPT TO ASSASSINATE GOVERNOR YATES OF ILLINOIS.—Governor Yates, of Illinois, was shot at through his window, while washing in his office, at his residence in Springfield, at a late hour on the 1st of July.

FAILURE OF INDIANA TO PAY INTEREST ON ITS DEBT.—The State of Indiana has made default in the payment of interest on its debt, due on the 1st of July, 1863. This is the first instance of default since its compromise with its creditors sixteen years ago.

Notwithstanding her eloquent appeal we still insist on our views being correct, and give it as the opinion of the whole male sex (and what lady does not dress with an eye to the admiration of we lords of creation) that a clean stocking on a well turned ankle, even incased in boys' or any other sort of shoes, is infinitely preferable to a long trail or filth-swab, which the fine gaiter *and so forth*, are left entirely to the imagination. Nothing is more repulsive to a gentleman than the untrammeled exercise of his imagination on a long trail in a muddy dirty thoroughfare.

A Spy Licked Up.

A few days ago a man calling himself Russell and claiming to be a correspondent of the Richmond *Examiner*, and an officer in the army, was in this city. His conduct excited the suspicion of some and he was placed for some time under arrest. Nothing however appearing positively against him, he was discharged and allowed to depart. A gentleman who has been concerned with the whole matter from the first appearance of Russell in this city, gives the following particulars of his career in this city, and his subsequent arrest. If the facts are developed as the following statement would indicate, we suppose he will pull hemp:

"This city was honored last week by the presence of a man hailing from Richmond, to whom it may be well to give a passing notice.—He arrived on the evening of the 28th June and immediately introduced himself to several as G. M. Russell, captain C S A, Associate Editor and Special army correspondent of the Richmond *Examiner*. He made himself known to several of the editorial fraternity by calling at their offices and introducing himself as the editor and correspondent of the Examiner, by which means he was courteously treated and allowed to look over their exchanges. He frequently expressed his opinion of certain military movements and sometimes plausibly criticised the ability of certain of our generals—all done so shrewdly and with such a natural air as not to excite suspicion that a *Spy* was among us.

"The day after he called at the store of W. F. Herring & Co, and purchased a dashing Confederate uniform. Rigged out in this new suit, he represented himself as a member of the lamented Stonewall Jackson's staff.

"This dashing major (or such was the style of his new uniform) next made a hasty trip to West Point, as he said, for the purpose of renewing his acquaintance with some old friends, returning to Atlanta the next day. After a day or two sojourning with us he was suspected and arrested, and his papers demanded. Papers however he had not, except passports from numerous Provost Marshals which he had, no doubt, obtained by lying and impudence.

"When arrested he voluntarily, and with perfect coolness gave his parole to remain 24 hours, till he could be identified by telegraph from his employers and friends in Richmond. At the end of the time no telegram had been received, and he gave himself up a prisoner, to be held till the desired information could be received. His boldness, frankness, and cool self possession were well calculated to deceive the most cautious. After being held for some time, and no charges appearing against him, he was discharged, obtained passports, and left the city.

"Subsequent to his departure despatches from those whom he had represented to be his friends in Richmond, disclaimed all knowledge of him. Our military authorities at once took steps to overhaul him, and (thanks to the magnetic telegraph) he was caught near Knoxville. He had in his possession a pocket instrument, and is doubtless the rascal who rendered the line on the East Tennessee & Georgia Railroad such an enigma to its experienced operators a few days ago, and caused the people of this city to suppose the Yankees were making another raid through East Tennessee.

"This same fellow introduced himself to Dr. Dennis in charge of the ambulance train from Tennessee as Maj Seymour of the regular army. He is very intelligent and had notes describing our operations, position, strength, and resources in every military department.—Justice demands that he be swung up immediately."

☞ A Louisville paper, alluding to the "Torped Expedition" of a party of our guerrillas, says: "There were rumors at Nashville that the Rebels, on Thursday, made a descent on the railroad south of Lavergne, and tore up a number of rails. It was also reported that the up-freight train, consisting of about twenty cars, fell into the hands of the Rebels, at the same place, and was utterly destroyed. After they had secured what they could, they made off with it. They also placed torpedoes on the track, which exploded under the cars, doing some damage.

vexation of spirit. However, seeing in this case, that you have sided with our enemies, I have summoned courage to address a short [illegible]

There are two things that always puzzled me—the moon and the Empress Eugenie. To see the moon, as she traverses the heavens, with her wan pale face, you would imagine you might tell her a "green cheese" to her face and she would [illegible] the spirit to answer you; and yet [illegible] absolute tyrant does not exist—[illegible] the earth, birds, beasts and fish, in [illegible] Bill Arp says "everything which don't spill when the earth turns upside down," stands in deadly terror of her. What possible concern it can be of hers whether a poor miserable man plants his vegetables in the "light" or in the "dark," I never could divine. But you dare to be indifferent on the subject and the consequences will be as terrible as if you should aver, in the very face of the Washington government, that your soul is your own. In either case that "foolishness would be stopped in short order."

The case of the Empress Eugenie is exactly similar. What on earth that woman has to do with my clothes I never could tell, but let her whisper, "high bonnets," and I would toil after one "as some men toil for virtue." Let her give the order "long dresses," and I would rush frantically to mine, and begin to tear out the hems and tucks, as though the sword of Damocles hung over me. Let her say, "short dresses," and if you think I would dare disobey her, I thank you for the compliment you pay my moral courage, but I do not deserve it. Macauley somewhere speaks of the Procrustian bed of public opinion. If he had only said the Procrustian bed of fashion, how much more touching would have been the simile.

I have painted my miserable condition before the war. After that began I flattered myself that the spoke of fortune's wheel to which I clung had got on the upper side, and I thought so long as the Emperor of France did'nt recognize us, I was safe. Whenever that subject was agitated,

"Fear at my heart, as at a cup
My life-blood seemed to sip."

But being quite lulled to peace, imagine how like a thunder-bolt came that decree, "*short dresses!*" I felt like Vulcan when he was kicked out of heaven. But when I found you—a Southern editor—were on the side of the Empress, my spirit quite left me.

I know you have decided on this question hastily, and there is one objection to your decision, which you have not considered, i. e., *shoes*. Some author has represented woman as hiding her sorrow from the world as a dove drops her wing over her wound. Now just consider our long dresses in this poetic light, and I know you will be reconciled to them.

If you only knew what I have suffered from the winds this spring! They began about the time I put on boys' shoes, and continued until, as the children say, they were "plum gone." I once heard a Dutchman who belonged to a brass band complain that he was required to blow and blow, until he blew his brains out, and I really had fears that the same accident would happen to old Boreas. And after all this we are expected to cut off six inches of our dresses! *six inches!* I'll tell you the honest truth—I have but one pair of shoes, and I am so afraid they will "evanish away" that I scarcely dare pull them off at night. Before I venture upon running such a risk I lock my door, and look under the bed, and up the chimney, and in every corner where could be hid one feloniously inclined.

Some one gave me two dog skins, but I had to kill the dogs to get them, and my humanity revolted. But if you continue to uphold the Empress Eugenie, I am afraid my humanity will go the way of Bob Acres' courage. If you are inexorable, at least be more reasonable. Say something less than six inches. Don't you hear a wail of sorrow? It's I and the dogs—howling together! Save us from our fate and we

"——will carve your name on bark of trees
With true love knots and flourishes."

EL ZAPATO.

OPINION ABROAD.—Rev. M. D Hoge, D. D., writes to the Richmond *Presbyterian* from Paris:

There are a great many people from the Northern States now residing in Paris—some of them to escape conscription, and others because of their Southern sympathies, and to [illegible] outraged by all that was passing around them that they were almost forced away. Nearly all the intelligent and educated people in England, France, and as I am informed, in Germany, are with us. That is they wish us success and desire our independence.

N. J. Cavalry, and John Flynn, of the 51st Indiana regiment. No day is fixed for the execution.

This community is disposed to await official confirmation before fully crediting the Martinsburg telegram; it is generally believed however that a decisive victory was achieved.

The report from City Point is regarded as partial confirmation of the news.

RALEIGH, July 6.—The House was deliberating on the Militia bill all day. No final action. The Senate passed a bill to punish the aiders and abettors of desertion.

RALEIGH, July 7th.—The Legislature passed the Militia Bill to-day—called out the men from 18 to 50 for home defense for the term of three months. All persons exempt from conscription are exempt from the regular militia.

RICHMOND, July 8.—The following dispatch was received here to-day:

"*Jackson, July 7.*—To Hon. J. A. Seddon, Secretary of War: Vicksburg capitulated on the 4th inst. The garrison was paroled, and are to return to our lines—the officers retaining their side-arms and personal baggage. this intelligence was brought by an officer who left the place on Sunday, the 5th.

(Signed) J. E. JOHNSTON."

SECOND DISPATCH

A special to the *Enquirer* from Winchester the 7th says: "There has been four days' fighting, commencing the 1st and ending on the night of the 4th, our men capturing the [illegible] fortifications of the enemy. Our loss is estimated at 10,000. Between 3,000 and 4,000 of our wounded are arriving here to-night. Gens. Scales and Pender are wounded, and have arrived. The hills around Gettysburg are covered with the dead and wounded of the (Yankee) army of the Potomac."

We have no official confirmation of the news from Martinsburg.

NATCHEZ, July 6.—A transport towing two barges loaded with coal passed down this morning, and one last night.

An officer of Gen. Smith's staff reports that Price was ordered on Sunday, 28th June, to take Helena. He moved immediately. Nothing from Port Hudson. All quiet.

SECOND DISPATCH.

An extra of the Natchez Courier says a letter from a member of the Conner battery dated last week near Lake Providence (a town on the west side of the Miss. river, some 60 miles above Vicksburg) reports that a battle had just occurred in which the enemy were severely punished, losing over 1,500 prisoners. The Conner battery was in the fight without damage.

A gentleman from the vicinity of Port Hudson reports that the movements indicate that Banks is about to raise the siege.

All the flats and skiffs in the river at Natchez were burned by order of Col. Smith (of Grant's staff.)

The river is rising—plenty of rain here—crops fine, weather pleasant—people confident—thermometer 90.

JACKSON, July 7th.—Vicksburg has fallen. It surrendered on the morning of the 4th, being in a starving condition, and being completely worn out from excessive fatigue. The terms of capitulation are, the officers were allowed their side arms, horses and all private property. They and the men were paroled immediately, and allowed to march out with all their colors. Immediately after the surrender, Grant sent a boat load of supplies to furnish the garrison. Some of our officers have arrived here.

SECOND DISPATCH (via Montgomery, 8th.)

But little more is known of the fate of Vicksburg. The officers who came out say that had Gen. Johnston reached there twelve days sooner, he could not have relieved the garrison, as they could not muster over 17,000 men for duty.

Many citizens are leaving here (Jackson) with their families, negroes, and stock. The *Mississippian* is packing up to leave.

THIRD DISPATCH.

Everything is in the wildest excitement here. The citizens are flying in every direction. The streets are filled with stock, negroes, families, ox carts and every species of conveyance. A terrible storm is prevailing. A report from Clinton says the enemy are burning every dwelling they pass. A fight here is hourly looked for.

All citizens had been ordered off. The troops were in the trenches all Thursday night.

The retreat was conducted in good order, and with but a trifling loss of stores and none of artillery.

A considerable number of Tennesseeans are reported to have deserted.

The army is hopeful and expect to fight.

The retreating General is violently abused by outsiders for permitting Rosecrans to outflank him.

I do not anticipate an early engagement.

DIRECT FROM CHAMBERSBURG.—We had an interview yersterday with Mr Cherry, of Georgia, who left Shippensburg, Pennsylvania, on Friday last. He had opportunities of seeing a large portion of our army, and reports that the troops are in the best spirits imaginable, and [illegible] flowing with peach and honey, [illegible] demoralized by the temptation [illegible] on the wayside. There is less [illegible] on any march heretofore, owing to the [illegible] discipline and to the earnest spirit pervading the army. The marches were easy—light and twelve miles a day. But little sickness was known, and what existed was caused principally by the carlessness of the individual soldier. The roads are generally good, but are being severely tested by our heavy trains; that between Chambersburg and Hagerstown is in very bad condition.

Those of the citizens along the line of march with whom our informant conversed, expressed the greatest surprise at the number and appearance of our troops. They were under the impression, they said, that most of the Confederates had been killed off, and what few remained were almost shirtless. They admitted, with expressions of gratitude, that they fared better in the presence of our own soldiers than in that of the Yankees.

The merchants who were compelled to sell goods at old prices for Confederate currency, were loudest in their grief. They were inconsolable, and no effort was made by our boys to mitigate their sufferings.

In Hagerstown we received one hundred and seventy-five recruits.

The road between Williamsport and Winchester was thronged with convalescent soldiers on the way to join their commands. It is understood that Gen Lee has ordered back all such now on their way to the army.

Our troops are anxious to get in *sight* of the "Melish," but fear the opportunity will not be afforded them, so long as the St Lawrence is passible.

More anxiety is felt for the safety of those left behind than for their own. The only news they now get is in the form of exaggerated rumors brought by convalescents joining their commands. Sometimes however a stray copy of a Richmond paper assures them that all is well "in the rear."—*Richmond Enquirer, July 4th.*

Simon Suggs Turned Up.

JACKSON, June 29, 1863.

Editor Mississippian:—A reliable gentleman has just arrived from Bay St. Louis, and brings intelligence of the taking of New Orleans by Magruder and the blowing up of the Customhouse and the hanging of 200 Union oath-takers. He then advanced on Carollton and took it by storm, and pressed all the gunboats and made a junction with Dick Taylor's forces at Donaldsonville, cut off all Banks' army, throwed Port Hudson into the river, took 11,000 woolly contrabands—forced them, at the point of the bayonet, to advance on Big Black; dammed up the Mississippi, and left Vicksburg high and dry—and the whole of Grant's army were very dry. They caught old Grant, put him in a bombshell, and were in the act of sending him to Abe's dominions and our informant left. Wires all down.

Yours, truly, SIMON SUGGS.

SUPPLIES FOR VICKSBURG.—Our people need have no apprehension about Vicksburg's being starved out, as we are informed upon very good authority, that there is on hand an abundant supply—and long before it is exhausted our army outside will open a way for the transmission of stores. We might mention the extent of our provisions there, but for prudential reasons refrain. This much we may say, however: If Vicksburg does not fall until her heroic garrison is "starved out," it will be many a long sultry month before the Yankee thieves will realize their dreams of capture.—*Mississippian, July 3d.*

☞ Three churches in Danville, Va, have contributed $3,969 for the New Orleans exiles.

Southern Confederacy

GEO. W. ADAIR,........J. HENLY SMITH,
EDITORS AND PROPRIETORS.
B. C. SMITH, M. D.,.................ASSOCIATE EDITOR.

ATLANTA, GEORGIA:

SATURDAY, JULY 11, 1863.

The Administration at Washington Boldly Defied for Suppressing and Infringing upon a Free Press—Lincoln Charged with Cowardice.

The Northern papers are beginning to throw off the slavish submission to the powers at Washington. In referring to the manner in which a Chicago mob forced Lincoln to repeal the order of his satrap, Burnside, for the suppression of the Chicago *Times*, the New York *World* openly charges Lincoln with combining the fears of the coward with the spirit of the tyrant, and uses the following language of defiance:

President Lincoln has never stood before the country in a worse light than at this moment. He has so deliberately committed himself against free discussion, by the transportation of Mr Vallandigham, that the reversal of General Burnside's order against the Chicago Times cannot be attributed to a returning spirit of justice or reverence for law. Mr Lincoln quails before the rising storm. He dares not carry out a principle to which he has given his deliberate sanction. He lost a golden opportunity to redeem the character of his Administration when he approved the proceedings against Mr Vallandigham. If he stops now in the career on which he then entered, it is not a retreat prompted by a sense of justice, but a concession extorted from his fears. He dares arrest nobody in this city for exercising the rights of free speech, for he knows that tens of thousands of brave men would resist it at the peril of their lives. He dared not permit matters to be carried to extremities at Chicago for a similar reason. The inconsistency, want of system and lack of principle which mark the proceedings of the Administration on this subject in various parts of the country are so glaring and indefensible that some of the most influential of its own party organs notice it, complain of it, and demand a consistent and settled policy.

The President assented to the suppression of the *World* in the four States which form Gen Burnside's department, but would not allow the suppression of the Chicago Times, which from its local position, circulates many more papers than we do in the same States. Why tolerate the greater mischief and suppress the less? It is simply because the subscribers to the World are not numerous enough in any one locality in those States to make a formidable show of resistance; while in the city of its publication the Times has too many friends to be put down without endangering the public peace. In other words the President goes as far in the suppression of free discussion as he dares; but his courage fails him when confronted with serious opposition.

THE EXAGGERATION IN THE ACCOUNTS GIVEN OF BATTLES—THE BOSH AND BLATHERUM OF MILITARY PHRASES—WHAT IS MEANT BY "FIGHTING LIKE FIENDS"—HOW RIDICULOUS ARE SUCH HIGH SOUNDING PHRASES.

The New York *World* makes the following sensible remarks on the ridiculous practice and hallucinations of the Yankee authorities in magnifying every little encounter into a desperate combat, and sending off the most bloody and savage accounts of every fight that takes place. The lecture that the *World* reads the government at Washington, impresses a good lesson, which might be heeded with profit by our own authorities. Says the *World:*

It is no disgrace *per se* to be beaten in a battle. Disgrace comes from want of brains in officers and want of pluck in men; when both these are shown, an accident or a slight mistake turns the the evenly poised scale. But it is a terrible disgrace to falsity, and a disgrace to accept, much more to welcome untruth. The American character has suffered in the eyes of the world from the ridiculous accounts of engagements where we have really displayed both military conduct and undoubted courage. One of these "boshes" appeared in the Times of yesterday over the signature of one Paul. Gen Pleasanton's cavalry had a brisk skirmish with Stuart's and it is said drove them. The fact is pleasant, and we willingly accept it as true. In the details it is stated that no less than four regiments of our cavalry, after charges by both sides alternately repulsed, contended hand to hand for *twenty* minutes, and that the officers and men fought on both sides like fiends. Our loss is about ten killed and 100 wounded. We very frequently see the phrase "fought like fiends," and have never yet obtained a very clear idea of the exact style of combat referred to. The story of this cavalry rencounter serves still more to puzzle us. Four thousand men, with all the destructive enginery of war with sharp-shooters in houses and behind walls, fighting twenty minutes, with only "about ten killed" on our side seems to us the most preposterous result possible. Put four New York companies in a "muss," take away the police and the fear of prosecution, give them no arms but fists, wrenches, and the trumpets of the foremen, and in ten minutes we will engage that the number of the killed and wounded will equal that of Pleasanton and Stuart's cavalry "fighting like fiends." There must be an untruth somewhere in this account; either the fighting or the loss is misrepresented. It is perhaps of no importance that a reporter, in a terribly excited condition, should treat us to such Bobadilisms; but it is of some importance that Americans, whom we delighted to think intelligent, reasonable and brave, should not be supposed by foreigners such consummate donkeys as to believe in such trash, or so weak as to be pleased with it. We want the truth; we are wise enough to be entitled to it, and we protest against that hallucination of the powers controlling the telegraph which persists in treating us like a parcel of children who will not take medicine without having it sugar-coated.—The paralyzing effect of imbecility seems to wither and shrink up everything, from the movements of an army to the clicking of a telegraph. We go to bed with the sense of having supplied money and men enough for the conquest of an empire, we wake up to find a great state in alarm and confusion at an irruption of a small flying column and learn that the administation has not a regiment to spare to meet it. Secretary Stanton has great faith in the Spirit of the Lord and the sword of Gideon; but are those instruments of combat surely in his hand? May he not mistake for them the eructations of aberration and the faith of harlequin?

A YANKEE PRISONER PLAYING THE SPY IN RICHMOND.

The New York *World* has the following paragraph, a very striking commentary on the loose discipline of our military prisons, which permits Yankee prisoners to "slip by the guard:"

Robert Flaven, a young Vermonter, eleven years of age, has just been released from imprisonment at the South, and has undergone some very sore experience. Several months since he was captured on the Mississippi river by a band of guerrillas and marched to Vicksburg, a distance of 175 miles. Thence he was taken to Richmond, and while there he determined to examine the gunboats, which he heard were constructing there. About ten o'clock in the morning, after the morning meal had been dealt out, he slipped by the guard and walked down to the navy, where two iron clads are in process of construction He remained there all day, with his wits about him and eyes wide open. He observed that the vessels were pierced for eight guns, and was told that they were to float on the 15th of June. After getting tired of the yard, he made his way to the Tredegar Iron Works, where they were casting shell and cannon.—This had been suggested to him by his fellow prisoners. He then went back to the prison, and slipping past the guard, returned to his companions, who plied him with questions as to his luck. Another day he was taken by a sergeant of police to the capitol, where he saw Jeff. Davis sitting in a red-covered chair. He also saw the "pretender" pass the train several times in a buggy. The little fellow has not seen or heard from his parents since his capture, and is consequently now enacting the role of "Japhet in search of a father."

PRACTICE vs. PREACHING BOWIE KNIVES vs CANNON.

From the New York Caucasian.

Our readers will recollect that a ranting Abolition member of Congress from Wisconsin, a few years since, was loudly proclaimed as a great hero for the part he played in an incipient duel with Roger A. Pryor, of Virginia. One would have supposed that such a valiant knight as he would have been off to the war at the first crack of the gun. Pryor has been illustrating his bravery at the cannon's mouth on the side of the South, but we learn that Potter has not even smelled gunpowder, though it will be seen from the following letter, [illegible] to us by a citizen of Wisconsin, that he promised not only to go, but to stay until the war [illegible].

EAST TROY, May 7, 1861

[illegible] A J LANGWORTHY—*Dear Sir:* I would like to [illegible] a private in your company, and if there [illegible] vacancy after your arrival in Washington, I [illegible] a transfer from Captain Clay's company to [illegible] transfer to train with the Wisconsin boys. I [illegible] to start, and am enlisted for the whole war [illegible] soon as the session of Congress is through—and [illegible] shortly shall join my command, and go where [illegible] and remain [illegible] we meet. I desire [illegible] I expect to leave for Washington in a day [illegible] gun, Maynard's carbine, is in prime order [illegible] I will soon be ready to march.

JOHN F POTTER.

The date of this letter is just after the firing on Fort Sumter. As Mr Potter's courage soon cooled out, his gun is supposed to be "in prime order" yet. As more soldiers are wanted, why don't he [illegible]?

(Correspondence of the Mobile Register and Advertiser.)

A Concise Report of Bragg's and Rosecrans' Movements.

CHATTANOOGA, Friday, July 3, 1863.

The restrictions which have been placed upon the telegraph is the cause of your not having been informed by the rapid messenger of the important army news from Middle Tennessee. So strict has been the surveillance, that a dispatch breathing of the "situation" had no hope of ever going further than the starting point.

THE LOSS OF THE GAPS.

In my last letter you were furnished with the intelligence of the evacuation of the position at Shelbyville, and the probable cause—The several important Gaps—Hoover's, Grey's and Liberty—were the key to that position—At each of these a brigade was placed, probably a mile in the rear, so as to be able to advance and quickly occupy them as soon as our cavalry should report the advance of the enemy. When the enemy did advance, they did so in heavy force, and either succeeded in eluding or cutting off the picket force, and reached the Gaps and possessed themselves of them before the forces which we had to hold them were aware of their approach. When their presence was ascertained, Liddell's Arkansas brigade was advanced to drive the enemy from Liberty Gap; Bates' Tennessee brigade to do the same for one of the other Gaps, and Bushrod Johnson's brigade to dislodge them from the third. These all advanced with spirit, and each suffered quite a severe loss, Liddell suffering heaviest. But the attempt was useless, although assistance had come to their aid, for the enemy had occupied in such heavy force that it would have required double their number to have dislodged them from such strong positions. Thus the enemy obtained by a surprise the key of our position, and compelled a withdrawal of Bragg's army. Who is responsible for the surprise remains to be developed by the proper investigation of it. Part of the of the brigades was enjoying a jollification at the time the enemy seized their position. The enemy advanced so rapidly that they succeeded in cutting off the retreat of our cavalry, which had been upon outpost beyond Shelbyville, and chased them into Duck river, which they were compelled to swim, and where many were drowned, killed, wounded and captured Several loads of commissary stores fell into their possession at Shelbyville.

THE POSITION AT TULLAHOMA.

When forced from Shelbyville or the first position, the army was withdrawn to Tullahoma, which every one had been led to believe was the very stronghold where the enemy would be met and annihilated. With confidence in our success in meeting Rosecrans' legions here, the army took position in the fortifications and impatiently awaited their arrival. Our Generals appear to have felt confident that if the enemy continued to advance, and really meant battle, he would accept the gage here. Every one, then, was astonished when it was learned that the enemy had passed around Manchester and outflanked us on the right. This movement compelled the evacuation of the boasted position of Tullahoma. Many marvelled why such experienced engineers as Gens Johnston and Bragg had not discovered, before the advance of the enemy, that their flank could be so easily turned. When the troops marched backwards from Tullahoma, the tents were left standing, and stores left behind, and no idea was entertained that they were abandoning the position.

THE POSITION AT ALISONIA AND COWAN

was the next occupied. Cowan is at the base of the mountains, the point at which the fall road tunnel penetrates through. This position is naturally very strong, and placed the mountains at Gen. Bragg's back, much the same as the position occupied by the forces at the battle of Sharpsburg. It was believed, too, that this position would prevent any flank movement of the enemy. The troops were mostly encamped at Alisonia, a few miles in advance of Cowan, but it was generally known that the latter was the desirable point for the coming engagement. Our troops had been in position here two or three days, the enemy continuing to advance carefully in force, and it was not known what hour would plunge the contending armies into a bloody battle. Again it was learned that Rosecrans, evading an open and pitched battle, was once more attempting the flanking process [illegible] Pikeville, over the mountains, and endeavoring to [illegible] the Tennessee river at Bridgeport, in the [illegible] of our forces, which would cut off their retreat.

On Tuesday, the 24 inst, the wounded, sick and stores were sent down by trains to Chattanooga, and our army commenced marching over the mountains, once more upon the retreat. Gen Bragg, who came down by the train, reached Bridgeport on Friday morning, and in the evening the advance of the army commenced pouring in. The citizens had all been ordered off to points of safety, and the troops had been in the trenches for two nights. The enemy sent a mounted force of 4000, with a view of reaching the river and destroying the bridge before our forces could arrive there, but learning that such a contingency had been provided for by the Confederate commander they desisted from their purpose, and continued to advance their main army.

* * * * *

I believe that Gen. Bragg would have fought the enemy at any time had they advanced *upon* him, but Rosecrans persistently continued to flank and out flank, and no alternative was left but to fight him under great disadvantages or retreat to a position which he could not flank.—It was believed that Cowan was such an one but even here he went miles and miles to the east to cover and get around the right flank, and forced further retirement to Bridgeport, where the river will prevent further flanking, without Rosecrans constructs bridges and crosses.

Of course the army, eager for the fray, are dissatisfied with the retreat, and deep imprecations are heaped on the head of the Commanding General for not giving battle. So it was when Albert Sidney Johnston retired to Corinth, Perhaps the one is as unjust as the other. Time will show whether General Bragg has acted with skill and discretion, and I forbear criticism on either the one side or the other.

The force under Rosecrans, as nearly as can be ascertained by military authorities, is 50,000 men.

Large numbers of Tennesseeans are reported as having deserted upon the abandonment of their homes.

The country evacuated was the richest portion of Middle Tennessee and North Alabama, and the largest and most favorable crops ever known were sown there. It is justly estimated that the country occupied by General Bragg's army would of itself have yielded it a full commissariat for the coming year.

* * * * *

NIMPOTE.

Mexico.

President Juarez and his Cabinet have evacuated the City of Mexico before the approach of the French, prefering not to risk a siege. On the 31st of May the Government was removed to San Louis Potosi, with a view of defending the mining regions against the French army.

The force that garrisoned the City of Mexico, said to number 20 000 men, was withdrawn to the Cuernavaca plaza and to intermidiate points around the city, for the purpose of carrying on guerilla warfare.

On the 1st of June a meeting was held in the city, at which the principal leaders of the church party was present. They sent a commission to Gen. Forey to offer their allegiance to the Emperor Louis Napoleon.

On the 5th, the French division, under Gen Bazaine, occupied the main entrance to the city, and afforded the church party protection against the excited populace.

The whole French army was expected to occupy the capitol on the 8th of June

Three newspapers had been established favoring the policy of the French.

One of these papers states that the occupation of the City of Mexico settles with absolute certainty that it is necessary to extirpate by the root, the democratic element, and no longer need there be even a dream of popular sovereignty.

Gen. Forey has issued a decree confiscating the property of all parties who have been or are in arms against the French.

FURTHER YANKEE ACCOUNTS OF THE BATTLE OF GETTYSBURG.

A correspondent of the New York *Times* writing from the battle field near Gettysburg, thus describes the battle of Thursday:

The position of our forces after the fight of Wednesday was to the eastward and southward of Gettysburg, covering the Baltimore pike, the Taneytown and Emmettsburg roads, and still being nearly parallel with the latter. The formation of the ground on the right and centre was excellent for defensive purposes. On our extreme left the ground sloped off until the position was no higher than the enemy's. The ground in front of our line was a level, open country, interspersed here and there with an orchard or a very small tract of timber, generally oak, with the underbrush cut away. During the day a portion of the troops threw up temporary breastworks and an abattis. General Meade's headquarters were at an old house on the Taneytown road, immediately in rear of the centre.

On Thursday morning there were strong premonitions of an early engagement with the enemy in force, but the day wore away and no positive exhibition was made by the enemy.

At 3½ o'clock, General Meade having received sufficient assurances to justify him in the belief that the rebels were concentrating their forces on our left flank, which all felt to be secure under the protection of the invincible Third corps. Our line was immediately strengthened on that flank, General Sickles' corps being sent to its support, and several batteries from the reserve being brought up and put in position.

At 4½ o'clock, P. M, the enemy sent his first compliments by a salvo of artillery, his first shells falling uncomfortably near Gen. Meade's headquarters. From this hour forth to 8½ o'clock, occurred by all means the most sanguinary engagements yet chronicled in the annals of the war, considering its duration. The artillery attack which was made by the enemy on the left and centre, was rapidly followed by the advance of his infantry. The Third corps received the attack with great coolness. The rebels at once made for our flank, and kept moving heavy columns in that direction. This necessitated support, which was quickly given by the Fifth corps. The division of Gen Barnes being sent to the right, and that of Gen. Ayres regulars, to the left, with General Crawford in reserve.

The battle now became perfectly fearful. The armies engaged each other at very short range, and for three long hours the war of musketry was incessant. I have heard more noise, louder crashes, in other battles, but I never saw or heard of such desperate, tenacious fighting as took place on this flank. The enemy would often bring up suddenly a heavy column of men and force our line back, only to be in turn forced back by our own line of glittering steel—The dispositions of the enemy were very rapid, for look where you would on that field a body of rebels would be advancing. Our dispositions were equally rapid. At half past six General Sickles was struck in the right leg by a piece of shell, and borne from the field. The injury was so great that amputation became necessary, and it was performed successfully—the limb being taken off below the knee.

The struggle grew hotter and hotter. The Second corps was called on for aid, and though its own position was strongly threatened yet the first division, bravely Gen Hancock's, flung themselves into the fight with desperation, and after a long and obstinate conflict, the enemy slowly and sullenly gave way. In this last charge the brigade of Gen Ca'dwell, Second corps, and that of Col Switzer, from the fifth corps, won great honors. The charges made by our men deserve mention, but want of time forbids. The rebels made frequent attempts to capture our artillery, and at one time had Watson's battery in their possession but it was retaken in a furious charge by Birney's division.

The battle lasted till fully 8½ o'clock, when the enemy fell back to his old position, and left our veterans the ensanguined victors of that field. Our pickets were thrown out, and our lines covered most of the field, including a great number of the enemy's dead and wounded.

I visited some portions of the line by moonlight, and can bear personal witness to the terrible ferocity of the battle. In front of General Webb's was found the body of Gen Barksdale, *that once haughty and violent rebel, who craved as dying boon a cup of water and a stretcher from an ambulance boy.* He is literally cut to pieces with wounds and must die.

A great and magnificent feature of this fight is the splendid use of artillery. Though our line of battle was only a mile and a half long, yet almost every battery belonging to the army of the Potomac was more or less engaged. Every one of the reserve batteries was brought in to action, the positions for use being numerous. The enemy also used artillery largely, but not to so great an extent as we did.

THE BATTLE OF FRIDAY—THE FIGHTING PERSEVERED IN—STILL GOING ON—GEN. BARKSDALE, [illegible]—CERTAINLY KILLED—THE LATEST.

On the first (Friday) morning, the battle was resumed, and was *still going on* up to the date of our latest advices from the North A dispatch dated at Gettysburg on Friday, the 3d, says:

The third day's battle began this morning at 4 o'clock. It is now 7 o'clock, and a circle of fire of musketry and artillery on the south side of Gettysburg describes the field of contest. The musketry fight is wholly within the woods; the artillery occupies the eminence shorn of timber.

The attack was commenced by the rebels on our right. The fight there has been unceasing, and the irregularity of the fire—slackening and scattering for awhile, and then heavy and continuous—indicates reinforcements of [illegible] sides.

[illegible] at this hour are in the best of spirits, and the general officers feel confident of the result. The battle has been planned and thus far fought by Gen. Meade with equal prudence (ably and energetically assisted by Gen. Butterfield, who has not left the army of the Potomac) and courage

The day is now overcast, and the air damp and cool. The sky threatens rain, and a fog already obscures the outer edge of the field of battle.

Gen. Barksdale, of Mississippi, wounded yesterday, is lying dead within our lines.—The rumor of the death of Longstreet, brought by rebel prisoners yesterday, is confirmed by prisoners taken this morning. Longstreet's and Hill's corps are said to be fighting on the right; Ewell's in front.

Sixteen hundred prisoners, thus far in the engagement, have been sent to the rear, and more are here.

What the result may be to day cannot now be predicted.

Important dispatches have been captured by Captain Dahlgren and the gallant scout Kline, from Jeff. Davis and Cooper to General Lee. They indicate anxiety for the position of Richmond. Both decline to send Lee the reinforcements from Beauregard he asked for.

The N. Y. *Tribune*, in its editorial summary of the latest news, thus sums up:

Our special telegrams give a clear understanding of the momentous events which have taken place at Gettysburg, Pennsylvania, within the past three days On Wednesday the action was brought on by General Reynolds, simply because he thought himself superior to the enemy. The action was not general, and was not intended to be so by General Meade. *Our forces engaged on that day were repulsed*, because overpowered but they subsequently fell back to a position which they held in the rear of Gettysburg. On Thursday there was no fighting until half-past 4 o'clock, P M. At that hour a bloody engagement was commenced, lasting until dark, and resulting in a substantial success to our arms The battle was commenced by the enemy with terrific force. Their entire army was engaged. Yesterday the third day's battle commenced, at 4 o'clock in the morning the field of contest being on the south side of Gettysburg and the musketry fighting being wholly within the woods, while the artillery was posted on eminences from which the timber had been cut.—The attack on this day, as on the day previous, was commenced by the Rebels, our right being the point aimed at. There the fight was unceasing, until the date of our last dispatches from the battle field—10 o'clock, A M. Longstreet's and Hill's corps were said to be engaged there, while Ewell was on the front The enemy, as well as ourselves, had suffered heavily in prominent officers. Prisoners on Thursday reported the death of General Longstreet, and prisoners captured yesterday confirmed the report Sixteen hundred prisoners had, up to 10 o'clock, been sent to the rear, and more were arriving. *The result of the day's battle could not then be predicted.*

Mr. Stephens' Reported Mission to Washington.

The Richmond *Examiner* of the 8th instant says:

THE MOVEMENTS OF THE VICE PRESIDENT, we have authority for stating, have no reference whatever to national affairs All the stories of his departure for Old Point and Washington with an *ultimatum* to submit to the Lincoln government in regard to the conduct of the war are stories built upon erroneous surmises without the foundation of truth. In company with Hon Robert Ould, Commissioner of Exchange, he visited City Point on Saturday, in an entirly unofficial character, and simply with a view to the enjoyment of the river scenery, and a relaxation from the cares of his station. The Vice President has probably ere this returned to the Capital. The fact that he was seen on Friday last, in company with several gentlemen, seated in a carriage, with a portmanteau strapped behind, going in the direction of the flag of truce boat, gave rise to the report among the idlers on Main street that he was en route for the kingdom of Abraham, with something portentous among his papers.

ATTEMPT TO ASSASSINATE GOVERNOR YATES OF ILLINOIS.—Governor Yates, of Illinois, was shot at through his window, while washing in his office, at his residence in Springfield, at a late hour on the 1st of July.

BY TELEGRAPH.

JACKSON, 9 o'clock, A M—The enemy is advancing rapidly on the Clinton road. Our cavalry are skirmishing with them three miles out from here and gradually falling back. Our force is in line of battle to receive them.

SECOND DISPATCH.

1 P M The enemy is still advancing slowly, shelling our cavalry. They are now within four miles of our works. There will probably be no engagement before [illegible].

THIRD DISPATCH.

9 P M A regular artillery duel has been going on for the past hour, three miles off. The Yankees are moving up steadily and steadily, and warm work is looked for at daylight.

RICHMOND, July 9.—The confirmation of the fall of Vicksburg, in connection with the reports from Yankee sources of the defeat of Lee's army, had a depressing effect on our community this forenoon, but later, it was learned that the reports were much exaggerated and unreliable, and has occasioned a much better feeling prevails. The President having received unofficial accounts by telegraph from Martinsburg, giving a more encouraging account of the position of affairs, Lee's army is still at Hagerstown.

The Potomac is falling.

Parties who left Washington on Sunday report much dejection there among the Unionists, and a number of them were preparing to move, believing that Gen Meade's army would be unable to prevent the occupation of the Capitol by Lee.

Specie, stocks, provisions, &c., are not materially affected here (Richmond) by the news today. Sugar sold at an advance of 20 to 30 cents on last week's rates. No excitement—the citizens hopeful and confident. This spirit animates official circles.

CHARLESTON, July 10.—An attack on this city has commenced. Four Yankee iron-clads are off the bar and one at the mouth of Stono river and one in that river. Forty transport vessels are off the harbor. There has been heavy firing from 5 o'clock A. M. Our Morris Island batteries have been replying for two hours. Yankee troops are landing at Grimball's Landing, on James Island. An iron clad and some gunboats have gone up Stono river to attack Fort Pemberton.

RICHMOND, July 10.—All the papers this morning gave more cheering accounts from our army in Maryland, and the uneasiness prevailing yesterday has given place to a feeling of confidence in the ability of General Lee to resume offensive operations.

The Martinburg correspondent of the Dispatch, writing on the 5th, says all the information concerning the battle of Gettysburg received there was brought by Maj. Hawks, of Ewell's corps, who left Gettysburg on Saturday morning, the 4th. He says our loss in the first two days (Wednesday and Thursday) was not very great, but on Friday it was heavy, especially in Pickett's division.

General Trimble lost a leg and General Hood an arm.

A gentleman who arrived at Richmond yesterday says our army fell back with the greatest deliberation. It is generally understood that the falling back was caused by the difficulty in obtaining supplies through so long a line of communication. The men are in fine spirits and ready for another fight.

MARTINSBURG, July 9th, via Richmond 10—The army is at Hagerstown—all quiet here to day. A cavalry skirmish occured yesterday.—We have no information from the Yankee army Maryland Heights are re-occupied by a small force of Yankees.

An Ordnance train has just passed by, going to Lee, who is waiting for it.

THE COWARDS.—A correspondent of a New York paper writes from Port Hudson:

"Our brigade has a skirt of hill level with the enemy's works—between us is a deep gully and a small bayou We could easily storm it if we could afford the loss of life. I made a reconnoissance along our right and have found a place where a storming party might carry the works. We are debating whether to try it. *The colored brigade probably will try it!*"

JACKSON, June 10, 8½ o'clock A. M.—The attack has begun. Our batteries have finally opened on them. The enemy is evidently in heavy force.

SECOND DISPATCH.

Heavy infantry and artillery skirmishing is going on. The enemy are shelling the city, and have killed several soldiers and citizens. No general engagement yet. Our troops are in excellent spirits, and if the enemy makes a general attack, it follows that we will be certain of success. Every man is at his post.

THIRD DISPATCH.

Heavy skirmishing continues on the Clinton road. The enemy are slowly working round our left. The attack may not become general before morning, though their troops are pressing forward. But few men have been hit on our side yet. The enemy must be suffering for water, as all the cisterns and ponds are destroyed. Thermometer 92.

Dispatches to the Mobile Tribune.

JACKSON, July 8.—A number of the Vicksburg heroes arrived here to day.

The privates praise Gen Pemberton in the highest terms. They say they went into Vicksburg prejudiced against him, but no man could have done more than he did. One man shed tears when he told me of what they had suffered, with no relief, and then for Vicksburg to fall.

The Yankees were led to believe that if they took Vicksburg the war was at an end, and they could then go home, and they would remark to our troops, "well, boys, we can all go home, now."

An officer who has arrived from Vicksburg tells me that the garrison had been living on pea bread and mule meat for two weeks.

He says that if it had been known that no relief was coming it would have held out longer.

It is stated that the officers of Pemberton urged him to surrender.

The garrison was at the point of starvation The men were without food for three days.—After the surrender, in marching to stack their arms, numbers of them staggered like drunken men from the effects of starvation and fatigue.

PASCAGOULA, July 7.—A friend just now from Biloxi informs me that since this morning the whole of Ship Island seems to be on fire. Occasional puffs of white smoke were seen, and afterwards thick black clouds. No reports were heard, the wind being unfavorable. Smoke was plainly visible for the last two hours at this point.

Correspondence of the Lynchburg Republican.

Gallant Exploit of the 8th Regt. Virginia Cavalry—They Capture Sixty Odd Prisoners and Disperse a Whole Camp of Yankees, With Very Small Loss.

CAMP 8TH VA. CAVALRY, July 1

Messrs. Editors:

On Saturday last, the 28th ult, one of the most brilliant as well as the most successful exploits of the war, was accomplished by a portion of the 8th reg't Va Cavalry, under the command of the gallant Capt C. J Lewis, of the Kanawha Rangers, near Gauley Bridge, Kanawha county.

On the 24th ult., Capt Lewis, with the Kanawha Rangers, Border Rangers, Border Grays, and Tazewell Troopers, making in all about two hundred effective men, took up the march for a place known as the mouth of Loup Creek, where were posted some several hundred Yankee Cavalry. They had quite an arduous march over trackless mountains, and through a sparsely settled country, most of the time having nothing for themselves or horses to subsist upon, yet the boys never uttered a single word of complaint, for they were too anxious to chastise a foe who had so ruthlessly lorded it over their homes for the last eight months.

Having ascertained from loyal citizens on their march the numbers and position of the enemy, Capt. Lewis knew that he must surprise and take the enemy at a disadvantage to whip them. So early on Saturday morning, coming upon the Yankee pickets, he charged them with his whole command, and followed right at their heels, smash into the middle of the Yankee camp. Then the work began, our boys using revolvers and sabres freely, and the Yankees fleeing in every direction, some on horseback, but the majority afoot, not having time to get their horses The scene at this point was grandly exciting; our boys might be seen in every direction, in squads and alone, pursuing the Yankees, and, when they came in striking distance, I could see from the flash of their eyes and by the mighty power with which they yielded their heavy sabres, that they were thinking of smoking houses, devastated plantations and outraged humanity.

We killed nine, captured some sixty prisoners besides sixty horses, one hundred navy revolvers, sabres, carbines, saddles, bridles, &c., and lost one man killed. Twelve Yankees attempted to swim the Kanawha, four were drowned and the rest about faced and were taken prisoners.

The 8th is commanded by Col J. M. Corns, a braver man than whom does not exist, and who prides himself in sharing equally the hardships with the private soldiers.

Yours, &c., J. E. L.

SUNDAY, JULY 12, 1863.

Financial and Commercial.

Comments under this head are rather uninteresting this week; they are overshadowed. Money is plenty in Bank, but owing to the unsettled and important military movements, traders are coy—not much disposed to trade.

The shape which the Impressment law has assumed has alarmed capital. It was the intention of the congress in passing it to seize goods, only when needed, and to provide just compensation for them when seized. The act was intended to put a check upon abuses, and protect the people from wrong. But the government has shorn it of its fair propositions and destroyed all hope of its doing any good, by an erroneous or forced construction, and by issuing orders for its execution in a manner never contemplated by congress. By the instructions of the War Department, it appears that the government, instead of impressing private property only when necessary, and only for the purpose of supplying its wants, has undertaken to control the prices of articles of necessity and regulate the markets of the country. In this it will signally fail. It has already done immense mischief, and will do a great deal more, unless it be speedily abandoned. No man nor set of men, nor even the government with all its power can control the prices of commodities, and should not if it could. This policy had better be stopped.

This act was passed to protect private rights and to prevent the taking of private property at an arbitrary and unjust price anything under the fair *overt* market value. It was intended also to furnish the government, when it needed supplies, and could not otherwise obtain them. The practice however is not to seize goods to meet the government's *necessities*, but to take articles that are held or offered at or above certain prices, or when found in the possession of a certain class of men; and not only so, but often, when the property of these men is seized ostensibly to supply the wants of the government, it is released and returned to the parties upon pledge to sell it at retail, or at certain prices Congress never contemplated this; and the whole government and congress combined can no more accomplish the herculean task of regulating the markets of the country than they can make water run up hill. Every effort will do mischief and mischief only

The manner in which this law is attempted to be enforced is creating wide spread dissatisfaction among the people, of all classes, and justly so They are not satisfied, and will not be, for an Impressing officer to take their property at a less price than what it will bring in open market. We earnestly appeal to the "Powers that Be," to cease this policy. Its damage will one day be felt—perhaps when it is greater than can be repaired, and its consequences must be endured.

But little change in the prices of leading articles. Tobacco sells freely to consumers. Owners have added on to their prices about enough to pay the Confederate tax. Blockade goods not so abundant, and prices stiffer. Lands, city property, and negroes are in good demand at high figures. The remainder of the sugar was seized here yesterday. Very little new flour come in yet. Corn is high All kinds of vegetables and fruit, considering their abundance, are excessively high—Peaches $1 per dozen; Watermelons, $5 each; Berries, 50 cents per quart; Cabbages, $1 per head; Cucumbers, $1 per dozen.

Cotton goods nominal Liquor in demand only by retailers—sells by the barrel at $15 per gallon. The whole country will soon be flooded with new Peach Brandy.

Gossip of the Week.

It is a positive fact that we have had two consecutive days without a *shower*. The sun is blazing down upon us to day as though he were angry at the fall of Vicksburg and wanted to scorch and blister the hands and backs of the vile Yankee invaders and robbers. We advise our female friends to put all their spoons and coffee pots in a cool place, lest they melt.

We never saw a better stand of grass and weeds than our farmers have now. The Corn generally looks well in the grass fields.

ARMY MOVEMENTS

Are very important. Lee has invaded Lincoln's dominions, and every one feels anxious to hear more of his operations. We must again express our doubts of the policy of invading the enemy's country. If it can be done successfully, we should rejoice at it, but in our judgment, it had better not have been attempted, than to fall short of a complete success But we must be patient, and know the final result before we can draw definite conclusions.

VICKSBURG.

Of course every heart is sad at the fall of the Hill city, and the cruel necesity of its gallant garrison to capitulate, though they came out with the honors of war. But as we have frequently said before, we do not consider its possession of that vital importance that others do. The holding possession of, and navigating a thousand miles of the river, whose banks are open at numberless points to the attacks of our brave guerrillas, will prove rather an expensive and unprofitable luxury to our North-western *brethren!*

TENNESSEE.

This State has almost passed from our hands. It draws horrid war yet a little nearer to our own doors, and it behoves every patriot at once to make arrangements to fight for and defend his wife and children.—Let the 8,000 called for and twice or three times that amount be raised, organized and equipped at once.—No time to stickle upon who you'll report to. Be ready when the time arrives, to shoulder your gun and see that your powder is dry!

CHARLESTON,

Too is again to be put to the test. Every one listens with the deepest anxiety for the next news from that gallant city—the special object of Yankee hatred. May she as heretofore, stand firm and bring her foes to confusion.

Protection of Private Property.

We notice that the Yankee correspondents of Northern papers have no standard by which to discriminate between those levies on property authorized by the rules of war and such as are made irrespective of any rules.—To their obtuseness in distinguishing the right from the wrong, according to principles of public law, they place in the same category the imposition of a fine on a community that has been conquered—and the indiscriminate pillage of the inhabitants individually. The rules of international law allow the former to prevent the latter. General Ewell has levied in money, and in kind, a contribution on the municipality of York, in Pennsylvania. This he is authorized to do by the laws of war.—The Yankees choose to call this plunder. It is a levy that grows out of the right of capture. It imposes the mulct in the least oppressive mode by levying it on the municipal government, the head of which is best able to distribute it equitably among its citizens.—Not to speak of the oppression of private license to soldiery to plunder, how much more conducive to justice than to leave the amount as well as mode of collection to the individual discretion of a number of officers, who divest or spoliate according to caprice or political animosities

Of the same character of complaint is the charge that we plunder private property at sea while we respect it on land. This is also authorized by public law. It has received the sanction of the most eminent names in our history. It has been acted on by every administration since the establishment of the government. The Yankees have derived the largest share of profit from it when the United States were at war with any of the powers of Europe. It is criminal and base now because they are the sufferers instead of being the gainers. The Federal Government, or rather Mr. Marcy in 1857, without authority from congress, in conformity with the recommendation of the Paris convention, offered to surrender it if the British Government would surrender the right of capturing private property at sea by their public armed vessels.—This they refused to do. This shows that the abstract right was made subservient to expediency. The distinction between private property on land and private property at sea as part of the public law, has been recognized in practice by all the maritime powers of Europe as well as the United States before the advent to power of the Lincolnites. And it will not do at this late day for the Yankees, in their sublimated morality—to denounce privateering after pocketing the profits of that practice whenever the occasion presented itself. C.

The Mayor of Charleston, on the 10th, issued three Proclamations:

1—Impressing all the Free Male Negroes, Mulattoes and Mestizoes, residing in that city, between the ages of 18 and 60 years of age, and all able-bodied male slaves within the same, to finish the defenses of Morris Island.

2—Ordering all business suspended within the city, from that day until the safety of the city is assured.

3—That all women and children be removed from the city, at the earnest request of General Beauregard.

Resolutions of Brown's Infantry on the Death of Sergt. S. D. Horne.

FORT GAINES, ALA., June 30, 1863.

At a meeting held by Brown's Infantry, of the First Confederate Regiment of Georgia Volunteers, at this place, to take into consideration the death of Sergt. S. D. Horne, 1st Lieut. T. B Cox was called to the chair, and Sergt. J. P. McKay requested to act as Secretary.

On motion of Sergt. W. H. Wagnon, a Committee of Five were appointed to draft suitable resolutions expressive of our feelings for the deceased and our sympathy for his bereaved family, consisting of Capt. Massey, Lieuts. Sanders and Small, Corpl. Price and Private A. S. C. Thornton.

On motion of Capt. Massey, Sergt. Wagnon and Private T. P. Thornton were added, when the Committee retired and prepared the following resolutions:

Whereas, it has pleased the Supreme Ruler in his divine wisdom to remove from our midst our beloved comrade Sergt S D Horne, who died on the morning of the 29th inst. Therefore, be it

Resolved, That in the death of Sergt. Horne disease for the first time has claimed its victim from our ranks; Georgia has lost a noble son and valuable citizen, and one who, had he lived, would have made a bright and shining light in society; our young Confederacy a noble and gallant defender, who left home and all that was dear to battle for the noble cause of his country's independence. The blood of another victim cries out for vengeance on the ruthless invaders of our soil and despoilers of our once happy homes.

Resolved, That we deeply sympathize with his family in this sad affliction—his wife has lost a kind and affectionate husband, and his little ones a protector whose loss is irreparable—and though we deeply deplore his sudden and unexpected death, yet we bow with humble submission to the will of Him who doeth all things well, and will be a father to the widow and the orphan.

Resolved, That the members of the Company wear the usual badge, and our company colors be draped in mourned for the space of thirty days, and that a copy of these proceedings be sent to the family of the deceased, and also to the Macon Daily Confederate, Dalton Times and Atlanta Confederacy, with the request to publish.

Capt. T. J. MASSEY,
2d Lieut. W. E SANDERS,
Jr. 2d Lieut. A. E SMALL,
Sergt. W. H WAGNON,
Corpl. DAVID PRICE,
Private A. S. C. THORNTON,
Private S. P. THORNTON,
} Committee.
J. P. McKAY, Secretary.

Gen. Meade's Official Dispatches.

The Philadelphia *Inquirer*, of the 4th inst, contains a dispatch from Gen. Meade to the War Department at Washington, dated on the 2d July, at 11 o'clock P. M, as follows:

"The enemy attacked me at 4 o'clock this afternoon, and after one of the severest contests of the war, was repulsed at all points.—We have suffered considerably in killed and wounded. Among the killed are Brigadier Generals Paul and Zook. Among the wounded are Gens. Sickles, Barton, Graham and Warren. Gen. Sickles' leg was amputated on the field. We have taken a large number of prisoners."

Gen. Meade's second dispatch, dated 8 o'clock Friday morning, says:

"The action commenced again at early daylight upon various parts of the field. The enemy thus far have made no impression upon my position. All the accounts agree in placing the entire rebel army in position in our front.

"The prisoners we have taken report that Longstreet's and Hill's force was much injured yesterday, and many general officers killed.—The dead body of Gen. Barksdale is within our lines. We have thus far about sixteen hundred prisoners, and a small number are yet to be started."

The correspondent of the Inquirer says it is reported that Gen Longstreet was killed.—The rebels still held Gettysburg at 1 P. M. on the 31 inst. Our loss was very heavy. The loss of the rebels cannot be far from twenty thousand, and the fight was still going on Friday The rebels, so far, have been repulsed in every attack, and the fight was still raging.

Gen. Lee had sent in a flag of truce asking a cessation of hostilities for two days to bury the dead. Gen. Meade refused to grant it.

The Inquirer says it breathes freely after reading Gen. Meade's dispatches.

Return of the Atlanta's Crew.

Yesterday morning a number of the crew of the *Atlanta* returned to this city. From Mr Veitch, one of the wounded sailors, we learn that all the crew, except the officers, were exchanged immediately, and sent to Richmond. The officers were sent to Fort Lafayette, where they now are. Some thirty of the crew took the oath of allegiance to the Lincoln Government, giving as a reason that their families and friends reside at the North. The remainder of the crew came South, and many of them have already joined the Confederate army, some at Richmond, and others at different places.

The account of the battle and surrender, as given by Mr. Veitch, differs but little from what we have already published. The first shot entered the *Atlanta's* starboard side, causing splinters to fly in every direction, and wounding ten marines and Lieut. Thurston. The second shot struck the pilot house, wounding Mr. Hernandez and Mr. Austin.—Mr. H. is but slightly hurt in the back; Mr. A. had his left arm broken, and a slight wound in the head, not very serious.

We learn that Capt. Webb was on the outside of his ship during the battle, and exposed himself very much. The crew were all in good spirits, and entertained the hope of a successful contest. Upon nearing the *Weehawken*, Capt. Webb asked the pilots if there was water enough for the *Atlanta* to make a dash at her. He was informed that there was, and he then ordered all steam up, in order to run into her, and blow her up with his torpedo. In a few moments after she had got under full steam, she brought to upon a sand bank, and careened over, which rendered her guns useless, and placed the *Atlanta* at the mercy of her two antagonists, at short range.

In this position, Capt. Webb found it useless to contend with the enemy, and informed his crew that his only course was to surrender the ship in order to save life. The officers and crew were then placed on board the *Weehawken*, and sent to Port Royal, where they remained four days. At this place they were well treated, and the wounded properly cared for. From Port Royal they proceeded to Norfolk, where they remained some days, and did not fare very well. They were then sent to City Point and exchanged.—*Savannah News, yesterday.*

Despatch from Rosecrans Announcing the Occupation of Tullahoma.

The Washington papers publish the following telegram from Gen. Rosecrans:

HEADQUARTERS, TULLAHOMA, TENN., July 1.—I telegraphed you on Monday the occupation of Shelbyville and Manchester. On Monday it rained hard all day, rendering the roads impassable. It was found impossible to move our artillery or get our troops into position until this morning, when a general advance was ordered at daylight.

Gen. Thomas yesterday made a reconnoissance on two roads, and Gen. McCook on one road, reporting the enemy in force at this place, with the addition of Buckner's division, which arrived Monday evening.

On advancing this morning it was found that the enemy had fled in haste last night, much demoralized. Their strong fortifications, a small quantity of stores, and three siege guns in our possession.

They took the direction of Winchester. General Thomas should be on their right flank to-night. General Sheridan and Brannan marched into town to day at 11½ o'clock, taking a few prisoners.

W. S. ROSECRANS, Maj Gen.

FAILURE OF INDIANA TO PAY INTEREST ON ITS DEBT.—The State of Indiana has made default in the payment of interest on its debt, due on the 1st of July, 1863. This is the first instance of default since its compromise with its creditors sixteen years ago.

BY TELEGRAPH.

RICHMOND, July 10.—The Baltimore Gazette, of the 7th, says: "What we really know in regard to the battles before Gettysburg amounts simply to this: The Confederates were attacked on Wednesday by two army corps, which they drove them back with great slaughter, capturing many prisoners. On Thursday afternoon the whole Federal force attacked the Confederates, and after a sanguinary conflict, repulsed them. On Friday the battle lasted through the day, and resulted in a more signal repulse than the previous day. The losses were extraordinarily severe on both sides—the Federals in General officers beyond precedent. On Saturday night Lee fell back towards the mountains What has followed since is almost wholly conjectural, but it is now admitted that Lee holds the passes of South Mountain, and will fight or retreat as circumstances may dictate."

The pontoon bridges at Williamsport are not destroyed.

The City of Washington has arrived, from Liverpool the 24th. The French mediation rumor is again prevalent. Roebuck and Lindsey, of the British Parliament, have had an interview with Napoleon, to whom he gave assurances that his views concerning the American war are unchanged, and he had decided again to interpose his good offices in conjunction with England. At a Cabinet meeting, Napoleon presiding, it was resolved to renew the French proposal to the English Government, for a joint diplomacy in relation to America.

Gold in New York 139-9. Nothing had been heard there of the surrender of Vicksburg.

SECOND DISPATCH.

Nothing additional from Maryland. The Central train has been detained by an accident and has not yet arrived.

THIRD DISPATCH.

A correspondence explanatory of Vice President Stephens' mission shows that he went to Fortress Monroe as Military Commissioner to obtain from the federal authorities an agreement to conduct the war hereafter according to the usages of civilized nations. After waiting for two days, Stephens was informed that the proposition for a conference was inadmissable. He therefore returned to this city. No news this morning.

MARTINSBURG, 9th, via Staunton and Richmond 10th—There was a heavy cavalry fight yesterday. We drove the enemy seven miles capturing a number of prisoners. Lee's army is quiet at Hagerstown.

JACKSON, July 10th P M—The artillery fire has ceased. The enemy's Sharpshooters and our skirmishers are blazing away. Our loss does not exceed 50.

CHARLESTON, July 10.—The firing on both sides ceased at 6½ o'clock P. M. The principal fighting has been with Battery Wagner on Morris Island. Four monitors were engaged from 5 A. M. to 2 P. M.—then withdrew for one hour. A tug boat then supplied them with ammunition and they renewed the attack at 5 o'clock

The infantry fight was also severe. The Yankees made two assaults on Battery Wagner and were repulsed Our casualties are about 150 killed, wounded and missing, including three officers killed: Capt's Haskell and Cheves, and Lieut Bee.

It is supposed the attack will be renewed tomorrow.

PETERSBURG, July 10—The Philadelphia Inquirer of the 8th says Secretary Welles had received notice of the fall of Vicksburg, from Admiral Porter. Pemberton sent a flag of truce to Grant on the morning of the 4th, offering to surrender if the men were allowed to march out. Grant replied that no man should leave except as a prisoner of war. After consultation with his command Pemberton unconditionally surrendered.

There is tremendous rejoicing over it all over the North Lincoln was serenaded and responded in a foolish speech.

The Inquirer has no news of special importance. Meade was closely watching his discomfited but wary antagonist, and an engagement was expected in a day or two.

The Inquirer claims 6000 prisoners, besides the wounded Confederates left behind. It says the worst feature of the disaster is so many federal officers—the most efficient—killed or incapacitated. General Butterfield is tough, worse than was anticipated, being injured internally.

The Cahawba, from New Orleans, says Donaldsonville, Ascension parish, Louisiana, (below Baton Rouge) was attacked by the Rebels in force on the 28th of June, commanded by General Greene. The Rebels were repulsed after three hours' hard fighting, with a loss of 600 men—the gun boats participating [A Yankee whopper!]
EDS. CONFED

Special to the Intelligencer.

CHATTANOOGA July 10—The enemy has made McMinnville his base of operations preparatory and with a view of invading East Tennessee, and occupies Tullahoma, Dechard and Winchester.

One column has moved to Huntsville.

McCann's command, on the first, burnt the bridges between Nashville and Franklin tore up the track and destroyed the telegraph, killed six and brought out 20 negroes.

A Remarkable Letter from Hon. Joseph Holt Just Come to Light.

WASHINGTON, Nov. 30, 1860.

My Dear Sir:—I am in receipt of yours of the 27th inst., and thank you for your kindly allusion to myself in connection with the fearful agitation that now threatens the dismemberment of our Government. I think the President's message will meet your approbation, but I have little hope it will accomplish anything in moderating the madness that rules the hour. The indications are, that the movement has passed beyond the reach of human control. God alone can disarm the cloud of its lightnings. South Carolina will be out of the Union, and in the armed assertion of a distinct nationality, probably before Christmas. This is certain; unless the course of events is arrested by some prompt and decided action on the part of the people and the Legislatures of the Northern States, the other slave States will follow South Carolina in a few weeks or months.

The border States, now so devoted to the Union, will linger a little while, but they will soon unite their fortunes with these of their Southern sisters. Conservative men have now no ground to stand upon—no weapon to battle with. All has been swept from them by the guilty agitations and infamous legislation of the North. I do not anticipate, with any confidence, that the North will set up to the solemn responsibilities of the crisis. by retracing those fatal steps which have conducted us to the very brink of perdition, politically, morally and financially.

There is a feeling growing in the free States which says "Let the South go!" And this feeling threatens rapidly to increase. It is, in part, the fruit of complete estrangement, and in part a weariness of this perpetual conflict between North and South, which has now lasted, with increasing bitterness, for the last thirty years The country wants repose, and is willing to purchase it at any sacrifice. Alas, for the delusion of the belief that repose will follow the overthrow of the Government.

I doubt not, from the temper of the public mind, *that the Southern States will be allowed to withdraw peacefully;* but when the work of dismemberment begins, we shall break up the fragments from month to month, with the nonchalance with which we break the bread upon our breakfast table.

If all the grave and vital questions which will at once arise among these fragments of the ruptured republic can be adjusted without a resort to arms, then we have made vast progress since the history of our race was written. But the tragic events of the hour will show that we have made no progress at all. We shall soon grow up a race of chieftains, who will rival the political bandits of South America and Mexico and who will carve out to us our miserable heritage with their bloody swords. The masses of the people dream not of these things.

They suppose the republic can be destroyed to-day and peace will smile over its ruins tomorrow. They know nothing of civil war.—This march in the desert of the pilgrimage of nations has happily been for them a sealed fountain. They know not as others do of its bitterness, and that civil war is a scourge that darkens every fireside, and wrings every heart with anguish. They are to be commiserated, for they know not what they do. Whence is all this? It has come because the pulpit and the press, and the cowering, unscrupulous politicians of the North have taught the people that they are responsible for the domestic institutions of the South, and that they can be faithful to God only by being unfaithful to the compact which they have made with their fellow men.

Hence those Liberty bills, which degrade the statute books of some ten of the free States, and are confessedly a *shameless* violation of the Federal Constitution, in a point vital to her honor. We have here presented, from year to year, the humiliating spectacle of free and sovereign States by a solemn act of legislation, *legalizing the theft of their neighbor's property.* I say THEFT, since it is not the less so because the subject of the despicable crime chances to be a slave instead of a horse or bale of goods.

From this same teaching has come the perpetual agitations of the slavery question which *has reached the minds of the slave population of the South*, and has rendered every home in that distracted land insecure. This is the feature of the irrepressible conflict with which the Northern people are not familiar. In almost every part of the South, miscreant fanatics have been found, and poisoning and conflagrations have marked their footsteps, Mothers there lay down at night trembling beside their children, and wives cling to their husbands as they leave their homes in the morning.

I have a brother residing in Mississippi, who is a lawyer by profession, and a cotton planter, but has never had any connection with politics.—Knowing the calm and conservative tone of his character, I wrote him a few weeks since, and implored him to exert his influence in allaying the frenzy of the popular mind around him. He has replied to me at much length, and, after depicting the machinations of the wretches to whom I have alluded, and the consternation which reigns in the homes of the South, he says it is the unalterable determination of the Southern people to overthow the Government, as the only refuge which is left to them from these insupportable wrongs, and he adds: "On the success of this movement depends my every earthly interest—the safety of my roof from the firebrand, and my wife and children from the poison and the dagger."

I give you this language because it truthfully expresses the Southern mind, which at this moment glows as a furnace in its hatred to the North, because of these infernal agitations. Think you that any people can endure this condition of things? When the Northern preacher infuses into his audience the spirit of assassins and incendiaries in his crusade against slavery, does he think, as he lies down quietly at night, of the Southern homes he has robbed of sleep, and of the helpless women and children he has exposed to all the *nameless horrors of servile insurrection?*

I am still for the Union, because I have yet a faint, hesitating hope that the North will do justice to the South, and save the Republic, before the wreck is complete. But action, to be available, must be prompt. If the free States will sweep the liberty bills from their codes, propose a convention of the States, and offer guarantees which will afford the same repose and safety to Southern homes and property enjoyed by those of the North, the impending tragedy may yet be averted, but not otherwise. I feel a positive personal humiliation, as a member of the human family, in the events now preparing.

If the Republic is to be offered as a sacrifice upon the altar of African servitude, then the question of man's capacity for self-government is forever settled. The derision of the world will henceforth justly treat the pretension as a farce, and the blessed hope which, for five thousand years, our race, amid storms and battles, has been hugging to its bosom, will be demonstrated to be a phantom and a dream.

Pardon these hurried and disjointed words. They have been pressed out of my heart by the sorrows that are weighing upon it.

Sincerely, your friend,
J. HOLT.

The Behavior of the Confederate Army in the Enemy's Country.

YANKEE TESTIMONY TO THE GOOD CONDUCT OF OUR SOLDIERS.

The New York *Herald* of a late date contains the following:

THE REBEL LEVY AT SHIREMANSTOWN.

SHIREMANSTOWN, PA., July 1.—The enemy did no particular damage here. They only made levy for something to eat.

REBEL OCCUPATION OF MECHANICSBURG.

MECHANICSBURG, PA., July 1.—The enemy agreeably disappointed the people here by his actions. General Jenkins preserved the best of order in town He had his headquarters at the Ashland House on Sunday, and ordered citizens to furnish rations for 1,500 men, and on Monday for only 150. The citizens complied as far as they could.

The rebels did not carry off the large amount of stores in warehouse here, and did no particular damage about town.

CARLISLE.

CARLISLE, PA, July 1.—The following speaks for itself. It was addressed to the troops:

HDQ'RS ARMY NORTHERN VIRGINIA,
Chambersburg, Pa., June 27, 1863.

General Orders,
No 73.

The commanding general has observed with marked satisfaction the conduct of the troops on the march, and confidently anticipates results commensurate with the high spirit they have manifested. No troops could have displayed greater fortitude or better performed the arduous marches of the past ten days. Their conduct in other respects has, with few exceptions, been in keeping with their character as soldiers, and entitles them to approbation and praise.

There have, however, been instances of forgetfulness on the part of some, that they have in keeping the yet unsullied reputation of the army, and that the duties exacted of us by civilization and christianity are not less obligatory in the country of the enemy than in our own.

The commanding general considers that no greater disgrace could befall the army, and through it, our whole people, than the perpetration of the barbarous outrages upon the innocent and defenceless and the wanton destruction of private property that have marked the course of the enemy in our own country. Such proceedings not only disgrace the perpetrators and all connected with them, but are subversive of the discipline and efficiency of the army and destructive of the ends of our present movements. It must be remembered that we make war only upon armed men, and that we cannot take vengeance for the wrongs our people have suffered without lowering ourselves in the eyes of all whose abhorrence has been excited by the atrocities of our enemy, and offending against Him to whom vengeance belongeth, without whose favor and support our efforts must all prove in vain.

The commanding general, therefore, earnestly exhorts the troops to abstain with most scrupulous care from unnecessary or wanton injury to private property; and he enjoins upon all officers to arrest and bring to summary punishment all who shall in any way offend against the orders on this subject.

R. E. LEE, General.

The following is a copy of a certificate for goods taken at Carlisle:

CARLISLE, PA., June 28, 1863.

This is to certify that I have this day received of Mr. John Noble, for the use of this division, ninty bushels of corn, at eighty five cents per bushel. JOHN A RODGERS,
Maj. and Chief Q'r 2d Div'n.

When the rebels came into town here they made an immediate requisition for twenty-five thousand pounds of bacon, one hundred sacks of salt, fifteen hundred barrels of flour, twenty five barrels of potatoes, twenty five barrels of molasses, five thousand pounds of coffee, five thousand pounds of sugar, twenty-five thousand pounds of dried fruit, and for various other articles in small quantities. Their design seemed to be to completely rid the town of these articles. They also made another requisition for three hundred ounces of quinine, ninety pounds of chloroform, fifty pounds of gum opium, &c. They took all the drugs and medicines they wanted, also surgical instruments.

The rebels did great damage to the railroad. They have destroyed a trestlework bridge, built on stone piers, near the town, completely, and have torn down the piers, bent the rails and burnt up all the wood work The track is also much torn up and much destroyed for nearly a mile out of town. A portion of the railroad is also destroyed between Carlisle and Newville The telegraph wires have suffered much.

A REBEL ADDRESS—GEN. EARLY TO THE CITIZENS OF YORK.

YORK, PENN., June 30, 1863.

To the Citizens of York:

I have abstained from burning the railroad buildings and car shops in your town, because, after examination, I am satisfied that the safety of the town would be endangered, and, acting in the spirit of humanity which has ever characterized my Government and its military authorities, I do not desire to involve the innocent with the same punishment of the guilty Had I applied the torch without regard to consequences, I would have pursued a course that would have been fully vindicated as an act of just retaliation for the unparalleled acts of brutality perpetrated by your own army on our soil. But we do not war upon women and children, and I trust the treatment you have met with at the hands of my soldiery will open your eyes to the odious tyranny under which it is apparent to all you are groaning

J. A. EARLY,
Major General, C S A.

See our new terms.

NEW YORK DAILY NEWS.

VOL. VII......NO. 182. NEW YORK, THURSDAY, JULY 16, 1863. PRICE TWO CENTS.

THE RIOT!!

Terrible Scenes in Nineteenth Street.

THE MILITARY AND THE MOB.

CHARGES AND COUNTER CHARGES

Colonel Jardine Mortally Wounded.

One Captain, Two Lieutenants and Fifteen Privates Killed.

HOWITZERS OPEN ON THE MOB

The Street Strewn with the Bodies of Men, Women, and Children.

SCENES IN THE ELEVENTH AVENUE.

THE MILITARY FIRE ON THE MOB.

THIRTY MEN AND WOMEN KILLED.

LIST OF THE SLAIN.

A Woman Shot Through the Heart.

DEATH OF COLONEL O'BRIEN.

RAID UPON THE BLACKS.

SEVERAL NEGROES HUNG.

ONE NEGRO DROWNED

BLOCKS OF NEGRO DWELLINGS BURNED

LETTER FROM GOV. SEYMOUR

Firemen and Citizens Organizing for Defense.

RIOT ON STATEN ISLAND.

Railroad Depot Burned—Lyceum Sacked, and a Negro Hung.

GREAT FIRE IN BROOKLYN

CONFLAGRATION IN NEWARK.

ARRIVAL OF TROOPS.

Gen. Dix to be Assigned to the Department of New York.

INCIDENTS, ACCIDENTS, &C.

[*For reports of riotous proceedings during the early part of the day, see second page.*]

Notwithstanding all that was done on Tuesday to satisfy the turbulent populace; and the confident hope of all good citizens that the riot would cease with Tuesday night's excesses, the riot raged yesterday more fiercely than on any previous day, although the personnel was greatly changed. There were but few, comparatively speaking, of those who rose for the purpose of opposing the draft in the ranks of the rioters yesterday. The mob seemed composed mainly of the vagabonds of the town—pickpockets, thieves, and the multitude of "prowlers about the streets." Many of the workingmen and firemen who had strenuously opposed the enforcement of the draft, as soon as its suspension was announced, joined the ward organizations for the protection of unoffending persons and property. The terrible scenes which occurred in Nineteenth street, in the Eleventh avenue, and elsewhere, exceed any which have occurred since the riot began. Arrangements have been made for the arrival of large re-enforcements of military to-day, and General Dix is to be assigned to the command of the Department of New York.

Yesterday's Proceedings.

The authorities in the City Hall fondly hoped on Tuesday night that the mob was crushed, that all apprehensions of further violence were groundless, and that peace absolute and serene would reign throughout the municipal borders and there would be naught to molest nor make afraid.

How near the truth came the prophecyings of these high officials, let the teeming columns of THE NEWS of to-day, filled as they are with the record of bloodshed and mischief, explain.

During the earlier hours of the morning, that is from one o'clock to six, that part of the city which is bounded by Wall street, the East and North Rivers, and the Battery, was comparatively quiet, although the authorities had every reason to believe that an attack upon certain public buildings in Wall street would be made at that time.

AT THE CUSTOM HOUSE.

One hundred of the clerks and a large number of other employees, fully armed, were kept on watch all night, expecting a visit from the fearful "mob." There are but two places into which the visitors could by any possibility have gone, and these were so guarded by well armed and determined men, that any attempt to break in would have resulted in an absolute failure, and in loss of life to whomsoever might make the foolish trial.

THE BANKS

are all safe and it is far more than likely that the fears of the officials at those necessary institutions are but the creations of their own lively imaginings; for to the best of our knowledge and belief, there has been no intimation nor thought of an attack upon them. The removal of the specie from several of them seems so absurd, that were we not familiar with the fact, we should regard the report as ridiculous in the extreme. No mob on earth, unprovided with artillery, could effect an entrance to the banks or their vaults, and it seems to us, that the less said about that, the better.

IN GREENWICH AND WASHINGTON STREETS,

however, affairs wore a far less peaceful look than in Wall street and Broadway. At about 2 o'clock in the morning a gang of men and boys, numbering perhaps sixty or seventy, went howling through the streets from the Battery up, rumaging even lager bier saloons, routing out the proprietors and other inmates, and playing grand havoc generally with everybody and everything. A German named Breussing, who keeps a small-sized restaurant near Morris street, had been in bed with his wife and children just long enough to reach the cheerful land of noddom, when he was awakened by a terrific pounding at his door and a stentorian voice thereat, intimating to him the propriety of an immediate opening. He went cautiously to the door and said he had closed for the night and did not propose to re-open. The order to "open and be d—d" was reiterated by half a dozen voices, and with trembling hands he obeyed the first part of the direction leaving the other portion to the decision of a more righteous tribunal. Instantly the scoundrel crew sprang in, seized the frightened Teuton by the throat and demanded a treat. This so soon as he was released he liberally gave, and his night-gowned frow came out to assist in doing the honors. The men, seemingly ashamed of their actions, the woman having quietly remonstrated with them, quietly retired, having done no damage save the upsetting of all the decanters, barrels and demijohns they could find, kicking the proprietor into his back room and saluting each for himself the indignant lady. Had they confined themselves to such pilferings as this, there would not have been so much cause for complaint, although that was bad enough, but we regret to say that

ARSON, in its worst form, was attempted and almost accomplished by the same set of ruffians, who made this section of the city hideous with their outrages for the space of three or four hours. Near the corner of Washington and Rector streets there is a large tenement and boarding house, occupied mainly by the poorest of the poor, against whom the rioters could by no possibility have even a pretended cause for hostility. On the lower floor, however, is a groggery, and in that commenced the row, which came near terminating in a most fearful calamity.

Having effected an entrance to the bar room the rioters made free with everything within reach, and then began to upset the liquor upon the floor. This the man in charge endeavored to prevent, but he was hustled into the street in short order, and the cry was raised, "Fire it! Fire it!" As is well known, but a spark is needed to set such tinder as these mobs are composed of into the most furious flames, and acting upon the suggestion they began to suit the action to the word.

Luckily, the main body of the gang had gone off into Greenwich street, "blackberrying," as they facetiously term their negro hunts, and but ten or a dozen of the fellows were left. These, however, proceeded to kindle a fire upon the bar room floor, when suddenly, and to their entire surprise, the barkeeper, accompanied by some half a dozen friends and neighbors, rushed in upon them and clubbed them most unmercifully. One of the rioters was so injured about the head and neck that he was unable to skedaddle with his friends, and was left upon the bar room floor, surrounded by broken bottles, puddles of rotgut and charred chips, until toward daybreak, when the liberal doucings of water he received and the fearful amount of brandy he was made to swallow, started up his faculties, and he was permitted to go in peace.

During the progress of the row the families in the upper part of the house became terribly alarmed and excited. They threw many of their effects from the windows and prepared to evacuate in full force. Had the fire been kept alive but a few moments longer, the house and all in it, and the tinder block which adjoins it, must have gone the way of destruction.

In the meantime the larger portion of the gang went from shop to shop "helling around" for no particular purpose, but just having a good time generally.

There was no one to stop them in their course, all the police being needed elsewhere, and they managed to scare all the women, batter a great many inoffending citizens, destroy any quantities of lager and other "beverages," and stir up the locality in a way which was new, startling and slightly disagreeable.

During the remainder of the day this portion of the city was very quiet, several gangs of men marched from the docks up toward the Park, and on further up town, but molested no one down town, nor did they create disturbance of any kind.

Toward eight o'clock this morning, a

NEGRO WAS CHASED

by a mob of half-grown men, every one of whom looked like a jail bird, from Burling Slip through South street, by the Fulton Ferry, and to the corner of Peck Slip. At this point, the man stumbled and his pursuers pounced on him with fiendish yells of triumph. In a struggle which ensued, the poor fellow got away again, and ran several yards, when the crowd again caught him, and beat him most unmercifully.

It seemed for a time as though the man's life was good for but a brief season, but fortunately for him a number of sailors belonging to vessels in the vicinity hearing the disturbance and the cries of the negro, rushed out from the eating house and charged the cowardly assailants pell mell and in true sailor style. As is always the case with miscreants, who war upon single individuals, the rioters were arrant cowards and ran from the stalwart thrashings of the men of the seas as if they had been whipped dogs. The negro was taken into the eating house, a glass of brandy was given him and he was sent home under a convoy of two of the noblest hearted men we have heard of in many a day.

In the house where this colored man lives there are five colored families, and of the seven men over nineteen years of age, five have been overhauled by mobs and cruelly beaten. The normal fruits of this savage treatment has not yet appeared. We have not seen a single negro who counseled opposition or spoke of revenge.

ONE OF THE MOST TERRIFIC FEATURES

of this riot was the double murder, which was committed yesterday morning, in Thirty-second street, near Sixth avenue. The facts, as gathered from a reliable reporter, are these, and as there are many exaggerations of the affair in circulation, which will, if believed, certainly cause trouble and bloodshed, we have taken great pains to get at the exact truth:

At half after six yesterday morning a middle-aged negro, named Potter or Porter, was passing quietly down Thirty-second street, near the avenue, when he was met by a fireman, an ex-Zouave, named Manney, who hailed him, asking where he was going. The negro, not understanding, apparently, what was said, made no reply, and Manney, with the most kind intentions, told him that the excitement was still very great, that the mobs would certainly be around to-day, and would doubtless kill him or severely beat him, if they should catch him. Still, apparently misapprehending Manney's intentions, and probably misunderstanding his language, the negro drew a revolver and discharged it with fatal effect. He shot twice certainly, each ball striking Manney full in the forehead, and entering his brain. He then started to run, but was soon overtaken by a crowd of excited and infuriated people, and by several of the firemen residing near by, who chased him a short distance, and soon overtook him.

The heart sickens at the recollection of the fearful and

DREADFUL SCENE

which followed. The negro was pounded, battered, kicked, pummeled, stoned, thrown down, trampled upon, and fairly bruised into jelly. A bloody pulp was all that was left of the mistaken murderer in a very few moments; but even this was considered slight revenge, and the mutilated mass of blood and bones and quivering flesh was carried brutally to a tree, to a limb of which it was hung, amid the cheers and jeers of the indignant crowd.

Poor Manney had the best of medical attendance, but probably for naught. Dr. Brooks, who was called to dress his wounds, declared that the case was a hopeless one, and that he would not probably live an hour. He was taken to Bellevue Hospital, and is probably gone to his last account long since.

In the tenement house where Manney lived, and in which some say the negro also lived, resided several Irish and negro families. Until now there has been but little trouble between them; in fact the house has been one of the most quiet tenement houses of the neighborhood. Since the present "uprising of the people," however, there has been considerable ill feeling, and during the day before yesterday the white families were moving out. Regardless of any fact, however, save the one all-convincing one that negroes were in the house, the crowd, which by this time had assumed the proportions of a mob, surrounded the building, and having saluted it with yells of unequalled fury and rage, set fire to it, and then moved on to other scenes of violence. Fortunately the fire was extinguished before it had got fairly under way, and the additional horror was thus spared.

In the afternoon about 3 o'clock, a large mob, among whom are many of the men who "assisted" at the foregoing outrage, gathered in the rear of the premises No. 147 East Twenty-eighth street, and inaugurated a renewal of

NEGRO OUTRAGES

which, for barbarity and recklessness of life and property, exceed anything before attempted. In the alley-way which leads from that point, reside a small colony of negroes, numbering in all about twenty-five families. To drive these people out and destroy their local habitation, was the least brutal of the intentions of the mob, which, with shoutings and profanity which do dishonor to the infernal regions, rushed unannounced into the very presence of their victims. Very many of the negroes had run off, but enough remained to invite the outrageous indecencies of the mob. For some minutes their search for the colored people was in vain, but they soon found one whom they

MURDERED WITH A CROWBAR

in the following manner: Van Clef (the negro) was found crouching behind a bedstead by two young men, one of whom had a large crowbar in his hand. The negro was at once hauled into the middle of the room, when he was pulled about by the hair, kicked and beaten over the head and finally punched and pounded with the crowbar until he was apparently lifeless. The crowd played with him for a little while, and then, as other victims were found, threw the mutilated and dying man into the alley, while they turned their attention to the other candidates for public notice. No other absolute murder was committed here, but many poor creatures were mercilessly beaten and thoroughly used up, so that when the crowd left them there was but little choice between life and death in their appearance or sensations.

From this place the mob went into Broadway alley, into a house kept by a black man named Dudley. They threw the furniture into the street and beat Dudley so badly about the head and chest, that he was not expected to survive. The women were frightened, as well they might be, out of their senses, and ran to and fro, crying for help and begging for protection, while their husbands and sons were beaten and murdered, their homes destroyed and their dwellings set on fire. Their attempts to save some of their goods were set at naught by the mob, and after suffering much from the brutal treatment of the rioters, they started with their little ones for the Central Office to seek a lodging and a protection from further violence.

TERRIBLE SCENES IN NINETEENTH STREET.

Over One Hundred Killed and Wounded.

At about 8 o'clock, as about one hundred citizens and returned soldiers, all armed, under the command of Col. Cleveland Winslow, late of the Duryee Zouaves, were passing through Nineteenth street, near Second avenue, they were attacked by a large number of rioters. Brickbats and other missiles were hurled upon them from the housetops. One man who had followed Col. Winslow's force, and had repeatedly fired into the ranks, was shot by one of the volunteer soldiers, who stepped from the ranks, leveled his musket and fired. The man dropped, and was left lying in the street. Two howitzers were then loaded and fired into the crowd, making great havoc and causing them to retire down First avenue. Col. Jardine, late of Hawkins' Zouaves, was severely wounded by a shot in the leg, and was taken to a house in 19th street, which the crowd afterward threatened to attack and take possession of the wounded officer. By a charge made upon Col. Winslow's force, one captain, one lieutenant and fifteen privates of his command were killed. Col. Winslow charged five distinct times upon the crowd. The effect of these charges were most terrific, the street was strewn with bodies, at least twenty or thirty dead and fifty wounded. As soon as the crowd dispersed, Col. Winslow came to the Central Office and reported the result of the engagement, which was the most desperate which has taken place since the commencement of the riots in the city. Capt. Ukell and Lieut. Brown were killed; Lieut. Upton and Col. Jardine were shot in the groin. Col. Winslow, as soon the crowd was driven off, marched his men down the Second avenue to Fourteenth street, thence to Third avenue, and thence to the Seventh Regiment Armory, to await further orders. He first reported to Gov. Seymour, at the St. Nicholas, and was ordered by the Governor to report to Gen. Brown, at Headquarters.

General Brown, as soon as the particulars of the fight were related to him, ordered a company of regulars, 200 men, commanded by Captains Putnam, Shelley and Rowolle, and a large body of policemen, to the scene of the slaughter, with instructions to use every effort to procure the body of Colonel Jardine and take it to a place of safety. The military carried two field pieces.

The Regulars arrived upon the ground about 10 o'clock. An immense crowd was found waiting to give them a warm reception. The house into which Col Jardine was taken, after he had received his wound, was surrounded by the rioters, who refused to disperse until they had contested the position with the soldiers. Capt. Putnam then ordered his men to turn the howitzers upon the crowd. The pieces, two in number, were loaded with canister and orders were at once given to fire. The artillerists then poured their death-dealing volley upon the crowd, which dispersed rapidly, bearing off their killed and wounded. The soldiers now marched to the house in the cellar of which Col. Jardine was lying, and removed the wounded man to a carriage in which he was taken to headquarters and afterward to the St. Nicholas, where he was attended by several physicians, who pronounced his situation extremely critical. Both of his legs were broken and he was severely wounded by a musket ball in the body. The other wounded officers were also taken to the St. Nicholas.

Frightful Scenes in 11th Avenue.

The following account, taken from the lips of an eye-witness, of a mission undertaken and successfully carried through by Judge McCunn on yesterday afternoon, presents the most astounding revelation of affairs in our city which has yet been presented to our readers:

It seems that Governor Seymour, who is doing all that he can to restore the quiet and peace of our city, sent for Judge McCunn yesterday afternoon, and after consultation with him upon the state of affairs in the upper districts of the city requested him to make a grand tour through the disaffected districts, that the true state of the internal sentiment of the people might be ascertained, and that so far as was possible, he (Judge McCunn) might allay the apprehensions of the citizens, and induce them to return to their ordinary avocations, and keep the peace of the city and county.

This mission, dangerous as it would seem to be, the Judge cheerfully undertook, and having ordered a carriage, drove first to the scene of the morning's conflict, concerning which, the most astounding accounts were circulating, all of which were calculated to do great damage to the cause of "law and order."

He first went to the corner of

SEVENTH AVENUE AND TWENTY-NINTH STREET.

where quite a large crowd had assembled, evidently intending to do further damage to the body of a negro who was crouching piteously at the foot of a large tree. A body of military under charge of a Lieutenant, whose name he did not gather, was stationed there, and the preparatory movements toward firing upon the crowd had been made when the Judge called out in an authoritative manner, "Lieutenant, don't fire!"

Col. Myers, under whose superior command the force was, demanded the name of the interrupter and wanted to know by what authority he presumed to interfere with the operations of the soldiers.

The Judge replied that he was the City Judge of New York and had come as a special messenger from Gov. Seymour; that he believed the crowd would be more easily dispersed by a word from him than by a volley from the soldiers, and that, if the Colonel had no objections, he would try the experiment and save the shedding of innocent blood.

The Colonel, of course, agreed to this course, and Judge McCunn, stepping forward, spoke as follows:

SPEECH OF JUDGE M'CUNN.

MY FRIENDS: You should not remain here longer. You are here for no lawful purpose, and I counsel you as your friend, to go to your quiet homes. You know who I am, and you know full well that to the extent of my power I will, as I always have, protect you. [Cheers.] Gov. Seymour [Cheers for Seymour] is in the city; he has already appealed to the President to retrace his steps in regard to the draft and has secured its suspension. The Courts yesterday afternoon decided that the draft was unlawful. [Applause] and if it is your pleasure, I will read you that decision. ["Go on, old boy."] (The Judge here read the decision rendered by him at Chambers, on Tuesday, which was received with cheers and applause.) Now, my friends, I have a message from the Governor.

The Governor, who is the people's friend, now as ever, has instructed me as his messenger, to say to you, that he will sustain the decision of the Courts of the State to his very utmost power: that the rights of no citizen shall be trampled upon, that if you are true and good men you will respect his advice, his counsel, and request that you go at once to your homes, and participate no further in these lawless proceedings. [Applause.]

At the conclusion of the Judge's speech the crowd slowly dispersed, giving cheers now and then for him and for the Governor.

For some unaccountable reason two of the soldiers discharged their muskets before the crowd had fully obeyed the direction of Judge McCunn, and immediately thereafter screams were heard from a large tenement house in the vicinity, and it was reported and believed that a man was killed. The Colonel promptly disarmed the soldiers and put them under arrest.

In the Eleventh avenue the Judge found a most terribly excited population. In many houses families were lamenting the death of husbands, sons and fathers from the effect of

THE MORNING'S FIGHT.

So near as the facts could be ascertained, the truth would seem to be that early in the day all along that portion of the avenue groups of men, women and children, gathered for the various purposes of discussion and observation. About noon, two companies of artillery passed along, making no disturbance, and causing no excitement. At 3 o'clock, or in that neighborhood, a force of soldiery marched up, under command (it was said) of Lieut. Ryer, whose presence attracted a still greater crowd, and called forth some hostile demonstrations.

Whatever may have been the immediate cause (and concerning this there are so many conflicting stories that we prefer to give none), the fact is that the troops

FIRED UPON THE CROWD

with fatal effect, instantly

KILLING SOME THIRTY

people, men, women and children. The effect was immediate, and the frightened people took to their houses and other shelter without waiting a second encounter.

The following is as correct a

LIST OF KILLED

as can be procured, and is long enough and fearful enough to enforce the advice and request of the Governor, as well as of all right-minded men, that the people would much better disperse and go quietly to their homes, than by riotous demonstration draw upon themselves and their families such fearful punishment as this.

Michael Ryan, Eleventh avenue, killed.
Daniel Kiernan, Eleventh avenue, killed.
Patrick Garvey, Eleventh avenue, killed.
John Grey, Forty-second street, killed.
John Kearney, Eleventh avenue, killed.
Patrick Quinn, Eleventh avenue, killed.
James Garrett, Eleventh avenue, killed.
Mrs. Thornton, Eleventh avenue, shot through the heart.
Child of Mrs. Thornton, Eleventh avenue, shot through both legs.
Patrick Casey, Eleventh avenue, killed.
Mrs. Lawrence, Eleventh avenue, killed.
Two Germans, names unknown, Forty-second street, killed.
Two Germans, names unknown, Forty-third street, killed.
Mrs. Lawrence and child, Eleventh avenue, killed
Mrs. Kirtland, Eleventh avenue, killed.
Richard Stafford, Eleventh avenue, killed.
C. Larkin, Eleventh avenue, killed.
Woman, name unknown, killed.
Lawrence Ryan, Eleventh avenue, killed.
Mr. Ackley, Eleventh avenue, killed.

The above twenty-three names are all that could be obtained up to the hour of going to press, but it is known that several others were mortally wounded. The greatest consternation prevails in the neighborhood, the women and children filling the air with their cries and lamentations, while the men who were happily spared from the dreadful fate of their friends and companions sat mournful and sullen.

The people, with what degree of fairness we know not, charge that the firing was reckless and wholly unjustifiable, but what the truth of the matter is, nothing but a legal investigation can determine.

At the request of Major General Sandford, Judge McCunn went over to the arsenal, whose adjacent precincts are picketted, sentinelled, and guarded with all the paraphernalia of war and strife.

While they were talking, firing was heard, and the General suggested that the mob was firing upon the pickets. Judge McCunn volunteered to go out and ascertain. He went to the corner of Thirty-first street and Seventh avenue (at 8 o'clock in the evening) in company with the Captain, and found that the pickets had been firing without orders. They were at once disarmed, placed under arrest and sent to the arsenal.

While the Captain and Judge McCunn were talking, a man named Henry Schultz, who said that he was a member of the Seventh regiment, came up to them and joined in the conversation. At this time, a woman started to cross the street; she was ordered back by Schultz; she continued her course, when Schultz levelled his gun, fired at her, and

SHOT HER DEAD.

in her tracks. The most intense excitement prevailed at once, and great trouble was anticipated, and would undoubtedly have ensued had not the murderer been instantly disarmed and sent to the Arsenal under arrest. The woman, whose name was Mrs. Thornton, was taken into an adjoining house, while a very natural gloom settled upon one and all.

A representation of these facts having been made to Gen. Sandford, he called in all the pickets and replaced them by others who were cautioned and counseled as to their duties and responsibilities by the General before they were sent out.

On the corner of Twenty-eighth street and Seventh avenue Judge McCunn, who was accompanied by Mr. Dunn, saw a large crowd gathered about a tree on which

HUNG THE BODY OF A NEGRO.

With his own knife Judge McCunn cut the rope which held the yet animate sufferer by the neck, and directed some men whom he recognized in the assemblage to take him into a house and care for him. This was done, and the Judge addressed the crowd in terms very similar to those in which he spoke before and accomplished the same results.

The above report was made to Governor Seymour by Judge McCunn in person. The Governor congratulated him on the good service he had done, and indorsed all that he had promised in his behalf.

A more extraordinary night's work has probably not been recorded in the annals of this most extraordinary outbreak of the people.

The Thirteenth Ward.

A mob gathered yesterday afternoon in Grand street, at the head of Mangin street, for the purpose of repeating some of the scenes of the previous night. Word was immediately brought to the Thirteenth Precinct Station House, when the police, under the command of Capt. Steers, proceeded to the scene of disturbance. When they arrived they were hooted by the mob, and some stones were thrown at them, when they immediately charged upon the mob, whom they succeeded in dispersing and arresting two of the ringleaders, named John Maher, who had a loaded pistol in his possession, and Francis Lamb. The arrests were made by Officer Johnson and Roundsman Holden, of the Thirteenth Precinct.

The police of the Thirteenth Precinct, under Capt. Steers, are patroling the Ward, and bringing all those who have had the misfortune to be born black to a place of safety, until the excitement shall have passed over.

A military vigilance committee, composed of citizens under command of Captain Huston, formerly of the Twelfth regiment N. Y. S. N. G., is forming in the Thirteenth Ward. Their headquarters are at the Thirteenth Precinct Station House. Already 400 names are enrolled. The following are the officers: William. H. Huston, Captain: John J. Tooker. Lieutenant; Bernard Rody, formerly of Wilson's Zouaves, Lieutenant; Frank Snyder, Lieutenant; Joseph T. Ellery, Lieutenant. They are to do duty under Captain Steers, of the Thirteenth Precinct Police, about 100 of whom, armed with muskets, patrol the ward.

In the Seventh Ward there is also another large armed patrol of citizens patrolling the ward.

Scenes at Harlem Bridge.

In Harlem and Yorkville all was quiet up to 12 o'clock. It was rumored that an attempt would be made to burn the bridge over the Harlem River, but the report was not verified up to the hour at which our reporter left Harlem. All the streets approaching the bridge were strongly guarded at favorable points, and long lines of policemen extended from the bridge to the different points where an attack was expected.

A large number of special officers were on duty, and strong detachments of these, intermingled with the regular police, were stationed at short intervals on all the avenues of approach. Near One Hundred and Twenty-sixth street, about one hundred men of the Twelfth Regular Infantry were stationed, ready to fall in at a moment's notice. The utmost vigilance was exercised to prevent any persons, not properly authorized, from approaching the bridge. Every carriage passing was closely examined, and any passer-by, who was unable to give an account of himself, was summarily arrested. Up to a late hour no disturbance was apprehended in this locality.

Firemen's Organization in the First Ward.

All is quiet here at 11 o'clock, P. M. Alder-

CONTINUED ON EIGHTH PAGE.

INVASION OF PENNSYLVANIA—BATTLE OF GETTYSBURG,

INVASION OF PENNSYLVANIA—BATTLE OF GETTYSBURG, THURSDAY EVENING, JULY 2, AS SEEN FROM ROCKY HILL, ON MEADE'S LEFT.—From a Sketch by our Special Artist, Edwin Forbes

ING, JULY 3.—From a Sketch by our Special Artist, Edwin Forbes.

INVASION OF PENNSYLVANIA—ACTION AT WRIGHTSVILLE AND DESTRUCTION OF THE COLUMBIA RAILROAD BRIDGE, JUNE 28.—From a Sketch by our Special Artist, A. Berghaus.

The Charleston Mercury.

DAILY PAPER—TWENTY DOLLARS PER ANNUM, PAYABLE HALF-YEARLY IN ADVANCE.

VINDICE NULLO
SPONTE SUA SINE LEGE FIDES RECTUMQUE COLENTUR.

COUNTRY PAPER—THRICE A WEEK—TEN DOLLARS PER ANNUM, IN ADVANCE.

VOLUME LXXXIII — CHARLESTON, S. C., MONDAY, JULY 20, 1863. — NUMBER 11,811

TELEGRAPHIC NEWS.

FROM GENERAL LEE'S ARMY.

WINCHESTER, July 17.—All quiet in the army. Nothing from the enemy. Heavy skirmishing today at Shepherdstown. The enemy attacked our cavalry with cavalry and artillery, and after a severe fight they were repulsed, leaving their dead and wounded on the field. We captured 17 prisoners and a number of horses. Our army is in splendid condition; but few sick, and no stragglers. General PETTIGREW is dead.

RICHMOND, July 18.—A special despatch to the *Whig*, dated Bunker Hill, 17th, says the cavalry fight yesterday, at Shepherdstown, lasted several hours, resulting in the defeat of the enemy, who retired to Harper's Ferry.

NEWS FROM RICHMOND.

RICHMOND, July 19.—Nothing of importance has transpired to-day. The chief topic of talk is the arrest of Mrs. ALLAN, wife of Mr. PATTERSON ALLAN, on a charge of communicating information to the enemy. The accused is a native of Ohio, and became united by marriage (in Europe) with one of the most wealthy and respectable families of Richmond. Letters written by her, to be forwarded by blockade runners, constitute the evidence of her guilt.

An officer from the Valley this evening states that MEADE's army is still in Maryland. The Yankee cavalry advanced on the 18th from Williamsport to within four miles of Martinsburg.

FROM THE WEST.

ATLANTA, July 18.—The *Appeal* has a special despatch from Okolona, which says that the Federals at Corinth are preparing six days' rations. A raid southward is anticipated.

On Sunday last the gunboats were repulsed at Yazoo City; subsequently the position was abandoned. The garrison has joined JOHNSTON'S army.

FROM EUROPE AND THE NORTH.

RICHMOND, July 18.—The Paris correspondent of the London *Times* says, on the authority of private letters from Madrid, that proposals for recognition have been made in behalf of the Southern States to the Spanish Government, with the sanction of the French Emperor.

The Chancellor of the Exchequer moved a vote of £100,000 for the purchase of an exhibition building at Bermington. After a stormy discussion, the vote was rejected, by a majority against the Government of 186. The result was received with loud cheering.

The debate in the British Parliament resulted in Mr. ROEBUCK's motion for the recognition of the Confederate States being adjourned to the 18th.

ROEBUCK stated in Parliament that the Emperor NAPOLEON had authorized him to say to the House of Commons that he (the Emperor) had instructed Baron GROS to propose a negotiation to the English Government, with a view to mediation in America. The London *Herald* says it was reported that RUSSELL had resigned on account of a disagreement with the Premier on the subject of the recognition of the South.

A block of warehouses in Liverpool and a large quantity of cotton was destroyed by fire. The loss was estimated at from £1,000,000 to £2,000,000 sterling.

A telegram to the Baltimore *American*, dated New York, 15th, says that the "rioters gutted about a dozen houses last night. This morning, a small row occurred in Cedar-street, but the police dispersed the ruffians. There was a serious riot at Staten Island last night, and six negros were killed. A perfect reign of terror prevailed. There was considerable disturbance in Brooklyn to-day, and the negros were horribly maltreated. Quite a number of troops are arriving. The general impression at this hour—noon of Wednesday—is that the worst is over, the mob fearing the tried troops from the seat of war. A large number of families have removed from the city and the exodus is unabated."

In Newark, N. J., on Tuesday, the office of the *Daily Mercury*, an Abolition sheet, was gutted by the mob.

The *Tribune*, of the 15th, is very severe on the *Herald* and *World*, and charges that their counsels excited the riot in that city. There is not a word of comment on the outbreak in the *Herald*, except a preface to a description of the scenes. GREELEY made a narrow escape on the first day. The crowd was informed that he was dining at WINDUST's, and they proceeded to that place. GREELEY was apprised of their approach, and escaped in a hack. Several men, supposed to be reporters for the *Tribune*, were severely handled—one killed. After making due allowance for the sensational reports in the New York papers, it is evident that the riot was the most formidable outbreak of the kind that ever occurred on this continent. It will encourage similar demonstrations in other Northern cities.

LOUISVILLE, July 8.—The steamers *Alice Dean* and *J. S. McCombs* were captured by about 200 rebels at Bradensburg, K., yesterday afternoon. Gunboats are in pursuit.

FOREIGNERS AND CONSULS.—Judge W. G. JONES, of the Confederate Court for Alabama, has lately given, at Mobile, a judgment and opinion on the liability of alien residents to the conscription. As to foreigners and Consuls, he says:

The petitioner, McKinn, produces a *certificate*, dated at Mobile, 26th May, 1863, signed by her Britannic Majesty's acting Consul at Mobile, and under the Consular seal, to the effect, that the acting Consul "has *good reason to believe*, after careful examination, that the bearer, Peter McKinn, a native of Monaghan county, who has never forfeited his claim to the protection of the Queen by becoming a subject, or a citizen of any foreign State or country whatsoever."

It is not for any Court to determine whether foreign Consuls are properly here or not. It is exclusively for the President to recognize foreign Ministers and Consuls, and when he recognizes a person as properly exercising the functions of a foreign Consul the Courts are bound to recognize him as such. Nor is it necessary, in these cases, to inquire into the powers and duties of Consuls. These powers are generally prescribed by laws and treaties. I know of no law or treaty which authorizes a foreign Consul to exempt any person domiciled in this country from obedience to our laws. The Consul's certificate, in this case, does not pretend to do any such thing. It merely states the *belief* of the Consul that the party named in it is a British subject, and as such entitled to the protection of the Queen. It is notice to any person to whom it is shown that the Consul considers him a British subject, and nothing more. If the person having such a certificate is really, and in fact liable, by law, to conscription, the certificate, would not of itself exempt him. But it seems to me that an enrolling officer ought to respect such a certificate so far as not to enroll the person having it without first making inquiries, and obtaining such information as satisfies him that the party is really a permanent resident of this country and liable to conscription.

The Mobile Tribune says the decision of Judge Jones in the Confederate States Court, respecting the liability of aliens, is regarded as one of the most important decisions that have yet been given, and will have a wonderful effect in bringing about a change in matters generally. For there is any quantity of these people who have resided in this city, married here, and have been doing business for years, and since the war have sworn that they never intended to become citizens, and were granted exemptions on this oath—men who are now engaged in every branch of speculation, and doing more to depreciate our currency than any other class in the community. We are told that there are hundreds in the interior who travel from towns to farms, buying up all the produce that they can get hold of and shipping it to the cities on speculation, which is partly the excuse for the exorbitant prices we have been paying all winter. Now that the Judge has declared them liable to conscription, the country will probably be rid of them, so far as their "business" qualifications are concerned at least.

THE MERCURY.

MONDAY, JULY 20, 1863.

The Struggle for Charleston.

The result of the tremendous bombardment and desperate assault of Saturday is exceedingly gratifying—not more from the glorious and bloody defeat of the enemy's designs, than from the small loss sustained by us in men and by the unimpaired condition of Fort Wagner. Let us not, however, deceive ourselves by the pleasing illusion that we have accomplished anything further than inflicting a heavy loss on the enemy and gaining time. So long as Monitors and the wooden gunboats are allowed to approach, the work is still exposed to a concentric fire of nearly half a circle by sea and land from the heavy artillery of the foe. His sharpshooters, too, are in occupation of rifle pits only some six hundred yards off. Renewed assaults at times and in ways of his own selection, it is still in his power to attempt. New batteries and new guns are likely to be put in position—perhaps means of reducing the fort other than either bombardment or assault may be tried. It is plain that men, materials, scientific labors and military contrivances will be exhausted by the active, scientific and ambitious commander of the Yankee forces in this Department. Either great exertions will have to be used to enable Battery Wagner to fight the battle of Charleston—to cope with the foe and beat him off successfully as long as he sees fit to attack, or the fight for the possession of Charleston harbor must be made elsewhere than on Morris Island, and by prompt and vigorous preparations. These questions, of course, we leave to the wisdom and experience of our military authorities to decide and meet. We wish merely to let our people see where we are, and the value of the great and glorious engagement of the 18th instant. While rejoicing with gratitude to God for this victory, we should not encourage false hopes and expectations. We should rather, by a knowledge of the truth, stimulate to every exertion for the lasting preservation of Charleston.

Oaths of Allegiance, Pledges and Promises.

In the late General Orders from the War Department at Washington, very adroitly issued on the 3d of July, just in time to nullify such paroles of sick and wounded prisoners as General LEE had granted on the field, and to embarrass him with the necessity of guarding through a long march the numerous other prisoners in his hands, the following declarations are embraced, which meet the cases of thousands of Confederate citizens upon whom the detestable oath of allegiance to the Yankee Government has been imposed by "ill usage and cruelty" or the fear of them, which is the same thing. According to these declarations all oaths taken, and all pledges and paroles given to avoid incarceration or secure release from imprisonment, or to protect property, or avoid any other sort of ill usage, are to be held as "not binding." The passages read as follows:

Any pledge or parole of honor extorted from a prisoner by ill usage or cruelty is not binding.

The obligations imposed by the general laws and usages of war upon the combatant inhabitants of a section of country passed over by an invading army close when the military occupation ceases, and any pledge or parole given by such persons, in regard to future service, is null and of no effect.

The Case of the Alexandra.

The decision of the British Court in the case of the *Alexandra*, puts an end to Mr. ADAMS' operations, through his spies, peering and prying into every British ship yard to ascertain if there were any ships building for the Confederate States. The decision gives perfect liberty to every shipbuilder to build as many ships as he pleases for the South. It will highly irritate the Yankees; but the English Court fortified itself by the highest Federal authority. It sustained its decision by citing the opinion of Judge STORY, who "laid it down that, although by the terms of the Foreign Enlistment Act a neutral State was precluded from equipping or arming vessels for the purpose of aggression against a friendly power, they were not precluded from equipping and arming them for the purpose of sale, to any one, belligerent or otherwise, who chose to purchase them." This, the Court assumed, authorized a neutral to equip a ship of war just as he may construct a cannon, if he intends not to use or have it used against a friendly power, but merely to sell it; and he might even sell it to either of the belligerents. But in the case of the *Alexandra* the question was not as "to arming and equipping," the testimony only proving the "building" of the ship. The jury gave a verdict for the defendants very promptly.

THE YANKEES IN NORTH CAROLINA.—The Kinston (N. C.) correspondent of the Raleigh *Journal* says that the Yankees at Newbern and Washington are organizing a force of mounted infantry, 3,000 strong, composed of whites and blacks, to advance simultaneously on both sides of the Neuse river. He adds:

I also learned last night, from a most reliable gentleman, who came up from below on yesterday, that the enemy are moving the most of their valuables from Newbern to Morehead City, as if they intended to evacuate the former place very soon, and take up their quarters at the latter place. Two heavy trains, loaded with ordnance stores, etc., were seen to leave the Newbern depot for Morehead City on last Thursday.

GENERAL EWELL STRUCK IN THE BATTLE OF GETTYSBURG.—During the battle of Gettysburg General Ewell reining in his horse and calling one of his aids to him said: "I have been struck; assist me to alight."

Having helped him from his horse, the aid inquired where the General had been hit.

"Here," said General Ewell, pointing to his wooden leg, "I'll trouble you to hand me my other leg."

The fractured artificial limb having been removed, and a fresh one put on in its place, the brave old General remounted his horse, and again rode to the front.

MAJOR GENERAL WHITING assumes command of the Department of North Carolina, with his Headquarters at Wilmington.

The Late Colonel DeSaussure.

Colonel WILLIAM DAVIE DESAUSSURE, 15th Regiment S. C. V., was killed on the 2d of July 1863, at the battle of Gettysburg. Descended upon both the paternal and maternal sides from Revolutionary ancestry, he fell a martyr to the cause of Southern Independence. He was a grandson of the late Chancellor DESAUSSURE, and the eldest son of Honorable WILLIAM F. DESAUSSURE, and SARAH, daughter of the late General WILLIAM DAVIE, and was born in Columbia, South Carolina, in 1819. He graduated at the South Carolina College in December, 1838, and after the necessary preparatory study was admitted to the bar. The Mexican war called into practice his strong military predisposition, and he raised a company for the Palmetto Regiment. From Vera Cruz to Garita de Belin he shared in the hardships of the campaign, and participated in every battle in which the Palmetto Regiment was engaged. Upon the close of that war he returned home, and was elected a member of the Legislature for Richland District. He then applied for and obtained a commission as Captain of Dragoons in the United States service. He was assigned to the 2d Regiment, and, with his command, was engaged in the Utah Expedition. While serving in the West he formed the acquaintance of General JOSEPH E. JOHNSTON, who conceived of him a favorable opinion as an officer, and expresses of him cordial feeling as a friend. At the time of the secession of his native State he was stationed near the Rocky Mountains, but as early as he learned what had occurred promptly resigned his commission, and by an arduous journey of over five hundred miles through the snow, returned to South Carolina. By Governor PICKENS he was appointed Major of a squadron of cavalry, and actively engaged in enlisting what now constitutes Major LUCAS' Battalion. Desirous of more active service than then appeared probable with that battalion, he resigned his commission, and sought to unite himself with another organization. In September, 1861, he was elected and commissioned Colonel of the 15th Regiment S. C. V. At the battle of Port Royal his regiment was the infantry support of the garrison. After several months of service on the sea coast of South Carolina his regiment was sent to the Army of the Potomac, and with that army he shared in the arduous campaign into Maryland, and was an active participant in the battles of Boonsboro and Sharpsburg. In this second campaign he is believed to have fallen.

Colonel DESAUSSURE was an amiable man. He was a firm friend, and a devoted brother, son, and husband. A high regard for truth was one of his eminent characteristics; and he scorned all that was dishonorable. He was constitutionally a brave man, and his spirit instinctively revolted at injustice or oppression.

THE NEW CALL FOR TROOPS.

The following is the proclamation of the President, extending the call under the Conscript Act, to embrace all residents of the Confederacy, between 18 and 45 years, not legally exempt. Under the terms of the proclamation and rulings of the Confederate Courts, foreigners, who are actual residents, will be called upon to do military service in defence of the country in which they reside:

PROCLAMATION BY THE PRESIDENT.

Whereas, it is provided by an act of Congress, entitled "an act to further provide for the public defence," approved on the 16th day of April, 1862, and by another act of Congress, approved on the 27th September, 1862, entitled "an act to amend an act entitled an act to provide further for the public defence, approved 16th April, 1862," that the President be authorized to call out and place in the military service of the Confederate States, for three years, unless the war shall have been sooner ended, all white men who are residents of the Confederate States, between the ages of eighteen and forty-five years, at the time the call may be made, and who are not, at such time, legally exempted from military service, or such part thereof as in his judgment may be necessary to the public defence.

And whereas, in my judgment the necessities of the public defence require that every man capable of bearing arms, between the ages aforesaid, should now be called out to do his duty in the defence of his country and in driving back the invaders now within the limits of the Confederacy:

Now, therefore, I, Jefferson Davis, President of the Confederate States of America, do, by virtue of the powers vested in me aforesaid, call out and place in the military service of the Confederate States, all white men residents of said States between the ages of eighteen and forty five years, not legally exempted from military service; and I do hereby order and direct that all persons subject to this call and not now in the military service, do, upon being enrolled, forthwith repair to the conscript camps established in their respective States of which they may be residents, under pain of being held and punished as deserters in the event of their failure to obey this call, as provided in said laws.

And I do further order and direct, that the enrolling officers of the several States proceed at once to enroll all persons embraced within the terms of this proclamation, and not heretofore enrolled.

And I do further order, that it shall be lawful for any person embraced within this call to volunteer for service before enrollment, and that persons so volunteering be allowed to select the arm of service and the company which they desire to join, provided such company be deficient in the full number of men allowed by law for its organization.

Given under my hand, and the Seal of the Confederate States of America, at the city of [SEAL.] Richmond, this fifteenth day of July, in the year of our Lord one thousand eight hundred and sixty-three.

(Signed) JEFFERSON DAVIS.

By the President:
(Signed)
J. P. BENJAMIN, Secretary of State.

IRON SHIPBUILDING ON THE MERSEY.—There are now in course of construction no less than twenty-three vessels of various sizes, not including gunboats for the Emperor of China, and the frigate for the English Government at Birkenhead. An improvement in the building of ships has lately been introduced, and the reports from the experimental vessels are very satisfactory indeed. We refer to the building of vessels of steel. It gives ships double the strength of iron with plates just one-half the thickness, thus allowing them to carry a cargo on a considerably less draft of water; it is also stronger than iron, and being of such light substance the vessels can be built with finer lines. So satisfactory have the experiments been that a keel has been laid down to build a ship of 1000 tons for Messrs. C. S. Lemon & Co., to trade between this port and the East Indies. The steel fleet are the steamers Banshee and Phantom (the latter now loading at this port for Nassau), and the schooner Domitila, now on her way to the Sandwich Islands. Mr. Laird has also on hand the two gunboats for the Emperor of China, but about whose ultimate destination so much has been said. They are in a very forward state, and their launch may soon be looked for. Some of the plates used are five inch ones, and are bent to the requisite angle by hydraulic power. The vessels are beautiful specimens of naval architecture, and very stong, built in Mr. Laird's well known style, and will certainly add efficiently to a fleet in either the China or Confederate waters. From these it will be seen that the trade is at present unusually brisk, and will bear favorable comparison with any other part of the Kingdom.—*Liverpool Journal of Commerce, June 3d.*

THE INVASION OF PENNSYLVANIA—THE BATTLE OF GETTYSBURG—THE RETREAT TO HAGERSTOWN.

The Richmond *Examiner* furnishes us with the following extract of a letter from an officer of the Army of Northern Virginia. It contains the only connected and intelligible account that has yet been given to the public of the movements of General LEE from his crossing of the Potomac to his return to Hagerstown, after the battle of Gettysburg.

THE GREAT PENNSYLVANIA CAMPAIGN.

"The advance of the Second corps crossed into Maryland on Thursday, June 18th, near Shepherdstown. Gen. Rhodes had already crossed below Martinsburg, and was occupying Hagerstown. General Jenkins was at Chambersburg, and Imboden about Cumberland. The Second corps (excepting Rhodes' division) occupied the battle-field of Antietam the 20th, 21st and 22d of June, and marched beyond Hagerstown on the 23d. The reception of these gallant victors of Winchester all through the lower valley was refreshing, and at Shepherdstown fair ladies crowded the streets, and welcomed the soldiers with flowers and smiles. Sharpsburg was black Union, but Hagerstown turned out with joy at our approach. On the 24th the corps pushed on through Greencastle to Chambersburg. I should say here that Early bore off to Waynesboro', and was at York when the rest occupied Carlisle.

"At Greencastle and Chambersburg the stores were taken possession of by the Quartermaster, the contents seized, so far as they were useful to the army (*i. e.* to the Quartermaster) and appropriated according to an accurate distribution by Chief Quartermasters and Sub-Quartermasters. A Major General got a hat, but as to the rest, hats, shoes, boots, calicoes, whisky, for the most part, that great unfathomable sponge, the active Quartermaster's Department, got them. At Shippensburg the track of the railroad was torn up and a bridge burned. The citizens, who turned out in large numbers to witness the passage of the rebels, were generally quiet. Occasionally you found a spirited girl, or a spunky parson. But, if one fact was more remarkable than any other, it is this: That portion of Pennsylvania which our army occupied was completely subjugated, very few having the courage to raise their heads. Foraging thrived. For a little Confederate note, and often for nothing, a soldier could get quantities of onions, apple butter, cow butter, ham, good Dutch loaves, cheese, and every delightful thing in the grand category of the productions of the great Cumberland Valley.

"On Friday, 26th, we took up the line of march through Chambersburg, on the Harrisburg road. The splendid band in the 4th Louisiana brigade, Colonel Williams, preceded the column, playing "Dixie" and the Marseillaise, whilst our red-cross banners flaunted proudly over the dark columns of our gallant troops. The scene subjugated that town. We passed through Shippensburg to the sound of martial music again, and went on to Carlisle. The troops were not allowed to plunder. Horses were taken and receipted for by authorized agents. So with cattle and flour. Foraging was tolerated, but the soldiers were expected to pay for their supplies. It was thought, and perhaps rightly, that licensed plundering would demoralize the army, and render it useless for great achievements. But this was occasionally carried to absurd lengths. We overheard an officer, with lachrymose countenance, deprecating the destruction of a cherry tree by some hungry rebels. The burning of rails was at first prohibited, but after a day or two it was generally permitted.

"We staid long enough at Carlisle to get what we wanted. Harrisburg was in a panic—and some of our engineer officers went to the banks of the Susquehanna, and found them fortifying the enormous heights on the southern side. Early and Jenkins were at York, and beyond, seeing after the bridges up as far as the river, all of which were destroyed. On the 30th Johnson marched back from Carlisle to Fayetteville, leaving Rhodes at Carlisle. On Wednesday, July 1st, A. P. Hill marched from South Mountain to the neighborhood of Gettysburg, followed by Johnson. Early reached the same vicinity on the same day from York, and Rhodes from Carlisle. Meade's advance of three or four army corps disputed the occupation of the town, giving battle to the north and east of the town from 10 a. m. to about 5 p. m. The result was a glorious victory to the Confederates. The invincible and gallant Early drove the force opposed to him for miles, and occupied the town. The 11th Corps, of Chancellorsville memory, gave themselves up by thousands. Gordon's brigade made what is regarded a most brilliant charge. It could but be successful with such men and such a leader. The Fayetteville Road was "cleaned out" by Hill. Rhodes swept down the Carlisle Road, and Early down the York turnpike. The loss of the Confederates in killed and wounded was probably 600. The Yankee loss in killed probably reached 400 and his wounded 2000.—We captured most of his wounded and 5280 additional prisoners.

"Gettysburg is in Adams county, Pennsylvania, some where near eight miles from the South Mountain which is the eastern boundary of the Cumberland Valley. It is a beautiful town of some 5000 inhabitants, and the centre of the following roads: A road from Baltimore; a road from Frederick, both on the southern side of the town, and the three roads just mentioned; between these two former roads and about three-quarters of a mile from the town were two tall hills, one wooded and detached, the other the front of a range that swept backward to the south. These positions boldly commanded the town and vicinity, and Meade occupied them Wednesday, heavily entrenching during the night. On Thursday morning, Ewell's corps lay beneath the first eminence and near the Baltimore road; A. P. Hill occupied a position to the west of the town and near it. Longstreet was not yet up. During the morning, occasional artillery and infantry skirmishing alone broke the silence that hung over the expectant hosts. The day was warm and beautiful. The enemy's cavalry stretched up to the south of the York road, threatening our rear, but was closely watched by the indefatigable Stuart, whose recent seven days and nights march from the vicinity of Washington was the most wonderful cavalry achievement of the war.

"At last Longstreet having passed to the south of A. P. Hill, opened at four p. m., followed by Hill and Ewell. Then ensued undoubtedly the fiercest cannonade of the war. This terrific fire lasted till night. About dark Ewell charged the position on the wooded hill. The enemy had several lines on this eminence and cannon in position, with abattis and planted sticks in rows to prevent our advance. The sides of the hill were rocky and precipitous to almost an inaccessible degree. Our lines, however, gallantly marched up under a fearful fire of musket balls and grape. A partial advantage was gained by Johnson's troops, and lost by accident. But it was beyond mortal endurance to stand before that terrific blast of shot, and the men were withdrawn, after suffering heavy loss. During the afternoon, the other corps had attacked the positions on the south without success. On Friday, July 3d, the battle was renewed early in the morning, and, with the exception of a lull from ten o'clock a. m., to one o'clock p. m., lasted all day. The Confederates did not succeed in holding any of the crests, although one or two were reached; and night again closed on the smoke-wrapped field. From 3½ to 5 p. m., General Stuart succeeded in driving back, very handsomely, the enemy's cavalry threatening our rear. The fight was quite severe and loss unknown.

"Thus ended the great battle of Gettysburg, the most remarkable conflict of the war. The loss of the enemy was probably 25,000 men—perhaps 30,000 during the three days. He was severely handled—for it is believed that he fell back with the greater portion of his force on Friday night, towards Boonsboro'. When I turn from this to our own loss my heart sickens. It was frightful. The loss in general officers was remarkably great. I believe the following to be correct:

"Brigadier General Garnett, killed; Major-General Trimble, leg amputated and captured; Brigadier-General J. R. Jones, severely wounded; Brigadier-General Jones, of the cavalry, captured; Brigadier-General Archer, wounded and prisoner; Brigadier General Armistead, wounded and prisoner; Brigadier General Barksdale, mortally wounded and left; Brigadier-General Kemper, killed; Brigadier-General Jenkins, slightly wounded.

"The list of Colonels and other field officers lost is enormous. The field officers of the First Maryland battalion were severely wounded. All of the field officers of Pickett's division, except the commander and one Lieutenant-Colonel, are killed and wounded. This division was almost destroyed in one brilliant charge; and, as its gallant commander looked over the pitiful remnant of his brave boys, he bowed his head and wept like a child.

"All our wounded that could be transported were removed beyond the Potomac. Those severely wounded had to be left. The Confederate loss in killed, wounded and prisoners (of which there are few) must be *twenty thousand*.

"All day long of July 4th our army lay in line of battle, in a new position overlooking the town. Scarcely a picket shot disturbed the day-long quiet. Meade was withdrawing, but we did not know it. Our trains were quietly moving back to Williamsport, and are now safely packed there, with the loss of but twenty vehicles, of various kinds, and teams! This was brilliantly executed.

"On the night of the 4th the army began quietly to fall back by Fairfield towards Hagerstown. The march back to Hagerstown, some twenty-four miles, occupied three days! The army took one road most of the way, and marched quietly and with dignity back. No defeat to the Confederates was shown in that proud, invincible tread, that spirited and bold heart, that grieved but proud and fierce array of freemen. The *morale* of our army was utterly unaffected; but Meade dare not say so much, as he points to his terrible loss, and his enforced retreat. One word here as to his greater loss. It may be said that the attacking army, especially when assailing such a position, must suffer more than the other. But the Yankees were crowded on their hills, and when our eighty cannon opened on them the slaughter was terrific. So when Johnson's division attempted the crest, nearly every shot of our men told among their compact ranks.

"Our army is yet numerous, and perfectly defiant. Witness even this fact: A few days ago the Yankees with three pieces of cannon attacked our park at Williamsport. Imboden, with his men, armed the teamsters and charged the enemy. The wagoners fought like devils, and took two pieces of artillery, and the enemy fell back.

"General Stuart, glorious, unconquerable Jeb, fought the Yankees yesterday morning a few miles from Hagerstown, on the Boonsboro' road, and drove them back after a furious fight, gaining a very handsome victory.

"The rear of our army was feebly attacked as far as South Mountain, eight miles from Gettysburg, on its retirement; but Meade has shown no disposition to trouble us with his main army.

"The battle of Gettysburg was a most remarkable conflict. It is strange that Lee attacked Meade where he was, when he had it in his power to choose his own position and compel Meade to fight him. As far as we can see (which isn't far) the battle as projected and executed on the 2d and 3d was a great military blunder. If Meade had been soundly defeated, he would have been on even ground or when he had attacked our heights, his army could have been cut to pieces and dissipated before he could reach Baltimore or Washington. The Monocacy could be his only hope, and this was too far off. As it is, we may yet beat him. Most persons adhere to the notion that we shall cross the river, but I cannot, will not believe it. The proud army of Northern Virginia will terminate this bloody campaign within the halls of the Federal Capital.

"We saw many a Pennsylvanian tired of the war. We met several Knights of the Golden Circle. One intelligent farmer told me that "we ought to be unsuccessful in the war unless we captured Abe Lincoln this trip, and that our advent in Pennsylvania was hailed with hearty joy by three million Northern Democrats." Take this for what it is worth. There is truth somewhere in it.

"You all complain of 'respecting private property.' Such was the order from headquarters, and attempted to be faithfully executed. But take your horse and follow the track of our army up the Cumberland Valley, thence to Gettysburg and thence to Hagerstown. You will find the route marked by the devastating trail—destroyed bridges, burnt fences, beat down wheat and rye fields, devoured clover fields, ransacked stores, horseless and cattleless farmers. At Gettysburg four houses were burnt, three large brick buildings, during the battle of the 1st by the explosion of shell. The vicinity of the city is desolate and trampled and cut up—being, I believe, the most *marked* field of the war. There has been no tendency to outrage. Our forces have not plundered, except in unauthorized squads, and these were few. Order has been enforced as much as possible, and well for us—but still there is the necessary, inevitable *trail*, which a great army leaves in its own country.

"Chambersburg or Carlisle should have been burnt by authority in retaliation for the ruthless destruction of Darien. Such destruction does not demoralize an army—whilst it gives the foe a wholesome lesson by which we vastly profit. How long will our Government pursue this weak-kneed policy of supinely receiving the enemy's cruelty and inhumanity and admitting it within the pale of civilized warfare by the sanction which this failure to retaliate inevitably carries with it? Burn! but by authority. Destroy! but through official proclamation and always with reference to some desecrated home or ruined city that once adorned a sunny landscape in the South. *Au revoir.*"

THE ENEMY'S LATE RAID ON THE BANKS OF THE COMBAHEE.

We take from the columns of the N. Y. *Tribune* the following gloating account of villianies that should make a savage blush, and which cry aloud, and cry not in vain, to Heaven for punishment:

What Stoneman and Grierson are upon the horse. Col. Jim Montgomery is upon foot. With but 250 negro soldiers, on board the gunboat John Adams and the transports Harriet A. Weed and Sentinel, he left Beaufort on the evening of the 1st inst., and at 2½ on the following morning anchored his little fleet in the Combahee River, 30 miles distant from the point of his departure, 20 miles from Charleston, and 15 from the village of Ashepoo, on the Charleston and Savannah Railroad. The Sentinel, unfortunately, got aground at the mouth of the Coosaw River, and was of no service to the expedition; the troops on board of her were transferred to the John Adams and the Harriet A. Weed.

The village of Ashepoo is approached from the Combahee by three different roads—one from Field's Point, where the rebels had constructed a battery, but had deserted it—one from Tar Bluff, two miles above Field's Point, and one from Combahee Ferry, six miles further up the river. In accordance with the plan fully determined upon before his departure, Col. Montgomery, almost at the same instant, took possession of the three approaches to Ashepoo, placing Capt. T. N. Thompson, with one company, in the earthworks at Field's Point; Captain Carver, with company E, in the rifle pits at Tar Bluff, and then with the balance of his force proceeded to Combahee Ferry, and with the guns of the John Adams and two howitzers, under command of Captain Brayton, completely covered the road and the approaches to the bridge. These points were all occupied without opposition. To deceive the enemy, and lead him to suppose his force was much larger than it really was, he instructed the officer in command at these difficult points to retain but a few men in reserve, and throw out nearly their entire strength as skirmishers.

At Ashepoo the rebels had three regiments of infantry, one battalion of cavalry, and a full battery of artillery. As Captain Thompson advanced up the road leading from Field's Point, cavalry came in sight, but a few well directed volleys soon sent them galloping back in confusion to their stronghold in Ashepoo. At half past seven a battery of six guns arrived and opened a brisk fire. Not a man flinched, but from such hiding places as they could find poured volley after volley upon the gunners, killing and wounding a number. In the midst of this little engagement the Harriet A. Weed came up, and a well directed shell from her guns, under the direction of Capt. Holden, caused a retreat of the rebel artillery. The raid upon this road then commenced in earnest. The soldiers scattered in every direction, and burned and destroyed everything of value they came across. Thirty-four large mansions, known to belong to notorious rebels, with all their rich furniture and rare works of art, were burned to the ground. Nothing but smouldering ruins and parched and crisped skeletons of once magnificent old oak and palmetto groves now remain of these delightful country seats.

After scattering the rebel artillery, the Harriet A. Weed tied up opposite a large plantation, owned by Nichols & Kirkland. Major Corwin, in command of companies B and C, soon effected a landing, without opposition. The white inhabitants, terrified at the sight of negro soldiers with loaded muskets in their hands, ran in every direction, while the slave population rushed to the boats with every demonstration of joy and gratitude. Three rice houses, well filled with rice, a large amount in ricks in the yard, and four large mills of different kinds, were destroyed. Mansions, negro quarters, and everything inflammable, was consigned to the flames. Sluices were opened, plantations flooded, and broad ponds and lakes made where, but a few hours before, luxuriant crops of rice and corn were putting forth their leaves.

Captain Carver, with Company C, landed at Tar Bluff. After a skillful disposition of his pickets, the enemy's cavalry appeared in sight, and threatened to overwhelm his little party, but upon throwing out his whole force he succeeded in repulsing them every charge, and finally drove them entirely out of sight. Upon this road SEVERAL LARGE STEAM RICE MILLS, THREE COTTON GINS, AND A FINE SAW MILL were destroyed, together with an immense amount of other property. Captain Hoyt, Company A, landed at Combahee Ferry, at 7½ a. m.—encountered cavalry pickets the moment he began to advance, but after a short engagement drove them back in disorder. The fine bridge across the Combahee River was then destroyed, together with all the ADJACENT PROPERTY.

Having brought within his lines nearly 800 valuable slaves, having destroyed property to the amount of TWO MILLIONS, most of which belonged to notorious leaders in this rebellion, Colonel Montgomery returned to Beaufort early on the morning of the 3d instant, without the loss of a man.

AN EXHIBITION OF THE DIFFERENT GROWTHS OF COTTON—THE TURKISH EXHIBITION.

[*From the Levant Herald.*]

The Egyptian samples, of course, take priority in class. A comparison of this with the other varieties exhibited, makes its great superiority manifest to the least skilled spectator. The Smyrna qualities range next, and several of their samples afford satisfactory indications of the improvement which has lately been effected in that province in the growth of the staple. Mr. Clarke, of Sokia, sends a specimen grown from New Orleans seed, which is in every respect satisfactory, both as to color, average length of staple, and cleanness. This gentleman, we may remark, is the only exhibitor who has appended any explanatory account of the crop sampled. From this we learn that it was planted in March last year, at rather an unfavorable time, and commenced to be ready for pulling in the following August, finishing in January. The earlier yield was of a short staple, and the latter of much superior length. The plants attained a height of seven feet, and produced from 100 to 500 pods, each of which contained on an average a drachm and a half of raw cotton. The success of this seed will have an important influence on the crop of the coming season. The Aidin cotton, though presenting the usual defect of the country—shortness of staple—is of excellent color and strength. From the use of the American and Egyptian seed, this district is likely to become a very important field of supply. One of the most interesting samples is from the Pashalik of Jerusalem; though rather short in staple, it has a silky glossiness and toughness of fibre which merit notice. The cotton from Damascus is of equal fineness to the short staples of Aleppo, Mossul, Adania, Konia and Rhodes, the relative difference being almost solely in the manner in which the wool has been cleaned. Hayrout sends samples grown from India seed, but they will not bear comparison with the Egyptian, or the better class of Smyrna. From Diarbekir, Moresh and Sivas, the qualities exhibited are, in every respect, most inferior. The district of Serres enjoys the reputation of being one of the most promising fields for the culture in the European provinces, and of six samples exhibited from it, two may be said to be of a fully average quality; the remainder are of a rather better description. Salonica, Phillippopli, Adrianople, Drama and Redosto, have severally sent specimens of good short staple, but not well cleaned. From the neighborhood of the capital, we notice some samples of a good quality from Kertulimi, which afford ample encouragement to the growers largely to extend the crop.

The samples of cotton manufactured goods in the Exhibition are so limited in number and so inferior in quality, as hardly to be worth notice. With the exception of some towels with fancy silk headings, made at Phillippopoli, and which are marked at the relatively high price of 16d., the other samples of the produce of the native looms are of the coarsest and most ill-woven description. These goods come from all parts of the empire, extending from Mossul to Philippopoli, and are of nearly uniform quality, the prices affixed compared with those of well-made British and French fabrics are so excessive—not less in any instance than 100 per cent. dearer than the latter—that any market competition is out of the question.

CORRESPONDENCE.

CHARLESTON, July 18th, 1863.

Capt. Ker Boyce, Charleston: I beg the pleasure of putting at your disposal ($2048) two thousand and forty-eight dollars, to be appropriated for the benefit of the Georgia Regiments now on duty on the Islands near the city—the amounts being subscribed in a few moments by the citizens. Below list of sub scribers.

Very respectfully, E. WILLIS.

H. H. DeLeon	$10.00	G. Mixer	$50.00
C. H. Cohrs	50.00	R. Douglass & Co	50.00
E. Willis	50.00	Hyatt, McBurney & Co.	50.00
Wm Stickney	10.00	Stevenson & Co	50.00
J. Gilliland	5.00	G. S. Cameron	25.00
C. J. & Co	150.00	A. Canhady	20.00
A. Milliken	5.00	A. J. Crews	20.00
R. A. Pringle	20.00	J. G. M. & Co	50.00
A. M. Happoldt	10.00	W. O. Cawtray	20.00
W. C. Corrie	5.00	H. Hart	1000.00
J. H. Taylor	50.00	Cash	20.00
B. D. Schur	3.00	E. B. Stoddard & Co	50.00
R. M. Welch	5.00	Capt. J. H. Baker	10.00
Wm. Cadow	20.00	J. R. Boylston	50.00
J. C. & Co	50.00	Jas. Purcell	50.00
J. G. Crane	50.00	Cash	10.00

CHARLESTON, July 19, 1863.

Major E. Willis:

DEAR SIR: It is with great pleasure that I acknowledge the receipt of your letter, with the accompanying liberal contribution of the citizens of Charleston on behalf of the Georgia troops on service on the Islands near the city. Be assured, sir, that it will be received with grateful emotions by all. Nothing is more pleasant than to feel that the sacrifices made and dangers incurred by the soldiers are appreciated by their fellow-citizens. Our wounded already have experienced the kindness and attention of the ladies of Charleston, and this tribute from the men of the city adds greatly to the emotions of gratitude which have been awakened. You state that the contribution was collected in a few moments of time. No wonder, when it was marked by such great liberality on the part of its donors. I notice that the donations of all are marked by a spirit of liberality worthy of the donors and the noble spirit at which they aim. It gratifies me to be the medium chosen for transmitting the contribution, which I will cause to be equally divided among the Quartermasters of the different Regiments and Battalions.

I have the honor of being,
Very respectfully, your ob't serv't,
KER BOYCE,
A. Q. M. 12th Georgia Battalion.

[FOR THE MERCURY.]

THE EIGHTH REGIMENT S. C. V.

This glorious old regiment may, with truth, be said to be extinct. The first organized regiment from any State to tread the soil of Virginia, she has ever maintained a spotless reputation. When on a bright day in May, 1861, she, numbering nine hundred and eighty men—the best young blood of the Pee Dee—took her departure for the heroic State (Virginia), high hopes and noble deeds accompanied and were expected of us. The blood stained fields of first Manassas, Williamsburg, Savage Station, Malvern Hill, Maryland Heights, Sharpsburg, Fredericksburg, Chancellorsville and Gettysburg, all attest her courage, her mettle and her glory. The field of Gettysburg was pre-eminently the field of her glory and her grave. She went into battle one hundred and seventy strong, and now, along the borders of Pennsylvania, their cool and gallant Colonel Henegan, has left him but forty men to rally around the old Palmetto flag, which she has borne safely through every campaign. It is a singular fact, that not a single sound member of this regiment has ever been taken prisoner, and there has never been a desertion. When the long roll of your lost is read around the hearths of your friends, every home in the swamps of the Pee Dee will find itself desolate—sadness will cover the land. Yes, true, our hearts are desolate, but still every bosom swells with proud emotion when your name and your immortal deeds are mentioned. I send you a list of the killed and wounded as far as they have reached us with certainty:

Major D. M. McLeod, killed; Lieut. H. R. Adams, Co. G, killed; Capt. J. R. McIver, wounded, severely; Capt. William Coker, wounded in foot; Capt. Thos. E Powe, lost left leg, wounded in right thigh and forehead, and in hands of the enemy; Sergt. Wilson, Co. F; Sergt. Stancel, Co. C; Corporal Craig, Privates J. R. Mallory, B. White, Rainwalers, Grimsby, and Axon, wounded, and Samuel Dixon, killed, all of Co. C; Privates McIntosh and J. R. Easterling, of Co. G, killed; Color Sergt. E. Adams, killed; Lieut. Bell Roger, Privates Hasken and Smith, Co. K, wounded.

PEE DEE.

A SUGGESTION.

To the Editor of the Mercury: Will not some one or all of our ministers come forward in this dark hour of need, difficulties and danger, and open their churches for the purpose of daily prayer to Almighty God in behalf of our sacred altars—our loved ones—our homes.

"Behold the Lord's hand is not shortened that it cannot save, neither his ear heavy that it cannot hear." "Call upon me and go and pray unto me, and I will hearken unto you." "Hath He said and shall He not do it? Hath He spoken and shall He not make it good." Surely "*the Lord will give strength unto his people, the Lord will bless his people with peace.*"

Let us arouse then to prayer, our most urgent duty and blood bought privilege, and our country, our cause, our city, shall be saved.

CAROLINA'S DAUGHTER.

AFFECTING SCENE.—Not many years since, says Fraser's Magazine, certain miners, working far under ground, came upon the body of a poor fellow who had perished in the suffocating pit forty years before. Some chemical agent to which the body had been subjected—an agent prepared in the laboratoy of Nature—had effectually arrested the progress of decay. They brought it to the surface, and for a while, till it crumbled away, through exposure to the atmosphere, it lay there, the image of a fine sturdy young man. No convulsions had passed over the face in death—the features were tranquil—the hair was black as jet. No one recognized the face. A generation had grown up since the day on which the miner went down his shaft for the last time. But a tottering old woman, who had hurried from her cot on hearing the news, came up, and she knew again the face which, through all these years, she had never quite forgot. The poor miner was to have been her husband the day after that on which he died. They were rough people, of course, who were looking on—a liberal education and refined feelings are not deemed essential to the man whose work it is to get up coals, or even tin—but there were no dry eyes there, when the gray-headed old pilgrim cast herself upon the youthful corpse and poured out to its deaf ear many words of endearment, unused for forty years. It was a touching contrast—the one so old, the other so young. They had both been young those long forty years ago. But time had gone on with the living, and stood still with the dead.

THE MERCURY.

BY R. B. RHETT, JR.

OFFICE NO. 4 BROAD-STREET, CHARLESTON.

THE DAILY MERCURY, ten cents per copy, $20 per annum.

THE TRI-WEEKLY MERCURY, issued on Tuesdays, Thursdays and Saturdays, ten cents per copy, $10 per annum.

ADVERTISEMENTS, Two Dollars per square of 13 lines.

MONDAY, JULY 20, 1863.

THE STRUGGLE FOR MORRIS ISLAND—AWFUL BOMBARDMENT OF BATTERY WAGNER—A NIGHT ASSAULT UPON OUR WORKS—SIGNAL AND BLOODY REPULSE OF THE FOE.

Saturday last was a day which will be forever memorable in the history of Charleston. The heavy rains had moderated the excessive heat of the preceding fortnight, the morning sky was cloudless, and the light breeze scarcely ruffled the placid waters of the harbor.

BOMBARDMENT OF BATTERY WAGNER.

About eight o'clock the desultory cannonade with which the experience of a week had made our community familiar was again heard. For nearly three hours the enemy's fire was maintained with the usual deliberation; but about eleven o'clock it was noticed that the reports came in far more rapid succession. By noon it became well understood that the foe was resolved to subject our position to an ordeal much more severe thon any which, up to that time, it had encountered. At that hour, as we learn by accounts from Morris Island, the converging fire of the enemy against the battery had become truly fearful. Five Monitors, the frigate *Ironsides*, seven wooden gunboats, with the land batteries which the Yankees had thrown up on the lower portion of the island, kept up a constant rain of shot and shell into our works. No less than sixty five heavy guns and eight mortars are known to have been in play against us. At one time, so rapid was the fire, that the reports averaged *twenty-seven per minute.* One of the Monitors lay north-east of Battery Wagner and two to the southeast, while the others, with the *Ironsides*, kept a position nearly opposite the sea face of the battery.—The wooden gunboats manœuvred at some distance outside the line of "turretted monsters," relying chiefly upon their long range rifled siege guns. There were two Yankee batteries on Morris Island—one, consisting of two guns and a mortar, was located at Craig's Hill, within about eight hundred yards of our battery; the other was beyond GRAHAM's House, and had an armament of eight rifled shell guns. It is estimated that during the day, no less than nine thousand shells were fired at the battery.

The bombardment, as viewed from eminences in the city, was a grand and terrible sight. The horizon, from Fort Moultrie to Vinegar Hill, was crowned with the shifting masses of the smoke of the conflict. Each moment the enemy's shells, sometimes singly, sometimes in clusters, could be seen bursting just above the site of Battery Wagner; but when, at intervals, the clouds of white smoke lifted for a time from the scene, the flag of the brave garrison could be seen still waving defiantly in the breeze, while with grim regularity and deliberation our guns kept replying to the foe.

For eleven consecutive hours the bombardment raged with more or less violence. About dusk the fire, which during the afternoon had been incessant (probably with the design of demoralizing our men and unfitting them for the expected night's work), began to slacken considerably, and at dark ceased almost entirely. The results, thus far, had been of a character to give us good cause for encouragement and gratulation. The damage to our Battery was insignificant and of a kind easily and speedily reparable. The bombproofs had afforded efficient protection to a large portion of the garrison, and our casualties at seven o'clock, p. m., were but four killed and fourteen wounded. Of the enemy's losses from our fire, if any, we have, of course, no trustworthy account. Fort Sumter, which bore a part in the action, sent several shells into the Craig Hill Batteries, and also into the camp of the enemy, about 3¼ miles distant, it is believed, with good effect.

THE NIGHT ATTACK.

At a few minutes before eight o'clock our pickets gave notice that the enemy, in heavy force was moving to the assault. The attack was not unexpected, and our men, though much jaded by the fatigues and exposure of the day, sprang to their places with zeal and alacrity. The enemy advanced in two columns of about 3,000 men each, the whole under the command of Brigadier General STRONG. The column which attacked our right was composed partially of negro troops, who were put in the advance. On our left, the other column advanced with spirit, under a severe fire from the Dahlgreen guns and columbiads of Fort Sumter. As the column advanced at the double-quick, the guns of Battery Wagner also opened, When the enemy had reached a point about sixty yards distant, our infantry, posted behind the parapet, poured a galling fire into the moving masses; the Yankees, nevertheless, in considerable force, succeeded in gaining the trench, and began to clamber up the sides of the Battery. At this moment, Lieut. WATIES, of Blake's Battery, who was in charge of two brass howitzers (belonging to a detachment of artillery under Capt. DEPASS, of White's Battalion) opened a raking fire which swept the strench, playing terrific havoc in the ranks of the assailants. The howitzers had been assigned to this position which they occupied so advantageously for us, at the instance of Col. HARRIS, of the Engineers, all the horses belonging to the section having been put *hors du combat* during the day. Twice the enemy was driven back at this part of our works (the left), and the trench filled with the enemy's dead attests the severity of the conflict there.

On the right, the negro troops were met with a terrible cross fire of musketry. Here were posted, among other troops, the Charleston Battalion, and these gallant men behaved in a manner worthy the fame their organization had so dearly won at Secessionville. The second assault was still more desperate than the first, but it was met and repelled in the same gallant style by the brave troops, Georgians, North Carolinians, and sons of our own city, who stood shoulder to shoulder in the fight.

In the centre of our lines a small body of the enemy succeeded in gaining a lodgment in a salient, the gun of which had been disabled. Here they maintained their position for more than an hour. A gallant but unsuccessful attempt was made to dislodge them, in which Captain RYAN fell, and it was not until a small force of Georgians had ascended the magazine and thus gained a position to command the salient that the audacious Yankees surrendered. At the time that this occurred the firing elsewhere had ceased, and the Georgians accomplished their purpose without firing a gun. The movement by which this was effected was undertaken at the suggestion of Colonel HARRIS.

THE RELATIVE LOSSES.

The fight lasted from 8 until 11 p. m., and was of a desperate character throughout. The enemy's losses were very heavy. His killed and wounded must have been at least 1500. The number of his dead left on the field and buried by us yesterday exceeded 600. We captured over two hundred prisoners, including a few of the negro troops.

Our own losses were comparatively light. It is estimated that our killed and wounded will not exceed 100. Among these, however, were some valuable officers, such as Lieutenant Colonel SIMKINS and Captain TATUM, of the 1st S. C. Infantry, and Captain RYAN. of the Charleston Battalion, killed, and Major RAMSAY, of the Charleston Battalion, severely wounded.

CASUALTIES IN THE CHARLESTON BATTALION.

To the Editor of the Charleston Mercury: Herewith I hand you a list of the casualties in Lieut. Col. Gaillard's Charleston Battalion, S. C. V., in the fight of Saturday, the 18th, at Morris Island:

COMPANY A—CAPTAIN J. A. BLAKE.

Killed—Sergeant Lambers.

Wounded—Privates Cheney, Ham, Wilder and Harvey.

COMPANY B—CAPTAIN T. Y. SIMONS.

Killed—Private S J Nesbit.

Wounded—1st Lieutenant Wm Clarkson; Jr. 2d Lieutenant Wm Sinkler, very slight; Privates T D Eskew, Wm Hill, M Hendricks, H R Fowler, H H Turner.

COMPANY C—CAPTAIN WM. H. RYAN.

Killed—Captain Wm H Ryan and Private M Twohill.

Wounded—Privates Callahan and Reynolds, dangerous; Corporal Preston, Privates Hill and Manin, slightly.

COMPANY D—CAPTAIN HOPKINS.

Killed—1st Sergeant W K Smith, Private S T Hyde.

Wounded—1st Lieutenant J A Cay, 2d Lieutenant J T Wells, Corporal H E Saylor, Privates T W Atkinson, J J Ball, W A Bailey, G P Ballentine, A Bumpus, W W Fowler, J F Harrison, W L Macbeth, J A Madden, R Owens, M Stone, J M Tims, E T Walker, W A J Ware.

COMPANY F—CAPTAIN SAMUEL LORD, JR.

Wounded—1st Lieutenant George Brown, Privates J W Glenn, J Brown Barry, H Schroder, J D Ashcraft and A Slant.

Major David Ramsay, severely wounded.

Respectfully,
W. D. WALTER, 1st Lieutenant,
Adjutant Charleston Battalion.

LIST OF WOUNDED IN THE TRAPMAN ST. HOSPITAL.

Willis Kinlock, 31st N C Vols, Co A—abdomen.
J Johnson, 1st S C Vols, Co I—lung.
J D Maloy, Lieutenant 51st N C Vols, Co D—neck.
L H Hill, Ch Bat, Co C—head.
Samuel Reynolds, Ch Bat, Co C—neck.
Arch Graham, 51st N C Vols, Co D.
H Hunter, 51st N C Vols, Co C.
Sergeant McArthur, 51st N C Vols, Co B.
H James, 51st N C Vols, Co C.
H H Turner, Ch Bat, Co B—leg.
Lieut G W Thompson, 51st N C V, Co F—leg; since dead.
G Ballentine. Ch Bat, Co D—wrist.
J J Ball, Ch Bat, Co D—arm.
Sergeant W B Bowden, 51st N C Vols, Co C—head.
Uriah Bass, 51st N C Vols, Co I—scalp.
S Granthem, 51st N C Vols, Co F—scalp.
B Porter, 51st N C Vols, Co I—scalp.
Lieut W E Reddick, 63d Ga Vols, Co B—arm.
J Abner, 51st N C Vols, Co C.
J Henderson, 51st N. C. V., Co F—bayonet wound.
E Walker, Ch Bat, Co D—thigh.
A Bumpus, Ch Bat, Co D—foot.
J Johnson, 31st N C V., Co B.
Lieut W T Means, 1st S C R I, Co H—contusion from shell.
Lieut James H Powe, 1st S C R I, Co H.
R M Wood, Ch Bat, Co B.
R L Wilder, Ch Bat, Co A.
J Falk, Ch Bat, concussion.
James Jones, 51st N C, Co C—hand.
H R Fowler, Ch Bat, Co B.
A Branch, 51st N C, Co K.
L M. White, 51st N C, Co D.
T J Thornton, 51st N C, Co B—side.

LIST OF WOUNDED IN THE CITADEL SQUARE HOSPITAL.

Private L Myers. Edisto Rifles—shot in right cheek—James Island—July 16.

Private W E Jones, Co. F, 19th Georgia—wounded in knee—James Island—July 16.

Captain E Sutherland, Co A, 51st N. C.—shot through thigh—Fort Wagner—July 18.

Corporal A G Maddox, Co A, 6th Georgia—shot through right arm—James Island—July 16.

Private T J Ramsay, Co I, 1st Regiment S. C. V.—shot through right thigh—Fort Wagner—July 18.

Private N Barber, Co F, 51st N. C.—wounded by a shell—Fort Wagner—July 18.

Private J Conners, Co A, 1st S. C. A.—shot through right thigh—Fort Wagner—July 18.

Private T W Atkinson Co D, Charleston Battalion—shot through right thigh—Fort Wagner—July 18.

Private A Nelson, Co H, 1st S. C. Artillery—contusion wounds Fort Wagner—July 18.

Private J Crawford, Co I, 1st S. C. Infantry—incised wound—bursting of shell—Fort Wagner July 18.

FACTS, INCIDENTS, ETC.

Fort Wagner occupies nearly the site of a small sea battery, constructed under the direction of the late Colonel THOMAS M. WAGNER. Indeed, a small portion of this sea battery is incorporated in the parapets and traverses of this fort. The importance of the site, as commanding the land approach to Cumming's Point, we are informed, induced Captain FRANCIS D. LEE, of the Engineers—then in charge of the harbor defences—to press the great necessity of the work. Captain LEE's designs having been approved by General PEMBERTON, the work was rapidly carried to completion under his direction, by the lamented Capt. LANGDON CHEVES.

Colonel SHAW, of Boston, who commanded the 54th Massachusetts (negro) regiment, was killed on our parapet. The Lieutenant Colonel of the same regiment, surrendered his sword to Colonel GAILLARD. The Major and one of the Captains were also killed. Another Lieutenant Colonel was killed just as he had mounted a bastion. Colonel H. S. PUTNAM, of the 7th New Hampshire regiment, (acting as Brigadier General) was left dead in front of our lines. Dr. DUCK, of the U. S. Navy, and the Adjutant of a Connecticut regiment were captured, and a Yankee Assistant Adjutant General was killed.

General TALIAFERRO commanded our troops on the Island during the fight and is universally commended for the gallantry, coolness and efficiency which he displayed on the occasion.

Major RAMSAY, commanding the Charleston Battalion, behaved with great bravery. He fell while leading a detachment of his command to occupy an angle the gun of which had been disabled.

Lieutenant-Colonel SIMKINS, who fell shot through the breast, commanded the artillery of the post. We learn that Lieutenant-Colonel DEL KEMPER, the distinguished Virginia artillerist, succeeds him.

The notes we have given above of the signal victory our troops have achieved are necessarily meagre and incomplete. We hope hereafter to be able to present our readers with a more detailed account.

THE BOILER EXPLOSION ON THE SOUTH CAROLINA RAILROAD.—Coroner WHITING, on Saturday, concluded his investigation of the boiler explosion on the South Carolina Railroad, by which the engineer, JOHN FITZHUGH, and the fireman, J. W. REIALS, were killed. The Jury rendered a verdict of accidental death in the cases mentioned, and gave it as their opinion that the explosion was caused by a lack of water in the boiler. The wood work encasing the boiler, and the signboard, gave evidence of this fact, as they were much charred, which could only result from the cause mentioned.

IN MEMORY OF—WHOM?—Two of the enemy's gunboats were observed with flags at half mast in the Stono on Friday. Probably some Yankee naval officer of high rank has lost his life during the bombardment of last week.

ELECTION OF STATE SENATOR.—JOSEPH DANIEL POPE, Esq, was, on the 14th instant, elected State Senator from St. Helena Parish, to fill the unexpired term of Hon. EDMUND RHETT.

THE "SIXTEENTH."—The Charleston correspondent of the Savannah *Republican* writes: "Just in front of the Charleston Hotel may be witnessed every afternoon, about 6 o'clock, a spectacle that should be photographed, as a lesson of patriotism for the generations to come. The living at the present day may also learn from it their duty. It is *The Old Men's Regiment*, made up of exempts, and composed chiefly of the old men of the city. Most of their heads and chins are "silvered o'er with years," and many with the infirmities incident to age upon them. A few foreigners are also among the number. All, fired by patriotism and the duty they owe, while life itself lasts, to the noble State that gave them birth or protection, have come up in the day of her distress from their counting rooms, their studios, their workshops, and quiet retirement for the evening of their days, to stake their lives, if need be, in defence of Charleston. With a proud mien and resolute tread, they shoulder their muskets and respond to the word of command. It is a glorious and most affecting exhibition. I commend their noble example to all the cities and towns of the South, and with especial earnestness to my own beloved Savannah."

THE FIGHT AT MORRIS ISLAND ON THE 10TH INST.—OUR MISSING MEN.—The following informatien in regard to the fate of our men missing after the fight of the 10th inst., at the south end of Morris Island, has been obtained, under flag of truce, from the enemy's lines:

LIST OF PRISONERS CAPTURED BY U. S. TROOPS ON 10TH JULY, 1863.

1. Capt J Ravenel Macbeth.
2. 1st Lieut J S Bee.
3. 2d Lieut J G Heyward.
4. Sergt W D Smith, Co I, 1st S C Artillery.
5. Sergt D Wieland, Co I, 1st S C Artillery.
6. Corpl James Smith, Co I, 1st S C Artillery.
7. Private F Hoffmann, Co I, 1st S C Artillery.
8. Private S Raney, Co I, 1st S C Artillery.
9. Private R Shine, Co I, 1st S C Artillery.
10. Private John Carroll, Co I, 1st S C Artillery.
11. Private John McNamara, Co I, 1st S C Artillery.
12. Private James Stone, Co I, 1st S C Artillery.
13. Private Asa Coker, Co I, 1st S C Artillery.
14. Private Thos. Dillon, Co I, 1st S C Artillery.
15. Private M S Lee, Co I, 1st S C Artillery.
16. Private W T Whitber, Co I, 1st S C Artillery.
17. Private Wm Stevens, Co I, 1st S C Artillery.
18. Private Peter Edlin, Co I, 1st S C Artillery.
19. Private John Edsols, Co I, 1st S C Artillery.
20. Private James Eskew, Co I, 1st S C Artillery.
21. Private Wm Goodwin, Co I, 1st S C Artillery.
22. Private Wm Brookbanks, Co I, 1st S C Artillery.
23. Private Michael Black, Co I, 1st S C Artillery.
24. Private E J Wiggins, Co I, 1st S C Artillery.
25. Private J L Carson, Co I, 1st S C Artillery.
26. Private J A Searcy, Co I, 1st S C Artillery.
27. Private Ed McKenna, Co I, 1st S C Artillery.
28. Private J A Aikens, Co I, 1st S C Artillery.
29. Private N B Jordan, Co I, 1st S C Artillery.
30. Private R Ferguson, Co I, 1st S C Artillery.
31. Private G W Banks, Co I, 1st S C Artillery.
32. Private Henry Holmes, Co I, 1st S C Artillery.
33. Private Andrew Carson, Co I, 1st S C Artillery.
34. Private Wm. Stewart, Co H, 1st S C Artillery.
35. Private James Laile, Co H, 1st S C Artillery.
36. Private Wm Hughes, Co H, 1st S C. Artillery.
37. Private John Tanner, Co H, 1st C Artillery.
38. Private Wm Fox, Co H, 1st S C Artillery.
39. Private J A Prince, Co H, 1st S C Artillery.
40. Private A Blackwell, Co H, 1st S C Artillery.
41. Private Elijah Brown, Co H, 1st S C Artillery.
42. Private D Jordan, Co H, 1st S C Artillery.
43. Private James Brown, Co H, 1st S C Artillery.
44. Private D O Sisum, Co H, 1st S C Artillery.
45. Private J F Corcoran, Co H, 1st S C Artillery.
46. Private J A Hicks, Co H, 1st S C Artillery.
47. Private Patrick Markey, Co H, 1st S C Artillery.
48. Corporal A B Strother, Co E, 1st S C Artillery.
49. Private John Flynn, Co E, 1st S C Artillery.
50. Private John Hagan, Co E, 1st S C Artillery.
51. Private John J Sullivan, Co E, 1st S C Artillery.
52. Private Joseph Maloney, Co E, 1st S C Artillery.
53. Private Barney Mulroney, Co E, 1st S C Artillery.
54. Private John Murphy, Co E, 1st S C Artillery.
55. Private W T Welsh, Co E, 1st S C Artillery.
56. Private H Desmond, Co E, 1st S C Artillery.
57. Private Mike Kenny, Co E, 1st S C Artillery.
58. Private C Hilliard, Co E, 1st S C Artillery.
59. Private Michael Kelly, Co E, 1st S C Artillery.
60. Private Michael Gorman, Co E, 1st S C Artillery.
61. Private Wm Haimes, Co E, 1st S C Artillery.

This list does not state which of the prisoners were wounded. Private J. H. Keziah's name also appears on the list as belonging to Company E, but there was no such man in the company. Of Company E the following men are unaccounted for, and must have been killed:

1. Private Barney Daugherty.
2. Private Jerry Halley.
3. Private Pat Brannon.
4. Private Daniel Burhe.
5. Private William Rogers.
6. Private Alexander Smealey.
7. Private Thomas White.

Lieutenant John S. Bee was severely wounded, and at last accounts was on his way to Hilton Head, attended by Surgeon Pressly, C. S. P. A.

Of Company I thirty-eight men were "lost in action." Thirty-one of these are accounted for as prisoners. The remaining seven must have been killed.

Of detachment Company H, 40 men, twenty-one were lost in action. Fifteen of these are prisoners.

S. CORDES BOYLSTON,
Adjutant.

THE HEAVY FIRING shortly after 10 o'clock last night was from the blockading fleet, supposed to be caused by a vessel trying to run in.

THE YANKEE FLOTILLA, consisting of two monitors, five gunboats and seven or eight transports, still cruises in James River. On Wednesday the monitors came up above City Point, but after a reconoissance and considerable blowing of steam whistles, dropped back down the river. The transports are not believed to contain any troops, as none have been seen on their decks. Some think it the design of the enemy to attack Drewry's Bluff; it is, however, more probable that the demonstration is an empty menace.

THE ENEMY'S MOVEMENTS AT WILMINGTON.—The Wilmington Journal of Friday says: "A report reached town late last night that the enemy was landing troops at Topsail Inlet. We cannot find any confirmation of this, although it is said that three vessels, apparently containing troops, were off Topsail yesterday. They may have been bound for Charleston or elsewhere."

THE FOLLOWING CONTRIBUTIONS have been received at this office since our last issue:

Fifty dollars from the Ladies of "Oak Lawn," St. Paul's Parish, for the soldiers on Morris Island.

One hundred dollars from the Ladies' Georgetown Aid Association for the 21st Regiment S. C. V., Colonel Graham.

Surgeon Witsell, of the 1st Division, Howard's Grove Hospital, acknowledges the receipt of $10 from E. B. F., $10 from N. A. F., $10 from J. A. F., and $5 from M. C. F. to supply reading matter for the sick and wounded in his charge.

SOLDIERS' RELIEF ASSOCIATION.—The ladies are again in need of cotton to fill beds for the hospitals. Will the patriotic supply them, and send to the Depository, Chalmers-street?

I GRATEFULLY ACKNOWLEDGE the receipt of $50 from Pinopolis—which I have sent to the Ladies' Relief Association, to be applied to the hospitals for the use of the sick and wounded soldiers,

Two hundred and twenty-five dollars from the Rev. Mr. GILBERT, now of Savannah, which, agreeable to directions, I have sent to the sick and wounded in Virginia—$225.

From Winter Brigade, near Georgetown, for the sick soldiers of South Carolina in General BRAGG's army, $100. I have ascertained that the sick are in various hospitals in Georgia. I have sent the amount to RICHARD PETERS, of Atlanta, who will see that the amount will be distributed.

J. BACHMAN.

SOLDIERS' RELIEF ASSOCIATION.—The ladies of the Soldiers' Relief Association acknowledge the receipt of valuable donations of refreshments for soldiers on Morris Island:

From Miss Brodie, Miss Cromwell, Mrs. Dr. Fitch, Mrs. Smyth, Mrs. Bachman Wilson, Mrs Blamyer, Mrs. James Gilliland, Messrs. Paul & Co., the Ladies of Pinopolis, through Mrs. T. P. Ravenel, Mrs. Snowden, Mrs. G. Robertson, Mrs. Reeder, Mrs. P. Wineman, Master Timmons, Mrs. Newton, Mrs. Blackwood, Mrs. Mary Robertson through Mrs. Forrest, Dr. Forrest, Mrs. Philip Porcher, Mrs. Minot, Mrs. M. Matthiesson, Misses Robb, Mrs. Carlin, Miss Taylor, Mrs. Farman.

The statement going the rounds, copied from the Richmond Examiner, that the Yankee batteries that knocked down one angle of Fort Pulaski were planted within six hundred yards of that work, is foolishly incorrect. Pulaski was fired upon from Tybee Island, and no part of Tybee Island is within less than a mile of Fort Pulaski. A careful examination of the Coast Survey Map convinces us of this.—*Wilmington Journal.*

The work was done by Parrott guns, at the distance of a mile and a quarter, as stated in the Savannah papers at the time.

Consignees per South Carolina Railroad. July 17.

1475 bushels Corn, 35 bales Fodder, 31 boxes, bbls and tierces Bacon, 480 bushels Meal, Mdse, Cattle, &c. To H C Guerin, H Lee, F J Pelzer, Ordnance Officer, Col Widdy, T Linning, Mrs E Edwards, J Ficken, Cotbran, Jeffers & Co, E M Grimke, C G Waller, E P Cuyler, E P Lemon, Fgarties & Stillman, D Barrow, W Kirkwood, and Order.

JULY 18.—200 bbls Flour, 520 bushels Corn, 46 tons Coal, Mdse, Cattle, &c. To H Lee, H C Guerin, E Will, Gas Company, Crenshaw Bros, D G Wayne, W Johnson, and Order.

☞ The Relatives, Friends and Acquaintances of Mr. and Mrs. WILLIAM RYAN, Mr. and Mrs. THOMAS RYAN, and Mr. and Mrs. JOHN RYAN, are respectfully invited to attend the Funeral Services of the late Captain WILLIAM H. RYAN, son of the former, at St. Mary's Church, Hasell-street, THIS AFTERNOON, at Five o'clock, without further invitation. July 20

—o—

☞ The Friends and Acquaintances of WM. KIRKWOOD SMITH, and of his Mother, Mrs. ELIZABETH SMITH, also of WM. KIRKWOOD, are invited to attend the Funeral Services of the former, at Trinity Church, Hasell-street, THIS AFTERNOON, at half past Three o'clock. * July 20

—o—

☞ The Relatives, Friends and Acquaintances of Mrs. E. MANGAN, of Mr. and Mrs. T. E. GILBERT, and Mr. and Mrs. R. H. WINNINGHAM, also the Congregation of St. John's Chapel, are respectfully invited to attend the Funeral Service of the former at St. John's Chapel, without further invitation, at Five o'clock, THIS AFTERNOON. * July 20

—o—

☞ The Friends and Acquaintances of Miss EVELINA STEEDMAN and Sisters, and of Mr. and Mrs. W. B. STEEDMAN, are invited to attend the Funeral Services of the former at Grace Church, THIS AFTERNOON, at half-past Four o'clock. * July 20

MARION AND LAFAYETTE ARTILLERY RESERVES

ARE ORDERED TO MEET, THIS DAY, AT 9 a. m., at Vigilant Engine House, State street.
By order Captain KIRKWOOD.
July 20 1*

MILITARY NOTICE.

HEADQUARTERS,
COLUMBIA, S. C., July 14, 1863.

I. BY ORDER OF GENERAL BEAUREGARD, WOMEN, children and non-combatants are prohibited from entering the City of Charleston. A guard will be stationed at Branchville, whose duty it will be to prevent all such from going nearer to the lines, unless they have passports from the General Commanding.

II. By order of General Beauregard, a guard will be placed on the railway trains, leaving and arriving at Charleston, Columbia and Augusta, who will examine the papers of all officers and soldiers; and will arrest those whose papers are not complete, reporting them to the Provost Marshal at Charleston, or the Commandant of the Post at Columbia or Augusta. The guard will be instructed to demand the passports of all persons travelling, and instantly report as above, all who are without them. All persons, therefore, are advised to obtain passports, either at Charleston, Augusta or Columbia, or elsewhere, before entering this Department. JOHN S. PRESTON,
July 17 10 Col. Commanding.

STATE OF SOUTH CAROLINA.
HEADQUARTERS, Charleston, July 14, 1863.

In consequence of a pressing call by General BEAUREGARD upon the Executive of the State for labor for immediate use, in addition to the call already made by Proclamation of this date, the following named persons are appointed and requested to make an earnest personal appeal to the citizens of their respective Parishes to furnish immediately, to be reported to Major ECHOLS, in this city, all the labor they can spare.

Overseers will be sent with every fifty hands, and the gentlemen named below are requested to see the negros promptly started to this place:

For St. James' Goose Creek—Messrs. KEITH BROWN and B. RHAME.

For St. Thomas and St. Dennis—R. K. FURMAN, Esq.

For Christ Church—Messrs. MORTIMER VENNING and GEORGE KINLOCH.

For St. Johns Berkley—Dr. S. W. BARKER.

For St. Stephens—P. C. KIRK, Esq.

For St. James Santee—DANIEL DUPRE, Esq.

For St George's Dorchester—Dr. JOHN MAY and Dr. M. T. APPLEBY.

For St. Andrews—Col. A. H. BROWN.

For St. Pauls—Col. HAWKINS KING, Hon. R. BOYLE and E. B. SCOTT.

For St. Bartholomews—Messrs. EUSTACE BELLINGER, B. SANDERS, Jr., JAMES G. VARN and REUBEN STEPHENS.

M. L. BONHAM.

—o—

STATE OF SOUTH CAROLINA.
HEADQUARTERS, CHARLESTON, July 15, 1863.

The following gentlemen are requested to act in concert with those heretofore appointed to procure negro labor for immediate use.

St. Bartholomews—Messrs. N. HEYWARD, O. P. WILLIAMS, J. P. A. DEVEAUX, W. OSWALD.

St. Pauls—R. S. BEDON, E. BARNWELL.

St. Andrews—W. I. BULL.

St. George Dorchester—I. M. DWIGHT, A. F. BROWNING.

St. James Santee—Hon. A. MAZYCK.

St. James, Goose Creek—Mr. C. W. GRAVES.

Christ Church—Col. P. P. BONNEAU.

M. L. BONHAM.

—o—

STATE OF SOUTH CAROLINA.
HEADQUARTERS.
CHARLESTON, July 13, 1863.

The following gentlemen are requested to act in concert with those heretofore appointed to procure negro labor for immediate use.

For St. James Goose Creek, for the section above Dean Swamp—SWINTON WARNOCK.

For the section between Dean Swamp and Wassamassaw—JAMES WIGGINS.

For Wasmassaw neighborhood—GEORGE C. OWENS. M. L. BONHAM.

HEADQUARTERS
DEPARTMENT OF SOUTH CAROLINA, GEORGIA AND FLA.,
CHARLESTON, S. C., July 18, 1863.

[*GENERAL ORDERS NO. 87.*]

WHILE THE COMMANDING GENERAL REGRETS that the enemy has succeeded in effecting a landing upon Morris Island, he acknowledges with satisfaction the conduct of the troops in their brave and prolonged resistance against a force largely their superior in numbers, and is specially gratified by the spirit and success with which the garrison of BATTERY WAGNER and the troops under Colonel GRAHAM repelled the assaults on that fortifica-

THE NIGHT ATTACK.

At a few minutes before eight o'clock our pickets gave notice that the enemy, in heavy force was moving to the assault. The attack was not unexpected, and our men, though much jaded by the fatigues and exposure of the day, sprang to their places with zeal and alacrity. The enemy advanced in two columns of about 3,000 men each, the whole under the command of Brigadier General STRONG. The column which attacked our right was composed partially of negro troops, who were put in the advance. On our left, the other column advanced with spirit, under a severe fire from the Dahlgreen guns and columbiads of Fort Sumter. As the column advanced at the double-quick, the guns of Battery Wagner also opened, When the enemy had reached a point about sixty yards distant, our infantry, posted behind the parapet, poured a galling fire into the moving masses; the Yankees, nevertheless, in considerable force, succeeded in gaining the trench, and began to clamber up the sides of the Battery. At this moment, Lieut. WATIES, of Blake's Battery, who was in charge of two brass howitzers (belonging to a detachment of artillery under Capt. DEPASS, of White's Battalion) opened a raking fire which swept the strench, playing terrific havoc in the ranks of the assailants. The howitzers had been assigned to this position which they occupied so advantageously for us, at the instance of Col. HARRIS, of the Engineers, all the horses belonging to the section having been put *hors du combat* during the day. Twice the enemy was driven back at this part of our works (the left), and the trench filled with the enemy's dead attests the severity of the conflict there.

On the right, the negro troops were met with a terrible cross fire of musketry. Here were posted, among other troops, the Charleston Battalion, and these gallant men behaved in a manner worthy the fame their organization had so dearly won at Secessionville. The second assault was still more desperate than the first, but it was met and repelled in the same gallant style by the brave troops, Georgians, North Carolinians, and sons of our own city, who stood shoulder to shoulder in the fight.

The Franklin Repository.

VOL. 70. | CHAMBERSBURG, PA., WEDNESDAY, JULY 22, 1863. | NO. 26.

Franklin Repository.

PHILADELPHIA.

The Alarm in Philadelphia—Prompt Organization of Regiments—The Loyal Sentiment of the City—The Clergy—Rejoicings Over the Union Victories.

Correspondence of the Franklin Repository.

PHILADELPHIA, July 18, 1863.

For several weeks there has been but one question on the lips of every person, old and young, and that the absorbing, the vital subject of the war. An apparently fatal apathy had taken possession of our people, previous to the entering of the rebel army into Pennsylvania, but when it was announced that the Capital of the State was in danger, and when all felt that, if it could not be successfully defended, the rebel hordes would appear on the banks of the Schuylkill, the excitement became intense. Recruiting for the defence of the State was vigorously pushed, and the city soon exceeded the requisition made by the Governor.

But those were anxious days and nights which preceded the battle of Gettysburg. Every person you met was agitated and alarmed, and fear of approaching calamity was depicted in every countenance. If Lee should be successful, what was to prevent him from marching on Philadelphia, or on Baltimore, or indeed enforcing a dishonorable peace, at the cannon's mouth, in the streets of Washington. Never did weightier issues hang on the result of a single battle; and, under Providence, the Army of the Potomac proved itself equal to the emergency. All honor to that army and its gallant leader. They saved a State from destruction and a Nation from disgrace, if they could not—what was perhaps too much to hope for—prevent the shattered columns of the enemy from recrossing the Potomac. The first report of Meade's victory was received here with every demonstration of joy. Never were the tidings of victory borne to more grateful ears. The sense of uneasiness, which had for days hung over the city like a pall, was removed. Men saluted each other in joyful strains, and a feeling of relief was apparent in every face.

This city, although troubled with a few Copperheads, has been thoroughly loyal ever since the opening of the rebellion, and the loyal sentiment never was stronger than at the present time. This fact was clearly manifested, during the dark days preceding the battle of Gettysburg. Many touching instances could be given in illustration, and I think none more worthy of mention than the calling of two hundred clergymen in a body on the Mayor, and tendering him their services in working upon the entrenchments of the city.

The draft is quietly progressing here, and no indication of trouble appears, nor is any apprehended.

The Union League have sent, under their auspices, three regiments for the defence of the State.

The news of the fall of Vicksburg, following so closely on the victory at Gettysburg, caused nearly a surfeit of good news. Besides the usual popular manifestations of delight, the State House bell was rung on the occasion, which is only done when great events occur. And now we have the victory of Port Hudson, which should about finish the Rebellion in the Southwest.

TUSCARORA.

BRIEF WAR ITEMS.

A dispatch dated Cairo, July 15, to the Cincinnati *Gazette*, says: "Parties from Helena represent that Gen. Blunt has captured Little Rock, with a large number of prisoners."

Lee is said to be pushing as rapidly as possible for Culpepper, and will hardly stop until he is beyond the Rappahannock. The necessity of feeding his army, which cannot well be accomplished at any great distance from Richmond, will hurry his movements.

General Sherman has advanced as far east from Vicksburg as Bolton, half way to Jackson. Johnson had his headquarters at that place at the last accounts. Sherman has been unable to find any traces of the main body of Johnston's army, and has been much delayed in the roads by obstructions placed there.

Gen. Sherman's victory over Johnston's rear guard turns out even more brilliant than first reported. Instead of capturing two thousand prisoners, it seems that he took the entire division comprising the rear guard, numbering some six thousand, infantry, cavalry and artillery. Johnston was in full retreat across Pearl river, with Sherman hotly in pursuit.

By a bearer of dispatches we have further details of the capture of Port Hudson, by Gen. Banks. He took possession of the town on the 9th inst. The garrison consisted of 7000 men, and we took also 35 field pieces, 25 siege guns, and 10,000 small arms. Amongst the prisoners were Major General Gardner, Brigadier General Beale, and Colonels Steadman, Mills, and others.

A few days since our black troops at Goodrich's Landing, on the Mississippi river, were attacked by the rebels. Two gunboats were sent up, and succeeded in driving off the attacking party, and shelled them for fifteen miles along the river bank. They also rescued a number of blacks who had been made prisoners. They were also pursued to Delphi, and many of them killed. In the flight they left all the plunder they had seized.

THE SEAT OF WAR IN PENNSYLVANIA AND MARYLAND.

Scene of the Great Battles betwean the Rebel Army under the Command of Gen. LEE, and the Army of the Potomac under the Command of Gen. MEADE. Showing also the Defensive position assumed by LEE's Army from Williamsport to Sheppardstown.

The following are Gen. Meade's official dispatches announcing the retreat of Lee:

Headquarters Army of the Potomac, July 14, 1863.—H. W. HALLECK, General-in-Chief:—My cavalry now occupy Falling Waters, having overtaken and captured a brigade of infantry, 1500 strong, with two guns, two caissons, two battle flags and a large number of small arms.

The enemy are all across the Potomac.

GEORGE G. MEADE, Maj. Gen.

Headquarters Army of the Potomac, July 14. 1863, 8.30 P. M.—To Major General HALLECK:—My cavalry have captured five hundred prisoners in addition to those previously reported.

Gen. Pettigrew, of the Confederate Army, was killed this morning in the attack on the enemy's rear guard.

His body is in our hands.

(Signed) G. G. MEADE, Maj. Gen.

General Gilmore's official despatch, dated July 12th, confirms the previously reported brilliant advance of that officer. He is on the right road to Charleston, and proceeding in the most effective way. Having cleared out all the lower batteries of the Rebels, and having captured eleven of their heavy guns, he has pushed forward his infantry within six hundred yards of Fort Wagner, which is situated on the northeast end of Morris Island, opposite to Fort Sumter, at a distance of twelve hundred yards. This brings General Gilmore within eighteen hundred yards of Sumter itself, quite within reach of the guns with which he battered down Fort Pulaski. At last the attack on Charleston gives bright promise of success.

General Heintzelman, desirous of ascertaining whether the rebels occupied the Shenandoah Valley in any force, sent out a reconnoissance of cavalry and artillery, some three days since, which discovered but few of the enemy. The expedition pushed on to Ashby's Gap, and found it held by a force of three or four hundred rebels. Col. Lowell gallantly dashed upon and drove them from the Gap, capturing a rebel adjutant general and a number of other officers.

THE Fulton, from Port Royal, brings news to the 15th inst. Gen. Gilmore had made an assault upon Fort Wagner, with a brigade composed of the 7th Connecticut, 9th Maine and the 47th and 48th New York, with the 76th Pennsylvania in reserve. The two first named regiments actually mounted the parapet, but were forced back by the murderous fire of the enemy. Our troops were badly cut up, losing near 300 men in the attack.—After the repulse Gen, Gilmore threw up intrenchments near the fort, and when the Fulton left Port Royal he was besieging it with a prospect of reducing it in a day or two. Six monitors, the New Ironsides and a number of gunboats were engaged in bombarding Fort Sumter, and the effect of their fire was plainly visible. Large breaches were made in the walls and as each shot struck clouds of dust and sand were thrown into the air. Gen. Terry held James Island up to Secessionville. There was much sickness among the troops at Port Royal and the adjacent posts.

RIOT IN NEW YORK!

COPPERHEADS RESISTING THE DRAFT!

Conscription Offices Destroyed!

A NUMBER OF CITIZENS KILLED!

Houses and Stores Plundered!

THE RIOT QUELLED!

On the 13th inst. a mob broke out in New York, ostensibly to resist the draft about to be made, and for three days it defied the civil and military authorities.

The several conscription offices were destroyed; the houses of the Mayor, Post Master and many other buildings burned, and a number of citizens killed. Every negro found on the street was brutally beaten and many fatally.

Gov. Seymour addressed the mob while rioting, plundering and murdering were going on in several parts of the city, and assured them that he was their friend—that they had been his friends. He assured them that he would stop the draft, and begged them in gingerly terms to go home. They did not go however, nor did Seymour get the draft stopped, and after three days of the most shameless parleying with a mob, he was compelled to issue a third proclamation declaring that the peace of the city must be preserved at all hazards.

The military were called out under the command of Gen. Brown, and in several instances had to fire on the mob to disperse them. Col. O'Brien, of the military, was most brutally murdered by the mob.

Thieves of every grade swelled the mob, and it finally became a mere plundering horde. After three days it was completely mastered and order reigns again in Gotham.

The government has given officiai notice that the draft will be made in New York, and elsewhere without delay.

THE RETREAT OF LEE INTO VIRGINIA.

ARMY OF THE POTOMAC, July 14.—The first news of the retreat of Lee and his army into Virginia was received at Hagerstown at four o'clock this morning, from a citizen who lived within their lines.

General Kilpatrick, commanding a cavalry division at that point, soon had his men in the road, and reached Williamsport at 7 o'clock, where he found 500 rebel soldiers who had deserted.

The news reached General Meade's headquarters at five o'clock, when Gen. Buford's division of cavalry was orderd to Falling Waters, where they engaged and captured a brigade of rebels under General Pettigrew, who was killed.

The position of the rebels was naturally a strong one, but their works were not of much account, consisting principally of hurriedly constructed rifle pits.

After Lee had retreated across the river it was ascertained that he commenced to move his artillery to the rear as early as yesterday morning, which was continued during the whole day, depending almost wholly upon the infantry and cavalry to hold our army in check.

Gen. Meade held a council of war on Saturday and Sunday evenings, consisting of his corps commanders, when the question of attack was freely discussed. All the Generals assembled were in favor of an immediate attack, except Sedgwick, Slocum, Sykes and French.

Gen. Meade himself was in favor of active operations, but finding his corps commanders equally divided, he hesitated to give the order, and the rebel army was allowed to make its escape.

An order was issued on Monday evening for a movement along the whole line at 7 o'clock this morning.

Yesterday afternoon about 2,000 of the Pennsylvania militia, which arrived in the vicinity of Hagerstown, were taken to the front and put into action. They were immediately ordered to charge the enemy, which was promptly done, but not without severe loss.

FALL OF PORT HUDSON.

The Mississippi Open.

Official Dispatches from Gens. Banks and Grant.

The Town Occupied by Union Troops on the 9th instant.

WASHINGTON, July 15.

The following dispatch has been received:

VICKSBURG, Miss., July 11—3 P. M.

To Maj. Gen. Halleck, General-in-Chief:

The following dispatch has just been received from Gen. Banks:

BEFORE PORT HUDSON, July 8th, 1863.

General:—The Mississippi is now opened.

I have the honor to inform you that the garrison of Port Hudson surrendered unconditional this afternoon.

We shall take formal possession at seven o'clock in the morning. (Signed)

N. P. BANKS, Maj. Gen.

U. S. GRANT, Maj. Gen.

THE BATTLE OF GETTYSBURG.

A Full Account of the Three Days' Conflict.

As a connected narrative of the memorable battles fought on Wednesday, Thursday and Friday, the 1st, 2d and 3d of July, near Gettysburg, in Adams county, Pennsylvania, will be valuable for reference, and also satisfactory as a *resume* of the details furnished in our despatches, we think the following carefully written account will be acceptable to our readers:

Gen. Meade took command of this army on Sunday, the 28th ult. At that time his headquarters were at Frederick, and Lee's at Hagerstown. It will be seen that he was in the southwest, and consequently in the rear of the foe, imminently threatening his line of retreat. The army of the Potomac began its campaign from that moment. Orders were issued to the several corps to move early in the evening, and on the morning of the 29th our whole brilliant and hopeful host was in motion towards Pennsylvania. The First, Third and Eleventh corps encamped on Tuesday at Emmettsburg; the Second and Twelfth also pitched their tents near by. The Sixth corps marched to Carlisle Wednesday morning, the first day of this month forever memorable. The First Corps, under Major-General Reynolds, and the Eleventh, under Major-General Howard, started for Gettysburg, Reynolds in command, where they arrived at 10 o'clock, A. M. The corps, in the advance, marched directly through the town. The enemy was discovered posted in a wood to the westward, near the Lutheran Theological Seminary. The beginning of the three days' conflict was at hand.

THE BATTLE OF WEDNESDAY.

One who has been in the presence, who now sits among the echoes, and whose brain teems with rushing memories of a conflict so recent and so vast, may well pause before attempting to indicate its magnitude or describe its progress. Rash as the advance of Gen. Reynolds has been pronounced by many brother officers who now lament his death, I question whether it was not after all for the best. It served at once as a reconnoissance, showing the enemy's exact position and probable force, and as a check upon any offensive movement which that enemy might have been intent upon. It secured the Army of the Potomac the commanding position on Cemetery Hill, from which the battles of the two succeeding days were chiefly fought, and which, had the rebel commander anticipated the engagement, he would doubtless have secured for himself. Not less, perhaps, than the skill of the generals who directed the battle on our side, gave us the victory. When, therefore, the heroic First Corps and its fated commander placed themselves in the terrible dilemma of Wednesday morning, they won a knowledge by their sacrifice worth all the world to us thereafter. The corps marched in the following order: First division, under Gen. Wadsworth; Third division, under Gen. Doubleday; five full batteries, under Col. Wainwright; Fourth division, under Gen. Robinson.

A portion of our artillery took position half a mile south of the Seminary. The enemy opened fire on it with such fierceness as forced the batteries to retire, which they commenced doing in good order. Gen. Wadsworth immediately came to their aid; two of his regiments, the 2d Wisconsin and the Twenty-Fourth Michigan charged the rebel infantry, forcing them in turn to retire. The batteries assumed an excellent position further in the rear, which they held during the day. Gen. Reynolds now rode forward to inspect the field and ascertain the most favorable line for the disposal of his troops. One or two members of his staff were with him. The enemy at that instant poured in a cruel musketry fire upon the group of officers; a bullet struck Gen. Reynolds in the neck, wounding him mortally. Crying out, with a voice that thrilled the hearts of his soldiers, "Forward! for God's sake, forward!" he turned for an instant, beheld the order obeyed by a line of shouting infantry, and falling into the arms of Capt. Wilcox, his aid, who rode beside him, his life went out with the words, "Good God, Wilcox, I am killed."

The command of the corps devolved upon Gen. Doubleday, who hurried to the front, placed it in position, and awaited a charge which it was seen the rebels were about to make. An eminence whereon stood a piece of woods was the important point thenceforth to be defended. The rebels advanced and opened fire from their entire line. They were instantly charged upon by Meredith's Western brigade, who, without firing a shot, but with a tremendous cheer, dashed forward with such swiftness as to surround nearly 600 of the feo, who were taken prisoners. A strong column immediately advanced against us from the woods, and, though volley after volley was pourded into them, did not waver. Their proximity and strength at last became so threatening that the brigades of the Second division were ordered to make another charge, which was even more successful than the first. Their momentum was like an avalanche; the rebels were shot, bayoneted, and driven to partial retreat, more than two regiments falling into our hands alive. Our ranks suffered fearfully in this demonstration, and it was evident that such fighting could not long go on. The Eleventh corps now made its appearance, and its General (Howard) assumed command of the forces. Steinwehr was ordered to hold Gettysburg and Cemetery hill —all his artillery being placed in the latter position. The other two divisions of the Eleventh corps, under Shultz and Barlow, then supported the First corps, on the right in time to resist two desperate charges by Ewell's troops. A third charge was now made by the entire rebel force in front, which comprised the corps of Hill and Ewell, sixty-two thousand strong. The shock was awful. The superior numbers of the foe enabled them to overlap both our flanks, threatening us with surrounding and capture. Their main effort was directed against our left wing and notwithstanding the gallant fighting done by our soldiers at that point, they at last obtained such advantage that Gen. Howard was forced to retire his command through the town to the east, which was done in good order, the compliments of the rebels meanwhile falling thick among it, in the shape of shells, grape and canister. The two corps were placed in line of battle on Cemetery Hill at evening, having withstood during the entire day the assaults of an enemy outnumbering them three to one. Not without grief, not without misgiving, did the officers and soldiers of those corps contemplate the day's engagement and await the onset they believed was to come. Their comrades lay in heaps beyond the village whose spires gleamed peacefully in the sunset before them. Reynolds the beloved, and the brave, was dead, and Zook slumbered beside him. Barlow, Paul, many field and scores of line officers had been killed. The men of the First corps alone could in few instances turn to speak to the ones who stood beside them in the morning without meeting with a vacant space. The havoc in that corps was so frightful as to decimate it fully one-half, and that in the Eleventh corps —nobly rescued from the suspicion which rested upon it before—was scarcely less great. Yet the little army flinched not, but stood ready to fall as others had fallen even to the last man. With what a thrill of relief Gen. Howard, who had sent messenger after messenger during the day to Slocum and Sickles, saw in the distance at evening the approaching bayonets of the Third and Twelfth corps, only they can tell who fought beside him. Those corps arrived assumed positions to the right and left of the First and Eleventh on the heights about Cemetery Hill at dusk. The enemy made no further demonstration that night. Gen. Meade and staff arrived before 11 o'clock. The commander then examined the position, and posted the several corps in the following order: the Twelfth (Slocum) on the right, the Eleventh (Howard) next, the Second (Hancock), First (Doubleday), and Third (Sickles) in the center, the Fifth (Sykes) on the extreme left. The situation was brilliant commanding. For almost the first time in the history of this army's career belonged the advantage in the decisive battles which ensued.

The heights on which our troops were posted sloped gently downward from our front. The line stretched in a semi-circle—its convex centre toward Gettysburg, the extremes toward the southwest and south. Ledges on the interior sides gave our soldiers in some instances a partial shelter from artillery. Every road was commanded by our cannon, and the routes by which Lee might otherwise soonest retreat in case of his defeat were all in our possession. At every one weaker than others reserves were judiciously posted, and the cavalry—an arm of the service scarcely brought into play in some recent and destructive battles—protected both our flanks in immense numbers.

Thus the great army lay down to sleep at midnight, and awoke on the morn of a day more sanguinary than the last.

THE BATTLE ON THURSDAY.

On what a spectacle the sun of Thursday rose, the memory of at least that portion of our forces who witnessed it from Cemetery Hill will linger forever. From its crest the muzzles of fifty cannon pointed toward the hills beyond the town. From the bluffs to the right and left additional artillery frowned, and away on either side, in a graceful and majestic curve, thousands of infantry moved into battle line, their bayonets gleaming like serpents' scales. The roofs of Gettysburg in the valley below, the rifs of woodland along the borders of Rock creek, the orchards far down on the left, the fields green and beautiful, in which the cattle were calmly grazing, composed a scene of such peace as it appeared was never made to be marred by the clangor of battle. I strolled out to the cemetery ere the dew was yet melted from the grass, and leaned against a monument to listen to the singing of birds. One note, milder than the rest, had just broken from the throat of an oriole in the foliage above me when the sullen rattle of musketry on the left told that skirmishing had begun. Similar firing soon opened along the entire rebel line, and although no notable demonstration was made during the forenoon, it was apparent that the enemy was feeling our strength preliminary to some decisive effort.

The day wore on full of anxious suspense. It was not until four o'clock in the afternoon that the enemy gave voice in earnest.

He then began a heavy fire on Cemetery Hill. It must not be thought that this wrathful fire was unanswered. Our artillery began to play within a few moments and hurled back defiance and like destruction upon the rebel lines. Until six o'clock the roar of cannon, the rush of missiles and the bursting of bombs filled all the air. The clangor alone of this awful combat might well have confused and awed a less cool and watchful commander than General Meade. It did not confuse him. With the calculation of a tactician and the eye of an experienced judge he watched from his headquarters on the hill whatever movement under the murky cloud which enveloped the rebel lines might first disclose the intention which it was evident this artillery firing covered. About six o'clock p. m., silence, deep, awfully impressive, but momentary, was permitted as if by magic to dwell upon the field. Only the groans unheard before of the wounded and dying, only the murmur—a morning memory—of the breeze through the foliage, only the low rattle of preparation for what was to come, embroidered this black stillness. Then, as the smoke beyond the village was lightly borne to the eastward, the woods on the left were seen filled with dark masses of infantry, three columns deep, who advanced at a quickstep. Magnificent! Such a charge by such a force—full 45,000 men, under Hill and Longstreet—even though it threatened to pierce and annihilate the 3d Corps, against which it was directed, drew forth cries of admiration from all who beheld it. General Sickles and his splendid command withstood the shock with a determination that checked, but could not fully restrain it. Back, inch by inch, fighting, falling, dying, cheering, the men retired. The rebels came on more furiously, halting at intervals, pouring volleys that struck our troops down in scores.

General Sickles, fighting desperately, was struck in the leg and fell. The 2d Corps come to the aid of his decimated column.—The battle then grew fearful. Standing firmly up against the storm, our troops, though still outnumbered, gave back shot for shot, volley for volley, almost death for death. Still the enemy was not restrained. Down he came upon our left with a momentum that nothing could check. The rifled guns that lay before our infantry on a knoll were in danger of capture. Gen. Hancock was wounded in the thigh, General Gibbon in the shoulder. The 5th Corps, as the 1st and 2d wavered anew, went into the breach with such shouts and such volleys as made the rebel column tremble at last. Up from the valley behind, another battery came rolling to the heights and flung its contents in an instant down in the midst of the enemy's ranks. Crash! Crash! with discharges deafening, terrible, the musketry firing went on; the enemy, reforming after each discharge with wondrous celerity and firmness, still pressed up the declivity. What hideous carnage filled the minutes between the appearance of the 5th Corps and the advance to the support of the rebel columns of still another column from the right, I can not bear to tell. Men fell as the leaves fall in autumn before those horrible discharges.—Faltering for an instant, the rebel columns seemed about to recede before the tempest. But their officers, who could be seen through the smoke of the conflict galloping and swinging their swords along the lines, rallied them anew, and the next instant the whole line sprang forward as if to break through our own by mere weight of numbers. A division from the 12th Corps from the right reached the scene at this instant, and at the same time Sedgwick came up with the 6th corps, having finished a march of nearly thirty-six consecutive hours. To what rescue they came, their officers saw and told them. Weary as they were, bare-footed, hungry, fit to drop for slumber as they were, the wish for victory was so blended with the thought of exhaustion that they cast themselves in turn *en masse* into line of battle, and went down on the enemy with death in their weapons and cheers on their lips. The rebel camel's back was broken by this "feather." His line staggered, reeled, and drifted slowly back, while the shouts of our soldiers lifed up amid the roar of musketry over the bodies of the dead and wounded, proclaimed the completeness of their victory Meanwhile, as the division of Slocum's corps on the extreme right left its post to join in this triumph, another column of the enemy, under command of Gen. Ewell, had dashed savagely against our weakened right wing, and as the failure to turn our left became known it seemed as if determination to conquer in this part of the field overcame alike the enemy's fear of death and his plan for victory elsewhere. The fighting was terrific, and for fifteen minutes the attack to which the three divisions of the 12th Corps were subjected was more furious than anything ever known in the history of this army. The 6th corps came to their support, the 1st corps followed; and from dusk into darkness, until half past nine o'clock, the battle raged with varied fortune and unabated fury. Our troops were compelled by overpowering numbers to fall back a short distance, abandoning several rifle-pits and an advantageous position to the enemy, who, haughty over his advantage and made desperate by defeat in other quarters, then made a last struggling charge against that division of our right wing commanded by Gen. Geary. General Geary's troops immortalized themselves by their resistance to this attempt. They stood like adamant, a moveless, death-dealing machine, before whose volleys the rebel columns withered and went down by hundreds. After a slaughter inconceivable the repulse of Ewell was complete, and he retired at ten o'clock P. M., to the position before referred to. The firing from all quarters of the field ceased soon after that hour, and no other attack was made until morning.

THE BATTLE OF FRIDAY.

As one who stands in a tower and looks down upon a lengthy pageant marching through a thoroughfare, finds it impossible at the close to recall in order the appearances and the incidents of the scene, so I, who sit this evening on a camp-stool beside the ruins of the monument against which I leaned listening to the robin of yesterday, find it impossible to recall with distinctness the details of the unparalleled battle just closed. The conflict, waged by 160,000 men, which has occupied, with scarcely an interval of rest, the entire day, from 4 A. M. until 6 o'clock this evening, contains so much, so *near*, and such voluminous matter of interest as one mind cannot grasp without time for reflection.

The last engagement has been the fiercest and most sanguinary of the war. It was begun at daylight by Gen. Slocum, whose troops, maddened by the loss of many comrades, and eager to retrieve the position lost by them on the preceding evening, advanced and delivered a destructive fire against the rebels under Ewell. That general's entire force responded with a charge that is memorable even beyond those made by them yesterday. It was desperation against courage! The fire of the enemy was mingled with yells, pitched even above its clangor. They came on, and on, and on, while the national troops, splendidly handled and well posted, stood unshaken to receive them. The fire with which they did receive them was so rapid and so thick as to envelope the ranks of its deliverers with a pall that shut them from sight during the battle which raged thenceforward for six dreary hours. Out of this pall no straggler came to the rear. The line scarcely flinched from its position during the entire conflict. Huge masses of rebel infantry threw themselves into it again and again in vain. Back, as a ball hurled against a rock, these masses recoiled, and were reformed to be hurled anew against it with a fierceness unfruitful of success—fruitful of carnage, as before. The strong position occupied by Gen. Geary, and that held by Gen. Birney, met the first and hardest assaults, but only fell back a short distance before fearful odds, to re-advance, to re-assume and to hold their place in company with Sykes' division of the Fifth corps and Humphrey's (Berry's old divison) of the Third, when, judiciously reinforced with artillery, they renewed and continued the contest until its close. It seemed as if the gray-uniformed troops, who were advanced and re-advanced by their officers up to the very edge of the line of smoke in front of our infantry, were impelled by some terror in their rear, which they were as unable to withstand as they were to make headway against the fire in their front. It was hard to believe such desperation voluntary. It was harder to believe that the courage which withstood and defeated it was mortal.

The enemy gradually drew forward his whole line until in many places a hand to hand conflict raged for minutes. His artillery, answered by ours, played upon our columns with frightful result, yet they did not waver. The battle was in this way evenly contested for a time, but at a time when it seemed problematical which side would gain the victory, a reinforcement arrived and were formed in line at such a position as to enfilade the enemy and teach him at last the futility of his efforts. Disorded, routed, and confused, his whole force retreated, and at 11 o'clock the battle ceased and the stillness of death ensued. The silence contined until 2 P. M. At this moment the rebel artillery from all points, in a circle radiating around our own, began a terrific and concentrated fire on Cemetery Hill, which was held, as I have previously stated, by the Eleventh and Second corps. The flock of pigeons, which not ten minutes previous had darkened the sky above, were scarcely thicker than the flock of horrible missiles that now, instead of sailing harmlessly above, descended upon our position. The atmosphere was thick with shot and shell. The storm broke upon us so suddenly that soldiers and officers—who leaped, as it began, from their tents, or from lazy siestas on the grass—were stricken in their rising with mortal wounds and died, some with cigars between their teeth, some with pieces of food in their fingers, and one at least—a pale young German, from Pennsylvania—with a miniature of his sister in his hands, that seemed more meet to grasp an artist's pencil than a musket. Horses fell, shrieking such awful cries as Cooper told of, and writhing about in helpless agony. The boards of fences, scattered by explosion, flew in splinters through the air. The earth, torn up in clouds, blinded the eyes of hurrying men; and through the branches of the trees, and among the grave-stones of the cemetery, a shower of destruction crashed ceaselessly. As, with hundreds of others, I groped through this tempest of death for the shelter of the bluff, an old man, a private in a company belonging to the 24th Michigan, was struck scarcely ten feet away by a cannon ball, which tore through him, extorting such a low, intense cry of mortal pain as I pray God I may never again hear. The hill, which seemed alone devoted to this rain of death, was clear in nearly all its unsheltered places within five minutes after the fire began.

Our batteries responded immediately.—Three hours of cannonading ensued, exceeding in fierceness any ever known. Probably three hundred cannon were fired simultaneously until 4 o'clock, when the rebel infantry were again seen massing in the woods fronting our centre, formed by the First and Second corps. Gen. Doubleday's troops met this charge with the same heroic courage that had so often repelled the enemy in his desperate attempts. The charge was made spiritedly, but less venemously than before. Gen. Webb, commanding the Second brigade, Second division of the Second corps, met the main fury of the attack with a steady fire that served to retard the enemy's advance for a moment. That moment was occupied by the rebel General Armistead in steadying his troops behind the fence. Gen. Webb immediately ordered a charge, which was made with such eagerness and swiftness, and supported by such numbers of our troops, as enabled us to partially surround the enemy, and capture Gen. Armistead and 3,000 of his men. The carnage which accompanied this charge and the terror inspired by it were so great as to reduce the foe to actual cowardice. They fell upon their knees and faces, holding forward their guns and begging for mercy, while their escaped comrades, panic-stricken and utterly routed rushed down across the ditches and fences through the fields and through Gettysburg. Not a column remained to make another start. The triumph fought for during these three terrible days belonged at last to the noble Army of the Potomac.

TRACES OF THE STRUGGLE AT THE CEMETERY.

Monuments and head-stones lie here and there overturned. Graves, once carefully tended by some loving hand, have been trampled by horses' feet until the vestiges of verdure have disappeared. The neat and well-trained shrubbery has vanished, or is but a broken and withered mass of tangled brush-wood. On one grave lies a dead artillery horse, fast decomposing under the July sun. On another lie the torn garments of some wounded soldier, stained and saturated with his blood. Across a small headstone, bearing the words, "To the memory of our beloved child, Mary," lie the fragments of a musket shattered by a cannon shot. In the centre of a space enclosed by an iron fence, and containing a half dozen graves, a few rails are still standing where they were erected by our soldiers and served to support the shelter tents of a bivouacking squad. A family shaft has been broken in fragments by a shell, and only the base remains, with a portion of the inscription thereon. Stone after stone felt the effects of the *feu d'enfer* that was poured upon the crest of the hill. Cannon thundered, and foot and horse soldiers trampled over the sleeping place of the dead. Other dead were added to those who are resting here, and many a wounded soldier still lives to remember the contest above those silent graves.

POSITION OF CEMETERY HILL—ITS IMPORTANCE.

The hill on which this cemetery is located was the centre of our line of battle and the key to the whole position. Had the rebels been able to carry this point, they would have forced us into retreat, and the whole battle would have been lost. To pierce our line here was Lee's great endeavor, and he threw his best brigades against it. Wave after wave of living valor rolled up that slope only to roll back again under the deadly fire of our artillery and infantry. It was on this hill, a little to the right of the cemetery where occurred the charge of the famous brigade of Louisiana Tigers. It was their boast that they were never yet foiled in an attempt to take a battery, but on this occasion they suffered a defeat and nearly annihilation. Sad and dispirited they mourn their repulse and terrible losses in the charge.

THE REBEL DEAD.

Retracing my steps, before reaching the extreme left, I returned to the centre of our position, on the Cemetery Hill. I do not follow the path by which I come, but take a route along the hollow, between the two ridges. It was across this hollow that the charges were made in the assault upon our position. Much blood was poured out between these two swells of land. Most of the dead have been buried where they fell, or gathered in little clusters beneath some spreading tree or beside clumps of bushes. Some of the rebel dead are still uncovered. The first that meets my gaze, I come upon suddenly, as I descend a bank, some three or four feet in height, to the side of a small spring. He is lying near the spring, as if he had crawled there to obtain a draught of water. His hands are outspread upon the earth, and clutching at the little tufts of grass beneath them. His haversack and canteen are still hanging • him, and his hat is lying near him. His musket is gone; either carried off by his comrades, taken by some relic seeker, or placed in the accumulated heap by our own soldiers.

The body of another rebel attracts my attention by a singular circumstance. The face is discolored in the extreme, black as that of the purest Congo negro. The hands are as delicate as those of a lady and of snowy whiteness. With the exception of the face, the body is but little swollen, and there are no signs of the commencement of decompotion. Several bodies that I find show blackened faces, but no others than this display such a contrast between the color of the face and hands. Near a small white house on the rebel line lies the body of an officer, evidently a lieutenant or captain. His right arm is extended as if to grasp the hand of a friend. All possible positions in which a dying man can fall can be noticed on this field.

SHELLING GENERAL MEADE'S HEADQUARTERS

The little farm house on the Emmettsburg road, where General Meade held his headquarters during the cannonade is most fearfully cut up. It is already known how Gen. Lee masked his artillery and opened with one hundred and thirty pieces at the same moment. Two shells in every second of time fell around those headquarters. The shells tore through the little white building exploding and scattering their fragments in every direction. Not a spot anywhere was safe. One shell through the doorstep, another in the chimney, a third shattering a rafter, a fourth cutting off the legs of a chair in which a staff officer was seated; others severed and splintered the posts in front of the house, howled through the trees by which the dwelling was surrounded, and raised deep furrows of the soft earth. At the fence in front of the building the horses of aids and orderlies were standing. A dozen of the frightened animals fell by the rebel projectiles, and others broke away and fled in the wildest fright towards the rear. One staff officer, and another, and another, were wounded. Strange to say, amid all this iron hail, no one of the staff was killed. Every man stared death full in the face, and had little prospect of escaping unhurt. Rarely in the history of war has there been a scene to equal this.

LEE'S ADDRESS TO HIS ARMY.

FREDERICK, July 12, 1863.—The following general order of General R. E. Lee to the Rebel army, issued from Hagerstown, on Saturday, was found when General Kilpatrick entered the town on Sunday morning:

GENERAL ORDERS—NO. 16.

HEAD-QUARTERS, ARMY OF NORTHERN VIRGINIA, July 11, 1863.—After the long and trying marches, endured with the fortitude that has ever characterized the soldiers of the Army of Northern Virginia, you have penetrated to the country of our enemies, and recalled to the defense of their own soil those who were engaged in the invasion of ours. You have fought a fierce and sanguinary battle, which, *if not attended with the success that has hitherto crowned your efforts*, was marked by the same heroic spirit that has commanded the respect of your enemies, the gratitude of your country, and the admiration of mankind.

Once more you are called upon to meet the enemy from whom you have torn so many fields, the names of which will never die. Once more the eyes of your countrymen are turned upon you, and again do wives and sisters, fathers and mothers, and helpless children, lean for defense on your strong arms and brave hearts. Let every soldier remember that on his courage and fidelity depends all that makes life worth having, the freedom of his country, the honor of his people and the security of his home. Let each heart grow strong in the remembrance of our glorious past, and in the thought of the inestimable blessings for which we contend; and invoking the assistance of that benign Power which has signally blessed our former efforts, let us go forth in confidence to secure the peace and safety of our country. Soldiers, your old enemy is before you. Win from him honor worthy of your right cause, worthy of your comrades dead on so many illustrious fields.

R. E. LEE, Gen. Com.

THE CONTEMPT IN WHICH THE REBELS HOLD PEACE SNEAKS.

We take the following remarkable article from the Richmond *Enquirer*, of June 12th, in which the whole tribe of Peace Sneaks, who are endeavoring to embarras the Government, and thus give aid and comfort to the Rebels, are brought under the old-time slave-driver's lash:

TWO YEARS HENCE.

In two years, as many persons hope, we may probably have peace—that is, always provided we continue to repulse and defeat the invading enemy. The Yankee "Democracy" is certainly arousing itself, and preparing for a new struggle (at the ballot-box,) in the *great cause of the "spoils,"* or as they call it, the cause of Constitutional Liberty. Those democrats are evidently beginning to *raise a Peace platform for their next Presidential election:* and if they have the good luck to be helped on and sustained by more and more serious disasters of the Yankee army in the field, there is no doubt that the present devourers of the said spoils at Washington may soon be so discredited and decried that our enemy's country would be ripe for such peaceful ballot-box revolution.

It is sincerely to be hoped that those earnest champions of constitutional freedom will be helped on and sustained in the manner they require—namely, by continued and severe reverses in the field; and it is the first and most urgent duty of our countrymen so to help and sustain that Democratic party.—It is nothing to us which of their factions may devour the "spoils;" just as little does it signify to us whether they recover or do not recover that constitutional liberty which they so wantonly threw away in the mad pursuit of Southern conquest and plunder. *But it is of the utmost importance to us to aid in stimulating disaffection among Yankees against their own Government, and in demoralizing and disintegrating society in that God-abandoned country.* We can do this only in one way—namely, by thrashing their armies and carrying the war to their own firesides. Then, indeed, conscientious constitutional principles will hold sway; peace platforms will look attractive; arbitrary arrests will become odious, and habeas corpus be quoted at a premium. This is the only way we can help them. *In this sense, and to this extent, those Democrats are truly our allies, and we shall endeavor to do our duty by them.*

But they evidently look for other and further help at our hands, and of quite a different sort. No doubt they are pleased for the present, with the efficient aid which the Confederate army is affording them. Chancellorsville was a God-send to them, and the tremendous repulse at Port Hudson is quite a plank in their plat form. Yet they understand very well that no matter how soundly their armies may be happily beaten; no matter how completely Lincoln's present war policy may be condemned by its results, yet all this will not be enough to enable the *unterrified Democracy to clutch the "spoils,"*—or, as they phrase it, to restore the Constitution of their fathers. This, of itself would never give them a Peace-Democrat President and Cabinet; it would only result in another Abolitionist administration, with a new Secretary of War, and a new Commander-in-Chief, and a slightly different programme for "crushing the rebellion." Those Black Republicans are in power; after long waiting, pining, intriguing in the cold shade of the opposition; and they have now the numerical preponderance so decidedly that they both can and will hold on to the offices with a clutch like death. The Democrats can do absolutely nothing withont "the South," as they persist in terming these Confederate States; and they cannot bring themselves to *admit the thought that we would refuse to unite with them (as alas! we used to do) in a grand Universal Presidential campaign, for a Democratic President, with a Peace platform, and the "Constitution as it is."* In fact, this whole two years' war, and the two years' more war which has yet to be gone through, is itself, in their eyes, only a Presidential campaign, only somewhat more vivacious than ordinary.

This explains the Vallandigham Peace Meetings in New York and New Jersey; and the "manly declarations" of Mr. Horatio Seymour and other patriots. "Do not let us forget," says Fernando Wood, writing to the Philadelphia meeting, "that those who perpetrate such outrages as the arrest and banishment of Mr. Vallandigham, do so as necessary war measures. Let us, therefore, strike at the *cause* and declare for *peace and against the war.*"

This would sound very well if the said "declaring for peace" could have any effect whatever in bringing about peace. If a man falling from a tower could arrest his fall by declaring against it, then the declarations of Democrats against the war might be of some avail. As it is, they resemble that emphatic pronouncement of Mr. Washington Hunt: "Let it be proclaimed *upon the housetops*, that no citizen of New York shall be arrested without process of law." There is no use of brawling from the housetops what everybody knows to be nonsense. Or this resolution of the New Jersey meeting:

Resolved, That in the illegal seizure and banishment of the Hon. C. L. Vallandigham, the laws of our country have been outraged, the name of United States disgraced, and the rights of every citizen menaced, and that it is now the duty of a law respecting people to *demand* of the Administration that it at once and forever desist from such *deeds of despotism and crime.* [Enthusiasm.]

Demand, quotha? The starling that Mr. Sterne saw in the cage, said only "I can't get out." It would have been more "manly" to scream, "I demand to get out—I proclaim on the housetops that I *will* get out."

Another of the New Jersey resolutions throws an instructive light upon this whole movement, and its objects.

Resolved, That we renew our declaration of attachment to the Union, pledging to its friends, *wherever found*, our unwavering support, and to its enemies, in whatever guise, our undying hostility, and that, God, willing, we will stand by the Constitution and laws of our country, and under their sacred shield will maintain and defend our liberty and rights, "peaceably if we can forcibly if we must." [Great cheering.]

This phrase, "wherever found," implies that there are friends of the Union in this Confederacy, and the resolution obligingly pledges to them the support of the New Jersey Democracy—not surely without an equivalent return.

To the same meeting, Gen. Fitz John Porter writes a letter, declaring, of course, for the Constitution and resistance to despotism, and ending thus:

"The contest of arms, however, will not be required; the certain and peaceful remedy will be found in the ballot-box. Let us all possess our souls in patience. The remedy is ours."

Gen. Fitz John knows well that the remedy is *not* theirs, unless "the South" consent to throw its votes into that same ballot-box; and it is for this, and this only, that the Democratic hook is bated with "Peace." But in a speech of Senator Wall, of New Jersey, before a Democratic Club of Philadelphia (which we find printed in *The Sentinel*), is a passage more fully expounding the Democratic plan than any other we have seen. He says:

"Subjugation and annihilation being alike impossible, I am in favor of an immediate cessation of hostilities, for an armistice—that amid the lull of the strife the heat of passion shall have time to cool, and the calm, majestic voice of reason can be heard. In the midst of such a calm I am for endeavoring to learn from those in arms against us what their demands may be, and inviting their co-operation in the name of a common humanity, to some plan of reconciliation or reconstruction by which the sections may unite upon a more stable basis—a plan in which the questions upon which we have differed so long may be harmoniously adjusted; and each section, by virtue of the greatness developed in this war, may profit by the experience. If it shall be found that sectional opinions and prejudices are too obstinate, and the exasperations of this war have burnt too deep to settle it upon the basis of reconciliation or reconstruction, then I know that separation and reconstruction are inevitable."

Here is the whole plan; an armistice, and then "inviting our co-operation." During that armistice they hope that the "calm, majestic voice of reason" and a "common Christianity" might do something considerable.—The game, as they calculate, would then be on the board, with stakes so tempting! Mr. Wall would endeavor "to learn from us what our demands are."

Anything in reason he would be prepared to grant us; but if we replied, our demands are, that you bring away your troops from every inch of our soil, that you leave the Border States free to decide on their own destiny, that you evacuate all our forts and towns which you now hold, and make us rid of you and the whole breed of you forever, then Mr. Wall would exclaim, What! do you call that the calm, majestic voice of reason? Is that your common Christianity? He would say, *when I spoke of the calm majestic, &c., I meant the spoils;* when I said a common Christianity, *I meant money.* Let us talk rationally—how much common Christianity will you take?

In vain is a net spread in the sight of any bird. We are aware of them; and we will watch them well, and the friends of the Union, "wheresoever found." *Our views go a little further than theirs—we hope to so disorganize and disintegrate society in their country that they will rush into armed revolution and anarchy. We spit upon their ballot-box.* We care not what they "demand" in resolutions, nor what helpless trash they proclaim on the housetops. We do not believe in their power to attain so much as an armistice for two years to come. If an armistice, indeed, were offered, and the invading troops were withdrawn, of course we should not object to it, and good use could be made of it.

But, mark well, *ye armistice mongers!* During that suspension of hostilities all negotiations must be between Government and Government. Our lines should be more strictly guarded than ever. No negotiations or fraternization of parties by public meetings or private conferences; *no bargaining with the calm voice of reason; no secret pocketing of Wall's "Common Christianity."*

But armistice there will be none, and we are glad of it. Our sovereign independence is already won and paid for with treasures of brave blood. *It shall not be sold by pedlers, to be built into a Yankee platform.*

THE LOUISVILLE JOURNAL—an intensely Conservative and pro-slavery, but not exactly pro-rebel sheet—thus tartly rebukes the more reckless Copperheads:

We look at the columns of the Philadelphia *Evening Journal;* we read the speeches of peace factionists and the resolutions of their meetings, and while they have no word of commendation or encouragement for those who are engaged in fighting the battles of this war for the preservation of the Union we find that they are equally and most significantly silent in condemnation and execration of the Rebellion and of those who are endeavoring to overthrow the Government. When such men propose an armistice, we can see, but little difference between them and the rebel in arms; the former would destroy the country by cunning strategy, and the latter by open assault The patriotic Democracy, to which we turn with hope and encouragement in these terrible trials, is firmly in favor of sustaining the Government in all these measures which it deems indispensably necessary to secure a peace by putting down the Rebellion, and the more steadily and resolutely it adheres to this policy, the more extended will be the scope of its usefulness, and the more brilliant the successes which it must achieve before the people.

We have voluminous extracts from rebel papers of late dates. On the 3d of July the people were told that Lee's army is marching towards Baltimore. A considerable number of his men were doing so as prisoners of war, as the Enquirer will learn very soon. After Grant had taken Vicksburg, his natural playfulness of spirit seems to have shown itself, by his sending out parties of negroes to inform Johnston's army that he intended to make an assault on the city on that day.

Franklin Repository.

CHAMBERSBURG:

Wednesday Morning, July 22, 1863.

☞ JOHN K. SHRYOCK is authorized to receive Subscriptions and contract for Advertisements for the REPOSITORY in the Eastern cities.

SINGLE copies of the REPOSITORY can be had at the counter with or without wrappers. Price five cents.

THE SITUATION.

The Old Flag of the Union waves in triumph at every point where patriots and traitors have confronted each other, to decide the future destiny of the Republic by the shock of battle.

Vicksburg and Port Hudson have fallen,—their rebel garrisons are prisoners, and the Father of Waters is open to the free navigation of loyal men from its source to the Gulf. Prentiss repelled the attack of Price at Helena, capturing some 2,000 of his men, and thus perished the last hope of rebel foothold on the Mississippi. Six month ago Jeff. Davis declared before the Mississippi legislature, that "the Confederacy must stand or fall "by the defence of the River!" The River has fallen from the cruel embrace of treason, and the Confederacy reels in the last violent throes of death.

Little Rock, the capitol of Arkansas, has just been captured by Gen. Blunt, and Jackson, the capital of Mississippi, has been captured by Gen. Sherman, with 6,000 prisoners. Johnston is now retreating upon Pearl River with his shattered and hopeless army.

Bragg has been driven nearly out of Tennessee by Rosecrans, with a loss of 4,500 prisoners, and Chattanooga and all of East Tennessee, with thousands of loyal souls, are now, or soon must be, under the protection of the Old Flag.

Lee has been retreating his defeated army toward Richmond as rapidly as possible, and Meade is pursuing him on the eastern side of the Ridge, and will, we trust, strike the rebel commander at Gordonsville and utterly route the demoralized and despairing remnant of his army. Invasion in force is ended, and the effort has given the deepest and keenest stab to the vitals of treason. If Meade shall reach Lee at Gordonsville, the rebel army of traitors will cease to exist save in history.

Charleston, the hot-bed of the rebellion, is about to pay the penalty of her causeless war upon the government. The doomed city is now closely besieged by land and water; the out-works of the enemy have been gained, and Fort Sumter, on which the first Flag was struck to traitors, must soon surrender to the gallant Gilmore.

In the brief period of thirty days, the monster treason has been discomfited at every point, and the cause of Free Government, under the guidance of Him who holds the reigns of Justice, seems to break upon the noontide of victory!

THE RETREAT OF LEE.

The popular disappointment at the retreat of Lee, with the remnant of his army, across the Potomac with comparative safety, is keen and undisguised. With many the unreasonable hope was cherished with confidence that Lee would be utterly destroyed or captured; but with the more reflecting there prevailed a conviction that Gen Meade would deliver battle with every chance of success, and that the rebel hosts would be routed and practically destroyed as an army.

It is possible that General Meade could have engaged Lee on Monday of last week, and routed him. Certainly had he known how helpless Lee was just then, with part of his artillery already across the river, the destruction of Lee could have been attained. But Gen. Meade must not be judged and censured rashly. A glance at the map given on our first page will show what an herculean task he had to perform. It must be borne in mind, too, that Lee had gained possession of the South Mountain passes from the Potomac up to the Gettysburg turnpike, before Gen. Meade had command of the Army, and that Lee's open line of retreat was in his own hands and beyond the power of Meade to interrupt.

Lee commenced his retreat on Saturday morning, July 4th, of course presenting a strong front to Meade until his artillery and baggage were safely out of reach. He then withdrew his rear guard, leaving his dead and wounded to the tender mercies of the Union commander. Lee had thus full twenty-four hours start of Meade in his movement, and he was falling back toward his base and shortening his lines, while the pursuit by Meade extended his lines and involved immense transportation of provisions and ammunition over two mountains and bad roads.

Lee had but to recross the South Mountain into Franklin county by the Gettysburg and Monterey passes, and from thence had a straight line to the river, reaching his new position in a march of thirty miles. On the other hand Meade's army had been brought to Gettysburg by the most exhausting forced marches, with the smallest possible amount of transportation, and the very hour his troops reached there the engagement commenced, and for three days it raged with the deadliest fury until full twenty thousand of his gallant warriors were numbered with the dead, wounded and captured. Although victorious in holding his position and utterly defeating and turning back the rebel hordes under Lee, still the shock of that battle, with the dead and wounded of both armies in his hands, left his army in a sorry condition for prompt pursuit. He did pursue, however, as rapidly as was possible to move and supply his men; but he had to march nearly thirty miles to Frederick, thence across the Catoctin and South mountains to Boonsboro, nearly twenty miles more, and then found the rebel lines extending from Shepperdstown to Williamsport, (as marked on the map by dotted lines) and also covering Hagerstown. He promptly made reconnoisances from Boonsboro to the Antietam, to Funkstown and Hagerstown, and Sedgwick compelled Lee to retreat from the Shepperdstown ford and shorten his line immediately around Williamsport.

The position thus chosen by Lee was one of singular strength naturally, and was fortified so as to make it almost impregnable. Meade *might* have attacked it successfully on Sunday, but at a sacrifice of nearly two of his brave veterans to one of the enemy; and even if successful in driving Lee from his chosen and fortified position—a success as yet never achieved by either side in this war, although attempted by Burnside at Fredericksburg and Lee at Gettysburg—Lee could still have retreated up the Potomac, and, if pressed, could have chosen a position at Hancock in the mountains from which double the force of Meade could not dislodge him. With an adequate force on the south side of the Potomac, he might there have suffered capture; but he could scarcely have failed to make good his escape across the river before the Union army could have been thus disposed to cut off his retreat.

We doubt not that Meade manœuvered his army under positive instructions from the Commander-in-Chief not to uncover Washington, or, in other words, not to deliver battle with the enemy between him and the National Capitol. The peril of this movement doubtless prevented Meade from throwing his army around from Boonsboro' to Hagerstown to attack Lee from the West on his comparatively unprotected left flank. But such a change in the Union forces could not have been made for an attack in less than twenty-four hours, and Lee would have simply declined battle by crossing the Potomac, as it was passable by the time Meade could have reached a position on his left.

It is due to Gen. Meade, who so nobly redeemed Northern soil from rebel invasion by his skill and heroism at Gettysburg, that the almost immeasurable difficulties which confronted him in the pursuit and attempt to engage Lee again, should be known and duly considered. Had he hurled his decimated army upon Lee's fortified lines on Saturday or Sunday and suffered a repulse, Lee would have been re-inforced and renewed his offensive movements upon our soil; and the fruits of the deeply crimsoned victory of Gettysburg would have been lost. Instead of Lee retreating with a shattered, dispirited and hopeless army upon Richmond, Meade would now be retreating with the gallant Army of the Potomac upon the defences of Baltimore and Washington. Disappointed as we must be that Lee has not been destroyed, let us be thankful for the rich fruits of Meade's signal though incomplete triumph, rather than ungenerous in our exactions.

We have read much, not only in this, but in other campaigns during this war of the certainty of "bagging" rebel armies; but in field operations such results are simply impossibilities. Burnside was defeated at Fredericksburg with a river in his rear, commanded by rebel batteries yet he withdrew his army safely, losing his dead and wounded. Hooker was defeated at Chancellorsville with a river in his rear swollen to the angriest tide, and Sedgwick was at the same time repulsed with fearful loss on the Fredericksburg heights,—yet both re-crossed their commands in safety in the very face and under the very guns of a rebel commander to whom masterly ability is conceded by friend and foe. Nor did Hooker and Burnside withdraw their commands from before an army worn out by forced marches, and just from fields dripping with the gore of full one-fourth their comrades who entered the battle. Lee's army was comparatively fresh and on its long occupied ground after the battles of Fredericksburg and Chancellorsville, and their loss in neither engagement equalled ours. Yet the Union army retreated in safety, as did Lee from the front of Meade, nor was Lee held as wanting in ability or energy because he did not "bag" Burnside and Hooker. And it is worthy of consideration that the repulses of Burnside and Sedgwick at Fredericksburg, and the disastrous repulse of Lee at Gettysburg, were the results of attacks against skillfully selected and fortified positions just such as Lee held, and Meade must have assailed at Williamsport. Let us deal justly if not generously with our heroes, and sustain and strengthen their hearts for future triumphs, rather than cripple them with ill-considered and unmerited criticism. Gen. Meade has done well—who has done better?

DEMOCRATIC FIRE IN THE REAR.

THE Harrisburg *Patriot and Union* is the central organ of the Democratic party of the State, and claims to favor the suppression of the treasonable and murderous rebellion now seeking to destroy the Republic—Few and heartless are the words of encouragement it gives to those who are shedding their blood to preserve the Government; and it announces the triumphs of the Union army with a confusion of terms that but too clearly betokens the sad disappointment that rankles in the breast that dictates its leaders.

But a few days ago the North stood appalled at the invasion of loyal soil by eighty thousand traitors in arms, seeking at once to desolate our fair land and deal a death-blow to our sacred Nationality. The stoutest and truest hearted quailed as the insurgent leader hurled his legions to the very doors of our capitol, and threatened to make the line of the Susquehanna the future battle-ground of the war. With clouded hope all eyes turned toward the Army of the Potomac as it made forced marches to meet the insolent foe, and earnest were the supplications to the God of battles that He might shield it and the Nation from disaster.

The gory field of Gettysburg attests how nobly the Army of the Potomac fought; how heroically its bravest warriors died; how its bronzed and tattered flags bore the signal of victory after three days of the deadliest conflict. The insolent invader was turned back upon his home, made waste by wanton, wicked war, and half his army was strewn in his bloody path as he retraced his steps to the dominions of treason. Thus was our State, our capital, our Nationality saved over twenty thousand fallen heroes of the Army of the Potomac.

Of that gallant army full eighty thousand are numbered with the dead, the wounded and the disabled by disease. Its shattered ranks appeal to the Nation by its many battles won and lost with honor; by its deeply crimsoned but glorious history, and by its bright hopes of future triumphs for the cause of Right—it appeals to every loyal impulse to fill its blurred and blotted rolls, and swell its columns until it shall be invincible in its holy war against the treasonable authors of this sanguinary fraternal strife.

The government responds to its call. Those who share the priceless blessings of free government—who owe to it life, liberty and every civil and religious privilege, are enrolled for conscription to give heart and hope and strength to the battle-scarred veterans of the Army of the Potomac. With a victory so costly in loyal blood, so decisive in its triumph, as that of Gettysburg to inspire the friends of the government, none but a craven or a traitor could interpose his voice against a measure fraught with the safety of the remnant of our noble army, and the safety of the Republic.

To this call the *Patriot and Union* responds as if driven to fiendish folly by the victories of Gettysburg and Vicksburg streaming on our old and honored flag. In its issue of the 14th inst., in an elaborate leader, abounding with the most reckless misrepresentations and appealing to the basest passions, it answers the call of the Army of the Potomac for men in this wise:—"Yes, the Conscription act MUST be enforced at once; *the altar of the modern Moloch needs a fresh "supply of victims.* Homes are to be "made desolate; fire-sides invaded; "children must be torn from their "parents; husband from wives; broth- "ers and sisters must be parted, and "the clasped hands of love of ev- "ery degree be wrenched asunder "by the rude force of military power! "Such is the fiat of Black Republic- "anism." In the same article it sighs "for the advent of a Woodward to "put an end to this groveling position "of our old commonwealth!" and groans in agony "for that glad and "speedy approaching day when she "(Pennsylvania) will take her stand "properly and proudly by the side "of New York, *with her admirable* "SEYMOUR!"

The same paper gives the sickening details of the legitimate fruits of the teachings and policy of the "admirable Seymour." An effort to swell our armies by conscription in New York resulted in a riot, inflamed by the men of whom the *Patriot and Union* is an humble echo. For four days the sworn officers of the law had their houses plundered and sacked and their lives jeoparded, and the "admirable Seymour" addressed the mob as his "friends;" assured them "their rights should be fully respected," and implored them to moderation in their stealing and butchery; but not a word did he utter looking to the enforcement of law or the strengthening of our armies in the field!

Thus drags along the slimy, loathsome reptile of treason in the North, —its path crimsoned with blood, and leaving plundered homes, convulsed cities, and anarchy in its tread. As yet it has a tangible footing only in New York, under the "admirable Seymour;" but the sigh for "the advent of a Woodward," who shall come with social chaos and butchery in his train, is wide spread amongst the leaders, of whom the *Patriot and Union* is the organ. The cloven foot is now stripped of all guise, and we rejoice that against "the advent of a Woodward" will be arrayed every heart that beats responsive to the dictates of humanity and of social order; and every patriot who would save our gallant army in the field; save untarnished the sacred memory of our heroic dead, save the great cause of American Nationality.

DEMOCRATIC NOMINATIONS.

The Democratic State Convention, which met at Harrisburg on the 17th ult., after several stormy sessions nominated Hon. GEORGE W. WOODWARD, of Luzerne, for Governor on the ninth ballot, and Chief Justice WALTER H. LOWRIE, of Allegheny, for Supreme Judge without the formality of a ballot. The contest for the Gubernatorial nomination seemed at the outset, to be between Hon. Heister Clymer, of Berks, and Hon. Wm. H. Wittee, of Philadelphia—the former having 33 votes on first ballot and 62 on the eighth, and the latter having 47 on the first and 51 on the eighth. Before the ninth and last ballot Hon. Frances W. Hughes, of Schuylkill, withdrew the name of Mr. Wittee, and urged the Wittee men to go to Woodward, who had then risen to but 13; and in obedience to orders, they gave Woodward 75 votes to 53 for Clymer, who on the previous ballot was within four votes of a nomination.

Judge Woodward is a man of conceded ability, and as subtle and dangerous as he is able. His official career commenced by his election as a Delegate to the Constitutional Convention in 1837, in which body he was one of the youngest members. He took considerable part in the able debates which characterized its proceedings, and made his mark especially in his earnest efforts to disfranchise all foreigners in Pennsylvania. He made one of his ablest speeches in favor of incorporating the denial of suffrage to foreigners with our organic law, but he failed,—so that the Irish and Germans who vote for him in October, can do so with the satisfactory assurance that if Woodward had succeeded in his efforts to amend our Constitution, they would now be without even the right to vote at all. In 1842, or thereabouts, Gov. Porter appointed him President Judge of the Centre District. In 1845, Mr. Buchanan vacated his seat in the U. S. Senate to accept the Premiership under President Polk, and the Democratic legislative caucus nominated Judge Woodward to fill the unexpired term. The legislature was democratic in both branches; but Woodward's ultra Free Trade doctrines were so offensive to a portion of the party, that thirteen bolted the nomination, and joining the Whigs elected Hon. Simon Cameron. In 1846 President Polk, desiring to heal Woodward's Senatorial wounds, nominated him to fill a vacancy in the Supreme Court of the United States. The Senate was largely Democratic, but the Judiciary Committee reported against him, and he was rejected by Democratic votes. In 1852 Gov. Bigler appointed him to a vacancy on the Supreme Bench of this State, and the same fall he was carried into an election by the immense popular tide that gave Pierce every State but four for the Presidency.

He has now been one of the members of our highest judicial tribunal for eleven years; but we believe that his decisions may be searched in vain for a single record pointing to the progress of freedom or the strengthening of our nationality. When the storm of treason gathered over us in 1861, because the people had chosen Mr. Lincoln President in strict conformity with our laws, instead of displaying the common manhood due from every citizen, and especially due from one charged with the maintenance of the laws, he temporized with and apologized for the murderous traitors in arms, and in a public speech in Independence Square, denied the power of the Government to preserve its own existence! In keeping with his settled purpose to weaken the loyal cause and blight the hopes of the brave defenders of our flag in the field, he delivered the opinion of the Supreme Court denying the right of our own soldiers to vote, although they had voted in the Mexican war without judicial hindrance. His nomination was the result of the implacable hatred between the leading contestants for the empty prize, and it took that turn mainly because no man in Pennsylvania has fewer attachments than George W. Woodward. He is a chilling accident on the ticket, and he will fall less lamented by friend and foe than any other man who could have been seriously thought of as a candidate. We thank the Convention for its work!

—Judge LOWRIE is a man of high personal integrity, of very moderate ability, of commendable industry, of wonderful self-appreciation and middling loyalty. He is the present Chief Justice of the State, and has been on the Supreme Bench for twelve years. He will rise or fall as a mere appendage to the Woodward kite, as the Gubernatorial contest will entirely overshadow the Judgeship. We charge him nothing for advising him to look out for strong gales about next October.

HENRY J. STAHLE, of the Gettysburg *Compiler*, was arrested by Gen. Meade as soon as he gained possession of the town, and sent as a prisoner to Fort McHenry. We cannot form any judgment as to the guilt of Mr. Stahle from the statements and denials in the Gettysburg papers. It is alleged that he gave the rebels information where the Union troops and property were concealed, and rendered himself in other respects useful to the enemy.

We trust that Mr. Stahle has not been arrested and imprisoned without a purpose. If he has been guilty of the charges preferred against him, he should be promptly tried by a military court, convicted and shot,—if innocent, he should be allowed an early opportunity to establish it and be discharged. It is high time that military arrests should be understood as meaning something beyond imprisonment without notice of charges and release without explanation. Had Daniel Dechert, of Hagerstown, been tried, convicted and inexorably executed, as he richly deserved, when he was detected as a spy within our lines, corresponding with and furnishing maps to bring the enemy to his own home, justice would have been vindicated and a wholesome practical lesson would have been learned by semi-traitors along the entire border. We insist that military arrests shall mean the prompt trial and conviction or acquittal of the accused, and that the penalty of treason, when clearly shown to extend to positive acts of hostility to the Government, shall be death. It is alike just and humane to the loyal people of the North that they shall not be the victims of cowardly spies and traitors at home; and if Mr. Stahle has by his acts brought himself within that class, he should die. But if he is the victim of personal or political prejudice, or of the inflamed public feeling naturally resulting from the shock of battle between the great armies at Gettysburg, he should have early and ample opportunity to vindicate himself, and be discharged to prove his devotion to the Government by an earnest support of the prosecution of the war. In this particular, we must confess, he has room for improvement.

THE Richmond *Enquirer* of the 6th inst. announced that "Lee defeated the enemy on Friday last," that "they (Meade) are retreating toward Baltimore and Lee pursuing," and that "Lee has 40,000 prisoners on their way to Richmond!" But a vein of sadness is manifested in the *Enquirer's* rejoicings because, as its calculation demonstrates, it will cost the confederacy $1.50 per man, or $60,000 per day, to subsist the 40,000 Yankee prisoners. Naturally inclined to love our enemies, we freely mingle our joy with the *Enquirer's* that its $60,000 per day is saved! It will doubtless sympathise with us when it is informed that Gen. Meade has imposed upon our Government the cruel task of subsisting some 15,000 of Lee's army; but it seems to be Gen. Meade's way and we must submit! When Gen Lee reaches Baltimore the *Enquirer* will oblige us by giving early information of the fact!

GOV. CURTIN spent Tuesday of last week in consultation with General COUCH, and on Wednesday and Thursday visited the Pennsylvania regiments of militia at different points south of this place. He was received with the liveliest enthusiasm by the troops and addressed them at a number of their camps. On Friday morning he returned to Harrisburg. It is his purpose to make arrangements for the prompt payment of the militia before they leave the field. The fruits of his ceaseless devotion to our troops are manifested in the singular order discipline and spirit of the men now upon our border. As a military organization it has never been surpassed in efficiency in the brief time employed to create it.

WE have unofficial but reliable information that Gen. Lee lost at the battles of Gettysburg fully 6,000 killed; 10,000 wounded left in our hands; 7,000 wounded taken with him on foot and in wagons; and not less than 12,000 in prisoners and deserters—making a total loss of not less than 35,000. He crossed but 41,000 men over the Potomac on his retreat, which, excepting a few cavalry, is the entire force he has taken back to Virginia. But a month ago he crossed into Maryland with over 80,000 men. Gen. Meade's loss at Gettysburg was about 4,500 killed, 10,000 wounded and 4,000 captured.

ANDREWS, the leader of the New York rioters, who maltreated or murdered every negro found on the streets, was captured on Wednesday at a house of ill-fame with a negro paramour. He was the chieftain of those whom Gov. Seymour addressed as "my friends," and to whom he gave positive assurance of friendship in a public speech, while rioting, butchery and plundering were going on all around him. Progressive Democracy that!

We give in to-day's paper a most accurate map, which shows the route of the rebel Gen. Lee in his invasion of the North, the great battle-ground at Gettysburg, the lines of retreat of Lee, and Meade's pursuit, and the rebel line as formed on the Potomac before the final retreat across the river. All the points threatened by Lee, including Harrisburg, Baltimore, Washington, and the several lines of Railroad are also accurately located. We shall henceforth publish maps as often as important movements in the war may render them useful and interesting.

Hon. Charles J. Biddle, Chairman of the Democratic State Convention, seemed ambitious to get out of an unfortunate command, and he asked Judge Woodward to please to allow him to go and help defend Pennsylvania. Woodward generously allowed him to resign and go, apparently recognizing the impropriety of a Democratic chairman taking any part in this war. Couldn't Woodward procure a special dispensation for a few of his copperhead friends in New York to go and help defend the life of the Republic?

It is worthy of remark that every New York city Journal that supports the administration of Gov. Seymour, denounced the draft in the most inflamatory terms the day before the riot. They *have* the "admirable Seymour" and seem to know their man. If the "advent of a Woodward" had occurred in this State last fall, we should now have a State in the throes of revolution and the whole government would be on the very verge of anarchy. Let us not be unmindful of the lesson.

The Richmond *Enquirer* of the 14th seems to have given up the idea of entertaining forty odd thousand Union prisoners at a cost of $60.000 per day. It seems at last to have acquired a clear conception of the helpless condition of the Rebellion. It says:

"The fall of Vicksburg, the retreat of Bragg, the repulse of Lee, and the advance on Charleston, are all serious disasters, the most serious that have attended our arms since the commencement of the war."

An interesting letter from one of our army correspondents, giving some important details of the gallantry of the Pennsylvania Reserves, and their heroic young commander, Gen. S. A. Crawford, is ommitted for want of room. It will appear next week.

We are indebted to the Hon Wm. D. Kelly for valuable public documents.

For the Franklin Repository.

UNION NOMINATIONS.

Having had considerable intercourse with leading men of every Election District in our county, I am glad to learn that there is a determination on the part of all loyal men to fill our County offices with wounded soldiers.

Col. J. G. Elder, for County Treasurer; Capt. J. H. Reed, for Prothonotary; Harry Strickler, for Register and Recorder, and, (let me suggest,) Lieut. Josiah W. Fletcher, for Clerk of the Courts. They are all wounded soldiers, and their election will prove the gratitude of their neighbors toward their Country's defenders. Patriotism.

Loudon, July 8, 1863.

The Democrats of Jefferson county have nominated J. B. Hutchinson for Assembly, subject to the approval of Clearfield, Elk and McKean counties.

The Massachusetts Democratic State Convention will meet in Worcester on the 3d of September.

PROCLAMATION OF THE PRESIDENT.

A Day of Thanksgiving and Prayer.

Washington, July 15.—By the President of the United States of America:

A PROCLAMATION.

It has pleased Almighty God to hearken to the supplications and prayers of an afflicted people, and to vouchsafe to the army and the navy of the United States victories on land and on sea so signal and so effective as to furnish reasonable grounds for augmented confidence that the Union of these States will be sustained, their Constitution preserved, and their peace and prosperity permanently restored.

But these victories have been accorded not without sacrifices of life, limb, health, and liberty, incurred by brave, loyal, and patriotic citizens. Domestic afflictions in every part of the country follow in the train of these fearful bereavements. It is meet and right to recognize and confess the presence of the Almighty Father, and the power of His hand equally in these triumphs and sorrows.

Now therefore be it known, that I do set apart Thursday, the 6th day of August next, to be observed as a day for national thanksgiving, praise and prayer, and I invite the people of the United States to assemble on that occasion in their customary places of worship, and in the forms approved by their own conscience, and render the homage due to the Divine Majesty for the wonderful things He has done in the nation's behalf, and invoke the influence of His Holy Spirit to subdue the anger which has produced and so long sustained a needless and cruel rebellion; to change the hearts of the insurgents; to guide the counsels of the government with wisdom adequate to so great a national emergency, and to visit with tender care and consolation throughout the length and breadth of our land all those who through the vicissitudes of marches, voyages, battles and sieges have been brought to suffer in mind, body or estate. And finally to lead the whole nation, through the paths of repentance and submission to the Divine will, back to the perfect enjoyment of union and paternal peace.

In witness whereof I have hereunto set my hand and caused the seal of the United States to be affixed.

Done at the city of Washington this the 15th day of July, in the year of our Lord one thousand eight hundred and sixty-three, and of the independence of the United States of America the eighty-eighth.

[L. S.] ABRAHAM LINCOLN.

Wm. H. Seward, Secretary of State.

LATEST NEWS!

Affairs in New York.

New York, July 20.—General Wool was relieved on Saturday by General Dix.

The draft in this city will not begin until the exact quota of the city has been definitely determined and publicly announced, by which time the Government will be prepared to execute it. Possibly a week may elapse before this is done.

The British Consul has notified the Police Commissioners that he has requested the ship-of-war Challenger to take a position in the river for the purpose of protecting colored seamen who are subjects of Great Britain.

A card is published from James T. Brady, Esq., against mob law, in which he states that the real authors of the late riots have been kept in secure secrecy.

Morgan's Raid into Ohio—An Unsuccessful Attempt to Cross the River—150 Rebels Killed and Drowned—1,000 Taken Prisoners—Cols. Dick Morgan and Ward Among the Prisoners.

Cleveland, July 20.—Morgan made an unsuccessful attempt to cross the Ohio river yesterday near Cooleyville, but was prevented by a gunboat.

One hundred and fifty rebels were killed and drowned. A thousand prisoners were taken with their artillery,

Among the prisoners were Col. Ward and Col. Dick Morgan, a brother of John.

The band scattered among the hills.

Gen. Judd is confident of the capture of the balance of the party to-day.

The War in Tennessee—Sharp Cavalry Skirmish at Jackson—The Enemy Sharply Punished.

Washington, Sunday, July 19.—Maj. Gen. Hurlbut telegraphs from Memphis, July 17, to the War Department, as follows:

"The enemy's cavalry was sharply punished at Jackson, Tenn., by Col. Hatch, on the 13th.

Their loss was 200 in killed, wounded and prisoners, 400 conscripts released, and about 250 horses taken, with more than that number of arms."

From Vicksburg—Jackson Occupied by Sherman—Johnston in Full Retreat.

New York, July 20.—A letter from Vicksburg, dated the 11th, says that all of Pemberton's troops have left our lines except a few stragglers.

Gen. Sherman occupied Jackson yesterday.

Gen. Johnston is retreating to the next river east of the Pearl.

Payment of State Troops.

Philadelphia, July 20.—Gov. Curtin was present at a meeting of the Bank Presidents to-day, and arranged for the payment of all the State troops called out for the emergency. They will be paid before being mustered out.

Lee's Army at Winchester.

New York, July 20.—A Washington letter says the bulk of Lee's army is still at Winchester. There are hopes entertained that the Union army may yet complete its destruction.

OUR ARMY IN VICKSBURG.

A correspondent in Grant's army describes at length the entree of the national troops into Vicksburg. From this account we extract the following interesting paragraphs:

HOW THE REBELS APPEARED.

All intercourse between the two armies was prohibited until the final act of surrender was consummated, but by the courtesy of Gen. Legget, who had command of the ceremonies on our side, your correspondent was permitted to pass our pickets and get among the rebs before our army passed in, and thus see how they endured the final pangs: and he must be faithful to the truth by saying that the rebels seemed to lay down their arms very much as though they were glad to get rid of them—very much like Christian getting loosed from his burden. He could not discern even the faintest ray of that proud regret at not having been permitted to die in the last ditch, which Southern assumption would have led him to look for. In fact, I noticed one company which marched out at a quick march, and marched back at the double quick, kicking up their heels, and generally enjoying the occasion as much as any of the "Yanks." And this was not a Tennessee, but a Mississippi company; not a Union man among them, but every one of them heartily tired of the siege, and tired, I think, of the war.

PLANTING THE STARS AND STRIPES.

As soon as the ceremony of stacking arms was over, Gen. McPherson, simply attended by his division Generals and staff, rode into the city, and took formal possession. No demonstrations of an insulting character were made by the citizens, as is usually the case when victorious armies enter conquered rebel towns. I have heard of but one instance of this kind occurring during the whole day, which I will mention hereafter Gen. McPherson proceeded to the Court House, and Col. Coolbaugh and Lieut. Col. Strong, of his staff, went up, and at half past eleven planted the Stars and Stripes on the cupalo of the building, gave three cheers, which were heartily repeated by the officers below, and then sang "The Battle Cry of Freedom." All of which was listened to with due (outward) respect by the dumb crowd of gaping secesh who witnessed the scene.

PEMBERTON'S IDEAS OF OUR FIGHTING.

The conference was conducted with good feeling, and Pemberton was rather disposed to be agreeable to the point of facetiousness. He freely criticised the manner in which we had fought, and made this remark: "Grant, you have n't but one division in your army that will fight worth a d—n, and that is this one," pointing to the front covering Logan's division. Perhaps I ought not to give this, as it might convey an invidious distinction; but I mention it merely to show that the rebels felt the loss of High Hill Fort, which was in Logan's front, seriously. If the men of the chivalrous and soldierly J. E. Smith, or of the persevering and intrepid Ransom, or any others, of the right or of the left, had been placed where Logan's men were, they would have done just as well.

AN IRON MINE AT VICKSBURG.

Vicksburg, or that portion of land enclosed by the fortifications, is almost literally a bed of iron. Pieces of mortar shells and shots of various sizes and shapes, some in pieces and some not, solid shot of many sizes, all in conglomerate mass, are everywhere visible.

I saw one pile of shells and solid shot of all sizes, used by our army, near the door of a fine residence a little back from the river, and estimated to be 300 in number. The proprietor of the house informed me that they were all gathered up in and about his house. By this statement your readers can form a judgement approaching correctness of the ordeal Vicksburg has passed.

GEN. LEE'S STRATEGY AND RETREAT.

The Frederick correspondent of the *Herald* gives the following graphic account of Lee's strategy to avoid an engagement and his subsequent retreat:

General Lee has retired, but notwithstanding, it has not been as successful a feat as represented by the disaffected; in fact, the affair has rather a consolatory rebel disaster appended to it which should cement the Gettysburg link of affection between the people, General Meade and the War Department. The facts of the case and the cause of the apparently successful retirement, may alter the first impressions of the people in regard to General Meade, who has really worked with remarkable assiduity for the consummation of the fondest hopes of the public. That he has not succeeded as fully as our wild hopes predicted, lies not with him, but with that overruling Providence who disposes all things

Throughout the days of the 12th, 13th and 14th, Gen. Lee preserved a large force in our front, intrenched in a commanding position. Wherever our forces turned they met resistance. At the same time the rebel chief was doubtless crossing his forces. Gen. Meade, anxious to bring the affair to a head, tried by every means in his power to draw the rebels out, or at least to show their front. This Lee could not be persuaded to do. At one time he presented a sort of a line of battle with his forces, apparently masked in the woods; but on our attempting to feel this line to discover its arrangement, preparatory to a general attack in force, it was always changed, withdrawn or its front located differently. Indeed to such an extent was this carried, that it seemed folly for our troops to rush blindly on the enemy's unknown position. Time was needed for our generals to ascertain what point was practicable and where the greatest degree of success was likely to ensue.

The occasion was momentous. The fate of a great nation once and yet destined to be the pride of the world hung on the action of a single man. The responsibility was immense, and General Meade would of course be held responsible for any rash act with such a stake. Caution could not be too excessive; for, with so wily a foe and so great a risk on our part, we would not expect of our chosen leader that he would rashly sacrifice our army for the sake of bowing to popular clamor. A general is supposed to be the judge of the actions of his own army and those of his enemy. General Meade did this. He did all man or general could, and wisely refrained from unnecessarily slaughtering his men. If he was mistaken it was not an entirely lucky mistake for the enemy; for the latter was in so narrow a strait, thanks to the vigilance of our commanders, that he was only too willing to sacrifice a small army from his active force for the sake of getting off the remainder.

With remarkable logic General Lee argued that captured men were always paroled, while rebel artillery and trains were not. Therefore he was compelled, in fact, owing to our vigorous pushing against his position, to leave a large force to keep up his camp fires and the pretended resistance to our advance until he could get his artillery and trains on the south bank of the Potomac. This done nothing under Heaven could save the force left to cover his retreat. This he well knew, and he was only too happy to be assured that the large force left behind would alone be captured, so bad was the condition into which Meade's and his own strategy had gotten him. This great sacrifice on the altar of the demon of secession is sufficient proof of the ability of Meade and the blunders of Lee. He flies to Virginia, it is true; but the cries of the dead and dying at Gettysburg are ringing in his ears. His pride is broken; his spirit crushed. He entered Maryland inflated, tattered, raged—a burlesque on his former self

Our army is enthusiastic, and will advance into Virginia with high hopes of finally annihilating the rebel ogre. Secesh citizens are depressed at the idea of General Lee evacuating under compulsion the soil of Maryland, and consequently—although it would have been prefer ble to have captured the rebel army entire on our soil—Union stock is at a premium, and we must not complain if our Utopian dreams are not verified by stern realities. Virginia is open to us, and General Meade—a live, active man—commands with such favorable auspices we can safely assert that the rebel General will not be able to attain a supporting distance of his columns at Richmond before he is cut to pieces by our eager troops.

Our troops are ready to do anything that is ordered. They have confidence in the General, as, indeed have the people; for Gettysburg in itself is prestige enough to warrant a lifetime's respite from the toils of the field to any officer. It must be understood further, however, in regard to this retirement of Lee, that a day or two previous to its final discovery General Meade was led to believe that reinforcements from General Beauregard to the extent of some forty thousand men, had reached the enemy. This fact in itself demanded caution on our part; and, moreover, since after our bold movements the enemy always showed a firm and strong front, it was very natural to suppose that he intended fight, and consequently it was determined to accommodate him, as the pugilists say. Our dispositions were made for whatever might transpire, though our advance was retarded through the misty nature of the rebel movements. Notwithstanding we pressed the rebels sore, and Lee was doubtless much distressed thereby; in fact we have learned that it became necessary for him to even reinforce the division which he expected to sacrifice for the balance of his army. That General Meade had so pressed the enemy that he has been forced to retire with great loss, while our forces, inflicting so severe a punishment on the enemy, met with no casualties whatever, is sufficient vindication of our commanding officers' conduct without one word from the pen of your correspondent.

There is not the slightest depression here on the subject, nor is there cause for any. Though there may be some disappointment at not being able to capture Lee's army entire, our soldiers are sensible men and understand that such affairs are not so practicable as set forth in the vaporings of the inexperienced. There are bright stars glistening for them in the South. Grant's and Banks' success is in itself a tower of strength to them, and through its influence they will advance with lighter hearts and higher hopes than heretofore. Demoralization must ensue in the rebel ranks from the reception of this adverse news; and the result of our victorious forces—elate with the prestige of late accumulating victories and their attendant laurels fresh upon them—advancing on the shattered remnants of the once proud and formidable rebel Army of Virginia, may be imagined though not easily described. Let as hope that it will bring them finally to their senses, through the medium of the bitter experience of which the last two years have brought. They see themselves gradually losing ground, the favorite projects of their skilful General foiled, and they themselves beaten and forced to fly in defeat ignobly and disgracefully from the soil which it was their proud boast they would overrun and disenthral from the power of the legitimate government. When the final blow shall have been given them by the gallant Army of the Potomac, within the next two weeks, what hope is there for them but to throw themselves on the clemency of the government they have so misinterpreted, and, casting from their pedestals the rotten idols which they have so long worshipped in poverty, starvation and disgrace, take up the old love once more and be themselves again? To this, in the present crisis of their fortunes, it must come at last.

The California Democratic State Convention has nominated the following ticket: For Governor, John S. Downey; Congressmen, John Bigler, John B. Weller, and Joseph M'Corkle; for State Printer, Beriah Brown.

We are credibly informed that Gen. Lee occupied a place on the steeple of the Seminary during the battle of Gettysburg, under the protection of a hospital flag, and there directed the movements of his troops.

The Governor of Rhode Island has issued a proclamation recommending all the cities and towns to make immediate provision for the support of the families of the men drafted from the State.

The Peace Democracy of Iowa have nominated Mr. L. Fisher for Governor; J. F. Duncombe for Lieut. Governor, and Charles Mason for Supreme Judge.

The Connecticut Legislature adjourned *sine die* on Saturday last.

MARRIED.

On the 15th inst., in Watertown, N. Y., by Rev. John Sessions, Mr. J. R. Kinney, of Chambersburg, Pa., to Miss Ella Sessions, daughter of the officiating clergyman.

DIED.

Recently, at his residence, in Antrim township, Mr. James Beatty, aged 74 years. He was an honest man and highly respectable citizen.

On the 11th ult., in this place, John Wesley, son of Jacob and Mary Shaffer, aged 15 years and 4 months.

On the 6th inst., at the residence of her brother, Mr. John Crawford, in Guilford township, Miss Nancy Crawford, in the 70th year of her age.

$25. $75.

Employment!—Agents Wanted!—We will pay from $25 to $75 per month, and all expenses, to active Agents, or give a commission. Particulars sent free.—Address Erie Sewing Machine Company, R. James, General Agent, Milan, Ohio. april 29, 63-1y

Prevention of Incrustation in Steam Boilers.—WINANS' ANTI-INCRUSTATION POWDER REMOVES AND PREVENTS THE DEPOSIT OF SCALE, AND WITHOUT INJURY TO THE IRON. Seven Years in Use.

References in all parts of the country, viz: Albany Gas Co.; Eaton, Gilbert & Co., and others, Troy; Syracuse. Rochester, Auburn, &c., &c.; John Gibson & Co., Phelps, Charles Ensign, John R. Evans & Co., Jewett & Root, and others, Buffalo: Cleveland, Columbus, Ranesville, &c., &c.; Geo. Shield, Miles Greenwood, Mitchell & Rammelsburg, and 40 others in Cincinnati; and throughout the West; Indianopolis, Dayton, Terre Haute, Logansport, Chicago. Springfield, St. Louis, St. Paul, &c., &c., &c. Cost about 40 to 60 cents per week. For circular, address H. N, WINANS, 11 Wall St., New York.

P.O. Box No. 6. [july 22, '63-6m.

Editor of Repository—Dear Sir: With your permission I wish to say to the readers of your paper that I will send by return mail to all who wish it, (free) a Recipe, with full directions for making and using a simple Vegetable Balm, that will effectually remove, in 10 minutes, Pimples, Blotches, Tan, Freckles, and all Impurities of the Skin, leaving the same soft, clear, smooth and beautiful.

I will also mail free to those having Bald Heads or Bare Faces, simple directions and information that will enable them to start a full growth of Luxuriant Hair, Whiskers, or a Moustache, in less than 30 days. All applications answered by return mail without charge.

Respectfully yours,

THOS. F. CHAPMAN, Chemist,

july22'63-3m. No. 831 Broadway, New York.

Madame Porter's Curative Balsam has long tested the truth that there are first principles in Medicine as there is in Science, and this Medicine is compounded on principles suited to the manifold nature of Man! The cure of Colds is in keeping open the pores, and creating a gentle internal warmth, and this is caused by the use of this Medicine. Its remedial qualities are based on its power to assist the healthy and vigorous circulation of blood through the lungs, it enlivens the muscles and assists the skin to perform its duties of regulating the heat of the system, and in gently throwing off the waste substance from the surface of the body. It is not a violent remedy, but emollient, warming, searching and effectivs. Sold by all druggist at 13s and 25 cents per bottle. [july 22.

The Confessions and Experience of an Invalid.—Published for the benefit, and as a warning and A CAUTION TO YOUNG MEN who suffer from Nervous Debility, Premature Decay of Manhood, etc., supplying at the same time THE MEANS OF SELF CURE, By one who has cured himself after being put to a great expense and injury through medical humbug and quackery.

By enclosing a post-paid addressed envelope, single copies may be had of the author.

NATHANIEL MAYFAIR, Esq., Bedford, Kings county, N. Y.

may 20, 63 1y

Ornamental Iron Works.—Wood & Perot, 1131 *Ridge Avenue, Philadelphia, Pa.*, offer for sale, upon the most Favorable Terms, *New* and *Beautiful Designs* in great variety of *IRON RAILINGS* for *Cemeteries, Residences, &c.*, of Wrought and Cast Iron, and *Galvanized Iron* and *Brass Tubing; Iron Verandahs, Balconies, Stairs, Counters, Fountains, Gates, Columns, Hitching Posts, Lamp Stands, Vases, Tables, Flower Stands, Sofas, Chairs, Statuary, Animals*, and all other Iron Work of Decorative character. Designs forwarded for selection. Persons applying for same, will please state the kind of work needed. june 3, 63-2m

Card to the Suffering.—The Rev. William Cosgrove, while laboring as a missionary in Japan, was cured of Consumption when all other means had failed, by a recipe obtained from a learned physician in the great city of Jeddo. This recipe has cured great numbers who were suffering from Consumption, Bronchitis, Sore Throat, Coughs and Colds, and the debility and nervous depression caused by these disorders.

Desirous of benefitting others, I will send this recipe, which I have brought home with me, to all who need it, free of charge. Address Rev. WM. COSGROVE, 439 Fulton Avenue, Brooklyn, N. N.

dec 5, 62-1y

To the Young or Old, Male or Female.—If you have been suffering from a habit indulged in by the YOUTH OF BOTH SEXES, WHICH CAUSES SO MANY ALARMING SYMPTOMS, *It unfits them for Marriage*, And is the greatest evil which can befall MAN OR WOMAN.

See symptoms enumerated in advertisement, and if you are a sufferer.

Cut out the Advertisement,
And send for it at once,
Delays are dangerous
Ask for Helmbold's,
Take no other.
Cures guaranteed.

Beware of Counterfeits and Imitations. july 15, 63-2m

The Confessions and Experience of a Nervous Young Man.—Published as a warning and for the especial benefit of young men, and those who suffer with Nervous Debility, Loss of Memory, Premature Decay, &c., &c., by one who has cured himself by simple means after being put to great expense and inconvenience, through the use of worthless medicines prescribed by learned Doctors. Single copies may be had (free) of the author, C. A. Lambert, Esq., Greenpoint Long Island. by enclosing an addressed envelope. Address CHARLES A. LAMBERT, Greenpoint, Long Island, New York.

July 22, '63-7t-

Wanted.—Local and Travelling Agents in every Town and County. Circulars, with Testimonials of Clergymen and Scientific men, in regard to the business, sent free. ISAAC HALE, Jr., & CO., Newburyport, Mass.

july 15, 63-3t

REPORT OF THE MARKETS

PRICE CURRENT OF EYSTER & BRO'S.

CORRECTED WEEKLY.

CHAMBERSBURG, July 21, 1863.

Butter	10	Washed Wool	50
Eggs	10	Unwashed Wool	33
Lard	8	Clover Seed	4 00
Tallow	8	Timothy Seed	2 00
Soap	4 to 6	Flax Seed	2 00
Bacon Hams	12	Pared Peaches	3 00
Bacon Sides	7	Unpared Peaches	1 50
Soup Beans	1 50	Dried Apples	1 00@1 50

CHAMBERSBURG FLOUR AND GRAIN MARKET.

CORRECTED AT CHAMBERSBURG MILLS.

Flour—White	$7 00
Flour—Red	6 50
Wheat—White	1 30
Wheat—Red	1 20
Rye	85
Corn	80
Oats	60

POTATO MARKET.

Mercer, New	80
Pink-Eyes	75

Philadelphia Markets.

PHILADELPHIA, JULY 18, 1863.

There is very little demand for Flour, either for export or home use. Sales comprise about 300 bbls Ohio family at $6.30@6.50; 100 bbls superfine at $5.50 and 300 bbls City Mills extra at $6.50 ℔ bbl. The retailers and bakers are buying moderately at $5.50@5.75 for superfine, $6@6.50 for extra $6.80@6.75 for extra family, and $7@8 ℔ bbl for fancy brands, according to quality. Rye Flour is dull at $4.50@4.75 ℔ bbl, Corn Meal is scarce and dull at $4.25 for Brandywine, and $4 ℔ bbl for Pennsylvania.

Grain.—There is very little demand for Wheat, and the offerings are light; small sales of Pennsylvania red are reported at 140@145c, and white at 150@155c ℔ bu., according to quality. Rye sells on arrival at 105c ℔ bushel. Corn is very dull; small sales of prime yellow are making at 86c, and Western mixed at 81@82 ℔ bushel. Oats are firmly held; 2,500 bushels of Pennsylvania sold at 78@80c, weight.

Whisky.—There is very little doing; small sales of bbls. are making at 47@47½c, and drudge at 45½@46c ℔ gallon.

New Advertisements.

THE ELEVENTH SESSION OF Sunny Side Seminary will open on Tuesday, September 1st. [july 22-6t.

ESTRAY.—Came to the residence of the subscriber, ½ mile East of Greenwood, near the Turnpike, on the 6th of July, 11 HEAD OF SHEEP, and 1 MULEY COW. Any person proving property and paying charges can have the same, by applying personlly or by letter to S. E. STALL

july 22, '63.

Bank of Chambersburg, July 20, 1863.

U. STATES 5-20 LOAN.—The Secretary of the Treasury, having extended the time for receiving subscriptions to this loan, the undersigned gives notice that he will continue to receive subscriptions and furnish the bonds with as little delay as possible. Persons having subscribed heretofore are requested to call, and receive their bonds.

july 22, '63-3t. G. R. MESSERSMITH.

NOTICE.—Whereas, Letters of Administration on the Estate of George A. Anderson, late of Quincy township, dec'd, have been granted to the subscriber, residing in Quincy township.

All persons indebted to the said Estate, are hereby requested to make immediate payment, and those having claims or demands against the Estate of said decedent, will make known the same without delay, to

july 22-6t. LEVI C. KEPNER, Adm'r.

NOTICE.—Whereas Letters Testamentary to the Estate of James Beatty, late of Antrim township, dec'd, have been granted to the subscribers.

All persons indebted to the said Estate are requested to make immediate payment and those having claims or demands against the Estate of the said decedent will make known the same without delay, to

JAMES NILL, T. B. KENNEDY, } Executors.

jnly 22.'63.

FORTY DOLLARS REWARD.—Stolen, from the pasture field of the subscriber, on the Riddle Farm, about a mile and a half North of Chambersburg, on Monday night, the 13th instant, A DARK ROAN MARE, medium size, and has two lumps on the withers. A reward of *Twenty Dollars* will be paid for the return of the Mare, or *Forty Dollars* for the recovery of the Mare and conviction of the Thief.

july 22, '63. SAMUEL BURNS.

$10 REWARD!—Strayed or Stolen from the premises of Mr. Etter, in Green Township, about four miles from Greenvillage, on Sunday morning, the 12th inst., a LARGE BAY MARE, with a star on her forehead, four black feet, and black mane and tail, also a slight scar on the right fore-shoulder. She left a sucking colt at home. The above reward will be paid to any one who discover and return said mare to JOHN C. AU, Newburg, Cumb'd Co., Pa.

July 22-3t.

AUDITOR'S NOTICE.—In the Court of Common Pleas of Franklin County, Pennsylvania: The Auditor appointed by the Court, to make distribution of the balance in the hands of Martin Heintzleman, Assignee of John Baughman, to among the creditors of said John Baughman, will meet the parties interested for the purposes of his appointment, on *Wednesday, the 5th day of August next*, at 10 o'clock, A. M., at the office of Stumbaugh & Stewart, in the borough of Chambersburg F. S. STUMBAUGH, Auditor.

July 20, 1863.-3t.

NOTICE.—The undersigned, with many others, have had their fence destroyed by the military occupation of this section, and are unable to repair them for some time to come. Their crops are therefore exposed to all stock that is permitted to run at large. They hereby give notice to their neighbors, and especially to the owners of cows, hogs, &c., in town, not to allow their stock to run at large, as in justice to themselves they must enforce the laws strictly. They appeal to all neighbors to respect their notice.

MICHAEL LE-HER,	LEVI OYLER,
WM. SKINNER,	DANIEL M'CLEARY,
JOHN HADE,	SAMUEL HEINTZELMAN,
WM. HEYSER,	G.R. MESSERSMITH,
S. GREENAWALT,	CHAS. M. BURNETT,
JOS. KELLER,	ALEX. MARTIN,
DR. E. CULBERTSON,	JOSHUA BEAR,
july 22-3t	ADAM HURST.

LIST OF LETTERS remaining in the Post Office at Chambersburg, July 21, 1863:

Arnheim Major	Fortna Cosmas K	M'Donald E A
Arnheim Gustave	Ford Mrs Alsinda	Miller Maggie C
BulkleyEdmundR	Fox Datton A	McElwee William
Barclay James J	GilmoreMrs Mary2	Millhouse Owen P
Burnet Eli S	Green Lieut Jos	McCarroll Benj.
Baxter Miss Anna	Gaul Samuel	Many James
Frinton Wm R	Gushart Miss	Rozell H
Barber Joseph	Sarah 2	Ripper Miss Mary
Brown Anthony	Grimm John B	Shell C M
Campbell Hon	Hayes Harry P	Stouffer Franklin
James H	Humberger Mrs J	Stouff Daniel
Cook Lieut J W	Hues David	Schmid John
CalliganMissMary	Hollabush Daniel	Stofer Miss Hetty
Evans Henry	Hunter C J	Snyder Rev M
Essinger Annie	Jimeson James 2	Sims Wm H
Eust Adam	Jessup A D	Schouten C M
Elflin Wm H	Keer Thomas G	Steward & Wheeler Messrs
Fleming James P	Luthead Robt S	
FrymireMiss Fannie D	Louth Miss Mary	Taylor C N
Fisher H S	Moore John H	Vauguntèn Geo W

Persons calling for the above Letters will please say that they have been advertised. J. W. DEAL, P. M.

july 22.

PROCLAMATION.—To the Coroner, the Justices of the Peace, and the Constables of the Different Townships in the County of Franklin, Greeting: Know all ye, that in pursuance of a precept to me directed, under the hand and seal of the Hon. JAMES NILL, President of the several Courts of Common Pleas, in the Sixteenth District, consisting of the counties of Somerset, Bedford, Fulton and Franklin, and by virtue of his office, the Court of Oyer and Terminer and General Jail Delivery for the trial of capital and other offenders therein, and in the General Court of Quarter Sessions of the Peace, and William W. Paxton and James O. Carson, Esqs., Judges of the same county of Franklin. You and each of you are hereby required to be and appear in your proper persons with your Records, Recognizances, Examinations, and other Remembrances before the Judges aforesaid, at Chambersburg, at a Court of Oyer and Terminer and General Jail Delivery, and General Quarter Sessions of the Peace, therein to be holden for the County of Franklin aforesaid, *on the Second Monday in August, being the 10th day of the month*, at 10 o'clock in the forenoon of that day, then and there to do those things, which to your several offices appertain.

Given under my hand at Chambersburg, the 15th day of July, 1863. SAMUEL BRANDT, Sheriff.

july 22-tc.

CAPITAL NEW BOOKS,

JUST PUBLISHED BY

JOHN BRADBURN,

(Successor to M. D. DOOLADY),

49 *Walker Street*,

(Near Broadway),

NEW YORK CITY.

LEAVES FROM THE DIARY OF AN ARMY SURGEON, by Doctor Thos. T. Ellis, Late Post Surgeon at New York, and Acting Medical Director at White House Va. Cloth. 350 pages. 12mo. Price $1. A Liberal Discount to the trade. Each copy contains an autograph letter from General McClellan.

DR. CUMMING'S REPLY TO BISHOP COLENSO.—*Bishop Colenso fully Answered*: His Errors refuted and the Mosaic authorship of the Pentateuch clearly established, by the Rev. John Cumming, D. D., in a series of Lectures. Cloth. 271 pp. 12mo. Price $1.

THE ACTRESS IN HIGH LIFE, *An Episode in Winter Quarters*, by a Lady of South Carolina. Cloth. 461 pages. 12mo. $1.25.

ADVENTURES BY SEA AND LAND OF THE COUNT DE GANAY; *Or, the Devotion and Fidelity of Woman.* An Episode of the Colonization of Canada. By H. Emile Chevalier. Cloth. 312 pp. 12mo. $1.

LES MISERABLES, by Victor Hugo. Five Vols. in One. Fantine, Marius, St. Denis, Cosette, Valjean. Cloth. 476 pp. 8vo. $1.50.

HANS OF ICELAND:—*The Demon of the North.* A Romance by Victor Hugo. Cloth. 187 pp. 8vo. 50c.

ARBITRARY ARRESTS IN THE SOUTH:—*Scenes in the Experience of an Alabama Unionist*, by R. S. Tharin, A. M. Native of Charleston; for thirty years a resident of the Cotton States; and commonly known in the West as "the Alabama Refugee." Cloth. 319 pp. 12mo. $1.

LIVES AND LETTERS OF ABELARD AND HELOISE by O. W. Wright. Cloth 319 pp. 12mo. $1.

THREE YEARS IN CHILI. Cloth. 158 pp. 12mo. 75c.

WOODS AND WATERS:—*The Saranacs and Racket.* By Alfered B. Street. Cloth. 341 pages. 12mo. $1.25

STORIES OF FRONTIER ADVENTURE IN THE SOUTH AND WEST. By Wm. T. Coggeshall, Author of "Home Hits and Hints," "Poets and Poetry of the West," &c. Cloth. 371 pp. 12mo. $1.

THE BATTLE OF WATERLOO. By Victor Hugo. Paper Covers. 75 pages. 16mo. 15c.

TRIPS IN THE LIFE OF A LOCOMOTIVE ENGINEER. Paper Covers. 224 pp. 12mo. 50c. Cloth, $1.

OUR FARM OF FOUR ACRES, *and the Money we made by it.* From the 12th London Ed. by Harriet Martineau. Paper Covers. 128 pp. 11mo. 25c. Cloth, 38c.

These books may be bought at retail from the Store of S. S. SHRYOCK. [July 22-3m.

New Advertisements.

CHAMBERSBURG FEMALE SEMINARY.—Arrangements have been made for opening the fall session at the time appointed, September 8. For particulars, address

juty 22-1t Rev. H. REEVES, Principal.

MUSICAL INSTRUMENTS.

WM. A. POND & CO.,

547 *Broadway, New York.*

(Late FIRTH, POND & CO.)

Manufacturers of and Dealers in all kinds of

MUSICAL INSTRUMENTS AND MUSICAL MERCHANDISE,

Publishers and Importers of Sheet Music, Musical Works, &c., &c., &c.

Messrs. W. A. Pond & Co. can furnish anything in the musical line at the shortest possible notice, and at prices that defy competition.

PIANO-FORTES (New) from $225 to $800.

PIANO-FORTES (Second-hand) from $75 to $300, according to size and style of case.

MELODEONS of all the celebrated makers, at manufacturers' prices.

FLUTES, from one to eight keys, and from 50c. to $125 in price.

GERMAN SILVER FIFES, in case, $7.

GUITARS, BANJOS, VIOLINS, VIOLONCELLOS, DRUMS, ACCORDEONS, CONCERTINAS, and all kinds of Musical Instruments.

A set of our very best VIOLIN STRINGS, 75c; GUITAR STRINGS, $1; BANJO STRINGS, $1; sent by mail postage-paid.

We publish one of the largest and most valuable Catalogues in America, and are daily adding to it. Our facilities for furnishing everything in this particular department are unlimited.

Every piece of Music published in the United States for sale, at wholesale and retail. We have constant exchanges with the European publishers, and can therefore supply any foreign music desired.

CATALOGUES SENT GRATIS.

Music Sent by Mail, Postage Paid, on Receipt of the Marked Price.

Dealers, Teachers, and Seminaries, can obtain their suppiies of Music by mail, at a postage of only Two Cents on each package of four ounces, or less, and four cents for each four ounces, or less, weight of books.

WM. A. POND & CO., 547 Broadway, New York.

july 22-1t.

A LIST OF GRAND and TRAVERSE JURORS, drawn for a Court of Oyer and Terminer, Court of Quarter Sessions of the Peace, and a Court of Common Pleas, to be held at Chambersburg, on Monday, the 10th day of August, A. D. 1863.

GRAND JURORS, *August Term*, 1863.

Hyssong John A. Mercersburg; Beard Andrew, Hamilton Township; Bauman John, Guilford; Barnhart Henry, Antrim; Brackenridge S G, Southampton: Crouse Benj. Fannett; Campbell Charles, Metal; Deardorf, John S, Guilford; Frey John, Montgomery; Feldman Peter, Chambersburg; Henderson Upton, Guilford; Kaufman Sam'l, Guilford; Lehman Jacob, Guilford; Leckrone Sam'l, Washington; McCurdy S O, Fannett; Stake Daniel, Fannett; Stouffer Daniel, Letterkenny; Stake William, Letterkenny; Shank Henry, Antrim; Shartle Samuel, Montgomery; Speck Joseph, Letterkenny; Snider Jacob C, Guilford; Wilson Andrew, Waynesboro'; Welsh Henry, Hamilton.

TRAVERSE JURORS.

Bosserman Joseph, Montgomery; Brewer Isaiah, Warren; Bushey Henry, Montgomery; Bonebreak Nicholas, Washington; Byers David C. Lurgan; Byers John W, St. Thomas; Bakener Daniel D, Quincy; Cressler, Joseph G, Southampton; Dull Peter, Quincy; Dittman George, Chambersburg; Elder Samuel, Fannett; Foreman Daniel, Greencastle; Fortney William, Quincy; Gilbert Joseph, Washington; Heintzleman Samuel W, Guilford; Huber Benjamin, St. Thomas; Harman Jeremiah, Guilford; Hawk John, Peters; Harbaugh George J, Quincy; Ho.singer Jacob, Guilford; Harbaugh Simon, Hamilton; Jones Jesse, Metal; Johnston William, Fannett; Leedy Jacob V B, Letterkenny; Leckrone Daniel M, Antrim; McLanahan A G, Antrim; McKee Mathew, Greene; McClain William, Metal; Morrow William, Fannett; McCune James A, Mercersburg; McGeehan Geo, Chambersburg; Miller William, Sr., Waynesboro'; McFerren Peter, Guilford; McColloh A S, Warren; Oyer Jacob, Hamilton; Peckman Frank, St. Thomas; Rebuck John, Lurgan; Ruthrauff William, Antrim; Small Benj. C, Guilford; Sentman Samuel L, Lurgan; Sellers John A, St. Thomas; Skinner John S, Metal; Snively Samuel, Antrim; Thomas John H, Warren; Waddel Thomas A, Mercersburg; Welch Jacob R, Waynesboro': West John, Chambersburg; Walter Henry, Washington.

CIRCULATE THE "GUARD."—We are now on the verge of one of the most important elections that has ever taken place in our State The great question is to be decided in October whether or not the State of Pennsylvania shall continue to give to the National Government a hearty and unconditional support in its efforts to crush the rebellion and restore the Union. It is of the most vital importance that the unconditional friends of the Union should carry our State, and there can be no doubt that such will be the case if proper candidates are selected, and the campaign properly managed. One of the most important things to be done is to circulate Union documents, such as newspapers, pamphlets, &c.

The National Guard being an unconditional Union paper and uncompromising in its support of the Government, is worthy of an extended circulation. It is universally admitted to be one of the handsomest and best conducted papers published in the country. Its pages are filled with useful and interesting matter, the ablest writers are employed upon its columns, and everything possible is done to make it what it is—a first-class paper.

The Guard will be furnished at the following moderate rates:—One copy, one year, $2. Five copies, one year, $8. Twelve copies, one year, $20. Twenty copies or more, one year, $30. One copy of the Guard will be sent for the year to the getter up of the club. To postmasters and canvassers we will allow fifty cents to every two dollar subscriber sent us. We offer the following

SPLENDID PRIZES

to persons getting up clubs for the Guard:—

First Prize.—To the person getting up the largest club over one hundred, a Melodeon, to cost not less than $75.

Second Prize.—To the person getting up the second largest club over one hundred, a Gold Watch, to cost not less than $50.

Third Prize.—To the person getting up the third largest club over one hundred, a Patent-Lever Silver Watch, to cost not less than $35.

In order that no one making an effort to obtain the prizes above named shall go unrewarded, we will give to every person who does not take a prize, twenty-five cents for every subscriber sent at our club rates.

The time of subscription to commence with our pictorial number of the Fourth of July, and the time in which these clubs must be gotten up to end on the 20th of September next. Subscriptions should be sent in as fast as obtained. Immediately after the 20th of September, the prizes will be forwarded to the parties who shall gain them. Everything will be conducted in the fairest possible manner, and our subscription books will be open for the examination of all who may contend for the prizes. [july 22-3t.

THE EVENING POST.

(ESTABLISHED IN 1801.)

A Thoroughgoing, Independent and Fearless Advocate of Freedom.

A COMPLETE FAMILY NEWSPAPER.

EDITED BY

William Cullen Bryant and Parke Godwin.

TERMS,

PAYABLE IN ADVANCE.

DAILY EVENING POST.

One Copy, one year, delivered by Carrier	$11 00
One Copy, one year, sent by mail	10 00
One Copy, one month	1 00

SEMI-WEEKLY EVENING POST

Is Published every Tuesday and Friday.

One Copy, one year	$3 00
Two Copies, one year	5 00
Five Copies, one year	12 00
Ten Copies, one year	22 50

An extra copy will be sent to any person who sends us club of twenty and over.

WEEKLY EVENING POST

Is Published Every Wednesday.

One Copy, one year	$2 00
Three Copies, one year	5 00
Five Copies, one year	8 00
Ten Copies, one year	15 00
Twenty Copies *to one address*, one year	25 00

And an extra copy to the getter-up of the club.

PREMIUMS.

Any person sending us $45 for twenty Semi-Weekly subscribers will be entitled to an extra copy of the Semi-Weekly one year; or $22 50 for ten copies, will be entitled to one copy of our Weekly one year.

Any person sending us $15 and the names of ten subscribers to our Weekly will be entitled to an extra copy of the Weekly one year for his services; for twenty names and $30 he will be entitled to one copy of our Semi-Weekly or two copies of our Weekly one year.

Each subscriber's name is printed on his paper.

CLERGYMEN are supplied by mail at the following rates: Daily, $8 per annum; Semi-Weekly, $2 50; Weekly $1 50. Money may be forwarded by mail at our risk.

SPECIMEN COPIES

Will be sent *free* to all who desire it.

WM. C. BRYANT & CO., Office of the Evening Post, 41 Nassau Street, Cor. Liberty, New York.

july 22, '63-tf.

ASSAULT ON A NEGRO

WOMEN PILLAGING.

THE FIGHT

DESTRUCTION of PROVOST MARSHAL'S OFFICE 3d Av

PROVOST GUARD

IN LEXINGTON AVENUE

The attack on Croton Cottage.

AT

THE GREAT RIOT IN NEW YORK—SCENES ON T

DAY AT 2D AV.

ANDREWS OF VIRGINIA & OTHER RINGLEADERS.

HANGING A NEGRO IN CLARKSON ST.

THE RIOTER'S

BURNING OF THE COLORED ORPHAN ASYLUM

BUNE OFFICE

BURNING OF THE 2D AV. ARMORY.

ANDREWS OF VIRGINIA HARANGUING THE MOB.

ND 14th OF JULY.—From Sketches by our Special Artists.

Emmettsburg, Md. Gen. Meade's Army pursuing Gen. Lee.

INVASION OF PENNSYLVANIA—BATTLE OF GETTYSBURG—CEMETERY HILL, DURING THE ATTACK OF THE REBELS, THURSDAY EVENING, JULY 2.

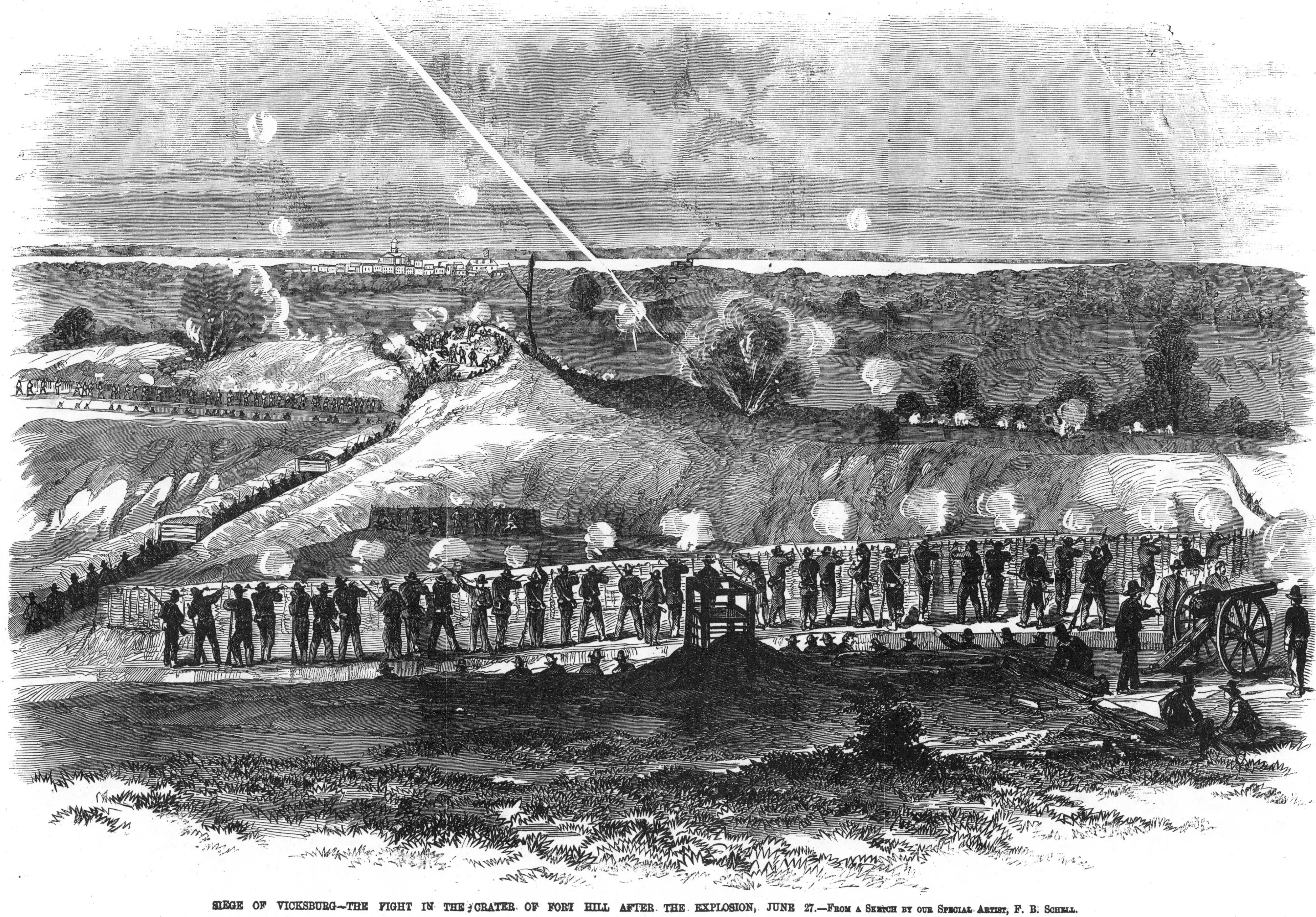

SIEGE OF VICKSBURG—THE FIGHT IN THE CRATER OF FORT HILL AFTER THE EXPLOSION, JUNE 27.—FROM A SKETCH BY OUR SPECIAL ARTIST, F. B. SCHELL.

INVASION OF PENNSYLVANIA—BATTLE OF GETTYSBURG—CHARGE OF THE REBELS ON CEMETERY HILL, THURSDAY NIGHT, JULY 2.—FROM A SKETCH BY OUR SPECIAL ARTIST, EDWIN FORBES.

Troy Weekly Times,

TROY, SATURDAY, JULY 26, 1863.

TO OUR SUBSCRIBERS.

You are aware that our office was sacked and destroyed by a mob of ruffians on Wednesday of last week. In consequence of this outrage, we were unable to print the WEEKLY TIMES last week, and now we can only furnish a half sheet which is printed at the office of the Albany Morning Express. Under the circumstances, we feel assured that our subscribers will indulge us. Next week, the publication of the WEEKLY TIMES will be fully resumed, with new material throughout and we trust with a vigor that shall at least render it quite as interesting and valuable as ever. We shall fully compensate for the necessary omissions, also, by furnishing subscribers with messages, &c., upon extra sheets, so that they may feel perfectly satisfied. Be assured, also, that, sufferers as we are from the demonism of a ruthless mob, the TIMES will maintain the Old Flag with a still more resolute purpose, and contribute its best ability towards crushing treason at the South and punishing mob traitors at home. We ask our friends to put forth renewed efforts to increase the circulation of the TIMES. If every loyal subscriber would make it a point to get additional subscriptions for the paper, our list might be doubled in a month. Can a better plan than this be adopted in evincing a determination to rebuke mob law, and to advance the cause of just principles.

THE NEWS.

We can give our readers but a brief resume of the exciting news of the past ten days.

The fall of Vicksburg and Port Hudson places the Mississippi in our possession, and cuts the traitor confederacy in two. Grant captured some 32,000 prisoners, about 200 cannon and 60,000 stand of arms; Banks 8,000 prisoners, 60 cannon and 10,000 small arms. Gen. Sherman has driven Johntson out of Jackson; Johnston's supplies have been captured, and our army is pursuing the fugitives. It is believed they will be entirely disorganized.

Rosecrans has driven Bragg into Georgia, and at last accounts was vigorously pursuing him. Bragg's army is greatly demoralized, and hundreds are daily deserting to our lines. Bragg is used up.

Lee commenced his retreat immediately after being whipped at Gettysburg, Meade pursuing him. Lee was badly cut up on his retreat and lost heavily; but he got into Virginia with a majority of his army, where Meade is now pushing him. The rebel loss has not been less than 35,000; ours has not been half as many. We captured 60 cannon.

A vigorous movement was commenced against Charleston on the 4th of July, and our forces have captured all but one end of Morris Island. There the rebels hold Fort Wagoner, but its fall is deemed certain, and with its fall we shall have such a sweep at Fort Sumter that this rebel stronghold must surrender. The rebel papers fear that Charlston must fall this time. The women and children have been cleared out. Gen. Gilmore is confident of success.

Gen. Prentiss has "kept on" whipping the rebel General Price in Arkansas, and there is now little left of the rebellion in that state.

The rebel Gen. Morgan with his band of 2000 of 3000 guerrillas made a raid into Ohio. He has been whipped, and most of his force captured. It is expected that we shall have the chief, also with his 400 or 500 skedaddlers.

Jeff. Davis has became alarmed, and ordered a conscription of every person in the confederacy between the ages 18 and 45. But we trust it is too late.

Everywhere we are pounding the Rebel Confederacy to pieces, and the only dark side of the glorious picture is the fact of the recent riots in New York and Troy, under the plea of resistance to the draft. In New York, the riot raged three or four days of last week, but it has been suppressed by the strong arm of military power, and probably not less than 400 or 500 of the rioters were killed. They destroyed several houses, including the orphan asylum for colored children, murdered Col. O'Brien, who was commanding a portion of the military against them, murdered several inoffensive colored men, and perpetrated other atrocities. In Troy, the mob destroyed the Times office, sacked the residences of Martin I. Townsend and Deputy Provost Marshal Laithe, broke into the jail and released all the prisoners, gutted several houses of ill fame, &c. They desisted from their work for the time being through the efforts of Rev. Mr. Havermans, and a few others. The authorities seemed to be perfectly paralyzed; indeed they did nothing to stay the mob. On Wednesday night the barn of Mayor Van Alstyne was set on fire and burned. Several horses were burned to death. It is believed that arrangements are now perfected, so as to check further outrages, and to properly punish the mob if it resumes its atrocities. Mobs cannot triumph; the draft will be enforced, and traitors both North and South will be crushed out.

One of the Boys.

Passengers who came on to New York with Gen. Kilpatrick last week were attracted toward a little fellow in his company, evidently quite a pet, who wore the dress of the cavalry service, with spurs and trappings, and a jacket bespattered with mud, showing the evidence of his late adventures among the rough riders of Kilpatrick's force. Upon inquiry of the General, the following story of the lad was told: He was born in England, where his parents still reside, and came to this country with an elder brother, who is now a member of an infantry regiment in the Potomac Army. Taking a fancy to the cavalry service, he managed to get a horse, and fell in as a soldier. After one of the recent fights, the General noticed him grieving over the loss of his horse. A day or two later, seeing him near his tent, he asked him to do an errand to his Adjutant-General. When he arrived at his destination, the officer asked, "Who are you, Sir?" "Aid-de-Camp to Gen. Kilpatrick, Sir," was the prompt reply. Now our young hero had made his point. He was at once adopted into the military family of the General, who assured the writer that no man in his command would better convey an order upon the field. At the battle of Gettysburg he took himself three prisoners, one being very tall, his head, while standing, being as high as the head of the young cavalryman seated upon his horse. Bringing his prisoners to headquarters, confronting the General, he says: "General, what do you think of *that?*" He has been in seventeen battles with his favorite General, who in turn now proposes to give his gallant and faithful young friend a good education. He is small of his age, which is 14, and his name is "Charley" Smith.

About 500 Rebel prisoners, all officers, arrived in Pittsburg on Monday, en route for Johnson's Island, where they will be detained until exchanged. They came from Fort Delaware, where there are now nearly 10,000 prisoners confined, and were in charge of a detachment of Young's artillery, under command of Lieuts, McConnell and Ahl. Among the prisoners were Gens. Archer and Jones, both of whom were captured at Gettysburg.

THE PURSUIT OF LEE.

His Army Near Winchester or Above that Point.

Gen. Meade's Army in a Position to Intercept Him.

A BATTLE EXPECTED SOON.

The Washington Republican of Wednesday evening contains the following:—"From the best information at hand, it appears that Lee's army is near Winchester, or above that point, while our own army occupies such a position that he cannot get back to Richmond without fighting at a disadvantage. The Rebel General is either holding his position to gather supplies from the crops in the Valley, or, with the aid of such reinforcements as he may have obtained, to give another battle or series of battles to the Army of the Potomac. Our army is ready to fight him—anxious, indeed, rather than return to another campaign in those districts of Virginia which have been so thoroughly devastated by war. We may expect stirring news from Gen. Meade's army soon."

Effect of Union Victories on the Southern Markets.

From the Richmond Inquirer, July 17.

The markets labor under the pressure of revived anxieties. The public has become used to the siege of Vicksburg, and even in the most critical hours of that ill-fated city, business pursued a passive tenor, and some began to think that it was regaining its natural channel. But Vicksburg went down, followed by Port Hudson; the fever of speculation broke out again, and sugar being the most plausible commodity to operate with, sugar was consequently marked for a furor. It went up like rockets. Men who had accumulated thousands upon thousands by speculation began suddenly to feel the insatiable grip of their gross cupidity squeezing their souls with refreshed strength. The interregnum of abatement seemed to have a period of lethargic repose, which they shook off as the wild beasts shake off their drowsy mood after long slumber. Then they sought for prey, and the community knows the consequence.

The financial market during this time held up. Little was done. The brokers refused to sell specie or foreign funds for several days, waiting to see more clearly ahead. But they bought all they could at slightly advanced rates. Gen. Lee went to Hagerstown, and the market made a feverish opening. The Yankees commenced the attack on Charleston, and the market was firmer, at advanced rates.

The market is now fairly reopened. We are again becoming used to critical impendences, and begin to breathe freer, though the rates are up. The condition of affairs in Virginia, however, renders it incompatible with the laws of trade for any advance to be made in any produce whatever for which we have to depend upon our own soil. Any advance, therefore, in the necessaries of life raised within the State would be the most heartless, unblushing and impudent speculation. It is, indeed, to be pitied that the people are not more minutely and critically acquainted with the principles of supply and demand. Popular intelligence in this branch of learning would break down many a scheme of disguised villainy with which even now the community is swindled.

We present yesterday's quotations:—Gold, buying $7.75 premium, selling $9; silver, do. 6 do., selling $7; sterling bills $8.50, do. $9.25. Wheat, $5.50 a $6. Corn, $10, scarce. Oats, sheaf, $9 a $10 per cwt. Hay, $9 a $10. Flour, superfine, $31 a $32; extra, $33 a $34; family, $37. Meal, $10.50 a $11. Bacon, $1.45 a $1.50. Tea, $8 a $10 for black, $10 a $12 for green. Sugar, $1.50 a $1.75 for brown—there are holders at $2; butter $1.75 a $2.25; molasses, $11 a $12.50; salt, 54c.; rice, 18c. a 22c.; soap, 60c. a 75c. for country made; candles, tallow, $2.75 a $3—few others in market; French brandy, $45 a $50 a $60; whiskey, $25 a $40—latter for pure; rum, $45; gin, $45; wines, port and sherry, $45. Leather—Soles, $3.50a$4; upper, $5a$6.25; harness, $4.25; calf skins, $400 per dozen.

Daring Robbery of a Banking House in Brockport.

A correspondent of the Journal, writing from Brockport, under date of the 22d says:

This afternoon, while George Gordon was alone in Waters, Bishop & Co.'s Banking House, a man came in and asked him to change a ten dollar greenback. While Gordon was in the act of complying with the request, the man jumped over the counter, and, by administering chloroform, or some other means, stunned him, put him in the vault, locked the door, took $4,400 from the counter, and left.

Mr. Bishop soon returned from dinner, found his money gone, and George locked up in the vault, half insensible.

In five minutes the whole town was in search of the robbers. There proved to be two or three of them, who had come up from Rochester. They ran to the Presbyterian Church, where they had left their horse and buggy, and started east. In hastily driving out of the yard, the buggy upset, throwing them out.

One was caught, but not the one who had the money. The other two took to their heels. The one taken is a well-dressed fellow, and had on a coat with an enormous pocket in the skirt, as big as a carpet bag, and made to button up. A revolver and cartridges was found on his person. He refuses to give his name, and says he lives in New York. He has, however, been seen in Rochester. Hundreds of men are scouring the woods in search of the other two.

Brockport will soon be entitled to a City Charter.

A Cargo of Prostitutes.

From the Cincinnati Commercial.

A few days since, General Mitchell, commanding at Nashville, peremptorily ordered all the prostitutes in that place to leave within twenty-four hours. On the day following, one hundred and six of the frail ones were shipped for Louisville on the Government steamer Idahoe. On arriving at the latter point, General Boyle ordered the Idahoe to Cincinnati, with her cargo. She arrived here yesterday noon, landing outside of several empty coal barges lying at the Newport wharf. General Boyle furnished a military escort, who are on guard, to prevent these women from going ashore. While on the trip several escaped from the boat—one by swimming ashore in the night. On arriving here the company numbered eighty-eight women and six children. An increase is hourly anticipated in the number of the latter. Several of the women have served in the Federal and Rebel ranks, one having performed the duties of a gunner with our artillery at Fort Donelson. The majority are inveterate chewers of tobaccacc and "up to snuff." Up to last night, we understand, the military authorities had not decided relative to the disposal of this cargo of frail humanity. It is possible they may be ordered back to Nashville.

The majority are a homely, forlorn set of degraded creatures. Having been hurried on the boats by a military guard, many are without a change of wardrobe. They managed to smuggle a little liquor on board, which gave out on the second day after leaving Nashville. Several became intoxicated and indulged in a free fight, which resulted without material damage to any of the party, although knives were freely used. They are nearly all strong Rebel sympathizers, and boast of their Southern blood. Two other steamers have also left Nashville with similar cargoes.

MYSTERIOUS DISAPPEARANCE—SUPPOSED MURDER.—Edward Warren, in the employ of Fuller, Warren & Co., of Troy, started at an early hour Tuesday evening, to repair a stove at a house on Thirteenth street, and reached there about eight o'clock, with his coat torn and face bruised. He reported that he had been attacked and beaten by three men, who set upon him, and from whom he narrowly escaped. After remaining until ten o'clock, he concluded that he could not remain there all night, and, although fearful that he would be attacked, started on his return to the lower part of the city. From that hour he has not been seen, and fears were entertained in Troy last evening that he had been murdered. The missing man was quite zealous in the cause of law and order, during the recent disturbance in Troy. It was a current report in that city last evening, that he had been found murdered, but we could not trace it to any reliable authority.

The Invalid Corps is rapidly reaching its prescribed dimensions. Twenty companies of the First battalion have already been organized, and also seven companies of the second battalion. Recruits are gathered at St. Louis, Washington, Michigan, Connecticut, South Carolina, and Fortress Monroe, and will all soon be brought into the organization. At least 2,500 men have already enlisted.

NEWS ITEMS.

Gen. Kilpatrick is at his house in Sussex county, New Jersey, recruiting from his recent exhausting labors in the field.

The New York Police are bagging vast quantities of plunder taken by the rioters last week.

Gen. Gideon Pillow has again turned up. He now figures as a guerilla leader at the head of a couple thousand ragamuffins.

A wealthy Marylander named Cashal has been arrested on charge of having acted as spy and informer for the Rebel General Stuart.

Five hundred pounds of minie balls were the other day, upon information given by a colored man, discovered secreted in a hole in one of the wharves of Boston.

It is rumored that the Major-Generalship in the United States Army, vacant by the retirement of Gen. Wool, will be tendered to Gen. Grant.

When the advance column of Gen. Meade's army passed through Westminster, the women-folks exhibited much sympathy for them, and one young lady created amusement by her ingenuous remark: "Poor fellows, how dirty their hands are."

Captain Ulric Dahlgren—son of the Admiral—is promoted to a Lieutenant-Colonelcy of Volunteers for gallant conduct at Gettysburg. Among his certificates of good behavior was a lost leg.

It appears that the intercepted despatches of Jeff. Davis to Gen. Lee contained an order to fall back into Virginia, as a sufficient number of troops could not be raised to protect Richmond.

A Federal spy has been arrested at Atlanta, Ga., calling himself Russell. He had passed for a Richmond correspondent, and had been on an extensive tour throughout the South. He had a telegraph instrument with him and was in the habit of tapping the Rebel lines, getting information and alarming the Rebels with strange despatches.

Nearly every gate in the city of Vicksburg is adorned with unexploded 12-inch shells placed atop of each post. The porches and piazzas (nearly every house has one) are also adorned with curious collections of shot and shells that have fallen in the yards.

A woman who was at Gettysburg in hope of recovering the body of her husband, reported killed, was overjoyed to find him alive, among a crowd of hobbling wounded men.

The Commissioner of Internal Revenue has decided that where Corporations make profits without declaring dividends, they must be taxed on these profits precisely as if a dividend had been declared.

An attempt was made last week at Holly Springs, Miss., to kill Dr. Peters, the slayer of Van Dorn. The would-be murderer fired at him through a window, while he was in bed.

Before the fall of Vicksburg, flour sold there for $5 a pound, which is equal to $980 a barrel, and butter was $4 a pound, with little to be had.

Several persons advertise themselves as substitutes for $250, in Providence papers.

News from the Southwest.

RETREAT OF BRAGG—ITS DISASTROUS EFFECTS.

From the Montgomery Advertiser, July 11.

The retreat of Bragg from Tullahoma to the Tennessee river is much to be regretted. We are confident that it will have a very judicious effect, not merely on the people, but on the troops, particularly those from Tennessee. The army correspondent of the Mobile Register stated in his letter of the 6th instant, that a considerable number of the troops from that State have already deserted, and we should not be surprised to learn that there has been still greater disaffection, from the fact that Middle and East Tennessee have been abandoned, for it would be impossible to keep a small body of troops at Knoxville after Bragg's army has left the State. Nor will the misfortune stop here. The retreat from Tennessee opens the northern counties of Georgia and Alabama to the incursions of the enemy. In our own State the Tennessee valley will be desolated, and raiding parties will penetrate the counties lying between the Tennessee and the Alabama, and east of the Bigbee rivers. This will bring the enemy to our own doors, and open the way to the rich counties of South Alabama. The incursions may not immediately occur, for Rosecrans may intends to fight Bragg, but the position assumed by the latter, south of the Tennessee river, will check his operations, and may, perhaps, hold him at bay for another six months. But if it be the object of Rosecrans to avoid a decisive engagement, then he will assuredly send his cavalry to destroy our crops and desolate the State.

But there is another view of this question which is important. Vicksburg having fallen, Grant has an army of eighty thousand men at his disposal. It will be impossible for Gen. Johnston to oppose this army with any hope of success, and as he retires towards the Bigbee, which we suppose he will do, Grant will close on him, and unite his army with that of Rosecrans. Here, then, will be an army of one hundred and sixty or seventy thousand men encamped on the soil of Alabama.

To face these facts it becomes the sacred duty of every man in Alabama to gird up his loins for the fight, and surely it will be a struggle for existence. Every man who has a gun, and every man who owns a horse, should be ready to do his duty to his country. The war, with all its brutality, is approaching our own homes. It would be criminal to disguise the fact that we are in great danger; but it would be equally criminal to whine about the horrors of war. The way to meet danger is to face it boldly. If we are vigilant, if we are prompt in organizing, if we muster our whole strength, if we give everything to the cause and resolve to conquer or die, all will be well. The time calls for action. The State demands our services, and sink or swim, survive or perish, live or die, we must rally to her support and drive back the invader dicomfited.

A Lament for the Loss of Tennessee.

From the Chattanooga Rebel, July 9.

Among the objects of repining to which the mind very naturally reverts in contemplating the loss of Middle Tennessee, none forces itself more persistently upon us than the rich crops of grain which our retreat threw into the hands of the enemy.

We share this sore reflection to some extent undoubtedly, but not so feelingly as some of our more despondent friends.

The crops of Tennessee, like the soil and all else therein, were fair to see. Many a time during the last three months have we cast a hopeful eye upon the teeming acres and their fruitful promise. But luxury, rather than absolute want, was the main figure in the prospect. We saw with gratification the energetic industry which was converting a thousand cotton fields to patches of corn and wheat in the far South, and at no time did we fear starvation or even need. Hence we have not regarded the Middle Tennesse crops—whilst to be greatly desired—as absolutely essential to our existence, nor do we at this time.

It would be wanton affectation were we to deny an extreme regret at the loss of so much produce; but we can continue to do without it; and, in any event, there is no use crying over spoiled milk.

A REPENTANT REBEL.—While our surgeons at Gettysburg were attending to the wounded as they were brought into the hospitals, without regard to the side upon which they had fought, a Rebel colonel, covered with blood, was ordered to be placed in a bath. He was lifted carefully in, and then, casting his eyes about him, upon those who had taken him up so tenderly, burst into a flood of tears, and wept like a child. Recovering himself, he said to those around him: "I hope I shall be forgiven for raising my hand against the Stars and Stripes, and if I recover from these wounds I will not only never do the like again, but try to make amends, so far as I can, for the wrong I have done."

GEN. GRANT'S HEADQUARTERS.—Gen. Grant's headquarters will probably remain for some time, as at present, at Vicksburg. He is not afraid to let his Lieutenants earn what glory they can in the campaigns on which they have gone. In connection with the large capture of cattle just made by one of Gen. Grant's expeditions, it deserves to be known that not more than two hundred of the beeves furnished to our large army during the siege of Vicksburg came from the North. The rest were found in Mississippi and Louisiana.

TELEGRAMS!

LATEST DESPATCHES.

IMPORTANT FROM THE SOUTHWEST.

Gen. Stanley Believed to be in Huntsville, Ala., and Gen. Sheridan in Chattanooga.

GEN. JOE JOHNSTON AT BRANDON.

Both His and Bragg's Armies Destitute and Demoralized.

They Give Up Mississippi and Advise the Planters to Make the Best Terms Possible.

THE REPORTS OF OUR SUCCESSES AT NATCHEZ, YAZOO CITY AND JACKSON FULLY CONFIRMED.

Special to the Philadelphia Inquirer.

HEADQUARTERS MCCOOK'S CORPS, WINCHESTER, Tenn., July 15.

It is believed here that Gen. Stanley is in Huntsville, Va., having entered it on Monday afternoon. I will write the particulars as soon as received. We will probably have definite information to-day.

The probability also is that Gen. Sheridan is in Chattanooga.

The enemy does not seem to design to make a stand anywhere; indeed, I presume he can not.

MEMPHIS, July 21, via CAIRO, July 23.

Gen. Hurlburt's scouts arrived to-day from Okolona, Miss., and report Johnston at Brandon, and Gen. Sherman in possession of Jackson.

The forces of the Rebel Generals Ruggles, Chalmers, Saunders and Ferguson are at Tupola. Ruggles is concentrating his forces, with the intention, probably, of making a dash into our lines.

Correspondence from Bragg's and Johnston's armies depict them in great destitution and greatly demoralized. They give up Mississippi, and advise the planters to stay and make the best terms possible. Our scouts report the majority of the planters anxious that we should get possession of the country before Jeff. Davis has time to conscript them.

Johnston's army is estimated not to exceed 30,000.

Great consternation exists throughout the whole Southern country.

The reports of our successes at Natchez, Yazoo City and Jackson are fully confirmed. Large quantities of munitions of war, especially of ammunition, have fallen into our hands with these places.

THE REBEL MORGAN CROSSES THE MUSKINGUM RIVER.

OUR FORCES IN FULL PURSUIT OF HIM.

The Citizens of Zanesville Turning out En masse to Resist his Progress.

CINCINNATI, July 23.

Morgan crossed the Muskingum river at Eaglesport, 18 miles below Zanesville, at 10 o'clock this morning. Scouts report his force 1,000 strong, with two pieces of artillery.

Col. Lamont, 86th Ohio, sent his regiment and a large number of militia after him. Col. Chandler, of Zanesville, and twenty-five citizen scouts were captured at Deerstown last night.

The latest reports from Eaglesport say the 86th Regiment, under Lieut. Col. McFarland, are fighting the Rebels and driving them up the river towards Zanesville. This is not entirely reliable.

Business is suspended at Zanesville, and the citizens are turning out en masse to resist Morgan's progress.

SECOND DESPATCH.

CINCINNATI, July 23.

Morgan, this afternoon, was in Guernsey county, near the Central Ohio Railroad, and was supposed to be making eastward for the Ohio river.

FROM WASHINGTON.

WASHINGTON, July 23.

Admiral Lee, in a communication dated off Newport News, encloses a copy of a report from Capt. Case, respecting the driving ashore of the Penobscot, and the subsequent abandonment, by her crew, of the steamer Kate on the 12th inst., at the south end of Smith's Island.

An attempt was made by the Penobscot crew to get her afloat under the guns of the blockade, but without success, and she was subsequently burnt. It is reported to have been a double screw, schooner rigged, iron steamer, with an assorted cargo of merchandize, and a notorious blockade runner.

To-day, in the District Court, a decree was granted confiscating the personal estate of Dr. Garnett, son-in-law of Ex-Governor Wise, during his lifetime, while his real estate is an absolute forfeiture. The same principles affect seventeen other cases, in which simtlar decrees were ordered to be issued.

The Draft in Auburn—An Enthusiastic Demonstration.

AUBURN, July 23.

The draft for the city of Auburn and seventeen sub-districts in the county of Cayuga, took place in this city to-day. The best of order was observed, and the best spirit was manifested.

The drafted men of this city have a dress parade this evening, headed by a band of music, and colors flying. The city is quiet and perfectly peaceful.

9 P. M.—There is a crowd of 2,000 persons now in front of the Exchange where the procession of conscripts has halted. They have been addressed by Hon. T. M. Pomeroy, Provost Marseal Knapp, and Mayor White. The drafted men are cheering for the Union, Old Abe, the draft, our recent victories, &c., &c. It beats any demonstration had in Auburn for years.

Highly Successful Cavalry Raid in North Carolina.

WASHINGTON, July 24.

The Petersburg Express of the 22d, referring to the cavalry expedition sent out by General Foster, says:

"The Yankee raiders burnt the railroad bridge over the Tar River, near Rock Mount. They destroyed the depot at that place, tore up two miles of track, and burnt 5,000 bales of cotton and a large cotton factory. The bridge over the Tar River was on the Wilmington and Weldon Railroad, and was about three hundred yards long. They also captured a train of cars, which contained two car-loads of ammunition and 30,000 pounds of bacon, which were destroyed."

The Philadelphia Common Council Refuses to buy Exemptions.

PHILADELPHIA, July 23.

The Common Council have negatived the bill appropriating $500,000 to pay exemptions for drafted men. The vote stood, 18 Democrats for the bill, and 18 Republicans and four Democrats against it. A bill subsequently passed, appropriating $1,000,000 for relief of the families of drafted men.

Mail Communication on the Mississippi.

WASHINGTON, July 23.

The Post-Office Department will resume mail communication between the West and New Orleans, by the Mississippi, as soon as it shall ascertain that it can be done with safety. The mails between the Atlantic cities and New York will continue to be carried in the usual way.

The Richmond Examiner Despondent.

FORTRESS MONROE, July 23.

The flag of truce boat New York arrived this evening from City Point with 1,200 prisoners of war.

The Richmond Examiner of the 23d says, editorially:—From the Mississippi we have no news which is good news.

From Northern Virginia, the lines of Gen. Lee extend to the old battle-ground of Manassas.

Of the Northern army we know notning, except that it cries loudly for reinforcements and has received none.

Vessels Captured by the Pirates.

NEW YORK, July 23.

Bark Zingarilla, from Rio Janeiro, reports ship Jabez Snow, from Newport, Eng., for Montividio, with coal, captured May 25th by pirate, and burned. Also, bark Amazonian, from New York, for Montividio, captur[...]
Crews arrived[...]
The ship G[...]
charging her[...]
pirate Georgi[...]
the vessel wh[...]
ing Englishm[...]

Unio[...]

Union Stat[...]
2d:—All pers[...]
ally sustainin[...]
prosecution[...]
suppressed, a[...]
enforcement[...]
call of Union[...]
ties, and cho[...]
meeting of[...]
meet at Syrac[...]

The[...]

The five mi[...]
pionship of A[...]
Pittsburg, and Ward, of Newburg, took place today. It was won by Ward, beating Hammil by two lengths. Time, 42 minutes 29 seconds.

TROY WEEKLY TIMES

SATURDAY AFTERNOON, JULY 25, 1863.

IN PURSANCE of an order of MOSES WARREN, Surrogate of the county of Rensselaer, notice is hereby given, according to law, to all persons having claims against Hannah May, late of the town of Pittstown, deceased, that they are required to exhibit the same, with the vouchers thereo, to the subscriber, Orin Sherman, at his residence in the town of Pittstown, on or before the 1st day of October next.—Dated March 14 h, 1863.
mh21-1 aw6m*   ORIN SHERMAN, Executor.

IN PURSUANCE of an order of MOSES WARREN, Surrogate of the county of Rensselaer, notice is hereby given, according to law, to all persons having claims against John Stover, late of the town of Pittstown, deceased, that they are required to exhibit the same, with the vouchers thereof, to the subscriber, Spencer A. Buckley, at his residence in the town of Easton, Washington county, on or before the 15th day of October next.—Dated April 2, 1863.   MARY E. STOVER, Adm'x.
ap4*6m   SPENCER A. BUCKLEY, Adm'r.

IMPORTANT FROM BRAZIL.

Difficulty Between Minister Webb and the Government.

NEW YORK, July 23.

Intelligence has been received here that the town of Fort Plata, St. Domingo, was totally destroyed by fire on the 30th of June.

The news from Rio Janeiro is to the 9th of June.

A difficulty is reported between Gen. Webb, the American Minister, and the Brazilian Government.

It was said that the General had demanded satisfaction from Brazil for having tolerated the Confederate corsairs Alabama, Florida and Georgia in the waters of the Empire at Pernambuco and Bahia.

It was also said that Gen. Webb had demanded indemnity for the burning of American vessels, and the dismissal of the Presidents (who answer to our Governors of Territories) of Bahia and Pernambuco.

Two newspapers printed at Rio de Janerio state that our Minister had presented a protest against the action of which he complained, and that the Imperial Government had consented to dismiss the two Presidents of the Provinces named, if the Government of the United States approved of Gen. Webb's course.

Brazil is supposed to be friendly to us; but having recognized the Confederates as belligerents, she could not deny her ports to their armed vessels any more than to ours.

ATTEMPTED RAID INTO MARYLAND.

Lee Moving Toward Winchester.

REBEL CAVALRY ABOUT HARPER'S FERRY.

BALTIMORE, July 23.

About 400 Rebel cavalry encamped near Nolan's Ferry, three miles from Point of Rocks, attempted to cross the Potomac last night with the intention of tearing up the rails of the Baltimore and Ohio railroad, but their designs were frustrated by a band of Independent Rangers, commanded by Captain Means, who drove them from the river. They remain still encamped at their quarters.

We learn further from headquarters that about 3 o'clock this (Thursday) morning Lee's entire army was in motion and moving rapidly in the direction of Winchester. Ewell, who had made a move in the direction of Cumberland, fell back and followed Lee.

There are no parties now at Martinsburg but a body of cavalry and some few horsemen scattered between that place and the Potomac.

Scouts report an increased body of cavalry near Harper's Ferry, supported by two regiments of infantry, one of which is dressed in Federal uniform.

Railroad Accident.

NEW YORK, July 23.

The passenger train which left Philadelphia on Tuesday night at 12 o'clock, containing about 500 passengers, ran off the track about nine miles east of Susquehanna at 2 o'clock on Wednesday morning. The engine, baggage car and express car were thrown off and completely smashed.

Fortunately the only injury inflicted was some slight bruises to a Lieutenant, whose name was not ascertained. All the others miraculously escaped.

The wife of Bishop Potter, of Pennsylvania, lies seriously ill.

Arrival of Rebel Prisoners, &c.

NEW YORK, July 23.

Eight hundred Rebel prisoners, taken at Gettysburg, arrived at David's Island to-day. Eight hundred more come to-night.

The Superior Court has ordered the United States Trust Company to pay to Mrs. Catharine M. Forrest the interest on a mortgage for $75,000, held by them for Edwin Forrest, on property of the Society of St. Vincent de Paul. Mrs. Forrest's allegation was, that he has failed to pay her allowance since August, 1860.

From San Francisco.

SAN FRANCISCO, July 22.

The Supreme Court has sustained the constitutionality of the law of the last Legislature requiring all attorneys to take the oath of allegiance to the National Government before being permitted to practice in the State.

The receipts of silver at San Francisco has been, for three months, at the rate of $1,000,000 a month.

Port Hudson After the Surrender.

The following description of Port Hudson after the surrender, is from the Herald's correspondent:

The works at Port Hudson were found to be fully as strong as represented, but every part of them had been searched by our shot and shell. Large trees had been cut down and the earth torn up in every direction. Only one house was uninjured, and that is now occupied as a telegraph office. The nine-inch shot and shell from the naval battery had done the most damage; the effects of them could be seen on every side. It is very evident—at least officers say so who are capable of judging—that had Vicksburg not fallen, and a supply of provisions could have been obtained, we might have knocked in vain at the door of Port Hudson. Any assault we might have attempted would have been repulsed with great slaughter. The amount of artillery we have captured is smaller than I anticipated. It is represented to be as follows:—Two ten-inch columbiads, one eight-inch columbiad, two thirty-two pounders, rifled; one forty-two pounder, rifled; one forty-two pounder, smooth bore; one thirty-two pounder, smooth bore; and four field batteries. Several other heavy guns were inside the works, but they had been disabled and rendered worthless by our fire. Six thousand stand of arms, with a large amount of ammunition, also form part of the spoils, and the number of prisoners will reach nearly six thousand, say fifty-five hundred at least. The troops that composed the garrison were the Tenth, Fourteenth, Fifteenth, Eighteenth and Twenty-third Arkansas, the First and Thirty-ninth Mississippi, the First and Forty-ninth Alabama, Mills' Legion of Louisiana troops, and Wingfield's cavalry. The loss sustained by the enemy during the siege they report to be six hundred and ten, and but a small portion only was occasioned by the use of artillery. Large caves had been dug in which the men slept, and covered themselves from the perfect hail storm of bullets and pieces of bursting shell. There does not appear to have been any females within the work, consequently the reports of two having been killed are without foundation.

THE ATTACK ON THE CHARLESTON FORTS.—The official advices received at the Navy Department from Admiral Dahlgren are to the morning of the 17th inst., on which day the attack on the harbor defences of Charleston was to be renewed. Everything was in readiness, and a favorable result was confidently anticipated.

The New York Police Commissioners have placed some three thousand of the hunted colored people under the care of Mr. John H. Keyser, who issues an appeal for clothing and food for them. He also solicits employment and board for them in the country. Mr. Keyser says, in his appeal:

"Parents are parted from children, and husbands and fathers have been either murdered or driven without the city. In one instance, a father, after rescuing his family from his burning home, was thrown back into the flames and burned to death. In another instance, a child was taken from its mother's arms and dashed into the rear yard some forty feet. Many are bruised and maimed for life by fiendish outrages. The old and decripid, in many instances driven from sick beds, are lying on bare floors, and the damp flag-stones of station-houses. They have been stripped of every article of clothing and furniture which now make comfortable the homes of their persecutors."

DIED:

[...]oungest child
[...]nonths and 8
[...]ck, from No.
[...]e 50th year of
[...] at 3 o'clock,
[...]he 1st day of
[...]E, (from Wa-
[...]6th Regiment
[...]ck, from the
[...] POHLMAN,
[...]egiment N. Y.
[...]l. WILLIAM
[...] the 86th year
[...]nly son of Ed-
[...]ear, 5 months

[...]3.

[...]ur merchants
[...]isiness on the
[...]ittle business
[...]ainly of a re-
[...] Rye steady, with sales of 500 bu. State at 1.00. Corn dull and 1c. lower, with a limited business doing in Western mixed at 65, in car lots. Oats unchanged in valne, with a limited inquiry: sales 3000 bu. State, in car lots, at 73, delivered.

FEED—A steady market, with a moderate demand; sales 11 tons medium at 1.20.

WHISKEY—Sales 67 bbls Prison at 45¼.

New York Markets, July 23.

FLOUR—Dull, unsettled and a shade lower, except for round hoop Ohio and extra State, which are scarce and in moderate request; sales 9200 bbls. at 4@4.45 for State and Western, 4,95@5,10 for extra State, 5,15@5,25 for choice do., 4,90@5,35 for common to medium extra Western, 5,60@5,75 for common to good shipping brands of extra round hoop Ohio, 5,90@7,25 for trade brands, closing dull. Canadian dull; sales 600 bbls.

WHISKEY—Dull; sales 250 bbls. at 45@45½ for State and Western.

GRAIN—Wheat less active and common grades 1@2c. lower; demand quite moderate and confined chiefly to choice grades; sales 106,000 bu. at 1,05@1,17 for Chicago Spring, 1,10@1,20 for Mil. Club, 1,21@1,23 for amber Iowa, 1,21@1,23 for Winter red Western, 1,24@1,28 for amber Mich., 1,28@1,30 for very choice Winter amber State, 1 24 for inferior white Ohio, 1,32 for good do. Rye dull, lower and nominal. Barley dull and nominal. Corn opened a shade firmer and closed dull at yesterday's prices; sales 123,000 bu. at 65½@66 for shipping mixed Western, nearly all at the inside price, and 64@65 for Eastern. Oats quiet at 70@76.

PROVISIONS—Pork opened dull and closed steady and more active; sales 2100 bbls. at 11,62½@13,62½ for mess, 10,50@11,12½ for prime. Beef quiet and steady; sales 250 bbls. Cut meats more active. Bacon sides dull and heavy. Lard dull; sales 250 bbls. at 9¾@10. Butter selling at 13@17 for Ohio, 16@21 for State. Cheese quiet at 9@11.

STOCKS—Better and moderately active. Chi & R I 104; C., B & Q 115; Tol & W 81½; Cleve & Tol 117; Gal & Chi 97⅞; Pacific Mail 232; N Y Cent 121; Erie 98¾; Reading 109½; Hudson 148½; Harlem 109¼; Mich Cent 111; Mich South 86; do. guar 114½; Ill Cent scrip 109¾; Cleve & Pitts 94¾; Del & Hud 143¼.

SECOND BOARD—Higher and closed firm. Chi & R I 104¼; Cleve & Tol 106½; Gal & Chi 98¾; Hudson 158; Harlem 111; do pref. 105; Reading 110; Mich Cent 111; Mich South 86; Cleve & Pitts 94½; Erie 99; do. pref. 104; N Y Cent 122½; Pacific Mail 234.

Government Stocks steady. U. S. 6s of '81, coupons, 106½@106¾; Treasury 7.30 106⅞@107.

MONEY—Easy 5@6 ₩ cent.

STERLING EX.—In moderate request at 138@138½ for first-class bills.

AMERICAN GOLD—Without material change, opening at 26¼, and closing at 26 ₩ cent.

Oswego Markets, July 23.

Flour unchanged. Wheat quiet; sales last night 7000 bu. Winter red Ind at 1,15½. Corn in limited demand; sales 12,000 bu. Ill. mixed at 57@58. Other grains scarce, quiet and nominal. Canal freights a shade easier on grain—Flour 38, Wheat 9½, to New York. Imports—200 bbls Flour, 34,000 bu. Wheat, 39,000 bu. Corn. Exports—574 bbls. Flour, 5000 bu. Wheat, 13,600 bu. Corn.

Vol. II. RICHMOND, SATURDAY, AUGUST 1, 1863. No. 4.

MAJ. GEN. GEORGE E. PICKETT

Was born in the city of Richmond, State of Virginia, and is the eldest son of the late Col. Robert Pickett, of Turkey Island, in the county of Henrico.

He entered West Point as a cadet in June, 1842, and graduated in June, 1846. In the fall of 1846, he entered the American army, then in Mexico, as a brevet second lieutenant. The celebrated battles of 1846 had been fought by Gen. Taylor previous to the arrival of the young lieutenant, and he consequently bore no part in them. In the winter following, the division of the army to which Lieutenant Pickett belonged was ordered to join the expedition, under Gen. Scott, against Vera Cruz. From Vera Cruz to the city of Mexico, Pickett served as second lieutenant in the Eighth Infantry (Gen. Worth's command), and was repeatedly noticed in the reports of General Scott for his gallant and meritorious conduct in the battles of Contreras, Cherubusco, Molina del Rey and Chapultepec. For his gallantry at Contreras, he was brevetted first lieutenant, and "for gallant and meritorious" conduct at Chapultepec was complimented with the position of captain.

From the end of the Mexican war, in 1848, until 1861, he continued almost constantly on duty upon the frontier—in Texas, New Mexico, Oregon and Washington Territory—his "leaves of absence" from his command being few and of short duration.

In March, 1855, he was appointed captain in the Ninth Infantry, United States Army. In 1859, the American settlers in San Juan Island having complained to General Harney, who was in command of that department, of outrages suffered from the Indians and aggressions threatened by the British authorities, Captain Pickett was ordered to take military possession of the island, which order was promptly obeyed, and a camp formed with a force of about sixty men. In this situation he was found by three British men-of-war, sent by the British Governor, Douglas, to enforce obedience to his authority. The three men-of-war anchored with their broadsides commanding his camp, and Captain Pickett was "warned off" the island, and afterwards "summoned" before a British magistrate. Upon refusal to recognise either of these notices, the British officers proposed to land a force equal to his own and establish a joint military occupation of the island. Acting upon his orders, Captain Pickett refused to consent to this, and, notwithstanding the disparity of force, declared that he would fire upon them if a landing were attempted. A collision of arms seemed inevitable, when the British Admiral, Baynes, arrived upon the spot, and by his orders the commencement of hostilities was postponed. Shortly after, Lieutenant-Colonel Casey reached the island with reinforcements, and took command of the post, which he named "Camp Pickett;" and, in the course of a few months, the difficulty was settled by General Scott in person, who consented to the joint military occupation proposed by the British officers. The conduct of Captain Pickett was pointedly approved by General Harney, and he was recommended by the same officer for a brevet for "the cool judgment, ability and gallantry" which he had displayed President Buchanan, in the instructions to General Scott, directed that Captain Pickett should remain in command of the United States forces upon the island, and these instructions were at first complied with; but afterwards, at the instance of the British Governor, Douglas, General Scott thought fit to remove him. He was subsequently replaced in command by General Harney, and remained there until 1861, when he resigned his commission and returned to Virginia, not without difficulty, to offer his services to the Confederate States.

He was immediately appointed to a colonelcy in the Provisional Army, and placed in command on the lower Rappahannock. In February, 1862, he was appointed to the command of a brigade, in Longstreet's Division, in the Army of the Potomac; and his brigade bore an honorable share in the campaign of that year, at Williamsburg, at Seven Pines, at Gaines' Mill, and the subsequent engagements. At Gaines' Mill, General Pickett received a severe wound in the shoulder, which disabled him for several months, and he did not rejoin his command until after the return of the army from Maryland. Soon afterwards, he was made Major-General of Division in the Corps of Lieutenant-General Longstreet, which command he now holds.

MAJ. GEN. GEORGE E. PICKETT.

FROM A PHOTOGRAPH BY J. R. ROCKWELL, PETERSBURG.

At the late battle of Gettysburg, Pickett's Division displayed courage, fortitude and discipline to a degree that has never been surpassed. Owing to the absence of two brigades, the division did not exceed five thousand in number. Yet this little body of men, advancing steadily over half a mile of broken ground, charged and carried the most formidable entrenchments, under a concentrated fire of artillery and musketry, and would have maintained the position but for the failure of the supports which they should have received. A correspondent of the "Enquirer" thus describes the charge—

"It is due to Gen. Pickett and his division that the country should know and properly appreciate the service rendered by them in the terrible action of the 3d of July.

"The day preceding, the division had made a long and toilsome march. At three o'clock of the 3d, they moved forward to the field of battle, and were in position very early on the morning of that eventful day. During a considerable portion of the forenoon, the division were exposed to the burning rays of a July sun and the terrible shelling from the enemy's batteries. Thus, very much exhausted by the intense heat, and seriously crippled by the enemy's fire, about 3 o'clock they were ordered to charge the heights. An eye witness testifies that they formed into line-of-battle as coolly and deliberately as if forming for dress parade. Headed by their gallant officers, the column being led by Gen. Pickett himself, they moved forward to the charge across a plain, some 500 yards in width, subjected to the action of guns smoking like a hurricane of death all over the field.

"The noble and gallant Pickett, commanding, then, pressed up to the ugly ramparts of the enemy. It is believed that a more gallant and heroic charge was never made on this contininent. Pickett's Division has been in the hardest fighting of this bloody war. The division have borne themselves well and nobly, always and everywhere. But the crowning glory of those patriotic heroes was achieved in the assault upon the iron-clad crest of Gettysburg. The list of casualties tells, in terms of truer eloquence, the bravery and patriotism of that blood-stained and scar-honored division, than can any figures of rhetoric or poetry. Every brigadier fell, and a long catalogue of colonels and other officers. The division went in from five to six thousand strong. Three days after the battle but fifteen hundred reported for duty. Well done, noble heroes, officers and men; your country will cherish the memory of your deeds and sufferings with a gratitude and affection which time can never obliterate. Major-General Pickett has well earned and will no doubt receive the meed of his country's praise. Without meaning to disparage any other officer or division, it is, indeed, a high honor to have belonged to Pickett's Division and to have fought under that gallant commander.

THE SOUTHERN SENTINEL.

T. G. COMPTON, PROPRIETOR. "ETERNAL VIGILANCE IS THE PRICE OF LIBERTY." $8 PER ANNUM, IN ADVANCE.

VOL. 1. ALEXANDRIA, LOUISIANA, AUGUST 22, 1863. NO. 25.

We are authorized to announce

Richard Charles Downes,

of the Parish of Iberville, as a Candidate to Represent the Fourth District of Louisiana in the next Confederate Congress.

Election First Monday in November by General Ticket

The News.

"Some tell, some hear, some make it. And he that lies most loud, is most believed."

We cannot even this week regale our readers with manufactured news at least to any extent. We have used and are still using every effort to give our readers reliable intelligence—but is is an uphill business. Now and then a stray paper arrives here—but it is most invariably carried to Headquarters, and its contents to the public generally are hermetically sealed until the next issue of the Government Organ—or an extra, if the case demands it. Well we must wait for the wagon, perhaps our day may come yet.

The Cincinnatti Commercial of the 6th inst., contains the statement, purporting to be authentic, that Secretary Seward has instructed Mr. Adams, Minister to England, to inform the English Government that if the vessels, now being built on their territory for the Confederates, are allowed to leave their ports, such permission will be considered as a declaration of war.

It is quite currently rumored that 2,000 Yankee Cavalry are at Trinity, and that Yankee troops are being landed near the mouth of Red River.

We understand and indeed have observed, that some feeling has been produced here by the republication in the Sentinel, of articles taken from Texas papers, respecting the purchase of cotton by government agents, as we were supposed to apply them to a particular person. This *is not so*, we copied the articles as items of interest—and we see in the same papers that there are other government agents in Texas of the same rank, as the individual alluded to. We make or copy no inuendoes against any one. But as we observe that an investigation is to be made of the charges relating to this matter, if anything is brought to light we will make it known.

Government Advertisements.

We notice in the Caddo Gazette of the 15th inst., three columns and a half of advertisements from Head Quarters in Shreveport—and at the bottom of each, *Louisiana Democrat* copy 4t—heretofore it has been *Louisiana Papers*. Well as we said before, it is perhaps better for us not to be favored.

For the benefit of our readers we give the following *free gratis for nothing*. It is to be hoped there will be no more winking.

CIRCULAR.

HEADQUARTERS BUREAU OF CONSCRIPTION,
Dept. Trans-Miss., Shreveport, La.,
August 10th, 1863.

To the People of the Trans-Miss., Department:

The President of the Confederate States, has called for all the able-bodied men between the ages of 18 and 45, to recruit our armies, so as to repel any invasion of this Department which our enemies may attempt. It is to be hoped that the people will discard all considerations of self, and with alacrity flock to their country's standard.—The necessity of a resort to coercive measures in this crisis, will be discouraging and humiliating, and they will not be employed unless circumstances absolutely demand them. If however, the people will not willingly battle for their families, their homes and their rights, it is well for them to be informed, that a military force has been provided to compel obedience to the law, and that the most rigid compliance with its requisitions will be exacted from all who claim exemptions from its provisions. Conscript Officers who wink at shifts or evasions, or who fail to discharge to the letter their duties will be promptly dismissed; and (if liable,) put in the ranks, and their places supplied with faithful men. One instance of wilful disregard of duty will be fatal to the delinquent, and Inspecting Officers will be sent out to enquire into their conduct, and report them for commendation or punishment. In this connection it is proper to state that Conscript Officers in this Department have not hitherto been paid as regularly as they should have been. but that measures have been adopted which will secure them prompt payment in future.

By command of Brig.-Gen. GREER.
W. STEDMAN, A. A. Gen.

II. All citizens between the ages of 18 and 45, in the employment of Quartermasters, Commissaries, Government Contractors, Purchasing Agents and other officers and agents of Government, are liable to conscription and must be enrolled as conscripts.

III. Soldiers in the employment of any of the above named officers and agents, who have not been detailed by the Commander of the Department or District, will report themselves to their commands if accessible, if not to the nearest camp of instruction, or be treated as deserters, unless they are, upon application to the proper authorities detailed anew.

IV. No detail hereafter of conscripts for any purpose, will be valid unless made from the Department Headquarters, or this Bureau, or a commandant of a District.

V. Officers and soldiers absent from their commands without leave, or after the expiration of their respective leaves of absence or furloughs and who are not laboring under disability, are deserters, and enrolling officers, are required to enroll and arrest such, and send them to the nearest camp of instruction. If resistance in such cases be made, the person resisting will be sent to the Department or District headquarters for trial.

GALVESTON July 27, 1863.

Editor News: SIR:—I have concluded to investigate the conduct of the agents of the Government who have been swindling the people and the Government in purchasing cotton for the Confederate States. If the planters who have sold cotton to persons representing themselves as the agents of the Government, will write to me and give me their names and their address, the names of the persons who claimed to be the agents of the Government, to whom they sold cotton, the number of bales sold, the date of the sale, and the marks on the bales, if any, so that I can determine who have been engaged in the business, I will be able to ascertain who have obtained the cotton by fraudulent pretences or who have appropriated the cotton to their own use or misapplied said cotton in order to bring them to justice. I hope every planter will afford me this aid as they are interested in the matter, being one of the parties swindled. I have no interest in the matter, except what every citizen ought to have who is in the army. Please insert in your paper for the information of the public, and much oblige, Yours truly,

FRED. BARNARD.

LESSONS OF THE PAST.

Now while there is a lull in the storm of war on this side of the great river, and no reliable information reaches us from the other, it is a good time to sit down and muse on the lessons of the past, and see what light they shed on our present condition and prospects. In doing this we shall surely discern facts which will encourage our hearts and strengthen our hands in the fearful struggle through which we are now passing.—There is one memorable case, which history has preserved on its immortal pages, that may fringe with the rainbow of hope the darkest clouds of [illegible] Whoever has read Grecian [illegible] with the name of Pyrrhus—a man of great military genius, of undaunted bravery, and untiring perseverance. To him is eminently appropriate the fine description of Johnson.

> "A frame of adamant, a soul of fire,
> No dangers fright him. and no labors tire."

To give full play to his vast energies and his boundless ambition, he determined to conquer the Romans and the warlike nations that were under their control, to press on with his victorious legions and seize upon the fertile and populous island of Sicily, and then to compel Libya and Carthage and Macedon and all Greece to acknowledge his sway.

At his Court of Epirus was an elegant and accomplished Thessalian named Cineas, who had been a pupil of Demosthenes, and was the only orator of his time who presented a lively image of the grace, and force and spirit of his illustrious master. He was an excellent diplomatist, too, so that Pyrrhus used to say that Cineas had gained him more cities by his address than he had won by his arms. Cineas was of course, therefore, a great favorite, and could take liberties with the King which would have been perilous for any other courtier.

When Pyrrhus was preparing for his famous expedition against the Romans (an ill starred enterprise, which ended with him very much as the Russian campaign did with Napoleon,) Cineas one day quietly interrogated the King as follows: "If it please heaven that we conquer the Romans, subjugate Italy, take possession of Sicily, annex Libya and Carthage to our dominion—when we have subdued *all these nations*, what are we to do then?" "Why, then, my friend," said Pyrrhus, "then—we will take our ease and enjoy ourselves." "*Why not do that now?*" rejoined Cineas, "when we have all the means of doing so that we ever shall have after we have waded through seas of blood. and encountered infinite toils and dangers, besides having caused the greatest miseries to others?"

Pyrrhus was silent and thoughtful. He was impressed by the force of the truth so powerfully, yet so delicately insinuated by Cineas. He was almost ready to abandon the stupendous project he had conceived. But his impression speedily vanished. How few are drawn from the fearful current of fatal passion and infatuated purpose which is sweeping them along, by the voice, however eloquent, of wise and earnest friendship! This man, endowed with so many splendid qualities, and among others with a magnanimity as rare as his valor and genius, was hurried on to ruin by the demon of military ambition. He embarked with a magnificent fleet and army in his expedition against the Romans. Pomp and splendor were exhausted in the glittering armament. And thousands of upraised hands implored the blessings of the guardian Minerva upon that brilliant and exultant fleet as it bore away before the breeze to swell with a new conquest the giddy Leader. Let them enjoy their triumph in *prospect*, they never will do so in *reality!*—After six years of fighting, with various successes, Pyrrhus was at last driven from Italy and Sicily, and was compelled to return, with shattered power, to his own country. That herculean frame, that had stood the shock of a hundred battles, at last received the fatal blow from a tile flung by the hand of a woman from the roof of a house in Argos, which (after having lost a son in the charge) he had just carried by assault. Such was his realization of those glorious visions of rest and enjoyment which, like a pleasant and peaceful shore ever seemed to be beyond the rocks and breakers of his stormy ambition.

The infamous dolt who sits on the throne at Washington and wields the sceptre of a despot, though destitute of the noble and splendid qualities which distinguished the royal Pyrrhus, is pursuing the same course to the same miserable end. Fired not by the lofty spirit of enterprise which animated Pyrrhus, but by the mean spirit of revenge he is sending forth his mercenaries by hundreds of thousands, to overrun our territory, carrying like the prairie fires of the West destruction in their bosom, and leaving desolation in their rear; and he expects, in this way, to force us back into the bosom of the old Union again.—Mistaken, foolish hope! There may be some who, by such infernal means, may be cowed into submission to the federal government. There may be some who, to save their cotton and their niggers, will swear allegiance to the despotism of the North—who, like Esau, will sell their birth-right for a mess of pottage. But such men are few. The spirit of resistance to Northern oppression, and of hatred to Northern barbarities, burns fiercely on the altar of nearly every heart, and it never will be extinguished till the last man of the present generation has gone down to the dust; and from the ashes of the race that now lives and fights will spring a stock as determined as they are to be free and indedendent. The men of the present, like stern old Hamilcar, will take their sons to the altar and make them swear eternal enmity to the despoilers of their homes, their institutions, and their peace.

If Lincoln shall be able to wrench one after another from our bright galaxy of States—what then? If he has the men and the means to subjugate the entire South (as well might he attempt to pluck the stars from their spheres)—what then? He is doomed in the end to an ignoble discomfiture and defeat. State after State will rally again under the proud banner of the Confederacy. The mailed heel of the oppressor cannot always remain upon their necks. And he and his minions will be hissed in disgrace from the theatre of their temporary triumph—this beautiful land which God has decreed shall be free. If nothing else a tile from the hand of a woman shall find for this cruel and cowardly tyrant and usurper, a grave. Our motto is, and let it be emblazoned on every banner that floats over our ranks—Freedom or Extermination.

Would that Lincoln had a wise friend like Cineas to whisper in his ear continually, "why not do that now?" Why not cease at once this brutal and impotent strife? Why not call off the dogs of war from a gallant and unoffending people before they turn and rend you? Why press on further in a course from which you will certainly return shattered and disgraced? why not "rest and enjoy yourself" in the country that acknowledges your rule, and which is large enough certainly to satisfy the ambitious cravings of the Macedonian himself? Why suffer yourself to be the dupe and puppet of that despicable buffoon and jester, who occupies your chair of state, and is kicking you on to inevitable destruction?

The thinking masses of the North are beginning to realize the fruitlessness of their struggle, and the perils of its issue, and hence the mobs and riots that are sending such consternation through their great cities, and causing them to heave as with the throes of an earthquake. The contagion of excitement is rapidly spreading, and soon the populace frenzy against the war will sweep over the whole territory of our enemies, like the waves [illegible] will cry out with one voice—a voice [illegible] their rulers, sound of many waters—"why not do that now?" Why not give us peace at once and forever?"

Not the Man for Galway.

The Democrat of last week, (12th August,) has amongst its editorial paragraphs the following:

"The croakers, sore-heads and swell-heads of our Parish leave no stone unturned to find fault with our best military commanders; Grosbecque says the only fault he finds with the President, is that he should have neglected Rapides in selecting Generals, &c. There are over one hundred here, if you take them by their own self-constituted military merits, would make far better and more successful military commanders than Lee—Let us hope their merits will yet be acknowledged in time to save the country."

We suppose this refers among others to the communication of "Creole" in our issue of 8th inst. We do not exactly know under what class to include sore-heads and swell heads, but as coupled to the word croakers, we suppose according to the definition of the Democrat, all who do not agree with it or the party it represents, are either croakers, sore-heads or swell-heads, (we copy the othography of the Democrat in the last words,) and our friend Creole can choose his own place among them—Creole, we find in referring to his article, blames only one General, and if he is the best or one of the best in the Confederacy, Heaven have mercy upon it, we say. Now if those who find fault with his Generals are to be designated by these polite and complimentary epithets, how must those be called who take the name of the President himself in vain, and yet a correspondent of the Democrat writing under the head, "Of an opinion upon the fall of Vicksburg," says, "that the only way by which Mr. Davis can escape the censure of the civilized world, will be to assert, what he (the correspondent) believes to be a *lie* and unless that lie *is asserted* he will proclaim himself a *miserable apology* for a general, and *altogether* unfit to hold in his hands the destiny of *this* or any *other* people—that is he must prove himself a liar or acknowledge himself a fool. Well if this is not blasphemy and heresy we would like to know by what name to call it. *Grosbecque* of the Democrat has but one fault to find with the President, and that is, that he neglected Rapides in selecting Generals, &c. Well we think also that Mr. Davis might (as he did do,) go farther and fare worse. We have an idea that if one son of Rapides had been selected for the command of this Department, (not District,) he would at least have done as well as has been done, and we judge so from analogy alone. A man who is active, energetic and *successful*, in private affairs, will be apt to be the same in charge of great public interests. We think at any rate he would have made a better showing towards doing something, and would never have been found hunting wild cats, catching crawfish, or picking black berries, whilst a yankee remained to be hunted, caught or picked off in the Trans-Mississippi Department. Richlieu the great Minister of Louis the 13th of France, in reply to an enquiry from the King, why he never hunted, said he was too busy hunting Spanish wolves and Hugnenot foxes, from his dominions, to have time for any less important sport, and so we think it should be with our Generals. That there was a most unfortunate and unaccountable mismanagement of military affairs in this Department at the time of the Federal raid, in May last. No one who takes the trouble to reflect, can for a moment doubt.

From the time that Banks retired from Port Hudson and Baton Rouge to his arrival here, upwards of two months elapsed. His destination was not or should not have been for a moment doubted, to military men—Gen. Taylor's force at Camp Bisland was say 5,000 men. Had the proper exertions been made this could have been increased by Walker's Division and other sources to an army sufficient to have prevented, if not the defeat of Taylor at Bisland, at least the advance of Banks farther than the Attakapas parishes. As it was, he marched almost unmolested through a hostile country nearly two hundred miles from his base of supplies—and then retreated unpersued, except when too late. The highest estimate put upon the force under his command which reached here, was about 15,000, half that number, according to our experience in this war, could have held them in check, and cut him up in detail, and as we said before, more than half that number might have been obtained had the proper exertions been made and we are therefore compelled to say despite of *Grosbecque*, that in our opinion the right man has not been sent to the right place, and that it is very clear, the one that's here, is not the man for Galway.

From a gentleman who crossed at Rodney, last Friday week, we obtain the following information. He read in a Mobile Tribune, an extract from the New York Tribune, to the effect that France intended to demand an armistice within thirty days. The same intelligence was contained in a Chicago paper received at Natchez, and the Federal officers at that place were betting high in favor of it. Gen. Ransom, on account of his leniency to the citizens of Natchez, has been superceded. The city is garrisoned by 4000 negroes and 2000 whites. Our forces, Logan, with his cavalry and mounted infantry is doing good work around Natchez. On the 28th ult., he burned three bridges on the St. Catharine, and captured some Yankee pickets. The loss on both sides was small.

At Rodney there is stationed a gunboat, to prevent persons crossing. Last Sunday week, sixteen transports passed down, loaded with troops One of the boats above Rodney was struck by lightning, causing her to blow up, and killing between 600 and 700.

Johnson is at Forrest, between Meridian and Morton, on the Southern Railroad; Hardee is with him.

Our cavalry were at Jackson at last accounts.

Gen. Bowen, of Missouri, is dead. He had just been made a Major-General.—[*Shreveport News, August* 14th.

A young lawyer, who had long paid his court to a lady without much advancing his suit, accused her one day of being "insensible to the power of love."

"It does not follow," she archly replied, "that I am so because I am not to be won by the *powers of attorney*."

"Forgive me," replied the suitor. "but you should remember that all the votaries of Cupid are *solicitors*."

Harper's Weekly.

We believe we have heretofore noticed, the utter mendacity and malignity which this journal manifests towards the South, which so liberally and so foolishly supports it and other Northern publications of a like character, to the prejudice alike of southern talent and southern enterprise. We have recently come across two or three numbers of the Weekly of June last, and it is really amusing to look at the illustrations purporting to be scenes of the war, taken on the spot, with all the natural features faithfully reproduced by accomplished artists, accompanying the Federal armies, and in the pay of the proprietors of the paper, while in fact they are mere fancy sketches having none, or scarcely [illegible] of the actual local traits of the places they are represented faithfully to represent. Two of these particularly attracted our attention—one a representation of General Logan crossing the Bayou Pierre, at Port Gibson, Mississippi—and the other, Cotton pouring into Brashear City. In the first, a long line of infantry is represented as crossing the Bayou on pontoons, and on their right the bridge burnt by the Confederates still in flames. This bridge is represented as a suspension one, swinging from abutments and towers of solid masonry. It has been a long time since we saw the locality, but from our recollection of it—no such a structure was practicable from the nature of the soil, and we are pretty certain no such a one as the picture represents ever was erected. How correct the picture of Brashear City may be, we cannot say, but that *seven* steamers, loaded with cotton have even been seen at the wharf in one day, during the past year we are certain is not so. The most correct and life-like feature of the scene is however, the unloading of the boats. A number of stalwart contrabands are represented in the foreground, each one, with a bale of cotton on his shoulder, which he is carrying to the train of cars seen a little in the distance, we give an extract from the letter press description, which equals in veracity the engraving which it refers to.

The quiet little town of Brashear, on Berwick's Bay—or "Brashear City," as it has been christened by courtesy—which we illustrate on page 380, has suddenly become the scene of vast commercial doing. Those people very much mistake the full scope of Major-General Banks' recent brilliant operation in the Attakapas region of western Louisiana who look upon them merely as among the most successful military events of the war. It is in their *material* results that they are about to gratify the country and startle the world.

General Banks, aided by the gallant Farragut, has not only disorganized and put to flight the whole rebel army west of the Mississippi River, from New Orleans to Alexandria, on the Red River, but opened up untold mines of wealth to the treasury of the United States. Almost hourly vessels are to be seen coming down the bay freighted with mountain loads of the precious materials of the region just regained by our arms—cotton, hogsheads of sugar, and countless heard of *mules* and cattle.

The treasures already discharged upon the landing of Brashear City up to this date (May 21) would amount to many hundred thousand of dollars; while this is but an installment of what remains behind, and which can only be counted by *millions* of dollars.

One significant fact has also been laid bare to the outer world by the probing process of our bayonets; and that is, that the planters in the newly-overrun regions had not the amount of "patriotism" which the rebel leaders either supposed or pretended they had—and which too many people in the North and abroad believed—and did not quite see the necessity of consigning to flames all the wealth they possessed in the world, merely for the sake of proving their devotion to the cause of Jeff Davis & Co.

Wherever our armies have penetrated they have found cotton and sugar carefully concealed in all sorts of remote corners; and as they seize these costly products a receipt is given to the owners, upon a fair valuation, in case they should hereafter be able to prove themselves of loyal antecedents, the *onus probandi* being entirely on the planter.

If any thing more were wanted to utterly overthrow the value of Confederate credit, and to prove to the gulled people of Europe that they have been making a bad bargain with traitors in this country, it will be found in Uncle Sam's so unceremoniously bought the very materials upon which the leaders have been staking their money. What Confederate credit was worth previous to this new and irreparable inroad upon it may be gleaned from the fact that our soldiers, in parley with rebel pickets, could at any time have received *ten dollars* of Confederate trash for *one dollar* of Uncle Sam's good, honest greenbacks.

The Invasion of Pennsylvania.

The following are the concluding remarks of a special correspondent of the Chicago Times—headed, "The Rebel invasion of Pennsylvania and Maryland. A scathing review by our special correspondent. Some facts for history, not flattering to the administration of President Lincoln." This correspondent asserts among other things, that the contemplated invasion of Pennsylvania by Lee was fully known, and could have been prevented—but that the Federal administration wanted to avail themselves of so good a plea to enforce their call for 300,000 fresh troops. He says:

The theory of how to do it—that is, how not to stop Lee—was most thoroughly studied and ably mastered by the central controlling power of our armies, and thus the rebel host was invited and led on to invade the North. It was simply a studied plot. and it succeeded admirably. It was a plot with a purpose, as all plots have have purposes. And that purpose was not, as military purposes usually are, the destruction of the enemy. The enemy was too useful to the central controlling power at Washington to be destroyed. The administration cannot yet afford to do away with the rebel army of Northern Virginia.

It might be profitable to take a limited glance at the results of this invasion. Great victories elsewhere, and successes where least looked for, have called the public mind from the consideration of this subject. But the theme will be revived. Maryland and Pennsylvania, at least, will not lose sight of it. Their desolated fields, ruined crops, wasted farms, sacked towns and villages, smoking ruins of hamlets burned, their impoverished people, the crowd of cripples that swarm their highways, the stench of battle-fields, desolation, general and wide-spread, from Gettysburg to the banks of the Potomac, will long continue to remind them that the administration at Washington is playing at war to subserve political purposes. When they remember how easily all this might have have been avoided; how the labor of the husbandman might have been gathered in, and the abundant crops on thousands and tens of thousands of acres, now destroyed, might have been secured; how their homes might not have been desolated, and their families not broken up and scattered by the din of war in their own door-yards; how their brothers need not have been slaughtered, their wives, and sisters and daughters not ravished, their children not turned houseless and homeless upon the cold charities of the world—when all this recurs to their mind, as it will oft and frequently in all its most glaring colors—and the picture here is but feebly painted—then their love and reverence for the administration will scarcely be found, and it will require a larger army than that which is now chasing Lee through Virginia, to enforce a conscription among them.

We notice that the Shreveport News of the 14th inst., copies the communication of Creole which appeared in our paper of the 8th, and which the Democrat attributes to a croaker, a sore-head or a swell-head.

THE LATEST NEWS.

Morton, July 31.—The gloom which has overspread the State since the fall of Vicksburg and the occupation of Jackson is rapidly giving way to a more healthy feeling.

Since the enemy retired to Vicksburg the Mississippians who had absented themselves from the army are returning to their commands and numbers of guerilla organizations are being perfected to render the navigation of the Mississippi impossible, some of which will soon be heard [illegible]

[illegible] large number of troops who were sent to the sick, after the severe exposure in the trenches of Jackson, are returning daily, and the morals of the army [illegible] under the discipline [illegible]

[illegible] States, and reminds them that there is no alternative but victory or subjugation to slavery and utter ruin. All that is necessary to insure victory is that those called to the field by every motive that can move the human heart, should promptly repair to the post of duty and standing by their comrades now in the front, and thus so strengthen the army of the Confederacy as to insure success. After referring to various causes of absence from the army, the President appeals to his countrymen to hasten to their camps in obedience to the dictates of honor and duty.

Richmond, Aug. 3.—A Liverpool letter says that one of Laird's iron-clad vessels was launched a short time since. She is most formidable and will have two turrets and a ram projecting seven feet. It is believed this vessel is designed for the "rebels."

Mosby's men made a raid on Fairfax Courthouse on Wednesday, capturing a number of sutler's wagons loaded with goods. Osterhaus was not killed as reported.

Charleston. August 3.—Slow firing on both sides continued yesterday and last night. Our casualties on Morris Island yesterday were two killed and fifteen wounded. All quiet this morning.

Halifax, August 3.—The steamer Arabia. from Liverpool 25th, via Queenstown 26th, arrived here this afternoon.

Gordonsville, Aug 8, via *Richmond*, Aug 9.—A gentleman just from Brandy Station says the enemy's force, for miles beyond that point from the direction of Rappahannock Bridge, is destroying everything. They are supposed to be three regiments of cavalry and eight regiments of infantry. The men are all fleeing, leaving the women and children.

Gordonsville, Aug 9.—An intelligent gentleman arrived to-day from Middleburg, who fled thence last Wednesday.

The Yankee raiders are burning the wheat and destroying everything.

They carried off what citizens they could capture, including two little boys caught plowing; also horses, cattle and sheep.

He reports Meade's headquarters at Catlett's Station, Sedgwick's at Warrenton, and Pleasanton's cavalry at Warrenton Junction.

The Yankees have sent back a certain number of each company to gather conscripts, who will remain where they are until the conscripts increase their force, when they will advance.

Richmond, Aug 9.—Baltimore papers of the 8th contain dispatches from Memphis of the 5th, which report all quiet on the river below.

An arrival at New York brings Vera Cruz advices to the 6th ult.

The Way it has been Done.

The letter referred to in the following extract from the Galveston News has already appeared in our paper. We see also that steps are to be taken to bring the fraud to light. It seems to us queer justice that innocent citizens should suffer for guilty government agents:

We copy the following letter from the Telegraph, and hope this example of showing up the financial operations of Government cotton agents will be followed by others. We invite free communications on all such operations, as they will afford instructive lessons in finance to most of our readers especially to those who desire to do an extensive business on a small capital, and make princely fortunes without drudgery of labor, and at the same time get the credit of serving their country with a most self sacrificing devotion. It will be quite interesting to the public to find out the modus operandi by which so many bales of cotton have slipped out of the hands of the Government into the hands of individuals We believe it to be the solemn duty of all those who are in possession of facts that will throw light upon this subject, to disclose them for the information of the public. According to the evidence now before us, the Government has been swindled out of several millions of dollars in this State and the consequence is an order for the impressment of several thousand bales of cotton. From all we can learn there was an absolute necessity for this order to protect the Government against the acts of its own agents. Every man in the Confederacy has a paramount interest in sustaining the credit of the Government. If we permit that credit to be sacrificed, all will be lost, for without credit our efforts to achieve our independence will be in vain; and even were it achieved it would be of very little value if its attainment has been at the expense of a national honor and violated faith.

No doubt the execution of this order of impressment will in some instances, fall heavily upon innocent parties, but they should bear in mind that they will in due time be fully remunerated.

The present necessity admits no delay. but there will be ample time for the Government to make equitable settlements with our own citizens. While we are all made to suffer from the swindling operations of speculators, and perhaps of high official functionaries. it becomes the more manifestly our duty to investigate those high handed frauds, fully without fear, favor or partiality.

The Telegraph says this letter is from a merchant of Houston, and the names are subject to the authorities. The public will therefore expect the "authorities" proceed in the investigation at once.

Of all the wares and commodities in exchange and barter, wherein so mainly consists the civilization of our modern world, there is not one which is so carefully weighed—so accurately measured—so plumed and gauged—so doled and scraped—so poured out in *minima* and balanced with scruples—as that necessary of social commerce called "an apology!" If the chemists were half so careful in vending their poisons, there would be a notable diminution in the yearly average of victims to arsenic and axalic acid. But, alas, in the matter of apology, it is not from the excess of the dose, but the timid, niggardly, miserly manner in which it is dispensed, that poor Humanity is hurried off to the Styx! How many times does a life depend on the exact proportions of an apology! Is it a hairbreadth too short to cover the scratch for which you want it? Make your will—you are a dead man! A life, do I say?—a hecatomb of lives! How many wars would have been prevented, how many thrones would be standing, dynasties flourishing—commonwealths brawling round a *bema*, or fitting out galleys for corn and cotton—if an inch or two more of apology had been added to the proffered ell! But then that plaguy, jealous, suspicious, old vinegar-faced Honour, and her partner Pride—as penny-wise and pound-foolish a she-skinflint as herself—have monopoly of the article. And what with the time they lose in adjusting their spectacles, hunting in the precise shelf for the precise quality demanded, then (quality found) the haggling as to quantum—considering whether it should be Apothecary's weight or Avoirdupois, or English measure or Flemish—and, finally, the hullabaloo they make if the customer is not perfectly satisfied with the monstrous little he gets for his money—I don't wonder, for my part, how one loses temper and patience, and sends Pride, Honour, and Apology, all to the devil. Aristophanes in his "Comedy of *Peace*," insinuates a beautiful allegory by only suffering that goddess, though in fact she is his heroine. to appear as a mute. She takes care never to open her lips. The shrewd Greek knew very well that she would cease to be Peace. if she once began to chatter. Wherefore, O reader, if ever you find your neck under the iron heel of another man's boot. heaven grant that you may hold your tongue, and not make things past all endurance and forgiveness by bawling out for an apology!

A WESTERN DUEL.

The following terrible account of a south-western duel is no work of fiction, but the history of an actual occurrence, that took place in a public tavern some years ago, and amidst a number of witnesses. To render the story intelligible, it should be premised [illegible] swaggering Western colonel, [illegible] that occasionly [illegible] swore that he would [illegible] do so, [illegible] lie, [illegible] a rencontre [illegible] the [illegible] jected or unattended to, a new proposition was made. It was distinctly—that in order to disarm one of the parties of his decided general advantages of a duelist—to prevent the other, as far as possible, from being butchered as well as wantonly insulted—and, in short, to place both upon as perfect an equality as possible, the following articles ought to he agreed to:—That the landlord should give up the use of a large empty room, which extended over the whole top of his house, and allow every window to be closely blocked up with shutters and boards. That when this was done, the duelists should be divested of every particle of clothing, armed each with a brace of pistols and a bowie knife, and then be let into the room, three minutes given, after the closing of the door, before hostilities commenced, the expiration of the time being announced to them by three rapid knocks upon the door.

"Will it be believed that this arrangement was instantly agreed to? But so it was. And a tolerable party immediately proceeded up stairs, some to make the needful arrangements, and others to listen to this unseen fight, and await its exciting result.

"Savage as men's spirits may be, such a scene of preparation was enough to silence, if not awe them. While it was passing, no man spoke; but all looked curiously upon the fine, muscular persons that were soon, in all probability, about to cut each other up alive.

"All things being ready, the door, which had cautiously been kept closed, to prevent the interior of the place being seen by the duelists, was opened, and they entered the room of death together. The old man, whose friend one of them was, wept in silent bitterness; but by an involuntary action, as the young man passed out of his sight, evidently besought heaven to assist the innocent. The door was closed. The time-keeper drew out his watch. and kept his eyes steadily fixed upon it. The assembled party employed that brief period in offering and accepting (in whispers) bets of from one to five hundred or more dollars, as to the result. According to sporting phrase, 'the colonel was the favorite,' though the backers of neither one nor the other appeared inclined to offer very large odds.

"The time-keeper closed his watch' and gave the signal; at the same moment, all the lights on the landing and staircase were extinguished, in order that no ray might pass through the least crevice into the inside of the room.

"Everybody expected, upon the giving of the signal, to hear the commencement of the strife; but they listened in dead silence to no purpose—not the remotest sound, even of a footstep, could be heard. And thus they waited five minutes, and ten, and twenty, and yet the combatants gave no sign. After the lapse, as near as might be conjectured of half-an-hour, or thereabouts one pistol was discharged; and although the listeners had been in continued expectation of it so long, yet, when it did come, a sudden start of surprise ran through them, as though each man had instantly felt that he might have received the contents himself. And then followed a hasty step across the floor—another pistol report—the clashing of knives, and a brief, but seemingly desperate, attempt to wrestle, which quickly terminated, and all again was quiet.

"It's all up!" whispered one, "I'll bet drinks for the crowd!"

"Taken!" said another. "I begin to want a julep."

"Fifty to forty the colonel has killed him!" remarked a third. "He was a very nice young man, but he can't come in this time."

"And thus they would have gone on, had not the third report been just then heard, followed by a prolonged conflict, hand to hand, and knife to knife, in the course of which the fourth pistol was exploded. The strokes of the knives began to grow less frequent, and more faint in sound; but ere they had entirely ceased, a heavy body dropped with a dead sound upon the floor of the room. Another instant, and there followed another heavy fall.

"Some individuals present were for opening the doors immediately; but this proposition was overruled on the ground that, if the fight was not yet over, the most able might take advantage of the appearance of the light to kill the other even lying on the boards.

"About half an hour was, if I recollect aright, allowed to pass in close and attentive listening, to catch the most distant sound from within. None was heard; and at the expiration of that period, amidst a crowd of the most horrible of anxious faces, the door was opened, and the whole party rushed in. Towards the remoter end, and not far from the wall, lay a heap like red cloth. It was composed of the gashed and bloody bodies of the duelists! One lay across the other. They were taken up; and something like a distant murmur of applause followed when it was discovered that the colonel was undermost!

"But many who best knew him spoke outright their gladness, when an examination proved that he was perfectly dead. Both bodies were so mangled that it was next to impossible to handle them without touching the wounds.

"The best of it was, however, that the conqueror of this fearful white savage was found to be still alive. He was taken down stairs instantly, stimulants were given, and he began to revive. His body was then carefully washed; after which. being cautiously wrapped up, he was conveyed away to the nearest surgeon's some time after midnight.

"The room exhibited a spectable not to be described.

"The young man eventually recovered entirely of all his wounds, and was often congratulated of having rid the country of a monster whom few dared to attack.

"This was not all. During his convalescence, inquiries were frequently made of him as to how the fight was managed; and he accordingly gave the following curious account, as nearly as the writer can remember:—

"When the door was closed," said he. "we were surrounded by the most profound darkness. It seemed for some moments to confound the senses and be close to my eyes. During the three minutes allowed before the battle might begin, my principal aim was to get away from my antagonist into another part of the room, without his knowledge, and to stand there by the wall, until, perhaps, he should make some movement, by the sound of which I could be directed in my attack. The crowd outside was as still as death. I held my breath, and treading so lightly that I could not hear my own footfalls, I stole away to that side of the room on which I entered. Whether he had calculated that I should naturally do so, and had, therefore, taken the same direction, nobody can now tell; but no sooner had I stood to listen for him, than I found he was somewhere about me—I could hear his breathing. With the greatest caution and silence, I hastened to another part, expecting every moment that he would run against me, or I against him. And in this kind of manœuvering, sometimes to get away, and sometimes to approach, if I fancied, though why I know not, that an advantage might be gained, the greater part of the silent half-hour you speak of was spent.

"At length, having safely reached the opposite side, I stood still, resolved not to move again, until he either approached, having, perhaps, found me out, or by some means or other I could discover his position in the room. Having now got beyond his reach, I felt that to be motionless on my part would be the wisest step, and calculated that his passion and fury would soon lead him on to the exhibition of less caution. Nothing of the kind occurred, and yet the first ball discharged was mine. A mouse could have been heard to stir: but we were perfectly lost to each other.

"Eventually, whether my eyes had become more accommodated to the blackness, or from whatever cause, but true enough it is, I perceived a pair of eyes on the other side, nearly opposite me. They shone like those of a hyena in the night. I fired instantly, and rushed forward. The flash showed me the colonel crouched down against the wall, and must have equally directed him to me. He fired as he advanced, but missed. We were almost close together. The empty pistols were thrown down, and the knives used. He rushed on with great ferocity, and tried to grapple with me, but I slipped out of his arms: and for an instant being quite separated, both stood still, listening for the place of the other. I think he must have heard me, for he fired a second time, with such effect as you have all seen. Nothing but his knife now remained. I had a knife and pistol. We were so close together that he was upon me almost as soon as the pistol-ball. The [illegible] staggered me a little at the moment, but I met him with the knife, and from that time we never separated again. My object was to keep him from closing upon me, until I could be as [illegible] would permit of using my last ball to advantage. In consequence of that I retreated in various ways, both still fighting, sometimes on the open floor, and sometimes knocking ousselves with violence against the wall.

"I was growing faint. I found my strength failing and then I fired my second pistol. The light instantaneously made, showed both men redder than the Indian on the field of battle. I heard that he staggered, and rushed with all my strength upon him. He still fought a little, but suddenly dropped defore me. and more than that I do not know."

"Such is the tale, as nearly as the writer can remember, that was related to him. Should it be said that he met with a romancist. in that case, his only hope is, that he may meet with another such every day of his life; though his firm and well-founced belief is that all the details are perfectly true."

The opening of the Mississippi is unlikely to produce any noticeable change in the general business of the Northwest the present season. Trade has accustomed itself to other channels, and cannot be instantly diverted, even when immediate advantages are offered. The commerce along the banks of the river below Cairo is almost entirely destroyed. At New Orleans the changes in business, and facilities for the transaction of business, are not less marked than in the country above. Had we an abundance of produce to ship, and means for its transportation, aside from the purchases which government will make for our armies, there would be no market. The planters have nothing to buy with. Their sugar and cotton have been confiscated, their plantations plundered, and slaves driven and enticed away from them. In a word, the country has been desolated, and, in its desolation the trade of the Northwest, which formerly sought that channel for an outlet has been deprived of a market. We can now realize the injury to ourselves which abolition policies have done along the banks of the Mississippi. The injury is permanent, and will be felt under the most hopeful circumstances for a quarter of a century. It has taken longer than that to improve the country laid waste. The destruction of the industrial system of the South, so far as it has already gone, now renders the opening of the Mississippi comparatively useless to us. Should that destruction be prosecuted as threatened, the Northwest will suffer in consequence as directly, and to nearly as great an extent, as the planters themselves. We have felt this when cut off from all trade with them, and shall feel it as sensibly when the channels of trade are opened, but the commodities which made it profitable are no longer in existence. The eastern States are entirely willing that our trade with South should be destroyed. It is profitable to them. But of course, inurging what they know will destroy it, they are only working in the "interests of God and humanity."

The order of Admiral Porter relative to convoying steamers down the Mississippi River gives a very clear idea of what is to be expected from the opening of that great artery of commerce, as it is familiarly called in buncombe speeches and editorials. No steamer will be allowed to go without convoy, for the simple reason that it would be continually molested, if not captured and burned, by the marauding bands which infest the banks from Memphis to New Orleans. Practically the river is no more open to legitimate commerce now than before the fall of Vicksburg. It is open to speculators in cotton and army goods, and goods intended for rebel use—of which last there are not a little—but to commerce it is still forbidden. And so it will remain so till the close of the war.—*Chicago Times.*

The following is the description of "the girl that any man would be proud to call his wife."

> Her hand's like a lily—
> But just at the tip
> It hath stolen a tint
> Like the hue of her lip!
> Her breath's like the morn
> When hyacinths blow;
> Her feet leave a blessing
> Wherever they go!
>
> For each one she's something
> To comfort or cheer;
> When her purse fails her wishes,
> She gives them a tear!
> E'en the sound of her step
> Seems to bring them relief!
> And they bless that sweet face
> Which speaks hope 'mid their grief!
>
> Her mouth's like a rose bud.
> Just budding half through,
> When it opens at morn
> Amidst fragrance and dew;
> And her heart is a dwelling
> When angels might rest,
> And forget their own Heaven
> In that of her breast!

HEADQUARTERS DEPARTMENT TRANS-MISS.
Shreveport, La., July 27th, 1863.

SPECIAL ORDERS, No. 96.

XI. Enrolling or recruiting officers are enjoined not to remove or interfere with employees in the Nitre and Mining Bureau, nor with employees of contractors with that Bureau engaged in hauling cotton to, and ordnance stores from, the Rio Grande and Gulf Ports.

By command of
Lieut.-Gen. E. KIRBY SMITH.
S. S. ANDERSON, A. A. G.

Arkansas, Louisiana and Texas papers copy four times. a8-4t.

VOL. II. RICHMOND, SATURDAY, AUGUST 29, 1863. No. 8.

Recollections of Stonewall Jackson.

Our readers are doubtless aware that we have recently issued from our presses a memoir of this great and good man. The book will be read by thousands, still there will remain many who will never have an opportunity of perusing its pages. For the benefit of such of our readers we make a few extracts from the work. The "Dispatch" of this city has truly remarked, "that the people can never be tired reading even the slightest unveiling of this mysterious man, whom they almost worshipped."

"JACKSON IS DEAD."

"Seldom have words penetrated more deeply to the heart of a great nation. The people of the Confederate States had begun to regard this immortal leader as above the reach of fate. He had passed unhurt through such desperate contests; his calm eyes had surveyed so many hard fought battle-fields, from the commencement of the combats to their termination, that a general conviction of the hero's invulnerability had impressed every heart—no one could feel that the light in those eyes of the great soldier would ever be quenched. But that Providence which decrees all things wisely at last sent the fatal bullet; and the South is called upon to mourn the untimely death of one who seemed to his countrymen the chosen standard bearer of liberty. After the battle of Chancellorsville and while the wound of the famous soldier attracted to him the warmest sympathy and drew forth the earnest prayers of many thousands for his recovery, the journals of the land contained many notices of his services and genius, and his death was alluded to as a calamity too frightful to be contemplated. Well has one of these journals in speaking of Lee and Jackson said: 'It is an honor to breathe the air they breathe. Together, they make up a measure of glory which no nation under Heaven ever surpassed. Other great leaders we have, to whom unstinted praise is due and everywhere gladly accorded; but the rays of their fame converge and accumulate but to add to the dazzling splendor that illuminates the names of Lee and Jackson.

"'The central figure of this war is, beyond all question, that of Robert E. Lee. His, the calm, broad military intellect that reduced the chaos after Donelson to form and order. But Jackson is the motive power that executes, with the rapidity of lightning, all that Lee can plan. Lee is the exponent of Southern power of command; Jackson, the expression of its faith in God and in itself, its terrible energy, its enthusiasm and daring, its unconquerable will, its contempt of danger and fatigue, its capacity to smite, as with bolts of thunder, the cowardly and cruel foe that would trample under foot its liberty and its religion.

"'Jackson was no accidental manifestation of the powers of faith and courage. He came not by chance in this day and to this generation. He was born for a purpose. In this conviction, he rests serenely, awaiting the healing of his wounds; willing once more to hear the wild cheers of his men as he rides to the front; or, if that be denied him, content to retire from the field, a maimed, humble, simple Christian man. Civil honor, were it the highest gift of the country, could not add one cubit to the stature of his glory.

"'Even should he die, his fiery and unquailing spirit would survive in his men. He has infused into them that which cannot die. The leader who succeeds him, be he whom he may, will be impelled, as by a supernatural impulse, to emulate his matchless deeds. Jackson's men will demand to be led in "Stonewall Jackson's way." The leader who will not or cannot comply with that demand, must drop the baton quickly. Jackson's corps will be led forever by the memory of its great chieftain.'

"Alas! the termination of his wound was fatal. The great soul has passed away from us: and we are left without his sagacious counsels, his splendid powers of execution; his unerring judgment, and that intuitive genius for war which made him, in his sphere, the first of living leaders, and ranked him with the greatest who have lived in all tide of time."

HOW HE GOT THE NAME OF "STONEWALL."

'Twas at the first battle of Manassas, when the Southern leaders "saw with irrepressible anguish the exhaustion of the troops, the waning fortunes of the day, and the countless reserves which the enemy hurled incessantly upon their thin and weary lines. Among these was the heroic General Bee, in command of the 4th Alabama and some Mississippians, who were nearly worn out by the terrible ordeal through which they had passed. Bee rode up and down the lines, cheering on the men, and beseeching them, by all they held dear, not to give way, when he met Jackson, and said, in the bitter despair of his heart, "*General, they are beating us back!*" The face of the stern, silent soldier betrayed no answering emotion. The keen eye glittered for an instant; the lips opened; and in the curt, peculiar tones of the speaker he said, "*Sir, we will give them the bayonet!*" Bee seemed to gather new inspiration from the words; he galloped back to the remnants of his command, and fronting to Jackson, called out to his men: "*There is Jackson standing like a stonewall! Let us determine to die here, and we will conquer. Follow me!*" * *

At Manassas, "the country had gained a splendid victory against enormous odds; and although he did not then know it, Jackson had gained a name with which he is forever inseparably identified. When the heroic Bee exclaimed, "There is Jackson standing *like a stonewall*," he unconsciously employed a term which thenceforth clung to Jackson more closely than his baptismal appellation. From that hot day of battle, the leader of the men of the Valley was known as "Stonewall Jackson,"—his command as the "Stonewall Brigade." Many are ignorant and few recall the fact, that the great soldier was christened "Thomas Jonathan." His veritable christening in the popular heart was on that evening of Manassas when Bee, about to surrender his great soul to his Maker, baptized him, amid blood and fire, "STONEWALL JACKSON!"

LIEUT. GEN. T. J. JACKSON.

PERSONAL APPEARANCE.

The outward appearance of the famous leader was not imposing. The popular idea of a great general is an individual of stiff and stately bearing, clad in splendid costume, all covered with gold lace and decorations, who prances by upon

ARMY  NAVY

GAZETTE OF THE REGULAR **JOURNAL.** AND VOLUNTEER FORCES.

VOL. I.—NO. 1. NEW YORK, SATURDAY, AUG. 29, 1863. FIVE DOLLARS PER YEAR. SINGLE COPIES, TEN CENTS.

CONTENTS OF NUMBER ONE.

THE MILITARY SITUATION.

THERE is not now the shadow of a doubt that Fort Sumter lies a heap of ruins. The entire course of the combined land and naval operations towards this end, from the time of the landing on Morris Island, six weeks ago, now stands forth a very complete and perfect piece of work, and presents the triple result of opening a new epoch in siege operations, seriously crippling the Rebellion in its material parts by closing for ever the leading inlet for blockade-runners, and throwing into the scales of the Union the weight of a moral prestige which will be profoundly felt both at home and abroad. It is true, Charleston is not yet taken, and we cannot share the popular illusions as to the immediate certainty of this achievement. The work still before the army and navy is immense. But enough has already been done to "shut up in measureless content" all who have at heart the speedy triumph of the cause of the Union.

General GILLMORE effected the landing of his force on Morris Island, under cover of the navy, on the 10th of July, and forthwith began that slow, difficult engineering labor of opening parallels, erecting batteries, etc., which, while it prepares the grandest results, is apt to pass unheeded by the public. In the meanwhile, the fleet of iron-clads and wooden gunboats has been assiduously engaged in firing at the enemy's works on Morris Island and at Fort Sumter, for the purpose of engaging their attention while the preliminary operations of the siege went on. When guns enough had been mounted, General GILLMORE began his operations on Fort Wagner, and after a vigorous shelling by his batteries and the fleet, an assault was made on that work with a view of carrying it. The attack miscarried. General GILLMORE then proceeded with his siege operations, resolving to leave Fort Wagner aside and concentrate his efforts on Fort Sumter, regarding that as the key to the whole situation, and confident that the reduction of the great sentinel-fort being accomplished, the minor works on Morris Island would fall by their own weight.

Monday the 17th inst. found the preliminary preparations complete, and the bombardment was begun at daybreak of that date. General GILLMORE opened all his batteries on Fort Sumter, firing over Fort Wagner and the intermediate space. The ordnance used consisted of two-hundred-pounders, one-hundred-pounder and eighty-pounder Parrot rifles, and eighty-pounder Whitworth guns rifled. At the same time, Admiral DAHLGREN moved up the entire available naval force, leading with the flag in the Monitor *Weehawken*, followed by the Monitors *Catskill*, *Nahant*, and *Montauk*—the *Passaic* and *Patapsco* in reserve for Sumter. The *Ironsides* was placed opposite Fort Wagner, and the gunboats *Canandaigua*, *Mahaska*, *Cimmarone*, *Ottawa*, *Dai-Ching* and *Ladona* at long range. After a steady and well-directed fire, Fort Wagner was silenced shortly after nine o'clock. The only casualty was the killing of the gallant Fleet-Captain, G. W. RODGERS, who had taken command of his old vessel, the *Catskill*, for the attack.

Meanwhile the fire of the shore batteries was working effectually upon the gorge of Fort Sumter, which appeared to have been strengthened in every possible manner. The Monitors *Passaic* and *Patapsco* now steamed up and devoted themselves for the rest of the forenoon to the attack of Fort Sumter, taking position at two thousand yards from the fort. The siege batteries continued the bombardment during the whole of the day. Fort Sumter scarcely replied. Of the result of Monday's work we have no precise information. Newspaper accounts, however, state that several craters "five or six feet in depth" could be observed in the south-west face. The sand traverse or barricade which the enemy had thrown up to protect the gorge about the sallyport was, at an early hour, penetrated by shell, which knocked out some of the lower tiers, and brought the pile tumbling down about the wharf in an irregular mass, but still in such a position as to protect the wall in a great degree.

On Tuesday the 18th, at four o'clock in the morning, the bombardment was renewed. Additional guns had been placed in position during the night. In consequence of a severe gale and high sea, however, the navy was unable effectually to coöperate in the attack. As before, Fort Sumter was all but silent, batteries Wagner and Gregg being the only assailants on the rebel side. As night closed in the effects of the firing was observable in "deep holes" in the south-west face, and only a portion of the parapet remained; the coping was torn off, and one corner knocked away completely.

The third day of the bombardment—Wednesday the 19th—witnessed a "continuation of the same," though the firing is stated not to have been as rapid as on the two previous days. The gunners, however, had got the range perfectly, and no ammunition was wasted. In the afternoon two of the Monitors advanced towards Fort Sumter for the purpose of attacking it at two thousand yards range, but the current was so strong that the vessels became unmanageable, and the officers were compelled to abandon the design. Fort Sumter fired but one gun during the day, and the new rebel batteries on James' Island were the only ones really alive. The firing was kept up regularly throughout the night. "Shots," say the accounts, "were now going through one side of Fort Sumter and passing out of the opposite side; we could see the channel through the apertures made." The siege batteries fired 130 rounds, 75 of which struck Fort Sumter. In the afternoon one of the eighty-pounders was disabled in the breech, the result of its own discharge.

It was now resolved to remove the Whitworth guns and replace them by Parrott rifles. At night a sap was constructed from the third parallel to within two hundred yards of Fort Wagner. The rebels were also building a sap from Fort Wagner towards our works. A dispatch from Charleston to the Richmond papers under date of the 20th inst., says: "Up to Monday night, the third day of the attack, 1,972 projectiles had struck Fort Sumter, and, including to-day, 2,500 have struck. The damage is, of course considerable; and for the last two days all the guns on the south face of the Fort have been disabled."

Thursday, the 20th, opened on the fourth day of the siege. The firing was still exceedingly heavy, though the Monitors did not even advance towards the rebel works. At about noon Fort Wagner opened heavily on the land batteries, but ceased after the *Ironsides* got fairly to work. In the morning the rebels commenced shelling the marsh battery from their works on James Island. During the day they fired 116 shots, with but trifling results. Our sappers were still approaching Fort Wagner. On the fifth day of the bombardment, Friday the 21st, says the Richmond *Sentinel*, "the fire of the enemy's land batteries has been kept upon Fort Sumter, and more guns are disabled." A heavy fire was also kept up on battery Wagner, both from the fleet and the land, and also upon battery Gregg. On Saturday the 22d, the land batteries opened on Fort Sumter from south to north, and the Monitors, coming within closer range, from east to west. The rebel papers report *six hundred and four shots fired that day at Fort Sumter, of which four hundred and nineteen struck inside and outside!*

As the results of this extraordinary week's bombardment—a siege unparalleled in military annals, it is announced that "Sumter is an immense ruin!" The surrender, however, had not taken place. "Col. Rhett," says a Charleston dispatch, "is ordered with his brave garrison to hold his outpost, even as a forlorn hope, until he is relieved or the place taken." On Sunday, 23d, at eleven o'clock, Gen. GILLMORE sent a communication giving notice that at eleven o'clock on Monday, the 24th, he would open fire on Charleston, and "in the meantime non-combatants would go out of the city." The loss of life on the rebel side, during the week's firing, appears to have been quite severe. The real work of the navy still remains to be done—to pass beyond Fort Sumter into Rebellion Roads, and reduce the batteries that line both sides of the water approach to the city. It is doubtless a task that will test to the full the powers of our iron fleet; but the public has implicit confidence that Admiral DAHLGREN and his gallant force will do all that can possibly be done. The only hope for the rebels now is that their interior batteries are still sufficiently formidable to repel our fleet; or that BEAUREGARD make his long promised attack "with the bayonet" on our land force on Morris Island. The denouement of this wonderful drama will of course be watched with the greatest interest.

—THE situation of the Army of the Cumberland is of a nature to attract the liveliest attention of all who have any adequate appreciation of the supreme strategic importance of the objective point towards which the operations of General ROSECRANS are directed. The great mountain system which runs like a wedge into the heart of the Confederacy has been aptly styled "the citadel of a large fortress, of which the walls are formed by the parallel ridges, the ditches by the rapid streams in the valley, and the doors by the gaps." Chattanooga is a natural bastion on the salient angle of the great line of rebel communications. The possession of this will give us the same advantage the enemy has so long had, namely, interior lines, while it will throw them back on exterior lines and permit their attack and defeat in detail. If General ROSECRANS shall be successful in his work, it will change the whole nature of military combinations and operations over the whole theatre of war. ROSECRANS' advance from the old position at Tullahoma and Winchester was commenced a fortnight ago, but the absence of details as to the lines of march leaves us in darkness as to a manœuvre of great military interest. The right column (McCOOK's corps) appears to have moved by way of Winchester and Cowan, striking the river at Bellefonte, Ala., twelve miles west of Stevenson. The

NOTICES TO CORRESPONDENTS.

The Editor of this JOURNAL will always be glad to receive from officers in the two services, correspondence and general communications of a character suited to its columns. It is necessary that the name of the writer should, in all cases, accompany his communications, not for publication, but as a guarantee of good faith.

Officers are especially requested to give us early notification of all personal matters of general interest; of the movements of vessels; of casualties among officers; and military and naval events.

The Editor will, at all times, be pleased to respond, in these columns, to enquiries in regard to tactical and other matters.

From gentlemen in the medical service we shall be glad to receive communications on military hygiene, practical surgery, and reports of notable operations and novel forms of treatment.

The subscription price of THE ARMY AND NAVY JOURNAL is FIVE DOLLARS a year, or THREE DOLLARS for six months, invariably in advance. The subscription price may be sent in United States funds, or Quartermaster's, Paymaster's or other drafts, which should be made payable to the order of the Proprietor, W. C. Church.

All communications should be addressed to the ARMY AND NAVY JOURNAL, New York.

U. S. ARMY AND NAVY JOURNAL.

NEW-YORK, SATURDAY, AUGUST 29, 1863.

THE ARMY AND THE NATION.

WE take it that one of the most important results in the great moral transformation of the American people effected by the War for the Union is the altered tone of public sentiment which has silently grown up in the minds of men in regard to our National Army, understanding, of course, by this term both services—the *Pallas armata*—the embodied war-power of the Nation on land and sea. For the future we are a military people. It is hardly possible that we shall henceforth lapse into the infinitely false and fatal delusions that for a generation or two, at least, have held possession of the public mind. To secure this beyond a doubt, it remains that theory shall consolidate what practice has taught, by the establishment of principles having all the force of a National creed touching the status, rights and relations of the National Army.

It has been often remarked, since the outbreak of the war, that if we had had a standing army of fifty thousand men, the Rebellion never would have occurred. This statement is doubtless quite correct; but it in reality begs the whole question. In order that we should have had an army of fifty thousand men, it was necessary that we should *not* have had the very order of sentiments and theories in which the Rebellion took root, and without which it never would and never could have seen the light.

To reach to the root of this matter would require a piece of historical analysis quite beyond the scope of the present article. The fact remains, that delusive notions have for many years held possession of the public mind regarding war, war establishments, the army, military education, and military men. Look at the course of our National Legislation for a generation or two: it has been, with but rare exceptions, repressive to the army and navy—marked by parsimony, and "bound in to saucy doubts and fears." And the tone of public sentiment, especially at the North, has been as bad, if not worse. Its whole tendency has been to frown upon the army, to isolate it from sympathy and honor, and throw it into an attitude of antagonism. Military men were looked upon as idle pensioners on the public purse, sporting their epaulettes in the fashionable circles of metropolitan society. And this indignity, too, in face of the fact that no service in the world has been so hard-worked as ours: a fact strikingly illustrated in the circumstance that insurance corporations long refused to take risks on army officers, as statistics proved, so severe were the duties and hardships imposed upon our small army, that the ratio of mortality in our service—even in so-called peace times—was greater than in that of any other service in the world, peace and war included!

Among the complexity of causes in which this prejudice had its origin, we may count as prominent ones, first, certain loose political theories and vicious social doctrines brought into the sphere of public thought by the French studies and sympathies of some of our earliest political writers; secondly, the spurious peace-sentimentalism that obtained such currency a few years ago. This notion, originating with a few European *doctrinaires*, was seized upon by many in this country, especially in the North, and particularly in New England. According to these visionaries, a new millennium of peace had dawned upon the world; war was henceforth to cease, and armies become useless and burdensome anachronisms. It was a curious bit of that Titanic irony we sometimes see in affairs that, just about the time these vagaries reached their climax, a great European war broke out, involving in it the leading Powers, and shaking the continent to its foundations.

In addition to the causes already enumerated as among the formative influences that gave this false bias to public opinion on military affairs, we should mention the entire absorption of our people in purely material interests. This is undoubtedly a tendency incident to all modern peoples. Our Political Economics tell us much of the Wealth of Nations, but very little of the Strength of Nations. They forget that cardinal truth set forth by BACON in one of his powerful aphorisms, that, "Neither is money the sinews of war (as is trivially said,) when the sinews of men's arms, in base and effeminate people, are failing." There appears to be in the life of modern societies a counter movement, so that, often, while their wealth goes on increasing, their strength declines. Now, we do not mean to intimate that the former is not good. This is the age of material developments. We do not expect to restore the age of chivalry, and would not if we could. Modern nations need vast wealth, vast resources. But there is a limit beyond which this tendency cannot safely go; and when it goes so far that Strength declines as Wealth advances, the decay of that nation has begun, and the time comes when even its wealth falls a prey to the invader. "When a strong man armed keepeth his palace," says the Good Book "his goods are in peace; but when a stronger than he shall come, he taketh from him all his armor wherein he trusted, and divideth his spoils."

The South, on these matters, it must be confessed, always held sounder doctrines than the North. The nature of their institutions was doubtless favorable to the military spirit, but there was, besides, always a strong sentiment in the same direction. It is sometimes charged on the *élèves* of our Military Academy that in their tastes and attachments, their political and social views, previously to the war, they very generally assimilated with the South. There is no wonder they did. And yet it is worthy of remark, so strong is the sentiment of loyalty which the service breeds, that, notwithstanding the South has always favored and the North always frowned on the army, the moment it came to be a question of the disruption of the nation, the proportion of those educated at our Military Academy who adhered to the flag was greatly in excess of what it would have been had the graduates from the North gone with the North, and the graduates from the South with the South, and had not a very considerable proportion of men over whom the sectional traditions of the South would be supposed to have peculiar sway preserved their fealty to the Union. And in regard to the body of the army and navy, President Lincoln, in his Inaugural Message, signalized the remarkable fact that not a single common soldier or sailor had abandoned his allegiance to the flag.

Let us hope that in the future history of our country, juster views in these regards will prevail—that a military spirit will be cultivated, that the army will be cherished. "In all grades," says Marshal MARMONT, "the profession of arms is noble, because, for all alike it is composed of sacrifices, and is rewarded, before all, by public estimation and glory. To speak disdainfully of those who compose the rank and file of armies is a kind of blasphemy, even to speak of them with indifference is to misconceive the very conditions of our nature." And more especially is this true in our country. Under our system the civil authority controls the military. The war-power is not the prerogative of the military but of the civil government. The prating, therefore, which is sometimes heard in regard to the dangers of Cæsarism or military despotism can arise only either from a knavish spirit, or from a fundamental misconception of the genius of our institutions. With us the army is simply the arm *of* the nation: not an arm *over* the nation. If it be truly its *arm*, therefore, its arm for protection and for vengeance, it is a living, incorporate part of the body politic, sharing its sympathies, motives, desires. In the great volunteer army which has been in the field during the past two years, a *million* of citizens have, for longer or shorter periods, borne arms in the public service. We believe their army life has made them better men and better citizens. That it has raised their sentiment of patriotism, no man who has seen our armies in the field will deny. The feeling of the army regarding the late attempts to discourage the conscription strikingly illustrates this. We doubt if these attempts would ever have been made if their originators had foreseen what contempt and indignation they were destined to stir up in the army—what white fury sat on the lips of men eager to leave the rebels in their front and come to settle accounts with those whom they regarded as worse rebels in the rear.

These tendencies are all profoundly encouraging, no doubt. And yet, powerful though the shock be which the old anti-military prejudices have received, and committed though we believe we are and will be by the whole current of events to correct practical action as to our war establishments, we readily foresee how strong the temptations to a relapse will be,—how strong will be the attempts, through the machinery of partisan politics, operating on the passions and interests of men quick to forget the lesson when the immediate material occasion is removed. While battles in the field go on, therefore, there is need of a battle for the army itself. The UNITED STATES ARMY AND NAVY JOURNAL is designed as an arena on which this contest may be fought. We shall bring what strength we can, entrenched behind what we believe to be impregnable positions, to the service of this cause. We believe in the army. We believe it is a necessity to the nation. This does not mean, perforce, that we favor bloated and expensive war-establishments or a huge standing army. What is important is that the spirit and temper of the nation be right on these great questions. This is the one paramount aim of this JOURNAL. We have no other creed than the army has—the creed of loyalty, the creed of nationality. Of party politics we know nothing and care nothing. With such aims our enterprise is launched forth, and committed to the consideration of both branches of the United Service.

THE REDUCTION OF FORT SUMTER.

IT is with no slight gratification that we are able to open the issue of the ARMY AND NAVY JOURNAL with the illuminated initial of the reduction of Fort Sumter. We have not, as yet, the tidings of the actual surrender: but this mere technicality is of small moment in the face of the crowning fact that the historic fort, whose possession was the first material triumph of the Rebellion, lies to-day a mass of ruins.

The facts thus far developed regarding the reduction of Fort Sumter are too scanty to permit of an appreciation of this notable and highly important piece of engineering. The relations of this to what remains to be done are also still too obscure for us to see the way clearly up to the aim of these operations—the possession of Charleston. It is announced that Gen. GILLMORE is shelling the city with his three-hundred-pounder Parrott rifle. The line of fire to the city is prodigious—four miles and a half: though not beyond the powers of this great engine. He can, no doubt, throw a certain number of shell into Charleston: but the task will ultimately reduce itself to the question of our ability to approach the city and meet the force of the enemy with the bayonet, or to move up the harbor with the fleet of iron-clads.

Fort Sumter, standing as a sentinel midway at the entrance of the harbor, was the key to the approach by water. It was absolutely necessary to eliminate this element from the problem before a single step could be taken. The attack by the iron fleet under Admiral DUPONT, last April, demonstrated conclusively the incapacity of that fleet unaided to reduce Fort Sumter. The weakest of the strongholds of Charleston in its powers of defence, Fort Sumter was the strongest of them all in its powers of offence. The offensive powers of the guns of the iron-clads measured against the offensive powers of the tremendous battery of Fort Sumter proved so inadequate that in the trial, five out of the nine vessels were in an hour so disabled as to be compelled to retire from the combat without having done the fort any considerable damage. This being definitively settled, the present attack has been wisely planned and conducted on different principles. The brunt of the work has been made, this time, to rest on the land force. The navy has, thus far, played a secondary part. The Monitors have been handled with an excessive delicacy; and even after Fort Sumter was half in ruins, Admiral DAHLGREN appears to have cautiously avoided exposing his vessels to its fire. Having obtained a footing on Morris' Island, Gen. GILLMORE immediately began the work of opening parallels and constructing batteries. Over a month was spent on this work, and after considerable practice at various times at Fort Wagner, aided by the navy, and an assault which turned out disastrous-

No 415—VOL. XVI.] NEW YORK, SEPTEMBER 12, 1863. [PRICE 8 CENTS.

Our Sketches.

HEADQUARTERS DEPT. OF THE SOUTH,
Morris Island, S. C., Aug. 24, 1863.

Having found it necessary to employ Mr. W. T. CRANE to make sketches of the progressive demolition of Fort Sumter by our batteries, I most cheerfully bear testimony to the general accuracy of his delineations.

Q. A. GILLMORE,
Brig.-Gen. Commanding.

We insert the above high testimony to the fidelity of the sketches which we have given of the operations of our army and navy in the Department of the South, the more readily as it was entirely unsolicited by us.

No reader of FRANK LESLIE'S ILLUSTRATED NEWSPAPER can now indulge any doubt as to the truth of what we occasionally say of the merit of our sketches, as actual living pictures of events passing around us.

We spare no expense in keeping at every important point competent Artists, all of whom could obtain from the Generals on the field similar testimonials. Such we have never sought; but when, amid the cares of so great a campaign, Gen. Gillmore can stop to commend our exertions, it is no vanity on our part to lay it before our readers.

THE LAWRENCE MASSACRE.

THE war has had its terrors. The deep hypocrisy of the Confederate leaders, who, hanging Union men in Tennessee and Missouri as bridgeburners, guerillas, or simply and nakedly as Union men, insulted Heaven and outraged humanity by their mendacious protests against the reprisals occasionally and too seldom made by our kindly-hearted authorities, reaches a climax in the fearful massacre at Lawrence, Kansas.

In atrocity, in bloodthirsty cruelty, in barbarity, rapine and fiendishness it has no parallel in our history. A town entered treacherously by night, nearly 200 of its people butchered without mercy, the city pillaged and fired, such is, in the eyes of the sanctimonious Davis and Beauregard, a part of civilized warfare. When Bishop Lynch chanted his Te Deum to thank the Almighty that civil war had begun, was it to ask the benediction of heaven on scenes like this?

The immediate perpetrator of the frightful massacre was Quantrell, who has, for the last two years, figured in guerilla war, in Missouri, and though often defeated, never captured. His force consisted of 300 picked men from Lafayette, Saline, Clay, Johnson and other border counties of Missouri. It started on the 20th from Middle Fork, Grand river, 15 miles from the Kansas border, and crossed the line near the town of Gardner, reaching Lawrence at four o'clock on the morning of the 21st. He posted a guard around the city and began the work of mur-

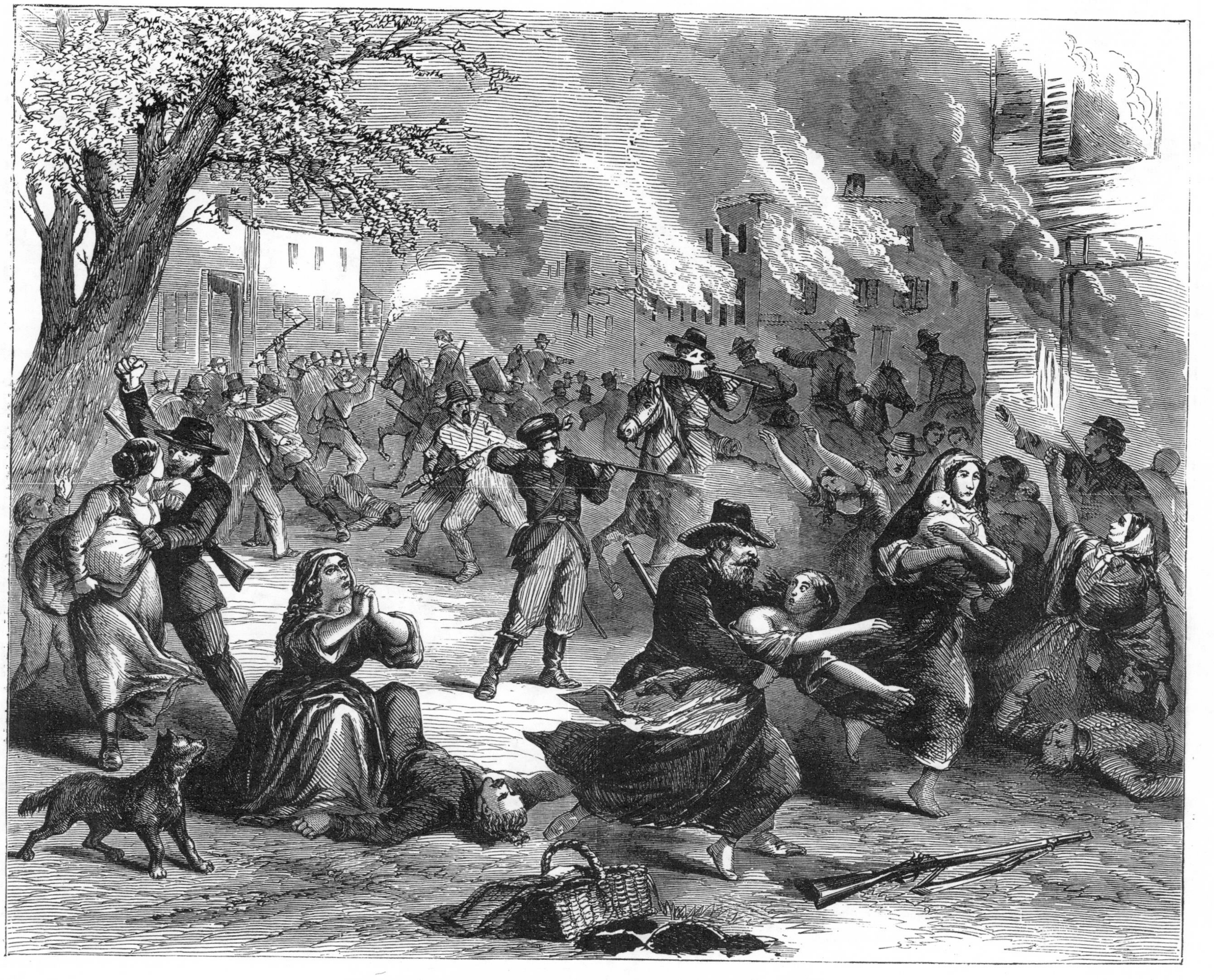

THE WAR IN KANSAS—FEARFUL MASSACRE AT LAWRENCE BY QUANTRELL'S GUERILLAS.

PUBLISHED BY JAMES GARDNER. AT SEVEN DOLLARS Per ANNUM.

NEW SERIES.] AUGUSTA, GA., SATURDAY, SEPTEMBER 12, 1863. [VOL. 1.---NUMBER 37.

[Written for the Southern Field and Fireside.]

GERALD GRAY'S WIFE.

BY THE AUTHOR OF "BUSY MOMENTS OF AN IDLE WOMAN," "LILY," "SYLVIA'S WORLD," &C., &C.,

"If ever I think I have the stuff in me to write an Epic, by Jove! I'll try. If I only feel that I am good enough to write a story of "sentimental feelings," I will do that."
PENDENNIS.

LORD ALFRED.—"Pray, sir, proceed
With your tale. My compatriot, what was his crime?"
STRANGER.—"Oh, nothing! His folly was not so sublime
As to merit that term. If I blamed him just now,
It was not for the sin, but the silliness."
LORD ALFRED.—"How?"
STRANGER.—"I own I hate Botany. Still, I admit—
Although, I, myself, have no passion for it;
* * * * * Yet, I cannot despise
The cold man of science, since he, I suppose,
Has some purpose beyond the mere mischief he does.
But the stupid and mischievous boy that uproots
The exotics, and tramples the tender young shoots,
For a boy's brutal pastime, and only because
He knows no distinction 'twixt heartsease and haws;
One would think for the sake of each nurseling so nipped,
To catch the young rascal and have him well whipp'd.
LUCILE.'

CHAPTER I.

A tall, pale, thin woman; she is not very ugly, and she is by no means pretty. Her eyes are large and dark, with thick, long, black lashes, and the shape of her mouth is graceful and classic. These are her only beauties. Even these are only perceived when you study her closely, for the eyes are so stony in their usual expression, so cold, so self-concentrated apparently, so defiant, and so distrustful, and the lips have a way of setting themselves firmly together, from which they rarely relax into the smile which can diffuse a charm over the plain, rigid face. She asks and takes nothing from dress to redeem her lack of good looks. Her father requires that she should wear rich stuffs, fine laces, handsome jewels. She chooses that she should be a parade for his wealth just as his houses, and equipages, and plate, and hot-houses are constantly displayed; so to-day, on this wild, sandy beach, she wears a costly muslin gown, each flounce heavy with rare mechlin, and about her thin, sun-burnt wrists are great gold bracelets, and in her ears two pearls are hung with diamonds encircling them, of which, when her father tossed them in her lap, on her last birth-day, he said:

'Here, my girl; these cost a cool three thousand.'

But the rich muslin is carelessly put on, and the shawl she has wrapped about her (for the evening grows chilly,) is a worn old tarltan plaid, thrown over her head and gathered up about her throat in dowdy folds, and she has shoved the bracelets out of sight, far up her arms, and the pure, lustrous pearls, which would have been so beautiful touching a snowy throat, I wot of, only make her's browner. So, to see her pacing along this strip of ocean-beaten land, with low dark clouds veiling the setting sun, the white sea-birds skimming the water crests of the angry waves, and a sullen wind murmuring hoarsely of the storm to come, you might have thought this solitary, sallow, stern woman was some desolate wayfarer, some miserable waif and stray on life's ocean; and not Ruth Desborough, the richest and most courted heiress in the whole State.

Ruth Desborough's mother died when she was still a child. She was a gentle, feeble woman, who always seemed to stand in awe of all the luxury which her husband heaped about her. She wore her jewels as if she were afraid of them; Ruth put on hers as if she were ashamed of them. Mrs. Desborough thought wealth a great and glorious thing—something too grand for her to enjoy—she, who had began life as a nursery-governess, and been wooed and won by the stout, jolly, purse proud Jacob Desborough long before he made his tremendous speculations, passed for a madman, lowered on the brink of ruin, and then set down his large feet firmly as a *millionaire*.

Of course, Jacob Desborough loved his only child. He saw she was not handsome nor stylish, but she was dutiful to him and proud to all the world. He liked the way she carried herself to the "a-*ris*-tocrats" as he called his neighbors. He rubbed his huge, red hands and chuckled when she looked over the heads of the Misses Seymours, and Cecil, and Clare—her companions and *friends*, as such acquaintances are called—and when saucy, smiling, sneering Mrs. Berners asked one day at dinner if the two pictures over the plate-laden side-board were "family portraits"—they were dame and cavalier in silk and satin, rouge and powder—Ruth fixed her unquailing eyes on the pretty questioner, and said calmly: 'Scarcely. Papa is an orphan-house boy, and my mother's parents kept a little corner-shop. Those portraits, bought for a song, at an auction lately. Their owner was a gambler and a swindler, came to grief, and had to sell his own father and mother. His name was Cressingham.'

Mrs. Berners dropped her eye glass, and colored scarlet. It was but three years since she used to write herself "Rosaline Cressingham." She had not recognized her own grand parents, disposed of by her own uncle.

'Why, you are a Cressingham,' said another guest, as obtuse as some people can be, while the rest of the party were aghast.

'I beg your pardon for my allusion,' said Ruth, with stately courtesy, and changed the conversation.

Ruth was now twenty-six years of age. She had had many offers of marriage—but, although more than one of her suitors would have readily been accepted for her by her father, she had never wavered for one moment.

I often have thought the man bold who dared to address Ruth Desborough. I have often wondered how they went about it. I think all the declarations must have been written ones. I cannot imagine a person of ordinary courage daring to sit or stand before that steel-faced woman, and make pretty speeches—speeches that, spoken or on paper, always meant to her mind—"you are very rich, and I want your money, so I'll take you."

That, of course, was the curse of her life; there was the secret source of bitter waters that from earliest childhood, had sprung up within her, and forcing its way into every vein, had mingled each throb of her heart with its acrid tide. From infancy her ears had been made familiar with the idea. Her father, in the kindly coarseness of his nature, constantly said: 'You mayn't be as pretty nor as smart as some girls, but I'll be hanged if you can't buy as good a husband as the best of them.'

Her husband was to be bought! As a child the idea amused and pleased her. Her dolls were bought for her. French dolls, with painted cheeks and elaborately dressed hair, tiny corsets, and whole suits of clothes; English dolls, just like real babies, with their fat, dimpled necks and infant heads turned on one side, their soft rings of flaxen hair, (not wigs,) and their long robes and caps; then when she grew up, instead of dolls, her papa would buy her a husband; a "true-for-true" husband—yes he would. So she confidentially said one day to one of her playmates, and this girl, barely ten years of age, answered scornfully: 'Buy a husband indeed! I would not have a bought husband.'

'Why?'

'Because I heard my mamma say that love can't be bought; and when I grow up and get married I want to be loved,' and the little precocious wife tossed her little nose in the air.

Ruth thought over this remark, and soon she went gravely to her father and repeated it.

Mr. Desborough laughed heartily, and patted her head, and told the story after dinner to his two guests, and they laughed, and Ruth, who was eating grapes at her papa's side, grew angry and sullen, and lifted her large dark eyes from her place, and looked seriously at both of her father's old comrades, and walked out of the room.

From that day the word "husband" never escaped the child's lips. When Mr. Desborough jested, as he had always done on the subject, she kept a sort of wounded silence; and when she was eighteen and a ball of great magnificence proclaimed the fact that she was now about to enter the market to buy, and not to be bought, her resolution was taken.

She would live and die Ruth Desborough. No purchased love for her. Since even her own father deemed her unworthy to inspire a passion, she would endure no sweet words to be paid for in dollars and cents; no lover's vows looking for return in bank-stock; no soft glances to match her diamonds.

And the canker of this thought did not extend alone to her views of wooer's motives. All mankind gradually came under the same leprosy.

She did not reject attentions from men or women, but she decided with unflinching severity that every kind word or action was given to the heiress not the woman. And what she took she paid back scrupulously. To society she extended an unbounded hospitality. She spared no pains that money could bring about to entertain those who entertained her.

On her more familiar acquaintances—friends, she had none—she lavished gifts, seeking carefully to choose what was pleasantest to receive; not as her father would have done, with loud-voiced disclosure of his reasons for offering, letting himself be guided by the cost in proportion to the intention. No; but with an inborn delicacy of thought and manner which often won for her affection and respect—unuttered half the time—for few dared to speak of affection, or respect, or interest to the cold, reserved, repellant Miss Desborough.

Such were her antecedents. Such was the morbid, unhealthy condition of her mind. No wonder she daily grew less and less sociable to herself and to the world. No wonder that on

A ROMANTIC INTRODUCTION.

THE NEW YORK HERALD.

WHOLE NO. 9864. NEW YORK, SATURDAY, SEPTEMBER 19, 1863.—TRIPLE SHEET. PRICE THREE CENTS.

IMPORTANT OPERATIONS IN GEORGIA.

Impending Battle Field of Major General Rosecrans—The Country Between Chattanooga and Atlanta.

THE NEW YORK HERALD.

WHOLE NO. 9867. | NEW YORK, TUESDAY, SEPTEMBER 22, 1863.—TRIPLE SHEET. | PRICE THREE CENTS.

THE BATTLE FIELD NEAR CHATTANOOGA.

Scene of the Terrible Conflict Between Gen. Rosecrans' Army and the Rebels Under Bragg and Johnston, Saturday and Sunday, September 19 and 20, 1863.

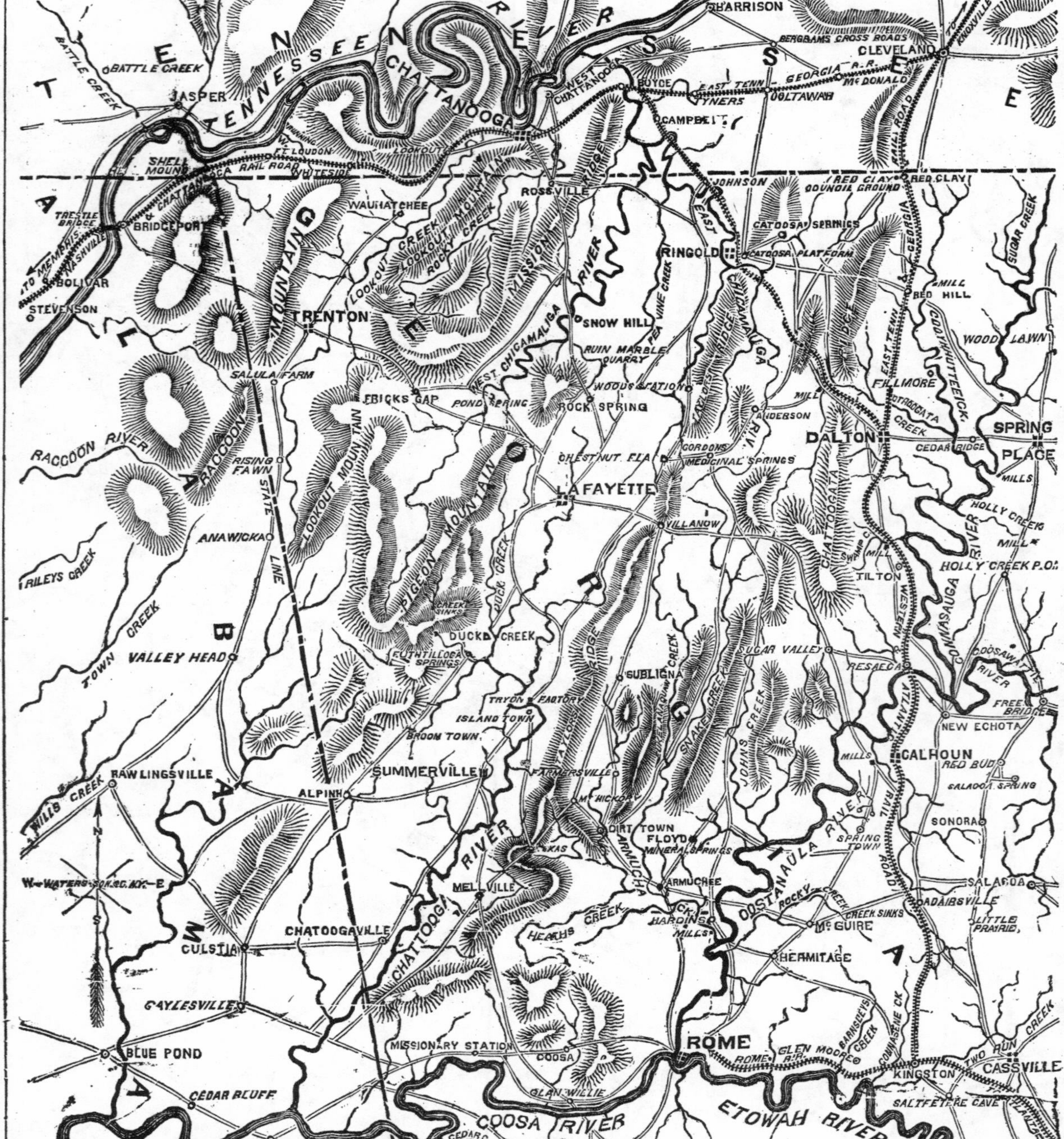

See Third Page for the Latest Particulars from the Battle Field.

SITUATIONS WANTED—FEMALES.

A YOUNG GIRL WANTS A SITUATION AS chambermaid and waitress. Can be seen for two days at 178 East 31st st., between 1st and 2d avs., top floor, front room.

A RESPECTABLE YOUNG GIRL WANTS A SITUATION as cook, washer and ironer. Has no objection to do general housework in a small private family. Can be seen for two days at 128 West 30th st., in the rear.

A SITUATION WANTED—BY A RESPECTABLE young woman as plain cook, and to assist in washing and ironing in a small private family. Can be seen for two days at 65 West 20th st.

AS COOK AND TO ASSIST AT WASHING AND IRONING.—An experienced cook wishes a situation as above, in a first class private family; best of reference given. Can be seen at 91 West 19th st. till engaged.

A YOUNG WOMAN WISHES A SITUATION AS chambermaid or to do general housework in a small family; fully understands her work in all its branches and can get good reference from her last employer. Call for two days at 283 1st av., corner of 17th st.

A YOUNG WOMAN IS DESIROUS TO OBTAIN A SITUATION as nurse and chambermaid; can be fully recommended by her last employer, where she has lived two years and a half. Can be seen at 435 Fulton av., near Adelphi st., Brooklyn, on the second floor.

AN EXPERIENCED AND TRUSTWORTHY YOUNG woman wishes a situation as chambermaid and to do fine washing and ironing; has the best of city reference from her last place. Can be seen for two days at 53 West 22d st., between 5th and 6th avs.

A RESPECTABLE YOUNG WOMAN WISHES A SITUATION in a private family, to do chamberwork, or is willing to assist in the washing and ironing; is fully competent. Understands her business. Best of city reference from her last place. Call for two days at 95 West 19th st.

A RESPECTABLE YOUNG GIRL WISHES TO GET A situation as chambermaid and waitress. Is one who thoroughly understands her business. The best of city reference can be given. Call for two days at 98 Front st., between Adams and Pearl sts., Brooklyn.

A RESPECTABLE YOUNG WOMAN WISHES A SITUATION to do general housework in a private family. Good references. Call for two days at 148 West 35th st., second floor, front room.

A SEAMSTRESS—A PERSON WHO UNDERSTANDS dressmaking, shirtmaking and needlework of all kinds, both plain and fancy, and is a married woman, wishes a situation. Address 111 Wooster st.

AS INFANT'S NURSE, OR CHILD'S NURSE AND seamstress. Has had the care of children for many years. Good city reference. Call at 26 East 28th st., between Madison ave. and 4th ave. Can be seen for a few days.

A SITUATION WANTED—BY A RESPECTABLE young woman, as good plain cook and will assist in the washing and ironing, and is an excellent plain baker. Good reference if required. Call at 178 Johnson st., Brooklyn. Can be seen at any time.

A RESPECTABLE GIRL WISHES A SITUATION AS chambermaid and plain sewer, or chambermaid and waitress. Would not object to do general housework in a small private family. Can be seen at 64 East 29th st., corner of 4th ave., first floor, over the grocery store.

A RESPECTABLE YOUNG WOMAN WISHES A SITUATION as chambermaid and to do fine washing and ironing, or as laundress. Can do French fluting. Best of city reference. Can be seen at 142 East 21st st., near 3d ave., second floor, front room.

A SITUATION WANTED—BY A COMPETENT PERSON, as good cook and to assist with the washing and ironing in a small private family. Good city reference. Call for two days at 89 West 19th st.

A SITUATION WANTED—BY A YOUNG GIRL, TO do general housework or as chambermaid. Call for two days at 366 8th st.

A SITUATION WANTED—BY A RESPECTABLE young woman, as cook, washer and ironer; is an excellent bread and biscuit maker. Has good reference from her last place. Can be seen for two days at 77 West 28th st., second floor, back room.

A RESPECTABLE GIRL WISHES A SITUATION AS chambermaid and to assist with washing and ironing or housework, in a small family; is honest and obliging, and has good reference from her last place. Call at 132 West 33d st., near 7th av.

A COMPETENT PERSON WISHES A SITUATION AS seamstress, to cut and fit ladies' and children's dresses and do all kinds of family sewing; would take care of children or assist with the chamberwork. Apply for two days at 40 West 13th st., between 5th and 6th avs., back room.

A SITUATION WANTED—BY A RESPECTABLE GIRL, as nurse and seamstress; can cut and fit children's clothes and do all kinds of family sewing. The best of city reference given. Call for two days at 14 East 11th st., near 4th av.

A RESPECTABLE PROTESTANT GIRL WISHES A situation to do general housework, or would do plain cooking, in a small private family. Has the best of city reference. Can be seen for two days at the grocery store 534 Columbia st., Brooklyn.

A RESPECTABLE WOMAN WANTS A SITUATION AS cook, and to assist in the washing; is an excellent bread maker. Has first class city references. Call for two days at 64 West 18th st., near 6th av., first floor.

A LADY WISHES TO PROCURE A GOOD SITUATION for a young woman to nurse a child and sew. Apply for two days at 61 West 19th st.

A SITUATION WANTED—BY A COMPETENT YOUNG woman, as nurse and seamstress; has the best of city reference from her last place. Can be seen for two days at 444 6th av., corner of 27th st.

A LADY, WHOSE TIME IS UNOCCUPIED, WISHES to make engagements to read aloud for ladies and gentlemen; writes a legible hand and would do writing or copying; is also a good chess player; or would accept the position of housekeeper to some wealthy person. Address Frances B., Herald office.

A RESPECTABLE GIRL WISHES A SITUATION AS chambermaid and waitress and to assist in the washing of a small family; can be recommended from her last place, where she lived four years. Can be seen for two days at 490 6th av., room 9.

A RESPECTABLE MARRIED WOMAN, WHO HAS lost her baby, wishes to take one to wet nurse. Apply in 53d st., third door from 2d av., between 1st and 2d avs., third floor.

A SITUATION WANTED—BY A RESPECTABLE German girl, as cook; is also a good washer and ironer; good reference given. Call at 243 7th av., near 26th st.

A SITUATION WANTED—BY A RESPECTABLE PROTESTANT girl, as chambermaid, or to take care of children, in a small family; never lived out before. Apply for two days at 98 Christopher st.

A SITUATION WANTED—BY A VERY RESPECTABLE girl, as plain cook, or as laundress; can be seen Tuesday and Wednesday. Call at 49 Bank st., in the front basement.

A RESPECTABLE PROTESTANT GIRL WANTS A situation to do general housework in a small private family. Can be seen at 121 East 20th st., in the basement.

A SITUATION WANTED—BY A RESPECTABLE young woman, to do chamberwork; would have no objection to do light housework; is capable of doing both. Has the best of city reference. Can be seen at 479 7th av. till suited.

AS SEAMSTRESS AND NURSE.—WANTED, BY A young woman of 12 years experience, a situation as seamstress and nurse; is capable of taking the entire charge of an infant from its birth; an excellent family seamstress; understands operating on Wheeler & Wilson's sewing machine. Good city reference. Can be seen at 36 West 13th st., between 5th and 6th aves.

A SITUATION WANTED—BY A YOUNG GIRL, AS nurse and to do light chamberwork, or chamberwork and waiting; can furnish three years' reference from last place employed. Inquire at 160 West 43d st.

A YOUNG GIRL WISHES A SITUATION AS CHAMBERMAID and waitress, or as nurse and seamstress, in a private family. Call for two days at 55 2d av., between 31st and 32d sts., top floor, back room.

A RESPECTABLE YOUNG GIRL WISHES A SITUATION to do general housework in a small family, or to go as chambermaid and waitress; has good city references. Can be seen at 166 22d st., between 1st and 2d avs., first floor, back room.

A RESPECTABLE GIRL WANTS A SITUATION AS good cook; she thoroughly understands her business; is willing to assist in washing. Best of city reference. Call at 223 West 33d st., second floor, back room.

AS COOK.—WANTED, BY A MOST EXPERIENCED woman, who has lived in some of the best families, a situation as cook in all its branches; understands all kinds of pastry, soups and fancy dishes; makes excellent bread and biscuit. Best of city reference. Call at 335 3d av., near 26th st., in the store.

COOK.—A SITUATION WANTED, BY A RESPECTABLE young girl, as cook, washer and ironer in a small private family. Best of references. Apply at 556 3d av., between 36th and 39th streets.

SITUATION WANTED—TO DO GENERAL HOUSEwork in a small family, by an honest, obliging girl; is a good washer and ironer and can give good city reference. Can be seen for two days at 314 Hicks st., South Brooklyn.

SITUATIONS WANTED—BY TWO RESPECTABLE young women; one to cook, wash and iron, the other to go as chambermaid and waiter. Has no objections to assist in the washing and ironing. The best of city and country reference. Call at No. 75 West 19th st., a few doors of 6th av.

SITUATION WANTED—BY A RESPECTABLE YOUNG woman, as cook or to do general housework; is an excellent washer and ironer. The best of city reference from her last place. Can be seen for two days at 109 6th st., room 12.

SITUATION WANTED—BY A GOOD COOK; NO OBjection to assist in washing and ironing in a private family; good reference. Call at 36 West 13th st.

TO TAKE CARE OF CHILDREN.—SITUATION WANTed, by a Protestant girl, to take care of children. Can give the best of recommendations. Apply at 343 West 23d st., this day.

TWO SISTERS WISH TO OBTAIN SITUATIONS; ONE as chambermaid and waitress, or waitress alone; the other as seamstress and to do light chamberwork; can do all kinds of family sewing, and is willing to make herself generally useful. Best of city reference can be given. Can be seen for two days at 203 West 22d st., in the rear, first floor.

TWO GERMAN GIRLS WANT SITUATIONS IN A private family, one to cook, wash and iron, the other as chambermaid. Call at 233 6th st.

WANTED—SITUATIONS IN A PRIVATE FAMILY, by two young ladies; one as cook and the other as chambermaid. Inquire at 48 Spring st., for two days.

WANTED—A SITUATION, BY A RESPECTABLE girl, to take care of children. Can be seen for two days, from 1 to 5, at 188 Dean st., Brooklyn.

WANTED—A SITUATION, BY A RESPECTABLE girl, as chambermaid and seamstress; good city reference can be given. Apply at 123 West 33d st.

SITUATIONS WANTED—FEMALES.

WANTED—A SITUATION, BY A YOUNG GIRL, TO do up stairs work or help in the kitchen. Best of reference from her last place. Call for two days at 99 Fulton st., Brooklyn, from 10 till 4.

WANTED—A SITUATION, BY A YOUNG SCOTCH woman, as stewardess. Excellent reference as to respectability, &c. Call at Mrs. Walton's, 689 Broadway.

WANTED—A SITUATION, BY A YOUNG WOMAN, AS wet nurse. Call this day at 361 Cumberland st., Brooklyn.

WANTED—A SITUATION, IN A SMALL FAMILY, AS good plain cook, washer and ironer; or would do general housework. Call at No. 111½ 24th st., between 6th and 7th avs.

WANTED—A SITUATION, BY A RESPECTABLE young girl, to do chamberwork or mind children; has no objection to travel with a lady; has three years' reference from her last place. Call at 192 7th av., between 23d and 24th sts., first floor, front room.

WANTED—SITUATIONS, BY TWO RESPECTABLE girls; one as plain cook and laundress, the other as waitress and chambermaid. Can be seen for two days at 417 3d av.

WANTED—BY A YOUNG WOMAN, A SITUATION AS lady's dressmaker and seamstress; can cut and fit do all kinds of family sewing on Grover & Baker's machine. Can be seen for two days at 125 West 24th st., near 7th ave.

WANTED—A SITUATION AS PLAIN COOK, WASHER and ironer in a private family, or to do waiting and assist at washing. Call for two days at 126 Clinton place, second floor, front room.

WANTED—BY A RESPECTABLE GIRL, A SITUATION as chambermaid and waitress, or as chambermaid and children's maid. Has good reference. Address 136 West 36th st., for two days.

WANTED—BY A RESPECTABLE YOUNG WOMAN, A situation as waitress in a hotel or private boarding house. Has good city reference. Call at 113 East 22d st., between 2d and 3d avenues, for two days.

WANTED—A SITUATION, BY A RESPECTABLE girl, to do chamber work and assist with the washing and ironing. Good city reference from her last place. Can be seen for two days at 512 3d av., between 38th and 39th sts.

WANTED—A SITUATION IN A SMALL PRIVATE family in Brooklyn, to do general housework, by a neat, industrious and capable girl. Reference from last place. Inquire at 175 Duffield st., Brooklyn.

WANTED—A SITUATION, BY A RESPECTABLE woman, in a small respectable family, to do general housework. Call at 285 West 28th st.

WANTED—BY A RESPECTABLE YOUNG GIRL, A situation to do general housework in a small private family; is willing to make herself generally useful. Can be seen for two days at 251 West 50th st.

WANTED—A SITUATION AS CHAMBERMAID AND waitress, by a respectable girl; she is efficient and can give the best city reference for honesty, &c. Call at No. 4 Sands st., corner Fulton st., Brooklyn.

WANTED—A SITUATION, BY A RESPECTABLE woman, as nurse and plain sewer or up stairs work; no objection to go in the country; best of city reference from her last place, where she lived three years and a half. Inquire for two days at 65 Douglass st., Brooklyn, first floor, front room.

WANTED—BY A RESPECTABLE YOUNG GIRL, who can give the best of city references, a situation as chambermaid and waitress or to assist in washing and ironing and take care of children; would have no objection to do general housework in a small private family. Apply at 390 4th av., second door above 28th st.

SITUATIONS WANTED—FEMALES.

WANTED—BY A RESPECTABLE YOUNG WOMAN, a situation as cook; understands baking and is capable of her business; good reference. Can be seen for two days at 365 6th av., near 23d st., top floor.

WANTED—A SITUATION, BY A RESPECTABLE and competent young woman, as first class cook in all its branches; the very best city reference can be given; is obliging. Can be seen for two days, if not engaged, at 116 West 27th st.

WANTED—A SITUATION, BY A RESPECTABLE girl, as plain cook, washer and ironer; has the best of city reference. Can be seen for two days by applying at 228 Schermerhorn st., Brooklyn.

WANTED—BY A PROTESTANT WOMAN, A SITUATION to cook, wash and iron in a small family. Best reference from her last place. Can be seen for two days at 287 Spring st.

WANTED—WASHING, BY A COMPETENT LAUNDRESS; ladies' or gentlemen's washing, or for families; can do up shirts in the best style. Call at 249 West 18th st., second floor, back room.

WANTED—BY A FIRST CLASS WASHERWOMAN, ladies' and gentlemen's washing, at 70 3d av. Inquire in the store.

WANTED—A SITUATION TO DO CHAMBERWORK and waiting or general housework in a private family, by a respectable woman. Best of references. Address 113 West 15th st.

WANTED—A SITUATION, BY A YOUNG WOMAN, to do general housework in a private family; is a good plain cook and excellent washer and ironer; has good city reference. Can be seen for two days at 564 2d av., up one pair of stairs, back room.

WANTED—A SITUATION, BY A YOUNG GIRL, TO DO chamberwork and sewing, or to take care of children. Best city reference. Call for two days at 208 West 16th st., between 7th and 8th avs.

WANETD—A SITUATION AS LADY'S MAID, OR seamstress, by a respectable woman, who has had several years experience. Best of city reference given. Address or call at 877½ Broadway.

WANTED—A SITUATION, BY A YOUNG GIRL, WHO can do general housework; good city reference given. Apply at 214 East 21st st., up one flight of stairs, back room.

WANTED—BY A DOUNG WOMAN, A SITUATION TO do general housework; is a good washer and ironer; can do plain cooking. Call at 25 Hester st.

WANTED—A SITUATION, BY A RESPECTABLE woman, as cook; has no objection to assist in the washing and ironing in a private family; can be well recommended from her last place. Can be seen for two days at 156, southwest corner of 37th st. and 2d av.

WANTED—BY A RESPECTABLE GIRL, A SITUATION as cook, washer and ironer in a small family. The best city reference. Call at 120 7th av., top floor, front room.

WANTED—BY A GIRL 14 YEARS OF AGE, A HOME in a respectable family; a situation to do light housework; is willing and obliging. Apply for two days at 124 Henry st.

WANTED—A SITUATION AS NURSE AND SEAMSTRESS; is competent to take charge of an infant; or as lady's maid. Good city reference. Address 120 West 20th st., near 7th av.

WANTED—BY A RESPECTABLE YOUNG WOMAN, a situation as chambermaid and waitress in a private family, or to do kitchen work; the best of reference. Call at 69 Butler st., Brooklyn.

WANTED—BY A RESPECTABLE GIRL, A SITUATION as good cook, washer and ironer. Good city reference. Call for two days at 2.1 West 21st st., between 8th and 9th avs.

THE TRADES

A GOOD TINSMITH WANTED—ACCUSTOMED TO sheet iron and brass work for ships. Apply at 231 West st.

A SITUATION WANTED—BY A SWISS WATCHMAKER, who thoroughly understands his business. Can give the best of references. Call at 113 West 15th st. on F Hauser.

A FIRST CLASS BONNET FRAMEMAKER WANTED—Also a few Apprentices to learn the trade. Apply at 602 2d avenue.

GILDERS WANTED.—INQUIRE OF B. PHILIPS French's Hotel, on Wednesday from 7 to 8 o'clock A.M.

PLUMBERS WANTED—SIX GOOD JOURNEYMAN plumbers, with good pay and steady employment. Apply to J. & H. Jones & Co., 38 and 40 White st., from 9 to 11 A. M.

TO BOOKBINDERS.—WANTED, THREE PLAIN FORwarders, three casemakers. Apply to Altemus & Co., northwest corner of 4th and Race sts., Philadelphia.

TO JEWELLERS.—GOLD VEST CHAIN MAKERS wanted immediately, on first class work. Also, three respectable boys to learn the trade. Apply to Jahne, Smith & Co., 95 and 97 Cliff street.

TO SHIRT MANUFACTURERS.—A FINE AND STYlish shirt cutter and fitter wishes a situation in a fine custom shirt department, or as head man in a shirt manufactory; understands the business from A to Z; has a long experience; best city reference. Address A. Z., Shirt Manufacturer, Herald office.

TWO TIN AND SHEET IRON WORKERS WANTED.—Steady employment and good wages will be given to two well recommended workmen. Apply this day, from two till five P. M., at the National Stove Works, 239 Water st.; or address Chadeayne & Brother, Yonkers, N. Y.

TIN AND SHEET IRON WORKERS WANTED—THOSE who understand furnace and hot air work preferred; good wages and steady work; also two or three boys who have worked two or three years at the trade; also a man who understands cleaning and repairing furnaces and ranges. Apply to W. C. Lesster, 1,279 Broadway, corner 34th st.

TO BOOKBINDERS.—WANTED, TWO FORWARDERS. Apply at 115 Franklin street. D. McLEOD.

TO KEROSENE OIL MANUFACTURERS.—WANTED, a situation as foreman in oil works, by a man who thoroughly understands the refining of petroleum oil. Good references. Address G. H. B., Herald office.

WANTED—SIX SILK HAT FINISHERS. EXPENSES paid to Philadelphia. Address immediately P. Herst & Co., 36 South 5th st., Philadelphia.

WANTED—SIX IRON MOULDERS FOR BENCH work. Apply at 87 and 89 Beekman st.

WANTED—AN EXPERIENCED LOCKSMITH AND Bell hanger, to go a short distance into the country. Apply at 26 Beekman street, between 12 and 2 P. M.

WANTED—A COMPETENT MAN TO TAKE CHARGE of a well established file manufactory in a Western city; also, a few good file cutters; none but those thoroughly posted in the business need apply. To the party taking charge of the factory liberal inducements will be offered. Apply to W. H. Sage, at the St. Nicholas, or to Louderback, Griswold & Co., 23 Park row, until the 24th inst.

WANTED—A GOOD HARNESS MAKER, PERMAnently. Apply at 23 West 13th st.

WANTED—A FIRST CLASS PANTS AND VEST cutter on customer work. Salary $1,500 a year. Address Granville Stokes, 609 Chestnut st., Philadelphia. Refer to R. Watkinson, at Brooks Brothers.

WATCHMAKER WANTED—ONE WHO THOROUGHly understands his business. Apply to Jos. Solomons, 427 Broadway.

THE TRADES.

WANTED—A GOOD JOURNEYMAN BARBER, TO GO to Orange, N. J.; steady employment. Inquire of Frank Wishart, with J. B. Bynnes, between 8 and 11 A. M., at 175 Broadway, up stairs.

WANTED—TEN GOOD SEGAR MAKERS; NONE BUT good workmen need apply to W. H. Vanderveer, 130th st. and 3d av., Harlem.

WANTED—ONE HUNDRED SEGAR MAKERS. APply at 356 Pearl st., fourth floor.

HELP WANTED—MALES.

AGENTS WANTED.—$2 POSITIVELY MADE FROM 20 cents; urgently needed by every person. Call and examine, or ten samples sent free by mail for 20 cents—retails for $2—by R. L. WOLCOTT, 170 Chatham square, N.Y.

A SALESMAN WANTED—IN A RETAIL DRY goods store in Jersey City. Apply to J. Allen, 205 Grove st., Jersey City.

A BOY WANTED—WHO UNDERSTANDS THE BUSIness, to attend bar, open oysters and make himself generally useful. The best of reference required. Apply corner of 59th st. and Broadway, Park House.

BOY WANTED—IN A LAWYER'S OFFICE; ONE who is accustomed to the business. Apply at 18 Wall st., room 31.

NOW THEN, BOYS, FOR PRIZE MONEY.—WANTED, for a gunboat going on the blockade, 20 landsmen, green hands, coal passers, machinists, blacksmiths and firemen. Ship for one year, unless sooner discharged. $19 50 to $31 50 a month; $54 to $90 advance.
F. GALLAGHER, naval rendezvous, 174 South street.

WANTED—A CANVASSER FOR A FIRE INSURANCE company. Applicants will please give their names, address and references. None need apply without unexceptional references. Address box 2,904 Post office, N. Y.

WANTED—A PRACTICAL, STEADY MAN, TO TAKE the full charge of my pianoforte manufactory. Also ten men to work at finishing and regulating. Apply to J. P. HALE, 478 Broadway.

WANTED—A PERSON OF EXPERIENCE, FROM 30 to 40 years of age, to conduct a general, domestic and foreign correspondence. Address box 493 New York Post office.

WANTED—A SALESMAN, WHO UNDERSTANDS THE fish and provision business. Address, with reference and particulars, Provisions, Herald office. Must be sharp and shrewd.

WANTED—IN A RETAIL DRY GOODS STORE, A young man, as salesman; one who speaks German preferred. Apply at 599 8th av.

WANTED—A BOY IN AN OFFICE.—APPLY, WITH references, at No. 195 Broadway, room No. 8, afer nine o'clock.

WANTED—A STRONG YOUTH, AS PORTER, REferences required. Apply at 579 Broadway, up stairs.

WANTED—A GOOD STABLE MAN, WHO UNDERstands the care of horses and washing wagons; also an experienced driver. Apply at 118 Clinton place, near 6th av.

WAITER WANTED—A STEADY SINGLE MAN, ACcustomed to waiting in private families, is wanted by a family in Baltimore. Those who can give unquestionable testimonials will apply at room 81 Fifth Avenue Hotel, on Tuesday and Wednesday, from 9 to 11 A. M., or 7 to 9 P. M.

FRENCH ADVERTISEMENTS.

ON DEMANDE—DEUX FILLES FRANCAISE, UNE de 16 a 20 ans, pour soigner deux petits enfants, et l'autre pour soigner un enfant et femme de chambre. Il faut qu'elle sache coudre. S'adresser au 36 Amity st., avant midi, Lundi et Mardi.

HELP WANTED—FEMALES.

A LADY GOING TO EUROPE WISHES A PERSON to take charge of children during the voyage; one who is not liable to sea sickness would be preferred. Apply to Mrs. Woolf, at Dr. Anderson's house, New York av., Clifton, Staten Island.

A NURSE WANTED—ONE ENTIRELY QUALIFIED to take entire charge of an infant six months old. Apply at 224 Wooster st., in the day time.

A GOOD COOK, WASHER AND IRONER WANTED—at 31 7th av. Apply from 9 to 2.

COLORED COOK WANTED—AT THE "WORTH House," corner of Twenty fifth street and Broadway; one who can bring the best recommendations as to cooking in all its branches. None others need apply.

GOOD SERVANTS AND GOOD SITUATIONS MAY BE obtained at Clinton Hall, on Astor place, a few doors east of Broadway, formerly at the Bible House. German, Dutch, Italian and French languages spoken.
Rev. WM. DEMAREST, Superintendent.

NURSE AND SEAMSTRESS.—WANTED, A PROTESTant woman, accustomed to the care of children, and with good city references. Apply at 82 10th st., near 5th av., between 10 and 5.

TWO COLORED GIRLS WANTED—A COOK AND chambermaid; must have good references. Apply at 48 West 33d st.

WANTED—IN A PRIVATE FAMILY IN BROOKLYN, two suitable young women, who can bring good references from their last places—one as chambermaid and waitress, and the other as nurse and seamstress. Apply to Mrs. Osborn, Clinton av., between Myrtle and DeKalb avs., Brooklyn.

WANTED—A RESPECTABLE FEMALE, TO SELL A popular article required in every family; an investment of four to eight dollars. Five dollars per day can be made; the money refunded if not sold. Call at No. 34 West 15th st.

WANTED IMMEDIATELY—A WOMAN TO TAKE care of a child and assist in housework; she must be strong and come well recommended. Apply at 313 East 30th st.

WANTED—A GIRL, AS CUTTER, IN BABCOCK'S cloak and mantilla store. Apply immediately at 111 Chambers st.

WANTED—20 OPERATORS, ON WHEELER & WILson's sewing machines to work on fine flannel shirts. None but first class hands need apply, at 22 Warren st.

WANTED—IN BROOKLYN, A NEAT, TIDY GIRL, TO do general housework. Apply in Clinton av., between Lafayette and Greene avs., west side.

WANTED—AN EXPERIENCED PROTESTANT COOK, who understands baking, and is willing to assist in washing and ironing. Apply before 12 o'clock on Monday or Tuesday, at 15 West 29th st.

WANTED IMMEDIATELY—FOR A SMALL FAMILY, without children, an entire Second or Third floor, with five or six rooms unfurnished, with all modern improvements, not above Fifteenth street, in a private house. Address, for three days, R. B., box 1,214 Post office.

WANTED—A YOUNG GERMAN GIRL, IN AN AMERIcan family, to take care of children and do plain sewing. Apply at 303 West Houston st.

WANTED—A HOUSEKEEPER, WITH GOOD REFErence, by a widower of respectability; either a single woman or a widow without children. To save time and trouble, address, stating age and qualifications, John White, box 106 Herald office.

WANTED—A MIDDLE AGED WOMAN, FOR NURSE and chambermaid. Must come with good references. Wages $7. Apply at 267 Pearl st., Brooklyn.

WANTED—A GIRL TO COOK, WASH AND IRON, and to do the housework of a small genteel family; no children; a good willing servant required; must come well recommended from last place, with city references. Apply this morning, from 10 to 1 o'clock, at 105 East 39th st., between Lexington and 3d avs.

WANTED—A TRUTHFUL, TIDY GIRL FOR GENEral housework. German preferred. Apply in the bakery 456 Greenwich st.

WANTED—A GIRL, FOR GENERAL HOUSEWORK. Apply this day at 18 Mansfield place, West 51st st., at basement, after 10 o'clock.

WANTED—A GOOD GIRL, GERMAN PREFERRED, as chambermaid in a small family. Apply at 200 2d ave., between 10 and 5 o'clock.

WANTED—TWO RESPECTABLE GIRLS; ONE TO cook, wash and iron, and the other as chambermaid and waitress; must come provided with good city reference. Apply at 162 West 34th st.

WANTED—TWO YOUNG LADIES, WHO THOroughly understand the business of ladies hair dressing and wig making. Apply at 251 Grand st., up stairs.

WANTED—A SEAMSTRESS, WHO UNDERSTANDS cutting and fitting; has to take care of a child two years old. Apply at 257 West 22d st., from 10 to 1 o'clock.

WANTED—A GIRL, WITH CITY REFERENCES, FOR general housework; must be a good cook, washer and ironer. Apply at the basement door, 162 West 11th st.

WANTED—A TRIMMER FOR A FIRST CLASS MILlinery establishment in Philadelphia. Address immediately E. G., Herald office.

WANTED—A GOOD ORDER COOK, EITHER MALE or female. Apply at dining saloon, 284 Greenwich st. None but competent persons need apply; also an experienced waiter.

WANTED—A SEAMSTRESS, BY THE MONTH, WHO understands sewing on Wheeler & Wilson's sewing machine. Apply this day at Bell Institute, 15 West 5th st., between 5th and 6th avs.

WANTED—BY A SMALL PRIVATE FAMILY, TWO colored women; one to cook, wash and iron; the other as chambermaid and seamstress. Apply at 115 East 12th st., near 3d av.

WANTED.—A GIRL, WHO SPEAKS OR UNDERstands Spanish, to attend a lady and children. Apply at room 4, No. 21 Broadway.

WANTED—LADIES OF GOOD ADDRESS CAN OBtain situations to wait on tables, at liberal salaries, by applying at the Reveille Saloon, during this week, from two to four P.M.

WANTED—A GOOD LAUNDRESS, TO ASSIST IN chamberwork; wages $6. Also a good waitress; wages $7. Best city reference required. Apply at 61 West 19th st., between 9 and 12 o'clock.

WANTED—IN A SMALL FRENCH FAMILY, A GOOD competent girl, to do the housework; must be a fine washer and ironer; wages $8. City references. Call at 92 East 31st st., Tuesday and Wednesday, Sept. 22 and 23, in the afternoon.

WANTED—A GOOD COOK, BAKER, WASHER AND ironer. Apply at 67 Willoughby st., Brooklyn, on Wednesday, from 10 A. M. to 4 P. M.

WANTED—IN A PRIVATE FAMILY, A PROTESTant girl, to cook, wash and iron; good references required. Apply for two days at 167 Amity st., Brooklyn.

WANTED—A FIRST RATE LAUNDRESS TO TAKE home the washing of a lady, child and maid; must understand fluting. $9 per month. Apply for three days, before 10 A. M., at 42 West 28th st.

WANTED—A COMPETENT WOMAN TO COOK, WASH and iron; must thoroughly understand cooking and be an excellent baker of bread; best of city reference required. Call at 32 West 34th st.

WANTED—A FIRST CLASS LAUNDRESS; GOOD reference required. Call at 76 West 42d st.

1,000 CLOAK MAKERS WANTED.—TO GOOD seamstresses, experienced hands, who thoroughly understand the work, we can give steady employment and the highest pay. Apply this day at the cloak manufactory (rear entrance) of Allen & Paine, 334 Broadway.

SITUATIONS WANTED—MALES.

A YOUNG MAN, LATELY FROM THE SEAT OF WAR, wishes a situation as entry clerk or assistant bookkeeper; can give the best of city reference. Apply to George Robinson, 270 9th street.

A YOUNG MAN OF SOBER AND INDUSTRIOUS habits wishes a situation as clerk or porter in some respectable business; satisfactory reference given. Address J. M., box 112 Herald office.

A SITUATION WANTED—BY A YOUNG MAN, AS valet to a gentleman, or would learn the druggist business, either in the United States or elsewhere, either with a surgeon or doctor; also is a good writer, waiter or servant; sober, honest, and willing to work. Good city or country reference given if desired. Call for four days at Peter Schubid's, for Thos. Quinn, No. 1 Greenwich st., N. Y.

DRUG CLERK.—THE ADVERTISER, A RESPECTAble young man, with seven years' experience and good city references, requires a situation in a first class retail store; understands the compounding of medicines thoroughly. Address Drug Clerk, Herald office.

SITUATION WANTED—BY A RESPECTABLE YOUTH 16 years of age (who resides with his parents), either in a wholesale grocery or hardware store; or any other genteel employment. The best testimonials as to character given. Address P. H., box 125 Herald office.

SITUATION WANTED—BY A YOUNG MAN OF INtegrity and good business habits, as clerk or salesman in a wholesale grocery or dry goods house, or in any position where strict attention to business and the interest of his employers would secure him a fair remuneration; has had considerable experience in bookkeeping, and is a good penman. The best of reference as to ability, character, &c. Address R. H. C., care of Williams & Co., 469 Broadway.

SITUATION WANTED—BY A GENTLEMAN, WHO has a knowledge of paper; would take the management of a warehouse or travel for a firm. He also has been accustomed to the publication of newspapers and periodicals, and could take a situation in that line. Address Selwyn, Herald office.

SITUATION WANTED—BY AN HONEST BOY, IN A store; he can bring good recommendations and is well acquainted with the city. Address L. M., box 207 Herald office.

THE ADVERTISER, HAVING HIS TIME ONLY PARtially occupied, would devote a few hours every afternoon to keeping a set of books, copying, or in any capacity requiring the services of an experienced business man. Terms reasonable. Address Industry, box 228 Herald office.

WANTED—A SITUATION, BY A YOUNG MAN, IS A Civil and Mining Engineer and Surveyor, is a good draughtsman, topographical and right line. For the last two years has commanded a light battery in the Army of the Potomac. Address F. P., Herald office.

A YOUNG MAN, 20 YEARS OF AGE, A GOOD PENman and quick at figures, wishes a situation as clerk or assistant bookkeeper. Can give good reference. Address W. M. T., Herald office, for three days.

WANTED—A SITUATION AS ASSISTANT BOOKkeeper, by a young man without experience, a graduate of a commercial college. Good reference relative to character given. Address H. V. S., box 127 Herald office.

For other wants see ninth page.

The Daily Journal.

VOL. 13.—NO. 15. WILMINGTON, N. C., WEDNESDAY EVENING, SEPTEMBER 23, 1863. WHOLE NUMBER 3,675

BY FULTON & PRICE, PROPRIETORS.

JAS. FULTON, Editor,...A. L. PRICE, Associate Editor.

TERMS OF SUBSCRIPTION—CASH IN ADVANCE.
12 months.......................................$10 00
6 ....5 50
3 ....3 00

The Daily Journal will be supplied by the month to soldiers only, for ONE DOLLAR.

Weekly Paper per year,..........................4 00

No subscription received for the Weekly Paper for less than 12 months.

The paper will be discontinued at the expiration of the time paid for unless renewed.

All letters on business connected with this office, must be addressed to the proprietors.

BUSINESS AND PROFESSIONAL CARDS

WM. P. CAMPBELL,
COMMISSION AND FORWARDING MERCHANT,
St. George's, Bermuda.
REFER TO
Maj. Norman S. Walker, St. George's, Bermuda.
Jno. Stewart, Esq., Richmond, Va.
Rickarby, Campbell & Co., Mobile, Ala.
A. F. Ravenel, Esq., President N. E. R. R. Co., Charleston, S. C.
DeRosset, Brown & Co., Wilmington, N. C.
Sept. 12th, 1863. 6-2m

[The Mobile Register, Montgomery Advertiser, Augusta Constitutionalist, Savannah Republican, Charleston Courier, Columbia, (S. C.,) Guardian, Petersburg Express, Richmond Enquirer and Richmond Dispatch, will please copy the above card for two months and forward bills *immediately* to this office for payment.] 6-tf

GEO. O. VANAMRINGE, SEN.,
COMMISSION MERCHANT,
Wilmington, N. C.
August 26, 1863. 270-1m*

WM. G. CRENSHAW, JAMES R. CRENSHAW.
JOSEPH H. CRENSHAW.
CRENSHAW BROTHERS.
GENERAL COMMISSION MERCHANTS,
Office with E. Murray & Co.,
NORTH WATER STREET,
WILMINGTON, N. C.
Aug. 14th, 1863. 261-2m*

W. H. LIPPITT,
WHOLESALE AND RETAIL DRUGGIST AND CHEMIST. Prescriptions accurately compounded.
N. CORNER FRONT & MARKET STS.,
Wilmington, N. C.
March 25, 1863. 141-1y.

WALKER MEARES,
WHOLESALE AND RETAIL DRUGGIST,
37 Market Street,
Iron Front Building,
Wilmington, N. C.
Feb. 27, 1863. 119-1y

"THE ST. GEORGE'S FANCY STORE,"
(BERMUDA,)
WM. HENRY GRISET,
DEALER IN PERFUMES, HAIR OIL, BRUSHES, PICTURES, STATIONERY, TOYS, FANCY ARTICLES IN VARIETY, WOOD AND WILLOW WARE, BOOTS AND SHOES, FRENCH WINES, &c., &c., &c.
Orders for Goods carefully attended to.
July 18th, 1863 238-3m*

OPEN AGAIN.
THE PALMETTO HOTEL is again open for the reception of visitors. The House has been thoroughly renovated.
JAMES H. BAILEY.
Nov. 24, 1862 38-tf

POTASH—POTASH.
A FIRST RATE ARTICLE for sale by the barrel. Orders solicited.
B. G. WORTH & CO.
June 26th, 1862. 220-3m.

SOAP—SOAP!
EQUAL TO ANY received through the blockade, is now manufactured in Wilmington, by the subscriber, and can be had by the pound or box, at the store on Market street, one door west of Bradley's old stand.
H. MARCUS.
May 1, 1863. 187-tf.

SALT FOR SALE.
APPLY at the Store of Mr. Geo. Myers', Front Street.
THOMAS EVANS.
Aug. 27th, 1862 297-tf

FOR RENT,
FOR ONE YEAR from the 1st of October next, that desirable residence on Front Street, opposite the Bank of Wilmington, lately occupied by Edward P. Hall, deceased.
For terms apply to H. A. Bagg or the subscriber.
ELI W. HALL.
Sept. 11th, 1863. 5-tf

VALUABLE SOUND LAND FOR SALE.
THE SUBSCRIBER will offer to the highest bidder, in the Town of Wilmington, on Saturday, the 26th of this month, a track of LAND in this County, situated on the Plank Road, eight miles from Wilmington, and generally known as the Eight Mile Place. The track contains seven hundred acres more or less, and joins the lands of Reuben Everitt, O. F. Alexander and Frederick Moore.
There are two tracts of this land, and will be sold seperate if desired. This is a rare chance for salt makers, as the lands are well timbered and not far from the Sound.—Terms made known on day of sale.
R. N. BLOODWORTH.
Sept. 16. 3-10t*

SALT PAN TAKEN BY MISTAKE.
A CAST IRON GRANULATING PAN was taken by mistake from the Wilmington and Weldon Railroad Depot, some time within the last two months. The pan was slightly cracked in casting and banded with bar-iron lengthwise on each side.
It is thought that the pan had the name of the subscriber on it, but this is not certain.
Any person having said pan will please communicate with James Anderson, Esq., Wilmington, N. C.
J. H. BURNETT.
Sept. 17. 10 6t

STATESVILLE MALE SEMINARY.
WILL RE-OPEN Monday, Sept. 14th, in charge of G. W. JEWETT, late Principal of Wilmington Male and Female Seminary.
For particulars address him at Statesville, N. C.
Aug. 26th, 1863 270-3w

$20 REWARD.
STRAYED OR STOLEN, from Camp Davis, about seven miles from Wilmington, on Saturday, the 19th inst., two HORSES, viz: One a medium size dark Bay, black feet and legs, a sore about one and a half inches in diameter on the top and side of the right shoulder. The other a medium size light Sorrel, being shod infront only; C. S. on the left shoulder, but the C. hardly visible. The above reward will be paid for their delivery at the above Camp, or for any information that will lead to their recovery. Address
P. T. WOODSON,
Asst. Surgeon 3d N. C. Battalion, or
A. M. DARDEN,
Lieut. Co. C, 3d N. C. Battalion.
Sept. 22. 14-4t*

RAIL ROADS.

WIL. & WEL. RAIL ROAD CO.,
Engineer & Superintendent's Office,
Wilmington, Sept. 19th, 1863.
WANTED IMMEDIATELY
25 GOOD CARPENTERS to work on cars, for which the highest market prices will be paid.
S. L. FREMONT,
Eng. & Supt.
Sept. 19. 12-tf

PRESIDENT AND DIRECTORS' OFFICE,
Laurinburg, Sept. 15th, 1863.
THE ANNUAL MEETING of the Stockholders of the Wilmington, Charlotte & Rutherford Rail Road Company will be held in the Town of Rockingham, on Wednesday, 21st October, 1863.
JAMES I. McCALLUM, Secretary.
Sept. 19th, 1863. 12-tm
Fayetteville Observer, Wadesboro' Argus and Charlotte papers copy till meeting and forward bill to this office.

TRANSPORTATION OFFICE, W. C. & R. R. R.,
Laurinburg, N. C., Aug. 5th, 1863.
PARTIES HAVING FREIGHT in warehouse at Old Hundred, will please come forward, pay charges, and remove their goods on or before the 15th inst., as the Depot will be discontinued on and after the 18th inst.
Freight will be received at 103, on and after the 13th inst. By order.
ROGER P. ATKINSON,
Master Transportation.
Aug 6, 1863. 254-tf

TRANSPORTATION OFFICE,
W., C. & R. R. R.,
Laurenburg, N. C., July 25th.
On and after the 27th day of July, 1863, the Freight Train on this Road will run as follows:
UP. DOWN.
Mondays. Tuesdays.
Thursdays Fridays.
All freight except live stock for up Train from Wilmington, must be delivered at the Warehouse on Tuesdays and Fridays by 2 o'clock P. M.
Live stock at Wilmington for up Train, must be delivered by 8 o'clock A. M., on Wednesdays and Saturdays.
Freight on down Train must be delivered at the Warehouse by 2 o'clock on Mondays and Thursdays.
Goods by Passenger Train taken only at option of Company; then at double rates.
By order.
ROGER P. ATKINSON,
Master of Transportation.
[244-tf]

WILMINGTON & WELDON R. R. CO.,
Superintendent's Office,
Wilmington, N. C., June 1, 1863.
NOTICE TO MECHANICS.
WANTED IMMEDIATELY, at the Shops of this Company, twenty-five good Finishers, two good Moulders three good Blacksmiths—one to be a master workman, for which the highest prices will be paid—per day of 10 hours good and faithful service. None need apply who are not willing to render such service. Apply to
S. L. FREMONT,
Eng. and Supt.
June 1st. 198-tf
Raleigh *Progress*, Charleston *Mercury*, Augusta *Constitutionalist* and Petersburg *Express* copy 3 times and send bills to Superintendent.

Wilmington, Charlotte & R. R. R.
ON and after Wednesday, the 20th inst., the Passenger Train on this Road will run as follows:

UP TRAIN. Tuesdays, Thursdays and Saturdays.		DOWN TRAIN. Mondays, Wednesdays and Fridays.	
Leave Wilmington	9:00 A. M.	Leave 103 at	7:30 A. M
Riverside	10:00 "	Laurinburg	8:37 "
Northwest	10:40 "	Shoe Heel	9:06 "
Marlville	11:28 "	Red Banks	9:22 "
Rosindale	12:17 P. M.	Moss Neck	9:57 "
Brown Marsh	12:52 "	Lumberton	10:36 "
Bladenboro'	1:27 "	Bladenboro'	11:35 "
Lumberton	2:23 "	Brown Marsh	12:10 P. M.
Moss Neck	3:03 "	Rosindale	12:45 "
Red Banks	3:39 "	Marlville	1:32 "
Shoe Heel	3:55 "	Northwest	2:20 "
Laurinburg	4:36 "	Arrive at Riverside	2:58 "
Arrive at 103	5:28 "	Wilmington	4:00 "

By order.
R. P. ATKINSON,
Master of Transportation.
May 16th, 1863. 185-tf

WILMINGTON & WELDON RAILROAD CO.
Office Chief Eng. & Supt.,
Wilmington, March 20th, 1863.
CHANGE OF SCHEDULE.
ON AND AFTER the 20th inst., the trains on this Road will run as follows:
PASSENGER AND MAIL TRAINS.
Leave Wilmington daily at 7 A. M. and 7 P. M.
Arrive at Wilmington daily at 5 A. M. and 4:20 P. M.
Leave Weldon daily at 4 A. M. and 4 P. M.
Arrive daily at Weldon at 8 A. M. and 7.35 P. M.
Passengers going to the North Carolina or Raleigh & Gaston Rail Roads may take either train and will lay over in Goldsboro' from 1.15 A. M. or P. M., until about 7.30 P. M. or A. M., and at Weldon from 8 A. M. or P. M., until 4 P. M. or A. M.
S. L. FREMONT,
Chief Eng. & Supt.
The Railroad time is 15 minutes faster than the town time.
March 20th, 1863 137-tf
Papers on the line please copy.

Office Gen'l Superintendent,
Wilmington and Manchester Rail Road Co.,
Wilmington, N. C., Feb. 18th, 1863.
CHANGE OF SCHEDULE.
ON and after February the 22d, double Daily Passenger Trains will be run on this road as follows:
Leave Wilmington daily, 5.20 P. M. and 6.15 A. M.
Arrive at Kingsville 7.20 A. M. and 7.28 P. M.
Leave Kingsville daily, 4.00 P. M. and 4.45 A. M.
Arrive at Wilmington 6.00 A. M. and 6.00 P. M.
Leave Florence (going South) 2.15 A. M. and 2.50 P. M.
Arrive at Florence (going South) 2.00 A. M. and 2.20 P. M.
The Steam Ferry Boat connecting with these trains leaves the Wilmington & Weldon Depot Wharf at 4.40 P. M. and 5.30 A. M. respectively.
Passengers going to Charleston should take the 6.15 A. M. train to make a close connection at Florence with the North Eastern Rail Road for that place.
HENRY M. DRANE,
Gen'l Sup't.
Feb. 25th, 1863 117-tf

MILITARY NOTICES.

CONFEDERATE STATES OF AMERICA,
Office of the Chief Commissary for the 4th District, Wilmington, N. C., Aug. 31, 1863.
IN ACCORDANCE with directions from the Commissary General, through the Chief Commissary of the State, this District, embracing the counties of New Hanover, Brunswick, Columbus, Bladen, Robeson, Cumberland, Richmond, Anson, Harnett, Moore and Montgomery, has been subdivided and the following officers have been selected as purchasing Commissaries for the various sub-districts, with authority to appoint agents for each county in their respective districts:
Geo. H. Kelly, Agent, Headquarters Lumberton, for the counties of Bladen, Robeson, Richmond and Anson.
J. B. Southerland, Agent, Headquarters Fayetteville, for the counties of Cumberland, Harnett, Moore and Montgomery.
O. Kelly, Agent for the district for the purchase of Beef Cattle.
Farmers having subsistence supplies of any kind for sale, are requested to apply to the Agent of the County in which they may reside.
C. S. McKINNEY,
Capt. & Chief Commissary 4th District.
Sep. 1, 1863. 275-4w
Fayetteville Observer and Presbyterian copy 4 weeks and send bills to this office.

Headquarters District of Cape Fear,
Wilmington, August 19th, 1863.
NOTICE.
THE PUBLIC ARE INFORMED THAT, until further orders, no passes will be given to visit the Forts at the mouth of the river.
(Signed,) W. H. C. WHITING,
Major General.
Official:
A. Vanderhorst, Maj. and A. A. General.
August 19th, 1863. 265-tf.

CAMP OF INSTRUCTION,
Camp Holmes, N. C.,
Aug. 15, 1863.
SPECIAL ORDER NO. 275.
THE FOLLOWING SLAVES have been captured by the military, in attempting to escape to the enemy, and are now in custody at this Camp, subject to the disposal of their owners:
CASON, about 28 years of age, dark complexion, 5 feet 6 inches high, belonging to the estate of Elijah Weeks, Carteret county, and employed by B. Blackman, of Duplin county; JOHN, about 8 years of age, dark complexion, 4 feet 2½ inches high, and NICY, about 30 years of age, dark complexion, 5 feet 3½ inches high, property of Mrs. Odom, of Pollocksville.
By order of
Col. PETER MALLETT,
Comd't of Conscripts for N. C.
J. M. Prior, Adj't. 264-30t

Engineer Department, Wilmington,
July 20th, 1863.
WANTED IMMEDIATELY,
THREE HUNDRED ABLE BODIED NEGROES FOR work on Defences.
For good hands $20,00 per month will be paid, clothing, rations and medical attendance furnished, with guarantee that in case of attack they shall be sent to their homes or a place of safety. A suitable number of overseers, not exceeding one to twenty-five negroes, will be also employed; such overseers to be selected by owners of negroes. First rate overseers will receive $100 per month.
By order of Maj. Gen. Whiting.
WM. H. JAMES,
Capt. and Chief Engineer.
July 23, 1863. 242-tf

CONFEDERATE STATES OF AMERICA,
Engineer Department, Dist. Cape Fear,
Wilmington, N. C., March 16th, 1863.
NOTICE is hereby given to all persons having claims against the Engineer Department, for services of slaves employed as laborers on the *land defences* near Wilmington, N. C., that the undersigned is authorized and prepared to pay the same at his office, on the second floor of the building next above Meares' Drug Store, Market Street.
Persons executing Powers of Atttorney will observe the following form—their signatures, in all cases, to be witnessed by two witnesses and signed in duplicate, or they may be witnessed before a Justice of the Peace or Clerk of any Court.
FORM OF POWER OF ATTORNEY.
I, ———, of ———, do hereby appoint ———, of ———, my true and lawful Agent to sign receipts for, and receive payment of all moneys due to me by the Engineer Department of the Confederate States of America, for the services of my slaves employed as laborers on the land defenses at ———, during the month of ——— 186
Witness, my hand and seal, at ———, this ——— day of ——— 186
(Signed in duplicate.)
———[Seal.]
Witnesses:
———
———
The signatures of colored persons should be witnessed by three witnesses.
There must be separate duplicate Powers of Attorney for each month. Blank forms can be had upon application at this office.
W. H. JAMES,
Capt. & Chief Eng.
July 2nd, 1863. 133-tf
Fayetteville Observer please copy till forbid.

Headquarters District Cape Fear,
Wilmington, N. C., June 28th, 1863.
General Orders,
No. 31.
THE attention of all concerned is called to the order of the Board of Navigation, published on the 26th inst.
The officer in command of Fort St. Phillip will communicate the regulations to all steamers arriving at this port.—He will ascertain and report the date of departure of all steamers from foreign ports, and will see that no vessel passes Fort St. Philip, on her way up, without special authority from these Headquarters, within the limits prescribed by the Quarantine Regulations.
By command of Maj. Gen'l Whiting.
JAMES H. HILL,
Maj. & A. A. General.
June 29. 227-tf

TO THE PEOPLE OF NORTH CAROLINA.
I REQUIRE LABOR for the defence of the State. I have resorted to all methods to procure a sufficient supply, except that of impressment. I now appeal to the patriotism of the citizens.
The last census, I believe, estimates the slave population of the State at upwards of 300,000. Surely, from this number you can supply me with all the force I need. For the present, let me have from 500 to 1000, and bring them forward immediately.
The Chief Engineer in Wilmington, Capt. James, will arrange for receipt, guarantee and terms of payment and provisions.
W. H. C. WHITING,
Major General,
Comd'g Dept. of N. C.
July 18th, 1863 238-tf

SALT—SALT.
A SUPPLY OF OCEAN SALT, a good article received daily, and for sale at lowest market rates.
J. M. MONK, 47 North Water Street.
September 26th, 1863. 17-tf

FOR RENT.
THE HOUSE AND LOT opposite the M. E. Church, on Front Street.
For particulars apply to
JAS. M. MIDDLETON,
Magnolia, N. C.
Aug. 29, 1863. 273-tf

ADVERTISEMENTS
Will be inserted daily at TWO DOLLARS per square of ten lines for the first, and ONE DOLLAR per square for each subsequent insertion—CASH IN ADVANCE.
Advertisements inserted once, twice, or three times a week, will be charged as new advertisements for each insertion.
Advertisements inserted as Special or Bishop Notices are charged one-half more than above rates—eight lines (leaded) or less counted as a square.
No publication made without a responsible name.

MILITARY NOTICES.

Headquarters District Cape Fear,
Wilmington, N. C., Sept. 9th, 1863.
Extract.
Special Orders,
No. 269.
I. SEAMEN belonging to Blockade Running Steamers, will not be allowed on shore after sundown. Major Gibbes will send strong patrols for the purpose of arresting all such found about the streets and loding them in jail.
By command of Maj. Gen. Whiting.
A. VANDERHORST,
Maj. and A. A. Gen'l.
Sept. 9th 3-tf

HEAD QUARTERS DISTRICT OF CAPE FEAR.
Wilmington, September 1st, 1863.
THE FOLLOWING REGULATIONS in regard to Steamers running the Blockade, from and to this Port will be enforced from this date:
I.—Yankee goods must not be imported, upon penalty of confiscation of the goods, except munitions of war and medicines.
II.—Improper or suspicious persons must not be taken as passengers to this port. They must be properly vouched for, and permission given to embark, by Major L. Heyliger, at Nassau, or Major Norman Walker, at Bermuda. Any passenger brought to this port, without proper credentials, will be sent back by the same Steamer.
III.—Steamers will not be permitted to bring in seamen, or other employees of the vessel, to be discharged upon arrival here. In all such cases special permission must be obtained from these Head Quarters.
IV.—Passengers outward-bound must obtain permits from Head Quarters. The officers in charge of boarding vessels will take out such persons as have no permits, and detain the vessel until further orders, if the party is on board by permission of the officers of vessel.
V.—All vessels, after obtaining proper clearances, must apply to Head Quarters for permission to sail, and without such permission will be stopped at the Forts and sent back.
VI.—Letters upon outward and inward bound vessels, must be sent to Head Quarters for inspection and approval. Failure to comply with this rule will involve the offending parties in considerable penalties.
VII.—Lists of the officers and crews of all vessels arriving, must be made out for the inspecting Officer. As spies can more readily ship as seamen or firemen, care must be taken by Captains in selecting their crews.
VIII.—Copies of manifests of cargoes of vessels arriving will be sent to Head Quarters.
IX.—All vessels from Nassau will remain at Quarantine until permission is given to come to the city.
X.—Persons, other than officers of vessels, must be on board by 9 o'clock, P. M., every night, unless by special permission from Head Quarters. Such persons violating this order will be arrested and lodged in guard house.
XI. All official business in relation to Steamers, will be attended to by Major Gibbes.
W. H. C. WHITING,
Major General.
(*Official.*)
J. H. Hill, Maj. & A. A. General. 276-tf

Headquarters Department N. C.,
Wilmington, N. C., Aug. 10th, 1863.
"Extract."
Special Orders
No. 18.
* * * * * *
VII. Hereafter, all officers arriving in the city and remaining over, will report in person at these Headquarters.
* * * * * *
By Command of Maj. Gen. Whiting:
T. BROWN VENABLE,
Maj. & A. A. General.
Aug. 10th, 1863. 257-tf

NAILS AND BI. CARB SODA.
22 KEGS NAILS, assorted sizes;
20 kegs Bi. Carb Soda. For sale by
WORTH & DANIEL,
4 North Water Street.
Aug. 28th, 1863. 272-tf

NOTICE.
PERSONS WISHING MEDICINES will please to send *Vials* and *Pill Boxes*.
WALKER MEARES,
Druggist & Apothecary.
July 30, 1863. 248-tf.

LIGHTERAGE.
ON and after this date, the rates of Lighterage will be as follows:

Bags of Salt, each	40 cents.
Bags Corn, Meal, Flour, Pea Nuts, &c., each	25 "
Barrels of Salt	75 "
Barrels of Spirits Turpentine	75 "
Barrels of Oil	75 "
Tierces of Rice	$1 00
Bales of Cotton	1 00
Bales of Fodder	75 "

Other articles in proportion.
ORRELL & HAWES.
Sept. 14th 7-1m

$30 REWARD.
Camp Davis, Sept. 21, 1863.
THE USUAL REWARD OF $30 each will be paid for the delivery at this Camp, or to the Commandant of the Garrison of Wilmington, of the following enlisted men belonging to Co. B, 1st Battalion N. C. Artillery:
Privates MARSHALL HUNTER and JOSHUA T. LEE, both residents of Duplin County.
Z. ELLIS, Lieut. Com'ndg Co. B,
1st N. C. Battalion Artillery.
Sept. 21. 13-6t*

FOR SALE.
THE MATERIALS FOR A SETT OF SALT WORKS, on Dutchman Creek, in Brunswick County, at Mr. Charles Dosher's Landing, consisting of brick and lumber, a first rate tank and good pump, Salt house, six pans, with wooden sides and very thick wrought iron bottoms; grates, and wrought iron doors. To any person putting up works on Lockwood's Folly, they will be found cheaper than they can buy and pay freight on the articles down there.
For further particulars, apply on the premises to Mr. Dosher, or to
JOHN K. CURRIE.
Sept. 18. 11-6t*

ADMINISTRATOR'S NOTICE.
THE UNDERSIGNED, at September Term, 1863, of New Hanover County Court, having qualified as administrator on the estate of Thomas Murphy, deceased, hereby notifies all persons indebted to the estate of the said deceased to make immediate payment and settlement; and all persons having claims against said estate will present them for payment within the time prescribed by law, or this notice will be pleaded in bar of their recovery.
This, the 17th day of September, 1863.
S. R. BUNTING, Adm'r.
Sept. 17, 1863. 10-6t

THE DAILY JOURNAL.

CONFEDERATE STATES OF AMERICA.

WILMINGTON, N. C., WEDNESDAY, SEPT'R. 23, 1863.

☞SEE READING MATTER, AUCTION SALES AND OTHER ADVERTISEMENTS ON 4TH PAGE.☜

☞Some matters intended for publication to-day, are unavoidably deferred until to-morrow.

THE fighting in Northwestern Georgia still continues, the tide of battle setting apparently towards the Alabama line, that is, assuming that ROSECRANZ is cut off from the route to Tennessee by our forces getting possession of, and holding, the road to Chattanooga. This is the report. If ROSECRANZ does not fall back towards Chattanooga, he will fall back towards Shell Mound or Bridgeport, lower down on the Tennessee. His line of retreat would be made much longer and more difficult, but running through a mountainous country it would afford any number of positions at which to make a stand.

If our latest reports are true, the fighting must have been very desperate and the carnage awful, and the end is not yet. If we have really achieved any important success, we presume that it will be pushed to the utmost, so as to secure all the advantages that can possibly be derived from it.

Yesterday it was expected that LONGSTREET would advance on the enemy's new position on Mission Ridge, which would appear to be eleven miles in the rear of his original position.

The Atlanta papers of yesterday have nothing that tends to throw any additional light upon the position or "situation." We know nothing certainly and can only hope that our loss is not so heavy as reported.

The rumors of General LEE's presence in the West were evidently unfounded. His name is not mentioned in connection with the recent battles.

The reported death of General HOOD is very much doubted in military circles, as the General was still suffering so much from the effects of a wound received at Gettysburg, that it is not believed he was in a condition to go on the field. It is remarked that General BRAGG, in his despatches of the 21st makes no mention of any injury to General HOOD, an omission which would hardly have occurred in regard to an officer of the rank and position of General HOOD, had he indeed been mortally or even seriously wounded. We shall soon learn definitely.

WE like scuppernong grapes very well indeed, and yet while the grape season lasts we are in constant danger of breaking our backs or violating several of the commandments. Night or day the unwary pedestrian is in danger of slipping up and falling *down* over a grape skin, or sundry grape skins, thrown broadcast over the pavement at all the most frequented corners in town. There *may* be saints who can refrain from an audible or at least a mental execration when they find themselves going! gone! but we have our doubts upon the subject, and truly we think the man who deliberately casts his grape skins on the pavements at street corners, to endanger the lives and limbs of men, women and children, deserves something worse than cursing; the huck-negroes who do so ought to be soundly thrashed. A little wholesome fining would do white men no harm. Of course we speak mainly in the interests of religion and morality and to remove the incitements to profanity which these grape-skins are always furnishing.—Finally, if people who slip and perhaps fall upon these things, can't help it, and *must* curse, we do hope that they will remember to curse the person that threw the skins down, and not the skins which has no souls to be cursed.

GOOD NEWS IF TRUE.—One of our citizens, just returned from Augusta, in this State, informs us that he heard, while there, a report, believed by him to be reliable, that a letter has been very recently received by Mrs. Maury from her husband, Lieut. Maury, of the Confederate Navy, from Nassau, stating that there were then three Confederate iron-clads at that port, and that four others were expected in a very short time. Mrs. Maury is now in Columbia, S. C., where she received the letter above mentioned. This intelligence would seem to be, in a measure, corroborative of a despatch from the Chicago Times, in reference to the same subject, which we published yesterday. Our readers will certainly join us in the hope that the report may be founded on fact. What a nice little diversion seven iron-clads might produce on our coast just now!

Columbus Times.

Alluding to the new Confederate rams, the Augusta *Constitutionalist* of Saturday says: "We have information of their whereabouts of a most cheering character, if true, and we are disposed to credit it. They are near enough to the Yankee blockaders to give them a serious butting before many days." We attach little importance to this report, but give it as one of the rumors of the day.

THE DAY OF ATONEMENT.—This (Sept. 23d,) is the Day of Atonement, the most solemn in the Jewish Calendar.—We presume it will be strictly observed by all the members of that denomination.

THE CHARLESTON COURIER states that the big Blakely gun at that place was *not* bursted by reason of its muzzle having been elevated, as learnedly surmised by the Richmond *Examiner*.

THEATRE TO-NIGHT.—"The Toodles," MILLER in his comicalities, and "Betsy Baker."

EARLY COLD.—Frosts have already been felt in Petersburg, Raleigh and Charlotte. This is at least three weeks sooner than the usual appearance even of early frosts. It has been quite cold here at nights but not near freezing.

For the Journal.

Messrs. Fulton & Price:—

Until lately, ever since the Yankees came to Newbern, the negroes in this quarter have had the Abolition fever, but *now* their *fever* has turned to an ague, since they have found out that instead of having been carried to the North and set free and *now* living in brick houses and riding in fine carriages, and eating ham and turkey and drinking French Brandy and Champagne, every negro that has run off to Newbern, since the Yankees came there, is there yet in a most ragged and beggarly condition, working on fortifications and railroads for 8 dollars per month, which pay, *they say themselves*, they have never received, and that Abraham Lincoln's orders are, that the Captain of every vessel that sails from Newbern to the North shall, before leaving that port, take an oath that he has not a negro on board, and the reason why *this* order has been made is, the Northern people have found out that every negro that was stolen from us in the wars of 1776 and 1812 by the *British*, had to be *paid for*, and they have *no idea* of being taxed to pay for our negroes, *especially* as about three-fourths of the people there are opposed to interfering with our institution of slavery. For instance, about *one-half* of the North ern people are *democrats* and *of course* are opposed to Abolitionism; and as for the *other half—the Black Republican party*—only *one-half* of *them* are Abolitionists, whilst *the other half* are *high tariff* men, who care *nothing about* our negroes, but promise the Abolitionists to assist *them* to free our negroes, if *they* would assist *them* to pass their high tariff laws. Yes, our negroes have found out all this; also, that the *New York Herald* has advised Abraham Lincoln to hunt up all the free negroes at the North and send them down South and put them in the front of battle and have *one half* of them killed, and let the *other half* run off and hide in our swamps as the most effectual means of getting clear of them, which plan *Abraham* was not slow to adopt, as his own State has passed a law to prevent free negroes from going there, and *he himself* having said that "the difference between the white and black races *is so broad* that it is *impossible* for the *latter* to ever aspire to a moral, social, and political equality with the *former*, and that he would rather see slavery extended from the *Rio Grande* to the *Saint Lawrence*, than to see the Union dissolved"—which proves how much *he* thinks of the negro.—Yes, our negroes, having found out all this, *now say* they have got enough of Yankee freedom—are *satisfied, especially* as they have also heard that the London *Times* says, "no matter which whips, the North or the South, the negroes are *doomed* to either *slavery* or *extermination*," and that the *Times* justifies our slavery institution on *Bible grounds*; also, that the London *Dispatch* says, "the negroes in *Louisiana* are better off in a state of *slavery*, than they are in *Dahomy free*; that the day the British government set their slaves in their West India possessions free, was the day both the *blacks* and the *whites* went to ruin; that every Journal in London, except a few under the influence of the *Exeter Hall* clique, are opposed to abolitionism; and that the great big Black Republic of *Liberia* is a *total failure*"—has *completely fizzled out*. Messrs. Editors, this war has caused the whole civilized world to enquire into the condition of our slaves, and the result of their enquiry is, that the negro in the Southern Confederacy, in a state of *slavery*, is better off than he is at the North or any where else on earth *free*. The truth is, it would puzzle the wisest statesman, Philosopher and Philanthropist on earth to determine which the negro most stands in need of—*an overseer*, on the account of *his idleness*, or a *guardian*, on account of his *improvidence*—he being *proverbial for both idleness* and *improvidence*. We believe that if our Legislature was to pass a law *to-day* to emancipate our slaves, that it would not be five years before they would desire the law to be repealed. Look at the free negroes all over the State, not half as well provided for as the slaves are, and frequently giving their indentures for life to some white man, or applying to the Legislature to be made slaves. The *negroes themselves* have got sense enough to know that two races, a *superior* one and an *inferior* one, cannot live in the same state on terms of *equality*; that the latter are obliged to be slaves to the former *in fact* if not in *law*. And the *only* difference in being a slave in *law*, and one in *fact*, is this: the *former* has but *one* master, and the latter has a *dozen*—every man in the neighborhood—and it is easier to serve *one* master than it is to serve a *dozen*. Look at the free negroes at the North—99 out of 100 of them the *poorest, raggedest*, and meanest vagabonds on this earth, one half of their time in the daily workhouses and Penitentiaries. And why is this the case? Why, *first*, because of their idleness and improvidence; *second*, because the Yankees cheat them out of what little *they do work for*.

TUCKAHOE.

Lenoir County, N. C.

For the Journal.

HEADQ'RS 1ST N. C. CAVALRY,
Sept. 18th, 1863.

Messrs. Editors: I transmit a list of the casualties in the 1st N. C. Cavalry in the fight of Culpeper, on the 13th of September, for the information of the friends of the Regiment:

Co. A—Killed—None.
Wounded—1st Lieut. J. L. Smith, seriously in right arm.
Missing—Privates J. D. Dixon and Thos. J. Laxton.
Co. B—Killed—None.
Wounded—Lieut. J. W. Peele, severely in left thigh.
Co. C—Killed—None.
Wounded—Capt. M. D. L. McLeod in right arm; Lieut. R. H. Maxwell seriously in arm; Corp. J. Lewallen.
Co. D—Killed—None.
Wounded—Bugler Smith F. Carroll severely in thigh and captured.
Co. E—Killed—None.
Wounded—Private Wm. Green slightly.
Co. F—Mortally Wounded—E. R. Sloan, since died.
Missing—D Harvey Purviance.
Co. G—Killed—None.
Wounded—None.
Missing—Sergt. E. S. Patterson.
Co. H—Killed—None.
Wounded—Privates W. H. Bailey and J. L. McKay, slightly.
Missing—Lieut. Bryan Whitfield, Privates B. F. Whitfield, L. Gurley.
Co. K—Killed—None.
Wounded—T. W. P. Davis.
Missing—Private John N. Arnold.

RECAPITULATION:

Wounded.........11
Missing.........8
Total.........19

D. F. ARMFIELD,
Lieut. and Act. Adjt.

State papers please copy.

For the Journal.

Messrs. Editors:—

I send you this communication, and desire that you will allow it a space in your paper, that the proper authorities may take the matter in hand, and correct, what I deem an abuse of privilege. How is it that the soldiers of certain artillery companies, or *company*, on Topsail Sound, are allowed to catch fish and bring them to market in Government wagons with Government horses and artillery harness, and sell them at one dollar for two and three fish, when our regular fishermen are deprived of the privilege of fishing. We all like fish in Wilmington, having been accustomed to them all our lives. *Is this right?*

Yours, STONO.

Sept. 23d, 1863.

FEDERAL RULE IN NATCHEZ.—Natchez is now completely under Federal rule and her citizens are experiencing that "great love" which Lincoln and his hordes have for those who reside in the South. The people are subjected to every species of indignity and annoyance that can be devised by their persecutors. One singular custom has been introduced that we suppose will be followed up elsewhere, that of compelling ladies who may wish to attend divine service upon the Sabbath day, to procure a Provost Marshal's pass, which must be presented to a pair of drunken Yankee bullies stationed at each door. The Selma *Reporter* comments thus on the matter:

Just think of it a moment, reader! Before our mothers, wives, sisters and daughters can have permission to worship Almighty God in the temples which have been dedicated to His name, they must pass the ordeal of insult at the hands of a dirty, thieving set of rapscallions, hardly fit to have their heads blown off and used as manure for the next cotton crop. And yet there are to be found men who occasionally hope that the glorious Union will once more be reconstructed. Could they be compelled to reside for a short time with their families within the corporate limits of Natchez, they would wish every puritanic knave who hails from Lincoldom plunged into a bath of boiling brimstone, with the privilege of knowing that their agonies were to prove eternal.

The Surrender at Cumberland Gap.

The Bristol (Tenn.) *Advocate* contains some particulars of the surrender of the Confederate force at Cumberland Gap. It says:

It is with deep mortification that we announce the unconditional surrender of Cumberland Gap to the Federal forces on Wednesday, the 7th inst. According to the best information we can gather there were 2,100 men in the garrison when it was surrendered. It is reported however, that something near a thousand refused to comply with the surrender, and made their escape. Of these latter it is said that some two hundred belonged to Col. Slemp's (64th Va.) regiment.—Our loss in stores, arms, &c., must be considerable.—Among them was Leyden's battery, of the 9th Georgia battalion—one of the most splendid batteries in the service. It was presented to the Confederacy by the merchants of Liverpool, and was stationed near this place for several weeks during the past summer. That splendid company, the Gilmer Grays, who were stationed here last winter, are said to be among the captured. But we will not persist in narrating the sickening details. We do not pretend to speak advisedly, but the thing is regarded in intelligent circles here as being one of the most disgraceful occurrences of the war. The garrison is said to have been in command of General Frazier, of whom we know nothing.

That noble regiment, the 1st Tenn., which had been recently placed on detached service in the vicinity of the gap, were ordered to this place, and took up their line of march hither on Sunday morning before the surrender, and reached here on last Sabbath. It is understood, since their arrival here, that the Yankees pursued them near Jonesville, Va.

As to the probable result of this surrender of the gap, we will not speculate further than to say that we are fearful that the enemy will prosecute his journey to the Salt Works. There is a turnpike road from the gap to Estillville, thence there are two parallel turnpikes to Saltville—one by way of Lebanon and Haytor's Gap, the other through the Poor Valley and by way of Abingdon. It is certainly a matter of vital importance that our authorities and people will look to the protection of this interest.

Nothing very important "from the front" since our last issue. In upper East Tennessee Maj. General Jones is in command. There was brisk skirmishing on Monday, and on Tuesday evening two wounded Confederates and four Yankee prisoners were brought up from below Jonesboro', where they were wounded and captured.

From later intelligence, received by the Advocate, the following list of regiments at the Gap is obtained:

The garrison consisted of four regiments, viz: 55th Ga., 64th Va., 62d and 64th North Carolina, a portion of Leyden's artillery, Capt. Barnes's company of Ga., also, Fain's Tennessee battery, commanded by Lt. Conner. The enemy's force at the Gap was commanded by Gen. Burnside in person. He left the Gap on Friday with his and Gen. Shackelford's brigade for Knoxville, leaving only two regiments to guard the Gap, the 104th and 98th Ohio. Up to Saturday morning the enemy had made no move up the Virginia Valley outside of their picket lines. Only about 300 of our forces escaped, the larger portion of whom were of Col. Slemp's command.

A SENSIBLE YANKEE SPIRIT.—In the *Spiritual Banner*, of Boston, the experience of a Wisconsin soldier, killed in battle, is thus given:

[Have you seen any battles?] Yes, all sorts, sizes and kinds. [Have you seen Lee's army?] Yes, I have been down there lately. You heard that he was to be trapped. Now, don't you believe it—don't you believe it. Now, with all the Yankee shrewdness your generals possess, Lee will out-general them all.—[Do you think he will get over the river?] Yes, he will. Now, see here; I've been looking at the two armies. The folks at the South, they are fighting for liberty, for their lives. Here, the Yankee is fighting for the almighty dollar, and, my God! he'd sell his soul, and country, too, for a dollar! It's so. It's my opinion that you won't beat the South in the way you think you will. I thought you would when I was here. I wouldn't have fought a day if I hadn't thought we should conquer them. But I don't think you will now.

LINCOLN TO BE RE-ELECTED.—The New York *Caucasian* reminds its readers that "the Constitution requires that the successful candidate for President of all the States shall have a majority of all their electorial votes; failing in this the election goes to the House of Representatives, and the House elects, voting by *States*. Now, it is scarcely within the reach of probability that any candidate will have a majority of *all* the electoral votes, as Mr. Lincoln had in 1860. The election, therefore, will go to the House of Representatives, where, the voting being by *States*, Mr. Lincoln is sure of his election."

From the Spirit of the Age.

The "Peace" Bubble.

The Peace Deception, we learn from various quarters, is fast giving way before Gov. Vance's recent Proclamation, and other exposures of its folly, its mischievousness, and its utter inability to accomplish any thing that its friends propose. On several instances, we learn, where a few persons (for all of these meetings have been gotten up and engineered by a few men) had been gathered to hold such meetings, they have been prevented by gentlemen going there and explaining the danger and fallacy of the course they were pursuing.

What has been done in these instances may be done again. Let some gentlemen in whom the people have confidence, attend at all these places where such meetings are proposed to be held, and let them state plain facts—the injurious tendency of these meetings—and the majority of the people will listen to reason, truth and patriotism, and scout the designing few who are misleading and deceiving them. And let the people converse calmly upon these things, and they cannot fail to discover that nothing can be more preposterous than the insane idea of acquiring a peace by negotiation, except by an agreement to entirely surrender our rights, our liberties and our property up to Abe Lincoln.

The "Peace" bubble has exploded; many of the few who have attended the so-called "peace meetings," have become ashamed of it, and denounce those who duped them; and soon North Carolina will be *unit* on this subject, excepting the few who for ulterior purposes inaugurated the movement. The North is becoming despondent of conquering the South, and old Lincoln himself says that he has accomplished no substantial advantages over us yet. A few more months, with a united people, and day will break on the South.

COULDN'T HOLD COURT.—Judge Shipp, Solicitor Merrimon, and other legal gentlemen who started to attend the Superior Court for Cherokee county, last week, returned, reporting it impracticable to make the attempt in the present condition of that county. Many of the Southern men are leaving the county.

Asheville News, 17th inst.

THE TITHE LAW DOES NOT REACH THE POOR MAN OR WOMAN AT ALL.—Every one is entitled first to reserve for his or her own use 50 bushels of sweet potatoes, 50 bushels of Irish potatoes, and 100 bushels of corn (or 50 bushels of wheat;) also 20 bushels of peas or beans. Here is, at present market rates, nearly a thousand dollars worth of produce of the farm upon which no tax whatever is levied. It is evidently more than many poor families make, and enough to bread a good sized family; and as for meats, the tax is one tenth of all the bacon estimated at 60 lbs. of bacon to 100 lbs. of pork, whereas 100 lbs. of pork will make nearly 70 lbs. of bacon besides the part not cured into bacon. So that out of every 100 lbs. of pork some 15 or 20 lbs. are untaxed. On cattle the tithe tax is not laid—it is 1 per cent only on the value.

It is manifest from this statement, (for the accuracy of which see the law itself,) that the tithe law does not reach the poorer class of farmers; though from the manner in which the matter is handled by some, it might be supposed that it was to protect this class from oppression and injustice that the law is denounced and its repeal demanded. The law operates only upon the larger farmers, who make a surplus to sell, *and who are not taxed in any other way*, by the law; that is, neither their lands nor their negroes, nor their incomes from the sale of the surplus productions of their farms, are taxed.—This tithe tax is therefore the only way in which these well-to-do farmers are called upon to contribute to the support of the Government and the war; and it is the only way in which their land and negroes can be taxed. The constitution forbids the taxing of lands and negroes till a census is taken. During the war, consequently, but for this tithe law, land and negroes, the great wealth of the South, would escape taxation at all.

Fayetteville Observer.

General Johnston.

It is a subject of very general complaint that Gen. Joseph E. Johnston should have been relieved of his command at a time when the very existence of the South depends upon the result of the movements along the Tennessee line. We read a statement some time since that the President finding himself embarrassed by the public opinion which demanded the removal of General Pemberton, determined to relieve both Pemberton and Johnston. By what process of reasoning this result was reached, we are unable to explain, but suppose there must be more military propriety involved in the decision, or it would not have been made. In reference to what has been said about the President's desiring to injure the reputation of Gen. Johnston, we do not believe it; on the contrary, we have reason to believe that President Davis has the highest estimation of General Johnston's ability and conduct as a soldier of superior talents. But we think, in common with our entire community, that the service has received a severe blow in the temporary retirement of General Johnston. It is rumored that he is to be placed in command at Mobile. We think that the larger and more important field of operations along the Tennessee line require just now the presence of such a man to direct the movements of our army. With Bragg at Mobile, and Johnston in command of the army of Tennessee, the country would feel confident of success, as the right man would be in the right place.

Montgomery Mail.

News from the Islands.

The force of Yankee workers at batteries Gregg and Wagner was apparently increased on Monday. The enemy seemed to be unusually active at Battery Wagner in throwing up sand embankments. A vigorous fire was kept up by Fort Moultrie and Battery Simkins. Our shells were thrown with great accuracy, continually falling and exploding among the Yankees, and driving them from their work. Whenever a shell is observed coming the Yankees drop their spades and dodge under cover, but resume work immediately after the shell has exploded or passed over. No response was made to our fire, the enemy again remaining silent throughout the day.

We learn from good authority that the Yankees are busy at work upon a battery on Black's Island. Considerable activity was manifested among the fleet Monday afternoon. Dispatch steamers were observed busily plying between the Monitors and Ironsides, transferring men, &c. Another strange craft, having somewhat the appearance of a Monitor, came up from the South Monday afternoon and joined the fleet inside.

Chas. Courier, 22d inst.

TO THE VOTERS OF THE 4th CONGRESSIONAL DISTRICT.

For several weeks past a card has appeared in the Fayetteville Observer and in the Wilmington Journal, suggesting my name as a candidate for Congress. Sometime before any one had been announced, I was frequently requested to become a candidate. I then stated that if this should appear to be the general wish of the District, I was willing that my friends should announce my name. Since that time I have been applied to by influential persons from every county in the District, and urged to become a candidate.—Under these circumstances I feel called upon to say that if my fellow-citizens shall see fit to elect me, I shall esteem it a very high honor to be chosen their representative, and would devote myself earnestly to the discharge of the important duties of that responsible trust.

There is one great question for the representative of the people at this time to consider, and that is how the entire energies of the Government, within its Constitutional limits, can be best exerted to secure an early and successful termination of this great struggle for the independence of the Confederate States. It is true, there may be divisions amongst us upon minor questions of policy, but I believe and trust that the great body of the people of North Carolina are firmly united in the resolution that "the separation from the late United States is final, and that for the Independence they have asserted they will accept no alternative."

Yours very respectfully,
ROBERT STRANGE.

Wilmington, Sept. 18th, 1863. 13-2t—52-1t*

CAMP IVERSON'S OLD BRIGADE,
Near Orange C. H., Va., Sept. 3d, 1863.

FOR CONGRESS.

Mr. Editor: The undersigned, voters from Halifax county, in this Brigade, beg leave most respectfully to offer for the consideration of the 1st District the name of Colonel BRYAN GRIMES, 4th N. C. T., of Pitt county, as a suitable candidate for Congress at the ensuing election. Colonel GRIMES is too well known throughout the District to need any encomiums at our hands. His fame forms a part of the history of the war, and his conspicuous gallantry and heroic devotion to our cause, and noble exertions in behalf of our independence, have won for him the respect and gratitude of every patriot. Moreover Colonel GRIMES will make us an able, influential and useful member; and being a man of firm intellectual attainments, solid worth and unbending integrity, the people of the District cannot entrust to safer hands their honor and confidence.

VOTERS OF HALIFAX COUNTY.

Sept. 18, 1863. 11-1t—52-1t*

BY TELEGRAPH.

Reports of the Press Association.

Entered according to the Act of Congress, in the year 1863, by J. S. Thrasher, in the Clerk's Office of the District Court of the Confederate States for the Northern District of Georgia.

ADDITIONAL PARTICULARS OF THE BATTLES IN NORTHWESTERN GEORGIA.

Atlanta, Geo., Sept. 22.

Two heavy trains of wounded arrived here this afternoon from the Burnt Bridge, near Ringgold, and we have further particulars of the battles, which enables us to correct the former unsatisfactory reports that have come in. The principal correction we have to make is, that the enemy's line was formed on the West of Chickamauga River, not on Pea Vine Creek, as reported. After two days' desperate fighting, Rosecranz was driven several miles from his position, and our right flank took and held the road to Chattanooga, by which he received his supplies. Last night our right was one and a half miles in advance of that road, cutting him off completely from Chattanooga, which was seven miles distant. On Sunday night Rosecranz abandoned the field and selected a new position in the mountains. On Monday morning skirmishing occurred, as our troops pushed forward, and about two 2 P. M. cannonading was heard in the front.

From the best information we can obtain the enemy has concentrated on Mission Ridge. Longstreet was to aduance against them this morning. Our loss is stated to reach from ten to fifteen thousand, that of the enemy much greater. In the killed we have to add Gen'ls Deshler and Hood, who died after amputation. Many General officers were wounded. The Yankee Generals known to be killed, are Little and Thomas.

Two trains, with twelve hundred prisoners, have arrived here.

Breckinridge's division fought nobly, and lost thirteen hundred out of sixteen hundred men.

MESSAGE OF THE GOVERNOR OF SOUTH CAROLINA.

Columbia, S. C., Sept. 22, 1863.

Gov. Bonham's message was read to-day at one o'clock, P. M. He recommends that a military force be raised of two regiments of infantry, one to be mounted, and a proportionable force of cavalry and artillery, to resist the apprehended raiding parties of the enemy. This force is to include all able-boded citizens between sixteen and sixty years not in the Confederate service, or otherwise legally exempted; those who have employed substitutes; those who are becoming citizens, and those having domiciles.

The Governor asks the Legislature to adopt a policy to mitigate the evils of impressment by the Confederate government; and also asks additional legislation so as to furnishing labor for coast defence, recommending the impressment of it, including free negroes. The topics of the message were appropriately referred.

Message number two was received and considered in secret session.

FROM VIRGINIA.

Richmond, Sept. 22, 1863.

Nothing by the Central train this evening, except the statement that firing was heard in the direction of the Rapidan.

Commissioner Ould, in an official interview with Commissioner Meridith, submitted a proposition for the exchange of officers, but no definite reply could be given until the authorities at Washington were counsulted.

The community was much elated to-day with the news from Northern Georgia.

Recognition rumors were current this evening, but not traceable to any reliable source.

FROM VIRGINIA.

Richmond, Sept. 23, 1863.

A special dispatch to the Enquirer states that a considerable cavalry fight occurred yesterday, beginning near Madison Court House. Our forces fell back some three or four miles. There was also artillery firing at several of the lower fords yesterday evening.

The Legislature has passed an act suppressing the circulation and issue of small notes as currency by courts, cities and towns.

LATEST FROM CHARLESTON.

Charleston, Sept. 23d, 1863.

Last evening our Parrott guns on Sullivan's Island opened a more rapid fire upon the enemy than has been heard here for the past fortnight. The fire was maintained all night and continues this morning.

Prepare for the winter, you that dwell in comfortable houses, protected from the desolation of the ruthless invader. Prepare clothing of all sorts for the soldiers. Not alone for your brothers and fathers and husbands and sweethearts, (we are appealing to the ladies now,) but to every Southern soldier, to whom you are bound by the holiest ties of liberty and home associations.— Organize yourselves, our fair countrywomen, into one grand Southern Relief Society; but without any little sub-associations, to beget quarrels and jealousies; establish one grand central depot, and let every body contribute. Never mind the style, nor the quality, nor whether it be old or new—the article contributed.— "Clothes for the Southern soldiers!" be the rallying cry. The chances of war may remove our brave defenders to a latitude much farther north than the borders of Tennessee, or even Kentucky. Let us clothe them well if we would keep them there. What is the expenditure of a few paltry dollars compared with the loss of a whole fortune? And whose property is secure if our army be reduced by disease superinduced from scanty clothing in the wintry weather? Clothe the army, as you value your liberty, and your home comforts, and as you love your native South. We are in for another winter campaign—in all probability the last one, for the North cannot keep up this miserable farce of subjugation another year. But we are now to deal with the momentous present. The winter is upon us almost.— Think of the noble young soldier scantily clad and barefoot upon the distant picket, and of the veteran grayhairs shivering and warming his gun barrel over the bivouac fire.

The soldiers will need more comfortable clothing this winter than the Government will be able to supply. Therefore, let every man, woman and child in the land contribute something to keep the soldiers warm. Our countrymen, go to work! Action! our countywomen. Up with your bristling needles of steel, and charge with balls of yarn. Be instrumental in the noble cause of your country, and reflect that every knitted stocking but clads another freeman's foot put forward to meet and press back the invader.

SPIRITS TURPENTINE

IN GOOD ORDER, FOR SALE BY

WM. R. UTLEY.

Sept. 3d, 1883. 277-tf

Surgeon Rat.

The Petersburg "Express," is responsible for the following:

We have heard and read a great many stories about the rat, but in all our experience, we never before had one brought before us in the character of a Surgeon. learn that at one of our large hospitals a night or two since, an operation was successfully performed upon an invalid soldier by a common rat, which the Surgeon in charge had himself delayed for a time, with the hope of causing less suffering to the patient. This patient was suffering from the effects of a fracture of the frontal home of the skull—a piece of which projected outwards to some length, and the healing of the fleshy parts depended upon its removal. The bone was so firmly fixed, however, as, in the opinion of the Surgeon, would cause unnecessary pain in its forcible removal, and such remedies were applied as would assist nature in eventually ejecting it. A soothing poultice was placed upon the part a night or two ago, a hole being made through the application for the insertion of the projecting bone.— The patient was soon asleep in his bed; but during the night was aroused by the sting of pain, and awoke to discover a rat making off with the piece of bone in his mouth. He struck at and hit the rat, but did not hurt him.

The rat had probably been drawn to the bed of the soldier by the scent of the poultice, which was pleasant to his olfactories; but on reaching it his keen appetite, no doubt, caused him to relish in a large degree the juicy bone so convenient to his teeth. He therefore seized and drew it from its position, and was made to scamper off by the patient whom he had aroused with pain. It was a skillful operation, quickly performed, and will result beneficially to the invalid. We understand the patient is getting on remarkably well.

Look Out for the Thieves.

On Saturday or Sunday night last some thieving villians entered our Press rooms and stole therefrom the valuable Leather Bands that connected our Prees and Engine. The Bands were some four or five inches broad, very thick and heavy and were fifteen or twenty feet long, keyed together by copper eyes. It was of the very best Belt Leather and would now sell for four or five hundred dollars. We will give any reasonable reward for its return to us, or for any information that may lead to the detection of the thieves.— And we call upon all leather dealers and workers to have an eye out for any such that may be offered for sale, either in this city or elsewhere. It may possibly be cut up into shrot strips to avoid suspicion; but from the character of the leather it can readily be detected.

A great many leather-made articles have been stolen in this city of late, and from the fact that no clue whatever has been discovered, it is believed they are sent off to other places for sale. Ours may have been sent on a trip of this sort: We hope therefore our exchanges will notice this paragraph and perhaps thus enable us to recover our Belt, without which our Engine must stand still.—*Spirit of the Age.*

What the Yankees are doing for the Slaves of the South.—A friend sends us the following extract from a letter received by a gentleman in this city from a former resident of Savannah, now in Havana. As onr friend remarks in his note, it is another corroboration of the charge against the Yankees, that while affecting to give liberty to the negro, they speculate on his condition and return him to slavery— in the West Indies, where his condition, physically, socially and morally, is tenfold worse than that from which he has been seduced by the falsehood and villany of his pretended friends. The poor negro who has been beguiled by the seductive promises and pretences of the lying Yankee abolitionists of the North to leave his Southern master, his home and relatives, to find himself basely betrayed and sold into Cuban slavery, is indeed to be pitied, though even such a fate is preferable to the bitter experiences of the liberty which they promise him. Even as a Cuban slave, his condition would be better than that of the Northern free negro, the victim of Yankee cupidity, villany and brutality. The following is the extract:

"While walking over the city, examining the different sights, I was stopped and called by name. Looking round, I saw a negro man with hat off and a broad smile on his face. He told me he was from Savannah, that he had gone from there to the Yankees, and was after a time sent by them, with a good many others, and sold near this place (Havana). Asking what price they brought, he told me that he heard they were sold at from four to five hundred dollars a head. It seems that they bring but very few women. This boy says that there was but one woman for about every fifteen men."—*Savannah News.*

Okra Coffee.

To those who, like ourselves, are too poor to drink coffee at seven or ten dollars per pound, we can recommend a substitute which is as good to our taste as the original. We received from Col. James B. Merriwether, of this county, a specimen of okra seed, ground and parched, which had so much of the appearance and odor of the genuine coffee that, notwithstanding our prejudice against substitutes, we had prepared in the usual way, and found it as good as the best. We do not believe anybody could discover the difference. There is no reason why okra coffee should not be a most wholesome drink, as it certainly is a most pleasant one to our palate. It was certainly used in this country as early as 1821, and it may be even at an earlier period.

Parch the seed slowly and carefully, so as not to burn them; then prepare the decoction properly, and, our word for it you have as good a cup of coffee as anybody but a Confederate quartermaster, a successful blockade runner, or a sugar speculator can afford to drink.—*Montgomery Advertiser.*

THE YOUNG LADIES AND GENTLEMEN

OF MAGNOLIA will hold a Concert for the benefit of sick and wounded soldiers, at Magnolia College, on FRIDAY NIGHT next, Sept. 25th.

Sept. 23. 15-2t.

[Advertisement.]

Messrs. Editors: Though not at all used to writing for the public eye, I feel constrained to notice a few erroneous statements contained in the card of Mr. Thomas I. Faison, published recently in your *Journal*. To follow the author in all of his labyrinthian meanderings, would occupy more space and time than could now be afforded, but there are some such glaring mistakes and inconsistencies I do not feel willing that they should pass unnoticed. His card reminds me of the old lady reading in the dictionary. She said the reading was mighty good, but the subject changed 'most too often. Mr. Faison, in this card—as always in his political course heretofore—is as near non-committal as he well can be. He believed that we ought to have seceded early, but eulogizes the course and opinions of those opposing the measure. Then he appears *awfully frightened* lest "Billy Seward" should ever find out his dubious opinions, or the secrets of the country. He next strikes a blow (I hope not deadly) at the Tax in Kind law; he calls it "an old Jewish law." I am not aware Messrs. Editors, that the tithing law was made by the Jews; but if I understand scripture—it was a law made by God himself, the great "I am," and given to Moses upon Mount Sinai. And next his quotation from St. Luke 11th, 42nd, "But woe unto you Pharisees! for ye tithe mint and rue and all manner of herbs" is irrelevant and out of place to prove anything, and especially in bad taste in a politician's card. As to his course in the State Legislature, but little has ever been seen or known. I have heard of only one measure of which he was the champion, that was a kind of "woman's rights" bill introduced by him, and the speech he made upon the merits of that bill was so ridiculous that the Legislature lost what little interest they had in the measure. He says he has every confidence in Jefferson Davis as President of the Confederate States. Who ought not to feel grateful to him for such great condescension. Just suppose he should happen to disagree with the President; how would the Confederacy survive? His next pathetic appeal is to his "Fellow-Citizens in the Army." How well he loves them—how very grateful he feels to them. He has shown his love and zeal by running in several regiments for every military position in the gift of the regiment, from Colonel down to "anything Lord." He says, in his last candidacy for Congress he was unsuccessful—"which was to be attributed more to my (his) limited acquaintance in the District than anything else," but he returns his heartfelt thanks to his "fellow citizens in the army" for the very handsome support they gave him two years ago. It was "no time for electioneering" and of course he did none. But he says "amends was made in part, if not entirely," for his defeat, by the citizen soldiers of his own county who knew him best and who elected him to the Senate of North Carolina without his being a candidate, "an honor equal if not greater than to have been elected to Congress." Now, Messrs. Editors, I happen to know something of Mr. Faison's not being a candidate; and here I would remark, if his election was so very honorable, he ought certainly (forever) to keep quiet about the manner in which that result was brought about. It is true, he did not have his name announced in the newspapers—he prefered to operate in a less open manner—no person supposes it necessary (in candidacy for office within the gift of the county) to have your card published in the newspapers, if, as was the case with Mr. Faison, you would go to almost every voter in the county and in the army; go with the conscripts of the county from home to the camp of Instruction at Raleigh, treating freely, staying with them till the election, and pulling the last man up to the polls, making many fair promises of influence and assistance entirely out of his power to wield or give— having numerous electioneering agents in the army for months previous to the election. If all such wire-pulling and electioneering agencies as these was not being a candidate, then Mr. F. was not one, and I admit freely that he was not in this instance, nor never was, a fair one—but in this he was indefatigable in season and out of season with the voters of Sampson County, and then after all of this exertion, just by the skin of his teeth was he elected. The Conscripts from the Southern portion of Sampson County, in the Camp of Instruction at Raleigh, who were almost to a man opposed to Mr. F, for some cause were ordered off the night previous to the election, or there is not a doubt but he would have been defeated. He next parades before the voters of the 3rd Congressional district a vast amount of Revolutionary ancestral pluck. Now, I dislike to doubt his patriotism, but he is an old politician. In all of his regards for and visiting the army, he has seemed to have some ulterior motive. We find him at one time visiting the army frequently, and soon we hear of his candidacy for some office, either Colonel, Lieutenant Colonel, Major or Congressman, and, failing in these, he feels very "grateful to the citizen soldiers of his own county" for the State Senate. In fact it has almost passed into a proverb in the army, if Mr. F. visits them oftener, or takes more interest than usual in the soldiers, "that he has an axe to grind."

In regard to the gentleman's high eulogium of the late lamented Capt. W. J. Houston, I heartily agree with him; but as to his not becoming a candidate against Captain Houston had he lived, I leave for his past history to answer. If I am not mistaken, after Capt. Houston had announced himself as a candidate, Mr. F., or his friends, had his name brought before the people of the district, published in several papers of this and one at least of an adjoining State, and I never heard the slightest hint of an intention on his part to decline. He speaks of sending five of his family into service, *two wounded.*

I cannot say how man sons went into service or how many came out of service. I do not propose to visit the sins of the father upon his children, but it will be impossible to send every man to Congress who has five or seven, for any other number of sons into service. Nor do I think the voters of the 3rd District would object to a man (if otherwise qualified) who had no sons old enough for service, provided he was himself in this, where Mr. F. says his mother's brother was in the old revolution.

I do not propose to extend this notice much farther. I should not have thought of noticing it at all, but it contains errors that can be proven as such, and misrepresentations again and again heralded through the press by Mr. F. or his friends. We caution the voters of the District in and out of the army to be careful how they cast their votes. It is a time that we need our purest and best men—men unacquainted with political trickery, wire-pulling or demagoguism.

A FARMER,
of the 3rd Congressional District.

Sept. 23d, 1863. 15-1t—52-1t*

MARRIED.

At the residence of George A. Smith, Esq., in Franklin county, on the morning of the 22nd inst., by the Rev. J. B. Cheshire, WM. H. McRARY, Esq., of Wilmington, to Miss PATTIE WIGGINS, of Scotland Neck.

WILMINGTON MARKET, SEPTEMBER 23, 1863.

Beef Cattle—Are in fair enquiry for butchering purposes, and the market is rather poorly supplied. We quote on the hoof at 60 to 70 cents per lb. for net meat, as in quality.

Bacon—Is brought to market slowly, and is in demand at high prices. We quote small sales from carts at $2 per lb. for hog round.

Butter—In demand at $3 to $3 50 per lb.

Corn—Sells by the quantity at $4 50 to $5 per bushel.

Corn Meal.—Supply light. Sells from the granaries at $5 75 per bushel, in lots to suit.

Copperas—Retails at $1 75 to $2 50 per lb., as in quality.

Cotton—60 to 65 cents per lb.

Eggs—Sell from carts at $2 a $2 25 per dozen.

Flour.—But little in market, and prices rule high. Small sales of superfine at $65 a $66 per lb.

Fodder—$8 to $10 per 100 lbs.

Hides—Green, 75 to 80 cents, and Dry $1 60 to $1 75 per pound.

Leather.—Sole $5 50 to $6, and Upper $6 50 to $7 00 per lb.

Lard—$2 per lb. by the bbl.

Molasses—Retails at $10 per gallon.

Nails—$1 per lb. by the keg.

Osnaburgs—$1 60 per yard.

Poultry.—Chickens $1 50 to $2 each, as to size, and grown fowls $2 50 to $3 each.

Potatoes.—New crop Sweet sell at $3 to $10, and Irish at $10 per bushel.

Rice.—Clean, 18 to 20 cents per lb.

Salt.—Sound made, $18 to 20 per bushel.

Sugar—Is scarce, and sells at $2 20 to $2 25 per lb. in bbls.

Sheeting.—Fayetteville factory, $1 60 to $1 65 per yard by the bale.

Spirits Turpentine—$2 to $2 50 per gallon.

Tallow—$1 35 to $1 40 per lb.

Yarn—Retails at $20 to $21 per bunch.

Wood—Is in demand, and but little arriving. We quote by the boat load at $18 to $20 per cord.

The anniversary of the Acclimatization Society, London, must have been a queer affair, as it is described in the English papers. The particular purpose of the banquet, we are told, was "to illustrate in the first place some of the special objects of the society—as, for example, the introduction of the Chinese sheep and the yam, or *diosorea batabus*; and in the second place, the food of other countries, which do not usually find their way to our (British) tables." Among the celebrities present were Captain Speke, and Captain Grant, and Mons. DuChallie. The peculiar dishes were the white soup of the Channel Islands, lucioperca, (?) gronouilles, or edible frogs, pepperpot, Chinese lamb, with piloff and Kuscoussou (?) pulets, a la emancipation des negres (can any one tell us what Abolition chickens are?) and ostrich eggs. Greek, Austrailian, Hungarian and California wines were drunk. The rooms were of a tropical temperature, and decorated with the horns and skins of many strange beasts.

SUPERIOR SALT.

I am constantly making a SUPERIOR ARTICLE OF SALT at my works; every care is taken in making it, and there is none to excel it in this market. For sale by

WM. R. UTLEY.

July 28th, 1863. 246-tf

HAVING confidence in the ability, integrity and patriotism of Col. ROBERT STRANGE, we respectfully present his name to the voters of this, the Fourth Congressional District of North Carolina, as a candidate to represent us in the next House of Representatives of the Confederate States.

Election first Wednesday (4th day) of Novembe.

VOTERS OF THE 4TH DISTRICT.

Aug. 26.

DIED.

At the Hospital of the 51st Regiment, N. C. T., at Mount Pleasant, opposite Charleston, S. C., on the 10th inst., of Typhoid Fever, Private EZRA LENNON, of Company H, 51st Regiment, N. C. T., a native of Bladen county, N. C., aged 20 years.

At the same place, on the 17th inst., of secondary hemorage, Private ATPHA BLACKMAN, of the same Company and Regiment, a native of Columbus county, No. Ca., aged 27 years. Said disease was caused by a severe fracture of the right arm, "which rendered amputation necessary," inflicted during the furious bombardment of Sullivan's Island, on the night of the 1st inst.

NEW ADVERTISEMENTS.

WILMINGTON THEATRE.

TO-NIGHT—THE

TOODLES,
TOODLES,
MILLER IN HIS COMICALITIES,
MILLER IN HIS COMICALITIES,
BETSY BAKER,
BETSY BAKER,
BETSY BAKER.

For particulars see small bills.

Sept. 23. 15-1t.

BEERYS' SHIP YARD.

The following men having deserted from this yard some time since. Militia and other officers are requested to arrest them wherever found.

W. F. COX, Columbus Co.
J. W. LONG, " "

B. W. & W. L. BEERY, Contractors.

Sept. 23, 1863 15–d1t w1t*

NOTICE.

CONFEDERATE TAX.

I WILL ATTEND at Mitchell's Sound, (Masonboro District) on Saturday, 26th inst., and at Fort Fisher, on Tuesday, 29th inst., to receive the Confederate Tax lists for the above districts.

E. MURRAY, Assessor.

Sept. 23, 1863. 15-6t

FOR SALE.

250 SACKS SUPERIOR SALT. For sale by

T. C. CRAFT,
No. 48 Market Street.

Sept. 23d 15-6t

AUCTION SALES.

BY S. M. WEST, Auct'r.

NEGRO BOY AT AUCTION.

ON THURSDAY, September 24, 1863, at 10 o'clock, A. M., at Exchange corner, will be sold,

1 likely NEGRO BOY, about 12 years old.

Sept. 23, 1863. 15-1t

BY S. M. WEST, Auct'r.

SALT PANS AT AUCTION.

ON SATURDAY, September 26th, 1863, at 10 o'clock, A. M., on the Wharf in front of my office, will be sold

5 SALT PANS,
1 WAGCON and 2 MULES.

Sept. 23, 1863. 15-ts

BY WILKES MORRIS, Auct'r.

HORSES AT AUCTION.

ON FRIDAY NEXT, 25th inst., at 10 o'clock, A. M., I will sell, at Exchange Corner,

FOUR HORSES.

By order C. W. STYRON,
Capt. & A. Q. M.

Sept. 23d, 1863. 15-ts

STEAM ENGINES, BOILER, &c.

1 LOCOMOTIVE BOILER, about 700 feet fire surface.
2 High Pressure Engines, 12 inch bore, 2 feet stroke.
Also, the Iron Hull of a Stern Wheel Boat, 100 feet long, 17 feet wide, 32 feet deep. For sale by

JOHN MYERS & SON.

Tarboro', Edgecomb Co., N. C.

Sept. 22, 1863. 14-4t*

TURPENTINE.

THE SUBSCRIBER will be in the market for Yellow Dip Turpentine, first of October next.

A. H. VANBOKKELEN.

Sept. 22, 1863. 14x52-1m*.

$100 REWARD.

RUNAWAY from the subscriber on the 21st inst., his negro man named ZION. Said negro is about 5 feet 4 inches high, stout built, not very black, and weighs about 160 or 170. He had on when he left a brown homespun suit and a greyish hat.

The above reward will be paid for his delivery to me, or for his safe confinement in New Hanover county Jail.

J. T. SCHONWALD.

Sept. 22d, 1863. 14-6t*

EXECUTOR'S NOTICE.

THE SUBSCRIBER having, at September Term, 1863, of the Court of Pleas and Quarter Sessions for New Hanover County, qualified as Executor upon the estate of Levin Lane, deceased, hereby gives notice to all persons indebted to said intestate to come forward and settle; and all persons having claims against the same are hereby notified to present them within the time prescribed by law, otherwise this notice will be pleaded in bar of a recovery.

THOS. H. LANE, Executor.

During my absence from Wilmington, Dr. W. W. Lane is my authorized Agent to settle all business against said estate.

T. H. LANE.

Sept. 18, 1863. 11-daw3*

THE TRI-WEEKLY TELE

VOL. XXIX—NO. 86 HOUSTON WEDNESDAY, OCTOBER 7, 1863. WHOLE NO. 3741

NEW ADVERTISEMENTS

HEADQUARTERS, HOXEY'S BATTALION,
Independence, Washington county,
September 28, 1863.

All volunteers recruited by W. M. Williamson, are hereby ordered to rendezvous at Independence, Washington county, on Friday the 9th day of October, on which day they will organize and immediately go into camps.

T. R. HOXEY, Major Cadets.

oct7-tw3t*

HEADQUARTERS, DISTRICT OF TEXAS,
NEW MEXICO AND ARIZONA,
Houston, October 6, 1863.

Special Orders, No. 271.

The companies of Minute men within the limits of the Northern Sub District, are hereby notified that their services are required on the northern frontier, and are requested to report with all the arms they can procure, and with the utmost promptness, to Brigadier General H. E. McCulloch, at Bonham.

Quartermasters and Commissaries are directed to furnish these companies with necessary transportation and subsistence on application of the commanding officers. By command of

Maj. Gen'l J. B. MAGRUDER.

EDMUND P. TURNER, A. A. G.

oct7tw3t

FEMALE TEACHER WANTED—In Port Sullivan College, (under the care of the Texas Annual Conference.) We have one hundred pupils, and the situation offered is a good one. None but those of ability and experience need apply. Address Rev. J. B. ALLEN, Wheelock, Texas.

oct7-tw2t*

PEACH STONES AND ONIONS.—I want from one to five bushels of Peach Stones; also, the same quantity of small Button Onions for setts.

oct 7-tw1t* PHINEAS J. MAHAN.

WANTED TO RENT a comfortable residence, for which a liberal price will be paid. Apply to [oct 7 tw1t*] W. B. SORLEY & CO.

NOTICE TO ENROLLING OFFICERS OF THE 4TH CONGRESSIONAL DISTRICT—I will attend for the purpose of examining Conscripts at the following named places and times, viz: At Liberty, Liberty county, on Monday, October 19th; Wallisville, Chambers county, Wednesday, October 21st; Beaumont, Jefferson county, Friday, October 23d; Orange, Orange county, Sunday, October 25th; Livingston, Polk county, Thursday, October 29th; Hardin, Hardin county, Tuesday, November 3d, and Woodville, Tyler county, on Thursday, November 5th. Enrolling officers of the above named counties will please use due diligence to procure the prompt attendance of conscripts.

THOS. A. STANWOOD,
Surgeon 4th Cong. District.

oct 7-tw4t

EXPRESS NOTICE.—The undersigned will leave Huntsville, Texas, on the 15th of October next, for Richmond, Va; and proposes to carry all letters and small packages forwarded to his care by hand or mail to Huntsville. Each letter must be accompanied with one dollar, and packages with a reasonable pay. I will also, attend to any business with the Departments of Government, or individuals. I was unavoidably prevented from leaving as was advertised in the Galveston News, but will, no providential hinderence be sure to leave on the 15th Oct. and understanding the difficulties in the way from traveling heretofore the same route, I am confident that I shall be able to go through.

ROGER PARSONS.

Huntsville, Oct, 6th, 1863. oct82t*

RANAWAY from my plantation in Wharton county, about the 1st of September, the following described negroes:

FRANK, aged 50 years, 5 feet 8 or 9 inches high, heavy set, should weigh about 150 lbs., dark copper color, grey headed, pleasant countenance, quick spoken and intelligent.

ISAAC, aged 30 years, 5 feet 8 or 9 inches high, should weigh 140 lbs., black, bow legged, very prominent eyes and red, very low forehead.

CHARLES, aged 1 years, 5 feet 10 or 11 inches high, color brown, would weigh 170 or 180 lbs.

Said negroes are trying to make their way to Louisiana. The boy Charles was separated from the other two before crossing the Brazos river. Frank and Isaac were seen near Montgomery. Any one taking up the above negroes will be liberally rewarded.

Address F. G. BANKS,
Chappell Hill, Texas.

oct7tw3t

HEADQUARTERS, DISTRICT OF TEXAS, ETC.,
Sabine Pass, October 1.

Special Orders, No. 266.

X. A misapprehension having occurred in reference to the question of permits for vessels leaving the country loaded with cotton, the following letter of instruction from these Headquarters, to Brigadier General Scurry commanding Eastern Sub-District, is published for the information of the public, and with a view to its correctness:

HEADQUARTERS, DISTRICT OF TEXAS,
NEW MEXICO AND ARIZONA,
Sabine Pass, Sept. 21, 1863.

Brigadier General Scurry,
comd'g Eastern Sub-District.

General—I am directed by Major General Magruder, to inform you that Mr. House's cotton vessels, Mr. Harris Hoyt's, and Mr. Marx Levy's can go to sea. Give them permits, and others who you are satisfied are good and loyal men. Keep the "Lizzie Bacon" and the "Enriquita," Rubrieux's vessel. Do not permit the latter two vessels to go to sea under any circumstances, nor their captains to leave the country. If Bacon, who ownes or sails the Lizzie Bacon, is not in Houston, send for him and keep him a prisoner of war and his crew of Yankees, or such as are Yankees. The rest foreigners can remain on board to take care of the ship, or be discharged. The vessel and cargo ought to be confiscated.

Very respectfully, your ob't servant,
(Signed) STEPHEN D. YANCEY, A. A. G.

XI. In consequence of the great press of military business, while the Major-General is in the field, no more permits will be issued from these Headquarters, but they will be given by the Sub-District commanders, as before directed in General Orders, No. 168.

By command of
Maj. Gen'l J. B. MAGRUDER.

EDMUND P. TURNER, A. A. G.

oct7tw3t

OFFICE CHIEF QUARTERMASTER, DISTRICT OF
TEXAS, NEW MEXICO AND ARIZONA,
Houston, Sept. 29, 1863.

No. 69 of official "Exemptions" to parties acting for me in the transportation of cotton to the Rio Grande, has been lost, mislaid or stolen.

Enrolling officers and all persons whatsoever are notified that any person using the said exemption, No. 69, has come by the same fraudulently. Enrolling officers are requested to arrest and conscript said person at once and notify me of the fact.

B. BLOOMFIELD,
Major and Chief Quartermaster.

Every paper in the State will publish and send bill to me.

B. BLOOMFIELD.

sep30€t. Major and Chief Quartermaster.

WANTED.—Ink bottles of all sizes. Deliver at this office.

sept. 28, tw3t.

PUBLIC SALE.—I will sell, at Millican's Depot, on Thursday, the 8th of October, to the highest bidder, twelve Ox Wagons and Teams, for cash.

o2-d5t* ADIN POWELL.

A SITUATION is wanted by a young man, in any active capacity, as travelling agent, or other out-door employment. References given. Address Box 55, Houston, Texas o6—tw2t*

SUBSTITUTE WANTED—For 4 months' service in the militia. Address A. B. C. at the drug store of George & Davidson, Houston. oct 3—trw 2t *

MILITARY NOTICE.—All persons having authority to raise companies for Fulkrod's Battalion, will report to me with their recruits at Brenham, Washington county, immediately, where they will be provided for.

J. A. RANDLER.

Brenham, Oct 5, 1863—o6-3t

SCHOOL BOOKS.—I can furnish several dozen of each of the following books: Texas Primer Speller, Reader. Arithmetics—Smith's, Smiley's, Ray's, Colburn's. Grammars—Clark's, Bailey's. Geographies—Monteith's, Olney's, Smith's. Botanies—Lincoln's, Darby's. Histories—Willard's School History; Universal do. Philosophy—Parker's and Comstock's. Chemistry—Porter's, Comstock's.

JAMES BURKE.

Houston, Sept. 30—tw2t&w1t*

HEADQUARTERS, DIST., TEXAS,
NEW MEXICO AND ARIZONA,
Sabine Pass, Sept. 16, 1863.

General Orders, No. ——

The following order is published for the information of all concerned:

"HEADQUARTERS, DEPT. TRANS-MISSISSIPPI,
Shreveport, La., August 26, 1863.

"General Orders, No. 38.

"In accordance with the Proclamation of the President, a general pardon and amnesty is hereby granted to all officers and soldiers now absent without leave, in the Department Trans-Mississippi, who will return to duty by the 30th of September, proximo.

"Officers and enlisted men absent from their commands East of the Mississippi River, will, under this amnesty, report as follows, viz: those from Arkansas at the Camp of Instruction at Washington, and District Headquarters; from Texas, at Bonham and Houston; from Louisiana, at Shreveport and District Headquarters; and will be permitted to join any regiment of their own corps they may select.

"This amnesty and pardon shall also extend to all who have been convicted and undergoing sentence for absence without leave, or desertion, except only those who have been twice convicted thereof. By command of

"LIEUT. GEN. E. KIRBY SMITH.
(Signed,) S. S. ANDERSON, A. A. G."

The commanding officers at Houston and Bonham will designate an officer to whom these officers and men will report. They will be allowed to select any regiment of their corps in the District, and will receive from the officers appointed for the purpose the necessary orders. Transportation and subsistence supplies will be furnished.

The Major General commanding calls upon all concerned to avail themselves of the amnesty within the time, or else they will be hunted down, brought in as deserters, and punished according to the law.

Col. N. C. Gould, of the 23d Texas Cavalry, has been assigned to the duty of executing this order.

The period of the amnesty for deserters in the Eastern Sub District of Texas, and those in Louisiana, within convenient distance of Texas, is hereby extended to the 15th of October, and those in the Western and Northern Sub-Districts, to the 31st of October, 1863.

By command of
Maj. Gen'l J. B. MAGRUDER,

EDMUND P. TURNER, A. A. G.

oct7-tw15t

HEADQUARTERS, DIST. OF TEXAS, NEW
MEXICO AND ARIZONA,
Sabine Pass, Sept. 27th, 1863.

General Orders, No. 166.

Maj. Geo. Williamson, A. A. G., and Capt. F. Ducayet, A. Q. M., having been ordered by Lieut Gen. E. Kirby Smith to this District to investigate thoroughly "the alleged cotton frauds," the following orders will be rigidly and promptly obeyed.

I. Maj. Dickinson and Capt. Waller, the Board heretofore appointed by the Major General Commanding, to make this investigation, will report for duty and instructions to Maj. Williamson, and will turn over to him all the instructions, correspondence and orders which they have, on the subject of the alleged cotton frauds.

II. All officers in this District will forthwith furnish to Maj. Williamson, at Houston, care of Maj. B. Bloomfield, a list of the Agents they have heretofore had, and who are now engaged in the purchase of cotton.

III. All officers in this District will forthwith furnish Maj. Williamson with an abstract of the contracts they have heretofore made, and now existing, which are to be paid in cotton, with a statement whether said contracts have been fulfilled in part or in whole, and the cause of the failure to fulfil, if known.

IV. All Quartermasters and Commanders of Posts in this District are hereby directed to afford Maj. Williamson and Capt. Ducayet every facility in their power to enable them to carry out their special instructions from the Lieut. Gen. Commanding the Department.

By command of
Maj. Gen. J. BANKHEAD MAGRUDER.

STEPHEN D. YANCEY, A. A. Gen. o6-3.

CIRCULAR.

OFFICE OF THE CHIEF COMMISSARY, T. S. T.
Houston, October 2d, 1863.

Assistant Commissaries of Battalions of State Troops will forward to Major H. B. Blair, Chief of Bureau of Subsistence, at Shreveport, La., all the accounts and returns required by the regulations to be rendered to the Commissary General.

Copies of the following Monthly and Quarterly papers will be sent to this office:

MONTHLY—Returns of provisions received and issued. Abstract of purchases. Report of Extra Duty Men employed. Summary statement of Funds received and disbursed.

QUARTERLY—Account Current. Abstract of all purchases of provisions in the quarter. Abstract of all other expenditures during the quarter. Estimate of Funds required for the next quarter (in duplicate). List of outstanding debts due and unpaid (in duplicate).

Estimates will be carefully revised and corrected by Commanding Officers before approval.

Funds will be turned over to bonded Commissaries on estimates properly approved.

J. E. OWENS, Capt. & Chief
Commissary State Troops.

Approved by command of
MAJ. GEN MAGRUDER.

J. D. MCADOO, A. A. Gen., T. S. Troops.

October 3-tw2w

NOTICE TO THE CITIZENS OF COLORADO COUNTY.—I am fully authorized to receive the Tax in kind for Colorado County. Planters are requested to bring in their corn and fodder while the roads are good. A reasonable compensation will be paid for transportation, in excess of eight miles, the distance required by law. Receipts will be given on the delivery of the corn and fodder at this place, or at Alleyton. Let it be turned in without delay, as it is much needed by the troops now in the field.

UDOLPHO WOLFE,
A. Q. M., C. S. A.

Post Q. M. Office, Columbus, Oct. 1, 1863.

oct5-tw3t

AUCTION SALE,

BY

A. C. McKEEN & CO.

On WEDNESDAY, Oct. 7th, 1863,

TO CLOSE CONSIGNMENTS

A lot of valuable field negroes; several cooks, washers and ironers; 43 cases boots; 800 lbs. shoe thread; 20 boxes choice tobacco; 20 bbls. Louisiana rum; 20 bbls. whiskey; 1000 lbs. powder; 2000 lbs. harness leather; 20 hhds. Louisiana sugar; 10 family clocks; horses, mules, wagons, buggies and other articles to be sent in. oct 2—tds

---

VALUABLE PROPERTY FOR SALE.—On account of ill health, I offer for sale for Confederate money or Negroes, the following property: The Columbia Ferry, with a new cypress boat 70 feet long, ropes and other fixtures; two or three drays and teams; one two horse freight wagon and team; my homestead, well situated in the town of Columbia, embracing three lots of ground, on which is a dwelling containing eight rooms, kitchen, smoke house, negro house, brick cistern, stables, crib, carriage house, peach orchard, &c. &c. The Houston Tap and Brazoria Railroad terminus being on the east side of the river at this place, the ferry connected with the draying business is very profitable, a quantity of freight is constantly awaiting transportation over the river.

oct 6-tw2w F. W. T. HARRISON.

$100 REWARD.—Ranaway from the subscriber, near Eagle Lake, Colorado county, Sept. 19th, a negro boy named Ephraim, 18 years old, black, medium height and spare make; said he was raised by a Mr. Linton, on Bayou Bœuff, La.; was bought, about two weeks since, of John A. Campbell, Houston, and is doubtless in or on his way to that place. Had on a thick Osnaburg shirt, striped cotton pants and shoes and other clothes with him. The above reward will be paid for his apprehension and delivery, and any information of him will be suitably rewarded.

o6-tw2t* W. G. FOOTE.

Our Alexandria Correspondence.

ALEXANDRIA, Sept. 29.

Dr. O. Teagarden, of Sumpter, Texas, arrived here day before yesterday, en route to Texas. He kindly loaned me the Chicago Times of the 12th and 14th and other papers from which I obtained the following dispatches.

WASHINGTON, Sept. 11.—The following report from Gen. Burnside concerning the capture of Cumberland Gap has been received at headquarters.

CUMBERLAND GAP, Sept. 9, 1863.

To GEN. H. W. HALLECK.

I have telegraphed you of movements up to the occupation by our forces of Knoxville. Since then a cavalry force has been sent up the railroad to within a few miles of Bristol, capturing three locomotives and two additional cars. Another force, composed of two regiments of infantry and two regiments of cavalry, I brought to this place, in person, to reinforce Gen. Shackleford, who is here with two regiments of cavalry, Col. DeCourcey being on the Kentucky side with a brigade which I started in that direction before leaving Kentucky. The infantry brigade marched from Knoxville to this place, 60 miles in 52 hours. The garrison here consisting of over 2,000 men and 14 pieces of artillery, made an unconditional surrender without a fight.

A. E. BURNSIDE.
Major General.

On the 12th inst, gold opened in New York at 29 and advanced to 30½.

FORTRESS MONROE, Sept. 12.—The steamer Massachusetts has arrived from Charleston Bar, which she left on the evening of the 9th.

On the 8th, the Weehawken sent a shell into Fort Moultrie's magazine, exploding it.

The Ironsides sent shells into Moultreville, firing and destroying half the town.

The Monitors and Ironsides bombarded Sullivan's Island four hours, doing extensive damage.

On the 8th, at 11 p. m., a boat expedition left the squadron to storm Sumter, but were repulsed with a loss of a number of killed, wounded and prisoners.

The following naval officers were captured on the walls of Fort Sumter: Lieut. E. P. Williams, Lieut. S. W. Preston, Lieut G. C. Reamy, Lieut. Tracy, Lieut. D. S. Meade, Lieut. Bradford, and Ensign B. H. Potter. The latter was wounded.

NEW YORK, Sept. 12.—The steamer Arago, from Charleston on Wednesday evening, has arrived. The Ironsides and Monitors are still shelling Moultrie. Sumter had not surrendered. The Union forces were erecting works to shell Charleston. No attack on the city had been made.

The World's Washington special says: We have authority for stating that Gen. Gillmore was determined when he got possession of Morris Island, if Gen. Beauregard did not surrender, that he would throw incendiary shells into the city for the purpose of destroying it as a cover and base of supplies for the Confederate forces.

The Tribune's Washington special says: It is not true, as stated in a London letter published by one of your cotemporaries, that one of the Anglo-rebel rams sailed from England during the last week of August. The Government official dispatches, of quite as late a date as any newspaper correspondence, positively state that all the rams whose departure was threatened, were still in the yards where they were built.

FORTRESS MONROE, Sept. 12—A flag of truce arrived from City Point this morning.

The Richmond Enquirer, of the 11th inst., says: The office, type and presses of the Raleigh (N. C.) Standard, edited by Wm. Holden, have been destroyed by a party of Georgia soldiers. Mr. Holden was in Petersburg at the time. In return for this outrage, the citizens and friends of the Standard destroyed the office of the State Journal. Gov. Vance reached the spot after the work of destruction was nearly completed, and begged the crowd to desist, rebuking them for the act, and telling them that no such example had been set in Lincoln's dominions.

SAN FRANCISCO, Sept. 12—Work on the San Francisco harbor defences was commenced yesterday by a large number of laborers, promising the speedy completion of very formidable fortifications.

Nearly complete returns make the majority for the Union State ticket a little below 20,000. 32 Union and 3 Democratic Senators, and 65 Unionists and 5 Democratic Assemblymen were elected.

ST. JOHNS, N. F., Sept. 12.—The following is the continuation of the news of the City of Manchester, which arrived off Cape Race yesterday evening, having left Liverpool on the 2d and Queenstown on the 3d.

The London Morning Herald understands that at a French Cabinet Council on the expediency of recognizing the South, the question was discussed, the majority being in favor of doing so, but that a final decision was not arrived at.

The Polish question remained without change.

The Congress of German princes had closed, and the result was satisfactory to the Emperor of Austria.

WASHINGTON, Sept. 13—The Navy Department has received information of the capture, on the 2d ult., in Lat. 26 50, Lon. 93 30, by the steamer Cayuga, the schooner Ware, which ran the blockade at San Louis Pass, near Galveston, bound to Vera Cruz. She had the Swiss Confederation flag flying, and is owned by J. C. Kuhn, Consul of Switzerland at Galveston. Her cargo consisted of 80 bales of cotton.

The Cuyuga also captured the schooner J. T. Davis off the Rio Grande, having run out of the same port. She had no colors, papers or log book. Her cargo consisted of 97 bales of cotton. Both vessels were sent to New Orleans for adjudication.

The following was received at the Headquarters of the Army to-day:

ST. LOUIS, Sept. 13th.

To Major General Halleck:

Col. Cloud routed the enemy near Fort Smith on the 1st inst., and now holds that place. Western Arkansas and the Indian country are now in our possession.

(Signed) J. M SCOFIELD,
Major General.

NEW YORK, Sept. 13.—The Times correspondent with the army of the Potomac writes on the 10th that it is believed that one corps of Lee's army, or about one third of his army, under Longstreet, is moving to Richmond, there to be transferred, two divisions of it to the South-west and one to Charleston. Hood's division left Fredericksburg on Tuesday last for Richmond and thence for Charleston. This seems to indicate that the rebels in Virginia will remain entirely on the defensive for the coming campaign, which every one here counts upon before winter.

ST. LOUIS, Sept. 13.—The line of railroad from Little Rock to Duvall's Bluff is in our possession, in complete order, and stock will be placed upon it to supply our forces, so that no mishap may take place, the Arkansas river failing us.

At dark this evening the splendid steamer Imperial took fire, and drifting down fired three others—the Jesse D. Bell, Hiawatha and Post Boy. All four were totally destroyed.

CHATTANOOGA, Sept. 12.—No details of Negley's engagement at Dug Gap have come to us. From all we can gather the casualties are eight. Negley retired three miles, to the foot of Lookout Mountains.

Baird's division also engaged Dug Gap four miles north, near Lafayette, where the main column of Bragg was at the time of the engagement.

Bragg fears to lose control over his line of retreat to Rome, and is retreating slowly, to avoid a repetition of the Tullahoma retreat, and prevent straggling.

NEW YORK, Sept. 13—The Paris Press positively denies that the American government has delivered any protest to the French government, or made any verbal complaints against the proceedings of the French in Mexico, and strives to prove that the Washington government has no right to make such a protest.

CHARLESTON, Sept. 15.—The weather here is variable and the equinoctial gale is daily expected.

The enemy is building a telegraph line from Tybe Island and Fort Pulaski along the Carolina coast to Cummings' Point.

Our batteries continue to annoy the enemy occasionally. No other firing is heard.

CHARLESTON, Sept. 15.—There was considerable firing to day from our batteries against the enemy. A magazine at one of our James Island batteries exploded, killing a Lieutenant and five men.

RICHMOND, Sept. 14—The report from Fredericksburg of a threatened attempt of a force of Yankees to cross the river at that place is not true.

There is nothing additional from the upper Rappahannock, except the report of a renewal of the fight at Culpepper Courthouse to-day.

It is understood that the exchange of prisoners at City Point will be renewed in a few days.

The Virginia Legislature has passed an act authorizing the reception of all issues of Confederate notes into the treasury in payment of taxes and other State dues.

The subject of punishment for desertion from the army is under consideration. The Senate has already passed a bill to punish with severe penalties persons harboring deserters. Another bill is pending.

RICHMOND, Sept. 15.—In the fight at Brandy Station on Sunday, Gen. Stuart lost two pieces of horse artillery.

The enemy had advanced to Rapidan. Skirmishing was going on all day yesterday between the cavalry and sharpshooters.

RICHMOND, September 15.—All is quiet on the Rapidan to-day. The prospect of an engagement is diminishing.

We lost twenty-three killed and wounded in the artillery duel at Raccoon Ford.

The flag of truce at City Point to-day brought three hundred and fifty paroled convalescent prisoners.

CHARLESTON, Sept. 15.—There has been considerable firing to-day from our batteries against the enemy.

ATLANTA, Sept 14—Advices from the front are that Gen. Sherrod Johnson and Gen. Forrest were skirmishing with the enemy near Dalton, Friday. Gen. Forrest was slightly wounded, but still kept his saddle.

The Yankee advance was at Tunnel Hill on Friday night. Our troops were concentrating to meet them.

There is a report that Gen. Wheeler had a skirmish near Lafayette on Friday.

The enemy being strong, Wheeler fell back.

On Saturday Gen. Buckner took 300 prisoners at McLemore's Gap.

CHARLESTON, Sept. 14.—There has been nothing to vary the monotony here to-day. Very little firing. Some anxiety prevails to hear from Bragg.

The enemy is perfecting his arrangements for the permanent occupation of Morris Island. He has erected a telegraph along the whole length of the Island, and is converting Battery Wagner into a powerful work—enlarging the bomb proof, &c.

The Yankees fire occasionally from Battery Gregg on boats plying in the harbor.

It is understood that the exchange of prisoners at City Point will be removed in a few days.

The enemy had advanced to Rapidan. Skirmishing was going on all day, between the cavalry and sharpshooters.

September 15.—All is quiet on the Rapidan to-day. The prospect of an engagement is diminishing.

We lost twenty-three killed and wounded in the artillery duel at Racoon Ford.

Baltimore papers of Saturday afternoon contain telegrams from Fortress Monroe, announcing an arrival from Charleston bar, with advices to the 6th.

The only allusion to the repulse of the attack on Fort Sumter, is that a small boat expedition left the squadron on the night of the 8th, to storm Sumter, but was repulsed with a loss of a number killed and wounded, and also some prisoners. It is reported that Burnside has tendered his resignation.

DETROIT, September 12.—Mr. Vallandigham has returned to Windsor, and was visited to-day by several distinguished citizens of Ohio, who represented the prospects in that State as daily growing in favor of the Democracy.

The U. S. steamer Michigan is lying at anchor in the river with steam up, watching Mr. Vallandigham's movements, to prevent, if possible, his making his appearance in the United States. She has already overhauled several suspicious craft, among which was the steamer Morning Star, a few miles below the city, on her way to Cleveland.

Reports have been current the last few days, in this city, that the draft will be immediately enforced in Michigan.

DETROIT, Sept. 12—11 p. m.—Mr. Vallandigham was serenaded to-night at his hotel in Windsor. A boat load of prominent citizens of Detroit composed the party that waited upon him.

Senator Pugh, of Ohio, is here, and remains for a few days.

The Democratic Association have issued a call for a grand rally of the democracy of the city and county, to come off Sept. 20th. Hon. S. S. Cox, of Ohio, is announced as one of the speakers

The N. O. Picayune of the 24th, reports a regular engagement between the Alabama and Florida, commanded by Com. Semms, and the U. S. frigate Wabash, 42 guns. The Wabash was compelled to surrender.

The Yankees are fortifying Vicksburg and Natchez, very strongly *next to the river*.

The cavalry on the other side of the Mississippi, annoy the enemy up to the very towns.

ALEXANDRIA, Sept. 27.

I suppose the readers of the Telegraph are all anxious to see Abraham's last little joke. Well, here it is:

LINCOLN'S LETTER.

WASHINGTON, August 26.

HON. JAS. C. CONKLIN—My Dear Sir:—Your letter, inviting me to attend a mass meeting of Unconditional Union men, to be held at the capital of Illinois, on the 3d day of September, has been received. It would be very agreeable to me thus to meet my old friends at my own home, but I cannot just now be absent from this city so long as a visit there would require. The meeting is to be of all those who maintain unconditional devotion to the Union, and I am sure that my old political friends will thank me for tendering, as I do, the nation's gratitude to those other noble men whom no partisan malice or partisan hope can make false to the nation's life. There are those who are dissatisfied with me. To such I would say—you desire peace, and you blame me that we do not have it; but how can we attain it?

There are but three conceivable ways: First, to suppress the rebellion by force of arms. This I am trying to do—are you for it? If so, so far agreed; if you are not, a second way is to give up the Union—I am against this. If you are, you should say so plainly. If you are not for force nor yet for dissolution, there only remains some imaginable compromise. I do not believe that any compromise embracing the maintenance of the Union is now possible; all that I learn leads to a directly opposite belief. The strength of the rebellion is its military—its army. That army dominates all the country and all the people within its range. Any offer of terms made by any man or men within that range in opposition to that army is simply nothing, for the present, because such man or men have no power to enforce their side of a compromise if one were made with them. To illustrate, suppose refugees from the South and peace men from the North meet together in convention and frame and proclaim a compromise embracing a restoration of the Union. In what way can that compromise be used to keep Gen. Lee's army out of Pennsylvania? Gen. Meade's army can keep Gen. Lee's army out of Pennsylvania, and I think can ultimately drive it out of existence, but no paper compromise to which the controllers of Gen. Lee's army are not agreed can at all effect that army.

In an effort to make such compromise, we would waste time which the enemy would improve to our disadvantage, and that would be all. A compromise, to be effective, must be made either with those who control the rebel army, or with the people first liberated from the dominion of that army by the success of our army.

Now, allow me to assure you that no word nor intimation from the rebel army, or from any of the men controlling it, in relation to any peace compromise, has ever come to my knowledge or belief. All charges and intimations to the contrary are deceptive and groundless, and I promise you that if any such proposition shall hereafter come, it shall not be rejected and kept secret from you. I freely acknowledge myself to be the servant of the people, according to the bond of service of the United States Constitution, and that as such I am responsible to them. But, to be plain, you are dissatisfied with me about the negroes. Quite likely there is a difference of opinion between you and myself upon that subject. I certainly wish all men could be free, while you, I suppose, do not. Yet I have neither adopted nor proposed any measure which is not consistent with even your views, providing that you are for the Union. I suggested compensated emancipation, to which you replied that you wished not to be taxed to buy negroes. But I had not asked you to be taxed to buy negroes, except in such a way as to save you from greater taxation to save the Union exclusively by other means.

You dislike the emancipation proclamation, and perhaps would have it retracted. You say it is unconstitutional. I think differently. I think the Constitution vests the Commander in Chief with the law of war in time of war.

The most that can be said, if so much, is that slaves are property. Has there been any question that by the laws of war property both of enemies and friends may be taken when needed; and is it not needed whenever it helps us and hurts the enemy? Armies, the world over, destroy the enemy's property when they cannot use it, and even destroy their own to keep it from the enemy. Civilized belligerents do all in their power to help themselves and hurt the enemy, except a few things regarded as barbarous, and among the exceptions are the massacre of vanquished foes and non-combatants, male and female. But is the proclamation law valid, or is it not valid? If it is not valid, it wants no retraction; if valid, it cannot be retracted any more than the dead can be brought to life.

Some of you profess to think that retraction would operate favorably to the Union. Why better after the retraction than before the issue? There was more than a year and a half of trial to suppress the rebellion before the proclamation was issued, the last one hundred days of which passed under an explicit notice that it was coming, unless avoided by those in revolt returning to their allegiance.

The war has certainly progressed as favorably to us since the issue of the proclamation as before. I know as fully as one can know the opinion of others, that some of the commanders of our armies in the field, who have given us our most important victories believe the advantageous policy of aid from colored troops, constituted the heaviest blows yet dealt to the rebellion, and that at least one of these important successes could not have been achieved when it was, but for the aid of black soldiers.

Among the commanders holding these views are some who have never had any affinity with what is called the Abolition or with the Republican party politics, but who hold them purely as military opinions.

I submit their opinions as being entitled to some weight against the objections often urged that emancipation and arming the blacks are unwise as military measures, and were not adopted as such in good faith.

You say that you will not fight to free negroes. Some of them seem to be willing enough to fight for you, but no matter, fight exclusively to save the Union. I issued the proclamation on purpose to aid you in saving the Union. Whenever you shall have conquered all resistance to the Union, and I shall urge you to continue fighting, it will be an appropriate time for you to declare you will not fight to free negroes.

I thought that in your struggle for the Union, to whatever extent the negroes should cease helping the enemy, to that extent it weakens the army in her resistance to you. Do you think different? I thought that whatever negroes can be got to do as soldiers, leaves just so much less for the white soldiers to do in saving the Union.

Does it appear otherwise to you? But negroes, like other people, act upon motives. Why should they do anything for us, if we will do nothing for them? If they stake their lives for us, they must be prompted by the strongest motives. Even the promise of freedom, and the promise being made must be kept.

The signs look better. The father of waters again goes unvexed to the sea, thanks to the great Northwest for it, nor yet wholly to them. Three hundred miles up they meet New England, the Empire State, the Keystone State and Jersey hawing their way right and left. The sunny South, too, in more colors than one, also lent a hand on the spot. Then part of the history was jotted down in white and black.

The job was a great National one, and let no more be barred who bore an honorable part in it, and while those who have cleared the great river may well be proud; even that is not all. It is hard to say that anything has been more bravely and better done than at Antietam, Murfreesboro, Gettysburg, and on many fields of less note.

Nor must Uncle Sam's webbed feet be forgotten. At all the water's margins they have been present, not only on the deep sea, the broad bay and the rapid river, but also up the narrow, muddy bayou, and where the ground was a little damp they have made their tracks.

Thanks to all the great Republic, for the principles by which it lives and keeps alive for man's vast future. Thanks to all peace does not appear so distant as it did.

I hope it will come soon and come to stay, and so come as to be worth the keeping in all future times. It will then have been proved that among free men there can be no successful appeal from the ballot to the bullet; and that they who take such an appeal are sure to loose their case and pay the cost; and then there will be some black men who can remember that, with silent tongue, and with clenched teeth, and with steady eye and well pierced bayonet they had helped mankind on to this great consummation, while I fear that there will be some white men unable to forget that with malignant heart and deceitful speech, they have striven to hinder it. Still let us not be over sanguine of a speedy final triumph—let us be quite sober—let us diligently apply the means, never doubting that a just God, in his own good time will give us the rightful result.

Yours, very truly,
ABRAHAM LINCOLN.

I said, a long time ago, that there never would be a "decisive" battle fought during this war, and that it would eventuate in a guerrilla warfare. Lincoln evidently has about arrived at the same conclusion. He, however, still entertains the opinion that we will ultimately be "subjugated." I do not Time will prove who is the better prophet.

One effect of Abe's letter was to send gold up in New York in two days from 124⅝ to 147 per cent! Wall street is a barometer on which there is no discount.

There is one peculiarity about this letter. Aside from the sentiment it embraces, it is the greatest botch of a letter that has eminated from a professed statesman this century. Every rule of grammar is violated in it. You can scarcely find in it a strictly grammatical sentence, and most of the sentences are such as ought to put to shame the ordinary run of flatboatmen and rail splitters.

THE CAUSE OF OUR TROUBLES.

A correspondent of the Richmond Whig makes a few home truths which might not miss the mark if aimed at some who now flourish in Texas as well as elsewhere. He says:

"To saddle our present troubles on the President must manifest to any attentive observer a profound degree of ignorance. To accuse Pemberton, D. H. Hill and Bragg of inefficiency, because of their want of success, and compliment Beauregard *because of his success*, shows a great want of knowledge of the facts of our history. Who ever had a greater run of bad luck than Beauregard, from Columbus, Island No. 10, Shiloh, Corinth? Who has a better disciplined army, or one that has fought better and manifested more attachment to its leader than Bragg? Who can boast of better fighting than D. H. Hill, from Richmond to Sharpsburg? And still President Davis is denounced for appointing these men. No, sir, the cause of our troubles is to be found principally among the people. They denounce the President for not concentrating our forces, and so soon as he begins to do so, the cry is raised that he is giving up large districts of country to the enemy. They denounce him for a want of energy in equipping and filling the ranks of our army, and yet they hold on to every bushel of grain, and many of the denouncers of the President, to my certain knowledge, conceal it to prevent the government from getting it, hoping thereby, to raise money from the afflictions and necessities of their country. They denounce our Generals and Government for not enforcing discipline in the army, and will keep their own sons at home as long as they can without ensuring them a deserter's fate. They denounce the Government for not securing provisions in certain exposed districts of country, and when the Government sends wagons there they refuse to sell forage at any price, declaring they have none to spare. They denounce the Government for not supplying the soldiers with better food and clothing, and yet they charge a poor soldier from one to two dollars for a very poor meal. If these croakers and fault finders would join the army and fight, we would gain our independence in two months.

Under the caption of "Greely's Stocks" a New York paper quotes the sales of some negroes in Georgia.

H. P.

ALEXANDRIA, Sept. 25.—The following letter is from the correspondent of the Chicago Times. All the Yankee papers admit that he is the most reliable and truth telling letter writer they have among them. Although lengthy, I give it entire on account of its merit:

WASHINGTON, Aug. 22.—Unless the signs of the times are utterly deceptive, the approaching month of September will open with very nearly the same military situation, near Washington, as was witnessed in the first days of September of last year. The Confederates are doing all in their power to bring on a collission between the armies of Gen. Lee and Gen. Meade, under circumstances that will result in the defeat of the latter, and that will place Washington in danger; and the administration is doing all in its power to assis them.

The movement of Gen. Lee's army from Winchester to Culpepper, between the 22d and 24th of July, was not the end of Lee's campaign, although the administration has been led to believe that it was. The object of that campaign, on the part of Gen. Lee, was the defeat of Meade's army and the capture of Washington. All of Gen. Lee's movements ever since he recently reached Gordonsville and Culpepper, have been made with the object still in view. The administration is so blind that it cannot see this.

At the time the two armies reached their present positions on opposite sides of the Rappahannock, say on the 25th ult., they were about equal in numbers; at least the disparity between them was not very great. What has been the course of the two Governments since? The one has been marked by wisdom, decision and activity; the other by hesitation, inactivity and stupidity. On the part of the Confederates, Gen. Lee has been reinforced to an extent that now gives him the command of 150,000 troops, and he has been spending the last three weeks in drilling and exercising, in the cool and shady dells of the Shenandoah Valley, fifteen squadrons of newly organized cavalry, and twelve batteries of newly organized artillery, the guns of which are new brass field pieces. Has anything of the kind been done to Gen. Meade's army? On the contrary, so far from acting on the offensive, it may well be doubted whether that army is even able to act on the defensive on the line of the Rappahannock. To keep that army where it is now is to expose it to attack from greatly superior numbers, and from an enemy who has, within a few days, showed both the ability and the inclination to get in Gen. Meade's rear. Do not be surprised, therefore, if, at any moment, you hear that the army of the Potomac has returned to Washington. If Gen. Meade is allowed to make this movement promptly enough, it will be in his power to occupy with his army the heights of Centreville. By doing this, he will not only cover Washington effectually, but he will also be able to prevent the enemy from coming north of Occoquan River, or east of the Bull Run Mountains, all winter. But, if the policy of vacillation and indecision prevails here many days longer, you may expect to see the heights of Centreville occupied by Gen. Lee's army, and Gen. Meade's army either defeated, or else retreating to the Washington forts. In this case, either the scenes of last September will be re-enacted, or else we will have another winter like that of 1861–'62, with Washington beleagured and the Capitol, or else this city will be at once attacked.

Such are the disgraceful alternatives that are presented to us. Such is the humiliating position to which we are reduced in consequence of the fact that the war on our part is managed by politicians, and solely with political ends in view.—Instead of reinforcing General Meade properly, the Administration, during the last four weeks, has been lending all its energies to the task of managing the next Presidential election, so as to secure a new lease of power, and of managing to defeat the election of a new Democratic Speaker in the next House of Representatives; and of plotting for the abolition of slavery in the Southern States!

The members of the Administration are greatly depressed at the nature of the dispatches from Charleston. In spite of the glowing accounts in the papers, and the fine promises made every day, but never fulfilled, that "Charleston will be taken in a few days; that "Fort Sumter will soon be ours," that "the nest of the rebellion will speedily be wiped out," it is well known that there is no prospect of immediate success there, and very little prospect of ultimate success at present. The popular idea, that the fate of Charleston depends upon Fort Sumter, is erroneous. If Fort Sumter were demolished to-morrow, the task of taking Charleston would only be begun. The city *cannot* be reached by vessels. The harbor has been rendered utterly *inaccessible*. This fact will be apparent after Fort Sumter is knocked to pieces, if that fate is in reserve for it. When Charleston is completely invested both by land and sea, and by a land force amounting to 200,000 troops, Charleston may be expected to fall.—But this has not been done; and the Administration has been informed to-day that enough troops have been sent from Richmond to Gen. Beauregard to insure the successful defence of the place.

The magnitude of the task of "subjugating the South," which the administration has undertaken, now begins to become apparent. The work is only begun yet; but see what it is costing the country already. Look at the matter of military force alone. We have already called out and put into the field one million five hundred thousand men. Of these 100,000 have returned to their homes at the expiration of the term of their enlistment, and 600,000 now compose our force in the field. Where are the rest? Where are the other 800,000 men? They have perished, either in battle or by disease. And how many of the troops that we now have in arms are available for active operations in the field? Not one half of them. It will require more than one-half of them—nay, it does require more than one-half of them—to "hold, occupy and possess" those points on the borders of the South that have already been captured. Look at Norfolk, Newbern, and the sundry points in North Carolina where the attempt is being made to develop "a healthy Union sentiment," by stealing slaves and "confiscating" private property. Can it be supposed that anything less than 15,000 troops would be enough to retain possession of those places? Look at the Peninsula. Even while General Dix was there with 30,000

THE NEW YORK HERALD.

WHOLE NO. 9889. NEW YORK, WEDNESDAY, OCTOBER 14, 1863.—TRIPLE SHEET. PRICE THREE CENTS.

THE MILITARY SITUATION.

Map of the Present Scene of Active Operations in Eastern Tennessee and Georgia.

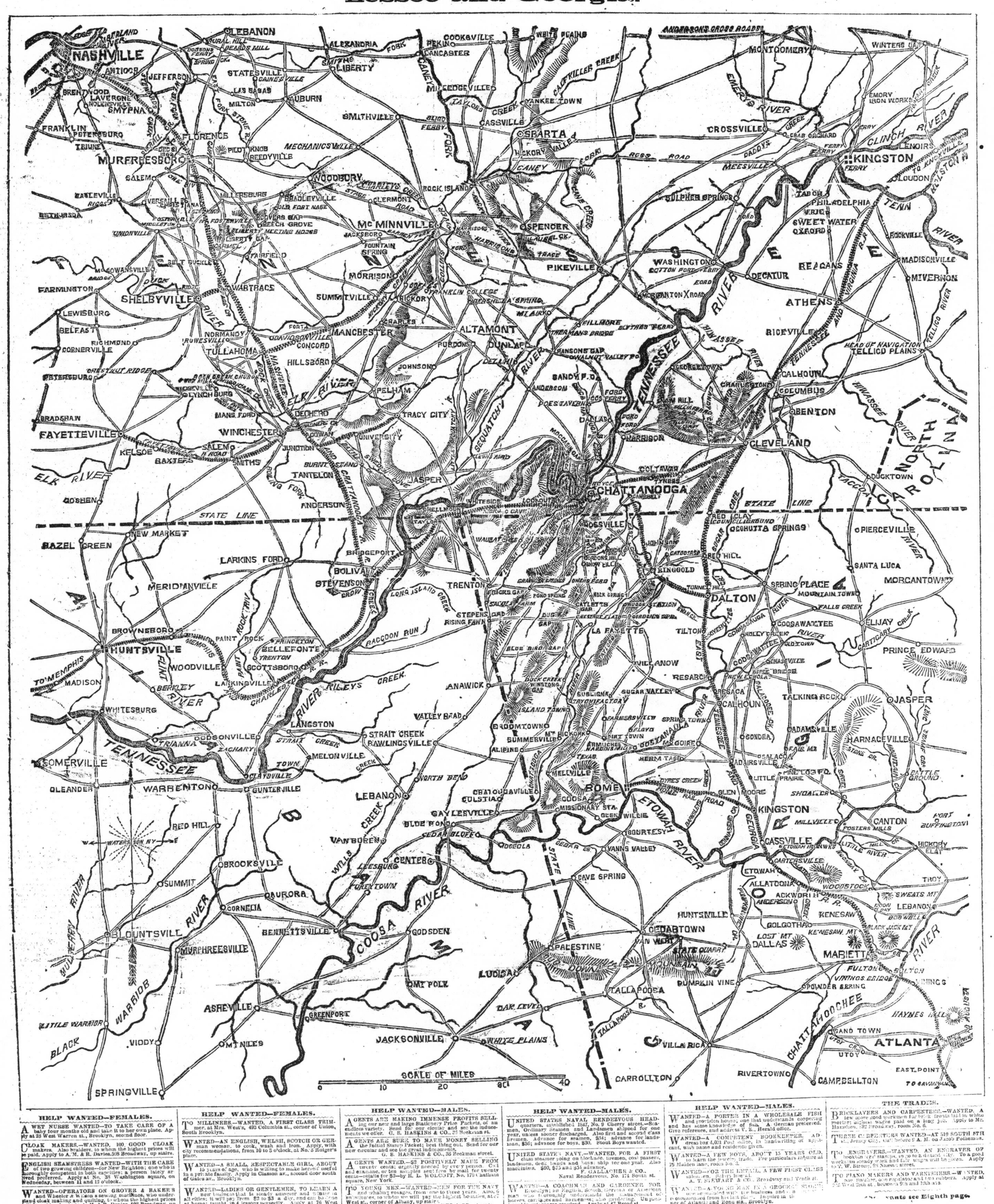

[illegible] wants see Eighth page.

The Daily Huntsville Confederate.

VOL. I. MARIETTA, GEO., FRIDAY EVENING, OCTOBER 16, 1863. NO. 104.

[No. 90.]

An Act to Authorize the Establishment of Express Mails.

The Congress of the Confederate States of America do enact, That the Postmaster General be, and he is hereby, authorized, if found practicable and necessary, to establish express mails for the conveyance of letters and Government dispatches only, as a means of securing greater dispatch than can be afforded by the regular mails; and the lines of express mails so established shall be deemed post routes.

SEC. 2. The rates of such postage on such lines shall be fixed by the Postmaster General, but shall not exceed one dollar on a single letter not exceeding in weight one half ounce, and at the same rate for any additional half ounce, or fraction of a half ounce, for any distance not exceeding five hundred miles, and for any distance exceeding five hundred miles double the said rate to be so fixed. Provided, This law shall not repeal the laws now in force regulating the ordinary mail service.

Approved May 1, 1863. [sept11—1aw2w.

[No. 92.]

Joint Resolutions to Provide for the Payment of certain Accounts of the Acting Quartermaster and other Officers of the Indian Troops.

Resolved by the Congress of the Confederate States of America, That the Quartermaster General audit and pay the accounts of the Acting Quartermaster and other officers of the Indian troops, for camp utensils, horse equipments, clothing, ordnance, and advance stores furnished by Jones and Thebo and R. M. Jones, for the use of said troops, upon the bills of particulars herewith filed, amounting to eleven thousand two hundred and sixteen dollars and seventy-five cents: Provided, That said accounts have been examined and approved by Brigadier-General Albert Pike.

Approved May 1, 1863. [sept11—1t.

[No. 93.]

An Act to Continue and Amend the Third Section of an Act Supplementary to an Act concerning the Pay and allowance due to deceased soldiers, approved February 15, 1862, and to provide for the prompt settlement of claims for arrearages of pay, allowance and bounty due deceased officers and Soldiers.

The Congress of the Confederate States of America do enact, That the third section of an act entitled "An Act supplementary to an act concerning the pay and allowance due to deceased soldiers," approved February 15th, eighteen hundred and sixty-two, and to provide for the prompt settlement of claims for arrearages of pay, allowance and bounty due deceased officers and soldiers, be continued of force until otherwise provided by Congress.

Approved May 1, 1863. [sept11—1aw4w.

[No. 94.]

An Act to amend an act entitled "An Act to organize Military Courts to attend the army of the Confederate States in the field, and to define the powers of said Courts," Approved October 9th, 1862.

The Congress of the Confederate States of America do enact, That in addition to one military court to attend each army corps in the field, as now authorized by an Act entitled "An Act to organize military courts to attend the army of the Confederate States in the field, and to define the power of said Courts," approved October ninth, eighteen hundred and sixty-two, one military court shall be organized in each of such military departments as, in the judgment of the President, the public exigencies may require; to be organized in the manner and with powers prescribed in the act of which this is an amendatory.

Approved May 1, 1863. [sept11—1aw3w.

[No. 95.]

An Act in relation to the custody of persons charged with Offences against the Confederate States.

The Congress of the Confederate States of America do enact, That whenever, from insecurity or other reason, a District Court Commissioner shall, in his discretion, deem it inadvisable to commit a prisoner to the jail of the county in which he shall be sitting, he shall commit him to any other jail within his district, or the district within which the offence is alleged to have been committed, which shall seem to him most convenient and safe.

SEC. 2. That whenever it shall appear to a Commissioner that good reason exists for the removal of a prisoner already committed, he shall order his removal and commitment to any jail to which he might have committed him under the first section of this act.

Approved May 1, 1863. [sept11—1aw2w.

[No. 96.]

An Act to provide for the election of Members of Congress for certain Districts of the State of Louisiana.

The Congress of the Confederate States of America do enact, That unless the Legislature thereof shall otherwise provide, the members of Congress for any district of the State of Louisiana in which an election cannot conveniently be held in consequence of the same being occupied wholly or in part by the troops of the enemy, may, on proclamation of that fact by the Governor of said State, be chosen by the qualified voters thereof, in such portions of the State as shall not be so occupied.

SEC. 2. The election provided for in the foregoing section shall be held at such time and places as may be prescribed by the laws of said State now in force, or as hereafter be enacted, and shall in all respects, not inconsistent with the provisions of this act, be conducted in the mode prescribed by said laws.

Approved May 1, 1863. [sept11—1aw2w.

An Act making appropriations for the support of the Government, for the period from February first, to June thirtieth, eighteen hundred and sixty-three, inclusive, and to supply deficiencies arising prior thereto.

The Congress of the Confederate States of America do enact, That there be appropriated and paid out of any money in the treasury, not otherwise appropriated, the following sums of money, and for the following purposes, viz:

Legislative.—For compensation and mileage of members and delegates of the House of Representatives, one hundred and seventy-four thousand, two hundred dollars.

For compensation of officers, clerks, &c., of the House of Representatives, five thousand, five hundred dollars.

For contingent expenses of the House of Representatives, ten thousand dollars.

For compensation and mileage of members of the Senate, twenty-nine thousand, nine hundred dollars.

For compensation of officers, clerks, &c., of the Senate, six thousand dollars.

For contingent expenses of the Senate, six thousand dollars.

Executive.—For componsation of the President of the Confederate States, six thousand, two hundred and fifty dollars.

For compensation of the Vice-President of the Confederate States, one thousand five hundred dollars.

For compensation of the private secretary and messenger of the President, one thousand and seven dollars and thirteen cents.

For compensation of the private secretary of the Vice-President, seven hundred and fourteen dollars and forty cents.

For contingent and telegraphic expenses of the Executive office, four thousand dollars.

Treasury Department.—For compensation of the Secretary of the Treasury, Assistant Secretary, Comptroller, Auditors, Treasurer, and Register, and clerks, and messengers in said department, three hundred and fifty-seven thousand, eight hundred and ninety-seven dollars and ten cents.

For incidental and contingent expenses of the treasury department, twenty-one thousand eight hundred dollars.

For interest on the public debt, twenty million dollars.

For engraving and printing treasury notes, bonds and certificates of stock, and for paper for the same, three hundred and fifty thousand dollars.

For the transfer of funds to foreign parts, five million dollars.

For the transmission of Confederate States funds, two hundred thousand dollars.

War Department.—For compensation of the Secretary of War, Assistant Secretary, Chief of Bureau, clerks, messengers, &c., in said department, ninety-six thousand, seven hundred and fifty dollars.

For incidental and contingent expenses of the war department, fifty-four thousand dollars.

Quartermaster's Department,—For the pay of the army one hundred and nineteen million, two hundred and seventy thousand, seven hundred and seventy-one dollars.

For the transportation of troops and their baggage, of quartermaster's stores, subsistence, ordnance and ordnance stores, from place of purchase to troops in the field, purchase of horses, mules, wagons and harness, purchase of lumber, nails, iron and steel for erecting storehouses, quarters for troops and other repairs, hire of teamsters, laborers, &c., forty-seven million, seven hundred and eight thousand, three hundred and eight dollars.

For pay for horses of non-commissioned officers and privates killed in battle, under act No. 48, section 7, and for which provision is to be made, one hundred and twenty-five thousand dollars.

For pay for property pressed into the service of the Confederate States, under appraisement, said property having been either lost or applied to the public service, one hundred and eighty-seven thousand, five hundred dollars.

For the subsistence of prisoners of war, under act No. 181, section 1, and the hire of the necessary prisons, guard houses, &c., for the safe-keeping of the same, or so much thereof as may be necessary, one million dollars.

For the bounty of fifty dollars to each non-commissioned officer, musician and private now in the service for three years or for the war, to be paid at the expiration of the first year's service, on the basis that sixty thousand men will have to be paid, three million dollars.

For pay of the officers on duty in the offices of Adjutant and Inspector General's Department, the Quartermaster General's Department, medical, engineer, ordnance and subsistence departments, three hundred and twenty-three thousand three hundred and fifty dollars.

Commissary Department.—For the purchase of subsistence stores and commissary property, forty-eight million, six hundred and fifty-six thousand five hundred dollars.

Ordnance Department.—For the ordnance service in all its branches, twelve million five hundred thousand dollars.

For the purchase of pig and rolled iron, three million dollars.

Engineer Department.—For the engineer service, three million dollars.

Medical Department.—For pay of private physicians employed by contract, one hundred and fifty thousand dollars.

For pay of nurses and cooks, not enlisted or volunteers, two hundred and forty thousand dollars.

For pay of hospital stewards, sixty thousand thousand dollars.

For pay of matrons, assistant matrons and ward matrons, two hundred and forty thousand dollars.

For pay of ward masters, one hundred and fifty thousand dollars.

For pay of hospital laundresses, fifty thousand dollars.

For medical and hospital supplies, two million five hundred thousand dollars.

For the establishment and support of military hospitals, one hundrod and fifty thousand dollars.

MISSISSIPPI.—A letter from Canton, Miss. dated the 28th ult., says:

Quite a number of small boats have passed down the Mississippi without loads. These boats are evidently intended to bring the soldiers down the Red, White, and other rivers, for the purpose of supplying the places of those who are being hurried North. Thus is Texas, Arkansas, and Louisiana, being relieved by events at Chattanooga, where the backbone of the Yankee campaign appears to have been effectually crushed. Their columns are staggering everywhere, and all that seems to be needed to prostrate them is to push them briskly before they recover from the shock.—There will soon be nothing to keep our hosts from the west bank of the river, and I have no doubt they will be there in due season, while on this side there is every indication that we will not be laggards in seizing the golden opportunity.

Dispatches from Washington, marked "approved" by authorities there, admit a severe reverse in Tennessee, and censure Burnside for it.

TELEGRAPHIC.

Reports of the Press Association.

CHARLESTON, Oct. 16.—This is the 98th day of the siege. A grand review of the troops, by Gen. Beauregard, will take place to-day.—Nothing new, this morning. Weather fair.

From our Morning Edition.

RICHMOND, Oct. 15.—The following telegram has been received from Meridian, 15th: Gen. S. Cooper: The following dispatch has been received from Oxford, 14th: Eleven regiments of cavalry, with 9 pieces of artillery pursued us. We skirmished with them all the way, fought them four hours near Byhalia, and at the river, when they were repulsed and retired, after burning Wyatt. Our loss is considerable—the number not known, on account of much straggling. We saved our train and captured property.

JOS. E. JOHNSTON.

CHARLESTON, Oct. 15.—Two French war vessels arrived off the bar to-day, and signified a desire to communicate with the French Consul. He will, probably, visit them to-morrow. Capt. Haulv and a crew of seven men, in a small boat, were drowned in harbor this mornmorning. Firing of our batteries continues; no response from the enemy.

RICHMOND, Oct. 15.—The Petersburg *Express* today, has an extra New York *Herald*, of the 12th. The news from Tennessee consists, chiefly, of confused reports of the movements of Wheeler and Wharton.

A telegram from Nashville, the 11th, announces the arrival of three hundred rebel prisoners, captured at McMinnville, and more expected. The same dispatch says, telegraphic and railroad communication with the front is uninterrupted.

A dispatch from Leavenworth gives the particulars of an attack on Gen. Blount and escort below Fort Scott, by three hundred rebels in Union uniforms. His escort broke. Out of a hundred men 78 were killed.

Maj. Curtis, a son of Gen. Curtis, was thrown from his horse, and found with a bullet hole through his head.

Gen. Blount escaped and meeting reinforcements below Fort Scoott, took command of them and started in pursuit of Quantrell in Cowskin Prairie, McDonald Co., Missouri. A letter from Fort Scott, 8th, says the rebel forces burned Carthage, Mo., that morning. Gen. Schofield telegraphed to Leavenworth, that 1800 Rebels, under Quantrell, Coffee, Gordon and Hunter, were marching on Fort Scott, and that he had ordered Col. Weir to remove all the force he could to Fort Scott

A telegram from Washington, 11th, refers to the failure of Buford's cavalry to ascertain whether the enemy had fallen back on Gordonsville, or was attempting some flank movement to get between Meade's army and Washington in a similar manner to Stonewall Jackson's movement on Pope over the same ground.

The prevailing impression seems to be that the Rebels have gone to Gordonsville and Richmond, where sufficient garrisons may be left, and the remainder of Lee's army sent to reininforce Bragg and Beauregard.

Another telegram, of the same date, says, it appears to be, generally, believed that the main body of A. P. Hill's corps passed from left to right of our front, pursuing an obscure route near the Blue Ridge, intending to make a demonstration on our right, for the purpose of cutting our railroad communications.—Measures are progressing to give him a fitting reception in that quarter. We are, also, prepared for an attack on our front. The advance of Hill's corps, probably, commenced moving from Madison C. H. Thursday morning.

A mob in Jackson, New Hampshire, 8th, burned the hotel, where the deputy provost marshal was stopping, while serving notices on drafted men.

Gold in New York, on Saturday, 149.

RAPPAHANNOCK, Oct. 14.—The bridge over the Rappahannock was badly burnt. The ruin is, still, smoking. Rapid firing has been heard here, during tqe day, in the direction of Warrenton.

There was a cavalry skirmish at Catlett's Station, on Tuesday, the enemy fleeing.

Our cavalry surrounded a body of Yankees, dismounted cavalry, acting as sharpshooters, at Jefferson, Tuesday, wounding several, and taking over 100 prisoners. More prisoners are coming.

The country, from Culpeper C. H., to this point, is desolated. The negroes are all carried off. Most of the houses, left untenanted, are pulled to pieces to build Yankee huts.

The battle-field about Brand'y's Station is literally strewed with dead with dead horses.

Botts is, again, paroled, and appears at Richmond.

The Bristol (Tenn.) *Advocate* of the 8th states that Mr. James H. Debtor, of Stickleysville, Lee county, Va., come to our town Monday night, with four prisoners—three Yankees or Kentuckians, and a Confederate deserter.—Debtor being the sole guard for 50 or 60 miles.

Mr. *Debtor* is entitled to great *credit* for this act!—*Knox. Reg.*

The Albemarle Movement.

A SUCCINCT EXPOSITION BY SENATOR WIGFALL, OF THE CAUSES AND EFFECTS OF HIGH PRICES, ETC.—PRACTICAL SUGGESTIONS.

The Central Committee appointed at the late meeting in Albemarle county, Va., has appointed various sub-committees to canvass their respective districts, and to obtain the written pledge of the people to carry out said resolutions. By request, Mr. Wigfall has furnished the following brief sketch of his remarks at the September Court:

Gentlemen: In compliance with your request, I herewith furnish briefly the reasons which induced me to advise the action lately taken by yourselves and others of this county.

It seems to me that the people do not properly realize the fact that their interests are identical with those of their Government. It is but their agent. It has and can have no interest which is antagonist to theirs. The President, members of Congress, Cabinet, Ministers and Judges, are all citizens of the country, chosen by other citizens to discharge temporarily the duties which belong to their respective offices.

The army is also composed of citizens. It has to be paid, clothed, subsisted and armed. This can be done only by the Government.—The heavy purchases necessary for this purpose must be made either on credit or for cash. The Government itself has no credit except that based on the property of the people. It has no money except that collected by taxation.

It follows, then, that it is the interest of the tax-payers that the war shall be conducted with as little cost as possible. In other words, that the Government should buy at the lowest prices.

The currency now reaches certainly five and possibly ten times the amount necessary for the convenient transaction of the business of the country. Prices have steadily risen as money has become abundant. Reduce the currency and prices will fall. The war debt will thus be lessened and the taxes be lightened in proportion.

Those who are now selling for high prices will receive less it is true; but they will pay less for what they buy, and on the whole their condition will not be materially changed.—The farmer now protects himself against what he considers the extortion of the merchant by the increased price of his produce. So the merchant protects himself against the farmer. All who have anything to sell seem to be growing rich. How is it with the Government who buys everything and sells nothing? It buys for the tax-payers and every note it issues must at some time be redeemed by them in gold or silver. When that time comes they will see that instead of riches they have been piling up a monument of debt to fall upon and crush them.

Their liberties have been invaded and their right to self-government denied. They have been involved in a most cruel war. An army has been put in the field. To arm and subsist it Treasury notes have been issued, and have become the currency of the country. They were issued in large amounts, and prices immediately began to rise. The higher the prices the larger the issues, and the larger the issues the higher the prices. The cost of the war the first year was one or two hundred millions of dollars, three or four hundred millions the next, and it will be eight or ten the third, if prices are not reduced. Must not such a debt swallow up not the incomes only, but the property itself of the tax payers, if prices continue to increase in the future as they have in the past? Let them no longer live under the fatal delusion that they are growing richer and richer by selling to each other and to the Government at prices steadily growing higher and higher. They will wake from that dream of prosperity when peace and the tax-gatherer come.

The remedy I suggest will certainly reach the evil if acted on. Then let every man at once resolve to invest every surplus dollar in Government bonds. Every dollar that is so invested will to that extent contract the currency and reduce prices. The cost of the war will then begin steadily to decrease. It has increased heretofore, it is now increasing, and it must be diminished, or the people will be ruined. The present debt can be easily handled if funded. The Government can well afford to pay eight per cent. interest on the cost of army supplies, when buying at from five hundred to one thousand per cent. less than it is now paying. Would any farmer give for a horse his note without interest for a thousand dollars, if he could buy the same horse for a hundred dollars and borrow the money at eight per cent. interest?

This is no "*Government Debt*" we are contracting. It is a debt which *we* shall have to pay. Every man who has one dollar's worth of property to be taxed will be called on for his share. Then let those who are interested at once turn over to the Government their one-tenth tax in kind, and to that extent relieve the Government from the necessity of further purchasing and further inflating the currency, by additional issues of treasury notes. Set aside also another tenth, and, if needed, sell it to the Government at old prices. The issue of treasury notes will thus, day by day, become less, and day by day those now in circulation will become absorbed. Prices then must soon fall. In the meantime sell to the soldier's family at reasonable prices. Deal not hardly with the wives and children of those who are fighting for the protection of our property. Upon the soldier the present high prices fall with peculiar hardship. The eleven dollars a month which he receives is scarcely worth one, and he cannot be relieved by an increase of pay. It would but still further inflate the currency and increase prices. If his pay were double, the twenty-two dollars would probably buy less than the eleven which he now receives.

Trusting, gentlemen, that the other counties will follow the noble example yours has set, and that, if they should do so, the people of the other States will not regard with indifference the action of the people of this great Commonwealth, I beg leave to remain,

Very respectfully,

Your obedient servant,

LOUIS T. WIGFALL.

To Messrs. W. W. Minor, T. J. Randolph, W. S. Dabney, J. J. Bowcock, S. W. Ficklin, W. H. Southall, Thos. Wood, Committee.

MILITARY CORPS.

EXECUTIVE HEADQUARTERS,
Chattanooga, Tenn., August 7, 1863.

General Orders, No. 15.]

I. The returns of the census provided for in an act of the General Assembly of the State of Tennessee, passed March 18th, 1862, entitled "An Act, to raise, organize and equip a provisional force, and for other purposes" having been made from those counties not occupied by the enemy; and under the legislation of the Confederate Government all those between the ages of eighteen and forty-five, having been called into service, the Governor directs the organization of all the able-bodied white male population (included in the counties named in this order) of the State, under the provisions of this act, into a military corps, for the defence of the State; and, for the purposes of said organization directs, that the militia districts for companies, as they existed in the militia, shall constitute districts for companies in the military corps, and that the boundaries, and limits of territory and population constituting a regiment, and in the militia law, shall constitute and form a regiment in the military corps of the State, which are numbered and laid off in this order, for the Eastern Division of the State, with a view of directing the election of regimental and company officers, viz:

Those persons constituting the military corps of the county of Johnson, shall compose the 1st regiment:

The county of Carter	2d	Regiment
The county of Sullivan	3d & 4th	"
The county of Washington	5th & 6th	"
The county of Hancock	7th	"
The county of Union	8th	"
The county of Green	9th & 10th	"
The county of Hawkins	11th, 12th & 13th	"
The county of Cocke	14th	"
The county of Jefferson	15th & 16th	"
The county of Grainger	17th & 18th	"
The county of Claiborne	19th & 20th	"
The county of Sevier	21st	"
The county of Blount	22d & 23d	"
The county of Knox	24th & 25th	"
The county of Anderson	26th	"
The county of Campbell	27th	"
The county of Monroe	28th & 29th	"
The county of Rome	30th & 31st	"
The county of Morgan	32d	"
The county of McMinn	33d, 34th & 35th	"
The county of Meigs	36th	"
The county of Rhae	37th	"
The county of Bledsoe	38th	"
The county of Hamilton	39th	"
The county of Marion	40th	"
The county of Sequatchie	41st	"
The county of Bradley	42d & 43d	"
The county of Polk	44th	"
The county of Scott	45th	"

II. These commands will be changed, modified, or consolidated whenever their efficiency may demand it.

III. Each company is entited to elect one Captain, and three Lieutenants, and each regiment is entitled to elect one Colonel, one Lieut. Colonel and one Major. Said officers will be commissioned by the Governor and will hold their offices during the existence of said military corps unless they shall become unnecessary by consolidation or reorganization.

IV. The Constables in each district, or such other persons as the Sheriff may appoint, shall hold the election for said offices, at the places heretofore designated under the militia law, for the election of officers of the militia of like grade. And said elections shall be held, and returns thereof made in all respects as required by the militia law, in regard to the election of officers of the militia of like grades.

V. Such inhabitants of the State, between 18 and 45 years of age as have been exempted from conscription into the service of the armies of the Confederate States, shall constitute a part of the military corps of the State for its defence.

VI. Sheriffs and Constables of the counties in the Eastern Division of the State, will open and hold an election for the officers of the military corps of said Division, on Tuesday the 27th day of August, 1863.

VII. Upon the organization of regiments, the commanders will report the strength of their commands by companies to the Adjutant General of the State.

VIII. Captains of Companies are directed vigilantly and constantly to police his district with his command or details therefor, to arrest and send forward to the nearest Confederate force, all stragglers and deserters from the army—and to perform such other duties as may protect their immediate country.

IX. In the event any command as organized by this order, shall fail to elect the officers required, the Governor will at once exercise the authority conferred upon him by the act of the General Assembly, and appoint the necessary officers.

X. Volunteer companies to be mustered into the Confederate service, for the period of six months, and for service within the limits of the State of Tennessee tendered in accordance with the terms prescribed by the Governor in his proclamation of July 22d, 1862, will be accepted if organized and offered on or before the 27th of August, 1863.

By command of ISHAM G. HARRIS, Gov., &c.

aug13—te. W. C. WHITTHORNE, A. Gen.

All the papers in the State, weekly and daily papers will publish semi-weekly till election.

OFFICE COMMANDANT CONSCRIPTS,
Talladega, Ala., July 28, 1863.

General Orders, No. 19.]

I. The following notice from the Bureau of Conscription is published for the information of all concerned particularly of enrolling officers:

NOTICE.

BUREAU OF CONSCRIPTION,
Richmond, July 21, 1863.

To answer numerous inquiries, and to correct errors not uncommon, the following notice is published to all concerned.

1. Under the recent call of the President extending the conscript age, all substitutions have ceased to be valid, if the substitute be less than 45 years old, and is not otherwise exempt by law.

2. Membership, unless as an officer duly accepted by the War Department, of local organizations for home defence, or special service, confers no claim to exemption from Confederate service: neither does service in the militia, unless in case of officers actually in commission who have been duly qualified.

3. Hereafter any one furnishing a substitute will become liable in his own person, whenever the services of the substitute are lost to the government from any cause other than the casualties of war.

4. Applications for exemption on any ground whatever must first be addressed to the local enrolling officer, who, if he has not power to act, or is in doubt, will refer them to higher authority, with report of the facts. All such addressed direct to higher authority will necessarily and invariably be referred back for local examination and report; and the applicants will, thus have uselessly lost time and prolonged suspense.

Appeals against adverse decisions by local officers, will be forwarded by them for hearing, when any plausible ground of appeal is set forth.

[Signed] G. W. LAY, Lt. Col. A. A. G.,
Acting Chief of Bureau.

II. The exemption mentioned in the circular of the Bureau published above, with regard to militia officers is not applicable to this State. All militia officers, not otherwise exempt are liable to conscription.

III. Medical officers engaged in the Conscription service in this State, are not authorized to extend leave of absence to officers or furloughs to soldiers.

IV. Par. III, General Order No. 12, from this office, is hereby revoked.

V. Overseers entitled to exemption under the provisions of the Act of May 1st, 1863, upon presentation of the affidavit required by that Act, and the receipt of any bonded Quartermaster, for the amount of five hundred ($500) dollars, will be exempted for twelve months, from the date of the receipt, by the commissioned enrolling officers of their respective districts, who will forward the receipt to this office. Enrolling Officers will be careful to give certificates of *exemption*, not of *detail*.

By order of Maj. W. T. WALTHALL.

G. A. CARY,
1st Lieut. and Adj't.

OFFICE COMMANDANT CONSCRIPTS,
Talladega, Ala., August 6, 1863.

"EXTRACT" * * * * * * *

General Orders, No. 20.]

I. Details of overseers heretofore granted under the provisions of Par. III, General Orders, No. 12, from this office, dated June 18th, 1863, being illegal, are hereby declared void. Persons, holding such details, can have them exchanged for *exemptions* for the same period, on application to the respective district Enrolling Officers.

By order of W. T. WALTHALL, Com'dt Ala.

G. A. CARY,
1st Lieut. and Adj't.

aug11—

GENERAL ORDER,

Organizing Volunteer and Conscript Bureau of Geographical Department No. 2.

HEAD QR'S. VOL. AND CON. BUREAU, DEP'T NO. 2, Marietta, Ga., July 27, 1863.

General Orders No. 5.]

THE undersigned having been by orders of General Joseph E. Johnston, in obedience to an order of the Secretary of War, placed in charge of the Conscript service in Department No. 2, and the officers and agencies of the Conscript Bureau of the Government within the States of Tennessee, Alabama and Mississippi, having been by the Secretary of War transferred and assigned to duty under me as Superintendent of Conscripts for this Department, it is ordered that

Those officers and the organizations as heretofor existing within this Department, will continue their labors without change until otherwise ordered. The President, by his proclamation, having called out all men liable to duty under the Conscript law to the age of forty-five years, all such are required to report themselves for duty to the enrolling officers of their respective districts, or to the officers of the recruiting bureau. Upon so reporting, they will be received and enrolled as volunteers. If they fail so to do until arrested, they will be enrolled as Conscripts. In addition to the camps of instructions established by order of the War Department, and now existing in the States composing this geographical department, the system of rendezvous established by the chief of the bureau of the army of Tennessee, will be continued. The officers engaged in the last named organization, belonging to the army of Tennessee, and subject to be withdrawn from this bureau by the exigencies of the service will not for the present be blended with the former organization. The two corps of officers will work in their respective spheres, and under the orders heretofore existing. Both organizations will arrest all deserters and stragglers, receive all volunteers who tender themselves, and will arrest all Conscripts between the ages of eighteen and forty-five.

The commanders of rendezvous will furnish the commandants of conscripts for their States with the names and descriptive lists of all Conscripts by them arrested and sent to the army.

Each class of officers will respect the decisions of the other, and while engaged in the same labor, will avoid all conflicts. Should any collisions of authority occur, they will be referred to the common su erio directing the operations of both corps. Each organ zation will keep a record of its proceedings, and wil make weekly reports to the General Superintendent both organizations.

The hopes of the country depend upon the labors o this Bureau in strengthening the armies of Tennessee and Mississippi. No higher motive to exertion could be presented to the patriot soldier. We have the population required for this purpose, and it is our duty to put it in these armies. Proper efforts will accomplish it and deliver our country from desolation and despotism.

GID. J. PILLOW, Brig. Gen. C. S. A.,
and Sup't Vol. and Con. Dep't, No. 2.

☞ Papers in East Tennessee, Montgomery Advertiser and Mail, Mobile Register and Tribune, Selma Reporter and Mississippi papers will publish one week, and forward their accounts to Major Cheatham, A. Q. M. at these Headquarters. [aug6—1w.

ATTENTION, CONSCRIPTS!

OFFICE COMMANDANT CONSCRIPTS, Talladega, Ala., July 21, 1863.

General Orders, No. 18.]

1. The President of the Confederate States having called for the services of all men between the ages of eighteen and forty-five years of age, not legally exempt, Enrolling Officers are hereby ordered to extend the operation of the Conscription Laws, and the orders regulating the same to all thus called into service.

By order of Maj. W. T. WALTHALL, Com't for Ala.
G. A. CARY,
aug6—6t 1st Lieut. and Adj't.

CASH FOR WHEAT.

THE highest market price will be paid for good Wheat delivered at the Chattanooga Steam Mills.
aug1—tf. JAS. S. SNYDER & CO.

NEGRO MEN WANTED.

WE wish to hire or buy ten good stout negro men.
JAS. N. SNYDER & CO.,
aug1—tf. at the Chattanooga Mills.

WANTED.

I WISH to hire a sprightly negro boy, to go into the army as cook. A liberal reward will be paid.
A. T. HAWKINS, Maj.
Com'g Hawkins's Sharp-shooters, Wood's Brig.
Tyner's Station, Tenn., July 29, 1863.
July 29, 1863.

LODGED IN JAIL.

THE following negroes have been seized and lodged in the jail of Chatham county, Ga.:

John Nelson, formerly belonged to Thos. Stevens, of Marshall county, Miss., belongs now to Isaac Houston, of Franklin county, Missouri.

Anderson, belongs to James Hamer, of Marshall county, Miss.

Fink, belongs to John B. Connelly, of Marshall county, Miss.

Sam, belongs to Jesse Woomers, of Marshall county, Miss. Sam is a native African.

Aaron, belongs to Reuben Jones, who lives fourteen miles from Holly Springs, Miss.

Huldah, a woman, also belongs to Reuben Jones.

King, belongs to Dr. McCargo, Desoto county, Miss.

These negroes represent that they were captured last year by the enemy, at various times, and, with eleven others, put to work on the Memphis & Charleston Rail Road, about seven miles from Memphis. About a month or six weeks ago they were re-captured by armed citizens of the Confederate States, and carried to Meridian and sold. From Meridian they were carried to Mobile by the purchaser; there some trouble arose with regard to them, and they were hurried forward to Atlanta and sold. The purchaser immediately brought them to Savannah, and re-sold them to a firm of brokers. Several facts coming to light which indicated that all was not right, at the instance of the purchaser the sale was rescinded and the moneys refunded. The negroes were then arrested and lodged in jail to await the claim of the real owners.

Savannah, June 20. WM. FRAY.

**The Jackson Mississippian and Huntsville Confederate will please copy one week with editorial notice and send bill to this office for collection.—*Sav. Rep.*
june27—d6t.

$100 Reward!

RANAWAY from the Round Mountain Iron Works, Cherokee Co., Ala., on Sunday, May 24th, ult., the following negro men: Enoch Coffee, of deep dark complexion, slim, about 5 feet 8 or 9 inches high, and 25 years old; Edmund Hall, black complexion, thick set, about 5 feet seven inches high, and 40 years old; Nedam Oats, copper colored, pretty well built, about 5 feet 8 inches high, 24 years old, and has lost two upper front teeth; and Elbert McLein, black complexion, stout built, about 5 feet 10 inches high, and 22 or 23 years old. The first two negroes were brought recently from near Wartrace, Bedford Co., Tenn., where they were hired, and Edmund Hall has a wife there. Enoch belongs to a man named Coffee, Edmund to Vance Davidson, of Wartrace, and the last two to the undersigned. All of them were seen near Guntersville, on Friday last, and are, probably, making their way to Wartrace.

I will give Twenty-five dollars for the apprehension of each of said negroes and his delivery to me, or confinement in jail, so that I can get him; or One Hundred Dollars for all of them. My Post Office is Blue Pond, Cherokee Co., Alabama.

W. L. CRIGLAR.

June 4, 1863.

Deserters---$90 Reward!

I WILL pay a reward of Thirty Dollars for each of the following named deserters from Company A., Snodgrass's Alabama Regiment, if delivered to me in camp, or lodged in jail, so that I can get them:

R. A. Hornbuckle, aged 24 years, 6 feet high sallow complexion, light hair, blue eyes. Resides near Vienna, Madison county, Ala.

John M. Lee, aged 24 years, 5 feet, 9 inches, high, fair complexion, light hair, blue eyes. Resides in Madison county, Ala.

M. L. Servel, aged 24 years, 5 feet, 11 inches high, sallow complexion, dark hair, blue eyes. Resides in the Big Cove, Madison county, Ala.

J. B. DICKEY, Capt. Co., A.,
Snodgrass's Ala., Reg't.

Camp on Big Black, Miss., June 15, '63.
june30—w4t.

Deserter---$30 Reward!

DESERTED from Company A., Snodgrass's Alabama Regiment, in the Army of Mississippi, **James Ragsdale**, about 31 years of age, 5 feet 10 inches high, dark hair and complexion. He was enlisted near Port Hudson, La., March 30, 1863, and resides near Maysville, Ala. I will pay Thirty Dollars for his apprehension and delivery to me, or his lodgment in any jail, so that I can get him.

J. B. DICKEY, Capt. Co. A.,
june24'63-w4t. Snodgrass's Ala. Reg't.

Daily Huntsville Confederate.

J. WITHERS CLAY, EDITOR.

Friday Evening, Oct. 16.

Subscription and Advertising Schedule.

TERMS OF SUBSCRIPTION.

For 1 month, ... 2 00

RATES OF ADVERTISING.

For one Square, (ten lines or less,) first insertion Two Dollars. For each subsequent insertion One Dollar. No deduction will be made from these rates. TERMS CASH.

OUR JOB OFFICE.—We have a superior Job Office and excellent workmen, with facilities for doing Job work in the best style. We have recently replenished our stock of folio, cap and letter paper, in Charleston. We make the announcement, as some of our friends have informed us that, until very recently, they were not aware that we had a Job Office in operation.

WANTED—One or two good compositors at this office.

THE 4TH AND 48th ALA. REGIMENTS.—On Wednesday, we published the casualties in "the Immortal Fourth" at the battle of Chickamauga, and, yesterday, those in the 48th Ala., which belongs to the same Brigade, Law's, Hood's Division, and from its brilliant services in Virginia, Maryland and Pennsylvania, deserves to be placed on the same roll of immortality.

These two regiments fought, side by side, in the late battle, and were, at one time, subjected to a heavy cross-fire of the enemy, which, they told us, surpassed any fire they had ever been under or witnessed. The 4th was led on the 19th by its gallant Lieut. Colonel, L. H. Scruggs, who has had the luck of being wounded in three battles, but only once severely, and was placed *hors du combat* by a ball, which struck him where it must have proved fatal, if it had penetrated, but most unaccountably, it ran round the left hip, barely cutting the flesh and leaving a black bruise for six or eight inches, disabling him for a day. Maj. T. K. Coleman gallantly led the 4th into the engagement of the 20th, and fell early, mortally wounded. We announced his death in this place, week before last. He is greatly lamented by the 4th, who speak of him in the highest terms.

The 48th Ala. was led by Col. James L. Sheffeld, who has illustrated his State on many a well-fought field. At Gettysburg, he commanded a brigade, and, again and again, when his command was beaten back by overwhelming numbers in a strong position, rallied them by impassioned appeals to their patriotism and State pride and led them back to victory at last.

It ministers both to our pleasure and pride to record the valorous deeds of these two commands, all of whom hail from our State, and two companies of the 4th from our city and county. We visited them last week, and found them in good health, cheerful and eager to engage the enemy again and open the way to their beloved homes.

NEWS FROM CHATTANOOGA.—A citizen of Chattanooga tells us, that he has received information that the Yankees have shot Dr. L. Y. Green, and hung David P. Swick, the former a practising physician, the latter a merchant of that place. It is said that Dr. Green had been visiting his patients between the outer and inner lines of Federal pickets, and was returning to the city, when the inner pickets, without challenging, fired on and killed him. Green has been a Surgeon in our Army, and continued true to our cause. Swick is said to have been hung for declaring his purpose to poison the wells of the city, to kill the Yankees. Jessee Allison, the City Marshal, is said to have pointed Swick out to the Yankees. Allison's known Union proclivities lead his acquaintances to credit this statement.

Our cause on the rising tide again.

"The Situation" is decidedly encouraging to the true Southern heart, just now. The tide of affairs seems to have changed, and "taken at the flood," may "lead us on to fortune"—the bright we seek, triumph of right, honorable peace, permanent independence. In Virginia, Meade's "best army on the planet" is retiring before Lee's "ragged, starving Rebels," who are flanking, pursuing, and capturing the enemy, in considerable numbers. The Yankees have burnt a bridge across the Rappahannock, to save their rear from our attack, and are in great trepidation lest A. P. Hill may "come Stonewall Jackson over them," as that lamented Christian hero did over the cowardly braggart, Pope, get between them and Washington and take the Capital.

The Yankee Lieut. Gov. Boreman, of Western Virginia, has issued a proclamation, calling on the militia to hold themselves ready to repel a contemplated movement of the forces of Gens. Imboden, Jackson and others through the mountains of that bogus State; and the Yankees are reported to have, almost completely, evacuated Norfolk and to be destroying public buildings and works, indicating a permanent evacuation, with the exception of two gunboats as a guard against re-occupation by Confederate troops. This will leave Fortress Monroe as, almost, the only bulwark of Yankee power in all Virginia, South of the Rappahannock.

In North Carolina there are said to be not enough Yankee troops left at Newbern and Washington to admit of the withdrawal of any of them, to make raids into the interior—the balance of the force, formerly there, having been sent to reinforce Gillmore at Charleston.

In South Carolina, Gillmore is making slow progress. Sumter, still, hurls defiance at him from her ruined battlements—grander, if possible, in her ruins, than in her entirety, while the batteries on Sullivan and James Islands retard his advance, with continuous shelling, and the grand old "city by the sea" challenges the admiration of the world by her calmness amid danger and heroic resolution to resist the savage vengeance of the devilish foe, even to the death of her citizens, the destruction of their houses, and the desolation of their hearthstones. There, however, the "peerless Beauregard," with his gallant officers and men, stand, faithful sentinel over the city and defies the ruthless foe, declaring he shall never take the city, and, from the energy, activity and nerve manifested, we believe he will keep his word.

Northern Georgia has been delivered from the enemy by the skill and energy of Bragg and his brave army, and Savannah, the only other point on the mainland threatened, is, as yet, intact from Yankee vengeance.

The yankees are quiet and making no progress in Florida. Alabama has, probably, no armed foe within her limits, except a few at Stevenson and Bridgeport, who must hold their positions very uneasy, now that their communication with Nashville is interrupted and Rosecrans is held in durance at Chattanooga. Mobile has resumed her former quiet, under a sense of, at least, present security.

In Mississippi, the enemy have possession of Port Hudson and Vicksburg, and very precarious positions on the Memphis & Charleston Railroad, and their operations are limited to sudden raids, often disastrously repulsed, while her capital, Jackson, is, once more, occupied by its citizens and is recommended by the *Mississippian* as a safe and proper place for assembling the next session of her Legislature.

Banks and his Abolition myrmidons have recently met with serious reverses in Lousiana, at the hands of Magruder, Dick Taylor, and Tom. Greene, stopping his progress, and the last named General having, again, it is said, as effectually blockaded the Mississippi river, against Yankee craft, as it was by the frowning battlements at Vicksburg; while Kirby Smith is watching Banks and throwing obstacles in his way, in Western Louisiana. Price is fulfilling a like duty towards the enemy in Kansas. In the mean time, the enemy's forces at Little Rock and Grant's army are forced by Bragg's success at Chickamauga to a serious depletion to reinforce Rosecrans.

In Missouri, Quantrell has inflicted a severe chastisement on Blount by his own confession, threatens Fort Scott and forces Blount to call loudly for reinforcements.

In Tennessee, Burnside is represented as falling back towards Cumberland Gap, demonstrating a purpose to abandon East Tennessee, while General Jones is said to be within nine miles of Knoxville, and likely soon to re-occupy it with Confederate terms. Rosecrans is cooped up in Chattanooga, with half rations for his troops, his supply trains destroyed, his communications with his base cut, his depots of supplies at McMinnville, Murfresboro' and Shelbyville and their guards and garrisons captured and millions of stores destroyed by the bold and energetic Wheeler, while Stephen D. Lee is operating in the vicinity of Winchester and Roddy on the Memphis and Charleston Railroad not far from Stevenson. This, certainly, places "the wily Dutchman" in a bad fix, proving the correctness of the surmise of a Yankee journal that "he had advanced too far into the bowels of Rebeldom."

West Tennessee is occupied by the enemy at Memphis and a few other points on the Memphis & Charleston Railroad, but they have not strength to depart far into the interior.—Nashville has a garrison of only 1,000 men, it is said, and Clarksville with only 150, and so with several other points. So that, on the whole, the capture or destruction of Rosecrans's army or its complete flight into Kentucky, is likely, soon, to be the *denouement* to his grand occupation of Chattanooga and North Georgia, and his magnificent boasts of a speedy and triumphant *entree* into the Gate City of Georgia.

The situation is, certainly, encouraging to the Confederate arms and our glorious cause.

A Yankee, named J. M. Bromagen, was printing the Winchester Army Bulletin (the property of our friend Slatter) at Stevenson, two or three weeks ago, and may be yet, if our cavalry have not interfered with his thievish adventure.

The Explosion at Bridgeport.

The New York *Herald* of the 5th contains the following in reference to the explosion of a Federal ammunition train near Bridgeport:

NASHVILLE, TENN., Oct. 4, 1863.

The Press of to-day says: A terrible explosion occurred near Bridgeport. A train of twenty army wagons laden with ammunition had camped near the city for the night. Two negroes quarrelled, one of whom seized a shell which he accidentally let fall among the ammunition, causing it to explode and communicate to the other ammunition, immediately wagon after wagon caught fire, the teamsters and attendants flying for their lives. The mules had been removed before the explosion.

Later reports say there are nine or ten killed and double that number wounded. The fire finally reached the magazine, exploding it, and destroying a vast quantity of ammunition.

MOBILE.—Several gentlemen of observation, recently from Mobile, inform the editor of the *Appeal* that the fears so lately entertained that the city would be assailed at an early day by the enemy, no longer prevail. The best information from the Mississippi river is to the effect that no preparations looking to a movement on the eastern coast of the Gulf are perceptible. On the other hand, the whole of the energies of the Federals seem to be directed toward West Louisiana and Texas, and they boast that their programme comprehends reaching the Rio Grande. In the meantime our friends are not idle.

Letter from the United States.

We give some selections from Northern papers, bearing date as late as the 6th inst:

THANKSGIVING DAY.

King Abraham has issued a proclamation, appointing the last Thursday in November, as a day of thanksgiving and prayer in Yankeedom. In his proclamation he says:

"In the midst of a civil war of unequalled magnitude, and severity, which has sometimes seemed to provoke the aggression of foreign States, peace has been preserved with all nations, order has been maintained, the laws have been respected and obeyed, and harmony has prevailed everywhere, except in the theatre of our military conflict; while that theatre has been greatly contracted by the advancing armies and navies of the United States.

Needful diversions of wealth and of strength from the fields of peaceful labor to the National defence, have not arrested the plow, the shuttle or ship. The axe has enlarged the borders of our settlements, and the mines are full of iron and coal and of the precious metals, and have yielded even more abundantly than heretofore.

Population has steadily increased, notwithstanding the waste that has been made in the camp, the seige and the battle-field; and the country, rejoicing in the consciousness of augmented strength and vigor, is permitted to expect a continuance of years with a large increase of freedom.

No human council hath devised, nor hath any mortal hand worked out these things. They are the gracious gift of the Most High God, who, dealing with us in anger for our sins, has, nevertheless, remembered mercy. It has seemed to me fit and proper, that they should be solemnly, reverently and gratefully acknowleged by the whole American people.

WHAT THE WASHINGTON DIPLOMATS THINK OF FRENCH INTERVENTION.

The Washington correspondent of the New York *Times* writes:

The "body of foreign diplomacy" here, as Burke once called the *personnel* of the embassies, did not, if we except the French portion of it, without a pang, read the pamphlet of M. Chevalier. The hand of the French Emperor was plain to them throughout all its parts, and inimical to our institutions as the European ministers are, they cannot, now that it appears a thing determined, look undisturbed on France reaching forward to the Mexican-Confederate combination, which gives that ambitious power all Mexico, and besides the first place in the alliance and affections of the Confederate States, the cotton producing power of the world. While they profess to believe that the Napoleon-Davis partnership will prevail, they console themselves in the conviction that there will be no permanency in the new alliance, and they are equally sure, that Davis in the end will get the best of the bargain, since if the Confederate States can secure their independence thro' French help, they will not be long in seizing Mexico on their own account.

They say that Louis Napoleon's mind is visible all through the Chevalier's pamphlet, and manifest from a similar test as that by which Dugald Dalgetty detected the Duke of Argyle, when that noble visited Scotland in disguise, to wit: that no one else would have spoken of him so well.

From East Tennessee.

CLEVELAND, Tenn., Oct. 12.

Editors Knoxville Register: Gen. Vaughn is at this point. He with others attempted to go as far as Sweetwater, but on arriving at Athens stopped. Gen. Forrest's pickets proceeded as far as Mouse Creek, and there drove back the pickets of Woolford's cavalry, and returned to this place. Woolford's headquarters are at Sweetwater; at which place and up to Louden are two Federal brigades, and constituting nearly all the force on this side of London. In a few days I think the Feds will all be driven across the Tennessee river. There are enough troops here to do it, if Gen. Bragg will give the order. All our troops are in fine spirits and eager to advance upon the enemy. Trains run as far as Charleston, and could go to Athens with safety, if the bridge was rebuilt at Charleston. It should be rebuilt at once.

Judge Gaut and son, Clegg, and other men of standing, having left for the North, is a strong indication that the Confederates are expected to re-possess East Tennessee quite soon. Many of the prominent citizens of Monroe and McMinn were made to believe that Bragg's army was captured, and the Confederacy had "gone up." They were shut out from all news, except what the Yankees saw proper to let them have, and being surrounded by Yankee troops were led to take the "oath" and submit to the Yankee yoke. Thanks to God, they will soon be relieved from it. The Confederate flag will soon wave over them. Those noble spirits who resisted the raising of a Union flag at Sweetwater, will feel a proud consciousness that their decision of character, manifested in a holy cause, has won for them immortal honor. More anon.

H. F. SMITH.

FROM FORT SUMTER.—The Rev. A. B. Stephens, Chaplain of the 11th S. C. Regiment, writes, September 23d:

"We now constitute the garrison of Fort Sumter. On the last fast day, I began a meeting which has been going on and increasing in interest all the while, till now God has honored us with a gracious revival of religion among the soldiery of this command. A few months ago but two officers in the regiment were members of the Church. Now but few more of that number are not professors of religion.—About two hundred have joined the Church, and a larger number have been converted and are now happy in the love of God. It would do your soul good to visit the old fort, battered and scarred as it is, and hear the soldiers make the tattered walls ring with the high praise of the living God. No camp meeting that I ever attended can come near it. I need ministerial help very much; am almost worn out."—*Christian Advocate.*

PRISONERS—LARGE FIGURES.—The Richmond *Enquirer*, of the 7th, states that on the previous day the Libby prison displayed a force of 8556 Federal prisoners, including 825 general, regimental, and other commissioned officers.—Of this number, 4850 were received from Chickamauga—which, including 2500 sick, wounded, and played out, paroled on the field, make the total number of captures on that famous field, as far as ascertained, 7850, including 299 officers.

NOBLE AND PATRIOTIC.—William Gregg, Esq., President of the Graniteville Manufacturing Company, offers to sell to the State of South Carolina, for the benefit of the poor of the State, 10,000 yards of their goods a week, at Government price, which is now $1 10 per yard, less than half what the goods are selling at.—The proposition was officially communicated to the Legislature by Gov. Bonham.

THE GOVERNOR ELECT OF MISSISSIPPI.—The returns from the recent election in Mississippi leave no room to doubt that Gen. Charles Clark has been chosen Governor. Notwithstanding the fact that the enemy have overrun nearly one half their State, not a single vote was polled, nor a single man run for office in favor of reconstruction or re-union upon any terms. Gen. Clark has always been extremely Southern in his political views, and fought the enemy from the commencement of the war to the battle of Baton Rouge, where he was desperately wounded; and permanently disabled from again taking the field.

New Advertisements.

CIRCULAR.

OFFICE COMMANDANT OF CONSCRIPTS FOR ALA., Talladega, Ala., Oct. 8, 1863.

ENROLLING Officers are instructed to be vigilant and active in arresting all absentees and deserters from the army within their districts, and to this end will invoke the aid of the civil authorities, and the people everywhere. It is the duty of every citizen to assist, and they will do so. The evil of desertion must cease, and those absent from their commands must be returned without delay. The country needs their services, and needs them *now*. Such as are now absent have been appealed to by the President of the Confederate States to return and receive pardon. Some have refused to do so, and, in many instances, have been committing outrages upon defenceless women and children whose husbands, fathers and brothers are fighting the battles of our country. They *can and will be* overtaken and brought to justice. This being part of my duties I am determined to prosecute it with the utmost vigor. Such as voluntarily report to me, or, to the Enrolling Officers under my orders will be forwarded to their commands and their pardon recommended.

Enrolling Officers are directed to report, and take proof against all citizens harboring, feeding, lodging, or in any way aiding soldiers absent from their command without leave. This is intended to apply, not only to deserters, but to stragglers and absentees.

Enrolling Officers are directed to see that their assistants are active and efficient, and *in no case will they be retained, if found slow to act or indifferent.* They must earnestly and zealously devote their *whole time* to the work of collecting conscripts, arresting deserters, absentees and stragglers.

Particular attention is directed to a class of persons offering themselves as substitutes. In many cases they have been found to be deserters holding *forged papers*. Some of them are believed to have substituted several times under different names.

I rely with confidence upon the patriotism of the people of Alabama, to aid in this work. I appeal to them to see that no soldier is absent from his command, and that no conscript remains out of camp.—Our independence is sure if we but unitedly reach forth our hands to receive it.

H. C. LOCKHART,
oct16—4t Lieut. Col. and Commandant.

HEADQUARTERS STATE TROOPS, ATLANTA, Oct. 8, 1863.

General Orders, No. 8.]

I. Commanding Officers of State Troops wherever stationed are requested to use their utmost efforts to arrest and return to their respective commands all persons absent from the army without leave.

II. In all counties where the State Troops have not been called into the field, the commanding officers are hereby ordered, when necessary, to call out a portion of their companies to arrest and return all such persons to the army.

The utmost diligence is enjoined upon them in the execution of this order.

By command of
Major General HOWELL COBB.
R. J. HALLETT, A. A. A. General.
oct16—1aw2w.

☞ Marietta papers copy once a week for 2 weeks.

EXPRESS NOTICE.

OFFICE SOUTHERN EXPRESS COMPANY, Marietta, Geo., Oct. 9, 1863.

IN order to avoid misunderstanding, and to make our charges conform to the liability assumed, this Company hereby gives notice, that from and after October 1st, 1863, shippers will be required to place their valuation upon each package, before it will be received.—Such valuation will be inserted in the Company's receipt and establish the liability of the Company for the amount—the act of God and the Public Enemy only excepted.

J. R. ANDERSON,
oct15—1m. Agent.

CIRCULAR.

CHIEF QUARTERMASTER'S OFFICE, GEORGIA STATE TROOPS, Atlanta, Ga., Oct. 10, 1863.

ALL officers of Georgia State Troops will report at once to this office the strength of their commands, showing both rank and file, that requisitions for funds may be made. It will be impossible to get funds to pay them, until this is done.

J. L. MORGAN,
Major and Chief Quartermaster G. S. T.
oct15—1w.

☞ Daily papers in Georgia copy one week.

NEGROES CAPTURED!

ON the 28th of September, 1863, were brought to the headquarters of Gen. Pillow at Marietta, Geo., by a detail of men from his Bureau, two negro men, in the possession of soldiers who said they had been captured on Chickamauga river, on the 21st of September inst., the day of the big fight. The negroes had on Yankee uniforms. One of them says his name is William, that he belongs to Benjamin Yeargain, a citizen of Williamson county, Tenn., a soldier in the 20th Tenn. Regiment, Col. Thomas B. Smith commanding; that he was waiting on his master and was captured by the Yankees at the Murfreesboro' fight last Winter, and has been with the Yankee army ever since, until his re-capture, as above stated. He is copper-colored, straight, athletic, about 5 feet, 10 or 11 inches high, weighs, probably, 160 pounds, is free spoken, intelligent, and says he is 30 years old. The other says his name is Benjamin Clark, belongs to Frank Milyry, of Gallatin, Tenn., that he and his master were, both, captured there by the Yankees, last Fall, that he has been with Rosecrans's army, ever since, until recaptured. He says, his master has a brother in a Geo. Reg't, the 4th, he thinks. He is black, has a peculiar physiognomy, protruding brow, thick eyebrows sprinkled with grey, is about 5 feet, 6 inches high, chunky and ungainly in appearance, weighs, probably, 135 or 140 pounds, quick spoken, of average intelligence, and, probably, 28 or 30 years old.

The owners of these negroes can get them by application to
Capt. Y. S. PATTON,
Post Quartermaster C. S. A. Marietta, Geo.
sept29—6t.

EXCHANGE NOTICE NO. 6.

RICHMOND, Sept. 12, 1863.

THE following Confederate officers and men, captured at Vicksburg, Mississippi, July 4, 1863, and subsequently paroled, have been duly exchanged, and are hereby so declared:

1. The officers and men of Gen. C. L. Stevenson's division.
2. The officers and men of Gen. Bowen's division.
3. The officers and men of Brig. Gen. Moore's brigade.
4. The officers and men of the 2d Texas regiment.
5. The officers and men of Waul's Legion.
6. Also, all Confederate officers and men who have been delivered at City Point at any time previous to July 25, 1863, have been duly exchanged, and are hereby so declared.

RO. OULD,
sept21—6t. Agent of Exchange.

☞ Southern papers copy six times and send bills to the War Department.

OFFICE COMMANDANT CONSCRIPTS, Talladega, Ala., Sept. 21, 1863.

General Order, No. 22.]

Pursuant to Special Order, No. 149, from Gen. Jos. E. Johnston, the undersigned hereby assumes command of the Conscript service of the State of Alabama.

Commandants of Camps of Instruction and Enrolling Officers will continue to be governed by the orders, heretofore issued from the office of the Commandant for the State.

The attention of Enrolling Officers is, particularly, invited to the character and efficiency of their assistants, a full descriptive roll of whom will be returned to this office as soon as possible.

II. 1st Lieut. G. A. Cary is assigned to the duty of Adjutant, and will be respected and obeyed as such.

H. C. LOCKHART,
sept28—4t. Lieut. Col. & Com't for Ala.

UNCONDITIONAL S. GRANT.

NEW IBERIA, PARISH OF ST. MARTIN, LA., SATURDAY, OCTOBER 24, 1863.

VOLUME I. BY THE ETERNAL,—THE UNION MUST AND SHALL BE PRESERVED.—*Andrew Jackson* NUMBER I.

Unconditional Grant.

PUBLISHED EVERY SATURDAY BY
SERG'TS THORPE & WHITLOCK.
OF THE 130th. ILLS. REGT.

Military Directory.

N. NILES, Colonel 130th Illinois, commanding post, New Iberia.
E. S. DEWEY, Acting Post Adjutant.
J. W. WILKINS, Captain Company "K" 130th Illinois, Provost Marshal.
J. W. HARRELL, 1st Lieutenant Company "C" 97th Illinois, Assistant Provost Marshal.

Roster of Officers of the 130th Illinois.

James H. Matheny, Lieutenant-Colonel, (on sick leave.)
John B. Reid, Major commanding 130th Illinois.
H. H. Harrington, Quartermaster.
Lewis H. Wilcox, Surgeon.
David Wilkins, Assistant Surgeon.
Wm. F. Sigler "

COMPANY A.

Wm. H Copp, Captain.
C. T. Mullen, 1st Lieutenant.
John Gall, 2d "

COMPANY B.

Wm. H. Prescott, Captain.
F. M. Pickrell, 1st Lieutenant.
J. W. Paulen, 2d "

COMPANY C.

James H. Robinson, Captain.
W. C. James 1st Lieutenant.
Frank Parker 2d "

COMPANY D.

Daniel DeCamp, Captain.
Abram May, 1st Lieutenant.
Robert Orr, 2d "

COMPANY E.

U. B. Harris, Captain.
Wm. C. Harned, 1st Lieutenant.
C. W. Johnson, 2d "

COMPANY F.

John D. Donnell, Captain.
F. D. Phillips, 1st Lieutenant.
John Murdock, 2d "

COMPANY G.

John J. R. Patrick, Captain.
Duff Lietch, 1st Lieutenant.
J. P. Colcord, 2d "

COMPANY H.

Jesse R. Johnson, Captain.
Clark S. Crary, 1st Lieutenant.
Jesse E. Harris, 2d "

COMPANY I.

John W. Watts, Captain.
R. S. Taylor, 1st Lieutenant.
W. J. Neill, 2d "

COMPANY K.

J. W. Wilkin, Captain.
W. C. Pool, 1st Lieutenant.
A. S. Martin, 2d "

Roster of Officers of the 97th Ills.

Lewis D. Martin, Lieutenant-Colonel commanding.
Victor Virquain, Major, (serving on General Burbridge's Staff.)
Wm. D. Turner, Surgeon.
Chas. Davis, Assistant Surgeon,
Geo. C. Cockrell, Quartermaster
Wm. M. Baker, Chaplain.

COMPANY A.

Richard M. Wood, Captain.
Wm. E. Best, 1st Lieutenant.

COMPANY B.

James G. Buchanan Captain.

COMPANY C.

P. Henry Pentzer, Captain.
James H. Harrell, 1st Lieutenant.
Selah W. Jones, 2d "

COMPANY D.

James W. Wisner, Captain.

COMPANY E.

Jonathan B. Denman, Captain.
George W. Larimer, 1st Lieutenant.

COMPANY F.

Andrew Ray, Captain.
Thomas M. McClanahan, 2d Lieutenant.

COMPANY G.

Fred. T. Lewis, Captain.
Levi Davis, 1st Lieutenant.

COMPANY H.

James M. Erwin, Captain.
Louis C. McNeil, 1st Lieutenant.
Wm. L. Martin, 2d "

COMPANY I.

Wm. Achenbach, Captain, (detached.)
Samuel R. Howard, 1st Lieutenant, (Acting Adjutant.)
Wilson Campbell, 2d " (on Brigade Staff.)

COMPANY K.

Benj. F. Slaten, Captain.
Thomas B. Spaulding, 1st Lieutenant.
Samuel B. Orem, 2d " (in command of Company I.)

The above includes all officers serving with their commands, or on detached service in the field.

The 97th Illinois Volunteers.

This Regiment was ogranized at Camp Butler, Illinois, and mustered into the service of the United States on the 16th of September, 1862, under command of Col. F. S. Rutherford. It was recruited principally in the Counties of Madison, Jersey, Macoupin, Coles Cumberland, Jasper, Fayette and Calhoun. Though in the service but little over a year the 97th has seen much active service, and its history, brief as it is, has nevertheless been eventful.

We received marching orders and left Camp Butler October 3d, 1862 ; and proceeded by rail to Cincinnati. ; lay at Covington till the 20th of Oct., then marched for the interior of Kentucky ; reached Nicholsonville, about one hundred miles from the Ohio, the 29th of the month ; remained there until the 11th of Nov., when we were put in motion for Louisville, where we arrived the 15th, and on the 17th embarked for Memphis. Landed at Memphis Nov. 26th and went into camp. Dec. 20th embarked at Memphis, as part of the force designed to operate against Vicksburg ; landed on the Yazoo Dec. 26th, and next morning marched to the battle-field ; were placed on the right,—stood picket or skirmished with the enemy during the five days following, when our forces were withdrawn and the attack abandoned. Next proceeded with the expedition against Arkansas Post, and took part in the battle of that place on the 11th of Jan.; were held in reserve until near the close of the action, when we were ordered to the front, and were advancing on the enemy's works with fixed bayonets when the fort surrended. The 97th was the first regiment, as a regiment, to gain the entrenchments, and to Lieut. Campbell, of this regiment, belongs the honor of hauling down the rebel flag. Our loss was not heavy, five being wounded, two of whom died ; Capt. John Tribble being one of the latter.

Arkansas Post being captured we again turned our course down the Mississippi ; lay at Young's Point from the 20th of Jan. till the 4th day of March, being engaged digging on the canal ; then moved to Milliken's Bend, where we remained until the 15th of April, when, as part of Gen. Grant's grand army, we again took up the line of march for Vicksburg, via Grand Gulf ; crossed the Mississippi on the 30th of April, at dark ; marched eighteen miles and took part in the battle of Port Gibson next day, with a loss of eight wounded. Was at the battle of Champion Hills, May 16th, where we had four wounded, two of whom died. Was on the field at Black River Bridge next day, but did not get into action. Come in sight of the formidable works at Vicksburg May 19th, and at 3 o'clock advanced in the first assault, in which we had one killed and about twenty wounded, several mortally ; in the advance next day the gallant Lieut. Atchinson, of Co. A; was killed, and nine or ten wounded. In the subsequent assaults, and during the seige we had a number wounded, some of whom have since died. But Vicksburg fell on the 4th of July, and early the next morning the 97th was seen wending its way, through dust and heat, towards Jackson. Arrived there on the 10th and aided in the investment of the place, until its evacuation on the 16th, when we returned to Vicksburg, and went into camp on the 22d. It is needless to narrate the many hardships and privations undergone from the time we left Milliken's Bend to the time of settling down in camp at Vicksburg ; those who were with us need not to have their memories freshened, but those who were not along would not credit the many tales of suffering that might be truthfully told.

One month of rest at Vicksburg and we again take the field Arrive at New Orleans and go into camp at Carrollton, Aug. 27th ; lay there until Oct. 4th ; go to Brashear City, eighty miles ; march from there to this place, (about sixty miles). From 889 men the 97th has been descimated by death, disease and causalities until she now musters but 537, all told. But with this residue, as a part of the column headed to the westward, we will go with our commander wherever duty requires.

***

New Iberia, La., Oct. 24th, 1863.

THE 130th Illinois Volunteers.

Mr Editor of the Grant :

Sir,—I, having been invited to furnish a history of this Regiment, will try to the best of my ability to comply with the request. In so doing I will give the town and county in which each company was organized, with a list of the original company officers. which may be at some future day of interest to their friends.

Company A. was organized in the town of Waterloo, Monroe County, on the 22d day of Aug., 1862, by W. H. Copp, Capt., W. H. Miller 1st Lieut., and C. T. Mullen 2d Lieut.

Company B. was organized in Camp Butler, Sangamon County, on the 20th day of Aug. 1862, by the election of Wm. Prescott Capt., F. M. Pickerll 1st Lieut. and J. W. Paulen 2d Lieut.

Company C. was organized in the city of Cairo, Alexander County, on the 8th day of Aug. 1862, by J. H. Robinson, Capt., W. James, 1st Liet. and F. Parker 2d Lieut.

Company D. was organized in Blueivlle Christian County on the 14th day of Aug. 1862, by D. DeCamp, Capt., A. May 1st Lieut., and J. B. Holford 2d Lieut.

Company E was organized in Millersburg Bond County on the 12th day of Aug 1862, by U. B. Harris Capt., W. Harlin 1st Lieut., and W. C. Harnard 2d Lieut.

Company F. was organized at Greenville, Bond County on the 7th day of Aug. 1862, by J. B. Reid Capt., W. M. Colby, 1st Lieut., and J. D. Donnell 2d Lieut. Capt Colby, who subsequently commanded this company was mortally wounded while gallantly leading his command in the charge on the rebel works at Vicksburg, May 22d 1863. Peace to his ashes.

Company G. was organized in Mattoon Coles County, on the 4th day of Sept., 1862, J. P. H. Keller, Capt., D. A. Crum 1st Lieut. and D. Leitch 2d Lieut.

Company H. was organized in Claremont, Richland County on the 14th day of Aug., by J. R. Johnson Capt., J. Gardener 1st Lieut., and J. Blow 2d Lieut.

Company I was organized in Sumner, Lawrence County, on the 14th day of Aug 1862, by J. W. Watts Capt., R. S. Taylor 1st Lieut. and W. J. Neill, 2d Lieut.

Campany K. was organized in Marshall, Clark County, by J. W. Wilkin, Capt., W. C. Pool 1st Lieut., and A. S. Martin 2d Lieut

The above companies were organized for three years, unless sooner discharged and assigned to the 130th Regiment, by Adjt. Gen. Fuller, and mustered into the service of the United States at Camp Butler, Illinois, on the 25th day Oct., 1862, by Capt. J. H. Rathbone, U S A.

The regiment received marching orders for Memphis on the 11th day of Nov. 1862 at which place we arrived on the night of the 17th ; was assigned to the 16th Army Corps commanded by Gen Hurlbut. The Regiment remained in Fort Pickering, near the city, until the 27th day of March, 1863, during which time the Regiment did Provost duty in the city nearly two months. much to the satisfaction of its citizens On the 27th day of March we embarked on the steamer J. C. Swon, for Milliken's Bend La., where we were assigned to the 2d Brigade, 10th Division 13th Army Corps, commanded by General John A. McClernand. The Regiment remained on duty from the time of our arrival at Milliken's Bend, which was the 31st day of March until the 15th day of April, when we received marching orders for Vicksburg. We crossed the Mississippi river at Bronesburg on the morning of the 1st of May. Marched immediately for Port Gibson, where our forces were engaged witn the enemy, arriving in time to see the close of the battle. This was the first time the Regiment was under fire, and they stood it like veterans, We continued with the army through Mississippi ; was at the battles of Champion Hills, Big Black River, and through the seige, until the surrender of Vicksburg, on the 4th day of July. On the 5th, the day after the surrender, the 13th Army Corps was ordered to Jackson, Miss., where it remained during the seige, and until the evacuation of that place by Johnson and Breckenridge.

After this was accomplished, and Johnson and his forces scattred, the regiment returned to the city of Vicksburg, and went into camp for rest, during the remainder of the summer ; affording some of the brave men a short furlough to visit home, which all accepted that were permitted to do so. On the 25th day of Aug. 1863, after one months rest, marching orders came for New Orleans, transfering us to the Department of the Gulf in Maj. Gen. Banks' command. The Regt. arrived at Carrollton La., on the 28th day of Aug, 1863. Our stay at this place was also short, for on the 4th day of October, orders to move, which we were so well used to, came, and in a few hours we were again on the father of waters, but for a short time. Arriving at Algiers we were transferred to the railroad and, at two o'clock A. M. arrived at Brashear City, some eighty miles from New Orleans. Crossing Burwick Bay to the city of Burwick, where we went into camp for two days. On the morning of the 7th again orders to the front, to be ready to march by 5 o'clock. next morning, which were complied with as well as orders are usually obeyed. This march continued for three days, Arriving in the vicinity of New Iberia, some sixty miles from Burwick Bay, where we are now pleasantly situated, Col. Niles commanding the Post, New Iberia is the head of steam-boat navigation on Bayou Teche, and the base of supplies for our army. When the friends of many of our brave men who have fallen read this their hearts will be drawn out toward us who are still at the mercy of the

THE TRI-WEEKL RAPH.

VOL. XXIX—NO. 94 | HOUSTON MONDAY, OCTOBER 26, 1863. | WHOLE NO. 3749

MARRIED—At Gonzales, on the 19th inst., by the Rev. Mr. Harris, Major O. Steele to Miss Lizzie, eldest daughter of Capt. Jno. C. Walker, all of Galveston.
oct 26—trw 1t*

MARRIED—On the 16th inst., at the residence of Chas. W. Brien, Esq., Liberty county, Lieut. S. W. Jones, of Pyron's regiment, to Miss Eulalie Salles, of the parish of St. Mary, Louisiana. oct 26 1*t

From Near Chattanooga.

The Mobile News makes the following extract from a private letter, dated near Chattanooga Oct. 1st:

"Our armies are in line of battle and close to each other, and with the exception of a little skirmishing and a few shots of cannon, are very quiet. We are digging rifle pits and throwing up some small field works for our artillery. Our picket along the east and slope of Missionary Ridge is so strong that I think it impossible for Rosecrans to dislodge us. Having driven back an invading army, and holding it closely confined in a position in which it will have great difficulty in supplying itself, may fall much short of the grand expectations entertained by many at home, and will doubtless be much criticised; but Gen. Bragg has certainly accomplished a great deal, and may be in a position to effect more, but all these grand movements require time. Our cavalry are across the river and will operate in the rear of the enemy, with what success, we shall soon know, but we must expect them to meet with serious opposition, as the wiley Rosecrans is fully alive to the great importance of keeping his rear open to bring forward supplies, which will have to be brought by wagons across the mountains from McMinnville, or by a very bad road over a mountain from Bridgeport—the first place 75 miles and the last 40 miles distant.

Yesterday was a day of great talk among the military, on account of the arrest of Gens. Polk and Hindman. I understand the circumstances to be as follows: On Sunday night, Gen. Bragg ordered Gen. Polk to attack the enemy at daylight on Monday morning vigorously, and follow him up, which was not done. This was reported to the President, and the order for arrest came from him. The order for Gen. Hindman's arrest came from the same quarter, and was for his failure to destroy the division of the Federal army in McLemore's Cove on the 11th ult. Gen. Hindman then had command of his own and two of Gen. Buckner's divisions, and Gen. Hill was assisting with two divisions from the other side of the mountain, through Dug Gap.

☞ A severe and wet Norther sprung up on Thursday night, reminding us that winter is coming on apace. The price of wood renders it quite certain that it will be a cold winter to, alas! too many of our people.

The Pennsylvania Campaign.

GENERAL LEE'S OFFICIAL REPORT.

The following is an authentic copy of General Robert E. Lee's official report of the "Pennsylvania campaign:"

HEADQ'RS ARMY NORTHERN VA., July 31st, 1863.

Gen. S. Cooper, A. and I. Gen., Richmond, Va:

GENERAL—I have the honor to submit the following outline of the recent operations of this army for the information of the Department:

The position occupied by the enemy, opposite Fredericksburg, being one in which he could not be attacked to advantage, it was determined to draw him from it. The execution of this purpose embraced the relief of the Shenandoah Valley, from the troops that had occupied the lower part of it during the winter and spring, and if practicable, the transfer of the scene of hostilities north of the Potomac.

It was thought that the corresponding movement on the part of the enemy, to which those contemplated by us would probably give rise, might offer a fair opportunity to strike a blow at the enemy therein, commanded by Gen. Hooker, and, that in any event, that army would be compelled to leave Virginia, and possibly to draw to its support troops designed to operate against other parts of the country. In this way it was supposed that the enemy's plan of campaign for the summer would be broken up, and part of the season of active operations be consumed in the formations of new combinations, and the preparations that they would require.

In addition to those advantages, it was hoped that other valuable results might be attained by military success.

Actuated by these and other important considerations that may hereafter be presented, the movement began on the 3d of June. McLaw's division of Longstreet's corps left Fredericksburg for Culpeper C. H., and Hood's division which was encamped on the Rapidan, marched to the same place.

They were followed on the 4th and 5th by Ewell's corps, leaving that of A. P. Hill to occupy our lines at Fredericksburg.

The march of these troops having been discovered by the enemy on the afternoon of the 5th and the following day he crossed a force, amounting to about one army corps, to the south side of the Rappahannock on a pontoon bridge laid down near the mouth of Deep Run. Gen. Hill disposed of his command to resist their advance; but as they seemed intended for the purpose of observation rather than attack, the movements in progress were not arrested.

The forces of Longstreet and Ewell reached Culpeper Court House by the 5th, at which point the cavalry under General Stuart, was also concentrated.

On the 6th a large force of Federal cavalry, strongly supported by infantry, crossed the Rappahannock at Beverly's and Kelly's Fords, and attacked General Stuart. A severe engagement ensued, continuing from early in the morning till late in the afternoon, when the enemy was forced to recross the river with heavy loss, leaving four hundred prisoners, three pieces of artillery and several colors in our hands.

General Jenkins, with his cavalry brigade, had been ordered to advance towards Winchester, to co-operate with the infantry in the proposed expedition into the lower valley, and at the same time Gen. Imboden was directed, with his command, to make a demonstration in the direction of Romney, in order to cover the movement against Winchester, and prevent the enemy at that place from being reinforced by the troops on the line of the Baltimore and Ohio railroad. Both of these officers were in position when Gen. Ewell left Culpeper Court House on the 16th. Crossing the Shenandoah near Front Royal, he detached Road's division to Berryville, with instructions, after dislodging the forces stationed there, to cut off the communication between Winchester and and the Potomac. With the divisions of Early and Johnson, General Ewell advanced directly upon Winchester driving the enemy into his works around the town on the 13th.

On the same day, the troops at Berryville fell back before Gen. Rodes, retreating to Winchester. On the 14th, Gen. Early stormed the works at the latter place, and the whole army of Gen. Milroy was captured or dispersed. Most of those who attempted to escape were intercepted and made prisoners by Gen. Johnson. Their leader fled to Harper's Ferry with a small party of fugitives.

Gen. Rodes marched from Berryville to Martinsburg, entering the latter place on the 14th, where he took seven hundred prisoners, five pieces of artillery, and a considerable quantity of stores.—These operations cleared the valley of the enemy, those at Harper's Ferry withdrawing to Maryland Heights. More than four thousand prisoners, 29 pieces of artillery, two hundred and seventy wagons and ambulances, with four hundred horses, were captured, besides a large amount of military stores. Our loss was small. On the night that Ewell appeared at Winchester, the Federal force in front of A. P. Hill, at Fredericksburg, recrossed the Rappahannock, and the next day disappeared behind the hills of Stafford.

The whole army of Gen. Hooker withdrew from the line of the Rappahannock, pursuing the roads near the Potomac, and no favorable opportunity was offered for attack. It seemed to be the purpose of Gen. Hooker to take a position which would enable him to cover the approaches to Washington City—with a view to draw him further from his base, and at the same time to cover the march of A. P. Hill, who, in accordance with instructions, left Fredericksburg for the Valley as soon as the enemy withdrew from his front. Longstreet moved from Culpeper Court House on the 15th, and advancing along the east side of the Blue Ridge, occupied Ashby's and Snicker's Gaps. His force had been augmented while at Culpeper by Gen. Pickett, with three brigades of his division.

The cavalry, under Gen. Stuart, was thrown out in front of Longstreet to watch the enemy now reported to be moving into Loudon. On the 17th his cavalry encountered two brigades of ours under Gen. Stuart, near Aldie, and was driven back with loss. The next day the engagement was renewed, the Federal cavalry being strongly supported by infantry, and General Stuart was in turn compelled to retire.

The enemy advanced as far as Upperville and then fell back. In these engagements Gen. Stuart took about four hundred prisoners, and a considerable number of horses and arms.

In the meantime a part of Gen. Ewell's corps had entered Maryland, and the rest was about to follow. Gen. Jenkins with his cavalry, who accompanied Gen. Ewell, penetrated Pennsylvania as far as Chambersburg. As these demonstrations did not have the effect of causing the Federal army to leave Virginia, and as it did not seem disposed to advance upon the position held by Gen. Longstreet, the latter was withdrawn to the west side of the Shenandoah, Gen. Hill having already reached the valley.

Gen. Stuart was left to guard the passes of the mountains and observe the movements of the enemy, whom he was instructed to harass and impede as much as possible should he attempt to cross the Potomac. In that event, Gen. Stuart was directed to move into Maryland, crossing the Potomac east or west of the Blue Ridge, as in his judgment should be best, and take position on the right of our column as it advanced.

By the 24th, the progress of Ewell rendered it necessary that the rest of the army should be in supporting distance, and Longstreet and Hill marched to the Potomac. The former crossed at Williamsport, and the latter at Shepherdstown. The columns reunited at Hagerstown, and advanced thence into Pennsylvania, encamping near Chambersburg on the 27th.

No report had been received that the Federal army had crossed the Potomac, and the absence of the cavalry rendered it impossible to obtain accurate information. In order, however, to retain it on the east side of the mountains after it should enter Maryland, and thus leave open our communication with the Potomac through Hagerstown and Williamsport, General Ewell had been instructed to send a division eastwards from Chambersburg to cross the South Mountains. Early's division was detached for this purpose, and proceeded as far east as York, while the remainder of the corps proceeded to Carlisle.

General Imboden, in pursuance of the instructions previously referred to, had been actively engaged on the left of Gen. Ewell during the progress of the latter into Maryland. He had driven off the forces guarding the Baltimore and Ohio Railroad, destroying all the important bridges on that route from Cumberland to Martinsburg, and seriously damaged the Chesapeake and Ohio Canal.

He subsequently took position at Hancock; and after the arrival of Longstreet and Hill at Chambersburg, was directed to march by way of McConnellsburg to that place.

Preparations were now made to advance upon Harrisburg; but on the night of the 29th information was received from a scout that the Federal army, having crossed the Potomac, was advancing northwards, and that the head of the column had reached the South Mountain. As our communications with the Potomac were thus menaced, it was resolved to prevent his further progress in that direction by concentrating our army on the east side of the mountains. Accordingly, Longstreet and Hill were directed to proceed from Chambersburg to Gettysburg, to which point Gen. Ewell was also instructed to march from Carlisle.

Gen. Stuart continued to follow the movements of the Federal army south of the Potomac, after our own had entered Maryland, and in his efforts to impede its progress, advanced as far eastward as Fairfax Court House. Finding himself unable to delay the enemy materially, he crossed the river at Seneca, and marched through Westminster to Carlisle, where he arrived after General Ewell had left for Gettysburg. By the route he pursued, the Federal army was interposed between his command and our main body, preventing any communication with him until his arrival at Carlisle.

The march towards Gettysburg was conducted more slowly than it would have been had the movements of the Federal army been known.

The leading division of Hill met the enemy in advance of Gettysburg, on the morning of the 1st of July. Driving back these troops to within a short distance of the town, he there encountered a large force, with which two of his divisions became engaged. Ewell, coming up with two of his divisions by the Heidlersburg road, joined in the engagement. The enemy were driven through Gettysburg with heavy loss, including about five thousand prisoners and several pieces of artillery.

He retired to a high range of hills south and east of the town. The attack was not pressed that afternoon, the enemy's force being unknown, and it being considered advisable to await the arrival of the rest of our troops.

Orders were sent to hasten their march; and, in the meantime, every effort was made to ascertain the numbers and position of the enemy; and find the most favorable point of attack. It had not been intended to fight a general battle at such a distance from our base, unless attacked by the enemy; but finding ourselves unexpectedly confronted by the Federal army, it became a matter of difficulty to withdraw through the mountains with our large trains. At the same time, the country was unfavorable for collecting supplies while in the presence of the enemy's main body, as he was enabled to restrain our foraging parties by occupying the passes of the mountains with regular and local troops. A battle thus became, in a measure, unavoidable. Encouraged by the successful issue of the engagement of the first day, and in view of the valuable results that would ensue from the defeat of the army of General Meade, it was thought advisable to renew the attack.

The remainder of Ewell's and Hill's corps having arrived, and two divisions of Longstreet's, our preparations were made accordingly. During the afternoon, intelligence was received of the arrival of Gen. Stuart, at Carlisle, and he was ordered to march to Gettysburg, and take position on the left. A full account of these engagements cannot be given until the reports of the several commanding officers shall have been received, and I shall only offer a general description

The preparations for attack were not completed until the afternoon of the 2d.

The enemy held a high and commanding ridge along which he had massed a large amount of artillery. Gen. Ewell occupied the left of our line, Gen. Hill the centre, and General Longstreet the right. In front of Gen. Longstreet the enemy held a position, from which, if he could be driven, it was thought that our army could be used to advantage in assailing the more elevated ground beyond, and thus enable us to reach the crest of the ridge. That officer was directed to endeavor to carry this position, while Gen. Ewell attacked directly the high ground on the enemy's right, which had already been partially fortified. Gen. Hill was instructed to threaten the centre of the Federal line, in order to prevent reinforcements being sent to either wing, and to avail himself of any opportunity that might present itself to attack.

After a severe struggle, Longstreet succeeded in getting possession of and holding the desired ground. Ewell also carried some of the strong positions which he assailed, and the result was such as to lead to the belief that he would ultimately be able to dislodge the enemy. The battle ceased at dark.

These partial successes determined me to continue the assault next day. Pickett, with 3 of his brigades, joined Longstreet the following morning, and our batteries were moved forward to the position gained by him the day before.

The general plan of attack was unchanged, except that one division and two brigades of Hill's corps were ordered to support Longstreet.

The enemy, in the meantime, had strengthened his line with earthworks. The morning was occupied in necessary preparations, and the battle recommenced in the afternoon of the 3d, and raged with great violence until sunset. Our troops succeeded in entering the advanced works of the enemy, and getting possession of his batteries; but our artillery having nearly expended its ammunition, the attacking columns became exposed to the heavy fire of the numerous batteries near the summit of the ridge, and, after a most determined and gallant struggle, were compelled to relinquish their advantage, and fall back to their original position, with severe loss.

The conduct of the troops was all that I could desire or expect, and they deserved success so far as it can be deserved by heroic valor and fortitude. More may have been required of them than they were able to perform, but my admiration of their noble qualities, and confidence in their ability to cope successfully with the enemy, has suffered no abatement from the issue of this protracted and sanguinary conflict.

Owing to the strength of the enemy's position and the reduction of our ammunition, a renewal of the engagement could not be hazarded, and the difficulty of procuring supplies rendered it impossible to continue longer where we were. Such of the wounded as were in condition to be removed, and part of the arms collected on the field were ordered to Williamsport. The army remained at Gettysburg during the 4th, and at night began to retire by the road to Fairfield, carrying with it about four thousand prisoners. Nearly two thousand had previously been paroled, but the enemy's numerous wounded that had fallen into our hands after the first and second day's engagements, were left behind.

Little progress was made that night, owing to a severe storm, which greatly embarrassed our movements. The rear of the column did not leave its position near Gettysburg until after daylight on the 5th.

The march was continued during that day without any interruption by the enemy, except an unimportant demonstration upon our rear in the afternoon, when near Fairfield, which was easily checked. Part of our train moved by the road through Fairfield, and the rest by the way of Cashtown, guarded by Gen. Imboden. In passing through the mountains, in advance of the column, the great length of the trains exposed them to attacks by the enemy's cavalry, which captured a number of wagons and ambulances; but they succeeded in reaching Williamsport without serious loss.

They were attacked at that place on the 6th by the enemy's cavalry, which was gallantly repulsed by Gen. Imboden. The attacking force was subsequently encountered and driven off by Gen. Stuart, and pursued for several miles in the direction of Boonsboro.' The army after an arduous march, rendered more difficult by the rains, reached Hagerstown on the afternoon of the 6th and morning of the 7th July.

The Potomac was found to be so much swollen by the rains that had fallen almost incessantly since our entrance into Maryland, as to be unfordable. Our communications with the south side were thus interrupted, and it was difficult to procure either communication or subsistence, the latter difficulty being enhanced by the high waters impeding the working of our neighboring mills. The trains with the wounded and prisoners were compelled to await at Williamsport, the subsiding of the river and the construction of boats, as the pontoon bridge left at Falling Waters, had been partially destroyed. The enemy had not yet made his appearance, but as he was in condition to obtain large reinforcements, and our situation, for the reasons above mentioned, was becoming daily more embarrassing, it was deemed advisable to recross the river. Part of the pontoon bridge was recovered and new boats built, so that by the 13th a bridge was thrown over the river at Falling Waters.

The enemy in force reached our front on the 12th. A position had been previously selected to cover the Potomac from Williamsport to Falling Waters, and an attack was awaited during that and the succeeding day. This did not take place, though the two armies were in close proximity, the enemy being occupied in fortifying his own lines. Our preparation being completed, and the river though still deep, being pronounced fordable, the army commenced to withdraw to the South side on the night of the 13th.

Ewell's corps forded the river at Williamsport, those of Longstreet and Hill crossed upon the bridge. Owing to the condition of the roads the troops did not reach the bridge until after daylight on the 14th, and the crossing was not completed until 1 P. M., when the bridge was removed. The enemy offered no serious interruption, and the movement was attended with no loss of material except a few disabled wagons, and two pieces of artillery, which the horses were unable to move through the deep mud. Before fresh horses could be sent back for them the rear of the column had passed.

During the slow and tedious march to the bridge, in the midst of a violent storm of rain, some of the men lay down by the way to rest. Officers sent back for them, failed to find many in the obscurity of the night; and these, with some stragglers, fell into the hands of the enemy.

Brig. Gen. Pettigrew was mortally wounded in an attack made by a small body of cavalry, which was unfortunately mistaken for our own and permitted to enter our lines. He was brought to Bunker Hill, where he expired a few days afterwards. He was a brave and accomplished officer and gentleman, and his loss will be deeply felt by the country and the army.

The following day the army marched to Bunker Hill, in the vicinity of which it camped for several days. The day after its arrival, a large force of the enemy's cavalry, which had crossed the Potomac at Harper's Ferry, advanced towards Martinsburg. It was attacked by Gen. Fitz Lee, near Kearneysville, and defeated with heavy loss, leaving its dead and many of its wounded on the field.

Owing to the swollen condition of the Shenandoah river, the plan of operations which had been contemplated when we recrossed the Potomac could not be put in execution, and before the waters had subsided, the movements of the enemy induced me to cross the Blue Ridge and take position south of the Rappahannock, which was accordingly done.

As soon as the reports of the commanding officers shall be received, a more detailed account of these operations will be given, and occasion will then be taken to speak more particularly of the conspicuous gallantry and good conduct of both officers and men.

It is not yet in my power to give a correct statement of our casualties, which were severe, including many brave men, and an unusual proportion of distinguished and valuable officers—among them, I regret to mention the following general officers: Major-Generals Hood, Pender and Trimble, severely, and Major-General Heth slightly wounded.

General Pender has since died. This lamented officer has borne a distinguished part in every engagement of this army, and was wounded on several occasions while leading his command with conspicuous gallantry and ability. The confidence and admiration inspired by his courage and capacity as an officer, were only equalled by the esteem and respect entertained by all with whom he was associated, for the noble qualities of his modest and unassuming character.

Brigadier Generals Barksdale and Garnett were killed, and Brig. General Semmes mortally wounded while leading their troops with the courage that always distinguished them. These brave officers and patriotic gentlemen fell in the faithful discharge of duty, leaving the army to mourn their loss and emulate their noble examples.

Brigadier Generals Kemper, Armistead, Scales, G. T. Anderson, Hampton, J. M. Jones, and Jenkins, were also wounded. Brigadier General Archer was taken prisoner. General Pettigrew, though wounded at Gettysburg, continued in command until he was mortally wounded near Falling Waters.

The loss of the enemy is unknown, but from observations on the field, and his subsequent movements, it is supposed that he suffered severely. Respectfully submitted,

(Signed) R. E. LEE, General.

List of Casualties.

1ST TEXAS REGIMENT—CAPT. D. K. RICE, COMD'G.

Capt D K Rice, commanding, missing.

Company A—Captain G S Toof, commanding; killed, Hugh Dougherty; wounded, Lieut W W Laney, leg; H H Robinson, arm; sergt A Campbell, leg; sergt E D Smith, shoulder and mouth; corp T Brewer, severe; T B Allen, leg; F E Blackburn, leg, amputated; Jno Veal, thigh; missing, corp Harkins.

Company B—Lieut W F Walker, commanding; killed, R R Ghout.

Company D—Capt H G Mossitt, commanding; wounded, Lt J M Thomas, severe in face; Lt A G Oliver, slight, arm; sergt E C Powell, severe, breast; sergt A J Wood, severe, arm; J P Cook, slight, side; W M Durham, severe, head; J J Durham, severe, breast; Wm Mose, mortally; A Miles, slight, ankle; J C Robinson, severe, mouth; J P Snodgrove, severe, foot; W M Snow, thigh; wounded and missing, W H Oliver, J P Dunklin.

Company E—Capt B W Webb, commanding; killed, R J Marshall; sergt J A Lindsay; A D Sanderson; wounded, sergt J Barefield, finger; J B Stephens, leg, amputated; J N Kirksey, hip; M E Donnelly, mortally; J M Canterberry, head, slight; missing, G H Johnson, supposed killed.

Company G—Lieut A W Buckner, commanding; killed, sergt J G McInnis; A D Harris; wounded, sert E B Series, slight; J P Neele, slight; J Rainey, severe; J W Armstrong, slight; S Sassester, slight; W T Stamper, severe; O Perry, hip; W D Prescott, side.

Company F—Lieut A J Rigsby, commanding.—Killed: E H Crier, G H Hicks. Wounded: Sergeant J E Perryman, shoulder; B Bradham, foot; Corp'l H C Jones, leg amputated; Serg't W V Smith, head, slight; W Poole, hip, slight; J H Tiner, face, slight; W M Gilder, arm, slight.

Company G—Capt E S Jemison.—Wounded: Lieu't W P Mynatt, Serg't Kyle, Corp'l E Day, Corp'l W T Haselwood, Corp'l Ira Parker, H F Bradley, S B Davis, H Darnhall, J R Keely, T F Mann, E Newsom, A T Ratliffe, H D Reed, J G Stenson, J M Stallcup, A Thompson, A J Watts, S R Burrows, M Hamby, Lewis Grooms. Missing: Serg't W G Wren.

Company H—Capt Bedford Parke, commanding.—Wounded: Capt B Parke, foot, slight; Lieut S P Torbell, bowels, slight; Serg't S W Small, knee, slight; J E Hickman, back, slight; Corp'l J E Erms, shoulder, severe; N A Menanhall, breast, severe; S L Scott, back, severe; M A Berry, ankle, slight; R R Birdwell, ankle, slight; J A Graham, ankle, slight; A F Erwin, hip, slight; J R Smith, finger off.

Company I—Lieut John H Wooters commanding.—Killed: Serg't I H Foster, Serg't G G Morris, W Y Salter, N B Mason, Joseph Rudical. Wounded: Lieut A E Aldrich, thigh; Serg'ts D B Bush, hand; R F Emmonds, ankle; Corp'l S J Boydston, slight; Corp'l J M Drawnosh, hip; S O Foster, thigh, serious; John Harris, slight; F M Morris, head; J W F Norford, severe; G P Mann, thigh; W Oliphant, slight; A D Oliphant, head. Missing: G M Weatherhead.

Company K—Capt J H Mason commanding—Killed: L M Mason. Wounded: Sergt J V Ruddell, severe; Corpl W J Cureton, slightly; Privates Jas Statings, severely; J O Noble, slightly; W H Watson, slightly; Jno Brandon, slightly; S M Peterson, slightly. Missing: Sergt H S Bennett, supposed prisoner.

Company L—Capt W A Bedell commanding—Killed: Corpl J Lewis. Wounded: Lieut R Armstrong, in arm; Sergt G H Kingsey, in arm; W B Robinson, in breast; Corpl J Pratt, leg; J Brand, face; E G Crawford, mortally; D Elmadorf, foot; John Fratish, arm; P S Gibbs, finger; A Kelso, both leg; Wm Leach, leg; S S Lazarus, leg; J Murphy, foot; J Nagle, face; W Shepherd, leg; Wm Schadt, arm; Schmidt, arm; A W Wood, leg. Missing: Lieut W P Randall, supposed prisoner.

Company M—Lieut Wm Cecil commanding—Killed: A J Adams, G W Orelsby, J Ratliff, J D Stephens. Wounded: Sergts W A Roach, F M Slater, J S Bailey, C Dunlap, E Diar, W E Forsyth, J A Jones, D M Morrow, S Morgan, E Pope, severely; Corpl J S Look, H H Penson, J A White, W T White, S Stubblefield, J R Stewart slightly. Missing: Sergt S B Landy.

RECAPITULATION—Killed: 19; wounded: 124; missing: 12. Total, 155. A. P. FORSYTH, Adjutant.

FOURTH TEXAS REGIMENT—LIEUT. COL. J. P. BANE COMMANDING.

Field and staff—Wounded: Lieut Col J P Bane, in arm; Capt R H Bassett, (acting field officer) slight in shoulder; Lieut T W Masterson, (acting adjutant) severely in leg.

Company A—Capt R M Bomar commanding—Killed: Color Sergeant Ed D Francis, Daniel McDonald. Wounded: Lieut J B Grundy, severely, hip; W A Cavitt, severely, leg amputated; John Clark, jaw broken; John Dean, severely and missing; G Derrington, slightly, shoulder; S A Dronnan, severely, leg amputated; Wesley Francis, leg; Geo Fletcher, head; Riley Hammon, finger shot off; J M Hopkins, severely, breast; Wm Walker, slightly, head; A G Futch, severely, arms; R B Lockridge, slightly, head. Missing: corporal N A Strong.

Company B—2d Lieut John T Price commanding—Killed: Corporal G R Nichols, J K P Jones, John Shuller. Wounded: 2d Lieut John T Price, slightly; sargeant T Colvin, slightly; F M Burnham, S W Hamilton, A Masterson, slightly; A A Durfee, severely; John Griffin, Uriah Gould, C M Phaul, slightly; S T C Stone, Alf George, severely; A J Howard, slightly. Missing: R A Davidge, C H Rushton, F Strahmer.

Company C—1st Lieut Livingston commanding.—Killed: Sergeant E D Wooding, corporal W Norton, G H Griffin, J J Jones, D Kinsey. Wounded: Lieut M Livingston, arm; sergeant W C Steele, leg amputated; Frank Burton, leg, severely; P J Barzza, breast, slightly; J J Mitchell, arm, slightly. J A Smith, breast, severely.

Company D—1st Lt W H McClaugherty commanding.—Killed; W R Smith, R T Sefferson, Jas Campbell. Wounded: Lt W H McClaugherty, severely; Lt R H Franks, finger shot off; E J Cody, mortal; John Rodgers, slightly; Julius Glazer, bayonet, severely; S A Jones, slightly: Wm Shumate, slightly; H D Flores, slightly. Missing: A G Green.

Company E—Capt J C Billingsley, commanding.—Killed: Capt J C Billingsley, 1st Lt A G Killingsworth, J D Miller, T L Norwood, C M Whitehead, W M Hicks. Wounded: Sergeant J H Manahan, shoulder and breast, slight; Sergt E Telly, leg, slight; Corp T M Mullens, leg, slight; Corp F M McKaig, neck, severe; S H Chambers, leg amputated; L D Hollaway, face, severe; W H P Burton, arm, severe; W A Pamplin, hand, severe; J B Chapman, thigh, severe; J C West, groin.

Company F—1st Lt Haywood Brahan, commanding.—Wounded: Sergts J D Murray, slightly in the foot; E R Crockett, slightly in thigh; P S Penn, slightly in hip; Jacob Quick, severely in breast and arm; Corp J H Currie, severely in leg, (amputated); James Alford, arm, slight; C Brooks, hip, slight; J L Brantley, finger shot off; A C Penn, through right breast, severely; T J McCann, thigh, severely; M Pickett, left arm, severely; M M Pengras, arm, slight; Jack Sutherland, shoulder, slight; H Dansby, arm, slight.

Company G—2d Lieut J M Bookman commanding—Killed: Lt J M Bookman, J D Barry, D Silverbaugh and Corpl J McGowan. Wounded: J J Atkinson, thigh, slight; Serg'ts D A Wood, side, severe; L H Barry, arm, slight; Corpl W E Barry, slight; J W Thomas, finger shot off; Thomas Churchwell, right breast, severe; J G Duke, left shoulder, severe; W M Bainee, head, slight; W R A Eckels, left arm amputated.

Company H—2d Lieut T J Tedford commanding—Killed: Privates Berry, Kirby and Wm Peacock. Wounded. Lieut R J Tedford, slightly in hand first day, severely in leg second day; Serg'ts J G W Cartwright, severely in body; Green Griggs, side, slight; Corpl R H Steward, leg, severely; Privates B Anders, leg, severely; L C Cartwright, side, severely; Wm Fisher, foot, severely; J H Hall, shell, slightly; J Lown, leg, slight; W J Landrum, shoulder, slight; M F Meyers, ankle, slight; John Smith, knee, severe, S Stanfield, leg, slight; John Taliaferro, shoulder, severe; A Taylor, head, slight; H Travis, arm, slight; J S Tucker, foot, slight.

Company I—1st Lieut J R Loughbridge commanding—Killed: Sergt L M Riggs, Corpl B F Childress; Privates W E Carroll, J C Walker. Wounded: Lieut Mat Beasly, hip, slight; Sergt P Smith, arm, severe; Corpl A J Brewster, foot, slight; Privates J H Asti, thigh, severe; J W Hollamon, side, slight; J B Lanham, head, slight; J H Massey, leg, severe, amputated, J M Polk, head, severe; L W Rice, thigh, slight; J L Utzman, side, severely; H E Walker, hip, slight. Missing: Privates J T Green, A Barry.

Company K—1st Lieut M O Clanahan commanding.—Killed: private J M Allen. Wounded: Serg't A H Rogers, foot, severe; Corp'ls M Antle, shoulder, severe; A J Lane, back, severe; privates A R Clanahan, leg, slight; J J Pickering, thigh slight.

Recapitulation—Killed, 26; Wounded, 102; Missing, 5.—Total, 133. HAYWOOD BRAHAN, 1st, Lieut.
Acting Adjutant, 4th Texas Regiment.

FIFTH TEXAS REGIMENT—MAJ. J. C. ROGERS, COMMANDING.

Field and Staff—Wounded: Maj J C Rogers, hip, severely; Capt J S Cleveland, Acting Lieutenant Colonel, leg, severely; Serg't Maj. J M Smithers, wrist, severely.

Company A—Lieut B S Fuller, commanding.—Wounded: W H Clark, color-bearer, leg, severely; R Campbell, arm, severely; J Morris, hand, severely; O O'Mally, arm, severely; D H Robbins, arm, severely; F W Stumer, back, slightly; C B Darndner, arm, slightly. Missing: M S Steele.

Company B—Lieut Ed Collier, commanding.—Wounded: Lieut Ed Collier, toe amputated; Lieut Ben Baker, thigh, severely; Serg't Obenchain, thigh, severely; Corp'l Sheppard, hip and ankle, severely; W L Burton, arm, slightly; John Deganworth, face, severely; D Harby, leg, slightly; John Leagh, abdomen, slightly; John Harvey, arm, severely; Auguste Eficke, wrist, severely; Ed Hart, foot. Missing: John Morriesy.

Company C, Capt J J McBride, commanding—Killed, R B Perry; wounded, Lieut G F Bunder, neck, slight; Lieut Z L Logan, thigh, severe; sergt J C Cox, (with colors,) side, severe; J J Gough, hand, slight; T M Robertson, thigh, severe; J D Stephens, arm; J S Skinner, thigh, severe; B Turner, thigh, slight; Eli Yow, thigh; missing, T M Lee.

Company D, Lieut O S Caldwell, commanding; killed, corporal T L Watson, M C Brown, John Tomlinson; wounded, Lieut O S Caldwell, wound unknown; sergt Robinson, leg amputated; T J Lewis, arm, slight; J Parker, thigh, slight; M L Gilbert, foot, severely; J E Gilbert, leg, slight; W B Rowe, head; J A Dickie, arm, slight; A H Trayler, arm.

Company E, Captain D A Baber, commanding—Wounded, sergt W B W George, thigh, slight; F A Eldridge, leg, severe; S T Collins, leg, slight; M A J Evans, shoulder, severe; J B Gee, breast; W C LeGrand, head, slight; T H Mullins, thigh, severe; J T Leugely, arm, severe; J Wallace, leg, severe; J E Maddox, bowels, (since dead); J W Spann, thigh, (since dead.)

Company F—Lieut L H McKinnon commanding—Killed: Sergeant W S Evans (with colors) J C Buxton. Wounded: sergeant H V Angell, severely; Thomas Cosgan, thigh amputated; F J Whittington, face, severely; D Toups, mortally, (since died) W L McCary, lungs, severely; Wm McVoy, knee, leg amputated; Julius Beckman, shoulder; J M Dillon, side and hand, severely; T W Bryan, shoulder, slightly; H L Taylor, hand and hip, slight; C McCally, neck, slightly.

Company G—Lieut Sam S Streetman commanding—Killed: Lieut S S Streetman, G L Bagwell. Wounded: J T Austin, hip, severe; A B Jones, leg, severe; F H Rowe, hip, severe, M D Garrett, knee, severe; J B Small, leg slight. Missing: R B Mayes J L Stewart, J H Odam.

Company H—Lieut William Robertson commanding.—Wounded: Lieut T B Spratt, ankle, slight; sargeant J A Jennings, head, mortal, since dead; T J Simmons, head, mortal; R E Lee, arm amputated; J Barber, thigh, slight; Harvey Rose, leg, slight; R Wilson, hand, slight.

Company I—Lieut. B J Franklin, commanding.—Killed: J W Kibby. Wounded: Corporal J W Graves, leg amputated; John Short, mortally, since dead; B J Baldwin, head, slight; Wm Crabtree, leg amputated, since dead; John Davis, leg, slight, J D Holmes, knee; W A Holmes, leg, slight; A W Holt, contusion in shoulder; R W Spence, abdomen, slight; J W Tooley, thigh. Missing: Stephen Driscoll, supposed to be wounded.

Company K—Lieut. Joe Turner, commanding.—Killed: Sergeant J C Beard, N Oats (with colors.) Wounded: Lieut. Joe Turner, arm, severe; Corporal L B Dortch, head, severe; F Butler, arm and side; A J Fairchilds, shoulder; W M McDonald, back, severe; T W McCrory, abdomen, slight; W D S Nibbetts, foot, slight. Missing: W D S McCoy.

Recapitulation—Killed 11, wounded 93, missing 3—112.
The regiment went into action with 225 men.
CHAS McCALLY, Acting Adj't.

From the Atlanta Confederacy.

We are highly gratified to learn that Dr. Darby, the surgeon of General Hood, reports to General Robertson that the crisis of General Hood's recovery is past, and he is out of danger. We hope that this valuable officer may soon be able to take the field again.

The Tri-Weekly Telegraph

HOUSTON, TEXAS.

E. H. CUSHING, Editor and Proprietor.

ARMY MAIL.—The next messenger will leave November 5th. Carriers charge on all letters to go beyond e Mississippi, $2. Remit only Confederate money. county scrip is current here.

W. Adams will carry the mail of Nov. 5th.

THE BATTLE OF SABINE PASS.

It has been sometimes said that we have made too much of the Sabine Pass fight, and that anybody else could have done as well if they only had a chance, and some have even gone so far as to profess that since nobody was killed or wounded, it was no great affair after all. We beg respectfully to differ with these people, and to still insist that in importance to Texas as well as the Confederacy, no one has yet begun to publish a full appreciation of that battle, while the skill and daring that won it are worthy the greatest praise we can bestow.

It is the spirit that led these brave forty odd men to stand to their colors, and face the overwhelming odds that was sent against them that we admire. A spirit indeed that has been wanting on our outposts from time to time since the war began—a spirit which if it had animated the defenders of so many other places we could enumerate, would have saved whole States from the ravages of the enemy, and fifty thousand lives that have since been lost in attempting to retrieve the errors that have thus been committed.

It is the spirit of the noble Bee, at Manassas, when he said, "My friends, let us determine to die right here," and which turned the fortunes of that memorable day. It is the spirit of the glorious Texas Brigade that stormed the heights of Gains' Mill, and wrested victory out of the jaws of death. It is the spirit that animated that other noble band, the 2d Texas, when at battery Robinet they with all the self-forgetfulness brave men can have, marched up and laid down their lives without inquiring whether others, who should have supported them, were doing their duty. It is the spirit of those noble old Texians in the Alamo, who did "die right there," but saved their country. Such a spirit makes heroes, and when we find them we claim the right to bestow upon them the laurels they have won.

But as to the importance of the affair to Texas what need we say, more than that our invaders were turned back upon our threshold, and a two months respite has been given us to prepare and meet them. What is more, it has thrown their movements so far back that now they will have to encounter almost impassable bogs, and that, too, so far from any base of supplies they can establish, as to render success on their part absolutely impossible. We cannot give a better idea of the damaging effect this blow has had upon the Federal cause than to quote from the N. Y. Herald, of Sept. 22d, as follows:

Gold ran up five per cent. yesterday in Wall street on the news of the naval and military disasters at Sabine Pass and Chattanooga. The uneasiness that appears to prevail in the public mind from the likelihood of a foreign war may also have had its effects upon the market. We do not participate in that apprehension. Mr. Lincoln's doctrine of 'one war at a time' is a sound one, and will be acted upon by our Government; and there is not the remotest danger that either England or France will voluntarily go to war with us.

But the criminal incapacity which led to the Sabine pass disaster, and the military bungling of the War Depatment which caused the repulse of Rosecrans, have naturally alarmed capitalists and speculators, and have produced this last Wall street panic.

The Government had calculated upon securing, as one of the results of the Texas expedition, and of the advance of General Rosecrans, into Georgia, some 200 or 300,000 bales of cotton, which were to be shipped to England and sold for specie. With the amount thus to be realized in hard cash, the Government might have been able to force the price of gold down to par, and possibly to have resumed specie payments. But this splendid financial plan has been frustrated by these two defeats in the Southwest. Capitalists and business men realize that their effect will be to protract the war much longer than they had calculated upon. The Government will need more troops and larger supplies, and will be forced, within the next two or three weeks, to come into the market for a loan of sixty, eighty, or a hundred millions of dollars. That must inevitably run up the price of gold still higher, and produce such a revulsion in financial matters as will swamp the specula'iors in all such fancy stocks as Hudson and Harlem. These stocks will then fall from the ridiculously high figures to which speculators have run them up, to the forty and sixteen per cent. at which they were respectively quoted a year ago, and which more nearly represented their real value.

Some of the princely fortunes which have been so rapidly made in Wall street within the last twelve months, will as rapidly melt away under the influence of the serious crisis through which the country is about to pass."

Thus it will be seen, that in the view of the shrewdest men in New York, the Sabine Pass affair assumes an importance equal to the great battle of Chickamauga, and the two together have turned the fortunes of the war for this year at least. Let us not, then, be criticised for bestowing upon our own heroes the credit that is their due. To have been in the Sabine Pass affair will be one of the proudest of the many proud memories the saldiers of this war will cherish.

☞ We have had the pleasure of meeting Gov-elect P. Murrah in town on Friday morning. He was on his way to Austin. In company with him were Col. A. W. Terrell and Dr. Hayden, chief medical officer of the Trans-Mississippi Department; and, we believe, only second in rank in the Confederate army. They left by the Central train on Friday.

☞ The official report of the Pennsylvania campaign, which we publish to-day, to the exclusion of much other matter of interest, will be read with satisfaction by everybody. It makes that whole affair perfectly clear, and leaves anything but the disagreeable impression on the mind which has hitherto attended the thoughts of that expedition.

☞ Col. Ashbel Smith, of the Second Texas, has been assigned to duty as Chief Inspector General of the State Troops. The assignment of this distinguished veteran of the Tennessee and Mississippi campaign to this position, not only shows the high estimate Maj. Gen. Magruder has of the State Troops, as a body, but his acceptance of the position shows that Col. Smith believes the material of which these troops are formed, gives promise of an efficient organization.

☞ At the battle of Sabine Pass six guns were fired 107 times in 35 minutes. So rapid was the firing that the Federals thought there must be two guns to each port hole. The guns were managed by six men each.

Letter from Alexandria.

ALEXANDRIA, Oct 18.

The Mobile Evening News of the 7th has come to hand. I condense its news items:

Several brokers in Richmond were victimized about the 1st inst., by a man calling himself Livingston. Representing himself as a member of the firm of J. J. North & Co., brokers, Savannah, Ga., he induced them to sell him gold for drafts on that firm to the amount of $150,000 and after securing the gold fled to parts unknown. It is believed he embarked for Nassau from Wilmington. Both his hands appeared to be malformed, and one was worn in a sling. This was probably done to prevent identification. He was accompanied by several women. The drafts returned protested.

THE DRAFT A FAILURE.

The authorities at Washington have come to the conclusion that the draft is a failure—that it will not pay. Under its process they obtain more money than men, and the character of the substitutes prevents the really worthy men who are drafted from serving. It is probable that the draft will be abandoned for a new plan of volunteering with bounties derived from the draft commutation fund. It has been ascertained that more men were obtained under the recruiting system than by the draft, and there is a strong disposition to return to the voluntary enlistment.—*Washington Paper.*

GOOD FOR OLD VIRGINIA.

The farmers of Virginia are holding county meetings, endorsing the late acts of the Legislature, and voluntarily offering all their surplus produce to the government, &c.

CHARLESTON.

The enemy is evidently making himself impregnable on Morris Island. Besides enlarging and strengthening Batteries Gregg and Wagner, he has erected palisades around his works to guard against any effort on our part to take the Island by assault. The enemy has teams of mules constantly transporting supplies to and from the south end of the island to Cumming's point notwithstanding our fire.

Our batteries continue to shell the works of Gregg and Wagner, doing considerable damage, notwithstanding they continue their digging operations. When the lookout man sees a flash, the signal is given, and all hands tumble into their boom proofs until the explosion has taken place, and immediately thereafter recommence work.—Now and then they are caught, not being sufficiently nimble of foot, and a shell drops in their midst, producing death and confusion. Not unfrequently a sudden puff of white smoke rising to view, tells of the explosion of an ammunition chest—and occasionally a team is sent flying like shattered corn about the floor.

These Yankees are determined, and will not cease their operations until they have made these works the strongest of the kind in the world.—When that is accomplished, look out for squalls and shells. They will come then and come in a heap.

The Yankees occupy pretty nearly every island around Charleston, besides Sullivan and James. On the latter the pickets are within hailing distance of each other. Upon some of these islands Yankee batteries are going up.

The city, as usual, is perfectly quiet, while the good people move to and fro, seemingly perfectly regardless of the danger that hangs over and around them.

The soldiers give evidence of a determination to hold the place at al hazards. Their easy, devil-may-care carriage and look tells, too, of the desire to meet and measure strength with the enemy, and that with a confidence that will certainly triumph when the trial comes, be that sooner or later.

There has been but one arrival here from east of the Mississippi, except from Natchez, during the last ten days. Nothing can exceed the dullness of this place (Alexandria) at present.

The Yankee force below is estimated by Gen. Green to be from fifteen to eighteen thousand. A battle is imminent. H. P.

☞ Now is the time to sow wheat. Let us urge upon the people of Northern Texas the importance of putting in the largest possible crops. We believe they will do so, with the exception of the tories. These, we understand, have determined to put in only enough for their own supplies, and will sow no more. Let the people of Northern Texas look to this. Let the measure of fealty to the Government be the amount of grain each man sows. Let traitors beware how they tempt the fate that is their due.

MUSICAL ACADEMY.—We are pleased to learn that Mr. Charles Otis has, after much labor and research perfected his long contemplated idea of a general school in the education of young children in the elements of music, vocal as well as instrumental. The vocal system with which the institution will be opened, is founded upon that introduced into England under the auspices of the Parliamentary Board of Education, by the celebrated Hullah. By it, in a very short period of time, the youngest children make surprising progress, while the elder learn with a facility almost magical. As a large number of children are taught at once, the expense will be almost nominal to each. It has been the object of Mr. Otis to make this a really popular and beneficial institution for the poor as well as the rich, and one which may in after-time become the nucleus of a great popular educational movement. The establishment will open early next month. The children of soldiers in the service will receive their education without charge, if desired.

CIRCULAR.

OFFICE OF THE CHIEF COMMISSARY, T. S. T.
Houston, October 2d, 1863.

Assistant Commissaries of Battalions of State Troops will forward to Major H. B. Blair, Chief of Bureau of Subsistence, at Shreveport, La., all the accounts and returns required by the regulations to be rendered to the Commissary General.

Copies of the following Monthly and Quarterly papers will be sent to this office:

MONTHLY—Returns of provisions received and issued. Abstract of purchases. Report of Extra Duty Men employed. Summary statement of Funds received and disbursed.

QUARTERLY—Account Current. Abstract of all purchases of provisions in the quarter. Abstract of all other expenditures during the quarter. Estimate of Funds required for the next quarter (in duplicate). List of outstanding debts due and unpaid (in duplicate).

Estimates will be carefully revised and corrected by Commanding Officers before approval.

Funds will be turned over to bonded Commissaries on estimates properly approved.

J. E. OWENS, Capt. & Chief Commissary State Troops.

Approved by command of
MAJ. GEN. MAGRUDER.
J. D. McADOO, A. A. Gen., T. S. Troops.
October 3-tw2w

HEADQUARTERS 2D REGT. TEXAS INFANTRY,
Camp Lubbock, Houston, Oct. 21, 1863.

General Order No. —.

Official information has been received at these headquarters that the officers and men of the Second Texas regiment, captured at Vicksburg and subsequently paroled, have been duly exchanged.

The attention of the members of this regiment is directed to the following order from Major General Magruder:

HEADQUARTERS DISTRICT OF TEXAS,
NEW MEXICO & ARIZONA,
Houston, Texas, Oct. 17th, 1863.

Special Orders, No. 282.

The officers and men of the 2d Texas regiment of infantry will rendezvous at Camp Lubbock, near Houston.

The enemy is now advancing on Texas. No delay will be tolerated, and active measures will be taken to bring into camp all who do not comply with this order promptly.

By command of
Maj. Gen. J. BANKHEAD MAGRUDER.
EDMUND P. TURNER, A. A. Gen.

In obedience to the above orders, *all* members of the 2d regiment will report *without delay* to Camp Lubbock for duty. By order of
ASHBEL SMITH, Colonel Comdg.
B. W. LECOMPTE, Lt. and Adjutant. oct 23—trw 3t

WANTED—Two copies of the 1st volume of Kent's Commentaries have been taken from my office. Please return them. GEO. GOLDTHWAITE.
oct 21—trw5t *

BY PONY EXPRESS.

OUR SPECIAL DISPATCHES.

Telegraphed from Beaumont.

ALEXANDRIA, Oct. 23d.—During the last six days, the following information has daily reached here through different channels. At first I did not heed the reports, but as each succeeding day fresh rumors seemed to confirm previous ones, I am induced to send them forward, though they need confirmation. They are these:

Burnside attempted to reinforce Rosecrans through the northern section of Georgia, but was cut off before he could form the junction and his army completely cut up. He himself barely escaped capture, all of Rosecrans wagons across the river were burned and his supplies cut off. Failing to be reinforced as he expected, after being shelled by Bragg six days he surrendered on the 12th.

This news is too great and joyful to be believed, unless backed up by the very best authority, hence I am slow to believe it.

I have as yet nothing but unpublished statements. The following appeared in the New Orleans Era of the 13th.

NEW ORLEANS, Oct. 13.—The city was thrown into considerable commotion yesterday afternoon by the arrival of the government transport J. A. Scott, which no sooner made her appearance off the city, her rigging gaily decorated with flags, than she was saluted by loud salutes of artillery from the other vessels in port.

People wondered what it would all mean until the news got abroad that she had on board Brig. Gen. A. J. Hamilton, the Military Governor of Texas and his staff. We had the pleasure of meeting the General during the evening and were delighted to find him in robust health.

During the past week, there has been heavy skirmishing below.

Reports came in last evening and to-day that the enemy has been heavily reinforced and is not advancing in this direction. They were last reported at Opelousas.

Our forces are falling back. If the enemy keep advancing, look out for blue blazes soon.

H. P.

HEADQUARTERS, BUREAU OF STATE TROOPS,
DISTRICT OF TEXAS, NEW MEXICO AND ARIZONA.
Houston, Texas, Oct. 17th, 1863.

General Orders, No. 29.

I. The Major General Commanding, in view of the absolute necessity for the consolidation of the cavalry and infantry of the State Troops into regiments and battalions, has determined, before the troops go into the field, to form them into cavalry and infantry regiments and battalions upon the most just and equitable basis, looking to the rights of the officers and the comfort and feelings of the men. In seperating the cavalry from the infantry, he has determined that the Major should go with the majority of his command, wherever the same is practicable. In consolidating the companies, he deems it just that the men of neighboring localities should go together. In assigning the various Majors to the consolidated commands, he leaves the question of rank to be settled by the regulations—by seniority where there is a difference in the date of election, and by lottery where there is not. In case of vacancy, he leaves the selection of the officer to the men. This plan having been submitted to the officers of the State troops reporting at Houston, representing some twelve battalions, cavalry and infantry, and having been unanimously endorsed by them after a full and fair conference, he trusts that the State Troops, as a body, will receive it in the same spirit. The alacrity with which they have responded to his call, their enthusiastic devotion to the cause, and their intelligence as citizens, and his fellow-soldiers convince him that the course he has pursued will meet their endorsement.

II. In all cases of dispute concerning rank of the officers, the question will be settled by priority of election, and when the date of the election is the same, by lottery.

III. Majors of present battalions will immediately forward to these headquarters a certificate showing the date of their election, or a copy of the same certified on honor.

IV. The Adjutant, Assistant Quartermaster and Assistant Surgeon, will go with their Major in case he becomes the Commander of a Regiment or Battalion by seniority. In Regiments, the Assistant Surgeon of the next Senior Major in rank will become Assistant Surgeon. All other Assistant Surgeons and Assistant Quartermasters, whose Majors do not become Regimental or Battalion Commanders, will report by letter for duty at these Head Quarters. Adjutants, whose Majors do not become Regimental or Battalion Commanders, will be assigned to duty as Lieutenants and Instructors of Tactics in the command of which their Major is a field officer.

V. Where elections are to be held for Field Officers, the Officer Commanding will order the election at such time as will afford the whole command an opportunity to vote.

VI. Transportation and Company property will go with the Companies who have it in possession. All other Quartermaster and Commissary property will be turned over by Assistant Quartermasters, who do not become A. Q. M's. of the Regiments or Battalions, to the A. Q. M. of the command to which the bulk of the Battalion is attached.

VII. Commanding Officers of Regiments and Battalions thus formed, will immediately forward to these Head Quarters' a list of their Staff Officers. In commands where elections are to be held, the present Battalion Staff of the senior Officer in Command will act until the new Staff is appointed.

VIII. Commanding Officers of Regiments and Battalions will immediately notify these Head Quarters as to the Postoffice of their Head Quarters, so that Companies may be notified where to send returns.

IX. Adjutants of present Battalions will continue to make returns to these Head Quarters until the Regimenty or Battalion to which the are attached is fully organized. Detached Companies will also make returns to these Head Quarters.

X. The Senior Officers of all Regiments and Battalions formed as above, will immediately assume command and report the fact and date to these Headquarters, with a statement of the other Field Officers of the command.

XI. The rank of Captains of companies will be decided according to the date of the muster of their companies. Where companies were mustered on the same day, the rank of the Captains will be decided by lottery. The companies will be lettered accordingly.

By command of
Maj. Gen. J. BANKHEAD MAGRUDER.
J. D. McADOO, A. A. G., State Troops.
oct 26-tw3t

HEADQUARTERS, DISTRICT OF TEXAS,
NEW MEXICO AND ARIZONA,
Houston, Texas, Oct. 20, 1863.

General Orders, No. 188.

A violation of the Revenue Laws by the Quartermaster and other Officers of Colonel Bates' Regiment, at Velasco, in having purchased and received certain goods from the super-cargo of the British schooner *Mary P. Burton*, before the Revenue Laws were complied with, having been reported to these Head Quarters, Commanding Officers are hereby directed to prevent the sale or delivery of any portion of the cargoes arriving in this District, to any officer or enlisted man of the army, until both vessel and cargo have been regularly entered at the Custom House.

The particular attention of Commanding Officers along the coast is called to this Order, and a strict compliance will be required by all.

By command of
Maj. Gen. J. BANKHEAD MAGRUDER.
EDMUND P. TURNER, A. A. G.
Oct 24tw3t.

CONFEDERATE ASSESSOR'S NOTICE.—All persons liable to pay a tax on sales, or property, or following any taxable occupation, are requested to hand in their lists for assessment, and register their business before the first of November next, or the penalty of the law will be exacted.

W. R. BAKER,
JAS. E. GREGORY, } Assessors.
Houston, Oct 24-tw2t

LAND FOR CONFEDERATE MONEY.—640 acres in Colorado county, a first rate stock range and a 20 acre lot of the "Texas Military Institute," in Fayette county. Address or apply to
A. L. D. MOORE,
LaGrange, Texas.
Oct 12tw3t*

HEADQUARTER'S ECTOR'S BRIGADE,
Near Meridian, Miss., October 4, 1863.

The Brigadier General commanding directs that I send the following list of casualties of this brigade, in the battle of Chickamauga, with the request that you give it a place in your columns. These brave spirits who have so nobly battled and bled for the common cause, while cut off from all communication with the loved ones at home, must attract the admiration of all.

The lists of killed and wounded on every field in which they have acted a part, speak with eloquence of truth of the stubborn courage and noble heroism with which they have ever borne themselves. Your generous heart must warm towards the gallant defenders of liberty.

I am, sir, very respectfully,
T. B. TREZEVANT, A. A. A. Gen.

List of Casualties.

Ector's Brigade in the Battles on the 19th and 20th of September, 1863.

General Staff—M D Ector,* Brigadier General, slightly wounded, arm; Capt C B Kilgore, A A General, severely wounded, thigh; Lt H M Lane,* A D C, slightly wounded, wrist.

9TH REGIMENT TEXAS INFANTRY—COL W H YOUNG, COMMANDING.

Field and Staff—Wounded, Col W H Young, severely, left breast; Sergt Major C W Moore, severely left foot.

Company A—Capt W H H Long,* commanding. Wounded: Capt W H H Long, slightly, groin; privates T J Calloway,* slightly, thigh; F G Evins, slightly, thigh. Missing: H Thurmond, Joseph Penall.

Company B—Lt G W Thompson, commanding. Severely wounded: Lt G W Thompson, hand: Privates N Lyles, shoulder. Slightly: Corp R Bass, foot; 1st Sergt J M Wallace, hip. Missing: Privates W R Harris, L K Masten, M V Gentry.

Company C—Capt L F Ely, commanding. Killed: Lt S C Fitch. Severely wounded: Privates D Fallis, leg; J T Garrison, leg; J C McLane, leg and hips. Slightly: M Chapin, arm; R D Reynolds, leg.

Company D—Capt J H McReynolds, commanding. Slightly wounded: Sergt W B Willis, foot; A C Reynolds,* shoulder; M F Fowler, hand and thigh; H F Freeman,* breast; T J Justice,* thigh; A J Moulton, thigh; J S Penly, head; C H Smith, arm. Severely: J M Hays, both legs. Missing: Privates J W Jones, J E Williams.

Company E—Lt Thos H Legon, commanding. Killed: Private W R Bruce. Severely wounded: Private J W Harris, foot. Missing: 1st Sergt J R Miller, Private E Peniman.

Company F—Lt J E Agee, commanding. Slightly wounded: Lt Agee,* breast and thigh; Private T J Vansickle, finger. Severely: Private M W Houston, head; W Clayton, shoulder.

Company G—Lt A L Hamilton, commanding. Killed: Lt Hamilton. Slightly wounded: Lt J B Terrel,* foot. Missing; P W Conner, M Grizzle.

Company H—Capt G W Daniels commanding. Wounded severely: Corpl M P Davis, arm. Slightly: Privates J P Bush thigh; J Mitchel, hand. Missing: Privates J S Batty, W M Yates.

Company I—Captain R M Boord, commanding.—Killed: Privates J M Burns, J M Harris. Wounded slightly: Privates J W Whisenant, neck; S Dobson, finger. Missing: Privates J Day, J F O'Dell.

Company K—Captain D Riddley, commanding.—Killed: Private B R Worthington. Wounded severely: Captain Riddley, thigh. Slightly: Privates B S Rowland, ankle; B S Roach, foot; Sergt J H Harmon, thigh. Missing: Lieut G W Bedford, Corp'l W H Owens, Private J G Terrill.

TENTH REGIMENT TEXAS (DISMOUNTED) CAVALRY—LT. COL. C. R. EARP COMMANDING.

Field and Staff—Killed: Assistant Surgeon M C Hillyard. Wounded: W J Sparks,* in arm; Sergt. Major J W Kelly, severe mouth.

Company A—Capt. J J T Wright, commanding—Wounded severely: Capt. J J T Wright. Slightly: Corp'l A J Waldroupe, arm; R H Noyes, leg; privates J M Shipp, arm; Z R Finley,* A McBride.* Missing: S C White, J R Butler, W L Essery. Killed: Thomas Green, Jas W McMillan.

Company B—J W Cannon, commanding—Killed; Private F M Rogers. Wounded severely: Capt. J W Cannon, since dead; Lt. J W Huggins, breast, dead; Corp'l J H Garrett, thigh; Private R A Linley. Slightly: Sergts J S Brown,* J L Shamberger.* Privates J D Attoway, foot; J W. Brown, arm; F A King,* W F Hanson.* Missing: C J Milsap.

Company C—Capt W G McGee commanding—Killed: Private J D Neal, C C Weir, A Hamilton. Wounded severely: Joh Wright, hand. Slightly: Capt W G McGee, knee; J B Hillyard leg; Sergt E S Phillips,* leg. Missing: J W Hicks, J J Spratts.

Company D—Capt R W Smith commanding—Wounded severely: Capt R W Smith, face; Sergt W C Calvert, loins; Private S T Wilson, face. Slightly: H Morris, thigh; W L Goss,* leg. Missing: E Shrum.

Company E—Lieut W F Young commanding—Wounded severely: Sergt W B Turner, leg amputated; Private Anderson Kelly, leg. Slightly: Lieut W F Young, Corp'ls J Eaton, L Lyd,* Privates John Davis, thigh; Wm Harvie, head; Wm Melton, knee; L H Oliver, ankle; W J Mathews, J J Spence. Missing: D S Melton D L Terry.

Company F—Capt Booty commanding—Killed: Privates J Shivers and J Boland. Severely wounded: C H Wall. Slightly wounded; Sergt A C Hillyard,* hip; privates A J Booty, thigh; S L Fite, leg; J N Gray,* J C Thompson,* W A McClanchan. Missing: Privates J M Murphy and W V Cogswell.

Company G—Lieut G W Tramwell commanding—Killed: Sergt B N Lay. Severely wounded: Privates J M Watson, Jas Anderson, arm amputated; C A Birdwell, leg; Reuben Goforth, leg; B W Hobson, shoulder; John Lee, hip. Slightly wounded: Lieut Tramwell,* Lieut E L Phillips,* Sergt J S Becton, leg; Corp'l H Gatlin, R M Monk, Wm Smith,* E Barthold,* Stoke Hutchings, arm; R B Irvin,* knee. Missing: Sergt Butler and Jas Wade.

Company H—Lieut R S Lisles commanding.—Slightly wounded: Lieut Lisles, Corporal A J Odun,* Corporal J T Hatton, in heel; privates T J Benton, in hand; R B Smith, D McBride. Mortally: W G Harper, leg broke. Missing: P Smith, Wm Losely and W A Allen.

Company I—Capt J F M Hall commanding.—Killed: Corporal J A Holmes. Slightly wounded: Capt Hall, arm; Lt J A Spaulding,* F M Weltch.* Severely: Corp'l J M Francis, in hip; J S Lowden, leg; J W Skurlock, back; Ball, in foot. Missing: J H Burks, J A Templeton, C J Odum, G T Egbert, M Walters.

Company K—Captain T K Gibson commanding.—Slightly wounded: Capt Gibson, head; Corp'l L Spear,* Corp'l D W Spear,* privates W R Glen and Ed Wooten.

14TH TEXAS CAVALRY (dismounted)—COLONEL J. L. CAMP, COMMANDING.

Field and Staff—Wounded: Major J H Garrison, slightly; Lieut J T Wells, Acting Adjutant, slightly.

Company A—Capt S V Lak, commanding.—Killed: Corp'l J H McCarty. Slightly wounded: Serg't Wm Burchfield; privates E H Egan. Missing: W Donoho, W S Fulton, C R Hurff, J A Hopkins, C T Rayburn.

Company B—Lieut. Tunnell commanding—Woended slightly: Lieut Tunnel, private G G Cole,* Severely: A Ledfin, J Stevenson, W B Tunnell.

Company C—Lieut Hynes commanding.—Killed: private Wm Gregg. Severely wounded: J E Myrick, J R Boteman, corporal J A Hart, privates C S Russell, J Grigsly, W W Youngblood. Slightly: S Higs,* Missing, J Hale, J J Patterson.

Company D—Capt Hoize commanding—Killed: Sargeant J C Hudson, W Friddle: Severely: private R H Gary. Slightly, Lieut C C Doyle, sargeant J L Hale,* corporals E Guinn, W C Nicholson,* J R Russell, H H Shadden,* Jones Williams,* C H Bailey. Wounded and missing: privates H C Horton, G W Robinson, missing.

Company E—Capt R H Harkey commanding—Killed, sargeant J S Irvin. Mortally wounded: R Ashbury, (since died.) Severely wounded: O D Richardson, Missing: James cooper. (also wounded.)

Company F—Capt L Purdy, commanding—Killed: Private J L Campbell. Severely wounded: W Spencer, corporal James Shegog.* Slightly wounded: Private George Washington Box*, James Spencer. Missing: Wm Graves, Wm Hamilton, M M Harkins and Dan McKey.

Company G—Captain A M Sanford, commanding. Killed: Privates Jas Arnold and B M Lynch. Severely wounded: Sergerants S M Gorum and Paul Potts. Missing: Capt A M Sanford, Sergeant J A P Hill, Corp S M Price, privates W L Taylor and J C Pierce.

Company H—Capt C W Merchant, commanding. Severely wounded: Sergt M B Wisdom. Slightly wounded: Sergt G W Thompkins: privates W E O'hair, B Case*, D Crites*, J L McLane*, Wm Welch*, U C Hurley*. Missing. Sergt C T Clayton and Wm Wells.

Company I—Dapt. S C Ragan, commanding. Severely wounded: Lt W L Russell, private Sefferson Rolland. Slightly wounded: Corp A P Grimsley*, privates W L Bearden*, O D Bell, Dan'l Morriss*, Sylas Poe, Alex Shelton*. Missing: Serget C L Fuller, Corp P H Hopson, privates J W Burks, Lordrich Holt and John Polvado.

Company K—Capt R H Harkey, commanding. Killed: Privates W W Gaston.

THIRTY SECOND TEXAS REG'T, COL. J. A. ANDREWS COM'D'G

Field and Staff—Wounded: Col J A Andrews, severely in thigh; Adjutant G M Lindsay, severely in hip.

Company A—Killed. Privates D W Howard and Solomon Simpson. Wounded: Lieut R H Hays, slightly in head; Privates G A Watson, slightly in head*: A J Fanning, slightly in leg; G W Crabtree, slightly in arm; E T Anderson, slightly in leg; Henry Hamilton, slightly in both thighs; W F Jolly, slightly in leg. Missing: L M Trailer.

Company B—Killed: Lieut L A Williams, Corp'l D R Despain, Serg't E D Posey. Wounded: Lieut H H Garrison, slightly in the back*; Lieut W H Vaden, slightly in foot and knee: private S S Midget, severely; S F Rowe, slightly in leg*; J M Ashcroft, slightly in thigh; L I Johnson, slightly in hip; W L Wolf, slightly in knee. Missing: John Hill, Marion Patrick.

Company C—Wounded: Capt E D Gayden, slight in arm; Lieut W C Williams, slightly in knee; Serg't T R Friddle, slightly in thigh*; private John Smith, slightly in knee.—Missing: J T Merchant, John C Cook, John Sanders, N R Hillin.

Company D—Killed: Serg't R H Huland, private W C Lyster. Wounded: Capt H E E Lyon, severely in leg; Lt H W Crawford, severely in leg; privates J R Mounce, slightly in abdomen and hips; J R Taylor, slightly in side*; W W Mathis, severely in shoulder; J C Wiley, slightly in side and hip; E L Anderson, slightly in thigh; J R Paul, severely in ankle; J A Williams, severely in arm and side. Missing: privates J M Harman, Robert Hestlewood, C C Payne, T J Elder, Amos Bean, T B McGill, S B McGill.

Company E—Killed: Capt J S Dixon. Wounded: Lieut E A Estes, severely in right hand; Sergt G T Johnson, finger off; private T N Mabes, slightly in foot. Missing: Sergeant W B Saughter; Privates Robt Tisdale, John Godsey.

Company F—Killed: Corp W D Oddell. Wounded: Lieut W L Richardson, severely in both arms; Sergt D M King, slightly in leg; Privates H C Hunter, severely in leg; W P Kelly, severely in hip. Missing: Privates J A Evans, J C Foberson.

Company G—Wounded severe: Lieut H H Hays, arm and breast; Corpl N Williams, leg; Privates John W Jones, Jr, neck; Robert Rowland, breast; N B Littlejohn, ankle. Slight: Ensign G James, leg; Privates Henry Wells, left arm; Geo W Wells, breast; J W McClure, leg, severe; C E Burns, shoulder; S E Smart, leg; W T Nixon, side;* Missing: Privates W R Long, D C Crosby, W W Johnson, E C Cavin, T N Griffie.

Company H—Wounded: Lieut Nordleet Smith, slightly in knee; Sergt James Moore, slightly in hip; Corp'l Marshall Smith, mortally in thigh; Privates John Burns, mortally in hip; Jas Tidwell, mortally in thigh; Wm A Walker, slightly in leg; Richard Wilbur, slightly in arm.* Missing: Privates H Gillespie, S D Poer, B Walker, Corpl J B Bardman.

Company I—Killed: Sergt J M Skelton; privates A G Garey, J R Brown, R T Barnes. Wounded: F M Lee, slight in thigh,* J M Fitzgerald, slight in hand; R L Graves, severe in elbow and amputated; L W Garrett, severe in arm and side. Missing: Ell Patton.

Company K—Wounded: Lieut J C Todd, slight in thigh; Sergts Wm M Dunn, slight in foot; J A Ferguson, slight in breast; Corp J G McCoun, slight in elbow;* privates, Wm Wingo, slight in thigh; J A Good, slight in hip and arm. Missing: Privates Geo Hughes, Thos Kerney, Biram McPherson, W A J Chesser, T S Ellington, Austin Bush, Samuel Gray, Wm Lorance, W B Gohlston, G T L Hurtt.

Recapitulation: Killed, 13; wounded, 65; missing, 40; total, 118.

All the mounted officers of the Brigade had their horses either killed or wounded.

Those marked thus (*) have returned to duty since the battle.

F. B. TREZEVANT, A. A. A. G., Ector's Brigade.

BY PONY EXPRESS.

OUR SPECIAL DISPATCHES.

ALEXANDRIA, Oct. 20, 1863.

No change, worthy of mention, has taken place in the armies below, since my last dispatches.

A general engagement is looked for soon.

Gen. Wm. R. Scurry and staff have left for below.

I have received no later Confederate papers, and consequently must send the following Yankee dispatches. Make due allowance for them.

CINCINNATI, Oct 6.—Rosecrans is still entrenched at Chattanooga, but it is making preparations to assume the offensive.—Bragg is already fortifying himself on the defensive.

WASHINGTON, Oct. 6.—The Republican, of this morning says that all rumors to the contrary notwithstanding, communication with Rosecrans is not cut off.

That a cavalry force crossed the Tennessee River at Washington to annoy Rosecrans' rear, there is no doubt, but whether that force ever gets back to rebeldom without suffering the fate of Morgan—defeat and capture—the greatest doubt does exist. Rosecrans, it adds, is master of the situation at Chattanooga.

LOUISVILLE, Oct. 6.—The Journal has received a special dispatch from Knoxville, considered entirely reliable, that Burnside holds the country south from Knoxville to Calhoun, on the Hiawassee River and Western and Atlantic R. R., only twenty-five miles distant from Kingston, the Junction of the Western and Atlantic and Rome R. R., and East of Knoxville as far as Greenville, on the East Tennessee and Virginia R. R., and also that he has possessed all the passes into North Carolina. Burnside's right wing is in communication with Rosecrans, and his position is all that could be desired. His army is in the best of health and spirits.

The Nashville Dispatch of to-day says the rebels burned the R. R. bridge at Stuart's Creek and another over Stone River.

After the capture of McMinnville on Saturday by the rebels under Wheeler, they burned one locomotive and ten cars, and took a number of Railroad men as prisoners, subsequently Col. McCook with a brigade of Federal cavalry, attacked them, scattering them in every direction.

The rebels left behind all the prisoners they had taken and several hundred horses.

McCook killed and wounded one hundred and twenty-five, and took ninety prisoners. On Sunday morning, the Confederates appeared before Murfreesboro' driving the Federals into the entrenchments.

After remaining all day and part of the night, they destroyed the Railroad bridge, crossing Stone River, and are now three miles distant, when it is said they will have to fight.

The Nashville Journal editorially says, Wheeler with near eight thousand rebel cavalry and mounted infantry has succeeded in getting into the rear of Rosecrans, and threatens to break his Railroad communication.

There seem to be rebel cavalry all along the Chattanooga railroad, watching for weak points.

NEW YORK, Oct. 6.—A special to the Herald, dated Nashville, 5th, says the enemy to-day destroyed the large bridge south of Murfreesboro'. They left one portion and cut the other. All is quiet at Murfreesboro' to night.

The Commercial's Washington correspondent states that the President has prohibited the further enlistment of Maryland slaves in the army. Also that Government will not allow any correspondents to telegraph any news relative to Rosecrans' army to the North, although extracted from the published columns of the Washington newspapers.

NEW YORK, October 6th.—A Fortress Monroe letter, dated October 4th, to the Herald, states an expedition on a large scale, consisting of artillery, cavalry and infantry, has been organized, and in conjunction with several armed gunboats, started from here yesterday afternoon. The weather is all that could be desired, hence the expeditionary corps will not suffer any from unfavorable wind and tide.

The destination is unknown, even to those participating in it.

WASHINGTON, Oct. 6.—Lieut. Comd'g Chandler, of the San Jacinto, informs the Secretary of the Navy, that on the 16th of September, in lat. 25:58 north, long. 85:11 west, the steamer Lizzie Davis, a rebel blockade runner was captured by that ship, after a chase of two hours.

She was bound from Havana to Mobile, and left Havana on the 14th. She was loaded with lead and other articles for the rebel authorities.

A band of guerrillas, under the famous White, of Loudon county, made a raid last night on Longley, six miles above Georgetown, driving in the pickets. They had two pieces of artillery

NEW YORK, Oct. 6.—The Herald's special from Nashville, dated yesterday, says an unusual degree of excitement prevails here to-day in consequence of the rebel General Forrest with a force of about 4000 mounted men, having made a raid on our line of railroad communication between this place and Bridgeport or Chattanooga.

Just at this particular time, no trains are leaving in the direction of the front.

Yet the circumstance need give no particular cause for alarm.

The enemy can do but comparatively little to injure our communication.

Forrest may succeed in intercepting our communications for a few hours, but we have not only a force to drive them back, but to defeat an immensely superior force.

There is no need to fear Gen. Rosecrans' success in holding his position at Chattanooga, and he is too strong at that place for Bragg to attack him with a show of success.

To-day skirmishing has been going on in the neighborhood of Murfreesboro'.

The enemy made an attempt to destroy a bridge of considerable importance to us in a railroad point of view.

Unless the enemy is very desperate, he will not attack Chattanooga. If he does, there is every likelihood that he will be defeated. If he attempts a flank movement on this place, he will meet a force that has been long and well tried in the field, and Gen. Rosecrans would be able to hold out several days against movements and attacks even of a very superior force. The present raid is not an unexpected one. We were looking for it. Cavalry movements do not worry us, as it is only when heavy bodies of infantry move on our lines of communication or flanks that we prepare for serious engagements.

Let me assure loyal people that fears for Rosecrans' rear, and for the safety of Murfreesboro' need not be entertained, unless the enemy move in our rear flank in full force, and a General well qualified to know, assures me that there is no information of an attack on Chattanooga, except as due to the cutting of the wires between here and Bridgeport, Alabama, said cutting having taken place this morning.

CINCINNATI, Oct. 6.—Private advices from Chattanooga, October 1st, represent the army in fine spirits, and the position impregnable.

H. P.

A hopeful disposition is a good thing, and the editor of the Memphis Bulletin seems to be well endowed with it. In his issue of September 25th, he says:

In another column we give our views upon the military situation in which Gen. Rosecrans is placed. It is best to be hopeful. The first reports of such an action are necessarily exaggerated and wild. Even taking the statements as published in our column, we captured ten guns and lost but six.

The Knoxville (Atlanta) Register of Sept. 30th says that Gen. Bragg had 250 guns in position that day ready to open on Rosecrans. It is rumored that our cavalry have captured Murfreesboro.

THE TRI-WEEKLY TELEGRAPH.

VOL. XXIX.--NO. 101 HOUSTON THURSDAY, NOVEMBER 12, 1863. WHOLE NO. 3756

NEW ADVERTISEMENTS.

WILL sell for Confederate money or exchange for negroes, one-third of a league of land, (1440 acres,) lying on the San Jacinto river, in Montgomery county. Inquire of A. Morrison & Co.

Also a lot of No. 1 negroes; Perry, 28 years old, first rate house servant; Driver, hostler, jockey and gardener; Caroline, his wife, 25 years old, cook washer and ironer; Emily, their child, 6 years old, smart and likely; Tom, 16 years old, field hand, strong and likely; Bill, 22 years old, field hand. nov 11—tw6t*

FOR SALE—My entire stock of horses and carriages, at seventy five per cent. on first cost. B. P. LANHAM.

Houston, Nov. 11, 1863 [tw3t*]

NOTICE is hereby given that all persons are warned not to purchase any of the property or effects of my late father, W. J. Mills, as no person is authorized as yet to do so. CAROLINE RICE.

Houston, Nov. 12—tw3t*

GENERAL HOSPITAL, P. A. C. S., Houston, Texas, Nov. 12, 1863.

PERSONS applying for medicines, on prescriptions of an army surgeon, must supply vials. I desire to purchase old vials, old linen and cotton rags—which are greatly needed in the Hospital. W. P. RIDDELL,

n12-tw6t Post Surgeon in charge of Hospital.

TEAMS WANTED.—I have bought, for the Engineer Department, C. S., by authority of Capt. Schleicher, of San Antonio, 500 bales of cotton, and teams are wanted to haul the same to Brownsville. I will pay ten cents per pound, in specie, for transportation, and teams guaranteed from impressment, by order of Lieut. Gen. Smith. Apply to O. A. Norwood, Washington, who is my agent during my absence.

nov 12-tw6t R. T. FLEWELLEN.

☞ News copy.

HEADQUARTERS, DISTRICT OF TEXAS, &C., Houston, November 7, 1863.

General Orders, No. 195.

No cotton bureau having been established, and the commanding General finding it impossible to perform his military duties if subjects of that sort engage his attention, he hereby temporarily relieves from duty Major B. Bloomfield, Chief Q. M. of the District, and assigns him to the duty of procuring cotton by purchase or impressment, as may be ordered by Lieutenant General Smith, and of transporting the same to the Rio Grande, to meet the obligations of the Government.

All communications on the subject of cotton, or contracts for supplies to be paid for in cotton, will be made to Major B Bloomfield.

Major Bloomfield is also authorized to make all purchases for the different Staff Departments, and will pay for the same in cotton or otherwise.

By command of

Major-General J. B. MAGRUDER.

W. A. ALSTON, Capt. & A. A. G.

Nov12-tw3t

DESERTED—Alexander Barckman, on the 12th of November from Capt. Bond's Company F, Brown's Battalion of Cavalry. Said Barckman was born in the State of Indiana, U. S.,—was, when elisted, a resident of Nevarro county, Texas, and by occupation a stock raiser. He is 21 years of age, 5 feet 6 inches high, fair complexion, blue eyes, dark hair; was enlisted on the 12th day of April, 1862.

[illegible] Said Donald was enlisted on the 12th day of April, 1862; is 23 years old, 6 feet 2 inches high, dark complexion, black eyes, black hair, a stock raiser by occupation, and a resident of Navarro county. He was born in Liberty county, Texas.

ALSO—John A. Garrison, a private of Captain Hargroves' Company B, Brown's Battalion, on the 1st of November. Said Garrison aged 21 years, hazel eyes, light hair, dark complexion, 6 feet 5½ inches high, was born in Lamar county, Texas; occupation, a farmer; enlisted May 8th, 1862.

ALSO—John C. Burk, of Captain Hargroves' Company B, Brown's Battalion. Said Burk is aged 28 years, blue eyes, light hair, fair complexion, 5 feet 6½ inches high; born in Louisiana; by occupation a farmer; enlisted May 8th, 1862.

A reward of $30 each will be paid for the apprehension and delivery of said deserters to any Provost Marshal or military authorities.

R. R. BROWN,

Lt. Col., Com'd'g Brown's Bat. of Cavalry.

nov12tw3t.

HEADQUARTERS, DIST. OF TEXAS, NEW MEXICO AND ARIZONA, Houston, Nov. 8, 1863.

GENERAL ORDERS, No. 194.

I The limited stock of clothing, camp and garrison equippage on hand at any one time requires that only the absolute necessities of the troops be supplied. To accomplish this, immediately on the reception of this order, the companies will be inspected critically by their commanders, superintended by the Regimental, Battalion or Post Commander, as the case may require, and both officers shall forward at once, to Capt. E. C. Wharton, A. Q. M., Chief of Bureau of Clothing and Equippage, Houston, a statement, certified on honor, showing at inspection:

1st. The number of men actually present.

2d. The quantity and character of Clothing in possession of the men, under the headings of "Hats or Caps," "Coats or Jackets," "Trowsers, Shirts, Drawers, Socks, Shoes, Blankets, Great or Overcoats.

3d. The quantity and character of Camp and Garrison Equippage in charge of the Company or its Commander.

4th. The quantity and character of Clothing and Equippage absolutely requisite to enable the men to take the field.

Any inaccurate statement will subject the Inspecting Officers to prompt punishment.

At the same time, Sub-District, Post, Regimental or Battalion Quartermasters will furnish Capt. E. C. Wharton, A. Q. M., with a certified Return of Clothing and Equippage in their charge, showing whether for issue or for transportation; and the Returns will be made to Capt. Wharton, monthly.

The troops enlisted for the war will be the first supplied by Captain Wharton, and the Clothing and Equippage Quartermasters under his control, as Chief of the Clothing and Equippage Bureau. Of these troops, those ordered for active service will have the preference.

Sales of clothing to officers will be confined strictly to absolute necessities for their own personal use, and must not interfere with the paramount duty of clothing the troops.

The funds received by Post, Regimental and Battalion Quartermasters, for sales of clothing to officers, will be turned over by them to Captain Wharton, A. Q. M., Houston; Capt. McKinney, A. Q. M., Tyler, or to Capt. Prescott, A. Q. M., San Antonio.

II. General Orders No. 193, Nov. 2d, 1863, from these Headquartes, are so far modified as to allow Commanding officers, in case of absolute necessity, to permit their Quartermasters, and Commissaries of Subsistence to leave their posts or commands on public business.

III. Officers are hereby positively prohibited from detaining a messenger beyond the schedule time, of the Pony Express, on any route in this District. This order is positive, and a strict compliance will be required.

By command of

Maj. Gen. J. B. MAGRUDER.

E. P. TURNER, A. A. G.

Nov12tw3t

FOR SALE.—A desirable homestead, containing 876 acres of land, sixty acres in cultivation; improvements good. It is unsurpassed as a stock farm; and will be sold with the place 450 head of cattle, and a few good mares, with corn and fodder, if desired. The place is within less than thirty miles of Houston, in Harris county, on the waters of Willow creek. Payments and terms easy. For particulars apply to

By the Shreveport Express.

From the Shreveport News Extra, Nov. 9th.

CAMDEN, Nov. 8.—We take the following from the Memphis Bulletin of the 29th October.

CHATTANOOGA, Oct. 23.—Gen. Grant arrived this evening. We have been visited by heavy rains and the traveling roads are in a horrid condition. All quiet.

LOUISVILLE, Oct. 25.—Gen. Rosecrans, accompanied by his staff, arrived here last night at ten o'clock, and took up his quarters at the Galt House. Shortly after his arrival, he was serenaded by the citizens of Louisville, and in response, made a short speech, thanking them for their attention and welcome.

The following farewell order was published to the army of the Cumberland after his departure:

Headquarters, Department of the Cumberland, Chattanooga, Tenn, Oct. 29, 1863.

Generel Orders, No. 242.

The General commanding announces to the officers and soldiers of the army of the Cumberland, that he leaves them under orders from the President. Major General George H. Thomas, in compliance with orders, will assume the command of the army and department. The chiefs of all the staff departments will report to him for orders. * * * *

Companions-in-arms, officers and soldiers farewell, and may God bless you.

(Signed) W. S. ROSECRANS, Major General.

He left to-day, at noon, for Cincinnati on the mail boat.

WASHINGTON, Oct. 25.—Ed. Baul sends the following to this bureau:

Head Quarters, Army Potomac, October 24.—The enemy's infantry recrossed the Rappahannock this morning upon two pontoon bridges, driving back Gen. Gregg's cavalry division, which lost very heavily. They had a short engagement with two brigades of our infantry, one belonging to the 2d corps and the other to the 3d corps. The enemy now occupy the line, the left of which rests on Beverly Fork, crossing the railroad near Ballard's Station, and extending towards Stafford Courthouse.

NEW YORK, Oct. 26.—The bark Urauca, from Cape of Good Hope August 29th, Helena Sept. 11th, arrived here, and reported the bark Sea Bird of Boston was captured by the Alabama in sight of the harbor; also reports the capture of the Anna F. Schmidt of Boston. The Florida and Tuscaloosa were cruising on the coast. Semmes had declared that he would hang Capt. Hasky, of the Urauca, for flying the stars and stripes in port, while anchored near the Alabama.

DANVILLE, Oct. 25.—A squad of guerrillas supposed to be a part of Richardson's, from the vicinity of Bardstown, numbering about 75, dashed into our town yesterday morning, seized the telegraph office, and cut the wires, but did no material damage to the instruments. They burned all Commissary and Quartermaster stores.

NASHVILLE, Oct. 25.—No news of importance from Chattanooga.

Hooker's corps has crossed the Tennessee river, and fighting was reported yesterday.

The river is rising, with five feet water on the shoals. No arrivals by the river.

KNOXVILLE, Oct. 23.—The rebels are still east of the Hiawassee. Nothing of interest from that direction.

All it quiet towards Virginia.

"EDITORIAL."—Dispatches from Chattanooga to Saturday evening, report the rebels as making a [illegible] News of Nov. 8th has the same dispatches received by us yesterday from Vienna, but somewhat more full. The London letter to the New York Herald, referring to the treaty said to have been made between the Confederate States France and Spain, says:

The writer says it is feared that if the Lincoln administration should conquer the South, it would undertake to rule all America by the sword, and eventually consider the whole civilized world too contracted for the field of its operations. He then intimates at some legth that the best policy of Lincoln, under the circumstances, is to make peace with the South, and 'let the two Republics work out the problem of man's capacity for self government.

The Herald closes its editorial allusion to the letter, to which it attaches importance, by urging another vigorous blow at the rebellion. "By prolonging the war," says the Herald, "we increase the dangers of European intervention, and war throughout Christendom."

MISSIONARY RIDGE, Oct. 24, via Chickamauga, 26.—Four brigades of the enemy moved down the river this morning to their picket lines as if for the purpose of making an attack on our forces at the base of Lookout mountain. After manoeuvering around for an hour, two brigades withdrew, the others remaining under cover of the banks of Chattanooga Creek. In the meantime the battery on Moccasin Point opened fire slowly throughout the morning without doing any damage.

ATLANTA, October 26.—Our cavalry continues active operations in the Sequatchie Valley, to the great annoyance of the enemy. On Friday they captured the notorious Colonel Clift, of Tennessee, with his escort and mails.

RICHMOND, October 27.—New York papers of the 24th say the report that Dahlgren has been removed, is now said to be certainly untrue.

Meade has returned to his command, after a satisfactory interview with the President, with instructions to follow up the attack on Lee. Meade's headquarters are at Warrenton. It will be some time before the army can advance.

The Etna has arrived from Liverpool, 14th, and Queenstown, 15th.

A guard of marines was placed on board the Rams seized on the Mersey.

The Liverpool cotton market continued excited.

The Courier de Etas-Unis says that the Cabinets of Washington and Richmond assented to the removal of the French tobacco stored at Richmond. Vessels were about repairing to City Point, when the Washington Administration suddenly withdrew the consent it had given.

CHARLESTON, October 27.—Firing by the enemy was renewed at 7 o'clock this morning from Gregg and Wagner, and the centre battery, upon Forts Sumter and Johnston, and occasionally upon Fort Moultrie, and the battery upon Sullivan's Island. It was heaviest upon Sumter.—Shot and shell were thrown—mostly 200 and 300-pounder Parrotts. Some of the James and Wiard's rifled cannon shot have been picked up.

GORDONSVILLE, Oct. 21.—Everything appears quiet in front. Most of the prisoners that were sent through here to Richmond last night were foreigners, and expressed themselves tired of the war. Many would take the oath of allegiance. Imboden is reported to have taken 700 prisoners in Charlestown.

CHARLESTON, Oct. 22.—All quiet this morning.

RICHMOND, Oct. 21.—Imboden entered Charlestown on Sunday, 18th inst., and surprised and brought off 430 prisoners and some valuable property. The prisoners captured during Lee's recent advance movement, 1200 in number, have arrived here.

HEADQUARTERS, DIST. OF TEXAS, NEW MEXICO AND ARIZONA, Houston, Texas, Nov. 10, 1863.

General Orders, No. 196.

All commanding Officers are hereby directed to use the men of their commands, and such means as may be at their disposal, to repair the roads and bridges in the immediate vicinity of their respective commands.

The roads and bridges are represented to be in a very bad condition, and growing even worse, and speedy repairs are absolutely necessary to enable the troops to move, as well as for the transit of citizens. By command of

Major-General J. B. MAGRUDER.

E. P. TURNER, A. A. G. [Nov12-tw2t]

FARM FOR SALE—530 acres of land, situated about 1½ miles north-east of Navasota Depot, on Central Railroad; about 120 or 150 acres open land. If not sold by 1st December the premises will be rented to a good tenant for the next year on reasonable terms. For particulars, apply to the undersigned or to E. B.

RIO GRANDE NEWS.

We have the Fort Brown Flag of the 30th ult. from which we take the following:

The Flag mentions the arrival there of Major Magruder, Lieut. Stacard, Major Howard, Major Ballard, S. Dunn, Capt. Ducayet, Capt. French and Lt. Canfield.

The Flag has the following account of an exciting affair there, which resulted in the death of nine men. We publish all the main facts in the matter:

"The garrison of Fort Brown and the citizens of Brownsville were thrown into an alarm on Tuesday night by the report that Capt. A. Vidal's company, heretofore stationed at the mouth of the Rio Grande, had revolted and were marching upon the city of Brownsville to capture the place. The military force hitherto left to defend this post, had been withdrawn during the day, and was then camped some distance from town, on the road to the interior. Col. Duff and his staff were still in town however, but were to leave next morning.

On Tuesday, after Col. Duff's regiment had left, two men from Co. A, Jerry Littoral and D. H. Dashiel, were sent on an express to Vidal, at the mouth of the river, with orders that he at once report to Capt. Taylor, commanding officer at Fort Brown. The expressmen met Vidal about twenty miles from town, already on the march, as he stated that he had already been informed that he would be ordered to Brownsville. The expressman delivered the order to Vidal, and at once joined the command on the march. Arriving within ten miles of town, Vidal requested Dashiel to drink with him, and while the latter was drinking Vidal and the Mexicans commenced shooting, at the two expressmen. Dashiel was instantly killed, but Littoral succeeded in mounting his horse and making his escape, bringing with him a horrid wound through the jaws.

Littoral rode for Brownsville, where he gave the information that the Mexican company were coming. The military at once made defensive preparations by calling all citizens inside of the garrison, by issuing arms to such as had none, and by placing the heavy cannon, consisting of one 24-pounder and one 8-inch siege howitzer, in such position as to command the arsenal and the main approach to the garrison. The citizens turned out with alacrity, and manifested the utmost willingness to do any and all duty necessary to the defense of the place. Old and young, native and foreign, alike responded to the emergency, and not a murmur was heard at the imposition of any task upon any man. Every man expressed his confidence in Gen. Bee, and the universality of the response arose in a great measure from the personal influence of the commanding general. Gen. Slaughter and his staff were prominent in the crowd and at one time we noticed the General in the ranks of the citizens, with a gun in his hands. Maj. Magruder took command of the 24-pounder, and soon drilled his men in the use of the gun. Capt. Greer commanded the howitzer, and soon brought the squad in charge of that gun into good exercise. Capt. Winston, of Gen. Slaughter's Staff, was at one time in command of the howitzer, but ultimately Mr. Kawolski came into charge of the pieces and commanded them until daylight. Serg. Gallagher was very efficient in placing and rendering useful the artillery, for the guns were of such immense weight that only a [illegible] could move them with the inex- [illegible]

Col. Duff took command of the [illegible] garrison, and made prompt and efficient arrangements to police the city and stop all irregular passing to and fro out of the place. There were probably three hundred men, of all arms, ready for the emergency, and the spirit of the force was ready and willing to meet the Mexicans if they attacked the place.

It may seem strange that all this array and alarm existed in presence of a simple company of Mexicans, 40 or 80 strong, led by a wild and reckless boy, as Vidal was considered; but this is easily explained when it is understood that he was believed to be in communication with the Yankee blockader off the mouth of the river, and that through the Yankees in Matamoros, he had been promised the assistance of a large number of Mexicans and renegades from Texas. The outbreak was so sudden, and the movement so daring, that every one at once admitted the possibility of a better leader and a larger force at the back of the attempt; and when parties circulated extravagant reports as to the strength of the revolt, the wisest heads could not deny them, and the firmest judgment only suggested the propriety of strengthening the garrison, to resist a well organized and powerful combination of renegade Texans, disaffected Mexicans and runaway negroes!"

Litterol's statements are corroborated by Lytoon Lengoria, who escaped from Vidal's party. He says that Vidal seized Messrs. Clark, Selkirk & King at the Boca; the two former he discharged, but King (firm of Kennedy & King) he [illegible] shot in cold blood, by a detail of six men.

The course of the outlaws was marked with blood. Fabio (of the Magruder coffee house) was shot, next two soldiers shared the same fate, next Antonio Cruz, next Bartelow of Santa Rita.

Colonel Duff's regiment was ordered back to town. Vidal's insurrection appears to have been a personal freak of a crazy young man. He is only about 20 years of age, but very daring. He was promoted from the ranks by Gen. Bee for his services in raising a company of Mexicans.

Of the conduct of Governor Ruiz, of Tamaulipas, the Flag speaks as follows:

In this connection, it affords us profound pleasure to announce that Governor Ruiz, of Tamaulipas has acted the part of the statesman, the soldier and the neighbor. The interest of both parties is peace, and the voice of humanity denounces murder and rapine. Vidal disturbed the public peace, and he murdered men and stole property. It was the duty of all officers, whether in Texas or Mexico, to arrest and suppress such proceeding. Accordingly when General Bee informed Governor Ruiz of the outrageous conduct of Vidal, Governor Ruiz at once made an offer of all the military force of Matamoros to repress the disturbance and to restore quiet. He dispatched cavalry forces to guard the river that he might not escape to Mexico without being arrested, and that he should not be reinforced from that side of the river.

In pursuance of the vigilant police instituted by Gov. Ruiz, a considerable number of Vidal's men were arrested, and the balance were prevented from crossing. The public will stand surprised and confused when we say that these arrests were made and this vigilance was exercised by Col. Juan Nepomuceno Cortina, so well and so fearfully known on this side of the river. Cortina was in command of the river police, and he seems to have acted with all his known energy and discretion in carrying out his instructions. We congratulate him on the new and laudable effort to atone for the evil which he long inflicted on this community. Gov. Ruiz was informed that the Yankee Consul was plotting to assist Vidal, and he at once sent a patrol of cavalry to keep the renegades in subjection to the law, and although there was some design to move the disreputable elements of Matamoros, in a general thieving expedition, the timely and judicious action of Gov. Ruiz at once suppressed it."

As the Flag goes to press the trouble seems to be all over.

AUCTION SALE by J. S. & J. B. SYDNOR, on Tuesday, the 10th inst., at 10 A. M., a large stock and large lots of assorted Merchandise, embracing five cases Prints and all other descriptions of Staple and Fancy Goods. nov 10-twtds

---

AUCTION SALE, by J. S. & J. B. SYDNOR, on Thursday, the 12th inst., at 10 A. M., the entire stock of Culmell & Co., at their store, adjoining the Rusk House, consisting of assorted merchandise, and every imaginable description of goods. nov 10-twtds

---

AUCTION SALE, by J. S. & J. B. SYDNOR, on Tuesday, the 17th inst., at 10 A. M., 35 likely negroes, and the usual variety of assorted merchandise, horses, mules, &c. The negroes are represented as a very choice lot, mostly field hands and some house servants. [nov 10-twtds]

ITEMS OF INTEREST.

A Yankee paper says:

Though fifty thousand rifled muskets have been sent to the army within the last month, there is still an accumulation at the armory in Springfield of over 125,000.

Better send them along. We shall want them soon.

Texas Beef, first quality, is quoted at $60 per head in New Orleans.

We note in the Era of the 15th notices of sale of 209 bales of cotton, cargoes of schooners Wave and Maccanfield, ex Galveston, come to grief in attempting to run the blockade.

From the New York Journal of Commerce.

The jolly tars attached to the Russian fleet are cruising about the city, and spending their money with the grand improvidence of the sea-faring men the world over. The apple stands and fruit stores are particularly patronized by them. When the Chinese fleet first came to New York, they invested all their money in omnibus rides up and down Broadway; but the Russian sailors seem to think their funds most judiciously laid out in peaches and apples. The sidewalk venders of these articles are doing a fine business with our strange visitors; and the pecuniary transactions involved are usually carried on in the center of a large crowd of curious spectators. It is difficult to say whether the Russians or the queer looking silver pieces which they pay out are regarded with the greater astonishment and interest. In the absence of any definite and known valuations of the Russian silver coin, the apple dealers estimate them by their size, compared with the dime and quarter of our own remote past, and give the Russians change accordingly, and the latter take what is offered them and pocket it trustingly. The postage currency staggers them a little, but they courteously accept it out of regard to the country and its institutions.

ST. LOUIS, Sept. 30.—It is understood that a plot has been discovered to burn all the government transports on the Western rivers.

Several men have been arrested and are now in irons, upon one of whom a cypher was found, which, upon being translated, disclosed instructions to destroy all the steamers that can be of any service to the government. The matter is being fully investigated.

It is marked as a sign of the times in New York that there is not a first class mansion on the Fifth Avenue for sale. Everybody there is so rich that nobody needs to sell, while many bodies rich enough (and such bodies are legion) are sighing to purchase to live there, to see at least the now great movements of carriages, equipages, &c., up and down.

The Senatobia correspondent of the Mobile Register states that five steamers, including the Imperial, have been destroyed on the Mississippi river. How, when or where, is not stated. Our river guerillas are promptly at work.

From the Columbus (Ga.) Times.

What is to be the end of the present extravagant rates for houses to live in, is difficult to foresee, unless it be the ultimate smashing up of all parties. The idea of a gentleman paying three hundred dollars a year rent for a little 8 x 10 room is the height of folly, yet it is asked and will have to be paid, unless a fellow choose to sleep under a bridge or on a cellar door or do as we heard a fellow did the other day, take up quarters on the river bank. The truth is we are running wild with excitement about the currency, and every man is endeavoring to get as huge a pile of notes as possible, so that if not rich when the war terminates he will have enough to make up for depreciation.

From the London Economist.

Louis Napoleon, then, has put himself deliberately and avowedly in opposition to the arrogant pretensions of the American republic. But that republic is no longer one and indivisible. With which section of it, therefore, will his occupation of Mexico bring him into collision? With which will he quarrel, and with which will he form, or seek to form, an alliance? There can be no doubt as to the *immediate* answer. The success of the secession movement, the severance of the old republic into two states, is essential to the permanent independence of Mexico as a powerful country under French protection; since the *real* restoration of the Union would once more make the American nation so mighty and so proud that all its old pretensions would be renewed, and it would probably be impossible for France ultimately to uphold her *protege* without a continuity of struggle, and a waste of men and treasure which she could not endure *en permanence*, and of which she would soon grow weary. His Mexican conquest thus entails upon Louis Napoleon almost the necessity of an alliance with the Southern Confederacy, and an alliance concluded in time enough to enable his aid to insure their success and their independence. If he delays till they are beaten, and if they are beaten in consequence of his delay, he will have to consolidate and maintain his Mexican enterprise, not against one enfeebled and diminished nation, by the help of that nation's exasperated foe, but without aid against the reconstructed Union, which in time would become as powerful as before. We comprehend, therefore, that he will, in his heart, be just as anxious to proffer aid as the hard pressed Confederates will be to accept it; and, between contracting parties thus mutually predisposed, terms of treaty are not difficult, and are seldom long protracted. Even before the Mexican conquest, as we are well assured, the sympathies and wishes of the French Emperor inclined him to recognize the South; and he was only withheld from doing so by the want of our co-operation. Those sympathies and wishes are fortified and vitalized by urgent political interests now.

NEW ORLEANS, September 30.—The headquarters of the 19th Army Corps, under Gen. Franklin, and part of the 13th Army Corps, under Gen. C. C. Washburn, are at Camp Bisland, fifty miles from Brashear City. They have met no enemy as yet. Foraging parties have gathered up large quantities of mules, horses and cattle, but the plantations are generally deserted. The advance of the army was delayed on account of obstructions in Bayou Teche. These obstructions were blown up, and the Bayou is now open for steamers to New Iberia.

The Cincinnati Commercial says:

Gen. Banks is rapidly recovering the territory of Louisiana Navigation on the Bayou Teche has been re-opened, and the army, at last accounts, was fifty miles from Brashear City, pushing into the interior. So far, they have met no resistance, or any enemy.

President Davis has promoted the following individuals to the rank of Brigadier General in the provisional army:

Col. G. C. Wharton, of Va., from July 8.
Col. W. A. Quarles, of Tenn., from August 25.
Lieut Col. Robert D. Johnson, of N. C., from Sept. —
Col. A. Perrin, of S. C., from Sept. 10.
Col. A. W. Reynolds, of Va., from Sept. 14.
Col. E. W. Pettus, of Ala., from Sept. 18.
Col. T. N. Waul, of Texas, from Sept. 18.
Col. A. L. Long, for artillery duty, on Gen. Lee's staff, from Sept. 21.
Col. B. R. Jackson, of Ga., from Sept 21.
Col. Wirt Adams, of Miss., from Sept. 23.
Col. James B. Gordon, of N. C., from Sept. 18.

The Atlanta Appeal says that Lieutenant General Pemberton was called on to make a speech some days ago at a village south of that place. There were present some two thousand of the exchanged Vicksburg prisoners. The General said that he felt much embarrassment because, for the time, a cloud rested upon him, and, besides, he was willing to wait the authoritive vindication of his character by a competent tribunal. "If, however," continued the General, "any of those exempts and gentlemen who have substitutes, and those speculators who have denounced me as a coward and traitor through the press, or otherwise, will organize themselves into regiment, brigade or division, and will march with me to the front, the world shall determine who of us are cowards and who are traitors. I have not been denounced by any brave soldier or officer from Vicksburg, neither have my soldierly qualities and patriotism been called in question by them, but by those carpers and critics at home who have already done infinite mischief."

We take the following from the Chicago Times of the 10th:

Burking was a crime that became frequent in England, notwithstanding its horrid nature and the extreme punishment which followed detection. It consisted in murdering persons for the purpose of selling their bodies for dissection, for which the perpetrators received only a few shillings. In this country another crime, scarcely less heinous, is becoming a matter of every day occurrence. It is the arrest of innocent persons charged with being deserters, for each of whom the criminal receives thirty dollars and assurances of freedom from punishment. For the *habeas corpus* is suspended, and, under the rulings of our military authorities, every man so arrested is presumed guilty until he is proved innocent, and no opportunity, or at best a miserable excuse for an opportunity, is offered the victim to prove his innocence. The liberty of every American citizen, therefore, unless he happen to be possessed of friends who are influential with "the government," is at the mercy of professional kidnappers. Burglary and other similar crimes are falling into disrepute, being more hazardous and no better paid than the business of "arresting of deserters."

We are living in the golden age of abolition "freedom to all men."

The Herald's Washington dispatch, Oct. 8th, states: "By the latest private advices from the South, it appears that Gen. Bragg's army has been reinforced since the battle of Chickamauga by the following troops: One division from Richmond, commanded by Gen. Arnold Elsey; one from Western Virginia, commanded by Gen. Sam. Jones; one from Petersburg and Weldon, commanded by Gen. Ransom; three brigades from Florida, commanded by Gen. Howell Cobb; and three famous batteries from Lee's army, viz: Catts', Blodgett's, and [illegible]alton's. In addition, Bragg has his original army, consisting of D. H. Hill's and Polk's corps, besides four divisions from Mississippi and one division from Charleston, one division of Georgia State troops, under Gen. Walker, one division from East Tennessee, seven divisions from Lee's army, 15 000 Georgia State militia under Gen. Wayne, 5,000 cavalry under Pillow, 15,000 cavalry under Gen. Wheeler, and 350 pieces of artillery. His whole force is estimated at 175,000. It is now represented that Joe Johnston's reserves at Rome, Resaca, Kingston, Costersville, and Etawah Bridge number 55,000.

Wilkes' Spirit of the Times is informed by a Colonel attached to the Department of the Gulf, that an intelligent loyal citizen of the United States, who resided at Bagdad, a little town near the port of Brazos, reported to him that in June last there were eighty-five sail collected there; that eight of the number were British men-of-war, and that he had stood on shore and seen these vessels unload their broadside guns, and sending them ashore for transportation to the interior, receiving cotton in exchange. That these operations were conducted on the part of the Confederates by the Captain who was in charge of the troops at Bagdad, and when he inquired of the Captain why the cotton was shipped on board these public vessels, the answer was, that it was to go to England, to make good the Confederate indebtedness in the cotton loan.

From the Vienna Press, Sept. 14.

The Mexican deputation which will formally offer Archduke Ferdinand Max the Imperial crown, voted by the Assembly of Notables, is expected to arrive here in a few days. It is asserted that the Archduke is greatly disposed to accept the offer; but it is a mistake to suppose that he will accept it unconditionally. He is firmly determined only to ascend the throne provided the powers interested in upholding the balance of power by the erection of a monarchy in Mexico, the dissolution of the North American Republic, and the prevention of the subjugation of Europe by America, will fulfill such conditions as shall afford the Mexican throne warrants of permanency.

These conditions are:

1. Guarantee of the throne by the three powers who originally undertook the Mexican expedition—England, France and Spain—that is to say, that they shall undertake to support the monarchy by arms in case of danger from within or without.

2. That all the Mexican municipalities shall declare themselves by free vote satisfied with the establishment of a monarchy and the choice of an Austrian Prince.

Upon these conditions, and as we are positively assured, upon these conditions only, Archduke Ferdinand Maximilian will set out for Mexico.

GOOD AND BAD NEWS.—Amongst the instructions, says Bourrienne's Memoirs, given by the first Napoleon to his confidential attendant, was the following rather singular: "At night," said he, "you will enter my chamber as seldom as possible. Never awaken me when you have good news to announce. With good news there is no necessity to hurry. When, on the contrary, you are the depositary of evil tidings, rouse me instantly; for on such occasions there is not a moment to be lost." Napoleon is said to have profited not a little by acting on this calculation. But it is evidently not upon such a calculation that the press in either section of the country, or its correspondents, base their practice in regard to good or bad news. They sleep on the bad, and give the public opiates to make it sleep also; while they rouse everybody with reports of the good, so enlarged by fiction that the sober reality is at last regarded with disappointment as if it were a disaster.

The Marquis de Gallifet, on his return from Vichy, proceeded at once to St. Cloud to deliver to the Prince Imperial the small cannon offered to the Prince by the French in Mexico. This piece of miniature artillery is of American manufacture, having been presented by the President of the United States to the Mexican Government. The young Prince appeared delighted with the present, and had it placed, with the thirty rounds of ammunition which accompanied it, under cover in the palace garden. The wounded officer was re[illegible] with great distinction.

Hall's Journal of Health gives the following sensible advice:

"Like the gnarled oak that has withstood the storms and thunderbolts of centuries, man himself begins to die at the extremities. Keep the feet dry and warm, and we may snap our fingers in joyous triumph at disease and the doctors. Put on two pairs of thick woolen socks, but keep this to yourself; go to some honest son of St. Crispin, and have your measure taken for a stout pair of winter boots or shoes; shoes are better for ordinary, every day use, as they allow the ready escape of odors, while they strengthen the ancles, accustoming them to depend on themselves. A slight accident is sufficient to cause a sprained ancle to a habitual boot wearer. Besides, a shoe compresses less, and hence admits of a more vigorous circulation of blood; but wear boots when you ride or travel. Give direction, also, to have no cork or India rubber about the shoes, but have placed between the layers of the soles, from out to out, a piece of stout hemp, or new linen, which has been dipped in melted pitch. This is absolutely impervious to water—does not absorb a particle—while we know that cork does, and after a while becomes "soggy" and damp for weeks. When you put them on for the first time, they will feel as easy as an old shoe,' and you may stand on damp places for hours with impunity."

Gov. Brown is re-elected in Georgia by 6,841 votes over both competitors.

By the exemption act, persons in the military service can procure the exemption of an overseer by the annual payment of $500, provided the overseer was really such on the 17th of April, 1862. The following order, from the Adjutant General in Richmond, shows how this exemption may be procured:

Overseers entitled to exemption will be exempted from military service for one year, when the owner of the slaves of whom the overseer has had charge, shall present to the enrolling officer the receipt of a quartermaster for the amount of the tax imposed in such cases by the act of Congress, approved May 1, 1863. Officers of quartermaster departments are directed to receive and receipt for money thus paid.

The Columbus (Ga.) Sun says that some wounded soldiers, from Tennessee, at the hospitals in Griffin, Ga., recently rode a Mr. Swayze, of the "Bugle Horn of Liberty," on a rail, on account of some indelicate flings at Mrs. Gen. Morgan and other Tennessee ladies, in a late number of the "Horn." Mr. Swayze has since published a card in the Atlanta papers, denying any intention to reproach the family of Mrs. Morgan, and says his purpose was to burlesque the "Illustrated News" and other similar newspaper enterprizes.

From the Charleston Courier.

In accordance with the action of the President, as lately reported in our columns, official notice has been given through the proper channel to the gentleman lately acting as British Consul for this port, that his official functions had ceased and could not be longer recognized. This action meets with very general approval on grounds of self-respect and public policy.

In reference to the Consuls thus relieved, different questions may arise as to their private and personal position after this official demise. In some cases these Consuls before or during their official career, have acquired and exercised the rights of citizenship. This was the case in this city.

The Richmond Examiner says that the repulse of twelve thousand Yankees at Sabine Pass, by forty-two Irish Confederates, eclipses the action of Leonidas at Thermopylæ.

The Louisville Journal states that the guerilla General, Richardson, who has so long been a terror to the Federals in West Tennessee, has been taken prisoner. He had ventured to Memphis in disguise, but was recognized and arrested.

Dr. F. C. Baur, the famous German Pantheist, died in Berlin recently. He was considered a much more powerful and dangerous opponent of the Christian religion than Voltaire. On his deathbed he renounced his previous belief and prayed for mercy.

The frigate Liverpool is left in the Mersey, it is reported, to watch the suspected iron rams.

A Georgian recently gave one thousand dollars to aid in sending ministers to the army.

A meeting of the Confederate Society of Enterprise, Mississippi, adopted a memorial for general signature, urging Congress to increase the taxes to an extent sufficient to absorb the currency and pay a large proportion of the present debt. The ground taken is, that it is easier for the people to pay the public debt in a cheap than in a dear currency, and, moreover, the payment of one-half the debt, is the paying into the treasury of one-half the currency in taxes, and will render the other half so much more valuable as not materially to lessen the value of the means the citizens may have There is a world of wisdom as well as patriotism in the suggestion.

Col. J. Ross Snowden, late director of the U. S. Mint in Philadelphia, made a speech in that city the other day in which he estimated the Yankee debt at this moment to be not less than two thousand millions of dollars. This tremendous sum if paid in gold would require 921 four horse wagons to transport it. We doubt if it will ever be transported.

Mr. ——, having on his plantation a field of oats, was desirous of paying his tenth as he hauled the crop in, so he told the negro to haul nine loads to the barn and the tenth to the quarmaster. Upon returning after a few days absence, he asked the servant if he had delivered the tenth load as ordered. "No massa," said the trusty boy with an air of having done something, "the government don't get nuffin—for dar warnt [illegible] tenth load, I done cram it all in nine!"

NATIONAL INTELLIGENCER.

THE MILITARY ELECTION IN MARYLAND.

By the following letter from the Hon. JOHN W. CRISFIELD, which we find in the Somerset (Md.) Herald of the 17th instant, it will be seen that the unlawful interference of the military with the election in that Congressional district has been brought to the notice of President LINCOLN, who promises to hold the offenders to a proper account:

PRINCESS ANNE, (MD.) Nov. 14, 1863.

The outrages perpetrated at the recent election demand investigation. The subject has been brought to the notice of the President of the United States, and he has responded in the following letter:

EXECUTIVE MANSION,
Washington, November 11, 1863.

Hon. M. BLAIR.

MY DEAR SIR: Mr. Crisfield's letter, which you enclose, is received. Let Mr. C. procure the sworn statements of the election judges, at any voting place, as to what may be deemed misconduct of any military officer, and present it to me, and I will call any such officer to account who shall by such statement appear to have violated or transcended his orders.

A. LINCOLN.

I invite all persons having knowledge of the misconduct of any military officer at or in reference to the recent election to give information thereof by affidavit duly attested. The sworn statements of the election judges are preferred; but, when these cannot conveniently be had, the sworn statements of any credible person competent by the laws of this State to give evidence will be received, and forwarded to the President.

Newspapers favorable to free elections will aid the preservation of that inestimable right by giving publicity to this notice.

J. W. CRISFIELD.

THE CEREMONIES AT GETTYSBURG.

CONSECRATION OF THE CEMETERY.

The consecration of the National Cemetery at Gettysburg, on Thursday last, was an imposing and very impressive affair. The town was crowded on the previous evening, and the tired multitudes were obliged to sleep in the churches and in the parlors of the citizens, every available resting place being occupied.

The special train conveying the President and his company, including Secretaries Seward, Blair, and Usher, of the Cabinet; the French and Italian Ministers, and other guests, reached there about half past six o'clock in the evening. The President was greeted at the depot with much enthusiasm by a large gathering of citizens, who followed him to his lodgings at the residence of David Wills, Esq., where soon after his arrival he was serenaded by the Band of the Fifth New York Artillery, in response to which the President spoke as follows:

"I appear before you, fellow-citizens, merely to thank you for this compliment. The inference is a very fair one that you would hear me for a little while, at least, were I to commence to make a speech. But I do not appear before you for the purpose of doing so, and for several very substantial reasons. The most substantial of these is that I have no speech to make. [Laughter.] It is somewhat important in my position that one should not say any foolish things if he can help it, and it very often happens that the only way to help it is to say nothing at all. [Renewed laughter.] Believing that that is my precise position this evening, I must beg of you to excuse me from saying one word."

The President's appearance was enthusiastically greeted, and at the close of his brief address he retired amid general and prolonged applause.

SPEECH OF MR. SEWARD.

After serenading the President, the band proceeded to the residence of Mr. Harper, adjoining, where Secretary Seward was stopping, and serenaded him also.

Mr. Seward acknowledged the compliment by making a brief speech, as follows:

"Fellow citizens: I am now sixty years old and upwards. I have been in public life, practically, forty years of that time, and yet this is the first time that ever any people or community so near to the border of Maryland was found willing to listen to my voice. And the reason was that I saw, forty years ago, opening before this people a grave-yard that was to be filled with brothers falling in mutual political combat. I knew that the cause that was hurrying the Union into that dreadful strife was slavery, and when I elevated my voice, it was to warn the people to remove that cause while they could by constitutional means, and so avert the catastrophe of civil war which has fallen upon the nation.

I am thankful that you are willing to hear me at last. I thank my God that I believe this strife is going to end in the removal of that evil which ought to have been removed by peaceful means and deliberate counsels [Applause.] I thank my God for the hope that this is the last fraternal war which will fall upon the country that has been vouchsafed to us by Heaven—the richest, the brightest, the most beautiful, the most magnificent, the most capable of a glorious destiny of any country that God has ever given to any human race; and that when that cause is removed, simply by perishing as the cause and the agent of a treason that is without justification and without parallel, thenceforth we shall indeed be a Union—one country, having only one hope, one ambition, and one destiny. [Applause.] Then, to-morrow, if we have not known it before, we shall know that we are not enemies, but that we are friends and brothers; that this Union is a reality, for it is one common country; and we shall mourn, I am sure, with equal sincerity, over the grave of the misguided insurgent whom we have consigned to his last resting-place, and pity him with the same sincerity and the same heartfelt grief that we mourn over the brother by whose hand, raised in defence of the Government to which we all owe allegiance, that misguided brother fell.

And when we part to-morrow night, let us remember that we owe it to our country, that we owe it to mankind, that this war shall have a triumphant conclusion in the establishment of a democratic Government upon the simple principle that whatever party or portion of the nation shall prevail in our election that party shall be respected and maintained in power until it shall give place, upon another trial, and after another verdict, to a different party of a different portion of the people. [Applause.] Without that let me tell you that you are drifting, at once and irresistibly, to the very verge of the destruction of all government. With that principle this Government of ours will be the best, the first, and the happiest in the world, and may be, and, so far as we are concerned, will be, immortal. [Cheers.] Fellow-citizens, good night.

Mr. Seward was warmly applauded at the conclusion of his address.

The same train that conveyed the President to Gettysburg had on it many other distinguished civilians and officers, amongst whom were noticed Governor Curtin, of Pennsylvania; Governor Morton, of Indiana; Governor Tod, of Ohio; Mr. Brough, the Governor elect of the same State; Gen. Cameron, late Secretary of War, and Gens. Stoneman, Doubleday, Stahl, and other officers in the military service. Governor Seymour, of New York, was also present, and made a patriotic speech in presenting a standard to one of his regiments.

Marshal LAMON, of the District of Columbia, and his special Aides, and many of the Assistant Marshals appointed by the Governors of the different States, had previously arrived.

THE PROCESSION.

At an early hour on Thursday morning the streets of Gettysburg were thronged with the gathering thousands. At nine o'clock the military portion of the procession began to assemble on Carlisle street, north of the public square, and the civic portion on York street. From a tall flag-staff in the centre of the square, and on all the public buildings and many private houses, the national ensign was displayed at half-mast, and soon the mournful booming of minute guns smote upon the ear, imparting to the otherwise joyous features of the occasion a touch of sadness that led the thoughtful to realize that as a nation we must sorrow whilst we rejoice for the great deliverance here achieved through the glorious success vouchsafed to our arms by the blessing of a merciful Providence

At ten o'clock the procession commenced moving over the route designated toward the Cemetery, according to the programme published in the Intelligencer of Tuesday last.

The military portion of the procession was headed by a squadron of cavalry, followed by Major Gen. Couch and Staff.

The Fifth New York Artillery Regiment, from Baltimore, with their fine battery, were next in line, presenting a splendid appearance.

Gen. Schenck and Staff were also present. Next came the Marshal-in-Chief, Ward H. Lamon, Esq., and his numerous staff of Aides. wearing yellow and white scarfs, with tri colored rosettes on the breast, and black and white shoulder knots.

Next came the President of the United States, and Secretaries Seward, Usher, and Blair, all finely mounted.

The remainder of the procession was chiefly composed of various civic bodies.

The head of the procession reached the platform erected in the centre of the cemetery a quarter before noon, and when all the different bodies had assumed their respective positions around the platform, B. B. French, Esq , one of the Chief Marshal's Aides, gave the signal, and the solemn ceremonies were commenced by the performance of a funeral dirge by the band.

A most impressive prayer was offered by Rev. Thomas H. Stockton, Chaplain of the House of Representatives, during which the most profound silence prevailed and very many were affected to tears. The touching pathos of the venerable divine, the occasion, and the scene presented, was at once most affecting, and not a few eyes not accustomed to weep were bathed in tears. The President evidently felt deeply, and, with the venerable statesman and patriot, Hon. Edward Everett, who was by his side, made no effort to hide his emotion.

The scene was a grand and imposing one. The battle-field lay like a panorama in full view, and the heroism there displayed on the opening of July seemed to be re-enacted in the imaginations of the beholders. The surrounding troops, the vast concourse, and the insignia of a nation's mourning made up a scene that can never be forgotten by those who were present.

At the conclusion of the prayer the band appropriately performed the grand old hymn of Luther, "Old Hundred."

Hon. B. B. French now introduced the Hon. Edward Everett, who advanced to the front of the platform and pronounced the eloquent oration which we had the pleasure of placing before our readers in yesterday's Intelligencer.

When Mr. Everett had concluded the following Hymn, composed by Hon. B. B. French, was sung with excellent effect by the Baltimore Glee Club:

'Tis holy ground!
This spot, where, in their graves,
We place our Country's braves,
Who fell in Freedom's holy cause,
Fighting for Liberties and Laws.
Let tears abound.

Here let them rest!
And summer's heat and winter's cold
Shall glow and freeze above this mould;
A thousand years shall pass away;
A Nation still shall mourn this clay,
Which now is blest.

Here, where they fell,
Oft shall the widow's tear be shed,
Oft shall fond parents mourn their dead,
The orphan here shall kneel and weep,
And maidens, where their lovers sleep,
Their woes shall tell.

Great God in Heaven!
Shall all this sacred blood be shed—
Shall we thus mourn our glorious dead,
Oh, shall the end be wrath and woe,
The knell of Freedom's overthrow—
A Country riven?

It will not be!
We trust, oh God, thy gracious power
To aid us in our darkest hour.
This be our prayer, "Oh Father, save
A people's freedom from its grave—
All praise to Thee!"

SPEECH OF THE PRESIDENT.

The PRESIDENT then appeared at the foot of the platform, and, upon being introduced by the Marshal, was vociferously cheered by the vast audience. He spoke as follows:

"Four score and seven years ago our fathers brought forth on this continent a new nation, conceived in liberty and dedicated to the proposition that all men are created equal. [Applause] Now we are engaged in a great civil war, testing whether that nation, or any other nation so conceived and so dedicated, can long endure. We are now on a great battle-field of that war. We are met to dedicate a portion of it as the final resting-place of those who here gave their lives that that nation might live. It is altogether fitting and proper that we should do this. But, in a larger sense, we cannot dedicate, we cannot consecrate, we cannot hallow this ground. The brave men, living and dead, who struggled here have consecrated it far above our poor power to add or to detract. [Applause.] The world will little note nor long remember what we may say here; but it can never forget what they did here. [Applause.]

It is for us, the living, rather to be dedicated here to the unfinished work that they have thus far so nobly carried on. [Applause.] It is rather for us here to be dedicated to the great task remaining before us; that from this honored day we take increased devotion to that cause for which they here gave the last full measure of devotion; that we here highly resolve that these dead shall not have died in vain. [Applause.] That the nation shall, under God, have a new birth of freedom; and that Governments of the people, by the people and for the people, shall not perish from the earth. [Long-continued applause.]

It was announced by B. B. French, Esq. that a letter had been received from Lieutenant General Scott regretting his inability to be present on the occasion.

After the ceremonies were concluded, a salute was fired by the artillery, and the military portion of the procession re-formed and escorted the President to his lodgings, where he was subsequently visited by a large number of citizens. He returned to Washington in a special train, which left Gettysburg about seven o'clock, and arrived here about one o'clock on Friday morning.

MARYLAND—AGAIN.

THE ELECTION IN BALTIMORE COUNTY.

It is well known that a controversy sprung up immediately preceding the late election between Gen. Schenck and Gov. Bradford, as to what should be required of persons offering to vote. The Governor objected to [illegible] of the military taking possession of the polls, (and we think very justly too,) from the fact, as the Governor said, that the plan was liable to abuse, and that it was abused in some cases in our county, is a fixed fact, as the following will show:

Soldiers were brought from Baltimore city by wagon loads to Catonsville to vote [illegible] voted the Independent ticket of course; and, not content with this fraud upon the honest and loyal voters of the county, the same men were loaded into ambulances, and led from Catonsville by one of the candidates on the disorganizers ticket to the polls of the Thirteenth district, and demanded their votes. The judges refused to receive them. The Union challenger, Mr. Edward Whittemore, was knocked down by a notorious character, the window broken in, and a fellow calling himself Capt. Boyle, who was in command of the squad of soldiers, entered the room, drew his revolver, laid it on the ballot-box and dared the judges to refuse the votes that his men would offer. The judges through fear and intimidation took therefore from this gang of infernal rowdies from Baltimore city thirty-one illegal votes.

In the Third district some little difficulty occurred, but it was all amongst the military. But in the Ninth (our own district) every thing was apparently "cut and dried." Provost Marshal Cathcart, acting under orders, sent to these polls Deputy Charles Rodgers with a squad of men, simply to preserve order, and we would fail to do our duty as a faithful chronicler of events if we did not say that his duty was performed in a manner highly creditable to himself as an officer.

THE ELECTION IN CHARLES COUNTY.

From the Port Tobacco (Md.) Times of November 12.

The election in our county on the 4th instant passed off quietly and without interruption or hindrance, except at Allen's Fresh. Early in the morning a squad of cavalrymen, acting under orders of Gen. Schenck, took possession of each of the four voting precincts in our county. No hindrance or difficulty, however, was offered to voters at Hill-Top or Coomes's. At Bryantown a few were, we understand, challenged, and then required to take the oath of allegiance previous to being allowed to vote. Instances of this kind were not frequent, and offered no serious obstacle to a full and fair vote. But at Allen's Fresh affairs took a widely different turn. At an early hour in the morning a guard was posted at the door leading to the room in which the judges held the polls, who prevented voters from entering. The lieutenant in command here required all who wished to vote (with few exceptions) to take an oath which he read to them, a copy of which has been already published. After the applicant had taken, or had signified his willingness to take the oath in question, it seems his difficulties were not ended. Then followed a series of cross questioning, such as "Are you a Union man?" This being answered in the affirmative, was followed by another, "Are you an unconditional Union man?" An affirmative answer to this, it seems, was not in all cases sufficient to entitle a person to vote. Further interrogatories were propounded, as "Are you in favor of a prosecution of the war?" "Do you approve the policy of the present Administration?" "Are you for emancipation in this State?" This latter question was put to a friend of ours, we are informed, and a failure to answer it in the affirmative precluded him from voting. These questions were put and insisted on, it will be remembered, after the person desiring to vote had proved his loyalty, or rather purged himself of disloyalty by taking the oath of allegiance. For this reason the vote taken was small, being considerably less than one half the usual number. With this exception, the vote taken in our county, as shown by the official returns, was a very fair average.

LATE EUROPEAN NEWS.

The steamer Persia, arrived at New York, brings news from England to the 8th instant.

In the British Court of Exchequer. on the 5th instant, the Attorney General moved for a rule to show cause why there should not be a new trial in the case of the gunboat Alexandra, on the ground of misdirection by the Judge, and also on the ground that the verdict of acquittal was against the evidence. After sundry explanations and arguments the court granted the application.

It is stated that the agent dispatched by Lloyd's Salvage Association to inquire into the capture of the steamer Sir William Peel by a Federal vessel will proceed in the first instance to Washington to communicate with Lord Lyons, and will afterward go to Matamoros and thence to New Orleans, where he will claim the ship and cargo in the prize court to be held there.

A Paris telegram had been posted in the Underwriter's room at Liverpool, to the following effect: "Don't ship any thing to Matamoros—blockade effective."

At London the Confederate loan was down to 63 a 65.

La France says that the acceptance of the Mexican crown no longer admits of doubt. Maximilian will embark for Mexico about the commencement of February. The Mexican deputation dined with Louis Napoleon at St. Cloud on the 3d.

THE POLISH QUESTION.

The London Gazette publishes a despatch from Earl Russell, dated October 20th, addressed to the British Ambassador at St. Petersburgh. It is short, and commences by stating that her Majesty's Government have no wish to prolong the correspondence with the Russian Cabinet for the mere purpose of controversy, and concludes by asserting that "the Emperor of Russia has special obligations with regard to Poland, and that the rights of Poland are contained in the same instrument which constitutes the Emperor of Russia King of Poland."

Numerous engagements continue to be reported. A large number of ladies were arrested for wearing mourning. The Polish Town Captain Warsaw, issued a proclamation advising ladies to cease wearing mourning, to avoid the brutalities of the soldiery. The exasperation of the population was extreme.

SPEECH OF THE FRENCH EMPEROR.

The speech of Louis Napoleon on the opening of the French Chambers, which we publish in another column, is the prominent topic of remark by the French and English journals. They construe it differently—some of them regarding it as pacific, while others view it as indicative of war.

The Paris Presse, in an article signed by M. de Girardin, wishes that the appeal of the Emperor may be understood in Europe, to open at last a new era of peace and liberty.

The Gazette de France thinks that the speech tends to the alternative of a congress reorganizing ancient Europe or to war.

The Pays applauds the speech and says: "If the Emperor has spoken of war it is not as a threat, but to impress upon sovereigns and nations the necessity of anticipating by recommending peace.

The Constitutionnel says; "The whole of France will join in the magnificent and patriotic language of the Emperor Europe will understand that this appeal was made by a clear-sighted and sagacious policy—proud without wishing to impose itself upon others, national without the spirit of conquest—the friend of order and of progress."

The Nation considers the Emperor's speech to show that the common action of the three Powers is at an end, and also does not believe that Europe will accept a Congress.

La France says: "The Emperor has condemned with equal firmness the rashness which endeavored to carry him away, and the system of egotism and decay which has overthrown other *régimes* and which his name rejects."

The London Times thinks the speech will tend to the reassurance of the European Powers. It says:

"Whether the Emperor, with so many schemes in hand, and with the winter before him, when the chief of them cannot be carried out, desires to preserve his freedom of action, or whether he really thinks that he will do best for France and his own fame by maintaining the peace of Europe, certainly his tone is such as to lessen the disquiet lately felt. Russia is, however, warned that if she refuses the way of peace, she may enter on another which, sooner or later, conducts to war; but we may look upon it as probable that the Emperor really desires to avoid an European contest if his own position and the impulses of France will allow him to remain at peace."

The Morning Post (Ministerial) says: "The Emperor's words are words of peace and conciliation, but, though well intended, we fear they will prove of little avail."

The Daily Telegraph remarks that a peremptory refusal on the part of Russia ensures a delay of some weeks, and during that delay the Polish question may receive that further development which, in the opinion of Napoleon III, it so urgently demands.

The Advertiser thinks that the speech will produce a profound and universal feeling of dissatisfaction in France, "and will, if we are not greatly mistaken, give a heavier blow and greater discouragement to imperialism than any thing that has occurred since the notable 2d December, 1852"

The Star says there is but too much truth in the Emperor's description of the alternative—either this or war. "Europe will act unwisely, indeed, if she again declines to listen to a Napoleon when he offers to initiate a general peace."

The Daily News opposes the idea of England's joining a Congress, and argues that the calling for one is purely a signal for the return of political chaos.

The Times also expatiates on the difficulties in the way of a Congress, and wonders if the Emperor really means that war is inevitable without one.

La France of the 17th says; "We are in a position to announce that the declaration contained in the Imperial speech will immediately be followed by diplomatic overtures. The Emperor Napoleon will address a letter to the Sovereigns who are friends and allies of France to submit a project of European arbitration for their approval. A European Congress may be considered as being convoked. We shall know in a few days whether the proposal is accepted or rejected. The Polish dispute is now merged in the European question."

Almost all the Viennese journals consider the speech of the Emperor calculated to create uneasiness. The official Weiner Zeitung of the 8th instant says:

"We cannot refrain from remarking that the treaties of Vienna have not ceased to exist because, according to international stipulations, they have been partially modified, or because their service upon isolated points have been shaken. The fact is that Austria has always honestly fulfilled the treaties. Even her endeavors to bring about German reform have been based upon European treaty rights, and were specially directed to appease the agitators of Germany. Austria can perfectly acquiesce in the main idea of the speech, viz. a mutual agreement between the Powers to demand the eventualities of war.'

The Paris Bourse on the 6th was dull, and rentes declined to 66 90. This was regarded as evidence that the Emperor's speech had by no means dispelled the prevailing want of confidence.

OPENING OF THE FRENCH CHAMBERS.

SPEECH OF THE EMPEROR.

The French Chambers were opened at one o'clock on the 5th of November instant by the Emperor NAPOLEON, who delivered the following speech:

Messrs. Senators and Deputies:

The annual assembly of the great bodies of the State is always a happy opportunity for bringing together the men who are devoted to the public welfare and for manifesting the truth to the country. The frankness of our mutual intercourse calms anxiety and strengthens our resolutions. I, therefore, bid you welcome.

The Legislative Body has been renewed a third time since the foundation of the Empire, and for the third time, in despite of some local dissents, I can only congratulate myself upon the results of the elections. You have all taken the same oath to me. That is a guarantee to me of your support. It is our duty to attend to the affairs of the country promptly and well, remaining faithful to the Constitution which has given us eleven years of prosperity, and which you have sworn to uphold.

The *exposé* of the situation at home will show to you that, despite the forced stagnation of labor in certain branches, progress has not been slackened. Our industry has contended successfully against foreign competition, and, in presence of undeniable facts, the fears engendered by the treaty of commerce with England have vanished. Our exports during the first eight months of the year 1863, compared with those of the corresponding months of the year 1862, show an increase of 233,000,000f. During the same period our shipping trade shows an excess over that of the preceding year of 175,000 tons, of which 136,000 are under the French flag. The abundant harvest of the present year is a blessing of Providence, which will assure to the population a cheaper price of food. It is also a proof of the prosperity of our agriculture. Public works have been actively carried on. About one thousand kilometers of new lines of railway have been thrown open to traffic; our ports, our rivers, our canals, our high roads have been continually improved.

As the session has met earlier than has been customary, the report of the Minister of Finance has not yet been published. It will be produced shortly. You will find therein that, if our expectations have not been fully realized, the revenues have followed a continous rise, and that without extraordinary credits we have been able to meet the expenses caused by the war in Mexico and in Cochin China.

I shall have to point out to you various reforms which are deemed advisable—among others, one relating to the freedom of the baking trade, one which will render the maritime conscription less onerous to the populations on the coast, a project for modifying the law on joint-stock companies, and one for suppressing the exclusive privileges for theatres. I have also ordered a bill to be taken into consideration with a view to increase the powers of the general and communal councils, and to remedy the excess of centralization—in fact, to simplify administrative formalities, to modify the laws applicable to the classes deserving of all our solicitude. This will be a step in advance to which you will gladly associate yourselves.

The sugar question will also be submitted to your consideration, a question which stands in need of a final solution by a more distinct enactment. The project submitted to the Council of State tends to grant to home produce the facility of exportation which is granted to sugars of other parts. A bill on registration will abolish the *double décime*, and will replace that impost by a more equitable repartition.

In Algeria, despite the anomaly which subjects the same populations, some to the civil, some to the military authorities, the Arabs have learnt to understand the mild and equitable sway of the French rule, while the Europeans do not place less confidence in the protection of the Government.

Our ancient colonies have seen removed the barriers which obstructed their transactions, but circumstances have not been favorable to the development of commerce. The recent establishment of credit institutions will, I trust, improve the state of affairs. In the midst of these material considerations nothing has been neglected which concerns religion and public morals. Religious and benevolent institutions, science, and public instruction have received great encouragement.

Since 1848 the population of the schools has increased one-quarter. At the present day nearly 5,000,000 children (one-third of them gratuitously) are admitted into the primary schools; but our efforts must not be slackened, as there are still 600,000 devoid of instruction. The higher class of studies has been encouraged in the secondary schools, where special instruction is under reorganization.

Such, gentlemen, is the substance of what we have already done and of what we still intend to do. Assuredly, the prosperity of our country would advance still more rapidly if political anxieties did not disturb it; but in the life of nations unforeseen and inevitable events occur which must be boldly and fearlessly faced and met without shrinking. Of this number is the war in America, the compulsory occupation of Mexico and Cochin China, and the insurrection of Poland.

The distant expeditions which have been the subject of so much criticism have not been the result of any premeditated plan; they have been brought about by the force of circumstances, and yet they are not to be regretted. How, in fact, could we develop our foreign commerce if, on the one hand, we were to relinquish all influence in America; and if, on the other, in presence of the vast territory occupied by the Spaniards and the Dutch, France was to remain alone without possessions in the seas of Asia? We have conquered a position in Cochin China, which, without subjecting us to the difficulties of the local government, will allow us to turn to account the immense resources of those countries and to civilize them by commerce.

In Mexico, after an unexpected resistance, which the courage of our soldiers and our sailors overcame, we have seen the population welcome us as liberators. Our efforts will not have been fruitless, and we shall be largely rewarded for our sacrifices when the destinies of that country, which will owe its regeneration to us, shall have been handed over to a Prince whose enlightenment and high qualities render him worthy of so noble a mission.

Let us, then, put faith in our expeditions beyond sea. Commenced to avenge our honor, they will terminate in the triumph of our interests; and if prejudiced minds will not see the good promise of the seed sown for the future, let us not tarnish the glory achieved, so to say, at the two extremities of the world—at Pekin and in Mexico.

The Polish question needs a fuller explanation. When the Polish insurrection burst out the Governments of France and Russia were on the most friendly footing. Since the conclusion of peace they were always agreed upon the great European questions, and I do not hesitate to declare so.

During the war in Italy, as well as at the time of the annexation of Nice and of Savoy, the Emperor gave me his most sincere and cordial support. This good understanding demanded forbearance, and it was only the Polish question, very popular in France, that could induce me not to hesitate to compromise one of the alliances of the continent, and to raise my voice in favor of a nation rebellious in the eyes of Russia, but in ours heirs to a right inscribed in history and in treaties.

Nevertheless, this question touched upon the most serious European interests. It could not be treated by France alone. An insult to our honor or a menace against our frontiers alone impress upon us the duty of action without preliminary concert. It therefore became necessary, as at the time of the events in the East and in Syria, for me to come to an understanding with the Powers who had equal rights and similar reasons as ourselves to express an opinion. The Polish insurrection, which from its duration assumed a national character, aroused sympathy on every side, and the aim of diplomacy has been to attract to its cause as much adhesion as possible, so as to bring to bear upon Russia all the pressure possible of the public opinion of Europe. This almost unanimous expression of wishes appeared to us to be the beast means of persuading the Russian Cabinet.

Unfortunately, our disheartened counsels have been interpreted as an attempt to intimidate; and the steps taken by England, Austria, and France, instead of putting a stop to the struggle, have only tendered to embitter it. Excesses are being perpetrated on both sides, which, in the name of humanity, must be equally deplored. What, then, is to be done? Are we reduced to the sole alternatives of war or of silence? No! Without having recourse to arms, and without remaining silent, one means remains us It is to submit the Polish question to a European tribunal.

Russia has already declared that conferences at which all the other questions which agitate Europe shall be discussed would in nowise offend her dignity. Let us take note of that declaration. Let it serve us to extinguish once for all the ferments of discord which are ready to burst forth on every side, and from the disquietude itself of Europe, which in every quarter is mined by the elements of dissolution, let a new era of order and of peace arise? Has not the moment arrived to rebuild on new foundations the edifice destroyed by the hand of time and piecemeal by revolutions? Is it not urgent to recognise by new conventions that which has been irrevocably accomplished, and to carry by common accord what the peace of the world requires?

The treaties of 1815 have ceased to exist. The force of circumstances has upset them. They have been discarded nearly every where—in Greece, in Belgium, in France, in Italy, as upon the Danube. Germany is agitating to alter them. England has generously modified them by the cession of the Ionian Islands, and Russia treads them under foot at Warsaw. In the midst of these successive infringements of the fundamental European pact ardent passions become over excited, powerful interests demand solution in the South as well as in the North.

What, then, can be more legitimate and more sensible than to convoke the Powers of Europe to a Congress, in which self love and resistance would disappear in face of a supreme arbitrament? What can be more in conformity with the ideas of the age, with the wishes of the greatest number, than to address ourselves to the conscience, to the reason of statesmen in all countries, and to say, Have not the prejudices and rancor which divide us already lasted long enough? Is the jealous rivalry of the great Powers incessantly to obstruct the progress of civilization? Shall we be constantly casting defiance at each other by exaggerated armaments? Are our most precious resources to be indefinitely exhausted in vain ostentation of our strength? Shall we eternally preserve a position which is neither peace with its security nor war with its chances of success? Let us no longer give factitious importance to the subversive spirit of extreme parties by opposing ourselves with narrow calculations to the legitimate aspirations of nations. Let us have the courage to substitute a regular and stable state of affairs for an unhealthy and precarious condition, even if it should cost sacrifices. Let us meet without a preconceived system, without exclusive ambition, animated by the sole thought of establishing an order of things based henceforth upon the well-understood interest of the Sovereigns and of the Peoples.

I cannot but believe that this appeal would be listened to by all. A refusal would lead to the supposition of secret projects which fear the light of day; but, even if the proposal should not be unanimously adopted, it would have the immense advantage of having shown Europe where lies danger and where safety. Two ways are open: the one leads to progress through conciliation and peace; the other, sooner or later, conducts fatally to war by the obstinacy of maintaining a past which is rolling away.

You know now, gentlemen, the tone which I propose to adopt toward Europe. Approved by you, sanctioned by the public assent, it cannot fail to be listened to, for I speak in the name of France.

The Virginian.

WEDNESDAY MORNING, DEC. 2, 1863.

No More Exchanges.

The Yankee General Hitchcock having rejected the last, and we may presume the only proposition that we can make for a fair exchange of prisoners, the question is now at an end, so far as we are concerned. The next proposition must come from the enemy, and there is little probability that he will make any overtures, so long as we allow him to feed the prisoners we now hold at Richmond. We must withdraw the privilege—one that never should have been granted—and put the Yankee prisoners up on the same allowance—short rations if necessary—that is provided for our soldiers in the field. They are not entitled to more; and as a question of policy, affecting the welfare of our own imprisoned countrymen, our Government should feel bound to pursue it.

If the Yankees believe that we are starving, and that our soldiers are on short rations; thereby creating the necessity for subjecting prisoners in our hands to the same deprivations—be it so; it will sooner effect the result we desire, and work the release of our unhappy countrymen now pining in Northern prisons. This is, perhaps, the only thing to bring our enemy to terms. Public opinion North; the clamor of the populace, and the friends of the soldiers would demand that their countrymen be released from a captivity that involved a want of the necessaries of life. The Government would thereby be forced to acquiesce in some plan of exchange. We repeat, that only such a pressure as this can, under present circumstances, bring about another exchange.

We hope to hear that our Government has taken its stand, and will refuse to allow any more Yankee provisions to be sent through the lines for the purpose indicated.

The French Tobacco.

The mystery is revealed, and it has transpired that the visit of the French vessel to Virginia waters has reference, as many supposed, to the removal of the tobacco owned by the French Government, and now stored at Richmond.

It would seem that the Lincoln Government has gotton into a more amiable mood with the French since the Emperor has partially turned his back upon the "rebels." Perhaps this slight concession, this suspension of the blockade to enable the Emperor to export millions of dollars' worth of a Southern staple, to the great advantage of his revenues, will set the two sovereigns to hobnobbing across the water, and induce Napoleon the Third to yield graciously to Abraham the First, in the matter of the Rams now building in French ports. One good turn deserves another, and Abraham is not the man to waive, through motives of delicacy, the assertion of his sense of the obligation conferred in opening our ports even partially, for the benefit of French commerce. Perhaps, as an honest people, we were bound to allow the the removal of this property for which the French Government had paid our citizens; but, we doubt not, the Yankee has overreached us in the material advantage to be derived from the transaction. Our people, and to that extent only our Government, will be benefitted in the enhancement of the value of the tobacco that may remain after the shipment of so large a quantity from our country—and it may even induce other heavy purchases by French agents, to await future shipments—but the Yankees will make all the capital out of it.—Even Mexico may no longer be a bone of contention, for the ENTENTE CORDIALE is perfect between their Majesties.

Abraham has done his cousin over the water a great service which may not be ignored.

After all, there has been a great deal of mere acting on the part of the Yankee Government about the French occupation of Mexico, and we may expect that Lincoln and those he represents, will acquiece in the measure with the most exemplary patience.

This matter of the French tobacco, after permission to ship it had once been granted and then refused, and is now granted again, satisfies us that we have been overreached by the Yankees. Be it so. If the whole world forsake us, let us be true to ourselves.

TERRIBLE FIGHTING!

DETAILS OF THE LATE BATTLE AT CHATTANOOGA

The Knoxville (Atlanta) Register, of the 27th, has the following account of the late battle at Lookout Mountain.

The morning of the 25th came very thick and foggy. During the night our forces had evacuated Lookout Mountain, and withdrawn to the right of Chattanooga creek. About 8 o'clock, A. M., the fog cleared and revealed an immense force of Yankees along the base of Missionary Ridge. Gen. Bragg had vacated his quarters during the night, hence when the enemy opened their terrific cannonading on that point, they found no game.

The fight continued furiously during several hours, when comparative quite reigned. We could not perceive the result, but from the fact that that point is only four and a half miles from Chickamauga Station, and that the enemy had not made any demonstration on that place they could not have gained much advantage over our left.

At 9'clock heavy cannonading was heard on our extreme right. Soon the battle raged furiously. General Cleburne had taken position during the night on the extreme right of Missionary Ridge and massed the greater portion of his forces near the Tunnel. At this point Swett's battery was posted and during the entire day it kept up its continuous music.

The Yankees marshalled their forces in long and broad columns from Chattanooga, and the various positions along the Citico creek, advancing like the cloud on the unflinching heroes of Cleburn's and Cheatum's commands. Sherman's corps, supposed to number 35,000 men, advanced to the assault, and made assault after assault aganst the impregnable position.

During the hours between 11 a. m. to 5 p. m., the firing of musketry and cannon was incesant. We have never heard it equalled on any field on which it has been our lot to do battle. But their charges were unavailing. They were beaten back time and again. At one time they came within fifteen feet of Swett's battery, when the 5th Arkansas, with a yell and a volley that echoed high above the din of war, drove them back. Numbers of the men finding their guns so fouled as to be useless, cast them away and threw rocks into the faces of the foe.

One Irishman whose left hand was so shattered he could not hold his gun, threw stones until he was exhausted and came back swearing that while Ould Pat was there the boys could whip all the damned Yankees they could bring against them.

The Second Tennessee also was supporting this battery, and for infernal stubborn fighting it has never been surpassed.

One more furious assault at 4 P. M., and Sherman's corps received a terrific punishment that made them turn and fly down the hill, and soon they were lost to view in the stinking murky clouds of war. Our forces pursued them rapidly and the last account we had from the foe was that they had crossed the Tennessee and we had destroyed his pontoons at the mouth of Chickamauga.

At half past four p. m., an attack was made some distance down the ridge towards our centre, and judging from the terrible and rapid firing of musketry our forces were slowly retiring over the crest of the ridge. The continuous and heavy firing was heard at half past 6 p. m. when the train left.

We can form no estimate of our loss, though we know a large number of wounded were received at the field and general hospitals. But the Yankees turned their pale and bloody faces to the setting of the sun on the western slope of the ridge by so many hundreds, that we are satisfied that hell had one of its grandest jubilees over its accessions from their ranks. The slaughter in the path of our batteries was awful and immense, but not one assault on us proved successful. ***.

EAST TENNESSEE—SENATOR HAYNES

The people of Knoxville, for ten days past, have been suffering all the horrors of famine. The Federal troops have pillaged every house and every town in Central East Tennessee.

The losses sustained by the Hon. Landon C. Haynes, were not greater than those visited upon all loyal Tennesseans. His residence in Knoxville is the headquarters of Gen. Sam. D Carter, an old schoolfellow of the eloquent Senator. His summer abode at Jonesboro' has been converted into a hospital. The Yankees have not left him an ear of corn nor a grain of wheat. His barns and stables emptied and burned, his household furniture destroyed, his bed clothing taken away, and there is nothing left to mark the scene of social pleasures for which the country home of the Tennessee Senator was distinguished, save the bare walls of a beautiful residence converted into a filthy hospital.—His neighbors all shared his fate. He lives now at Wytheville Va—Knox Register

LATEST FROM THE U. STATES.

We have received the following summary of news from the Baltimore "Gazette" of the 25th and 26th inst.:

FROM CHATTANOOGA.

The following official despatches have been received at the War Department:

CHATTANOOGA, Nov. 24, 12 P. M.—Yesterday, at half-past 12 o'clock, Gens Granger's and Palmer's corps, supported by Gen Howard's, were advanced directly in front of our fortifications, drove in the enemy's pickets, and carried his first line of rifle-pits between Chattanooga and Carter's Creek. We captured nine commissioned officers and about 200 enlisted men. Our loss was about one hundred and eleven men.

To day Gen Hooker, in command of Geary's division of the 12th corps, and two brigades of the 14th corps, carried the north slope of Lookout Mountain, with small loss on our side, and a loss to the enemy of five or six hundred prisoners. The killed and wounded are not reported.

There has been continuous fighting from 12 o'clock until after nightfall, but our troops have gallantly repulsed every attempt of the enemy to retake the position.

Gen Sherman crossed the Tennessee river before daylight this morning at the mouth of South Chickamauga, with three divisions of the 15th corps, one division of the 14th corps, and carried the northern extremity of Missionary Ridge. Our success so far has been complete, and the behavior of our troops admirable.

(Signed) GEO H THOMAS, Maj. Gen.

CHATTANOOGA, Nov 24, 6 P. M.—The fight to-day has progressed favorably.—Gen Sherman carried the end of Missionary Ridge, and his right is now at the Tunnel and his left at Chickamauga Creek

The troops from Lookout Valley carried the point of the mountain, and now hold the eastern slope and the point high up. I cannot yet tell the amount of casualties, but our loss is not heavy.

Gen Hooker reports 2,000 prisoners taken, besides which a small number have fallen into our hands from Missionary Ridge.

(Signed) U. S. GRANT, Maj. Gen.

CHATTANOOGA, Nov. 22.—Bragg evacuated the summit of Lookout Mountain last night, and our troops occupy it.—The enemy, however, still holds the rifle pits on the base of Missionary Ridge.

LETTER FROM JOHN MINOR BOTTS.

A letter from John Minor Botts to the Richmond "Examiner," dated Oct., is published in the Yankee papers. He denies having proclaimed himself a Union man without any ifs or buts, and having said that he wished the Federal Generals knew half that he knew of the rebels and their resources and intentions. He says his earnest prayer is that the revolution may result in whatever may contribute most to the permanent peace and happiness, prosperity and freedom of the people of Virginia—if by the success of the revolution, then he prays God the revolution may succeed; but if by a restoration of the Union, then he hopes the Union may be restored. The letter closes with the following paragraph:

"I cannot be induced to swerve one hair's breadth from the line of conduct which my own judgment and conscience may dictate, which is to take no lot, part, or share in the responsibility that rests upon those who have brought this whirlpool of desolation and war upon my unfortunate country; but, if to adhere firmly and consistently to the opinions and principles that I have maintained for thirty years, and, if to prefer living as I did before the war to living as I have done since the war makes me a traitor, then a traitor's life let me live, or a traitor's death let me die."

THE YANKEE PRISONERS ON BELLE ISLE.

We have a few interesting facts with reference to the Yankee prisoners on Belle Isle which show how false are the statements which teem through the Yankee press touching the treatment and the condition of these prisoners.

With a view to the proper distribution of clothing and provisions sent by the North to these prisoners, a board of officers—nay, two boards of Yankee officers, have been organized; one for the Quartermaster's and another for the Commissary's department, under whose direction the distributions are made.—We were present and saw a considerable lot of clothing in the course of distribution among the prisoners. It was conducted entirely by the Yankee board. Col. Sanderson, a former hotel keeper in New York of a popular Southern house, or a house much patronized by Southerners, was chief of the proceeding, and managed it in a business like style. It was plain that every facility that could be expected from the most liberal administration of authority over prisoners was given for a fair, complete appropriation to those men of everything that is sent to them from their homes. Coming here to invade and desolate the homes of our people they have been captured, and they are treated with all the humanity and consideration that could be meted out to enemies coming in the form most in accordance with civilized warfare, and least abhorrent to humanity.

They generally look healthy, and though they may not at all times get the most liberal allowance of food, they get precisely the amount and the quality that is given to our own soldiers. They certainly show no indication of suffering on acount of food.

A fact which we gathered, among others of considerable importance, was the following: In five months sixty five men have died on the island, and yet during the first three of that time only one died! At the termination of those three months it was ascertained that the Yankee government had broken off the exchange of prisoners, and a feeling of despondency prevailed at once among the prisoners. Trifling cases, immediately assumed a serious phase, and deaths increased most remarkably. Thus it is seen in this fact how the inhuman Northern Government is persecuting its own soldiers by its deliberate and atrocious plan to starve out the metropolis of the Southern Confederacy by compelling an accumulation of Yankee prisoners there to be fed and guarded.—R. Dispatch.

TRIBUTE OF RESPECT.

The following preamble and resolutions are published by an order of Mackey Lodge of Free and Accepted Masons, at its regular communication, on the 9th of Nov., A. L. 5863:

WHEREAS, it has pleased the Almighty Father to take from us our highly esteemed and well beloved brother, Dr. JOHN A. NELSON, who fell mortally wounded at Raccoon Ford, on the 11th of October:

Resolved, That, whilst it becomes us to submit with resignation to all the decrees of Providence, our hearts are yet bowed in sorrow at this sad affliction, and we cannot refrain from the expression of a heartfelt conviction that his untimely death is a common calamity to the country and to this fraternity, of which he was a valued and cherished member—with a heart full of human kindness, ever conciliating in his conduct, liberal in his impulses, and generous in all his associations, he was loved and admired in every relation of life, but it was here, in "this sacred retreat of friendship," that we learned to love and honor him most, in the exemplification of many virtues which ennoble and adorn the human character. Thus loved and honored, in the prime and vigor of early manhood, and on the threshhold of an honorable and successful career, he has fallen a martyr to his country's cause, and faithful at the post of duty.

Resolved, That whilst deploring for ourselves the loss of our lamented brother, we cannot withhold our heart-warm sympathies from those who were bound by the nearer and dearer ties of affection.

Resolved, That as a further testimonial of respect to his memory, the usual badge of mourning will be worn by the members of this Lodge for thirty days, and the Lodge be draped in mourning for the space of three months.

EDWIN R. PAGE, W. Master.
W. A. CLEMENT, Sec'ry.

1. Rebel Graves. 2. View of Gettysburg from Cemetery Hill. 3. Graves of Union Soldiers. 4. The Dedication of the National Cemetery by the Pre

THE CONSECRATION OF THE GREAT NATIONAL CEMETERY NEAR GETTYSBURG, THURSDAY, NOV. 19,

ited States. 5. General Meade's Headquarters. 6. Round Top Mountain, the "Slaughter Pen" of Gettysburg, from Granite Top. 7. Graves of Union Soldiers, Gettysburg.

AM LINCOLN, PRESIDENT OF THE UNITED STATES, AND HIS CABINET.—From Sketches by our Special Artist, Joseph Becker.

GOLD HILL DAILY NEWS.

VOL. 1. GOLD HILL, N. T., WEDNESDAY EVENING, DECEMBER 23, 1863. NO. 62.

THE EVENING NEWS

Is published every Evening, (Sundays excepted,)

— BY —

LYNCH & MUNDALL.

PHILIP LYNCH. J. H. MUNDALL.

Office:—South Main Street, Gold Hill, in the building lately occupied by Wells, Fargo & Co.'s Express.

TERMS:

One Year, by Mail or Express.............$16 00
Six Months.............................10 00
Three Months............................6 00

THE DAILY NEWS

Is delivered in Gold Hill, Virginia and Silver City, at FIFTY CENTS PER WEEK.

AGENTS:

L. P. FISHER..........................San Francisco
MR. LARABEE, News Agent....San Francisco
EDWARDS & CO..........................Sacramento

ASSESSMENTS LEVIED.

Office of the Jewett & Shepard Gold and Silver Mining Company.—At a meeting of the Trustees of the above Company, held December 10th, 1863, an assessment, No. 2, of one ($1) dollar per share on each and every share of the capital stock was duly levied, payable immediately, in United States gold coin, to the Secretary, at his office in Gold Hill, opposite the Odd Fellows' Hall. By order of the Board of Trustees.
de10 1m ALONZO JEWETT, Sec'y.

Gilmore Gold and Silver Mining Company.—Notice is hereby given that an assessment of twenty-five (25) cents per share has this day been levied upon each and every share of the capital stock of the above named company, payable immediately to the Secretary, at his office, Burlington House, south B street. Delinquent shareholders are requested to pay in their assessments without delay. By order of the Board of Trustees. W. DOOLIN, Sec'y.
Virginia, Nov. 30, 1863. del-1m

South Ophir Gold and Silver Mining Company, Notice.—At a meeting of the Board of Trustees of the above company, held to-day, an assessment, No. 6, of Fifty Cents per share, was levied on the capital stock of said company, payable immediately to the Secretary, at his office in Gold Hill.
By order of the Board of Trustees.
V. LEMERY, Secretary.
Gold Hill, Nov. 20, 1863. no27 1m

Notice is hereby given that the Board of Trustees of the Colorado Gold and Silver Mining Company, at a meeting of said Board held December 2d, 1863, levied an assessment (No. 1) of One Dollar on each and every share of the capital stock of said Company; said assessment payable immediately in gold coin, to the Secretary, at the office of the company—office of H. H. Flagg & Co.—Gold Hill, N. T.
By order of the Board of Trustees.
de3 1m H. H. FLAGG, Secretary.

Carson Gold and Silver Mining Company.—Notice is hereby given that at a meeting of the Trustees of the Carson Gold and Silver Mining Company, held Dec. 2d, A. D. 1863., an assessment of One Dollar was levied on each and every share of the capital stock of the company, payable immediately, in Gold Coin, to the Secretary, at his office in Gold Hill.
By order of the Board of Trustees.
WM. W. BISHOP,
Sec'y Carson G. & S. M. Company.
Gold Hill, Dec. 3, 1863. de3 1m

Crœsus G. and S. M. Co.---Assessment Notice.—At a meeting of the Board of Trustees of the above named company, held this day, an assessment of Five Dollars per share was levied, payable immediately to the Secretary at his office, at the store of Korn Bro.'s, Gold Hill, N. T. By order of the Board of Trustees.
J. PFOUTZ, Sec'y,
Gold Hill, Dec. 3, 1863. de3-1m

Knickerbocker Gold & Silver Mining Company.—At a meeting of the Board of Trustees held this day an assessment, No. 2, of Fifty Cents per share on the capital stock of said company was levied, payable immediately to the Secretary, at H. H. Flagg & Co.'s office (Post Office building).
GEO. W. TURNEY, Secretary.
Gold Hill, Dec. 2, 1863. de3 1m

Notice.—At a meeting of the Board of Trustees of the Challenge Silver Mining Company, held this day, an assessment, No. 2, of Ten Dollars ($10) per share was duly levied upon each and every share of the capital stock of said company, made payable in United States gold coin as follows: one half immediately to the Secretary, at his office in Gold Hill, and one half in thirty days at same place.
A. D. BROOKS, Secretary.
Gold Hill, Nov. 28, 1863. no28 1m

Crittenden Gold and Silver Mining Company—Notice.—At a meeting of the Trustees of the Crittenden Gold and Silver Mining Company, October 13th, 1863, an assessment of fifty (50) cents per share was duly levied, payable within ten days, in gold and silver coin of the United States, to the Secretary, at his office in Como; and the shareholders are hereby notified to come forward, pay their assessments, and receive their stock, and thereby save further expense in advertising. By order of the Board of Trustees. J. S. CROSMAN, Sec'y.
Como, Nov. 25th, 1863. no28 1m

Winegardner Gold and Silver Mining Company.—At a meeting of the trustees of the Winegardner Gold and Silver Mining Company, it was duly authorized that an assessment of One Dollar per share be levied on each and every share of the capital stock of the company, payable immediately to the Secretary at his office in Gold Hill.
By order of the Board of Trustees.
GEORGE W. BROWN, Secretary.
By WM. W. DENNY, Acting Secretary.
Gold Hill. N. T., Nov. 28, 1863. no30 1m

Office of the Abell and Key Gold and Silver Mining Company.—Notice is hereby given that at a meeting of the Trustees of the Abell and Key Gold and Silver Mining Company, held at the office of the company, November 14th, 1863, an assessment of fifty (50) cents a share was levied on each and every share of the capital stock of the company payable immediately to the Secretary at his office in Gold Hill, in United States gold coin. By order of the Board of Trustees.
WM. W. BISHOP, Sec'y.
Nov. 16, A. D. 1863. no16 1m

Last Chance Gold and Silver Mining Company.—Notice is hereby given that at a meeting of the Board of Trustees of the above company, of Devil's Gate District, held on the 15th day of November, A. D. 1863, an assessment of Fifty Cents was levied on each and every share of the capital stock of the company, payable immediately to the Secretary, in Gold Hill.
By order of the Board of Trustees.
W. R. UPHAM, Secretary.
Gold Hill, Nov. 20th, 1863. no20 1m

White House G. & S. M. Company. Notice is hereby given that at a meeting of the Trustees of the above company it was duly authorized that an assessment of one dollar be levied on each and every share of the capital stock of the company, payable immediately to the Secretary at his office in Odd Fellows building.
By order of the Board of Trustees.
J. J. DENNY, Secretary.
Gold Hill, N. T., Dec. 5, 1863. de5 1m

Lee Gold and Silver Mining Company.—Notice is hereby given that at a meeting of the Board of Trustees, held this day, an assessment of One Dollar per share was levied on the capital stock of the above company, payable immediately, to the Secretary, at H. H. Flagg & Co.'s office, (Post Office building).
GEO. W. TURNEY, Sec'y.
Gold Hill, Dec. 10th, 1863. del1 1m

Union Gold and Silver Mining Company.—Notice is hereby given that at a meeting of the Board of Trustees of the above company held this day, an assessment of five dollars ($5) per foot, or two dollars and fifty cents ($2 50) per share, was duly levied, payable immediately, to the Secretary, in Gold Hill, or to J. F. Nesmith, No. 10, Armory Hall, Montgomery street, San Francisco. By order of the Board.
WM. E. HALE,
Sec'y. Union G & S. M. Co.
November 27th, 1863. no27 1m

Yellow Jacket Company Assessment. An assessment of three (3) per cent. upon the capital stock of the above company has been levied by the Board of Trustees, payable, Dec. 15th, to the Secretary at Gold Hill, or to Wm. M. Lent, San Francisco. No transfers will be made or stock issued after that date, upon which this assessment is unpaid.
CHAS. BONNER, President.
SAM'L HYATT, Secretary.
Gold Hill, Dec. 12, 1863. de17

Office of the Golden Eagle Gold and Silver Mining Company No. 1.—Notice is hereby given that at a meeting of the Board of Trustees held this day, an assessment of Fifty (50) Cents per share was levied on the capital stock of the above named company, payable in United States gold coin to the Secretary at his office in Gold Hill. J. N. B. CARVER,
Sec. Golden Eagle Co. No. 1.
Gold Hill, N. T., Nov. 24, 1863. no24 1m*

Winfield Scott Gold and Silver Mining Company—Notice.—At a meeting of the Trustees of the Winfield Scott Gold and Silver Mining Company, October 12th, an assessment of Ten (10) Cents per share was duly levied, payable within ten days to the Secretary, at his office, in Como, in gold or silver coin of the United States. The shareholders are hereby notified to come forward, pay their assessments, and receive their stock, and thereby save further expense in advertising.
By order of the Board of Trustees.
J. S. CROSMAN, Secretary.
Como, Dec. 7th, 1863. de9 1m

English G. and S. Mining Co.—At a meeting of the Board of Trustees of the above Company, held November 7th, 1863, an Assessment of Twenty-five (25) Cents per share was duly levied on the capital stock of said Company, payable immediately to the Secretary, at his office in Como, Palmyra District, in gold or silver coin of the United States. By order of Board of Trustees. J. S. CROSMAN, Secretary.
Como, Dec. 7th, 1863. dec9 1m

ASSESSMENTS LEVIED.

Emigrant No. 2 Gold and Silver Mining Company, Devil's Gate District, Lyon county, N. T.—Office No. 712 Montgomery street, San Francisco.—Notice is hereby given that at a meeting of the Board of Trustees of the above named company, held on the 14th day of November, A. D. 1863, an assessment of One Dollar on each and every share of the capital stock of the company was duly levied—the same now, due and payable immediately, in U. S. gold coin, to the Secretary.
no21 1m WM. WILLIS, Sec'y.

Prima Donna Gold and Silver Mining Company, Devil's Gate District, N. T.—Notice is hereby given that the Board of Trustees of the Prima Donna Gold and Silver Mining Company, at a meeting of said Board held November 18, 1863, levied an assessment (No. 4) of Fifty Cents on each and every share of the capital stock of said Company—said assessment payable immediately, in gold coin, to the Secretary, at the office of the Company, No. 621 Washington street, San Francisco.
By order of the Board of Trustees.
no24 1m H. B. CONGDON, Sec'y.

Argo Gold and Silver Mining Company.—At a meeting of the Board of Trustees held this day, an assessment of Fifty (50) Cents per share was levied on the capital stock of the above company, payable immediately at H. H. Flagg & Co's office [Post Office building.]
GEO. W. TURNEY, Secretary.
Gold Hill, Dec. 11th, 1863. del1 1m

War Eagle Gold and Silver Mining Company.—At a meeting of the Trustees of the War Eagle Gold and Silver Mining Company, held at the office of the Company, at the American Flat Hotel, November 25th, 1863, an assessment of Four Dollars per foot was duly levied, payable immediately in United States gold or silver coin to the Secretary, at his office, at the American Flat Hotel. By order of the Board of Trustees.
no27 1m* C. T. BOQUIST, Secretary.

Peerless Gold and Silver Mining Company.—Notice is hereby given that at a meeting of the Board of Trustees of the above named company, held on Wednesday, December 9th, 1863, an assessment of One Dollar per share was levied on the capital stock of the company, payable immediately to the Secretary, at his office—Blue Wing Saloon, Main street, Gold Hill.
de10 1m V. FRANK VALLE, Secretary.

Michigan Mining and Mill Company.—At a meeting of the Trustees of the above named Company, held November 23d, 1863, an assessment of Ten dollars was levied upon each and every share of the capital stock of the company, and made payable immediately, to the Secretary, at his office in Gold Hill.
no23 1m S. H. ROBINSON, Sec'y.

American Flat Mining Company.-- NOTICE.—At a meeting of the Board of Trustees held on the 21st day of Novemner, 1863, an assessment of Twenty-five (25) Cents per share was duly levied on the capital stock of the above named company, payable immediately to the Secretary, at his office, American Flat, or to Dr. D. K. Korn, the President of the Company, Gold Hill. By order of the Board of Trustees.
n24 1m* J. H. JESSEN, Sec'y.

Oncoto Consolidated Gold and Silver Mining Company.—At a meeting of the Board of Trustees of the above Company, held the 30th of November, 1863, an assessment of twenty (20) cents per share was levied, payable immediately, to the Secretary, at his office, on the Michigan Company's claim, Gold Hill.
GEORGE SWENSON, Sec'y.
Gold Hill, Dec. 2. 1863. de2 1m

Sunrise Gold and Silver Mining Company—Notice.—An assessment of fifty (50) cents was this day levied, payable immediately, to the Secretary, at his office, in Gold Hill. By order of the Board of Trustees.
PLATT KETCHAM, Sec'y.
November 28, 1863. no28 1m

Dardanelle Gold and Silver Mining Company—Notice.—At a meeting of the Board of Trustees held this day, an assessment of $1 50 per share on the capital stock of the company was levied, payable to the Secretary, immediately at his office.
GEO. W. TURNEY, Secretary.
Gold Hill, Dec. 16, 1863. de17 1m

Dardanelle Gold and Silver Mining Company.—An assessment of One Dollar per share was this day levied on the capital stock of the above company, payable to the Secretary immediately, at his office.
By order of the Board of Trustees.
GEO. W. TURNEY, Secretary.
Gold Hill, Dec. 8th, 1863. de9 1m

North American Mining Company— Assessment Notice.—Notice is hereby given that an assessment of ten dollars per share on all the capital stock of the North American Mining Company, was this day levied by the Board of Trustees, payable in United States gold coin, immediately, to the Secretary, at the office of the company, No. 13 North B street, Virginia, N. T., and that no stock will after this date be transferred on the books of the company without the previous payment of said assessment.
By order of the Board of Trustees,
J. R. PLUNKETT, Sec'y.
Virginia, Oct. 19, 1863. [oc20 tf]

Excelsior Gold and Silver Mining Company.—An assessment of One Dollar per share was this day levied, payable immediately, to the Secretary, at his office.
By order of the Board of Trustees.
de11 1m E. CUSHING, Sec'y.

Continental Gold and Silver Mining Company.—At a meeting of the Board of Trustees of the above company, held this day, an assessment of Fifty Cents per share was levied, payable to the Secretary immediately, at H. H. Flagg & Co's Office (Post Office building).
GEO. W. TURNEY, Secretary.
Gold Hill, Dec. 9th. de9 1m

Office of the Independent G. & S. M. Company No. 2—Gold Hill, Dec. 12, 1863.—At a meeting of the Independent Gold and Silver Mining Company No. 2, held at the office of the company Dec. 12, 1863, an assessment of Fifty Cents per share was levied on the capital stock of the company, payable immediately to the Secretary of the company.
de18 1m E. E. PHILLIPs, Sec'y.

Central Hawkeye Company.—At a meeting of the Trustees of the above named company, held Dec. 16, A. D. 1863, an assessment of Two Dollars and Fifty Cents per share was levied on each and every share of the capital stock of said company, and made payable immediately to the Secretary, at his office in Gold Hill.
de18 1m S. M. JOHNSON, Sec'y.

Office of the Miantonomoh G. & S. Mining Company—Gold Hill, Dec. 12, 1863.—At a meeting of the Trustees of the Miantonomoh Gold and Silver Mining Company, held this day, an assessment of Fifty Cents per foot was levied, payable immediately to the Secretary.
de18 1m H. C. BROOKE, Sec'y.

St. Charles G & S. M. Co.--Office D street, opposite Maguire's Theater.—At a meeting of the Trustees held this day, an assessment (No. 6) of one dollar per share on the capital stock of the company was levied, payable immediately to the Secretary at his office.
ALBERT CRAMER, Secretary.
Virginia, December 15th, 1863. de21-1m

Notice.—At a meeting of the Trustees of Confidence Gold and Silver Mining Company, held Dec. 12, 1863, an assessment of $25 per foot, or $2 08⅓ per share, on each and every share of said company was levied, payable immediately, in gold coin, at the banking house of Almarin B. Paul & Co.
D. L. BLISS, Secretary,
de14 1m Confidence G. & S. M. Com'y.

War Eagle Gold and Silver Mining Company.—At a meeting of the Board of Trustees of the above company, held November 28th, 1863, an assessment of Fifty (50) Cents per share was levied on the capital stock of said company, payable within ten days to the Secretary, at his office in Como, in gold or silver coin of the United States. J. S. CROSMAN, Secretary.
Como, Dec. 7th, 1863. de9 1m

Massillon G. & S. M. Company.— Notice is hereby given that at a meeting of the Board of Trustees of the Massillon Gold and Silver Mining Company, held this day at the office of the Secretary, an assessment of One Dollar ($1) per share was duly levied on each and every share of the capital stock, made payable immediately to the Secretary, at his office in Gold Hill, N. T., opposite Odd Fellows Hall.
By order of the Board of Trustees.
G. A. HART, Secretary.
By A. J. GOULD, Deputy. de4 1m

SPECIAL MINING NOTICES.

CAUTION!

NOTICE IS HAREBY GIVEN TO CAUTION all persons against purchasing or otherwise negotiating for any of the following certificates of stock in the Johanna Gold and Silver Mining Company, issued in the name of J. D. Emersley, as said stock was sold at public auction for delinquent assessments, and will not be transferred on the company's books:

Certificates 22, 41, 42, 43, 44, 45, 46.
JOHM WHITE,
de7 1m Sec. J. G. & S. M. Co.

SPECIAL MINING NOTICES.

Caution.—The public is hereby cautioned against purchasing or negotiating for the following certificates of stock in the Laboring Gold and Silver Mining Company, as the same were sold for assessments, at public sale, in front of Hart's Sample Rooms, Gold Hill, on the 16th day of December, 1863, and will not be transferred by the Secretary:

Names.	*Shares.*	*Certificates.*
F McMahon	8	15
G W F Vosburg	10	54
H Harricourt	7	105
J M Neall	3	71
E Scharff	10	2
B Cordes	18	104
C McVicar	10	129
W Burk	1	83
J Leconey	24	70,71,87
W H Beegan	3	64
M O'Connell	5	84
Sam King	12	62
H Sullivan	5	80
W B Harris	12	111,130
E F Child	35	121,122,123

By order of the Board of Trustees.
W. W. VAN VLIET, Secretary,
By A. J. GOULD, Deputy.
Gold Hill, N. T., Dec. 17, 1863. de17 1m

CAUTION!

THE PUBLIC IS HEREBY CAUTIONED not to purchase any of the following certificates of stock in the Louisville Gold and Silver Mining Company, as the same were sold according to law on the 14th day of November, A. D. 1863, for assessments due thereon, and will not be transferred on the books of the company, to wit:

Names.	*Cert.'s.*	*Shs*
Charles Satchell	9, 101	10
John Williams	20, 25	30
James Dailey	38, 138	20
W H Wilkinson	74, 76, 77, 78	40
James J Phillips	85, 86	25

J. A. APPERSON, Secretary.
Gold Hill, Nov. 18, 1863. no18 1m

CAUTION!

ALL PERSONS ARE HEREBY CAUTIONED against purchasing or negotiating for two certificates of stock in the Dardanelle Gold and Silver Mining Company, Gold Hill, numbered as follows: No. 202, of 15 sharas, and No. 203, of 10 shares, standing in the name of L. W. Lee, and obtained from me by fraud. Notice has been given to the Secretary, and they will not be transferred on the books. L. W. LEE.
Gold Hill, Dec. 8th, 1863. de8 1m*

NOTICE.

A SAFETY VALVE, SOME GUY RODS FOR smokepipe, and a couple of iron rollers, marked "B. F. Sherwood," belonging to the Yellow Jacket Company's machinery, have been delivered elsewhere by mistake. Any information about them will be thankfully received by SAML. HYATT, Sec'y.
Gold Hill, Dec. 7th, 1863. de8 tf.

Lucerne Mining Company.--Notice is hereby given that at a meeting of the Board of Trustees of the Lucerne Mining Company, held this 27th day of November, 1863, an assessment of Three Dollars on each and every share of the capital stock of the Company was duly levied, and made payable immediately, in United States gold coin, to Jos. S. Paxson, at the office of the City Treasurer of San Francisco; and notice is further given, that by order of the Board of Trustees all assessments remaining unpaid on the FIFTH DAY OF JANUARY, 1864, will be declared delinquent, and the stock standing in the name of delinquent shareholders will be advertised for sale at public auction, in accordance with the laws of the State of California. By order of the Board.
de1 1m JOS. S. PAXSON, Sec'y.

Notice is hereby given to L. Ott, that in accordance with an act of the Legislature of Nevada Territory, approved December 19, 1862, entitled An Act Empowering Corporations and Associations for Mining to Sue Individual members, there will be suit brought by the Knickerbocker Mining Company to recover the sum of Thirty-seven 50-100 dollars, being the assessment now due upon Three (300) Hundred shares of the capital stock of the company, standing in the name of said L. Ott upon the company's books, unless the above amount, including costs of advertising, be paid on or before the Thirteenth day of January, A. D. 1864.
By order of the Board of Trustees.
GEO. W. TURNEY, Secretary.
Gold Hill, December 12, 1863. dec14 1m

NOTICE.

PROPOSALS WILL BE RECEIVED UNTIL the 22d instant, for sinking a 150 foot shaft on the Prima Donna Ledge, Devil's Gate District. For particulars apply to F. Morgan, at Silver City, who will also receive the proposals.
F MORGAN, Acting Supt.
P. D. G. & S. M. Co.
Silver City, N. T.. Dec. 15, 1863. de 15 td*

Caution to the Public!

THERE IS IN THE MARKET, AND HAS been offered and sold at the Stock Board in Virginia, a mining stock purporting to be that of the Crœsus Gold and Silver Mining Company. The stock so offered is bogus and worthless. The stock of the Crœsus Gold and Silver Mining Co., of Gold Hill District, is all signed by Wm. Arrington as President, and by either H. H. Flagg or J. Pfoutz as Secretary. This is to caution buyers of Crœsus stock that all stock otherwise signed is spurious.
Gold Hill, Nov. 20, 1863. no20 1m

Lost,

ON TUESDAY EVENING, DECEMBER 15th, between American Flat and Gold Hill, a pocket book containing two certificates of stock in the Navigation Gold and Silver Mining Company, and other papers of value to the owner. The finder, by leaving the same at the Fountain House, Gold Hill, will be suitably rewarded.
de16 1w* LOUIS WAGNER.

Notice is hereby given that at a meeting of the trustees of Confidence Gold and Silver Mining Company, held December 1st, 1863, an assessment of $4 16⅔ per share was levied (or $50 per foot) on each and every share of the capital stock of said company, payable immediately at the banking house of Almarin B. Paul & Co., in gold coin.
D. L. BLISS,
de2 1m Sec'y Confidence G. & S M. Co.

Winfield Scott Gold and Silver Mining Company.—Notice is hereby given that an Annual Meeting of the Stockholders of this Company, for the Election of Trustees, and the transaction of other business, will be held at the store of Sears & Witherall, in the Town of Como, Lyon County, N. T., on SATURDAY, January 9th, 1864, at 7 o'clock, P. M. J. S. CROSMAN, Sec'y.
Como, December 7th, 1863. dec9 1m

LOST.

CERTIFICATE NO. 28, OF FIFTY SHARES in the Polhemus Company, standing in the name of S. T. King. The finder will please return the same to the Secretary. no23 1m

Notice To Contractors.

PROPOSALS WILL BE RECEIVED BY the Natoma Mining Company for sinking a shaft on their ground, on the American Flat Road, near Reed's Mill; said shaft to be four feet six inches by eight feet nine inches, and one hundred feet deep. The Company will furnish all material used in timbering said shaft. Bids will be received by the undersigned at the Banking House of B. F. Hastings & Co., Virginia, until Monday, December 21, 1863.
H. A. THOMPSON, Supt.
Virginia, Dec. 15, 1863. de16 tf

Winegardner Gold and Silver Mining Company.—Notice is hereby given that the annual meeting of the Winegardner Gold and Silver Mining Company, for the election of officers to serve the ensuing term, will be held at the office of the Secretary, in Gold Hill, on MONDAY, the 21st day of December, 1863, at 3 o'clock, P. M.
By order of the Board of Trustees.
GEO. W. BROWN, Secretary.
WM. W. DENNY, Acting Secretary.
Gold Hill, N. T., Nov. 20, 1863. no20 1m

POSTPONEMENT.—The above meeting has been postponed until MONDAY. January 4th, at 3 o'clock P. M. de22 td

CAUTION.

THE PUBLIC IS HEREBY CAUTIONED not to purchase any of the certificates of stock in the several below designated companies, and standing in the names of the following persons on the books of the said several companies, the same having been sold on the 17th and 18th instant, at public auction, according to law, for the payment of assessments due thereon.

WIDE AWAKE G. & S. MINING COMPANY.

Names.	*Cert.*	*Shs.*
Linn & Folsom	132	5
G W Melzner	125 & 153	15
E Grandbois	33	10
H H Flagg	139	5
J Campbell	94 & 95	25
P Barry	62	25
W P Roberts	90	6
H N Hanchett	91, 92, 93	20
A S Rogers	108	10
D J Rogers		5
A McGraw	147	10
J T Keepers	150	10
J Mathewson	152	5
POTOMAC G. & S. M. COMPANY.		
C H Simpkins	11	15
MAJOR G. & S. M. COMPANY.		
J H Hetteker	29	10

A. LUKIN, Sec'y.
Gold Hill, Dec. 19th, 1863. de19 1m

SPECIAL MINING NOTICES.

CAUTION.

THE PUBLIC IS HEREBY CAUTIONED not to purchase any of the following certificates of stock in the American Flat Gold and Silver Mining Company, as the same were sold according to law on the 10th day of December, A. D. 1863, for assessments due thereon, and will not be transferred on the books of the company, to-wit:

Names.	*No. Cert.*	*No. Ass't.*	*No. Shs.*	*Amt.*
Harry Green	6	3	5	$ 1 25
W W Ward	53	2 3	25	11 25
Amos Roach	62, 63, 64	2 3	50	22 50
Julia Jones	25	2 3	25	11 25
J W Belamy	18	2 3	10	4 50
M Wheaton		1 2 3	25	13 75
James Brackan	52	2 3	25	11 25
John Allen		1 2 3	25	13 75
J W Hill	24	2 3	12½	5 62
H P Harris	69	2 3	25	11 25
Arnold Dale & Co	60	2 3	10	4 50
D W Kelly	50, 51	2 3	20	9 00
H H Ackors	82	2	5	2 00
G A Moore	66	3	5	1 25

[de11 1m*]

Notice. The delinquent stockholders of the Palo Alto Gold and Silver Mining Company are hereby notified that in accordance with the by-laws of said Company and an order of the Board of Trustees, there will be sold at public auction, in front of the post office, Gold Hill, N. T., on the 10th of January, 1864, between the hours of 12 M. and 3 P. M., so much of the interest of each delinquent stockholder as will be necessary to pay their delinquent assessments and costs of sale and advertising.
J. S. WATKINS,
Sec'y P. A. G. & S. M. Co.
Gold Hill, Dec. 9th, 1863. de9 1m*

FOUND.

CERTIFICATES NO. 25, 26, 27 and 28, for fifty-five shares of stock in the Spring Valley Gold and Silver Mining Company, standing in the name of John Holmes. The owner is requested to call at the office of the DAILY NEWS, pay for this advertisement and take them away.
Gold Hill, Dec. 10th. del6 toc

Fuller Company.—The Stockholders of the Fuller Gold and Silver Mining Company are requested to meet at the office of the company, on the 28th day of December, 1863, at one o'clock P. M., to attend to business of importance.
By order of the Board. de14 td

Kentucky G. & S. M. Co.--The members are requested to meet at the American Flat Holel, at 6 o'clock P. M., on SATURDAY, 26th ins., being the adjourned annual meeting.
de21-td* WM. HUNT, Sec'y Kentucky Co.

LEGAL ADVERTISEMENTS.

OFFICE OF INTERNAL REVENUE DIST., N. T. }
VIRGINIA, December 8th, 1863. }

ALL PERSONS DOING BUSINESS IN THIS trict without license for the year of A. D. 1863, and delinquent in the payment of their monthly duties as manufacturers, are respectfully directed to the following provisions of the Revenue Law, which will be strictly enforced if payments are not made to the 25th inst.:

"All persons who shall neglect to pay the duties and taxes as aforesaid assessed upon them, to the Collector, within the time specified, shall be liable to pay ten per cent. additional upon the amount thereof."—Sec. 10.

"That if any person or persons shall exercise or carry on any business hereinafter mentioned, for the exercising or carrying on of which trade or business a license is required by this Act, without taking out such license as in that behalf required, he, she or they, shall, for every offense respectively, forfeit a penalty equal to three times the amount of the duties or sum of money imposed for such license."—Sec. 59.

"That for neglect or refusal to pay the duties provided by this Act on manufactured articles, as aforesaid, the goods, wares and merchandise manufactured and unsold by such manufacturers, shall be forfeited to the United States."—Sec. 70.

"That it shall be the duty of the Collector aforesaid, or his Deputies, in their respective Districts, and they are hereby authorized, to collect all the duties and taxes imposed by this Act, however the same may be designated, and to prosecute for the recovery of any sum or sums which may be forfeited by virtue of this Act."—Sec. 80

"The duties on legacies and inheritances are payable whenever shares in the same become distributive."

All persons who may be delinquent at the expiration of the above notice, and no property can be found to satisfy such claims, names will be published, and suit commenced immediately in the Circuit Court under section 24 of amendatory Act of March 3d, 1863.

The undersigned, Collector of Internal Revenue, District N. T., having received the Annual List, (1863) from the Assessor of said District, gives notice that he will be in the following places in the several counties of said District, in person or by Deputy, on the following days, to wit:

Storey county—Virginia, at Collector's office, Medan Building, 15th to 25th December.

Storey county—Gold Hill, at A. B. Paul's bank, 18th and 19th December.

Lyon county—Silver City, at Collector's office, 21st December.

Lyon county—Dayton, at Post Office, 22d and 23d December.

Ormsby county—Carson City, at County Collector's office, 25th and 26th December.

Douglas county—Genoa, at Deputy Collector's office, 15th to 25th December.

Washoe county—Washoe City, at Deputy Collectors's office, 15th to 25th December.

Humboldt county—Unionville, at Deputy Collector's office, 15th to 25th December.

Lander county—Austin, at Deputy Collector's office, 15th to 25th December.

For the purpose of collecting the Taxes and Licenses assessed and due; and that the law in reference to collecting the same will be strictly enforced. JAMES S. DILLEY,
del1td Collector District N. T.

PROCLAMATION.

WHEREAS, A REQUISITION HAVING been made upon me by Brigadier General Wright, U. S. Army, commanding the Department of the Pacific, for one (1) regiment of Volunteer Infantry and two (2) companies of Cavalry, for service in the employ of the General Government of the United States.

Now, therefore, I, JAMES W. NYE, Governor of the Territory of Nevada, and Commander-in-Chief of the Militia thereof, by virtue of the authority in me vested, do issue this my Proclamation, calling upon the people of this Territory to forthwith proceed to organize a regiment of Infantry, consisting of ten (10) companies, and (2) companies of Cavalry, in full compliance of said requisition.

All applicants for line officers will present themselves before the Army Examining Board for examination, and report to me with certificate of such examination as soon as practicable.

Given under my hand and seal, at Carson, N. T., this fourth day of December, A. D. 1863.
JAMES W. NYE.
Attest: Gov. of the Territory of Nevada.
ORION CLEMENS, Sec'y of the Territory.

Each company of Infantry consists of one (1) Captain, one (1) First Lieutenant, one (1) Second Lieutenant, five (5) Sergeants, eight (8) Corporals, two (2) Musicians, one (1) Wagoner and sixty-four (64) Privates.

Each company of Cavalry consists of one (1) Captain, one (1) First Lieutenant, one (1) Second Lieutenant, one First Sergeant, one (1) Quartermaster Sergeant, one (1) Commissary Sergeant, five (5) Sergeants, eight (8) Corporals, two (2) Farriers or Blacksmiths, two (2) Trumpeters, one (1) Saddler, one (1) Wagoner, and not less than sixty (60) Privates. de7 1m

Summons.

UNITED STATES OF AMERICA, TERRITORY of Nevada, County Storey—ss. Jacob Reim, Plaintiff, against James Ford, Defendant. The people of the United States of America, Territory of Nevada, to James Ford, greeting: You are hereby summoned to appear before me, a Justice of the Peace in and for Gold Hill Precinct, County and Territory aforesaid, at my office, on the NINETEENTH DAY OF JANUARY, A. D. 1864, at 10 o'clock, A. M., of that day, to answer the complaint of Jacob Reim, wherein he claims to recover from you fifty-two (52) dollars, for lager beer to you sold and delivered, as per complaint on file in my office; and you are notified that if you fail to appear and answer the complaint as aforesaid, judgment will be taken against you for the said sum of $52 and costs of suit.

To the Sheriff or any Constable of said county, greeting: Make legal service and due return hereof. Given under my hand this 16th day of December, A. D., 1863.
S. A. KELLOGG,
Justice of the Peace of Gold Hill Precinct, Storey County, N. T. de16 1m

Notice.

UNITED STATES OF AMERICA, TERRITORY of Nevada, county of Storey.—Civil Probate Court. KORN BROS. vs. M. MEIGHAN and C. MEIGHAN.—Notice is hereby given to all persons holding or claiming liens upon that certain piece or parcel of land, situate, lying and being in the town of Gold Hill, Storey county, Nevada Territory, situate on the east side of Broadway, and bounded as follows, to wit: On the north by premises owned by one Berry; on the west by Broadway; on the south by premises owned by — Deland; on the east by a line parallel with Broadway, five hundred feet distant; said premises being in front one hundred and five feet on Broadway, and five hundred feet deep. To be and appear before the Civil Probate Court of the county of Storey, on the 13th day of January, A. D. 1864, and exhibit then and there the proof of said lien, or the same will be taken as waived. M. KORN, L. KORN.
By BISHOP & COOPER, Attorneys.
December 21st, 1863. de21-1aw3w

PROFESSIONAL CARDS.

D. K. KORN,
ATTORNEY & COUNSELOR-AT-LAW,
GOLD HILL, N. T.
OFFICE—Main street, opposite Odd Fellows' Hall. no16 tf

DR. TH. EHRENBERG,
PAYS SPECIAL ATTENTION TO LADIES' and Children's Diseases. Office, Rooms and Residence in Wells, Fargo & Co.'s New Building, north entrance, Virginia.
Rooms--Nos. 4 and 5.
Consultations in English, French and the German languages. no30 1m

A. A. C. WILLIAMS,
(Late Surgeon United States Army,)
SURGEON AND PHYSICIAN.
OFFICE—No. 12 Taylor's new building (up stairs), entrance on Taylor street. Virginia, o16 tf

WAKE BRYARLY,
SURGEON AND PHYSICIAN.
OFFICE—No. 57 C street, south of Taylor, Virginia. no16 tf

C. GREENWICH HOWARD,
ATTORNEY & COUNSELOR-AT-LAW.
OFFICE—No. 10 Union Block, corner Taylor and B streets, Virginia. no16 1w*

DR. HEWLETT,
SURGEON DENTIST,
OFFERS HIS PROFESSIONAL SERVICES to the citizens of Gold Hill and vicinity. After an experience of fifteen years, he feels assured that he can give entire satisfaction, in any operation pertaining to the dental art, would respectfully solicit your patronage.
OFFICE—In Union Block, corner B and Taylor streets, Virginia City. no18 tf

WM. W. BISHOP..............WM. B. COOPER
BISHOP & COOPER,
ATTORNEYS-AT-LAW,
GOLD HILL, N. T.,
Will attend to all business intrusted to their care in the several Courts of this Territory. Also, the Supreme Court, and the Court of Claims of the United States. de15 tf

DR. S. T. WATTS.
OFFICE—Virginia Hotel, North B street, Virginia City. de12 tf

W. W. COPE. } { J. F. HUBBARD.
COPE & HUBBARD,
-LAW OFFICE,-
Enterprise Building, No. 22 South C street, Virginia. de12 tf

DR. J. U. HALL,
PHYSICIAN AND SURGEON.
OFFICE—Main street, second door below Wells, Fargo & Co.'s Express office, Gold Hill. 6e20 1m*

BURBANK & EDGERTON,
ATTORNEYS-AT-LAW.
OFFICE—No. 15 and 17 Taylor's Building, corner Taylor and C streets, Virginia. oc12 tf

QUINT & HARDY.
ATTORNEYS-AT-LAW,
OFFICE—Over the Post Office, Virginia.

STEWART, BALDWIN & RISING,
ATTORNEYS-AT-LAW,
Virginia, N. T.

J. B. HARMON,
ATTORNEY-AT-LAW.
OFFICE—B street, corner of Taylor, Virginia. oc12 tf

CHAS. H. S. WILLIAMS,
ATTORNEY AND COUNSELOR.
OFFICE—In Taylor's new building (up stairs) —entrance on Taylor street—Virginia. [oc12 tf

W. GASTON,
PHYSICIAN AND SURGEON.
OFFICE—Corner of Main and Blanchard sts., Gold Hill. oc12 tf

W. G. ALBAN, M. D. } { C. C. GREEN.
DRS. GREEN & ALBAN,
PHYSICIANS AND SURGEONS.
OFFICE—In Taylor's Building, No. 11, entrance on Taylor street, between B and C. Residence—E street, near Sutton Avenue. [oc12 tf

SAMUEL ARNOLD,
TOWN MARSHAL,
OFFICE—With Judge Kellog.

W. H. HOWARD,
Sheriff Storey County, N. T.
PHILIP STONER, Under Sheriff.
LEE McGOWAN, } Deputy Sheriffs.
F. A. ELLIS, }
Office in the new Court House building, No. 14 South B street, VIRGINIA.

NO PERSON EXCEPT THE ABOVE-named officers, is authorized to serve any Process coming from or through the office of the Sheriff of Storey county, Nevada Territory. W. H. HOWARD,
o26tf Sheriff Storey county, N. T.

PARDEE, BARSTOW & CO.,
STOCK BROKERS.
OFFICE—24 South C Street, Enterprise Building, Virginia.
MINING STOCKS BOUGHT & SOLD.
Orders promptly attended to. oc12

J. W. PHILLIPS,
STOCK & EXCHANGE BROKER,
Gold Hill and Virginia.
OFFICE—24 South C street, Enterprise Building. de12 tf

F. A. TRITLE. DANIEL ST. C. STEEVENS.
TRITLE & STEEVENS,
SEARCHERS OF RECORDS,
Conveyancers, Notaries Public, etc.
OFFICE, NO. 48 B STREET, OVER BRYAN AND SEELY'S.

DANIEL ST. STEEVENS, late of Sacramento, takes this opportunity of informing his friends and the public, that he has become a permanent resident of Virginia, and has associated himself with Mr. F. A. Tritle as above. Having been exclusively engaged in the business of "Searcher of Records" the past 14 years, he is thoroughly conversant with this profession in all its branches, and will guarantee perfect and reliable abstracts of Title and Incumbrances, and correct recapitulations thereof, in all cases when engaged and required.
Virginia, Oct. 12, '63. o12

LEE BROTHERS,
GOLD HILL, NEVADA TERRITORY,
— DO —
MILL WORK,
And guarantee satisfaction. Also, HOUSE, SIGN and ORNAMENTAL
PAINTING!
In all its branches, executed in a style unsurpassed in the Territory.
Main St. opposite Odd Fellows' Hall.
de5 tf

THE EVENING NEWS.

MY HONEST FRIEND.

He came to me so smilingly,
And shook me by the hand,
And spoke to me so silvery,
In tones so smooth and bland,
That, though I did not know him yet,
His way and mein so kind,
Proclaimed at once the gentleman
We now-a-days seldom find.

He spoke to me so cordially
About his home affairs;
He spoke to me so willingly
Of all his business cares;
He told me most that happened from
The moment of his birth;
I grasped his hand in joy to find
I'd found a soul of worth.

He drew me now so lovingly
A little way aside, he
Then whispered me confidingly,
With air so bona fide,
And said it was with deep chagrin
That he did ask of me—
But did I have about me then
So small a thing as a "V?"

I slipped the sum right eagerly
Into his honest hand,
He bowed to me so tearfully.
My friend he'd ever stand.
We parted, but death soon, alas!
O'ertook this nature's prince;
That is—I think he must be dead,
For I've not seen him since!

Taxing the Mines.

The San Francisco *Bulletin* thinks the General Government ought not to tax the mines, even in the present strait for the sinews of war. It unreservedly admits, however, that the mineral lands belong to the Government. Suppose we amend by striking out the word "tax," and insert "rent," would there be anything objectionable or wrong in that? Men rent farms, houses, etc. They do not expect to get fertile fields, and crop them year after year, until they become exhausted and worthless, without paying something for the privilege. They pay rent for them, and then they pay taxes on the wealth they take out of them. Some farms are good, some indifferent, some bad, and rents are graduated accordingly. Is it more unreasonable to ask rent for a mine than for a farm or garden? The *Bulletin* thinks that miners ought to be favored above all producing classes in the State, that mining is the predominating interest, and that the State is rich principally because of its mines; that when they languish, agriculture and all other pursuits droop or perish. Perhaps so. Mining advertisements would certainly fall off greatly. If the entire State were made up of mineral land, instead of a comparatively small portion of it, we would no doubt have a very rich State, but under the *Bulletin's* plan where would the money be had to carry on the Government? As a "half-agricultural, half-mining county," as she is designated by a San Francisco journal, Sacramento is interested on both sides of this question; and it can, perhaps, be better viewed from her stand-point than from that of counties more exclusively mining or agricultural; and from that stand-point the proposition seems not unreasonable but right, and a column of pettifogging sophistry, such as that in the *Bulletin*, is well calculated to convert many doubting ones to that view of the matter. The Nevada *Transcript*, published in the heart of one of our richest mining counties, and the editor of which was, in former times, a practical miner, indorses the recommendation of the Secretary of the Interior, that the mines should yield the Government which owns them and protects their operators, their fair quota towards the general burden of taxation, and says. "We agree with the Secretary. We have on more than one occasion indicated our opinions on the question at issue. We maintained them in the face of all opposition when a miner ten years ago, and adhere to them now. It is no new question with us, as our readers well know. Difficulties may be suggested in the way of a law taxing mines, but they never seem to us insuperable." But the miners of California are a patriotic and an eminently practical and just-minded class of our population; and recognizing right and duty, will look at and discuss this matter aside from and above a mere dollar-and-cent point of view.—*Sac. Bee, Dec. 19th.*

REESE RIVER CANAL.—We have before alluded to this enterprise, projected by Messrs. Gould and Farley, but since the plans have been perfected, and a large amount of work done, its importance deserves at our hands another notice. The canal commences at a point on Reese river about one mile below Jacobsville, and extends northeast towards the foot hills until it reaches its most extreme point of divergence from the river, about two miles from Amador, when it turns towards the west and again taps the river. It will be of a capacity sufficient to carry all the water in the river when at an ordinary stage. The ground is quite favorable for the completion of this work, as the canal can pursue a pretty straight course, necessitating cuts of much depth at only a few places. The running of this canal was rendered necessary, not only by the great distance of Reese river from the mines, but by the fact that the soil for some distance on each side of the river is so miry that it would be impossible to secure a good solid foundation for a mill. This, however, extends to the foot hills, where fine mill and building sites can be secured, and will be also much nearer and easy of access to the mines of Amador, Yankee Blade and Reese River. The roads from all these places will be descending grades for the whole distance, and will extend along the foothills so that they will be at all times good. There are sites enough along the banks of this canal, and a sufficient quantity of water will be conveyed for all the mills that will, probably, be erected in this section for a number of years. Two gates will be erected where the ditch leaves the river, so that the water in the river can be turned into or off from the canal at pleasure. Messrs. McDonnell & Dillon have contracted to complete this work by the first of next April, and they are now pushing it forward rapidly, under the general superintendence of Mr. C. B. Harwood, the agent of Messrs. Gould & Farley. They employ about twelve or fifteen men daily. So far there have been no deep cuts necessary, the average depth being about three feet and a half. It is also very encouraging that so far only one place has been found where it will be necessary to flume, and at this point only for a short distance. The canal will be about three miles in length. Messrs. Gould & Farley are now in San Francisco making arrangements to bring up a mill early in the Spring. Several mill sites have already been applied for. This enterprise will do much, very much towards developing our mines, and advancing the interests of this whole section of country, and we hope that its projectors will be magnificently rewarded.—*R. R. Reveille.*

BASALT.—A naval officer has offered the following solution for that tough geological problem, the origin of basalt. He thinks that the columns never were lava, or molten matter of any sort, Wherever naturally ball and socket jointed columns are exposed to view in cliffs, or in separate groups, or mounds, in plains far away from volcanic districts, there the bamboos, from which the columns derive their form and features, really did grow. The fact of coal, fossil wood, and pillars of basalt being so often found in contact, one above another, or side, arises from the fact of their having all once been growing vegetable matter. Instead of basaltic columns being protruded upwards through the coal beds, the bamboos which formed those columns grew before the surrounding horizontal or overlaying strata of coal or other matter were formed.

THE mother of a little fellow who was taking a ride in the Hartford-horse cars, asked him as he scrambled in "why aren't you going to kiss your mother before you go." The little rogue was in such a hurry that he couldn't stop, and hastily called out: "Conductor. won't you kiss mother for me?"

THE city of Philadelphia is in debt to the amount of $20,000,000.

Our State Constitution.

It seems that there is to be an organized opposition to the adoption of our State Constitution, having its headquarters at Virginia.

Our limited space will not permit us, in this issue, to enter into any extended argument on this subject, but we think that such opposition, if successful, would prove materially injurious to the interests of our Territory. Everything indicates that Congress is about to take some action in regard to taxing the mines on the Pacific coast. If there is ever likely to be a time when there is urgent necessity for Nevada being fully and ably represented in Congress it is during the present session, as the mining interests are now represented by the delegation from only one State—California. We need men there whose energy, ability, and eloquence can influence Congress to adopt measures, which, instead of retarding, will assist and advance the development of the vast mineral resources of this Territory.

Litigation is increasing, too, and growing in importance, and it is necessary that our Judiciary system should be so extended and organized as to meet the wants of our rapidly growing Territory, and this can only be done under a State organization.

The objection that the Convention have incorporated into the Constitution a clause, which provides that all mines shall be taxed, prospecting holes as well as bullion producing ones, is totally without force, as any one who reads the clause will see that the matter is left almost wholly to the discretion of the Legislature. The Legislature may say that no mine shall be taxed unless it pays a dividend of fifty or one hundred thousand dollars per month. Some portions of the Constitution may be objectionable, but we venture that a second attempt will prove exceedingly lucky if it succeeds as well, and, in our opinion, the people of the Territory will do themselves a gross wrong by suffering these trivial objections to defer our admission as a State for two more years.

The argument that a State organization would be so expensive, that we would be unable to bear its burdens, is too silly to need a refutation. The large amount of bullion that is daily shipped from the Territory, and the rich discoveries that have been recently made in various portions of the country conclusively prove the contrary. Why was this objection not urged at the election last September? A country which pays out annually over twenty millions of dollars for freight alone, too poor to bear the burdens of a State Government! It is absurd. Did any of the States which have been admitted within the last twenty years possess, at the time of their admission, the wealth of Nevada? This objection is a mere cloak to conceal the cloven foot of disappointed politicians, penurious capitalists, and grasping monopolies.

Nevada, rich in unequalled mineral resources, and rich in a population unsurpassed in industry, enterprise, activity and intelligence, should no longer suffer her expanding energies to be contracted, and her growth retarded by being bound up in Territorial swaddling clothes. Let the people send their fiat forth on the third Tuesday of January that the Constitution shall be adopted, and Nevada can then rear her head by the side of the proudest of our States.—*Reese River Reveille.*

At Gettysburg.

The dedication of the National Cemetery at Gettysburg took place November 19th. The ceremonies were most impressive and the concourse immense. President Lincoln, Edward Everett, and Secretary Seward, spoke on the occasion. The President's brief, but feeling and suggestive address, we append:

"Four score and seven years ago our fathers established upon this continent a Government subscribed in liberty and dedicated to the fundamental principle that all men are created equal by a good God. [Applause.] Now we are engaged in a great contest—the question whether this nation, any nation, so consecrated, so educated. can long remain. We are met on a great battlefield of the war; we are met here to dedicate a portion of that field as the final resting place of those who have given their lives that the nation might live. It is all right, befitting and proper that we should do this, but in a larger sense we cannot dedicate; we cannot consecrate; we cannot hallow this ground. The brave men, living and dead, who struggled here, have consecrated it far above our power to add or detract. [Great Applause.] The dead will little heed. Let us long remember what we have, but not forget what they did here. [Immense applause.] It is for us, rather —the living—to be dedicated here to the unfinished work that they have thus far so nobly carried forward. ['Good,' and great applause.] It is better for us to be dedicated to the great task remaining before us—for us to renew our devotion to that cause for which they gave the full measure of their devotion. Here let us resolve that what they have done shall not have been done in vain; that the nation shall, under God, have a new birth; that the Government of the people, founded by the people, shall not perish."

Reese River Items.

The following items we clip from the *Reveille* of the 19th:

PROSPECTING PARTY.—A party consisting of five or six persons left this place yesterday for San Antonio District. This is the second trip of some of them, but they go this time well prepared with provisions, horses, &c., and they intend thoroughly prospecting the district. Some of them expect to remain in that section during the winter, but the others will return in a few weeks. We hope that each one of the boys may strike a ledge that will make him his pile.

VESTA LEDGE.—A contract has been let to sink an incline upon this ledge to the depth of twenty feet. The work will be commenced immediately, and pushed forward as rapidly as possible. The prospects still continue good that the owners will realize their expectations. They are determined to develop it without regard to expense.

THERE SHE BLOWS!—We witnessed an exciting spectacle a few days since. Three graybacks were raised close in shore. A brace of boats put off in pursuit. The weather was very fine and calm, and but a brief period elapsed ere a harpoon was fastened to one of the triad; when, darting like a courser under whip and spur, the light chariot of the Sea Kings leaped like a thing of life over old Neptune's course, accompanied by the balance of the herd as outriders. Leaping into bright sunshine they lashed the waters to madness with their mighty flukes and far-extending fins. "Master of the situation," as we say on the Potomac, the bold harpooner, with quick eye and cool nerve, darted the keen lance into the quivering flesh again and again, until the stream of life ascending in successive crimson jets was exhausted, when the whale, with a ponderous throe rolled heavily to the leeward--his great heart broken, his last race ended.—[*Monterey Gazette.*

WE use but very few words compared with the number in the language, amounting to about 125,000. Shakspeare, who displayed a greater variety of expression probably than any writer in the language, produced all his plays with about 15,000 words. Milton's works are composed with 8,000; and the Old Testament utters all its history, its poetry, and its divine teachings with 5,642 words.

The Ladies' Knapsack.

No. 5.] CINCINNATI, DECEMBER 31ST, 1863. [5 CTS. A COPY

The Ladies' Knapsack,
Miss MARTHA M. THOMAS, Editor,
Assisted by the Ladies of the COMMITTEE ON POST-OFFICE AND TELEGRAPH. *It will be issued* TRI-WEEKLY, *during the continuance of the Fair. Office of Publication,* POST-OFFICE, GREENWOOD HALL, MECHANICS' INSTITUTE BUILDING. *The* KNAPSACK *can be found at the "Ladies' Bazaar," Fifth Street Market Space; "Art-Hall and Curiosity Gallery," Mozart Hall, Catholic Institute Building; "Produce and Machinery Hall," Sixth Street Market Space, and at "Merchandise Hall," Palace Garden.* Price, 5 cents.

Refreshment Table.

The dainty viands; e'en the sight
Must surely tempt your appetite;
The tender partridge cooked with care;
The jucy Ham, the Ven'son rare;
Beef a la mode, and beef that's not;
Ducks, turkeys, chickens, cold or hot;
Fresh oysters, fried, stewed, or raw,
The finest ones you ever saw.
Pickles and Cheese of every kind;
Tea, Coffee, Chocolate, you'll find—
And other dainties, too, are there,
To tempt the gentle ladies fair,
Who may with more etherial mind,
Be less substantially inclined.
There's Chicken-salad, very nice,
We'll help you ladies in a trice;
Ice-creams and Sherbets, Punch-romaine,
Just try them, and you'll come again.
Bon-bons; fresh Peaches, brandied too;
Cakes, Nuts and Raisins; take a few—
And fairy bow'rs and temples gay,
All wrought of sugar, so they say—
For little ones, there's sugar candy,
Like that which tempted Jack-o'-Dandy,
And Pop-Corn Balls, and Sugar toys;
Come buy them, little girls and boys—
Come every one, we'll serve you all,
Beaux, belles, wives, husbands, good and small.

Steamboat Ohio Belle.

The steamboat Ohio Belle, owned by Capt. John Sebastian, was among the first boats captured by the rebels. It fell into their hands at Napoleon, Arkansas, and was recaptured at Island No. 10, and is now in our docks, and, having undergone repairs, is as good as new.

Capt. Sebastian is a gallant officer and patriotic man; he lost his arm at the mouth of Yazoo river on the gunboat Tylor, in her fight with the rebel ram Arkansas. We congratulate him on the recovery of his boat.

We are glad to see that this fine steamer is advertised for New Orleans. We hope that she will be loaded with freight and crowded with passengers.

ADVERTISEMENTS.

The Ladies' Knapsack.

EDITED BY

Miss MARTHA M. THOMAS,

ASSISTED BY THE TELEGRAPH AND POST-OFFICE COMMITTEE.

CINCINNATI, DECEMBER 31, 1863.

☞ We will pay twenty cents per copy for a half dozen copies of the *Knapsack* of the 24th.

The highest praise is due to the Committee on Lectures and Readings, for the quality and quantity of Entertainments and amusement they have offered the public, and which their receipts will show the public have appreciated Mr. S S. Smith, with his usual taste and judgment, has given all his energies to the cause, and been most successful in the enterprise.

The closing Soiree of the Fair will take place on Friday evening at the Bazaar. The ladies will be dressed in Calico, which dresses they afterwards donate to the Fair, to be distributed among soldiers' families.

[For the Knapsack.]

A Growl from a Bachelor.

Washington Irving was a bachelor. So am I. He was once in love, and his biography reads none the worse for the youthful incident. I am superior to Irving in this respect, for I have been in love a half dozen times. I may have good reasons for not marrying, yet the unfeeling world is always taunting me with what no enlightened tribunal has ever decided to be a crime. If I choose to remain a bachelor, I don't see why people will not let me alone.

My Christmas Presents were designed not to please but to annoy me. The first was an image of the Evil-one-himself, with hoofs, horns, and a grinning countenance suggestive of concentrated wickedness and malignity. This nice little piece of mantle furniture was intended for a match-box, and would have pleased me much had it taken any other form. But what a fiendish thing!

My second present was a baby in a basket, all exquisitely carved from a single *butternut*. And, to my additional horror, the handle of the basket was made to represent a vipor of the Copperhead type. These choice gifts were accompanied with notes, wishing me "A Merry Christmas." The worst wish I have for such friends is, that they would get married and mind their own business.

A SUFFERER.

[For the Knapsack.]

Woman's Rights.

Yes, I *think* we have rights. We are jostled on the streets by the men, our dresses half torn off us, and the offender turns round almost with a look of contempt, but there is no apology offered us. We are permitted to stand in cars while men keep their seats, or if one does *chance* to offer it, and does not get in return the most grateful thanks, he seems to think he has received some personal injury.

Why, I heard a man scold like another Xantippe, the other evening, for a half hour, because a woman did not thank him for his seat. Of course, every *lady* will thank a *gentleman* who gives up his seat to her, but every gentleman should offer it.

I saw a lady come into the car the other night from the Fair, looking tired and worn, and among a half-dozen men who had seats, not one offered to give up his. After holding on for some time to the strap, she seated herself on the floor of the car, at the feet of a burly wretch of a man, who never thought of offering her his place. O, yes, we have our rights, if being trodden on, jostled, allowed to stand when men are seated, constitute any part of them.

ONE OF THE FAIR.

Wanted,

A clergyman, a D.D., President of a Southern College, and a bachelor, has been indulging in gambling at the Fair. He won a child's dress and some other garment, and desires to advertise, through the colums of the "Knapsack," for a widow, (for a wife, we suppose,) who has a child the garments will fit. Plenty of widows have offered, but none have the necessary belonging.

[For the Knapsack.]

A Soldier's Soliloquy.

I am married to my country now,
She is a fickle dame:
I to her every mandate bow,
In hopes 'twill lead to fame.

Now, if I fret, or scold and fume,
At her coquettish way,
She tells me I must not presume,
For she will surely pay.

Then to her lovers far and near,
I notes of *promise* see;
But not one word of love I hear,
No billet-deux for me.

Salt pork and beans we have for dinner,
Bean soup, 'tis not the best:
A fellow grows thin and thinner,
He can't such stuff digest.

I am tired of leading such a life,
It would be no loss,
To get a bill from such a wife,
Alas, ther's *no divorce*.

REPLY.

I have heard say, that love was blind,
You have no love for me:
Such trifles would not vex your mind,
My faults you would not see.

I've dressed you nice in suits of blue,
The tailors promised well;
They said the cloth was strong and new,
Such awful lies they tell.

You've traveled far at my expense,
By rail and steamer too;
And may I ask, without offence,
What more you'd have me do?

And now if you'll stand by me,
I'll promise you a horse;
And then I'm sure you'll never see
The want of a divorce.

Horticultural Department, &c.

GREENWOOD HALL,

[For the Knapsack.]

While loitering near a table of exquisite plants, at Greenwood Hall, a few days since, I chanced to hear an exclamation from one of a group of gentlemen—"What an Eden of delight is Greenwood Hall! With its floral decorations—well supplied tables—intelligent and affable ladies, it is certainly a charming place to spend an evening."

As I was returning from the table, an officer accosted me with—"Will you have a beetle, madame?" Have what, said I? A beetle, he replied—(at the same time showing me a horrid beetle, of which he had eaten at least one half.)

Why, Captain B—— are you insane? What possessed you to eat beetles? What possessed me? Why, I like them—and I assure you I was never more sane in all my life. Now, do just taste this? (Handing me the remaining half.)—Ugh! I refused, with a shudder.

He deliberately ate it with apparent gusto, and said, "You see I have just returned from Libby Prison, and assure you this is a delicate morsel, compared to the *soup* we poor fellows had to take while guests of that inhospitable mansion; and besides, this is not as repugnant to the taste as you seem to imagine." This beetle is made of *chocolate* and *sugar*, and came from Mrs. W.'s table. She has a few more left, and as a special favor, will doubtless let you have one or two.

AUBURNIAN.

Chivalrous.

The *gentle*man who ran against a lady on Greenwood Hall stairs, the other evening, nearly throwing her over and scattering her parcels, then continued his way without as much as a "Beg pardon," leaving her to collect her scattered articles, lacked one great characteristic of the American gentleman—gallantry to women.

One suggests, that he had seen an importunante creditor in the Hall above.

Thanks.

The ladies having the "Knapsack," in charge at Palace Garden, wish us to thank the gentlemen officiating there, for their kind courtesy which has lightened an otherwise arduous duty. Also, to thank those dining there for their liberality in purchasing the paper.

Fruit.

Upon the Refreshment Table at Greenwood, is seen a most beautiful display of fruit, donated by Gen. M. S. Wade, and raised upon his farm. There are five varieties of Apples and six of pears, most tempting and refreshing.

Found,

At the Ladies' Bazaar, a heart frightfully mutilated. From its peculiar organization and great flexibility, supposed to be the property of a gentleman's heart. Inference—Rejected by a *fair* one, incapable of appreciating its noble qualities.

Lost,

By a young lady, her voice. As it can be of no use to any but the owner, the finder will please return it to Greenwood Hall Post-Office.

Stolen,

By a young lady, a gentleman's heart. If not immediately returned, she will be sued—for her hand.

Better than Pin-Money.

Miss Kidd, yesterday, sold two copies of the "Knapsack" for $5.

In the collection of Jacob Hoffner, Esq., on exhibition in Greenwood Hall, is a fine specimen in bloom of the Stanhopea, one of the species of the Geneva "Orchidaea," or Air Plants. Description would fail to convey to the reader the singularity and beauty of this interesting plant.

By some the flower is said to resemble a *Flying Dragon*. One lady we heard compare it to a *Crab*—see its *Claws*, she remarked. Its formation is of that anomalous character that it would be a work of amusement to stand by and listen to the varied expressions of the different individuals on first seeing the flower, and hear their varied and sometimes most opposite comparisons. Its form, as we remarked, we will not attempt to describe; in color it is a delicate creamy white, speckled with circular spots, of a chocolate color, whilst its odor of a delicate *Vanilla*, permeates and diffuses itself through the atmosphere for a considerable space. This interesting class of plants, to which the foregoing belongs, are natives of *Tropical* regions, generally growing in thickly wooded swamps, where they are found attached to the limbs of trees, in the same manner that we see the mistletoe growing in this vicinity.

This rare specimen should be seen by every visitor to the Fair.

We hope the gentlemen will inaugurate the New Year by purchasing liberally. The flower tables at Greenwood will be generously supplied with bouquets, which will be dispensed, with the graceful compliments of the season, by the ladies attending, to any wishing to procure them as an offering from the Fair to the *fair*. There can be no more beautiful New Year's present.

A friend at our elbow, says, it strikes him as very remarkable, that so many and such fresh evergreens, should be procurable in mid-Winter, as are seen at Greenwood Hall. It certainly is a most elegant place of resort.

The vase donated by Mr. Athingers, which stands at the head of Greenwood Hall, attracts much attention, from its large proportions, and the beauty of the mosses and immortals, with which it is filled.

Mrs. Dr. John Davis, the untiring Secretary of the Horticultural Department, is always to be found at her post, ready and willing to give any information in her power. She is a favorite with all.

☞ Mr. Hopkins' beautiful statues are on exhibition at Greenwood Hall. The Infant Floral by Palmer, has been added to the others.

Mr. Cyrus Garett has paid the highest price yet paid for a letter at the Post-Office in Greenwood Hall.

Don't forget to call at Greenwood Hall and see the Statues.

Ladies' Bazaar,

FIFTH STREET.

We have heard of ladies losing handkerchiefs, gloves, muffs, victorines, &c., and know one lady who lost her bonnet from her head; she had put it on at the milliners, and on reaching home, walked into the parlor, saying, "How do you like my new bonnet." When lo! she had no bonnet on, and she has not heard of or seen it since. But we never heard of a lady losing her cloak from her person on a cold night, and not discovering it, as we are told was the case with a lady at the Bazaar on Christmas night. She had just purchased it at Wilson's, and is much chagrined at its loss. We have heard it suggested, that perhaps her interest in the cause, or her company, kept her warm.

The table of the Fifth Presbyterian Church in the Bazaar, is still amply supplied with necessaries of every description

VOL. II. JANUARY, 1864. NO. 10

PUBLISHED BY THE AMERICAN TRACT SOCIETY, BOSTON.

For the Christian Banner.

THE TWO CAPTAINS.

BY JENNY BRADFORD.

"May I tell you of just one thing that mars my pleasure in these delightful talks?" said Captain Hunter to his friend, as they were taking their usual stroll along the wooded ridge which overlooked the camp, the river, and the sunset beyond.

Captain Thayer answered, "Certainly;" but there was a chill in his voice, and his hand grew considerably lighter on his friend's arm.

"Now, Ned, you needn't take it that way. You know perfectly well that I like you better than any body else in the whole brigade, and that your society is my chief solace in this barbarous life we live. I am sure you are welcome to tell *me* any of my faults that annoy you."

"Safe enough for you to say that," replied Thayer, "when you know you haven't any. The fact is, I hate abominably to hear any thing against myself; but I suppose it is useful, and I know you are the best friend I have in the world, beside my mother; so pitch in."

"Well, then," said Captain Hunter, "it hurts me to hear you swear."

"Oh, pshaw! is that all?" looking relieved.

"*All!*" repeated Hunter, with a sad smile. "That is altogether too much, Ned."

"Well, I know it is a bad trick," replied his friend, "and I wish I were well rid of it. In fact, I have tried three several times to break off; but the first I know, my mouth lets fly an oath, and I have come to the conclusion that it's no use trying. If ever I get back to civilization, I reckon it will die out of itself."

"Don't you believe it," cried Hunter. "That is one of the Devil's own lies. The habit never will die a natural death. You will have to uproot it with a desperate effort."

"Then it will have to stay, I'm afraid," replied Thayer, with a shrug. "I don't feel equal to any thing very desperate in the home department. Any how, George, the habit hurts nobody but myself; and if I am willing to take the risk, where is the harm?"

"Every oath is a direct insult to your best friend."

"An insult to you!"

"To a far nobler and older friend than I," was the answer.

"Oh, I understand. All that seems very real to you, I suppose; but I can't see it. Jesus Christ is no better than a myth to me," said Captain Thayer.

"There it is!" exclaimed his friend. "You have bandied about his sacred name till it has lost all meaning for you. Is it no harm to have the most pure and holy things in the universe dragged in the dirt, until there is nothing left for you to reverence and adore? Where is the foundation of morality, even, let alone religion, when the name of the eternal God himself is kicked about like a foot-ball?"

"I am not so bad as all that!" exclaimed Thayer.

"Not yet, my friend; but you have started on the straight road for it. God forbid you should ever go to the end. You have fine instincts, a careful education, and an adored Christian mother to keep you back; but you know what our army is; to all this coarse, horrible blasphemy which disgusts you, you, a thorough-bred gentleman, the only son of a Christian home, are giving your influence. Oh, Ned," he added, with strong feeling, "I can not tell how shocked and pained I was to hear you swear at your company yesterday."

"Now, George, don't blame me too much. I didn't intend to do it; but when men act so like dunces, you can't help it."

"Beg your pardon; I *can* help it," said Captain Hunter.

"*You!* Of course you can. You that can make a man cower with a look or a tone have no occasion to swear. It would be very reprehensible, Captain Hunter, if you did; but just you give me that magnificent voice and eye and figure of yours, and maybe even you would feel the need of a little ballast to your orders."

"Then I would throw up my commission," said Hunter. "I never would insult my men by swearing at them. I would as soon strike them in the face."

"Now, George, I declare to you, I think it really does them good to bolt an oath at them once in a while, — starts them up."

"Does them good!" exclaimed Hunter, turning on his friend a look which shamed him into sincerity. "Think of your Sergeant B., as good a Christian as there is out of heaven; think of swearing at him! There's your Corporal H. could heap black oaths mountain high above all your lips ever could be brought to utter; is it any particular use for you to swear at him? Is it good for the mother's boys who are just learning to swagger and swear and drink? Ah, Ned, you know better! I am sure you can not forget, more than I, that we are responsible, not only to see that our brave fellows do their duty to the country, but to return them in as good condition as we found them, body and soul, if it is a possible thing."

"But what if I can't make them obey without?"

"You can. The higher moral tone there is among them, the easier discipline will be. Every oath a company hears from the captain goes to confound his best ally, — their own consciences. Authority does not depend on those little advantages of voice, etc., as much as you think, Ned. If men are sure that an officer understands himself, that he isn't afraid of any thing, that he looks out for their comfort, and that he doesn't feel too important, he can do almost any thing with them. One thing is certain: they will neither fear nor love him any the more for flinging oaths in their teeth."

For a moment they walked on in silence; then Hunter went on, —

"All this while, we have not spoken of the absolute wickedness of the thing. Profanity is put, by the Judge of all the earth, in the same decalogue with stealing and murder. My dear friend, He will not hold you guiltless, neither will your own conscience, neither do I that love you."

The words were spoken with deep seriousness, and it was hardly less gravely that Captain Thayer replied, —

"Indeed, George, I would stop if I could; but I am afraid it is too late."

"The only sure way to leave off swearing is to begin praying," said his friend.

"It would be only a mockery for me to pretend to pray. I should just speak into space. There is no one there for me."

"Still, you do believe there is a God whom you have grossly offended, and a bleeding Redeemer who waits to make peace between you."

"Yes, I believe it all, but I can not feel it," Thayer answered.

"Only the Holy Spirit can make real to you those grand realities, and that Spirit comes in answer to prayer. You will have to take the bare word of the Eternal for it, Ned, that he not only is, but is the Rewarder of them that diligently seek him. Ask him in the dark for pardon and salvation, live as though you meant it, and you will not have to wait long before there will be some 'one there.' Ned, shall we begin here and now?"

THE NEW YEAR'S ADDRESS

OF THE

NEWSMEN

OF THE

NEW YORK HERALD,

To its Subscribers and Readers, Jan. 1, 1864.

HOW swiftly roll the years away,
  Like waves along the shore!
'Twas Sixty-Three but yesterday,
  And now 'tis Sixty-Four.
And while again the Newsman sings
  The year's auspicious dawn,
We hail the promises it brings,
Upon its broad and shining wings,
  From the grand old year that's gone.

This very day, twelve months ago,
  Came forth the Proclamation,
To some three million Southern slaves,
  Of their emancipation.
And "Father Abraham" now declares,
  With pride and exultation,
That it has opened wide the gates
Of Freedom, in the Southern States,
  Insuring our salvation.

Last New Year, resting from the shock
  Of a disastrous fight,
Our grand Potomac army lay
  In a melancholy plight.
While all around the Vicksburg hills,
  And far along the shore,
The rebel great guns, looking down,
Barr'd our approaches to the town,
  And shut up every door.

It was, too, on last New Year's morn,
  Magruder with his fleet
Of steamboats, clad with cotton bales,
  And all his plans complete,
Pounc'd on our ships at Galveston,
  While sleeping, I'm afraid;
For, otherwise, the daring Turk
Could not have done the bloody work
  Of that foolhardy raid.

Again, 'twas on last New Year's night,
  Driven back and held at bay,
Rosecrans reformed his broken lines,
  For yet another day.
'Twas well. He turned the battle's tide,
  Snatch'd victory from defeat—
Bragg, driven to the right about,
Barely escaped a final rout,
  In his forlorn retreat.

And here commenced our victories
  Of the glorious year gone by—
Glorious, from the auspicious signs
  Of the crowning triumph nigh.
Vain were the task here to recount
  The feats our boys have done,
On every field—on every wave,
Link'd with some story of the brave,
  And names immortal won.

How at the Post of Arkansas,
  An ugly rebel den,
The whole concern was "gobbled up,"
  With full five thousand men;
How Hindman, Price, and Holmes & Co.,
  Were found, chastised, and quelled,
Within Missouri's borders, and
In Arkansas, till scarce a band
  Remains to be expelled;

How, down in Louisiana's swamps,
  And fields of corn and cane;
And lakes, and bayous, Gen. Banks—
  In a dashing Spring campaign—
Routed the rebels, hip and thigh,
  And with but little slaughter,
Successfully, on every hand,
Clearing their "graybacks" from the land,
  Their gunboats from the water;

How, on the hills of Gettysburg,
  Lee's bold and grand array,
One hundred thousand strong, were met,
  And how they lost the day;
How, less than sixty thousand men,
  Straggling through mud and rain,
That bleeding, shattered host retired;
How from that day its hopes expired,
  Never to rise again.

And we might tell how this event,
  Throughout the mighty North,
Crowned the rejoicings of the day
  We call "the Glorious Fourth;"
And how Grant and his army had
  Their celebration, too,
With thirty thousand rebel troops,
Defiling by in solemn groups,
  As in their last review.

How Vicksburg fell into our hands,
  On "Independence Day,"
Army, forts, batteries, magazines,
  In all a grand display;
How next—Port Hudson caving in,
  "Old Massassip" was free
To the East and the great West again,
While the rebel States were cut in twain
  From Memphis to the sea.

Of all these things, we might, for hours,
  Like an old time minstrel sing,
Had we the task assigned us, and
  An ancient listening king;
And tell how Thomas saved our cause
  At Chickamauga, and
How, from wild Chattanooga's heights,
The great North wakes to new delights,
  Which thrill throughout the land;

How Longstreet up at Knoxville found,
  Gave Burnside quite at home;—
How Hooker fought above the clouds,
  On Lookout's lofty dome;—
How Sherman stormed a beetling cliff,
  [illegible] the sight;—
How Mission Ridge was next convulsed;—
How Bragg was utterly repulsed,
  And routed left and right.

And we might sing the gallant deeds
  Done by our bold Jack Tars,—
Those generous, daring, fearless boys
  Of Neptune and of Mars—
On Mississippi's ample flood,
  Red River and Yazoo;—
And how they made the rebels break,
From many a troubled inland lake,
  And jungle-bound bayou.

And how along the Atlantic line
  Bold Jack has cleared the coast;
How Sumter's walls have ceased to be
  The Charleston rebels boast.
But of these themes and many more,
  Worthy the poet's song,
The HERALD files the facts impart,
And every needful map and chart,
  And so we pass along.

Old Abe says "Johnny Bull's a trump,
  Look at those rebel rams!"
Jeff. Davis says "John Bull's a cheat,
  Look at his tricks and shams;"
That Southern independence now
  Depends on Southern arms;
That Louis Napoleon's fighting shy,
That "he refuses—can't tell why—
  To take us to his arms."

King Jeff. in fact gives up his case,
  With many tears and groans,
Is there no spot reserved, where he
  May rest his broken bones?
Hemm'd in—how can he now escape
  The terrors of the law?
Let Welles look sharp, or the knowing blade
May slip the Wilmington blockade,
  And turn up at Nassau.

Jeff's cause is lost—the end draws nigh
  Our armies, pressing on,
Will still contract their tightening lines,
  Till his last chance is gone.
How restoration is to come,
  In truth we cannot tell.
We trust that wise and wholesome rules,
Will cut out fanatics and fools,
  And all will yet be well.

Napoleon's scheme in Mexico—
  How goes it? What's the chance?
Well, the Frenchman plays his fiddle, but
  His Dutchman does not dance.
For he knows the Mexicans at best
  Are a slippery, dangerous few;
And that the Yankees may come down,
And kick out Dutchman, throne and crown,
  And the jolly Frenchman too.

Napoleon in this thing, you see,
  At length is fighting shy;
Because, much nearer home, he finds
  He has other fish to fry.
Good. Let him pass. Now what about
  Great Heenan and Tom King?
We can't do justice to the case,
We leave it in its proper place,
  In the records of "the Ring."

What of the Russian ball? Hi—Hi!
  It was a grand affair.
The beaux were fine, the belles divine,
  And all the world was there.
But what would Barnum call it? Well,
  A humbug, if you please;
Like the Dickens ball—"long time ago,"
Or that grand Aldermanic show
  Of the astonish'd Japanese.

What of the year's elections? Good!
  The Copperheads are dish'd.
How's Congress? Guess it's pretty much
  As "Father Abram" wished.
What of our new Lord Mayor—run in
  Contrary to all rule?
They say that Mozart chuckled, while
Old Tammany smiled a ghastly smile—
  Good-bye to Brudder Boole.

How's gold? To buy it or to sell,
  You run some little risk.
And "greenbacks?" Plentiful and cheap.
  How's trade? Brisk—very brisk.
And how about our taxes? Well,
  We are gaining on John Bull.
Shall we be call'd to drain his cup?
Can't say. How's cotton? Cotton's up,
  And shoddy, pork and wool.

Fun, fashion, folly, and finery reign,
  In the midst of blood and crimes.
'Tis strange that this most frightful war
  Should bring such jolly times!
We hope the day of peace draws nigh,
  That when we next appear
The season's compliments to pay,
The States, from Maine to Texas, may
  Join in the glad NEW YEAR.

THE ARMY OF THE CUMBERLAND—GENERAL BAIRD'S DIVISION CAPTURING THE REBEL GUNS ON THE LEFT OF MISSIONARY RIDGE.—FROM A SKETCH BY MR. THEODORE R. DAVIS.—[SEE PAGE 11.]

Daily Chronicle & Sentinel.

BY N S MORSE & CO AUGUSTA, GA., THURSDAY MORNING, JANUARY 7, 1864. VOL XXVIII NO 9,

CHRONICLE & SENTINEL.

[FROM OUR EVENING EDITION OF YESTERDAY.]

HOME RESOURCES.—The good of our country, the advancement of our cause, the comfort of our brave defenders in the field, self-interest—in fact a hundred reasons combine to urge upon every family to look to its own resources. The hand card and the hand loom and the spinning-wheel, should be found every where—in every family. All who can, should grow their patches of flax and cotton. All who can should have sheep, if but a few. Our forests furnish dyes as various and as bright as the tints that make their foliage as glorious at "the turn of the leaf." With these materials, there is no reason why our ladies should not be clad in beautiful apparel, the product of their own industry and taste; while they also may clothe their husbands and sons. There is not a planters wife who may not easily provide clothing for all her servants, and make some to sell besides. Ladies in the cities also can do much towards providing cheap and substantial clothing for their families, if they only had the mind so to do. Where there is a will, there is generally a way. A little energy, a little determination, a little effort put forth in the right direction by ladies who now do nothing, would accomplish a great deal.

How much more independent and happy we should all be if we thus provided for ourselves as we ought to. Much more now, than heretofore, should all housekeepers and heads of families make their arrangements for meeting all their wants by home industry and enterprise. Earnestly, therefore, do we advise all to use every means in their power to provide for themselves and their families from their own resources.

FROM TRANS-MISSISSIPPI.

The editor of the Mobile Advertiser has had a conversation with Hon. A. M. Branch, member of Congress from Texas, and obtained the annexed news from him:

The enemy were at Matagorda, Texas, moving along the coast in a column about 6,000 strong, accompanied by their naval force. Their immediate destination was Velasco, which they were expected to reach about the 8th, but it was doubtful whether they would succeed, as Magruder's force was ample to meet them.—The General himself was in the saddle, and the Texans, minded of the days and deeds of 1835 and '36, were turning out to a man. Velasco is at the mouth of the Brazos, in close proximity to the southern extremity of Galveston Island, and the object of the Yankee movement is to flank Galveston.

The Federals have fallen back from New Iberia, La.

Kirby Smith left Shreveport with Price, who was moving on Little Rock with about 15,000 men. The enemy at Little Rock are said to be 5,000 strong, the rest of the force, some 7,000, being at Pine Bluff. They have increased their force at the latter place since Marmaduke's raid, in which he captured 150 negroes and 300 horses and mules, and burned their commissary stores, with a loss of only 12 men. The Yankees, it will be remembered, reported this as a repulse of Marmaduke.

On Saturday Dec. 12th, Capt. Adams, of Capers' command, with 50 men surprised a party of Yankees and negroes on Boeuf river, killing 40 or 50, and capturing 12 prisoners and 20 odd horses, arms, &c, with the loss of one man.

Gen. Cooper was returning towards the Arkansas river from the Indian nation with two Texas regiments and a force of about 5,000 Indians, composed of two Choctaw, two Creek and two Cherokee regiments, and a battalion of Seminoles. The Cherokees and Creeks are mostly expatriated, and have taken refuge in the Choctaw nation, but maintain their position.

It is very difficult now to cross the Mississippi river. The Federals destroy every boat and and dug out they can find, and keep a sharp look out.

The Federal main brigade lately made a descent on Bruinsburg; where they seized a quantity of salt and 200 packages of tobacco, which they distributed among the negroes, and ended by plundering everybody, the negroes included, whom they robbed of their blankets. A lieutenant of this brigade with some of his men was captured by our troops a short time since, and hung.

It will be impossible for Banks to injure the interior of Texas. Few men penetrate it. Before the Federals can reach it, they will have to march through deserts of sand where there is no water, and almost nothing, in the form of food for man or beast. Banks, therefore, is not likely to win such glory, and neither Texas nor the Confederacy is likely to be much hurt.

FROM THE FRONT.

General Johnston has quietly rssumed command of the forces and with his usual unostentations style of proucedure is doubtless engaged in all which can be done. He is regarded by every one in and out of service with affectionate confidence as a patriotic man of great abilities.

A gentleman just from upper East Tennessee states that the condition of the campaigns in East Tennessee is prosperous and hopeful. It is considered that Burnside will not be able to hold his position at Knoxville. Our forces have completely cut off his communication with Cumberland Gap, and his troops are on short rations.

At Chattanooga the enemy is reported on allowance, by parties recently out from that vicinity. On the Lower Tennessee, bodies of Federal cavalry seem to be organising for the coming spring campaign. Our scouts in the regions of the Tennessee lines are said to be well regulated.

Only one cotton mill is now running at Lowell, Mass.

FROM VIRGINIA.

The Federals have made a raid through Page county, Va., destroying much property and stealing many negroes.

Gen. John H. Morgan is at Danville, Va.

The bill of the "Currency Committee" was on Thursday, read before the House of Representatives in secret session. We understand the bill relies upon taxation, and not upon funding, for the reduction of the present inflated currency. It is said it proposes to levy a tax of four per cent. upon the present valuation of property, a very heavy discount being offered as an inducement to tax-payers to pay in their taxes within a short given period.

In Richmond, the price of gold and silver has not been nearly so much enhanced by the passage of the "substitute bill" as was expected. It is an absolute fact that gold has since risen only about two dollars.

Some statistical statements, says the Richmond Enquirer, have been afforded Congress of the amount of cotton burnt on Government account in the Southwest and elsewhere. But there are yet very uncertain data as to the amount destroyed on individual account, and recent observations in the South assure us that it is much less than is generally supposed. At the time of the capture of Memphis, and when the enemy had then got fairly into the cotton region, there was some cotton burnt; but it was done without any organization or system. Since then there have been some instances of burning private cotton, but very few in the immediate vicinity of the enemy, where there was the greatest necessity for its destruction. In the Mississippi bottom a great deal of cotton has passed into possession of the enemy by theft or purchase. It is stated that when Grant got possession of Helena, the cotton-burrers were known to burn cotton in the seed, while baled cotton, on adjoining places, was allowed to be hid in the canebrakes. But little cotton has been burnt near Memphis and the line of the Memphis and Charleston railroad, and it is in this vicinity that the enemy has secured large quantities of cotton through the cupidity of planters. It is also stated that the enemy secured considerable supplies of the staple north and south of the Tallahatchie river. The traffic with the enemy in cotton has been very demoralizing in Mississippi; and it is not unusal to hear the argument there that the people in the northern counties who are suffering, do quite well to exchange their cotton for money or supplies, and are excused by their necessities.

RICHMOND GOSSIP.

The Richmond correspondent of the Atlanta Confederacy writes thus concerning some resolutions about to be introduced into Congress by Senator Hill, of Georgia:

It is reported that Mr. Hill, Senator from Georgia, will soon introduce important resolutions before the Senate, which may explain several passages in his letter urging the election of Hon. Joshua Hill for Governor, and in his Macon letter, where he speaks of an honorable door of compromise being opened at no distant day, &c.

The purport of these resolutions are said to be expressive of a willingness on the part of the people of the South to meet the conservative element of the North in Convention, to discuss the issues between us, but in no wise compromising the spirit of the revolution.

Holding Mr. Lincoln and the Republican party responsible for the fanaticism at the North which has produced and continued the war, he would refuse to treat with him or his party otherwise than on the field of battle; but respecting a dignified spirit of conservatism which would hear the voice of reason, he would meet it in council, and determine the issues between us in a spirit of conciliation and compromise.

FROM MISSISSIPPI.

On December 21, Gen. Wirt Adams had a little skirmish at Fayette, Miss., with three columns of the enemy, who moved from Rodney and Natchez with the expectation of catching him. He repulsed them.

Late advices from Vicksburg state that the new line of works has been completed, and are reported to be very strong. The garrison has been considerably increased since the battle of Missionary ridge. Col. Colbaugh, who superintended the railroad, has resigned, and contemplates moving to Mexico—charges of a disreputable character having been preferred against him. A committee for confiscating Confederate property have commenced operations.

The Yankee bridge over Big Black was swept away recently by the heavy rise in that stream, and persons have now to cross in skiffs and flats. The Yankees, it is said, intend throwing another and more substantial bridge across at an early day.

Lieut. Gen. Leonidas Polk will make his head-quarters at Enterprise, Miss., and leave the army stationed at Brandon in charge of Major-General French.

NATIONAL FORTITUDE.—"If there is anything more astonishing than another in the history of the Roman Republic, it is the unconquerable spirit, the persevering energy, the invincible determination with which, under every calamity, and often in the very extremity of adverse fortune, they combined to struggle for the superiority, and at length attained it—not so much by conquering as by wearing out their adversaries. In no period of their long and glorious annals was this transcendant quality more strikingly evinced than in the second Punic War, when, after the battle of Cannæ Corpus, the second city of Italy, yielded to the influence of Hannibal, and nearly a half of the Roman Colonies, worn out by endless exactions in men and money, refused to send any further succors. The heroic spirit the Roman Senate then evinced, the extraordinary sacrifices they made, may, without exaggeration, be pronounced without parallel in the annals of mankind, if we reflect on the length of time during which these sacrifices were required. But while this invincible spirit augments our admiration of the Roman character, and makes us feel that they indeed deserved that mighty dominion which they afterwards attained, it takes much from the merit of their individual commanders. It was almost impossible to avoid ultimate success, with such armies to lead and so heroic a people to sustain the efforts and furnish the munitions of war."—*Blackwood's Magazine, June*, 1863.

FOREIGN ITEMS.

The American house, at Liverpool, of Messrs James McHenry & Co., which failed several years ago, have recently sent to Mr. Mosely a check for £47,000, principal and interest, of a debt owing at the time of this failure. The English papers rightly describe the circumstances as an instance of American commercial honor.

A bankruptcy of 110 years ago was recently in courts in England—owing to about £400 coming into the hands of the official assignee. The survivor of one of the creditors applied for part of the money, and as she seemed to be the only person alive concerned, she was given some. The last time the attorney in the bankruptcy was heard of was in 1775.

The renowned paddle and screw steamship Great Eastern, 22,791 tons, 679 feet in length, 92 feet in breadth and having four paddle engines of 1,000 horse and four screw engines of 1,600 horse power, is to be sold at auction, by order of the mortgagees, at the sale rooms of Messrs. Cunard, Wilson & Co., Liverpool.

Prince Napoleon's son was only half baptized at his birth, and now that his father wishes the baptism completed it cannot be done, as the proposed godfather, Victor Emanuel, is excommunicated, and the Prince refuses to have any body else.

There have been 225,042,000 francs spent by the French Government since 1852 in beautifying Paris.

NEWS SUMMARY.

Several buildings in Newnan, Ga., occupied as hospitals were burned, Dec. 2.

A machine has been invented by Rev. Mr. Davis, of Montgomery, Ala., which will make about twenty-five pairs of cotton cards per day.

The Mobile Register says that there has been a dead silence about Fort Jackson for a number of days—not a breath of tidings to indicate how the negro revolt against the Yankees terminated. The Northern papers aver that it only lasted half an hour. We have positive information that this account is false, and we have no information to show that it is even yet over.

A correspondent of the Atlanta Appeal says the Lincoln authorities have seized all the gold on deposit in Memphis. Most of it belonged to parties who had sold cotton to the Lincolnites. They have met with a deserved fate.

The total receipts of cotton at New Orleans from the 1st of September to the 13th Dec. were 47,878 bales. The stock on hand at the latter date was 9,900 bales, of which 2,500 were captured at sea. The receipts of sugar from the 1st of September to 13th December were 20,403 hogsheads.

The Lockville Mining and Manufacturing Company contemplates the manufacture of iron and the casting of railroad wheels, rolling of iron, &c. The works will be erected on Deep river, Chatham county, North Carolina, a locality secure from invasion, plentiful in provisions, with a boundless supply of iron and coal. It offers not only a safe investment, but one which will enable the prosecution of an enterprise of the utmost importance to the country.

Major Denis, under the orders of the War Office, assumes the duties lately vacated by Gen. Pillow, in Alabama, who has been ordered to the Army of Tennessee.

Under the authority of an Act "to provide for the issue and sale of State Bonds, and for other purposes" approved the 8th of December, 1863, bids will be received at the Executive Department, at Montgomery, until 12 M., on the 20th day of January, 1864, for $600,000 of 6 per cent. State of Alabama Bonds, $1,000 each, having twenty years to run from the 1st day of February, 1863, renewable at the pleasure of the State, with coupons attached for interest thereon, payable annually at the State Treasury on the first of February in each year. The Department, however, reserves to itself the right to reject all bids which shall not prove to be satisfactory. Upon all bids which may be accepted, the person or persons offering the same will be allowed until the 1st of February thereafter to make payment for the same at the State Treasury and receive the bonds as bid for and accepted. Said bonds may be paid for in Confederate States Treasury notes.

The Raleigh Standard, the organ of the Conservative party of North Carolina, scouts and repudiates the terms of the Lincoln's proclamation as insulting and degrading, and urges an uncompromising prosecution of the war to resist a peace on such a basis.

NORTHERN NEWS.

A large number of counterfeit treasury notes have been put in circulation in Cincinnati. Eleven counterfeiters have been arrested.

The Yankee papers say that the Choctaw chief, McCurtain, has declared for peace, says his tribe is for peace, and asks for an interview with the Yankee General McNeill.

The army correspondent of the New York News says Meade's army will not move again this winter. Its bridge builders and railroad repairers have been sent to another department.

The New York Mayoralty election cost the candidates $105,000. Gunther the successful one spent $50,000. Boole about $30,000. Blunt not less than $25,000. Here is "purity of the ballot box" for you.

The Governor and Legislature of Kentucky have requested Lincoln to postpone the draft until corrections are made in the enrollment papers.

The expenditures for the United States Capitol extension, during the year ending October 31, 1863, were $373,296, leaving a balance in hand of $33,712. The total expenditures from the commencement to the present time, were $6,399,909. This sum does not include the amount expended in the new dome.

UNCALLED FOR TELEGRAPHIC MESSAGES.—The following messages remain in the office and cannot be delivered for want of the proper direction:

Mrs M C Terrill, W H Cooper, E J Wright.

CONSIGNEES.

Per Augusta & Savannah Railroad, Jan. 6.—Merchandise—John Schley, J J Wall, W H Hilliard, G J Anderson, E Campfield, E W P[illegible]tey, Maj Norman, W Smith, S C Dwine, M[illegible] F Winnemore, Plumb & Leitner.

SPECIAL NOTICES.

City Guard Attention!—You are commanded to be and appear at your parade ground on Green street, in front of St. James' Church, THIS (Wednesday) AFTERNOON, at 3 o'clock. By order of Capt. Holleyman,

Punctual attendance will be enforced.

ja6 1d JOHN U. MEYER, O. S.

Attention, Young Men!—Company D, Augusta ARSENAL BATTALION, to be stationed at Augusta for Local Defence. Having received authority to raise a Company for the above Battalion, I invite all young men under the age of Conscription to join me. Those wishing to join will please come forward and fill up the ranks of this Company.

For further particulars apply to me at Augusta,

M. C. DAUGHERTY, or
GEO. S. ROBBINS,
jan6 12d Planters Hotel.

Blankets for the Soldiers!—OFFICE OF THE GEORGIA RELIEF AND HOSPITAL ASSOCIATION.—*To the People of Georgia.*—DECEMBER 7TH, 1863.—In view of the fact, now well ascertained, that our soldiers cannot be supplied during the present winter with a sufficient number of blankets, the Georgia Relief and Hospital Association, by its Executive Committee, has determined to try and supply this want to some extent by the manufacture of what are called Comforts or Comforters. These can be made out of our thinnest factory cloth, padded with bats of carded cotton, and quilted. The cloth should be as light as possible and the padding not too thick, otherwise the article will be too heavy for transportation. Even with these precautions they may not be easily transported by the soldier, and may be soon lost; still we hope that with the increased experience of our troops, this may not be an invincible inexperience; and that at all events, they may secure warmth for the present winter. If no more be effected, this result will amply repay the cost and trouble.

The undersigned have been appointed a committee for the purpose of invoking the aid of our people in this work. We have already sought and found the assistance of the ladies Augusta and its vicinity, whose energy during this unhappy war has been as untiring as their patriotism is ardent. These ladies, according to their custom, have responded to our call with an alacrity which has inspired our hearts with thankfulness and our minds with increased zeal, and which encourages us to call upon patriotic citizens, especially the women, in all parts of our State, and invite them, wherever such cloth and cotton-batting can be procured, to unite with us in this enterprise, this effort to protect our gallant defenders from the cold of the winter's night. The officers of the Augusta Factory in a spirit of the most liberal patriotism, have offered to furnish us with the materials upon very low terms, and in such quantities as will enable us if all will assist who can do so, to send forward to the army several thousands of these comforts in a week or ten days. Other factories in our State will do the same, we doubt not, if application be made. The articles when finished, can be sent to our rooms in this city, and will be immediately forwarded to the troops. A vigorous effort on the part of our people can thus almost entirely remedy the grievance which we desire to remove, certainly among our own soldiers. Past experience teaches us not to doubt but that this effort will be made elsewhere in Georgia with energy like to that which inspires it here.

The cloth used by us here is thinner than shirting. Shirting will do—and is cut seven and a half or eight feet long by six feet wide. It would be better if dyed some color, but we have no time to wait for this to be done.

All packages sent to be forwarded by the Association should be addressed W. H Potter, General Sup't. Augusta Ga.

E. STARNES,
C. J. JENKINS, } Com,
dec9 tfd

Clerk of Council's Office, Augusta, Ga., Dec. 24. [illegible] TITLE DEED, or the City Council Bond for titles to Lot No. 42, southeast corner of [illegible]fair and Wilde streets, are requested to present the same at this office as soon as possible. L. T. BLOME,
dec25 1md Clerk of Council.

Notice.—HEADQ'RS 2d DIST. GA. STATE GUARD,—SAVANNAH, Dec. 30th, 1863.—GENERAL ORDERS, No. 6.

I. Officers commanding Regiments and Battalions comprised in the 2d District G. S. G., will, forthwith rendezvous their respective commands at points most convenient for railroad transportation to this point.

II. They will report to these Headquarters the time and places of rendezvous and the number of men for whom they require transportation.

III. The horses belonging to cavalry organizations will be left in their present localities until further orders.

By command of Brig. Gen. H. R. JACKSON, commanding 2d District G. S. G. H. JACKSON,
ja1 6d Captain and A. A. G.

Tax Notice.—CLERK OF COUNCIL'S OFFICE, City Hall, Augusta, Ga., Jan. 3d, 1864.—All persons liable for City Taxes are hereby notified that the City Tax Digest for the present year is now open at my Office, and will remain open until the first day of March, 1864, by which time all returns must be made. All those who fail to make their returns by the time above specified will be double taxed.

Office hours, daily, (Sundays excepted) from 9 o'clock A. M. to 1 o'clock P. M., and from 3 to 5 o'clock P. M.

L. T. BLOME.
ja5 47d Clerk of Council.

[CIRCULAR.]

Chief Quartermaster's Office, Georgia State TROOPS, Atlanta, Ga., Oct. 10, 1863.—All Officers of Georgia State Troops will report at once at this office the strength of their commands, showing both rank and file, that requisitions for funds may be made. It will be impossible to get funds to pay them unless this is done. J. L. MORGAN,
oct 28 tfd Major and Chief Qr Master, G. S. T.

Blankets.—The appeal for blankets for our suffering troop in Tennessee will doubtless meet with a ready response from the ladies of Augusta and its vicinity. The General Superintendent of the Georgia Relief and Hospital Association has kindly offered to see that any contributions of this kind, shall carefully forwarded tfd nov 8

The Highest Market Price
PAID FOR
OLD ROPE, OLD BAGGING, RAGS, WASTE COTTON, &c.,

500,000 Pounds
IN LOTS OF TEN POUNDS AND UPWARDS,
Wanted Immediately
AT THIS OFFICE.

PLANTATION FOR SALE.

ONE of the most valuable COTTON PLANTATIONS in Southwest Georgia for Sale, lying seven miles from the Atlantic and Gulf Railroad, and will be within three miles of the Macon and Brunswick Road when completed: is bounded by the Altamaha River on the North; has one of the best Hog and Cattle ranges in that section of country—having exclusive control of the extensive swamp attached thereto; and bounded on the East by Big Goose Creek, which is navigable to the river for timber rafts—is a fine stream for fishing for trout and rock—the small lakes and ponds attached to the swamp abound in fine fish; Shad fishing is to a considerable extent carried on in Altamaha. It contains nineteen hundred acres of which about two hundred acres are cleared and partly under fence; has an Oat crop planted of ten acres; also, a bearing Orchard of superior fruit—consisting of Peaches, Figs, Pomegranates, Plums Mulberrys, &c. The improvements with some repair can be made substantial. There is a large new double Crib and Stables, and logs and boards just prepared for a new dwelling. The public road from Darien to the interior of the county runs near its Southern boundary. With the Plantation will be sold about thirty head of Stock Cattle and fifty Hogs, Goats, &c. Apply to E. C. WADE, Augusta Ga.
dec31 3tawd 1m

Dancing School.---A New Session.

MONS. BERGER respectfully informs his patrons and the public in general, that the Second Session will begin the 8th of JANUARY. Assemblies will open during the same month.

A NIGHT CLASS will open on the 7th at seven o'clock if a sufficient number of Pupils are present.

A PRIVATE CLASS for grown Ladies is now forming. Terms $20, in advance. For particulars apply at the Masonic Hall at the time of Tuition. dec31 eod4d

WANTED,

AT Telegraph Office, TWO BOYS to deliver Messages.
ja6

Blockade Goods,
Blockade Goods,
Blockade Goods,
Blockade Goods,

In Great Variety,
In Great Variety,
In Great Variety,
In Great Variety,

In lots to suit Purchasers,
In lots to suit Purchasers,
In lots to suit Purchasers,
In lots to suit Purchasers,

At less than Auction Prices,
At less than Auction Prices,
At less than Auction Prices,
At less than Auction Prices.

Call and Examine our Stock!
Call and Examine our Stock!
Call and Examine our Stock!
Call and Examine our Stock!

CHURCHILL & JOHNSTON.
CHURCHILL & JOHNSTON.
CHURCHILL & JOHNSTON.
CHURCHILL & JOHNSTON

233 Broad Street.
233 Broad Street.
233 Broad Street.
233 Broad Street.
dec15 tfd

ADDITIONAL.

100 pair WOOL CARDS
100 suits English Uniform COATS and PANTS
200 pair BLACKSMITH'S TONGS;
100 pounds SEWING SILK
100 French Felt HATS;
50 gross HAIR PINS;
1 case SHEET
50 cases GOLD LACE
1 case Colored COBURGS;
1 case MOIRE ANTIQUE;
1 case 6-4 Black MERINO
50 dozen SHIRT COLLARS;
48 dozen Bone CROCHET NEEDLES;

White and Fancy SHIRTS, &c., &c.

FOR SALE AT

LONG & CO'S.
dec17 tfd

INTEREST NOTES, &C.

$10,000 Interest Bearing NOTES;
$5,000 STATE BANK NOTES.

FOR SALE BY
dec15 tfd E. B. LONG & CO., 286 Broad St.

ENGLISH UNIFORMS.

100 SUITS COATS and PANTS.

For sale by
dec29 tfd LONG & CO.

Brass Handle Shovel and Tongs,
CONCAVE AUGURS,
LONG SHARP AUGURS,
SOCKET CHISEL.

ONE CASK, FOR SALE—A BARGAIN—BY
dec29 tfd LONG & CO.

ON CONSIGNMENT,

2 bales Ladies' HEAVY CLOTH OVERCOATS;
1 case WELLINGTON BOOTS;
1 case CAVALRY BOOTS;
2 cases CONGRESS BOOTS;
2 cases HEAVY BROGANS;
20 cases FELT HATS.

FOR SALE BY
LONG & CO.
dec29 tfd

Wanted Immediately to Hire,

A GOOD COOK, WASHER and IRONER. Apply to M. S. KEAN, at the old stand of Hickman, Hills & Crews.
ja1 6d

Der Texas Demokrat.

Jahrgang 4. Houston, Freitag, den 22. Januar 1864. **Nummer 8**

Die deutsche Sprache.

Muttersprache, Mutterlaut,
Wie so wonnesam, so traut!
Erstes Wort, das mir erschallet,
Süßes, erstes Liebeswort,
Erster Ton, den ich gelallet,
Klingest ewig in mir fort.

Ach! wie trüb ist meinem Sinn,
Wenn ich in der Fremde bin,
Wenn ich fremde Zungen üben,
Fremde Worte brauchen muß,
Die ich nimmermehr kann lieben,
Die nicht klingen als ein Gruß.

Sprache, schön und wunderbar,
Ach, wie klingest du so klar!
Will noch tiefer mich vertiefen
In den Reichthum, in die Pracht,
Ist mir's doch, als ob mich riefen
Väter aus des Grabes Nacht.

Ueberall weht Gottes Hauch,
Heilig ist wohl mancher Brauch.
Aber soll ich beten, danken,
Geb' ich meine Liebe kund,
Meine seligsten Gedanken,
Sprech' ich wie der Mutter Mund.

Notizbuch eines föd. Marine-soldaten.

(Fortsetzung.)

2. Dez. — Der Monat hat mit Wind und regnerischem Wetter begonnen, so daß Alles an Bord feucht und höchst ungemüthlich ist. Gestern Abend wurden wir etwas überrascht, als unsere bei der Stadt gelegenen Schiffe auf dieselbe ein ziemlich lebhaftes Feuer eröffneten. Es scheint, daß die Union Einwohner, die auf einem der untern Warfs der Stadt, unter dem Schutze der Geschütze unserer Schiffe, ihre Lager aufgeschlagen haben, von einer Abtheilung Rebellen vom Pointe die auch auf die Schiffe feuerten, angegriffen wurden. Sie wurden bald, mit Verlust einiger Todten und Verwundeten vertrieben.

4. Dez.—Die Ruhe letzter Nacht wurde wieder durch Abfeuern schwerer Geschütze und pyrotechnische Aufführungen unterbrochen, aber Rebellenthum hatte nichts damit zu thun. Der Dämpfer Tenessee kam vor dem Hafen an und kündigten auf diese Weise seine Ankunft an. Er brachte Vorräthe für die Galveston Flotte und eine kleine Post von New-Orlens. Gestern landete ein Foragirungs-Abtheilung von unserem Schiffe auf Bolivar Point um, uns mit frischem Fleisch zu versehen. Das Schicksal der Foragirungs-Partie von der Owasco an derselben Stelle einige Wochen zuvor machte uns vorsichtig genug, vor dem Landen eine Bombe in die Büsche zu senden. Ob dies die Rebellen von einem Angriffe auf uns abhielt, oder nicht, können wir natürl. nicht sagen, wenigstens ließen sie uns in Ruhe, aber das Rindvieh schien dadurch in nicht unbedeutenden Schreck versetzt worden zu sein, denn sobald wir uns ihnen näherten, nahmen sie alle Reißaus. Eine Kuh war jedoch zu langsam und wurde bald in Rinfleisch verwandelt. Die Zähigkeit, mit der sich das Fleisch heute beim Mittagessen allen Anstrengungen von Messern und Gabeln widersetzte, zeigte deutlich warum dieses Thier hinter seinenen Gefährten zurückblieb. Junges Texas Rindvieh ist so leichtfüßig, wie Texas Soldaten.

7. Dez — Gerüchte von Angiffen, die von den Rebellen von Virginia Point auf uns gemacht werden sollen, sind so zahlreich wie Muequtoes im Sommer, indem die Union Einwohner jede Nacht uns neue bringen. Obgleich derartige Nachrichten uns keineswes Furcht einjagte, halten sie uns doch wachsamer. Heute erhielten wir einen Besuch von den Sezessions Offizieren vom Point unter Parlementärflagge; was sie aber wollten, hat die Mannschaft noch nicht erfahren. Sie verließen uns in sehr gutem Humor— dasselbe bemerkten wir von unseren Gästen, die wir in Powderhorn empfingen. Wir dachten damals, dort sei die Union gesichert, fanden aber ein paar Tage später aus, daß dem nicht so war, weshalb wir auch jetzt keine Meinung aussprechen wollen, um nicht wieder getäuscht zu werden. Gesteren erhielten wir Nachricht von Sabine Paß, daß mehrere Dampfer und ein Ram einen Angriff auf unsere Blockade Schiffe daselbst beabsichtigen. Die Clifton wurde zur Verstärkung dorthin gesandt. Wir erfreuen uns wieder angenehmer Witterung.

11. Dez. — Noch immer in Galveston und Alles ruhig trotz der immer wiederholten Gerüchte, angegriffen und von hier vertrieben zu werden. Die Clifton kam Sonntag Nachts vom Sabine Paß zurück mit der Nachricht, daß dort Alles in Ordnung sei. Montag Morgens fuhr sie nach der Brücke hinauf, die Galveston Insel mit dem Point verbindet, wo die Rebellen eine Batterie zu bauen schienen, und feuerten einige Bomben ab. Ein Ausreißen unter den Sezessionisten war die Folge und sie haben sich an dieser Stelle seither nicht mehr sehen lassen. Gestern waren wir den ganzen Tag an Bord mit Ziehen und Heben beschäftigt. Wir schafften unsern alten 100 Pfünder aus dem Wege und nahmen eine 9 zöllige Dahlgreen Kanone von der Clifton an Bord. Die Westfield ist nun wieder so ziemlich zum Kampfe gerüstet, obgleich nicht ganz so vortrefflich, als wo wir zum ersten Male ausliefen. Was uns aber an Metall fehlt, wiegt vielleicht unsere lange Erfahrung in der Handhabung schwerer Geschütze auf. Die Teunesse fuhr vor einigen Tagen nach New Orleans ab

14. Dez. — Ein ruhiger, aber umwölkter Sabbah endigt eine andere monotone Woche. Es ist nichts von Bedeutung vorgefallen und im Sturme des Krieges scheint eine Windstille eingetreten zu sein. Anfangs letzter Woche wurde den Einwohnern von Galveston durch Plakate, die an den Straßenecken der Stadt angeklebt waren, mitgetheilt, daß nach Donnerstag Abend alle Communication zwischen der Stadt u. Virginia Point aufgehoben würde und Allen, welche die Stadt verlassen wollten, die letzte Gelgenheit dargeboten sei. Die Union Einwohner auf den unteren Wherften legten dieser Notiz verschiedentlich aus und wurden lauter in ihrem Geschrei um Schutz vom Commodore, der Allen die es wünschten, eine Passage nach New-Orleans anbot. Die Kohlenbarke „Island City", die gerade leer war, wurde zu diesem Zweck gemiethet und Freitags begaben sich etwa hundert an Bord. Als Vorsichtsmaßregel wurden die Harriet Lane und Owasco" weiter an der Stadt hinauf gelegt, um die Bewegungen der Rebellen besser übersehen und ihr allzu nahes Vorrücken verhindern zu können. Der Umstand daß sämmtliche Unionsmänner die Stadt verließen, erweckten Bedenklichkeiten in uns über das unterhalb der Stadt befindliche Fort und das Geschütz daselbst zu zersprengen, aber ohne Erfolg. Es wurde jedoch zum Gebrauche untauglich gemacht und das Magazin niedergebrannt. (Fortsetzung folgt)

Houston, den 18. Januar.

Die Yankeezeitungen haben die Nachricht verbreitet, Longstreet sei umzingelt und getödtet worden; Niemand aber glaubt es. — Kein Schiff und kein Mensch darf ohne Paß vom Distrikts-Marschall den Hafen von New York verlassen. Man will mit dieser Maßregel eine Wiederholung der Chesapeak-Affäre vermeiden. — Lee's Armee wird ihre Winterquartiere in der Nähe von Hanover Courthaus nehmen. — Die „News" hat die Nachricht von Shreveport erhalten, daß New Yorker Zeitungen vom 24. Dez. schreiben: „Meade und Lee haben eine neue Schlacht geschlagen. Meade hatte nicht die Absicht, sich in ein Gefecht einzulassen; er wollte nur sein Winterquartier näher an die Front verlegen, da wurde er plötzlich von Lee angegriffen und geschlagen. Keine weiteren Spezialitäten." —In Chattanooga ist Alles ruhig. Das Conscribiren der Bürger allein verursacht einige Aufregung. — Gold steht in NYork 52½ und Baumwolle 79 Cents. — Von NYork wird geschrieben, daß Longstreet sich mit Lee vereinigt, daß Lee über den Rapidan gegangen und daß Meade zurückgefallen ist. — In Westtennessee haben sich mehrere Guerilla-Corps vereinigt und den Big Hatchie überschritten. Forrest erhebt Contributionen von den Farmern der Umgegend. Er liegt mit 4—5000 Mann einige Meilen von Paducah Andere Nachrichten melden, er habe sich mit Faullner vereinigt und ihre vereinigte Macht belaufe sich auf 1500-2000 Mann. — Wheeler arbeitet zwischen Chattanooga u. Harrison, nimmt Yankeesoldaten gefangen, reißt gehißte Unionsflaggen herunter u. steckt Unionisten unter seine Armee. — In den ersten Tagen dieses Monats kamen viele Yankeesoldaten den Mississippi herab und machten nach NOrleans. Der Redriver ist bedeutend hoch bei Shreveport gestiegen. — Contrabande hat den Yankees am Potomac die Nachricht gebracht, die Rebellen schicken ihre flüssigen Kräfte alle an Lee und werde derselbe einen Hauptschlag gegen Meade ausführen. — Die Yankees sollen bei Atlanta und Dalton die Eisenbahn zerstört und die Verbindung zwischen Bragg's Armee und Richmond durchbrochen haben. — Die Conscription ist im Yankeethum um 20 Tage hinausgeschoben worden. Biele Gouverneure protestiren gegen die Aufhebung der $300exemption und glaubt man, der Congreß werde die Exemption auf $500 erhöhen. — Gen. Polk wird an der Stelle Holmes das Commando in Arkansas übernehmen. An Provisionen soll es unsern Leuten dort nicht fehlen, aber an Kleidern. Die Frauen machen ihrer Familie Kleider von Fußteppichen. — Der Gouverneur Yates von Illinois hat seine Legislatur auf ein Jahr vertagt. Die Supreme Court erklärt diesen Schritt für illegal; seine abolitionistische Freunde behaupten, es sei dies eine nothwendige Maßregel, da die Majorität der Legislatoren Landesverräther seien — Longstreet's Leute leiden stark bei der Kälte; viele derselben sind barfuß und der Schnee liegt fußtief im Gebirg. — Am 23. Dez. passirte John Morgan durch Columbia und ging nach Walhalla, SC. — Jackson McCurtin, der Häuptling der Chactaw Indianer kam mit mehreren Häuplingen zu Gen. McNeil und erklärte, daß er die Sache der Conföderation verlassen und die Amnestie Lincoln's für sich und seinen Stamm beanspruche Ihr Beispiel wird einen mächtigen Einfluß auf die übrigen Stämme ausüben. — Gen. Thomas hat unter'm 24. Dez. nach Washington berichtet, daß er dem Gen. Banks 17,000 gut ausgerüsteter Negersoldaten geschickt habe. Ueberhaupt habe er 51,000 Männer, Weiber u. Kinder unter seiner Aufsicht, von denen er viele an die benachbarten Farmer vermiethet habe Auch hat er die verlassenen Plantagen an Farmer und zwar gegen $4 von jedem gelieferten Ballen Baumwolle, 1 Cent von jedem Pfund Zucker und 4 Cents von jedem Bushel Mais oder Potatoes verrentet. Der Ueberschuß fällt in die Staatskasse. Man ist allgemein mit diesem Arrangement zufrieden. Thomas wird später nach Philadelphia und NOrleans gehen, um Neger zu bewaffnen. Zehn Regimenter sind fertig, an Grant geschickt zu werden. — Eine föderale Flotte liegt vor der Mündung des Redrivers mit der Absicht, die Wachita heraufzusegeln und den Rebellen allen möglichen Schaden zu thun. Die Yankees unter Washburn in Texas wollen sich in San Antonio conzentriren und von da aus Magruder anzugreifen. — In Hallifax sind Verhaftungsbefehle gegen acht von den Leuten, welche die Chesapeak kaperten, herausgenommen; man glaubt aber nicht an die Ausführung derselben, da die öffentliche Meinung für die Leute ist. — Culpepper und Umgegend ist von den Yankees occupirt und mit Batterien besetzt. Die Conscription ist nicht hinausverschoben worden; sie beginnt am 5. Januar; das Handgeld fällt von da ab weg. (H. Tel.)

Marktpreis von Richmond: Speck $3,25 per Pfund; Rindfleisch 75Cts; Schweinefleisch $2,25 p Pfund. Eine Richmond Zeitungzeitung schreibt, bis zum 1. Februar innerhalb der Conf. Linie in Virginien eine Million Pferde, 400,000 Stück Schlachtochsen, 100,000 Schweine und 550,000 Stück Schafe sein würden.

Mexiko. — Der Erzbischof von Mexiko hat die dortige französische Armee, vom höchsten Offizier bis zum gemeinen Soldaten, in Kirchenbann gethan, weil ihr Kaiser sich weigerte, die von den früheren mexikanischen Regierungen confiszirten Kirchengütern wieder der Kirche zu überben. Er ließ bei Abhaltung eines Hochamtes die Kirchthüren vor den Franzosen verschließen, der französische Commandant ließ dieselben aber aufsprengen und nöthigte den Erzbischof, das Amt fortzusetzen. — 26,000 Franzosen sind in Vera Cruz gelandet, um die Kaiserlichen zu verstärstärken. Eine starke Macht der neuen Regierung marschirt auf San Luis, wo Juarez mit seiner Armee steht. Juarez scheint aber nicht gewillt sein, seinen Stand zu vertheidigen; er soll bereits auf der Flucht nach Monterey sein. Der Gouv. Vidauri will zwar den Bürger Juanrez erlauben, in Monterey zu wohnen, nicht aber den Präsidenten Juarez — Mit jedem Tag erwartet man den Ausbruch von feindlicher Thätlichkeit zwischen Ruiz und Cortinas in Matamoras. Ruiz ließ neulich 14 Leute Cortinas' erschießen und Cortinas will die That rächen. Gouv. Serna u. viele Andere haben sich zu Gunsten der Franzosen erklärt. Der Weg ist also den Franzosen vollkommen geebnet und glaubt man, daß bei der Ankunft Maximilian's, die Anfangs Februars erwartet wird, sich auch sie Differenzenzen mit den V Staaten heben werden. — Die NOrleans „Bee" bringt folgende Correspondenz aus dem Inneren von Mexiko: Fast alle Hauptstädte des Landes sind von den französisch-mexikanischen Truppen besetzt. Gen. Miramon, von seinen zwei Brüdern begleitet, hat mit mit 200 Kriegobersten die Hauptstadt Mexiko verlassen, um nach Durango, die Region der Silberbergwerke, zu gehen. Man erwartet, daß San Luis bis zum 25. Dez. ohne Widerstand occupirt sein wird. Juarez' Regierung ist nur noch ein Schatten; Niemand beachtet ihre Befehle. Er hat zur letzten Stunde noch eine Zwangsanleihe erhoben; San Luis, Ortaga und Gonzales haben je $400,000 und Zacatelas $500,000 bezahlt. Gen. Uraga hatte mit 10,000 M. die Straße nach San Luis besetzt, zog sich aber bei der Annäherung der Franzosen zurück. Gen. Mijia führt die Avant der vereinigten französisch-mexikanischen Armee und er wird der erste in der San Luis betritt. Er hat den [illegible] Befehl, die Straße nach Tampico von den Guerillas zu säubern. Die Uneinigkeit der Führer in Tamaulipas wird es den Franzosen leicht machen, ihrer Herrschaft dort Geltung zu verschaffen. Viele alte Partisgänger von Juarez werden sich ihnen anschließen. Der erste Akt des Dramas ist beendigt und werden wir nun im zweiten sehen, welche Rolle Napolean mit dem perfiden u. meineidigen Hause Habsburg spielen wird.

Magruder hat die Ordre erlassen, daß alle Fuhrleute, die zur Armee gehören und detaillirtwaren, ohne Verzögerung in die Armee und unter ihr Commando sich zu stellen hätten, widrigenfalls sie als Deserteure behandelt werden würden.

Der Soldat von Büchel's Regiment, der am 8. ds auf der Halbinsel getödtet wurde, heißt Wilhelm Behrens.

Ein Yankee-Offizier, der unter Parlementärflagge nach Sabine Paß kam, erzählte daß die Chesapeak den britischen Autoritäten übergeben sei; daß die französische Regierung die Rappahannock freigegeben und dem Capitän erlaubt habe, zu segeln, wohin er immer wolle, und daß die Alabama, Georgia u. Florida noch immer den Ocean durchforchten.

In Rücksicht der dermaligen Lage der Conföderation, wo sie die Hülfe aller derer bedarf, die militärpflichtig sind, hat der Congreß zu Richmond folgenden Gesetzvorschlag angenommen: Sei es beschlossen, daß keine Person auf dem Grund, einen Substituten gestellt zu haben, vom Militärdienst eximirt ist; und sei es beschlossen, daß diese Clausel nicht so erklärt werden soll, als werde der Substitut von seinen contrahirten und übernommenen Verpflichtungen und Verbindlichkeiten dadurch befreit; auch soll dieser Act sich nicht auf solche Personen beziehen, die, selbst nicht militärpflichtig, Substituten stellten.

Gen. Magruder hat folgende Order erlassen: Es sind häufig Klagen über gesetzwidrige Wegnahme von Privateigenthum seitens Offiziere und Agenten dieses Distriktes bei dem kommandirenden Generalmajor erhoben worden, und wird hiermit bekannt gemacht, daß, wo irgend ein Beispiel dieser Art beim Hauptquartier constatirt wird, so ist der kommandirende Offizier des Detaschements welches des Raubes beschuldigt wird, verantwortlich, wenn die Thäter nicht ermittelt werden können. Die Bürger werden besonders aufgefordert, eine Copie des Attestes jeglichen Impreßments ihres Eigenthums an das Hauptquartier einzuschicken, um, wenn das Impreßment ungerecht wär, den Thäter sofort zur Strafe zu bringen. Anderntheils sin die Offiziere ermächtigt, ihre Pflicht mit Festigkeit, aber mit Höflichkeit und immer strikt nach dem Impreßment-Gesetz auszuführen.

Die Nachricht von der Niederlage Meade's scheint ungegründet zu sein, desgleichen das hier in der Stadt verbreitete Gerücht daß die Yankees 15 Meilen unter Caney gelandet seien.

Am 12. Jan. ging Major Breckinridge mit 135 Mann von Port Lavaca in die Nähe der Yankees bei Alt-Indianola. Er hatte ein lebhaftes Scharmützel mit ihnen u. wenigstens die Genugthuung, sie aus ihrer Ruhe aufgeschreckt und ihre Stärke ermittelt zu haben. Die Hauptmacht des Feindes liegt in Neu-Indianola oder Powderhorn. Bei Annäherung unseres kleinen Detaschements strömten sie in ganzer Stärke von Powderhorn herauf. Es mochten ihrer gegen 5000 sein und hatten sie 9 Stück Kanonen verschiedener Art bei sich. Ueber das Scharmützel wollen wir nichts sagen und nur bemerken, daß dasselbe zur Befriedigung unsrer braven Jungens ausfiel. Vor einigen Tagen wurden mehrere Yankees zwischen Lavaca und Alt-Indianola gesehen Ob sie jagten oder fischten oder den Canal untersuchten, weiß man nicht. Sie haben noch keine Cavallerie; doch ist nicht zu zweifeln, daß sie Verstärkung in der nächsten Zeit erhalten werden. Ob sie dann beabsichtigen, von dieser Seite ins Innere zu dringen, oder ob sie mit ihrer dermaligen Position dem Gen. Magruder Sand in die Augen streuen wollen, wollen wir der Beurtheilung Anderer überlassen.

Aus Matamoras wird unter'm 29. Dez. geschrieben: Die Yankee-Armee jenseit des Flusses besteht ungefähr aus 7000 Mann. Gen. Ord kam am 28. in Brownsville an u. übernahm das Commando. Sofort erließ er den Befehl, daß die Truppen sich innerhalb dreier Tage marschfertig machn sollten. Wahrscheinlich aber wurde er in Folge der kalten Witterung in seinen Bewegungen aufgehalten. Brownsville ist mit Redouten versehen und Point Isabel und San Brazos haben einige schwere Geschütze erhalten. Die Yankees werben Mexikaner dies- und jenseits des Flusses an und halten sie der Sache der Union ergeben. Die Mexikaner sind aber mit ihren amerikanischen Offizieren nicht zufrieden. Man spricht, die Mexikaner und ein Theil der regularen Armee bleibe als Besatzung in Brownsville und der Rest gehe an den Nueces.

800 Pferde haben die Yankees in Mexiko gekauft und 2080 in Cameron County von den dortigen Viehzüchtern erhalten. In Mexiko herrschte eine Zeitlang die Ansicht, daß Texas für die Sache der Conföderation verloren sei und confiszirte man in Folge dessen sämmlichen dort befindlichen Cotton der Conf. Regierung und 15 Millionen Conf. Bonds; Magruder aber hat sie neuerer Zeit eines Bessern belehrt. In Monterey hegt man trotz der Intriguen der Yankee-Agenten Conf. Sympathien. Diese Agenten bieten den nordöstlichen Staaten von Mexiko eine Allianz, Waffen und Hülfstruppen gegen die Franzosen an. Man sagt man, daß, falls es zu einem Kampfe zwischen den beiden Gouvernören von Tamaulipas, Ruiz und Serna, kommen sollte, die Yankees Matamoras besetzen würden.

Aus dem Victoria Advocate: Seit dem Einfall der Yankees in Port Lavaca haben wir nichts Weites von Wichtigkeit von ihnen gehört. Sie beschwerten Niemand während ihrer Anwesenhei in Lavaca; nur das Eigenthum des Col. Bradbury behandelten sie mit mit wenig Schonung. Am Chocolate drangen sie in das Haus des Hrn. Norris, dessen Frau und Kinder allein zu Hause waren und zerstörten alle Speisevorräthe, schnitten die Betten auf, zerbrachen die Möbel rc. Wären 200 bis 300 unserer Leute dort gewesen, die Burschen hätten Anderes zu gehabt, als Krieg mit Weiber und Kinder zu führen — Die Bürger von Lavaca, Dr. Hughs, Rev. McRae, Dr. Rosenkranz, und McKee benutzten die Anwesenheit der Yankees sich in Abraham's Schoos zu flüchten. Wir gratuliren unseren Mitbürgern von Lavaca, daß sich dadurch ihr geselliges Leben von diesen Schmutzflecken gereinigt hat. — Es scheint, die Yankees wollen sich in Powderhorn häuslich einrichten. Sie haben bereits Handelsgeschäfte eröffnet und geben dort selbst eine Zeitung heraus. Wir erwarten nächstens zu hören, daß sie ein Auskunftsbureau und eine Lebensversicherungsbank errichtet haben. — Ihre Zeitung erscheint in einem halben Bogen und benutzen sie das Druckmaterial des verstorbenen Yancey. Wir bringen folgende Auszüge aus derselben: Siehe die Anzeige: „Rhein-Wein bei H. Runge & Comp." in einer andern Spalte. Wo ist Runge? Wie die Leute in Cincinnati zu sagen pflegen: „er ist über den Rhein". — Wie sind in unserem neuen Wohnplatz über die Thatsache erstaunt, keine „ungeb leichten Amerikaner" zu treffen, Ein neuer Zug von Großartigkeit in den Dixie-Städten. Wir hören, daß die farbige Bevölkerung und einige gelbe Herren durch den Einfluß der letzten schaurigen „Norder" auswanderten. — Gen. FitzHenry Warren hat neulich eine strenge Ordre gegen Herumstreichen und Marodiren der Truppen unter seinem Commando erlassen. Oberoffiziere sind für das Betragen ihrer Leute verantwortlich. Eine sehr gute Ordre. Es ist nicht unser Wille, wehrlose Bürger zu belästigen. Wir haben unser Geschäft mit den bewaffneten Rebellen abzumachen. Der kommandirende General wird alle Bedürfnisse der Soldaten auf militärischem Wege befriedigen. Unser Besuch in dieser schönen Stadt war plötzlich, unerwartet und unceremoniös, aber nichtsdestoweniger angenehm. Wirklich, der Platz gefällt uns nach der kurzen Bekanntschaft schon ganz vortrefflich, und haben wir uns vorgenommen nach dem Krieg uns ganz hier niederzulassen.

Freund Michel in Indianola machte neulich mit den Yankees eine Jagdpartie und wurde aufgefordert, das angeschossene Wild über eine kleine Bayou zu verfolgen. "Das thue ich nicht", rief er aus, „es könnte ja, bei Gott, ein salpeteriger Torpedos in der Pfütze sein."

Port Lavaca, den 4. Jan. Seit einer Woche sind wir ohne Post aus dem Osten u. wir wissen darum nicht, ob die Yankees ihre Drohung, Galveston wieder zu nehmen, ausgeführt haben; doch ist wahrscheinlich dort nichts vorgefallen, da die Yankees noch ihre ganze Mannschaft und ihre Munitionen in Powderhorn haben. Sie erwarten noch Leute und Sachen und würden sie gewiß nicht so lange an diesem wüsten, wasserlosen Küstenstrich mit der angeblichen Stärke sich aufhalten, wenn sie nicht dazu genöthigt wären. Ihre Emissäre verbreiten beständig falsche Nachrichten und wundere ich mich nur, wie irgend ein vernünftiger Mann nach so vielfacher Erfahrung noch ein Wort davon glauben kann Sie betrachten diese Art Lügen als einen Theil ihrer Strategie und streuen sie mit verschwenderischer Hand aus. So z. B. sagten sie ihren Vertrauten in Lavaca, daß sie so u. so viel Truppen an den u. den Plätzen hätten, was sich später als unwahr herausstellte. In gleiche Kategorie gehört wohl auch ihre Angabe, daß eine starke Colonne von Brownsville und eine andere via Shreveport kommen werde. Ich führe diese Sachen an, um das Volk zu warnen, dergleichen Gerüchten keinen Glauben zu schenken; denn dergleichen Lügen schwächen die Knie der Schwachen, machen die Verräther kühner und die Spione verwegener. — Gestern brachte unsere Streifwache die Nachricht, daß ein kleiner Scharmützel zwischen den Pickets in der Nähe von Alt-Indianola stattfand. Sonst nichts Neues von Belang.

Die Quartiermeister der Armee scheinen im Congreß zu Richmond nicht besonders gut angeschrieben zu sein. Ein Mitglied äußerte sich folgendermaßen: „Sehen Sie sich um, meine Herren, und Sie werden überall Quartiermeister sehen, die in Reichthum und Ueppigkeit leben. Sie besitzen die schönsten Häuser und Landsitze, halten sich Leibdiener und herrliche Pferde, kleiden sich nach der feinsten Mode, tragen Tausende von Dollars am Leibe, sind die ersten Gambler und setzen Tausende auf eine Karte. Woher kommt dieser plötzliche Reichthum? Dieselben Männer waren meistens vor wenig Jahren noch arm, wohnten in kleinen Hütten und machten kaum ihr Leben. Doch das Uebel besteht ja noch!

Die Preise der Lebensmittel und der Kleidungsstoffe steigen hier in Houston von Woche zu Woche und gehört für die einfachste Haushaltung schon eine wöchentliche Einnahme von mehr als hundert Dollars dazu, die Ausgabe zu decken. Weizenmehl kostet per Pfund $1,25 und ist dasselbe kaum zu haben, und doch fehlt es im Land weder an Weizen, noch an Mahlmühlen, wohl aber an Fuhrwerk, um Mehl beizuschaffen. So schreibt uns Herr E. Baum aus Parker County: „Sie schreiben in Ihrer Zeitung von dem hohen Preis und dem Mangel an Weizenmehl in Houston. Bei uns kostet der Bushel Weizen $5 und haben wir hier noch große Vorräthe und zwei Dampfmühlen erster Klasse. Schicken Sie uns nur Fuhrwerk herauf und wir wollen Houston reichlich mit Flour versorgen."

(Correspondenz.) Lieber Onkel! Seitwir Houston verließen, sind wir beständig auf dem Marsch. In Columbia erhielten wir den Befehl, nach Lavaca zu gehen. Als wir nach Matagorda kamen, hörten wir, daß Saluria von den Yankees bedroht werde. Wir, Wood's und Pyron's Reg., trafen Vorbereitungen, per Dampfer den Unseren bei Saluria zu helfen. Unsere Pferde sollten zu Land nach Lavaca gebracht werden. Als wir eben bereit waren, abzudampfen, erhielten wir die Nachricht, daß Saluria geräumt und in den Händen der Yankees sei. Seit dieser Zeit liegen wir westlich von Caney, 12 Meilen von Colorado und 30 Meilen von Matagorda. Wir lauern hier, daß die Yankees landen möchten, um ihnen eine Lektion in gutem Texanischen zu geben. Unsere Armee fühlt sich stark genug dazu. In der Neujahrsnacht erfror ein Mann auf unserem Vorposten. In Houston wird man sich wahrscheinlich von Schlachten und Gefechten erzählen, von denen die Armee nichts weiß. Die Yankees beschießen von ihren Schiffen aus täglich unsere Festung am Caney, bezwecken dabei nichts mehr, als daß sie die Neger, die an den Werken arbeiten, erschrecken. Ein Mann von Büchel's Leuten, Behrens mit Namen, wurde beim Postenstehen auf der Schanze erschossen. Col. Büchel agirt hier als Brigarde General und hat das Commando am Caney. Nach Velasco haben die Yankees bisjetzt nur wenige Bomben geworfen. In Powderhorn sollen 2000 Yankees gelandet sein. Sie treiben schon Handel u. geben 8 Pfund Koffee für $1. Flour schenken sie den Armen und vor die Häuser der Frauen, deren Männer im Conf. Dienste stehen, haben sie Wachen gestellt, um sie gegen Insulte zu schützen—doch werden auch viele Unwahrheiten verbreitet. Duff's Reg. liegt in Victoria; wir werden wahrscheinlich auch noch nach dem Westen beordert werden; die Yankees scheinen es zunächst auf Westtexas abgesehen zu haben.

Letzte Nachrichten.

Bomb Hole, 19ten Jan — Das gewöhnliche Beschießen des Bernad von den Yankees begann diesen Vormittag um 7 Uhr und dauerte 3 bis 4 Stunden. Wir hörten, Indianola sei von unseren Leuten niedergebrannt und bei Port-Lavaca habe ein Gefecht stattgefunden. Beide Gerüchte sind unwahrscheinlich und ungegründet. Die Bomben der Yankees haben ihren Schrecken für unsere Leute verloren. Ihre Schüsse zeigen, welch armselige Kanoniere sie sind. Unsere Befestigungswerke werden in den nächsten Tagen fertig und wir zum Tanz bereit sein.

In Bonham wurden in diesen Tagen zwei Verräther kriegsgerichtlich erschossen.

Die Pocken sollen in Lagrange herrschen.

Magruder war in diesen Tagen in Houston anwesend.

Der Little Rock Democrat ist jetzt ein Yankeeblatt.

In Kentucky will man die Legislatur nach Louisville verlegen.

Europa. In Deutschland rüstet sich Alles gegen Dänemark, und der Kriegsdonner wiederhallt vielleicht schon heute an den Gestaden Schleswig Holstein's. Durch den Tod des Königs von Dänemark ist die Frage entstanden: Wer ist der eigentliche Herzog von Schleswig Holstein? Nach dem salischen Gesetze und dem Wunsche des Volkes mußte Prinz Augustenburg das Herzogthum erhalten. Nach einem Vertrag der europäischen Mächte, worin der Prinz Christian als Erbfolger des kinderlosen Königs von Dänemark ernannt wurde, wurde ihm auch der Besitz der Herzogthümer Schleswig und Holstein garantirt. Prinz Augustenburg wandte sich an den deutschen Bundestag, die Frage zu entscheiden. Derselbe, zu dem auch Oesterreich und Preußen gehört, welche das salische Gesetz zu Gunsten Christians abzuwenden versuchten, entschied sich zu Gunsten Augustenburgs. Preußen und Oesterreich wurden überstimmt. Einstweilen wird die Sache auf diplomatischem Wege verhandelt.

Copenhagen, 5ten Dez '63 — Folgendes ist die Proklamation des Königs Christian an die Holsteiner: „Wir beabsichtigen, den Thron von Dänemark in Frieden zu besteigen, ohne Ehrgier und nur mit den besten Wünschen für das Land. Die Integrität der dänischen Monarchie ist ein Gesetz Europa's, weil dieselbe nothwendig für den Frieden Europas ist. Unter dem Vorgeben erblicher Rechte hat sich eine Opposition gebildet, die beabsichtigt, die dänische Monarchie zu zerrißen. Dieselbe hat große Aufregung in Holstein hervorgerufen. Die Erhaltung der Monarchie ist aber eine unserer heiligsten Pflichten.

Bei der letzten städtischen Wahl zu Houston wurde W. Anders zum Mayor, W. E. Thomas, G. Frazer, H. Fox, W. D. Roberson zu Aldermen, St. Brewster zum Assessor und Collektor, J. B. Hegan zum Recorder, J. C. Lord zum Stadt-Marschall und H. G. Penton zum Sexton gewählt. Bei der Installirung der städtischen Behörden sprach der Mayor in einer Rede namentlich über die Finanzangelegenheiten der Stadt und sagte unter Andern: „Ich bin glücklich, Ihnen mittheilen zu können, daß der Zustand unser städtischen Finanzen ein sehr guter ist, was wir der Weisheit und der Energie des Boardes von letzten Jahr besonders zu danken haben. Sie haben auf gesetzlichem Wege die Einkünfte der Stadt bedeutend vermehrt und verfuhren sehr haushälterisch damit und wandten jeden Dollar zweckmäßig, gemäß ihres Rechnung-Etats an. Am 1. Jan. '64 waren nach dem Bericht des Sekretärs und Schatzmeisters $30,000 vorräthig in Kasse. Diese bedeutende Summe würde Verbesserungen an den Straßen und am Markthause gestatten und rechtfertigen, aber der nichtgeordnete Zustand unseres Landes erlaubt keine außerordentliche Ausgaben, da durch den gestörten Handel die Steuereinnahme geringer und durch das Steigen der Preise und Arbeitslöhne verhältnißmäßig die Ausgaben sich erhöhen und vermehren."

Wir hören, daß G. W. Paschall von Austin als Gefangener hieher gebracht wurde.

Herr J. Coller ist unser Hauptagent in den Counties Victoria und Goliad und nimmt Gelder für uns in Empfang.

„Südliche Blätter."

Unter obigem Titel werden wir von nun ab eine Unterhaltungsschrift—mit Vermeidung aller Politik—herausgeben. Aufforderungen von vielen Seiten bewogen uns zu diesem Unternehmen, welches wir bisjetzt aus Mangel an Papier nicht ausführen konnten. Da wir aber in den letzten Tagen durch die Bemühungen des Herrn Veitt und anderer Freunde Gelegenheit fanden, wieder eine bedeutende Quantität weißen Papieres anzukaufen, so sind wir nunmehr in den Stand gesetzt, dem Wunsche des Publikums zu entsprechen und in 14 Tagen die erste Nummer derselben herauszugeben. Der Preis beträgt per Nummer 10 Cents in Silber oder im Verhältniß in Papiergeld; dies ist unter den jetzigen Verhältnissen, wo wir $300 für das Rieß Papier, welches früher soviel Cents kostete, und für Druckerschwärze $10 bis $15, die früher 20-25 Cents kostete, die anderen Ausgaben gar nicht zu rechnen, bezahlen, gewiß sehr billig, billiger als irgend ein anderer Artikel auf dem Markte. Das Blatt wird in Buchformat, 8 Oktavseiten stark, halbmonatlich publizirt, und umfaßt, wie schon oben bemerkt, ausschließlich Unterhaltungsstoff, wie laufende Novellen u. s. w. Bestellungen mögen baldigst gemacht werden, damit es uns nicht gehe wie bei unserm diesjährigen Kalender, indem wir durch verspätete Bestellungen dieselben unvollständeg oder gar nicht ausführen konnten. Wegen dem Verhältniß von Silber zu Papier mögen Diejenigen, welche auf die „Südlichen Blätter" zu abonniren wünschen, sich an uns wenden. Der Houstoner Geldmarkt wird jedoch als Norm angenommen.

Fr. & O. Dietzel.

Bestellungen auf den Kalender für '64 mögen eingestellt werden, da beide Auflagen (2000) bereits bestellt und versandt sind.

Antwort an Correspondenten.

D Volk, Victoria. Werden unser Mögliches thun, konnten jedoch bisjetzt nichts bezwecken.

L Constant, M. $10 empfangen.

E N Clarke, Catspring, Received $10.

Mad Bender, N. B. Uebergeben Sie unsere Gelder Herrn P Butz.

Hausmann, M. $80 empfangen.

F Seydler, HH. $40 empfangen.

Keßler, HH. $15 empfangen.

J Bauer, Goliad, Der verstorbene Müller erhielt von uns 12 Kalender; bitten um Zusendung des Betrags von $30.

J Berends, S A. Briefe vom 8ten 12ten und 15ten nebst Inhalt empfangen.

Eli Baum, Weaterford. Ihre Bestellungen erhalten.

C C Koch, J. $40 durch J Veitt empfangen.

L Miltahler, Galveston, Konnten Ihnen Sendung nicht machen, da uns Ihre Adresse verloren ging. Bitten um dieselbe.

Nach Eagle Paß.

Eine Ambulance geht am 15ten Februar von hier nach Eagle Paß. 2 bis 3 Mitreisende werden gesucht. Näheres ist zu erfahren bei Heinrich Wiener.

Houston, 20ten Januar 1864. n8m3°

The Peninsula.

VOL. I. FERNANDINA, FLA., THURSDAY, FEB. 4, 1864. NO. 38.

THE PENINSULA;

Published Every Thursday at Fernandina, Florida.

BY W. C. MORRILL.

TERMS.

Two dollars a year in advance; single copies, five cents.

Advertising—Fifty cents per line for each insertion.

Imperishable.

The pure, the bright, the beautiful,
That stirred our hearts in youth,
The impulse to a worldly prayer,
The dreams of love and truth;
The longings after something lost,
The spirit's yearning cry,
The striving after better hopes,
These things can never die.

The timid hand stretched forth to aid
A brother in his need,
The kindly word in grief's dark hour,
That proves a friend indeed—
The plea for mercy softly breathed,
When justice threatens high;
The sorrow of a contrite heart—
These things shall never die.

The memory of a clasping hand,
The pressure of a kiss,
And all the trifles sweet and frail,
That make up love's first bliss:
If with a firm, unflinching faith,
And holy trust and high,
Those hands have clasped, those lips have met;
These things shall never die.

The cruel and the bitter word,
That wounded as it fell;
The chilling want of sympathy
We feel but never tell;
The hard repulse that chills the heart
Whose hopes are bounding high;
In an unfading record kept—
These things shall never die.

Let nothing pass, for every hand
Must find some work to do;
Lose not a chance to waken love—
Be firm, and just and true.
So shall a light that cannot fade,
Beam on thee from on high,
And angel voices say to thee
These things shall never die.

-- Those who alwas have a good story to tell, as President Lincoln's last, are responsible for the following:

A few days since, so they say, a New England gentleman called at the White House to propose a new plan for capturing Richmond

"I know, Mr. President," said he, "that the Union men in the rebel capital with the prinoners and the contrabands there, are able to overpower the garrison —so all that you have to do is to let General Meade make a diversion against Lee's army, and then let General Butler go up the James river, to co-operate with the Unionists."

"I have great confidence in General Butler,' replied Mr. Lincoln, "but I am not so sure about Richmoud. Your plan reminds me of a story told of a lot of Methodist ministers, who were the trustees of a Western college. It so happened that this college was connected with a neighboring town by a bridge, and that this bridge was subject to be carried away by freshets. At last they held a special session, to receive the plans of a noted bridge builder, a good mechanic; but rather a profane man. 'Can you build this bridge?' asked a reverend gentleman. 'Build it,' bluntly replied the mechanic, 'I could build a bridge to'—[the infernal regions] This horrified the trustees, and after the bridge builder had retired, the minister who had recommended him thought proper to apologize. 'I feel confident,' said he, 'that our energetic friend could build a safe bridge to Hades, although I am not so sure of the abutment on the other side.' "

"And so with your plan, concluded the President, I have great confidence in General Butlor, but doubt the strebgth of the Unionists at Richmond."

U. S. SALE OF LANDS,
for unpaid Direct Taxes,
DISTRICT OF FLORIDA

NOTICE is hereby given that the several Tracts or lots of land, situate in the State of Florida, hereinafter described, have become forfeited to the United States, by reason of the non-payment of the Direct Tax charged thereon, under the Act entitled "An Act to provide increased revenue from imports, to pay interest on the puulic debt, and for other purposes," approved August 5, 1861, and An Act entitled "An Act for the collection of Direct Taxes in insurrectionary districts within the United States and for other purposes," approved June 7, 1862, and "an Act to amend an Act entitled an Act for the collection of Direct Taxes in insurrectionary districts within the United States, and for other purposes, approved June 7, 1862, and approved February [illegible] 1863, and [illegible] the same will be sold at public auction on MONDAY the EIGHTEENTH day of January, A. D., 1864, at the city of FERNANDINA, in the county of Nassau, State of Florida, and that said sale will be continued from day to day until all are sold.

CITY OF FERNANDINA.

Block.	Lot.	Tax & Penalty.
1	1	$3 24
1	2	2 70
1	3	2 70
1	4	2 70
1	5	2 70
1	6	2 70
1	7	2 70
1	26 8	8 64
1	9	2 43
1	10	2 43
1	11	2 43
1	12	2 43
1	13	2 43
1	14	2 43
1	15	2 43
1	16	2 43
1	17	2 70
1	18	2 70
1	19	2 70
1	22	13 50
1	23	2 70
1	24	2 70
1	25	7 02
1	27	16 20
1	28 29	24 30
1	30	2 70
1	31	2 70
1	32	2 70
1	33	4 59
1	34	4 59
2	1	2 43
2	2	2 43
2	3	2 43
2	4	2 43
2	5	2 43
2	6	2 43
2	7	2 43
2	8	2 43
2	9	2 43
2	10	2 43
2	11	2 43
2	12	2 43
2	13	2 43
2	14	2 43
2	15 16	9 72
2	17	2 70
2	18	2 70
2	19	2 70
2	20	2 70
2	21	2 70
2	22	2 70
2	23	2 70
2	24	2 70
2	28	3 24
2	29	2 70
2	31	2 43
2	32	2 43
2	33	2 43
2	34	2 43
3	1	2 70
3	2	2 70
3	3	2 70
3	4	2 70
3	5	2 70
3	6	8 10
3	7	2 70
3	8	8 10
3	9 10, 11 25, 26	16 20
3	12	2 70
3	13	2 70
3	14	2 70
3	15	2 70
3	16	2 70
3	17	2 70
3	18	2 70
3	19	2 70
3	20	2 70
3	21	2 70
3	22	2 70
3	23 24	6 75
3	27	2 70
3	28 29	16 20
3	30	2 70
3	31	2 70
3	32	2 70
3	33	2 70
3	34	2 70
4	1	2 70
4	2	2 70
4	3	2 70
4	4	2 70
4	5	2 70
4	6	2 70
4	7	2 70
4	8	2 70
4	9	2 70
4	10	2 70
4	11	2 70
4	12	2 70
4	13	2 70
4	14	2 70
4	15	2 70
4	16	2 70
4	17	2 70
4	18	2 70
4	19	2 70
4	20	2 70
4	21	2 70
4	22	2 70
4	23	2 70
4	24	2 70
4	25	2 70
4	26	2 70
4	27	2 70
4	28	2 70
4	29	2 70
4	30	2 70
4	31	4 32
4	32	2 70
4	33	2 70
4	34	2 70

Block.	Lot.	Tax & Penalty.
5	1	1 62
5	2	1 62
5	3	1 62
5	4	1 62
5	5	1 62
5	6	1 62
5	7	03
5	8	03
5	9	03
5	10	03
5	11	03
5	12	03
5	13	03
5	14	03
5	15	03
5	16	03
5	17	03
5	18	03
5	19	03
5	20	03
5	21	03
5	22	03
5	23	03
5	24	03
5	25	1 62
5	26	1 62
5	27	1 62
5	28	1 62
5	29	1 62
5	30	1 62
5	31	1 62
5	32	1 62
5	33	1 62
5	34	1 62
6	1	1 62
6	2	1 62
6	3	1 62
6	4	1 62
6	[illegible]	1 62
6	6	1 62
6	7	1 62
6	8	1 62
6	9	1 62
6	10	1 62
6	11	1 62
6	12	1 62
6	13	1 62
6	14	1 62
6	15	1 62
6	16	1 62
6	17 18	11 34
6	19	1 62
6	20	1 62
6	21	1 62
6	22	1 62
6	23	1 62
6	24	1 62
6	25	1 62
6	26	1 62
6	27	1 62
6	28	1 62
6	29	1 62
6	30	1 62
6	31	1 62
6	32	1 62
6	33	1 62
6	34	1 62
7	1	2 70
7	2	2 70
7	3	do
7	4	do
7	5	do
7	6	do
7	7	do
7	8	do
7	9	do
7	10	do
7	11	do
7	12	do
7	13	do
7	14	do
7	15	do
7	16	do
7	17	do
7	18	do
7	19	do
7	20	do
7	21	do
7	22	do
7	23	do
7	24	do
7	25	do
7	26	do
7	27	do
7	28	do
7	29	do
7	30	do
7	31	do
7	32	do
7	33	do
7	34	do
8	1 2 & 34	15 12
8	3	2 70
8	4	2 70
8	5	2 70
8	6	2 70
8	7	2 70
8	8 9	8 10
8	10	2 70
8	11	2 70
8	12	2 70
8	13	2 70
8	14	2 70
8	15	do
8	16	do
8	17	do
8	18	do
8	19	do
8	20	do
8	21	do
8	22	do
8	23	do
8	24	do

Block.	Lot.	Tax & Penalty.
8	25	do
8	26	do
8	27	7 02
8	28 29	11 88
8	30	2 70
8	31	2 70
8	32	2 70
8	33	2 70
9	2	2 70
9	3	do
9	4	do
9	5	do
9	6	do
9	7	do
9	8	do
9	9	do
9	10	2 85
9	11	2 70
9	14	2 70
9	15	do
9	16	do
9	17	do
9	18	4 05
9	19	2 70
9	20	do
9	21	do
9	22	do
9	23	do
9	24	do
9	25 26	7 02
9	27	2 70
9	28	do
9	29	do
9	30	do
9	31	do
9	32	do
9	33	do
10	1 & 34	21 60
10	2	8 10
10	3	4 59
10	8	8 10
10	9	2 70
10	10	do
10	11	do
10	12	do
10	13	do
10	14	do
10	15	do
10	16	do
10	17	do
10	18	do
10	19	do
10	20	do
10	21	do
10	22	do
10	23	do
10	24	do
10	26	3 24
10	27	3 24
10	28	10 80
10	29	10 80
10	32	2 70
10	33	2 70
11	1	1 62
11	2	do
11	[illegible]	do
11	4	do
11	5	do
11	6	do
11	7	do
11	8	do
11	9	do
11	10	do
11	11	do
11	12	do
11	13	do
11	14	do
11	15	do
11	16	do
11	17	do
11	18	do
11	19	do
11	20	do
11	21	do
11	22	do
11	23	do
11	24	do
11	25	do
11	26	do
11	27	do
11	28	do
11	29	do
11	30	do
11	31	do
11	32	do
11	33	do
11	34	do
12	1	3 24
12	2	1 62
12	3	do
12	4	do
12	5	do
12	6	do
12	7	do
12	8	do
12	9	do
12	10	do
12	11	do
12	12	do
12	13	do
12	14	do
12	15	do
12	16	do
12	17	do
12	18	do
12	19	do
12	20	do
12	21	do
12	22	do
12	23	do
12	24	do
12	25	do
12	26	do
12	27	do
12	28	do
12	29	do
12	30	do
12	31	do
12	32	do
12	34	2 70
13	1	4 32
13	2 3	3 78
13	4	8 10
13	5	1 62
13	6	do
13	7	do
13	8 9	11 34
13	10	1 62
13	11	do
13	12	do
13	13	do
13	14	do
13	15	3 42
13	16	1 62
13	17	do
13	19	do
13	20	do
13	21	do
13	22	do
13	23	do
13	24	do

Block.	Lot.	Tax & Penalt
13	25	do
13	26	do
13	27 28	14 04
13	29	1 62
13	30	do
13	31	do
13	32	do
13	33	do
13	34	do
14	1	do
14	2	do
14	3	do
14	4	do
14	5	do
14	6	do
14	7	4 86
14	8	1 62
14	9	do
14	[illegible]	do
14	11	do
14	12	do
14	17	do
14	18	do
14	19	do
14	20	do
14	21	3 78
14	22	1 62
14	23,24,25	15 66
14	26	1 62
14	27	1 62
14	28	do
14	29	do
14	32	do
14	33	do
14	34	do
15	1,33,34	23 76
15	2	1 62
15	3	1 62
15	4	3 78
15	5	1 62
15	6	do
15	7	do
15	8	do
15	9	do
15	10 11, 12 13, 14	10 35
15	15	1 62
15	16	do
15	17	do
15	18	do
15	19	do
15	20	do
15	21	do
15	22	do
15	23	do
15	24	do
15	25	do
15	26 27	4 59
15	28	1 62
15	29	1 62
15	30	do
15	31	do
15	32	do
16	1	do
16	2	do
16	[illegible]	do
16	4	2 43
16	5	1 62
16	6	9 18
16	7 8 9, 10 11	27 00
16	12	1 62
16	13	do
16	14	do
16	15	do
16	16	do
16	17	do
16	18	1 78
16	19	1 62
16	20	do
16	21	do
16	22	do
16	23	do
16	26	do
16	27	do
16	28	do
16	29	do
16	30	do
16	31	do
16	32	do
16	33	do
16	34	do
17	1	do
17	2	do
17	3	do
17	4	do
17	5	do
17	6	do
17	7	do
17	8	do
17	9	do
17	10	do
17	11	do
17	12	do
17	13	do
17	14	do
17	15	do
17	16	do
17	17	do
17	18	do
17	19	do
17	20	do
17	21	do
17	22	do
17	23	do
17	24	do
17	25	do
17	26	do
17	27	do
17	28	do
17	29	do
17	30	do
17	31	do
17	32	do
17	33	do
17	34	do
18	1	do
18	2	do
18	3	do
18	4	do
18	5	do
18	6	do
18	7	do
18	8	do
18	9	do
18	10	do
18	11	do
18	12	do
18	13	do
18	14	do
18	15	do
18	16	do
18	17	do
18	18	do
18	19	do
18	20	do
18	21	do
18	22	do
18	23	do
18	24	do

Block.	Lot.	Tax & Penalty.
18	25	1 62
18	26	do
18	27	do
18	28	do
18	29	do
18	30	do
18	31	do
18	32	do
18	33	do
18	34	do
19	1	do
19	2	do
19	3	do
19	4	do
19	5	1 62
19	6	do
19	10 11	3 51
19	12	3 24
19	13	1 62
19	14	do
19	15	do
19	16	do
20	2 13, 14 15, 16	24 30
20	3	1 08
20	4	1 08
20	5	03
20	6	03
20	7	03
20	8	03
20	9	03
20	10	1 08
20	11	1 08
20	12	do
21	2	do
21	3	do
21	4	do
21	5	do
22	1	2 16
22	2	1 08
22	3	1 89
22	4	5 40
22	5	2 97
22	6	1 08
22	7	11 61
22	8	1 08
22	9	do
22	10	do
22	11	do
22	12	do
22	13	do
23	1	do
23	2	do
23	3	do
23	4	9 18
23	5	1 08
23	6	do
23	7	do
23	8	do
23	9	do
23	10	do
23	11	do
23	12	do
23	13	do
23	14 15	11 88
[illegible]	[illegible]	[illegible]
24	1	do
24	2	do
24	3	do
24	4	do
24	5	do
24	7	do
24	8	do
24	9	do
24	10 11, 12	8 64
24	13	2 16
24	14	1 08
24	15	1 08
24	16	10 80
25	1	1 08
25	2	do
25	3	do
25	4	do
25	5	do
25	6	do
25	7	do
25	8	do
25	9	1 89
25	10	1 08
25	11	do
25	12	do
25	13	do
25	14	do
25	15 16	2 43
26	1	1 08
26	2	do
26	3	do
26	4	do
26	5	do
26	6	do
26	7	do
26	8	do
26	9	do
26	10	do
26	11	do
26	12	do
26	13	do
26	14	3 78
26	15	2 62
26	16	1 08
27	1	95
27	2	95
27	3	95
27	6	95
27	7	95
27	8	95
27	9	95
27	10	95
27	11	95
27	12	95
27	13	95
27	14	95
27	15	95
27	16	95
28	1 & 16	2 31
28	2	1 35
28	3	1 62
28	4	1 08
28	5	2 16
28	6 7	2 97
28	8	1 49
28	9	2 70
28	10	1 49
28	11	1 08
28	12	1 62
28	13	3 78
28	14 15	2 70
29	1 & 16	2 97
29	2 & 3	4 59
29	4	1 35
29	5	1 49
29	6	95
29	7	95
29	8	95
29	9	2 03
29	10	1 35
29	11	1 08

Block.	Lot.	Tax & Penalty
29	12	2 81
29	13	95
29	14	6 48
29	15	1 08
30	1	do
30	2	do
30	3	do
30	4	do
30	5	do
30	6 7	[illegible]
30	8	1 08
30	9	do
30	10	do
30	12	do
30	13	do
30	14	do
30	15	do
30	16	do
31	1 & 16	3 78
31	2	1 08
31	3	do
31	4	do
31	5	do
31	6	do
31	7	do
31	8	do
31	9	do
31	10	do
31	11	do
31	12	do
31	13	do
31	14	1 35
31	15	1 03
32	1	do
32	2	do
32	3	2 43
32	4	78
32	5	1 08
32	6	1 08
32	7	3 78
32	8	3 78
32	9	1 08
32	10	1 08
32	11	do
32	12	do
32	13	do
32	16	2 70
33	1	1 08
33	2	do
33	3	2 43
33	4	1 08
33	5	do
33	6	do
33	7	do
33	8	do
33	9	do
33	10	do
33	11	do
33	12	do
33	13	do
33	14	do
33	15	do
33	16	do
34	1 2	3 24
34	3 4	8 37
34	5	95
[illegible]	6	[illegible]
34	7 8	2 16
35	1 8	10 13
35	2 7	7 56
35	3	1 08
35	6	do
35	7	do
36	1 2	6 48
36	3	1 08
36	4 5	28 89
36	6	1 08
36	7 8	2 43
37	1,2,7,8	4 59
37	3	1 08
37	4	do
37	5	do
37	6	do
38	1 2	26 46
38	3	1 08
38	4	do
38	5	do
38	6	do
38	7 8	2 70
39	1	2 16
39	2	3 78
39	3	1 22
39	4	1 08
39	5	do
39	6	do
39	7	2 70
39	8	6 48
40	1	1 62
40	2	1 08
40	3	1 08
40	8	2 03
41	1	1 08
41	2	do
41	3	do
41	4	do
41	5	do
41	6	do
41	7	do
41	8	do
42	1	do
42	2	do
42	3	do
42	4	do
42	5	do
42	6	do
42	7	do
42	8	do
43	1	1 78
43	2	1 49
43	3	3 08
43	4	do
43	5	do
43	6	do
43	7	do
43	8	3 65
44	1	95
44	2	1 62
44	3	do
44	4	95
44	5	95
44	6	95
44	7	1 22
44	8	6 48
45	1,2,7,8	8 10
45	3	95
45	4	95
45	5	2 43
45	6	95
46	1 8	9 99
46	2	95
46	3	95
46	4	95
46	5	1 75
46	6	95
46	7	2 16
47	1	1 08
47	2	95
47	3	95
47	4	95
47	5	95
47	6	

Daily Huntsville Confederate.

VOL. I. DALTON, GEO., SATURDAY MORNING FEBRUARY 6, 1864. NO. 174.

MEMBERS OF THE CONFEDERATE CONGRESS.

The first session of the 2d Congress will commence on the 19th February next. The following is a list of the Senators elect and those holding over, with the year annexed in which their respective terms of office expire, (18th of February each year); also, a list of the members elect of the House of Representatives, as far as ascertained:

SENATE.

ALABAMA—Richard W Walker, 1870; Rob't Jemison, 1868.

ARKANSAS—Robert W Johnson, 1870; Charles B Mitchell, 1868.

FLORIDA—James M Baker, 1870; A E Maxwell, 1866.

GEORGIA—Herschel V Johnson, 1870; Benjamin H Hill, 1868.

KENTUCKY ——, 1870; H C Burnett, 1868.

LOUISIANA—Edward Sparrow, 1868; Thomas J Semmes, 1866.

MISSISSIPPI—J W C Watson, 1870; Albert G Brown, 1868.

MISSOURI——, 1870; ——, 1866.

NORTH CAROLINA—Wm A Graham, 1870; Wm T Dortch, 1866.

SOUTH CAROLINA—James L Orr, 1868; Robert W Barnwell, 1866.

TENNESSEE——, 1870; Langdon C. Hayne, 1868.

TEXAS—W S Oldham, 1868; Louis T Wigfall, 1866.

VIRGINIA—R M T Hunter, 1868; Allen T Caperton, 1866.

HOUSE OF REPRESENTATIVES.

ALABAMA—1, Thomas J Foster; 2, William P Smith; 3, [illegible] W Cobb; 4, *M H Cruikshank; 5, Francis S Lyon; 6, W P Chilton; 7, David Clopton; 8, James L [illegible]; [illegible], *J S Dickinson.

ARKANSAS—We have no information of the election of Representatives to the next Congress.

FLORIDA—1, S St John Rogers; 2, R B Hilton.

GEORGIA—1, Julian Hartridge; 2, William E Smith; *Mark H. Blanford; 4, *Clifford Anderson; 5, *J T Shoemaker; 6, *J H Echols; 7, *James M Smith; 8, George N Lester; 9, *H P Bell; 10, *Warren Akin.

KENTUCKY—No election for next Congress.

LOUISIANA—1, Charles J. Villere; 2. Charles M Conrad; Duncan F Kenner; 4, Lucien J Dupre; 5, Henry Marshall; 6, John Perkins, Jr.

MISSISSIPPI—1, *J A Orr; 2, *W D Holder; 3, Israel Welch; 4, Henry C Chambers; 5, Otho R Singleton; 6, Ethel Barksdale, 7, *J T Lampkin.

MISSOURI—The present delegation were elected to hold office until their successors were elected. The question of qualification will be decided by the next Congress.

NORTH CAROLINA—1, W H N Smith; 2, R R Bridgers; 3, *J T Leach; 4, *Thomas C Fuller; 5, Josiah Turner, Jr; 6, *John A Gilmer; 7 *Samuel H Christian; 8, *J G Ramsay; 9, B S Gaither; 10, *George W Logan.

SOUTH CAROLINA—1, *James H Witherspoon; 2, W Porcher Miles; 3, Lewis M Ayer; 4, W D Simpson; 5, James Farrow; 6, W W Boyce.

TENNESSEE—1, J B Heiskell; 2, William C Swan; 3, *[illegible]; 4, *John P Murray; 5, H S Foote; 6, E A Keeble; 7, *James M Cullom; 8, *Thomas Menees; 9, J D C Atkins; 10, John V Wright; 11, David M C[illegible].

TEXAS—1, John A Wilcox; 2, Claiborne C. Herbert; [illegible] Branch; 4, Frank B Sexton; 5, J R Baylor; [illegible] S H Morgan.

VIRGINIA—1, *Robert L Montague; 2, Robert H Whitfield; 3, *Williams C Wickam; 4, Thomas S Gholson; 5, Thomas S Bocock; 6, John Goode, Jr; 7, Wm C Rives; 8, D C Dejarnette; 9, *David Funsten; 10, *F W M Holliday; 11, John B Baldwin; 12, Walter R Staples; 13, *Fayette McMullen; 14, Samuel Miller; 15, Robert Johnston; 16, Charles W Russell.

The asterisks (*) indicate new members—forty as far as ascertained.

[NA]MES OF THE MEMBERS OF THE PRESENT, OR FIRST CONGRESS.

We subjoin a list of the members of the Senate and House of Representatives of the present Congress:

SENATE.

President—Alexander H Stephens, of Georgia. *Cl'k*—J H Nash, of South Carolina. *Sergeant-at-Arms*—Lafayette H Fitzhugh, of Kentucky.

ALABAMA—*Clement C Clay, Robert Jemison, (elected to fill vacancy.)

ARKANSAS—*Robert W Johnson, Charles B Mitchell.

FLORIDA—A E Maxwell, *James M Baker.

GEORGIA—*Benjamin M Hill, Herschel V Johnson. (Elected to fill vacancy.)

KENTUCKY—H C Burnett, *William E Simms.

LOUISIANA—Edward Sparrow, Thomas J Semmes.

MISSISSIPPI—Albert G Brown, *James Phelan.

NORTH CAROLINA—*George Davis, William T Dortch.

SOUTH CAROLINA—Robert W Barnwell, James L Orr.

TENNESSEE—Langdon C Haynes, *G A Henry.

MISSOURI—John B Clark, (vacancy.)

TEXAS—Louis T Wigfall, W S Oldham.

VIRGINIA—R M T Hunter, Allen T Caperton.

Total number, 26. *Term of office expires on the 17th of February, 1864.

HOUSE OF REPRESENTATIVES.

Speaker—Thomas S Bocock, of Virginia—*Clerk*—Albert R Lamar, of Georgia. *Sergeant-at-Arms*—R H Wynn, of Alabama.

ALABAMA—1, Thomas J Foster; 2, William R Smith; 3, *John P Ralls; 4, *J L M Curry; 5, Francis S Lyon; 6, W P Chilton; 7, David Clopton; 8, James L Pugh; 9, *E S Dargan.

*ARKANSAS—1, Felix I Batson; Grandison D Royster; Augustus H Garland; 4, Thomas B Hanly.

FLORIDA—1, *James B Hawkins; R B Hilton.

GEORGIA—1, Julian Hartridge; 2, *Charles J Munnerlyn; 3, (vacant); 4, *Augustus B Kenan; 5, *David W Lewis; 6, *William W Clark, 7, *Robert P Trippe; 8, *Lucius J Gartrell; 9, *Hardy Strickland; 10, *Augustus R Wright.

KENTUCKY—1, W B Machen; 2, J W Crockett; H E Reed; 4, George W Ewing; 5, J S Chrisman; 6, T L Burnett; 7, H W Bruce; 8, G B Hodge; 9, E M Bruce; 10, J W Moore; 11, R J Breckinridge; 12, J M Elliott.

LOUISIANA—1, Charles J Villere; 2, Charles M Conrad; Duncan F Kenner; 4, Lucien J Dupre; 5, Henry Marshall; 6, John Perkins, Jr.

MISSISSIPPI—1, *J W Clapp; 2, *Reuben Davis; 3, Israel Welch; 4, H C Chambers; 5, O R Singleton; 6, E Barksdale; 7, *John J McRae.

*MISSOURI—1 (vacant); 2, Thomas A Harris; 3, Caspar W Bell; 4, A H Conrow; 5 George G Vest; 6, L W Freeman.

NORTH CAROLINA—1, W N H Smith; 2, Robert R Bridgers; Owen R Kenan; 4, F D McDowell; 5, Archibald H Arrington; 6, *J R McLean; 7, *Thomas S Ashe; 8, *William Lander; 9, B S Gaither; 10, *A T Davidson.

SOUTH CAROLINA—1, John McQueen; 2, W Porcher Miles; [illegible] Ayer; [illegible] Simpson, (elected to fill vacancy); [illegible] Farrow; W W Boyce.

TENNESSEE—1, J B Heiskell; 2, W G Swan; 3, *W H Tibbs; 4, *W L Gardenhire; 5, H S Foote; 6, *Meredith P Gentry; 7, *G W Jones; 8, Thomas Menees; 9, J D C Atkins; John V Wright; 11, David M Currin.

TEXAS—1, John A Wilcox; 2, Claiborne C. Herbert; 3, *Peter W Gray; 4, F B Sexton; 5, *Malcolm D Graham; 6, William B Wright.

VIRGINIA—1, M R H Garnett; *John R Chambers; 3, James Lyons; 4, *Charles F Collier; 5, Thomas S Bocock; [illegible] John Goode, Jr; 7, James P Holcombe; [illegible]; 9, David Funsten, (elected to fill vacancy); 10, Alexander R Boteler; 11, John B Baldwin; 12 Walter R. Staples; 13, *Walter Preston; 14, Samuel A Miller; 15, Robert Johnson; 16, Charles W Russell.

The whole number, one hundred and five.—The asterisks (*) indicate the members who have not been reelected [illegible] Arkansas, Kentucky and Missouri.

Miss Rebecca Cox, of Amite county, Mississippi, a little girl about thirteen years of age, has sent to [illegible] soldiers within the past two [illegible] two hundred yards of jeans, several [illegible], and many pairs of socks, [illegible] of her own fair hands. She [illegible] example and deserves [illegible].

A [illegible] is [illegible] to go into operation at Columbus, Geo.

Gen. McClellan's Report.

We find in late Northern papers frequent allusions to the Official Report of General McClellan, a volume of twelve hundred pages. We can only furnish our readers with a brief extract. It appears that the spirit that actuated this ablest of Federal leaders was not appreciated at Washington. The popularity of Gen. McClellan as a candidate for the Presidency is the measure of the conservatism of the Northern masses. The cause of his removal by President Lincoln is made apparent by the appended letter addressed to the Northern autocrat:

"Mr. President: You have been fully informed that the rebel army is in our front, with the purpose of overwhelming us by attacking our positions or reducing us by blocking our river communications. I cannot but regard our condition as critical, and I earnestly desire, in view of possible contingencies, to lay before your Excellency, for your private consideration, my general views concerning the existing state of the rebellion, although they do not strictly come within the scope of my official duties. These views amount to convictions, and are deeply impressed upon my mind and heart.

If secession is successful other dissolutions are clearly to be seen in the future. Let neither military disaster, political faction, nor foreign war shake your settled purpose to enforce the equal operation of the laws of the United States upon the people of every State.

"The time has come when the Government must determine upon a civil and military policy covering the whole ground of our national trouble. The responsibility of determining, and declaring, and supporting such civil and military policy, and of directing the whole course of national affairs in regard to the rebellion, must now be assumed and exercised by you or our cause will be lost. The Constitution gives you power sufficient even for the present terrible exigency.

"This rebellion has assumed the character of war; and as such it should be regarded, and it should be conducted upon the highest principles known to Christian civilization. It should be a war looking to the subjugation of the people of any State in any event. It should not be a war upon population, but against armed forces and political organization. Neither confiscation of property, political executions of persons, territorial organizations of States, or forcible abolition of slavery should be contemplated for a moment. In prosecuting the war all private property and unarmed persons should be strictly protected, subjected only to the necessity of military operation. All private property taken for military use should be paid or receipted for; pillage and waste should be treated as high crimes; all unnecessary trespass sternly prohibited, and offensive demeanor by the military toward citizens promptly rebuked. Military arrests should not be tolerated, except in places where active hostilities exist, and oaths not required by enactments constitutionally made should be neither demanded nor received. Military government should be confined to the preservation of public order and the protection of political rights. Military power should not be allowed to interfere with the relations of servitude, either by supporting or impairing the authority of the master, except for repressing disorder, as in other cases. Slaves contraband under the act of Congress, seeking military protection, should receive it. The right of the Government to appropriate permanently to its own service claims of slave labor should be asserted, and the right of the owner to compensation therefor should be recognized. This principle might be extended upon the grounds of military necessity and security to all the slaves within a particular State, thus working manumission in such State; and in Missouri, perhaps in Western Virginia also, and possibly even in Maryland, the expediency of such a measure is only a question of time.

"A system of policy thus constitutional and conservative, and pervaded by the influences of Christianity and freedom, would receive the support of almost all truly loyal men, would deeply impress the Rebel masses and all foreign nations, and it may be humbly hoped that it would commend itself to the favor of the Almighty.

"Unless the principles governing the future conduct of our struggle shall be made known and approved, the effort to obtain requisite forces will be almost hopeless. A declaration of radical views especially upon slavery, will rapidly disintegrate our present armies.

"The policy of the Government must be supported by concentration of military power.—The national forces should not be dispensed in expeditions, posts of occupation, and numerous armies, but should be mainly collected into masses and brought to bear upon the armies of the Confederate States. Those armies thoroughly defeated, the political structure which they support would soon cease to exist.

"In carrying out any system of policy which you may form, you will require a commander-in-chief of the army, one who possesses your confidence, understands your views, and is competent to execute your orders by directing the military forces of the nation to the accomplishment of the objects by you proposed. I do not ask that place for myself. I am willing to serve you in such a position as you may assign me; and will do so as faithfully as ever subordinate served superior.

"I may be on the bank of eternity, and, as I hope forgiveness from my Maker, I have written this letter with sincerity toward you, and from love for my country."

New Orleans papers, received at Mobile, report that the cold spell at the beginning of the year in Louisiana, destroyed the ratoons of the sugar plant, and perhaps much of the cane bedded for planting. This will seriously affect the sugar crop of next year. It was also thought that the extensive orange groves of the State had been killed. It was the coldest spell known for at least thirty years.

There is a prospect of an abundance of salt in Alabama the present year at very low rates. A large stock is now on hand, with the salting season closed, some of it purchased on speculation at higher prices than those now ruling.—In addition to this stock, contracts are being entered into between parties and the Governor nearly every day, for the manufacture of salt at as low as four and even three dollars per bushel.

A Federal opinion of the Prospects this spring.

A correspondent of the Chicago *Times* writing from Washington, gives his views upon the prospects of Lincoln's Generals the coming campaign. It will be seen that while he is confident that no headway can be made in Virginia, he is not at all sanguine of any success in the West:

From all that can be learned of the plans and resources of the Confederates, it is evident that they are fully prepared for a vigorous spring and summer campaign. Their armies are much less numerous than ours. It cannot be shown that they have quite 400,000 troops, but they are all well disciplined and in a defensive war are equal to 700,000 acting offensively. It seems to be understood that at the opening of the spring campaign, they will be divided between Gen. Lee, on the line of the Rapidan, and Gen. Johnston, between Chattanooga and Atlanta, with a small force under Beauregard, at Charleston. The general features of the war, on their part, will be strictly defensive Our armies, when they advance, will meet with little resistance until they are down into the interior of the country, but then they will be assailed with what the Confederates will try to make overwhelming numbers. Military men understand perfectly that, until Richmond falls, Charleston cannot be taken. In the East, therefore, the exertions of the Confederates will be confined chiefly to the defence of their capital; and it is not likely that any change will be made in the mode of conducting that defense which has hitherto been so successful.

In the West, it is likely that our operations will carry us into what has hitherto been *terra incognita*. It will be seen, on examining a good map, that between Chattanooga and Atlanta there are two rivers. The first is the North branch of the Coosa River, which extends from Rome to Ellijay, a distance of sixty miles. The second is the Etowah River, which extends from Rome to Dahlonega, a distance of seventy miles. Both of these rivers cover Atlanta, and both form admirable defensive lines against an army advancing from Chattanooga. It is probable that it is the design of General Johnston to make use of these two defensive lines to their fullest extent. It seems that an army, advancing from Chattanooga to Atlanta, must cross both these streams at some point.—If Mine Run, in its insignificance, formed an insurmountable barrier to the advance of Meade's army, what cannot be done with two, as small streams as these? The practicability of turning them will, of course, occur to Gen. Grant. But to turn them will require a circuitous march through the untrodden defiles and across the trackless mountains of North Georgia—an operation quite as hazardous to an army as an attempt to cross the two rivers in the direct line of its march. There is no doubt, however, that the conqueror of Vicksburg will be found equal to all the exigencies of the campaign. Progress in the war may be made in the West, but there is little hope of any progress in the East.

House of Representatives.

Tuesday, Feb. 2.—Mr. Garland, of Arkansas, from the Committee on the Judiciary, reported a bill to amend the act to prohibit the transportation and sale of certain articles in any port or place within the Confederate States in possession of the enemy, and to prohibit the barter and sale of certain articles therein named to alien enemies.

The following is a copy of the bill:

"That in all cases where persons have furnished or may hereafter furnish, by contract, with the officers of the Confederate States, by the advice or consent of the Secretary of War or President, to the Government, supplies for the use of the army and navy of the Confederate States, such person shall be exempt from the operation of the act to which this is an amendment."

The bill was taken up and passed.

MILITARY COURTS.

Mr. Dargan, of Alabama, from the Committee on the Judiciary, reported a bill to amend an act to organize military courts to attend the armies of the Confederate States in the field and to define the powers of said courts.

The bill authorizes the President to establish a military court in North Alabama, which shall set at such times and places as said court may direct, and shall have all the powers and jurisdiction given to the military courts by the said act; the said court to cease to exist after one year from the passage of this act, unless longer continued by Congress.

The bill was taken up and passed.

Mr. Gray, of Texas, from the Judiciary Committee, reported a bill supplementary to the several acts in relation to military courts.

The bill proposes to abolish the office of provost marshal in said courts; to give to the clerks the rank and pay of captains of cavalry; to give all military courts the power to compel the attendance of witnesses, and by the same processes as provided by the laws of a State; to authorize the President to organize military courts when required, not exceeding one for each State; to allow the right of challenge as to the competency of members of courts to the same extent as now allowed by law; and to cashier any member of a court who shall be intoxicated while on duty, or so as to prevent his attending to his duties.

Mr. Gray asked the immediate consideration of the bill, and it was, after various propositions and suggestions, laid on the table and ordered to be printed, on motion of Mr. Baldwin.

SLAVE IMPORTATIONS INTO KENTUCKY.—The Legislature of Kentucky, on the 13th, passed a bill prohibiting the importation of slaves into that State. The influx of slaves, says the despatch has had the effect of cheapening the price of the stock on hand, and overflowing the market.

LARGE PAYMENT.—The Mobile and Ohio Rail Road Company paid to the Treasurer of Mississippi, a few days ago, the sum of $230,000, the amount due the State by the company. If we mistake not, says the *Clarion*, this money was borrowed a few years ago in gold and silver, from the Chickasaw School Fund. The Mississippi Legislature, at its last session, passed a bill to receive our present currency in payment.

Mirabeau thus wrote to a young lady who had fallen in love with his genius, and wished to know how he looked: "Fancy his Satanic majesty, after having had the small-pox—and such am I."

TELEGRAPHIC.

Reports of the Press Association.

CHARLESTON, Feb. 5.—Eighty-five shots were fired at the city, to-day. No firing at Sumter. The enemy have been at work, all day, hauling ammunition to Gregg's and Cumming's Point batteries.

There has been a large fire on Folly Island, to-day, supposed to be the burning of a Yankee hospital.

A gunboat, in Edisto River, is lying high and dry. It is believed she will be destroyed.

MORRISTOWN, Feb. 5.—Private W. H. Roberts, Co A., 21st Mississippi Regiment, Humphries's Brigade, was shot, to day, for deserting his regiment to join a cavalry regiment.—Trains are, now, running to Rogersville Junction. We have nothing of interest to report from the front.

ORANGE C. H. Feb. 2.—Kinchloe's Prince William Cavalry sent in a batch of prisoners, captured near Kettle Run, Fauquier Co., Va., on Sunday last. They belong to the fifth corps, and report everything quiet in their lines. Our scouts report the enemy granting furloughs, quite liberally, to re-enlisted men.

RICHMOND, Feb. 5.—In Senate, to-day, the House bill to increase the efficiency of the Army by the employment of negroes in certain capacities, was reported upon favorably, by the Senate Military Committee, and placed on the calendar.

Several appropriation bills were amended and passed. One amendment proposed that no salary should be paid an officer appointed under the Provisional Government, unless he had been re-appointed and confirmed since the permanent Government was established; but, at the solicitation of several Senators, it was withdrawn.

The Bill, exempting farmers and planters, who furnished substitutes, was, on motion, taken up from the table—yeas 14, nays 8—and made the special order for Tuesday next, one o'clock.

In the House, the evidence of the re-enlistment of large numbers of troops from various States was presented and resolutions of thanks were adopted.

The Senate bill to organise a General staff for the army was discussed, but not disposed of. Both Houses were in secret session the most of the day.

MOBILE, Feb. 5.—A special to the *Evening News*, from Clinton, Miss., Feb. 4th, says that Sherman's two corps, under McPherson and Hurlburt, are advancing. Gen. Jackson has fought them all day. They made but two miles to-day. Their camp, to-night, is six or eight miles below Clinton. The prisoners report 30,000. Gen. Ross whipped them on the Yazoo yesterday, hand to hand, with pistols.

A special to the Registor from Jackson, 4th, says, the enemy commenced crossing Big Black yesterday, and threw over six regiments of infantry, two of cavalry and two batteries, on the railroad bridges, and attempted to cross at Messenger, but failed. They are now, attempting to cross at Birdsongs. The city is full of rumors and excitement, but confident.

☞ Government has established a horse infirmary for broken down stock in the army. It is located in Laurens County, Georgia, twelve miles from Oconee Station, on the Central railroad. Three thousand acres of land are employed for the purpose; the stables are adapted to peculiar diseases; fifty negroes and eight white men are employed and two professional veterinary surgeons. Thirty cases of glanders, heretofore supposed to have been fatal, have been cured in these hospitals, and of the whole number of broken down horses who would have died in the field, eighty five per cent. have been saved. A similar institution should exist in every State in the Confederacy.

Yankee Peace Resolutions.

On the 14th ult., Hon. I. Rogers, of New Jersey, introduced a resolution in the House, that the Federal Government should appoint commissioners to meet rebel commissioners as equals and to concoct measures of peace with them.

The resolution was rejected, but received 42 votes in its favor.

"How is it," said a gentleman to Sheridan, "that your name has not an O attached to it? Your father is Irish, and, no doubt, illustrious."

"No family has a better right to an O than ours," said Sheridan, "for we *owe* everybody."

BURNT.—We regret to learn that the gin house of Judge Martin, on the Line Creek road, some four or five miles from the city, was burnt on Sunday last—and also some fifty bales of cotton.—*Mont. Mail, 3d.*

The frost went to the flower to marry, and said to the flower, "Wilt thou?" and the flower *wilted*.

HIGH PRICES OF NEGROES.—Mr. A. J. Salinas, Broker and Auctioneer, made the following sales, Monday morning, at auction [belonging to an estate:] Jim, 22 years of age, field hand and ploughman, $6100; Sam, 20 years of age, field hand and ploughman, $5850. Average, $5975 each.

A literary reputation is to be built at this day like the walls of Jerusalem with a trowel in one hand for plastering friends—a sword in the other for smiting enemies.

News Summary.

The forces under Maj. Lee, of Atlanta, are very effective in arresting deserters and stragglers in that city.

There are several hundred cases of small pox among the Federal prisoners at Saulsbury, N. C.

The Government has adopted measures to perfect our communications with the Trans-Mississippi. The transit of the river will be effected at several points, and letters will be safely transferred to their destination.

A man in battle is not allowed to whistle to keep his courage up, and the whistling of the bullets doesn't have that tendency.

That young man who drinks, bets, swears, gambles and idles away his time, is on a thin place in the ice.

An author, ridiculing the idea of ghosts, asks how a dead man can get into a locked room.—Probably with a skeleton-key.

Horace Walpole tells a story of the Lord Mayor of London in his time, who, having heard that a friend had the small-pox twice, and died of it, inquired if he died the first time or the second.

THE VALUE OF GOLD.—The Richmond Sentinel states that a gentleman from abroad is now boarding at one of the hotels in that city, and enjoying its handsome accommodations, who pays his bills in specie at sixty cents per day. From which the Sentinel argues, and correctly, that the difference between gold and Confederate notes is not altogether a depreciation of the latter, but in great part an appreciation of the former.

Gold is no longer a correct standard of value. It is wanted for blockade running. So much of it has been carried off in that way that it has become scarce, and sixty cents of it will buy the equivalent of five dollars at the old value. In this view of the matter—undoubtedly the correct view in the main—treasury notes have not depreciated more than two-thirds, that is, three for one.

A new commotion has been excited in the New York custom-house, by the arrest and confinement in Fort LaFayette of Mr. A. N. Palmer, charged with being in collusion with parties engaged in contraband trade with the Southern States, and abusing his position in the collector's office to further that trade. Mr. Palmer is a member of the Republican [N. Y.] State Committee.

GENERAL ORDER,

Organizing Volunteer and Conscript Bureau of Geographical Department No. 2.

HED QR'S. VOL. AND CON. BUREAU, DEP'T NO. 2,
Marietta, Ga., July 27, 1863.

General Orders No. 1.]

THE undersigned having been by orders of General Joseph E. Johnston, in obedience to an order of the Secretary of War, placed in charge of the Conscript service in Department No. 2, and the officers and agencies of the Conscript Bureau of the Government within the States of Tennessee, Alabama and Mississippi, having been by the Secretary of War transferred and assigned to duty under me as Superintendent of Conscripts for this Department, it is ordered that

Those officers and the organizations as heretofore existing within this Department, will continue their labors without change until otherwise ordered. The President, by his proclamation, having called out all men liable to duty under the Conscript law to the age of forty-five years, all such are required to report themselves for duty to the enrolling officers of their respective districts, or to the officers of the recruiting bureau. Upon so reporting, they will be received and enrolled as volunteers. If they fail so to do until arrested, they will be enrolled as Conscripts. In addition to the camps of instructions established by order of the War Department, and now existing in the States composing this geographical department, the system of rendezvous established by the chief of the bureau of the army of Tennessee, will be continued. The officers engaged in the last named organization, belonging to the army of Tennessee, and subject to be withdrawn from this bureau by the exigencies of the service will not for the present be blended with the former organization. The two corps of officers will work in their respective spheres, and under the orders heretofore existing. Both organizations will arrest all deserters and stragglers, receive all volunteers who tender themselves, and will arrest all Conscripts between the ages of eighteen and forty-five.

The commanders of rendezvous will furnish the commandants of conscripts for their States with the names and descriptive lists of all Conscripts by them arrested and sent to the army.

Each class of officers will respect the decisions of the other, and while engaged in the same labor, will avoid all conflicts. Should any collisions of authority occur, they will be referred to the common superior directing the operations of both corps. Each organization will keep a record of its proceedings, and will make weekly reports to the General Superintendent of both organizations.

The hopes of the country depend upon the labors of this Bureau in strengthening the armies of Tennessee and Mississippi. No higher motive to exertion could be presented to the patriot soldier. We have the population required for this purpose, and it is our duty to put it in these armies. Proper efforts will accomplish it and deliver our country from desolation and despotism.

GID. J. PILLOW, Brig. Gen. C. S. A.,
and Sup't Vol. and Con. Dep't. No. 2.

☞ Papers in East Tennessee, Montgomery Advertiser and Mail, Mobile Register and Tribune, Selma Reporter and Mississippi papers will publish one week, and forward their accounts to Major Cheatham, A. Q. M. at these Headquarters. [aug?—tw.

The Daily Southern Guardian

VOLUME VI. COLUMBIA, S. C., MONDAY MORNING, FEBRUARY 8, 1864. NUMBER 224

Notice.

Subscribers to the *Guardian* are respectfully informed that on and after Monday, the 11th instant, the following will be the terms of subscription and advertising:

Daily Guardian, 6 months	$15 00
For any less time, per month	3 00
For *Tri-Weekly Guardian*, 6 months	10 00
For any less time, per month	2 00
Weekly Guardian, 6 months	4 00

ADVERTISING.

Two Dollars a Square of ten lines, for each insertion.

Terms in all cases CASH.

January 9, 1864.

TELEGRAPHIC.

REPORTS OF THE PRESS ASSOCIATION.

Entered according to the Act of Congress in the year 1863, by J. S. THRASHER, in the Clerk's office of the District Court of the Confederate States for the Northern District of Georgia.

From Charleston.

CHARLESTON, Feb. 7.—The enemy have ceased firing on the city, but continue working on their batteries and hauling ammunition. Nothing else of interest.

From Virginia.

RICHMOND, Feb. 7.—There is a report that the Yankees are advancing in considerable force towards this city from the Peninsula. Heavy firing was heard this morning in the direction of Bottom's Bridge. No particulars received.

RICHMOND, Feb. 7.—Information from below is meagre and conflicting. A force of the enemy, estimated at about 5 regiments, is reported moving in this direction. One report is they were repulsed. Another that they crossed Chickahominy near White Oak Swamp. No apprehension exists here of their further approach. The enemy's movements is believed to be a raid for the destruction of property, or a diversion to draw attention from movements elsewhere.

Official Dispatch from Gen. Lee.

RICHMOND, Feb. 5.—The following dispatch has just been received:

ORANGE C. H., Feb. 6.—*Gen. S. Cooper:* On the 30th, Gen. Rosser captured a train of 93 wagons, loaded with United States stores and forage, on the way from New Creek to Petersburg. They also captured 300 mules and 20 prisoners. The guard of 800 infantry escaped to the mountains. Our loss was 250 killed and wounded.

Information of an advance upon Petersburg having been received, the garrison evacuated it during the night. On the 2d, Rosser destroyed the bridges over Patterson Creek and captured 40 prisoners. 270 prisoners, 50 wagons, 1,200 cattle and 500 sheep have been brought off. Gen. Rosser has shown great energy and skill, and his command deserve great credit.

(Signed,) R. E. LEE, General.

From East Tennessee.

MORRISTOWN, Feb. 6.—Private Geo. Smith, Company A, 48th Alabama Regiment, was shot to-day for desertion.

Maj. Giltness' Brigade made a dash upon the enemy's outposts on Thursday and captured 11 and killed 8. Trains now run to this point.

Latest Northern and European News.

RICHMOND, Feb 6.—A flag of truce boat arrived at City Point to-day. The Baltimore *American*, of the 4th, says Denmark absolutely rejects the ultimatum of Prussia and Austria calling for the withdrawal of the movement relating to the Constitution, upon the penalty of their occupation of Schleswig. In consequence of this refusal, the envoys of those powers left Copenhagen.

The proposition for the new French loan, of £12 000 000 sterling met with extraordinary success, the bids exceeding thirteen times the amount required.

The London stock exchange was feverish, in consequence of the warlike aspect of affairs in Germany.

Austrian troops were on the way to occupy Schleswig Holstein.

The Confederate loan has advanced to 44.

The Baltimore *American* says Averill overtook Rosser near Springfield, when a severe engagement ensued. On the 3d, the rebels were defeated, and a number of prisoners taken. Patterson's Creek was recaptured. The rebels have captured the burnt steamer Serge, on the Kanawha. Brigadier General Schommon and one of his staff were captured with the boat.

The attempt of the rebels to take Newbern was handsomely repulsed. It is believed the Union forces are able to hold the city. On the 26th, Col. Phillips drove Roddy to the North side of the Tennessee, captured his train, 200 cattle, and 600 sheep.

Gold unchanged, $1.46.

RICHMOND, Feb. 7.—The Yankee House of Representatives has passed the bill reviving the grade of Lieutenant General, and recommended Gen. Grant for the position.

James B. Clay died recently in Canada.

A New Orleans letter in the *Herald*, dated 24th, says in all parts of this city it is believed Mobile is about being attacked by Farragut on water and the troops of Banks on land.

La France says the Florida has challenged the Kearsage to a fair fight, and the latter having accepted, they intend to go a few miles out to sea and settle their differences at cannon range.

The Alabama has destroyed the Yankee ship Contest in the Straits of Sunda. Vessel and cargo valued at one million dollars.

WILMINGTON, Feb. 4.

To General S. Cooper:

On the 2d instant, Gen. Martin, with the 17th and 42d, and Col. Jackson's command from Kenansville, broke the railroad at Shepherdsville, driving the enemy from their works at Newport barracks and across Newport river.

W. H. C. WHITING, Major-General.

DALTON, Feb. 4.—A flag of truce has just arrived at Catoosa, two miles this side of Ringgold, with twenty-eight persons from Knoxville, ladies and gentlemen, sent out as violent secessionists.

The enemy are reported to have evacuated Knoxville, and are retreating to Maysville.

Gen. Jo. Johnston's Chief of Staff.

General W. W. Mackall arrived in Macon on Thursday, on a short visit to his family in Vineville. He has accepted the position of Chief of Staff to General Johnston, and for that purpose has resigned his command in Mississippi. Gen. Mackall was Chief of General Bragg's staff in the same army up to a time a little subsequent to the battle of Chickamauga.

The European Exodus.

The number of emigrants who arrived at New York last year was 155,223—more than double the number of the year preceding. We get from a Washington letter, dated 23d ult., in the New York *Journal of Commerce*, the following particulars of this vast tide of humanity setting towards America. The statement is for the eleven months of 1863, omitting December, and is copied from the official records at the Yankee capital:

From Ireland	36 691
From Germany	32 801
From England	16 898
From Denmark	1,567
From Switzerland	1,078
From France	1,195
From Wales	1,083
From Scotland	1,664
From Sweden	1,359
From Italy	405
From Holland	379
From Belgium	456
From West Indies	242
From Spain	152
Various others	374
Total	148,519

It is difficult for a plain man to understand why the emigration has been more than doubled within the twelvemonth, without assuming that it is stimulated by the Yankee Government.

From the North.

From the New York *Herald* of the 1st inst. we copy the following account of the capture by Gen. Early of a Yankee army train in a severe fight in Hardy county, Va. It may be taken as confirmatory of the report of Gen. Early's success in the movement which he is known to have made:

HEADQ'RS DEP'T WESTERN VIRGINIA, January 31, 1864.

Again we are in the midst of excitement and activity, caused by a severe conflict that took place yesterday afternoon in the neighborhood of Williamsport, Hardy county, and which lasted, with considerable persistence and severity, for four hours.

On Thursday night a train of about eighty wagons was sent out from New Creek, heavily laden with commissary stores for the garrison at Petersburg, and accompanying the train was an escort of 800 men, being detachments from the 23d Illinois, (Irish Brigade,) 4th Virginia cavalry, 2d Maryland, 1st and 14th Virginia infantry, and 100 of the Ringgold cavalry battalion, the whole under command of Colonel J. W. Snyder.

Nothing unusual occurred until the train got about three miles south of Williamsport, when it was suddenly set upon at different points by open and concealed forces of the enemy.

Although somewhat surprised by the suddenness of the attack, the guard at once formed and deployed for action. Then it was that a hand fight ensued, commencing at 3 o'clock in the afternoon and lasting for over four hours, at the expiration of which time it was found that we had about 80 in killed and wounded, rank and file. The enemy's loss is said to be about 100.

In the early part of the fight the rebels opened fire from four pieces of artillery. The superiority of the enemy's strength—there being in all about 2 000 men—also gave them an advantage in outflanking movements, and the enemy exercised his ingenuity simultaneously to operate on the front, rear and flanks of Col. Snyder's command.

The enemy, however, completely failed of his object, which seemed to be to try to surround, and, if possible, to capture the whole party. Several times the rebel lines were broken, and several times the rebel charges were repulsed.

At last, as night closed, the superior numbers of the rebels, and not their great fighting qualities, gained them a success.

At one time the train was in a fair way of being entirely saved; but owing to the excitable skedaddling propensities of some few of the teamsters, and the effect of their conduct on others, a kind of panic was the result. A portion of the train was saved, notwithstanding the above mentioned misfortunes. On hearing of the engagement, Col. Mulligan at once sent reinforcements to Col. Snyder.

A later dispatch than the above, says that the command of Col Thorburn, which comprised the garrison at Petersburg, had succeeded in making their escape by a mountain road, passing between two of our columns, with all their trains, guns, &c.

The dispatch says that next morning General Early shelled the evacuated fortifications.

A dispatch from Washington states that dispatches had been received at the Yankee War Department, from General Kelly, confirming the capture of the trains above alluded to.

FROM EAST TENNESSEE.

The latest dispatch from Knoxville announces that the rebels had captured and driven off 800 head of cattle. Longstreet has "changed his front," and occupied the rich Valley of Tennessee, upon which the Union army depended for subsistence.

From Mississippi.

MOBILE, February 5.—A special dispatch to the *Evening News*, dated Clinton, the 4th, says that Sherman's two corps, under McPherson and Hurlbut, were advancing.

Gen. Jackson has fought them all day. They made but two miles to-day, and camped to-night six or eight miles below Clinton.

Prisoners report them thirty thousand strong.

Gen. Ross whipped them on the Yazoo yesterday hand to hand with pistols.

The enemy commenced crossing the Big Black yesterday.

They threw over six regiments of infantry, two of cavalry, and two batteries at the railroad bridge.

They attempted to cross at Messenger's, but failed.

They are now attempting to cross at Birdsong's.

DALTON, Feb. 4.—Information from Sand Mountain this morning states that the Federals there or in Wili's Valley, are four thousand strong, on this side of the river, at Larkin's Landing, near Coffeetown, foraging. There is one regiment at Stevenson, two at Bridgeport, two at Shell Mound, and two at Running water.

On the 27th, the enemy sent two brigades of negroes to reinforce Knoxville.

The enemy expects to abandon Knoxville.

Their artillery is being removed from Chattanooga towards Stevenson, probably for forage.

Out of three Yankee brigades only forty men re-enlisted. The Kentuckians, to a man, refused to re-enlist.

The Yankees say they will have to fall back to the north side of the river.

The steamer Advance brought, on her recent trip, 10,000 pairs of shoes, 12,000 blankets and 8,000 pairs of cards.

NAPOLEON AND MEXICO.—The Paris correspondent of the *Courier des Etats Unis*, M. Gaillardet, in his last letter, gives the following interesting particulars of the reception of Marshal Forey by the Emperor:

The marshal had hardly reached Paris when he was authorized to visit Compiegne, where he had an interview with the Emperor. At the close of this interview His Majesty seemed quite anxious and thoughtful. There are two signs by which the Emperor may be known to be anxious. He twists the ends of his long moustache, or slips from one finger to another the two rings which he commonly wears, one of them a present from his mother, and the other from his wife. When these rings are seen flying from one hand to another, and his hands are crossed behind his back, everybody knows that this concentrated and self commanded nature is undergoing one of the greatest agitations of which it is susceptible.

The Emperor dislikes to be watched and have people divine what he is thinking about. Just before the Italian war he said to the Duke of Montebello, "I am tired this morning; I have a headache," "Your Majesty's anxiety is intelligent," replied the Duke, "when one thinks how complicated the political situation is." The Emperor curtly replied, "I have a headache because I worked till 2 a. m., on my Life of Cæsar."

COMFORT FOR SUBSTITUTE MEN.—The substitute men, who are now so miserable at being forced in the army, should take courage from the following paragraph from a late Mississippi paper:

A son of a Mrs. Forrest, about thirteen years of age, residing in Choctaw county, Mississippi, committed suicide one day last week. It appears that this boy was exceedingly anxious to go to the army, and had become a great annoyance to his mother about going, which she was decidedly opposed to—he being too young. So his mother whipped him, and he then took down a double barrel shotgun, cocked it, put the muzzle to his head, pulled trigger with his big toe and shot his brains out.

Congressional.

RICHMOND, Feb. 5.—In the Senate to-day the House bill to increase the efficiency of the army by the employment of negroes in certain capacities, was reported upon favorably by the Senate Military Committee, and placed upon the calendar.

The General Appropriation bill was amended and passed. One amendment proposed that no salary be paid any officers appointed under the Provisional Government unless they have been reappointed and confirmed since the Permanent Government, but, at the solicitation of several Senators, this was withdrawn.

The bill exempting farmers and planters who have furnished substitutes was, on motion, taken up from the table—yeas 14, nays 8. It was made the special order for Tuesday next at one o'clock.

SIEGE MATTERS—TWO HUNDRED AND TWELFTH DAY.—The enemy's firing upon the city continues steady. Eighty five shots were fired from half past five o'clock Thursday to half-past five Friday evening. There has been no further firing on Fort Sumter. The monitors and land batteries ceased firing on the wreck Thursday night, the former moving back to their usual anchorage.

The Yankees are still working on Battery Gregg, and were also very busy during Friday hauling ammunition to Gregg and the Cummings' Point batteries. Our batteries kept up a slow but steady fire at their working parties with some effect. A large fire was observed on Folly Island all day, supposed to be the burning of a Yankee hospital. A Yankee gunboat in North Edisto was also reported hard aground Friday, lying high and dry. The Yankees were making great efforts Friday night to release her, but had not succeeded up to a late hour.

The number of vessels inside the bar continues about the same.—*Courier, 6th.*

The following official dispatch from Commander Wood, gives the particulars of the destruction of the gunboat mentioned in the dispatch of Gen. Pickett:

KINSTON, Feb 4, 1864.

Hon. S. R. Mallory:

The force under my command boarded and captured, last night, the United States gunboat Underwriter, four guns and ninety men and officers.

Her position was within musket range of several strong works; one of which was raking the vessel during the time we had possession, and her not having steam up caused me to burn her.

Our loss is twenty killed and wounded, and four missing; the enemy's unknown.

J. TAYLOR WOOD.

We learn by a gentleman who came up on the York river railroad, that two transports, convoyed by a gunboat, were near West Point yesterday. The Yankees, reported to be three thousand strong, are said to be advancing up the Peninsula. On Friday last, twenty-five of our cavalry were captured at a ball in Gloucester county. They had been home recruiting, and the house where they were receiving the hospitality of their friends was surrounded, and the party taken.—*Rich. Sentinel, 4th.*

RATHER BE HUNG.—Force, recently convicted and sentenced to the penitentiary for the murder of Dixon, bears his fate with manly resignation. On his way to the jail, after the verdict had been announced, he expressed his regret that the jury, if they believed him guilty of murder, did not sentence him to be hung, as he greatly preferred that to an ignominious imprisonment in the penitentiary.

Yankee naval officers assert that Charleston cannot be taken this winter.

RECRUITS WANTED FOR THE 1ST S. C. CAVALRY, COL. J. L. BLACK, COMMANDING.

THE detachment sent home under my command to procure remount horses, will rendezvous at and leave Chesterville, S. C., on the 15th of February next, for Virginia. This will afford Recruits an excellent opportunity of sending their horses through. Any one wishing to attach themselves to this Regiment, can address me at Yorkville, S. C., or report at Chesterville on the above mentioned day.

J. WILSON MARSHALL, Lieut., com'g Detach. 1st S. C. C.

jan 15—fmw13

NOTICE.

ALL persons having demands against the Estate of Rev. ELIAS B. HORT, deceased will present them duly attested, and all indebted to the same will make payment in Charleston to

dec 31—1am3m* I. E. HOLMES, Adm'r.

NOTICE.

BIDS for furnishing WOOD will be received at the office [Robert Bryce's Store] of the Columbia Mutual Supply Association.

jan 21—thstu H. P. GREEN, Chairman.

STRAYED,

FROM THOS. and B. W. TAYLOR'S plantation, a HOUND DOG PUPPY, about six months old—white, with small black specks; around the right ear and eye he is black, around the other, white. I will pay a suitable reward for his recovery, or any information leading to the recovery of him. H. R. TYLER.

feb 3—6*

ANNUAL MEETING OF THE STOCKHOLDERS OF THE South Carolina Railroad Company. AND OF THE SOUTHWESTERN RAILROAD BANK

THE ANNUAL MEETING OF THE STOCKHOLDERS of the above institutions will be held in the city of Columbia, on the SECOND TUESDAY in February next, it being the ninth day of the month.

Place of meeting—City Hall, on Main street. Hour of convening—11 a. m.

On the day following (Wednesday), there will be an election held at the same place, between the hours of 9 a. m. and 3 p. m., for FIFTEEN DIRECTORS OF THE RAILROAD COMPANY and THIRTEEN DIRECTORS OF THE BANK. A committee to verify proxies will attend.

The attention of the Stockholders is called to the following resolution, adopted at the Annual Meeting in 1854:

Resolved, That every Stockholder who shall have owned his stock for three months previous to the General Annual Meeting of Stockholders, be permitted to pass on the Road to and from said meeting free of charge, and that every Stockholder who shall have owned five or more shares for three months previous to General Annual Meeting of Stockholders, be permitted to pass on the Road to and from said meeting, with his immediate family, free of charge, and that the resolution of February 12, 1851, upon the subject, be and is hereby rescinded.

J. R. EMERY, Sec'ry.

jan 18—mwf10 tu1

A CALL FOR VOLUNTEERS For Twelve Months' Confederate Service in the State!

COLUMBIA, S. C., Jan 22, 1864.

HAVING received instructions from the Bureau of Conscription at Richmond, thro' the Commandant of Conscripts for South Carolina, to raise SIX COMPANIES OF MOUNTED MEN for the purpose of arresting Deserters and delinquents from Conscription, and also for the purpose of resisting any "local invasions" or raids that may be attempted by the Abolitionists; Such authority on my part is thus made known to the citizens of the State in order that this most important service may be rendered the great cause of Southern Independence.

It is proposed to form the Battalion from "Exempts and Non-conscripts." Each company to consist of not less than sixty, nor more than one hundred, rank and file; to elect its own officers, and to furnish its own horses. Arms (sabre and carbine) and accoutrements will be furnished by the Confederate Government; and persons desirous of joining the corps can report, either individually or in organized companies, to the nearest District or Congressional Enrolling Officer, who is authorized to muster in and report them to me at these Headquarters.

The above Card is issued with the full consent of the State authorities.

The term of service will be for twelve months, and its sphere of action local—that is, within the State. ALLEN J. GREEN,

jan 22—fmw12 Major and Enrolling Officer.

☞ *Carolinian*, Charleston *Mercury* and *Courier* publish three times a week and all country papers once a week for one month and forward bills to *Guardian* office.

WANTED,

A WELL furnished ROOM. Highest price paid. Call at Express office.

jan 2—5*

ESTATE NOTICE.

THE Estate of Col. J. H. IRBY, deceased, will be settled in the Ordinary's Office for Laurens District on the 1st day of March next. All persons having demands against the said Estate, must render them in to me or to J. WISTAR SIMPSON, Esq., on or before the said day or they will not be paid by me as Administrator.

J. W. BARRINGTON,

jan 14—37 Administrator.

ESTATE NOTICE.

THE Estate of Capt JOHN D. GARLINGTON will be settled in the office of the Ordinary for Laurens District on TUESDAY, the 9th day of February next. All persons having demands against the said Estate, must present them to me on or before the said day or they will not be paid by the Administrator.

H. W. GARLINGTON,

jan 19 1* Administrator.

ADMINISTRATRIX'S NOTICE.

ALL persons having demands against the Estate of WILLIAM BOLLINGER, will present them duly attested, and all indebted will make payment to

MARGERY A. BOLLINGER,

dec 2—ms42m4* Administratrix.

EXECUTOR'S SALE.

A. R. PHILLIPS, Auctioneer.

WILL be sold, at the Courthouse, on THURSDAY, the 11th February, at 11 o'clock, The FOLLOWING STOCKS belonging to the Estate of Whiteford Smith, deceased,

20 New Shares BANK OF CHARLESTON
87 shares Bank of South Carolina
35 " Farmers' & Exchange Bank
20 " State Bank
8 " People's Bank
10 " Greenville & Columbia Railroad.

By order of Whiteford Smith, Executor.

Terms cash. F. D. FANNING,

jan 26—28 29, f11 22 Main street.

$120.

I WILL pay the above reward for the apprehension and delivery of the whole, or Thirty Dollars each, of the following named Deserters from my company, from Camp near Russelville, Tennessee, December 25th, 1863, to any Conscript Officer in the State so that I can get them:

Sergeant A. D. SPEARS
Private W. T. CUDD
" WM HAWKINS
" LEMUEL SPROUSE.

The above Deserters live in Union District, S. C.

JOHN L. BAILEY, Lieut., comd'g Co. H, 15th S. C. Reg't.

jan —12

ONE OF THE MOST BEAUTIFUL RESIDENCES IN THE UP COUNTRY FOR SALE.

LOCATED in the best improved section of the up country, with 1000 acres of Land, bounded on two sides by public market roads, 4 miles from New Market, 6 miles from Greenwood. DWELLING HOUSE brick granitized, form most approved cottage style, two porticos, pillared, roof tin, nine rooms, eight large, with fireplaces and closets in each; pantries, cellar unsurpassed in the State; barn, gin house, large and well arranged; negro houses and all other buildings good, and the entire improvement new; first class male and female academies convenient; churches fine and numerous; society of the best; location healthy; fine well water. Possession given immediately if required. Apply soon or miss a rare opportunity. Address the subscriber at New Market, Abbeville District, S. C.

jan 26—12* J. S. CHIPLEY.

☞ Charleston *Mercury* please copy and forward bill to this office.

NEGRO LABORERS WANTED.

I WISH TO HIRE about 40 ABLEBODIED NEGROES to extend and complete the military works on the Upper Santee River, at Taylor's point. I will want them for about one month or six weeks, and will pay $40 per month for good hands and furnish them with rations and transportation down and up. Owners of negroes willing to hire their hands to me, will please state the number of hands they can hire out, and leave their names at my office at the New State House, or with Mr. G. T. BERG, at the same place, on or before the first day of February.

JOHN R. NIERNSEE, Major of Engineers S. C. A.

feb 2

Adjutant and Inspector General's Office, RICHMOND Feb. 4, 1864.

GENERAL ORDERS NO. 14.

THE following Order is published for the information of all concerned;

CONFEDERATE STATES OF AMERICA, WAR DEPARTMENT, RICHMOND VA., Feb. 1, 1864.

EXCHANGE NOTICE, NO. 8.

I. All prisoners heretofore held by the United States authorities, whether officers, soldiers or civilians received at City Point, before the first of January, 1864, are hereby declared exchanged.

II. All officers and men of the Vicksburg capture, who reported for duty at Enterprise, Miss. at any time prior to the 14th November, 1863, and whose names were forwarded to me by Major General John H. Forney, are declared exchanged.

III. All officers and men of the Vicksburg capture belonging to the 1st Tennessee Heavy Artillery, who reported for duty at Marietta, Ga., and whose names were forwarded to me by Col. A. Jackson, are declared exchanged.

RO. OULD, Agent of Exchange.

By order:

Signed S. COOPER, Adj't and Insp'r Genl.

feb 6—6

LAW NOTICE.

THE subscriber may be consulted by his friends—In Charleston at Hayne & Miles, Postoffice building; and in Columbia at Col McMaster's Office, Law Range.

feb 6—tf WM. E. MARTIN.

RECENT IMPORTATION.

POCKET INKSTANDS.

A neat and convenient article, portable and secure, by wholesale or retail.

MOURNING LETTER PAPER AND NOTE of superior quality.

MOURNING ENVELOPES in considerable variety and of latest style.

PROPELLING PENCILS, Ivory, of very fine quality.

CARMINE INK In 1, 1½ and 2 oz. bottles.

STEEL PENS A great variety and of the best manufacture.

VIOLIN STRINGS Extra fine Italian and German manufacture.

Mucilage, Lead Pencils, India Rubber, Memorandum and Pass Books, and many other articles for the Counting Room, for sale at

P. B. GLASS & CO'S Bookstore.

feb 6—6

COTTON CARDS! COTTON CARDS!!

DIRECT IMPORTATION.

2000 PAIRS superior No 10 English COTTON CARDS, on leather at wholesale or by single pair, at 20 per cent. less than auction prices, at

D JACOBS',

229 Main street, opposite Nickerson's Hotel, 2 doors below J. K. Friday's Store.

feb 5—3

TAKEN UP,

WITH my cattle yesterday, two SMALL YEARLINGS—one red and the other white. The owner is requested to prove property, pay expenses and take them away. JAMES M. CRAWFORD.

feb 4

PEANUTS WANTED.

WE will pay the highest market price for two thousand bushels PEANUTS to be delivered at Muller & Senn's, in Columbia

feb 4—12* HOWLAND & CO.

$200 REWARD

WILL be paid for the apprehension and delivery of MIKE, the property of W. D. FARLEY, dec'd. Said boy is about 37 years of age, medium size, copper-colored, very likely, and a bricklayer. He has been in the habit of working at his trade, on small jobs, by my permission, in this District, Spartanburg, Union and Greenville, and may be still engaged in one of those Districts, without creating any suspicion that he is now absent without leave.

P. M. FARLEY, Administrator.

LAURENS C. H., Feb. 1, 1864.

feb —

HILLSBORO MILITARY ACADEMY

THE Sixth Academic Year of this Institution will begin on WEDNESDAY, February 3, 1864. For circulars or information, W. GORDON, Superintendent H. M. A.

OYSTERS! OYSTERS!

OYSTER DEPOT AT THE French Coffee House!

THE proprietors of this establishment are glad to announce that they are able to furnish **Fresh Oysters Every Day, by the Quart and Bushel!**

dec 5—smwtf A. GEORGET & CO.

FINAL NOTICE.

ALL persons having claims against the Estate of R. O. FERGUSON will present them, properly attested, on or before the 23d February next, as a final settlement of said Estate will be made in the Ordinary's Office on that day.

E. B. FERGUSON,

jan 19—31 Administrator.

PROVISIONS.

THE Mutual Supply Association having opened their Store, at No. 87 Richardson street for the purchase and supply of PROVISIONS are ready to receive offers from planters and others, for all kind of provisions, for which their Superintendent will pay fair prices in cash, or barter Salt and other groceries.

Persons bringing any of those articles to this market, either in wagons or by Railroad, would do well to apply there before selling.

ROBERT BRYCE, Chairman Committee on Provisions.

Columbia, S C., Dec. 22, 1863. dec 23

HEADQUARTERS, JAMES' BATTALION,

KERSHAW'S BRIGADE, Camp near Russelville, East Tenn., Jan. 15, 1864.

ALL Officers and Privates now absent from this command are earnestly expected to report without delay, as by remaining away they deprive those who have endured the hardships of the last three months from visiting their families and homes.

Enrolling Officers and Army Surgeons will use all means in their power to send on promptly all absentees able for duty.

W. C. HARRIS, Adjutant.

jan 28

OFFICE CHARLOTTE AND SOUTH CAROLINA RAILROAD COMPANY.

COLUMBIA, Jan. 15, 1864.

ON and after MONDAY, Jan. 18th, PASSENGER TRAINS will leave Columbia for Charlotte daily at 7.30 a. m. and 5.30 p. m., Columbia time.

THOMAS R. SHARP, Sup't

jan 16

SUNDAY TRAINS.

FROM this date, the SUNDAY TRAINS on the Spartanburg & Union Railroad will cease until further notice.

jan 9 THOMAS B. JETER.

Plantation, Provisions, Implements, Cattle, Mules, Hogs, &c.

By B. McCall, BROKER AND AUCTIONEER.

ON THURSDAY, the 11th day of February, instant, commencing at 10 o'clock, at the farm formerly owned by D. B. Rhett, and more recently by Mr. Arthur Middleton, being five miles from Walhalla, on the middle road to Pickens Courthouse, will be sold, without any manner of reserve, to the highest bidder, the entire PERSONAL PROPERTY on said farm,

CONSISTING OF;

CORN, PEAS, BACON, Irish and Sweet Potatoes, Seed Potatoes, Tobacco, Turnips, Hay, Fodder, Shucks, Straw, Wagon and Harness, Ploughs of various kinds, Hoes, Spades, Shovels, Pick and Club Axes, Crow Bars, Harrows, Ox Yokes, Trace and Log Chains, two fine Mules, four head Cattle of imported stock, Hogs of fine breed, and many other articles too numerous to mention.

Terms cash—articles to be removed immediately after sale. Unlimited property will be received at the place on the morning of the sale.

feb 3—3d, 5th, 8th, 10th*

☞ *Carolinian* copy 4th, 6th, 9th, 10th.

AT PRIVATE SALE.

A COMMODIOUS and eligible RESIDENCE, with forty acres of land attached, in one of the healthiest portions of Orangeburg District, about eight miles from the line of the S. C. Railroad, and within easy reach of two depots. The Dwelling House which is well built and in good order, contains six rooms, with fire places, a pantry and a wide hall, and has double piazzas in front. On the premises are a kitchen, store-room, stable, &c., with ample accommodations for servants.

ALSO,

An unfailing Spring of very pure and very cold water. To families from the coast, desirous of securing a safe convenient and healthy residence, this place offers superior attractions.

For terms, apply by letter to the subscriber at the office of the Camden *Journal*, Camden, S. C.

feb 3—wlm3 D. D. HOCOTT.

☞ *Courier* and *Mercury* insert three times, and send bill to Camden *Journal*.

OPERATIVE DENTISTRY.

THE FOLLOWING PRICES are charged at the office of the undersigned for DENTAL OPERATIONS:

Extracting	$ 1
Gold Fillings	$10 to 25
Tin "	3 to 6

All Neuralgic cases treated and advice given on reasonable terms.

jan 27 tf I. D. DURHAM M. D.

CENTRAL ASSOCIATION.

CARS WILL BE DISPATCHED

For Johnston's Army on the 3d February.
" Longstreet's " " 9th "
" Lee's " " 14th "

M LABORDE,

jan 26 Chairman C. Association.

EXCHANGE.

A PLANTER of Lancaster District proposes to exchange FLOUR for SALT, to be sent to Rock Hill Depot, on the Charlotte Railroad. His address can be had at this office.

feb 3—tf

$180 REWARD.

I HEREBY offer the above reward for the apprehension and delivery of the whole, or Thirty Dollars each, of the following named Deserters from my company, from Camp near Russelville, Tennessee, on the 25th December, 1863, to any Conscript Officer in the State so that I can get them:

Sergeant G. S. SPEARS, Privates JOHN FOWLER, JAMES KNOX, J. M. LENNARD and JAMES SPENCER. The above Deserters live in Union District, S. C.

GEORGE STEEN, 1st Lt., comd'g Co. F, 15th S. C. Reg't.

jan 25 12

SPLENDID HOUSE AND LOT FOR SALE IN THE VILLAGE OF ANDERSON.

A TWO STORY brick DWELLING HOUSE with six rooms, five of which has good fireplaces, and portico in front, good brick kitchen, new stables and all other necessary outbuildings, an excellent well of pure water, splendid garden with some choice fruit trees of various kinds; the whole is in good repair and situated in the most fashionable part of the town.

The above Lot contains ... if not disposed of before ... in February at public auction on that day.

J. B. McGEE.

jan 6—wfm12

☞ Charleston *Courier* please copy and send bill.

FEMALE ACADEMY, ANDERSON COURTHOUSE, S. C.

I WILL open a FEMALE SCHOOL in this place on the FIRST WEDNESDAY in February (3d day of the month). Young ladies committed to my care will receive every attention. The patronage of the public is respectfully solicited.

The scholastic year will be divided into two sessions of 20 weeks each. French or any of the Languages $5 per session, extra.

For further information, apply to

THOMAS HALL, A.M.

Anderson Courthouse, S. C., Jan. 22, 1864.

jan 22—fmw6

STATE OF SOUTH CAROLINA.

Adjutant and Inspector General's Office. COLUMBIA January 27, 1864.

GENERAL ORDERS NO. 2.

[EXTRACT.]

* * * * * * *

II. ALL persons, except those above the age of fifty years, claiming exemption from State military service, are required to present their claims to the District Enrolling Officer on or before the day above mentioned, or they will be liable to forfeit their right to the same, in pursuance of the Act of the General Assembly; and persons claiming exemption on the ground of physical disability will be examined by the Surgeon of the District at such times as he may publish in orders on or before the day above specified.

* * * * * * *

By command:

[signed] A. C. GARLINGTON, Adjutant and Inspector General S. C.

Official: G. A. FOLLIN, Captain and A. A. G.

feb 2—33

☞ Papers of State publish till March 10.

STATE OF SOUTH CAROLINA. LAURENS DISTRICT—IN ORDINARY.

AMANDA KNIGHTS, applicant, vs. LEWIS GANT and others, defendants.

IT appearing to my satisfaction that Lewis Gant, John Gant, Allen Gant, Reubin Gant, Mancil Owens, Toliver Owens, Robert Owens, William Summerel, husband of Nancy Summerel, defendants, reside without this State. It is therefore ordered that they do appear and object to the division or sale of the Real Estate of NANCY GANT, on or before the 6th day of February next, or their consent to the same will be entered of record.

Given under my hand and seal 6th day of November, 1863. W. H. LANGSTON, O. L. D.

nov 9 m8m

WANTED TO PURCHASE.

A PAPER CUTTING MACHINE. Apply at the office of the *Southern Guardian*.

STAUNTON SPECTATOR.

VOL. XL. STAUNTON, VIRGINIA, TUESDAY, FEBRUARY 9, 1864. NO. 37.

Staunton Spectator.

RICHARD MAUZY, Editor & Proprietor.

THE SPECTATOR IS PUBLISHED EVERY TUESDAY MORNING, AT THE FOLLOWING RATES:

FOR 1 YEAR, $5.00 IN ADVANCE.
" 6 MONTHS, $3.00 " "
" 3 " $2.00 " "
SINGLE COPY 25 CENTS.

ADVERTISEMENTS of eight lines (or less) inserted at the rate of TWO DOLLARS *per square for each insertion. Larger advertisements inserted in the same proportion.*

☞ *Annual advertisers will be limited to their immediate business, or the advertisements charged for at transient rates.*

All advertising for a less time than three months, will be charged for at the usual rates—$2.00 per square for each insertion.

Unless the number of insertions be marked upon the manuscript, they will be inserted until forbid, and charged accordingly.

COMMUNICATIONS.—Announcements of Candidates for Office, and all Communications or Notices of a personal or private character, or intended or calculated to promote any private enterprise or interest, will be charged for as advertisements.

OBITUARIES will be charged for at the rate of TEN CENTS *per line. They must in all cases be accompanied by the money.*

1864. CALENDAR. 1864.

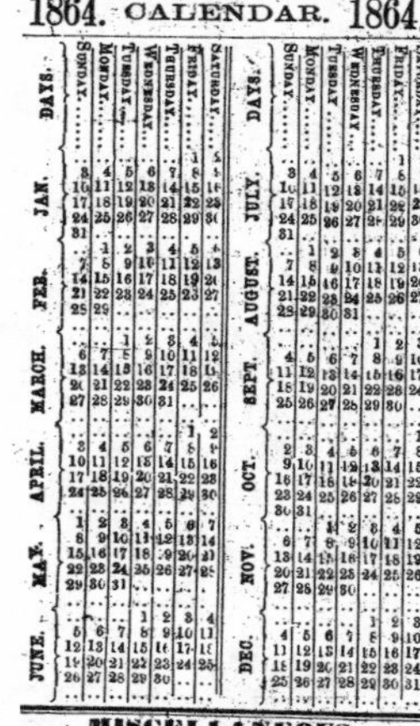

DAYS.	SUNDAY	MONDAY	TUESDAY	WEDNESDAY	THURSDAY	FRIDAY	SATURDAY	DAYS.	SUNDAY	MONDAY	TUESDAY	WEDNESDAY	THURSDAY	FRIDAY	SATURDAY
JAN.						1	2	JULY.						1	2
	3	4	5	6	7	8	9		3	4	5	6	7	8	9
	10	11	12	13	14	15	16		10	11	12	13	14	15	16
	17	18	19	20	21	22	23		17	18	19	20	21	22	23
	24	25	26	27	28	29	30		24	25	26	27	28	29	30
	31								31						
FEB.		1	2	3	4	5	6	AUGUST.		1	2	3	4	5	6
	7	8	9	10	11	12	13		7	8	9	10	11	12	13
	14	15	16	17	18	19	20		14	15	16	17	18	19	20
	21	22	23	24	25	26	27		21	22	23	24	25	26	27
	28	29							28	29	30	31			
MARCH.			1	2	3	4	5	SEPT.					1	2	3
	6	7	8	9	10	11	12		4	5	6	7	8	9	10
	13	14	15	16	17	18	19		11	12	13	14	15	16	17
	20	21	22	23	24	25	26		18	19	20	21	22	23	24
	27	28	29	30	31				25	26	27	28	29	30	
APRIL.						1	2	OCT.							1
	3	4	5	6	7	8	9		2	3	4	5	6	7	8
	10	11	12	13	14	15	16		9	10	11	12	13	14	15
	17	18	19	20	21	22	23		16	17	18	19	20	21	22
	24	25	26	27	28	29	30		23	24	25	26	27	28	29
									30	31					
MAY.	1	2	3	4	5	6	7	NOV.			1	2	3	4	5
	8	9	10	11	12	13	14		6	7	8	9	10	11	12
	15	16	17	18	19	20	21		13	14	15	16	17	18	19
	22	23	24	25	26	27	28		20	21	22	23	24	25	26
	29	30	31						27	28	29	30			
JUNE.				1	2	3	4	DEC.					1	2	3
	5	6	7	8	9	10	11		4	5	6	7	8	9	10
	12	13	14	15	16	17	18		11	12	13	14	15	16	17
	19	20	21	22	23	24	25		18	19	20	21	22	23	24
	26	27	28	29	30				25	26	27	28	29	30	31

GENERAL ORDERS.

ADJ'T & INSP'R GENL'S OFFICE, Richmond, Jan. 23d, 1864.

GENERAL ORDER, No. 7

I. Paragraph IV, General Orders No. 3, current series, is hereby revoked.

II. Enrolling officers will proceed as rapidly as practicable in the enrollment of *all persons* made liable to military service. Previous to enrollment as conscripts, all such persons will be allowed to volunteer, provided—

1st The company selected was in service on the 16th April, 1862.

2d The company selected is, at the time of volunteering, below the minimum number prescribed by regulations.

3d. No person made liable to service under this order will be permitted to join, or will be assigned to any company which has more than sixty-four privates on the roll until all the companies in service from the State of which the volunteer or conscript is a resident shall have the minimum number prescribed by regulations.

4th. Upon the company being selected, the volunteer will receive from the enrolling officer a certificate to the effect that he has so volunteered; and no volunteer will be received in any company except on such certificate.

III. Persons who fail to make selection, according to the provisions of this order, and at the time of enlistment, will be assigned according to existing regulations ... organized under this order to receive conscripts or volunteers will forthwith send to the commandant of conscripts of the State accurate certified rolls of their companies: and without such roll, showing that they do not exceed sixty-four privates, there will not be assigned any conscript or volunteer.

By command of the Secretary of War.
(Signed) S. COOPER, Adjutant and Inspector General.

POETRY.

WAIT.

CHRISTIAN, wait—the nations tremble,
Shaken to their utmost bound—
Men their terror ill dissemble,
Dread and panic spread around;
There's no prophet now to call us
To behold, in vision true,
What events will soon befall us—
Wait, and see what God will do.

Christian, wait—the mutt'ring thunder
Gathering in the sky afar,
Need not bring dismay or wonder,
Doubt, or fright, or pallid fear;
Stay your soul on His protection,
He will guide you safely through—
Banish every sad dejection,
Wait, and see what God will do.

Christian, wait—Jehovah reigneth
On his throne of mercy still,
And the wrath of man restraineth
When it would not do His will;
Be assured [illegible]
[illegible]
[illegible] do.

CONFEDERATE STATES' CONGRESS.

In the Senate, on Saturday, the 30th, Mr. Read, of North Carolina, offered the following, which was unanimously agreed to:

The Congress of the Confederate States having learned, through the public press, of the re-enlistment, for the war, of the North Carolina Brigade in the army of Northern Virginia, serving under General Robert D. Johnston: Therefore,

Resolved by the Confederate States of America, That the patriotism and spirit of the North Carolina troops evinced by this prompt and voluntary devotion of themselves afresh to the service of the country, are beyond all praise, and deserve the unbounded gratitude of the Government.

In the House, the following bill, alluded to last week, was adopted by a vote of 44 ayes to 31 nays:

SECTION 1. The Congress of the Confederate States of America do enact, That the above recited act shall not apply to farmers and planters engaged on the 5th of January, 1864, in the production of grain and provisions, either by their own manual labor or in superintending the labor of others: Provided, The exemption herein contemplated is granted subject to the following conditions:

I. That the person availing himself thereof shall devote himself, and the labor of which he has the control or superintendence, exclusively to the production of provisions and family supplies.

II. That there shall be paid and contributed from the farm, or, if more than one farm, from each of the farms which the person thus exempted owns or superintends, in addition to the tithe required by any tax law, an additional tenth of the pork or bacon produced on said farm or farms (beginning with the product of last year) for the use of the army.

III. That the person thus exemped will, if so required, sell all his surplus provisions, now on hand or her after raised, for the use of soldiers' families, or for the use of the army, at prices not greater than those fixed for the time being by the commissioners appointed under the impressment act.

IV. That the person seeking to avail himsef of the benefit of this act shall have furnished a substitute not liable to military duty, who is now in the service, or who has been legally discharged therefrom, or who has died therein.

V. That the benefit of this act shall not apply to persons on farms or plantations on which ... to military duty.

SEC. 2. Nothing contained in this act shall be construed as limiting the power of the President, under existing laws, to exempt such persons as he may deem proper on grounds of equity, justice, or necessity.

The following bill establishing an invalid corps was also adopted:

Section I. *The Congress of the Confederate States* of America, do enact, That all officers, non-commissioned officers, musicians, privates and seamen, who have or shall become disabled by wounds or other injuries received, or disease contracted in the service of the Confederate States and in the line of duty, shall be retired or discharged from their respective positions as hereinafter provided. But the rank, pay and emoluments of such officers, and the pay and emoluments of such noncommissioned officers, musicians, privates and seamen, shall continue to the end of the war or as long as they shall continue so retired or discharged.

Sec. 2. That all persons claiming the benefits of his act shall present themselves for examination to one of the medical examining boards now established by law. Upon the certificate of such board that such permanent disability exists, such persons shall be retired or discharged as aforesaid.

Sec. 3. That all persons retired or discharged, as aforesaid, shall, periodically, and at least once in six months, present themselves to one of said boards for further examination, the result of which examinations shall be reported by such board to the Secretary of War. And if any such person shall fail so to report himself to such board, whenever he shall be required so to do, he shall be dropped from said retired or discharged list, and become liable to conscription under the terms of the law, unless such failure shall be caused by physical disability.

Sec. 4. That the Secretary of War may assign such officers, and order the detail of such non-commissioned officers, musicians, privates and seamen for such duty as they shall be qualified to perform. If any such noncommissioned officers, musicians, privates and seamen, shall be relieved from disability they shall be restored to duty.

Sec. 5. That the Secretary of War shall make all needful rules and regulations for the action of the medical boards, as aforesaid.

Sec. 6. That vacancies caused by the retirement of officers under this act, shall be filled as in case of the death or resignation of such officers.

Sec. 7. This act shall be in force from its passage.

The House then adjourned

In the Senate on Monday, the 1st of February, resolutions complimentary of the Louisiana troops, who have re-enlisted for the war, were adopted; and the House bill to establish an asylum, to be called "The Veteran Soldiers' Home" was adopted. The Senate then resolved into secret session to resume the consideration of the "currency question."

The House passed the bills to allow rations in kind to commissioned officers of the army by conscribing free male negroes and slaves as teamsters, cooks, &c., both under certain conditions and limitations.

The latter bills reads as follows:

"Whereas, the efficiency of the army is greatly diminished by the withdrawal from the ranks of able-bodied soldiers to act as teamsters, and in various other capacities in which free negroes and slaves might be advantageously employed; therefore,

"SECTION 1. *The Congress of the Confederate States* of America do enact, That all male free negroes, not including those who are free under the treaty of Paris of 1803, or the treaty with Spain of 1819, resident in the Confederate States, between the ages of eighteen and fifty years, shall be held liable to perform such duties with the army, or in connection with the military defences of the country, in the way of work upon fortifications, or in State works for the production or preparation of material of war, or in military hospitals, as the Secretary of War may from time to time prescribe; and while engaged in the performance of such duties shall receive rations and clothing, and compensation at the rate of eleven dollars per month, under such rules and regulations as the said Secretary may establish: PROVIDED, That the Secretary of War, with the approval of the President, may exempt from the operations of this act such free negroes as the interests of the country may require should be exempted, or such as he may think proper to exempt on grounds of justice, equity or necessity.

"SECTION. 2. Be it further enacted, That the Secretary of War is hereby authorized to employ, for duties similar to those indicated in the preceding section of this act, as many male negro slaves, not to exceed twenty thousand, as in his judgment, the wants of the service may require, furnishing them while so employed with proper rations and clothing, under rules and regulations to be established by him, and paying to the owners of said slaves wages at the rate of eleven dollars per month for their use and service, and in the event of the loss of any slaves while so employed, by the act of the enemy, or by escape to the enemy, or by death inflicted by the enemy, or by disease contracted while in any service required of said slaves, then the owners of the same shall be entitled to receive the full value of such slaves, to be ascertained by agreement, or by appraisement under the laws regulating impressments at the time, to be paid under such rules and regulations as the Secretary of War may establish.

"SECTION. 3. Be it further enacted, That when the Secretary of War shall be unable to procure the services of slaves in any military department in sufficient numbers for the necessities of the department upon the terms and conditions set forth in the preceding section, then he is hereby authorized to impress the service of as many male slaves, not to exceed twenty thousand, as many be required from time to time to discharge the duties indicated in the first section of this act, according to the laws regulating the impressment of slaves in other cases: PROVIDED, That slaves so impressed shall, while employed, receive the same rations and clothing in kind ... owners, and in the event of their loss, shall be paid for in the same manner, and under the same rules established by the said impressment laws: PROVIDED, That if the owner have not one male slave between the ages of eighteen and fifty years, he shall not be impressed without the consent of the owner."

"SECTION. 4. Be it further enacted, That impressments of slaves shall, as far as praticable, be made in counties and districts the productions of which are least available for the use of the army, or remote from facilities for transportation; and shall be apportioned, as nearly as practicble, among the owners, according to numbers of laboring hands: PROVIDED, that in making the impressments, not more than one in every five male slaves, between the ages of eighteen and forty-five years, shall be taken from any owner: Provided further, That free negroes shall be first impressed, and if there should be a deficiency it shall be supplied by the impressment of slaves, according to the foregoing provisions.

In the Senate, Tuesday, the 2nd, the House joint resolutions to the heroic defenders of Sabine Pass and of Charleston, S. C., were unanimously concurred in. Two bids relative to the Engineer Corps were introduced and referred, after which, the Senate went into secret session on the currency question.

The House of Representatives went into secret session very soon after the regular hour of meeting, on the special order, which is understood to be the military bill. Nothing of interest was transacted in open session, save the passage of a bill to establish certain post routes in several States.

Feb. 3 The principal business before the Senate, [Wednesday] was the bill to provide and organize a general staff for armies in the field.—The bill was perfected and passed. A bill introduced by Mr. Phelan, creating the office of ensign in the army, was also considered and passed. The House joint resolutions of thanks to Gen. Patrick R. Cleburne and the officers and of his command, were unanimously agreed to.—The Senate went into secret session to consider the bills regulating our foreign commerce.

The House was engaged, most of the time in open session, in the agreeable duty of adopting resolutions of thanks to various organizations of troops, who continue to re-enlist for the war.

A few bills and resolutions relating to other subjects, were introduced.

The House met at night and went into secret session on the Military bill.

In the Senate, on Thursday, the 4th, nothing of importance was done in open session. A motion was entered to reconsider the vote by which the bill creating the office of ensign in the army was passed, and several resolutions of thanks to troops who have re-enlisted for the war were concurred in.

The House passed a bill to increase the compensation of the Treasurer, and Clerks in the Treasury Department, at Richmond, the Assistant Treasurer, at Charleston, and extending the provisions of the act to the Clerk and employees in the Department, at Columbia, South Carolina.

The bill from the Senate to establish a volunteer Navy was also passed; and a bill to authorize the President to establish a Military Court for each Division of cavalry in the field, and one for each State in military department; whenever the public interest may require it.

The Senate, Friday, Feb. 5th, was cheifly occupied in the discussion of an amendment to the "Appropriation Bill," withholding the pay of officers appointed under the Provisional Government who have not been renominated and confirmed by the Senate. After a lengthy debate, the proposition was withdrawn. The House bill to exempt farmers who have furnished substitutes from military service, was made the order of the day for Tuesday next.

Nothing of importance was transacted by the House in open session. Soon after it was called to order, a motion was made to go into secret session, but it was withdrawn to allow the introduction of some memorials to re-enlisted troops. The motion was then renewed, and the House went into secret session to consider the business before it, which, it is understood, has been increased by the adoption of the Financial bill, which has been sent from the Senate.

LINCOLN'S DRAFT CONSOLIDATED.

Lincoln has issued the following call for troops:

EXECUTIVE MANSION,
Washington Feb. 1st, 1864.

Ordered, that a draft for 500,000 men to serve for three years or during the war, be made on the 10th of March next, for the military service of the United States, crediting and deducting therefrom so many as may have been enlisted or drafted into the service prior to the 1st day of March and not heretofore credited.

ABRAHAM LINCOLN.

The Herald says:

The new order is but a consolidation of the two calls previously issued for 300,000 men, nearly half of whom were obtained by volunteering and re-inlistments, and which number, as well as those enlisted up to the first of March next, will be credited. Therefore, the call virtually demands only 200,000 men. If the enlistment of soldiers is properly and vigorously advanced, there will be no need of any draft to fill the quota demanded by Mr. Lincoln.

THE WRIT OF HABEAS CORPUS IN GEORGIA.—The State of Georgia, at the last session of the Legislature, passed the following resolution unanimously:

An Act to amend the Habeas Corpus laws of this State.

Section 2. The General Assembly of the State of Georgia do enact, that when any person shall apply for the writ of Habeas Corpus to any Judge of the Superiour, or Justice of the Inferior Courts, whose duty it is to grant the same, shall forfeit to the party aggrieved the sum of twenty-five hundred dollars, to be recovered in any court of law in the State having jurisdiction of the same.

Section 2. Repeals all conflicting laws.

DISTANCE MAKES A DIFFERENCE.—We learn from a gentleman direct from Bermuda, that Yankee greenbacks were selling at that place for sixty-two and a half cents on the dollar, and Confederate graybacks at seventy cents, the latter being seven and a half cents more valuable in the estimation of the Bermudians than the "promise to pay" of the Lincoln Government.

Joe Coburn, a New York pugilist is out with a challenge to Tom King, the victor over Heenan, for $5,000 a side, and offering him $1,000 towards defraying his expenses to fight in this country.

Of the slaves who have fallen into the hands of the enemy during the present war, not less than one-half perished by want, disease and violence.

THE LEGISLATURE.

In the Senate, on Saturday, the 30th, House bill for the relief of families of soldiers in counties within the lines or under the control of the enemy, was reported with amendments.

In the House the bill was received from the Senate and made the order of the day for Monday at 1 o'clock.

Mr. Baker introduced a resolution looking to the convoking of a convention of the farmers and planters of Virginia, and the other Southern States, through their Legislatures, for the purpose of increasing the production of food, and regulating the price of the same.

The bill to regulate the transportation on rail-roads, previously under discussion, was passed. Adjourned.

In the Senate, on Monday, the 1st of February, the report of the Committee on Confederate Relations as to the liability of the Confederate Government for the slaves lost in the service was taken up, when a discussion ensued which lasted some time. The first resolution was agreed to and the second rejected.

In the House, Mr. McCue's bill for the protection of sheep and to encourage the growth of wool was taken up on its third reading, and after various amendments, ryders, &c., all of which were rejected, the bill was passed—ayes 50,—noes 46. ... was commenced ... of the militia bill ... Senate, and consumed the remainder of the day.

In the Senate, on Tuesday, the 2nd, the House bill providing for the protection of sheep and to increase the growth of wool, and the bill, presented by leave, authorizing an increase of the salaries of the professors of the University of Virginia, and providing for the education of persons disabled by wounds received in the public service, were reported from the appropriate committees without amendment.

In the House, Mr. Anderson, from the Committee on Military Affairs, reported a bill to authorize the appointment of an agent by the Governor, whose duty it shall be to make out a list of all the officers, non-commissioned officers and privates who have been conscripted in the State of Virginia, and who have died or been killed in the army.

On motion of Mr. James, the Senate joint resolutions against extending the provisions of the conscript act were taken up.

Mr. James said it was important that this subject should be disposed of. As far as he had opportunities of learning the sentiment of the people of this State, they were opposed to the extension of the conscript law, as proposed to be carried out by the Confederate Congress. They did not believe such a measure necessary.

Mr. Melvin offered the following as a substitute for the Senate resolutions:

Resolved, In the opinion of the General Assembly, Congress should pass a law enrolling all men between the ages of forty-five and fifty-five years—from that number should be detailed the non-producing class [and not to be taken beyond the limits of their respective States] to act as provost guards, gather conscripts, and to fill such other positions as are now filled by able bodied men between the ages of eighteen and forry-five years, the residue to be organized and held as a reserve to meet and repel raids, and perform such other duty as can be rendered without calling them from their agricultural pursuits, so as to seriously interfere with said pursuits.

The resolutions were debated at much length by Messrs. James, Fleming, Jones and others.

In the Senate, on Wednesday, the 3rd, the bill authorizing an increase of the salaries of the Professors of the University of Virginia, and providing for the education of persons disabled by wounds received in the service, was passed.

And a bill to amend the 10th and 11th sections of chapter 184 of the Code of Virginia, as amended by the Act passed March 21, 1863, entitled "an act increasing the compensation of Clerks of Courts during the existing war."

After a recess the Senate closed its doors and had a brief secret session which was followed by the presentation of a petition of Col. Taliaferro in regard to the recent election in the 23d Senatorial District. Referred. Adjourned.

The House resolved itself into secret session shortly after the hour of meeting, and so continued till the hour of adjournment.

In the Senate, on Thursday, the 4th, a joint resolution, looking to the election of 1st and 2d Auditors, a Treasurer, Secretary of the Commonwealth, and other State officers, was submitted. Laid over under the rules.

After the adoption of several resolutions of inquiry, the Senate passed the bill providing for the preservation of the records of the counties of Warwick, Elizabeth City, James City, and the city of Williamsburg.

The Senate went into secret session on the same subject which engaged their attention on the previous day.

Adjourned.

In the House, the Committee on Confederate Relations reported a joint resolution, as a substitute for the Senate resolution upon the same subject, urging upon Virginia representatives in Congress to secure the passage of an act providing remuneration to Virginia slave holders and others who have lost slaves in the service of the Confedeaate States.

The joint resolution of the Senate, remonstrating against the extension of the conscript act by Congress, to which a substitute has been offered in the house, gave rise to considerable discussion. On motion, the subject was indefinitely postponed.

The substitute of the House for the joint resolution of the Senate relating to the subject of payment for slaves lost in the Confederate service, was amended and discussed; pending which The House adjourned.

The Senate, on Friday, the 5th, shortly after meeting, resolved itself into secret session, in which condition it remained until 3 o'clock P. M.

The Senate's resolution in regard to the liability of the Confederate Government for slaves lost in the public service, was reported back with a substitute therefor from the House. Tabled.

The bill to incorporate the Richmond Insurance Company was reported with amendments.

A bill of the House, with amendments, was reported, in relation to the sale of certain slaves in the Penitentiary.

Adjourned.

HOUSE.—After prayer by the Rev. Dr. Pettigrew, the bill for indemnifying the owners of tobacco destroyed by fire at the public warehouse with the refusal of the Senate to recede from their amendment, was taken up, when, on motion, a committee of conference was ordered.

A committee reported a bill for disbanding the 179th regiment militia of the line, and providing for the more efficient organization of the 19th regiment of the line, and the first regiment of the second class militia was offered—(which is understood as a sort of amendment to the militia bill to the Senate, inasmuch as the Senate's bill exempts the 179th regiment, and this bill disbands that body.) A lengthy discussion ensued, in which almost every member of the House participated.

A bill authorizing and directing the payment of the "Dixie Boys," an independent company of scouts and rangers operating in Virginia, was presented.

Adjourned.

LINCOLN'S CALL TO RE-ELECTION.—The New-York World says Lincoln is a proper candidate for the Presidency on the part of Black-Republicans, for the following reason:

"1 He proclaimed as a necessity of party action an "irrepressible conflict" between the interests of one section and the fanaticism of the other.

2 He has announced that there is no law in the United States but the will of the majority.

3 He writes worse English than any President we have ever had.

4 He is as great a strategist as he is a statesman, and has distinguished himself equally in war and in jurisprudence.

5 Since Archy, the king's jester, no man has used such an abundance of stories, from the broad smutty to the diluted Joe Miller.

"Shall parts so various aim at nothing new?
He'll shine a joker and a ruler too."

6 He is used to ... all the violations of the Constitution that are possible to any President, and by a frequent practice does ... easily that which may come awkwardly to any other man.

7 There never has been an official ... true to his party, ... of shoddy and ... inate him."

FOR THE SPECTATOR.

INFORMATION WANTED!

Don't imagine, gentle reader, that my wife or daughter has eloped with some gentleman with bars or stars upon his collar, for I have neither. Nor that my brother or some other near relative has been missing for months, of whom nothing can be heard; but the information wanted is this: 1st, Why is it that Quartermasters and Commissaries with the rank and pay of Captain or Major can dress finer, ride finer and fatter horses than company or field officers of the same rank and pay? 2d, Why is it that Commissaries can feed their horses on corn-meal at the rate of from two to three gallons per day, and themselves on ham, sweet potatoes, molasses and every other good thing that the country can afford, while a private or company officer does not know that there is such a thing in existence? 3d, Why is it that a certain gentleman who volunteered for the war in the Spring of 1862, has been at home ever since that time without doing one day's duty and without putting a man in his place, has never been reported by the officers of his company or regiment, while another member of the same company who has over a hundred thousand dollars less to fight for than the other gentleman referred to, has been reported by the same officers as a deserter, because he happened to be detained on his way to the army by Gen. Lee's order?

I do not pretend to know anything about military law, nor civil jurisprudence; but I claim a little COMMON SENSE, which has always enabled me to distinguish right from wrong; so when I see a man with the rank of Captain or Major exposing himself to the enemy's balls as well as to all the trials and perplexities of camp life, and then at the close of each year finds himself in debt from five hundred to a thousand dollars, while another man, with the same rank and pay, lives upon the fat of the land, never heard a minnie, and at the end of each year buys a farm for twenty or thirty thousand dollars cash down, when every body knows that before the war he couldn't pay his liquor bills, I am forced to conclude that all is not right. So, also, when I see a man, no difference what his age may be, volunteer for the war and then go home and remain there unmolested and unreported by the officers under whom he volunteered, while all others are reported as deserters, if they happen, from any cause whatever, to remain a day or two over their time, am I compelled to come to the same conclusion. And when I see that same man riding around through the country buying everything he can get hold of and then selling it for double what he gave, while the other man, who is no more a volunteer than he, and who stands upon precisely the same footing in his company, has to have his name banded around, not only through the army, but in his native county as a deserter, simply because he failed to report up to time owing to the fact that Gen. Lee had ordered all men to be stopped at Gordonsville, I am constrained to believe that JUSTICE has fled from her temples on earth and awaits us only on high to measure out what is right between man and man! I do not pretend to say that these things are not right in the eyes of the MILITARY, but from where I stand, beneath a musket and forty rounds of cartridges, IT DOES NOT LOOK SO; consequently, any information on the subject will be gratefully received by

JUSTICE, Co. F, 5th Va. Infantry.

FOR THE SPECTATOR.

RICHMOND, Feb 1, 1864.

MR. EDITOR:—The County Court of Augusta at the December term conferred upon me the authority to purchase a quantity of corn for the use of the families of soldiers and others, to the extent of 10,000 bushels, provided the cost and expense of transportation does not exceed $4.00 per bushel. I have made use of all the facilities which my position gives me here, to get the information needed, to enable me to carry out the wish of the Court. I regret to say that in consequence of the great demand in Virginia and North Carolina for corn, to say nothing of the wants of the army, that the price has enhanced so much in the extreme South as to render it utterly impossible to meet its wishes. Last evening, I met an intelligent Commissary of General Lee's army just from South Alabama and Georgia who informs me the price of corn there is $2.25 per bushel, to which $4. for transportation must be added.

Permit me to say I am gratified at the refusal of the Court to make the levy of the negroes.—I learned at Drewy's Bluff, on Saturday last, from an officer high in command there, that no more negroes were wanted in that quarter, that the soldiers could do all that was necessary to be done, and that he fully concurred in General Lee's view of the matter, who said he thought the negroes had better be left on the farms to RAISE corn and let the soldiers RAISE the embankments.

Yours truly,
J. M. McCUE.

For the Spectator.

To the Churchville and Hebron "Soldiers Aid Societies:

LADIES:

Your kind donation of socks to Col. Wm. S. Jackson's Brig., were taken by J. F. Heizer and myself and delivered over to Cpt. Walker, commandant of Post at Millboro Depot, to be forwarded immediately to the Brigade.—Col. Jackson was prevented, however, from receiving the socks for some weeks afterwards, by the raid of Averill.

On my recent visit to the Brigade, the Col. informed me that he had written twice expressing his gratitude at the reception of so invaluable a present; but his communications, I presume, were mislaid, as they have never been received; consequently, I take pleasure, by his request, in announcing to you that he received the socks at the proper time, and distributed them to those who needed them most in his Brig. He tenders you his most profound thanks for your kindness to the exiled soldiers of his command, who are cut of from all communications with their own dear ones at home, and who will ever remember the Ladies of Augusta for their kindness, patriotism and zeal for our cause.—Your present calls forth the praise of the entire Brig., and renerves them to endure the hardships and privations of a soldier's life, and to use all of their energies to drive the vandals and cut-throats from our soil. It is a great source of pleasure to our soldiers to know that though they are cut off from home and friends, yet they are not forgotten by the kind, noble and generous Ladies of the South, who alone possess the power of softening our natures and building up in our hearts again the sacred EDEN of LOVE, where perennial flowers forever bloom, and crystal waters gush from inexhaustible fountains.

Yours Respectfully &c.
J. GORDON RILEY.
Capt. P.A.C.S.

CHURCHVILLE VA. Feb. 2nd, 1864.

FOR THE SPECTATOR.

Mr. Editor:

I am under the impression that there is a law imposing a fine upon any one refusing to receive Confederate Money. Why is it that many farmers having corn for sale refuse to receive it for corn. I know many who desire to purchase corn, and other grain, for their horses and families & cannot procure it with out the gold, or silver,—which few can command. Confederate money has been denounced as trash,—worth nothing. I refer the present generation to the good old honest days of the ... How about the resources of the revolution ... the present time. Are country then, and ... now than not our resources infinitely ... then. I wish to God there was as much patriotism now, as there was then. I hope some steps will be taken by Congress to put a stop to such proceedings. A great deal of suffering will be experienced by the poor, as well as by those better off from this very cause. Many tillers of the soil need grain for their horses, who cannot procure it, for the want of gold and silver.

A FARMER.

Sharp.—The Mississippian is responsible for the annexed sharp and truthful statement of facts;

"It is said that there are only three ways to get out of a quarrel—fight out, write out, or back out; but the safer mode is to keep out. By the same four ways, also, a man may get out of the army. The soldiers fight out, the editors write out, the substitute buyers back out, and the members of Congress keep out."

The [illegible] have [illegible] they [illegible]

Staunton Spectator.

STAUNTON, VA.

TUESDAY, ... FEBRUARY 9, 1864.

YANKEES NEAR RICHMOND.

A few days since, a force of Yankees with 12 guns, two regiments of cavalry and three or four more of infantry crossed the York River Railroad, near Dispatch Station, twelve miles East of Richmond. They soon went back.

MOVEMENTS ON THE RAPIDAN.

The enemy crossed in large force, on Saturday, at Morton's ford, but, after a sharp contest, were repulsed by Gen. Ed. Johnson's division, and driven back over the river and pursued. The enemy also attempted to cross at Barnett's ford, but were repulsed by Gen. Scale's North Carolina brigade and Lomax's cavalry. The casualties on our side were slight. The enemy have all retreated.

THE SPIRIT OF THE ARMY.

The spirits of the people have revived within the past several weeks, and a general impression seems to prevail that we will defeat the enemy in the chief engagements which will take place in the ensuing campaign. Our armies are in fine spirits and our soldiers in all of them are re-enlisting with a spirit which reflects great credit upon their bravery, fortitude and patriotism. The soldiers in the armies of the enemy are re-enlisting slowly and reluctantly, whereas the noble soldiers in our armies are re-enlisting with a "perfect rush." The armies of the enemy will, it is thought, be recruited chiefly by *raw levies*, who will be unable to stand before our brave and tried veterans, whose flags have waved in triumph over so many bloody fields of battle. Whilst we will be stronger in the next campaign than ever before, the enemy will be weaker than at present. We cherish the hope that we will be able, in the next campaign, to recover all of the territory of the South now in the possession of the enemy. If this hope be realized, the enemy will see that we will be able to continue the war for an indefinite period.

The result of this war will not be determined by numbers or bravery so much as by fortitude and persistent determination. We must be prepared to continue the war, and must submit to its evils with patient endurance. Time will crown that party with success which will exhibit the greater fortitude. We have not so much to dread from the enemy as from our own people. We can meet the enemy without dread, but the apprehension of unwise Legislation on the part of our Congress creates a feeling of alarm which the armed hosts of the enemy fail to inspire. We should not expend all of our strength one deperate effort. We should not abstract too many from labor, for it is as necessary that the army should be fed as that it should be armed. We must, also, retain a reserve of men for military service to supply the places of those who may fall in battle or be disabled by disease. The next campaign may end the war, but wisdom dictates that we should make preparations to continue it for a longer time, for it is just as probable, ay more so, that the next campaign may *not* terminate it. When the enemy learns that we are not only disposed and willing, but *prepared* to continue the war for an indefinite period, they will think of stopping the further effusion of blood, but not before.

We should show the enemy that we are not relying solely upon the operations of a single campaign, but that we intend to protract the struggle, if necessary, for years, and will transmit it, if needs be, as a woful inheritance to our children and children's children to the third and fourth generation. We should show them that we have faith in the sentiment that,

> "Freedom's battle, once begun,
> Bequeathed from bleeding sire to son,
> Though baffled oft,
> Is ever won."

ROSSER'S CAPTURE.

We have been informed that, in his last raid, Gen. Rosser captured 1000 head of cattle, 300 hogs and a considerable number of sheep, in addition to the wagons and mules noticed in another article. He captured a large quantity of stores, and what he was unable, for want of transportation, to get away, he destroyed. At Petersburg, in Hardy County, he destroyed the works of the enemy, and broke up completely the snug nest the foul birds of prey had built there.

SUBSTITUTE QUESTION.

The first decision under the law of Congress conscripting the principals who had hired substitutes, was made by Judge French, at Lumberton, N. C., on Friday last, in a case of *habeas corpus* from Moore county. The Judge affirms the constitutionality of the law, and remands the applicant to the custody of the Enrolling Officer. It appears to be sustained by the analogous decision of the highest courts of North Carolina and the United States.

SENTENCE OF ROB'T S. FORDE.

It will be remembered that in April last, in Richmond, Robert S. Forde, of Kentucky, shot and killed Robert Emmet Dixon, of Georgia, Clerk of the C. S. House of Representatives.

Last week the jury rendered the verdict that he was guilty of murder in the second degree and sentenced him to the Penitentiary for eighteen years.

EXCHANGE NOTICE.—It will be seen by the notice in to-day's paper, that our commissioner has made a further declaration of exchange of both citizens and soldiers.

WIRT ADAMS AT WORK.—It is reported that Gen. Wirt Adams captured on the 22d inst., at Selsertown, near Natchez, thirty-five pisoners and sixty wagons and teams loaded with cotton going to Natchez, and about eighty negroes.

RENNOLD'S PILLS.

Those who have been using the compounded by Dr. T. Rennolds, dec'd., will be pleased to learn that they can still be had at Dr. Fuqua, at this place.

GOOD NEWS FROM NORTH CAROLINA.

For several days the N. C. papers have been hinting at an attack on Newbern, N. C. On Monday last the movement on that town commenced, and the result is given as follows in an official telegram from Major-General Pickett:

KINSTON, Feb. 3d, 1864.

To Gen. S. Cooper:

I made a reconnoissance within a mile and a half of Newbern, with Hoke's brigade and a part of Corse's and Clingman's, and some artillery, met the enemy in force at Batchelor's Creek, killed and wounded about 100 in all, captured 13 officers and 280 prisoners, 4 negroes, 2 rifled pieces and caissons, 300 stand of small arms, 4 ambulances, 3 wagons, 55 animals, a quantity of clothing, camp and garrison equipage, and 2 flags.

Commander Wood, C. S. N., captured and destroyed the U. S. gunboat Underwriter.

Our loss was 35 killed and wounded.

(Signed,) G. E. PICKETT,
Major-Gen. Commanding.

We regret to learn that in the earliest part of this engagement Col. Henry N. Shaw, of the 8th North Carolina, was shot through the head and killed by the enemy's pickets. He was in command at Roanoke Island when that post fell, and was a member from North Carolina in the old U. S. Congress. His body arrived at Weldon Wednesday. The following [illegible]

WILMINGTON, Feb. 4

To General S. Cooper:

On the 2d instant Gen. Martin, with the 17th and 42d, and Col. Jackson's command from Kenansville, broke the railroad at Shepherdsville, driving the enemy from their works at Newport Barracks and across Newport river.

W. H. C. WHITING, Major General.

The following official despatch from Commander Wood, gives the particulars of the destruction of the gunboat mentioned in the despatch of Gen. Pickett:

KINSTON, Feb. 4, 1864.

Hon S. R. Mallory:

The force under my command boarded and captured, last night, the United States gunboat Underwriter, four guns, and ninety men and officers.

Her position was within musket range of several strong works; one of which was raking the vessel during the time we had possession, and her not having steam up caused me to burn her. Our loss is twenty killed and wounded, and four missing; the enemy's unknown.

J. TAYLOR WOOD.

THE RECONNOISSANCE TO NEWBERN.

The reconnoisance to Newbern under Gen. Pickett proved very successful. Our forces left Kinston on Sunday morning, the 31st ultimo. On the next morning they encountered the enemy at Batchelor's Creek, seven miles from Newbern, and here, in laying down the pontoons for the Confederates to cross, Col. Shaw and three privates, of the 8th N. C. regiment, were killed, and fifteen wounded. The enemy were driven from here, as stated in the official telegram.

All the other particulars of this fight were given in Gen. Pickett's telegram. A good many rumors were afloat that the town of Newbern had been invested, but none of them are as yet true. On the contrary, an official despatch has been received that our forces under Gen. Pickett have returned to Kinston. They succeeded in bringing off safely all the captures mentioned in the telegram.

CAPTURE OF A YANKEE TRAIN.

The Rockingham "Register" learns from a member of Co. H. 7th Regt., Gen. Rosser's Brigade, the following facts concerning the capture of the Yankee train by that command on Saturday, the 30th ult.:

The train was captured near Wiliamsport, on the turnpike between Petersburg and Burlington. One informant states that we captured 110 wagons, between 300 and 400 mules, and about 20 prisoners, [one of whom is a Federal Major,] and 60 head of cattle. The wagons were loaded with sugar, coffee, molasses, pickled pork and flour, and corn and oats. We brought of 65 of the wagons well loaded with the necessary articles spoken of. We killed 7 or 8 Yankees, and lost 3 killed, and 7 or 8 wounded. Of the killed, one belonged to the 11th Regt., and 2 to the 12th.—Of the wounded, Lieut. Howell, Co. G, 7th Regt., was most severely wounded, a shot through the upper part of his arm rendering amputation necessary.

We failed to capture the Yankees at Petersburg for the very good reason that they "vamosed the ranche" before we reached there. They left in a hurry on Sunday night at about 12 o'clock, having received intelligence of our approach through a young man belonging to our command whom they had captured.

The enemy had the road leading from Moorefield to Patterson's Creek pretty effectually blockaded, and guarded by two companies of infantry; but our gallant pioneers cut their way through, and led by Rosser, who dismounted and went ahead, they soon drove the enemy off. The gallantry of Rosser is greatly praised by all of his men, who know him to be a courageous leader, and willing to go wherever duty calls, whatever dangers stand in his path.

FROM GEN. LONGSTREET'S ARMY.

A correspondent, writing from Carter's Station, Tenn., the 22d ult., to the Columbia Carolinian, says General Longstreet is being rapidly re-inforced. More than 7,000 have already passed through Bristol to join their respective commands. So I am informed by the Quastermaster at that place.

"Last Saturday and Sunday the enemy made an attempt to drive General Longstreet from his comfortable winter quarters, but they were gallantly met and briven back with considerable loss. Our own loss was quite small. The full particulars are not yet known here.

"Full supplies of clothing and shoes for Gen. Longstreet's troops are rapidly arriving; also money to pay them off. Many of the men have suffered much from the want of those things.—I hear that the feet of some of the men have been so badly frost-bitten as to necessitate amputation."

SPIRIT OF THE TENNESSEE ARMY.

A Chaplain in the Tennessee army, writing from Dalton, Ga., to a friend in Richmond, gives the most cheering intelligence as to the patriotic and enthusiastic spirit of that army. As he has visited extensively among the troops, his opportunities of observation have been unusually favorably. Last fall he was accustomed to write gloomily; now, he expresses himself as follows: "A glorious, patriotic spirit now prevails in our army. About all the Tennessee soldiers have re-enlisted for the war, and other State troops are catching the fire. This is noble, glorious! God bless those brave men who have left home and all behind, and now, driven from their State, are still determined to fight on, till all is won.

"We are safe. The enthusiastic spirit of 1861 is speading abroad. We expect to whip Grant's army next spring, when the great fight comes off."

A RAID TO MADISON COURT-HOUSE.

A body of Yankee cavalry made a dash to Madison Court-House on Sunday week, picking up fifteen or twenty of our loose soldiers, and seizing as many horses. They staid only a few min- [illegible] by a traitor named Robinson, who had gone off with the Yankees, and the object of the visit was probably to enable him to remove his family, which he did.

YANKEES REFUSING TO RE-ENLIST.

A scouting party from the neighborhood of Cumberland Gap, states that Wilcox's ninth army corps has been mustered out of service and gone home, very few having re-enlisted, notwithstanding the large bounties and land warrants offered them. The enemy's cavalry force has thus been very much diminished.

GOOD NEWS FROM THE BLACKWATER.—An official dispatch from Colonel Jordan, at Ivor Station, on the Petersburg and Norfolk Railroad, Monday night, the 1st inst., says:

"The whole Yankee force, about one hundred and fifty men, are our prisoners, and their gunboat, Smith Brigg, destroyed. No one hurt on our side. Four Yankees killed and two or three wounded. The prisoners are now at Broadwater. Send down a train for them to-morrow.

It is understood that this party were sent out by Beast Butler to destroy a Cotton Factory at Smithfield, Isle of Wight county.

FROM EAST TENNESSEE.—On the 26th ult. Major Day captured Tazewell, East Tennessee, with a number of prisoners and stores. Tazewell is within twelve miles of Cumberland Gap.

We have noticed the arrival of two hundred and sixtyfive prisoners in Lynchburg within the last few days, captured by our forces in East Tennessee. They were shipped "on to Richmond."

FROM KENTUCKY.—Persons who have recently come from Kentucky [illegible] that a vast change has taken place among the people of that State in reference to the war—that a large number of citizens, formerly opposed to the Southern movement for separation and independence, have changed their views and the Southern cause is stronger than ever, and getting stronger every day.

ANOTHER CAPTURE IN LEE COUNTY.—The Abingdon Virginian, of the 28th ult., learns that General Jones' and Giltner's command captured a foraging party of Yankees in Lee county a few days ago, comprising about 100 prisoners, with their arms and equipments, horses, mules, wagons and all.

Change of Commanders.—The management of the Department of Southwest Virginia, under command of Major-General Samuel Jones, has been changed. The President has relieved Gen. Jones and assigned Major-General John C. Breckinridge to the command of the department in question. It is to be hoped that this new appointment will prevent the recurrence of those raids by the enemy which have so lately been made a feature of Southwestern Virginia, or may result in the capture of some of the raiders.

GEN. MORGAN arrived in Columbia, S. C., Saturday week and was serenaded at night, which drew together a large assemblage of ladies and gentlemen. The General briefly addressed the audience, tendering his thanks for the honor conferred, and uttering the resolve that when he was once more in the field, he would, with his sword, make good those sentiments of patriotism and of devotion to the common cause which he was not able to express on the occasion.

The Adjutant-General of the Confederate States has found it necessary to publish a general order forbidding the impressment of supplies of provisions *in transitu* to arsenals, armories and ordnance depots, under the order of the commanding officers of the same. It appears that the mania of impressment has gone to such extent that even the Government has to protect itself against the violence of its own officers.

EFFECTS OF THE RAID.—Some of the Union people who fell into the hands of their Yankee friends on the occasion of Averill's raid in Western Virginia, were effectually cured of their treasonable propensities by the treatment they met with. One Union man named Wolf, in Alleghany, whose property was not respected by the freebooters under Lincoln's banner, is ready to bushwhack his former champions. One defenceless widow, who protested her unwavering Unionism, and alleged in corroboration that her sons were deserters from the Confederate army, on pleading with the vandals to leave her one horse to ride to mill, was met with the reply, "Ride your d—d cowardly sons to mill!"

CANVASS IN YANKEE LAND.

A young lady who arrived here last week from within the lines of the enemy gave us a copy of the "New York Freeman's Journal and Catholic Register" dated the 9th of January. In the leading editorial, that paper says:

"We are ready to act with the powerful organizations forming in various States, for putting in the field, after other nominations are made on un-Democratic platforms, an electoral ticket for Vallandigham, Thos. H. Seymour, or any other stern and consistent Democrat. If he cannot be elected—and some States may elect him—at least the beacon-light of free principles of Government, as upheld by the Jeffersonian Democracy, will be kept burning, that, when the distress and agony come, the people may have a banner of hope, round which to rally.

There are one million of voters who may be relied on to vote for the man that avows, and pledges himself to carry out in good faith, the ancient Democratic principles of State supremacy, and of constitutional nullity of all attempted coercion of a State [illegible] Federal power.—There are one m[illegible] who will [illegible] deserts these pr[illegible] palters about adopting them.

Through this "return to first principles," only, lies the way of hope to restoring fellowship between the disrupted States."

ARREST OF GEN. ROBT. TOOMBS.

The circumstances attending the arrest of Gen. Toombs, as reported to the Richmond "Enquirer," are as follows:

General Toombs had taken the cars in Savannah *without a passport.* The officer on the train, whose duty it was to examine passports, called, in the discharge of this duty, upon Mr. Toombs for his passport. Mr. Toombs had no passport, and so informed the officer, and said that he would not procure any, adding that he was General Robert Toombs, and owed allegiance to Georgia and no other Government, and that his State did not require her citizens to travel with *passes and passports* and that he would not procure a passport.—The officer informed General Toombs that his orders allowed him no discretion, but required of him not to permit *any man* to pass without a passport.—General Toombs, still refusing to procure a passport, was ejected from the cars by the guard. A crowd of citizens and soldiers having collected, General Toombs proceeded to harangue them in an excited and bitter manner, and in disloyal and treasonable language.—General Beauregard being in Savannah, and hearing the facts, ordered the arrest and confinement of General Toombs, and he was taken in charge by a guard.

RETALIATION.—Major Webber, of General Morgan's command, and one of the prisoners confined in the Ohio pententiary, recently wrote a letter to some person in the Confederacy, in which he took the high ground, that, no matter whether they suffered a life-long imprisonment or died in prison, the Confederate Government should preserve its integrity of principle, and never recognize negroes as soldiers and prisoners of war. For this expression of his sentiments, Major Webber was placed in a dark cell and subjected to other indignities. This coming to the knowledge of General Morgan, he communicated the fact to the Confederate Government, and an order has been issued consigning Major White, the member of the Pennsylvania Legislature now held a prisoner at Salisbury, North Carolina, as hostage for the human treatment of Major Webber.—*Examiner.*

GENERAL LEE ON THE WAR.—A gentleman who has just arrived in Columbia, from Richmond, brings the cheering intelligence that General Lee, in conversation with a bevy of friends, recently made the remark that, with 20,000 additional men in his army, and 40,000 additional troops in the army of General Johnston, we could whip all the Yankee tribes that may be brought against us. He further observed, that if the contest was prolonged until September next, and we should meet with no grave disaster, (which General Lee did not anticipate,) the greatest crisis of the war would be successfully passed.—*South Carolinian.*

The N. Y. Herald has recovered from its fright, or it would not dare to express the following opinion of Lincoln's Administration:

The discussions in Congress on the proposed amendments to the confiscation act are so much time thrown away. There can be no doubt as to the unconstitutionality of any enactment which assumes that treason runs in the blood. It matters but little, however, how Congress may legislate on this or any other constitutional question. The war policy of the present administration has entirely superseded the constitution, and we now live under a regime as purely military as that of Rome under the Cæsars.

NOBLE LITTLE GIRL.—Miss Rebecca Cox, of Amite county, Miss., a little girl about thirteen years of age, has sent to our sildiers, within the past two years, over two hundred yards of jeans, several home-made blankets, and many pairs of socks, mostly the work of her own fair hands. She has set a most noble example, and deserves much praise.

VICE PRESIDENT STEPHENS.—This distinguished gentleman is now at his residence in Crawfordville, Georgia, and has recovered from his late illness, so as to be able to walk about, and resume, to some extent, correspondence with his friends.

Col. Crozet, long known and distinguished as a Civil Engineer in this State, died on Friday last at the residence of his son-in-law, Dr. C. S. Mills, near Richmond.

The Blue Ridge Tunnel was excavated under his superintendence.

THE BIRTH OF A PRINCE.

The papers by the last mail from Europe give full reports of the circumstances attending the accouchment of her Royal Highness, the Princess of Wales. This interesting event was not expected till March, this infant Prince being, like George III and Louis Napoleon, a seven months' child.

The "happy event" occurred about nine o'clock at night, and the Princess had been on the *same* evening to a skating party on the lake at Frogmore, and was enabled to take part in the sports and to witness the animated scene in which the Prince of Wales played a conspicous part, and did not return to the royal residence at Frogmore till a late period of the afternoon. In a few hours after the return of her Royal Highness, the following official bulletin was issued at Frogmore:

FROGMORE, Friday Evening.

Her Royal Highness, the Princess of Wales, was confined of a healthy prince at *two minutes before nine, P. M.* Her Royal Highness and infant prince are doing perfectly well.

E. H. SIEVEKING, M. D.
H. BROWN, M. D.

NOTICE TO EXEMPTS AND PERSONS NOT ENROLLED.—It may not be generally known that all persons who have been exempted from military service heretofore from any cause whatever, are required to report themselves with the evidence of their claims to exemption, for the purpose of having their exemptions revised.

Persons between the ages of 18 and 45 years, and now regularly detailed; those who have at any time been discharged from the army; those who have been discharged by Medical Boards for the examination of conscripts as well as those who have furnished substitutes, are also required to report themselves for examination and enrollment.

THE NEW CONSCRIPTION.

We learn that, by general orders of the Adjutant-General, examining boards for conscripts will be at once organized, and be composed of two medical officers and one employed surgeon. In all cases where there are two medical officers on the boards for examination of conscripts, recommendations and certificates must be concurred in and signed by both medical officers.

HELD AS A HOSTAGE—The Rev. Dr. A. H. Boyd has been arrested by the Yankees in Winchester, and is held as a hostage for Wm. Dooley, a Union man, now confined in Castle Thunder. Dr. B. is an able and distinguished minister of the Presbyterian Church, and has long been in charge of a Congregation in Winchester. He is a brother-in-law of the Hon. C. J. Faulkner.

Mrs. S. C. Law, at the head of a delegation of ladies, passed through Atlanta last Thursday, in charge of five hundred blankets and fifteen hundred pairs of socks, designed for the needy soldiers [illegible]. This munificent donation to the gallant men of the Tennessee army, says the Atlanta *Appeal*, is the free will offering of the ladies of Columbus, Georgia.

MAJOR LAMAR FONTAINE—This brave young officer, author of "All Quiet Along the Potomac To Night," was, as many of our readers are aware, captured by the enemy in a skirmish near Lawrenceburg, Tenn. He was dismounted at the time of the attack, and made a gallant resistance, but was overpowered by numbers.

A YANKEE paper says that a despatch from Knoxville announces that the rebels had captured and driven off 800 head of cattle. Longstreet has "changed his front," and occupied the rich Valley of the Tennessee, upon which the Union army depended for subsistence.

PRISONERS ESCAPED.—Seventy Yankee prisoners escaped from the Danville prison post last week. The escape was accomplished by the improved tunneling process. Eleven were re-taken immediately, but fifty-nine were at large at last accounts.

There were large accessions to General Johnston's army, at Dalton, during the month of January, and the discipline of the army is said to be very fine.

For the Spectator.

FOR SHERIFFALTY.

It is the desire of the citizens in the lower end of the county that Mr. John Batis should announce himself as a candidate for the Sheriffalty of Augusta county. MANY VOTERS.

Feb 9—1t*

FOR THE SPECTATOR.

FOR MAGISTRATE.

The citizens living in the New Hope Magisterial District would be pleased to have an opportunity to vote for Mr. John Hanger for the office of Magistrate, and hope that he will announce his willingness to be voted for. X.

Feb 9—1t*

FOR THE SPECTATOR.

FOR COUNTY CLERK.

The citizens of the lower end of the county desire to vote for Wm. A. Burnett for the office of Clerk of the County Court, and hope that he will soon announce himself. His qualifications are so well known as not to need an advocate. Y. D.

Feb 9—1t*

FOR THE SPECTATOR.

FOR SHERIFF.

GREENVILLE, Feb 6, 1864

MR. EDITOR:—As the time is nearly at hand when we must select a suitable man for Sheriff of this county, and beliving JOHN J. LAREW, as well qualified to fill that office as any one that can be brought out, we call upon him announce himself as a Candidate for the office of Sheriffalty in the County of Augusta. If he will consent to be a Candidate he will be cordially supported by MANY VOTERS.

Feb 9—1t

MARRIED.

On the 4th instant, by the Rev. Mr. Dice, Mr. JNO. J. DUNLAP, C. S. A., and Miss CATHERINE A. KNOWLES, of Staunton, Va.

On the 4th inst., by the Rev. Mr. Dice, Mr. ANDREW M. DAY, C. S. A., and Miss LIZZIE C ST. CLAIR, of Staunton, Va.

On Thursday, the 4th inst., by Rev. Martin Garber, Mr. ARCHIBALD S. RIFE and Miss ELIZA JANE BARGER, daughter of Jacob Barger, all of Augusta County.

NEW ADVERTISEMENTS.

NEW ADVERTISEMENTS.

MISCELLANEOUS.

HAMMOND GAZETTE.

[TRUTH, JUSTICE, MERCY,—UNION, LIBERTY, COUNTRY.]

VOL. 2. NO. 13. POINT LOOKOUT, MD., FEB. 10, 1864. WHOLE NO. 65.

Poetry.

Cavalry Song—the Starlight Charge.

Our good steeds snuff the evening air,
Our pulses with their purpose tingle;
The foeman's fires are twinkling there,
He leaps to hear our sabres jingle!
HALT!
Each carbine sent a whizzing ball;
Now, clang! clang! forward all
Into the fight!

Dash on beneath the smoking dome,
Through level lightnings gallop nearer;
One look to heaven! No thoughts of home—
The guidons that we hear are dearer.
CHARGE!
Clang! clang! forward all!
Heaven help those whose horses fall;
Cut left and right!

They flee before our fierce attack!
They fall! they spread in broken surges.
Now, comrades, bear our wounded back,
And leave the foeman to his dirges.
WHEEL!
The bugles sound the swift recall.
Clang! clang! backward all!
Home, and good-night.

THE SOLDIER BLOUSE.

BY M. T. CALDOR.

CHAPTER III.

The correspondence commenced in this romantic manner was not likely to be suspended by either party, and as Mrs. Weston insisted upon seeing every letter, and found nothing in any of them to censure, her approval ensured their establishment as a matter of course. Perhaps could the anxious mother have looked into Katie's day dreams, and read them also, she might have found the unknown soldier correspondent, taking almost too dear a place in her darling's thoughts; and yet, so implicitely did she share Katie's confidence in the integrity and worth of the unseen Philip Lisle, even then she might have been content to await the result of events without foreboding of evil.

And so Katie followed Philip Lisle, by means of his eloquent letters, along the eventful campaign, thrilled with horror as she read of the dangers imminently escaped; gay as he, to learn his steady promotion, from sergeant to orderly, from second to first lieutenant.

And he did not abuse the trust reposed in him. Never a line hinted aught beyond the most respectful friendliness; never an appeal to win any unguarded expression from her, marred the gentlemanly refinements of the whole—they were letters the whole town might have read, and none found cause for criticism. Why Kate was so charry of them, and allowed none but her mother and Cousin Mary to read them, is not for me to say.

"Oh, Katie, you must be sure and be early at your table at the fair," called out Belle Winsor, as she tripped lightly past the open window where Kate was leaning to watch a brilliant sunset. "And we have quite an unexpected attraction too—an invalid captain, fresh from the battle grounds, has arrived at the hotel, and made known his intention of visiting our soldier fair. Young, handsome, and a hero—what a conquest for somebody! So be sure and look your prettiest."

Kate answered carelessly. All her interest just now was verged in lieutenants. What was a captain more than a soldier, how much less than one lieutenant. So she forgot the captain entirely, until he was recalled to her mind by seeing her Uncle Hugh approaching her fancy table, with a pallid, but very handsome officer, in a captain's uniform, on his arm.

"So that is the stranger; he is very fine looking," was her inward comment, while she responded gracefully to the introduction, and hunted up the cigar case he desired to purchase.

She handed him the residue due him, as he laid the bank note beside her, but with a smile he refused it.

"I, who can so many times testify to the worth and efficiency of the Sanitary Commission, should be ashamed to take it," answered he.

And to her surprise he still leaned against her table, and began a conversation relating to the fair and its object. It was not long before they had strayed off to the war and its battle grounds. She listened with earnest attention until he referred in some way to Malvern Hill.

"Ah, were you there?" asked she breathlessly.

"In all the battles before Richmond. I belonged to the Army of the Potomac. Had you friends there?"

She smiled, and colored a little, but answered readily,

"I have had a vivid description from one who was there, and have a strong interest therein. Did you tell me your regiment?"

He named it. She started and asked again,

"And the company?"

"D."

The rose on her cheek burnt deeper and deeper.

"*His* superior officer," thought she. But he evidently did not perceive her embarrassment, nor mistrust the question that rose again and again to her lips and died away unspoken.

And so he talked on, and she could not help listening with respectful interest, often involuntary admiration. When at last he turned away, she beckoned her uncle to her side.

"What did you call his name—Captain—what?"

"Captain Guile, I understood the landlord. He's a fine specimen of a soldier, isn't he?"

"I should judge so. I believe the whole regiment bears a fine reputation," answered she.

The captain found his way to her side once more, toward the close of the evening, when her empty table gave her liberty to attend solely to his conversation, and she found he had made the acquaintance of her mother in the interval, and accepted an invitation from her to dine with them on the following day.

"I found your mother as patriotic as yourself," said he smilingly. "She said something about having followed our regiment's movements quite closely, and your interest therein.",

Kate colored again. "Yes," answered she; "although I have never seen him, I have known as much as one can learn from constant correspondence of one of your under officers."

He waited for more information, but as it was not given, politely turned the topic.

Capt. Guile lingered two weeks in G——, and scarcely a day passed that he was not in some way present wherever Kate Weston was to be found. He was extremely gentlemanly and agreeable, if she had wished, Kate would have found it difficult to avoid him. Nevertheless, neither her mother, nor Kate herself, were so very much startled when the latter received, one morning, a written declaration of love, and offer of marriage from him.

"What shall I say?" exclaimed Katie, in utter confusion.

"What you think, my dear," answered her mother smilingly.

"But it is so short an acquaintance," stammered Kate.

"Is he agreeable to you, my child? does he seem worthy of your affections—"

"Oh, yes, indeed, but then—"

"But what, my child, I scarcely understand you, for you seem pleased and pained alike."

"And so I am. I like him very much, but I thought—"

"He says he will prove satisfactorly to us his position and character—you need not fear imposture, what did you think?"

Kate hid her face on her mother's shoulder

"I like Capt. Guile very much, mother, but I can't feel sure, for I used to think before he came, that—that—"

"Well, Kate."

"That I loved Lieut. Lisle—that is all, mother."

"Hark! there is the door bell; there is no time to discuss the matter. It is Capt. Guile himself, I am sure, come for your answer. Act as your own pure heart dictates, dear Katie, and go, for it is cruel to keep him waiting."

Kate went slowly and timidly to the parlor door. Capt. Guile had heard her step and came forward to meet her.

"It is too important a subjent not to be the first thing mentioned, dear Kate," said he. "I have come for my answer.

Kate's soft brown eyelashes clung perversely to the glowing cheek, and she faltered,

"It is so sudden—I am so confused and surprised."

"That is true, but in times like these, we can waive the old rules of etiquette. A soldier's furlough will not admit of idle dallyings. May I hope, may I venture to believe my proposal is not disagreeable to you?"

Poor Katie was twisting a ring on her finger, and desperately struggling for calmness, but only grew more hopelessly nervous, as she exclaimed in almost ludicrous distress.

Concluded on fourth page.

HAMMOND GAZETTE.
WEDNESDAY MORNING, FEB. 10, 1864.
GEORGE EVERETT, Publisher.
TERMS.—One copy, for three months or less, fifty cents, IN ADVANCE; single copy, five cents.

ERRATA.—In our last issue we published the name of our new Quartermaster as Capt. "Gregory," it should have been Capt. "Godfrey."

ON Wednesday last about one hundred and seventy more rebel prisoners arrived at this place from the old Capitol prison in Washington.

GREENBACKS.—Maj. Green, Paymaster U. S. V., paid this place a visit during last week, and while here paid Uncle Sam's boys their hire, commencing with the N. H. regiments and ending with the Hammond Hospital inmates.

DROWNED.—On Friday morning, a patient in ward A, by the name of M. Noak, belonging to Co. A, 78th regiment N. Y. V., was found drowned in front of the hotel building. For several days previous the unfortunate man was considerably deranged in his mind. He was a German, with no relatives in this country, but leaves a wife in Prussia.

GENERAL McClellan's report is now out, and has created considerable comment in Congressional circles, and the democratic members are generally desirous of having a large number of copies printed, relying upon it as an influential document in the coming political campaign, and some have already referred to McClellan as their candidate for President. We shall see what we shall see.

IT affords us much gratification to learn that our friend Sergt. J. K. Whittier, of Co. G, 12th N. H. regiment, has been promoted to 2d Lieutenant of that Company. It will be remembered that he was for some time in command of the hospital guard here, and by his gentlemanly bearing made many warm friends who will rejoice with us upon learning of his merited advancement.

ON Monday night, 1st inst., a corporal and three privates who were on guard at the wharf deserted by means of a boat and canoe, one of which they obtained by bribing a boy to bring it from a schooner in the harbor. When ready to start they forced the boy to go with them, and then separated into two parties, the corporal and one of the privates forming one, and the other two privates and the boy forming the other.—The latter boat drifted down the river and was picked up by the guard at the light-ship, one of the men having perished from the effects of the cold, and the other one and the boy being in a helpless condition from the same agency. They were brought to this place on Friday morning. The other boat was subsequently found capsized, and the inference is that its two occupants were drowned. Truly the way of the transgressor is hard, and the wages of sin is death.

Negro Recruiting Camp.

A squad of about a dozen negroes, under the command of Lieut. Smithson, are now stationed in this village, for the purpose of recruiting. They reached here on Saturday evening last, and have, we learn, obtained three recruits since their arrival. The slaves in this vicinity are quite free in their intercourse with them, but a disposition to enlist does not seem to prevail. It may be proper to add, however, that Government officials—or persons claiming to be such—have already enlisted, or seduced away, a very large proportion of the young negro men of this county. We mention this fact, that public opinion at the North may not do our "colored friends" an injustice. They are unquestionably imbued with an average degree of "patriotism," and if enlistments are not more rapid among those that remain, it must not be attributed to a want of reverance for the "flag." Unaccustomed, heretofore, to the performance of military duty, and possibly not fully appreciating the exigencies of the Government, their tardiness may be more properly attributed to a want of knowledge of their duty, than an indisposition on their part to "serve their country." Let there be, therefore, no unjust discrimination against the negro recruits obtained in this county. Let them stand fair and square with their white brethren from Massachusetts, and let no man dare question their claims to equality! In conclusion, we move the arrest and *banishment* of the editor of the New York *Times*, for insinuating, in a late issue of his paper, that "there *might* be some persons at the North, that did not think a nigger as good as a white man."

Three weeks ago we had occasion to publish an article from the St. Mary's Gazette, on Negro soldiers, and comment thereon, and we had hoped that the disloyal editor of that sheet would give us no more occasion to refer to them, by carrying out the southern doctrine of "let them alone." But this Mr. Downs seems determined not to do, but to slander and villify them, and all who have anything to do with them, by vulgar slurs and sneers. The above article is from the last issue of the Gazette. We do not wish to quarrel with its editor, but it is no more than just that the people should know how to credit his statements. We do not advocate negro equality neither in social nor political affairs, yet we do say, and challenge a *reasonable* contradiction, that *some* negroes are more than equals of *some* white men, except in *color* only. And as regards that, at present, inestimable quality "patriotism," they are, in this county, by far the superiors of the whites. They are imbued with vastly more than an average degree of patriotism, taking that of the whites of this county as the standard. But this is not to be wondered at, for there has been but one paper published in the county, and that has been continualy blatting treasonable sentiments in the ears of the people, and being brought up to worship the golden calf of slavery, they are very naturally loth to turn from their idol. But all that is necessary is for the people to comprehend the true nature of the present struggle, and we think they will not be long in arraying themselves upon the side of right and freedom, against slavery and oppression. The colored portion have already seen that it is going to effect their freedom, and it is useless for the editor of the Gazette to assert that they have no disposition to enlist. The squad arrived in Leonardtown on Saturday, and the above article was probably written on Tuesday or Wednesday, and he records but three enlistments. Very good, we think, for the first three days of location in a neighborhood where no pains have probably been spared to make the negroes believe the government would do something awful with them should they ever leave their masters. How is it by this time, Mr. Downs? Have a large portion of the young negro men of that vicinity been "seduced away?" Please give us the precise number, and we venture to say it will do honor to their reverence for the "flag," as you sneeringly quote it.—They, black, swarthy and ignorant, as they are, have more reverence for that glorious emblem of our nationality, than you, white, free, educated, and possessing all the glorious privileges of an American citizen dare boast.

They, at the call of the government, rush to uphold its authority against the assaults of traitors, but you seek to disgrace it by endeavoring to keep back its defenders, and thus allow the traitors to trail it in the dust. They seek liberty, natural to all men, and you blat and jeer at them for so doing. It has well been said that, "in ignorance is bliss," and "where ignorance rules, 'tis folly to be wise," for the editor of the Gazette evidently acts upon those principles. The one he seeks to impose upon the blacks, the other upon the whites, of this county.

As we have said before, we do not advocate negro equality, and have not, therefore, the least sympathy with those who do, come they from Massachusetts or from South Carolina; but what is the use in continually "blowing" about the government for calling, and the negroes for giving, their assistance in putting down this foul rebellion. We say to the editor of the Gazette as Gamaliel said to the men of Israel, "Refrain from these men, and let them alone: for if this counsel or this work be of men, it will come to naught: but if it be of God, ye cannot overthrow it," and you may be found fighting against God as well as against your country. In conclusion we would say to the editor, be not over much zealous, either in contemptuous or earnest language, for the banishment of editors, whether loyal or disloyal, for "the dogs may be turned to their vomit, and the swine to their wallowing in the mire."

WE are furnished the following list of Medical Officers and attendants connected with the Medical department of the Prisoners' Camp by Dr. E. W. Walton:—

Surgeon in charge, James H. Thompson, Surg. U. S. V.

Ex. Officer and in charge of Hospital Department, L. F. Russell, Act. Asst. Surg, U. S. A.

Surgeon in charge of Divisions, E. W. Walton, Act. Asst. Surg U. S. A.

Examining Surg. for rebel recruits, W. Childs, Asst. Surg. 5th N. H. V.

Hospital Stewards, J. J. Gasser, C. Martin, (acting).

Confederate Hospital Assistants, Drs. Wm. Powell, Texas; R. A. Atkins, Va.; J. B. Munnerlyn, La.; J. F. Jones, Va.

Confederate Division Assistants,—1st, Wm. Godwin, N. C.; 2d, T. E. Stratten,

Va.; 3d, R. W. Gatlin, N. C.; 4th, Wm. Hale, Tenn.; 5th, B. Brown, Ga.; 6th, Wm. G. Robbets, Ga.; 7th, E. N. McCaulay, N. C.; 8th, E. F. Yong, Va.; 9th, W. H. Sibley, Va.

"DEAR GAZETTE":—I am told that you have a population of fifteen thousand on the Pint. Please inform me how in the world so many persons manage to live on a Pint of land?

I also desire to know if the last charge against the the rebs has been collected? and if the large guns were discharged on account of their demoralizing tendency?

Why do the officers file off their men? I should think they would shrink enough by being continually wet and dry.

Ike, the rascal, says they are always *dry* on a *Pint*, and the danger is, that they will dry up and blow away by the high winds.

How cruel the officers are to drill the men with muskets. Ike says it's because they want the men more *holy*.

Your early information will much oblige
Your friend
MRS. PARTINGTON, JR.

P. S.—When I call you *dear* I do not mean to be blunt, and intimate that you are *high*. MRS. P., JR.

The above questions and suggestions are from young Mrs. Partington, who was recently made such by marrying the rascally Ike, only son of the old lady's, but as we have no column for 'notices to correspondents' we decline to attempt answering them; however, we have no objections to her asking as many as she wishes.

THE town is laughing at an amusing story of a recent interview between the Secretary of War and the President of the Baltimore and Ohio railroad. It is too good to be lost, and I give it as I find it afloat:

"The draft has fallen with great severity upon the employees of our company."

"Indeed?"

"If something is not done to releive us, it is hard to foresee the consequences."

"Let them pay the commutation."

"Impossible! the men can't stand such a tax."

"[illegible] have a rich company at their back and that's more than other people have."

"They ought to be exempted, because they are necessary to the working of the road for the government."

"That can't be."

"Then I will stop the road."

"If you do, I will take it up and carry it on!"

The discussion is said to have been dropped at this point, and the very worthy President is still working the road as successfully as ever.—*Wash. Cor. N. Y. Eve. Post.*

TO ALL WHO HAVE FRIENDS IN THE ARMY.

MEMBERS OF CONGRESS, Soldiers' Aid Societies, clergymen, editors and others are respectfully requested to aid in disseminating the following notice, which is of interest to all who have friends in the army:

DIRECTORY OF THE HOSPITALS.

The Sanitary Commission have made arrangements for supplying gratuitously information with regard to patients in the United States General Hospitals at the following points, (others will be added:)

Eastern Departments:—For information address "*Office Sanitary Commission, Washington.*"

Washington, D. C.	Cumberland, Md.
Georgetown, D. C.	Point Lookout, Md.
Alexandria, D. C.	Frederick City, Md.
Baltimore, Md.	Fairfax, Va.
Annapolis, Md.	Aquia Creek, Va.
Annapolis Junction, Md.	York, Penn.

Philadelphia Department.—For information, address "*Office Sanitary Commission, No. 27 South Sixth street.*"

Philadelphia, Pa.	Chestnut Hill, Pa.
Chester, Pa.	Reading, Pa.
Germantown, Pa.	Harrisburg, Pa.

New York Department.—For information, address "*Office Womans' Central Union, No. 10 Cooper Institute.*"

New York, N. Y.	Portsmouth Grove, R. I.
Albany, N. Y.	Boston, Mass.
Newark, N. J.	Burlington, Vt.
New Haven, Conn.	Brattleboro, Vt.

Western Departments.—For information, address *Office Sanitary Commission, Louisville, Ky.*

Columbus, Ohio.	Louisville, Ky.
Cleveland, Ohio.	Covington, Ky.
Camp Dennison, Ohio.	Lexington, Ky.
Gallipolis, Ohio.	Danville, Ky.
Cincinnati, Ohio.	Perryville, Ky.
Quincy, Illinois.	Bowling Green, Ky.
Cairo, Illinois.	Memphis, Tennessee.
Mound City, Illinois.	Clarksville, Tenn.
Jeffersonville, Ind.	Jackson, Tenn.
Evansville, Ind.	Murfreesboro, Tenn.
New Albany, Ind.	La Grange, Tenn.
Saint Louis, Missouri.	Gallatin, Tenn.
Ironton, Missouri.	Nashville, Tenn.
Rolla, Missouri.	Vicksburg, Miss.
Springfield, Missouri.	Corinth, Miss.
Keokuk, Iowa.	Helena, Arkansas.
Davenport, Iowa.	Grafton, Virginia.
Paducah, Ky.	Point Pleasant, Va.
Bardstown, Ky.	Parkersburg, Va.
Lebanon, Ky.	Clarksburg, Va.
Columbus, Ky.	Charlestown, Va.
Columbia, Ky.	

Information will, under ordinary circumstances, be given to any person who may apply for it, in answer to any or all of the following inquiries. If the application is by letter, the answer will be sent by return mail; if in person, it will be answered at once

1. Is ——— [giving name and regiment, and state where when last heard of:] at present in the hospitals of ———?

2d. If so, what is his proper address?

3d. What is the name of the Surgeon or Chaplain of the hospital?

4th. If not in hospital at present, has he recently been in hospital?

5th. If so, did he die in hospital, and at what date?

6th. If recently discharged from hospital, was he discharged from service?

7th. If not, what were his orders on leaving? More specific information as to the condition of any patient in the District of Columbia hospitals will be furnished within twenty-four hours after a request to do so is received at the Washington office.

The office of the Directory will be open daily from 8 o'clock A. M. to 8 o'clock P. M., and in urgent cases applicants ringing the door bell will be received at any hour of the night.

Much inconvenience in conducting the business of the Directory having arisen where visitors have been given direct access to the record books themselves, this practice will hereafter be discontinued; nor can lists of wounded in hospitals, by States, counties, regiments, or otherwise, be hereafter furnished from these records.

The Sanitary Commission, under special authority from the President of the United States maintains an extensive system of agencies for securing the safe conveyance to and distribution of goods put in its charge for the sick and wounded at points where they are most wanted. It operates with equal care and generosity at all points—at New Orleans and at Washington, before Vicksburg and at Nashville—its distributions being governed by a comparison of the wants of the patients in all cases. To ascertain the relative character of these wants in a trustworthy manner, and to secure an equitable distribution and honest use of goods distributed, besides the unpaid services of the members of the Commission, twenty physicians of high professional and moral character and more than fifty lay-agents are employed, under pecuniary securities for responsible and efficient service. The cost of these arrangements have thus far been about 3 per centum of the value of the goods distributed. The Commission has not been able to obtain authentic evidence of losses, miscarriage, or misappropriations, to the value of one dollar in ten thousand, of goods which have been once *received* at its shipping depots. The following are the names of these depots, to which auxilliary societies and all disposed to aid the sick and wounded, without reference to States or localities, but simply to their relative necessity for assistance, are invited to send their offerings:

Sanitary Commission, Branch Supply Office, 22 Summer street, Boston, Massachusetts.

Sanitary Commission, Branch Supply Office, 10 Third Avenue, New York.

Sanitary Commission, Branch Supply Office, 27 south Sixth street, Philadelphia, Penna.

Sanitary Commission, Branch Supply Office, Cincinnati, Ohio.

Sanitary Commission, Branch Supply Office Bank street, Cleveland, Ohio.

Sanitary Commission, Branca Supply Office, Chicago, Illinois.

Sanitary Commission, Branch Supply Office, Louisville, Kentucky.

The Commission receives no pecuniary aid whatever from the Government, and is wholly dependant on the voluntary contributions of the public for the means of sustaining its operations. Contributions to its Treasury are solicited, and may be transmitted to GEORGE T. STRONG, Esq., Treasurer, 68 Wall street, New York.

The names of the following gentlemen, commissioners of the President of the United States are pledged to the public for the economy, integrity, and efficiency with which whatever is entrusted to the Sanitary Commission will be administered:

H. W. Bellows, D. D.	George T. Strong. Esq.
A. D. Bache, LL. D.	Horace Binney, Jr., Esq.
G. W. Cullum, U. S. A.	Rt. Rev. T. M. Clark, D. D.
A. E. Shiras, U. S. A.	Hon. Joseph Holt.
R. C. Wood, M. D., U. S. A.	Hon. R. W. Burnett,
S. G. Howe, M. D.	Hon. Mark Skinner
W. H. Van Buren, M. D.	Rev. John H. Heywood.
Wollcott Gibbs, M. D.	Prof. Fairman Rogers,
C. R. Agnew, M. D.	Hon. Schuyler Colfax.
Elisha Harris, M. D.	Fred Law Olmstead Esq
J. S. Newberry, M. D.	

CENTRAL OFFICE OF SANITARY COMMISSION,
244 *F street Washington, February 7, 1863.*

"I don't know, oh, I wish I did."

He might well look surprised, and a little pained.

"You don't know whether you can love me or not, is that what you mean, Kate?"

The little touch of sadness in his voice had a salutary effect. She raised her eyes and looked directly into his face.

"Something like that, I mean certainly. I like you very much indeed, only I am afraid—"

"I wrote that when I received your sanction, I would prove to your mother my standing, and give her ample facility for enquiring into my circumstances and character; of what can you be afraid, dearest Kate?"

"Of your lieutenant; what is he like, Capt. Guile? I have never seen him, but I am afraid I am more in love with him than with you."

She spoke the words hurridly, a blending of smiles and tears on her face, but she dared not look at him, and sat waiting to hear what he would answer.

"Then you know my lieutenant; what is the name you call him by?"

"Philip Lisle, of course," answered Kate.

"There is no such lieutenant in our regiment, Miss Weston. Are you sure you have not been imposed upon?"

Kate drew a long breath. "It cannot be. I could almost stake my life on his integrity, though I have only known him by his letters."

The captain caught her hand, and showered his kisses upon it.

"God bless you, Kate, for a true, leal-hearted woman."

It was Kate's turn to look astonished. She scarcely anticipated his praise for her faithfulness to the lieutenant.

"It is cruel to cheat you longer, my noble Kate; there is no Lieut. Lisle, but Capt. Philip Lisle, your humble servant, faithful correspondent, and devoted lover, stands before you."

Kate's little shriek of delight, and gesture of thanksgiving, was pleasent and pretty for him to witness.

"And now," asked he archly, "can you give me my answer, can you tell me if you love me well enough, being both lieutenant and captain, to stand up before that worthy pastor of yours, and answer in the affirmative that all-important question?"

Kates answer was inaudable, but her mother guessed it readily enough, as she came gliding silently into the room, and laid a hand on each, saying, with a stifled sob,

"God bless my children."

"But, mamma," began Kate eagerly, "you do not know—" and then she paused abruptly.

A look of significance upon her mother's face explained it all.

"Oh, mother, you were in the plot, you knew who he was all the time."

"Do you think I would have sent you from me in such a quandary if I had not?" returned the mother tenderly.

And a quiet wedding followed speedily, and Cousin Mary was there with her earnest congratulations and gentle sympathy.

"Oh, Mary, dear Mary, it is half due to you," whispered the lovely bride; and then with a wistful quivering of the lip she added—"How little you thought I should have such a precious gift to offer my country. I can do better now than sewing on the soldier's garment. I can give my husband's strong arm to wield the sword that shall lead his company on to battle. Oh, Mary, dear Mary, pray for me, that I have strength to yield him trustfully and bravely!"

But Kate was equal to the trying ordeal.—Thrusting down the sharp pang and rising sob, she, like many another loving wife, bade her beloved one God speed upon his way, and calmed her anguish with the consoling cry,

"It is for my country. I too am working for the righteous cause. I will bear lonliness, and dreariness, and bitter anxiety for my country's sake, and God can save and preserve."

Her anxieties for her husband's safety are ended now. From Gettysburg the thrilling words flashed to her along the wires,

"Capt. Philip Lisle wounded severely and dangerously."

Smothering her wild fears, Kate hastened to the distant hospital, and nursed him back to life. She has him at home now. It will be months and months before he can stir without a crutch, and it may be he will never walk again with the old free step and easy gait, but a happier couple you cannot find, than Kate and the recipient of her first Soldier Blouse!

JOSH BILLINGS.—The following is worthy of the "great showman" himself;

The most oneasy critter I ever pursued was a hobtail bull in fly time.

I am prepared tu say tu seven of the rich men out of every ten, "make the most of your money, for your money makes the most of yu."

A big soul makes a man look like an old-fashioned tin lantern with a kandle in it.

The meanest man I ever nu was the one that stole a sugar whistle from a niggar baby, to sweeten a kup of rye coffee with.

When you have seen trouble, du as the dogs du when they get whipped. go in secret and lick your sores till they git well, and then look up another fite.

There is this differance between rusting out and wearing out: if you rust out, when yu git thru yu ain't worth a cuss; but if yu wear out, what's left of yu is fustrate.

Official List of Officers and Patients.

The following is an official list of officers and patients (Union) now in connection with, and in, the Hospital at this place:

Surgeon in Charge---ANTHONY HEGER, Surgeon, U. S. A.

Assistant Surgeons--W. H. GARDNER, U. S. A., Executive Officer, GEO. MCC. MILLER, U. S. V.

Activg Asst. Surgeons---GEO. JOHNSON, T. LIEBOLD, R. N. WRIGHT, M. A. BOOTH, WM. F. BUCHANNAN, W. W. BIDLACK, W. A. HARVEY, J. GILMAN, H. S. COLSTON, F. GIESDORF.

Chaplain---Rev. J. A. SPOONER.

Hospital Stewards---H. C. ARCHIBALD, Chief Steward, J. P. STAMBAUGH, R. L. WERNWAG, J. E. MCGOWAN.

NEW YORK.

1 D W Smith G, art., L Smith F,
J C Torney C, art, 88 P Rian I,
sgt. T Coyne B, art. P Mehan A,
2 C Brill L, art. 94 L Ellithorpe K,
J J Laich L, art, W Skellen F,
6 S Smalley L, 95 J G Pratzen E,
J Smalley G, 97 E M Huntley D,
A H Tompkins G 102 J W Gilbert K,
7 C Isar F, cav. 104 C Tanner G,
9 J DeLong G, art, 107 A Noles G,
11 J J Clark C, bat, W T Warner G,
13 J Kenigan F, cav. 108 cor E Fisher I,
14 F Learn I, J Neary K,
15 cor J Daly, bat, P Weldon K,
A McCrutchen id bty, B Stump I,
16 S Fordham C, sgt J H Warden G,
39 C Butger B, E Durand B,
W Fritzsch D, 114 L S Talbert C,
42 P Gorman F, 120 G Woener I,
J Scanlon F, 121 W Dengman H,
B Butler A, cor A Harrington H
43 L Shephard K, J Severn K,
H Goldsborough H, T G Shephard F,
W Prate I, M S Tanner H,
44 W H Wheeler D, J C Peasley G,
S Ziela F, W H Rinehart G,
52 C Gilbert I, 122 D Hall K,
J Hass A, 123 J Tellier E,
J Marder D, 124 W H Dill D,
P Ruff E, J N Hazen F,
C Berrum E, G G Taylor C,
C F Miller A, 126 W B Brando D,
F Weisner I, 127 A L Romaine C,
G Korten A, 136 J Henrick F,
57 A Baker K, J Kelley F,
60 K Dygert C, C B Rhodes B
cor H Steward F, 137 J A Burrows A,
61 B Delong I, T Potts A,
P Finigan I, 140 W Eichorn B,
M Burns A, 141 S Ankle G,
64 F Cleaveland D, corp W Moore H,
W F Roffey A, 146 F Gillaume D,
J Sanders G, W S Roberts K,
69 E Quirk A T E Jepson K,
70 S W Cook B, R Kelly H;
71 P McKeon E, 147 C G Willis G,
73 C Houghtaling A, 149 J F Knoop A,
corp C D Bouton F, 150 C Dolan D,
76 G W Stout C, D Moon C,
E Field K, 151 G Cooper B,
77 W Wyatt K, M N Cole H,
E C Bryan A, W H Huie K,
W H Wildey K, M W Stockwell A,
78 M Noah A, 154 J Conant E,
82 T Foley I, W S Teft C,
T Hall F, Scott's 900 P Conly B,
86 sgt J Love E,

ILLINOIS.—12 R H McKapsley G cav.

PENNSYLVANIA.

3 E Shade A, 102 cor G O'Meally F
6 J M Pauling M, cav, A Stevens F,
8 G Holtz F, cav., 106 J Maloney K,
11 T Mulligan H, T Otto H,
23 J H Sharp B, 116 W S Kite F,
46 J H Price C, 118 E F Hubbs G,
57 E W Terry A, 119 R Nelson B,
63 G W Graham C, W Spicer C,
69 J Murry B, 121 J R Hunus G,
71 N Carty D, 138 E Y Imler E,
72 J Harbison I, 140 D H Weaver F,
W Garson H, 142 sgt G Clark B,
W Carlin F, 145 S Parrish F,
73 N Kiser —, 148 A B Rose G,
82 H Milson I, J N Rathford K,
N H Pippet A, B Simmerman A,
83 J P Ford C, A L Whitehill C,
84 W Diebart H, R Lyle I,
91 R A Wakefield I, 149 W A Price I,
96 P McNiley H, 150 J Sluffer A,
98 G Geisler B,

MASSACHUSETTS.

1 T Kennedy G, W S Sampson C,
2 I H Sawyer G, 19 J Smith I,
7 E S Elliott F, L Boyle F,
H Graff I, W B Fisher G,
H H Stevens F, J Q A Fergason B,
G Standley F, 20 E Lamprecht A,
10 C H Lather K, 22 L Ball I,
11 H H Anderson I, 28 N R Hennessy E,
sgt P Kennedy H, S Woolsencroft B,
12 J McCabe A, 32 S W Dunham D,
15 G G Taylor B, 33 G Brown D,
16 G Lovell G, E Bolton I,
18 L S Weston E,

MAINE.

1 A J Colcord C, cav, 16 G A Getchel F,
3 G W Lamont A, 17 E J Bracket D,
W O Clark E, 19 cor W Stackpole F,
4 J Hynes F, M Smith K,
5 C Dunham I, 20 H D Brown I,
H Sargent H, C A Jones I,
6 W Kelly F, J Soule A,
D Doyle B, H B Thorndike I,
H Ricker A, J S Bearse B,
7 S Crooker D,

MARYLAND.

1 J G Bowen K, 3 J F Brown K,
B A Dean E, 4 G H Foley B,
G W Morgan A, 5 C Hoffman G,
A M Trice E, 6 A J Wilkins K,
W E Lee D, 8 W W Morris E,
J Martin B, P L.G W Gunzel B, cav
2 J T Baldwin H, E. S.

UNITED STATES.

2 J Spohn E, cav. H Hackett.
J Putnam B, cav. Eng.—E Marr A,
B A Edmuns A, cav. Navy—S Smith.
J Pluck K, cav. J Adams
J Donovan G, cav. J Ellington,
J S Foster G s s. J Stevens,
S. S. E Havens B, S Capall,
J Rrandon 1st Berdan S. S.

INDIANA.

7 W H Hamilton E, R F Daniels H,
14 N Cale A, H Davis C,
M Shank G, W C Harbison K,
W S Coleman A, 27 R Sum[illegible] B,
J Towhey B,

DELAWARE.

1 J A Potter F, J Coneham C,
W H Michael K, C Kinsler A,
J Shaffner B, cor V Piereth F,
corp J B BooneD, 2 H Holden H,
W Adkins E,

RHODE ISLAND.

1 E D Pendleton F, art. D B Allen F, art.
W W Kenyon F, art. 7 W H Dakin I,
J H Chester F, art. J Shipper C,
A Grinnell F, art.

CONNECTICUT.

1 D F Crocker C, cav, 20 S L Hall A,
17 A N Allen A, H J Tibbals D,
S A Lester A,

MICHIGAN.

16 H Lawrence A, 24 T A Woodworth A,
A Bechaud A, H N Hughes C,
17 A W Kent K,

OHIO.

1 cor I Parker H, 6 W O Grover
4 G H Beddon I, 7 S G Cone D,
5 H Walker C, 107 C Boersman E,

WISCONSIN.

3 H Wood A, 26 P Lersh D,
7 T Price F,

NEW JERSEY.

3 N J Pittiuger D, 8 T A Hedden B,

VIRGINIA.—7 T O Cline D,

MINNISOTA.—1 J White H.

TRI-WEEKLY MERCURY.

BY R. B. RHETT, JR.

OFFICE NO. 434 KING-STREET, CHARLESTON

THE DAILY MERCURY, fifteen cents per copy, $15 for six months.

THE TRI-WEEKLY MERCURY, issued on Tuesdays, Thursdays and Saturdays, fifteen cents per copy, $8 for six months.

THURSDAY, FEBRUARY 25, 1864.

SIEGE MATTERS—TWO HUNDRED AND TWENTY-NINTH DAY.

Yesterday, being WASHINGTON's birthday, was celebrated by the enemy with as much *eclat* as if the *Pater Patriæ* had been a Yankee. The blockading vessels had all their colors fluttering in the breeze, and fired a "national" salute at sunrise, noon and sunset. From the calibre of the guns used in this salute it is inferred that the *Ironsides* participated.

Forty-eight shells have been fired at the city since Sunday afternoon. Four Parrott shots were also fired at Fort Sumter, three of which struck. The practice of our mortar batteries on Sullivan's Island yesterday was excellent, speedily silencing the fire of a thirty pounder Parrott gun at Gregg.

TWO HUNDRED AND THIRTIETH DAY.

Since our last report the bombardment of the city has again become quite brisk. From 5 30 p. m., on Monday, until the same hour on Tuesday, one hundred and twenty-three shells were thrown at the city. Two shots have also been fired at Fort Sumter, both of which struck. Two of the enemy's picket boats were discovered on Monday night within five hundred yards of the fort.

A large fire on Folly Island was noticed by our lookouts on Monday afternoon.

Three prisoners and eight Yankee deserters from the enemy's force on Kiawah Island were brought to the city yesterday.

THE DEATH OF NELSON MITCHELL.—The illness of this gentleman, which has been of a very serious character for more than a week past, terminated fatally a little before one o'clock Monday morning.

NELSON MITCHELL was born in Charleston on the 15th of January, 1812. Graduated in South Carolina College in 1832, with the second honor of his class—JOSEPH W. LESESNE, of South Carolina, subsequently of Alabama, and Chancellor of the Southern Division thereof—succeeding Chancellor one of the earliest graduates of the South Carolina College. He was particularly distinguished for his Greek, whilst at College, ranking, in the opinion of Professor HENRY, with any who had graduated at that Institution. He was accomplished in almost all the languages of Europe—German, French, Spanish, Italian—speaking German, French and Spanish. He entered the Legislature in '46, and remained in, we believe, until '58. Although a Union man, he was Chairman of the Committee on Federal Relations, in for four years, commencing in '50. He was subsequently Chairman of the Judiciary Committee as long as he was in the Legislature. He was the acknowledged leader in judicial reform, and in its advocacy delivered a very able argument. His displays of legal knowledge and professional judgment were such, at the Bar and in the Legislature, that he was nominated for the Chancery Bench. His career at the Bar is familiar to our people. It was such as to give him their respect for his acumen and learning, and uncorruptedness.

ACKNOWLEDGEMENTS.—We have received from Mr. B. T. SELLERS, a box containing thirty dozen of eggs and a barrel of grists, for the use of the hospitals, which have been properly disposed of. Mr. SELLERS will oblige by sending a duplicate list of contributors, which we will cheerfully publish, the former having been mislaid.

Mr. SELLERS will also accept our thanks for his kind remembrance of ourselves.

THE RE-ENLISTMENTS.—We are indebted to Capt. H. W. FEILDEN, A. A. G., for copies of the following gratifying despatches:

COOSAWHATCHIE, S. C., February 18, 1864.

Capt. James Lowndes, A. A. A. G.:

CAPTAIN: I beg leave respectfully to inform you that the Lafayette Light Artillery, originally enlisted in Confederate service for three years on the 13th March, 1862, have re enlisted, unconditionally, for the war.

I have the honor, Captain, to remain
Very respectfully,
Your obedient servant,
(Signed) J. T. KANAPAUX,
Capt. Commanding L. L. Artillery.

HEADQUARTERS PARTISAN RANGERS, POCOTALIGO, February 17, 1864.

Captain James Lowndes, A. A. A. G.:

CAPTAIN: At a meeting of my command, held this afternoon, at their encampment, they to a man re-enlisted for the war.

Very respectfully, your obedient servant,
(Signed) M. J. KIRK,
Captain Commanding P. R.

HEADQUARTERS 25TH REGIMENT S. C. VOLS., 20th February, 1864.

Brig. Gen. Thos. Jordan, Chief of Staff and A. A. General:

GENERAL: I have the honor to inform you that a majority of Co. C, (Captain Chind) have re-enlisted for the war.

Very respectfully, your obedient servant,
(Signed) JNO. G. PRESSLEY,
Lieutenant Colonel Commanding.

The following preamble and resolutions were unanimously passed by the members of Schultz's Light Battery, stationed at Willtown Bluff, on the 22d February:

On motion, Corporal W. A. Kesler was called to the Chair and Mr. H. L. Williams requested to act as Secretary.

WHEREAS, we, the members of Chesnut Light Artillery, Company F, Palmetto Battalion Light Artillery, being attached to an organization which was originally and unconditionally mustered for the war, and we are thereby debarred the necessity of thus repeating our devotion to the cause in which we are struggling, we nevertheless deem it a privilege to give expression to our renewed and unfaltering determination and readiness to re-dedicate our lives, our fortunes and our sacred honor to the service of our beloved Confederacy.

Resolved, That whilst admiring the patriotism of our brethren in arms, in Virginia and the West—the heroes of many battles, who have re-volunteered for the war—we pledge ourselves likewise to remain in service so long as an armed foe pollutes the soil of our sacred homes.

Resolved, That we trust that the war will be prosecuted until the full measure of our rights are secured and we are left regenerated and disenthralled.

THE STOCK MARKET.—We give below the prices obtained Monday at the Stock auction of Mr. JOHN S. RIGGS:

Four Thousand Five Hundred Dollars in Confederate States Eight Per Cent. Bonds, redeemable in 1873, $140.
Sixty Thousand Dollars in Confederate States Eight Per Cent. Bonds, redeemable in 1868, $137.50 to $135.
Three Thousand Dollars in Confederate States Eight Per Cent Bonds, $141.
One Share Chicora Steamship Company, $4625.
Ten Shares Palmetto Steamship Company, $805.
Five Shares Atlantic Steamship Company, $2950 to $3050.
One Thousand Dollars in South Carolina Railroad Bonds of $500 each, $325 per the hundred.
Five Hundred Dollars in Greenville and Columbia Railroad Bonds, $220 per the hundred.
Two Shares Georgia Steamship Company, $2010.

SOLDIERS' RELIEF ASSOCIATION.—During the past week the following donations have been received:

From Miss Cecile Mordecai—2 pairs socks.
From Misses Simpson—2 pairs socks.
From Misses Cohen—2 pairs socks.
From Miss Mills—2 dozen eggs.
Through Express—1 bundle of rags.
From a Friend—1 bundle linen rags.
From a Lady, through Rev. C. P. Gadsden—$100.
From Mrs. Just, through Dr. Bachman—$5.
From G. E. Mills—$5.

The following have been given to seamen and soldiers in various hospitals:

4 pairs pants, 14 flannel shirts, 18 pairs drawers, 24 pairs socks, 10 pocket handkerchiefs, 2 cotton shirts.

The English Court of Exchequer on the Alexandra.

The London *Index*, of the 14th January, devotes a long editorial article to the above case, upon which it sheds some light not already given to the Confederate public. Our space will not permit us to copy the whole article. We, therefore, confine ourselves to a statement of such new facts as it may contain.

It will be remembered that the British Government, at the instigation of C. F. ADAMS, LINCOLN's Minister at London, and upon information furnished by LINCOLN's spies at Liverpool, seized the steamship *Alexandra*, then in the river Mersey, on the allegation that she had been built and was to be fitted out as a ship of war for the service of the Confederate States, in contravention of the provisions of the Foreign Enlistment Act. The case was tried before the Chief Baron and a jury. The jury, under the direction of the Chief Baron, found for the claimants of the vessel and against the Government. The Government took an appeal to the Court of Exchequer from this ruling of one of its Judges. This appeal came before the Court during the last term, and it was supposed that the decision would be given in November. The arguments in the case were heard then on a motion for a new trial. The Court took time to consider its judgment, which was pronounced on Monday, January 11th, the first day of the present session.

The Chief Baron adhered to his former ruling. Mr. Baron BRAMWELL, the senior of the puisne judges, agreed with him. Mr. Baron CHANNELL dissented, holding that the direction of the Chief Baron to the jury had not been satisfactory, and that, on this account, a new trial ought to be granted. The junior of the Court is Mr. Baron PIGOTT. Mr. Baron PIGOTT was, when this case commenced at Liverpool, a member of Parliament for the borough of Reading, and known to entertain opinions favorable to the Government, and opposed to the parties claiming the ship. He was appointed, *pendente lite*, by the Government, one of the parties to the suit. His opinion was given in favor of a new trial; but, as the Court was thus evenly divided, he, being the junior, according to custom, withdrew his judgement, and the rule for a new trial was refused. The effect of this decision will be to leave the Government at liberty to appeal to what is called the Court of Exchequer Chamber, where, in this case, the Judges of the two other Courts (Queen's Bench and Common Pleas) will review the decision of the Court of Exchequer; and from them there lies a further appeal to the House of Lords.

It is not supposed that the English Government has any hopes of condemning the *Alexandra*, but, by detaining her, they equally serve the purposes of SEWARD. They know that her release at this time would bring them insolent despatches from Washington, and they fancy that it might lead to a declaration of war; and therefore it is their policy to postpone that event as long as possible. In this point of view, the division of opinion in the Court of Exchequer is just what they wanted, and planned to bring about, when they appointed Mr. PIGOTT to the fourth seat on the Exchequer bench. It gives them good cause for a further appeal, and it does not give them a new trial, which would be final, and would, in all probability, terminate in favor of the defendants the claimants of the vessel, and against the Government.

The *Index* does not charge or even hint that Mr. Baron PIGOTT was influenced in his opinion in any way by political feeling. But it plainly intimates that a knowledge of his opinions on this case, then pending before the Court of Exchequer, was mainly influential with the ministry in causing his nomination to the vacant place in that court.

Considerable dissatisfaction, remarks the Wilmington *Journal*, no doubt exists in England, caused by the mean, pettifogging course of the Admistration, which is more consonant to the dealings of the lower sort of attorneys than to the usage of great nations in important causes of this character. Still to any questions propounded in Parliament, RUSSELL or PALMERSTON, or any of their strikers, will have the all-sufficient answer that the question is before the courts on its legal merits. Those who know anything of the resources of legal chicanery and delay may form some idea of how long it will *stay* there.

RETREATED.—The Rome *Courier*, of Saturday states that the Federal force, a division of infantry under General OSTERHAUS, and a brigade of cavalry, commanded by General WILDER, that recently occupied Wills Valley, have all retired beyond the Tennessee River. They recrossed last Tuesday night, and have fortified on the north bank of the river, opposite Larkin's Ferry. Their pontoons had not been taken up on Wednesday. Our scouts now go to Larkin's Ferry, and also Gunterville.

MAJOR GEN. GILMER, second in command of this Department, has been tranferred temporarily from Savannah to Mobile. The following official announcement of the fact appears in the papers of the former city:

Under orders from the War Department, Major General Gilmer repairs for temporary duty to Mobile. During his absence, Brigadier General Mercer is assigned to the command of the Military District of Georgia and Third Military District of South Carolina.

NEWS FROM BERMUDA—MOVEMENTS OF THE BLOCKADE RUNNERS.—We take the following from the Bermuda *Royal Gazette* of February 8:

The steamer Don, which left here on Sunday morning last for Nassau, N. P., is reported (falsely of course), to have been captured on leaving Nassau by the United States steamer Tioga. From the 3d to the 6th ult., the steamers Fannie, Syren, Scotia and Hansa had arrived there from Wilmington. The Presto and the Wild Dayrell had also arrived.

The steamer City of Petersburg hence for Wilmington, N. C., was captured off that port on the morning of the 18th ult., by the United States ship Connecticut.

The steamer Red Jacket, from Mobile, with 500 bales of cotton and a quantity of rosin, had been captured by the United States steamer Kennebec. The Red Jacket is valued at $100,000.

The steamer Isabel, under Spanish colors, arrived at Havana from Mobile on the 15th ult., laden with cotton.

The blockade runners Cumberland, Alice, and Little Lola were at Havana on the 16th ult.

It was reported at Havana that the steamship Harriet Lane, formerly the United States gunboat of that name, had been fitted up at Galveston, Texas, for blockade running purposes, and was expected at Havana with a full cargo of cotton.

The steamers Index, Emily, Minnie and Caledonia had arrived at Bermuda from England. They were supposed to be intended for blockade running.

Editor Mercury: Permit me to acknowledge through your colums the following donations to Hospital Encampment, Summerville, S. C., Surgeon E. E. JENKINS in charge:

From the Misses Tuckers, 10 dozen eggs and 1 ham.

From Mrs. Clayton, 1 can lard and 1 ham.

Through Rev. J. W. Miller, Post Chaplain, 19 pounds lard, 48 pounds bacon, 3 sacks peas and 2 pounds butter.

Respectfully,
R. M. FROST,
Steward Hospital Encampment.

The Gibbons House, in Savannah, was nearly destroyed by fire, February 19th. The premises were occupied by the Confederate Government, and used as a Naval Hospital. All the bedding, furniture, medicines, &c., were saved; some of the furniture and bedding were damaged. All the patients were saved and removed to General Hospital No. 1. The property is owned by Mr. Horace Morse, and is valued at over $100,000. An insurance of $20,000 is on the building, in the Southern Insurance and Trust Company. The building is very much damaged generally, and it cannot at the present time be repaired so as to be occupied.

The United States Supreme Court has decided that Vallandigham was legally arrested, tried and banished.

THE VICTORY IN FLORIDA.

We are glad to say that the news of our victory in Florida is fully confirmed. General BEAUREGARD yesterday received a despatch from General FINNEGAN, dated Lake City, February 20th, and giving additional details. We took five cannon and drove the enemy from the field, on which he left his dead. Our loss was 250 killed and wounded. COLQUITT's brigade, we learn, distinguished itself. ANDERSON's cavalry had not yet arrived, but the rest of our cavalry were in full pursuit of the retreating foe.

The Yankee force beaten in this fight is estimated to have been 3000 strong. They landed at King's Ferry, on the St. Mary's River, and were about midway on Saturday between that point and the Satilla Bridge. A despatch to the Savannah papers, dated Lake City, Saturday afternoon, says:

A severe battle has been going on all this p. m., near Olustee, thirteen miles east of this place, the enemy slowly retreating, and our forces pressing them. Their dead and wounded lay thick on the field. But few casualties are yet reported—among the gallant Lieut. Col. James Barrow, of the 64th Georgia Regiment, killed; the Colonel and Major of same regiment were wounded. Col. Clinch was wounded. Col. Carraway Smith had his horse shot from under him.

The Savannah *News* of Monday contains the following:

On Friday night last eight deserters from the Yankee army in Florida arrived in this city by the Gulf train. They state that they left their regiments on the 13th instant, previous to their advance on Sanderson, and therefore had no knowledge of any movements of importance. They are all conscripts, and give as a reason for their desertion ill treatment and the deception practiced upon them. They, with their regiments, left Riker's Island, New York harbor, on the 8th of October, and with one or two exceptions, have received no pay from the Federal Government up to the present time. They state that the Yankee force which landed at Jacksonville, Florida, numbered from four to five thousand men, and among them are the 48th New York Infantry, 7th Connecticut, 7th New Hampshire, 115th New York, 47th New York, and two negro regiments. These troops are commanded by General Seymour, of New York. One of the negro regiments is the 40th Massachusetts. They are mounted infantry, and number about six hundred. The 1st Massachusetts negro cavalry numbers about two hundred and forty men. They have also a small force of negro infantry called the 3d South Carolina, and the 54th negro regiment from Pennsylvania, from eight to nine hundred strong.

They stated that the main object of the expedition, as they learned from their officers, was to devastate the country and destroy the railroads in that section. They represent that they lived on half-rations, and were instructed to live off the country through which they passed. If the statements which they give are true, there is great dissatisfaction in the whole Yankee army in Florida. One of the deserters, a German, informed us that his whole regiment would desert if they thought they could reach our lines in safety and not be recaptured. They are very hostile to the negro troops, and assert that they are not to be trusted in battle, but will retreat on the first fire. Their officers instructed them to capture all the negroes they could, asserting that it was the intention of the Federals to colonize Florida with blacks.

FROM EAST TENNESSEE.

Private letters from Bristol announced the forward movement of Longstreet. It is said that he passed Knoxville, which is effectually garrisoned by small pox. The number of troops in the place is very small. Our scouts say that Thomas is reinforcing Foster. On yesterday it was reported by Unionists and others, that a fierce conflict had taken place near Knoxville. The fight continued through two days. On the first day the battle was indecisive, on the second, the Federals were routed. Such are the stories brought in by our scouts. Our readers may judge of their credibility.

On yesterday, two pieces of artillery and three hundred cavalry and infantry came out from Chattanooga and attacked our pickets. Two of these were captured. No other reported losses on either side.

The roads about Dalton are in a horrible condition. Of the ninety prisoners brought in from Alabama, one is a woman in man's apparel. She goes on crutches, and belongs to the 16th Illinois. So says the Knoxville Register of the 21st.

THE AMERICAN WAR IN ENGLAND.

[*London Correspondence of the New York Times, February 12.*]

A few days more, and the session (of Parliament) will open. Lord Palmerston has issued cards for his full dress dinner to open the session, and Mr. Disraeli, the conservative leader, will soon do the same. Nothing can be begun, carried on or ended here without eating dinners.

As the premium on gold goes up in New York, Confederate stock rises in London. It has been down to 30 It is up to 50. There are some quiet movements going on here that are producing confidence in those who "sympathise with all rebellions but their own." The speeches of Mr. Spence, published by Bentley, are sown broadcast.

Active agents are going round among the business houses of London, and every commercial town in the Kingdom, getting signers to petitions to the Government to do something to stop the war. These petitions, I believe, are signed by almost every one who is asked. I was told a few days ago in a business house in Leicester square that two or three hundred signatures were obtained in single establishments. There is a hard pinch now on commercial and manufacturing classes. The cost of cotton is draining the country of specie, the discount rates having gone up to eight per cent., which is simply ruin to men trading with a small margin of profit. I am more and more convinced that a far stronger effort will be made at the coming session than heretofore for recognition. Even Mr. Scholefield, the colleague of Mr. Bright, in the representation of Birmingham, is an officer in a "Southern Independence Association," where he figures with the most noble Marquises of Bath and Lothain, with Lords Robert and Eustace Cecil, with the Right Honorable Lords Wharncliff and Campbell, &c., &c. This and similar associations had not been idle during the recess, and I shall be much disappointed if a very strong pressure is not brought to bear upon the Government, in which case the resignation of Earl Russell, should it be accepted, will be no common misfortune. No doubt he is one of the most unpopular of ministers, but he is also one of the most respected, and his dogged obstinacy of character is not easy to get over. * * * * *

If ever a decided policy was needed, it is now. I know that, in the opinion of many, the rebellion is already crushed and the South ready to submit, so that the Union will be fully restored before the next election, and no war needed, unless with some foreign power—but that is not my opinion. I look forward to a year of severe and terrible conflicts in the South, and there are some indications that there may be serious difficulties in the North. If not, it will not be for lack of the disposition to foment them. * * *

England feels, in view of a probable defeat of the Confederates much as a sympathizer with the beaten side would be likely to, when the victor was about to turn round with his—"now that job's done, and if you don't like it, I'm ready for you." And the first thought of England has been, and is, "if we let these Yankees beat, after all we have said and done, they are sure to turn round and pay us off for it." It is human nature.

Great efforts are now making to stop the emigration from Ireland to the United States, so far, at least, as its object is to strengthen the Northern armies. I mentioned the letter of John Mitchell to a leading paper in Dublin! The letter of His Holiness the Pope, though but a pious expression of a wish for peace suitable to the Head of the Church, also has its influence, as it seems a recognition of Mr. Davis' official position. And now we have an officer of the Confederate army in Ireland, with letters to several Bishops, whose mission is to induce them to use their influence in favor, at least, of non-intervention.

MORE EXECUTIONS OF DESERTERS AT KINSTON.—The execution of seven deserters at Kinston, N. C., on the 13th, has been published. On the 16th, thirteen more were hanged. The correspondent of the Raleigh *Confederate* says:

J. S. Brock Wm. Reddock, C. Huffman, Stephen Jones, A. J. Britton, J. J. Summerlin, William H. Daughtry, Lewis Taylor, Lewis Freeman and John Freeman, of Nethercutt's battalion; and W. D Jones, of Wright's battalion, and Jos. Brock, of the 27th North Carolina regiment, and C. R. Cuthrell, of Latham's battery, were all hanged in this place on yesterday, by order of court martial, for deserting their comrades and taking up arms on the enemy's side.

BRIGADIER GENERAL MCGOWAN, having partially recovered from the effect of his wounds, resumed the command of his brigade on the 4th instant.

ADDRESS OF CONGRESS

TO THE PEOPLE OF THE CONFEDERATE STATES.

In closing the labors of the First Permanent Congress, your Representatives deem it a fit occasion to give some account of their stewardship; to review briefly what, under such embarrassments and adverse circumstances, has been accomplished; to invite attention to the prospect before us, and the duties incumbent on every citizen in this crisis; and to address such words of counsel and encouragement as the times demands.

Compelled by a long series of oppressive and tyrannical acts, culminating at last in the selection of a President and Vice-President by a party confessedly sectional and hostile to the South and her institutions, these States withdrew from the former Union, and formed a new Confederate alliance, as an independent Government, based on the proper relations of labor and capital. This step was taken reluctantly, by constraint, and after the exhaustion of every measure that was likely to secure us from interference with our property, equality in the Union, or exemption from submission to an alien Government. The Southern States claimed only the unrestricted enjoyment of the rights guaranteed by the Constitution. Finding, by painful and protracted experience, that this was persistently denied, we determined to separate from those enemies, who had manifested the inclination and ability to impoverish and destroy us, we fell back upon the right for which the colonies maintained the war of the revolution, and which our heroic forefathers asserted to be clear and inalienable. The unanimity and zeal with which the separation was undertaken and perfected, finds no parallel in history.

The people rose *en masse* to assert their liberties and protect their menaced rights. There never was before such universality of conviction, among any people, on any question involving so serious and so thorough a change of political and international relations. This grew out of the clearness of the right so to act, and the certainty of the perils of further association with the North. The change was so wonderful, so rapid, so contrary to universal history, that many fail to see that all has been done in the logical sequence of principles, which are the highest testimony to the wisdom of our fathers, and the best illustration of the correctness of those principles. This Government is a child of law instead of sedition, of right instead of violence, of deliberation instead of insurrection. Its early life was attended by no anarchy, no rebellion, no suspension of authority, no social disorders, no lawless disturbances. Sovereignty was not for one moment in abeyance. The utmost conservatism marked every proceeding and public act. The object was "to do what was necessary, and no more; and to do that with the utmost temperance and prudence." St. Just, in his report to the Convention of France, in 1793, said:

"A people has but one dangerous enemy, and that is government." We adopted no such absurdity. In nearly every instance, the first steps were taken legally, in accordance with the will and prescribed direction of the constituted authorities of the seceding States. We were not remitted to brute force or natural law, or the instincts of reason. The charters of freedom were scrupulously preserved. As in the English Revolution, of 1688, and ours of 1776, there was no material alteration in the laws beyond what was necessary to redress the abuses that provoked the struggle. No attempt was made to build on *speculative* principles. The effort was confined within the narrow limits of historical and constitutional right. The controversy turned on the records and muniments of the past. We merely resisted innovation and tyranny, and contended for our birthrights and the covenanted principles of our race. We have had our Governors, General Assemblies and Courts; the same electors; the same corporations; "the same rules for property; the same subordinations, the same order in the law and in the magistracy." When the sovereign States met in council, they, in truth and substance, and in a constitutional light, did not make, but prevented, a revolution.

Commencing our new national life under such circumstances, we had a right to expect that we would be permitted, without molestation, to cultivate the arts of peace, and vindicate, on our chosen arena, and with the selected type of social characteristics, our claims to civilization. It was thought, too, by many that war would not be resorted to by an enlightened country except on the direst necessity. That a people, professing to be animated by Christian sentiment, and who had regarded our peculiar institution as a blot and blur upon the fair escutcheon of their common Christianity, should make war upon the South for doing what they had a perfect right to do, and for relieving them of the incubus which, they professed, rested upon them by the association, was deemed almost beyond belief by many of our wisest minds. It was hoped, too, that the obvious interest of the two sections would restrain the wild frenzy of excitement and turn into peaceful channels the thoughts of those who had but recently been invested with power in the United States.

These reasonable anticipations were doomed to disappointment. The red glare of battle, kindled at Sumter, dissipated all hopes of peace, and the two Governments were arrayed in hostility against each other. *We charge the responsibility of this war upon the United States.* They are accountable for the blood and havoc and ruin it has caused. For such a war we were not prepared. The difference in military resources between our enemies and ourselves; the immense advantages possessed in the organised machinery of an established Government; a powerful navy; the nucleus of an army; credit abroad, and illimitable facilities in mechanical and manufacturing power, placed them on the "vantage ground." In our infancy we were without a seaman or soldier, without revenue, without gold and silver, without a recognized place in the family of nations, without external commerce, without foreign credit, with the prejudices of the world against us. While we were without manufacturing facilities to supply our wants; our ports were blockaded; we had to grapple with a giant adversary, defend two thousand miles of seacoast, and an inland frontier of equal extent. If we had succeeded in preventing any successes on the part of our enemy, it would have been a miracle. What we have accomplished, with a population so inferior in numbers, and means so vastly disproportionate, has excited the astonishment and admiration of the world.

The war in which we are engaged was wickedly, and against all our protests, and the most earnest efforts to the contrary, forced upon us. South Carolina sent a commission to Washington to adjust all questions of dispute between her and the United States. One of the first acts of the Provisional Government was to accredit agents to visit Washington, and use all honorable means to obtain a satisfactory settlement of all questions of dispute with that Government. Both efforts failed. Commissioners were deceived and rejected, and clandestine but vigorous preparations were made for war. In proportion to our perseverance and anxiety have been the obstinacy and arrogance in spurning offers of peace. It seems we can be indebted for nothing to the virtues of our enemy. We are obliged to his vices, which have enured to our strength. We owe as much to his insolence and blindness as to our precaution.

The wager of battle having been tendered, it was accepted. The alacrity with which our people flew to arms is worthy of all praise. Their deeds of heroic daring, patient endurance, ready submission to discipline, and numerous victories, are in keeping with the fervent patriotism that prompted their early volunteering. Quite recently, scores of regiments have re enlisted for the war, testifying their determination to fight until their liberties were achieved. Coupled with and contributing greatly to this enthusiastic ardor, was the lofty courage, the indomitable resolve, the self denying spirit of our noble women, who, by their labors of love, their patience of hope, their unflinching constancy, their uncomplaining submission to privations of the war, have shed an immortal lustre upon their sex and country.

Our army is no hireling soldiery. It comes not from paupers, criminals or emigrants. It was originally raised by the free, unconstrained, unpurchaseable assent of the men. All vocations and classes contributed to the swelling numbers. Abandoning luxuries and comforts to which they had been accustomed, they submitted cheerfully to the scanty fare and exactive service of the camp. Their services above price, the only remuneration they have sought is the protection of their altars, firesides and liberty. In the Norwegian wars the actors were, every one of them, named and patronymically described as the King's friend and companion. The same wonderful individuality has been seen in this war. Our soldiers are not a consolidated mass, an unthinking machine, but an army of intelligent units. To designate all who have distinguished themselves by special valor would be to enumerate nearly all in the army. The generous rivalry between the troops from different States has prevented any special pre-eminence, and hereafter, for centuries to come, the gallant bearing and unconquerable devotion of Confederate soldiers will inspire the hearts, and encourage the hopes, and strengthen the faith, of all who labor to obtain their freedom.

For three years this cruel war has been waged against us, and its continuance has been seized upon, as a pretext by some discontented persons to excite hostility to the Government. Recent and public as have been the occurrences, it is strange that a misapprehension exists as to the conduct of the two Governments in reference to peace. Allusion has been made to the unsuccessful efforts, when separation took place, to procure an amicable adjustment of all matters in dispute. These attempts at negotiation do not comprise all that has been done. In every form in which expression could be given to the sentiment—in public meetings, through the press, by legislative resolves—the desire of this people for peace, for the uninterrupted enjoyment of their rights and prosperity, has been made known. The President, more authoritatively, in several of his messages, while protesting the utter absence of all desire to interfere with the United States, or acquire any of their territory, has avowed that the "advent of peace will be hailed with joy. Our desire for it has never been concealed. Our efforts to avoid the war, forced on us as it was by the lust of conquest and the insane passions of our foes, are known to mankind."

The course of the Federal Government has proved that it did not desire peace, and would not consent to it on any terms that we could possibly concede. In proof of this, we refer to the repeated rejection of all terms of conciliation and compromise, to their recent contemptuous refusal to receive the Vice President, who was sent to negotiate for softening the asperities of war, and their scornful rejection of the offer of a neutral Power to mediate between the contending parties. If cumulative evidence be needed, it can be found in the following resolution, recently adopted by the House of Representatives in Washington:

"*Resolved*, That as our country and the very existence of the best Government ever instituted by man are imperilled by the most causeless and wicked rebellion that the world has seen, and believing, as we do, that the only hope of saving this country and preserving this Government is by the power of the sword, we are for the most vigorous prosecution of the war until the Constitution and the laws shall be enforced and obeyed in all parts of the United States; and to that end we oppose any armistice, or intervention, or mediation, or proposition for peace, from any quarter, so long as there shall be found a rebel in arms against the Government; and we ignore all party names, lines and issues, and recognize but two parties in this war—patriots and traitors."

The motive of such strange conduct is obvious. The Republican party was founded to destroy slavery and the equality of the States, and Lincoln was selected as the instrument to accomplish this object. The Union was a barrier to the consummation of this policy, because the Constitution, which was its bond, recognized and protected slavery and the sovereignty of the States. The Union must, therefore, be sacrificed, and to ensure its destruction, war was determined on.

The mass of the Northern people were not privy to, and sympathized in no such design. They loved the Union, and wished to preserve it. To rally the people to the support of the war, its object was proclaimed to be "a restoration of the Union," as if that which implied voluntary assent, of which agreement was an indispensable element and condition, could be preserved by coercion. It is absurd to pretend that a Government, really desirous of restoring the Union, would adopt such measures as the confiscation of private property, the emancipation of slaves, systematic efforts to invite them to insurrection, forcible abduction from their homes and compulsory enlistment in the army, the division of a sovereign State without its consent, and a proclamation that one-tenth of the population of a State, and that tenth under military rule, should control the will of the remaining nine tenths. The only relation possible between the two sections, under such a policy, is that of conqueror and conquered, superior and dependent. Rest assured, fellow-citizens, that although restoration may still be used as a war cry by the Northern Government, it is only to delude and betray. Fanaticism has summoned to its aid cupidity and vengeance; and nothing short of your utter subjugation, the destruction of your State Governments, the overthrow of your social and political fabric, your personal and public degradation and ruin, will satisfy the demands of the North. Can there be a man so vile, so debased, so unworthy of liberty as to accept peace on such humiliating terms?

It would hardly be fair to assert that all the Northern people participate in these designs. On the contrary, there exists a powerful political party, which openly condemns them. The Administration has, however, been able thus far, by its enormous patronage and its lavish expenditures, to seduce, or by its legions of "Hessian" mercenaries to overawe the masses, to control the elections, and to establish an arbitrary despotism. It cannot be possible that this state of things can continue. The people of the United States, accustomed to freedom, cannot consent to be ruined and enslaved, in order to ruin and enslave us. Moral, like physical epidemics, have their allotted periods, and must sooner or later, be exhausted and disappear. When reason returns our enemies will probably reflect, that a people, like ours, who have exhibited such capabilities, and extemporized such resources, can never be subdued; that a vast expanse of territory, with such a population cannot be governed as an obedient colony. Victory would not be conquest. The inextinguishable quarrel would be transmitted "from bleeding sire to son," and the struggle would be renewed between generations yet unborn. To impoverish us would only be to dry up some of the springs of Northern prosperity—to destroy Southern wealth is to reduce Northern profits, while the restoration of peace would necessarily re-establish some commercial intercourse. It may not be amiss in this connexion, to say, that at one time it was the wish and expectation of many at the South, to form a treaty of amity and friendship with the Northern States, by which both peoples might derive the benefits of commercial intercourse and move on side by side, in the arts of peace and civilization. History has confirmed the lesson taught by Divine authority, that each nation, as well as each individual, should seek their happiness in the prosperity of others, and not in the injury or ruin of a neighbor. The general welfare of all is the highest dictate of moral duty and economic policy, while a heritage of triumphant wrong is the greatest curse than can befall a nation.

Until some evidence is given of a change of policy on the part of the Government and some assurance is received that efforts at negotiation will not be spurned, the Congress are of opinion that any direct overtures for peace would compromise our self-respect, be fruitless of good, and interpreted by the enemy as an indication of weakness. We can only repeat the desire of the people for peace, and our readiness to accept terms consistent with the honor and integrity and independence of the States, and compatible with the safety of our domestic institutions.

Not content with rejecting all proposals for a peaceful settlement of the controversy, a cruel war of invasion was commenced, which, in its progress has been marked by a brutality and disregard of the rules of civilized warfare, as stand out in unexampled barbarity in the history of modern wars. Accompanied by every act of cruelty and rapine, the conduct of the enemy has been destitute of that forbearance and magnanimity, which civilization and Christianity have introduced to mitigate the asperities of war. The atrocities are too incredible for narration. Instead of a regular war, our resistance of the unholy efforts to crush out our national existence is treated as a rebellion and the settled international rules between belligerents are ignored. Instead of conducting the war as betwixt two military and political organizations, it is a war against the whole population. Houses are pillaged and burned. Churches are defaced. Towns are ransacked. Clothing of women and infants is stripped from their persons. Jewelry and mementoes of the dead are stolen. Mills and implements of agriculture are destroyed. Private salt works are broken up. The introduction of medicines is forbidden. Means of subsistence are wantonly wasted to produce beggary. Prisoners are returned with contagious diseases.

The last morsel of food has been taken from families who were not allowed to carry on a trade or branch of industry. A rigid and offensive *espoinage* has been introduced to ferret out "disloyalty." Persons have been forced to choose between starvation of helpless children and taking the oath of allegiance to a hated Government. The cartel for exchange of prisoners has been suspended and our unfortunate soldiers subjected to the grossest indignities. The wounded at Gettysburg were deprived of their nurses and inhumanly left to perish on the field. Helpless women have been exposed to the most cruel outrages and to that dishonor which is infinitely worse than death. Citizens have been murdered by the Butlers and McNeils and Milroys, who are favorite Generals of our enemies. Refined and delicate ladies have been seized, bound with cords, imprisoned, guarded by negroes, and held as hostages for the return of recaptured slaves. Unoffending non-combatants have been banished or dragged from their quiet homes to be immured in filthy jails. Preaching the Gospel has been refused except on condition of taking the oath of allegiance. Parents have been forbidden to name their children in honor of "rebel" chiefs. Property has been confiscated. Military governors have been appointed for States, satraps for provinces, and Haynaus for cities.

These cruelties and atrocities of the enemy have been exceeded by their malicious and blood thirsty purposes and machinations in reference to the slaves. Early in this war, President Lincoln averred his constitutional inability and personal unwillingness to interfere with the domestic institutions of the States, and the relation between master and servant. Presidential considerations may have been veiled under conscientious scruples, for Seward, in a confidential instruction to Mr. Adams, the Minister to Great Britain, on 10th March, 1862, said: "If the Government of the United States should *precipitately* decree the immediate abolition of slavery, it would reinvigorate the declining insurrection in every part of the South." Subsequent reverses and the refractory rebelliousness of the seceded States caused a change of policy, and Mr. Lincoln issued his celebrated proclamation, a mere *brutem fulmen*, liberating the slaves in the "insurrectionary districts." On the 24th June, 1776, one of the reasons assigned by Pennsylvania for her separation from the mother country was that, in her sister colonies, the "King had excited the negroes to revolt," and to imbue their hands in the blood of their masters, in a manner unpractised by civilized nations. This, probably, had reference to the proclamation of Dunmore, the last royal Governor of Virginia, in 1775, declaring freedom to all servants or negroes, if they would join "for the reducing the colony to a proper sense of its duty." The invitation to the slaves to rise against their masters, the suggested insurrection caused, says Bancroft, "a thrill of indignation to run through Virginia, effacing all differences of party, and rousing one strong, impassioned purpose to drive away the insolent power by which it had been put forth." A cotemporary annalist, adverting to the same proclamation, said "it was received with the greatest horror in all the colonies."

"The policy adopted by Dunmore," says Lawrence in his notes on Wheaton, "of arming the slaves against their masters, was not pursued during the war of the Revolution; and when negroes were taken by the English, they were not considered otherwise than as property and plunder." Emancipation of slaves as a war measure has been severely condemned and denounced by the most eminent publicists in Europe and the United States. The United States, "in their diplomatic relations, have ever maintained," says the Northern authority just quoted, "that slaves were private property, and for them, as such, they have repeatedly received compensation from England."—Napoleon I. was never induced to issue a proclamation for the emancipation of the serfs in his war with Russia. He said: "I could have armed against her a part of her population, by proclaiming the liberty of the serfs. A great number of villages asked it of me, but I refused to avail myself of a measure which would have devoted to death thousands of families." In the discussions growing out fo the treaty of peace of 1814, and the proffered mediation of Russia, the principle was maintained by the United States that "the emancipation of enemy's slaves is not among the acts of legitimate warfare." In the instructions from John Quincy Adams, as Secretary of State, to Mr. Middleton, at St. Petersburg, October 18th, 1820, it is said: "The British have broadly asserted the right of emancipating slaves (private property) as a legitimate right of war. No such right is acknowledged as a law of war by writers who admit any limitation. The right of putting to death all prisoners in cold blood, and without special cause, might as well be pretended to be a law of war, or the right to use poisoned weapons, to assassinate."

Disregarding the teachings of the approved writers on international law and the practice and claims of his own Government in its purer days, President Lincoln has sought to convert the South into a St. Domingo by appealing to the cupidity, lusts, ambition and ferocity of the slave. Abraham Lincoln is but the lineal descendent of Dunmore, and the impotent malice of each was foiled by the fidelity of those who, by the meanness of the conspirators, would only, if successful, have been seduced into idleness, filth, vice, beggary and death.

But we tire of these indignities and enormities. They are too sickening for recital. History will hereafter *pillory* those who committed and encouraged such crimes as immortal infamy.

General Robert E. Lee, in a recent battle order, stated to his invincible legions that the "cruel foe seeks to reduce our fathers and mothers, our wives and children to abject slavery." He does not paint too strongly the purposes of the enemy or the consequences of subjugation. What has been done in certain districts is but the prologue of the bloody drama that will be enacted. It is well that every man and woman should have some just conception of the horrors of conquest. The fate of Ireland at the period of its conquest, and of Poland, distinctly foreshadows what would await us. The guillotine, in its ceaseless work of blood, would be revived for the execution of the "rebel leaders." The heroes of our contest would be required to lay down their proud ensigns, on which are recorded the battle fields of their glory, to stack their arms, lower their heads in humiliation and dishonor, and pass under the yoke of abolition misrule and tyranny.

A hateful inquisition, made atrocious by spies and informers; star chamber courts, enforcing their decisions by confiscations, imprisonments, banishments and deaths; a band of detectives, ferreting out secrets, lurking in every family, existing in every conveyance; the suppression of free speech; the deprivation of arms and franchises; and the ever present sense of inferiority would make our condition abject and miserable beyond what freemen can imagine. Subjugation involves everything that the torturing malice and devilish ingenuity of our foes can suggest. The destruction of our nationality, the equalization of whites and blacks, the obliteration of State lines, degradation to colonial vassalage and the reduction of many of our citizens to dreary, hopeless, remediless bondage. A hostile police would keep "order" in every town and city. Judges like Busteed would hold our courts, protected by Yankee soldiers. Churches would be filled by Yankee or tory preachers. Every office would be bestowed on aliens. Absenteeism would curse us with all its vices. Superadded to these, sinking us into a lower abyss of degradation, we would be made the slaves of our slaves, hewers of wood and drawers of water for those upon whom God has stamped indelibly the marks of physical and intellectual inferiority. The past of foreign countries need not be sought into to furnish illustrations of the heritage of shame that subjugation would entail. Baltimore, St. Louis, Nashville, Knoxville, New Orleans, Vicksburg, Huntsville, Norfolk, Newbern, Louisville and Fredericksburg are the first fruits of the ignominy and poverty of Yankee domination.

The sad story of the wrongs and indignities endured by those States which have been in the complete or partial possession of the enemy, will give the best evidence of the consequences of subjugation. Missouri, a magnificent empire of agricultural and mineral wealth, is to-day a smoking ruin, and the theatre of the most revolting cruelties and barbarisms. The minions of tyranny consume her substance, plunder her citizens, and destroy her peace. The sacred rights of freemen are struck down, and the blood of her children, her maidens and her old men, made to flow, out of mere wantonness and recklessness. No whispers of freedom go unpunished, and the very instincts of self-preservation are outlawed. The worship of God and the rites of sepulture have been shamefully interrupted, and, in many instances, the cultivation of the soil is prohibited to her own citizens. These facts are attested by many witnesses and it is but a just tribute to that noble and chivalrous people, that, amid barbarities almost unparalleled, they still maintain a proud and defiant spirit towards their enemies.

In Maryland, the judiciary, made subservient to executive absolutism, furnishes no security for individual rights or personal freedom; members of the Legislature are arrested and imprisoned without process of law or assignment of cause, and the whole land groaneth under the oppressions of a merciless tyranny.

In Kentucky, the ballot box has been overthrown, free speech is suppressed, the most vexatious annoyances harass and embitter, and all the arts and appliances of an unscrupulous despotism are freely used to prevent the uprising of the noble patriots of "the dark and bloody ground." Notes of gladness, assurances of a brighter and better day, reach us, and the exiles may take courage and hope for the future.

In Virginia, the model of all that illustrates human heroism and self-denying patriotism, although the tempest of desolation has swept over her fair domains, no sign of repentance for her separation from the North can be found. Her old homesteads dismantled, her ancestral relics destroyed, her people impoverished, her territory made the battle ground for the rude shocks of contending hosts, and then divided, with hireling parasites mockingly claiming jurisdiction and authority, the Old Dominion still stands with proud crest and defiant mien, ready to trample beneath her heel every usurper and tyrant and to illustrate afresh her *Sic Semper Tyrannis*, the "proudest motto that ever blazed on a nation's shield or a warrior's arms."

To prevent such effects, our people are now prosecuting this struggle. It is no mere war of calculation, no contest for peculiar kind of property, no barter of precious blood for filthy lucre. Everything involved in manhood, civilization, religion, law, property, country, home, is at stake. We fight not for plunder, spoils, pillage, territorial conquest. The Government tempts by no prizes of "beauty or booty," to be drawn in the lottery of this war. We seek to preserve civil freedom, honor, equality, firesides, and blood is well shed, when "shed for our family, for our friends, for our kind, for our country, for our God." Burke said: "a State, resolved to hazard its existence rather than abandon its object, must have an infinite advantage over that which is resolved to yield, rather than to carry its resistance beyond a certain point." It is better to be conquered by any other nation than by the United States. It is better to be a dependency of any other power than of that. By the condition of its existence and essential constitution, as now governed, it must be in perpetual hostility to us. As the Spanish invader burned his ships to make retreat impossible, so we cannot afford to take steps backward.—Retreat is more dangerous than advance. Behind us, are inferiority and degradation. Before us is everything enticing to a patriot.

Our bitter and implacable foes are preparing vigorously for the coming campaign. Corresponding efforts should be made on our part. Without murmuring, our people should respond to the laws, which the exigency demands. Every one capable of bearing arms, should be connected with some efficient military organization. The utmost energies of the whole population should be taxed to produce food and clothing, and a spirit of cheerfulness and trust in an all-wise and overruling Providence should be cultivated.

The history of the past three years has much to animate us to renewed effort, and a firmer and more assured hope. A whole people have given their hearts and bodies to repel the invader, and costly sacrifices have been made on the altar of our country. No similar instance is to be found of such spontaneous uprising and volunteering. Inspired by a holy patriotism, again and again have our brave soldiers, with the aid of Heaven, baffled the efforts of our foes.

It is in no arrogant spirit, that we refer to successes that have cost us so much blood, and brought sorrow to so many hearts. We may find in all this an earnest of what with determined and resolute exertion, we can do to avert subjugation and slavery—and we cannot fail to discern in our deliverance from so many and so great perils, the interposition of that being who will not forsake us in the trials that are to come. Let us, then, looking upon the bodies of our loved and honored dead, catch inspiration from their example, and gather renewed confidence and a firmer resolve to tread, with unfaltering trust, the path that leads to honor and peace, though it leads through tears and suffering and blood.

We have no alternative but to do our duty. We combat for property, homes, the honor of our wives, the future of our children, the preservation of our fair land from pollution, and to avert a doom which we can read, both in the threats of our enemies and the acts of oppression, we have alluded to in this address.

The situation is grave, but furnishes no just excuse for despondence. Instead of harsh criticisms on the Government and our Generals; instead of bewailing the failure to accomplish impossibilities, we should rather be grateful—humbly and profoundly—to a benignant Providence for the results that have rewarded our labors. Remembering the disproportion in population, in military and naval resources, and the deficiency of skilled labor in the South, our accomplishments have surpassed those recorded of any people in the world. There is no just reason for hopelessness or fear. Since the outbreak of the war the South has lost the nominal possession of the Mississippi River, and fragments of her territory, but Federal occupancy is not conquest. The fires of patriotism still burn unquenchably in the breasts of those who are subject to foreign domination. We yet have in our uninterrupted control a territory which, according to past progress, will require the enemy ten years to overrun.

The enemy is not free from difficulties. With an enormous debt, the financial convulsion, long postponed, is surely coming. The short crops in the United States, and abundant harvests in Europe, will hasten what was otherwise inevitable. Many sagacious persons at the North discover in the usurpations of their Government the certain overthrow of their liberties. A large number revolt from the unjust war waged upon the South, and would gladly bring it to an end. Others look with alarm on the complete subversion of constitutional freedom by Abraham Lincoln and feel in their own persons the bitterness of the slavery which three years of war have failed to inflict on the South. Brave and earnest men at the North have spoken out against the usurpation and cruelties daily practiced. The success of these men over the radical and despotic faction which now rules the North, may open the way to peaceful negotiation, and a cessation of this bloody and unnecessary war.

In conclusion, we exhort our fellow-citizens to be of good cheer, and spare no labor nor sacrifices that may be necessary to enable us to win the campaign upon which we have just entered. We have passed through great trials of affliction, but suffering and humiliation are the schools in which that lead nations to self-reliance and independence. These disciplinary providences but mature and develop and solidify our people. We beg that the supplies and resources of the country, which are ample, may be sold to the Government to support and equip its armies. Let all spirit of faction and past party differences be forgotten in the presence of our cruel foe. We should not despond. We should be self denying. We should labor to extend to the utmost the productive resources of the country. We should economize. The families of soldiers should be cared for and liberally supplied. We entreat from all a generous and hearty co-operation with the Government in all branches of its administration, and with the agents, civil or military, in the performance of their duty.

Moral aid has the "power of the incommunicable," and by united efforts, by an all comprehending and self-sacrificing patriotism, we can, with the blessing of God, avert the perils which environ us, and achieve for ourselves and children peace and freedom. Hitherto, the Lord has interposed graciously to bring us victory, and in His hand there is present power to prevent this great multitude which come against us, from casting us out of the possession which He has given us to inherit.

T. J. SEMMES,
J. L. ORR,
A. E. MAXWELL,
Committee on the part of Senate.

J. W. CLAPP,
J. L. W. CURRY,
JULIAN HARTRIDGE,
JOHN GOODE, Jr.,
W. N. H. SMITH,
Committee of House of Representatives.

THOMAS S. BOCOCK, Speaker H. of R.	R B HILTON,
WALTER PRESTON,	CHARLES J VILLERE,
JOHN McQUEEN,	J W MOORE,
CHARLES W. RUSSELL,	LUCIEN J DUPRE,
W LANDER,	JOHN C ATKINS,
A H CONROW,	ISRAEL WELSH,
C J MUNNERLYN,	WM G SWAN,
THOMAS S ASHE,	F B SEXTON,
O R SINGLETON,	T L BURNETT,
J L PUGH,	GEO G VEST,
A H ARRINGTON,	WM PORCHER MILES,
WALLER R STAPLES,	E BARKSDALE,
A R BOTELER,	CHARLES F COLLIER,
THOMAS J FOSTER,	P W GRAY,
W R SMITH,	W W CLARKE,
ROB'T J BRECKINRIDGE,	WM W BOYCE,
JOHN M MARTIN,	JOHN R CHAMBLISS,
PORTER INGRAM,	JOHN J McRAE,
A H GARLAND,	JOHN PERKINS, Jr.,
E S DARGAN,	ROBERT JOHNSTON,
D FUNSTEN,	JAMES FARROW,
THOS D McDOWELL,	W D SIMPSON,
J R McLEAN,	LUCIUS J GARTRELL,
R R BRIDGERS	M D GRAHAM,
G W JONES,	JOHN B BALDWIN,
B S GAITHER,	E M BRUCE,
GEORGE W EWING,	THOMAS B HANLY,
W D HOLDER,	W P CHILTON,
DAN W LEWIS,	A H KENAN,
HENRY E READ,	C M CONRAD,
A J DAVIDSON,	H M BRUCE,
M H MACWILLIE,	DAVID CLOPTON,
JAMES LYONS,	W B MACHEN,
CASPER W BELL,	D C DeJARNETTE,
	H C CHAMBERS.

MARRIED.

On the 12th November, 1863, at "Pooshee," St. John's Berkley, by the Rev. P. F. STEVENS, Dr. R. Y. DWIGHT (Lieut. 1st S. C. Infantry) to Miss R. E. RAVENEL, third daughter of Dr. HENRY RAVENEL, all of Charleston District.

☞ Richmond papers please copy.

OBITUARY.

DIED, at Society Hill, S. C., CONSTANCE WILLIAM STOCKTON, daughter of Lieut. E. C. STOCKTON, C. S. Navy, and of the late EMMA W. STOCKTON, aged 2 years and 6 months.

DIED, of Typhoid Fever, in Nassau, N. P., on the 29th December, 1863, HENRY STINDT, a native of Geestendorff, Germany, at the age of 19 years, 8 months and 11 days.

DEPARTED THIS LIFE, on Tuesday, the 16th instant, at 12, m., near Graham's Turnout, S. C., CURTIS CORNELIUS, infant son of CURTIS C. and ANNIE C. FAUST, aged 14 days.

"Suffer the little children to come unto me, and forbid them not, for of such is the Kingdom of God."

VOL. 11.]

THE OPELOUSAS COURIER.

[No. 48.

OPELOUSAS:

SATURDAY, : : : : : : MARCH 5, 1864.

☞ We refer the reader to the card of Capt. McCutcheon, to be found elsewhere. The Captain is a native of Lower Louisiana, and speaks both French and English; he will be in town in a few days, when persons desirous of joining his corps will have an opportunity to do so.

☞ Five Federal gunboats entered Red River on Tuesday last and ascended it up to the mouth of Black River, thence up that river, bombarding the woods near Fort Beauregard. We have not heard what was the result of this first incursion.

THE FIGHT NEAR NEWBERN.—The following are the official reports of the recent brilliant action near Newport N. C.:

KINGSTON, Feb. 3, 1864.—To Gen S. Cooper:—I made a reconnoissance within a mile and a half of Newbern with Hoke's brigade, and a part of Corse's and Clingman's and some artillery, met the enemy in force at Batchelor's Creek, killed and wounded about a hundred in all, captured thirteen officers and two hunded and eighty prisoners, fourteen negroes, two rifled pieces and caissons, three hundred stand of small arms, four ambulances, three wagons, fifty-five animals, a quantity of clothing, camp and garrison equipage and two flags. Commander Wood, C. S. N., captured and destroyed the U S gunboat Underwriter. Our loss 35 killed and wounded.

(Signed) G. E. PICKETT,
Major General Commanding.

KINGSTON, Feb. 4.—Hon. S. R Mallory:—The force under my command boarded and captured, last night, U. S. gunboat Underwriter, four guns, and ninety men and officers.

Her position was within musket range of several stong works, one of which was raking the vessel during the time we had possession, and her not having steam up, caused me to burn her.

Our loss is twenty killed and wounded, and four missing; enemy's loss unknown.

(Signed) J. TAYLOR WOOD.

ORANGE C. H., Febrary 6, 1864.

To Gen. S. Cooper:

On the 30th ult., Gen. Rosser captured a train of ninety-three wagons, loaded with commissary stores and forage, on the way from New Creek to Petersburg; also three hundred mules and twenty prisoners. The guard of eight hundred infantry escaped to the mountains. Our loss was twenty-five killed and wounded.

Information of the advance upon Petersburg having been received, the garrison evacuated it during the night.

On the 2d inst., Gen. Rosser destroyed the bridges over Patterson's Creek and north branch of the Potomac and canal, and captured forty prisoners. Two hundred and seventy prisoners, fifty wagons and teams, twelve hundred cattle and five hundred sheep have been brought off

Gen. Rosser has shown great energy and skill and his command deserves great credit

R. E. LEE.

SALE OF STATE BONDS.

EXECUTIVE OFFICE,
SHREVEPORT, February 23d, 1864.

IN accordance with the provisions of an Act of the General Assembly of the State of Louisiana, entitled: An Act "To authorize the sale of Bonds for the relief of the Treasury, and final liquidation of the principal and interest thereof," approved February 8, 1864.

Sealed proposals will be received at my office, in the city of Shreveport, until the first of September next, for the sale or exchange of State Bonds, having not less than twenty nor more than fifty years to run from their dates, and to be issued in amounts of not less than two hundred nor more than one thousand dollars each, at the discretion of the Governor, with six per cent. per annum, payayble semi-annually at the office of the State Treasurer.

These Bonds will be sold for the benefit of the State, or exchanged for any of the Confederate or State Treasury notes.

The General Assembly in authorizing the sale or exchange of these Bonds, has provided for the payment of the current interest semi-annually, and the redemption of the bonds at maturity, by the creation of an ample sinking fund.

On the first Monday of every month the sealed bids received, will be opened and the Bonds awarded to the highest bidder, at the discretion of the Governor.

H. W. ALLEN,
Governor of the State of Louisiana.

March 5, 1864.—48—3m.

Louisianians!

I have been appointed Captain of Cavalry by His Excellency H. W. Allen, with authority, under Act No. 32 of General Assembly, to raise a company of one hundred mounted men.

I am directed to recruit from persons liable to military duty between the ages of 16 and 18, and 55, and also from those who have furnished substitutes in C. S. A., provided they shall enlist in the State service before the 1st of March. Each man shall furnish his horse, saddle, bridle and shot-gun, for which he will receive same compensation as in Confederate service.

Come forward promptly to defend your homes and your rights, and do not wait until you are called out in the militia. Your Governor, who has seen service and has suffered much from the cruel effects of this war, now calls upon you to rally around him. Let it not be in vain.

Lieutenants will be elected by the company. Volunteers will be received at ——.

SAML. McCUTCHEON,
Captain State Guard.

March 5, 1864.—48—tf.

Attention Hays' Louisiana Brigade.

BY virtue of authority received from the Secretary of War in Special Orders No. 15, all men belonging to this Brigade wherever they may be in this Department, in whatever arm of the service they may now be serving, are ordered to report to Capt. W. K. JOHNSON, at Alexandria, or Capt. C. M PILCHER, at Minden, La., on or before the 10th March, 1864, for the purpose of making the arrangements necessary to insure a safe and speedy return to their command in Virginia, otherwise they will be published as deserters.

WM. K JOHNSON,
Captain Co. I, 8th La Regiment.
C. M. PILCHER,
Captain Co. H, 6th La Regiment.

March 5th, 1864. 48—2t.

NOTICE.

JOSEPH BLOCH, at the old stand of Bloch, Firnberg & Co, Opelousas, has opened a store where he will endeavor to keep articles of general family and plantation use. He has now an assortment of Flour, Salt, Sugar, Molasses, &c., and will soon receive other goods of a general use.

JOSEPH BLOCH.

Opelousas, December 19 1863. 37—tf

THE OLD BANK HOUSE,

NEAR the Court House, Opelousas, kept by Mrs Stuart, where boarders will be received and well entertained.

Opelousas, January 2, 1864.

HEAD QUARTERS TRANS-MISSISSIPPI DEPARTMENT,
SHREVEPORT, LA., February 4, 1864.
[*Extract.*]

SPECIAL ORDERS No. 29.

VII. The following schedule of prices for articles and labor herein named, adopted by Commissioners appointed pursuant to law for the State of Louisiana, is announced for the information of all concerned.

This schedule of prices established every two months or oftener, will be published for the information of parties making impressments; and no officer or agent will pay or approve for payment any local appraisement materially in excess thereof, but will always refer the same to the Board for its rivision and a final valuation.

Commissary Stores.

Articles.	Quality.	Description.	Quantity.	Price.
Wheat,	Prime,	White or Red,	per bush. 60 lbs.,	$ 5 00
Flour,	Superfine,		do do 100 do	20 00
Corn,	Prime,	N. Shreveport to State line,	do do 56 do	1 00
do	do	On Ouachita,	do do do do	1 00
do	do	S. Shreveport to Caushatta,	do do do do	1 25
do	do	From Caushatta to Grand Ecore,	do do do do	1 50
do	do	From Grand Ecore to Cotile Landing.	do do do do	1 75
do	do	From Cotile Landing South,	do do do do	2 25
Corn Meal*	Good,	N. Shreveport to State line,	do do 45 do	1 00
Oats,	do		per bus. 32 lbs.,	1 50
Rye,	do		do do 56 do	3 00
Peas,	do		do do do do	2 00
Bacon,	do	Sides Clear,	do lb.	50
do	do	do Ribbed,	do do	45
do	do	Hams,	do do	45
do	do	Shoulders,	do do	40
Pork,	do	Fresh,	do do	20
do	do	Salted,	do do	25
Hogs,	Fair,	Gross Fattened,	do do	15
Lard,	Good,	Nett,	do do	45
Beef Cattle,	4 years old and upwards,	do	do do	10
Mutton,	Fair,	Wethers,	do head	9 00
Tallow,	Good,		do lb.	40
Candles,	do	Tallow,	do do	60
Potatoes,	do	Sweet,	do bushel 60 lbs.,	2 00
Sugar,	Fair,	Hogshead,	do lb.,	25
do	Good Common,	do	do do	20
do	White Clarified	do	do do	60
Molasses,	Good,	Barrel,	do gallon,	80
Vinegar,	do	Manufactured,	do do	50
Salt,	do		do bushel 50 lb.,	2 50
Soap,	do	Hard,	do lb.,	40
Whisky,	do	Barrel,	do gallon,	5 00

Quartermasters' Stores.

Articles.	Quality.	Description.	Quantity.	Price.
Fodder,	Good,	Blade,	per 150 lbs.,	$ 2 50
do	do	Baled,	do do do	3 00
Hay,	do	Grass,	do do do	2 50
Leather,	do	Sole,	do lb.,	1 00
do	do	Upper,	do do	1 25
do	do	Harness,	do do	1 25
Shoes,	do	Russets,	do pair,	6 00
Hides,	do	Dry,	do lb.,	20
Wool,	do	Washed,	do do	1 50
do	do	Unwashed,	do do	75
Jeans,		Half Wool,	do yard,	7 50
Linsey,		do	do do	6 00
Cotton Cloth.		Striped or Plaid,	do do	3 50
do		Plain,	do do	3 00
Socks,	do	Woolen,	do pair,	2 25
do	do	Cotton,	do do	1 50
Hats,	do	Woolen,	do dozen,	48 00
Work Oxen,	No. 1,		do yoke,	200 00
Horses,	No 1,	Artillery,	do head,	650 00
do	Good,	Cavalry,	do do	600 00
Work Horses,	do		do do	450 00
Mules,	No. 1,		do do	450 00
do	No. 2,		do do	350 00
do	No. 3,		do do	200 00
Wagons,	Mule, Road,	Iron Axle,		650 00
do	Oxen,	do		650 00
do	do	Wooden Axle,		500 00
do	Mule,	do		500 00
Ambulances,	Good,	Two Horse,		550 00

*To which is to be added the same increase of price for the localities as made in the value of corn.

In measuring corn in cribs or pens, four cubic feet should be allowed for each barrel of slip-shucked corn. The prices of corn apply to the valleys of Red river and the Ouachita and their tributaries.

When articles are impressed in any parish not produced or raised in that parish, the authorized transportation or other necessary expenses are to be added.

The following scale of prices for the service, &c., hereinafter specified, will be paid by officers of the army and Government Agents:

For hauling the Tax in kind to depots established by the Government Agents, four cents per hundred pounds per mile, when the distance exceeds eight miles from the place of production, the owners to furnish rations for drivers and forage for teams.

For other hauling, ten dollars per day for six mule and four yoke ox teams, eight dollars per day for four mule and three yoke ox teams, and six dollars per day for two mule and two yoke ox teams. The Government to furnish rations for drivers and forage for teams. The distance fixed for each day's travel, to be eighteen miles for mule, and fourteen miles for ox teams; or six cents per hundred pounds per mile, for distances over fifty miles, the owners to furnish rations and forage.

For the hire of Grist and Saw Mills, one dollar per day for each horse-power, the Government to furnish everything, and repair all damages beyond the usual wear and tear.

For the rental of stores or other tenements, twelve per cent. per annum on the State Tax assessment, and pro rata for portions of buildings, to take effect on the first of January, 1864.

For the hire of Negro men, thirty dollars per month, the Government to furnish rations, shelter and medical attendance. Any time lost by sickness, to be deducted from the amount due the owners.

☞ It is respectfully recommended to the ladies to form parish and neighborhood associations for the purpose of furnishing woolen and cotton cloth and socks for our soldiers in the field, who are much in need of all those articles, and for which the Schedule prices will be paid Address at Natchitoches and Alexandria, La.

RICHARD NUGENT,
JOS. H HYNSON,
Commissioners.

By command of
Lieut. Gen. E. KIRBY SMITH.

S. S. ANDERSON, Ass't. Adj't. Gen.

Feb. 27 —47—4t.

REGISTRY TAX! REGISTRY TAX!!

CONFEDERATE STATES TAX COLLECTOR'S OFFICE, DISTRICT ST LANDRY,
Opelousas, 27th February 1864.

THE attention of those named in the 5th Section of an Act entitled "An Act to lay taxes for the common defence and carry on the Government of the Confederate States," approved April 24th 1863, is called to the following Sections of the same Act:

"SEC 2. Every person engaged or intending to engage in any business named in the fifth Section of this Act, shall, within sixty days after the passage of this Act, or at the time of beginning business, and on the first day of January in each year thereafter, register with the district collector, in such formas the commissioner of taxes shall prescribe, a true account of the name and residence of each person, firm or corporation engaged or interested in the business, with a statement of the time for which, and the place and manner in which the same is to be conducted, and of all other facts going to ascertain the amount of tax upon such business for the past or the future, according to the provisions of this Act. At the time of such registry there shall be paid to the collector, the specific tax for the year, ending on the next thirty-first of December, and such other tax as may be due upon sales or receipts in such business, at the time of such registry, as herein provided; and the collector shall give to the person making such registry a copy thereof, with a receipt for the amount of tax then paid.

"S c. 3 Any person failing to make the registry, and to pay the tax required by the preceding Section, shall, in addition to all other taxes upon his business imposed by this Act, pay double the amount of the specific tax on such business, and a like sum for every thirty days of such failure."

The following are the occupations, trades and persons taxed under the provisions of the fifth Section of the Tax Act:

Auctioneers, Apothecaries, Bankers, Brewers, Brokers, Butchers, Bakers, Bowling-alleys, Billiard Rooms, Commission Merchants, Commercial Brokers, Cattle Brokers, Circus, Confectioners, Dentists, Distillers, Distillers of fruit for 90 days or less, Hotels, Inns, Taverns, Eating Houses, Jugglers and exhibiters of shows, Livery Stable Keepers, Pawnbrokers, Pedlers, Physicians, Photographers, Retail Dealers, Retail Dealers in liquor, Surgeons, Theatres, Tobacconists, Wholesale Dealers and Wholesale Dealers in liquor

NOW THEREFORE, in pursuance of the provisions of the said Tax Act, I do hereby give notice to all parties concerned, to come forward, make their registry, and pay their taxes to me at my office in the town of Opelousas, within the thirty days next ensuing the date of this notice. In case of failure to comply with the law within the time specified, the penalties attached to such failure will be strictly enforced against all delinquents.

THEO. C. LITTELL,
District Collector.

47—5t]

NOTICE.

THE undersigned having made a small issue of small bills about 18 months ago, in order to facilitate the change, and it having been reported to him, lately, that some persons were offering, and did give a premium for said bills,—he hereby invites the holders of the same to have them presented to him, at Washington, to be there redeemed in the shortest delay possible, as they will be redeemed only in Confederate notes, as therein stipulated, and not in specie, as certain misinformed persons seem to believe

T. HERBERT.

Washington 20th February 1864. 46—3t

Notice.

ALL parties holding accounts against the undersigned will please present them immediately for settlement.

GEO. D. LOGAN, Capt.
and A. Q. M 2d Reg't. La. Cavalry.

February 27, 1864 —47—2t.

TO HUNTERS

GAME SHOT of all dimensions for sale by the undersigned at $3.50 per pound.

LOUIS VATTER.

Opelousas, February 6, 1864. 44—tf.

Public Sale.

Estate of Marie Louise Gilbert.

THE public are hereby informed that there will be sold at public sale, to the last and highest bidder, by the undersigned Administrator, or by a duly commissioned Auctioneer, at the last residence of Marie Louise Gilbert, deceased, at Queue Tortue, in the Parish of St. Landry, on

Tuesday, 22d day of March

next, 1864, the following described property, belonging to the succession of said deceased, to wit:

A CERTAIN

TRACT OF LAND,

situated on Queue Tortue, in said Parish, containing one hundred and forty-seven superficial arpents, bounded North by Norbert Blanchard, South by Theolin Lalande, East by Théodule Mire and Mme. Firmin Breau, and West by lands of Hypolite C. Guidry, together with all the buildings and improvements thereon.

SIX SLAVES.

A lot of wild horned cattle;
2 pair work oxen;
One mule;
One pair young oxen;
One lot of gentle horned cattle;
Household furniture;
Kitchen utensils;
About 400 pounds of cotton in the seed, and many other articles the enumeration of which would be too tedious.

Terms and conditions:—One, two and three years credit, from the 1st of April next, 1864.—Purchasers furnishing their notes with two good and solvent security in solido, to the satisfaction of the administrator of the Estate. Said notes made payable to his order, and bearing interest at the rate of eight per cent per annum from time due until paid. And moreover, the land and the slaves remaining specially hypothecated unto said estate until full and entire payment of capitel and interests which may accrue thereon.

DRAUZIN BREAU, Adm'r.

Opelousas, February 20, 1864.

ADJ'T & INSPECTOR GEN'S. OFFICE,
RICHMOND, Jan. 19th 1864.

General Orders No. 2.

I. The following Acts of Congress and Regulations are published for the information of all persons concerned therein:

ACTS.

AN ACT to prevent the enlistment or enrollment of Substitutes in the military service of the Confederate States.

The Congress of the Confederate States of America do enact, That no person liable to military service shall hereafter be permitted or allowed to furnish a substitute for such service, nor shall any substitute be received, enlisted or enrolled in the military service of the Confederate States.

[Approved December 28, 1863]

AN ACT to put an end to the exemption from military service of those who have heretofore furnished substitutes.

Whereas, in the present circumstances of the country, it requires the aid of all who are able to bear arms.

The Congress of the Confederate States of America do enact, That no person shall be exempted from militar service by reason of his having furnished a substitute; but this act shall not be so constructed as to effect persons who, though not liable to render military service, have, nevertheless, furnished substitutes.

[Approved January 5, 1864]

II. Persons rendered liable to military service by operation of the preceding Acts, are placed on the same footing with all other hitherto held liable by acts of Congress

III. Persons herein rendered liable to military service, are required to report as volunteers or conscripts, without delay, to the enrolling officers; and all who delay beyond the 1st day of Feb. 1864, will be considered as having renounced the privilege of volunteering, and held for assignment according to law.

IV. Enrolling officers will proceed as rapidly as practicable in the enrollment of persons herein made liable to military service. Previous to enrollment as conscripts, all such persons will be allowed to volunteer in companies in service on the 16th of April 1862, provided the company chosen does not at the time of volunteering, reach the maximum number allowed, and upon such company being selected, the volunteer will receive from the enrolling officer a certificate to the effect that he has so volunteered, and no volunteer will be received into any company except on such certificate. Persons who fail to make their selection at the time of enrollment, will be assigned according to existing regulations.

V. Persons who report to the enrolling officer will be enrolled, and may be allowed a furlough of ten days before reporting to the Camp of Instruction

VI. All persons, whether volunteers or conscripts, under this order, will pass through the Camp of Instruction of the State to which they belong, and be forwarded thence to the companies which are selected, or to which they may be assigned

VII The Bureau of Conscription is charged with adopting proper regulations for the enforcement of this order

VIII. All exemptions heretofore granted are subject to revision, under instructions from the Bureau of Conscription, and if found to be improper or unauthorized by law, will be revoked.

By order of S. COOPER, A. & I. Gen.

Feb. 20. 1864.

Notice.

THE undersigned having lost all the notes subscribed by purchasers at the sale of property of the Estate of John H. Maggee, her late husband, hereby gives notice to those who may be interested therein, that payment of the same has been stopped, and she therefore cautions the public not to negotiate nor trade for any of said notes.

WIDOW JOHN H. MAGGEE,
Administratrix.

St. Landry, Feb. 6, 1864.—44-5t.

NOTICE.

MY negroes have killed as mine, a black cow branded thus: O-N, on the rightside of the rump. The ear brand is an underbit in each ear. The proprietor is requested to come forward and receive payment for his cow.

HENRY L. GARLAND

Opelousas, February 13, 1864. 45—4t.

FOR SALE FOR CASH,

THE BEAVER CREEK SPRINGS, situated 35 miles North-West of the Town of Opelousas, measuring 200 arpents of wood land, together with the improvements.—Also a good Billiard table with its apparatus.

For the particulars apply to
H. PROVENT, proprietor.

Opelousas January 16th 1864. 41tf

OLD TYPE METAL,
Suitable for making shot, for sale at this office.

PUBLIC SALE.

Succession of Ursule Boutin.

BY virtue of an order from the Honorable the Judge of the Eighth Judicial District Court of the State of Louisiana holding its session in and for the Parish of St. Landry, the undersigned a public Auctioneer for said Parish, will offer for sale at public auction, to the last and highest bidder, on the plantation of said deceased, being her last residence, situated at Gros Chevreuil, about twelve miles from the Town of Opelousas, on

Tuesday, 22nd of March next,

the following described property, belonging to the succession of the late Ursule Boutin, deceased widow of George Lalonde, to wit:

9 Slaves:

PRUDENT, mulatto man about 65 years.
JOE, negroman aged about 40 years.
ETIENNE, (Sambo) black boy about 13.
LIZA, negrowoman aged about 30 years, with her five children, viz: Marie, a girl about 9 years old, Flore, a girl 7 years old, Ben, a boy 5 years old. Charlotte, a girl 3 years old, and Azema, a girl 15 months old.
17 head of gentle cattle;
One pair of work mules;
One mule;
One creole horse;
One work ox;
A lot of cotton in the seed;
A four seat carriage with harness;
A corn mill, and a large quantity of other articles the enumeration of which would be too tedious.

Terms and conditions:—All and every adjudications payable on a credit of one, two and three years, from the 1st day of April 1865. Purchasers furnishing their notes with security in solido to the satisfaction of the administrator of said estate, and made payable at the store of Mr. Michel Emonet, in Gros Chevreuil, and in case of non-payment at maturity, said notes to bear interest at the rate of eight per cent per annum from time due until paid And moreover the slaves remaining specially mortgaged unto said Estate until full and entire payment of capital and the interests which may accrue thereon.

JEAN BOUFFARTIGUE,
Auctioneer.

St. Landry February 20th 1864.

PUBLIC SALE.

SUCCESSION OF CELESTINE CORMIER.

BY virtue of an order from the Honorable the 8th District Court of the State of Louisiana, holding its session in and for the Parish of St. Landry, the undersigned will offer for sale at public sale, to the last and highest bidder, on the Plantation of the deceased, situated about 12 miles South-East of Opelousas,

On Tuesday, 8th March 1864,

the property hereinafter described belonging to the community heretofore existing between the said late Célestine Cormier and her surviving husband, Théodule Lalonde, to wit:

A Negroman

named Narcisse, aged about 45 years.
One horse; one cow and calf;
One work ox; 9 head of sheep;
One hog; a stilyard and a looking glass.

Terms and conditions:—Each adjudication of ten dollars and under payable cash; and each adjudication upwards of ten dollars payable upon a credit of one and two years from the day of sale. Purchasers furnishing their notes with two securities in solido to the satisfaction of the Administrator of said Estate, and made payable at the office of Jean Bouffartigue, Notary Public at Gros Chevreuil; said notes to bear interest at the rate of 8 per cent per annum from maturity until paid. And moreover the slave remaining specially mortgaged unto said Estate until full and entire payment of capital and interest which may accrue thereon.

J. BOUFFARTIGUE,
Auctioneer.

Gros Chevreuil, St. Landry, Feb. 6, 1864.

Public Sale.

ESTATE OF EDWIN M. SMITH.

THE public are hereby informed that there will be sold by the undersigned Auctioneer, at public sale, to the last and highest bidder, at the residence of Chs. B. Smith, on Upper Plaquemine, on

***Saturday 5th March next,* 1864,**

the following described property, belonging to the Estate of said Edwin M. Smith, deceased, to wit:

A Small Plantation,

situated in Bellevue, Parish of St. Landry, joining that of Mrs. Widow Jean F. Richard, measuring about 94 superficial acres of land, together with all the buildings and improvements thereon erected.
Plantation implements;
Household furniture;
Horses; Cows;
A branding iron;
A surveying Compass and chain;
A lot of books and many other articles the enumeration of which would be too tedious.

Terms and Conditions:—All adjudications of ten dollars and under payable cash; all adjudications upwards of ten dollars payable in one, two and three years credit from the day of sale; Purchasers furnishing their notes with good and solvent security in solido, to the satisfaction of whom the right; said notes made payable to the order and at the domicil of the administrator of said Estate, and bearing interest at eight per cent. per annum from time due until paid. And moreover, the land remaining specially mortgaged unto said Estate until full and entire payment of capital and the interests which may accrue thereon.

JOHN F. SMITH,
Auctioneer.

Opelousas, January 30, 1864.

THE OPELOUSAS COURIER.

Published on Saturday by Joel H. Sandoz.

CONDITIONS:

Subscription, for one year, payable in advance, TEN dollars if paid at the end of the year, *twelve* dollars. A subscriber wishing to discontinue, must give a *written notice* to that effect, and settle up all arrearages.

Advertisements will be inserted at twenty-five cents per line for each of the first three publications, and TEN cents per line for each and every subsequent insertion. A liberal discount will be made for standing advertisements.

All the advertisements will be inserted in french and english until the editor shall judge it convenient to discontinue the publication.

Twenty dollars in advance will invariably be required for the announcement of candidates for office.

No advertisements or subscription will be stopped until all arrearages are paid, unless at the option of the publisher.

VOL. 11.] LE COURRIER DES OPELOUSAS. [No. 48.

OPELOUSAS:

SAMEDI MATIN : : : : : 5 MARS 1864

☞ Cinq gunboats fédéraux sont entrés dans la Rivière Rouge Mardi dernier, ont remonté Black River en bombardant les bois jusques près du fort Beauregard, à Harrissonburg. Nous ne savons quel a été le résultat de cette première incursion. Le Gén Polignac est à Harrissonburg.

☞ Voyez l'avis du capitaine McCutchon dans une autre colonne. C'est un natif de la Louisiane, parle français et anglais, et sera ici probablement aujourd'hui ou demain.

☞ Les nouvelles de la Baie sont contradictoires; cependant, il est certain que les fédéraux ont toujours des forces là et à Franklin. On s'attend à les voir avancer sur nous sous peu.

FAIRE ARGENT DE TOUT.

On se rappelle que lorsque l'armée de Lee passa le Potomac et s'élança sur la Pennsylvanie, il y eut, dans cet Etat, comme un mouvement d'hésitation qui étonna tout le monde, dont s'indignèrent les honnêtes âmes, qui ont le culte sincère de la patrie. Les Pennsylvaniens, surpris par cette expédition si pleine d'audace, ne jouèrent pas un rôle exactement Spartiate. Ils furent lents, très lents à prendre les armes pour la protection de leur propre sol, et si scandaleuse fut cette lenteur, que de tous les Etats voisins, un tolle s'éleva contre ces patriotes en théorie, qui ne pouvaient se décider à la pratique. Il fallut leur adresser des appels sans nombre pour qu'ils remplissent enfin leur devoir—il fallut leur faire entrevoir des dangers bien plus grands encore, dans un avenir prochain, afin de les déterminer à faire face, comme des hommes, au danger du présent.

Souvent, afin d'enhardir un enfant à avaler la drogue qui lui fait horreur, un parent y met la dent ou la lèvre... Ce fut un peu l'expédient auquel il fallut avoir recours pour décider les Pennsylvaniens à prendre le mousquet, et à placer leurs poitrines entre les envahisseurs et leur capitale. New-York, le premier, se chargea de donner l'exemple,—sous les yeux des Pennsylvaniens, il goûta à la médecine qui leur répugnait tant, et ceux-ci, regaillardis par ce fait, stimulés par ce dévouement, se résignèrent enfin, et formèrent des contingents à peu près décents.

Seulement, si la venue des Newyorkais à la rescousse, provoqua, enfin, chez les Pennsylvaniens un tardif accès de patriotisme, pendant l'attente duquel l'armée confédérée gagnait toujours du terrain, ces héros [illegible] en témoignèrent étrangement leur reconnaissance à leurs voisins de New-York.

Le contingent New-Yorkais amenait sur le sol envahi un surcroît de population—des consommateurs nouveaux par conséquent. De nombreux négociants Pennsylvaniens se rendirent compte immédiatement de la situation, et, immédiatement aussi, ils voulurent en bénéficier, l'exploiter. Si la fibre patriotique vibrait en eux, la fibre commerciale n'en résonnait pas moins aussi—toute deux chantaient en duo dans leur être; seulement, la fibre commerciale faisait la première partie

La pensée dominante de ces citoyens, républicains, mais négociants, fut donc consacrée au calcul des profits qu'ils pourraient réaliser dans ces circonstances *malheureuses*. Ils furent vite fixés sur ce point, et a peine les troupes New-Yorkaises étaient-elles sur la terre Pennsylvanienne que le prix des denrées montait d'une façon anormale, scandaleuse.

En d'autres temps, en d'autres pays, les habitants de la région secourue auraient cru faiblement payer ceux qui venaient à leur aide, en leur prodiguant au moins les articles de première nécessité. A cette époque de lucre, et dans certaines catégories de la Pennsylvanie, on ne pense pas ainsi. On laisse ces beaux mouvements là aux [illegible] du sentiment. Ce sont de ces fantaisies qu'un homme sérieux, un homme, qui s'est développé derrière un comptoir, ne saurait transporter dans la vie réelle. Il est prudent de brider la générosité, afin qu'elle ne prenne pas le pas de la prodigalité.

La chose fut facile aux Pennsylvaniens, et, comme nous l'écrivions plus haut, le tarif de leurs marchandises fut soudainement élevé dans des proportions honteuses, pour souhaiter la bienvenue aux vrais patriotes de New-York. Ceux-ci consentaient à donner leur sang—mais ce n'était pas assez de ce sacrifice, on voulait encore leur extirper leur argent.

Cela eut lieu effectivement, et on n'a pas encore oublié les justes et sanglantes flagellations que l'on fit subir à ces Shylocks ébontés. Chose incroyable, et qui est cependant une vérité, des fermiers de la Pennsylvanie vendirent de l'eau à ceux qui venaient d'affronter, à Gettysburg, bombes, boulets, balles et baïonnettes. Ils firent payer, et chèrement encore, leur soif à ces hommes accourus d'un Etat voisin pour tacher de compléter leur courage plus qu'imparfait—ils spéculèrent indignement sur les fatigues de ceux qui avaient permis à leur couardise de se cacher au fond de la pièce la plus reculée de leurs demeures.

Ce souvenir est une flétrissure, et il eut été bon de tout mettre en œuvre afin de le racheter, de l'effacer à jamais. Il paraît que telle n'est pas encore l'opinion des Pennsylvaniens—ce sont là des délicatesses qu'ils prennent en pitié. De l'audace, encore de l'audace, et toujours de l'audace! disait un révolutionnaire fameux; des chiffres, encore des chiffres, et toujours des chiffres! disent les pères conscrits du commerce pennsylvanien.

Insatiables dans leurs appétits d'argent, ils trouvent que ce n'est pas assez des profits réalisés par les commerçants, au tardif dont il est question plus haut; pas assez des greenbacks empochés par ces fermiers de Gettysburg, qui, pour la circonstance, s'étaient transformés en bornes-fontaines, versant l'eau, mais à bon prix.—Ils veulent aller plus loin encore.

A cette heure, les Pennsylvaniens sont en voie de commettre une infamie aussi curieuse que honteuse Par l'intermédiaire de leurs représentants au Congrès, ils demandent à être indemnisés des dépenses qu'ils ont faites, pour aider à repousser l'invasion de leur propre sol.

Enoncer la proposition, c'est stigmatiser ceux qui ont eu l'impudeur de la faire. Où trouver, en effet, dans l'histoire le pendant de pareille réclamation? Comment admettre que la passion du gain puisse arriver à ce degré, à ce délire d'immoralité! Ne faut-il pas admettre que la gangrène morale est au sein de la population chez laquelle se trahissent semblables symptômes?

L'impunité enhardit vraiment, et si de nombreux précédents ne l'établissaient, ce fait isolé suffirait pour vous le prouver Il est des moments où les masses outragées ont peut être le droit de se faire justice elles-mêmes, surtout, quand elles savent que certains actes—véritables crimes pourtant—ne peuvent être atteints par la loi. L'un de ces actes était les boutiques ouvertes par les trafiquants Pennsylvaniens, autour des cadavres de leurs défenseurs—l'un de ces moments a été celui où l'on méconnaissait ainsi le dévouement, le courage.

A cette heure-là, nous eussions compris que les troupes new-yorkaises, dont on retournait ainsi les poches, eussent mis à bas boutiques et boutiquiers. Elles ne l'ont pas fait,—elles se sont contentées de signaler la turpitude, de la clouer au mépris public, comme on clouait autrefois un malfaiteur à sa croix. Pour des spéculateurs de cet étage, le mépris n'est pas un châtiment. L'impunité a donc enhardi ceux-là, comme nous l'écrivions tout à l'heure, et c'est pourquoi ils ont eu l'audace de cette demande au Congrès.

M. Fernando Wood s'est indigné en l'entendant formuler, et voulant en mieux faire ressortir tout l'odieux, il a déclaré à la chambre qu'il lui semblait que l'Etat de New-York avait droit aussi à faire une saignée au trésor fédéral, puisqu'il avait si largement contribué à secourir la Pennsylvanie.

Un autre représentant, M. Rogers, du New Jersey, a demandé, satiriquement aussi, que son Etat ne fut pas oublié dans les munificences du Congrès, puisqu'il avait fourni sa bonne part d'aide à la Pennsylvanie.

Il y aurait, selon nous, deux moyens de répondre à cette [illegible] réclamation; le premier serait de la rejeter en la flétrissant [illegible] dont elle est digne [illegible] second—et celui-là serait peut-être le meilleur—serait de payer, en effet ce moment de courage auquel se sont décidées les milices Pennsylvaniennes. Mais non; car il n'y aurait pas là le châtiment si bien mérité—l'encaissement de l'indemnité consolerait de la flétrissure tous ces Shylocks.

LOUISIANAIS!!

Le soussigné a été nommé par Son Ex. le Gouverneur Allen, Capitaine de Cavalerie, avec l'autorité de lever une compagnie de cent hommes à cheval, armés et équipés.

Il est autorisé à recruter parmi les hommes sujets au service militaire entre 16 et 18 ans et entre 45 et 55 ans, ainsi qui parmi ceux qui ont fourni des substituts dans l'armée Confédérée, pourvu qu'ils s'engagent dans l'armée de l'Etat avant le 1er de Mars. Chaque homme devra fournir son cheval, selle et bride, et un fusil double, pour lesquels il recevra la même compensation que dans le service des Etats Confédérés

Présentez vous donc promptement pour défendre vos foyers et vos droits, et n'attendez pas que vous soyez mis dans la milice. Votre Gouverneur, qui a eu du service et qui a beaucoup souffert des effets cruels de la guerre, fait aujourd'hui un appel pour que vous vous réunissiez autour de lui. Que cet appel ne soit pas fait en vain!

Les Lieutenants seront élus par la compagnie.
Les volontaires seront reçus par

SAM'L McCUTCHON,
Capitaine dans la Garde d'Etat.

5 mars 1864. 48—2t.

Attention Brigade de Hays.

EN vertu d'autorité reçue du Secrétaire de la Guerre, dans les Ordres Spéciaux No. 15, tous les hommes appartenant à cette Brigade partout où ils se trouvent dans ce Département, dans quelque branche du service que ce soit où ils servent maintenant, sont ordonnés de se rapporter au Capitaine W. K JOHNSON. à Alexandrie, ou au Capitaine C. M. PILCHER, à Minden, Lne., le 10 mars 1864, ou avant, afin de faire les arrangements nécessaires pour s'assurer un retour sûr et prompt à leur commandement en Virginie, autrement ils seront publiés comme déserteurs.

W. K. JOHNSON,
Capitaine Co. I. 8e Rég. de la Lne.
C M PILCHER.
48—2t. Capt Co. H, 6e Rég. de la Lne.

BUREAU DE L'ADJ. ET INSP. GENERAL,
Richmond 19 Janvier 1864.

ORDRES GENERAUX No. 2.

I. Les actes du Congrès ainsi que les Réglements qui suivent sont publiés pour l'information de ceux que cela concerne.

ACTE pour empêcher l'enrolement des substituts dans le service militaire des Etats Confédérés.

Le Congrès des Etats Confédérés d'Amérique décrète: Qu'aucune personne sujette au service militaire ne pourra, dorénavant, être admise à fournir un substitut pour le service militaire, ni aucun substitut ne pourra être reçu ni enrôlé dans le service militaire des Etats Confédérés.

[Approuvé le 28 Décembre 1863]

ACTE pour mettre fin aux exemptions du service militaire pour cause de substituts antérieurement fournis.

ATTENDU que dans les circonstances actuelles, le pays réclame l'aide de tous ceux qui peuvent porter les armes:

Le Congrès des Etats Confédérés décrète: Que personne ne sera exempt du service militaire pour raison d'avoir fourni un substitut; mais cet acte ne sera pas interprété de manière à affecter les personnes qui, quoique non sujettes au service militaire, ont néanmoins fourni des substituts.

[Approuvé le 5 Janvier 1864.]

II. Les personnes sujettes au service militaire par l'opération des actes précédents, sont placées sur le même pied avec toutes celles jusqu'ici frappées par les actes du Congrès.

III. Les personnes par les présentes rendues sujettes au service militaire sont requises de se rapporter comme volontaires ou conscrits, sans délai, aux officiers enrôleurs; et ceux qui ne l'auront pas fait au 1er Février 1864 seront considérés comme ayant renoncé au privilège de volontaire et tenu pour assignation d'après la loi.

IV. Les officiers enrôleurs procèderont aussi rapidement qu'il est possible à l'enrôlement des personnes rendues par les présentes sujettes au service militaire Auparavant de l'enrôlement des conscrits, les dites personnes auront le droit de se joindre comme volontaires aux compagnies dans le service au 16 Avril 1862, pour que la compagnie choisie n'atteigne pas le maximum accordé, et quand on aura fait choix de sa compagnie, le volontaire recevra de l'officier enrôleur un certificat à cet effet, et aucun volontaire ne sera reçu dans aucune compagnie excepté que d'après un tel certificat. Les personnes qui négligeraient de faire leur choix au moment de l'enrôlement, seront assignées d'après les réglements établis.

V. Toutes les personnes qui se rapporteront à l'officier enrôleur seront enrolées, et pourront obtenir un furlough de dix jours auparavant de se rapporter au Camp d'Instruction.

VI. Toutes les personnes soit volontaires ou conscrits, d'après cet ordre passeront devant le Camp d'Instruction de l'Etat auxquel elles apartiennent, et seront acheminées de là aux compagnies qui seront choisies, auxquelles elles auront été assignées

VII. Le Bureau de Conscription est requis d'adopter des réglements convenables pour la mise en vigueur de cet ordre.

VIII. Toutes les exemptions jusqu'ici accordées sont sujettes à une révision, d'après les instructions du Bureau de Conscription, et si elles étaient trouvées défectueuses ou non autorisées par la loi, elles seraient rejetées. Par ordre de

(Signé) S COOPER,
[illegible] Général

47—

Taxe des Etats Confédérés!!!

BUREAU DU COLLECTEUR [illegible] DISTRICT DE LA TAXE DES ETATS CONFEDERES POUR LA PAROISSE ST LANDRY,
Opelousas 27 Février 1864.

L'ATTENTION des personnes dénommées dans la Section 5 d'un acte du Congrès intitulé "Acte pour imposer des taxes pour la défense commune et pour le maintien du Gouvernement des Etats Confédérés," approuvé le 24 Avril 1863, est appelée aux Sections suivantes du dit acte:

SECT. 2. Toute personne engagée ou ayant intention de s'engager dans aucune des branches d'affaires dénommées dans la cinquième section du présent acte, devra, dans les soixante jours qui suivront la date de l'adoption du présent acte, ou à l'époque où elle commencera ses affaires, et ensuite le premier jour de Janvier de chaque année, enrégistrer, au bureau du Collecteur de District, en telle forme que le Commissaire des taxes pourra le prescrire, un état fidèle du nom et de la résidence de chaque personne, société ou corporation engagée ou intéressée dans les affaires, ainsi qu'un état du laps de temps, du lieu et de la manière avec lesquelles ces affaires seront conduites, comme aussi tous autres faits qui pourront faire connaître le montant de la taxe sur telles affaires pour le passé et pour l'avenir, conformément aux stipulations du présent acte. A l'époque de l'enregistrement il sera payé au Collecteur la taxe spécifique pour l'année terminant le trente-et-un Décembre prochain, ainsi que telle autre taxe qui pourra être due sur les ventes ou reçus dans telles affaires, à l'époque de l'enrégistrement, ainsi qu'il est ici pourvu; et le Collecteur devra donner à la personne qui fera tel enregistrement une copie d'icelui ainsi qu'un reçu du montant de la taxe par elle payée.

SECT 3 Toute personne qui manquera de faire cet enregistrement et de payer la taxe requise par la section précédente devra, en outre de toutes autres taxes sur ses affaires imposées par le présent acte, payer un montant double de la taxe spécifique sur telles affaires, ainsi qu'une somme semblable pour chaque trente jours qu'elle aura ainsi manqué."

Ce qui suit est la dénomination des occupations, métiers et personnes taxés conformément à la 5e section de l'acte relatif à la taxe:

Encanteurs; Apothicaires; Banquiers; Brasseurs; Courtiers; Bouchers; Boulangers; Jeux de Quilles; Cafés-Billards; Marchands. Commissionnaires et Agents de change; Marchands Commissionnaires en betes à cornes; Cirques; Confiseurs; Dentistes; Distillateur; Distillateurs de fruits, pour 90 jours ou moins; Hotels, Auberges; Restaurants ou autres maisons où l'on vend à manger; Jongleurs et autres exhibitions de ce genre; Avocats; Ecuries publiques; Prêteurs sur gage; Colporteurs; Médecins; Artistes en Photographes; Marchands en détail; Détaillants de liqueurs; Chirurgiens; Theâtres; Fabricants de tabac; Marchands en gros; Marchands de boissons, en gros.

EN CONSEQUENCE, conformément aux stipulations dudit Acte, le soussigné donne par les presentes avis à tous ceux que cela concerne, de venir faire leur enregistrement et payer leurs taxes, à son Bureau, en la ville d'Opelousas dans les TRENTE JOURS qui suivront la date du présent avis. Dans le cas où on manquerait ou négligerait de se conformer aux stipulations de la loi dans le laps de temps spécifié, les peines appliquées seront rigidement mises en force contre tout délinquent.

THEO C. LITTELL,
Collecteur de District.

47—5t]

AVIS.

TOUTES les personnes qui ont des réclamations contre le soussigné sont invitées à les lui présenter immédiatement pour réglement.

GEO. D LOGAN,
Capitaine et A. Quartier-Maitre du 2e Regiment de Cavalerie de la Louisiane.

27 Fevrier 1864. 47—2t

Vente Publique.

SUCCESSION DE MARIE LOUISE GILBERT.

LE public est par le présent averti qu'il sera vendu en vente publique, au plus offrant et dernier enchérisseur, par le soussigné Administrateur, ou par un Encanteur dûment commissionné, à la dernière résidence de feu dame Marie Louise Gilbert, à la Queue Tortue, dans la Paroisse St. Landry, le

Mardi, 22 Mars 1864,

les propriétés ci-dessous désignées, dépendant de la succession de ladite défunte, à savoir:

UN CERTAIN

Morceau de Terre,

situé au quartier de la Queue Tortue, dans la Paroisse St Landry, mesurant cent quarante-sept arpents de superficie, borné au Nord par Norbert Blanchard, au Sud par Théolin Lalande, à l'Est par Théodule Mire et Madame Firmin Breau, et à l'Ouest par les terres d'Hypolite C. Guidry, ensemble avec toutes les bâtisses et améliorations qui en dépendent.

SIX ESCLAVES.

Un lot de bêtes à cornes farouches;
2 paires de bœufs de tire;
Un mulet;
Une paire de jeunes bœufs;
Un lot de bêtes à cornes douces;
Meubles de maison;
Ustensiles de cuisine;
Environ 400 livres de coton en graine, et une infinité d'autres articles dont l'énumération serait trop longue.

CONDITIONS:—Un, deux et trois ans de crédit, à compter du 1er Avril prochain, 1864; c'est à dire, un tiers le 1er Avril 1865, un tiers le 1er Avril 1866, et le dernier tiers le 1er Avril 1867. Les acquéreurs fournissant leurs obligations avec deux bonnes cautions solidaires à la satisfaction de l'administrateur de la succession; lesquelles obligations seront faites payables à son ordre, et porteront intérêt à raison de 8 pour cent par an à compter de l'échéance. Et en outre, la terre et les esclaves demeurant spécialement hypothéqués à la succession jusqu'au paiement final et définitif, tant du principal que des intérêts qui auront pu s'accroître.

DRAUZIN BREAU,
Administrateur.

Opelousas, 20 Février 1864.

$600 de recompense.

PARTIS MARRONS du soussigné, à environ 5 milles du pont de Lloyd, sur la route du chemin du Ferry de Burr, dans la nuit du 9 au 10 d'Aout, les esclaves ci-dessous décrits, savoir:

Un nègre nommé TYREE, couleur griffe, âgé d'environ 36 ans, taille d'environ 5 pieds neuf pouces.

Un nègre nommé WILSON, couleur griffe foncé, âgé d'environ 35 ans, taille d'environ 5 pieds 8 pouces, fortement construit. Il lui manque une dent de devant.

Un nègre nommé McCOY, âgé de 19 ans, et taille d'environ 5 pieds 8 pouces de haut.

Une négresse nommée ROSETTA, âgée de vingt ans, environ.

CENT PIASTRES seront payées pour l'appréhension de chacun d'eux et sa livraison à moi à un point quelconque entre le Bayou Bœuf et le Ferry de Burr.

Sont aussi partis marrons, de mon habitation, sur le Bayou Bœuf:

Un nègre nommé GEORGE, âgé d'environ trente [illegible]

Un autre nègre nommé ALLEN, âgé d'environ 26 ans.

Cent piastres de récompense seront payées pour la livraison à moi de chacun de ces esclaves, à un point quelconque entre ma résidence et Burr's Ferry Les deux esclaves dernièrement mentionnés sont sans doute sur mon habitation ou dans le voisinage; et les autres tenteront probablement de retourner au même quartier sous peu.

GEORGE R KING.

St. Landry 12 Septembre 1863. 28tf

Avis.

LE soussigné ayant fait une petite émision de billets, il y a environ 18 mois, dans le but de favoriser le change, et ayant appris dernièrement que quelques personnes offraient une prime pour ces billets; invite les détenteurs de ces dits billets à les lui présenter à Washington pour être remboursés dans le plus court délai possible, attendu qu'ils ne seront remboursés qu'en billets Confédérés, conformement à la stipulation qu'ils contiennent et non en espèces, comme quelques personnes mal informées, le croient.

T. HERBERT.

Washington, 20 Février 1864. 46—3t.

AVIS.

JOSEPH BLOCH, à l'ancien établissement de Bloch, Firnberg & Co, à Opelousas, vient d'ouvrir un magasin où il s'efforcera de tenir des articles à l'usage général des familles et des habitations. Il a en main un assortiment de farine, sucre, mélasse, sel, et recevra incessamment un envoi de marchandises d'un usage général

Opelousas 19 Décembre 1863.—tf

AVIS.

LA soussignée ayant perdu toutes les obligations souscrites par les acquéreurs à la vente des biens de la succession de John H. Maggee, son époux, décédé, donne par les présentes avis à ceux que cela concerne, que le paiement en a été arrêté, et elle avertit en même temps le public de ne pas négocier lesdites obligations

VEUVE JOHN H. MAGGEE,
Administratrice.

St. Landry 6 Février 1864. 44—5t.

A vendre au comptant.

LES SOURCES DE BEAVER CREEK, situées à 35 milles d'Opelousas, contenant 200 arpents de terre boisée, avec les améliorations:—Plus, un Billard avec ses accessoires.

Pour les particularités, s'adresser à

H. PROVENT, propriétaire.

Opelousas 16 Janvier 1864. 41tf

Maison Vieille Banque.

CET Hotel, situé près de la Maison de Cour, à Opelousas, est tenu par Mm. Stuart, qui s'efforcera de satisfaire ceux qui voudront bien l'encourager.

Opelousas, 2 Janvier 1864.

Aux Chasseurs.

PLOMB à giboyer, de toutes dimensions, à vendre par le soussigné, à $3.50 la livre.

LOUIS VATTER.

Opelousas 6 Février 1864. 44—tf.

AVIS.

MES nègres ont tué, [croyant être pour moi] une vache noire marquée sur le côté gauche O-N. La marque à l'oreille est une entaille à la partie inférieure de chaque oreille.

Le propriétaire est prié de se présenter et recevoir le paiement de sa vache.

HENRY L. GARLAND.

Opelousas, 13 Février 1864. 45—4t.

VENTE PUBLIQUE.

Succession de Ursule Boutin.

EN vertu d'un ordre de l'Honorable la Cour du 8e District Judiciaire, siégeant à Opelousas, Paroisse St. Landry, le soussigné offrira en vente publique, au plus offrant et dernier enchérisseur, sur l'habitation de la décédée, à Gros Chevreuil, à environ 12 milles de la ville d'Opelousas, le

MARDI, 22 MARS 1864,

les propriétés ci-après décrites, dépendant de la succession de feue Ursule Boutin, veuve décédée de feu George Lalonde, savoir:

9 Esclaves,

SAVOIR:

PRUDENT, mulâtre	âgé d'environ	65	ans;
JOE, nègre	" "	46	"
ETIENNE, (Sambo)	" "	13	"
LAIZA, négresse	" "	30	"
et ses cinq enfants: Marie,	âgée de	9	ans;
Flore,	"	7	"
Ben,	"	5	"
Charlotte	"	3	"
Azéma,	"	15	mois.

Un lot de coton en grain;
Une voiture à quatre places avec harnais;
Une paire de mulets;
Une mule;
17 têtes de bêtes à corne douces;
Un cheval créole;
Un bœuf de tire;
Un moulin à gruau, et une infinité d'autres articles dont l'énumération serait trop longue.

Termes et Conditions:—Toutes adjudication payable à un, deux et trois ans de crédit à compter du 1er Avril 1865. Les acquéreurs fournissant leurs billets avec caution solidaire à la satisfaction de l'administrateur de ladite succession, et payable au magasin de M. Michel Emonet, à Gros Chevreuil. A défaut de paiement des dits billets à leur échéance, ils porteront intérêt au taux de 8 pour cent l'an, en outre les propriétés sujettes d'hypothèques demeureront spécialement hypothéquées à la succession jusqu'au paiement final tant du principal que des intérêts qui auront pu s'accroître.

JEAN BOUFFARTIGUE,
Encanteur.

Gros Chevreuil, St. Landry, 20 Fév. 1864.

VENTE PUBLIQUE.

SUCCESSION DE CELESTINE CORMIER.

EN vertu d'un ordre émanant de l'Honorable La Cour du Huitième District Judiciaire de l'Etat de la Louisiane, siégeant dans et pour la Paroisse St. Landry, le soussigné offrira en vente publique, au plus offrant et dernier enchérisseur, sur l'habitation de la décédée, à environ 12 milles de la ville d'Opelousas, le

Mardi 8 Mars 1864,

les propriétés ci-après décrites, dépendant de la succession en communauté entre feu Célestine Cormier et Théodule Lalonde.

Un Negre,

nommé Narcisse, âgé d'environ 45 ans.
Un cheval alezan, quart américain;
Une vache et son veau;
Un bœuf de tire;
Une romaine poids;
Neuf moutons,
Un cochon et un miroir.

Termes et Conditions:—Chaque adjudication de 10 piastres et au-dessous, payable comptant, et chaque adjudition au-dessus de 10 piastres, payable [illegible] ans de crédit à partir du jour de la vente. Les acquéreurs fournissant leurs billets avec deux cautions solidaires à la satisfaction de l'administrateur de la succession, et payables au bureau de M. Jean Bouffartigue, Notaire, à Gros Chevreuil. A défaut de paiement des dits billets, ils porteront intérêt à raison de 8 pour cent l'an à partir de leur échéance à leur entier paiement, en outre les propriétés sujettes à hypothèques demeureront spécialement hypothéquées à la succession jusqu'à leur parfait paiement tant du capital que des intérêts qui auront pu s'accroître.

J. BOUFFARTIGUE,
Encanteur.

Gros Chevreuil, 6 Février 1864.

VENTE PUBLIQUE.

SUCCESSION DE FEU EDWIN M. SMITH.

LE public est averti qu'il sera vendu en vente publique, au plus offrant et dernier enchérisseur, par le soussigné, Encanteur public, sur l'habitation de Charles B Smith, au haut de Plaquemnié en cette Paroisse,

Le Samedi 5 Mars prochain,

1864, les propriétés ci-après mentionnées, dépendant de la succession dudit feu Edwin M. Smith, décédé, à savoir:

Une petite Habitation,

située dans le quartier de Bellevue, Paroisse St. Landry, joignant l'habitation de Mme. Veuve Jean F. Richard, mesurant environ quatrevingt-quatorze acres de terre de superficie, ensemble avec toutes les bâtisses et améliorations qui en dépendent.

Un petit lot de chevaux et de vaches;
Meubles de ménage;
Un lot de livres;
Instruments d'habitation;
Instruments d'arpenteur;
Un fer à marquer, et une infinité d'autres articles dont l'énumération serait trop longue.

CONDITIONS.—Toute adjudication de dix piastres et au-dessous payable comptant, et toute adjudication au-dessus de dix piastres, payable à un crédit de un, deux et trois ans, à compter du jour de la vente. Les acquéreurs fournissant leurs obligations avec caution solidaire à la satisfaction de qui de droit; lesquelles obligations seront faites payables à l'ordre et au domicile de l'administrateur de ladite succession, et portant intérêt à raison de huit pour cent par an, à compter de l'échéance de chaque terme. Et en outre la terre demeurant spécialement hypothéquée à la succession jusqu'au paiement final tant du principal que des intérêts qui auront pu s'accroître.

JOHN F. SMITH,
Encanteur.

Opelousas 30 Janvier 1864

LE COURRIER DES OPELOUSAS,
Publié le Samedi par Joel H. Sandoz.
CONDITIONS:

L'abonnement est de DIX piastres par an payables d'avance ou *douze* piastres à la fin de l'année. Aucun abonnement ne sera arrêté avant que les arrérages ne soient payés, à moins que l'éditeur ne le juge convenable.—Et les abonnés qui désireront arrêter leur abonnement devront en donner avis *par écrit* au moins quinze jours avant le terme de leur abonnement.

Les avis seront insérés à raison de vingt-cinq cents la ligne pour chacune des trois premières publication, et dix cents la ligne pour chaque publication subséquente. Quand on traitera de gré à gré avec l'Editeur, une déduction libérale sera faite pour les avis permanents.

Tout avis, à moins qu'il n'en soit autrement ordonné, sera publié en français et en anglais jusqu'à ce qu'il soit retiré, ou jusqu'à ce que l'Editeur juge convenable de le retirer.

Les annonces de candidats se paieront vingt piastres pour chaque candidat, et d'avance.

THE HOUSTON DAILY TELEGRAPH

VOL. XXIX—NO. 175. HOUSTON, SATURDAY, MARCH 19, 1864. WHOLE NO. 2830.

Address of the Richmond Congress to the People of the Confederate States.

To the People of the Confederate States:

In closing the labors of the first permanent Congress, your representatives deem it a fit occasion to give some account of their stewardship; to review briefly what, under such embarrassments and adverse circumstances, has been accomplished; to invite attention to the prospect before us and the duties incumbent on every citizen in this crisis; and to address such words of counsel and encouragement as the times demand.

Compelled by a long series of oppressive and tyrannical acts culminating at last in the election of a President and Vice President by a party confessedly sectional and hostile to the South and her institutions, these States withdrew from the former Union, and formed a new Confederate alliance, as an independent government, based on the proper relations of labor and capital. This step was taken reluctantly, by constraint, and after the exhaustion of every measure that was likely to secure us from interference with our property, equality in the Union, or exemption from submission to an alien government. The Southern States claimed only the unrestricted enjoyment of the rights guaranteed by the constitution. Finding, by painful and protracted experience, that this was persistently denied, we determined to separate from those enemies, who had manifested the inclination and ability to impoverish and destroy us, we fell back upon the right for which the colonies maintained the war of the revolution, and which our heroic forefathers asserted to be clear and inalienable. The unanimity and zeal with which the separation was undertaken and perfected, finds no parallel in history. The people rose *en masse* to assert their liberties and protect their menaced rights. There never was before such universality of conviction, among any people, on any question involving so serious and so thorough a change of political and international relations. This grew out of the clearness of the right so to act, and the certainty of the perils of further association with the North. The change was so wonderful, so rapid, so contrary to universal history, that many fail to see that all has been done in the logical sequence of principles, which are the highest testimony to the wisdom of our fathers, and the best illustration of the correctness of those principles. This government is a child of law instead of sedition, of right instead of violence, of deliberation instead of insurrection. Its early life was attended by no anarchy, no rebellion, no suspension of authority, no social disorders, no lawless disturbances. Sovereignty was not for one moment in abeyance. The utmost conservatism marked every proceeding and public act. The object was "to do what was necessary, and no more; and to do that with the utmost temperance and prudence." St. Just, in his report to the convention of France, in 1793, said, "a people has but one dangerous enemy, and that is government." We adopt no such absurdity. In nearly every instance, the first steps were taken legally, in accordance with the will and prescribed directions of the constituted authorities of the seceded States. We were not remitted to brute force or natural law, or the instincts of reason. The charters of freedom were scrupulously preserved.—As in the English revolution of 1688, and ours of 1776, there was no material alteration in the laws beyond what was necessary to redress the abuses that provoked the struggle. No attempt was made to build on *speculative* principles. The effort was confined within the narrowest limits of historical and constitutional right. The controversy turned on the records and muniments of the past. We merely resisted innovation and tyranny, and contended for our birth-rights and the covenanted principles of *our race*. We have had our Governors, General Assemblies and Courts; the same electors, the same corporations, "the same rules for property, the same subordinations, the same order in the law and in the magistracy." When the sovereign States met in council, they, in truth and substance, and in a constitutional light, did not make, but prevented, a revolution.

Commencing our new national life under such circumstances, we had a right to expect that we would be permitted, without molestation, to cultivate the arts of peace, and vindicate on our chosen arena and with the selected type of social characteristics, our claims to civilization. It was thought, too, by many, that war would not be resorted to by an enlightened country, except on the direst necessity. That a people, professing to be animated by Christian sentiment, and who had regarded our peculiar institutions as a blot and blur upon the fair escutcheon of their common Christianity, should make war upon the South for doing what they had a perfect right to do, and for relieving them of the incubus which, they professed, rested upon them by the association, was deemed almost beyond belief by many of the wisest minds. It was hoped, too, that the obvious interest of the two sections would restrain the wild frenzy of excitement and turn into peaceful channels the thoughts of those who had but recently been invested with power in the United States.

These reasonable anticipations were doomed to disappointment. The red glare of battle, kindled at Sumter, dissipated all hopes of peace, and the two governments were arrayed in hostility against each other. We charge the responsibility of this war upon the United States. They are accountable for the blood and havoc and ruin it has caused. For such a war we were not prepared. The difference in military resources between our enemies and ourselves; the immense advantages possessed in the organized machinery of an established government; a powerful navy; the nucleus of an army; credit abroad, and illimitable facilities in mechanical and manufacturing power, placed them on the "vantage ground." In our infancy we were without a seaman or a soldier, without revenue, without gold and silver, without a recognized place in the family of nations, without external commerce, without foreign credit, with the prejudice of the world against us. While we were without manufacturing facilities to supply our wants our ports were blockaded; we had to grapple with a great adversary, defend 2,000 miles of sea coast and an inland frontier of equal extent. If we had succeeded in preventing any successes on the part of the enemy it would have been a miracle. What we have accomplished, with a population so inferior in numbers, and means so vastly disproportionate, has excited the astonishment and admiration of the world.

The war in which we are engaged was wickedly, and against all our protests and most earnest efforts to the contrary, forced upon us. South Carolina sent a commission to Washington to adjust all questions of dispute between her and the United States. One of the first acts of the provisional government was to accredit agents to visit Washington, and use all honorable means to obtain a satisfactory settlement of all questions of dispute with that government. Both efforts failed. Commissioners were deceived and rejected, and clandestine but vigorous preparations were made for war. In proportion to our perseverance and anxiety have been the obstinacy and arrogance in spurning offers of peace. It seems we can be indebted for nothing to the virtues of our enemies. We are obliged to his vices, which have assured to our strength. We owe as much to his insolence and blindness as to our own precaution.

The wager of battle having been tendered, it was accepted. The alacrity with which our people flew to arms is worthy of all praise. Their deeds of heroic daring, patient endurance, ready submission to discipline, and numerous victories, are in keeping with the fervent patriotism that prompted their early volunteering. Quite recently scores of regiments have re-enlisted for the war, testifying their determination to fight until their liberties were achieved. Coupled with and contributing greatly to this enthusiastic order, was the lofty courage, the indomitable resolve, the self denying spirit of our noble women, who, by their labors of love, their patience of hope, their unflinching constancy, their uncomplaining submission to privations of the war, have shed an immortal lustre upon their sex and country.

Our army is no hireling soldiery. It comes not from paupers, criminals or emigrants. It was originally raised by the free, unconstrained, unpurchasable assent of the men. All vocations and classes contributed to the swelling numbers. Abandoning luxuries and comforts to which they had been accustomed, they submitted cheerfully to the scanty fare and exactive service of the camps. Their services above price, the only remuneration they have sought is the protection of their altars, firesides and liberty. In the Norweigan wars, the actors were, every one of them, named and patronymically described as the King's friend and companion. The same wonderful individuality has been seen in this war. Our soldiers are not a consolidated mass, an unthinking machine, but an army of intelligent units. To designate all who have distinguished themselves by special valor, would be to enumerate nearly all in the army. The generous rivalry between troops from different States has prevented any special pre-eminence, and hereafter, for centuries to come, the gallant bearing and unconquerable devotion of Confederate soldiers will inspire the hearts and encourage the hopes, and strengthen the faith, of all who labor to obtain their freedom.

For three years this cruel war has been waged against us, and its continuance has been seized upon as a pretext by some discontented persons to excite hostility to the government. Recent and public as have been the occurrences, it is strange that a misapprehension exists as to the conduct of the two governments in reference to peace. Allusion has been made to the unsuccessful efforts, when separation took place, to procure an amicable adjustment of all matters in dispute. These attempts at negotiation do not comprise all that has been done. In every form in which expression could be given to the sentiment—in public meetings, through the press, by legislative resolves—the desire of this people for peace, for the uninterrupted enjoyment of their rights and property, has been made known. The President, more authoritatively, in several of his messages while protesting the utter absence of all desire to interfere with the United States, or acquire any of their territory, has avowed that the "advent of peace will be hailed with joy. Our desire for it has never been concealed. Our efforts to avoid the war, forced on us as it was by the lust of conquest and the insane passions of our foes, are known to mankind."

The course of the Federal government has proved that it did not desire peace, and would not consent to it on any terms that we could possibly concede. In proof of this, we refer to the repeated rejection of all terms of conciliation and compromise, to their recent contemptuous refusal to receive the Vice-President, who was sent to negotiate for softening the asperities of the war, and their scornful rejection of the offer of a neutral power to mediate between the contending parties. If cumulative evidence be needed, it can be found in the following resolution, recently adopted by the House of Representatives in Washington:

"*Resolved*, That as our country and the very existence of the best government ever instituted by man, are imperiled by the most causeless and wicked rebellion that the world has seen, and believing as we do, that the only hope of saving this country and preserving this government is by the power of the sword; we are for a vigorous prosecution of the war until the constitution and laws shall be enforced and obeyed in all parts of the United States; and to that end we oppose any armistice or intervention, or mediation, or proposition for peace from any quarter, so long as there shall be found a rebel in arms against the government; and we ignore all party names, lines and issues, and recognize but two parties in this war, patriots and traitors."

The motive of such strange conduct is obvious. The republican party was founded to destroy slavery and the equality of the States, and Lincoln was selected as the instrument to accomplish this object. The Union was a barrier to the consummation of this policy, because the constitution, which was its bond, recognized and protected slavery and the sovereignty of the States. The Union must therefore be sacrificed, and to ensure its destruction war was determined upon.

The mass of the Northern people were not privy to, and sympathized in no such design. They loved the Union and wished to preserve it. To rally the people to the support of the war, its object was proclaimed to be "a restoration of the Union," as if that which implied voluntary assent, of which agreement was an indespensable element and condition, could be preserved by coercion. It is absurd to pretend that a government, really desirous of restoring the Union, would adopt such measures as the confiscation of private property, the emancipation of slaves, systematic efforts to invite them to insurrection, forcible abductions from their homes and compulsory enlistment in the army, the division of a sovereign State without its consent, and a proclamation that one-tenth of the population of a State, and that tenth under military rule, should control the will of the remaining nine-tenths. The only relation possible between the two sections, under such a policy, is that of conquerer and conquered, superior and decendent. Rest assured, fellow citizens, that although restoration may still be used as a war cry by the northern government, it is only to delude and betray. Fanaticism has summoned to its aid cupidity and vengeance; and nothing short of your utter subjugation, the destruction of your State governments, the overthrow of your social and political fabric, your personal and public degradation and ruin, will satisfy the demands of the North. Can there be a man so vile, so debased, so unworthy of liberty, as to accept peace on such humiliating terms?

It would hardly be fair to assert that all the northern people participate in these designs. On the contrary, there exists a powerful political party, which openly condemns them. The Administration has, however, been able thus far, by its enormous patronage, and its lavish expenditures to seduce, or by its legions of "Hessian" mercenaries to overawe the masses, to control the elections, and to establish an arbitrary despotism. It cannot be possible that this state of things can continue. The people of the United States, accustomed to freedom, cannot consent to be ruined and enslaved, in order to ruin and enslave us. Moral, like physical epidemics, have their allotted periods, and must, sooner or later, be exhausted and disappear. When reason returns, our enemies will probably reflect, that a people, like ours, who have exhibited such capabilities, and extemporized such resources, can never be subdued; that a vast expanse of territory, with such a population, cannot be governed as an obedient colony. Victory would not be conquest. The inextinguishable quarrel would be transmitted "from bleeding sire to son," and the struggle would be renewed between generations yet unborn. To impoverish us would only be to dry up some of the springs of northern prosperity—to destroy southern wealth is to reduce northern profits, while the restoration of peace would necessarily re-establish some commercial intercourse. It may not be amiss, in this connection to say that, at one time, it was the wish and expectation of many at the South, to form a treaty of amity and friendship with the northern States, by which both people might derive the benefits of commercial intercourse, and move on side by side, in the arts of peace and civilisation. History has confirmed the lesson taught by Divine authority, that each nation, as well as each individual, should seek their happiness in the prosperity of others, and not in the injury or ruin of a neighbor. The general welfare of all is the highest dictate of moral duty and economic policy, while a heritage of triumphant wrong is the greatest curse that can befall a nation.

Until some evidence is given of a change of policy on the part of the government, and some assurance is received that efforts at negotiation will not be spurned, the Congress are of opinion that any direct overtures for peace would compromise our self-respect, be fruitless of good, and interpreted by the enemy as an indication of weakness. We can only repeat the desire of the people for peace, and our readiness to accept terms consistent with the honor and integrity and independence of the States, and especially with the safety of our domestic institutions.

Not content with rejecting all proposals for a peaceful settlement of the controversy, a cruel war of invasion was commenced, which in its progress, has been marked by a brutality and disregard of the rules of civilised warfare, as stand out in unexampled barbarity in the history of modern wars. Accompanied by every act of cruelty and rapine, the conduct of the enemy has been destitute of that forbearance and magnanimity which civilization and Christianity have introduced to mitigate the asperities of war. The atrocities are too incredible for narration. Instead of a regular war, our resistance of the unholy efforts to crush out our natural existence, is treated as a rebellion, and the settled international rules between beligerents are ignored. Instead of conducting the war as betwixt two military and political organizations, it is a war against the whole population. Houses are pillaged and burned. Churches are defaced. Towns are ransacked. Clothing of women and infants are stripped from their persons. Jewelry and mementoes of the dead are stolen. Mills and implements of agriculture are destroyed. Private salt works are broken up. The introduction of medicines is forbidden. Means of subsistence are wantonly wasted to produce beggary. Prisoners are returned with contagious diseases. The last morsel of food has been taken from families who were not allowed to carry on a trade or branch of industry. A rigid and offensive *espionage* has been introduced to ferret out "disloyalty." Persons have been forced to choose between starvation of helpless children and taking the oath of allegiance to a hated government. The cartel for exchange of prisoners has been suspended and our unfortunate soldiers subjected to the grossest indignities. The wounded at Gettysburg were deprived of their nurses and inhumanly left to perish on the field. Helpless women have been exposed to the most cruel outrages, and that dishonor which is infinitely worse than death. Citizens have been murdered by the Butlers and McNeils and Milroys, who are favorite generals of our enemies. Refined and elegant ladies have been seized, bound with cords, imprisoned, guarded by negroes, and held as hostages for the return of captured slaves. Unoffending non-combatants have been banished or dragged from their quiet homes to be immured in filthy jails. Preaching the gospel has been refused, except on condition of taking the oath of allegiance. Parents have been forbidden to name their children in honor of "rebel" chiefs. Property has been confiscated, military governors appointed for States, satraps for provinces and Haynaus for cities.

These cruelties and atrocities of the enemy have been exceeded by their malicious and blood thirsty purposes and machinations in reference to the slaves. Early in this war, President Lincoln averred his constitutional inability and personal unwillingness to interfere with the domestic institutions of the States and the relation between master and servant. Presidential considerations may have been veiled under conscientious scruples, for Seward, in confidential instructions to Mr. Adams, the Minister to Great Britain, on the 10th of March, 1862, said:

"If the government of the United States should *precipitately* decree the immediate emancipation of slavery, it would reinvigorate the declining insurrection in every part of the South." Subsequent reverses and the refractory rebelliousness of the seceded States caused a change of policy, and Mr. Lincoln issued his celebrated proclamation—a mere *brutum fulmen*—liberating the slaves in the insurrectionary districts." On the 24th June, 1776, one of the reasons assigned by Pennsylvania for her separation from the mother country was, that in her sister colonies, the "King had excited the negroes to revolt" and to imbue their hands in the blood of their masters, in a manner unpracticed by civilized nations. This, probably, had reference to the proclamation of Dunmore, the last royal Governor of Virginia, in 1776, declaring freedom to all servants or negroes if they would join for the reducing the colony to a proper sense of its duty." The invitation to the slaves to rise against their masters, the suggested insurrection, caused, says Baucroft, "a thrill of indignation to run through Virginia, effacing all differences of party and rousing one strong, impassioned purpose to drive away the insolent power by which it had been put forth." A cotemporary annalist, adverting to the same proclamation, said "it was received with the greatest horror in all the colonies."

"The policy adopted by Dunmore," says Lawrence in his notes on Wheaton, "of arming the slaves against their masters, was not pursued during the war of the revolution; and when negroes were taken by the English, they were not considered otherwise than as property or plunder." Emancipation of slaves as a war measure has been severely condemned and denounced by the most eminent publishers in Europe and the United States. The United States, "in their diplomatic relations have ever maintained," says the northern authority just quoted, "that slaves were private property, and for them, as such, they have repeatedly received compensation from England." Napoleon I. was never induced to issue a proclamation for the emancipation of the serfs in his war with Russia. He said: "I could have armed against her a part of her population in proclaiming the liberty of the serfs. A great number of villages asked it of me, but I refused to avail myself of a measure which would have devoted to death thousands of families." In the discussion growing out of the treaty of peace of 1814, and the proffered mediation of Russia, the principle was maintained by the United States that "the emancipation of enemy's slaves is not among the acts of legitimate warfare." In the instructions from John Quincy Adams, as Secretary of State, to Mr. Middleton, at St. Petersburg, Oct. 18, 1820, it is said: "The British have broadly asserted the right of emancipating slaves (private property) as a legitimate right of war. No such right is acknowledged as a law of war by writers who admit any limitation. The right of putting to death all prisoners in cold blood and without special cause, might as well be pretended to be a law of war, or the right to use poisoned weapons, or to assassinate."

Disregarding the teachings of the approved writers on international law and the practice and claims of his own goverment in its purer days, President Lincoln has sought to convert the South into a St. Domingo, by appealing to the cupidity, lusts, ambition and ferocity of the slave. Abraham Lincoln is but the lineal descendant of Dunmore, and the impotent malice of each was foiled by the fidelity of those who, by the meanness of the conspirators, would only, if successful, have been seduced into idleness, filth, vice, beggary and death.

But we tire of these indignities and enormities. They are too sickening for recital. History will hereafter *pillory* those who committed and encouraged such crimes in immortal infamy.

Gen. Robert E. Lee, in a recent battle order, stated to his invincible legions that the "cruel foe seeks to reduce our fathers and mothers, our wives and children to abject slavery." He does not paint too strongly the purposes of the enemy or the consequences of subjugation. What has been done in certain districts, is but the prologue of the bloody drama that will be enacted. It is well that every man and woman should have some just conception of the horrors of conquest. The fate of Ireland at the period of its conquest, and of Poland, distinctly foreshadows what would await us. The guillotine, in its ceaseless work of blood, would be revived for the execution of the "rebel leaders." The heroes of our contest would be required to lay down their proud ensigns on which are recorded the battle fields of their glory, to stack their arms, lower their heads in humiliation and dishonor, and pass under the yoke of abolition misrule and tyranny. A hateful inquisition, made atrocious by spies and informers; star chamber courts, enforcing their decisions by confiscation, imprisonments, banishments and death; a band of detectives, ferreting out secrets, lurking in every family, existing in every conveyance; the suppression of speech; the deprivation of arms and franchise; and the ever present sense of inferiority would make our condition abject and miserable beyond what freemen can imagine. Subjugation involves everything that the torturing malice and devilish ingenuity of our foes can suggest. The destruction of our nationality, the equalization of whites and blacks, the obliteration of State lines, degradation to colonial vassalage, and the reduction of many of our citizens to dreary, hopeless, remediless bondage. A hostile police will keep "order" in every town and city. Judges, like Busteed, would hold our courts, protected by Yankee soldiers. Churches would be filled by Yankee or tory preachers. Every office would be bestowed on aliens. Absenteeism would crush us with all its vices. Superadded to these, sinking us into a lower abyss of degradation, we would be made the slaves of our slaves, hewers of wood and drawers of water for those upon whom God has stamped indellibly the marks of physical and intellectual inferiority. The past of foreign countries need not be sought into to furnish illustrations of the heritage of shame that subjugation would entail. Baltimore, St. Louis, Nashville, Knoxville, New Orleans, Vicksburg, Huntsville, Norfolk, Newbern, Louisville and Fredericksburg are the first fruits of the ignominy and poverty of Yankee domination.

The sad story of the wrongs and indignities endured by these States which have been in the complete or partial possession of the enemy, will give the best evidence of the consequences of subjugation. Missouri, a magnificent empire of agricultural and mineral wealth, is to-day, a smoking ruin and the theatre of the most revolting cruelties and barbarisms. The minions of tyrants consume her substance, plunder her citizens, and destroy her peace. The sacred rights of freemen are struck down, and the blood of her children, her maidens and her old men, is made to flow, out of mere wantonness and recklessness. No whispers of freedom go unpunished, and the very instincts of self-preservation are outlawed. The worship of God and the rites of sepulture have been shamefully interrupted, and, in many instances, the cultivation of the soil is prohibited to her own citizens. These facts are attested by many witnesses, and it is but a just tribute to that noble and chivalrous people, that, amid barbarities almost unparalleled, they still maintain a proud and defiant spirit towards their enemies.

In Maryland the judicary made subservient to executive absolutism, furnishes no security for individual rights or personal freedom; members of the Legislature are arrested and imprisoned without process of law or assignment of cause, and the whole land groaneth under the oppression of a merciless tyranny.

In Kentucky the ballot box has been overthrown, free speech has been suppressed, the most vexatious annoyances of an unscrupulous despotism are freely used to prevent the uprising of the noble patriots of "the dark and bloody ground." Notes of gladness, assurances of a brighter and better day, reach us, and the exiles may take courage and hope for the future.

In Virginia the model of all that illustrates human heroism and self denying patriotism, although the tempest of desolation has swept over her fair domains, no sign of repentance for her separation from the North can be found. Her old homesteads dismantled her ancestral relics destroyed, her people impoverished, her territory made the battle ground for the rude shocks of contending hosts, and then divided, with hireling parasities mockingly claiming jurisdiction and authority, the Old Dominion still stands, with proud crest and defiant mien, ready to tramp beneath her heel every usurper and tyrant, and to illustrate afresh her *sic semper tyrannis*, the "proudest motto that ever blazed on a nations shield or a warrior's arms."

To prevent such acts our people are now prosecuting this struggle. It is no mere war of calculation, no contest for a peculiar kind of property, no barter of precious blood for filthy lucre. Everything involved in manhood, civilization, religion, law, property, country, home, is at stake. We fight not for plunder, spoils, pillage, territorial conquest. The government tempts by no prizes of "beauty or booty," to be drawn in the lottery of this war. We seek to preserve civil freedom, honor, equality, firesides, and blood is well shed when "shed for our family, for our friends, for our kind, for our country, for our God." Burke said, "a State, resolved to hazard its existence rather than abandon its object, must have an infinite advantage over that which is resolved to yield, rather than carry its resistance beyond a certain point." It is better to be conquered by any other nation than by the United States. It is better to be a dependency of any other power than of that. By the condition of its existence and essential constitution, as now governed, it must be in perpetual hostility to us. As the Spanish invader burned his ships to make retreat impossible, so we cannot afford to take steps backward. Retreat is more dangerous than advance. Behind us are inferiority and degradation. Before us is everything enticing to a patriot.

Our bitter and implacable foes are preparing vigorously for the coming campaign. Corresponding efforts should be made on our part. Without murmuring our people should respond to the laws, which the exigency demands. Every one capable of bearing arms should be connected with some effective military organization. The utmost energies of the whole population should be taxed to produce food and clothing, and a spirit of cheerfulness and trust in an all-wise and overruling Providence should be cultivated.

The history of the past three years has much to animate us to renewed effort and a firmer and more assured hope. A whole people have given their hearts and bodies to repel the invader, and costly sacrifices have been made on the altar of our country. No similar instance is to be found of such a spontaneous uprising and volunteering. Inspired by a holy patriotism, again and again have our brave soldiers, with the aid of Heaven, baffled the efforts of our foes. It is in no arrogant spirit that we refer to successes that have cost us so much blood, and brought sorrow to so many hearts. We may find in all this an earnest of what, with determined and resolute exertions we can do to avert subjugation and slavery—and we cannot fail to discern in our deliverance from so many and so great perils, the interposition of that Being who will not forsake us in the trials that are to come. Let us, then, looking upon the bodies of our loved and honored dead, catch inspiration from their example, and gather renewed confidence and a firmer resolve to tread, with unfaltering trust, the path that leads to honor and peace, although it lead through tears and suffering and blood.

We have no alternative but to do our duty. We combat for property, homes, the honor of our wives, the future of our children, the preservation of our fair land from pollution, and to avert a doom which we can read, both in the threats of our enemies and the acts of oppression, we have alluded to in this address.

The situation is grave, but furnishes no just excuse for despondency. Instead of harsh criticisms on the government and our generals; instead of bewailing the failure to accomplish impossibilities, we should rather be grateful, humbly and profoundly, to a benignant Providence, for the results that have rewarded our labors. Remembering the disproportion in population, in military and naval resources, and the deficiency of skilled labor in the South, our accomplishments have surpassed those recorded of any people in the annals of the world. There is no just fear of hopelessness or fear. Since the outbreak of the war, the South has lost the nominal possession of the Mississippi river and fragments of her territory, but Federal occupancy is not conquest. The fires of patriotism still burn unquenchably in the breasts of those who are subject to foreign domination. We have in our uninterrupted control, a territory which, according to past progress, will require the enemy ten years to overrun.

The enemy is not free from difficulties. With an enormous debt, the financial convulsion, long postponed, is surely coming. The short crops in the United States and abundant harvests in Europe, will hasten what was otherwise inevitable. Many sagacious persons at the North, discover in the usurpations of the government, the certain overthrow of their liberties. A large number revolt from the unjust war waged upon the South, and would gladly bring it to an end. Others look with alarm upon the complete subversion of constitutional freedom by Abraham Lincoln, and feel in their own persons, the bitterness of the slavery which three years of war have failed to inflict on the South. Brave and earnest men at the North have spoken out against the usurpation and cruelties daily practiced. The success of these men over the radical and despotic faction which now rules the North, may open the way to a peaceful negotiation, and a cessation of this bloody and unnecessary war.

In conclusion, we exhort our fellow citizens to be of good cheer, and spare no labor nor sacrifices that may be necessary to enable us to win the campaign upon which we have just entered. We have passed through great trials of affliction, but suffering and humiliation are the schoolmasters that lead nations to self-reliance and independence. These disciplinary providences but mature and develop and solidify our people. We beg that the supplies and resources of the country, which are ample, may be sold to the government to support and equip its armies. Let all spirit of faction and past party differences be forgotten in the presence of our cruel foe. We should not despond. We should be self-denying. We should labor to extend to the utmost, the productive resources of the country. We should economise. The families of soldiers should be cared for and liberally supplied. We entreat from all, a generous and hearty co-operation with the government in all branches of its administration, and with the agents, civil or military, in the performance of their duties. Moral aid has the "power of the incommunicable," and by united efforts, by an all-comprehending and self-sacrificing patriotism we can, with the blessing of God, avert the perils which environ us, and achieve for ourselves and children, peace and freedom. Hitherto the Lord has interposed graciously to bring us victory, and in his hand there is present power to prevent this great multitude which come against us, from casting us out of the possession which he has given us to inherit.

J. L. ORR,
T. J. SEMMES,
A. E. MAXWELL,
Committee on the part of the Senate.
J. W. CLAPP,
J. L. M. CURRY,
JULIAN HARTRIDGE,
JOHN GOODE, JR.,
W. N. H. SMITH,
Com. of House of Representatives.

The New Conscription Act.

Section 1 provides that all white men, residents of the Confederate States, between the ages of 17 and 50, shall be in the military service of the Confederate States during the war.

Section 2 provides that all between the ages of 18 and 45, now in the service, shall be retained during the present war in the same organizations in which they were serving at the passage of this act, unless they are regularly discharged or transferred. Companies from one State who were put into organizations from another State shall be transferred, provided they expressed their dissent at the time they were placed in said organization. Individual soldiers are allowed the same privilege.

Section 3 provides that, at the expiration of six months from the 1st of April next, a bounty of one hundred dollars in a six per cent. Government bond, shall be paid to each non-commissioned officer and private then in the service.

Section 4 provides that no person shall be relieved from the operation of this act by reason of having been discharged, where no disability now exists, or by reason of having furnished a substitute; but no person who has been hitherto exempted on account of religious opinions, and paid the required tax, shall be required to render military service.

Section 5 provides that all between 17 and 18 years, and 45 and 50 years of age shall form a reserve corps, not to serve out of the State in which they reside.

Section 6 provides that the last named persons shall elect their own regiment and company officers, and be entitled to the same pay and allowances as troops in the field.

Section 7 provides that any person of the last named failing to attend at the place of rendezvous within thirty days, as required by the President, without a sufficient reason, shall be made to serve in the field during the war.

Section 8 provides that all the duties of provost and hospital guards and clerks, and of clerks, guards, agents, employees, or laborers, in the Commissary and Quartermaster Department, in the Ordnance Bureau and Navy Department, and all similar duties, shall be performed by persons who are declared, by a board of surgeons, as unable to perform military service in the field. The President may detail such bodies of troops or individuals required to be enrolled under the sixth section of this act (between the ages of 45 and 50) as may be needed for the discharge of such duties. Persons between seventeen and eighteen years of age shall not be assigned to such duties. The President is empowered to detail artisans, mechanics, or persons of scientific skill, to perform indispensable duties in the departments or bureaus herein mentioned.

Section 9 provides that any Quartermaster, or Assistant Quartermaster, Commissary, or Assistant Commissary (other than those serving with organizations in the field.) or other officer in the Ordnance Bureau, or Navy Agent, or Provost Marshal, or officer in the conscript service, who shall hereafter retain or employ any person subject to military duty, as herein provided, shall be cashiered.

Section 10 repeals all existing exemption laws, and exempts the following:

1. All who shall be held unfit for military service, under rules to be prescribed by the Secretary of War.

2. The Vice President of the Confederate States, the members and officers of Congress, of the several State Legislatures, and such other Confederate and State officers as the President or the Governors of the respective States may certify to be necessary for the proper administration of the Confederate or State Governments, as the case may be.

3. Every minister of religion authorized to preach according to the rules of his church, and who, at the passage of this act, shall be regularly employed in the discharge of his ministerial duties; superintendents and physicians of asylums of the deaf, dumb, blind and insane; one editor for each newspaper being published at the time of the passage of this act, and such employees as said editor may certify on oath to be indispensable to the publication of such newspaper; the public printer of the Confederate and State Governments, and such journeymen printers as the said public printers shall certify on oath to be indispensable to perform the public printing; one skilled apothecary in each apothecary store who was doing business as such apothecary on the 10th day of October, 1862, and has continued said business without intermission since that period; all physicians over the age of thirty years, who are now and have been for the last seven years in the practice of their profession, but the term physician shall not include Dentist.

The old law exists covering professors and teachers.

All superintendents of public hospitals established by law before the passage of this act, and such employees as the said superintendent shall certify on oath to be essential to the management thereof.

4. There shall be exempt one person as owner or agriculturalist on each farm or plantation upon which there are now, and were on the first day of January last, fifteen able-bodied field hands between the ages of sixteen and fifty, upon the following conditions: 1st, This exemption shall only be so granted in cases in which there is no white male adult on the farm or plantation not liable to military duty, nor unless the person claiming the exemption was on the first day of January, 1864, either the owner and manager or overseer of said plantation, but in no case shall more than one person be exempted, on one farm or plantation. 2d, Such person shall first execute a bond, payable to the Confederate States of America, in such form and with such security, and in such penalty as the Secretary of War may prescribe, conditioned that he will deliver to the Government at some railroad depot, or such other places as may be designated by the Secretary of War, within twelve months next ensuing, one hundred pounds of bacon, or at the election of the Government, its equivalent in pork, and one hundred pounds of net beef, (said beef to be delivered on foot) for each able-bodied slave on said farm or plantation within the above said ages, whether said slaves are in the field or not, which said bacon, or pork and beef, shall be paid for by the Government at the price fixed by the Commissioners of the State under the impressment act. *Provided*, that when the person thus exempted shall produce satisfactory evidence that it has been impossible for him, by the exercise of proper diligence, to furnish the am't of meat thus contracted for, and leave an adequate supply for the subsistence of those living on said farm, the Secretary of War shall direct a commutation of the same to the extent of two-thirds thereof in grain or other provisions to be delivered by such persons as aforesaid at equivalent rates.

Such person shall furthermore bind himself to sell the marketable surplus of provisions and grain now on hand, and which he may raise from year to year while the exemption continues, to the government or to the families of soldiers at prices fixed by the Commissaries of the State, under the impressment act: *Provided*, That any person exempted as aforesaid, shall be entitled to a credit of twenty-five per cent. on any amount of meat which he may deliver within three months from the passage of this act: *Provided further*, That persons coming within the provisions of this exemption shall not be deprived of the benefits thereof by reason of having been enrolled since the first day of February, 1864.

In addition to the foregoing exemptions, the Secretary of War may, under the direction of the President, exempt or detail such other persons as he may be satisfied ought to be exempted on account of public necessity, and to insure the production of grain and other provisions for the army and for the families of soldiers. He may also grant exemptions or details, on such terms as he may prescribe, to such overseers, farmers, or planters, as he may be satisfied will be more useful to the country in pursuits of agriculture than in the military service: *Provided*, That such exemption shall cease whenever the farmer, planter, or overseer shall fail diligently to employ, in good faith his own skill, capital, and labor exclusively in the production of grain and other provisions, to be sold to the Government and the families of soldiers at such prices not exceeding those fixed at the time for the articles by the Commissaries of the State under the Impressment Act.

The old law is re-enacted relating to railroads.

6. Nothing herein contained shall be construed as repealing the act approved April 4, 1863, exempting contractors for carrying the mails of the Confederate States, and the drivers of post coaches and hacks, from military service: *Provided*, That all the exemptions granted under this act, shall only continue while the persons so exempted are actually engaged in their respective pursuits or occupations.

Section 11. That the President be, and he is hereby authorized to grant details, under general rules and regulations to be issued from the War Department, either of persons between forty-five and fifty years of age, or from the army in the field, in all cases where, in his judgment, justice, equity, and necessity require such details, and he may revoke such orders of details whenever he thinks proper: *Provided*, That the power herein granted to the President to make details and exemptions shall not be construed to authorize the exemption or detail of any contractor for furnishing supplies of any kind to the Government by reason of said contract, unless the head or Secretary of the department making such contract shall certify that the personal services of such contractor are indispensable to the execution of the contract: *Provided further*, That whenever such contractor shall fail diligently and faithfully to proceed with the execution of such contract, his exemption or detail shall cease.

Section 12. That in appointing local boards of surgeons for the examination of persons liable to military service, no member composing the same shall be appointed from the county or enrolling district in which they are required to make such examination.

THE TAX LAW.

Section 1. *The Congress of the Confederate States do enact*, That in addition to the taxes levied by the "act to lay taxes for the common defense, and to carry on the government of the Confederate States," approved 24th of April, 1863, there shall be levied, from the passage of this act, on the subjects of taxation hereafter mentioned, and collected from every person, copartnership, association or corporation liable therefor, taxes as follows, to wit:

I. Upon the value of property, real personal and mixed, of every kind and description, not hereinafter exempted or taxed at a different rate, at five per cent., *Provided*, That from this tax on the value of property employed in agriculture shall be deducted the value of the tax in kind delivered therefrom as assessed under the law imposing it, and delivered to the Government, *Provided*, That no credit shall be allowed beyond five per cent.

II. On the value of gold and silver wares and plate, jewels, jewelry and watches ten per cent.

III. The valued property taxed under this section, shall be assessed on the basis of the market value of the same, or similar property in the neighborhood where assessed in the year 1860, except in cases where land, slaves, cotton or tobacco have been purchased since the 1st day of January, 1862, in which case the said land, slaves, cotton and tobacco so purchased, shall be assessed at the price actually paid for them by the owner.

SEC. 2. On the value of all slaves or interests held in any bank, banking company or association, canal, navigation, importing, exporting, insurance, manufacturing, telegraph, express, railroad, and dry-dock companies of every kind, whether incorporated or not, five per cent.

The value of property taxed under this section shall be assessed upon the basis of the market value of such property in the neighborhood where assessed, in such currency as may be in general use at the time, in the purchase and sale of such property, at the time of assessment.

SEC. 3. I. Upon the amount of all gold and silver coin, gold dust or silver bullion, whether held by the banks or other corporations, or individuals, five per cent.; and upon all moneys held abroad, or upon the amount of all bills of exchange drawn therefor on foreign countries, a tax of five per cent.; such tax upon money abroad to be assessed and and collected according to the value thereof at the place where the tax is paid.

II. Upon the amount of all solvent credit, and of all bank bills, and all other papers issued as currency, exclusive of non-interest-bearing Confederate Treasury notes, and not employed in a registered business, the income from which is taxed, five per cent.

Section 4.—Upon profits made in trade and business as follows:

I. On all profits made by buying and selling spirituous liquors, flour, wheat, corn, rice, sugar, molasses, or syrup, salt, bacon, pork, hogs, beef or beef cattle, sheep, oats, hay, fodder, raw hides, leather, horses, mules, boots, shoes, cotton yarns, wool, woolen, cotton or mixed cloths, hats, wagons, harness, coal, iron, steel or nails, at any time between January 1, 1863, and January 1, 1865, ten per cent in addition to the tax on such profits as income under the "act to lay taxes for the common defence, and carry on the Government of the Confederate States, approved April 24, 1863."

II. On all profits made by buying and selling money, gold, silver, foreign exchange, stocks, notes, debts, credits, or obligations of any kind, and any merchandize, profits or effects of any kind, not enumerated in the preceding paragraph between the times named therein, ten per cent, in addition to tax on such profits as income, under the act aforesaid.

III. On the amount of profits exceeding twenty-five per cent. made either of the years 1863 and 1864, by any bank or banking company, insurance, canal, navigation, importing and exporting, telegraph, express, railroad, manufacturing, dry dock, or other joint stock company of any description, whether incorporate or not, twenty-five per cent. on such excess.

SEC. 5.—The following exemptions from taxation under this act shall be allowed, to-wit:

I. Property of each head of a family, to the value of five hundred dollars; and for each minor child of the family to the further value of one hundred dollars; and for each son actually engaged in the army or navy, or who has died or been killed in the military or naval service, and who was a member of the family when he entered the service, to the further value of five hundred dollars.

II. Property of the widow of any officer, soldier, sailor, or marine, who may have died or been killed in the military or naval service, or where there is no widow, then of the family, being minor children, to the value of one thousand dollars.

III. Property of every officer, soldier, sailor, or marine, actually engaged in the military or naval service, or of such as has been disabled in such service, to the value of one thousand dollars; provided, that the above exemptions shall not apply to any person whose property, exclusive of household furniture, shall be assessed at a value exceeding one thousand dollars.

IV. That where property has been injured or destroyed by the enemy, or the owner thereof has been temporarily deprived of the use or occupancy thereof, or of the means of cultivating the same by reason of the presence or proximity of the enemy, the assessment on such property may be reduced in proportion to the damage sustained by the owner, or the tax assessed thereon may be reduced in the same ratio by the district collector on satisfactory evidence submitted to him by the owner or assessor.

Sec. 6. That the taxes on property laid for the year 1864 shall be assessed as on the day of the passage of this act, and be due and collected on the first day of June next, or as soon after as practicable, allowing an extension of ninety days west of the Mississippi river. The additional taxes on incomes or profits for the year 1863, levied by this act, shall be assessed and collected forthwith; and the taxes on incomes or profits for the year 1864 shall be assessed and collected according to the provisions of the tax and assessment acts of 1863.

Sec. 7. So much of the tax act of the 24th day of April, 1863, as levies a tax on incomes derived from property or effects on the amount of value of which a tax is levied by this act, and also the first section of said act, are suspended for the year 1864, and no estimated rent, hire or interest on property or credits herein taxed *ad volorem*, shall be assessed or taxed as incomes under the tax act of 1863.

Sec. 8. That the tax imposed by this act on bonds of the Confederate States heretofore issued shall in no case exceed the interest on the same, and such bonds when held by or for minors or lunatics, shall be exempt from the tax in all cases where the interest on the same shall not exceed one thousand dollars.

—

SUSPENSION OF THE WRIT OF HABEAS CORPUS.

A bill to suspend the privilege of the writ of *habeas corpus* in certain cases.

Whereas, The Constitution of the Confederate States of America provides, in Article 1, section 9, paragraph 3, that "the privilege of the writ of *habeas corpus* shall not be suspended, unless when, in case of rebellion or invasion, the public safety may require it;" and, whereas, the power of suspending the privilege of said writ, as recognized in said Article 1, is vested solely in the Congress, which is the exclusive judge of the necessity of such suspension; and, whereas, in the opinion of the Congress the public safety requires the suspension of said writ in the existing case of of the invasion of the States by the armies of the United States; and, whereas, the President has asked for the suspension of the writ of *habeas corpus*, and informed Congress of the condition of the public danger which renders the suspenson of the writ a measure proper for the public defence against invasion and insurrection; now, therefore,

Sec. 1. That during the present invasion of the Confederate States the privilege of the writ of *habeas corpus* be, and the same is hereby suspended; but such suspension shall apply only to the cases of persons arrested or detained by order of the President, Secretary of War, or the General officer commanding the Trans-Mississippi Military Department; by the authority and under the control of the President. It is hereby declared that the purpose of Congress in the passage of this act, is to provide more effectually for the public safety by suspending the writ of *habeas corpus* in the following cases, and no other:

I. Of treason or treasonable efforts or combinations to subvert the Government of the Confederate States.

II. Of conspiracies to overthrow the Government or conspiracies to resist the lawful authority of the Confederate States.

III. Of combining to assist the enemy, or of communicating intelligence to the enemy, or giving him aid and comfort.

IV. Of conspiracies, preparations and attempts to incite servile insurrection.

V. Of desertions or encouraging desertions, of harboring deserters and of attempts to avoid military service: *Provided*, That in cases of palpable wrong and oppression by any subordinate officer, upon any party who does not legally owe military service, his superior officer shall grant prompt relief to the oppressed party, and the subordinate shall be dismissed from office.

VI. Of spies and other emissaries of the enemy.

VII. Of holding correspondence or intercourse with the enemy, without necessity, and without the permission of the Confederate States.

VIII. Of unlawful trading with the enemy and other offenses against the laws of the Confederate States, enacted to promote their success in the war.

IX. Of conspiracies, or attempts to liberate prisoners of war held by the Confederate States

X. Of conspiracies, or attempts or preparations to aid the enemy.

XI. Of persons aiding or inciting others to abandon the Confederate cause, or to resist the Confederate States, or to adhere to the enemy.

XII. Of unlawfully burning, destroying or injuring, or attempting to burn, destroy or injure any bridge or railroad, or telegraph line of communication, or other property with the intent of aiding the enemy.

XIII. Of treasonable designs to impair the military power of the Government by destroying or attempting to destroy the vessels or arms, or munitions of war, or arsenals, foundries, workshops, or other property of the Confederate States.

Sec. 2. The President shall cause proper officers to investigate the cases of all persons arrested or detained in order that they may be discharged if improperly detained, unless they can be speedily tried in the due course of law.

Sec. 3. That during the suspension aforesaid no military or other officer shall be compelled, in answer to any writ of *habeas corpus*, to appear in person, or to return the body of any person detained by him by the authority of the President, Secretary of War or the general officer commanding the Trans-Mississippi Department; but on the certificate, under oath of the officer having charge of any one so detained that such person is detained by him as a prisoner under the authority aforesaid, further proceedings under the writ of *habeas corpus*, shall immediately cease and remain suspended so long as this act shall continue in force.

Sec. 4. This act shall continue in force for ninety days after the next meeting of Congress, and no longer.

HEADQUARTERS, DIS. TEXAS, NEW MEXICO AND ARIZONA.
Houston, Marh 16, 1864.

Special Orders, No. 76

XII. Lt. Col. J. J. Meyers, DeBray's regiment, will collect all the absentees of the regiment, not on extra duty by order of the Maj. Gen. Commanding, causing them to be assembled at such place as the may designate, and proceed with hem to Alexandria, La., and join the regiment at that place or wherever it may be.

By command of
Major-General J. B. MAGRUDER
(Signed) L. G. ALDRICH, A. A. G.

HOUSTON, March 17, 1864.

All commissioned, non-commissioned officers and privates belonging to and absent from De Bray's regiment will, in obedience to the above order. report to me at Hempstead without delay.

J. J. MYERS,
mar18d3t Lt. Col. DeBray's Reg. T. C.

$100 REWARD will be paid for the apprehension and confinement in jail so that I get him, of my negro man Brister. H is 5 fee, one inch high, stout, active, and quick in speech, and will probably say he belongs to Jas. Hauks of Anderson county. GEO. T. BEALL,
mar 16-tw&w3t near Brazoria.

JAMES H. DOWLAND, General Commission Agent, for the sale of Negroes, Real Estate, Produce, and all classes of Merchandise, at the "Green Store," Houston. mar 16-d2t
mar16

HEADQUARTERS, DISTRICT OF TEXAS, NEW MEXICO AND ARIZONA,
Galveston, March. 1, 1864.

General Orders, No. —.

Capt. John Kelso having reported to these Headquarters for duty, he is hereby announced on the staff of the Major General Commanding as Assistant Inspector General, and will be obeyed and respected accordingly.

By command of
Major Gen. MAGRUDER.
E. P. TURNER, A. A. G, mal7 2t

The Daily Telegraph

HOUSTON, TEXAS.

E. H. CUSHING, Editor and Proprietor.

TERMS.—Daily, per month, $4; per quarter, 10. Daily, every other day, per month, $2; per quarter, $5. Weekly, per month, $1; per quarter $3 Advertising $1 per line, each insertion. Nine words make a line. The money must accompany the advertisement.

OUR ARMY MAIL.—Our next mail will be carried by Mr. Adams at $5 a letter. Money will be taken at 10 per cent. in kind, either specie or currency. Send your money without delay.

Those men of capital who at the beginning of the war locked up their money, shut up their shops, and declared they would have nothing to do with speculating, nor anything else, to make money, are entitled to no credit. Their patriotic showing of being unwilling to trade on the necessities of the country, was really founded on an unwillingness to risk their means in the uncertainties of the times. They are like the servant who hid his Lord's money in a napkin.

It is the fashion of the times to abuse traders, speculators, blockade runners, etc., as being the enemies of the country. This abuse is both unnecessary and unjust. Look for instance at these classes of our citizens. They have to be sure brought in some rum, some calico and some gimeracks, but they have brought in besides, before the Yankees cut off their trade at Brownsville, vast stores of arms, of gunpowder, etc., without which our armies in this Department would be sadly fitted to take the field at this juncture. They have also found a use for money, and thus while keeping it in circulation have prevented its value being lost by stagnation. There is more in this than our people are aware of. If there is no use for money, its value is lost. The more use there is for it, the more will its value be increased; and if there was any call for the use of twenty millions in this State instead of two, the value of the currency would rise with the demand for it.

It has been the fashion to charge upon the Rio Grande trade in this State the depreciation of the currency here. Never was a wider mistake. The Rio Grande trade, on the contrary, has been a benefit to the currency, by keeping it in circulation; and it is a fact that may be proved by refence to quotations that *there has been no time in the last two years when gold was not higher by from five to twenty per cent in Richmond, Atlanta, Mobile, Charleston, etc., than in Houston*. Even to-day it is undoubtedly cheaper here than in any of the above places, though the difference is not so manifest since the interruption of the Brownsville traffic.

Were we asked to point out the most useful man in Houston to-day, we should point to such men as House, etc., of this city, and Mills, Ball, etc., of Galveston, who have been instrumental in introducing so much of value to the armies and the people, and who, if they have added to their wealth by their enterprise, are certainly entitled to any thing else than the envious sneers of those whose money has been locked up in their safes for the last three years. By all means if we are to sustain a chronic war, let no energy of the people sleep. Let what planting, what trading, what mechanic arts, what literary pursuits we can have, be cultivated with all assiduity.

In the last number of the News we see an article (which though published without credit was taken we believe from a Shreveport paper) the "Texas Militia," which pays a left-handed compliment to the State Troops, which they must highly appreciate. It speaks of them as a helpless body of brave men, who marched and countermarched along our line of defence. This ridiculous farce was prosecuted with a zeal worthy of a better cause. We are under the impression that the State troops believed that they were not enacting a part in a "ridiculous farce," but were in the field for a good cause, than which none could be better, and that they could render "efficient assistance to the Confederate army."

We know that Maj. Gen. Magruder frequently complimented the State troops upon their soldierly bearing and upon their efficiency in drill and discipline. Col Ashbel Smith, an old veteran soldier, and a strict disciplinarian, in a letter to Col. Sayles, compliments his regiment as surpassed by no regiment of the line in discipline and drill; and no old regiment marched with more alacrity to meet the enemy than did the regiment of State troops when stationed upon our coast.

Although a small portion of the State Troops were unarmed last winter, that deficiency has now been supplied, and there are arms sufficient to place a musket in the hands of every soldier.

We are willing to bank heavily upon the State Troops, and have no doubt that they will sustain their well earned reputation of last winter. We thought of noticing the article when we first saw it, but it slipped our attention. Its reproduction in the News in a form that may lead the public to regard it as expressive of the sentiments of the editor of that paper, done we imagine, inadvertently, calls we think for the notice we have given it.

BAYLOR UNIVERSITY, INDEPENDENCE.—We are requested to notify each Trustee of this Institute, that a meeting will be held at 11 o'clock, on Saturday, the 26th of March. It is hoped that every member will be present. A general attendance of citizens and friends, is also requested at the same time, at the Baptist Church. Males entered classes since September, 1863, 85, females 170.

☞ We endeavored to say in our last that Banks had twenty thousand available men in Louisiana, and that the three columns would number fifty thousand men. The printer, however, fixed it the other way, and made anything but sense of it.

A. SESSUMS IN ACCOUNT WITH THE BENEVOLENT FUND S. S. S. E — Por amount received, proceeds Concert on the evening of the 14th inst., $3430,00
Amount donated by J. S. Perkins, 100 00

Contra, $3530,00
Expenses per vouchers, $1047 00
Balance net proceeds, 2483 00

$4530 00.

ALEX. SESSUMS, Treasurer.

WANTED—By a young lady, a situation as Governess in a small family. Address
Miss CORA LEE MONTGOMERY,
march16 3t* Victoria, Texas.

Letter from High Private.

SHREVEPORT, March 15th, 1864.

The following order may be found in a late New York Times:

HEADQUARTERS DEPARTMENT OF THE SOUTH
HILTON HEAD, S. C, Jan. 31st, 1864.

GENERAL ORDER, No. 16.—

In accordance with the provisions of the Presidential Proclamation of pardon and amnesty, given at Washington on the 8th day of December, in the year of our Lord, 1863, and in the pursuance of instructions received from the President of the United States, Major John Hay, A. A. G., will proceed to Fernandina, Fla., and other convenient points in that State, for the purpose of extending to the citizens of the State of Florida, an opportunity to avail themselves of the benefits of that Proclamation, by offering for their signature the oath of allegiance therein prescribed, and by issuing to all those subscribing to said oath certificates entitling them to the benefits of the Proclamation. Fugitive citizens of the State of Florida within the limits of said department will have an opportunity to subscribe to the same oath and secure certificates at Hilton Head, S. C.

By Command of
Maj. Gen. Q. A. GILLMORE.
ED. W. SMITH, A. A. G.

How many "availed themselves of the benefit of that Proclamation" during Gillmore's last effort in Florida the record of the last battle will show. Mr. Ed. Smith, no doubt carried away about as many blank certificates as he took them, provided they did not fall into the hands of the "rebels." One thing is certain the amnasty has not worked well there so far.

The Alexandra case was taken up to the British Exchequer Chambers on the 6th of Feb. The appeal was dismissed on the ground of want of jurisdiction, and the case has, therefore, been carried up to the House of Lords.

Earl Russell stated, in the House of Lords, that Mr. Adams, the American Minister, had thought it prudent to withhold Secretary Seward's dispatch in relation to the Alabama, at which Lord Derby was so indignant that it had never been presented.

Mr. Laird said that America had made no demand, either written or verbal, for indemnity for the doings of the Alabama.

Three-fourths, at least, of the dispatches in the Northern papers, from Cairo (Ill.) are concerning the doings of guerrillas. Truly they must be a troublesome set.

A letter from Calcutta, Jan. 5th, says the British ship Peast, at this port, spoke, on the 3d inst. the pirate steamer, Alabama, 30 miles south o Sand Head. H. P.

SHREVEPORT, March 15, 3 P. M.

A letter writer in Alexandria has stirred up the good and bad people of this town amazingly to-day, by sending word that a Captain Cleveland, of Hood's brigade, has arrived there with the news that Grant, or rather Thomas and Gen. Johnston have had three engagements between Dalton and Chattanooga, and that Thomas has been defeated at all points and driven to Chattanooga; that Longstreet has driven Foster from Knoxville and was crowding him towards Chattanooga, &c., &c.

That Chattanooga must be a big place to hold so many people all at one time! Don't you think so?

Of course I can send no such news as this over the wire. When I do you may believe it. I have no doubt—with due respect to "Captain Cleveland," and the Alexandria letter writer,—that a portion of Johnston's and Thomas' forces have been skirmishing at different points between Chattanooga and Dalton, and I presume we got the better of them, compelling them to fall back to the main body, but I feel certain there has been no general engagements, and as to Longstreet whipping Foster I don't believe a word of it.

We have just whipped the scoundrels bad enough in Florida, and I don,t believe in "crowding the mourners" quite so fast as some of our "reliable" news-mongers are disposed to do. If we have really whipped the enemy in Tennessee as bad as is reported, they will stay whipped until I have time to get at the truth of the matter, and then I will send it on. So don't be in a hurry about ringing the bells.

I am inclined to believe that the Federals have evacuated and destroyed Fort Smith in Arkansas. But wait. H. P.

SHREVEPORT, March 15.—The Chattanooga correspondent of the Chicago Times, under date of the 20th ult., says:

"Contrary to the general expectation here one week ago, no forward movement of our troops from this point has yet occurred. At that time everything was in commotion, and a large column of troops were under marching orders for several days. Rumor assigned their probable destination as Dalton; but day after day slipped away, and with them all hopes of surprising the rebel forces at that point. General Johnston was then reported to have but few troops at Dalton.

His command was scattered widely through the country contiguous, and it was not thought possible to push to that point and dispossess him before his scattered army could be collected for successful resistance. For some reason it was not done and our latest accounts from there report Johnston on the *qui vive*. His brigades have been hastily drawn together there within a week, as if expecting an attack, and deserters and scouts estimate his force variously at from 25,000 to 40,000. The impression here is, that, in the absence of so many veteran regiments, our available force is too small to warrant an advance to that point. A battle might ensue, and a large additional force would be necessary to re-build and guard the railroad in any event. The veterans are returning already from the different States. Two weeks more will place most of them in the field again. Active operations will probably follow immediately."

A special dispatch to the Chicago Times from Cincinnati, Feb. 27, reads thus:

All advices to the contrary, you may depend upon it that Sherman having taken Selma will attack Atlanta and Montgomery, and, after tearing up the railroad, will move upon Mobile, and co-operate with Banks and Farragut in the capture of that city. He has already secured a large quantity of cotton, and the Confederates are greatly alarmed at his daring movements and successes. While Sherman is thus operating in the South West, Thomas is moving on Johnston at Dalton, to hold him in check, and Schofield is after Longstreet, expecting to drive him into Western Virginia. Sherman's force numbers at least 60,000.

(Who says Sherman did not intend to reach Mobile?)

The Richmond Enquirer, of the 22d says: "If Grant defeats Johnston, Georgia and Alabama are open to him, and Mobile will fall without a struggle."

MEMPHIS, Feb. 26.—Reports of stragglers that Gen. Smith's expedition had been cut up, prove false. The General arrived here at 11 o'clock last night. From an officer's diary, kept during the progress of the expedition, I condense the following particulars in addition to those already furnished:

"On the 18th, the expedition reached Okolona on the Mobile and Ohio Railroad, 70 miles south of Corinth, and 130 miles south-east of Memphis Here we heard that Sherman had captured Meridian, and was advancing east.

"On the 19th, we marched to Egypt Station, on the Mobile and Ohio Railroad, where we captured and destroyed a vast quantity of Confederate corn. One column went through Aberdeen, and the other west of the railroad, concentrating at Prairie Station. The Aberdeen column, under Gen. Grierson, had considerable skirmishing near that place. We destroyed over 100,000 bushels of corn at Prairie Station; also, a large lot of Confederate cotton.

"On the 20th, broke camp at 5:30 a. m. Forrest was reported in force at West Point. At 11 a. m., the advance skirmished heavily with the enemy. At 3 p. m., halted within a mile of West Point. Lost one Lieutenant killed and five men wounded in the skirmish; killed one rebel Captain and captured a wounded rebel Major and one private.

"On the 21st, moved west and found that Forrest, Lee, Chalmers and Roddy were combined against us. They tried to cut our column in two, but without success. Very heavy fighting occurred, both rear and advance. The 2d Iowa had a number killed and wounded in a gallant charge. 2000 to 3000 rebels on each flank. We have lost three pieces, 4-pounder steel guns, which were spiked before captured. All their ammunition was saved Smith now fell back slowly, our troops ambushing the rebels as they advanced. Rebel loss quite heavy. Smith burned every trestle on the Mobile and Ohio Railroad, and destroyed miles of track and a very large amount of corn as he fell back.

"On the 22d, broke camp at 1 A. M., after resting only two hours. Some fighting at the rear all day. The rebels lost heavily, as the road were ambushed at every available point. Volley after volley were poured into them at short range as they advanced, but having so much the larger force they continued to pass our rear heavily a rebel column moving on each flank with the evident design of reaching the Tallahatchie in advance of our forces, forming a junction to prevent our crossing, and capturing our whole command, but by forced marching Smith pressed both flanking columns, and marching all night crossed safely at New Albany.

"On the 23d the van guard had skirmished all the way.

"On the 24th skirmishing continued. On the 25th we marched 52 miles, arriving at Memphis at 11 p. m. Most of the expedition, however, stopped at Collierville.

"The expedition was successful in every point and in every particular, except the important one of making a junction with Sherman."

In other words, the expedition was a successful failure. No sooner had our forces time to concentrate than these "successful" Yankees commenced a retrograde march, commencing at 1 p. m. and running as if the devil was after them, at the rate of 52 miles a day until they reached the point they started from. No wonder Sherman never heard from them during his entire "raid" A more frightened and used up set of devils never found themselves so far from home, and none ever made better time in reaching it. I always told you that Forrest had given Smith and Grierson more than they bargained for, and when the truth comes out it will be found that the balance of Sherman's force was equally well used up.

That Longstreet has fallen back there is no longer any doubt, but for what purpose remains to be seen. He will turn up all right before the 1st of April.

Our Alexandria correspondent send the following dispatches. Although not as late dates as those sent on they will be found of some interest:

ALEXANDRIA, March 13

Since my last communication I have perused the Daily Missouri Democrat of the 24te ult. From it I extract the following items:

Special dispatch to the Missouri Democrat.

FORT SMITH, Feb. 23.—A bearer of dispatches from the expedition sent into the Indian Country has reached Gen. Thayer's headquarters. The troops are now 100 miles south of Fort Gibson, the rebels having retreated to Red River, where they are massed in force.

Gen. Maxey was present with the Choctaw Legislature ten days ago, and urged the Indians to remain at home and raise crops.

Delegates were present from the Choctaw, Cherokee, Creek, Chickasaws, &c. The Choctaws urged a separate Confederacy, as the rebel Confederacy was unable to protect them. The rebel Creeks were prepared in the Wachita mountains.

All the Canadian Valley and its tributaries are clear of rebels. The upper Seminole country has been completely swept out, so that all rebel supplies must come from Red River in any movement towards Arkansas. The rebel Indians are entirely disheartened, Gen. Maxey having failed in his promise to place a force between the Canadian and Gibson. Maxey has either to content himself with defending Northern Texas, in which case he will lose his Indian allies, or recover the prestige which he has lost by attacking our forces on the Arkansas river.

The Indian brigade, under Col. Phillips and Wattles, had a lively skirmish with the rebel Indians and Texans on Middle Boggy river, 100 miles south-east of Fort Gibson, on the 14th inst. The entire rebel force was about 3,000, but a small proportion of the army was engaged. Rebels killed, 40; our loss, 1. Our forces pursued the enemy to near old Fort Arbuckle, and then fell back to the Canadian.

The following orders explain themselves:

LITTLE ROCK, Ark., Feb. 18.

Brig. Gen. Thayer, Commanding District of Frontier, you will establish your headquarters at Van Buren or Clarksville until further orders, and assume command of all troops heretofore belonging to the District of the Frontier, and now in the Department of Kansas, reporting to these headquarters. FREDERICK STEELE,
Maj. Gen. Com'd'g Dep't Ark.

LITTLE ROCK, ARK., Feb. 22.

TO BRIG. GEN. THAYER:

By authority from the War Department, the town of Fort Smith is included in the Department of Arkansas. You will still designate your command the District of the Frontier. You can take your choice between the towns of Ft. Smith and Van Buren for your headquarters.

By order of Maj. Gen. F. STEELE.
GEO. A. SAKALSKI, A. A. A. G.

HEADQ'RS DIST. OF THE FRONTIER,
Ft. Smith, February 22, 1864.

General Orders, No. 1.

In compliance with the foregoing orders from Major General Steele, commanding Department of Arkansas, the undersigned hereby assumes command of all troops heretofore belonging to the District of the Frontier, and now in the Department of Arkansas, including the town of Fort Smith, with the troops in and around it, with headquarters in the town of Fort Smith. Commanders of posts, brigades and detachments will report to these headquarters.

JOHN M. THAYER,
(Official) Briadier General Comm'g.
W. G. WHITTON, Capt. and A. A. G.

NEW YORK, July 23.—A Washington letter says advices from near Charleston report that some 15,000 troops have been dispatched by the rebels to Tallahassa, Florida, for the purpose of disputing the advance of our forces upon that place.—Part of these troops are said to have been sent from Georgia, and the remainder from Beauregard's army. If the number of the rebel troops be correctly stated, the opposing armies will be very nearly matched, should they meet.

FORT MONROE, Feb. 22.—Fifty of the escaped officers from the Libby Prison, Richmond, have arrived here safely. The Richmond papers of today state they have recaptured 48—this leaves 11 out.

BOSTON, July 23.—A vessel arrived here brings news from Capetown, Dec. 31. that the rebel privateer, Tuscarora, has been seized by the British authorities, for violating the neutrality laws, by landing a portion of her cargo on that coast."

H. P.

From Flakes Bulletin.

From the N. Y. Daily News, Feb. 23.

FORT MONROE, Feb. 22.—The Richmond Examiner of Feb. 20, has the following:

Spencer Dayton has been arrested, tried, condemned, and hung as a Yankee spy at Castle Thunder.

MOBILE, Feb. 19.—Farragut has not renewed his attack on Grant's Pass. His fleet lies in the sound, the weather being too bad for action. No landing is reported yet in the direction of Pascagoula.

Major General Scammon and staff have arrived in Richmond, and are lodged in Libby Prison, which is a pleasing offset for the loss of Col. Straight.

Fifty-eight escaped Yankee officers have been returned to Libby Prison.

Three deserters who went to Newbern and took up arms against the Confederacy, were captured and hung at Kingston on the 12th inst.

ST. LOUIS, Feb. 22.—The iron clad turreted gunboat Ozark made a trial trip to Cairo on Saturday, to the satisfaction of the naval officers. She will be immediately armed and equipped for active service.

BALTIMORE, Feb. 22.—The Unconditional Union State Convention, which met here to-day, adopted the following resolutions:

Resolved, That the delegates elected by this Convention to the National Convention, be and are hereby instructed to vote for Abraham Lincoln first, last and all the time.

Resolved, That this Convention is in favor of the entire and immediate abolition of slavery in this State and the States in rebellion, and is opposed to any organization of State Governments in those States which do not recognize the immediate abolishment of slavery as a precedent.

FORT MONROE, Feb. 22.—Fifty of our officers escaped from the Libby Prison in Richmond, have arrived here. Richmond papers of to-day state that they have recaptured fifty-eight. This leaves eleven still out.

A PETITION TO THE MISSOURI LEGISLATURE FAVORING POLYGAMY.—Mr. Jamison, one of the Representatives in the General Assembly from the county in which the city of St. Louis is located, has presented the petition of numerous unmarried ladies, praying that body, in view of the depopulation of males in that State consequent upon the war, that a plurality of wives be legalized.

Fourteen Federal vessels of war are now waiting for seamen, being ready in all other respects, to proceed to their respective points of destination. It is thought that the amendments to the enrollment bill lately passed will remedy this evil.

A long paper, prepared by Admiral Davis of the Bureau of Navigation, goes to show that it was not an impossibility for the Wyoming and Alabama to have been at Amboy at the time stated by telegraph, but that it was somewhat improbable.

The farmers near Hagerstown, Maryland, apprehending a Confederate raid in the spring, are selling their farms and stocks preparatory to moving West.

Two Confederate prisoners escaped from the barracks in Cincinnati, on the 12th instant, by digging a tunnel 12 feet in length, from the cellar to the prison.

From the New Bedford (Nass.) Mercurry, Feb. 26.

CHATTANOOGA, February 24.—In the engagement at Tunnell Hill yesterday, General Palmer captured over 300 prisoners, who have been brought in.

We lost about 75 killed and wounded.

BY TELEGRAPH.

Special to the Telegraph.

SHREVEPORT, March 18.

The enemy's gunboats arrived at Alexandria on the 16th, and immediately demanded a surrender, which was granted.

WASHINGTON, March 6.—Sherman it is said has returned to Mississippi again.

DALTON, March 4—The enemy's line of skirmishers was two miles this side of Tunnell Hill last night.—It is not believed they will make a general attack on our front. The enemy's force has fallen back from Lafayette to Ringgold. We captured several prisoners, who report their regiments do not average 300 men. It is expected the enemy will await reinforcements.

DALTON, March 4, 2 P. M.—The enemy continue to fall back. Gen. Wheeler has advanced beyond Tunnell Hill with a view of cutting off the enemy's trains. Our line of battle is advanced.

Gen. Johnston is continually in the saddle. There is no prospect of a general engagement.

LATER.

The enemy has disappeared from the front, going towards Chattanooga. Wheeler is in pursuit.

The Raleigh Confederacy says the recent attack of Newbern is only a diversion to be soon followed by heavier demonstrations.

RICHMOND, March 2.—Three thousand prisoners have been sent to Americus, Ga.

KNOXVILLE, March 4.—Scouts report that Longstreet has shipped his wagons to Richmond—mounting his men. The rebel cavalry still scour the country south and east. Morgan is feared on the Railroad.

SHREVEPORT, March 18.—We have whipped and repulsed the enemy at every point east of the Mississippi during the last three weeks—in Florida, Sherman, Smith, Grierson, at Dalton, Tunnell Hill; Virginia; at every point. Gen. Price is in command of the District of Arkansas. His headquarters are at Camden.

From the News.

SHREVEPORT, March 18.

DEAR NEWS:—I am in possession of five or six days' later intelligence, through the Little Rock Bulletin of March 9th:

NEW YORK, March 17.—Killpatrick's raid on Richmond was a signal failure and his command cut to pieces. Two hundred and four of his men and five of his officers were taken prisoners. Lt Col Pollard and seventy or eighty of his men were captured, they were on the way to Richmond.

The Richmond Sentinel of the 5th inst. says Col. Dalghgreen was shot dead in a reconnoitre with the 9th Va. Cavalry. Gen. Grant is to take Halleck's place immediately, and Hooker to take command of the army of the Potomac.

NEW YORK, March 8.—The World's special says our relations with France are in a very critical condition. Grant, it is said, will totally change the militarp plans of Lincoln. Commodore Wilkes is to be tried by a naval court martial, for, among other things, permitting the Alabama to escape.

WASHINGTON, March 7th.—Resolutions were introduced into the Senate to-day by Sherman, looking to a solution of the Presidential election difficulties; they declare a quorum of the Senate to consist of a majority, and a majority of the presidential electors, duly qualified, are competent to elect a president. In case the election goes to the House a majority of States represented in that body are competent to elect.

KNOXVILLE, March 7.—Twenty-six votes only were cast in Knoxville at the recent Yankee election. The vote, it is said, would have been larger, but many loyal men refused to take Johnson's oath.

In Hickman, Ky., Confederate guerrillas prevented an election by destroying the ballot-box.

NEW YORK, March 7.—The World's special from New Orleans says General Banks has sent a large cavalry and infantry force into the Teche country.

It is rumored that the 2d Louisiana cavalry were captured by the rebels.

The same correspondent says the attack on Mobile was a mere demonstration on Fort Gaines, to prevent troops being sent to aid Polk.

It is reported that several of the vessels were crippled and the Calhoun sunk.

Seymour was considered strong enough to repel any attack upon his position at Jacksonville, Fla.

NEW YORK, March 7.—Rumors are afloat here of the capture of Newbern, N. C., by the rebels. M. E.

LIST OF LETTERS

Remaining in the Post Office at Houston, Texas, 15th March, 1864.

Autny Miss M	Goodrich C A	Noble Dr
Ardo John	Grippon Capt	Posey B
Adler Miss S	Geu Miss H E	Patten Mrs E A
Brashears F S	Garnett H T	Perry Miss L A
Berlol er B	Gibson E A	Rutter E J
Beasely H	Heller Louis	Siley & Churchill
Bennett J W	Harman Mrs C	Riley Mrs M A
Benton Mat	Huling M	Row Wm
Barsanter E H	Hall W P	Saunders E B
Behrens Mrs M	Hurd S C	Stevenson J A
Beazley W H	Hogue Mr	Simpson Mrs S E
Binson Mr	Henderson Lt	Smith Sam
Bradshaw W R	Hildebrandt F	Sawyer F A
Brown J B	Howerton Capt	Steadman H
Byler W L	Hoffman J	Schadt Miss L
Bowers J	Harrall Mrs S J	Solomon L J
Burress E E	Holly Miss F	Senter C D
Brooks N B	Haly Mrs F	Schneider G
Brasher Miss E L	Hibberts Mr	Smith Mrs C
Bliss C E	Inge Dr J C	Scherrer F
Brackad S	Ingram R	Settegast J
Birchett Geo	Johnson W R	Steel A
Battaile J F	Jones Ike	Squyres J W
Curran Miss K	Johnson J W	Thomas W A
Cray John	Jacobs B	Tiers W O
Cochran G C	Jerman Mr	Tobyn D
Carnes R S	Jennings Mrs M	Talley W
Cassedy W G	King G A	Talley A
Crawford Mary	Kirkman Dr W H	Thomas J
Chilcort Mrs S C	Kahmody J K	Turner Miss E
Coney D W	Kuykendall M	Walsh Miss M
Camby Rob	Lemman R A	Winterfeldt Miss
Carter G W	Lynn & Williams	Watkins W D
Cos ley Mrs M J	Lauftin R M	Wilson M D
DeBast Miss E	Leverhahn H	Wilson I
Dunn Mrs Sarah	Liverhuhn F	Williams A E
Englehard Mr	Lee S J	Wilsen B
Elberling C	Miller Mrs M	Waller O
Edwards Miss Z	Manger S S	White Mrs S E
Fulton G W	McLeary J H	Wells Mrs E J
Furguson Mrs H	Morgan L	Wells Mrs E
Farrell J B	Morgan M P	Wagner A J
Flowers A	McKenzie M E	Woods A
Florence J	Meeckel J D	Williams Miss J E
Faville T D	Mathews E T	Wadley H
Givens W P	Moody J F	Webster Mrs N.
Good Dr G G	McClain M M	Yarborough G W
Grouch Mrs D	Miller C G	
Gallagher Mrs B	Meyers S	
Gordon G.	Noble J M.	

Persons applying for the above list of letters, will please say that they are advertised.

O. L. COCHRAN,
Post Master.

☞ We are authorized to announce R. O LOVE, as a candidate for Recorder of the City of Houston. Election 22d March, 1864.

NEW ADVERTISEMENTS

WANTED—To hire a likely and careful negro girl about twelve years old. Inquire at
HORACE CONE,
mrch19 d1t Main Street, Houston.

☞ For County Clerk of Harris County, STERLING FISHER. tde*

OFFICE ASS'T CH'F COMM'Y, T., N. M. & A.
Houston, March 18, 1864.

Special Orders, No. —.

All Depot and Post Commissaries, of the Eastern Sub-District of Texas, will make the following returns to this office, within the first ten days of each month:

Form No. 1.—Return of Provisions received and issued.

Form No. 2.—Report of Persons and Articles hired.

Form No. 3.—Monthly summary statement.

In addition to the above, they will send a weekly statement of rations on hand, enumerating the different kind of rations.

ROB'T W. KEYWORTH. Major
mar 19-d3t A. C. Com., T. N. M. and A.

HOUSE SERVANT WANTED—A good Cook, Washer and Ironer, for whom the highest wages will be paid monthly. Apply to Mrs. Majors Boarding House, near the Central Railroad Depot. mar 19-d2t*

OBITUARY NOTICE.

HOUSTON, March 17th, 1864.

Died, at Virginia Point, on the 13th inst., of conjestion of the brain, EDMUND P. FRAZIER; aged 27 years, a private in Company E, Col. Geo. Madison's Regiment, Gen. Majors' Brigade. The body was brought to this city and interred. The deceased was a native of Sabine County, in this State, and at the breaking out of hostilities, was residing in Arizona, and was among the first to enroll himself in a company of Confederates raised in that territory by his brother, Maj. Geo. Frazier, and continued in the service of his country until the time of his death. Edmund fought in all the battles of Arizona and New Mexico, and through the brilliant campaign in Louisiana, and returned with his command to his native State, to defend its cherished hearthstones and firesides. He was a dutiful son, an affectionate brother and a kind friend, and was beloved by all who knew him; and though it was not his fate to fall where the brave and intrepid most desire—in the heat of battle and the smoke of consuming conflict—yet, under all the pangs of the disease of which he died, he bore up with that manly fortitude that ever marked his course under the most trying circumstances. Peace to his ashes. And though his many friends may not refrain from shedding a tear to "poor Ned's" memory and untimely fall, yet we have the consolation to believe that he has gone to reap that reward treasured up in Heaven for those who have "fought the good fight."

"But no, the brave die never—
Being deathless, they but change
Their country's arms for more—
Their country's glory."

march19 1t* A FRIEND.

DIED—Of Consumption, on the 29th of February, at the residence of Mr. Blunt, in Houston, Texas, Capt. F. P. CLARKSON, of Farquar county, Va., in the 37th year of his age.

Descended from an illustrious family, whose scions have done noble service in the army of Virginia, and rendered the "Blank Horse" Cavalry historic, the present revolution found the subject of this notice a temporary sojourner in the malfated State of Missouri. Participating in all those glorious achievements of Price, which the good qualities of the illustrious dead have shielded from a strict criticism, he acquired a repute for gallantry and patient endurance of excessive hardships, which elicited the unqualified commendation of his superior officers, and endeared him to his comrads and secured for him the certainty of high promotion. But the exposures of life and disregard of personal comforts which attracted the attention of his superior officers, invigorated the incipiency of the disease of which he died.

Ordered south on recruiting service, in the hope that change of air and a milder climate would reinvigorate and strengthen him, he came to Houston only to sicken and die.

Friends gathered around him and soothed his last moments. Gentle women and brave men wiped the death damp from his brow and followed him to his last resting-place.

Peace to thy ashes, brave Clarkson? One who has seen thee tested in the crucible of California trials in its early day—has heard thy name on every lip in the army of Missouri, and who has witnessed thy patient endurance under the heavy hand of disease and death, and always found thee ever true and noble, pays to thee this last tribute of his admiration and love.

"None knew thee but to love the;
None named thee but to praise."

S. P. B.

☞ Mobile and Richmond, Va., papers please copy.

HEADQUARTERS 6TH BRIGADE TEXAS S. T.,
Brenham, March 16, 1864.

General Orders, No. 2.

All exemptions, furloughs and discharges granted to the State Troops in this brigade district, who were in the service at the time of the examination, by the examining board of physicians, are hereby revoked and annulled. All who hold such papers will report without delay to their respective companies.

Applications for discharges on account of disability must be made through the regular regimental or battalion Surgeon or assistant Surgeon.

By command of
Brig. Gen. J. D. McADOO,
Com. 6th Brigade T. S. T.
B. E. TARVER, A. A. G. mar19 2t

LOST—A Produce Loan Certificate, No. 103. issued by Henry Sampson for $2000 in favor of J. L. Farquar, dated Feb. 3d, 1868. J. L. FARQUHAR.
mar18d3t*

GARDEN SEEDS SENT BY MAIL PAID—12 papers for ten dollars. The following seeds may yet be planted—Melons, Squash, Cucumber, Beans, Tomatos, Egypt Plant, Cabbage, Pumpkins, Spring Turnips, Radish, Lettuce, Cabbage Indigo. JAMES BURKE.
mar-19w&tw1t*

ELECTION NOTICE.

WHEREAS the office of City Recorder has become vacant by the death of James B. Hogan, late Recorder. Therefore, I, William Anders, Mayor of the City of Houston, by virtue of the power vested in me by law, do hereby order that an election be held by the qualified voters of the City on Tuesday the 22d day of March, A. D. 1864, for one Recorder to fill the vacancy aforesaid.

Said election will be held at the City Council Room, Aldermen Fraser, Burnett and Fleishman are appointed managers of said election and will conduct the same and make returns thereof as required by law.

Given under my hand and the seal of said City this 11th day of March, 1864.

WILLIAM ANDERS,
mar12 td Mayor.

$200 REWARD—Ranaway on the 13th inst. my negro woman Elizabeth, 40 years old, short, thick set, sullen look, and slow spoken—bought of Duncan Linten, of Louisiana Had on when she left, a blue check dress, a new pair of heavy shoes, and spotted calico head-handkerchief. Any one returning her to me or the City Marshal, will receive the above reward.

J. M. JONES, at
mar 17-d3t* Lippman & Kopperl's.

☞ We are authorised to announce MARTIN T. KURTZ, as a candidate for Recorder, at the ensuing special election. marh17-dte

AVERTISEMENT.—Henry Crane is anxious to learn the whereabouts of his mother. She was formerly a resident of Galveston. Her son can be heard of by enquiries of Alexander Brown, on board the schooner Velocity. Address care of House & Co., Houston. mar17-3t*

☞ A. BERTALLOT is a candidate for the office of City Recorder. Election on Tuesday, the 22d inst. tde*

WM. FERGUSON is a candidate for re-election to the office of City Recorder. Election on Tuesday, 22d March, 1864. mar18d4t

HARPER'S WEEKLY.
A JOURNAL OF CIVILIZATION.

Vol. VIII.—No. 377.] NEW YORK, SATURDAY, MARCH 19, 1864. [$1,00 FOR FOUR MONTHS. $3,00 PER YEAR IN ADVANCE.

BRIGADIER-GENERAL GEORGE A. CUSTER.—Photographed by Brady.—[See Page 187.]

FRANK LESLIE'S ILLUSTRATED

NEWSPAPER

Entered according to Act of Congress in the year 1864, by FRANK LESLIE, in the Clerk's Office of the District Court for the Southern District of New York.

No. 442—Vol. XVII.] NEW YORK, MARCH 19, 1864. [Price 8 Cents.

GEN. CUSTER'S EXPEDITION.

Capt. Ash, with the 5th Regulars, charging into Stuart's Camp.

Gen. Custer, with 1,500 picked men, in light marching order, left Culpeper Court-house about two o'clock on Sunday afternoon, Feb. 28th.

The 6th and 3d corps marched from their winter quarters earlier in the day, the former halted at Madison Court-house and threw out a strong cordon of pickets, while the latter bivouacked in the neighborhood of James city, and held the line of Robertson's road.

About two A. M. the raiders left their resting-place near James city, and took the road for Charlottesville. The men had been picked from Merritt's and Gregg's divisions, and were well mounted. When they marched up the steep banks of the Ravenna river their coming was unknown and altogether unexpected.

Before us (a correspondent says) was a large cavalry camp, the huts arranged with mathematical precision and soldierly regularity. On one side the horses were quietly standing; on the other side pieces of artillery were parked, with all the appurtenances neatly arranged and in close proximity to the caissons.

The 5th regular regiment of Gen. Merritt's old brigade led the van. Capt. Ash, with one squadron, dashed in among the comfortable-looking huts with reckless precipitancy, and scattered the occupants in all directions.

He ordered the men to destroy all they could, and they obeyed their instructions to the very letter. Neither axes nor rat-tailed files could be found in his command. It was found impossible to spike the guns or chop the gun-carriages to pieces, so they contented themselves with blowing-up the caissons and destroying the camp.

Custer's raid was well conducted. After effecting his purpose, by a masterly movement, masked under another charge which Custer headed in person, he decoyed Stuart from his position, flew past him on a side road, recrossed the river at Banks's mills, and halted safe. His trophies are 60 prisoners, numerous valuable horses, and samples of the ashes of three grist-mills, eight wagon-loads of commissary stores, six caissons, two forges and a set of artillery harness.

RECRUITING IN THE PARK, NEW YORK.

The recruiting service which, for a time, dotted the Park with tents of all shapes and sizes,

THE WAR IN VIRGINIA—GEN. CUSTER'S 5TH REGULARS, CAPT. ASH, CHARGING INTO J. E. B. STUART'S CAMP NEAR CHARLOTTESVILLE.—FROM A SKETCH BY OUR SPECIAL ARTIST.

THE CLARENDON BANNER.

Terms: $4.00 in Advance.] Manning, S. C., Tuesday March 22, 1864. [Vol. vi.—No. 49.

CIRCULAR.

TO THE SEVERAL SOLDIER'S BOARDS OF RELIEF IN THIS STATE.

Comptroller General's Office,

Columbia, S. C., December 23, 1863.

The Soldiers' Boards of Relief in the several Districts and Parishes of this State, are hereby notified that, under the requirements of the Act of December 17, 1863, entitled "An Act to make provision for the support of the families of soldiers from this State in the Confederate and State service," the amount appropriated by said Act has been apportioned upon the basis of the white population, shown by the census of 1859, as set forth in the schedule below. The Act aforesaid requiring the provisions of the "Act to make appropriations in aid of the families of soldiers," &c., ratified December 18, 1862, to be observed, notice is also hereby given that after one-fourth of the amount now subject to the draft of the Chairman of each Board has been drawn from the Treasury, a statement of the transactions of each Board is required to be made to the Treasurer of the Division in which the Board is located, before any further payment can be made, which will be thereafter upon quarterly drafts upon the Treasury.

Chairmen of the respective Boards are particularly requested to communicate with this office as soon as they are prepared to proceed in the discharge of their duties. *Particular* attention is called to the Act of December 17, 1863, (published in the *Guardian* of 21st inst.,) in all respects, and *especially* as to the reports to be made to this office before the first day of February next, which reports should give the information required in tabular statements in conformity with the provisions of said Act.

JAMES A. BLACK,
Comptroller General.

APPORTIONMENT.

Abbeville,	$18,316 67
Anderson,	23,400 48
Barnwell,	20,823 47
Chester,	12,044 00
Chesterfield,	12,483 30
Clarendon,	6,992 86
Darlington,	16,601 93
Edgefield,	25,205 02
Fairfield,	11,965 62
Greenville,	27,504 42
Kershaw,	8,995 03
Lancaster,	10,570 96
Laurens,	17,392 36
Lexington,	14,250 29
Marlboro'	8,426 72
Newberry,	11,465 89
Orange,	9,542 12
Pickens,	24,675 91
Richland,	11,673 29
Spartanburg,	31,311 13
Sumter,	10,335 79
St. Matthews,	3,215 54
Union,	13,819 16
York,	20,619 33
All Saints,	2,018 50
Christ Church,	1,637 99
Horry,	9,352 68
Marion,	18,708 62
Pr'ce Geo. Winyah,	4,497 52
Prince Williams,	2,919 96
St. Andrews,	692 43
St. Bartholomews,	9,012 99
St. Geo's Dorchester,	3,863 88
St James' Goose Creek,	3,093 07
St. Jamos' Santee,	798 58
St. Johns Berkely,	1,918 88
St. Johns Colleton,	1,041 91
St. Helena,	2,077 29
St. Lukes,	2,418 60
St. Pauls,	1,693 51
St. Peters,	3,205 75
St. Phillips and St. Michael,	49,593 52
St. Stephens,	1,169 30
St. Thomas and St. Dennis,	440 94
Williamsburg	8,212 77
	$500,000 00

January 12, 1864

ADJUTANT AND INSP. GEN'S OFFICE.

RICHMOND, VA., Feb. 4, 1864.

General Orders No. 14.

The following order is published for the information of all concerned:

Confederate States of America.
War Department, Richmond, Feb. 1, '64.

EXCHANGE NOTICE, No. 8.

1. *All prisoners* heretofore held by the United States authorities, whether *officers, soldiers or civilians*, received at City Point, *before the* 1st *of January*, 1864, *are hereby declared exchanged.*

2. All *officers and men of the Vicksburg capture*, who reported for duty at Enterprise, Miss., at any time *prior to the* 14*th of November*, 1863, and whose names were forwarded to me by Maj. Gen. John H. Forney, *are declared exchanged.*

3. All officers and men of the Vicksburg capture, belonging to the 1st Tennessee Heavy Artillery, who reported for duty at Marietta, Ga., and whose names were forwarded to me by Col. A. Jackson, *are declared exchanged.*

RO. OULD,
Agent of Exchange.

By Order
(Signed) S. COOPER,
Adjutant and Insp. Gen.

Feb. 10, 1864. 6t.

☞ Confederate newspapers publish six times and send bills to the war Department.

NOTICE IS HEREBY GIVEN

TO ALL PERSONS who are indebted to the estate of *J. S. Tindal*, late deceased, to come forward and make settlement. All those having demands against the said deceased, are requested to hand them in properly attested, within the time prescribed by law.

ELIZA A. TINDAL, *Executrix.*

WAYSIDE HOME.

IN view of the increased demands upon the *Wayside Home*, the Executive Committee charged with its management have appointed the following gentlemen Agents of this institution to solicit contributions in Money and Provisions, and beg that these friends will act promptly without further notice. The Conductors of the various Rail Roads will give their generous aid in the transportation of all supplies.

JAMES S. GIBBES,
Chairman pro tem., and Treasurer Wayside Home.

Dr. Lewis Dantzler, Vance's Ferry, (Orange Parish.)
T. Zimmerman, St. Matthew's, S. C.
C. Whittemore, Orangeburg C. H.
Rev. T. O. Frierson, Kingstree.
J. H. Dingle, Sumter.
Rev. B. N. Suares, Barnwell.
Col. J. J. Ryan, Blackville.
E. L. Kerrison, Columbia.
Rev. J. R. Dow, Aiken.
Silas Johnstone, Newberry.
H. B. McMaster, Winnsboro.
Rev. J. B. Adger, Pendleton.
Rev. W. A. Gamewell, Marion.
A. O. Norris, Esq., Anderson.
Rev. C. McCortha and F. M. Lawton Abbeville.
Lieut. Col. J. A. Bradley, Chester.
W. A. Latta, York.
J. Kyle, Esq., Laurens.
Rev. J. D. McCollough, Union.
C. J. Elford, Greenville.
Rev. W. C. Kirkland, Spartanburg.
Etsel L. Adams, Society Hill.
Capt. Wm. A. Courtenay, Hardeeville.
C. J. Colcock, Grahamville.
George Martin, Pocotaligo.
Rev. W. O. Prentiss, Adams Run.
Capt. L. Wm. Trenholm, Coosawhatchie.
Col. Johnson, Bluffton.

Dec 22 4t

☞ All papers in the State copy four times.

The Good we Might Do.

We all might do good,
Where we often do ill—
There is always the way
If we have but the will;
Though it be but a word,
Kindly breathed or supprest,
It may guard off some pain,
Or give peace to some breast.

We all must do good,
In a thousand small ways,
In forbearing to flatter,
Yet giving due praise;
In spurning ill humor,
Reproving wrong done,
And treating but kindly
The heart we have won.

We all might do good,
Whether lowly or great,
For desert is not gauged
By the purse or estate;
If it be but a cup
Of cold water that's given,
Like the widow's two mites,
It is something for Heaven.

SUSPENSION OF THE WRIT OF HABEAS CORPUS.

The following bill passed both houses of Congress, and is now a law of the land:

A Bill to Suspend the Privilege of the Writ of Habeas Corpus in Certain Cases.

Whereas, the Constitution of the Confederate States of America provides in article 1, section 9, paragraph 3, that "the privilege of the writ of *habeas corpus* shall not be suspended, unless when in case of rebellion or invasion, the public safety may require it;" and whereas the power of suspending the privilege of said writ, as recognized in said article 1, is vested solely in the Congress, which is the exclusive judge of the necessity of such suspension; and whereas, in the opinion of the Congress, the public safety requires the suspension of said writ in the existing case of the invasion of these States by the armies of the United States; and whereas, the President has asked for the suspension of the writ of *habeas corpus*, and informed Congress of conditions of public danger which render the suspension of the writ a measure proper for the public defence against invasion and insurrection; now therefore:

1. That during the present invasion of the Confederate States, the privilege of the writ of *habeas corpus* be and the same is hereby suspended; but such suspension shall apply only to the cases of persons arrested or detained by order of the President, Secretary of War, or the general officer commanding the Trans-Mississippi Military Department, by the authority and under the control of the President. It is hereby declared that the purpose of Congress in the passage of this act is to provide more effectually for the public safety, by suspending the writ of *habeas corpus* in the following cases, and no other:

I. Of treason, or treasonable efforts or combinations, to subvert the government of the Confederate States.

II. Of conspiracies to overthrow the Government, or conspiracies to resist the lawful authority of the Confederate States.

III. Of combining to assist the enemy, or of communicating intelligence to the enemy, or giving him aid and comfort.

IV. Of conspiracies, preparations and attempts to incite servile insurrection.

V. Of desertions or encouraging desertions, of harboring deserters, and of attempts to avoid military service; Provided, that in cases of palpable wrong and oppression by any subordinate officer, upon any party who does not legally owe military service, his superior officer shall grant prompt relief to the oppressed party, and the subordinate shall be dismissed from office.

VI. Of spies and other emissaries of the enemy.

VII. Of holding correspondence or intercourse with the enemy, without necessity, and without the permission of the Confederate States.

VIII. Of unlawful trading with the enemy and other offences against the laws of the Confederate States, enacted to promote their success in the war.

IX. Of conspiracies, or attempts to liberate prisoners of war held by the Confederate States.

X. Of conspiracies, or attempts or preparations to aid the enemy.

XI. Of persons aiding or inciting others to abandon the Confederate cause, or to resist the Confederate States, or to adhere to the enemy.

XII. Of unlawfully burning, destroying or injuring, or attempting to burn destroy or injure any bridge or railroad, or telegraph line of communication, or other property with the intent of aiding the enemy.

XIII. Of treasonable designs to impair the military power of the Government by destroying or attempting to destroy the vessels or arms, or munitions of war, or arsenals, foundries, workshops, or other property of the Confederate States.

Sec. 2. The President shall cause proper officers to investigate the causes of all persons so arrested or detained, in order that they may be discharged if improperly detained, unless they can be speedily tried in the due course of law.

Sec. 3. That during the suspension aforesaid, no military or other officer shall be compelled, in answer to any writ of *habeas corpus*, to appear in person, or to return the body of any person detained by him by the authority of the President, Secretary of War or the general officer commanding the trans-Mississippi Department; but upon that certificate, under oath, of the officer having charge of any one so detained, that such person is detained by him as a prisoner under the authority aforesaid, further proceeding under the writ of *habeas corpus*, shall immediately cease and remain suspended so long as this act shall continue in force.

Sec. 4. This act shall continue in force for ninety days after the next meeting of Congress and no longer.

He is but half prepared for the journey of life who takes not with him that friend who will forsake him in no emergency, who will divide his sorrows, increase his joys, lift the veil from his heart, and throw sunshine around the darkest scenes.

The Clarendon Banner.

MANNING, S. C.,

TUESDAY, MC'H 22, 1864.

H. D. MACHEN,
EDITOR

The mails heretofore due at Manning on Monday and Thursday evenings now arrive on Tuesday and Friday mornings, and leave same days.

Adjutant Gen. Cooper has published general orders No. 92, for the enforcement of the military bill, to which all interested should give immediate attention. All persons between seventeen and eighteen, and forty-five and fifty, are to be at once enrolled. Camps of instruction are to be established at suitable points, under the charge of "commanders and enrolling officers and drill-masters." Applications for exemption are to be made in general to the enrolling officer of the county or district and shall be supported by the affidavit of the party, and other testimony under oath. If the enrolling officer approve the application, he may grant an exemption of sixty days—provided it is not countermanded by the commandant of the conscripts, to whom the certificate of exemption has to be forwarded. In case both the enrolling officer and the commandant of conscripts reject the application for exemption or detail, there is an appeal to the bureau of conscription and the Secretary of War.

Editorial Synopsis of the past week.

The aspect of affairs with England and France has created much uneasiness in the North.

Mrs. General Beauregard is reported to have died in New Orleans on the 23d ultimo.

Dispatches from Washington to the Abolition journals of New York and Philadelphia indicate that the rumored recognition of the Confederate States by France is not entirely groundless.

The dwelling house and furniture of Mr. Boyd, and the old depot and forty-five bales of Government cotton were destroyed by fire at Manchester, S. C., on the 12th instant—supposed to be accidental.

Mr. William B. Hicks, who was wilfully shot down in the street at Columbia, S. C., on the 9th inst., by William D. Morris, died on the 12th from the effects of his wound.

The operator at Baldwin telegraphs that our forces have been fighting the enemy all day at Jacksonville, (Fla.,) and that we had captured two thousand prisoners.

The movement against Lincoln for re-election of President, is rapidly gaining strength.

A Mrs. H. L. Knox, from Mobile, Ala., has been committed to prison in Richmond charged with being a spy, and communicating treasonable information to the enemies of the Confederacy.

The Macon *Confederate* says it is very clear that the Yankees will endeavor to concentrate upon Chattanooga the baffled, whipped and demoralized army of Sherman, and from thence sally forth to give battle to Gen. Johnston. Grant cannot advance from Chattanooga now, for he has not men enough, and Sherman's army will not be able to take the field again in three months. The new draft will not yield available men enough by one-third that will go out of service. The *Confederate* says we have little doubt that North Georgia is the next objective point to the enemy. We ought to be able to concentrate a powerful army under Johnston, as the time that will be given is ample to make every preparation necessary.

The *Tuscumbia*, a monster iron-clad at St. Louis, had broken her back by her own weight while laying at the wharf. She is, therefore, useless.

The report of recognition by France was generally believed in Baltimore, and occasioned great rejoicing among the friends of the South in that city.

The official statement of the Yankee Provost Marshal General says, the last draft has not added 50,000 men to the ranks of their army; and another statement made by letter writers, says that not 40,000 of the veterans had enlisted. The Richmond *Dispatch* says: "With our strengthened armies in the field, let our people take courage and do all in their power to sustain them in comfort. The stage is cleared. The curtain is slowly rising on the spring campaign. Already we see the shining sandals of victory, and as it rises higher it will disclose to our view the glorious crown which encircles her brow."

A reunion of the Democracy of Ohio recently took place at Columbus, with a supper. Judge Van Trump presided, and speeches were made by a number of persons. Among the toasts are the following:

The Union of the States—Formed by the consent of the several States, acting in their sovereignty capacity, it cannot be perpetuated by force, but must rest upon the continued assent of the parties to the compact.

The Virginia and Kentucky Resolutions—The true exposition of the nature of the Federal Government.

C. L. Vallandigham—The exile, patriot and statesman—time will vindicate his course and confound that of his revilers and persecutors.

The West—The equal not the vassal of the East, demands equal immunities, with no more than her equal burdens of men and taxation

The Duty of the Hour—To appeal from the confusion occasioned by the war, to the sovereign people with reference to *State Rights and peace.*

Miscellaneous Items.

Price's Army.—The latest accounts represent Gen. Price to be only a few miles back of Washington, Ark., with a fine army—numbers it is needless for well known reasons to name. The army is in fine plight and most excellent spirits.

The Paris Presse computes the population of the globe at one thousand millions, speaking three thousand and sixty-four languages, and having eleven hundred different forms of religion.

A resolution has been offered by Hon. Linton Stephens, in the House of Representatives of the Legislature of Georgia, declaring that peace shall be officially offered the enemy after every Confederate victory, on the principles of 1778, leaving each doubtful State to decide her association by a Convention of the people.

There is a further decline in Richmond in manufactured and smoking tobacco, sugar and other articles.

A correspondent writes: "The small pox in Washington City is prevailing to a degree before unknown. There are over six hundred cases in the 5th and 6th wards alone. Many persons are afraid to ride in the street cars, or attend church, for fear of contracting the disease."

The New Currency Coming.—Within one week from this date there will be sent to Richmond from the presses of Columbia ten millions of the new currency. The number of signers has been largely increased. Many of these are ladies. We learn that the issue from the "mills" will be at the rate of two millions a day.—*Charleston Mercury, March.* 12.

Salmon P. Chase, the Yankee Secretary of the Treasury, who has been prominently mentioned as a candidate for the Presidency against Lincoln, has withdrawn his name from the canvass.

Rich, Racy and Ridiculous.—A correspondent of the London *Herald*, writing from New York, on the 25th of December, is the author of the following:

"It is the first time in six years that I have seen large quantities of *roasted apples* sold in the market. They are *roasted on the trees* by the heat of the sun, (!) and then gathered and brought to the market. They sell at fifteen cents the peck, roasted."

The fellow must have seen persimmons.—*Carolinian.*

GEN. BEAUREGARD.

No graver error could be committed by our authorities than the adoption of the views suggested by a portion of the Mobile and Richmond press, namely: That Gen. Beauregard should be detached from his present useful position and assigned to the command of the department of Mississippi.

Sent to Charleston for the purpose of gratifying the whim or prejudice of the Executive, at a period when it was not foreseen that his great abilities would be called into play; buried, as it then seemed, beneath all hope of a future useful career; in short, imolated upon an altar on which his past alone was to shine in glorious lustre, Providence has seen fit to confound the ways of man, and to assign to General Beauregard, a grander opportunity of proving himself one of the greatest generals and the most heroic defenders of our cause and our country who have yet appeared upon the stage during this struggle.

Assuming the command of Charleston at a time when its exterior defences, if not virtually abandoned, had been materially contracted; at a time when our sagacious citizens saw everything to tempt the invader and little to encourage our defence, his very presence became a sudden beam of light, and his name added a new born strength to the hearts of the people.

With an energy characteristic of the man, he at once commenced his noble labors, and from that hour until the present—whether we fix our observation upon the cannon-crowned fortifications of Charleston and of Savannah—whether we contemplate his operations on land or water—we find everywhere that energetic, zealous skillful direction of will, industry and science, which place him at once in the first rank of the great captains of the age. These labors have their fruition in the glorious defence which for two hundred and fifty days has baffled a persevering and powerful enemy, and saved to us all that we hold dear.

The question that now recurs is, can we spare such a benefactor? Although, as is set forth by the Mobile Register, his presence in Mississippi would add prestige to our cause there, South Carolina has a right to claim this son of Louisiana as her defender, first and last, in preference to any other General who may be chosen to take his place.

He was identified with her at the outset of the war. His name is linked with all that is great or grand in her present career, and while she is trembling in the throes of her second birth, she looks to him for her safe deliverance from the perils by which she is environed.

But there is another view of this question. Gen. Beauregard has made himself minutely familiar with every detail of the large and responsible department of which he is the chief. No portion of the Southern coast presents so many openings to an enemy, by which he may penetrate its interior, as does that between Wilmington and the Southern edge of Florida.

To become acquainted with this serrated ocean boundary, to learn the depths of its streams, the width of its inlets, and the capacity of the whole for defence, is not the work of a day or week. To suppose that a new man can suddenly familiarize himself with these several facts, or can, in an emergency, use that complete chain of communication which now works so successfully to our advantage, or that he can, by the exercise of the best abilities, take the place of Gen. Beauregard and fulfil the duties now performed by him, is absurd and preposterous. Beauregard may be needed in Mississippi, but he is more needed in the large department which he now commands.

The fate of Florida, South-western Georgia, and the interior of South Carolina, with its valuable railroad communications, depends upon the manner in which this coast is defended, and while we have before us the memory of a past thickly crowded with heroic defences like those of Wagner, Sumter, Moultrie and James' Island, we are content to trust our destinies for the future in the hands of one who stands with Robert E. Lee, at home and abroad, the representative of the military greatness, glory and success of our country.

Finally, we are satisfied that the assignment of Gen. Beauregard elsewhere, and the appointment of any other officer in his place, would be unwelcome to the mass of our people. We trust the change will not be made.—*South Carolinian.*

Letter from Gen. Beauregard.—Recently Gen. Beauregard received a present from a lady of Mobile. The following is the response to the gift:

CHARLESTON, S. C., Feb. 14, 1864.

To Miss Mary Weldon, Mobile, Ala.:

Dear Miss: Your favor of the 4th ult., I have received, together with a beautifully embroidered velvet smoking cap and pair of slippers, which compliment I fully appreciate. The beauty of the work and the work itself are greater testimonials of taste and skill than I can well describe.

Permit me to acknowledge through you my indebtedness to Miss Denny, for the flattering condition attached to her donation to the Orphans' Fair. My thanks to her for her kind intention are many and true.

Hoping your delightful city may be forever spared the terrific ordeal through which heroic Charleston is passing, I remain, yours, very sincerely.

G. T. BEAUREGARD.

FROM NORFOLK.

An Episcopal Clergyman Sentenced to Sweep the Streets!

Every arrival from Norfolk brings some new and additional proof of the horrible tyranny practiced by the Yankees upon the people of that unfortunate and conquered city. The latest instance of the merciless vengeance of the Yankee tyrants is an edict sentencing the Reverend Mr. Wingfield, an Episcopal clergyman, to the degrading punishment of *sweeping the streets!* This infamous and dastardly act of tyranny pleads as its excuse that its victim is an "avowed secessionist!" The *Old Dominion*, published at Portsmouth, contains the official order, from which the following is an extract:

Headquarters Norfolk and Portsmouth,
Norfolk, Va., February 25, 1864.

Special Orders, No. 44.

IV. It having been reported to the General commanding that S. H. Wingfield, of Portsmouth, is an avowed secessionist, and that he takes every opportunity to disseminate his traitorous dogmas, much to the annoyance of his loyal neighbors, and that on one occasion, at a place of worship, while the prayer for the President of the United States was being read, his conduct was such as to annoy and disgust the loyal portion of the congregation, and believing a wholesome example is necessary for the benefit of Mr. Wingfield in particular, and the class in this community he represents in general, men of education and ability, who use the talents God has given them for the purpose of stirring up strife against the Government of the United States.

It is therefore ordered that the Provost Marshal arrest Mr. S. H. Wingfield, and that he be turned over to Colonel Sawtelle to work for three months *cleaning the streets* of Norfolk and Portsmouth, thus employing his time for the benefit of that Government he has abused, and in a small way atone for his disloyalty and treason.

By command of Brig. Gen. E. A. Wild.

GEORGE H. JOHNSTON,
Capt. and A. A. G.

From the South Carolinian.

Camp Song of the 23d Regiment, S. C. V., in Virginia.

We come from the land of the cypress and pine,
From the home of the brave and the true,
To win from the foe green laurels to twine
Round the staff of our banner so blue.

CHORUS.

On hill-top and valley, by river and rill,
Let the crack of our rifles be heard;
And with bayonets bright, in the thick of the fight,
"Make room for the Twenty-Third."

Like our own Palmetto, which stands by the shore,
We'll brave the war-cloud in its wrath;
We'll charge the foe with a wild hurrah,
And scatter their dead in the path.
On hill top and valley, &c.

The breath of the fanatic poisons the air;
Our suffering women appeal;
Remember New Orleans, boys, and swear
By the blood on your [illegible] steel.
On hill-top and [illegible], &c.

MISCELLANY.

The Christian Soldier in Death.

It was just after the battle where hundreds of brave men had fallen, never to bear arms again, and where hundreds more were wounded, that a soldier came to the tent and said, "Chaplain, one of our boys is badly wounded, and wants to see you right away."

Hurriedly following the soldier, I was taken to the hospital, and led to a bed upon which lay a noble young soldier. He was pale and blood-stained from a terrible wound above the temple. I saw at a glance that he had but a few hours to live upon earth. Taking his hand, I said to him, "Well, my brother, what can I do for you?" The poor dying soldier looked up in my face, and placing his finger where his hair was stained with blood, he said, "Chaplain, cut a big lock from here for mother; for mother, mind, Chaplain!" I hesitated to do it. He said, "Don't be afraid, Chaplain, to disfigure my hair. It's for mother, and nobody will come to see me in the dead house to-morrow."

I did as he requested me. "Now Chaplain," said the dying man, "I want you to kneel down by me and return thanks to God!" "For what?" I asked. "For giving me such a mother. Oh! Chaplain, she is a good mother; her teachings comfort and console me now. And, Chaplain, thank God that by His grace I am a Christian. Oh! what would I do now if I wasn't a Christian? I know that my Redeemer liveth. I feel that His finished work has saved me. And, Chaplain, thank God for giving me dying grace. He has made my dying bed feel soft as downy pillows are. Thank Him for the promised home in glory. I'll soon be there—there, where there is no war, no sorrow, nor desolation, nor death—where I'll see Jesus, and be forever with the Lord!"

I knelt by the dying man, and thanked God for the blessings he had bestowed upon him—the blessings of a good mother, a Christian hope, and dying grace to bear testimony to God's faithfulness.—Shortly after the prayer, he said "Good-bye, Chaplain; if you ever see mother, tell her it was all well!"

THE WORTH OF THE BIBLE.—Near the close of his life, Patrick Henry laid his hand on the Bible, and said to a friend: "Here is a book worth more than all others; yet it is my misfortune never to have read it with proper attention until lately."

William Pitt, when he came to die, said: "I fear that, like many others, I neglected my religious duties too much to have one ground of hope that can be efficacious on my death bed."

DON'T FAIL TO EDUCATE CHILDREN.—If amid the excitement and tumult of war, the education of your children is neglected, the whole nation will reap the bitter fruits of this negligence for many years to come. The boys that are now running wild about the streets, will in a few years have control of the country, and will have the management of all affairs both in Church and State. A very heavy responsibility then rests upon parents and guardians of the present day if they do not educate them in such a manner as to prepare them for the important places they will have to fill in the future destiny of the country. Education is a companion which no misfortune can depress, no crime can destroy, no despotism enslave. At home, a friend—abroad, an introduction—in solitude a solace, and in society an ornament. It chastens vice, it guides virtue; it gives at once grace and government and genius.

An Incident.—A Yankee taken prisoner at Lake City, says a correspondent of the *Enquirer*, stated that he saw a negro boy, about eighteen years of age, refuse to fire, replied, "I can't shoot thar; my young master is thar; and I played with him all my life, and he has saved me from getting a many whipping I would have got, and I can't shoot thar, for I loves my young master still." He was then told if he did not fire when the word to fire was given again, that he would be shot himself. He still refused to fire on his young master, when a Yankee officer drew a pistol and shot him down.

HOW THEY GOT HIM.—A fellow was brought into the conscript office the other day who pretended to be totally deaf.—They tried all sorts of sudden and unexpected noises on him all to no purpose. Just as they were about to dismiss him a new plan occurred to one of the examining board. He took two silver quarters and rattled them behind him. No sooner was the sound made than the fellow turned and exclaimed, "I'll give ye ten dollars fur them."—*Macon Confederacy.*

A PROPHECY.—Rev. John Gilbert, aged 100 years, writes from Clay county, Ky., to a friend in Franklin: "During the revolutionary war corn blades had seven points to them; that is, the blade grew in such a manner as to have seven distinct points or ends corresponding with the sharp points of the blade: These seven points indicated the duration of the Revolutionary war. Now, there are but three separate and distinct points to many of the blades, and this indicates very clearly, to my mind, that the duration of the present war will be three years—the points of the blades representing years."

How Coffee Came to be Used.—It is somewhat singular to trace the manner in which arose the use of the common beverage of coffee, without which, few persons, in any half or wholly civilized country, in the world, now make breakfast. At the time Columbus discovered America it had never been known or used. It only grew in Arabia or Upper Ethiopia. The discovery of its as a beverage is ascribed to the superior of a monastery in Arabia, who, desirous of preventing the monks from sleeping at their nocturnal service, made them drink the infusion of coffee, upon the reports of the shepherds, who observed that their flocks were more lively after browsing on the fruit of that plant. Its reputation spread through the adjacent countries, and in about two hundred years it had reached Paris. A single plant brought there in 1814 became the parent stock of all the French coffee plantations in the West Indies. The Dutch introduced it into Java and the East Indies, and the French and Spanish all over South America and the West Indies. The extent of the consumption now can hardly be realized. The United States alone annually consumed it at the cost, on its landing, of from fifteen to sixteen millions of dollars.

An Interesting Love Letter.

The Mobile *Tribune* publishes the following love letter received by a soldier in the [illegible] of Tennessee, and appended to his application for a furlough. General Johnston granted a leave of absence for fifteen days. How could he avoid it?

FEBRUARY 13, 1864.

My Most Esteemed Friend: I am awair that you will be surprised to hear that father and mother has consented for myself and you to get married, which affords me pleasure; for I don't feel as though I could ever give my consent to marry any other gentleman, for you know yourself that I always esteemed you higher than any one els.

Mr. * * * bear in mind—you know you once said that you never could live an see me in the armes of Another man. Know is the time to prove it. You will haf to come home immediately. I am shore that the commanding officers will not object to your haveing a fur low to come onn such important business as that. Ma an pa has give thair consent, thinking that you would hardly get a fur low, an then they could say it was not thair fault; but I want you to take them onn a surprize. I know, if you love me as you you say you do, you will not fail to come. Give my kindest regards to General Johnston, and tell him to be a friend to matrimony this time for my sake.

Nothing more until I hear from you, an be asshured that I shall await your arrival with the greatest anxiety.

Yours, as ever, * * * *
Ton ami, H. T. W.

ECONOMY.

DRIED POTATOES.—We have been shown some potatoes, of the yam species, and crop of 1861, which are in a state of preservation, and though hard, contain all their sweetness and nutriment. They were baked over two years ago, and then dried. Apparently they will remain sound for an indefinite time. The experiment is suggestive in this time of scarcity, and perhaps could be turned to a good account. A half bushel of potatoes thus dried, could be carried readily in a soldier's haversack, and a little hot water would doubtless soften and prepare them for food.

The friend who exhibited these specimens to us, suggests that a cake made of potatoes, rice and parched corn, and well seasoned with pepper and salt, would be excellent rations for a long march.—*Savannah Republican.*

Raise Hogs.—Now is the time to feed and attend well to the pigs which came last fall. At twelve or fourteen months old, you will have to kill them, and make your meat, next winter. By proper care, you can make them weigh from 100 to 200 pounds, at the age mentioned. Don't let them get poor, stunted and mangy now, for if you do, it will be almost impossible to get them started again. There is no telling how much meat can be raised by proper management, even when corn is scarce. The slops and waste from the kitchen will make many a pound of meat. Every house keeper whether he or she has much or little of this world's goods, can go far towards raising his or her own meat. If you have no pigs, obtain one or more, as soon as you can, and go to feeding them. You can accomplish wonders with them in twelve months.

OBITUARY.

MARY J. C. JOHNSON, daughter of William and Mary Johnson, died in Clarendon District, S. C., Dec. 26, 1863, of pneumonia, in her 23d year.

From early life she exhibited very lovely traits of character, which endeared her to all who knew her. In her 14th year she joined the Methodist Church, of which she continued a consistent member until her death. She was a dutiful and obedient child, a kind and affectionate sister, and a sincere and faithful friend. During her last illness, though she suffered a great deal, she murmured not, but bore her sufferings with Christian patience. A short time before she died, she spoke of her spiritual prospects, and expressed strong confidence in regard to the blessedness and glory, that awaited her in the realms of light and immortality. Her trust was in the adorable Redeemer, and she was sustained and comforted to the end, by the presence and grace of her Lord. She died in great peace and without a struggle, praising the Lord even to the end.

PASTOR.

CLARENDON, S. C.,
MARCH 16th, 1864.

PURSUANT to orders from R. B. JOHNSON, State Agent, each Road Commissioner is hereby required to collect from each slave owner in his jurisdiction the number of hands liable to road duty, and also the amount of coast labor already furnished, and make a report of the same to me at Fulton P. O., S. C., as soon as practicable.

W. H. B. RICHARDSON,
Chairman.

March 22. 1t

NOTICE.

I FOREWARN all persons from trading for a note given by me in favor of Warren Rhame, for $110—payable in January next. Said note was for hire of a negro, and has been paid.

T. M. MIMS.

March 22, 1864. 1t*

Administrator's Notice.

THE subscriber having administered upon the estate of *Aaron Mitchum*, deceased, notice is hereby given to all persons indebted to the said estate to make payment; and all those having demands against said deceased, are required to hand in their claims, duly attested, within the time prescribed by law.

JOSEPH SPROTT,
Administrator.

Sept. 8, 1863.—tf.

CIRCULAR.

To the Tax Collectors of the State

Comptroller General's Office,

COLUMBIA, S. C., March 1, 1864.

The Tax Collectors of the several Districts and Parishes of this State are here by notified that, in conformity with the following Instructions, they will be required to make a deduction of Thirty-three-and-one-third per cent. on all "Confederate Treasury Notes" bearing date prior to 1st April, 1864, received by them from and after the 1st day of April next, in payment of Taxes due to this State. They are also required, after the 1st of April next, to send their certificates to this office of the amount of Taxes received by them respectively before that date.

JAMES A. BLACK,
Comptroller General.

March 8, 1864. 2t.

☞ All the papers in the State will publish twice.

Office of Attorney General,

COLUMBIA, March 1, 1864.

To His Excellency Governor Bonham:

SIR: In reply to your enquiry as to the kind of money in which Tax Collectors shall require payment of State Taxes after 1st April next, I answer that the Tax Collector is required to receive Confederate Treasury notes or other current funds, but, in my opinion, after the 1st April Confederate Treasury notes being, by Act of the Confederate Congress, reduced in value as currency 33⅓ per cent., these notes, instead of being received at 100 cents in the dollar, should be taken at the value as currency fixed by law, viz: 66⅔ cents on the dollar.

I am, very respectfully,
Your ob't serv't,
I. W. HAYNE, Att'y Gen'l.

To James A. Black, Esq., Comptroller General:

SIR: You will issue instructions to the Tax Collectors in conformity with the above opinion of the Attorney General.

M. L. BONHAM,

EXECUTIVE DEPARTMENT, Columbia, March 1, 1864.

NOTICE.

CONFEDERATE STATES OF AMERICA War Department, Bureau of Conscription,

RICHMOND, Va., Jan. 28, 1864.

PARAGRAPH X of General Orders No. 82, Adjutant and Inspector-General's Office, of 1862, requires that applications for exemption must in all cases be made to the Enrolling Officer. If the local Enrolling Officer has not the power to act, or is in doubt, he will, after investigation, under Circular No. 3, current series, refer such application, through the proper official channels, to this Bureau.

All such applications addressed to this Bureau will necessarily and invariably be returned for local investigation, and the applicants will thus have uselessly lost time and prolonged suspense.

Appeals from adverse decisions of the local officers, and of the Commandant of Conscripts for the States, will be forwarded by them for hearing, when any plausible ground of appeal is set forth.

By order of
Col. JOHN S. PRESTON, Sup't.
C. B. DUFFIELD, A. A. Gen.

March 8, 1864. 3t.

☞ All papers in the State copy three times and send accounts to Commandant of Conscripts for S. C.

SOUTH CAROLINA'S DEAD.

Biographical Roll of Honor.

HAVING received frequent applications from the friends of deceased soldiers to place in a permanent form and make it accessible to all who might desire a copy of the "ROLL OF HONOR," on which I am engaged for the State, I propose to publish a work more extended in its scope and design than the State Roll, embracing Biographical Sketches of the officers and men from this State who have fallen or died in service during the present war, and whose friends may furnish me with the necessary materials for such sketches.

The plan is this: The friends of the deceased soldiers desiring a place in this work will forward to me the necessary information to make up for publication the biographical sketches, or send me the notices they wish inserted, when they will be revised and compiled for publication. Each biographical sketch must be accompanied by the name of at least one subscriber, and Ten Dollars to defray the expense and labor involved in the preparation and compilation of the sketches, for which a receipt will be given entitling the holder to a copy of the work at the subscription price.

I am perfecting arrangements with a leading publishing house for the publication of the work. It will be published in monthly numbers, and issued in the best style of letter press printing, on fine white English book paper and printed with the best English Ink. Each number will contain one or more portraits of officers and men who have distinguished themselves during the war. The twelve numbers will make four handsome volumes.

Terms $50 per annum or for twelve numbers, payable on the publication of the first number, of which due notice will be given. The work will be continued until the roll is completed. Those intending to subscribe or furnish biographical sketches, should do so without delay, as the first edition will be limited to the number of subscribers.

Address
WILLIAM B. JOHNSON,
Columbia, S. C.

☞ The Editors of the State will please copy this prospectus, and call attention to it, for which they will be furnished with a copy of the work as it appears.

Feb. 23, 1864. tf.

Candidates,

For Clarendon District.

:o:

Capt W. S. BRAND, the gallant and able defender of our rights upon the field of battle, is announced as a Candidate for *TAX-COLLECTOR*, at the ensuing election, by his MANY FRIENDS.

November 17, 1863.*

We are authorized to announce WILLIAM O. CHEWNING, as a candidate for the office of *SHERIFF* of Clarendon District at the ensuing election.

November 10, 1863.*

FOR SHERIFF,
ELIAS G. DuBOSE,
D. J. BRADHAM.
FOR TAX COLLECTOR,
JOHN C. BAGNAL.
RUFUS M. THAMES.
FOR CLERK,
JOSIAH M. FELDER,
G. D. RHODUS,
R. M. SKINNER.

NOTICE.

THE NOTES AND ACCOUNTS due the concern of *Kelly, Pack & Co.* having been placed in the hands of *Y. N. Butler* for collection, those indebted will please come forward and settle the same with him.

H. KELLY,
C. S. PACK.
H. A. KELLY Admr'x
Estate J. D. KELLY.

July 21, 1863. 14tf.

NOTICE.

WE WILL attend at the following times and places to receive the returns of all hogs slaughtered between the 24th *April*, 1863, *and* 1st *March*, 1864. Tax-payers will return the number of pounds of net pork. No deduction allowed for head, back bones, &c.; all must be returned. Those who are unable to come out will please get some friend, as it will be unpleasant for us to enforce the law and double-tax delinquents.

At Samuel Chandler's, Monday 22d March.
S. B. Coker's, Tuesday 23d.
J. J. McFaddin, Wednesday 24th.
Doggett's Shop, Thursday 25th.
C. G. Capell's, Friday 26th.
Brewington Church, Saturday 27th.
Manning from the 29th of March to the 5th of April; at which time the books will close.

J. B. DuBOSE'S APPOINTMENTS.

Fulton, Wednesday 17th March '64.
M. L. Haryin's, Thursday 18th.
Packsville, Saturday 20th.
Friendship, Monday 22d.
Summerton, Wednesday and Thursday 23d and 24th.
Junesville, Friday 25th.
Manning, Saturday 26th.

J. B. DuBOSE,
D. D. BRADHAM,
Assessors.

March 8. 1864. tf

BLANKS---BLANKS.

THE SUBSCRIBER has on hand a number of the following printed blanks Any one needing the same can be furnished on application. Terms reasonable

LAND TITLES, MORTGAGES for LAND, BONDS for MONEY, MORTGAGES for PERSONAL PROPERTY, &c., &c.

W. R. BURGESS, Sr.

Dec. 22, 1863. 6m*

New Drug Store.

THE UNDERSIGNED would respectfully inform his friends and patrons that he has now in store, corner Brooks and Boyce streets a full and complete stock of

DRUGS AND MEDICINES,

which he offers for cash at the lowest market prices, consisting in part as follows:—

CASTOR OIL,
EPSOM SALTS,
RHUBARB,
CALOMEL,
BLUE MASS,
QUININE,
COPPERAS,
OPIUM,
MORPHINE,
SPTS. TURPENTINE,
LINSEED OIL,
EXTRACT OF LOGWOOD, for dyeing,
TOILET SOAP,
ENGLISH TOOTH BRUSHES,

A fine lot of TOBACCO, &c.
Prescriptions carefully compounded.

G. A. HUGGINS, M. D.,
Druggist and Apothecar

Sept. 22, 1863.

State of South Carolina.

ADJ'T AND INSP. GEN'S OFFICE,
COLUMBIA, Feb. 10, 1864.

GENERAL ORDERS NO. 3.

I. BY an Act of the General Assembly of the State, entitled "An Act to amend the law in relation to the general staff," it is provided "that the duties heretofore performed by the Ordnance Office be hereafter performed by the Arsenal Keepers of Charleston and Columbia, under the supervision of the Adjutant and Inspector-General." The Keepers of the Arsenals will, therefore, make their reports and address their correspondence to the Adjutant and Inspector-General, and obey all orders from that officer.

II. The State Works at Greenville having been assigned, by orders heretofore issued from this office, to the Ordnance Department, all orders and instructions for the Superintendent of said Works, and all communications from him, will be made to the Adjutant and Inspector-General, except when the urgency of the case will not admit of delay. By order:

A. C. GARLINGTON,
Adjutant and Inspector-General S C

Feb 23, 1864.

Administrator's Notice.

THE subscriber having administered upon the estate of *Aaron Mitchum*, deceased, notice is hereby given to all persons indebted to the said estate to make payment, and all those having demands against said deceased, are required to hand in their claims, duly attested, within the time prescribed by law.

JOSEPH SPROTT,
Administrator.

Sept. 8, 1863.—tf.

Nickerson's

SOUTHERN STATES

HOTEL,

COLUMBIA, S. C.

State of South Carolina.

EXECUTIVE DEPARTMENT,
COLUMBIA, S C, Feb. 6, 1864.

COL. Robert B. Johnson is appointed the State Agent for the supply of negro labor for coast defence, *vice* Col. Wm. M. Shannon, resigned.

By order of the Governor.
B F ARTHUR,

Bureau of Central Association Columbia.

Cars will be Dispatched

For Johnston's Army, March 16,
" Lee's " 18,
" Longstreet's " 23

M. LaBORDE,
Chairman C. Association.

March 8.

Headquarters,

COMMISSARY GEN'S DEP'T S. C.
COLUMBIA, S. C., March 5, 1864.

THE Boards of soldiers' relief throughout the State, who have not remitted the amounts for sales of CARDS and CLOTH in full, are hereby requested to do so before 1st April next. All amounts received by them after said date for sales of above, will be subject to the deduction of thirty-three-and-a-third per cent., and will be so received by this Department.

By order of the Governor.
RICHARD CALDWELL,
Lt. Col. and C. G. S. C.

March 15, 1864. 3t.

☞ All papers in the State will please insert three times and send bills in duplicate, with copy of advertisement attached, to this Department for payment

CAROLINA SPARTAN.

WM. H. TRIMMIER, — Devoted to Southern Rights, Politics, Agriculture, and Miscellany. — $5 PER ANNUM

VOL. XX. SPARTANBURG, S. C., THURSDAY, MARCH 31, 1864. NO 49

The Object of this War.

In the United State Senate on Tuesday last, Mr. Wilson reported the following bill, (as a substitute for Mr. Carlisle's resolutions,) which may be taken as the final declaration of the views of the Republican party:

That the object of the war are the subjugation of the rebels in arms to the rightful authority of the United States and the re-establishment of such authority; that, in the prosecution of the war, the United States may adopt whatever measures, not in consistent with the rules of civilized warfare, as may be deemed necessary to secure the public safety now and hereafter, that any person born and residing in the United States, whether bond or free, owes allegiance to the United States, and this allegiance is paramount to any duty which such person may owe to any State or individual; that the Constitution of the United States does not recognize slaves as property but as persons owing service or labor in certain States under the laws thereof, and it is the right and duty of the United States to offer such persons such inducements as are best calculated to enable them to give to their country the paramount allegiance which their owe, and that the proclamation of emancipation issued by the President of the United States on the 1st day of January, 1863, was a measure necessary for the common defence, sanctioned by the spirit of the Constitution, and by the law and practice of nations, and said proclamation is hereby declared to have the force and effect of law, anything in the law or Constitution of any State to the contrary notwithstanding.

HEAVY LOSS.—We learn from prisoners in our hands that out of thirty seven officers from the New York regiments that went into the battle, only four escaped being killed, wounded or captured.—*Florida Columbian.*

Contemn not poor acquaintances, not flatter rich friends.

Betray no trust, divulge no secret.

The Raiders in King and Queen.

On Wednesday, during the late raid, the rumor reached "Traveler's Rest," in King and Queen county, that the Yankees had crossed the Pamunkey, and were advancing in the direction of Aylett's. Three young men, B. Fleet, jr., and Wm. Talliaferro, of King and Queen, and Mr. Sizer, of King William, determined to make a reconnoissance in that direction. After proceeding about a mile from Aylett's, they perceived three soldiers in Confederate uniform advancing to meet them, and concluding they were Confederate soldiers, continued to advance until within about thirty yards of them. They then called out, "Are you friends or enemies?" The three men replied, "Friends!" Perceiving the Yankee column in the rear, they turned their horses and endeavored to escape. The Yankees fired on them, and Fleet was so badly wounded that, although he escaped into the woods, he was found dead next morning. Talliaferro was dangerously wounded. Fleet is represented to have been a noble youth, of seventeen, and intended the same day to join the gallant Mosby's command.

Talliaferro, also a youth, who had recently joined the Signal Corps, was shot through the body after he had nearly stopped his horse to surrender. The savages in the advance guard did not stop to render him any assistance—not even to plunder him. But the main body coming up, one of the wretches started to to take his hat off remarking, "he would have no further use for it." He was by this time lying on the ground, and the demons as they dashed by, covering him with dirt thrown up by the horses' feet, tauntingly inquired "What is the matter old fellow?" At length an officer, more humane than the rest, directed a Lieutenant and one of the men to take him to the next house. He raised his head and sustaining it on his lap, offered to carry his messages to his mother. They finally bore him to a house about a mile distant, and left him after sending for a physician. We are gratified to learn that there is a prospect of Talliaferro's recovery.

Sizer, the third party, threw himself from his horse, and it is believed, escaped unhurt, so intent were the Yankees on capturing his fine steed.

The murder of Fleet, added to the wounding of Talliaferro, has thrown a gloom over the community in which they lived. Fleet was a universal favorite, the idol of his parents, and time alone can mitigate the agony of their terrible bereavement. The question may very pertinently be asked if Yankees in the guise of Confederate soldiers, are to be allowed with impunity, to pass through the country, and to numberless other outrages of the usages of civilized warfare, add that of clothing themselves in the guise of Confederate soldiers, and murdering our unoffending people. The country reasonably awaits and expects some official action in relation to the late raid, so that if the offenders will not be brought to justice, others at least may be deterred from the repetition of their outrages.—*Richmond Whig, 12th*

From the North.

ORANGE C. H., March 14.—The Washington Chronicle of the 10th contains Seward's celebrated letter of July 11, to Minister Adams. It says the United States Government will be satisfied with the decision in the Alexandria case if affirmed. It becomes parliament to pass laws to prevent the fitting out of similar vessels. If it is not done the United States vessels will be compelled to pursue vessels of character even into British ports. This may lead to war. Great Britain will alone be responsible.

Davis, Kentucky, introduced in the Senate a resolution that no person whose mother or grandmother is a negro shall be a citizen eligible to office; also that Maine and Massachusetts shall constitute one State, and be called East New England; Vermont, New Hampshire, Rhode Island and Connecticut another State, and be called West New England.

HARRISONBURG, March 14.—We have Delaware papers of the 10th. The Washington correspondent of the Philadelphia Inquirer says a special messenger from Dayton, minister to France, had arrived. Nothing was known officially of the dispatches, but he told his friends that France had determined to recognize the Southern Confederacy. The report was generally believed in Baltimore, and occasioned great rejoicing among the friends of the South in that city.

RICHMOND, March 14.—Vague rumors of the speedy recognition of the Confederacy, under which the Confederate loan advanced to 59, were current in London on the 19th ult. The London Post mentions the report on the 24th, reiterated it on the 26th, and, up to the time of the departure of the last steamer, the report had not been contradicted.

A son of Minister Dayton arrived at New York with dispatches from his father and proceeded immediately to Washington. He stated to friends that the Emperor Napoleon had announced his conclusion that something should be done with a view of terminating the civil war in America, raging long enough with no definate result.

DALTON, March 14.—Northern papers state that Adj't. Gen. Thomas was at Nashville, pushing forward the work of organizing negro troops. Several reinlisted regiments passed through Nashville, returning to the field. Sherman's command was at Vicksburg on the 8th, making preparations for another grand movement, Chattanooga being the probable destination. The Yankees are much alarmed in regard to Longstreet's whereabouts. One account represents him *en route* to Lee, another to Johnston.

We paint our lives in fresco. The soft and fusile plaster of the moment hardens under every stroke of the brush into eternal rock.

From Norfolk.

Every arrival from Norfolk brings some new and additional proof of the horrible tyranny practiced by the Yankees upon the people of that unfortunate and conquered city. The latest instance of the merciless vengeance of the Yankee tyrants is an edict sentencing the Reverend Mr. Wingfield, an Episcopal clergyman, to the degrading punishment of sweeping the streets! This infamous and dastardly act of tyranny pleads as its excuse that its victim is an "avowed secessionists!" The Old Dominion, published at Portsmouth, contains the official order, from which the following is an extract:

"HEADQUARTERS,
NORFOLK, VA., February 25, 1864.
Special Orders No. 44.

IV. It having been reported to the General commanding that S. H. Wingfield, of Portsmouth, is an avowed secessionists, and that he takes every opportunity to disseminate his traitorous dogmas, much to the annoyance of his loyal neighbors, and that on one occasion, at a place of worship, while the prayer for the President of the United States was being read, his conduct was such as to annoy and disgust the loyal portion of the congregation, and believing a wholesome example is necessary for the benefit of Mr. Wingfield in particular, and the class in this community he represents in general, men of education and ability, who use the talents God has given them for the purpose of stirring up strife against the Government of the United States.

It is therefore ordered that the Provost Marshal arrest Mr. S. H. Wingfield, and that he be turned over to Colonel Sawtelle to work for three months cleaning the streets of Norfolk and Portsmouth, thus employing his time for the benefit of that Government he has abused, and in a small way atone for his disloyalty and treason.

By command Brig. Gen, E. A. Wild.
GEORGE H. JOHNSTON, Capt. and A. A. C,

The New Prison Depot for Yankees.

From all accounts it would seem that Camp Sumter, on the Southwestern Railroad, in Georgia, is destined in point of magnitude to become the Camp Chase of the Confederacy. A correspondent of the Macon Telegraph says of it:

In returning from Americus on yesterday, I stopped for a short time to examine the camp, and was kindly shown around by the officers. The enclosure is a parallelogram of eighteen acres, through the centre of which runs a clear, beautiful stream, with gently sloping hills on either side. The stockade is composed of hewn pine logs, 21 feet long, with six feet in the ground. They are very closely set together, as well as strongly set in the trenches. A large bakery has been erected just outside the stockade. It is made of brick and capable of making, at one time, near two thousand pounds of bread.

The stockade is not completed, Capt. Winder, under whose efficient management the work was begun and thus far finished, tells me it would have been completed two weeks since, but for the impossibility of procuring negro labor. A sentinel walk is to be placed around near the top of the stockade. The encampment for officers and men is on the hill near the south end of the enclosure.

Capt Winder, late of Richmond, planned and carried into execution the work, and deserves the thanks of the country for the skill and energy displayed. The grounds have been enlarged from the original design, and will accommodate twelve thousand prisoners. There are to be two regiments stationed there to guard them, Colonel A. W. Parsons is at present in command of our troops. There are four hundred prisoners at the camp. In company with some of the officers, we walked among them, and conversed with some. As a general thing, they looked haggard, and their physical habiliments were decidedly of the earth earthy."

A Lady in the Yankee Lines.

A lady writing from Cleveland, Tennessee, to the Atlanta Register, thus speaks of the treatment of her sex in the Yankees lines.

We think the gifted pen of Sir Walter Scott would fail to portray the proceedings of these vandal hordes. Allow me, sister Georgians, to tell you that you will never know what constitute the Yankee army until you see the path of desolation and destruction carved by their ruthless hands, and feel the wants of the comforts of life, even the essential necessaries of life, deprived of your wardrobes and reduced to half rations. I have seen and felt, the wants of all

I have seen six or eight Yankees enter the house, demand the keys, and before they could be produced, burst the door (of a locked room) down, search every trunk, drawer and box, and if you inquire what they are in quest of, they tell you contraband property, and continue to search every little nook about the room. On one occasion an officer was engaged in this daring bravery, when he seized a box four inches square, containing a set of jewelry. A young lady standing by, looking on in disgust, gently touched the arm of the miscreant officer, saying, "Captain, do you think that little box contains a cavalry horse or saddle?" His reply was no! and he dropped the jewels, and retired from the room, ashamed of his cowardice, in stooping to such a petty action. I might relate many such trying incidents, but I will desist, at least for the present.

Too many Christians mark the distinction between Sunday and other days, by praying for each other on Sunday, and praying for each other throughout the week.

Those who endeavor to imitate us we like much better than those who endeavor to equal us. Imitation is a sign of esteem; but competition of envy.

From the North.

We are indebted to the Exchange Bureau for United States papers to the 10th inclusive. Those who dont believe that the Yankees will destry by fire what they cannot take away, will change their opinion, when they have read all the particulars of the Raid Around Richmond. Here is a small specimen of Col. Dahlgreen's exploits up to the time he was killed.

THE RAID ON RICHMOND.

The account of the late raid are very voluminous, and, as usual, teem with exaggerations. The New York Times' correspondent says the special object of the raid was a failure, but in every other respect it was a "complete success." Millions of dollars, worth of property were destroyed; miles of railroad torn up; six or seven grist mills and saw mills burnt; six canal boats and several locks on James River Canal destroyed. The failure of the principal object of the expedition is attributed to the treachery of the negro guide, who was immediately hanged. So secretly and well-planned was the expedition that the rebels had not the most distant idea of its whereabouts until the command was almost within sight of Richmond, and a few hours later was "hurling leaden messengers of death from a battery inside the defences of the city into its very suburbs." The men were in the saddle four days, during which time they were supplied from rebel larders and the horses from rebel granaries. Nearly three hundred prioners were captured, several hundred horses, and hundreds of negroes.

The Latest from Suffolk.

We have received no further official information of the movement of our troops in the vicinity of Suffolk, and the accounts given by passengers by the train from Ivor yesterday afternoon, were rather conflicting and unsatisfactory. After comparing all the statements, we set down the following as about as near the truth as we could reach.

Gen. Ransom, learning that the Yankee troops had occupied Suffolk on Sunday, moved his force from the neighborhood of Somerton, and reached Bethlehem Church on Wednesday morning. About 10 o'clock in the day his skirmishers advanced to the Merry Oak two miles from town, where some negro pickets were posted. They fled and were pursued into the town, where a regiment of negro cavalry were stationed. The fight took place in the streets, the negroes dismounting after the first fire and flying in every direction. Several were killed in the streets, and many took shelter in a vacant house, just beyond the limits of the town, on the east. This house was charged by our men, and all but four captured. These four refused to surrender and the house was fired. When the flames were well under way, one came out firing upon our men as he did so, and was killed. The other three remained and were consumed in the flames. The flying negroes were pursued to Jericho Run, where they tore up the bridge; also the bridge at the Canal, a quarter of a mile distant. Ransom's forces pursued and charged the camp at Bernard's Mill, the Yankees running as though the arch fiend of the regions of wo was after them. Having only a small force of cavalry they could not be followed. The camps and quartermaster's stores were destroyed, the men first supplying themselves with overcoats and other articles, which they could bring off conveniently.

We lost three men in the engagement, and the number killed of the enemy was about thirty. We had two men captured and have not learned how many prisoners we took. The affair is regarded a very brilliant one.

Gen. Ransom has fallen back this side of Suffolk, and the Yankees, have again advanced, and there was some skirmishing Thursday morning at Cowling's Landing, two miles west of Suffolk. Should the Yankees be reinforced and make any further advance, they will find the gallant Ransom in the right place.

Several of the negro soldiers killed in this battle belonged to a gentleman in Suffolk, and died in a few hundred yards of their old homes.

Gen. Ransom obtained from the enemy some fine horses, a piece of artillery, and many small arms.—*Petersburg Express, 12th.*

Yankee Straggler's in Florida.

Many Yankee deserters are wandering through Florida, and when opportunity offers come into our camps. Some of them are in a wretched condition, and report that they have been nearly starved since they deserted. They assert that their black allies are terribly frightened since the battle at Ocean Pond, in which they were nearly all cut to pieces. The negro regiments from Pensylvania and Massachusetts, which entered the battle with full ranks, and were forced on by the Yankees behind them, now do not number more than two companies each. The prisoners stated that their officers assured them that they would meet with no opposition in their march through the state, and that in a few weeks they would occupy Tallahassee, and establish a government there, when each soldier would be entitled to a farm for his services in conquering the State. Some had even gone so far as to write to their families in the North, advising them to make arrangements to move South.

Another account, speaking of the terrible havoc made of the negro troops, says:

Persons living on the line of road through which the Yankees passed on their way to Lake City, state that out of two full regiments of blacks who passed up, but about one hundred and fifty of the number returned on their retreat. *Sav. News.*

SURE TONIC FOR BLOCKADERS.—What tonic is a sure remedy for blockaders? *Housatonic,*

OUR CAMP JOURNAL.

NO PEACE WHILE TRAITORS ARE IN ARMS.

VOL. 1.—No. 6.] Headquarters, First Division, Second Army Corps, Va., April, 1864. [PRICE 10 CTS.

THE LATE COL. E. SHERRILL, 126th N. Y. VOLS.

COL. ALFORD B. CHAPMAN, 57th N. Y. VOLS.

CAPT. JAMES MAGNER, 28th MASS. VOLS.

CAPT. J. M. FAVILL N. Y. 57th VOLS.

BRIG. GEN. JOHN C. CALDWELL.

FIRST LIEUT. C. A. ALVORD, 11th MAINE VOLS.

FIRST LIEUT. CHARLES E. GRISSON 26th MICH. VOLS

FIRST LIEUT HENRY DOPSON 26th MICH. VOLS.

FIRST LIEUT. J. B. HALENBECK, 61st N. Y. VOLS.

Our Camp Journal.

APRIL, 1864.

EDITOR:
Lieut. L. D. BURCH, 26th Mich. Vols.

CONTRIBUTORS:

First Brigade.
Capt. A. W. ACHESON, 140th Penn. Vols.

Second Brigade.
Private WM. H. GIBSON, 116th Penn. Vols.

Third Brigade.
Serg't-Major C. L. MOORE, 57th N, Y. Vols.

THE CHANGE IN OUR PAPER.

By advice of many of our friends in the regiment, and beyond it, we have decided to *double* the size of our paper. In doing this we are compelled to give it a more general and less regimental character than heretofore. We shall not, however, forget the men who have so cheerfully sustained the JOURNAL up to the present; but with its enlargement and embellishment, it will simply be *impossible* for any single regiment to support it. So we are obliged to extend its circulation by making it of interest to the entire Division, and even beyond it. The JOURNAL is the only army paper that has outlived the first campaign of its publishers; and while we have started out with the experiment of its enlargement to a Division paper, and the increased expenditure consequent thereon, we dislike to think of taking the back track. We hope all the friends of the experiment will do what is in their power to sustain it. We have no commercial, or advertising, nor any political patronage to fall back upon, but depend wholly upon the sale of the paper in our Division to keep it in existence. We design to continue its publication at its present dimensions and price, and shall do so, with the liberal patronage of our brother officers and soldiers. While we shall be careful to publish nothing that is contraband, we shall endeavor to make the JOURNAL a faithful reflection of the views and feelings of the men whose patronage determine the measure of its success.

THE POTOMAC ARMY.

If there is one army of this half century to which posterity will accord greater honor than to any other, it is the Army of the Potomac. We mean not by this that it has fought more valiantly, won more victories, or achieved greater success than any or all other armies of the same period, but simply, that in the same space of time, there is not an army of history even that may produce a record of so many great battles—so much loss of life and limb—so many rapid, extended, and fatiguing marches, and such extreme trials of human endurance as this same Potomac Army. It has been charged by many grumblers in civil life, and to some extent by aspirants for military honors in other departments, that it has been unsuccessful, or, to say the least, *unfortunate;* that the Western troops could take its place and sweep Virginia with the besom of sure destruction in a single campaign, and much other talk of the same sort, all of which may be as true as it is possible to transform eternal verities into myths, or to make the first spasmodic impulses and excitements of popular opinion the final rule by which men and events are to be judged. There are *some facts* patent to men of common sense which *possibly* might enlighten these chronic fault-finders.

The Army of the Potomac has been opposed from first to last by the very choicest troops of the Confederacy, under the command of men confessedly its ablest generals, and indeed among the best of their time. It is generally conceded that Virginia troops have given the most stubborn and persistent resistance to our advance of any in the rebel service. Beside this, the Potomac Army has fought an enemy always its equal, generally its superior in numbers, with the vast advantage of a *defensive* warfare in a region made up of the strongest natural defenses to be found upon the continent. An officer of high rank, recently from the Western army on a visit to the Second Corps, remarked in our hearing: "I am only surprised that an army *invading such a country* has not been wholly destroyed." These jungles of cedar and bramble, bottomless roads, interminable ranges of hills, with the endless succession of rivers and "runs" which make up the topography of Virginia, render even ordinary military resistance hard to be overcome. And then, too, it has repeatedly been forced, by the inexorable demands of an excited, half-frenzied, and exacting public opinion, to fight the enemy in his strongholds against the judgment of its commanders. Each and all of these forced movements have resulted in unfortunate failures, out of which came unjust criticisms, calumnies, and indignities from the press, the rostrum, and the pulpit, not to say the people; but in the midst of which this noble army has marched on, fought on, and suffered on, through a succession of campaigns such as would blot from the map of Europe half its old "principalities and powers," still unshaken in its faith in the final triumph of our arms, still unshorn of its strength, to fight and win the battles of other campaigns. The men whose wholesale denunciations of this army, on the plea that its great battles are without corresponding good results to our cause, have been systematic and persistent, will sleep in their forgotten graves when other men are learning that *temporary success* is no proof of personal greatness, any more than of the legitimacy or truthfulness of the logic of events. He is a happy man—and a philosopher—who, in the midst of the buffetings and misfortunes of the present hour, can hold steadily on his way of well doing, content to leave with destiny the judgment of his works and the keeping of his fame. Happily for the Potomac Army it is quite satisfied to leave its honor in their keeping, and accept its legitimate meed of praise at the hands of those men who, far removed by time and change from the jealousies, strifes, and rancor of cliques and parties, will learn the lesson of its heroism from the fearless and impartial teachings of history. It is folly to talk of any special merit arising out of mere *locality*. In a population like ours, eminently homogeneous, its character and geographical boundaries have little to do with the fighting qualities of men. Men, under the same circumstances of training and leadership, actuated by similar purposes, and inspired by the greatness and justice of a common cause, fight equally well in its defense. Western troops in the Eastern army have fought just as well (no better) as Eastern men. Eastern men in the Western army have shared all the dangers and sacrifices with the honors of those great campaigns with the same courage and grace as their brothers in arms. Who but the men of the 9th and 23d Army Corps, under Burnside and Hartsough, mutilated and nearly destroyed Longstreet's Army at Knoxville, and expelled the rebels from East Tennessee? Who fought any better than the men of the 11th Corps under Hooker at Lookout Mountain? And yet these generals and men are graduates from the old Potomac Army, and will never be ashamed of their Alma-Mater. Fighting on the vast plains of the West, with the advantages equally distributed, is quite a different thing from dislodging an enemy from *a chain of continuous natural and artificial defenses covering an area of 60,000 square miles*. When Gen. Grant shall ask for the relief of Burnside, Hooker, Hartsough, Howard, and Averill, with the gallant men they led from the East, we shall be quite satisfied that the talkative gentlemen who have so unscrupulously criticised the weak points of this great army, forgetting its good ones, are partially justified by *facts*. For the present, we are content to believe in the men and their leaders who upon the plains of Gettysburg fought and won the grandest battle of the century, saved the fortunes of the Republic, and are calmly watching and waiting by the Rapidan the coming of their last campaign.

COURAGE.—Many men walk with trembling step upon firm ground; when one has a tranquil conscience and a good purpose, he ought to walk with a firm step upon trembling ground.—*Victor Hugo.*

ABRAHAM LINCOLN.

We love Abraham Lincoln, and in this are not singular. Go where you will, and you find him *first* in the hearts of the people. On the rail-car—in the cabin of the steamer—in the closely packed omnibus, and the crowded thoroughfare—by the hearthstones of the lofty and lowly—in the editorial columns, and the conventions—and by the camp-fires of the all-pervading army—the mention of his name is greeted with an enthusiasm unparalleled since the days of Washington. He is the guardian, guide, and watchword of *eight hundred thousand soldiers*, who look upon him with feelings akin to reverence, and would peril their lives in defense of his honor. Few men are less soldierly, and yet none have moulded the great heart of the army, and fashioned it into sympathy with their own, so effectually as he. With little knowledge and less practice of the doubtful arts by which sharp politicians make and control opinion, and without assistance of the President makers, he has unconsciously made himself master of the political forces about him, and stands before the political community "a stumbling block and rock of offense" to crafty and designing leaders of factious men and their factious aims. Early a stranger to the higher walks and arts of learning, he has risen above the promise and prophecy of his pioneer life, and gathers to his hearthstone and councils the friendship and wisdom of the most elegant and learned men of his country and time. Burdened with an excess of public cares and responsibilities, and surfeited with numberless and flattering attentions of the great, he has never forgotten to open his purse and extend his hand, while his heart has warmed toward the lowly and unfortunate Walking up the aisles of the great hospitals with noble words and moistened eye, wounded and languishing soldiers from a hundred battle-fields bless his passing shadow; and on the street the glad freedman points to him as the liberator of a wronged and forsaken race. He is the personal embodiment of the grandest idea of the century; *the political regeneration of the Republic*. Possessed of rare intuitive knowledge of men and things around him, he has given liberality and comprehensiveness to his opinions of them by a close and elaborate study of systems, their advocates, and practical workings, until, it may be conceded, he knows as well how to manage them as any statesman of his day. Entering upon his executive career with a higher trust—and greater obstacles in the way of its faithful keeping—than was ever entrusted to the care of any civil ruler, he has held steadily and persistently to the helm of his imperiled Government, directing its destinies in the midst of the faithlessness and faltering of his friends—the perfidy and treason of secret enemies—the threats of avowed disloyalists and the frowns of their foreign sympathizers—until an honest policy and victorious army have at last dispelled the danger that threatened us, reassured the wavering, and inspired every lover of liberty and law with a determined purpose to crush treason everywhere, and "restore the Government to its original purity and integrity."

It is not at all strange that in the fullness of his success, under all the remarkable circumstances of the rebellion, there should be a wild excess of enthusiasm for him; for to the hastily judging multitude *success* is the measure of greatness. But barring all this, there is in Mr. Lincoln's composition a native goodness, an overpowering honesty of purpose and sincerity, and independence of action, with an all-conquering faith in the ultimate triumph of justice, that have drawn the hearts of the people toward him by the sympathetic magnetism of a great nature that embodies all the excellence that is in themselves. And so the people love him to-day, and believe in him as the leader who is to bring them forth to peace, prosperity, and a higher civilization for all the suffering and tears and blood of this sad war. The saying of Jefferson, "*Vox populi, vox Dei,*" is the truthful philosophy of this hour. The eyes of the people are turned to Abraham Lincoln, their hearts are warming toward him, and he is becoming each hour

TENT LIFE IN VIRGINIA,

On the Rapidan, the beautiful, winding Rapidan, and in tents, too, with all the paraphernalia of war in order about you! Not *one*, *two*, or *three* tents merely—such as would make up the encampment of a hunting or fishing party—but vast villages of white tents stretching away over the country for miles, all filled with the best heart and muscle of the land. Who would have ventured the prophecy of all this three years ago this March? *Then* the lordly barons of this historic "Old Dominion," with high words and imperious air, dictating the policy of the Government, or threatening its ruin. *Now*, this endless city of tents, their folds idly flapping in this soft Southern breeze, and its camp-fires lighting the evening skies over the lands and homes of their proud old realm, and themselves homeless wanderers in a land of want and graves.

SELF DESTRUCTION

is a thankless task. These "lords of the manor" who sought to create a false deity for their country and the world, before which politics and commerce were to humble themselves in self-acknowledged abasement, have in three short years become the creatures of that higher and inevitable law of justice by which God ultimately regulates the nations. Their mightiest weapons have been turned against them; they stand adjudged by the moral sense of Christendom of a great crime against humanity; and while they are sinking beneath the sullen waters which themselves have "troubled," *self-destruction* is being written on the proud temples of their godless civilization. To one who admires the Virginia of the olden days, with its social elegance and political purity, the royal old Virginia of the Fairfaxes, Berkleys, and elder Lees; of the Wirts, Henrys, and Randolphs; of Washington, Jefferson, and Madison, and comes now to look on all the degeneracy of their sons, the wasted fortunes and faded splendor of that heroic age, with the sad blight of war that hangs like a pall upon the Virginia of to-day, there is left only a sense of utter melancholy. The skies are still bright and warm, and the mountains robed in the purple beauty they wore in the century agone, but their liberty-tree is hewn down by the hands of the children whose sires nurtured it; and their beautiful rivers flow only through valleys of dry bones to the Great Bay. But this wide waste of early fruitfulness will not last forever, surely, and soon will come.

A NEW ORDER OF THINGS.

The heart of the world pulsates quick and strongly. The march of ideas is rapid and onward. Henceforth, humanity goes no more backward. Where yesterday the swarthy slave groaned beneath the burden of the imperious taskmaster, to-day is war with its historic lesson of morals and politics. To-morrow shall plant here the germs of liberty and law, and the sun of the future will shine upon a vast and happy people planting in these valleys and mountain-aisles the foundation stones of a free and Christian civilization. . . . Forgetting these changes—forgetting that we are *human*, and were made to *bless*, not to *kill* each other—forgetting the homes, and loves, and all the arts of peace we left behind—forgetting *everything* but the stern facts of war—we come with stout heart and steady nerve to talk of

LIFE AT THE FRONT.

The winter has passed quietly, with no sound of hostile or friendly gun on the Rapidan, until Saturday, February 6th, when we were ordered, with "three days' ration," to march, nobody knew where. The best feature of military movements in these later days of the war is their celerity, and the still better fact of the success with which commanding generals keep their own counsels. In the early part of the war, every movement of the army was canvassed in New York and Chicago before it was half completed—often before it was undertaken. Now armies awake in the morning to a consciousness that they are *moving*, but *where* and for *what* is better known when they have fought a battle, and night with its darkness and hot coffee brings on a canvass of the day's procedure. In our case, however, it only wanted an hour's march to satisfy us that we were bound for

MORETON'S FORD.

The 3d division was already there, and, with Gen. Hayes at their head, had forded the river, dispersed, or captured the picket, and as we came in view, were in line of battle in front of the enemy's works. There seems to have been no design of bringing on a general engagement, as only the 3d division was thrown across the river. There was little musketry firing during the day. The enemy shelled the line at intervals, with little or no effect, and so the day passed without any of the high excitement of battle, until toward evening, when, as is the uniform custom of Virginia weather on the eve of battle, the "heavens opened,

THE RAIN DESCENDED,"

and up went shelter tents and oil blankets. Either the rebel war-god controls the elements for the especial benefit of their king, his Royal Highness Jeff. Davis, or there is something in the atmospheric influence of exploding gunpowder, or still some other phenomenon that ought in part to account for the endless and overwhelming *rains* of campaign life in Virginia. John Howard once remarked to a friend, who asked why he always rode in the rain, that "it was the only cleansing his clothes ever got." A wag suggests to the "Journal," that "Providence interferes, on the hard marches, to wash the dust out of the blue uniforms." A good joke on those soldiers who insist on putting Providence to all that trouble, but not so pleasant to that better, and larger class who are obliged to come under the same *wet* rule. But coming back to the noble old

THIRD DIVISION,

we find them engaged about dusk in a spirited and brilliant fight. Ewell has come down upon them in the darkness of fog and smoke, and at night a rebel corps close in upon them. These brave and undaunted men hurl back the rebel horde to their works, and an hour later recross the river. They have fought well—fighting is no new thing to them—and left another battle-field to be added to the map of their campaigns. When battles are fought men yield up blood and life. So here, beside the intrenchments of Moreton's Ford, sleep some of their honored dead, and in the hospitals are some of their uncomplaining wounded. But we are all this side the river now, and it is ten o'clock. The darkness is dense, the rain has chilled our spirits just a little, and a dozen of us are sitting around a cheerful fire, each telling his story, singing his song, or making his speech, as is the custom at such places,

"To drive dull care away."

Before we have gone to rest, Major Saviers calls on the election of candidate for the next Presidency.

WHICH WAY THE WIND BLOWS.

Eleven for Lincoln; *one* for Gen. Grant. All speak in praise of the hero of Vicksburg, and would make him Lieutenant-General. All but one want Abraham Lincoln for the next President. Politics are dropped by common consent, and here, on the banks of the beautiful Rapidan, in the darkness and rain of this starless night, around a dying camp-fire we revive the memory of all the great-hearted President has done for the army and country, and *elect him to the honors of another term.* We elected him, because ours was the choice, and ours the views of the "grand army"—because all we *thought* and *did* was *representative.*

ASLEEP IN THE RAIN!

It is very agreeable to sit in a club-room or parlor idealizing the

"Glorious pomp and circumstance of war;"

but here among the camp-fires of the Second Corps, "*en bivouac;*" here where no choice of resting place is left to aching heads and weary limbs; here beside the sullen stream—hitherto, alas! our rubicon—in the drenching rain, sleep the war-worn veterans of many campaigns, who are yet to rescue, at some Runnymede, the "Magna Charta" of our liberties; here, side by side, lie sleeping the pampered children of wealth and pride, and the sons of penury and want. The officer and servant, mayhap under the same blanket, sharing a common couch—the bosom of their mother earth—nor heeding the storm as they dream of mother, maiden, wife, and child. These same men, wet to the skin, will awake in the morning full of the cheerfulness and

GOOD HUMOR OF ARMY LIFE,

and shaking off rain and dullness, sit down to a cup of coffee, some bacon, and hard tack with the same happy smile and confident chat that greets you in the sunnier places of home life. Few words of complaint will be spoken, for these are men who are trained to the self-sacrifice of army life, who march and fight as if bred to the life-long profession of war. With all its fatigue and loss of life and limb—with its melancholy days and memories of home—there is no place in the wide world of pleasure so brim-full of music and fun as volunteer army life in America. Joking is chronic with the soldier, and he indulges in it at the expense of himself and every body else.

ARMY SHOES.

Of all the unmitigated nuisances patent in these "days of shoddy," army shoes take rank—not of necessity, for the genuine shoe worn by the American soldier is a most refreshing relief to the feet that have been compelled to march all day in the high, stiff, puritanic boots of the latest pattern, until with blushing galls they reproach you at every step. But the *shoddy shoe*, furnished by some of the contractors for the men of iron nerve and heroic soul, who are braving numberless perils of camp and field to keep inviolate the heritage of liberty—the *spongy, brown paper shoe*, that affords the wearer protection from stub and stone on the outward bound side of a ten days' expedition, with the inexpressible pleasure of returning with shoeless feet. This is the shoe we dislike, and that every body who ever wore it dislikes; and while the Government is hauling swindlers of every grade over the coals, we hope it may pay its respects to some of the "army shoe"

CONTRACTORS.

The Duke of Wellington once brought an offender against the rights of his soldiers to summary justice, by *hanging* him in presence of the men he had wronged. It might be a healthful policy to inaugurate the hanging of soulless contractors for our own army, and if among the many reforms which happily characterize the present administration of the War Department, the proper authorities will hang half a dozen of the miscreants who are revelling in ill-gotten wealth on Fifth Avenue, or Beacon street, at the expense of many a foot-sore soldier's happiness, and hang them on a pine tree in front of the "Journal" office, the "Journal" man—who does'nt believe in hanging—will write their obituaries for the special edification of those who go unhung. Speaking of these days of

"SHODDY,"

reminds us that there are shoddy men and women other than "army contractors." He was happy in his selection of a theme for story writing, who entitled his book "Days of Shoddy." While men and women wear shoddy apparel, unfortunately they are leading shoddy lives. In the army and out of it—especially out of it—each vies with the other in the extent and degree of fashionable folly and senseless pleasure that unfortunately mark the present hour as one of the most foolish and brainless extravagance in our American history. One half the nation is fighting the battles of constitutional liberty, while the other, with brainless head and jubilant heart, is lost in the intoxication of short-lived pleasures, at the end of which may come bitter, bitter weeping, and remorse. Pearls, diamonds, brocades, and operas, club-rooms, pleasure tours, fast horses and wine! Over against these are battle-fields, graves, hospitals, wounded and dying men, widowhood, orphan-

THE NEW YORK HERALD.

WHOLE NO. 10,073. NEW YORK, SATURDAY, APRIL 16, 1864.—WITH SUPPLEMENT. PRICE THREE CENTS.

APPALLING DISASTER IN THE HARBOR.

Explosion of a Boiler on Board the Gunboat Chenango.

Over Thirty of Her Crew Scalded Terribly.

Prompt Assistance of the Revenue Cutter Bronx, Gunboat Rose and Transport Tilley.

SCENES AT THE MARINE HOSPITAL, BROOKLYN.

DESCRIPTION OF THE VESSEL,

&c., &c., &c.

A most terrible accident occurred in the lower bay yesterday afternoon, owing to the explosion of one of the boilers of the United States gunboat Chenango, Lieutenant Commander T. S. Fillebrown. She was proceeding to the mooring buoys at the Horseshoe, for the purpose of correcting her compasses, and was to have taken the iron-clad Onondaga in tow this morning and gone to sea, Fortress Monroe being her destination. When opposite Fort Hamilton, at a quarter past four P. M., her port boiler suddenly exploded, blowing up the decks and severely scalding all connected with the engineer's department—thirty-three in all. One was blown overboard, but subsequently recovered, but badly injured; one has died, and the remainder are in a very critical state. Several of them will probably die. The United States revenue cutter Bronx, being in the vicinity, immediately repaired to the scene of disaster, and proceeded to the Quarantine, where she procured a number of physicians, and took them on board the Chenango to relieve the sufferers. The United States steam transport Tilley, Captain Bourne, from Alexandria, while coming up witnessed the explosion, and immediately went to the Chenango's assistance, doing a great deal of good. Also the United States steamer Rose, which was near at hand, rendered all the aid in her power. The Tilley and Rose and the cutter Bronx took her in tow and brought her to the Navy Yard.

Among those severely scalded are:—First Assistant Engineer Joseph N. Cahill, in charge; Second Assistant Engineer Albert S. Murray, and Second Assistant Engineer Frank P. Root.

When the Chenango left the Navy Yard the yards of the North Carolina were manned by order of Captain Meade, and three cheers were given in compliment to the crew of the new vessel. The salute was returned by the sailors on board the Chenango, and amidst loud and prolonged huzzahing the gunboat glided out into the stream and proceeded on her voyage down the bay. Hardly two hours had elapsed from the time of her departure when news of the shocking disaster was received at the Navy Yard, producing the most intense excitement among the seamen, and casting a deep gloom where all had been life and activity.

On arriving at the hospital we found quite a number of surgeons present, who were attending the injured men. Among the number we noticed Surgeons Smith, Breslan, Bates, Zeuzen, Rhoades, Bogert and others. The hospital steward, Mr. Currier, was exerting himself to the utmost, as were the nurses and attendants, as well as all the convalescent patients. The sailors were working like heroes to alleviate the agony of their shipmates.

It was reported that Lieutenant Commander Fillebrown was missing; but we know that he was uninjured, and wrote a letter to Commodore Radford after the explosion took place. Therefore he could not have been hurt at that time. He did not come on shore last night, which may explain the cause of the rumor.

The wounded men were transferred to the Rose as soon as possible, and she steamed up to the Navy Yard, to have them sent to the Marine Hospital. Commodore Radford immediately sent for all kinds of comfortable conveyances, and the men were sent up to the hospital as rapidly as circumstances would allow. The groans of these poor fellows were heartrending, and elicited the warmest sympathy from all who were present at the sad spectacle. Every exertion and every device that humane people could think of was put in requisition to alleviate the sufferings of the unfortunates, and a hundred hands were busy for some time in forwarding them to the place where the best of medical attendance was awaiting them.

At the hospital the scene was of the most intense excitement. About thirty noble men, in all stages of suffering and torture, were lying outstretched upon beds, their bodies a mass of raw and burning flesh—some screaming in intense agony, others moaning pitifully, while others were quiet and subdued, their blackened and swollen faces plainly showing the acute suffering within. As soon as they arrived they were stripped of their clothing and bathed in oil and lime water, and covered with a copious covering of flour, which kept the air from the raw flesh. Everything that medical skill and science could afford was done for the poor unfortunates. Seldom does one witness such a heart-rending scene. Men who but a few short hours ago were in the enjoyment of all that makes life happy, were now but a mass of living fire and agony. The cries of some of them were terrible. Some had lost their reason in consequence of the excruciating suffering they were undergoing. Others were hurriedly and feebly drawing their last life-breath. One lay a corpse, having died in being transferred from the Navy Yard to the hospital. We noticed one man's head which was so swollen that it might have been taken for the head of an enormous giant. One poor fellow, a landsman, uncomplainingly said to us, "Why did Heaven send such a calamity to us? I had just shipped. What, oh what, will my poor mother say?" Scarcely any of them could talk much—in fact so little that it was impossible to gain any reliable particulars of this sad accident. One young man told us that the vessel was terribly shattered, the spar deck as well as the hurricane deck being torn to fragments over the boiler. Further than this little could be learned. Scarcely a man could be found who knew the names of half a dozen persons on board of the ship at the time of the disaster, owing to the fact that the vessel had but recently been put in commission, and they had not become acquainted.

No list of names was sent on shore by the paymaster in the excitement, and the surgeons would not be able to obtain their names until some time to-day. It is the opinion of the surgeons that most of the sufferers will recover. Possibly some half a dozen will die. There are at least four of them who seem to be marked with death. It will require some thirty-six hours to ascertain who have inhaled sufficient steam to cause their death. Our reporter did not leave the hospital until a late hour, when all the severely injured had arrived, and were as comfortable as circumstances would allow.

—— Welsh, a fireman, residing in Water street, was taken to his residence, where he lies in a precarious condition.

The cause of the accident is at present unknown, and we cannot at this time pretend to account for it. It was impossible to learn the amount of steam pressure on the boilers, and this part of the details must remain in doubt until a future time.

The Chenango was a side-wheel steamer, known as a double-ender. She had an armament of ten guns, and was built by Jere. Simonson, at Greenpoint, L. I., and launched in 1863. The following are her dimensions:—

Length over all	240 feet.
Extreme breadth	35 feet.
Depth of hold	12 feet.
Tonnage	974 tons.

Her engines were built at the Morgan Iron Works, and had a fifty eight inch cylinder, with eight feet stroke. She had two of Martin's boilers, and was considered a fast vessel.

She was put in commission in February, 1864, and has been ready for sea several weeks, waiting only for her crew. She was destined for special service, and was a first class vessel of the kind.

The following is a list of her officers:—

Lieutenant Commander—T. S. Fillebrown.
Acting Master—William McGlain.
Acting Assistant Surgeon—David P. Goodhue.
Acting Assistant Paymaster—Bailey Hascall.
Paymaster's Clerk—Rufus Stephens.
Surgeon's Steward—Erskine B. Mudge.
Paymaster's Steward—John J. Corbitt.
Engineers—First Assistant, James N. Cahill; Second Assistant, Albert Murray; Acting Second Assistant, Frank P. Root; Acting Third Assistants, John White, James F. Sullivan.
Acting Ensigns—George B. Mott, F. G. Adams, James A. Crossman, Alfred S. Leighton.
Acting Master's Mates—D. F. McKenzie, G. H. Goodmanson, F. R. Jastebe.
Gunner—Hegman Peters.
Yeoman—James C. Hanson.
Master-at-Arms—F. W. Fuller.

THE FAIR.

Undiminished Success of the Exhibition—Nearly $35,000 Received Yesterday, &c.

The delightful weather attracted thousands to the Fair yesterday, and both buildings overflowed with visitors during the afternoon and evening. The interest felt in this great charitable enterprise, so far from being on the wane, seems rather to be in the zenith of its glory. If the same crowds flock to the doors next week the committee will have to change their determination of closing up finally on the 23d. Half the people who desire to see it have not yet done so, owing to a variety of causes. No premature resolution should deprive them of an opportunity of satisfying their wishes. Hundreds are likewise pouring into the city by every train from the rural districts. It would be worse than injudicious to send back such strangers ungratified. The committee, or some of its members, talk of having a grand five dollar day, for the especial benefit of the *haut ton*, the *bon ton* and all the other tons. Why not have it? The novelty of the idea would perhaps fill both buildings, capacious as they are, with people anxious to exhibit themselves and not particularly solicitous about the attendant expense.

All the extra admission places were liberally patronized.

THE CURIOSITY SHOP

in the second story still forms a great object of attraction. Among its rich variety of oddities, from an assortment of the old clothes of history to a Japanese mermaid, one always finds something new to interest. The mermaid is, of course, one of the most wonderful objects in nature or anywhere else, and is kept in a glass case. It has a head that is woolly, a chest that bespeaks the presence of lungs and the necessity of air; but it tapers to a tail that is very decidedly fishy. Curiosity shops make odd associations. Near to the mermaid is a magnificent bronze vase made in the time of Louis XIV., once the property of the great Earl of Chatham, and once used in a church as a baptismal font. Over this vase lies a hickory cane from the Hermitage home of Old Hickory, and on one end of the vase hangs a heavy haversack—a stout and serviceable leather bag that carried the rations of Charles XII. Over the way from this and turned towards it is the grand face of Napoleon from the cast taken after death. Under the brass nose of the Emperor, and between him and the relic of the Northern hero, is a nugget of gold from California that Professor Silliman values at forty thousand dollars.

One might moralize considerably over this odd juxtaposition of the past and the present in leather, brass and gold; but the crowd presses, a young lady declares—to the horror of all antiquarians—that the great Swede's haversack is "a disgusting thing," and we are borne on by the current out of the Curiosity Shop, casting a lingering look at that ancient tapestried chair that came from France during the French Revolution, and that looks as if it ought to have some stories to tell.

IN THE RESTAURANT

one may see that the thousands of angels, fays, fairies, sprites, sylphs, sylphides, &c., that make the Fair so brilliant with their presence, do not eat ambrosia, at least exclusively. Ice cream may be and often is an airy and immaterial diet; but oysters are real, and so is chicken salad, so are sandwiches, and even pies, especially mince. And all of these things are found and eaten in this well managed and well furnished restaurant. Nothing is so likely to astonish a visitor to the Fair as the perfect order that reigns in this department of it, though it is, especially near mealtimes, so full that one has to wait for a seat.

THE INDIANS

have been but slightly noticed since the opening, although they have proved a great attraction, and have been the means of adding immensely to the treasury. No feature, in fact, of the Fair is more successful than these Indians, who have introduced a most refreshing variety into the style of the human countenance, and who have also introduced several dances that must become the rage. One of them is the Raccoon dance. It has been said that the Jerusalem artichoke is so called because it doesn't come from Jerusalem and isn't an artichoke. In the same way the Raccoon dance, perhaps, has that name because it isn't a dance ex[illegible] any raccoon in it. Our knowledge of the [illegible] language is so slight that we couldn't see what [illegible] coon had to do with the performance; but it was, nevertheless, a performance full of life and spirit and with a wild, natural music, and rhythm wonderfully attractive. The Indians, it is said, perform so often in the day and night that the Fair to them is by no means a matter of joking. They are well kept, however, and eat plenty of tripe, even on Friday.

THE VOTE ON THE SWORD

was spirited yesterday. Nearly nine hundred votes were cast, and at the close of the polls McClellan was 533 ahead of Grant. The total vote was 9,637, which was divided as follows:—

McClellan	5,062
Grant	4,529
Scattering	46

—One of the voters paid $160 for an equal number of votes for Grant.

The receipts yesterday, up to three o'clock in the afternoon, from most of the departments of both buildings, amounted to $34,759 40. It is believed that the total receipts up to date exceed $600,000. A blundering contemporary foots up an aggregate of nearly one million dollars.

CINDERELLA AT NIBLO'S GARDEN.

The public must not forget Cinderella this afternoon at Niblo's Garden. Rumor has it that the pretty little fairy tale will be presented in the most finished manner as regards costume, scenery, &c.; but the fact that the performers will be exclusively children is decidedly the most interesting feature of the affair. Who will not desire to see the lovely Cinderella personified by a little Miss not out of her teens, and the *role* of the Prince enacted by a youth not much older. Miss Cropsey, a daughter of the artist, and Master Charlie Fremont, are the names of these two juvenile amateurs. The Herald will be done by a son of Prof. Morse, and the Queen by a beautiful little girl. We predict that Niblo's Garden will be crowded this afternoon, and that thousands will have to go away without seeing the performance. At two o'clock the curtain will rise. Go early and get a good seat.

THE COUNT JOANNES TO DO HIS SHARE.

The Count Joannes is to make his contribution to the Fair fund this evening, when he will deliver his lecture on "Napoleon and the French Empire," at Cooper Institute. The entertainment will wind up with a vote by the audience on the question "Shall his Excellency Abraham Lincoln or Major General Geo. B. McClellan be the next President of the United States?" The Count declares that the ladies shall have a vote, and that the affair will be conducted according to strict parliamentary rule, without the "Speaker" leaving the chair "to move a vote of expulsion of any member of the representatives of the people" who may happen to be present. The net proceeds will be handed over to the Treasurer of the Fair fund.

THE UNION SQUARE BRANCH—CHILDREN'S DEPARTMENT.

The entertainments of yesterday afternoon at the children's department delighted the young folks exceedingly. The hall was crowded with children. Mr. Seagrist, from the Hippotheatron, repeated his remarkable exhibition of Saturday last with his trained dogs, through the kindness of Mr. Platt, who, on both occasions, has refused to receive any compensation. The famous Punch and Judy from the Academy of Music, under the direction of Mr. Abiette, entertained the children for nearly an hour with its novel and comical performances.

News from San Francisco.

SAN FRANCISCO, April 14, 1864.

Arrived, ship James R. Keeler, from New York.

Business is very dull.

The weather has been very warm for several days.

There is no news.

The universal topic of conversation centres on the question what has caused the recent great advance in the price of gold in the Atlantic cities, for which our people are unable to account.

The Steamer Caledonia.

PORTLAND, April 15, 1864.

The steamer Caledonia, from Glasgow, sailed for New York last evening.

City Intelligence.

A FIVE CENT STAGE FARE.—The Bleecker street and Broadway line, running from Twenty-third street and Eighth avenue to the South ferry, has hoisted on the top of each of its stages a board, lettered in plain, large characters, with the words, "Fare Five Cents." This board presents a very respectable and honest appearance, and the stages of the line have been consequently very well patronized, as indeed they have always been. After nightfall yesterday, however, they suffered some in company with the extortionists, as many casual travellers on Broadway did not see, or could not read, the signboard.

SACRED CONCERT AT THE CHURCH OF THE IMMACULATE CONCEPTION.—A grand musical vespers and sacred concert will be given to-morrow evening at the Church of the Immaculate Conception, at Yonkers, under the direction of Mr. R. Gonzalez, assisted by a number of competent artists. The proceeds are to be applied for the benefit of the church.

THE FUNERAL SERVICES over the remains of the late A. A. Bovett, Superintendent of the Peoples' Line of Telegraph, took place yesterday afternoon, and were conducted by Rev. Dr. Osgood. A very large number of the friends of the deceased were present. The remains were forwarded last evening by the land route for Boston, escorted by a deputation of the operators of the line from this and other cities. The final ceremonies will take place at Beverly, Mass., where the remains will be

IMPORTANT FROM THE MISSISSIPPI.

Capture of Fort Pillow by the Rebels.

Reported Massacre of the White and Black Troops.

Women and Children Murdered in Cold Blood.

The Dead and Wounded Negroes Burned.

SKETCH OF THE FORT,

&c., &c., &c.

CAIRO, April 14, 1864.

On Tuesday morning the rebel General Forrest attacked Fort Pillow. Soon after the attack Forrest sent a flag of truce demanding the surrender of the fort and garrison, meanwhile disposing of his force so as to gain the advantage. Our forces were under command of Major Booth, of the Thirteenth Tennessee (United States) heavy artillery, formerly of the First Alabama cavalry.

The flag of truce was refused, and fighting resumed. Afterwards a second flag came in, which was also refused.

Both flags gave the rebels the advantage of gaining new positions.

The battle was kept up until three o'clock in the afternoon, when Major Booth was killed, and Major Bradford took command.

The rebels now came in swarms over our troops, compelling them to surrender.

Immediately upon the surrender ensued a scene which utterly baffles description. Up to that time comparatively few of our men had been killed; but, insatiate as fiends, bloodthirsty as devils incarnate, the rebels commenced an indiscriminate butchery of the whites and blacks, including those of both colors who had been previously wounded.

The black soldiers, becoming demoralized, rushed to the rear, the white officers having thrown down their arms.

Both white and black were bayoneted, shot or sabred. Even dead bodies were horribly mutilated, and children of seven and eight years and several negro women killed in cold blood. Soldiers, unable to speak from wounds, were shot dead, and their bodies rolled down the banks into the river. The dead and wounded negroes were piled in heaps and burned, and several citizens who had joined our forces for protection were killed or wounded.

Out of the garrison of six hundred but two hundred remained alive.

Among our dead officers are Captain Bradford, Lieuts. Barr, Ackersbrout, Wilson, Revel and Major Booth, all of the Thirteenth Tennessee cavalry.

Captain Poston and Lieutenant Lyon, Thirteenth Tennessee cavalry, and Captain Young, Twenty-fourth Missouri, Acting Provost Marshal, were taken prisoners.

Major Bradford was also captured, but is said to have escaped. It is feared, however, that he has been killed.

The steamer Platte Valley came up at about half-past three o'clock, and was hailed by the rebels under a flag of truce. Men were sent ashore to bury the dead and take aboard such of the wounded as the enemy had allowed to live. Fifty-seven were taken aboard, including seven or eight colored. Eight died on the way up. The steamer arrived here this evening, and was immediately sent to the Mound City Hospital to discharge her suffering cargo.

Among our wounded officers of colored troops are Captain Porter, Lieutenant Libberts and Adjutant Lemming.

Six guns were captured by the rebels and carried off, including two ten pounder Parrotts and two twelve-pounder howitzers. A large amount of stores was destroyed or carried away.

The intention of the rebels seemed to be to evacuate the place, and move on or towards Memphis.

The Position of Fort Pillow on the Mississippi.

Diagram of the Fort.

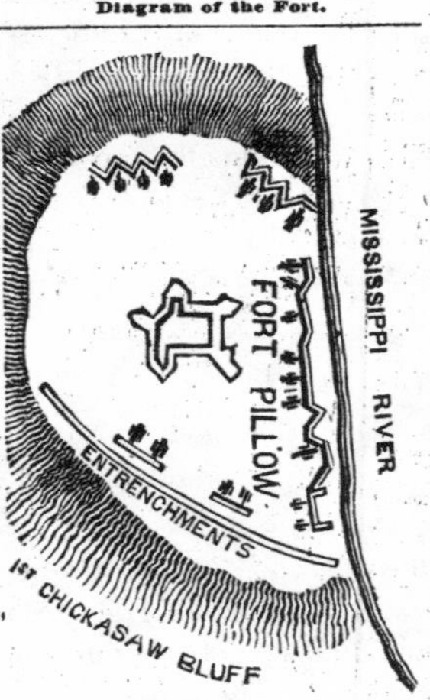

Fort Pillow.

LOCATION AND DESCRIPTION OF THE FORT.

Fort Pillow is one of the formidable forts constructed by the rebels on the Mississippi river soon after the commencement of the war. It is situated on the first Chickasaw Bluffs, on the Tennessee shore of the Mississippi river, about seventy miles above Memphis. The course of the bluffs is nearly north and south. Above them the river makes a bend at nearly right angles, the upper end of the bluffs being just at the beginning of the bend. At this point a small stream, called Coal creek, flows into the Mississippi, separating the bluffs from the bottom and beyond. The position is shown in the accompanying diagram. From the stream the bluffs rise abruptly to the height of about a hundred feet, and at all points are very difficult of ascent. Along the base of these bluffs and about twenty feet above the level of the river, the rebels constructed a line of powerful works about three-fourths of a mile in length. The glacis is at the highest possible angle for earth to be placed, and could be ascended only in places where the men had dug small steps or footholes. At regular intervals along the whole distance the work was properly bastioned, most of the bastions being built of sandbags, planking and rammed clay. Some of them were designed for mounting two guns, but most of them for but one. All of the guns were protected by embrasures, though none of them were casemated. The walls of the embrasures were constructed in the strongest manner possible, one of them, and in fact the entire bastion, being of granite, chiselled and built up with great care and neatness. The guns were mounted on firm plank floorings, and commanded the entire river between the fort and Craighead Point, on the opposite shore. The batteries were built on a bench at the base of the cliff, upwards of half a mile in length by fifty yards in width. Several springs gush from the base of the bluff, and afforded clear water to the men within the fort. Four bombproof and well constructed magazines were placed at intervals in rear of the batteries, in the least exposed positions. Near some of the guns were holes in which the men could retire whenever threatened by the bursting shells from the Union gunboats operating against the fort. The slope of the face of the bluffs forms an angle of fifty or fifty-five degrees. On a bench or shelf about half way up the bluffs there was a work mounting two guns, which swept the river in their front. On the summit of the bluffs there was a series of extensive field works, extending in the aggregate from five to seven miles, and all provided with a ditch in front. These works followed a zigzag course over a series of ridges and hills that stretch back from the river into the interior, and they extended from Coal creek, on the northern point of the bluff, to a point below the lowest of the water batteries. A few batteries were constructed on the summit of the bluff, one overlooking the river and mounting six guns; one of them a hundred and twenty-pounder of recent manufacture. The road from the river to the top of the elevation is cut in the side of the cliff, and has a steady though not steep ascent throughout. Steps for footmen had been cut in the bluff at various points. The trees for half a mile in the rear of the works had been cut down by the rebels to destroy all chance of shelter for an approaching enemy.

EVACUATION BY THE REBELS IN 1862.

Fort Pillow was the third fortified point on the Mississippi river, descending from Cairo, which yielded to the advance of the Union arms. After retiring from Columbus in February, 1862, the rebels halted at Island No. 10, and for a time stayed our progress toward the Gulf. Simultaneously with the battle of Pittsburg Landing this second stronghold was taken, and the insurgent forces fell back to the first Chickasaw Bluffs, nearly a hundred miles below, and completed those powerful works described above, which had already been begun, and named Fort Pillow. On the 4th of June this place was evacuated also, and the grand highway of the great valley of the West was again open from St. Louis to Memphis, after a fourteen months' blockade.

A fleet of Union gunboats had been stationed in the river a short distance above Fort Pillow, anxiously awaiting a propitious moment for moving upon the works. On the 10th of May, 1862, the rebel gunboats came past the fort and attacked the Union fleet. A desperate naval engagement ensued, in which both sides sustained considerable damage. But finally the rebel gunboats were driven off, and ours justly claimed the victory. Affairs then assumed a quiescent state, and another month was passed in idleness, with an almost daily rumor that the position was being evacuated. On Sunday, June 1, a deserter came from the fort and stated that the upper battery was being dismantled, and that the land pieces were soon to be moved away. It was currently believed in the fort that the destruction would be completed by evening, and that the whole garrison would leave by their transports, under cover of the night. The story [illegible] generally credited throughout the fleet, and Commodore Davis prepared to fall upon the rear of the retreating rebels and take immediate possession of the works. [illegible] reconnoissance was made by one of the tugs to within a short distance of the fort; but, though no shots were fired, it was thought that a considerable force was still in possession, and prepared to dispute any advance that might be made against it.

On Tuesday afternoon three of the rams were sent down to reconnoitre, and on nearing the fort were fired into by the rebel gunboats. They then returned, and in about an hour's time were followed by the rebel boat Jeff. Thompson. The latter passed around Craighead Point, and came speedily within range of the Cairo, the foremost boat of the Union fleet. Six or eight shots were fired at the Jeff. Thompson, eliciting no reply from the latter, which soon turned and went back to the fort. Observations made by the rams convinced Commodore Davis that the fort was nearly, but not quite, deserted. Tuesday night was passed in listening for explosions; but not a sound was heard.

Next morning a little tug proceeded down close to the fort, and, returning at dark, reported that the works were evidently evacuated. As it was then too late to reach the fort until long after nightfall, the movement was delayed till morning. About seven o'clock P. M. two explosions were heard in quick succession. Two or three like explosions were heard previous to ten o'clock P. M., and several others near morning. Several fires were seen through the trees on Craighead Point. They were evidently in the neighborhood of the fort. The commander of the infantry forces on the southern shore of Craighead Point sent word to Commodore Davis late in the afternoon of Wednesday that the fortifications were deserted, and the fires and explosions during the night confirmed the opinion of all that Fort Pillow was evacuated. On Thursday morning the Union gunboats moved down past Craighead Point, and then outward towards the frowning cliff in their front. The landing was soon reached, and a party of soldiers, springing on shore, climbed the parapet of the works, and unfurled the Union flag for the first time from Fort Pillow. A cheer rose from the advancing gunboats and transports, and in a short time the rebel fortifications were alive with Union soldiers.

THE LATEST NEWS.

Additional Particulars of the Fight.

CAIRO, April 15, 1864.

No boats have been allowed to leave here for points below Columbus since the first news of the Fort Pillow affair.

Several of the guns captured by Forrest at Fort Pillow were spiked before falling into his hands. Others were turned upon Gunboat No. 7, which, having fired some three hundred rounds and exhausted her ammunition, was compelled to withdraw. Although a tin-clad, she received but slight injury.

Gen. Lee arrived and assumed the command at the beginning of the battle, previous to which Gen. Chalmers directed the movements. Forrest, with the main force, retired after the fight to Brownsville, taking with him the captured funds.

Many of those who had escaped from the works and hospitals, who desired to be treated as prisoners of war, as the rebels said, were ordered to fall into line, and when they had formed were inhumanly shot down.

Of three hundred and fifty colored troops not more than fifty-six escaped the massacre, and not one officer that commanded them survives. Only four officers of the Thirteenth Tennessee escaped death.

The loss of the Thirteenth Tennessee is eight hundred killed; the remainder were wounded and captured.

General Chalmers told this correspondent that, although it was against the policy of his government to spare negro soldiers or their officers, he had done all in his power to stop the carnage. At the same time he believed it was right.

Another officer said our white troops would have been protected had they not been found on duty with negroes.

While the rebels endeavored to conceal their loss, it was evident that they suffered severely. Colonel Reed, commanding a Tennessee regiment, was mortally wounded. There were two or three well filled hospitals at a short distance in the country.

While the steamer Platte Valley lay under flag of truce, taking on board our wounded, some of the rebel officers, and among them General Chalmers, went on board, and some of our officers showed them great deference, drinking with them and showing them other marks of courtesy.

Singular Resurrection of Two Negro Soldiers.

CAIRO, April 15, 1864.

Two negro soldiers, wounded at Fort Pillow, were buried by the rebels, but afterwards worked themselves out of their graves. They were among those brought up in the Platte Valley, and are now in hospital at Mound City.

The officers of the Platte Valley receive great credit from the military authorities for landing at Fort Pillow at imminent risk and taking our wounded on board, and for their kind attentions on the way up.

The Bloodthirstiness of the Rebels.

ST. LOUIS, April 15, 1864.

A correspondent who was on board the steamer Platte Valley, at Fort Pillow, gives even a more appalling description of the fiendishness of the rebels than our Cairo despatches. Many of our wounded were shot in the hospital. The remainder were driven out, and the hospital was burned.

On the morning after the battle the rebels went over the field, and shot the negroes who had not died from their wounds.

ANOTHER ATTACK ON PADUCAH.

Activity of the Rebels in Kentucky.

One Division Under Buford Operating on the Ohio.

Threatened Gigantic Raid by Morgan.

IMPORTANT MOVEMENTS,

&c., &c., &c.

Mr. DeB. Randolph Keim's Despatch.

CAIRO, April 12, 1864.

The rumors received yesterday, and which we have been prone to disbelieve, come better founded in official messages. No attack as was reported has yet taken place, though a large number of rebel troops have returned to the vicinity of Paducah and are threatening the place.

A heavy reinforcement of troops is about leaving here to strengthen the garrison at Paducah. With all their apparent intentions to attack, it is doubtful whether Forrest will undertake the job again. If he does, there can be but one result.

The Press Despatches.

CAIRO, April 14, 1864.

Another demand was made this afternoon for the surrender of Paducah, giving one hour for the removal of women and children. Colonel Hicks declined to surrender, and prepared to meet the anticipated attack.

LOUISVILLE, April 14, 1864.

Colonel Pratt telegraphs that he is informed that Paducah has been attacked, and that the town is full of rebels.

The Operations of the Rebels.

It has for some time been stated that General Forrest has been threatening Paducah and Columbus, and other accounts have reported that he was operating in front of Fort Pillow. Still other despatches have reported that General Buford commands the rebels in the vicinity of the last named place, and that Forrest is in Kentucky. Paducah is at the mouth of the Tennessee river, where it empties into the Ohio, above Cairo, and Columbus is on the Mississippi river, below Cairo. The distance between these places overland is inconsiderable—although much greater by the river—and could easily be marched in a day by mounted forces. The rebels, having the inner lines, could therefore move from one place to another before transports [illegible] the water route.

It would, however, be impossible for forces operating before Fort Pillow, which is a short distance above Memphis, to reach either Columbus or Paducah in any such time as they have been reported to have so moved. It is, therefore, perfectly plain that the attacking party at Paducah and Columbus is entirely separate from that moving upon Fort Pillow.

The following order clearly shows who was at that date in command of a division of the rebels at Mayfield, which is a few miles east of Columbus and midway between that place and Paducah:—

GENERAL ORDER—NO. 2.
HEADQUARTERS, SECOND DIVISION, FORREST'S CAVALRY,
MAYFIELD, Ky., March 28, 1864.

The general commanding returns to the officers and troops of this division his congratulations upon the success which has thus far *attended the campaign in Kentucky*. The hardships you bore upon a march almost unprecedented, from Libbie station to Paducah, in a week, the devotion you have exhibited to the cause of freedom, and valor in the attack upon Fort Paducah, calls for the highest admiration and praise of your commander. At the very doors of their homes some of your comrades laid down their lives to rescue Kentucky from the iron heel of abolition despotism and the vote of the negro. Among those whose faces are gone from us forever we are forced to pay a lasting regret to the memory of one brave, courteous and beloved, whose merits as a citizen, as a friend and as a soldier we all felt and appreciated. He fell as a soldier desires to fall—at the head of his command—a hero, regretted by all. Colonel A. P. Thompson, Second regiment, commanding Third brigade, will long be remembered by all who know his noble deeds and heroic death. With a force less than that of the enemy, within a stockade, and in an exposed condition with skirmishers, silenced his guns, caused one of his gunboats to withdraw from the action, fearful of the accuracy of your fire; captured and destroyed immense stores, quartermaster, commissary and ordnance; inflicted upon him the loss of twenty-seven killed, from seventy to eighty wounded, besides capturing sixty-four prisoners, our own loss being ten killed and forty wounded. *The General commanding feels proud of the division. He relies upon your courage, fortitude and discipline to hold this portion of the State of Kentucky, aided as you will be by the friends now flocking to your ranks.*

C. A. BUFORD,
Brigadier General P. A. C. S.

Official—THOS. M. CROWDU, Captain, A. A. G.

It is also certain that the same rebel officer is in command in the same vicinity at the present time by the following correspondence, which took place at Columbus, Ky., on the morning of the 13th inst:—

HEADQUARTERS, CONFEDERATE STATES ARMY,
BEFORE COLUMBUS, Ky., April 13, 1864.

TO THE COMMANDER OF THE UNITED STATES FORCES, Columbus, Ky.—

Fully capable of taking Columbus and its garrison by force, I desire to avoid shedding blood. I therefore demand the unconditional surrender of the forces under your command. Should you surrender, the negroes now in arms will be returned to their masters; should I be compelled to take the place by force, no quarter will be shown negro troops whatever; white troops will be treated as prisoners of war. I am, sir, yours,

A. BUFORD, Brigadier General.

To this the commandant of the forces replied as follows:—

HEADQUARTERS OF POST, COLUMBUS, KY.,
April 13, 1864.

Brigadier General BUFORD, Commanding forces before Columbus, Ky.—

GENERAL—Your communication of this date has come to hand. In reply, I would state that, being placed by my government with adequate force to hold and repel all enemies from my post, surrender is out of the question.

I am, General, very respectfully,

WM. HUDSON LAWRENCE,
Col. Thirty-fourth N. J. Vols., Commanding Post.

Officers who arrived at Cairo on the Maria Dunning on the evening of the 13th report the enemy as having left the vicinity of Columbus. Doubtless this explains the attack upon Paducah. Buford, finding he could not take Columbus, at once moved his forces, by way of Mayfield, to Paducah, which place is now threatened by the rebel troops. He is, without doubt, the rebel commander in that district, while General Forrest is operating in person in the vicinity of Memphis.

Another feature of the rebel movement is set forth in the following extract from a paper published in Kentucky:—

[From the Louisville Journal, April 13.]

A distinguished officer in the federal service, who is now in command of a division of the Army of the Mississippi in Georgia, has written to us to say that our warnings of an intended rebel raid in this State have been most proper. He feels confident that it will be made on the most gigantic scale, and require extraordinary exertions to repel it. Deserters, our secret service men, and rebel papers, all concur in the one idea that Longstreet aided by Breckinridge, Buckner *and Morgan*, will burst into the State, while at the same time Johnston will threaten our advance before Chattanooga to keep our whole army employed there. *John H. Morgan is at this present time somewhere in the neighborhood of Abingdon, Virginia, fitting out and remounting his command.* This fact is almost indisputable, from circumstances which we will state. His men went from the front in Georgia some time since by rail to Richmond, and he refused a donation from the ladies of Columbia, S. C., of money to fit out his command, *in a letter which was dated at Lynchburg*, saying "the government had kindly undertaken to furnish all necessary equipments for his intended expedition." Though we do not know exactly where the blow will be struck, or in what numbers the rebels will be prepared to assail us, the "intended expedition" must be set down as a fixed fact.

This confirms the following statement, published yesterday by us, taken from a rebel paper:—

[From the Raleigh (N. C.) Confederate.]

General Morgan is about to undertake one of the boldest expeditions he has ever yet made, which, if successful, will be productive of great good to our cause.

It is, therefore, perfectly plain that three distinct rebel cavalry forces are already busily engaged in the military division of the Mississippi, each acting independently of the other.

Preparations to Resist the Enemy.

From other sources we learn that reliable information reached Cairo that Forrest, with a very heavy force from Mayfield, was again advancing on Paducah. Colonel Hicks and force had once more retired within the fort, and telegraphed there for reinforcements, which were promptly sent.

The following order has been issued in reference to a portion of the Seventeenth army corps, which has arrived there from Vicksburg and encamped:—

GENERAL ORDERS—NO. 5.
HEADQUARTERS OF THE POST OF CAIRO,
April 10, 1864.

In accordance with instructions received from the district headquarters, the troops belonging to the Seventeenth army corps who may be temporarily at this post will be encamped on grounds designated by the General commanding the district. The senior officer present with such troops will command the camp. Regiments and detachments will be governed and report as if in the field. A strong camp guard will be kept. Persons and trade will be excluded at the discretion of the commanding officer. Intoxicating drinks, however, are not to be admitted in any case. The duties and privileges of sutlers belonging to the command are to be as in the field. The officer commanding will order that not more than two enlisted men to each company shall be absent from camp at one time, nor more than two hours; that no passes be given to men who have been guilty of drunkenness or disorderly conduct. All keepers of drinking saloons will be required to close their establishments at twelve o'clock every night, and will not open them until six in the morning. All men found outside the camp without properly approved passes will be arrested by the Provost guard.

The Provost Marshal will see that this order is carried into effect in regard to soldiers being in the city without properly approved passes, and in the closing of all saloons at the time mentioned.

By order of Colonel JOHN I. KINAKER,
One Hundred and Twenty-second Illinois infantry, commanding post.
JNO. H. MUNROE, Assistant Adjutant General.

THE LATEST NEWS.

The Rebels Shelled Out of Paducah, &c.

CAIRO, April 15, 1864.

The attack on Paduch yesterday proved to be a mere raid for plunder made by a couple of hundred men, who were shelled out by the fort and gunboats after occupying a portion of the city in squads. About noon they left, taking away a number of horses and considerable plunder, and leaving behind about six of their wounded. No one was hurt on our side.

THE ARMY OF THE POTOMAC.

Soldiers Killed by Guerillas—Sudden Dash of Mosby Near Bristoe Station—Capture of Union Troops—Expedition to Occoquan—The Mud Dried Up—Nothing to Hinder An Advance of the Army, &c., &c.

OUR SPECIAL CORRESPONDENCE.

ALEXANDRIA, Va., April 15, 1864.

About ten o'clock this morning privates Samuel Cook and Thomas B. Ford, of Company D, Tenth regiment Pennsylvania Reserves, while on duty as guard to a wood hauling party, were killed by a party of guerillas, about a mile from Manassas.

Colonel J. W. Fisher, commanding the brigade of Pennsylvania Reserves stationed at that point, immediately sent a detachment of the Thirteenth Pennsylvania cavalry in search of the marauders, but I have not learned with

Early this morning Colonel Mosby, at the head of about five hundred rebel cavalry, made his appearance on the line of the Orange and Alexandria Railroad, near Bristoe Station, so suddenly as to take by surprise the patrol for the protection of the road between that place and Manassas. From twenty to twenty-five of our soldiers were captured and carried into captivity. The rebels went away in the direction of Fredericksburg.

Last night Lieutenant Colonel Gustin, with a detachment of the Twelfth regiment Pennsylvania reserves, of Colonel Fisher's command, went on an expedition to Occoquan and vicinity. The party returned this morning with five prisoners, two of whom, named Henry T. Tillett and John Marshall, belonged to the Fifteenth Virginia cavalry. These men were captured at the house of one Wm. Moore, a short distance from Occoquan. Some horses were also captured, having U. S. in large and distinct characters branded upon their shoulders. These horses were brought to Manassas with the prisoners; but Mrs. Moore came on after them, and claimed that they were her husband's property, were raised by him from colthood, and that the U. S. were her husband's initials, and stood for Wm. Moore. Colonel Fisher did not see the similarity in names and initials, and retained the property and sent the prisoners to Washington.

Having left the Army of the Potomac at eleven o'clock A. M. to-day, I can speak knowingly of the prospects. The roads are so dried as to allow the freest locomotion, and there is nothing to hinder an early movement. The streams have all assumed their wonted dimensions, and the roads are passable, to say the least.

Successful Union Raid in Virginia.

BALTIMORE, April 15, 1864.

The *American* has a letter from Point Lookout, which says General Hinks, commanding that post, returned on Thursday from an expedition across the Potomac into Virginia, having captured fifty thousand dollars' worth of tobacco on its way from Richmond to Baltimore, and also having taken prisoners a gang of blockade runners.

The United States Ship Mohican—A Long Cruise, &c.

PHILADELPHIA, April 15, 1864.

The United States steamship Mohican, from Brazil via St. Thomas, which sailed hence October 23, 1862, has been at sea two hundred and eighty-two days. She sailed under steam alone 13,344 miles, and under steam and sail 36,381 miles. All are well on board of her. Captain A. S. Glisson is her commander.

Conclusion of the South Street Tragedy.

BROOKS, THE COLORED MAN, SENT TO THE STATE PRISON FOR FOUR YEARS—OTHER SENTENCES, ETC.

COURT OF GENERAL SESSIONS.

Before City Judge A. D. Russel

APRIL 15.—In the Court of Sessions this morning, City Judge A. D. Russel on the bench, a number of convicted prisoners were brought up for sentence. Among them was Daniel Brooks, the quadroon, who on Friday had been convicted of manslaughter in the third degree, on an indictment charging him with having caused the death of William Smith, a bartender in Mr. McKinley's saloon, at the corner of Fulton and South streets, by shooting him with a pistol on the morning of the 2d of February last. The court room was crowded with spectators, among whom were a number of colored people, who had come down to see Brooks previous to his departure for the State Prison. The wife and children of the prisoner were also in court.

BROOKS SENTENCED.

When Brooks was called to the bar and asked by Mr. John Sparks, Clerk of the Court, what he had to say why judgment should not then be pronounced against him, according to law, he smiled at the Judge, shook his head and said he had nothing to say.

Judge Russel, addressing the prisoner, said:—Brooks, you were charged with the homicide of William Smith; you were ably defended and tried by a jury of your own selection, by whom a verdict was found against you of manslaughter in the third degree. The circumstances detailed by the witnesses on the stand show you did not act as a good citizen should have done, and as your companions did, who immediately left, as it was your duty to have done after the altercation in the street. They ran away, and did not return. After the discussion Smith ran into the store and you after him, and then the pistol was fired. In view of all the circumstances of the case it becomes my duty, for the welfare of the community at large, to impose on you the highest punishment the law provides. The sentence of the court is that you be confined in the State prison for four years. Brooks heard his sentence pronounced with the greatest composure.

OTHER SENTENCES.

Louis Andressen, who pleaded guilty on Friday last of receiving goods, knowing them to have been stolen from the store of Messrs. H. B. Claflin & Co., was sent to the State prison for two years.

Louis Sasa, a German, who had pleaded guilty of grand larceny, was also sent to the State prison for two years.

The court then adjourned until Monday next at eleven o'clock.

MILITARY GOODS!!

G. W. WILEY, & CO.,

MARKET STREET,

One Door Above News Depot,

CHATTANOOGA, TENN.

ARE receiving daily a LARGE ASSORTMENT of—

OFFICERS' FINE

Regulation Uniforms,

Light Summer Blouses;

French Flannel Pants;

New Regulation Hats and Caps;

Furnishing Goods;

Regulation Swords,

For Line and Field Officers.

English Sabres, Sword Belts,

Sashes, Wreaths, Bugles,

Gauntlets, Gloves,

Haversacks, Canteens,

Sole Leather Valices,

Pellissier Bags,

Trunks and Trimmings,

Officers and Veteran Badges,

Non-Commisioned Chevrons. Spurs,

Presentation Goods

of all descriptions.

GEO. W. WILEY & CO.

Chattanooga, March 18, 1864. tf.

Great Thoroughfare!

THE

BALTIMORE & OHIO RAILROAD.

THIS is the safest shortst and quickest route from Chattanooga to

Washington,

Baltimore

Philadelphia,

New York,

And other points East The Road is entirely safe.

☞ No change of cars. from VVheeling to Baltimore. 3tf

GARDEN SEEDS.

AN assortment of Garden Seeds from the *PENN. RELIEF ASSOCIATION FOR EAST TENNESSEE*, will soon be received at the rooms of the *United States Sanitary Commission* in Chattanooga, for distribution to citizens of the vicinity. Families of Loyal persons and of those who are in the service of the Government will be first supplied.

Applications for seeds may be made to the Commission in writing, stating the name of the applicant., residence, number of persons in the family, amount of land to be cultivated, and the kinds and quantities of seeds needed.

☞ Address, Agent U. S. Sanitary Commission, Chattanooga, Tenn.

March 13th, 1864. tdf.

WINNIE HOUSE.

COR. 3d St. & BROADWAY, CINCINNATI, OHIO.

By MRS. MARY J. HOOD.

Persons visiting Cincinnati, will find this House as convenient to the business portions of the city and prices as reasonable, as the times will admit

THE

DAILY GAZETTE

WILL CONTAIN THE

LATEST WAR AND POLITICAL

NEWS.

PRICE ONE COPY FIVE CENTS.

Liberal Discounts made to Dealers.

MILITARY GOODS!!

SCOTT, KEEN & CO.,

ARMY CLOTHIERS,

WILL KEEP CONSTANTLY ON HAND AT HEADQUARTERS

OF THE

ARMIES

OF THE

Cumberland and Tennessee,

A LARGE ASSORTMENT OF

OFFICERS' FINE DRESS AND FATIGUE

UNIFORMS,

DOESKIN, KERSEY, BEAVER, CORDUROY AND FLANNEL PANTS,

LINEN AND MERINO UNDER SHIRTS AND DRAWERS,

VALISES, PELISIERS AND HAVERSACKS,

CLOTH, BEAVER & FLANNEL BLOUSES,

CLOTH AND BEAVER JACKETS,

SWORDS, SASHES AND BELTS,

FINE WOOL OVER SHIRTS,

BOOTS AND SHOES,

HATS AND CAPS,

RUBBER GOODS,

GLOVES, GUANTLETS, etc., etc.

SCOTT, KEEN & CO.,

Chattanooga, Tenn.,

Cleveland, Tenn.,

Bridgeport, Ala.,

Huntsville, Ala.,

Corner Sixth and Main Streets, Louisville, Ky.

18 Public Square, Nashville, Tenn.

Market Street, Chattanooga.

THE ELEGANT WAR MEMENTO.

ANNALS

OF THE

ARMY

OF THE

CUMBERLAND.

FOUR EDITIONS SOLD IN FOUR MONTHS—THE FIFTH EDITION IN PRINT.

"I have received and examined your beautiful work, 'Annals of the Army of the Cumberland.'—It exceeds my highest expectation, as an elegant memento of our Army, and you have my hearty thanks and earnest wishes for its success."

Maj.-Gen. WM. S. ROSECRANS.

"I am indeed rejoiced to hear of the success of your book. It was undertaken for a noble purpose, and deserves the unbounded patronage of the people of the whole country."

Maj.-Gen. GEO. H. THOMAS.

"Your book is a beautiful memento of our Army, and I hope it will receive, what it justly merits, the liberal support of the Army, and of friends at home."

Maj.-Gen. JNO. M. PALMER.

THIS BEAUTIFUL AND POPULAR WORK is now being sold, from Maine to California, and has been sent to England, as a sample of an American War Book. No volume of the war, nor for years previous has been so well received, by the press and the public, as has this.

A limited number of copies of the last edition has just been received in Chattanooga, it containing a very valuable addition—to-wit:

THE CHATTANOOGA CAMPAIGN,

AND THE BATTLE OF CHICAMAUGA,

With an elegant Map, etc.

The work is now complete, as the Annals of the Cumberland, under Major-General Rosecrans.

A more beautiful and appreciative gift, from the soldier to his family, at home, or to friends, cannot be found, at double the cost. They will esteem it because of its beauty as well as its peculiar relation to the donor. And it is an undying record of patriotism for each soldiers family, that will live to succeeding generations.

Subscribers, and all soldiers desiring the work, will apply to the authors agent, at Chattanooga, near the Post office.

Also, for sale, the elegant pamphlet: SPIES AND REBEL EMISSARRES OF THE ARMY OF THE CUMBERLAND.

And also, the New and Elegant Pamphlet defending the Army of the Cumberland, entitled—

"Chicamauga, the Price of Chattanooga."

Also, Steel Plates of Generals and Staff Officers.

Chattanooga, March 16th, 1864. 3tf

DAILY GAZETTE JOB OFFICE

Is prepared to do all kinds of

Plain and Ornamental

JOB PRINTING

In the latest styles.

LETTER HEADS,

ARMY BLANKS,

BILL HEADS,

PROGRAMMES,

HAND BILLS,

CIRCULARS

CARDS

ETC., ETC.

TERMS, CASH.

OFFICE OVER THE POST OFFICE.

EMBALMING THE DEAD

DR. PRUNK,

Offers his improved method of

EMBALMING BODIES.

IT RESTORES

THE NATURAL

COLOR, ARRESTS

DECOMPOSITION,

AND EFICTUALLY

ERADICATES ALL INFECTION WITHOUT

MUTILATION,

and leaving the Corps free from all unpleasant oder and in a fit conditon for

Home Obsequies.

Bodies can be embalmed even after they have been interred for weeks, and then shipped in wooden boxes, saving the expense of Metalic cases.

TO OBTAIN DECEASED FRIENDS!

Address DR. PRUNE who will give information promptly, at Chattanooga Tenn., Box No. 18.

METALIC CASES AND ZINC COFFINS on hand.

☞ OFFICE No. 61 Union Street, Nashville, Tenn.

Branch Office, Market Street, opposite Military Prison, Chattanooga.

D. H. PRUNK, M. D.

March 15, 1864. 6m*

DRY GOODS,

R. CHANDLER, of Chattanooga. S. I. KNIGHT, of Nashville.	JAS. CAMERON, of Chattanooga. CHAS. T. GRIER of Etna

A LARGE

AND

COMPLETE ASSORTMENT

OF

Foreign & Domestic

DRY GOODS!

CAMERON, KNIGHT & CO'S,

S. E. Cor. College St. & Square,

NASHVILLE, TENNESSEE.

We take pleasure in informing our friends and the public generally, that we are now receiving our

SPRING AND SUMMER STOCK OF DRY GOODS

which has been selected with great care, from the importers direct in New York and Philadelphia markets, and which we now offer to citizens of East Tennessee and North Georgia, at a small advance. Our stock consists of

Prints,
Brown Domestic,
Bleached Domestic,
Irish Linens,
Lawns,
Bed Ticking,
Denim,
Hickory Stripe,
Cotton Check,
Gingham,
Flannels,
Poplins,
De Laines,
Foulards,
Check Mohairs,
Check Valencia,
Barages,
Gradanines,
French Chintzs,
English Calicoes,
Mozambiques,
Colored Alpacas,
Black Silks,
Fancy Dress Silks,
Foulard Silks,
Shawls,
Table Cloths,
Napkins,
Hoop Skirts,
Hosiery,
Gloves,
Pins,
Needles,
Threads,
Trimmings and Linings of every description.

Also, a fine assortment of Jeans, Cassimeres, Doe Skin, Broad Cloth, Linen, Duck, Linen Drill, and Marsailes for Gentlemen's wear.

We would request the attention of merchants to call and examine our Wholesale Rooms.

SPECIAL NOTICE.

Particular attention is given to filling orders by mail. All orders must come *approved by the necess Board of trade, or officer in command of the Post*, and also be accompanied by the CASH to insure a speedy delivery.

CAMERON, KNIGHT & CO.,

S. E. Cor. College St. & Square

[Wm. S. & S. Eakin & Co's old stand.]

March 16 1864. 3tf

SUPPLEMENT
TO THE
SOUTH CAROLINIAN.

Columbia, S. C, Saturday April 23, 1864.

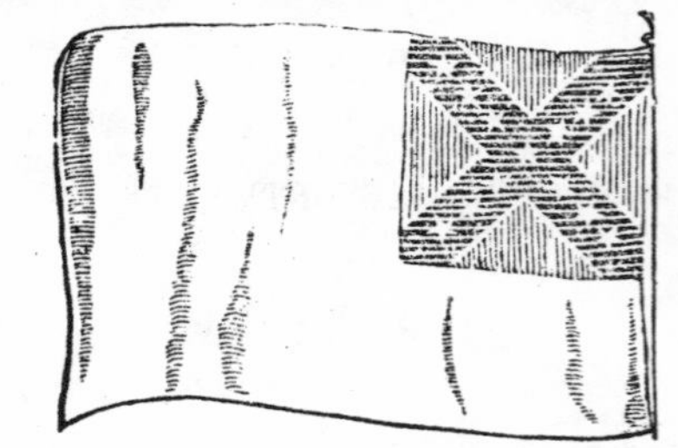

Grand Demonstration
IN HONOR OF
GEN. HAMPTON'S TROOPS!

STIRRING SPEECHES
BY
DR. PALMER, GEN. HAMPTON & COL GARY!
The Barbecue!
BANNERS, BOOTHS & BEAUTY!

The presence of a large number of soldiers in Columbia having given to our citizens the opportunity of displaying the esteem in which they hold their brethren of the camp, the chance was at once appropriated by the ladies, and a barbecue in honor of the returned members of HAMPTON'S Legion was unanimously resolved upon. Meetings were called by the fair enthusiasts, and active preparations immediately set afoot to make the *fete* as brilliant a one as possible. It was decided that a committee of gentlemen should be appointed to assist in carrying out the conceptions of the gentle patriots. By this committee, the following sub committees were named: Messrs. DeSaussure and Johnston to request Dr. Palmer to welcome the soldiers in an address; Dr. Parker, Col. Sims and Col. Davis to superintend the arrangements of the table; Messrs. McKenzie, Heise, Wright and Col. Childs to superintend the barbecue; Messrs. Wright, Wells and D P. McDonald to act as a committee on supplies; Messrs. Johnston, Brown and Arthur on finances; Col. Childs, Sims, Davis and Dr. Parker to provide music; and Messrs DeSaussure and Johnston to act as a committee on invitations. It will be seen, by these systematic proceedings, that the intention was that nothing should be omitted which might insure success, and we are happy to state that the most complete success was attained. Every body unites in declaring that a more magnificent tribute to our soldiers has never yet been laid before them.

The festival, of course, was not confined to the Legion alone. All officers and soldiers in Columbia, and all who had been honorably discharged, were invited to dine with their gallant brethren in arms.

The day appropriated for the festival dawned as if nature herself was in keeping for the occasion—and the dame donated from her wardrobe twelve as fairy spring hours as ever graced the necklace of the season.

Bright and early the ladies were all alive to the business of the *fete* Wagons loaded with provisions, evergreens and flags, servants with sundries, gentlemen lovers, and husbands with hammer, nails and string were on hand, or wending their way, and long before noon, the interior of the broad enclosure at the Lunatic Asylumn which, by reason of its high brick walls and convenient dimensions, had been selected for the purpose, was a scene of busy enterprise and ingenuity. The hour announced for the addresses was one o'clock, and the enclosure rapidly began to fill. Ladies and gentlemen who had contributed were admitted freely, others were provided with complimentary tickets, while soldiers one and all were gladly welcomed without restraint.

The scene on entering was striking, if not beautiful, for the eye could rest scarcely anywhere without being attracted by some pleasing device which woman's taste had discovered was required to fill a niche. From one of the centre windows of the Asylum was suspended a large Confederate flag. From poles and trees were suspended flags. The ladies wore flags, and, in a word, the eruption of bunting was as healthy and generous as the most sanguine diagnostic critic could desire.

To enter more particularly into a description of the arrangements—three large tables, each from two to three hundred feet long, ran parallel with each other, in the centre of the enclosure The speaker's stand was erected at the South end of these tables, and surmounted by a superb silk banner, presented to the HAMPTON Legion by the ladies of Havana. In rear of this position was a large mound, on the summit of which was a fountain, enclosed in a circular arbor, almost buried in evergreens and flowers, above which floated the torn and battle-stained flag which has been borne through so many victorious battles by the brave men of the HAMPTON Legion. A fine band was stationed at this point, and in addition to the other music provided, performed appropriate airs during the day. At the opposite end of the long tables an immense arch of green was erected and decorated with colors captured in battle. Under this arch the troops marched as they came in to take their places around the festive board.

The cooking department was located a little to the rear of the mound, far enough away from the crowd to prevent the aroma from acting as too pungent an appetizer, and consisted of a trench three feet wide and about forty feet in length, together with sundry gigantic pots and kettles and a corps of ebony cooks. Here, at half past 12 o'clock, a visitor might have seen from thirty-five to forty good-sized pigs and half as many sheep—in all about thirty five hundred pounds of meat—singing, cracking, sputtering and "doing" good generally in a manner that would have tickled the olfactories of the daintiest Chinese.

The gems of the place, however, consisted of some twelve or fifteen booths, which had been erected along the wall or scattered at intervals in other parts of the enclosure. All of these were as attractive as feminine fancy could make them.

Each was different from the other, and it is not a sweeping compliment to say that each contained, in addition to an abundance of delicacies, from one to a half dozen fairies in evergreen frames, who were in themselves the most beautiful ornaments of the place. The other decorations consisted chiefly of mottoes, festoons, flowers, pictures, busts and bunting. At one table, we observed attached to a miniature ship the motto, "Our Cavalry—a Terror to the Enemy on Water as well as on Land." Twined in an arch of flowers above the table (to which were attached a profusion of tobacco bags) was another motto, "Go forth to honor and to victory." "Our brave defenders, our prayers go with you." Over another booth was the word "Welcome!" written in leaves. A third had "Welcome home, our brave defenders—our HAMPTON forever!" A fourth, "Brandy Station!" (we immediately stationed ourselves at this point, but didn't see any brandy) A fifth, "None but the brave deserve the *fare!*" A sixth, "Trust in God, and keep your powder dry." "Millions for defence, but not one *gent* for tribute."

The eatables at these side tables embraced almost everything an appetite could suggest—pies and patties, pigs and poultry, chocolate, coffee, cakes and custards, salads, syllabubs and sausages, blanc mange, bread and butter, pies, pickles and preserves.

In spite of the crowd, the utmost good order prevailed. Indeed, too much cannot be said in praise of the behavior of the soldiers. It had been feared by some that the demoralization of the camp would lead many to forget that they were in the presence of ladies; but, to the agreeable surprise of all, not a single impropriety marred the enjoyments of the day. Each private conducted himself with as much decorum as if he thought that upon his own demeanor depended the honor of the whole Confederate army.

About one o'clock, the troops, consisting of the 1st and 2d Regiments South Carolina Cavalry and HAMPTON'S Legion, escorted by the Arsenal Cadets, Capt. Thomas, with their bands playing, entered the enclosure and took their places at the tables.

The troops having taken their places, Hon. W. F. DESAUSSURE came forward and made the following graceful introduction of the speaker announced for the occasion:

FRIENDS AND FELLOW CITIZENS: I have the honor of introducing to you the Rev Dr Palmer—a gentleman whose name has been a tower of strength throughout our land from the inception of the war, and who will address you on the issues involved in this gigantic contest. His patriotic heart has always been alive to the duty of enlightening our people as to the vital interests connected with the struggle, and his whole energies have been directed to the encouragement of our people and to the stimulation of those exertions essential to the success of our cause.

The Rev. Dr PALMER then addressed the concourse as follows:

SPEECH OF THE REV. DR. PALMER.

SOLDIERS OF THE LEGION AND GENTLEMEN OF THE ARMY: The graceful and delicate office is assigned to me by the ladies of South Carolina to bid you, after a long separation, a welcome to your native State.

Ever since the commencement of this heroic struggle, you have been in the presence of the foe. To-day, these tables are spread to remind you that you are in the presence of those whose hearts beat towards you only with kindness, gratitude and love. On your lonely and fatiguing marches, when you have been bivouacked by the side of your camp-fires; when as sentinels picketing in the presence of a treacherous foe, and still more in the awful shock and rage of battle, though you may not have known it, many an eye has been moistened with tears of sympathy for your privations—many a heart accustomed to hold communion with Heaven has invoked the watchful providence of Almighty God to throw around you the shield of protection; and to day, in your glad return to your native State, and to the scenes so familiar to you, we find, in part, the answer to our prayers.

Three years ago, a venerable mother may have laid her hand in benediction upon your head, never expecting to greet you again except in the land of the blessed; many a loving wife sobbed her last farewell upon your breast as you tore from her embrace; affectionate sisters may have girded on your sabres, smiling amid their tears, as you have seen the sheen of Heaven's own bright sun dancing among the drops of dew; and your little ones may have grouped around you, and wondered as they gazed upon their fond and gentle father to see you transformed into the grim visaged and determined soldier. The necessities of war may not permit you to renew, at present, these associations of a happy past; but here, all around you, are mothers and sisters, who, with one voice and with one heart, claim you as their sons and brothers, and stand here as the representatives of your homes. Welcome, soldiers! welcome to our hearts; and gallant General, (turning to Maj Gen. Hampton, who was seated on the platform,) thrice welcome to you and your comrades, among those who bear in grateful remembrance your noble deeds in defence of South Carolina and her Confederate sisterhood. (Applause)

Soldiers! we are too near the great events which stir the age in which we live to behold the grandeur of their proportions. Just as when we stand at the base of an over hanging mountain and lift our eyes to the precipices that are beetling above, we are unprepared to scan the proportions which are thrown in such gigantic outlines upon the canvass of the sky, so must we, with the philosophic historian of future years, look back upon these human events before we can behold them in their grandeur or have our hearts stirred by their sublimity.

It is not long since, when you and I indulged the grand dream of an American Empire which should spread its power from ocean to ocean. The generation now living have seen the tide of emigration rolling from the Atlantic board until it lay in the lap of the broad valley of the Mississippi; and then, over-leaping that barrier, sweeping onward in its flow, until breaking itself across the mountains, it rested on the edge of the Pacific sea, and the voice of California echoed to the voice of the Atlantic States. There were not wanting proud dreamers among us then, who looked even beyond this gigantic swell of growing humanity to the time when the entire continent should be absorbed from the waters of the Southern sea to the Northern pole, when

"No pent up Utica should contract our powers,
But the whole boundless continent be ours"

But that fond delusion has been dispelled. The baseless fabric of a vision has faded from our sight. The stern decree of God came down; that proud nation was cloven in twain, and now we see what we recked not before—that we had become too great for our good. Alas! the day had passed by when the noble statesmen of the country were too pure to become the hacks of party; and the time arrived when placemen wield the baton of power. Thus the demoralization of our country stood forth embodied in the last election. But when the coarse jester of the West occupied the seat once hallowed by Washington, Jefferson and Madison, and the crafty politician of New York stood before the world showing that coarseness and cunning were to be ruling genii of the land—almost too late—just when the finger of the clock upon the dial-plate pointed to the very hour and moment of our destiny, South Carolina in the van, but followed shortly after by other sisters of equal courage and magnanimity, dissolved the bonds of that which had become a profane alliance; and these banners, to-day, wave over a land that is resolved to be free, and over a people who have sworn to pass through the most fearful baptism of blood to secure the rights and privileges which were about to be wrested from our grasp. Fellow-citizens, that event is an epoch of our history, for it separated us from a section of our country that had become bloated in party corruption, and was destined soon to fall into premature decay. And upon an issue ordered by Almighty Providence, the confederate South and the North measured arms in the sight of the nations of the earth. We may not see the end of it, but when the work of disintegration shall have gone forward, it will be found that three in probably five grand republics will stand forth, and constitute a congress of nations on this American Continent, like that family of nations now seated on the Continent of Europe. I think it is well to live in an age which looks forward to such a future, and which has brought out actors whose deeds will be hereafter signalized by historians as incidents introduced in this grand change of the economy of Providence.

But I must pass to another grand feature of this struggle in which we are embarked. We are contending for the preservation of the Republican principles for which our fathers fought, and which they have transmitted to us as a legacy. I must not be tempted into the discussion of a theme so fruitful as this; but I apprehend that what may be the difficulties we are called upon to grapple, there is not a heart through all of this broad land which is not resolved to work out under God the sublime problem of a free Republican Government. So far as the North is concerned, she is disabled from taking part in this mighty enterprise. I will not advert to her rapid demoralization, but only point you to the single fact that in the whole structure of Northern society there is not a class which represents the conservative element, and therefore it is that the wild Democracy of the North—and I use the term in its broad and philosophical sense, and not as a technical application—like Mazeppa, tied to his Tartar steed, bounding through the forests and breasting the broad rivers, will at last fail in its mad career only when it falls exhausted upon the earth. But as for us of the South, we place our back against that institution which lifts itself up from the bed of history like a mighty rock in the midst of the broad ocean; and though the fanaticism of the age in which we live, like a wave of the sea, dashes itself against this rock, it is only to be broken into spray, and to prove how powerless are human agencies when they wage war against the decrees of God. I believe, as I believe the fact of my being, that the only hope of Republican institutions on this continent, is to be found in the perpetuation of that institution which has been made the occasion of this war. (Applause.)

We are then contending for the very principles of our fathers; and, gentlemen, permit me to say, that when the Convention of South Carolina, in that sublime vote which withdrew her from the old Federal alliance, threw off the shackles by which she was bound, it did seem to me as though the spirits of our fathers were in that hall—that the Rutledges, the Laureus, the Pinckneys, and the Haynes of the past had re-appeared in those grave and reverend counsellors, who, with their hearts solemnly impressed with the fear of God, were not afraid to pit their State against all the fortunes of this fearful and bloody war. And when my thoughts have followed the soldiers of our armies on their lonely march and on the field of strife, it has seemed to me that the spectres of those who suffered at Valley Forge had risen from their revolutionary bed to hover around you, and testify to you that you were contending for the principles for which they fought, and for which they willingly surrendered their lives. Notwithstanding all the privations and hardships of the times, I rejoice that I live abreast of these mighty scenes, and that it is permitted me to lift my poor voice in the assertion of those immortal principles; and may this right hand forget its cunning, and this voice be hushed in death, ere it ceases to proclaim beneath Heaven's own dome, that it is for a free, happy and glorious Republican Government that we are as prepared to strive and die as were our fathers before us. (Applause.)

Once more. There is an awful grandeur in this struggle in the loneliness with which it is conducted. All the nations of earth have turned away their eyes of sympathy from us. All alone, but upon a platform as high as our own Blue Ridge, a spectacle to the world, and immediately under the eye of the Great God of Hosts and God of Battles, we are fighting for the right and for the true. Alone—all alone—upon the face of the earth! Let England and France coquette as long as they may—as it has been their policy through all the past to coquette until the balance of power can be grasped by them—but with a firm faith in the integrity of our principles, and with a religious trust in the power of Almighty God, we of the South, in our infancy, all alone, will grapple with our foes until God, in his own time, shall grant us our freedom, and we shall sit beneath our own vine with none to molest or make us afraid.

I cannot enter here into the discussion of the questions involved in these foreign affairs; but I must not deny myself the privilege of saying a word more as to the issue of this struggle. Let none but the deist doubt. I am free to say to you that so long as there is a God, in whom I can believe, and whose hand, I know, is stretched out in the righteous administration of human affairs, so long will I hope for my country and for my country's future; and when that hope shall die out of my heart, the spring of life will be broken. I shall die with the dying of my hope. What though odds be great against us? They are less now than they have been. For three years we have held the bloodhounds at bay, and for three years to come, so help us God, we are able to hold them still at bay. (Cheers.) Does not heaven spread its broad arch? Is not the early and the latter rain gathered by God into its cisterns in the sky? Do not our feet tread the fertile earth which has given seed time and harvest to man? Where, then, is the danger of famine in such a land as this? When you shall gather around these ample boards, and receive the welcome of Carolina's fair daughters to the repast which they have prepared, you will understand that we are, at least, by a quadrant or ninety degrees removed from all danger of starvation. And when in turn they look upon these brave men assembled here, and remember that the Confederacy is girdled by thousands of such noble hearts, will have no fear for the result.

Soldiers! do you remember that stirring incident in Grecian history, when the hosts poured through the narrow defile of Thermopylæ, how Themistocles—perhaps the greatest name in all Grecian history—assembled the fighters of Athens upon the ships which he had prepared, and standing upon the prow of a vessel, extended his arms over the fleet, and exclaimed, "This now is Athens!" Have you forgotten the Dutch war, when the Silent William, regarded as the great hero of history, never won a single battle, was always worsted, encountered almost insuperable difficulties in maintaining the organization of his army, and yet through an indomitable will conducted the conflict, until to day all Europe recognizes the Dutch Republic as being the saviour and guardian both of the civil and religious liberties of the continent. Shall I draw your attention nearer home, and tell you how, through seven years of bloody war, our forefathers, with immeasurably less resources than we command, wearied out an importunate and powerful foe, and after he had occupied all of our cities, drove him at last from his strongholds and became the victors and possessors of the soil? So will it be with us; and when you are called again to face the enemy, remember the benediction of your countrymen and the preciousness of the treasure you bear; and when next you return to Carolina's fair soil, may it be our happiness to welcome you not as now, simply defenders, but as mighty conquerors over those who have fallen beneath your prowess. (Applause)

And now, General, (turning to Gen. Hampton,) I have an individual confession to make. It has been my privilege, as you know, through three and twenty years to hold forth to my fellow-men the Gospel of the peace and grace of God, and I have not seldom been startled at the sound of my own voice, when I have been called upon again and again to lift aloft the red brand of war, and, like the monk of another age, who came from his humble cloister, to summon my countrymen to arms in defence of all that was dear to the human heart. Sir, there is a spirit within this breast which I should perhaps be ashamed to avow, for it has sometimes chafed at the restraints of my calling; and I have almost wished that the decree which has gone forth, had not reckoned the priests among the women. There have been times when I wished there was a spur on my heel and a sword in my hand; and yet I must yield to these restraints that have been put upon me by Divine Providence, and continue in the sphere to which I have been assigned. In this capacity, let me say that to you is allotted a noble destiny. It is given to you, with your brave command, to carve your name with the point of your sword upon the history of your country. The day will come when that blade, which gleams so brightly by your side in the hour of battle, will be hung as a relic upon your ancestral walls, and there will come forth some fair haired urchin who, as he takes it down and springs the rusty blade from its scabbord, will say this was the sword with which my great grand-father passed through the many battles of the revolution of 1860 and '64. Mark you, he will not call it "the great rebellion," as neither you nor I do, but a mighty and stupendous revolution, which gave freedom to our land. At the same time, there may be a flaxen-haired girl who, as she turns over the old family pages of her history, and her eye falls upon the name of "Hampton," will call to remembrance a family tradition, that on a certain April day, some seventy-five or eighty years ago, her great grandfather pinned the emblem of South Carolina and the Confederacy as near as he could get it over Gen. Hampton's heart.

[Suiting the action to the word, the reverend speaker advanced to Gen. Hampton, and with a grace that cannot be described in language, attached to his breast an exquisite Palmetto badge, interwoven with a miniature Confederate flag. There was scarcely a dry eye in the vast assembly, and the brave soldier himself could not restrain the tears, which the act and its associations involuntarily called forth.]

And now, General, (resumed Dr. Palmer,) this is a secret which neither you nor your honored lady must ask to be revealed. A daughter of Carolina pins that symbol of the State and the Confederacy on your heart. I have only to say, in the name of the fair lady, see to it that South Carolina and the Confederacy are saved; and (turning to the concourse) I now point to you, ladies of South Carolina, the Chevalier Bayard of the South—the chivalric knight, "without fear and without reproach." (Great cheers.)

Cries of "Hampton," "Hampton," now rolled from every lusty throat in the crowd, and the General, visibly affected by the heart felt demonstrations of his men, responded as follows:

SPEECH OF MAJOR-GENERAL HAMPTON.

Ladies of Columbia, and Brother Soldiers: These brave men to whom you have extended so warm a welcome have requested that, in their name, I should thank you for your kind reception. I feel my inability to do justice either to their feelings or to respond in fitting terms to the graceful compliment that has been paid; but I cannot refuse a request so gratifying to me, while, at the same time, I take occasion to bear testimony to the courage and patriotism of my noble troops. I do this, fellow-soldiers, because, before I leave you, I desire, in the most public manner, to express my thanks to those upon whose tried discipline and valor I have so often depended, and whose constant exhibition of soldierly qualities has ever been my pride. I do so for the additional reason that I may look, for the last time, upon the brave men I have led, and whose confidence has repaid me all the affection I have given them. These motives have impelled me to come, to-day, to speak to you and for you, and to thank my fair countrywomen, who in doing honor to you have honored themselves.

Three years ago, a band of soldiers assembled on this spot. They were small in numbers, but largely represented the patriotism and intelligence of our State. They were untried, unexperienced men, knowing little of the perils or privations of war; but they felt that their State had called them, and they had prepared to respond with their lives. Most of that little band are gone from among us forever, but the survivers have gathered here to-day—a mere handful. How they have borne themselves let that banner, (pointing to the battle flag of the Hampton Legion,) which bears upon it the names of the most glorious battle-fields of the Confederacy, testify. They have done their duty in the fullest sense, and deserved the praise of their country. They have returned home, some to seek rest from their toils, and others to prepare again to take their places in the approaching campaign. But, as at first, our noble women are here to bless, encourage and cheer them on the way. Let not these fair daughters of our State imagine that they are not exercising a material influence upon the soldier in manifesting the interest which has become proverbial among the sex. Far from it. Demonstrations of this character cheer the soldier on his lonely march, and under all the circumstances of his varied life. But there is something more that woman does. I have seen her nursing in the hospitals, caring for the wounded, wiping the cold sweat from the brows of the dying, and when the fight was sweeping by their very doors, I have seen them rush out and wave their white arms, while the bright sabres of my men were flashing by, and join their voices in the wild shouts that cheered our men on to victory. You do well, therefore, ladies, in extending this welcome to these brave men. Brother-soldiers, although our official connection is about to be severed, and the ties broken which bound us together, let me take this opportunity of saying that the associations between us have been of no ordinary character. We have together shared the perils, privations, and victories of the soldier. I have been honored by your confidence, and I have given in return an affection warmer than I entertain for anything beyond my own immediate family, an affection which, I am proud to believe, was reciprocated, for never have troops sustained their commanding officer better than you have sustained me.

It has been the fashion, fellow citizens, to speak lightly of the services of the cavalry, and to say that our fights have been bloodless. The best answer to these statements is to be found in the reports of the last year's campaign. This will show that your little brigade took into the first engagement of the campaign fourteen field officers. When that campaign ended, every one of those brave men were killed or wounded. These vacancies were filled, and the number increased to twenty-three; and of that number, twenty-one have been placed in the same mournful list. I cannot say what has been the loss in the brigade, but I have been informed that the casualties in this cavalry division during the last campaign exceed those of any other division in the army. I refer to these facts to show to these ladies that they are not welcoming mere holiday soldiers, but tried patriots, whose aim has been to sustain their country. I have seen you during the dreary winter watching, while our army slept in security behind you. I have seen you sleeping upon the frozen ground without tents, shoes, over shoes or blankets, only waiting for the morning's light to attack the enemy, whose fires lighted our own bivouack, and yet I have never heard a murmur. Such, ladies, are the men whom I have the honor to command; and I tell you, they are worthy of a nation's gratitude and a nation's love. While referring to this subject, I am reminded that our distinguished Chief Magistrate, in a letter which he wrote to his Excellency the Governor, has alluded to these two regiments which are here, and by the kindness of the Governor I am permitted to read an extract. Speaking of the difficulty of mounting cavalry, and the reason for sending them away, "No one sooner than yourself will respond to the claim of these brave men to be shielded from circumstances which will depreciate their hard won reputation in the cavalry of Northern Virginia." (Cheers)

I am sure I need say nothing more to the ladies to prove that their kindness has been well bestowed. The task only remains for me to bid you, my soldiers, an affectionate farewell. It was not by my consent that you were taken away. You have seen those who are to take your place, and, like myself, have been pleased at their appearance. They will do all that men can do to honor their State, but I can never forget, wherever I may be assigned to command, the old brigade from whom I now part. During our association, I know that you will do me the justice to say that I have done all I could to shield you from harm, and I feel assured that there is not a man who will claim that I can send a soldier to a place where I would not go myself. (Cries of "that's so.") May your future be peaceful and happy. May God bless and protect you in danger, and when you are again called to the field, that it may be not only with full ranks, but with hearts animated by the same spirit you have ever manifested in the past. Should you be restored to the army of Northern Virginia, you know there is no place where you would be more welcome than to my own command.

(Turning to Dr. Palmer.) To your flattering remarks, I can scarcely find words to respond. Whatever credit may be due to me, is due alike to my men; their successes have been my own, and it has only been my good fortune to have such troops under my command.

To the lady who has done me the honor to present through you this emblem, I can only say that where it has been placed, there it shall be worn, and it shall be my aim to ever carry it where honor dictates and glory may be found. (Cheers. Music.)

Col. Gary, of the Hampton Legion, being called for, His Excellency Gov. Bonham, in one of his fascinating little speeches, which, when he wills it, are like a woman's eyes—say nothing, but mean a great deal—introduced that officer to the audience. He spoke as follows:

SPEECH OF COL. GARY.

Ladies and Gentlemen: I had thought that the eloquent and heartfelt response of our brave and distinguished leader on so many battle-fields, in behalf of his veteran followers, would have relieved us from any part in this pleasing ceremony. But I find that here, as upon the field of battle, every man is expected to do his duty. I congratulate myself and my brave command, whom I have the honor to represent here, that such an auspicious opportunity has been afforded us of acknowledging in person, that noble heart offering, that patriotic spirit, and public sympathy, which has been the characteristic of the State, and especially of our beautiful and glorious ladies. It is an acknowledgment, not merely for the bestowal of present favors, but one which extends back to the past. We have not forgotten your kind benedictions, given when with eager and confident spirits we rushed to the field of action. We still treasure up those elegant souvenirs of your regard, having worn them as talismen on the bloody fields of battle. Nor have we forgotten, and never can forget, the donors of that splendid and sacred flag, presented through the President of the Confederate States of America, by fair daughters of South Carolina. Its bullet-rent folds, and the long list of brave men that have fallen under it, attest the high appreciation that we place upon this patriotic gift, and the great principles which it symbolizes. After an absence of three years, animated by your approving expression of *well done*, we renew, to-day, our allegiance to that sacred doctrine, "that only Southern men shall rule the South."

I participate in that common feeling of confidence which now, more than ever, inspires the army in the final triumph of our arms—a fighting and bloody triumph, independent of moral and political causes. It will be a triumph, sanctified by the protracted and terrible character of the struggle, and enriched by episodes of daring deeds of bold men and patriotic devotion of noble women, such as former times do not record; and cherish the hope that the day is not far distant when our beloved country, converging like Venus from her sea of blood, shall take her position among the nations of the earth, when she will command the respect and admiration of an enthusiastic world.

We have returned to our homes not for the purpose of enjoying luxury and ease, but to fit ourselves for the new field of duty to which we have been assigned. We are now girding on our armor to renew the conflict, and I trust that the return to our native soil will give to us, like Antæus, new energy and strength for the coming contest. I know that the ladies of this State will never grow weary in this great and glorious cause, and so, too, with the ladies of the South. I can speak advisedly of the ladies of the noble Old Dominion—they have watched at the bedside of your fathers, comforted your wounded brothers, and wiped with their gentle hands the death damp from the brow of your lovers.

A distinguished patriot divine of our sister State, Georgia, has suggested that a monument be erected to the unknown dead who have fallen in this war. Simultaneously should be raised by its side one to perpetuate the patriotism, the courage and generosity of the ladies of the South, whose charities, like the dews of Heaven, have fallen broadcast upon the soldiers of the Confederacy.

I again thank you in behalf of my command for this unexpected and appreciative compliment.

When the speeches were concluded, Mayor Goodwyn advanced to the front of the platform, and announced that the food would be immediately placed upon the table. Upon this, the soldiers moved up in a column of fours, and ranged themselves along the ample boards. From that time until the feast ended, the supplies were of the most bountiful character, and not a man departed unsatisfied. The barbecue being disposed of, straightway all the happy guests adjourned to the booths and the ladies, where they were regaled with articles before enumerated.

Great praise is due to the respective committees, and especially that which superintended the tables and barbecue proper, for the admirable judgment displayed in every detail connected with their departments.

Before concluding this sketch, we must not omit to express our unqualified approval of the festival and its object. There are not wanting some who maintain that a more practical and useful mode of testifying the gratitude we owe to our brave defenders might have been found than the fleeting demonstration of the day. Yet, if they will look at the matter from another point of view, they will probably come to the conclusion that the good feeling, the cordiality and the enthusiasm engendered by such a gathering are likely to prove in reality far more permanent in their good results than a merely utilitarian generosity. Months hence, the brave men whom we have welcomed here will recur to this entertainment as an evidence that their services are not forgotten at home. Not one gay smile, not one blue glance of all the favors lavished upon them by the ladies of Columbia will soon be forgotten. The recollections which they will carry away may be the inspiration of many a heroic deed in many a far away battle field, and more than one foe may have to thank, for the blow which cleaves him to his chine, or the bullet which speeds with unerring aim to his heart, the lessons learned, yesterday, from those not less unerring missiles which dart from beneath many a beautiful brow, or are shot forth from the Cupid's bow of many an exquisite mouth. Nor, in all probability, will the happy influences of the occasion be confined to the gallant guests alone. The enthusiasm which the fair hostesses have sought to kindle will react upon themselves, as they may discover in the renewed and hopeful spirits by which they will hereafter be repaid for the hospitalities of the moment. There will thus be a mutual interchange of benefits between the entertainers and the entertained, and each may part from the other delighted in having added to their stock of pleasant memories one of the few perfectly happy days which the times permitted them to enjoy.

The following list of names of ladies who had charge of tables has been handed us: Mrs. Snowden, Leland, Caldwells, Bower, Stenhouse, Sims, Berry. Hopson, Sutphen, G. M. Thompson, M. A. Shelton, J. Ingals, J. J. Cohen, Wineman, B. F. Moise, Wolfe, G. M. Goodwin, Cassedy, Wilbur, Price, Howe, Crawford, McMaster, McFee, Barnes, Squier, Friday, Farley, James Cathcart, Morrison, Steele, McKenzie, Speck, J. H. Cathcart, R. S. Cathcart, Guignard, Davis, Trezevant, Shand, Nichols, Hunt.

From Longstreet's Army.

A correspondent of the Atlanta *Confederacy* writes the following encouraging letter from Bristol:

Longstreet's corps has certainly had a severe time this winter in the mountains of Tennessee. In the number of miles marched, engagements fought, and hardships endured, the last campaign excels all others, and only needed the prestige of success to eclipse the famous valley campaigns of the lamented Jackson.

It seems as if the rest and comfortable winter quarters enjoyed by the balance of the army is denied to us. Last winter we were engaged in active operations on the Blackwater, and this winter we have been ever on the wing. However, we are the boys that can stand it, and uncomplainingly, too; for whilst we hear echoes of certain growlings and grumblings at home, here none but the most hopeful expectations for the coming campaign are entertained. Many of us expect to bite the dust, but yet a few will live to enjoy the peace their valor won. Just kill off the enemies of our cause at home, and Longstreet's corps do promise you to take care of their share of the open enemies in the field.

The army, as a general thing, is very badly clothed, and but poorly fed. So was the army of Italy, and so was the army of Valley Forge. We are none the worse for that, though we would prefer to have a little more to eat and a little cloth to patch our only pair of pantaloons; and I would very willingly give a month's pay (old issue) for an onion or a potato.

Our new General, Fields, the successor of Hood, has created a tolerable good impression in the division, but he will have to exert himself to prove himself worthy of being the successor of Gen. Hood. We love Hood's very name, and in our partiality regret that promotion which deprived us of his leadership.

From Gen. Forrest.—The Mississippi *Clarion* publishes the following despatch received by the Governor from Gen. Forrest:

Dresden, Tenn., via Okalono, Miss., April 3, 1864.—*Gov. Clark, Macon, Miss.:* Left Jackson on 23d—captured Union City on 24th, with 450 prisoners, among them the renegade Hawkins and most of his regiment, about 200 horses and 500 small arms. Also took possession of Hickman, the enemy having vacated it. I moved myself, with Gen. Buford's division, marching from Jackson direct to Paducah in fifty hours, attacked it on the 26th, drove the enemy to their gun boats and forts, held the town for ten hours, could have held it longer, but finding the small pox was raging, and vacated the place. Captured many stores and horses, burned sixty bales of cotton, one steamer on the dry dock, brought out fifty prisoners. My loss at Union City and Paducah as far as known is twenty-five killed and wounded, among them Col Thompson, commanding Kentucky brigade, killed; Lieut. Col. Langham, Faulkner's regiment, mortally wounded; and Col. Crossland, of the 7th Kentucky, and Lieut. Col. Norton, of the 2d Tennessee, slightly wounded. Enemy's loss in Paducah fifty-five killed and wounded, prisoners in all 500. Have despatched Gen. Gholson at Tupelo to meet prisoners at Corinth and take them to you. Hold possession of all the country except posts on the river. Think if I can remain here unmolested for fifteen days, will be able to add 2,000 men to my command. I would urge upon you the importance of repairing the railroad to Corinth, as well for the welfare of the citizens as for the good of this Department.

Gen. Grant a Pork and Beans Man.—They tell us now that Gen. Grant is a genuine pork and beans man—a regular Saturday night New England man. It is said that he does not fancy the luxurious style of living prevalent in the Army of the Potomac. He says he can maintain his physical integrity on pork and beans, as soldiers do out West, and believes it can be done by them here. Caterer to the delicate palates of our officers are in spasms at the report that the Lieutenant General is about to banish their wares from the line.

[*Schenectady* (*New York*) *Star*.

The corn crop in Georgia last year was forty millions of bushels. In South Carolina it was over fifteen millions. In Alabama, thirty millions, and yet meal is held at thirteen dollars and thirty-three cents a bushel. Will there not be a long chapter in the history of the American war, entitled "Planters—their diligence in the hour of trouble?"

CONTRABAND NEWS.

NEWSPAPERS AT HOME.

THE FIELD
SKETCHING.
A CORRESPONDENT.
RELIABLE INFORMATION.
Th. Nast.
ON.
AFTER THE BATTLE
HARPER'S
THE NEWSPAPERS IN CAMP.
BOOK.

BUTLER, THE BEAST, AT WORK.

[Written for the Illustrated News.]

Lines.

By a Rebel Prisoner at Johnson's Island, 1864.

BY ASA HARTZ.

To———

Star of the evening,
Star of my love,
Beaming serenely
On me from above,
Fondly I gaze on thee,
Shining afar,
And think of my loved one,
My beautiful star!

Star of my best beloved,
Comely and bright,
Say, does she gaze on thee
Sadly to-night?
And do the tear-drops
Of love in her eyes
Reflect back thy brightness,
Dear gem of the skies?

Star of my brightest hopes,
Brilliant and pure,
Let thy rays enter
Her breast to its core!
Watch o'er my loved one—
Dispel all her gloom,
While the flowers of night
Distil their perfume!

Star of my future life,
May thy bright rays
Illumine her pathway
Throughout all her days!
Drive from her dear heart
All grief and regret,
And shine ever brightly
On ASA and BET!

The Drama.

"All the world's a stage,
And all the men and women merely players;
They have their exits and their entrances,
And one man in his time plays many parts!"

MR. E. R. DALTON closed his engagement in this city last Saturday night, on which occasion he appeared as "Richelieu," in the five act play of that name. The picture which Mr. DALTON gave of the crafty minister contending with all the difficulties of his station—now exulting—now sinking under the weight of physical infirmities—at one moment stern and unrelenting, the next tender and loving, yet at all times cunning, scheming and crafty—was effective in the extreme. The interview between the Cardinal and "De Mauprat," in the first act, the tempestuous passages towards the close of the fourth, and the highly dramatic scene near the end of the fifth, were particularly good, and elicited great applause from the large audience.

We noticed on this night, as on several others of late, that some of the younger actors were guilty of the very grievous and annoying practice of "winging their parts," or in other words, studying their lines between exits and entrances. If an actor has not committed the lines of the the author to memory, he certainly cannot portray the character with any degree of truthfulness or spirit. Look to it, Mr. Stage Manager. Compel your actors to know their lines when they come to rehearsal in the morning. One of the best rules in the world for the government of a theatre, is that which compels each member of the company to go through the morning's rehearsal with as much care and attention as he does the evening performance. The Stage Manager then knows, in the morning, what he may expect at night.

During the present week we have had a revival of several old pieces, among them—"by request"—(as the Manager announces,) the "Virginia Cavalier," written by that unknown Captain, "booted and spurred." "Camille" was produced on Monday night to a fair house, Mr. OGDEN appearing as "Armand," and Miss BRIDGES as "Camille." On Thursday night that terribly bloody drama of the "Jibbenainosay," was produced, with Mr. OGDEN as the "Avenger." The play was well put on the stage. "Miscegenation," (the saints be praised,) didn't pay, and was withdrawn.

Rumor has it that Mr. DALTON will shortly revisit this city, bringing with him his company from Macon—that the company, under his direction, will play a short engagement at the Richmond Theatre, while Manager OGDEN, with ap ortion of the Richmond company, will go to Macon and Savannah and play short engagements in both of these cities. The play-going public will thus have an opportunity of judging of the relative merits of the two companies.

THE GHOST! THE GHOST!

The "Ghost," which has astounded and confounded the people of both Europe and America, will shortly be produced in this city, the necessary articles having been procured by the Manager of the Richmond Theatre, at an expense of some seven thousand dollars. The "Ghost" will first be exhibited in the play of the "Skeleton Witness," and will doubtless be quite effective. The Ghost on the stage is an optical illusion, produced by means of a strong reflected light. The plan is exceedingly simple. A very large plate of transparent glass is set at an angle on the stage in front of the actors; an opening is made through the floor of the stage in front of the glass, and the skeleton is placed beneath the floor in front of the opening. As soon as a strong light is thrown upon the skeleton, the light passes upward through the opening in the floor, and is reflected from the glass, producing an image in the rear. The glass is an invisible mirror producing its image among the actors who are visible directly through the bones.

The Manager deserves especial commendation for the spirit he has evinced in the production of novelties of late. The "Ghost" will doubtless have a long run. It may possibly be produced during the coming week.

BENEFIT OF THE COMEDIAN.

JAMES WELLS, the Comedian at the Theatre, has a benefit one night next week. This young gentleman has been on the stage but a short time, but during that brief period, has, by close application and study, attained an excellent position in the profession which he has adopted. He deserves the most liberal encouragement, and we trust his first benefit may be a *substantial* one.

METROPOLITAN HALL.

The Dramatic company at this Hall has been augmented by the addition of Miss JENNIE POWELL, who is well known to the playgoers as a vivacious and sprightly young actress.

PETERSBURG THEATRE.

HARRY MACARTHY, who closed his engagement in this city last Saturday night, appeared at Phœnix Hall to a good house, on Monday night following.

CONCERT HALL, AUGUSTA.

The above Hall has been re-opened, with a fine dramatic company, with A. WALDRON as Lessee and Manager, and WALTER KEEBLE as Stage Director. On the 14th, the Comedy of the "Honey Moon" was performed with Mr. THEO. HAMILTON as "Rolando," Mr. KEEBLE as "Duke Aranza," Mr. D. F. ANDERSON as the "Mock Duke," Miss ELLA WREN as "Julianna," Miss FANNY as "Volante," and Mrs. D. T. ANDERSON as "Zamora." The pieces produced have been such as the "The Wife," "Fazio," "Camille," "Richelieu," and "Ingomar," in all of which Miss WREN and Mr. HAMILTON assumed the principal characters.

YANKEE THEATRICALS.

We notice little of interest in Yankee dramatic circles. A critic in one of the New York sporting papers, in speaking of the Gottschalk Concert, says:

"CARLO PATTI'S violin solas served to fill up the interstices, though the delay he made in putting on an appearance somewhat provoked the patience of the audience.—This is inexcusable in a great artist, whilst in such a mediocre performer it is unbearable. This young importation from secessia, though he be ADELINA PATTI'S brother, should be, and we trust will be, taught better manners in future, or else he will have to be returned to fiddle to the Confederates (whence, if we mistake not, he came,) and there play his solo 'La Melancholie.'"

CARLO PATTI was, at the commencement of the war, attached to an Alabama regiment. He made his escape from Charleston harbor.

JULIA DEAN HAYNE is engaged for the season at Portland, Oregon.

Miss MARY SHAW made her first appearance in New Orleans on the 19th inst.

HELEN WESTERN is in Boston.

WALLACK'S "Rosedale" has reached one hundred nights. It has also been produced with success in Boston.

BARRY SULLIVAN still has charge of the Theatre Royal, at Melbourne. He lately had a benefit, on which occasion was performed "The Lady of Lyons," and the "Spectre Bridegroom."

JOEY GOUGENHEIM and Mr. and Mrs. CHAS. KEAN are also at Melbourne.

KATE DENIN is at the Howard Athenæum, Boston. She has seven new plays: "Eleanor's Victory," "The Outlaw," "Very Hard Cash," "The Yellow Passport," "Heart of Gold," "Bohemian Mother," and "Marian Willobey."

LYNCHBURG VIRGINIAN.

NOTICE.—The cross mark appended to the names of certain subscribers indicates that the term fo which they subscribed will soon expire. They are thus notified in time to renew their subscription if they desire.

ALEXANDRIA MATTERS.—The following named residents of Alaxandria died in that city recently, viz: D. B. Smith, Isaac Buckingham, Betty Pugh, Mrs. H. Claugett.

Lincoln has approved of the joint resolution temporarily increasing the duties on imports fifty per centum. It is, therefore, a law.

We have been requested to inform the country people that contributions of articles suitable for sick and wounded soldiers would be very acceptable. There will be great demand for such articles within the next few days. They may be left at the residence of David E. Spence, Esq.

THE VERY LATEST.—From information received at a late hour last night we learn that the enemy were also landing at Wilcox Wharf, in Charles City county, and that the force at Bermuda Hundreds, in transports, was estimated at 9,000.

Our force at Forge Bridge, below the Chickahominy, were driven off by superior numbers.

A number of houses were burned by the enemy at New Kent C. H., and it is supposed that the Courthouse was also burned.—Dispatch.

MISCELLANEOUS.

A letter from Kanawha Court-House states that the rebels are committing serious depredations in the vicinity. The writer says: "On Tuesday night they took seventy horses from the bank of the Ohio river, opposite Gallipolis. On Wednesday they captured some twenty or thirty mules, within twelve or fourteen miles of this town, where a pretty large military force is encamped. And on Thursday they got four horses belonging to Judge Summers, and took the contents of two stores from Red House Shoals."

The joint resolution which unanimously passed the United States House of Representatives, about a month ago, protesting against the French occupation of Mexico and the establishment of Monarchial institutions on this Continent, still sleeps in the Senate's Committee on Foreign Relations, which it is permitted to do for reasons of state policy.

The Boston Courier, ever ready to defend the barbarities of the slaveholders, triumphantly cites two cases to show that eighty years ago the practice was permitted of the butchery of a garrison which had defended, an untenable post. The Courier could scarcely have found a humane person to justify or praise the practice, which has been discontinued as barbarous in more recent wars.

INVESTIGATION OF THE FORT PILLOW AFFAIR.

Senator Wade and Mr. Gooch, the Sub-Committee on the Conduct of the War, who went to Fort Pillow to ascertain the facts as to the alleged massacre of coloured troops there, have returned, and report that the stories have not been exaggerated. That great cruelty was practiced by the rebel troops, after the surrender of the fort, there can be no doubt.

FRANCE THE EMPEROR'S LETTER.

The Emperor had addressed the following letter, dated April 16, to M. Fould, Minister of Finance: "The happy solution of the Mexican affair creates in me a desire to see the country profit by the first repayment of the the expenses of the war, by diminishing taxes. Be good enough to see if it be not possible to effect the immediate suspension of the second decime registration fee, only preserving of the general law prepared by the Council of State those arrangements which may be strictly necessary for balancing the budget. This measure together with the hopes of peace, which every day becomes more certain, will contribute, I trust, to the development of prosperity."

DEATH OF COMMODORE W. D. PORTER

Commodore W. D. Porter. the eldest son of old Commodore David Porter, and the elder brother of Admiral David D. Porter, Red river, died on Sunday morning at St. Luke's Hospital, New York, of disease of the heart.

Two years ago Commodore Porter was severely scalded by an explosion on the Essex, and dated the commencement of his breaking down to that event. While in the discharge of his duty he passed through four attacks of yellow fever, one of which was so severe that his coffin was made, in certain anticipation of his death.

OFFICERS CASHIERED.

Nine officers of a colored regiment at Fortress Monroe, having resigned for insufficient causes at the approach of active operations, General Butler has forwarded their resignations to the President with a recommendation that they be remanded to their former regiments to serve out their time as private soldiers. Lieutenant J. Wilkinshaw, 62d Pennsylvania Volunteers, Army of the Potomac, having resigned under similar circumstances, has been dishonorably discharged.

The "World's" correspondent says Chase had a long conference with Lincoln on the 1st instant, and it is understood that he remains in the Treasury, pending the investigation about to commence by the Special House Committee into his department. Had not this been ordered, there is little or no doubt but that Mr. Chase would have resigned last Thursday.

To the Citizens of Lynchburg and County of Campbell.

HEADQUARTERS,
Lynchburg, May 2d, 1864.

I. The following list of the names of parties who are to furnish Slaves to work on the Fortifications at this point under the provisions of General Order, No. 188, (late series.) Adj't and Insp'tr General's Office, Richmond, (which is hereto appended,) is published for the information of those concerned:

1st District.

James Farmer	1	Richard Morgan	1
Benj Wyatt	1	Josiah Stepherson	1
Jno W Stone	1	Thos H Allen	1
Jno D Alexander	2		

2d District.

A G Hancock	1	A G Dabney	1
G M Rucker	1	Jno M Warwick	1
J W Stone	1	O G Clay	1
Ed Burton	1	Dr Floyd	1
H F Bocock	1	Maj G C Hutter	1
H F Barksdale	1	Samuel Miller	1
Judge Wm Daniel	1		

3d District.

R A Hunter	1	Est. Judge Saunders	1
Jno Andrews	1	Maj Ro Saunders	1
Dr M Haden	1	Jesse Irvine	1
B T White	1	C H Lynch	1
Thos Dillard	1	Edward Dillard	1
Benj Tardy	1	Charles Anthony	1
A A Arnold	1	W L Pannill	1
D H Creasy	1	S C Tardy	1
James Brown	1		

4th District.

Thos P Johnston	1	D C Moorman	1
Christian Mohr	1	John C Ward	1
John H Sweeny	1	John W Fore	1
R H Walthall	1	J S Payne	1
J H Farmer	1	J B Dabney	1
Bowling Clark	1	John Pannill	1
B M Payne	1	James Conley	1

5th District.

Armistead Hamlet,	1	Dr Ro Smith	1
Clem Clark	1	Thos F Poindexter	1
Langley J Talbot	1	W H Cook	1
John J Young	1	R Tweedy	1
J C Spencer	1	Jas McIver	1

6th District.

James Hamlet	1	G A Burks	1
S D Chambers	1	Lynch Jones	1
T P Elliott	1	W W Jones	1
D B Hancock	1	W A Poore	1
Christopher Clark	1	John Cardwell	1
Thos B Harvey	1	S B Tweedy	1

7th District.

C J Jones	1	G Ashlin	1
Jesse Thornhill	1	S S Railroad	1
Davidson & Martin	1	John H Tyree	1
G S Diuguid	1	Col M Langhorne	4
R Crawford	1	F B Deane, jr	2
R H Staten	4	R J Wade	1
J J Burkes	4		

8th District.

Timothy Fletcher	1	J N Anderson	1
W H Ogden	1	So Express Co	1
J E Owens	1	Shelby Johnson	1
W A Clement	1	Est Dr Saunders	3
John M Warwick	1	Jesse Clark	1
Va & Tenn R R	7	J G Meem	1
James Morgan	1	Col A Leftwich	1
John Oyler	1	P D Christian	1
J L Harrison	1	J L Claytor	1
James M Booker	3	S McCorkle	1
T F Grimaldi	1	J H Flood	1
Untermeyer & Shelton	1	C L Mosby	1
J M Speed	1	A B Rucker	1
M Moore	2	Bocock & Parrish	1
C S Langhorne	1	A B Hall	1
J Franklin	1	Wade & Haynes	1
McDaniel & Irby	1		

II. The above mentioned parties are notified to deliver the number of Slaves indicated opposite their names, to Lieut. MASON, Engineer in Charge, at Lynchburg, as follows: Those residing in the 8th District, on Thursday, the 5th day of May, (inst.) and those in the remaining Districts, on Thursday the 11th day of May, (inst.) Lieut. Mason will make all suitable arrangements for the subsistence, management and custody of said Slaves.

III. The Commandant of the Post hopes that the above requisition will be complied with promptly and cheerfully, as it will save much annoyance to all concerned; and particular attention is directed to Par. IV, of the General Order hereafter recited.

By order of
Brig. Gen. FRANCIS T NICHOLLS
Commanding Post.
G. W. LATHAM, Asst. Adj't Genl.

[EXTRACT.]

ADJUTANT AND INSPECTOR GENERAL'S OFFICE,
RICHMOND, Oct 24, 1863.

GENERAL ORDERS,
No. 138.

The following instructions are published for carrying into effect the 9th section of the Act of 26th March, 1863: To regulate impressments in respect to labor on fortifications and other public works:

* * * * *

4. The ordinary period for impressment shall be sixty days, but if the owner of any slave shall fail to bring the slaves impressed to the place of rendezvous within five days after the time appointed, the slaves so withheld may be detained for ninety days, and for a longer term of ten days for every day of default, unless a reasonable excuse be given for the delays that have occurred.

6. Notices shall be given of the number and character of the slaves required, the time and place of their delivery, the time for which the service is required, and of the arrangements made for the subsistence, management and custody of the slaves so required; and if the masters of the slaves, shall agree to furnish subsistence for their slaves, and a suitable overseer or agent to superintend them, they shall have the privilege of so doing. But such overseers shall be subject to the control of the officer in charge, and may be dismissed for any misconduct by him.

7. The sum of twenty dollars per month for each slave delivered in pursuance to requisition, and fifteen dollars per month for each slave held in consequence of failure of his master to obey requisition made as herein before provided, shall be paid by the Confederate States, and soldiers rations, medicins and medical attendance furnished, and the value of all such slaves, as may die during their time of service or thereafter from injuries received or diseases contracted, in such service or may not be returned, shall be paid by the Confederate States. Such value shall be conclusively established by a formal appraisement by a Board of Experts mutually agreed upon at the time the slaves are received into the Confederate service—Compensation shall also be made for all injuries to slaves arising from the act of the public enemy, or from any injury arising from a want of due diligence on the part of the authorities of the Confederate States. But the Confederate States will not be liable for any slave not returned by reason of fraud or collusion on the part of the owner or his agent, or the overseer selected by him to superintend them, nor if his death should be caused by the act of God, or by disease existing when the slave is received by Confederate authorities.

8. Subsistence and provisions furnished by the owner shall be commuted for at the rates allowed soldiers in service. All slaves sent voluntarily to the Confederate authorities, and accepted by them without other special contrast, shall stand on the same footing as those delivered under requisition, and the owners of all slaves delivered or taken under requisition shall be entitled to regard the Confederate States as contracting with them to comply with the obligations and conditions herein expressed.

9 In case there should be any disagreement on the subject of the value of any slave impressed, or in case the impressing officer shall not be satisfied of the accuracy of any valuation or valuations, the appraisement shall be referred to the appraisers appointed under the 5th section of the act concerning impressments according to the provisions of the act of Congress approved 27th April, 1863, and published in Orders No. 53, current series.

By order;
(Signed,) S. COOPER.
A., & I., General
may3—d&ct11may

LATEST BY TELEGRAPH

Reports of the Press Associatio

FURTHER FROM THE FIFHT.

ORANGE C. H., May 6.

The attack by the enemy this morning was very violent, but they were repulsed in every instance. A strong effort was made to turn our right. We drove them back on our left, but they was stubborn on our right—but, Longstreet finally forced them to give way.

Gen'l Longstreet received a severe wound in the shoulder.

Gen'l Paul Jennings was mortally wounded.

The fighting was principally with musketry, the ground being unsuitable for artillery.

Col. Brown, of the Virginia Artillery, killed.

The battle fought was near the Wilderness.

The enemy have been pushed back near Chancellorsville.

The Yankee General Wadsworth was killed.

Seventeen hundred prisoners have reached here.

LATER.

ORANGE C H. May 6.

The following additional particulars of the fight received yesterday. Heth and Wilcox in the fight yesterday: they checked and drove back three corps' and two divisions of the enemy.

Laws' N. C., brigade last night surprised and captured three hundred prioners.

Gen Pegram was painfully wounded in the knee.

From 3 o'clock until night there was heavy musketry fighting and but little artillery engaged. Cooks brigade fought well and loses heavily. Thomas and McGowan's brigade also, suffered considerably.

Rosser fought Wilcox's whole division of Yankee cavalry yesterday with a single brigade, driving them back at all points. They are fighting again this morning, mostly musketry. It is reported and believed that we are driving them.

Gen Benning slightly wounded in the arm in the fight this morning.

The battle field is 25 miles below here.

About 300 more prisoners received here, and 300 more are on the way.

The Richmond Ambulance Committee arrived here this morning.

The Press correspondent left for the battle field this morning.

2D DISPATCH.

RICHMOND, May 7th.

The following received this morning:

HEAD'QRS ARMY NORTHERN VA.,
May 6th, 1864.

To the Sec. of War:

Early this morning as the division of Gen. Hill engaged yesterday were being retired, the enemy advanced, creating some confusion, but the ground lost was recovered as soon as fresh troops got into position, and the enemy were driven back to the original line, afterwards. We turned the left of his fresh line, drove it from the field, leaving large numbers of dead and wounded in our hands, among them Gen Wadsworth. A subsequent attack forced the enemy into his entrenched lines on Brook road, extending from the Wilderness tavern on the right to Trigg's mill.

The enemy advanced on us fast, and, thanks be to a merciful God they have been repulsed.

Our loss in killed is not large, but we have many wounded; most of them slightly—Artillery being but litte used on either side.

I grieve to announce Lieut-General Longstreet severely wounded, Gen'l Jenkins killed, and Gen'l Pegram badly wounded yesterday.

Gen'l Stafford, it is hoped, will recover.

(Signed.) R. E. LEE, Gen'l.

3D DESPATCH.

RICHMOND, May 7.

The Chief Monitor in the James river is the Oneida, just finished at New York.

The Yankee gunboat destroyed by a torpedo yesterday was blown into fragments. An official despatch says that there was hardly a piece left as big as a row boat. After the explosion, the rest of the fleet stopped.

Nothing heard of the situation of affairs this morning.

Grant's plan was to turn our right and get between Lee and Richmond.

Longstreet had turned the enemys left, and was pressing him back steadily when severely wounded. He was shot by Mahone's brigade through mistake. Jenkins was killed by the same brigade. Kershaw commanded McLaw's division with great honor.

In the late battles the Alabama and Gordon's Georgia brigades suffered severely.

FROM TRANS-MISSISSIPPI.

MOBILE, May 7th.

A special to the Tribune, dated Jackson the 5th, says an officer left Taylor's camp, 15 miles from Alexandria, on the 28th and confirms the report of Banks' retreat to Alexandria.

The gunboat, Eastrop, blown up with two transports captured. The remainder of the fleet is above the Rapids—no chance to escape.

Taylor captured four thousand prisoners.

Price's sucesses consists in Marmaduke capturing Steele's train.

Steele was surrounded and Price demanded his surrender. Steele agreed on condition that the negroes be treated as prisoners of war. Price refused the terms and referred to Smith who replied that the negroes be sent to their owners.

Steele refused to surrender on these terms. The further action was unknown. It is believed that the whole force would capitulate. Smith is reinforcing Price.

THE FIGHT COMMENCED.

ORANGE C. H. May 6th.

A considerable engagement occurred 20 miles below here near Parker's Store, in Spottsylvania county, on the Plank road, between a part of Ewell's corps and five corps of the Yankee infantry, including Sickels' regulars. The engagement lasted from 12 o'clock until night. Our troops repulsed the enemy most handsomely, capturing nine hundred and eighty-one prisoners, and forty commissioned officers, who have arrived here. Gen J M Jones, and Col Warren, 10th Va., killed, and Gen Stafford mortally wounded.

FROM RICHMOND.

RICHMOND, May 6th.

The fleet in James river came up yesterday to Bermuda Hundreds above City Point, and landed several regiments. The enemy's force is estimated at about 9000. It is believed the plan is to attempt to cut the railroad between Richmond and Petersburg, or move against Fort Drewry.

The enemy on the Peninsula is reported advancing.

2D DESPATCH.

RICHMOND, May 6.

The following was received this morning

HEAD'QRS ARMY NORTHERN VA.,
May 5th, 1864.

Hon. Sec. War:

The enemy crossed the Rapidan at Ely's and Germana Fords. Two corps of this army moved to oppose him—Ewell by the old turnpike and Hill by the plank road. They arrived this morning in close proximity to the enemy's line of march. A strong attack was made on Ewell, who repulsed it, capturing many prisoners and four pieces of artillery.

The enemy subsequently concentrated upon Hill who, with Heth's and Wilcox's divisions, successfully resisted repeated and desperate assaults. A large force of cavalry and artillery on our right were driven back by Rosser's brigade.

By the blessing of God we maintained our position against every effort until night when the contest closed.

We have to mourn the loss of many officers and men.

The gallant Gen J M Jones was killed, and Brig Gen Stafford, I fear, mortally wounded, while leading his command with conspicuous valor.

R. E. LEE, Gen.

FROM JOHNSTON'S ARMY.

DALTON, May 5th.

Contrary to all expectation, the enemy has advanced but little to-day.

A division of Hooker's corps are at Lee and Gordon's Mills, and Palmer's corps and one division are in front of Tunnell Hill, occupying our old picket stations. Howard's corps, two divisions, are between Varnel's Station and Red Clay. All are busy engaged cutting roads and causeways and building bridgeways. Their advance will be necessarily very slow.

Numbers of deserters have come into our lines to-day and given themselves up, saying that their time expires from the 10th to the 12th, and none of them will fight in the approaching engagement.

FROM GEN. LEE'S ARMY.

2ND DESPATCH.

RICHMOND, May 6.

The fight between Lee and Grant was resumed this morning.

Several telegrams received represent the news from the front to be cheering. About two thousand prisoners were captured yesterday.

The train on the York river railroad returned this morning after proceeding to Meadow Station, in consequence of a report that our troops had fallen back, and the Yankees having crossed the Chickahominy at South Bottom bridge.

The steamer Shultz, with Yankee prisoners for City Point was turned back by the enemy this morning.

Reported additional transports with troops came up the river to-day.

Quite a large force landed on the South river, opposite City Point. No uneasiness is felt in official circles on account of the aspect of affairs.

One Yankee gunboat on James river was blown up this afternoon.

FROM MISSISSIPPI.

DEMOPOLIS, May 6th.

Information from Mississippi states that the enemy, with ten thousand infantry and two batteries of artillery and 280 cavalry, all under Geu'l McCarther, were advancing towards Yazoo City. They encamped the night before last, eight mile below Mechanicsburg.

FROM TRANS MISSISSIPPI.

MERIDIAN May 6.

Information from Trans Mississippi confirms former rumors of a battle between Price and Steele, in which, the Confederates gained a complete victory. Steele is said to have lost his entire wagon train.

Nothing further from the fight in East La.

The cars resumed their regular trips to Brandon on Sunday.

3D DESPATCH.

DALTON, May 6.

The enemy have been almost at a stand still to-day. They are repairing both Rail Roads and have a chain of pickets which render it impossible to learn what is going on inside. The enemy's lower pickets $1\frac{1}{2}$ miles from Tunnel Hill at 2 o'clock.

Gen Johnston has issued an order granting pardon to all persons under arrest except those for plundering and pilfering.

CONGRESSIONAL.

RICHMOND, May 6th.

Both Houses of Congress held a short session to-day. In the Sonate Wigfall introduced resolutions defining the powers of the Confederate States Government—made the order of the day for Monday next. Adjourned until Monday.

The House adopted resolutions for the appointment of a committee to inquire into the expediency of employing stenographic reporters.

FROM GEORGIA.

MACON, May 6.

A disastrous fire occurred in East Macon to-day, which burned two large cotton warehouses and several other buildings and about five thousand bales of cotton, also a small amount of Government cotton.

THE MILITARY SITUATION.

Public attention is just now completely engrossed with the two great movements supposed to be pending. The march of Grant against Lee, and that of Thomas against Johnston, are of the most significance. The fate of Virginia and Georgia in the estimation of the enemy, will be determined by these movements. Indeed, they imagine that the whole Confederacy will be at their feet, and the subjugation of the South be virtually secured, if they shall be successful in Virginia and Georgia. Seeing, therefore, the importance they attach to these two movements, and remembering that Chickamauga was won by the timely arrival of detachments from the army of Lee, they have determined to mass, as far as practicable, their forces against Lee and Johnston, and make a simultaneous attack in order to prevent reinforcements being sent from one to the other. This purpose is clearly avowed in the following extract from the Nashville correspondence of the Chicago Journal.:

"It is evident that the spring campaign is to begin within a fortnight—perhaps by the first of May. The object is, evidently, to press the enemy every where at the same time, to prevent him from concentrating all his troops in Virginia, as he is evidently attempting. I am fully convinced that, unless a demonstration is made towards Atlanta within a very short time, Northern Georgia will be evacuated and the troops sent to reinforce Lee."

Accordingly, we perceive that simultaneously with the advance of Grant, Thomas makes a demonstration towards Dalton with a view of occupying the attention of Johnston. Our reporters supposed that a battle between those two commanders was imminent and could not be postponed more than a day or two. We may, therefore, reasonably expect to receive stirring news from Dalton ere long.

All the information we have been able to gather concerning the condition of the army under Gen. Johnston, is encouraging. In numbers it is large, whilst its *morale* is represented to be greatly improved. Still, we do not feel the same confidence of success in that quarter that we entertain respecting events nearer home.

It may be, however, that that our repeated misfortunes in the West have operated to impair confidence and create distrust.—But our troops at Dalton are commanded by a skilful and wary leader, and doubtless will render a good account of themselves. Thus far, the situation wears a cheerful aspect.

May the God of justice crown our arms with success, and give us an early, honorable, and lasting peace.

LYNCHBURG VIRGINIAN.

Notice.—The cross mark appended to the names of certain subscribers indicates that the term for which they subscribed will soon expire. They are thus notified in time to renew their subscription if they desire.

RAGS WANTED.—The highest market price will be paid at this Office for Clean Cotton Rags. They will be purchased in any quantity.

About 300 Campbell militia arrived in this city yesterday to take a hand in guarding the Yankee prisoners.

The Richmond *Sentinel* says that General Beauregard has charge of the defences of the Southside.

The *Dispatch* speaking of the explosion of the Yankee gun boat, says that it occurred at Deep Bottom, near Aikin's Landing, 12 miles below Richmond and that not a soul on board survived the disaster.

Gen Robert Toombs was in Columbus, Georgia, a few days ago. In conversation he stated that "the present is the brightest day which has ever dawned upon our Confederacy."

A locomotive belonging to the Va. & Tenn. Railroad, blew up in their yard yesterday, badly scalding the engineer and throwing the fragments up into the city. Nobody else hurt that we heard of.

Force of the Enemy.—The Yankee prisoners in this city say that Grant had 200,000 men and that Lee had but 60,000. Let this be remembered when they attribute their defeat and route to overwhelming rebel numbers. They express great astonishment that Grant has not yet occupied Richmond.

Rags Wanted.—We are requested to say that linen or cotton rags are badly wanted to dress the wounds of the soldiers at this Post. All persons having old rags large enough to bind up wounds or to be serviceable in dressing the same, are requested to send them to Dr. Taylor, at the Medical Purveyor's office.

Ladies Relief Hospital.—The Lady officers of this hospital earnestly request their friends in the city and county to send them rags and slipperyelm bark. Their hospital is filled with very sick and many wounded soldiers. They crave buttermilk.

Our friends abroad who have telegraphed us for news are informed that our failure to respond promptly, in all cases, is attributable to the refusal of the telegraph office to receive dispatches, owing to the great pressure of public business. It gives us pleasure to satisfy, as far as we can, the anxious inquiries of the people.

The debate in the Yankee Congress relative to the propriety of giving the rebel States a republican form of government, reminds one of the old formula for dressing a hare. It begins with, "first catch the hare." Our Yankee brethren had better wait until they catch the hare. They are catching fits just now, and the probability is that they will soon have no government of their own.

Lieut. Gen. Longstreet.—It is no secret that this gallant officer has been removed from the army to the interior. He arrived in this city on Sunday night, and the country will be gratified to know that though severely, he is not dangerously wounded. He is very cheerful and hopeful of the results now pending. The General is very comfortably provided with lodgings at the residence of his kindswoman, Mrs Caroline Garland, and expects to be able to take the field in a short time.

Gen'l Jackson's Grave.—Mr. Hugh Sheddon, of Liverpool, having presented to the Governor of Virginia, through the Secretary of War, a Confederate Flag of his own manufacture to be raised over the grave of the lamented Lt. General T. J. Jackson, the ceremony of raising the Flag will take place to-day, this being the anniversary of the death of Gen. Jackson.

Governor Letcher will deliver an address appropriate to the occasion.

Help for the Wounded.—We are requested to say that the article of buttermilk is in great demand with the wounded soldiers arriving here. They crave it. Cannot the farmers send in of their abundance? Our own citizens are doing all they can. Committees are in waiting at the cars day and night, supplying the wounded men as the trains arrive, with all the comforts that can be had, even at the present enormous prices. The towns people are heavily taxed, in this regard, and the country people should contribute to the wants of the gallant men who have suffered so severely in the common defence.—The poor fellows evince great gratitude at these manifestations of concern for their comfort, and even those who are too feeble to do more than look the thanks they feel, do it in the most expressive manner.

The line was so much occupied with Government business last night that we did not receive our usual despatches, but there was a rumor that there was fighting yesterday at Drewry's Bluff, the enemy endeavoring to flank the works. We have, also, good reason to believe that a whole corps of the enemy was terribly cut up near Fredericksburg on Sunday. We could not get the particulars but the corps is supposed to be the Fifth, formerly commanded by Sickels. Ewell is reported to have been their opponent.

It is said that a dispatch was received at the War Office from Gen Lee, saying that his victory was complete.

Information was received here yesterday to the effect that the enemy, supposed to be under Averill, had reached the neighborhood of Dublin and that a fight was progressing. A company under Crawford had fought them all the way from Rocky Gap, a distance of about forty miles. They are said to consist of five regiments of infantry and one company of cavalry. Reinforcements were hurrying to McCausland who commanded our forces, that we may rest satisfied that every effort will be made to defeat the object of the enemy. From what we have heard of the position of Gen. Breckenridge, we should not be surprised to hear that the Yanks have found themselves uncomfortably hemmed in.

LATER.

Since writing the above we learn that the Yankees occupy Dublin and that McCausland is disputing their passage to New River Bridge. This party is said to be commanded by one-eyed Powell, who was captured last summer at Wytheville. The force under command of Averill was divided, one party going to the Salt Works, from which they were driven by Morgan and whipped badly yesterday. We regret to hear that Major Blake L. Woodson of this city was killed.

The Five Dollar Notes.—We are reluctantly compelled to decline receiving these notes except at the established rate of depreciation. We did all we could to keep up their credit, and have received them at par until within a day or too, hoping that Congress would do something to restore their credit. Since it has refused to do anything, these notes have been under the ban and are not taken by town or country people at par. Under these circumstances, and finding ourselves unable to purchase supplies of any kind with these notes, at par, we are compelled to yield to the force of circumstances and go with the tide. We would, however, advise all persons who have not provided themselves with enough of the four per cent bonds, to hold on to the fives rather than submit to the shave.

It is amusing to read such extracts as the following by the light of events that have transpired since this was written. The immense preparations made by the enemy to give the final and decisive blow, show the ground of their confidence and the extent of the combinations which our glorious army, by the blessing of God, has overcome:

[From the Washington correspondent of the New York Tribune.]

THE PROSPECT OF THE COMING CAMPAIGN.

"The plan of the campaign resolved upon by the commander of the army of the Potomac should, and with God's favor will, substantially quell the rebellion and end the war. The army is in the best possible condition and spirit. Rivalries between commanders and corps are at an end. The army is at last a unit. Its commander is in perfect accord with the head of the War Department. A difference of opinion that was not angry, respecting the disposition to be made of the invalids, was promptly harmonized by an explanation. Secretary Stanton has the fullest confidence in General Grant's capacity, and in the wisdom of his plans. Their relations are entirely harmonious. A sun of Austerlitz is rising for freedom."

FUNERAL NOTICE.

The funeral services of the late Mrs. N. R. Bowman will take place at the residence, on Court Street, this morning at half past 9 o'clock.

The friends of the family are invited to be present.

LATEST BY TELEGRAPH

Reports of the Press Association.

Entered according to Act of Congress, in the year 1863, by J. S. Thrasher, in the Clerk's Office of the District Court of the Confederate States for the Northern District of Georgia.

FURTHER PARTICULARS OF THE GREAT FIGHT.

OUR ARMS STILL VICTORIOUS.

THE ENEMY DRIVEN BACK.

&C., &C., &C.

Orange C. H. May 7th.

The Press Correspondent left the front at 4 o'clock a. m., bringing the following reliable intelligence:

Ewell again repulsed the enemy yesterday, who advanced on his front with five lines of battle.

The enemy's loss was terrible, especially in Early's front.

Ewell's loss very small.

About 12 o'clock yesterday, the enemy having previously attacked Heth and Wilcox and drove them back, Longstreet planned and was in the act of executing a flank movement on the enemy's left wing, when, by mistake, our men fired into Lt Gen Longstreet and staff, instantly killing Brig Gen Jenkins, of S. C., and seriously; though not mortally, wounding Gen'l Longstreet in the shoulder. So say the physicians with whom the Press Correspondent conversed, and who examined his wound.

Our troops continued to press the enemy until about 4 o'clock, driving back the enemy's left and centre some two miles, our left standing fast in its position.

Last night our men held possession of the enemy's battle-field on the left and centre, capturing a number of the enemy's wounded and some dead.

The enemy fought yesterday most obstinately. On all parts of the field our successes were very great, though not decisive.

The charge of Gordon's Brigade on Thursday is represented as the grandest of the war. Just before daylight there was some picket firing in front of Hill's corps, and about 6 a m cannonading on Ewell's line.

Our loss thus far is about 5000, of whom, a large portion are slightly wounded.

The proportion of officers to privates killed and wounded is very much larger than in any previous fight.

The Yankee Gen Hays is reported killed, and, a dead Yankee Gen with the inuitials, H H C., supposed Courch or Case, was found on Ewell's front.

The fight occurred in a densely wooded country, hence little or no artillery was brought into action.

At one time yesterday, when the enemy was heavily pressing Hill's men, Gen Kershaw opportunely, by doublquicking, with his troops, arrived on the field, checked, repulsed and pursued the enemy, thus turning the fortunes of the day on that end of the line.

The battle-field extended a space of eight miles in length.

LATER—THE ENEMY FALLING BACK.

Orange C H. May 8.

Advices from the front to sunrise this morning state that there were no general engagement yesterday, only heavy skirmishing. There was an impression last night that the enemy were falling back towards Culpeper or Fredericksburg.

The negro troops occupying Brandy Station, advanced out to Culpeper C. H. Friday, and occupied it yesterday, but went back to Brandy Station, set fire to the stores, principally Quartermasters, and marched to join Grant. Scouts say the enemy have abandoned the line of the Orange and Alexandria railway, and no cars are running on it. It is supposed that Grant intends now to make Fredericksburg his base.

Ewell holds the road leading to Germana Ford, but the enemy still have two fords by which to cross the river to Culpeper if they wish.

Stewart yesterday was engaged with the enemy on our right, and it is reported was compelled to give back until Hampton joined him, when he forced the enemy to retire.

The enemy's loss thus far is estimated at 18000. Ours will reach 7000.

The Yankee Gen. Hays is certainly killed; Gen. Wadsworth wounded, and a prisoner. He may recover. Gen. Oglesby is reported killed.

Twenty four hundred privates and one hundred commissioned officers have been registered here, not including the Yankee wounded, of whom we captured some 1,500, chiefly in front of Hill and Longstreet, on Friday.

Our men began yesterday evening to bury our own and the Yankee dead.

Siegel occupied Winchester on Friday with 5,000 infantry and 2,000 cavalry.

The country between the Rappahannock and the Potomac is reported to be filled with Yankee deserters.

Gen. Longstreet's condition is much improved. He left for the interior today.

Mosby captured ten wagons heavily laden, and horses attached, near Martinsburg, last Thursday.

The latest from the front, at 12 M. represents the enemy falling back towards Fredericksburg, our troops pursuing them closely.

Rosser's cavalry fought the enemy yesterday all day on our extreme right, losing heavily and gaining nothing important.

Ewell captured 2 pieces of artillery in the fight. On Thursday 1200 wounded arrived here, and received every attention.

Gen R. H. Anderson now commands in place of Gen. Longstreet.

[SPECIAL DESPATCH.]

BALTIMORE & OHIO RAIL ROAD TAPPED.

FIVE MILLIONS DOLLARS WORTH OF PROPERTY DESTROYED.

Harrisonburg, May 8th.

On Monday 2d instant, McNeal, with 60 men, struck the Baltimore & Ohio Railroad at Piedmont, burned a bridge, destroyed the Machine Shops, and two freight trains of Government stores.

Intercepted and destroyed the Express; overhauled important mail matter; secured nine engines; burned 3; six were sent up the road under full steam, without Engineer.—Piedmont is within six miles of New Creek, where there is a Yankee force.

McNeal's loss, one man and two horses killed. The damage will amount to four or five millions. Thirty two horses taken.—Hundred and fifteen prisoners taken and paroled.

BATTLE AT PORT WALTHALL JUNCTION.

THE ENEMY REPULSED, &c.

Richmond, 8th.

On Friday afternoon a force of the enemy landed at Port Walthall, and advanced to Port Walthall Junction of the Richmond and Petersburg Railroad.

After a sharp skirmish, the enemy were repulsed, leaving about 100 killed and wounded on the field. The enemy having been reinforced, renewed the attack yesterday afternoon. The engagement lasted several hours, resulting in a second repulse of the enemy with heavy loss. Nothing definite has been heard this morning.

It is reported the enemy have again returned to the attack, and it is believed that our forces are equal to the emergency.

All the Yankee officers confined at Libby prison were sent to Danville on Saturday, to make room for fresh arrivals.

Richmond, May 8th.

The following received this morning:

Head'qrs Army Northern Va., May 7th, 1864.

To the Sec. of War:

Gen. Gordon turned the enemy's extreme right yesterday evening, and drove him from his rifle pits.

Among the prisoners captured are Generals Seymour and Sheler. A number of arms were also taken.

The enemy has abandoned Germana Ford road, and removed the pontoon bridge towards Ely's Ford.

There has been no attack to-day—only slight skirmishing along the line.

(Signed.) R. E. LEE, Gen'l.

ANOTHER YANKEE GUNBOAT CAPTURED AND BURNT.

Richmond, May 8.

An official dispatch from Chaffin's Bluff states that one of the enemy's gunboats was attacked, disabled, boarded and burned, on the 7th.

Two iron clads bore down on our forces, but they returned.

No particulars given. No loss on our side.

THE FIGHT AT PORT WALTHALL—BUTLER COMMANDING IN PERSON.

Petersburg, May 8, 1864.

The battle fought in the vicinity of Port Walthall Junction yesterday, raged from eleven to half-past four o'clock, with an intermission of half an hour. The enemy greatly outnumbered us but were handsomely repulsed, and retreated from the field leaving some dead and wounded. The heaviest fighting was on our left, near the railroad, where chiefly South Carolinians were engaged. Our casualties are one hundred and seventy-five—about 30 killed. The prisoners taken say they belong to Gilmore's corps recently in Florida, and that Butler commanded in person. The enemy lost very heavily. Prisoners say two thousand. All quiet to-day, save slight firing from gunboats in the Appomattox.

DEATH OF GEN'L STAFFORD.

Richmond, May 8th.

Brig. Gen'l Stafford, of La., died this morning at No. 4 Hospital.

The report of the ... Richmond, May 7th. represents the actual circu... of the Treasury of April, seven hundred and fifty... the first About two hundred and fifty millions were funded on the East of the Mississippi—presumed to be fifty millions more than have been funded West of that river. Less than one-half of the notes are hundred dollar notes, leaving unfunded of that denomination about one hundred and twenty-eight millions, after the deduction tax of one-third. Actual currency left in circulation, two hundred and fourteen millions. The Secretary earnestly advises against the further issue of Treasury notes.

Flake's Bulletin.

TRI-WEEKLY.

F. FLAKE.......S. RINKER

PUBLISHED BY F. FLAKE & CO.

GALVESTON:

Wednesday Morning, May 11th, 1864.

THE BLOCKADE.—A schooner came up from the eastward on Sunday morning. A gunboat went West on Monday morning and returned at 12:40 same day. A gunboat arrived from the N.-East Monday morning, also barque-propeller Virginia from the West. The side-wheel left during the [illegible] same day. [illegible] yesterday morning, and a gunboat during yesterday morning and returned in the evening. At anchor at sundown, flag ship, propeller Virginia, 4 gunboats, a brig and a schooner.

BY TELEGRAPH!

[SPECIAL TO FLAKE'S BULLETIN.]

SHREVEPORT, May 10th, 1864.

General Taylor has since April 21st driven the enemy seventy-five miles, fought them every mile, destroyed or captured one heavy iron-clad, two wooden gunboats and seven transports, killed, wounded and captured 2,000.

Nothing from Arkansas to-day.

SHREVEPORT, May 10th, 1864.

The iron-clad Osceola, which could not get down to the falls with the fleet, is in our possession with nine guns, the guns from the Eastport also. We will probably capture all the fleet.

Yankee Steele was wounded at Jenkin's Ferry, and his right bower, Major Thayer, killed.

Our cavalry since the fight have captured 180 wagons and several ambulances filled with enemy's wounded.

Enemy still retreating.

SHREVEPORT, May 10th, 1864.

LATER.—From a strictly reliable source I am enabled to send you the following:

General Banks has been partially reinforced. One of his regiments, the 120th Ohio, was captured on the City of Baltimore on the river below Alexandria, en route to that place. The boat was captured and [illegible] Warner was also captured and sunk while going down, and the Anna captured and burned. These three are transports.

The gunboats Signal No. 6 and Covington No. 25 attacked our batteries on the 5th near Wilson's Landing. The latter was fired and consumed, the former captured, her guns removed and the boat sunk.

The river is thus obstructed and Banks' communication with New Orleans cut off.

The enemy are short of provisions, as is apparent from the enclosed letter which I send by courier. Foraging parties, supported by heavy forces, are thrown out daily on the roads and driven back by our troops.

Ten boats are still above the falls. The Yankees with characteristic energy and ingenuity are attempting to construct a dam to get them over the falls.

The Mississippi and Atchafalaya are falling; therefore, even if they succeed in crossing the falls, it is doubtful whether they can cross the bar or Snaggy Point.

FROM ARKANSAS.

Letter to Major Guy M. Bryan:

"News established of death of Thayer and wounding of Steele. Enemy destroyed and abandoned all his transportation, 250 wagons, within 4 miles of Jenkin's Ferry. His retreat was complete. If our cavalry could have crossed Saline in force, his destruction would have been inevitable." H. P.

HOUSTON, May 10th, 1864.

One hundred and seven privates, twenty three officers and three niggers (Yankees) captured by Col. Griffin on gunboats at Calcasieu, arrived here to-day from Beaumont by rail. C.

☞ We are informed that scouts belonging to Brown's regiment picked up about 40 bales of cotton on the Gulf shore, near the Three Trees, on Saturday and Sunday last.

HEAD QUARTERS BUREAU OF CONSCRIPTION
Trans-Mississippi Department,
Marshall, Texas, April 28th, 1864.

Special Orders No. 65.

Enrolling officers of this State will suspend the execution of General Orders No. 9, current series, until further orders from this Bureau.

By command of Brigadier-General GREER.

A. POPE, A. A. Gen'l.

General Orders, No. 9, were instructions to enrolling officers to carry out immediately all the requirements of the conscript acts passed by the late Congress.—ED. BUL.

THE BATTLE OF SALINE RIVER, ARK., APRIL 30TH.—P. P. gives an account of this battle to the Galveston *News*, from Tulip, Ark., May 2nd, from which we condense:

General Smith commanded our army in person. Numbers about equal on each side. Yankee army composed principally of Dutch and negroes. There has been no more stubbornly contested battle in this war. We were frequently driven back, and advanced again. At last the Yankees gave way and crossed the river, throwing 2000 Enfield rifles and 2 cannon captured from us into the river. The rifles we recovered again. Yankee loss not known. They took most of their killed and wounded with them, left 135 mortally wounded on this side and another lot on the other side of the river. Yankees destroyed 103 wagons at Camden and 250 more in Saline bottom. Our loss very heavy, particularly in officers, estimated at from 400 to 1000. I think that it will come nearer the latter figure. I cannot say that we achieved a great victory. We kept the ground, but the Yankees accomplished their object, that is they escaped with about 500 negroes [illegible] a number of families that left Camden with them.

From the Mobile *Tribune* of the 14th we learn that Forrest had an engagement after leaving fort Pillow, with the Yankees at White's station, three miles from Memphis, in which he killed and wounded a large number of them. The Southern R. R. depot and other buildings in Vicksburg have been destroyed by fire. General Polk is about making his headquarters again at Meridian. The *Clarion* has been re-established at Meridian. Meridian is being rebuilt where it was burnt by Sherman. A good deal of trade has been done between Vicksburg and the Yazoo in cotton, but Ross has interfered with it. Telegraphic communication has been re-opened with Holly Springs. Letters from Europe state that Dr. E[illegible]oni, who is a large property holder in Texas, is to accompany Maximilian as counsellor, with the title of Duke. He is said to be very urgent for the recognition of the Confederacy, and at the bottom of the machinations to re-annex Texas to the Mexican Empire.—*Houston Telegraph, 9th.*

THE CASE OF THE ALEXANDRA FINALLY DECIDED AGAINST THE CROWN.—Wilmer & Smith's *European Times* of April 9th contains the final decision of the highest tribunal in England in the case of the Alexandra. It is the decision of the House of Lords in the case. "The Attorney General vs. Sillem and others," claimants of the Alexandra, as to whether the Court of Exchequer Chamber had or had not the right to entertain the appeal sent to them from the Court of Exchequer, relative to the verdict given against the crown in the case of that vessel. The Lord Chancellor, Lord Cranworth, Lord St. Leonards, Lord Wensleydale, Lord Chelmsford, and Lord Kingsdown delivered lengthy judgments. Four of the Lords, including the Lord Chancellor, were against, and two for the crown. The appeal of the Attorney General was dismissed with costs. The public were present in large numbers.

On the subject of the removal of the British Consuls from the Confederate States, the Marquis of Clanricarde said, in the House of Lords on April 5th, that though he did not go so far as to desire the recognition of the Confederate States, yet the want of accredited officials had been productive of great inconvenience and loss. In his opinion the want could be supplied without recognizing the Confederates. Earl Russel said he had endeavored to devise some plan of supplying the place of Consuls for the protection of British subjects and their interests in the Confederate States, and had entered into communication with Mr. Mason for that purpose; but as yet there had been no results.

There is a considerable excitement in Lancashire about "Federal recruiting." It appears that men, with families, are engaged as mill hands and receive an advance which they bind themselves to repay in ninety days, that is in about two months after they get to America. Of course they cannot pay the amount in that time, and in default are obliged to enlist. Such, at all events, is the statement made by the "Central Relief Committee," which is not a political body, and the members of which are men of very high standing.

The Confederate Government has sent the Hon. J. P. Holcombe, of Va., to Halifax, as its special Commissioner, to look after the affair of the Chesapeake. Mr. Holcombe's instructions are said to be very definite. The Confederate Government assumes the entire responsibility, and demands the unconditional release of the men. The restitution of the vessel is demanded on the ground that it was a lawful capture.

The London *Army and Navy Gazette* has, for the last year, been strongly Federal. Its faith is shaken. It observes: "We have through good and evil held to the faith that the North must succeed. But ignorance and incapacity, faction and corruption, may counterbalance all the influence which should operate in producing a natural result. The Union, let us say it for the twentieth time, can never be restored. It begins to be doubtful at last if the means which the Northerners employ to subjugate the South, are equal to the work."

SHREVEPORT, May 4th.—*Dear News.*—Nothing additional from Arkansas, at least nothing worth reporting. A letter has been received from General Taylor to the effect that he is infesting Alexandria, and that a skirmish occurred a few days since on Bayou Robert, which was a complete success. Also, that we had captured and destroyed a transport below Alexandria, and 2000 bales of cotton, which were also destroyed.

Gov. Allen of La. calls on the refugees from that State, not engaged in cropping, to promptly return, with their teams and hands, and secure a full crop for that redeemed State. He adds: while "thus employed, provisions will be furnished by the State at cost."

Results of Amalgamation.

From The Richmond Dispatch, April 14.]

The Yankee project of commingling their breed with the African race is open to this dreadful objection—What will become of the Yankees?

We feel assured they have never weighed the awful consequences of such a catastrophe. The Yankee race blotted out of existence! They have threatened to exterminate the South, and behold, they are about to exterminate themselves! Alas! what will become of the cause of civilization, of humanity, of progress, without Yankees? What will the world do for steam engines and wooden nutmegs, philanthropic associations, and paper soled shoes, and patriotism, and patent medicines, puritanism and pumpkin pies, cuteness and codfish, without Yankee Doodles?

Did that blessed Mayflower cross the wide ocean for such an end? Was Pilgrim Rock consecrated for such a superstructure? Did the saintly Pilgrim Fathers fit out slave ships for the coast of Africa, and sell the cargoes to the south, with any idea that these sable heathens were to be united in wedlock to the descendants of the true believers? We wish that their grim old spectres could revisit the earth, and receive the due reward of their deeds in beholding the final result of their notable system for improving the morals, religion and politics of mankind.

It is not for us to complain of the great loss which mankind at large must suffer from the deprivation of Yankees. Three years of selfdenial have enabled us to dispense with even such luxury as their companionship. We find that, by dint of manly fortitude and abstemiousness, we can manage to exist without Harper, Beecher, Greeley, Everett, or any of their works. But how can Yankeedom give itself up in this wholesale suicide, immolate the memory of its ancestry, and slaughter that "manifest destiny" which was to appropriate the whole continent of America to the Yankee race?

The Confederacy can look with philosophical composure upon this tragical performance. We are not to be astonished at this time of day at any exhibition which Yankees may make. After all the atrocities and diablerie which for three years we have beheld and suffered, winding up in the effort to make a bonfire of a city of fifty thousand souls, we are not to be amazed by any new wickedness which Yankee ingenuity can invent. Having cohabited spiritually with the devil till their souls have become as black as the ace of spades, it is right and proper that they should adopt some process by which their bodies will approximate the complexion of their souls. Our only sympathy is with the sable medium of this national transformation. The polishing of Yankee boots, which has hitherto been their chief occupation in the free States, will now give place to the polishing of the entire Yankee nation, an achievement which no human power has yet been able to accomplish. A quarter of a century hence, the United States bids fair to be an empire of mullattoes, inheriting some improvement, perhaps, upon its abolition blood; but a sad depreciation of the African stock, which, in its lowest thraldom, was never so debased as when its "rich currents" commingled with the vile spawn of Black Republicanism.

From the Nassau Guardian of the 26th ult.

The steamer Helen (formerly Juno) left Charleston about half past eight P. M. on Wednesday, March 9, for this port. The weather was moderate on starting, but about midnight a stiff breeze sprang up, which increased to a gale at noon the next day. The wind was blowing from south to southwest. The vessel was then in the Gulf Stream. About forty five or fifty bales of cotton on deck, besides coal, &c., were thrown overboard to lighten ship, and she was put before the gale about four o'clock in the afternoon. She had previous to this taken in a considerable quantity of water, but this was pumped out. A fresh leak however, was started in the midship compartment, which extinguished the fires. At six o'clock P.M. the gale had not abated, and the steamer, which was then under sail, unfortunately parted amidships and sunk in three minutes. All hands were on deck at the time, and it is feared that many of them went down with her. Two of the officers [Messrs W. J. Burke and J. H. Dent] saved themselves by clinging to a piece of the bridge deck to which they held on from six o'clock in the evening till ten the next morning, when they were picked up by Capt. Habernicht, of the schooner Petrel, from Charleston, bound also to this port. Some of the crew got into two of the boats, but one of them was capsized by the falling of the smoke stack, and the other was swamped. There were eight officers, including the captain, belonging to the Helen, and twenty-two seamen, &c., besides one stowaway who, it is feared, all met with a watery grave. The bridge on which the two who were taken on board the Petrel saved themselves was not more than eight feet long by about four feet wide, and this parted in the night, and it was with great difficulty kept together again.

Capt H's attention was first directed to the survivors by seeing some of the cotton and pieces of the wreck floating about, when he tacked ship and stood towards them.

A correspondent of the Chattanooga *Gazette* says he learned from a rebel citizen that Johnston's force numbers 140 regiments, about 60,000 men. He will assume the offensive in a few weeks.

LYNCHBURG VIRGINIAN.

NOTICE.—The cross mark appended to the names of certain subscribers indicates that the term fo which they subscribed will soon expire. They are thus notified in time to renew their subscription if they desire.

RAGS WANTED.—The highest market price will be paid at this Office for Clean Cotton Rags. They will be purchased in any quantity.

A Yankee lieutenant who jumped off the train about thirty miles North of this place was recaptured and brought to this city today.

INCENDIARISM.—The stable of Mr Jas W. Wright, in Campbell, was fired on Wednesday night and burned to the ground, consuming four horses, harness, &c.

The quantity of bacon destroyed by the Yankees at Beaver Dam Depot, was 160,000 pounds. So says the Richmond *Enquirer*.—We could illy spare it.

THE 8TH VA. REGIMENT.—We have been requested to say that the 8th Va. has not been in any engagement as yet. Persons having friends in that Regiment may, therefore, feel easy about them. They are all safe.

FROM JOHNSTON'S ARMY.—A report was brought here from Richmond, yesterday, based upon a telegram said to have been received in that city, to the effect that Gen'l Johnston had encountered the enemy near Dalton and gained a signal advantage. The fruits of this advantage are said to be from six to nine thousand prisoners and a position of great strength gained by masterly strategy. We shall look with much anxiety for fuller accounts.

FROM SOUTHWESTERN VIRGINIA.—It is now ascertained with certainty that the enemy burnt New River bridge on the Va. & Tenn. R. R., destroyed the Company's Depot, a very fine structure at Christiansburg, and also the Machine shops of the Company at Central Depot. The fine mansion of Dr. Jno. B. Radford was also fired by a shell and burnt to the ground. In the list of casualties at Dublin Depot, is the name of Gen Albert G. Jenkins, said to be mortally wounded. It is reported that the Yankees have ten regiments and eight pieces of artillery. They were at Blacksburg yesterday, 7 miles from Christiansburg, where they were reinforced by two thousand cavalry. These are all the facts that we could glean with any certainty.

TORPEDOES IN JAMES RIVER.—We learn that Mr Britton who so gallantly guided the torpedo that lately blew a Yankee gunboat to atoms in James river, says the Petersburg *Register*, perished by the hands of the enraged foe in a few minutes after. When he had succeded in attaching the torpedo to the boat he was retiring when it exploded without injury to himself; but a volley from another boat wounded him. The enemy overtook him and stabbed him repeatedly with bayonets and beat him with the butt-ends of their muskets until life was extinct. The name of Britton will be long remembered as that of a hero who sacrificed himself in the service of his country.

GEN JONES, whose funeral took place at the Baptist Church in this town on yesterday evening, says the Charlottesville *Chronicle*, was a son of Col Jones, (deceased.) The Colonel was for many years a prominent citizen of this place. Gen Jones was educated at West Point; was an officer in the old U. S. Army, and was killed in the late battle of the Wilderness while gallantly leading his Brigade, which was of Gen Edward Johnson's Division, Ewell's Corps. His untimely fall is mourned by a large number of surviving relatives and friends in this place, in Orange, in Louisa, and in South Carolina.

AVERILL'S RAID.—A telegram says the Richmond *Dispatch*, was received at the War Department yesterday evening, announcing that Averill, with a very large force of mounted infantry, had the day before attacked the Confederates under Gen Jenkins, at Dublin Depot, in Pulaski county, and after a severe engagement forced them to fall back to this side of New river.

On our side Gen Jenkins was wounded, Col Hand was killed, Maj Tyler wounded, and a number of other officers killed and wounded. Among the wounded was Lieut Col Thomas Smith, a son of Gov. Smith, who fell shot through the thigh while gallantly leading his regiment—the 36th Virginia infantry.—He was left at the house of Mr Guthrie, three miles from Dublin, and fell into the hands of the enemy.

All the Government stores at Dublin were brought off in safety.

PETERSBURG SAFE.—Although Grant has announced that Petersburg is in his possession, the Petersburg "Register" of that city, in speaking of the defence of Fort Clifton, and the situation of Petersburg, has the following:

The enemy's attack on Fort Clifton was repulsed in the most gallant style. After the destruction of their gunboat the balance of the boats moved off and the Island batteries withdrew. The fort was uninjured and no casualties occurred to the garrison. The wind of a shell stunned two men temporarily, which was the only damage sustained.—On the night of Monday the garrison was reinforced and the works strengthened. The brave defenders are now ready and anxious for another brush with the enemy.

On every side Petersburg is prepared for successful resistance. Every hour adds to the efficiency of our defences, and increases the numbers of our veteran defenders. Our citizens are aware of all that is passing, but for the information of our readers at a distance, we state that brigade after brigade is passing through, formed of battle scarred veterans, bearing the tattered remnants of flags that have witnessed a score of fights. There is no apprehension entertained here of the Yankee invaders, and our country friends who receive this paper may rely that Petersburg is impregnable to Beast Butler and his plundering minions.

ACKNOWLEDGEMENTS.—The Surgeon in charge of General Hospital No. 2, on behalf of the sick and wounded soldiers, returns thanks to the ladies, in the Elon District of Amherst county, for the following contributions:

Mrs. B Shelton, 1 bunch Asparagrass.
" Ambler, 1 bundle rags.
" R D Rucker, 1 " "
" Wm Hawkins, 1 " "
" D B Cheatwood, " " and 5 pounds butter.
Miss M L Terry, 1 bundle rags.
W R Shelton, 1 bunch Asparagrass.
Miss M Clark, " bundle rags.
Mrs Shelton, " " " and 1 peck of potatoes.
Mrs R S Barton, 1 " "
Miss Keeton, " " "
Mrs R G Scott, " " "
Mrs Smith and Miss Rucker, one bundle rags.
Mrs M J Wortham, one bundle rags and 2 bunches Asparagrass.
Mrs M Wortham, a lot nice fish and 3 lbs butter.
Mrs R Woody, one chicken and one bunch slippery elm. Also, from the same, 30 fresh fish and one bundle rags.
Miss St John, one chicken and one bundle rags.
Miss Kellumns, one bundle rags.
Mrs V H Rucker, two loaves of bread and six chickens.
Mrs W Terry, one hundred buisquit, 1½ pounds butter and one ham of bacon. By the same, one chicken.
Mrs E J Hewett, one bundle rags.
Miss S W Mason, one bundle rags.
" Sallie W Scott, " " " and one ham and bread.
Miss Caroline Old, one bundle rags.
" Silvy Evins, " " "
" Sallie W Scott, " " ", ellum and comfrey.
Miss R W Woody, one bunch red pepper.

W. C. N. RANDOLPH,
Surg't in charge Gen. Hos. No. 2.

A FEMALE VAMPIRE.

There is a young married woman in the city, a native of the Canton of Berne, Switzerland, who is afflicted with a disease which she calls "a dancing of the heart," and which the physicians pronounce incurable. The lady with the "dancing heart" firmly believes that she can be cured by drinking a few drops of the blood of a man who has been executed.

Her name is Elizabeth Mund, and she is 23 years of age, and has been a mother of three children, none of whom survive. She has made numerous applications at the jail to inquire when there would be an execution, and as there has been no case of capital punishment at that institution for several months, her desire for human blood has not been gratified. She heard that John Abshire, sentenced by court martial to be hung by the neck, was to be executed in the jail yard on the 18th (yesterday) as it was stated in the papers. The execution of the sentence, however, was suspended, and on being informed that the man was not to be hung, Mrs. Mund appeared to be greatly disappointed and chagrined. Captain Bishop cheered her drooping spirits, however, by telling her that on the fifteenth of April a man would be hung by the neck until he was "dead, dead, dead," and that she might then appear and obtain a dose of the blood of Valentine Hansen, the murderer, provided Governor Hall did not pardon or respite the criminal, and the physician would allow her to extract the curative fluid. With this pleasing assurance, Mrs Mund took her departure, greatly consoled. This is a curious case of modern superstition.—*St. Louis Democrat*, 19.

NOTICE.—To the Tax-payers of the City of Lynchburg and one mile beyond the corporate limits. You are hereby notified, that I shall commence, on Monday the 16th day of this Month, at my office, over A. B. Rucker's Store, taking the assessments or general list of all property, real, personal or mixed, which embraces all classes of persons. Free persons of color are especially called to this notice, both male and female, as they have to pay the Confederate Taxes as well as whites; therefore, I hope all will come forward at once, with a list of their property or effects of any kind, and give it to me, as my time is very limited, and don't wish to enforce the law. as you will find the Taxes ample without any additional for non-compliance with this notice.

JNO. J. MITCHELL, Assessor
may 12 1w for the City of Lynchburg.

WE have for sale, on commission, a few barrels of FINE OLD APPLE BRANDY.
apl 14 d2w SPENCE & SLAUGHTER.

LATEST BY TELEGRAPH

Reports of the Press Associatio

Entered according to Act of Congress, in the year 1863, by J. S. THRASHER, in the Clerk's Office of the District Court of the Confederate States of the Northern District of Georgia.

FROM GEN'L LEE'S ARMY.

BATTLE-FIELD, NEAR SPOTSYLVANIA C H,
via Louisa C. H., May 11th.

There was heavy cannonading all day yesterday. About 12 o'clock yesterday the enemy having got possession of the road leading to the main road to Louisa Court House with a large force, Heth's division, was sent to drive them off, which was accomplished with slight loss to us. Our troops drove the enemy back some three or four miles, and out of their lines of breastworks, capturing one piece of artillery, one caisson, and some one hundred and fifteen prisoners.

Among those wounded on our side was Brig. Gen. H H Walker, of Va.; foot amputated.

Between 10 o'clock and night-fall the enemy made repeated assaults upon Field's division, but were handsomely repulsed in every instance by our line of skirmishers; Fields' line of battle never finding it necessary to engage them. Fields' loss very trifling.—Very near dusk the enemy made a most vigorous and determined assault on Rodes' line of battle, driving Daniels' and Doles' line of battle from their breastworks, and capturing six pieces of our artillery. Johnston's N C, Walker's (Stonewall) Va. and Gordon's Ga. Brigades, however, quickly came to their assistance, driving the enemy back and recapturing our lost guns.

The enemy's loss is said to be very heavy, especially in Fields' and Rodes' front.

The enemy is certainly fighting with great desperation and nerve.

General Sedgewick is certainly killed. It is reported that Warren and Stevens were killed on other parts of the line.

Yesterday there was nothing but heavy skirmishing.

Gen Hays, of Louisiana, was wounded in the leg yesterday, but not dangerously.

Fredericksburg was occupied by the enemy on Sunday night.

The enemy has three pontoons over the Rappahannock. The town is said to be filled with Yankee wounded; the number estimated at 15,000.

The enemy's loss, thus far, is believed to be fully thirty thousand; some have it forty thousand.

Stuart's cavalry have been incessantly fighting and persuing the enemy; have done excellent service.

Our position is very strong.

Grant has issued orders congratulating his troops on their success; telling them that Petersburg is in Yankee hands, and urging them to fight hard.

Our troops, though wearied, are in good fighting plight, and confident of final success.

The enemy, on the raid around our lines, captured a few of Ewell's ordnance wagons and recaptured some of their prisoners on their way to Richmond.

Up to noon to-day there has been no general engagement; only some skirmishing and occasional discharges of artillery on our right.

Everything is progressing well and the army is in no danger of suffering for want of supplies.

LATER FROM LEE'S ARMY.

BATTLE-FIELD, NEAR SPOTSYLVANIA C H.,
May 10th, via Gordonsville, 12th.

The last heavy fighting on the Wilderness battle-ground occurred on Friday evening.

During the day Saturday, nothing occurred save skirmishing.

Grant began leaving our front near Parker's Store at Wilderness on Saturday night. Gen Lee about the same time sent forward some troops to watch the enemy's movements and to keep between Grant and Richmond. Our infantry encountered the enemy about ten o'clock Sunday morning near Spottsylvania; Fitzhugh Lee's cavalry having previously been heavily engaged at the same place all the morning. A severe fight resulted, in which, our forces, under Gen Kershaw, repulsed the enemy, inflicting upon them heavy loss, the enemy's killed and wounded being estimated at ten to our one. At the same time we captured some prisoners and lost some.

Later in the day, Kershaw was again engaged and also Rodes, both of whom repulsed the enemy. During Kershaw's fight on Sunday the Yankee Gen Robinson, commanding the second division, 5th corps, was killed. Our loss in Sunday's fight not over 400 killed and wounded.

During the night, Sunday, our forces formed line of battle around Spottsylvania C. H., our right resting about one mile beyond Spottsylvania C H, towards the Fredericksburg railway. Both sides threw up fortifications on Sunday night. Yesterday and Monday there was skirmishing at intervals all day. Johnson's N C brigade and the Stonewall Va brigade, repulsed an attack of the enemy, and about night they succeeded in getting the road over which our wagon train was passing, but our trains had all gotten safely by.

The enemy doubtless occupied Fredericksburg as a new base on Sunday night, or yesterday morning. The enemy now hold Fredericksburg and Spottsylvania C H, and the telegraph roads; the latter some 12 miles out.

Lt Gen A P Hill is sick, and Gen Early is commanding his corps.

The enemy was continually shifting troops from the right to the left yesterday, requiring similar movements on our part.

Lt Col Collins, 15th Va Cavalry, was killed in the fight Sunday, and Maj Wooldridge, 8d Va Cavalry, was wounded in the leg yesterday. The troops are much fatigued, but in good spirits and confident of success.

Large quantities of small arms and *debris* of all sorts were left in the trenches on the Wilderness battle-field.

Gen. Anderson's Division on Sunday captured a battalion of cavalry, with the line of sharpshooters.

It is not believed that Mahone's Brigade wounded Gen. Longstreet.

The Yankee General Wadsworth died in our hospital yesterday.

It is reported that Gens. Warren and Sedgwick, also, were killed.

Brig. Gen. Gordon has been promoted to Maj. Gen., for gallantry on the field.

There has been heavy cannonading on our left and centre, from early this morning until 2 P. M., when the telegraph operator left for the station.

Field's line of skirmishers had been warmly engaged with the enemy, and had repulsed him three times. Fitz Lee had also driven the enemy back two miles on the road.

The weather is exceedingly oppressive and the roads deep in dust. The Yankees fought with great obstinacy on Sunday, and actually bayonetted our men at their breastworks whilst our men, their ammunition being exhausted, had to use the buts of their muskets to repulse the enemy.

ENROLLING OFFICE,
Lynchburg, May 12, 1864.

THE Advisary Board for Campbell will be met again, at Campbell C. H., on Tuesday, the 17th. Applicants for details will be expected to attend punctually with their witnesses.

E. J. ANDERSON, Capt.
may 12 4t and Enrolling Officer.

OFFICE SOUTHERN LITERARY MESSENGER,
May 1st, 1864.

NOTICE.—On and after May 1st, 1864, and until July 1st following, remittances in five dollar bills of the old issue will be subjected to discount according to their market value in Richmond at the time of receipt, and the period of subscription limited accordingly.

WEDDERBURN & ALFRIEND,
may 11 2t Proprietors.

$100 REWARD.—I will give one hundred dollars for the apprehension of WINSTON, who left my house on the 23d. He has a family at Gordonsville, and is well known in Richmond and on the Canal, having been a boatman for many years. He is upwards of 6 feet high, well made, dark complexion and good countenance. He must be delivered to me or put in some jail.

apl 27 ts MAYO CABELL.

NOTICE.—Ranaway from my plantation, in Bedford county, on the night of the 14th inst., my negro man, BOOKER. He is about 38 years old; about 5 feet 10 inches high; of a brown gingerbread color. It is believed said negro is lurking about Lynchburg, or some where in the county of Campbell or Bedford. I will give a liberal reward for the apprehension and delivery of said negro, or secure him in jail so that I can get him again.

mar 18 dts WM. C. MITCHELL.

RUNAWAY IN BEDFORD COUNTY JAIL. Was lodged in the Jail of Bedford county in July last, a dark mulatto man about 30 years old, and about 5 feet 10 inches high, and rather spare made and slow of speech when spoken to, who says his name is LUNSFORD, and that his master's name is Welfinbarger, of Granger county, East Tennessee. The owner will come forward, prove property, pay charges, or the said slave will be sold agreeably to law.

WM. H. PREAS,
apl 13 d6w Sheriff Bedford County.

$100 REWARD.—We will pay one hundred dollars for the apprehension and delivery of our office boy, "FERDINAND," who ran away on the night of the 2d int. He is about 12 or 13 years of age; very bright color; light colored straight hair; and will no doubt attempt to pass himself off as being a white boy; had on when he left a mixed jeans suit of clothes, roundabout coat, black hat, fastened up on one side with a military button. He reads well; is very sprightly and intelligent.

feb 8tf J. B. HARGROVE & CO.

$500 REWARD.

RANAWAY from the Subscriber, last night, 22d inst. near Liberty, Bedford county, Va., two Negroes, JIM and ELLEN. Jim is some 25 years old, dark complexion rather bow-legged, and about 5 feet 6 inches high. He had on, and took with him when he left a pair of cavalry boots, a jacket, a gray overcoat, a slouch hat, a blue frock military coat, and a portmanteau to carry his clothes in. Jim has been in the army, and may try to pass himself off as the servant of an officer.

Ellen is some 30 years old, light complexion, stout, and rather genteel. She had on, and took with her when she left, a plaid linsey; a black striped mourning calico, a black hood, and a bundle with her blankets, &c.

As they have recently been purchased of Mr. John F. Taliaferro, of Culpeper county, they will, no doubt, make their way in that direction to the enemy's lines. The above reward will be paid for their apprehension, in the new currency, if delivered to Wm. Winston, at Richmond, or to myself, at Liberty, or secured so that I get them, or $250 for either one.

JOS. P. WINSTON,
Liberty. Bedford county, Va.
ap 30 d1w sw4w

CARD.—As successor to Messrs. Lee, Rocke & Taylor, No. 105 Main Street, I shall be pleased to see my former patrons, as also those of the former concern, intending to continue the Commission Business in all its branches as well as to keep a general assortment (as far as possible) of Groceries, Domestics, Cotton Yarns, Sugar, Coffee, Nails, Iron, Soda, Pepper, &c. &c., at wholesale and retail.

mar 19ts MARTIN HOLLINS.

IMPORTANT NOTICE.

I am instructed by the City Council to take a census of the city of Lynchburg, including all white persons, refugees, all free negroes and slaves—old and young—who are either hired or reside in the corporation.

This is important to all citizens, as the distribution of Salt and domestic supplies will be made by this census; and those failing to register now, will be excluded, as the supplies will be obtained by these returns.

my 3 4t L. L. ARMISTEAD.

HOLLINS INSTITUTE.

IN consequence of the aggravated rumors relative to the sickness at the Institute, I avail myself of the earliest opportunity to state the facts of the case as they really exist. I have paid two visits to the school, and on each visit met the Physicians in attendance on the Patients. The session of the School opened under inauspicious circumstances, as the weather has been unusually bad during the months of March and April. Many of the young Ladies reached the place with bad colds The consequence was, there were several cases of Pneumonia, two of which terminated fatally.—Two servants have died, one from an attack of Pneumonia, brought on and increased by her own imprudence, and the neglect of a careless servant with her The other from a disease no human skill could avert. From all the circumstances and surroundings, I am satisfied, no local cause exists for disease of any kind at that place. The professors, female teachers, ladies and children are all well The health of the place is proverbial; that of the country around never better. I therefore see no cause for alarm, and I hope in a few weeks the School will be again opened under more propitious circumstances I will add, those now sick are convalescent, and the disease is of mild...

GEORGE P. TAYLOR,
may 10 3t Pres't of the Board of Trustees.

$250 REWARD.—I will pay the above reward for the apprehension or delivery to me of my body-servant, FOX, who ranaway from my house, in Amherst, about the first March. Fox has light brown skin and short hair; is 5 feet 8 or 9 inches high; short built; weighs one hundred and seventy five pounds; has a small scar on his forehead He is the boy that accompanies me on all occasions, and is generally known by that fact. I am inclined to believe that he is harbored in the neighborhood of Robt Martin's, in Amherst.

JNO. M. WILLIAMS,
del 21 dts Lynchburg P. O.

100 DOLLARS REWARD.

STOLEN from my Farm, in the county of Bedford, on the night of the 8th of April, a large dark brown or black MARE, about ten years old, has a very little white on her forehead. She had a sore back, was shod all round, walks well, and paces a little. She was in good working order. Also a blind bridle and a pair of plough lines.

Any information concerning her will be thankfully received, and the above reward paid for her delivery to me.

Address Lynchburg, Va., care Ro W Crenshaw.
my 3 d&tw2w SAM'L McDANIEL.

AMHERST COUNTY BONDS FOR SALE.—There will be offered for sale to the highest bidder, at Amherst May Court, (3d Monday) $50,000 interest bearing County Bonds.

SAM'L M. GARLAND,
may 9 d7t For Amherst County.

$200 REWARD.—Ranaway from the subscriber, on the 22d of April, a negro boy, named NATHAN, about 19 years old, some five feet six or 7 inches high, very stout built and black. Had on when he left a raged black coat; a new oznaburgs shirt, and an old pair of shoes and a grey cap. He was raised near Farmville, and has been working about the Iron Works, in Botetourt county, near Buchanan, and on the Catawba. He may be found at one of the three places. I will give the above reward for his apprehension and lodgment in Jail.

Address J. C. DEYERLE,
Big Spring Depot,
may 2tf Montgomery Co., Va.

OFFICE SOUTH-SIDE R. R. Co.,
Lynchburg, May 6, 1864.

NOTICE.—On and after this date, I will receive notes of the New Issue only in payment of Freight and Passenger fare, and five dollar notes of the Old Issue at a discount of thirty-three and a third per cent.

W. B. GRIGG, Agt.,
may 7ts South-Side R. R. Co.

To the Patrons of the late Dr. Jno. H. Patteson.

DR. PATTESON has died, leaving a large and dependant family. He has kept no account of his services rendered for some years I am reluctantly compelled to adopt this mode of calling upon those for whom he has rendered service. to come forward and pay over to me, as his Executor, the amounts due him.

ED. D. CHRISTIAN,
may 6d1w Executor, &c.

POLICE NOTICE.—Notice is hereby given to all owners of lots in the city, that they are required to have all impurities removed from the same immediately. A failure to comply with this requirement will subject all delinquents to a fine.

may 6 1w JOHN MITCHAM, M. P.

WANTED.—Four No. 1 Mules or Horses. Apply to

MRS. DR. JAS. SAUNDERS,
Lynchburg, or
MR. R. POLLARD,
may 6 7t Box 77, Liberty P. O.

$400 REWARD.—The above reward will be paid for the arrest and jailing of my two negro boys, NELSON and HARVEY, or $200 for either one of them. They have worked for some years as factory hands in Lynchburg, and may be lurking in or about the city, though I think it more probable that they are with the army, upon forged passes.

Nelson is about 6 feet tall; very spare and black, and 25 years of age, with a sore on one of his legs.

Harvey is of a copper color, 16 years of age and very pleasant and smiling when spoken to; usually wears a frock coat, buttoned up to the chin, and his boots outside of his pantaloons.

WM. A. READ,
apl 2 1m Forest Depot, Bedford Co., Va.

ATLANTA, GA., April 1, 1864.

I HAVE turned over to Mr. PAUL JONES, an old Virginian and Tobacco Manufacturer, the Tobacco trade of my house. Mr Jones will do justice to consigner and purchaser. I ask for him a liberal patronage from my friends and the public. Mr. Jones can be found as heretofore, at the Store of

L. B. DAVIS,
Commission Merchant,
may 6 1m Peach-tree Street.

MEETING OF STOCKHOLDERS.—A meeting of the Stockholders in the Virginia and Tennessee Rail road Company will be held in the city of Lynchburg, on the 11th inst, (second Wednesday,) pursuant to adjournment. As business of importance to the stockholders will be submitted for their consideration, it is desirable that a quorum should be present in person or by proxy.

CHAS. W. CHRISTIAN, Sec'ry
may 2 dt11m to the meeting.

PHOTOGRAPHS, CARTE VISITES, &C.
The Whitehurst, or Kyle's Picture Gallery, has been supplied with Photographic materials, which will enable the proprietor to furnish Photographs and Carte Visites in the best style of the art, in addition to Ambrotypes and Ivorytypes.

Call and see specimens, at
No. 132, MAIN STREET,
apl 30 2w Lynchburg, Va.

EXCHANGE NOTICE, No. 9;

RICHMOND, VA., May 2d, 1864.

ALL Confederate officers and men who have been delivered at City Point, Virginia, at any time previous to the 20th of April, 1864, are hereby declared to be duly exchanged.

RO. OULD,
may 4 d6t Agent of Exchange.

NOTICE.—The co-partnership heretofore existing under the firm and name of Moss & Day is this day dissolved by limitation, one of the parties having to go in the army the other living in the country. All persons having claims against the concern will present them for settlement to Jos. Grimes, and those indebted to them will please call on the same promptly and settle their bills.

JAMES W. DAY,
apl 1 deod2w JAMES S. MOSS.

NOTICE.—I wish to hire FIVE NEGRO MEN for General Hospital No. 2.

C. N. RANDOLPH, Surg in Ch.
may 7 1w Gen'l Hospital No. 2.

LYNCHBURG VIRGINIAN

NOTICE.—The cross mark appended to the names of certain subscribers indicates that the term fo which they subscribed will soon expire. They are thus notified in time to renew their subscription if they desire.

RAGS WANTED.—The highest market price will be paid at this Office for Clean Cotton Rags. They will be purchased in any quantity.

POSTPONEMENT OF SALE OF GOVERNMENT BONDS.—In consequence of the interruption of business operations, the sale of the 6 per cent bonds, advertised for the 12th inst., has been postponed by the Secretary of the Treasury until the 26th inst.

LIEUT. GEN'L LONGSTREET.—We are gratified to be able to state that the Gen'l is still improving. He was sitting up on Saturday and his Surgeon expects that he will be in the saddle again by the first of July. His right arm is partially paralized, but it is expected that time will restore to the limb the usual vitality and power.

HON. W. C. RIVES has been appointed Chairman of the Committee on Foreign Relations in the House of Representatives, and is also on the Committee on Flag and Seal. We had supposed that this last matter was disposed of finally by the adoption of the present flag. and seal. Only three other members from Virginia; viz: Russell, on the Judiciary, McMullin, on Public Buildings and Montague, on Ordnance and Ordnance Stores, are chairmen of committees.

AVERILL DEFEATED BY GEN MORGAN AND WOUNDED.—Information received from a gentleman who witnessed it, says, General Morgan's command met Averill's with his forces at a very favorable position, and, within 7 miles of Wytheville, on the Tazewell Court House Road, in Wythe county that a severe engagement ensued, in which Averill's force suffered a loss of two hundred in killed and wounded—Averill himself being wounded through the head was borne off by his men.

The Mobile *Advertiser* says that five dollar bills are in great demand in that city, and that brokers pay for them a premium of 33⅓ per cent.

This was the case in Richmond a few weeks since, except as to the rate of premium paid; but the fives ran down faster and lower than the brokers intended. whereby, we suspect a good many of these worthies have been caught, to the intense satisfaction of all honest people.

CASUALTIES IN THE 2D VA. CAVALRY.—Capt. Ro. W. Snead, who reached here from the battle field yesterday, reports the following casualties in the 2d Va. Cavalry:

Privates Yancey, of Lynchburg, and Roderick Davis, of Amherst, killed; Wm. Chiles wounded badly; John Chiles and John N. Eubank, wounded slightly; Wm. Pettit and Paul Knight missing.

We learn from the same authority, that the following members of Capt. R. H. Eubank's (Co. F, 50th Va. Reg'm't, of Amherst,) were captured by the enemy, when deployed as skirmishers, in the first day's fight at Parker's store:

Richard S. Ellis, Wm. P. Snead, James Gardnor, Wm. Ridgeway, Ro. Rodgers, Geo. Feagans, Ro. L. Hicks, Wm. Gillespie, Jno. Gillespie and Geo. Burton.

BUTTERMILK FOR THE SOLDIERS.—We are requested by a public-spirited and humane citizen of Appomattox, to say, that if an agent could be sent down the South-side road with proper vessels, every day, they could be filled at the different depots with buttermilk and returned here, and thus a large supply of this article could be secured, free of cost, for the sick and wounded soldiers.—Let this arrangement be understood, and the farmers would bring or send supplies to the different depots, daily.

The following points have been named:—Concord, Spout Spring, Appomattox and Pamplin's depot.

We trust that the Surgeons or others having charge of the hospitals, will confer together and unite on this plan or some other, to secure the much needed supplies of the refreshing and greatly coveted beverage.—The people are willing to help all they can to alleviate the sufferings of the gallant men that, fresh from the battle-fields of Virginia, are now crowding all our hospitals.

"THOMASITES."—The Richmond *Examiner* says this is a new denomination of "so-called" Christians, brought into notice by the emergencies of the hour, one of the articles of their religious manuel prohibiting the manuel of arms, and forbidding the exercise of the right and duty of self-defence against invasion from the common enemy. A number of this meek tribe were hauled up yesterday by the guards, and paraded their religious scruples as a barrier to exercise the highest and noblest duty of patriotic citizens. They were sent to the guard house, where several paid the five hundred dollars exemption money, under the law which exempts other non-combatant religious denominations, and were discharged."

We regret to learn that Major Samuel Hale, Inspector General on Early's staff was killed on Thursday last.

A gentleman who reached here on Saturday night, saw a copy of the New York *Herald* of the 9th, which stated that Gold had gone up to 203, and the *Herald* says Grant had better retire to the North side of the Rappahannock before he loses all his men.

MAJOR BLAKE L. WOODSON.—This gentleman denies the truth of the report that he was killed in the late fight near Dublin. Of course he ought to know and we are therefor happy to retract our publication which was to that effect.

DEATH OF ENSIGN HENRY D YANCEY.—We regret to announce the fall of this young gentleman, son of our townsman, W. T. Yancey, in one of the recent battles. Ensign Yancey was a member of the 2d Va., Cavalry and a youth of high promise. Alas! that so many of the young men who were the hope of the country should thus be cut off.

What a country we should have if all christians recognized these doctrines! We might be overrun and subdued by Yankees, Mormons, Pagans, or Devil-worshippers of any kind, and compelled to conform our religious opinions or worship to their notions. Such are not the doctrines taught in the Holy Scriptures.

CASUALTIES IN THE 2D VA. CAVALRY,
From the 5th to the 9th May, 1864.

Co. A—Killed, C. G Clay.

Wounded—Privates T Ferrill, severely; J. Franklin, do.; John Caddle, slightly.

Missing—T W Hatcher.

Co. B.—Killed, W H Stratton; H Locke; W C Bradley.

Wounded—Lt. Thornhill, severely; Lieut. Isbell, slightly; private A Boyd, do.

Co, C—Wounded, Lieut. E Brugh, severely; privates Noell Bishop, slightly; A Shafer, severely: M Stanley, slightly; W C Givens, severely.

Co. D—Killed, privates C H Calloway, S S Pasley.

Co. E—Killed, private J R Wingfield; color corp'l H D Yancey; private Geo. Eiserman.

Wounded—Corp. C E Watts, severely; privates W H Childs, do; R L Thomas, do; R L Davies, mortally; W Armstrong, severely; J N Eubank, slightly; J H Ackers, do., J T Ware; D Eiserman; P M Knight.

Missing—W H Pettit.

Co. F—Killed, private L H Johnson

Wounded—Capt. Graves, slightly; priv'ts C T Hubbard, mortally; Geo Johnson, slightly; J S Board, do.; E D Nance do.; J T Morgan, do.; W D Fields, mortally; J W Creutz, severely; sergeant S Murrell, do; privates C P Walker, do.; J A Farres, slightly.

Missing—Serg't Jones, captured.

Co. G—Wounded, Lieut. J A Douglas, severely; serg't C E Adams, do.; corp'l J G Childs, slightly; privates W Cocke, do.; S Winfield, severely; O McCardle, slightly; J A Bigbee, do.

Co. H.—Killed; Serg't W H Glover.

Wounded—Lt Saunders, severely; Serg't D W Gills, slightly; privates, D McKinnir, slightly; Geo L Ferguson, slightly.

Co. I.—Killed; privates W D. Dupriest, J D Lipscomb.

Wounded; Cap't Graham, slightly; privates T S Payne, slightly; Jno. J Puckett, severely. Missing; E Hayes.

Co. K.—Wounded; Corp'l T W Gentry, slightly; privates W A Garth, severely; J W Mroton, severely; E Payton, slightly; T E Tucker, slightly; W D Wood, slightly.

Captured; T D Garth.

Recapitulation.

Killed..13
Wounded....................................52
Missing.......................................5

Total..70

[Signed.] J. W. TAYLOE,
Adj't 2d Va. Cav'y.

There was quite an alarm in Richmond on Wednesday, and the following appeal from the Governor was posted all over the city:

"To the Citizens of the State and the People of Richmond:

"The enemy are undoubtedly *approaching the city*, and may be expected at any hour, with a view to its capture, its pillage, and its destruction. The strongest consideration of self and duty to the country, *calls every man to arms!* A duty which none can refuse without dishonor. All persons, therefore, able to wield a musket, will immediately assemble upon the Public Square, where a regiment will be found in arms, and around which all can rally, and where the requisite directions will be given for arming and equipping those who respond to this call.

"The Governor confidently relies that this appeal will not be made in vain.

"WILLIAM SMITH,
"Governor of Virginia."

The *Examiner* adds: Nor was the appeal in vain. In a short time the entire arms-bearing population of Richmond turned out, and repaired to the Capitol Square, where they awaited information from the enemy, before they should march to the field.

This is an example which all other cities and towns should, in like emergency, imitate.

LATEST BY TELEGRAPH

Reports of the Press Association

Entered according to Act of Congress, in the year 1864, by J. S. THRASHER, in the Clerk's Office of the District Court of the Confederate States for the Northern District of Georgia.

LATER FROM LEE'S ARMY.

RICHMOND, May 11th.

Nothing official from Lee's army.

It is confidently believed that every thing is progressing favorably in that direction.

Several divisions of Yankee cavalry were approaching Richmond by the Brooke road this A. M., Stuart's cavalry pressing their rear advance. The enemy was whipped at Ashland this A. M; quite a number killed and captured. At last accounts the enemy were at Yellow Tavern, 6 miles from Richmond. It is believed our forces are adequate to repel them. An attack on the city defences is hourly expected. Nothing from Chesterfield this A. M.

2D DESPATCH.

RICHMOND, May 11.

The Yankee cavalry have not yet made their appearance at the city defences. Their exact position is unknown at present; hopes are entertained that the entire force will be captured. It is supposed the Yankees in Chesterfield have retired from the immediate vicinity of the Railroad.

No fighting to-day.

Private telegrams from Guinna say that Grant's army was repulsed yesterday with terrible slaughter.

3D DESPATCH.

RICHMOND, May 12.

A conflict occured between Stuart's cavalry and the raiders yesterday afternoon, at Yellow Tavern, 6 miles from Richmond, in which Col H Clay Pate, 5th Va cavalry was killed, and Gen J E B Stuart seriously wounded in the left leg.

Severe skirmishing along the lines of defences since daylight this A M.

Our cavalry is in the rear of the enemy on the north side of the Chickahominy.

It is believed that a large number of the raiders will be captured.

Nearly 100 prisoners were brought in this A M.

The fight was progressing at 1 o'clock.

4TH DESPATCH.

RICHMOND, May 12.

The Yankee raiders are still in the vicinity of the city, but latest reports indicate that they will endeavor to leave to-night.

Heavy rains fell last night.

This A M no news from Gen Lee's army.

GUINNA'S STATION, May 12.

Very little of interest transpired yesterday. Last night heavy skirmishing occurred at intervals all night. This morning at daylight the enemy having massed heavy forces in front of Johnston's division, made most vigorous assaults upon Johnston's brigade. For a while our line of battle was broken, they pressed over the breast works, gaining possession of several pieces of our artillery—capturing a number of prisoners. Forces however, were quickly sent to the relief of those thus engaged and the enemy was driven back.

About 10 o'clock this, A. M. the enemy made most vigorous and repeated assaults upon Field's division, but were driven back with great slaughter. At 2 P. M. the enemy were making a most desperate fight in Ewell's front, but all accounts concur that we are driving them back and punishing them with great slaughter. The musketry to-day is the heaviest of the war. The battle has extended along our whole lines to-day and has been fought by the Yankees with more vim and bravery than any other fight in Virginia.

Among our casualties are Brig Gen Herin, killed; Brig Gen Walker, Stonewall brigade, wounded in the arm; Col Garrett, 5th N C., killed; Brig Gen McGowan, reported wounded, slightly.

We captured 2,000 of the enemy's wounded, left by them at the Wilderness.

Yankee papers of the 7th, contain letters written from Grant's Headq'rs, acknowledged a loss of 20,000 men in the Wilderness fights.

The fighting to-day is regarded as the most desperate of the war.

Yankee prisoners say that Gen Grant is putting fresh troops in the field to-day.

At 2 o'clock, severe and continuous fighting had occurred all along our lines, but the enemy had been every where repulsed and in some cases we have driven the enemy before us.

Heavy rain has been falling all day and greater part of last night to add to the discomfort of the troops, but our men are buoyant and resolute.

So far, we have achieved grand results, but the enemy is still pressing the battle with desperation.

Our loss to-day not very heavy.

We are fighting mostly behind breastworks and the enemy in the open field; their loss must be terrible.

Hill's corps has been extensively engaged all day recovering—in some instances—ground lost by other troops. Manson's and Lawsons' brigades about 2 o'clock made a most gallant charge, capturing about 300 prisoners and numbers of stands of colors.

Gens Ed Johnston and G H Stuart are missing and supposed to be captured.—About 3 o'clock p m the firing ceased, in a great measure, all along the lines, and, it is supposed, the enemy are gradually falling back.

2D DESPATCH.

RICHMOND, May 14th.

Thursday afternoon a force of the enemy, consisting of cavalry, infantry and artillery, crossed the Richmond and Petersburg Railroad, struck the Danville Railroad at Coal Field, doing considerable damage to property in that vicinity, also tore up a part of the track and the telegraph.

The raiders on the North side of the city crossed the Chickahomany at Mechanicsville, followed the course of battles around Richmond, recrossing the Chickanomany at Grapevine Bridge with the supposed purpose of reaching James River opposite City Point.—The raiders on the Danville Railioad attempted to destroy the bridge across the Appomattox, but were repulsed. They went in the direction of the High Bridge above.

This embraces the latest information from either party.

3D DESPATCH.

RICHMOND May 14.

Gen Stuart died Thursday night from injuries received in the fight at Yellow Tavern. His funeral took place yesterday.

A battle between the Confederate forces and Butler's troops, was progressing this morning about midway between Richmond and Petersburg. The people here are confident of our complete victory. Nothing occurred to produce the slightest despondency.

BATTLE-FIELD SPOTTSYLVANIA C. H., May 13
VIA GUINNA'S STATION, 14th.

The battle yesterday lasted all day and late into last night.

Our men, after a temporary repose in front of Johnston's division, successfully resisted every onset of the enemy, who repeatedly assaulted our lines with troops massed in, as some say, as many as ten columns. Our boys stood nobly to their work, piling the enemy's dead thickly before our breast works.

The lowest estimate of the enemy's loss in the battle yesterday is 20,000. These figures are corroborated by a Yankee Colonel, wounded and in our hands.

The Yankee General Stevenson was killed on the 10th.

Our losses yesterday, in killed and wounded, is estimated at 1,000; among the casualties on our side yesterday, was Gen Gordon, slightly wounded; Col Baker, 16th Miss., killed; Lt Col Pelters, same Regt., killed; Col Harding, 19th Miss., killed; Lt Col Miler, 1st Va., killed.

There was continuous figting for ten hours yesterday, and so severe was the musketry fire that the trees were cut down by it. Prisoners say that Grant expressed a determination not to recrss over the river while he has a man left.

Reports from Fredericksburg say the enemy is arresting all male citizens as hostages for prisoners alleged to have been captured by citizens on Sunday last. It is also stated that the enemy had a force of 10,000 men on Monday busily putting the Railroad, between Fredericksburg and Acquia Creek, in running order.

The Yankee prisoners say that Grant is issuing whiskey rations to his troops.

Our troops yesterday fought with more than usual gallantry, and the enemy fought more stubbornly than ever. Thus far, today, no general engagement; only slight skirmishing and occasionaly discharges of artillery.

A heavy rain has been falling since 4 A M, and the roads are deep in mud.

It is supposed this will be called the battle of Spottsylvania C. H.

Our men are all as resolute as ever, whilst accounts from the Yankees show that their troops are growing dispirited.

The enemy yesterday bayonetted some of our men in the breast works. The enemy to-day is still on our front, strongly fortified, and shows no signs of falling back.

FROM RICHMOND.

RICHMOND, 14th.

Congress has met daily, as usual, during the past week, but no business of importance was done. It is believed an adjournment will take place about the first of June.

The Herald of the 12th claims Grant victorious, and says he had advanced his lines 12 miles. Gold 171.

The Raiders on the Danville Railroad have been driven off—nothing heard from the other party.

The flag of truce boat arrived is the Curtis Peck, yesterday afternoon, for any prisoners we have to deliver.

No papers received yet.

The battle on the south side of Drewry's Bluff has been progressing all day. The firing is distinctly heard here. Nothing auspicious yet received, but all reports are favorable.

Private dispatches confirm the main facts of the battle on Thursday at Spottsylvania given in the press dispatches.

No further fighting since Thursday.

A WIFE WORTH HAVING.

A TRUE STORY.

The distinguished William Wirt, within six or eight months after his first marriage, became addicted to intemperance, the effect of which operated strongly upon the mind and health of his wife, and in a few months more, she was numbered with the dead. Her death led him to leave the country where he resided, and move to Richmond, where he soon rose to distinction. But his habits hung about him, and occasionally he was found in jolly and frolicsome spirits in bachanalian revelry. His true friends expostulated with him, to convince him of the injury he was doing himself. But he still persisted. His practice began to fall off, and many looked upon him as on the sure road to ruin. He was advised to get married, with a view of correcting his habits. This he consented to do, if the right person offered. He accordingly paid his addresses to a Miss Gamble. After some months' attentions, he asked her hand in marriage.—She replied:

"Mr Wirt, I have been well aware of your intentions for some time back, and should have given you to understand that your visits were not acceptable, had I not reciprocated the affection which you evinced for me. But I cannot yield my assent until you make a pledge never to taste, touch or handle any intoxicating drinks."

This reply to Mr Wirt was as unexpected as it was novel. His reply was, that he regarded the proposition as a bar to all further considerations on the subject, and left her.—Her course to him was the same as ever—his, resentment and neglect. In the course of a week, he went again and solicited her hand. But her reply was, her mind was made up. He became indignant and regarded the terms proposed as insulting to his honor, and avowed it should be the last meeting they should ever have. He took to drinking worse and seemed to run headlong to ruin.

One day while lying in the outskirts of the city, near a little grocery or grog shop, dead drunk, a young lady, who it is not necessary to name, in passing that way to her home, not far off, beheld him with his face upturned to the rays of the scorching sun. She took her handkerchief with her own name marked upon it, and placed it over his face. After he had remained in that way for some hours, he was awakened, and his thirst being so great, he went into the little grocery or grog shop to get a drink, when he discovered the handkerchief, which he looked at, and the name that was on it. After pausing a few minutes, he exclaimed.

"Great God, who left this with me? Who placed it on my face?" No one knew. He dropped his glass, exclaiming:

"Enough! enough!"

He retired immediately from the grocery, forgetting his thirst but not the debauch, the handkerchief or the lady—vowing, if God gave him strength, never to touch, taste or handle intoxicating drinks.

To meet Miss G. was the hardest effort of his life. If he met her in her carriage or on foot, he would dodge the nearest corner. She at last addressed him a note in her own hand, inviting him to the house, which he finally gathered courage enough to accept. He told her if she still bore affection for him, he would agree to her own terms. Her reply was:

"My conditions now are what they ever have been."

"Then," said the disenthralled Wirt, I accept them."

They were soon married, and from that day he kept his word, and his affairs brightened, while honors and glory gathered thick upon his brow. His name has been enrolled high in the temple of fame, while his deeds, of patriotism and renown, live after him with imperishable lustre. How many noble minds might the young ladies save, if they would follow the example of the heroine hearted Miss G., the friend of humanity, of her country, and the relative of LaFayette.

THE SWAMP ANGEL.

Vol. I. Morris Island, S. C., May 26, 1864. No. 2.

THE SWAMP ANGEL.

The salutatory below was prepared for our first issue, but was crowded out by the glorious news from Virginia.

About mid-way between our office and Charleston, may be seen a small basin-like mound, breaking the otherwise dead level of the far surrounding marsh. That little pile is made of sods and bags of sand. Its merits have been discussed by the London *Times*, the *Moniteur*, and other Continental journals. The nation and the world was startled by its sudden appearance.

When an Engineer officer made requisition for a detail of men, fifteen feet tall, to operate in the marsh, Gen. Gillmole was not able to fill the requisition, and some of the men who aided in performing the service are now on Morris Island. The incessant shelling received at the time, from the rebel "Bull of the Woods," are to them, among the reminiscences of the past. Nor will Beauregard ever forget his night-mare vision of the last Judgement, and utter bewilderment and terror when he learned that the loud *Trumpeter* was an Angel, not "flying through the midst of the heavens," but crouched low in the salt marsh, only five and a quarter miles from his doomed city.

This was the "Swamp Angel." Some had supposed its day was past. Not so, gentle reader. We propose to catch its falling mantle and preserve a measure of its spirit. As that name will long live in history, so its power and daring must burn in the breast of the army and animate the whole Republic. We intend to make it still speak, though in a softer tone, through these columns.

The project of issuing this humble sheet was a happy conception. We only regret that Col. Davis, with whom it originated, is not present to give it his personal attention.

No pains will be spared to make it worthy of general patronage. We leave our readers to form, from personal inspection, their opinion of its character.

SAD CATASTROPHE AT A FUNERAL.---At Port Allegany, Pa., a few weeks ago, a funeral procession was passing over a bridge to bury a child of Mr. George Moore, when the bridge gave way, and precipitating the mourners into the water, another child belonging to Mr. Moore was drowned, together with three of his brothers children, and one or two other lives were lost.

What is the merriest Sunday in the year?----Wits-Sunday.

SOUTHERN NEWS.

FEMALE CLERKS IN THE TREASURY DEPARTMENT.—A recent number of the Petersburg *Express* says, one hundred and thirty ladies, employed as note-signing clerks in the Treasury Department, passed through this city yesterday morning en route for Columbia, S. C., where they are hereafter to conduct their peculiar branch of the business. It has been ascertained that living is cheaper in Columbia—how much we do not know—than it is in Richmond, and the policy of the Government, which is an economical one, is to remove their field of operations thither. The ladies filled three coaches, and were conveyed from the depot in Pocahontas to the Southern depot, where they attracted much attention until the train left for the South. A good many of them found friends and acquaintances waiting for them, who entertained them during the several hours of their stay, in front of Jarratt's Hotel.

It is an unfortunate necessity that compels the removal of these ladies so far away from their homes and friends, and the sympathy of the public is very naturally extended to them. Many of them are young, handsome and intelligent, but by the force of circumstances are forced to labor for their living, and as matters now turn out, not at home where the company of family and friends is enjoyed, but hundreds of miles distant, where everything is strange and everybody a stranger.

——oo——

A MODEL LOVE LETTER.—The following is a copy of a letter appended to an application for a furlough, forwarded a few weeks since to Joe Johnson's head-quarters. This application for indulgence was made for the purpose of getting leave to go to Georgia to carry out a matrimonial engagement, and was approved by the Rebel General for fifteen days. The writer's orthography is retained:

"FEBRUARY, 13th, 1864.

My Moast Esteemed Friend: I am awair that you will be surprised to hear that father and mother have consented for myself and you to get married which affords me great pleasure; for I don't feel as though I could ever give my consent to marry any other gentleman, for you know yourself that I always esteemed you higher than any one else.

Mr. ——— bear in mind—you know you once said that you could never live and se me in the arms of Another man. Know is the time to prove it. You will haf to come home immediately. I am shore that the commanding officers will not object to your having a furlow to come home on such important business as that. Ma and pa have give thair consent, thinking that you would hardly get a furlow, and then they could say it was not thair fault; but I want to take them on a surprize. I know if gou love me as you say you do, gou will not fail to come. Give my kindest regards to General Johnson, and tell him to be a friend to matrimony this time for my sake.

Nothing more till I hear from you; an be assured that I shall await your arrival with the greatest anxiety.

Yonrs, as ever, *Ton Ami*, H. T. W

——oo——

☞ The printers of Atlanta, Georgia, having "struck" for $1 87 per thousand ems, the four journals published at that place have been compelled to temporarily suspend the publication of their papers. As soon as the printers quitted work, the conscript officers siezed and marched them off to camp, the "typos" thus getting "from the frying pan into the fire."

——oo——

☞ An alarming riot of females—demanding "bread or blood"—took place in Savannah on the 17th ult. The amazonian band appeared armed in the streets, seizing all the food they could find. The military were called out and suppressed the tumult. The ringleaders were consigned to prison.

——oo——

SUPERSEDURE OF GENERAL BANKS —General Canby has been promoted to be Major General of Volunteers, and ordered to the command of all the troops west of the Mississippi, thus superseding General Banks. He leaves at once to assume the command.

The navy are now in receipt of large numbers of recruits daily, under the law recently passed authorizing transfers from the army to the navy, and in a short time all the vessels will be put in commission.

A Prussian letter from Mexico, published in Berlin, expresses the highest hopes of the prospects of the new empire, and says that if the North Americans oppose it, the republic will be surrounded "on all sides" by monarchial institutions.

☞ The number of printing presses now in operation or ready for use in the Treasury building in Washington, is so large that if placed in a line, they would extend a quarter of a mile.

☞ A dealer in ready made linen advertises his shirts and chemisetts under the mellifluous appellation of "male and female envelopes."

Major Generals French and Keyes have been mustered out of the volunteer service by order of the President.

The Swamp Angel.

OUR PEACE MAKER.

MORRIS ISLAND, May 26,::::::::::::1864.

THE SWAMP ANGEL, printed by the Post Printers, will appear semi-occasionally, as circumstances offer themselves.

☞ The laborers who were sent to the Guard House last week, for refusing to work, sent in a petition on Monday, to Quartermaster Weidensaul, agreeing to work till the first of July. He allowed them to return to work.

——oo——

☞ Capt. Gurney, 127th N. Y. V., commanding Boat Infantry, assisted by Lieuts. Leonard, 54th Mass. Vols., and Sammis, 127th N. Y. Vols., recently made a most daring reconnoisance to Fort Sumter, advancing as it were to the very mouth of the howitzers stationed on its mass of ruins. They received four charges of grape and retired without the loss of a man.

——oo——

TERRIFIC HAIL STORM.—On the 18th inst., we were visited by one of the most terrific storms of hail and rain, that it has been our province to witness in this Department; stones falling as large as hazel nuts, and in some places they could be taken up by the shovel full. The storm broke forth about three o'clock in the afternoon and continued with the greatest fury for half an hour, when it subsided, and the sun coming out warm and genial, very soon converting the icy particles into water, and had we not occular demonstration of the fact we would not have known there had ever been such a storm on Morris Island.

——oo——

UNPARALLELED.—A small work entitled "the Philanthropic Results of the War," prepared, as we have good reason to believe, from the most reliable data, exhibits a record of generosity without a parallel in the history of the world. It appears that the total contributions of states, towns, and cities, in our land for the relief of soldiers and their families, are over one hundred and eighty-seven millions of dollars; the contributions for the same purpose by individuals and associations are over twenty-four millions; the contributions for the same time for sufferers abroad have been over three hundred and eighty thousand, and over half a million has been given for the sufferers by the July riot in New York; making altogether over two hundred millions of dollars, exclusive of Government expenditures.

☞ He bids fair to grow wise, who discovers that he is not so.

FORT PILLOW.

The country has been recently thrilled and horrified by recitals of the massacres of Fort Pillow and Plymouth; and no events have occurred during the existence of the war which throw a clearer light upon the character of the rebellion, or tend more to justify the soldiers of the Union, white or black, in deeds of retributory vengeance. "Strike back, and stronger," might seem the proper motto to adopt in regard to such cases, and, under the circumstances, our natural impulses would prompt us to deeds, which if we lived under the old Mosaic dispensation, might be considered just and righteous; but in this enlightened and more Christian age, the "eye for eye, and tooth for tooth" doctrine, even in warfare, is looked upon as partaking somewhat of barbarism, and is never upheld save by those who take counsel of their excited passions and predjudices rather than their better reasonings. Why should we perpetrate horrors, because the brutal followers of a reckless leader have done so? Why should we render less black the infamy which attaches to the cause that attempts to sustain itself by such atrocious acts, by copying the bloody example? These things will live in history—to be read and meditated upon when the excitements of war no longer distort the judgement, nor arouse the passions—and how much better it will appear to find the defenders of the Union placed on the living record as soldiers, who did not unite brutality with bravery, nor carnage with victory—who, spurning the traitors' method of warfare, withheld the vengeful bayonet from the prostrate foe, and retaliate deeds of blood by offices of mercy. The brave and chivalrous soldier, cherishes no cruel resentments, mindful of his country's glory as well as her success, he will do nothing in the encounter and clash of arms to tarnish the lustre of her victories, or give weight to the arguments of the assailants; but, fearless as an old crusader in the strife when the foe is overcome, and victory achieved, he offers his hand to the vanquished, and staunches the blood his trusty weapon has caused to flow. *Vincet, qui se vincet!*

——oo——

SKEDADDLING OFFICERS TO BE REDUCED TO THE RANKS.—Among the skedaddlers from the army of the Potomac, says the Washington *Star* of the 12th instant, who have come up here under the pretence of being wounded in the recent battles, are several officers. These it is understood to be the intention of the War Department to reduce to ranks, and compel them to serve out the remainder of their time as privates. About four hundred altogether have reached here, who are either entirely unhurt or so slightly wounded as not to incapacitate them from duty. These will be immediately returned to their places, and it is probable that they will not find their lot very much improved by the cowardly and disgraceful course they have pursued.

MILITARY AFFAIRS.

We have received full reports of several reconnoisances made since our last issue.

On the evening of the 19th, Captain James W. Gurney, a dashing officer of the 127th N. Y. V., headed a party making a cruise of exploration out into the harbor. While the main party waited near the telegraph poles, running from Sumter to Johnson—now minus wire, as climbing them proves and bringing one of them away certifies—Sergeant Bennett, of Co. E, with two men, paddled quickly on towards Johnson. We understood his orders were to go till fired on and see all he could. The tide was running strongly towards the fort, thus making capture certain in case of any accident to the boat. But the sergeant pushed boldly on till a sentry saw him and commanded "Halt! where you going?" "Up to the dock," was promptly answered. "D———d if you are!" impolitely replied the sentry, and let go his musket at him.

The Sergeant concluded he had obeyed orders—had gone till he was fired on and had seen a large rebel ram anchored about 300 yards from Johnston—so he put his boat about, fired his pistol at the sentry and returned to the waiting party. They then moved northward till they encountered a large ten-oared picket boat about 200 yards from the main obstructions and 400 yards from the Fort Johnston shore. The tide setting so strongly towards Charleston, going at the rate of four or five miles per hour, it was deemed imprudent to attack and the order given to retire.

As they approached Sumter they saw a number of men on the wharf and others placing a small howitzer in position on the parapet. As they came abreast of the fort, the howitzer opened with grape and cannister, coming rather near but doing no damage to any one. A musket was fired back at Sumter, and Putnam gave the rebs orders to cease firing in the shape of a couple 30 lb shells which was promptly obeyed and the howitzer carried below. Our party returned safely to camp much pleased with their midnight adventure

From Coles Island we learn that Col. Von Gilsea with a small force crossed to to Battery Island, drove in the rebel pickets, captured three strong breastworks and pursued the flying enemy on towards Secessionville and took his first line of rifle pits. A detachment of the 55th Mass. crossed a small stream, wading to their necks, holding their muskets and cartridge boxes over their heads and concealed themselves in the grass, while the remainder of the force crossed at a bridge gotten up. A rebel regiment came charging up to the place where the 55th lay, who held their fire till the rebs were close on to them and then poured in such a destructive volley, that all who were not killed or wounded, fled in confusion. On Monday afternoon quite a spirited fight took place between our gunboats in the Stono and Secessionville

THE
North-Carolina Standard
WILLIAM W. HOLDEN,
EDITOR AND PROPRIETOR.

TERMS OF THE STANDARD.

The terms of the *Standard* are as follows:

Semi-Weekly, six months,	$7
" " three months,	4
Weekly paper, six months,	5
" " three months,	3

The government through its financial agents, and the various corporations and trading men, having estimated five-dollar Confederate bills at two-thirds of their value, we are compelled to do the same. Persons sending five dollar bills will be credited for two-thirds of their face and no more, and no bills due the office can hereafter be paid in fives, save at such discount. Twos and ones and new issue preferred.

Advertisements inserted at two dollars per square of ten lines or less, for first insertion, and one dollar for each subsequent insertion. The very large circulation of the *Standard* renders it a valuable medium for advertising.

Weekly Standard.

VOL. XXX.—NO. 12. RALEIGH, N. C., WEDNESDAY, JUNE 1, 1864. WHOLE NUMBER 1515.

RALEIGH: FRIDAY, MAY 27, 1864.

We give elsewhere to day the latest news from the armies in Virginia and Georgia. Gen. Lee, it will be seen, was at Taylorsville, within fifteen miles of Richmond, on the 25th; and Gen. Johnston was supposed to be in a secure position west of Atlanta to meet Sherman. It is not known whether Gen. Lee will give battle where he is, or fall back to the fortifications near Richmond. The Richmond *Sentinel* says it is believed that Grant is endeavoring to get to West Point, on the Pamunkey, where he will be in communication with his gunboats.

All was quiet on the 24th between Petersburg and Richmond. The federals are behind their fortifications near Bermuda Hundreds.

We may expect soon great battles near Richmond and Atlanta. The armies on both sides have been reinforced, and the conflicts will be prolonged and terrible. The whole country looks with the deepest anxiety to the result, and every Southern man hopes that, in the end, our banners may be crowned with success. There is ground for hope. Our enemies are numerous, well provided, and powerful, but we have the utmost confidence in Generals Lee and Johnston and the glorious troops under their command. They will accomplish all that can be accomplished.

Both houses of the General Assembly of this State have resolved to adjourn on Monday morning next.

HABEAS CORPUS IN THE LEGISLATURE.—On Wednesday, after some debate, the House of Commons passed the resolutions reported by the majority of the committee, as published in our paper of to-day, protesting against the suspension of *habeas corpus* and calling for the repeal of the act, by a vote of 64 to 32. For vote see Wednesday's proceedings.

Similar resolutions were discussed in the Senate on the same day, by Messrs. Warren, Brown, Boyden, Hall and others. We have heard the speeches of Messrs. Warren, Brown, and Boyden referred to as very able, eloquent, and conclusive on the whole subject. We give to day a synopsis of the remarks of Messrs. Hall, Brown, and Warren, and shall publish the speech of Mr. Boyden hereafter in full. We trust Messrs. Brown and Warren will also prepare their remarks in full for the press. [illegible] will no doubt finally pass both Houses by [illegible]

Political Agitation in the Legislature.

Early in the present session Mr. Smith, of Macon, an intimate friend of Gov. Vance, introduced a resolution in the Senate endorsing his administration, and the resolution was passed and sent to the Commons. On Monday the resolution was taken up in the Commons, and on motion of Mr. Cobb, of Edgecombe, amended so as to endorse President Davis, yeas 45, nays 42. Gov. Vance and President Davis were thus united and commended in the same series of resolutions; but some of the friends of Gov. Vance, fearing that he would lose votes by this *public* coalition, were anxious to disunite them. Accordingly, on Tuesday Mr. Amis moved to reconsider the resolutions. Mr. Carpenter moved to lay the motion to reconsider on the table, believing that the House had placed the two functionaries very properly together, and having no wish to disturb their unity; but the House refused the motion and reconsidered. An animated debate then took place, in the course of which Mr. Person very emphatically told the Vance Destructives that if it was their purpose to make war on the Richmond administration, he would advise his party to abandon Gov. Vance and run a candidate of their own. To this Mr. Waddell replied, daring Mr. Person to run another candidate. It was altogether an interesting time between the piebald supporters of his Excellency. After much tribulation, on motion of Mr. Cobb, of Edgecombe, the whole subject was postponed until Thursday. Time was thus given for *negotiation* between the Vance and Davis men, and we may expect that they will, in the end, endorse the former in one series of resolutions and the latter in another. But the trick will be too apparent to deceive any one. The coalition was plainly *admitted* by the declaration of Mr. Person, that if the Vance wing should pursue a certain course the Davis wing would abandon Vance and run a third candidate. This much of the coalition is public. What the private, secret understanding is we have no means of knowing.

We call the attention of the people to the fact that no small portion of the time of the present session is being consumed in political resolutions intended to promote the election of Gov. Vance, and break down the true Conservative party. Mr. Smith, Gov. Vance's intimate and confidential friend, appears to be primarily responsible for this agitation; and we leave it to our readers to infer whether Gov. Vance himself is not also responsible, whether primarily or not is best known to himself and Mr. Smith. These resolutions will consume at least four days of the session, and will cost the people in taxes not less than *fourteen thousand dollars!* And all to bolster up a sinking candidate for Governor, and that too at a time when the country is bleeding at every pore and many of our people are suffering for the necessaries of life.

WHO IS RESPONSIBLE FOR AGITATION?—While the capital of the Confederacy is threatened by hundreds of thousands of the enemy, and while the vast forces of Lincoln are attempting to close in upon us and subjugate us, the Governor of this State is absent from his post, haranguing for votes, neglecting his business, and stirring up strife among the people; and his friends in the Legislature are wasting precious time and thousands of dollars in a controversy as to whether they will endorse him and President Davis in the same, or in a separate series of resolutions. "Nero fiddles," or rather piddles "while Rome is burning." Wo, wo unto this people! Like Simon and John, when Titus thundered at the gates of Jerusalem, they fight the enemy all day, and then fight each other all night. Who is responsible for this strife? Certainly *we* are not. We are here at home, quietly engaged in our business. Let the people judge between us.

Another Falsehood Exposed.

A friend writing us from Smithfield, under date May 23d, says:

"In Gov. Vance's speech in this place to-day, he said he could prove, by two or three as respectable members as there are in the Legislature, that you had made propositions to them to introduce resolutions calling for a Convention for the purpose of seceding from the Confederacy; and that if you had any friends present, which he knew you had, they were at liberty to communicate his statement to you. Please let me hear from you on this particular point—not that I believe the statement, but to meet it when used against you."

The above is from a gentleman whose word may be implicitly relied on.

This charge against us appeared in the *Confederate* of Tuesday last, which was printed Monday night, the day on which the Governor spoke at Smithfield.

We now say to our correspondent and to the public that there is no shadow of foundation for Gov. Vance's statement. We have never supposed nor stated that a Convention would be called for the purpose of seceding from the Confederate government. We have made no propositions to members of the Legislature to introduce resolutions or bills calling for a Convention for any such purpose; nor have we any recollection of having suggested to any member the propriety of such a bill or resolution for any purpose. We have thought, and still think, that it would be well for this State and all the Confederate States to have Conventions in being, if not in session during the war—not to secede from or embarrass the common government, but to aid that government in obtaining an honorable peace, as recommended by the Legislature of Georgia; and at the same time to see to it that the administrators of that government do not subvert or change its character, or trench fatally on the reserved rights of the States and the liberties of the people. *We are not afraid to trust the people, as Gov. Vance is.* No one supposes that the present Legislature will submit the question of Convention to the people; but, with our views of the subject, and looking to the condition of the country, we would support no man for the next Legislature who would not pledge himself, if the emergency required it, to consult the people at the ballot-box as to whether they would have a Convention. If it be true that the people can be trusted at all times with the management of their own affairs, then a Convention could do no harm, and it might do much good; and even if it should do harm, which we do not believe, the people themselves, who would have to bear it, would be to blame for it.

In the *Standard* of February 24, 1864, we published a letter from Robert P. Dick, Esq., in relation to the Greensborough meeting, which letter met, as it still meets our warm approval. Among other things Mr. Dick said:

Secession will always bring war; and war produces bloodshed, desolation and sorrow. Civil war always engenders sectional strife and unrelenting hate, and it is the prolific source of want, corruption and crime. A dire necessity made North-Carolina secede from the old Union, and she has reaped an abundant harvest of bitter fruits. She could not remain neutral. She was compelled to assume her present position, and nobly has she maintained her honor and her fame. Secession now would be utter folly and madness, and such an act could only be justified in a "life and death struggle" for her liberty. I desire a convention to prevent any necessity for secession. The State in her full sovereignty might check any usurpations and abuses of the common government by firm and determined remonstrance.

Conventions in all the States would greatly strengthen the Confederate government by granting it needful powers in every emergency, which if assumed without their consent would be the usurpation of unwarranted authority.

I further desire a State Convention to inaugurate negotiations for peace. I do not propose that this State shall treat with the Lincoln government. An honorable peace can never be obtained from that source. I scorn any proposition which Lincoln has made, and I feel assured that the fanatical hatred of his friends will never allow us any honorable terms of adjustment.

I desire that this State in Convention shall invite a conference, through commissioners, with her sister States of the South to see if some plan cannot be devised to stop the war by negotiation. I am opposed to any separate State action, and if the other States will not heed the voice of North-Carolina for peace, then she will have done her duty to God and her people, and be free from any of the responsibilities of the future.

While our heroic soldiers are fighting and falling in the "deadly breach" and defending every inch of their native land, I want to see a grand council of sovereign States, in a spirit worthy of the civilization and Christianity of the age, receiving, proposing and calmly considering propositions for an honorable peace.

A strong peace party at the South, sustained by the action of sovereign States, would greatly increase the power of the peace men at the North and enable them to overturn the hateful Black Republican dynasty at Washington. I feel sure that we could successfully treat with the conservative men at the North, if they were in power, and obtain such terms as would be honorable and acceptable to the whole country.

Negotiations for peace would greatly encourage our people at home, and make them use every energy to sustain our cause; and they would cheer and strengthen our gallant army in the field; for then they might have some hope that the sword would not devour forever. I feel that it is a higher evidence of patriotism *to save the life of one citizen than to destroy a thousand enemies.*"

Time again have we announced similar views in the *Standard*, from the moment the Convention question was first discussed up to the present. The charge of Gov. Vance falls to the ground. There is no truth in it.

Since the above was written we have received the *Conservative* of Wednesday, containing a communication from which we make the following extract:

"But the important fact stated by Gov. Vance, was, that Mr. Holden had declared to two or three members of the Legislature that he advocated a Convention of the State, for the purpose of carrying the State out of the Southern Confederacy. And stated further, that if Mr. Holden denied it he would prove it on him by certificates from those gentlemen, and desired any friend of Mr. Holden to tell him he had said so; another feature in this Smithfield trip was, the abandonment of the cause of Mr. Holden by the members of the Legislature from Johnston county, and I could see the powerful effect it had on the crowd whilst Gov. Vance was speaking. The same facts which were eviscerated by Vance, had startled the members from Johnston the week before, and they came out with a card, but when the Governor himself told these people the facts in regard to Holden, and they saw Woodall and Avera and Sanders, all had left Holden for the same cause, they shifted their *range and changed their dress, too*, and now *to-morrow* Vance will beat Holden so badly in Johnston county that the *Georgia soldiers* would not know him."

We repeat our denial of this charge in the most emphatic terms. When we see the certificates referred to we shall be prepared either to pronounce them unqualifiedly and wilfully false, or the result of some unaccountable misunderstanding or perversion of our views.

And now, a word or two in relation to Messrs. Sanders, Woodall, and Avera.

Mr. Sanders has not left us, for he has not been with us since the meetings held in Johnston to promote the cause of peace. He refused to attend those meetings, and thus forfeited to a considerable extent the confidence of the party; but he has lost all of that confidence by announcing himself a candidate on the Stallfederate or Destructive ticket.—The explanation in relation to Messrs. Avera and Woodall is equally plain and easy. Some time since it was announced that the Conservatives [illegible] Johnston would hold a mass meeting in Smithfield on the 28th instant, to nominate a ticket for the Legislature. About the 12th instant Mr. Avera came to Raleigh and handed us a notice for publication containing the name of Thos. D. Snead, Esq., for the Senate, and his own name and that of Mr. Woodall for the Commons. This announcement, which was signed "*Many Conservatives after the straitest sect,*" he requested us to publish in the *Standard*, and also in handbill form and send to various persons in Johnston, which we did. It occurred to us at the time that Messrs. Avera and Woodall were rather hasty, especially as the announcement was made without reference to the proposed meeting; and also, that they were not indisposed to strengthen themselves by associating their names with that of Mr. Snead. Soon after this we heard from several influential Conservatives of the County that Messrs. Avera and Woodall *had* acted hastily—that they had not shown proper respect for the party, and that it was more than probable they would not be nominated at the proposed meeting. The result was, these gentlemen, despairing of a nomination, and having determined to run at all hazards, after sundry consultations with various Stallfederates and blockade runners in Raleigh, concluded to drop Mr. Snead, indentify themselves with Mr. Sanders, and take their chances on the Vance or Destructive ticket. We should like to know where they got their timber out of which they constructed their *spring-board*, on which they cut such a sudden, keen, and ridiculous somerset. We call them the *spring-board* candidates. After the first Thursday in August they will rest quietly on their political *cooling-board*.

Mr. Avera has assured us, quite recently, that our vote in Johnston would be as large as that of Dr. Leach, and that of Gov. Vance about equal to Col. McRae's. We are the same man now we were then. *We* have not changed, and yet Messrs. Avera [illegible] into the support of Vance by the charge against us that we had proposed a Convention for the purpose of seceding. It is also pretended by the *Conservative* that they deserted their principles and identified themselves with the crooked sect and the Destructives, because we would not consent to be *caucused* out of the field by certain "*leaders*" in the Legislature! These are poor excuses for the abandonment of principle and the breaking of plighted faith. But we leave these gentlemen to the tender mercies of the Conservatives of Johnston County. They will know what to do with them.

Our readers will observe that the *Conservative*, the mercenary organ of Gov. Vance, sneers at us in connection with the Georgia mob. Let this be remembered. *The Governor and his minions are amused when they recur to the fact that our office was mobbed and our life put in jeopardy by an armed band of Confederate soldiers, acting under orders, because we had boldly advocated negotiations for an honorable peace.* Is this the way in which Gov. Vance protects loyal citizens from violence, and vindicates the insulted majesty of the State?

Col. McRae's Accounts.

In the latter part of the year 1862, Gov. Vance appointed Col. Duncan K. McRae a Commissioner to proceed to Europe with George N. Sanders, Esq., to inspect certain goods to be purchased by the latter for this State in exchange for naval stores, and to verify the bonds of the State to be delivered in accordance with such contracts as Mr. Sanders might make. It seems that the contract for this business was solemnly made by Gov. Vance *with Mr. Sanders;* but the sequel shows that Gov. Vance abrogated the contract with Mr. Sanders, and Col. McRae *did the business*, returned home, and left Mr. Sanders to "meditate on the mutability of human glory, and sigh over the miseries of ungrateful man." Col. McRae no doubt found it a good thing, and had a good time generally in transacting this business. Mr. Sanders published Col. McRae at much length for his conduct, appealing to the Governor for justice, which he is not likely to get. We reprinted the pamphlet for Dr. J. T. Leach, with sundry very truthful and appropriately severe remarks by the latter, in an Appendix to the same: for which Col. McRae has sued Dr. Leach and ourself in damages each to the amount of $20,000.—Our bond is filed, and we await the issue with as much equanimity as possible under the circumstances.

But this is somewhat by the way. Col. McRae returned from Europe just in time to run for Congress in the 3d District. He was beaten, as a matter of course. He always is. So brilliant, and yet so unappreciated. But this is also somewhat by the way. He stated, on the stump, that he would be a conscript *as soon as his accounts as State Commissioner should be settled;* and he kept on stating and acting this up to the time the *Confederate* was established by the "patriots and property holders" to "save the State from disgrace," when he suddenly became the Editor of that interesting journal—jumped the ropes into the charmed circle of exempts, and commenced to laud Gov. Vance as the best Governor, the greatest orator, and most versatile genius of the age. Indeed, he said the Vance "grapes" were so delectable they "melted in his mouth." Golden fruit, no doubt. But still the accounts of Col. McRae as Commissioner remained unsettled. He signed his name to his letters as follows: "I am, very respectfully, D. K. McRae, *Colonel* and Commissioner for the State of North-Carolina." His pay, therefore, was that of a Colonel in the Confederate service, in gold. The law of the State provides that *all* accounts and claims against the State shall be audited and adjusted by the [illegible] Auditor; but the report in Raleigh is that Gov. Vance, disregarding this law, which is a highly important and useful one, some months since appointed a couple of gentlemen of this City as a sort of private committee to examine and adjust Col. McRae's accounts; that the committee met and acted under this appointment; that Col. McRae claimed *eleven thousand dollars in gold* for his services, in addition to his pay as Colonel; that the committee allotted him *five thousand dollars in gold*, but that Col. McRae indignantly refused this amount, and appealed to the Governor for relief, like "Oliver asking for more." And Gov. Vance, in his late message, says, "A report of the operations of our other Commissioner, Col. D. K. McRae, necessarily incomplete, is also submitted, and will, I believe, be [illegible] satisfactory, and creditable to him as Commissioner," and then advises the appointment of a committee to investigate all matters appertaining to the blockade-running of this State, &c. He says nothing about his disregard of the law which places Col. McRae's accounts before the Auditor—nothing as to the importance of waiting until Mr. Sanders returns, and evidence in relation to the manner in which Col. McRae has transacted the business can be obtained from Europe. We do not charge or insinuate that Col. McRae has acted dishonestly in the matter, but we make the following points:

1st. His accounts have remained unsettled eight months. During this period, up to the time he became Editor of the *Confederate*, he has been saved from conscription by Gov. Vance; and he, a Destructive, supports Vance, a professed Conservative for Governor.

2d. Gov. Vance has disregarded the law of the State, which required Col. McRae to settle with the Auditor. If it be answered that the laws under which Col. McRae acted were passed in secret session, and therefore it is not proper that the Auditor should examine and adjust his accounts, the answer is, the law says *all* accounts shall be passed upon by the Auditor, and a private committee could have no more right, if as much, to pass upon the accounts as the Auditor.

3d. As a settlement of the accounts has been so long delayed, no matter from what cause, they ought not now to be settled in hot haste, but ample time should be allowed to obtain testimony from Europe, to shed light upon the manner in which Col. McRae transacted the business which Mr. Sanders charges he induced the Governor to take from his into his own hands.

4th. Col. McRae himself, now that he is happily an exempt, and as his business capacity, and his reputation, as Mr. Sanders thinks, are somewhat involved, ought to be anxious that his whole conduct should undergo the strictest scrutiny by the State Auditor, so that justice may be done to Gov. Vance, to himself, and to the State.

[illegible] favor of repealing the act suspending the writ of *habeas corpus*, was laid upon the table by a vote of 57 to 24—the yeas and nays called for by Dr. J. T. Leach.

YEAS—Messrs. Aiken, Anderson, Atkins, Barksdale, Blandford, Boyce, Bradley, Branch, E. M. Bruce, H. W. Bruce, Chambers, Chilton, Chrisman, Clopton, Colyar, Conrad, Dejarnette, Dickinson, Dupre, Echols, Foster, Funsten, *Gaither*, A. H. Garland, Hanly, Hartridge, Heiskell, Hilton, Holliday, Johnston, Keeble, Lyon, Machem, McCallum, McMullen, Menees, Miles, Miller, Montague, Moore, Perkins, Pugh, Read, Russell, Sexton, Shewmake, Singleton, J. M. Smith, W. E. Smith, Staples, Swan, Triplett, Villere, Welch, Whitfield, Witherspoon, Mr. Speaker—57.

NAYS—Messrs. Ayer, Baldwin, Bell, Cruikshank, Farrow, Foote, *Fuller*, Gholson, *Gilmer*, Holder, Lamkin, *J. M. Leach, J. T. Leach*, Lester, *Logan*, Marshall, Murray, Orr, *Ramsay*, Rives, Rodgers, Simpson, *Smith* of North-Carolina, *Turner*—24.

Mr. Gaither, it will be seen, darkles as a lone star in the firmament of despotism. The Conservative party of the State has at length got rid of him, and we are glad of it. Mr. Bridgers, who voted against the suspension at the last session, was absent.

Missouri and Kentucky have some twenty-two members of the House, nearly all of whom voted against the repeal, to say nothing of the members from West Virginia and other localities represented in the federal Congress. The two States first named have full representations in the federal Congress, and they have contributed greatly more men and means against us than for us. Still their votes exert a controlling influence in the Congress on great questions of taxation and civil liberty.

The Speaker laid before the House the following message from the President on the subject:

MESSAGE OF THE PRESIDENT ON THE HABEAS CORPUS.

To the House of Representatives of the Confederate States of Amrrica:

The following resolution passed by the House of Representatives, on the 14th inst:

"*Resolved*, That the President be requested to inform the House, if not incompatible with the public interest, whether the reasons given in his special message for suspending the writ of *habeas corpus*, still exist, and what additional reasons now exist to such extent that the public safety requires the continuance of the suspension thereof."

In my opinion, the reasons given in the special message transmitted to Congress at its last session, recommending the suspension of the writ of *habeas corpus*, still exist in undiminished force, and the present juncture especially requires the continuance of the suspension. The effect of the law for that purpose has been most salutary, and to that law, in no inconsiderable degree, are we indebted for the increased efficiency of the military preparations which have enabled our gallant armies, under the providence of God, to beat back the invading forces which still threaten us.

In my judgment it would be perilous, if not calamitous, to discontinue the suspension while the armies of the enemy are pressing on our brave defenders with persistent effort for their destruction and for the subjugation of our country.

It is a source of gratification to be able to inform you, that the mere passage of the law suspending the writ, was so effectual in restraining those who were engaged in treasonable practices and in dangerous complicity with our enemies, that the instances are extremely few in which arrests were found necessary.

The effect of the law in preventing the abuse of the writ, for the purpose of evading military service, by men, whose plain duty it is to defend their country, can hardly be over-estimated.

The sensitiveness exhibited in different parts of the country to the legislation on this subject, is indicative of the love of freedom which is innate among the people, and which should ever be cherished as the sole guarantee for the preservation of their constitutional liberties. It is not doubted, however, that if those who have expressed dissatisfaction with the law had been in possession of the information which it was my duty to communicate to you, and which may not yet be revealed without injury to the public interests, they would fully have approved the exercise of the power of suspending the writ, which was entrusted to Congress by the Constitution. All trusts impose duties. The power was entrusted expressly with the intent that it should be used when necessary to the public safety in case of invasion.

Congress concurring with me that the exigency had arisen which required the exercise of the power, performed but a plain duty in passing the law, and such will, I doubt not, be the judgment of the people when the facts can be made known without detriment to their interests.

JEFFERSON DAVIS.

RICHMOND, VA., May 20, 1864.

The Latest News from Virginia and Georgia.

FROM RICHMOND.

RICHMOND, May 24.—Official information has been received that Sheridan's raiders crossed the Pamunkey at White Post yesterday and moved up between the Pamunkey and Mattaponi, probably to rejoin Grant.

The corps of Cadets of the Virginia Military Institute were reviewed on the Capitol Square this afternoon by President Davis.

[SECOND DISPATCH.]

RICHMOND, May 24.—The following dispatch has just been received here.

HANOVER JUNCTION, 10, p. m.—About noon today the enemy approached the bridge over the North Anna. In the afternoon he attacked the guard at the bridge and drove it to its place.—About the same time the 5th corps (Warren's) at Jericho Ford on our left, was attacked by A. P. Hill, and his advance checked.

(Signed) R. E. LEE.

[THIRD DISPATCH.]

RICHMOND, May 25, A. M.—The following was received this morning:

TAYLORSVILLE, 8:30, P. M., 24.—*Secretary War:* The enemy has been making feeble attacks upon our lines to-day, probably with the view of ascertaining our position. They were easily repulsed. Gen. Mahone drove their right across the river, capturing a stand of colors and some prisoners, among them one aid to Gen. Laidley.

(Signed) R. E. LEE.

LATEST FROM THE NORTH.

PETERSBURG, May 24.—Northern dates to the 21st received. Grant telegraphs that an effort was made Thursday evening by Ewell's corps to turn the Yankee's right. It was promptly repulsed. Three hundred prisoners fell into the Yankee's hands, besides many killed and wounded. Yankee loss 600 killed, wounded and missing.

Staunton assures the Northern press that over twenty-five thousand veteran reinforcements have been sent Grant. No reports from the battle.

The Red river is blockaded at many points by rebel batteries. Gen. Canby, who is about to resume command, promises to move them early.

Seigel has been removed and Maj. Gen. Hunter succeeds him.

A dispatch from Sherman, dated Thursday night at Kingston, states that he was driving the enemy, and that day had pushed a column beyond Kingston in pursuit of Johnston as far as Cass Vaila. A hard fight for Atlanta it looked for.

The *Herald* states that among the passengers on board the prize Rebel steamer *Grayhound*, just arrived at Boston, was Edward A. Pollard, of Richmond. He is [illegible] in Fort Warren.

The homeless people of Northern Georgia are said to be crowding into Atlanta, to await the result of the impending battle.

It is stated that movements looking to a secure base for Johnston's army have been made. The federals are moving up to Dallas in force. Several days, it was thought, would elapse before a general engagement would take place.

Congress.

On Monday last, in the House of Representatives, Dr. J. T. Leach introduced the following resolutions:

"*Whereas*, The unconstitutional enactment of laws by the Congress of the United States from time to time upon subjects of vital importance to the harmony and independence of the States, the happiness and prosperity of the people, the preservation and perpetuation of the Union, against the demands of justice, the appeals and admonitions of her best and wisest statesmen, made it our painful duty to fall back upon the rights for which the colonies maintained the war of the revolution and which our forefathers asserted and maintained to be clear and inalienable. Therefore.

Resolved by the Congress of the Confederate States, That the delegations from each State, acting in its sovereign and independent character, for the purpose of adding moral to our physical force, and placing ourselves properly before the civilized world, do most earnestly appeal to the President, by and with the advice and consent of the Senate, to appoint commissioners whose duty it shall be to propose an armistice of ninety days to the proper authorities of the Federal government, preliminary to negotiations for peace upon State sovereignty and independence, and that said commissioners shall report in writing to the President the answer received from the Federal government upon the subject.

Resolved, That should the peace-making power of the Federal government accede to the proposition for an armistice of ninety days, the President be requested to convene the Congress of the Confederate States for the purpose of appointing Commissioners, by and with the advice and consent of the Senate; and that he also be requested to notify the Executives of the several States of the fact, and ask their co-operation by appointing commissioners, either by the Legislature or Convention, to co-operate with the Commissioners appointed by the President to negotiate with Commissioners appointed by the Federal government upon such terms of peace as will be consistent with the honor, dignity, and independence of the States, and compatible with the safety of our social and political rights.

Resolved, That in maintaining the rights guaranteed to us by the blood and treasure of our Revolutionary fathers, and dearest at all times to free men, we desire to be let alone—we ask no man's property—we fight not for conquest, but for our rights: the independence of the States, our equality, our civil and religious liberties.

Resolved, That such terms of peace as are agreed to by the Commissioners ought to be endorsed by the President and Senate, and submitted to the people for their ratification or rejection."

On motion of Heiskell, these resolutions were laid on the table by the following vote:

YEAS.—Messrs. Anderson, Atkins, Ayer, Baldwin, Barksdale, Blandford, Boyce, Bradley, E. M. Bruce, H. W. Bruce, Chambers, Chilton, Chrisman, Clopton, Colyar, Conrad, DeJarnette, Dickinson, Dupre, Farrow, Foster, Funsten, *Gaither*, Gholston, Goode, Hanly, Hartridge, Heiskell, Hilton, Holder, Holliday, Johnston, Keeble, Lyon, Machen, McCollum, McMullin, Menees, Miles, Miller, Montague, Morgan, Murray, Orr, Perkins, Pugh, Read, Rogers, Rives, Russell, Sexton, Shewmake, Simpson, Singleton, J. M. Smith, Staples, Swan, Villere, Welsh, Whitfield, Witherspoon, Mr. Speaker.—62.

NAYS.—Messrs. Akin, Bell, Cruikshank, Echols, Foote, *Fuller*, A. H. Garland, R. K. Garland, *Gilmer*, Lamkin, *J. M. Leach, J. T. Leach*, Lester, *Logan*, Marshall, *Ramsay*, W. E. Smith, *W. N. H. Smith*, W. R. Smith, Triplett, *Turner*.—22.

It will be seen that these resolutions contain the true view as to the plan of negotiations, as advocated by this journal, and which has, substantially, the approval of the Legislature of Georgia, to wit, *co-operation between the common government and the sovereign States in the effort to procure an armistice—then a treaty of peace, and then a vote of the people on the treaty, after its endorsement by the President and Senate.* We are gratified at the introduction of these resolutions by our friend, Dr. Leach, and we regard the vote against laying them on the table as a happy indication of the growing peace feeling in Congress. It will be seen that Mr. Gaither voted by himself to table, and that Messrs. Fuller, Gilmer, J. M. Leach, J. T. Leach, Logan, Ramsay, Smith, and Trrner voted against laying on the table.

On Tuesday last Mr. Graham presented his views at some length to the Senate on the *habeas corpus* question, opposing its further suspension.

The communication of "A Western Farmer," with others unavoidably crowded out by the pressure of legislative proceedings, shall appear soon.

While many of the soldiers' families throughout the State are reduced to bread and water, we learn that shade officers who surround Gov. Vance receive their supplies from the State storehouse by the wagon load at a time. These things may be denied, but it is generally known in this community that these shade officers—some of them wealthy men who are able to buy—are regularly supplied at government prices.—*Progress.*

We are glad to see that Mr. Rogers, of Wake, has introduced a resolution of inquiry in the House on this subject.

Soon after Gov. Vance came into office he abolished this Stallfederate system. He did so at our earnest suggestion, and the understanding was that the system would not be revived. But the "Rolly Click" was irresistible,—the Governor yielded, and now, while the families of our soldiers are crying for bread, pampered shade officers like Col. George Little not only run the blockade and thus procure Yankee and English luxuries, but they draw their supplies of rice, and sugar, and meal, and bacon, and other articles from the State at low prices. Is this to be endured? Will not the Legislature direct Gov. Vance, in the most emphatic terms, to discontinue this system? How can Vance men face their constituents, and ask a renewal of their confidence with this load upon their shoulders?

The Very Latest from the North.

The New York *Herald*, of the 16th, was received Saturday night. It contains very little of interest not even the closing quotation of gold on the 14th, which we presume was published in Sunday's issue.

The *Herald's* army correspondent, under date of 14th, gives the following mild statement of the losses in Grant's army to that date:

The 2d corps has lost 1100 killed, 7000 wounded, 1400 missing. The 5th corps has lost 1200 killed, 7500 wounded and 1300 missing. The 6th corps has lost 1000 killed, 6000 wounded, and 1200 missing. The total losses of these three corps amount to 27,700. Burnside's losses are nearly in the same proportion, and swell the total to about 35,000.—The proportion of slightly wounded is extraordinarily large.

The only allusion to the terrific fight of Thursday, 12th, is contained in the following extract from the same letter:

Hancock captured 4000 prisoners, as stated, and my informant counted 18 pieces of cannon taken by him, and believes there were others. The prisoners and guns were mainly from Gen. Ned Johnson's command. His cannon had been taken from their first position, by order of Lee, to strengthen another point. At Johnson's urgent solicitation, they were turned to him on Wednesday night, and his men were engaged in putting them in position at 5 [illegible] success was uniform along the whole line all day—no reverse at any point.

Considerable space is devoted to particulars of Sheridan's movements, but they contain only exaggerated accounts of facts already known here.—The *Herald's* situation summary says:

On the 13th the whole command encamped at Bottom's Bridge, after accomplishing the most splendid cavalry movement of the war. At 3 o'clock on Saturday afternoon Sheridan formed a junction with Butler's army at Turkey Bend, on the James river. His whole loss was not over 300 in killed, wounded, and missing.

There is nothing later from Gen. Butler.

A telegram dated Fortress Monroe, 15th, says:

Gen. Sheridan arrived at the James river yesterday afternoon.

He had heavy fights, in which he was very successful. He got inside of the rebel works around Richmond and could have taken the city, but was ignorant of Gen. Butler's position. Our men could see the gas lights in Richmond. They took three hundred prisoners.

Capt. Hower, A. A. G., of rebel Gen. Ruggle's staff, and seventeen officers and three hundred rebel prisoners, have arrived from Belle Plain in charge of Capt Hood, of the 18th veteran corps, *en route* to Fort Delaware. Among them are Major Gen. Edward Johnson, Brig. Gen. Geo. H. Stuart; Col. Pebbles, of Georgia; Col. Davidson, of New Orleans; Colonel Hardeman, of Georgia; Colonel Harrell, of North Carolina; Colonel Fitzgerald, of Virginia; Colonel Parsley, of North-Carolina; Colonel Davant, of Georgia; Major Carson, of Georgia; Major Enett, of North-Carolina; Major Wilson, Louisiana; Major Warnum, of Louisiana; Colonel Vanderventer, of Virginia; Colonel Cobb, of Virginia; Colonel Haynes, of Virginia; Major Nash, of Georgia; Major Perkins, of Virginia, and Major Anderson, of Virginia.

Many reports were in circulation yesterday in regard to the situation of affairs in Northern Virginia, but the only reliable information from that quarter is given in the letters of our army correspondents and the telegraphic dispatches which we publish this morning. It is believed that Grant, having thrown away 50,000 men in front of Gen. Lee, without accomplishing anything, is now endeavoring by a strategic movement to reach the Peninsula, with a view of advancing on Richmond from that route, taking for his base West Point, which he might have occupied at the commencement of the campaign without the loss of a man. Be this as it may, we have a General in command whose eye is constantly watching the movements of the invader, and who will not fail to take advantage of every opportunity to meet and circumvent them.—*Richmond Dispatch of Monday last.*

MARRIED,

On the 22d instant, at the residence of the bride's mother, by A. R. Perry, Esq., MR. JOHN MORGAN to MISS HASTY HALL, all of Wake County.

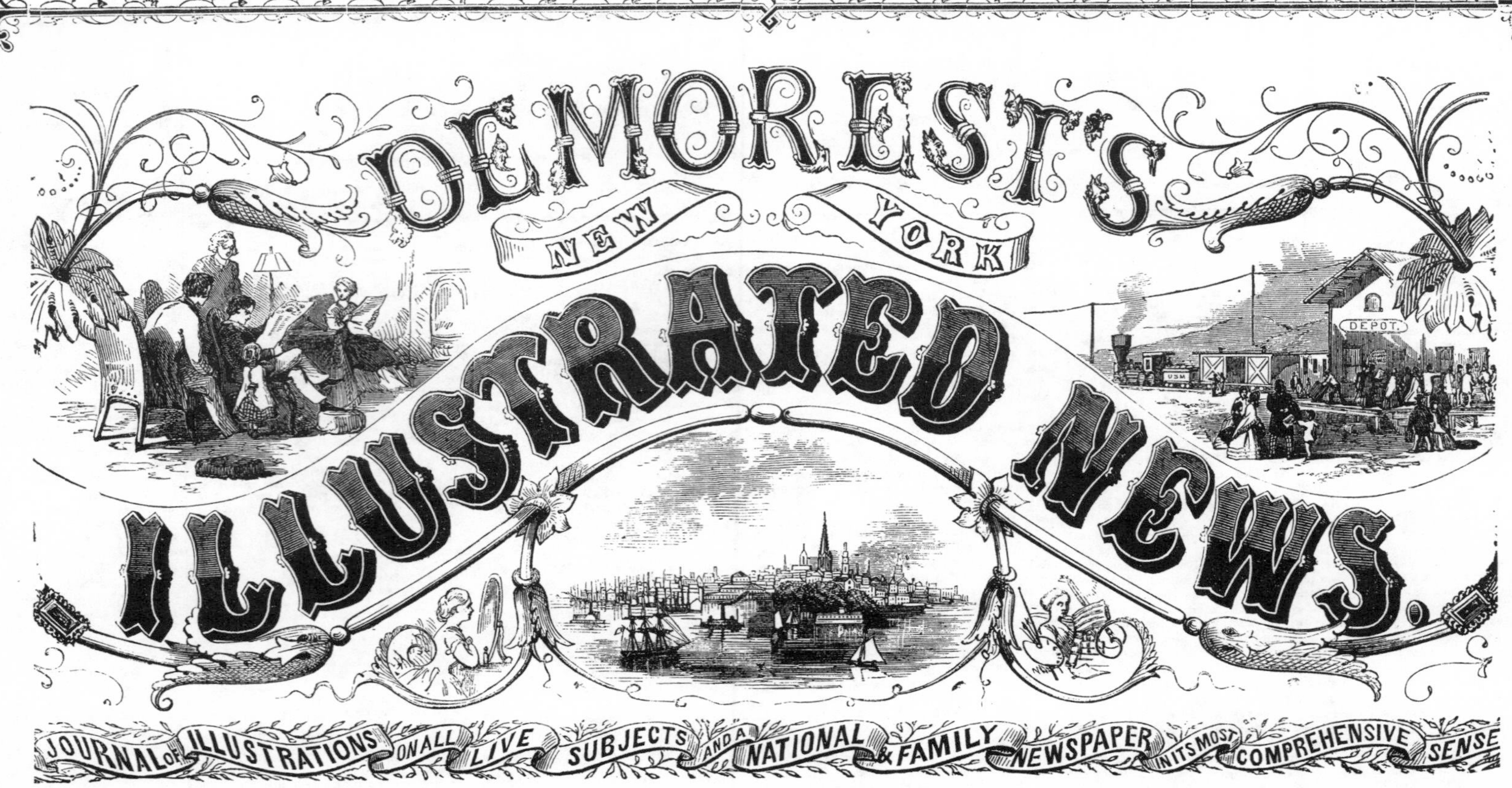

VOL. X.----No. 240.] NEW YORK, SATURDAY, JUNE 4, 1864. SINGLE COPIES, TEN CENTS, $4 00 Per Year, In Advance.

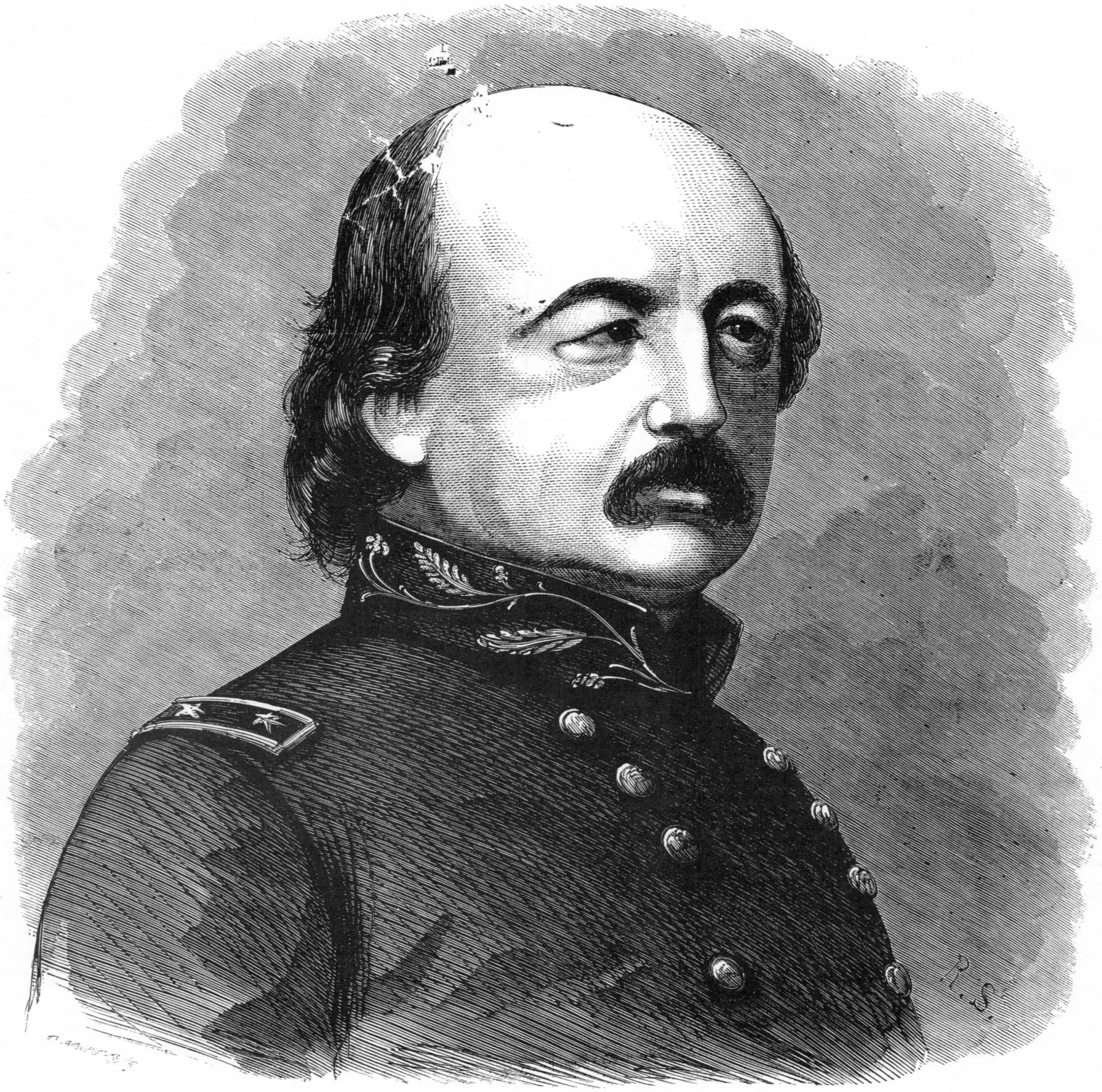

MAJOR-GENERAL BENJ. F. BUTLER.

LYNCHBURG VIRGINIAN

Monday Morning, June 13, 1864.

THE VIRGINIAN

Is published Daily, Tri-Weekly, and Weekly, by

CHARLES W. BUTTON.

TERMS OF SUBSCRIPTION.

Daily Virginian, one year,	- - -	$30 00
Do. do. six months,	- - -	15 00
Do. do. three months,	- -	8 00
Do. do one month	- -	3 00
Tri-Weekly, one year	- - - - -	$20 00
Do. six months,	- - -	10 00
Do. three months,	- - - -	6 00
Do. one month,	- - -	2 00
Weekly, one year,	- - - - -	$10 00
Do. six months,	- - -	6 00

☞ No paper will be sent without the subscription is paid in advance.

RATES OF ADVERTISING

ADVERTISEMENTS are inserted at $2.00 per square of 8 lines or less for each insertion.

OBITUARY AND MARRIAGE NOTICES charged for at the same rates.

TAXES: FOUR PER CT. BONDS.

It may not be generally known that under a decision of Mr. Memminger, contained in recent instructions to tax collectors, the four per cent. bonds which were secured by the people with a view to paying all taxes for the year 1864, will not serve that purpose in all cases. The second section of the currency act declares that, "The Secretary of the Treasury is hereby authorised to issue the bonds required for the funding provided for in the preceding section, and until the bonds can be prepared he may issue certificates to answer the purpose. Such bonds and certificates shall be receivable without interest in payment of all Government dues *payable* in the year 1864, except export and import dues." Now, the inference to be deduced from the wording of this act is clearly, that all taxes *accruing* in the year 1864, no matter at what particular time they might be payable, could be paid with the four per cent. bonds. Acting upon this belief, many persons estimated their probable income for the present year, and supplied themselves with bonds sufficient for the purpose of paying the tax thereon. It turns out now, however, that only the ad valorem tax, and the tax paid by merchants on their first three quarters' sales, can be paid with these bonds. The tax on their last quarter's sales, returnable after the expiration of the year, must be paid in new currency. Even in this, however, they are much better off than many other persons whose incomes are derived in a different way.

Under the decision of Mr. Memminger, persons whose incomes are derived from salaries or rents, from investments in stocks, from trading, or from the pursuit of any business not registered and required to have account thereof made quarterly to the tax collector, will have no use whatever for their four per cent. bonds. They will not answer the purpose for which they were provided, if that purpose was to use them in the payment of taxes. Consequently, the sharpers who can pay their taxes during the progress of the year, with bonds that may be bought for two-thirds, or less, of the amount expressed upon their face, will have that advantage over the other class we have described, who will have to pay their taxes, for the whole year, in a currency worth at least a third more. Is this equal, just, or right? Is it not taking an advantage of the people and making discriminations against certain classes that ought not to be made?

No reason is assigned by the Secretary, in the circular that we have seen, for the decision he has reached. We presume, however, that his instructions to the tax collectors are based upon two clauses, taken together, one in the tax and the other in the currency bill. The second section of the currency act provides that these bonds shall be receivable, &c, for "all Government dues PAYABLE in the year 1864." Now, the 6th clause of the 7th section of the tax bill which enumerates the forms of income taxable under the act, concludes thus: "The tax levied in this section shall be PAID on the first day of January next, and on the first day of January of each year thereafter." The income tax, therefore, for 1864, cannot be paid till the first day of January, 1865, and Mr. Memminger, taking advantage of a technicality, determines that one description of taxes which accrued during the year 1864, can not be paid with the bonds which Congress declared should be received in payment of "all taxes payable in 1864, except export and import dues." While the letter of the law may justify the position taken by the Secretary of the Treasury, it is evident that Congress intended that all taxes accruing in the year 1864, might be payable in these bonds or certificates, which they declared should "be receivable without interest in payment of all Government dues payable in the year 1864, except export and import dues." The whole question turns upon the construction to be given to the term "payable" as above; but as these bonds or certificates were issued with no view to their use in the payment of the taxes of 1863, but were intended for the liquidation of those accruing in the present year, no matter when paid, as the people supposed; Congress should see that no advantage is taken of the tax payers, and adapt the phraseology in question to the spirit of the law as the people apprehended and acted upon it. We hope that this matter will be set right when Congress comes together again in December.

THE YANKEES IN THE VALLEY

The diversion in the Valley was doubtless a part of Grant's masterly strategy for the accomplishment of his great purpose of taking Richmond. It is one of the combinations that, thus far, have signally failed as a whole. Butler was to advance by the South Side, Crook and Averill were to hold South West Virginia, and Siegel the Valley; whilst Grant and Burnside, cooperating more immediately together, were to drive Lee before them and march straight into Richmond.

But, the scheme has failed in every essential particular. Butler was whipped back; Averill and Cook were driven out of the South-west; the flying dutchman went "kiting" down the Valley, and the great Lieutenant-General Grant, after the loss of some seventy or eighty thousand men finds himself unable to stand before the invincible army of Lee. The disaster in the Valley has been but partially repaired and the second and more successful expedition under Hunter will ultimately come to grief. This Yankee has penetrated into a country that is comparatively easy of defence, abounding in mountain passes and gaps which will be used to dispute his farther advance. But more than this; he is about one hundred and twenty miles from his base of supplies, with all the intervening country filled with a hostile population and his deadly enemies. Mosby and McNeal, hovering in his rear, to cut off his trains. These daring partizans will give him a vast deal of trouble and when the gallant Breckinridge again gets him on the tilt, he will strive to emulate his swift-footed dutch predecessor. We cannot believe that Hunter can hold his position in the Valley, and, therefore, look for an early evacuation of Staunton and a retrograde movement with heavy loss on the part of the enemy. If Breckinridge had been retained in the Valley after the defeat of Siegel, as he should have been, the prestige of his success and the spirit of his troops would have prevented our late disaster.—But even that blunder may be partially repaired and the enemy be driven out of that beautiful country.

VANDALISM OF SHERMAN'S ARMY.

[From the Mississippian.]

It is a well known fact that whenever the Federal army have penetrated the Confederacy they have stolen negroes, horses, mules, wagons, bacon, corn, beef cattle; burning towns, private dwellings, churches, &c. But many of their most atrocious acts will never be known to the world. I regard it the duty of every citizen having cognizance of their heinousness to report them to some newspaper, that their doings may be published to World. For this reason, I here give you a brief sketch of facts gleaned from reliable and authentic sources. When Sherman's army was in the vicinity of Meridian, Mississippi, they took up a Mrs. Rushing at Marion station, and whipped her very severely, in order to make her tell where her husband's money was; but failed to extract the information from her. They afterwards caught Mr Rushing, her husband, and with a rope around his neck they swung him to the limb of a tree, swearing that they would hang him until he was dead, unless he would tell where his money was, which he finally did to save his life.

On their retreat from Meridian, they were piloted by deserters from our army to the residences of Dr Davis and his brother, and destroyed everything they possessed, handcuffed them, chained them to the tail of their wagons and took them off with them, for no other crime than that of having aided our cavalry in putting deserters into the army.

As they passed farms along their route, they took off negro men, women and children; many of the childrin were dropped by the wayside; but when they reached Tuscalameter and Pearl rivers, they drowned the balance of the little negroes in those streams.

Orders were given that all the negroes who wished to go back to their homes to step out in front of the army; many hundreds stepped out, and were there shot down for wishing to go back to their masters.

Mr. Stephens and others along the route went out and met the army with a smile, and extended the hand of friendship to them, and informed them that they were "great Union men." The Yankees replied that, "if they were Union men, they could afford to take liberties with them," and suiting their actions to their words, destroyed all they possessed.

THE DARING ATTEMPT OF KAUTZ'S CAVALRY TO CAPTURE PETERSBURG—THEY CHARGE AND TAKE THE BREASTWORKS—THEIR FINAL REPULSE AND DEFEAT.

FULL PARTICULARS OF THE AFFAIR.

We obtain from the "Express" the following full account of the attempt of the enemy to capture Petersburg.

At nine o'clock, our pickets on the Jerusalem Plank Road, were driven in, and before ten, the enemy showed himself in overwhelming numbers, filling the road, and the woods on both sides. Our breastworks here extend from the residence of Timothy Rives, Esq., on the left to and across the road, and beyond the house of Mr. Wm. A. Gregory, on the right. The enemy manœuvred for a while, thinking probably that our raw troops would abandon their position without a fight. But never were the Yankee invaders more mistaken. Our men were made of sterner stuff, and inspired by the cool determination of their leaders, Gen. Colston and Col. F. H. Archer, maintained their ground like veterans. Finally, the enemy ordered a charge, and came down to our breastworks with a yell, their drawn sabres flashing in the sunlight. When within forty paces of the fortifications, the order to fire was given, and the Yankees recoiled and fell back. A prisoner taken, subsequently, states that in this charge, the notorious Speare led, and that they had forty wounded and two killed. This charge was repeated twice, but with like results, when the enemy resorted to the flanking process, which by reason of his overwhelming numbers, he was enabled to do with much ease. A short time afterwards a regiment came around Rives' house on our left, another appeared on our right, and a large body came down in front. We had but 170 men all told, and it was impossible with this number to guard centre, right and left, along a length of three quarters of a mile or more. The order was given to retreat, and in a few minutes the enemy had possession of our works, our camp, and were in full pursuit of our men. Couriers had been dispatched for reinforcements, but they did not come up in time to save our fortifications, and many of Petersburg's best and most gallant sons, who fell in the affray, some killed, and others wounded.

The enemy came on in double column, with sabres drawn, until they reached the hill opposite the Water Works, where they planted a cannon for the purpose of shelling the city. They then started down the hill, and their advance column actually took possession of a bridge which crosses Powell's Run, at the foot of the Water Works Hill.

They were almost in Petersburg—could see its spires and steeples, and many of the houses on our suburban limits—but again that Divine arm which has been so often outstretched in our behalf, was barred, and our city was saved from the tread of the ruthless invader. Just at this opportune moment, Graham's Battery reached the Reservoir Hill, unlimbered in an instant, and with a precision and rapidity which we have heard spoken of as being almost without precedent, threw into the ranks of the enemy a shower of shell. The missiles of death coming so unexpectedly to the foe, he at first seemed overwhelmed with surprise and halted, neither advancing nor retreating. But a minute or two later, another branch of our service made its appearance, which quickly determined the enemy as to the best course for him to pursue. Dearing's Cavalry Brigade quickly dismounted, and descending the hill with a yell, charged upon the enemy in beautiful style. This was more than they expected (since they had encountered but a few militia in the breastworks, and had advanced nearly a mile, without seeing any regulars) and they instantly wheeled their horses, and started back up the hill in great confusion. Graham's Battery continued to play upon them, and Dearing's men crossed the ravine and ascended the opposite hill, in gallant style, their carbines keeping up a regular and most musical fusilade upon Kautz and Speare, and their rapidly retreating followers. Upon reaching the top of the opposite hill, the enemy hoped to make a stand, as here another column, which they had sent on to the city for the purpose of entering by the Blandford Church road, hove in sight. But this column had also started on a retrograde movement, for to their surprise too, they had encountered Sturdivant's Battery, which had gone out by another road, and the two columns met and continued their retreat at a speed not at all slackened by the Confederate shell and balls which were falling thick and fast among them. In Jackson's field, a mile or so from the Blanford Church, we captured a handsome cannon and six horses, which the enemy were compelled to abandon in their flight. Our forces pursued them for a few miles, killing and wounding many, and taking some prisoners.

Yesterday afternoon late, our pickets extended for several miles out on the Jerusalem Plank Road, but no signs of the enemy could be seen, and it is supposed they have retreated to the river. This is only supposition, however, and the vandals will bear constant and vigilant watching.

Gen. Kautz was in command of this force, and prisoners taken, variously estimate it at from three to five thousand.—None put the number at less than three thousand, and some say that it was even more than five thousand. There is no doubt but that it was intended to capture this city, and all the circumstances are strongly corroborative of this view.—Thanks to a kind Providence, who has nerved the hearts and strengthened the hands of our brave men, we have been again preserved.

The enemy crept up behind the residence of Mr Wm. A. Gregory, ascended to the roof, and knocking off the shingles, were enabled not only to obtain an excellent view, and ascertain the number of our forces, but through the openings thus made, fired upon and killed many of our men behind the breastworks.

The residence of Timothy Rives, Esq., fell into the possession of the invaders, after our forces retreated, and the scoundrels not only ransacked, and robbed it of all its valuable contents, but then applied the torch, and burnt it to the ground.—They also carried Mr Rives off a prisoner.

The foregoing are substantially all the facts connected with this bold attempt to capture Petersburg, so far as we have been enabled to collect them, but the saddest part of our statement yet remains unrecorded. Petersburg's bravest and best blood flowed freely yesterday, and many a household has been plunged into the most inconsolable grief. We witnessed scenes yesterday afternoon, which we trust we may never witness again. All who have been so stricken, have the consolation—a sad one it is true—but nevertheless, it is consoling to know, that those who have been so suddenly snatched from them, fell in a glorious cause. Their memories will ever be held in grateful recollection by our people, and this whole community deeply sympathize with the bereaved.—The following is a list, of the killed and wounded, which with great care, we have obtained, and which we believe to be corret:

KILLED.

Prof Staubly, Professor of French in the Petersburg Female College, formerly of Randolph Macon.

Lieut Wales Hurt, aged 18, a son of the late Branch T Hurt, and gallant youth.

John E Friend, eldest son of our late Postmaster, Wm N Friend, Esq. Deceased leaves a wife and one child.

Wm C Bannister, for many years an accountant in the Exchange Bank and one of our best citizens. He leaves a large family.

George B Jones, a prominent druggist, of Petersburg, and a most excellent man.

John Crowder, of this city, a noble youth.

George R Conway, of Prince George.

Wm Daniels, of Prince George, a youth. He was killed by a bayonet thrust through the breast, and his head was severely mutilated with the butt of a musket.

E P Brown, of Stuardivant's Battery, from Albemarle.

WOUNDED.

Henry A Blanks, of this city, seriously body and arm.

Dr Wm Bellingham, of Petersburg, a prominent dentist, severely in side.

Wm Howard, a clerk at the bookstore of Richard Riches.

Wm A Meanley, of this city, shot in three places, severely.

Robert A Martin, of the firm of Martin, Tannahill & Co., shot in the arm.

Wm T McCandlish, merchant of this city, shot in the hand and prisoner.

Rich'd A Harrison, of this city, shot through the hand.

Samuel Hall, hat merchant of Petersburg, shot in the thigh, severely.

W H Hardee, merchant of Petersburg, in the leg below the knee—since amputated.

Lieut Geo V Scott, of this city, severely in face and leg.

Norbourne T Dage, of this city in the hand.

Adjutant Guy G Johnson, shot in the bowels—feared mortally wounded.

Joseph Cooper, son of Joseph H Cooper, Esq., of this city, wounded and a prisoner.

A C Harrison, of this city, slightly in the arm

Richard M Cary, formely of Hampton, but now of Petersburg, in the thighs in two places—not mortal.

C L Bartlett, Professor of Music, in three places, severely.

A S Shafer, of Petersburg, in leg slightly.

Nathan Pritchard, of this city, slightly.

Wm F Johnson, of Albemarle, (Sturdivant's Battery,) through the head—supposed mortally.

Wm Griffith, of Prince George, wounded in both thighs.

Jas. Kane, of Prince George, in the leg.

CAPTURED.

Rev Wm A Hall, Chaplain Washington New Orleans Artillery.

Prof. Carr, of the Petersburg Female College.

James Boisseau, merchant of this city.

James Kerr, of Petersburg.

Timothy Rives, of Prince George.

Sam'l Jones, of Prince George—6.

PRISONER CAPTURED.

The following prisoners were brought in at an early hour yesterday afternoon:

William Tompkins, Co. F 11th Penn. Cavalry, commanded by Colonel Speare; Solomon Saxton, do; John Logan, Co. D same regiment, and Peter White, bugler, of the same regiment.

These men all agree that the expedition was for the purpose of capturing Petersburg: They say that Gen. Kautz was in command, and that Col Speare was along.

They left Bermuda Hundreds at halfpast 10 o'clock, on Wednesday night, and crossed on a pontoon bridge three miles this side of City Point.

FINE CLAY AS A DRESSING FOR SORES.

Dr. Schreber, of Leipsic, recommends clay as the most "energetic, the most innocent, the most simple and the most economical of palliative applications to surfaces yielding foul and moist discharges." He moreover considers that it has a specific action in accelerating the cure. Clay softened down in water, freed from all gritty particles, is laid, layer after layer, over the affected part to the thickness of about a line. It it become dry and fall off, fresh layers are applied to the cleansed surface. The irritating secretion is rapidly absorbed by the clay and the contact of air prevented. The cure thus goes on rapidly. This clay ointment has a decisive action in cases of fœtid perspiration of the feet or armpits. A single layer applied in the morning will destroy all odor in the day. It remains a long time supple, and the pieces which fall of in fine power produce no inconvenience.

HOW BURNSIDE'S NIGGERS FIGHT—NOTICE TO OUR SOLDIERS.

Cap't J James, of the 11th Ala. regiment, sends us a Yankee letter taken off the battle field on the 3d of June. The writer, one William Reardin, Company K, 164th N. Y. S. V., 4th brigade, 2d division, 2d corps, army Potomac," writing from the camp of his regiment, "on the battle field." May 20th, to a friend, speaks of the rough times he has had, his regiment losing 130 men, the prowess of said regiment, and the writer's lucky escape from bursting shells. He adds: "We are driving the Rebs all the time. Our regiment charged on four tiers of rifle pits, and captured them. Our brigade has done so well that it is the whole talk of the Army of the Potomac. We have just received good news from Burnside's corps. His niggers fight like devils. They neither ask or give quarter, and take no prisoners, but kill all. We are in the same corps as Meagher's brigade," &c. We hope our soldiers will remember Burnside and his "niggers" the first available opportunity, and doubt not they will do so.

LYNCHBURG VIRGINIAN

Tuesday Morning, June 21, 1864.

THE VIRGINIAN

Is published Daily, Tri-Weekly, and Weekly, by

CHARLES W. BUTTON.

TERMS OF SUBSCRIPTION.

Daily Virginian, one year,	$30 00
Do. do. six months,	15 00
Do. do. three months,	8 00
Do. do one month	3 00
Tri-Weekly, one year	$20 00
Do. six months,	10 00
Do. three months,	6 00
Do. one month,	2 00
Weekly, one year,	$10 00
Do. six months,	6 00

☞ No paper will be sent without the subscription is paid in advance.

RATES OF ADVERTISING

ADVERTISEMENTS are inserted at $2.00 per square of 8 lines or less for each insertion.

OBITUARY AND MARRIAGE NOTICES charged for at the same rates.

Very much to our regret, but for causes that all must see are clearly justifiable, we suspended the issue of the "Virginian," for a whole week. Every man connected with the office, including an old man 70 years of age, deaf as a post, and blind in one eye, shouldered arms and went to the field. We hope that another such interruption will not occur. Our office is but partially re-organized now, and we could not publish as much news to-day as we desired.

THE BATTLE OF LYNCHBURG.

Another has been added to the many names that will be illustrious in history. Southern valor and prowess have once more been tested by our demoniac foe; and these, by the blessings of Almighty God, have been sufficient to prevent that saturnalia of demons to which all the conquered cities of the South are doomed. The fiends who have perpetrated murder, arson, pillage and rape during their whole march from Staunton to the neighborhood of this city, were signally discomfited within sight of the goal of their wishes on Saturday last: and thus, the high carnival they expected to hold here has been postponed indefinitely.

Since Monday, the 13th inst., nearly every able-bodied man, (except a few skulkers whom no appeal to patriotism could move—men upon whom the band of disgrace should be indelibly stamped,) was under arms or busy making trenches from which to hurl leaden death upon the armed marauders that were daily expected.

Stationed at all the passes by which ingress to the city was afforded, it was not doubted that the militia, the reserves, the convalescent soldiers and the volunteers would be able to keep the enemy at bay until reinforcements could arrive. Accordingly, during the interval between the first alarm and the arrival of the forces under Major General Breckinridge, our people, though anxious, were calm and collected. Every man, with the exceptions above named, seemed to be determined to do his duty and to defend the town to the last extremity. Day by day, and almost hour by hour, scouts would arrive and report the progress and precise locality of the foe. They were advancing slowly, whilst every foot of their way was disputed by the brave and indomitable Gen. McCausland, to whom we owe a debt of lasting gratitude. With fifteen hundred men, he fought twenty thousand Yankees and materially retarded their progress from Staunton to this place.

On Friday morning it was ascertained that the enemy had approached within a few miles of the city, and in the afternoon the booming of artillery was heard on the Lynchburg and Salem Turnpike road, near the old Quaker Church, about three miles distant. It was McCausland, with some of Imboden's cavalry, disputing the further advance of the enemy. A gun on our side, was disabled at this point, which, report said, had fallen into the hands of the foe. Our troops then fell further back. We should have stated, in the proper place, that McCausland had a very heavy skirmish with the enemy on Thursday, near New London, in which he suffered considerably.

After the fight at the Quaker Church, on Friday afternoon, further hostilities were suspended until Saturday morning when, about 7 o'clock, our batteries on the Salem Turnpike opened with an occasional shot. At 11 o'clock precisely, a furious cannonading set in, and, with some brief intervals of silence, was continued until late in the afternoon. Occasionally the roll of musketry was heard as an accompaniment to the deeper toned thunders of artillery.

The line of battle extended from about half a mile above the toll gate, (two and a half miles from Lynchburg,) on the Lynchburg and Salem Turnpike, moving in a direction a little West of North, including portions of the land of Dr. Owen, Charles Moorman, Jno. B. Lee, H. S. Barksdale, and terminating on the farm of Seth Halsey, near the Blackwater creek. The distance embraced by this line must be two and a half to three miles.

From the character of the ground over which the battle raged it is impossible to give any thing like an accurate description of all its parts. Persons familiar with the topography of Lynchburg and its environs will readily understand this. The whole country is a succession of hills, gorges, and streams. The former are broken and precipitous, and in many places thick woods intervene to break the view; so, that, a position that would command a prospect of one part might not avail to afford a view of any other. At the point where we were stationed with the volunteers, on the Lexington road, we could only observe portions of the scene of combat, and had to judge from the sound of our guns and the responses thereto, of the localities held by the respective combatants.

Dr. E. H. Murrell, who was in a good position to observe a portion of the fight, has informed us that a battery stationed on Halsey's farm did great execution. He distinctly saw a large body of cavalry, which he supposed to be about 4000, drawn up in line of battle in Capt. Barksdale's field, on the Forest road. They charged upon our fortification with great spirit, yelling defiance and at the top of their voices, which were borne to the point where the Doctor stood concealed, he heard them cry, "come out of your holes you d——nd rebels, we've got you now! come out of your holes." When these infuriated wretches got within reach of our grape and canister, our boys let fly a volley at them which did terrible execution. Two other volleys were poured into them, when they broke and fled.

We hear that the old Stonewall brigade acted very gallantly, and we have heard some other commands very highly spoken of also; but as no accurate account can be given by any single spectator of the fight, we forbear, lest we seem to be invidious, by singling out any particular troops for special encomium. When all the reports shall have been collected, and the truth fully elicited, it will give us great pleasure to publish all the particulars of the battle of Lynchburg. The battle ended on Saturday afternoon, and the enemy retreated in great haste on Saturday night. Had they remained until the next day, we are satisfied, from the dispositions that had been made by Gen. Early, that they would have been captured. Their safety is not now an assured fact by any means.

We rode over the battle field on Sunday observing the results of the previous day's work. On two or three contiguous fields, on the farms of Doct. Owen and Jno. B. Lee, we counted some forty odd dead Yankees, who lay stiff and stark and nude, a spectacle of horror. They had been denuded, it was said, by their particular friends, gentlemen of "African decent." Most of them were supposed to be sharp-shooters who fell in advance of the enemy's lines, and quite near to our rifle pits and intrenchments. Fully three-fourths of them were shot through the head, and others through the heart; thus showing the accuracy of that unerring aim which sent them to their last account. Some of them were fierce looking, heavily bearded cut throats, whilst a few were smooth-faced boys. We noticed one who seemed to be a stripling of scarce seventeen summers. He had a good countenance and must have been under the influence of wicked advisers. Alas! for the mother who will never learn the fate of this misguided and unhappy boy. Stranger hands have now buried him out of sight, and his dust will mingle with mother earth in the land of those he came to despoil. These were the dead of Saturday and many more, we were told, were lying about over the extensive field and in the woods. The enemy, with their accustomed inhumanity, left them to be buried by their foes. This proves too, the precipitancy of their flight.

On the left of the Salem turnpike, near the Quaker Meeting House, we saw five graves. On the wooden boards placed at their head was, Geo. Straup, 1st Lt. co. D, 91st Ohio Vol. In.; Wm. Randall, co. F, 91st O. V. I.; Sam'l McKee, co. I, 91st O. V. I.; Wm. Emmons, co K. 91st O. V. I.; Lewis Graham, co. C, 91st O. V. I.. The record stated that these were all killed on Friday, the 17th. On the other side of the road, a man was laid out in a blanket with a piece of white paper pinned on his breast, marked Ro. J. Simpson, co. I, 1st Va. Light Infantry. These memorials show the States from which these troops came. The track of the enemy was marked by the usual amount of destruction. Dressed chickens, a dead sheep, large portions of beef thrown away, all attest the robberies perpetrated upon our people, many of whom have been plundered of all their flocks and herds, whilst even their furniture has been wantonly destroyed. We shall speak of these hereafter. We subjoin a few facts of interest, which give an inside view of the expectations and purposes of the enemy.

Gens. Hunter, Crook, Averill and Sullivan put up with Major Hutter, about four miles from town, whose beautiful home was used as headquarters. In their suit were the notorious Dr. Rucker and David H. Strother (Port Crayon), the former attached to Crook's staff. Major Hutter being an old army officer was well acquainted with Hunter and talked freely to him respecting his expedition. Hunter said that he had fifty thousand men and could take Lynchburg easily; that we had better make no resistance. When Major Hutter informed him that it would be no easy task, and that our people, in the last resort, would retire to the Amherst heights and fire upon them, Hunter replied that, in such event he would help them to destroy the town. The general officers were in very high spirits at the supper table on Friday night, and boasted that they would be in Lynchburg the next day. On Saturday night they took their meal at the same board in perfect silence. Gen. Averill retired to the back porch after supper very moody, and remarked to Miss H. that "the battle of Lynchburg would be one of the bloodiest records of this war for the time it lasted." He said that the loss was very heavy on both sides, theirs being not less than eight hundred to a thousand. The General was mistaken as to ours, which is six killed and 95 wounded.

Sullivan said they had some 25 or 30,000 men, and reinforcements were expected under Pope, who, with other troops, had 4000 contrabands. The Yankees avowed it to be their purpose to capture Lynchburg and then proceed to the assistance of Butler. They placed their signal officers on the top of Major Hutter's house, and as the battle progressed on Saturday the "look out" declared that the cavalry were charging splendidly; after a while however, he said that they were giving away, and finally left his eyry in disgust.

When Miss H. remonstrated with Gen. Hunter for his vandalism in burning the Military Institute, he replied, "You need not make a fuss about that, for I intend to burn the University of Virginia also."

After the melancholy supper referred to, Hunter told Maj Hutter that they wanted to hold a council. They thereupon appropriated two rooms, the doors of which they locked carefully. Major H. having retired to a back chamber of his house attemptad to pass out of the building, when he was informed that he was a prisoner. When the Yankee officers retired they said that they were going to the front and thus took up the line of retreat before Major Hutter was aware of their intentions.

Some of the Yankee soldiers repaid the hospitality of Maj. Hutter by plundering Miss H's chamber, searching trunks and drawers, and carrying away various ornaments and valuables. Some 90 odd wounded Yankees were left in Maj. Hutter's barn. Four or five of them died on Sunday. These wounded were rather the best looking Yankees we have yet seen, being mostly Western men. Other wounded were left at different points amongst the families of the people they had robbed, whilst many of the slightly wounded were doubtless carried off.

We are obliged to close our narrative here, by adding that the Yankees retired by the way they come, and are hotly pursured by Gen. Early, who is but two miles behind them. We trust that he will bag the whole party.

THE LATE BRILLIANT ACHIEVEMENT OF HAMPTON'S CAVALRY.

We have received a more detailed account of the defeat of Sheridan's forces by our cavalry under Generals Hampton and Fitz Lee, which not only confirms previous intelligence, but shows that the enemy were thoroughly beaten and demoralized. As heretofore stated, skirmishing commenced on Saturday, the 11th instant, a few miles this side of Trevillian's depot, on the Central Railroad; and while Hampton engaged the enemy on the front, in the vicinity of the railroad, Fitz Lee attacked them in the flank, this side of Louisia Court House. This was about 10 o'clock in the forenoon. At noon the Yankees succeeded in capturing our wagon train, several led horses and a number of prisoners; but their triumph was of brief duration, for Rosser's brigade, which was posted on the Gordonsville road, being immediately ordered to the rescue, not only recaptured all the wagons, horses and prisoners, but captured two hundred and fifty of the enemy also. On the same day, Gen. Fitz Lee took one hundred and fifty prisoners and three pieces of artillery, and captured the headquarters of the Yankee Gen. Custar.

Our troops, having thus gained signal advantages, rested quietly through the night, but the enemy being still in their front, breastworks were hastily thrown up, and other preparations made for a renewal of the struggle on the following day. Meanwhile, Generals Hampton and Fitz Lee united their divisions and calmly awaited an attack. The fighting commenced about noon on Sunday. The enemy, rendered desperate by their losses on the previous day, charged our breastworks three times, and were as often repulsed with heavy loss. By nightfall the Yankees were driven from the field, which remained in possession of our troops. Being thus utterly discomfitted, they concluded not to renew the contest, and about midnight commenced retreating in the direction of the Rapidan, which stream, it is said, they succeeded in crossing. They left their dead and wounded in our hands—among the latter two Lieutenant Colonels. In all, 517 prisoners were captured, who were subsequently sent to Charlottesville; and the entire loss of the enemy is estimated at 1,500. The Yankees were much demoralized, and being without rations or forage, and their horses broken down, they could not be brought to face our men the third time. Many of the horses were rendered useless, and on the retreat a large number of the men were dismounted. Sheridan's force consisted of Wilson's and Gregg's divisions, (six brigades,) numbering in all some ten thousand men, with several pieces of artillery. Captured officers admit that it was their design to make a raid upon Gordonsville and Charlottesville, and destroy the public buildings and stores at those places, and form a junction with Crook and Averill.—Thanks to the gallantry of Hampton and his brave command, their nefarious purposes have been signally defeated.

A gentleman from Spotsylvania states that on their retreat through that county, the raiders destroyed everything in their way, and carried along with them a considerable number of negroes. To destroy and rob is the object of these expeditions, and the main design of this party having been thwarted, they probably sought revenge by the infliction of atrocities upon the defenceless inhabitants of Spotsylvania.—Richmond Dispatch.

SHELLING THE CITY.

If anything were wanting to establish the barbarity and inhumanity of the Yankee army in this war, the attempted shelling of Petersburg would complete the measure. Grant wants the city, but to get it, he must pass over the gallant army defending it. This he cannot do, and hence his batteries are placed in commanding positions, and a portion of the city is exposed to his shells. The thousands of women and children here were exposed to this danger without a moment's warning, and for an entire night and parts of two days there has been but little cessation in the flying and bursting of these missiles. To tell where every one strikes, where hundreds are thrown, would be a tedious task. The eastern suburbs of the city, of course, suffer the most, and in consequence that portion of the town has been much depleted of its inhabitants.

Surprising to say, however, but litttle damage has been done to life or property in comparison with the number of shells thrown. Some few buildings have been struck, and some few persons have been injured. It is the anticipation of danger more than the reality that disturbs the remaining populace.

Yesterday morning early, a shell broke through the rear wall, second story, of the building on Sycamore street, occupied as a bakery and dwelling by Mr. Chas. Brown. It exploded with tremendous force after its entrance into the room, scattering the plastering from the walls and disarranged the furniture generally. Mr. Brown's family, consisting of several ladies and children, were in the room at the time of the explosion, but very miraculously and providentially escaped serious injury. One of the ladies received a slight scratch on the face.

We hear also of one or two other houses that have been slightly damaged.

A few accidents occured yesterday, the most serious of which happened to two negro children in Blanford. While lying asleep in their mother's house, near Spicer's factory, a shell bur[...]

[...] as were declared exchanged by Exchange Notices, numbered six, seven and eight.

RO. OULD, Agent of Exchange

June 21—6t

FROM GRANT'S ARMY—DEPARTURE OF EXPIRED TIME REGIMENTS.

A dispatch from the headquarters of Grant's 5th corps, says, "I have been compelled to chronicle the departure of some regiments whose term of service has expired in nearly every recent letter," and goes on to notice the departure of the 2d Wisconsin, which carried away 128 men and 15 officers, including two surgeons. It had been in fourteen battles, and lost 793 killed and wounded.

Gen Ferrero and his "colored infantry" is represented to have gobbed up by 50 rebel cavalry on the 10th instant.

The rebel sharpshooters are stated to be very fatal to the officers, and any one wearing shoulder straps pays his life for attempting to walk about the fortifications. Lieut Col Burfee, of the 2d Conn., and Lieut Col Corning, of the 14th New York, are among the latest victims.

The Louisville Journal notices the mortifying fact that ten of Morgan's men threw a train off the track near Smithfield, Ky, and captured 26 Federal soldiers, to whom they administered an oath to support the Southern Confederacy. They were polite to the ladies, and did'nt take any money except Government or company funds, except in a few instances, where they borrowed some change from the male passengers to be returned "after the war." The cars, with the exception of the ladies' coaches, were burned. The conduct of the rebels was "strangely marked by a show of gallantry and an exhibit of desperado."

Very much to our regret, but for causes that all must see are clearly justifiable, we suspended the issue of the "Virginian," for a whole week. Every man connected with the office, including an old man 70 years of age, deaf as a post, and blind in one eye, shouldered arms and went to the field. We hope that another such interruption will not occur. Our office is but partially re-organized now, and we could not publish as much news to-day as we desired.

LYNCHBURG VIRGINIAN.

NOTICE.—The cross mark appended to the names of certain subscribers indicates that the term for which they subscribed will soon expire. They are thus notified in time to renew their subscription if they desire.

RAGS WANTED.—The highest market price will be paid at this Office for Clean Cotton Rags. They will be purchased in any quantity.

We would be glad if our friends in the country would inform us of all the atrocities committed by the Yankees in their late movements. We hear of a great number of reports, but will not publish mere rumors.

THE VA. MILITARY INSTITUTE.—General Smith of the Institute informs us that all the apparatus, books, maps, &c., belonging to the Institute were saved, whilst a new supply of books is now at Wilmington, having run the blockade. The walls of the Institute are not much injured and the buildings can be easily restored.

FROM HUNTER'S ARMY.—We have reliable authority for stating that the rear guard of Hunter's army was overtaken Sunday evening this side of Liberty, driven through the town and pursued until night, when they reached their main body and formed in line of battle. Our forces rested until morning, when the enemy were found to have retreated. Gen Early immediately commenced the pursuit, and from the fact that heavy cannonading was heard in that direction, it was supposed that he had overtaken them and the two forces were engaged in a fierce contest.

So soon as it was known here that the raiding party of the enemy from the Valley had passed Lynchburg, coming in this direction, the reserve forces at this place were ordered under arms and placed in the fortifications opposite the town, on the North side of the river. Cannon were also planted upon the heights, to welcome the marauders, should they incline to pay us a visit.—Danville Register.

LIEUT. GENERAL LONGSTREET.—and family arrived at Danville, on the Richmond train Thursday. He is the guest of E. B. Estes, Esq.—Ib.

FROM SUFFOLK AND VICINITY.—Raiding parties, says the Christian Sun are going out in every direction from Suffolk, robbing the farmers of horses, provisions, etc. Butler has issued orders to have all the horses taken in Nansemond, Isle of Wight and Gates county, N. C., so as to prevent the making of crops. A party came into Suffolk last Friday, with 114 horses and mules taken from their owners. Another party was at Chuckatuck, and captured Dr. Wm. T. Jordan, of the Signal Corps, and a citizen, carrying them off. Great distress and consternation pervades the whole section of country now given up to the ravages of the cruel enemy.

The following is the latest from Staunton to Dix:

SECRETARY STANTON TO DIX.

WAR DEPARTMENT, Washington, June 12—12 M.

Major Gen. Dix:

A despatch from Gen. Hunter, dated at six o'clock, on the morning of the 8th instant, at Staunton, reports that—

"We met the enemy at Piedmont last Sunday, the 5th instant, killing Wm. E. Jones, their commanding General, and totally routing them after a battle of ten hour's duration. We have captured one thousand five hundred prisoners altogether, one thousand men and over sixty officers on the field of battle—also three thousand stand of arms, three pieces of artillery and a vast quantity of stores. We have to day effected a junction with Generals Crook and Averill."

It is stated in another despatch, unofficial, dated at Staunton, June 9, that "our infantry is now engaged burning ties and bending rails, east and west. All government and railroad buildings have been burned at Staunton. We leave to-morrow."

A despatch from Gen. Grant's headquarters dated yesterday at 4 P. M., reports that "rebel cavalry having yesterday made a dash into Wilson's lines, near the Lenny House, Wilson this morning sent out a part of McIntosh's brigade to see where the enemy was. Their pickets were driven back and their outer lines forced, the cavalry passing over the intrenchments about a mile west of Bethesda church, McIntosh came upon Field's division of infantry, and, having accomplished the purpose of his reconnoissance, retired. He killed and wounded a number of rebels in his progress, and brought away four or five prisoners. He had sixteen men killed and wounded.

Despatches from General Sherman, dated at his headquarters, Big Shanty, Georgia, this morning, have been received. They state that our lines were within four or five hundred yards of the enemy; but no fighting yet.

EDWIN M. STANTON, Secretary of War.

TERRIFIC CANNONADING AND MUSKETRY FIRING—THE ENEMY REPULSED.

There was now quite a cessation of hostilities, until six o'clock, when heavy cannonading again commenced, the reverberations of the guns roaring through the city, and jarring the windows of every house.

As night approached, the cannon firing grew more incessant, and the rattle of musketry, which was continuous, was distinctly audible to every ear.

The fight, we learn, commenced on our right near Batteries 17, 18, 19 and 20, at Col. Avery's farm, but gradually extended around to our extreme left, and by dark, the engagement was general along the whole line, a distance of about five miles.

As the contestants in the vicinity of the New Market Race Course became engaged, the booming of the cannon, and the popping of musketry, fell upon our people with a distinctiveness which aroused the entire city to the highest pitch of excitement, and every street and alley, and all the surrounding hills, were crowded with people, listening with breathless anxiety to hear the result.—The moon was high in the heavens and shone with unusual brilliancy, and the flashes of the big guns and the blaze of musketry, could be seen from the Blandford Church and Bolling Hills with great distinctness.

For a half hour the battle raged and roared, and during this time, from the nearness of the sound, many became impressed with the idea that the invaders of our soil were getting the advantage of our troops, but all of a sudden there was one universal blaze of musketry along the entire length of our line, and then fell upon the ears of the listening multitude, a shout from the throats of our brave boys, which none were slow to interpret. It was the shout of victory—a glad and welcome sound to the fathers, mothers and daughters of this city. Couriers soon arrived, announcing the glad tidings that we had repulsed the enemy along the entire line, and occupied the lines which we held at early dawn yesterday. Never were a people more relieved than ours, and many a venerable matron and fair daughter, wept profuse tears of gratitude. It was now 10 minutes to 10 o'clock, and the firing gradually slackened, until 11 o'clock, when it had almost entirely ceased. About 11 o'clock there was a renewal of the musketry firing, and a few discharges of cannon, but it did not last more than 15 minutes. As we now write, at 12 o'clock, the firing has entirely ceased, with the exception of that 32-pounder Blakely gun which the Yankees fired during all of Thursday night at intervals of five minutes.

We have been unable to obtain any details, or very little reliable intelligence, but parties who participated, inform us that Hoke's Division stood like a wall of adamant, never receding an inch from their position. In front of their breastworks all accounts agree that the slaughter of the enemy was fearful, and an ordnance officer who came in for ammunition, informs us, that he has been present at all the great battles of Lee's army, but that he has never witnessed greater mortality in the ranks of the enemy.

On the right, occupied by a portion of Bushrod Johnston's Division, we hear that the enemy came up in seven lines of battle, and so great was the pressure of overwhelming numbers, that there was a temporary wavering among our men, who upon the first shock gave way. They were soon rallied, however, our lines restored, and the enemy made to pay fearfully for their temporary success.—Petersburg Express of Saturday.

LATEST BY TELEGRAPH

Reports of the Press Association

Entered according to Act of Congress, in the year 1863, by J. S. THRASHER, in the Clerk's Office of the District Court of the Confederate States for the Northern District of Georgia.

FROM THE SOUTH SIDE.

PETERSBURG, June 20th.

Since yesterday nothing of great interest has transpired. To-day there has been some cannonading, also slight skirmishing yesterday.

Gen Meade sent a flag of truce to General Beauregard, requesting permission to bury his dead, which was not granted.

The City Council to-day held a meeting and sent a committee to Gen Beauregard to ask his advice in regard to the removal of non-combattants. Gen B replied that no notice had been given by the enemy of their purpose to shell the city, but it would be prudent for those who could to leave the lower part of the city, and for women and children to remain in cellars. Very few shells have been thrown into the city to-day.

Grant's lines reach from James river across the Appomattox to within two miles of the Weldon railroad.

Advices from Liberty this morning says that Hunter had been pursued through that place; that he was retreating towards Buford's Gap in considerable disorder; that some prisoners had been taken, and more doubtless would be.

The enemy at this writing seem to be moving towards the Weldon railroad. Our Generals will doubtless be prepared for them.

PETERSBURG, 19th.

Grant's whole army is in front of this place in line of battle. More or less fighting every day since Wednesday. The enemy have been generally repulsed, gaining little or no ground since Wednesday, when they got within one and a half miles of the city, taking some of our works, which they now hold. Occasional shells have been thrown into the city, doing however but little damage.

Grant's new base is City Point, on the James River, 12 miles distant.

The enemy have constructed an immense observatory, about 11 miles below from which to observe operations hereabouts.

The enemy yesterday attempted to advance on our lines, but our troops opened upon them with artillery and musketry, inflicting loss upon the enemy equal to any of the campaign. The enemy at no time got nearer than 400 yards of our lines. To-day some cannonading and heavy skirmishing.

The people of Petersburg are quiet and resolute; all able to bear arms being in service.

The most of Grant's army is south of the Appomattox.

FROM RICHMOND.

RICHMOND, 20th.

Sheridan is reported in Hanover to-day, moving towards James river, with the remnant of his command. The capture of the entire party is confidently anticipated.

RICHMOND, June 17.

Authentic information from Sheridan's raiders has been received. He passed through New Town, King and Queen county, on yesterday, where it is reported he was again attacked by Hampton. Sheridan is evidently aiming to reach Gloucester Point. His wagon train is reduced to 23 wagons. Prisoners taken confess a thorough defeat of the expedition.

No official despatches received at the War department to-day.

NORTHERN NEWS.

RICHMOND, 19th.

United States papers of the 16th have been received. A telegraph from Lexington says, Burbridge defeated the rebels at Cynthiania on the 12th, killing three hundred and taking four hundred prisoners.

Maximillian arrived at Vera Cruz on the 28th, and would proceed at once to the city of Mexico.

Grant has commenced a new campaign against Richmond on the South Side of James River. His headquarters are at Bermuda Landing.

Sturgis' defeat by Forrest is confessed officially as a disaster.

European advices to the 1st. Lindsay's motion for recognition of the Southern Confederacy was postponed to the 17th.

There was a report that Napoleon had sent two Commissioners to America to report the progress of the war, and renewed overtures to England for a cessation of the carnage.

The proposition of the London Conference is to detach Holstein and the Southern part of Schleswig from Denmark. Rejected by the latter.

Gold in New York 15th opened and closed at ninety seven and a half.

PETERSBURG, June 19th.

The Express has Northern dates to the 14th.

Stanton telegraphs to Dix that Burbridge telegraphs here that he had a fight, lasting an hour, with Jack Morgan, at Cynthiania, Ky., on the 12th, completely routing Morgan, killing 300, wounding nearly as many, and capturing near 400 prisoners. Burbridges' loss 150. Of Morgan's forces his dispatch farther says, they are flying in all directions; have thrown away arms, out of ammunition, and wholly demoralized.

Morgan had previously whipped Hobson, commanding at Cynthiania, capturing 1500 prisoners.

The correspondent of the Tribune, writing in regard to the fight, June 3d, at Cold Harbor, says, the regiments engagement all loss from one-third to one-half of their commands.

Gold closed on the 13th at 198.

FROM THE SOUTH-WEST.

MOBILE, 18th.

A special dispatch to the Register, dated Senatobia 17th, says Morgan's forces, estimated at from three to five thousand, whipped Gen Hobson and captured his whole command, 1500, at Cynthiania. Frankfort attacked and the barracks burned. The attacking party were repulsed.

It is reported that Burbridge routed Morgan on the 12th, but it is not credited.

Wild excitement in Louisville. Morgan dispatched to the city authorities that he would attack. The Federal forces were inadequate for defence.

Gen Sturges reported arrested by charges from Grierson.

TWO MILES WEST OF MARIETTA, June 18th.

The enemy has removed large numbers of his forces on our left. Cannonading and musketry constant, amounting almost to an engagement.

The rain continues to render the roads unfit for military operations.

There are indications that our left and centre will be attacked.

The army is in splendid spirits, and ready for an attack.

Deserters came in this morning drunk.

But few casualties yesterday on our side. Several prisoners captured this morning.

CLINTON, LA., 18th, *via* MOBILE.

The steamer Progress, loaded with 1300 bales cotton, was burned on the Mississippi; no lives lost.

Ex-Mayor French, of New Orleans, died on the 14th.

Thursday night our batteries attacked the steamer Laudal, another transport, loaded with troops, and struck her ten times. Three shells exploded on deck. She whistled a signal of distress, and a gunboat came up and towed her off. The Yankee cavalry from Port Hudson pursued our batteries, but a few shells drove them off.

North Carolina Times.

Liberty and Union — Now and Forever — One and, Inseparable.

VOL. 1. NEW BERNE, N. C., WEDNESDAY, JUNE 22, 1864. NO. 44.

BY GEO. MILLS JOY:

The NORTH CAROLINA TIMES will be published WEDNESDAY and SATURDAY mornings, on Craven Street, New-Berne, N. C.

TERMS OF THE PAPER.

$5,00 per year in advance; **$1,25** for 3 months; **50 cts.** per month.

SINGLE COPIES FOR SALE

At the office of publication, and by the different news dealers in the District.

The Miser's Bequest.

The hour hand of Philip Acre's old fashioned silver watch was pointing to the figure eight—the snug red curtains shut out the rain and darkness of the March night, and the fire snapped and crackled behind the red hot bar of the little grate in the most cosy and comfortable sort of a way, casting a rosy shine into the thoughtful, brown eyes that were tracing castles and coronets in the burning coal.

For Philip Acre was, for once, indulging himself in the dangerous fascination of a day dream.

"If I were only rich?" he pondered to himself. "Ah, if. Then good bye to all of those musty old law books; good bye to the mended boots and thrice turned coats, and all the ways and means that turn a man's life into wretched bondage! Would'nt I revel in new books and delicious paintings and high stepping horses? Would'nt I buy a set of jewels for Edith—not pale or sickly emeralds, but diamonds, to blaze like links of fire on her royal throat? Would'nt I—what nonsense I'm talking though!" he cried, suddenly rousing himself. "Phil. Acre, hold your confounded tongue! I did suppose you were a fellow of more sense! Here you are, neither rich nor distinguished, but a simple law student, while Edith Wyllis is as far above your moonstruck aspiration at the Queen of night herself!

"She loves me though—she will wait—and the time may one day come. If only Dr. Wyllis was not so distrustful of a fellow! However, I must prove myself worthy of the sweetest prize that ever—Halloo! come in there whoever you are."

It was only the serving maid of the establishment carrying a letter in the corner of her apron, between her finger and thumb.

"Please, sir, the postman just left it —two cents to pay.'

"Here are your two coppers, then Katy—a pretty fair equivalent for any letter I may receive. Now," said he, as the door closed behind Katy's substantial back, "lets see what my unknown correspondent has to say. A black seal eh? Not having any relations to lose I am not alarmed at the prognostic.

He broke the seal and glanced leisurely over the short business-like communication contained within, with a face that varied from incredulous surprise to sudden gladness.

"Am I dreaming?" he murmured to himself as if to insure complete possession of his senses. "No, I'm wide awake, visions! But who would ever suppose that old Theron Mortimer, whom I haven't seen since I was a boy of sixteen, and picked him out of the river half dead with fright, would die and leave me all his money. Why, I'm not even the shadow of a relation; but, then, I never heard that the old man had neither kith or kin, so I can't imagine any harm in taking advantage of his odd freak. Rich—am I really to be rich? Oh, Edith! Edith!"

He clasped both hands over his eyes, sick and giddy with the thought that the loved, far-off star of his adoration, would be brought near to him at least by the magnet of gold. All those years of heartless waiting were to be bridged over by the strange bequest; he might claim Edith now!

How full of heart sunshine were the weeks that flitted over the head of the accepted lover—brightened by Edith's smiles—made beautiful by the soft radiance of Edith's love! There was only one alloying shadow—the most imperceptible touch of disgust and suspicion with which stern old Dr. Wyllis regarded his future son-in-law!—Ah! he feared to trust his only child to the keeping of any man who had not been proved in the fiery furnace of trial.

It was precisely a week before the wedding, and the soft lights veiled by shades of ground glass ware just lighted in Dr. Wyllis's drawing room, where Edith sat among her white roses and heliotrope, working on a bit of cambric ruffling, and singing to herself. She was a slender, beautiful girl, with violet grey eyes. A blue veined forehead, and glossy abundant curls of that kind old painters love to portray.

"I wonder if Mortimer Place is so lovely," she said to a silver-haired lady who sat opposite. "Philip is going to take me there, when we return from our wedding tour, aunty; he says it is the sweetest spot a poet's fancy could devise, with fountains and shrubberies and green delicious copses? Oh! shall we not be happy there?

She started up with a bright sudden blush, for even while the words were trembling on her lip, Philip Acre came into the room, his handsome face looking a little troubled, yet cheerful withal, Mrs. Wyllis, with an arch nod at her niece, disappeared into the perspective of the conservators, leaving the lovers to themselves.

"You are looking grave, Philip," said Edith as he bent over and kissed her cheek.

"I am feeling so, darling. I have a very unpleasant disclosure to make tonight—our marriage must be postponed indefinitely."

"Philip! for what reason?"

"To enable me to labor diligently at my profession to realize sufficient means to support you, dearest, in a manner satisfactory to your father's expectations and my own wishes."

"But, Philip, I thought——"

"You thought me heir to Theron Mortimer's wealth? So I was Edith, a few hours since, but I have relinquished all claim to it now. When I accepted the bequest, I was under the impression that no living heir existed. I learned to-day that a distant cousin, a woman, is alive, though in ignorance of her relationship to Theron Mortimer. Of course I shall immediately transfer all the property to her."

But Philip, the will had made it legally yours."

"Legally, it is; could I reconcile it to my ideas of truth and honor to avail myself of old Mortimer's fanciful freak, at this woman's expense, I might take the hoarded wealth, but I should never respect myself again, could I dream of legally defrauding the truthful heir.—Nay, dearest, I may lose name and wealth, but I would rather die than suffer a single stain on my honor as a Christian gentleman!"

"You have done right, Philip," said Edith, with sparkling eyes. "We will wait, and hope on, happy in loving one another more dearly than ever. But who is she? What is her name?"

"That's just what I didnt stop to inquire. I will write again to my lawyer to ask these questions and to direct that a deed of conveyance be instantly made out and then darling—

His lips quivered a moment, yet he manfully completed the bitter sentence: —"Then I will begin the battle of life over again."

And Edith's loving eyes told him what she thought of his noble self-abnegation—a sweet testimonial!

"Hem!' said Dr. Wyllis polishing his eye-glasses majestically with a crimson silk pocket handkerchief; 'I didnt suppose the young fellow had so much stamina about him—an honorable thing to do Edith, I never felt exactly certain about Phil Acre's being worthy of you before—"

'Papa!'

'But my mind is made up now. When is he coming again?'

'This evening, sir,' faltered Edith, the violet eyes softly drooping.

'Tell him Edith he may have you next Wednesday just the same as ever! And as for the law practicing—why there's time enough afterwards. Child, don't strangle me with your kisses—keep 'em for Phil.'

He looked after his daughter with eyes strangly dim.

'Tried and not found wanting!' he muttered distinctly.

The perfume of orange blossoms had died away, the glimmer of pearls and satin were hidden in velvet caskets and traveling trunks—and Mr. and Mrs. Acre, old married people of nearly a week's duration, were driving along the shores of the Hudson in the amber glow of a glorious sunset.

'Haloo; which way is Thomas going?' said Philip, leaning from the window, as the carriage turned out of the shore road.

'I told him the road to take Phil!' said Edith with bright sparkling eyes. 'Let me have my own way, just for once. We are going to our new home.'

'Are we?' said Phil, with a comical grimace.

'Wait until you see sir!' said Mrs. Acre, pursing up her little rosebud of a mouth. And Philip 'waited' dutiously.

'Where are we?' he asked, in astonishment, when the carriage drove up in front of a stately pillored portico, which seemed not unfamiliar to him,—'Surely this is Mortimer Place.''

'I shouldn't be surprised if it was,' said Dr. Wyllis, emerging from the door way. Walk in my boy—come Edith! Well how do you like the looks of your new house?'

'Our new house?' repeated Phillip. 'I do not understand you sir.'

'Why I mean that your little wife yonder is the sole surviving relative of Theron Mortimer, although she never knew of it until this morning. Her mother was old Mortimer's cousin, but some absurb quarrel had caused a total cessation of intercourse between the two branches of the family. I was aware of the fact all along, but I was'nt sorry to avail myself of the opportunity of seeing what kind of stuff you were made of Phil Acre. And now as the deed of conveyance is'nt made out I don't suppose your lawyer will trouble himself about it. The heiress won't quarrel with you I'll be bound.'

Phillip Acre's cheeks flushed and then grew pale with strong emotion, as he looked at his fair wife, beside him, the sunset turning her bright hair to coils of shining gold, and thought how unerringly the hand of Providence had straightened out the tangled web of his destiny.

Out of darkness had come light.

From Washington Cor. Cincinnati Commercial.

A Man who Works Without Pay.

A few weeks since I wrote of a man who didn't want an office. Now I have a still more startling fact to announce—a man who holds an office under the Government, works hard, and wont take any pay for it. The *rara avis* is Mr. Whiting, Solicitor of the War Department, and the case as related to me by an intimate friend of his, is as follows:

About two years ago Secretary Stanton wrote to Mr. Whiting, whom he had known well and favorably as a lawyer for many years at his home in Massachusetts, informing him, that he was about to create the office of Solicitor of the War Department, tendering him the position, at a salary of $5,000 a year, I believe. Mr. Whiting replied that he would be glad to serve the Government in the capacity named, and would accept the office on one condition, that he receive no pay or emoluments of any kind, and have the privilege of bearing his own expenses at the Capitol. This was finally, though reluctantly acceeded to by Mr. Stanton, and Mr. Whiting left his palatial home in New England, and took up his abode in Washington city.

Not content with his refusing to receive compensation himself, he drew up an instrument in writing, and filed it in the War Department, stipulating that in case of his death while here, his family should not be entitled to one dollar, for the service he may have rendered. Mr. Whiting is a rich man, can afford to do all he has magnanimously agreed to, but it should be remembered there are hundreds of others equally rich and who could afford it, who would hesitate for a long time before accepting such a non-remunerative berth. There are positions under the government in which a man can work for nothing and yet make a fortune every year, but I am told, by those well informed on the subject, that Mr. Whiting is not one of them. So let us congratulate ourselves that in these days of shoddy—when the grab-game seems to be so immensely popular—when hundreds are getting rich by swindling soldiers, while soldiers are getting killed by fighting rebels—there is one man who says to the powers that be, "Throw greenbacks to the dogs, I'll have none of them."

Whenever any general or public officer springs suddenly into public favor, a set of sensation scribblers and penny-a-liners rush into print with not only exciting panegyrics upon the new hero, but with also a lot of racy reminiscences of his former career and anecdotes illustrating certain characteristics which the aforesaid Alcibiades is supposed to possess. In their haste to be first before the admiring gaze of the worthy populace, these cachexics jumble up "facts" in a most ridiculous manner, forgetting the old proverb:—

"Lest men suspect your tale untrue,
Keep probability in view."

Anecdotes in the Clouds.

The Cincinnati Commercial is responsible for the following, published some months ago:

"General Grant, yesterday morning, asked a hackman at the Spencer House what he would charge to take him across the river to Covington. The reply was, three dollars. General Grant said that it was too much—he would rather walk—and walk he did."

Now that is *rather* steep. In days gone by, a famous Indian chief, named "Walk-in-the-Water," used to make frequent visits to his Great Father at Washington; and in one of his accustomed forays he mysteriously disappeared. Can it be that the Egyptian theory of transmigration of souls is true, and that the spirit of "Walk-in-the-Water" has entered the body of our noble General? If so, he is a bigger brave than ever, and could walk across the Ohio without ever wetting his galoshes, as it appears "walk he did," for *there is yet no bridge at the place mentioned.*

We are sorry to see that Mrs. Harriet Beecher Stowe has fallen into this habit of cachexcy; and in her late brilliant panegyric on President Lincoln, she has sought to elevate her hero at the expense of our credulity. In her elaborate sketch of the "Defender of the Faith,' she treats us to the following morceau:—

In 1836 our backwoodsman, flat-boat hand, captain, surveyor, obtained a license to practice law, and, as might be expected, arose rapidly. One anecdote will show the esteem in which he was held in his neighborhood. A client came to him in a case relating to a certain land claim, and Lincoln said to him:—

"Your first step must be to take thirty thousand dollars and go and make a legal tender; of course it will be refused, but it is a necessary step."

"But," said the man, "I haven't the thirty thousand to make it with."

"Oh, that's it. Just step over to the bank with me, and I'll get it."

So into the bank they went, and Lincoln says to the cashier: "We just want to take thirty thousand dollars to make a legal tender with. I'll bring it back in an hour or two.

The cashier handed across the money to "Honest Abe," and without a scratch of the pen in acknowledgment, he strode his way with the specie, all in the most sacred simplicity, made the tender, and brought it back with as much nonchalance as if he had been borrowing a silver spoon of his grandmother.

In the days in which the above incident was supposed to have transpired, no bank in the Northwestern country, except the Bank of the State of Missouri, ever saw or imagined they saw any such sum of specie. In those times gold, too, was a scarce commodity, and not to be had, even in the Atlantic cities, except at a premium of one per cent. over silver; and our own experience and recollection leaves no shade of doubt but that any coin held by any such bank must have been in silver dollars.—Now $30,000 in silver weighs just 2500 pounds troy—*twenty-five hundred pounds* is a pretty good burden for even "Old Abe" to trot off with, and we think Mrs. Stowe drew the arrow rather tight that time.

It is almost equal to the narrative of the graceful and well known writer of household stories, wherein a thoughtful and prudent wife saved up the odd change from her market money, and when her husband in 1837, was just toppling off the precipice of ruin for the want of $7000 to pay the last note with (it's always the *last* note,) this charming helpmate trips gayly up stairs and brings down $8500, all in five and ten cent pieces, *in her apron*, to the delight and astonishment of her spouse.

This story ran the rounds of the papers, until some growling old bachelor of an editor discoved that the little pile weighed about *seven hundred pounds*, and remarked that he would like to know something about "them ere apron strings."

It is to be earnestly hoped that the fair record of General Hancock, and the new heroes who are niching themselves into Fame, will not be smouched by any such gauzy adulation.

THE DEAD PICKET.—On the field, yesterday, on the left near Tilton, where our cavalry engaged the enemy, a beautiful garden, clothed in all the loveliness that rare plants and Southern flowers could give it, attracted my attention and I was drawn to it. The house had been deserted by its owners, and the smiling magnolias and the roses seemed to stand guard over the deserted premises. I entered through an open gate, stooped to pluck a rose from the bush, when I discovered one of the enemy's pickets lying partially covered by the grass and bushes, dead. He was a noble looking man, and upon his countenance there seemed to rest the remnant of a smile.

The right hand clasped a rose, which he was in the act of severing from its stem when he received the messenger of death. In the afternoon, the cavalry dug a narrow grave, and with Federal soldiers for pall-bearers, and the beautiful flowers for mourners, he was laid to rest, the rose still clasped in his stiffened hand. Nothing was found to identify him, and in that lonely grave his life's history lies entombed. No sister's tears will baptize the grave among the roses where the dead picket fell.—*Letter from Resaca.*

CAPTURE OF A PRUSSIAN BLOCKADE RUNNER.—The Navy Department has received information of the capture, by steamer Clocura, Lieut. Com. Bancroft, off Gherardi, Brazos river, Texas, on the 3d of May, of the Prussian schooner Frederick II, She had run the blockade off Brazos river, in company with the British schooner Agnes. She had on board 114 bales of cotton, and was sent to New Orleans for adjudication.

HARPER'S WEEKLY.
A JOURNAL OF CIVILIZATION

Vol. VIII.—No. 392.] NEW YORK, SATURDAY, JULY 2, 1864. [$1,00 FOR FOUR MONTHS. $3,00 PER YEAR IN ADVANCE.

GEN. ROBERT EDMUND LEE.

General Robert E. Lee, Commander-in-Chief of the Rebel Armies, whose portrait we give on this page, is unquestionably a consummate master of the art of war. That superiority, indeed, was acquired at the expense and under the patronage of the Government he is now endeavoring to destroy; but this does not alter the fact. His career, prior to his desertion of the flag of the country, may be briefly stated. Born in 1808, he was regularly educated at West Point. In the Mexican campaign he served with the Engineer Corps, and was twice promoted for gallantry. At Chapultepec he was severely wounded. In 1852, while holding the rank of Major, he was appointed Superintendent of the Military Academy; but three years afterward he was sent to Europe with M'Clellan, then a Captain, to study the proceedings of the French and English armies in the siege of Sebastopol. About that time he was advanced to the rank of Lieutenant-Colonel of the Second Regiment of Cavalry, and this was his position when he traitorously forsook his country and entered the rebel service.

General Lee, now in his fifty-sixth year, is six feet in height, erect, well-formed, and of imposing appearance; has clear black eyes, dark-gray hair, and a heavy gray beard. He is plain in dress, wearing a black felt hat with a narrow strip of gold around it, and a plain Brigadier's coat with three stars on the collar. He is said to be popular with his army, but the conviction is growing that in General Grant he has met his match; and the confidence now entertained in him is not, probably, as great as formerly. In the present campaign he has displayed great tenacity and skill in the management of his army; but in all the elements of strategy Grant has proved more than his equal.

The photograph from which our engraving is made is one taken by Messrs. Minnis & Cowell, of Richmond, which bears the stamp of its legal registration in 1863, "in the District Court of the Confederate States for the Eastern District of Virginia."

GEN. SHERMAN'S CAMPAIGN.

We continue our illustrations of General Sherman's campaign in Georgia, which is only second in importance to that of General Grant in Virginia.—On pages 424 and 425 we present a stirring picture of the Rebel Assault on General Logan's Position in the battle at Dallas, May 28. The first attack of the enemy was made upon General Harrow's Division, and a portion of the incomplete earth-works on the extreme front were carried by the assailants and a part of a battery captured. This success, however, was but momentary; Walcott's Brigade immediately charged, driving back the enemy and recapturing the battery. The assault then became general. General Logan, seeing the importance of the crisis, dashed along the lines with words of cheer and encouragement, and in a few minutes his troops were swarming over the works and rushing resistlessly down upon the now retiring foe. The rebel assault was made by Cheatham's, Bates's, and Walker's divisions of Hardee's Corps. The men said they were told the assault was to be made upon a negro brigade and a few hundred-days' men. Their loss in the assault was 3000 men. Our picture shows General Morgan L. Smith's Division on the extreme left, General Osterhaus's Division next on the right, and General Harrow's on the extreme right.

On page 421 we give a sketch, showing General Hooker's Escort charging through the Woods, and opening the battle near Dallas, May 25. In approaching Dallas this corps marched in three columns, General Hooker being with the centre column, under the command of General Geary. Just as the head of the column reached Pumpkin Vine Creek a few shots were fired by a small force of rebels. The escort under Captain Duncan dashed across the bridge, which had been fired but not consumed, and a sharp skirmish ensued, the rebel force (of cavalry) being driven back until the ammunition of the body-guard was exhausted. Then a charge was made, led by Captain Duncan of the escort and Colonel Fessenden of General Hooker's staff. Just at this time the head of General Geary's column came up and was soon heavily engaged. Thus opened the battle of Dallas. Before night of the same day the commands of Generals Williams, Butterfield, Howard, and Palmer were all in position.

Another sketch, illustrative of the same battle, is given on page 428. It shows General Williams's Division of Hooker's Corps driving the rebels through the woods. Colonel Robinson's Brigade is on the left, General Ruger's in the centre, and General Knipe's on the right. On page 420 we give five sketches, showing the scene of several important events in Sherman's campaign. One sketch shows the Eighth Missouri Regiment of Logan's Corps reaching the railroad bridge at sunrise on the 16th of May. The enemy having evacuated Resaca on the night of the 15th, our advance was made at dawn by General Logan's Corps, and Resaca very shortly entered by the Eighth Missouri, the men dashing through the town toward the bridges. The railroad bridge was destroyed, together with the old wooden bridge just fired by the enemy. The rebels had departed so quickly that they had left a caisson on the bridge, and four guns in a small earth-work near by.—Some of the soldiers went on to the bridge and threw into the water the planks already on fire. Of the towns of which our artist gives sketches he writes as follows:

"Adairsville is a small hamlet on the Dalton and Atlanta Railroad. Woodlands, as the map gives it, is the residence of Mr. Bairdsley, an Englishman who has made some money in this country, and has since the commencement of the war been a purchasing agent for the "Confederate Government."—A slight skirmish took place on the afternoon of 18th directly in front of the house, in which the Colonel of the Second Pennsylvania was killed by the Brigade of Colonel Wilder. This Colonel was a very gallant man, and was only killed because he would not surrender. Kingston, like the railroad towns of the South, has few houses. Since the battle of Chicamauga it has been used as a hospital. The inhabitants having been removed further south, it is now the last station on the railroad, and is likely to be the scene of much activity."

On page 426 we give a topographical Map illustrative of General Sherman's campaign since the capture of Resaca. After that event the army crossed the Oostanaula River in two columns—one column, under Hooker and Schofield, crossing just below Resaca; and the other, under M'Pherson, Thomas, and Butterfield, at New Echota, a little to the left of Resaca. This latter column separated itself into two after crossing the river, Thomas and Butterfield moving on the left, and M'Pherson on the right flank; while in the meantime Hooker and Schofield kept the centre, moving toward Kingston, along the line of the Chattanooga Railroad. The rebel line of defense, stretching along the line of the railroad connecting Rome and Atlanta, north of the Etowah River, not being able to resist this combination, was broken up.—Kingston and Cassville thus came into our possession, though not without some sharp fighting. As a matter of course, Rome was no longer tenable by a rebel force. After resting for a few days and obtaining fresh supplies the Etowah was crossed, and Dallas—in the rear of which Johnston was intrenched—was made the objective of the new lines of approach. Altoona Pass, through which the Western and Atlantic Railroad runs to Atlanta, was taken by our cavalry; and this success, together with the victory of May 28, forced the rebels to adopt a new line of defense covering Marietta, along Lost and Kenesaw mountains. On the night of June 18 this line was partly withdrawn, but still covered the advance to Marietta.

THE REBEL GENERAL ROBERT EDMUND LEE.

TWENTY-SIXTH.

No. 4. NEW LONDON, CONN., JULY 8, 1864. Vol. 1.

Our Term of Service.

In former numbers of the Twenty-Sixth, it was asserted that our term of service would not expire until August 10, 1863. This statement was not credited by many persons, and some still maintain that our regiment would have been at home and mustered out on the 25th of June, "if Port Hudson had been taken."

In order to sustain our former assertions we publish the following:

1. Our regimental muster rolls read "mustered into service Nov. 10, 1862."

2. The United States did not pay our officers for services rendered previous to Nov. 10th.

3. The following note was written to the wife of a member of Co. D.:

STATE OF CONNECTICUT,
Executive Department,
Hartford, April 5, 1863.

In reply to your enquiry I would say that the 26th Reg't was mustered and accepted into the service on the 10th of November, and the term will expire on the 10th day of August.

Yours Truly,
WM. A. BUCKINGHAM.

4. In May, 1862, an Official document for the use of Major General Banks was seen at his headquarters by Orderly Haven, of Co. C. 26th C. V., which gave the date of muster of each of the nine months regiments. It stated that there were twenty-one nine months regiments in the department, and that the 26th C. V. was mustered Nov. 10, 1862.

5. During the siege of Port Hudson considerable dissatisfaction existed in a few of the nine months regiments. The 4th Massachusetts laid down their arms. Their Officers and such of the soldiers as finally refused to do duty were arrested and severely punished. About this time the following *printed circular* was sent to the Commanders of all the nine months regiments in the Department:—

HEADQUARTERS DEPARTMENT OF THE GULF,
19th Army Corps,
Before Port Hudson, June 18, 1863.

SIR:

In order that the period when the term of service of your regiment will expire may be definitely fixed, the Commanding General directs that you immediately report the date when your regiment was mustered into service, as a regiment; or, if no such formal muster was ever made, the date of muster into service of the field and staff.

Very respectfully,
Your most ob't serv't,
RICHARD B. IRWIN,
Assistant Adjutant General.

Commanding Officer
26th Conn. Vols.,
through Genl Dwight.

Our regiment was then under command of Lieut. Col. Selden, Col. Kingsley being at Baton Rouge, wounded. Col. Selden replied as follows:—

HEADQUARTERS 26TH REG'T CONN. VOLS,
In Field before Port Hudson,
June 19th, 1863.

COLONEL:

The 26th Regiment Conn. Vols. was mustered into the service of the United States, at Camp Russell, Norwich, Conn., on the Twenty-fifth day of September, 1862, by United States Mustering Officer Watson Webb, Jr.

Respectfully your ob't serv't,
JOSEPH SELDEN,
Lieut. Col. Commanding Regiment.

Deeming the matter of more importance than ordinary orders, Col. Selden forwarded the circular to Col. Kingsley, who sent the following to Headquarters:

CONVALESCENT HOSPITAL,
Baton Rouge, La., June 19, 1863.
R. B. IRWIN, Esq., Assistant Adj. General:

The 26th Reg't Conn. Vols. were not all sworn into service on one day. The Privates were sworn into the U. S. service on the 25th day of Sept., 1862, and never since. The Adjutant of the Reg't was sworn at the same time. The officers were sworn into service on the 10th day of November. The mustering officer said the officers were required to take an oath different from the privates, and he had not the oath with him, but would come and administer it at some future time, and did not do it until November 10, 1862.

Respectfully, your ob't serv't,
T. G. KINGSLEY,
Col. 26th Reg't C. V.

There are some drafted men in the Reg't who were drafted by an order from Gov. Buckingham, Sept. 3d, 1862, and all the members of the Reg't are in lieu of drafted men.

Yours, T. G. K.

Shortly after the reply of Col. Kingsley was received, Lieut. Col. Selden was ordered to report to headquarters. Having arrived there, the following conversation occurred. (We give the substance of what was said.)

Col. Irwin. Why did you not inform me when your staff officers were mustered in?

Col. Selden. You did not order me so to do unless there "was no general muster of the regiment."—There *was* a general muster on the 15th day of September.

Col. Irwin. I have received a message from Col. Kingsley in which he states that the Officers of the regiment were not mustered until Nov. 10th.

Col. Selden. The statement of Col. Kingsley is correct, sir.

Col. Irwin. Then you will understand that the term of service of your regiment will not expire until the tenth day of August.

Col. Selden. Is there no appeal from that decision?

Col. Irwin. No, sir.

Extracts from my Diary.

New Orleans, La., Tuesday, July 21, 1863.—Met Col. Kingsley and Quartermaster Tracy at Bell's Livery stable.

Quartermaster said the regimental stores could not be collected within ten days, and therefore the regiment could not leave for home within that time. Decided to remain here until next steamer arrives from the North and then join the regiment with a mail.

Wednesday, July 22.—Called on Lieut. Col. Selden at Carrolton. He is quite sick with a fever but anxious to join his regment. He informed me that our Colonel, Major and Quartermaster called last night and advised him to rest a few days before joining the regiment. His physician advised him to go home via the Ocean, but Col. Selden replied that he will go with the regiment if it costs his life. He agrees to wait until Monday and then join the regiment with me so that I can take care of him until we reach Port Hudson.

Thursday, July 23.—Have been assisting some of our wounded to leave the hospitals for the regiment.

Friday, June 24.—As some of our wounded are not able to walk, but are otherwise well enough to go home, I visited Col. Selden for advice. As he was too sick to write I penned a letter to the Medical Director which was signed by the Lieut. Col., stating the case and asking that they may be sent to the regiment next Monday in my care. The M. D. replied that our regment would not probably leave for home within two weeks; that as we had so many sick and wounded it would probably be sent by the Ocean; that it is customary to send such wounded by hospital steamers, but if our Commanding Officer would agree to have suitable accommodations, and have the transport which would convey us home (via Ocean) stop at New Orleans, he would send us our wounded on board.

Monday, July 27.—While in the post office this morning assisting the clerks distribute the mail which arrived from the north last night, I was called upon by Mr. Royce, formerly of Co. B. 26th C. V., but now of the signal corps, and informed me that our regiment left for home yesterday via Cairo! Went to Carrollton and was surprised to learn that Col. Selden left Carrollton for Port Hudson on Saturday! His physician thinks the journey will kill him, as he still has a high fever. He has not sit up an hour during the last ten days. (I afterwards learned that Col. Selden did not reach Port Hudson until the regiment had left, but he followed, arriving at Cairo a few days later.) About one dozen of our wounded and a few detached men are left here.

Tuesday, July 28.—Being somewhat acquainted in Medical Department. I there obtained a certificate which procured me transportation to New York on any government steamer.

Have visited our wounded and promised to do what I can for them. The 42d Mass. sails direct for New York to-day and I can go with them, but have not yet obtained transportation for the wounded.

Thursday, July 30.—After working three days I have obtained transportation for the wounded on the hospital steamer *Pioneer*, and I am to accompany the vessel as acting hospital steward. The Pioneer is a flat-bottomed boat, formerly used on the North River, and afterwards as an armed transport in the Burnside expedition.

Sunday, August 2.—While in the dead house of the Barracks hospital I noticed ths clothes of Col. Bailey of Co. B. 26th C. V. The hospital records show that he was brought here from Baton Rouge and died four days later. I have with me about 1000 letters for our regiment which have arrived since the 26th left for home. (Delivered these letters to the regiment on the 19th of August, at Norwich, Conn.

Monday, August 3.—Sailed from the wharf near the Barracks hospital at 1 P. M. We have on board 165 men of various regiments, all of whom [illegible] are from hospitals except two surgeons and myself. Five members of the 26th are with me, viz.:—Wallace Fuller and John Phillips of Co. D., Caleb F. Noyes of Co. F., Edwin Shirley and A. B. Frazier of Co. H. I was obliged to leave Benj. Sweet, Russell Bogue, George Brewster and a few others of our regiment who were not able to stand the voyage. Mr Bogue could not stand alone. (He died four days later of chronic diarrhea.)

Friday, August 7.—Ebenezer Norman of the 12th Conn. died of chronic diarrhea and was buried with appropriate services.

Monday, August 10.—Two men died, one of dropsy, the other of lung disease.

Tuesday, August 11.—Two men died last night, one of chronic diarrhea and one of dropsy.

Thursday, August 13.—Two men died last night of chronic diarrhea.

Friday, August 14.—Arrived in New York, having had very good weather during the entire passage. Invaluable assistance was rendered to us to-day by Col. John H. Almy, Agent of the State of Connecticut. He was at the wharf when we arrived, with carriages for the sick and wounded. Agents of other States were also present. They came on board and carried those who were too weak to walk to the carriages.

Saturday, August 14—John Phillips of Co. D. died last night in the New England rooms, New York.

The remaining members of the 26th who came with me are still alive and doing well.

Norwich, Conn., Wednesday, June 19.—Was mustered out of service with the regiment, receiving pay to the 17th inst.

THE TWENTY-SIXTH.

PRICE THREE CENTS.

In accordance with the wish of many members of our regiment, we issue this the fourth number of the "26th." It is our intention to issue *one* number more in a few weeks, in which we shall publish the deaths of Companies C, D, E, F and H. The deaths of the other five companies may be found in another column. This paper is issued on the anniversary of the surrender of Port Hudson. Persons wishing to contribute to the last number will address Box 321, New London, Conn.

WHEN SHALL WE MEET AGAIN.—Would it not be a pleasant gathering if our regiment should meet in Norwich this fall? We suggest that such a meeting shall take place on the 12th day of next November, two years from the day we left Connecticut. What do our readers think of the proposal?

RE-ENLISTED.—About one hundred members of the 26th have re-enlisted. We will endeavor to publish their names in our next under this heading:

ROLL OF HONOR.

Twenty-four Hours in a Field Hospital.

It was about 3 P. M. of May 27th, 1863, when an ambulance arrived at the Field Hospital of Gen. Sherman's division, before Port Hudson. A voice called me to it and then Orderly Albert Smith of Co A, 26th C. V., said: "Good bye: remember me to friends at home; tell them I have done my duty and am prepared to die. It is all right here, (placing his hand on his heart) and I hope you will all meet me in heaven." We carried him into the hospital which was soon filled with wounded soldiers. The "Hospital" was an old cotton press, built much like northern cider mills—a roof, but no floor or sides. Our wounded friends were carefully laid on the ground under the roof, which was the best place that could be found in the vicinity.

Three long tables were [illegible] one side of the place and on these were placed our friends to have their wounds dressed. The surgeons did their work quickly and carefully. For instance: A member of the 165th N. Y. was placed on a table. His shattered leg was examined by the surgeon of the 6th Michigan and one from the regular army—the senior surgeons. It took but a moment to decide that the limb must be amputated. The hospital steward of the 165th N. Y. administered choloroforms, the surgeons laid aside their cigars, and in a few minutes the leg was off, and the arteries, &c., duly tied. The soldier was removed and the surgeons resumed their smoking and joking until the next patient was placed before them. (This cheerfulness on the part of the surgeons was necessary for themselves and patients. No person can work for wounded men unless he is cheerful and calm.) During the afternoon I noticed Capt. Randall, Corp. Siegneious and others of Co. K in charge of Wm. O. Tift. There were a few of us there who were not wounded and we were busily employed in supplying calls for water, &c. The lamented Commissary Manning was constantly relieving wants. At about sundown I was called by Edwin Shirley of Co. H, who was wounded in both legs "just as he expected." "Now," said he, "if I live to get home we will see if those patriotic men in Stonington will assist me as they promised. I guess it is lucky for me that my bounty money is in the bank." Shirley was supplied with water and wine and then wanted nothing except a "blanket to keep these pesky ant from crawling into my wounds." A. B. Frazier made a similar complaint, so I went to a box which was sent us by the Norwich Soldiers Aid Society and obtainee two quilts which made them comfortable. Sergt. Sherman was mortally wounded and wished me to carry messages to his wife. "Tell her that I was a good soldier and a true husband. I had been off the field twice with wounded and had been slightly wounded myself before the fatal ball hit me." He kissed his wife's ambrotype many times before delivering it to me.

Wm. P. Latham (musician), said: "I am in no pain but am mortally wounded; tell my mother that I have read my testament every day." We have not space to even notice many interesting scenes.

Twenty-Sixth Conn, Volunteers.

Casualties during the Siege of Port Hudson.

FIELD AND STAFF.

WOUNDED.

May 27.—Col. Thomas G. Kingsley, through the jaw, buck shot in wrist and struck by piece of shell in back.

June 14.—Lieut and Adjutant S B Meech, in knee.

COMPANY A.

KILLED.

May [illegible]63.—Joseph A. Tillotson, James Lomba[illegible]

June [illegible]ohn O Chapell, Joseph Flike, Orrin E Lyon, James F Thompson.

WOUNDED.

Capt J C Maynard, in chest; Lieut H A Smith, in right arm; 1st Sergeant, Albert Smith, mortally; Corporal J S Niles, mortally; Thomas Charlton, right arm; Chas Burdick, contusion; R D Holt, left lung; R Andrews, slightly; J Ackley, great toe; Michael Tangney, slight; Joseph A Austin, leg.

June 13.—Charles Lamb, thigh, slightly.

June 14.—Sergt. John W Bogue, shoulder, slightly; Corp. Sherwood Fuller, leg, slightly; Wm J Br[illegible]n, mortally; George H. Chapel, mortally; [illegible]omas Hughes, leg; O W Rathbone, kn[illegible] Stephen H Austin, hand; Wm Martin, le[illegible] B R Sweet, leg; Geo B Fuller, stunned by shell; W. W. Mitchell, stunned.

COMPANY B.

KILLED.

June 14.—Philip Hendrick.

WOUNDED.

May 27.—Lieut Martin R. Kenyon, left shoulder; Serg Vine S Stetson, neck; Corp. Thomas B Conger, bruised by shell; E E Fish, thigh; Wm P Irish, right hand; J P Case, right hand; Privates Thomas Kerrigan, left leg; James Parkerson, mortally; Charles P Crandall, mortally; J. Kimball, finger; H Worthington, finger; Edwin Bailey, chest and shoulder; S C Bennett, dangerously; Elisha Bennett, hand and arm; G H Lamphere, slight; Horace and Henry Worthington, slightly. Jas S Maples, slightly.

June 14.—Corp. C. J. Green, shoulder. Privates Perry Burdick, finger; John Charlton, slight; James M Pierce, shoulder; Steven Burdick, hand.

Myron W Sterritt. Missing.

COMPANY C.

KILLED.

May 27.—Joseph R. Barker.

WOUNDED.

Corp. T. R. Harding, both legs; James D Ferriter, leg; A G Rowland, mortally; H L Chapel, neck and jaw; S W Bramble, jaw; Leroy Noon, thigh; D Holmes, mortally; D W Main, slightly.

June 14.—Sergt, F B Banta, shoulder and head; Charles Schneider, mortally; Horace P Tucker, hand; Corp. Chas H. Willey, mortally; Chas J Beckwith, mortally, Charles H Main mortally.

COMPANY D.

KILLED.

June 13.—Rudolph Slater.

WOUNDED.

O E Hilderbrand, arm and side; Wallace Fuller, thigh; Peter Sauer, leg; J. L. Christie, shoulder; Patrick O Sullivan, chin; Wm E Chapman, mortally; J. Lane, hand; J G Hoxie, slight; Wm Smith, slight; Peter Farrelly; slight; Isham Bromley, slight; Thos H Frink, slight.

June 14.—Herman Kamp, hand; Sabart M Porter, foot; Alex. Driscoll, neck.

COMPANY E.

KILLED.

June 14.—James Cooney.

WOUNDED.

May 27.—Simon Newmark, leg; B. Carter, leg; Phineas B. Sterry, mortally; D. Miller, Elbow; C. W. Bailey, thigh; Joseph Holt, leg; M. Gross and N. Linicus, bruised; Joseph Kohl—mortally.

June 13.—William Dunn, slightly.

June 14.—Serg't. James Jerome, foot; Corporal P. Daicey, Wrist.

COMPANY F.

WOUNDED.

May 27.—Chas. Miller, chest and right arm; C. M. Geer, mortally, H. Brooks, arm; Norman Phillips, mortally, N. S. Rogers, side; Corporal Jno Geer, slight; Edwin Hill, leg; Charles Miner, breast; E. B. Luther, head: Wm H Bogue, slight.

June 13.—1st Serg't. Henry G. Gay, thigh.

June 14.—Lieut. Hervey F. Jacobs, mortally; Corporals E Button, mortally; Joseph W Dowley, wrist; Privates Nathan York, foot; Ulysses Warner, leg; H. C. Wright, hand; E. T. Hills, thigh and hand; Geo. A. Haskell, slight; H. C. Wright, finger; L. Dixon, hand; Daniel Frazer. face.

COMPANY G.

KILLED.

May 27.—Capt. John L. Stanton.

WOUNDED.

May 27.—Sergeants H. W. Whitmore, arm; Edwin R. Keys, mortally; Privates N. A. Keables, shoulder; John N Redhead, mouth; Michael Moore, finger; Julius Williams, neck; G. P. Weeks. thumb; Alexander Buck, shoulder.

June 13.—Dyer Copeland, leg; James Dugan hand.

June 14.—Corp. S. A. Wait, arm; W. H. Kenyon, hand; A. F. Smith, head; H. J. Marshall, arm; J. P. Lewis, hand.

COMPANY H.

KILLED.

May 27.—John Nye; Nathan S, Sheffield.

WOUNDED.

May 27.—Lieut. S. K. Tillinghast, arm; Serg't Wm M Sherman, mortally; Corporals A H Brown, mortally; Geo E Brayton, finger; Chas Bennett, leg; Privates Wm. F. Ecclestone, finger; A B Frazer, severely: C W Taylor, contusion; Edwin N Shirley, both legs badly; W P Thompson, shoulder; Thaddeus M Weems mortally.

June 13.—Henry L Babcock, severely.

June 14.—David Galliver. leg off; Thomas Crowley, hand; D. S. Burrows, finger; James A Lord, hand.

COMPANY I.

WOUNDED.

May 27.—Oliver Nason, side; Samuel Flanders, left shoulder; Wm Elkington, hand; Geo Harvey, finger.

June 13.—Joseph I Bailey.

June 14.—Serg't Daniel Penhallow, leg; Corporals Walcott Hobron, mortally, Wm D Osborne, mortally; Privates George Brewster, foot; Joseph Kelly leg; Isaac Comstock, hand, slightly.

COMPANY K.

WOUNDED.

May 27.—Chaplain Jedediah Randall, mortally Sergt Horace Clift, shoulder; Corporals John L Seignious, mortally, Thomas S. Carroll, finger; Privates John Watson, leg; Geo Beebe, slightly; Warren Burnett, thigh; Ezra Roath, right arm; Wm P Latham, (musician,) mortally; E York, slight; A Stafford, slight; A Destin, slight; C H Niles, slight.

June 13.—John Tufts, leg.

June 14.—Caleb H Burdick, hand.

Record of Deaths.

TWENTY-SIXTH CONNECTICUT VOLUNTEERS.

COMPANY A.

First Sergeant Albert Smith, at New Orleans, La., May 31st, 1863, of wounds.

Corporal David G. Bogue, at Toledo, Ohio, of disease.

Corporal John A Niles, at Baton Rouge, June 5, of wounds.

Joseph Flike, killed before Port Hudson June 14, 1863.

O E Lyons killed before P Hudson June 17, '63
J O Chapel, " " " " " "
J F Thompson, " " " " " "
J. Lombard, " " " " " "
J Tillotson, " " " " " "
W J Brown, " " " " " "
G Chappell, " at Baton Rouge, of wounds.
Thomas H Hues, " " " "
Russell Bogue, " " N Orleans, Aug 7, disease
Joseph Shelley, " " Wa erford, Ct " "
Peter Mulligan, " " Norwich, " " "

Total deaths in Co. A, to July 1, 1864, - 15

COMPANY B.

Lieut. M. R. Kenyon, in Preston, Conn., of Wounds.

Corporal H C Bailey, at New Orleans, July 24, of disease.

Edwin W. Bailey, at New Orleans, July 16, of wounds.

Montgomery Gray, at Camp Parapet, May 10, of disease.

James W. Johnson, at Camp Parapet, Mch 6, of disease.

Chas P Crandall, at Port Hudson, May 28, of wounds.

B L Fuller, at P Hudson, May 28, of disease.

Phillip Hendrick, at Port Hudson June 14, killed.

James Parkerson, at Port Hudson, June 1, of wounds.

Myron W Sterritt, at Port Hudson, missing since May 27.

Rodman Ellis, at Mound City, Illinois, of disease.

S T Johnson, at Mound City, Ill. of disease.
D W Main, " " " "
Wm A Main, " " " "
G D Chapman, at Norwich, Conn., "
E. Erskine, " " " "
M W Russell, " " " "

Total to July 1st, 1864, - - - 19

COMPANY G.

Henry L Smith, of disease, at Camp Parapet, La.
George France, " " " "
Lucius J Snow, " " " "
Andrew M Chapman " " " "
Albert J Burlingame " " " "
Jared Griffith, " " " "
Allen H Franklin, " " Carrolton, "

Corporal Cortland C Avery, of disease, before Port Hudson La.

Capt John L Stanton, killed in action, before Port Hudson, May 27.

Sergeant Edwin R Keys, at Baton Rouge of wounds.

George F Edgartown, of disease at Port Hudson.

James Dugan; of disease on board steamer South Western.

Albert F Young, of disease in Norwich, Ct.

Sylvester R J Hines, of disease in Sterling, Conn.

Ira B Carpenter, of disease in Woodstock, Conn.

Andrew J Rrunt, of disease, Woodstock, Ct.

Total to July 1, 1864, - - - 16

COMPANY I.

James C Tinker, of diseese, at Camp Parapet, La, April 17.

Corporal Wolcott Hobron, in New Orleans, June 20, of wouuds.

Corporal Wm B Osborn, wounded June 14, died at Baton Rouge, La. June 23d.

Fife Major John C Daniels, died of fever, in Port Hudson, July 23.

John Barber, of fever, at Cairo, Ill, Aug 3d.

Geo S Gray, of fever at Chicago, Ill, Aug 5.

Samuel P Beebe, of fever, in New London, Conn, Aug 15.

Gilbert Keeney, of chronic diarhea, at Chicago, Aug 17.

David Roach, of fever, in New London, Conn Aug 19.

Isaac H Comstock, re-enlisted, died Sept 8, in New London, while at home on a furlough.

COMPANY K.

Capt Jediah Randall, at Baton Rouge.

Lieut H E Maxon, of Groton, of disease.
Thomas Shirley, at Camp Parapet, of disease.
Adam Bentley, " "
Wm. P. Latham, at N. Orleans, of wounds.
John L. Seignous, at B. Rouge, of wounds.
Prucius Bailey, " of disease.
Wm. Watrous, " "
Thomas Manice, at Port Hudson, "
Wm. Fellows, on Mississippi river, "
Thomas Maloy, in Groton, of disease.
John Parks, (re- enlisted,) in Groton, disease.
Charles Keeney, in New London, "
Armand Stafford, in Groton, of disease.

Total to July 1st, 1964. - - 14.

Why we are Fighting.

This war is often spoken of as a "nigger war." Those persons who use this refined expression probably intend to say that the civil war in which our nation is engaged, was opened and is prosecuted for the sole purpose of improving the condition of the slaves. A little reflection must convince any reasonable man that there is no ground for such a charge.

We are fighting for the purpose of defending our own liberties, which had been attacked by the secessionists with the avowed design of reducing ALL LABORERS to the condition of slaves.

This statement is proved by the conduct of the leading men of the South, and by editorials which appeared in southern journals *before the war was opened.*

Read the following, which appeared in the Richmond (Va.) *Examiner* in 1856:—

"Until recently, the defence of slavery has labored under great difficulties, because its apologists took half-way grounds. They confined the defence of slavery to mere *negro* slavery; thereby giving up the slavery *principle*, admitting other forms of slavery to be *wrong*.

"The line of defence, however, is now changed. The South now maintains that *slavery is right, natural, and necessary, and does not depend upon difference of* COMPLEXION. The laws of the slave states *justify* the holding of WHITEMEN in bondage."

Another Southern paper, about the same time, published the following:—

"Slavery is the natural and normal condition of the *laboring man*, whether WHITE or black. The great evil of Northern *free* society is, that it is burdened with a *servile* class of MECHANICS and LABORERS, *unfit for self-government*, and yet clothed with the attributes and power of citizens. Master and slave is a relation in society as necessary as that of parent and child; and the Northern States will yet have to introduce it."

It seems to us that the above extracts indicate plainly enough that this terrible war was intended to make slaves of laboring whites. But here is additional evidence. It appeared in the Richmond *Examiner* in 1857:—

"Repeatedly have we asked the North, 'Has not the experiment of universal liberty failed? Are not the evils of FREE SOCIETY INSUFFERABLE?' Still no answer. This gloomy silence is another conclusive proof, added to many other conclusive evidences we have furnished, that *free society* in the *long run* is an impracticable form of society.

We repeat, then, that policy and humanity alike *forbid the extension* of the evils of *free society* to new people and coming generations.—Two opposite and conflicting forms of society cannot co-exist and endure. The one must give way and cease to exist while the other becomes universal."

And the South not only intended to degrade and enslave white laboring men, but was then and is now determined to destroy everything free. The articles quoted were published in the first year of Buchanan's term, or earlier, when southern men controlled all branches of the government. Here is something to the point from a leading Georgia paper:—

"Free society! we sicken at the name. What is it but a conglomeration of GREASY MECHANICS, FILTHY OPERATIVES, SMALL-FISTED FARMERS, and moon-struck THEORISTS. All the Northern States are devoid of society fitted for well-bred gentlemen. The prevailing class are hardly fit for association with a southern gentleman's body servant."

The following is an extract from an article which was published in a Virginia paper while our dear southern brethren were trying to force slavery into Kansas—a deed which they almost accomplished with the aid of President Buchanan and his cabinet, border ruffians and the bowie knife:—

"We hate everything with the prefix FREE, from free negroes up through the whole catalogue—FREE farms, FREE labor, FREE society and FREE schools. But the worst of all these *abominations* is the New England system of FREE SCHOOLS."

These rebels, who were then traitors at heart, hated everything free and were determined to make our country a nation of rich masters and poor slaves. Long before the political campaign of 1860, the Charleston *Standard* said:—

"If WHITE MEN accept the office of menials, it should be expected that they will do so with an apprehension of their relation to society, and the disposition quietly to encounter both the responsibilities and the liabilities which the relation imposes."

The legislators of the South have for years advocated that POOR WHITES should be sold at auction. When Mr. Downs of Louisiana was a United States Senator he made a speech in which occurred the following passage:—

"Poverty is unknown to the southern slave, for as soon as the master becomes too poor to provide for them, he SELLS them to others who can take care of them. This, sir, is one of the excellences of the system of slavery, and this the superior condition of the slave over the white laborer."

It is very plain that those men who have controlled the legislation of the southern states, long since determined to *exterminate free society* and make slavery the condition of *all laborers* either by fair means or foul. They fought the Presidential campaign of 1860 on that platform and were defeated; then *they made war* upon our government which is ourselves; and we determined to defend that system which our fathers gave us, which makes ALL men free and equal.

We are fighting to defend free labor, free schools and FREE MEN against the attacks of those who "hate everything free." And we are determined to maintain the rights of laboring men and crush all opposition to our cause, if there is power enough in the country to accomplish this object. We agree with LEWIS CASS, an honored democratic statesman, when he says:—"It is better to crush every institution and every living thing in the South, than to see our system of free government destroyed and the establishment of another in its stead which would make slavery its chief corner-stone.

The Southern Banner.

THE INDEPENDENCE OF THE SOUTH.

ONE DOLLAR PER MONTH. ATHENS, CLARK COUNTY, GEO. JULY 13, 1864. VOLUME XXXIII---NUMBER 19

Children—What are They?

BY JOHN NEAL.

What are *children?* Step to the window with me. The street is full of them. Yonder is a school let loose, and here, just within reach of our observation, are two or three noisy little fellows, and there another party mustering for play. Some are whispering together and plotting so loudly and so earnestly as to attract everybody's attention, while others are holding themselves aloft, with their satchels gaping so as to betray a part of their plans for to-morrow afternoon, or laying their heads together in pairs for a trip to the islands. Look at them, weigh the question I have put to you, and then answer it as it deserves to be answered: *What are children?*

To which you reply at once, without any sort of hesitation, perhaps—"Just as the twig is bent, the tree's inclined;" or, "Men are but children of a larger growth;" or, peradventure, "The child is father of the man"—And then, perhaps you leave me, perfectly satisfied with yourself and with your answer, having "plucked out the heart of the mystery, and uttered without knowing it, a string of glorious truths. * * *

Among the children who are now playing *together*, like birds among the blossoms of earth, haunting all the green shadowy places thereof, and rejoicing in the bright air, happy and beautiful creatures, and as changeable as happy, with eyes brimful of joy, and with hearts playing upon their little faces like sunshine upon the water.—Among those who are now idling together on that slope, or pursuing butterflies together on the edge of the wood, a wilderness of roses, you would see not only the gifted and the powerful, the wise and the eloquent, the ambitious and the renowned, the long-lived and the long-to-be-lamented of another age; but the wicked and the treacherous, the liar and the thief, the abandoned profligate and the faithless husband, the gambler and the drunkard, the robber, the burglar, the ravisher, the murderer, and the betrayer of his country. *The child is father of the man.*

Among them and that other little troop just appearing, children with yet happier faces and pleasanter eyes, the future—the mothers of nations—you would see the founders of states and the destroyers of their country, the steadfast and the weak, the judge and the criminal, the murderer and the executioner, the exalted and the lowly, the unfaithful wife and the broken-hearted husband, the proud betrayer and the pale victim, the living and breathing potents and prodigies, the embodied virtues and vices of another age and of another world, *and a'l playing together!* Men are but children of a larger growth.

Pursuing the search, you would go forth among the little creatures as among the types of another and a loftier language, the mystery whereof had just been revealed to you, a language to become universal hereafter, types in which the autobiography of the Future was written ages and ages ago—Among the innocent and helpless creatures called children, you would see warriors with their garments rolled in blood, the scepters of kings and princes, poets with golden harps and illuminated eyes, historians and painters, architects and sculptors, mechanics and merchants, preachers and lawyers; here a grave digger flying a kite with his future customers; there a physician playing at marbles with his; here the predestined, the early and violent death for cowardice, fighting the battles of a whole neighborhood; there a Cromwell, or a Cæsar, a Napoleon or a Washington, hiding themselves for fear, enduring reproach and insult with patience, a Benjamin Franklin higgling for nuts or gingerbread, or the "old Parr" of another generation sitting apart in the sunshine and shivering at every breath of wind that reaches him. Yet we are told that "just as the twig is bent, the tree's inclined." * * *

Even fathers and mothers look upon children with a strange misapprehension of their dignity. Even with the poets, they are only the flowers and blossoms, the dew drops or the playthings of earth. Yet "of such is the kingdom of heaven." The Kingdom of Heaven! with all its principalities and powers, its hierarchies, dominions, thrones! The Saviour understood them better; to him their true dignity was revealed. Flowers! They are the flowers of the invisible world; indestructible, self-perpetuating flowers, with each a multitude of angels and evil spirits underneath its leaves, toiling and wrestling for dominion over it! Blossoms! They are the blossoms of another world whose fruitage is angels and arch-angels! Or dew drops!—They are the dew drops that have their source, not in the chambers of the earth, nor among the vapors of the sky, which the next breath of wind or the next flash of sunshine may dry up forever, but among the everlasting fountains and inexhaustible reservoirs of mercy and love. Playthings! God! If the little creatures would but appear to us in their true shape for a moment! We should fall upon our faces before them, or grow pale with consternation, or fling them off with horror and loathing.

What would be our feelings to see a fair child start up before us a maniac or a murderer, armed to the teeth? to find a nest of serpents on our pillow? a destroyer or a traitor, a Harry the Eigth, or a Benedict Arnold, asleep in our bosom? A Catharine or Peter, a Bacon, a Galileo, or a Bentham, a Napoleon, or a Voltaire, clambering up our knees after sugar plums! Cuvier laboring to distinguish a horse-fly from a blue bottle, or dissecting a spider with a rusty nail? LaPlace trying to multiply his own apples, or to substract his playfellow's gingerbread?—What should we say to find ourselves romping with Massalina, Swedenborg, and Madame de Stael? or playing bo-peep with Murat, Robespierre, and Charlotte Corday? or "puss in the corner," with George Washington, Jonathan Wild, Shakspeare, Sappho, Jeremy Taylor, Alfierie, and Harriet Wilson? Yet stranger things have happened. These were all children but the other day, and clambered about the knees and rummaged in the pockets, and nestled in the laps of people no better than we are. But *if* they could have appeared in their true shape for a single moment, while they were playing together! What a scampering there would have been among the grown folks! How their fingers would have tingled!

Now to me, there is no study half so delightful as that of these little creatures, with hearts fresh from the gardens of the sky, in their first and fairest, and most unintentional disclosures, while they are indeed a mystery. And I have an idea that if we only had a name for the study, it might be found as attractive and as popular; and perhaps—though I would not go too far—*perhaps* about as advantageous in the long run to the future fathers and mothers of mankind, as the study of shrubs and flowers, or that of birds and fishes. And why not? They are the cryptogamia of another world, the infusoria of the skies?

Then why not pursue the study for yourself? The subjects are always before you. No books are needed, no costly drawings, no lectures, neither transparencies.

Your specimens are all about you. They come and go at your bidding.—They are not to be hunted for, along the edge of a precipice, on the borders of the wilderness, in the desert, nor by the seashore. They abound not in the uninhabited or unvisited place, but in your very dwelling houses, about the steps of your doors, in the very street of every village, in every green field, and every crowded thoroughfare.—They flourish bravely in snow-storms, in the dust of the trampled highway, where drums are beating and colors flying, in the rear of cities. They love the sounding sea breeze, and the open air, and may always be found about the wharves and rejoicing before the windows of the toy-shops. They love the blaze of fire works and the smell of gunpowder; and where that is they are, to a dead certainty.

You have but to go abroad for half an hour in pleasant weather, or to throw open your widows or doors on a Saturday afternoon if you live anywhere in a neighborhood of a school-house, or a vacant lot, with here and there a patch of green or a dry place in it; and steal in behind the curtains or draw the blinds, and let the fresh wind blow through and through the chambers of your heart for a few minutes; winnowing the dust and scattering the cobwebs that have gathered there while you were asleep, and lo! you find it ringing with the voices of children at play, and all alive with the glimmering phantasmagoria of leap-frog, prison base, or knock-up-and-catch.

Let us try the experiment. There! I have opened the windows, and I have drawn the blinds, and hark! already there is the sound of little voices afar off, like "sweet bells jangling." Nearer come they, and now we catch a glimpse of a bright faces, peeping round the corners, and there, by that empty enclosure, a general mustering and swarming, as of bees about a newly discovered flower-garden. But the voices we now hear proceed from two little fellows who have withdrawn from the rest. One carries a large basket, and his eyes are directed to my window; he doesn't half like the blinds being drawn. The other follows him with a tattered book under his arm, rapping the posts, one after the other as he goes along. He is clearly on bad terms with himself. And now we can see their faces. Both are grave, and one rather pale, and trying to look ferocious. And hark! now we are able to distinguish their words.—"Well, I ain't skeered o' you," says the foremost and the larger boy. "Nor I ain't skeered o' you," retorts the other; "but you needn't say you meant to lick me." And so I thought. Another, less acquainted with children, might not be able to see the connection; but I could—it was worthy of Aristotle himself or John Locke. "I *didn't* say I meant to lick ye," rejoined the first; "I said I *could* lick ye, and so I can." To which the other replies glancing first at my window and then all up and down the street, "I should like to see you try it." Whereupon the larger boy begins to move away, half-backwards, half sideways, muttering just loud enough to be heard, "Ah, you want to fight now, 'jest 'cause you're close to your own house." And here the dialogue finished, and the babies moved on, shaking their little heads at each other, and muttering all the way up street. Men are but children of a larger growth!—Children but empires in miniature.— * * * * *

"Ah, ah, hourra! hourra! here's a fellow's birthday!" cried a boy in my hearing once. A number had got together to play ball, but one of them having found a birthday, and not only the birthday, but the very boy to whom it belonged, they all gathered about him as if they had never witnessed a conjunction of that sort before. The very fellows for a committee of inquiry!—into the affairs of a national bank, if you please.

Never shall I forget another incident which occurred in my presence between two other boys. One was trying to jump over a wheelbarrow. Another was going by; he stopped, and after considering a moment, spoke.—"I'll tell you what you can't do," said he. "Well, what is it?" "You can't jump down your own throat." "Well *you* can't." "*Can't I though!*" The simplicity of "Well, you can't," and "Can't I though!" tickled me prodigiously. They reminded me of a sparring I had seen elsewhere—I should not like to say where—having a great respect for the temples of justice and the halls of legislation. * * *

I saw three children throwing sticks at a cow. She grew tired of her share in the game at last, and holding down her head and shaking it, demanded a new deal. They cut and run. After getting to a place of comparative security, they stopped, and holding by the top of a board fence, began to reconnoitre. Meanwhile, another troop of children hove in sight, and arming themselves with brickbats, began to approach the same cow. Whereupon two of the others called out from the fence, "You, Joe! you'd better mind! that's our cow!" The plea was admitted without a demurrer; and the cow was left to be tormented by her legal owners. Hadn't these children the law on their side? * * *

But children have other characters. At times they are creatures to be afraid of. Every case I give, is a fact within my own observation. There are children, and I have had to do with them, whose very eyes were terrible; children, who after years of anxious and watchful discipline, were as indomitable as the young of the wild beast, dropped in the wilderness, crafty and treacherous and cruel. And others, I have known who, if they live, *must* have dominion over the multitude being evidently of them that, from the foundations of the world, have been always thundering at the gates of power.

Freedom of the Press in New York State.

An Important Letter From Governor Seymour.

STATE OF NEW YORK,
Executive Department,
Albany, May 23, 1864.

To A. Oakly Hall, Esq., District Attorney of New York:

SIR: I am advised that on the 12th inst., the office of the Journal of Commerce and that of the New York World were entered by armed men, the property of the owners seized, and the premises held by force for several days. It is charged that these acts of violence were done without the sanction or the State or national law.

If this be true, the offenders must be punished.

In the month of July last, when N. York was a scene of violence, I gave warning that "the laws of the State must be enforced, its peace and order maintained, and the property of its citizens protected at every hazzard." The laws were enforced at a fearful cost of blood and life.

The declaration then made was not intended merely for that occasion, or against any class of men. It is one of an enduring character, to be asserted at all times and against all conditions of citizens, without favor or distinction. Unless all are made to bow to the law, it will be respected by none; unless all are made secure in their rights of person and property, none can be protected. If the owners of the above named journals have violated State or national laws, they must be proceeded against and punished by these laws.—Any action against them, outside of legal precedure, is criminal.

At this time of civil war and disorder the majesty of the law must be upheld or society will sink into anarchy. Our soldiers in the field will battle in vain for constitutional liberty, if persons, or property, or opinions are trampled upon at home. We must not give up home freedom, and thus disgrace the American character, while our citizens in the army are pouring out their lifeblood to maintain the national honor. They must not find, when they come back, that their personal and fireside rights have been despoiled.

In addition to the general obligation to enforce the laws of the land, there are local reasons why they must be upheld in the city of New York. If they are not its commerce and greatness will be broken down. If the great centre of wealth, business, and enterprise is thrown into disorder and bankruptcy, the national Government will be paralyzed. What makes New York the heart of our country. Why are its pulsations felt at the extremities of our land? Not through its position alone, but because of the world-wide belief that property is safe within its limits from waste by mobs and spoilation by Government. The laborers in the workshop, the nine, and in the field, on this continent and in every part of the globe, send to its merchants, for sale or exchange, the products of their toil. These merchants are made the trustees of the wealth of millions living in every land, because it is believed that in their hands, property is safe under the shield of law administered upon principle, and according to known usages.

This great confidence has grown up in the course of many years by virtue of a painstaking, honest performance of duty by the business men of your city. In this they have been aided by the enforcement of laws based upon the solemnly recorded pledges that "the right of the people to be secure in their persons, houses, papers and effects against unreasonable searches and seizures, shall not be violated, and that no one shall be deprived of liberty or property without due process of law." For more than eighty years have we as a people been building up this universal faith in the sanctity of our jurispendence. It is this which carries our commerce upon every ocean, and brings back to our merchants the wealth of every clime. It is now charged that, in utter disregard of the sensitiveness of that faith, at a moment when the national credit is undergoing a fearful trial, the organs of commerce are seized and held, in violation of constitutional pledges; that this act was done in a public mart of your great city, and was thus forced upon the notice of the commercial agents of the world, and they were shown in an offensive way, that property is seized by military force and arbitrary orders.

These things are more hurtful to the national honor and strength than the loss of battles. The world will confound such acts with the principles of our Government, and the folly and crimes of officials will be looked upon as the natural results of the spirit of our institutions. Our State and local authorities must repel this ruinous interference. If the merchants of New York are not willing to have their harbors sealed up and their commerce paralyzed, they must unite in this demand for the security of persons and property. If this is not done, the world will withdraw from their keeping its treasures and its commerce. History has taught that all official violation of law in times of civil war and disorder goes before acts of spoilation and other measures which destroy the safeguards of commerce.

I call upon you to look into the facts connected with the seizure of the Journal of Commerce and of the New York World. If these acts were illegal, the offenders must be punished.—In making your inquiries and in prosecuting the parties implicated, you will call upon the sheriff of the county and the heads of the police departmedt for any needed force or assistance. The failure to give this by any official under my control will be deemed a sufficient cause for his removal.

Very respectfully, yours, etc.,
HORATIO SEYMOUR.

A Combat.

Once on a time, a quarrel arose, and a fight began, between two men, one of whom was a giant in size, and strength, while the other was not nearly so large as his antagonist, but was courageous and active, so that, all things considered, he had reasonable hopes of defending himself successfully against the mad assaults of his enemy. Besides, he was in the right, and this nerved his arm to the utmost. In fact, his adversary had made the attack, and he was only striving to ward off the blows aimed at him—to save his own life—and having no idea or intention of pushing the fight, provided he were let alone. Before the combat began, as soon as he saw matters leading that way, he had attempted to address the giant, and tried to settle the quarrel by negotiation. The latter pretended, at first, that he would listen, but all the time he was merely preparing to strike, and so soon as he deemed himself ready, strike he did, with all his might, announcing to the other that he would listen to nothing.

Seeing this, the smaller man had but to address himself to the task of defence. A long while they fought; and at length the smaller man again spoke.

"I will listen to nothing you have to say," replied the giant, "so long as you retain your weapons. Lay down your arms, if you wish to converse with me."

"And will you," enquired the other, "lay down yours?"

"No!" was the emphatic answer; "I will not. You must lay down yours, but I shall retain mine. You must put yourself completely in my power. I must be at liberty to work my will on you. I will give you no guarantee whatever. I shall probably take your property away. I may make you a slave. I do not even promise to spare your life. By daring to take up arms against me, your have forfeited your rights, and now I am free to do as I please with you. Lay down your arms, or say nothing more!"

So the constest continued. Some of the by-standers urged the smaller man to ask for peace.

"But do you not see," said he, "that he will not listen to me unless I throw aside my arms, and put myself in his power—that he expects to take my property, and will not even promise to spare my life?"

"No matter," was the reply; "propose peace every time you have stricken a good blow, and then you cannot be suspected of cowardice."

All the while, the giant continued to assure his antagonist and all the world, that he would listen to no proposition, unless the other should resign all means of resistance—should, in short, own himself subjugated, and that he *must not* even promise to spare his enemy's life. This he reiterated, and the smaller man continued to declare that all he wanted was to be let alone, and that he would be satisfied with this; so that at last all the world understood the position of the two parties. Still the same spectators insisted that the smaller man should ask for peace. At length, for the third time, he raised his voice to speak to the giant. Nobody knows what he wished to say, for the giant thundered out again:

"I will not hear, until you lay down your arms! Silence!"

So the fight went on, and is still raging. Will the small man ever be fool enough to throw away his weapons, and allow himself to be knocked on the head by the giant? We believe not; but if he must lose his life, we believe he will die with arms in his hands, and die resisting.—*The Countryman.*

THE SITUATION.

The Richmond Whig of the 20th has the following editorial on "The Situation":

As we surmised would be the case, Grant has definitely established himself on the South-side. The scene of immediate assault is transferred from Richmond to Petersburg. The mass of the Federal army is now south of the Appomattox, and is about 15 miles further from this city than when it made its last effort on the north side of the James. For one thing we must give Grant credit. He seems to be in just as much of a hurry as we are to get through with this campaign. To be sure he is hastening to a very different conclusion from that which he had hoped to reach, but after all, it is a conclusion. He had at his command a certain number of men, and a definite amount of resources. He has no sort of hesitation in sacrificing the men and expending the resources within the shortest possible space of time. When he has solved this little problem nothing more can be done. Richmond will still stand a monument to the skill and constancy of the one side, and to the unrelenting but fruitless vindictiveness of the others and—*vioa la fin.* But Grant will at least have done one thing in which his predecessors have failed. He will have exhausted the means of the Yankee nation. He is resolved to differ in something from that long list of fugacious chieftains who educated the Army of the Potomac to defeat and safety. If the beginning of every Yankee campaign in Virginia had for its object to capture Richmond, the end of every campaign had for its purpose to save the army. So when McClellan made his famous change of base; when Burnside recoiled from the heights of Fredericksburg; when Hooker rushed frantically back across the Rappahannock, the Yankee papers could say with some truth that these Generals had accomplished their objects—they had saved the army. Grant evidently thinks that if Richmond cannot be taken the army is not worth saving. With dogged resolution be led to slaughter at the Wilderness, at Spottsylvania. and at Cold Harbor, and managed in these fruitless assaults to dispose of as many men as McClellan took away from the Chickahominy, or as Hooker saved from the shambles of Chancellorsville. With the battered remnant he is now making his last effort on the south side of James. *Laus Deo!* when that is over; Grant and the Army of the Potomac will pass away into the debts of history together.

But in the meantime he will doubtless strike heavy and furious blows. The assaults on our lines at Petersburg, in the early part of last week, were but a prelude to a more ferocioes attack on Friday. It appears that on the morning of that day the enemy gained a partial success in the capture of one of our batteries; but heavy and repeated charges on the others were successfully repeled. In the evening a general advance was attempted; but was met by our troops with their resolute courage, and after severe fighting the Yankers were drivon from the ground they had gained, and our lines were re-established in their original integrity. Of the operations of Saturday in that quarter, we have at the moment of writing, no definite information.

Rumors were current yesterday that there had been severe fighting; but up to a late hour, no official, or even authentic information to this effect had been received. We imagine that, after the repulse, of Friday, Grant took at least a day to rest his forces and modify his plans.

On the line between this city and Pertersburg the schemes of the enemy have signally failed. It was no doubt, Grant's intention and his hope to interpose a force on our line of communication before a sufficient number of men could be concentrated in Petersburg for its protection against the sudden assault which he meditated. It was for this object that the Yankees advancod from Bermuda Hundreds and occupied the lines which we had temporarily abandoned. But there must have been some notable defect in this part of the scheme, for a very slight effort sufficed to eject the Yankees from their threatening position and to force them back into their works at Bermuda. When Grant marched against Petersburg in force he found, of course much to his mortification and chagrin, that he was again confronted by the redoubtable troops who have stood between him and Richmond like a wall of brass. It is useless to try strategy, Lieut. Gen. Grant, Lee is your master in that, just as the army of Northern Virginia is the master of the army of the Potomac in valor and endurance.

Movements of Maximilian.

The Atlanta Confederacy, in noticing the movements of Maximillian, speaks thus of the appointments made by him:

Two little things Maximillian has done look well for us. He has made Santa Anna a Field Marshal, and recalled him home; and he has created Dr. Gwinn Duke of Sonora, with the office of Governor General of that blooming Province. Both of these dignitaries are truly and loyally inclined to us and our cause. As far back as 1861, Santa Anna was betting high on Southern valor, at Havana, and did win, it was said, several thousand pistoles upon the result of the first battle of Manassas. He wrote a letter to his agent in New Orleans just before its fall. offering a large sum to be applied to the Confederate Hospital Fund, and subscribed to $50,000 worth of Goverament stock. His partisans in Mexico are anti Lincoln to the score. and his interest will be thrown in our favor wherever he can find a chance. He is to be made Prince of Matamoras, it is said and placed in charge of the military department of the Rio Grande. In this event he will have many occasions to show his kindly disposition, and we do not doubt that he will redeem his expressions of sympathy. If he had no other motive, the interest invested in our success would be a sufficient inducement.

Dr. Gwinn is a Confederate by birth. He was born in Tennessee, raised in Mississippi, and schooled in an extreme school of Southern politics. A Democratic member of Congress from the State of his adoption, he emigrated to California in the beginning of the gold fever, and flourished there. He made a fortune, married and became an American Senator. At Washington City he held the position of a bold, unscrupulous leader, a dashing financier and a lucky adventurer. When the Yankee element in California deprived him of his place in the Senate he went to Paris. He has been there until recently, and the result of his mission is as above stated.

It is not heard to decipher out of the situation of Maximilian, and these two appointments, where his interests and sympathies incline, and the day is almost in sight when a close bond of fellowship will exist between his floral Empire and the Sunny South, a union which we heartily approve as natural expedient and right.

The Bible

Sitting alone in my study I fell into a train of reflections on the preservation of the Bible and its influence on the history of man. Here before me lies an unpretending little book.—What a volume of thought does it suggest? It is by many centuries the oldest book in the world. More than three thousand year ago the first word of it was written in the desert of Arabia; more than seventeen hundred the last word was written on the rocky isle of Patmos. It has been read by more people than all other books in the world put together. More of it is remembered by men than all the books that were ever written. It treats of questions of the highest moment to all men, and proposes to reveal that for which the wisest of all ages have sought in vain—the secret of true happiness. These very letters that pass under my eye are the same as those traced by the finger of God on the tablets of stone amid the thunders and lightnings of Mt. Sinai. The language in which the New Testament was written is the same in which Solon, Plato, and Demosthenes wrote and spoke.

This book has survived the revolutions and changes of three thousand years. It has seen Nineveh, Babylon, Memphis, Thebes, Tyre, Sidon, Carthage, Rome, Athens, and a thousand other cities, rise, flourish and fall. It has lived amid wars the most bloody, amid desolations the most complete, amid tyranny the most grinding, amid darkness the most profound; amid superstitions the most degrading, amid idolatry the most repulsive, amid blasphemy the most heaven daring; and has been against all these the great witness of God. This book has outlived all the efforts made to shake the faith of man in its revelation and to

The York river road, being now useless, will, it is understood, be made subsidiary to the repair of the Danville, and the connection on this with the South, broken by Wilson's depredations, it is expected will be restored in the course of a few days.

Beyond a very limited extent, the James' river and Kanawha canal is now inoperative. Alleged ca u — Government impressment of stock and forage.

From Virginia.

FROM PETERSBURG AND VICINITY.

The Petersburg express of July 5 confirmed the rumored stir and commotion in Grants army, and reports that considerable change has been made in Grant's front. It says:

It is positively known that Grant has greatly contracted his lines around the city, having withdrawn an army corps or more from his extreme left, which, until Saturday, extended to Dr. Gurley's farm, within four miles of Reams station, and about two miles to the east of the Petersburg and Weldon road. His reasons for this contraction are not known, but two or three causes suggest themselves. His idea of circumvallating the city so as to include the Weldon, Southside and Danville railroads, has been completely exploded by the recent disastrous termination of his grand Wilson raid.

Again the point to which he had extended his left offered such a tempting bait to Mahone that it had been twice flanked and a large number of prisoners captured. It is said, too by persons who know the country, that in that particular section there is always a great scarcity of water, but since the present protracted drought it has been next to an impossibility to procure it. Prisoners taken confirm this, and say that there has been great suffering in camp for water. During one of the late engagements in that section a General barely escaped capture while endeavoring to slake his thirst over a mud puddle in the woods. Two of his Aids were not so fortunate, and our soldiers captured them on the spot.

Our cavalry have also contributed somewhat to this recent contraction of Grant's lines. A day or two more will fully develop the intention of Grant.

It was also rumored in Petersburg that the enemy had embarked a large number of troops at City Point on Thursday last. The men occupied five transports, and the boats appear d o be crowedd to overflowing. Whether these were men whose terms of service has expired, or whose removal from Grant's army has been rendered necessary for operations elsewhere, was not known.

Tremendous cannonading commenced Sunday night, about 10 o'clock on our left. One of the guns used was a whopper, and each explosion shook the city.

MOSBY'S RAID ON THE BALTIMORE AND OHIO RAILROAD.

On the 27th ult., Colonel Mosby, with a portion of his battallion—43d Virginia—surprised a Yankee camp at Duffie's Depot, a station on the Baltimore and Ohio Railroad, eight or ten miles above Harper's Ferry, and captured the whole command consisting of thirty-nine infantry, including two Lieutenants. On coming in range of the camp, Col. Mosby sent in a flag demanding a surrender, in reply to which the Yankee Lieutenant in command, and to whom the whole business was a novelty, said he was unable to make up his mind whether or not to comply he would take the matter under advisement and see what his men thought about it.

He was taken before Col. Mosby, and after a moment's interview concluded to give up unconditionally. The captors proceeded to tade possession of the depot with army supplies, as also of some sutler's in the vicinity, which they disposed of in their ustially expeditious style. The booty was plenty and valuable. Whilst engaged in bringing off the spoils a force of forty or fifty cavalry come up and charged a detachment of Col. Mosby's command, and succeeded in leaving twenty-six of their number, including a lieutenant, prisoners in our hands, besides several of their dead on the field.

REMOVAL OF TROOPS.

We hear from a source entirely reliable, that the enemy embarked a large number of troops at City Point on Thursday last. The men occupied five large transports, and the boats appeared to be crowded to overflowing. Whether these were men whose terms of service has expired, or whose removal from Grant's army have been rendered necessary for operation elsewhere, we are unable to say.

HUNTER'S LOSSES.

Hunter is estimated thus far to have had 3,000 men put *hors du combat*, exclusive of his losses near Staunton. In addition he has lost nearly, if not quite, all of his artillery and his entire wagon train, numbering some 800 or 1,000 wagons. Our cavalry at last accounts were still harrasing him, and the drain upon his forces was constant. Before he reaches a place of assured safety he will be made to suffer still more severely.

KAUT'S RAIDERS.

The latest news from these brigands is that the remnant of them were making their way in a scattered and disorganized condition towards Grant's rear. Their expedition, begun so gaily and conducted so haughtily till they reached Staunton river bridge, ended in disaster. At Sapponi church, Reams' station and stony creek they lost the entire fruits of their campaign, all their artillery, and more than one-third of their men.

Besides the negroes, wagons, ambulances and other stolen property, we are said to have taken from them upwards of 3,000 horses.

VARIOUS ITEMS.

Those who are well acquainted with the country around Petersburg say the scarcity of water will compell Grant to move his army.

In a late fight near Petersburg we captured several hundred small arms and sixty thousand rounds of ammunition.

About 3,000 horses have been captured from the various Yankee raiding parties.

The canvalescent soldiers in the hospitals at Lynchburg, on Hunters recent approach to the place turned out and assisted in driving him off. Our cavalry have succeeded in finding two more cannon in the Nottoway river, between Stony Creek and Jarrat's Depot—this makes fifteen pieces taken; which prisoners say is all they had.

Wilson's raiders not only stole jewelry from the hands of ladies, but also stole their dresses, under clothing &c.

A captured officer states that both Wilson's and Hunters raiding parties were composed of picked men, and fully equiped in every particular They numbered about 8,000 men. Great things were expected of them by Grant, but he has been disappointed.

From Virginia

In late Virginia papers we find the annexed news:

CAVALRY FIGHT AT TREVILLIANS.

Our two divisions under General Fitz Lee and Wade Hampton, achieved a victory June 12th, over Sheridan's cavalry corps, which, for its results and extent, has no superior in the history of this war. On the evening of the 9th information was received that a large body of their cavalry and twenty-four pieces of artillery had passed around our left and were moving up the South Anna in the direction of Gordonsville, with the evident intention of destroying our stores at Charlottsville and tap the railroad from that place to Lynchburg. Gen. Hampton, with two divisions of cavalry and Major Breathead's artillery set out during night, and by a rapid march, got ahead of them at trevillian's depot, four or five miles above Louisa C. H. Early on the morning of the 11th. their advance coming up, a simultaneous attack on their front and left flank was commenced by Gens. Hampton and Fitz Lee, which lasted, with terrible fury during the entire day, with a decided success on our side.

During the engagement Custar's brigade charged through Rosser's line, but were cut off and scattered through the woods in every direction, with a loss of five hundred and forty prisoners, one piece of artillery and a great many horses. The remainder of the party, in attempting their escape, passed out of the woods near Gen. Hampton's trains, capturing several ordnance wagons. ambulances and a portion of Butler's lead horses. This having been reported to Gen. Lee, he immediately ordered the second and fifteenth Virginia regiments to charge them mounted which they did, recapturing Hampton's train, four caissons, one hundred prisoners, and fifty horses and mules. They also captured four pieces of artillery, but the Yankees ran off with the limbers and they had no means of bringing them out, as they already had as much as they could guard safely into our lines.

The main bodies on both sides being dismounted and in regular infantry line of battle, kept up a continuous fire regardless of these mounted dashes untill closed the game. During the hottest of the battle Fitz Lee's right was forced back by an overwhelming force, and Lieut. Col. W. R Carter, commanding the Third Virginia, was severely wounded in the leg and hand, and while two men of his regiment was carrying him off they too were wounded and had to leave Carter on the field, where he was captured. Everything remained quiet during the night; next morning Gen. Hampton having sent out scouting parties, found the enemy in his same position and commenced a heavy skirmish, which lasted until about 4 o'clock, p. m., at which time Gen. Lee having moved around from the enemy's flank to his front with Hampton, both divisions were dismounted and a general and almost as desperate engagement ever witnessed was made along the whole line, and lasted until about eight o'clock at night.

The Yankees fought with a courage and determination worthy of a better cause. They charged our line again and again, but were repulsed every time, leaving their killed and wounded in a few steps of our line.

After making desperate assaults upon our flanks without success, they abandoned their intended raid, made a hurried retreat during the night; leaving over a hundred badly wounded, together with Col. Carter and the rest of our wounded, which they had captured the evening before, besides a number of Sharp's rifles, Colt's pistols, two caisons and every thing in the way of equipments. Their dead covered the entire battlefield, and in their retreat they admitted to the citizens they were badly "used up."

They marched rapidly down the river the way they came, and their wounded left at citizens houses on the road, their unburied dead, broken down ambulances, and wagons and dead horses which strew the road upon which they retreated; all mark the extent of our victory. Our loss was very heavy in wounded, but moderate in killed. From the best estimates, the Yankees must have lost more killed than we did in killed and wounded together. We left the battle field in pursuit of them, bringing over 700 prisoners, a number horses and mules, and a piece of artillery, four caissons; several waggons, including Custar's headquarters wagon and his Adjutant General. Our wounded have been all well attended to and left in the Green Spring neighborhood, where there is plenty of everthing. besides the patriotic attention of the ladies who had already crowded our hospitals with good things before we left.

A CAVALRY FIGHT NEAR SAMANA CHURCH.

A severe engagement occured near Forge Bridge on Wednesday June 23; in which one of our brigades drove back a brigade of the enemy upon Sheridan's main body, who were at the time crossing the Chickahominy. After this affair, our men withdrew in the direction of Richmond, and rejoined the rest of Hampton's force at Samana church, near Nance's shop, it seems that Sheridan was completely deceived by this manoeuvre, Believing that this brigade was the entire force we had in this neighborhood, he determined to cut them off. With this design he halted with two divisions at Charles City Court House, and despatched Gregg and Custar with their divisions to get in our rear.

During Thursday night these Yankees, by following the direct road from the Court House to Long bridge, put themselves in Hampton's rear at a point between Hawes' shop and Samana church, and no doubt congratulated themselves exceedingly upon the success of their plans for our certain capture. To make assurance doubly sure, and to provide against the possibility of our escape, they spent most of the day in throwing up heavy double lines of earthworks in front of thems lves and between us and Richmond.

General Hampton also threw up entrenchments. At three o'clock Friday evening the hostile forces were half a mile apart, a thick wood and a narrow field being between them, the enemy fronting south east, our forces northwest Chambliss was on the left of our line, then Young, Wickham and Lomax, and Butler on our extreme right. Each side had a skirmish line thrown out some two hundred and fifty or three hundred yards in front, between whom skirmishing began about noon.

About four o'clock, P. M. all of our men being dismounted, Gen. Hampton sent Chambliss to turn the enemy's right flank and take him in the rear, and soon after ordered the rest of our force to leave their breastworks and charge the enemy. When our troops reached our skirmish line they were opened on by the enemy's cannon with canister and grape. at a distance of three hundred yards. Not wavering for an instant, our men pushed forward, firing volley after volley, their fire being mostly directed against the artillerists. When we got into the field before mentioned, just beyond which were the enemy's entrenchments and cannon, a large body of the enemy's cavalry charged upon us. Our men were order d to halt and receive their onslaught. They dashed up to us in handsome style, but on receiving two steady volleys broke and fell back in confusion. Again being rallied they were brought to the charge, but this time with much less steadiness and impetuosity. A volley or two scattered them and they came back no more but scampered away to our right.

Our men resumed their charge upon the enemy's works, but observed, with regret, that his cannon had disappeared. It had been withdrawn during the diversion created by the cavalry charge, and was at that moment clattering away towards Charles City Court House. But the enemy's dismounted men kept up a hot fire from his breastworks upon our advancing line, a fire which we returned with good effect.—On our getting near the enemy's first line of intrenchments his men deserted them and fled, leaping and running over the men in the second line. Our men scaled the outer works and dashed up to the second, from which not a shot was fired upon them, and where they found the Yankees seeking safety by crouching behind the intrenchments. As we scaled this line its occupants fled, and joined pell-mell in a regular race for Charles City Court House. Simultaneously with our advance Chambliss had struck them in rear.

Our men pressed them closely, pouring into them a galling fire. The pursuit was kept up till we arrived within two miles of the Court House, when, night having come on, we halted.

Immediately on the arrival of his beaten divisions, Sheridan made a hasty change in his plans. Instead of attempting to reach Harrison's landing, as he had proposed, he immediately started for Wyanoke, a point on James river, five or six miles below Charles City Court House. At this place, on Saturday, he crossed on pontoons for the Southside of James river.

In this battle the enemy lost not less than five hundred killed and wounded, two hundred prisoners, and a large number of horses. One hundred will cover our casualties. Most of the enemy were killed after they had been driven from their works and were in retreat, when we fired into them from rear and flank.

Among the enemy's killed who were left on the field, were two lieutenant colonels, a major and several captains.

The Position in Georgia.

Thursday says the Intelligencer of the 9th, the greater part of the enemy's demonstrations were made against our position in the neighborhood of Green's Ferry. Heavy musketry firing and cannonading occurred during the day, but no heavy movement was made by the enemy to march on the position to take it by assault.

Sherman has sent a large force to threaten our left, and doubtless to divert our attention from other and more important positions. His movements down the river in the direction of West Point cannot be very extensive or safely made, for the reason that if an isolated force gets away in that direction too far from their depots of supplies on the railroad, they subject themselves to great privations without securing any advantages. Such a force will be doubtless broken up by our cavalry, who are watching the operations. One object of the movement is probably to destroy our railway line to West Point. The enemy have been surprisingly quiet along the greater portion of our lines. Doubtless, they are seeking for the most available positions from which to dig up to our front again, and if necessary, lay seige regularly to our position. It seems to be a determined policy with Sherman not to fight a regular battle, but to take this city by strategy and merely outweighing us. Surely the turning point must be nearly reached.

From the Atlanta Confederacy, 10th inst

Crossing the Chattahoochee.

The latest interesting items from the front is the crossing of a force of the enemy, artillery, infantry and cavalry at Roswell. The Yankee force on this side as yet, is comparatively small and prompt measures have been taken to give them a reception worthy of so commendable an undertaking.—We presume, that having "made the landing," they are still crossing, and will endeavor to make the passage of the river with their whole army at that point, which we predicted in a recent issue. At all events, as Netherland used to say in his canvas for the Governorship of Tennessee:

> Part of the host have crossed the flood,
> And part are crossing now.

We trust the movement on our part to anticipate this advance may not be so precipitate as to frighten these fellows back before they receive the whipping their temerity deserved. We should prefer about one-half or two-thirds, of Sherman's army to cross before General Johnston pitches into them, for another Leesburg and Ball's Bluff affair. From the appearance of some of the Federal prisoners who passed our window last evening, they would be all of them none the worse for a little clean water, and we predict that when our boys hear the charge sounded, the raiders will go into the Chattahoochee as precipitately as did the negro workman the other day when a Yankee shell fell amongst them.

There was some firing along the lines to-day, but of the result we can learn nothing yet. About half a dozen prisoners were brought in last evening.

[Special Dispatch to the Constitutionalist.]

Charleston, July 9, A. M.

The following dispatch was received at headquarters this morning from John's Island:

"We attacked the enemy, who was expecting us, at daylight this morning, and are driving him at all points. We have passed the line of works occupied by the enemy yesterday.

B. H. ROBERTSON, Brig Gen."

ION.

Clinton, La., July 6, via Mobile, 9th.

A gentleman of this town, just from the other side of the river, reports the capture of Little Rock by Price, with all of Steele's supplies, ammunitions and transportation, and all his army except 4,000.

Our army is marching on Fort Smith. The enemy has been driven entirely out of Arkansas, except around Helena.

Our informant says the news was officially received at Alexandria.

Lieutenant General Kirby Smith has ordered the impressment of half of the cotton in the Trans-Mississippi department for the purpose of buying military supplies.

Mobile, July 8.

The reporter at Jackson reports that the force which moved from Rodney simultaneously with the one from Vicksburg was commanded by Col. Ellit, of the Marine Brigade, numbering 500 white cavalry, and 1,500 negro infantry, and was met at Coleman's Cross Roads, ten miles South of Port Gibson, by Colonel Wood, with his regiment, Morman's battalion, and a few State troops, all being a portion of Adam's brigade, numbering 1,000.

They were driven back after a sharp and decisive fight. The enemy's loss 47 killed and a large number wounded.

We captured many horses, small arms and equipments. Our loss six killed. The number wounded is unknown.

Mobile, July 9.

A special dispatch to the Register, dated Senatobia, July 7th, says that Northern dates announce Wilson's return after destroying sixty miles of railroad and burning bridges on the Danville road for twenty miles.

Ewell's corps is in the vicinity of Harper's Ferry.

Hunter and Seigel have evacuated Martinsburg.

The Herald's Bermuda Hundred's correspondent says the armies are taking their last repose before girding up for battle.

Fessenden has not yet accepted the position of Secretary of the Treasury.

Seven steamers under convoy were fired into near Clarenden without damage.

Sherman's advance is bulletined as a great success. His army is in fine spirits.

The New York Herald's Washington correspondent says:

Lincoln will call for half a million of men immediately on the adjournment of Congress.

Washburn has issued Special Order No. 60, taking 40 citizens as hostages for guards on railroad trains.

Special Dispatch to the Constitutionalist.

Charleston, July 9.

The enemy have been driven steadily on John's Island to day, and are supposed to be abandoning the Island.

Our loss is heavy. The enemy's much greater. No definite particulars have been received.

The Georgians have been the greatest sufferers.

The enemy are keeping up a bombardment on Sumter and on battery Pringle, on James Island.

ION.

FRUITS OF MORGAN'S RAID.

We need not enumerate the towns taken by Morgan, for a full account of his movements gleaned from the Northern papers has been published already. The fruits are these: Twenty-one hundred men carried into Kentucky, upwards of eighteen hundred brought back. Seven hundred dismounted men procured good horses, and all the command were supplied with fresh horses. Twenty-seven hundred Yankees were captured and paroled, amongst them General Hobson, the man who captured Morgan in Ohio. Hobson was sent in company with one of Morgan's Majors, to Cincinnati, to negotiate the exchange of 7000 of Morgan's men now in captivity. In the event of his failure to accomplish a favorable result he has to come within our lines and deliver himself up to Morgan. Such are some of the substantial fruits of Morgan's work in Kentucky, in which his destruction of Yankee property is not included.

The Southern Banner

JAMES A. SLEDGE,

EDITOR AND PROPRIETOR.

ATHENS, GEORGIA

WEDNESDAY MORNING, ... JULY 13, 1864

Ley Wanted.

Strong Hickory or Oak Ley wanted at the Southern Banner office. A liberal price will be paid for it. We hope some of our country friends will accomodate us.

Latest News.

We have reports by passengers, which we consider reliable, that both armies have crossed the Chattahoochee river, and are now confronting each other about four miles from Atlanta. A day or two will decide whether Gen. Johnston intends to fight or give up the city. Should he do the latter, this place and all North-East Georgia will be within the enemy's lines.

From Virginia it is reported that Gen. Early is at Hagerstown Maryland. It is certain that he has captured Martinsburg; and taken in connection with the fact that Grant has withdrawn some of his troops from Petersburg, and sent them to Washington, the report of Gen. Early's presence in Maryland is highly probable. Everything looks bright in Virginia.

A Paying Trip.

Col. Andrew Young, with fifty men, left this place last week, and went to a point within the enemy's lines, and brought out twenty-one wagon loads of leather—thirteen hundred and eighty sides. The estimated value of it is over $300,000. The manner in which this affair was conducted, reflects great credit upon the skill and daring of Col. Young and the brave men who accompanied him.

The Colonel has great energy and perseverance and is bound to put things through.

The Militia to be Called out.

The special correspondent of the Atlanta *Confederacy* writes on the 7th inst. that he learns that Gov. Brown is going to call out the Militia of Georgia. This will add greatly to the strength of our army. They will be under the command of Gen. G. W. Smith, a brave, experienced and skillful officer.

Pleasant Yankee News.

The New York Herald of the 4th inst. says Secretary Stanton has telegraphed to Dix that Kirby Smith has crossed the Mississippi. We are inclined to believe this report. We have heard rumors some time since of such a movement. It will be remembered that at the first battle of Manassas, Gen. Smith came in with reinforcements just in time to turn the tide in our favor. If he can do the same thing now, and contribute to as decisive a victory over Sherman, it will wind up the campaign in this department.

☞ Capt. D. B. LANGSTON, of the Athens Guards, is at home. He was wounded at Spottsylvania. We are pleased to learn that his wound is doing well. The Captain has been in command of the 3d Ga. Regiment about six months.

To be or not to be—a Refugee.

Many persons are now much interested upon this question. We take the following sensible remarks upon the subject from the Atlanta *Confederacy*—the writer, we believe, being a refugee himself, and therefore speaks from experience:

To be a refugee or not to be a refugee, that is the question. For some time we have been acquainted with the fact that numbers of our people had their household goods ready packed preparatory to a flight to a more tranquil and less warlike atmosphere. We know that there are many who entertain doubts of the safety of Atlanta, and who are pluming their wings for migration to the interior or points closer to the Gulf

We have a word of advice for all such people. In the beginning we disapproved of the practice of constantly flying before the enemy. The non-combatants throughout the country would be much better off to remain where they are, and by so doing would best serve the interests of the cause. There is not a more senseless or useless thing, than the blocking up of transportation trains with women and children and household plunder in the panic to avoid the enemy. Every additional family of refugees into the farther South, takes so much more of the sustenance which the army requires. Neither the cause, nor the soldier nor the individual are benefitted. On the contrary, the inconvenience of all is increased. As the invasion gradually encroaches upon our territory, people swarm Southward, abandoning house and home, trusting to the genius of adventure, seeking a resting place they know not where, and for a purpose they cannot explain, save that they are flying from the Yankees.

We have witnessed many retreats, we have experienced many evacuations of city and village. The depredations of the enemy, even, are not so saddening as the needless sufferings these helpless refugees entail upon themselves by flying before the army and cumbering its movements.—The man who urges that non-combatants should crowd the railroads and other public avenues in their refuge from the enemy, as a patriotic principle, is without reason, candor or humanity.—They are far better where they are. Nine cases out of every ten have proven that the non-combatant remaining quietly at home suffered less than the friendless refugee seeking hospitality among strangers who have not the means, if they had the inclination, to tender their hospitality.—Cool reflection upon these matters

> "Puzzles the will,
> And makes us rather bear the ills we have,
> Than fly to others we know not off."

Those who are able to go, and have the means of subsistence in the new homes they may select, should certainly make refugees of themselves if they choose, but in doing this they by no means enhance the cause of the South. Our advice to those who are not able to subsist themselves in a strange country, is, to remain where they are. After all, the chances are in many instances that removal may not be necessary at all. A great deal of anxiety, a great deal of inconvenience and incalculable privation may be avoided by the exercise of a little philosophy and reason.

Lincoln's Letter of Acceptance.

The following is Lincoln's reply to the letter informing him of his nomination by the Baltimore Convention:

EXECUTIVE MANSION, WASHINGTON, June 27th, 1864:

Hon. Wm. Dannison and others, a committee of the National Union Convention.

Gentlemen: Your letter of the 14th inst., formally notifying me that I have been nominated by the convention you represent, for the *Presidency* of the United States, for four years from the 4th of March next, has been received. The nomination is gratefully accepted, as the resolutions of the convention, called the platform, are heartily approved. While the resolution in regard to the supplanting of the republican government upon the Western continent is fully concurred in, there might be misunderstanding were I not to say that the position of the Government in relation to the action of France in Mexico, as assumed through the State department, and endorsed by the convention among the measures and acts of the Executive, will be faithfully maintained so long as the state of facts shall leave that position pertinent and applicable.

I am especially gratified that the soldiers and the seamen were not forgotten by the Convention, as they forever must and be remembered by the grateful country whose salvation they devote their lives

Thanking you for the kind and complimentary terms in which you have communicated the nomination and other proceedings of the Convention, I subscribe myself.

Your obedient servant,

A. LINCOLN.

Tribute of Respect.

UNITY LODGE, NO. 36, F. A. M.
July 9th, 1864.

Providence, in His mysterious dealings with his creatures, has again called upon us to mourn the loss of a worthy brother, JAMES A. SMITH.—And this dispensation has shrouded our hearts in mourning, and his afflicted family are now suffering in grief their irreparable loss. Brother Smith was a member of our Lodge for some time—not a great while since was with us, rejoicing in the strength and vigor of manhood, and hopeful of the future; but alas! his remains lie encased in the tomb, and what remains with us, is the recollection of his many virtues. He died at his residence in Jackson county, on the 17th day of June 1864, in the forty-fourth year of his age.

1st. Resolved, therefore, That in the death of our brother, James A. Smith, his wife and children have lost a kind husband and father, this Lodge a clever member, and the community a good citizen.

2d. Resolved That our sympathies are due and are hereby tendered the bereaved family of the deceased; and that these proceedings be spread upon the minutes of the Lodge, and that we wear the usual badge of mourning for thirty days.

3d. That a copy of these proceedings be furnished the Athens Banner for publication.

Resolved, That a copy of the above be forwarded to the family of the deceased.

JOHN SIMPKINS,
JAMES E. RANDOLPH } Com
HENRY J. LONG,

A true extract from the Minutes.

P. F. HINTON, Clerk.

DIED,

Died, on the morning of the 10th, FIDELEA JOHNS, daughter of Dr. R. D. Moore, aged 16 years, 3 months and 19 days. "Blessed are the dead, who die in the Lord."

NOTICE.

ALL persons having leather at my tan-yard, are notified that they must call and take it away immediately. If not attended to, it must remain at their risk. J. BANCROFT.

July 13 3t

FOR SALE.

ONE of the best harness horses which has been in market for some time. He is 7 years old, works gently in double or single harness. I have owned him since he was a colt. He has never been injured.

Also, a beautiful Rockaway and harness, never used but very little. Curtains fine enameled leather—cushions covered with black morocco. A good article

Also, an excellent two-horse wagon, never used but a little, and harness. Also, a good second-hand top-buggy and single harness. Enquire of Capt. Dorsey, or Capt. Ewing, or

July 13 AT THIS OFFICE.

MR. MAHONY will resume the exercises of his school, on Monday the 18th instant, for one session of 20 weeks. He will confine himself exclusively to a few paying scholars, males and females.

Terms of tuition for classics,	$40 00
Advanced branches of English,	30 00
Minor branches or rudiments of Eng.	25 00

One-half of the tuition fee to be paid at the entrance, and one dollar from each pupil as a contribution for winter fuel There will be an examination of the pupils at the end of the term, that parents may know their progress. Mr. M. solicits a share of public patronage, and respectfully refers to Mrs. Hamilton, whose husband, Col. Thomas N. Hamilton, had been formerly one of his Trustees, during some years at the Appling Academy, Columbia county.

July 13-1t

GEORGIA, Hart County.—All persons having demands against the estate of Barnabas Barron, late of said county, deceased, will present them in terms of the law. Those indebted, will come forward and settle.

SANDFORD C. BARRON,
One of the Executors.

July 13 6w Printer's fee $6 50

THE HOLDERS OF BONDS against the county of Clarke, NOW DUE, are requested to present them to John Calvin Johnston, County Treasurer.

By order of the Inferior Court.

JOHN CALVIN JOHNSON, Clerk.

July 13—3t

UNIVERSITY HIGH SCHOOL

ATHENS, GEORGIA.

THE Summer term of this School, consisting of 20 weeks, will commence on Wednesday the 13th of July, and end the 7th of December next.

☞ Cadets of the School between 17 and 18 years of age, are specially exempted from Confederate service.

CHARGES.

For board, tuition, washing, Fuel and Lights per term of 20 weeks, One Hundred Dollars *in specie*, or an equivalent in provisions *at specie prices*, or $600 in Confederate currency.

For day scholars, per term, $150 in Confederate currency.

☞ Payments to be made one half on entrance, and one half at the expiration of the first 10 weeks.

For circular, detailing plan of school, address

B. R. CARROLL,
July 6 tf Pres. U. H. S. Athens, Ga.

COWS LOST!

TWO COWS LOST—One a small red cow; the other a clay-ground with dark spots.—The finder will be handsomely rewarded. Enquire at this office. June 29 2t.

TO GARDENERS & FARMERS.

THE army is suffering with Scurvy for the want of vegetables. I am directed to obtain all I can by purchase or otherwise. I will receive daily at my office under the Franklin House, and forward by express. It is hoped that none will omit this their duty to aid in this call of humanity.

By order of Major J. F. CUMMINGS, C. S.

JNO. W. NICHOLSON,
June 29 3t Gen'l Agent C. S.

BLUESTONE! BLUESTONE.—A genuine article, for sale by
june 29 I. M. KENNEY.

BLACK PEPPER, Spice, Brimstone, Epsom Salts, BORAX, Extract Logwood, Soda, by june 29 I. M. KENNEY.

FACTORY THREAD, Country Stripes, Socks, Beeswax, Tallow, Flour, for sale by
june 29 I. M. KENNEY.

WANTED.—Old Bank Notes and Georgia State issues, by I. M. KENNEY.
june 29

NOTICE.—Two months after date, application will be made to the Court of Ordinary of Banks county, for leave to sell the lands belonging to the estate of Robert Allan, late of said county, deceased.

E. J. ALLAN, Adm'x,
May 13 2m Printer's fee $8 50

NOTICE.—Application will be made to the Court of Ordinary of Franklin county, at the first regular term thereof, after the expiration of two months from this date, for leave to sell the negroes belonging to the estate of William N. Swift late of said county, deceased.

YOUNG DAVIS,
SAMUEL KNOX, } Adm's
May 25 2m Printer's fee $8 50

GEORGIA, Franklin County.—Whereas, Martin L. Looney, administrator of Lydia Dortch, deceased, applies for letters of dismission from said estate,

These are, therefore, to cite and admonish all persons concerned, to be and appear at my office on or before the first Monday in September next and show cause, if any they can, why said letters should not be granted the applicant.

Witness my hand and official signature, this March 16th, 1864.

JAMES A. HARRISON, Ordinary.
March 30 6m Printer's fee $9 00

TO BRIDGE BUILDERS.

THE contract for repairing Mitchell's Bridge is not yet taken. The public are cautioned not to cross said bridge as it is unsafe. F. M. McLeroy is authorized to contract for the necessary repairs.

By order of the Inferior Court.

J. C. JOHNSON, Clerk.
June 8, 1864. 4t

The Conservative.

SATURDAY MORNING, JULY 16, 1864.

FOR PRESIDENT:

ABRAHAM LINCOLN,

Of Illinois.

FOR VICE-PRESIDENT:

ANDREW JOHNSON,

Of Tennessee.

Republican Union State Convention.

The Republicans of Kansas, together with all those who indorse the President's Emancipation Proclamation, and who are in favor of an earnest, vigorous and uncompromising prosecution of the war for the suppression of the slave holders' rebellion, the principles enunciated in the platform adopted by the National Republican Union Convention at Baltimore, on the 8th of June, 1864, and who are in favor of the election of Abraham Lincoln and Andrew Johnson for President and Vice-President of the United States, are requested to meet at Topeka, in delegate convention, on Thursday, the 8th day of September, 1864, at 12 o'clock M., for the purpose of placing in nomination candidates for the following offices: A Governor, Lieutenant Governor, Secretary of State, Auditor, Treasurer, Superintendent of Public Instruction, Attorney General, Judge of the Supreme Court, Representative in Congress, and three Presidential Electors for the State.

The ratio of representation will be one delegate for each Representative District. Delegates will be elected in each Representative District, on Saturday, September 3d, 1864.

To prevent the abuse of the proxy system which has been practiced in former State Conventions, the Committee would recommend to the people that the Delegates be instructed not to appoint persons as proxies who reside outside of the District which they are elected to represent.

By order of the Republican State Central Committee.

SIDNEY CLARKE, Ch'n

J. STOTLER, Secretary.

[Republicnn papers in the State please copy.]

PETERSBURG CAPTURED.

An official dispatch received at the Fort last night stated that Grant was in full possession of Petersburg. Sheridan had cut off the rebel invaders and the capture of the entire force was confidently expected.

THE BUSHWHACK HUNT IN MISSOURI; PROGRESS OF THE UNION "RAID."

The troops sent out from this point in pursuit of Thornton's gang of bushwhackers making very commendable progress. We yesterday gave a brief account of the fight at Camden Point where the guerrillas were thoroughly routed by Col. Ford, who afterwards burned the village. It comprised between forty and fifty houses, all of which were burned with the exception of the Female Academy and the house of Col. Hale, the only Union man in the place.

On Thursday pursuit was resumed and the bushwhackers widely dispersed. At Platte City one building was burned on Thursday night and several others yesterday morning. The Union troops were determined to clean out the secesh element, and could not be restrained, but did not molest the property of or person of any loyal man. The following is a list of the buildings burned:

Private houses—W. C. Remnington, Dr. Moore, Dr. Guthrie, Robert Robinson, Mr, Adkins, and Mr. Lykins.

Cabinet Shops—Philip Lutz, M. Brady.

Churches—Methodist, and Presbyterian (both unanimously secesh.)

Four law offices and Dr. Moodie's office.

Two printing presses, including the Platte City *Sentinel*, and the law offices of Thomas Herndon (loyal), and Praxton and Merryman, also loyal men,, besides the Odd Fellows' Lodge.

The clothing and dry goods store of Mr. L. C. Holmes, formerly of this city and to whom we are indebted for this information, was also destroyed, but it contained no goods—the bushwhackers having appropriated his entire stock, on Sunday, valued at $4,000.. Mr. Holmes narrowly escaped with his life from the guerillas, but afterwards recovered several hundred dollars worth of his goods. He states that Cols. Ford and Jennison left Platte City yesterday morning, for Parkville, where they intended to "do so some more." The Colorado boys are rampant and hard to be held in check, but they do not intend to meddle with Union men.

The first building fired at Platte City was the *Sentinel* printing office. The editor and publisher is A. F. Cox, formerly of Weston, where the *Sentinel* was published about a year ago. Cox's Weston office was destroyed by soldiers. Since his residence in Platte City he has been extremely conservative in politics.

When Camden Point was burned, on Wednesday night, two wagon loads of negroes were carried off to Weston. They belonged to a "sympathizer."

The guerillas have been thoroughly routed and are now fleeing through the country in small squads, waylaying travelers, robbing farmers, and committing all sorts of depredations. On Thursday afternoon several farmhouses were visited in the neighborhood of Weston, the guerillas helping themselves to whatever suited their wishes or caprice. The citizens generally are arming to protect their property.

Col. Ford is vigorously pursuing the bushwhackers, and the indications are that secession sympathizers will come in for a share of retaliation. Col. F. is reported to have said that he did not intend to hold any correspondence with superior officers until after he finished his job. What between the bushwhackers and the Union troops the Platte country is likely to come to grief. The former have plundered the loyal citizens without stint or mercy, and if the latter do not now scorch the disloyal, we mistake the temper of the avengers. They will certainly never have a better opportunity.

—Empress Eugenie is out against high bonnets, which she says must come down. She ought to be the last person to wish the fall of crowns.

FROM THE LOWER MISSISSIPPI.

[Correspondence of the Leavenworth Conservative.]

GUNBOAT STATION, ONE MILE BELOW MOUTH OF WHITE RIVER, July 7, 1864.

According to promise I sit down to let you know my whereabouts. We have made very slow progress since leaving Leavenworth, having laid at St. Louis a day and a half, Memphis two and a half, at Helena twelve hours, and by order of the Government to be detained here several days. There is here a small stockade, manned by three companies of the Twelfth Iowa Infantry' and upon whom the rebels made an attack a few days ago, which resulted in the loss of some twenty-five of their number; our forces losing two killed—no wounded. Some five thousand rebels are reported back of here; and last night as I slept on the hurricane deck I distinctly heard cannonading below us on the Arkansas. The gunboats are fighting every day, and we are looking for an attack on this post, and also expect some rough usage on our way up the White river. The river is said to be narrow, and as we have in tow a barge and a ferry boat, loaded with horses, Shelby will probably make an effort to capture us.

Since we have laid in port here, some twenty boats have come in loaded with cavalry and infantry, most of which have departed to places we know not where. There is not so much singing among the boys here as when at home on furlough. They settle down to their work, and expect to get into business. Here grim-visaged war has put on his "wrinkled front;" the dead solitude of the bottom lands shows it; the absence of people along the river, homesteads deserted, and blasted fields, betray too plainly the sad fact.

Our voyage on the way down was of but little interest, passing old, dilapidated dwellings, and still more dilapidated towns. July 5th we arrived at Helena, a small village some eighty miles below Memphis, and about the same distance above here. It is a place of considerable historical interest, having played an important part in this war's battles. The town is surrounded by chains of bluffs, with intervening valleys. An old frame building, the picture of a country printing office, bears the old rebel words, "States Rights *Democrat*"—now pretty well "played out," and a living memento of the folly of the rebels. High and dry on a sand bar opposite Helena, laid a gunboat, still manned by her crew. How she got there and how she will get away from there this summer is a knotty question.

Traveling back a little, I might say that I was in Memphis on the Fourth, and could not help contrasting the celebration with a Fourth of July in Leavenworth. Everything felt dead; a few packs of fire crackers and a few torpedoes in the hands of secesh urchins, was all I could see. There were, however, speeches at night, bnt I could not hear them, being on board the boat. The town is secesh to the core. You can see it in the lowering countenances of the natives.

Refugees, or as the soldiers call them, "refugeesuses," are plenty at military stations. They are principally the poor, ignorant class of whites you see so much in Arkansas, and who say "we uns" and "you uns." I wish I had some news to write you, but we are lying here ignorant of most that is transpiring around us. As soon as we get into duty, I will redeem my promise and send you something for THE CONSERVATIVE, as I shall then be among Kansas troops, I am in good spirits—eat my "sow belly" and "hard tack" with a relish—and am hearty as a buck. Give my respects io the boys. Yours truly,

J. D. GRINNELL.

ALL SORTS.

—There have been 92 dead bodies recovered from the wreck of the train at the scene of the disaster on the Grand Trunk railway, and twelve persons are still missing.

—An afflicted husband was returning from the funeral of his wife, when a friend asked how he was. "Well," he said, pathetically, "I think I feel better for that walk."

—The total number of officers for colored regiments examined by the proper board up to this time, is 2,471. Of these 985 have been rejected and 1,486 recommended.

—The rebel General Winder is reported to be "sick unto death." If Satan don't give him a side-Winder when he claps claws on him, it will be because he knows nothing of his outrages upon Union prisoners.

—The steamer Belvidere sailed from New York a few days since with the following very acceptable supplies for the Army of the Potomac: Four hundred barrels of onions, three hundred barrels of turnips, twenty one barrels of beets, fifty boxes of lemons and from seven to ten thousand heads of cabbage.

BUYING NOMINATIONS.

We find the following in the editorial column of the *Times*:

"How sad it is to reflect that a man cannot, in our country, get a nomination for public office unless he buys it, and cannot be elected without resorting to all manner of dishonorable tricks and expedients!"

No one is better qualified than the owner of the *Times*, Thomas Carney, to speak on the question of political corruption. He has bought everything he ever had Without ability or integrity he has relied entirely upon money for political position.

ALMOST everybody seems to have guerilla on the brain. A band of these fellows were reported within six miles of St. Louis on Tuesday last, whereupon a Capt. Clifford went in pursuit with a squad of cavalry and captured twelve men. When they were brought into St. Louis they were proved to be simple minded farmers and dairymen, thoroughly loyal and patriotic. One of the unfortunates, while attempting to escape from the soldiers, was shot and killed.

St. Louis, July 15.

The steamboats Welcome, Sunshine, Glasgow, Cherokee, Dix and Northener were burned at the levee this morning. Loss on boats and cargoes will foot up half a million dollars. Origin of fire not known.

BY TELEGRAPH.

EVENING REPORT.

New York, July 14.

The Commercial says prominent banking houses in Wall street have received a dispatch from their Washington branches this morning, which states that Grant's forces have occupied Petersburg. We have received nothing confirmatory of this statement.

The Commercial also says a private dispatch to a Wall street banker states that Sheridan with his entire cavalry force has been dispatched to intercept the rebel raiders, and has reached Hanover C. H.

New York, July 14.

A Washington dispatch to the Philadelphia Inquirer, dated the 14th, 3 p. m., says the enemy began their retreat across the Potomac at about 2 o'clock last night. They had held Rockville, about five miles from the Potomac, as a base. This morning our forces started in pursuit, and we may yet be able to intercept their retreat. They are carrying their plunder, as well as impressed citizens, with them. We made considerable captures.

Baltimore, July 14.

When Franklin was captured he was seated in the car by the side of a wounded Lieutenant Colonel, when a rebel officer came up and asked the Colonel if he was Franklin; the officer replied that he was not. The rebel then asked Franklin, who disclosed himself, feeling convinced that he had been pointed out by one of the passengers. In a few moments Gilmore came in and told Franklin that he must consider himself as his prisoner. The General was then put in a carriage and taken to Reistertown, where they stopped for the night. The General feigned sickness and sleep until his guards were asleep; he then made the best of his way, as near as he could, in the direction of the city for three-quarters of an hour, when being broken down by fatigue he crept into a thick wood, and remained the balance of the night and all next day, frequently seeing rebels scouting for him. About sunset, being nearly famished, he ventured out, and shortly met some men, who proved to be friends, one of whom took him to his home, and finally provided means for the General to reach the city.

Baltimore, July 14.

The Washington Chronicle of this morning states that the private papers of Mr. Blair, composed of correspondence with Henry Clay, Andrew Jackson, and other men of mark, were not destroyed, and his plate had been transferred to the residence of Mr. Wilson, with a note to him by Gen. Breckinridge, while the furniture and other personal effects of Marshall Bonnifant were destroyed. A large quantity of hay and wood is saved from the torch. The cattle, horses, etc., of the residents were carried off. The dead were left undressed, and the badly wounded uncared for. About seventy of the latter were left at the house of F. P. Blair.

It is stated that the bulk of the rebel force commenced retreating at 11 o'clock, a. m. The residence of Hon. Montgomery Blair was destroyed with all its contents,, causing a heavy loss.

New York, July 15.

A special to the World from Washington, 14th, says the rebel columns have continued their retreat toward the Upper Potomac fords since their abandoment of the position held in front of Washington, and some say their force is reported as having crossed into Virginia, though indications this morning were that the main army seemed disposed to make a stand between Rockville and Poolesville, either accept battle or cover the crossing of their vast quantities of supplies. Our forces are in close pursuit.

The military authorities have information that the enemy intended on Monday to attack the weakest point in our lincs in large forces but abandoned it on unexpectedly finding veteran troops.

The rebel General Holmes was severely wounded at the battle of Monocacy.

New York, July 15.

A Washington special details information received in Washington concerning the invasion, from which it appears that Halleck, on the 5th, received an intercepted letter from a rebel Colonel, saying Ewell's corps with Hampton's cavalry, making over 50,000, were ordered to march upon Harper's Ferry. My own belief is we will go directly to Washington.

Washington was to be attacked Saturday night, but delayed till Monday. when Early received such information as to make him abandon the attempt causing great dissatisfaction among subordinate officers and men, who believed everything entirely safe.

Military men estimated the rebels at 30,000. A Union scout avowed to Secretary Stanton that he slept the night before in Longstreet's camp, and his force was encamped near Manassas Junction.

The Washington Star of yesterday says our pursuing force were in Montgomery county, Md., near Yalto Cross Roads, the rebels crossing the Potomac with their main force opposite Poolesville.

Washington, July 14.

There are probably to-night no rebels in Maryland. This morning their rear guard was at Rockville and sufficient time elapsed to enable them safely to recross the Potomac. Our treops doubtless have reached the ferry by this time, and may have been in season to attack the enemy while crossing, but of this nothing is known.

The fisst intimation the rebels received of the presence of veteran troops, was given them on Monday evening by a charge of part of the 6th corps at dark. Their wagon trains were starfed back in great haste, citizens reporting drivers lashing their teams, and making every effort to get out of the way of of the retreating columns. Their badly wounded was left at houses along the line of retreat. Many of them were abandoned on the field. From facts in our possession there is no doubt that their casualties greatly exceed ours. There is little doubt that had the enemy attacked our defences previous to Monday night, they could have been taken with comparative ease.

Washington, July 14.

Details received last night announce Sherman's army within six miles of Atlanta. Up to 10 o'clock this a. m., nothing has been ascertained.

The rebels recrossed the Potomac, and it was thought had sent over most of their plunder.

An extra says information accumulated strengthens the conclusion that the rebel force was 35,000 strong, all armed, and that they entered Maryland with thirty-four pieces of cannon. Many of their troaps were dismounted cavalry.

Cannonading was heard in the neighborhood of Seneca early this morning. Our cavalry have been harrassing and annoying the rebels. There was no definite result of our operations yet been received other than a number of prisoners have been captured. Nothing known here of the occupation of Petersburg by Grant. Nor have we any intelligence as to the intention of Gen. Sheridan.

New York, July 15.

The latest news nws from Sherman is as follows:

Chattanooga, July 1.—The rebels burned Chattanooga railrod and common road bridges across the Cattahoochee river yesterday. Sherman cossed above and below the bridges, and effeted a secure lodgment on the south bank. The rebels have abandoned their strong fortfications on Chattahoochee Heights, beirg again effectually flanked. Do not know in what direction they have gone. Our communications are in a favorable condition.

The latest news frcn Petersburg is to Wednesday morning, when heavy skirmishing was going on.

Official dispatches from the rebel General Jones to the 4th, report the repulse of the Federal forces near Charleston, with a loss of six hundred men. He confirms the capture of two rebel guns, but states that the rebel picket line is established—the Federals hastily falling back. Monitors and gunboats were firing on the rebel lines heavily.

Louisville, July 14.

The Nashville Union says dispatches had been received there stating that Sherman had crossed the Chattahoochee, and his advance on Tuesdy last was within three miles of Atlanta.

A passenger by the Mollie Able, leaving New Orleans on the 7th, states that they were detained thereby six hours, towing the gunboat Mound City to White river. The gunboat Benton was waiting for a steamer to tow her to the same point. The two boats had been ordered to White river to dislodge the rebel batteries at the Cut Off. All quiet along the river. The 19th army corps was embarking on steamers. Their destination was supposed to be Fort Monroe.

Fortress Monroe, July 14.

The steam-tug Navy, left Cherrystone, yesterday noon, for this place, and was due here at 3 o'clock this same day. She has not been heard from up to four o'clock this afternoon. There are suspicious that she has been captured and swamped or disabled.

Washington July 14.

Reports from the Army of the Potomac say the rebels have maneuvred their troops in a manner which seem to augur an attack on our rear. From last accounts Hill's corps was massing around our left with the intention, say military men, of getting in our rear.

Tuesday morning the rebels made a demonstration on Jerusalem road, apparently for the purpose of attacking our troops, but being confronted by ample force, changed their design.

Interesting Account of Things in the Gold Regions.

[Correspondence of the St. Joe Herald.]

VIRGINIA CITY, IDAHO TERRITORY, June 14th, 1863.

I arrived here the fifth day of this month, and find the miners that have claims all doing well; but the mining district is very limited, and all the claims that are considered good are taken up and the emigrants as they arrive here cannot get any unless they buy them, and that at ruinous rates. Those who can get work by the day do so, those that can't, and have means skedaddle for the States again. You may look for a heavy stampede from here this fall.

The party that left here this spring to prospect the Yellow Stone country have nearly all returned disappointed enough; found no mines to pay, and still worse, the Indians stole all their ponies and they had to foot it back to Virginia—some two or three hundred miles. There has been no new discoveries made near here recently.

There has been, and is still, quite an excitement about a discovery recently made, called Kurthey Mines, some place up in the British possessions, about five hundred miles from the United States line. A good many have already left here for those mines, and more are leaving daily.

You can go by wagons from here to within two hundred miles of the mines; then you have to pack the balance of the way; but those who, have returned from there say, with a little work a good road can be opened through to the new discovery. I have seen some of the gold. It is very fine and the mines are said to be extensive. All that I have seen from there have returned here to sell what interest they have in this section and return immediately.

Flour in those mines is worth one dollar per pound, bacon 37c per pound; sugar and coffee the same; and all kinds of goods in proportion, because they have to be packed so far; but there is already thousands of goods here, and the big trains have not yet begun to arrive. Coffee here is selling from forty-five to fifty cents by the sack.

Look out for some broken merchants this fall from these parts. No buildings here to put goods in; everything is full. They charge $5 a ton per month for storage and ten per cent per. month for money advanced on goods. Every merchant that has goods coming in here will be compelled to build him a house, for if he could rent one fit to put a few goods in, it would cost from $200 to $500 per month, which would soon take all the goods. I am building me a good store 24x75, all lathed and plastered. I expect to stay here two or three years and possibly longer: in fact I will be compelled to. if I wish to sell my goods so as to save myself. I think there are goods enough here and on the road to last this country for the next three years, with the exception of a few certain articles.—Cattle, mules and wagons of all kinds are low here. I saw a good new Chicago wagon sold yesterday at auction for forty dollars.

The Guerillas Around Us.

[From the St. Joe Herald.]

After all that has been said, written, and published concerning the proximity of guerillas, it is now perfectly evident that the wolf is at our doors. Scouts have been sent out in all directions, and their reports agree perfectly in all essential particulars. One Captain saw the body of men which entered Taos last Sunday. He says they numbered thirty-three. As villainous a gang of scoundrels never before entered county. They are thieves and murderers. They are intent upon getting horses, provisions and greenbacks, and we think they are not extremely particular as to the mode of operating, or the parties operated upon.

The Pawpaws in Platte county were very generally sworn into the rebel service on the arrival of J. C. Calhoun Thornton with his ragged brigands and thieves, Captain Johnson is unquestionably a traitor, and many of his men are of the same stripe. When Capt. Johnson's men were sworn in, and the outward forms of traitor-making were through with, they went to their tents, unpacked their trunks, took out new Confederate uniforms, put them on, and came into the streets in full feather. These devils have had these uniforms on hand and in waiting for this very event. It is all useless for these men to assert that they were compelled to enlist or die. That is all pure gammon. There were troops and citizens enough in Platte City and vicinity to have made Thornton's ragamuffins bite the dust; but not a man lifted a finger there toward meeting them, except to embrace them as friends. The guns, ammunition, and other stores in possession of the Pawpaws were cheerfully turned over to the bushwhackers. May God forgive us if we do not forever hereafter fight to the utmost of our ability against allowing men, of known disloyalty, or patriotism which is not above a breath of suspicion, to be armed in our midst.

We understand that Thornton advised his new recruits to kill every Union man they met. He told them they "must learn to do this work." Such advice is quite generally followed by those who engage in the service of the rebels. We expect to hear that the very men who clothed their traitorous carcasses in rebel uniform in Platte City, are in Platte county attending to their usual avocations, after Thornton leaves, swearing that they have always been good Union men, but in favor of the Constitution and laws.

Scouts report that many guerillas have gone up into Gentry, and the Northern counties. We expect soon to hear of trouble up there. They will obtain few recruits in that portion of Missouri, for the rebels have been driven out there, till a real, live sympathizer is a curiosity.

This Morning's Advertisements.

HEADQUARTERS PROVOST MARSHAL, NORTHERN DISTRICT OF KANSAS, LEAVENWORTH CITY, July 12, 1864.

In pursuance of Circular No. 24, War Department, Provost Marshal General's Office, June 25th, 1864, public notice is hereby given, that copies of the Enrollment lists of this District will be open for the examination of the public, at all proper hours, and any person enrolled may appear before the Board of Enrollment and claim to have a name stricken off the list, if he can show to the satisfaction of the Board that the person named is not properly enrolled on account of: 1st, Alienage. 2d, Non-residence. 3d, Over age. 4th, Permanent Physical Disability of such degree as to render the person not a proper subject for enrollment under the law and regulations.

Civil Officers, Clergymen and all other prominent citizens are invited to appear at all times before the Board to point out errors in the lists and to give such information in their posession as may aid in the correction and revision thereof.

J. McCAHON

Capt. and Pro. Mar. North'n Dis't Kan., and Pres't Board of Enrollment

july13d&w3t

General Order No. 9.

HEAD QUARTERS 1ST BRIGADE DISTRICT, Leavenworth, July 13th 1864.

I. The following companies of Kansas State Militia are hereby ordered into active service for the term of fifteen days: Company C of the 19th Regiment; Company D of the 1st Regiment; Company C of the 7th Regiment.

II. Colonels of Regiments, or officers commanding regiments will be held responsible for the strict enforcement of this order.

III. Guard House and camp is hereby established at the Third ward or South Leavenworth school house. Details of officers for duty will be made by Col. M. S. Grant Commanding Post.

By order of PETER McFARLAND, Col. Com. 1st Brig. Dist.

A. HASTINGS, A. A. Gen. jul4 tf

GENERAL ORDER NO. 8.

HEADQUARTERS 1ST BRIGADE DISTRICT, LEAVENWORTH, July 11th, 1864.

I. General S. A. Drake having accepted a Commission in the 17th Kansas Regiment, has resigned the command of this Brigade District.

II. As ranking Colonel I hereby assume command. Commanders of Regiments, Battalions and Detachments will report to me at these Headquarters until further orders.

PETER McFARLAND, Col. Commanding 1st Brigade.

A. HASTINGS, A. A. Gen.

Cavalry Horses Wanted.

HORSES FOR CAVALRY service will be purchased in Open Market at

Fort Leavenworth, Kas.,

Until Further Notice,

In lots of not less than eight, and for which $150 00 PER HEAD will be paid. Payment made on delivery and acceptance of horses. Horses MUST BE SOUND, active, well-formed, not under fifteen hands high, not more than NINE nor less than FIVE years old, and subject to ridgid inspection.

M. H. INSLEY, Capt. and Chief Q. M. Dep't. of Kansas

july 12d&wtf

Proposals for Indian Supplies.

OFFICE SUPERINTENDENT INDIAN AFFAIRS, SOUTHERN SUPERINTENDENCY, LEAVENWORTH, Ks., July 11th, 1864.

SEALED PROPOSALS, endorsed "Proposals for Indian Supplies," to be delivered at Fort Smith, Arkansas, at the Cherokee Agency, Cherokee Nation, Ohio City, and Neosho Falls, Kansas, will be received at this office ... 12 o'clock M. Monday, the 25th day of July next, for furnishing in such quantities, and at such time or times, during the months of August, September, October, November, and December, 1864, and January, Februray, and March, 1865, as may be required or ordered by me, or the Agent or Commissary at each of the above named points, may require and direct, the following articles:

10,000 Sacks Superfine Flour, put up in good Osnaburg Sacks.
20,000 Bushels Shelled Corn, put up in New Strong Gunny sacks.
500 Head of good Beef Cattle, none to weigh less than 900 pounds.

The above articles are to be delivered at Fort Smith and the Cherokee Agency, and the following at points named in Kansas, viz:

1,000 Sacks Superfine Flour.
2,000 Bushels Corn in the Ear
150 Head of Beef Cattle, none to weigh less than 900 pounds, and 20 Parrels Salt

All the aforesaid articles are subject to inspection and weight at the place of delivery. It is to be understood that the right will be reserved to require a larger or less quantity of any of the articles named than that specified in the above schedule, and to reject any or all bids offered, and that none from persons who have failed to comply with the requirements of a previous contract with the United States, will be considered.

The right will also be reserved to terminate the contract at any time, as far as Kansas is concerned, on the removal of the Indians to their homes.

Bidders must be present at the opening of their bids and must have the guarantee of at least two responsible parties for the fulfillment of the contract, if awarded.

Deliveries will commence upon notification of award of the contract.

Bonds will be required in the amount of the bid, for the faithful performance of the contract, with two or more sureties, whose sufficiency must be certified by a United States Judge or District Attorney.

Bids will be considered for all the supplies required by this advertisement, or for the points named in Kansas, and for those at Fort Smith and the Cherokee Agency, separately.

Proposals must be in Duplicate, and none will be considered except from loyal persons, and that do not strictly conform, in all particulars, to the terms and directions of this advertisement.

W. G. COFFIN, Superintendent Indian Affairs, Southern Superintendency.

july12dtd

ATTENTION VOLUNTEERS!

I AM now Recruiting a Company for the One Hundred Days Regiment, recently called for by his Excellency Governor Carney.

The time for raising the Company is limited; it is therefore necessary that you enlist at once. The time of service is short, and every true patriotic citizen in favor of protecting the border and their homes and property can find time to turnout and enlist at once for 100 days. You will find me at all hours of the day at my office, corner of Shawnee and Main street, up-stairs. Entrance on Shawnee street.

EBENEZER N. O. CLOUGH.

jy9d20d.

200 TEAMS WANTED!

TO haul hay to Fort Leavenworth. Highest prices will be paid. Apply to William Tholen, at THE CONSERVATIVE Office, or the undersigned at Brown's Livery Stable. HENRY STILL.

50 Mowing Machines Wanted!

TO cut hay upon the Delaware Reservation. Apply as above to Still or Tholen.

WE will pay full market price for good Hay, delivered at the Fort, and contract with parties for the delivery in lots of not less than ten tons.

H. STILL, W. THOLEN.

july6d&wtf

Attention Merchants and Dealers.

YOUR attention is specially directed to General Curtis' General Order, No. 29; published this morning. The police force have stringent orders from me to watch closely and report every violation of said orders. Persons detected in violation of the same will at once be turned over to the military authorities.

JAMES L. McDOWELL, Mayor.

je23dtf

DAILY CAROLINA WATCHMAN.

VOL. 1 SALISBURY, N. C., JULY 20, 1864. NO. 55

TELEGRAPHIC.

REPORTS OF THE PRESS ASSOCIATION.

Entered according to act of Congress in the year 1863, by J. S. Thrasher, in the Clerk's office of the District Court of the Confederate States for the Northern District of Georgia.

DEATH OF GENERAL GRANT?

Petersburg, July 19.

Yankee flag in fleet on James River has been at half mast for two days. Yankee pickets say Grant was wounded, and died from the effects of amputation.

To go to Salisbury.—A large number of a particular class of prisoners confined in Castle Thunder are to be forwarded to Salisbury, North Carolina, in a few days, as soon as a proper classification of them can be made. This exodus will relieve the prison of several hundred inmates, and leave more food for the consumption of the city's defenders and the citizens.—*Rich. Examiner.*

NOTICE.

IN answer to numerous applications for admission to my school from persons at a distance, I will just say, that for one barrel of flour and twenty pounds of bacon per month, (furnished monthly in advance,) I will board, instruct in the highest branches, and furnish with all needful books, stationary, washing, fuel, and lights, any boy or girl, in the best manner that I am able. EDWARD PAYSON HALL.

July 2, 1864. dtf41

500 BUSHELS CORN.

WE will purchase and pay for in New Issue or Specie.

G. V. ANCKER & CO.

July 7, 1864. tf44

Commission and Brokerage Office.

THE subscribers keep constantly for sale, Farm and House Negroes, among which may be found valuable Mechanics.

We will devote particular attention to disposing of and buying NEGROES, STOCKS, BONDS AND REAL ESTATE.

☞ Liberal Cash advances made.

G. V. ANCKER & CO.

Salisbury, N.C., June 27, 1864. dtf35

Wanted to Purchase.

$20,000 *N. Carolina Bank Notes.*
$20,000 *Greensboro Mutual Insurance Notes.*

G. V. ANCKER & CO.

july 9. tfd46

To Candidates

AND OTHERS DESIRING A PUFF—Bruner is in the shade beside our fine *Orono Smoking Tobacco.*

15 Boxes and 10 Barrels for sale.
7 Boxes Cigars.
10 " Fine Chewing Tobacco. Wholesale or retail.

WM. E. EDWARDS & CO.

Salisbury, July 13. dtf50

New Auction and Commission STORE.

W. H. & R. S. TUCKER and W. R. ANDREWS have this day associated themselves together under the name and style of

TUCKER, ANDREWS & CO.,

for the purpose of conducting a general Auction and Commission business. All business entrusted to them will meet with promptness and dispatch.

TUCKER, ANDREWS & CO.

Raleigh, June 22d, 1864. 3wd34

NORTH CAROLINA, Davie County. } In Equity.

James M. Ijams,
vs.
Philip C. Booe and Denton Ijams.

WHEREAS, affidavit has been made before me, that Philip C. Booe, one of the defendants in the aforesaid suit, is not an inhabitant of this State: Notice is hereby given to the said Philip C. Booe, to appear at the next Court of Equity to be held for the County of Davie, at the Court House in Mocksville on the 4th Monday in August next, and plead answer or demur, to complainant's bill, or the same will be taken pro confesso, and the cause for hearing ex parte, as to him.

Witness, L. Bingham, Clerk and Master of said Court, at Office, the 29th day of June, A. D. 1864.

6w8pradv$17 L. BINGHAM, CME.

Pigs Wanted.

THE undersigned wishes to purchase a few well grown Pigs, suitable for fattening this Fall, for which he will pay in coin. Apply soon. J. B. BEARD, Agent.

July 12th, 1864. 4tw8

STRAY HOGS.

STRAYED from my premises about two weeks ago, three black and white spotted hogs, about 50 lbs. weight, each. Mark, a slit in one ear and a hole in the other. They were bought of Mr. Gaskey, near this place. A suitable reward will be paid for their recovery. Apply to JAMES B. BEARD.

June 9, 1864. 5tw8

WEIGHTS AND MEASEURS.

BUSHELS.	POUNDS.
Wheat,	60
Shelled Corn,	56
Corn in the ear,	70
Peas,	60
Rye,	56
Oats,	32
Barley,	47
Irish Potatoes,	60
Sweet Potatoes,	55
White Beans,	60
Castor Beans,	46
Clover Seed,	60
Timothy Seed,	45
Flax Seed,	56
Hemp Seed,	44
Blue Grass Seed,	44
Buckwheat,	52
Dried Peaches,	38
Dried Apples,	24
Onions,	57
Salt,	50
Stone Coal,	80
Malt,	38
Bran,	20
Turnips,	55
Plastering Hair,	8
Unslacked Lime,	80
Corn Meal,	48
Fine Salt,	55
Ground Peas,	24

A box 24 by 16 inches, 22 deep, contains one barrel.
A box 16 by 16½ inches, 8 deep, contains one bushel.
A box 8 by 8¼ inches, 8 deep, contains 1 peck.
A box 4 by 4 inches, 4½ deep contains ½ gallon.
A box 4 by 4 inches, 2½ deep contains 1 quart.
Ten gallons Pickled Onions, 83 pounds.
Ten gallons Sour Krout 81 pounds

FOR SALE.

500 Bunches Cotton Yarn,
100 Sacks Virginia Coast Salt.
300 Gallons Brandy.

G. V. ANCKER & CO.

july 9. tfd46

Corn! Corn! Wanted.

I WILL exchange one bushel salt for two bushels corn. MICHAEL BROWN.

Salisbury, July 4, 1864. 43dtf

$300 REWARD.

I WILL PAY the above reward of three hundred dollars for the apprehension or confinement in Jail either North Carolina or Virginia, my negro boy HENRY, so that I can get him. Said boy is 23 years old, was raised in Orange county Virginia, and has been in Richmond for the last four years with Mr. Davis; he is 5 feet 9 or 10 inches high, dark mulatto, complains of rheumatism in both legs and arms, spare made. Said boy left my plantation in Davie county, North Carolina on 19th inst., and may be trying to make his way back to Virginia.

T. N. COOPER.

Eagle Mills, Iredell Co., N. C.

June 25, 1864—d33&w4tf.

☞ Daily Confederate, Raleigh, copy ten times and send bill to this office,

FOR SALE AT AUCTION!

25000 LBS. DAMAGED HAY.—WILL be sold at public auction, in the town of Salisbury, N.C., at or near the Government Hay lot, on the 1st Thursday (4th day) of next August, twenty-five thousand pounds (more or less) damaged Hay. This Hay is worth the attention of farmers and those having stock—this most of it can be put to some use.

J. M. GOODMAN,
Capt. & A. Q. M.

Salisbury, July 4, 1864. 5wd&w4t

Piedmont Springs,

BURKE COUNTY N. C.

THESE springs will be open for the reception of visitors on the 1st of July. The Company have obtained the services of Capt E Barton, a gentleman well calculated to take charge of the House.

During the month of July, a good and comfortable four horse stage will leave Morganton on Tuesday, Thursday and Friday; August and September, it will leave Morganton daily, so that passengers leaving Salisbury in the morning, will arrive at the Springs the same afternoon.

Board $13 per day by the month; $15 per day by the week, and $20 per day less than a week.

E. BARTON, Proprietor.

June 25, 1864. w2m7.

Enrolling Office, Rowan County,

Salisbury, N.C., July 8, 1864.

All persons exempted at the last enrollment in this county, (except those exempted by the Board of Surgeons) will appear at this Office without delay, that certificates of exemption, under the new form, may be given them. All other certificates of exemption are hereby declared of no effect.

The Board for investigating applications for detail and exemption will meet, until further notice, on Thursday and Friday of every week. All persons whose applications have not been investigated, will be expected to attend on those days. JNO. K. HOYT,

july 9:1w1d46] Lieut, & E. Officer.

FOR SALE.

150 lbs. English refined Borax. Also, an assorted lot of Homespun Cloth, striped and checked.

J. M. JOHNSON,
Mocksville, N. C.

June 22.—6td31.

OFFICE C. S. ORD. WORKS,

Salisbury, N.C., July 5, 1864.

WANTED to hire, a Watchman for these Works. A disabled soldier prefered, to whom liberal wages will be paid. Apply at once to A. G. BRENIZER,
Capt. Art. Com'ding.

July 8. 6td45

Olin High School,

IREDELL CO., N. C.

THE Fall Session will begin on Monday the 18th of July, 1864, and continue twenty weeks.

Tuition per Session. In the Primary studies $40.00; in the higher English $60.00; Ancient and Modern Languages $10.00; Music on Piano $45.00.

Board per session $375 in new issue; or $8 00 per month if paid in provisions at old prices.

The two departments, Male and Female, are kept entirely distinct and separate. Miss Maggie Tucker has charge of the Female School. Miss Rosinda Daughtry, Teacher of Music.

For further information address the undersigned: S. MILTON FROST.

July 7th, 1864. 5td45pd

FOR SALE.

1 Barrel refined Sugar,
1 " Brown do
70 Kegs Nails, 4, 6, 8, 10 and 12,
2 Kegs Soda,
Cast Steel,
Iron and Shovel moles,
Refined Borax,
Writing Paper,
Rifle Powder,
Spun Cotton Nos. 8, 9, 10, 11, 12,
Salt. MICHAEL BROWN.

Salisbury, June 29th, 1864. tfd37

CALICOES! CALICOES!!

ANOTHER supply of Calicoes just received and for sale. MICHAEL BROWN.

Salisbury, July 4, 1864. 43 dtf

OFFICE W. N. C. RAILROAD,

Statesville, N.C., July 7th, 1864.

Notice to Stockholders:

This Company will make returns of all the Stock and pay the Confederate Tax on same.

By order of the Board,
R. F. SIMONTON,

July 7-12td45 Treasurer.

TOBACCO, TOBACCO.
150 BOXES.

JUST RECEIVED ON CONSIGNMENT and for sale, 150 Boxes, Manufactured Chewing and Smoking Tobacco.

MICHAEL BROWN.

Salisbury, April 25, 1864. tf49

PROSPECTUS OF "THE AGE,"

A SOUTHERN MONTHLY MAGAZINE.

The undersigned has commenced in the City of Richmond the publication of a Monthly Magazine, under the above title.

It will present to its readers, selections from the best European Periodicals, of Literary and Scientific articles, of Novels and Sketches, which, having already received the imprimature of an enlightened taste, cannot but prove acceptable to the Southern public. The effort will be made to keep the readers of the Magazine as nearly as possible abreast of the literary progress of the age. Arrangements have been made which, it is hoped, will enable the proprietors to secure this end.

The Magazine will also present original articles from our best writers, in all departments, and a special aim of the proprietors of this periodical will be to foster Southern authorship by offering an adequate and remunerative field for its exercise. They will not, however, under the plea of this design, encourage, by reproduction in its columns, that class of compositions which create a vivid and unhealthy taste, to be stated only by that hybrid literature which Yankee ingenuity has contrived, under the name of sensational romance.

The Industrial Resources and the Educational Interest of the Confederacy—the twin foundations of true independence—will receive the important share of attention they deserve. In the developement of these questions, its object will be to make a practical application of the doctrine of States Rights to the policy of the country. It will endeavor to explain the mission of the Confederacy, which is to demonstrate liberty regulated by law, to exhibit a system of States, each supreme within its foundation, and only bound by a voluntary alienation of powers. It will vindicate those elements of National Independence, which are secured by a high standard of intelligence and refinement, by accumulated capital, varied industry and by abundant facilities of intercommunication. It will promote the adoption of all those measures in which the Confederate States are now deficient. And, whilst the Constitution of the Confederate States forbids the General Government to organize and operate enterprizes of a nature calculated to attain these results, the projectors will consider it their duty to urge upon the States the developement of interests so indispensable to the national welfare. It is thus that, through the aggregate ability of the separate States, the power of the Confederate States will be made manifest. It is thus that the collision of sectional interest and the oppression of a common head will be avoided.

The various departments of literature to which the Magazine will be devoted, may be named as follows:

1. Essays, original and selected, political literary and scientific, and biographical sketches.
2. Novels, Tales and Sketches, original and selected.
3. Reviews of Books.
4. Educational Essays and News.
5. Notices of the progress of Science and Art.

In the fourth section, it is the design to afford to Teachers information needed in their profession, and a field for the interchange of ideas on that subject, to which end, their assistance and collaboration is invited. Southern School Books will be noticed and reviewed; and the Southern system of Education as opposed to New England empiricism and practicalism, dupheld, developed and defended.

Terms—Each number $1.50. For three months $4. For six months $8.

The trade will be supplied by GEORGE L. BIRGOODS, 161 Main Street.

ERNEST LAGARDE & CO.,
Proprietors.

Wm. M. Burwell, Chief Editor.
Ernest Lagarde, Associate Editor.

January 1, 1864.

THE Southern Literary Messenger

FOR 1864.

This long established and well-known Journal of Literature having been recently purchased by the subscribers, will, in future, be conducted exclusively under their control. In all its departments, both business and editorial, the Messenger will be under the management of an entirely new regime, and the Proprietors are sanguine of success in the future, which the Magazine has never yet realized, if their friends and the public shall yield them a support worthy of so important an enterprise, looking to the advancement of the highest literary interest of the Confederacy.

Argument or appeal in behalf of the importance of an elevated literature to our country, the absence of which has hitherto made us a by-word of reproach among the older nations, and even now militates against our interests abroad, need not be addressed to those whom this circular is designed to reach.

But to the attainment of this great end, something more is necessary than mere verbal expressions of sympathy and encouragement.— The friends of Southern Literature must foster the efforts of our literary men to secure for us a worthy position in the world of letters.

We design the Messenger to be an enterprise worthy of support of all classes of our people. We shall aim chiefly to secure for our pages the productions of the highest order of genius and scholarship, and at the same time such articles as will contribute to the instruction and amusement of the public at large. To this end we shall give our attention to and solicit contributions from Southern writers in all the departments of Literature. Poetry, Romance, Review, Criticism, in short, every subject whose prominence is sufficient to entitle it to notice will have its due share of attention.

We earnestly solicit the assistance of our friends throughout the Confederacy in the enlargement of our subscription list, which must be increased to enable us to meet the heavy pecuniary outlay to which we shall be subject.

Terms, $12 for twelve months, $8 for six months. This increase will not affect those who subcribed before the 1st of March. Orders must be accompanied with the money.

Mr. George C. Wedderburn, formerly of New Orleans, now of this city, will control the business interests of the Messenger, and Mr. Frank H. Alfriend, of this city, will direct its editorial management. Communications connected with the literary conduct of the Messenger will be directed to the editor; other communications should be directed to the Proprietors.

WEDDERBURN & ALFRIEND,

June 10, '64. Richmond, Va.

GOVERNMENT OF NORTH CAROLINA.

His Excellency, Zebulon B. Vance, Buncombe, Governor.
Col David A Barnes, Northampton, Aid.
do George Little, Wake, do
Richard H Battle, Jr, Anson, Private Secretary.
Dr Edward Warren, Chowan, Surgeon Gen'l.
John P H Russ, Wake, Secretary of State.
Jonathan Worth, Randolph, Public Treasurer.
Curtis H Brogden, Wayne, Comptroler.
Samuel F Phillps Orange, Auditor.
Oliver H Perry, Wake, State Librarian.
Major General R C Gatlin, Lenoir, Adjutant General.
Major William B Gulick, Beaufort, Paymaster.
Major John Devereux, Wake, Quartermaster.
Major Thomas D Hogg, Wake. Commissary and Ordnance Officer.
Major James Sloan, Guilford, Quartermaster.
Major Henry A Dowd, Edgecombe, do
Major James H Foote, Ass't Adjt Gen, (Roll of Honor.)
Major William A Graham, Jr., Ass't Adjt General.
Lieut Josiah Collins, Washington county, Ordnance Department.
Lieut John B Neathery, Wake, Ass't Adjt General.
Lieut Thomas White, Franklin, Ass't Quartermaster.
Lieut Isaac W Garrett, Edgecombe, Ass't Quartermaster.
Lieut Thaddeus McGee, Wake, Ass't Commissary.
Lieut Charles H Thompson, Wake, Ass't Commissary.

JUDICIAL.

Supreme Court—Richmond M Pearson, Yadkin, Chief Justice,—Wm H Battle, Orange, and Mathias E Manly, of Craven, Judges; Sion H Rogers, Wake, Attorney General; Hamilton C Jones, Rowan, Reporter; Edmund B Freeman, Clerk. [Meets in the city of Raleigh second Monday in June each year. The Morganton term has been discontinued]

Superior Courts—Judges—Edwin G Reade, Person, Romulus M Saunders, Wake; Robert R Heath, Chowan; Robt S French, Robeson; James W Osborne, Mecklenburg; George Howard, Wilson; Robert B Gilliam, Granville; Wm M Shipp, Henderson.

Solicitors—1st Circuit, Jesse J Yeates, Hartford; 2nd, Charles C Clark, Craven; 3rd, Sion H Rogers, Wake, Attorney General; 4th, Thomas Settle, Rockingham; 5th, Ralph Buxton, Cumberland; 6th, Robert F Armfield, Yadkin; 7th, Wm P Bynum; 8th, Augustus S Merrimon, Buncombe.

Council of State—F B Satterthwaite, Pitt; Robert P Dick, Guilford; Dr James Galloway, Wilkes; L Eldredge, Johnston; J R Hargrave, Anson; Jesse R Stubbs, Martin.

Literary Board.—His Excellency, Governor Vance President *Ex Officio*, Rev Wm E Pell, Wake, and Professor Richard Sterling, Guilford; Dr Wm Sloan, of Gaston; Richard H Battle, Jr, Secretary.

Board Internal Improvements—His Excellency, Gov Vance, President, *Ex Officio*, Wm Eaton, Jr, of Warren, J H Flanner, of New Hanover, and Montford McGehee. Richard H Battle, Jr, Secretary.

Commissioners of Sinking Fund.—Hon Thomas Ruffin, Alamance, Hon Weldon N Edwards, Warren, and Hon David L Swain, Orange.

The University of North Carolina is at Chapel Hill. Hon David L Swain, President. Rev Calvin H Wiley is Superintendent of the Common Schools of the State.

Willie J Palmer, A M, is Principal of the N C Institution for the Deaf, Dumb and the Blind at Raleigh.

Dr Edward C Fisher is Superintendent of the Insane Asylum.

CONFEDERATE STATES GOVERNMENT.

LOCATED AT RICHMOND, VA.

The Executive:

Hon. Jeff. Davis, of Miss, President.
Hon. A. H. Stephens, of Ga., Vice-President.

The Cabinet:

J P Benjamin, of La., Secretary of State.
C G Memminger, of S C., Sec'y of Treasury.
Jas A Seddon, of Va., Sec'y of War.
S R Mallory, of Fla., Sec'y of the Navy.
Hon Geo Davis, of N C., Attorney General.
John H Reagan, of Texas, Postmaster Gen'rl.

Heads of Bureaus.

Rufus R Rhodes, Commissioner of Patents.
G E W Nelson, Supt of Public Printing.
Gen Sam Cooper, Adj't and Inspector Gen.
John S Preston, Chief of Bureau of Conscription.
Brig-Gen A R Lawton, Quartermaster Gen.
S P Moore, Surgeon-General.
E W Johns, Medical Purveyor.

North Carolina Representation in Congress.

Senate.

Wm T Dortch and Wm A Graham.

House of Representatives.

First District—Martin, Hertford, Gates, Chowan, Perquimans, Pasquotank, Currituck, Camden, Northampton, Washington, Tyrrell and Bertie—W N H Smith.

Second District—Halifax, Edgecombe, Beaufort, Wilson, Pitt, Green, Lenoir and Hyde—R R Bridgers.

Third District—Carteret, Jones, Craven, Onslow, Duplin, Wayne, Johnston and Sampson—J T Leach.

Fourth District—New Hanover, Brunswick, Columbus, Bladen, Robeson, Cumberland Richmond and Harnett—J C Fulcher.

Fifth District—Warren, Franklin, Granville, Wake, Orange and Nash—Josiah Turner.

Sixth District—Alamance, Person, Caswell, Rockingham, Guilford, Stokes and Forsythe—J A Gilmer.

Seventh District—Randolph, Davidson, Chatham, Moore, Montgomery, Stanly and Anson—J M Leach.

Eighth District—Rowan, Cabarrus, Union, Mecklenburg, Gaston, Lincoln, Catawba and Cleaveland—J G Ramsay.

Ninth District—Ashe, Alleghany, Wilkes, Caldwell Alexander, Yadkin, Surry, Davie, Iredell and Burke—B S Gaither.

Tenth District—Clay, Cherokee, Macon, Jackson, Madison, Buncombe. Transylvania, Henderson, Polk, Yancey, McDowell, Rutherford, Mitchell, Haywood and Watauga—G W Logan.

CONFEDERATE STATES COURTS.

The District of North Carolina is divided into three Judicial Districts, and the times and places of holding the courts appointed by the Judge.

Hon. Asa Biggs, of Martin, Judge.
Geo. V. Strong, of Wayne, Dist. Attorney.
Wesley Jones, of Wake, Marshall.

The Court of the District of Albemarle is held at Halifax, on Wednesday next after third Monday in May and November. Joseph Ramsey, clerk, Rocky Mount.

The Court for the District of Pamlico is held at Goldsboro' on the fourth Monday in May and November. William M Watson, clerk, Warrenton.

The Court for the District of Cape Fear is held at Salisbury, the Monday next after the fourth Monday in May and November. Daniel Coleman, clerk, Concord.

E A Thompson of Charlotte, E B Borden of Goldsboro, W S Mason of Raleigh, Thos W Brown, Jr., of Wilmington, Confederate States Commissioners.

Head-Quarters C. S. Military Prison,

Salisbury, N. C., May 24th, 1864.

List of Officers and Attachees at the Confederate States Military Prison, Salisbury, N. C:

Col. John A. Gilmer Jr., commandant of Post
Capt. J. A. Fuqua, Ass't "
Lieut. F. D. Stockton, Adjutant.
J. M. Abernathy, Assistant Surgeon.
G. B. Paulson, Hospital Steward.
James Martin, Sergeant Major.
J. L. Lyerly, Prison Clerk.
B. James Best, Commandant's Clerk.

PRISON GUARD.

Capt. C. D. Freeman, Co. A, 116 men.
1st Lieut. J. L. Shirley "
2d " J. A. Moore "
Jr 2d " M. C. Davis, "
Capt. H. P. Allen, Co. B, 108 men.
1st Lieut. G. A. Latham, "
2d " C. H. Snead, "
Jr 2d " G. T. Allen, "
Capt. E. D. Snead, Co. C, 112 men.
1st Lt. R. H. Watlington, "
2d " W. R. Snead, "
Jr 2d A. M. Whitsett, "

Prisoners confined in the C. S. Military Prison, Salisbury N. C.:

Confederates serving out sentences of Court Martial,	310
Yankee deserters,	95
Political prisoners,	164
Prisoners of War,	00
Total,	569

Battle of Kennesaw Mountain—Yankee Account.

We find in the war correspondence of the Cincinnati papers full accounts of the repulse of General Sherman's forces at Kennesaw mountain. Some of the incidents of the terrible fighting on the mountain are interesting:

A TERRIBLE CHARGE.

The grand attack took place June 27th. At a given signal, five thousand devoted men fixed their bayonets, bounded from their intrenchments, and with a loud cheer, rushed toward the foe. The rebel skirmishers scarcely made an attempt at resistance, but instantly a sheet of vindictive fire from the enemy's works flashed in our soldiers' faces. Ten thousand muskets hurled their bullets amongst them. From twenty pieces of cannon a deluge of canister was poured upon them. A demoniac yell saluted them as they approached. As lightning withers a tree, so was their front withered by the blast from the enemy's guns, while an inconceivable deadly fire of both musketry and artillery tore in pieces their long and exposed flanks. But those heroic soldiers never faltered in their career until simultaneously and with a shout they carried the first line of the enemy's works.

A FAILURE.

Not a moment did our columns halt in the outer works they had taken. Deploying into line as rapidly as possible, they moved straight upon the enemy's main defences, heedless of wounds, heedless of death, heedless of aught save victory. Beneath the now redoubled fire of the enemy it seemed impossible that any man should live. It made me weep with anguish to see our columns reel and stagger while deploying under those murderous volleys. But up to the very foot of the ramparts our soldiers pressed, and some actually climed upon it. Others lay down within a score of yards of the breastworks, and maintained upon them a steady fire. But at last human courage and endurance could effect no more. The rebel works were too strong to be taken by assault, and all the columns retired, torn and bleeding, but in order and undemoralized, some to a greater and some to a less distance from the enemy's works.

DEATH OF GENERAL HARKER.

When Harker perceived that his column had halted, and that the men were lying under the crest of the ridge, he rode forward and asked Colonel Bradley, (Fortieth Indiana,) who commanded one wing of the brigade, if he did not think it best to venture another charge. Colonel Bradley replied that he believed the men's energies had already been tested to the utmost. "At least," said Harker, "we may try what can be done!" Saying which, he galloped up to his men, took off his hat, waved it, and called upon them to follow him. Animated by the voice of their beloved leader, the soldiers sprang to their feet and rushed after him up the crest of the hill. Alas! the first volley from the rebel works disabled every man near the general, and the heroic Harker himself reeled and fell from his saddle. A bullet had shattered his arm, entered his side, and passed through his body. There were those that loved him, who, in spite of death and danger, bore him from the field. A few hours afterwards he breathed his last, dying as he had lived—a soldier, a patriot, and a christian.

COOLNESS OF OUR TROOPS.

Colonel McCook had led his soldiers to the very edge of the ditch. They had no time to hesitate under the tremendous fire poured upon them, when McCook jumped across the ditch, climbed upon the summit of the works and defiantly waved his sword! The loud shout of exultation which burst from his men was frozen in the utterance, as the Colonel immediately fell, pierced through the shoulder and lungs by a rifle ball.

A momentary dismay seized a portion of his line. The right of it gave way, leaving Mitchell's left exposed to a destructive cross as well as direct fire, before which it melted like snow. Like an indignant wave both columns rolled back a short distance from the works. It was short indeed; for, incredible as it may seem, they halted at a distane of from forty to sixty paces from the rebel bulwarks, between the line they had carried and the main line, commenced fortifying themselves, and held their position spite of all efforts to dislodge them.

It was at first feared that McCook's wound was mortal; but better hopes now prevail.

Mitchell, cool and steady under the enemy's works as when in his tent, seemed to bear a charmed life, and came out entirely unhurt.

Thus ended the battle in the centre.

OPERATIONS ON THE LEFT—MOUNTAIN FIGHTING.

On the left wing, which was formed immediately around the northwestern, northern and northeastern bases of Kenesaw, a series of gallant actions took place, rivalling the fighting in the centre. To the army of the Tennessee had been confided the task of driving the rebels from Kennesaw, and taking possession of that mountain if it were possible to do so.

The order was to attack the enemy at 6 A. M. Promptly to the hour General Logan moved out the troops intended to operate along his front. Three brigades constituted the attacking force.

This superb force moved forward in order, under the eye of General Logan himself, and encountering the rebel pickets, drove them three-fourths of a mile.

THE ENEMY'S FIRST LINE CARRIED.

The advancing line soon came to the abattis and palisades which the rebels had constructed along nearly their entire front. We suffered some loss at these, but our men went gallantly through and attacked the first line of the rifle pits. Here the fighting was severe; but the rebels were at length dislodged, and the works occupied. The retreating enemy attempted to make his way into a gorge which runs down the side of the Kennesaw. Our troops followed up the foe so closely that more than a hundred prisoners fell into our hands. Up the side of the mountain and along the slopes of the gorge our soldiers continued to skirmish, driving the rebels slowly before them.

A GRAND SPECTACLE.

The scene now became one of exciting and solemn grandeur. The dozen pieces of artillery which the enemy had upon the top of the mountain thundered so incessantly, shooting forth in every direction fierce gushes of flame and smoke, that Kennesaw seemed to have revived its long extinguished fires. Our batteries replied—with tireless vigour. Thunder above was answered by thunder from the plain below; and underneath that "sulphurous canopy" one might well imagine the ancient fable realized, and that the Titans contended with the demons of the upper air.

The rebels threw shells principally, but our own artillerists confined themselves exclusively to solid shot, lest the bursting of the shells upon the sides of the mountain might injure our own troops as they were clambering up. The incessant explosion of musketry all along the sides of the mountain added to the novel and awful character of the scene.

OUR ADVANCE ARRESTED.

Our troops had now pushed their way until they found themselves at the foot of a perpendicular cliff, some thirty feet in height. Here they waited for Colonel Barnhill to bring up two regiments Along the crest of the cliff the rebels formed in order of battle, and in addition to a destructive fire of musketry which was poured upon us they rolled down huge stones and trunks of trees. Colonel Barnhill was killed at the foot of the cliff. Of course it was impossible for the troops to go further. It had taken them just one hour and a quarter's continued fighting to reach the cliff, and they heard gladly the word to retire a short distance and throw up such works of earth and stones as might be necessary to protect them from the rebel missiles. The Eighty-third Indiana had two color-bearers killed while ascending the hill. Sixty officers fell in the fight, seven of them commanding regiments. Of rank and file probably five hundred were killed and wounded.

Thus ended what I shall call the battle of Kennesaw mountain. Everywhere had we carried the first line of the enemy's works; nowhere had we made an impression upon the second. Never had men fought more bravely than ours; and he who in any quarter of the world admires courage must regret that such courage was unavailing.

ALL IMPORTANT.

The most impartant election that has been held, or that ever will be held in North Carolina, will take place on Thursday, the 4th day of August. The candidates for Governor, are well known to the people, and there would seem to be no difficulty to decide between them. Gov. Vance has been tried, and not found wanting, either on the field or in the Chair of State—he has emphatically made a "good Governor," Holden, his opponent, has kept aloof from the post of danger, although he did more than any man in the State to bring on the war. Holden has no experience as a stateman—he cares not a cent for the success of the South, if he can but get elected Governor, and would sell his country to consumate the hopes of his unhallowed ambition. Let the people with one accord spurn this tory aspirant for gubernatorial honors.—*Iredell Express.*

"HEROES OF AMERICA."

We wonder if there are not some of these "heroes" in the County of Iredell? If there are we warn them to come out of this mischievous society and renounce the damnable league against the Confederate cause and their kindred. The law is swift in its retribution, and the "heroes" know not how soon they may be caught in its meshes.

A word to the wise is sufficient.—*Iredell Express.*

We have been told that there are many in Iredell.

THE
DAILY WATCHMAN

J. J. BRUNER, EDITOR AND PROPRIETOR,

SALISBURY, N. C.

WEDNESDAY, JULY 20, 1864.

TERMS:

Daily Watchman 6 months	$12 00
" " 3 "	7 00
Weekly Watchman 6 months	$5 00

ADVERTISING IN DAILY:
Two dollars per square (of 12 lines or less) for each insertion.

WEEKLY:
Two dollars per square for the first and $1 for each subsequent insertion.

ATTENTION! GIRLS AND BOYS!!

The meeting for singing will be held in the Methodist Church this morning at 8½ o'clock. Come one! Come all!!

☞ We observe that the *Progress* remains *silent* as the grave in regard to Mr. Boyden's card announcing that he adheres to Gov. Vance. That paper had said—"holding the views he" (Mr. Boyden) "does, he cannot support the Governor; and in contradiction of our assertion that he would, it said again, "we have it from the distinguished gentleman's *own lips*, that it (the Watchman) had no right to speak for him." But Mr. Boyden came out and took his position at length, against that assigned to him by the *Progress*, since when that print remained silent, either determined that its readers shall never know the truth in the case, else because it "*knows a thing or two*" which had better not be uttered in the faces of those who are deliberating as to how they shall cast their votes. In the meantime, a highly respectable gentleman of Morganton publicly asserts in the streets of that town that he had, on *two* occasions, heard Mr. Boyden say he could not support Gov. Vance for re-election.

This State of facts, to say the least of it, precludes the idea that the distinguished gentleman has pursued such a course on the subject of the Gubernatorial election as to admit of no doubt. On the contrary, it is strongly suggestive that he has swayed in his views, has hesitated, and, perhaps, has calculated the results of a final dicision on certain ambitious aspirations the breath of suspicion has imputed to him. There is a Confederate Senator to be elected by the next Legislature, and why may not he fill the place? The only difficulty in the way is in getting votes enough to put him in it. And the only difficulty in that is, in pursuing such a course as that he can obtain the support of the Vance conservatives and the Holdenites. Like some others we know of, was he not *afraid* to commit himself openly to the support of the Gubernatorial candidates, lest the man of his choice might not be in the ascendancy in the Legislature! Or, again, anticipating that the contest between the two "conservative" wings might be close, an available man for Senator, should hold a position admitting of a *compromise* between them, one in whom each party either had confidence or mutually detested. A compromise man being the desideratum, there is a motive for, and a prize tempting, sharp, calculating men to shape their course in reference to it. Whether Mr. Boyden aimed at this in the way and in the case suggested, is a question to be judged of by the best lights before us. It is quite certain he had a motive for telling the *Progress* that *we* had no right to speak for him, and we charge that it was a deliberate purpose to conceal his preference of the two candidates. He knew that Holden was claiming him as one of his supporters; he knew that we had claimed him for Vance; and that when called on by Holden's friends to know how he stood, he simply declared that the *Watchman* had no right to speak for him, leaving it to be inferred, as most naturally it was, that he was a Holdenite. The *Progress* drew that inference and published, as he had the right to do, an article assigning the distinguished gentleman to a place among the Holdenites.

False Alarm.—The Telegraph flashed over the wires from Charlotte, yesterday afternoon about 4 o'clock, that a Courier had arrived at Lincolnton, with intelligence from Morganton, that yankees and tories, to the number of 2000, had entered that town the evening before, and were burning it when the messenger left. The news came from a credible source, and Captain James E. Kerr, of the volunteer company recently organized here, caused the Court House bell to be rung, and the alarm was soon spread over town. Citizens turned out; the Commandant of the C. S. Prison was out taking steps to bring out his forces, Capt. Brenizer of the Foundry, had out his men, and the details from the Car Shops, and from every other quarter in town, were speedily under arms and ready for the emergency. It is surprising how much of preparation was made in so short a time. But just about the time all were ready to march, the regular down train from Morganton, at 7½ o'clock, arrived and put an end to the excitement. Morganton, we were told, was all safe, and totally unconscious of the needless alarm manifested here. It was welcome intelligence, and our little improvised army disbanded, and returned to their respective quarters.

In conclusion, we would admonish citizens that when these sudden emergencies arise, and it is believed that our homes and dear ones are imperiled, it is expected that *every* man able to bear arms, will promptly respond to the call. Let all assemble at the place of rendezvous, at least, and show by their acts that they are willing to do the part of true and brave citizens, whether able or not to go on a march.

A Yankee Account of Forrest's Victory.—A Federal officer who accompanied Gen. Sturgis in his last advance from Memphis speaks thus of the great victory gained by Forrest over him:

We have had a terrible time—having been cut all to pieces. Out of five regiments of infantry and one battery, but about three hundred and eighty have been saved, all the rest being killed, wounded or taken prisoners. Col. Humphreys, of the 95th Illinios, and Col. McKeag, of the 12th Illinios, were killed. I saw Col. Humphreys, when he was shot, and afterwards saw his body at Ripley. Col. McKeag was shot during our retreat. It is impossible to tell who are killed and wounded now, and will be for some time to come. The 113th regiment left here with about three hundred men—the balance being on duty at this place as a guard to Irying block—only eighty-eight have returned.

It has been a great disaster. We have lost not less than three thousand men including 1200 wagons, 16 pieces of artillery, and a large quantity of supplies and ammunition, and 5,000 stand of small arms. The fight took place about two miles west of Baldwin, a town on the Mobile & Ohio railroad, forty miles south of Corinth.

A CARD.

To the Voters of Rowan and Davie Counties and Soldiers in the Army:

FELLOW-CITIZENS:—Having announced myself as a candidate to represent you in the Senatorial District, composed of said counties, in the next General Assembly of North Carolina, and being a citizen of Davie, and comparatively unknown to many citizens of Rowan, and finding it impossible to thoroughly canvass the District, I have thought proper to issue a short Card.

Though I have taken no very active part in the political contests, it is known to many of the people of these counties, that in the political differences which formerly distinguished the two parties in the country, I was a member of the Whig party. The true conservative and patriotic views of that party are now acknowledged by all men since the wise counsels of Mr. Clay and his compeers ceased to govern the counsels of the nation, and the wild and fanatical views of the North on the subject of Slavery have gained the ascendency which was consummated in the election of Mr. Lincoln, I have known no party except that which was best calculated to release us from the tyranny and oppression of Yankee dominion, and secure to us an independent Southern nationality.

If elected I shall use every effort in my power to secure our independence and to supply the wants of the soldiers and provide for the comforts of their families. I will cheerfully support any appropriations that may be necessary for the comfort and welfare of soldiers' families.

I shall support the Hon. Z. B. Vance for Governor.

I anxiously desire peace, and will use all the influence which my position as a member of the Legislature will give me in securing an honorable peace—one consistent with our independence and such as will vindicate the memory of our noble dead, and alike honorable to our brave soldiers in the field.

Very Respectfully,
W. B. MARCH.

July, 1864.

First Regt. Junior Reserves.—The organization of Junior Reserves, composed of the First and Sixth Battallions and Capt. John A. Mannings company, of that corps, was effected on the 16th, and the following officers were elected:

F. S. Armstead, Colonel;
Charles W. Broadfoot, Lt. Colonel;
Walter McKay Clark, Major.

Another Battallion was also organized by the consolidation of the Second and Fifth battallions; John H. Anderson, Lieut. Colonel and Wm. F. Beasley, Major.—*State Journal.*

Going Over to the Enemy.—Three members of the Nineteenth Virginia infantry, militia of the Reserves, Francis Burns, Charles Gibbons and John Morris, were committed to the Castle yesterday, having been detected in the act of going over to the common enemy.

ANNOUNCEMENTS.

THE Freemen of Rowan County will vote on Thursday, August 4th, for Hon. N. BOYDEN, to represent Rowan and Davie in the Senate of the next General Assembly of North Carolina—and F. E. SHOBER and MOSES L. HOLMES, to represent Rowan in the House of Commons. june 18, 1864. pdte

WE are authorized to announce WM. B. MARCH, Esq., a candidate to represent Rowan and Davie counties in the Senate of the next General Assembly. july 7, 1864. p'dte

WE are authorized to announce Dr. JOHN F. FOARD a candidate to represent Rowan county in the Commons of the next General Assembly. june 21, 1864 te

AT the request of many citizens, I, THOMAS W. HAYNES, announce myself a candidate to represent Rowan county in the House of Commons of the next General Assembly of North Carolina. I presume my views are generally known concerning public affairs and particularly speculation and extortion. Should the citizens and soldiers elect me I will do all I can for them and their country. july 2, 1864 te

WE are authorized to announce WILLIAM H. CRAWFORD a candidate to represent Rowan county in the House of Commons of the next General Assembly July 8th, 1864 te

WE are authorized to announce DAVID FLEMING a candidate for a seat in the House of Commons to represent the people of Rowan county in our next Legislature. july 8th. te

Senatorial candidate in Lincoln, Gaston and Catawba.

WE are authorized to announce M. L. McCORKLE Esq, as a candidate to represent the Senatorial district of Lincoln, Gaston and Catawba, in the next General Assembly of the State. 12td:40

Commoner for Davidson County.

TO the soldier and citizen voters of Davidson county: We are permitted to announce Lt. Col. C. W. BRADSHAW, of the 42d Regt N C Troops, who has been a faithful soldier for three years, as a suitable candidate to represent the people of Davidson county in the Commons of the next General Assembly of the State. june 24. dte:33] MANY VOTERS.

WE are authorized to announce WM. A. WALTON, Esq, as a candidate for re-election to the office of Sheriff of Rowan. june 18. tepd

WE are authorized to announce THOS. J. MERONEY a candidate for the office of Sheriff of Rowan county, at the ensuing August election. te

Charleston Daily Courier.

NO. 19,830 — CHARLESTON, S. C., CONFEDERATE STATES OF AMERICA, MONDAY MORNING, AUGUST 1, 1864. — VOL. LXIII.

BY TELEGRAPH.

REPORTS OF THE PRESS ASSOCIATION.

[Entered according to Act of Congress, in the year eighteen hundred and sixty-three, by J. S. Thrasher, in the Clerk's Office of the District Court of the Confederate States, for the Northern District of Georgia.]

IMPORTANT FROM PETERSBURG.

ENEMY SPRING A MINE—SHARP FIGHT IN THE TRENCHES—ENEMY DRIVEN BACK WITH LOSS—BRILLIANT FIGHTING OF MAHONE'S DIVISION—CAPTURE OF BRIGADIER GENERAL BARTLETT AND STAFF, AND TWELVE STANDS OF COLORS.

RICHMOND, July 30.—A special dispatch to the Richmond *Whig*, from Petersburg to-day, says: "The enemy shelled the city with great vigor this morning for several hours. Several houses were burnt. Between four and five o'clock this morning the enemy sprung a mine under a portion of our works on the Baxter road, blowing up a portion of the works. A large force of Yankees charged through the breach, making some captures of prisoners and guns, but after a sharp fight they were driven back. The seventeenth and eighteenth South Carolina Regiments lost a number of men. Considerable activity pervades along the lines.

RICHMOND, July 31.—Official dispatches to the War Department from Petersburg state that "at five A. M. Saturday the enemy sprung a mine under one of our salients on our front. He opened his batteries upon our lines and the city of Petersburg. In the confusion caused by the explosion he got possession of a salient, which was afterwards retaken, and the enemy driven back to his lines with loss."

A later official telegram says: "When we drove the enemy from the salient, we recovered the four guns with which it was armed, captured twelve stands of colors, seventy-four officers, including Brigadier General BARTLETT and staff, with one hundred and fifty-five enlisted men. Upwards of five hundred of the enemy's dead are lying unburied in the trenches. Our loss is slight.

PETERSBURG, July 30.—About two o'clock this afternoon, everything being aroused, General MAHONE threw forward SANDERS' Alabama brigade, which charged the enemy in gallant style, recapturing the rest of the breastworks temporarily lost, taking about five hundred prisoners, including one hundred and fifty negroes, thirty-five officers and Brigadier General BARTLETT, commanding First Division of the Ninth Yankee Corps, besides two stands of colors and the four pieces of artillery lost by us this morning. Over six hundred of the enemy's dead are lying in our trenches

MAHONE's and WRIGHT's brigades, besides the prisoners captured this morning, took ten stands of colors. Our lines are identically the same as before the fight this morning. All the lost ground has been reclaimed Not over a hundred and thirty lives are believed to have been lost in the blowing up of the mine. The losses in MAHONE's division are not over two hundred killed and wounded Among the killed is Col. EVANS, of the 64th Georgia and Capt. RUTH, commanding 22d Georgia regiment. Col. WILLIAMS, of the 6th Virginia, was slightly wounded. All is quiet to night.

YANKEE NEWS.

PETERSBURG, July 29.—We have received Northern dates of the 27th instant.

The New York *Tribune* has dispatches announcing ROSSEAU's return to Marietta, after having burnt all the road bridges North of Marietta and twenty miles South of it. Dispatches also say that GARRARD's expedition was also successful, destroying the bridges at Covington, forty miles East of Atlanta. Dispatches also say that the Federals have buried a thousand dead rebels since the late fight; and that the situation is also favorable.

McPHERSON's remains had reached Nashville *en route* to Louisville.

A steamer struck a snag and sunk on the Mississippi river, fifteen miles below Greenville, Miss., on the 21st instant, losing fifty lives, principally of the 10th Federal Missouri Cavalry.

Very little had been heard from EARLY's force in the Valley. Orders have been sent to remove everything from Frederick.

Dispatches from Baltimore say it is supposed that the enemy intend making a raid into the Southern counties of Pennsylvania. The loyal leaguers have been called out in Baltimore. The Baltimore and Ohio Rail Road was again cut. The Washington *Chronicle* says: "Commanding Generals have requested the utmost secrecy in regard to military operations, and GRANT's operations especially demand secrecy."

No gold quotations are given.

A rumor was current at Cherbourg, France, that the Federal and Confederate officers had agreed to fight off Cherbourg in ten days.

The Confederate loan had advanced to seventy-eight.

The London *Herald* says MASON had an unofficial interview with Lord PALMERSTON. He was introduced by Mr. LINDSAY. The meeting was satisfactory to all parties, and the withdrawal by Mr LINDSAY of his intended recognition motion in Parliament is said to have been the result of the interview, Lord PALMERSTON having given out an implied proviso that he would support the motion at a more opportune moment.

List of undelivered messages at John-street Telegraph Office, July 31st, 1864:

Capt. S. L. Percival, E. Stille, R. H. Riker, R. Spinse, C. Backman, Rev. R. Barnwell, Mrs. L. Crager, Capt. J. F. Wheaton, L. Caldwell, O. H. Williams, Jr., Holmes, J. H. Skines, Mrs. E. J. Johnson, E. A. Caldwell, P. Fitzpatrick.

BRITISH CONFEDERATE PUBLICATIONS.—Many readers of the *Courier* will receive with expectant eyes and ears the announcement we copy from the *Index*, of June 30th:

In the Press, post 8vo, Vol. I., Life of Lieutenant General Thomas J. Jackson, ("Stonewall Jackson,") derived from authentic sources, by his personal friend and Chief of Staff to his Corps, Professor R. L. Dabney, D.D., of Richmond, Virginia, with additions by Rev. W. Chalmers, A. M. Dr. Dabney has been selected to write this memoir by the General's widow and friends; by his successor and devoted comrade Lieutenant General Ewell; and by the advice of the service in general. All the materials in the hands of his widow and relations have been placed at the disposal of Dr. Dabney, and unlimited access to the papers of the Confederate War Department has been granted to him. The First Volume brings the memoir down to the battle of Bull Run; the Second Volume, concluding the work, is in preparation

London: James Nisbet & Co., 21 Berners-street, W.

Next week will be published, in two volumes, post 8vo. The Cruise of the "Alabama" and "the Sumter," from the Private Journals, etc., of Capt. Semmes, C. S. N., and other officers, with illustrations, correspondence, &c.

London: Saunders, Otley, & Co., 66 Brook-street, W.

SHIPPING IN SPANISH PORTS.—BOARD OF TRADE, WHITEHALL, June 24.—The Committee of Privy Council for Trade have received a copy of a dispatch from her Majesty's Minister at Madrid, enclosing a translation of a Spanish Royal decree, abolishing the exclusive privileges hitherto existing at Spanish ports with regard to the lading and unlading of vessels in those ports.—*Gazette.*

RICHMOND, July 29.—The following, among over one hundred other casualties in McGowan's brigade shortly to be furnished, occurred in yesterday's fight near Malvern Hill. Killed: Ensign D. Lee McClintock and Lieut. M. T. Hutchin. Wounded: Sergeant J. W. Mottc, mortally in the bowels, Sergeant Dishilds, severely in the breast, all of the 14th S. C. V. John Adams, 3d S. C., severely.

S. L. HOLMES.

CHARLESTON.

MONDAY MORNING, AUGUST 1, 1864.

Siege of Charleston.

THREE HUNDRED AND EIGHTY-EIGHTH DAY.

Five hundred and eighty-three shots have been fired at Fort Sumter since last report. Our batteries have kept up a brisk reply. Sullivan's Island fired at Gregg on Sunday one hundred and eleven shots, to which Gregg responded, firing thirty six shots at Sullivan's Island. Six shots were fired by the enemy at Castle Pinckney, doing no damage. Considerable firing was heard in the direction of Stono Saturday and Sunday. About six o'clock on Saturday evening, a large double smokestack side-wheel steamer from the North passed the bar and went into Stono Inlet. She is believed to have had troops on board. The enemy's troops on Morris and Folly Islands were moving about with considerable activity Sunday.

Only two shells have been fired at the city since Friday evening.

There has been no change of importance in the fleet.

Thirty-six of the escaped Yankee prisoners have been recaptured and brought back to the city.

UNDERMINING.—Our friends of the press in Richmond and Petersburg have indulged very confidently in sneers and sceptical comments on the reports of GRANT's mining operations which have been made by prisoners and deserters for some weeks. It is probable, if our dispatch approaches the truth, that these editors may change their opinions and the notions of the word "impossible," which has been too easily and readily applied by our editors ande genrals. Some who considered themselves masters of all that West Point knew or had taught concerning military projectiles pronounced it impossible for Yankees or any other persons to throw shells from any part of Morris' Island to any part of this city—and many rested quietly under this belief for days and weeks that could and had have been employed in prevention or preparation. Almost everything marked or apparently decisive that has been accomplished on either side in this war has been done after it had been pronounced impossible by some of those stereotyped minds who never learn anything after they leave school, and no great amount at school.

We are sick and tired of the word impossible, and of other words fondly used by military editors in the rear, and by some officers who should be in front. Let us away with it and go to work—work—work—in deep earnest, taking a lesson from the enemy whom we have been and are too prone to imitate in many matters less commendable and worthy than his constant and thorough use, appreciative and applicative, of the mechanical and engineering resources of war. Let us hear no more of this or the other result being impossible, unless it can be demonstrated so by reference to known and established laws of nature, and not merely to what has been done by followers of routine and red tape. What is possible at all, or under any circumstance, will be attempted by the Yankees against us if we allow them time enough, and what is attempted in engineering or constructive warfare by GRANT, aided by GILLMORE and backed by mercenaries more willing to work than to fight, will be probably achieved.

MORE ROBBERIES.—The store of S. D. JACUBOSKY, on Meeting-street, near John-street, was broken open Saturday night and robbed of about three thousand dollars worth of property.

A Boot and Shoemaker, a Mr. KUNE, in Sires-street, on Friday night was also robbed of a considerable stock of leather, ready made shoes, &c.

RAID ON THE GEORGIA CENTRAL RAIL ROAD.—A private dispatch from Savannah, July 30th, received in this city Saturday, says: "From three to eight hundred Yankee raiders cut the Central Road at Gordon at eleven o'clock last night. They burnt all of the Company's buildings and a Central and State Road train."

[Gordon is on the Central Rail Road, at the junction of the Milledgeville Rail Road, twenty-one miles East of Macon.]

The last accounts we have from Atlanta state a heavy fight was progressing. No particulars as yet have been received as to the result.

A good lager beer has at length been made in this State, and if people will or must drink qualified or modified or medicated water, it will be found more wholesome than much of the vile products from the stills which, beside using good corn turn into mean whiskey much of the condemned and rotten grain of the country. T. C. CLAFFY, on King, near Vanderhorst street, has the lager referred to.

GRANT AND THE TELEGRAPH.—GRANT has established a line of telegraph from his headquarters, near City Point, to Portsmouth and Norfolk, and thence to Fortress Monroe. Ever since the line was put up the wires have been cut on an average about three times a week, which has been a source of no little annoyance to the irascible Lieutenant General.

He has endeavored to find out in vain the perpetrators of the mischief, but, as a retaliatory measure, has confined in Fort Powhatan the Rev. E. C. MURDAUGH, WILLIAM RUFFIN, old Mr. BARHAM and JOHN J. DEAL, Esq., the Postmaster at Cabin Point. These citizens, he declares, shall be held as hostages, and if the wires are again cut they are to be executed, and every building within five miles of Cabin Point committed to the flames. Mr. MURDAUGH is widely known as a Minister of the Protestant Episcopal Church, and the other three gentlemen named are represented to be most worthy and estimable citizens.

GRANT has not the shadow of proof that either of these gentlemen have ever interfered with his telegraph wires, and yet he drags them ruthlessly from their homes and places them in confinement. The Petersburg *Express* thinks that in this, and all similar cases, the Government ought to retaliate, and that too very promptly. It says: "Let four prominent Yankee officers be immediately placed in close confinement, and if GRANT does execute his threat, let the Yankee officers swing *instanter*. The *lex talionis* must be rigidly enforced. An eye for an eye and a tooth for a tooth, is the only way to deal with the semi-barbarous foe we are now fighting."

The North Carolina soldiers who voted for Governor on the 28th ult., have so far as heard from given Governor VANCE a rousing majority for re election, preferring very sensibly VANCE to HOLD on, rather than HOLDEN.

The citizens (and if not closely watched some other persons) will vote on Tuesday, 2d instant, when we hope to hear a large advance on the part of VANCE.

LINCOLN, with an arrogance and pretension not equalled by that hereditary monarch, GEORGE the Third, absolutely refuses to recognize us in any way, and addresses his late communication "To all whom it may Concern." Even GEORGE the Third admitted JOHN ADAMS, the Commissioner of the Colonies, to his presence, to state the grievances of the people whom he represented; but his High Mightiness, ABRAHAM the First, will not condescend to recognize Southern gentlemen by name!

Correspondence.

CHARLESTON, July 27, 1864.

Colonel—The ladies of the "Soldiers' Relief Association" being desirous of showing their high appreciation of the very valuable services rendered by your gallant regiment in the late brave defence of Battery Pringle, have prepared the accompanying "substantial refreshments," hoping they will be acceptable to yourself and your men.

The ladies cannot express the confidence they feel in the troops which now surround their city, defying the entrance of an insolent but powerful foe, and they feel assured, with the blessing of Heaven and the determined efforts of these braves, the old city by the sea will ever be safe

It is a pleasure to the ladies to know that the gallant sons of Georgia are side by side with the troops of Carolina in this noble struggle.

With high considerations of esteem, very respectfully,

F. M. BLAMYER,
L. S. PORTER,
Corresponding Secretaries Ladies' Relief Association.

Col. EDWARDS, 47th Georgia Regiment.

HEADQ'RS 47TH REG'T GEORGIA VOLUNTEERS,
James' Island, July 28, 1864.

To the Ladies of Charleston, S. C.:

In the absence of Col. EDWARDS, it becomes my pleasing duty to acknowledge the receipt of a supply of refreshments for the soldiers of this Regiment from the ladies of the Soldiers' Hospital Relief Association of Charleston, together with a letter expressing eloquently their confidence in Georgia "veteran troops."

On the 10th and 16th of June, 1862, this Regiment sealed its devotion (on this Island) to the cause of Southern Liberty and Southern Independence with its best blood.

From the barren hills of North Carolina to the sunburnt islands around Charleston, on the beautiful plains of our Savannah, rich fields of Alabama, and bottom lands of Mississippi, the classic battle ground around Jackson, to the bloody fields of Chickamauga, Missionary Ridge, Oostinaula, the dead of this gallant regiment fill soldiers' graves. Four hundred young and patriotic who marched out with us to do battle with all the patriotism and love of country ever known in the days of "chivalry," now fill low but honored graves.

It was again our pleasing duty to aid "materially" in driving back the despoilers of the old "City by the Sea," on John's Island, July 9th, 1864.

Though many of this command feel that their services are appreciated only by you, still I speak the unanimous sentiment of my command when I say that they are ready to be sacrificed at any moment, and on any battle field, in defence of the fair daughters of our sister State.

I am, ladies, very respectfully,
Your most obedient servant,
J. S. CONE,
Major Comd'g 4th Reg't Ga. Volunteers.

To the Ladies of the Soldiers' Relief Association, Charleston, S. C., through Misses F. M. BLAMYER and L. S. PORTER, Corresponding Secretaries.

The Second Regiment of Artillery, S. C. V.

This splendid command, raised in 1861 by the co-operative efforts and influence of the late Col T. G. Lamar and Col. A. D. Frederick, its present commander, still retains, we are pleased to learn, the first place in the affections of the people of that State, and maintains the reputation for gallantry and usefulness which it acquired under the leadership of the "Hero of Secessionville," who was so well known and beloved by the people of this community.

Composed as it is of some of the best citizens of South Carolina, many of whom having their plantations here, and connections [illegible] in this city, are well known to us, we consequently take great interest in its prosperity, and have more than common interest with the people of that State in the success of the organization. We learn that it now numbers over fourteen hundred men, and have no doubt that the popularity of its gallant commander could, if he desired and it was allowed, soon raise it to a brigade. Indeed, it now numbers more effective men than many of our brigades, and considering the great and many services which it has been rendering to the country for the past three years, under its former and present able commanders, we should be pleased to hear that it has been done

The Lieut. Col. J. Welsman Brown, one of the most brilliant ornaments that formerly graced the halls of the Citadel, is an officer of high military endowments and qualifications; and Major E. F. Warley, who was wounded at Battery Wagner, and captured on returning at night to the city, and still a prisoner, is also a most able and gallant officer.

The regiment has been intimately identified with the defences of Charleston from the beginning, being always at the posts of honor and danger on James' Island—as at Batteries Simkins and Cheves, Secessionville and the new Line—always doing splendid execution in their particular arm of service, and performing faithful duty in whatever capacity and whenever called upon to act, and never having had a deserter from its ranks, it has always enjoyed, under trying circumstances, the unlimited confidence of all general officers who had the good fortune to command it, and while we have recently seen frequent allusions to the services of other deserving corps, we are surprised not to have seen some mention of the services of this one—for in point of discipline, morale, usefulness and efficiency as artillerists, it has no superior in the service. Its present commander, Col. Frederick, has generally commanded a brigade on Eastern or Western division of the island, and during the recent active operations there he was continued in command of a splendid brigade, having the artillerists of his own regiment posted at the batteries of the new lines, against which the advance of the enemy was expected to be made.

The enemy, however, were so soon brought under the fire of these accurate artillerists, that they were driven back from their positions, and forced to leave the Island. For a time they seemed not to know that they were confronted by the gallant defenders of Secessionville—against which it will not soon be forgotten the vast hordes of the best of the enemy's troops made so unsuccessful an advance on the memorable 16th of June, 1862—of which the whiz of their shell soon convinced them, and they prudently concluded to try some more easy route to Charleston.

Col. Frederick's energetic attention to his duties and ability as a commander, added to his thorough familiarity with the topography of the Island, makes him peculiarly valuable as a commander there, and we are highly pleased to have heard that the distinguished services lately rendered there by him in that capacity have been properly appreciated. Whilst he has ever maintained fine discipline among his troops, his kind and generous nature has endeared him to his command, and his zealous and able discharge of duty have secured the esteem and confidence of his superiors. These are uncommon qualities in an officer, and we happen to know that he possesses them.

When upon the untimely death of the gallant and lamented Col Thomas G. Lamar, the mantle of command descended upon his shoulders, he resolved that the good name already attained by the regiment should never suffer while he was in command; and right gracefully has he worn that glorious mantle, and right faithfully has be maintained that trust.

In taking leave of this pleasant subject I cannot refrain from bowing my head in respect and honor to the memory of one of its former "brightest lights" who "went out" in a blaze of glory, manfully defending his Battery, on the 16th of June, 1862, Capt. Samuel J. Reed, who was well considered one of the most promising officers of the Regiment. All hail to its gallant dead and to the glorious chivalric spirits now composing the 2d Regiment of Artillery, South Carolina Volunteers.

A GEORGIA VOLUNTEER.

The Richmond correspondent ("Tyrone Powers") of the Augusta *Constitutionalist* writes:

The new Secretary of the Treasury is winning golden opinions from all men, and with the hope of some financial change for the better and the good news, political and military, that is pouring in upon us, it is long since Richmond has been so cheerful or exhibited so gratifying a revival of public hope and confidence.

American Affairs in Europe.

NO HOPES OF RECOGNITION.

[*London (July 6) Correspondence of Manchester Guardian.*]

A friend, who is in confidential official communication with both sides in the American civil war, speaks of the difficulties of the South as far greater than are allowed to appear on the surface In his opinion, notwithstanding all the gallantry of Confederate resistance, the Federal Government, so long as it can command a General like Grant to carry out the policy of "man for man," and has at its back the as yet unexhausted recruiting fields of Ireland and Germany, to say nothing of a practically unlimited command of greenbacks, ships, stores and munitions of war, must progress towards a conquest, which can only be retarded by all that Confederate determination and skill can accomplish. I mention this as it is the opinion of one who enjoys, I believe, almost unequalled opportunities of coming to a sound conclusion, and whose sympathies are in many respects with the South, all the more as he considers that slavery—the real obstacle to English good wishes for the Confederacy—is practically at an end, whatever be the issue of the present conflict.

DESPERATION OF THE NORTH—THE FEARFUL CARNAGE OF THE WAR—WITH WHOM RESTS THE RESPONSIBILITY.

[*From the London Morning Herald.*]

The North and South have been busy during three and a half years past—the one designedly, the other unwillingly—in proving, after a melancholy fashion, their claims of being able to do some things on a grander scale than other men. To one at a distance it would appear at first sight that the resources of both States must be indeed boundless, for, in as far as war consists in wholesale [illegible] countless as the sands of the sea, this American war is without a parallel in history.

There is no peculiar plan of raising men in the North that can save that country from utter exhaustion if the struggle be continued much longer. A far lesser drain of men for the Napoleonic wars left France enfeebled and powerless for thirty years. Mr. Lincoln has announced another call for 500,000 men, which will make up a sum exceeding 2,000,000 required since the commencement of the war. The losses of North and South, taken together, are more than half a million yearly by death on the battle field and disease in camp. Taking the whole fighting population of a country as one in six of the inhabitants, at the close of 1866, there will be nothing left to recruit from unless the women and aged men are to be sent into the field.

* * * * *

If the South is fighting with as much desperation as the North, it is because gigantic efforts call for energies as gigantic to oppose them. The South has a better cause—it is fighting for independence, for very existence. It would be craven and unmanly in a Southerner if he refused to take up arms for a country which he loves with a fervor unknown to the cold-blooded and calculating politicians of the North. Yet the South does not desire war. It only wishes for peace, and to be let alone.

In the correspondence between Mr. Davis and Governor Vance, of North Carolina, which was published, the Southern President tells us that on three successive occasions he has attempted to open negotiations for peace, but each time the Northern Government has arrogantly and insultingly refused to receive his envoys or to communicate with him in any way. Both parties in the North are bent on the prosecution of the war.

The Convention at Baltimore, which re-nominated Mr. Lincoln for President, and the Convention at Cleveland, which has nominated General Fremont, are agreed in this article of their "platform," that the subjugation of the South must be accomplished at whatever cost. The South has always wished for peace, and desires it most earnestly still. The whole blame of this wicked and bloody war rests entirely on the heads of the leaders of the Northern people.

PEACE MUST PREVAIL.

[*From the London Morning Post.*]

If we are right in concluding that Grant's expedition against Richmond is virtually at an end, our next enquiry must be respecting the consequences of this failure upon the duration of the civil war. The present is the fourth year of hostilities, and it is also the last year of Mr. Lincoln's Presidentship. The circumstance that the present [illegible] spring, and that the largest and most perfectly organized army which the North have ever succeeded in bringing into the field has been unable to force an entrance into the Capital of the neighboring State of Virginia, cannot fail to convince some at least in the Northern States of the folly of the task which they have undertaken.

Serious as were the losses sustained in the previous campaigns in Virginia, they bear no comparison in respect to magnitude with those entailed upon General Grant's army during the short month which elapsed between the first collision of the rival armies on the 5th of May, in the Wilderness, and the repulse of the Federals on the banks of the Chickhominy on the 5th of June.—Previous to the crossing of the Pamunkey it was estimated that the Federals had lost, in killed, wounded and missing, upwards of sixty thousand men, and as their subsequent losses may probably be set down at twenty thousand, the total is raised to a figure almost fabulous.

SPEECH OF EARL RUSSELL.

The following passage from Earl RUSSELL's speech in the House of Lords on the future of the Confederacy is significant His Lordship said:

It is no longer a question with reference to the balance of power in Europe. There are other parts of the world in which our interests may be as deeply involved, and in which we may have, some day or other, to maintain the honor and interests of this country. The civil war now waging in America, ending how it may, whether by the establishment of an independent republic in the South, or whether it ends most unexpectedly as it would be to me, I confess, by restoring the Union, still the United States of America, or the Northern States, or whatever they may be called, will then be in a totally different position to that which they were in a few years ago A great army will then be maintained by the United States. A formidable navy will also be kept up. Our relations with that power are liable at any moment to interruption I hope and trust that our friendly relations may be maintained, and those friendly relations must be considered and kept in view as well as our interest in the maintenance of the balance of power in Europe.

THE VIRGINIA WAR NEWS.—It seems very well settled that GRANT is about to throw his army against Richmond from this side of the river instead of operating against it from the vicinity of Petersburg. The history of the movement may be stated in the following facts: On Tuesday night he crossed about three corps over the pontoons below Deep Bottom, which were followed at an early hour Wednesday morning by their large wagon trains. Shortly after sunrise, our troops near New Market, distant about ten miles from Richmond and about five from his pontoons, were attacked and four guns of the Rockbridge Artillery captured. The capture was effected by the enemy extending his line (having a largely superior force) and flanking our forces. There was no fighting, and the men of the battery succeeded in bringing off their horses with them.

His lines now extend from James river, at a point about twelve miles from Richmond, on the left, to White Oak Bridge, a distance of seven miles Malvern Hill is about five miles in his rear. He has succeeded in putting his army this side of the Chickahominy, and with the same repulse in store for it that it experienced at Cold Harbor. As he has torn up the York River Rail Road, it is likely that he will make James river his base of supplies.

There was nothing of interest transpiring in front of Petersburg Thursday evening A little shelling from Battery No. 5, the "bungs" striking near the planing mill, in Blanford, and doing no injury, has been the only occurrence worthy of note within the last forty eight hours.

The *Illustrated London News*, published Saturday, 18th June, an admirable portrait of Major General J. E. B. STUART. In the preceding week the same journal contained a portrait of Major General LONGSTREET, and in the week before that a portrait of General ROBERT E LEE, commander-in chief of the army of the Confederate States.

Who will furnish copies?

Latest from Georgia.

From our Augusta exchanges of Sunday morning we make the following extracts:

THE SITUATION.

The news and rumors which come in on us at this time are, to say the least, startling. Since the Yankees have crossed the Chattahoochee, although they have attempted to enter Atlanta, their grand object and aim seem to be to convert their whole army into mounted infantry, and to so override the State. They have appeared in large numbers on every hand mounted; and to every place they go, if nothing else is taken, the horse does not escape

On the Georgia Rail Road, fifty miles Southeast of Atlanta, they have appeared, cut the rail road and stolen all the horses. On the Montgomery and West Point Rail Road they damaged the road most seriously, and stole indiscriminately, but never forgetting the horse. On the Central Rail Road, eighteen miles East of Macon, they now appear in force, burn bridges and destroy the rail road, and take away all horses, while a still larger force is reported to the West of Macon, enquiring the route to Andersonville and Columbus.

Now, the important question, not only for the army, but the whole people of the State, is: Will the enemy be permitted to raid in this manner unchecked through the State, and thereby carry off every horse fit for service? The question is, shall we leave the horses exposed to the seizure of the enemy, and so mount the whole of Sherman's army?

That this is the intention of Sherman is plain. The war on his part, since he has secured his present position, is changed into a war of raids, the most distressing and destructive of all wars.

Will the people rest supinely in fancied security, until the enemy are at their very doors? Send your horses out of danger upon the report of the advance of the raiders, or mount them and harass and bushwhack them at every defile, every cross roads, every bridge.

And unless Gen. Hood has a force of eight or ten thousand men, that can be thrown to Andersonville at short notice, we will have a whole army of prisoners turned loose upon us, only wanting guns to become mounted raiders.

Affairs in Georgia are reaching a culminating point. The daring of Sherman's raiders is beyond all precedent, and his success in this endeavor will warrant its continuance.

It is our bounden duty, therefore, to meet them on equal footing, and in a condition to keep up with them. Let our authorities, therefore, at once, take all the horses of the country, of every character, and mount veteran infantry of General Hood's army. This should not be delayed an hour. We must have more mounted men or Georgia will be a ruin—the very home of desolation. Mount men, and mount twenty thousand at once. The horses can be had. We should not stand upon the order of doing this thing, but do it at once.

The only chance, in our humble judgment, for the protection of Georgia now, is an army of cavalry. Our infantry, however gallant and brave, are useless when once in the rear of the raiders.

We await with anxious solicitude news from Macon concerning the large force reported passing South of that place.

THE RAIDERS.

We learn that a force of Yankee cavalry, numbering from five to eight hundred, made their appearance at Gordon, on the Central Rail Road, at the junction of the Milledgeville branch, about 10.30 Friday night, burned the depot and were destroying the track when our informant left.

It is supposed that this party was sent out from the force operating near Covington, on the Georgia Rail Road.

The interruption of communication between here and Macon prevents us from obtaining any positive information as to the extent of the operations of the enemy on the Macon and Western Rail Road. It is reported that a large portion of the track has been torn up. From the information received we are of opinion that there are three distinct parties operating on the Central and Macon and Western Roads—one in the vicinity of Jonesboro', one at Griffin, and another at Gordon.

We are informed that our troops were on the alert at Macon yesterday, and were moving towards the enemy in such force as to warrant us in stating that the raiders will be effectually disposed of

V. Feugas for the use of the following telegram:

TENNILLE, July 30.

To H. V. Feug, Agent:

Gordon was burned last night by the Yankees. Force not ascertained.

N. M. SMITH,
Major and Chief Inspector F. T.

After the foregoing was in type, we were furnished by Col. Raines with the following information:

Col. Raines:—Hearing of the return of the Yankees to Covington, I went up Friday morning, and returned this morning from Rutledge. There I met a responsible citizen whom I know. He was in Covington when Gen. Stoneman entered, and passed freely among the Yankees He was informed by several officers that the force amounted to two divisions, under Guerrard and Tillinghurst—the whole commanded by Stoneman, about 8000 strong; four batteries, four guns each, and two Parrot 24 pounders, which he saw in Covington

They were *en route* for Macon, and expected to make a junction there with Rosseau and march on Andersonville. A.

P. S.—Stoneman left Covington on Thursday at noon—his rear guard marched out on Thursday night on Monticello road.

Guerrard crossed, with his division, Yellow river, and marched towards McDonnough. They were making enquiry as to the distance from Macon to Andersonville and Columbus. A.

We learn officially that the raiders on the Central Road burned the depot at Gordon, the junction of the Milledgeville and Eatonton Rail Road.

It is stated that the Yankees have cut the Macon and Western road in two places at Griffin and Jonesboro'. The amount of damage done is not yet ascertained.

The Yankees hope probably to interfere with Gen. Hood's commissary department. True, they may cause a little inconvenience. Those who know best say that he is in no danger of wanting rations, as he has a two weeks' supply on hand This is good news. Before that time expires, Sherman's raiders will be disposed of and communication with our gallant army again opened.

From all accounts from Central Rail Road we collect the following:

The raiders made their appearance at Gordon about half-past ten Friday night. It is supposed they numbered from eight hundred to one thousand Several cars were burned, also the depot.

After completing their work of destruction at Gordon, it is rumored that the Yankees proceeded down the road towards Savannah, burning depots and tearing up the track in their course, until they came to the Oconee bridge. This it is reported they also destroyed. If the report is correct we have truely suffered a great loss, as the bridge and trestle work is over a mile in length.

We have not heard what route was taken from this point.

A large number of troops left Macon in pursuit of the raiders on Friday. Troops, we understand, have been sent after them from other sections.

FROM THE RAIDERS.

We learn that there is some doubt about the burning of Oconee bridge, near Station No. 14, on the Central Rail Road, though it has been asserted that a gentleman saw it in flames.

The cars on the Georgia Rail Road went up as far as Madison yestesday. The raiders were still at Covington in considerable force, and fortifying, with the expressed determination of spending the summer in that locality. We presume, however, that their anticipations in this respect will be seriously interfered with ere long, and that they will have to seek summer quarters in a more Northern latitude.

A bill has just passed the Connecticut Legislature providing for a fine of twenty-five dollars upon rail road companies that neglect to carry a certain quantity of good drinking water in passenger cars.

IMPORTANT DECISION.—After a full argument before Judge Cadwallader, in reference to the naval stores captured at Newbern, North Carolina, by the combined land and naval forces of the United States, the Court has decided that the captured goods are not prize goods, and therefore do not belong to the naval captors.—*Philadelphia Ledger.*

A private letter received by a gentleman of Boston, from London, gives a fact which we have not seen before published: "At the great commemoration day at Oxford, last week, a Confederate officer appeared on the platform in his uniform, and was cheered to such a degree as to rise several times and bow to the galleries in acknowledgment of the honor."—*Washington Chronicle.*

The Treasury Investigation.

YANKEE MORALS—A PEEP BEHIND THE CURTAIN.

During the session of the Yankee Congress, Hon. JAMES BROOKS, of New York, declared that the Treasury Building at Washington had been turned into a bawdy house, where Government officials, in responsible situations, disported with lewd women, and otherwise conducted themselves in a manner that brought disgrace upon the Department.

The New York *Sun* says of this statement and what came of it:

When Mr Brooks made this statement the opposition laughed derisively, and the "loyal press" of the country immediately published a series of indignant editorials, denouncing the Copperheads for this "weak invention." A Committee of Inquiry was demanded, and refused by the Republican members. Subsequently an investigation was ordered, and a Committee appointed. These gentlemen sent for forty persons and a large pile of papers; spent many weeks in their investigation, and finally prepared two reports The majority report was a whitewashing document The minority in their report said that "they were not permitted to examine into but a very small portion of the allegations made by Mr. Brooks on the floor of the House." The testimony taken before the Committee has just been published, and from it any intelligent reader may form his own conclusions Affidavits are made showing that Superintendent Clark used his position for the purpose of prostituting the young girls employed in his Department; drinking ale with them in his private office in the Treasury building, where acts were committed, the particulars of which are unfit for publication in these columns.

As to the morality or immorality of the Treasury, the public will judge, not only from the affidavits published, but from the verification of them by the Solicitor of the Treasury, another Republican. Read as follows:

I have further, in obedience to your (Mr. Chase's) order, called before me most of the persons whose affidavits are herewith transmitted by Provost Marshal Baker, and made such other enquiries as it has been in my power to make touching the matter stated in the affidavits, and the result is an entire conviction that the most material of these statements are true; particularly those contained in the affidavits of Ella Jackson, Jennie Germon and Laura Duvall. What action, if any, ought to be taken, in view of these facts, is, of course, not a question for me to consider. I have the honor to, with high respect,

(Signed) EDWARD JORDAN,
Solicitor of the Treasury.

The Slave Market Outdone.

A WHITE MAN SELLING HIS OWN SONS.

Sumner and his followers may prate as loudly as they please about "the barbarism of slavery," and Mrs. Stowe may rack imagination to create a monster like the brutal Legre, but we had an exhibition in this town during the examination of those recently conscripted, which, for inhuman and barbarism, we defy any slave mart in the world to match. A father, who had already sold one minor son as a substitute to the human shambles, where he fell a victim, appeared in our town on last Monday, dragging at his heels two half-grown, ill-shaped boys. They were all the sons he had, and he had contracted to sell them both as substitutes. They had been bargained for by "loyal" men. The smaller one, almost a mere child, was prospectively the property of a loud-mouthed and pestilent Abolitionist—a huge beast of a man, who stood six feet two in his stockings, and weighed over 200 pounds.

This intensely "loyal" and "patriotic" fellow, when his own son, a sturdy, well grown young man, enlisted, followed him to Chambersburg, and brought him back home on the plea that he was a minor, and had enlisted without his father's consent. Yet he is always full of war, and eager for fighting so long as it is at the expense of the blood of some one else than himself or his own family Being drafted, however, and wishing to lessen the probability of such a misfortune befalling him again speedily, and impelled at the same time to save a little money, he had bargained with a brutal father to pay a less sum than three hundred dollars for the body, the bones, the blood, nay more, the life of a child.

The father was actuated solely by a sordid desire for gain; the purchaser was moved by the sneaking, white-livered cowardice that forbade his risking his own worthless carcase in a war for the prosecution of which he howls daily, and by the mean selfishness of his nature, which prompted him to make a cheap bid when bartering for a human victim. A plot had been made up by the parties to this disgusting transaction by which they hoped to deceive the Board. The boys were made to lie as to their ages, and represented themselves as older than they really were. So immature and youthful, however, was the appearance of the little wretches, that the Board refused to believe the statements made to them, even though the father himself lied as to their ages in order that he might be enabled to effect a sale of his offspring They were both rejected for this reason, as entirely too young for the service

The overgrown human brute, who had expected to save himself in this way, sorrowfully and reluctantly paid over his money to save his carcase for a time, and the wretched father, after reeling about our streets for a day or so in drunkenness, went home, much disappointed, no doubt, in being balked in the sale of his sons. There is no coloring about this story, no fictitious glossing. It is true, just as we tell it, and known to be so to the very letter by many who will read this statement. We need make no comment We have seen negroes sold on the block to the highest bidder, but that only involved a change of service. Here was a white man, with one son whom he had sold dead already, endeavoring to sell two more boys to what was almost certain death. He found loyal Abolitionists ready and eager to become the purchasers of cheap substitutes Let us hear no more about the barbarism of slavery, when the barbarism of this war can exhibit such a revolting spectacle in the light of heaven, on the free soil of Pennsylvania.—*Fulton (Pa.) Democrat.*

LAUNCH OF TWO STEAMERS.—Yesterday there were launched from the building yard of Messrs. Jones, Quiggin & Co., two splendid steam ships, which are intended for the Nassau and Wilmington trade. The vessels, which are exactly of similar size, were both launched from the same slip The first of the vessels launched was christened the Owl. She is 770 tons burthen, 230 feet long, and 26 feet in breadth. Her lines are exceedingly fine, and she has been constructed with a special regard to fast sailing properties. The vessel went beautifully off the stocks, and was immediately followed by the Bat, her exact sister ship. The Owl was taken into Messrs. Laird's Graving Dock at Birkenhead, where she will receive her engines and other fittings. The Bat was towed into the Great Float, where her engines, which are being constructed by Messrs Watts & Co., of London, will be placed on board. Messrs. Jones, Quiggin & Co.'s yard is at present in a state of very great activity, there being no less than twelve vessels on the stocks, four of them being swift paddle steamers, for which Messrs. Watts & Co., of London, are constructing the engines. One of the ships nearly ready for launching is a very fine vessel of about 1600 tons burthen, built upon Mr Jordan's original plan of iron frame work, with wooden planking, in every respect similar to the celebrated Tubal Cain. We also understand that the large ship of between 3500 and 4500 tons burthen, intended for the Australian trade, the keel of which was laid a few weeks ago, will at once be proceeded with. This vessel, which is upwards of 400 feet in length, is the largest merchant ship ever constructed on the banks of the Mersey.—*Liverpool Journal of Commerce, 22d June.*

It is generally believed in the army, and so reported by Yankee prisoners, that Major General Frank Blair was captured by our forces in the fight of Friday, and that he is now concealing himself in the disguise of a private, with the view, probably of getting an earlier exchange than he would get if his rank was known. The crowd of prisoners should be thoroughly searched and the rascal ferreted out. No one who has ever seen his face could forget it, for it is the embodiment of brassy impudence and assurance. Hon. George W. Jones and Col. John H. Savage, now in this place, we believe served in the old Congress with him, and would be able to identify his hang dog countenance. The prisoners, we are informed, will pass through Griffin on their way South to-day For want of transportation they are on foot.—*Chattanooga Rebel.*

A destructive insect, called the "midge," is making sad havoc with the Canadian crops.

Conundrum by the author of the forged proclamation.—Why are cross dogs like ladies in summer? Because they need muslin.

LYNCHBURG VIRGINIAN.

NOTICE.—The cross mark appended to the names of certain subscribers indicates that the term of which they subscribed will soon expire. They are thus notified in time to renew their subscription if desired.

FOR PEACE.—The Abingdon Virginian learns from persons just in from Kentucky, that 9 out of the 10 members of the Yankee Congress from that State, are out-and-out peace men.

ORPHAN ASYLUM FOR SOLDIERS' CHILDREN.—We learn that steps are being taken to organize a plan for the establishment of an orphan asylum, under the auspices of the Methodist Church of Virginia, for the benefit of the children of deceased soldiers; and that as soon as the arrangements are completed, the members and friends of that denomination will be called upon to contribute funds for that purpose.

FROM EAST TENNESSEE.—The Bristol Gazette says: "We learn from a reliable scout just from the vicinity of Knoxville, that all remains quiet in our front. The forces supposed to be reinforcing Knoxville have left for the 'lower country.' He asserts positively that there are now not more than 500 Yankees between Knoxville and this place. Bushwhackers—East Tennessee Tories—are abundant."

In addition to the above we have private intelligence from East Tenn. of an interesting character, which we do not deem it prudent to publish at this time.—ED. VIRG'N.

A STEAMBOAT ON THE CANAL.—A beautiful little side-wheel steamer, called the "Minnie Gorgas," has recently been put upon the James River Canal, at Richmond, and in point of appearance and speed presents a lively contrast to the slow-moving, clumsy-looking boats that have heretofore had undisputed sway of this valuable source of communication. She was built at the Bellona Arsenal, and is the property of the Confederate Government.

FROM MOBILE.—In view of the exciting news from Mobile and the critical situation of affairs there, the following list of the enemy's ships off that city will be read with interest:

Hartford (flag ship) 20 guns, Richmond 18, Brooklyn 24, Monongahela 12, Lackawanna 14, Oneida 10, Metacomb 10, Gennessee 8, Sebago 10, Port Royl 8, Kenebec 5, Pindola 4, Luseo 4, Phembina 6, Penguin 7, Tennessee 5, Conemagh 9, Ossipee 12 and Galena 14; Cowslip, Phillippi, Glassan, Jasmine, Buckhorn—tugs.

TRANS-MISSISSIPPI.—Yankee papers say Gen Kirby Smith is crossing the Mississippi to the east side, but at what point they do not know. Gen Marmaduke, they say, was crossing his men in small parties in the neighborhood of James' Landing. On the 10th inst., Shelby, who was at Searcey, between Little Rock and Batesville, captured 180 of the 10th Illinois cavalry, including eight or nine commissioned officers. Gen Carr was in command of the Federal troops at Little Rock, whilst Gen's Lee and Gordon, from Louisiana, were at the mouth of White river with reinforcements for Gen Steele.

NEWSPAPER MEN IN THE FIGHT.—In the fight before Atlanta on the 22d ult., Captain Farris, known for many months past as "Marshall" of the Atlanta and Knoxville Register, was killed.

Captain Mathews, known to the readers of the Appeal as "Harvy," lost a leg early in the fight.

Captain Cluskey, editor of the Memphis Avalanche, now of Gen Vaughn's staff, received a dangerous wound in the side.

Virginius Hutchen, formerly editor of the Kentucky Reporter, passed through the fight unscatched.

ADMISSIONS OF THE ENEMY.—The New York *World*, in an editorial, admits that Richmond cannot be taken, and in commenting on the repulse at Petersburg, says:—"Thus terminates the summer campaign."

"Gen. Grant is a tenacious military leader, and intends to get all the work he can out of his soldiers; but troops who are so constantly disappointed of victory, after undergoing terrible sacrifices, cannot be expected to be in proper *morale* for immediately pushing on the campaign. Indeed, the problem is no longer the destruction of Lee's army, and the capture of Richmond, or even the capture of Petersburg, but the defence of the loyal States against the rebel armies.—No doubt Gen. Grant will keep a large force operating on the James, but we can never afford to present to the world the spectacle of an enemy marching unhindered through our own territory."

FROM THE UNITED STATES.—The Richmond *Sentinel* says:

"We had a pleasant interview last evening with a gentleman just arrived from the United States. He gives a most gratifying account of the changes in public sentiment with regard to the prosecution of the war.—In Pennsylvania the reaction in favor of peace is very great; and he is confident, without some unforseen occurrence arises, that the peace candidate will be triumphantly elected next fall.

We are satisfied from data exhibited to us, but which it would not be prudent to publish, that the call of Lincoln for troops, will furnish two white men from Maryland to the Confederate armies for one to the Federal."

HUNTER'S WAR ON WOMEN.—Hunter, the monster, openly proclaims a war on the women of the South. Read the following extract, from a lady to her daughter, written from the Sweet Springs, under date of the 1st of July, and published in the *Enquirer*. One of the first ladies of the land went to the scoundrel Hunter to ask him for a guard to protect her house. He told her to go home, for he had determined to burn the house; that he intended to burn every house within five miles of any spot at which any of his men had been bushwhacked. She said:—"Surely, General, you cannot be in earnest in saying that you intend that women and children are to suffer such a calamity in addition to all besides that is the natural consequence of war." He replied in these remarkable words: "I do intend that the women shall suffer; I organized this raid for that especial purpose; the women of the South are the fiends that have kept up this war; they have thrust their fathers, sons and brothers into the rebel army, and have endured everything that could incite the men to go on with the war, and I intend to crush the proud, rebellious spirit of you Virginians. I am coming back to burn your grain fields, to make a desert of the pride of the earth, to desolate your country, and to starve women and children, but that they shall come back to their lawful Government—the best Government on the face of the earth."

A PLEA FOR THE DOGGERIES.—We have received a letter from one "John Lucas, 32d Georgia Battalion," who is evidently much displeased with our strictures on the doggeries. He thinks that the soldiers "ought to be let alone, and have places to get a drink when they feel like it." No doubt John loves a dram and would be loath to have his grog stopped. We pity him. The writer objects to our mentioning negroes and soldiers in the same connection, and we deem it due to ourselves to say that we meant no offence to [illegible]ers, nor designed to put them upon a [illegible] of condition with an inferior race.—We have as high a regard for our country's defenders as any man in it, and rather more than those have who would poison them with mean whiskey.

"John Lucas, 32d Georgia Battalion," adds, "I would wish you for one, to direct your attention to a higher grade than the soldiers. Eight days ago, a *gentleman* with and wearing the uniform of a commissioned officer of the Confederate army was carried along the streets between two negroes to his home, after imbibing this so-called poison, and in large potations I presume, to all appearance." To this we would simply remark that the negroes should have been ashamed of their companion.

"John Lucas, 32d Georgia Battalion," thinks that "the large hotels, where a man gets poisoned in the most approved style," should receive a share of our condemnation. They will: If this charge could be proven we would advise that their licenses for keeping houses of entertainment be taken from them.

"John Lucas, 32d Georgia Battalion," concludes his letter with a threat. Would you harm us John for wishing you well? Be it so then: we are always in place. But seriously; we half suspect that this fierce Georgian is a myth and that same keeper of a low doggery and has assumed a name that does not belong to him. How is it John? are you a fiction or a reality?

EFFORTS OF REPUBLICANS TO HAVE GENERAL M'CLELLAN RESTORED TO COMMAND.

A despatch from Washington says:

A very strong effort is making by Republican politicians to induce the Administration to give General McClellan the command of the defences of Washington, as urged by the Herald. They say that his appointment is demanded by expediency; that if he can rally an army of a hundred thousand or a hundred and fifty thousand men for the defence of Washington, and to operate on Lee's flank, the advantage done to the cause will compensate for the sacrifice of personal feeling towards him, while if, as they believe, he should fail to secure any considerable support from the people, it will dispose at once and forever of his claims as a leader, either military or political. Hon Henry J. Raymond arrived here this morning, it is understood for the purpose of urging this matter upon the President.

LATEST BY TELEGRAPH

Reports of the Press Association.

Entered according to Act of Congress, in the year 1863, by J. S. THRASHER, in the Clerk's Office of the District Court of the Confederate States in the Northern District of Georgia.

IMPORTANT FROM MOBILE

AN ENGAGEMENT WITH THE ENEMY'S FLEET.

ONE MONITOR SUNK.

TWO CONFEDERATE VESSELS CAPTURED.

ADMIRAL BUCHANAN WOUNDED AND TAKEN PRISONER.

THE ENEMY'S FLEET APPROACHED THE CITY.

RICHMOND, Aug. 7th.

The following was received yesterday, dated Mobile, Aug. the 5th:

Hon. J. A. Seddon—Seventeen of the enemy's vessels, 14 ships and 3 ironclads, passed Fort Morgan this morning.

The Tecumshe, a monitor, was sunk by Fort Morgan.

The Tennessee surrendered, after a desperate engagement with the enemy's fleet.

Admiral Buchanan lost a leg and is a prisoner.

The Selma was captured and the Gaines was beached near the hospital.

The Morgan is safe and will try to run up to-night.

The enemy's fleet has approached the city.

A monitor has been engaged at Fort Powell all day.

Signed, D. H. MAURY, Maj-Gen'l.

2D DISPATCH.

MOBILE, Aug. 6.

A special to the Advertiser from Fort Morgan, the 6th, says the enemy's gun boat, with wounded, has left for Pensacola. We communicated with her.

Admiral Buchanan's wound is doing well, he may be saved.

On the Tennessee two were killed and eight wounded; on the Selma eight killed, including Lieut. Comstock, and seven wounded; on the Morgan one slightly wounded.

The garrison at Fort Morgan are in fine spirits; loss slight; enemy firing wildly.

A gunboat came up last night; also, the crew of the Gaines.

The enemy lost one monitor and one gunboat.

In Mobile business is generally suspended and the city is a military camp.

Three gunboats came within a few miles of Dog River Battery yesterday evening; they went back. The enemy have merely carried the out posts.

FROM PETERSBURG—MORE ABOUT THE COUNTER-MINE.

PETERSBURG, Aug. 7th.

It having been definitely ascertained several days since that the enemy were mining in front of an important position on our centre, counter-mining was at once commenced and rapidly pushed forward for the purpose of preventing the consummation of his object. The enemy's tap was approached some distance in front of his breastworks and beneath his picket line, where chambers were dug and powder deposited. All being in readiness, and while the enemy's diggers were still excavating beneath and his skirmishers firing above, the mine was sprung, causing a heavy explosion and throwing the earth upwards to some height. The enemy was much confused by the unexpected event, but soon manned their cannon and sprung to their breastworks. No infantry attack was made on our side, none having been intended. The object of the mine was fully gained in destroying the enemy's sap, which it is believed was effectually done with some loss to the Yankees. Immediately after the explosion the enemy opened a fierce cannonading on our lines, which was replied to by our artillery. Everything was very quiet yesterday and to-day.

FROM ATLANTA.

ATLANTA, August 6th.

Brisk skirmishing continued throughout yesterday and last night on our left; lively artillery duel took place last evening between our batteries on Peach Tree and the enemy.

Comparative quiet reigned in the city last night.

The enemy continue to concentrate their force on our left—Palmer's corps occupying the extreme right, his headquarters on the Longtown road, and Staily's on the left, his pickets extending to the Georgia Railroad.

About 75 prisoners, including a Captain and Lieutenant, were brought in yesterday and last night.

Gen. Wheeler has issued a congratulatory order to the Cavalry, on the defeat and rout of the enemy's raiding party.

All quiet save some sharpshooting this morning.

2D DISPATCH.

RICHMOND, August 7.

The following was received this morning:

ATLANTA, Aug. 6.

Hon. J. A. Seddon:

The enemy made two assaults, to-day, on Findley's and Lewis' brigades, of Bates' Division, in Lee's corps, both of which were handsomely repulsed with loss to them.

Signed, J. B. HOOD, General.

LATER FROM THE NORTH.

RICHMOND, Aug. 7.

The New York Times of the 5th received.

No intelligence of importance from either of the main armies.

A Court of Inquiry is about to be convened, to inquire into the causes of the late disaster at Petersburg.

The exact number of Federal losses is ascertained to be five thousand six hundred and forty.

No gold quotations, the 6th being fast day.

The Washington Chronicle, of the 6th, says Kelly repulsed the rebels under McCausland and Bradly Johnson, at New Creek, the 5th.

The rebel loss was severe, ours slight.

Another force of rebels occupied Hagerstown, the 5th.

Gov. Curtin calls for thirty thousand militia.

He says, I cannot too earnestly urge upon the people of this State the necessity for the immediate presence of this force.

A telegram says the greatest consternation once more prevails along the Cumberland Valley.

The population are panic stricken, and the farmers hurrying off stock.

Foreign advices to the 26th are unimportant.

2D DISPATCH.

RICHMOND, Aug. 8.

The following is additional from the Chronicle of the 6th.

The City Council, of Philadelphia, voted to pay four hundred dollars bounty to every volunteer.

The most extensive gang of counterfeiters ever known in the United States, were broken up at St. Louis. A large amount of counterfeit greenbacks was secured.

Great excitement exists in Montgomery county, Illinois, in consequence of attempts to capture a band of guerrillas and deserters in that county.

The citizens of Hillsboro' fear the rebels will execute their threats to burn the town.

A regiment of infantry is ordered to Hillsboro.

Stirring times are anticipated. Wade, of Ohio, and Davis, of Maryland, have published a letter in the Tribune strongly animadverting upon the refusal of Lincoln to sign the bill for re-organizing the Rebel State Governments.

FROM THE SOUTHWEST.

CLINTON, LA., Aug. 5th.

New Orleans papers state that the enemy have entirely evacuated Brownsville Texas, removing everything.

Our batteries in sinking the steamer Clara Bell killed and wounded 13 Yankees; the balance escaped.

A National negro convention is to be held at New York on the 4th of October.

Yesterday morning at 8 o'clock Col Scott captured the Stockade at Doyle's plantation, on the river below Baton Rouge, without the loss of a man. We have over 100 prisoners and a large amount of military stores.

FROM PETERSBURG.

PETERSBURG, Aug. 8.

Since the explosion, Friday evening, nothing of interest has occurred.

Some picket firing and mortar shelling today, but resulting in nothing.

Grant is certainly sending more troops from his command to the Valley.

Grant. however, is not believed to have abandoned mining, but is still persevering in digging.

THE CAMDEN WEEKLY CONFEDERATE.

"KNOWLEDGE IS POWER, AND THE PRESS IS THE ROYAL THRONE UPON WHICH SHE SITS, AN ENTHRONED MONARCH."

Vol. III. CAMDEN, S. C., WEDNESDAY MORNING, AUGUST 10, 1864. [No. 19.

The Confederate

IS PUBLISHED AT CAMDEN,

EVERY WEDNESDAY MORNING,

BY

J. T. HERSHMAN.

☞ Terms of subscription—**Five Dollars per annum.**

☞ Rates of Advertising—**Two Dollars, per square** of twelve lines, for first insertion, and **One Dollar and Fifty Cents** for each subsequent one.

☞ Communications calculated to advance the interest of our District and State, published free of charge.

Johnston and Hood.

The Lynchburg Republican has the following able editorial on the recent removal of Gen. Johnston from the command of the Army of Tennessee:

We are compelled to regard the removal of General Johnston from the command of the army of Tennessee as a most fortunate circumstance, if indeed, it has not been effected too late to avert impending disaster in Georgia. He assumed command at Dalton several months ago under the most favorable auspices which never marked the assumption of power by any officer. From causes which it is needless now to discuss, but which are mostly attributable to the shameless conduct of the Atlanta press, General Bragg had so far lost the confidence of the country, and to some extent of his officers and men, as to make it prudent and desirable even in his own judgement, that he should be relieved of his command. It is true he had defeated Rosencrauz with almost double his numbers, at Murfreesboro." He had held the overwhelming numbers of that wily General in check at Tullahoma and on the banks of the Tennessee, for months. He had fought the brilliant battle of Chickamauga, and won one of the most glorious victories of the war. But by the unexpected miscarriage of Longstreet's expedition to Knoxville and the factious exposure of his plans by the Atlanta press, Bragg lost the battle of Missionary Ridge and was compelled to fall back to Dalton. At this point and under these circumstances, Bragg retired from the field and Johnston mounted into his stirrups. The whole country—even Bragg's best friends—rejoiced in the change and gave their warmest sympathies to the new commander, simply because the peculiar circumstances of the case rendered a change desirable, and a more auspicious state of things was eagerly anticipated as the result.

Johnston was given several months to re-organize and dicipline his army, and was heavily reinforced by Gens. Polk, Loring and other commands. The press which had ruthlessly pursued Bragg to his death, now eagerly came to the support and applause of Johnston, and predicted for the army of Tennessee under his direction, a far more brilliant fame than it had been able to win under the bad management of his fallen predecessor. On all occasions, and from every source, the country was constantly electrified with the glad tidings that our army was in splendid trim and eager for the gauge of battle to be thrown down by the enemy. It had been the army of defeat and of retreat under Bragg—it has now to be the army of victory and of advance under Johnston. Such was the predictions of friends and such the hopes of the country. No one dreamed that there would be any falling back from Dalton, but no sooner did the enemy advance than Johnston, with a splendid army, nearly as large as General Lee's proceeded to execute one of those brilliant retrogade movements which alone have given him all the fame he has ever won in this war, and all to which he is entitled. He fell back to Resaca and then to Etawah river to prevent the enemy from flanking him. The country was startled but it did not complain. Johnston it is said, had given up a weaker for a stronger position, and had placed a formidable river between himself and his adversary. It was here, we think, that he issued one of his stirring addresses to his troops, in which he promised them that there was to be no more "retreats," and that the enemy was to be met and vanquished upon the banks of that stream. But no sooner did the enemy advance than Johnston again retreated, first to Altoona, then to Ackworth, and afterwards to the Kennesaw mountains. It is not strange that the confidence of the country began to be shaken by those repeated retreats; but this feeling was suppressed by the confident assurance that Johnston had at last reached an impregnable position from which he could neither be whipped nor flanked. Here in the mountain fastnesses of the Kennesaw, was to be the Waterloo of Sherman. But the amazement and deep chagrin of the country could no longer be disguised when, a few indecisive combats, our gallant army was put in motion to the river, and the mountain passes of Kennesaw abandoned for the lowlands of the Chattahoochee river, only five miles from Atlanta! This might have been tolerable, and even pardonable, had there been any room for belief that Johnston would join battle and arrest the further advance of the enemy. But the whole tenor of the press and off all the news from that quarter, made perfectly certain that Johnston was still alarmed for his "flank," and that he was ready to abandon Atlanta and again fall back to the interior.

At this critical stage of the campaign he has been superceded by Gen. Hood. We know nothing of Hood's intellectual calibre, and cannot pronounce upon his fitness to succeed to the command of a great army. But we know that he has a splendid reputation in the army and in the country, that the Fabian policy is none of his policy, that he will keep his eyes to the front and not exclusively to his flanks, and that when he retreats it will be because his men cannot stand. We fear Atlanta will fall, because Johnston has permitted the enemy to reach its environs, but we have the utmost confidence that the day is far from being lost in that quarter, and that in less than a month the fortunes of battle will be turned in our favor, and the hosts of the enemy sent howling back to the banks of the Ohio.

Scenes in Wilson's Raid.

A Yankee correspondent who accompanied Wilson on his last raid, gives the following sketch of the conduct of the negroes seduced by the raiders from their homes?

We had scarcely marched ten miles on the late expedition when the negroes began to rally aound our flag, and the number rapidly increased, still, I feel perf ectly safe in saying, two thousand contrabands of all ages followed the expedition.

It was an amusing sight to witness the manner in which they came in, and to see the taste they displayed in selecting articles to carry along into the promised land; for it seemed to be a settled opinion with them that when once they reached 'Yankeedom' they were in the land of promise "sure 'nuff." A wench dressed in some cotton stuff, coarse enough for gunny bags, dirty and greasy withal as the sacks pork merchants encase sides of bacon in, would steal her mistress, fashionable bonnet, ornate with marvellous ribbons and wonderful plumes and flowers, and with this upon her head she would trudge along through the dust, supremely proud of her finery, and thinking herself as attractive as an African Venus.

Some of the women would take articles along with them of no earthly utility. Occasionally one could be seen carrying a huge mirror, another a china washbowl or pitcher or some other article of crockery ware of equally doubtful utility. Some boy, whose master had skedaddled, would steal his clothes, even to his cane, gloves and hat, and mounted on a gay and prancing steed which he had purloined, he would ride about, swelling like a peacock, and looking down upon his walking companions with the imperious air of a Magnus Apollo. How the women and children managed to keep up with us I cannot conceive. From the 22d of June till the present they have followed us, notwithstanding the fact that at times we scarcely rested for an hour in forty eight; and in twenty-four hours we have marched more than sixty miles. Yet the poor creatures followed, panting and perspiring, still keeping up.

Many of them joined us mounted on either horses or mules, and as these were wanted in the batteries and wagons they were taken from them. A large number of carts, wagons, carriages, coaches, barouches, and vehicles of every description were brought into the hands of the enemy. The rebel cavalry sabred many of the negroes who fell into their hands when they made their charge near the wanty. It was really appalling to hear the heart-rending shrieks of the women and children as the rebels dashed into them, firing their carbines among them and cutting them down with their sabres. Probably a thousand men, women and children followed us to our lines.

As Far from the End as Ever.

The Chicago Times acknowledges that efforts of the North in this war have proved a disastrous failure, and that really the Government at Washington is no nearer the subjugation of the rebellion than it was two years ago. It speaks thus boldly:

The three main causes upon which the Administration and its adherents have relied for assistance in the suppression of the rebellion, viz: starvation, financial ruin and demoralization, have all failed to render the Union causes the slightest assistance. With ample supplies, with armies that are a unit in their resistance, the South opposes us everywhere to-day with as much determination and in as great force as ever. The rebel armies are nowhere demoralized; on the contrary, they are everywhere a unit in their resistance to the North, and, in addition, present at every point a strength as numerically great, in spite of continued and enormous losses, as that with which they have opposed us at any time during the war. Practically we are not one rood nearer the subjugation of the rebellion than we were one year to two years ago. We have captured a few forts and other strongholds, but we have not conquered the people; we do not hold the country; nor have we suppressed, to any extent, the spirit of the rebellion.

The parties now attempting the task are utterly unable to effect what they have undertaken. They have spent some two thousand million dollars; have plunged the nation into practical bankruptcy; have had an armed force of nearly or quite two million men; have sacrificed a quarter million lives, and incapacitated an equal number of men from their duties as citizens; have demoralized the whole country—and yet, despite all these tremendous sacrifices, have accomplished scarcely anything towards subjugation of the rebellion.

J. T. HERSHMAN—Editor.

Camden, Wednesday, August 10.

Fort Sumter.

The Ladies, Aid Association proposes, sending vegetables on Thursday next, 11th inst., to the gallant defenders of Fort Sumter; and requests those who feel disposed, to send their contributions to the store of R. M. KENNEDY, who will take charge of them until shipped.

The Attack on Macon.

The Atlanta *Appeal* says that when the enemy made the advance on Macon that Gen. J. E. Johnston took the field promptly at the head of the impromptu forces that were raised to defend the city, and the number at his command proved equal to the emergency. Hurrah for the gallant old chieftain.

The rush of emigrants from Ireland to New York is so great as to entirely surpass all of transportation offered by steamers or sailing vessels.

SUICIDES IN FRANCE.—More than ten suicides take place every day in France; last year 4000 persons committed suicide.

Prince Edmond de Polignac, brother of the Prince in the Confederate army, is to marry a daughter of Baron Sina, the wealthiest man in Austria; his fortune is estimated at $43 000,000.

The anual Convention of the Bible Societies of South Carolina will be held at Spartanburg C. H., on the third Tuesday of September, 1864. The opening sermon will be preached by the Rev Dr. BACKMAN, of Charleston.

In the Northern States the coming harvest promises to be very slender. In this country and in Europe it is directly otherwise. In England and Ireland, according to last accounts, the fields were offering the greatest abundance, and in France it was the same.

It is believed by knowing ones that Gen. Hood is very busily engaged just now in Hood-winking Gen. Sherman, and that that shrewd Yankee conquerer will wake up some fine morning to find himself in the fix of Sam Weller's sweetheart—"circumvented."

A private letter to the editors of the Lynchburg *Republican* says that the Baltimore and Ohio railroad has been effectually destroyed. For a distance of fifteen miles the ties have been burnt and the iron cut in two so as to render it totally unfit for any future use.

Chambersburg is the county seat of Franklin county, Pennsylvania, in the Vally of the Conecocheague, a tributary of the Potomac. It is 22 miles from Hagerstown, Maryland, and 42 from Harrisburg. It contains a population of about 5,000, and was a flourishing place.

THE GREAT SOUTHERN CENTIPEDE.—The *Tribune* says: "The rebellion is visibly on its last legs, and tottering at that., To which the Boston *Courier* replies: "Though not much of an entomologist, we venture to suggest that the rebellion, in extremities, resembles the lobster more than the centipede, inasmuch as when it looses its last legs new ones grow.

The old remark of "an engineer being blown up with his own petard" is applicable to the Yankee attack on Saturday week last. Their sapping and mining cost them about two thousand five hundred men, in killed, wounded and prisoners. Grant is in a fair way to find out that the "cocade city" is a harder nut to crack than Vicksburg. His Mississippi laurels are getting soiled in the mud of the Appomattox.

It is not a fact generally known, that CHARLES SUMNER, FESSENDEN and WILSON, the three arch devils of the Abolitionist party, were illegimate children. SUMNER is not recognized by the members of his family, and WILSON does not wear his true name. JOHN C. FREMONT is the son of a French fidler, was born in Charleston, and unsanctified by marriage. HAMLIN, the Yankee Vice President, is a mulatto. LINCOLN is in the same catalogue.

It is pleasant to read the speculations of the Northern press upon the "safety of the National Capital," and in the same light to detect the unmistakable symptoms of fright and dismay. Hardly have their last words of gratulation, for their timely deliverance from the "audacious rebels," died away, when they are again fleeing for safety before the same mighty sword which smote them, carrying awe and terror among them.

LATEST ARMY NEWS.

From Petersburg

RICHMOND, August 6.—Special to the *Whig* from Petersburg. It having been ascertained that the enemy were mining extensively in front of Gracie's Brigade, on our centre, it was determined to stop their operations by countermining—our culvert being completed. Yesterday between 6 and 7 o'clock p. m., our mine was sprung, blowing up the enemys skirmishers line, demolishing his mine. The affair was a great success, completely frustrating the design of the enemy at that point, throwing troops along his line. Great confusion ensued. No infantry attack was intended or made on our side. Artillery firing along the lines were very rapid, for the space of an hour. Numbers of the enemy were killed by the explosion of the mine. A few shells were thrown into the city, after the explosion of the mine.

Everything resumed its usual quiet this morning.

Northern News.

CLINTON, August 5.—New Orleans papers say that the enemy have entirely evacuated Brownsville, Texas, removing everything.

Our batteries in sinking the steamer Clara Bell, killed 3 and wounded 13 Yankees. The ballance escaped to Skipmith Landing.

The National Democratic Convention is to be held in New York on the 4th of October.

Yesterday morning at 3 o'clock Col. Scott captured the stockade at Doyle's plantation on the river, below Baton Rouge, without the loss of a man. We have taken over 100 prisoners and a large amount of military stores.

The New York *Times* of the 5th has been received. No news of importance from either of the main armies. The Court of Inquiry to inquire into the late disaster at Petersburg had met. The exact number of Federal loss has been ascertained to be 5,640.

No gold quotions given, the 4th being a day of fasting.

The Washington *Chronicle* of the 6th says Reilly repulsed the rebels under McCaslin and Bradley Johnson at Tow Creek, on the 4th. Entire loss 7.

Another force of rebels occupied Hagerstown on the 5th. Gov. Curtin call for 3000 militia forces, and earnestly urges on the people the necessity of immediate preparation for defence.

A portion of the Cumberland Valley are completely panic stricken, and the farmers are hurrying off their stock.

From Richmond.

ATLANTA, August 7.—The following was received this morning:

To the Hon. J. A. Seddon, Secretary of War: The enemy made two assaults on Findley's and Lewis' brigade, of Bates Division, Lee's corps. both of which were handsomley repulsed, with heavy loss to the enemy.

(Signed.) J. B. HOOD.

ATLANTA, Aug 7.—Brisk skirmishing continued throughout yesterday. Last night on our left a lively artillery duel took place between our batteries on the Peach Tree and the enemy. Comparative quiet reigns. The enemy continued concentrating forces on our left—Palmer's forces occupying our extreme right. His headquarters on Sand Town road, and Staley's on the left—his pickets extending to the Georgia railroad.

About 75 prisoners, including Captains and Lieutenants were brought in last night.

Gen. Wheeler has issued a congratulatory order to the cavalry on the defeat and route of the enemy's raiding parties.

All quiet, except some sharpshooting this morning.

From Mobile.

MOBILE, August 6.—In an engagement with the monitors we had two killed and eight wounded on the Tennessee, and seven wounded at fort Morgan. The garrison of the fort is reported to be in fine spirits. Lieut. Comstock was killed in the engagement, and Admiral Buchanan wounded severely in the leg, though it was thought amputation unneccessary.

Our loss is considered slight. The enemy continues firing. The crew of the Gaines and other gunboats came up last night. The enemy lost one monitor and one gunboat in the engagement.

Business in Mobile generally suspended, and the city military all in camp.

Three gunboats came within a few miles of Dog River Bar on yesterday evening, and went back. The enemy have barely carried our out-post.

MOBILE, August 7.—To the Hon. J. A. Seddon Secretary of War: Seventeen of the enemies vessels, 14 ships and 3 iron-clads, passed Fort Morgan this morning.

The monitor Tecumseh was sunk by Fort Morgan. The Tennessee was compelled to surrender after a desperate engagement with the enemy's fleet.

Admiral Buchanan loss a leg, and is a prisoner.

The Selma has been captured.

The Gaines was beached near Hospital at Fort Morgan.

The enemies fleet has approached the city, and the monitors have been engaged with Fort Powel all day.

MOBILE, August 8.—On Friday night, Lieut. Col. Williams, commanding Fort Powell, evacuated it and blew it up. The enemy have been shelling fort Gains yesterday and to-day. The people of Mobile are all ready for the fray. Great confidence prevails. The people are satisfied with the conduct of Buchanan, Murphy and Bennett of the Navy.

STILL LATER.

MOBILE, August 8.—We are pained to announce that Fort Gains was surrendered at half past nine o'clock this morning by it's commander Col. Charles Anderson of the 21st Alabama. The Fort was provisioned for six months and had a garrison of six hundred men.

The followin are the particulars of the surrender, as far as known:

Col. Anderson communicated with the enemy's fleet, by flag of truce, without consulting Gen Page. Gen. Page inquired, by signals, what Anderson's purpose was, but received no answer. He then repeatedly telegraph to Anderson to the fort. At night the general visited Fort Gaines and found that Anderson was on board the flag ship of the Yankee commander, arranging terms of capitulation. He was obliged to return shortly after to the city, but left orders relieving Anderson of command, and peremptory orders to defend the fort the last extremity.

Fort Morgan signalled Fort Gaines this morning, but received no answer except from Yankee officers on the ramparts. Anderson's conduct is officially denounced as inexplicable and shameful

From Ohio.

Wade of Ohio and Davis of Maryland have published letters in the *Tribune*, strongly animadverting on the refusal of Lincoln to sign the bill for the reorganization of the rebel States.

From Richmond.

RICHMOND, August 8.—Additional from the Washington *Chronicle* of the 6th:

The City Council of Philadelphia have voted to pay $400 bounty for every volunteer.

The most extensive counterfeiters ever known have been discovered. The United States is broken up. In St. Louis a large amount of the counterfeits have been secured.

Great excitement prevails in Montgomery county in consequence of an attempt to capture a band of guerrellas and deserters in that county. The citizens of Hillsboro' are fearful that the rebels will burn the town. A regiment of infantry has been ordered to Hillsboro.' Stormy times anticipated.

From Petersburg.

PETERSBURG, August 8.—Since the explosion of the mine of Friday evening, nothing of interest has transpired. Some picket firing and mortar shelling to-day, resulting in nothing of importance.

Grant is certainly sending more troops from his command to the Valley. He is not believed, however, to have abandoned mining, but still perseveres in digging.

A Mormon Settlement in Western Virginia.

The Wheeling (Va) *Intelligencer* says: We learn that there is in the town of South Wheeling a society of Mormons, who practice all the doctrines of that sect except that of polygamy. We have had a conversation with an Englishman who belongs to the society, and who firmly believes in all the peculiar notions of the Latter day Saints. He says he was converted to the faith since his arrival in this country. In his opinion, all the churches to which Gentiles usually attach themselves are wonderfully corrupt. He has not had a physician in his house for five or six years. Cases of sickness are cured by anointing and by laying on of hands, according to the customs of the New Testament.

Complimentary.

Senator Hale, of New Hampshire, said some time ago, that the stealings under the Lincoln administration were more than the entire legimate expenses of the government,

Johnston, Forrest and S. D. Lee.

The friends of Johnston complain that Forrest and Lee have not been sent to cut Sherman's lines of communication; to do for Johnston what he had ample force to do for himself, and to take care of and save his army. Wheeler's large and splendid cavalry force would long since have cut those lines of communication had they been ordered to do so.—But General Johnston is one of those singular overwise men whose comprehensive, intellectual vision and great foresight sees all the dangers, all the chances of failure, all the difficulties ahead, and who will never go forward so long as there is a single obstacle in his way, or a single chance of failure. His wisdom and great accomplishment as a scientific soldier paralizes his action. He is ever standing still, with folded arms, as during the siege of Vicksburg, or retreating, as from Manassas, Yorktown and Dalton. He will never risk a battle until every possible advantage exists on his side; every possible disadvantage on the side of the enemy. Such overwise, apprehensive men are rare in public life, for wholly wanting confidence in themselves, they seldom win the confidence of others. In private life, they are more common; and hence we find that bold, daring, enterprising men, of mean capacity and little learning, much oftener succeed in business than the meditative, the learned, and the wise.

In fact, however, Lee and Forrest have all the while been fighting Johnston's battles, and saving his army from annihilation. But for their splendid achievements in defeating and driving back, with terrible loss, the large reinforcements on their way to join Sherman, he (Johnston) would have long since had much of his supplies cut off, and been overwhelmed by superior numbers.—*Richmond Sentinel.*

Financial matters.

Some of our subscribers want us to give weekly reports of the wholesale markets in New York. How can we? With the circulating medium ranging, in one day, up and down, twenty, thirty and more per cent, any attempt at quotations, in a weekly paper, must mislead. That is why we discontinued it. In our paper dated June 18th, we said greenbacks were down to but a shade above 50 per cent, and were dear at that! Gold was ranging at a nominal average of near 190 to the gold dollar. We were remonstrated with by a good friend, who agress with us in politics, but thought we were extravagant. Well, it is less than one month that has passed. We then pronounced gold the best investment any one could make. It was quoted at one hundred and ninety-nine cents, compaired with greenbacks. Now, in less than one month, ago, were valued at a shade more than fifty cents on the dollar. To-day they are hawked on the streets at thirty-six cents on the gold dollar, and no buyers at that! In another week, perhaps, woman may be pedling greenbacks in baskets on the street, crying: "Three for a dollar, gentlemen, pick them out!"

Merchants are to-day, buying extensively coffee, tea, etc, to ship to Europe, in place of gold. What does this mean? It means that Lincoln's management of Lincoln's war has so impoverished the people of the North that these must drink herb tea, and rye coffee—and without sugar—for that is going away, too.

Well, what of it? Are you not, as the reason of this poverty killing American citizens down South? Is this not "glorious?" Don't the abolition preachers and the abolition papers tell you that it is "glory" to be killed, by those that you lately called "fellow-citizens?"

Poverty is upon you, fooled, deluded people! It is poverty that will come, not as a sacrifice, but as a necessity. It will not be as a free will offering, but will be a punishment on you for letting you rulers handle you as they have done! Will you wake up? Will you demand a stop to this slaughter and impoverishment? Or is America going to sink into the apathy of Asia? Now to day, this week, is the time for you to consider of this?—*From the New York Freeman's Journal!*

The Confederate States and China.

We referred some time ago to a decree issued by the Chinese Government, at the request of the United States Minister in Pekin, against the admission of Confederate vessels to any Chinese port.—The decree is of course, not to the liking of the British residents in China, and one of their organs threatens the Chinese with the wrath of President Davis. "The decree of Prince Kung" it says, "amounts to a casus belli, and if it should suit President Davis to make trouble about it he will have an excellent opportunity of doing so. If he selects to retaliate, there is no power except the United States that would care to interfere, and that power could do but little. Confederate cruisers might open communications with the Talpings, and with ease sweep the present dynasty from the throne. We know of nothing which could be more easily effected; and as, speaking with reference to the law of nations, the Confederate States would have right on their side, unless Prince Kung should select to eat the leek, there would be little difficulty in creating such a complication as might produce most important, perhaps disastrous results."

[*New York Tribune.*

The Siam Times.

VOL. 1., BANGKOK, THURSDAY, AUGUST 12, 1864. NO. 3.

PROSPECTUS.

The Siam Times

A WEEKLY JOURNAL, will be issued from the Printing Office in the rear of the Portuguese Consulate every Thursday, containing such POLITICAL, SHIPPING, COMMERCIAL and LOCAL information as may render it deserving of general support.

The want of such a Journal has been long felt in Bangkok, and the Proprietor feels confident the establishment of a well conducted newspaper, advocating matters connected with the advancement of the country will show, that, an absolute necessity has at last been successfully provided for. The growing importance of Siam, its political situation, located as it is between the prosperous provinces of British Burmah, and the recently acquired French possessions in Cochin China render it imperative that some channel should be introduced to keep those interested in the Country fully acquainted with events transpiring in it.

THE SIAM TIMES will be open for contributions or correspondence under the usual restrictions. As an Advertising medium another want will be supplied.

Orders for advertisements will be received at the Office, and should be directed to the Proprietor, from whom rates of charges can be ascertained, personally or in writing. The Editor will be happy to receive and enter the names of subscribers.

Rates of Subscription.
(*Payable in advance.*)

QUARTERLY, ...	Dollars	5,00
HALF YEARLY, ...	,,	9,00
YEARLY, ...	,,	18,00

Single Extra Copies.

To SUBSCRIBERS	0,30
To NON do.	0,45

J. H. CHANDLER.

๏ วิไสยใจมนุษอยากจะรู้เหตุทุกอย่าง ที่เกิดขึ้นในบ้านเมืองของคน แลใน บ้านเมืองอื่น ๆ ด้วย แลเพราะเหตุการ ที่เกิดขึ้นมักฦๅไปอยู่เอง แลครั้นจะเล่า ฦๅกัน ลางคนก็จะเติมบ้าง ลางคนก็ จะเว้นเสียบ้าง ทำให้ความเสียไป แล เพราะเรื่องความมักเสียไปดังนี้ ลาง คนในทวีปยุรบ ได้รับเปนธุระเก็บเอา เรื่องความที่เกิดมีขึ้นในที่นั้น ๆ เขียน ลงเปนหนังสือแล้ว ก็แจกขายกันต่อ ๆ ไป ภายหลังครั้นมีเครื่องพิมขึ้นแล้ว ก็ได้เอาเรื่องความนั้นตีพิมลงแล้วขาย เหมือนกัน แลทุกวันนี้การนั้นก็เปน การใหญ่ขึ้นแล้ว บัดนี้ในประเทศ สยาม มีหนังสือสัญญาไมตรีทางค้าขาย กันกับหลายประเทศ แล้วก็มีการค้า ขายหลายอย่างหลายแห่ง มีกำปั่นไป มาค้าขายเสมอ แลมีพ่อค้าอาไศรยอยู่ มากแล้ว จึ่งอยากจะรู้เหตุข่าวแลเรื่อง ความในประเทศนี้ แลประเทศอื่น ๆ ด้วย แลเพื่อจะได้รู้เรื่องความต่าง ๆ นั้น เหนควรจะตั้งแต่งหนังสือจดหมาย เหตุในกรุงสยามนี้ แลหนังสือนั้นจะ เรียกว่า สยามแตม แลหนังสือสยาม แตมนี้จะตีพิมทุก ๆ วันประหัศ แล้วก็จะ บอกราคาของสินค้าต่าง ๆ กับทั้งเหตุ การที่เกิดขึ้นทั้งเมืองนี้ แลเมืองนอก ด้วย ถ้าผู้ใดมีของอยากจะขาย หฤๅ อยากจะซื้อ ถ้าจะประกาศไว้ในหนังสือ นี้จะขายได้เร็ว แลจะหาได้ง่าย จะจับ ตีพิมกลางเดือน ๘ นี้ ฯะ

๏ ราคาหนังสือจดหมายเหตุนี้คือดัง นี้ว่า ฉบับหนึ่ง ๓ เดือนเปนเงิน ๕ เหรียน ๖ เดือน ๙ เหรียน ปีหนึ่ง ๑๘ เหรียน แลเงินราคานี้ต้องใช้ให้เงิน ล่วงน่าก่อน ถ้าจะซื้อปลีก แลเปน คนเคยรับตั้งแต่ ๓ เดือนขึ้นไปก็จะ ขายใบละ ๒ สลึง ถ้าเปนคนไม่เคยรับ ก็จะขายใบละ ๓ สลึง เชิญท่านทั้ง หลายที่อยากจะได้ให้มาลงชื่อไว้ที่โรง พิมใต้วัดแก้วฟ้าลงมา ฯะ

NOTICE.

THE UNDERSIGNED BEGS TO inform the Ship owners and Agents of Bangkok, that he has been appointed Surveyors to the Register Maritime or International Loyd's, and is prepared to grant Certificates of Classification on vessels according to their rules.

DANIEL MACLEAN.
Bangkok, 4th August, 1864. tf

๏ ข้าพเจ้ามิศมะเกลน ขอแจ้งความ แก่ท่านทั้งหลายที่เปนเจ้าของเรือกำปั่น ด้วย มีพวกหนึ่ง เปนพวกใหญ่ในเมือง อังกฤษที่เรียกว่า อินเตอแนซันแอลลออิก เปนธุระจะตรวจดูเรือกำปั่นทุกอย่าง ให้รู้ว่ากำปั่นที่ตรวจดูนั้น จะดีชั่ว ประการใด แล้วให้จดไว้ในบาญชีเพื่อ พวกที่รับอินซุแรนคือรับประจำกำปั่น แลของสินค้าซึ่งบันทุกกำปั่น จะรับ ประจำอย่างไร ก็พวกนี้ได้ตั้งข้าพเจ้า ให้เปนเจ้าพนักงานตรวจดูในเมืองไทย แลใคร ๆ มีกำปั่นซึ่งอยากจะให้ตรวจดู นั้น ข้าพเจ้าก็จะมาตรวจดู แล้วก็จะ ให้มีหนังสือบอกให้รู้ว่ากำปั่นเปนอย่าง ไรตามทำเนียมกฎหมาย พวกอินเตอแน ซันแอลลออิดนั้น ฯะ

NOTICE.

PILOT REGULATIONS
for the
Port of Bangkok.

The above Regulations have been cancelled by me from this date, due notice of my doing so, having been made in open Court, before His Excellency, the PHRA-KLANG, Minister of Foreign Affairs.

JOHN BUSH.
HARBOUR MASTER and MASTER ATTENDANT.

N. B.—All Masters of Vessels engaging Licensed Pilots, or other Pilots, must do so at their own risk and responsibility.

JOHN BUSH
HARBOUR MASTER, and MASTER ATTANDANT.
Bangkok, 21st July, 1864. uc

WAR VESSELS

PREPARING AT THE PORT OF NEW YORK.

During the week ending May 10th a considerable number of essels have left the port, and several others are now in commission and will take their departure within a few days. Great difficulty has, however, been experienced in securing the proper class of men for the vessels sailing.

The various departments of the Navy Yard are very busy, and are turning out more work within the same period of time than was ever done there before. Between six and seven thousand men are employed.

The Ticonderoga, of fifteen hundred tons burthen, carrying twenty guns, left the dry dock last evening, and will depart as soon as she receives her battery, probably on monday.

The Brooklyn, carrying twenty-six guns, which has been lying in the North River for a few days will soon take her departure.

The double-ender Mendota, carrying ten guns, will probably leave on sunday.

The Queen, carrying seven guns, left yesterday.

The Gettysburg (Lieutenant Roswell H. Lamson), five guns, and the Cactus (Acting Master Newell C. Graham) two guns, were ready to sail yesterday afternoon.

The Heliotrope (Commander Farley Hop kins), two guns; the Tritonia (Commander George Wiggins), two guns, and the double ender Osceola, left the port in the early part of this week.

A large number of men are at work on the screw frigates Matawassa and Wampanora. The construction of the iron-clad Kalamazoo is going on egularly.

The various yards in and near the city, engaged in constructing vessels for the government, are pushing the work as rapidly as possible. At the yard of Mr. Webb, the Lunderberg, to carry ten guns, is making much progress, having a part of her armour already on. It is expected that she will be launched next month.

At the New York iron ship-yard of Mr. J. J. S. Underhill, Greenpoint, the light-draft monitor Moduc is nearly completed, and will be launched in a few weeks. This vessel is two hundred and twenty-five feet long, forty-five feet wide, carrying two guns, and nineteen feet deep. An important improvement has been made in the construction of the Moduc. Her deck is rounded, the centre being twenty-one inches higher than at the edges, and when she is submerged nothing but this round surface will be visible. The balls will be prevented ripping up the deck plates. She will be launched in September, completely equipped and ready for service. The vessel has a duplicate steering apparatus, and in case the one in the pilot-house becomes disabled, the one under the deck can be used with facility. The bow forms a ram, descending three feet below the top of the deck, and is very strong and sharp.

At the Continental Works, Greenpoint, the light-draft monitor Cohoes is building rapidly, and will be finished in three or four months. Her dimensions are about the same as those of the Moduc.

The Puritan, of the same class as the Dictator, and to carry four guns, is also rapidly completing, and will be launched about the first of July.

The iron double-ender Muscoota, carrying ten guns, will be finished in a few months She is one of the five new iron vessels of her class ordered by government, and will be 255 feet long, 34 feet beam and 12½ feet deep, with side wheels. She is fifteen feet longer than the Chenango class.

The iron-clad Dictator is preparing for a trip to Europe.

Messrs. Secor & Co., of Jersey City, have about four hundred men engaged on the vessels now constructing by them. The Manahatta, 235 feet long, 42 feet wide and 14 feet deep, and carrying two guns, has been launched, with her turret up, and a large number of men are busily engaged in fitting her for service. Her engines and boilers have been tested, and by the 15th she is expected to make her trial-trip, when she will go to the Navy Yard to be put in commission. The Mahopac is nearly ready for launching, which will take place on the 21st inst. She is 235 feet long, 42 feet wide and 14 feet deep, and has two guns. Captain Ericsson has applied a valuable invention to this vessel—a sounding-well—the leadsman standing inside of the turret, and dropping his line through a hole in the bottom of the vessel, thus having his person protected. She will be ready for commission in about eight weeks from the time she is launched. Her engines, forty-eight inch cylinder by eleven inch stroke, are in, and ready to receive the copper pipes and connections. The double-ender Mohongo, carrying ten guns, is completed, with the exception of the side wheelhouse and coal bunkers. She will be built of iron, will have great strength and light draught of water, and is intended for river and inlet service. In two years the Messrs. Secor & Co. have built the following vessels, at a cost to the government of two millions and four hundred thousand dollars: Weehawken, Comanche, Tecumseh, Manahatta, Mahopac and Mohongo; with the exception of the last, which is a double-ender, all of them iron-clads.

The above taken from the New York *Evening Post* gives some idea of what the United States is doing to prepare herself for any emergency at home or abroad. Nearly all the above are iron clads.

PETROLEUM AS FUEL.

(London Times.)

Steam is now generated by the combustion of coal, and generated effectively, but under conditions so onerous as to govern the whole form and dimension of a steamship. The Great Eastern herself, that miracle of marine architecture, took her shape and size exclusively from the capacity required for her coal bunkers. The problem was to build a steamer capable of running at a stretch from England to India, or, in other words, of carrying coal enough for a voyage of that length. It turned out on computation that this condition could only be satisfied by a vessel of 22,000 tons, carrying 10,000 tons weight of coal. The proportion of coal tonnage to aggregate tonnage is not quite so great in ordinary steamers, but it is still very large indeed. The Persia, of 3,500 tons, one of the finest Atlantic packets afloat, gives 1,400 to her fuel; the Warrior, our strongest ironclad, gives about 1,400 out of a gross tonnage of 6,000. Generally speaking, a war steamer can carry coals for about ten day's steaming, but not more. That is the limit of a capacity attained at so great a sacrifice, and it has been urged as a reason for encumbering our steamers with the masts and hamper of sailing ships. All such fittings detract from the speed and handiness of the vessel herself; but as she may any day, from the exhaustion of her fuel, be unable to steam and be compelled to sail, she must be furnished with those supplementary means of locomotion against emergency.

It is obvious, then, that if a substitute could be found for this bulky and ponderous material, which would lie in a small compass and make less demand upon space and tonnage, the conditions of steam navigation would be entirely changed. It is this substitute which has now been indicated in the rock oil or earth oil, known by the name of petroleum, and it does happen, so far as we can judge, that petroleum is nearly as common a production of the earth as coal itself. This preliminary and indispensable condition appears actually to be satisfied. Petroleum, if it answers the purposes of coal, is plentiful enough to be used in its place. Whether such substitution will prove really practicable or not we cannot venture to foretell, but we can state what has been done towards the verification of the theory. The Americans appointed a Commission to investigate the subject, and on this Commission was placed the chief engineer of the United States' Navy. In due time the Commissioners reported, and they said that petroleum was beyond doubt more than twice as powerful as anthracite coal in the production of steam, and that steam could, by the use of this fuel, be produced in less than half the usual time. This much they do say, but they say no more. How it is to be applied to the boilers, whether in small burners, or in some more special form imparted to it for the purpose, we do not learn, though we are told that an American firm has patented a process for the adaptation of the material to the use, and that the patent article was the article to which the inquiry was directed. Practically, however, after recording the great evaporative powers of the fuel, the Commissioners recommend that the very necessary information still desirable should be obtained by further actual experiment.

However, leaving this very critical question to be elucidated by the American experiment, let us glance at the results which would follow if this not quite improbable theory should be actually established. In the first place, at least two-thirds of the space now required for fuel might be saved in the designs for a steamship, or, if the ship were built upon the old scale, she might keep the sea at least three times as long as before. We may conclude, too, that the little army of stokers and firemen now maintained for the service of an engine room might be materially reduced; and as these savings would determine the model of the vessel a new and improved steamship would at once compel a fresh fleet. Dispense with coal bunkers, and you may revolutionise the form of a steamer. Here is change enough, in all conscience; but there is a great deal more to come. Steam on this principle could be applied to the longest lines of ocean navigation, for steam-packets would be independent of coal depots. Nor would the revolution be less on land, for this substitution of oil for coal would relieve our fuel from a most devouring consumption, and enable us to economise that precious article, the exhaustion of which has recently been foreshadowed.

ED.—Petroleum is abundant in Burmah, and we doubt not would be found in Siam if sought for.

THE NEW YORK HERALD.

WHOLE NO. 10,192. NEW YORK, SATURDAY, AUGUST 13, 1864. PRICE THREE CENTS.

NEWS FROM NEW ORLEANS.

ARRIVAL OF THE EVENING STAR.

Successful Expedition Up Grand Lake.

Destruction of Flatboats and Capture of Valuable Property.

A Battalion of Scott's 900 Surrounded by the Rebels.

They Refuse to Surrender and Cut Their Way Through.

Repulse of the Rebels in an Attempt to Cross the Atchafalaya.

Union Pickets Driven In at Donaldsonville.

THE NEW TRADE REGULATIONS, &c., &c., &c.

The steamship Evening Star, Captain Wimpenny, from New Orleans on the 6th instant, arrived at this port yesterday morning. Among her passengers are Mrs. General Banks and family.

We are under obligations to the purser of the Evening Star for favors.

Our gunboats made an expedition up Grand Lake on the 26th ult., and destroyed a large number of flatboats just completed by the rebels and several in course of construction. They also captured a considerable number of small arms and accoutrements left by rebel skedaddling cavalrymen.

On the 28th the same gunboats destroyed two sawmills, captured two boatloads of valuable lumber, and returned to Beswick Bay.

On the 29th a party of General Ullmann's scouts had a fight with some rebels near Morganzia, resulting in the flight of the rebels, leaving a rebel captain and several men dead and a number wounded, besides several prisoners, in our hands.

General Canby issued important new trading regulations on the 2d inst., by which no trading boats are allowed below Cairo, no commercial intercourse beyond the national lines, and trade stores restricted to permanent military posts.

General Banks issued an order on the 2d enlisting all able bodied colored men in the department between eighteen and forty years of age, the same to be put in existing colored regiments.

Six steam transports, from Brazos Santiago, arrived at New Orleans on the 5th inst., probably laden with troops withdrawn from Texas.

Cotton active at $1 65 a $1 67½ for middling. Flour advanced to $16 per barrel for choice. Sugar dull. Molasses steady.

Colonel Appleton, of the Eighty-first colored infantry, formerly of the Twelfth Maine, has resigned.

It is reported that the steamer Rob Roy, with one thousand bales of cotton, was captured and burned in Washita River by Texan guerillas.

An order was issued by General Canby, on the 30th of July, enrolling all citizens in the militia, expelling all families of rebel soldiers, all persons liable to rebel conscription to be kept within our lines, and all foreigners claiming to be neutrals to be enlisted as policemen.

Mr. Wm. Young's Despatches.

NEW ORLEANS, August 2, 1864.

ANOTHER RAID UPON THE COLORED PEOPLE.

Emancipation day was celebrated yesterday, and while they were enjoying themselves hugely the military authorities made a raid upon the able bodied colored men fit to become soldiers, and abruptly terminated their pleasure by marching them off to the barracks where colored candidates for military glory and renown are forced to congregate. A regiment of cavalry is on duty now making further raids upon colored men.

GUERILLAS HANG A UNION SOLDIER—HE IS REVENGED.

The guerillas who dashed into the pickets of Scott's Nine Hundred several nights ago captured one private of that regiment, whom they hung, and then secreted his body. It was ascertained at what houses these guerillas quartered, and a force was sent out by direction of Colonel Sherburne, who in boiling eggs under the corners of these houses were so unfortunate as to communicate the flames to the combustible buildings. The place where these houses did stand is marked by ashes.

SUSPENSION OF TRADE.

There is a temporary suspension of trade with the localities up the river, inside the limits of what is known as the trade district. This is done in conformity with orders from Washington, and it is stated no clearances will be granted for what is known as the coast trade until new trade regulations are prepared to carry out the intentions of the recent Congressional enactment regulating or prohibiting trade with insurrectionary districts.

THE PLANTERS IN TROUBLE.

The planters are in trouble about the military order providing for the enrolment of plantation negroes. It is feared that the force remaining will be insufficient to gather the growing crop of cotton.

CAVALRY SURGEON GOING NORTH.

Dr. Skilton, Surgeon-in-Chief of the cavalry division, goes North to-day on the steamer Gladiator, by the river route.

BATTERY GOING HOME.

Hebard's First Vermont battery, to be mustered out of service, goes up the river on the Gladiator.

NEW ORLEANS, August 6, 1864.

THE REBEL COLONEL SCOTT ATTACKS SCOTT'S NINE HUNDRED CAVALRY.

From the following telegrams, furnished for publication by Major Gamble, it will be seen that Colonel Scott, commanding a brigade of rebel cavalry, demanded yesterday morning the immediate surrender of Major Remington's battalion of Scott's Nine Hundred, or the Eleventh New York cavalry; that the Major did not surrender, but cut his way through, abandoning his camp equipage and leaving his sick behind; that he subsequently concentrated his force and moved out in pursuit of the enemy:—

FIRST DESPATCH.

TELEGRAPH STATION, OPPOSITE DONALDSONVILLE, August 5, 1864.

Colonel J. P. SHERBURNE, Chief of Cavalry, Department of the Gulf:—

We were attacked this morning by Colonel Scott with a brigade of cavalry and a battery of artillery. He demanded an unconditional surrender; his forces were stationed in the cornfields and completely surrounded my camp. I succeeded in cutting my way through with but small loss, excepting the sick. My horse was shot under me and Captain Norris was shot through the shoulder. S. P. REMINGTON, Major Commanding Eleventh New York cavalry.

The following is a copy of a note received this morning from Colonel Scott, C. S. A.:—

SECOND DESPATCH.

HEADQUARTERS, CAVALRY BRIGADE, August 5, 1864.

TO COMMANDING OFFICER FORCES AT DOYALS' PLANTATION:—

To avoid an unnecessary effusion of blood, I hereby demand an unconditional surrender of the stockade and the forces under your command. I have at my immediate disposal a brigade of cavalry and a battery of artillery. Your refusal or acceptance of this demand must be made within five minutes after its reception. Yours, respectfully,

J. S. SCOTT, Colonel Commanding.

I have cut my way through to the telegraph station.

S. P. REMINGTON, Major Commanding Eleventh New York cavalry.

The above despatch was received here at five minutes past nine A. M. Major Remington's camp, or the stockade, was about seven miles from the telegraph station, opposite Donaldsonville.

THIRD DESPATCH.

TELEGRAPH STATION, August 5—10:50 A. M.

Major T. T. GAMBLE, A. A. G., Cavalry Division, Department of the Gulf:—

I am just moving in the direction of Doyals' with the larger part of my force concentrated here. Within three hours will give you further information. Loss of men, as far as known, is mostly sick taken prisoners.

S. P. REMINGTON, Major Commanding Eleventh New York cavalry.

Up to ten o'clock last evening no further information was received from Major Remington. The loss in Scott's Nine Hundred in prisoners captured by the rebels is estimated at from forty to sixty sick men.

NEWSPAPER CONTROVERSY.

A spirited newspaper controversy has been progressing between the venerable and patriotic Jacob Barker, a well known banker who was true to the Union when others faltered, and Dr. A. P. Dostie, the State Auditor. Neither of the controversialists spares the other in their unpleasantly severe personalities. It is the general conviction that Mr. Barker gets the best of the discussion.

CONGRESSIONAL CANDIDATES.

The only candidate for representative to Congress thus far publicly named is Thomas M. Welles, who is suggested as a candidate for the Fourth district.

ADOPTION OF THE CONSTITUTION.

It is thought that there will be but very little opposition at the polls to the new constitution of Louisiana, and its almost unanimous adoption is therefore regarded as quite certain.

CONTRABANDS COMING IN.

One of the Brashear City gunboat fleet lately brought in a large number of contrabands who had left the enemy's lines.

CONTRABANDS GOING OUT.

After the promulgation of the order enrolling all able bodied men between the ages of eighteen and forty five, guards were stationed at the various avenues to prevent embryo soldiers from decamping. On one avenue one hundred and fifty colored men were arrested in one night, who had sought to decline the honor of fighting for equality and freedom.

OBSERVANCE OF FAST DAY.

The observance of Fast Day on Thursday was very general and spontaneous. Fewer business establishments were open than is usual on Sunday.

THEATRICAL INTELLIGENCE.

The St. Charles theatre is open for a short season under the direction of Mrs. J. W. Thorpe. With somewhat unattractive bills, large audiences are attracted to the interior of the only place of amusement in New Orleans.

HEALTH OF NEW ORLEANS.

Mayor Hoyt is indefatigable in his exertions to keep the city in good sanitary condition. The consequence is that New Orleans is now the healthiest city in the Union. There have been no cases of yellow fever. With the approach of autumn the heat becomes less intense, and there is only now and then a day that is uncomfortably warm. The nights are deliciously cool.

THE NEW TRADE REGULATIONS.

The legislation supposed to have been proposed by Mr. Chase, which was enacted by Congress, near the close of the session, forbidding trade with and in the States in insurrection, amounts to only this and nothing more: that trade stores in localities liable to be raided upon by the enemy will be abolished, and that trade with persons outside of the lines will not be permitted. So far as the effect of the legislation goes, its tendency is to create a policy widely different from that founded in wisdom, which would restore loyal citizens and loyal districts to the condition of unrestricted trade and commerce enjoyed before the war. The tinkering policy of hedging in loyal communities with embarrassing regulations for ordinary trade, requiring permits, and imposing taxes where there should be no restrictions, is not popular in the Department of the Gulf.

PERSONAL.

Major Gamble, of Scott's Nine Hundred, has been relieved from duty as adjutant general of the cavalry division, Department of the Gulf, and appointed Inspector General in the same division. General Heron, lately in command of the Union forces at Brownsville, is expected here to-day.

SECOND MAINE CAVALRY.

The Second Maine cavalry regiment has been transferred to Pensacola. It is expected they will have an opportunity to distinguish themselves in that vicinity.

DICK TAYLOR AND STAFF FOR RICHMOND.

General Dick Taylor and staff crossed the Mississippi, probably *en route* for Richmond, three or four days since.

ALL QUIET ON THE LINES.

With the exception of the demonstration made against Scott's Nine Hundred, all is quiet elsewhere along the lines.

PROSPECT OF THE COTTON CROP.

The prospect of the cotton crop continues to be good. There is, however, a scarcity of labor on the plantations.

RECRUITING COLORED TROOPS.

The order promulgated by General Banks, providing for recruiting colored troops, closes thus:—

In order that mechanics whose services are indispensable to their employers may be retained, one-fifth of the men liable to conscription under this order will be exempted, it being left to the discretion of the Provost Marshal and the employer which of them to exempt.

If consistent with the interest of the government and the defence of the Department of the Gulf, at the time the crops now under cultivation become ready for harvesting, the laborers taken from the various plantations under this order will be temporarily returned.

Mr. Henry Thompson's Despatches.

NEW ORLEANS, August 2, 1864.

ANOTHER EXPEDITION LEAVES NEW ORLEANS.

As it is well known in this city that an expedition of considerable force left here on transports on Sunday evening last, it cannot be contraband to inform your readers of that fact. As to their destination, I cannot at present state it.

GUNBOAT RAID UP GRAND LAKE.

On Tuesday last the gunboat Glide, Acting Master L. S. Fichett commanding, left Brashear City for a reconnoissance to Grand Lake, information having reached Lieutenant S. B. Washburn (commanding the fleet in Berwick Bay) that the rebels were engaged in building a fleet of large flatboats in the neighborhood of Lake Fausse Pointe, near the upper part of Grand Lake, and distant from New Iberia about five miles.

On reaching the above place, which was accomplished without creating alarm, by the Glide rounding a point of woodland, a large party of rebels were discovered busily at work building flatboats, while a company of cavalry were on guard.

Fire was immediately opened upon them from the Glide's thirty-two pounders, and the surprised rebels fled with great alertness to the woods, leaving tools, clothes, tents and provisions behind.

A boat's crew was then landed from the Glide, when it was discovered that the rebels had actually built several flatboats, and were in the act of finishing two others when the Glide so unceremoniously appeared to stop the work. It is estimated that the whole would carry nearly one thousand men. After setting them on fire the Glide returned to Brashear City.

Two days after, the Glide left Berwick Bay for another trip to Grand Lake, for the purpose of destroying two large sawmills which were reported to be then running and turning out immense quantities of lumber daily. She was accompanied by the steamer A. G. Brown, and it was the intention to load her with lumber in case the mills were discovered. As the steamers passed the point of woodland before mentioned it was found that the rebels had again placed a guard there; but this time they were more vigilant, and fled at the first appearance of the boats, without waiting for the iron messengers, which, however, immediately opened upon them.

The mills were discovered and destroyed. This was not done, however, before the Glide and A. G. Brown were well laden with lumber, when they returned to Brashear City. On the way there a skiff, containing two exchanged rebels, was captured and brought in. They were from Mobile, and were on their way to Alexandria for the purpose of joining their regiments.

Whether this building of flatboats was intended simply as a raid on Brashear City or a part of a programme to retake New Orleans I am unable to state.

ENGAGEMENT NEAR MORGANZIA.

A very lively skirmish occurred near Morganzia on Friday last.

A considerable body of rebels, under the command of a captain, organized undoubtedly for the purpose of destroying the telegraph and firing upon unarmed transports, was met by a larger body of Union troops, and the consequence was that a fight ensued, in which the rebels were repulsed, after losing their captain and four or five others killed, and several wounded.

Our loss was slight.

NEW ORLEANS, August 6, 1864.

REPULSE OF THE ENEMY NEAR THE ATCHAFALAYA.

News having arrived that the enemy in considerable force were crossing the Atchafalaya on the 28th ult., Gen. Ullmann received instructions to make a reconnoissance, and a brigade of infantry, two regiments of cavalry and a battery of artillery were at once despatched for that purpose, when it was discovered that the enemy, to the number of twelve or fifteen thousand, were actually in the act of crossing the Atchafalaya, and that a large portion were already on this side.

There was no general engagement, though several skirmishes ensued between the two parties, which finally resulted in the falling back of the enemy to the opposite side of the river.

Our loss was two privates killed and some twelve or fourteen wounded. Col. Chrysler, of the Second New York cavalry, was severely wounded in the neck. The loss of the enemy is unknown.

Two days later a company of rebels were repulsed with severe loss. They had assembled in considerable numbers for the purpose of destroying the telegraph, having organized themselves into a company under the command of a captain.

A scouting party of Union soldiers discovered them, and a fight was the consequence, in which the rebels were repulsed, after having lost their captain and five or six privates killed, besides several wounded. Our loss was small.

STEAMER ROB ROY BURNED.

News has reached us that the steamer Rob Roy has been destroyed by the rebels on the Washita river, and that Captain Griffin and his entire crew were captured. The Rob Roy is said to have had over one thousand bales of cotton on board.

COLLISION—LOSS OF THE SCHOONER LIZZIE BACON.

On the 1st inst. the Matanzas, Captain Liesgang, collided with the schooner Lizzie Bacon, Captain Parmele. The latter sunk on the bar at the Southwest Pass. No lives were lost.

PERSONAL.

Mr. Raphael Beamis has been appointed by the Governor Judge of the Fourth Judicial district.

Dr. M. F. Bruzano, lately appointed from Washington one of the three commissioners for the collection of taxes, arrived here on Sunday on the Evening Star.

News from Memphis.

CAIRO, Ill., August 11, 1864.

Memphis papers of the 9th instant are received; but they contain no news of importance.

The supply of cotton in the Memphis market was entirely out.

FARRAGUT.

THE ATTACK ON MOBILE.

Fort Powell Evacuated by the Rebels.

The Monitor Tecumseh Blown Up by a Torpedo.

THE UNION FLEET IN MOBILE BAY, &c., &c., &c.

Despatch to the Navy Department.

WASHINGTON, August 12, 1864.

The government has received official telegraphic advices from Dauphin's Island, Mobile harbor, up to the 6th inst. The only point of interest or importance contained in addition to what was previously known through rebel sources is, that the Monitor Tecumseh was sunk by a torpedo, instead of the guns of Fort Morgan, which is more satisfactory to the friends and advocates of the Monitors than if she had gone down under the fire of the fort.

Despatch from General Banks.

Mrs. General Banks, who arrived here yesterday on the steamship Evening Star, from New Orleans, received the following despatch at Southwest Pass from the General:—

OFFICE UNITED STATES MILITARY TELEGRAPH, WAR DEPARTMENT, NEW ORLEANS, August 6, 1864.

Mrs. N. P. BANKS, on steamship Evening Star:—

The following despatch has just been received from Fort Pike:—

The steamer Clyde passed here this morning from the fleet. She reports that fourteen gunboats and three Monitors passed the forts at Mobile yesterday at eight A. M. One Monitor was blown up opposite the forts by a torpedo. The rebel ram Tennessee was captured. Admiral Buchanan lost a leg in the fight. This gives us possession. I have no other particulars.

N. P. BANKS, Major General Commanding.

Mr. Henry Thompson's Despatches.

DEPARTMENT OF THE GULF, UNITED STATES MILITARY TELEGRAPH OFFICE, SOUTHWEST PASS, August 6, 1864.

The fleet under Admiral Farragut passed the forts at the entrance of Mobile Bay at eight o'clock on the morning of the 5th inst.

The Monitor Tecumseh was blown up by a rebel torpedo. No other vessel was lost.

The rebel ram Tennessee surrendered after an obstinate resistance.

Admiral Buchanan lost a leg in the action and is now a prisoner.

The land forces, under Major General Granger, invested Fort Gaines, and with the light batteries opened upon the fort simultaneously with the passage of the forts by the fleet, taking the water batteries in rear and silencing them.

Our loss is not reported.

Fort Powell, in Mobile Bay, was blown up and evacuated by the rebels.

NEW ORLEANS, August 6, 1864.

ORDERS FOR THE ATTACK ON MOBILE GIVEN.

On Wednesday last orders were promulgated to the fleet off Mobile by Admiral Farragut that the attack on the forts would take place at three o'clock the following morning. This is reliable.

Up to this writing nothing further has arrived, though official despatches are expected from the Admiral to-day.

THE UNION MILITARY FORCES OCCUPY DAUPHIN ISLAND.

The attack on the forts commenced yesterday morning. Our military forces now occupy Dauphin Island.

Mr. Wm. Young's Despatch.

NEW ORLEANS, August 6, 1864.

NEWS FROM THE MOBILE EXPEDITION.

The steamer J. M. Brown arrived last evening, having landed troops at Dauphin Island, on one extremity of which Fort Gaines is situated. When the J. M. Brown left the gunboats were shelling the woods on the island. At six o'clock yesterday morning Admiral Farragut had not commenced operations against the forts at the entrance to Mobile Bay. Some of our Monitors were lying within a mile of Fort Morgan.

THE GUERILLAS.

Operations of the Guerillas at Brandenburg, Ky.—They are Driven Off by Five of the Home Guard—Demand for the Surrender of the Town—A Fight Reported to be Going On, &c., &c.

LOUISVILLE, Ky., August 11, 1864.

About daylight yesterday morning twenty guerillas, under Dupaster, entered Brandenburg, and were driven out by five of the home guard, armed with double barrelled shotguns.

The guerillas then sent in the following note:—

HEADQUARTERS OF THE SEVENTH KENTUCKY CAVALRY.

HOME GUARD—We demand an immediate surrender of the town, and if there is a shot fired at us from any person in the town we will burn the place and shoot every citizen who is caught bearing arms.

Captain DUPASTER,
Captain BRYANT,

Commanding the Confederate forces in Mead county, Ky.

The home guard refused to comply with the demand, and prepared to defend the town.

As the mail boat passed up the river, about sunset, firing was heard, and it was supposed that an engagement was progressing.

Further particulars of the affair are not obtainable to-night.

Sixty guerillas passed through Grayhamtown, Mead county, yesterday morning, with a detachment of thirty Union troops, under Captain Carr, in pursuit of them.

Last night thirty guerillas robbed the stores of Messrs. Allone and Longrun, in this county.

The remains of General Greathouse, recently Colonel of the Forty-eighth Illinois, passed here for home this evening.

Guerilla Operations Near Lafayette, Tenn.

MEMPHIS, August 9, 1864.

Yesterday a citizen came into our lines near Lafayette, and applied to the commandant of the post for protection and permission to remove his household goods inside our lines.

A guard of men was immediately sent out with him to protect him in bringing in his goods; but after entering the house the man fled, and on attempting to come out the guard were surrounded by twenty-five or thirty guerillas.

Five of our men escaped and the other three surrendered, after which the guerillas murdered them. They belonged to the One Hundred and Fortieth Illinois infantry.

The Guerillas on the Cumberland River.

ST. LOUIS, August 12, 1864.

Sadina, on the Cumberland river, twelve miles above Smithland, was attacked by two hundred rebel cavalry Sunday morning. The rebels were repulsed with a loss of six killed and twenty wounded.

One thousand guerillas are reported to be in Union county, Ky., under Col. Johnson; also a large number in the Western part of the State, near the Tennessee line. Gen. Payne has gone down there to clear them out.

Personal Intelligence.

Mrs. Major General N. P. Banks and family, from New Orleans; Hon. H. C. Denning, of Hartford; Hon. E. C. Cleaveland, of Hartford; Charles E. Waters, of Baltimore, and General J. T. Stead, are stopping at the Astor House.

Dr. E. Sackett, of Rochester; H. F. Sweetzer, of Meadville, and General Hamilton, of Texas, are stopping at the Metropolitan Hotel.

Gov. Hahn, of Louisiana, is stopping at the St. Nicholas.

Major General Sickles arrived at the Brevoort House last night from Washington, where he passed several days in frequent communication with the President on the condition of the Southwestern States, that he was appointed some four months since to visit and report upon. The General has laid before the President much valuable material connected with the situation of the vast section of country he has lately traversed, and we trust the Executive will see the necessity of prompt action on many points that call for it most urgently. It is said the services of General Sickles will be shortly required in another still more important field of action.

SHERMAN.

GENERAL STONEMAN'S RAID.

Mr. D. P. Conyngham's Despatches.

MARIETTA, August 5, 1864.

While sending an account of General McCook's raid yesterday, I little thought I would have to apprise you of such a signal disaster to General Stoneman and his command. There was no cavalry officer here, or in the Army of the Potomac, in whom the public and the country in general have more confidence than in Major General Stoneman. Though first reports are generally the worst, and men who escape imagine every one killed or captured but themselves, I believe, making all allowance for exaggeration, there is no doubt but that General Stoneman, several officers of his staff and the most of his command have been captured.

WANT OF CO-OPERATION.

The enemy seemed perfectly aware of our movements and were fully prepared to meet them. Somehow, there seemed to be a want of co-operation among the different raiding parties that started out under such favorable auspices. The only one that succeeded effectually being Rousseau, who went out on his own hook. There was to be a co-operation between Stoneman, Garrard and McCook. McCook destroyed a large share of rebel stores and returned, owing his safety to desperate fighting, but losing a larger portion of his command.

As for Stoneman, all the officers who have returned agree in stating that he did all that a brave man could do under the circumstances. He fought desperately, recklessly exposing his life to save what now only remained to a soldier—his honor. I will not wait now to question who is to blame, or by what mismanagement we have lost the use of such a splendid cavalry force.

THE LOSS NOT VITAL—STONEMAN'S OBJECT.

As all our communications are well guarded, and we still have sufficient cavalry to operate on our flank, Sherman will not suffer materially from such a heavy loss. We know that Stoneman aimed at liberating our prisoners. The poor unfortunates themselves were aware of this; but how their hearts must have sunk within their Bastile when their expected deliverer and his men were thrown in chains among them, to rot in their fetid dungeons.

RETURNED OFFICERS.

Lieutenant Colonel Smith, Chief of Stoneman's Staff, and Lieutenant Root have both returned, and confirm the sad news. From the officers who have returned I have learned the following particulars:—

THE START—STONEMAN'S FORCE.

Major General Stoneman started from Decatur on the morning of the 27th July, with the following force:—The First brigade, commanded by Colonel Adams, who has returned; the Second brigade, comprising the Fifth and Sixth Indiana, commanded by Colonel Biddle. The Fourteenth Illinois, Eighth Michigan and McLoughlen's Ohio squadron formed the Third brigade, commanded by Col. Capron.

THE ROUTE.

The command took the Georgia Railroad towards Covington, thence south by Monticello towards Macon, capturing a large number of horses and about 300 negroes, whom they mounted on the prizes. At Macon a battalion of the Fourteenth Illinois made a dash on a station called Gordon, near the Oconee river, destroying eleven locomotives and several trains loaded with quartermaster and commissary stores. We also destroyed the bridge at Macon, a locomotive and one train loaded with horses and hogs.

WHEN NEAR MACON

General Stoneman learned that all the prisoners had been sent to Charleston the previous day. From this it is evident that they were fully apprized of our movements. Up to this time we encountered only slight skirmishing, but we now ascertained that the garrison was largely reinforced, and that a heavy force was moving on our flank. About three o'clock on Saturday, after skirmishing all the morning with the enemy and developing their strength, Stoneman decided on returning. He encountered the enemy's skirmishers all the evening of Saturday, and on Sunday morning (31st), finding a heavy force of the enemy in our front, he deployed a heavy line of skirmishers. This was between Clinton and Hillsborough, and about fifteen miles from Macon.

THE LOCALITY—THE REBELS.

The country around there was very unfavorable for cavalry operations, and he soon found that Allen's brigade of infantry had wheeled from our flank and had taken up position along the main route, thus heading us off.

Armstrong's brigade of cavalry, comprising the First and Second Kentucky, had come down on our left flank at the same time, thus with the troops in our rear completely surrounding us. Here it happened by a strange coincidence that the First and Second Kentucky of Adams' brigade were pitted against their rebel namesakes.

THE TROOPS DISMOUNTED—THE FIGHT.

Stoneman now dismounted some of his troops, who repeatedly charged the enemy in front, but were each time repulsed. The troops were now giving way, but were rallied by Stoneman and staff, who charged at their head.

The enemy now burst out on our flank, creating a regular panic. Despite the example and exhortations of their General, the lines wavered—broke.

MAJOR KEOGH.

Here Major Keogh, of his staff, dashed in front, trying to rally the men, and having partially succeeded, dashed right upon the enemy; but he was soon deserted, except by some of the officers. This small Spartan band swept down upon the enemy, and for a moment checked their onward course; but many a saddle being emptied, the few survivors had to return, among whom was the gallant Major, whose reckless bravery all who have returned bepraise.

THE ENEMY

were now sweeping our lines on all sides with artillery, infantry and cavalry. The led horses and scared negroes considerably added to the confusion.

THE SURRENDER.

General Stoneman seeing all chances of resistance now fruitless, ordered all who could to escape, and finally surrendered. As stragglers and squads are coming in it is hard to ascertain our real loss.

THE PRISONERS.

The following have reported at Marietta:—Colonel Adams' First and Second Kentucky; also about seventy-five men from other regiments and twenty from the Eighth Michigan, making in all about four hundred.

Colonel Capron's brigade effected its escape, but has not as yet reported.

Our loss will considerably dwindle down when all the stragglers come in.

The brave Stoneman and the gallant Keogh are deeply regretted. It is to be hoped that such gallant officers will not be long detained from their country's service. As far as I can learn Stoneman's whole effective force was only about two thousand.

What have returned are so used up as to be unfit for service for some time.

NEAR ATLANTA, August 6, 1864.

REVIEW OF THE SITUATION.

The Army of the Tennessee having wheeled round from the left encountered the enemy on the right while taking up position on the 28th.

Our left being strengthened by cavalry, and refusing the Fourth corps, the Twenty-third followed and took up position on the right. While doing so a skirmish took place with the enemy on the 3d, in which we lost some thirty men, but punished the enemy severely. On the same evening the Fourth corps, principally Wood's division, skirmished briskly with the enemy and advanced their lines.

GALLANT AFFAIR OF THE FOURTEENTH CORPS.

Next day, August 4, the Fourteenth corps made a demonstration, General Palmer throwing out a heavy line of skirmishers which advanced close on the enemy's works but were repulsed, the rebels taking possession of their rifle pits. Our men made a dashing charge recovering their pits and capturing near two hundred prisoners. There was also some skirmishing and brisk artillery fire in front of Schofield, in which Lieutenant Julius A. Kerulsh, of his staff, was killed.

GENERAL ADVANCE BEGUN, BUT COUNTERMANDED.

It was expected that a general advance would take place along the line yesterday, and that the right would press on for the railroad, which is less than two miles distant, but strongly defended.

GENERAL STANLY

opened the proceeding by making a heavy demonstration, in which Newton's and Wood's divisions were principally engaged. There was heavy artillery firing, particularly in front of Gibson's and Wagner's brigades. The casualties were light, and no material advantage gained. The skirmishing extended along the Twentieth corps to the right, but no regular assault took place.

SHERMAN'S TRAINS ACROSS THE CHATTAHOOCHEE.

Trains passed over the Chattahoochee bridge yesterday afternoon. Heavy fighting is daily expected. Captain Walker, Seventy-seventh Pennsylvania, and Lieutenant Skenaker, One Hundreth Illinois, were killed.

REBEL ACCOUNTS.

[From the Augusta Chronicle, August 4.]

From all accounts from up the road we gather the annexed:—

A party of raiders made their appearance at Athens on Tuesday—about one thousand in number. They were met by a force under Colonel Dribble, and retreated, it is said, without making much show of a fight. A large force of Confederate cavalry it is stated was in their rear. This probably was one reason why they left without making an attack.

The raiders have left Madison. The fire seen in that direction on Tuesday was not the Oconee bridge, but was a large lot of commissary stores which had been piled up and fired by the Yankees.

The country above Madison is said to be full of scattered bands of federals moving round and making their way towards Sherman's army.

From all reports, it appears that one body of the raiders has been badly whipped, demoralized and scattered in all directions.

There may, however, be other parties still in other sections that have not been properly attended to. Those whose duty it is should be on the lookout.

Among others who have suffered by the vandalism of the Yankee raiders at Madison, we learn that honorable Joshua Hill was a heavy loser in horses, mules and other property.

THE REBEL PIRATES.

The New Pirate Steamer Tallahassee.

The Vessel Built in London and Probably Owned by Englishmen.

Her Operations at the Entrance to Our Harbor.

Capture of the Pilotboat James Funk, No. 22, of New York.

Destruction of the Brigs Carrie Estelle and Richards, Bark Bay State and Schooners Sarah A. Boyce and Atlantic.

The Schooner Carroll Bonded and Loaded with Paroled Prisoners.

Statements of the Pilots and Captains of the Captured Vessels.

DESCRIPTION OF THE TALLAHASSEE, &c., &c., &c.

A new rebel pirate, known as the Tallahassee, commanded by Captain John Taylor Wood, C. S. N., has made her appearance off the mouth of our harbor, sinking, burning and destroying no less than six vessels in as many hours. The news did not reach the city yesterday in time to despatch any vessels in pursuit of her; so that she will have another twenty-four hours' unmolested career. We give below some very interesting details of her operations up to the latest moment, as far as is known.

ARRIVAL OF THE PIRATE'S PRISONERS AT FIRE ISLAND.

FIRE ISLAND, August 12, 1864.

While one of the sailing boats attached to the Surf Hotel was cruising outside this morning it discovered a yawlboat making for the shore.

Upon coming alongside of this boat sixteen persons were found on board, who belonged to the pilotboat James Funk, of New York; the brig Estelle, the brig Sarah Boyce, the brig Richards, the bark Bay State and the schooner Atlantic.

All these vessels had been captured and burned by the rebel steamer Tallahassee, commanded by John Taylor Wood, off the coast, yesterday afternoon.

The sixteen men who were found in the yawlboat will start for New York this afternoon.

STATEMENT OF THE PILOTS AND CREW OF THE PILOTBOAT JAMES FUNK.

The pilotboat James Funk, No. 22, left New York August 10, with the following pilots on board:—Messrs. Yates, Fryer, Smith, Handrew. At nine P. M. put Mr. Handrew on board of the brig Cora. On Thursday morning, at half-past seven, Fire Island bearing northwest, distant thirty miles, discovered a steamer steering west. Kept off for her and set our colors. On approaching her we perceived that she flew the pennant and Union flag. On nearing us she stopped. Thinking she wanted a pilot, we hove our yawl out, and Mr. Smith and two men went alongside of her. As soon as the yawl got alongside of the steamer down came the Stars and Stripes and up went the rebel flag. The pilot and men who were in the yawl were taken on board as prisoners, and they lowered two boats full of armed men, who came and took possession of the pilotboat in the name of the Confederate States.

Before taking us he had captured the schooner Sarah A. Boyce, of Great Egg Harbor, bound from Boston to Philadelphia. At nine A. M. the privateer captured the brig Carrie Estelle, of Boston, bound to New York. She was burned. At eleven A. M. she captured the bark Bay State, from Alexandria to Boston, and burned her also. At one P. M., captured brig A. Richards, of Boston, from Glace Bay, C. B., bound to New York. She was burned also. At three P. M., captured schooner Atlantic, of Addison, and burned her.

At half past three o'clock she boarded the schooner Carroll, from East Machias, bound to New York. She was released on signing bonds for $10,000, she taking all the crews of the captured vessels to New York. All of the prisoners were paroled, and during all of this time the privateersmen would not give us anything to eat or drink. August 12, off Fire Island, fifteen of the paroled men left the schooner Carroll in a rowboat, and steered for Fire Island Inlet, where we were kindly taken in tow by the yacht Lily, Captain Johnson, who brought us into the inlet. We feel greatly indebted to Mr. Sommers, of the Surf Hotel, and his guests, for their kind treatment while at the house, and regret that we could not pay the compliment to the captain of the steamer from the hotel to Panataquit, as an agent of the Long Island Railroad, who charged us twenty-one dollars for a passage to New York, and we had difficulty to get this man to accept an order on the pilot office.

WILLIAM SMITH, pilot.
E. FRYER, pilot.
ROBERT YATES, pilot.
ALFRED BAUDIER, boatkeeper.
CHARLES HARBINSON, boy.
ED. FRANKEL, seaman.
T. MURPHY, seaman.
Capt. A. S. ADAMS, schooner S. A. Boyce.
GEO. MARINER, mate, schooner Boyce.
Capt. T. C. SPARROW, wife and servant.
G. A. GOULD, mate, bark Bay State.

CARD OF THANKS.

NEW YORK, August 12, 1864.

We, the undersigned paroled prisoners, released from the Confederate States steamer Tallahassee, desire to return our thanks to Capt. Johnson, of the yacht Lily, also to Messrs. Barmend, Fuller and Rev. Messrs. Potter and Tucker, and to the proprietors and company of the Surf Hotel, Fire Island, for the kind and generous treatment we received at their hands.

W. SMITH, R. YATES, E. FRYER, } Pilots of Jas. Funk.
A. BAUDIER, Boatkeeper.
CH. HARBINSON, ED. FRANKEL, T. MURPHY, T. HEWSON, } Crew of pilot boat Jas. Funk.
Capt. THOS. C. SPARROW and family, of bark Bay State.

STATEMENT OF CAPT. ADAMS, OF THE SCHOONER SARAH A. BOYCE.

We left Boston on Friday, August 5. On Thursday, August 11, at half-past four o'clock in the morning—Fire Island N. W. thirty miles—saw a steamer about thirty yards to windward of us, who hailed us and told us to heave to. On coming on board the officer informed me that my vessel was a prize to the Confederate steamer Tallahassee, and ordered me and my crew on board as prisoners. They then scuttled the schooner and bore down to a vessel which proved to be the James Funk, a New York pilotboat, No. 22. At four o'clock in the afternoon we were paroled and sent on board the schooner Carroll, which I left this morning, at ten o'clock, and landed at Fire Island and proceeded to New York.

FROM OUR SHIP NEWS REPORTER.

Mr. Abraham Jones, a Sandy Hook pilot, came in from outside the Hook yesterday afternoon, and reported speaking a bark which had seen a rebel cruiser on Thursday morning, 11th inst., sixty miles southeast from Sandy Hook. She had captured the pilotboat James Funk, New York pilotboat No. 22, at nine A. M. The cruiser is a steamer, schooner rigged, painted white, with red bottom, and had two smokestacks.

STATEMENT OF MR. JAMES WATSON, OF PILOTBOAT EZRA NYE, NO. 2.

Mr. Watson brought in the Italian bark Teolinda, which reports:—Thursday morning, about nine o'clock, when sixty miles southeast from Sandy Hook, saw a steamer to windward, showing the Stars and Stripes; came close under the bark's stern, but did not hail. The pilotboat James Funk, No. 22, was to windward, and, those on board the steamer seeing her, immediately steered for her, at the same time hauling down the American ensign and running up the rebel flag; saw her send a boat on board the James Funk, and put a crew on board of her, when she got under way again and steamed off east, going in toward Montauk Point, the James Funk following. Mr. Watson at the same time saw a schooner about three miles to the windward with all her sails apparently cut adrift and sinking. Supposed the privateer had captured and scuttled her. Mr. Watson describes the steamer as small and English built, straight stem, square stern, fore and aft schooner rigged, painted white (not black), red bottom, carries a pivot gun forward and another aft, and thinks four broadside guns; is not very fast. Had a large number of men on deck. The pilotboat could apparently outsail her.

THE PILOTBOAT JAMES FUNK, NO. 22.

The James Funk was built by Webb & Bell, at Greenpoint, three years ago; is about one hundred and thirty tons burthen, and is very fast. She was owned by Messrs. Martin Lyons, Henry Devere, William Smith, Edward Fryer, Albert Malcolm and Robert Yates, pilots. Messrs. Smith, Fryer and Yates were on board at the time of her capture. The latter pilot had his little son with him.

DESCRIPTION OF THE TALLAHASSEE.

The privateer Tallahassee is an iron steamer, painted white, with two smokestacks, two screws, about two hundred and thirty feet in length, twenty feet beam, and draws about nine feet of water. Her bell is marked "Tallahassee, of London, 1864." Engine marked "J. & W. Dudgeon, London."

She is fore and aft schooner rigged; mounts three guns—one small one on the topgallant forecastle, a long thirty-two pounder amidships and a twenty-four-pounder aft. She carries four waist boats. Her crew consists of about one hundred and twenty persons, including the officers. Men of all nationalities are represented on board, most of whom are said to be soldiers from Lee's army.

She is said to have run out of Wilmington about six days ago, without having been seen by any of Admiral Lee's blockaders. She has quite a quantity of cotton on board to protect her boilers, and there are four barrels of turpentine on deck to be used in firing vessels.

She is commanded by John Taylor Wood, C. S. N. The Surgeon, Sheppardson, says he was one of the Chesapeake pirates.

A Mr. Hall is the boarding officer. The crew are dressed in rags and tatters. Some of them wear their pistols tied to them with Manila rope yarns. They are a hard looking set. The Chief Engineer says he is a Boston man, or that he was born and brought up in that city.

LATEST TIDINGS OF THE TALLAHASSEE.

The last seen of the privateer she was steering southeast, with the pilotboat James Funk in tow as a tender.

All of the officers and crews of the vessels captured by the privateer were paroled, and signed a document promising not to take up arms against the rebels until regularly exchanged. The following is a copy of the form of parole signed. These poor fellows, who have lost everything they had, can at least console themselves with the fact that, being prisoners of war, they cannot be drafted:—

FORM OF PAROLE.

C. S. STEAMER TALLAHASSEE, AT SEA, August 11, 1864, Lat. 40 19 N., long. 72 27 W.

I, B. F., do agree, in consideration of being released as prisoner of war by Commander John Taylor Wood, C. S. N., not to take up arms or serve against the Confederate States of America, either by land or sea, until regularly exchanged. B. F.

Witness—
WM. SHEPPARDSON, C. S. N, Surgeon.
C. LUCIAN JONES, C. S. N.

SHERIDAN.

Occupation of Winchester by Our Troops.

THE REBELS RAPIDLY RETREATING.

A Battle Expected at Strasburg, &c., &c., &c.

Mr. T. C. Wilson's Despatch.

WINCHESTER, Va., August 12—10 P. M.

The last of Early's rebel forces left here yesterday morning about ten o'clock. His train was over three miles long. Our cavalry charged into the town yesterday as the rebel rear guard went out. Early established his headquarters last night at Newtown.

Yesterday morning there was heavy skirmishing between our forces and a portion of the rebels on the Milford and Front Royal roads, at a point about two miles from this place. We drove the rebels

Early is well protecting his front and rear, and making up the valley as fast as ever he can go. I cannot learn that he expects to be materially reinforced. His train is very heavily loaded.

Early will make a stand at Strasburg, if he must; but he is trying hard to reach a point where the valley is narrower.

Everything is very quiet here to-day. There are no rebel forces between here and Martinsburg and Hagerstown, and the road from here to the above named places is clear.

Rebel Account of the Fight Near Moorefield.

[From the Richmond Sentinel, August 10.]

There was an unpleasant rumor in circulation yesterday, to the effect that Generals McCausland's and Bradley Johnson's cavalry had met with a reverse at Moorefield, Hardy county, Virginia, in which they lost four hundred prisoners, four pieces of cannon and a number of horses. Moorefield is in Hardy county, on the east side of the south fork of the Potomac river, one hundred and thirty-one miles northwest by north from Richmond, forty-one miles west of Winchester and forty five south of Cumberland, Maryland.

There was also a rumor that General Early had gained another victory over the enemy. We are certainly more inclined to believe in the last than in the first rumor.

Letter from Secretary Chase—His Resignation.

[From the Paulding (Ohio) Gazette.]

The following letter from Mr. Chase is in reply to one from Hon. Joseph Cable, inquiring for the reasons which led to the former's resignation:—

WASHINGTON, July 11, 1864.

MY DEAR SIR—We have not written each other frequently of late, but my regard for you has by no means diminished. Hard at work, I have not had time for correspondence, but my heart still holds to my old friends.

I trust there is no ground for the fear that the country is again to be cursed with the miscellaneous currency of local corporations, but it is impossible to foresee what is to come. It was one of my strongest desires to give the people a uniform currency, made in the end equivalent to gold everywhere. My efforts were stoutly resisted outside, and had not earnest support inside of the administration. They were steadily prevailing, however, when a sense of duty to myself and the country alone compelled me to resign. I hope they will not be abandoned.

Your friend, S. P. CHASE.

Hon. JOSEPH CABLE.

Fires in Massachusetts.

BOSTON, August 12, 1864.

A fire in Northampton, Mass., this morning, destroyed Damon's gristmill and sawmill. Loss twenty-five thousand dollars; insurance ten thousand.

The loss by the fire in East Boston last night, which was reported to be above one hundred thousand dollars, will not exceed forty thousand.

A fire in East Boston last night destroyed the joiner's establishment and planing mill of Manson, Paterson & Co., No. 88 Border street; also two or three wooden buildings adjoining. A large stock of valuable lumber was consumed. Loss $100,000, of which Manson, Paterson & Co. lose $75,000, which is mostly insured.

THE NEW YORK HERALD.

WHOLE NO. 10,194. NEW YORK, MONDAY, AUGUST 15, 1864. PRICE FOUR CENTS.

FARRAGUT.

Details of the Passage by Our Fleet of Forts Morgan and Gaines.

The Rebel Forts Silenced by the Fire of Our Wooden Vessels.

Daring Dash and Brilliant Victory.

The Naval Engagement in Mobile Bay.

Desperate Resistance of the Rebels.

Triumph of Our Wooden Vessels Over Rebel Iron-Clads.

The Ericsson Monitor Iron-Clad Tecumseh Sunk by a Torpedo.

The Screw Sloop Oneida Seriously Injured by a Ram.

The Rebel Gunboat Selma Attempts to Escape, but is Captured by the Metacomet.

HORRIBLE SLAUGHTER ON BOARD OF HER

The Hartford and Monongahela Ram the Tennessee.

The Iron-Clad Ram Tennessee Forced to Surrender to Wooden Ships.

ADMIRAL BUCHANAN LOSES A LEG.

Fort Gaines Surrendered, Fort Powell Blown Up,

&c., &c., &c.

By the arrival of the United States mail steamer Creole, Captain Thompson, at this port yesterday we have our first instalment of the glorious news from Admiral Farragut's victorious squadron. The reports furnished by our own correspondents, as well as those from other sources, are full of the most intense interest; and this latest achievement of the "Old Salamander" will place him at the head of the list of all naval commanders in the world. The consummate coolness and spirited dash evinced on this occasion have only their counterpart in his movements in the spring of 1862, when he passed up to New Orleans with an insignificant wooden squadron. The loss of life would have been quite small in comparison to the number of men engaged had it not been that one of the miserable Ericsson Monitors was blown up by a torpedo, carrying with her to the bottom of the bay nearly five score of precious souls.

The details of the engagement as narrated cannot fail to create a widespread sensation, disproving as it would seem to do the alleged superiority of iron-clad vessels. This little fleet of wooden vessels, not materially aided by cheese boxes or wonderful machines, not only silenced two heavy forts, but actually broke up and captured an entire iron-clad flotilla opposed to them, and subsequently caused the destruction of a formidable earthwork and the surrender of a regular built casemated work; and from the latest accounts it would not be long before the victorious Admiral would be on his way to the city of Mobile.

The attack commenced on the morning of the 5th inst., and before afternoon he had gained a foothold in Mobile bay which cannot by any means be wrested from him.

Mr. Henry Thompson's Despatch.

OFF MOBILE, August 5, 1864.

PASSING THE FORTS—LINE OF BATTLE.

Admiral Farragut has again fought and won. Mobile bay is ours.

About eight o'clock this morning the attack commenced, the iron-clads Tecumseh, Manhattan, Winnebago and Chickasaw leading, closely followed by the wooden vessels Hartford, Monongahela, Tennessee, Metacomet, Oneida, Itasca, &c., eighteen in all, lashed two and two, in the same manner as when the Port Hudson batteries were passed. The Brooklyn was the first following the Monitors and the Hartford (flagship) second. The Richmond, Lackawanna, Ossipee, Monongahela, Oneida, Galena, Port Royal, Metacomet, Octorara, Seminole and Itasca followed.

When the fleet was fairly under way the line headed directly for Fort Morgan, the enemy opening a terrific fire from Forts Morgan and Gaines, and assisted by the guns from the rebel ram Tennessee and four other vessels at the entrance of the bay.

Our only reply to the enemy from this range was the sending of a few shells from one hundred-pounder Parrotts, stationed at the bows of the vessels; but when the fleet arrived at within a biscuit's throw of Fort Morgan every vessel was ready with her broadside, and as the fleet passed they opened a terrible fire, the cannon rattling in volleys similar to an infantry fire of musketry, driving the gunners from their guns and silencing both fort and water battery.

ENGAGING THE REBEL RAM—LOSS OF THE TECUMSEH.

As soon as the bay was reached the rebel ram Tennessee gunboat Selma and three others attacked the fleet, and almost before the first gun was fired in the action with them the Monitor Tecumseh struck a torpedo, which fairly blew her, or rather lifted her, out of the water, when she descended and disappeared. Nearly all on board were lost, but eight or ten escaping. They were picked up by a boat from the Metacomet while the fight was going on. The fighting was terrific for a time; but it was soon evident that we had the best of the action, though the smoke rendered the engagement very indistinct.

As the Tennessee and other rebel vessels were engaging the fleet several of the smaller vessels passed them, when the Tennessee would attempt to run them down. The Oneida was cut to the water's edge by her formidable ram, and to prevent her from sinking she was run into shoal water. This vessel also received a shot in her boiler.

The rebel gunboat Selma attempted to leave the fleet quietly and steam to Mobile, but the Metacomet discovered the movement and hastened after her. When the former saw that escape was impossible she surrendered to Captain Jarrett, of the Metacomet. The rebel vessel had lost fearfully in killed and wounded, and when her decks were reached the dead and dying lay around, while her scuppers ran with blood. Her Commander, Lieutenant Comstock, formerly of the United States Navy, was lying dead across the breech of a gun, with his bowels torn out. He was evidently in the act of sighting the piece when shot.

The engagement with the enemy's fleet took place on the west side of Mobile bay, in the direction of Fort Powell, and out of range of the guns of Fort Morgan.

The Tennessee boldly steamed in the direction of our fleet, as if for the purpose of running down and destroying the wooden vessels, without paying attention to the Monitors, except to keep out of their way; but they persevered in following her and cutting her off, when her whole attention was forced to be directed to them. The fighting did not last long between them, however; for the flagship and the Monongahela steamed in the direction of the Tennessee, the Monongahela striking her amidships with her terrible prow, causing the huge rebel monster to reel like a drunken man.

The Hartford then grappled the Tennessee; but further bloodshed was saved by the latter hoisting the white flag from the pilothouse.

Captain Pierre Giraud led the party who boarded the ram, and the rebel Admiral Buchanan delivered up his sword to him.

The same horrible slaughter was observable all around as on the Selma, and Admiral Buchanan had a leg shot off during the action. His life is despaired of.

Captain Giraud, the former commander of the United States steamer Tennessee, now commands the captured ram of that name.

The Tennessee is reported to have surrendered on account of the demoralization of her crew.

Our loss in this action is about two hundred and fifty, including nearly one hundred who perished on the Tecumseh.

We have captured nearly three hundred prisoners.

A portion of our fleet are operating on Fort Gaines.

REPORTED CAPTURE OF FORT GAINES AND DESTRUCTION OF FORT POWELL.

We have received news of the capture of Fort Gaines and the destruction of Fort Powell.

It is certain that a terrific explosion occurred in the direction of Fort Powell, and a bright light was seen in the direction of Fort Gaines.

The despatch boat is known to have taken forty men of the United States sloop-of-war Vincennes (which drew too much water to enter Grant's Pass) and placed them on board the United States steamer Stockdale, which started to go through Grant's Pass; but whether she passed through or not I am not able to tell. This occurred after the explosion in the direction of Fort Powell took place.

The outbuildings of the latter are said to have been fired by the rebels previous to their evacuation of the fort, and that the land forces, under command of Major General Gordon Granger, invested and compelled an unconditional surrender.

The army has also possession of Dauphine Island and the telegraph leading to Mobile.

WHY THE ATTACK WAS POSTPONED.

It was intended that the passing of the forts should take place yesterday morning, and orders were issued the day before by the Admiral for all to be in readiness; but the military failed to co-operate in time, and the attack was postponed to this morning.

On Wednesday the Monitor Winnebago, Captain Stevens, sent a few shells into Fort Morgan, and yesterday steamed in front of Fort Gaines and fired several shots at the rebel steamer Natchez, which was lying near the fort, landing troops and ammunition. The latter steamer left in a hurry.

TOWING OFF AN OBSTRUCTION.

Lieutenant Commander Peters, of the Chickasaw, at the close of the action in the bay, steamed off in the direction of Fort Powell, and discovered anchored, a few hundred feet from the fort, a barge filled with stone. The intention was to sink this and obstruct the channel.

Passing in between the fort and the barge, the Chickasaw made fast to her, slipped the cable and towed the obstruction off. During this time the fort fired only one gun.

THE INJURY TO OUR FLEET.

The Hartford (flagship) is probably injured more than any other vessel of the fleet, with the exception of the Oneida.

The former unfortunately received a stroke intended for the rebel ram Tennessee. She had just struck the ram with her prow, and was turning round for the purpose of delivering a broadside, when the Metacomet, which had not been observed on account of the smoke, was upon her before either vessel could change her course, and the side of the gallant flagship was crushed in. The Hartford was also badly injured in the engagement, and it will be necessary for her to go North for repairs.

LOSS OF THE DESPATCH BOAT PHILIPPI.

The Admiral's despatch boat, Philippi, was destroyed by fire to-day in sight of the fleet. The cause is unknown. She was commanded by Captain Seevers.

She accompanied the Hartford to the rebel forts, but was ordered off when the firing commenced.

The fate of her officers is unknown, but it is supposed that they escaped in their boats.

FORT MORGAN TO BE INVESTED.

A large body of our soldiers marched in the direction of Fort Morgan, from Pensacola, for the purpose of heading off the garrison from escaping to Mobile and investing the fort.

ADMIRAL FARRAGUT TO COMMODORE PALMER.

The following is a synopsis of a letter from Admiral Farragut to Commodore Palmer, received in New Orleans a few hours before the steamer sailed. He says in substance:—

At an early hour on Friday, our fleet, lashed two and two, sailed into the Pass, close up under the guns of Fort Morgan, pouring in broadside after broadside of grape and canister—thus driving the gunners of the fort from their pieces and leaving our vessels exposed only to the fire of Forts Gaines and Powell, which were, of course, less effective on account of distance. At the same time General Granger's land batteries enfiladed Gaines and caused the evacuation and blowing up of Powell. In passing the forts the Oneida received a shot which temporarily disabled her machinery, but she was safely towed through the fire by her consort.

Our Monitor Tecumseh was one of the foremost. A torpedo exploding beneath her bottom she sunk almost instantaneously, carrying down all her officers, only ten of her crew escaping. She was commanded by Captain Tunis A Craven. Our loss on this vessel was about one hundred. The gunboats having passed the forts, and being out of their reach, were pursued by the formidable ram Tennessee and three iron-clad gunboats—the Selma, Gaines and Morgan. Our vessels immediately attacked the ram and battered him so effectually that he surrendered in a few minutes by hanging out the white flag. Admiral Buchanan, the commander, lost a leg, and, with all his crew, are prisoners in our hands. There were only three killed on the Tennessee. She was but slightly damaged, and it is probable that Farragut has made her fit for action by this time. We also captured the Selma, of which Captain Murphy was the commander. Lieutenant Prentiss, of the Monongahela, lost both legs. He is a gallant officer, and has a young wife in this city. Captain Malaney, of the Oneida, lost an arm. All the wounded will be sent to Pensacola. Our loss is two hundred and forty killed and wounded. The two remaining rebel gunboats fled under the guns of Fort Morgan, for protection; one of them is aground, and the Admiral is confident that he can destroy them today. He has not the slightest doubt of his ability to reduce the forts. But their capture will not give us command of the city, which is extensively fortified at Dog river and elsewhere.

The Press Despatches.

NEW ORLEANS, August 7, 1864.

Intelligence was received at headquarters yesterday, announcing that the fleet under Admiral Farragut passed the forts at the entrance of Mobile bay at eight A. M. on the 5th instant.

The Monitor Tecumseh was blown up by a rebel torpedo.

No other vessels were lost.

The rebel ram Tennessee surrendered after an obstinate resistance.

The rebel Admiral Buchanan lost a leg in the action and is now a prisoner.

The land force, under Major General Gordon Granger, invested Fort Gaines, and with light batteries opened simultaneously with the passage of the forts by the fleet taking the water batteries in reverse and silencing them.

Our losses are not reported.

NEW ORLEANS, August 7, 1864.

Later advices from Admiral Farragut's fleet may be summed up as follows:—

Fort Gaines has surrendered.

Fort Powell was blown up by the rebels. (This was at Grant's Pass, at the opposite end of Dauphin Island from where the fight occurred.)

Four Monitors went in first, followed by the steam war vessels Brooklyn, Hartford, Metacomet and others. The principal fighting was with the ram Tennessee, inside the bay.

The Metacomet, in attempting to ram the Tennessee, struck the Hartford and stove in her side timbers. The Hartford will go North for repairs.

The rebel gunboat Selma was sunk by the Metacomet.

The gunboats Chickasaw and Winnebago chased two rebel gunboats—the Gaines and Morgan—into Navy Cove, and they are blockaded there without a chance of escape.

Only ten persons are known to have survived the destruction of the Monitor Tecumseh by the torpedo.

The despatch boat Philippi was burned at sea while the fight was in progress.

Admiral Farragut will push right on for Mobile city.

NEWSPAPER ACCOUNTS.

[From the New Orleans Times.]

WEST GULF BLOCKADING SQUADRON, OFF FORT MORGAN, August 3, 1864.

The fleet for the reduction of Mobile, commanded by Admiral Farragut, and composed of the Winnebago, Chickasaw, Manhattan and Tecumseh, of the Monitor fleet, and the Hartford (flagship), Brooklyn, Oneida, Itasca, Tennessee and Metacomet, of the wooden fleet, will commence to-morrow morning to pour their iron hail into the rebel Fort Morgan.

The ball was opened this afternoon by the Monitor Winnebago, who steamed defiantly up to the fort and threw in a shell or two to give the rebs a taste of our quality. She is a splendid specimen of Monitor naval architecture, and is as buoyant as a cork. On her your correspondent is located, and we expect to be first into the fight to-morrow. Her officers are every one of them gentlemen, and have afforded and will afford me every opportunity to witness the fight.

Captain Thomas Stevens is well known as an officer "chock full of fight," and he is ably seconded by Volunteer Lieutenant W. F. Shankland, Paymaster Girard, Chief Engineer Simon Shultes, First Assistant Engineer John Purdy, Ensigns Morrissy, Murphy and Whitworth, Acting Master Megathlin, and Robert Sherman, gunner. To this latter gentleman I am indebted for favors to be remembered hereafter.

Of the fighting qualities of this noble vessel I shall speak more fully at some future time. The guns in her forward turret are worked by steam, and that they are terrible in execution the rebs will bear me witness.

ON BOARD STEAMSHIP WINNEBAGO, August 4, 1864.

This morning opened beautifully. Contrary to expectations, the land force under General Granger failing to co-operate, we did not attempt the reduction of the forts to-day. But Captain Stevens, determined not to be balked of his share of the fight, steamed up in front of Fort Gaines, and at half-past eleven o'clock this morning threw his first shell at the transport Natchez, which was unloading troops and ammunition at the landing in front of the fort. You should have seen her leave. In less than a minute after the shell burst in her neighborhood the smoke of burning bacon and rosin was plainly visible. We gave and received about a dozen shots, but nobody was hurt on our side.

That you may fully understand the position of affairs let me explain. As we lie, head up the bay, Fort Morgan stands on our right, by and around the lighthouse well known to many of your readers. Immediately opposite, and about five miles off, on the northeast end of Dauphin Island, is Fort Gaines. Running across from Morgan to Gaines is driven a tier of piles, fastened together by a network of chains. Opposite each fort a channel is left open, of about fifteen hundred yards in width, for the use of blockade runners. In the channel, in front of Morgan were placed a lot of buoys, on which the guns of her water battery are trained. I say were, for our boys destroyed about half of them last night. Outside of the piles are placed the torpedoes.

Just inside of the obstructions is lying the rebels' pride and hope—the ram Tennessee and three gunboats. Neither of these have dared to show themselves outside while we were firing into their transports, but contented themselves with throwing a shot at us at long range—say about five miles—when they could have no hope of hitting us.

LATER.

Orders have just come on board for us to go into the fight to-morrow, and from the quantity of fight in the captain and officers of the Winnebago, and of the fleet generally, I can assure you we shall see fun.

Everything now betokens success on our part, and before this reaches you Mobile, I am convinced, will have fallen.

WEDNESDAY, August 5, 1864.

The glory is ours. The victory is with us. I have only time to say that we have passed Fort Morgan and are anchored in the bay.

The rebel ram Tennessee is ours, and also one of their gunboats. Buchanan, the rebel commodore, is wounded, and I hear is dying.

The Monitor Tecumseh was run on a torpedo opposite the obstructions and sunk immediately. All but eighteen of her officers and crew went down with her. Captain Cravens, I believe, was her commander.

The Chickasaw is shelling Fort Powell. In the action to-day we have lost about one hundred and fifty killed and wounded

The bearer of the above letter informs us that Fort Powell was blown up and Fort Gaines taken. We learn from another source that the fleet which passed the forts consisted of fourteen gunboats and four Monitors.

LETTER FROM AN OFFICER ON BOARD THE GUNBOAT PORT ROYAL.

The following account is furnished us by A. C. Sterrett, who was on board the gunboat Port Royal at the time of the fight:—

FRIDAY, August 7, 1864.

The fleet, consisting of the Hartford, Brooklyn, Richmond, Lackawanna, Ossipee, Monongahela, Oneida, Galena, Port Royal, Metacomet, Octorara, Seminole, Itasca, and the Monitors Tecumseh, Manhattan, Chickasaw and Winnebago, and the Admiral's steam barge Loyal, got under weigh at the anchorage off the entrance to Mobile Bay at sunrise, the Monitors in advance and the wooden vessels going together in pairs, the flagship taking the lead. When within point blank range of Fort Morgan the vessels ahead were slowed down to enable the line to close up, and at this time the fort and rebel vessels opened fire on the fleet, which was returned from the one hundred-pounder Parrotts placed on the bows of our vessels in the advance.

The Admiral waited until directly abreast of Fort Morgan, when he delivered a succession of broadsides from the nine-inch guns of the Hartford with such precision and galling effect that the rebels were driven away from their guns, and the water battery and fort were silenced. At this time the Monitor engaged the rebel iron-clad ram Tennessee, which was discovered lying in position to advance on our noble Admiral.

At this moment the Monitor Tecumseh struck a torpedo, and was seen to rise and disappear beneath the water almost instantly. The firing now became terrific, and the fleet, although steaming ahead at a full rate of speed, was completely enveloped in flame and smoke. The rebel ram made several attempts to run our passing vessels down, but failed to do so, and in the midst of all this a boat was lowered from the Metacomet to pick up the survivors of our ill-fated Monitor. It was a beautiful and appalling sight to witness this boat rowing around on its sacred mission to rescue our drowning men, with its beautiful flag flowing to the breeze, and the missiles of death and destruction striking and ricochetting all around it. But the gallant officer (an ensign, whose name I forget) heedlessly kept on his way, and succeeded in rescuing the pilot, one of the officers, and three men, belonging to the Tecumseh.

With the exception of the Monitor our fleet had by this time succeeded in passing Fort Morgan, only to be subject to a galling, raking fire from the three rebel gunboats—Selma, Morgan and Gaines

Our vessels, which were secured together in pairs, were now cast off, and the engagement became general, which in a short time resulted in driving the ram and two gunboats under the guns of Fort Morgan, while the Selma steamed up the bay, with the evident intention of escaping to Mobile. After a chase of about forty minutes the Selma hauled down her flag to Captain Jarrett, of the Metacomet. On boarding her the cause of her surrender was soon apparent—the decks were covered with the dead and dying, and her scuppers were running with their blood. Among others I recognized the body of Lieutenant Comstock, with his bowels torn out and lying across the breech of a gun, which he was engaged in sighting at the time of his death. He once belonged to our navy. Language is not adequate to describe the soul-stirring cheers which went up from the throats of our brave tars, and was re-echoed from one vessel to another all through this terrible ordeal; and our brave, noble Admiral has exemplified in this fight that his theory of "iron hearts and wooden ships" is a correct one.

At this time, while our fleet, with a few exceptions, had collected together on the west side of the bay, in the direction of Fort Powell, and out of the range of Morgan's guns, the ram Tennessee was discovered steaming in the direction.

The Monitors closed with her when in range, and one of the most interesting naval engagements of the war succeeded, and we, in the smaller wooden vessels, were the spectators.

A fight of some minutes ensued, when Admiral Farragut, anxious to close the engagement in a summary manner, started toward the Tennessee at full speed; at the same time Captain Strong, in the Monongahela, struck the Tennessee amidships, and withdrew in time to give room to our Admiral to grapple his antagonist, Buchanan. When the smoke cleared away from the two vessels a white flag was seen to wave from the Tennessee's pilot house, in token of submission, and Captain Jeraud, who went in as a volunteer on the Ossipee as a representative of Admiral Farragut, received the sword of Admiral Buchanan, and that terrible engine of destruction was ours, although gained at a great loss of life.

Our loss in this fight is about two hundred and forty wounded, including the brave Captain Craven, of the Monitor, and one hundred of his crew, who went down with him. Admiral Buchanan, of the Tennessee, was shot through the leg, below the knee, and the leg will have to be amputated.

Fort Powell, in Grant's Pass, was blown up last night after dark, and Fort Gaines will soon follow. The rebel gunboats, which sought protection under the guns of Morgan, will be destroyed or captured by our Monitors today, and the investment and capture of Morgan must follow.

We have, by this great victory, effectually closed the port of Mobile, and its capture is only a question of time, and Admiral Farragut and the gallant officers and men under his command have established another claim to the admiration and respect of their countrymen and those who love liberty.

[From the New Orleans Picayune, August 7.]

We are indebted to the courtesy of an officer of the navy, who witnessed the naval engagement in Mobile Bay on Friday last, for the following interesting particulars:—

Between seven and eight o'clock on that morning the fleet moved in the following order:—Four Monitors and fourteen wooden vessels, the Tecumseh leading the former and the Hartford (flagship of Admiral Farragut) the latter, advanced. The Monitors were the Tecumseh, Manhattan, Winnebago and Chickasaw. The wooden vessels followed in pairs.

The rebel ram, the Tennessee, and gunboats Selma, Morgan and Gaines were lying in wait under the guns of Fort Morgan, ready to attack the federal fleet as it approached; it opened upon them with grape and canister—the Hartford and other vessels—with such severity that nothing could withstand the force of the terrific attack. The gunners of Fort Morgan, in the meantime, were driven from their guns, so fierce was the fire from the federal fleet.

The Tecumseh, in passing the forts, was blown up by the explosion of a torpedo. The captain and all on board, with the exception of ten, sank with her. The Confederate ram Tennessee, after first attacking the fleet as it advanced, seemed to return for shelter under the guns of Fort Morgan; but, after the fleet had proceeded some distance up the bay, stood towards them as if to give battle; whereupon the Hartford, the Monitors and the wooden vessels of the fleet stood for her and a most terrible engagement commenced. The Tennessee was rammed by the Hartford, the Lackawanna and the Monongahela, the Lackawanna striking her under full headway, and all the vessels delivering a heavy fire at the same instant. The Manhattan, meantime, put one solid fifteen inch shot at her, which penetrated her armor through and through and lodged on the opposite side.

Admiral Farragut, during the engagement, was stationed in the maintop, where he had lashed himself in case he should receive a wound, communicating his orders below through speaking tubes. After a most determined and gallant engagement the Tennessee showed a white flag as a token of surrender. An officer of the federal fleet then boarded the Tennessee and demanded the sword of Admiral Buchanan, which that officer surrendered, and it was taken on board the flagship. The Confederate Admiral was wounded severely, and will probably have to suffer the amputation of a leg.

The Confederate gunboat Selma, in the meanwhile, retreated up the bay, and was followed by the Metacomet, Lieutenant Commander Jewett, and Port Royal, Lieutenant Commander Gherardi. The Selma surrendered to Lieutenant Jewett. The two other rebel gunboats, Morgan and Gaines, took refuge under the guns of Fort Morgan, and (says our informant) would probably be captured in the course of yesterday.

The United States Monitor Chickasaw, Lieutenant Commander Perkins, steered gallantly up to Fort Powell, and took in tow a steam barge from immediately under the guns of the fort. After taking the barge out of range, she returned and pelted the fort vigorously for half an hour with eleven-inch shell. Fort Powell was finally evacuated, and at eleven o'clock at night was blown up by the rebels.

Of course, as the rebel vessels concentrated their fire principally upon her, she suffered the greatest loss. The total federal loss, including that of the Tecumseh (which was blown up by the torpedo and sunk), in killed, wounded and missing, was about two hundred and forty.

On the Tennessee there were twenty officers and about one hundred and twenty men, Admiral Buchanan commanding. Among the officers besides were Captain Johnston and Lieutenants Bradford and Wharton.

Details From Other Sources.

[From the New Orleans Era.]

THE LINE OF BATTLE.

The Union fleet passed the forts in the following order:—First came the four Monitors, two of them the same which recently lay in front of New Orleans; then came the Brooklyn, with a steamer lashed to her side—the side farthest removed from the enemy; following her came the flag-ship Hartford, with the Metacomet lashed to her. In what order the others followed we have not yet ascertained.

HOW THE HARTFORD WENT IN.

The noble old ship-of-war Hartford had, of course, to perform some deed of more than common daring—something different from the gallant exploits of her consorts. When it came to her turn to run the fiery gauntlet Admiral Farragut directed her to be steered in as close to Fort Morgan as the depth of water would permit; and as the shore at this point is very abrupt very short range was thus obtained.

The battle tried vessel moved steadily down towards the rebels and received the first fire without injury, when her heavy broadsides were opened upon the fort. Grape and canister were literally rained upon the enemy, at once stopping all work at his guns and causing the artillerymen to seek safety in ignominious flight. So fierce and well sustained were the Hartford's broadsides that the rebel fire was nullified, and all the damage that vessel received was in the subsequent fight in the bay, of which more hereafter.

ADMIRAL FARRAGUT'S POSITION.

The position chosen by the Admiral, and which he maintained throughout the contest, was a novel but most commanding one. Desiring at once to overlook the enemy and watch the movements of his own fleet, he ascended to the maintop of the Hartford and was there lashed fast.

A speaking trumpet was run down to the deck, and an officer was stationed at the lower end to receive the Admiral's orders and pass them to the person whose duty it was to see them executed. This proved to be a most admirable arrangement, and we may expect ere long for the commanders of fleets to have comfortable quarters built for themselves on the top of the masts of their flagships.

THE FLEET PILOT.

Elevated as was the station of the Admiral, the Fleet Pilot rivalled him, for he, too, was far up in the rigging, and from his high position communicated his orders to his subordinates.

THE WAY THE TENNESSEE WAS TAKEN.

The great rebel iron clad ram Tennessee, which the rebels have so often boasted could, and would if opportunity presented, sink the whole federal fleet, has had a trial, fought well, but was forced to succumb to superior skill and prowess. After the fleet had passed the forts, all the vessels made direct for the Tennessee and completely surrounded her. Then followed the fiercest part of the combat. Ship after ship was driven against the iron sides of their formidable adversary, and broadside after broadside poured in upon her, until she was overpowered, and the bastard stars and bars gave place to the glorious flag of the free.

HOW THE HARTFORD WAS INJURED.

It is with pain that we inform our readers that the Hartford—the ship that has so often hurled defiance in the very teeth of the rebels in their boasted strongholds, received some rather serious injuries in this fight, but the enemy cannot claim credit for having performed the deed.

The Hartford took a leading part in the struggle with the Tennessee, and it was while manœuvering to injure her enemy that the accident occurred which we are about to relate.

With a full head of steam on the Hartford rushed down upon the great iron-clad, and the concussion shook the rebel vessel to the centre, but without damaging the stout sides of the flagship. Swinging around, after butting her opponent, it was the intention to deliver a broadside into her. Just at this critical moment a vessel was discovered rushing upon the Hartford from the other side.

It proved to be the Metacomet, which had the exact range of the ram, but the Hartford had swung across her path, and the smoke which enveloped the combatants was so dense that, until the moment before they collided, the unfortunate position of the Hartford was not discovered. As soon as the latter was discerned, the engines of the Metacomet were stopped and reversed, but still the momentum was sufficient to crush in the side timbers of the Hartford.

This accident will compel the Hartford to go North for repairs. Admiral Farragut is said to be exceedingly grieved at this misfortune—that is, as much grieved as a man who has won a great victory can be.

THE TECUMSEH.

As before stated, the Monitor Tecumseh was blown up by a torpedo and sunk; but it is thought that she can be raised and repaired. It grieves us to state that, as far as known, only ten men were saved; but we hope and believe that later and positive accounts will place a more favorable aspect upon this affair.

REBEL LOSSES.

It is, of course, impossible to give the losses sustained by the rebels; but it is supposed their casualties will greatly exceed ours. The fire upon the fortifications was very severe.

BELOW EXPECTATIONS.

Our highest naval authorities are greatly surprised at the small loss inflicted upon the Union fleet. Admiral Farragut, it is said, fully expected to lose half a dozen of his vessels; but as it is the ram Tecumseh is the only one that can be called lost. We surely have prize vessels sufficient to offset this.

ADMIRAL BUCHANAN.

Latest accounts say that this brave but misguided officer is very low, and that it is almost impossible that he can recover. Admiral Franklin Buchanan is the only officer of his rank in the rebel navy. He is an old and experienced officer having originally entered the United States Navy on the 28th of January, 1815. On the breaking out of the rebellion he deserted his country's flag, and on the 5th of September, 1861, entered the service of the so-called confederacy. On the 26th of August, 1862, the organization of the rebel navy was completed, and he, on that date, received his commission as admiral. Buchanan is a native of, and was appointed from, Maryland. He served twenty-one years and five months sea service in the United States Navy, and nine years on shore. He has been naval commandant at Mobile nearly the whole time since leaguing with traitors.

Should the present incumbent of the position of senior officer in the rebel navy not survive, a chance to testify their regards for the pirate Semmes will be opened to the rebel authorities.

LOSS OF THE PHILLIPPE.

We are sorry to record the loss of the despatch steamer Phillippe, Capt. Seevers. She burned in sight of the fleet, but the affair is as yet enveloped in mystery. The Phillippe was a beautifully finished, sharp prowed, light draught steamer, built expressly for speed, and for some time past has been employed as Admiral Farragut's despatch boat.

She accompanied the Hartford until within range of the rebel works, but when firing began she was ordered away. After getting some distance out flames were observed to burst suddenly from her, and it is supposed she was totally destroyed. The fate of Capt. Seevers, and the other officers and men of the Phillippe, is unknown, but it is thought that they took to the boats and pulled to some of the blockading squadron in Mississippi Sound, a distance of nearly thirty miles. The destruction of this vessel is a severe loss, as she was extremely useful to our naval commanders.

Our Losses.

Up to the time the despatch steamer Glasgow left the fleet off Mobile for New Orleans, Admiral Farragut had sustained a loss of two hundred and forty-nine killed and wounded.

CASUALTIES ON BOARD THE FLAGSHIP HARTFORD.

The following is a list of some of the killed on board the flagship Hartford, August 5, 1864.

—— Higgingbotton, Fleet Captain's Secretary.
Benjamin Harper, seaman.
James B. Osgood, ordinary seaman.
Charles E. Schaffer, ordinary seaman.
Louis McLane, landsman.
Adolphus Pullo, seaman.
Thomas Bayne, ordinary seaman.
John C. Scott, ordinary seaman.
Thomas Stanton, seaman.
James Alexander, landsman.
Henry Clark, first class boy.
Wm. E. Andrews, captain of afterguard.
Wm. Smith, landsman.
Frederick Munsell, landsman.
Thomas Wildes, landsman.
George Stillwell, nurse
David Morrow, quarter gunner.
Peter Duncan, coalheaver.
Andrew E. Smith, coalheaver.
Francis Campbell, second class fireman.
George Wallace, landsman, and two others, and twelve wounded.

CASUALTIES ON BOARD THE MONONGAHELA.

Lieutenant Prentiss lost both legs.

CASUALTIES ON BOARD THE ONEIDA.

Commander Mullany lost one arm.

The gunboat Oneida was struck by a shell from the ram Tennessee. It passed through the Oneida's boiler, scattering hot water and scalding thirty of her men, some severely.

CASUALTIES ON THE TECUMSEH.

Commander T. A. Craven and all hands, except ten or eighteen—accounts conflicting.

Description of the Tecumseh.

The Tecumseh was one of Mr. Ericsson's improved Monitor batteries, and was built by Secor & Co., under the superintendence of George Birkbeck, Jr., at Jersey City. She was launched on the 12th of September, 1863, at eight o'clock A. M. She was christened by Mrs. Kate Gregory, daughter-in-law of Admiral Gregory, U. S. N. She made her final trial trip on the 28th of March, 1864, and was put in commission at the Brooklyn Navy Yard on the 25th of April, 1864, and arrived at Hampton Roads on the 28th of that month. After a few weeks' stay in the James river, with Acting Rear Admiral Lee, she was sent to Mobile for Admiral Farragut. Her career has been brief and her finale horrible. Heaven save us from any more Monitor disasters!

The Tecumseh was of the following dimensions:—Extreme length over armor, 235 feet; length of hull proper, 190 feet; extreme beam over armor, 46 feet; beam of hull proper, 37 feet; depth of hold, 13 feet; armament, two fifteen inch guns.

The following was the list of officers of the iron-clad Tecumseh:—

Commander—T. A. M. Craven.
Lieutenant—J. W. Kelly.
Acting Assistant Surgeon—Henry A. Danker.
Acting Assistant Paymaster—George Work.
Acting Master—Charles F. Langley.
Ensigns—F. H. de Estamanville, G. Cottrell.
Engineers—Chief, John Farron; First Assistants, Chas. Pennington, W. L. Penell; Third Assistants, F. Scott, W. D. Kay.
Clerk to Captain—Isaiah Conley.

Sketch of Commander T. A. M. Craven, U. S. N., late Commander of the Tecumseh.

Tunis Augustus Macdonough Craven entered the naval service of the United States as a midshipman on the 2d of February, 1829. He was born in New Hampshire, and was appointed from New York State, of which he was a citizen. In 1830 he was ordered to the sloop-of-war Boston, attached to the Mediterranean squadron. He remained in her until 1833, when he was granted a leave of absence for a few months. In 1834 he joined the sloop-of-war St. Louis, under Master Commandant Thomas M. Newell, on the West India station. He returned from her during the close of that year.

On the 3d of July, 1835, he was warranted as a passed midshipman, and waited orders until 1836, when he was ordered to duty in connection with the surveying of our coast. His aptitude for this kind of work induced the Navy Department to keep him in this service until 1842. At an extra session of Congress in 1841, he was promoted to be a Lieutenant, his commission bearing date September 8, 1841. His first orders after being a lieutenant was to the sloop-of-war Falmouth, of the Home squadron. He was attached to this vessel until 1843, when he was ordered to the receiving ship North Carolina, at New York. He remained there but a short time when he was ordered to the storeship Lexington. He was relieved from her in January, 1844, and granted a furlough.

In 1847 he was ordered to the sloop-of-war Dale, Commander W. W. McKean, of the Pacific squadron. He made a full cruise in her and left her in August, 1849, and waited orders, until ordered to the Coast Survey in 1850 and 1851, where he remained until 1858, when he was ordered to the command of the Atrato Expedition, whose duty it was to explore and verify the surveys previously made of a ship canal near the Isthmus of Darian, to connect the waters of the Pacific and Atlantic by the Atrato and Turando rivers. In 1859 we find him again attached to the Coast Survey in the steamer Corwin. He left the Coast Survey in June, 1859, and was ordered to command the steamer Mohawk, of the Home squadron, under Flag Officer W. J. McCluny, his station being off the coast of Cuba, to intercept slave traders. When the rebellion broke out he was in command of her, but shortly afterwards he was placed in command of the Crusader. His services were of such value in these vessels that the Board of Underwriters of this city presented his wife with a service of plate and forwarded to him the following complimentary letter:—

OFFICE OF THE BOARD OF UNDERWRITERS, NEW YORK, Oct. 19, 1861.

DEAR SIR—The Board of Underwriters of the city of New York have observed that while in command of the United States steamers Mohawk and Crusader you have always evinced a desire to render such assistance to the commerce of our country as could properly be extended in the performance of your duty, and that on several occasions you have rendered important services to American vessels in distress in the vicinity of Key West, Florida. Appreciating these services, the Board, by a resolution, have requested me to convey to you its acknowledgment and thanks; and in doing so, permit me to add that you have their best wishes for success and advancement in your profession and in the service of your country at this trying hour, and that they will continue to feel a deep interest in your welfare. Very respectfully, your obedient servant,

T. B. SATTERTHWAITE, President.

Captain T. AUGUSTUS CRAVEN, United States Navy.

Commander Craven received his present commission April 24, 1861, and in September, 1861, he left the Crusader and took command of the new screw sloop Tuscarora, which was despatched across the Atlantic to cruise for rebel pirates. He returned in July, 1863, after performing much valuable service for the Union abroad. Early this year he was ordered to the command of the Ericsson battery Tecumseh and sailed in her for Hampton Roads to join Acting Rear Admiral Lee's James river flotilla. He was among the first to reach City Point; and, after a somewhat lengthened stay in the James river, he was ordered to join Admiral Farragut, and in the passage of the Mobile forts his vessel was blown up by a torpedo and he perished in a most horrible manner, no doubt having been drowned in the pilot house.

He was an officer of rare merit, and a great favorite. Socially, he was genial and affable and won friends in all classes. No one knew him but to love him. He was full of inventive genius, and was apt and quick in anything he undertook. He was opposed to the Monitor system in all its details, yet he would not request any other command, feeling, as he did, that they were unsafe under almost any circumstance. Commander Craven will be a great loss to our navy, and one not easily repaired. He leaves a very interesting family behind him to mourn his loss. Wherever he was known his loss will be felt. He stood number three on the list of commanders, and has served his country faithfully for over thirty-six years; nearly twenty years of this time has been at sea. He was just in the prime of life, and full of bright promise. He has fallen a victim to the Monitor interest. Peace to his ashes.

REBEL ACCOUNTS.

Official Report of the Naval Battle in Mobile Bay.

The Richmond *Examiner* of the 12th has the following:—

MOBILE, August 9, 1864.

Hon. S. E. MALLORY, Secretary of the Navy:—

The enemy steamed in through the main entrance with four Monitors and about sixteen heavy vessels of war. The Tecumseh, Commander T. A. M. Craven, was sunk with nearly all her crew; and also another gunboat, the Philippi, which I subsequently burned.

The Richmond, Hartford and Brooklyn, in line of battle, followed by the remainder of the fleet, pushed by Fort Morgan under full headway, when they were encountered by the Tennessee, the Morgan, the Gaines, and the Selma.

The Tennessee and other vessels steamed in close range of the advancing force and poured a heavy fire into the leading ships. After a desperate struggle between the fleets the Gaines retired to Fort Morgan in a sinking condition. The Selma, cut off, surrendered, and the Morgan escaped to Fort Morgan.

The Tennessee, so far uninjured, steamed toward the whole fleet, and after an obstinate fight surrendered, her rudder disabled, her smokestack carried away, and, as we suppose, her crew in an exhausted and smothering condition.

On the Tennessee Admiral Buchanan was severely wounded by a splinter in the leg. Two were killed and several wounded among her crew. On the Gaines two were killed and two wounded. On the Morgan one was wounded. On the Selma eight were killed, including the executive officer, Lieutenant J. H. Comstock, and seven were wounded.

The enemy suffered severely, and requested permission to bury his dead.

Respectfully, &c.,
G. W. HARRISON, Confederate States Navy.

The *Examiner* also gives a list of the twenty-eight Union vessels engaged, having two hundred and twelve guns, with the four Confederates having thirty-two guns. It says:—

It was a most unequal contest, in which our gallant little navy was engaged, and we lost the battle; but our ensign went down in a blaze of glory.

OUR NORTHERN FRONTIER DEFENCES.

Preparations of Governor Seymour to Repel Rebel Raids from Canada,

&c., &c., &c.

SYRACUSE, N. Y., August 14, 1864.

The following important order has been issued by Governor Seymour with regard to the frontier defence:—

Brigadier General Green publishes a general order in which he assumes command, and is making details to patrol the borders of the State:—

STATE OF NEW YORK, INSPECTOR GENERAL'S OFFICE, ALBANY, August 12, 1864.

To Brigadier General JOHN A. GREEN, Commanding Twenty-fourth brigade National Guard, Syracuse:—

GENERAL—The Governor, being informed that refugees, deserters and other evil disposed persons are gathered in considerable numbers in the adjoining Canadian provinces, and that there is danger that they may elude the vigilance of the Canadian authorities and make an attack upon some of our frontier towns, the northern boundary of the State, from the east line of the county of Monroe to the west line of the State of Vermont, is placed under your military charge. This will embrace the counties of Wayne, Cayuga, Oswego, Jefferson, St. Lawrence, Franklin and Clinton, and this order will continue in force, unless revoked, until the brigades in the several districts embraced in the above counties shall respectively report at least two organized regiments. You will immediately make such arrangements as will secure to you the earliest information and as will, in your judgment, best enable you to guard against any invasion of our territory by marauders. If it shall become necessary to maintain a patrol at any point, you will make such details from the organized regiments of the National Guard in your brigade, or from the district patrolled, as may be required for that purpose, reporting your action in the premises to the Commander-in-Chief. Contracts for subsistence, should any become necessary, will be made by you pursuant to instructions from the Adjutant General, who will issue such other and further orders in the premises as the exigency of the service may require.

Very respectfully, your obedient servant,
JOSIAH T. MILLER, Inspector General.

SHERMAN.

There was a report in town last evening that General Sherman had been engaged on the 9th inst. shelling the city of Atlanta from all parts of his line, and that the Union right rested near East Point. If that place has been occupied the railroad communication is thereby cut off between Atlanta and the South, at the junction of the railroads leading to Montgomery via West Point and Macon, and renders further raids along those lines perfectly unnecessary.

Rebel Accounts of Affairs at Atlanta.

[From the Richmond Examiner, August 12.]

Up to Thursday night nothing of interest had occurred before Atlanta. Major General Bates received a flesh wound in the leg. The enemy is massing on our right and endeavoring to extend his lines in the direction of the Western Railroad.

A few shots were fired at the city yesterday (9th). Brisk shelling commenced at 11 o'clock last night and continued four hours. No personal casualties are reported

NEWS FROM WASHINGTON.

WASHINGTON, August 14, 1864.

ABSENCE OF WAR NEWS IN WASHINGTON.

Nothing has transpired here to-day in relation to operations either at Atlanta or in the valley. The city, under the influence of the extreme heat prevailing and the absolute dearth of news, has been very quiet. A thunder shower this afternoon cooled the atmosphere somewhat; but it is still uncomfortably sultry. The attendance at the churches was rather slim, the heat preventing the usual attention to their religious interests by people generally.

THE SEVEN AND THREE-TENTHS LOAN.

The subscriptions to the seven-thirty loan reported to the Treasury Department yesterday amounted to $1,028,500. The aggregate amount to date is $13,067,750.

THE SECOND NEW YORK CAVALRY.

Major Brinton, of the Second New York cavalry (Harris light) is here, *en route* for New York, for the purpose of recruiting. No regiment in the service has a more brilliant record than this, or is more admired in the Army of the Potomac. Three generals—Kilpatrick, Duffie and Davies—have been appointed from it, each of whom begged to have the regiment assigned to their command.

PAYMENT OF TROOPS IN THE HOSPITALS.

Four hundred thousand dollars have been paid to patients in the hospitals here and at Alexandria for the last term of two months. This is the largest payment that has been made in these hospitals during the war.

SENT TO THE DRY TORTUGAS.

H. A. Burnham, Company B, Fiftieth New York Engineers; Jesse Sheres, Twentieth New York State Militia; James Norman, One Hundred and Twenty-fifth New York, and W. J. Evans, Fourteenth New York State Militia, were sent from here yesterday to the Dry Tortugas, in punishment for military offences.

THE NON-ESTABLISHMENT OF IDENTITY BY PENSION AND OTHER CLAIMANTS.

Great complaint is made by the several departments, particularly at the Pension Bureau, of the failure on the part of applicants for pensions and other claims to establish their identity, according to the published rules. Hundreds of claims of whose justness no one entertains the least doubt have been on file many months, and must remain there until the claimants present more satisfactory credentials. To those seeking the settlement of the accounts of relatives killed in the service, this subject is of the greatest importance, and all should understand that their failure to accomplish their object in this respect is attributable solely to the incompleteness of their papers.

THE GUERILLAS AGAIN AT ANANDALE.

The guerillas made their appearance again at Anandale yesterday, killing a sergeant of the Sixteenth New York cavalry, whose name has not been obtained.

THE CROPS ON THE ARLINGTON ESTATE.

An immense force of contrabands is employed securing the harvests of the government farms near Arlington, under the superintendence of Colonel Green, Chief Quartermaster of the Department. It is estimated that the net profits from these farms for the present season will exceed fifty thousand dollars.

News from Havana.

HAVANA, August 10, 1864.

A new censor, Senor Carada, is to be appointed in place of Senor Apolinar del Rato; and the *Siglo* has resumed publication.

The *Siglo* refutes the recent falsehoods of the *Diario de la Marina* and the New York correspondent in regard to the war in the United States.

The rector of the University here has resigned, and Senor Duran has been appointed his successor.

A fire in Matanzas on Saturday night destroyed Springer's cooper shop. Loss heavy and uninsured.

The heat continues oppressive. Though the yellow fever is decreasing, there are many cases of typhoid fever.

The Congressional Committee in Maine.

BANGOR, Me., August 14, 1864.

The Congressional Committee was joined at Bath by Hon. Sidney Perham, ex-Governor Washburn, Collector of Portland and Hon. John A. Poor. They left Rockland at five P. M. and arrived at eleven P. M., where they were greeted by a salute of artillery and received by the hospitable citizens, who provided accommodations for the whole party at the hotels and private residences. To-morrow the party will visit Indian Old Town, the residence of the remnants of the Penobscot Indian tribe.

Personal Intelligence.

Major General Q. A. Gillmore, who was seriously injured by his horse falling upon him while leading a column in pursuit of Breckinridge during the recent raid on Washington, has so far recovered as to be able to leave Brooklyn to-day for West Point, where he will remain until able to take the field again. It will yet be some time before General Gillmore can enter upon active service, his injuries being of such a nature as to preclude a rapid recovery; otherwise the General is in excellent health and spirits.

The Conservative.

WEDNESDAY MORNING, AUG. 17, 1864.

FOR PRESIDENT:

ABRAHAM LINCOLN,

Of Illinois.

FOR VICE-PRESIDENT:

ANDREW JOHNSON,

Of Tennessee.

THE INDIAN TROUBLES.

The following dispatch gives a pretty correct account of matters relating to Indians on the Blue. Some of Gen. Curtis' troops must be at Beatrice by this time.

NEBRASKA CITY, Aug. 15.

Major General Curtis:

A reliable citizen of this place has just arrived from Beatrice. He left there at 6:30 last evening. He says the Indians have committed no depredations except on the stage road on the Little Blue, and only in small parties on the road. The main force of the enemy, 2,000 strong, are on the Republican, southwest of Fort Kearney. Informant had a brother killed on Little Blue. Small parties first attack trains and if repulsed return in greater force. A citizen company of fifty men, commanded by Captain Gilbert, is on the Little Blue. Several ranches have been burned. There are two hundred families at Beatrice, and about two hundred men, but they have but few arms and little ammunition. People are a good deal excited and reports are exaggerated. Heard nothing of an attack on the Otoe Agency except report of fire in that direction, which was prairie burning. Twenty-two scouts sent there, went to Blue Springs; report no enemy there.

OUR RAILROAD INTERESTS.

Kansas City has just cause for rejoicing this week, and its spirited little newspaper, the *Journal*, for once, gets into a rhapsody upon adequate provocation. The present week witnesses the opening of the Pacific Railroad east to Independence, and the opening of the Union Pacific west to Lawrence. The *Journal* remarks:

"We will have the only railroad west of the Missouri border—forty miles in extent, and lengthening each season as it stretches away to the Golden Spurs of the Rocky Mountains. Even now it will arrest and divert the rich trade of Western and Southern Kansas, and make it tributary to this city. Eighty miles of wagon transportation will be saved to much the largest portion of Western trade, and the four days time and enhanced cost will be saved for other and more profitable pursuits, cheapening in a double ratio the comforts and necessities of the population to the west of us."

We hope that such facts as these will stimulate our own people to a vigorous and determined effort in behalf of the project of connecting Leavenworth with the North Missouri Railroad. The apathy hitherto exhibited concerning this measure is unaccountable. With a public spirited city administration, the people would have been aroused through the agency of public meetings—or at least some official appeal.

But the diversion of trade from the interior by the completion of the road from Kansas City to Lawrence, and the opening

LETTER DE KOTCH IT--NO. 2.

POPE CLEMENT TO ST. THOMAS.

EXE-KEW-TIV MANSHUN, DAYTON,
NORTH WESTERN CORNFEDERACY,
Orgust 16th, 1864.

MY DEAR GUV'NER: I must confess to no leetle surpries on larning through a privit telagrim from Faithfil Tra that yew hed maid mi sealed lettur of instruckshins (to yew) public, through the kolems of a jurnal professidly opposed to the progress of dimmycratic idees and principels. Dogonned ef it don't look to me as ef yer week pint was a illeegitemate hankerin after notoryety.

Now, ef as how sich should proove tew be the case, I wish tew sa tew yew, in the very acmy of emfasiss, that no purson in the North Western Cornfederacy is entytled tew notoryety, save and eksept miself—who am chief baker, butcher, butler and bottell kracker, the fairest snake among a hundred thousand, and the wun alltergether luvly. And as I am oncapable of dewin ennything further that would create surprize in the minds of our ennymees, I ekspect all my transactshuns for the present tew be kep profoundly a secret.

Your unwarrantable perceedins smak sumwhat of onfare pla, and I shall hev tew titen the skrews on yew; and I haarby warn yew tew bee keerfull not tew give further cos fur suspishun. Howsumever it may bee as how them ar' Conservativ' chaps got holt un that ar' dockyment in a onreg'lar manner, and, ef that should bee the trew state o' the case, of coarse it 'ud bee agin the laws o' conshense to blame yew. I shall resarve enny further opinyun till I haar from yew.

Thar ar' a leetle bit o' skandal floatin' around these diggins in regard to your right and left bowers, and I think it 'ud bee well—arter tha' hev fullefillid thar mishun—to leeve 'em out in the Linkum draft. That leetle poodle dorg o' yourn, (Fitz Hindoo,) that does your barkin fur the stra' crums from yer table, was interdewsed too me a few days ago, when he sed that thar had been so much talk about me that when he hearn that I had accomplished mi pillgrimige to the land of the blessid Eske-moes and had returned safely to mi Exe-kew-tiv' Manshun, despite o' the keen scented bloodhounds o' Mr. Linkum, he had sich a oncoptrolable pan-shong tew sea me, that he jist tuk the fust cattle train that left Weston and cum right along without stoppin' tew dress fur dinner, and that I must ekskewse his ruff lookin' exterior, fur he'd been doin' considerable durty work fur a long back.

I told him I had hearn so, and that his appearance didn't in the least detract frum mi hearsay testimonee. Then, wishing tew git at the trewth of sertin not very creditable on dits, I adroitly axed him ef he was ackquaneted with the good ole abolishenist of thirty years standin'.

"Thirty yeers!" sez he. "Your hig'ness ar misstooken; he's bin a abolishner ever sence he's bin ennything."

"Why, what do you meen?" sed I.

"Well," sez he, "he's a abolishener by consanguine relashunship."

"Please explane yourself," sed I.

"Wal," sez he, "I think as how his ab'rijurnal fust mammy wur a feminine shemale African wimin of the kuller'd fare seks."

"You don't sa' so?" sed I. "Has he got wool?"

"Beware O' ... borned, cradel ... the brest of fr... and has worn ... varietee of cos...

Hoping to ... shun from yew ... tripidashun, ...

Pop...

—The City ... thorized the ... to put the for... immediate rep...

—The loyal ... N. Y., had a F... and wounded ... Christian Com...

—Philadelph... fense, $315,93... $2,005,250; ... Total, $6,668,... can go far bey... half exhausted...

—A package ... of the Sons o... office that Dar... in Terre Hau... thing drop, le... exposed.

—The Roun... dressing a lad... at $4,310. No... on $310. the s... absorb the wl... wanted by the...

—The New ... doubled their ... the quality an... you object to ... the high cost o... meat, they asl... price?

—Col. Mulli... of his memory ... his strongest ... prompting the ... down and sav... citizen say, "I... my country i... 'save the flag.'

—The New ... says that con... weigh twenty-... four shillings ... one dollar in ... present price ... 953-4 in currer...

THE INI...

Luke Ben...

[Fro...

Mr. James ... night received ... Pifer, dated F... states that th... Benham's tra... Creek massac... not been hear... Benham's l... 000. Sam. Ro... was in charge...

We learn by ... on the 10th in... ed Pawnee Sta... Fort Kearney, ... purpose of cap... quantity of sto... fight ensued, v... being driven ... their number ... tacking band l... white men, at ... Several over... out by the co...

The Bushwhackers in Missouri.

[From the St. Joe Herald.]

We noticed yesterday that a fight was expected with Bill Anderson. at a camp ten miles north of Liberty. A dispatch received by Gen. Fisk last night, states that Anderson was overtaken near Fredericksburg, Ray county, by a company of militia under Capt. Colly. A severe fight ensued in which several of the guerillas were killed. On our side Captain Colly and four of his men were killed.

The 6th cavalry, M. S. M.. are pursing the fiends. Messengers from that section report the citizens as failing utterly in their duty to report the whereabouts of the guerillas. Gen. Fisk tells us that General Retribution will be placed in command down that way.

Another dispatch received at Headquarters says Anderson is threatening the railroad near Hamilton. Gen. Fisk is concentrating his troops near Kingston, Caldwell county, and hopes to surround and capture the whole gang. Major McDermott, with a detachment of the 1st Iowa cavalry left here by a special train last night for Hamilton, the point which it is presumed Anderson is making for.

TO ARMS! TO ARMS!

The Foe, They Come! They Come!

Colored Men Arouse!

AVENGE FT. PILLOW!

MAJ. GEN. S. R. CURTIS has been authorized to raise a

COLORED BATTERY

With Black Commissioned Officers.

Lieut. W. D. Matthews has been regularly mustered and authorized to recruit the Battery. His office is in the Waverly House, two doors south of the Post Office, Main Street, Leavenworth, where he will receive recruits, swear them in and issue clothing.

Recruiting Offices will be opened at Wyandotte and Lawrence—Lieut. P. H. Miner will have charge of the office at Wyandotte. The recruits will receive the same Bounty, Pay, Clothing and protection as white Volunteers.

Bounty and Pay same as to White Recruits.

The necesities for State defence, and the duty and honor of Colored Men, require this Battery to be filled up immediately, in the next ten days if possible.

Able Bodied Men Fall In!

MAJ. R. H. HUNT,
Chief of Artillery.

Lieut. W. D. MATTHEWS,
Recruiting Officer.

P. S.—All influential colored men are earnestly requested to aid in filling up this Battery. THIS IS YOUR DUTY.
jy19dtf

...y west from ... ke the Yellow-... r. The Dakota ... Sully. Four ... onsin and two ... eft at Fort Rice ... at post. ... st, a messenger ... Fort Berthold, ... at there were ... s in camp near ... the arrival of ... ed to give him ... mated that the ... thousand war-... , and eager for ... Rice immedi-... nce to General ... er, who, it was ... e expedition in ... eral deem the ... ubt was enter-... rn his column ... d direct his ... f the painted ... battle has ere ... icinity of Fort

...iagara Falls.

...rier.] ... ini, the funam-... was Blondin's ... gara Falls, was ... rd the rapids ... a pair of iron ... pose. The ex-... ff on the 15th. ... we learn, the ... o rehearse the ... ded in getting ... the point be-... Island bridge, ... , or gave way, ... rapids. ... his accident ... on's Island, a ... which lies to ... and very near ... Fall. He suc-... shore of this ... f from the wa-... stained a pain-... s. ... about 800 or ... fore spoken of, ... uld be floated ... le, perhaps, be ... an is not too ... he might be ... s feared, how-... done he will ... d and nervons ... ctly descried, ... t making not ... t attention or ... is tights and ... uently to rub ... imb. A more ... he is in, could

Thursday, September 1st, 1864,

—AT—

Turner's Hall,

and will continue Tuesday and Thursday of each week during the season.

Hours for instruction of Young Ladies and Misses from 2 to 5 o'clock, P. M. Gentlemen, for the first four lessons, from 7 to 10 o'clock in the evening.

Mr. Lee pledges himself to devote his best exertions to the care and instruction of those who may favor him with their patronage.

Ladies and gentlemen wishing to form a private class can be accommodated by applying at the hall. Good music will be in attendance. aug16d3m

GENERAL ORDERS, NO. 17.

HEADQUARTERS STATE OF KANSAS,
ADJUTANT GENERAL'S OFFICE,
TOPEKA, August 5th, 1864.

I. In view of the threatening attitude of Guerilla bands upon our Eastern border, and of the actual Indian troubles within the limits of our State, it is ordered—

II. That the entire Militia of the State hold themselves in readiness for immediate active service when ordered to take the field.

III. Commandants of Regiments, and Battalions, will perfect their organizations at once, so that no delay occur. They will also see that *all* the Companies constituting their respective commands are provided with the necessary arms, ammunition and equipments for immediate active service.

By order of the Commander-in-Chief.

C. K. HOLLIDAY,
aug16d4t Adjutant General.

PROPOSALS.

CHIEF QUARTERMASTER'S OFFICE,
Fort Leavenworth, August 16, 1864.

SEALED PROPOSALS, in duplicate, will be received at this office until 12 o'clock M., of Saturday, the 3d day of September next, for the delivery at Fort Larned, Kansas, of

25,000 Bushels of Shelled Corn,

clean and of the best quality, in good gunny sacks securely sewed with linen twine.

10,000 bushels to be delivered by the 15th day of October, and the whole quantity by the 30th day of November, 1864.

Proposals for 5,000 bushels will be received.

Bidders must be present at the opening of the bids, and successful bidders be in readiness with good and sufficient securities to enter into contracts and execute required bonds, as soon as awards are made.

The right is reserved to reject any and all proposals that may be offered. M. H. INSLEY,
Capt. & Chief Qu'r'mr Dept. of Kansas.
aug16dtd (Bulletin copy.)

For Sale.

I HAVE some Forty Lots in Latta's Addition some of which are 60 by 140 feet, one 150 by 336 feet, which I will sell up to the 10th of September for one-half in hand, the balance in one year, with interest.

Also a large two-story frame building on Cherokee street, a good location and well calculated for a Grocery Store, Boarding House or Country Hotel.

EDWARD T. LATTA,
Delaware Street, near Broadway.
August 13, 1864. aug14d4w*

Lost.

LOST on last Friday, a small, black Cow, with a star on her forehead and about six or seven years old. I will pay five dollars for her delivery to me, at the next house to the corner of Miami and Third streets.

aug12d1w MEYER GREENSPAN.

THE CONSERVATIVE OFFICE is at 13 and 15 Shawnee street.

whom the contract may be awarded.

Given under our hands and seals this ——— day of ——— 1864.

——————— [seal.]
——————— [seal.]

——————— Witness.

The responsibility of the guarantors must be shown by the official certificate of a United States District Attorney, or any other officer under the United States Government, or responsible person known at this office.

Bidders must be present at the opening of the bids, and in readiness to close contracts, as soon as awards are made, and their particular attention is called to the requirements of this advertisement.

The undersigned reserves the right to reject any or all bids that may be offered.

Proposals must be made in triplicate, on separate sheets of paper, and endorsed "Proposals for Artillery Horses." HENRY C. HODGES,
aug12dtd Captain and Depot Quartermaster.

LEAVENWORTH CITY AND FORT LEAVENWORTH PACKET.

THE STEAMER ELLA

WILL commence making regular trips between Leavenworth City and Fort Leavenworth on Thursday, August 11th, leaving the Levee at the foot of Shawnee street, as follows:

Hours of Departure for the Fort.

At	6 o'clock,	A. M.
"	8 "	"
"	10 "	"
"	12 "	"
"	2 "	P. M.
"	4 "	"
"	6 "	"

Returning, Leaves the Fort.

At	7 o'clock,	A. M.
"	9 "	"
"	11 "	"
"	1 "	P. M.
"	3 "	"
"	5 "	"
"	6½ "	"

The packet will make a landing on the Missouri shore every trip.

For the accommodation of workmen, the six o'clock morning packet will land at Skelton's Mills.

RATES OF FARE:

Civilians and Officers.......... 15 cts.
Soldiers and Laborers.......... 10 "
aug12dtf

Wanted for Adoption.

A RESPECTABLE FAMILY having just lost their only child, is desirous of adopting a female infant from six to ten months old; must have black eyes. Address MRS. SARAH M. LYNCH,
aug12d1w* Leavenworth P. O., Kansas.

WANTED.

FIFTY YOKE of good, well broke Work Cattle, for which the highest cash price will be paid.

A. CALDWELL & CO.,
aug11d1w 104 Delaware St., Leavenworth, Ks.

Business Chance.

ANY one wishing to invest a small capital in a good paying Business will do well by calling at No. 11 Shawnee street, one door east of this office.
aug11d4t*

Leather Belting

OF ALL

SIZES,

FOR SALE AT

W. C. LOBENSTEIN'S,
No. 20 Cherokee street,
Between Main and Second Streets,
Leavenworth, Kansas.
aug11d&w6mos

TO ARMS! TO ARMS!

The Foe, They Come! They Come!

Colored Men Arouse!

AVENGE FT. PILLOW!

MAJ. GEN. S. R. CURTIS has been authorized to raise a

COLORED BATTERY

With Black Commissioned Officers.

Lieut. W. D. Matthews has been regularly mustered and authorized to recruit the Battery. His office is in the Waverly House, two doors south of the Post Office, Main Street, Leavenworth, where he will receive recruits, swear them in and issue clothing.

Recruiting Offices will be opened at Wyandotte and Lawrence—Lieut. P. H. Miner will have charge of the office at Wyandotte. The recruits will receive the same Bounty, Pay, Clothing and protection as white Volunteers.

Bounty and Pay same as to White Recruits.

The necesities for State defence, and the duty and honor of Colored Men, require this Battery to be filled up immediately, in the next ten days if possible.

Able Bodied Men Fall In!

MAJ. R. H. HUNT,
Chief of Artillery.

Lieut. W. D. MATTHEWS,
Recruiting Officer.

P. S.—All influential colored men are earnestly requested to aid in filling up this Battery. THIS IS YOUR DUTY.
jy19dtf

Great Bargains.

AT

No. 52 Delaware Strt.

Notwithstanding the late extraordinary advance in goods

Daniels, Millington & Co.

In order to make room for a

LARGE STOCK

Of Goods to arrive, offer their STOCK OF

SUMMER GOODS AT COST,

Consisting of

Lawns,	Parasols,
Jackonets,	Ladies' Hats,
Organdas,	Misses Summer Hats,
Brilliantes	Men's Summer Hats,
Challis	Boys' Summer Hats,
Bereges,	Summer Coats,
Mozambiques,	Summer Pants,
Tissuaes,	Summer Vests,
Grenadines,	Light Summer Suits,
Summer Shawls,	Summer Cassimeres,
Silk Mantillas,	Summer Vestings,
Sum'r Bamoral Skirts,	Wall Paper,
&c. &c.,	&c.

Now is the Time to Buy.

LEAVENWORTH, July 16th, 1864. jy16-30t

Balloon Ascension!

POSTPONED TILL

Monday, August 22d,

AT

2 O'CLOCK, P. M.

aug16d2t

ST. BENEDICT'S COLLEGE,

ATCHISON, KANSAS.

THE object of this Institution is to impart to young men a thorough education, which will make them capable of filling any situation in life. The Collegiate Department comprises two distinct courses of study—the Classical and the Commercial.

No student will be received for a shorter space than a session, and no deduction will be made for absence, unless occasioned by protracted sickness.

Payments must be made semi-annually in advance.

Boarders are permitted to go into the city once, and only once a month, on the first Saturday of each month.

The Academic year consists of two sessions, the first beginning on the first Monday of September, and ending on the 1st of February; the second beginning with the 1st of February and ending with the 1st of July.

TERMS:

Entrance Fee	$ 5.00
Board and Tuition for one Session	75.00
Washing and Bedding	10.00
Music Lessons and use of Instrument	25.00

Doctor's Fees and Medicines form extra charges.

All communications should be addressed to

aug11d3w REV. AUGUSTINE WIRTH,
O. S. B., President.

BAIN CITY.

Four Hundred Acres

OF THE

Munsee Lands

COMMENCING at the Missouri river and running west 1½ miles on the southern boundary of Leavenworth city, to Messrs. Tanner & Lecompt's farm, thence south half a mile, which includes a

Great Variety of

SCENERY AND SURFACE.

Splendid sites for fine Residences, Gardens, Graperies, &c. "Sugar Loaf" is on the south of these lands. From many points a view of the city, Fort, river and adjoining beautiful country is obtained.

Railroads, Depots, Shops, &c., are adjoing, and State buildings below. The tendency of the city is, and in future will be, to the south. Far-seeing and liberal gentlemen will secure these desirable five-acre lots.

There are 160 acres now laid off with two such lots on a block, and each block

Surrounded with a Street.

No part of the whole city is so liberally and regularly supplied with streets.

Gentlemen residing here will be exempt from tax, and still be one half mile nearer the foot of Dealaware street than the western boundary of Leavenworth.

To persons wishing to improve, these lots are now offered at low prices, and on liberal terms.

Apply to Mr. J. Hall, No. 8 Delaware street, or to real Estate Agents generally.

je28dtf J. W. BAIN.

COUGH NO MORE.

TRY

Strickland's

Mellifluous

COUGH BALSAM.

DR. STRICKLAND'S

Mellifluous Cough Balsam.

CURES COUGHS, COLDS, SORE THROAT, Asthma, and Consumption. It is only necessary for any one troubled with these complaints to try one bottle of

Strickland's Mellifluous Cough Balsam

to convince them that it is the best preparation ever used. It not only cures the above affections of the Throat and Lungs, but it cures Night Sweats and Spitting of Blood, and is an excellent gargle for any kind of Sore Throat. It is pleasant to take, and a safe medicine for infants. Price 50 cents per bottle. Fo sale by Druggists generally.

General Depot, 6 East Fourth street, Cincinnati, Ohio.

For sale by EDDY & ARNOLD, and Dr. G. C. PARK, Leavenworth, Kansas. july3d&wly-is

200 TEAMS WANTED!

TO haul hay to Fort Leavenworth. Highest prices will be paid. Apply to William Tholen, at THE CONSERVATIVE Office, or the undersigned at Brown's Livery Stable. HENRY STILL.

50 Mowing Machines Wanted!

TO cut hay upon the Delaware Reservation. Apply as above to Still or Tholen.

WE will pay full market price for good Hay, delivered at the Fort, and contract with parties for the delivery in lots of not less than ten tons.

H. STILL,
july6d&wtf W. THOLEN.

DR. WRIGHT'S

Rejuvenating Elixir!

Or, ESSENCE OF LIFE.

Prepared from Pure Vegetable Extracts, containing nothing injurious to the most delicate.

"As the Phoenix rises from the ashes of its fire, animated with new life"—so does this Elixir rejuvenate the system and overcome disease.

The Rejuvenating Elixir is the result of modern discoveries in the vegetable kingdom; being an entirely new and abstract method of cure, irrespective of all the old and worn out systems.

This medicine has been tested by the most eminent medical men of the day, and by them pronounced to be one of the greatest medical discoveries of the age.

One bottle will cure general Debility.

A few doses cures Hysterics in females.

One bottle cures Palpitation of the Heart.

From one to three bottles restores the manliness and full vigor of youth.

A few doses restores the appetite.

Three bottles cure the worst case of Impotency.

A few doses cures the low spirited.

One bottle restores mental power.

A few doses bring the rose to the cheek.

This medicine restores to manly vigor and robust health the poor debilitated, worn-down and despairing.

The listless, enervated youth, the over-tasked man of business, the victim of nervous depression, the individual suffering from general debility, will all find immediate and permanent relief by the use of this Elixir or Essence of Life.

Price $2 per bottle or three bottles for $5, and forwarded by Express, on receipt of money, to any address.

All such orders must be sent to C. A. COOK, Chicago, General Agent for the West. P. O. Box 6524.

Sold in Chicago, by FULLER, FINCH & FULLER, Wholesale Druggists, and by all Druggists everywhere.

C. A. COOK, CHICAGO, General Agent for the States of Illinois Iowa, Wisconsin, Michigan and Indiana.

DR. W. R. MERWIN & CO.,
SOLE PROPRIETORS,
No. 59 Liberty street, New York.

CHEROKEE PILLS!

SUGAR COATED.

Female Regulator.

Health Preserver.

CERTAIN AND SAFE.

For the Removal of Obstructions, and the Insurance of Regularity in the Recurrence of the Monthly Periods.

They cure or obviate those numerous diseases that spring from irregularity, by removing the irregularity itself.

They cure Suppressed, Excessive and Painful Menstruation.

They cure Green Sickness (Chlorosis).

They cure Nervous and Spinal Affections, pains in the back, and lower parts of the body, Heaviness, Fatigue on slight exertion, Palpitation of the Heart, Lowness of Spirits, Hysteria, Sick Headache, Giddiness, etc., etc. In a word, by removing the Irregularity, they remove the cause, and with it ALL the effects that spring from it.

Composed of simple vegetable extracts, they contain nothing deleterious to any constitution, however delicate, their function being to substitute strength for weakness, which, when properly used they never fail to do.

They may be safely used at any age, and at any period, EXCEPT DURING THE FIRST THREE MONTHS, during which the unfailing nature of their action would infallibly PREVENT pregnancy.

All letters seeking information or advice will be promptly, freely and discreetly answered.

Full directions accompany each box.

Price $1 per box, or six boxes for $5.

Sent by mail, free of postage, on receipt of price.

All such orders must be sent to C. A. COOK, Chicago, our General Agent for the West. P.O. Box 6524.

Sold in Chicago, by FULLER, FINCH & FULLER, Wholesale Druggists, and by all Druggists everywhere.

C. A. COOK,

CHICAGO,

General Agent for the States of Illinois, Iowa, Wisconsin, Michigan and Indiana.

DR. W. R. MERWIN & CO.,
SOLE PROPRIETORS,
No. 59 Liberty st., New York.

JOB PRINTING neatly and cheaply done at THE CONSERVATIVE OFFICE.

THE CONSERVATIVE JOB OFFICE IS THE most complete in Kansas.

The Palmetto Herald.

BY S. W. MASON AND CO.

PORT ROYAL, THURSDAY, AUGUST 18, 1864.

FROM MORRIS ISLAND.

Destruction of a Blockade-Runner.

The Firing on Fort Sumter,

From Gen. Schimmelfinnig's command we have the news of the sinking of another blockade-runner.

On the morning of the 9th a large propeller was discovered aground not far from the pier on Sullivan's Island, near Fort Moultrie. It seemed that she had run in during the night, through this channel, and had got aground at this point, where it is very narrow.

She was lying with her stern towards the beach, and the rebels were very busy carrying her cargo ashore.

Several vessels of the fleet opened on her, but their distance was so great they did not succeed in hitting her. The batteries on Morris Island, as soon as she was perceived, began to fire on her, and with excellent effect. One shot went through her smoke-stack, another struck her in the bow, and injured her so she began to sink, and a third exploded her boiler. She was made a complete wreck of, so that nothing further was saved from her except some floating goods, which were gathered from the shore at considerable risk. It is possible that the steamer was running out instead of in, and that she had been turned about by the tide, after grounding.

The steamer was clipper-shaped, and evidently a valuable one to the blockade-runners. It is judged also that her cargo was important, and that a very large venture resulted most unprofitably to some one, just as a success was nearly achieved.

Since writing the above we have received a Charleston Courier of the 10th, which gives the following account of the sinking of the steamer:

The steamer Prince Albert, Captain Coombs, which left Nassau last Wednesday, 3d inst., in attempting to run into this port Monday night, ran against the wreck of the steamer Minko, and grounded fast nearly opposite Fort Moultrie, Sullivan's Island. Finding it impossible to get her off the officers and crew removed their baggage and a part of the cargo in small boats to Sullivan's Island. About daylight the Yankee batteries opened heavily upon the Prince Albert, completely riddling her with shot and shell, and several times setting the vessel on fire, rapidly reducing her to a total wreck. Only a small portion of the cargo, which consisted chiefly of medicines and other light articles, was saved.

The Prince Albert belonged to the Richmond Importing and Exporting Company, and had made one successful trip to this port from Nassau, and another outward. This was her second trip to this port.—*Charleston Courier, Aug. 10.*

The firing on Fort Sumter is kept up slowly but with much accuracy. A deserter recently arrived informs us that Gen. Foster's knowledge of the fort, acquired while stationed there, is resulting in great damage to the work, from the selection of the weakest points as the objects of our careful fire. The casemates are already becoming unsafe, and the rebels apprehend serious damage from the constant weakening of important parts of the structure which they cannot readly repair.

In addition to our batteries at the northern extremity of Morris Island, two more are being built, in which six 11 inch and 9-inch guns furnished by Admiral Dahlgren are to be mounted. They will be manned from the navy, and will make quite an important addition to our offensive strength.

The rebels admit that our prisoners are confined in open lots and poorly fed and clothed, but declare this treatment the best they can give, and say the rations to prisoners are the same that our troops have.

A Court of Inquiry is investigating the circumstances of the failure to capture Fort Johnson during the recent expedition, when that project was so nearly accomplished.

600 MORE UNION PRISONERS UNDER FIRE IN CHARLESTON.

GEN. FOSTER TO RETALIATE.

When Gen. Foster brought Gen. Jones to terms in regard to the fifty Union Generals and officers placed under fire in Charleston and effected their exchange, it was supposed that all troubleon that point would cease. But it seems that what the rebels could not acomplish by a *coup de main* they are stiving to effect by a *coup d'etat*. At thetime of and soon after the exchange welearned by returned prisoners, deserters and refugees that six hundred Union prisoners were in Charleston, exposed to our fire. A communication to the rebel authorities on the subject, resulted in a disavowal of the object attributed in such a disposition of the prisoners, and a declaration that they were merely held therein *transitu*.

The reports that they were still confined continuing, Gen. Foster wrote to Gen. Jones a letter in which he deprecated his conduct, and threatened immediate retaliation.

So it is probable that within a short time we shall have six hundred rebel prisoners here, to be placed under fire in the most exposed portions of Morris Island. The residences erected there being insufficient for the accommodation of so large a number, they will be placed in tents, in a large lot, surrounded by a high fence, well-guarded.

It is doubtful if Gen. Jones has an opportunity to obtain these prisoners until a baptism of fire has been administered, and they are allowed a taste, at least, of the hardships which our prisoners in rebel hands are forced to undergo.

FLAG OF TRUCE.

Supplementary Exchange of Prisoners.

COL. HOYT, SURGEON ROBINSON AND OTHERS RELEASED.

On Tuesday last Major Anderson had charge of a flag-of-truce party which met a rebel one, under command of Major Lay, at Port Royal Ferry. The principal object of the interview was the reception of the balance of prisoners due us under the terms of the recent exchange of generals and field officers off Charleston.

The meeting resulted in the delivery over into our hands of Col. H. M. Hoyt, of the 52d Pennsylvania, Surgeon Robinson, of the 104th Pennsylvania, Assistant Surgeon Terrell, of the 12th Conn., Capt. Robbins, of a Kentucky regiment, Lieut. P. O. Rogers, of the 39th Illinois, and eight enlisted men.

The Surgeons were simply released as non-combatants. without exchange, Gen. Jones having concluded to consent to such an arrangement, which he at first disapproved.

Col. Hoyt gives us some additional information in regard to his capture at Fort Johnson on the 3d of July, which is of great interest,

The attacking party had intended to reach the landing place before daylight, but were detained at a bar for an hour. They then proceeded directly up towards a point, about 400 yards from Battery Simpkins. For some distance they had to pass through a narrow channel in single file, but met with no difficulty. Col. Hoyt, with less than one hundred men, promptly landed, and the rebels fled without a show of resistance. Battery Simpkins was occupied, and while proceeding towards Fort Johnson, another battery was stumbled upon, from which the enemy fled, and which was occupied by about twenty-five of Col. Hoyt's force. He then kept on with his column, but on the way encountered two obstacles in the way of marshes, one of which was waded and the other avoided by a detour.

About four hundred yards distant the fort opened with artillery and musketry, doing them but little damage however.

On arriving at Fort Johnson, no resistance was encountered, excepting a scattering musketry fire, but the garrison was found to consist of about two hundred, and Col. Hoyt's little party was too weak to cope with them. So they retired from the work, and being joined by about sixty more who had come up, made an attack at another point.

But it was finally ascertained that the balance of the force so confidently relied on, had not landed at all, and by this time the rebels had been reinforced to four hundred strong. So Col. Hoyt was reluctantly compelled to give the order of surrender, to save the slaughter of his men, all chance of holding the Fort being lost by the failure of the rest of the force to come up.

A rebel force then went down to take the force left in Battery Simpkins, and who were included in the surrender. The occupation of the work was entirely bloodless, but the rebels claimed it as a recapture, and a glorious victory.

The prisoners were taken to Charleston immediately, and as they marched through the streets were treated with perfect civility, They found a stronger Union sentiment prevailing there than they anticipated.

Col. Hoyt has since been a portion of the time at Macon.

Lt. Col. Conyngham is now at Charleston, and will probably soon be exchanged.

The casualties in the 52d in the attack on Fort Johnson numbered only 21.

LATE REBEL PAPERS.

DATES TO AUG. 15th.

LATER NEWS FROM MOBILE.

The Rebel Papers Talking Peace.

By flag of truce, on Tuesday, General Foster received files of rebel papers to Aug. 15, from which we are permitted to make extracts.

Nearly all the papers are discussing the subject of peace, and it is evident that Grant's starving process, Sherman's pressure in Georgia, Farragut's victory at Mobile, and Federal successes everywhere, are gradually bringing them to terms.

The following are extracted from the latest papers:

As a retaliatory measure, for the confinement of Yankee officers in Charleston, Gen. Foster, commanding the enemy's forces, had huts constructed on Morris Island and Cummings' Point, where he intended to imprison our officers, thus subjecting them to the fire of all our batteries. Gen. Sam Jones promptly notified him that in case he put his barbarous threat into execution, every one of the Federal officers then in Charleston would be transferred to Sumter and there exposed on the ramparts to the fire of Gregg and Wagner, and the other works on Morris Island. This had the desired effect. Gen. Foster, unwilling to assume the responsibility, under the circumstances, referred the matter to the Washington authorities, who instructed him to endeavor an exchange. A correspondence ensued between Gens. Foster and Jones, the result of which was that our officers confined in the transports at Hilton Head were brought to Morris Island and exchanged for the Yankee officers in Charleston. Gen. Jones having proven himself such an excellent officer of exchange, we understand that the Government has sent to Charleston five or six hundred Federal officers to be exchanged for the same number of Confederates.—*Richmond Paper.*

Col. Anderson, the officer who figures so infamously in the surrender of Fort Gaines, is said to be a native of South Carolina. He entered West Point from Texas, but remained only two years, and, of course, did not graduate. He was appointed Second Lieutenant in the old army in 1856, and being stationed in the South, joined the Confederate army at the commencement of the war.—*Charleston Mercury, Aug. 15.*

Atlanta, August 13.—The enemy yesterday evening, advanced his right about one mile, at the same time extending his left a short distance, but hurridly withdrew both this morning, from a cause unknown, to the original position. Their line officers attempted frequently, at different points along the line, to communicate with ours; in several instances they proposed a cessation of picket firing, which was not entertained, in consequence of not coming through the proper channel. No shells thrown at the city during last night or today, with the exception of slight artillery firing.

Brigadier General John C. Brown, of Tennessee, has been promoted temporarily to the rank of Major General. Lieutenant Colonel James Kennard, C. S. A., has been assigned as Chief of Ordnance of the Army of Tennessee.—*Charleston Mercury, Aug. 15.*

Mobile, August 9, 1864.—Hon. S. R. Mallory, Secretary of the Navy: The enemy steamed in through main entrance with four monitors and about sixteen heavy vessels-of-war. The Tecumseh, Commander T. A. M. Craven, was sunk with nearly all her crew. and also another gunboat—the Philippi, which I subsequently learned. The Richmond, Hartford and Brooklyn, in line of battle, followed by the remainder of the fleet, pushed by Fort Morgan under full headway, where they were encountered by the Tennessee, Morgan, Gaines and Selma.

The Tennessee and the other vessels steamed in close range of the advancing force, and poured a heavy fire into the leading ships. After a desperate engagement between the fleet the Gaines retired to Fort Morgan in a sinking condition; the Selma, cut off, surrendered, and the Morgan escaped to Fort Morgan. The Tennessee, so far uninjured, steamed towards the whole fleet, and after an obstinate fight, surrendered—her rudder disabled, her smoke-stack carried away, and, as we suppose, her crew in an exhausted and smothering condition. On the Tennessee, Admiral Buchanan severely wounded by a splinter in leg, two killed and several wounded. On the Gaines, two killed and two wounded. On the Morgan, one wounded. On the Selma, eight killed, including her executive officer, Lieut. J. H. Comstock, and seven wounded. The enemy suffered severely, and he requested permission to bury his dead. Respectfully, G. W. Harrison, Confederate States Navy."—*Charleston Mercury, Aug. 15.*

Whilst we deprecate discussions of terms of peace by our Press, and all serious overtures from Government at this present juncture of of affairs, we do not mean to say that diplomacy should be wholly set aside in bringing hostilities to a close, or that any overture coming from the enemy with apparent sincerity, should not be met with a corresponding sentiment of accommodation on our part. The Richmond Sentinel, which is supposed to reflect, at least in some degree, the sentiments and policy of the Administration, has recently given publication to several articles of this character, called forth by certain unusually liberal remarks in the Washington Chronicle. The Sentinel makes no direct proposition regardterms of peace that can be construed as binding either on itself or the government, but simply throws out certain hypotheses as subjects for consideration on the part of both belligerents. The articles were wholly diplomatic, and originated, as any well-balanced mind would see at a glance, in the very best and most patriotic motives. It is believed by many wise men that the war once stopped and negotiations for peace begun, the former can never be revived, even though the terms of settlement demanded by the South may not be wholly acceptable to the present Government at Washington—that the people will compel it to do what is right, or take the matter into their own hands. It is for this reason, possibly, that the Sentinel, and we may add some of our most far-seeing statesmen, are willing to set forth propositions as matters for negotiation, when they would be among the last to make a concession that is dishonorable or injurious to their country.—*Savannah Republican, Aug. 14th.*

Hasty Censure.—We cordially unite with our contemporary of the Columbus Enquirer in condemning the hasty judgment of "treason and cowardice" that has been entered up so generally by the press and telegraph against Col. Anderson, for the surrender of Fort Gaines. The case has a bad aspect with our limited view of the reasons that led to it, but it is evident that the public knows too little of the circumstances of the capitulation, to enable it to form a just opinion of its real character. Col. Anderson and his men are in the hands of the enemy, and cannot be heard; and so long as their lips shall be closed in their own defence, we protest against all attempts to blacken their character as men, and sully their fame as soldiers. An Alabama commander of Alabama troops is not the man to disgrace his name and state in a struggle for liberty. It is not in the blood, and we believe that a satisfactory explanation will yet be made of the extraordinary and lamentable occurrence. Let us hear before we strike.—*Savannah Republican, Aug. 14th.*

Gen. Jones having made so excellent a commissioner of exchange, our Government has sent six hundred Yankee officers to Charleston to be exchanged on the same terms, and under a cartel that is somewhat unusual. Our Commissioner of Exchange in Richmond will have to look to his laurels, or Gen. Jones will eclipse all his achievements in the exchange business.—*Richmond Sentinel.*

Mobile.—Charleston has been assailed from the beginning of the war by the most powerful armament that the enemy could bring against it. She has been bombarded nearly four hundred days, and is now as safe as when the enemy first began the siege. In fact no city has yet been taken by the enemy after time and preparation for its defence, with the exception of Vicksburg, which was not taken by force, but starved into subjection. And why should Mobile fall, after over three years preparation for its defence. Fort Morgan, one of its strongholds, is the most formidable work of the kind, next to Fortress Monroe, on the American continent, besides her other defences are strong and tenable. We can't believe the Yankee flag will ever float over the city of Mobile.—*Savannah Republican, Aug. 14th.*

Maj. Gen. Gillmore, late commander of the 10th Army Corps, U. S. Army, was thrown from his horse, while charging a detachment of Gen. Early's command near Washington, and fractured his ankle. Pity it wasn't his neck.—*Savannah Republican.*

NAVAL MATTERS.

We have a few naval items in addition to the account of the brilliant exploit in Doboy Sound, given elsewhere. Admiral Dahlgren has recently been on a tour of inspection to the southward. He is now in this harbor, with the flag-ship Philadelphia.

The Admiral has recently published a touching letter, vindicating the character of his son, the gallant Col. Ulric Dahlgren, from the aspersions of his brutal rebel murderers, and proving the document alleged to have been found on his person, and put forth as a justification for his murder and the mutilation of his body, to have been a forgery.

Lieut. Commander L. S. Phythian, commanding the Commodore McDonough, has been ordered North on court martial duty.

Lieut. Commander J. C. Chaplin, commanding the Dai Ching, has been ordered temporarily to the command of McDonough.

Acting Master A. S. Gardner, has been detached from the barque Ironsides, and ordered to the steamer Patapsco as harbor master.

Act. Asst. Paymaster A. McVey, has been detached from the New Hampshire and ordered to the John Adams.

Act. Ensign A. Hartshorn of the New Hampshire, has been ordered on special duty.

Act. Ensign T. E. Chapin has been promoted to Act. Master, and granted a leave of absence for thirty days.

Acting Master's Mate Chas. H. Hanson has been promoted to Act. Ensign.

The following are recenent announcements in the official gazette:

Ordered—Lieut.-Commander Jas. Stillwell, to command the Ottawa.

Detached—Lieut.-Commander S. Livingston Breese, from the command of the Ottawa, and ordered North.

Second Asst. Engineer Jas. J. Noble, and Third Asst. Engineer Henry C. Beck-

ARRIVAL OF THE ARAGO.

New York Dates to Aug. 11th.

GREAT SUCCESSES BY FARRAGUT AT MOBILE.

Important from other Points.

By the arrival of the Arago on Monday morning, we received full files of New York papers, for which we are indebted to Purser Fred. W. Ely. The following extracts embrace the most important news;

War Department, Washington, Aug. 7, 1864. To Major-General Dix, New York—Major-General Sheridan has been assigned temporarily to the command of the forces in the Middle Military Division, consisting of the Department of Washington, the Middle Department and the Department of the Susquehanna and Southwest Virginia. He transmits the following intelligence:

Headquarters, Middle Military Department, Harper's Ferry, Va., Aug. 8—4:40 P. M. Major-General Halleck, Chief of Staff—Brigadier-General Kelley reports that a scout has just arrived at New Creek, and reports that General Averill overtook the enemy near Moorefield yesterday and attacked him, capturing all of his artillery and five hundred prisoners. Nothing official has been received from General Averill, however.
P. H. Sheridan,
Major-General Commanding.
E. M. Stanton, Sec'y of War.

War Department, Washington, Aug. 8—9 P. M. To Major-General Dix, New York—The following announcement of the successful operations against Mobile appears in the Richmond Sentinel of this date, and is transmitted by Major-General Butler to the President:

From Headquarters of Gen. Butler, Aug. 8—3 P. M. To His Excellency A. Lincoln, President—The following is the official report taken from the Richmond Sentinel of August 8th.
B. F. Butler, Major-General.

"Mobile, Aug. 5, 1864. Hon. J. A. Seddon, Secretary of War—Seventeen of the enemy's vessels (fourteen ships and three iron-clads) passed Fort Morgan this morning. The Tecumseh, a monitor, was sunk by Fort Morgan this morning. The Tennessee surrendered, after a desperate engagement with the enemy's fleet. Admiral Buchanan lost a leg and is a prisoner. The Selma was captured. The Gaines was beached near the hospital. The Morgan is safe, and will try to run up to night. The enemy's fleet has approached the city. A monitor has been engaging Fort Powell all day.
D. H. Maury, Major-General."
E. M. Stanton, Sec'y of War.

Washington. Aug. 8, 1864.—Richmond papers of Saturday last announce that our forces have taken possession of Dauphin Island, on the south side of the harbor of Mobile and in the rear of Fort Gaines.

Washington, Aug. 8, 1864.—The Navy Department yesterday engaged a fast steamer at New York, which is to be immediately loaded with ice and fresh provisions and despatched to the fleet off Mobile.

War Department, Aug. 10—10:30 P. M. To Major-Gen. Dix, New York: The following report of the success of our operations at Mobile, extracted from the Richmond Enquirer of this morning. has just been received by this Department from Major-General Butler:

"Mobile, Aug. 8, 1864.—Friday night Lieutenant Colonel Williams, commanding Fort Powell, evacuated and blew up the fort. Yesterday and to-day the enemy are shelling Fort Gaines. The people of Mobile are all ready for the fray. Great confidence prevails. The people are satisfied with the conduct of Lieuts. Buchanan, Maury and Burnet, of the navy."

SECOND DESPATCH.

"Mobile, August 8, 1864.—It is painfully humiliating to announce the shameful surrender of Fort Gaines at half-past nine o'clock this morning, by Col. Chas. Anderson, of the Twenty-first Alabama. This powerful work was provisioned for six months, and had a garrison of six hundred men. He communicated with the enemy's fleet by flag of truce, with the sanction of Gen. Page. Gen. Page inquired by signal what his purpose was, but received no answer. His attention was attracted by signal guns. Page repeatedly telegraphed, 'Hold on to your fort.' The same night he visited Fort Gaines, and found Anderson on board the Yankee fleet arranging the terms of capitulation. He left peremptory orders for Anderson, on his return, not to surrender the fort, and relieved him of his command. Fort Morgan signalled this morning; but no answer was received except the hoisting of the Yankee flag over the ramparts of Fort Gaines. Anderson's conduct is officially pronounced inexplicable and shameful."

Despatches just received from General Sheridan report his forces moving against the enemy up the Shenandoah. At four P. M they were skirmishing about ten miles from Winchester.

This morning Gen. Grant reported the explosion of an ordnance boat yesterday, loaded with ammunition, at City Point wharf. No details have been received. Col. Babcock, of Gen. Grant's staff, was slightly wounded.

No operations before Atlanta of consequence are reported to-day. Portions of Stoneman's command are continuing to arrive, and the total loss will not exceed one thousand.
Edwin M. Stanton, Sec. of War.

Washington, August 10, 1864.—The Navy Department to-night received a despatch containing the following from the Richmond Examiner of the 9th: "A despatch from Mobile, dated August 7—two days later than our previous advices—states that the situation had not materially altered since the enemy's victory over our iron-clads on last Friday. The Navy Department received a telegram yesterday morning announcing that the Morgan, the only gunboat of our fleet which was not either sunk, beached or captured, had succeeded in getting over the bar and reaching Mobile."

The U. S. Transport Arago, Henry S. Gadsden, commanding, left New York at 1 P. M. Thursday, August 11, and arrived at Hilton at 6 A. M. Monday, Aug. 15. The following were passengers by the Arago: Lieut.-Col. Bennett, Major W. W. Hart, Captain Hambrick, Lieut. Hardenburgh, Asst. Surg. H. R. Silliman, Rev. D. O. Jones, Captain Campbell, J. Goodbye, J. Arnold, J. H. Hewston, J. T. Gleason, G. S. Batchieldor, J. W. Hamcox, J. R. Martin, J. T. Steele, F. Nichols, Philip L. Mars, Jas. Gardner, — Kendall, P. Haas, L. Haas, H. Haars, G. T. Davis, H. Friend, J. T. Long, D. Post. A. H. Barber, C. F. Williams, W. A. Alden, T. N. Williams, J. Wilson, L. D. Cunningham, Capt. J. H. King. T. D. Curry, John K. Stimson, and 59 others in the steerage.

FORT PULASKI METEOROLOGICAL OBSERVATIONS.

Resume of meteorological observations made at the Post Hospital daily at s. r., 2. p. m. and 7 p. m. during the month of July, 1864:

Temperature.—Maximum, 93°; minimum, 68°; maximum daily mean, 85°; minimum daily mean, 71°; monthly mean, 81°; two warmest days, 7th and 21st; temperature of both being the same; coldest day, 24th.

Prevailing Winds.—First ten days, S. W.; second ten days, E.; last eleven days, E.

Rain—On the 4th, 15-100 in.; 9th, 1 16-100 in.; 10th, 22-100 in.; 13th, 78-100 in.; 14th, 15-100 in.; 16th, 46-100 in; 18th, 2-100 in.; 20th, 1-100 in.; 22d 2-100 in.; 24th, 22-100 in.; 28th, 18-100 in.; 30th, 3 55-100 in.; whole amount, 7 31-100 inches.

[Official.]

COMMERCIAL INTERCOURSE WITH AND IN STATES DECLARED IN INSURRECTION.

Treasury Department,
Fourth Special Agency,
Beaufort, S. C., August 1, 1864.

The attention of traders in this Department is respectfully called to the following letter in relation to the purchase and transportation of merchandise, and all existing rules and regulations not in accordance herewith are hereby suspended:

"Treasury Department, July 16, 1864.

"Sir: By the recent act of Congress the purchase of products in States declared in insurrection is altogether prohibited, and the transportation of goods, wares and merchandise into such States is greatly restricted, and confined to the necessary supplies of loyal citizens within the lines of actual occupation by the military forces of the United States,

"To meet the provisions of this act, regulations are now being prepared, and, until they are completed and put into effect and you are notified thereof from this Department, you will grant no more authorities for the purchase or transportation of products in or from those States, nor to transport to or sell within such States any goods, wares or merchandise whatever, either under existing trade regulations or otherwise.

"No boat or other vehicle of transportation will be cleared by you, or permitted to go to an insurrectionary State with any goods, wares, or merchandise on board, except such as belong to the United States, or are being transported under contract of sale to them, and except sutlers' supplies, the shipment of which you will carefully restrict to the provisions of the present rules and regulations in regard thereto.

"Respectfully,
"(Signed) GEO. HARRINGTON,
"Acting Sect'y of the Treasury.

"To John H. Pilsbury, Esq., Asst. Spl. Agt., Beaufort, S. C."

The method of obtaining necessary supplies for loyal citizens will be immediately announced, and all applications must be made at the office of the Treasury Agency, Beaufort, South Carolina.
JOHN H. PILSBURY,
Assistant Special Agent.

[Official.]

Headquarters, Dept. of the South.
Hilton Head, S. C., Aug. 10, 1864.

General Orders, No. 116.

I. THE MAJOR-GENERAL COMMANDING the Department has learned that leaves of absence and furloughs, granted from these Headquarters, have been in many instances interpreted as allowing the time stated therein to be counted from the arrival of the officer or soldier at New York until his departure therefrom. This interpretation seems to be based upon the idea, that because General Order No. 276, from Adjutant General's Office, series of 1863, places all officers and soldiers upon duty while on Government transports, therefore the time spent by them in going to and returning from the North, on such transports, is not to be charged against their leaves and furloughs. The duty imposed by such General Order does not relieve them from the operation of their leaves, but is to be regarded as a partial equivalent for the transportation furnished by the Government.

To avoid further misconception, it is ordered that the time granted in all leaves of absence and furloughs shall begin when the officer or soldier leaves the Department, and that all officers and soldiers absent on leave shall be required to be *within the Department* at the expiration of the time specified in their leaves or furloughs.

II, Capt. Jesse Merrill, U. S. Signal Corps, is announced as Chief Signal Officer of the Department, and will be obeyed and respected accordingly.

By Com'd of Major-Gen. J. G. FOSTER,
W. L. M. Burger,
Asst. Adjutant General.

Official:
Thomas J. Robinson,
1st Lieut. 21st U. S. C. T.,
Act. Asst. Adjt. General.

[Official.]

Headquarters, Dep't of the South,
Hilton Head, S. C., Aug. 15, 1864.

General Orders, No. 118.

A NATIONAL SALUTE OF THIRTY-FIVE guns, will be fired from Fort Welles, at 12 o'clock, M., this day, in honer of the late glorious achievement of Admiral Farragut and his gallant Fleet, at Mobile.

Although the details of this brilliant victory have not been received, enough is known to make sure that the Union Fleet successfully passed the Forts, at the entrance of Mobile Bay; that it engaged, captured, sunk, or destroyed, a large number of the enemy's fleet,—the remainder taking refuge in flight; that it forced the evacuation and blowing up, after a furious bombardment, of Fort Powell; and that, finally, it forced Fort Gaines, after a terrific bombardment of two days, to surrender, with its garrison, stores, and guns; thus opening the whole bay for reinforcements to our gallant Fleet.

The surrender of Fort Morgan, and the capture of Mobile itself, must soon follow such heroic efforts.

By Command of Major-Gen. J. G. FOSTER,
W. L. M. Burger.
Asst. Adjt. Gen'l.

Official:
Thomas J. Robinson,
1st Lieut. 21st U. S. C. T.,
Act. Asst. Adjt. General.

[Official.]

Headquarters. Dep't of the South,
Hilton Head, S. C., Aug. 13, 1864.

General Orders, No. 117.

I. PROCEEDINGS OF A GENERAL COURT Martial which convened at Jacksonville, Fla., pursuant to Special Orders No. 131, dated Headquarters, District of Florida, Department of the South, Jacksonville, Fla., June 22, 1864, and of which Lieut.-Col. Ulysses Doubleday, 3d U. S. C. T., is president, was arraigned and tried:

Capt. Wm. Harrison. 107th Ohio Vols.

Charge 1st—"Neglect of Duty."

Specification 1st—"In this; that Captain Wm. Harrison, 107th Regiment Ohio Vols., being in command of the Provost Guard, did neglect to take the proper precaution to secure John Aleck Williams, private 35th U. S. C. T., who was condemned to suffer death; although he, the said Capt. William Harrison, had been repeatedly cautioned and warned of the more than ordinary necessity for watchfulness and care in respect of said prisoner, and that in consequence of such neglect on the part of said Captain William Harrison, said prisoner did escape."

All this at Jacksonville, Fla., on or about the 24th day of June, 1864.

Specification 2d—"In this; that Capt. William Harrison, 107th Regt. Ohio Vols., being in command of the Provost Guard, did cause certain private soldiers to be arrested and confined in the Guard House, without removing from them their side-arms."

All this at Jacksonville, Fla., on or about the 24th day of June, 1864.

Charge II.—"Conduct prejudicial to good order and military discipline."

Specification—"In this; that Captain William Harrison, 107th Regt. Ohio Vols., being in command of the Provost Guard. when the Sergeant of the Guard did arrest and bring to the Guard House, a commissioned officer, to wit, Lieut. Charles L. Rundell, 3d U. S. C. T., in uniform, and charged with no offence, did justify the said arrest."

All this at Jacksonville, Fla., on or about the 24th day of June, 1864.

Charge III.—"Breaking his arrest."

Specification—"In this: that Captain William Harrison, 107th Regt. Ohio Vols., having been placed in arrest by order of the Commanding General, did leave his quarters and the limits of his camp, and proceed to various houses and places within the city of Jacksonville, without proper authority."

All this at Jacksonville, Fla., on or about the 28th day of June, 1864.

To which Charges and Specifications the accused, Captain William Harrison, 107th Ohio Vols., pleaded as follows:

Charge I.
To the 1st Specification, "Not Guilty.
To the 2d Specification, "Not Guilty."
To the Charge, "Not Guilty."
Charge II.
To the Specification, "Not Guilty."
To the Charge, "Not Guilty."
Charge III.
To the Specification, "Not Guilty."
To the Charge, "Not Guilty."

And the Court, after maturely considering the testimony adduced, is of opinion that the accused, Captain William Harrison, 107th Ohio Vols. is of

Charge I.
Of the 1st Specification, "Guilty."
Of the 2d Specification, "Guilty."
Of the Charge, "Guilty"
Charge II.
Of the Specification, "Guilty."
Of the Charge, "Guilty."
Charge III.
Of the Specification, "Guilty," but attach no criminality thereto.
Of the Charge, "Not Guilty."

And do therefore sentence him, Capt. William Harrison, 107th Ohio Vols., "To be suspended from rank and pay for one year."

II. The proceedings, findings, and sentence in the case of Captain William Harrison, 107th Regt. Ohio Vols., having been approved by the officer ordering the Court, and submitted to the Major-General Commanding, they are hereby approved and confirmed, excepting the findings on the second charge and specification thereof, which are disapproved, as being unsupported by the evidence.

Captain William Harrison, 107th Regt. Ohio Vols., is accordingly suspended from his rank and pay for one year from this date.

III. The action of Brig.-Gen. R. Saxton, Commanding U. S. Forces, Port Royal Island, S. C., in the case of Private Billy Eddy, Co. D, 1st Regt. S. C. Vols., (now the 33d U. S. C. T.,) as published in General Orders No. 71, from Headquarters U. S. Forces, Port Royal Island, dated Beaufort, S. C., December 20th. 1863, is approved. But in consideration of the long confinement of Private Eddy in the Guard House, at Beaufort, S. C., the sentence in his case is hereby commuted to four months' imprisonment at Fort Clinch, Fla., where he will be sent under proper guard.

By Command of Major-Gen. J. G. FOSTER,
W. L. M. Burger,
Asst. Adjt. General.

Official:
Thomas J. Robinson,
1st Lieut. 21st U. S. C. T.,
Act. Asst. Adjt. General.

THE SIEGE OF PETERSBURG—CHARGE OF THE 2ND DIVISION, 9TH ARMY CORPS, INTO THE CRATER, JULY 30.—FROM A SKETCH BY ANDREW McCALLUM.

EXTRA.

ATLANTA, GA.

THURSDAY, SEPTEMBER 1, 1864.

THE IMMEDIATE FRONT.

THE LINES.—Important events, it [illegible] known, were occurring in the vicinity of [illegible] Macon railroad yesterday, and the most exaggerated reports thereof continued to reach the city until late at night. The true situation we have reason to believe to be, that the main body of the enemy, consisting of three of his army corps, were making an effort to reach the railroad a short distance this side of Jonesboro; and that heavy skirmishing took place between them and our forces under Gen. Hardee. Nothing like a general engagement took place up to three o'clock, P. M.; but one was anticipated without any great delay. Gen. Hardee has adequate force, who are eager for the fray, under him; and as they will understand the vital importance of their good behavior when the hour of trial does come, they will patriotically fullfil the expectations that we entertained of them.

In addition to the principal movement of the enemy, reported above, another detachment of Federals, consisting of about four thousand infantry, cavalry and artillery, moved in the direction of Rough and Ready yesterday morning. They were met by a mixed command of our troops near Mt. Gilead Church, about eight o'clock A. M., who skirmished with them, falling back slowly, until about two o'clock, when the enemy reached the road about a mile below Rough and Ready. Our force consisted only of about six hundred. Col. Lindsay, of the 16th Louisiana, was killed during the day. We lost a few killed and wounded; eight of the latter were brought to the city last night.

Our men continued to retire slowly up the railroad, the enemy cautiously advancing, and at last accounts the latter were at Rough and Ready, having torn up the track a short distance behind.

At a very early hour this morning heavy artillery firing was heard in the direction of Rough and Ready, and from what is known of the situation yesterday, the impression generally prevails that a fight is progressing.

THE CITY.—We enjoyed another quiet day yesterday, after the excitement consequent upon the movements of the night previous. Being aware of the fact that the defenses of the city are adequately manned to protect against raids, or even any force the enemy can possibly spare from his movements below, our citizens are resting easy. The feature in our situation most regretted is that we are compelled to do without news from abroad.

NO DISPATCHES.—The line through to Macon was not repaired yesterday previous to the appearance of the Yankees in the vicinity of Rough and Ready, therefore we are without dispatches from abroad.

FROM THE TRANS-MISSISSIPPI.—We had the pleasure yesterday of meeting with Governor Lubbock, of Texas, and Major Tom Ochiltree, of Gen. Dick Taylor's staff, who bring cheering news from "over the water." There are no Yankees in Texas, and West Louisiana is almost free from the vandals. A small force is stationed at Morganza and several points along the river.

Gen. Buckner has relieved Gen. Walker of the command of West Louisiana. Gen. Walker relieves Gen. Magruder of the department of Texas, who in turn relieves Gen. Price in Arkansas, and Gen. Price, with a strong force, has gone to Missouri, where he will be heard from.

The governor represents affairs generally in that department as very prosperous, and the army in splendid condition as regards equipments, morale, etc.

Governor L. has recently been appointed aid-de-camp to the President, with the rank of colonel.

NARROW ESCAPE.—The last train that left the city yesterday, narrowly escaped falling into the hands of the enemy, a short distance below Rough and Ready. It was stopped only on coming in sight of the foe on the road below, and before whom our forces were slowly falling back. The engine was nearly out of steam, and altogether out of wood, and it was at one time thought the train would have to be abandoned; but the passengers went to work and procured a supply of fuel as speedily as possible. We are assured, too, that the demolition of fence rails was greatly accelerated by the explosion of a couple of Yankee shells in the vicinity of the train, and a back out was accomplished in time to prevent capture.

☞ All the trains that left the city yesterday went through, except one, which was turned back a short distance below Rough and Ready in the afternoon.

PRISONERS.—Twenty prisoners, captured in the vicinity of East Point, were brought in yesterday.

☞ Capt. Wynne, of Gen. Morgan's staff, has been transferred to the command of Gen. Forrest, with the rank of major.

Congratulatory Order of Gen. Jackson to his Troops.

General Orders, No. —.

HEADQUARTERS JACKSON'S CAVALRY DIVISION, Atlanta, Ga., August 24th, 1864.—The brigadier-general commanding, desires to congratulate the officers and men of his command, also Gen. Reynolds and brigade, on their successful expulsion of the large and well appointed raiding party under Kilpatrick, boasting to "destroy our rear communications, and compel the army of Tennessee to retire from Atlanta," and to tender his good thanks for their energy and fighting. He takes pleasure in noticing the part performed by Gen. Ross, and his gallant Texans, in resisting with the most determined courage, the entire force of the enemy, not less than four thousand, hurled upon his brigade as a "dernier resort" to cut their way through, continuing to fire upon them till the last one had passed—inflicting heavy loss upon them and capturing one piece of artillery and four stands of colors; reflecting the highest credit upon himself and brigade. As, also, Gen. Armstrong and brigade, for very vigorous pursuit, compelling the enemy to abandon wagons, horses and ambulances.

He takes this occasion to make special mention of the daring bravery displayed by Lieut. George B. Young, of Croft's battery, who alone continued to serve his howitzer, when completely surrounded by the enemy, within a few paces of him, and refused to abandon it till ordered away by his brigade commander.

Soldiers: In meeting and repelling this, the largest raiding party ever sent to your rear, you have won the lasting gratitude of your commanders and countrymen, and have reflected fresh glory upon the proud appelation of the Confederate army.

You inflicted upon the enemy a loss of five hundred killed, wounded and prisoners, captured two pieces of artillery, four stands of colors, a number of horses, equipments and small arms, besides wagons and ambulances, with small loss to yourselves.

He returns thanks to Gen. Armstrong, Ross and Reynolds for prompt action, hearty co-operation and skillful handling of their commands.

By command of W. H. JACKSON,
Brigadier-General.

E. T. Sykes, A. A. General.

TIMELY PROVISION.—Governor Brown, on behalf of the State, has forwarded to this city one thousand bushels of meal, which is now being distributed to the necessitous of Atlanta. Rations are issued, as to soldiers, upon application being made, supported by proof of necessity. The distributing depot is at the old business rooms of Messrs. Brown, Fleming & Co., on Decatur street.

MISSISSIPPI.—We have cheering tidings of the spirit with which Mississippi is answering to the call of her patriotic governor. Her men are rushing to arms at the various rendezvous appointed for their assemblage. Numbers have already gone forward to reinforce Gen. Forrest, and several thousand cavalry and infantry are on different points of the Mobile and Ohio railroad, ready to move wherever they are needed.

MOBILE.—We learn from the Register of the 27th that the enemy continues his movements in the vicinity of Mobile. Troops were thrown from a number of transports on Mon Louis Island, the force being estimated at four thousand. They had also landed in some force at Cedar Point, on the most southerly point of the coast of the bay, and half a mile from Fort Powell. This looks like a trial of our strength on our land front. With steady men behind the intrenchments, they will find it a hard road to travel. The Register says it is certain the enemy has no force adequate to the investment of the city. They will try a sudden dash to scare us out of the city. The citizens, without the troops, can block that game; for one man inside the works is worth ten outside of them. All engineers pronounce these works the strongest in the Confederacy.

☞ Two Richmond traders, A. Osiper and Wm. J. Haywood have been examined and ordered for trial, for trading in greenbacks with Yankee deserters. One of them gave three hundred dollars for a fifty dollar greenback, and the other sold two pair of shoes for sixty dollars of the same money.

FAITHFUL NEGROES.—Some fifteen or twenty negroes, captured at Fort Gaines and brought over to Fort Morgan side of the bay have escaped and reached Mobile, Ala. As a reward for their fidelity, Gen. Maury has granted them fifteen days' furlough, which they will pass in a visit to their plantation homes in the interior.

RAILROAD ACCIDENT.—The Selma Reporter says that on the 24th inst., two messenger trains on the Alabama and Tennessee River railroad collided near Silver run, killing Mr. Jerry Covill, the engineer on one of the trains, and severely wounding three or four other persons. Both engines were completely demolished.

☞ A Cincinnati dispatch says the first train from Sherman's front to Chattanooga, after Gen. Wheeler struck the railroad, arrived on the 21st. Six heavy trains left there at once for the front, the last of which was reported to have been captured near Kingston, by a small force detached from Wheeler's command.

GEN. EARLY RETALIATING.—The brute Hunter arrested and carried off six Southern gentlemen from Hedgesville, and as soon as Gen. Early was informed of it he took six of the most prominent Union men of Hagerstown, and held them as hostages for the release of our citizens. This is the proper way to do—the lex talionis should be carried out in its strictest sense, for it is by this means only that our foe can be brought to conduct the war against us on principles of humanity and the recognized rules of civilized warfare.—Lynchburg Republican.

TELEGRAPHIC DISPATCHES.

Late from New Orleans and the Southwest—Delayed Dispatches.

EAST PASCAGOULA, August 26.—New Orleans papers to the evening of the 24th received by flag of truce.

The family of President Juarez, of Mexico, have arrived in New Orleans from Brazos Santiago.

The Interventionist forces under Gen. Douai, had occupied Saltillo, and expected soon to be at Catarina, whence, to Monterey, there will be stubborn resistance.

Accounts from Vera Cruz of the 7th state that the French and Imperialists will advance simultaneously as far as New Leon, Coahuila and Tamaulipas.

On one side they have already taken Durango, and on the other have reached Victoria.

Monterey and Matamoros will soon be attacked.

Gen. Canby has ordered the correspondents of the New York Herald and Tribune, who were permitted to accompany the troops operating in Mobile bay, to be sent beyond the limits of his command for having abused the confidence reposed in them by giving public information to the enemy, and engaging in controversy calculated to disturb the harmony of the troops.

Gen. Banks has ordered, as the banks of the State of Louisiana have so far failed to comply with the provisions of law as to justify the forfeiture of their charters, that they are required as a condition of any further transaction of banking business, to receive United States treasury notes at par in exchange for their own issues. Any institution aggrieved by the order may demand an investigation of its affairs, and show its credit superior to that of the United States.

The Era says the recent gunboat expedition to Chicot Pass, at the head of Grand Lake, La., completed its work, destroying property consisting of the saw mills and houses of Capt. Fuller, the notorious "Paul Jones of the South," who was captured when the Star of the West was destroyed, and who died a prisoner on Johnson's Island.

The reported riot in New Orleans against the draft is without foundation.

☞ The Tallahassee left Halifax on the 20th. A list of twenty-four vessels destroyed and seven bonded by her is published.

☞ The Selma Reporter learns that several individuals in that city have attempted to discount the old currency 10 per cent. in addition to the legal discount.

☞ Two hundred Yankees captured by Forrest at Memphis, passed through Selma, Ala., on the 26th en route to some Confederate prison.

☞ The Montgomery Advertiser hears that Warren Adams, the trans-Mississippi courier, was captured while attempting to cross the Mississippi river last week.

☞ The Selma Dispatch of the 27th, states that the regular trains over the Montgomery and West Point railroad would commence running through on the 30th ult.

☞ Secretary Mallory has assigned Commodore French Forrest to an important position connected with the Navy Department.

☞ Dr. Pride Jones, of Hillsboro, has received the appointment of Confederate States marshal of North Carolina, vice Wesley Jones, resigned.

ARRESTED.—Mr. John Mullaly, the editor of the Metropolitan Record, a Catholic paper published in New York, has been arrested by the Abolition authorities. The warrant sets forth that the said Mullaly, in an issue of the Metropolitan Record of the 6th of August last, caused to be printed, issued and published, an article entitled "The Coming Draft" and other articles, in which he counsels one Seymour and other persons to resist the draft ordered by the President of the United States, to take place in September next.

SERVED HIM RIGHT.—Some seven months ago a fool, of this city, bought of "the Government" a confiscated rebel estate in Mississippi, and moved his whole family on to it. The family were five in number, and the dead bodies of all have been sent back to this city for burial. They were killed by guerrillas supposed to be friends of the owner of the property. Cheerful prospect for Uncle Abe's customers. We pity the man's family, but not him. The man who will consent to occupy the property of another on such terms is not a whit better than a thief.—New York Day Book.

THE SOUTHERN EXPRESS COMPANY.—P. W. A., the well known correspondent of the Savannah Republican, pays the following tribute to the efficiency of the Southern express company. It is a well merited compliment, and we heartily endorse the praise bestowed:

The people in Georgia and Alabama can now realize the great inconvenience resulting from the interruption of the railway lines and postal communication of the country. I do not know what the Government, the army and the people of Virginia would have done this summer when all the railways were cut but for the Southern express company. This company not only surmounts difficulties at which the agents of Government stand appalled, but it actually keeps up some sort of mail communication in spite of the sword of the public enemy and the torch of the bridge burners. It carries paper from one newspaper office to another, when the post office has ceased to operate; it delivers valuable packages when all other means of transportation have ceased; it receives and transports packages of food and apparel for the soldier in preference over all other freight; it has entered into an arrangement by which it is required to convey all funds belonging to Government to any part of the Confederacy, and for the safety of which the company is responsible. The Government has not lost a cent out of the many hundreds of millions of dollars entrusted to the company. Indeed, the Southern Express company is a public benefactor. It is indispensable to Government and of incalculable advantage to the people. Its agents and employees are really agents and employees of Government and are rendering more important service to the great cause where they are, than they possibly could if they were in the field.

THE SUN.

IT SHINES FOR ALL

THIRTY-FIRST YEAR. NUMBER 10,033.

NEW YORK SATURDAY, SEPTEMBER 3, 1864.

PRICE ONE CENT—IN GOLD
TWO CENTS IN CURRENCY.

The Latest News

By Telegraph to the N. Y. Sun.

GLORIOUS NEWS!

ATLANTA OURS!!

Great Battle Fought.

HOOD'S ARMY CUT IN TWO.

Our Forces Entering the City.

Gen. Hardee Killed.

Another Piece of Good News.

NO DRAFT IN THIS CITY.

Naval Enlistments to be Allowed

Only 300,000 Men Required.

Sec. Stanton on the Situation.

REBELLION TOTTERING TO ITS FALL.

&c., &c., &c.

GENERAL SHERMAN.

Glorious News!—Atlanta Ours!!

[OFFICIAL DISPATCH.]

WAR DEPARTMENT,
WASHINGTON, September 2—8 P.M.

To Major-General Dix, New York:

This Department has received intelligence, this evening, that General Sherman's advance entered Atlanta about noon, to-day. The particulars have not yet been received, but telegraphic communication during the night with Atlanta direct is expected.

EDWIN M. STANTON, Secretary of War.

SECOND OFFICIAL DISPATCH.

Great Battle Fought—The Rebel Army Cut in Two.

War Department, Washington, Sept. 2.—*To Major General Dix:*—The following telegram from Major General Slocum, dated this day *in Atlanta*, and just received confirms the capture of that city.

"General Sherman has taken Atlanta. The 20th Corps occupies the city. The main army is on the Macon road near East Point.

"A battle was fought near that point in which General Sherman was successful. Particulars are not known.

(Signed) H. W. SLOCUM, Major-General."

An unofficial report states that a battle was fought near East Point by General Sherman with Hood. The rebel army was cut in two, with very heavy loss to the enemy, and General Hardee was killed. Our loss is not known.

EDWIN M. STANTON, Secretary of War.

Confirmatory Accounts.

Philadelphia, Sept. 2.—The Philadelphia EVENING TELEGRAPH has just received a dispatch from a source of the highest credit, dated Marietta, Georgia, stating that our advance guard entered Atlanta this morning.

SECOND DISPATCH.

Louisville, Sept. 2.—Brigadier-General Ewing, commanding the Western District of Kentucky, has just received a telegram from the front, announcing that Sherman's advance entered Atlanta at 9 o'clock this morning.

No further particulars have been received.

THIRD DISPATCH.

Nashville, Sept. 2.—General Sherman's advance entered Atlanta this morning, at 11 o'clock. The whole Federal force will enter to-day.

FOURTH DISPATCH.

Nashville, Sept. 2.—Several miles of the Nashville and Chattanooga Railroad were burned by Gen. Wheeler's forces yesterday. Gen. Rosseau drove the rebel force within three miles of Lavogne late in the afternoon of yesterday. He met with a stubborn resistance. Late intelligence reports that the head of Wheeler's column left the Murfreesboro pike, going to the right at 10 o'clock, and the rear about 3 o'clock, the whole force moving from the Tennessee and Alabama Railroad in the direction of Franklin. Rosseau is in close pursuit. A person just in from Franklin reports that the town is in the hands of Wheeler's forces, he having entered and captured it last night. Particulars have not yet been received. Our casualties in yesterday's skirmishing were 5 killed, and 50 or 55 wounded. A small body of rebels fired on a train at Brentwood, eight miles from here. The rebel loss, yesterday, was 8 killed, and 15 wounded. We captured a number of prisoners.

The river is falling.

Value of the Victory.

The details published in yesterday's SUN respecting the operations of the opposing armies at Atlanta, will have prepared our readers for the glorious news of the capture of that place. We stated that General Sherman had swung his army around to the Macon railroad on the south, threatening Eastpoint, a strongly fortified place, five miles from the city, on the junction of the Macon and Montgomery railroads. This movement reduced the enemy to the necessity of choosing between fighting for a vital position, retreating from the city, or else being shut up in it to stand a close siege, with the certainty of the ultimate loss of the place and the army. Our view of the position has been fully realized. The enemy were forced to fight as Eastpoint as indicated, were beaten of course, and Atlanta is now ours. This is really better news than the capture of Richmond would be. The possession of Atlanta, though it does not end the war in the cotton States, gives us a secure vantage ground for doing so. No other point in the South is so favorable to the rebels for concentration and defence. Atlanta is the centre of the great lines of railroads which radiate thence to all the principal cities in the cotton States. From its railroad facilities it was selected to be the great arsenal, foundry, and manufacturing depot of the Confederacy, and as such has grown to be a place of immense importance. Its possession opens to us the back door to Charleston, Savannah and Mobile. The rebels will, of course make a stand at Macon, Montgomery, and other places, but their chances will diminish as they recede from Atlanta, while ours will increase. The following table of distances will enable our readers to appreciate General Sherman's great victory, and anticipate the probable movements of the shattered fragments of Hood's army, and our invincible Western heroes:

From Atlanta to

Macon	80 miles.
Milledgeville	85 "
Mobile	310 "
Chattanooga	100 "
Nashville	210 "
Charleston	270 "
Savannah	225 "
Knoxville	160 "
Memphis	340 "
Montgomery	150 "

General Sherman's victory places the various guerrilla bands operating in his rear, in a bad position, and Wheeler, Roddy and Forrest are likely to speedily disappear from the vicinity of Nashville and Chattanooga. These desperadoes are likely to be struck either in their advance or retreat, by General A. J. Smith's column of thirty thousand men, which left Memphis some time since to effect counter demonstrations upon Hood's line of communications, and cover General Sherman's.

Rejoicing.

Poughkeepsie, Sept. 2.—Great excitement exists here, consequent upon the reception of the news of Sherman's victory. Although the hour is late, the air is filled with fireworks, and the streets with bonfires, and cheers can be heard in every part of the city.

Rebel Operations in Sherman's Rear.

Nashville, August 30.—Rousseau's district has been invaded by the cavalry commands under Wheeler, Forrest and Roddy. Wheeler crossed the Tennessee with the main force, at Kingston, on the 28th, and reached Sparta the same night. Here he divided his force and sent Colonel Detrill against McMinnville. Detrill attacked Colonel Waters, East Tennessee, at McMinnville yesterday, and forced him from the town. Waters lost twenty men, killed and wounded, but punished the enemy so severely that he was unable to pursue Waters in his retreat to Tullahoma. Wheeler with the rest of the force reached Lebanon at 3 o'clock A. M. to-day, surrounding the College building, in which was Captain Rush's company of East Tennessee Cavalry, and succeeded in capturing the greater part of the force; only a few escaped. A son of Gov. Campbell, who escaped, reports Gen. Milligan captured. A report from Silver Springs reports a company of white and two companies of colored troops engaging the enemy near the fords of the Cumberland. A dispatch to-day to Col. Donaldson, Chief Quartermaster, reports Wheeler across the Cumberland River, where he captured a Captain Hunter, A. Q. M. This is the latest we have from Wheeler or Detrill. The former is doubtless making for the Louisville and Nashville Railroad, near Gallatin, on the South Tunnel, and Roddy has rendezvoused at Moulton, Alabama, for some days past. He has been joined by Forrest, and both crossed the Tennessee yesterday at Savannah and Tuscumbia. They have a large force. Colonel Nixon, of Roddy's command, held the advance and was enforcing a wholesale conscription. We are hourly expecting to hear of the breaking of the railroad to Chattanooga and to Louisville.

SECOND DISPATCH.

Nashville, Tenn. Sept. 1.—A rebel force, estimated at ten thousand strong, with twelve pieces of artillery, were within seventeen miles of Nashville, on the Murfreesboro' Pike, at daylight this morning. At last accounts Gen. Rosseau had driven the rebels under Wheeler, Roddy and Forrest, three miles towards Murfreesboro'. Messengers from our advance report that Gen. Wheeler's whole force is now between this city and Murfreesborough. There is a considerable force of rebels also at Lebanon.

THIRD DISPATCH.

Louisville, Ky., Sept. 1.—Passengers from Nashville say that the rebel forces under Generals Wheeler, Forrest and Roddy, are engaged in tearing up the track of the Great Western Railroad, between Nashville and the Tennessee. Fifteen guerrillas, under Billy McGander, are reported to have thrown an engine off the track of the Lebanon Branch Railroad, this afternoon, six miles from New Haven. They burned the express and baggage car, robbed the passengers of all their valuables, and left in the direction of Bardstown.

GENERAL GRANT.

A Big Gun Opened on Petersburg, Etc.

Washington, Sept. 2.—Yesterday passed without any changes in the relative positions of the opposing armies that can be of any interest to the general reader. The monster 15-inch mortar, mounted on a railroad car, has recently been run up the road opposite to Petersburg, and a few shells thrown into the city. The object of this was to deter the rebels from firing on our pickets, and it seems to have been partially successful.

SECOND DISPATCH.

Philadelphia, Sept. 2.—A special despatch to the PRESS contains the following:

"Before Petersburg, Sept. 1st.—The enemy were reported to be moving artillery to their right in the afternoon. Slight skirmishing began along the Weldon road. The Fifth Corps was placed under arms and marched into the breastworks. Some deserters come into the works during the day and said we were to be attacked at four o'clock in the afternoon. With the exception of a slight skirmish along the railroad, there was no disturbance. Our men waited with anxious expectation, but no rebels made their appearance. The quiet along the entire front is as wonderful as it is unaccountable. There is something oppressive about it. We seem to be continually expecting a fight, and know not the time or place of its occurrence."

GENERAL SHERIDAN.

Early Still in the Valley, Etc.

Baltimore, Sept. 2.—A special dispatch to the AMERICAN, dated Charleston, Va., Sept. 2d, says: Reconnoissances have established the fact that Early has not left, and has no intention of leaving the Valley. His headquarters are at Bunker Hill, half way between Martinsburg and Winchester. He is busily engaged in repairing and putting up a telegraph line, and he has already telegraphic communication with Richmond from this side of Woodstock. He is also receiving reinforcements, and Fitzhugh Lee is known to have received 500 horses for his cavalry, which is said to number 7,000. There is a regular stage from Winchester to Staunton, which runs every day, and several officers and soldiers are receiving short furloughs to go home and return to Winchester, which does not look as though the enemy intend leaving the Valley.

ADMIRAL FARRAGUT.

Capture of Fort Morgan.

The capture of Fort Morgan took place on Tuesday, August 23d, when the garrison marched out and surrendered to our forces. The bombardment commenced on Monday morning, all the preliminary operations having been completed. The army under General Granger, had taken a position on Mobile Point, and planted a battery in the rear of the fort. The fleet invested the place from two sides towards the sea, so that the fort was open on one side only. A battery from the fleet had also been planted on the shore, and manned by Jack Tars, who enjoyed hugely the fun of peppering the rebels from *terra firma*, did good execution. On Sunday night, August 21st, the land batteries were all in order, and word to that effect was sent to Admiral Farragut. At daylight on Monday morning the entire fleet stood in towards shore. The Monitors, for nearly two weeks previous, had been doing picket duty by firing on the fort night and day, so as to occupy the garrison and prevent it from disturbing the operations of the land forces on their rear. On Monday morning, however, both wooden and iron vessels participated in the fight. About 5 o'clock the fleet opened with thirty guns of different calibre, and sixteen eight and ten inch mortars. The land batteries also commenced a brisk cannonade, and the firing continued with great precision and without intermission until dark. The effects were soon visible. Early in the afternoon smoke issued from the fort at intervals, as if something were on fire, which resisted only partially the efforts to repress it. At dark, the smoke burst out into a broad sheet of flame, which was supposed to originate from a fire lit by the garrison, to give notice of attempts at assault. By others it was surmised that the citadel was in flames, and this view proved to be correct. It subsequently appeared that the rebels made an attempt to communicate signals of surrender during the night, but the movements were either not seen, or were mistaken by our forces. Early on Tuesday morning, a party bearing a white flag, and carrying a boat marched out of the main sally-port, fronting Fort Grimes, and attempted to put off to negotiate terms of surrender with the fleet. But this was not permitted by the General commanding. It was then arranged that the garrison and all public property should be surrendered on the terms usually accorded to honorable antagonists. General Paige asked and obtained an extension of time till two o'clock to surrender, in order that his officers and men should have an opportunity of collecting their private property. At the appointed time the garrison, to the number of six hundred, marched out without music or banners, and were met by two Union regiments proudly bearing the colors of the United States and their respective States, and accompanied by a band of music playing "Yankee Doodle" and "Hail Columbia." The rebels halted within a few paces of our lines, and stacked arms; when our troops swept past, entered Fort Morgan, tore down the rebel flag, hoisted the "Stars and Stripes," and spread the "Star Spangled Banner" to the breeze. Sixty heavy guns were found inside the rebel fort, and a large quantity of stores and munitions. It appeared that on Monday night the enemy passed a most uncomfortable season in the fort. They were greatly alarmed lest the flames of the Citadel would explode the magazine, and flood it with water. A large quantity of powder was also thrown into the wells. About a thousand shells exploded in the fort, and the walls were fearfully battered, the citadel being reduced to a mass of ruins. On Tuesday afternoon Admiral Farragut issued an order for the firing of a salute of a hundred guns in honor of the victory, for which he awarded equal credit to the army and navy.

In a dispatch to the Navy Department dated August 25th, Admiral Farragut complains in terms of great indignation of the displcable conduct of the rebels, in attempting to rob our forces of the legitimate fruits of victory after the flag of truce had been hoisted, and the surrender had virtually occurred. The particulars are given in the following letter of Admiral Farragut;

I regret to state that after the assembling of the rebel officers, at the appointed hour, 2 P.M., for the surrender outside the fort. It was discovered on an examination of the interior, that most of the guns were spiked, many of the gun carriages wantonly injured, the arms, ammunition, provisions, &c., destroyed, and there was every reason to believe this had been done after the white flag had been raised. It was also discovered that General Page and several of his officers had no swords to deliver up, and further that some of those which were surrendered had been broken. The whole conduct of the officers of Fort Gaines and Fort Morgan presents such a striking contrast in moral principle, that I cannot fail to remark upon it. Col. Anderson, who commanded the former, finding himself in a perfectly untenable position, and encumbered with a superfluous number of conscripts, many of whom were new troops, determined to surrender a fort which he could not defend, and in this determination was supported by all his officers, save one. But from the very moment he hoisted the white flag he scrupulously kept everything intact, and in that condition delivered it over, whilst Gen. Page and his officers, *with a childish spite*, destroyed guns which they said they would defend to the last, but which they never defended at all, and threw away or broke those weapons, which they had not the manliness to use against their enemies, for Fort Morgan never fired a gun after the commencement of the bombardment, and the advanced pickets of our army were actually on the glacis. As before stated, the ceremony of surrender took place at 2 P. M., and that same afternoon all the garrison were sent to New Orleans in the U. S. steamers Tennessee and Bienville, where they arrived safely.

Very respectfully, your obedient servant,
D. G. FARRAGUT,
Rear-Admiral Com'g W. G. B. Squadron.

Hon. Gideon Welles, Secretary of the Navy, Washington.

The Indian War.

The Savages Routed.

St. Louis, Sept. 2.—The Sioux City (Iowa) REGISTER of the 27th ult., says Mr. Sell, of the Quartermasters' Department, just arrived from Fort Union, reports that a battle occurred between Gen. Scully's command and about 5,000 Indians, near Knife River, on the 25th of July, in which the latter were defeated, with a loss of 150. Our loss was 5 killed, and 20 or 30 wounded.

News via Washington.

Washington, Aug. 2.—An official dispatch received here to-day says the murders and depredations on the Plains are committed by comparatively few of the several Indian tribes. It is understood that the Indian Bureau has sent thither a special agent with a view to the pacification of the disaffected savages. The fact may not be generally known that the Governor of Colorado has issued a proclamation urging either individuals or armed organizations to kill and destroy the hostile Indians and seize their property, distinguishing between them and those who are friendly. This proceeding of the Governor is independent of the Federal authorities, and may increase rather than lessen the calamities to which settlers and emigrants are now exposed.

From Europe.

Six Days Later News.

The steamship Hecla from Liverpool 23d, and Queenstown 24th of August, arrived at Halifax yesterday. The Calidonia from Glasgow August 26th, also arrived at St. Johns, N. F. The news is six days later. The steamship Jura from Liverpool 18th, and Londonderry 19th of August, passed Farther Point yesterday on her way to Quebec.

The Commissioners of Customs in London have issued a General Order to Collectors, that in pursuance of instructions from the Lords of the Treasury, no ship-of-war belonging to either of the belligerent powers in North America, shall be allowed to enter any of her Majesty's ports for the purpose of being dismantled and sold.

A Lisbon telegram, of the 18th, says that the Federal frigate Niagara is in the Tagus. It is said that her mission is to intercept a steamer bought at Liverpool, ostensibly for navigation between Lisbon and Liverpool. The Portuguese papers further assert that the steamer will not sail, as the intentions of the Federals have become known. This, doubtless, refers to the steamer Georgia, which recently left Liverpool for Lisbon.

The New York correspondent of the London TIMES, writing from Niagara Falls, under date of August 8th, says:

"Clifton House has become the centre of negotiations between the Northern friends of peace and Southern agents, which promise a withdrawal of differences from the arbitrament of the sword." The correspondent then goes on to explain that an effort is to be made to nominate a Democrat for the Presidency, upon a platform for an armistice, and a Convention of States, and to thwart by all possible means the efforts of Mr. Lincoln for a re-election.

The TIMES winds up an editorial on the present situation of the war in America, as follows:

"As regards the final issue of the war, we consider the prospects of the Confederates to be as good as ever; but the Federals have shown such an insensibility to defeat, and such an inflexible tenacity of purpose, that we cannot anticipate any early termination of the strife. Perhaps the success of Sherman in Georgia, or Farragut at Mobile, might counteract the disappointment produced by the failures of Grant in Virginia, and once more inspire the Federals with expectations of absolute success. But in Europe we can only employ the lessons of eventful campaigns, to confirm our convictions of the hopelessness of war and the necessity of speedy peace."

The DAILY NEWS says there are rumors of a projected new Confederate loan.

Order has been restored in Belfast, where there has been no rioting since the 19th.

Electioneering riots with bloodshed had occurred at Geneva, but they had subsided, and quiet was restored.

Tuesday's second edition, TIMES City article, says:

The discount market shows no alteration. Among the more significant points in the present accounts from New York is the change of tone becoming observable with regard to the new order of things in Mexico. Reports sent from Americans in Mexico fully confirm the hopeful description obtained from other quarters of the rapid consolidation of the new government. Advices from Frankfort state that recent facts have suddenly begun to disturb the eager faith of investers in United States bonds. Some letters received by German houses speak of the existing decline as owing to the fear of importers to enter goods at the present rate of duties. It was known at Frankfort that many German orders had been countermanded, apprehensions beginning to be experienced that the new November dividend may be lost, and that it will not be paid in specie. The distrust was being increased by the circumstance that large sales were being pressed by parties hitherto looked upon as being best informed on American affairs.

The King of Spain has left France for Spain. He visited Queen Christina prior to his departure.

The INDEPENDENCE BELGE announces a prospective marriage between Prince Humbert and the Princess Anna Murat, and says that it will strengthen the bonds between France and Italy.

The occupation of Holstein by the Prussians and Austrians is said to be decided upon.

The Czar of Russia has ordered a reduction of the army, and immediate and unlimited discharge is granted to soldiers whose service expires on the 1st of January next.

Commercial Intelligence.

Liverpool, Aug. 24.—Cotton—Sales to-day, 3,000 bales. Market irregular.

Breadstuffs are quiet; Provisions are dull. Produce Market is quiet, but steady.

London, Aug. 24.—Consols 88⅛a89 for money. American Stocks—Illinois Central shares, 45½a44½ discount; Erie shares, 41a42.

THE official statement of the public debt on the 30th of August, shows the amount outstanding to be $1,878,565,234, and the interest in both coin and lawful money, $77,447,122, or an increase of the public debt since the 2d of August, of $53,073,000, and of interest, $1,029,000. The debt bearing interest in coin is now $389,899,492; the debt bearing interest in lawful money, $469,197,000; the debt on which interest has ceased, $357,470; the debt bearing no interest, $619,111,267. The unpaid requisitions are $78,785,000, and the amount in the Treasury $17,189,518. It further appears that since the 2d of August, the six per cent. bonds under the acts of July 17th and August 5th, 1861, exchanged for seven-thirties, have increased to the extent of $75,000,000; that the seven-thirty three-year notes under the act of July 17th, 1861, have been reduced about the same amount; and the six per cent. certificates of indebtedness under the act of May 1st, 1862, increased nearly $28,000,000.

NO DRAFT!

Naval Enlistments Allowed—Only 300,000 Men Required to End the Rebellion.

WAR DEPARTMENT,
WASHINGTON, Sept. 2—8 P. M.

To Major General Dix: It is ascertained with reasonable certainty that the naval and other credits required by the Act of Congress will amount to about 200,000, including New York, which has not been reported yet to the Department; so that the President's call of July 18th is practically reduced to 300,000 men, to meet and take the place of

First—The new enlistments in the navy;

Second—The casualties of battle, sickness, prisoners and desertion; and

Third—The hundred days' troops and all others going out by expiration of service this Fall.

One hundred thousand new troops, promptly furnished, are all that General Grant asks for the capture of Richmond and to give a finishing blow to the rebel armies yet in the field. The residue of the call would be adequate for garrisons in forts and to guard all the lines of communication and supply, free the country from guerrillas, give security to trade, protect commerce and travel, and establish, peace, order and tranquility in every State.

EDWIN M. STANTON,
Secretary of War.

An Explanation Regarding the President's Call.

Washington, Sept. 2.—Little, Brown & Co's. last volume of the Statutes at Large, contains an error in the act further to regulate and provide for the enrolling and calling out of the National forces. It states that in case the quota shall not be filled within the space of sixty days after the call, the President shall immediately order a draft for one year, etc.; but the official rolls from which a copy of the act was furnished to the authorized newspaper publishers of the laws of the State Department, provides that fifty days (as stated in the President's proclamation) shall elapse after the call before a draft, in the contingency mentioned, shall be ordered.

News Items.

[By Telegraph to the New York Sun.]

THE subscriptions to the Seven-Thirty loan, as reported to the Treasury Department, yesterday, amount to $616,000; and the Ten-Forty loan, $353,400.

THE N. Y. State Sunday School Convention adjourned at Buffalo last evening, after a three days' session. The attendance was large and the proceedings unusually interesting.

TEN privates have recently been tried and convicted at Washington, of desertion, and sentenced to imprisonment at hard labor at Fort Delaware for two or three years, and to forfeit all pay and allowances.

THE messenger of the Mutual Redemption Bank of Boston called at the Shoe and Leather Bank, of that city, yesterday, and placed a small trunk on the counter, and while he was temporarily engaged the trunk was stolen. It contained $40,000, mostly in small bills on country banks.

KING KAMAHAMEHA on the 13th of August, after an excited speech, abrogated the Sandwich Islands Consitution of 1852, and declared the Constitutional Convention dissolved. This arbitrary act was regarded as a regular *coup d'etat* by the King, and if submitted to by the Hawaiian people will render the kingdom nearly an absolute monarchy.

OUR troops stationed in Fairfax and Loudon counties, Va., having been greatly molested of late by bushwhackers, it has been determined to put a stop to the disorder by arresting the disloyal citizens of the neighborhood, many of whom are believed to be connected with these rebel gangs. On Thursday thirty-two alleged warm rebel sympathizers residing in these counties, were taken to Washington and committed to the Old Capitol, to await investigation. Thirty of the sixty rebel sympathizers and suspicious characters arrested in Loudon county a week or two ago, were released from the Old Capitol on Friday, upon their parole of honor.

General Intelligence.

[By Mail to the New York Sun.]

FARMERS and horse dealers will take notice that government are now paying $175 for cavalry and $180 for artillery horses.

A "LIFE" convict, who had lived 15 years in solitary confinement, died last week in the State Prison of Michigan. He murdered his father 17 years ago.

THE generous Gail Borden, of Winsted, Conn., condenses all the blackberries sent him for the army gratuitously, and furnishes all the sugar at his own expense.

THREE lieutenants in a New York regiment have been dismissed the service by General Butler for tendering their resignations on the ground of incompetency to comply with a certain order of their brigade commander.

A LOCOMOTIVE got loose on the Brighton, (Eng.) Railway, recently, and tore along fearfully, made a clean hole through the station house, carried away a tailor's shop, part of a house, and an entire wall, and at last brought up against a building substantial enough to arrest its progress.

THE enlistment of seaman at Calcutta for the federal cause in America has attracted the notice of the authorities there, who are on the watch for the detention of some federal agents who are believed to have already freighted one ship for the northern states with unemployed sailors.

THE rebel General Hood, who commanded at Atlanta, is described by a person who has recently seen him, as a "white-headed, homely, spindle-shanked fellow, about thirty-two years of age, and over six feet tall, had been pretty well hacked in pieces: one leg gone, an arm useless, a lot of bruised ribs, and a broken collar-bone."

THERE is now a complete organization of the miners throughout Illinois, Ohio, and Pennsylvania, under the style and title of "The American Miner's Association. The Association will hold an annual convention at Cincinatti on the 7th of September. They have an organ, the WEEKLY UNION, at Belleville, Illinois.

A LATE number of the PACIFIC COMMERCIAL ADVERTISER, published at Honolulu, Sandwich Islands, states that at a recent election in one of the Districts, the ballot-box was stuffed, only 373 votes being recorded, while 788 were found in the box. This indicates progress in "the arts of civilization," rather more rapid than we expected to see.

(Continued on last page.)

THE NEW YORK HERALD.

WHOLE NO. 10,233. NEW YORK, SATURDAY, SEPTEMBER 3, 1864. PRICE FOUR CENTS.

EUROPE.

The Hecla at Halifax, the Jura at Father Point, the Caledonia Off Cape Race and the Mails of the Europa at New York.

FIVE DAYS LATER NEWS.

No American War Vessels to be Dismantled or Sold in British Ports.

British Speculations on Peace After the Chicago Nominations.

Important Rebel Reasons for Peace and Independence North and South.

Heavy Fall in United States Bonds in Germany.

THE FRIGATE NIAGARA AND THE PRIVATEERS

RIOTS IN SWITZERLAND.

Joe Coburn and Jem Mace in Training,

&c., &c., &c.

The steamship Hecla, Captain Macauley, from Liverpool at two o'clock on the afternoon of the 23d, via Queenstown on the 24th ultimo, arrived at Halifax at two o'clock yesterday morning, on her voyage to New York.

The steamship Caledonia, from Glasgow on the 26th, passed Cape Race at half-past seven o'clock on Thursday evening, September 1. Her news has been telegraphed to the HERALD via Port Hood, and is published in our columns this morning.

The advices are five days later than the report of the Europa.

No commercial advices have been received by the Caledonia.

The steamship Jura, from Londonderry on the 19th of August, reached Father Point yesterday on her voyage to Quebec.

The mails of the Europa reached this city from Boston last evening. Our European files and correspondence are dated to the 20th of August. The papers contain interesting details of our telegraphic report from Halifax, published in the HERALD last Thursday.

Our Paris correspondent, writing on the 19th of August, says:—Americans in Paris are busy hoping for a fall in gold. In fact, certain indications seem to give at least a coloring of reason to this hope. It is certain that the present rate of exchange and the increased tariff have combined to greatly diminish the usual exports from Paris, and I am credibly informed that many New York houses are shipping back to France goods recently imported and still in bond—a phenomenon never before seen in Paris. This certainly should have the effect of bringing gold to its senses.

Persons wishing to return home from Paris are a good deal exercised in their minds by the sort of circular printed in the papers by the consuls at Liverpool and Havre, to the effect that in future passports, properly vised, are necessary in order to land in the United States. The Havre consulate appears to be the only one in France at which instructions of this nature have been received from Washington.

The rebels and rebel sympathizers in London were exulting over reports of General Grant's want of success before Petersburg. The rebels said the Union cause was "caving in."

Three uncommonly fast steamers were in the London market for sale, and likely to be placed in the blockade running trade.

Order has been restored in Belfast, where there has been no rioting since the 19th of August.

The difficulty between the American Consul and the Egyptian government has been satisfactorily adjusted.

Electioneering riots, with bloodshed, had occurred at Geneva; but they had subsided and quiet was restored.

A despatch from General Cameron, dated Headquarters, Auckland, June 7, says:—During the next three months active operations will hardly be practicable in any part of New Zealand. A greater part of the troops have hutted themselves for the winter.

The ship Frank Pierce was abandoned at sea June 7.

The ship Ontario, from New York for Hong Kong, put into Simon's Bay, damaged.

The American Question.

TRADE IN BELLIGERENT WAR VESSELS STOPPED IN BRITISH PORTS.

The Commissioners of Customs in London have issued a general order to collectors, that in pursuance of instructions from the Lords of the Treasury, no ships-of-war belonging to either of the belligerent Powers in North America shall be allowed to enter any of her Majesty's ports for the purpose of being dismantled and sold.

THE NIAGARA WATCHING A NEW PRIVATEER.

A Lisbon telegram of the 18th says that the federal frigate Niagara is in the Tagus. It is said that her mission is to intercept a steamer bought at Liverpool ostensibly for navigation between Lisbon and Liverpool.

The Portuguese papers further assert that the steamer will not sail, as the intentions of the federals have become known. This, doubtless, refers to the steamer Georgia, which recently left Liverpool for Lisbon.

THE PEACE MOVEMENT—BRITISH OPINION OF THE PROBABLE NOMINATION AT CHICAGO.

The New York correspondent of the London *Times*, writing from Niagara Falls under date of August 8, says:—Clifton House has become the centre of negotiations between the Northern friends of peace and Southern agents, which promise a withdrawal of differences from the arbitrament of the sword. The correspondent then goes on to explain that an effort is to be made to nominate a democrat for the Presidency, upon a platform for an armistice and a convention of the States, and to thwart by every possible means the efforts of Mr. Lincoln for a re-election.

[illegible]GENT REASONS OF THE REBELS FOR PEACE—INDEPENDENT BUT UNITED AMERICANS RETALIATING FOR THE "SELFISH" POLICY OF EUROPE—MR. LINCOLN'S PRESIDENTIAL CHANCES.

[From the London Index (rebel organ in London) August 20.]

Our readers will acquit us of having ever been unduly sanguine in our appreciations of the events of the American war. While we have never for an instant doubted the *ultimate triumph of Confederate independence*, and while we have seldom been deceived even transiently by the boastful impostures of federal newspapers and diplomatic documents, we may modestly claim the credit of having been substantially correct in the few predictions we have ventured, and of never having encouraged the hopes of peace based upon either the exhaustion of the North, its financial collapse, its return to reason, or even the successes of the Southern arms. We have steadily held to the conviction that the war, left to its own course, whatever might be its vicissitudes, must be a long one; *that no influence from within, at least during the time of Mr. Lincoln's administration, would be potent enough to end it;* and that the only hope of shortening this fated period lay in the wisdom and justice of European Powers, if, by recognizing an incontestable political fact, they had exchanged a false for a true neutrality. Within the last two years and a half this only hope seemed several times on the point of realization. To-day *none but a visionary will deny that the idea of recognition is practically less present to men's minds than it was twelve months ago.* Whether this arises from the frequent disappointment of well founded expectations, or from a strengthening conviction that the South now stands in less need than formerly of even such aid from abroad we need not here inquire. Certain it is that the South itself has long ceased to expect, scarcely to desire, recognition; and in like proportion has grown the proud confidence in its own Heaven aided ability to accomplish the work of national salvation. Yet at this very moment when we once more acknowledge the fallacy of the only hope upon which we had heretofore dwelt seriously, we are able to say with all calmness and soberness *that the prospects of speedy peace were never so promising, unless some absolutely certain.* It is our sincere belief that, before the [illegible] disaster befalls the Confederate arms [illegible] this month, *the democratic party then assembling in convention at Chicago will nominate a peace candidate for the Presidency, and within three months thereafter there will be an armistice.*

It is not because the military situation presents unprecedented features that we stake our judgment upon so bold a prediction. Another Confederate invasion might possibly end in another Sharpsburg or Gettysburg. Another period of reciprocal inactivity might ensue, affording time for recruiting another army in Ireland and Germany. Nor is it because the financial condition so unmistakably indicates that the bottom of the nation's pocket has been reached. Federal finances have so often defied rational calculations, so many grave crises have been passed—not safely, but still passed—so buoyant and sanguine is the American temperament, that we would hesitate to deny the possibility of another miracle, and, given a drawn battle or two, or some illusory success, we are not sure but even this last crisis might be tided over, and the inevitable ruin, carefully concealed by "shoddy" flowers from public view, might be staved off for another season. These embarrassments have become periodical ever since the battle of Bull run, aggravating with each year. To a cool observer at a distance they seemed fatal in 1861; they were worse in 1862: still worse in 1863. It is not because they are worst in 1864 that we look for peace, but because in 1864 they coincide with embarrassments of quite another kind—with a quadrennial civic revolution which, even in ordinary times, puzzled and perplexed the acutest understanding of European statesmanship. The curious feature of the American federative system is its affectation of mathematical mechanism. The federal government is wound up, warranted to run four years. It may run as wildly fast or as tamely slow as the materials of its clock-work will admit, but at the striking of a certain hour its motive power is exhausted. At one second after twelve o'clock on March 4 the four years king is dead—four years life to the new king. Alas! however, for human ingenuity, there is an interval between the winding up again and running down, and this interval is an interregnum. The new king is elected in November, the old one dies in March. In the four months intervening, unless he happens to be his own successor for another "term," the courtiers desert the setting sun to worship the rising one. The federal government has only a nominal head. At noon on March 4 of next year Mr. Lincoln, unless re-elected, loses the last semblance of power; four months and four days earlier, on the first Tuesday of November next, the entire substance. In the meanwhile the semblance and the substance remain irremediably disunited, and therefore dormant.

How slim are Mr. Lincoln's chances of re-election may be seen by *the indecent alacrity with which the rats are scampering away from his ship.* Already he is opposed by a candidate of his own party, one who is not only the first love of that party—its candidate when Lincoln was not yet known outside his own village—but one who represents that very section of the party which by its rabid radicalism leavened the rest, and in the heat of the fermentation flung Mr. Lincoln into power. Even the convention which lately nominated Mr. Lincoln, composed as it was of his own officeholders, deemed it necessary to save the appearance of self-respect by insulting him in his Mexican policy. The most important committee of his own Congress has denounced him for the attempted usurpation of arbitrary power for the purpose of manufacturing fictitious votes from the "rebellious" States; and the two houses of Congress, as one body, have given practical effect to this denunciation by a legislative enactment that the vote of the "rebellious" States shall not count in the ensuing election. *In open feud with his Congress, at variance with his party, deserted by his mercenary friends, ridiculed by the press, despised by the public, his favorite generals defeated in the field, his pet schemes ending in disaster, Mr. Lincoln is not a very formidable competitor for the Presidency.* Add to this that the democratic opposition, keenly alive to the possible turns of fortune in their favor, have adjourned the nomination of their candidate to the decision of the issue of the summer's campaign, fixing it at a date barely eight weeks prior to the November election. At that election the successful candidate requires, since the votes of one third of the States are counted out, a numerical majority of the actual votes cast, such as no President since Washington has ever obtained.

The personal triumph or humiliation of Mr Abraham Lincoln is, however, merely an incident—and in no sense an element—in our calculations for peace. If the war against the South is to be prosecuted, we prefer him as President of the United States to any one of the four millions of adult males in the population of federal America. Our prognostication rests upon the fact that a new idea has entered the Northern mind, and that this idea is the only practicable bridge from war to peace. This idea scores of newspapers, which before were eagerly clamoring for a more vigorous prosecution of the war, have within the last few weeks taken up with utterance more or less distinct. It is in the minds and mouths of men of all parties, defended or denounced, but familiar to all. It is reflected in the public correspondence of the European press from America; it is sharply mapped out in nine-tenths of the private letters which fill the American mail bags. It is like the confused sound of many voices; unless a providential event hushes it, it will have swollen, ere our printed pages reach the other side of the Atlantic, into the deafening chorus of millions of men. It is an idea all the more powerful because it flatters American vanity without being altogether chimerical and impracticable. *It is an idea which implies solution and not defeat.* It is an idea which gratifies vague popular longings for revenge, and which yet promises solid material advantages.

This idea, *in which we recognize the mustard seed of a lasting and prosperous peace,* may, when stripped of its surplusage of words and extravagancies of drapery, be succinctly described somewhat as follows. The North says to itself:—"In the event of success (and no true Northerner permits himself to doubt of eventual success), what shall we gain? The experience of over three years of war has demonstrated that the chances of success upon which we most counted either never did or certainly do not now exist. Thanks to an administration as imbecile as it has been ferocious, there is neither 'latent Union feeling' nor 'negro-rising,' and there will be none. If, therefore, we succeed, after incalculable further expenditure of blood and treasure, in conquering the South, we shall find ourselves chained to a corpse. We are persuading ourselves that we are fighting for the Union—that is to say, for commercial prosperity at home and power and prestige abroad. If, after years of war, we subdue the South, our prosperity at home will consist in having the productive portion of our national territory laid waste, and the industrial portion of it burdened by a debt which it is equally ruinous to repudiate or to pay. Our prestige abroad will consist in having the flower of two thirds of our manhood employed in keeping under subjection the mutinous remaining third. The price in our own liberties which we have already paid, for the mere attempt, gives the standard of what success will cost us; and if we shall be further called to strike an average of the amount of liberty suitable equally to white American freemen and emancipated black slaves, the future is sickening to contemplate. Viewing all this, three years of war have greatly changed circumstances. If we were right then, we are not now. It is the part of wisdom to make the most of circumstances as they are. The nations of Europe, by their own short-sightedness and cowardice, have let a golden opportunity pass. *It presents itself to us now; let us be wiser than Europe. The South is neither conqueror nor conquered; let us have the credit of doing generously what some day we may have to do by compulsion.* North and South, since the formation of the Union, have ever been recognised entities. We nominally classed both under a varying number of States, and we lived prosperously when these States numbered thirty-four. *Why should we not live prosperously if the Union meant two States instead of thirty-four?* In or out of the Union, as contiguous empires who have tested each other's strength, we must live together upon some sort of terms. The South has war debts as well as we. *There will, therefore, with a little concession on both sides, be no insuperable obstacle to an identical commercial policy, much as Southerners talk about free trade.* The South owes no favors to Europe, neither do we. There is no obstacle, therefore, to a permanently identical foreign policy. Why should not the Union become a marriage between two great States, a marriage without possible divorce, admitting a distinct individuality and independent rights in both, but representing a unit to the outside world.

Such is the substance of the argument which, at the family fireside, in the club, at the domestic breakfast table, or at the public *table d'hote*, now forms the staple of discussion—for and against—throughout the Northern States. We have transcribed it almost textually from the mass of Northern correspondence, unconnected and even antagonistic in its sources, which has reached, us directly or been submitted to us. We have awakened to its importance through the coincidence in many essential points which forced itself on our attention in our Southern correspondence. It is not for us to pronounce on the merits of this argument. *The North, being the aggressor, must initiate the terms of peace.* But this much we are free to say. In the heart of the population of the Confederate States, wearied of war, though undaunted in the confidence of its issue, proposals of this sort must touch a responsive chord. The men of authority may see the inconveniences of so close an alliance with the North, but the people will see that they must choose their allies from between the Western European nations or their nearest neighbors; and neither England nor France, nor even Gallic Mexico, has done aught to interfere with the natural claims of that formidable nearest neighbor. *In spite of their habitual self-restraint, Southerners are disgusted at the imbecility of the English government of the day, and at the inconsistency, not to say treachery, of that of France.* If they are forced to choose between Europe and America, they might very well choose their own hemisphere, provided the first word of every treaty of alliance was always unchallenged confederate independence.

There is only one logical conclusion to these reflections; it is, that if *any selfish hope of exhausting both American belligerents has animated the policy of Europe, that policy will have its just reward.* Neither has lost the restorative energies of youth. Both have only just learned their own strength. Debt burdened and bled as they may be, the day that they make an honorable peace, with amity and an identical foreign policy, the twin confederations will be physically and morally stronger than ever was or could have been the undivided Union, with its materialistic tendencies, and its external strength neutralized by an internal sectional balance of power.

PROSPECTS OF THE WAR.

The London *Times* winds up an editorial on the present situation of the war in America as follows:—As regards the final issue of the war, we consider the prospects of the Confederates to be as good as ever; but the federals have shown such an insensibility to defeat and such an *inflexible tenacity of purpose*, that we cannot anticipate any early termination of the strife. Perhaps the success of Sherman in Georgia or Farragut at Mobile might counteract the disappointment produced by the failures of Grant in Virginia and once more inspire the federals with expectations of absolute success. But in Europe we can only employ the lessons of eventful campaigns to confirm our convictions of the hopelessness of war and the necessity of speedy peace.

UNITED STATES BONDS IN GERMANY—LOSS OF FAITH IN THE INVESTMENT AND DECLINE IN THE STOCK.

By the Hecla we have the following on this subject:—The London *Times* (City Article) says:—Frankfort advices show a loss of faith in United States bonds, large sales having depressed prices to 38, which is three per cent below the last quotations from New York.

The report of the Caledonia, dated the 26th of August, says:—Advices from Frankfort state that recent facts have suddenly begun to disturb the eager faith of investors in United States bonds. Some letters received by German houses speak of the existing decline as owing to the fear of importers to enter goods at the present rate of duties. It was known at Frankfort that many German orders had been countermanded, apprehensions beginning to be experienced that the new November dividend may be lost, and that it will not be paid in specie. The distrust was being increased by the circumstance that large sales were being pressed by parties hitherto looked upon as best informed on American affairs.

A NEW REBEL LOAN SPOKEN OF.

The London *News* says there are rumors of a projected new Confederate loan.

The Mexican Empire.

ENCOURAGING REPORTS OF ITS CONSOLIDATION.

Tuesday's (August 23) second edition of the London *Times'* city article says:—The discount market shows no alteration. Among the more significant points in the present accounts from New York is the change of tone becoming observable with regard to the new order of things in Mexico. Reports sent from Americans in Mexico fully confirm the hopeful description obtained from other quarters of the rapid consolidation of the new government.

The Danish Question.

The King of Prussia arrived at Vienna on the 20th on a visit to the Emperor of Austria.

The occupation of Holstein by the Prussians and Austrians is said to be decided upon.

France.

The King of Spain has left France for Spain. He visited Queen Christina prior to his departure.

Prince Humbert, Crown Prince of Italy, who is on a visit to Copenhagen, is shortly expected in Paris.

The *Independance Belge* announces a prospective marriage between Prince Humbert and the Princess Anna Murat, and says it will strenghten the bonds between France and Italy.

Advices from Algiers via Paris confirm the rumors of fresh disturbances in the province of Oran.

The Bourse flat and lower, rentes 66f. 35c.

Russia.

The Czar has ordered a reduction of the army, and immediate and unlimited discharge is granted to soldiers whose service expires on the 1st of January next.

The Prize Ring.

JOE COBURN AND JEM MACE IN STRICT TRAINING.

[From Bell's Life in London, August 20.]

A further deposit of £50 a side for this match was made at Mr. Ward's, the Princess of Wales, Stepney Green, on Tuesday last, according to agreement. The next—of £50 a side—will be due at Nat Langham's, Mitre, Upper St. Martin's lane, on Tuesday week.

Coburn writes good accounts of himself at his training quarters.

Mace took a farewell benefit on Thursday evening last at the Grecian theatre, when he had a regular bumper. He has now gone into strict training, and has left his interests in the hands of Harry Brunton, George and Dragon, Beech street, Barbican, at whose house Jem's new colors may now be obtained on receipt of a "sov." Jem wishes us to say that he cannot let them go on any other terms.

THE CHAMPIONSHIP.

Andrew Marsden and Joe Wormald have again posted a fiver each in our hands. The next deposit of £5 a side must be forthcoming on Thursday, August 25, at Bob Travers', Sun and Thirteen Cantons, Castle street, Leicester square.

Cape of Good Hope.

Dates have been received from the Cape of Good Hope up to July 13. The news is unimportant. Trade was dull. The recent alarm in regard to a possible Kaffir war proves groundless.

India.

CALCUTTA, July 30, 1864.

Cotton goods improving. Accounts of the indigo crop are better. Exchange 2s. 1d.

BOMBAY, July 30, 1864.

Cotton and cotton goods dearer. Exchange 2s. 1⅜d.

China.

CANTON, July 11, 1864.

Cotton goods unchanged. Tea higher. Exchange 4s. 11⅜d.

SHANGHAE, July 5, 1864.

Shirtings quiet. Silk drooping. Exchange 7s. 1d.

No new movements by the rebels are reported.

The Portuguese have been unable to obtain a ratification of their treaty with the Chinese government.

Commercial Intelligence.

THE LONDON MONEY MARKET.

Discount market unchanged. Funds depressed. Consols still falling.

LONDON, August 23, 1864.

Consols closed at 88⅝ a 89 for money.

AMERICAN SECURITIES.

The sales on the 23d were Illinois Central at 45 a 44 discount; Erie Railroad 40½ a 41.

LONDON, August 24, 1864.

The latest sales were Illinois Central shares at 45½ a 44½ discount; Erie Railroad, 41 a 42.

LIVERPOOL COTTON MARKET.

LIVERPOOL, August 23, 1864.

The sales of cotton yesterday and to-day were 10,000 bales, including 2,500 to speculators and exporters. The market is irregular and inactive. Quotations are generally unchanged, only choice parcels maintaining previous rates.

LIVERPOOL BREADSTUFFS MARKET.

The breadstuffs market is generally steady, and slightly firmer. Messrs. Wakefield, Nash & Co., and Richardson, Spence & Co., reports:—Flour steady. Wheat firmer; amber, 8s. a 8s. 1d. Corn steady; mixed, 30s.

LIVERPOOL PROVISION MARKET.

The provision market is very dull. Circulars report:—Beef very dull. Pork very dull and unchanged. Bacon inactive. Lard firm, and partially advanced 6d. Tallow quiet.

LIVERPOOL PRODUCE MARKET.

Ashes quiet and steady. Sugar firm. Coffee steady. Rice steady. Rosin quiet and steady. Spirits turpentine easier at 67s. Petroleum steady; refined 2s. 1d. a 2s. 3d. per gallon.

LONDON MARKETS.

LONDON, August 23, 1864.

Breadstuffs upward. Sugar quiet and steady. Coffee quiet. Tea firm. Rice buoyant. Tallow quiet and steady. Spirits turpentine quiet at 68s.

THE LATEST MARKETS.

LIVERPOOL, August 24, 1864.

COTTON.—Sales to-day 3,000 bales. Market closing irregular, with fair demand for good qualities at full previous quotations.

BREADSTUFFS.—The market is quiet and steady.

PROVISIONS.—The market is dull except for lard, which is firmer.

PRODUCE.—The produce markets are generally quiet and steady.

Personal Intelligence.

ARRIVAL OF GENERAL BUTLER IN THIS CITY.

Considerable excitement prevailed for a time yesterday in the crowded thoroughfare of Nassau street on the circulation of a rumor, which spread on the very wings of rumor herself, that Major General Butler was then and there mysteriously closetted in an upper room of 82 Nassau street. Madame had not sped upon her errand ere she was forestalled by the ubiquitous HERALD reporter, who, being there just in the nick of time as usual, had noted the fact, and all the pregnant circumstances connected with it. Rumor was, for a miracle, right this time, and, *maugre* the speculations she flung widecast on her way, the facts are simply these:—About one o'clock an open barouche drove up to the door of 82 Nassau stret, from which a rather heavy, uncouth looking personage hastily descended and made his way to the door, as quickly followed by two staff officers in uniform. At once our reporter recognized General Butler. The latter proceeded up stairs to the rooms of the Corporation Counsel, where he remained some considerable time, the crowd gathering thicker and thicker every moment. After some time the General reappeared with his attendant officers, and, entering the carriage, was driven hurriedly off. The crowd looked on as at the passing of a meteor, "held their breath for a time," and wondered what was to come of it. The General and staff are stopping at the Fifth Avenue Hotel.

The Muller Case and the Police.

CORRESPONDENCE BETWEEN INSPECTOR TANNER, OF THE LONDON DETECTIVE POLICE, AND SUPERINTENDENT KENNEDY.

EVERETT HOUSE, NEW YORK, August 29, 1864.

SIR—Permit me to return my sincere thanks, both to yourself and Mr. Inspector Carpenter, for the attention, advice and assistance which have been given to me during my visit to New York to arrest the man Muller for the murder of Mr. Briggs, in London. And I beg to assure you that I shall ever have a grateful remembrance of your kindness. Permit me also to thank you for the assistance of detective officer Tieman, whom you so kindly placed at my disposal. Tieman rendered me very valuable assistance; he was very anxious and zealous in the discharge of the duty entrusted to him, and I beg to inclose for him a gratuity of ten pounds (English), if you will be pleased to allow him to receive it. I am, sir, your obedient servant,

RICHARD TANNER,
Inspector of the Detective Police, London.

MR. KENNEDY, Superintendent of Metropolitan Police, New York.

OFFICE OF THE SUPERINTENDENT OF POLICE,
300 MULBERRY STREET, NEW YORK,
August 31, 1864.

MR. TANNER, Inspector of Detective Police, London:—

SIR—I have to acknowledge the receipt of your note of the 29th inst., and to assure you that whatever has been done by myself or any of my officers in aiding you in the prosecution of your duty has been as much prompted by a feeling of respect for the department to which you are attached as by a sense of duty on our part.

The ten sovereigns you have the kindness to offer as a gratuity to detective Tieman he will be permitted to receive. Very respectfully yours,

JOHN A. KENNEDY, Superintendent.

The Steamship Asia.

HALIFAX, Sept. 2, 1864.

The steamship Asia arrived from Boston at two o'clock A. M. and sailed for Liverpool at five o'clock A. M.

GRANT.

THE PETERSBURG COURT OF INQUIRY.

Mr. Finley Anderson's Despatch.

HEADQUARTERS, BEFORE PETERSBURG, August 31, 1864.

The Court of Inquiry concerning the unsuccessful assault on Petersburg on the 30th of July continued its investigations to-day, taking the testimony of Generals Ferrero and Wilcox, commanding divisions in the Ninth corps; General Humphreys, Chief of Staff, and General Hunt, Chief of Artillery of the Army of the Potomac, and Lieutenant Benyard, of the Engineers. Their testimony had reference to the movements and conduct of troops on that occasion, the manner of their withdrawal from the crater caused by the explosion of the mine, the preparations for the debouche of troops to take part in the assault, and the probable chances of success if other dispositions and arrangements had been made.

THE FIFTH CORPS.

Mr. James B. Wardell's Despatch.

HEADQUARTERS, FIFTH ARMY CORPS, SIX MILE HOUSE, Sept. 1, 1864.

ALL QUIET ON THE LEFT

Since the late assault by the rebels upon the works across the Weldon Railroad, held by the Fifth corps, an unusual quiet has prevaded the entire left of the line, not even an occasional shot between the pickets breaking in upon it. That this will continue for any length of time—the enemy permitting us to hold undisputed possession—is not probable, although they received a very strong intimation of our strength and ability to hold the road when they made their last demonstration.

VALUE OF THE WELDON RAILROAD—THE PREPARATIONS TO RETAKE IT.

The importance to the rebel cause of again possessing themselves of the Weldon road is fully appreciated by us, as it is by them, and doubtless the most strenuous exertions will be put forth by the enemy to retake it, which will be met by a resistance and determination on our part, resulting doubtless in the most complete success to our arms. That the enemy are preparing to make another assault is no doubt true; but that they will meet with a reception warmer than they can well stomach is also true. Breastworks, fortifications and redoubts of the largest kind have been thrown up, enabling us to punish and drive back the most formidable force that can be brought forward to dislodge us. The troops are in the finest physical condition and the highest spirits, not only anticipating, but heartily wishing, for an attack upon their position. Not the faintest doubt is expressed as to the result.

ALONG THE LINE.

Up to this time there is a quiet all along the line, from left to right, only an occasional shot being fired on either side. Last Monday the firing was quite brisk, and towards evening, and sometime after dark, very heavy. Since then but little has been done on either side—a quiet and a rest that will soon be broken in upon by the roar of artillery, musketry and the bursting of murderous shells.

CAPTAIN DALY NOT DEAD.

In the despatch giving an account of the recent battle in which the Fifth corps was engaged it was stated that Captain Daly, of General Warren's staff, was shot dead by the rebel General Heyward, whom he had supposed, from certain indications, was about to surrender his force. This, I am happy to state, is so far untrue, that Captain Daly at this present writing is still alive, in hospital, seriously, though not dangerously wounded.

THE CHICAGO NOMINATION IN CAMP.

A great deal of interest is manifested here upon the nomination at Chicago. Groups of officers and men have been talking excitedly, discussing the relative chances of one and another, but generally settling upon one point unanimously—the merits of their candidate. These groups are to be seen at all hours. Last evening, when the papers came up to camp, it was amusing to witness the eagerness with which the newsboys were beset, and when one of the soldiers succeeded in getting a paper he immediately became the centre of an excited group anxious to learn what were the chances for their favorite. Later in the evening the news arrived by telegraph that McClellan had been nominated, when the most general satisfaction was expressed.

THE WEATHER

still continues fine, and the roads are becoming very dusty. The nights are quite cool, making one or more blankets very necessary.

The Washington Despatch.

WASHINGTON, Sept. 2, 1864.

The last information from the Army of the Potomac is that yesterday passed without any changes in the relative positions of the opposing armies that can be of any interest to the general reader.

The monster fifteen-inch mortar, mounted on a railroad car, has recently been run up the road opposite to Petersburg, and a few shells thrown into the city. The object of this was to deter the rebels from firing on our pickets, and it seems to have been partially successful.

The Fortress Monroe Despatch.

FORTRESS MONROE, Sept. 1, 1864.

A schooner, name unknown, ran the blockade yesterday, and got safely to Smithfield, Va.

A small force was sent to Smithfield yesterday with orders to make a reconnoissance, but was met by a party of guerillas and prevented from landing.

The mail steamer John Brooks has arrived from City Point with twenty prisoners. She brings no news from the army.

The Philadelphia Despatch.

PHILADELPHIA, Sept 2, 1864.

A special despatch to the *Press* contains the following:—

BEFORE PETERSBURG, Sept. 1, 1864.

The enemy were reported to be moving artillery to their right in the afternoon.

Slight skirmishing began along the Weldon road. The Fifth corps was placed under arms and marched into the breastworks.

Some deserters came into the works during the day and said we were to be attacked at four o'clock in the afternoon.

With the exception of a slight skirmish along the railroad there was no disturbance. Our men waited with anxious expectation; but no rebels made their appearance.

The quiet along the entire front is as wonderful as it is unaccountable. There is something oppressive about it. We seem to be continually expecting a fight, and know not the time or place of its occurrence.

General McClellan at Home.

SERENADE BY THE CITIZENS OF ORANGE—THE GENERAL'S REPLY, ETC.

[From the Newark (N. J.) Journal, Sept. 1.]

The reception of the news of the nomination of George B. McClellan was the occasion of great rejoicing in Orange. The General and his family being at his beautiful rural home on the crest of the Orange mountain, it was decided in the evening to give him a serenade. Accordingly a band was procured from Newark, and at about ten o'clock a large concourse of people assembled in front of General McClellan's residence, where a selection of patriotic airs was admirably played. On the conclusion of the music the crowd cheered vehemently for the General, who made his appearance on the front portico, when another outburst of cheers waked up the slumbering echoes of the mountain. General McClellan then briefly thanked the assemblage in the following words:—

MY FRIENDS—The events of the day are so new and of such vital importance to us, to our children and to our country, that I cannot as yet realize them; nor do I yet fully comprehend the position in which I am placed. I thank you sincerely for coming here, for I know from daily experience the fatiguing walk you have taken and the difficult hill you have had to climb. I am sure that you will not expect me to make a speech. If the action of to-day leads to the results we all expect, I think that you will have no cause to regret what has been done. Most sincerely do I thank you, my friends and neighbors, for this kind visit and these hearty congratulations.

THE GENERAL'S RESIDENCE.

It is supposed by many that General McClellan is only a temporary sojourner on the soil of New Jersey. This impression is erroneous, the General having resided in Orange more than one year, and recently he has purchased property on the Orange Mountain, whereon he intends to build another house for the permanent residence of himself and family.

Police Intelligence.

A MAN SERIOUSLY SHOT.—The police of the Fifth precinct report that a man, who gave his name as Chas. Daly, was arrested on Thursday night in Thompson street, near Canal, on the charge of shooting John Robinson, residing in Plymouth street, Brooklyn. It seems that officer Gale, while patrolling his beat, heard several pistol shots fired in quick succession. He proceeded at once to the spot, in Canal street, near West Broadway, where he found Daly. The latter upon seeing the officer ran, but was pursued several blocks, and finally caught. Daly was taken to the station house, and search was then made for the wounded man. Several hours after it was ascertained that he was in the New York Hospital, and was very dangerously wounded in the abdomen. Yesterday Coroner Wildey visited Robinson for the purpose of taking his ante mortem examination, but the victim was found to be in too exhausted a condition to converse. Daly was committed by Justice Hogan to await the result.

A DISHONEST DOMESTIC.—Sarah Hagerman, a domestic, in the employ of Mrs. Flora Jacobs, of 269 Bleecker street, was brought before Justice Ledwith yesterday on the charge of having stolen from her employer a black silk dress, valued at $40, a pair of sleeves worth $10, and a gold breastpin, $3. The accused was seen coming out of complainant's apartments with a bundle containing the above named property. She was committed to answer, in default of $500 bail.

Lighthouse Burned.

HALIFAX, Sept. 2, 1864.

Flint Island lighthouse, in Cow Bay, was burned on Wednesday night.

SHERMAN.

FALL OF ATLANTA.

Brilliant Strategic Movement of the Union Commander.

HOOD HOODWINKED.

A BATTLE FOUGHT NEAR EAST POINT

GENERAL HARDEE KILLED.

The Rebels Assisting Sherman's Plans.

Operations of Wheeler, Forrest and Roddy.

Rousseau in Close Pursuit of the Cavalry Raiders.

Georgia Virtually Redeemed from Rebel Rule.

The "So Called" Confederate States Reduced to Three,

&c., &c., &c.

Secretary Stanton to General Dix.

WAR DEPARTMENT, WASHINGTON, Sept. 2—8 P. M.

To Major General DIX, New York:—

This department has received intelligence this evening that General Sherman's advance entered Atlanta about noon to-day. The particulars have not yet been received, but telegraphic communication during the night with Atlanta direct is expected.

EDWIN M. STANTON, Secretary of War.

Secretary Stanton's Second Despatch.

WAR DEPARTMENT, WASHINGTON, Sept. 2—11 P. M.

To Major General DIX:—

The following telegram from Major General Slocum, dated this day, in Atlanta, and just received, confirms the capture of that city:—

General Sherman has taken Atlanta.

The Twentieth corps occupies the city;

The main army is on the Macon road, near East Point.

A battle was fought near that point, in which General Sherman was successful. Particulars are not known.

H. W. SLOCUM, Major General.

An unofficial report states that a battle was fought near East Point by General Sherman with Hood. The rebel army was cut in two, with very heavy loss to the enemy, and General Hardee was killed. Our loss is not known.

EDWIN M. STANTON, Secretary of War.

Sherman's Victory in Washington—His Masterly Strategetic Movement.

WASHINGTON, Sept. 2, 1864.

There is great rejoicing in Washington this afternoon over the news that Atlanta is in the possession of the Union forces. It appears that while the rebel cavalry was operating upon General Sherman's rear, that officer was prosecuting his movements successfully, and at eleven o'clock this morning entered the city of Atlanta, and found that his combinations had compelled its evacuation by Hood. Transmission of this intelligence over the wires, which have been cut for several days, proves that Rosseau has been successful in his effort to dislodge the cavalry expedition of Forrest, Wheeler and Morgan, and driven them from the road. The capture of Atlanta secures the possession of the whole State of Georgia, and renders the condition of the rebel leaders more desperate than ever before.

It was by an apparent retreat—one of those masterly strategic movements for which this general has been so noted—that he has been enabled to achieve so brilliant a result. For some time past it has been apparent, not only to General Sherman but to the majority of his officers, that the position could not be taken by direct assault. The works which Johnston was enabled to build around Atlanta during the time he occupied Sherman's attention by his slow retreats, are represented to be of the most formidable character and strength. On the other hand, a complete investment of the place was impossible from a want of men—General Sherman's army being too small to establish the line around the city as strongly as would be necessary to prevent successful sallies of the enemy. It is now well known that Hood has added materially to his strength by the conscription of numerous boys and old men, who behind works could render very good service. Outside of the works this very strength would prove a great weakness and a terrible cost of powder and provender.

The purpose of General Sherman in the movement which began on the night of the 26th was to deprive the rebel commander, General Hood, of this strength and of his protection of the works at Atlanta. In other words, Sherman hoped by flanking Atlanta and cutting off his supplies to force Hood out to fight, and thus, with his largely preponderating force of veteran troops, to whip him in an open field. With this view Sherman moved on the night in question with twenty days' rations, and all his army, except the Twentieth corps (Slocum's), which had been withdrawn from the front of Atlanta to Chattahoochie bridges, there to remain as a corps of observation, and to occupy Atlanta in the event of Hood abandoning it. It was also employed to look after the communications and hurry forward the railroad and supplies to whatever new position Sherman might assume.

The army is reported to have moved in the following order:—The Twenty-third corps (Schofield) in advance, followed the Fourteenth (Davis), Fifteenth (Logan), Sixteenth (Ransom), Seventeenth (Blair), and the Fourth (Stanley), in the order named, all making the flank movement with strong skirmish lines on either flank and front and rear. East Point was left to the east, and at dawn Hood found Sherman gone; at least the following from the Richmond papers of August 29 looks like it:—

It was rumored yesterday that official intelligence had been received that Sherman was retreating from Atlanta, and that Hood was pressing him heavily. We are much disposed to believe this report, though no information on the subject has been given the press. Wheeler and others have been playing such pranks in Sherman's rear as must have rendered his position before Atlanta dangerous and extremely uncomfortable.

The Nashville Despatches.

NASHVILLE, Sept. 2, 1864.

General Sherman's advance entered Atlanta this morning at eleven o'clock. The whole Union force will enter to-day.

NASHVILLE, Tenn., Sept. 1, 1864.

A rebel force, estimated at ten thousand strong, with twelve pieces of artillery, was within seventeen miles of Nashville, on the Murfreesboro pike, at daylight this morning.

Major General Rousseau, with a body of cavalry and infantry, started yesterday afternoon, and met the enemy's advance early this morning. Sharp skirmishing commenced, with varying success.

At last accounts General Rousseau had driven the rebels three miles towards Murfreesboro.

Messengers from our advance report that General Wheeler's whole force is now between this city and Murfreesboro.

There is a considerable force of rebels also at Lebanon.

Prisoners and some wounded have been sent from General Rousseau's front.

NASHVILLE, Sept. 2, 1864.

Several miles of the Nashville and Chattanooga Railroad were burned by General Wheeler's forces yesterday.

General Rousseau drove the rebel force within three miles of Lavergne late in the afternoon of yesterday. He met with a stubborn resistance.

Late intelligence reports that the head of Wheeler's column left the Murfreesboro' pike, going to the right, at ten o'clock, and the rear about three o'clock, the whole force moving from the Tennessee and Alabama Railroad in the direction of Franklin. Rousseau is in close pursuit.

A person just in from Franklin reports that the town is in the hands of Wheeler's forces, he having entered and captured it last night. The particulars have not yet been received.

Our casualties in yesterday's skirmishing were five killed and fifty or fifty-five wounded.

A small body of rebels fired on a train at Brentwood, eight miles from here.

The rebel loss yesterday was eight killed and fifteen wounded. We captured a number of prisoners.

The river is falling.

The Louisville Despatches.

LOUISVILLE, Sept. 2, 1864.

Brigadier General Ewing, commanding the Western district of Kentucky, has just received a telegram from the front announcing that Sherman's advance entered Atlanta at nine o'clock this morning.

No further particulars have been received.

LOUISVILLE, Ky., Sept. 1, 1864.

Passengers from Nashville say that the rebel forces under Generals Wheeler, Forrest and Roddy are engaged in tearing up the track of the Great Western Railroad between Nashville and the Tennessee.

The Nashville *Union* says that General Rousseau has made such a disposition of his forces that these rebel commands cannot injure the railroad, and that he has gone out to give them battle.

Railway Outlawry of the Guerillas in Kentucky.

LOUISVILLE, Ky., Sept. 1, 1864.

Fifteen guerillas under Billy McGauder are reported to have thrown an engine off the track of the Lebanon Branch Railroad this afternoon, six miles from New Haven. They burned the express and baggage car, robbed the passengers of all their valuables, and left in the direction of Bardstown.

Jessey's gang of two hundred guerillas returned this forenoon from a raid to the Ohio river, and encamped four miles from Newcastle. The inhabitants of that town momentarily apprehended an attack.

Rejoicing Over the Capture of Atlanta.

POUGHKEEPSIE, Sept. 2, 1864.

Great excitement exists here consequent upon the reception of the news of Sherman's victory. Although the hour is late the air is filled with fireworks and the streets with bonfires, and cheers can be heard in every part of the city.

REBEL ACCOUNTS.

Official Despatch of General Hood—Wheeler's Movements—He Captured Dalton, with Large Quantities of Stores, Prisoners and Mules, &c., &c.

[Telegram to the Richmond Whig, August 31.]

ATLANTA, August 28, 1864.

Hon. J. A. SEDDON:—

The enemy have changed their entire position, the left of their line resting near the Chattahoochee, about Sandtown, and their right extending to a point opposite and near the West Point Railroad, between East Point and Fairburn. They hold all the crossings on the Chattahoochee, but not with a continous line. Despatches from General Wheeler, of the 19th, report the capture of Dalton, with large quantities of stores, about two hundred prisoners, and two hundred mules. He destroyed three trains of cars and twenty-five miles of railroad. His command is in good condition.

J. B. HOOD, General.

NEWS FROM THE PACIFIC.

California Political Affairs—Loss of the Ships Mary Robinson, Lady Washington and St. Charles—Abrogation of the Sandwich Islands Constitution by the King, &c., &c.

SAN FRANCISCO, August 31, 1864.

Arrived, ships Sumatra, Belvidere and Daniel Marcy, from New York; Winged Hunter, from Boston. Sailed, ship Mary L. Sutton, for Baker's Island.

The Union Republican State Convention has nominated for Presidential electors:—J. G. McCallum, Sam Brannan, Rev. C. C. McClay, J. Wing Oliver and William Crane, and as a matter of precaution have instructed them to cast the vote for Lincoln and Johnson.

A *nolle prosequi* has been entered in the case of Mr. Smiley for keeping the treasure received from the steamer Golden Gate.

SAN FRANCISCO, Sept. 1, 1864.

J. C. McRuer, of San Francisco, has been nominated by the Union Republican Convention for Congress from the Southern District of California; William Higby, from the Middle District, and John Bidwell from the Northern District. This is regarded as an excellent ticket.

Arrived, ship Milan, from New York. Sailed, ship Rival, from Hong Kong.

An arrival from Honolulu brings dates of the 13th of August, which state that the ship Mary Robinson became a total loss at Howland's Island on the 28th of June.

The ships Lady Washington and St. Charles became a total loss at Baker's Island on the 8th of June.

Sailed from Baker's Island, June 26, ship Skylark, for England.

King Hamehameha, on the 13th of August, after an excited speech, abrogated the Sandwich Islands constitution of 1852, and declared the Constitutional Convention dissolved. This arbitrary act was regarded as a regular *coup d'etat* by the King, and if submitted to by the Hawaian people will render the kingdom nearly an absolute monarchy.

Defeat of the Indians by General Sully.

ST. LOUIS, Sept. 2, 1864.

The Sioux City (Iowa) *Register*, of the 27th ult., says Mr. Sell, of the Quartermaster's Department, just arrived from Fort Union, reports that a battle occurred between General Sully's command and about five thousand Indians, near Knife river, on the 25th of July, in which the latter were defeated, with a loss of one hundred and fifty. Our loss was five killed and twenty or thirty wounded.

The Love Poisoning Case.

TO THE EDITOR OF THE HERALD.

NEW YORK, Sept. 2, 1864.

In your issues of the HERALD of this date and yesterday we notice a report of the proceedings before Coroner Ranney of the alleged poisoning of Mrs. John Love. We beg to ask for a suspension of public opinion as to any guilty connection of either Mrs. O'Neil or John Love with Mrs. Love's death; and beg to state that, when a full, fair and impartial investigation of the whole case is had, both of the accused will be proven and judicially declared entirely innocent of the horrible and grave charge made against them. By giving this an insertion in your paper you will be doing but justice to the unfortunate accused. Yours, &c.

ALEX. H. REAVEY,
J. C. LANG,
Counsel for Mr. Love and Mrs. O'Neil.

The New England Fair.

SPRINGFIELD, Mass., Sept. 2, 1864.

Every train, thus early, brings people and stock for the great New England Fair, which will begin here Tuesday. An immense crowd, as well as a very large exhibition, is promised. Among the famous horses, Draco, Gen. Knox, Ashland and Actacon will trot. There will be an extraordinary show of implements of all kinds.

NEW YORK HERALD.

JAMES GORDON BENNETT, EDITOR AND PROPRIETOR.

OFFICE N. W. CORNER OF FULTON AND NASSAU STS.

TERMS cash in advance. Money sent by mail will be at the risk of the sender. None but bank bills current in New York taken.

THE DAILY HERALD, FOUR cents per copy. Annual subscription price $14.

Volume XXIX..............................No. 245

AMUSEMENTS THIS EVENING.

NIBLO'S GARDEN, Broadway.—CAMILLE.

WINTER GARDEN, Broadway.—EVERYBODY'S FRIEND—ROUGH DIAMOND.

NEW BOWERY THEATRE, Bowery.—REPROBATE—HANDSOME JACK—BEAR HUNTERS—LOVE AND MURDER.

BOWERY THEATRE, Bowery.—SIGNET OF KING SOLOMON—BASEMENT BELLE—MAURICE THE WOODCUTTER.

BROADWAY THEATRE, 485 Broadway.—MARRIED LIFE—PEOPLE'S LAWYER.

BARNUM'S MUSEUM, Broadway.—LIVING WHALE, TWO GIANTS, TWO DWARFS, ALBINOS, SARPENTS, &c., at all hours. JOCLO—At 11 A. M., 3 and 7¾ P. M.

WOOD'S MINSTREL HALL, 514 Broadway.—ETHIOPIAN SONGS, DANCES, &c.—THE CONTRABANDS COLLEGE.

CAMPBELL MINSTRELS, 199 and 201 Bowery.—VARIED AND EXCITING MELANGE OF ETHIOPIAN ODDITIES.

AMERICAN THEATRE, No. 444 Broadway.—BALLETS, PANTOMIMES, BURLESQUES, &c.—VOL-AU-VENT.

NEW YORK MUSEUM OF ANATOMY, 618 Broadway.—CURIOSITIES AND LECTURES. from 9 A. M. till 10 P. M.

HOOLEY'S OPERA HOUSE, Brooklyn.—ETHIOPIAN SONGS, DANCES, BURLESQUES, &c.

New York, Saturday, September 3, 1864.

THE SITUATION.

The most vital news of the day is the capture of Atlanta by General Sherman, which he accomplished yesterday by a very clever flank movement. The Twentieth corps occupied the city at noon yesterday. The main army was occupying a position on the Macon road, near East Point, where, it is said, a battle occurred, in which General Sherman succeeded in cutting the army in two, and inflicting heavy loss upon them. General Hardee is reported among the killed. Sherman appears to have made a fine strategic movement. Keeping the enemy employed with his cavalry while he was apparently retreating, he forced General Hood to come out and fight him at a terrible disadvantage. Thus while he seemed to be abandoning the siege of Atlanta, he was in fact securing its capture.

Our despatches from Louisville and Nashville yesterday show that the combinations in Tennessee coincided with Sherman's movements. A force of ten thousand rebels, with twelve pieces of artillery, under Generals Roddy, Wheeler and Forrest, made an attempt to destroy the railroad between Nashville and the Tennessee river. They got within seventeen miles of Nashville on the Murfreesboro' road. General Rousseau advanced to meet them, and, it is said, drove them three miles towards Murfreesboro'. At last accounts Wheeler was in Franklin.

The Navy Department received Admiral Farragut's official account of the surrender of Fort Morgan, yesterday. The Admiral complains of the conduct of the rebel Gen. Page and his officers. He states that the guns were spiked and the ammunition destroyed after the white flag was hoisted; also that neither General Page nor several of his officers had swords to deliver up, while the weapons of many of those who had any were found to be broken. Admiral Farragut draws a contrast between this conduct of General Page and that of Colonel Anderson, of Fort Gaines, very much to the disparagement of the former, who, it will be remembered, denounded Colonel Anderson for surrendering Fort Gaines.

No change has taken place in General Grant's army [illegible] mishing, and a threatened attack of the rebels, which has not yet taken place, everything was perfectly still.

The Secretary of War has forwarded an important despatch to General Dix relative to the draft, which we publish to-day. He announces that the naval and other credits which had not yet been reported to the Department reduce the call of the President last July to 300,000 men. He says, furthermore, that 100,000 more fresh troops are all that is required by General Grant to give a finishing blow to the rebellion, and that the residue will only be required to garrison forts, guard the lines of communication and protect travel and commerce from the assaults of guerillas in the different States now infested with them.

EUROPEAN NEWS.

By the arrival of the steamships Hecla at Halifax and Caledonia off Cape Race we have telegraphic reports of European news to the 26th of August—five days later than the advices by the Europa.

The Hecla is on her voyage to New York.

The British government had ordered that American war vessels, belonging to either of the belligerents, should not be dismantled or sold in British ports.

The frigate Niagara was in the Tagus watching the movements of a new privateer, supposed to be the Georgia, which it was thought would soon sail under pretence of a voyage to Liverpool. The Portuguese government had declared the vessel should not leave the port of Lisbon.

We publish to-day an important article from the London *Index*, the special organ of the rebels in Europe, on the subject of the prospect of a peace resulting from the action of the Chicago Convention. The writer says that the nominations by that body will be followed by an armistice, which will lead to the adjustment of our difficulties by the organization of two American governments, independent in executive functions but united in sentiment, finance, trade and military objects, and ready to reward the "selfish policy," or "treachery," or "cowardice" of any nation of the Old World which worked for their mutual exhaustion. The *Index* thinks that Mr. Lincoln's chances of re election are very "slim;" but if the war is to continue the rebels prefer him to any other person for President of the North.

Despatches from Niagara Falls to the London *Times* express the conviction that peace would soon ensue in America—by an armistice and convention of the States—after the nomination of a democratic candidate for the Presidency at Chicago.

The London *Times* thinks that the war prospects of the rebels are as good as ever, if the operations of Sherman and Farragut do not counterbalance what it calls the failures of Grant.

A new rebel loan was spoken of in London.

United States bonds had experienced a decline of three per cent in Frankfort; and it was said that Germany was "losing faith" in the investment in consequence of advices from New York and an eagerness to sell evinced by many houses well informed on American affairs.

The financial affairs of the Mexican empire were much brighter in England, it having been reported that the monarchy was rapidly consolidating.

The King of Spain had left Paris. He visited Queen Christina on his way to Madrid.

It was thought that Prince Humbert, of Italy, would be married to the Princess Anna Murat, of France.

Prussia and Austria had decided on taking possession of Holstein.

The Czar of Russia had commenced a large reduction in his army.

The difficulty between the United States Consul and the Egyptian government was amicably adjusted.

Election riots, terminating in shedding of blood, had taken place in Geneva, Switzerland.

No disturbance had occurred in Belfast, Ireland, since the night of the 19th of August.

The British army in New Zealand had gone into winter quarters.

There is no commercial or financial report (to August 26) by the Caledonia. The latest markets are dated to the 24th of August. Consols closed in London at 88⅞ a 89 for money. The Liverpool cotton market closed irregular, but good qualities were in fair demand, previous quotations being fully maintained. Breadstuffs were quiet and steady. Provisions were generally dull.

MISCELLANEOUS NEWS.

There was a special meeting of the Board of Aldermen called for yesterday, but a quorum failing to attend, no business was transacted. A number of the Aldermen officiated as delegates at the Chicago Convention, and have not yet returned to their homes.

Monday next, the 5th instant, is the day that was appointed by the President for the draft to take place in all districts throughout the country which shall not have filled their quotas of the call for five hundred thousand men prior to that time; but up to last evening General Hays, the Assistant Provost Marshal General in this city, had received no orders to commence drafting on the day named.

Major General Benjamin F. Butler arrived in this city yesterday from Fortress Monroe, on a short leave of absence from his command.

The Sixty-fifth regiment of New York Volunteers, who arrived home from the seat of war on Thursday last, after a three years term of service, had a formal reception and parade yesterday. They were escorted by three companies of the Seventh regiment, National Guard. In the evening they were entertained at a supper in the armory of the Seventh regiment.

The Constitutional Union General Committee met last evening at the Sinclair House, Mr. J. L. Noyes in the chair. Most of its members were announced to be absent still at Chicago, and the business was of a trivial nature. The chairman announced also that in the Twenty-first ward a new campaign hall has been erected, near the Harlem depot, by a few citizens of the ward.

The Dry Goods Protective Association held a meeting at No. 110 Grand street last Thursday evening, the President, Mr. Chaddocks, in the chair. A number of new members having been admitted, the question of an increase of salaries was discussed. The President advocated a gold basis as the only proper one when the currency fluctuations were so uncertain as at present. Mr. Altman proposed a committee of conference to meet such from other societies, and deemed fifty per cent a sufficient advance for a beginning. A member of the Early Closing Association stated that his society were carrying forward the resolves of the late Dry Goods Clerks' mass meeting, and it was resolved that this Association cordially endorse the resolutions of the said mass meeting so far as an increase of salary to fifty per cent is concerned. The general opinion was that the gold basis is the only true one; but a majority believed that it would not be conceded at present. A committee was appointed to inform the Early Closing Association of the concurrence in the rate demanded for the present.

In the United States Commissioner's office yesterday Commissioner Stillwell discharged two men, named Richard Turner and John Wilson, who, with another previously discharged, were charged with enticing a colored man to desert, the government failing to produce any witnesses or testimony in the case.

By a fire at the Troy (N. Y.) Nail Works on Wednesday morning property to the value of $20,000 was destroyed.

The ups and downs of gold yesterday had a very unfavorable effect on the market for general merchandise, and values were completely unsettled. Some of the merchants would not name prices at which they would either buy or sell, and prices of nearly everything were merely nominal. The transactions elsewhere chronicled are, in the present stage of the markets, of especial value. Cotton was steady. Petroleum was irregular. On 'Change the flour market was 15c. a 30c. higher. Wheat was 2c. a 4c. higher, with only a moderate business doing. Corn was 1c. higher, and oats were a shade firmer. Pork opened active and firmer, but closed dull and heavy. Beef was quiet. Lard was quite active and firmer. Whiskey quiet. Freights were a shade firmer.

Brilliant Strategical Movement of Sherman—Fall of Atlanta—The Progress of the War—Our Prospects, &c.

General Sherman on the night of the 26th ult. raised the siege of Atlanta, and moved from his position in front of it to draw Hood from his defences and force a fight in the open field, which would give him the benefit of his old troops and necessarily rob Hood of the service of his recent reinforcements of militia; for these, though effective enough in the position at Atlanta, would be useless, or worse, in open battle. One corps of Sherman's army—the Twentieth, under Gen. H. W. Slocum—was left on the Chattahoochee to hold Sherman's line of communication. With the rest this enterprising commander turned Hood's left, flanked the im[illegible] where the Montgomery [illegible] Jonesboro—a point [illegible] twenty miles south of Atlanta. This movement of course cut Hood's line of communication and broke up the deadlock at Atlanta by compelling Hood to come out and fight, just as Grant has lately compelled Lee to do on the Weldon road. The result of this strategical movement is the fall of Atlanta, and its occupation by the Twentieth corps under General Slocum. Sherman engaged Hood near East Point—the junction of the two railroads—and is reported to have cut the rebel army in two. The enemy's loss was very heavy, and General Hardee was killed. Our telegraphic communication is now complete with Atlanta direct.

All accounts agree as to the present almost hopeless condition of the rebel cause. Accounts from rebel papers, no less than the accounts of our own correspondents, indicate that the rebel armies are worn out with the incessant toil and battle of the last four months. Militia—a contemptible crowd of trembling, nerveless old men and barefooted boys—are now the principal reliance for the defence of certain important points in the confederacy. All the able bodied men were long since forced into the army, and the vast majority of these have been slain in battle. Union soldiers, that have escaped from rebel prisons and traversed sections of the Southern States greater in extent than the space between New York and Philadelphia, unanimously declare that they never saw an able bodied man. The armies to compose which the Southern country has been thus swept are used up, and there can be no renewal of their numbers. This is now acknowledged in the acts of the rebel authorities. Southern Governors and generals no longer pretend to force more men into their armies; but they call upon the population to rise and do what can be done. Mobile is now held by these collections of feeble old men, and boys that can hardly carry a musket. Hood could only be reinforced with the same material. For such work as Lee has lately done on the Weldon road, or as Hood required of his men when Sherman first crossed the Chattahoochee, this material would of course be a great deal worse than useless. But yet some effective service may be gotten out of them in defending intrenched positions like Atlanta and Mobile. And it is now the tactics of the rebel leaders to carry on the war so as to make them effective in just that way. The rebel plan now is to make the longest fight that is possible in their intrenched positions, and to drag out the struggle in that way till the last possible moment, in the hope that Vallandigham and his fellow laborers may be able to bring about a revolution in the North, which will do more for their cause than all their great armies have been able to do. Jeff. Davis has done all that he can do, and the confederacy now only waits to see what Vallandigham can do, and cherishes the faint hope that it may be able to hold out till this succor from its Northern friends can reach it.

How different are all the appearances at the North. Men were never more plentiful, nor was the activity in military preparation ever greater than now. Three and four columns of military advertisements appear in our paper every day. Many of these are advertisements for substitutes, for which many persons are now giving a thousand and twelve hundred dollars. This is not a government expense—it is the munificent price that private individuals pay to be rid of the draft in advance. And this large price brings forward good men—men that are physically of the very best quality; for, under these circumstances, the surgeon who examines the offered man makes his standard of acceptance pretty high. Thus, under the present excellent management, the call for men is yielding the government a full regiment a day of robust and willing soldiers, and these, many of them veterans even, are going forward to our armies with great rapidity. Our armies also are handled as they have never been hitherto. On the James river the fighting has been such that the rebels could trust no militia there. They have kept in that field the best men they had. Yet even with these the position is now immensely in our favor. At Atlanta they have trusted to militia. In the immense intrenchments with which that place is fortified they did good service, and it would have been a bloody business to carry the place by storm. But General Sherman, as we have seen, has done better. And with such operations as that now in progress under Sherman; with Grant's activity on the James, and with old Farragut and Granger at Mobile, our prospects are so good that the country can afford to scorn the labors of the Vallandigham plotters, certain that if they can even effect an apparent change in Northern sentiment, that change will come too late to save the rebellion.

The Presidential Question—Shall We Have an Insurrection at the North?

During the political canvass in 1860 we warned both parties that the election might be followed by a revolution. Our warnings were not heeded then, and the consequence was that the election of Lincoln was quickly succeeded by the secession of the Southern States. Now, at the opening of the canvass in 1864, we have the same warning to utter; but it is in regard to an insurrection at the North. The experience of the past four years ought to have taught the American people that the HERALD does not predict rashly, and that its prophecies are worthy of the most earnest attention. When every other paper said that there was no danger of disunion, we assured the people that disunion would certainly be the result of Mr. Lincoln's election. Now we as solemnly assure them that, unless careful precautions are taken, a Northern insurrection will be the certain result of Mr. Lincoln's re-election.

We have not the slightest doubt that there is a mutual understanding between the Seymours, the Woods, Vallandigham and the rebels. This understanding is shown in the secession platform adopted by the Chicago Convention, and in the nomination of Mr. Pendleton, of Ohio—who is a practical secessionist—for Vice President. We have now driven the rebels completely to the wall. General Grant has the best of them at Richmond, and General Sherman has succeeded in capturing Atlanta. This is not the time, then, that any reasonable man would be talking about "an immediate cessation of hostilities." We are in favor of an armistice, like that between Prussia and Denmark, where both sides hold their ground and are ready to begin the conflict at any moment; but there is a vast deal of difference between such an armistice and the "immediate cessation of hostilities" which the Chicago platform requires. Nothing can explain such a platform except the hypothesis that it was dictated by Jeff. Davis to the peace democrats, and that these peace men [illegible] price of their endorsement of General McClellan's nomination.

For three years past the HERALD has sustained and defended the hero of Antietam. We have done full justice to his generalship, his statesmanship, his honesty and his patriotism. But when McClellan takes his stand upon a cowardly peace platform we are at a loss how to follow him and defend him. This the General has not yet done, and we hope that he will never be foolish enough to do it. We advise and urge him to come out boldly and declare that his only platform is his past record as a Union general, and that his sentiments are those expressed in his letter from Harrison's Landing and his oration at West Point. If he hesitates to do this he is lost. There must be no prevarication nor equivocation. The rotten Chicago platform must be kicked to pieces and McClellan's own platform substituted. He had better a thousand fold decline the nomination than to accept it upon such conditions as those imposed by the Convention. The Chicago platform invites defeat, and it must be broken up, either by McClellan himself or by the voice of the people at the polls.

We candidly and sincerely believe that the peace copperheads at the North do not desire the election of McClellan any more than the Southern secessionists desired the election of Douglas or Breckenridge in 1860. They bitterly opposed McClellan at Chicago, and openly denounced him as a tyrant and a usurper. Finally they accepted him, upon condition that they should have the platform and the Vice President. But even now the copperheads are not earnest in his support. Like the rebels, they want to see Lincoln re-elected. There is no saying but that Mr. Lincoln may be elected by a small majority, and in that event the copperheads intend to raise a revolution at the North. This they can very readily do if the people do not beware of the trap. Suppose the election to be decided by only a few thousand votes, then the democratic minority will be nearly as strong as the republican majority. In fact the minority will be stronger; for the democrats will fight, while the abolitionists will not; and so a thousand democrats are more than equal to two thousand abolition republicans. What, then, is to hinder a revolution? Is it the army? The moment the army is withdrawn to put down an insurrection here the rebels will come out of their intrenchments and capture Washington. This, as we understand it, is part of the copperhead plan, and if successful it will put an end to the government and the country.

That this idea of a vast Northern conspiracy between the copperheads and the rebels is no mere bugbear is evident from the fact that the Chicago Convention, instead of adjourning *sine die*, as conventions usually do, adjourned to meet again at the call of the Executive Committee. This is equivalent to the organization of a revolutionary body. Our merchants and capitalists so consider it; for they are closing up business, shipping their goods back to Europe, turning their property into gold, sending their money across the water, and in every way preparing to leave the country as soon as the revolution begins. These movements are not to be lightly considered. They mean mischief, and show that trouble is brewing. Gen. McClellan can avert that trouble and restore public confidence if he have the pluck and sagacity to ignore the Chicago platform and come out boldly as a Jackson democrat on the platform of his past record. Then he will have a fair chance of election, because he will not be bound to a cowardly policy if he be elected. But what could Washington himself do if he were pledged to negotiate for "an immediate cessation of hostilities?" The Chicago platform will encourage the rebels to hold out until election, and, as things stand at present, the peace copperheads have promised them one of two things: either the re-election of Lincoln and a Northern insurrection—in which case the rebels will have the upperhand of us; or, in the event of McClellan's election, "an immediate cessation of hostilities," in which case the rebels will have everything their own way. Gen. McClellan can destroy these schemes by framing his own platform out of sound Union timber and being elected upon it. Then a Northern insurrection will be impossible; and, if the people do their duty in the meantime, there will be no rebellion left to make terms with, and no Jeff. Davis in existence to receive an offer for "an immediate cessation of hostilities." This is as great a crisis as that at Harrison's Landing or at Antietam. Let Little Mac reflect deeply and act wisely.

THE EXTRAVAGANCE OF THE DAY.—For four years we have been engaged in a war which has greatly taxed the resources of the country, cost the lives of hundreds of thousands, and entailed the expenditure of an immense amount of treasure. Still the metropolis has given no signs of this. More than ever brilliant and gay, New York society revels in amusements of every description with an ever increasing zest. The extravagance of the so-styled *beau monde* knows no bounds. High prices do not affect the newly enriched, nor cannot subdue shoddy. Ladies now sweep along Broadway with dresses which cost hundreds of dollars; their bonnets alone represent a price which a few years since would more than have paid for an entire outfit. Silks, satins and laces have risen in price to an extent which would seem beyond the means of any save millionaires, and yet the sale of these articles is greater than ever. The wonder of it all is where do people procure the means to indulge in the frightful extravagancies of the day.

This war may last years yet, and, to judge from what has occurred up to the present time, prices will increase as the war lasts. With the decrease of the value of our currency the luxuries above mentioned will increase in price, until it will cost a fortune to equip a lady in such style as may now be witnessed at every step on Broadway. In the South the ladies, who are by far more bitter secessionists than the men, have long since discarded the use of silks and satins. They wear cotton goods, and, we dare say, appear quite as pretty in them. With us the same sentiment has not as yet obtained. A few ladies of fashion, who were anxious to get up a sensation, did, it is true, make last season a show of a dress reform; but then the whole affair was a humbug. The ladies got up meetings where they wore cheap dresses, but covered them with laces and diamonds. They went to these meetings in splendid carriages, with liveried servants in waiting upon them, and, by the contrast with the object they seemed to have in view, made themselves and the subject ridiculous.

What the ladies we refer to undertook as a pastime will, ere long, become a matter of not play at a reform in dress. The time for extravagance is rapidly drawing to a close. Economy will force itself upon the consideration of all. Even shoddy will have to succumb to high prices if this fearful civil strife is to continue much longer. To urge that what seems inevitable should be met half way is, we know, labor lost. The people will not reform until dire necessity forces them to such a course, and it is merely as a chronicle of the day that we point out the wasteful extravagance of the metropolis.

PARTY PRESS AMENITIES.—The *Tribune* says that General McClellan is a traitor to his country and has offered his sword to fight for the rebels. The *World* says the White House at Washington is "filled with infamy." Who are responsible for such atrocious charges in a contest that should be conducted in a mild and gentlemanly spirit? Greeley, with his seventeen joints, is responsible for the malignant abuse of McClellan. Barlow, with his mining stocks and gold speculations in Wall street, and Belmont, the agent of the Rothschilds, are the financial controllers of the *World*, and responsible for the vileness of the Bohemians in that concern. We advise these gentlemen to overlook their organs and make them decent, or take the responsibility of the filth and grossness that besmear their columns.

CAUTION.—We had occasion a few days since to caution the public against the operations of a Mr. Joyce. We find another advertisement from him to the following effect in the Boston *Herald* of Sept. 1:—

THE NEW YORK NEWSPAPERS FORWARDED FROM NEW YORK DAILY AT GREATLY REDUCED PRICES.—Terms for one year, payable in advance:—For the HERALD $7, instead of $10; *Tribune*, $7; *Times*, $7; *World*, $7; *Daily News*, $7; *Evening Post*, $9; *Evening Express*, $6 50. Address, with remittance, to A. Joyce, No. 62 West Thirty-sixth street, New York.

We repeat that this Joyce has no authority to offer the HERALD for sale, and that it is impossible to furnish this journal at the prices named in his advertisement. People should, therefore, take care how they bite at the bait held out to them.

THE GREAT PEACE NEGOTIATORS.—The Rev. Jaquess & Co. (Gilmore and Greeley being the company) are in a sad bother at being repudiated by Lincoln's organ in Washington, edited by the handsome man. The great peace negotiators will doubtless relieve their feelings as follows:—The Rev. Jaques will drone out a solemn sermon on the subject; Gilmore will indite a long and tedious article to the *Atlantic*, and Greeley will whine and snuffle through a column and a half.

LINCOLN OBSTINATE.—If Mr. Lincoln does not throw out the rotten timber in his Cabinet he will find that even his friends will not support him. He must comply with the demands of the Baltimore Convention.

City Intelligence.

FIRE IN TENTH AVENUE.—About nine o'clock last night a fire broke out in the packing house of Lippincott & Martin, No. 511 Tenth avenue, near Forty-second street. The firemen were promptly on the ground; but before the fire was extinguished damage to the extent of about $10,000 was done; said to be insured. The origin of the fire is at present unknown.

FIRE IN BROADWAY.—Between one and two o'clock on Friday morning a fire broke out in a tailor's store, No. 1,348 Broadway, corner of Thirty-sixth street. The contents of the store were destroyed. Loss about $500; insured for $800 in the Globe Insurance Company, and owned by Marks Witkoski. The upper part of the building is occupied by Mrs. Cox. Damage to her furniture about $200; no insurance. The building is owned by General T. A. Davis. It is damaged about $400, and fully insured. The origin of the fire is under investigation by Fire Marshal Baker.

SHERIDAN.

Mr. Francis C. Long's Despatches.

HEADQUARTERS, FIRST CAVALRY DIVISION,
NEAR HARPER'S FERRY, Va., August 27, 1864.

AN APOLOGY.

Having been with the Third Cavalry division, I have not been able to give a correct account of the operations of the First until the present moment, and, although a few days have elapsed since the reconnoissance occurred, I trust it will not be devoid of interest to the readers of the HERALD.

THE ADVANCE OF MERRITT'S DIVISION.

The First division marched from its camp, at Shepherdstown, at seven o'clock A. M. on Thursday, the 25th instant, on the Winchester road, General Custer taking the advance, followed by the brigades of Colonels Cesnola and Gibbs. At Walper's crossroads the division met Wilson's command, as I stated in a former despatch. The First and Second brigades massed on the right of the road, while the Third dismounted, leaving their horses in the road. The crossroads mentioned were reached at eleven o'clock A. M. Soon after Custer's brigade moved out towards Karneysville, followed by the reserve brigade, while Colonel Cesnola, with the Second, advanced through the fields on the right in a line parallel with Custer.

THE REBEL ADVANCE MET.

About three hundred yards from the railroad (the Baltimore and Ohio) we met the enemy's advance, which was coming up the road evidently to meet us. They were driven back about half a mile into the woods. Custer then dismounted his command and went into the woods after the enemy, and soon became hotly engaged. The Third division soon came up and formed on his left, as I have previously stated. The other two brigades formed in the rear, facing to the right, to hold the Winchester road and guard against a flank movement. Ransom's battery was put in position a little to the left, and shelled the woods, briskly firing over a part of General McIntosh's line. Custer engaged the enemy for about an hour, when he was ordered to fall back, which he did, the reserve brigade covering the rear, and the First United States cavalry being deployed as skirmishers to allow the dismounted men to retire. Major James Starr, with his regiment (Sixth Pennsylvania), also formed in close column of squadrons near the wood, with the First New York dragoons upon his left, until the dismounted men could leave the field; after which Cesnola, with his brigade, retired, followed by Custer a little to the right. The enemy seeing that we were retiring, advanced rapidly, but were gallantly met and held in check while the First New York dragoons and Sixth Pennsylvania retired to the railroad, followed by the skirmishers. At the railroad the two regiments mentioned broke into column of fours and retired under a sharp fire from the left, the enemy having taken possession of the ground where Wilson's division had lately been formed.

THE PLACE TO BE HELD.

The division fell back, skirmishing sharply, Captain A. P. Morrow, with a squadron of the Sixth Pennsylvania, covering our left flank until we reached a point within a mile of Shepherdstown. At this point orders were received from General Merill to hold this place until Custer could establish a picket line Soon after the First United States was relieved by the First New York dragoons, who then joined the brigade—Major Smith having orders to hold the position if possible; but if too hotly pressed, to break across the country to the Charlestown road.

THE ATTACK—CUSTER CUT OFF.

The regiment was soon attacked in heavy force, both in front and on both flanks, and to avoid capture Major Smith was obliged to retire through the town, and down the Charlestown road for about half a mile, the enemy following with infantry in the immediate rear and cavalry on the right flank. Here the regiment halted and formed in line, and succeeded in holding the enemy until General Custer came up. Meanwhile Colonels Gibbs and Cesnola had moved on some distance towards Halltown, leaving a considerable interval between themselves and General Custer, which the enemy took advantage of, and threw a column of his infantry between them, thus effectually severing the latter from his division.

RANSOM'S BATTERY ENGAGED.

Hearing the firing in the rear, Custer turned the head of his column about and went back to see what was the matter, and found the rebels in the act of charging upon Ransom's battery, who was gallantly defending himself, discharging his guns into the ranks of the advancing rebels as fast as they could be shotted. When support arrived Ransom removed his battery some two hundred yards to the rear, to the crest of a hill which commanded the whole field, when he again unlimbered and commenced a fierce fire, under cover of which the brigade was formed on either side of the battery.

THE ENEMY.

The position being defended with so much determination, the enemy appeared to waver and hesitate. Finally he sent a column of infantry off upon our left to take possession of the Harper's Ferry road, and another at the same time on our right to bar our retreat to Shepherdstown ford.

ESCAPE OF CUSTER.

The moment was a critical one for the brigade, as it was almost surrounded; but, fortunately, Gen. Custer had already perceived the intention of the enemy, and without delay he hastened with his gallant little band to the river, the First New York dragoons taking the advance, followed by the battery, with a regiment on the left as flankers, to protect the column from a sudden [illegible] rear, taking the hottest part of the pursuing enemy's fire. The brigade crossed the Potomac without difficulty, and encamped for the night midway between the ford and Sharpsburg, which is about two miles distant, leaving a heavy picket force at the river.

GENERAL AVERILL

was engaged with the enemy further up the river, as the booming of his cannons could be distinctly heard. Learning of Custer's proximity, he sent to him requesting his co-operation, to which he (Custer) readily assented. Hearing firing in the direction of Williamsport, the brigade moved out on the Hagerstown road, intending to go to Averill's support. But at Sharpsburg a despatch was received from General Merritt ordering the brigade to join the division at Harper's Ferry. Custer instantly started for Harper's Ferry, compliant to the order; but he had not marched his command far when a fresh order came for him to remain with his command at Antietam ford until further orders. Accordingly he repaired to that place, where he still remains.

The First New York dragoons, which belongs to the reserve brigade, with the First, having been cut off from the column with Custer, left him at Antietam ford and rejoined its brigade near Harper's Ferry yesterday afternoon, and this, with a list of the casualties, brings me to the end of the reconnoissance.

HARPER'S FERRY, August 28, 1864.

COLONEL GIBBS' RECONNOISSANCE.

Colonel Gibbs, with the Second brigade, went out on a reconnoissance yesterday, but did not meet any considerable force of the enemy. The brigade broke into columns of regiments and scoured the country pretty thoroughly for a number of miles. Captain Sweitzer, with the First United States cavalry, charged through Shepherdstown, which was occupied by a small force of rebels, killing two of them and wounding and capturing a number more. The citizens of Shepherdstown say that the rebels suffered severely in their engagement at Kearneysville with our cavalry. Two colonels are known to have been killed. The First division started on an expedition of some kind this morning, leaving their wagons and pack trains behind, and taking subsistence for three days with them.

Mr. Theodore C. Wilson's Despatch.

FALLING WATERS, August 31—Evening.

GENERAL AVERILL'S MOVEMENTS—MARTINSBURG.

For two days past General Averill has been demonstrating against the enemy, feinting, with a view of facilitating the execution of the plans and the carrying out of the orders of General Sheridan. To-day we attacked the enemy on three different roads for the purpose of making him develop his strength. On the Charlestown and Gerrardstown roads there was nothing but very light skirmishes, while on the Winchester pike there was all that we had hoped for and desired. On this road, early in the morning, we attacked the enemy's outposts and drove his pickets in upon their reserves, and towards Darksville. In the afternoon, again, we made another attack on the same line, when the rebels placed a division of infantry into line and advanced, no doubt to ascertain the strength of the party so persistently annoying them. Between one and two o'clock the enemy's line had reached the outskirts of Martinsburg. At this time we opened fire from two sections of Wier's battery—Battery D, Fifth United States artillery. Soon after the enemy returned the fire from four guns, planted on an eminence somewhat to the right of Martinsburg from the rebel position. At this time the rebel infantry line pressed our right and centre, where was deployed a portion of Colonel Jas. M. Schoomaker's brigade. On our left, where was stationed Colonel Powell's brigade, there was not so heavy a pressure. The shells from both the rebel and the Union guns passed over the town without striking any of the houses in it.

Some of the scenes and incidents of the occasion were of rather an amusing character. The United States mail coach made its exit out of town, full of passengers, while the guns on both sides were booming, and at a rate of speed highly favorable to a flying trip between Martinsburg and Hagerstown.

The Press Despatch.

CHARLESTOWN, Va., Sept. 2, 1864.

Reconnoissances have established the fact that Early has not left, and has no intention of leaving, the valley. His headquarters are at Bunker Hill, half way between Martinsburg and Winchester. He is busily engaged in repairing and putting up a telegraph line, and he has already telegraphic communication with Richmond from this side of Woodstock.

Early is also receiving reinforcements, and Fitzhugh Lee is known to have received five hundred horses for his cavalry, which is said to number seven thousand.

There is a regular stage from Winchester to Staunton, which runs every day, and several officers and soldiers are receiving short furloughs to go home and return to Winchester, which does not look as though the enemy intend leaving the valley.

Music at the Park.

The Park Commissioners announce that there will be music on the Mall to-day, commencing at four o'clock in the afternoon, if the weather is fine, by the Park Band, under the leadership of H. B. Dodworth.

THE DRAFT.

Official Despatch from the Secretary of War.

Our Naval Enlistments to be Credited on Our Quota.

Grant Asks but One Hundred Thousand Men to Give the Rebellion Its Finishing Blow, &c., &c., &c.

Secretary Stanton to General Dix.

WAR DEPARTMENT, WASHINGTON, Sept. 2, 1864.

To Major General DIX, New York:—

It is ascertained with reasonable certainty that the naval and other credits required by the act of Congress will amount to about 200,000, including New York, which has not been reported yet to the Department; so that the President's call of July 18 is practically reduced to 300,000 men, to meet and take the place of—

First—The new enlistments in the navy;

Second—The casualties of battle, sickness, prisoners and desertion, and

Third—The hundred days troops and all others going out by expiration of service this fall.

One hundred thousand new troops, promptly furnished, are all that Gen. Grant asks for the capture of Richmond and to give a finishing blow to the rebel armies yet in the field. The residue of the call would be adequate for garrisons in forts and to guard all the lines of communication and supply, free the country from guerillas, give security to trade, protect commerce and travel, and establish peace, order and tranquility in every State.

EDWIN M. STANTON, Secretary of War.

No Orders Yet Received for the Enforcement of the Draft on the Appointed Day in This City.

Provost Marshal General Hays has not yet received any orders for the enforcement of the draft on Monday next; but something relative to the matter will probably be known to-day. Every arrangement, however, has been made for the drawing to take place on the above day, should the authorities at Washington give the necessary instructions.

Preparations for the Draft in Brooklyn.

The Provost Marshal of the Third Congressional district, which consists of a large portion of the city of Brooklyn, is now fully prepared for the draft, which is expected to take place on Monday next. A large number of persons, physically disabled, have thus far been exempted by the surgeon, and all others not liable are requested to present themselves before eleven o'clock to-day. After that no person will be examined with a view to exemption until after the draft.

The total number of men required under the last call in the Third district is 3,574. Of this number nine hundred and forty-five only have been enlisted and accredited to the quota, leaving 2,629 men still to be raised. The following figures show the deficiency in each ward:—

Ward.	No. of Men.	Ward.	No. of Men.
1	77	11	380
2	247	13	423
3	13	15	249
4	191	19	104
5	390	20	283
7	322		
Total			2,629

At a meeting of committees of the joint Boards of Aldermen and Supervisors, held yesterday morning, Supervisor Bloom and Alderman Turton were appointed a committee to proceed to Washington for the purpose of procuring, if possible, either a postponement of the draft or securing a furlough of thirty days for drafted men, in order to give time to make a revision of the enrolment lists, which are claimed to be excessive. They are likewise to obtain credit for recruits enlisted in the navy prior to February, 1864. Hon. Messrs. Odell and Kalbfleisch will probably accompany the committee.

Increase of the Bounty in Jersey City.

A [illegible] City was convened last night, at the City Hall, for the purpose of considering the subject of bounties.

A communication was received from Mayor Cleveland setting forth that a new regiment is now being raised in the district, which could be readily filled if the same inducements were offered in Jersey City as are offered in Newark and Bergen county, and recommended that the bounty for volunteers be increased to five hundred or six hundred dollars for one year men.

Alderman Gafney offered the following preamble and resolution which was adopted:—

Whereas, Other counties, cities and townships in our State are paying higher bounties than our city; therefore

Resolved, That to place our city in as favorable a position as other localities, the Committee on Enlistments be authorized to offer such bounty as they may deem expedient, not to exceed six hundred dollars, for one year volunteers or substitutes, to the extent of the quota.

POLITICAL AFFAIRS.

The Proposed Withdrawal of Lincoln and Fremont.

OUR SPECIAL ST. LOUIS DESPATCH.

ST. LOUIS, Sept. 2, 1864.

A call is being privately circulated for a mass convention at Cincinnati on the 28th of this month, with the design of bringing sufficient pressure to bear to secure the withdrawal of Lincoln and Fremont and the nomination of a consolidated ticket. The call is without signature, but the movement is understood to be in the Chase interest.

McClellan and Pendleton Ratification Meeting in this City.

The Democratic Union Association, with the aid of the various county organizations and McClellan clubs, will hold a mass meeting at Union square on Thursday evening next, the 8th instant. A number of the Chicago delegates from this and other States will be here to address the meeting, including Governor Seymour, Governor Bigler, of Pennsylvania; Senator Weller, of California; Hon. James Guthrie, of Kentucky; Hon. Wilson Shannon, Senator Buckalew, of Pennsylvania, and a large number of prominent men from all parts of the Union. There will be eight stands erected around the square and immense preparations made for the reception of the distinguished gentlemen expected.

Intended McClellan Mass Meeting in Brooklyn.

The democracy of King's county are making arrangements for a grand McClellan mass meeting, to be held some time next week. The time has not yet been designated. The Union Democratic General Committee have placed a fine banner and transparency in front of their headquarters at Montague Hall, bearing the names of the candidates nominated by the Chicago Convention. At a late meeting of the committee a resolution was unanimously adopted endorsing the candidates and the platform.

The Brooklyn Delegates to the Republican State Convention.

The King's county republicans have selected the following delegates in the several Assembly districts designated, to represent the party in the State Convention at Syracuse:—

First District.—Delegates—Charles W. Goddard, Alonzo H. Gale, John McDermott. Alternates—D. C. Winslow, George W. Stilwell, John L. Spader.

Second District.—Delegates—John Cashow, W. S. Gove, Jas. Johnson. Alternates—Benjamin Haskell, J. Walter Stoops, C. M. Felt.

Third District.—Seth B. Cole was elected delegate, after which the Convention adjourned.

Fourth District.—Delegates—Henry Quigley, George J. Hardy, Wm. W. Halleck. Alternates—A. G. Becade, Sidney Sanderson, Dennis Downey.

Fifth District.—Delegates—Charles L. Benedict, M. H. Roberts, A. F. Campbell. Alternates—John Truslow, Francis C. Kirby, Wm. G. Boggs.

In the Sixth district no nominations were made.

Seventh District.—Delegates—G. H. Rose, D. Maujer, Wm. Cobb. Alternate—George W. Platt.

McClellan Ratification in Philadelphia.

PHILADELPHIA, Sept. 2, 1864.

The first public demonstration in this city in favor of the Chicago nominees was made to-night at the Continental theatre. The building was crowded, and speeches were made by Messrs. Charles Ingersoll, Richard Vaux, Charlton Burnet, and others. The meeting was very enthusiastic, and adjourned to meet the Keystone Club, which is expected to arrive from Chicago at midnight. The procession was quite large, notwithstanding the short notice given of the expected arrival of the Club. Preparations are making for a ratification meeting at an early day.

Base Ball.

MUTUAL VS. ATLANTIC.

The grand match between these two crack clubs—the former of New York and the latter of Brooklyn—will take place on Monday next, at the Capitoline Ball Grounds, Bedford, L. I. The interest in this game among the ball playing fraternity is at the highest pitch. As this is a championship game, there is little doubt that thousands will be present to witness the contest.

LYNCHBURG VIRGINIAN.

NOTICE.—The cross mark appended to the names of certain subscribers indicates that the term of which they subscribed will soon expire. They are thus notified in time to re new their subscription if desired.

RAGS WANTED.—The highest market price will be paid at this Office for Clean Cotton Rags. They will be purchased in any quantity.

Printing Presses for Sal .—We have an Adams Power Press, and a No. 5 Washington Press, (the latter nearly new) that are offered for sale. Apply at the *Virginian* Office.

TELEGRAPHIC.—All the Richmond papers, except the Whig, have withdrawn from the Press Association, and no longer receive telegraphic dispatches. The Virginian still receives them from every quarter of the Confederacy, and will continue to do so, though at an enormous expenditure of money.

MAIL CONTRACTS.—We are informed that the mail contractor between Bonsack's depot and the Greenbrier White Sulphur Springs has failed to deliver the mail except about once a month, since the raid on this place. The contract requires the mail to be carried tri-weekly, except in the months of July, August and September, during which time it is to be carried daily. The people in that section are without mail facilities, and we would, as requested, call the attention of the Postmaster General to the fact, and trust some arrangements may be made to deliver their mails in future.

THE DEATH OF GEN. MORGAN.—It adds to the regrets which the death of Gen. Morgan has caused to know that he fell a victim to treachery, and did not fall in fair and open fight. A woman, at whose house he was spending the night—a Mrs. Williams, said to be a native of this city—rode to the nearest camp of the enemy, and informed them of his whereabouts. Eager on securing so illustrious a prize, they lost no time in repairing to the spot, surrounded the house, and, while thus in their power, the noble chief received his death wound through the heart. The enemy were afterwards driven out of the town. The false creature who thus, in violation of all the soft and gentle promptings of her sex, has brought the blood of our princely hero upon her head, deserves the execrations of friend and foe, the ceaseless lashings of conscience—if she has one—and anathemas for time and eternity.

FROM THE VALLEY—A RAID BROKEN UP.—A correspondent of the Charlottesville Chronicle gives the following: On Thursday Anderson's troops relieved ours in front of Charlestown, and Early with his forces moved to the left to Shepherdstown. About midway we encountered all the cavalry force of the enemy, who had started out—splendidly equipped—to make a grand raid behind us. They told the citizens in Shepherdstown as they passed, that they intended to destroy our reserve ordnance and other trains at Winchester, and then pass up the Valley to Staunton, destroying everything as they went.—They were in great spirits, and spoke confidently of success—saying that Early would be compelled to leave the Valley at once, and stay out of it. They stumbled on us unexpectedly, and their pride had a tumble. We smashed them up considerably, and drove them partly across the river, and partly back to Harper's Ferry. So ended that chapter very luckily. Poor Arrington, (General R.'s Aid) was wounded in this affair, just above the knee. The bone was badly crushed.

SIEGE OF CHARLESTON—EXPLOSION OF A TORPEDO.—About nine o'clock on Sunday night, (says the Courier of August 30th,) a terrific explosion, which shook the buildings in this city, took place. Many supposed it to be a two hundred pounder Parrott time fuse shell. It appears, however, that about nine o'clock some musketry firing was heard at Fort Sumter. Upon examination Capt. Huguenin discovered that the firing was about two hundred yards from the fort, in the direction of Fort Johnson. The firing continued a few seconds only, when three Yankee barges were seen coming in towards the West face. Col. Lewis, with a detachment of the Thirty-second Georgia, mounted the parapet and opened a fire of small arms upon the parties, but had not fired more than one or two rounds before a tremendous explosion occurred about thirty feet from the West face of the fort, near the wharf. After the explosion the enemy were seen in rapid retreat towards Morris Island. Our men kept up the fire of small arms until the enemy had gotten entirely out of sight.

The Yankees it seems had floated down a torpedo from the direction of fort Johnson. The torpedo exploded near the wharf of the fort. No damage was done to the works. The shock was distinctly perceptible all over the fort, and some of the officers on the Southwest angle were knocked down.

Col. Wm. E. Peters, wounded at the surprise at Moorefield, has reached this city.—He is doing well.

Col. Ro. W. Withers, of the 45th Va. regiment, was badly wounded at or near Shepherdstown recently—shot through the lungs. Col. W., is a citizen of this county.

A friend is in great distress over the loss of a favorite dog. Whoever may now "hold and possess" the animal will confer an act of real humanity by returning it to its sorrowing owner. He advertises his bereavement in another column.

STANTON has commenced telegraphing bulletins to Dix again. The following is a specimen:

"One hundred thousand new troops, promptly furnished, is all that Grant asks for the capture of Richmond, and to give a finishing blow to the rebel armies yet in the field.

The residue of the call would be adequate for garrisons in forts and cities, and to guard all the lines of communication and supplies, free the country from guerrillas, give security to trade, protect commerce and travel, and establish peace, order, and tranquility in every State."

THE SITUATION AT PETERSBURG.—Grant turned loose his big guns with fury on Petersburg again Sunday night, and our batteries replied with equal spirit. The Express says the bombardment was terrific, and the cannonading was heard to a great distance in the country. Many citizens could not resist the belief that a general engagement was pending, and quickly enrobing themselves, hurried into the streets to await the result. At one o'clock, however, the sound of the last gun had ceased to reverberate, and all was quiet on the lines, save an occasional discharge of musketry from the opposing pickets.

We are pleased to hear that there were no casualties on our side in the trenches or in the city, from this fierce discharge of big guns.

Monday afternoon early, the Express adds, there were several demonstrations at different points on our extreme right, in the vicinity of the Weldon Railroad, but beyond a little cannonading and musketry firing, we could not learn that it amounted to anything. The enemy evidently has a hankering after the South Side Railroad, but is afraid to venture, after the sad experiences which he has been recently undergoing.

It is most probable that the next fight will be for the possession of this road.

FROM THE VALLEY.

There is very little authentic news from the Valley. The accounts are confused and contradictory. The Baltimore American thus sums up the latest intelligence of the situation in the Valley:

In the first place Early has not left, and has no intention of leaving the Valley.—His headquarters are at Bunker Hill, half way between Martinsburg and Winchester.

He is busily engaged in repairing and putting up the telegraph wires, and already has telegraphic communication with Richmond from this side of Woodstock.

Early is receiving reinforcements, and Fitzhugh Lee is known to have received five hundred fresh horses for his cavalry, who are said to number 7,000.

There is a regular stage from Winchester to Staunton, which runs every day, and several officers and soldiers are receiving short furloughs to go home and return to Winchester, which does not look as though they intended leaving the Valley.

NEW RIVER AND OTTER BRIDGES.

EDITORS VIRGINIAN:—Articles have appeared in several of the papers in this State on the rapidity with which the Va. and Tenn. Railroad was again put in order after the extensive damages done to it by the enemy on the advances of Crook and Hunter in May and June last, which do not justice to all the parties concerned.

New River bridge, 800 feet long, was rebuilt in 19 days, from timber standing in the forest, by the engineer forces of the department of West Va., and the railroad forces jointly, all under the direction of Capt. R. C. McCalla, C. S. engineer, by virtue of an order from the brave Gen. W. E. Jones, then commanding department as a military necessity. Maj. Goodwyn, Superintendent of the railroad, neither planned or directed that work.

In the first place, extensive facilities had to be established, for the transhipment of freight, passengers, &c. across the broad and rapid river. This engaged the engineer forces nearly a week's time. They then built two-thirds of the bridge in the balance of the nineteen days, while the railroad forces built the other third in the entire time.

Nor is the entire credit for rebuilding the Otter bridges due the railroad company and their superintendent. It is true that they exercised, with great energy, the lesson they had learned at New River on bridge building. Besides, Capt. McCalla, with his veteran engineer troops, was there also, "boiling in the hot sun," to the extent of any one, none the less useful again, with his skillful appliances than with the heavy blows of his large mechanical and laboring force, and teams, &c. WEST.

THE REASON OF McCLELLAN'S REMOVAL FROM THE ARMY OFFICIALLY DECLARED.

At the great meeting in New York, a few days since, Hon Eli. P. Norton said:

The administration would not have denounced him if he had merely been a soldier but Geo B McClellan had his own ideas as an American citizen. He did not believe in abolition, confiscation, and a war against the population of the South. Within two weeks, he (Mr Norton) knew that Mr McClellan had been offered the highest command in the army, if he would give in his adhesion to the policy of the Administration. He refused. Governor Dennison, of Ohio, who presided at the Baltimore Convention, which nominated Abraham Lincoln, had declared, of his personal knowledge, that McClellan was removed, not from any doubt of his military ability, but because the Administration believed the democratic party would make him their next candidate for President. Governor Dennison made the remarks in his (Mr Norton's) presence.

LATEST BY TELEGRAPH

Reports of the Press Association.

Entered according to Act of Congress, in the year 1863, by J. S. THRASHER, in the Clerk's Office of the District Court of the Confederate States in the Northern District of Georgia.

FROM NORTHERN GEORGIA—WHEELER'S OPERATIONS—&c., &c.

MACON, Sept. 6th.

No material change in the situation at the Georgia front.

It is rumored that the enemy are repairing the Railroad and advancing, but this is not credited.

A courier from Rome reports that Wheeler destroyed the tunnel at Tunnel Hill, several days ago. The last heard from him at headquarters, was that he was operating on the Nashville & Chattanooga Railroad, this side of Murfreesboro.

After a drought of six weeks, we had a refreshing rain to-day.

Governor Brown issued a Proclamation to-day, setting apart the 15th inst., as a day of fasting and prayer, and calling upon the people and army to observe it.

2D DISPATCH.

RICHMOND, Sep. 7.

Gen. Hood reports officially that the enemy have withdrawn from his front, retreating to Atlanta.

3D DESPATCH.

MACON, 7th.

The enemy continues to retire his main force on the M and W Road trains to Atlanta. We drove them out of the Junction yesterday and retook a good many wounded prisoners.

Our loss from all causes in the battles of last week is now ascertained to have been 1500.

FROM PETERSBURG.

PETERSBURG, Sep. 7.

This morning Lomax's North Carolina pickets surprised, by a flank movement, and captured 12 infantry Videtts, near the Davis House on the Weldon Railroad. Nothing else of interest.

SHERMAN'S OFFICIAL REPORT OF THE CAPTURE OF ATLANTA.

The Herald of the 6th received.

Stanton telegraphs to Dix Sherman's official report.

Sherman withdrew from Atlanta and made a break on the West Point Railroad, reaching a good position on the 30th from which to strike the Macon Road. The right commanded by Howard near Jonesboro, left under Scholfied, near Rough and Ready and the centre under Thomas, is at Couch's Station. Howard drove the enemy from their position near Jonesboro, after a hard fight.

Sherman broke the railroad from Rough and Ready to Howard's left, throwing his whole army between Jonesboro and Atlanta, and made a general attack on the enemy at Jonesboro Thursday, the 14th corps, General Jeff Davis, carrying the works splendidly, taking ten guns and 1,000 prisoners.

In the night the rebels retreated to Lovejoy's Station, the Federals following. Hood finding Sherman between him and a considerable portion of his army blew up his magazine and left, when the 20th corps occupied the place.

Sherman says his losses will not exceed 1200. Have over 300 rebels dead and 250 wounded and over 1500 prisoners.

Slocum, under date of the 3d, telegraphs that the rebels destroyed 7 locomotives, 81 cars loaded with ammunition, small arms and stores and left 14 pieces artillery and a large number small arms in Atlanta.

The Herald says a division of rebel cavalry under Lomax attacked a portion of Sheridan's near Bunker Hill Saturday and resulted in their being defeated and driven 5 miles towards Winchester.

The rebel artillery barely escaped capture.

The Herald says the victory at Atlanta has put down the rebellion, though the mountains of Virginia may be unpleasant to travel in for years to come.

Great rejoicing in Burlington, N. J., Utica, Auburn, and New York city, because exempted from the draft.

Gold two hundred and forty and a half.

[We received two pages of foolscap from Senatobia last night, giving *news* from Northern papers of the 31st ult. and 1st inst., nearly a week *older* than we have already had. The press reporter at that point must have just waked up from a long nap. We will not inflict his stale rehash upon our readers, though we will have to foot the bill. Unless the Senatobia reporter can do better, we advise him to resign and join the army. Will Col. Thrasher look after him? His two pages contain one bare item which has not before been published, which is, that Kirby Smith and Price have invested Little Rock.]

The World

CAMPAIGN EDITION.

NINE NUMBERS. NEW-YORK, TUESDAY, SEPTEMBER 20, 1864. NO. 3.

THE GRAND RATIFICATION

Democratic New-York Beating Herself.

A Hundred Thousand Patriots in Convention.

A SEA OF HUMANITY

Oratory and Music, Patriotism and Pyrotechny, Torch-Light Processions, and Salvos of Artillery.

EVERYBODY FOR "LITTLE MAC."

The Tocsin of Doom for the Shoddy Party.

LINCOLN'S KNELL RUNG

How the Metropolis Greets the Nation.

THE BEGINNING OF THE END

The largest meeting in point of numbers, the most magnificent in point of display, and the most enthusiastic in view of the zest, unanimity, and universality of the popular expressions of approbation, ever held in this city, took place on Saturday evening, at Union Square, pursuant to the suggestion of the Chicago Convention, in celebration of the anniversary of the adoption of the Constitution, the anniversary of the battle of Antietam, and, primarily, in ratification of McClellan for President. The demonstration comprised all the attributes of a great meeting, and each feature was especially developed to its fullest capacity, so that no part of [illegible] details, was a failure.

To the hundred thousand of our citizens who witnessed the scene the vivid recollection which they have of it cannot be enhanced by anything that can be written concerning it; and to those who did not witness it, it is impossible to convey any adequate idea of it by a description.

Ten platforms were erected around the inclosed space of Union square, facing outward upon the open street, making an entire circuit of the square and opposite respectively to lower Broadway, the Maison Dorée, Fourteenth street on the west side, Fifteenth street, Sixteenth street, Seventeenth street; and upper Broadway, the Everett House, Fourth avenue, Sixteenth street, on the east side, and the Washington monument. The arrangements for illumination and decoration were appropriate and tasteful, and on the most elaborate scale. Each of the stands was hung with banners and furnished with lights, and each contained on its front some extract from McClellan's letter, thus forming a succession of patriotic mottoes around the square. Around the whole circuit from stand to stand, and from lamp post to lamp-post, was stretched a line upon which were hung countless brilliant Chinese lanterns colored red, white, and blue, and most of them bearing the illuminated motto: "McClellan and Liberty."

The excitement of the scene commenced soon after dusk, when the people began to assemble in front of the stands and in front of the Maison Dorée. An hour after the speakers began to take their places on the platforms, the plain lights, and tri-drummond lights, plain lamps, and tri-colored lanterns, were lit, fireworks began to be sent up and the ward processions began to appear on the ground. The crowd then rapidly augmented and continued to increase to ponderous proportions until 9½ o'clock. The whole male population of the city seemed gathered into the space designated for the meeting.

The cars found it impossible to pass through it, and the stages were obliged to take circuitous routes, and even then were often stopped to await the passage of processions. At one time there was a solid mass of human beings filling the whole vast space on every side of the square, a scene never before witnessed in New-York. From the stands, a sea of swaying faces, interspersed with lanterns, banners, and mottoes, made clearly visible by the illuminations of the lanterns and the glare of fireworks, was seen on every hand. Passage could hardly be made for the ward processions that passed with trucks, firing cannon, ringing bells, and shouting. The crowd surged into the surrounding streets, upper and lower Broadway, Fourth avenue, University Place, Fourteenth, and all the surrounding streets. Ladies and children lingered upon the outskirts of the crowd, but dared not enter it, because of its density. At the lower end of the square a young lady, unable to get through, was badly crushed, and had to be carried out by friends.

Many houses, stores, and public buildings in various parts of the city were illuminated. As processions passed, ladies, with McClellan badges, waved their handkerchiefs or McClellan flags from the windows. On Union square many of the houses and hotels were illuminated from the inside, the windows and every available space for observation being occupied by ladies who waved their handkerchiefs, and, in some cases, table-cloths and sheets. The Maison Dorée was filled with ladies. The large eagle of gas jets on the front of the house blazed in light. Many soldiers were in the crowd and wore McClellan badges. The New-York State Soldiers' Depot, in Howard street, was appropriately decorated and illuminated. Flags and streamers floated from parts of the building, and the sight was at the same time picturesque and novel.

The Processions.

The feature of the whole celebration was the procession of clubs. So universal a turnout was never before known. The remote wards of the city were depleted of men to swell the concourse. All of them bore banners, lanterns, and transparencies; most of them were accompanied with wagons and trucks; many of them carried loads of fireworks, which they discharged with utter profusion, filling the air with glittering sparks and brilliant emblems, and flashing jets of flame. Everywhere the processions were welcomed in shouts. Dozens of bands did their best to add to the universal acclaim of noise; now came hosts of mounted riders, followed by triumphal cars, and after these, the infantry of Democracy, moving with solid and measured tread. The fire companies too, made a splendid display of their red shirts drawing ornamented "machines," and the shrill whistles of fire steamers were heard ever and anon from all sides. One of the trucks carried a bell, which at regular intervals tolled a dismal sound as though it were the funeral of an arbitrary, imbecile, abolitionized, and corrupt administration. One banner was inscribed:

BILL SEWARD'S BELL.	
KEY.	KEY OF FORT LAFAYETTE.

One of the wards had a representation of the Temple of Liberty in red, white, and blue, inside of which was a young lady representing the Goddess of Liberty. The First Ward Union McClellan Club, John Fox, president, had with them a large ship, fully rigged and manned, which was mounted on a large truck, drawn by men in red shirts; those in the ship were dressed in red shirts, and carried the signal lights. The club had also several large trucks, on which they carried banners, transparencies, etc., and were accompanied by a cavalcade of horsemen, numbering some three hundred men. Many of the clubs found it impossible to reach the square, and were content to improvise meetings of their own, or parade through the adjoining streets.

Besides the regular platforms for speakers there were many stands improvised on the trucks of fire companies and on the steps of the houses in the vicinity from which young and adept politicians held forth to enthusiastic crowds. Companies of half a dozen or more wandered about the adjacent streets, stopping at public places and continually cheering for McClellan. Often in all parts of the city over-zealous individuals would be heard pulling and shouting all the way for McClellan and Seymour.

The mottoes and representations on transparencies were most pungent and laughter-provoking, and made up half of the intellectual furniture of the meeting, counting the speeches as the other half. They were so numerous that it would take columns to give them all, but we append a number that were noticed among the many.

One banner, with picture and words, was as follows:

ONE OF OLD ABE'S JOKES.	
CROSS BONES AND SKULL.	COFFIN MARKED DEATH.

Another bore the emblem of a Scotch cap and cloak.

Another represented a kicking contraband suspended by a pair of hand scales hooked into the posterior portion of his apparel held by Old Abe, with the words underneath, "All that is precious hangs trembling in the balance."

At 10½ o'clock the clubs left the square, and the proceedings wound up by a magnificent pyrotechnic spectacle. The pieces consisted of a large spread-eagle, a splendid American flag, an equestrian statue of McClellan, and the motto, "McClellan, the People's Choice." Each called forth loud and prolonged cheers, and, when the fire of the last died out, the multitude adjourned, cheering for "Little Mac."

THE SPEECHES.

Of those who addressed this monster meeting, many bear names honorably familiar to all Democrats. Among others were Governor Joel Parker, of New Jersey; Hon. Robert C. Winthrop, of Massachusetts; Judge George F. Comstock, Hon. August Belmont, Hon. F. A. Tallmadge, and Judge Daly, of New-York. Mayor Gunther also addressed the people from one of the stands. We regret exceedingly that of all the patriotic, eloquent, and conclusive speeches delivered, we are only able to give those of Hon. George F. Comstock and Robert C. Winthrop:

Speech of Robert C. Winthrop.

Mr. Winthrop spoke as follows:

I thank you, fellow-citizens, for this friendly and flattering reception. I thank your honored president for the kind words in which he has presented me to you. I feel glad in being here under the lead of one who, as the gentleman who called the meeting to order said, has added new honor to a name that was already associated with so much of true and tried patriotism, with so much of spotless integrity, and with so much of financial and commercial wisdom. You know me, men of New-York—if I may presume to imagine that you know me at all—as a member of the old Whig party of the Union, as long as that party had any organization or existence. (Cheers.) And I cannot help recalling the fact, on this occasion, that among my earliest political efforts, nearly thirty years ago, was a speech in this city against the Democratic candidates of that day. I fear that my faculty of making a speech, or certainly an open-air speech, is somewhat impaired by the lapse of years; but such as I can make is heartily at the service of the Democratic candidates of to-day. (Applause.) I could not find it in my heart to refuse the request of your committee of arrangements, seconded as it was by an old and valued friend, whom I knew so long ago as the tried and trusted friend of Daniel Webster, that I would at least be present as a witness of this great demonstration. Nor, being here, can I refuse to respond to the call which has been made on me by your honored president, and to bear my humble testimony to the cause in which you are engaged. It was promised me that I should see the greatest meeting ever held in America; and no one can doubt, I think, that the promise is fulfilled. ("So it is." Cheers.) It is, indeed, a glorious sight—this vast assemblage of American citizens; unseduced by patronage, unawed by power—in the great commercial metropolis of the Union—itself one of the noblest products of that Union—all rallying beneath a common banner, all animated by a common resolve; that banner, the Stars and Stripes—that resolve, to do all that in us lies for the rescue of our country from the dangers by which it is encompassed. (Cheers.) You are assembled in Union square, and I am glad to know that you all intend to stand square on the platform of the Union. (Laughter and applause.) You are assembled on the anniversary of the day on which the Constitution of the United States received the attesting signatures of its framers; and I rejoice to be assured that you are all resolved to uphold the authority and vindicate the supremacy of that Constitution. (Applause.) Yes, my friends, in yonder city of Philadelphia, which we are glad to remember, in this connection, was also the birthplace of George B. McClellan, (cheers) on the 17th day of September, 1787, that sacred instrument was perfected, which has secured union and peace to our land for more than seventy years past, and which, if this day's ratification shall be successfully carried out, may still, I fondly hope and believe, secure union and peace to our land for seven times, or even for seventy times seventy years to come. (Enthusiastic applause.) You are assembled, too, on the anniversary of the day when the noble candidate whose nomination you are about to ratify completed his great work of rescuing the capital of his country from the confederate hosts by the glorious victory of Antietam. You have not forgotten those memorable days of September, 1862, when the fate of our republic seemed just trembling in the scales, when almost all men's hearts were failing them for fear, and when the gallant McClellan, forgetting the unmerited indignities to which he had just been subjected—forgetting everything but his country's dangers and his own determination to stand or fall with its flag, and responding without a murmur or a moment's delay to the personal appeal of the President, gathered up the scattered fragments of his brave but broken army, reorganized their shattered battalions, as by the waving of a magician's wand, drove back the invaders across the Potomac, and once more secured the safety of Washington and of the government. (Loud cheers.) I would not disparage the successes which have been achieved on other days and under other commanders. We all remember with grateful admiration the splendid victories which have been won, on the land and on the sea, by Meade, and Grant, and Sherman, by Porter, and Kearsarge Winslow, and the heroic Farragut, and by so many others of our generals and admirals. All honor to the heroes of Vicksburg and Chattanooga, of Gettysburg and Atlanta, of Mobile bay, and of the blessed waters, whatever they are called, which at last ingulfed the Alabama; and all gratitude to the soldiers and sailors by whose brave hearts and stout arms these victories were achieved. (Applause.) But none of them have eclipsed, or even dimmed the brilliant record of the Army of the Potomac and its leaders during those eventful days which ended at South mountain and Antietam. For that gallant leader it is glory enough that it may be said of him, as the result of that brief but almost miraculous campaign, that, born in the birthplace of the Constitution, he was privileged, by an auspicious and beautiful coincidence, to commemorate its seventy-fifth birthday, by saving the capital of his country. But who of us is not ready to accept the omen that it is still reserved for him who saved the capital on that day to save the country itself at this? (Loud [illegible]

And now, fellow-citizens, you have not forgotten that this was the last military service which General McClellan was permitted to perform in the defense of the Union. You have not forgotten that, only a few weeks afterward, he was summarily deprived of his command, and sent into that retirement from which no patriotic offers of his own, and no persistent solicitations of his friends, have prevailed on the administration to recall him. But the day is at length at hand when the people of the United States have the constitutional opportunity and the constitutional right to revise and reverse the decrees of the administration; and most heartily do I hope that this one of their decrees, if no other, will be revised and will be reversed. (Applause.) Most heartily do I hope that, disregarding all consideration of parties and platforms, and with the single and simple view of restoring Union and peace to our distracted land, the people of the loyal states would resolve, by their votes in November next, to take upon their own shoulders this leader whom the rulers have rejected, and to bear him triumphantly into that same White House from which the rejection has emanated. ("We will, we will." Cheers.) That, as I understand it, is the proposition before this meeting; and for one, certainly, I gladly avail myself of this earliest opportunity which has been presented to me to express my approval of it. (Cheers.) Young men of New-York, and of the nation, will you not take it in special charge, and see to it that this is done? ("Yes, yes.") The candidate whom we support is eminently a young man's candidate; the youngest in years, I believe, that was ever nominated for the presidency; but who has won more laurels in the field, and shown a discretion and a wisdom in civil affairs, which would have done honor to the oldest. It ought to be the pride of Young America not only to see that he has fair play and a generous support, but to secure him an opportunity of showing what young men can do, and are destined to do, in the high places of the land, as well as on the field of battle. (Loud applause.) And yet let me not seem for a moment, fellow-citizens, to put the great issue of the approaching election on any personal grounds. The question before us is not about candidates, but about our country; not about the relative claims or merits of Abraham Lincoln and George B. McClellan, but about the nation's welfare, and the nation's life. (Three cheers for McClellan.) In whose hands will that precious life be safest? That is the question; and I do not forget that it is a question of opinion, on which every man has a right to form, and every man has a right to follow, his own opinion. I do not forget, either, how many honest and excellent men, in my own and other parts of the land, with whom I have heretofore delighted to take counsel in private and in public affairs, have come to different conclusions from my own. But I have not been able to resist the conviction, my friends, that the best interests of the country, and the best hopes of restoring the Union of the country emphatically and urgently demand a change of administration at the approaching presidential election. (Cheers.) I cannot resist the conviction—or certainly the deep and earnest apprehension—that if the policy adopted and pursued by President Lincoln and his supporters during the last two years is to be persisted in for four years to come, we shall find ourselves plunged irretrievably into the fearful and fathomless abyss of disunion. I can enter into no detailed discussion of that policy on this occasion; nor can it wisely be discussed, on any occasion, in the hearing of our southern enemies. I can only say, that in my humble judgment it has been a policy fatally calculated to divide and weaken the councils of the North, to unite and concentrate the energies of the South; and, beyond all question, it has accomplished that result, if no other. Why, my friends, the all important end of re-establishing the Union has been almost shut out of sight; so mixed up and complicated has it been with schemes of philanthropy on the one side, and with schemes of confiscation, subjugation, and extermination on the other. Instead of the one great constitutional idea of restoration, we have been treated to all manner of projects and theories of reconstruction. There would almost seem to have been a willingness, in some quarters, to vie with our enemies themselves in discarding and destroying the old Constitution of our fathers. At one time, we have had solemn propositions for annihilating whole states, whole systems of states, and blotting out their stars from the national banner. At another, we have heard open declarations from the high places of the land, that we never, as now, were to be permitted to have "the Constitution as it is and the Union as it was." Good heavens, what else are we fighting for? What other Union are we striving to establish? What other Constitution are we struggling to vindicate? What other Constitution are our rulers and legislators solemnly sworn to support? We might expect such declarations as these from rebels in arms against the government, but who can listen to them from loyal lips, without recalling the warning words of a great English statesman and orator, when he bade us "look with horror on those children of their country who are promptly rashly to hack that aged parent in pieces, and put him into the kettle of magicians, in hopes that, by their poisonous weeds and wild incantations, they may regenerate the paternal Constitution and renovate their father's life!" Heaven save us from any such regeneration and renovation as that. (Great applause.)

Fellow-citizens, we all know that it was the success of the Republican party, with its avowed sectional organization and sectional objects, which furnished the original occasion, four years ago, for that atrocious and ungodly assault upon our government which initiated this gigantic civil war. ("That's so." Applause.) We all know that the secession leaders of the South, who had so long been meditating the movement in vain, exulted in the election of Abraham Lincoln at that day—as I fully believe they will exult again, if he is re-elected in November—because it supplied the very fuel which was needed for kindling this awful conflagration. That assault upon the government can never be characterized in terms of too severe condemnation; and, if railing at the rebellion or its authors would do any good this evening—if it would be any thing better than baying at yonder moon—I would join with you in denouncing it until the vocabulary of condemnation was exhausted. But we all know that the whole North rose nobly up, as one man, without distinction of party, to repel that assault; and that they have sustained the government—Democrats, Republicans, and conservatives alike—with all their hearts and hands, pouring out their blood and money like water from that day to this. And the loyal states will continue to sustain the powers that be in all their constitutional action, until the end of their term, whatever may be the result of the pending election—not all of them by any means, as approving the policy of the administration, but all of them as recognizing its rightful possession of the authority of the government. But no considerations of loyalty, or of patriotism, call upon them to go further. ("No," and cheers.) No considerations of loyalty call upon us to prolong the supremacy of a party whose action and pars it has so eminently been to extinguish almost every spark of Union sentiment in the southern breast, and to implant there in its stead a desperate and defiant determination never to be reconciled, never to submit or yield, never again to come under rulers, whom, reasonably or unreasonably, they have learned to hate. No considerations of patriotism call upon us to renew the official term of an administration whose peculiar policy, by inspiring this spirit of desperation and hate, has rendered the victories of our armies a hundred-fold harder to achieve, and has robbed them of so many of their legitimate results [illegible] they have been achieved. For never, my friends, do victories cost so much, [illegible] when they are wrung [from] despair. This sort of goading and maddening process my answer, well enough for increasing the sport of a bull fight, but it has certainly involved us in at least one Bull Run. ("Good," laughter, and cheers.) And I fear the day is still distant when it will secure us that sort of victory which we can reasonably hope to see followed by union and peace.

Nothing could be further from my purpose, in these remarks, than to cast the slightest imputation upon the patriotism of President Lincoln, or anybody else. No one can doubt that he wishes to write his name on the roll of history as the restorer of the American Union. It is a title which might satisfy the most exalted ambition. He may well be excused for his eagerness to remain in office until he has accomplished the work. He may almost be pardoned for wielding the enormous patronage and power which belongs to the executive in a war like this for securing his own nomination and his own election, if he really believes he can accomplish it. And those who are of opinion that he is just about to succeed—whether within sixty days or ninety days—before Christmas or after—are right to give him their support. We would all support him if we were of their opinion, for we want the country saved, no matter who is to have the glory. But President Lincoln is evidently looking forward to another title in the history of the future. He desires to be enrolled as the great liberator of the African race—a glorious title, also, if it could be legitimately obtained. But I greatly fear that in aiming at the second he has lost the first. No man, I think, can help perceiving that he is so embarrassed and entangled by his proclamations, and commitments, and pledges in regard to slavery, as to be almost incapacitated for bringing this terrible struggle to an early or successful termination. (Applause.) He has contrived to weave a Gordian knot, which he himself is unable to untie, and which the truest and sharpest swords seem thus far powerless to cut asunder. No one can have forgotten, certainly, that recent and extraordinary manifesto "To whom it may concern," in which, in reply to the first suggestions of peace, he felt obliged to insert a condition which discomfited his best friends, and rendered all such efforts hopeless.

Fellow-citizens, we need a change of counsels ("That's true." Applause.) We need a change of counselors. We need a return to the policy on which the loyal states first rallied so unanimously to the suppression of the rebellion. We must go back to the principles embodied in the resolution adopted by the Congress of the United States, not far from the fourth day of July, 1861, and worthy to have been adopted on that hallowed anniversary itself, adopted in the Senate, on motion of Andrew Johnson, and adopted in the House of Representatives on motion of the lamented Crittenden. That terrible repulse at Bull Run had then just taught us wisdom. Would to Heaven that we had not so soon forgotten that lesson! If we had never departed from that resolution—if we had never recanted vows made in pain"—firmly believe that union and peace would have been our blessed portion at this moment. You all remember that resolution. It embodied the simple policy of a vigorous prosecution of the war for no purpose of subjugation or aggression, in no spirit of revenge or hatred, with no disposition to destroy or impair the constitutional rights of any state or any section, but for the sole end of vindicating the Constitution and re-establishing the Union. (Cheers.) That was the policy which would have divided the South and which ought to have satisfied and united the North. Let me rather say it was, and is still the policy which steadily pursued, under the lead of men against whom the whole southern heart, and mind, and soul have not become hopelessly embittered and poisoned; under the lead of men, too, who are not ashamed to avow the readiness for reconciliation which is the highest ornament of the Christian character, and without which we cannot rely on the blessing of God; this, I say, is the policy which thus pursued will again, if anything earthly ever will, unite both North and South in the bonds of constitutional fellowship, and exhibit our country and its flag once more in the face of all the world, with "a star for every state and a state for every star." What a glorious day that will be, my countrymen, for us and all mankind. If to yearn for it, and pant for it, and pray for it, be a subject for reproach as exhibiting too great a willingness for peace, I am the guiltiest man alive. (Cheers.) And how can we hasten that day more effectively than by supporting the candidate who is the very impersonation of the policy I have described? Our noble candidate has enforced and illustrated it a thousand fold better than any one else can do, in his memorable dispatch from Harrison's Landing, in his brilliant oration at West Point, and still more recently in his admirable letter accepting the nomination we are assembled to ratify. (Three cheers for General McClellan.) These are the true platforms for the hour, and not for the hour only but for all time. ("That's so.") We need no other, and some of us certainly, can recognize no other. (Voice, "They're good enough.") I rejoice to see so many of their noble sentiments and golden sentences emblazoned on the countless banners and illuminations around me. Let us cherish them in our memories and write them on all our hearts. (Applause.)

Yes, my friends—if anybody is disposed to cavil with you about your platform, tell him that General McClellan has made his own platform, and that it is broad enough and comprehensive enough for every patriot in the land to stand upon. Tell him that you should as soon think of holding General McClellan responsible for not taking Richmond, when he was so rashly interfered with, and so cruelly stripped of his troops on the right hand and on the left, as you should think of holding him responsible for any equivocal or any unequivocal words of Chicago conventions, or any other conventions, which malicious partisans may attempt to assert to his injury. Tell him that you should as soon think of the brave Army of the Potomac having been frightened from following their gallant leader to the field by the quaker guns on the roadside, as of his supporters for the presidency being scared from their position by any paper pellets of the brain, wise or otherwise, which ever came from the midnight sessions of a resolution committee in the hurly-burly of a national convention. (Cheers.)

General McClellan, I repeat, has made his own platform, which ought to be satisfactory to everybody. His letter of acceptance especially, ought to be hailed with delight and with gratitude even by those who are too far committed in other directions to give him their support. (Applause.) It is worth an army with banners to the cause of the Union. It has the clarion ring to rally a nation to the rescue. (Cheers.) It speaks, too, in trumpet tones to our deluded brethren in rebellion, warning them that there is to be no cessation of hostilities upon any other basis than that of Union, but proclaiming to them that the door of reconciliation and peace is open on their resuming their allegiance to the Constitution and laws of the United States. And, certainly, my friends, that letter of acceptance has turned the flank of his revilers as handsomely as the gallant Sherman has turned the flank of Hood at Atlanta. (Laughter and applause.) It has taken away every pretext for those indecent and unjust insinuations against the patriotism and loyalty of all the opponents of the administration, which have fallen from so many ruthless partisan pens and so many reckless partisan tongues. It has destroyed every pretense for the imputation that there is a party at the North ready for a precipitate and ignominious abandonment of the great struggle in which we are engaged, and willing to entertain propositions incompatible with the restoration of the Constitution and the Union. The Union—"the Union at all hazards"—is as distinctly the whole import of George B. McClellan's letter of the 8th of September as "the Union in any event" was of that Farewell Address [of George Washington which is so] nearly associated with the day on which we are assembled. (Loud cheers). "The Union—it must be preserved"—is as clearly the maxim of McClellan in '64 as it was of Andrew Jackson in '32. (Applause). A Democratic President saved the Union then, and I believe a Democratic President can save the Union now. (Cheers.) Let us rally, then, to the support of that great principle of unconditional Unionism which is common to Washington, Jackson, and McClellan. Let us go for the flag, the whole flag, and nothing but the flag. (Cheers.) Let us vindicate the rights of free opinion, of free speech, of a free press, and of free and unawed elections (loud cheering), even in a time of civil war, and show to all the world that we are, and still mean to be, a free people. (Voice—"We mean to be.") Let us bring no railing accusations against the patriotism of others, and let us treat all which are brought against our own patriotism with the contempt and scorn which they deserve. (Applause.) Let us furnish all the men and all the money which are required for the aid of our gallant defenders in the field, and bear the welfare of our soldiers and sailors ever uppermost in our hearts. And as we throw out our McClellan banners to the breeze, let the word still and ever be, alike to friend and foe, "The Union is the one condition of peace. We ask no more. But the Union must be preserved at all hazards."

Mr. Winthrop closed amid loud applause, followed by three cheers for the speaker.

Speech of the Hon. George F. Comstock.

FELLOW-CITIZENS OF NEW-YORK: The condition of my voice is such that I can hope to be heard by only a small portion of this vast audience, and I am quite certain that I shall not be able to address you at any considerable length. But in the little I do say I will endeavor to bring distinctly to view the issues this people has to determine. The direct question is whether Abraham Lincoln or George B. McClellan shall be elected President of the United States? (Cries of "George B. McClellan." Cheers for McClellan.) If the choice were to turn upon the personal qualities of the two candidates, we should point you proudly to the lofty patriotism, the noble achievements, the ripe cultivation, the elevated statesmanship, the pure and upright character, and the stainless record of the youthful soldier who is our standard bearer. (Cheers.)—To whom, indeed, can the nation more safely intrust the supreme control of its armies than to the hero who twice saved its capital from destruction, and whose march to the capital of the enemy was only arrested by political faction and hatred. (Cheers.) I say nothing of the personal qualities of his opponent—I have no taste for caricature. His own political friends have frequently drawn that picture in colors stronger and more repulsive than I myself should like to paint it. But these two candidates for the highest office in the nation—an office upon the manner of filling which the destiny of thirty millions of people at this moment depends—have each made a platform to stand upon; have each indicated to all the world the policy on which he proposes to administer the government, if intrusted to his hands for the next four years. "To all whom it may concern." (Hisses.) Mr. Lincoln announces, after more than three years of the most shocking war known to history, that he will receive proposals for peace embracing "the restoration of the Union *and the abandonment of slavery.*" On other points he says he will be liberal—yes, liberal; but on these points he insists. This is a very short and a perfectly intelligible platform. Equally brief is that of General McClellan, which I also give in his own words: "Union is the one condition of peace; we ask no more." These are noble words, which might well be written on the sky above us. They prescribe but one condition of peace, and that is the preservation of our glorious Union, for which the war was commenced. (Cheers.)

But Mr. Lincoln, in language equally explicit, lays down two conditions—Union, and the abandonment of slavery. Is the Union certainly one of these conditions? You answer yes. Is not the other just as clearly the abandonment of slavery? No man can answer no. If both are not, neither is, because both are inseparably connected, and they stand or fall together. If the President means the country shall not have peace without the Union, he also means the country shall not have it without the abandonment of slavery. When he lays down the precise conditions on which he says he will receive proposals for peace, the common sense of all mankind declares that he will not receive them except on these very conditions.

I appeal to the whole bench and bar of this country to say if this is not the true, the only interpretation. I will submit the question to any Republican judge or lawyer in the land. If Mr. Lincoln were on trial before the Senate of the United States, as the high court of impeachment, charged with a usurpation of an authority unknown to the Constitution, to wit, carrying on war to abolish slavery in the Southern States, he could not escape a conviction. His manifesto over his own hand would be his sure condemnation. If he were tried before judge and jury acquittal would be impossible. I know there is not a judge in this country who would not charge the jury to find the meaning of this manifesto to be that the President will not make peace until slavery is abolished.

Now the country was struck with great astonishment some six weeks ago, when the President issued this extraordinary document. The public judgment was formed upon it instantaneously. It was understood and condemned. A nation anxious for peace after the unspeakable desolations of war protested against this pretension of an imperial usurper to use the fleets and armies of the Republic for a purpose unknown to its Constitution and laws. Nothing could exceed the consternation of the political leaders and guides who were thirsting for four years more of power to enjoy the ruin they had brought upon the nation. You have witnessed the efforts since made to allay the storm by concealing the issue, even by denying that Mr. Lincoln meant exactly what he said. But Abraham Lincoln has a record older than the manifesto which stamps him as unfit to be the President of the Union of states. In 1858, in a speech to a political convention in Illinois, he announced the monstrous doctrine that a Union could not permanently exist between slave and free states. And why not? Our glorious Union peacefully existed in this manner for over seventy years. Its fundamental nature is an alliance between co-equal states for certain objects of national importance—an alliance which presents them as one to the other nations of the earth, but leaves to each the control of its domestic affairs. No one state, nor any class of states, is responsible for the institutions of any other state. If New England had felt less responsibility for the sins and errors of other states the Union to-day would have been at peace and the nation would have been saved from the revolution which threatens to overwhelm it. Abraham Lincoln, then, is the first secessionist. His record as such is older than that of Jefferson Davis. I say a secessionist. Union, he says, cannot endure between free and slave states. What then? To what result does it lead? Why certainly that the Union ought not to exist at all, and the states ought to separate. If they cannot live together in peaceful union, each enjoying its own right to control its own affairs, they ought not to live together at all. If there is such a necessary antagonism between a slave and a free state that they cannot unite peacefully for purposes common to them both, then they should never form a Union. No southern secessionist ever uttered a sentiment more hostile to the Union. Mr. Lincoln said the states could not live together. He became President. The South said, "we take you at your word. You say the Union cannot permanently endure as our fathers made it; therefore we will divide now." If Mr. Lincoln was right, then the South was right, and ought to have been allowed to depart in peace from a Union impossible to be maintained.

Did the President intend just what he said when in the late manifesto he declared the abolition of slavery to be one of the conditions of peace? My fellow-citizens, he could not say, he could not intend anything less, without reversing his policy for the last two years. Look at his proclamation of emancipation. Two years ago, by a stroke of his pen he liberated all the slaves in the rebel states. He declared them forever free and he pledged the army and the navy to maintain their freedom, in other words, he pledged himself to carry on the war until the negroes were emancipated. Resistance to the Constitution and laws might cease in every rebel state. The federal duties might be collected in every southern port. The mails regularly transmitted, the forts and places of the government surrendered [into his] possession, in short, every lawful object of the [war might be accomplished] and yet the fearful struggle must go on to carry out the proclamation and redeem the pledge given to the negro. History must resume the story of battles, of sieges, of conflagration and desolation. Since that pledge has been given more than a million of men have been called to arms for the purpose of maintaining it. In the struggle to maintain it the nation is now tottering on the verge of bankruptcy and ruin!

Now the President, in his latest annual message, has said that he will not take a step backward, that he will never will revoke this proclamation. Do I misinterpret its meaning? I am certain that I do not. When this imperial dictator declares that the slaves are and "*shall be from thenceforward forever free,*" there is but one possible or conceivable interpretation. I will submit this question to all the lexicographers, to all the judges, to all the lawyers in the country. And having pledged the army and navy to maintain such freedom, the very necessity of his position compelled him, in his last manifesto, to prescribe "the abandonment of slavery" as one of the conditions of peace.

But all doubt upon this subject disappears, if we look at Mr. Lincoln's plan of reconstructing the Union. This plan is exhibited in his so-called amnesty proclamation. May I beg your attention, fellow citizens, a few moments, to this extraordinary document? The attention of the whole nation ought to be at once turned to it. It contains the exact policy on which Mr. Lincoln is carrying on the war, the very policy to maintain which he demands your treasure and your blood. Its grand features are these: (1.) It assumes that all the people of the rebellious states, without trial or judgment, are in the situation of convicts and outlaws, without any rights of citizenship, even the right to be tried according to the Constitution. (2.) As President he pardons them, except civil and military officers, on condition that they will take an oath to support the proclamation of emancipation, and all other proclamations and acts of Congress relating to slavery. (3.) The people who take this oath, if they amount to one-tenth of the voters of the state, may form a new state constitution based on the proclamation, and organize a new state government; and to support this state government of one tenth, he pledges all the power of this nation. (4.) The existing constitutions and governments of eleven states are overthrown, and the nine tenths of the people who may refuse to take the oath, remain in the condition of convicts and outlaws, without a single right of citizenship. Even if they lay down their arms their property is confiscated, and even the right of suffrage is taken from them.

Now by this plan, and by the military power in his hands, and which he asks to be continued in his hands four years longer, Mr. Lincoln proposes to reorganize one third of all the states, and then restore them to the Union. Their existing state governments, their existing constitutions are to be overturned, and new constitutions and laws are to be enforced by arms upon nine-tenths of the people. And thus we are to have a new Union of free states. Being in possession of a small part of Louisiana and Arkansas, the plan has been actually put in operation in those states, the requisite number of votes being obtained from a few of those inhabitants and from soldiers and followers of the camp. I notice a similar movement on foot in Tennessee, and these states I suppose are expected to be in readiness to vote in November for the author of their existence. The experiment was also tried in Florida, but an army was sacrificed without any result.

To this plan the President so far as we know, adheres with unflinching tenacity. Congress passed an act presenting a different scheme, but he refused to sign it because he declined to abandon his own.

It is impossible, therefore, for any candid and intelligent mind, to mistake the policy of Abraham Lincoln in conducting this war and under which he proposes to conduct it hereafter. The fundamental principle is in the proclamation of emancipation which he declares he will never revoke. It is to be practically worked out and by revolutionizing the government of eleven states according to his amnesty, and forcing upon new constitutions and laws which shall prohibit slavery, and as he never expects to obtain even by armed power the consent

(Continued on Fourth page.)

THE SUN.

IT SHINES FOR ALL

THIRTY-FIRST YEAR. NUMBER 10,052.

NEW YORK, SATURDAY, SEPTEMBER 24, 1864.

PRICE ONE CENT—IN GOLD: TWO CENTS IN CURRENCY.

The Latest News

By Telegraph to the N. Y. Sun.

VICTORY AGAIN!!

"Little Phil. Sheridan" Strikes Another Deadly Blow.

EARLY'S ARMY ROUTED.

Sixteen Guns Captured—Also a Great Many Caissons, Artillery, Horses and Prisoners.

OUR FORCES PUSHING ON.

THE WAR WESTWARD.

Fighting Going on in Missouri.

REPORTED CAPTURE OF LITTLE ROCK.

FROM THE RIO GRANDE.

Cortinas Fighting the French.

IMPORTANT FROM WASHINGTON.

CHANGE IN THE CABINET.

Resignation of Postmaster Blair.

&c., &c., &c.

GENERAL SHERIDAN.

Review of the Advance.

The preliminary operations which resulted in the brilliant victories in the Shenandoah Valley commenced during the latter part of last week, by a reconnoissance under General Getty, in the direction of the Opequan. On Friday the enemy were found to have fallen back in the direction of Winchester, presenting a weak line upon our right wing. This opening was promptly taken advantage of, and on Sunday General Averill's cavalry attacked and drove the rebel General Gordon's division of infantry from Martinsburg. General Early manifested a disposition to advance in force to sustain Gordon, when General Sheridan determined to fall upon his rear, in the direction of Berryville. The entire army was placed in marching order on Sunday night, and before daylight on Monday morning the Nineteenth and Sixth corps advanced, followed by General Crook's command a few hours later. The two corps moved in parallel columns along the Winchester road, while General Crook's moved in a south-westerly direction across the open country, to form a junction with the two Army Corps at a point on the road. While these movements were going on against the enemy's right, the cavalry, under General Averill, demonstrated on the left, so as to divert the attention of the enemy. The entire movement was splendidly executed, only a slight derangement occurring from the failure of the infantry to connect at the proper time, and the delay afforded time to General Early to bring up part of his forces.

The battle commenced at noon with the advance of the Sixth and Nineteenth Corps across the Opequan, General Crook's force remaining as a reserve on the east bank. The enemy opened with a furious fire, which compelled our men to fall back and await the reserve, which was ordered to cross the river and support our advance. About three o'clock General Sheridan was joined by his various cavalry divisions, and advanced along the entire line, the infantry and artillery on both sides being engaged. The infantry moved on the centre, supported by cavalry on the left and right flanks.

About four o'clock a splendid infantry charge was made by the Army of West Virginia under General Crook. The enemy were pushed back from the First, but retired in comparatively good order, until our cavalry under General Torbert, coming down on the enemy's right, struck their flank a mile or two north of Winchester, and drove it completely off the turnpike, with the loss of several hundred prisoners. The cavalry under General Averill now joined in the battle, and about dark the route was complete. The enemy fled at all points, hurrying through Winchester under cover of the darkness, and pressed by our cavalry. At night our troops rested in the town. Our losses in this engagement are estimated at from three to four thousand. The enemy lost more than twice that number. In this engagement all arms—artillery, infantry and cavalry were equally engaged. The enemy fought with great courage and desperation. The cavalry made some of the finest charges in the war. In no case did the rebel cavalry venture to cross sabres. At one time General Torbert chased them a distance of eight miles. The infantry, of course, offered the most serious opposition. A splendid charge of General Custer's and Lowell's brigades a little before dusk resulted in the capture of three guns, nine stands of colors and eight hundred men, including sixty officers. Three thousand rebel wounded were found in Winchester, and their dead and wounded lined every road and field. An hour or two more of daylight would have rendered the destruction of the rebel army complete.

During the night, the enemy retired towards Fisher's Hill, where it was subsequently discovered they had made a stand. This place is about three miles from Strasburg and twenty miles from Winchester, and is defended by formidable entrenchments constructed long since. It is defensible against a largely superior attacking force in front, and the pursuit was so vigorous that our army opened fire upon the place on Tuesday night. On Wednesday morning our forces occupied the neighboring heights. Desultory cannonading took place during the forenoon, with a view of demoralizing the enemy pending the progress of the operations for forcing the position. About noon the line of battle was formed with the Sixth corps on the right and the Nineteenth on the left of the Strasburg turnpike, and General Crook's army of Western Virginia in reserve. General Averill's cavalry were posted on the extreme right. At daylight General Torbert's cavalry had been sent round the mountains in the direction of Front Royal with a view of striking the enemy's rear, through the gap in the Luray Valley, and thus compelling them to evacuate the position. The results of this movement will appear in our telegraphic dispatches.

During the afternoon of Wednesday our forces pressed the enemy closely and developed him in strong position on the crest of the hill. A strong skirmishing line of the Sixth Corps drove the rebels from a position at the bottom of the hill, where our artillery was then planted. Our batteries opened and continued firing until night, but failed to elicit any response. The enemy did not fire a single gun. This partial activity on one side and inertness on the other continued until near dark when Warner's brigade, of the Sixth Corps, charged up the crest of an eminence commanding the hill, under a furious fire of musketry and artillery, and carried it in splendid style. This terminated the operations of the day, leaving our army inspired with the utmost enthusiasm and confidence, and animated by the most confident hopes of achieving the complete destruction of the rebel army.

BY TELEGRAPH.

Another Glorious Victory.

War Department, Washington, Sept. 23—3 P. M.—Major-General Dix: The following telegram, announcing another victory of General Sheridan over Early, has just been received;

Harper's Ferry, Sept. 23.—Hon. E. M. Stanton: Sheridan has again beaten the enemy at Fisher's Hill, capturing sixteen guns and many prisoners. This is in all probability the *finale* of General Early. J. D. STEVENSON, Brig.-Gen.

The Surgeon-General this morning reported that our wounded were all cared for at Winchester, with adequate arrangements and supplies. The number of our wounded, prior to the battle of yesterday was estimated not to exceed two thousand.

EDWIN M. STANTON, Secretary of War.

SECOND DISPATCH.

War Department, Washington, Sept. 23d, 1864, 3.30 P. M.—Major-General John A. Dix:—Sheridan's victory proves to be signal and complete. Nothing but the coming night saved even a remnant of Early's army. The following dispatches of General Stevenson, and Major-General Sheridan's official report to General Grant, give all the particulars thus far received:

Harper's Ferry, Sept. 23.—To the Hon. E. M. Stanton:—The military telegraph line is down. The affair is complete and overwhelming.

Respectfully,

JOHN D. STEVENSON, Brig.-Gen.

HEADQUARTERS M. M. DIVISION, 6 MILES FROM WOODSTOCK, 11:30 P. M., Sept. 22d, 1864.

Lieut.-General Grant, Commanding Armies U. S., City Point.—I have the honor to announce that I achieved a most signal victory over the army of General Early at Fisher's Hill to-day. I found the rebel army posted with its right resting on the north fork of the Shenandoah, and extending across the Strasburgh Valley westward to North Mountain, occupying a position which appeared almost impregnable. After a great deal of manœuvering during the day, General Crook's command was transferred to the extreme right of the line on North Mountain and he furiously attacked the left of the enemy's line, carrying everything before him. While Crook was driving the enemy in the greatest confusion, and sweeping down behind their breastworks, the 6th and 7th Army Corps attacked the rebel works in front, and the whole army appeared to be broken up. They fled in the utmost confusion. Sixteen pieces of artillery were captured, also a great many caissons, artillery horses, etc., etc.

I am to-night pushing on down the Valley.

I cannot say how many prisoners I have captured, nor do I know either my own or the enemy's casualties. Only darkness has saved the whole of Early's army from total destruction. My attack could not be made till 4 o'clock in the evening, which left but little daylight to operate in. The 1st and 5d Cavalry divisions went down the Luray Valley to-day, and if they push on vigorously to the main valley the result of this day's engagement will be still more signal. The victory was very complete. A more detailed report will be made as soon as I can obtain the necessary data.

P. H. SHERIDAN,
Major-General Commanding.

It will be remembered that Early's command embraced the "Stonewall Jackson Brigade," and the troops constituting "Stonewall" Jackson's corps, and was the *elite* of the rebel army.

E. M. STANTON, Secretary of War.

The Last of Stonewall's Brigade.

Washington, Sept. 23.—The battle-flags captured by General Sheridan were deposited in the War Department to-day. "Stonewall" Jackson's old brigade were all killed or taken prisoners in the battle near Berryville.

The Battle Flags.

Washington, Sept. 23.—To-day Capt. Ellis, the Acting Inspector General of General Torbett's division of cavalry, reached here from the front in the Valley, bringing eight rebel battle and regimental flags, captured by that division in the engagement of Monday last. He proceeded immediately to the War Department, where they were formally presented in the name of General Sheridan. Seven of the men bearing them were the actual captors of the flag each carried. The Adjutant General will take charge of the flags, and will by direction, furnish the captors with medals with their names inscribed upon them.

GENERAL SHERMAN.

Exchange of Prisoners—Extension of the Truce.

Chattanooga, Sept. 22.—Gen. Sherman, by special arrangements with the rebel General Hood, has effected the exchange of 2,000 prisoners. Out of the batch of 900 rebels, 17 refused to be exchanged, and took the oath of allegiance. Of 100 picked rebels, on duty at Rough and Ready, 21 deserted. This is a fair indication of the demoralized condition of Hood's army. The truce between Sherman and Hood expired to-day, but will be extended several days, to complete the removal of families.

The War Westward.

Fighting Going on in Missouri.

Cairo, Sept. 22.—Citizens just from Charleston, Missouri, state that the 2d Missouri militia, fearing an attack from a superior force of Shelby's rebels, evacuated Bloomfield, and retreated in the direction of White Water River. It was reported at Charleston that the enemy, several thousand strong, had overtaken the militia, and a fight was going on at White Water River last night. Great excitement existed at Charleston, but it is not thought that any considerable number of rebels have been in that vicinity.

Reported Capture of Little Rock.

New York, Sept. 23.—We have New Orleans papers to the 15th inst. The most important item they contain is a report brought down by the steamer Sultana, by some passengers who got on board at Gaines' Landing, that the rebels had captured Little Rock, but as no particulars are given, the New Orleans ERA is disposed to question it. The passengers referred to came on board the Sultana on the 10th. The previous advices from Little Rock were to the 7th, when there was no prospect of a fight.

(By Mail.)

Fort Smith, Aug. 15.—The rebels are still making inroads upon us every day, and menacing us in every quarter. We are still between hope and fear. A sad affair happened last Friday, about 15 miles east of Van Buren. A mail party consisting of 49 persons were fired upon suddenly; 10 of them were instantly killed, 18 escaped, and the rest were captured. All the mail was taken by them. It was the largest ever brought, amounting to 600 pounds. Capt. Beeler, of the 13th Kansas, was killed the same evening, while trying to capture some bushwhackers that he found in a house near Van Buren. He shot the captain of the gang, and, after he fell, he in return shot Capt. Beeler. No more of either party were killed. The 13th captured several horses already saddled, one of which had Col. Bowen's saddle on him. I should have said that not one of the party who captured the mail was killed. They made a complete thing of it. Van Buren is now threatened by the rebels, and you need not be surprised to hear that it is taken soon, as they are hovering around it.

From New Orleans.

Later from the Rio Grande.

New Orleans, Sept. 16, via Cairo, Sept. 23.—Some additional particulars of the recent capture of Brownsville by Cortinas has been received, but they embrace nothing important beyond those sent you on the 12th. Col. Day, of the 91st Illinois, commands the Federal troops at Brazos Santiago. It is rumored in military circles here that Gen. Banks leaves this department next week. He is now more popular with the Free State party than ever before. A McClellan organ is to be started here, if his friends cannot purchase one of the city papers.

LATER—The transport Alabama has just arrived from Brazos, with intelligence that another fight has occurred at Bagdad, between the French and Cortinas. A private letter, within ten minutes before the Alabama sailed, says, "the fight is now progressing. Artillery is used on both sides. The French marines are good gunners, and are entrenched. The result is purely conjectural."

Late Rebel News.

Dates to Wednesday Last.

Washington, Sept. 23.—A copy of the Richmond EXAMINER, of Wednesday, received here to-day, says:

There was no news of interest from any quarter yesterday. Lincoln's campaign, which was to have crushed the "Confederacy," hangs fire at the season of the year most favorable to active military operations. We may, however, with certainty expect his armies to be again put in motion before the next snow.

The EXAMINER says there was a rumor current last night that Major General Robert Rhodes had been killed in the Valley, and that his body had reached Staunton. We did not learn whether he was killed in battle, or skirmish, nor any particulars whatever. [*Note.*—From the above it would appear that accounts of Sheridan's victories had not at that time reached Richmond.]

The flag-of-truce steamer New York, Major Mulford, arrived off Varina yesterday evening, with one thousand sick and wounded Confederate prisoners on board. Among the officers, of whom there were a number aboard, was Gen. Walker, of what brigade and corps is unknown.

In the Richmond City Councils, Mr. Scott offered a resolution to offer a reward of $1,000 for the detection of the incendiaries engaged in kindling the fires now of nightly occurrence in Richmond, and suggesting the co-operation with the police of the members of the fire brigade as patrolmen. Mr. Glassbrook wanted the reward increased to $5,000. The subject was referred to the Committee on Police.

A letter from Camden county, N. C., says: "The Yankees have just made a raid out here, committing the most fiendish acts of cruelty upon the people. They were not satisfied with subsisting upon the people, carrying off horses, &c., but they burned some fifteen or twenty houses turning the defenceless families out of doors, with a total loss of furniture, clothing, &c."

The EXAMINER complains that there are citizens of Winchester, and of the neighborhood, calling themselves Confederates, who refuse to supply General Early's commissaries and quartermasters with food for man or horse, except on the terms of being paid in Mr. Fessenden's green paper, and who utterly refuse to sell to a soldier an egg or an apple for any quantity of the paper which serves us for money in this country, and the EXAMINER is sorry to learn that there are planters and merchants in Winchester and vicinity who do absolutely refuse to touch their country's legal currency, and who demand to be paid for everything in that of the enemy's country. It concludes by saying:—The policy of being gentle and indulgent to open traitors and of encouraging them to violate the laws, is perhaps a little characteristic of our government, which is stern and austere enough with honest citizens who are straining every nerve and risking everything they have in the world, together with their lives and their children's lives to uphold the said government, but it is a policy which will scarcely recommend itself to straightforward confederates.

Mobile, Sept. 19.—A Yankee force from Pensacola is reported to be making a raid on Pollard.

The following extracts are made from Georgia and South Carolina papers, from files up to the 17th inst.:

The Macon CONFEDERATE says it is currently rumored on the streets that Gen. Beauregard is to take command of the Army of Tennessee.

The Macon TELEGRAPH remarks if the reader will consult the map he will come to a realizing sense of the ease with which Sherman can repeat from Atlanta the combined movement by which he backed Johnston down from Dalton to the heights of Altoona. It shows how Sherman can move by different roads, flank Barnesville, and thence southward, they would flank Macon with the same ease. Hence there is an overwhelming necessity for such reinforcements as shall prevent a repetition of the Sherman strategy from Dalton to the Etowah.

The Charleston MERCURY of the 17th, says: "We have little to report to-day. The enemy's bombardment of the city yesterday was quite brisk, about fifty shells having been thrown. There will we understand be another communication with the enemy by flag of truce on Monday next.

The Savannah REPUBLICAN says "if Sherman is to be allowed to hold peaceable possession of Atlanta until he has time to fortify the place, and make it impregnable, then the citizens of Georgia may look out for large and formidable raiding parties from that place, making extensive excursions through the State.

Change in the Cabinet.

Resignation of Postmaster-General Blair at the President's Request.

Washington, Sept. 23.—When the resolution of the late Baltimore Convention, declaring that they "deemed it essential to the general welfare that harmony shall prevail in the national councils, and regarding as worthy of public confidence and official trust those only who cordially endorse the principles proposed in the series of resolutions, and which should characterize the administration of the Government," was, shortly after its passage, read to Postmaster-General Blair, he at once verbally tendered his resignation, which was not formally made and accepted until to-day, as will be seen from the following correspondence. It is understood that Ex-Governor Dennison, of Ohio, will be his successor:

EXECUTIVE MANSION,
WASHINGTON, Sept. 23, 1864.

Hon. Montgomery Blair:

MY DEAR SIR—You have generously said to me more than once that whenever your resignation could be a relief to me, it was at my disposal. The time has come. You very well know that this proceeds from no dissatisfaction of mine with you personally or officially. Your uniform kindness has been unsurpassed by that of any friend, and while it is true that the war does not so greatly add to the difficulties of your department as to those of some others, it is yet much to say, as I most truly can, that in the three years and a half during which you have administered the General Post Office, I remember no single complaint against you in connection therewith. Yours as ever,

A. LINCOLN.

MR. BLAIR'S REPLY.

POST OFFICE DEPARTMENT,
Sept. 23d, 1864.

My Dear Sir—I have received your note of this date referring to my offers to resign whenever you should deem it advisable for the public interests that I should do so, and stating that in your judgment that time has now come. I now, therefore, formally tender my resignation of the office of Postmaster General. I cannot take leave of you without renewing the expressions of my gratitude for the uniform kindness which has marked your course towards

Yours very truly,

M. BLAIR.

The President.

The Peace Movement.

The rumored peace negotiations continue to attract general attention, and, in the absence of positive official information, the reports are necessarily vague and contradictory. A Washington dispatch positively denies that General Sherman has entered into any peace negotiations, except those involved in the ten days' truce for the removal of the inhabitants of Atlanta. The tone of the Richmond press, however, indicates that the movement was regarded as highly important in that city, and excited considerable apprehension. The DISPATCH has the following significant article on that subject:

There is no mistaking the object of Sherman in desiring to hold a conference with Vice-President Stephens and Governor Brown. It is to detach the State of Georgia, if possible, from the Confederacy, through the agency of these two gentlemen, whom, from their course with regard to the *Habeas Corpus* Act and other measures, he takes to be at heart well disposed to promote such a measure. We are confident that he will find himself disappointed in his estimation of these two gentlemen, yet we very much regret that they should have advocated any line of policy which the Yankee general can, by any possibility, thus interpret. We trust the meeting will not be accorded. It can answer no good purpose, and is designed for no good end. If there were no other objection to it, the very fact that it is proposed by Sherman is sufficient of itself to indicate its impropriety. No good citizen ought, especially at a time like this, to do anything which may, in the slightest particular, serve to indicate that there is a difference, in his opinion, between the interests of his State and the interests of the Confederacy. The Governor of Georgia ought at least to recollect that his State was one of the first (the first after South Carolina) to secede from the Union, and that if she now treats of peace on her own terms, as a sovereign State, she withdraws from the Confederacy, and leaves her sisters the bag to hold, after having got them into this scrape. We make these remarks because separate State action has been agitated of late in more quarters than one. The late deplorable peace delusion gave rise to it, and the depression consequent upon the disappointment of hopes raised by it has kept it up. We hope it has not spread to any great extent; but we may be assured that Sherman has heard of it, and that it encourages him to seek this conference. The Constitution confers upon the President, by and with the consent of the Senate, authority to make peace. If a State make peace on her own account she withdraws from the Confederacy. Sherman knows this, and thinking he has his heel upon the State of Georgia, he hopes in this way to bring her back into the Union. Are the people not the politicians—are the people of Georgia prepared for this step? Will they consent to abandon Virginia, which entered into this Confederacy because she was determined to share the fate of her sister? Will she abandon Virginia now, after having dragged her into this war? We cannot and will not believe it of the gallant State of Georgia. Her sons have fought too gallantly to warrant such a belief.

A "peace" movement has started from a different quarter, and is vouched for as follows by the Washington REPUBLICAN, an administration journal:—

We learn from a source so reliable that we believe the statement, that Mr. Jacob Thompson, ex-Secretary of the Interior, now residing at Niagara Falls, received a few days since a proposition from Jefferson Davis, to be submitted to our government, for a peaceable settlement of the present difficulties. Davis proposes that the rebel armies shall lay down their arms, return to their allegiance to the United States, and that the Union of the States shall be preserved as formerly. Slaves that have been made free during the rebellion to remain so, and slaves now in slavery in the rebellious States to remain as they are. This letter of Davis was handed on Monday last to a responsible and wealthy manufacturer, (a Democrat) of New York State, who left Niagara that day en route for this city. If he has arrived here, he has not yet communicated with the Government. That such a letter exists and is in the hands of a party authorized to present it to the Government of the United States, we have not the slightest doubt.

News Items.

[By Telegraph to the New York Sun.]

THE subscriptions to the 7-30 Loan for the last two days amount to $1,705,000. Thus far the entire amount subscribed is $39,500,000.

GENERAL DIX is at Sandusky for the purpose of inquiring into the recent rebel piracy on the lake and take effectual measures for the future.

GEN. GILMORE is in Washington. It is thought that he will receive a command immediately.

A SALUTE of one hundred guns was fired from the Capitol at Nashville, Tenn., on Thursday, in honor of Sheridan's recent victory, by order of General Grant.

THE Atlantic Club of Brooklyn defeated the Ontario Club of Rochester, at a game of base-ball yesterday in the latter city, by a score of 54 to 5. The Atlantics play the Utica Club on Saturday morning.

THE "owl" train from New York, on the Philadelphia and Trenton Railroad, was run into at three o'clock yesterday morning by Adam's Express train near Towisdale. The passenger train was waiting for the latter to cross the bridge. The locomotives were damaged. None of the passengers were injured. The engineer and greaser were scalded.

THE N. Y. State Fair at Rochester closed yesterday afternoon. The aggregate receipts are $6000. In the afternoon Hon. Lewis F. Allen of Black Rock, read a memorial on the late Gen. James S. Wadsworth, and appropriate resolutions were offered by Ex-Gov. John A. King. Hon. A. B. Conger of Rockland read a memorial on the late Hon. E. G. Vaile, ex-President of the Society, and an address was delivered by Dr. Anderson of the Rochester University. The fair has been a very great success.

General Intelligence.

[By Mail to the New York Sun.]

A YOUNG woman in Milton, Wis., died last week from the sting of a bee on her wrist. She survived the sting only twelve hours.

THE St. Joseph HERALD says that the streets of that city are filled with women with cigars in their mouths.

IT is said of the recent operations in the valley of the Shenandoah, that the "Early bird" has got his "Phil."

Two women who have been confined in prison at Washington, upon the charge of repeatedly aiding soldiers to desert, by furnishing them with citizens' clothing, have been sent to the Female Prison at Fitchburg, Mass.

A JUROR lately held out against his eleven companions in Santa Cruz, California, and the others, after trying all other means, finally agreed to send in a verdict of guilty, with the addition, that the obstinate member was a great rascal and confederate of the prisoner. He caved.

A BOY eleven years of age, at Berks county, Pa., last week, enticed another boy only seven years of age, into the garret of a house, and then shot him, and afterwards drew the body into the yard, placed it upon a pile of shavings and fired them. The neighbors, alarmed by the smoke, discovered the crime.

THE Lancaster (Ohio) GAZETTE states that the citizens of Lancaster design presenting their distinguished townsman, General Sherman, the celebrated horse "Bronze," now owned by Messrs. Reber & Kuntz, of that place, as an appropriate testimonial of their appreciation of the General's services.

U. S. TRANSPORT steamer N. W. Thomas arrived at New Orleans on the 13th inst., from Red River. She left that place a few days before with a supply of clothing for the Union soldiers held in confinement by the rebels at Tyler, Texas. The N. W. Thomas proceeded to Red River Landing, where she met the Confederate flag-of-truce boat Thos. S. Conley, and the supplies were transferred to that steamer.

THE rebel sympathisers in England have resorted to a new dodge for the Confederacy, by circulating a "peace" document, purporting to be an appeal of the English people to the Northerners to stop "the cruel war." The London STAR and other journals friendly to the United States expose the cheat, and show that the petition to which the free working men of England are asked to attach their names is entirely in the interests of the Confederacy, and calculated to build up a slave empire on the ruins of freedom and progress.

THERE are now exposed to public view, on the Capitol grounds, at Harrisburgh, Pa., about fifty pieces of brass cannon, which belong to the State. They are said to be pronounced unfit for service, and are to be disposed of, and rifle cannon to be supplied in their place. There are two brass pieces also on these grounds that once belonged to Lafayette, and two that were captured in the Mexican war, but these will be retained as relics of the olden time.

THE election of a Member of Congress from Chicago is invested with something of a representative interest, nearly similar to the famous struggle in Illinois between Lincoln and Douglas for the Senatorship. The candidates are McCormick, the famous reaping machine man, on the Democratic side, and the celebrated "Long John Wentworth" on the other. Both are Chicago institutions, and immensely wealthy, and very popular in and outside their respective parties, and the contest already excites immense local interest.

THE Canadian papers denounce the seizure of the two steamers on the lakes by secession refugees in Canada as an infamous abuse of the privileges of asylum. They complain that such attempts from Canadian ports tend to compromise the neutrality of the Lakes, and call for severe punishment on the guilty parties. The steamer Parsons was towed to Detroit on Wednesday, badly and wantonly damaged by the pirates, who, it appears, were nearly all escaped rebel prisoners, aided by "respectable" Southern persons and Canadian sympathizers.

A PARIS letter in the INDEPENDENCE BELGE says: "Negotiations have been opened with the Archbishop of Paris for the purpose of removing the obstacles opposed to the baptism of the children of Prince Napoleon. As is well known, the situation in which Victor Emanuel, the intended godfather, is placed in relation to the Church, had prevented the first baptism. The Emperor's cousin will not consent to the ceremony for the second of the princes taking place before the obstacles to the baptism of the first shall have been removed. To obtain this result is the object of the present negotiations, and there is no doubt that it will be attained."

FRESH complications are apprehended in Germany in consequence of the probable demise of the reigning Duke of Brunswick without heirs, in which case Hanover expects to annex that ancient Duchy. The question of succession attracts great attention, and an attempt has been made to submit the question to the arbitrament of the Diet, but the Brunswickers object to being disposed of without their consent, and demand that their destinies shall be disposed of by the States General of the Duchy to

(Continued on last page.)

THE NEW YORK HERALD.

WHOLE NO. 10,269. | NEW YORK, SUNDAY, OCTOBER 9, 1864. | PRICE FIVE CENTS.

THE DEFENCES OF RICHMOND.

The Scene of Operations on the North Side of James River and the Defences of the Rebel Capital, from a Map Found on the Body of the Rebel General Gherardie.

NOTES OF REFERENCE.

[illegible] Works on New Market Heights and Road, carried by General Birney September 29.

C C—Continuation of same, previously taken by General Ord September 29.

B B—Works unsuccessfully assailed by General Birney September 29.

D D—Points reached by [illegible]'s reconnoissance October 1.

See Fifth Page for Late and Important News from the North Side of the James.

The Conservative.

TUESDAY MORNING, OCT. 11, 1864.

City and Country.

READ the military orders that were rushed into our paper last evening, and make your arrangements accordingly.

THE city was yesterday morning placed under martial law—S. A. Marshall, provost marshal.

A VERDANT chap lost his bayonet yesterday, and coming toward us with a disconsolate air and a forlorn grasp upon his empty scabbard, asked if he should have to pay for it. We assured him that he would have to pay nothing, as they always "charge, bayonets!"

FENCIBLES, ATTENTION!—Some members of the Fencibles yesterday failed to report. We meet this morning at seven o'clock, near Laing's Hall. Every consideration of patriotism and honor should lead our men to promptly respond.

THE FENCIBLES.

FRIENDS have importuned us to give such and such individuals "fits" who have engineered themselves out of the reach of the summons to arms. We shall never descend to comment upon the acts of able-bodied men who shield themselves behind exemption papers, and refuse to fight in defense of their homes and their families.

DO NOT expect much of us this morning. We were in the ranks all day yesterday, and last night we came up to the *scratch* with reluctant fingers. There were other causes that served to disable our battery. A keg of beer mysteriously made its appearance in our company, (Co. F) and the exigencies of the hour were a sufficient justification for a charge on its contents by "prompt movement." And, besides, we are now a Sorehead—got it yesterday, through the awkwardness in drill of our "file leader," who, in bringing his piece to a "right shoulder shift," brought it rapidly down at an angle of depression, thumping us on the head heavily.

AT a meeting of the Republican Township Convention, held at High Prairie, on the 8th day of October, A. D., 1864, Prof. W. Foster was elected President, and James Orr, Secretary.

The meeting was called to order by the chair and then proceeded to nominate a candidate as Representative in the next State Legislature.

It was moved that Mr. S. D. Ewing be the candidate. Carried unanimously.

Moved and carried, that we elect by ballot four delegates to the County Convention to be held at Leavenworth, October 10th. The Chairman announced the following:

S. P. Hawkins, John C. Temple, John Hutchison and James Orr.

Motion carried that H. P. Keller, Henry Donehoo and James Orr be the committee for Stranger Township for the ensuing year.

On motion, the meeting adjourned *sine die*.

W. FOSTER, Ch'n.

JAMES ORR, Sec'y.

FROM ARKANSAS.

[Correspondence of the Leavenworth Conservative.]

LITTLE ROCK, ARK., Sept. 25.

Thinking a line from me may not be entirely unacceptable, I will attempt to give you an item concerning matters and things in this Department.

For some three or four weeks we were expecting an attack on this post from the rebel army, said to be in large force under Magruder. All was hurry and bustle. Entrenching parties were at work all around the city, strengthening the fortifications, and that old trump, the spade, was made to do heavy duty. The scare blew over and Little Rock is now considered in as little danger as St. Louis or Leavenworth. Excepting the bustle of the military Little Rock is to-day as peaceful and quiet and unconcerned as any Northern city. It is Sunday evening, and long before I commenced this epistle the bugles were sounding the retreat. From one camp the echo has scarcely died away before a distant bugler takes it up, and it passes backwards and forwards, through and around the fortifications which encircle us, until lost in the distance. The division and brigade bands and the fife and drum, all mingling and hammering away, independently, help to convince the Rackensacks that Uncle Sam is represented here. The only objection I have to the music is, that the time is bad. They must have set their watches in Leavenworth, as they seem to disagree like Leavenworth jewelers.

I have noticed quite a number of Leavenworth people here—Captain Haskell, A. Q. M., A. S. Addis, John Templeton, and others of the old Leavenworth theatre stock. There is one thing I haven't noticed—a Leavenworth newspaper. Why can't you send me a copy of the WEEKLY CONSERVATIVE once in a while. If we only had a live newspaper like it published here it would serve to wake up the dry bones.—The two papers published here are milk-and water sheets—one of which is edited by a former rebel surgeon in Hindman's army. His editorials are almost entirely devoted to proving his loyalty. Some of the brigades who have small army presses allow the printers to get out a little sheet occasionally, and which are generally pretty well spiced, although odd in title. One brigade issues the "Hard Tack," and a rival brigade calls theirs the "Sow Belly."

There are a number of Kansas troops in this Department, yet I only know of the Ninth Cavalry being at Little Rock at present. I was up to see some of them a few days ago, and found them in as good, or rather better condition than the majority of troops in this Department. The men want to see more fighting down here. There were quite a number of troops expecting to be mustered out, and some of them may now be on their way to Leavenworth. The regiment lost four men in the fight with Shelby at Bull creek, some three or four weeks ago.

J. D. G.

Price on His Way to Kansas!

Avows his Intention to go to Leavenworth!

His Columns Widely Spread for Subsistence!

HEADQUARTERS DEP'T OF KANSAS, Fort Leavenworth, Oct. 10.

EDS. CONSERVATIVE:—The following has just been received by Major General Curtis:

HEADQ'R'S, ST. LOUIS, Oct. 10.

Price's movements are not known, but he has avowed his intention to go to Leavenworth. If he will try this it will enable our columns under Mower and Smith and our cavalry to get between them and the Osage, and they will suffer. They spread and stretch out for subsistence; therefore your cavalry can forcibly strike the heads of their columns and hurt and retard their march. The telegraph lines are so interrupted it will be difficult to communicate with you.

(Signed) W. S. ROSECRANS, Major General.

Yours, &c., L. B. FLEAK.

FROM FORT SCOTT.

Lamar Burned by Bushwhackers.

HEADQUARTERS DEP'T OF KANSAS, Fort Leavenworth, Oct. 10.

The following telegram has just been received:

FORT SCOTT, Oct. 10.

To Major General Curtis:

Lamar was burned last night entire—not a house left. Supposed to be done by a large force of bushwhackers. Lamar is forty-six miles southeast of here.

(Signed) C. W. BLAIR, Col.

Respectfully, L. B. FLEAK.

FROM PAOLA.

PAOLA, Oct. 10.

Col. A. C. Ellithorpe:

Publish the following in your issue tomorrow morning:

J. G. BLUNT.

OLATHE, Oct. 10.

[General Orders No. 1.]

1. In obedience to instructions from Headquarters Department of Kansas, the undersigned assumes command of the District of South Kansas, Headquarters at Paola and in the field.

2. Capt. Geo. S. Hampton is announced as Assistant Adjutant General, and will be obeyed and respected accordingly.

JAS. G. BLUNT, Maj. Gen.

HEADQUARTERS, DEP'T OF KANSAS, Fort Leavenworth, Oct. 10, 1864.

ED. CONSERVATIVE: The following telegram has just been received:

"HEADQUARTERS, ST. LOUIS, Oct. 10, 1864.

To Major General Curtis:

I notice in the Leavenworth papers a dispatch to you from Gen. Brown, saying that the rebels captured four guns from Ewing, and at last accounts, nearly his entire command. I am happy to inform you that Ewing made good his retreat to Rolla, with all his guns and his entire command. Please publish this.

(Signed,) W. S. ROSECRANS, Major-General."

HEADQUARTERS, ST. LOUIS, Oct. 9, 1864.

To Major General Curtis:

Price has left Jefferson City, and is marching West. I shall follow him wherever he goes. W. S. ROSECRANS, Maj. Gen.

SELF-PRESERVATION is a good law—in fact "the first law of nature;" and our citizens yesterday sprang to arms in a manner that testifies their determination to exercise the prerogatives of the law. But every rule has its exceptions, and a few sneaks succeeded in displaying their cowardice and avoiding the patrol, while a few others were smoked out of their holes and jostled into the ranks, where, armed and equipped, they looked as bold as a sheep.

DEATH OF A DISTINGUISHED MAN.—Hon. Thomas F. Marshall died at his house in Woodford county, Kentucky, on Thursday, the 22d ult., of disease of the heart and lungs. Mr. M. was widely known as one of the most gifted men of his day, and for the last thirty years had occupied a large share of the public attention. Few men surpassed him in varied learning and elegant literary acquirements, which, with his splendid genius, made him one of the most attractive orators of the age in which he lived.

IT is stated that five Federal officers, consisting of a colonel, lieutenant-colonel, major, and two captains, who were dishonorably expelled by Gen. Sherman from his army and sent into the Confederate lines for speaking disrespectfully of the President of the United States in the presence of the enemy, while accompanying a flag of truce, have arrived in Richmond, where they are to be confined during the war for fighting against their principles.

THE largest single payment ever made an author was the check for £20,000 paid by the Longman's to Macaulay for the third and fourth volumes of his history.

LOCAL NOTICES.

THE thoroughbred Stallion "Little Arthur," that belonged to Sam Smith, of Independence, is for sale at my stable, corner of Second and Seneca. WM. PHILLIPS.

WHOLESALE OYSTER DEPOT, No. 11 Shawnee street, four doors west of Main, Leavenworth city, Kansas. I am now receiving Maltby's and Hart's celebrated fresh oysters, daily, by express. Families, saloons, and others supplied at Baltimore prices, (freight added.) Orders from the country promptly attended to.

sept8d3m H. R. CAMP, Agent.

KANSAS FREEDMEN'S HOME.—There are at this Institution, a number of colored females, desiring places, for service, either in the City or Country.

Families, wishing "help" for a reasonable compensation will be able to secure it here.

The home at present occupies the old U. S. Hospital Buildings, at the north end of Seventh Street.

Leavenworth, Aug. 29, 1864. aug30dtf

SPECIAL NOTICES.

DO NOT expect much of us this morning. We were in the ranks all day yesterday, and last night we came up to the *scratch* with reluctant fingers. There were other causes that served to disable our battery. A keg of beer mysteriously made its appearance in our company, (Co. F) and the exigencies of the hour were a sufficient justification for a charge on its contents by "prompt movement." And, besides, we are now a Sorehead—got it yesterday, through the awkwardness in drill of our "file leader," who, in bringing his piece to a "right shoulder shift," brought it rapidly down at an angle of depression, thumping us on the head heavily.

LYNCHBURG VIRGINIAN

Saturday Morning, Oct. 15th, 1864.

THE VIRGINIAN
Is published Daily, Tri-Weekly, and Weekly, by
CHARLES W. BUTTON.

TERMS OF SUBSCRIPTION:

Daily Virginian, one year,	$30 00
Do. do. six months,	15 00
Do. do. three monts,	8 00
Do. do. one month,	3 00
Tri-Weekly, one year,	$20 00
Do. six months,	10 00
Do. three months,	6 00
Do. one month,	2 00
Weekly, one year,	$10 00
Do. six months,	6 00

☞No paper will be sent without the subscription is paid in advance.

RATES OF ADVERTISING:

ADVERTISEMENTS are inserted at $2 00 per square of eight lines or less for each insertion.

OBITUARY AND MARRIAGE NOTICES charged for at the same rates.

SECESSION OF THE WEST.

We have understood, through a source entitled to confidence, that the opinion prevails to a considerable extent, in official circles, that the re-election of Lincoln will be likely to precipitate a further disintegration of the so-called United States. Especially is this result apprehended in case the election should be warmly contested and Lincoln be elected by a small majority—if that majority appear to be due to any interference of his partizans with the most perfect and unconstrained freedom of the ballot box. The precaution which has already been taken in Tennessee, under the administration of Andrew Johnson to prevent the framing of an electoral ticket for McClellan and Pendleton, is indicative of what the Administration of Lincoln will do wherever military organization prevails. Thus, not only in Tennessee; but in Maryland, Louisiana, and West Virginia, the military satraps of Lincoln will take charge of the election and either keep the Democrats from the polls, or, multiply the votes of their own supporters to a prepondering extent.

A fair election, in no event, is to be expected; and Lincoln will, by some means or other, be likely to get all the votes he may need. This will add to the rancor and bitterness with which the West already regard the New England States, and serve to promote disunion.

The feeling that now exists between these two sections of the Union and the estimate, in which the West holds the North, may be inferred from the following extract of a letter from the editor of the Hartford *Times*, dated at Chicago. He says:

"There is, throughout the West, a wide spread and growing feeling of dislike towards New England. I find this feeling to be bitter, and that it is largely shared in by Western republicans as well as democrats. The feeling that to New England fanaticism the country is largely indebted for this calamitous war, and that Eastern men have been getting an undue share of the profits, while the West has sustained the conflict with its blood and treasure, is more generally entertained and freely expressed than is pleasant for me to hear. In this sweeping condemnation, there is but little liability that justice will be done to those in the Eastern States who have never countenanced fanaticism, but have suffered from its persecutions. If, by any unpropitious fate Lincoln should be re-elected and the South gain a separate independence, there is but little hope that the West would consent to remain with New England."

In this view of the case it is difficult to determine whether we should prefer the election of Lincoln or that of McClellan. If the latter should be elected the Republicans might grow luke-warm upon the war question, preferring secession and disunion to a restoration of the Union with slavery. It is comforting for us to know however, that we cannot be worsted in any event; and that, result as the election may, it will serve to widen the breach that already exists between the geographical and political parties in the United States.

The Ohio, Pennsylvania and Indiana elections were to take place on Tuesday last. The New York Times (Republican) is certain of Ohio, but rather doubtful about Pennsylvania and Indiana, in the latter of which States there are organizations "openly arrayed" against the Government.

CONFINEMENT OF OUR OFFICERS AT MORRIS ISLAND.

The Palmetto Herald, a Yankee sheet, published at Port Royal, South Carolina, gives a description of the prison and treatment of our officers confined on Morris island. It says:

"The place of confinement is located between Fort Strong and Putnam, in the dangerous district, where shells fly freely, in full view of all the rebel works, and closely under our own guns. Within an immensely strong palisade of heavy timbers, deeply imbedded in the sand, twelve or fifteen feet high, and firmly strapped together, and surrounding an area of perhaps an acre and a half, are the tents of the prisoners, laid out in regimental style, with wide streets and abundance of room between them. Entirely surrounding the camp, although at some distance from the tents, in order to give the prisoners breathing room, is a rope attached to posts, about fifteen feet from the palisades, which marks the extreme verge and limit of the camp, and beyond which no one crosses, save under the pain of instant death at the hands of the guards, who have imperative orders to shoot down any one who attempts to cross the death line. Within the space between the 'dead line' and palisades are the sentries, who patrol their beats night and day without intermission. Upon a platform, erected on the outside of the palisades, is the second line of sentries, who can look down and maintain the closest watch upon the prisoners in all their movements. Beyound these are other sentries and pickets, properly stationed, and forming successive cordons of guards, to prevent escape, if the inner lines have been passed by those who may be insane enough to attempt an escape. Light artillery, in position at different points, bear upon the prisoners, to be used if any combined effort should be made to surprise and overpower the guard, and rush out en mass. Besides, the heavy guns of Fort Strong bear upon every part of the camp, and could be used with deadly effects should the situation of affairs demand it. There is little danger of such an attempt being made, as the most reckless of the prisoners must observe the utter futility of an effort of the kind; but all the precautions are wisely taken, and the greatest vigilance is always observed.

"The prisoners have rations of precisely like quantity furnished by the Confederates to Union prisoners in Charleston, and of like kind as near as may be.—They are cooked by detailed men, and distributed to them in camp. They would have been compelled to do their own cooking, if such an arrangement would not have occasioned embarrassment and trouble. The plan had too many serious disadvantages to be adopted just at present.

"The prisoners are divided into eight detachments, each commanded or in charge of a negro sergeant, who brings them into line at roll call three times a day and when they receive their food. The prisoners do not particularly fancy their immediate commanders, but are compelled to put up with them. The sergeants are proud of their position, and are exceedingly strict in enforcing obedience to all proper orders. They treat their charge with a proper degree of politeness and no more, but carry out their orders promptly and to the letter.

"The rebels pronounce their present situation as far preferable to any they have yet been placed in, and seem to be enjoying themselves as well as persons can under like circumstances. They enjoy the heavy artillery contest, which is going on night and day, and exhibit great satisfaction when the rebel shells fall into our works, or a paticularly good shot is made by the rebel gunners. A few fragments of shell have fallen in the enclosure, but none of the prisoners have been injured. They sleep upon the ground, wrapped in a single blanket, but suffer no discomfort from that sort of lodging.

"They are quiet and tractable, and have not exhibited the first sign of a mutinous or turbulent spirit since they have been ashore. They are all in a tolerable good state of health, and are patiently awaiting the day of exchange and a transfer to the streets of Charleston, towards which they turn many a long and wistful gaze.

HEAVY DEMOCRATIC GAINS IN THE NORTH.

The New York World sees a great victory for the democratic party in the late election in Connecticut. The World says of the result:

In Connecticut, as in Maine, every engine of official patronage and social despotism has been remorselessly set to work against us, yet town after town records the swelling majority of the people over the placemen, of the lovers of the Union over the fetish worshippers of abolition.

Of the fifty-five towns already heard from in Connecticut, thirty have been carried by the Democracy, and in all others the Democratic vote has been largely increased over the vote of last spring, in many cases doubling upon that vote!

The State has already repudiated Lincoln! In seven towns alone a Democratic gain of one thousand votes knells the doom of the fanatics at Washington who have dared to forget that the administration exists for the nation, not the nation for the administration. Bridgeport, for several years overwhelmingly Republican, gives this year a Democratic majority of 117. Derby, on the largest vote ever polled there, gives a Democratic majority for the first time in fifteen years; Norwich gives a Democratic gain of 264 since last spring; Greenwich, a Democratic majority of 167; New London, a Democratic gain of 132; Meriden, a Democratic gain of 200—and so on.

SEYMOUR ON THE STUMP IN PHILADELPHIA.

Seymour has been making a speech in Philadelphia, which the Black Republican press stigmatizes as being full of cant and demagoguism. We make the following extracts of this speech, which are taken from the Philadelphia Age:

Now, you know that that monstrous army that we gave them nine months ago has been so nearly annihilated that another call for five hundred thousand men is made upon us, and we are not in as good a condition as we were then. That part of Louisiana and of Arkansas, west of the Mississippi river, that was wrested from them, has resumed the offensive and invaded Missouri itself. The great army of Sherman that attacked and captured Atlanta, has its rear communications attacked and endangered by large bodies of rebels. Go into Virginia and what do you find there? Instead of the army of Lee reduced down to a skeleton, as it was a year ago, it has sustained itself thus far with full force and great power, and it is strong in numbers to day. Now, I believe that, notwithstanding your political views and political prejudies, you will admit that our armies have done their work. We, in common with our Republican friends, have honored the names of Grant, and Farragut, Sherman, Sheridan, and all the heroes of the war; but we all cannot deny that their efforts have been unsuccessful, and the blame is not with our armies.

Speaking of Missouri, he thus defines the duties of the Northern people towards that State. Perhaps there is another side to this question of choice on the part of Missouri which the spirit of the dead ruffian Lyon could explain could the dead speak, and, speaking, tell the truth, which they never told when living:

You are compelled, at the expense of the people of Missouri, and of every other Northern State, of contributions of men an money, to hold in the Union a State which originally was with us of its own will.

What he says about Kentucky, from the conduct of that State towards its Southern brethren, does not deserve rebuke.—Kentucky merits all the contumely heaped upon her name:

When armed resistance to the authority of the Government first began, the people of Kentucky resolved to stand by us. They severed the dearest ties, the ties of consanguinity; they broke away from the dearest of relationship; they said they would not go with those who were bound to them by the dearest ties of earth. They said they would not go with them. And do you not remember with what joy we hailed such men as Wickliffe, Guthrie, and Crittenden, of Kentucky, who stood by the flag and Constitution of our land? But since the Government at Washington has taken the control of that State in hand, the position of things has changed. The presence of vast armies there is now required, and those men who were with us at heart at the outset now come here to tell you of the injury and insult to which they have been subjected.

A REGIMENT OF TRAITORS.

Private Jonathen Ford, an exchanged prisoner, informs the correspondent of the Columbus Enquirer, that about seven hundred of the prisoners (out of seventeen hundred) at Atlanta had taken the oath, and had gone into the service of the enemy as cavalry, and here known as the 1st Georgia Cavalry. In this organization nearly every State in the Confederacy is represented. The 1st Alabama infantry has thirty-one; 37th Georgia, two, 11th Tennessee, eleven; Keyes' and Sweat's batteries from Arkansas, twelve; Barry's battery, commonly known as the Lookout battery, from Chattanooga, every man that was captured [twenty-one] took the oath and joined this organization.

Each man is to receive a splendid outfit, including a fine horse. Their operations by special permit are to be confined to the rear, guarding trains and bridges. It will be a black day for the miserable traitors when Forrest's troopers meet them. They should each carry an extra halter for their own accommodation.

AN ALLIGATOR EATS A MAN.

A correspondent of the Wilmington Journal, writing from Onslow county, on the 11th instant, says:

On the 4th of this month I found in a creek, known as "Hadnot's Creek," the body of a man cut off at his lower ribs, all below that being gone. I got all the people together that I could, took it up and had it burried. It had been in the water some time, as it smelled very offensive. No information could be ascertained as to where it came from.

This morning, while talking with Mr E W Pelletier, I heard an alligator catch one of my hogs; I caught my gun and ran to the scene of action, and found the alligator with a large hog of mine in the creek. I shot and killed him. On getting him out, I found him to be one of the largest I had ever seen; he was also uncommonly full. We cut him up and found in his stomach the foot and leg and the lower part of the trunk of a man.—These parts doubtless belonged to the same body of which the upper parts have already been found. Where the man came from, or who he was, I have no means of ascertaining. It is believed that he was a deserter from our side or from the enemy's, and was caught by the alligator while trying to swim the creek.

RECEPTION OF THE MEXICAN ENVOY BY THE QUEEN OF SPAIN.

[By telegraph to the English papers.]

MADRID, Sept 3.—The reception of Senor Francisco Frazio, Envoy Extraordinary and Minister Plenipotentiary of the Emperor Maximilian to this Court, took place to-day. In delivering to the Queen the letter from the Emperor, announcing his accession to the throne, and attesting the diplomatic character of his envoy, Senior Frazio said:

"YourMajesty: My august Sovereign has deigned to honor me with the high mission of placing in your Majesty's hands the letter announcing his accession to the imperial throne of Mexico, to which he has been solemnly called by the nation. Sincerely desiring that the Empire and Spain may maintain good and friendly relations, he has also appointed me his Envoy Extraordinary and Minister Plenipotentiary to your Majesty, as confirmed by the letter that I have the honor to present to your Majesty.

"I shall consider myself fortunate, if, in the discharge of my official functions, it is given me to continue by all possible means to strengthen the bonds of sympathy, amity and interest that should unite the two nations. Great also is my satisfaction at the distinguished honor of being the first envoy to your Majesty of a Government from which the noble portion of the New World expects its regeneration, and the assurance, by God's favor, of the inestimable benefits of religion and monarchy, which are those that will give the rising empire peace, prosperity and greatness.

"Full of zeal and hope, I shall unceasingly labor to this end, and my wishes will be fulfilled if I have also the honor to merit your Majesty's goodness."

The Queen replied:

"Sir—I am interested in the well-being and prosperity of the Mexican nation as in that of every people forming the civilized world. I desire that the anarchy of which that country has been the victim may cease, and that it may generate in the bosom of religion, order, and true liberty. If the empire which has just been established is the base of this future, I salute the empire with sincere sympathy, as well as the distinguished prince who has accepted and assumed its crown. Spain, which over held to Mexico a friendly hand, cannot deny or withdraw it now.

"I am equally gratified at the selection which has been made of you to reside near my person, in the quality of envoy extraordinary and minister plenipotentiary of the new emperor. I receive the assurance you give me of your sentiments and offer you a sincere welcome. Let us hope that with the favor of Providence the relations between the two states will be uninterruptedly good and friendly. They should be so from the identity of origin, by the similarity of customs, and the evident concord of all their interests."

POLITICAL RIOTS IN MISSOURI.

The St Louis Republican, in noticing the political outrages committed throughout the State of Missouri, says:

"If Mr Lincoln or his friends have really the slightest regard for the freedom of elections, it is about time they should show it in Missouri. So far, at this early stage of the canvass, their supporters, in the shape of mobs, have interfered with the demonstrations, meetings and speakers of the party opposed them. In St Louis a procession was assailed and partially broken up one night, and a club room demolished, and a meeting dispersed with damage to limb, if not life, in another. On two succeeding evenings the office of the Republican was threatened by riotous demonstrations for merely hanging out a banner inscribed with sentiments which every patriot must approve, and none but a man totally lost to all his obligations as a good citizen or member of society would condemn. In Kansas city, Judge Birch was unable to proceed with his canvass, his life being threatened by a mob. In Troy, Lincoln co., a McClellan meeting was fired into by some soldiers, no doubt set on by low demagogues more responsible than the soldiers; and among the peaceable, good citizens there assembled for a lawful purpose, and in the exercise of rights which no man should dispute, one individual was killed and two wounded. In Jefferson city, an attempt was made to break up a McClellan meeting by rowdies, who were incited by well known demagogues, who plied their tools with whiskey. On that occasion, George Dingham, State Treasurer, and a most estimable man, was assailed, and by accident only escaped with his life. In Moniteau county, we are informed that two persons, who were prominent at a McClellan meeting, were murdered on their way home, after the meeting broke up. Probably these instances comprise but a portion of the outrages committed by men who, while committing them, profess to be acting in the interests of Mr Lincoln.

"It was predicted by some, before the canvass opened, that terrorism would be used to prevent the opponents of Mr. Lincoln from conducting an active canvass and from voting in Missouri. We are sorry to say that, from the indications so far, these predictions are likely to be realized."

THE WAY THE ENROLLING OFFICERS ARE TREATED IN PENNSYLVANIA.

A dispatch from Easton, Pennsylvania, dated the 4th instant, shows that the place of enrolling officer in Pennsylvania is not a bomb-proof:

Private Leader K. Dease, of Capt Stroud's cavalry, of Philadelphia, was shot through the head with a ball, and in several parts of the body with buck-shot, and instantly killed, near the house of Jacob Miller, in Price township, Monroe county, Pennsylvania, yesterday. A squad of men, he being one of them, had gone out as a guard to the person who was to serve notices upon the drafted men of that township, and, while riding along the road, they were fired upon from the bushes, with the result above named. Miller, and a man named Secoe, were arrested by the comrades of the deceased and brought to Stroudsburg last evening, and were taken to Philadelphia to-day. Dease was a highly respectable young man, and a resident of Philadelphia.

DEATH OF COLONEL PATTON.

A letter in the Norfolk (Va.) Regim speaking of the death of Colonel Patton (late of Richmond,) after the battle of Fisher's Hill, says:

"He was mortally wounded in the fight on Monday, and carried to Mr. William's house, in this town, from whence we will be buried some time to-day.—General Early sent a flag of truce to General Sheridan to inquire respecting him. Believing that he was mortally wounded and not likely to recover, he requested that he might be buried in such a manner that a citizen designated in his communication would be able to identify his remains, at the same time requesting such information concerning his condition as General Sheridan might find it convenient to communicate. In accordance with instructions from General Sheridan, Colonel Edwards has forwarded all the facts in the case, which will doubtless be conveyed to Early in due season by flag of truce."

LYNCHBURG VIRGINIAN

Notice.—The cross mark appended to the names of certain subscribers indicates that the term of which they subscribed will soon expire. They are thus notified in time to renew their subscription if desired.

RAGS WANTED.—The highest market price will be paid at this Office for Clean Cotton Rags. They will be purchased in any quantity.

Col. T. T. Munford, acting Brigadier, arrived in this city Thursday night, from the Valley. He is suffering with a painful carbuncle, which renders him unfit for duty at present. His services entitle him to a brigadier's commission, which we hope he will soon receive.

The Yankees in the Valley.—The Yankees do not even attempt to disguise their wholesale and infamous vandalism in the Valley. They boldly proclaim the commission of acts sufficient to damn them forever in the estimation of enlightened nations.—Yet, heartless and shameless as they are, they seem to glory in their enormities.

A Northern correspondent referring to the execution of Grant's recent order to destroy everything in the Valley—"to make it one barren waste"—says:

"The rebels will cry out against what is now being done in the Valley. Yet it is only since we have commenced this work that we fairly see how necessary it is. Many of the mills were found to contain thousands of bushels of wheat, which the millers were grinding up as fast as they could for the use of the rebel army. The amount of wheat which we find in the Valley is astonishingly large. The mills are full of it. The barns are stored with it. Stacks as high as houses are found in the fields. Besides, there is an abundance of oats in the sheaf and enormous quantities of corn. Almost every barn we come to is loaded with wheat, hay and oats. The destruction of these barns is being accomplished as fast as possible."

There is one article of subsistence which is bound to be cheap. It is sorghum.

The Columbus *Enquirer* notices the sale at auction in that city, of a very fine article of syrup at $3:05 per gallon, and adds: "There has been an exceedingly large amount of this syrup made in this section the present season, and we would not be at all surprised if it went still lower. We hear of farmers who never made more than from three to five bales of cotton, who will make this year from twenty to twenty-five barrels of syrup, and whose families cannot consume more than one or two barrels of it. There is hardly a farmer or planter but will have more or less of it to sell."

Sorghum syrup is selling in Charlotte, North Carolina, at $5 per gallon.

SORGHUM FLOUR.

We would advise planters to save all the seed from the present crop of Chinese Sugar Cane, as it is known by those who have tried it, that the grain when ground and bolted the same as wheat, makes a good substitute for buckwheat. It may also be used as a substitute for coffee. A trial of either or both might be a beneficial experiment.

The Newspapers.—In an able article on the indispensable importance of the Press to the country and society, especially in our great pending struggle for independence, the Augusta, Ga., Register remarks: "Our honest opinion is that no class of our countrymen, except our soldiers, have done more for our success than newspaper men. This is our candid opinion after maturely considering the subject. They have given tone to public sentiment, and aroused the patriotism of the people to every demand made upon them. In the emergencies of our country, may harsh and grievous laws have been passed—many orders and regulations hard to be borne have been adopted. In some cases designing men, in others well meaning ones, supposing they were doing their duty, have done much to arouse all the feelings of prejudice and opposition by the people to these supposed usurpations and tyrannies. Just here the press have come in, and by their daily pleadings, their patriotic appeals, reconciled apparant differences and allayed all opposition. They have educated the minds of the people to every great and important change in the policy of our Government, and have, with rare exceptions, with all their powers sustained the cause of our country.

Blot out the newspapers of the country and you will have no general policy among the people. There will be as many opinions as there are individuals and as many leaders as there are communities. Rumors will be rife all over the land and in the absence of reliable information, as now obtained, the people will be subjected to imposition and will always be depressed by dangers real or imaginary. Newspapers form a kind of bond of union—a common medium of the interchange of ideas, and next to our organized armies are the most powerful engines within our country for the attainment of its independence, by holding up the duty of the citizens on the one hand, the rights of the Government on the other; the grounds for encouragement on the one hand and the necessity for endurance on the other. From the President to the humblest citizen—from the General to the private—the high and the low, the rich and the poor, would all feel the need of this common source of information and of comfort. Woe be unto our country when it is destroyed!"

From the Valley.—We have authentic information from the Valley. The account which we published of the cavalry reverse on Sunday last was, in the main, correct. Rosser, commanding a division, had driven the enemy beautifully for three days, making valuable captures, and killing not a few of the enemy. On Saturday evening he pursued them to within two miles of Fisher's Hill, far ahead of the infantry supports.—Early Sunday morning three divisions of the enemy's cavalry moved to attack Rosser.—Notwithstanding the disparity of numbers our forces stood their ground, and received the attack. The unequal contest was kept up for some time successfully by our side, but by strategy the enemy threw a brigade around our left, which opened on the rear, throwing our men into confusion and causing a retreat, which soon partook very much of the nature of a disorderly flight. The right of our line, commanded by Col. Munford, held its ground as long as possible, and fought well, but was compelled, by the giving way on the left, to retreat. This occurred on the back road. On the main pike, Lomax at the same time engaged another force of the enemy, with a like result. Rosser lost six pieces of artillery, twelve wagons, including ordnance and head quarter wagons, some ambulances, and about one hundred and seventy-five men, killed wounded and missing. Lomax lost three pieces of artillery. Shoemaker's battery was not captured, as reported.

The following are all the casualties of the 2d Va. Regiment that we could obtain:

Killed. ———Singleton of Campbell Co., R. Y. Oliver, Roanoke, M. Anderson, Albemarle, Lt. H. Hatcher, Bedford.

Wounded. Lt. Haythe, company C, Lieut. Davis, Lynchburg, severely, Sandy White, Roanoke, lost a leg and captured.

Captured. T. P. Taylor, Company B.

Notwithstanding their misfortune our men were in good spirits and anxious to give the foe another turn, confident that they would regain their lost laurels. The enemy's cavalry in the Valley is supposed to number from eight to ten thousand, and is splendidly mounted and equipped.

The scene of desolation which the Valley presents is said to be appaling and sickening. Scarcely anything but charred and blackened walls and heaps of ashes meet the eye. Barns, stables, mills and dwellings have alike been devoted to the flames. Hundreds of families are roofless and homeless. For miles around the track of the enemy was lighted up with the wild glare of the devouring element. Thousands on thousands of bushels of grain were consumed, and the implements of husbandry destroyed. Grant's inhuman instructions have been literally fulfilled, and that beautiful and bountiful region made a barren waste. Yet, the noble and long-suffering people are only truer and firmer in their fealty and allegiance, as their sufferings increase. May the day of their permanent deliverance be near at hand.

LATEST FROM THE VALLEY—SHERIDAN'S REPORT OF HIS DESTRUCTION OF PRIVATE PROPERTY—REPORT OF THE FIGHT WITH ROSSER.

The despatches from Gen Sheridan to Stanton we give in full as a specimen of the warfare he is boasting of carrying on and the lying he can do officially. This is the first:

Woodstock, Virginia, Oct 7—9 P. M. }

Lieutenant General U. S. Grant:

I have the honor to report my command at this point to-night. I commenced moving back from Port Republic, Mount Crawford, Bridgewater and Harrisonburg yesterday morning.

In moving back to this point, the whole country from the Blue Ridge to the North mountain has been rendered untenable for a rebel army.

I have destroyed over two thousand barns, filled with wheat and hay; and farming implements; over 70 mills, filled with flour and wheat; have driven in front of our army over four herd of stock, and have killed and issued to the troops not less than three thousand sheep.

This destruction embraces the Luray Valley and Little Fort Valley, as well as the main Valley.

A large number of horses have been obtained, a proper estimate of which I cannot now make.

Lieutenant John R. Meigs, my engineer officer, was murdered beyond Harrisonburg, near Dayton. For this atrocious act all the houses within an area of five miles were burned.

Since I came into the Valley from Harper's Ferry, every train, every small party, and every straggler, has been bushwhacked by the people, many of whom have protection papers from commanders who have been hitherto in the Valley.

The people here are getting sick of the war. Heretofore they have had no reason to complain, because they have been living in great abundance.

I have not been followed by the enemy to this point, with the exception of a small force of rebel cavalry that showed themselves some distance behind my rear guard to-day.

A party of one hundred of the 8th Ohio cavalry, which I had stationed at the bridge over the North Shenandoah, near Mount Jackson, was attacked by McNeil with 17 men while they were asleep, and the whole party dispersed or captured. I think they will all turn up. I learn that 56 of them had reached Winchester. McNeil was mortally wounded and fell into our hands. This was fortunate, as he was the most daring and dangerous of all the bushwackers in this section of the country.

P. H. Sheridan, Maj-Gen'l.

His second dispatch:

Strasburg, Va., October 9—Midnight. }

Lieut. Gen. Grant, City Point:

In coming back to this point, I was not followed up until late yesterday, when a large force of cavalry appeared in my rear. I then halted my command to offer battle by attacking the enemy. I became satisfied that it was only all the rebel cavalry of the Valley, commanded by Rosser, and directed Torbert to attack at daylight this morning and finish this Saviour of the Valley.

The attack was handsomely made. Custer, commanding the Third cavalry division, charged on the back road, and Merritt, commanding the First cavalry division, on the Strasburg pike. Merritt captured five pieces of artillery; Custer captured six pieces of artillery, with caisons, battery forage, &c.

The two divisions captured 47 wagons, ambulances, etc. Among the wagons captured are the headquarter wagons of Rosser, Lomax, Wickham and Col Pollard. The number of prisoners will be about 330.

The enemy, after being charged by our gallant cavalry, were broken, and ran. They were followed by our men on the jump 26 miles, through Mt Jackson and across the north fork of the Shenandoah. I deemed it best to make this delay of one day here and settle this new cavalry general.

The 11 pieces of artillery captured to-day make 36 pieces captured in the Shenandoah Valley since the 19th of September. Some of the artillery was new and never had been fired. The pieces were marked "Tredegar works."

P. H. Sheridan, Maj-Gen'l.

LATEST BY TELEGRAPH

Reports of the Press Association.

Entered according to Act of Congress, in the year 1863, by J. S. Thrasher, in the Clerk's Office of the District Court of the Confederate States in the Northern District of Georgia.

DESPATCH FROM SHERMAN.

Richmond, Oct. 14th.

The Whig has received the Herald of the 11th.

Sherman telegraphs Hallack, from Alatoona the 9th, that he reached Kenesaw the 6th instant in time to witness the distant attack at Altoona. He anticipated the attack, and ordered Gen Corse from Rome with reinforcements. The attack was met and repulsed—the enemy losing 200 dead and a 1000 wounded and prisoners. Our loss 700 aggregate.—The enemy captured the small garrisons at Big Shanty and Acworth and burnt 7 miles of Railroad. Have abundance of provisions at Alatoona and Atlanta. Hood moved back to Dallas. Van Wert was watching him, in case he tries to reach Kingston and Rome.—Atlanta is perfectly secure.

Sheridan is at Woodstock; has destroyed everything in the way of provisions.

Gold 199½.

[The reporter might have saved himself some trouble and us some expense if he had withheld the above. It came to us by the Richmond papers several hours in advance of the telegraph.]

PRESS ASSOCIATION.

Augusta, Oct 12.

The Board of Directors of the Press Association having adjourned from Columbus to Augusta, met here to-day. A quorum was present. Telegrams were received from absent directors giving assurance of co-operation in the action of the board. A resolution was adopted, directing the President to correspond with the President of the Southern Telegraph Company, with a view to arrange fair and equitable commutation for the payment of tolls for press reports; also a resolution directing the President to send a circular to the members explaining matters considered at the present meeting, apprising them of the proposed action of the Telegraph Companies and embarrassment to the Press that may result therefrom, at the same time assuring them of the entire confidence felt in the useful permanance of the present organization.

PENNSYLVANIA, INDIANA AND OHIO GONE FOR THE REPUBLICANS.

Richmond, Oct 14.

To-night Northern papers of the 12th were received. Pennsylvania, Indiana and Ohio have gone Republican by large majorities.

Sheridan is at Fisher's Hill.

The Governor General of Nova Scotia is on a visit to Grant.

Nothing later from Sherman.

DESTRUCTION OF A PORCELAIN FACTORY.

Augusta, Oct. 14th.

The Factory of the Porcelain Company at Roaline, six miles from Augusta, was destroyed by fire last night.

FROM RICHMOND.

Richmond, Oct 14.

The fight was not resumed to-day on the North sides of the James, as expected.

Nothing at the War Department or in any quarter.

Cazenovia Republican.

Vol. XI. CAZENOVIA, N. Y., WEDNESDAY, OCTOBER 19, 1864. No. 25.

REBELS ROUTED IN OHIO! INDIANA! PENNSYLVANIA!

The Cazenovia Republican,

PUBLISHED AT

Cazenovia, Madison County, N. Y.,

BY

IRVING C. FORT,

EDITOR AND PROPRIETOR.

☞ Office in the second story of the Post-office building, on Albany street. Entrance through the Post-office.

Terms:

FOR THE NEWSPAPER: To Village Subscribers, having their papers left at their doors, $2.50 a year. To Mail Subscribers, $2.00 a year, or at the same rate for any shorter time. Advance payment is always insisted on.

RATES OF ADVERTISING:

	1w.	2w.	3w.	1m.	3m.	6m.	1y.
1 Square,	$ .75	$1.00	$1.25	$1.50	$3.00	$5.00	$ 9
2 Squares	1.25	2.00	2.50	3.00	4.00	7.00	12
¼ Col'mn	1.75	2.25	3.00	3.50	5.00	10.00	18
½ Col'mn	3.00	4.00	5.00	6.00	10.00	18.00	30
1 Col'mn	6.00	8.00	9.00	10.00	18.00	30.00	50

Business Cards of not more than five lines, $4 per year.

Special notices leaded and made up next to the reading matter fifty per cent. higher than the above.

Notices of Marriages and Deaths are inserted free, but where more than the customary mention is made, fifty cents will be charged for the first ten lines and five cents for each additional line.

Legal advertising at statute prices.

⁂ Payment considered due when the advertising is half finished.

Lawyers.

D. W. CAMERON, Attorney and Counsellor at Law—office in Hough's block, corner Albany and Lincklaen streets, CAZENOVIA, N. Y. ☞ All business entrusted to him will be promptly attended to.

W. L. STORKE, Attorney, Justice of the Peace and Government Claim Agent. Office, in the Hearsy Block, near the Park House. 10-50y1

CHARLES STEBBINS, Jr., Attorney and Counsellor at Law, Insurance Agent, and Notary Public. CAZENOVIA, N. Y.

Boots, Shoes, Hats, Caps.

REMOVAL. H. J. WEED has removed his Hat and Cap Store to the building second door west of the Post Office, where may be found

HATS AND CAPS

in all their varieties, and of the LATEST STYLES.—Call and examine his stock, before purchasing.

H. J. WEED.

Cazenovia, May 3, 1864. /13tf

NEW CUSTOM SHOP.—The subscriber has again taken up the hammer and last. Old Friends and New will find him at

WEED'S NEW STAND,

ready to make to order

EVERYTHING IN THE BOOT AND SHOE LINE.

None but the best of workmen employed, nothing but the best of stock used, and

GOOD FITS AND PERFECT SATISFACTION

guaranteed to every customer. A splendid stock of

Ready-Made Boots and Shoes

just received. ☞ Call, examine, and purchase, if you desire good bargains. JOHN G. TODD.

Cazenovia, May 11, 1863. 13tf

A. DARDIS. Has just received a large and well-selected assortment of BOOTS & SHOES of the newest fashions and best city manufacture, which will be sold for cash, or its equivalent, as cheap as ordinary work sold in other markets. Call and see before purchasing elsewhere. We will not be undersold.

For CUSTOM WORK of all kinds; for style and durability, he has never been excelled, even in any city in Western New York.

Gentlemen's French Calf Sewed Boots, do. Peg Boots, do. Balmorals, do. Congress Gaiters, Glove Balmorals, Brogans, Calf and Kip, Stoga, Slippers of all kinds.

Ladies' Prunella Button Gaiters, Glove do., Glove Congress Gaiters, Balmorals, 3 soled; Opera Congress Bals., Calf Cong., 3 soled; Slippers with heels.

If treated with the indignity they deserve by treading well under foot, the subscriber will feel grateful.

Cash paid for Hides. (9-18tf) A. DARDIS.

BOOTS AND SHOES!

The Subscriber has just received a

FRESH SUPPLY

of Boots and Shoes for the

FALL AND WINTER TRADE.

In proportion to the price of merchandise generally,

WE WILL SELL CHEAP!

Our terms are Cash, for we have tested the old adage that "A nimble sixpence is better than a slow shilling."

F. HAWLEY.

Cazenovia, Aug. 16, 1864. 11-16

Furniture.

CAIN KILLED ABEL.

Cane seats and chairs can have repairs
If taken where they can do it;
Spring seats covered with cloth of hair,
And sofas still added to it.

But not to mention all things done,
Bring on whate'er you want fixed up,
And I will suit you well and soon—
All will be done in my own shop.

As cheap as the cheapest, as good as the best, three doors west of the Post Office. M. J. TROWBRIDGE.

August 1st, 1862.

PEACE DECLARED.—The Subscriber having resumed his old business of Cabinet Making,

Three Doors West of the Post Office,

wishes to say to the public generally that he may be found at all times ready to wait on all who may favor him with a call for work in his line. He intends keeping on hand a good assortment of

CABINET WARE AND CHAIRS,

and will make or furnish to order, on short notice anything in the trade.

COFFINS.

A full assortment of sizes of Coffins already on hand. Particular attention paid to repairing old work. Prices for all to suit the times.

WANTED—In exchange for work: CASH, most kinds of Lumber, and Products of the Farm.

Please give me a call before purchasing elsewhere.

M. J. TROWBRIDGE.

Miscellaneous.

CAZENOVIA LIVERY STABLES. The Subscriber has bought the Barns, Sheds, &c., in rear of the Lincklaen House, and has permanently located his Livery Stables there. He has recently been making Extensive Additions of

FRESH HORSES, NEW CARRIAGES, NEW BUGGIES, NEW HARNESSES, &c.,

to his stock, and is prepared to furnish as Complete and Handsome Equipages, and at as REASONABLE PRICES as can be desired. Strangers and others carried to any part of the country, promptly, by night or day.—Public patronage solicited. H. S. KEELER.

May 5, 1863.

CIGAR MANUFACTORY!

The subscriber would respectfully inform the citizens of Cazenovia and vicinity that he has opened a

CIGAR MANUFACTORY AND TOBACCO STORE

on Lincklaen Street, opposite Concert Hall, where he will keep constantly on hand every variety of

CIGARS OF THE BEST QUALITY!

AND

THE BEST BRANDS OF TOBACCO!

☞ Call and examine his stock, and satisfy yourselves. M. YALE.

Cazenovia, June 22, 1864. 11-8m1-

THE SUBSCRIBER has now on hand a large lot of

STOVE AND EGG COAL,

which he will sell as low as can be bought in any market.

COAL WILL BE SCREENED

at Yard, or no sale.

Also, a large lot of

CEDAR AND SPRUCE SHINGLES.

FAY H. HUTCHINS.

Chittenango, July 18, 1864. 11-12m6

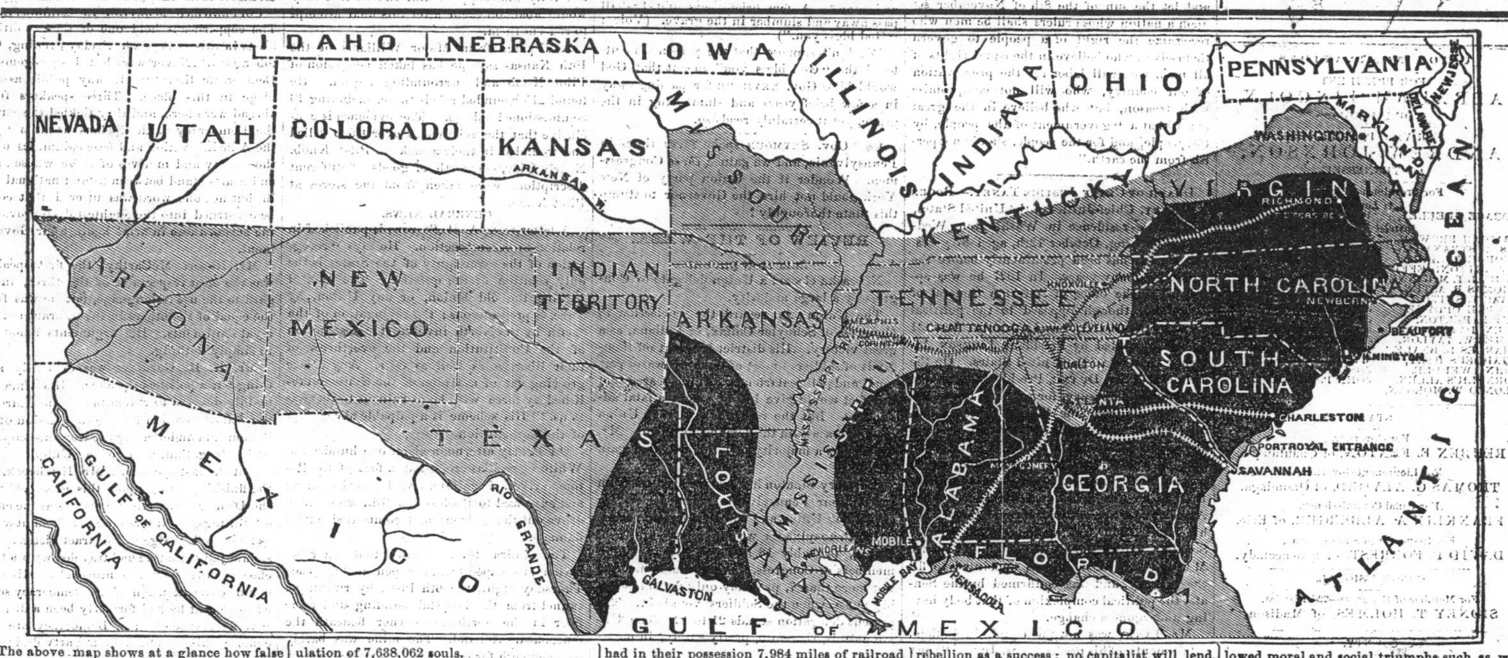

The above map shows at a glance how false is the assertion, that "the experiment of war" is a failure. When the news of the attack, surrender, and evacuation of Fort Sumter first reached the President, the territory in possession of the rebels embraced all that exhibited by the dark black and shaded lines—or all the slave States, except the little State of Delaware. According to the tables of the last census, the States and Territories then in the possessian of the rebels contained an area of 1,653,852 square miles, and a population of 12,121,294 souls.

The parts of States now held by the rebels comprises an area of only 342,668 square miles and a population of 4,453,232.

We have recovered to the Union a region comprising 1,311,184 square miles and a population of 7,638,062 souls.

When the rebels commenced the war they held every fort and port of entry from Fortress Monroe to the mouth of the Rio Grande. Now they hold but *four* forts and *one* entry, and the four forts and the one port of entry are besieged and blockaded by our army and our navy.

When the rebels commenced the war, they had undisputed possession of more than two-thirds of our sea coast, and a large tonnage of commerce. Now, they have not one merchant vessel to raise their flag; and they have no port that any vessel dare attempt to enter by daylight. They have not a single vessel of war that would venture to meet a vessel of our Navy.

When the rebels commenced the war, they had in their possession 7,984 miles of railroad—all well equipped and in thorough running order. Now they have only 1,485 miles, and what they have would not be deemed fit for commercial and passenger traffic in any Free State.

When the rebels commenced the war, they held the navigation of the Mississippi from Columbus, Ky., to its mouth. Now they do not hold one foot of either shore.

There is not a State or Territory of the old Union over a large portion of which the Government does not hold possession. Its vessels of war are before every port—its armies are constantly advancing—the beams of the rising sun welcome the old flag, where yesterday flaunted the bastard emblem of rebellion.—No Government on earth dare recognize the rebellion as a success; no capitalist will lend it a farthing; no dealer will trust it for a keg of gunpowder or a barrel of meat. It is bankrupt in credit, exhausted of material; it has "robbed the cradle and the grave," and has an existence to-day only as a reckless adventurer, "waiting for something to turn up," viz., the election of MCCLELLAN, and the accession to power of those who will again bind the giant North in chains, and sell their birthright of freedom for pieces of silver.

With a few exceptions, the ravages of war have been confined to the territory of those who commenced it. *To-day not a rebel footstep profanes the soil of the Loyal States, except that of a prisoner of war.*

These are the material victories we have gained. But in the wake of these have followed moral and social triumphs such as war rarely brings, of which we may be more proud than of all our other conquests. We have taught the rebels, who had for years reviled us as a community of cowards and speculators, to regard and respect us as a nation of brave, patriotic men, and true and devoted women. We have, by due process of law, abolished slavery in Louisiana, Maryland, Missouri, Arkansas, and in a large portion of Virginia. Our armies have struck the chains from hundreds of thousands of men and women in Kentucky, Tennessee, Mississippi, Alabama, North Carolina, South Carolina, Florida, and Texas, and should the war stop now, as stop it soon must, from the steady onward march of GRANT, and SHERMAN, and SHERIDAN, and CANBY, and FARRAGUT, no human power could reconstruct the blighting fabric of human slavery.

EQUINOCTIAL.

BY OLIVER WENDELL HOLMES.

The sun of life has crossed the line,
The summer shine of lengthened light
Faded and failed, till, where I stand,
'Tis equal day and equal night.

One after one, as dwindling hours,
Youth's glowing hopes have dropped away,
And soon may barely leave the gleam
That coldly scores a winter's day.

I am not young, I am not old;
The flush of morn, the sunset calm,
Paling and deepening, each to each,
Meet midway with a solemn charm.

One side I see the summer fields
Not yet disrobed of all their green;
While westerly along the hills
Flame the first tents of frosty sheen.

Ah, middle point, where cloud and storm
Make battle-ground of this my life;
Where, even matched, the night and day
Wage round me their September strife.

I bow me to the threatening gale
And know that, when its fury's past,
Among the peaceful autumn days
An Indian summer comes at last.

WON AT LAST.

The wedding ceremony was just over.

Through the arches of Trinity the tumultuous sweetness of the organ rolled in billows of sound, while the tinted splendors of stained glass casements streamed like shivered rainbows across the path of the bridal cortege. And Karl Chesney, looking down at the fair face shrined in a silver mist of tulle and jasmine blossoms, felt his strong heart thrill within him with a new-born happiness.

"My wife—my darling!"

Was it but a sickly fancy, or did the rose-leaf hand shrink away from his arm as he pressed it closer to his heart? Surely she loved him, this little wild flower he had transplanted from the wilderness to his palace home—there could be no doubt about *that*. Yet the mere possibility that for an instant flashed across his mind seemed to curdle the warm currents of life around his heart.

"Does not she look like a freshly gathered rose-bud?"

There was a momentary stoppage in the crowded vestibule, and Karl Chesney heard the low-spoken words from one of the bridesmaids beyond.

"Yes; I was afraid the sleepless night and all those tears would spoil her beauty."

"Did she weep much?"

"Poor thing! if you could only have seen her sobbing on my shoulder after the wreath and veil were on. She don't love him—she can't, poor, child! Just consider how brief the acquaintance has been."

"That is true," acquiesced the bridesmaid.

"But then it was such a splendid match, and her mother insisted on it. She would never have married him, though, if it were not for the fact that his regiment marches to-day. He will be away some time, and in fact who knows what may happen before he returns? In any event time will reconcile her to the marriage."

The words had been spoken in a whisper, but every syllable fell on Karl Chesney's ear as distinctly as if pealed through a trumpet's brazen throat—fell like fiery rain on the upspringing blossoms of his heart.

So he had been blinded, trifled with, deceived. A bright, brief dream! But he was rudely waked at last with a pang than which death would have been far sweeter. It was well that he was so soon to leave the young wife who detested him; and the dangerous fire blazed into his eyes as he thought of the words he had just heard—"Who knew what might happen before he returned?"

"Good-by, Cecile!"

He touched his cold lips to the fair forehead overhung with radant ripples of golden hair, and held for an instant the soft hand in his own. How lovely she was! how innocent! A bride, yet a widow; a wife, and no wife!

For Karl Chesney had sworn within his inmost mind a solemn oath that he would never return to claim an unloving heart. And Cecile looked shyly up into the dark, stern face and wondered if it was wrong to be glad that her husband was going off to the wars within an hour of his bridal. Poor child! she was not much to blame after all.

So Captain Chesney left his beautiful wife. If all our soldiers carry such reckless desperation, such sick hearts into the tumult and carnage of the battle-field, it is no wonder that they fight with the fierce abandon that makes a world stand by in awed wonder.

"There, I thought how it would be. Allen is down. What on earth possessed the General to send *him* of all other men!"

Col. Playfair spoke the short, fierce words between his teeth, as he sat on horse-back, grimly surveying the confused field through his glass. Karl Chesney struck his spurs into his horse's flanks and rode up alongside with a curious gleam in his eye.

"Who is to take his place, Colonel?"

"Whose? Allen's? Nobody that cares a fig for his life. I tell you, man, anybody that rides beyond the hill rides into the jaws of death."

"Nevertheless, the orders must be carried. You have a duplicate; give it to me."

Col. Playfair dropped his glass and stared blankly at Chesney.

"Man! are you tired of your life that you would throw it away from you?" he asked, hoarsely.

Karl Chesney snatched the paper from Playfair's hand and spurred his horse furiously on, while a strange exultation curved his lip into something like a smile.

"There goes the bravest fellow on the staff!" ejaculated Playfair, clenching his hand over his sword-hilt. "Struck from his horse! I knew it—I warned him! Poor Chesney! and he was married only the day we marched!—Oh, my God! how much longer is this massacre to last before retreating orders come?"

At that instant a young aid-de camp galloped up with a whispered message. Playfair turned sharply on him.

"At last. Well, it is not my business to criticise. Tell the General that Frank Allen and Chesney are gone, and I don't much care what else happens!"

It was a heavy heart that throbbed behind the blunt old man's battle-tarnished uniform as he rode slowly at the side of his decimated regiment that night—a heavy heart and a sore, for he had liked the two brave boys that were down.

"Where am I? What are you doing to me?"

The red stream of lantern-light seemed to burn across Karl Chesney's eyeballs like molten fire, as it revealed the swarthy faces bending over him.

"Turn him over, Benson—gently, gently! Now a long strip of bandaging and a tuft of lint. I wonder how long it will be before the ambulances are here.

The surgeon spoke indistinctly with a sharp steel instrument between his teeth. Chesney snatched his arm from the kindly touch, and tore the bloody ligatures away.

"Leave me alone! why cannot you let me die in peace? I *was* dying."

"Hallo!" ejaculated the Confederate surgeon. "Here's a new aspect of things!—Steady, my lad! it isn't my business to let people die if I can help it."

"Then go to some one that needs you."

"I am of the opinion that *you* need me," said the surgeon, coolly striking the revolver from Chesney's hand. "We don't require that little instrument, and it is not exactly grateful to point it at my head. Tie his hands, Benson! I see we shall have to do him good against his will."

"Ain't he game!" ejaculated the admiring cadet. "Want's to die, just because the Yankees have got the worst of the little skirmish. I say, doctor, it's all I can do to hold him."

"Why do you torture me back into life? I tell you I have no desire to live."

"For several reasons," said the surgeon, quietly. "One is, that I don't choose to have you Yankees say that you don't receive proper attention within our lines. Another is, were you aware that this cut across your upper lip is likely to prove rather an awkward affair for your beauty? Did you ever wear a moustache? because you'll have to now. A curious zigzag scar; I should think it might change the whole expression of your face.—There! are you easy now? Benson, lend a hand here, and help lift him into the ambulance. My boy," he added, in a lower tone, as he softly laid the wounded man's head on the cushions, "I have a son about your age in the ranks; I have done for you what I would fain have some charitable soul do for him, were he in your place; and I say to you what I would say to him, don't forget that you have no right to throw away the life God gave you!"

"What a delicious breeze there is from the Atlantic to-night!"

Harper Talboys was sitting on the long hotel piazza at Newport, smoking an evening cigar with the dark-faced fellow-traveler who had come in the same steamer with him from Cuba. Mr. Streighton did not reply, but then he was not a man that talked much at any time, and Talboys was used to his grave taciturnity.

"Lots of people here, Jenkins tell's me, and pretty girls enough to drive a fellow distracted. But the belle of the season is a young widow, Mrs. Chesney."

"Chesney did you say?"

"Ay, the widow of an officer who fell in that unfortunate affair at ——, a year ago. A beauty and an heiress—now there's a fine chance for you and me, Streighton. I just saw her at the dinner table, and—I'll be hanged if here she don't come now on horseback! See what a sensation she makes among those young fellows on the steps! By Jove, what a beauty!"

Streighton rose deliberately up and walked forward a step or two, leaning back against a column of the piazza to get a good view of the reigning beauty.

Like a shower of gold the fair curls floated away from under the black plumes of her riding-hat, while the liquid blue eyes sparkled with healthful exercise, and the color on her cheek was deep and soft as the velvet petal of a pomegranite blossom as she rode up to the hotel steps in the carmine glow of the August twilight.

"Who is that dark gentleman on the piazza?" she asked, looking rather earnestly at the stranger.

"A new-comer, I believe," replied her cavalier. "Streighton, I think his name is, from Cuba. Take care, Mrs. Chesney; it is never safe to drop your reins like that, and Selim is inclined to be a little gay."

The words were yet trembling on his tongue when Selim gave a forward spring. Cecile caught at the reins; but it was too late, and the next moment the horse was checked with a firm hand like iron, and she was lifted from the saddle by the dark stranger.

As he bowed and turned away she laid her hand timidly on his arm.

"May I not know whom I am to thank?"

"Mr. Streighton has had the pleasure of being useful to you, madam."

Cecile was used to the adulation of the male sex; but there was something in that olive face, with its dark, melancholy eyes and heavy moustache, that made her breath come quicker and brought the roses back to her blanched cheek.

All that evening Streighton watched her bright, innocent vivacity with grave, dreamy eyes—watched her girlish happiness and unconscious beauty, while his heart ached with unspoken pain.

"She cares little enough for the husband who fell in battle," he pondered. "I wonder if I could make her care for Charles Streighton. It is worth the trial. I love her in spite of everything, and in spite of everything, she *shall* love me!"

Those were bright days at the sea-side—days of golden air and blue quivering sunlight, with silver shimmers on the snowy beach and pulses of liquid music rolling up against the rocky battlements beyond; bright days, but they came to an end, like all bright things.

"Going to-morrow, Mr. Streighton?"

Her lip quivered in spite of her resolute effort at self-control, and he could feel the tremble of the little hand that lay on his arm.

"Yes."

"Oh, I am so sorry!"

They were alone in the moonlight shadows of the garden, while the merry music of viol and flute streamed from the brilliant windows of the house beyond, and died away in delicious cadences among the moving leaves.

"Do you care, Cecile?"

"Do I care, Charles?" she said reproachfully.

"Oh, Cecile!" he exclaimed, turning to her with an almost passionate intensity of fervor, "is it possible that you have learned to love me at last?"

"At last?" she repeated, vaguely.

"Tell me, love," he went on, "could you feel for me what a wife should feel for her husband? Do you love me in very truth, Cecile?"

He trembled now—she saw the quiver that ran through his whole frame.

"Are you mine, Cecile? mine in heart and soul? Love, do not deceive yourself or me, tell me the truth."

She put her hand on his shoulder and looked frankly and lovingly into his white, agonized face.

"Yours, dearest! yours forever!"

He drew her close, close to his breast with a strong, convulsive sob.

"Oh, my wife, my darling! did no warning impulse tell you that it was your husband who sought the priceless gift of your affection? Oh, Cecile! my blue-eyed dove, I have won your heart at last!"

So Cecile Chesney had two wedding days—one for her hand and the other for her heart.

THE TIMES ON FARRAGUT'S VICTORY.—The London *Times*, of September 17, in summing up the results of Admiral FARRAGUT's victory, says:

We think the reader will admit that this is a most extraordinary battle, and, perhaps, the most wonderful part of it is the comparative impunity with which it appears that wooden ships can still engage an iron-clad.—It is obvious to surmise that the result might have been different if the Tennessee had attacked her antagonists with shells insteed of with rifle bolts, which merely cut clean holes through their sides, but it is also clear that "ramming" cannot be tried, as it was in Hampton Roads, if ships can only so move as to elude the ram. What destroyed the Congress and the Cumberland was that they were mere sailing vessels, and could not evade the shock, whereas Farragut's vessels, by aid of their screws, escaped fatal damage, and at last, being fourteen to one, actually beat their great antagonist at his own proper game. In fact, the Tennessee was literally hustled into surrender. Her crew were knocked off their feet every five minutes, and were no longer fit for fighting, though their ship was substantially uninjured. Finally what are we to think either of Confederate plating or Federal guns when such enormous pieces fail to produce any effect on armor at ranges measured, not by yards, but by feet or even inches?—These are questions which will be asked with considerable interest, and the battle in Mobile Bay will, perhaps, add one more lesson to those which we have received from the American war.

THE RECORD OF ABRAHAM LINCOLN.—We find the following record of our noble President in the Syracuse *Journal*. Those who are constantly asserting that he cares nothing for the Union and would sacrifice all for the negro, should read and remember:

I hold that, in contemplation of universal law, and of the Constitution, the Union of these States is perpetual.—*Inaugural Address, March 4th*, 1861.

I appeal to all loyal citizens to favor, facilitate, and aid this effort to maintain the honor, the integrity, and existence of our national Union, and the perpetuity of popular government.—*Proclamation of the 15th of April*, 1861.

Now and ever I shall do all in my power for peace consistently with the maintenance of the Government.—*Letter to the Governor of Maryland, April 29th*, 1861.

You will in no case listen to any suggestions of compromise by this Government, under foreign auspices, with its discontented citizens.—*Instructions to Minister Adams, April 10th*, 1861.

It is with the deepest regret that the Executive found the duty of employing the war power in defence of the Government forced upon him. He could but perform this duty or surrender the existence of the Government.—*Message of July 4th*, 1861.

The Union must be preserved; and hence all indispensable means must be employed.—*Message of December 3d*, 1861.

Our common country is in great peril, demanding the loftiest views and boldest action to bring a speedy relief. Once relieved, its form of Government is saved to the world; its beloved history and cherished memories are vindicated, and its happy future fully assured and rendered inconceivably grand.—*Appeal to Border States, July 12th*, 1861.

My paramount object is to save the Union, and not either to save or destroy Slavery.—*Letter to Horace Greeley, August 22d*, 1862.

Whatever shall appear to be God's will I will do.—*Reply to Chicago Clergymen, Sept. 13th*, 1862.

Hereafter, as heretofore, the war will be prosecuted for the object of practically restoring the Constitutional relation between the United States and each of the States.—*Proclamation of September 22d*, 1862.

Upon this act, sincerely believed to be an act of justice, warranted by the Constitution upon military necessity, I invoke the considerate judgment of mankind, and the gracious favor of Almighty God.—*Proclamation of Emancipation, January 1st*, 1863.

Must I shoot a simple-minded soldier boy who deserts, while I must not touch a hair of a wily agitator who induces him to desert.—*Reply to Albany Resolutions, June 13th*, 1863.

You claim that men may, if they choose, embarrass those whose duty it is to combat a giant rebellion, and then be dealt with only in turn as if there was no rebellion. The Constitution itself rejects this view.—*Reply to Ohio Resolutions, June 29th*, 1863.

My purpose is to be in my action just and constitutional, and yet practical, in performing the important duties with which I am charged, of maintaining the unity and the free principles of our common country.—*Letter to Horatio Seymour, August 7th*, 1863.

This nation under God shall have a new birth of freedom, and government of the people, by the people, and for the people, shall not perish from the earth.—*Speech at Gettysburg, November 19th*, 1863.

I freely acknowledge myself to be the servant of the people, according to the bond of service, the Constitution of the United States.—*Springfield Letter, August 26th*, 1863.

While all contribute of their substance, the soldier puts his life at stake, and often yields it up in his country's cause. The highest merit, then is due to the soldier.—*Speech at Washington, March 16th*, 1864.

—Gen. Frank Fessenden, son of the Secretary of the Treasury, has put on a Palmer leg and gone to the front again.

CLEVELAND DAILY PLAIN DEALER.

VOLUME XX. CLEVELAND THURSDAY EVENING, OCTOBER 20, 1864. NUMBER 283

THE ROAD THAT ABE BUILT.

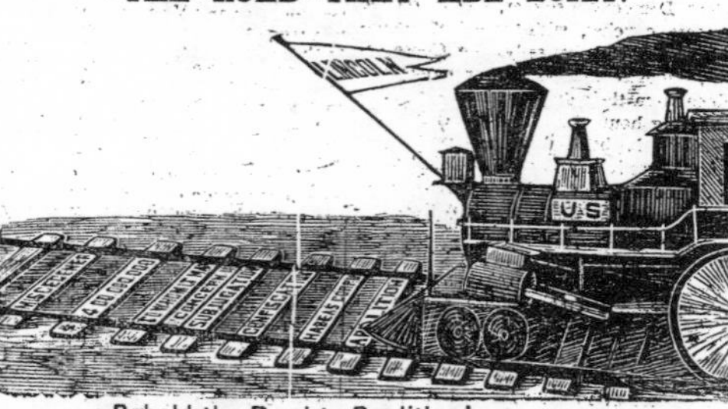

Behold the Road to Perdition!

Behold! they who preached Abolition!
Who laughed in glee o'er the graves of the slain,
Helped lay the track and started the train
On the terrible road to perdition.

Behold the vermin that stole the gold,
Perjured their souls and consciences sold,
And joined those that preached Abolition!—
And laughed in glee o'er the groans of the slain,
Helped lay the track and rode on the train,
On the terrible road to perdition.

This creature laughed when the battle was strong,
And cried: "Lamon, sing us another song,"
He winked at the men who for silver and gold
Perjured their souls and consciences sold,
And joined those who preached Abolition—
Laughed and joked o'er the graves of the slain,
Laid the track and guided the train
On the dread road to perdition.

This is the beast that with hoof and horn
Plotted and planned both night and morn.
And backed up the creature that jeered with the throng,
And cried: "Lamon, sing us a Negro song,"
And baught up the men who for silver and gold
Perjured their souls and consciences sold,
And told them to preach Abolition—
Dug open graves that gaped for the slain,
Levelled the track and urged on the train,
On the dire road to perdition.

This is the soldier who fought in the field,
The Statesman and Hero whose wisdom revealed
The plan of the beast that with hoof and horn
Plotted and planned both night and morn.—
He'll hurl out the creature that jeered with the throng
And cried: "Lamon, sing us another song,"
Along with the ghouls who for silver and gold
Perjured their souls and consciences sold,
And preached, long and loud, Abolition—
He'll weep o'er the graves, and honor the slain,
He'll tear up the track, and switch off the train
And save the land from perdition.

THE POET ON A TRAIN,
—OR—
The Romance of the Railroad.
By the author of the "Fair Inez," "The Prince of Wales," "The Ghost Hunters," &c., &c.

(CONTINUED.)

CHAPTER XXV—SOLDIERS AND ODD CUSTOM.

Now the air is filled with music,
And the sound of many feet,
For a regiment of soldiers
Is now marching down the street.
They are coming, "Father Abraham,"
But not to join the war,
And fill the city's quota for
"Five Hundred Thousand More."

They are only Broadway Soldiers,
Where they make a grand display,
As they march for target practice,
Or to have a gala day.
One to see them dressed so splendid
With their martial band so grand,
Would think no braver soldiers
Could be found in all the land.

They have passed, and omnibusses
Fill the street from every side;
And, as I must go a distance,
One I'll stop, and take a ride.
As I entered, an odd custom,
Which I noticed, I must pen,
Though no credit to New York men.

A young and handsome lady
Went into the Bus with me;
The Bus was filled, she looked in vain
A vacant seat to see;
I thought for sure some man there would
His seat at once resign,
And offer it, as I'd been taught,
To any feminine.

But New York men don't do such things,
They do not deference pay
To females who ride in a Bus,
Or on a street railway;
And old and young, and rich and poor,
Must stand up when they ride,
If they don't chance to find a seat,
Though men fill up each side.

☞ [TO BE CONTINUED.]

DAILY CONSTITUTIONAL UNION.

The Constitution and The Union, one and inseparable, now and forever.

VOL. III. WASHINGTON, SATUDRAY AFTERNOON, OCTOBER 22, 1864. NO. 120

DAILY CONSTITUTIONAL UNION,
PUBLISHED EVERY AFTERNOON.
[SUNDAYS EXCEPTED,]
No. 330 E Street, near Grover's Theatre,
BY
THOMAS B. FLORENCE.

To subscribers in the City it will be served for FIFTEEN CENTS PER WEEK; to mail subscribers EIGHT DOLLARS PER YEAR, payable in advance.

We also publish "The Weekly Constitutional Union," which will be furnished at the following terms: Single copies, $2.00; two copies, $3.50; ten copies, $17.50; twenty copies, $30.00.

TERMS OF ADVERTISING.

One Square,	1 day,	50	Do.	1 month	6 00
Do.	2 days,	75	Do.	2 do.	8 00
Do.	3 do.	1 00	Do.	3 do.	10 00
Do.	1 week,	1 75	Do.	6 do.	18 00
Do.	2 do,	2 75	Do.	1 year,	30 00

Six lines constitute a Square. If an advertisement exceed a square, the price will be in exact proportion. For the insertion of advertisements on alternate days the prices differ from the above scale, according to the days ordered; and when published but once a week, full price will be charged for each insertion.

Dentistry.

NEW INVENTION OF ARTIFICIAL CHEOPLASTIC

BONE TEETH

BY

DR. S. B. SIGESMOND & HAYWARD,

360 Pennsylvania Avenue, between 12th and 13th streets Washington.

Drs. S. & H. calls the attention of the public to the following advantages of their improved system:

1st. The teeth of their manufacture will never corrode nor change color by any acids, and are three-fourths lighter than any other.

2d. No teeth or roots need be extracted, as the artificial ones can be inserted over them.

3d. The roots will be made inoffensive and never to ache.

4th. No temporary teeth are needed, as permanent ones can be made immediately, thereby preserving the natural expression of the face, which, under the old system, is frequently disfigured.

This work has been fully tested for over five years, by many of the first chemists and physicians of his and the old country.

Drs. S. & H. has also invented a white indestructible metal filling, with which the most sensitive teeth can be filled without pain, and can build up a perfect round tooth on any side roots, which will last through a lifetime.

TEETH EXTRACTED WITHOUT PAIN!

With Innoxious Vapor, by Drs. Sigimond & Hayward, 61 Pennsylvania avenue, inventors and sole manufacturers of Anaestic Innoxious vapor, (not Laughing Gas, nor Chloroform, or Ether,) but strictly an Anaesticagent, entirely free from exhilarating effects and perfectly harmless, causing a quiet sleep, with pleasant sensations and perfect insensibility to pain.

The best of references given, if required.

Call and examine for yourselves. de10-1y

GREAT DISCOVERY IN DENTISTRY.

TEETH EXTRACTED WITHOUT PAIN WITH THE MURITE OF OXYGEN.

I would advise all persons having Teeth to extract to call at DR. LEWIE'S OFFICE and have them taken out by this new and harmless process. Also, call and examine the Doctor's new and improved method of inserting ARTIFICIAL TEETH. If you once see the great improvements in his Teeth, you will have them in no other style than this new and valuable one.

No. 242 Pennsylvania avenue, between Twelfth and Thirteenth streets. S. R. LEWIE, M. D., Dentist.
te19-1y

Attorneys and Agents.

A CARD.

M. JORDAN,

ATTORNEY AND COUNSELLOR AT LAW,

Has opened an Office in this city for the purpose of practicing his profession.

He will prepare and prosecute claims before Congress, in the Court of Claims, or against either of the Executive Departments of the Government.

Having had large experience in the management and prosecution of cases before Courts Martial, he would appear as counsel for the accused before those Courts, for the trial of either military or civil cases.

Conveyancing in all its branches promptly attended to.

REFERENCES:

Hon. Solomon Foot, of Vermont.
Hon. Wm. A. Richardson, of Illinois.
Hon. Lucian Anderson, of Kentucky.
Hon. W. H. Randall, of Kentucky.
Hon. R. K. Williams, Judge of Supreme Court of Kentucky.
H. M. Moffitt, Esq., Baltimore.
Seth J. Thomas, Esq., Boston.

Washington City, Sept. 9, 1864. s9 tf

REAL ESTATE AGENCY.

JAMES F. HALIDAY,

(LATE COLLECTOR OF CITY TAXES,)

WASHINGTON,

Devotes his entire attention as an Agent for RENTING and COLLECTING OF RENTS on Real Estate, BUYING and SELLING the same, and to all business connected with the management of Real Estate. Charges moderate; Business of non-residents solicited, and will be carefully attended to.

OFFICE—515 ELEVENTH STREET, six doors south of Pennsylvania avenue.

By permission, he REFERS TO

James C. McGuire & Co., Auctioneers.
John C. Rives, Esq., Editor of Globe newspaper.
L. Johnson & Co., Bankers.
Hon. Jas. G. Berret, Hon. W. W. Seaton, Hon. Peter Force, } Ex-Mayors of Washington.

Several fine Farms and a number of Building Lots and Improved Property for sale. s14-tf

JOHN F. ENNIS,

ATTORNEY AT LAW,

No. 22 LOUISIANA AVENUE,

NEARLY OPPOSITE CITY HALL,

WASHINGTON, D. C.

The Collection of Claims, and all other Professional Business, will receive prompt attention.
te19-tf

THOMAS H. FORD,

ATTORNEY AT LAW,

WASHINGTON, D. C.

Office, 443 Ninth street.
Residence 341 F street. e12-tf

E. E. WHITE,

No. 63 LOUISIANA AVENUE,

Between Sixth and Seventh streets, Opposite the Bank of Washington,

Wholesale and Retail Dealer in

FINE FAMILY GROCERIES,

WINES, LIQUORS, SEGARS, ETC.

N. B.—Goods delivered free of charge in any part of the city. jel1-1y

HOMŒOPATHY.

DR. J. GREEN

Has REMOVED from C street to

NO. 6 FOUR-AND-A-HALF ST.,

el-tf Near Dr. Sunderland's Church.

Amusements.

GROVER'S NEW THEATRE,

Pennsylvania avenue, near Willard's Hotel.

LEONARD GROVER .... Director
C. D Hess .... Acting Manager

FAREWELL NIGHT OF MR. AND MRS. BARNEY WILLIAMS.

THIS (SATURDAY) EVENING, OCT. 22,

The performance will commence with the thrilling Serio-comic Irish Drama, entitled,

IRELAND AS IT WAS.

Ragged Pat (the original)........Mr. Barney Williams
Judy O'Trot (the original)........Mrs Barney Williams

To conclude with the excellent Irish Comedy of

BARNEY THE BARON.

Barney the Baron ....Mr. Barney Williams

On Monday next, our old favorite Comedian,

MR. DAN SETCHELL,

will commence a brief engagement, by appearing in his great characters of CAPTAIN EDWARD CUTTLE and HUGH DE BRAS.

FORD'S NEW THEATRE,

TENTH STREET, ABOVE PENNSYLVANIA AVE.

JOHN T. FORD..............Proprietor and Manager.
(Also of Holliday-St Theatre, Baltimore.)

GRAND DOUBLE PERFORMANCE.

MR. JUNIUS BRUTUS BOOTH IN TWO OF HIS FAVORITE CHARACTERS.

THIS (SATURDAY) EVENING, OCT. 22,

Will be presented Tom Taylor's startling play of

RETRIBUTION; OR, A HUSBAND'S REVENGE.

Count Priuli . . . . Mr. J. B. Booth
Madame de Beaupre . . . . Miss Alice Gray

To conclude with Shakspere's Comedy, in three acts, of

KATHERINE AND PETRUCHIO.

Petruchio . . . . . Mr J B Booth
Katherine . . . . . Miss Alice Gray

Time altered—Curtain rises quarter to 8 o'clock.

CANTERBURY HALL,

LOUISIANA AVENUE, near Sixth street.
GEORGE LEA..............Manager and Proprietor.

EXTRAORDINARY ATTRACTION!

The Manager is proud to announce an engagement for a brief season with

CHERRY BELLE,

the Star of the West, Pantomimist, Banjoist, Vocalist, Guitarist, Comedienne, and altogether the most versatile and most beautiful woman on the American Stage.

First appearance of

MISS LAURA LE CLAIRE, Protean Actress and Vocalist,

JOSH HART, the celebrated Negro Comedian. Also of

MISS NAOMI PORTER, the Champion Female Jig Dancer

Szollosy's Ballet Troupe, composed of

SIXTEEN BEAUTIFUL LADIES, in a variety of Solo Dances, Ballets, etc., etc,

John Mulligan every night, with

THE BURNT CORK BRIGADE, in a choice selection of Funny Negro Acts.

Second week of the INFANT ACROBATS.

Admission 25 and 50 Cents. Private Boxes $5.

GRAND FAMILY MATINEE—Saturday Afternoon, at 2 o'clock. Admission—Ladies 25 cents; Children 15 cts.

MARINI'S

FASHIONABLE

DANCING ACADEMY,

TEMPERANCE HALL,

E street, between Ninth and Tenth streets.

This Academy is now open for the reception of pupils.

DAYS OF TUITION.

For Ladies, Misses, and Masters—Tuesdays, Thursdays and Fridays, from 3 to 5 p. m.

Gentlemen's Class—Tuesdays, Thursdays and Saturdays, from 8 to 10 p. m.

Those desirous of joining may do so by applying at the Academy during school hours. Quarter commencing on entry. o10 1m

THE BALL SEASON IS NOW UPON US.

TEMPERANCE HALL

Has been newly refitted, and is now the HANDSOMEST and LARGEST HALL for

BALL PURPOSES

in the city. Terms moderate. Apply to
JOS. F. WANNALL, Janitor,
oc19 3t at the Hall, on E st., betw. 9th and 10th.

BRADY'S GYMNASIUM.

Will open at 82, 84, and 86 Louisiana Avenue, adjoining the Central Guard House, about the middle of October.

Term $30 per year, $21 for six months. For gentlemen purchasing their subscription tickets prior to October 5, the terms will be $25 per annum.

Subscription lists have been left at Messrs. Jay Cooke & Co.'s, Fifteenth street, and at Messrs. Philp & Solomon's, 332 Penn. av., Galt & Bro.'s, 354 Penn. av., Hinton & Teel's, 358 Penn. av., Metropolitan Hotel, and at the Gymnasium.

s21 1m ABNER S. BRADY.

MOUNT VERNON MARBLE WORKS.

LARGE STOCK OF MARBLE MONUMENTS.

WILLIAM RUTHERFORD,

E STREET NORTH, between Sixth and Seventh streets, near the Postoffice Department,

Keeps constantly on hand a large and most extensive assortment of

STATUARY, ORNAMENTS,

Italian Marble Monuments, Grave-Stones, &c.,

and a complete variety of

Marble Mantels, Counter Slabs and Tiles,

which he offers low for cash. He respectfully invites the attention of purchasers to an inspection of his stock, which is constantly receiving additions. s27 3m

JAY COOKE & CO.,

BANKERS,

have this day

REMOVED

TO

THEIR NEW OFFICE,

FIFTEENTH STREET, NEAR G,

OPPOSITE

UNITED STATES TREASURY.

au1-M,T,F

McCLELLAN PUBLICATION DEPOT OF NEW YORK.

The following Campaign Documents are ready for circulation. They are in sheet form, adapted to general distribution, and particularly for enclosing to the Soldiers in sealed envelopes:

"McClellan's Platform." $1 per 100.
"McClellan's West Point Oration," $1 50 per 100.
"The Potentous Threat of Secretary Seward," $1 per 100.

All orders addressed to the Office of the COSTITUTIONAL UNION, or to

HENRY C. FARR,
280 Pearl Street, New York,

will receive immediate attention. o11

CITY RAILROAD

STOCK AND BONDS.

We have for sale
150 SHARES STOCK, and
$10,000 MORTGAGE BONDS
of the WASHINGTON AND GEORGETOWN RAILROAD COMPANY

The Bonds bear six per cent. interest, payable semi-annually, and, with the Stock, offer a safe and desirable investment.

JAY COOKE & CO., Bankers.
au22-tf

Personal.

COMMUNICATIONS BETWEEN THE NORTH AND SOUTH.—During the existing troubles THE CONSTITUTIONAL UNION offers a good medium, through its "Personals," to persons who wish to communicate with each other in regard to their health and whereabouts. The charge for inserting Personals for the South will be One Dollar for a single insertion, or Two Dollars for five insertions. We would advise that all notices should be inserted five times, as making it more certain of reaching the party.

FOR THE SOUTHERN JOURNALS.

MRS. SARAH E. HALBERT, Steel's Tavern, Augusta County, Va.—Dear Wife: I am enjoying the greatest of blessings health; and am at present working at Kendall Green, Washington City, D. C. Let me hear from you soon. Yours,
ALEX. HOLBERT.
New York Daily News and Richmond papers will please copy.

INFORMATION IS WANTED OF CAPTAIN WOODFORD STONE, of Washington City, D. C., who sailed in his vessel, the schooner Alert, from Baltimore, Maryland, on the 15th February last, 1864, with a cargo of sutler's goods, bound to Folly Island and Port Royal, since which time nothing has been heard of or from Captain Woodford Stone or his vessel. His wife and family, who are distressed at his long absence, will be grateful for any information communicated in relation to him or the fate of his vessel.
MARY STONE,
No. 606 Sixth street, corner of E street, (Island.)
(New York News and Southern Papers please copy.)

INFORMATION WANTED of the present whereabouts of MISS MARY ELLEN PIERCE, who, when last heard from, was living in Richmond, Va., but who formerly resided in Washington city. Also, where JOSHUA B. PIERCE at present resides, if living, his residence having been for the last ten years in the city of Richmond. Your sister, residing in the city of Washington, is earnestly anxious to hear from either her sister or brother, above named. Address
S. E. PIERCE,
No. 290 F street, betw. 1st and 2d streets, (Island,)
Washington City, D. C. o10 tf
New York News and Southern papers please copy.

INFORMATION WANTED of THEODORE T. HARRY, by his Mother. He was captured 11th May, 1864, at the Wilderness of Belle Plains; supposed to be in Richmond. An anxious Mother waits an answer.
MRS. MARY ANN HARRY.
Tennallytown, D. C.

OCTOBER 5, 1864.

DEAR WIFE:—I am at Eastern Branch Park, near Washington, D. C., and quite well. Wish that you would come on as soon as possible.
HENRY SOEFKER.
New York News and Richmond Examiner please copy.

TO SOUTHERN AND OTHER NEWSPAPER CORRESPONDENTS AND OTHERS.—Information wanted of JOHN R. MEADOWCROFT, Company D, 8th Pennsylvania Cavalry, missing since the battle of Trevillon Station, June 11th, 1864; supposed to be a prisoner. Any information will be thankfully received by his mother.
S. MEADOWCROFT,
No. 25 North Tenth street, Philadelphia, Pa.
New York News and Richmond papers please copy.

WASHINGTON, D. C., Sept. 28, 1864.

DEAR WIFE:—I take this opportunity of addressing you a few lines. We are in this city safe and well. We are residing at present on Twentieth st., No. 213. Kiss Jimmy for me. Tell Henry's friends that he is well and very anxious to hear from home. I remain your affectionate husband,
JOSEPH T. DAVIS.
New York News and Richmond and Petersburg papers please copy.

GEORGETOWN, D. C., Sept. 29, 1864.

ASST. SURG. BODISCO WILLIAMS, C. S. A.—Your "Personal" received. Also two letters and your card per flag of truce. All well at home.
Yours truly, A.
New York Daily News and Richmond Enquirer please copy.

SEPTEMBER 19TH.

T. S. EVERETT:—Your family is well, and anxious to hear from you. The last received was May 2d. Do let me hear from you. Taken Prisoner, April 20th, at Plymouth, N. C.

TO SOUTHERN ARMY CORRESPONDENTS AND REPORTERS.—Will you oblige a mother by making known through the Southern papers whether GEORGE A. CHILDS, Private of Company I, Ninth Maryland U. S. Infantry, captured at Charlestown, Va., on or about the 7th of September, 1863, and sent prisoner to Belle Island, and transferred to Andersonville, Georgia, is still alive. A distressed mother anxiously awaits a reply.
New York News and Southern papers please copy.

FROM THE SOUTHERN PAPERS.

GOOCHLAND COUNTY, Va., Sept 27, 1864.

TO WM. H. GREEN, (supposed to be in some of the Northern States.)—Dear Husband: Are you ever going to let us hear from you any more? Your mother, Laura, and myself, are well, and most anxious to know your whereabouts; have never heard a word from you. Settle yourself and write to us. Answer through New York News, requesting the Richmond Semi-Weekly Enquirer to copy.
ELIZA JANE GREEN.
New York News, Philadelphia, Baltimore, Washington, and Norfolk papers, please copy.

RICHMOND, Sept. 29, 1864.

J. P. MAZEEN, Washington or Baltimore.—Dear Chum: Let me know how times are, and how you are getting on. Give my love to George Mc., Sam Hunt, and the rest of the boys, and tell them I hope to see them soon. If you see "Fright" Mullen in your travels, tell him his wife and children are well, and send love. Answer through New York Daily News, requesting Richmond Enquirer to copy.
Truly yours. "CYRUS."
New York News and Washington and Baltimore papers please copy.

RICHMOND, Sept. 28, 1864.

AUNT ADDIE, Washington, D. C.—I observed your notice inquiring about George D. Thirslow, and have written to several officers on the subject, but have received no intelligence of him. When any information may reach me, I will at once communicate it. Nothing has been heard in regard to him since the date mentioned. Your many friends here are well, and be assured I often recur with much pleasure to the agreeable hours passed with you and yours, and continue to hope that the time will yet come when the association of former days can be renewed. My love to J. B. and Sammy.
Sincerely yours, THOS. E. MARTIN.
New York News please copy.

MARIUS, Washington City.—Your cheering letter of the 11th September received and sent to Auburn. M. still there. All well a week since. Seen Aaron B.; he gives a good account of Spragner. Leigh Priddy slightly wounded. Charles at home—wishes you were all here. What has become of friend C. J.? Wrote you of the sale of the place, purchased in Caroline. Expect to stop here some time. Well and happy as we can be without Dick, whose health is not better; he is doing guard duty at Chimborazo. M. A. B. A.

TO DR. E. TUCKER BLAKE, Washington, D. C.—Died, of consumption, contracted in the service of his country, on the 5th of July, ult., at the residence of his aunt, Miss Sarah F. Davidson, in Charlotte, N. C., Lieut. JOS. DAVIDSON BLAKE, of the C. S. Navy. The deceased was a gallant, energetic, and able officer, one of the most amiable of men, and in his intercourse with his brother officers and others was a thorough and elegant gentleman. He bore his long and painful sickness with great patience, and committed his soul to the merciful keeping of the blessed Redeemer. A FRIEND.
New York News please copy.

ANY INFORMATION OF PRIVATE F. BEAZLEY, Company I, Sixth Virginia Cavalry, captured at Summitt Point, near Charlestown, Virginia, August 30, 1864, will be thankfully received by his sister. Wish to hear from W. W. D. and S. V. C. also.
S. A. BEAZLEY.
New York News, Baltimore Sun, and Washington papers, will please copy.

RICHMOND, September 19, 1864.

IF MR. SAMUEL J. MILLS is in Washington City, he will please let me hear from him through the Richmond Enquirer. KATE.
Washington papers please copy.

GUINEA'S DEPOT, Caroline County, September 16, 1864.

DEAR COUSINS:—We saw your personal, and were glad to hear you were well; had not heard for long months till then. Our family circle is yet unbroken. Aunts H. and J. are still with me. Father and family well. We lost less than we expected; have written full particulars. Much love to each one of you.
A. P. C.
New York News and Washington papers please copy.

CLARENCE PERCIVAL, Washington, D. C.—If you have not forgotten your "old friend," address "ZOE," through New York News and Richmond Enquirer
New York News and Washington papers please copy.

RICHMOND, VA., September 15, 1864.

MR. HAUSER, Washington, D. C.—I received your advertisement in the Richmond Enquirer. Children and myself are well. Please let me hear through the Enquirer every month. I received only one letter from my husband. Your
LOUISA GUVERNATOR.
New York News and Washington papers please copy.

PETERSBURG, September 5, 1864.

DR. F. B. CULVER, Washington, D. C.—I am with Major J. B. Hill, Quartermaster Evans' South Carolina Brigade. Eddie is in the Fourth Maryland Artillery. Cousin Charles is at Mooresboro, North Carolina. Major H. sends his thanks for your attention to Lieut. Hulgins, and for the personal. Write by flag of truce, care of Major H. WILLIE.

CONSTITUTIONAL UNION

SATURDAY AFTERNOON, OCT. 22, 1864.

PRESIDENT,

GEORGE B. McCLELLAN.

VICE-PRESIDENT,

GEORGE H. PENDLETON.

Truth in Dreams.

"James Russell Lowell never penned a more graphic or wittier sentence than his description of the late Democratic gathering at Chicago:

"'The convention was a rag-bag of dissent. All the odds and ends of personal discontent, every shred of private grudge, every rag snipped off by official shears, scraps of rebel gray, the leavings of Union blue—all had been gathered, as if for the tailoring of Joseph's coat.'"

How unfortunate for James Russell Lowell, in his attempt to be "witty and graphic," that he should have directed attention to the 37th chapter of Genesis. Some one of those reverends whose consciences are seared with teh secret letter A, (Abolitionists,) should have admonished him to read on. Truly, it is proven a little learning is a dangerous thing. Ye who subscribe to the higher law, "Go ye into all the world and shout my doctrine." Thus reads the History of Joseph:

"Now Israel [the People] loved Joseph, [McClellan,] more than all his children; and he made him a coat of many colors.

"And when his brethren saw that their father loved him more than all his brethren, they hated him, and could not speak peaceably unto him.

"And Joseph dreamed a dream, and he told it his brethren, and they hated him yet the more.

"And he said unto them, 'Hear, I pray you, this dream which I have dreamed:

"'For, behold, we were binding sheaves in the field, and lo! my sheaf arose, and also stood upright; and, behold, your sheaves stood round about, and made obeisance to my sheaf.'

"And his brethren said to him, Shalt thou indeed reign over us? or shalt thou indeed have dominion over us? And they hated him yet the more for his dreams and for his words.

"And he dreamed yet another dream, and told it his brethren, and said, Behold, I have dreamed a dream more; and, behold, *the sun and the moon and the eleven stars made obeisance to me.*" [Lincoln, Johnson, and the Confederate States.]

And now, Mr. Russell Lowell, you and your brethren conspire against our Joseph—our *George*, or, as we choose to call him for *shortness*, "Little Mac"—as malignantly as ye dare; know that, despite of "pitfalls," and "evil beasts," aye, and Pharoah's "captain of the guard," and all the "company of Ishmaelites," with their bribes of spices, balms and myrrhs from Gilead, even "Egypt" will acknowledge the sway of Joseph; ye shall fall down round about, while he stands upright, and through love, *not* fear, shall even "the sun, moon, and eleven stars make obeisance to him." W. H. D.

[*Sunday* Chronicle please copy.]

THE NOVEMBER ELECTIONS.—The whole number of votes in the Electoral College, (not counting Tennessee or Louisiana) is 231, of which 116 are required to give a clear majority and elect a President. Now, can Gen. McClellan secure one hundred and sixteen votes? We think—nay, we are sure, he can and will.

STATES CERTAIN TO VOTE FOR M'CLELLAN.

California,	5	Missouri,	11
Delaware,	3	New Jersey,	7
Illinois,	16	New York,	33
Kentucky,	11	Pennsylvania,	26
Maryland,	7	Oregon,	3
Minnesota,	4		
Total,			126

But the Administration may put a forcible stop to elections in Missouri, Kentucky, Maryland and Delaware; so it becomes a question whether there are not some other States which will probably vote the Democratic ticket. That there are such will be seen by the following list:

STATES WHICH WILL PROBABLY VOTE FOR M'CLELLAN.

Connecticut,	6	Rhode Island,	4
Indiana,	13	West Virginia,	5
Michigan,	8	Wisconsin,	8
New Hampshire,	5		
Total,			49

STATES CERTAINLY FOR LINCOLN.

Iowa,	8	Massachusetts,	12
Kansas,	3	Vermont,	5
Maine,	7		
Total,			35

STATES WHICH MAY BE LINCOLN.

Michigan,	8	Rhode Island,	4
New Hampshire,	5	Wisconsin,	8
West Virginia,	2		
Ohio,	21	Total,	51

It will thus be seen that if Lincoln carries the doubtful Republican, as well as the certain Republican States, he will still fall far short of the needed 116 votes.

It is easily demonstratable that the same percentage of increase of this fall's vote in Connecticut, Pennsylvania and Ohio, as compared with last year, will give us all the States in November save those indicated above as being certain for Lincoln.

To Those Who Expect Peace Through Subjugation.

Do you flatter yourselves that with the overthrow of the organized military power of the Confederacy we shall have peace and harmony? This hope is a delusion. They who would cause you to trust therein point you to the historical examples of England and France as illustrative of the facility with which the ravages of war are obliterated after its termination.

It may be true that during the civil wars in these countries personal animosities were as bitter and as intensified as those now witnessed by us, and that these feelings soon subsided after peace was once established. But you must recollect that in those cases the antagonist parties were not separated by geographical lines, but were intermingled throughout the entire country.

We have often witnessed more exasperation between opposing political parties in Presidential elections than was exhibited in 1860. But in previous cases those parties were interspersed throughout every State and neighborhood in not very unequal proportions. The political hurricane was succeeded within a few days by a calm which left scarcely a trace of the recent convulsion. Intelligent men understood this difference *then*. We can all appreciate it *now*.

Examples more pertinent and suggestive than those above referred to might readily be found in English history. In the year 1172 Henry II succeeded in establishing, by force of arms, his claim to the sovereignty over Ireland. The independence of the latter country was thus "crushed out," and, as it was then thought, forever. But the two parties to that contest were geographically separated, and for more than six hundred years has the fury of national and individual hatred sometimes blazed and sometimes smouldered, but has never been for a moment extinct.

Time and again has rebellion reared its head in that devoted country with temporary success, and as often has England vindicated the "right" of oppression by the sword. The people have shown themselves ever ready to co-operate with a foreign foe for the overthrow of a Power which held them in unwilling subjection, but the military and naval power of England would at length prove triumphant and Ireland would be again quelled, though unsubdued. Every expedient that vengeance or ambition could suggest has been exhausted—devastation and cruelty and starvation, but all in vain. Colonization has been attempted with a view of supplanting the whole population by another race between whom and their fellow-countrymen on the other side of the channel no "irrepressible conflict" of religious opinion should exist, but all to little purpose, until England, despairing of success through measures of mere force, has finally resorted to those of toleration and justice. But even now the traditional memory of seven hundred years of wrong still lives in the bosoms of her children wherever scattered on the earth, and the eye of every hod-carrier and ditch-digger will still sparkle with the treasured feelings of hatred unavenged, at the mention of a name which he always couples with the idea of national wrong and individual oppression.

But the example of Scotland is still more pertinent and analagous, inasmuch as the two people inhabited the same country, and in point of population, wealth and power stood more nearly towards each other in the relation of the two belligerents here.

Towards the close of the thirteenth century Edward I, of England, claimed to be the legitimate sovereign of Scotland—holding all those to be traitors who resisted his rule. His claims were stoutly resisted by the "rebels," under the leadership of the celebrated William Wallace. In 1299 they were defeated at the decisive battle of Falkirk. Their military power was "crushed" and Scotland was subjugated and "loyal."

Three years later Wallace had become again as formidable as before, and Edward had to commence his work of conquest anew. He moved northward with the whole military power of his realm, accompanied by his navy, which had the entire command of the sea. After a war of two years the Scotch were entirely overwhelmed, and Wallace taken prisoner and executed. The conqueror marched in triumph from one end of the country to the other. All vied in their professions of allegiance; all bowed to the sceptre of the conqueror. He attempted to abrogate the Scottish customs, to abolish the Scottish name, and even to substitute English for the Scotch inhabitants of the kingdom. All seemed peace and security.

Two years later the rebellion broke out afresh under Robert Bruce. In 1307, at the fatal battle of Methven, the organized military power of Scotland was again annihilated and Bruce became a fugitive and a wanderer. Eight years later he found himself at the head of another army. The battle of Bannockburn was fought and Scotland was again free.

Under the weak successors of Bruce the domination of England was again claimed and enforced. For three hundred years Scotland often raised the standard of rebellion, and seized upon every opportunity that presented itself for co-operation with the enemies of England. The two nations came to be regarded as natural enemies until James VI, of Scotland, at length ascended the English throne. The more powerful country thus united itself to the weaker, and national animosities became extinguished by peaceful appliances which would never have yielded to force. The lapse of more than two hundred and fifty years has seen that union constantly growing stronger, which centuries of war and mutual injury has seemed to have rendered wholly impossible.

These teachings of the history of the past are confirmed by the lessons of our own experience. The State of Missouri, once reduced to quiet and held in a constrained loyalty by military power, is again rising in successful rebellion, and must be conquered anew. The same may be said of a great portion of Louisiana, Texas, Arkansas, as well as some of the States on this side of the Mississippi.

Mere conquest never extinguishes national antipathies, but gives them edge and venom. The mild influences of peace and kindness effect what could never be attained by violence in the production and preservation of national unity. They accomplish their purposes, not by resisting the power to separate, but by removing the wish and the motive for doing so. Is the lesson to be lost upon us? Shall we continue vainly to pursue the phantom "Union" over fields of carnage, when it is ready to nestle in our bosoms as a blessed reality, if, discarding the brutal, savage, and fiendish propensities of our nature, we invoke the peaceful influences of intellect and reason and the teachings of the Divine Master. We may soon have peace and union if we choose, but not by war, however successful.

The conquest of all the cities and the dispersion of the armies of the Confederacy will only bring increasing difficulties and enshroud the country in a deeper gloom. Your means of support will be abstracted by increasing taxation, your sons snatched from you by frequently recurring conscription. Large standing armies will be necessary to preserve the country in its forced allegiance. The simplicity of your republican institutions will disappear, and in their stead the costly machinery of a Government which enforces obedience by the fear it excites rather than by the affection it induces. For your own sake and for that of your posterity we conjure you to turn back from the path of danger in which you are now rushing forward to your ruin.

By order of the Resident Committee:
CHARLES MASON, Chairman.

McCLELLAN.

The soldier stands aloof—not now
He seeks the crest of fame;
His country's love bound on his brow,
Her blessings on his name:
He served her well when foemen threw
The gauntlet in her face,
And fierce the strife that brought to view
The manhood of our race.

His strong right arm was nerved to lead
Potomac's gallant men—
Brave sons of every clime and creed,
From rugged mount and glen—
With him they fought and bled and fell,
And struck the foemen down;
And blood-stained Antietam speaks well
The soldier's bright renown.

Though Catalines infest our land,
As in the Roman time,
And stay the might of him whose hand
Brands treason as a crime;
Though reckless men now sorely press
The hero's dear-bought fame,
A nation's throbbing heart will bless
McCLELLAN's honored name.

Boston, May 6, 1863. R.

[For The Constitutional Union.]

THE SNAKE SONG.

AIR: THE BOB-TAILED HORSE.

There is a viper, and no mistake;
That's so—that's so.
'T is the Northern Leaguers' big black snake;
That's so—that's so, too.
CHORUS.—They 'll spill the nation's blood,
And call themselves true blue;
They 'll fight for Lincoln shinplasters,
And for the darkie too.

This snake he tries to work by charms,
That's so—that's so.
And when he fails he cries to arms;
That's so—that's so, too.

This snake is dangerous, but seldom bites;
That's so—that's so.
He is just like the sneaking Lincolnites;
That's so—that's so, too.

He'll wrap himself round you and stop your breath;
That's so—that's so.
If you don't cut him loose he'll cause your death;
That's so—that's so, too.

This snake has been working for thirty years,
That's so—that's so.
For naught but widows' and orphans' tears;
That's so—that's so, too.

There's one thing sure about this snake—
That's so—that's so.
He dare not venture across the lake;
That's so—that's so, too.

This snake he works on various schemes
That's so—that's so.
To free the darkie, so it seems;
That's so—that's so, too.

This snake would still work many ways;
That's so—that's so.
But McClellan will rout him from where he lays;
That's so—that's so, too.

This snake's in league with hell I believe;
That's so—that's so.
He's the self-same breed that tempted Eve;
That's so—that's so, too.

That snake brought terror on mortal man;
That's so—that's so.
And so will this one, if he can;
That's so—that's so, too.

This snake lies concealed under rotten logs;
That's so—that's so.
You'll find him in thickets and in the bogs;
That's so—that's so, too.

There's another place those serpents stay;
That's so—that's so.
In waste houses at night, ashamed of day;
That's so—that's so, too.

They should change their names from black to white;
That's so—that's so.
For such cowardly dogs they will not fight;
That's so—that's so, too.

They do very often change their name;
That's so—that's so.
They sugar-coat the pill, but it's still the same;
That's so—that's so, too.

There's one thing I'm sorry to relate;
That's so—that's so.
That we have such serpents in our State;
That's so—that's so, too.

When Little Mac beats them, as you diskiver;
That's so—that's so.
Then Abe and his Cabinet will go up Salt River;
That's so—that's so, too.

When Mac takes his seat it will all be right;
That's so—that's so.
He'll knock Abolitionism out of sight;
That's so—that's so.

Just one more verse, and then I'm done;
That's so—that's so.
I hope I have offended none;
That's so—that's so, too.

WILL VOTE FOR LINCOLN.—Every man who agrees with the following sentiment, uttered on the floor of the Connecticut House of Representative, by Rev. Mr. Gilbert, an abolition member, Jan. 15th, 1864, will vote for Lincoln: "For one, I am not afraid to say, that I had rather lie down and die in the tracks to-day, than see any restoration of the Union as it was."

ANOTHER VOTE.—A vote was taken on the Central Railroad train coming east, leaving Buffalo at 5.45, Oct. 17th, with the following result:

McClellan,	152
Lincoln,	58

Forty-eight soldiers voted for Little Mac, and twelve for Lincoln.

Walton's Morning Journal.

BY E. P. WALTON. MONTPELIEB, MONDAY OCTOBER 24, 1864. NUMBER 1094.

Special Notices.

From the army hospital—the bloody battle-field—the mansion of the rich and humble abode of the poor—from the office and the sacred desk—from the mountain top, distant valleys and far off islands of the ocean—from every nook and corner of the civilized world—is pouring in the evidence of the astonishing effects of DRAKE'S PLANTATION BITTERS. Thousands upon thousands of letters like the following may be seen at our office.

REEDSBURY, WIS. Sept. 16, 1863.

"* * * * have been in the army hospitals for fourteen months—speechless and nearly dead. At Alton, Ill., they gave me a bottle of Plantation Bitters. * * * Three bottles restored my speech and cured me * * * *

C. A. FLUTE.

SOUTH WARSAW, O., July 28, 1863

"* * * One young man who had been sick and not out of the house for two years with Scrofula and Erysipelas, after paying the doctors over $150 without benefit, has been cured by ten bottles of your Bitters.

EDWARD WOUNALL.

The following is from the Manager of the Union Home School for the children of Volunteers:

HAVEMEYER MANSION, FIFTY-SEVENTH-STREET, New York, August 2, 1863.

"DR. DRAKE: Your wonderful Plantation Bitters have been given to some of our children suffering from weakness and weak lungs with most happy effect. One little girl, in particular, with pains in her head, loss of appetite, and daily wasting consumption, on whom all medical skill had been exhausted, has been entirely restored. We commenced with but a teaspoonful of Bitters a day. Her appetite and strength rapidly increased, and she is now well. * * * *

Respectfully, MRS. O. M. DEVOE."

"* * * I owe much to you, for I verily believe the Plantation Bitters have saved my wife.

REV. W. H. WAGGONER, Madrid, N. Y.

"* * * Thou wilt send me two bottles more of thy Plantation Bitters. My wife has been greatly benefited by their use.

Thy friend, ASA CURRIN, Philadelphia, Pa."

"* * * I have been a great sufferer from Dyspepsia, and had to abandon preaching. * * * The Plantation Bitters have cured me.

REV. J. S. CATHORN, Rochester, N. Y."

"* * * Send us twenty-four dozen more of your [Plant]ation Bitters, the popularity of which are daily in[creasin]g with the guests of our house.

SYKES, CHADWICK & CO.
[Pr]oprietors Willard's Hotel, Washington, D. C.

* * * I have given the Plantation Bitters to [hu]ndreds of our disabled soldiers with the most astonishing effect.

G. W. D. ANDREWS,
Superinten dent Soldier's Home, Cincinnati, O.

"* * * The Plantation Bitters have cured me of liver complaint, of which I was laid up prostrate and had to abandon my Business.

H. B. KINGSLEY, Cleveland, O."

"* * * The Plantation Bitters have cured me of a derangement of the kidneys and urinary organs that has distressed me for years. It acts like a charm.

C. C. MOORE, 254 Broadway, N. Y.

&c. &c. &c. &c. &c. &c.

The Plantation Bitters make the weak strong, the lan guid brilliant, and are exhausted nature's great restorer. They are composed of the celebrated Calisaya Bark, Wintergreen, Sassafras, Roots, Herbs, &c., all preserved in perfectly pure St. Croix Rum.

S. T.—1860.—X.

Persons of sedentary habits troubled with weakness, lassituude, palpitation of the heart, lack of appetite, distress after eating, torpid liver, constipation, &c., deserve to suffer if they will not try them.

They are recommended by the highest medical authorities, and are warranted to produce an *immediate* beneficial effect. They are exceedingly agreeable, perfectly pure, and harmless.

NOTICE.—Any person pretending to sell Plantation Bitters in bulk or by the gallon is swindler and impostor. It is put up only in our patent log cabin bottle.—Beware of bottles refilled with imitation deleterous stuff for which several persons are already in prison. See that every bottle has our private United States Stamp over the cork unmutilated, and signature on steel plate side label.

Sold by respectable dealers throughout the habitable globe.

P. H. DRAKE & CO., 202 Broadway, N. Y.

91:42—d&w

MEASLES ARE PROSTRATING

the Volunteers by hundreds, the hospitals are crowded with them. Soldiers, be warned in time. Holloway's Pills are positively infallible in the cure of this disease; occasional doses of them will preserve the health even under the greatest exposures. 27:daw

If the reader of this "notice" cannot get a box of Pills or Ointment from the drug store in his place, let him write to me, 80 Maiden Lane, enclosing the amount, and I will mail a box free of expense. Many dealers will not keep my medicines on hand because they cannot make as much profit as on other persons' make. 35 cts., 88cts., and $1,40 per box or pot. daw:ly

REVOLUTION
IN THE DRESSING ROOM!

By the almost unanimous action of the parties interested, *CRISTADORO'S HAIR DYE* has replaced the old worn-out inventions for coloring the hair, which the better experience of years had proved to be ineffective and deleterious. Unlike the compounds that

MAKE WAR

upon the health of the hair and dry up and consume the juices which sustain it, this mild, genial and perfect dye is found to be a vitalizing as well as a coloring agent.

Cristadoro's Hair Preservative,

a valuable adjunct to the Dye, in dressing and promoting the growth and perfect health of the hair, and of itself, when used alone, a safeguard that protects the fibres' decay under all circumstances and under all climes. 27:30

Manufactured by J. CRISTADORO, No. 6 Astor House, New York. Sold by all Druggists. Applied by all Hair Dressers. daw:ly

Manufactured by J. CRISTADORO, No. 6 Astor House, New York. Sold by all Hair Dressers. dawly

PHYSICIANS WILL FIND PURE Drugs and Chemicals at WOOD, BIXBY & CO.'S, Druggist, 11 State Streeet,

SOFAS, WHAT-NOTS, CHAIRS, BUREAUS, at BABCOCK & CO'S.

TO THE LADIES OF AMERICA.

LYON'S PERIODICAL DROPS,
LYON'S PERIODICAL DROPS,
THE GREAT FEMALE REMEDY
THE GREAT FEMALE REMEDY!

LYON'S PERIODICAL DROPS Cure all complaints incident to the sex, and remove all obstructions of nature from whatever cause, producing health, vigor and strength.

LYON'S PERIODICAL DROPS are better than all Pills, Powders and nostrums; being a fluid preparation, their action is direct and positive, and it needs nothing but good common sense to see and understand the reason why they cure all those ills to which the female system is subjected, with dispatch and degree of certainty which nothing but a scientifically compounded fluid preparation could reach; they are, in the most obstinate cases,

RELIABLE, AND SURE TO DO GOOD!
RELIABLE, AND SURE TO DO GOOD!
AND CANNOT DO HARM,
AND CANNOT DO HARM,

to the most delicate constitutions.

LYON'S PERIODICAL DROPS will certainly pro duce the regular return of nature, if taken a day or two before the expected period, and it is a maxim in the profession, that prevention is better than cure.

LYON'S PERIODICAL DROPS have been used by over twenty-five thousand ladies, within the past six months, and the testimony of all is, "It surely cures."

CAUTION!! CAUTION!!!

Bear in mind that I guarantee my DROPS TO CURE Supression of the Menses, from whatever cause, though care should be taken to ascertain if pregnancy be the cause, as these DROPS would be sure to produce miscarriage, if taken whilst in that situation, and all are cautioned against using them, as I wish it distinctly understood that I do not hold myself responsible when used under such circumstances.

TO MARRIED LADIES!

They are peculiarly adapted, as they bring the monthly period with such perfect regularity.

I could furnish any quantity of testimonials of its efficacy from my own patients, but the practice of parading bought and fictitious ones before the public is so prevalent, I do not deem it advisable.

BE WISE IN TIME
BE WISE IN TIME
BE WISE IN TIME
BE WISE IN TIME

Let no disease destroy your constitution. Try a bottle of my PERIODICAL DROPS, and you will be satisfied that I am no imposter. Tell your afflicted friend what restored the bloom of health to your cheeks, and thereby confer a favor more valuable than gold. For painful or scanty Menstruation it is just the thing. I have now in my mind an instance of a lady who had been suffering from painful Menstruation two or three years, confining her to her room each time. She had applied to several eminent physicians, without relief, when one bottle of my DROPS entirely cured her.

ONE BOTTLE CURES
ONE BOTTLE CURES
ONE BOTTLE CURES
ONE BOTTLE CURES

In almost every case.

It is impossible to enjoy the bloom of health and vivacity of spirits, unless the Menses are regular as to the time, the quantity, and quality. When they are obstruc ted, nature makes her efforts to obtain for it some oth er outlet, and unless these efforts of nature are assis ted, the patient usually experiences Despondency, Nervousness, and generally, CONSUMPTION assumes its sway, and prematurely terminates a miserable life.

Do not suffer from these irregularities when an invest ment of one dollar in Lyon's Periodical Drops will reguate and restore nature to its healthy course; and

DO NOT BE IMPOSED UPON
DO NOT BE IMPOSED UPON!

by those who have other preparations, which they desire to palm off upon the strength of the popularity of my Drops. But when the Druggist you apply to has not got them, either make him buy them for you, or else enclose one Dollar to the nearest general wholesale agent, who will return you a bottle by return Express.

See that the name of Jno. L. Lyon is written upon the directions which are wrapped around each bottle. None others are genuine. Therefore, beware of counterfeits. They are for sale by every druggist in city and country, If you wish relief take no other

The trade generally sell the above article at one dollar and twenty-five cents ($1 25) per bottle:

DR. JNO. L. LYON,
Practicing Physician, New Haven, Conn.

Who can be consulted concerning all diseases, either [perso]nally or by letter.

[C]. C. Goodwin & Bo., Boston; D. S. Barnes & Co., [Ne]w York; Lord & Smith. Chicago, Wholesale Agents.

For Sale by WOOD, BIXBY & CO., Nontpelier, Vt.

mar4:daw:eowly

A CARD TO INVALIDS.

A Clergyman while residing in South America as a missionary, discovered a safe and simple remedy for the Cure of Nervous Weakness, Early Decay, Diseases of the Urinary and Seminal Organs, and the whole train of disorders brought on by baneful and vicious habits Great numbers have been already cured by this noble remedy. Prompted by a desire to benefit the afflicted and unfortunate, I will send the recipe for preparing and using this medicine, in a sealed envelope, to any one who needs it, *Free of Charge.*

Please inclose a stamped envelope, addresed to your self.

Address

JOSEPH T. INMAN,
98:49:daw Station D. Bible House, *New York City*

HAVING PURCHASED THE STOCK AND INTEREST —OF— Mr. J. C. EMERY we propose to continue the FURNITURE BUSINESS at his old stand.

In inviting the attention of the purchasing community, we assure them that it

Will be our Aim
To keep the best qualities!
The most approved and latest Styles!
And give satisfaction to every customer!
To do this

Our prices will be as low as possible, and we shall not abuse the confidence of one customer by selling to another at a less price, but shall confine ourselves strictly to

One Price, and no Variation,

thus doing full justice to all.

Our Stock is complete of

FURNITURE,
CARPETS,
ROOM PAPERS,
CURTAINS AND
FIXTURES,
MIRRORS,

and everything pertaining to the business.

Repairing of Furniture promptly done.

BRAINERD & CO.,
Successors to J. C. Emery.
Montpelier, Vt.

GEORGE BRAINERD,
FRED. E. SMITH.
October 4th, 1864. daw:6m

Walton's Daily Journal.

OCTOBER 24, 1864.

MORNING EDITION.

THE ST. ALBANS RAID.

The following description of the "decidedly cool" manner by which the robbery of the Franklin County Bank was effected is from statements of the cashier, M. W. Beardsley and Jackson Clark, a wood sawer, in the bank at the time: The bank was entered a little after three o'clock by four men, well dressed and apparently middle-aged. One of them came up to Clark and said—"You are my prisoner, and if you move an inch I'll blow your brains out," at the same time showing a pistol They then told him to step back towards the vault. The leader of the party who had but a little while before been endeavoring to purchase some gold of Mr. Beardsley, stepped up to him and very coolly remarked "Sir, we are confederate soldiers. We have come to rob the banks in this place and there is *one hundred* of our gang here now. You must keep quiet, make no noise, and hand over in the first place, all the greenbacks you have on hand, and then all the other monies in your bank." These "terse" remarks were followed by the speaker presenting a pistol to Mr. Beardsley's head and insisting on his compliance with their demands. The bank was soon cleaned when the rascals made Mr. Beardsley and Clark step into the vault, when they locked them in. These gentlemen remained in the vault about half an hour when they were released by some citizens who had heard their cries for assistance. The vault was terribly close and it is wonderful that they were not stifled to death before being released.

The robbery of the other banks was conducted in a similar manner.

Seven of the raiders are in custody at St. Johns, Canada, and four have not been delivered up by the magistrate at St. Aubridge, but probably will be. Nearly all the stolen horses have been recovered and some $70,000 ef the money. If identified, as some if not all will be, the facts will be proved,and Judge Corsoul will so report to Governor General Monk, when a requisition willl be made.—The decision will be of such magnitude as a precedent that the status of the rebels will not unlikely be referred to the Governor General and subsequently by him to the home government for instructions. The Canadian authorities show every disposition to administer the law impartially.

Mr. E. J. Morrison, wounded by the rebele at St Albans, has since died, and his remains taken to Manchester, N. H.

DANVILLE, Va., Aug. 2, 1864.

P. T. Washburn, Adj t. and Inspector Gen:

Sir:—Having been taken prisoner with others I deemed it proper to send you a list of those taken from the 17th Vermont regiment:

Capt. Frank Kenfield, Company C; Sergt. Worthington Pierce, D; Corp W. G. McClintock, C; Corp. J M. Chaplin, C; Corp. Omri Atherton, C; Corp. Thompson Stoddard, C; Privates E. D. Carter, C; H. M. Bray, G; W. E. Howard, G; E. M. Morton, E; John Henry Wakefield, E; Chas. Carlton, G; D. C. Brown, A; Corp. Lewis Minor, A; Priv. Milo Dean, A; and Corp. Chas. Rivet, F.

Of these there are wounded, viz.: corporal Stoddard, in shoulder, corp. Atherton, in hand, private Caston, sabre cut in hip. One man from A, wounded in hand, but unable to give his name. The wounded have gone to hospital, and the remainder are prisoners here, all in good health and fareing well.

Respectfully, your ob't. servant,
Capt. FRANK KENFIELD.

HEADQUARTERS ARMY OF POTOMAC, Oct. 21.

Quiet has prevailed in front of Petersburg for the past wesk, unintterrupted only by occasional picket firing, which was renewed Thursday night and was kept up with spirit until daylight along the centre. Heavy firing was also heard in the direction of the James river, but the ebject is eot known,

The dispatch announcing another Union victory in the valley caused most hearty rejoicing among the troops.

The President has issued a proclamation setting apart the last Thursday of November for a day of thanksgiving and praise to Almighty God for, among other things, vouchsafing to us many and signal victories over the enemy, and recommending his fellow citizens to humble themselves in the dust, and from thence offer up penitent and fervent prayer and supplications to the Great Disposer of events for the return of the inestimable blessings of peace, Union and harmony throughout the land.

BOSTON MARKET—OCT. 22.

Corn Exchange—The receipts since yesterday have been 4935 bbls Flour, 4000 bush Corn 5200 bush Oats and 2000 bush Shorts. The market for Flour remains without material change; we quote Western superfine at a $8 75 $9 00; common extras at $9 50 a $9,75; medium do at $10 00 a $10 50; and good and choice, including favorite St. Louis brands, at $11 00 a $14 Southern Flour continues quiet and prices nominal. In Corn there have sales at $1 58 a $1 69 per bush for Western mixed, but held mostly at $1 60 and upward. Oats range from 90 a 92c for Northern and Canada. Rye $1 55 a $1 60; Shorts $38 a 40; and Fine Feed at $47 a $50; and Middlings $60 per ton.

Subsequently Western mixed Corn has been sold at $1 63, and is now held at that price and upward; and Western yellow is held at $1 74 a $1 75 per bush.

Provisions—Pork is steady at $40 for prime; $42 50 a $43 50 for mess; and $45 a $47 per bbl for clear cash. New Beef is held at $24 a $26 per bbl for Chicago. Lard 22 a 22c in bbls. and tierces; and Smoked Hams 18 a 20c per lb, cash. Butter ranges from 42 a 50c per lb as to quality, and is scarce. Cheese is 15 a 18c per lb as to quality.

FARNSWORTH'S *MINISTRELS AND BRASS BAND* ARE COMING!

VILLAGE HALL;

Monday, Tuesday, and Wednesay, evenings October 24th, 25th and 26th.

The above celebrated Troupe are now on their Second Annual Tour through the New England States, and will have the honor of appearing in one of their inimitable, and ever popular entertainments introducing a new and Brilliant Programme.

Tickets 25 Cents.

Doors open at 7 to commence at quarter before 8 o'clock.

A Serenade by the Band each evening previous to the opening of the doors.

For full particulars see Programme and Large Bills.

F. E EDWARDS, Gen. Business Agent.
E. D GILMORE, Advertising Agent.
October 30th 1864 d:1w

APPLES AND CIDER.—200 bbls of Fall and Winter Apples for sale by L. B Huntington, under the Vt. Bank, Montpelier. Also, 100 bbls. of Cider in any quantity from a glass to a bbl. Send in your bbls, Kegs and Jugs for the next four weeks, as I shall have it sweet from the mill twice a week.

October 22nd, 1864. d:tf

FIRST COLLECTION DIS'T. OF VT.
UNITED STATES ASSESSOR'S OFFICE,
Fair Haven, Oct 20, 1864.

Special U. S. Income Tax for October 1864.

The undersigned hereby gives public notice, that the special income tax, provided for by the Joint Resolution of Congress, approved July 4, 1864, has been duly assessed against persons liable to said duty residing in the 1st, 2nd and 3rd divisions, in the district aforesaid, in the county of Washington and State aforesaid, and that said assessment with a list of taxes assessed against each of such persons, has been this day deposited in the office of Hon. Joseph Poland, in Montpelier, for examination by all whom it may concern, and also, that said list will remain open for inspection for the space of ten days from this date in said Poland's office.

Given under my hand on the day and year first above written.

WM. C. KITTREDGE, *Assessor*,
oct21:daw:1w 1st Collection District of Vt.

FIRST COLLECTION DIS'T. OF VT.
UNITED STATES
Special Income Tax Notice!

The undersigned hereby gives public notice to all whom it may concern that he will attend at the office of Hon. Joseph Poland. in Montpelier, in the County of Washing on, on the 8th day of November, A. D 1864, when and where appeals will be heard and determined relating to any erroneous or excessive valuations assessments or enumerations, by the Assessor or Assistant Assessor, returned in the Special Income List of Taxes made and assessed for the month of October, instant, under a Joint Resolution of Congress, approved July 4, 1864.

Given under my hand, at Fair Haven, this 20th day of October, 1864.

WM. C. KITTREDGE, *Assessor*,
oct21 daw:1w 1st Coll. District of Vt.

LANE'S IMPROVED PATENT LEVER SET CIRCULAR SAW MILLS,

one of the great improvements of the age Also patent Headblocks for Mills now in use to take the place of Screw Headblocks; Rose's Water Wheels Box Stoves, Arch-mouths, Pan-bars, Grates, Plow-points and other Plow-castings of various patterns to suit almost any Plow now in use, Cultivator Teeth, Stone and Post Hammers, Wagon boxes, Iron Fence, and all kinds of Mill work and Machinery, manufactured at the Montpelier Foundery and Machine Shop.

D. LANE, Proprietor.
Montpelier, Sept. 29, 1864. daw:tf

OFFICE A. A. PRO. MAR. GEN.
BRATTLEBORO, Vt., Oct. 8, 1864.

[CIRCULAR No 84]

The following letter is published for the information and guiance of all concerned:

"WAR DEPARTMENT,
"Provost Marshals General's Office.
"Washington, 6th Oct. 1864.

"Brig. Gen. T. G. PITCHER,
"Supt. Vol. Recruiting Services,
"Brattleboro, Vt.

"GENERAL:

"The Provost Marshal General directs that you immediately notify the public, by advertising in the newspapers of your State, authorized to publish advertisements for the War Department, that all claims for premiums for presenting recruits must be presented to Maj. W Austine, U. S. A., mustering and Disbursing Officer, Brattleboro, Vt, for payment, before October 31, 1864, and that no claims for said premiums presented after that date, will be paid.

"I am, General,
"Very Respectfully,
"Your ob't servant,
"(Signed) C. McKEEVER,
"A. A. Gen'.

By order of Brig. Gen.
T. G. PITCHER,
A. A. P. M. General.

GEORGE W. DEBEVOISE,
Lieut. Vet. R. Corps and
Act. Insp. P. M. Gens. Bureau.

Official,
C. R. CRANE,
Capt and Provost Marhal,
oct13;d;t:oct31 1st District Vermont.

FAMILY DYES at BROWN'S

THE DAILY WANDERER.

Railroad Edition.

VOL. 1. NO. 10.

AMITE, October 25. 1864.

Terms of the Daily:

Single copies, fifty cents ...Per month, five dollars, in advance.

Advertisements inserted on moderate terms.

In consequence of the absence of the Telegraph Operator there will be no telegraphic reports to-day. He will be absent a day or two. During his absence we have made arrangements to receive the reports by mail. The absence of our young friend, Henry C Davis, at this time is to be regretted, as we were in hopes to receive something contradictory to the reports we published in yesterday morning's edition. We hope that our subscribers will make allowances for our *little sheet* until the enlargement takes place which will be in eight or ten days.

We are permitted to make a few extracts from a private letter, from Richmond, which tells us how they do things there:

In the Trenches, Oct 2d 1864.

DEAR FRIEND—Ere this you have no doubt heard of the onward move of the enemy on this side for Richmond. Also the fort—which is simply a battery manned—Harrison being in the possession of the foe. It fell, not for lack of bravery of the troops, but the want of numbers **Our battery was ordered to fill up Fort** Gilmore, which it did about ten a m; about two p m we were charged three times, but successfully repulsed the enemy in every attempt. The carnage was terrible. One whole negro regiment succeeded in getting into the ditches, which encircles every fort; we lit the fuse of some thirty-two pound shell and rolled them in the trench. You can better imagine the carnage than I can describe it.

Destruction of a Yankee Gunboat.—The Wilmington Journal, of the 12th inst says:

It is generally known that the large, three-funneled steamer Condor, from Halifax, N S, in entering New Inlet Bar a week ago, was deceived by the wreck of the Night Hawk and ran aground. It appears that it was in attempting to come ashore from her in a boat that Mrs Rose Greenhow was drowned. The Condor has been slowly unloading under the guns of Fort Fisher, and a guard, as usual, has been kept on her all night. On last Friday night the Yankees made an attempt to board the Condor to destroy her, but were gallantly repulsed by Lieut. Sewles, of Co A, 20th N C Troops, and a detachment of men.

As soon as the attempt was made Lt Seweles communicated the fact to Fort Fisher, when her heavy guns burst forth to right and left of the Condor. The second shell fired to the left of the Condor struck a gunboat that had accompanied the party in, and so completely ruined her that she was run ashore on the south breaker of the bar and abandoned The enemy set fire to her in several places, and before morning she was totally destroyed, her magazine having exploded and torn her to pieces. Since this occurrence on Friday night last, we are informed that there has not been a sign of the enemy off the bar at night, and the fleet is hull down during the day.

THE VICTORY.

LINCOLN RE-ELECTED.

He Has Nearly All the States.

ALL NEW-ENGLAND FOR HIM.

New-York Close but Pretty Sure.

NEW-JERSEY FOR McCLELLAN.

Pennsylvania Union on Home Vote.

DELAWARE AND MARYLAND UNION.

The West All Right.

COPPERHEADS NOWHERE.

New-York  Tribune.

VOL. XXIV....NO. 7,362. NEW-YORK, WEDNESDAY, NOVEMBER 9, 1864. PRICE FOUR CENTS.

NEW YORK.

Complete Vote of the City.

Ward.	Dist.	Vote for President 1864. Lincoln Union.	McClellan Dem.	Vote for Governor 1862. Wadsworth Union.	Seymour Dem.
I	1	42	604	74	344
	2	63	491	37	365
	3	34	640	42	332
	4	40	116	43	89
	5	34	311	37	152
Total		213	2,162	218	1,282
II	1	127	144	88	134
	2	59	194	108	115
Total		186	338	196	249
III	1	77	223	58	188
	2	86	121	61	103
	3	53	112	50	91
	4	11	44	9	52
Total		207	500	178	434
IV	1	162	259	92	263
	2	77	506	53	408
	3	34	369	25	271
	4	85	324	13	198
	5	17	255	8	182
	6	14	323	7	178
	7	45	343	17	250
Total		434	2,379	215	1,750
V	1	92	198	90	187
	2	92	159	48	128
	3	103	285	98	249
	4	277	229	152	187
	5	85	351	63	230
	6	137	269	92	181
	7	158	269	96	189
	8	78	278	70	218
Total		1,022	2,038	709	1,569
VI	1	18	64	7	47
	2	32	247	12	113
	3	41	338	35	231
	4	55	382	33	251
	5	21	518	20	392
	6	61	655	33	420
	7	28	259	16	142
	8	45	295	35	202
	9	28	699	18	354
Total		329	3,457	209	2,152
VII	1	108	367	73	195
	2	56	596	45	358
	3	120	301	60	220
	4	70	269	30	154
	5	96	413	77	354
	6	275	405	167	288
	7	146	221	88	187
	8	119	342	77	235
	9	118	370	92	215
	10	50	475	40	365
	11	72	331	44	251
Total		1,230	4,090	793	2,822
VIII	1	130	244	65	164
	2	177	410	115	362
	3	110	266	64	196
	4	131	182	86	154
	5	76	186	51	134
	6	180	176	62	156
	7	221	380	103	302
	8	220	334	140	247
	9	156	264	94	204
	10	71	290	53	219
	11	101	255	67	158
	12	46	215	33	168
Total		1,619	3,202	933	2,464
IX	1	246	475	160	336
	2	363	314	208	269
	3	513	463	301	395
	4	297	272	190	208
	5	311	291	226	241
	6	223	183	132	163
	7	364	242	220	225
	8	268	328	149	251
	9	208	281	120	207
	10	217	281	133	203
	11	288	408	127	303
	12	190	306	109	249
Total		3,488	3,844	2,075	3,040
X	1	292	331	162	284
	2	315	422	155	327
	3	278	457	136	426
	4	201	396	105	297
	5	316	402	166	357
	6	288	339	117	318
Total		1,690	2,347	841	2,009
XI	1	119	353	44	267
	2	112	572	45	273
	3	144	362	81	274
	4	178	369	108	283
	5	152	317	94	247
	6	84	157	45	143
	7	75	410	22	316
	8	109	345	53	283
	9	140	190	108	157
	10	94	183	55	152
	11	140	203	82	159
	12	85	299	54	249
	13	78	405	29	284
	14	156	263	90	238
	15	50	186	23	121
	16	107	311	63	236
	17	48	254	31	175
	18	57	311	30	234
Total		1,928	5,490	1,057	4,191
XII	1	93	249	63	203
	2	298	440	131	415
	3	293	679	205	488
	4	411	389	293	381
	5	89	404	52	349
	6	181	337	161	273
Total		1,365	2,498	905	2,109
XIII	1	199	366	109	295
	2	174	414	123	349
	3	122	525	76	400
	4	119	409	92	348
	5	153	306	106	244
	6	139	267	99	159
	7	58	133	43	132
	8	142	297	104	224
Total		1,106	2,767	752	2,151
XIV	1	59	187	33	164
	2	29	670	23	328
	3	102	620	21	226
	4	41	609	31	324
	5	130	363	64	182
	6	139	356	62	246
	7	115	259	53	166
	8	80	319	30	157
	9	82	561	38	331
	10	82	285	42	190
Total		859	4,229	397	2,314
XV	1	289	260	214	221
	2	271	275	155	172
	3	137	294	108	235
	4	341	225	221	192
	5	161	88	108	90
	6	273	127	181	117
	7	159	85	114	100
	8	251	285	150	247
	9	209	160	146	114
	10	153	171	87	140
Total		2,244	1,970	1,484	1,628
XVI	1	307	278	160	252
	2	302	454	179	316
	3	364	470	246	373
	4	303	351	217	308
	5	183	393	207	292
	6	424	382	263	341
	7	212	463	141	339
	8	29	125	7	83
	9	387	275	276	244
	10	235	287	154	227
Total		2,746	3,478	1,850	2,775
XVII	1	251	248	130	197
	2	254	377	126	328
	3	252	352	134	285
	4	257	358	147	295
	5	319	409	198	296
	6	287	228	162	197
	7	403	327	256	289
	8	104	364	74	228
	9	61	489	22	313
	10	66	210	43	146
	11	108	412	58	253
	12	141	426	51	314
	13	155	290	97	224
	14	43	451	26	321
	15	95	404	48	280
	16	213	361	81	317
	17	99	435	40	316
	18	106	446	53	355
	19	211	444	101	326
Total		3,425	7,031	1,848	5,280
XVIII	1	356	214	262	224
	2	452	371	306	252
	3	488	287	310	255
	4	178	124	108	112
	5	176	154	133	145
	6	206	355	137	280
	7	181	290	115	196
	8	87	200	76	132
	9	158	243	94	171
	10	68	306	61	207
	11	154	317	87	236
	12	46	346	53	570
	13	34	488	34	357
	14	36	318	27	190
	15	58	411	—	—
Total		2,678	4,424	1,803	3,327
XIX	1	203	507	131	354
	2	157	434	74	325
	3	247	392	183	350
	4	240	467	224	468
	5	163	299	92	254
	6	191	281	152	432
	7	191	477	139	264
	8	302	348	143	198
	9	247	369	—	—
Total		1,941	3,574	1,138	2,645
XX	1	83	440	47	286
	2	189	303	116	215
	3	273	588	153	376
	4	173	360	108	205
	5	101	506	56	331
	6	328	245	220	225
	7	321	224	206	212
	8	164	419	79	320
	9	170	474	91	261
	10	169	367	104	261
	11	224	507	133	400
	12	186	336	146	299
	13	182	357	93	255
	14	311	427	237	315
Total		2,874	5,553	1,789	3,936
XXI	1	159	310	114	207
	2	127	426	74	227
	3	164	414	112	274
	4	141	446	94	251
	5	125	437	88	254
	6	84	278	48	174
	7	66	334	39	195
	8	185	145	128	142
	9	205	255	148	177
	10	238	309	166	214
	11	287	258	195	217
	12	290	204	187	208
	13	376	185	212	198
	14	320	176	193	182
Total		2,767	4,177	1,798	2,920
XXII	1	135	396	59	259
	2	248	420	96	306
	3	248	394	170	245
	4	281	280	172	222
	5	169	227	95	186
	6	137	165	69	105
	7	144	278	96	215
	8	200	218	129	200
	9	232	356	151	273
	10	163	313	113	304
	11	187	434	101	453
	12	60	306	29	229
	13	78	216	21	163
	14	78	133	47	105
Total		2,360	4,136	1,348	3,265

RECAPITULATION BY WARDS.

Wards.	1864. Lincoln.	McClellan.	1862. Wadsworth.	Seymour.	1860. Lincoln.	Fusion.
I	213	2,162	218	1,282	504	1,442
II	186	338	196	249	223	408
III	227	500	178	434	285	570
IV	434	2,379	215	1,750	498	2,037
V	1,032	2,038	709	1,569	1,144	2,147
VI	329	3,457	209	2,152	397	2,827
VII	1,230	4,090	793	2,822	1,435	3,365
VIII	1,619	3,202	933	2,464	1,641	3,130
IX	3,488	3,844	2,075	3,040	2,944	3,956
X	1,690	2,347	841	2,009	1,463	2,192
XI	1,928	5,550	1,057	4,191	1,943	4,224
XII	1,365	2,498	905	2,109	991	2,068
XIII	1,106	2,767	752	2,151	1,347	2,357
XIV	859	4,229	397	2,314	748	2,830
XV	2,244	1,970	1,484	1,628	1,737	2,528
XVI	2,746	3,478	1,850	2,775	2,473	3,418
XVII	3,425	7,031	1,848	5,280	2,975	5,690
XVIII	2,678	4,424	1,803	3,327	2,130	4,242
XIX	1,941	3,574	1,138	2,645	1,180	1,852
XX	2,874	5,553	1,789	3,936	2,822	4,386
XXI	2,767	4,177	1,798	2,920	2,269	3,596
XXII	2,366	4,126	1,348	3,265	2,141	3,039
Total	36,737	73,734	22,536	54,312	33,290	62,298

McClellan's majority.............36,997
McClellan over Seymour.........19,422
McClellan over Fusion............23,976
Net Democratic gain.............. 7,988

Vote for Governor, by Wards.

	1864 Fenton. Union.	Seymour. Democrat.	1862 Wadsw'th. Union.	Seym'r. Democrat.
I	207	2133	218	1282
II	188	335	196	249
III	221	500	178	434
IV	396	2422	215	1750
V	1012	2030	709	1569
VI	348	3429	209	2152
VII	1199	4061	793	2822
VIII	1520	3264	933	2464
IX	3495	3814	2071	3040
X	1614	3361	841	2009
XI	1948	5533	1057	4191
XII	1273	2485	905	2109
XIII	1077	2769	752	2151
XIV	809	4247	397	2314
XV	2227	1970	1484	1628
XVI	2864	3425	1850	2775
XVII	3349	7052	1848	5280
XVIII	2261	4370	1803	3327
XIX	1918	3575	1138	2645
XX	3071	5689	1789	3936
XXI	2785	4133	1798	2920
XXII	2340	4130	1348	3265
Total	36,122	73,727	22,536	54,312

Seymour's maj. over Fenton..........37,605
Seymour's maj. over Wadsworth......31,776

New-York State.

KINGS COUNTY.

Ward.	Dist.	McClellan.	Lincoln.	Ward.	Dist.	McClellan.	Lincoln.
I	1	252	235	XII	1	687	52
	2	335	150		2	735	126
II	1	400	96	XIII	1	278	385
	2	653	257		2	376	465
III	1	208	311		3	307	466
	2	299	398		4	278	490
	3	207	478	XIV	1	575	90
IV	1	287	375		2	532	230
	2	419	424		3	378	176
	3	344	343		4	247	218
V	1	545	84	XV	1	—	—
	2	487	227		2	409	542
	3	402	242	XVI	1	—	—
	4	460	205		2	368	415
VI	1	774	304		3	—	—
	2	354	295		4	548	241
	3	573	389	XVII	1	472	464
VII	1	317	232		2	311	465
	2	—	—	XVIII	1	261	163
	3	240	238		2	209	260
	4	177	276	XIX	1	129	152
VIII	1	367	255		2	183	333
	2	511	263		3	283	297
IX	1	741	260	XX	1	150	335
	2	240	215		2	245	532
	3	488	419		3	332	481
	4	295	200		4	167	240
X	1	238	343	New-Lots		—	—
	2	588	270	Flatbush		—	—
	3	302	343	Flatlands		—	—
XI	1	351	352	New-Utrecht		299	126
	2	538	213	Gravesend		136	98
	3	181	289				
	4	656	310	Total		23,515	18,191
	5	173	336	McClellan's majority, 5,324			

ORANGE COUNTY.

Lincoln majorities. Towns.	1860	1864	*Democratic majorities.* Towns.	1860	1864
Bloom'g G've	69	123	Deerpark	—	102
Mount Hope	—	40	Goshen	7	197
Southfield (new)		55	Mount Hope	1	—
Newburgh	—	150	Newburg	56	—
Wolkill	135	280			
Deerpark	39	—			

ERIE COUNTY.

Buffalo gives from 400 to 500 majority for McClellan, two districts yet to come. Returns from 8 towns in the county show a Democratic gain of about 60 over the vote of 1862.

MONROE COUNTY.

Riga, 47 Union majority.

Churchville, McClellan 147; Lincoln 226.

NIAGARA COUNTY.

Lockport, 66 Union majority.

LIVINGSTON COUNTY.

Mount Morris, 145 Democratic majority.

Dansville, McClellan 44; Lincoln, 246.

Geneseo, Lincoln 196; McClellan 144; Fenton, 196; Seymour 144.

ORLEANS COUNTY COMPLETE.

Union majority on Electoral Ticket 1,314. Fenton's majority will be about the same.

LIVINGSTON COUNTY.

West Sparta, McClellan 140; Lincoln, 139; Seymour 141; Fenton 138.

Ossian, McClellan, 124; Lincoln, 117.

MONROE COUNTY.

Greece, McClellan 292; Lincoln 148; Seymour 291; Fenton 149.

Sweden, 1st Dist, Lincoln 203; McClellan 86; 2d Dist. Lincoln 324, McClellan 241.

NIAGARA COUNTY.

Niagara, 1st Dist. Lincoln 216; McClellan 305,

WESTCHESTER COUNTY.

Eastchester, First District: Lincoln, 269; McClellan, 368; Fenton, 269; Seymour, 367. Radford, Democrat, for Congress, has 97 majority. Second District, McClellan, 92 majority.

Pelham, 78 Union majority.

NEW-ROCHELLE, N. Y., Tuesday, Nov. 8, 1864.

Special Dispatch to The N. Y. Tribune.

Town of New Rochelle, complete—Seymour 373; Fenton 231. Congress—Radford, Democrat, 373, Larkin, Union. 228. Assembly—Lockwood, Democrat, 364; Cornell, Union, 228. P. C. B.

STEUBEN CO.

Adrian, 76 Union majority.

Hornellsville, 66 Democratic majority.

TOMPKINS CO.

Trumansburg, 54 Union majority.

Ithaca, 43 Union majority.

CORTLAND CO.

Homer, 480 Union majority.

ONONDAGA CO.

Syracuse, 72 Union majority.

WESTCHESTER CO.

Sing Sing gives McClellan 134 majority. Brandreth (Union) is probably reëlected to the Assembly.

ALLEGHANY CO.

Phillipsville, 154 Union majority.

Frenchville, 122 Union majority.

Scio, 26 Union majority.

STEUBEN CO.

Rathboneville, 76 Union majority.

CHAUTAUQUA CO.

Forestville, 47 Union majority.

ALLEGHANY CO.

Alfred, 245 Union majority.

Andover, 210 Union majority.

Alleghany, 78 Democratic majority.

TOMPKINS CO.

Danbury, 150 Union majority.

CHAUTAUQUA CO.

Perrysburg, 130 Union majority.

CHAUTAUQUA COUNTY.

Sheridan, 79 Union majority: Fenton, 92 majority.

Fredonia, 173 Lincoln majority; Fenton, 168 majority

Randolph, Lincoln, 116 majority.

Jamestown, Lincoln, 649 majority.

Westfield, Lincoln, 231 majority,

Chautauqua, Lincoln, 172 majority.

Ripley, Lincoln, 92 majority.

Portland, Lincoln, 87 majority.

ALLEGANY COUNTY.

Cuba, Lincoln, 116 majority.

CATTARAUGUS COUNTY.

Little Valley, Lincoln, 74 majority.

STEUBEN COUNTY.

Cameron, Lincoln, 127 majority.

Addison, Lincoln, 10 majority.

Canisteo, Lincoln, 174 majority.

ALLEGANY COUNTY.

Belvidere, Lincoln, 14 majority.

Hinsdale, Lincoln, 33 majority.

Angelica, Lincoln, 180 majority.

ORANGE COUNTY.

Newburgh, 150 Union majority.

Goshen, 196 Democratic majority.

Blooming Grove, 123 Union majority.

Southfield, 55 Union majority.

Mount Hope, 40 Union majority.

Deerpark, 102 Democratic majority; Seymour, 112 majority; Winfield (Dem.) for Congress, 76 majority.

OSWEGO COUNTY.

Oswego City and ten towns in the County give a Union majority of 1,702. The remainder will probably increase this to 2,500. Three Union members of Assembly are elected.

ST. LAWRENCE COUNTY.

Potsdam, 786 Union majority.

Lawrence, 364 Union majority.

Oswegatchie, 275 Union majority.

Madrid, 267 Union majority.

These towns show a Union gain of 75 over last year.

FRANKLIN COUNTY.

Malone, 523 Union majority—a gain over 1860 of 260.

ST. LAWRENCE COUNTY.

Chateaugay, 20 Democratic majority; Union gain, 64.

Constable, 62 Union majority; Union gain, 83.

OSWEGO COUNTY.

Volney, 190 Union majority.

Granby, 102 Union majority.

Palermo, 264 Union majority.

Schroeppel, 73 Union majority.

WAYNE COUNTY.

Savannah, 122 Union majority.

Fenton, 119 Union majority.

Butler, 194 Union majority.

Lyons, 94 Democratic majority.

Arcadia, Third District, 15 McClellan majority.

KINGS COUNTY.

New Utrecht—Lincoln, 126; McClellan, 299.

Gravesend—Lincoln, 98; McClellan, 136.

TOMPKINS COUNTY.

Ithaca, 39 Union majority.

TIOGA COUNTY.

Waverly, 150 Union majority.

Owego, 205 Union majority.

Campville, 22 Democratic majority.

ALLEGHANY COUNTY.

Friendship, 144 Union majority.

Wellsville, 66 Union majority.

Cuba, 116 Union majority.

ONTARIO COUNTY.

Canandagua, 66 Union majority.

STEUBEN COUNTY.

Corning, 22 Democratic majority.

Bath, 184 Union majority.

Levonia, 96 Union majority.

Avoca, 123 Union majority.

Liberty, 73 Union majority.

Wayland, 79 Union majority.

BROOME COUNTY.

Binghamton, 353 Union majority.

CHEMUNG COUNTY.

Elmira (township), 43 Union majority.

Big Flats, 68 Democratic majority.

SULLIVAN COUNTY.

Highlands, 33 Democratic majority.

Fremont, 123 Democratic majority.

ORANGE COUNTY.

Walkill, 280 Union majority.

DUTCHESS COUNTY.

Rhinebeck, 88 Union majority.

Fenton, 96 majority; Ketcham (Union) for Congress, 87 majority.

WESTCHESTER COUNTY.

Yonkers gives McClellan 233 majority; Seymour, 244 majority; Radford, (Dem.) for Congress, 194 majority.

Tarrytown, 4 for Lincoln.

Beekmantown, McClellan, 71 majority.

Manhattan, 314 Dem. majority.

Peekskill, 22 Democratic majority.

QUEENS COUNTY.

Newtown, 2d district, Lincoln, 218; McClellan, 353.

KINGS COUNTY.

Flatbush, Lincoln, 191; McClellan, 214.

Flatlands, Lincoln, 164; McClellan, 119.

WESTCHESTER COUNTY.

West Farms, McClellan, 58 majority; Seymour, 36; Radford, (Dem.) for Congress, 53 majority; Strang, (Union) for Assembly, has 12 majority.

Votes of the Towns for President and Governor.

	President 1864 Lincoln.	McClellan.	Governor 1862 Wadsworth.	Seymour
Ithaca	43	—	37	—
Waverley	150	—	—	—
Owego	205	—	154	—
Campville	—	22	—	—
Friendship	144	—	90	—
Wellsville	66	—	51	—
Cuba	116	—	77	—
Canandaigua	66	—	—	3
Corning	—	22	—	3
Bath	184	—	174	—
Livonia, 1st district	96	—	89	—
Avoca	123	—	79	—
Liberty	73	—	37	—
Wayland	—	79	—	88
Binghamton	353	—	258	—
Elmira Township	43	—	190	—
Big Flats	—	68	—	16
Highland	—	33	—	48
Fremont	—	123	—	42
Walk Hill	280	—	141	—
Rhinebeck	88	—	60	—
Yonkers	—	233	—	153
Tarrytown	4	—	—	—
Beekman	71	—	78	—
Manhattan	—	314	—	—
Peekskill	—	22	—	106
Newtown, 2d Dist	218	353	163	54
Flatbush	191	214	121	166
Flatlands	164	119	75	98
West Farms	—	58	—	172
Sheridan	79	—	9	—
Fredonia	173	—	—	—
Randolph	116	—	101	—
Jamestown	649	—	476	—
Westfield	231	—	160	—
Chautauqua	172	—	152	—
Ripley	92	—	31	—
Portland	81	—	23	—
Little Valley	74	—	61	—
Cameron	127	—	87	—
Addison	10	—	—	2
Canisteo	174	—	156	—
Belvidere	14	—	—	—
Hinsdale	33	—	33	—
Angelica	180	—	207	—
Newburgh	150	—	—	164
Goshen	—	196	—	117
Blooming Grove	123	—	91	—
Southfield	55	—	—	—
Mount Hope	40	—	—	25
Deerpark	—	102	—	29
Adrian	76	—	—	—
Hornellsville	—	66	—	55
Trumansburg	54	—	—	—
Horner	480	—	467	—
Syracuse	72	—	—	294
Sing Sing	—	134	—	—
Philipsville	154	—	—	—
Frenchville	122	—	—	—
Scio	26	—	31	—
Rathboneville	76	—	39	—
Forestville	47	—	20	—
Alfred	245	—	189	—
Andover	210	—	138	—
Allegany	78	—	—	45
Danbury	150	—	—	—
Perrysburg	130	—	111	—
Attica	14	—	41	81
Rochester	—	62	—	418
Lima	59	—	55	—
Orleans County	1314	—	1159	—
Eastchester	—	191	—	147
Pelham	—	78	—	81
Genesee County	1283	—	932	—
Oneida County	1300	—	481	—
Buffalo	—	500	—	1523
Riga	47	—	69	—
Lockport	66	—	—	154
Mt. Morris	—	145	—	123
Danville	202	—	—	—
Geneseo	52	—	150	—
West Sparta	—	1	—	1
Ossian	7	—	25	—
Greece	—	144	—	81
Sweden	117	—	195	—
Niagara	—	89	—	134
Tonawanda	—	182	—	270
Scott	172	—	136	—
Marathon	135	—	66	—
Lisle	270	—	305	—
Triangle	160	—	170	—
Mamaroneck	—	25	—	6
Cortland	485	—	443	—
Oswego	2500	—	2000	—
Potsdam	786	—	689	—
Lawrence	364	—	292	—
Oswegatchie	275	—	298	—
Madrid	267	—	225	—
Malone	523	—	103	—
Chateaugay	—	20	—	149
Constable	62	—	—	11
Volney	190	—	71	—
Granby	102	—	22	—
Palermo	264	—	209	—
Schroeppel	73	—	40	—
Savannah	122	—	72	—
Butler	194	—	195	—
Lyons	—	94	—	84
Arcadia, 3d District	—	15	—	9
Dewit	79	—	76	—
Fabius	253	—	181	—
Geddes	34	—	36	—
Lafayette	55	—	162	—
Lysander	236	—	209	—
Camillus	10	—	—	17
Manlius, 2d dist	224	—	—	—
Clay, 1st dist	146	—	—	—
Onondaga, 1st dist	137	—	—	—
Pompey, 1st dist	64	—	—	—
Van Buren	71	—	—	—
Spofford, 1st dist	70	—	—	—
Onondaga Co	2700	—	1553	—
Poughkeepsie	266	—	114	—
Albany City	—	2300	—	2162
Troy	—	900	—	1006
Utica	—	259	—	353
Palmyra	40	—	—	36
Arcadia, 2d Dist	78	—	77	—
Walworth	179	—	79	—
Marion	326	—	255	—
Batavia	117	—	113	—
Lenox	209	—	164	—
Rome	—	471	—	465
German Flats	6	—	14	—
Herkimer	—	164	—	101
Lichfield	126	—	91	—
Warren	—	40	—	9
Columbia	94	—	116	—
Stark	49	—	83	—
Little Falls	—	228	—	110
Manheim	—	60	—	8
St. Johnsville	—	95	—	107
Minden	81	—	80	—
Canajoharie	—	11	—	77
Root	—	172	—	143
Palatine	—	156	—	115
Mohawk	—	53	11	—
Amsterdam	125	—	183	—
Schenectady	—	229	—	185
Greene	—	23	—	34
Oxford	34	—	18	—
Norwich	3	—	—	8
Sherburne	245	—	218	—
Smyrna	236	—	180	—
Columbus	208	—	226	—
Hamilton	156	—	172	—
Eaton	138	—	128	—
Cochocton	—	295	—	359

We find by the above figures, and those of the cities of New-York and Brooklyn, a net gain of **7,641** in the State over the vote for Wadsworth in 1862. Should this proportion hold out through the State, Lincoln's majority will reach **10,000** or more.

Congressmen Probably Elected.

Dist. I..*Stephen Tabor.*
II..*Tunis G. Bergen.*
III..James Humphrey, gain.
IV..*Morgan Jones.*
V..*Nelson Taylor.*
VI..Henry J. Raymond, gain.
VII..*John W. Chanler.*
VIII..William E. Dodge.
IX..William A. Darling, gain.
X..*William Radford.*
XI..*Charles H. Winfield.*
XII..John A. Ketchum, gain.
XIII..*E. N. Hubbell.*
XIV..*Charles Goodyear.*
XV..John A. Griswold, gain.
XVI..Orlando Kellog.
XVII..Calvin T. Hurlburd.
XVIII..James M. Marvin.
XIX..Demas Hubbard, jr.
XX..Addison H. Laflin.
XXI..Roscoe Conkling, gain.
XXII..Sydney T. Holmes.
XXIII..Thomas T. Davis.
XXIV..Theodore M. Pomeroy.
XXV..Daniel Morris.
XXVI..Giles W. Hotchkins.
XXVII..Hamilton Ward.
XXVIII..Roswell Hunt.
XXIX..Burt Van Horn.
XXX..Samuel J. Holley, probably gain.
XXXI..Henry Van Arnam.

Republicans in Roman. Democrats in *Italics.*

22 Union, 9 Democrats; in the present Congress, 15 Union, 16 Democrats.

BUFFALO, N. Y., Tuesday, Nov. 8—1 p. m.

The voting is proceeding here quietly. The day is rainy. The indications are that a very large vote will be polled.

Special Dispatch to The N. Y. Tribune.

PITTSBURG, Tuesday, Nov. 8—2 p. m.

The prospect at all the polls is very favorable. Increased majority certain. C. D. B.

ELMIRA, Tuesday, Nov. 8

This city goes Lincoln—162 majority.

Special Dispatch to The N. Y. Tribune.

NEW ROCHELLE, Tuesday, Nov. 8.

Vote of New Rochelle complete: McClellan, 381; Lincoln, 229. P. C. B.

RICHMOND COUNTY.

First District of Middletown—109 majority for McClellan.

First District of Castleton—189 majority for McClellan.

Seymour's majority in both the above districts the same.

WYOMING COUNTY.

Attica, 14 Union majority.

MONROE COUNTY.

Rochester City, complete, 62 Democratic majority; Union gain over last year, 127, and 200 over 1862. Hart, Union, is elected to Congress.

LIVINGSTON COUNTY.

Lima, 59 Union majority.

ORLEANS COUNTY.

Two-thirds of the County give a gain for the Union ticket thus far over last year, when the majority in the County was 1,164. This indicates a majority in the county of 1,300.

RICHMOND COUNTY.

Six districts give McClellan 1,058 majority.

SULLIVAN COUNTY.

Mount Hope, 4 Democratic majority. The following is the vote for Governor: Seymour, 193; Fenton, 193—a tie. Marvin, for Assembly, has 1 majority.

DUTCHESS COUNTY.

Amenia—Lincoln, 311; McClellan, 211; Fenton, 312; Seymour, 211; Ketcham, for Congress (Rep.), 333; Nelson, for Congress (Dem.), 195.

North Salem—Lincoln, 236; McClellan, 110; Fenton, 236; Seymour, 110; Brandeth (Rep.), 129 majority.

North-East—McClellan, 188; Lincoln, 136; Seymour, 187; Fenton, 136; Nelson (Dem.), for Congress, 183; Ketcham (Rep.), 236.

RENSSELAER COUNTY.

Sandlake—First District—Union majority, 89.

North Greenbush—Democratic majority, 59.

Grafton—Union majority, 73.

PUTNAM COUNTY.

Four towns give McClellan 78 majority, and Seymour 79. The Democratic majority in the County will be about 250.

ERIE COUNTY.

The Democratic majority in Erie County will be about 400, or a trifle less. The towns of Clas[illegible] give about the Republican gain, w[illegible] up the Democratic gains in the strong towns.

QUEENS COUNTY.

Jamaica—McClellan's majority 234; Seymour's, 238.

Hempstead—Lincoln's majority 338.

Newtown—Democratic majority 576.

North Hempstead—Union majority 95. Fenton's 109.

Queens County, complete, will probably give 1,000 Democratic majority.

SUFFOLK.

River Head—Union majority 73.

Southold—Union majority 164.

Southampton—Union majority 263

Easthampton—Union majority 9.

Shelter Island—Union majority 26.

PENNSYLVANIA.

PHILADELPHIA, Tuesday, Nov. 8, 1864.

We have returns from six wards, which stood up to 12 o'clock as follows:

Majority for Lincoln, 1,397. The same wards in October gave a Union majority of 1,534 at the close of the polls.

Special Dispatch to The N. Y. Tribune.

PHILADELPHIA, Tuesday, Nov. 8, 1864—2 p. m.

Our election is passing off quietly. There is every indication of an increased Union majority. J. N.

Special Dispatch to The N. Y. Tribune.

PHILADELPHIA, Tuesday, Nov. 8—3:40 p. m.

The Eighth Ward, up to this hour, gives four hundred and ten Union majority, within forty-six votes of her majority at the October election.

The Fourteenth Ward had 530 majority at ten a. m. —an increase of 250 over the same hour in October.

Various precincts in various wards increase their Union October majorities by forty per cent. The first precinct of the Twenty-first Ward had 23 majority at 11 a. m., for the Union, against 50 Democratic at the same hour in October.

The Ninth Ward, up to 1 o'clock, gives the Union 210 majority, against 70 in the October election at the same hour.

The first three precincts of the Second Ward give 325 Union majority, a gain of 60, up to 1 p. m., over the Union majority in October.

Both parties are hurrying up their voters. A large increase over the October vote is indicated. A.

Special Dispatch to The N. Y. Tribune.

PHILADELPHIA, Tuesday, Nov. 8—10 p. m.

The returns of the City of Philadelphia show a gain for Lincoln over October vote of three thousand votes, which will give Lincoln a majority of ten thousand in the city. The returns from the interior show gains for Lincoln in all the Counties thus far heard from.

Special Dispatch to The N. Y. Tribune.

WESTCHESTER, Tuesday, Nov. 8, 1864.

Seventeen townships show a Union gain in all but three, and indicate a Union majority of 2,500 in Chester County.

Special Dispatch to The N. Y. Tribune

LANCASTER, Tuesday, Nov. 8, 1864—10 p. m.

Twenty districts throughout the County show a Lincoln gain of 712. This indicates that Lancaster Co. gives about 5,400 majority for Lincoln. J. J. C.

PHILADELPHIA, Tuesday, Nov. 8—11 p. m.

The vote in this city stands as follows:

Union majorities—IId Ward, 172; gain, 62. IXth Ward, 257; gain, 17. XIIIth Ward, 826; gain, 146. XVIth Ward, 25; gain, 6.

Democratic majorities—IIId Ward, 236; Union gain, 23. IVth Ward, 1341; Democratic gain, 376. Vth Ward, 135; Union gain, 162. VIth Ward, 100; Union gain, 74. XIth Ward, 215; Union gain, 358. XVIIth Ward, 1114; Union gain, 239.

It is reported that returns from all but two wards give a Union majority of 10,200.

Union majority in Ist Ward, 1928; do. gain, 60. In XVIIIth Ward, 1375; do. gain, 269. XIXth Ward, 154; gain, 44. XXVIth Ward, 767; gain, 123.

Union majorities—VIIth Ward, 900; Union gain, 91. VIIIth Ward, 554; Union gain, 123.

Eleven wards give a Union gain of 924. The entire majority will be about 10,000.

Chester Co.—Nine Districts show Union gains of 120.

Bedford Co.—Saxton gives 35 Democratic majority; Union gain, 2.

Northampton Co.—Fremansburg, 10 Democratic majority; Democratic gain, 7.

Carbon Co.—Mauch Chunk, Democratic majority, 88; do. gain, 21.

Lehigh Co.—Allentown, two wards give Democratic majority of 50; Union gain, 12.

Carbon Co.—Franklin Township, Union majority, 3; do. gain, 31.

York Co.—Hanover Borough, Union majority, 110; gain, 8.

Adams Co.—Gettysburg, Union majority, 81; Democratic gain, 22.

Franklin Co.—Chambersburg, one ward shows Union gain of 23.

Lancaster Co.—Lancaster City, Democratic majority, 197; gain, 54.

Eight small Districts show over 200 Union gain. Large Union gains throughout the county.

Berks Co.—One ward in Reading gives 117 Union majority; gain, 23.

Schuylkill Co.—Scattering returns show Union majority of 640; gain, 68.

Lebanon Co.—About 1,000 Union majority; no change.

Carbon Co.—Summit Hill Borough, 313 Union gain.

Chester Co.—Union majority over 2,500; gain over 700.

Private dispatches say Delaware gives Lincoln her electoral vote. Philadelphia Union Clubs are parading the streets; Democratic headquarters darkened. Pennsylvania is generally conceded as having given her vote for the Administration.

Union majorities—Twentieth Ward, 995; gain, 293; Twenty-third Ward, 400; gain, 11.

This completes the vote in this city, which gives a Union majority of 9,396.

NEW-JERSEY.

SUMMIT, N. J., Tuesday, Nov. 8, 1864.

New Providence township gives Lincoln 98; McClellan, 136.

For Congress—Charles Scranton, (Union), 97; Charles Sitgreaves, (Dem.), 137.

For Assembly—Joseph T. Crowell, (Union), 96; Scudder, (Dem.), 138.

Chatham Township—McClellan, 9 majority; Little (Union), for Congress, 2 majority; for Assembly, Democratic majority 19.

Mendham Township (in Morris County)—Lincoln, 10 majority; Little, 18 majority; Gage (Union), for Assembly, 36 majority.

Newark—Full returns from four wards give a Union majority of 108.

Newark—Later—Nine out of fourteen wards show Republican gain of 368. The Democrats carry the city by reduced majorities.

Morris, Union and Essex Counties—The returns show indecisive Republican gains.

Springfield—McClellan, 25 majority; Sitgreaves (Democrat), for Congress, 25 majority; Scudder (Democrat), for Assembly, 7 majority.

Delaware Township (in Camden County)—Union majority, 97; gain, 52.

Pequannock (in Morris County)—Lincoln, 359 majority; Little (Union), for Congress, 362 majority.

MILBURN, Tuesday, N. J., Nov. 8, 1864.

Lincoln, 141; McClellan, 88.

Theodore Little (Union), for Congress, 141; Andrew J. Rogers (Dem.), 87.

Legislature—Rufus F. W. Harrison (Union), 142; Joel D. Mead (Dem.), 88.

NEWARK, Tuesday, Nov. 8, 1864.

Essex County has gone Union by over 150, making a Union gain of over 1,000 over last year. The Legislative delegation is six Union to three Democrats.

Gloucester County—Milville, Union majority, 114. Star for Congress, 111.

Morris Township, McClellan, 80 majority;

See Fourth Page.

CITIZEN EXTRA:

CANTON, MISS.:

THURSDAY NOV. 10, 1864.

LATEST BY TELEGRAPH

SYNOPSIS OF

PRESIDENT DAVIS' MESSAGE.

RICHMOND, 7th.—Congress met to-day, pursuant to adjournment. The message from the President was received and read. It begins with a review of the military operations since the adjournment of Congress in June, and recognizes protection from Providence in enabling us to successfully withstand the utmost efforts for our subjugation.

We have recovered Texas from the enemy, and Arkansas, with the exception of a few fortified posts. Nearly the whole of northwestern Mississippi, northern Alabama and western Tennessee are again in our possession. All attempts to penetrate from the coast have been baffled. In south-western Virginia, a succession of armies have been routed and a portion of eastern Tennessee reconquered by our troops.

The main army, after serious defeats and constant repulses of repeated assaults, is still engaged in the effort to capture Petersburg.

The army of Sherman succeeded in obtaining possession of Atlanta, but is unable to secure any ultimate advantage from this success. Had we been compelled to evacuate Richmond, as well as Atlanta, the Confederacy would have remained as defiant as ever. No military success of the enemy can accomplish the destruction of the Confederacy, nor save the enemy from the constant drain of blood and treasure which must continue until he shall discover no peace is attainable unless based on the recognition of our independence and rights.

No change in the conduct of foreign powers can be announced. The recognition of our independence is withheld from the assumption that recognition would be valueless without intervention. We wish no intervention, for we know ourselves fully competent to maintain our rights and independence. Peace is impossible without independence, and is not to be expected until the enemy will anticipate neutral in the recognition of that independence.

The total amount of public debt on the 1st of October was one billion one hundred and twenty million dollars.

No additional appropriations for meeting the needs of the public service up to the first of June are needed.

The Secretary of the Treasury recommends that the faith of the Government be pledged that the notes shall ever remain exempt from taxation; that no issue be made beyond that already authorized, and that a portion of the receipts for taxation and tax in kind be pledged for the gradual redemption of the entire circulation.

Referring to the report of the Secretary of War the President says, that exemption from military duty of persons of certain specified pursuits, or professions, is unwise and not defensible in theory. Discretionary power should be vested in the military authorities, so that the requisite number of those essential to the public service might be detailed to continue, and exercise their pursuits or professions, but exemptions from service of entire classes should be wholly abandoned.

Various recommendations of the Secretary of War are referred to and approved, among which is the reorganization and consolidation of reduced regiments.

In regard to prisoners of war the President says, each government hereafter will be allowed to provide necessary comforts for its citizens held in captivity by the other.

The subject of employing negroes in the army is discussed at some length. The President dissents from those who advise a general levy and arming of slaves for duty as soldiers, but recommends the employment of forty thousand as pioneers and engineer laborers, in addition to the duties heretofore performed by them. He favors acquiring for the public service the right of property in the labor of slaves, the government engaging to liberate the negro on his discharge after service faithfully rendered.

The President closes by reiterating the willingness of the Government to negotiate for peace which is manifestly impossible unless desired by both parties to this war. A disposition for negotiation among our enemies will be the better and more certainly invoked by the demonstration of our ability to defend our rights.

"NEWS" BULLETIN.

VOL. I. HOUSTON, SATURDAY, NOV. 12, 1864. No. 83.

CONDITION OF THE POOR WHITES IN THE NORTH —HOW THEY LIVE—A VIVID PICTURE.—The whole North is continually howling about the "horrors" of slavery. But where can we find in the whole South such a picture of misery and suffering as is given below by the New York Sun, while describing life in the "tenement houses" of New York "Uncle Tom's Cabin" even, with all its false and imaginary paintings of "slave pens," &c., does not present half so vivid and frightful a picture of misery and anguish. The Sun, after urging a reform in these abodes of poverty and wretchedness known as "tenement houses," proceeds to relate what its reporter saw and gathered on making a visit to some of them:

"In Washington and Greenwich streets these houses are more thickly populated than in almost any other part of the city. Here the casual observer will find a little room, about twelve feet square, with a bed-room attached, from which light and air are as scrupulously excluded as if they were injurious instead of beneficial to the health. In some of these little rooms our reporter, who permits nothing to escape him, saw at one time no less than *thirteen* individuals, all breathing the same impure and unwholesome air, while the stench from the accumulated filth in the yard below was intolerable. The family residing in these "apartments"(?) consisted of a widow, with a daughter over eighteen years old, and three sons, aged respectively sixteen, fourteen and eight years, and all occupying the same bed on the floor. The widow took in lodgers, and in one corner of the same floor lay two sisters, who paid two shillings each per night for their bed, such as it was, and in another corner lay the niece of the widow, a married woman, while the dark bed-room was occupied by a man, his wife, and three children. Sickness, as a matter of course, followed, and, as usual in such cases, the younger children suffered the most.

Beneath these apartments was a damp cellar, 'with ground for the floor,' where about a dozen 'boarders,' men and women, lay like pigs in a sty, and the family who boarded them consisted of five individuals, making *seventeen* in all.

A case came before Justice Hogan on Thursday in which a woman was summoned by two unmarried ladies for pawning their clothes. On enquiry the fact came to light that the women in question were lodgers, and she detained the clothes for their rent, which was fifty cents per night each. Now, the woman and her three children, and these two girls, occupied a room and bed-room in a rear house on Prince street, which, both together, were not sixteen feet square. Our reporter subsequently went to look at the place, and only wondered how six individuals managed to live in it, although the bed-room was light, and to do the woman justice, although she was was washing in one corner of the room, (she takes in washing for a living,) and had her dinner boiling on the stove in another part, the place was very clean, but so hot that our reporter was glad to beat a hasty retreat. Like the other, she is "a poor widow," and says she is compelled to take in lodgers to help pay her rent.

Now, in apartments of this kind there are even worse things done than eating, sleeping, washing and cooking all in the same room. Many of these women can be seen entering corner groggeries with their ginger-beer bottles, which they get filled with "the best brandy" for five cents—a material difference between that and a liquor store on Broadway, where "the best brandy" is two shillings a pony glass. If these poor women are asked why they drink, they reply: "It's so hot and stifling inside that if we did'nt take a little drop we would faint," and thus what is earned by hard work goes into the pockets of the vender of colored flavored alcohol and camphene.

When sleeps overtakes them they have to lay down and herd together like cattle"

CUTTING A LION'S CLAWS.—The Brussels journals give an account of a curious surgical operation just performed on the great African lion belonging to the Zoological Society of that city. For some time past the animal has been suffering from disease in the feet, which necessitated the cutting of its claws. In order to do this without danger, a large box was prepared with a grated bottom, covered by a wooden floor, which could be withdrawn so as to allow the lion's feet to pass between the bars. The top of the box was also made to descend by means of screws, so as to press on the animal and prevent it from drawing in its foot. When the lion entered the box the latter was turned on its side and the sliding bottom withdrawn. The paws then slipped between the bars, and the screws above were tightened. M. Thiernasse, assisted by five pupils of the Veterinary School, then proceeded to cut away the claws. The patient bore the operation tolerably well, only uttering a short roar occasionally, and seemed relieved when the first paw had been cut and dressed. A keeper, to whom the lion is much attached, sat near its head and endeavored to calm it by talking, evidently not without effect. The operation was successfully performed, and there is every reason to believe that the cure will be complete.

WAR DEPARTMENT,
WASHINGTON, Sept. 29, 7:45, A. M.

The draft is quietly progressing in all the States But desperate efforts will be made by the enemy to force Sherman from Atlanta, by destroying his communications, and volunteer enlistments being more speedy than the draft, all loyal and patriotic people should urge forward rapid enlistments, in order to reinforce Sherman, and enable him not only to hold his position, but also, without delay, to push on his campaign.

(Signed.)
EDWIN M. STANTON, Secr'y War.

The Military Prospect—How we Progress in the work of Subjugation.

General Grant has written two letters, one to Mr Washburne, the other to Mr Stanton. The first states that the enemy's army is composed of boys of a tender age and old men; the other calls for 500,000 more men in the shortest possible time. Gen. Sherman has also written a letter to Mr. Stanton, which calls for more men. As both of these letters to Mr. Stanton were evidently written at the instigation of the Government, else how should Sherman know "the draft was about to proceed." We append them hereto:

CITY POINT, 10:30 A. M., Sept. 13, 1864.

HON. EDWIN M. STANTON, Sec of War:—We ought to have the whole number of men called for by the President in the shortest possible time. Prompt action in filling our armies will have more effect upon the enemy than a victory over them. They profess to believe, and make their men believe, there is such a party North in favor of recognizing Southern independence, that the draft cannot be enforced. Let them be undeceived.

Deserters come into our lines daily, who tell us that the men are nearly universally tired of the war, and that the desertions would be more frequent, but that they believe peace will be negotiated after the fall election. The enforcement of the draft and prompt filling up of our armies will save the shedding of blood to an immense degree.

U. S. GRANT, Lieut. General

ATLANTA, GA., Sept. 13, 1864, 6:30 P. M.

HON. EDWIN M. STANTON, Sec'y of War:—I am very glad to hear that the draft will be enforced First, we need the men; second, they come as privates to fill up our old and tried regiments, with their experienced officers already on hand; and third, because the enforcement of the law will manifest a power resident in our Government equal to the occasion. Our Government, though a Democracy, should in times of trouble and danger be able to wield the power of a great nation. All well.

W. T. SHERMAN. Major-General.

Two very pertinent questions arise. If the Southerners have only boys and old men to fill up their ranks, why have we not whipped them? And how is it that, on the contrary, Grant has permitted himself to be invariably repulsed by them during an entire campaign? It seems that we are no match for these juveniles and these infirm old Confederates. Again, if, as Grant says, their "men are nearly universally tired of the war," why do he and Sherman write for more? It seems to us, if these generals told the truth we need only march forward and conquer the South.

But the miserable deception is plain enough. "Our Government, though a democracy, should in times of trouble and danger be able to wield the power of a great nation." That is it—"power!" God save a nation, whose generals in the field write political letters!

Read these two letters over, and blush for the nation that is so humbled as to receive them without protest.

After a campaign almost, if not entirely, unparalleled for its disasters and tremendous loss of life, Gen. Grant reaches Petersburg, a post thirty miles south of Richmond, his true objective point, and between which and the latter there are several lines of formidable defences, fortified heights west of the Appomattox, a frowning fortress on the James, completely encircled by earthworks, and a brave and veteran army fully equal in numbers to his own, and fighting upon the defensive. There he stops. His retreat is covered by a fleet of two hundred armed vessels. His vessels are held in check; his army beaten in detail at Lynchburg, at Deep Bottom, at Reams' Station and twenty other points, and his own existence hanging on a hair; and, while calling for five hundred thousand more men, tells us, in the same breath, that the enemy is enfeebled and only awaits the final *coup de grace*

At the same time Sherman advances along a line of railroad towards his objective at one end, 150 miles from his base on the other, running through a hostile country filled with armed parties of the enemy, and seizing his objective with unparalled temerity, turns round to the country and, exhibiting his dearly bought, blood-won triumph, asks it, almost as the grave is closing over him and his army, to send him more men!

The entire results of last year's campaign is Atlanta.

Let us see what Atlanta has cost us:

Skirmishing from Chattanooga to Resaca	2,700
Battle of Resaca	8,400
Skirmishing from Resaca to the Altoona Range	1,200
Battles at and near Dallas	4,100
Repulse at New Hope Church	4,300
Skirmishing near and battle at Lost Mountain	4,000
Skirmishing in front of Kennesaw before and after the defeat of 27th	4 500
Unsuccessful assault upon Kennesaw	7,200
Heavy skirmishing near Marietta	2,320
Crossing the Chattahoochee	750
Skirmishing at Peachtree Creek	1,500
Battle of 20th July	5,000
Battle of 22d July	10,200
Battle of 28th July	3,500
Skirmishing in front of Atlanta from the 28th of July to 28th August including affair at Jonesboro' and Schofield's repulses on 6th, and repulse of 14th corps on 7th August	5,600
Total killed, wounded and missing	65,070
Grant's losses in killed, wounded and missing from the battle of Wilderness to battle of Weldon Railroad	180,000
Maryland campaign	5,000
Red River expedition	25,000
Arkansas campaign	3 000
Captured, &c, at Plymouth, N. C., and Washington	5,000
Total	283,070

Besides this, there is Bank's disastrous retreat from Alexandria, and abandonment of Western Louisiana to the enemy; the loss of Texas, Florida, Arkansas and Plymouth, N. C., and of the Shenandoah Valley and Western Virginia, which we held last Spring.

This is what we have paid for Atlanta, which fell into our hands after it had been completely gutted and rendered untenable. Nearly 300,000 men, to say nothing of sickness and desertion.

Now, what is the prospect for winter? Grant's army is confessedly defeated Its commander says "we ought to have the whole number of men called for by the President (500,000) in the shortest possible time." Sherman also writes, "we need more men." Grant cannot advance and he dare not fall back. The moment he embarks his shattered regiments from City Point the North will lose heart, and the Confederates will cross the Potomac for another Washington campaign. Sherman has penetrated to Atlanta. He has 150 miles of communication to protect. The enemy have got possession of one portion of it (Dalton,) and have blown up a tunnel through which it runs, and destroyed 50 miles of its length. The least mishap would overwhelm him, and he is running a tremendous risk. If Mobile is taken by the Federals, and a line of communication established between it and Atlanta, the case is not bettered, for instead of one enemy in front, we shall have two armies to fight, one on each flank. Hood's on the east and the Confederates from the Trans-Mississippi on the West. This splitting of the Confederacy in two will merely compel us to fight in detail what we have hitherto fought with large masses of men.

To suppose the Confederates with a territory 2000 miles long and 500 wide, yet unimpaired, and an army 300,000 men in the field, are used up, is absurd.

Beauregard's Corps at Petersburg	20,000
A. P. Hill's Corps	18,000
Anderson's Corps, one division	5,500
Cavalry	12,200
Artillery, 300 guns	6,000
Early has in Shenandoah Valley	30,000
Troops at Lynchburg	12,000
Troops at Wilmington and Weldon	8,000
Hood's army in Georgia	62,000
Troops at Charleston and Savanah	20,000
Troops at Mobile	20,000
Troops in Texas, Louisiana, Arkansas and Missouri	65,000
Troops and guerrillas raiding in Mississippi, Kentucky and Tennessee, &c., and forces at Galveston, Brownsville, and along the Red River and the Mississippi	21,000
	300,000

It is barely possible we over-estimate them twenty-five or fifty thousand men. But is a veteran army of two hundred and fifty thousand to be despised? The truth is, it is we, who, as Grant writes to Washburne, are "robbing the cradle and the grave." It is we who are losing "a regiment a day."

All we want to establish is this: The South is not beaten, or nearly beaten, or weakened, or discouraged, or anything but strong and defiant. We say this to save further bloodshed.

It is a mistake for the South to think the North is relenting. It is equally a mistake for the North to think the South is repenting.

These mistakes we shall bewail and mourn in sackcloth and in ashes. The widow and the orphan's cry shall rise above all this contention, but only when it is too late—too late.

As for the future, they have plenty of resources, both in men and money. We discussed the money question the other day. We now exhibit their resources in men:

The seceded States had, in 1860, men from 18 to 45. 1.602,000; youths between 14 and 18, in 1860, 200 000; troops furnished by the States up to Aug. 16th, 1864, 818,000.

The 200,000 youths of 1860 are now 200,000 men of the fighting age. Add this to 1,602,000, and we have 1,802,000, less the 818,000 furnished, of whom 300,000 still survive. This leaves 984,000 yet in reserve, besides the present army and the natural increase. Then there are 4 000,000 negroes, useful as laborers, teamsters, cooks, servants, &c., and as producers of sustenance in the field and clothing and arms in the workshops.

The estimates for the Border States are based upon the sub-division of each as at present exists.

In a word, while the Administration is exhausting every device to recruit our armies, in order to perpetuate its power and renew the war, while they represent the military prospect as having been never before so assuring, we see in it nothing but a long and bloody war, capable of lasting for ten years longer. We have given four years of time, two millions of men, three thousand millions of money, and all our civil liberties, for Memphis, Vicksburg, New Orleans, and Atlanta. At this rate it would take a century, and the sacrifice of the entire nation, to subjugate the South. If we separate our forces we should be defeated; if we concentrate them we shall continue to fare as we have already fared with concentration—lose one place where we gain another—lose Brownsville, Gloucester, Plymouth, Washington, &c., and the entire Trans Mississippi for the barren victory of Atlanta.

To us, the military prospect never looked gloomier for the North.—*Metropolitan Record*.

Yankee Facts.

Brig. Gen. Nagle, one of McClellan's aids, who was dismissed from the Yankee service, has published a letter in the Yankee papers, defending his chief from the aspersions of the Lincoln party. The following extract from it in relation to Grant's losses is interesting:

The preference of General McClellan for the Peninsula campaign and the condemnation of the President's plan have been fully sustained. The families and friends of the 120,000 men lost South of the Rapidan, since the 4th of May last, proclaim it every where. Mr. Stanton told the country, at that time he had a hundred thousand men more than he wanted, and now he tells you he wants a hundred thousand more men.

Gen. Grant crossed the Rapidan with an army variously estimated from one hundred and eighty thousand to	120,000
He afterwards added Butler's	40,000
He was reinforced	45,000
Making, exclusive of Siegel's 30,000	205,000
On the 1st of September our forces were estimated, exclusive of Sheridan's thirty thousand, at	50,000
General Lee had on the Rapidan, after he had concentrated his army	85,000
Beauregard joined him in Richmond with his forces from the South, which, with those near Petersburg, amounted to	30,000
Breckinridge brought	10,000
And Lee was reinforced propably	30,000
Making in all	155,000
On the 1st of September his forces were estimated at Richmond, at	45,000
Exclusive of Early's command	30,000
Showing the discharges and loss from Grant to be	150,000
And that of Lee to be	85,000

According to these figures, General Grant had 235,000 men, of whom, on the 1st September, but 80 000 remained—50,000 at Petersburg and 30,000 with Sheridan, showing a loss of 155,000 men. According to this Gen. Grant has lost in battle as many men as General Lee had during the campaign.

If Grant had, on the 1st of September, but 50,000 men at Petersburg, his reinforcements since that time have amounted to but 30,000 while his losses from expiration of term of enlistment, hundred day men going home, and the casualties of battle, may be set down at 15 000 men—leaving him now about 60,000 at Petersburg. It is said that there are now awaiting transportation in the cities, from 35 to 40,000 men, which will be sent forwaad by the 25th inst—making his force 100,000 men. Of these not more than 40 000 are old soldiers the rest are new recruits.

THE BATTLE OF DARBYTOWN ON FRIDAY—THE REBEL LOSSES.—Yesterday morning broke upon one of those clear, bright days of autumn which are the glory of the declining year. The Yankee host, forty thousand strong, lay encamped on the north side of James river, the main body in the neighborhood of Fort Harrison, ten miles southeast of Richmond, the Tenth (Birney's) army corps and Kautz's cavalry being five and a half miles nearer the city, and in position between the Darbytown and Charles City roads.

With the first early light, General Gary's brigade of cavalry and a considerable force of our infantry struck the enemy's right, resting on the Charles City road, at a point from four and a half to five miles from the city. The Yankees were completely surprised, and with little resistance fled into their intrenchments, a short distance in their rear. Here they were in strong force and prepared for a desperate resistance; but our troops, following up their first blow with great impetuosity, carried the works and drove the Yankees out, capturing nine pieces of cannon, one hundred artillery horses and several hundred prisoners.

THE SUN.—Astronomer Leverrier has discovered an error in the sun's parallax, as stated by Encke, and hitherto followed by astronomers. Instead of 8,57 seconds, it is really 8,95 seconds. As the parallax, together with the earth's semi-diameter, is the basis on which the earth's distance from the sun is calculated, a change in the parallax must be attended by a change in the figures expressive of the sun's distance from us. Thus, the sun, instead of being 95,000,000 of miles from us, is, in reality, distant only 91,328,000 miles. The velocity of light, the distances and sizes of the heavenly bodies, &c., being calculated by comparison with the earth's distance from the sun, must also be changed correspondingly. Thus, light travels 183,470 miles per second, instead of nearly 192,000, as heretofore supposed. The sun's diameter must be reduced 38,000 miles. The distance of the planet Neptune from the sun is less by 122,000,000 of miles.—*Richmond Sentinel*.

INDIAN BARBARITIES.—A gentlemen who recently arrived at Leavenworth from New Mexico, saw at Fort Larned a boy of about seventeen years of age, a resident of Osawkee, Jefferson county, Kansas, who has received seventeen shots in his body. He was also scalped, and in their endeavors to get the scalp off his head they had torn the skin as far down as his shoulder blades. After this was accomplished, and in order to ascertain to a certainty whether life was extinct, they stuck their arrows and knives into the flesh laid bare by the removal of the scalp and skin. The boy endured this torture without moving a muscle, conscious that if he showed the least signs of life they would kill him. He is in a fair way of recovery, and has resolved on revenge, and says Indian killing will be his future occupation.—*St. Louis Union*.

BROWNLOW'S KNOXVILLE WHIG,

AND REBEL VENTILATOR.

VOLUME I. | KNOXVILLE, TENN., WEDNESDAY, NOVEMBER 16, 1864. | NUMBER 44.

The Knoxville Whig.

W. G. BROWNLOW, Editor.

Banner of freedom, by freemen unfurled!
Beacon of hope to a waiting world!
Shining above is the starry throng,
A rife in the murky clouds of wrong—
Clouds that shall roll from their beams of light,
Till the [illegible]

Knoxville, Wednesday, Nov. 16, 1864.

Our Poor Women.

We have, in East Tennessee, a great many suffering, toiling, destitute women, whose husbands and sons, their only natural protectors, are either in the Federal army or have gone from the ranks to their graves, on the field of battle, with no slab or board to mark the resting place of their ashes. These sufferers have been abused and robbed by the heartless rebels, because they were the wives, sisters and mothers of what they chose to call d——d Lincolnities! We know something of the fearful straits to which many of these poor women are reduced in these times of high prices, scarcity and swindling; and we are for them—so ought the Military and Relief Association, and against the infernal Shylocks who live and riot on their blood and tears.—God knows that if we had the power and means, we would make them all comfortable, and imprison their enemies and oppressors.

We have seen some of these suffering women *bare-footed* on our streets, within the last ten days, begging for something for themselves and children to eat, while their husbands are in the Federal army facing rebel bullets. At the same time, we have seen certain she-devils upon our streets, of the "female persuasion," dressed in silk, who scorn to walk under the American flag, *and walk round it to avoid contamination.* We have given a many a poor Union woman five and ten dollars, and if we had the fortune to sustain us, not one of them, in all the length ann breadth of East Tennessee, should want for anything. But what can a few individuals of limited means do, among such an army of sufferers?

If a rebel woman of means and distinction gets into any trouble, or has been deprived of her effects to any extent, our citizens, of the *Constitutional* and *Conservative* class, become greatly troubled, and consider her greatly outraged. Our sympathies, we confess, are for the poor Union women, and will continue to flow in that channel as long as we have a soul. And we would to God that our Government, our leading men in civil and military life, could be more warmly enlisted in behalf of these helpless women and their suffering children! What can be done for them as the winter blast approaches? What, O Merciful One? Are these desparing women—many of them sickened, nearly famished—to perish with cold and hunger, while their sons and husbands are out fighting the traitors who got up and have led on this hell-born and hell-bound rebellion?

Thanks to God, labor is everywhere renumerative, and when this war is over the scornful, proud, and bitter rebel woman will find herself upon a level with the poor Union woman, without a gang of negroes at her command. Our women will then be in a field together, where the rich and poor, the loyal and disloyal, can compete with each other, and where it will not be a disgrace to labor.

We hope to see the day in East Tennessee when it will no longer be dishonorable for young ladies to *sew* and work in the *kitchen.* Nay, we desire to see the day come when the honest and virtuous poor, who have been pinched and persecuted by the hateful aristocracy, will be called upon, in mercy, to give their descendent employment!

Difference of Opinion.

A correspondent of the Asheville (N. C.) *News,* a vile rebel sheet, writing from East Tennessee, thus expresses his views of our merits:

> Brownlow's course is becoming more vindictive and hostile daily; hence the outrages of the soldiers can be accounted for. Humanity blushes at the infamous and cruel conduct of this monster. * * * * * * Rev. Mr. Robinson, of Rogersville, was forced to leave his church on account of Brownlow's persecutions. His malice seems directed, of late, towards the clergy and the women. Let our iniquities be what they may, I can't think that God will suffer such a demon in the form of man to live to domineer over a gallant and noble people.

About the same date, the Chaplain of the 2d Ohio Heavy Artillery, thus concludes a letter to the Cincinnati *Christian Advocate:*

> The great advocate of the church and champion for the Federal Government, Parson Brownlow, is with us, moving among the hills of Knoxville city, with his regular old Damascus blade in hand, smiting without mercy all rebels, butternuts and copperheads. He is manifested to the people of this country, like Jupiter on Olympus, amid clouds and smoke, smiting down the "rebel Titans with the thunderbolts of his wrath." No man has done as much to keep East Tennessee loyal, and no man is now doing more to bring back the church, than Parson Brownlow. His fierce invectives, his scathing rebukes and bitter ridicule, have a marvelous influence and power upon the minds and hearts of the people.

The Murder and Starvation Policy.

From the very commencement of the war the rebels have starved Union prisoners, and placed them in pens, and on islands, depriving them of fire, clothes, and shelter, as a means of killing them off, and by these means they have murdered thousands, and made it certain they could never be exchanged, or again enter the Union army!

From the beginning until now, they have amputated the arms and legs of all Federal prisoners, who have had any sort of wound that afforded a pretext for this course. The patients have protested—alleged that they would get well if let alone. But no, the order was to *amputate,* and they were forced to submit. The object was to either kill the patient by the operation, or render him forever unfit for the service.

Hell is too comfortable a place for such men, but as we have no power to send them to a worse place, we ought to see that they go there upon short notice, and by the most direct route!

Slanderous Assault from a Dirty Quarter.

We have on our table the Asheville (N. C.) *News,* of the 28th of September, 1864—a dirty, treasonable sheet, edited and published by a pair of scoundrels who were born and raised in this town, *T. W. and S. Atkin,* the former rather notorious for his sneaking, mean, cowardly and two-faced propensities, which he cloaks with authority to preach in the Methodist Church, South. A leading article in the paper, prominently paraded, is in the following words and figures, to-wit:

> COL. JIM BROWNLOW.—It has been said that this Yankee, the wicked son of a blackguard father, on one occasion had committed to his charge fifty Confederate prisoners, and that before they had traveled twenty miles they were all lost. This fact was stated by Federal officers to a reliable Confederate then within their lines. These officers did not hesitate to express the wish that Brownlow might be taken by us and [illegible] never took a prisoner. He knows his deserts if taken by us, hence his desperate and successful attempt to escape at Newnan. It is possible that he may be captured. If so, as he will be in a strange country, let him be placed in a condition in which there will be a certainty of his being lost. He is beyond the pale of humanity, and should be treated as a wild beast.

Now, we meet the foregoing article, prepared with some care, and under the influence of still greater malice, by the broad assertion that it does not contain one word of truth. No Federal officers ever stated what is attributed to them. Colonel Brownlow has been endorsed repeatedly, and complimented in the highest terms, verbally and in writing, by such men as Major Generals Rosecrans, Schofield, Steadman, Brannon, and others, under whose command he has fought his regiment of cavalry during the last three years. We give one of these endorsements from the brave and gallant Schofield, who commanded the Federal forces, including Colonel Brownlow's regiment, at the time of writing, and when the Colonel was only Lieutenant Colonel in command of the First Tennessee Cavalry:

> NASHVILLE, May 21, 1863.
>
> *Governor Johnson:*—Having been informed that Lieutenant Colonel Brownlow, of the First Tennessee Cavalry is spoken of for Colonel of one of the new regiments to be raised in your State, I desire to recommend him as eminently qualified and deserving.
>
> I have rarely seen a cavalry officer who excited my admiration in so high a degree. He is energetic, daring and skillful. Success with him and his gallant command is the invariable rule.
>
> I am, Governor,
> Very respectfully,
> Your obedient servant,
> J. M. SCHOFIELD,
> Major General.

These two *Atkins* are the brothers of *Samuel T. Atkin,* of this city, one of the most bitter and unrelenting rebels in East Tennessee, His house is the resort of rebels here under bonds. He himself has the houses lots, or such interests in them as these two North Carolina rebel brothers may own, in his care and in his name. One stays here and takes the oath so as cloak and shield the property, while the two tory brothers run to North Carolina and strike at Union men through their newspaper.—Not only so, but this man *Sam. Atkin* has the machinery of two loyal men driven out of Loudon by the rebels and refuses to give it up; and what is more strange, the Federal authorities have failed to make him give it up. Nay, this man is in the employ of the Government and is receiving pay from the Government. We are looking for him and his brothers to procure an order for our removal from the country. We are not expecting them to succeed, but to attempt the project. The most impudent and brazen-faced devils we have here are *galvanized* rebels, who have taken the oath to protect their property.

We may owe the public an apology for occupying so much space in defending one who needs no defense against assaults *instigated here* and made by scoundrels in North Carolina who dare not return to this country again.

The Plot Thickens.

The subjoined dispatch from the Secretary of State, at Washington, was not without foundation. About 2,000 picked rebel desperadoes were detailed from the rebel army to go round into Canada and cross over in disguise, and instigate the firing of the principle cities North. This is their last desperate card. They know they can't prevent the election of Lincoln and Johnson, and they know that when elected they will put down the rebellion at all hazards. Nay, they know more—they know they can't hold out much longer, and that we can and will.—But to the dispatch:

> WASHINGTON, November 2.
>
> *To the Mayor of Buffalo:*
>
> This department has received information from the British Provinces to the effect that there is a conspiracy on foot to set fire to the principal cities in the Northern States on the day of the Presidential election. It is my duty to communicate this information to you.
>
> W. H. SEWARD.

Murder of Russell Gregory.

Old man Gregory, in his 73d year, with one arm, lame in one leg, and nearly blind, was deliberately murdered a short time since, in Cade's Cove, in Blount county, for his Union sentiments, by Welch's guerrillas, numbering about twenty. After cruelly murdering the poor old man, they robbed his family of all they had. Amony the men engaged in this horrible murder we have been furnished with the following names: *Capt. Jim. Welch, Nathan Birdfield, Bill. Anthony, Tom. Johnson, Jim. Colbert,* (citizen,) *Bill. Shurt, Ara Carver,* and a young *Foust,* and *Charles Gregory,* the latter the son of the murdered man!

We give the names of these "wild beasts," as furnished by men from Blount county, that they may be known should they fall into the hands of our men. Whoever may come up with any one of them, should see to it that he goes "the way of all the earth."

The Third and Last Prop.

When this rebellion was inaugurated, the Southern leaders depended for success upon England and France to *intervene* in their behalf. Loosing all hope of aid from that quarter, they have relied upon the Peace Democracy of the North. Lincoln having been most triumphantly elected, and all hopes of "aid and comfort" from Northern traitors having fled, the Southern leaders now turn to the *nigger* for relief. They call him into the field and offer him his freedom and 50 acres of land, if he will fight for the rebellion. This is the last card, and it will play out in 1865. Mark what we say!

[COMMUNICATED.]

East Tennessee.

BY CYRUS WICK, CO. 'F,' 17TH INDIANA VOLUNTEERS.

I stood upon yon mountain, far above
The waters of the winding Tennessee,
To view the land that well deserves our love,
A land whose fame can never cease to be,
Whose people are the true, the brave and free.
Their love of country was of purer glow,
Their love for freedom was of that degree
That left all mean ambitions far below,
And nerved them for the fight against the haughty foe.

The history of these long, weary years,
The sorrows that these faithful people met,
Shall cause the eyes of beauty to shed tears,
And manly faces even to be wet.
In spite of all the perils that beset,
They were more true than such as we might be—
LOYAL MEN AND WOMEN OF EAST TENNESSEE.

But now we know their night is nearly past,
Even while it seems so darkly to enshroud,
Although the sky is thickly overcast,
A light is seen behind the gloomy cloud;
THIS VERY DAY HAVE LOYAL MILLIONS VOWED
THAT TREASON SHALL BE CRUSHED, AND THERE SHALL BE
A TIME THAT HUMBLES MANY OF THE PROUD,
And traitors shall be made to die or flee,
When we avenge our loved and wronged East Tennessee.

Chattanooga, Tenn., November 8, 1864.

[From the Methodist.]

Disloyalty of the Jesuits in the United States.

Dr. Brownson, the able and eccentric champion of Roman Catholicism in the United States, announces in the October number of his Review, which we have just received, that this number may possibly be the last. The experience which he has, of late, had in his church is an extremely painful one. Having embraced the doctrines of the Church of Rome with a sincerity which no one has doubted, he has devoted to the defense of the Catholic interests, for many years, a talent which has no equal in the Roman Catholic Church of this country, and which has secured for him the admiration of both Catholics and Protestants, and for his pleas in behalf of his church an attention on the part of Protestants commanded by no other Roman Catholic writings. Perhaps it is this very intellectual superiority over the bulk of his co-religionists which has recently drawn upon him violent attacks from most of the Catholic papers, and at the close of his literary career, put him in danger of being read out of the church to whose defence he has devoted the best part of his life.

We can sincerely sympathize with such a fate, though we have long foreseen that Dr. Brownson would not ultimately be allowed to utter, on any subject, opinions which do not agree with those of the majority of the bishops. He has especially made himself obnoxious by his opinions on the temporal power of the Pope, the abolition of which he thinks it permissible for a good Catholic to advocate, and by his views on our war, on which question Brownson does not sympathize with either of the two great parties, having supported to the last Gen. Fremont for the presidency. On both questions, especially on the latter, he differed from every, or nearly every Catholic organ in the United States.

The attack made upon Brownson by some of his Catholic contemporaries have led to some curious revelations regarding the political attitude of the Roman Catholics in this country, which we commend to the attention of all Protestants. In reply to a statement made by the Catholic papers of Philadelphia, the Universe, that he had been forbidden one of the houses of the Jesuits, Dr. Brownson gives the following interesting information on the political bearing of the American Jesuits:

"That we were forbidden," he says, "one of their houses, which we had entered to seek our confessor, is true; but he who did it was one of the warmest and truest of our personal friends, and whom ever since we have known him we have loved and venerated. We never blamed him; he only did what he felt was expected of him by his superiors. We had just given a lecture before the Emancipation League in Boston, and as the Jesuits held property in the seceded States, it was feared, if they entertained us at one of their houses, the rebel government might take offense and confiscate it. They wish to give Mr. Davis of the Confederacy no occasion to charge them with misprision of treason, or of hostility to his government. The rector who excluded us, though personally sympathizing with us, felt that under the circumstances he was officially bound to exclude us, and he did so with tears in his eyes. That the incident affected us unpleasantly, we do not deny, but not in the way assumed, nor because we were the party excluded. As a personal matter we could never have given it a second thought, and the unpleasantness it occasioned was the regret that simple, worldly prudence or property considerations had more influence with the Jesuit body than we expected from a mendicant order, and that the education of the Catholic youth of the nation should be intrusted to a society so destitute of loyalty that it could look on with indifference and see the nation rent asunder and destroyed by a rebellion which every principle of our religion, as we have learned it, condemns. It was important only as one proof among many others, that the society, is, if not disloyal, at least unloyal."

This is the most extraordinary testimony of the kind which we have recently met with. The Jesuits, it appears, are so anxious to secure the patronage of the leader of an insurrection against the government, that they, in the most ostensible manner, discountenance anything that may be unpleasant to this chief of the rebellion.—Whether the views advocated by Dr. Brownson are correct or not, has nothing to do with this question; the main point is, whether it is compatible with the loyalty due to the government of the United States to show such a deference as the Jesuits have done to the avowed enemies of the country. Let us suppose we were involved in a war with France, Austria, Spain, or Mexico; must we not conclude from this example that the Jesuits would turn their face against every American Catholic who would plead the cause of his country against these Catholic powers, and thus do as much as lay in their power to give aid and comfort to the enemy?

There is one circumstance connected with this case which makes it look still worse.—The Jesuits have not acted thus where oppressed nations rose for the recovery of their rights from Catholic despots. They have never thought of disavowing an Austrian Catholic who had supported his government in the war for the suppression of the Hungarian revolution; or a Neapolitan Catholic who espoused the cause of the last Bourbon of Naples against the king whom the voice influence, open and secret, was used for strengthening the cause of the governments with which they sympathized. The reason of this difference is clear. They hate freedom; they sympathize with despotism.—They oppose the former and aid the latter.

Hitherto the immense majority of the American people have been in favor of allowing to the Jesuits, and other monastic organizations, a liberty of association which very few, even of the Catholic counties, allow to them. These communities will have to thank their own disloyal conduct if this sentiment of the American people should undergo a change. If in political matters they do not regard their duty toward their country as supreme, but as subordinate, to other considerations, they become a public nuisance and a danger to the welfare of the republic, and they fully deserve to be treated as such.

Another Fight in Carolina.

Our one hundred day men, under Capt. Divine, are doing a good work, as the following report will show:

> HEADQUARTERS U. S. FORCES,
> Madisonville, Nov. 6, 1864.
>
> *Dr. W. G. Brownlow*—SIR: About 150 men from this place, belonging to a battalion of one hundred day men, have just returned from an expedition into North Carolina. Lieut. Lyons was in command.—About sixty of the men were mounted.
>
> We had intended to surprise the rebels, but some zealous friend of Jeff. ran ahead and informed them of the approaching force. So they were ready for us. The rebels began the fight near Thomas' Mill, in Cheoah, N. C., and were gloriously whipped.—They left seven dead upon the field, and their retreat was trailed with blood, showing that they carried away some dead or badly wounded. Among the killed are the notorious bushwhackers Jesse Kirkland, Thomas Mashburne, and a John Strutton. Four Indians make out the list.
>
> On our side not a solder was hit. A deserter who was fighting with us was shot through the leg.—Many of our brave boys were shot through the clothing. We brought out three prisoners. By order
>
> Capt. Comd'g. One Hundred Day Men.
> D. V. CALVER, Lieut. and A. A.

The Knoxville Whig.

W. G. BROWNLOW, Editor.

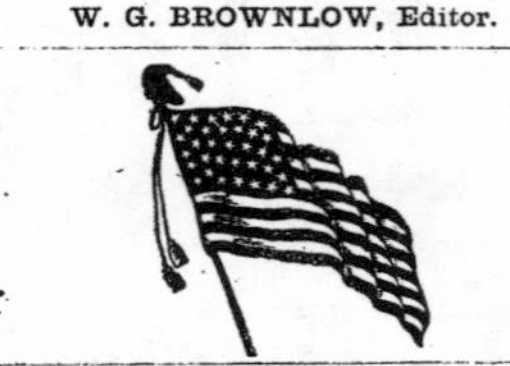

"The union of lakes—the union of lands—
The union of States none can sever—
The union of hearts—the union of hands—
And the flag of our Union forever."

Knoxville, Tennessee, Nov. 16, 1864.

LOUIS MCGLAUFLIN is authorized to act as our agent along the whole Pacific Coast. His address is San Francisco, California.

C. S. HUBBARD, of New Haven, Connecticut, is our regularly appointed agent to receive subscriptions for our paper in that State.

Advance in our Charges for Subscriptions.

In consequence of the increased cost of paper, ink, wages, fuel, and other materials, the Proprietor of the KNOXVILLE WHIG has been compelled to advance the price of subscriptions and advertising.—This step has been taken reluctantly, but from absolute *necessity*, and after mature deliberation. We have had either to do this or suspend publication, and we know that our Union friends don't want our paper to stop. A few facts stated may serve as an excuse for this reform.

The paper laid down to us here, before the rebellion, at $4 per ream, now cost us ELEVEN DOLLARS. Ink is *double*; labor is *double*; fire-wood is *double*; and all we purchase to live upon, or carry on the office, costs *twice* or *thrice* the prices paid before the rebellion. We were the first Publisher in East Tennessee, in 1839, to put down a weekly paper to TWO DOLLARS per year, and we have been the last to raise to a higher rate. As soon as circumstances will justify it, we will return to old prices. This war will be put down in the course of the year 1865, and then the country will be relieved of the high prices which are draining the resources of business men, and we shall be among the first to return to the old rates.

In future we must have THREE DOLLARS per year; and those sending us ONE or TWO DOLLARS, will have the paper furnished for a *third* or *two-thirds* of a year. Our advertising rates will be advanced in proportion. In the meantime we solicit the continued support of the friends of the Government and the enemies of the Rebellion; and in turn, we promise to fight for the one, and the other, until victory perches upon our standard.

W. G. BROWNLOW,
Editor and Proprietor.

November 16th, 1864.

Call of a State Convention.

The heavy loyal vote cast in Tennessee shows the sentiments of the people, and their desire to put down the rebellion and restore Civil Government. We are entitled to *eight* Representatives and *two* Senators in the Congress of the United States, as well as to a Governor, and other officers to be elected, and the interests of our people are suffering for the want of these representatives in Congress.

The undersigned, acting as the Executive Committee for East Tennessee, have designated the THIRD MONDAY IN DECEMBER (19th) for a preliminary State Convention to be held at Nashville, to form a ticket to be run for a Constitutional Convention by the loyal men of the State, the Governor designating the day for the election by proclamation, after the preliminary Convention makes out the ticket.

We call upon West and Middle Tennessee to act in concert with us, and at once appoint their delegates to the Convention of the 19th of December.

SAMUEL R. RODGERS,
R. K. BYRD,
W. G. BROWNLOW,
D. T. PATTERSON,
PEREZ DICKINSON,
Executive Committee.

November 12, 1864.

Convention in Knoxville.

The loyal men of all the counties in East Tennessee are requested to meet in Convention in Knoxville, the FIRST MONDAY IN DECEMBER, (5th,) to appoint Delegates to a Preliminary State Convention. A general attendance is desired, and men are requested to serve who are prepared to go to Nashville, and we promise them free transportation to and from Nashville. Counties remote from here are requested to appoint their own delegates, if they find it inconvenient to attend at Knoxville, and if they prefer it, they can appoint citizens expected to go, as their *proxies*—for instance, they can designate the Delegates from any one county to represent them. But, as the Federal Court will be in session here, we shall expect a large turn out on the 5th of December.

W. G. BROWNLOW,
SAM. R. RODGERS,
PEREZ DICKINSON,
DAVID T. PATTERSON,
R. K. BYRD,
Executive Committee.

November 12, 1864.

Gen. Gillem's Command.

It is known to the country, that BRIG. GEN. GILLAM, has for months, been in command of a Brigade of State and United States troops, sent here by GOV. JOHNSON, consisting of the 8th, 9th, and 13th Tennessee Cavalry. With this command he fought and whipped MORGAN, and subsequently VAUGHN, and, in short, rendered valuable services.

Last Friday he was attacked at Bull's Gap, by the rebel forces commanded by BRECKINRIDGE, and handsomely repulsed the rebels. The attack was renewed on Saturday, and a terrible battle insued, in which our forces repulsed them again, with a loss of *twenty-seven dead rebels* left on the ground, the enemy carrying off their wounded. Our loss was *eight* killed, and *nineteen* wounded. The fight continued for *seven hours*.

On Sabbath evening, GEN. GILLEM, finding the rebels were about to surround him, commenced a retreat, bringing his artillery and wagons out, with a portion of the 8th, and with the 9th, leaving the remainder of the 8th and the 13th, to protect the rear. The men and horses had now been three days without rations, except fresh beef without salt.

At the west end of Morristown, the rebels fired on our troops from the woods—the packed mules, some 150 of them, took fright and broke in every direction, and a panic seized upon our troops, and they broke in every direction, the result of which was, that we lost our Artillery, and wagons, and many of our men their horses and guns. Gen. Gillem threw himself into the front rank, and assisted by the officers of the Regiments labored to form his men into line, to make a stand, and give battle, but all to no purpose. The men were panic stricken, so were the numerous citizens along, and the very men who had fought so bravely, and so daringly, but the day before, and on former occasions, could not be brought to a stand.

The captured, killed, and missing, of our command, will not exceed *two hundred*. The command have all encamped west of the Plains, and the missing men are coming up. There are a thousand and one rumors afloat, as to the forces opposing us, and as to the conduct of our men, but we have stated the leading facts as detailed to us by different officers in the command, who were present and witnessed all that occurred.

The following order found in the pocket of *Capt. Hardy*, a rebel, after he was killed in the fight of Saturday, shows that Breckinridge regarded his force as equal to the occasion:

HEAD QUARTERS, ARMY OF EAST TENN.,
Rheatown, Nov. 10, 1864.

COL. W. O. PALMER:

The Maj. Gen. Commanding, desires that you move your whole command so as to form a junction with Gen. Vaughn near New Market on the 12th inst. The Maj. Gen. Commanding, in company with Gen. Duke, of the Cavalry, will move on the Gap on the same day, and if the two forces will operate promptly the enemy can be badly whipped and mostly captured. Have your men in good fighting order and move rapidly. Answer by return courier.

By order of
MAJ. GEN. BRECKINRIDGE,
D. O. PARK, A. D. C.

The Infantry Reinforcements.

On Sabbath evening, a train with five days rations, with ammunition, and three hundred reinforcements of the 10th Michigan, of Ohio troops, and of Kirk's command, were sent up by Gen. Ammon to reinforce Gen. Gillem, under command of Maj. Smith, a brave and gallant officer. These men and supplies got no further than Morristown, and then, after night, as we understand it, met with the troops of Gen. Gillem retreating, and fired into by the rebels from the woods, and from the tory houses in Morristown. This brought our own men in collision, for the moment, but the infantry were formed in line on the hill this side of Morristown, and fought the enemy with obstinacy. We understand that there were but three of this command lost, and that none were wounded. They have come in in good order, and brought their arms all with them.

The train that had the ammunition and rations, finding things as they were, returned without any further delay, and got into our city that night.—These are the facts, as we gather them from those who were along.

Rejoicing Over Our Defeats.

When the news came into our town of the disaster to Gen. Gillem's command, the rebel women rejoiced aloud, and talked out treason defiantly. Rebel traitors of the *male* pursuasion, who had taken the oath to save their property, were so rejoiced that they could not conceal their feelings. Old Secession *Rips*, who can't live at home, and have come here to save their lives, were on the streets exulting, and showing that they expected to have their tory friends in possession of the country soon.

What we want, and what justice demands, is, that these traitors, male and female, all be sent South, and their property confiscated. The military authorities have either to expell these spies, informers and traitors, from the country, or they will drive the authorities, and the rest of us, North of the Ohio River. The rebels still swear that but one party can live here!

Rewarding Treason.

Upon our first page we allude to the employment of *Sam. T. Atkin* by our military authorities, one of the most bitter and uncompromising rebels in East Tennessee. He went early into the rebellion, and continued active in [illegible]. He is now receiving of the Government $150 per month for the use of his foundry, made up in part of machinery taken from loyal men, driven out from Loudon for their Union sentiments. He is receiving $150 per month for superintending the work, and $50 per month for extra machinery. Total per month, $350, and for the year, FOUR THOUSAND TWO HUNDRED DOLLARS.

This is what our Government is doing in Knoxville for *one* rebel, and he one who ought to be in Camp Chase during the war. We don't know *whose fault it is*, nor do we care. We denounce *this infamous policy of rewarding treason*. If we were as ready to pay needy and destitute Union families for what they have furnished the Government, as we are to give employment to these *long-tried* enemies of the Government, and notorious secessionists, it would be a little more creditable to us. This man was concerned in making iron for the rebel government, under contract, before the Federal army came in, and it would be well for those who desire to promote the *interests* of avowed rebels, to hire him to start his iron-works again!

Still another case, *Samuel B. Haines*, of Sweetwater, late an *oppressive Enrolling Officer*, in the rebel service, a *volunteer conscript*, as he is sixty years of age—was brought into this city on Monday and lodged in jail by the United States Marshal, upon an indictment for treason by the Federal Grand Jury. Where does the reader, the loyal reader, and the Union refugee, wanting work, suppose the Marshal found this old traitor? He was arrested while at work, as *foreman in hay-packing*, employed by our Government right where he had been arresting Union men, *at Sweetwater*. We don't know whose fault this is, nor do we care—we denounce it as disgraceful, as unjust, unwise and impolitic.

Election Returns.

The votes of counties in our State come in slowly, owing to the want of mail facilities. The vote, under all the circumstances, has been large, and shows the feeling of the people to be deep and wide. They have voted for the war candidates, and for the crushing out of the rebellion. And all the votes polled were for Lincoln and Johnson.

The votes of certain counties show, with unerring certainty, the purposes of the people. And the votes cast, in view of the numbers in the Union army, show a large vote:

Knox county	2,537
Anderson county	760
Bradley county	1,024
Campbell county	649
Roane county	900
McMinn county	1,000
Greene county	800
Sevier county	1,174
Blount county	1,225
Morgan	250
Total in the ten counties	10,269

New York all Right.

The Union majority in the great State of New York is from 5,000 to 7,000. This secures the defeat of Seymour, the great Democratic trickster, of known rebel proclivities. McClellan is more overwhelmingly defeated than any man that ever run. There is no certainty of his having carried more than *one* State.

The Presidential Election.

Delaware has gone for McClellan by 450 votes. New Jersey has gone for him by 4,000 to 5,000, and Kentucky, though doubtful, is supposed to have gone for him. If he has carried the three States, he carries 21 electoral votes, and is the worst beat man that has ever run for the office for a quartery of a century!

Their Own Confessions.

A friend has sent us a package of the Southern *Confederacy*, published at Atlanta, in 1861, and from the paper of December 10th, we take a letter entire, written by a member of Stovall's Battalion, then stationed at Greeneville. The writer *boasts* of the hanging of *Fry and Hensie*. The same writer gives the proclamation of that soulless, christless, thief, liar and murderer, LEADBETTER.

When we announced, in our speeches at the North, two years ago, the hanging of *Fry and Hensie*, at Greeneville, by *Leadbetter*, and the substance of his proclamation, the Copperheads, Democrats and Peace-loving traitors, denied that any such hanging had ever transpired, or that any such Proclamation had ever been issued. Even EDWARD EVERETT had to defend us in a speech in Boston, and state that he had a confirmation of what we had said from gentlemen he knew to be reliable.

This is an old document, but we publish it for the benefit Northern traitors:

ALL THE PARTICULARS ABOUT HANGING THE BRIDGE-BURNERS—ITS EFFECTS—ANDY'S HOUSE FOR A HOSPITAL—COL. LEADBETTER'S PROCLAMATION—DEATH OF PRIVATE M'GRATH—WINTER QUARTERS AT GREENEVILLE.

GREENEVILLE, TENN., Dec. 2, 1861.

Dear Confederacy: The excitement caused by our hanging two bridge-burners has in some measure subsided, and every body seems satisfied that the sentence was just, and that the Government and its laws *shall be* recognized by the disloyal people in East Tennessee. True, some of Johnson's votaries and Brownlow's rag-tag and bobtail Union men condemn this execution. They may howl in their mountain gorges, and heap imprecations upon our heads, but it will only be for a season. We will surely keep up this novel amusement until the supremacy of our god and glorious Confederacy is fully established.

The two doomed culprits were not aware of their doom until a few moments before the hour, 4 o'clock, p. m., and short as the time was, they busied themselves in speaking on oath their full confession of guilt before the Court Martial. Fry confessed that he poured the turpentine on the bridge, and afterwards set fire to this combustible material, carried the sentinel off some half mile, and made him swear never to reveal the names of the offenders. Providence has saved the sentinel the trouble, for they have met the fate so justly meted out to them. They came in sight of the gallows—a temporary affair erected on the hillside in full view of the town—and a large oak limb was substituted as the cross-beam for this novel engine of death, and a shudder passed over them, which was perceptible by all.—They then knew that in a few moments they must die the death of a felon. The whole battalion under arms was drawn up around the ground, and the ropes were adjusted by Corporal McVay of our company—the caps drawn over their pale faces, the ladder was taken from the tree—the stillness of death pervaded the whole throng—the minute-hand was in a few seconds of 4 o'clock—the watch still went tick, tick—the knees shook visibly—the whole frame was ready to give way to nature's spirit—hark! it is 4 o'clock! The trigger is touched—and lo! dangling at the rope's end, between heaven and earth, are seen two struggling human beings! The struggles of one were short; the other seemed a little loth to give up the spirit from its tenement of clay, but in a few short moments they were both dead.

By order, they were left to hang all night and a portion of next day, when they were buried beneath the tree upon whose giant limb they hung, and where their wretched lives were brought to an end. Could that old and honored oak have spoken, it would no doubt have beseeched us not to tarnish its good name and old age by the touch of such miserable tories.

It has had a wonderful effect on unionism here, and scores are coming in night and day, taking the oath of allegiance to our Government, and by this serious service, proclaim to the world that they will defend it agrinst *all* of its enemies.

We have taken Andy Johnson's house as a hospital, and it has created some little fuss among his relatives, but we have occupied it, and it makes a splendid receptacle for our sick. I hear that Andy wept bitter tears in Louisville when he heard that our forces had occupied East Tennessee.

Enclosed I send you a proclamation by Col. Lea[illegible] can see for yourselves who is likely to be spared in this contest:

"PROCLAMATION TO THE CITIZENS OF EAST TENNESSEE.

"So long as the question of Union or Disunion was debatable, so long ye did well to debate it and vote on it. You had a clear right to vote for the Union, but when Secession was established by the voice of the people, you did ill to distract the country by angry words and insurrectionary tumult. In doing this you commit the highest crime known to the laws.

"Out of the Southern Confederacy no people possess such elements of prosperity and happiness as those of East Tennessee. The Southern market which you have hitherto enjoyed only in competition with a host of eager Northern rivals, will now be shared with a few States of the Confederacy equally fortunate, politically and geographically.—Every product of your agriculture and workshops will now find a prompt sale at high prices; and so long as cotton grows on Confederate soil, so long will the money which it brings flow from the South through all your channels of trade.

"At this moment you might be at war with the United States, or any other Foreign nation, and yet not suffer a tenth of the evils which pursue you in this domestic strife. No man's life or property is safe—no woman or child can sleep in quiet. You are deluded by selfish demagogues who take care for their own personal safety. You are citizens of Tennessee, and your State one of the Confederate States.

"So long as you are up in arms against these States, can you look for any thing but the invasion of your homes, and the wasting of your substance? This condition of things must be ended. The Government commands the peace and sends troops enough to enforce the order. I proclaim that every man who comes in promptly and delivers up his arms will be pardoned on taking the oath of allegiance. All men taken in arms against the Government will be transported to the military prison at Tuscaloosa and be confined there during the war. The bridge-burners and destroyers of Railroad tracks are excepted from among those pardonable. They will be tried by drumhead court-martial and be hanged on the spot. D. LEADBETTER,
"Col. Commanding.

"Head Quarters,
"Greeneville, Tenn., Nov. 30, 1861."

I chronicle with sorrow the death of one more of our soldiers—Priv. McGrath, of Capt. McDowell's company, of Barnesville. I knew Mc. well. I have enjoyed many an hour of song and jest with him, and his good temper and jovial ways won our heart. A good soldier—a dutiful one—we mourn his loss, and our only regret after his death is, that he died by disease, and not by the hand of our enemy, for he often expressed his desire to meet them. Farewell, Mc! comrade! friend! I drop a tear often when I think of my fellow-soldier.

T. D. W.

Capt. John Q. Arnold.

This rebel Captain is said to have been killed at the Gap, in the fight of Saturday. Among the papers found in his possession is the following letter by a rebel officer he had challenged to fight a duel:

ABINGDON, VA., May 25, 1864.

Captain John Q. Arnold:

Your communication of the 18th inst. has been considered; and in reply I must say that, under all circumstances, your request is most extraordinary. By what principle can an officer who is the accuser in a case pending in the military, send a challenge to the accused, before the termination of the trial? If I were even disposed to accede to your request, you, sir, must know that being under charges I can not resign in order to wave the "Rank" you mention.

Moreover, when you and myself entered the army we both took an oath to support and obey the Articles of War. If you can so far forget that oath as to send a challenge, let me assure you, sir, that I yet fully recognize its binding force, and consider it the highest duty of a soldier during this bloody struggle for independence, to dedicate his service, and if need be his life, to his country's cause.

When this war is over—when peace is restored to our destracted land, and my bleeding country no longer demands my services, being then released from all obligations, I would duly consider such a request as yours coming from a *gentleman*, and if necessary give him the satisfaction which you claim—but in no event, nor under any circumstances, would I accept a challenge from one whose social relation and unfortunate military antecedents have been such as to exclude him from the pale of honor.

This reply will be handed to your friend, Captain Hardy, by Lieut. John R. Rucker.

Your obedient servant,
G. W. DAY,
Major 12th Tenn. Bat. Cav.

[COMMUNICATED.]

News from East Tennessee Soldiers.

HEADQ'RS 1ST BRIG. 4TH DIV. CAV. A. C.,
Decatur, Ala., Nov. 5th, 1864.

Dr. W. G. Brownlow: SIR—We have had quite a calm at this place since Forrest's exit from north of the Tennessee river, until the 26th ult., when the rebel forces under Beauregard, Hood & Co. attacked us; but the enemy visiting this section of country have learned by experience that Brig. Gen. R. S. Granger is not to be thwarted by bold fronts or threatening tales.

The enemy was met about 12 M. by the 2d Tennessee Cavalry, Lieut. Col. W. F. Prosser, 10th Indiana Cavalry, Major ——, and one section of Battery A, 1st Tennessee Light Artillery, Captain Albert F. Beach, the whole under the immediate command of Lieut. Col. Prosser. The enemy opened on us with a full battery, partially masked in the woods. The fight was hard, and lasted until dark, when the firing ceased. Next morning it was again renewed, and continued until about noon on the 29th, making four days.

On the morning of the third day Captain Beach dismounted one of their guns and blew up two caissons, causing a considerable destruction of life among them. The same day, forty-seven of the 18th Michigan Infantry, under a Captain, (whose name I have forgotten,) charged and captured five commissioned officers and one hundred and seventeen enlisted men, making an aggregate of one hundred and twenty-two men captured in their rifle-pits by forty-seven men in the open field. This was a little over two and a half rebels that one Yankee *did* whip, instead of the "chivalry" whipping five, as they told us at the beginning of the war they were going to.

The 4th U. S. Colored Infantry, Colonel Morgan, charged a rebel battery and spiked two guns, killing and wounding a great many. It is quite common among the pro-slavery portion of the country to agree that the negroes are cowards and will not fight. I would just say to them, they never saw any fighting, neither do they know anything about it, consequently we can excuse them on account of their arguments, but cannot on account of ignorance.

I transmit herewith the list of casualties of our brigade:

2D TENNESSEE CAVALRY.

Co. D.—Killed—Captain A. G. McReynolds.
Co. C.—Killed—Sergt. Jesse Collins. Wounded—Corp. John Coward.
Co. B.—Killed—James McFall.
Co. A.—Killed—James M. Robertson.
Co. K.—Wounded—Rufus L. Mize, Andrew Reaves.
Co. H.—Wounded—Joseph J. Hearout.

BATTERY A, 1ST TENN. LIGHT ARTILLERY.

Killed.—Patrick Carroll and James Newberry.
Wounded.—Terrence Grimes and Michael Type.

The 10th Indiana Cavalry was temporarily attached to the Brigade, but they have not been required to report through Brigade Headquarters, consequently we have no list of casualties from that regiment.

WILL. A. MCTEER,
Adjutant 3d Tenn. Cav. and A. A. A. G.

(COMMUNICATED.)

To the Common People.

The great presidential contest is now over, and the result most glorious in its character. Although rebels and guerrillas invested many portions of our State, yet the vote of Tennessee, and especially East Tennessee, is eminently gratifying to the friends of the Union and freedom. The magnitude of the political struggle through which we have just past can scarcely be realized. Upon it hung the destiny of this vast Republic; and in its issue was involved the hopes of the lovers of liberty throughout the world.

The welfare of the bustling millions of the future was at stake. McClellan is defeated. Lincoln is re-elected, and "all the fond hopes of the rebellion dashed to the ground." The *fiat* has gone from the ballot-box, that the national soil should be maintained in all its integrity, and the great slaveholders insurrection crushed out by the powers and prowess of our army and navy. The re-election of Lincoln decides that there will be no Southern Confederacy—that the flag of the Union shall protect and defend the States and territories, from the silver lakes of the North to the golden sands of the Gulf of the South. This fixes the destiny of Tennessee *in the Union*, subject to its laws and bound by its authority.

The man who now entertains a doubt as to the success of the national cause, or possesses one gleam of hope for the rebellion, would adorn the chambers of a mad house, rather than enlighten the world in the arena of public debate.

In view of the present condition of public affairs, what should be the policy of the people? And by "*the people*" it is not intended to convey the idea of a few leaders, or would be leaders, assuming, as in the past, to direct the people what the will of the politicians is, but it is meant that the period has arrived in our history as a *free* Republic, when the great mass—"the common people," as they are called—shall arouse from the state of vassalage in which they have been held by the *Slave Lords*, and their instruments, the *politicians*, and assert the political equality of the white race. This is not a war for negro equality, as we are told by the Copperhead orators and press. It is a war to vindicate the rights of the plebeian population, and make the poor the equal of the rich—to place all men upon an equality, whether it be the peasant of the fields or the slave lord of the parlor, who counts his negroes by the hundred.

What, then, should the sovereigns of the land do in order to restore our State and people the immense blessings of the national Union? Our State Government has been subverted. We are without civil authority to administer to the wants of the citizen. The great civil war that has swept over the land for three years and more, has worked many changes, as already intimated, in our political and social system. Indeed, they are so great that many laws quite appropriate and necessary in the past, are now obsolete by force of circumstances, and if enforced would work incalculable hardships, and in some cases even ruin. For instance the Slave Code cannot be enforced, and it would be improper, not to say supremely unjust, to attempt such a thing.

These evils and inconsistencies exist in the organic law of the State.

The Constitution contains them, and as a wise, statesmanlike people we should learn to profit by experience, and prepare for our present protection and future prosperity, and greatness as a State, by reorganizing our State Government upon a basis more consistent with the principles of the Union.

To do this, the people who have stood by the flag of their country should take steps *immediately* to elect a Constitutional Convention, to reconstruct a loyal State Government by amending their Constitution, and removing the inconsistencies it contains.

Especially should slavery be wiped from its pages, and forever prohibited.

The people have indicated their desire to do this by their recent endorsement of Mr. Lincoln's administration.

Another question worthy of consideration is, whether we will provide for the election of a Lieutenant Governor, in addition to the officers already provided for in our Constitution. Tennessee is one of the few States without such an officer. He is the presiding officer of the Senate, and the convenience and services of such an official is potent to the minds of every statesman.

More on this subject in the future. H.

Testimony Against Slavery.

Through the columns of the WHIG, for twenty-five years past, we have given the testimony in favor of slavery, and the arguments in support of the institution. We now commence publishing the evidence on the other side, and now introduce a strong chapter:

Slavery is inconsistent with the genius of Republicanism—it lessens the sense of the equal rights of mankind, and habituates us to tyranny and oppression.—[Luther Martin, of Missouri.

It (slavery) is so odious that nothing can be sufficient to support it but positive law.—[Lord Mansfield.

Slavery is contrary to the fundamental law of all societies.—[Montesquieu.

It is injustice to permit slavery to remain for a single hour.—[William Pitt.

Slavery in all its forms, in all its degrees, is a violation of divine law, and a degradation of human nature.—[Brissott.

Those are men-stealers who abduct, keep, sell, or buy slaves of freemen.—[Grotius.

Slavery is detrimental to virtue and industry.—[Beattie.

Slavery is a system of outrage and robbery.—[Socrates.

Slavery is a system of the most complete injustice.—[Plato.

[illegible] abhor blood, they will reject with indignation the wild and guilty fantasy that man can hold property in man.—[Brougham.

Slavery is a state so improper, so degrading, so ruinous to the feelings and capacities of human nature, that it ought not to be suffered to exist.—[Burke.

No man is by nature the property of another.—[Dr. Johnson.

A system (slavery) which is not only opposed to the principles of morality, but, as it appears to me, is pregnant with appalling and inevitable danger to the Republic.—[Baron Humboldt.

Every man has a property in his own person; this nobody has a right to but himself.—[Locke.

It prevents human reason, and induces men endowed with logical powers to maintain that slavery is sanctioned by the Christian religion.—[John Q. Adams.

I never would consent, and never have consented, that there should be one foot of slave territory beyond what the old thirteen States had at the formation of the Union. Never, never!—[Daniel Webster.

It (slavery) ought not to be introduced nor permitted in any of the new States.—[John Jay.

Natural liberty is the gift of the beneficient Creator of the whole human race.—[Alexander Hamilton.

Slavery is an atrocious debasement of human nature.—[Franklin.

It (slavery) impairs our strength as a community, and poisons our morals at the fountain head.—[Judge Gaston, of North Carolina.

The evils of this system (slavery) cannot be enumerated.—[George W. Summers, of Va.

So long as God allows the vital current to flow through my veins, I will never, never, never, by word or thought, by mind or will, aid in submitting one rood of free territory to the everlasting curse of human bondage.—[Henry Clay.

Sir, I envy neither the heart nor the head of that man from the North, who rises here (in Congress) to defend slavery from principle.—[John Randolph.

We have found that this evil (slavery) has preyed upon the very vitals of the Union, and has been prejudicial to all the States in which it has existed.—[James Monroe.

[illegible] abolition of domestic slavery is the greatest object of desire in these Colonies, where it was unhappily introduced in their infant state.—[Thomas Jefferson.

I can only say, that there is not a man living who wishes more sincerely than I do to see a plan adopted for the abolition of it (slavery.)—[George Washington.

Extracts from a Rebel Letter.

We have a long letter from the pocket of *Ed. Gammon*, after he was killed in the late fight at Morristown, written by *R. M. Rhea*, the youngest son of Samuel Rhea, of Sullivan county. He writes from Chaffin's Farm, Va., August 25th, 1864. One rebel writing to another thus discloses his venom, and the falsehoods circulating among them as news:

"I would like to dash into Knoxville first rate, and liberate the oppressed people there. Thomas A. R. is in jail, and Mr. Snapp is to be hung. A very nice fix to be in, but they brought it on themselves, so let "em rip." Brownlow ought to be hung for six hours every day, by a hook through his old skin, until he is dead."

"I am glad to hear that Vaughn's Brigade will get to East Tennessee. If it does, Ed., see that every one of *Morgan's thieves is shot*, who in the least inform on the people there. Treat all the people with respect, and I think most of them will come to their senses. I am afraid old Brownlow is going to ruin everything down in East Tennessee. He is a fiend incarnate, and hell is too good for him."

"Well, Ed., things look prosperous for us, a great discord is certainly working in the North—they are going to have a war up there if they don't watch. I don't care how soon they do, for then it will turn it off of our shoulders. What does your father think of a speedy peace? I hope troops may be sent to East Tennessee, sufficient to retake and retain it."

"Where is Miss Kate Sneed? My regards to her. My love to Miss Mollie, when you go down to Jonesborough. Stop at Bristol and see Mr. James and Levitee Johnson. Tell her I have not forgotten sweet music. Kindest regards to friends.

Your friend,
R. M. REA.

Future Trade Regulations.

By order of the Treasury Department, the Supply Stores for East Tennessee will be given out to soldiers and sailors, who have lost their limbs or health in the service, they furnishing us the necessary papers upon which to act. If the allowance for each town is not taken up by them, the next preference will be for men who have served as long as two years. The third class preferred will be loyal men who are in the business.

The last class preferred, and the class we shall take a pleasure in denying, and forcing to retire, is that class of free-spoken men who oppose the Administration, and denounce the war policy of the Government. They can wind up their stores, or sell out, and this notice is given that they may prepare for a change. Men who are not for the Government are against it, and have no claims upon its bounty. The Government has *friends* enough in the country to do the business of the country, without the services of its *enemies*.

Circular.

Whereas, the Synod of Tennessee failed to meet on its last regular adjournment: and whereas, it is now deemed important to have a meeting of that body at as early a day as practicable:

I, therefore, as the last Moderator now in our bounds, by the authority in me vested by an act of the General Assembly of 1796, do hereby require the Synod of Tennessee to convene in the Presbyterian Church in Sweetwater, Tenn., on the 2d day of December next, at 11 o'clock, A. M.

The members are requested to be punctual in their attendance, together with as many ruling elders, representing the different churches, as may find it convenient to attend.

THOMAS BROWN, Moderator.
Philadelphia, Tenn., November 8, 1864.

BY TELEGRAPH.

Sheridan Again Victorious.

Prisoners and Cannon Captured.

Plymouth, N. C., Re-captured.

Rebel Army Attempting to Cross the Mississippi.

DANVILLE, KY., Nov. 10, 1864.

The majorities for Lincoln are variously estimated as follows:

In Pennsylvania from 10,000 to 15,000, exclusive of soldiers' vote; Maine from 15,000 to 18,000 Rhode Island from 5,000 to 6,000; Maryland from 5,000 to 7,000, on home vote; Connecticut from 2,000 to 4,000; Indiana from 20,000 to 40,000; Ohio from 30,000 to 40,000; New Hampshire from 4,000 to 8,000.

Lincoln has large majorities in Illinois, Wisconsin, Minnesota, Iowa, Michigan and Missouri.

McClellan's majority in Delaware is from 500 to 1,000; in New Jersey from 5,000 to 6,000; in New York City from 30,000 to 35,000.

Both parties claim New York State.

It is estimated that Kentucky will give McClellan a small majority.

The pirate *Florida* was captured on the coast of Brazil.

Reported capture and sinking of the *Tallahassee* near Hilton Head.

Reported resignation of General McClellan.

There is considerable excitement in Chicago caused by the discovery of a rebel plot to burn the city and release the prisoners. Gold [illegible]

LEBANON, Nov. 11, 1864.

The Philadelphia Bulletin estimates the Republican majority at from 10,000 to 15,000, to be swelled to over 35,000 by the soldiers' vote.

Rhode Island gives 5,061 majority for Lincoln, exclusive of soldiers' vote.

McClellan carries Delaware by 450 majority.

New York has gone Republican by 5,000, and Pennsylvania by 15,000 majority.

Eighteen Pennsylvania regiments in Grant's army gave 4,700 votes for Lincoln, and 2,300 for McClellan.

Lincoln has carried every State except New Jersey, Delaware and Kentucky.

The Herald says New York and Pennsylvania have both gone Republican.

The indications are that Seymour is defeated.

Next Congress will be overwhelmingly Republican.

Congressional delegations from States yet to elect members to Congress, to stand the same as at present, will be three more than two-thirds Republican on joint ballot.

LEBANON, KY., Nov. 11.

New Jersey gives McClellan about 5,500 majority.

The majority in Pennsylvania for Lincoln will be from 15,000 to 20,000 without counting the soldiers' vote in the field.

[Signed] SIMON CAMERON.

The Democrats claim New York State, but do not appear very strong in their figures.

The Republicans claim the State at from 5,000 to 9,000.

BALTIMORE, Nov. 9.

The Republicans have a majority in the House. The Senate is doubtful. The Republican majority in the State is about 7,000.

ALBANY, N. Y., Nov. 11.

The Union ticket in New York State is elected by from 5,000 to 7,000 majority.

Gen. Wright, member elect to Congress from New Jersey, is not dead.

ST. LOUIS, Nov. 11.

A tornado at Chester, Ills., destroyed $60,000 worth of property.

A part of Gen. A. J. Smith's command is at Rodney.

The rebel Gen. Meredith will be assigned to the command of Kentucky.

NEW YORK, Nov. 11.

The *World's* special report of the attack on and capture of Fort Morgan, with 19,000 prisoners, is pronounced false.

The *Commercial's* Washington special insists that Gen. McClellan has resigned his commission in the army.

The report of the rebel Secretary of the Treasury is very despondent. He says that he can only obtain $180 in specie for a $1,000 Confederate bond.

Gen. Ripley has been assigned to command at Pensacola.

Cotton 142; Gold 242.

The rebels again whipped in the Shenandoah Valley. Many prisoners and two cannon captured.

Official confirmation of the recapture of Plymouth, N. C., by our forces.

The rebels are terribly alarmed about the movements of Sherman and Grant.

The arming of slaves urgently advocated.

The Texas army is attempting to cross the Missippi river to reinforce Hood.

Stampede of cattle for Hood's army. Over 1,000 head captured by our forces.

Gen. Banks is to return to Louisiana.

Nothing from Hood.

Beauregard is with Hood at Florence, Ala.

Gold closed in New York at 244½.

New York gives a small majority for Lincoln and Fenton.

Delaware, New Jersey and Kentucky are the only States McClellan has carried.

The election on the Pacific has resulted gloriously.

Lincoln's majortiy in California is 25,000.

Oregon and Nevada are both for Lincoln. Heavy majorities in both States.

Important Foreign news. The Danish and German question has been settled.

Cock-a-my-Doodle-doo.

The great political game cock was pitted and spurred at Chicago, he flapped his wings, crowed out lustily, by way of acceptance. He comes out of the political cock-pit "un-heeled" and "quarter-clipped." His voice is heard in under-tones in the barn-yard, and none but *old setting hens* give audience! The *dung-hills* of the North, and the *shanghais* of Europe, all crowed on his side when he first dashed out from Chicago; and their echoes reverberated from the Aurora Borealis of Northern traitors, to the Southern Hell of rebel fiends!

And after all, what does it amount to? The *Peace Chickens* found one State willing to be converted into a barn-yard for *Dung-hill Roosters* to splurge in and crow over their own disgrace. Even the old roosters of monarchial Great Britain and imperial France, will refuse to do honor to such *Domineckers*.

The old *Illinois Rooster*, Abraham, is a popular chicken. He is a cock from Tippacanoe.

Cock-a-my-doodle-doo!

Whereabouts of Sherman.

Gen. Sherman is all right, and will wake up some body ere long, "away down South in Dixie." If the rebel forces want to find him, they will have to go South of Atlanta! And if they want to see where Atlanta "used to was," they can see by "passing by on the other side," as the good Samaritan did!

We don't know what Gen. Sherman's programme is, but ours is to lay rebeldom waste in all its parts, and from this out!

The Knoxville Whig.

"The union of lakes—the union of lands—
The union of States none can sever—
The union of hearts—the union of hands—
And the flag of our Union forever."

STAND BY THE OLD FLAG.

"The conspiracy is now known. Armies have been raised, war is levied to accomplish it. There are only two sides to the question. Every man must be for the **United States, or against it. There can be no neutrals in this war—only patriots or traitors."**—Stephen A. Douglas, at Chicago, April 11, '61.

"Whenever they (the Rebels,) have the power, they drive before them into their ranks the Southern people, as they would also drive us. Trust them not. Were they able, they would invade and destroy us without mercy. **Absolutely assured of these things, I am amazed that any one could think of 'peace on any terms.' He who entertains the sentiment is fit only to be a slave, and he who utters it at this time, is, moreover, a traitor to his country, who deserves the scorn and contempt of all honorable men."**—General Rosecrans.

"What right has the North assailed? What justice has been denied? And what claim, founded in justice and right, has been withheld? Can either of you to-day name one single act of wrong, deliberately and purposely done by the government at Washington, of which the South has a right to complain? I challenge the answer."—Hon. A. H. Stephens, 1861.

"Let Truth and Falsehood grapple; who ever knew Truth put to the worse in a free and open encounter."—Milton.

"If any man attempts to haul down the American Flag, shoot him on the spot."—John A. Dix.

Butchery of the Union Wounded Men at Saltville.

[Correspondence of the Philadelphia Inquirer.]

Headq'rs Army of the James,
October 17, 1864.

The rebel flag of truce boat William Allison brought down to Cox's Landing this morning about five hundred paroled Union prisoners, in exchange for a batch of paroled rebel prisoners sent up on Saturday. The boat left Richmond about 6 A. M., and reached the landing at about half-past 9.

A number of men (between thirty and forty, I believe) belonging to Burbridge's command, captured at Saltville on the 2d instant, were among the prisoners who arrived to-day. One of them, a gentleman of the Teutonic persuasion, gave me his opinion on the result of that expedition in the following somewhat laconic style: "We gets not mooch salt dere," said he, "but we gets peppered like der tuyfel!" The following regiments of Burbridge's command were represented: 12th Ohio Cavalry, 11th Michigan Cavalry, 11th and 13th Kentucky Cavalry, and 35th, 39th, 40th and 57th Kentucky Mounted Infantry.

According to the accounts of several officers and surgeons with whom I conversed, the conduct of a portion of the rebel troops, subsequent to the engagement at Saltville, was utterly lawless and brutal. In two field hospital near the scene of the battle [illegible] twenty-three wounded negroes of the 1st Colored Cavalry—fifteen in one and [illegible] the other. All but th[illegible] of them were murdered in cold blood by the rebel soldiers, who called there for that special purpose; and these fiends in human form boasted, while doing this hellish deed, that they had been engaged in this same work all day. They claim to have buried one hundred and twenty-five colored soldiers, of whom nearly all must have been slaughtered in the same way, as it is said scarcely a dozen were killed in the battle. This was on the 3d inst. The three negroes who had been spared (it is to be presumed through oversight,) were removed, with the rest of the wounded, to the Emory and Henry College Hospitals. Four days later, or on the 7th inst., a party of cut-throats, in rebel uniforms, entered the building and shot two of those dead. The other was fired at twice, and left for dead, but the would-be murderer, it appears, did not look critically to the effects of his shots, and the negro was but slightly grazed on the head. He was afterward removed to the house of a citizen in the vicinity, and concealed until he could be removed to a safer place.

But these demons had not yet appeased their thirst for blood, and on the day succeeding the outrage just related, the 8th instant, a band of fifteen men, led by the notorious Champ Ferguson, appeared. Ferguson himself wrested his musket from the hand of a sentry (rebel) who stood at the door of the hospital, and leaving two men to guard him, entered the building with the rest of his gang, and went straight to the room of Lieut. Smith of the 13th Kentucky cavalry. His men passed through the door in two files, and Ferguson, walking up between them, approached the bed on which the wounded lieutenant was lying.

"How are you, Smith?" "How are you, Captain?" were the salutions first exchanged, when Ferguson, balancing his musket on his hand, said tauntingly, "Look here, Smith, do you see this?" "For God's sake, Captain, don't shoot me," implored the lieutenant; but he had scarcely uttered the words before the other had raised the gun and shot him through the head. The gang then inquired for Col. Hanson of the 37th Kentucky mounted infantry (commanding a brigade) and Capt. Dagenfield, of the 12th Ohio cavalry, declaring their intention to shoot them both.

By this time the surgeons and hospital attendants had become aware of what was going on, and they hastened to the spot.—By persuasion, and almost by force, they endeavored to restrain these desperadoes from carrying out their savage purpose.—Ferguson was on the point of shooting the rebel surgeon in charge, Dr. Murphy, for daring to interfere, and one of his men actually presented a revolver at the breast of a major, who chanced to be visiting at the hospital at the time, and had volunteered his assistance. By argument and resistence combined, the ruffians were induced to leave without having fully carried out their murderous designs, but swore to return at night and complete their work.

Col. Hanson was immediately removed to the house of a citizen to await other arrangements for his safety, and a guard of convalescents was raised and placed around the hospital to resist another incursion.—During the succeeding night Col. Hanson, Capt. Dagenfield, Surgeon L. C. Woodman, 11th Michigan cavalry, Surgeon Gardner, 13th Kentucky cavalry, Assistant Surgeon Hunt, 12th Ohio cavalry, and Acting Assistant Surgeon Cronage, 11th Michigan cavalry, were placed upon the train and sent eastward by order of Gen. Breckinridge. Whether that officer did not feel himself able to afford them protection against the lawless violence of his own men, I know not.

My informants had not heard of any punishment having been meted out to the parties engaged in these outrages, although the name of the ring-leader, if not of others, was well known. It is but just to state in this connection, that the rebel surgeons, attendants and others connected with the hospitals, used their utmost exertions to prevent these lawless and barbarous acts, and resisted them at the risk of their own lives.

Letter From Hon. Robert J. Walker.

A letter from Hon. Robert J. Walker, written at London, has appeared. He urges very strongly the support of the Baltimore Candidates, and says of the influence which a Union triumph at the polls in November would have abroad:—

"There will be no recognition of the South by France, or England, or any other power, if Abraham Lincoln should be re-elected in November next. The American people will then have loudly proclaimed through the ballot box that they can and will subdue the rebellion by force of arms, and that they will continue to negotiate from the mouths of our cannon until the Southern armies shall have been dispersed and vanquished. Upon the news of the re-election of Mr. Lincoln reaching Europe the Confederate stock, now waiting the success of the Chicago candidates, will fall like Lucifer to rise no more. American securities, including those of the Federal Government and loyal States, railroads and other companies with real capital, will all be immensely appreciated. The difference in favor of our country, including the rise in greenbacks, would be equivalent in a few months to hundreds of millions of dollars. Nor is it only our stocks that will rise at home and abroad, but the national character will be immensely exalted."

ATTACHMENT.

O. F. Hill vs. John Crozier and others.

THE PLAINTIFF ON AFFIDAVIT SAYS THE DEFENDANTS, John Crozier, W. P. Crisp and W. M. Cocke are severally indebted to him and so abscond that the ordinary process of law cannot be served upon them, having obtained original attachments against them, made returnable before R. D. Jourolmon, a Justice of the Peace for Knox county, and the same having been levied on his property: It is ordered by said Justice that the defendants appear before him at his office in Knoxville on the 22d day of February, 1865, or it will be proceeded with ex parte. It is further ordered that this notice be published for four successive weeks in the Knoxville Whig.

o26-4t pf$5* R. D. JOUROLMON, J. P.

ATTACHMENT.

Martha E. Newman vs. Samuel W. Wallace.

THE PLAINTIFF ON AFFIDAVIT SAYS THE DEFENDANT is indebted to her, and so absconds that the ordinary process of law cannot be served upon himm, having obtained an original attachment against the defendant, made returnable before Joseph Ambrister, a Justice of the Peace for Blount county, and the same having been levied on his property: It is ordered by said Justice that the defendant appear before him at his office in Maryville, on the 18th day of March, 1865, or the same will be proceeded with ex parte. It is further ordered that this notice be published in the Knoxville Whig for four successive weeks.

o26-4t pf$5* JOSEPH AMBRISTER, J. P.

ATTACHMENT.

W. T. Manson vs. J. G. M. Ramsey.

THE PLAINTIFF ON AFFIDAVIT SAYS THE DEFENDANT is indebted to him, and so absconds that process cannot be served upon him, having obtained an original attachment against the defendant, made returnable before Charles Morrow, a Justice of the Peace for Knox county, and the same having been levied on his property: It is ordered by said Justice that the defendant appear before him at his office in Knoxville, on the 6th day of April, 1865, or it will be proceeded with ex parte. It is further ordered that this notice be published for four successive weeks in the Knoxville Whig.

o26-4t pf$5 CHARLES MORROW, J. P.

County Court—Knox County.

Benj. Wilkins, Adm'r, vs. Martha Wilkins and others.

IT APPEARING FROM THE AFFIDAVIT of the complainant filed in this case that Charles S. Wilkins, one of the respondents, has, since the filing of the bill in this cause, left the State of Tennessee: It is ordered that publication be made in the Knoxville Whig for four successive weeks, requiring said Charles S. Wilkins to appear at a County Court to be held for Knox county at the Court House in Knoxville on the first Monday of December, 1864, to answer said bill, or the same will be taken as confessed and the cause set for hearing ex parte as to him.

o26-4w pf$5 WM. CRAIG, Clerk.

Notice to Refugees—Applications for Labor.

REFUGEES WISHING EMPLOYMENT will be assisted in obtaining it by applying at this office—General Store East Tennessee Relief Association, Main street, first door east of the Court House. Persons wishing to employ hands, will please file in this office statements showing names, residences, kind of labor and length of time employment will be given.

o26-tf E. E. GILLENWATERS, General Agent E. T. R. Association.

ATTACHMENT.

James Henry vs. James Carnes.

THE PLAINTIFF ON AFFIDAVIT SAYS THE DEFENDANT is indebted to him and so absconds or conceals himself that the ordinary process of law cannot be served upon him, having obtained an original attachment against the estate of the defendant made returnable before W. H. Anderson, a Justice of the Peace for Blount county, and the same having been levied on his property: It is ordered by said Justice that the defendant appear before him at his office in Blount county on the 2d day of May, 1865, or it will be proceeded with ex parte. It is further ordered that this notice be published in the Knoxville Whig, for four successive weeks.

nov2-4t pf$5 W. H. ANDERSON, J. P.

ATTACHMENT.

John W. Cates, surviving partner of the late firm of Pride & Cates, vs. J. C. Fagg.

THE PLAINTIFF ON AFFIDAVIT SAYS THE DEFENDANT is indebted to him and so absconds that process cannot be served upon him, having obtained an original attachment against the defendant made returnable before Joseph Ambrister, a Justice of the Peace for Blount county, and the same having been levied on his property. It is ordered by said Justice, that the defendant appear before him at his office in Maryville, on the 10th day of December, 1864, or it will be proceeded with ex parte. It is further ordered that this notice be published for four successive weeks in the Knoxville Whig.

nov2-4t pf$5* JOS. AMBRISTER, J. P.

Attention, 3d Tennessee Cavalry.

ALL ABSENTEES FROM THIS REGIMENT will report to me at Nashville, Tenn., immediately.

BEN. CUNNINGHAM, Major 3d Tenn. Cavalry.

nov2-3w*

PROSPECTUS
OF
BROWNLOW'S KNOXVILLE WHIG
AND
REBEL VENTILATOR.

The undersigned is now publishing a Weekly Journal, bearing the above title, at Knoxville, East Tennessee. The paper I propose to send out for $2 per annum, *invariably paid in advance.* The cost of paper, materials of all kinds, and of labor, has so increased, since the inauguration of the rebellion, that I am not able to furnish the paper for less, or to hold out any inducements to clubs.

Two years ago, my paper, then the last Union sheet, and the only *religious* one floating over Jeff. Davis's ungodly dominions, was crushed out by that God-forsaken mob, familiarly known as the *Confederate Authorities.* I glory in opening my batteries from my old fortifications, beginning with this hell-born and hell-bound rebellion where the traitors forced me to leave off my "work of faith and labor of love."

The Whig and Ventilator will be Independent in all things and Neutral in nothing, taking a liberal hand in all the controversies of the day. This shall be an *unconditional* Union journal, holding up all participants in the *late* Rebellion—now almost played out—as a choice collection of men for a Rogues' Gallery. At the same time, I will make war upon all gamblers and thieves North and South—all whose trade it is to rob the public crib, as well as private pilferers; the whisky bloats; the bullies in elections; the oppressors who grind the face of the poor; extortioners in trade who swindle by wholesale and retail; and all foul mouthed Secession sympathizers and other disturbers of the peace in the various sinkholes of society, North and South. I will not fail to do justice to the worst class of men who make tracks upon Southern soil—*Secession preachers,* of all denominations.

I repeat, that in the rule of my editorial conduct, I shall abjure that servility which destroys the independence of the press, and cast from me that factious opposition which gives to *party* what is due to *country.* And while the name of my paper indicates in unmistakable terms, its politics, I shall, as a faithful sentinel, lose sight of Whigs, Democrats and Republicans, and remember only my Government and the preservation of the Federal Union, as richly worth all the sacrifices of blood and treasure their preservation may cost, even to the extermination of the present race of men, and the consumption of all the means of the present age.

Intervention, national jealousy and hatred, double dealing, and piratical cowardice have been governing principles with England; and when our home troubles are settled, I will advocate giving England a turn. The whole course of the Emperor of the French has been characterized by *diplomatic insincerity;* and a truly loyal American journal can entertain no other feelings toward Napoleon than those of hatred and contempt.

The *everlasting Negro question* brought on this war—the corrupt leaders of the South alleging that it was necessary to render the "peculiar institution" *secure,* when it *was* secure under the Constitution, and could never be secure anywhere else. It is now no longer the *local,* but the *traveling* institution of the country; and I have no sympathy with any Southern Disunionist who has lost his slaves. Slavery has been destroyed, and the South has done it, without any provocation whatever. This position I will openly take and stubbornly maintain.

RATES OF ADVERTISING.

One square, ten lines nonpareil, one insertion...	$1 00
Each continuation of same advertisement.	50
One square, six months.........	10 00
One square, per annum.........	15 00

Liberal discounts will be made to those who advertise liberally. Having lost thousands by advertising, no advertisement will be inserted without payment *in advance,* or some responsible man to assume payment. The extensive circulation of my paper will make it a desirable advertising medium.

October, 1863. W. G. BROWNLOW, *Editor and Proprietor.*

LAW PARTNERSHIP.

THE SUBSCRIBERS HAVE ENTERED into partnership in the practice of Law in the Circuit and Chancery Courts at Rogersville, and in the Supreme Court at Knoxville, in all cases in which they may be retained, and which may be taken to said Supreme Court from the counties of Hawkins, Hancock, Grainger, Claiborne and Campbell.

Our partnership extends also to all cases, civil or criminal, in which we may be employed in the Federal Court at Knoxville; and we will attend in said Court to the collection of claims in any county in East Tennessee, where the claimants reside out of the State, and see proper to entrust them to our management.

The style of the firm is Nelson & Netherland.

John Netherland will continue as heretofore, to attend the Circuit and Chancery Courts in Grainger, Hancock, Claiborne and Campbell counties.

THOS. A. R. NELSON.
Knoxville, Tenn. jel1-1y J. NETHERLAND.

LAW PARTNERSHIP.

THE SUBSCRIBERS HAVE ENTERED into partnership in the practice of Law in the Circuit and Chancery Courts at Jonesboro', Greeneville, Dandridge and Knoxville, and also in the County, Circuit, Chancery and Supreme Courts at Knoxville, in all cases in which we may be employed, taken to the Supreme Court from either of the Courts at Jonesboro', Dandridge, Greeneville or Knoxville.

S. T. and J. M. Logan, under the firm of Logan & Logan, will attend to any causes which may be entrusted to their management in the Federal Court. And Thomas A. R. Nelson will attend, individually, to any cause in which he may be employed in the Supreme Court at Knoxville, not embraced in his partnerships with Col. John Netherland, and Messrs. Logan & Logan.

The style of our firm is Nelson, Logan & Logan.

THOS. A. R. NELSON.
SAM'L T. LOGAN.
Knoxville, Tenn. jel1-1y JOS. M. LOGAN.

The Palmetto Herald.

VOLUME I. No. 38. PORT ROYAL, S. C., THURSDAY, NOVEMBER 17, 1864. PRICE Five Cents.

THE PALMETTO HERALD

IS PUBLISHED BY

S. W. MASON & CO.,

EVERY THURSDAY MORNING,

AT PORT ROYAL, S. C.

Office cor. Merchants' Row and Palmetto Avenue.

Terms:

Single Copy.........................Five Cents.
One Hundred Copies $3 50
Per Annum to any Address..................$2 00

Payment invariably in Advance.

A limited number of ADVERTISEMENTS received at Twenty-five Cents per Line. JOB PRINTING executed neatly and promptly.

Jefferson Davis' Message.

THE POLICY OF ARMING AND EMANCIPATING SLAVES RECOMMENDED.

In the Savannah papers of the 12th we find the Message of Jeff Davis to the rebel Congress, from which we make the following extracts:

THINGS TO BE THANKFUL FOR.

Cause for devout gratitude is found in the fact that Texas contains no Federals except as prisoners, and that the Yankees have not accomplished nearly as much as they evidently expected to elsewhere.

ATLANTA NO GREAT LOSS—RICHMOND, CHARLESTON, SAVANNAH AND MOBILE NOT VITAL POINTS.

Mr. Davis says:

The lessons afforded by the history of this war are fraught with instruction and encouragement. Repeatedly during the war have formidable expeditions been directed by the enemy against points ignorantly supposed to be of vital importance to the Confederacy. Some of these expeditions have, at immense cost, been successful; but in no instance have the promised fruits been reaped. Again, in the present campaign, was the delusion fondly cherished that the capture of Atlanta and Richmond would, if effected, end the war by the overthrow of our Government and the submission of our people. We can now judge by experience how unimportant is the influence of the former event upon our capacity for defence, upon the spirit and courage of the people, and the stability of the Government. We may, in like manner, judge that if the campaign against Richmond had resulted in success instead of failure; if the valor of the army under the leadership of its accomplished commander had resisted in vain the overwhelming masses which were, on the contrary, decisively repulsed; if we had been compelled to evacuate Richmond as well as Atlanta, the Confederacy would have remained as erect and defiant as ever. Nothing could have been changed in the purpose of its Government, in the indomitable valor of its troops, or in the unconquerable spirit of its people. The baffled and disappointed foe would in vain have scanned the reports of your proceedings, at some new legislative seat, for any indication that progress had been made in his gigantic task of conquering a free people. The truth so patent to us must ere long be forced upon the reluctant Northern mind. There are no vital points on the preservation of which the continued existence of the Confederacy depends. There is no military success of the enemy which can accomplish its destruction. Not the fall of Richmond, nor Wilmington, nor Charleston, nor Savannah, nor of Mobile, nor of all combined, can save the enemy from the constant and exhaustive drain of blood and treasure which must continue until he shall discover that no peace is attainable unless based on the recognition of our indefeasible rights.

UNCHRISTIAN CONDUCT OF EUROPEAN POWERS.

Mr. Davis finds much fault with the Christian nations of Europe, for their disregard of just, humane, and Christian duty, in refusing to recognize the Confederacy, thereby encouraging its enemies.

ENCOURAGING STATE OF THE REBEL FINANCES.

The public debt on the 1st of October was only $1,147,970,208, with the trifling exception of a foreign debt of £2,200,000, and another little item of County funds, the figures of which are not given; so the state of the finances is regarded as encouraging. Some little trouble is anticipated from the depreciation of Treasury notes, caused by redundancy and lack of confidence in redemption.

SLAVES AS SOLDIERS—SHALL EMANCIPATION BE USED AS AN INDUCEMENT?—THEIR EMPLOYMENT JUSTIFIABLE ON THE CONFEDERATE SIDE, AND BARBAROUS ON THE OTHER.

Viewed merely as property, and therefore as the subject of impressment, the service or labor of the slave has been frequently claimed for short periods in the construction of defensive works.—The slave, however, bears another relation to the State, that of a person. The law of last February contemplates only the relation of the slave to the master, and limits the impressment to a certain term of service. But for the purposes enumerated in the act, instruction in the manner of camping, marching and packing trains is needful, so that even in this limited employment, length of service adds greatly to the value of the negroe's labor. Hazard is also encountered in all positions he can be assigned to service with the army, and the duties required of them demand loyalty and zeal. In this respect the relation of person predominates so far as to render it doubtful whether the private right of property can consistently and beneficially be continued and it would seem proper to acquire for the public service the entire property in the labor of the slave, and to pay therefor due compensation, rather than to impress his labor for short terms; and this the more especially as the effect of the present law would vest this entire property in all cases where the slave might be re-captured after compensation for his loss had been paid to the private owner. Whenever the entire property in the service of the slave is thus acquired by the Government, the question is presented under what tenure he should be held. Should he be retained in servitude, or should his emancipation be held out to him as the reward for his faithful service, or should it be granted at once on the promise of such service; and if emancipated, what action should be taken to secure for the freed man the permission of the State from which he was drawn to reside within its limits after the close of his public service. The permission would doubtless be more readily accorded as a reward for past faithful service; and a double motive for the zealous discharge of duty would thus be offered by those employed by the Government, their freedom, and the gratification of the local attachment which is so marked a characteristic of the negro, and forms so powerful an incentive to his action. The policy of engaging to liberate the negro after service faithfully rendered, seems to me preferable to that of granting immediate manumission, or that of retaining him in servitude. If this policy should recommend itself to the judgment of Congress, it is suggested that, in addition to the duties heretofore performed by the slave he might be advantageously employed as pioneer and engineer laborer; and in that event, that the number should be augmented to forty thousand.

Beyond this limit and these employments it does not seem to me desirable, under existing circumstances, to go. A broad, moral distinction exists between the use of slaves as soldiers in the defence of their homes, and the incitement of the same persons to insurrection against their masters. The one is justifiable if necessary, the other is iniquitous and unworthy a civilized people; and such is the judgment of all writers on public law, as well as that expressed and insisted on by our enemies in all wars prior to the one now waged against us. By none have the practices of which they are now guilty been denounced with greater severity than by themselves in the two years wars with Great Britain in the last and in the present century; and in the Declaration of Independence of 1776, when enumeration was made of the wrongs which justified the revolt from Great Britain, the climax of atrocity was deemed to be reached only when the English monarch was denounced as having "excited domestic insurrection amongst us."

The subject is to be viewed by us therefore, solely in the light of policy and our social economy. When so regarded, I must dissent from those who advise a general levy and arming of the slaves for the duty of soldiers. Until our white population shall prove insufficient for the armies we require and can afford to keep in the field, to employ as a soldier the negro who has merely been trained to labor, and as a laborer the white man, accustomed from his youth to the use of fire-arms, would scarcely be deemed wise or advantageous by any; and this is the question now before us. But should the alternative of subjugation or the employment of slaves as soldiers ever be presented, there seems no reason to doubt what should then be our decision. Whether our view embraces what would in so extreme a case be the sum of misery entailed by the dominion of the enemy, or be restricted solely to the effect upon the welfare and happiness of the negro population themselves, the result would be the same. The appalling demoralization, suffering, disease and death which have been caused by partially substituting the invader's system of police, for the kind relation previously subsisting between the master and slave, have been a sufficient demonstration that external interference with the institution of domestic slavery is productive of evil only. If the subject involved no other consideration than the mere right of property, the sacrifices heretofore made by our people have been such as to permit no doubt of their readiness to surrender every possession in order to secure their independence. But the social and political question which is exclusively under the control of the several States, has a far wider and more enduring importance than that of pecuniary interest. In its manifold phases it embraces the stability of our republican institutions resting on the actual political equality of all its citizens, and includes the fulfilment of the task which has been so happily begun—that of christianizing and improving the Africans who have, in the will of Providence, been placed in our charge. Comparing the results of our own experience with those of the experiments of others who have borne similar relations to the African race, the people of the several States of the Confederacy have abundant reason to be satisfied with the past, and to use the greatest circumspection in determining their course. These contingencies, however, are rather applicable to the improbable contingency of our need of resorting to the element of resistance than to our present condition. If the recommendation above made for the training of forty thousand negroes for the service indicated shall meet your approval, it is certain that even this limited number, by their preparatory training in intermediate duties, would form a more valuable reserve force in case of urgency, than three-fold their number suddenly called from field labor, while a fresh levy could to a certain extent, supply their places in the special service for which they are now employed.

THE WELL KNOWN DISPOSITION OF THE CONFEDERATE GOVERNMENT FOR PEACE.

The disposition of this Government for a peaceful solution of the issues which the enemy has referred to the arbitrament of arms has been too often manifested, and is too well-known to need new assurances. But while it is true that individuals and parties in the United States have indicated a desire to substitute reason for force, and by negotiation to stop the further sacrifice of human life, and to arrest the calamities which now afflict both countries, the authorities who control the Government of our enemies have too often and too clearly expressed their resolution so make no peace except on terms of unconditional submission and degradation, to leave us any hope of the cessation of hostilities until the delusion of their ability to conquer us is dispelled. Among those who are already disposed for peace, many are actuated by principle and by disapproval and abhorrence of the iniquitous warfare that their Government is waging, while others are moved to the conviction that it is no longer to the interest of the United States to continue a struggle in which success is unattainable. Whenever this fast growing conviction shall have taken firm root in the minds of a majority of the Northern people there will be produced that willingness to negotiate for peace which is now confined to our side. Peace is manifestly impossible unless desired by both parties to the war, and the disposition for it among our enemies will be best and most certainly evoked by the demonstration on our part of ability and unshaken determination to defend our rights, and to hold no earthly price too dear for their purchase. Whenever there shall be on the part of our enemies a desire for peace there will be no difficulty in finding means by which negotiation can be opened, but it is obvious that no agency can be called into action until this desire shall be mutual. When that contingency shall happen, the Government, to which is confided the treaty making power, can be at no loss for means adapted to accomplish so desirable an end.

SINKING OF THE RAM ALBEMARLE.

REPORT OF LIEUTENANT CUSHING.

Admiral Porter has communicated to the Secretary of the Navy the following interesting particulars from Lieut. Cushing, in regard to the sinking of the rebel ram Albemarle:

ALBEMARLE SOUND, MONDAY, OCT. 30, 1864.—SIR: I have the honor to report the rebel iron-clad Albemarle is at the bottom of the Roanoke River. On the night of the 27th, having prepared my steam launch, I proceeded up toward Plymouth with thirteen officers and men, partly volunteers, from the squadron. The distance from the mouth of the river to the ram was about eight miles, the stream averaging in width about 200 yards, and lined with the enemy's pickets. A mile below the town was the wreck of the Southfield surrounded by some schooners, and it was understood that a gun was mounted there to command the bend. I therefore took one of the Shamrock's cutters in tow, with orders to cast off and board at that point, if we were hailed. Our boat succeeded in passing the pickets, and even the Southfield within twenty yards, without discovery, and we were not hailed until by the look-outs on the ram. The cutter was then cast off and ordered below, while we made for our enemy under a full head of steam. The rebels sprung their rattle, rang the bell, and commenced firing at the same time, repeating their hail and seeming much confused. The light of a fire ashore showed me the iron-clad made fast to the wharf with logs around her about thirty feet from her side. Passing her closely we made a complete circle so as to strike her fairly, and went into her, bows on. By this time the enemy's fire was very severe, but a dose of canister at short range seemed to moderate their zeal and disturb their aim. Paymaster Swan, of the Otsego, was wounded near me, but how many more I know not. Three bullets struck my clothing, and the air seemed full of them. In a moment we had struck the logs just abreast of the quarter port, breaking them in some feet, our bows resting on them. The torpedo boom was then lowered and by a vigorous pull I succeeded in driving the torpedo under the over hang and exploding it at the same time that the Albemarle's gun was fired. A shot seemed to go crashing through my boat and a dense mass of water rushed in from the torpedo filling the launch and completely disabling her. The enemy then continued his fire at fifteen feet range and demanded our surrender, which I twice refused, ordering the men to save themselves, and removing my overcoat and shoes. Springing into the river I swam with others into the middle of the stream, the rebels failing to hit us. The most of our party were captured; some were drowned, and only one escaped besides myself, and he in another direction. Acting-Marshal's mate, Woodman, of the Commodore Hull, met him in the water half a mile below the town, and assisted him as best he could, but failed to get him ashore. Completely exhausted I managed to reach the shore, but was too weak to crawl out of the water until just daylight, when I managed to creep into the swamp close to the fort. While hiding, close to the path, the Albemarle's officers passed, and I judged from their conversation that the ship was destroyed. Some hours travelling in the swamp served to bring me out well below the town, when I sent a negro in to gain information and found that the ram was truly sunk. Proceeding through another swamp I came to a creek and captured a skiff belonging to a picket of the enemy, and with this, by eleven o'clock the next night, I made my way out to the Valley City. Acting Master's Mate Wm. L. Howeth, of the Mouncello, showed, as usual, conspicuous in bravery. He is the same officer who has been with me twice in Wilmington harbor. I trust he may be promoted when exchanged, as well as Acting Third Assistant Engineer Stolsbury, who, being for the first time under fire, handled his engine promptly and with coolness. All the officers and men behaved in the most gallant manner. The cutter of the Shamrock boarded the Southfield, but found no guns there. Four prisoners were taken there. The ram is now completely submerged and the enemy have sunk three schooners in the river to obstruct the passage of our ships. I desire to call the attention of the Admiral and Department to the spirit manifested by the sailors on the ships in these Sounds. But few hands were wanted, but all hands were eager to go into the action, many offering their chosen shipmates a month's pay to resign in their favor. I am, sir, respectfully, your obedient servant,

W. B. CUSHING, Lieut. U. S. N.

Rear-Admiral D. D. Porter, Commanding N. A. Squadron.

The name of the man who escaped is Wm. Hoftman, seaman, on the Chicopee. He did his duty well, and deserves a medal of honor. Respectfully,

W. B. CUSHING, U. S. N.

"A YOUNG woman in Jackson, Michigan, has been carrying on the recruiting business in an original and highly peculiar manner. She marries a man on condition that he will enlist and give her his bounty. She being strikingly handsome, the man consents. After he is gone, she marries another. Four men has she thus wedded and sent to the army. On the fifth occasion she was detected."

It is possible the young lady may have been animated by the most fervent patriotism, and that it would be well to issue to her a recruiting commission.

WASHINGTON  DEMOCRAT.

THE ADVOCATE OF JUST PRINCIPLES FOUNDED UPON A STRICT ADHERENCE TO THE CONSTITUTION AND THE LAWS.

VOL. 1. OLYMPIA, WASHINGTON TERRITORY, NOVEMBER 19, 1864. NO. 3.

The Washington Democrat.
URBAN E. HICKS,
EDITOR AND PROPRIETOR.

Agents of the Washington Democrat.

The following named gentlemen are authorized to receive and receipt for subscriptions, advertisements, job work, &c., for the WASHINGTON DEMOCRAT:

Dr. E. Shiel, Hon. Frank P. Dugan	Walla Walla.
Hon. Louis Sohns, A. J. Lawrence, Esq.	Vancouver.
John Catlin	Portland, Or.
Hon. Columbia Lancaster	St. Helens.
Dr. N. Ostander	Monticello.
Henry Jackson	Cowlitz Co.
Hon. O. B. McFadden, Henry Miles	Lewis Co.
Dr. J. N. Johnson	Pacific Co.
Stephen Guthrie, Major Jas. Tilton	Thurston Co.
Stephen Judson, George Gallagher,	Pierce Co.
E. A. Wilson	Mason Co.
C. C. Terry, A. B. Rabbeson	King Co.
M. S. Drew, Jared S. Hurd	Kitsap Co.
Dr. P. M. O'Brien, Hon. J. J. H. Vanbokkelin.	Jefferson Co.
George W. Beam	Island Co.
H. C. Barkhousen	Whatcom Co.

Jeffersonian Democratic Platform.

LAID DOWN BY THOMAS JEFFERSON IN 1801.

"*Equal and exact justice to all men, of whatever State or persuasion, religious and political.*

Peace, commerce, and honest friendship with all nations—entangling alliances with none.

The support of State governments in all their rights, as the most complete administration for our domestic concerns, and the surest bulwarks against anti republican tendencies.

The preservation of the General Government in its whole constitutional vigor, as the sheet anchor of our peace at home, and safety abroad.

A jealous care of the right of election by the people—a mild and safe correction of the abuses which are lopped off by the sword of revolution where peaceable remedies are unprovided.

Absolute acquiescence in the decisions of the majority—the vital principle of Republics—from which there is no appeal, except to force, the vital principle and immediate parent of despotism.

A well disciplined militia—our best reliance in peace and war, till regulars may relieve them.

The supremacy of the civil over the military authority.

Economy in the public expenses, that labor may be lightly burdened.

The honest payment of our debts and sacred preservation of the public faith.

Encouragement of agriculture, and of commerce as its hand-maid.

The diffusion of information and the arraignment of all abuses at the bar of public reason.

Freedom of religion.

Freedom of speech.

Freedom of the press.

Freedom of persons under the protection of the habeas corpus and trial by juries impartially selected."

[From our Extra of Monday last.]

WE regret to be again compelled to ask the indulgence of our subscribers for another week in the non-appearance of the DEMOCRAT. We hoped to have had all things completed sufficiently to enable us to resume its publication on yesterday, but in consequence of the extreme length of the late laws of Crngress, which Mr. Prosch was compelled to finish before the transfer of the printing establishment to us, we have been delayed two weeks longer than was anticipated. This, together with the extra labor attendant upon the removal of our material from Steilacoom to Olympia, is a sufficient excuse. We are now however, "all right," and our friends and patrons may confidently expect the regular reception each week, of the DEMOCRAT from and after Saturday next.

BY some mysterious operation in the Telegraph Office at Portland, our regular telegraphic reports failed to reach us in time for this extra. We are disposed to believe that the telegraph machine, under the control of an operator, employed by Republican journals in this place to make up late dispatches for them, has become so extremely "loyal" that dispatches to a Democratic press cannot be sent along the line, even though an extortionate price was offered and would have been readily paid for every word and syllable. We do not wish to be hasty in our conclusions, but at this hour we are totally unable to account for the failure upon any other grounds.

We have not time now to acquaint our readers with the facts in the case, but shall do so in full in our issue on Saturday next. In the meantime, our patrons may rest assured that no effort will be spared to furnish them the very latest news—provided, hard Democratic money will buy dispatches as readily as greenbacks.

ACCIDENT.—An accident occurred at Tumwater on Saturday evening last, by the premature discharge of a cannon, which was being fired by the friends of "Old Abe," wounding Mr. Dudley Barnes in the left arm. The injury is said to be painful though not serious.

GREAT EXCITEMENT!
NEW GOLD AND SILVER DISCOVERIES

The people of Puget Sound are now in the midst of the greatest excitement ever before witnessed in this country, consequent upon recent discoveries of extensive and rich gold and silver-bearing quartz ledges, on the western slope of the Cascade Range, not more than 40 or 50 miles distant from this place, and within 20 or 30 miles of water navigation on the Sound. The discovery was made by Mr. Geo. Carpenter, in company with two other "prospectors," on their way across the Cascades from the Eastern side, coming over the Natchess Pass. The party had by accident travelled off of the main road some two or three miles to the south, when their attention was attracted by an unusual show of quartz rock exposed near the surface by the upturning of the roots of large fallen trees. Upon examination of the quartz, they discovered plain indications of both gold and silver, and having secured a few specimens for the purpose of testing, they hurried into Steilacoom and immediately sent the specimens to Victoria to be assayed. The assay return being even better than anticipated, Mr. Carpenter immediately started in return to the place of discovery, taking with him Hon. Sam. McCaw, of Steilacoom, and one or two other friends, but before reaching the ledge, however, the news had spread, and some 40 or 50 persons met there almost simultaneously. Claims were immediately taken up and mining laws enacted—copies of which we hope to receive soon for publication.

About 1,000 pounds of the quartz was brought into Steilacoom last week by Messrs. McCaw and uggins, and is now on the way to San Francisco to be thoroughly tested.—There is no doubt of the existence of gold and silver in this rock, as particles of gold can be distinctly seen with the naked eye in many places. The ledge lies North-west and South-east, and is said to be from 75 to 150 feet in width, and has already been traced a distance of more than three miles, in an unbroken lead, and we doubt not can and will be traced much further in a few days. It is probable that 400 or 500 claims have already been located, and perhaps several thousand will be before Spring. Intense excitement has seized upon our people, and almost every one who can leave home has either gone, or is about to go out in a day or two. The distance is but short, and the route easily travelled, as a good wagon-road leads from Steilacoom to within a dozen miles of the mines, already. Much strife and speculation has commenced regarding town sites and trading points, and a lively race has begun between Steilacoom, Seattle and Olympia [illegible] of each, claiming pecuniary advantages over the other. With this, however, we have nothing to do, only rejoicing in the fact that a discovery has at last been made which will unquestionably benefit and build up the whole country and every section and town thereof. More anon.

SEIZED.—The ship *Clara Morse*, Capt. Lawrence, recently loaded at Freeport Mills, for London, was seized by the Captain of the *Jenny Jones*, at Port Townsend on the 4th inst. The circumstances, as related to us by Capt. Lawrence, are as follows: The *Jenny Jones* engaged to be in readiness, on the morning of the 3rd, to tow the above vessel to Port Angelos, not arriving, however, the ship was sailed to Port Townsend, anchored and Capt. Lawrence proceeded to Victoria in search of a crew. Capt. Jones, arriving at Freeport a few hours after his appointed time and finding the ship had sailed, also proceeded to Port Townsend, seized, and entered suit against the ship for libel and towage.

The *Clara Morse* is one of the largest vessels that ever visited Puget Sound—carrying nearly one million feet of lumber and spars.

Upper Columbia Items.

We clip the following items from the *Walla Walla Statesman* of Nov. 4th:

RETURNING HOME.—A party of Walla Walla-ans, who left here last Spring to seek their fortunes in the auriferous fields of Kootenai, returned this week. Among them is Mr. H. Ackley, who, as he says, "has sold out and has no further interest in British Columbia." Mr. A. thinks that not over two or three hundred men will winter in the mines. Work is about suspended for the season. The chief mining operations have been on the famous Wild Horse Creek. Nothing could be done on Finlay Creek on account of high water.—He met several hundred pack animals going in. Flour was worth $36 ℔ cwt.; bacon, 75 cts ℔ lb; sugar, 60 cts. ℔ lb; cogee, 60@65 cts. ℔ lb; potatoes, 10@15 cts. ℔ lb; onions, 35@40 cts. ℔ lb.

We are informed by Mr. Bledsoe, of Wells, Fargo & Co.'s Express, that a man by the name of Strong, in Powder River Valley, was killed one night last week in an affray growing out of some domestic difficulty. He was literally hewn to pieces with a hatchet.

Large numbers of miners are now arriving from Warren's, Florence, Oro Fino, Elk City and other camps above, to remain during the winter. Very few go below, as they can make wages for the winter by remaining at Lewiston.

Marion Thomas, writing to his brother Newton Thomas, a packer belonging to this place, under date of October 5th, from Wild Horse creek, in speaking of the names and prospects of the country, says: "A piece of gold was found about one and a half miles above town weighing nine pounds, which would be $1,944 solid gold." Gentlemen of this place, knowing Mr. Thomas, vouch for the correctness of the statement. Kootenai gold is current at $18 per ounce in our market. This is a little the largest piece taken out north of California.

LATE EASTERN NEWS!

The *Times'* Atlanta dispatch says that Atlanta has been completely isolated for several weeks. At one time it was feared that our provisions were giving out. No danger is apprehended from that source now. Forage for animals was wanted some weeks ago, but foraging parties in the surrounding country have supplied all immediate wants.

The latest dispatches from Sherman state that the road is clear, and that railroad communication has been re-established.

NASHVILLE, Nov. 5.—A rebel force attempted to cross the Tennessee at the mouth of the Bluewater, on the 3d, but were repulsed with loss. Three regiments of rebel cavalry are reported between Decatur and Courland. Forrest, with a cavalry force, is reported near Johnsonville.

NEW YORK, Nov. 6.—It is officially announced to-day that Gen. Butler is to command the Department of the East. Over 10,000 troops have arrived here within the past two days, and they will report to Butler. The authorities possess information of a plan for a riot on election day, which was fully matured. A large number of Southerners who have been in the city for several months, will be here for that purpose.

The *Herald's* correspondent from Nashville says that Sherman has sent the 4th corps to Decatur to operate against Hood, while with the remaining five corps he moved to Atlanta, and is probably about to inaugurate an offensive campaign from that point, ignoring the existence of Hood, or leaving him to prosecute his campaign in Tennessee at his leisure.

SUSPENSION BRIDGE, Nov. 6.—Great excitement exists on the American side in regard to the anticipated raid. Citizens are arming themselves, goods and valuables are being removed, and a special train with troops is expected here to-night.

BUFFALO, Nov. 6.—The following extract is from a letter received by the editor of the *Express*, from Danville, C. W., Nov. 5:

"Look out for a raid on Buffalo from Toronto and Hamilton on the 8th. The advance guard is at Fort Erie and Suspension Bridge, or will be on Monday 7th. The headquarters of the army are at Toronto. Some leading Canadians direct the movement. The raiders are not all Southerners. The writer asserts that most of them are Northern Democrats. The letter is signed by John B. Halley.

HEADQUARTERS, Army of the Potomac, Nov. 6.—A lively time occurred between the pickets on the left of our line on the night of the 4th, resulting in the loss of men on each side. Yesterday there was a good [illegible] Jerusalem plank road without loss to us. Last night the pickets in the same vicinity opened fire shortly after dark and kept it up sharply all night. At 11 o'clock, A. M., the rebels attempted to advance their picket line and recover the ground taken last week, but failed. A citizen of Richmond arrived in our lines yesterday morning to escape conscription. He tells a story of want and destitution in that city; riots occurring daily in the streets, and of the high prices of the necessaries of life, etc. He says the rebels in front of Petersburg are mining under our works. Little faith is put in the report.

WASHINGTON, Nov. 7.—It is estimated that during the last week fifty thousand persons left here to vote at the Presidential election.

A letter received from an officer commanding one of the vessels of the Trans-Mississippi Squadron, dated Chattanooga, Nov. 1st says: My boat had two brushes with Hood's forces and repulsed him both times. He has now gone below the shoals. A large portion of his army has arrived at Florence for the invasion of Middle and Eastern Tennessee. Hood is represented as being tyranical in the extreme. His men dined for two days on corn and water with an occasional addition of some pumpkins stolen by the way. He suffers by desertion of these people who say he intended moving southward but was prevented by the threats of his soldiers to desert if he did not give them the promised harvest in East Tennessee. He will likely be bagged. Sherman is pursuing, Gen. Cross flanking and General Thomas is ahead.

CHICAGO, Nov. 7.—The *Journal* says: Yesterday telegrams were received announcing the coming of a large number of Bushwhackers. Colonel Sweet. commanding Camp Douglas, was communicated with and orders were immediately issued for arresting the desperadoes on their arrival. The fact soon leaked out and the faithful found means to apprise their friends. The Bushwhackers left the train at the city limits and scattered in the city in various directions. The military and police are constantly scouring the country and have succeeded in picking up hundreds of them. A propeller having on board nearly one hundred suspicious characters arrived this morning from Canada. The military and police are after them and all will be captured. Col. Sweet has long been aware of the existence of a rebel plot to release the prisoners in Camp Douglas and burn the city. His detectives have been at work with success, though the evidence obtained is insufficient to warrant the arrest of the conspirators, and it was deemed necessary to strike at once such as were unquestionably treasonable. Sweet has proof of a plan of the rebel conspirators to release the rebel prisoners and burn the city. Camp Douglas was to have been attacked on two sides to-morrow night, the prisoners released and the city pillaged and burnt. The police made a raid early this morning on the Donelson House, Canal street, and captured forty Bushwhackers, who had been tracked there. All were armed to the teeth. A mounted patrol of five hundred men has been organized by the citizens for the protection of the city, which will be on duty all night. There is enough military force here to prevent an outbreak.

Hancock, agent of the New York line of propellers, received a dispatch to-day stating the Canadian steamer *Georgian*, fitted out as a pirate, is on Lake Huron.

NEW YORK, Nov. 7.—The *Commercial's* Washington dispatch says: California officials express fears that the secession refugees in Mexico will endeavor to expel the American Minister from Sonora and excite a tumult between the two countries.

The Richmond *Enquirer* of the 3d announced the capture of Plymouth, North Carolina, by our gunboats after three hours fighting. The forts being passed all the guns were dismantled, and the rebels evacuated under a severe fire.

The express train from Dunkirk to New York &c., was thrown down an embankment 40 feet by the displacement of a switch. The engineer was seriously hurt, also forty others injured. A number who were dangerously wounded were under the debris could be seen but could not yet be recovered.

EUGENE CITY, Nov. 10.—A serious affray occurred at Long Tom this afternoon, in which two persons were severely wounded. It appears that a married couple, named Brown, having one child, agreed to live separately, Mrs. Brown taking with her the child, which she sent to school. Mr. Brown went to the school-house to obtain possession of the child, but the teacher refused to deliver it up to him. Mrs. Brown, hearing of this occurrence, hastened to the school-house, accompanied by a Mr. and Mrs. Childers, to prevent her husband from taking the child. Some angry words ensued, which resulted in Childers shooting at Brown, wounding him severely in the neck. Brown returned the fire, but missed Childers, the ball striking Mrs. Brown, and inflicted a dangerous wound.

The telegraphic reports of the Presidential election say, Lincoln has carried nearly, if not quite all the States. We acknowledge, with deep felt sorrow, the belief that he has been elected, though we place but little reliance in the reported majorities. Sufficient time has not yet elapsed to sum up the whole vote, and hopes are entertained that the Democracy have carried Pennsylvania, New York, Kentucky, New Jersey and Deleware.

Letter From Leslie Coombs.

FRANKFORT, KY., Sept. 19, 1864.

MY DEAR SIR:—Your letter of the 8th, being directed to Lexington, did not reach me till Saturday, when I had my weekly visit to my family of children and grandchildren. You may remember that, in 1860, the Union party, with the writer as their candidate, carried this State by over [illegible] majority, against the whole power of the National and State Administrations, and of course I could not allow myself to neglect my official duties then assumed. Our court commenced an adjourned term a week since, and will probably hold on for three weeks yet to come; after that I shall be footloose, and feel disposed to devote my whole time and energy to the great cause in which our hearts and judgments are all engaged. I have never spoken to an audience in your State, and should be especially pleased to meet my old Whig friends and counsel with them freely on the terrible state of the times, and the eventful future soon to constitute history.

In my deliberate judgment, if Mr. Lincoln is re-elected we shall have a military despotism fastened upon us and our children, with a standing army of free negro jannissaries. At first, they may be confined to locations south of the Susquehanna and Ohio, but unless we agree to be taxed also with a standing army of white men several thousand strong, they will, now and then, be sent across those rivers just preceding important elections, in order to preserve order at the polls and enforce obedience to power. The Government is now erecting strong, permanent fortifications, at the cost of millions of dollars, throughout Kentucky, which the Abolitionists consider a troublesome Border State, and filling them with negro soldiers, mainly recruits from loyal citizens in the State. The same thing is being done, you know, from Cairo to Balize, so that when the rebellion is crushed out, and the white rebels "extirpated"—for that is the programme—the whole southern country will be under the exclusive control of free negroes, with State lines obliterated or held for naught. The western and northwestern States will find, to their sorrow, when the Mississippi river is thus under this ignorant African control, they will be forced to submit to the degradation and danger, or abandon all southern trade.

The black troops are everywhere the pets and favorites of Lincoln & Co. Every Abolition political General lauds them to the skies.

An instance of naked favoritism came under my own observation in Lexington within the last three days. On Saturday, as I landed from the cars, a large negro regiment, mainly Kentucky slaves, were parading the streets, with full music, mounted on good, fat horses, finely dressed and with fancy caps, armed *cap a-pie*.

Yesterday I saw three regiments of white cavalry or mounted infantry as they were termed— I think from Illinois and Indiana—just returning from Stoneman's raid, pale, sallow and leg-weary, (for they were all on foot,) with ragged clothes and dirty shirts, wending their way slowly through the city to some temporary camp, until they could be sent on another expedition to the front, while the negroes would be left behind, marauding through this country to bedevil our citizens and keep our families in constant terror. I think my old Whig friends north of the Ohio, if they could witness what I have described, would rush in solid masses to the polls in November, and help to save the country, by voting once for a Democratic ticket, as I intend to do.

I fully reciprocate your kind expressions of personal regard, and subscribe myself,

Very truly yours,

LESLIE COOMBS.

D. H. PINNEY, Joliet, Ill.

[From the New York Evening Post.]

AN EXPLANATION BY GENERAL EARLY.

BURNING OF CHAMBERSBURG.

The substance of the following explanatory statement from the rebel Gen. Early was published in the *Evening Post*. We now give the statement in full as a bit of current history. It appears in the form of a speech delivered to the men carried off as hostages:

"GENTLEMEN:—I have had you arrested merely as 'hostages' to secure the release of six gentlemen residing near Hedgesville, in Virginia, who are now imprisoned by the Federal Government in consequence of the burning of the house of a Mr. Cookus by Confederate troops.

"I have examined the facts in the case, and am thoroughly satisfied that the burning was purely accidental; that, in burning some railroad property which they had been ordered to destroy, the fire, in spite of their efforts, was communicated to the house of Mr. Cookus, not far distant. And yet those six gentlemen, a Rev. Mr. Tongue, a Methodist preacher in that village, who was remarkable as a pious, good man, who did not interfere with politics, and five other gentlemen in the neighborhood, who were just as ignorant of the approach or purpose of the troops as any of you, are now in prison in consequence of the burning of that house. The families were stripped of all their personal property, and having no means of conveyance, the daughter of the preacher and the neice of one of the others walked eight miles to my headquarters, and with streaming eyes and sad hearts implored my aid in some manner to afford relief. They first wished me to arrest some of their Union neighbors; but I did not feel it proper for the Southern Confederady to retaliate upon its own citizens. Those men, however misguided they may be, are still citizens of the State of Virginia and under the protection of her laws; and we hope and trust they will soon see their errors, and yield a cordial allegiance to her government. But if they should not, it must devolve on the State of Virginia to deal with them according to her own laws. A mere difference of political opinion ought not and must not subject them to military rule. And, therefore, inflexibly opposed as I always have been to the destruction of private property, or the molestation of non-combatant citizens, yet it is always in the power of one army to force the other into retaliation.

"To illustrate my own views on that subject, permit me to say that, very recently, a short distance across the river, I approved a very severe sentence of two years in the penitentiary, passed upon a soldier for stealing the horse of a notoriously decided Union man. I will further remark that this is the fifth time I have been in Maryland at the head of an army; yet I believe not one private house has been injured nor non-combatant molested. Once I marched almost to the banks of the Susquehanna at Harrisburg, and thence down to Wrightsville, when the Federal troops, to escape our pursuit, set fire to the bridge in the middle, whence the flames rapidly extended westward, and from its proximity placed the town of Wrightsville in very imminent peril. My troops had just heard of the burning of the town of Darien, in Georgia, by the Federal army; a large number of my men were from that region, and very naturally felt a strong impulse for retaliation; but at my very urgent appeal they all, with alacrity and energy, joined in a united effort and actually extinguished the flames in time to save the town, and were richly rewarded by the grateful thanks of its citizens, who also bitterly denounced their own troops for exposing them to such danger. In York, Pennsylvania, I found two large manufactories engaged in making railroad cars for the Government, which of course it was my duty to destroy; but a slight examination satisfied me that to burn these would seriously endanger a large portion of the town; and hence I spared them for a moderate ransom. On my return I partly retraced my advancing track, and was greatly surprised to find so little evidence or trace of the passage of so large an army. In fact, except in horses and forage for the army, very little damage had been sustained

"Recently, in Maryland, the house of Governor Bradford was burned without my orders. But I must add that I approved it; and had I been present would have ordered it in retaliation for the burning of the house of Governor Letcher, whom I know to be a very poor man, and whose family were not allowed five minutes to remove clothing or other valuables. Afterwards, when in front of Washington, some of my troops were very determined to destroy the house of Mr. Francis P. Blair, and had actually removed some of its furniture, probably supposing it to belong to his son, the member of the Federal Cabinet. As soon as I came up I immediately stopped the proceedings, and compelled the men to immediately return every article as far as I knew, and placed a guard to protect it. The house of his son, Montgomery Blair, a member of the Cabinet was subjected to a different rule, for obvious reasons.

Gen. Hunter, in his recent raid to Lynchburg, caused wide-spread ruin wherever he passed. I followed him about sixty miles, and language would fail me to describe the terrible desolation which marked his path. Dwelling houses and other buildings were almost universally burned; fences, implements of husbandry, and everything available for the sustenance of human life, so far as he could do so, were everywhere destroyed. We found many, very many familes of helpless women and children who had been suddenly turned out of doors, and their houses and contents condemned to the flames; and in some cases, where they had rescued extra clothing, the soldiers had torn the garments into narrow strips, and strewn them upon the ground for us to witness when we arrived in pursuit.

"Gen. Hunter has been much censured by the voice of humanity everywhere, and he richly deserves it all; yet he has caused scarcely one-tenth part of the devastation which has been committed immediately in sight of the headquarters of Gen. Meade and Gen. Grant, in Eastern Virginia. For example, in Culpepper county, where Gen. Meade held his headquarters, almost every house and building has been burned; very few have escaped the flames; and utter desolation is seen on every hand. Even a small tannery in sight of Gen. Meade's headquarters, where a poor man tanned a few hides for his neighbors on the shares, to furnish shoes for the poor women and children who were necessarily left there, was burned by the army, and the half-tanned skins drawn from the vats and cut into narrow strips to prevent the possibility of their being useful.

"Recently they have burned the residence of Andrew Hunter, near Charlestown, with all its contents, requiring his family to stand by and witness the destruction of their home. They did the same with the house of Edmund J. Lee, near Shepherdstown, and repeated it on the buildings of Hon. Alex. R. Boteler.

"Such things, of course, cannot be long endured, and must provoke retaliation whenever it is possible. Accordingly I lately sent Gen. McCausland to Pennsylvania. I did not wish to retaliate in Maryland, because we all hope and believe that Maryland will eventually be a member of the Southern Confederacy. I therefore sent him to Pennsylvania, with written instructions to demand of the authorities of Chambersburg a sum which would be sufficient to indemnify those gentlemen, and also pay some other damages, which I specified in the order; and on default in their compliance, he was instructed to burn the town, which I learn was done. I was very reluctant, and it was a very disagreeable duty to inflict such damages upon those citizens; but I deemed it an imperative necessity to show the people of the Federal States that war has two sides. I hope and believe it has had, and will have, a good effect. I saw with much pleasure, since then, an able article in the *National Intelligencer*, which called upon the North to consider gravely whether such a mode of warfare as they had inaugurated is likely to yield a success commensraute to its cost.

"And now, gentlemen, I will repeat my sincere regret that I am obliged to subject you to this inconvenience. I have no object but to procure the release of these six citizens of Virginia who are now wrongfully imprisoned, and therefore will make you as comfortable as possible. It is notorious that many of our most respectable citizens, who have been imprisoned by your Government for similar and less serious causes, have been confined in the same room with condemned malefactors. Gentlemen, you need have no fears of such treatment whilst in my custody. I propose to retain four of you, and release the fifth on his parole that he will use his utmost efforts to procure the release of those six gentlemen. If he succeeds you will be discharged at once; but if he fails to accomplish this within two weeks he must surrender himself again to my custody.

"In conclusion, I will add that no citizen or resident of Maryland had any previous knowledfie of my purpose to arrest you; that your names were furnished by one connected with my army, and without reference to the greater or less intensity of your feelings. The fact that you are reputed to be Union men causes no bitterness of feeling on my part, for I do not forget that I was a Union man myself so long as I deemed Union possible. I was an old line Whig and voted for Bell and Everett. I was a delegate from Franklin county in the Virginia Convention, and zealously opposed and voted against the ordinance of secession from the beginning to the end. But the course of events has since thoroughly satisfied me of my error. I now conscientiously believe that it was an absolute necessity; that the salvation of Virginia depended upon it."

SOME LOYAL TALK.—Let us see what the "loyal" party thinks of the Constitution and the Union. We will here quote from some of their leaders—we have quoted from others, and will yet occasionslly show what they say of the Union:

"Who in the name of God wants the Cotton States, or any other States this side of perdition, to remain in the Union, if slavery is to continue."—[Bingham, of Ohio.]

"Mark the man who prates about the inviolability of the Constitution. He is a traitor."—[Sumner of Massachusetts.]

"This talk of restoring the Union as it was, under the Constitution as it is, is one of the absurdities which I have heard repeated until I have become about sick of it. The Union can never be restored as it was. There are many things which render such an event impossible. This Union never shall, with my consent, be restored under the Constitution as it is, slavery to be protected by it."—[Stevens of Pennsylvania.]

"I trust in God never to see this war end with the Constitution as it is and the Union as it was. Slavery must perish, or we will have fought in vain."—[Conway, of Kansas.]

"The Democracy say they want the Union as it, but God forbid that the Union shall be restored until that which was the cause of the rebellion be destroyed. Blow after blow has been struck on its front, and blow thall follow blow until slavery shall be wiped out, and freedom shall pervade the nation."—[Higby of California.]

Al. Ripson arrived on Monday evening direct from Florence and Warren's. The miners are still at work in Warren's. Mr. Ripson estimates that nearly one hundred men will winter in Warren's. At Florence, mining operations had nearly suspended. About three inches of snow had fallen at Warren's, and six inches at Florence.

An Affecting Incident.

During the proceedings of the Chicago Convention, and calling the roll of States for the presentation of credentials, the chairman of each delegation came forward and presented the credentials of himself and colleagues. Commencing with Maine, the Secretary called one State after another, until he reached that of Kentucky. There were two delegations from that State, and the Secretary paused a moment, as if in doubt whether to proceed further, but finally announced the name of the State. In answer to the call, Hon. Charles A. Wickliff and Hon. James Guthrie, Chairmen of the respective delegations, arose in their places at the extreme rear of the platform, and locking arms, advanced with slow and trembling steps to the Secretary's table.

There was that in the bearing of those venerable men, full of honors and associated for years past with their country's history, that told plainer than words, the purpose which brought them there—something which said those gray hairs and those aged forms, trembling and tottering upon the very verge of the grave, had not come up from their homes to that strange city for any less purpose than to assist in rescuing the honor and hopes of the country which had made their names great and honorable. As they advanced slowly up the broad aisle, one leaning upon the other, a deep emotion thilled that vast audience of thousands.

At last the Secretary's table was reached, and, surrendering each other's arms, these two old men, bowed beneath the weight of years, turned and faced each other in silence—and then, as if realizing suddenly the happy, peaceful days of their earlier manhood, when their country's glory was reflected upon them, and reviewing year by year, and step by step each advance to the present time, finally taking in at a rapid glance all the wide-spread ruin and devastation—these groans and tears, these widows and orphans, these millions of graves, the oceans of blood, this divided country—as if comparing the past with the present, and realizing, perhaps, stronger than ever before how unhappy is the great country they came from the very verge of the grave to try and save—these two old men fell upon each others' shoulders and wept over this ruin and appreciation of the terrible responsibilities resting upon them.

The vast audience was hushed—the sobs of the two old men who after years had palsied their tongues and wasted their strength, were about to undertake the greatest and grandest work of all their lives, alone thrilled the hearts of the thousands who gazed upon them. They did not weep alone, eyes that had known tears long since theirs, were wet too; heads which the frosts of winters had not yet clothed with the emblem of purity and peace were bowed with theirs. Ten thousand hearts swelling with one impulse thanked God that He had spared these two old men to this work, that He had willed that the heads already wreathed in honor should not be bowed down forever, until they had participated in the last great effort to rescue their country from irretrievable ruin, had been crowned with laurels before which all others pale and wither. A moment, that vast audience, rising to its feet, was silent before the sublime grandeur of the scene—a moment, and admiration for that noble grief carried it into the wildest applause, and ten thousand voices mingled in one, attesting the sympathy and admiration of the people.—*Newark* (N. J.) *Journal.*

American Women and the War.

The women of Carthage, when the Romans were at the gate, gave their hair to be made into bow-strings; the Countess Isabelle vowed never to change her chemise until the beseigers had been driven from her ramparts; and the butcher's wives of Newgate Market, declared they would drink no more burnt sack until King Charles' head was cut off—but I question whether either ancient or modern history can furnish an example of a conflict which was so much of a "Woman's War" as this. The bitterest, most vengeful of politicians in this ensanguined controversy are the ladies. They differ in opinion, but in exasperation and implacability they are unanimous. You have on one side, if you please, the pretty, timid, shrinking Puritan, Alice Bridgnorth—the pious, well-meaning, tract-distributing, flannel-petticoat-sewing, novel-writing, poetry-reading, chapel-haunting, parson-petting, negro-loving lady of New England, transformed into a termagant and a virago; and, on the other side, you have the haughty and defiant Flora M'Ivor, the embodiment of the indomitable will, and the constant mind of the South, ready to fasten the white cockade to the bonnet of her lover as he rides down the Conon-gate with Prince Charlie, but just as ready, and with fingers as firm, to stich at the shroud which is to enwrap the mangled remnants of that lover, after he has been hanged, drawn and quartered at Carlisle.—*Letter from America, in the London Times.*

Six thousand such "active preachers" as Tyng, Bellows and Beecher, are enough to raise hell and rebellion in the best government on the face of the earth. We've got a few of that stripe in this neck of woods, who follow as close to the heels of the bell weathers of the flock as their feeble abilities will allow. If they don't get badly singed in the next world, then there is no virtue in hell-fire, and future punishment is sheer humbug.—*Aurora Times.*

We learn that the friends of a young French officer, named Charles Sambeau, who served with distinction in our armies through the past three years, and was taken prisoner at Petersburg in July, recently applied to the War Department to obtain his exchange. Secretary Stanton, hearing the name Sambeau, and mistaking it for "Sambo," supposed that the captive was a black, and forthwith negotiated for his release.—*Phil. Age.*

WASHINGTON DEMOCRAT

OLYMPIA, W. T.

Saturday, November 19, 1864.

"Truth crushed to earth will rise again:
The eternal years of GOD are hers;
But error, wounded, writhes in pain,
And dies amid her worshipers."

THE WASHINGTON DEMOCRAT has more than double the circulation, and contains from two to three times more reading matter than any other newspaper in the Territory.

Lincoln's Election.

There is now no further doubt that the late Presidential canvass has resulted in the re-election of Abraham Lincoln, the Republican, Abolition and Miscegenation candidate. The contest was waged with energy and power, not to say with bitter and unrelenting severity. The whole force and talent of the Nation was enlisted in the strife. A stronger, more exciting, and important Presidential contest never, perhaps, took place since the formation of our Government. On the one hand was arrayed an implacable army of officers and appointees, numbering more than fourteen hundred thousand, besides a still greater army of shoddy contractors, paymasters, &c., which, together with the army of volunteer soldiers—most of whom are known to have been under the control of the President and his Major-Generals—all together numbering, at least, one to every five voters in the States allowed a vote in the election, and we see by the partial telegraphic dispatches that the result has been as was anticipated by many. While upon the other hand were arrayed the lovers of civil and Constitutional liberty—men who are opposed to the new-fangled doctrine of miscegenation—who believed that this Government was intended as a white man's government—men who believed that when the purposes for which the war was instituted were accomplished, that it should close, and those who believe that the youth, strength and wealth of this country should not be exhausted in the prosecution of a wild and miserable fantasy; and although these patriots and pure statesmen have been found in the minority, yet the principles for which they battled still remain as fixed and immutable as ever, resting, as they always have, upon the eternal rock of truth, justice and equality.

While Mr. Lincoln received the support of those who were hired and paid from the public treasury, or were bought with promises of reward hereafter, the Democratic candidate relied solely upon the justice and purity of the policy espoused, and could only expect support from those who believed that policy the safest and surest to accomplish what each professed to desire, and who realized the responsibility in deciding aright a question of so much importance, with such fearful consequences awaiting a wrong decision.

The emancipation and elevation of the negro was foreign to the purposes of this war. It was instituted for the sole purpose of restoring the bond of Union to a broken and dismembered Confederacy; a Union for which our patriotic fathers imperilled everything that man holds dear. The cry was, "you who are in rebellion, lay down your arms, yield obedience to the mandates of the Constitution, and your inalienable rights shall remain intact." But no sooner were the "dogs of war" let loose, than the scene shifted. Instead of a war for the restoration of the Union of our fathers,—a war in defence of the Constitutional rights of the States, and of the people, we find a war in which father is arrayed against son, brother against brother, neighbor against neighbor; and already tens of thousands of the prime manhood of the country have been slaughtered upon more than a hundred battle-fields, and their bleaching bones left to whiten the hills and valleys, swamps and mountain-tops of a country once inhabited by a friendly people. And what is the result of all this? A Union dissolved,—a great and wealthy nation ruined in finances,—a once happy people shrouded in grief and mourning,—the widow's cry and the orphan's wail resounding throughout a desolate land,—the great bulwarks of civil liberty torn down,—the Constitution of the country ignored,—law and order, no existence,—freedom of speech and of the press, a myth, and by the arbitrary and dictatorial sway of a President and his satellites, who, we were told, would bring peace, happiness and joy to a distressed and excited people, the best men of the Nation—men of talent and moral worth—patriotic in their love of country, have been immured for months and years in political dungeons, the Federal Bastiles, erected by the command of the man who gave his pledge, and swore to maintain, protect and defend American citizens in all their Constitutional rights. Against such a President, and against the further ruin and devastation of our country, the gallant, the heroic, the chivalrous Democracy, at the peril of their lives and liberties, arrayed themselves in the late contest, and, although defeated, we thank GOD they are not, and can never be vanquished. Democracy still lives, and will, as in the past, continue to outlive all opposition springing from corrupt sectional fanaticism and erroneous national policy. The influence of military and civil dictation—of shoddy-contractors—of money, and the more direct attacks of the bayonet, on the freedom and purity of the ballot-box, has, for the time being, crushed out the almost expiring spark of civil liberty.

But, if we have fallen, we have fallen gloriously, with our banner still floating to the breeze, and we call upon the Democracy to close up the ranks, stand firm and unflinching, ever remembering that

"Truth crushed to earth will rise again:
The eternal years of GOD are her's."

ALL RIGHT.—We take pleasure in announcing the fact that, after some delay and consequent vexation, we have at length succeeded in establishing our newspaper enterprise and now present our readers with the third issue of the WASHINGTON DEMOCRAT. Although some apology is due for the long delay, yet we cannot refrain from indulging in the expression of pride felt over our success, notwithstanding the various means resorted to by our political enemies to prevent another issue of the paper, as also the discouraging results of the Presidential election just past. Many prophecies have been made against the success of the enterprise,—either that the Democracy cannot support a party paper, or that the paper would be suppressed, or the establishment torn down before the year is half out;—yet, notwithstanding all this, we have met with even better encouragement from all parts of the country than was anticipated in the commencement, and we now announce to the world that the WASHINGTON DEMOCRAT IS A PERMANENT ESTABLISHMENT—A FIXED FACT. We have no fears of either mobs, bayonets, or suppression, because we mean to pursue and maintain a just, fair and honorable course. We intend to obey the laws of our country; we shall not countenance disloyalty or rebellion, but patiently submit to the constituted authorities of the land. In the discussion of political questions, we shall be governed by what we honestly deem best calculated to do the greatest good to the greatest number. We shall maintain our liberty and independence, unbiassed by prejudice and unawed by threats. Our establishment is bought and paid for, and we are free from all incumbrances. We start clean handed and clear footed; and although we are under much obligation to many friends for their liberal support, yet we owe no man any special favors. Starting thus, we hope to maintain our responsible position with credit to ourself and honor to the cause espoused and the party supporting us. In conclusion, we would further say, for the benefit of "whom it may concern," that there is but *one of us*, and when the plural pronoun "we" is used in our editorials, it simply means the editor of this paper, and no one else.

FIRE.—The building occupied by us as an office for the DEMOCRAT came very near being destroyed by fire on Tuesday morning last. The fire caught in the roof from a stove pipe, which became unjointed, being hurriedly put up a day or two previously and not securely fastened. By the early discovery and prompt and ready assistance of a number of friends, the fire was soon extinguished with little or no damage. We return our thanks to those who came to the rescue and saved us from a realization of a hasty prophecy made against our establishment by a political opponent.

INDIAN MURDER.—A man and his wife by the name of Castro, and a neighbor visiting Mr. Castro, were murdered and horribly mutilated by a party of four Indians, on Monday night, 6th inst., near Squak Lake, King county. It is supposed the deed was done in retaliation for the murder of two Indian men and a squaw, a short time previous, by a notorious desperado named Jim Riley. Superintendent Waterman took a force of 20 soldiers with him on the 13th, and went in search of this man Riley and the Indian murderers, but nothing definite has been heard from him since. It is hoped he will bring the guilty parties to just punishment.

NO MAILS.—By the accidental breaking of a shaft on the steamer *Rescue* last Wednesday, we failed to receive our regular mail on Thursday night, and are therefore unable to furnish any additional news from the East, except that found in our special telegraphic dispatches.

NEW ADS.—We call attention to the new advertisements from Victoria, in this issue. The parties named, we have good reason to believe, are liberal, just and honorable in their dealings, and no doubt offer the best bargains.

APOLOGETIC.—We again have to apologize for the mechanical appearance of our paper this week, owing to the confusion and extra labor attendant upon the removal of our office from Steilacoom to Olympia.

GIVE CREDIT.—We notice a long extract from our extra of Monday last, copied into the *Vancouver Times* without credit.—"Honor to whom honor is due," if you please.

BOB. RIDLEY.—This colored individual gave one or two exhibitions of his natural eccentricities before a fair audience, in this place, during the week past, and we are informed, acquitted himself satisfactorily to those who witnessed the performance.

CONVALESCENT.—Mr. Joseph Brannan the gentleman connected with the affray on White River, an account of which we published some time ago, has so far recovered from his wound as to be able to walk about his house.

A LIBERAL REWARD will be given to the finder of a gold sleeve-button, large size and elegantly mounted, by leaving the same at this office. 3:3w.

ARRIVED.—The *Eliza Andercon* Capt. Finch, left Victoria on Thursday, 8 P. M. and arrived here on Friday 9. P. M.

The wife of Geo. H. Pendleton is the daughter of the author of "the Star Spangled Banner."

The New Quartz Mines.

The excitement about the new discoveries of gold and silver bearing quartz in the Cascade range, near the Natchess Pass, still continues unabated, and parties are flocking there daily. From a gentleman just returned from there we gain the following additional particulars since the publication of our extra of Monday last.

The quartz is not found in ledges as in California, Nevada, and other places, but the whole mountain seems to be composed of the same character of rock as that in the discovery claim. The discovery claim is on the highest point of the mountain, the summit of which is perhaps 300 feet above the waters of White river, which run at its base. About eight miles of the mountain has been explored and claimed. The quartz from no other part, except the discovery claim, has been tested. Much depends upon the essay return from the half ton of quartz sent last week to San Francisco. Capt. Hale, late Superintendent of Indian Affairs, returned from this mountain on Wednesday last, and he says there is no doubt about the richness of the quartz. The Captain is said to be a good judge of the article, having had some experience in Washoe stocks, and his judgment is much relied on. Many parties have gone out there, located claims and returned to await further development and favorable weather to begin operations. The people of Steilacoom and Pierce county have commenced the opening of a wagon road direct to the mines. Hon. S. McCaw and party are exploring a new route to avoid the crossing of "Mud Mountain," that terror to all who have crossed the Natchess Pass. A town has been laid out at the foot of the mountain, and we learn that one trader by the name of F. Marks has already a large assortment of necessary supplies on hand, which he offers to dispose of at very fair rates.

We take the occasion to remind our merchants and traders at the several starting points on the Sound, that now is a good time to advertise, as parties from a distance will soon be looking out the most favorable chance to procure necessary supplies and equipments for a thorough and continuous working of these mines.

To those who contemplate coming to these mines, we would say, look at our advertising list, and be sure that those who advertise therein will furnish them all they need as cheap or cheaper than can be purchased elsewhere.

COPPERHEAD COMPLAINTS.—Can any of our readers guess what document contains the following complaints? The Abolitionists will readily say it is the "disloyal" platform of some Copperhead Convention:

"He has obstructed the administration of justice.

He has made judges dependent upon his will alone.

He has erected a multitude of new offices.

He has kept among us, in time of peace, standing armies, without the consent of Legislatures.

He has even effected to render the military independent of and superior to the civil powers.

He has combined, with others, to subject us to a jurisdiction foreign to our Constitution and unacknowledged by our laws, giving his assent to their acts of pretended legislation.

For quartering large bodies of armed troops among us.

For protecting them, by mock trial, from punishment for any murder which they should commit on the inhabitants of these States.

For depriving us, in many instances, of the benefit of trial by jury.

For taking away our charters, abolishing our most valuable laws, and altering fundamentally the forms of our Government.

He has incited domestic insurrections among us."

These are not extracts from any latter day political gatherings, but are taken from a renowned old document, signed by John Hancock and fifty-three others, written by Thomas Jefferson, engrossed by the order of Congress, and familiarly known as the Declaration of Independence.—*Cincinnati Enquirer.*

"Earnest—Yankee Jims."—Mr. Lincoln is a native of Kentucky. He is not a fit man to be Chief Magistrate of this great Republic. He may be a second edition or imitator of Joe Miller. On passing over the bloody field of Gettysburg, and in presence of the heaps of dead and mangled bodies covering the ground, he called upon one of his attendants to sing "Jim along Josie." Nero fiddled while Rome burned, Lincoln had no thought of the sufferings of wounded men before his eyes. A comic song is the true criterion of his heart and his head.

"X."—We understand that there is at present residing in San Francisco, an Irishman, who aided in the escape of the present Emperor of France from the Fortress of Ham. In fact, Louis Napoleon was indebted for his liberty perhaps life, to the gentlemen to whom you refer. —*Answers to correspondents in the S. F. Monitor.*

ADVICE TO OLD-LINE WHIGS.—The Louisville *Journal*, in the course of an article eulogistic of Mr. Winthrop's speech, says:

"The Whig who now refuses to act with the Democratic party, is an apostate. He refuses to stand just where he always has stood. He renounces his principles. He deserts his colors. He turns his back upon the wise teachings, and upon the high examples of Clay and of Crittenden. Such a man has no shadow of right to be called or to call himself a Whig. If he is an honest man and understands the English language, he will neither claim nor accept the honored name."

AH, THERE YOU ARE!—At last our friend of the *P. Tribune* has consented to be drawn into a controversy, and yields as gracefully as a "maiden of sixteen." We hope hereafter to hear from him often. We trust he does not take to heart the unkind remarks of the *Democrat.* If that sheet finds any relief in throwing Holloway's Pills at you, let him; and console yourself with the reflection that he might throw something infinitely worse. More anon. Be virtuous and be happy.—*Standard.*

Just so.

A CENSUS just taken by the Italian Government gives the population of their territories at 21,777,334 souls, the fifth population in Europe.

THE ABOLITIONISTS DO NOT WANT THE UNION RESTORED.

It is very natural, says the California *Express* that the Abolition party should be, as they are, opposed to a restoration of the Union, for such a restoration would result in their immediate overthrow as a party. A Union of the States that would secure to the inhabitants thereof all the rights of the elective franchise, guaranteed by the present Constitution, would sweep from office every Abolitionist from Maine to California. It would not only throw them into a hopeless minority, but would fasten upon them the brand of eternal disgrace, making the name of Black Republicanism as odious in America as ever Red Republicanism, with the guillotine as its symbol, came to be in Europe.

Every candid Abolitionist knows this to be true and will admit it to be true; at the same time it may be useful to demonstrate it by figures. At the last Presidential election the total vote given in all the States was 4,680,193; of these Abraham Lincoln received 1,866,452; the other candidates 2,813,741. By an unfortunate division of parties Lincoln was thus constitutionally elected President, though receiving only a little more than one-third of the votes of the people. These arch-conspirators against the Union, whose previous record shows that they preferred a dissolution, had the shrewdness to perceive that they could not conduct the government upon the principles they had avowed if the Southern States remained in the Union; for though in possession of the executive branch of the government, the people would return a majority of members of Congress hostile to their policy, and the judicial department would be a powerful barrier against their unconstitutional and revolutionary designs. Seeing clearly that they could not retain power or abolitionize the government with all the States in the Union, they determined to destroy the Union and drive out those States known to be hostile to their purposes. When these States asked Mr. Lincoln whether he intended to conduct his Administration according to the Constitution, or according to the principles upon which he was elected, he replied that the Chicago Platform was a law to him. Lincoln then held in his hands the future destiny of his country. All he had to do was to say that he would, as President, maintain the rights of all sections, and be the President of all the people, and war would have been averted and the Union maintained; but he did not want this.

Finding they had no security under the Administration of Mr. Lincoln, the Southern States asked for a Convention of the States, that the Constitution might be amended in the way provided in the instrument itself, in order that the new Administration might be restrained from violating their rights by giving to the Constitution a meaning never designed by its authors. The Democrats of the North favored this, but the Republicans all opposed it. They were determined on dissolving the Union. Refusing all terms of compromise, they invited secession by affirming, as Lincoln did in his Inaugural Address, that any people had a right to change their form of government whenever it did not suit them and establish another in its place, and also by declaring through Seward, then the chief oracle of the party, that of all forms of government, ours was the least adapted to the purpose of holding insurrectionary States in the Union by force. Even after all these menaces and invitations to secession, a permanent dissolution of the Union was doubtful. There was danger at any moment of a compromise being effected that would save the Union and overthrow abolition, and alarmed lest it might be effected, they determined to throw the Southern States into the position of belligerents. History will record how this was done through precipitating a fight in Charleston harbor. The South, thus cut off by secession ordinances and by the relation of public enemies from any further participation in the civil control of the Government of the old Union, the Abolition party, in the place of being a minority party, all at once came to be in the [illegible], thus securely enthroning itself in power in all the departments of the Government.

From the instant the first hostile shot was fired in Charleston harbor there never has been, and there never will be the least possibility of a restored Union under Abolition rule. To let the South come back would be fatal at once to Lincoln and all his partisans. To consent to a Convention of the States would be fatal to them. Any action that would restore the voice of the South in the conduct of the Government would at once hurl the Abolitionists from power forever.

Proof of so self-evident a proposition can hardly be needed, yet let us look at it from facts. Lincoln, when elected in 1860, received in all the Southern slaveholding States 36,430 votes. Trifling as was this vote, if Lincoln was voted for for President by the people of those States now, he would, at a fair election, receive a still smaller support. How is it at the North? At the Presidential election the popular vote stood as follows in the Northern States:

Lincoln	1,840,022
Douglas	1,211,633
Breckinridge	277,082
Bell	74,608
Total	3,403,345

Lincoln majority over all, 276,699.

Thus it will appear that in the non-slaveholding States Lincoln in 1860 only had a majority of less than three hundred thousand. When, however, we take into account the vote of the Border States yet remaining in the Union, viz: Kentucky, Missouri, Maryland and Delaware, we find that in them the combined vote of Douglas, Breckinridge and Bell exceeded that for Lincoln by three hundred and seventy-seven thousand four hundred and seventy-three votes. The result is that Lincoln received one hundred thousand seven hundred and seventy-four votes less than a majority of the people voting at the last Presidential election, in the States now in the Union. Let it, therefore, be remembered that Lincoln was never the choice of a majority of the people of the United States, even throwing out altogether the States which have seceded from the Union.

But it may be said that Lincoln has increased his strength in the non-slaveholding and border States, but an impartial examination of the State elections held since that time, will convince any one to the contrary. Taking that State which is regarded as the truest index to popular opinion, Pennsylvania, and how stands the case. In 1860 Lincoln received 60,000 majority over the combined opposition; now the Lincolnists are known to be in the minority by 20,000 votes.

It is therefore almost certain that the Abolitionists will be defeated by the Northern States alone. But if by fraud and force Lincoln can by any possibility be returned as re-elected we honestly believe that in order to render their domination more secure, they will not only continue hostilities against the seceded States, but will drive the border States into secession, in order that the popular will in those States may be cut off from all influence in the Federal Government, and the Northern Democracy be deprived of this valuable aid in combatting Abolition. To suppose that the Abolition party will ever let any one of the Southern States back into the Union on terms giving the people a voice in the Government is disproved by all their acts and all their declarations.

TO PICKLE GREEN TOMATOES.—Wipe the tomatoes clean; slice them, if large, twice in two—if small, only once. Sprinkle a thin layer of sugar on the bottom of a stone jar, then a layer of tomatoes, and then a sprinkling of sugar, and so on. When the jar is full, set it in a warm place. In a few weeks they will be good pickles. The tomatoes must be kept under the vinegar, and the jar tightly covered.

MANY ladies, when walking, are angry if they are gazed at, and sadly disappointed if they are not.

Questions For Freemen.

The theory of our Government is, that it is a Government of the people, in which all its citizens have equal rights and equal voice. He who seeks to restrain or coerce any citizen in the expression of his political opinions, or the exercise of the electoral franchise, violates the fundamental principle of freedom and is an enemy of free government. These are political axioms which no one will attempt to controvert. From these premises it is very easy to distinguish the false from the true friends of freedom and free institutions, whatever may be their professions.

Which party is it that assails the freedom of the press and the liberty of speech—suppresses the one and imprisons citizens for the exercise of the other within the constitutional and lawful limit?

Which party is it that proscribes men in their business and private relations for differences of opinion upon political questions?

Which party is it that attempts to coerce men, through their necessities or their fears, to renounce their honest political convictions and vote for those with whom they disagree in sentiment?

Which party is it that compels its members by secret oath to discharge from their employment all persons, however capable or faithful who do not subscribe to their party test and vote for their party candidates?

Which party is it that joins its members in secret League, pledged to carry the elections by proscription, intimidation, bribery, fraud or force?

Which party is it threatens the use of military power to control the ballot-boxes, and boasts of its ability to corrupt the electors to its purposes by the use of money?

Which party is it that recognizes military necessity as paramount to the rights and liberties of the people?

Which party is it that glories in the name of "loyalists," in contradistinction to that of "freeman," and holds precisely the same principles and advocates the same unconditional submission to arbitrary power, as the loyalists who denounced our rebel fathers in the revolutionary war?

"By their fruits shall ye know them." No honest man will pretend that the party which endorses any of the acts enumerated in the foregoing questions is the party of freedom, of popular rights, or of constitutional liberty. That man or that party is no friend to free government who will not defend the rights of all and concede to others all the rights which he demands for himself.

We ask now, when and where has the Democratic party invaded the freedom of speech or of the press? When has that party counselled or countenanced proscription for opinion's sake, or attempted to violate the freedom of the ballot-box? In what instance did the party attempt coercion, intimidation or bribery to secure a party success at an election? When did they ever claim any right for themselves which they did not concede to every other citizen of every other party? Does any one know of a Democratic employer who feels bound by his party obligations to compel his employees to join in party processions and vote the party ticket or to discharge them? Did you ever hear of a Democratic office-holder being compelled by his party to prescribe to all his clerks and subordinates a party test-oath to support the party in whatever measures or policy it might choose to adopt? Does any one know of an individual now acting with the Democratic party through fear or the promise of personal reward? Is it not a notorious fact that all of the mercenaries, time-servers and place-seekers who are willing to sell their liberties for a price are already retained by the Administration party? Take from that party its ability to buy and its power to coerce, and no intelligent man would presume to claim for it a majority of the electors in more than two States in the Union. The fact that its leaders dare not leave the contest to the unbiassed [illegible] of their purpose to overthrow our free Constitution and subvert the liberties of the people. It is a monstrous absurdity to suppose that the liberties of a people are to be perpetuated by corruption, intimidation and fraud practiced upon themselves. That man who takes the bribe or suffers himself to be coerced into the support of a party which seeks success by such means, is a traitor to his own liberties and to the liberties of his children.—*S. F. Dem. Press.*

[COMMUNICATED.]

How Republicans Officially Discharge their Duties.

PORT TOWNSEND, Nov. 10th, 1864.

A judgment, obtained at the last term of the Court, of the 3d Judicial District held at Port Townsend, in which M. H. Frost was Plaintiff, and Victor Smith, Ex-Collector of Customs (the protege of Solomon P. Chase, Ex-Secretary of the Treasury,) and H. S. Plantz, Mr. Chaser, Private Secretary, were defendents, disclose a system of designing villainy in keeping with the other acts of the precious trio.

It appears that Dr. P. M. O'Brien, of Port Townsend, had a power of Attorney from Frost, to collect his rents at Port Townsend and dispose of his interest in the town site of Port Angelos, to which the Custom House had been removed under the manœuvering in Congress, of Chase, Plantz, and Smith.

The Doctor sold through Smith, as agent for Plantz, the said interest of Frost to Plantz, giving a deed for the same which was witnessed by W. H. Taylor, Deputy Collector under Smith at the time of sale, and also by one Pinkham, an Inspector.

Smith gave his note payable in four months for the deed. The note was not paid at maturity; Frost sued for the amount and got judgment. Judge Hewitt was the Judge of the Court on the occasion.

The proceedings in the Port Angelos speculation it appears was not confined to this little operation. Smith who was in the habit of denying that he held any partnership in the business at all, had purchased from Lieut. White, formerly of the Revenue Cutter *Jeff Davis*, his interest, and Dr. Thomas of the Marine Hospital, purchased W. H. Taylor's interest, ostensibly for himself but according to Thomas's own admission, for Smith & Co.'s, use and benefit. There they go, Smith, Plantz, and Chase, whose averment in Washington city, that, after paying off all the claims of the owners of the town site, the sale of lands therefrom would yield to the National Treasury at least half a million dollars.

Can our Republican friends in the Land Office, inform us how much was realized by the sale of lands at Port Angeles?

Could they enlighten us as to the amount allowed to pay the holders of interest in the aforesaid port of entry.

Perhaps the *Standard* could gratify our curiosity, for that paper was the first we believe, to intimate to the President that there was something rotten in the motives which led to the removal of the Custom House from its former convenient port to its present location in the Straits of Fuca, and to the serious detriment of the commercial and shipping interests of Puget Sound.

Verily Republican officials are pure, patriotic men, unselfishly so, and honest.

A LOOKER ON.

GOV. ANDREW OF MASS., AN AMALGAMATIONIST.—In April, Gov. Andrew of Mass., gave a complimentary dinner at the Parker House, in Boston to *two negroes from Louisiana.* It was the anniversary of the firing on Fort Sumter. Gov. Andrew sat at the table, *one negro each side of him.* Long ago, however, Andrew declared himself an amalgamationist. In 1860 he said:

"Slavery will die out, because the day shall surely be when there will be one whole family of man upon a sanctified earth as there will be in Heaven. *But I do not intend to wait for the providence of God to work it out.*"

What it Costs in Money.

Now at the close of the fall campaign of the fourth year of the war, we may take a review of the position, and judging the future by the light of the past, calculate the possibility or probability of prosecuting the war three years more—which Mr. Lincoln said in his Philadelphia speech would be necessary to finish it up according to his plan. If the war should be closed within the next thirty days, the public debt of the adhering States alone cannot be estimated at less than $4,000,000,000 in addition to the current revenues derived from the most onerous system of taxation ever imposed on any people under any form of Government, which in its various applications absorbs not less than one-third of the products of labor, or in other words, taxes the laboring man to the extent of two days labor out of every six, and if continued at the same rate of increase for three years to come, would compel each laboring man to work two days of each week for the support of himself and family and four days for the Government for the emancipation of the negro. It must also be borne in mind that the expenses of the war increase in proportion to the decrease of the public credit which is now sixty per cent. below par, or two dollars and fifty cents of Government currency being only equal to one dollar of the universal standard, and the productive industry of the country is being constantly depleted at the rate of ten per cent. per annum at least. We need not go into a detailed statement of population and resources from official sources, but throw out general facts which any intelligent man may test by comparison, to show that the plan and policy of the present Administration for the continuance of the war for another three years can only end in ignominious failure and bankruptcy, after exhausting all the resources of the country, North and South, sacrificing the lives of a majority of the able-bodied men of both sections and reducing their families to beggary. Mr. Lincoln and his party offer the country no alternate short of this—no terms of peace which the people of the South could possibly accept without utter degredation to which annihilation would be preferred by any brave and intelligent people, as we are forced to acknowledge they are, for they are our own kindred, and have a common inheritance in the glorious achievements of our common ancestry and common country; and their subjugation is our common shame and the utter annihilation of the principles which formed our bond of Union. It is proposed to destroy ourselves and all that we hold valuable in our common institutions, for the sake of humiliating our opponents in this contest. The perpetuity of our Government, the honor of the nation, the restoration of the Union, are all staked upon the emancipation of the negroes—upon an impossible contingency. The cost in money alone renders it entirely unachievable. Compare the expenditures of the United States for sixty-eight years with the expenditures of the present:

Washington's term of four years,	$ 3,797,493
Washington's second term of four years,	12,083,205
Adams' one term	21,388,351
Jefferson's first term	17,174,483
Jefferson's second term	23,927,244
Madison's first term (including war)	36,147,856
Madison's second term (including war)	108,587,066
Monroe's first term	58,698,087
Monroe's second term	49,869,475
Jackson's first term	56,249,879
Jackson's second term	87,180,428
Van Buren's one term	112,188,691
Tylor's one term	81,216,623
Polk's one term	146,924,402
Filmore's one term	194,617,610
Pierce's one term	211,099,307
Total	$1,266,139,330

The total expenditure of the Government for sixty-eight years preceding the Administration of Mr. Buchanan, averaged but $18,619,696 per annum, including two foreign wars and many Indian wars; and we have the Republican testimony of members of a Congressional investigating committee that the frauds upon the public treasury during the first year of Mr. Lincoln's term amounted to more than the entire expenses of the Government for any one year under Mr. Buchanan's Administration. The expenditures of Mr. Lincoln's Administration for one term, for only a portion of the Union, will be nearly four times as much as the entire expenses of the Government for sixty-eight years. Senator Hall well said in his place in the Senate, that "we have more to fear from the corruptions of the Administration than from the rebellion." A party Congress voted to Mr. Lincoln a "secret fund" of $15,000,000, to be used if he thinks proper in carrying the Presidential election; a sum nearly equal to the whole expenses of the Government through eight years of Washington's Administration, and more than the civil expenses of the Government for any one year up the time the population of the whole country exceeded that of the present adhering States. There is no country, on earth, that could stand this pressure without ending in bankruptcy and ruin.—*S. F. Democratic Press.*

A Scene of Desolation in Georgia.

A correspondent of the Boston *Journal*, who has visited the region fought over in Georgia, writes as follows:

"Georgia, as seen from Marietta to Chattanooga—about one hundred and fifty miles—is totally swept of its male inhabitants. In the still standing cottages (mostly near the depots) and selling peaches, apples and pies, around the cars, you see the lean, lank, yellow-skinned women of the lower class, with their tow-headed children—a few boys under twelve and some unmanagable girls—all clad in the commonest of female or of homespun male garments; but never by any chance, excepting near the lines, and then very rarely, an able-bodied man. Every able-bodied man wears the Federal uniform. Every able-bodied negro is in the service of the army. Georgia here is abandoned, excepting by its women. All—every man of the adult male population is in the Southern army.

"I have seen in the letters of correspondents accounts of the fields of waving corn and wheat that would perish for want of men to cut them down. These fields were said to exist on this route. I did not see them, nor traces of them. It is a lovely land, with its gentle undulations, gracefully receding toward the forest covered mountains; it is a well watered and fertile soil capable of being made a paradise in point of beauty, and for fruitfulness another Egypt; but there has been comparatively a very small portion of the ground redeemed yet, and the cultivation that existed, meagre, rude, and limited as it was, has disappeared before the desolating march of the two great armies. Here and there you see patches of corn; but to call the country an uninhabited and uncultivated region, held by the military power, is the truest description to be given to it.

"All along the railroad you seldom lose sight of the great fact of the war. The country is cut up with breastworks and dotted over with rifle-pits. Had the 'chivalry' and the 'poor white trash' united in doing as much work in ploughing and otherwise cultivating the fields as they have done in their vain but persistent attempts to stop the progress of civilization as represented by Sherman's army, Georgia, instead of being now way down in the list of wealthy States, would have run up like gold—suddenly and far. But that would have been degrading themselves, while to ruin their State is ennobling!

"All along the railroad you see the black embers and charred timbers, and chimneys standing alone, that show where houses have been burned down by Johnston's or our army. The few little villages that are on the road are utterly deserted. You see large hotels, all open, with broken panes of glass, doors and blinds (of these last a few only) off their hinges, emptied of furnitnre from cellar to ceiling. So of all the stores, excepting those occupied by our troops or the Sanitary Commission.

"At every bridge, however small the stream it crosses, there is a block house or stockade, built or building, and a guard of soldiers."

The correspondent of the Columbus (Georgia) *Times*, writing from Atlanta on the 26th ultimo, says:

"On Wednesday night a large 42 pound shell entered the Presbyterian Church on Marietta street, and after passing through the pulpit, exploded in the basement or Sunday School room. Several families living in the vicinity, having taken refuge there, were more or less stunned and injured through the explosion, and one man had his right arm taken off. The scene in the room was frightful; it was after midnight, and all the inmates were sleeping peacefully, perfectly confident of security. Mothers caught up their children hurriedly and rushed frantically into the streets, screaming, though without any definite purpose in view, save that of escaping for the time from the scene which had struck such terror into their souls; and there, out upon the open street, they stood crouching, with their little families clinging around them, and knowing not where to fly for safety. Shell after shell in rapid succession came screaming through the air, and as the light of each terrific explosion, like lightning flashes quivered over them, the figure of one pale-faced mother could be described with bare, out-stretched arms, vainly hoping to shield her little ones from the fragments. Oh! the mighty depths of a mother's love! Assistance came at last, however, and the panic-stricken mother and children were huddled off in the bombproofs of kind neighbors in more secure localities, and the wounded properly cared for."

[From the Richmond Examiner, Sept. 9.]

WANTED, A HUNDRED THOUSAND MEN.

Wanted, a hundred thousand men!—only one hundred thousand! Just the little matter of a hundred thousand men is all that is required to finish up completely and handsomely [illegible] What are a hundred thousand human cattle? It is a mere trifle; it is all that General Grant demands. What a slander to speak of that excellent man as a butcher! What a rebuke to his copperhead revilers is this little call of his for only a hundred thousand more! It would take him fully a fortnight to get them all slaughtered—only a fortnight; let him do his best; and he promises that this trifling requisition shall be his last—positively his very last. Who will grudge the glorious Grant so trifling a hetacombe as this hundred thousand more mere human beings, counting negroes and foreigners. Give him just this many more, and think of the return. The glorious Union will be saved—all at the inconsiderate cost of this diminutive addition to the slaughtered little million or two already buried in this war.

Since King Richard's advertisement for a horse, never has there been such a chance for saving a Kingdom at a small cost. What was a horse to a King? What are a hundred thousand men to Stanton and Grant? It is only a few thousand more than Wellington or Bonaparte had at Waterloo. And what were those little Napoleonic wars to the grand affair which engages the attention of the universal Yankee nation? A hundred thousand are only about as many troops as Marlborough ever commanded; the man who conducted some campaigns in Europe which the vain-glorious English are in the habit of exalting into undue importance. This last demand is only for double as many men, or such a matter, as that roving bandit, Cæsar, was in the habit of taking with him in his raids into Germany, Gaul, and Britain.—Everybody knows that the Yankee nation is mightier than any potentate of antiquity, and yet it is notorious that Xerxes crossed into Greece with, at least, ten times as many people as Grant now demands to be sent over to Petersburg; and is Xerxes to outdo Lincoln?

What a reasonable demand is this! A hundred thousand men to complete the capture of Richmond, a town of thirty thousand inhabitants, the capital of a rebellion, now absolutely and without any further doubt, on its very last legs. Since A. Lincoln called out his first seventy-five thousand militia, and benignantly advised the rebels to disperse, the prospect has never been so good, of crushing out the rebellion. This positively last and merely supplemental requisition for recruits is only twenty-five thousand greater than the original army prepared for suppressing the insurrection in a campaign, "short, sharp and decisive," which was not, by any possibility, to last longer than "ninety days." The Yankees never were deceived by their government. Every one of its long chain of promises has been realized to the letter. It is, therefore, a moral as well as a mathematical certainty that the rebellion is to go under with the forwarding of this last squad of a hundred thousand reinforcements to Grant. Sherman has taken Atlanta, and thus half the rebellion is extinguished. Grant calls for a little more help to take Richmond and to extinguish the other half—only a hundred thousand men.

Well, the North will supply this last call; the Administration at Washington will raise these reinforcements; they cannot afford to fail in so important a matter; a thousand millions of dollars a year in patronage, for four years, are at stake; and what are a hundred thousand lives to four thousand millions, or even a twentieth part of the sum? The men will be furnished; but what then? Did the first army of seventy-five thousand men subdue the South? Did the two millions of men subsequently recruited accomplish the undertaking? Are we then to fall under the onset of a hundred thousand recruits, inferior in every moral and physical attribute to the hosts that preceded them? Such a contingency is not possible. But we have saved our cause heretofore by standing manfully to our duty. The same recipe—every man to his post—will save us again.

ABOUT 25,000 widows are receiving pensions under the laws passed with reference to the present American war.

LYNCHBURG VIRGINIAN

Tuesday Morning, Nov. 29, 1864.

THE VIRGINIAN
Is published Daily, Tri-Weekly, and Weekly, by
CHARLES W. BUTTON.

TERMS OF SUBSCRIPTION:

Daily Virginian, one year,	: :	$40 00
Do. do. six months,	: :	20 00
Do. do three months,	: :	12 00
Do. do. one month,	: : :	5 00
Tri-Weekly, one year,	: : :	$25 00
Do six months,	: : :	15 00
Do. three months,	: : :	8 00
Do. one month,	: : :	3 00
Weekly, one year,	: : : :	$15 00
Do six months,	: : : :	8 00

☞ No paper will be sent without the subscription is paid in advance.

RATES OF ADVERTISING:

ADVERTISEMENTS are inserted for $3 00 per square of eight lines, for the first insertion and $2 00 per square for each additional insertion.

OBITUARY AND MARRIAGE NOTICES charged for at the same rates.

SHERMAN'S MOVEMENTS.

The great interest attaching to the novements of Sherman and the points upposed to be aimed at by the Yankee rmy, will justify the publication of the ollowing table of distances between the rominent places regarded as objective oints. When last heard of, Sherman's eadquarters were at Gaylesville, in herokee county, Alabama, on the stage oad from Rome, Georgia, to Gunter's anding, on the Tennessee river, about quidistant from both points, say thirty iles from Rome, and forty miles from e Landing. Gaylesville is 150 miles om Montgomery, Alabama. Say to ome 30 miles. From Rome to Atlan by rail road 99 miles—total 129.

The following are some distances from lanta:

lanta to Macon, - - - -	103
acon to Savannah, - - -	190
Atlanta to Savannah, - - -	293
lanta to Augusta, - - -	171
gusta to Charleston, - -	137
Atlanta to Charleston, - -	308
lanta to Montgomery, - -	166
" to Columbus, - - -	203
" to Americus, - - -	173
anta to Augusta, - - -	171
gusta to Columbia, by Railroad,	143
Atlanta to Columbia, by Railroad,	314
anta to Augusta, - - -	171
gusta to Columbia, (stage) -	75
Atlanta to Columbia, - -	246
anta to Florence, - - - -	353

verland from Augusta the distance ld probably be less.

ndersonville is not far from Ameri- we believe. Montgomery is distant miles by water, and 197 by land n Mobile.

hese figures, taken from the Rail- l Guide and Gazateer, may be useful. y give the distances from Sherman's known headquarters to every lead point at which his talked of move- t could possibly be expected to aim.

IAT PEACE COMMISSION.

is rumored at the North that Lin- will shortly send peace commis- ers to Richmond. Ex-Governor s. H. Seymour, of Connecticut, one e purest and best public men in the th—who has opposed the war from ception, and denounced unsparingly policy of the Black Republicans first to last; will, it is said, be in- d in the commission. We don't ve it. In the first place, we have ea that Lincoln seriously contem- s such a movement at present; and, e next place, we feel entirely satis- hat Seymour would not consent to e medium of communication, for terms as Lincoln would propose.— ould not insult the Southern peo- ith a repetition of the "To Whom ay Concern" proposition; and he l be authorized to submit no other. en we shall have disposed of the of Sherman, and General Lee has istered the castigation he is pre- for Grant, then the people of orth may bring such influences to pon their Government as will l it to sue for peace. But, sup. as he was in the late election, and rse endorsed by all the provinces realm, save three, it is hardly to be expected that Lincoln will manifest any particular desire to make peace at this time, or agree to the terms which Congress so emphatically laid down in the unanimous vote of the House of Representatives a few days since.—The war must go on until it shall be demonstrated to the satisfaction of Lincoln and his party, that the object for which it was undertaken can never be accomplished. One would think that they ought to be fully convinced of its inutility already, and sick of the slaughter and misery it has produced. But pride of opinion may bolster them up for some time yet, for they are not willing to admit that they erred so egregiously in their convictions, and predictions with respect to the possibility of subduing the South and of restoring the Union. We reiterate the prediction that it will require still further reverses and failures to induce Lincoln and his party to make peace with us upon the only terms that we can or would accept.

FOREIGN NEWS.

The latest arrival from Europe was to the 11th, and a brief summary of the news was given yesterday. We give the following additional:

LORD PALMERSTON ON THE AMERICAN WAR.

The new Lord Mayor of London was inaugurated on the 9th inst, with the usual ceremonies, terminating with a grand banquet at Guild Hall.

The leading members of the British Cabinet and other high dignitaries were present.

Lord Palmerston, in an eloquent speech, spoke cheeringly of European politics.

As regards America, he said:

"There is one dark spot in the picture which the affairs of the world present. That spot is on the other side of the Atlantic. We grieve, and every man of right mind must grieve, that that bloody and disastrous war which broke out more than three years ago among the kindred nations of Northern America, still rages, still lays waste the fertile plains of that continent, still bedews with the blood of its people those forests and tracts of territory which ought to be cultivated and become sources of wealth, pleasure and happiness to mankind.

"We may earnestly trust that human nature will not long permit that deadly and disastrous strife to continue—that the contending parties within some period not remote will find it much better to be reconciled than to fight—and that these disputes which have bedewed the continent with fraternal blood, will be settled by an amicable arrangement between themselves. [Loud cheers.]—The beginning of the strife was expected to be attended in this country with most disastrouse results to manufactures. At all events, out of evil may come some good, and I trust in future our sources of supply will be spread over a great portion of the globe, and that we shall no longer be dependent on any one country for materials so essential to the industry and prosperity of our own country."

THE FLORIDA.

The London "Times" City Article says:

Advices from New York, with regard to the mode in which the Washington government have received the news of the capture of the Confederate steamer Florida, are awaited with the greatest interest by the mercantile as well as the political world. One reason for the importance attributed to these advices consists in the inference that if the affair be palliated or condoned by Lincoln's government, it will henceforth entirely extinguish any power on the part of the United States to assail by privateers the commerce of any nation with which they may be at war, since the precedent will establish a claim to the right to pursue and destroy every such vessel whatever may be the port in which she may seek shelter or supplies.

THE BURNING OF ROME, GEORGIA—SCENES AT THE CONFLAGRATION.

A correspondent of the New York Tribune writes that paper an account of the destruction of Rome Georgia. He says:

Owing to the great lack of railroad transportation, General Corse was obliged to destroy nearly a million of dollars worth of property, among which was a few thousand dollars worth of condemed and unserviceable Government stores. Nine rebel guns, captured at Rome by our troops, were burst, it being deemed unsafe to use them One thousand bales of fine cotton, two flour mills, two rolling mills, two tanneries, one saw mill, an extensive foundry, several machine shops, together with the railroad depots and storehouses, four pontoon bridges, built by General Corse's pioneer corps for use on the Coosa and Etowah rivers, and a substantial trestle bridge nearly completed for use, were destroyed.—This trestle was construced by the engineer corps, and, I am told, would have cost fifty thousand dollars North. Recollecting the gross outrages which I alluded to above as being perpetrated upon Colonel Streight by the "Romans," our troops, as soon as they learned that the town was to be abandoned and a portion of it burned, resolved to lay Rome in ashes in revenge for insult offered to our prisoners. General Corse, however, had taken the precaution to station guards through all parts of the city, with orders to shoot down the first man caught firing a building without proper authority. Stringent orders were also issued to arrest all citizens or suspicious persons found on the streets after the conflagration commenced. The roaring of the flames, as they leaped from window to window, their savage tongues of fire darting high up into the heavens and then licking the sides of the buildings, presented an awful but grand spectacle, while the mounted patrols and the infantrymen glided along through the brilliant light like giant spectres of horrid war. The citizens were horribly alarmed, expecting that the high wind would set fire to the hundreds of old wooden buildings with which the town abounds, and their fears were increased by the incessant cracking and roar of the flames, which resembled in sound the near approach of a long railroad train.

A later letter says:

Rome was evacuated at 10 o'clock this forenoon by our forces, but not until the Etowah House, a respectable three-story brick hotel, was consumed by fire. Stragglers managed to ignite a lot of straw in the building, and there being no fire-engines in the town, it was impossible to subdue the flames. A block of four brick stores was also wantonly destroyed by skulking stragglers, who are always in the rear when there is an opportunity to plunder and pillage private dwellings, but forever absent from the front when the musketry rattles. All the barracks were laid in ashes, and a black veil of dense smoke hung over the war-desolated city nearly all day, arising from the smouldering ruins. A few of the enemy's cavalry scouts hove in sight south of Coosa river, on Cemetery Hill, just as the rear guard was withdrawing, evidently for the purpose of watching our movements. A few shots were exchanged, but the river intervening, prevented the following up our rear guard to harass our operations. We strike tents at four o'clock to-morrow morning, and will march direct for Altoona, twenty-one miles distant where we will encamp for the night, resuming our march as far as Marietta on the following day.

SHERMAN'S MOVEMENTS IN GEORGIA.

The Augusta "Constitutionalist" of the 19th, in an article on the Georgia situation, views the present movement of Sherman as a retreat, forced upon him by irresistible and overpowering circumstances, and believes that if Georgia acts promptly, his hour has come. The "Constitutionalist" says.

Our gloomy faces are gradually assuming the cheerful hue, as the real situation begins to be thoroughly understood. As we write (9 o'clock p. m., Friday) it is fully believed that General Sherman, finding his way north entirely closed and a bold and defiant army confronting him, has determined upon making a bold retreat to the rear, where no army of consequence could impede his movement.

In our judgment it is the Anabasis of Sherman. It is plain his only object can be the making of a certain and secure base, He must move fast and obtain his object speedily, or he is lost—unless the whole State of Georgia are cowards and poltroons In a state of war we must not all expect to escape unscathed. Where the enemy marches he will leave his work of destruction

Sherman has cut loose from his base—Georgians must see that he makes no other.

Forrest having destroyed his stores at Johnsonville, and cut his communication north, this movement has been forced upon him and if our local and reserve force can hold him in check, impede his progress, burn and destroy in advance of his colnms, long ere he reaches his objective point (the base he looks to) his ammunition will be exhausted, his horses starved, and his army an easy prey to fresh and veteran troops.

Sherman has many weary miles to march in obtaining his object. It is absurdity to talk about his making a winter campaign with no communication with his government. How long will the ammunition he carries last him. He is retreating, simply retreating. He will destroy as he goes, but that makes it none the less so.

This movement is the modern Anabasis, and, like the Greek of old, he has only one object at heart, and that is to reach the sea; and as Xenophon's weary and long suffering ten thousand sent up shout after shout, "Thalatta! Thalatta!" so Sherman will gladly cry, The sea! The sea!

AN EXHORTATION TO THE GEORGIANS.

The utility of the Press is illustrated in the following telegram, which we copy from the Augusta Constitutionalist. It was directed to the Daily Press of the State of Georgia:

RICHMOND, Nov 18

To the People of Georgia:

You have now the best opportunity ever yet presented to destroy the enemy. Put everything at the disposal of our Generals. Remove all provisions from the path of the enemy and put all obstructions in his path. Every citizen with his gun, and every negro with his spade and axe, can do the work of a good soldier. You can destroy the enemy by retarding his march. Georgians be firm, act promptly and fear not.

(Signed) B H HILL

I most cordially approve the above.

JAMES A SEDDON,
Secretary of War.

SHERMAN'S RAID—THE YANKEE INTELLIGENCE FROM HIM.

The New York Herald gives a summary of all the Yankees know about Sherman's movements as follows:

Advices were received in Washington yesterday from General Sherman's army which show that he was, on Saturnay last, within thirty miles of Macon, Georgia, which place is supposed to be now in his possessien. He had met with but little opposition, and his campaign was progressing in the most successful manner. Intelligence from Richmond shows that the rebels have already learned sufficient of Sherman's operations to produce great consternation in their minds. They will probably soon be informed of much more, as there is but little force to oppose his advance besides the hastily-raised Georgia militia, under Howell Cobb, and these will be but slight hindrance in the path of the Union veterans.

The latest intelligence represents General Hood, with two corps, numbering together about thirty five thousand men, to be still in the vicinity of Florence, Alabama, on the Tennessee river. There are reports that Dick Taylor has joined him with an additional force of ten thousand. His latest movements do not indicate an intention of early offensive operations. Beauregard, with the rebel Gen. Stewart's corps, was still at Corinth, Mississippi, when last heard of. Gen. Thomas, commanding the Union army designed to check Hood's advance, is rapidly concentrating his forces, as though disposed to make an attack on the rebels in some direction. As we have already stated, the rebel reports of the destruction of government property at Johnsonville, on the Tennessee river, by Forrest, weae immensely exaggerated. We now learn that there was only one building in the place destroyed. It is still held by a division of Union troops.

THE ADVANCE OF THE ENEMY—BURNING OF ATLANTA, &c.

The Augusta (Georgia) Sentinel has the following:

A gentleman who arrived on Thursday evening from Stone mountain reports that the Yankee column moving down the Georgia railroad, divided at Decatur, one half going down the Covington road and the other the Rockbridge road. At Stone mountain they burned all the unoccupied houses, comprising some two-thirds of the town, and were laying waste the country as they progressed. They march in hollow squares, their trains in centre. They united at Baker's mill, near Covington, and it was not known whether they would strike for Eatonton or Athens.

This gentleman says that the view from the summit of Stone mountain of the conflagration of Atlanta was awful beyond description. The Gate City was "an ocean of flame" as the fiery waves rose and fell throughout its whole extent.

Passengers on the Georgia railroad last night reported that about 100 Federal cavalry made their appearance at Social Circle on Thursday and burned the railroad platform. It is not believed that they have come down any further than the Circle.

Their infantry encamped at or near Old Sheffields on Wednesday night, and from their movements it is thought they are en route to Eatonton.

It is also reported that they have burned Monticello and Hillsborough, which, if true, indicates clearly that they design tapping the Central railroad at Gordon, or some other point.

The passenger train on the Georgia road yesterday only came from Union Point.

FROM GRANT'S ARMY.

THE GREAT BATTLE TO COME OFF SOON.

The news from Grant's army is important. The Herald says:

All the Union iron clads previously lying at Fortress Monroe were, on last Friday morning, sent up the James river to Dutch Gap, and this and other significant movements lead to expectations of stirring events in that vicinity shortly.

[From the Alexandria (Va.) State Journal.]

Yesterday (Friday) morning the iron-clads previously stationed at Fortress Monroe, moved up the James river to Dutch Gap, and the indications were very strong a heavy movement being in operation. We may, therefore, look for very startling news from that quarter by the arrival of the steamer to morrow, and who can doubt that it will be of a most favorable character.

REPORTED INVASION OF KENTUCKY BY BRECKINRIDGE—THE FATE OF LIEUTENANT GOVERNOR JACOBS.

Gen. Breckinridge is suspected of a design to march from East Tennesse on an invasionary expedition into Kentucky and Gen. Burbridge is making rapid dispositions of his forces to prevent the movement.

The Baltimore American has the following about the Lieutenant-Governor of Kentucky, lately arrested by the Yankee military:

The arrest of Col. Jacobs, Lieutenant Governor of Kentucky, was reported a day or two ago by telegraph. The further report, however, that he had been sent to Washington city under guard, proves to be untrue.—Gen. Burbridge, it seems, has taken summary action in the case without the formality of sending the accused to Washington, and has decreed his banishment beyond the Federal lines. Col. Jacobs passed through Covington on Saturday last en route to the South, in accordance with the order above named.

AN EDITOR ARRESTED FOR TREASON

Dr John McElwee, editor of the Hamilton (Butler county, Ohio,) True Telegraph, was arrested on the 15th instant and taken to Cincinnati, in pursuance of an indictment found against him by the grand jury of the United States Court. He is charged under the act of July 17, 1864, section two, with giving aid and comfort to the rebels through the columns of the paper which he was editing. The articles specified are found in the Telegraph of July 21, 1864. The first, which is addressed "To the Patrons of the True Telegraph," and signed by John McElwee, is an editorial article, and advocates a separation of the States. The second, headed "The Ground Swell," protests against the draft, and suggests rasistance to it. The third and last mentioned, headad "Lincoln's Government," is abusive of the same, discourages enlistments, and opposes the draft. He was held to bail in three thousand dollars.

MARRIED.

On the 23d instant, by Rev. Jas. A. Davis, Col. THOS. N. COBBS to Miss LOU. B. TAYLOR, all of Washington co., Va.

FUNERAL NOTICE

The funeral of CHISWELL D. MAHONE will take place, at his residence in Amherst, this (Tuesday) evening at 3 o'clock.

The friends and acquaintances of the family are invited to attend.

OBITUARY

Departed this life, Sep. 3d, 1864, at the residence of her father's, OCTAVIA, eldest daughter of J R and L J Staton, of Albemarle county, age 14 years.

OCTAVIA, in the bloom of youth and pride of intellect, bade farewell, for awhile, to the endearments of home and went to Lynchburg to resume her studies; but, alas, had been there only a few months before she was taken ill and carried home, and, in a few weeks, death claimed her for his victim. She was possessed of a good mind, was studious, amiable and interesting. She was reared by pious parents. She was early taught the principles of christianity. Her end was calm, peaceful and triumphant; she talked of death as if it had no sting, and of the grave as if it had no victory. She spoke of dieing with great calamness. Her father asked her if she had any request to make; she said none at all except respecting her funeral. She told him whom she wished to preach her funeral, also selected a hymn. She said that day was a day of happiness to her. She then bade them fare-well and ceased speaking. Thus passed away a pure spirit in glorious triumph to the mansions of bliss. She leaves a father and monther, sister and brothers, with many relations and friends to mourn her death. But they mourn not as those who have no hope, for the bright angels were present to convey her happy spirit home to God. She rests in hope of a glorious resurrection. May her fiends prepare to meet her in Heaven.

M. M. S.

ATLANTA DAILY INTELLIGENCER--EXTRA.

ATLANTA, GA., DECEMBER 10, 1864.

TO OUR PATRONS.

In a few days we will again in this city resume the regular daily and weekly publication of the Intelligencer. Nearly all the material for the same has arrived. Until then we will give them only a synopsis daily of current events.

THE MAILS.

We understand from our efficient Post master, Col. Howard, that we will have daily mails from up the Macon Road, as well as on the West Point Road, and in a few days also on the Georgia Road.

TELEGRAPH.

We have been informed that in the course of ten or twelve days, telegraphic communication will be resumed between here and Macon, when we will furnish our readers with daily press reports, as usual.

☞ To our country friends who have been fortunate enough to escape the clutches of the Yankee hordes, and who have any produce to dispose of, we would advise them to bring it in, as there is a great scarcity of everything in the city. Col. Glenn, Commandant of the Post, has given us assurance that their teams will not be molested.

GEORGIA RAILROAD.—The Augusta Constitutionalist says: "We learn this road will be complete and in running order to Atlanta in forty days, if not interrupted.

We think it due to the public that the Government should lend every assistance requisite to the earliest possible completion of the road, in view of the fact that thousands of exiles may then return to their long lost homes.

THE CITY.

We doubt if the annals of history can furnish a passage in regard to the destruction of property as our city presents. For the information of those who are absent we will give them a hurried synopsis.

Whitehall street from Roark's corner up to Peachtree street is one entire mass of ruin.

Alabama street from Bridge to Pryor is destroyed. The property standing embraces the block of buildings from the Planter's Hotel to the Confederate smoke house.

On Pryor street the buildings from Hunter street are all standing.

Lloyd street.—With the exception of the block on which the Washington Hall was situated, the buildings are all standing.

Hunter street—From Whitehall to the Court House and beyond, all the houses are standing.

Mitchell street—All the residences on this street, with few exceptions, are standing.

Marietta street—From Dr. Powell's residence nearly all the houses are standing.

Peachtree street—From Wesley Chapel nearly all the houses are standing.

Washington street—From Col. Calhoun's residence to Knox's lot all the houses are in a good state of preservation.

Decatur street—From Hunnicutt & Taylor's Drug Store up to Masonic Hall the buildings have been destroyed. The balance of the street from the Masonic building, with some exceptions, the residences are standing. The residences on this street in the rear of the Trout House are all destroyed.

McDonough street—With the exception of Judge Clark's house and two others, all the buildings are standing.

Walton street—Nearly all the dwellings on this street are standing.

All the churches with the exception of the Episcopal Church, on Walton street, are preserved.

The depots of the four connecting roads, together with the car shed, are destroyed.

We have thus only given a description of those portions of the city we have visited, and will in a future number notice more. To our absent citizens we would say return as soon as possible, and with one mind commence to extricate ourselves from the ruin detailed upon us by the God-forsaken, miserable and deluded Yankee crew.

☞ On yesterday we had the pleasure of a visit from Gen. Tyler, at present commanding post at West Point.

☞ We understand from a reliable source that an Express between here and Griffin will shortly be started.

☞ We are indebted to Mr. Mitchell, of this place, for a late Augusta paper, for which he will please accept our thanks.

☞ A large lot of Yankee prisoners arrived at Augusta from Waynesboro', a few days ago, and were sent to Columbia, S. C., for safe keeping.

☞ Vice-President, Alexander H. Stephens, is at present in Richmond, presiding over the Confederate Senate.

☞ Gov. Joseph E. Brown is at present sojourning at Savannah, Geo.

MOBILE, Dec. 3.—A special to the Advertiser and Register from Senatobia, December 2d, says the St. Louis Republican of the 26th ult., and Memphis Bulletin of the 30th are received.

The New York dispatches of the 24th says it is a fixed fact that S. P. Chase is to be Chief Justice.

Gen. Lee is contracting his lines to send troops to Georgia.

Gen Early's headquarters are between Toomoeville and New Market, with his flanks well covered with cavalry.

A cavalry fight had occurred in the Shenandoah Valley, in which the Federals claim a victory.

The New York Herald publishes Sherman's order to his army before his march commenced. Howard commands the right wing, consisting of the 15th and 17th corps, Slocum the left, consisting of the 18th and 20th corps. Habitual order of march, when ever practicable, will be by four roads as nearly parallel as possible.

Kilpatrick commands the cavalry, and a day's march will be 15 miles. The cavalry will forage on the country, and not destroy property in localities where they are unmolested. Horses, mules, wagons, and able-bodied negroes will be appropriated freely.

A Nashville dispatch of the 24th says that Duck River has been adopted as the Federal line of defence.

A Louisville dispatch of the 25th says Pulaski is evacuated, and a battle was expected at Columbia that day.

The Louisville Journal thinks Breckinridge has his foot on Kentucky and moving in that direction, and Stoneman watching him.

Memphis papers notice the capture of Capt. Ned Montgomery, whilst attempting to cross the Mississippi river with a train of tobacco, and a quarter of a million of Sterling Exchange was found on his person.

NORTHERN ITEMS.

Mrs Greenhow, the lady who gave the Government so much trouble at the commencement of the war, acting as a rebel spy, was recently drowned in endeavoring to escape from the blockade runner Condor, at New Inlet Bar.

The charter election in Newark, N. J., yesterday, went for the Democrats by a reduced majority. The Union men gained one or two Aldermen and several School Commissioners.

An attack on the passenger train of the Kentucky Central railroad was made by 25 guerillas, midway between Parsons and Lexington. The engine was thrown from the track, the cars were burned, $2,700 were taken from the Adams' Express Company, and all the passengers were robbed.

Intelligence has been received at headquarters at St. Louis, that Price's army went from California to Booneville, Cooper county, yesterday, and Shelby sent 2,000 cavalry across the Missouri at that point.—Fisk has gone to Lexington to take command there. Gen. Sanborn is still pursuing the enemy. Reports were extensively circulated yesterday that Magruder, with 5,000 infantry, had entered Southeast Missouri, and occupied Fredericktown, but they proved to be unfounded. Business is suspended at St. Joseph, the citizens having been called to arms by Gen. Fisk, in anticipation of a visit from Price.

CAPT. WILLIAM BARNES.—The Savannah Republican of a late date, describes an incident which occurred at the capture of Cumberland Gap by the Yankees. Capt. Barnes is a citizen of this place, but now a prisoner of war at Fort Pulaski, and is the hero of our story.

Capt. Barnes commanded a Light Battery at the Gap, and when he was ordered to raise the white flag in token of the surrender, he refused to obey, saying that he had come there to fight, and not surrender, that he believed the position could, as he knew it ought to be, held. The order was repeated, and he again refused to raise the flag over his portion of the work—and when it was raised by one of his subalterns, by command of the Colonel in command, poor Barnes threw away his sword and wept like a child.

MILITARY DIRECTORY.

Col. LUTHER J. GLENN,
Commandant of Post.

Capt. THOS. L. DODD,
Provost Marshal.

Capt. R. L. MOSS,
Post Commissary.

HEADQ'RS GA. RESERVES,
AND MILITARY DIST. OF GA.,
Macon, Nov. 26, 1864.

SPECIAL ORDERS,
No. 145.

§ 11. Lieut. Colonel L. J. GLENN, Cobb's Legion, is assigned to the Command of the Post at Atlanta, Ga. This order to take date from the 24th inst.

By Command of
MAJ. GEN'L HOWELL COBB,
R. J. HALLETT, A. A. Gen'l.
Approved,
G. T. BEAUREGARD,
dec10–d1t. General.

HEADQ'RS, MILITARY POST,
Atlanta, Dec. 2, 1864.

GENERAL ORDER,
No. 1.

In obedience to the above order, the undersigned this day assumes command of this Post.

L. J. GLENN,
dec10–d1t Lt. Col. Com'g.

HEADQ'RS, MILITARY POST,
Atlanta, Ga., Dec. 3, 1864.

ORDER
No. 1.

§ I. No person will be allowed to carry any public or private property, until further orders, beyond the limits of this city, without a permit from these Headquarters.

§ II. All persons having in their possession any property belonging to the Confederate Government, or which may have been abandoned by the enemy, are hereby required to report the same to these Headquarters.—Against those failing to do so, the law will be rigidly enforced.

L. J. GLENN,
Lt. Col. Com'd'g Post.

HEADQ'RS, MILITARY POST,
Atlanta, Dec. 8, 1864.

ORDER
No. 2.

§ I. All persons who have taken possession of houses whose owners have gone within the enemy's lines, are hereby required to report to these Headquarters with the names of the owners and an accurate description of the property

§ II. All persons who own dwelling houses within the city or vicinity, and who are now occupying as tenants or agents the premises of others who have gone within the enemy's lines, are hereby required to vacate the same.

§ III. All persons who have in their possession negroes, furniture or other property belonging to parties who have gone within the enemy's lines, are hereby required to report a full and complete description of the same to these headquarters without delay.

L. J. GLENN,
Lt. Col. Com'd'g Post.

HEADQUARTERS, CITY HALL,
Atlanta, Dec. 8, 1864.

In obedience to the Proclamation of Governor Brown, of the 19th ult., all persons in Fulton County, between the ages of 16 and 55, are subject to Militia duty except those who are exempted in the Proclamation. All who are subject will report at the City Hall without delay at Judge Manning's Office for further orders.

Z. A. RICE,
dec10–d2w Lt. Col. F. C. M.

PROVOST MARSHAL'S OFFICE,
Atlanta, Dec. 5, 1864.

Special Orders,
No. 1.

In pursuance of Special Order No. 4, Headquarters Military District of Georgia, I have assumed the duties of Provost Marshal of this Military Post.

THO. L. DODD,
Capt. and Provost Marshal.

HEADQ'RS GEORGIA RESERVES,
AND MILITARY DISTRICT OF GEORGIA.
Macon, Ga., December 7th, 1864.

General Orders,
No. 30.

I. The following military organizations, raised under the authority of Governor Brown, and afterwards received into the Confederate service by General J. B. H[illegible], to wit: the Regiment commanded by Col. Findlay, the Battalions commanded by Majors Beall, Murkinson, Graham, McCallum and Ledford, and the battalion lately commanded by Lt. Col Glenn, of Pickens county, (whose commission was revoked because he was reported to Gov. Brown as a deserter,) under the person who may have been elected to command it, will be maintained for sixty days from date in discharge of such duties as they may be called upon to perform.

II. After the expiration of the sixty days, all men between the ages of 18 and 45, subject to conscription will report to the proper enrolling officer for assignment to the army in the field—those liable either to militia duty or to service in the Reserves, will remain in the present organizations

III. All persons now in these organizations absent without leave from the Confederate Army will return promptly to their commands, with the assurance that their cases will be recommended to the most favorable consideration of their respective commanding Generals in view of the services rendered by them in these organizations, and to carry out this object, the officers under whom they have been serving will furnish each one with a statement of his services. After this opportunity further indulgence to absentees will not be granted.

IV. The officers in command of these organizations are enjoined to be vigilant in the arrest of all deserters and absentees, and will forward them without delay to the Conscript Camp at this place.

By command of
Major General HOWELL COBB.
R. J. HALLETT, A. A. Gen'l.

EXECUTIVE DEPARTMENT,
Macon, Dec. 7, 1864.

I. The above orders of Major General Cobb have been submitted to my inspection, and I concur in the order that the persons in said organizations who are subject to my command as militiamen remain in the same organization with those subject to his command as Confederate Reserves, till further orders, and I direct all such organizations to report to General Cobb and obey its orders in future as they have heretofore beyed the orders of General Hood, till further directions from these headquarters.

II. All persons in said organizations, who belong to the State line, or the company of State scouts, who are now absent without leave, will report immediately to their respective commands. Those who obey this order by reporting to their commanding officers, or if they cannot reach them, to these Headquarters, within the next twenty days, will receive a free pardon except the deduction of their wages for the time they have been absent, and one months' additional deduction.

III. All other persons not in said organizations who are so absent without leave, will also report to their respective commands within twenty days, and will be excused from any degrading punishment.

JOSEPH E. BROWN.

☞ Papers in the 9th, 7th, 8th and 9th Congressional District publish three times dec10–d3t.

H'DQ'RS, MIL DIV. OF THE WEST,
Macon, Ga., Nov. 29th, 1864.

Special Orders,
No. —.

All supernumerary Officers of this Military Division not otherwise assigned to duty, will report Commandant of the Post, Macon, Ga.

By command of General Beauregard,
A. R. CHISOLM,
A. D. C. and A. A. G.

☞ All papers in Military Division will publish three times a week for two weeks, and send bill to Chief Quartermaster.

Dec. 10. A. R. C., A. D. C.

WAR FORNEY'S PRESS

TWO DOLLARS PER ANNUM. PHILADELPHIA SATURDAY, DECEMBER 10, 1864. VOL. IV.—NO. 5.

[From the Evening Telegraph.]

THE BIRD OF BATTLE.

[During the fierce cannonading at Nickajack, a small bird came and perched upon the shoulder of an artilleryman—the man designated, we believe, as "No. 1," whose duty it is to ram down the charge after the ammunition is put in the gun. The piece was a Napoleon, which makes a very loud report. The bird, as we have stated, perched itself on this man's shoulder, and could not be driven from this position by the violent motions of the gunner. When the piece was discharged, the poor little thing would run its beak and head up under the man's hair at the back of the neck, and when the report died away would resume its place upon his shoulder. Captain Babbitt took the bird in his hand, but when he released his grasp it immediately resumed its place on the shoulder of the smoke-begrimed gunner. The scene was witnessed by a large number of officers and men. It may be a subject of curious inquiry, what instinct led this bird to thus place itself. Possibly frightened at the violent commotion caused by the battle, and not knowing how to escape or where to go, some instinct led it to throw itself on this gunner as a protector. But, whatever the cause, the incident was a most beautiful and pleasing one to all who witnessed it.—*New Albany (Indiana) Ledger.*]

Upon the gunner's shoulder,
(Union gunner, Number One,
None deadlier or bolder,)
Burned the red beams of the sun.
Down breast, and back, and arms of might,
Rolled the sweat of desperate strength;
And a fiery mist, and a lurid light,
Shone round his straining length.

The cannon, thunder-throated,
The swift and swooping shell,
Laughed murderingly, and gloated
O'er the work they did so well.
And many a limbless trunk they hurled
O'er many a bloody track,
Before our Flag its folds unfurled
From the heights of Nickajack.

Whilst round that gunner's shoulder
The deadly fire bolts whirred,
There, seen by many a soldier,
Lit a fairy little bird.
Its wings against its panting breast
It flapped, with terror smote,
And its golden songs were all at rest
In its soft scarlet throat.

Its wings like leaflets trembled,
A little flying flower
That tiny bird resembled,
Borne rudely from its bower—
As though a flower had felt what fright
Could mean, that all life through
Had only fed upon the light,
And only drunk the dew.

Perhaps, as thus it nestled
Round the gunner's sturdy neck,
Whilst at his post he wrestled
And held the foe in check,
Could it have put its thoughts in words,
It would have said, "Not long
Ago the air was full of birds,
And the birds were full of song."

And when, with each fresh thunder,
Sore hurt with new despair,
It hid its small self under
The gunner's tangled hair,
Quick memories of the summers dead,

who was recommended to me the other day for housekeeper. You and Clyde stay here until I come back."

This speech Miss Flipper delivered with amazing volubility. Before Alice could utter a word, we were ushered into the dining-room. Then Miss Flipper suddenly took a notion that she should want me to go with her, to carry back some purchases she intended making.

Alice, all that morning, had been in a dreamy, half-pensive mood. I have mentioned the strange affliction to which she was subject. Although it never gave certain indications of its approach, and returned at no regular intervals, still there was something in her general air that led me to fear a crisis was approaching. With one whom I loved as I loved her, I was extremely watchful, affection creating a spirit of solicitude and observance beyond my years. Miss Flipper and I were ready to start, when I looked back to take a last glimpse of Alice. She had thrown aside her cloak and bonnet, and had seated herself at a small centre-table which supported a rare collection of white roses, preserved in spirits of wine. One hand was resting lightly on one of the dainty vases which held them; the other hung carelessly by her side. Her rapt, contemplative air seemed to separate her from all the world. Her attitude was that of repose, of introspection. I see the mellow light tinging the atmosphere of the room and hesitating ere it gathers round her delicate form. She seemed to me the very muse of silence, her attitude and air imposing upon all around her a dumbness which seemed waiting for her to speak.

"Alice!" I exclaimed.

But wrapt up in that dreamy state, she did not hear my voice. Her eyes cast down and fixed, her hands listless and inactive, she sat still, and so we left her.

Now, at the gate, Miss Flipper, who from sunrise to sunset was in as many moods as

ARMY OF THE POTOMAC—SCENE IN CAMP BEFORE PETERSBURG, VA.—SOLDIERS PLAYING AT TENPINS.

quickly and fiercely. "You cannot silence me as you have silenced others. The tongues of all the dead are in my mouth when I see you. Speak! Let me be sure that it is you. Do you remember years ago the misery you caused me. Do you forget that you have caused the misery I suffer now. Do you not know that through you I am a beggar, an outcast, dependent for the bread I eat on the charity of others? Speak, for God's sake!"

Alice crossed one hand over her brow in a perplexed and dreamy manner. Then an air of self-possession marked her features and her attitude.

"You mistake me for some other, Mr. Lawrence," she said, softly. "We never met before this day."

were my artful Alice, and are none the less so now. But it will not do. You are changed, too. You are not the flashing, brilliant, relentless creature you once were. Your eyes are soft, and your voice is low, and your looks are modest, and your face is sad. But you are the same Alice Arlyle, notwithstanding, and you can bring your arts to your aid as well now as then. I do not care to know the circumstances by which you are transformed from the penniless teacher into the affluent lady; I do not care to renew the curiosity of the past at all. But I cannot let it rest when my eyes behold you. Never let me see you, never let me hear of you, and perhaps the remembrance of it will cease to madden me, except at moments when it reappears to

and her hands clasped. A look of intense interest and half terror was upon her face.

It had been many a year since I had seen that face, but I knew it. As I gazed, hardly able to repress a cry of surprise, a long-forgotten scene came out from the mists of the past, and unscrolled itself before me. I saw, in remembrance, a shaded room, all of whose contents were reduplicated in a large mirror at the far end. I saw a crouching, supplicating figure, and heard sobbing, deprecating accents; and then I saw a bowed figure—the selfsame figure that I confronted now—moving down the sunlit avenue on the morning of a sweet June Sabbath. The face had been turned from me then, though I knew the eyes were shedding bitter tears. It was Janet, who had thus left me years ago; it was Janet whom I saw before me now.

She recognized me, too, but was more self-possessed. She did not blush nor start, nor indeed betray any emotion. She did not move for a few seconds. Then she laid one hand upon my shoulder, and with the other hand took hold of one of mine, leading me toward the door. We passed through it silently, and found ourselves in the garden.

Janet's first words were not as romantic as they might have been.

"How little, how very little you are!" she said.

I was indeed not larger than a child of half my age, but I deprecatingly insinuated that it was not my fault.

"And you, Janet," I exclaimed, my surprise scarcely over, "what brought you here? where have you been so long?"

"I was in the conservatory when you first came in, behind the oleanders," said Janet.

A strange look in Janet's face caused me to look up.

"Janet," I asked, "what does Mr. Lawrence mean by talking in this way; is he not out of his head?"

"No—yes—I don't know," answered

ago," I answered. "Who is the lady that has been looking for me, uncle?"

"Mrs. Jim Restive," he answered.

Then I learned that Mrs. Jim and Mrs. Charles, after six consecutive years of trial of each other's natures, had finally concluded that their souls were not in sympathy; that they had parted from each other never to be reunited as sisters any more; that Poplar Grove had been abandoned, and that Mrs. Jim had persuaded her husband to allow her to recuperate her exhausted nature (sorely tried by Mrs. Charles) by a trip to Beddoes, to join my Uncle Ned and me. So my Uncle Ned and I were left alone for that day, as there was no knowing when either of the ladies would be back. My Uncle Ned, after having recovered from his surprise at my meeting with Janet, proposed making a holiday of it, and taking a general jaunt round the town.

So we went. In that sleepy old town of Beddoes we visited everything that was worth or that was not worth visiting. We went to the Corridor of the Arts, and there we saw the standard collection of sleepy pictures and a gallery of somnambulent statuary. We went to the Institute of the Sciences, and pondered over fossils and skulls to our hearts' content. Then we went to a fair in the neighborhood, and here my uncle, I fully believe, would have gone on buying until night-time but for the fact that his pockets were not equal to his wishes. In the afternoon, too, we went to the theatre. In that quiet old town of Beddoes, unlike any other in the world I should suppose, they gave theatrical entertainments once in a while in the afternoon. I do not know whether the manager was incited thereto by any regularly defined and devoutly adhered to principle, or whether those sleepy entertainments—not sleepy to me then, however, were improvised to please the fantastic caprices of his managerial will. Neither do I recollect what the play was, but the little theatre was full of happy faces, children's faces mostly, and the applause was most vociferous. Looking at it after this lapse of years, I firmly beltieve that the whole performance was as professionally unique as private theatricals would be, publicly performed, and that the manager reaped a golden harvest from one of the sleepiest and most stupid humbugs in the world.

That was the first day since my acquaintance that I had been

LYNCHBURG VIRGINIAN

Tuesday Morning, Dec. 20, 1864.

THE VIRGINIAN

Is published Daily, Tri-Weekly, and Weekly, by

CHARLES W. BUTTON.

TERMS OF SUBSCRIPTION:

Daily Virginian,	one year,	:	$40 00
Do. do.	six months,	:	20 00
Do. do.	three months,	:	12 00
Do. do.	one month,	:	5 00
Tri-Weekly,	one year,	:	$25 00
Do.	six months,	:	15 00
Do.	three months,	:	8 00
Do.	one month,	:	3 00
Weekly,	one year,	:	$15 00
Do.	six months,	:	8 00

☞No paper will be sent without the subscription is paid in advance.

RATES OF ADVERTISING:

ADVERTISEMENTS are inserted for $3 00 per square of eight lines, for the first insertion and $2 00 per square for each additional insertion.

OBITUARY AND MARRIAGE NOTICES charged for at the same rates.

Seward has dispatched a United States Marshal to Montreal, to look after the interests of the Government, in the case of the St. Albans raiders. Why this step should have been taken after the prisoners were acquitted, we are at a loss to know. The duties of such an officer are simply executive. It is his business to enforce law under the direction of the supreme authority; but what law of the United States does Seward propose to enforce on British soil?—The court decided that it had no jurisdiction in this case, and so far from proposing to deliver the prisoners into the custody of the Marshal of the United States, set them at liberty.—Does Seward intend to arrest them within Her Majesty's dominions and bring them to the United States for trial? Taking the instructions issued by Dix, as to all future raids, it might be assumed that this is the purpose. This Yankee Major General commanding the Northern district of the United States proposes to extend the exercise of his functions within the British territory. He has ordered his subalterns to pursue any raiding parties in future into Canada, to arrest them there and, under no circumstances, whatsoever, to release them. Bravo! for Dix and Seward. They have quite forgotten that little affair of the Trent; when two obnoxious Confederates, protected by the British flag, were captured, and carried to a Northern bastile; but, upon the demand of her Majesty's Government, were promptly released. Is Seward anxious for another opportunity to strike the gridiron flag at the growl of the British lion? He may be gratified. Nor will it be necessary for him to obtrude his insolence much longer. Great Britain has endured a good deal, and in the language of one of her own poets, may yet show that even

"Mercy knows the appointed bound,
And turns to vengeance there."

The spectacle of a nation torn and rent like that of the North, unable, during four years of war to put down "a rebellion," so called, at home—attempting to bully a Power like England, is ridiculous. The pity which has been excited by such a scene, and the forbearance that has been indulged towards a people struggling "for the preservation of the national life," as Seward expresses his sense of that condition, may give place to another and very different feeling. The English are a proud people, and though a brace of driveling dotards, in the last stages of senility have succeeded thus far in compromising the dignity of the nation, its honor may not be forfeited. Palmerston and Russell may be swept from power rather than that the British lion shall be humbled by a nation that has shown its incompetency to suppress insurrection at home. The British, though slow to move, can be fired up to an intensity of passion that will prompt them to make any sacrifice to vindicate the cause of their nation. It cannot be, either, that the people and Government of Great Britain are so ignorant of the sentiment of the Southern half of what was once the United States, as to imagine, as the Yankees seem to do, that the first blast of the bugle which announces a war with our ancient enemy would be the signal for re-union, that we might join against the common foe. We say that this Yankee delusion cannot prevail over the water; nor is it possible for the British people to imagine that they would find us other than firm allies in the event of their entering into war with a people whom we hate worse than ever Briton was hated by his worst enemy.

The people of the South would rejoice to see the British navy batter down every city in Lincolndom. When it may be too late, Seward will find that we are more "debased" in this regard, than his letter to *Adams*, when denouncing the effort to distribute "British gold" amongst the Confederate prisoners, would indicate. So far as affection for our "Northern brethren" and "the best government the world ever saw," are concerned, we are shockingly "debased." We have not one generous or elevated emotion for either. In this respect we are utterly "debased." Let Seward and his royal master blunder into a war with England as, in all probability they will; and then they may learn the extent of our debasement.—The "blue lights," to signal British vessels, will then be seen on Southern coasts; and the sympathy which Yankee States alone, manifested for the British during the war of 1812, will be repaid with usury by the much wronged countrymen of the pure and patriotic Madison.

"Blood letting Chandler," the bellicose Senator from Michigan, wants to make England pay for all the destruction which Yankee commerce has sustained by our privateers or vessels of war. This is a magnificent conception of the illustrious Michigander. Make England pay? Certainly! Why not? It is the easiest thing imaginable. The word is only to be spoken, and the thing is done. Let Old Abe seize Canada as indemnity and a guarantee for the fulfillment of the obligation imposed on "perfidious Albion." Nothing is easier. But who will pay for the blood shed which this cowardly Yankee miscreant—one of the meanest looking mortals we ever beheld—advised, before one drop had been shed? "A little blood letting" was Chandler's prescription for "cementing" the Union; but the miserable quack has murdered the patient! Blind as ever, he would now invite England to bury it. Gather up the manes.—"Blood letting" has brought them to this, and now a little forced tribute from England will finish the work, and cover up all that is mortal of the American Union. We go for Chandler's proposition, and want to see England play both undertaker and sexton. It could do the last honors decently. We sincerely hope that the advice of the "blood letting" quack will be taken by the nation whom the gods would destroy and have first made mad.

OUR ROYAL PRESIDENT—ABE LINCOLN.

Under the above caption the New York Day Book gets off the following back handed compliment to the Illinois blackguard now filling the chair at Washington once occupied by patriots, christians and gentlemen:

A Philadelphia Miscegen paper gives an account of a sumptuous sixteen wheeled car, just finished for the "widow maker." It is the most elegant and costly thing of the kind ever seen in this country. It has sleeping apartments, a parlor, and a Secretary's office, and the ernamental work, executed by artists especially chosen for the work, is beyond conception, gorguons. Thus it is that our royal ruler proposes to prepare for his next four years' reign, if in the meantime, all his "plans" work just as he expects them to. The total cost of this new royal extravagance is eight thousand dollars! The grotesque appearance that Old Abe will make in this new and elegant car can be more easily imagined than described.

A gentleman of this city, who called upon him last summer at the White House, during the very warm weather, found him sitting in his room with nothing on but his shirt and pantaloos, and his bare feet sticking out of the window! The royal joker declared he was trying the experiment to see if it would not cool them! Whether he intends to travel around the country in his new car, in the same style of refinement, remains to be seen. A flat boat, with one pole such as he formerly owned, would evidently be more in accordance with his antecedents and habits. But, we suppose, he thinks he must get up something to dazzle the eyes of his subjects—the poor base born thralls who lay down their necks for him to trample upon.

Washington rode into New York on horseback when he was inaugurated President. Mr Jefferson refused to ride in a carriage from his residence to Congress, and trudged his way on foot, like the commonest workman going to his daily labor. But now a vulgar buffoon, who grins ghastly jokes over the grave of the Union, rides in a sumptuous sixteen wheeled car, at a cost of eighty thousand dollars of toil and sweat of the masses.—Are not the people robbed sufficiently now by his excises—his conscriptions, detectives, Provost Marshals, Assessors. Collectors, &c, but they must be taxed for a sumptuous car of royal magnificence, with "furnished parlor," luxurious "sleeping apartments," its elegant "secretary's office," such as no King, Emperor, Czar, Kasler, or even despotic Caesar himself ever indulged in! Where is the manhood of the American people?—Can it be possible that they will re-elect such a vulgar imitator of royalty—one who insults every white man by making negroes their equals, and who sits at Washington, joking over the downfall of a Republic, ruined by his vile attempt to carry out the disgusting and beastly doctrine of Miscegenation!

ATLANTA.

City Marshal O H Jones communicates to the Augusta Register, an account of the condition in which Atlanta was found by the returning exiles. After enumerating the private houses destroyed, either by name or locality, he adds:

All the hotels in the city are destroyed except the Gate City.

All the livery stables are burned except mine.

All the business houses are burned except Boark's corner and one little building opposite the Express Office and block, Masonic Hall building, and Col Z A Rice's house on Lloyd street.

The city hall is standing. The jail and calaboose are burned.

The fire engines are all shipped off except No 3; that is badly damaged.

Wesley Chapel and Trinity, the First and Second Baptist, First and Second Presbyterian, and Catholic Churches are standing. The First Episcopal Church is standing, but badly damaged. The Yankees used it, I have been told, for a ten pin alley.

Every depot, railroad turn table, water tank, pump, cross tie, bridge, blacksmith shop, (except one) and all the mills are burned.

I think more than two thirds of all the residences in the city are destroyed, but I can give but a faint idea of the destruction.

The cemetery fence is all destroyed.—The Yankees have buried their dead all over the city, and have taken the fence from around the cemetery to build some separate lots for themselves. They have put their dead in private vaults, and have stolen tombstones from Mr Oatman's marble yard to put at their heads. They have taken the moss and shrubbery from other graves to cover the graves of their dead. And have robbed our dead in the vaults of the silver coffin plates to make finger rings.

As if the Yankees had not plundered the unfortunate citizens enough, their houses were robbed by the people of the surrounding country after Sherman left. The following is to us the most sickening part of Marshal Jones's whole story:

From the best information I can get there have been from fifty to three hundred wagons per day in Atlanta, since the Federals left, hauling off iron, furniture, wagons, window blinds, door locks, books, lumber, &c., amounting to about fifteen hundred wagon loads. They came from fifty to one hundred miles in every direction. They broke open all the houses that were left, including the churches in which the exiles' furniture was stored, and plundered indiscriminately.

IMPORTANT FROM CANADA.

THE RELEASE OF THE ST. ALBANS AND LAKE ERIE RAIDERS.

The following despatches are published:

TORONTO, Dec. 13.

The Lake Erie raiders were again before the court to-day, and discharged on the ground that the court had no jurisdiction. The result causes much excitement.

MONTREAL, Dec. 13.

The case of the St. Albans raiders was reopened to day before Justice Coursal. The court room was well filled with spectators. The appearance of the prisoners was much the same as at their last appearance.

After some discussion between the counsel, the Court said this was a matter of most grave importance, involving his right of jurisdiction, and consequently the validity of these proceedings from their commencement. He should, therefore, take time to consider it before proceeding further and for this purpose the court would adjourn until 2 P. M.

The court reassembled at three o'clock this afternoon, and was densely crowded.

Mr. Justice Coursal, on taking the bench, said the matter in question was most important, since his authority had been denied. He had given the arguments on both sides his most serious consideration, and had come to the conclusion that the case came under the imperial act, and that he was bound to obey the imperial authority. In a national question like the one under consideration, the imperial act was supreme, and must be his guide. Our own provincial act to carry into effect the Ashburton treaty had not received the special royal sanction requisite. The case was a most exceptional one, and, being a treaty matter between the two nations, he could do no other than allow our own act to give way before that of the imperial legislature. The revised imperial act must rule, herein: and that act required that the warrant under which the prisoners were arrested should be signed by the Governor General. If the Court could have reserved the point for a higher tribunal, it would most gladly have done so. But since the liberty of the subject was involved, there admitted of no delay; and since he had not had the warrant of the government, he had come to the conclusion that the Court possessed no jurisdiction in the case, and he must order the immediate release of the prisoners.

This announcement was received with applause by a number of persons present, but the demonstration was instantly checked.

Mr Rose, counsel for the United States, wished to speak. He said he did not intend to call his Honor's judgment just delivered in question.

The Court declined to hear further, saying that if he had no right to arrest these men on the charge—as he held that he had not—then neither had he the right to detain them on any others. These men had been arrested on magistrates warrants, upon his own, and then on motion of the public; and now, when his Honor's own jurisdiction was called in question because his warrants were null and void he saw that he had been mistaken. And it was the duty of every British judge, on finding that, to rectify his errors. The Court, therefore, ordered that the prisoners be immediately discharged, and was prepared to incur the responsibility of its own act.

Applause again broke forth in the court but it was again instantly checked.

In a few moments the prisoners walked through the court room, and were congratulated by a few of their acquaintances, and when they emerged from the building a few voices were raised in something meant to be a cheer. They then separated, looking pleased at their enlargement, and the crowd at once dispersed.

AVOIDING THE DRAFT.

The Daily News rejoices over the following:

"Of three hundred substitute men who have been sent to the front from Columbus, Ohio, under a strong guard, the number who had escaped on the way from that city to Louisville, Ky., is said to have reached one hundred! The remainder, or at all events, those of them who will not have run off before they reach Nashville, will, we presume, take the earliest opportunity of finding the way within the lines of the Confederates.—The war has demonstrated no truth so clearly as that conscription of hundreds of thousands of unwilling men, will add but little to the numerical, and nothing to the physical, strength of our armies."

TOM THUMB.

The London papers of November 18th announce the arrival of "General Tom Thumb" and family in that city. They are holding daily levees in a hotel near St. James' Palace. The Star says: "The baby is a pretty little girl, with light silken hair and a vivacious disposition. She will be a year old next month, and it may interest our readers to know that she weighs precisely seven pounds and three quarters."

It is expensive to get sick; there is a Lincoln tax on sickness. It is expensive to be healthy; there's a Lincoln tax on health. It is expensive to die; there's a Lincoln tax on death.—*Louisville Journal.*

But the Journal has one consolation left. There is no tax on lying.—*Washington Chronicle.*

That is because the party that does the lying does the taxing.—*Louisville Journal.*

OBITUARY.

DIED, of remittent fever and bronchitis, in Harrisonburg, on the 1st of Dec., 1864, CHARLES H. SHIPMAN, aged 25 years—a member of Co. H., 49th Va. Volunteers, and a citizen of Nelson County. After being in the hospital a few days, he was removed to the house of strangers, who received and treated him with all the tenderness and solicitude which would have been expected from old acquaintances.

About seven weeks before his death, Charlie left home for the service. His clear, bright face, and compact form gave promise of a safe and happy return to his friends.—The only apprehension was the disasters of the battle-field. When he was brought back the victim of disease, the community in which he lived was painfully shocked, for he had the confidence and respect of all who knew him. Nature formed him for domestic and social life—he loved his friends, but he loved his family and home supremely.—His genial temper, cordial manners and sincere warm attachments, combined with a contented spirit and habits of industry, made him a useful and happy man at home and in his family. He was a good neighbor and a good citizen. His loss is a serious one to the community, and irreparable to his young family. Our Father in Heaven has promised to be a father to the fatherless, and a God of comfort to the widow; to his gracious care we commend this bereaved and helpless family. From the beginning of his attack our young friend had a presentiment that it would prove fatal. He gave himself to prayer and solemn meditation. He said to his Pastor or brother "I want you to pray for me, but do not pray for my recovery, but pray that God may give me grace to submit to His will, whatever that may be." Subsequently, he prayed himself to God to give him some unmistakable evidence of his pardon and acceptance; and while the prayer was on his lips he received the fullest assurance that it was heard and answered, and he seemed to be full of peace and joy. In the last days of his attack he became wild with delirium—in this state his mind unconsciously wandered back to the happy scenes of home—thus showing in death the ruling passion of his life. It is sad to contemplate the career of a friend thus prematurely and distressingly ended; but it is delightful to feel that the cares of life, the terrors of death, and the gloom of the grave are all swallowed up in victory and triumph through our Lord Jesus Christ.

P. C. C.

☞Republican copy.

IN COUNCIL OF THE CITY OF LYNCHBURG, December 12th, 1864.

The following preamble and resolutions were adopted and ordered to be published.

JAS. O. WILLIAMS,
Clerk of the City Council.

Whereas, under an ordinance of the 28th of December, 1849, passed in pursuance of the act of the General Assembly, of the 24th of March, 1848, incorporating the "Virginia and Tennessee Railroad Company," certain Stockholders in said Company, were, by the City of Lynchburg, guaranteed six per centum per annum on the par value of their Stock; and they, to indemnify the City therefor, executed powers of attorney, authorizing its Treasurer to demand and receive from the said Company all dividends declared upon such guaranteed stock.

And, whereas, the Stockholders at their last annual meeting, on the —— day of ——, 1864, declared a dividend of 110 per cent.; $100 thereof to be paid by the issue of certificates of new stock, and $10 in currency, on the 1st of January, 1865, to which, and all future dividends, so long as that gurantee and the said powers of attorney remain in force, the city of Lynchburg is, and will be, entitled.

And whereas, by the 5th Sec. of the ordinance aforesaid, the holders of the said guaranteed stock or any of them are authorized, when they elect so to do, to give up the guarantee and hold the stock with right to dividends as though it had never existed; in which event the powers of attorney aforesaid, are to be cancelled, and the city from the guarantee discharged; and whereas, to all such as may now so elect, the city is willing and offers to surrender the divided of 110 per cent. declared as aforesaid.

And, whereas, by the 6th Sec. of said ordinance, the Treasurer of the city is directed when so required by holders of said guaranteed stock, over and above thirty shares, to take a transfer thereof to the city, and in lieu thereof to give its bonds, bearing six per cent. interest, payable half yearly redeemable in 30 years and afterwards at its pleasure; and whereas, in the opinion of the Council, the time has arrived when the relations of these stockholders and the city of Lynchburg to this stock should be defined, and their respective future rights permanently fixed.

Therefore Resolved:

1st. That all holders of the said guaranteed stock be and they are hereby invited and requested, on or before the 29th day of December, instant, to make known in writing to the Treasurer of the city of Lynchburg, whether they choose to hold their stock *as now guaranteed,* leaving all future dividends to be received by the city; *or,* in accordance with the offer above made, elect to cancel their powers of attorney, discharge the guarantee and henceforth to hold the stock *unconditionally; or,* prefer, as provided for in the 6th Sec. of the ordinance, to exchange it for city bonds.

2d. That as to all such as elect the second proposition, the Treasurer of the city is directed at once to cancel the guarantee and powers of attorney aforesaid, and such stock holders may demand and receive the dividends aforesaid of 110 per cent. and all future dividends upon their stock declared.—As to all such as prefer the last proposition, the Treasurer is directed to issue bonds and take transfers, as provided for in the said 6th Sec., and as to those who accept neither, the Treasurer is directed to take no future step (except to pay the guaranteed 6 per cent.) unless in obedience to an express order of the Council.

3d. That the Treasurer keep an accurate account of his action hereunder and report the same to the Council, to be spread on the minutes.

4th That the Secretary cause the foregoing preamble and resolutions to be published semi-weekly in the city newspapers until the 29th day of December, inst., and semi-weekly in Richmond to same date.

dec14—swt29

THE NEW YORK HERALD.

WHOLE NO. 10,343. NEW YORK, THURSDAY, DECEMBER 22, 1864. PRICE FOUR CENTS.

SHERMAN.

The Gallop Through Georgia.

Forty-two Counties of the Rebel Empire State Laid Waste.

The State Capital Formally Surrendered to Ten Scouts, who Stampede Two Hundred Rebel Soldiers.

THE COUNTRY STRIPPED OF EVERYTHING

All the Railways Destroyed and Iron Burned.

THE BATTLE OF GRISWOLDVILLE.

Walcott Almost Annihilates Three Rebel Brigades with One and Captures the Rebel Commander.

Sherman Subsists on the Fat of the Land and Does Not Lose a Wagon or Gun.

The Spoils of the Campaign 4,000 Prisoners, 15,000 Horses, 10,000 Negroes, Thirty Pieces of Artillery, &c.

MILLIONS WORTH OF COTTON BURNED.

Sherman's Total Loss Only Fifteen Hundred.

STORMING OF FORT McALLISTER.

The Garrison and Twenty-four Guns Captured.

THE FLEET GOES UP TO THE NEW BASE.

The Siege of Savannah Opened.

MUTINY OF THE PEOPLE OF SAVANNAH!

They are Ready to Give Up---Warehouses Thrown Open and All Told to Help Themselves,

&c., &c., &c.

The United States steam transport Fulton, Capt. Wotton, from Port Royal on the 18th, via Fortress Monroe on the 20th inst., arrived at this port yesterday morning.

The Fulton touched at Fortress Monroe to land Lieutenant Colonel O. E. Babcock, bearer of despatches from Gen. Sherman to the War Department. Also Colonel A. H. Markland, General Sherman's mail agent.

Savannah was still in possession of the rebels. Its surrender had not been demanded by Gen. Sherman up to the time of the sailing of the Fulton.

Among the passengers per Fulton are Col. W. Gurney, One Hundred and Twenty-seventh New York Volunteers, nineteen other officers of lesser grade, who were wounded in the late battle at Pocotaligo, South Carolina, and our correspondents who accompanied General Sherman in his march through Georgia.

SHERMAN'S TRIUMPHANT MARCH.

Routes of the Army from Atlanta to the Atlantic----The Investment of Savannah.

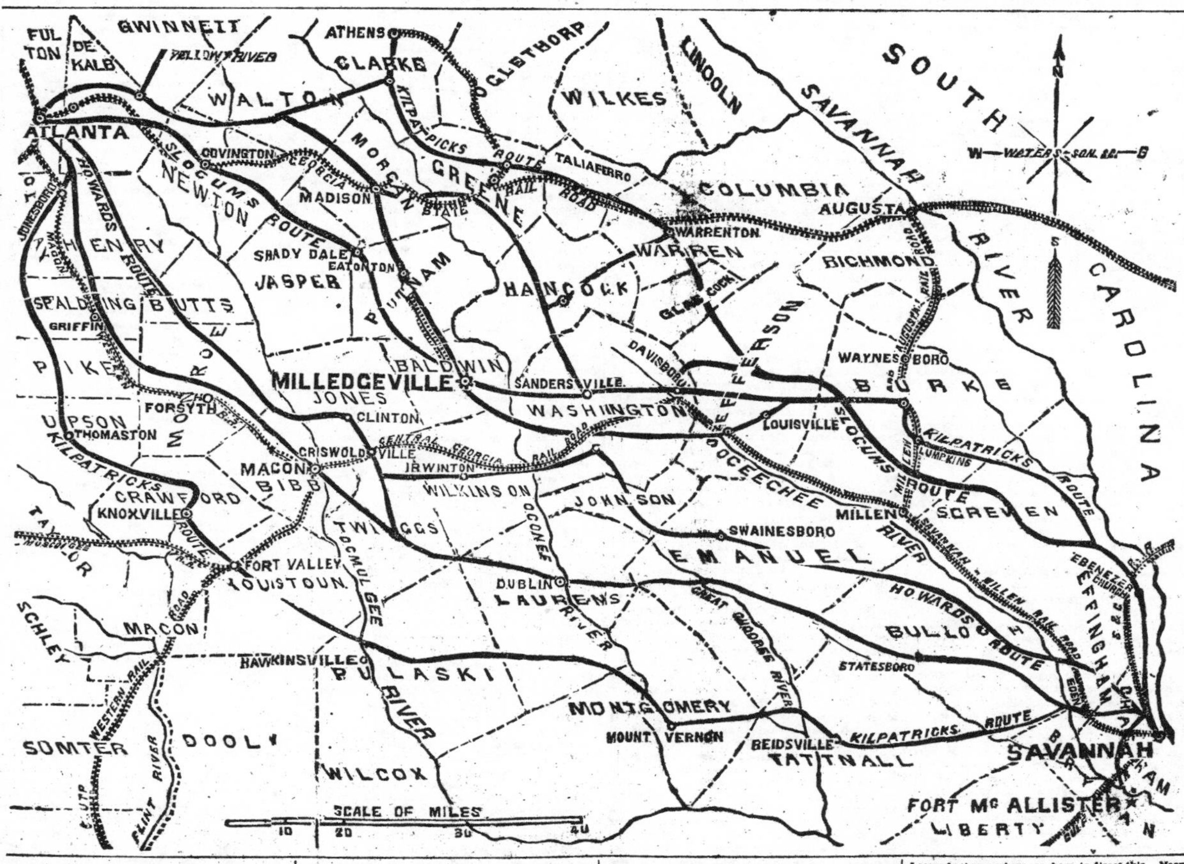

THE GRAND MARCH THROUGH GEORGIA.

Our Expeditionary Correspondence.

FORT MCALLISTER, OGEECHEE RIVER, Dec. 1, 1864.

The winter campaign of Sherman, which for the past two weeks has caused so much anxiety in the minds of the loyal people of the nation, and spread terror and alarm throughout the confederacy, from Richmond to Arkansas, may now be considered ended for the present. To the casual observer its importance in a military point of view may not be at first apparent; but a careful study of the route traversed, and the situation previous to its inauguration, will exhibit the fact that Sherman's month of raiding in the confederacy has produced results even greater than that which followed the fall of Atlanta. I propose, briefly, to inform the reader of

THE GENERAL SITUATION.

Previous to the commencement of this bold and audacious movement through the enemy's country, going as far back as the commencement of the spring campaign, I will renew the situation and record what seems to me to have influenced the recent movements of Sherman.

On assuming command of the Military Division of the Mississippi, Sherman found Johnston in force at Dalton, and Longstreet wintering in East Tennessee, confronted by Schofield. Before the campaigning season arrived Longstreet withdrew, leaving but one large army (Johnston's) in the Southwest to be assailed. Military men all agree that the East Tennessee route to Virginia is the most feasible mode of investing Richmond, by the capture of Lynchburg, the key to the whole military position in the East; and I believe that Sherman's keen sagacity pointed that way. But he had no alternative. With an army of only a hundred thousand he could not hold his long line of supplies from Louisville and protect Middle Tennessee from invasion while operating from Knoxville, consequently he was forced to follow Johnston into Georgia further and further from his base, until Atlanta fell into our hands, and Sherman found that Hood's army was still formidable for mischief. With Atlanta we severed the railway communications for a time, but the branch roads around Milledgeville and Macon still enabled the enemy to draw supplies from Florida, Southern Georgia, Alabama and Mississippi, for the subsistence of their armies, while it gave us one hundred and forty miles more of railway to guard against raids upon our flanks and guerilla depredations in the rear.

The further pursuit of Hood, consequently, seemed frought with danger and perplexity, and Sherman seems to have studied well the problem how to shorten his line of supplies, and at the same time hold Chattanooga, the key to Tennessee. The campaign of the summer had ended, Hood's army being not less than thirty thousand, while the draft had very largely swelled Sherman's ranks. It was then that the great genius of the man solved the question; and this campaign was created and worked out upon the map. The moment he could draw Hood away from his front, beyond the reach of railway communication with the rebel base of supplies, Sherman saw that by dividing his large army he could with the one wing keep Hood employed and by bold and rapid movements strike the coast and open up a new line of supplies, via some of the large rivers, from which he could operate against the interior of Georgia, Alabama and the Carolinas.

I have the best authority for saying that the subsequent advance to the coast was of Sherman's own conception, submitted and explained by him to General Grant and the War Department, and by them heartily approved.

With the subsequent movement of Hood to Sherman's rear, the cutting of his communications, the apparent tardiness of Sherman in pursuit, and the escape of Hood into Northern Alabama, the reader is familiar, and at the time, no doubt, felt like censuring Sherman for not showing more determination and energy against inferior numbers. But they must now see that this was a part of Sherman's well matured plan.

While Hood was boldly pushing away from his base Sherman was gathering all his strength for a desperate blow that was destined to break the outer shell of the rebellion and expose its vitals.

PREPARATIONS FOR THE MARCH.

Sending the Fourth and Twenty-third corps to Thomas as a nucleus for a new command, a new army was organized under that well tried general, and then Sherman bade the North good bye, destroyed the railroad from Atlanta to Chattanooga, refitted his army at Atlanta and cut loose—destination, the coast; object, a new base.

Loading his wagons with sixteen days rations for a march of over three hundred miles through an enemy's country, he first divides his command into four columns, marches via the Augusta and Atlanta Railway, destroys it in his march as well as the road to Macon. While his right wing threatens Macon the left occupies the capital of the State and lays waste the railways, cotton mills, foundries and machine shops. In his march he subsists his armies upon the fat of the land, branches off, threatens Augusta, cuts the railway communication with Savannah; then rapidly turns south, crosses the Ogeechee river, and concentrating his command covers his flanks with the two streams and moves direct upon Savannah and the coast, completely destroying the railways of Georgia, leaving not enough subsistence behind him to winter a kid, invests Savannah, and in thirty days from the time he cut loose, opens up a new line of supplies with his base only ten miles from his army.

And all this marching of over three hundred and fifty miles through an enemy's country is performed without the loss of a wagon or mule, a gun or a pound of ammunition.

The intelligent reader will now see the importance of this campaign in a military point of view. With Georgia stripped of all its summer crops, the railways all destroyed, Hood's army cannot subsist upon or occupy it until the return of another crop, and with Thomas confronting him he cannot hurry to the relief of Savannah and Charleston, which are now tottering to their downfall.

With a large army under Sherman and a grand navy under the gallant sea dog Dahlgren threatening them, their possession by us is only a question of a few weeks.

But it has had another important effect upon our common enemy. Heretofore Lee has drawn a large amount of subsistence from Florida, Georgia, Alabama, Mississippi and Texas. This raid of Sherman's has not only cut every line of communication with the Southwest, but blotted out the machine shops and iron works that furnished the material for repairing these railway arteries and veins. Hence for the future Lee must depend entirely upon the Carolinas and Virginia for subsistence for his army. He may endeavor to invade East Tennessee and obtain supplies from that quarter, but the withdrawal of any considerable force for that purpose would endanger Richmond and open the gates to Grant.

Taken as a whole, I am forced to the conclusion that this campaign of Sherman's own creation and execution is one of the most fruitful the war has produced. It is a blow from which Davis and his satellites will never recover; the effects of which will be felt from one end of the country to the other.

But there is still another effect it will have. It demonstrates to European Powers the weakness of the rebels and the power of the national government to cope with armed treason and rebellion.

But to the detailed narrative, which opens with

THE CONCENTRATION OF THE ARMY.

On the 11th the army was located as follows:—The Twentieth corps at Atlanta, the Fifteenth and Seventeenth corps at Powder Spring road, on the Chattahoochee river, and the Fourteenth corps at Kingston, Ga. Sherman's headquarters were at the latter place.

On the morning of the 12th the army commenced concentrating around Atlanta. The Fourteenth corps, Brevet Major General Davis commanding, remained at Kingston to cover the shipment north of the government property and rolling stock of the railway, and at noon of that day the Third brigade of the First division, Colonel H. A. Hambright, Seventy-ninth Pennsylvania, commanding, who, by the way, was the first commandant at Kingston, moved out, and the place was evacuated. Notwithstanding that the Colonel took every precaution to prevent a wanton destruction of the place, the negroes, who brought up the rear, fired several buildings, which were consumed. The corps reached Cartersville at night, and, after provisioning the troops, the public property was destroyed, and on the following day (the 13th) Big Shanty was reached, and the troops bivouacked for the night. Next day the corps reached the Chattahoochee river, and on the 15th Atlanta.

CHATTANOOGA RAILWAY DESTROYED.

The railway was torn up from Chattanooga to Atlanta, and all the bridges laid in ashes, as well as every building that could be of benefit to the enemy. The straggling negroes and cavalry destroyed quite a number of uninhabited houses, and, I regret to say, three or four churches.

On the 14th and 15th, the Fifteenth and Seventeenth corps, under General Howard, marched to a camp one mile south of Atlanta, to which point Slocum, commanding the left wing, moved on the morning of the 15th, leaving the city entirely empty, except a few citizens, who remained scattered over the city, preferring to dwell in the city until the return to its ruins of their disloyal friends than to accept of free transportation to the land of "Yankee mudsills" and "Puritanical abolitionists." The afternoon was spent in emptying the storehouses of clothing, commissary supplies, &c., and their transfer to the persons of the troops of the Fourteenth corps.

During the entire day Atlanta presented a very busy appearance, every street of importance being blockaded by wagon trains and mounted officers and men. Quite a number of houses were fired during the day, and regular detailed parties from the Twentieth corps destroyed all the public buildings of value to the enemy.

GENERAL SHERMAN'S ORDERS TO HIS TROOPS.

After the men had bivouacked for the night the following orders, issued by General Sherman, were read to the troops, and were greeted with many manifestations of approbation by the veterans, who, in so many bloody battles, have followed the lead of Sherman:—

SHERMAN'S ORDERS.

Special Field Orders—No. 119.

HEADQUARTERS, MILITARY DIVISION OF MISSISSIPPI, IN THE FIELD, KINGSTON, GA., Nov. 8, 1864.

The General commanding deems it proper at this time to inform the officers and men of the Fourteenth, Fifteenth, Seventeenth and Twentieth corps, that he has organized them into an army for a special purpose, well known to the War Department and to General Grant. It is sufficient for you to know that it involves a departure from our present base, and a long and difficult march to a new one. All the chances of war have been considered and provided for as far as human sagacity can. All he asks of you is to maintain that discipline, patience and courage which have characterized you in the past, and he hopes, through you, to strike a blow at our enemy that will have a material effect in producing what we all so much desire—his complete overthrow. Of all things the most important is, that the men, during marches and in camp, keep their places and not scatter about as stragglers or foragers, to be picked up by hostile people in detail.

It is also of the utmost importance that our wagons should not be loaded with anything but provisions and ammunition. All surplus servants, non-combatants and refugees should now go to the rear, and none should be encouraged to encumber us on the march. At some future time we will be enabled to provide for the poor whites and blacks who seek to escape the bondage under which they are now suffering.

With these few simple cautions in your minds, he hopes to lead you to achievements equal in importance to those of the past. By order of

Major General W. T. SHERMAN.

L. M. DAYTON, Aid de camp.

MILITARY DIVISION, MISSISSIPPI, IN THE FIELD, KINGSTON, GA., Nov. 9, 1864.

Special Field Orders—No 120.

I. For the purpose of military operations this army is divided into two wings, viz:—

The right wing, Major General O. O. Howard commanding—the Fifteenth and Seventeenth corps.

The left wing, Major General H. W. Slocum commanding—the Fourteenth and Twentieth corps.

II. The habitual order of march will be, whenever practicable, by four roads, as near parallel as possible, and converging at points hereafter to be indicated in orders. The cavalry, Brigadier General Kilpatrick commanding, will receive special orders from the Commander-in-Chief.

Paragraph III. relates to the position in the line of the ambulances and wagons.

IV. The army will forage liberally on the country during the march. To this end each brigade commander will organize a good and efficient foraging party, under command of one or more discreet officers, who will gather near the route travelled corn or forage of any kind, meat of any kind, vegetables, corn meal, or whatever is needed by the command; aiming at all times to keep in the wagons at least ten days' provisions for the command and three days' forage. Soldiers must not enter the dwellings of the inhabitants, or commit any trespass, but during a halt or in a camp they may be permitted to gather turnips, potatoes and other vegetables, and to drive in stock in sight of their camp. To regular foraging parties must be entrusted the gathering of provisions and forage at any distance from the road travelled.

V. To army corps commanders alone is entrusted the power to destroy mills, houses, cotton gins, &c., and for them this general principle is laid down:—In districts and neighborhoods where the army is unmolested no destruction of such property should be permitted; but should guerillas or bushwhackers molest our march, or should the inhabitants burn bridges, obstruct roads, or otherwise manifest local hostility, then army commanders should order and enforce a devastation more or less relentless, according to the measure of such hostility.

VI. As for horses, mules, wagons, &c., belonging to the inhabitants, the cavalry and artillery may appropriate freely and without limit, discriminating, however, between the rich, who are generally hostile, and the poor, or industrious, usually neutral or friendly. Foraging parties may also take mules or horses to replace the jaded animals of their trains, or to serve as pack mules for the regiments or brigades. In all foraging, of whatever kind, the parties will refrain from abusive or threatening language, and may, when the officers in command think proper, give certificates of the fact, but no receipts, and they will endeavor to leave each family a reasonable portion for their maintenance. * * * *

By order of Major General W. T. SHERMAN.

L. M. DAYTON, A. D. C.

ATLANTA ON FIRE.

"Now negress night came solemn down" upon the city, and as the flames spread from the public buildings and the depot that had been fired the whole heavens became illuminated by the lurid glare, while the unexploded shells in the dwellings and storehouses became heated, and as they exploded in rapid succession one almost imagined that the scenes of August last, when one hundred thousand heroes confronted the rebel stronghold, were being re-enacted.

Standing upon an eminence overlooking the doomed city, I had an excellent view of the conflagration, and never had I beheld so grand a sight. As night waned the gentle breezes carried the destroying element from house to house, and block to block, until one-half of the rebel city was in flames, the glare of which was so bright that the soldiers a mile distant read their last letters from home by the light. Next morning I rode over the city among the ruins, where nothing remained to tell the tale but tottering walls and blackened chimneys, that, like gravestones, stood there as monuments of departed glory.

ON THE WAR TRACK AGAIN.

On the morning of the 16th, at daylight, the whole army once more took up the line of march—the Seventeenth corps on the McDonough road, the Fourteenth on the Augusta road (running parallel with the railroad), with the Twentieth on the left and the Fifteenth on the right flanks. I accompanied the column of the Fourteenth corps, which passed out through Decatur, and the same evening encamped in Lithonia—a small town twenty miles southeast of Atlanta—without encountering any enemy.

On the 17th the march was resumed at daylight, through a country teeming in stock, vegetables and grain, that were found in abundance on all the large plantations that lined the route. This part of the State gives evidence of wealth and prosperity, and as we moved further into the interior the works of war's ravages became less frequent.

THE COUNTRY

is quite open, well watered, good roads and delightful climate. About half-past nine o'clock in the morning,

CONYERS,

a town of about five hundred inhabitants, was reached, but no halt was made, and the troops continued the march without interrupting the citizens, who flocked in large numbers to the doors and windows to see the long expected and much feared Yankees, and listen to the music of a score of bands that gave forth their martial strains. Only one man was seen in the town. All the others had "refugeed," as the ebony children classically expressed themselves. A rebel lieutenant, named Lewis A. Middleton, who acted as provost marshal at that place, left very hurriedly, forgetting to call at the post office for several letters, which were taken possession of by an aid-de-camp, and turned over to General Sherman for examination. The letters disclosed the fact that the Georgia militia accompanied Hood as far as Gadsden, Ala., when Governor Brown ordered them back to the State, where they arrived on the 6th, after a march of nearly five hundred miles.

One of the letters is worth producing here:—

A REBEL LETTER.

MONTGOMERY, August 13, 1864.

MY DEAR BROTHER—I have deferred writing to you for the past two weeks, daily hoping to get a few lines from you to tell us where you are and how you fared during and after the Yankee raid—but in vain; so I'll venture to write, even though my letter never reaches you. In fact, I scarcely know where or how to direct this. Mary is down at Greenville on a visit to Miss King, where she has been over two weeks. She went for her health, which had been very bad all the spring and summer. She writes me that she has improved and is enjoying herself very much; but no wonder, for she says she gets so well fed; that no one at Greenville seems to feel the war, but live in full and plenty, as they did before; though Margaret King always did live well; but she has plenty of money and nothing to do with it but support herself.

We had a terrible alarm the night the raiders were expected in Montgomery. This is the most excitable family the world ever produced, from the Judge down to the smallest negro child in the lot. Words of mine would fail to give you an idea of the time we had. Sufficient to say that the Judge snatched up his papers and money, flew down to the cars to take care of his own precious self, leaving orders that we all should follow at the first alarm bell, &c. Such a scene of confusion I never saw, and, without stopping to reflect, I jumped out of bed and commenced gathering together my clothes, for I was determined to try and save them, as I never expected to get any more, and where to get trunks or boxes to pack in I knew not. So I was up the whole night long, flying here and there, half dressed, and six o'clock came in the morning before I even sat down. Of course my servants were of no use whatever, and the Judge's, whom he thinks paragons, were in open rebellion. What influence they would have had on Polly when the time came to leave I cannot tell. Fortunately they were not tried, as the vandals did not get here; but when the excitement was over, and I had time to reflect, I thought how foolish it was in me to worry about running away any more, especially with Judge Jordan; for, in any great danger, he is a broken reed to lean upon—self is No. 1, and I have resolved hereafter to just stay where I am, and only regret that I was induced by the entreaties of the Judge to leave my all in Pensacola, not that I would have taken the Yankee oath. Selfish motives were at the bottom with the Judge. I hope I may do him injustice. The day after the alarm I was taken with a violent, nervous pain in my head, which seemed to get worse daily for about ten days, until I suppose the climax came, and then such excruciating pains run down the back of my head and neck that I was senseless for some time. A powerful remedy was administered—opiates and quiet—and in a few days I was myself again. In any great alarm, or excitement or rumor, I seem composed and do all that I can; but afterwards the reaction comes and prostrates me. But after this I think I shall have to stand my ground and take the Yanks as I find them. Now, I have reserved the *bonne bouche* for the last. On Monday, greatly to my surprise, a letter came from the post office, directed to Mary. It was so like your handwriting, though from Wilmington post office, that I was sure it was from you, and, while breaking the seal, wondered how you came to be there. Just think! it was a blockade letter from dear Peyton, written ever since the 20th of January—only seven months since. He had just arrived at Panama and found in the post office there two letters from Mary and one from you, dated, I think he said, 22d of July. It seems he has been in New York for the last two years. His health had been wretched, and after seeking and travelling about to various places in search of a climate to suit him, found that New York was the only place. His intention was to come into Dixie, but could not succeed; and after the fall of Vicksburg had to give up. Some of his good friends tried hard to get him in Fort Lafayette, but failed. His pecuniary matters are as usual; but it takes all he can raise to pay travelling expenses. He expected to meet his agent at Panama; but as he was not there he should go to Nicaragua, from thence to California, or perhaps accompany his agent to Europe; but would write and let us know; that we must write to him and direct our letters as we used to, to his agent in New York, and he would forward them to him, no matter in what part of the world he was. I have lost and forgotten his direction. I know it was a Mr. Sidell, Wall street; but what were the initials of the Christian name or the number of Mr. Sidell's house I have forgotten. Do you remember? If so, write and let me know; though if I write I don't see how we can get a letter to him; and as so much time has passed he may be dead. Write as soon as you can. The servants say, "Give their love to Massa Lewis." Goodby. May God bless and take care of you is ever the prayer of your affectionate sister.

I'll adopt Peyton's plan and not sign my name, in case it should fall into other hands. Love to Mary when you write.

The afternoon of the 17th was spent in destroying the Atlanta and Augusta Railway from Conyers to Yellow river, where Davis' column halted for the night, and Colonel Buell, of the Pioneer corps, threw down pontoons, upon which the army crossed on the following morning.

THE REBELS APPEAR IN OUR FRONT.

To-day the First brigade, First division, Colonel Hobart commanding, had the advance, with Major Fox, of the Twenty-first Michigan, in command of the advance guard. While riding in advance of his command, he was suddenly confronted by a rebel cavalryman, who demanded his surrender. The Major was unarmed and on the point of surrendering when his regiment appeared in sight, and the rebel and his companions, who had come up, retreated without taking the Major.

AN ADVANCE BY THE LADIES.

On the 18th the army moved at half-past six, the First division in the advance, and the Seventy-ninth Pennsylvania, Lieutenant Colonel Miles, the advanced guard. The first place of importance encountered was the beautiful little town of

COVINGTON,

noted, as geographers say, for its water power and pretty women. As Hambright's brigade entered the town the Lancaster (Penn.) band struck up "Dixie's Land," when two hundred women rushed to the piazzas and doors to view the Yankee invaders of whom they had so often read. Every window and door swarmed with blooming war widows, stately matrons and shy virgins in homespun and coarse linen. But when the band had finished "Dixie" and broke off on "Yankee Doodle," oh, what a retreat. The piazzas were cleared of their beautiful inhabitants, windows came down with a slam and doors closed very abruptly, until not a fair face was visible. The troops as they moved at the right shoulder shift, the State and national colors floating in the silken Southern breeze, and the nicely paved streets resounding to the tread of the soldiers of the Union, presented an imposing appearance, not soon to be obliterated from the memories of the rebellious sympathizers with Davis and the Devil. The column encamped at eleven o'clock A. M. near Allachovie river, distant ten miles north of Social Circle, and halted for the day.

FORAGING PARTIES

were sent out in the afternoon, and at night returned to camp with a large amount of fine stock, grain and vegetables.

THE RIGHT WING.

To-night (18th) Howard's (right) wing is encamped at Jackson, and has met no enemy. Slocum, on the left, is parallel with Howard, and has had no fighting.

SHERMAN'S HEADQUARTERS.

General Sherman makes his headquarters with Thomas' veteran corps, now commanded by Brigadier General Jeff C. Davis.

SHERMAN TASTES SORGHUM.

Many little incidents occur daily that go to show a leader like Sherman can make himself familiar with his soldiers, and still retain their confidence and maintain thorough discipline. A colonel commanding a regiment, who witnessed it, informs me that to-day a number of soldiers who were filling their canteens from a molasses barrel, near Sherman's headquarters, were quarreling over the division of the syrup, when Sherman passing by cooly crowded in among them, and dipping his finger in it put it to his lips, remarking, "Don't crowd, boys, there is enough for all."

A PLANTATION SCENE.

About six miles south of Covington we struck the plantation of Judge Harris, who is a Massachusetts man and owns over two hundred negroes. The plantation is one of the most extensive in Central Georgia for the production of cotton and serials of all descriptions. As the column moved past the Third brigade First division band struck up a quick step, when from the village of negro huts the dusky sons of Ham swarmed forth in large numbers and rushed to the fences. A rich scene followed. The negroes—men, women and children—struck off into a dance, swinging themselves round and twisting themselves into grotesque shapes that called forth peals of laughter from the soldiery, while shouts of "Glory be to de Lord, de Lincoom's hab come!" "Won't we go long wid yous!" "Ize off to glory!" "Bress de Lord!" were heard on all sides. They followed the troops for half a mile, making the air resound with their exclamations of gladness, until driven back to the rear.

ANOTHER REBEL ATTACK.

On the 19th the column moved at daylight, Morgan's division leading, Baird next and Carlin covering the rear. The column took the Sandtown road, and when out about three miles, were fired upon by a few rebel scouts, who retreated.

WET WEATHER AND BAD ROADS.

Up to this time we had beautiful weather, but at daylight the roads were found almost impassable from the rain that had fallen in torrents during the night. Nevertheless, nine miles were made through a pouring rain, and we encamped at eight o'clock in the evening three miles south of Sandtown.

On the 20th the command moved at the usual hour, rain still falling, and the roads in a horrible condition. About noon we arrived at Shady Dale, the plantation of an old man named Matthew Whitfield, who owns nearly the whole of Putnam county, and an abundance of stock and crops. There we found

ANOTHER VILLAGE OF NEGROES,

who worked the large plantation upon which Mr. Whitfield resided, and where another scene similar to that enacted at Harris' greeted the men. About twenty-five women followed the column a mile, and were driven back by the staff officers. Nearly all the male negroes went with the army voluntarily. At night the command encamped near Eatonton, and on the morning of the 21st resumed their march, making

MURDER CREEK

before night closed in upon them and rendered marching over muddy roads and swollen rivers too dangerous to be attempted. The country through which we passed was the garden of Georgia, the plantations furnishing an abundance of everything necessary for the subsistence of man and beast, which was very generally appropriated by the foraging parties, who obtained so much potatoes and meat that the commissary wagons were not called upon to disgorge a portion of their hard tack and bacon.

THE ARMY TEAMS

had become thoroughly rejuvinated by the acquisition of hundreds of fine mules captured from the wealthy nabobs who had hidden them in the woods, where they were found by the aid of the negroes. Some of the finest horses I have seen in the South, were also impressed into the United States service.

HOWELL COBB'S "NAG" GOBBLED.

Among the blooded stock captured was General Howell Cobb's celebrated pacing mare, that cost $25,000. She was found in a swamp near Milledgeville, by private Walter Burns, Company E, Twenty-first Ohio, who, ten or twelve days after, was captured while riding her and murdered. He was acting as orderly, and when his companions dug open his grave they found that the enemy had cut his throat after shooting him through the head.

THE APPROACH TO MILLEDGEVILLE

The rain cleared off on the 20th, and the cold north winds came down like good spirits to aid the onward march of the victors by drying up the roads and relieving the faithful friend of the soldier—the mule. The bracing wind and warm sun were balm to the toiling veterans, whose clothes for four days had been drenched with Georgia rains and mud, and as they were near Milledgeville—the capital of the State—where was passed the ordinance of secession, increased speed was plainly discernable in the movement of the men.

At twelve o'clock noon, Davis' advance, composed of Baird's division, encamped in the city, and by dark the woods and shrubbery around the city were illuminated by the camp fires of Sherman's grand army of "invaders."

But let me here dwell a moment upon the

OPERATIONS OF THE TWENTIETH CORPS,

which formed the left, and moved from Atlanta on a road parallel with Davis' route, through Decatur, Madison, Eatonton, &c. General Williams, of Michigan, commanded the corps; Jackson, the First; Geary, of Pennsylvania, the Second; and Ward, of Kentucky, the Third divisions. The corps made excellent time from Atlanta to Milledgeville, encountering no enemy, not even firing a shot, except at venturesome swine and cattle which strayed too near foraging parties.

NEW YORK PLANTS ITS COLORS ON THE CAPITAL.

Major General Slocum, the well tried commander of the left wing, accompanied the corps, which moved on a better road than that travelled by Davis, and reached the city one day in advance of him, planting upon the State House of Georgia the national colors of the One Hundred and Fourth New York regiment, which regiment, with the Third Wisconsin, who fought in the Valley of Virginia under Banks, were detailed as provost guard.

These, however, were not the first troops to enter the capital. The news that "Old Lightning" (which is now applied to Sherman) was coming spread like the wind, and on Saturday Governor Brown and the Legislature, which was in session, packed up their valises and vamosed the ranche, leaving about 1,000 rebel cavalry to cover their retreat to Augusta, where they hoped to find rest for their wearied feet.

CITY CAPTURED BY SCOUTS.

The cavalry left the same night, and on Sunday, the 20th, Captain Duncan rushed into town on a "free" cavalry charge, frightening the old granny who occupied the Mayor's chair into a surrender and stampeding all the male population, with a small squad of ten men. One rebel lady, whose husband is a high official in the State, and whose family is among the *bon ton*, described the surrender in the following words:—

"Early in the afternoon five Yankee scouts came dashing pell mell into the town, when the men—the mean, craven-hearted wretches, fully two hundred strong—skedaddled, leaving our baby Mayor to go out and surrender the place unconditionally to five greasy Yankees, ten miles in advance of their army. Oh, the men are mean, chicken-hearted wretches, and the Mayor a puffed up old fool. Had I been in town I'd collected all the women and driven the skunks out with mop handles and broom sticks."

This is the whole story in a nutshell. The craven-hearted bipeds of the masculine gender ran away and left their wives to the tender mercies of the Yankees, who, they have time and again asserted, came here to ravish, burn and plunder indiscriminately.

THE REBEL CAPITAL

is a very pretty little city, capable of accommodating

THOMAS.

THE BATTLES BEFORE NASHVILLE

Our Special Details of the Three Days Engagements in which Hood was Routed and Destroyed.

His Army Outflanked, Himself Outgeneraled.

His Losses Fully Twelve Thousand Men and Fifty Pieces of Artillery.

His Retreat Intercepted by Our Cavalry and the Gunboats on the Tennessee River,

Our Losses Not Over Three Thousand Men,

&c., &c., &c.

Mr. D. P. Conyngham's Despatch.

NEAR NASHVILLE, Dec. 17, 1864.

THE PRELIMINARY MOVEMENTS.

For several days past there have been exciting rumors. The heavy cavalry force on the north side of the river crossed over on the 12th, crowding the streets and giving currency to extravagant rumors. A council of war was held by Thomas and his generals, and they decided to attack next day, the 13th. The weather was so severe that the attack was deferred. Hood, as if apprised of what was transpiring, moved from his first line of works to a stronger position in front of the long range of hills that connect the bend of the Cumberland river which circles round Nashville.

General Lyon was now threatening the Louisville line, and Breckinridge giving indications of sweeping down on the Chattanooga line. It was therefore Hood's interest to take up a strong position and await Thomas' attack. Hood held a council of war at General Harding's house, where he had his headquarters a few days since, and it was agreed to take up a strong position and invest Nashville, while Forrest and his other raiders would cut off our supplies and thus compel us to attack him on his own terms or evacuate Nashville. On the 11th Forrest's and Page's cavalry commands attacked Murfreesboro, so as to draw off part of our force from Nashville. They were repulsed after a hot contest, and failed in interfering with Thomas' plans.

A SECOND COUNCIL OF WAR.

On the evening of the 14th Thomas and his corps and division generals held a second council of war at the St. Cloud Hotel, at which the following programme was decided on for the following morning:—

The artillery from the forts and advanced batteries to open all along the line. Major General Steedman, who commanded on the extreme left, was to make a heavy demonstration, so as to attract the enemy's attention to that point. Schofield, who connected with Steedman's right, was to hold himself in readiness to move as necessary. Wood's corps, the Fourth, was to move on the Hillsboro pike, keeping up a connection with A. J. Smith's, and pierce the centre, while A. J. Smith was to attack the extreme left. Hatch's division of cavalry connected with Smith's right.

Some of Major General Wilson's cavalry had wheeled on the enemy's rear, towards Brentwood, so as to cut off the rebel retreat. This was the programme for action, and was admirably carried out.

THE BATTLE BEFORE NASHVILLE.

The First Day's Fight, December 15.

The booming of guns from Forts Negley and Cassino and several batteries awakened the inhabitants to the terrible reality that a battle was raging outside their city. There was great anxiety and hurrying to and fro, for the fate of thousands hung upon the issue. Defeat would be ruin, for it meant the fall of Nashville. Thomas knew this, and therefore decided on attacking Hood before he had time to fortify his new position. At early dawn Steedman's troops were in motion. The First and Second brigades, colored troops, commanded by Colonels Thompson and Morgan—took up position to the right and left of the Chattanooga line. These were supported by an Indiana battery. Colonel Grosvenor, commanding a brigade formed of detachments of the Fourteenth corps, took up a position on their left. The colored troops drove back the enemy's skirmishers to their main lines, but wavered under the assault. Grosvenor's brigade charged, taking the advance line of works.

As it was not the intention of bringing on a general engagement at this point, and the enemy developing heavy lines, General Steedman ordered them to fall back to their original position, still keeping up a brisk skirmish fire. I met one of those sable warriors—a regular mud pie—returning from the front. "Are you hurt?" I exclaimed. "Oh, lor, massa, yes. Cannon ball struck this 'ere nigger right on de brest, and rolled me over, killing Jim, at de oder side."

He looked very well for a man whom a cannon ball had made a shuttle cock of.

THE ATTACK ON THE CENTRE.

Precisely at six o'clock the Fourth corps commenced its line of march along the Hillsboro pike, and soon formed. The Second division, commanded by General Elliot, moved *en echelon* to Smith. The First division, commanded by General Kimball, moved *en echelon* to the Second division, with the Third—General Sam Beatty's—*en echelon*. The corps moved forward in this order, guiding their movements by those of General Smith's command. General Garrard's division, Sixteenth corps, formed on the right of the Fourth corps, with McArthur's division connecting on his right.

Our line of action now extended from the left of the Granny White pike clear away to the river. Heavy skirmishing soon took place, and the batteries along the front hurled shot and shell over our men's heads into the rebel lines.

The rebels had now fallen back to their first line of works, in front of Mrs. Montgomery's house. General Wood, who was all the time actively engaged along the whole line, guiding and directing movements, seeing the importance of this position, ordered General Sam Beatty to assault the position and take it.

BEATTY'S ASSAULT.

Beatty formed his division, Colonel Post's brigade Second, on the right; Colonel Straight's on its left, with Kneffer's brigade held in reserve. The Forty-first Ohio followed by the Seventy-first Ohio, One Hundred and Twenty-fourth Ohio and Fifty-ninth Illinois, formed Colonel Post's line. The Eighth Kansas and Fifty-first Indiana, supported by the Eighty-ninth Illinois, and Fifteenth and Forty-ninth Ohio, formed Colonel Straight's line. The batteries of the corps, under Major Goodspeed, occupied the following positions:—Zeigler's Second Pennsylvania battery on the left, the First Illinois next, with the Sixth Ohio, Twentieth Indiana and Battery E, First Michigan, a little retired.

THE REBEL LINE.

From the best information I could glean, Cheatham occupied the left of the rebel line, Stewart in the centre, and S. D. Lee on the right. The disputed position, from which the rebels annoyed our lines, is a commanding eminence on the Granny White pike. On the crest of this stood the house of a Mrs. Montgomery. It had been burned down, and both it and Couen's were in ruins from our shot and shell.

Like the famed "*La Haye Sainte*" of Waterloo, it has its history; like it, too, its ruined walls and shattered trees attest the fierce nature of the conflict that raged around them. Perforated walls, heaps of bricks and rubbish, with fragments of splintered trees and unsightly corses, are its trophies of the victory. About two o'clock the line advanced to the assault. As soon as the order was given, "Forward, charge," the Second brigade rushed forward in double quick time, giving one loud cheer. The First brigade, fired with the enthusiasm of the thing, also dashed forward in solid phalanx and delivered a withering fire on the enemy, and followed it by a charge, dashing in on the rebel works. The rebels fled in confusion, delivering a straggling fire on us from the shelter of the ruined houses.

We had now gained the crest of the hill. Our men, fired with enthusiasm, dashed after the enemy, capturing over two hundred. Our loss in killed was light. Captain John M. Farquher, Inspector of the First brigade, and Captain Cobb, Inspector of the Second brigade, had their horses killed under them.

The Fourth regular battery, Lieutenant Canby, and Battery E, First Michigan, Captain De Vraes, soon occupied the hill, opening on the retreating enemy. Generals Kimball and Elliot were also sharply engaged on the right, and were steadily pressing the enemy in their front. The Fifteenth and Nineteenth Ohio captured a battery, which they had charged. Schofield, who had been in reserve during the early part of the fight, had now wheeled to the extreme right, with Hatch's division of cavalry between him and A. J. Smith. The battle now raged fiercely on our right. Schofield and Smith were desperately engaged; Garrard's and McArthur's divisions of Smith's command, had charged on the enemy's works, capturing them. Cox's division was also hotly engaged. Wilson's cavalry now swept on the rebel flank and rear, rendering important services and capturing a large number of wagons. To add to the infernal din of shrieking shot and shell, the gunboats on the river opened their brazen throats, hurling shot and shell through the woods on the rebel flanks.

THE LAST ASSAULT OF THE DAY.

The rebels were now giving way. Our right was doubling them up. Several of their guns were in our hands. The Sixteenth corps alone had captured eight.

The Fourth corps now prepared for a general assault along the centre. The First and Second brigades of Beatty's division occupied the left, formed in single line. Kimball's and Elliot's formed into column by brigade. The advance of this long line of battle was magnificently grand. In their front lay a long slope of open country bounded by belts of wood. An increasing slope ran to the woods now occupied by the rebels. Over this the line moved in one solemn, steady column. The crest of the hill in front partly sheltered it from the enemy's artillery. A dense volume of smoke rose from the valley shrouding the hills and rebel lines in our front.

The roar of the rebel artillery was becoming fainter, while the sound of our guns rang nearer and nearer. The Fourth corps for a moment halted and lay down to have Smith connect. We could soon see the rebels breaking pell mell from their works. Infantry, cavalry and artillery were sweeping across the plain. What does it mean?

A wild cheer rang from our lines, and the batteries redoubled their iron storm. Soon a column was seen emerging from the woods on the rebel flanks. Who are they? The Stars and Stripes float proudly in their front. They are our right, which has swung around their flank. Louder grow the huzzas—hats are flung in the air—civilians rush forward, helping the gunners. The Fourth corps jump to their feet and sweep right on the flying enemy. Alas! darkness was setting in. Oh, for a Joshua to command the sun to stand still!—just two hours!

The battle was fought, the victory won; Nashville was saved and Hood was repulsed, shattered and broken.

The victory was ours, sure and certain.

THOMAS.

General Thomas viewed the battle from a high hill in the centre of our position, with his usual imperturbable coolness. One could not judge by him how great an issue was at stake.

WEBSTER.

He was accompanied by Brigadier General Webster, Chief of General Sherman's staff. Webster is an excellent artillery officer, and rendered efficient service during the fight by his selection of locations and guiding artillery movements.

WOOD.

General Wood, who commands the Fourth corps in the absence of Major General Stanley, was active and vigilant as usual. I remarked his aids, Major Danson and Captain Chafer, riding along the hottest part of the line with despatches. It is hard to compute the losses as yet, but you will have them by telegraph before you receive this. We have certainly captured seventeen guns and over one thousand prisoners.

It is thought that Hood has been too badly used to renew the battle to-morrow.

THE BATTLE OF BRENTWOOD HILLS.

The Second Day's Fight, Dec. 16.

It was thought that Hood's severe repulse on yesterday, had so crippled him that he would not dare to renew the conflict to-day, and thus risk a signal defeat and repulse of his army. Hood is remarkable for his dogged pertinacity and perseverance. Men are mere machines in his hands. These are excellent military qualities in a wise general, whose plans are laid with prudence and foresight. With a general of Hood's unthinking impetuosity, they generally prove fatal.

Hood's intentions were to blockade the Cumberland, cut the Louisville and Nashville road, and thus compel Thomas to evacuate. With this intention he had fallen back from his works before the city, to intrench himself in the Overton range of hills. In this position he could keep Thomas hemmed up in the city, divide him from Rousseau at Murfreesboro, and with his cavalry and Breckinridge's forces, cut off Bridgeport and Chattanooga.

This programme looked very fine, but Thomas' feelings had to be consulted, and he took into his head to spoil Hood's well laid scheme altogether, and attacked him before he had time to fortify himself in his new position.

HOOD'S IDEA OF THE SITUATION.

At a council of war held a few days previous Hood gave free expression to his opinions, and remarked,

"All these stories about Thomas' army are false. He has but the Fourth and Twenty-third corps, which we have already whipped, and some conscripts. We must take Nashville. We shall take it, and then, gentlemen, turning to his officers, "how we'll feast on the rich Yankee spoils."

"We have taken stronger places, and by God we will take it," exclaimed Cheatham, rather chafed; for his native city lay before him, and the vision of past days of social conviviality rushed on his mind. Lee was thoughtful. It was the council of the fallen ones plotting to gain their lost State. Hood had swelled our prudent retreat from Pulaski into a disaster on our side and a grand strategic success on his part. He was fulfilling Jeff. Davis' predictions at Macon and driving the Yankee marauders out of Tennessee. He had now hemmed them in their last stronghold and was gathering his meshes around them. Let Nashville but fall, and Chattanooga and Knoxville, with their immense stores of supplies would follow. Then the rebel army would again occupy its former position in Tennessee, Alabama, Kentucky and Western Virginia, besides restoring their communication with Georgia. The prize was great. The result should be disastrous to the vanquished. Hood knew this, and felt this, and therefore fired up his army to the highest pitch by the promise of certain success and vast spoils. Our falling back on Nashville confirmed his troops in this belief, and they were in the highest spirits at the prospect before them. Hood knew too well that to retreat from Nashville after all his boastful promises would be the certain demoralization of his army. The men would feel that they were entrapped, and desert him in wholesale. Besides, Hood had a very large wagon train, carrying all his ammunition and supplies. The great distance from his base at Florence compelled him to do so.

THE BRENTWOOD RANGE OF HILLS

are about six miles south of the city, and run from the left of the Granny White pike about a mile beyond the Franklin pike, the latter passing right through them to Brentwood. These hills are rather conical and separated by deep wooded valleys, making it very difficult for an army to keep up its organization while making an assault. During the night Hood had contracted his lines back to this range, massing on the Franklin pike to keep it open in case of retreat and to cover his large wagon train, which was moving by byroads from off the Granny White into the Franklin pike.

THURSDAY NIGHT IN NASHVILLE

was an anxious one. Troops were moving through the city, officers and orderlies riding to and fro, and eager groups crowded the hotels and saloons, discussing the events of the day. Officers returned from the fight grasp one another's hands in mute congratulation.

The true Union men are wild with exultation, while rebel sympathizers—whose lips swear loyalty while their hearts hatch treason—grow faint hearted.

It was an anxious night, too, to the officers and soldiers who slept upon the battle field. They lay in dark masses around, covered with their blankets and watchcoats, scarcely recognizable from their dead companions around. Deep was their sleep; but ere to-morrow's sun go down, many of them shall sleep a deeper sleep—the solemn sleep of death. The bayonets of the stacked arms glittered in the soft moonbeams.

Early on Friday morning the whole army was in motion. A thick fog and drizzling mist obscured our advance.

THE REBEL LINES OF BATTLE.

S. D. Lee occupied the right of the rebel line, partly massed on the Franklin pike, with Stephenson's and Johnson's divisions, in front of Kimball and Elliot. Stewart occupied the centre, in front of A. J. Smith, with Cheatham on the extreme left, considerably out of line, and running nearly parallel with the Hillsboro pike, and about half a mile east of it, in order to cover their flank.

Our position remained unchanged from the first day—that is, Steedman on the extreme left, Wood connecting with him on the left of the Franklin pike. Garrard's division, of A. J. Smith's corps, connected on the right of Wood; next came McArthur's; then Colonel Moore, connecting with Schofield's left. Cox formed Schofield's right and Couch his left. Wilson's cavalry came up on Schofield's right, along the Hillsboro pike, with orders to operate south of the hills, and if possible to turn the rebel flank and cut off his retreat. Schofield occupied a deep valley, with his flank extended well towards its head, and facing the rebel line, which was drawn like a bow along the slope of the hills; Couch's division ran diagonally across a spur of the hills at an angle with Cox. About ten o'clock the mist cleared away, revealing the sombre forest trees crowning the steep bluffs, with their crests and sides scooped into murderous rifle pits and ridged with grim batteries.

Steedman's corps was the first to advance. He moved out on the Murfreesboro pike, with instructions to connect with Wood and outflank the rebel right. His command consisted of two colored brigades, under Colonels Thompson and Morgan, and a division of white troops, under General Cruft.

Our skirmishers advanced without opposition for a considerable distance, but as soon as they struck the belt of wood in front of the enemy's position brisk skirmishing commenced.

THE BATTLE FIELD.

Between the Granny White and Franklin pike is a kind of plateau, sloping towards the range of bluffs which seem to be bounded by Little Harper and Mill creeks. Fine residences and well cared plantations cover the landscape back to Nashville. Here the city is shut out from your view by the hills, crowned with forts and batteries, and their sides dotted over with white tents, and the dark forms of citizens crowding to see the battle, or at least hear its din.

Behind these rose the houses and steeples of the city. The cupola of the Capitol was crowded with anxious spectators.

We had now struck the rebel skirmishers, and the fierce musketry fire soon commenced. Our batteries opened along the line, shelling the woods and advanced position. The rebel skirmishers fell back slowly on their works. Between Whitaker's and Grose's brigades, Kemball's division, and Garrard's division lay on a hill, on the top of which were a farm house and out offices. From shelter of these the rebel skirmishers and a section of artillery harassed our advance. Whitaker's brigade, comprising the Ninety-sixth and One Hundred and Fifteenth Illinois, Forty-fifth and Fifty-first Ohio, Twenty-first and Twenty-third Kentucky and Thirty-fifth Indiana, were ordered to take this position, supported by the left of Gerrard's line, and on the right by Grose.

The brunt of this gallant charge fell upon Brigadier Generals Whitaker's and Grose's brigades. Nobly did they behave. There seemed to be a laudable spirit of State rivalry between them. They formed into column in double lines by brigades, and moved forward in quick pace. They had nearly crossed the plain in front of the enemy's works when a withering fire of artillery and musketry swept, in one sheet of lead and flame, right in their face. It has ever been the rebel tactics to suffer our troops to advance close on their works, so that their volleys would have more effect. The men received this with a taunting cheer and a regular volley along the line. Still on we advanced, until just closing upon them, when the works in our front seemed to belch forth one sweeping, withering fire, more deadly than before, that thinned our lines and made the stoutest veterans reel, and created a temporary confusion. The rebels in front loudly cheered, and some jumped on the parapet. Our men rallied, turned and fired, thinning the number of spectators. The momentary reaction nerved our men, and on they fought, in double quick time rushing over the works, and bayoneting the rebels in them. It was a gallant charge, and gallantly led, for both Kimball and Whitaker were conspicuous in the thickest of the bloody strife. Here the rebels left two of their guns and an arsenal of small arms in our hands.

The Fourth corps had now driven the rebels from their advance lines, and was pressing them back on their reserves. Beatty's division occupied the right of the Franklin pike, the Second division on the left of the pike, and the First division connecting with Garrard.

We were now closing in on the enemy's main works, and it was evident that the grand charge would soon take place. Our batteries, having advanced close to the enemy's work, now opened from over one hundred guns one fierce, continuous fire upon the rebel lines, making the air hideous with the horrid din of shrieking shot and shell, and obscuring the valley with a thick, sulphurous canopy of smoke.

The Ninth Indiana battery, from the hill in Garrard's front, swept the rebel lines, which were open on its range.

Near this stood General Thomas and his staff, accompanied by General Webster. Thomas surveyed the position with his usual cool calmness, closely scrutinizing every movement of the enemy and taking the necessary precautions to frustrate their designs. He conversed with the officers around him on the situation, evincing a full and clear appreciation of the rebel general's movements and intentions. All the time preparations were making for a general assault and our batteries were covering the advance by one of the fiercest artillery fires I have ever heard.

Our artillery all through did excellent service, running their guns close up to the rebel works, tearing them to pieces and making the rebels fly from their intrenchments. Major Goodspeed, Chief of Artillery, Fourth corps, worked his different batteries admirably, placing them in the most effective positions.

In front of the Fourth corps I remarked the Fourth regular battery, Captain Cornly; Battery B, Independent Pennsylvania—this had two guns dismounted and trunnions smashed; Sixth Ohio, Lieutenant Baldwin, and several others prominent in front of our lines, hurling their missiles of death upon the enemy, blasting their lines with their volcanic breath. It was now near two o'clock. General Thomas J. Wood surveyed the rebel position from a hill to the left of the Franklin Pike, near Mr. Mullen's house. Steedman, looking fiercely calm and resolved; General Beatty, unmoved and calm, as if nothing of importance was transpiring; Kimball and Elliot, both looking resolute to act their part, were all in consultation with him, but soon moved to their different commands.

In front of the rebel lines, commanding the Franklin pike, was a strong fort. This occupied the crest of the hill, with strongly intrenched works all round and slashed trees in front.

This hill is the first important one of the Overton range—the extreme western spur of the Cumberland range of mountains. It is about one mile in front of Mr. Thompson's house, where S. D. Lee had his headquarters, and about five miles from Nashville.

From this position the rebels not only checked the advance of Beatty's division, but also commanded a salient fire on our advancing columns. Wood, calm and rigid, sat his horse, for some time surveying the hill. He sent for Colonel Post, of the Seventy-fourth Illinois. Acting Brigadier Post, young, brave and chivalrous, came dashing up.

"Well, Post," said Wood, "what do you think of that hill; can you take it?"

"Yes, General," was his reply.

"Well, then, do," said the General; and, turning to his chief of artillery, he said "You, Goodspeed, give it to them."

Away went Colonel Post, cheerfully, to honor, but to death.

Off went Goodspeed, and the hellish roar of artillery that soon followed told that he, too, was fulfilling his death dealing mission. As yet the rebels had used their artillery very sparingly, except on Whitaker's and Grose's advance, evidently saving their ammunition or unwilling to reveal their batteries until they could rake our advancing columns.

COLONEL POST ASSAULTS.

Colonel Post's brigade, composed of the Forty-first, Seventy-first and One Hundred and Twenty-fourth Ohio and Fifty-ninth Illinois, formed into column by brigade. Colonel Straight's brigade, comprising the Fifteenth and Forty-ninth Ohio, Fifty-first Indiana, Eighth Kansas and Eighty-ninth Illinois, formed on his right. They were supported on the left by Colonel Thompson's Second brigade of colored troops, comprising the Twelfth, Thirteenth and One Hundredth United States Colored Volunteers. To the left of these were the First brigade of colored troops, and Colonels John Morgan's and Cruft's division of white troops, all of Steedman's command. The hill in their front was partly conical, and sparsely covered with trees. The troops moved grandly and proudly across the intervening valley and were ascending the slope when the rebels opened on them with musketry and artillery, ploughing up their line. The men advanced for a time under face of this until their ranks became sadly decimated. They faltered, wavered, and began to get into confusion; but their officers rallied them and cheered them on to the charge. The roar of musketry and artillery—the sweep of shot and shell from the hill was now terrific. A sheet of flame and a stream of lead seemed to burst from it Vesuvius-like, vomiting forth flaming, fiery missiles of death, more fatal than the burning lava that buried Herculaneum with its molten tide. Despite this murderous fire, which seemed to blast life with its breath, the troops rushed up the hill but to strew its sides with their dead bodies. Post fell mortally wounded while rushing on at the head of his men. He paid the sacrifice of his gallant bravery with his life. Straight was slightly wounded, and many of our officers either killed or wounded. The troops, unable to stand this fell back to their works, the rebels not daring to pursue. Gen. John J. Wood was fiercely riding along the lines, himself and his staff exposing themselves at all points. He oftentimes threw himself forward, calling on the troops to follow. Wood fell back, still vowing that the hill should be taken, for repulse seemed but an incentive to him. He did not understand failure; it had no place in his vocabulary. In this charge the colored troops bravely participated; but the rebels seemed to mark them for destruction with a fiendish malignity. All this time the roar of artillery and musketry, that echoed along the valleys from Smith's, Schofield's, Elliot's and Kimball's lines, was perfectly deafening. It came

Nearer, clearer, deadlier than before.

Steedman was now closing up on the rebel right. In front of Smith the men were engaged throwing up breastworks, when the order came, "Fall in." The veterans threw aside their picks and spades, for well they knew what the order meant.

This advance was first through an open cornfield with a strong stone fence on their front. All this time the rebels were pouring shot and shell among them. Cool and undismayed they advanced under this fire, hurling back the rebel skirmishers on their main lines and charging right up after them, driving them pell mell from their works, capturing large numbers of prisoners, artillery and battle flags. McArthur's gallant division captured six twelve-pounder Napoleon guns and four flags, besides a whole battalion of prisoners.

THE TWENTY THIRD CORPS

had to advance up a steep hill, directly in face of a rebel battery (Second Maryland), which they not only captured but turned the rebel flank.

MAJOR GENERAL WILSON'S CAVALRY

were all this time engaged on our right, sweeping down on the enemy and driving them back to their works. Generals Johnson and Hatch's divisions were chiefly engaged here while General Knipe had swept round on the rebel rear to harass their retreat. In this charge the cavalry captured a large number of prisoners and General Rucker.

A lull—a fearfull lull—of some ten minutes took place in the centre after Beatty's repulse. It was only momentary.

"We must take that hill," exclaimed General Wood, as he fearlessly rode in front of the lines encouraging his troops and watching every movement of the enemy, and turning to his aids he exclaimed, "Go, Major Dawson, and order Kimball and Elliot to renew the charge."

Major Dawson did so, participated in the gallant charge that followed and fell wounded. With such division generals as Beatty, Elliot and Kimball, supported by able brigade commanders and officers, and such troops as he commanded, Wood knew he could not fail.

Thomas still looked on calmly and listened to the fierce roar of artillery and musketry circling round the hills to the right and left of the enemy. He smiled, for he knew that the net was hauling in. Our lines were now closing in like a horseshoe around the enemy—they occupying the hollow and massed back to a contracted line of about two miles. Their right was already falling back for shelter behind J. D. Lee's corps. Steedman had now swung round and was pressing them.

Wood was again charging. Grose's and Whitaker's brigades, which had done such good service in the morning, were now surging down the enemy's lines, while Garrard was pressing them on their right, and Elliot on their left, and McArthur, the Scottish Campbell, fiercely thundering against their centre. These five columns were animated by a spirit of revenge for the loss of their brave companions. Post's men were eager to avenge his fall, and they nobly did so.

This was the tide which, taken at the ebb, led to fortune and victory. A ringing cheer from our right proclaimed Generals Smith and Schofield victories, as they doubled up the enemy's flank. A concentrated, converging fire now swept along the rebel works on the hill.

One desperate roll of artillery, one fierce volley of musketry, one wild huzza and on, on swept our men dashing over the rebel works and hurling them from them in wild panic, and capturing them wholesale. The rebels broke and fled. The Forty-first Ohio jumped over the bodies of their fallen comrades, which lay thickly piled around, and rushed after the retreating rebels, who left their guns, flags and four pieces of artillery. It was the Thirteenth Mississippi battery, Captain Sandford commanding.

The rebel rout now commenced. Our artillery and infantry pressed after them, delivering volley after volley in their rear. We pursued them along the Franklin pike, through the Brentwood Gap, picking up whole squads of prisoners and deserters. The darkness of the night at length compelled us to desist from the pursuit. Kimball's division, Fourth corps, captured an entire battery and a battalion of troops commanded by Major Johnson, of Maryland. Most of the prisoners taken by them were from J. D. Lee's corps and Stephenson's division.

CAPTURES.

We have certainly captured over four thousand prisoners, including General John K. Jackson, of Georgia, and Brigadier General Smith, with a large number of staff and field officers, with twenty-five pieces of artillery—making, with the sixteen the previous day, forty-one in all.

THE BATTLE ON THE HARPETH.

The Third Day's Operations, Dec. 17.

RETREAT.

To-day our cavalry are vigorously reaping the fruits of our glorious victories of the past two days, for Hood's shattered, demoralized army is breaking over the country, with our infantry and cavalry like vengeful furies hanging on their flanks and rear.

It cannot be called a battle—it is a disastrous rout of panic-stricken men, who no longer retain the discipline or *esprit de corps* of troops. All the fine promises of their leaders have ended in disaster and defeat. Instead of feasting on the rich spoils of the Philistines, they are hurled back, naked, hungry and dispirited. They now see that instead of entrapping Thomas and his army—as both Hood and his arch-priest, Jeff. Davis, told them they would do—Thomas had left the trap for them, and was calmly awaiting his stupid victims to mesh themselves in his snares.

PURSUIT.

At eight o'clock our infantry was in motion in pursuit, Smith and Schofield moving on the Granny White pike and Steedman and Wood on the Franklin. The fighting was mainly confined to the cavalry; for the rebels made good use of the long night to get out of reach of our infantry. In our line of march towards Franklin we captured a large number of wounded, whom we found in the houses—among them a rebel general—also a rebel hospital, containing nearly two thousand patients, including some of our own, who were left.

Our cavalry fiercely harassed the enemy, scattering any rebel force that offered resistance and picking up rebel stragglers and prisoners in squads.

Knipe's division had wheeled around the rebel right flank the previous day and struck their column at night, and was now pressing them vigorously, also trying to head them off.

CAVALRY SUCCESSES.

Hatch had been engaged the previous evening on the left of the Hillsboro pike, and had captured General Rucker and some three hundred prisoners, and pressed the enemy back on the Overton hill, and moving through the gaps, harassed Hood's retreating columns all Saturday morning and sweeping down on them at Spring Hill, where he captured three pieces of artillery and such a number of prisoners that they soon outnumbered his command.

General Knipe so hotly pressed their rear guard that they had to abandon their hospitals, with about three thousand inmates, among them General Quarles, of Tennessee, and five battle flags. General Johnston had wheeled round Franklin and struck the retreating rebels' flank, capturing their men in squads.

In fact, Hood's whole army was now one demoralized, panic stricken herd seeking safety in flight. They have lost all hope now that they see that, instead of loading them with the spoils of Nashville, as he so vain-gloriously promised, Hood only led them to slaughter, for never had an army been so badly managed.

Just at the moment Hood wanted his cavalry most he sent them to support a column of Pat. Cleburn's old troops, under Bates, to attack Murfreesboro; but Rousseau was prepared for them, for while Thomas was whipping Hood in front of Nashville on the first day, Rousseau and Milroy were paying the same compliment to Forrest and Bates, by routing them with a loss of about one thousand one hundred.

Hood did not expect an attack so soon from Thomas, and thought that by attacking Murfreesboro he would compel Thomas to throw his army down there. But Thomas was too cunning, and left Rousseau to take care of himself, and suddenly swept upon Hood, now that he had little cavalry to cover his flank. Of the little he had he dismounted some the first day to go in the trenches. His flank was now exposed. He saw his error when too late. After the first day's repulse he contracted his line to the shelter of the hills, called back his cavalry, but to partake in the general ruin.

On the night of Saturday, as well as I could ascertain, the rebel loss in killed and wounded numbered about two thousand, and about ten thousand prisoners, with ten battle flags, several small banners and guidons and artillery—first day sixteen pieces, second day twenty-five, third day eight—total forty-nine. Hood is said to to have had only about eighty pieces in all. If so, the most of his artillery is in our hands, besides a regular arsenal of small arms.

We are also to bear in mind that the pursuit is still going on.

GUNBOATS GOING UP THE TENNESSEE.

I heard from good authority—almost official—that a flotilla of gunboats was moving up the Tennessee river to Florence to destroy the bridge there. If they arrive in time *nothing can save Hood from total destruction*; for the Cumberland and Tennessee are so flooded by the late rains that nothing could ford them. Besides, from the way we picked up stragglers on all sides, it was evident that they were trying to break home in all directions. They were merely following Jeff. Davis' instructions and going home. When I left the army on Saturday night the Fourth corps had crossed the Harpeth river. It was expected that the cavalry would so detain Hood that our infantry would force him to fight or surrender.

Of the forty five thousand troops Hood was supposed to have on his vain-glorious march into Tennessee, I fearlessly state that he has not half of them to-day.

When near Franklin I went into the house where Pat. Cleburne's body was laid after the battle. His heart's blood yet stained the floor. I said to a rebel colonel in our hands:—

"Colonel, how has your army fared?"

"Oh!" he exclaimed, "it is a disastrous battle to us." Such were the sentiments of all the prisoners.

OUR WOUNDED MEN RESCUED.

I should have stated that as the cavalry swept by the hospitals, our men rushed from the houses, cheering most lustily for us. It was a pleasing sight to see our brave wounded, pale and emaciated, some half dressed, some with crutches, others leaning on some support, but all sending up one loud, hearty round of cheers for us. If any of our men halted to look after them their cry was, "Go on, boys—go-in; we are all right."

Indeed the fighting was almost entirely confined to the cavalry. Our infantry was only partially engaged, and then but skirmishing in front of the dashing Fourth corps, which was not of much importance.

With Sherman's army so gloriously victorious, and the great rebel Army of Tennessee scattered into guerilla bands and broken, ought we not to feel that we are near the beginning of the end, and give glory to God for thus saving the nation under such a fiery ordeal!

SCENES ON THE BATTLE FIELD.

A battle field is a sad and sickening sight. The dread contest of the day is now robbed of all its glory and chivalry. The marching hosts in hostile array—the wild tumult of battle—the din and roar of musketry and artillery have died away. Its pomp and strange attractions have now departed and fail to gild the painted sepulchre, leaving nothing behind but its ghastly harvest of dead and maimed fellow creatures.

It was just night, the rain was pouring down, and the din and roar of battle had ceased. Still rose in the distance the cheer and shout of our men as they dashed after the retreating foe, mingled with the deep boom of our guns which were still sending a parting shot after the enemy.

I was standing on the hill upon which was enacted the bloodiest drama of the fight. It was the hill of slaughter. The dead and dying lay thickly strewn around in all conceivable shapes. In one place were piled together the bodies of two white soldiers and three colored. They must have clung together for shelter, and were mowed down together.

Black and white lay side by side just under the rebel works; there was no distinction now—brothers in the fiery storm of battle, they slept together in death

The hill presented a ghastly picture of the wreck and debris of battle.

Bent and broken muskets piled beside the dead bodies of those who had used them—pigments of shell and round shot scattered in every direction, with broken artillery and exploded caissons—the ground furrowed and ploughed and scattered over with lopped branches of trees, were some of the realities that made up the ghastly picture; add to this the piercing groans of the wounded, whose mangled bodies writhed in torturing agony, and you have some idea of the horrors of a battle field when stripped of all its pomp and tinsel. Behind the intrenchments lay the rebel dead and wounded, some crushed and torn in the most unsightly manner by our shot and shell. So accurate was our artillery practice that our shot tore off the heads of some with the top of the parapet.

I was attending one poor fellow whose arm had been dreadfully shattered, giving him a drink of whiskey and of morphine, when Surgeon A. E. Jelnser, Fifth Ohio, came over to dress his wound. "Ah, gentlemen," exclaimed the poor fellow, "I have a wife and five children in Georgia, whom I had to leave helpless when I was conscripted. Save my arm for their sake."

Dr. Jeinser could hold out no hopes for him, but thought he could save his life.

I remarked the kind doctor's Christian attention to the unfortunate rebel wounded. But then our doctors make no distinction between friend and foe when once they are stricken down. Near him lay an officer with a leg shattered and his arm torn off from the shoulder. Though we made a bed with blankets for him he was rather sullen, and would not allow us to move him out of the trench where he lay doubled up. It mattered little; for a few hours terminated his earthly pain. As I rode away from this hill, over which the charnel house smell of death was already breathing, I saw a huge Kentuckian weeping bitterly over a dead rebel.

"Sir!" I exclaimed; "look at your dead comrades lying all around."

"True," he said, as he wiped his eyes and pointed to a dead Union officer; "there is my brother, shot by this man. I shot him in return. He is my cousin and boyhood companion. I weep for my brother and bosom friend." This is but one of the many affecting scenes I have witnessed on the battle field.

HOW THE COLORED TROOPS FOUGHT.

Though not afflicted with the disease called "Nigger on the brain," nor a Horace Greeley or Harriet Beecher Stowe advocate of miscegenation, I must in justice state that the two brigades of colored troops, under Colonels John Morgan and Thompson, did well. It is true they broke, but not until their piled bodies, lying beside their officers—who were most all killed or wounded—attested how well they fought and bled. They entertain a kind of reverential devotion for General Steedman. And now "They'll fight for massa general wherever he'll go."

A PROVIDENTIAL ESCAPE.

It is strange the hair-breadth escapes one will have on the battle field. I have often seen men rolled over, their clothes perforated, and yet not hurt. Among the many escapes of the late fight I must mention that of

FATHER P. P. COONEY.

He was administering the last sacrament to a wounded soldier, when a round shot plunged between them, burying the father alive, and sending his patient, I hope, to heaven.

THE CASUALTIES.

Killed.

Colonel J. G. Hill, 35th Iowa.
Captain E. Grosvenor, command, 18th Ohio.
Captain G. H. Ayers, Co. E, 17th United States colored troops.
J. H. Aldrich, 17th United States colored troops.
Lieut. J. W. Watson, Co. H, 5th Iowa cavalry.
Lieut. John Lecrist, Co. K, 123d Indiana.
Lieut. Jas. D. McBride, Co. H, 44th Missouri.
Lieut. D. H. Shanks, Co. H, 7th Illinois.
Colonel Post, commanding brigade, 4th corps, mortally wounded.
Captain Parker, 7th Ohio, mortally wounded.
Lieut. Lylle, 7th Ohio, mortally wounded.
Major Dawson, General Wood's staff, slightly.
Lieut. H. G. Baily, Co. D, 5th Minnesota, severely.
Captain C. C. Bateman, Co. C, 17th United States colored troops, slightly.
Lieut. Col. E. J. Bond, 112th Illinois, slightly.
Lieut. J. B. Erney, Co. B, 2d Ohio, slightly.
Capt. D. M. Henderson, Co. K, 121st Ohio, severely.
Lieut. Jesse Newman, Co. H, 12th Illinois, severely.
Capt. Wm. Artestine, Co. E, 11th Missouri, severely.
Lieut. M. Inman, Co. H, 17th United States colored troops, shoulder.
Lieut. Samuel Timmons, Co. H, 78th Illinois, side.
Lieut. E. D. Fish, 22d Indiana, elbow.
Lieut. F. A. Voufiet, Co. D, 27th Michigan, neck.
Lieut. Cobb, Aid-de-Camp to Col. Post, slightly.
Lieut. Clark, Acting Assistant Adjutant General, 2d brigade, severely.
Lieut. Dempsy, 124th Ohio, killed.
Lieut. McGrath, Acting Assistant Adjutant General, 1st brigade, severely.

SCHOFIELD IN COLUMBIA.

The army is still rapidly pursuing Hood's demoralized fugitives. Thomas intends, if possible, to strike them in the rear with his infantry before they reach Florence, while his cavalry are banging on their flanks with the intention of heading them off between Columbia and Florence. Should they succeed in this and destroy Hood's pontoons on the Tennessee, or should the expected gunboats arrive in time for this part of the ceremony, Hood's whole army will be captured; for the rivers are so swollen by the late heavy rains that he cannot ford them at any point, though there were no foe to interrupt him.

As I write this I am officially informed that Schofield's column has reached Columbia—a distance of forty-two miles from Nashville and about seventy-five from Florence. Though our men are much fatigued they march on cheerfully; for they feel that the annihilation of Hood's army is the death blow to the war in the West.

Our engineers and their hands are busy at work getting up the wires, and putting the railroad in order to Franklin, which they will have done by to-morrow. We can thus follow up the army with supplies. Hood's retreat has been along the line of railroad and the roads running parallel with it.

I should have stated that after the battle of Friday we found coarse stones, used in the old Roman fashion for crushing corn, which appeared to have been the chief food of Hood's *les misérables*.

REBEL ACCOUNTS.

Hood's Defeat.

A TERRIBLE TIRADE AGAINST JEFF. DAVIS AND HOOD.

[From the Richmond Examiner, Dec. 19.]

The accounts from Nashville are the statements of the enemy, and must be received with much caution. It is probable that the real facts are somewhat colored; that the number of prisoners and captured guns will be discovered to have been somewhat smaller than supposed, and the loss of General Thomas much greater than he would like to state in a bulletin. But it is *difficult to doubt that after gaining an expensive and worthless victory at Franklin through the valor of his troops, and in spite of the most reckless generalship or no generalship, Hood has now sustained a defeat before Nashville, where he had no business to go*. If it be true that his men were actually driven from their breastworks, it is proof that they have suffered great deterioration in his hands. But there is no reason in laying blame on the troops. Defects at headquarters, now as at Missionary Ridge, explain all. Since Beauregard was ordered off to stop Sherman without troops by his individual presence, the condition of the army which was so left without a general could not be remembered without a shiver. Thomas, the renegade Virginian, is one of the most intelligent men in the federal army, while Hood's only title to command was the circumstance that he did not approve the policy of General Johnston. Until lately Thomas had inferior numbers; but while Hood has been trenching before Nashville his opponent's ranks were filling, and behold the result. Those who could be surprised at any military plans of Hood or Davis were surprised at a campaign for Nashville and Kentucky at this late season. If that army could have cleaned out Middle and East Tennessee and regained Chattanooga and Knoxville the condition of the Confederate cause in the West would have been better than it has been since the battle of Murfreesboro. But even if Nashville had fallen, an *eclat* would have been the only gain. The place could not be held without Kentucky, and a campaign in Kentucky at this season would have been certain ruin. The battle of Nashville appears to be a piece with the campaign. All of Hood's army were engaged except his cavalry. Where was Forrest and his cavalry? We do not know, but it may be fairly supposed that they were employed as Wheeler was when Atlanta was evacuated. When Johnston had the army he kept his cavalry on his flanks, and the flunkeys and parasites of the government reviled him for doing so. When Hood took command he sent off the cavalry to raid on the enemy's rear, and until the consequences were seen great glory was given to General Hood for doing it. But the absence of the cavalry enabled Sherman to reach Jonesboro without Hood's knowing anything about it, and Atlanta was thrown away in the panic which ensued. Then God, in His mercy, gave him Forrest, and while we do not know the fact, it appears extremely probable that he has thrown away his services in Tennessee as he did those of Wheeler in Georgia. Viewed by the light of events now accomplished, who can justify the removal of Johnston from the head of that army? What melancholy significance is given to that point of past history by every successive event in the beginning of the year that is now closing. The enemy has formed two powerful armies and planned two parallel campaigns. The goal of one was Richmond; of the other Atlanta. To meet them we had inadequate armies; but against Grant and Sherman we had Lee and Johnston, princes of the military profession on this continent. Their defence against superior numbers was equally successful, and the incidents on the two scenes of action were marked by an uncommon similarity. The result was the same, except that Grant reached the banks of the James from the Rapidan in much less time than Sherman touched the Chattahoochee. At that moment Sherman's campaign was as great a failure to his position, more perilous than that of Grant. Atlanta was a dead lock on the Army of the Cumberland, not less effectual than Richmond on the Army of the Potomac. There is every human probability in the supposition that had Johnston, like Lee, retained the command of his army, Sherman's column, if not forced to retreat, would have been held in Northern Georgia like Milo in the Cloven Oak. The Confederate army in Atlanta was then fully equal to that in Richmond. It was as well organized, as harmonious, as confident in itself and in its leader. It was only too eager for battle. At that moment all was well in the confederacy. No sensible observer doubted that both Atlanta and Richmond would resist all efforts, and that the conclusion of the year would be rendered memorable by the undeniable failure of the greatest military effort of the energy. Unhappily and disastrously Mr. Davis mistook the cause of that Georgian army's enthusiasm for a clog upon its enemy. He got possessed of the notion that if Johnston, who would not fight, was taken off, the government, under the name of somebody or other, would just go out with that fine army, whip Sherman in a minute, gather all the glory to itself, and gratify all its grudges against the great officer who had lifted it and him from the depths of despair. So all the hurdy gurdies ground out the death song of Johnston. In three weeks the army had lost more men in killed and wounded than during all the month of Johnston's command. It lost Atlanta without knowing how or why, and it was reduced to the same state of helpless demoralization in which it once reached Dalton from Missionary Ridge. Such was the immediate and direct result of Johnston's removal.

Then followed the President's harangues containing the plan of the new campaign, which is just now concluding at Savannah and Nashville. We have never trusted the pen to make any remarks upon the harangues; and the chronicle of events which a painful duty compels us to publish day by day furnishes an ellucidation and a commentary which no words and no pen will ever rival. Enough it is to say that fortune fled from the Southern standard when Johnston's hand was removed from the staff; and the evil spirit which had haunted Bragg returned into the army when Hood assumed command.

CANADA.

More Arrests of the St. Albans Robbers.

QUEBEC, Dec. 21, 1864.

Young, and two others of the St. Albans raiders, were recaptured to-day at St. Francois, sixteen miles from Rivere du Loup, on the way east. It is thought that all will be arrested. It is evident they are making for New Brunswick by different routes.

A special messenger has arrived from Washington, with despatches from Secretary Seward.

It is understood that immediately after issuing the proclamation in reference to the rebel-Canadian raiders Major General Dix despatched a confidential agent to Canada.

This gentleman returned to New York satisfied that the Canadian authorities were taking every necessary step to perform international obligations.

The best understanding prevails between the Quebec and Washington governments.

Mr. Potter, the American Consul, is unwell, and has gone to Wisconsin to recuperate.

Mr. Thurston, the Vice American Consul, is also ill.

The Governor's proclamation, which was published yesterday, offers a reward for the arrest of the raiders.

MAILS FOR THE PACIFIC.

The mail steamship Ocean Queen, Captain Seabury, will leave this port at noon to morrow for Aspinwall. The mails for Central America and the South Pacific will close at half-past ten o'clock to-morrow morning.

THE NEW YORK HERALD—Edition for the Pacific—will be ready at ten o'clock in the morning.

Single copies, in wrappers, ready for mailing, six cents.

The Canada Outward Bound.

BOSTON, Dec. 21—7:30 P. M.

The steamship Canada for Liverpool, remains detained by the thick snow storm. She will probably leave this evening, as the wind has changed to the south, with light hail and rain.

Court Calendar—This Day.

SUPREME COURT—CIRCUIT.—Part 1—Court opens at ten o'clock A. M. Nos. 3277, 3279, 3281, 3283, 3289, 3291, 3293, 2796, 2800, 2802, 2804, 2806, 2812, 2814, 2816, 2818, 2820, 2826, 2828, 2830. Part 2—Court opens at ten o'clock A. M. Nos. 2046, 1753, 1860, 2394, 2258, 3001, 3015, 3107, 3025, 2191, 1988, 2526, 3013, 3019, 1870, 2189, 2749, 3127, 623, 2268. Part 3—73 Duane street. Court opens at ten o'clock A. M. Case on. No calendar.

NEW YORK DAILY NEWS.

VOL. VIII.....NO. 306. NEW YORK, MONDAY, DECEMBER 26, 1864. PRICE FOUR CENTS.

"SAVANNAH, Ga., Dec. 22, 1864.
'*His Excellency, President* LINCOLN:
"I beg to present you as a Christmas gift, the City of Savannah, with one hundred and fifty heavy guns and plenty of ammunition, and also about twenty-five thousand bales of cotton.
"W. T. SHERMAN, Major General."

THE CAPTURE OF SAVANNAH.

Wednesday, December 21.

ITS ALMOST BLOODLESS OCCUPATION.

GENERAL HARDEE AND TROOPS ESCAPE.

Gen. Hardee Blows Up the Iron-Clads and Burns the Navy Yard.

One Hundred and Fifty Guns, Ammunition, Twenty-five Thousand Bales of Cotton, Three Steamers, and Eight Hundred Prisoners Taken.

Christmas Present to President Lincoln

GENERAL SHERMAN'S DISPATCH.

DISPATCH OF GENERAL FOSTER

[OFFICIAL.]
WAR DEPARTMENT, WASHINGTON, Dec. 25—8 P. M.

Major General JOHN A. DIX, *New York:*

A dispatch has been received this evening by the President from Gen. Sherman. It is dated at Savannah, on Thursday, the 22d inst., and announces his occupation of the City of Savannah, and the capture of one hundred and fifty guns, plenty of ammunition, and about 25,000 bales of cotton. No other particulars are given.

An official dispatch from General Foster to General Grant, dated on the 22d inst., at 7 P. M., states that the City of Savannah was occupied by Gen. Sherman on the morning of the 21st, and that on the preceding afternoon and night, Hardee escaped with the main body of his infantry and light artillery, blowing up the iron-clads and the navy yard.

He enumerates as captured 800 *prisoners*, 150 guns, 13 locomotives in good order, 190 cars, a large lot of ammunition and materials of war, three steamers and 33,000 bales of cotton. No mention is made of the present position of Hardee's force, which had been estimated at about 15,000.

The dispatches from Gen. Sherman and Gen. Foster are as follows:

"SAVANNAH, Ga., Dec. 22, 1864.

"*His Excellency, President* LINCOLN:

"I beg to present you as a Christmas gift, the City of Savannah, with one hundred and fifty heavy guns and plenty of ammunition, and also about twenty-five thousand bales of cotton.

"W. T. SHERMAN, Major General."

STEAMER GOLDEN GATE, SAVANNAH RIVER, 7 P. M., Dec. 22, 1864.

To Lieutenant General GRANT *and Major General* H. W. HALLECK:

I have the honor to report that I have just returned from General Sherman's headquarters in Savannah.

I send Major Gray, of my staff, as bearer of dispatches from General Sherman to you, and also a message to the President.

The city of Savannah was occupied on the morning of the 21st. Gen. Hardee, anticipating the contemplated assault, escaped with the main body of his infantry and light artillery on the morning of the 20th, by crossing the river to Union Causeway, opposite the city. The rebel iron-clads were blown up and the navy yard was burned. All the rest of the city is intact, and contains twenty thousand citizens, quiet and well disposed.

The captures include eight hundred prisoners, one hundred and fifty guns, thirteen locomotives in good order, one hundred and ninety cars, a large supply of ammunition and materials of war, three steamers and thirty-three thousand bales of cotton safely stored in warehouses.

All these valuable fruits of an almost blodless victory have been, like Atlanta, fairly won.

I opened communication with the city with my steamers to-day, taking up what torpedoes we could see, and passing safely over others. Arrangements are made to clear the channel of all obstructions. Yours, &c.,

J. G. FOSTER, Major General.

The Richmond papers of yesterday state that on the 23d twenty-six vessels of the Wilmington expedition had reappeared.

The dispatch of General Bragg, as published in the Richmond papers, is as follows:

WILMINGTON, Dec. 23, 1864.

"Twenty-six vessels of the Federal fleet reappeared this morning. There has been no change since last dispatch."

This is the latest intelligence received from that expedition. EDWIN M. STANTON, Secretary of War.

Fall of Savannah—Wilmington Supposed to be Attacked—Rumored Fall of Fort Fisher.

BALTIMORE, Dec. 25, 1864.

The Associated Press letter from Fortress Monroe, dated 5 P. M. on the 24th instant, says:

"The mail steamer Thomas Collyer has just arrived.

"A telegraph operator named Baker, belonging to one of the chief offices in Richmond, escaped the night before last, and having succeeded in eluding the vigilance of the Rebel pickets, made his way successfully into our lines yesterday afternoon.

"He was subjected to a severe examination by Gen. Grant, and stated that intelligence of the fall of Savannah and the capture of the entire force, 15,000 in number, commanded by Gen. Hardee, had reached Richmond a few hours before he made his escape.

"There was a report prevailing at the same time that Fort Fisher, commanding the entrance to Wilmington, had also fallen through a combined attack by General Butler's and Admiral Porter's forces, but this could not be traced to any trustworthy source.

"The spirits of the citizens of Richmond he describes as in a very depressed state, and it was with difficulty that the authorities could exercise any influence whatever over the press and citizens, such were the public manifestations of contempt for the action of the rebel Government.

"Gen. Griffin is a passenger in the Thomas Collyer, and places the utmost confidence in the statement of this clerk, and is of the opinion that the report of the capture of Fort Fisher is true, the extensive preparation made by Gen. Butler on the sailing of the expedition warranting this early surrender."

THE WAR IN KENTUCKY.

Gen. Lyons on the Louisville and Nashville Railroad at Elizabethtown—A Force in Pursuit of Him—The Morning Star Boarded at Lewisport by Guerrillas—Losses by the Passengers—Two Soldiers Killed—The Vessel Released.

LOUISVILLE, Ky., Dec. 24, 1864.

Gen. Lyons's rebel forces, estimated at from 2,000 to 3,000 cavalry and six pieces of artillery, struck the Louisville and Nashville Railroad at Elizabethtown, and destroyed a few unimportant spans over Bacon Creek, a small stream. They then turned northward, and are now threatening the important trestle works and Muldraugh's Hill. LaGrange's Brigade of McCook's Division is close upon Lyon's rear, and our military authorities are prepared to give Lyons a warm reception.

Yesterday evening the steamer Morning Star, Captain Ballard, bound upward from Evansville to Louisville, put in at Lewisport, where she was boarded by fifty guerrillas under Captain Davidson. They robbed the passengers of about $3,000 in the aggregate, and fired shots while on the boat at persons in the cabin, injuring no one, but subsequently killed two discharged soldiers on the deck. They then compelled Captain Ballard to transport them to Cloversport, where they released the boat.

FROM WASHINGTON.

WASHINGTON, Dec. 25, 1864.

THE TEN-FORTY LOAN.

The subscriptions to the ten-forty loan for the week ending with Saturday, amounted to $29,658,550, and to the seven-thirty loan $5,334,000.

RESTITUTION MONEY.

Three cases of conscience have recently been brought to the notice of the Treasury Department. An officer of the United States being in doubt as to the propriety of having drawn a requisition for $125, has returned the money with the request that one half be considered as the property of the Government, and the other as his individual contribution to the cause of "Uncle Sam."

Another anonymous correspondent returns $152 50, but desires no publication of the fact; while the third, transmitting $23 75, requests its receipt to be acknowledged through a New York newspaper.

From San Francisco.

SAN FRANCISCO, Dec. 22, 1864.

Business at a stand still.

Owing to the blockade of the roads by mud, freight communications across the Sierra Nevada are prevented.

The Overland mail has arrived with St. Louis dates of the 26th.

The steamer Golden Age sailed to-day with a small number of passengers and $1,053,000 in treasure, of which only $383,000 is for New York; the remainder goes to England and Mexico.

The sailing of the next steamer is postponed to Jan. 4, on account of the holidays.

Order of Gen. Dana.

CAIRO, Dec. 24, 1864.

Gen. Dana has ordered all army ammunition and military pyrotechnics held by private citizens by military permission, to be shipped south of Cairo previous to the 1st of January. Persons found south of Cairo with such property, or materials used for their manufacture, after that date, will be arrested and imprisoned.

From St. Louis.

ST. LOUIS, Dec. 24, 1864.

The formal opening of the Union Pacific Railroad from Kansas City to Lawrence, Kansas, took place on Monday and Wednesday. A grand jollification was had at each end of the road. Daily trains are now running between the points named.

Death of James M. Wood.

BOSTON, Dec. 24, 1864.

The Hon. James M. Wood, formerly member of Congress from Maine, died this morning at the Revere House, from an attack of lung fever. He was forty-nine years old.

Marine Disasters.

BOSTON, Dec. 24, 1864.

The schooner James Barbour, from Ellsworth for New York, was wrecked on an island near Georgetown, on the coast, while trying to make a harbor. Vessel and cargo are a total loss. Crew saved and badly frost bitten.

SQUANKUM, Dec. 24, 1864.

The schooner Fowler, Captain Isaac Almer, of Baltimore, from New York for Baltimore, with merchandize, came ashore at Barnegat, on Friday night. She is full of water. All her cargo is damaged.

Weather at Montreal.

MONTREAL, Dec. 24, 1864.

It is snowing slightly this morning. Thermometer 20 degrees below zero.

Sailing of the Hibernian.

PORTLAND, Me., Dec. 25, 1864.

The steamship Hibernian sailed at 9.30 last evening for Londonderry and Liverpool.

The Cleveland and Pittsburgh Railroad Disaster.

CLEVELAND, Dec. 24, 1864.

The following is a list of the casualties caused by the disaster on the Cleveland and Pittsburgh Railroad yesterday:

KILLED—John Robinson and wife of Petersburg, Mich.; O. H. Perry of Cleveland; Dr. Miller of Minerva, Ohio.

Wounded—George Fenoyer, of Massilion, badly; Wm. Thompson, of Hudson, badly; Mrs Golyer, of Philadelphia; Capt. King, of Winchester, Ohio; W. H. Cooper, of Reading, Penn.; E. S. Stevens, of the Indian Bureau, Washington, badly; Mrs. Thompson, of Mansfield; B. H. Graham, of Millersburg; C. Kenworthy, of Philadelphia; P. Hammend, of Cleveland; Mrs. Embsteter, of Cleveland, Dr. Boch, of Pittsburgh; H. Gilman, of Cleveland; W. H. Baldwin, of Elmira; Mrs. A. Baldwin, of Cleveland, and a few others slightly.

Marine Disaster.

PHILADELPHIA, Dec. 25, 1864.

The British schooner Isabel, from Curacoa for Boston, with salt, sunk Thursday night off Fenwick Island.

General Preston's Family.

BOSTON, December 25, 1864.

The wife, son, and daughter of the rebel General Preston, of Kentucky, came as passengers in the Africa. Orders from the War Department refused them permission to land, and also declined their request to leave by rail for Canada. They therefore remain on the steamer, to be carried back whence they came.

Fire.

TAUNTON, Mass., Dec. 25.

The passenger depot of the Taunton Branch Railroad was burned on Saturday night. Loss, $10,000; insurance, $3,500.

FROM LIVERPOOL.—The steam-ship Erin, Capt Grase, arrived here yesterday. She left Liverpool on the 6th inst., via Queenstown the 8th. The Erin brings 459 passengers.

FIVE DAYS LATER FROM EUROPE.

BY THE PERUVIAN OFF CAPE RACE.

OPINIONS ON AMERICAN AFFAIRS

ADVICE TO QUEEN VICTORIA

Dullness of the European Continent.

Financial and Commercial Matters.

ST. JOHNS, N. F., Dec. 24, 1864.

The steamship Peruvian, from Liverpool at 11:30 on the morning of the 15th, via Londonderry on the 16th inst., passed Cape Race en route to Portland at 3 o'clock this afternoon. She was boarded by the news boat of the Associated Press, and a summary of her news obtained, which is five days later than that by the Canada, at Boston.

The steamship Nova Scotian, from Portland, arrived at Liverpool on the morning of the 15th inst.

The steamship Etna, from New York, arrived off Crookhaven early on the morning of the 15th inst.

Great Britain.

American advices in view of Sherman's operations in Georgia, and Hood's operations in Tennessee, were regarded with the greatest interest.

The London Globe thinks that at no period of the war wer greater interests at stake.

The disaster to the Florida was generally regarded as design, and Southern sympathizers indignantly denounce the American Government.

The London Times has an editorial to-day urging the opening of negotiations in America, and says it must come to that at last, and the sooner it does come it will be the better for America and the world at large. It empathically disclaims all selfish motives, but for the interests of humanity urges pacific advances. It believes that the war, unless ended by negotiations and mutual compromise, must go on until the South is made a howling wilderness and the North prostrated financially and commercially for years.

The 14th of December being the anniversary of the death of Prince Albert, Queen Victoria, accompanied by the royal family, paid a protracted visit to the royal mausoleum, and spent a day in complete retirement.

The London Times, in alluding to the subject, trusts that now three years have elapsed, and every honor that a nation and gratitude could pay to the memory of the Prince has been offered, the Queen will now think of her subjects claims, the duties of her station, and not postpone them longer in the indulgence of unavailing grief.

It was rumored that Federal agents were at work at Preston, seeking to beguile the factory operatives there to emigrate to America.

France.

The news is unimportant.

The Paris Bourse, on the 14th, was buoyant, but closed quieter at 66f. 30c.

Continental News.

The news from all parts of the Continent was exceedingly meagre and uninteresting.

Portugal.

It was reported that the Minister of Marine and Public Works had resigned.

Turkey.

A Constantinople dispatch says that the Porte had accepted the proposal, previously refused, for the appointment of a Commission by the great powers to replace the police of the Danube under international control.

London Money Market.

Gold continued to flow into the Bank of England, but there were large withdrawals for export to Egypt, which countermanded the receipts, and a further immediate reduction in the Bank rate of discount was considered doubtful. The demand for discount continued unimportant. The funds closed flat on the 14th inst.

Satterthwaite's Circular reports a steady market for American securities. Quotations were almost unaltered, except for Eries, which have declined two dollars. Five-twenties, after touching 42, slightly improved, closing firmer at 42¼@42½.

Advices from Frankfort state that American stocks remained firm, but the demand for them has decidedly ceased, and they are now always a fraction below New York prices.

Shipping Intelligence.

Arrived from New York October 17, Centurion, at Melbourne; 20th, Guiding Star, at Woosung; 12th, Queen of the Seas, Costa Rica and Jubilanne, at do.; December 10, Plymouth Rock, at Deal; 11th, Elizabeth Jenkins, at Flushing; 12th, Orient, at Liverpool; 13th, John Bunt, at do.; 11th, Ewsteron, at Broad Stairs.

Arrived from Boston Sept. 27, Lady Dufferin, at Melbourne; Oct. 20, Ocean Rover, at Melbourne.

Arrived from Callao Dec. 13, steamer Blanchard, at Queenstown.

Arrived from San Francisco Sept. 29, Colmwood, at Melbourne; Oct. 20, Helvetia, at do.

MEMORANDUM.

The American brig General Ward blew up at Shanghai on the 21st of October. All the crew were killed except one.

The ship Asia, from New York Sept. 30 for the Clyde, lost sails and boats.

The ship New York, from Sunderland for New York, founded off Dagger Island. Crew saved

Commercial per Peruvian.

LIVERPOOL, Dec. 15, 1864.

COTTON—The sales of the three days foot up 18,000 bales, of which 5,000 were taken by speculators and exporters. The market has been quiet, and prices are easier on some descriptions, though quotations are unchanged.

STATE OF TRADE.—The Manchester market is steady and quiet.

BREADSTUFFS are steady. Wakefield, Nash & Co. report: Flour quiet and steady; wheat firm; rice 7s. 6d @8s.; corn very dull, and 6d. lower: mixed, 27s. 6d.

PROVISIONS tend downward. Gordon, Bruce & Co., and Wakefield, Nash & Co. report: Beef has a declining tendency; pork quiet, at 65s @70s.; bacon inactive; butter firm; tallow steady; lard quiet, and steady, at 50s.@53s.

PRODUCE.—Ashes, small sales at 30s. for pots, and 29s. 6d. for pearls. Sugar dull. Rice inactive. Coffee steady. Resin quiet. Spirits turpentine quiet and steady. Petroleum firm at 1s. 10d.@1s. 11½d. for refined.

LONDON MARKETS.—Wheat steady, except the lower qualities, which have declined. Sugar active and firmer. Tea steady and unchanged. Rice steady.

Tallow firm at 41s. 6d.

Consols closed on Wednesday at 89⅝@89¾ for money.

LATEST, VIA LONDONDERRY.

LIVERPOOL, Dec. 16, 1864.

COTTON.—The Brokers' Circular reports the sales of the week 42,000, of which 11,500 were to speculators and 4,750 to exporters. The market is easier, and quotations barely maintained. The authorized quotations are:

	Fair.	Middling.
Orleans	28d.	26½d.
Mobile	27½d.	25½d.
Uplands	27d.	25½d.

The sales to-day (Tuesday) were 6,000 bales, the market closing quiet and unchanged. The stock in port is estimated at 376,000 bales, of which 12,500 are American.

Breadstuffs quiet and steady.

Provisions quiet and steady, except lard, which is slightly lower and flat, and bacon, which is easier.

LONDON, Dec. 16, 1864.

Consols for money are quoted 89¼@89⅜.

The bullion in the Bank of England has increased £28 ...

... contrary, it is just the way to make all thought of reunion impossible. But let it be conceded that the restoration of the Union is not the object of the war, and that the design is to conquer the country, no one can imagine that the work of conquest can be advanced by acts which incense a people and tell them that they have no choice between utter ruin and a desperate resistance. And let me add, that these deeds of barbaric warfare are not only injudicious in a military point of view, but also in their political effect. Europe is appalled at their recital, and I say advisedly that they are leaving the United States without a friend in the whole world.

The question of recognition is still the talk in political and diplomatical circles. It is urged by the friends of the Confederacy that on the fourth of March next, an entirely new government will be inaugurated at Washington; that Mr. Lincoln has been elected by the North only; that by a secession ordinance the Federal Congress declared the Southern States ineligible to take part in the election of President, and that neither in theory, nor in fact, is Mr. Lincoln the ruler over the South. It is therefore contended that European powers will be compelled to recognize the Confederate Government.

It will, perhaps, rather startle some of your readers to know the ground on which Mr. Cobden, Mr. Foster, and Mr. Laylor justify their support of the war among their private friends. They say that the restoration of the Union may be impossible, but one result of the war must be that slavery will be abolished, and that being accomplished, it signifies not about the reconstruction of the Union. Well, if this is what you are fighting for, I would suggest a more humane and far more economical way for your purpose. Buy every Southern slave at the highest market price, and it will cost you less *than to free* them by the prosecution of this war.

As usual at this season of the year, we have had one or two reform meetings, and some rather strong speeches in favor of an extended franchise, but you must not conclude that there is any real agitation on the question. The people display perfect apathy—those who have votes don't record them unless it is quite convenient to do so, and those who have not votes don't care about the exclusion. When the people want an extended franchise they will get it without any difficulty and without much agitation.

M. Mocquard, the Private Secretary of the Emperor Napoleon, died yesterday morning. His loss will be sincerely deplored by the Emperor. Throughout his life he was a devoted adherent of the Napoleon dynasty. He took an active part in the restoration of the Empire, and his services as private secretary were invaluable. All those who had business at the Imperial Court—I particularly allude to Englishmen and Americans—will bear willing testimony to the courtesy and tact of the deceased gentleman. The Emperor has ordered a magnificent funeral, and is about to confer marked favor upon the bereaved family.

At the funeral service of Mr. Dayton, the minister who officiated indulged in a political harangue, in which he denounced the South with much bitterness. Surely, in a solemn service for the dead, it was unseemly to drag in politics and to indulge in cursing. In one respect, the minister was exceedingly unhappy. He referred to the generous sympathy of France for the United States, and inferred—which is not true—that France is opposed to the Confederates. The witty Frenchmen were highly amused at this sermon, and remarked that France had commenced her connection with the United States when they were rebels, and that the preacher had given them a hint to commence a friendship with the Confederates under like circumstances.

PARIS CORRESPONDENCE.

The Funeral of Mr. Dayton—Political Harangues Mark the Ceremonies—M. Mocquard's Death—Court News and News of Courts.

[From Our Own Correspondent.]

PARIS, Dec. 8, 1864.

Official honors were paid to the remains of Mr. Dayton on Tuesday. The funeral service was read over the body at the little chapel in the Rue de Berry, in presence of the Northern colony here; a part of the Corps Diplomatique, orderly officers representing the Emperor and Prince Napoleon, and a detachment of infantry attended, such being the etiquette when a Foreign Minister dies at the French Court. With that utter want of taste and tact for which it is so remarkable, The Semi-Official Constitutionnel, on the day of the funeral, publishes a short necrological article, comparing the deceased gentleman with Washington and Franklin! There was one feature in the ceremony at the chapel in singularly bad taste.

After the reading of the noble funeral service which is common to America and England, and as those present were thinking of retiring, the officiating minister thought fit to improve on the occasion and deliver a lecture on the war, anathematizing what he was pleased to call the rebellion, and, in short, doing what he could to emulate that rare specimen of a New World theologian, the Rev. Mr. Beecher. The Corps Diplomatique stood aghast, and a few Englishmen that were present wondered at this commingling of the sacred duties of a minister of Christ with the peculiarities of a rowdy stump orator. But more was to come. The officiating clergyman having resumed his seat, up started to his legs Consul Bigelow, whilem editor of The New York Evening Post. He set off in a rambling, halting, hemming and hawing, hesitating speech, glancing at the career of Mr. Dayton, and a great deal (to use the words of your pet Abolition minstrel) about

"—Your patriotic pa's and the star spangled banner,
Your country's bird a sittin by and crying out hosannah!"

The assemblage who had come to attend a funeral service, not a lecture about the American war, were perfectly disgusted. The parson had astonished—the consul bored them. It was, therefore, with a feeling of relief that after watching him stumbling through his speech, he was observed to sink into his seat. His oration, be it observed, lasted nearly three quarters of an hour. The European portion of the company present naturally fancied their patience would be put to no further trial, and there was that general rustle preparatory to a move. But to their consternation, the example of the clergyman and the consul had fired the emulation of M. Laboulaye, a French litterateur, who, on the strength of his having once written a smart south "Paris en Amerique," thought ...

... induced the frocked and lay politicians not to indulge in splenetic garrulity.

M. Mocquard died this morning. He had been a *sous-prefet* under Louis Philippe, but always entertained Napoleonic tendencies, and kept up a correspondence with the present Emperor and his mother, Queen Hortense. In 1839 he gave up his administrative functions and started a newspaper, The Commerce, to advocate Bonapartism.

On the election of Prince Napoleon as President, in 1848, he became his secretary, and took a prominent share in the Coup d' Etat. He retained the post ever since. He was a witty and epigrammatic old man, well known in American society here, and generally. He was 73 years of age.

The Court continues at Compeigne, engaged in private theatricals and other pastimes of that kind. The presence among the guests of the Duc de Mouchy has caused a feeling of profound astonishment in Paris, and thereby hangs a tale—of too delicate a nature to be even hinted at.

The Court of Appeals has confirmed the sentence of the court below, convicting Garnier Pages, and twelve others, on the charge of "forming an illegal association of more than twenty-one." This monstrous decision has apperently produced no impression. Truly the patience of the France almost equals that of the American people—"*profecto magnum dedimus patientiæ documentum*," quoth Tacitus, alluding to the degenerate Romans of his day. What would he have said seeing the great American nation crouching beneath the wand of Lincoln and putting up with a Butler?

VIDETTE.

FROM HAVANA AND NASSAU.

Movements of Blockade-runners.

The steamer Corsica, from Havana, via Nassau, arrived here on Saturday.

Rawson Wm. Rawson, the new Governor of the Bahama Islands, had arrived at Nassau.

Rev. Dr. Nicholson, of the Episcopal Church of the United States, had left for Havana. He is on his way to Mexico, on a religious mission.

A General Lee is reported by The Nassau Guardian to have left Nassau on the 15th inst., in the steamer Darien, for Bermuda.

The blockade-runners Old Dominion, Wild Rover, Little Hattie, Banshee and Agnes E. Fry, had arrived from Wilmington; the Syren had arrived from Charleston; the Gem, Marmion and Kenilworth had returned in distress; and the Virginia, Hansa, Ella, Kate Gregg, Charlotte, Will o' the Wisp, Stormy Petrel, Little Hattie, Syren and Star had sailed to run the blockade.

Interesting Correspondence.

It appears that the Supervisors, in appreciation of the services of Mr. Orison Blunt in saving this county from the threatened draft under the call preceding the present, voted that gentleman a testimonial of the value of $50,000.

The Citizens' Association, it seems, have awakened to the fact of this presentation, and have written Mr. Blunt a letter, the impertinence of which is simply amusing. Mr. Blunt has written a reply quite fitting and equal to the occasion. The correspondence is decidedly rich, and will be read with interest:

THE CITIZENS' ASSOCIATION OF NEW YORK, Office No. 813 Broadway, Dec. 20, 1864.

ORISON BLUNT, ESQ.—*Dear Sir:* The Citizens' Association having been informed that the Board of Supervisors had voted to yourself as Chairman of the Volunteering Committee a testimonial of $50,000, directed an investigation, and were assured, upon what seemed to be satisfactory authority, that a resolution had been passed to give you such testimonial for your services upon that Committee, and that such testimonial was subsequently either by the Board or the Committee itself, of both of which you are a member, put at the sum of $50,000, and that a warrant for the amount had been drawn and paid to you.

They were also informed that you had previously received from the same source, and for similar service, a valuable service of plate.

Before, however, giving credence to such an accusation, however apparently well founded, the Executive Committee directed that a communication should be addressed to you requesting from yourself a statement of the facts.

They desire to know whether a testimonial of any kind has been voted to you either by the Board of Supervisors or by the Volunteering Committee, and if so, what was the nature or amount, and whether you have received and retained such testimonial?

Very respectfully,
ROBERT B. ROOSEVELT, Secretary.

REPLY.

NEW YORK, Dec. 23, 1864.

R. B. ROOSEVELT, *Esq., Secretary, etc., Citizens' Association:*

SIR: Your communication of the 20th inst., desiring to know whether a testimonial of any kind had been voted to me, either by the Board of Supervisors or by the Committee on Volunteering; and, if so, what was the nature or amount, and whether I have received and retained such testimonial, has been received and contents duly noted.

In reply, I have the honor to state that I have been voted a testimonial by the County of New York, of which testimonial I have received as yet a portion only, consisting of engrossed resolutions, gold medal, and silver plate. As soon as I have received the testimonial in full, I shall be pleased to exhibit the same to you and my fellow-citizens generally, and submit the cost thereof.

I have not received money or moneys as a testimonial from the County of New York, or from any other source.

As Chairman of the County Committee on Volunteering, I have received nearly seven millions of dollars in amounts drawn by the Controller for volunteering purposes, and over four hundred thousand dollars in deposits from the citizens of the County of New York for substitutes, every cent of which has been duly accounted for.

The warrants drawn by the Controller have varied in amount from one hundred dollars to sixty thousand dollars, for which I have returned vouchers for the amount expended, and vouchers for the expenditures on the account of citizens have also been duly filed.

I have been informed from various sources considered reliable, that the citizens of New York are desirous of presenting me a testimonial for saving them from a draft under the last call of President Lincoln for 500,000 men, and obtaining credits of over 20,000 men who had previously enlisted in the United States Navy, thereby saving over twenty millions of dollars to the County Treasury, which, but for my successful efforts, must have been paid for volunteers or substitutes for drafted men.

If your association is desirous of presenting me a testimonial on behalf of the citizens of this city, which I infer from your letter, I shall be pleased to confer with your Executive Committee, and make such suggestions as may be deemed advisable.

I remain, yours truly,
ORISON BLUNT,
Chairman of County Volunteer Committee.

Christmas Carol.

Mr. W. Francis Williams, organist of St. George's Church, in this city, has composed and published a very pretty, yet simple, carol, entitled "The Heavenly Stranger," which is well adapted to children, schools, etc., in the celebration of Christmas. It is in the key of three sharps, common time, and, as originally composed, is to be sung as a duet for soprano and alto. Sold at No. 183 Broadway.

FROM THE SOUTH.

Reported Evacuation of Plymouth, N. C., by the Federals.

Proclamation of Gov. Harris to the Tennesseeans.

APPEAL IN BEHALF OF THE MISSISSIPPIANS.

Important Operations of General Sheridan—The Virginia Central Railroad Threatened—Federal Cavalry at Madison Court House—Early's Troops Marching.

[From The Richmond Examiner, Dec. 22.]

It was currently reported yesterday that two divisions of the enemy's cavalry had crossed the Blue Ridge and were moving toward Madison Court House. They will gain nothing by this movement, as the condition of the roads will seriously impede their progress toward the Central Railroad, and long before they can reach it we will have an ample force of cavalry and infantry in their front.

LATER.

Sheridan's infantry have come up the Valley to a point between Harrisonburg and New Market. His advance is supposed to be intended as a diversion in favor of the cavalry movement on this side of the mountains. Early has marched out to meet him.

The mounted force which has crossed the mountains is four thousand in number, and have four pieces of artillery. They were yesterday in Madison County.

[From The Richmond Whig, Dec. 22.]

The Central Railroad is again threatened by a raiding party, who crossed the Blue Ridge yesterday, eight thousand strong, and are reported to be moving in the direction of Gordonsville. We have a large force of cavalry in the Valley, who will hasten to pay their respects to these marauders.

[From The Richmond Sentinel, Dec. 22.]

It was reported yesterday that two divisions of the enemy's cavalry had crossed the Blue Ridge at Chester Gap, had arrived at Madison Court House, and were moving on Gordonsville. We also learn that the telegraph wires were cut on Tuesday night, seven miles from Gordonsville, it is supposed by a Yankee spy.

No apprehension is felt for the safety of Gordonsville, if the above is not greatly exaggerated, as there had been ample time to concentrate a force to meet the raiders.

Grant's Forces Again Moving.

[From The Richmond Dispatch, Dec. 22.]

Our scouts report that Gen. Palmer, with a division of infantry and a battalion of artillery, has occupied Bower Hill, eight miles east of Portsmouth. It is suggested that this force is intended to operate against Weldon.

From Southwest Virginia—Railroad Attack on Bristol—Government Stores and Railroad Trains Destroyed.

LYNCHBURG, Va., Dec. 14, 1864.

Passengers by the Western train to-night report a raid on the Virginia and Tennessee Railroad at Bristol, Tenn.

The enemy are supposed to be a portion of Burbridge's command.

From Bean Station they advanced rapidly, and entered the town at 5 o'clock in the morning. They destroyed a considerable amount of Government stores; an engine and train on the East Tennessee and Virginia Railroad, and an Eastern bound train on the Virginia and Tennessee Road between Bristol and Abingdon, were destroyed.

No positive intelligence of the enemy's number had been received, but they are supposed to have been five or six thousand. A portion of the forces is said yet to occupy the town. A body of the enemy returning toward Bean Station, encountered our forces at Zollicoffer, a station on the East Tennessee Railroad, nine miles west of Bristol, where a fight was said to progressing at last accounts.

[From The Richmond Examiner, Dec. 23.]

We have no Southern news of Stoneman's operations in Southwestern Virginia. There has been no confirmation of the report that Breckinridge had beaten the raiders near Glade Spring, though the intelligence received on Tuesday relative to the fight at that place may be correct. Nothing in contradiction of it has been heard. From the nature of the case, it is difficult to get any authentic information from points beyond Bristol Station. An unofficial dispatch from Lynchburg, yesterday, states that the damage done to the lead-works by the enemy was slight, and will be speedily repaired.

The Resources of the Confederacy—Seven Hundred Thousand Men—Fighting Men—Interesting Statistics.

The Richmond Whig of Dec. 23 says editorially:

"The idea has been expressed abroad, and studiously enforced at the North, that the resources of the Confederacy, as to arms-bearing men, are on the point of exhaustion. Many well meaning people among ourselves have yielded to the delusion. Yet no proposition is more erroneous than that the Confederacy is exhausted, or nearly exhausted, in its arms-bearing population."

The Whig then goes on at great length with statistics, and shows that according to these figures the Confederacy has now a force of seven hundred thousand fighting m... allowance for details by the ...

LYNCHBURG VIRGINIAN

Monday Morning, Dec. 26, 1864.

THE VIRGINIAN.

Is published Daily, Tri-Weekly, and Weekly, by

CHARLES W. BUTTON.

TERMS OF SUBSCRIPTION:

Daily Virginian, one year,	:	$40 00
Do. do. six months,	:	20 00
Do. do. three months,	:	12 00
Do. do. one month,	:	5 00
Tri-Weekly, one year,	:	$25 00
Do. six months,	:	15 00
Do. three months,	:	8 00
Do. one month,	:	3 00
Weekly, one year,	:	$15 00
Do. six months,	:	8 00

☞ No paper will be sent without the subscription is paid in advance.

RATES OF ADVERTISING:

ADVERTISEMENTS are inserted for $3 00 per square, of eight lines, for the first insertion and $2 00 per square for each additional insertion.

OBITUARY AND MARRIAGE NOTICES charged for at the same rates.

CHRISTMAS.

For seven hundred years the Roman commonwealth had endured amidst almost incessant wars, when He whose mission it was to proclaim "Peace on earth, good will to men," was announced by shining heralds from a better world.—That scripture was about to be fulfilled which declared that, "The sceptre shall not depart from Judah, nor a lawgiver from between his feet, until Shiloh come." Judea was then a Roman province. It had yielded to the conqueror of the world; but the Jews were still an embodied people, and the emblems of authority remained with them. The sceptre had not departed from Judah, nor was the once favored nation peeled and scattered in all lands until after the destruction of their city and temple by Titus; when the Saviour of mankind had left the world. "He came to his own, but his own received him not;" and that wonderful event described by their native historian, Josephus, of the departing host proclaiming, "Let us remove hence," was the complete fulfillment of this remarkably prophecy. Then the sceptre and the lawgiver departed from Judah forever. This people had long been expecting the advent of the Messiah. Wearily had the years passed, and He whom they "trusted would restore Israel," still delayed His coming. But when, "in the fullness of time," "the word was made flesh" and dwelt amongst men, the mystery of incarnate Deity was as a sealed vision to them. Though "He was fairer than the children of men," and "spake as never man spake," the pride of their hearts revolted at His apparently humble origin. Whilst angels heralded His birth, and the multitude of the heavenly hosts attested His character and mission, they deliberately rejected Him. They expected a temporal deliverance, and a born king with all the insignia of royalty and power.—Little wist they of that reign that was to be spiritual, and destined to be of wider range than the universe itself. They could not recognize in the humble babe of Bethlehem the sublimest of sovereigns; in a sad and suffering man, crushed beneath the weight of a world's redemption, the anointed of God; "He which is, which was, and which is to come." They crucified the Lord of life and glory; and throughout all the ages since, and in all lands whither they were dispersed, that fearful imprecation; "His blood be upon us and upon our children," has been ringing in their ears and settling upon their hearts. Such is the solemn attestation of the truth of Holy Writ.

We have sketched briefly some of the scriptural references to, and attestations of the Messiah; and it is eminently proper on this day, which in all Christian lands is observed in commemoration of the greatest event in the world's history, to note the condition of the world at the period of the Advent. It was the Augustan age, the Golden Age of literature; the grandest the world had then seen. Weary of war and strife, the ruler of the nations comprising the most extensive empire that has ever acknowledged the sway of a single potentate, had turned his attention to the arts of peace. The Temple of Janus was closed, and that most beautiful of Latin poets, Virgil, in his Eclogne, addressed to the Emperor, referring to the approaching Golden Age, seems to have been almost inspired when speaking of that glorious Messenger who should come during the reign of this favored prince. Not only Virgil, but Terence and Varro, Atticus and Cicero, Sallust and Livy, Horace and Ovid had illumined with the splendor of their genius the country of their birth. Homer and Pindar, Solon, Lycurgus and Demosthenes, with Euclid, Aristotle and Longinus had made Greek literature imperishable. Seneca the moralist, Lucan the poet, Quintus Curtius the historian, Pliny the elder, and other distinguished men lived when, "in the days of these kings the God of heaven set up a king dom."

But, "the world by wisdom knew not God." In the language of a distinguished writer; "Across the night of paganism, philosophy flitted on, like the lantern-fly of the tropics, a light to itself, but alas! no more than an ornament of the surrounding darkness." "Life and immortality were brought to light through the gospel." But it is favorable to the claims of Christianity that it was introduced in a period of unequalled light and civilization. Its claims stand vindicated against the charge that it shrinks from the light and courts not investigation.

Again: the period chosen for the Advent was one of profound peace. In the language of England's divinest poet:

> No war, or battle's sound
> Was heard the world around;
> The idle spear and shield were high up-hung,
> The hooked chariot stood,
> Unstained with hostile blood,
> The trumpet spake not to the armed throng,
> And Kings sat still with awful eye,
> As if they surely knew their Sovereign Lord was by.

It was a fitting season for the advent of Him who said, "I came not to destroy men's lives, but to save them." His mission was Peace; his ministrations, Mercy. Alas! how sadly the world was wandered from the ways of Him who "went about doing good"!

In this nineteenth century of the era called Christian, man combats his fellow man with the fury of a demon, while the earth shakes beneath the tread of armed legions arrayed in deadly strife. Can this hellish work at which angels weep, be an acceptable sacrifice in the eyes of Him with whom we have to do? And shall we not blush for the civilization and Christianity of an age that can find no means of peaceful arbitrament that could avert the dire catastrophe of war, with all its attendant horrors? Both must be radically defective. They are not what He who, nineteen hundred years ago, trod the hills and vales of Judea ministering to the suffering, healing the sick, restoring sight to the blind, calling the dead from their graves—not peopling those dreary mansions—came to establish. When shall the world be wiser and better? Not until the light of Christianity shall cast its serene and steady radiance over all the earth, inducing every man to regard his fellow as a brother.

God speed that day!

SAN SALVADOR AIDING REBELS.

THE CASE OF BRADSHAW AND REYNOLDS.

Washington, Dec. 16.—A despatch from Acting Rear Admiral Pearson, dated Panama, Nov. 5, received at the Navy Department to-day, calls attention to the action of the government of Salvador in regard to the rebel pirates Bradshaw and Reynolds arrested at San Salvador on suspicion of being emissaries of ex-President Barries, but discharged on their declaration that they were in the employ of the Confederate States, and only there for the purpose of destroying and injuring, as far as possible, American commerce in the Pacific. He says, "I judge that the authorities of these Central American ports would gladly give them up to Commander Devenport, as there plan was to capture the very steamers so useful to them for commercial purposes and the accommodation of passengers; but the cool announcement that the pirates had but to inform the authorities that the sole object of their visit was the destruction of American commerce in order to obtain from them, in effect free passes to do as they pleased has somewhat changed the aspect of affairs in this particular." Naval vessels will soon be at Panama and in the Pacific, to replace the slow going craft on which American honor and interests are obliged now to depend for protection, of sufficient speed and capacity to prevent further possibility of danger from rebel pirates, whether afloat or concocting plans on shore to ? the unarmed commercial steamers.

THE SECRET INSTRUCTIONS TO THE COMMANDER OF THE REBEL PRIVATEER FLORIDA.

The following important rebel document has now, for the first time, been made public, having been received at the Navy Department in the safe of the Wachusett:

PARIS, Jan. 25, 1864.

SIR—When the Florida, now under your command, is ready for sea, you will sail on a cruise against the enemy's commerce.

Your position is an important one, not only with reference to the immediate results to the enemy's property, but from the fact that neutral rights may frequently arise under it. Reliance, however, is placed in your judgment and discretion for meeting and promptly disposing of such questions.

Since the sailing of the Sumter on her very successful cruise, Federal owners of ships and cargoes have adopted the practice of placing them under British protection, and this may at times cause you embarrassment. The strictest regard of the rights of neutrals cannot be too sedulously observed; nor should any opportunity be lost in cultivating friendly relations with their naval and merchant services, and placing the true character of the contest in which we are engaged in its proper light.

It is not deemed advisable to precribe too rigidly your cruising ground. You are recommended, however, to cover a large field of action; beginning on the equator, between the longitudes 18 deg. and 28 deg, to intercept the vessels that may be on return from California and the East Indies. About the 1st of April make for the northern coasts of the Confederacy, say in the neighborhood of Cape Hatteras—where you will most likely fall in with transport vessels carrying supplies of provisions, men and munitions to their stations in North and South Carolina.

Having made your mark in that region, it will be well, if circumstances permit, to make a dash on the New England coast, taking care not to be caught too near the enemy's coast on a short allowance of fuel.

You will not hesitate to assume responsibility whenever the interests of your country may demand it; and should your judgment ever hesitate in seeking the solution of any difficulty, it may be aided by the reflection that you are to do the enemy's property the greatest injury in the shortest time.

Authority is vested in you to make acting appointments to fill any vacancies that may occur.

You will communicate with your government as frequently as possible through any safe channel that may offer, always taking care to use the cypher agreed upon in any word that might betray what you desire to conceal.

The maintenance of strict naval discipline will be essential to your success, and you will enjoin this upon your officers, and enforce its rigid observance, always tempering justice with humane and kind treatment. I am, sir, very respectfully your obedient servant,

S BARRON, Flag Officer.

Lieutenant Commander Charles M. Morris, C. S. Navy, Confederate steamer Florida, Brest, France.

OUTRAGES BY YANKEE GENERALS

In the raid of Sherman through Georgia, all of the outrages were not perpetrated by privates and subordinate officers.—In proportion to their number, the officers of high rank were as guilty of as many acts of infamy as the scum comprising their commands.

The Macon Telegraph says that in the county of Burke, General Kilpatrick stopped at the house of an estimable lady and demanded a dinner for himself and others. When the dinner was ready, the lady of the house was required to sit by the fireside, while Kilpatrick, with three negro wenches, who were his travelling companions, took their dinners together, indulging during the report in the most familiar and indecent conversation.

The day after Kilpatrick dined at the house of another lady of similar character, and when he had finished his dinner, turned his hireling escort loose upon the furniture and other contents of the house, destroying with their sabres the fine cutlery, glass and china ware, &, &c, winding up the scene by ordering the corn cribs and other out-buildings to be fired. A faithful servant put it out, when one of the vandals threatened to shoot him; but at this moment the cry of "Wheeler's men," caused the party to depart precipitately, and thus the buildings and contents were saved.

To leave nothing undone, to complete the infamy of this Yankee General's conduct—he caused all the sugar of the lady whose hospitality he had forced, to be filled with sand, as well as her jars of sweet meats and preserves. Such was the conduct of Gen. Kilpatrick. We can well understand what the lower officers and privates of such a General would do. At the plantation of General Cobb, in Baldwin county, where General Sherman made his headquarters for thirty six hours, everything was destroyed by his order, and his soldiers robbed the negroes of their shoes, blankets, clothing, knives and forks and cooking utensils. Negro women were thrown down and their shoes taken off their feet, and their cabins pilfered of everything they could put their hands upon. As none of his negroes could be induced to go off with them they stole a boy about twelve years old and carried him in spite of the fears and entreaties of the child and his mother. A widow lady, whose plantation joined General Cobbs, was found guilty of being the nearest neighbor of this notorious rebel, and she was made to suffer for it. Though a defenceles widow —advanced in years and confined to her house by sickness, she was robbed of all that Yankee rapacity could find and then the torch was applied to the balance, and in a few moments she and her dependents were deprived of their last morsel of bread. This was at Sherman's temporary headquarters.

These incidents are mentioned because of the connection of their leading Generals with them; others far exceeding those inenormity and brutality by lesser officers and privates could be enumerated without number.

THE CANADIAN IMBROGLIO.

REVOCATION OF DIX'S ORDER—NEW PASSPORT REGULATION.

WASHINGTON, Dec. 18, 1864.

The following was to-day officially promulgated:

DEPARTMENT OF STATE, Washington, Dec. 17, 1864.

The President directs that, except immigrant passengers directly entering an American port by sea, no traveller shall hereafter be allowed to enter the United States from a foreign country without a passport. If a citizen, the passport must be from this Department, from some United States minister or consul abroad; and, if an alien, from the competent authority of his own country—the passport to be countersigned by a diplomatic agent or consul of the United States. This regulation is intended to apply especially to persons proposing to come to the United States from the neighboring British provinces. Its observance will be strictly enforced by all officers, civil, military and naval, in the service of the United States; and the State and municipal authorities are requested to aid in its execution. It is expected here that no immigrant passenger coming by sea in the manner aforesaid will be obstructed, or any other persons who may see our on their way hither before intelligence of this regulation could reasonably be expected to reach the country from which they may have started.

WILLIAM H. SEWARD,
Secretary of State.

The disapproval by the President of General Dix's order relative to future raids from Canada has excited some surprise here, as the order met with almost universal approbation. It is understood, however, that it was induced by official assurances from the Canadian authorities that every possible effort should be made to bring the St. Albans raiders to justice, and that such measures should be taken as would prevent any similar demonstration in future, and promises to keep rebel refugees under strict surveillance hereafter.

A proposition has been seriously urged here to accept the proffered services of the Fenian Brotherhood to form a corps of observation for the protection of the North ern frontier from rebel raiders. It is feared, however, that a corps as constituted would not be content with acting upon the defensive, but would promptly carry the war into Canada.

FROM EUROPE.

The steamship Hibernian has arrived with five days later news from Europe:

Earl Russell has made the following reply to the dispatch of the Confederate Commissioners and manifesto of the Southern Congress:

"FOREIGN OFFICE, Nov. 25, 1864.

Gentlemen—I have had the honor to receive the copy which you sent me of the manifesto issued by the Congress of the so called Confederate States of America.

Her Majesty's Government deeply laments the protracted nature of the struggle between the Northern and Southern States of the formerly United Republic of North America.

Great Britain has since 1783 remained, with the exception of a short period, connected by friendly relations with both the Northern and Southern States.

Since the commencement of the civil war which broke out in 1861, her Majesty's Government have continued to entertain sentiments of friendship equally for the North and for the South.

Of the causes of the rupture her Majesty's Government have never presumed to judge.

They deplored the commencement of this sanguinary struggle, and anxiously look forward to the period of its termination.

In the meantime they are convinced that they best consult the interests of peace and respect the rights of all parties by observing a strict and impartial neutrality. Such neutrality her Majesty has faithfully maintained, and will continue to maintain.

I request you, gentlemen,
To accept, etc.

[Signed] RUSSELL.

To J. Slidell, Esq., J. Mason, Esq., A. Dudley Mann, Esq."

The London Times fears that Earl Russell's letter will find no favor either with the North or South. First he snubs the Confederates. They are only "so-called Confederate States," and have yet to establish their right to the appellation. This, too, is a compliment to the United States; but then follows a counter snub to the United States.—They are the formerly "United Republic." But to say they were "formerly united," is to imply they are now "disunited," and to acknowledge, therefore, the "existence" of the Confederate States. Earl Russell seems to fear no danger of forgetting that "neuter" does not mean "both." Therefore, if he would maintain, even in the words, strict neutrality, it is necessary to avoid any demonstration of friendship to either belligerent.

A CHRISTMAS CAROL.

BY COLERIDGE.

> The shepherds went their hasty way,
> And found the lowly stable-shed
> Where the virgin mother lay:
> And now they check'd their eager tread,
> For to the babe, that at her bosom clung,
> A mother's song the virgin-mother sung.
>
> They told her how a glorious light,
> Streaming from a heavenly throng,
> Around them shone, suspending night!
> While, sweeter than a mother's song,
> Blest angels heralded the Saviour's birth,
> Glory to God on high! and peace on earth.
>
> She listen'd to the tale divine,
> And closer still the babe she press'd;
> And while she cried, the babe is mine!
> The milk rush'd faster to her breast:
> Joy rose within her, like a summer morn;
> Peace, peace on earth! the Prince of peace is born.
>
> Thou mother of the Prince of peace,
> Poor, simple, and of low estate!
> That strife should vanish, battle cease,
> O why should this thy soul elate?
> Sweet music's loudest note, the poet's story,—
> Didst thou ne'er love to hear of fame and glory?
>
> And is not war a youthful king,
> A stately hero clad in mail?
> Beneath his footsteps laurels spring;
> Him earth's majestic monarchs hail
> Their friend, their playmate! and his bold bright eye
> Compels the maiden's love-confessing sigh.
>
> "Tell this in some more courtly scene,
> To maids and youths in robes of state!
> I am a woman poor and mean,
> And therefore is my soul elate.
> War is a ruffian, all with guilt defiled,
> That from the aged father tears his child!
>
> "A murderous fiend, by fiends adored,
> He kills the sire and starves the son;
> The husband kills, and from her board
> Steals all his widow's toil had won;
> Plunders God's world of beauty; rends away
> All safety from the night, all comfort from the day.
>
> "Then wisely is my soul elate,
> That strife should vanish, battle cease:
> I'm poor and of a low estate,
> The mother of the Prince of peace.
> Joy rises in me, like a summer's morn:
> Peace, peace on earth! the Prince of peace is born!"

RECEIVING COMPANY IN BED.

The old French custom of receiving company in bed is well depicted in the sketch which follows. It would shock an American lady to carry out this habit, at least, of Parisian fashionable life:

Our conversation drifted along to the old French custom of receiving company in bed. It was so highly correct that the newly made wife of the Duc de St Simon went to bed, after the early dinner hour of those days, in order to receive her wedding visits. The Duchess de Maine, of the same date, used to have a bed in the ball room at Sceaux, and to lie, or half sit, there watching the dancers. I asked if there was not some difference in dress between the day and night occupation of the bed; but Madame A seemed to think there was very little. The custom was put an end to by the revolution; but one or two great ladies preserved the habit until their death. Madame A. had often seen Madame de Villette to receiving in bed; she always wore white gloves, which Madame A. imagined was the difference between the toilet of day and night. Madame de Villette was the adopted daughter of Voltaire, and as such all the daring innovators upon the ancient modes of thought and behavior came to see her and pay her their respects.

She was also the widow of the Marquis de Villette, and as such she received the homage of the ladies and gentlemen of the ancient regime. Altogether, her weekly receptions must have been very amusing, from Madame A's account.

The old Marquise lay in bed; around her sat the company; and at the crisis of the visit, she would request the femme de chambre to hand round the heart of Voltaire, which he had bequeathed to her, and which she preserved in a little golden case. Then she would begin and tell anecdotes about the great man—great to her and with some justice; for he had been traveling in the south of France, and had stopped to pass the night in a friend's house, where he was very much struck by the deep sadness on the face of a girl of seventeen, one of his friend's daughters, and, on inquiring the cause, he found out that, in order to increase the portions of the others, this young woman was to be sent to a convent—a destination which she extremely disliked. Voltaire saved her by adopting her, and promised to give a "dot" sufficient to ensure her a respectable marriage.

DESERTERS HUNG IN DALE COUNTY.

The Montgomery Mail says, a gentleman from Dale, informs us that the citizens of that section recently caught a deserter named Crim and a citizen named Myers, who had for a long time been connected with an organized band of deserters and thieves, and hung them both to a limb. Crim and Myers were suspected as being the murderers of Lt. Spears who lately went down there with a lot of ammunition.

LYNCHBURG VIRGINIAN

NOTICE.—The cross mark appended to the names of certain subscribers indicates that the term of which they subscribed will soon expire. They are thus notified in time to re new their subscription if desired.

RAGS WANTED.—The highest market price will be paid at this Office for Clean Cotton Rags. They will be purchased in any quantity.

In accordance with the usual custom, and to facilitate family re-unions, we suspend labor in this office to-day; consequently no paper will be issued until Wednesday morning. If there should be interesting news by telegraph, it will be posted at our office for the benefit of city readers.

KILLED.—A negro man was killed at the depot of the Va. & Tenn. Railroad Friday night, by the cars running over him. His master resides in Henry county.

ROBBERIES are increasing in boldness and frequency. Not a night passes without some depredation being committed. The store of Mr. J. L. Brown, on Main Street, was entered a few nights ago, and robbed of several thousand dollars worth of goods. The guardians of the city must double their vigilance, and their number should also be increased—or the freebooters will take the town.

OUR LITTLE CARRIER BOYS will make their usual Christmas visits to our city subscribers this (Monday) morning. We beg to commend them to the kindly remembrances of those whom they have served during the year. Their services have been arduous and wearisome, and some token of appreciation will be grateful and pleasing to them. Let the condition of the currency be thought of in making your gifts. Five dollars will be no more to them now than twenty-five cents was before the war.

FALL OF THE SALT WORKS.—We have to communicate the unpleasant intelligence of the fall of the Virginia Salt Works. The news was received here Saturday, but was not accompanied by any of the details. As the works were held by a considerable garrison, and were well fortified, we suppose they fell only after a severe engagemnnt. We know that Col Preston's regiment of reserves and Witcher's command were there, besides other troops. The blow is a heavy one, but can be borne. The country is well supplied with salt, and there are considerable quantities on store in the cities. Enough is no doubt on hand to last until the Works can be again put in operation. In the meantime the people must economise their stocks, and make them last as long as possible. We suppose it is hardly probable that the enemy will attempt to hold the Works, destitute as they must be of supplies and with no safe communication with their base.

LATER.

By the western train Saturday night we received some particulars of the fall of the works. They were attacked about 1 o'clock Tuesday, by the whole force of Burbridge, numbering about 5,000. The fight was kept up all the evening, mainly with artillery, our forces being commanded by Col Ro T Preston and numbering, it is said, not more than three hundred and fifty. When night sat in they still held their own, but under cover of the darkness the Yankees succeeded in reaching fort Breckinridge, one of the main defence of the place, in overpowering numbers and captured it.

Col. Preston deeming it impracticable to hold the works longer, then ordered the evacuation. He and three hundred of his men are known to have escaped safely. It was believed that some others would succeed in working their way out. The works were fired the next morning. It is believed, however, that no serious damage has been done, and that they will be in operation again in a month. The Yankees did not remain long, and are reported to have left for East Tennessee. At Abingdon we understand they destroyed two entire blocks of buildings, including the Courthouse and jail, oNce of the Virginian, and private residences, beside the railroad buildings.

THE MOVEMENTS ON MOBILE.—The Appeal of the 13th inst., says that various sensational rumors as to the situation around Mobile, were current in Montgomery that day, but it is convinced that the Yankees have no force at Mobile, as yet, unless it was landed from their fleet. The raiding party in Southern Mississippi had not reached the Mobile and Ohio Railroad on the 10th, as the despatch from Senatobia shows the lines were undisturbed on that day. They did not leave Augusta, Perry county, Miss., until Friday last. This point is about fifty miles from railroad.

The Clarion, of the 11th says:

They will hardly be able to reach the Mobile road before to-day or to-morrow. Gen. Gardner is still accumulating troops to meet them, and we presume Gen Maury is doing the same thing at Mobile. * * * They are marching for Mobile, 5,500 strong. Scott and others have turned up in the right place and warm work may be expected in two or three days.

Unless there is a strong column to co-operate with the one referred to by the Clarion, Mobile is in no danger. The Federals have not designed an attack, in all probability.

The latest official intelligence received at Montgomery stated that the raiders above mentioned had, at last accounts, changed their course, and were marching in the direction of Pascagoula.

The Governor, issues a stirring appeal to the people to rally to the defence of Mobile.

GENERALS WHO FELL AT FRANKLIN.

Of the Generals who fell at Franklin in the recent battle we make the following brief mention:

Major General Pat Clebarne was a native of Ireland. He had resided in Arkansas many years before the war, and was a lawyer by profession.

Brig. Gen. Strahl was, we believe, a native of Ohio, but was residing in Tennessee at the commencement of the war.

Major General Gist was a South Carolinian.

Brig. Gen. Gordon was a Tennessean by birth, but until the commencement of hostilities had resided some years in Texas. At that time he returned to Tennessee and raised a company.

Brig. General Granberry was from Texas, but whether a native or not we do not remember.

Maj Gen Quarles was a Virginian by birth, but from boyhood had been a residen of Tennessee. He was a lawyer by profession, and had only recently received his promotion as Major General. He is reported mortally wounded.

Maj Gen John C Brown, a Tennessean and a lawyer by profession. He is reported only slightly wounded.

PRESENTATION AT BERMUDA.

The following paragraph, from the Bermuda Advocate of the 9th instant, explains itself:

"The Government of the Confederate States presented the Hon J W Ritchie, today, with a beautiful and massive service of silver plate, as a testimonial of their gratitude for his valuable and gratuitous professional services in connection with the Chesapeake case. The presentation took place in the Halifax Hotel, in presence of a large number of our leading citizens, and others whom sympathy with the Southern cause, or a spirit of curiosity, called thither. Mr Holcombe, well known as one of the late Niagara peace negotiators, prefaced the ceremony with a very appropriate address. He had been sent by President Davis to inquire into the particulars of the Chesapeake affair. He was delighted to find that the Confederate interest had been looked after, and Confederate rights asserted with as much zeal and ability as if their own law officers had been present; and that, too, without any official or un official retainer."

ESCAPE OF REBEL PRISONERS FROM JOHNSON'S ISLAND.

The Sandusky [Ohio] Register of Wednesday says:

About one o'clock yesterday morning, by a preconcerted arrangement, a rush was made by 24 prisoners upon the centre of the guard line, on the northwest side of the prison on Johnson's Island. The prisoners had improvised eight scaling ladders by attaching cleats to boards and strips, very light, easily carried, and just the thing for scaling the high prison fence. The rush upon the guard at once occasioned the proper cry 'turn out the guard' accompanied by quite a rattling fire from the guard line, but the rush was impetuous and by so many prisoners that in spite of the guard four men out of the 24 scaled the fence, passed the guard, escaped from the Island, crossed the north channel of the bay, and went some distance upon the Peninsula. Of the others who did not get through, one received a shot cutting away his coat pretty severely at the waist, and was knocked down and captured. Another, Lt J B Bowles, son of the President of the Louisville Bank, Ky., was shot twice through the body about the same instant, and killed. The other 18 found the work too hot, and retreated to the barracks.

HIGH PRICES OF NEGROES.

At a public sale of negroes in Raleigh a few days ago the following prices were obtained: For one negro girl seventeen years old, $6,000; one girl fourteen years old, $5,600; one girl fourteen years old, $4,825; one girl seventeen years old, $5,225; one girl nineteen years old, $7,300; one girl seventeen years old, unlikely, $4,550; one boy ten years old, $3,750; one woman and three children, $9,200; one woman and three children, $9,000; one woman thirty years old, $3,075; one woman forty five years old, $2,710; one woman fifty years old, $1,005; one woman, unlikely, and four children, $7,675.

THE FRONTIER TROUBLES.

The Herald in its news summary, says:

The official correspondence relative to the troubles on our northern border, lately called for by the House of Representatives, was yesterday sent to that body by Secretary Seward. It commences with the beginning of our civil war, and is very voluminous.—Mr. Seward says that the difficulties to which this correspondence relates are not merely local, but have mainly arisen from the attitude assumed towards our Government by that of Great Britain soon after the rebellion broke out. In connection with the Canadian imbroglio, a Quebec despatch states that thirty companies of provincial volunteers were sent to the frontier during the last week.

The Montreal Chief of Police, Lamothe, who figured in the case of the St. Albans raiders, has resigned. There was a report that Coursol, the magistrate who ordered their release, had also resigned, but it is now pronounced untrue. Gen. Dix has authorized the raising in New England of a regiment of cavalry for service on our Northern border.

IN COUNCIL OF THE CITY OF LYNCHBURG,
December 12th, 1864.

The following preamble and resolutions were adopted and ordered to be published.

JAS. O. WILLIAMS,
Clerk of the City Council.

Whereas, under an ordinance of the 28th of December, 1849, passed in pursuance of the act of the General Assembly, of the 24th of March, 1848, incorporating the "Virginia and Tennessee Railroad Company," certain Stockholders in said Company, were, by the City of Lynchbuig, guaranteed six per centum per annum on the par value of their Stock; and they, to indemnify the City therefor, executed powers of attorney, authorizing its Treasurer to demand and receive from the said Company all dividends declared upon such guaranteed stock.

And, whereas, the Stockholders at their last annual meeting, on the —— day of ——, 1864, declared a dividend of 110 per cent.; $100 thereof to be paid by the issue of certificates of new stock, and $10 in currency, on the 1st of January, 1865, to which, and all future dividends, so long as that gurantee and the said powers of attorney remain in force, the city of Lynchburg is, and will be, entitled.

And whereas, by the 5th Sec. of the ordinance aforesaid, the holders of the said guaranteed stock or any of them are authorized, when they elect so to do, to give up the guarantee and hold the stock with right to dividends as though it had never existed; in which event the powers of attorney aforesaid, are to be cancelled, and the city from the guarantee discharged; and whereas, to all such as may now so elect, the city is willing and offers to surrender the divided of 110 per cent. declared as aforesaid.

And, whereas, by the 6th Sec. of said ordinance, the Treasurer of the city is directed when so required by holders of said guaranteed stock, over and above thirty shares, to take a transfer thereof to the city, and in lieu thereof to give its bonds, bearing six per cent. interest, payable half yearly redeemable in 30 years and afterwards at its pleasure; and whereas, in the opinion of the Council, the time has arrived when the relations of these stockholders and the city of Lynchburg to this stock should be defined, and their respective future rights permanently fixed.

Therefore Resolved:

1st. That all holders of the said guaranteed stock be and they are hereby invited and requested, on or before the 29th day of December, instant, to make known in writing to the Treasurer of the city of Lynchburg, whether they choose to hold their stock *as now guaranteed,* leaving all future dividends to be received by the city; *or,* in accordance with the offer above made, elect to cancel their powers of attorney, discharge the guarantee and henceforth to hold the stock *unconditionally; or,* prefer, as provided for in the 6th Sec. of the ordinance, to exchange it for city bonds.

2d. That as to all such as elect the second proposition, the Treasurer of the city is directed at once to cancel the guarantee and powers of attorney aforesaid, and such stock holders may demand and receive the dividend aforesaid of 110 per cent. and all future dividends upon their stock declared.—As to all such as prefer the last proposition, the Treasurer is directed to issue bonds and take transfers, as provided for in the said 6th Sec., and as to those who accept neither, the Treasurer is directed to take no future step (except to pay the guaranteed 6 per cent.) unless in obedience to an express order of the Council.

3d. That the Treasurer keep an accurate account of his action hereunder and report the same to the Council, to be spread on the minutes.

4th That the Secretary cause the foregoing preamble and resolutions to be published semi-weekly in the city newspapers until the 29th day of December, inst., and semi-weekly in Richmond to same date.

dec14—swt29

LATEST BY TELEGRAPH

Reports of the Press Association.

Entered according to Act of Congress, in the year 1863, by J. S. THRASHER, in the Clerk's Office of the District Court of the Confederate States in the Northern District of Georgia.

CAPTURE OF THE SALT WORKS—THE RAID IN ORANGE.

RICHMOND, Dec. 24.

The following official despatches was received to night: Head Quarters, Army Northern Va., 24th.

Hon. Jas. A. Seddon:

Breckinridge reports that the enemy after having been roughly handled in engagements Saturday and Sunday, near Marion, many having been killed and wounded, gained possession of Saltville during the night of the 20th. The garrison retreated up Rich Valley.

The head of his advance arrived at daylight, the 21st, and the enemy retired that night, and the morning of the 22d towards Hector's Gap; they are being pursued.

Our troops are bearing their fatigue and exposure with great cheerfulness.

The damage to the works can soon be repaired.

Many bridges and depots on the railroad have been burned.

R. E. LEE, Gen'l

Fitz. Lee reports that the forces which attacked Lomax yesterday consisted of two divisions of the enemy's cavalry under Torbert. Lomax was posted across the Madison turnpike, two and a half miles from Gordonsville. The enemy was handsomely repulsed and retired about 3 P. M., leaving some of his dead on the field. He traveled too rapidly last night to engage his rear, having passed Jack's shop, 12 miles from Gordonsville, one hour after dark. Thirty-two prisoners captured at Liberty Mills on the 22d, being unable to keep up on the retreat, were released. Lomax's loss is slight.

NORTHERN NEWS.

RICHMOND, Dec. 24.

The Baltimore American, evening edition of the 22d received.

Three more of the St. Albans raiders have been arrested by the Canadian authorities, and are undergoing examination.

Farragut has been appointed Vice-Admiral in the Yankee Navy.

The Mary, formerly the Alexandria, has been seized at Nassau for violation of the neutrality laws, being an armed vessel. She will probably be released.

A telegram from Hopkinsville says McCook struck part of Lyons' command at that place at day light the 16th, capturing his train of artillery.

Gold 222.

EVACUATION OF SAVANNAH.

RICHMOND, Dec. 24.

[Copied from the Evening Whig.]

Reliable information has been received here of the evacuation of Savannah, an event which the military authorities decided upon some time since. The evacuation was effected without loss, except of such material as could not be transported.

The last troops crossed the river at 3 A. M., Tuesday.

The Engineer troops held the bridges until after 6 o'clock, when the latter were destroyed. At that time the enemy occupied the city, which had been surrendered by the Mayor about five o'clock under flag of truce.

FROM WILMINGTON.

WILMINGTON, Dec. 24.

Seventy vessels of the enemy's fleet are reported off Fort Fisher this morning. No demonstration of landing yet.

Weather mild. Wind West North West.

A Yankee gunboat grounded last night near Fort Fisher and was blown up by the enemy.

GUNBOATS REPULSED ON THE ROANOKE.

WILMINGTON, Dec. 24th.

The Yankee gunboats were repulsed six miles below Fort Branch on the Roanoke river on Friday. Col Whitfield was severely wounded. The fight is expected to be renewed this morning.

Idaho Tri-Weekly Statesman.

VOL. 1. BOISE CITY, THURSDAY, JANUARY 12, 1865. NO. 74.

Idaho Statesman.

PUBLISHED EVERY TUESDAY, THURSDAY & SATURDAY BY
JAMES S. REYNOLDS & CO.
T. B. REYNOLDS. JAS. S. REYNOLDS. R. W. REYNOLDS
Proprietors.

Terms of Subscription:

One copy one week, payable to Carrier..	$1 00
One copy one month by mail or express..	3 00
One copy three months by mail or express	6 00
One copy six months by express by mail or express..	10 00
One copy one year by mail................	20 00

Agents supplied on liberal terms.
Terms--Invariably in Advance.

Rates of Advertising:

One square (10 lines or less) 1 insertion	$ 3 00
One square two insertions..............	4 00
One square one week....................	5 00
One square one month...................	10 00
One square two months..................	15 00
One square three months................	20 00
One square six months..................	30 00
One fourth column one insertion........	5 00
One fourth column one week.............	10 00
One fourth column one month............	15 00
One fourth column three months.........	30 00
One fourth column six months...........	50 00
One half column one insertion..........	8 00
One half column one week...............	15 00
One half column one month..............	25 00
One half column three months...........	60 00
One half column six months.............	90 00
One column one insertion...............	15 00
One column one week....................	30 00
One column one month...................	45 00
One column three months................	90 00
One column six months..................	150 00

Transient Advertisements to insure insertion must be paid for in advance.

Special Notices charged for at the rate of one dollar a line each insertion.

Office--Corner of Idaho and Seventh Streets.

AGENTS FOR THE STATESMAN.

The following is a list of the authorized Agents for the STATESMAN, to whom all dues for subscription are payable:
H. M. SWINNERTON—Idaho City.
P. W. JOHNSON—Centreville.
H. D. MARTIN—Pioneer City.
M. B. MOORE—Placerville.
J. C. HOLGATE—General Agent Owyhee County.
JOHN CUMMINS—Ruby City.
C. W. WALKER—Rocky Bar.
KELLY & JOHNSON—Walla Walla, W. T.
OLIVER WHITE—Dalles City, Oregon.

FRANK MILLER. CHAS. C. DUDLEY.
MILLER & DUDLEY.
Attorneys and Counselors at Law.
Office south west corner Wall and Montgomery streets, next door to Froats & Co.'s Packer's depot, Idaho City, I. T. n1

M. KELLY,
Counsellor at Law
BOISE CITY, I. T. n1tf

GEO. I. GILBERT, *Notary Public.* | GEO. C. HOUGH, *District Attorney.*
GILBERT & HOUGH,
Attorneys at Law,
WALL STREET, above Main, IDAHO, CITY I. T

A. G. COOK,
Attorney at Law and Notary Public,
BOISE CITY, I, T. no1tf

I. N. SMITH,
Attorney & Counselor at Law
Boise City, I. T. au16

L. P. HIGBEE,
Attorney & Counselor at Law
Ruby City, Owyhee County, I. T. au18tf

Daniel MLaughlin,
Attorney at Law,
Idaho City, I. T.

W. R. KEITHLY,
Attorney at Law and Notary Public
IDAO CITY, I. T.
OFFICE—Montgomery Street near Wall. no1-tf

D. G. CAMPBELL.
Physician and Surgeon.
Office on Main Street, opposite STATESMAN office, Boise city. au13tf

SCRANTON & SOUTHALL,
HOUSEBUILDERS AND CONTRACTORS. Also jobbing done on the shortest notice. Charges moderate.
Boise City, July 26, 1864. n1-tf

D. G. HIMROD,
Physician and Surgeon,
Office at the City Drug Store, Boise City, I. T. n1 tf

DR. J. B. ISBAIL,
DENTIST.
HAS REMOVED HIS OFfice, and taken rooms at the International, up stairs. on Main street, Idaho City. All operations guaranteed to give the best satisfaction. I shall visit Boise City, and the surrounding camps at stated periods, of which I shall give notice. oc13tf

H. MARTIN. J. M. MURPHY.
MARTIN & MURPHY,
Attorneys at Law,
OFFICES at Ruby City, and Idaho City. oc4tf

JOHN CUMMINS,
Attorney and Counselor at Law,
OFFICE—Court House, Ruby City, Owyhee County, I. T. n5tf

DR. F. C. CLARK,
DENTIST,
TWO DOORS ABOVE the Idaho Hotel, has recently located at Boise City, and is prepared to perform all kinds of work in his profession in the most satisfactory manner. All the most useful improvements applied when required, and all work warranted. n29

DRS. CLARK & PARKER,
Homœopathic Physicians.
Office on Main street, opposite Poujade House, Idaho City.
THIS TREATMENT will cure all diseases that any other treatment can cure, quicker and more permanently. Also, many that are considered incurable. Particular attention paid to CHRONIC DISEASES, and all diseases of Women and Children. Consultations at all hours, day and night.
J. R. CLARK. M. D. [n176m] C. B. PARKER, M. D.

A. H. COCHRANE,
Physician & Surgeon, U. S A
OFFICE—At the Garrison Hospital. nov3

C. JACOBS & CO.,
BRICK BUILDING,
Corner Main and Seventh sts., Boise City, I. T.,
WHOLESALE AND RETAIL DEALERS IN
FOREIGN AND DOMESTIC DRY GOODS,
CLOTHING,
Gents' Furnishing Goods,
BOOTS, SHOES, HATS AND CAPS,
Staple and Fancy Groceries
CIGARS AND TOBACCO,
Carpeting & Wall Paper
BLANK BOOKS AND STATIONERY,
Fine Brandies, Wines and Liquors,
CROCKERY, GLASSWARE,
TINWARE,
BLASTING POWDER,
STOVES,
SAFETY FUSE,
PAINTS,
OILS,
BRUSHES,
AND GLASS,
Mechanic's & Miner's Tools,
with a full assortment of Shelf Hardware,
IRON AND STEEL,
WHIP AND CROSS CUT SAWS,
PLAIN AND SELF RISING FLOUR,
Bacon Sides, Hams and Lard.
All of which will be sold at the lowest market prices.
au11tf C. JACOBS & CO.

Administrator's Notice.
ESTATE OF A. M. ADDINGTON, deceased.—In the Probate Court of Boise county, I. T.—Notice is hereby given that on the 16th day of November, A. D., 1864, I was appointed Administratrix upon the above named Estate; and all persons having claims against the deceased, are hereby notified to exhibit them, with the necessary vouchers, to the undersigned, in Boise City, within ten months from the publication of this notice, or be forever barred.
HANNAH ADDINGTON.
Administratrix.
Boise City, December 14, 1864. de154w

COOKING STOVES AND BLANKETS, for sale at
CRAWFORD, SLOCUM & CO.'S

JAS. M. BLOSSOM,
North East corner Main and Eight streets,
BOISE CITY, I. T.,
WHOLESALE AND RETAIL DEALER IN
BOOTS, SHOES, HATS,
CLOTHING,
Dry Goods, Groceries, Shelf
AND HEAVY HARDWARE,
PROVISIONS.
Farmer's, Mechanic's, and Miner's
TOOLS,
Cigars, Tobacco & Pipes,
POWDER, SHOT, LEAD,
Caps, Nails, Blankets,
GRIND STONES, STATIONERY, &c.
For sale at the
LOWEST MARKET RATES FOR CASH.
se24tf JAMES M. BLOSSOM.

NOTICE.
THE undersigned has opened an office at Portland, Oregon, for the purchase, sale, and transfer of Mining Stocks and Quartz Claims, and the transaction of business generally connected with the mining interests of Owyhee and Boise mines. L. P. Higbee, Esq., of Ruby City, and Edward Nugent, Esq., of Idaho City, will be his correspondents, through whom all business matters may be arranged and perfected.
Oct 4. 1864. [oc11tf] GEO. L. CURRY.

DuRell & Moore,
B. M. DURELL. *Boise City, I. T.* } Ruby City AND Boonville. { C. W. MOORE. *Ruby City, I. T.*
Owyhee Mines I. T.
WHOLESALE AND RETAIL DEALERS IN
Dry Goods, Groceries, Liquors
STOVES, TINWARE, CLOTHING,
BOOTS, SHOES, HATS & CAPS,
MINING TOOLS, BLASTING POWDER,
Fuse, Steel, Quicksilver,
FLOUR, BACON, BUTTER, LARD,
CHEESE, DRIED FRUITS.
Together with a general assortment of
Miner's and Packer's Outfits.
Goods received on Storage. Liberal cash advances, made on consignments.
DuRell & Moore.
Ruby City, August 16, 1864. au18tf

WALDRON BROS.,
WHOLESALE AND RETAIL
DRUGGISTS,
MAIN STREET,.......DALLES OREGON.
DEALERS IN
DRUGS, PATENT MEDICINES,
KEROSENE, TURPENTINE,
ALCOHOL, WINES AND LIQUORS,
Toilet Soaps, Pomades, Hair Oils, Flavoring Extracts, Lubin's Handkerchief Extracts, etc., etc.
Prescriptions carefully compounded. Having purchased a new and complete Stock in San Francisco for cash, we are enabled to sell at the lowest rates. Orders from the upper country are solicited, and will receive prompt attention. H. J. WALDRON,
no1-tf G. W. WALDRON.

PACIFIC IRON WORKS.
THE undersigned continue to manufacture STEAM ENGINES, BOILERS,
Quartz Mill Machinery
of every description, including the celebrated
BRYAN BATTERY,
Varney's and Wheeler's Amalgamators and Separators, Water Pipe, &c., &c. They are the sole manufacturers on the Pacific coast of the "GREENE" ENGINE, the best and most economical Steam Engine made in the United States.
Having largely extended their works and increased the machinery, the undersigned are able to turn out work in the best style, at the lowest prices, and with the greatest dispatch.
GODDARD & CO.
San Francisco, Oct. 24, 1864. 123m

NEW GOODS! NEW BOOKS!
JUST RECEIVED, AT THE OLD stand, a new and complete stock of
Blank Books & Stationery,
a large variety. Also, Miscellaneous BOOKS, a new lot. Novels, Fancy articles, Perfumery, etc., etc. All the popular
Magazines and Pictorials
kept constantly on hand. Post Office Book Store, Main Street, Idaho City.
oc26tf H. M. SWINNERTON.

B. M. DuRell & Co.,
DEALERS IN
Exchange and Gold Dust,
Will pay the highest rates for
Gold Dust, Legal Tenders,
QUARTERMASTER'S VOUCHERS,
Assist. Treasurer's U.S. Checks.
WILL SELL
Sight Drafts on Ruby City, Idaho,
VIRGINIA CITY AND EAST BANNACK,
MONTANA, AND
GREAT SALT LAKE CITY, UTAH.
ALSO ON
Portland Oregon,
AND
San Francisco, California.
Collections Made in all the above Named Places.

REVENUE STAMPS for SALE.

Money Received on Deposit.
B. M. DuRell & Co.,
Fire Proof Brick Building,
Corner Main and 8th sts.,
a2tf Boise City, I. T.

Stoves! Stoves! Stoves!
A LARGE lot of COOKING STOVES, all sorts and styles, with furniture and pipe complete. Also, twenty-five BOX STOVES, with pipe and drums complete, just received, and for sale
CHEAP FOR CASH
By B. M. DuRell & Co.,
Corner Main and Eighth streets,
se10tf Boise City, I. T.

School Books! School Books!
JUST RECEIVED a large lot of SCHOOL BOOKS, ordered expressly for this country; among which may be found READERS all grades, SPELLERS, common school, high school and mental ARITHMETICS, ALGEBRAS, GEOGRAPIES, &c. Also constantly on hand a good assortment SCHOOL STATIONERY and DRAWING PAPER, of all sizes and grades.
B. M. DuRell & CO.,
se10tf Boise City, I. T.

H. H. HILL. A. J. KANE.
HILL & KANE,
Wholesale and retail dealers in
Dry Goods, Groceries,
CLOTHING, HARDWARE,
CROCKERY, LIQUORS,
AND FARMING UTENSILS.
UMATILLA, OREGON.
Forwarding to all Parts of the Mines.
REFERENCES AT PORTLAND:
H. W. Corbett, Richards & McCraken, Allen & Lewis, Baum, Bros. & Co., Knapp, Burrell & Co., Cohen, Lyon & Co. jy28tf

Bloch, Miller & Co.,
Dalles City, Oregon.
Importers and wholesale dealers in
ALL KINDS OF DRY GOODS,
CLOTHING,
BOOTS AND SHOES,
HARDWARE,
MINERS' TOOLS.
Also, a good assortment of all kinds of
Groceries and Provisions.
Wines and Liquors,
Constantly on hand. no1-tf

Attention, Farmers.
JUST RECEIVED AND FOR SALE,
10 Large Peoria Breaking PLOWS.
10 Small Two Horse PLOWS.
10 Hinge HARROWS. Complete.
10 Doz. GARDEN HOES.
10 Doz. Garden SPADES, Long and short handles.
All of which will be sold cheap for CASH.
de6tf **B. M. DuRell & Co.**

BLANK DEEDS OF ALL KINDS,
BILLS OF SALE,
Mortgages and Power of Attorney,
For sale at H. M. SWINNERTON'S,
Post Office Book Store,
oc26tf Main Street, Idaho City.

LUMBER.
We are now prepared to furnish Lumber of all kinds, either at our mill in the mountains, or at our yard in Boise City.
n1tf ROBIE & BUSH.

JUST OPENED, a new Stock of Gents' Clothing and furnishing goods, at
CRAWFORD, SLOCUM & CO.'S

HARROWS, HARROW TEETH BEETLE-Rings and Iron Wedges. For sale by **B. M. DuRell & Co.**

Idaho Statesman.

MONEY MARKET.

Gold.. 231
Legal Tenders.................................46½@47½

EASTERN NEWS.

BY OVERLAND STAGE.

ONE DAY LATER.

Dates to December 31st.

The Rebels Gobble up Vouchers.

Report of Gen. Burbridge's Raid.

Habeas Corpus in Dixie.

Jeff. Davis Issues a Bull to Legalize Piracy.

The London Times Improving.

From the Daily Salt Lake Telegraph:

CINCINNATI, Dec. 29.—A package of quartermaster's vouchers, amounting to nearly $200,000, and approved, were taken from a train captured by the rebels on the Louisville and Nashville railroad, on the 23d.

LOUISVILLE, Dec. 29.—A reliable telegram from Guest's station on the 28th, represents Burbridge's command in good shape, returning to Lexington, after a most successful expedition. Burbridge destroyed the railroad ten miles beyond Wytheville. Breckinridge was badly whipped and left for North Carolina. The rebel department of North-western Virginia has no longer any efficiency.

NEW YORK, Dec. 29.—Per the Australasian, from Liverpool the 17th and Queenstown the 18th. The London Times applauds Secretary Seward for the well-merited snub which he gave to Mr. Parker, the would be presenter of the peace address to President Lincoln.

According to rebel reports our gunboats on the Roanoke are having poor success. The rebels claim to have repulsed them three times near Fort Bratnet, the last time on Friday last.

Steamers from Havana on the 14th say reports had been received at that place via Porto Rico, that the San Domingo rebels had submitted to the Spanish government.

NASHVILLE, Dec. 28.—Union prisoners, who escaped from Florence, and arrived on the 27th at Columbia, state that Hood's army arrived at the Tennessee river on the 21st. Next day his infantry crossed on the pontoon, which he had removed above the shoals, out of reach of our gunboats. One of the prisoners states that Hood entered Tennessee with 110 cannon. He counted 25 on his retreat.

On Saturday, when twelve miles this side of the Tennessee river, they heard heavy firing in the direction of Florence, probably Steadman's force was engaged with Forrest.

WASHINGTON, Dec. 29.—The following report of Burbridge's operations has been received: Pittsburg, Ky., Dec. 18th.—I have the honor to report that my mounted force, 4,000 strong, in conjunction with Gen. Gillem's brigade, the whole under the command of Gen. Stoneman, marched from Bean's station on the 12th of December at daylight. They met Duke's brigade at Kingsport. I sent two regiments to support Gen. Gillem, who flanked the enemy, routing them, killing, wounding and capturing a hundred rebels, taking their wagon train, and pursuing them to Bristol, which place was attacked and captured, with 280 prisoners, two trains of cars, five engines, and immense quantities of stores. I learned that Vaughn was at Zollicoffer, twenty miles below. I marched to attack him, but he slipped away in a dense fog and made for the Salt Works. I discovered his flight in time to head him off at Abingdon, which place I captured on the night of the 14th, taking one gun, a large amount of stores, and an engine with rolling stock. Gillem continued the pursuit of Vaughn, coming up with him from a strong position, and capturing 50 prisoners. I sent Brown's brigade to support Gillem, who again came on the enemy at Mount Airy, and drove him in confusion, capturing somd prisoners, seven pieces of cannon, and a large wagon train.

Col. Brown's brigade, later in the day, charged the home guard, capturing five pieces of cannon and eight caissons.

Major Harrison, of the 12th Kentucky, who had been detached by order of Gen Stoneman, with 300 men, struck the Virginia Railroad on the 15th, near Glade Springs, capturing two trians of cars, when he got in Vaughn's front; continued along the line of this railroad, destroying all the bridges and depots as far as Wytheville, a large amount of rolling stock and the great iron works near Marion. Col. Brown destroyed the bridges for ten miles above Wytheville.

When the expedition started on its return, the men and horses being nearly worn out, we came on Breckinridge, who was following. An engagement of 36 hours ensued, at the close of which Breckenridge retreated towards Saltville. But Col. Buckley, with his brigade, forced him in confusion towards North Carolina.

Col. Buckley effectually destroyed the lead mines near Wytheville on the night of the 20th, and after some resistance our united forces captured the Salt Works, with 8 pieces of cannon.

The expedition has been entirely successful and will be more felt by the rebels than the loss of Richmond. The Salt Works and lead mines are in ruins and cannot be repaired during the war. My forces are now at this place safe.

BURBRIDGE.

NEW YORK, Dec. 30.—The latest rebel newspapers received contain a manifesto from Jeff. Davis, giving notice that the pirate, Bennet J. Burley, concerned in the capture of vessels on Lake Erie, and an attempt to sieze the United States steamer Michigan, and liberate the rebel prisoners on Johnson's Island, who was recently released from arrest in Toronto, is a regular commissioned officer in the rebel navy and was dispatched from Richmond specially for the purpose of executing the work which he endeavored to carry out.

Some Richmond papers are urgent in the demand that Gen. Lee should be made Commander in Chief of all the rebel armies, or dictator.

In the rebel House of Representatives on the 24th, a resolution declaring that the writ of habeas corpus ought not to be suspended, was defeated by ten majority.

The Richmond Sentinel foresees a formidable winter campaign by the national armies against Charleston and Augusta, and says the evacuation of Savannah by our troops and the occupation of the city by Sherman's army, will simply give the enemy another point on our coast, and the ocean front of Georgia will be exposed like the ocean front of North Carolina and Virginia to a species of hostility that will annoy, without strengthening the foe. It is probable, however, that a formidable attempt on Charleston will be an early consequence of the fall of Savannah. Foster already holds a fortified position.

AN ACT TO ORGANIZE THE COUNTY OF ADA.

Be it enacted by the Legislative Assembly of the Territory of Idaho, as follows:

SEC. 1. That all that portion of Boise county, in the Territory of Idaho, included within the following lines, to wit: Commencing at the point where Moore's creek forms a junction with Boise river, on the westerly line of Alturas, and on the easterly line of Boise county, and running thence in a northwesterly direction to a point on Payette river known as Picket Corral; thence in a westerly direction to a point on Snake river, known as the Central or Moore's Ferry; thence up the middle of the channel of Snake river to the point where the westerly line of Alturas county intersects the same; thence in a northerly direction along said westerly line of Alturas county, to the place of beginning, be and the same is hereby organized into a county, to be called the county of Ada, and the county seat of said county is hereby located at Boise City

SEC. 2. The said county of Ada shall, from and after the passage of this Act, be exempt from all jurisdiction and control of the officers of Boise county, except that all taxes heretofore levied upon any person or property by the county last named, and which have not been paid, may be collected in the same manner as though this Act had not been passed.

SEC. 3. The recorder of the county of Ada, who shall be hereafter elected, is hereby authorized to transcribe into books to be provided for that purpose, such parts of the records and files of Boise county, as relate to matters within the county created by this Act, and the same shall have the same force and effect, and be of the same degree of evidence as the original files and records.

SEC. 4. J. S. M'Iteeny, L. D Montgomery and D. Stuart are hereby appointed county commissioners for said county of Ada, and the county commissioners so appointed, or a majority of them, shall meet at the county seat of said county on the first Monday in February, 1865, and appoint all county and precinct officers for the said county of Ada, and the officers so appointed, including the county commissioners, shall hold their respective offices until their successors shall be elected and qualified.

SEC. 5. An election shall be held at the various precincts of said county of Ada on the first Monday of March, 1865, subject to the laws and regulations governing general elections; at which election all county and precinct officers for said county shall be chosen; and the several officers so chosen, shall, within twenty days thereafter, duly qualify according to law, and enter upon the discharge of the duties of their respective offices.

SEC. 6 The term of office, of all officers elected under the provisions of this Act, shall expire on the first Monday in January, 1866.

SEC. 7. The county of Ada shall pay to the treasurer of Boise county, a just and equitable proportion of the debts for which the said county of Boise is now liable, and the auditors of said counties shall, on or before the first Monday of September, 1865, meet at Idaho City, and apportion the same, and ascertain the amount to be paid as aforesaid, from the assessment rolls of said county which may be assessed in 1865; and in case the said auditors shall be unable to agree as to such apportionment, they shall refer the matter in difference between them, to the judge of the second judicial district, who shall determine the same, and such determination shall be final.

SEC. 8. This Act shall take effect and be in force from and after its approval by the Governor.

THE LONDON SAUSAGE MARKET—A SCENE IN COURT.

The following extract is a report of the proceedings before the Middlesex County Court, London:

Jemmy Hosking, a gentleman wearing a red cap, remarkable greasy flannel jacket, and immensely thick grey overhaul stockings, appeared to sustain a claim for £1 18s 6d, against Thomas Tubbs, a wholesale dealer in beef and pork sausages, black puddings, and saveloys and young Germans. It is impossible to say which was the dirtiest, the plaintiff or the defendant; the whole of the auditory very readily and politely made way for the savory vendors.

Commissioner—What's this claim for, sir.

Jemmy Hoskins—For makin' o' sassingers, sir.

Defendant—You means for spilein on 'em, Jemmy.

Jemmy (knowingly)—I'll spile you afore I'm done. (Laughter.)

Commissioner—Did you mean to say that this is for wages?

Jemmy—Yes, sir, one week, in which I made a matter of three tons o' sassingers and young Garmins. (Laughter)

Commissioner—Three tons of sausages and young Germans! Why, what do you mean? Explain yourself. How do you make them?

Jemmy—Does yer honor mean what on? what did we make 'em on? cos if I was to tell that, why, per'aps——(Laughter.)

Commissioner—Sir, you are bound to answer anything I ask. From what did you manufacture so many sausage and young Germans, as you call them? Of beef—

"Beef," said Jemmy, reflectively. "Beef—yes—why, there certainly was some beef that week; and, let me see, we had two green 'uns, and no less than three luckies!"

Commissioner—And pray, sir, what is a green 'un?

Jemmy—Vy, a hunfortunate pig, to be sure; a pig as don't die a natteral wiolent death—one as goes off without being stick'd. (Laughter)

Commissioner—Then how does he die?

Jemmy—Oh, various ways. Sometimes a pig gets the measles, and sometimes they get smothered, and dies that way. (Great symptoms of nausea in court.)

Commissioner—But surely you don't use such unwholesome stuff for food?

Jemmy—No, sir, we chops 'em up for sassingers (roars of laughter), and wots werry bad, indeed we makes 'em inter savelors and Germans We season up all on 'em well, and dries 'em over burnin' saw dust!

Commissioner—Upon my word, you are a clever fellow. Pray, what do you mean by a lucky?

Jemmy—A lucky sir, is a oss as meets with a accident in the street—sich as breaking a leg, getting a shaft run inter him, and sich likes. (Laughter) We're sure to buy him cheap cos he must be sold. Meat's beautiful, sir, you wouldn't know it from beef. Why, we picks out the prime parts for the cheap soup houses and penny pie shops (Roars of laughter)

Commissioner—Well, Mr. Thomas Tubbs, and what do you say to all this?

Say, sir, (said Mr Tubbs,) I say as how this ere man's a lying warrant. The werry last day as he left me he spiled about three hundred weight of stuff.

Commissioner—Stuff! what stuff!

Mr. Tubbs—Why, the sassige meat, to be sure. Instead of running the proper licker inter the skins, he'd run in cold water, and in course the sassige hadn't got no taste nor flavor in 'em at all (Laughter)

Commissioner—You hear this, Mr. Jemmy Hoskins?

Hear him, (said Jemmy indignantly,) in course I hears him The mornin' as he speaks of I was going to fill the skins, and he comes up to me, and taking a handful of sassige, he smells to it, and then a shakin his head, he ses, 'Jemmy," ses he, "this yere's rather too strong; you'd better give a rince over with the licker in the bilers" "Why that's for making ketchup," ses I, "and that's my perquisite"

Commissioner—What, make catsup from water that horseflesh has been boiled in?

Jemmy—Yes, sir, the best mushroom ketch up in the world. (Roars of laughter.) (A sleek-headed juryman turned very sickly.) Mr. Jemmy Hoskins continued: Fact, sir, nobody don't know what they eats in London. I wants my money that's all. I ain't said nothin' about puddins yet, nor young Germans, nor ——(Laughter.)

Commissioner—For heaven's sake, say no more. Will you pay this man his claim?

After some altercation, Jemmy Hoskins agreed to take £1 10s in liquidation of all demands.

THE SUN.

IT SHINES FOR ALL

THIRTY-THIRD YEAR. NUMBER 10,159.

NEW YORK, WEDNESDAY, FEBRUARY 1, 1865.

PRICE ONE CENT—IN GOLD. TWO CENTS IN CURRENCY.

The Latest News

By Telegraph to the N. Y. Sun.

SLAVERY DEAD!!

PASSAGE OF THE AMENDMENT

Several Democrats Vote For It.

EXCITING SCENES IN THE HOUSE.

Salute Fired at Washington.

A NEW PEACE EXCITEMENT.

A REBEL TRIO COMING.

Reported Arrival of Stephens, Hunter and Smith at Annapolis.

Foot Footing Along the Same Road.

IMPORTANT FROM HILTON HEAD.

Porter's Fleet at Charleston.

LATER FROM NEW ORLEANS.

Reported Rebel Evacuation of Mobile.

PRICE'S FORCES STARVING

NEW YORK LEGISLATURE.

Passage of the Bounty Bill.

&c., &c., &c.

Peace! Peace!! Peace!!!

A New Batch of Reports.

Philadelphia, Jan. 31.—A rumor is current here that three rebel Peace Commissioners have arrived at City Point, and are on their way to Washington. Gold is falling here.

SECOND DISPATCH.

Washington, Jan. 31.—The city is full of rumors concerning the Peace Commissioners who are said to be on their way to Washington, and the story is credited in many quarters.

THIRD DISPATCH.

Washington, Jan. 31.—Nothing can be obtained confirmatory of the report that rebel Peace Commissioners had arrived at City Point, on their way to Washington.

FOURTH DISPATCH.

Baltimore, Jan. 31.—It was currently reported here last night, and is reported this morning, that Peace Commissioners are now on their way to Washington. According to the rumor they are expected to arrive at Annapolis.

FIFTH DISPATCH.

Baltimore, Jan. 31.—The AMERICAN has the following special dispatch from Annapolis this morning:

Annapolis, Jan. 31.—Col. Taylor, of the 2d Maryland regiment, who arrived here this morning, says that on Sunday Alexander H. Stephens, R. M. T. Hunter, and two others, reached our lines, and requested to come within our lines at Fort Hell, but were refused, and were awaiting permission from Gen. Grant, who was then absent.

N. B.—I think the Commissioners were admitted nevertheless, and are now on their way to Washington. Hope to have something definite soon.

SIXTH DISPATCH.

Philadelphia, Jan. 31.—A special dispatch to the EVENING TELEGRAPH says:

Washington, Jan. 31.—It is known in the best informed circles here that a commission from Jeff. Davis, consisting of Vice President Stephens, R. M. T. Hunter and Gen. G. W. Smith, have arrived at Annapolis, with full power to arrange a settlement of our national difficulties. It is believed, from the understanding between Mr. Blair and Mr. Davis, that the terms will be entirely satisfactory to the Administration and to Congress, and will chiefly consist of an amnesty to all offenders and a withdrawal of the confiscation proclamation.

SEVENTH DISPATCH.

Baltimore, Jan. 31.—The AMERICAN this afternoon publishes the following despatch:

"The report has been current on the street since last evening, to the effect that the Richmond SENTINEL had announced the departure of three Peace Commissioners for Washington. Up to noon to-day we have no official confirmation of the rumor, though the assertion has been varied this morning by an equally positive announcement that Peace Commissioners, consisting of the rebel Vice-President, Alexander H. Stephens, and Senators R. M. T. Hunter and Campbell, had arrived at City Point, and were expected to reach Annapolis to-day. They are not spoken of as commissioners representing the rebel government, but as citizens representing the people, on their way to Washington to confer with President Lincoln on the subject of peace, precisely in the same capacity that Mr. Blair visited Richmond."

EIGHTH DISPATCH.

Philadelphia, Jan. 31.—The TELEGRAPH of this city in its last evening's issue says: "On last Friday afternoon a special dispatch was published in the EVENING TELEGRAPH from our Washington correspondent, announcing the entire success of Mr. Blair's mission to Richmond, and the pledge of Jefferson Davis to send three Commissioners immediately to Washington to negotiate the terms of peace on a basis which would be satisfactory to Mr. Lincoln and to Congress. *We assure the public that the hour of peace is at hand.* We again affirm the truth of the statement which we published on Friday, notwithstanding the falsehoods so industriously kept afloat in the New York newspapers."

Foote, the Rebel Peace Man, Coming Along.

Washington, Jan. 21.—A note from Alexandria says ex-Gov. Foote was opposite Point of Rocks, on Saturday, intending to cross the Potomac at Berlin.

Wade Woefully Worried.

During the debate on the retaliation resolutions, while Mr. Wade was speaking about Mr. Blair's mission to Richmond, Mr. Johnson asked how he came to go there. Mr. Wade replied: I would like to know; yes, sir, I intend to know if there is power in the United States Senate, to be informed on that subject. I intend to know why it was that any man was permitted to go with impunity through our lines, and confer with the arch traitor of the Confederacy, and come back here and go again. Mr. Johnson said he went in a Government vessel the last time. Mr. Wade responded: Yes, I understand he went in a Government vessel. He had no more right to be on that vessel, on a mission to hold communication with this arch-traitor and Devil, than he had to be on his road to the lower regions in a vehicle furnished by the Government.

The Constitutional Amendment.

Salute Fired at Washington, Etc.

It will be seen by reference to our Congressional report that the House of Representatives yesterday passed the amendment to the Constitution, forever prohibiting Slavery in the United States. The following dispatch gives an analysis of the vote on this great measure;—

Washington, Jan. 13.—Soon after the passage of the anti-Slavery Constitutional amendment this afternoon, a salute was fired in honor of that event. The vote last June, when it was defeated for the want of the required two-thirds majority, was—yeas, 96; nays, 65; absent, 21. Those who at that time voted against the amendment, but who changed their votes and cast them in the affirmative to-day, are Messrs. Baldwin, Mich., Coffroth, McAllister, Ganson, Herrick, Radford, Steele, King, Rollins, Mo., and Hutchins. Those who were absent on the former occasion, and who now voted aye, are as follows: Messrs. Brown, W. V., Davis, Md., Davis, N. Y., Grinnell, McBride, Nelson, Pomeroy, Randall, Worthington, and Yeaman. The following, who were absent or not voting when the June vote was taken, now voted "No:" Messrs. Hall, Harris, Md., Harris, Ill., Winfield, Ben. Wood and Townsend. Those who voted against the resolution, and were absent or not voting, are Messrs. Lazear, Lebloud, McKinney, Marcy, McDowell and Rogers.

Important from Hilton Head.

A Portion of Porter's Fleet off Charleston, Etc.

The Port Royal NEW SOUTH, of the 23d ult., has been received.

The arrival of a portion of the fleet formerly with Admiral Porter, in Charleston Harbor, is noticed, and the naval movements in that quarter were giving the enemy no small amount of uneasiness.

The occupation of Salkehatchie by our troops is confirmed. The rebels evacuated that position on the approach of the advance of our forces, and retreated to Ashepo, where it is thought they will make a stand.

The brig Waltham, Capt. Wylie, which arrived at Port Royal on the 15th inst., reports taking from the brig Experiment, of New York, the captain and crew, in lat. 36.30 N. and long. 65 W. The brig was in a sinking condition.

The new gunboat Savannah had arrived at Hilton Head.

From New Orleans.

Reported Evacuation of Mobile, Etc.

Cairo, Ill., Jan. 30.—The steamer Magenta, from New Orleans on the 24th inst., has arrived here. A steamer had arrived at New Orleans from Mobile Bay, bringing the report of the evacuation of Mobile by the rebels. The report was received from the flag-ship of our squadron, off Mobile, on the 20th inst.

A Natchez letter, dated the 23d instant, to the New Orleans DELTA, has the following:—"News from the trans-Mississippi Department says that the rebels are fortifying Grand Ecore, and have an entire division stationed there. One division of rebel cavalry has been sent to Texas lately, with orders to be dismounted for infantry service. The headquarters of the rebel Gen. Kirby Smith are still at Shreveport, but there is no considerable body of rebel troops garrisoning there."

The main body of the old army of Gen. Price was reported to be at Fulton, on the upper Red River, near the borders of the Indian country, suffering all the horrors of starvation, cold and nakedness, having returned from their recent campaign very poorly supplied with the necessaries of life, a large quantity of which they anticipated securing.

The Memphis BULLETIN says that the steamers Chippewa and Anne Jacobs, two of the fleet which went up the Arkansas River to Fort Smith, were captured and burned at White Oak Shoals by the rebels, and that two others were damaged, but managed to escape.

Guerrilla Movements in Kentucky.

Louisville, Ky., Jan. 31.—Captain Clark, of the Fourth Missouri Rebel Cavalry, entered Danville with forty men on Sunday at 9 o'clock, and after swopping horses with several of the citizens, helped themselves to boots and shoes and other things that they stood in need of, when they departed. They were followed by Captain Bridgewater and seventy or eighty Federals, who overtook them about four miles from Harrodsburg, where a fight occurred. Two of the rebels were killed and four or five wounded. Two of Bridgewater's men were wounded, but none killed.

Major Jones, with a band of two hundred guerrillas, is reported, to-night, within nine miles of Elizabethtown. Quantrell, of Kansas notoriety, is said to be co-operating with Jones, and has a force of two hundred and ten men.

On Friday afternoon, Captain Berry, leading five guerrillas, approached within a short distance of Bardstown. They were fired upon by a party of Federal soldiers, and it is reported that Berry was killed. On Saturday evening the outlaws, being reinforced, made another raid on the place, but were repulsed, after a brisk fight.

A LETTER has been received from a reliable gentleman in the interior of the State of North Carolina, stating that a large number of Union soldiers and citizens are now in Saulsbury, N. C., many having been removed from Georgia and South Carolina to escape General Sherman. The letter states that the rebels are becoming more inhuman and barbarous, having actually taken additional measures to starve our men; the number of deaths from actual starvation being on an average of fifty per day.

Congressional Proceedings.

XXXVIIIth CONGRESS—Second Session.

SENATE.

Washington, Jan. 31.—Mr. Wade presented a joint resolution of the Ohio Legislature protesting against the passage of the bankrupt law, which was ordered to be printed, and laid on the table.

Mr. Wade.—I notice that the Secretary of War in replying to a communication of the Senate, about the employment of Generals, has made a mistake, which I wish to correct. He says among other things, that Genls. Banks and Lee are before the Committee on the Conduct of the War. This is a mistake, and one which I wish to rectify, because it seems to be a standing one. I think it interferes with the disposition which the Executive wishes to make of these officers. Mr. Wade further stated that on the 14th of December, General Banks was before the Committee for about two hours, to give testimony concerning the Red River Expedition. One day in January, the Committee found him in the city, and called on him for a few minutes to explain some matters. General Lee had not been before the Committee since the 13th of January, when he gave testimony for about two hours. He (Wade) wished it to be understood that neither Genl. Banks nor Genl. Lee were detained here by the Committee on the Conduct of the War.

Mr. Sumner offered the following resolution:

Resolved, That the President of the United States be requested, if not incompatible with the public interests, to furnish to the Senate any information in his possession concerning any recent personal communications with the rebel Jefferson Davis, said to have been under Executive sanction, and also copies of any correspondence relating thereto.

Mr. Johnson offered the following as an amendment, by way of a substitute for Mr. Sumner's proposition:

Resolved, That the President of the United States be requested, if not incompatible with the public interests, to inform the Senate if any person has, with his authority and assent, been in Richmond negotiating with the President of the so called Confederate States, or with any other person or persons in that place, in relation to the termination of the present war, or with a view to ascertain from such persons in authority, upon what terms, if any, they would be willing to have said war terminated; and if so, to inform the Senate; also what information he has obtained from such agent or person; also if such person was in Richmond as aforesaid; whether he was authorized or permitted by the President of the United States to represent to the Confederate authorities upon what terms or conditions the President would negotiate in relation to peace; and if so what such terms and conditions were.

Mr. Sumner said that the resolution he offered was much briefer and simpler than that of the Senator from Maryland. There were some words in Mr. Johnson's resolution which he did not like. He did not like to see the Senate adopt such a phrase as the Confederate authorities.

Several Senators—The resolution says "So-called Confederate authorities."

Mr. Sumner said he preferred to speak of them as rebel authorities.

Mr. Doolittle suggested that both resolutions be printed and called up to-morrow. This was agreed to, and it was so ordered.

The Senate proceeded to consider the resolution appointing a Standing Committee on the Corruptions of the Government.

Hr. Hale said he was opposed to appointing any more committees to investigate corruptions until some action was taken on frauds already discovered. He read at length from a report made by Hon. John Sherman, when a member of the House, on the subject of naval contracts, to show that while Congress had heretofore gone to great trouble and expense to discover frauds, yet none of the guilty parties had ever been punished.

The morning hour having expired the Chair decided that the retaliation resolution was in order on the proposition to recommit the papers on the subject to the Military Committee.

Mr. Saulsbury said that if all the allegations against the rebels as to their treatment of our soldiers be true, it was but another argument for peace. He was not ashamed to stand up in the Senate and advocate peace. He was not in the habit of endorsing what the President did. But if, as he heard, Commissioners were on their way here to treat for peace, and this was the result of promises held out to the Confederates by the President, he was willing to endorse him so far.

The question was then taken on the motion to recommit the subject, and the Senate refused so to do. Ayes 10; nays 26.

Ayes—Messrs. Carlile, Davis, Hendricks, Powell, Richardson, Riddle, Saulsbury, Sumner, Van Winkle and Wright.

The question then recurred on the amendment making retaliation conformable to the law of nations.

Mr. Sumner moved further to amend by making it conform also to the usages of war as practiced among civilized nations. Mr. Sumner called for the yeas and nays on his amendment, and it was adopted by a vote of 26 yeas against 13 nays.

NAYS.—Messrs. Chandler, Clark, Collamer, Conness, Dixon, Farwell, Hale, Howard, Hovey, Ramsay, Trumbull, Wade, Wilkinson.

Mr. Hendricks offered as an amendment an additional resolution, declaring the sense of the Senate to be in favor of an exchange of prisoners.

The amendment was adopted.

Mr. Henderson offered an amendment, advising the appointment of Commissioners of Prisoners, to look after the condition of our prisoners in the future.

The resolution as amended was then passed, and the Senate adjourned.

HOUSE OF REPRESENTATIVES.

Mr. Fernando Wood asked leave to offer the following resolution:

Resolved, That it is the duty of the President to maintain, in every constitutional and legal manner, the integrity of the American Union, as formed by the Fathers of the Republic, and in no event, and under no circumstances, to proffer or accept negotiations which shall admit, by the remotest implication, the existence of any other Federal or Confederate Government within the territory of the United States.

Mr. Farnsworth, of Illinois, objected to the reception of the resolution.

Mr. Fernando Wood gave notice that he would, next Monday, move a suspension of the rules to introduce the resolution.

The House resumed consideration of the Senate joint resolution proposing amendments to the Constitution of the United States.

Mr. McAllister (Dem., Pa.) said: When this subject was before the House, on a former occasion, I voted against the measure. I have been in favor of exhausting all the means of conciliatian to restore the Union as our fathers made it. I am for the Union, and utterly opposed to secession or dissolution in any way or shape. The result of all the peace missions, and especially that of Mr. Blair, has satisfied me that nothing short of recognition of their independence will satisfy the Southern Confederacy. It must therefore be destroyed, and, in voting for the present measure, I cast my vote against the corner-stone of the Southern Confederacy, and declare eternal war against the enemies of my country.

Mr. Coffroth, (Dem. Pa.) addressed the House in favor of the amendment, not, however, speaking for or against slavery. He argued the power of Congress to submit the amendment to the Legislatures of the States; that the South could defeat the amendment; that it must be submitted to the seceded States, or it would be recognizing their independence; that if this was done, it would apply only to those which adopted it. He also argued that the South would not remain in the Union under the Constitution as it now is, and that they would not come back after four years fighting. All relating to slavery should be stricken from our statute books, and then when the people of the South were tired and sick of this barbarous and inhuman war, and demand a cessation of hostilities until it be ascertained if peace cannot be obtained, there will be no obstacles in the way of giving new guarantees to every person who shelters himself under the American Constitution. He also argued that slavery was the fruitful theme for the opponents of the Democracy. It breathed life and existence into fanaticism, and unless that which sustained and fed fanaticism be removed from the political arena, the country would be entirely destroyed. He was in favor of removing it, and then the people would place in power the Democracy. He gave this vote after much consideration, and as a Democrat, and would consistently stand by the organization of his party. No power on earth should prevent him from voting for the candidates of his party. His desire was the triumph of the party which has made this country great.

Mr. Miller (Dem., of Pa.) said he owed it to himself and his constituents to reply to the sentiments of his colleagues, just uttered on this floor. He wished to so act that when he returned home, he would not be found derelict to the duty with which he had been entrusted, having taken an oath to protect, defend and preserve the Constitution of the United States. Long as the matter had been discussed here, it was very strange that no man had answered the question, what was to be done with the freed people, should such an amendment to the Constitution prove effective? Gentlemen on the other side had failed to make out a case. During this administration the Constitution had been violated in all its important features.

Mr. Herrick (Dem., of N. Y.), in the course of his speech, said it was inconsistent to remain stationary when all the rest of the world is moving. Change is the universal law of nature. What he had heretofore regarded as impolitic had ceased to operate. Having at the last session voted against the proposed Constitutional amendment, he would now vote for it. He had no doubt of the power to make the amendment in the manner proposed. In amending it, three-fourths of the States represent the whole. The time has arrived to exercise the power. He believed that if Democratic policy and measures had been adopted, we should not now be engaged in war; but in the late Presidential election the people had endorsed the anti-slavery issue. He was prepared to follow it. The question had been settled by the verdict of the people, and so far as the National Government was concerned, it was not now a political issue. The adoption of the amendment would tend to restore all that is desirable to the prosperity of the country. He believed the best good of the Democratic party would be enhanced by the passage of the proposition, and it will open up a way to its triumph in the future.

Mr. Brown, of Wisconsin, opposed the proposition, and gave notice of a substitute for gradual emancipation and compensation to Union men.

Mr. Harding said truth and principle never change, but men change, and from time to time adopt opinions just as readily as they change their garments. But he would rather hold on to the Constitution, which was the only ark of safety. He denied that there was any constitutional power to deprive any State in the Union of its local self-government. Kentucky had been treated in bad faith. Not one of the pledges made to her had been fulfilled. She had been betrayed, and now it was sought suddenly to emancipate all her slaves. The policy would result in the destruction of the slaves, and the men who proposed to carry it out had no more love for the slave than Satan has for sinners.

Mr. Kalbfleisch also opposed the proposition. He maintained that all our political misfortunes are attributable to a disregard of the Constitution. He denied that the result of the Presidential election was in favor of abolishing slavery everywhere. No such issue was made up in New York.

COMING TO A VOTE.

The debate having closed, Mr. Ashley demanded the previous question, which was on the motion heretofore made by the gentleman, to reconsider the vote of last session, by which the Constitutional amendment was lost for the want of the requisite two thirds majority.

The question was then taken on the motion to reconsider, and it was decided in the affirmative, yeas 112; nays 57.

The question was then taken on the adoption of the following Senate joint resolution, submitting to the Legislatures of the several States, a proposition to amend the Constitution of the United States.

Be it Resolved, By the Senate and House of Representatives of the United States of America, two-thirds of both Houses concurring, that the following articles be proposed to the Legislatures of the several States as an amendment to the Constitution of the United States; when ratified by three-fourths of said Legislatures, shall be valid, to all intents and purposes, as a part of the said Constitution—namely:

ARTICLE 13.—Section 1—Neither Slavery nor involuntary servitude, except as a punishment for crime, whereof the party shall have been duly convicted, shall exist within the United States, or any place subject to their jurisdiction.

Section 2—Congress shall have power to enforce this article by appropriate legislation.

There was much confusion throughout the proceedings, amid which the Clerk proceeded to call the roll on the passage of the joint resolution.

The Speaker said—Call my name as a member of this House.

When the Speaker answered to the name of Schuyler Colfax, applause followed his response, and also burst out at other parts of the proceedings, which, however, the Speaker checked, and calling the House to order, said he hoped a better example would be set to preserve the decorum of the House.

Several members on the Democratic side of the House said those on the other side were as noisy as the persons in the galleries.

Mr. Ganson, who had voted "No" on the question of reconsidering the vote by which the joint resolution was heretofore lost, now voted "Aye," and Messrs. Radford and Steele, of New York, changed their votes in the same manner. These changes gave rise to applause, which was promptly checked.

The utmost interest was manifested throughout the calling of the roll, and there was strict attention on the part of the members to their responses; for on the previous vote to reconsider two-thirds of the members present had not voted in the affirmative; but a large majority of the members present had carried that question. It was therefore somewhat doubtful whether the pending joint resolution would be passed. The votes of Mr. Baldwin (of Mich.) and the gentlemen above mentioned however gave additional hopes to the friends of the measure.

SLAVERY DEAD.

When the calling of the roll was completed, the Clerk proceeded to read the names, first of those who voted in the affirmative and next of those who had voted in the negative. The House was now comparatively silent. The result of the votes was noted on a piece of paper and handed by the Clerk to the Speaker, who then announced the passage of the joint resolution by a vote of 119 yeas, against 56 nays.

REJOICINGS.

Thereupon arose a general shout of applause. The members on the floor huzzaed in chorus with the deafening and equally emphatic cheers of the throng in the galleries. The ladies in the dense assemblage waved their handkerchiefs, and again and again the applause was repeated, intermingled with clapping of hands and exclamations of "Hurrah for Freedom!" "Glory enough for one day!" &c. The audience were wildly excited, and the friends of the measure jubilant. Never was a scene of such a joyous character witnessed in the House of Representatives; certainly not within the last quarter of a century.

There was extensive hand shaking and congratulation in every direction. The proceedings had attracted thousands of persons of both sexes, and having been brought to a close, those on the floor, who had been admitted by the favor of the members, and the occupants of the gallaries, hastily departed.

The vote on the passage of the joint resolution is as follows:

YEAS—Messrs. Alison, Ames, Anderson, Arnold, Ashley, Bailey, Baldwin, Mich.; Baldwin, Mass.; Baxter, Beaman, Blaine, Blair, Blow, Boutwell, Boyd, Brandagee, Broomall, Brown, West. Va.; Ambrose W. Clark, Freeman Clark, Cobb, Coffroth, Colfax, Cole, Cresswell, Davis, Md.; Davis, N. Y.: Dawes, Denning, Dixon, Donnelly, Driggs, Dumont, Eckley, Eliot, English, Farnsworth, Frank, Ganson, Garfield, Gooch, Grinnell, Griswold, Hale, Herrick, Higby, Hooper, Hotchkiss, Hubbard, of Iowa; Hubbard, Connecticut; Hubbard, Hutchins, Ingersoll, Jenckes, Julian, Kasson, Kelley, Kellogg, Mich.; Kellogg, N. Y.; King, Knox, Littlejohn, Loan, Longyear, Marvin, McAllister, McBride, McClurg, McIndoe, Muller, N. Y.; Moorhead, Morrill, Morris, N. Y.; A. Myers, L. Myers, Nelson, Norton, Odell, O'Neill, Pa.; Orth, Patterson, Perham, Pike, Pomeroy, Price, Radford, Randall, Ky.; Rice, Mass.; Rice, Me.; Rollins, N. H.; Rollins, Mo.; Schenck, Scofield, Shannon, Sloan, Smith, Smithers, Spalding, Starr, Steele, N. Y.; Stevens, Thayer, Thomas, Tracy, Upson, Van Valkenburgh, Washburne, Ill.; Washburne, Mass.; Webster, Whaley, Wheeler, Williams, Wilder, Wilson, Windham, Woodbridge, Worthington, and Yeaman—119.

NAYS—Messrs. J. C. Allen, W. J. Allen, Ancona, Bliss, Brooks, Brown, Wis., Chanler, Clay, Cox, Cravens, Dawson, Denison, Eden, Edgerton, Eldridge, Finck, Grider, Hale, Harding, Harrington, Harris, Md., Harris, Ill., Holman, Johnson, Pa., Johnson, O., Kalbfleisch, Kernan, Knapp, Law, Long, Mallory, Miller, Pa., Morris, O., Morrison, Noble, O'Neil, O., Pendleton, Perry, Pruyn, Randall, Pa., Robinson, Ross, Scott, Steele, N. J., Stiles, Strouse, Stuart, Sweat, Townsend, Wadsworth, Ward, C. A. White, J. W. White, Winfield, Ben Wood, F. Wood—56.

The absentees, or those not voting, were, Messrs. Lazear, Lebloude, Marcy, McDowell, McKinney, Middleton, Rogers and Vorhees—8.

A motion to adjourn was carried, amid the greatest confusion—Yeas, 121; nays, 24.

New York State Legislature.

Senate.

Albany, Jan. 31.—A bill was reported to incorporate the New York and Union Yacht Club.

Bills were noticed to incorporate the State Temperance Society, and for the construction of a pier in the North River, New York.

Bills were introduced to regulate the fees of physicians and surgeons in certain cases, and authorizing the Supervisors of New York to raise money to pay such bounty to volunteers as they may deem proper.

Bills were passed amending the charter of the German Savings Bank, and changing the name of More's Patent Firearms Company.

The State Bounty bill, which provides a State bounty of $300, $400 and $600, for one, two and three years' men, prohibits all local bounties, and authorizes the creation of a debt of $30,000,000 for the purpose, was also passed.

[The bill passed the Assembly last week, and now goes to the Governor.]

A bill was also passed appropriating $200,000 for the relief of the sick and wounded soldiers of this State in the service of the United States.

Bills were ordered to a third reading, providing for the appointment of five Commissioners of Appeals, and amending the charter of the Brooklyn Mercantile Library Association.

Assembly.

Mr. Reed introduced a bill to authorize the Board of Supervisors of New York to provide means to encourage enlistments and pay bounties to volunteers. The bill was referred to the following special committee: Messrs. Reed, Bemis, and Ingraham.

Bills were ordered to a third reading to amend the charter of the Washington Insurance Company of New York; to increase the compensation of Supervisors to $3 per day; to legalize the ordinance of the Board of Supervisors of New York, passed June 25th, 1864, relative to bounties; in relation to common schools in the city of New York.

Mr. Van Buren reported a bill for the better protection of seamen in the port of New York. Adjourned.

News Items.

[*By Telegraph to the New York Sun.*]

MRS. H. S. Foote, wife of the rebel Senator, arrived at Nashville, Tenn., on Monday evening.

OVER a thousand bales of cotton arrived at Cairo, Ill., yesterday, from Memphis for Cincinnati.

A DESPATCH from the Army of the Potomac, dated the 29th inst., says there is nothing to report except the arrival within our lines of squads of deserters daily, who repeat the stories of want and demoralization prevailing in the rebel ranks.

A PASSENGER train on the Galena and Chicago railroad, when near Cherry Valley Station, Monday night, was precipitated down a fifty foot embankment. Five cars were wrecked and several persons were injured.

THE Alexandria, Va., JOURNAL says the civil government has been restored on the Eastern shore of Virginia, and that in a few days civil government will be restored in every county where it was suppressed by the action of Gen. Butler.

THE financial arrangements just concluded between the Treasury Department and Jay Cooke contemplate the continuance of subscriptions to the Seven-thirties through the National Banks in New York, Philadelphia, Boston and elsewhere as heretofore.

N. B. DAVIS, identified at Newark, Ohio, some days since, as keeper of the Andersonville Ga., military prison, and who confessed on his arrest being the bearer of dispatches from Richmond to

Continued on the last page

Notice.—The cross mark appended to the names of certain subscribers indicates that the time for which they subscribed will soon expire. They are thus notified in time to renew their subscription if desired.

RAGS WANTED.—The highest market price will be paid at this Office for Clean Cotton Rags. They will be purchased in any quantity.

NOTICE TO CITY SUBSCRIBERS.—The accounts of all our city subscribers are now made out and in the hands of the collector.—We trust that no excuse will be made by those indebted to us, and that one call will suffice. Those who fail to pay will not be continued on our list.

THE PEACE fever is abating. Men begin to think, and allow reason to exercise its functions. The credulity with which the first rumors were received begins to give place to doubts; and the childish enthusiasm and excitement which they inspired are fast being succeeded by a calmer and less hopeful feeling. It is fortunate that this is so, as the reaction and depression will not be so great and sudden when the movement fails as fail it almost surely will.

It seems that the public have been laboring under a mistake as to the capacity in which the so-called "commissioners" go to Washington. All that can be said is that they go at the *suggestion* of the President, without any official appointment or authority. Of their mission the "Examiner" says:

"It is positively known that these 'Commissioners' (as they are called in the streets) were not nominated to the Senate; that their names were not in any way sent in to that body, or that they received any commission or appointment from the President; and that thus, therefore, their mission is without any official qualification.

The provisions of the constitution which apply to such matters are plain and indispensable. The President has power to negotiate treaties, but only that they may be submitted to the action and determination of the Senate; he may appoint Commissioners when Congress is not in session; but when that body is sitting, he can do nothing more than nominate them to the Senate."

Again that paper says of these gentlemen:

"They are not negotiators, and have no power to treat. They are not even commissioners from our Government; nor are they empowered to represent, or to speak for the country; inasmuch as there has been no appointment by the President or by the Senate. In short, just as Jacquess and Kirk, and after them Mr Blair, came to Richmond, to talk with any one who would converse with them, and were but too successful in getting themselves received at the Executive mansion, so these three Confederate gentlemen go to Washington to have a conversation with the enemy; though it is doubtful whether they will have equal success in being admitted to the White House."

This version of the capacity in which the Commissioners go is confirmed by the Enquirer, which says that "they have, with the knowledge and approval of the President, determined to visit Washington to see what can be done."

The Examiner thus notices another delusion which has possessed very many persons of late, and on which they are building high expectations:

"People say, and repeat to one another, rubbing their hands with an innocent glee, that there must have been some intimation conveyed to Seward from Europe, which makes the enemy so eager now to wind up the war; in fact, that England and France might, could, would or should have informed Lincoln that if on the fourth of March he be not inaugurated President of the whole of the old States, they, England and France, will then recognize him only as President of those States which concurred in his election. There is not the slightest evidence or foundation of fact for this or any kindred rumor. It is a blunder altogether. Not only is there no single symptom that those European Powers are changing their policy in a manner favorable to us, but no occasion will arise at the fourth of March for recognition of any person or anything. The European Powers know nothing about the Fourth of March; they do not renew their recognition of the United States on the inauguration of a new President, and will not be called upon for any action whatsoever that day, more than any other day. That delusion may be dismissed."

CAPTURE OF A RAILROAD TRAIN.—On Thursday last, Major Richards of Mosby's command, says the Sentinel, with a force of sixty men, struck the Baltimore and Ohio railroad between Duffields and Martinsburg, and captured a train of fifteen cars propelled by the engines and loaded with supplies for Sheridan's army. The engines were blown up and the cars consumed by fire. Our adventurous soldiers loaded their horses with such articles as they could bring away; many of them possessing themselves in this manner of sacks of coffee, besides other desirable supplies.

THE NEWS.—Gen'l Lee has at last been confirmed as Commander-in-Chief of all our armies. This event will have a most salutary effect on the people and the army, and great good may be expected from it.

Thomas' troops are reported passing over the Baltimore & Ohio Railroad, which means that they are going either to Grant or Sherman.

A deputation from the North Carolina Legislature have been to Richmond to consult with the Congressional Delegation from that State. What does it mean? We hope not mischief.

The war spirit is still buoyant at Richmond. A large meeting was held there Tuesday night in the interest of the war, at which great enthusiasm prevailed. Addresses were delivered by the Hon Thos S Flournoy and other prominent gentlemen, all of whom declared in favor of prosecuting the war until our independence is achieved. That's the talk. If we think less of peace and more of war, it will be better for the cause and country.

ASSISTANT SECRETARY OF WAR.—It is reported that Colonel Drinkard, of Richmond, will be appointed Assistant Secretary under General Breckinridge's administration of the War Department. Col Drinkard occupied a similar position in the old Government, when Governor Floyd was Secretary of War at Washington.

The North Carolina Commissioners who visited Richmond were Messrs D M Carter, S J Pearson, E D Hall and John Poole.—They are said to have been appointed by the North Carolina Legislature to come on business touching the more vigorous prosecution of the war. They held a conference with the North Carolina Congressional delegation at the Spotswood House.

GEN. J. D. Imboden is in command of all the military prisons in Georgia, Alabama and Mississippi.

FUNERAL NOTICE.

The funeral services of the late SAMUEL McALDEN will take place this (Thursday) morning, from the residence of his father-in-law, Mr. James C. Walton. The corpse is expected to arrive at the Presbyterian Grave yard about 1 o'clock. Friends wishing to attend the services will find an omnibus at Mr. S. A. Boyd's store, this morning, at 9 o'clock.

LATEST BY TELEGRAPH

Reports of the Press Association.

Entered according to Act of Congress, in the year 1863, by J. S. THRASHER, in the Clerk's Office of the District Court of the Confederate States in the Northern District of Georgia.

GEN'L LEE CONFIRMED AS COMMANDER-IN CHIEF.

A DEPUTATION FROM NORTH CAROLINA.

APPEAL FROM GENERAL LEE.

THOMAS' TROOPS PASSING OVER THE BALTIMORE AND OHIO RAILROAD.

GREAT WAR MEETING IN RICHMOND.

RICHMOND, Feb 1st.

The nomination of General Lee as General-in-Chief was confirmed yesterday by the Senate.

Reports from the Valley represent troops from Thomas' army passing over the Baltimore & Ohio Railroad.

A deputation from the North Carolina Legislature arrived here yesterday and had an interview last night with the Congressional Delegation from that State.

Gen Lee has issued an appeal for the surrender of all cavalry arms and equipments in private hands. He says prompt compliance with his call will greatly promote the efficiency and strength of the arm, particularly the cavalry.

A large public meeting held last night in the Hall of the House of Delegates was addressed by Hon Thos S. Flournoy and several members of Congress from Virginia and Georgia. Great enthusiasm prevailed. The meeting broke up at a late hour. All the speakers declared in favor of the prosecution of the war until our independence is achieved.

SHERMAN'S PROGRESS.

CHARLESTON, Jan 31.

All movements of the enemy indicate Augusta and Branchville as their points of destination.

The 20th army corps occupy Robertsville; a heavy force of infantry, artillery and cavalry is reported encamped near the Junction of Salkehatchee and old Union Road. The force is believed to be the 15th and 17th army corps. Yesterday morning the enemy advanced in considerable force of infantry and artillery from White Point and drove in our skirmish line 3 miles to Kings Creek; our infantry advanced and drove the enemy back to White Point re-establishing our picket lines. Since this, all has been quiet on the Combahee. At that point the enemy made a demonstration on our position. They threw pontoon brides over the Seakehatchee this afternoon but without result. 'Tis reported they burnt McPhersonsville last night.

CONGRESSIONAL.

RICHMOND, Feb. 1.

In the House Mr Gholson submitted the following:

Resolved, That the people of the Confederate States have ever been and are now ready to make peace on terms honorable to both parties, yet, tis the judgement of this House that while we should manifest willingness to treat for peace we should not omit to vigorously prepare for war.

Resolved, further, in the judgement of the House, this preparation can best be made by using every effort to place at once in the army every man liable under our laws to render military service; by causing Commissaries, Quartermasters and other departments to be administered with renewed energy; and since Lee has been made General-in Chief to assign him our best and most acceptable Generals to command our seperate armies; and by ceasing to agitate the policy of employing negro troops, a measure which has already divided public sentiment and produced much despondency. Gholson spoke at considerable length in support of his resolution. He incidentally paid a tribute to the Press, which he thought had accomplished more in aid of our struggle than an hundred fold the number of its employees could have done if armed and placed in the field.

Mr. Gholson occupied the morning hour, at the expiration of which the Currency bill was referred to a committee of conference.—The House then resolved into secret session.

The Senate passed the Senate bill to abolish the office of all Quarter Masters and Commissaries on duty at posts and depots, and provide for the appointment of bonded agents in their place. The act also repeals all authority to detail persons between 18 and 40 in said departments. Resolved into secret session.

No Yankee papers received to-day.

FROM GEORGIA.

MACON, Feb. 1.

A special to the Columbus Enquirer, from Marianna, Fal. 30th, says the enemy, 100 strong, came to Rice's Bluff in Apalachicola River and captured a Lieutenant and 40 negroes on the 25th, and then left. On the 29th the enemy were again reported advancing on Rice's Bluff; number unknown.

The Charleston Mercury.

DAILY PAPER—TWENTY DOLLARS FOR TWELVE MONTHS—PAYABLE IN ADVANCE. | VINDICE NULLO SPONTE SUA SINE LEGE FIDES RECTUMQUE COLENTUR. | COUNTRY PAPER—THREE A WEEK—Fifteen Dollars for Three Months—Payable in Advance.

Volume LXXXVI. CHARLESTON, S. C., TUESDAY, FEBRUARY 7, 1865. Number 12,287.

TELEGRAPHIC.

CONGRESSIONAL NEWS.

RICHMOND, February 2.—The House passed the Senate bill increasing the compensation and emoluments of the President, and increasing the salaries of officers and employees of the Government in Richmond, also adopted resolutions expressing the gratification of Congress for the additional evidence of patriotism of the different commands who have declared their purpose to maintain the war for independence.

FROM THE NORTHERN PAPERS.

THE GUNBOAT FIGHT IN JAMES RIVER—FARRAGUT GONE TO THE JAMES.

The most fanciful accounts of the naval excursion down James river, last week, are given in the New York papers. A correspondent of the New York *Tribune*, telegraphing from Washington on the 25th, says:

News reached here yesterday afternoon, from Grant's headquarters, that rebel rams and war steamers (we understand six in number) came down early in the morning from Richmond, and drove our armed vessels down the river, and [illegible] transports, and everything afloat, as far down as City Point. Details have not transpired here; but the emergency was deemed to be so great that Admiral Farragut was summoned to the James river, by telegraph, instantly.

Yesterday morning, at 2 o'clock, taking advantage of the high water in the Potomac, five rebel war vessels, including, we understand, two rams, ran past the obstructions we had placed in the river with the purpose of destroying our transports and warehouses at City Point. Our batteries on the shore opened fire at one of the rams, which had got aground, and was so hotly peppered that the rebels blew it up, setting a slow match to the magazine and escaping in their boats. Two others also got aground and were shelled warmly. It was doubtful whether they could escape. The fourth ram returned toward Richmond.

One is said to have got below our batteries. She caused a sensation, certainly, at least. If she did damage, and how much, if any, is not yet known. There will probably be a removal from command in the James River flotilla as a punishment for the negligence in this case.

The Washington *Star* says:

Despatches received here state that, yesterday morning at 2 o'clock, a rebel fleet of five vessels—the Richmond squadron, so long being prepared—came down the river to destroy our depots and works at City Point.

The high water caused by the freshet enabled them to pass the obstructions which our commander had placed above City Point for the better protection of the place.

A battle quickly opened between the rebel fleet and our nearest battery or fort, in which one of the rebel vessels was blown up and instantly and entirely destroyed, while two others were so badly damaged by shot and shell as to compel them to seek safety by speedy flight back in the direction of Richmond, accompanied by the other two, which escaped damage to speak of.

Admiral Farragut left here yesterday evening for the scene of action, and it is understood that he will at once assume naval command there.

STOPPAGE OF THE WILMINGTON BLOCKADE RUNNING.

A telegram from Halifax, Nova Scotia, announces the arrival of a steamer there from St. Thomas and Bermuda, and gives the following intelligence about blockade running:

The blockade runner Owl succeeded in reaching Fort Caswell the night it was evacuated, an immediately returned to Bermuda, arriving on the 21st, with the news of the capture of Fort Fisher and stopping the Maud, [illegible], Dominion, Florence, Deer, and Virginia, all ready to sail. The Charlotte and Stag sailed for Wilmington at the same time with the Owl, and the Rattlesnake, Chameleon and Stag between the 18th and 20th, and had not since been heard from.

The bark Sacramento, from New York for Rio Janeiro, put into Bermuda on the 16th instant, to land the captain and crew of the ship Ganges, which was fallen in with on the 7th instant, latitude 35, longitude 60, in a sinking condition.—The above is probably the brig Ganges, Captain Johnson, from Cadiz, November 4, for Boston.

The island of St. Thomas has been declared an infected port.

THE BURNING OF THE SMITHSONIAN INSTITUTE.

The losses by the burning of the Smithsonian Institute, at Washington, on Tuesday night, were quite heavy. A Washington letter says:

The fire in the Smithsonian Institute had probably been smouldering for days in the loft at the west end of the main building. The pipe of a stove had been placed in a flue in the south wall, and there was a joist running directly into this flue. But four or five pictures were saved in this gallery. "The Dying Gladiator" (a copy by John Gott) was utterly ruined, crushed to pieces and burned to lime. The books and records in the Regent's room, over the south door of the building, including the effects of the founder of the building, James Smithson, consisting of silver plate, the library of Bishop Johns, of Virginia, and the Beaufort, South Carolina, library, placed in the institution by the Governor for safe keeping, were totally destroyed. The sarcophagus brought from Syria by Commodore Elliot for President Jackson was damaged. The large collection presented to the institute by Dr. Robert Hare, of Philadelphia, was mostly destroyed.—Some that was got out was broken, and many of the pieces are missing. In the offices over the north front entrance, with but little exception, all the correspondence of the institution and a large number of back reports were burned. The east wing was not in the least injured, although the staircase leading from the professors' apartments to the apparatus rooms was several times in flames. The lecture room is gutted completely. The towers on the north front appear to be cracked, and some of the walls are warped. The library in the east end was uninjured, and much of the apparatus, having been stored below, was also saved. There was no insurance on the building or effects.

HORACE GREELEY ON THE BLAIR MISSION.

[From the New York Tribune, January 29.]

There are men who talk as if the war were a normal condition, and who stare at the suggestion of peace as if some wrong was done the nation. But all wars must have an end, even those carried on as so few ever have been, for the highest good of the people, though all may not be attained which the victorious party, at the outset, promised itself. Ordinarily it is a struggle of endurance. It is a question of pluck and resources, and resources, as in all human affairs, are the ground work of courage. Which can hold out the longest? Which can hold out the longer? There comes always a time when the last is the vital question, and when it comes, peace is inevitable. We may or we may not have reached that point; but the signs are, at least significant, and wise men will give them due consideration. Unwise, or at least, thoughtless men, remember only that we have been at war but four years, while other nations have, with more or less patience, endured its calamities ten, twenty, thirty years; with far less at stake. They do not remember that one year of modern warfare, in the exhaustion attending it, in its enormous expenditure of blood and treasure, is equal to five years of war a century or half a century ago.

The desolation that followed the thirty years of war in Germany was not greater, probably not so great, as that which, in the last four years, has been visited upon the rebellious States of the South. Half of Virginia is a desert; Tennessee is a barren waste; the young men of the South are in their graves; the old men are reduced to poverty; the industrial system of all the slave States is destroyed; from Mason and Dixon's line to the Rio Grande, desolation covers the land.

In the natural course of things, then, peace is imminent. It may be the imminence of weeks or of months; certainly it cannot be delayed beyond the duration of one more campaign. The North wants peace, provided the terms and conditions shall suit it. There is unquestionably a party at the South that demands it, caring little what the terms are; ready to accede to anything that we demand. It is ready to grasp our utmost demand—lay down its arms and submit. Some facts are known to us which it is not safe now to make public. But they must be known ere long, and from that moment our public affairs will assume a new aspect.

Mr. Blair's first visit to Richmond was neither fruitless nor useless, or it would not have been repeated. Without pretending to know anything of its details, we, in common with every body else, arrive at this conclusion. Not less significant is the gradual but steady decline in the price of gold.

We are not more sanguine than our neighbors, nor are we more hopeful of or anxious for peace, neither do we pretend to more wisdom. But we hail the flash of those bright streaks of the coming day, and do not choose to shut our eyes to them because others, with closed eyelids, keep out the light. We do not prophesy immediate peace, because we do not mean to prophesy at all; but we believe the utter exhaustion of the rebels portend the result which exhaustion always brings to all wars.

THE MERCURY.

TUESDAY, FEBRUARY 6, 1865.

A Tandem Team!

The whole country was horrified yesterday to hear by the telegrams from Richmond that "Commissary General NORTHROP has not resigned, as reported."

We are really so much astonished at this information that we are confounded. We don't know exactly how to begin to express ourselves on the subject. The fact is, the matter is beyond the reach of any words. It is a matter for *action*, not for words. It is a matter, if we comprehend it, for which somebody should be hurt.

Everybody knows that Mr. DAVIS' Cabinet are but his head-clerks of the several Departments, to record his wills and pleasures. Everybody knows that if Mr. NORTHROP stays where he is, after the expression of official opinion that has just taken place, it is because he is held there by Mr. DAVIS. It is a maxim in Kingly Governments that the King can do no wrong—(notwithstanding Mr. CHARLES STUART lost his head, because it was thought in England that he *did* wrong). Now, if Mr. DAVIS has already ascended to the title of JEFF. 1st, Autocrat of the Confederate States, in God's name let us hold somebody responsible, as was done in England with STRAFFORD. To what pass have we come, when the people of the Confederate States in Congress assembled, are to be treated with the defiance and the scorn with which Mr. JEFF. DAVIS undertakes to treat them now.—What are we all—white negroes, or serfs, or what? What is this little man JEFF. DAVIS? Where did he come from? What authority has he? Where did he get it? Is this man one of the CÆSARS [illegible] Can it be so? Or is he indeed that little backwoodman from Mississippi that performed that wonderful and immortal military feat of the figure V,—made the worst and most meddlesome Secretary of War ever known under the old United States Government—and is now making the very worst Executive officer known in the modern world, since the time of his prototype, JAMES 2d, of England. Is this really the man who has the audacity thus to defy the authority of the People of the Confederate States, and to spurn their expressed wishes? Impossible! Surely, surely, the thing is utterly impossible! Has the monomania of this man's egotism utterly overthrown his whole reason, and reduced him to the condition of a mere lunatic? What does the man mean?

And what is Congress after? Have they forgotten the power of the people to impeach? Is there no high toned gentleman in the land, like General LEE, or General JOSEPH E. JOHNSTON who could be raised by Congress to the position now held by this incompetent man, tried now for four long years, and always found equally wanting in capacity and in patriotism? Can not this body, if composed of men too insignificant, individually, to have any respect for themselves, entertain and summon up some respect for the entire people in their official capacity?

Is the millennium coming or the day of judgment? What is the matter?

HABEAS CORPUS.—The following is the vote of the Confederate House of Representatives on the suspension of the writ of *Habeas Corpus:*

Yeas—Messrs Anderson, Atkins, Ayer, Baldwin, Boyle, Branch, Clopton, Colyar, Cruikshank, Darden, Echols, Farrow, Foster, Gaither, Garland, Hanly, Herbert, Holden, Lampkin, Lester, Marshal, Manees, Miles, Simpson, J M Smith, W E Smith, Smith, of Ala; Smith, of N C; Wickham and Witherspoon—31.

Nays—Messrs Aiken, Barksdale, Batson, Blanford, E M Bruce, H W Bruce, Chilton, Chrisman, Clarke, Clusky, Conrad, Dickinson, Dupree, Elliot, Ewing, Funsten, Gholson, Goode, Hartridge, Hatcher, Holliday, Johnson, Keeble, Kenner, Lyon, Machen, Norton, Perkins, Pugh, Sexton, Shewmake, Snead, Swan, Triplett, Vest, Villere, Welsh, Wilkes and Mr. Speaker—41.

A SAMPLE OF SAVANNAH RULE.—We find in New York *Commercial* the following paragraph, which will show how delightful the Yankee rule in Savannah is becoming:

A Savannah belle stepped off the sidewalk the other day to avoid walking under the American flag, which hung in front of an officer's headquarters. General Geary, military commandant of the city, immediately gave orders to have her promenade back and forth under the hateful symbol for an hour, as a warning for similar offenders."

LIEUT. GEN. PEMBERTON is in town, it is said, upon official duty of inspection. Our city is glad to welcome him back.

FIRE AT MIDWAY.—At four o'clock last Saturday morning, a fire broke out, at Midway, in the dwelling house of Dr. HOPSON PINCKNEY, which was rapidly consumed, with its entire contents, the family escaping with only a portion of their clothing. The flames quickly communicated to the Post and Telegraph offices, and the dwelling of the Postmaster, Mr. SEASE. Fortunately the contents of these buildings were saved. The fire originated in a defective chimney.

The Governor of the State To the People of South Carolina.

The doubt has been dispelled. The truth is made manifest; and the startling conviction is now forced upon all. The invasion of the State has been commenced! our people driven from their homes; their property plundered and destroyed; the torch and the sword displayed, as the fate to which they are destined. The threats of an insolent foe are to be carried into execution, unless that foe is checked and beaten back.

I call now upon the people of South Carolina to rise up and defend, at once, their own rights and the honor of their State. I call upon every man to lay aside selfish considerations, and prepare to do his duty to his State. Let the suggestions of ease and comfort become inglorious and unworthy; let those ends only be honorable which conduce to the defeat of the foe; let all who falter now, or hesitate, be henceforth marked. All who have lived under the protection of the State, who have flourished under its laws, and shared its prosperity, will gladly arm to protect it from subjection. If any seek escape from duty and danger at this time, let them depart. The hour approaches when all who are true to the State will be found in the ranks of those who arm in its defence. There is no room in the State but for one class of men; they are the men who will fight in her cause.

I give now timely warning to all. The period is near when private business must be for a season suspended. While there is yet time, let all prepare to set their houses in order. Let us hope that the interval may be short in which we will pass from doubt to hope; let us feel that, as we grapple danger, we will pluck safety. In every district of the State the men will be organized. From a portion of these districts only will the militia be drawn. In others, more [illegible] will be left for protection to persons and security to property. In such cases, the duty will be as imperative as in others, where the men are called from home.

In every quarter of the State, in every district, village and town, let the men stand with their arms in their hands. When required to move, let them do so with expedition and hope. Until required to move, let them be vigilant, and prepared to repress disorder, and put down all violence.

It is the duty of every man to oppose all the resistance he can to the approach of the enemy. It is the command of the State that he shall do so. The foe now upon the soil of the State is here to kill; let him be killed. The foe now upon the soil of the State is here for rapine and lust; let him meet resistance unto death. That foe devotes us to a doom worse than death; let him receive the fate he designs for us.

If any one is so ignorant of the temper with which this war has been waged by the foe, as to suppose that resistance provokes punishment, which unarmed he would not incur, let him be quickly undeceived. He is only safe who is armed; he is only spared who defends himself. The stale, and not unsuccessful practice of the foe, is to promise pardon and threaten punishment. The threat is always executed when he dares; the promise never. Moreover, the State, your country, requires you to arm in its def[illegible] It is not given to any man [illegible] territories to choose whether they will arm or not. When a merciless foe is abroad ravaging the fields, wasting the property, taking the lives of the people, insulting the sovereignty, and impeaching the independence of the State; where the State plants its banner, there will all true men gather. When the State calls, as it now does, to arms, all will echo that call; all must obey that summons.

Remove your property from the reach of the enemy; carry what you can to a place of safety; then quickly rally and return to the field. What you cannot carry, destroy. Whatever you leave that will be of use to your foe, what he will not need, that will he destroy. Indulge no sickly hope that you will be spared by submission; terror will but whet his revenge. Think not that your property will be respected, and afterward recovered. No such feeling prompts him. You leave it but to support and sustain him; you save it but to help him on his course. Destroy what you cannot remove. He will make your return to your homes over a charred and blackened road; prepare you the same way for him as he advances. Let him read everywhere and in everything, that in this State, from one portion of it to the other, there is but one purpose and fixed resolve—that purpose is to meet him at every point; fight him at every road; that resolve is to undergo all suffering, submit to every sacrifice, welcome any fate, sooner than subjection by his army, or submission to his terms.

You have led the way in those acts which united the people of your sister States in this confederation of States, and their secession from the Government of the United States. You first fired the gun at the flag of the United States, and caused that flag to be lowered at your command. As yet, you have suffered less than any other people. You have spoken words of defiance—let your acts be equally significant. In your sister States, with the people of those States, you have a common sympathy in the determination to be free, and in your hatred of the foe: you will not falter in that stronger sympathy which is derived from a common suffering.

You have defied a tyrant; do not apprehend his power. You have dared to do; fear not to die. No worse fate can befall him who has pride in the ancient honor of his State than to see it governed by those who hate it; and insult, with their vices, the virtues we have been taught to cherish.

Once more I say to you your State is invaded. Once more I call upon you to arm in its defence. All who unite with us are more than brothers; all who desert us are as false as the foes which assail us.

It is said there are some who think they are not bound to fight with us; who affect a desire not to forfeit what they call their allegiance to some foreign Power. It may be that there are some who hitherto have been misled. I will not believe that there lives in South Carolina now, any man who, having been under the protection of the State and treated as that State treats its own citizens, will, at this time, attempt to find in this affected zeal for an allegiance he has practically abjured, an excuse for the succor he is bound to render. If there are such, let them depart. They shall not remain here and be the cold witnesses of the sufferings which others endure, while they are secure from danger. If they remain, they will do so with the full knowledge that the State expects and intends that every man shall do his duty.

Be as resolute as your cause is just, and triumphant success awaits you. What right have they to expect success in the sight of God who pursue, with unrelenting hatred, you, who seek nothing more than the privilege of accomplishing the great ends for which your God has given you being? You have not invaded their soil, nor sacked their cities, nor wasted their fields; nor murdered their relatives, nor violated their wives and daughters. They pretend not to the plea of visiting upon you the terrible punishment of retaliation. They claim a right to reduce you to subjection—to hold you in bondage—to strip you of more than life, when they deprive you of the privileges dearer than existence. Rise, then, with the truth before you, that the cause in which you are to arm is the cause of Justice and of Right! Strike, with the belief strong in your hearts, that the cause of Justice and of Right is the cause which a Power superior to the hosts seeking to oppress you will not suffer to be overthrown. And even upon the soil of the State in which this monstrous tyranny was first defied shall it meet the fate it deserves, while imperishable honor will be awarded those who contributed to that great consummation, in which humanity will rejoice.

By the Governor:

A. G. MAGRATH.

Official—HENRY BUIST, Lt. Col. and A. D. C.

February 7 2

I give now timely warning to all. The period is near when private business must be for a season suspended. While there is yet time, let all prepare to set their houses in order. Let us hope that the interval may be short in which we will pass from doubt to hope; let us feel that, as we grapple danger, we will pluck safety. In every district of the State the men will be organized. From a portion of these districts only will the militia be drawn. In others, more [illegible] will be left for protection to persons and security to property. In such cases, the duty will be as imperative as in others, where the men are called from home.

In every quarter of the State, in every district, village and town, let the men stand with their arms in their hands. When required to move, let them do so with expedition and hope. Until required to move, let them be vigilant, and prepared to repress disorder, and put down all violence.

It is the duty of every man to oppose all the resistance he can to the approach of the enemy. It is the command of the State that he shall do so. The foe now upon the soil of the State is here to kill; let him be killed. The foe now upon the soil of the State is here for rapine and lust; let him meet resistance unto death. That foe devotes us to a doom worse than death; let him receive the fate he designs for us.

HEADQUARTERS, CITADEL, CHARLESTON, January 17, 1865.

[GENERAL ORDERS NO. 1.]

I. THE UNDERSIGNED, ON ENTERING UPON the responsible duties of Provost Marshal of the City of Charleston, respectfully invites the cordial cooperation of the Military [illegible] Civil Authorities, and of all classes of citizens [illegible] to secure to ALL the fullest enjoyment [illegible] leges consistent with a due regard to the [illegible] The duties of a Provost Guard, especially [illegible] instanced as this is, are of a very delicate a[illegible] character, and should be performed with an [illegible] to the general good.—The safety of the city a[illegible] security of its inhabitants are especially confided to their keeping. It is an important and solemn trust; yet, with concert of action and the hearty co-operation of those most immediately interested, [illegible] the good results seen and felt by all. My Sentinels, Guards and Patrol will be required to demean themselves as gentlemen, and to treat all persons with the utmost courtesy and respect, exacting reciprocal respect from all classes of persons. This rule will be strictly enforced, and all violators, whether citizen or soldier, will be held to strict accountability.

II. In order to avoid confusion or annoyance all Passports, Passes or Permits, except those granted for a few hours to my own command, must be presented at the Office of the Provost Marshal General, on King street, for approval by Captain WM. J. GAYER, A. A. G. and P. M. G.

III. All persons knowing just cause of complaint against any officer or man of my command, will confer a favor by reporting the name of the party and facts in the case to these Headquarters.

C. R. HANLEITER, Captain Commanding.

January 18

HEADQUARTERS, 2D AND 3D SUB DISTRICT SOUTH CAROLINA, CHARLESTON, December 10, 1864.

GENERAL ORDERS NO. 96.]

* * * * * *

IV. NO RICE WILL BE SHIPPED FROM THIS city until otherwise ordered. The Agents of Railroad and Express Companies will see that this order is rigidly enforced.

* * * * * *

By command of Major General RANSOM.

December 12 WM. F. NANCE, A. A. Gen'l.

STATE OF SOUTH CAROLINA.

ADJ'T AND INSPECTOR GENERL'S OFFICE, [EXTRACT.] COLUMBIA, January 26, 1865.

[SPECIAL ORDERS No. 30.]

CAPT. WM. F. NANCE, A. A. GENERAL, P. A. C. S., having been assigned for temporary special service with these Headquarters, will be obeyed and respected accordingly until otherwise directed.

* * * * *

By order of the Governor.

(Signed) A. C. GARLINGTON, Adjutant and Inspector General S. C.

Official—G. A. FOLLIN, A. A. General.

January 30

STATE OF SOUTH CAROLINA.

EXECUTIVE DEPARTMENT, January 21, 1865.

TO THE PEOPLE OF SOUTH CAROLINA:

GENERAL BUTLER, WITH HIS DIVISION, IS ON his way to the aid of our State. General HAMPTON is with him. He needs horses, and I have told him he shall have them. You will not hesitate to give up your horses when your friends and brothers require them to defend your State from invasion, your property from pillage, your wives and daughters from insult. Put aside your pleasure-carriages for the time, cease your ordinary pursuits for this occasion, and bring or send in your horses to Columbia!

Colonel CHRISTOPHER F. HAMPTON is charged by me with the duty of receiving, with thanks, all that will be sent; of taking all that are withheld. The horses will be paid for. No one shall suffer from his devotion to the State.

By the Governor: A. G. MAGRATH.

Official: HENRY BUIST, Lieut. Col. and A. D. C.

January 26

Soldier's Letter.

THE FLAG WE FIGHT UNDER.

SECOND COLORADO CAVALRY.

VOL. 1 A REGIMENTAL PAPER----TO ACCOMPANY THE REGIMENT. NO. 15

OLIVER V. WALLACE,
Editor and Proprietor.

From the Steuben Republican.

THE SKEDADDLE RANGERS.

Come all ye brave fellows
Oppressed with the blues,
Ye fair weather patriots
Who shake in your shoes;
Come pour thro' your numbers
The thrill of a song,
As sneakingly you skulk with the cowardly throng.
Oh never mind stopping
This side of the sea;
Get anywhere out of
The land of the free:
We want not the men
That are weak in the knees!
So send for the North,
Or the South, if you please.
And when you're once gone out,
Don't curse us again,
In a land that was not made
For cowards, but men!
Don't skulk along back
When the old flag on high
Is shaking again
Its bright stars to the sky.

—Lieutenant A. L. Gooding has taken to himself a "better half!" Long life to them; and other GOODIES "too numerous to mention!"

☞ Our Gallant Colonel has been breveted a Brigadier General. We are sorry to lose him as our Colonel, although highly gratified at his promotion. None is more deserving!

—A large number of Sherman's soldiers have pledged themselves not to drink any intoxicating liquors for one year- Can't the "Second" follow suit?

—Captain Boyd is announced as Assistant Inspector of this District, vice Captain Booth relieved.

—The Paymaster starts West today.

COMPENDIUM OF HISTORY.

[Continued from No. 14.]

In pursuing the course taken by the enemy, it was necessary to exercise caution, in order to avoid being ambushed by the foe, which might prove fatal to our party; and in order to guard against this, Major Pritchard threw out flankers for a considerable distance on each side of the road, who were compelled to pick their way through the dense underbrush, through fences, and over logs, ravines, and hillocks—necessarily causing tardy movements on the part of our forces. Pursuing the trail for about five miles farther, they came to the ground where the enemy had camped, and fed their horses; but had moved on sometime before our troops came up, according to information obtained from citizens on the road, who seemed anxious to impart anything they knew, that would be of service to our troops, in their endeavours to overhaul the enemy: when within three miles of the town of Knoxville, the dead body of a citizen was found lying by the roadside—killed by the *Banditti*; and on pushing on two miles farther, a large amount of destroyed mail matter was found on the road, where the coach had been plundered, and the mail bags rifled, and their contents strewn about over the ground: being within one mile of the town, the Major ordered a charge, and the Battalion moved forward at a gallop, with drawn revolvers. Upon reaching Knoxville, the birds had flown, much to the chagrin and disappointment of our troops, who were anxious to give them a severe chastisement for their many evil deeds committed through that country. Moving in advance of our column the enemy had the advantage of securing all the best horses in the country, and by so doing, could bid defiance to the pursuers, whose horses had well nigh given out—having traveled over 100 miles, with very little rest. Taking into consideration the wearied men, and the jaded condition of the horses, the Major deemed it advisable to give over the pursuit, and return to camp, which, after a brief halt was carried into effect—the command reaching Liberty that night. In service of this nature, it was impossible to have wagons at all times, for the transportation of subsistence, and the troops were obliged—along with what provisions they carried in their haversacks—to subsist upon the farmers throughout the country, who had abundance of everything required; nor were our men slow to help themselves to what they needed to satisfy their appetites, while passing through a country whose inhabitants were so notoriously rebel in their sentiments, and actions. Up to the time of the invasion by our troops, they had never experienced the evil effects of war, brought to their own doors, and while the counties of Jackson, Cass, Bates, and others across the river, suffered all the terrible consequences of being overrun, and devastated by the contending forces—*they* had reaped all the benefits of the scarcity of provisions in market, and consequent rise in prices; at the same time allowed the secession element to flourish unmolested in their midst, until it manifested itself in such gigantic magnitude that it became intolerable, and had to be crushed. And now, having the war brought to their own doors, and realizing some of its blighting effects, they were obliged to take measures for their own peace and safety. Meetings were held, and resolutions passed, and bodies of men were organized to keep down *bush-whacking*, and preserve order throughout the country—preferring to take the matter into their own hands, rather than have their country laid waste; by the soldiers, who showed very little leniency for rebels against the United States Government, and still less for *bush whackers*. Matters having become quiet, and somewhat settled in that part of the country, Col. Ford and command returned to Kansas City—after assuring the people of Clay county that very severe measures might be expected, should he be obliged to pay them another visit.

HISTORY OF THE

First Colorado Battery.

On the 17th day of September, 1862, Col. Jesse H. Leavenworth, of the Second Colorado Volunteers, appointed W. D. McLain Captain, and George S. Eayre, 1st Lieutenant, to raise a Company—to be part of his regiment. C. S. Burdsal was appointed Orderly Sergeant of the Co. On the 15th day of December, '62; at Denver, Colorado, Captain Alley, Third U. S. Infantry, mustered the Company (84 strong) into the service, as "Captain McLain's Company" of the Second Colorado Regiment of Volunteers. Second Lieutenant Horace W. Baldwin, (chosen by the Company, and appointed by the Governor,) was also mustered in. It is proper to state that the word "Battery!" appears before the word "Company" in the Company's certificate attached to the Muster-roll.—Although not, perhaps, intended on the part of the Company officers, the muster was a fraud on the men; they having enlisted under the express understanding that they were to belong to the Artillery Arm of the service. Immediately after their muster, the company was put on the march to Ft. Lyon, where they arrived on the 29th day of the same month. No guard duty was performed, by any of the men, until the 1st of the ensuing April; although efforts were not wanting to induce them, by some act of their own to recognize their existence as an Infantry company. These efforts signally failed, calling forth in each instance, an earnest protest directed to the Chief Military authorities of the District.

Sometime in March, 1863, orders were received by Col. Leavenworth—then at Fort Lyon—to proceed with several companies of his regiment to the States. Ours was designated by the Col., as one of the said companies. But the men—conscious of their strength in the Right though anxious to go to the front—feared that by "footing" it to the States, they would sacrifice then and forever, their every hope of being equipped as a Battery, as repeatedly promised; and therefore, imposed such conditions on the Colonel as obliged him to leave us in the quiet possession of our *Sibleys on the Sand-banks of the Arkansas*—in this the men were backed by their officers. It was at this time that Post guard duty was first imposed upon the men, to which—without a murmer—they submitted; and only a few days subsequent to the departure of the companies destined for the States (6th April, 1863) that muskets were attempted to be forced into our hands–by order of the Commander of the Post, Captain Johnson, Ninth Wisconsin Battery—doubtless encouraged by the presence of Leavenworth—who still tarried here—and perhaps instigated to the act by him. The written statement of the conditions related to the arms, were accepted, and we took the muskets. In substance they were: "That no man should be required to do guard duty with a musket; that such arms should only be used for purposes of drill, and after each drill, returned immediately to the Arsenal." Simultaneously with these occurrences, a full statement of the grievances of the company was made out, and presented to Col. Leavenworth; and likewise, with a supplement of remarks to Col. Chivington—Commanding the District—and through him to Governor Evans, and the Secretary of War. The men never had but one object in view—*Fair play, and a Battery.*

Be patient, and you will find out whether or not they got it.

[To be continued.]

VanMetre.

WHY HE SHOULD NOT BE DRAFTED.

Petroleum V. Nasby gives the following cogent reasons why he should not be drafted

"I see in the papers last nite, that the Government has institooted a draft, and that in a few weeks hund reds uv thousands uv peaceable citizens will be dragged to the tented field. I know not wat uthers may do, but ez for me, I can't go. Upon a rigid eggsaminashun uv my fizzikle man, I find it wood be wus nor madnis fer me 2 undertake a campane, to wit:

"1—I am bald-headed, and hev bin obliged to wear a wig these 22 years.

"2—I hev dand-ruff in what scanty hair still hangs around my venerable temples.

"3—I hev a chronic katarr.

"4—I hev lost sence Stanton's order for draft, the use of one eye entirely, and hev chronic inflamashun in the other.

"5—My teeth is all unsound, my palit aint eggsactly rite, and I hev had bronkeetis 31 years last June.

"6—I'm holler-chested, and short-winded, and hev allers had panes in my back and side.

"7—I'm afflicted with kronic diar-rear and kostive ness. The money I hev paid for Jayneses karminnitiv balsam and pills wood astonish almost ennybody.

"8—I'm rupchured in six places, and am entirely enveloped with tresses.

"9—I hev very cose vanes, hev a white swelling on wun leg, and a fever sore on the uther—also one leg's shorter than tother, tho' I handle it so expert that nobody never noticed it.

"10—I hev korns and bunyons on both feet, which wood prevent me from marchin.

"I don't suppose that my political opinions, which are ferninst the prosekooshun uv this unkonstitooshunal war, wood hev any wate with a draftin orsifer, but the above reasons why I can't go, will, I maik no doubt, be suffishunt

"Petroleum V. Nasby."

Fort Scott,
Jan. 25th, '65.

Friend Wallace:

Being one of the scattered, I thought I would write, to let you know that some of the "Second" are luxuriating in the walls of the Hospital at Fort Scott. There are four of us here; three of Co. L, and one of Co. I; all reverely wounded. We are waiting for fair weather, to rejoin our Regiment. I sometimes console myself with the idea, that we escape the suffering caused by the severe weather, but when I think of the *hole through my breast*, I try to make myself think its all right as it is. I am taking two copies of the "Letter," as I value it highly as a history of the Regiment. With the best wishes for your prosperity, I remain yours. &c.,

Miles Jain,
Sergt. Co. I, 2d Col. Cav.

—It is said that the important rebel movement which is to "astonish the world," and which has been so mysteriously alluded to in recent Richmond papers, is designed to consist of a grand combination in Virginia of nearly all the rebel military forces, and march thence into the Northern States, where they propose to conquer a peace or die in the attempt.

TERMS OF SUBSCRIPTION.

Six months, or 25 Numbers, $1,75
Two copies six months, $3,00
Three " " $4,50
Four " " $6,00
☞ CASH IN ADVANCE. ☜

Fort Zarah,
Feb. 5, 1865.

Mr. Editor:—Having a few moments to spare, aside from the duties of a soldier, I have concluded to devote them to you and your readers, for the purpose of informing you in regard to matters transpiring at this Post.

On Wednesday, Feb. 2d, a small party of men were detailed to cut and haul some dry wood from an Island in the Arkansas river, about the distance of a mile from the Post. They had been on the Island but a short time before the report of fire-arms were heard, and, much to the surprise of all, one of their number came running toward the wagon, not reaching them, however, before he fell to the ground. But very few of the party were armed, and supposing there were Indians in the vicinity, and not knowing their numbers, they concluded to hasten to the Post, and give the alarm. Lt. Coy was immediately sent out with a party of men, and on arriving at the spot, found Pvt. Dutton, of Co. "C." 2d Colorado Cav., severely wounded in three places. The wounded man was moved to the Post Hospital, and there is some hopes entertained of his recovery. It is supposed that there were not more than three Indians on the ground, as the Lieutenant could see no trail to warrant a different opinion. Hereafter, when the boys are out on such duty, it will be well for them to keep their eyes and ears wide open, as there is no telling when the red scoundrels are skulking around.

The Battery boys are making great progress in their drill, under the instruction of Lt. Baldwin. They have target practice occasionally, and I have noticed that their shots are very accurate for green hands. They may yet have a chance to give the Indians a few shells, mixed up with a little grape and cannister, during the coming Spring.

Lt. Crane, of the 1st Colorado Cavalry, is at this Post. Before the arrival of Capt. Green and his command, he was acting in the capacity of Po. Adjutant.

Hoping that the LETTER is in a prosperous condition, I will close for the present.

J. H.

GENERAL NEWS, Is good news. Grant has sent peace messengers in earnest. The army of the Potomac is on the move. By our afternoon dispatches we have information of the movement of the Fifth Corps towards Ream's Station, on the Weldon road, about ten miles below the "Cockade City." The 2nd Corps has moved across the Appomattox River. It would seem as if the army was swinging around Petersburg by the "left flank," Grant's favorite movement. Considerable fighting occurred. Col Murphy, of the 69th New York, was severely wounded. A great battle is expected.

MAINE has ratified, unanimously, the Constitutional Amendment.—*Conservative.*

—Secretary Fessenden, in his instructions to Cock, says he intends to rely wholly, hereafter, upon taxes and the sale of 7-30 bonds, to pay the expenses of the war.

—The Court Martial at Fort Leavenworth is now engaged in the trial of Col. Jennison, on charges of insubordination, &c.

☞ We cannot furnish any more back Numbers!

FORT LARNED, Kansas,
Feb. 7th, 1865.

FRIEND WALLACE:

Company L left their comfortable mud chimnies and "cayote" holes at Fort Ellsworth, the 31st of January, and marched for Fort Larned, where we arrived on the 2nd ult., at dark. It had rained during the day, and we were wet, cold, and disposed to be quarrelsome: The *latter* disposition, finally found vent in what "Paddy" called a "discooshin," between two of the boys:—"Knock-down" arguments soon decided the matter.—This affair—as we would say of a thunder shower—"cleared the atmosphere," and restored good nature. The duty here, is very heavy, and the constant calls for "details" has so affected our Orderly, that his sleep is filled with visions of a country "more capacious than cool," wherein he is constantly making details for guard, from fresh arrivals—Number 14 has just come to hand. M. WISNER.

—The Department of Kansas is merged into that of Missouri; Headquarters at Leavenworth; Gen. Dodge in command. Gen. Curtis is transferred to the department of the Northwest; Hd. Qrs. at Milwaukie.

Major-General Pope is appointed to the command of the Military Division of the Missouri, including the Departments of the Missouri, and the Northwest; Hd. Qrs at St. Louis.

—We have just returned from Leavenworth, after an absence of 8 days; were taken sick on our way home, and compelled to lie over two days—hence the unavoidable delay of the present issue.

—A colored lawyer J. S. Rock, of the Massachusetts bar, has been admitted to practice in the Supreme Court of the U. S.

—The Mobile *Argus* publishes a letter denying the report of Gen. Price's death. A person who left Price's headquarters December 8th, avers that he was then still living.

—Col. Ford arrived from Leavenworth, Friday, accompanied by his wife's cousin—Mrs. Weary—who came up on a visit. The Co. is enjoying good health, and is looking well. Mrs. Ford is quite unwell.

—If you want to get an idea of the churning effects of "riding in a stage," just read the following lines, written while on our return from Leavenworth:

i e l v n i a a e |
ꟻI ʞ ¡ ¡ 8 u ɔ 8
h s i i g i a t g
E ¡ ɹ p u u s ɐ e.

—There is a report that Joe. Hooker has been "hooked"—and will commit matrimony.

—Opportunities, like eggs, must be hatched when they are fresh!

—Lieutenant George F. Crocker, is acting Post Adjutant, to fill vacancy occasioned by the severe illness of Lt. Roe.

—Clearwater, or Gillette's Ranche, nine miles above Julesburg, N. T., has been burnt by the Indians.

—H. S. Foote, rebel Congressman, succeeded in making his escape, and arrived in New York on the 7th inst.

—The President has a message prepared upon the late peace interview.

—General Curtis started on the 9th inst., for his new command. Major Curtis accompanied him.

—We have received so many letters, that we cannot find room for them all.

—The 11th Kansas have been relieved from duty at this Post, with orders to report to Fort Kearney.

—It is rumored that Gen. Rosecrans has been appointed to an important command in the field.

MILITARY DIRECTORY.

Fort Larned, Kansas.

Capt. Thomas Moses, Jr., Commanding.
Lt. W. H. Pierce, Adj't and C. S.
Lt. C. A. Allen, Q. M.
J. Williams, Surgeon.
James Blakey, Hosp. Steward.
Joseph Baker, Sergt. Maj.
W. B. Lawrence. Q. M. Sergt.
A. W. Means, A. Com Sergt.
H. H. Norris, Ord. "
Jesse Crane, Sutler.

The Philadelphia Inquirer.

PRICE TWO CENTS. | PHILADELPHIA, WEDNESDAY, FEBRUARY 15, 1865. | PRICE TWO CENTS.

THE LATEST NEWS

OFFICIAL WAR GAZETTE.

Despatch from General Grant.

SHERMAN ACROSS EDISTO RIVER

Hardee's Position at Branchville Turned.

UNION ARMY ADVANCING RAPIDLY.

Columbia its Destination.

ADMIRAL PORTER AT WORK.

Despatch from Com. Cushing.

MORE OF HIS BRILLIANT NAVAL FEATS.

He Finds the Woods Full of Rebel Deserters.

Despatch from General Grant.

WASHINGTON, Feb. 14.—It is stated that the substance of a despatch from General Grant to the Government, received to-day, is that the Richmond papers of Monday (Feb. 13), say that Sherman has crossed the Edisto, which was the line held by the Rebel General Hardee in defending Branchville. According to the same Rebel authority a portion of Sherman's forces are two-thirds of the way from the Edisto to Columbia—an important point, forming the junction of the Charlotte and South Carolina and Greenville and Columbia Railroads, connecting with the railroads to Richmond.

Despatch from Commander Cushing.

Admiral Porter has forwarded to the Navy Department the following:—

UNITED STATES STEAMER "MONTICELLO," OFF WILMINGTON, N. C., Feb. 7, 1865—Sir:—I have the honor to report that I entered Little River, S. C., on the night of the 4th inst., and proceeding about eight miles with four boats and fifty men, landed in a small town of All Saints Parish, on Little River. The town was placed under guard without the knowledge of its inhabitants, and I succeeded in capturing some soldiers and arms. I held the place all the next day, and discovered and destroyed about $15,000 worth of cotton. I also captured two flats at the mouth of the river containing twenty-three bales of cotton, which had some time before been removed from a blockade-runner to lighten her. This we brought off, together with some negroes.

The North Carolina planters, and all the men I met professed to be willing to come back under the Government, and most of them seemed to be loyal men and only awaiting emancipation from military rule.

On the 6th inst. I sent two boats' crews ashore in Charlotte Inlet, under command of Acting Master C. A. Pettit. He surprised and routed a Rebel force detailed to collect provisions in that county, capturing six soldiers with their arms and equipments, and destroyed the stores that had been gathered for the enemy at Flanderson.

The soldiers lately stationed at Charlotte had been withdrawn to assist in the defense of Wilmington. One hundred Rebels are still at Lockwood's Folly. The woods are full of deserters.

Very respectfully, your obd't serv't,

W. P. CUSHING,
Lieutenant-Commanding.

Rear-Admiral D. D. Porter, commanding North Atlantic Blockading Squadron, Cape Fear River, N. C.

REBEL ACCOUNTS.

RAILROADS LEADING FROM BRANCHVILLE ALL DESTROYED—A COLUMN OF UNION TROOPS MOVING RAPIDLY TO COLUMBIA, S. C., ETC.

WASHINGTON, Feb. 14.—Richmond papers of Monday, the 13th inst., announce the tapping of the railroad by Sherman's forces, north of Branchville, and between that place and Kingsville, thus destroying every road centring at Branchville.

Sherman Moving on Columbia.

WASHINGTON, Feb. 16.—Richmond papers of Monday announce that Sherman has flanked Branchville on the north, and is marching on Columbia.

FORTRESS MONROE AND THE SOUTH.

FORTRESS MONROE, Feb. 11.—The steamship *Atlantic* arrived this morning with mails and passengers from Fort Fisher. There is no news to communicate from General Terry's forces. Captain Arnsworth is still at Fort Fisher, superintending the building of wharves for the landing of stores for our troops.

The flag-of-truce steamer *New York*, in charge of Colonel Mulford, left here this afternoon for Varina with one thousand one hundred Rebel prisoners for exchange. Among them are quite a number of officers. She also carries about two tons of private stores for our Union soldiers in the Rebel prisons, which have been here some time, waiting an opportunity to be sent to Richmond.

The steamer *Cahawba* has arrived from Beaufort, N. C., and sailed this afternoon for New York.

FORTRESS MONROE, Feb. 12.—The steamer *Alhambra* arrived this morning from Beaufort, North Carolina, with the mails. The steamer *Escort* sailed this afternoon for Beaufort, taking freight, mails and passengers.

Lieutenant-General Grant arrived this afternoon on the steamer *Mary Brown*, from Baltimore, and proceeded to City Point.

DEPARTMENT OF THE GULF.

EVACUATION OF PASCAGOULA BY OUR TROOPS—NEW ORLEANS COTTON MARKET, &C.

CAIRO, Feb. 13.—The steamer *Missouri*, from New Orleans, has arrived with dates of the 5th. She brings a large cargo of sugar and molasses for St. Louis and Cincinnati.

The burning of Pascagoula is contradicted, but the place has been evacuated by our troops. Several gun-boats remain off the coast, however.

Cotton in New Orleans was in fair demand with a limited supply, prices being in favor of the sellers. Middlings are quoted at 70 cents; low do., 66@68 cents. Nearly 1000 bales of cotton have arrived here since Saturday morning for St. Louis.

Refusal to Permit the Recruiting of a Regiment.

Special Despatch to the Inquirer.

HARRISBURG, Feb. 14.—A despatch from Provost Marshal-General Fry announces that the application of the citizens of Dauphin county, made some time ago, to raise a volunteer regiment, cannot be granted.

GEN. SHERMAN'S GRAND ADVANCE.

Map Showing his Line of March from Savannah, Georgia, via Branchville, to Columbia, South Carolina.

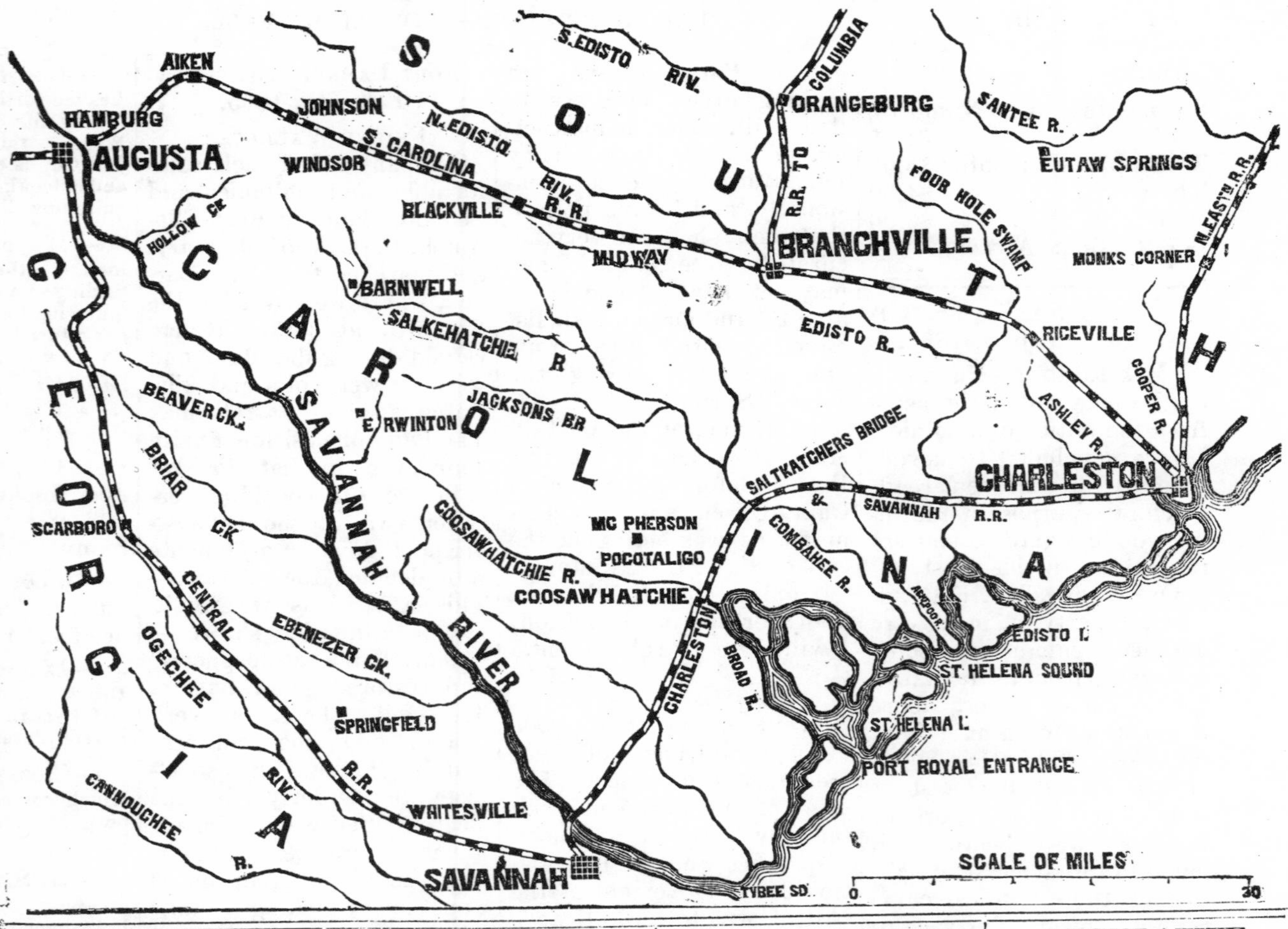

HARRISBURG.

TROOPS ASSEMBLING AT CAMP CURTIN—IMPROPER CONDITION OF THE RENDEZVOUS—COMPANIES ENLISTING IN VARIOUS PLACES—RECRUITING BRISTLING UP—TEMPORARY POSTPONEMENT OF THE DRAFT, ETC.

Special Despatch to the Inquirer.

HARRISBURG, Feb. 14.—Several hundred volunteers are again in Camp Curtin, but are very much dissatisfied with the accommodations. Many of them have visited the Governor with complaints. One would suppose that by this time the authorities would be prepared for the arrival of more troops, but this morning Major Dodge was requested to allow two soldiers to enter the hospital, their feet having been frozen for want of sufficient covering during last night. Blankets have not yet been furnished.

It is alleged that were it not for the unnecessary obstacles thrown in their way there would now be several thousands of volunteers in camp. The Lewistown Company have indicated their desire to return and enter the service as soon as a certain difficulty is removed, and when they have reason to expect that they will be treated better. Two companies at Pittsburg are said to be holding back, as they telegraph, until they are in like manner assured.

A company of volunteers from Reading despatched to the Governor this morning to know if they could be transferred to the Union League Regiment of Philadelphia. They were ready to start, but were deterred by the startling reports of the Legislative Committee on Camp Curtin. The State authorities, under the order, could not make such a transfer. There is no doubt in the world but that, with a proper system of recruiting and due encouragement to volunteer, our quotas could be filled without a draft.

The draft cannot take place in this District to-morrow, nor for some days, as arrangements for carrying it out have not been perfected.

CENTRAL AND SOUTH AMERICA.

SPANISH-PERUVIAN DIFFICULTIES ADJUSTED—NONE BUT AMERICAN TROOPS TO CROSS THE ISTHMUS—SALVADOR OPPOSES MAXIMILIAN, ETC.

NEW YORK, Feb. 14.—The steamer *Ocean Queen*, from Aspinwall on the 5th instant, arrived at this port to-day with $250,000 in treasure.

The steamer *Peru*, from Callao on the 28th of January, had arrived at Panama, with news that the Spanish-Peruvian question had been settled. The terms are said to be that Peru shall pay three millions of dollars for the expenses of the Spanish expedition.

Peru obtains possession of the Chincha Islands, admits a Spanish Envoy, and admits the interests of the Spanish. The settlement has been forwarded to Madrid.

Richard M. Jessup, of New York, one of the California dancers, died of neuralgia, at Aspinwall, on the 4th inst.

The small-pox continues its ravages at Kingston, Jamaica.

The Government of Bogota has issued an order prohibiting the passage of foreign troops across the Isthmus in future. Exception is made with regard to the United States troops, owing to the situation of their territories on the Pacific.

The President of Salvador, in his message to the Legislature, refutes indignantly the charge that he is in favor of annexing Central America to Mexico.

The Constitutional Amendment Passed by Indiana.

INDIANAPOLIS, Feb. 13.—The resolution indorsing the Constitutional Slavery Amendment having passed the State Senate by a vote of 25 to 24, passed the House to-night by a vote of 57 to 29. A salute of 100 guns is being fired at the State House in honor of the event.

Arrival of Prize Cotton.

NEW YORK, Feb. 14.—The United States steamer *Flag*, with a convoy of twenty-one vessels loaded with cotton, captured by Sherman at Savannah, arrived here this morning. The *Flag* brings no news.

WASHINGTON

OUR SPECIAL DESPATCHES

An Important Financial Bill.

FUNERAL OF THE LATE SENATOR HICKS.

Foote Abandons the Rebel Cause.

HIS DEPARTURE FOR EUROPE.

GOOD NEWS FROM TECUMSEH SHERMAN.

[SPECIAL DESPATCHES TO THE INQUIRER.]
WASHINGTON, Feb 14.

The New Financial Bill.

HIGHLY IMPORTANT MOVEMENT TO SECURE ADDITIONAL FUNDS FOR THE USE OF THE GOVERNMENT.

The Committee on Ways and Means will report a bill in accordance with the wishes of Secretary Fessenden, which provides for an issue of bonds or other obligations, prohibiting legal tender notes, not exceeding six hundred millions of dollars, payable at not over forty years from date, or redeemable at the pleasure of the Government, at not less than five nor more than forty years, and the amount issued in other forms and the bonds may be converted into bonds redeemable, &c., as the Secretary of the Treasury may deem expedient.

Principal or interest, or both, may be payable in coin or in any other money or currency declared by Congress to be lawful money or legal tender. Interest in coin shall not exceed six per cent., or if in currency, not to exceed seven and three-tenths per annum.

Another section gives the Secretary power to sell bonds in any market he chooses, here or in Europe, and on such conditions as he may deem advisable, for coin, lawful money, Treasury Notes or Certificates of Indebtedness, &c.

Another section exempts these bonds from State and municipal taxation.

The cost of printing not to be allowed to exceed one per cent.

Power is given to issue more gold interest bonds, in order to guard against any failure in future to raise money, should the Secretary fail to raise money enough by the sale of Seven-Thirties.

Funeral of Senator Hicks.

The committee of arrangements, pall-bearers, Knights Templars, escort and mourners will attend at the late residence of Senator Hicks, deceased, Metropolitan Hotel, at one o'clock P. M., on Wednesday, 15th instant, at which time the remains will be removed, in charge of a committee of arrangements, attended by the pall-bearers, mourners and escort, and Sergeant-at-arms of the Senate, to the Senate chamber, where, at 2 o'clock, Divine service will be performed. When these ceremonies are completed the funeral will move from the Senate chamber to the place of interment in the following order:—

Chaplains of Congress for the occasion.
Physicians who attended the deceased.
Committee of Arrangements:—Mr. Foot, Mr. Anthony, Mr. Willey, Mr. Buckalew, Mr. Morgan and Mr. Wade.
Escort of Knights Templar.
Pall-bearers:—Mr. Collamer, Mr. Davis and Mr. Doolittle on the left.
Mr. Lane, of Indiana, Mr. Foster and Mr. Hale on the right.
Family and friends of the deceased.
Senators and Representatives from the State of Maryland.
Governor Bradford and Aids.
Lieutenant-Governor Lewis.
Senate and House of Delegates and Court of Appeals of said State, and Mayor and City Councils of the City of Baltimore as mourners.
Sergeant-at-Arms of the Senate of the United States.
Members of the Senate, preceded by the Vice-President of the United States and Secretary of the Senate.
Sergeant-at-Arms of the House of Representatives.
The Members of the House of Representatives, preceded by the Speaker and Clerks.
President of the United States, with the Heads of Departments and Diplomatic Corps.
Judges of the United States.
Officers of the Executive Departments.
Officers of the Army and Navy.
Mayor of Washington, Citizens and Strangers.

The funeral orations will be delivered in both the Senate and House, and both bodies will adjourn. No business whatever will be transacted.

"Hangman" Foote Gone to Europe.

"Hangman" Foote, on arriving within our lines, communicated with the Secretary of State, desiring to remain in the country with a view to use efforts for the purpose of bringing about peace, with the overthrow of the Rebellion and the restoration of the Union upon the basis of the gradual removal of slavery, but Mr. Foote, while declaring that he had forever abandoned the Rebel cause, did not propose to accept the terms of the President's proclamation of amnesty. Permission, therefore, was given him either to return within the enemy's lines, or to leave the United States, not to return during the continuance of the war without permission from the Government. Mr. Foote has embarked for Europe.

Secretaryship of the Treasury.

No new name was sent in to-day for the portfolio of the Secretary of the Treasury. The chances are still in favor of ex-Gov. Boutwell, of Massachusetts, as Mr. Lincoln is disposed to select an Eastern man. Should Mr. Controller McCullough be selected, Judge Usher will retire from the Department of the Interior on the 4th of March, and Gov. Randall, of Wisconsin, will be appointed Secretary of the Interior. Secretary Fessenden has requested Mr. Lincoln to name his successor at an early date, as he desires to resume his seat in the Senate on the 4th of March next.

Important News from Sherman.

The Richmond papers of Monday say that Sherman has occupied Orangeburg, on the railroad from Branchville to Columbia, having passed by Branchville, thus completely misleading the Rebels as to his purposes. On Friday last he was but two days' march from Columbia. That city has now fallen, in all probability, into our hands.

The Rebels to be Surprised.

Important news is looked for daily from the South, and it is thought that the Rebel papers cannot long conceal an important move now being made upon their lines at a point where they had hoped for temporary respite.

The Air Line Railway Scheme.

A large lobby of speculators from Wall street, New York, arrived here yesterday to push the Raritan Bay scheme through the Senate. Horace Greeley has been inveigled into it by designing persons, (though it is not supposed he has any pecuniary interest), and he is busily at work. Senator Hale made a rather scathing reply to Senator Sumner's defense of the bill. It is claimed by the lobby that the passage of the bill will increase the value of the Raritan Bay stock from twenty dollars to one hundred dollars per share.

This accounts for the great interest manifested by Wall street, where the stock is all held, it having been bought up at low figures from the original holders. The bonds are held by the same parties in Europe who are said to hold stock in the Confederate Loan. This scheme, like the six-million-dollar swindle for a canal around Niagara Falls, and the Illinois Ship Canal, cannot pass the Senate. Much valuable time, however, needed for necessary legislation, may be wasted upon them.

Arkansas and Louisiana in Congress.

The House Committee on Elections have reported in favor of admitting Mr. Bonsall to a seat as Representative from Louisiana, and have also decided to report in favor of admitting Messrs. Johnson and Jackson as Representatives from Arkansas.

LEGISLATIVE.

HARRISBURG, February 14, 1865.

Senate.

Mr. WALLS read an act supplementary to an act incorporating the Susquehanna Boom Company.

Mr. DONOVAN, one incorporating the Colorado Mining and Exploring Company.

Mr. SCHALL called up the act incorporating the Northampton County Mutual Horse and Carriage Insurance Company. Passed.

Mr. FLEMING called up the bill making the counterfeiting of United States notes and postage currency punishable by State Courts. Passed.

Mr. LOWRY called up the bill compelling Railroad Companies to report accidents.

Mr. CLYMER offered the following substitute, which passed a second reading, and was laid over:—

Section 1. *Be it enacted, &c.* That in all cases of accident on any railroad in this Commonwealth, causing death or injury to individuals, whether to passengers or employees, it shall be the duty of the conductor or other person having charge of the train, to give immediate notice by telegraph to the principal office of said company, stating the extent of such injuries, and the names of the persons killed or injured, as far as they can be ascertained, which said notice the said company shall cause to be posted in a conspicuous place in all the telegraph stations of such company; and a failure on the part of the conductor or person having charge of said train to give such notice, shall be deemed a misdemeanor, punishable by fine or imprisonment, or both, or either, in the discretion of the Court of Quarter Sessions of the county in which said accident shall occur; and a neglect on the part of the company to post said notice, as aforesaid, shall cause said company to be liable to a fine of five thousand dollars, to be paid into the Treasury of the Commonwealth, and if not paid within sixty days after such accident, to be sued for and collected in the name of the Commonwealth, by the Attorney-General, in the Court of Common Pleas of Dauphin county.

The act to revive and continue the law graduating lands on which purchase money is due to the Commonwealth was considered and discussed at length in Committee of the Whole.

Mr. CLYMER called up the bill authorizing the election of one citizen of the United States, who may be a non-resident of Pennsylvania, as a Director of any Railroad company incorporated by this Commonwealth. Passed.

The supplementary bill allowing the Farmers' and Merchants' Insurance Company to take lawful money of the United States in place of gold and silver, and repealing the section which confined their operations to York county. Passed. Adjourned.

AFTERNOON SESSION.

Mr. NICOLS read a bill relative to the publication of legal advertising in Wayne county.

Mr. CLYMER called up the bill releasing the Lebanon Valley Railroad Company from the provisions of the act of April 12, 1864, which extended the provisions of the act relative to the making of lateral and branch roads by the Pennsylvania Central to the Reading and Lebanon Valley roads. Passed.

Mr. CONNELL called up the bill authorizing Mrs. Rebecca C. Pemberton to sell certain real estate. Passed.

The bill incorporating the Independent Red Men's Hall Association of Philadelphia. Passed. Adjourned.

House of Representatives.

The following bills were considered:—

Providing that when apprentices are over seventeen years of age, and have received an education, their indentures shall not be declared void, because the clause requiring the masters to furnish additional education has not been complied with. Passed.

Incorporating the Episcopalian Publishing Company to print a weekly newspaper in Philadelphia. Passed.

Incorporating the Homeopathic Medical College of Philadelphia. Passed.

Authorizing the Frankford and Philadelphia Passenger Railway Company to extend their road to Vienna street. (Amended by Mr. Donnelly so as to require them to make the same exchanges with the Second and Third as with the Union Passenger Railway.) Passed.

Increasing fees of jurors in Philadelphia to two dollars per diem, and of witnesses to one dollar per diem. (Amended by Mr. Ruddiman so as to give witnesses and jurors who attend from distant parts of Philadelphia, five cents per mile circular as milage). Passed.

Allowing sewers to be constructed in Philadelphia, when required by judgment of surveyors, without obtaining petition of a majority of property holders. Passed.

Empowering Ninth Presbyterian Church of Philadelphia to sell certain real estate, from Race to Cherry, west of Nineteenth. Passed.

Extending the privileges of the Market Street Railway beyond twenty years. (Amended by Mr. Thomas so as to restrict the Company to five cents fare. This amendment was opposed by Messrs. Smith and Ruddiman, and favored by Mr. Thomas, and was finally stricken off and the bill passed.

Providing a public park for Philadelphia. (Amended by Mr. Miller so as to insert Wilson Kerr, Daniel M. Fox and Wm. V. McGrath, as additional commissioners, as well as Chief Engineer and Surveyor, Chief Engineer of Water Works and Presidents of Councils; also, requiring assent of Councils before improvements are commenced). The bill was laid over, there not being the requisite two-thirds in its favor to supend the rules. Adjourned.

The Philadelphia Inquirer.

PRICE TWO CENTS. | PHILADELPHIA, MONDAY, FEBRUARY 20, 1865. | PRICE TWO CENTS.

SOUTH CAROLINA.

Sherman's Great March through the State. Charleston, Branchville, Augusta, Ga., Orangeburg, Columbia, and Florence, S. C. Map of Sherman's Grand Advance.

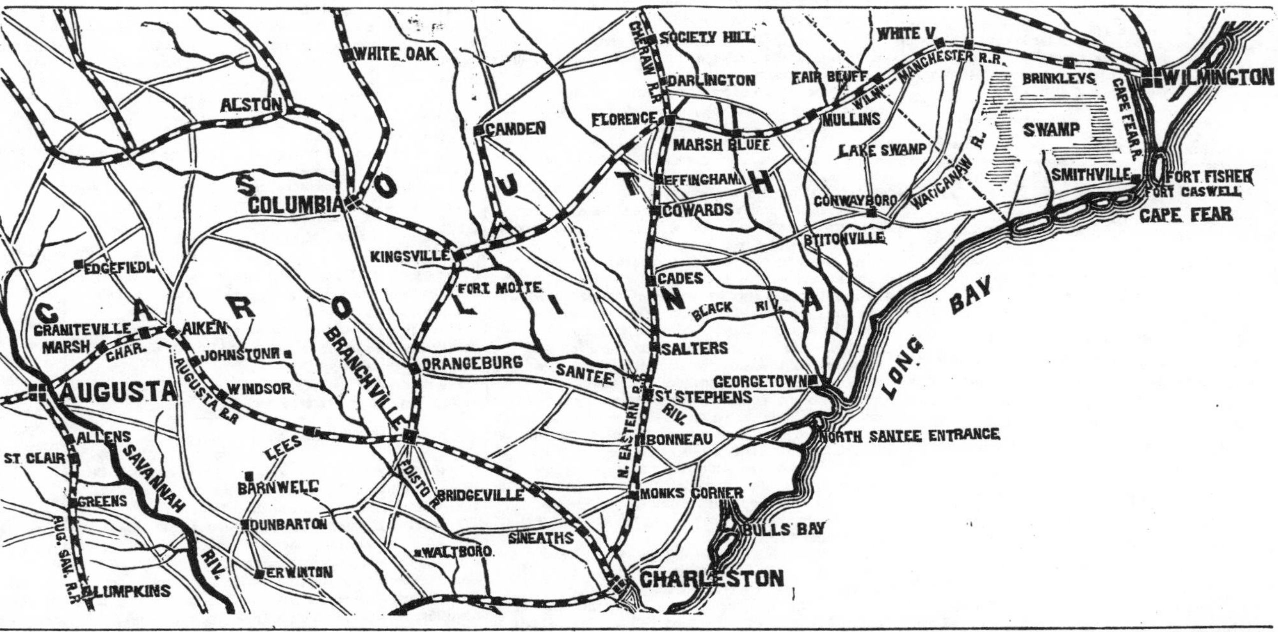

GOOD NEWS

WM. TECUMSEH SHERMAN.

Another Splendid Triumph.

SOUTH CAROLINA'S CAPITAL OURS.

The Capture of Columbia

VICTORY ACCOMPANIES SHERMAN'S BANNERS.

Beauregard Hunting Another Ditch.

GENERAL CONSTERNATION IN COMMAND.

The Chivalry Seized With Terror

CHARLESTON BEING EVACUATED

The City Probably in Our Possession

WHERE WILL SHERMAN GO NEXT?

Alarm for Raleigh and Wilmington.

THE REBELS FINDING NO PEACE

Latest Official War Bulletin.

DESPATCH FROM LIEUT.-GENERAL GRANT

WASHINGTON, Feb. 18, 1865—10 o'clock P. M.—Major-General Dix, New York:—The announcement of the occupation of Columbia, South Carolina, by General Sherman, and the probable evacuation of Charleston, has been communicated to this Department in the following telegrams just received from Lieutenant-General Grant. EDWIN M. STANTON, Secretary of War.

CITY POINT, Feb. 18—4·45 P. M.—Hon. Edwin M. Stanton, War Department:—The Richmond *Dispatch* of this morning says that Sherman entered Columbia yesterday morning, and its fall necessitates, it presumes, the fall of Carleston, which, it thinks likely, is already being evacuated. U. S. GRANT, Lieutenant-General.

CITY POINT, Feb. 18.—Hon. Edwin M. Stanton, War Department, Washington. The following is taken from to-day's Richmond *Dispatch*:—

The Fall of Columbia.

"Columbia has fallen. Sherman marched into and took possession of the city yesterday morning."

"This intelligence was communicated yesterday by General Beauregard in an official despatch.

"Columbia is situated on the north bank of the Congaree River, just below the confluence of the Saluda and Broad Rivers.

"From General Beauregard's despatch, it appears that on Thursday evening the enemy approached the south bank of the Congaree and threw a number of shells into the city.

"During the night they moved up the river, and yesterday morning forded the Saluda and Broad Rivers.

"Whilst they were crossing these rivers our troops, under General Beauregard, evacuated Columbia. The enemy soon after took possession.

"Through private sources we learn that two days ago, when it was decided not to attempt the defense of Columbia, a large quantity of medical stores, which it was thought impossible to remove, were destroyed.

"The female employees of the Treasury Department had been previously sent off to Charlotte, North Carolina, a hundred miles south of Columbia.

"We presume the Treasury Lithographic establishment was also removed, though as to this we have no positive information.

"The fall of Columbia necessitates, we presume, the evaeuation of Charleston, which, we think likely, is already in process of evacuation.

"It is impossible to say where Sherman will next direct his columns. The general opinion is that he will go to Charleston and establish a base, but we confess that we do not see what need he has of a base. It is to be presumed that he is subsisting on the country, and he has had no battle to exhaust his ammunition. Before leaving Savannah he declared his intention to march to Columbia, thence to Augusta, and thence to Charleston. This was uttered as a boast, and to hide his designs. We are disposed to believe that he will next strike at Charlotte, which is a hundred miles north of Columbia, on the Charlotte and Columbia Railroad, or at Florence, South Carolina, the junction of the Columbia and Wilmington and the Charleston and Wilmington Railroads, some ninety miles east of Columbia.

"There was a report yesterday that Augusta had also been taken by the enemy. This we do not believe. We have reason to feel assured that nearly the whole of Sherman's army is altogether at Columbia, and that the report that Schofield was advancing on Augusta is untrue." *From the Richmond Whig.*

Removal.

The Charleston *Mercury* of Saturday announces a brief suspension of that paper, with a view to its temporary removal to another point. This is rendered necessary by the progress of military events cutting it off from the mail facilities for distributing its paper to a large portion of its subscribers, while the lack of transportation renders its supply of paper precarious. Semmes has been made Rear Admiral, and will take command of the James River Squadron. U. S. GRANT, Lieutenant-General.

Columbia.

Columbia, the capital of South Carolina, is a pleasant city of 12,000 or 15,000 inhabitants. It lies on the east bank of the Congaree River, just below the confluence of the Saluda and Broad rivers, one hundred and twenty-four miles northwest from Charleston. The place is situated on a broad plain, is regularly laid out with wide streets, bordered with ornamental trees, and contains many elegant residenees. Among the public buildings are the State Government buildings, South Carolina College, the State Insane Asylum, &c. Columbia is the head of steam navigation, and has direct railroad connection with Charleston, Wilmington and Richmond. It is the terminus of railway branches from Yorkville, Laurens, Spartanburg, Anderson, and other points in the northwestern part of the State, and its capture by the Federal forces, from its central position, will give General Sherman the control of the entire State. With both Florence and Columbia in the hands of Sherman, they become important bases for movements to the interior of North Carolina and Virginia, and by cutting off the main sources of supply to Charleston, will compel the speedy capitulation of that city, if it does not fall before the advance of Gillmore.

A Table of Distances.

The following table shows the distances from each other of the places which are now the chief points of interest in the military field:—

From	*Miles.*
Branchville to Charleston	62
Branchville to Kingville	45
Branchville to Florence	108
Branchville to Columbia	68
Branchville to Augusta	75
Branchville to Wilmington	216
Branchville to Charlotte	174
Charleston to Florence	102
Wilmington to Florence	107

ARMY OF THE JAMES.

HEAD-QUARTERS ARMY OF THE JAMES, Feb. 15, 1865.—Deserters from the Confederate army arriving at head-quarters state that this morning, between 12 and 1 o'clock, a company from each regiment of Stewart's Brigade, of Pickett's Division, were sent out to advance their picket line about one hundred and fifty yards in order to strengthen as well as straighten their line on the Bermuda Hundred front, opposite the position held by the Second Pennsylvania Heavy Artillery.

On being discovered they were fired upon by our pickets, and after about twenty shots, they retired to their own lines. The party making the attempt are reported as having been supplied with intrenching tools to throw up works for their defense, and when fired upon retreated in the utmost disorder, not waiting to return our fire. Their loss is not known.

Nine hundred and eighty-three Union prisoners, including ten officers, from Danville, came down from Richmond on the Rebel steamer *Wm Allison*, to Cox's Landing. They were received and cared for by Lieutenant H. S. Merrill, Acting Assistant Quartermaster at these head-quarters.

About 5 o'clock, as the *Allison* was on her return trip to Richmond, and when a short distance above Fort Brady, she struck a torpedo, which exploded and completely wrecked her. She had on board two hundred and thirteen packages of blankets, and a number of other articles for the prisoners belonging mostly to the State of Indiana. The loss of life is unknown. There is no change in the weather, and the roads are very bad, owing to the continued rains.

FORTRESS MONROE.

FORTRESS MONROE, Feb. 17, 1865.—The steamers *New York* and *George Leary* arrived here last evening with released Union prisoners from Richmond, and sailed for Annapolis. Colonel Mulford remained at Varina to effect the exchange of prisoners as fast as they arrive. Other steamers have gone up the James River with Rebel prisoners, and the exchange will be made as rapidly as possible.

The steamer *Ariadne* arrived here to-day from Fort Fisher. Her captain reports that our forces had expected to have made an attack upon Fort Anderson on the 13th inst., but failed to do so for some cause to him unknown. Before he left Fort Fisher he saw a bright light in the direction of Fort Anderson, and the supposition was that the fort had been abandoned and burned by the Rebels.

The steamers *Northerner* and *Ellen S. Terry* sailed from here, this afternoon, for Fort Fisher, with colored troops for General Terry.

The steamer *Louisiana*, of the Bay Line, arrived here to-day, from Baltimore, the ice being broken up sufficiently for travel to be again resumed between here and Baltimore.

Several more schooner loads of coal are anxiously looked for here.

The steamer *Blackstone* arrived here this afternoon from Savannah, stopping at Hilton Head, S. C. The Captain of the *Blackstone* brought despatches from General Sherman for the authorities at Washington, which were telegraphed from here to the Capital.

The Captain of the *Blackstone* was not informed of the nature of the despatches, and knew nothing important of Sherman's movements.

News from Memphis.

CAIRO, Feb. 18.—The steamer *Liberty* passed up to-day, from Memphis, with eighty bales of cotton, for Evansville.

General Washburne had arrived at Memphis from Vicksburg, *en route* for the Army of the James, but meeting with countermanding orders would return to Vicksburg.

The draft to fill the quota of the District of Memphis, under General Canby's order, passed off quietly. Three hundred and eighty-seven names were drawn.

Movements of General Palmer.

LOUISVILLE, Feb. 18.—Major-General Palmer arrived here this morning.

REBEL NEWS

YANKEE MOVEMENTS IN THE CAROLINAS.

Preliminaries to the Capture of Columbia.

ARMING OF THE NEGROES.

The Question in the Rebel Congress

IT IS DEBATED IN SECRET SESSION.

Opinions of Two Rebel Newspapers.

RICHMOND WHIG VS. CHARLESTON MERCURY

Wanted, "Courage and One More Effort"

THE COLUMBIA PAPERS ON THE SITUATION.

Great Boasting and Little Realization

[SPECIAL DESPATCHES TO THE INQUIRER.]

WASHINGTON, Feb. 19.—From Richmond papers of Friday, delivered at the Washington office of THE PHILADELPHIA INQUIRER, we send the following:—

Yankee Movements.

From the Richmond Sentinel of Friday.

The Augusta (Ga.) *Chronicle*, a paper in the interest of the enemy, of the 10th inst., says:—From a gentleman who arrived on a special train last night, we gather the annexed news:—The Federals, on Thursday morning, were at Windsor, about fifteen miles from Aiken. It is not known in what force. No movements were made by them on Thursday. The cause of this is not ascertained. The troops in the vicinity of Winsor are Kilpatrick's Corps. It is reported that Generals Hampton and Wheeler engaged the enemy on the seventh and eighth, repulsing them at all points. Our loss was about seventy killed, wounded and missing; that of the enemy much greater.

The enemy are reported to be moving towards Congaree river. A gentleman from Columbia states that Slocum's corps is moving on that city on this side of the Edisto. His main line when last heard from was on the railroad. It is stated in Columbia that Kilpatrick's corps is protecting Slocum's left. It is ascertained that Porter is again moving on Charleston. When last heard from he was at Green Pond. It is not known where General Sherman himself is. Barnwell Court-House was burned on Monday night. The roads are teeming with vehicles, stock, and all kinds of movable property, fleeing from Georgia and upper Carolina.

Marching to the Front.

The Columbia (S. C.) *Guardian* of the 12th instant, in view of the vandalism perpetrated by the enemy, urges every man capable of bearing arms to march at once to the front, and adds, if there is a man in the State, who, after reading the future by the ghastly light of the burning village of Allandale, can expect to save his home in any other way than by shouldering his musket and hurrying to the field, he deserves to be classed with that sagacious quadruped of Alsop, who planted his clumsy hoofs upon the shoulder of his master in the hope of being caressed like a dog, when lo, instead of the gentle touches he was looking for, he received such a shower of blows as soon reminded him that he was nothing better than an ass.

The Negro Soldier Bill in the Rebel Congress.

In the Rebel Congress, on Thursday last, the only important proceedings were in the Senate.

The Senate bill to provide for raising 200,000 negro troops was taken up.

Mr. JOHNSTON (Ga.) moved to transfer the bill to the secret calendar.

Mr. WIGFALL opposed the motion, but before there was any decision on the question the doors were closed, to enable Senators to debate the propriety of transferring the bill to the secret calendar.

In the House, Mr. Barksdale had the floor, but before commencing his speech, on motion of Mr. ATKINS (Tenn.) the House went into secret session by a vote of 38 yeas, to 35 nays.

The doors being opened the House adjourned.

The bill of the House to abolish the fifteen-negro clause; to take from the President and Secretary of War the power to make details and exemptions, excepting mechanics and artisans in the employ of the Government; to revoke all exemptions and details heretofore granted by the President and Secretary of War, and to revoke all exemptions of mail contractors not permanently engaged in performing the contracts—was recommitted to the Military Committee, with instructions to inquire into the expediency of bringing a more liberal bill.

There is a strong disposition on the part of the Senate to preserve untouched the present exemption law.

Arming the Negroes—Difference of Opinion.

A *Whig* editorial says:—We regret to see in the Charleston *Mercury* an article on the subject of arming negroes, which has a tendency to provoke resentments and animosities among our people just at a time when harmony and good feeling are most imperatively needed. We can very well account for decided differences of opinion on this important question, for without such differences what now appears to be the prevailing sentiment in favor of the proposition could never have been reached. A sudden conversion from unanimous opposition to unanimous support on the part of reflecting people, would be an extraordinary phenomenon in the history of public questions. But the very fact that this question exhibits those phases of transition which seem to indicate an approaching affirmative decision should, we think, have suggested to so candid a journal as the *Mercury* the propriety of abstaining from unqualified impeachments of the integrity and patriotism of those who support the measure.

There can be no doubt that the expedient of using the services of negroes in some direct way against the common enemy, has grown in popular favor the more thoroughly it has been debated. The highest military authorities recommend it, and the people—just as sagacious as any other in the country—urge it upon Congress. The *Mercury* is simply mistaken in assuming that this originated in Virginia, or that it is a reflection of unsoundness in this State on the subject of slavery. It was a natural development of the necessities of the crisis; one among many projects and devices, to which the uneasiness of the past few weeks has given birth. If most others have fallen still-born, while this one has survived and grown in strength, that fact shows that it possesses superior vitality, and is more congruous with the demands of the times.

The *Mercury* does indeed limit its denunciations to those who propose to confer emancipation on the negro as a compensation for his military services, but it seems to infer that emancipation is the real object of those who favor the measure, thus attributing a kind of abolitionism to a very large number of our people, while in fact emancipation is suggested only as an incident by those who imagine that in this way alone could the main expedient be rendered effective.

In regard to this point, also, there may be a latitude of opinion which does not by any means imply treason or abolitionism, either on one side or the other. People who think that the gift of emancipation would better enable us to utilize the resources presented by our supply of negroes are not therefore abolitionists.

The expedient of arming the slaves being once adopted the question might present itself, how best can we render this expedient effective? The question would not be as it has been asserted, whether freedom or slavery is best for the negro, but whether the negro himself would so consider it. That large numbers of them do think it a desirable boon is proved by the fact that they run off to the Yankees in quest of it. That almost all of these would return to us with the same inducement, we think unquestionable; but we sincerely hope that we shall not be driven to any such alternative. We may accomplish all that we desire by using the negroes simply as slaves, but we do say that we would not hesitate to use them in any way whatever to get rid of Yankee domination.

We say this in order to meet fully the *Mercury's* assertion that South Carolina entered into this struggle for no other purpose than to maintain the institution of slavery, that Southern independence has no other object or meaning, and that independence and slavery must stand together or fall together. We do not pretend to dispute the *Mercury's* assertion, but we protest against applying it to other States. It is true that to preserve African slavery, menaced as it was by an unprincipled and imperious ochlocracy, was the proximate object of secession.

It is true that the stamp act and the tea tax were the proximate causes of the American Revolution, but we have yet to learn that the patriots of that day would have submitted to England after declaring independence, if England had guarantied to them free tea and unstamped paper forever, nor do we believe that this people would or ought to return to the Yankee Union, even if Lincoln could and would guarantee the perpetuity of African slavery.

The *Mercury* will have it that slavery and independence must stand or fall together. That neither of them can stand alone. As to slavery, it is true, without independence it must fall. How should we suffer then should we, in case of necessity, sacrifice it for the sake of independence? We hope to preserve it. We believe we can preserve it. So do we hope to preserve a portion, at least, of our houses and our lands. Would the *Mercury* declare that we should succumb to the Yankees rather than sacrifice any more of our property? or must we be told that it is our duty to give everything for independence, houses, lands, life itself, but not our slaves? These, to be sure, we shall lose at once should we be conquered; but is it better to be conquered, even to submit to the yoke so much dreaded, and against which we have so desperately struggled, than to make use of this last, and it may be, this most effective resource?

Going North.

From the Richmond Dispatch.

All Yankee privates, prisoners, confined in this city will be sent North by a flag of truce, this morning. At the same time ten or twelve officers will also go off.

Once More unto the Breach.

From the Mobile Register and Advertiser.

Blue as things now look, or as black as they present themselves to the vision of some, it is nevertheless an undeniable truth that we hold in our hands the means of sudden and perfect deliverance. No one doubts that the cause languishes and suffers, not from a deficiency of resources to maintain a war of defense, but from the poverty of spirit to breast reverses and of fortitude to endure triumph.

The people are not whipped, but cowed. Their souls, and not their hands, are disarmed. Our strength is not sapped, but our courage is oozing out at the ends of our fingers. As a lady from Georgia writes, in a letter we read this morning, "The people are whipped, but the army and the women are not, and, by the blessing of God, never will be." And what is wanting to change the leaden aspect and to drive away the clouds which hang like a pall over the Confederate situation? Courage and one more effort.

One single flash of that noble, warlike enthusiasm, which in 1861 spread its halo of crimson battle-light over the Southern land, now revived, and inspiring all hearts to answer with life in hand the sacred calls of duty and country, and these shadows now darkening all hearts with gloom would be lifted like a curtain, and unveil a scene of hope, and joy, and deliverance.

Rebel Prophecies About Columbia—Words of Comfort.

From the Columbia Carolinian.

We have had no Loydon, no Derry, no Saragosa as yet. Nay, we need not go any further than our cotemporaries of Mexico to find an example of heroism which, at least in the defense of our towns, we have not yet displayed. Few can have forgotten the events which belonged to the taking of Puebla. The Mexicans, according to an authentic report, defended their city inch by inch. They piled barricades in the streets, and fought behind them till the ground was covered with their dead. They converted each of the square blocks of the houses which composed the city into a separate fortress, and defended it till it fell and buried them in the ruins. The French were utterly unable to take some of these blocks, and therefore blew them up, defenders and all. Some of them were blown up by the desperate defenders themselves. At last Puebla fell; but, as a British writer remarks, the desperate courage of its defenders went far to redeem, in the eyes of the world, the many faults of their national character. Where have we anything to show like this? So far, indeed, as she has been tried, Charleston has done well, and it is possible that, under the same circumstances, she might do as much; but the fact remains, however it may be explained, that until we have fought in defense of one city, at least, as the Mexicans fought at Puebla, we shall not be able to deny that we have been surpassed in heroism by a people of whom we have been wont to speak as a degenerate offshoot of the degenerate Spanish race. Shall this reproach be made a permanent one? Here, at least, in South Carolina—here, above all, in Columbia—if the occasion should come, let the answer be, No!

From South Carolina.

From the Richmond Enquirer, Feb. 16.

Official intelligence was still wanting on yesterday. Our news by mail, however, states the position up to the 12th. The *Carolinian*, which arrived last night, says:—

The facts, briefly, are, that a portion of the enemy's forces have crossed the South Edisto at Bennaker's Ferry, and are slowly pushing forward towards the north branch of that river. The probabilities, briefly, are that this movement is made for the double purpose of cutting the Columbia and Charleston Road and Wilmington and Manchester Road, at or near Kingsville.

This done, Sherman will have achieved what he may deem an important object, preliminary to the capture of Charleston, namely, the bisection of the three important branches of supply. That he will succeed in doing this we have doubts, very grave doubts, for we know something of the dangerous operations of an army in the hands of Beauregard. But admitting Sherman's success to the extent named, what reason is there to anticipate an immediate advance on Columbia? We can recall none. True, Columbia is the Capital of the State, the abode of wealth, the theatre of much enterprise, but beyond these attractive features it is nothing compared to the grander game of Charleston, on the capture of which the energies of the whole Yankee army below us are now bent.

They cannot operate on Charleston from Columbia, and they will not leave Columbia on a northward march while Charleston stands. To believe it is contrary to common sense, contrary to a knowledge of Sherman's character and confessed determination, and contrary to all military strategy. *Possibly a raid* may be made here for the purpose of creating a diversion. It will not find us unprepared.

Long before Columbia falls we look for a battle

Continued on the Eighth Page.

The Daily Journal.

VOL. 14.——NO. 142. } WILMINGTON, N. C., TUESDAY EVENING, FEBRUARY 21, 1865. { WHOLE NUMBER 4,108

THE DAILY JOURNAL.

CONFEDERATE STATES OF AMERICA.

WILMINGTON, N. C., TUESDAY, FEB. 21, 1865.

CLOSED UP.

With the exception of the movement of troops, there is nothing to disturb the quiet of our town. Every store, every shop, every shanty is closed up, and one unacquainted with the circumstances of our position at this time, would infer that the inhabitants were respecting the Sabbath day, and keeping it holy. Will not our readers join us in praying that the Lord of hosts will let this bitter cup pass?

☞ We received no mails this morning and we are entirely without any news except what we present in our Telegraph column, and even that is of little importance to our readers. Of course the movements of the armies in our immediate front, conscientious scruples prevents us from saying anything about. We would advise our citizens, however, to be calm and considerate. But, then, considering our belliguered situation, we must say that we have never read of a more quiet community.

We would advise those in want of something good to eat to go to PORTER'S, on the corner of Front and Princess streets, where they will be sure to get something—he has mutton, beef, pork, and other things in abundance. Call upon him; he'll take your Confed.

The action taken by the authorities and people of Edenton, with reference to the robbers that infest them, is the right action. The counties of our State are infested with these banditti. Murders of peaceful citizen occur almost daily, arson and buglary, and other outrages are as common as night. Let our people band together and make short work of these depredators.—There are times when the self defence of communities is as impertive as that of individuals. Such times are these when gaols are insufficient to hold criminals, because of armed associates in league, to rescue them.—If communities will organize to resist and punish such characters, it will rid them of their presence, and it will have the good effect of sending deserters back to their commands.—*Raleigh Confederate.*

HOT-CROSS BUNS.—Rub four ounces of butter into two pounds of flour, four ounces of sugar, one ounce and a half of ground allspice, cinnamon, and mace, mixed together. Put a spoonful of cream into a cup of yeast, and as much good milk as will make the above into a light paste. The buns will bake quickly in tins set them near the fire to rise previoulsy to putting them into the oven. When half proved, press the form of a cross in the centre, with a tin mould.

WHAT GENERAL FORREST WANTS.—Gen'l Forrest favors arming 200,000 negroes. He declares if he ever had any inclination to fight for revenge, that time and feeling have past. He now only contends for principle, for home, wife and children, to prevent subjugation, but desires peace and is tired of scenes of blood. Ross' brigade of his corps is yet at Corinth; Bell's brigade is in West Tennessee, recruiting.

A modest young soldier, not long since, while tarrying a short time away from his command, left a portion of his wardrobe with his hostess which he subsequently wrote for, and his astonishment can only be imagined by perusing the following poetic response:

I hope, dear sir, you won't get hurt—
I'll frankly tell you all about it—
I have made a SHIRT of your old SHIRT,
I hope you may make a SHIFT without it.

What is the difference between a sailor and a soldier? One tars his ropes, the other pitches his tent.

The "coat-of-arms" on a steam fire-engine, just brought to Lynn, Massachusetts, is a lady's giater boot.

The United States has one square mile of coal-field to every fifteen square miles of territory.

Always heed a baby's cries. They are the poor little fellow's only signals of distress.

Knowledge and timber shouldn't be much used till they are seasoned.

An English soldier has but four cents a day for spending money.

DEATH OF A VERY OLD NEGRO.—A very old negro woman, Charlotte, recently died in Davidson county, N. C. She had reached the venerable age of one hundred and twenty-five years. A longevity that very few attain in these degenerate times. She was the property of M. C. Pendleton, and was long a faithful servant in that family.—*Salisbury Watchman.*

"Good morning, Patrick," said a gentleman to an Irish laborer. "Slippery this morning." "Slippery? Be jabbers it is nothing else, your honor. Upon my word, and I slid down three times without getting up once."

MR. LONG, OF OHIO.

The evening of the 7th instant having been set apart for making speeches, the following interesting debate occurred. The noble and patriotic sentiments of Mr. Long are those of a christian and statesman. Had there been more men like him in the North, this war would not have occurred, for the necessity which forced it on us would not have arisen:

Mr. Broomall (Pa) expressed his views on the financial questions, the President's message being nominally under consideration.

Mr. Long (Ohio) expressed himself as against this war, as wrong in principle, and must, if continued, result in the ruin and inpoverishment both of the North and South. War for separation has always been found successful on the side of those who wished to separate, and it has been found impossible to hold the two parties together in common bonds.

The coercion policy has failed, and it must fail under the providence of God, because it is in derogation of law. If any cause cannot survive the truth it ought to perish. Our armies have done all that brave men could do, and brave as they are and able as their commanders are, they have not yet overcome the South, because to do so is an impossibility. War has widened the breach it was intended to heal, and was appropriately denominated in the Chicago platform as a failure.

He spoke of the late Presidential election as a farce, occasioning emotions of sadness, and making the decadence of the old spirit of our country. There never could be a Union based on the coercion of sovereign States. War in that case was unjustifiable, improper and inexpedient. If it was still further prosecuted as preferred it should be under the auspices of those who now conduct its management. He had been strengthened in the opinions he had heretofore expressed.

Mr. Broomall—Does the gentleman say that a State has the right to secede?

Mr. Long replied that he did so believe, and there was nothing in the Constitution to prevent it. It is unconstitutional to coerce a State.

Mr. Broomall—Wherein does the gentleman differ from Jefferson Davis. Does he believe that Davis is wrong in trying to get the States out of the Union?

Mr. Long—I am not here to answer for the opinions of Jefferson Davis. I am not here to say whether he is right or wrong. I am not here to curse or praise him. If abuse would do anything, I should prefer that the gentleman, and Andrew Johnson and Parson Brownlow, the leaders of the Republican party, should curse him out of his boots. That would put down the rebellion in short order.

Mr. Long gave his views on the right of secession, saying that the war for extermination, but God would not allow an act of such atrocious vengeance. In taking his leave of this House, there was no part of his political life which he looked on with more satisfaction than the efforts he had made to arrest the madness which prevails, and avert the doom with which the country is threatened.

CAPITAL.

Here are some capital remarks from somebody, in answer to the wish we hear so often from the lips of young men who have large ambition, but little taste for patient industry—"*I wish I had Capital!*" Why, capital does not bring ultimate success once in a score of times; the capital, we mean, that is not made by the individual who uses it:

"Now, suppose you had capital—what would you do with it? Let me tell you, you have capital.—Haven't you got hands and feet, and body and muscle, and bone and brains, and don't you call them capital! Oh! but they are not money, say you. But they are more than money. If you will use them they will make money, and nobody can take them from you. Don't you know how to use them? If you don't it is time you were learning. Take hold of the first plow, or hoe, or jack-plane, or broad-axe that you can find, and go to work. Your capital will soon yield you a large interest. Aye, but there's the rub; you don't want to work, you want money or credit that you may play the gentleman and speculate, and end by playing the vagabond, or you want a plantation and negroes, that you may hire an overseer to attend to them while you run about over the country and dissipate and get in debt; or you want to marry some very rich girl, who may be foolish enough to take you for your fine clothes and good looks, that she may support you.

"Shame upon you, young man! Go to work with the capital you have; you'll soon make interest upon it, and with it to give you as much money as you want and make you feel like a man. If you can't make money upon what capital you have, you couldn't make it if you had a million of dollars in money. If you don't know how to use bone and muscle and brains, you would not know how to use gold. If you let the capital you have lie idle, and waste and rust out, it would be the very same thing with you if you had gold: you would only know how to waste."

From the Raleigh Confederate.

MR. EDITOR: A Yankee correspondent of the Cincinnati *Commercial*, in a description of the city of Savannah, its public places, cemeteries, &c., makes the following allusion to Gen. Francis S. Bartow, one of the hero martyrs of the first battle of Manassas, who lies buried in Laural Grove Cemetery, near Savannah:

"And there is a handsome monument erected over the remains of General Francis S. Bartow, of Savannah, who was killed at the first battle at Mannassas, and brought home for burial. A brave man no doubt he was, and a chivalric he may have been; but now that he fills a traitor's grave, it ought to be so marked if at all."

Fathers, brothers, mothers, sisters and companions of the brave martyrs who have fallen in defence of your homes and liberty, so would our inhuman foe have the tombs of *your* loved ones marked, if marked at all—"*a traitor's grave.*"

And yet, under your very eyes, here in the city of Raleigh, a vile and infamous sheet, in alluding to Yankee rule in Savannah, says the people "are rejoiced at the change of rulers," and fain would persuade you, notwithstanding your "passion and predjudices," that your condition would be improved under Yankee rule.

Truly, the Confederate authorities are merciful and forbearing, all such open treason would not go unpunished.

Raleigh, Feb. 16, 1865. A SOLDIER.

An old bachelor says the most difficult surgical operation in the world is to take the jaw out of a woman.

BY TELEGRAPH.

NORTHERN NEWS.

RICHMOND, Feb. 20th, 1864.

Northern papers of the 17th instant, including the evening edition of the Baltimore American, has been received.

Gen. Ed. Johnston has been sent to Fortress Monroe for exchange—he is nearly blind.

Four hundred guerrillas were within six miles of Nashville on the Murfreesboro' turnpike on the 15th.

A Cairo telegram of the 16th says that late news from Kirby Smith's army says his troops are very much scattered, for the purpose of obtaining food and forage; it would be impossible to concentrate them in any force during the present season.

Price is reported to have gone to Mexico on an important confidential mission under orders of Kirby Smith.

The imperial forces under Vega had been badly defeated at Sonora. Vega was captured and shot as a traitor.

LATER NORTHERN NEWS.

RICHMOND, Feb. 20th, 1864.

The New York World of the 18th says Lincoln has issued his proclamation convening the Senate on the 4th of March in extraordinary session.

The Senate adopted resolutions declaring that the rebel debt or loan can never be recognized by the United States in any part or any way.

The reprieve of Capt. Beall, sentenced to be executed on Saturday, was considered certain.

CONFEDERATE CONGRESS.

RICHMOND, Feb. 20th, 1864.

In the House Mr. Perkins reported back from the Committee of Foreign Affairs a preamble and resolutions, a condensed report of which reads as follows:

WHEREAS, The Congress of the Confederate States has ever been desirous for an honorable and permanent settlement, by negotiation, of all matters of difficulty between the Confederacy and the United States, and to this end sent three Commissioners in February, 1861, to Washington to negotiate friendly relations between the two governments; and whereas, these having been refused reception, Congress in June, 1864, adopted and published to the civilized world a declaration of its continued desire for an honorable peace, to which the only response from the Congress of the United States was a rejection by large majorities of all resolutions for an amicable settlement of the existing difficulties; and whereas, President Lincoln has recently announced to three eminent citizens that the authorities of the United States would hold no negotiation with the Confederate States, or any of them separately; that no terms except such as the conqueror grants to the subjugated would be extended to the people of these States. Therefore,

Resolved, That while Congress regrets that no ultimatum is left to the people of the Confederate States but a continuance of the war, or submission to terms of peace alike runinous and dishonorable, it accepts in their behalf the issue tendered them, and solemnly declares its unalterable determination to prosecute the war with the United States until that power shall desist from its efforts to subjugate them, and the independence of the Confederate States established.

The second resolution compliments the army for various patriotic resolutions recently adopted.

The third resolution invites the people to assemble in public meetings and renew their vows of devotion to the cause of independence, etc.

The fourth resolution pledges Congress to the passage of most energetic measures to secure our ultimate success.

Mr. Gilmer offered the following additional resolution:

Resolved, That notwithstanding all this, we believe the Confederate States would consent—First to a separation between the United States and the Confederate States, each one perfectly free and independent of the other with rights of navigation, trade, transit, etc., fairly agreed on. Second—That an American Diet be created, to which each party shall be at liberty to send delegates, each being its own judge as to number and manner of election, each party paying its own expenses. Third—The privileges of this Diet to be clearly and definitely settled. Fourth—Each section to have one vote, binding on the parties only when ratified by Congress and the President of each. The resolutions of the committee and proposed amendment were ordered to be printed.

The House resolved itself into secret session on the negro bill.

In the Senate the appropriation bill was passed, also the bill abolishing the office of provost marshal, except within the lines of the army in the field.

SPEAK TENDERLY.—"When, some three weeks since, some forty of the children in charge of the Children's Aid Society of New York, were arranging for removal to the west, a boy was folding, with great care, his old cap, having previously taken out its lining—a small piece of faded calico. 'John,' called a friend, 'what are you going to do with that greased calico?' 'Please sir, it is not greased; it is all that I have to remember my dead mother by; it's part of her dress, which I cut off when she lay dying in the garret in——street.' The question and the answer were too much for the little fellow, and putting the strip under his shirt, next to his breast, he buried his face in his hands, and filled the room with his sobs.

"Man, woman, whoever you be, speak tenderly to that boy across the way. He may be an orphan.—His mother and his father may both be in the graveyard yonder. Dear child! he has none but his own little hands by which to work his way in the world.—Speak kindly to him. Perhaps some day an orphan may walk the earth whose name and yours shall spell alike."

General Sherman is sending the negroes who followed him into Savannah to Beaufort. With the first ship load he sent this message to General Saxton: "Please find enclosed seven thousand contrabands, the first instalment of fifteen thousand. Many of them are from far up in Georgia, and a long, weary and sorrowful tramp they have had. Many of them with little children have not brought a thing with them, and have most miserable covering. Bales of clothing can be disposed of among them."

DAILY LIFE.

"But evil is wrought by want of thought,
As well as by want of heart."

We suppose that no one who has not an *educated* conscience, and a high ideal of life, can rightly interpret the true meaning and awful force of those words of Thomas Hood's.

For it isn't in great actual deeds, in sudden heroic impulses, or occasional lofty purposes, that life consists—it is in the general temper of the heart, the loving, trustful soul that looks out with watchful eyes upon every hour and circumstance, seeking to do good, to bless, and be blessed, as one has opportunity.

And yet, what a frightful mistake most people make in this matter—good sort of people, we mean, or those that are considered so—people who simply live to enjoy themselves from day to day, good-natured, agreeable, good hearted, ready at any time to do you a courteous, or obliging act—and yet what real richness or perfume, what real depth or graciousness, is there in their lives.

And what will become of these good sort of folks when their lives are opened before them by the angel of the Lord, and their eyes are opened, too, to see, and their hearts to understand, what a true ideal of life is; what are its solemn relations and duties, and sanctities; what will they think of themselves when they see what a poor, miserable unfruitful work their living has been? How will they answer the voices which must call to them on every side—"what has your life been worth?" "With how many good, just, true, self sacrificing deeds have you filled it? How much better is the world because you have lived in it?" Yet these very same people would be terrible shocked at being called selfish, indolent, ineffective.

Now, it is very certain that God calls very few of us to do great deeds in life; very few days furnish us with opportunities for high and heroic accomplishment, but it is equally certain that as a "man thinketh in his heart so is he," and to have a broad, generous, loving spirit, a soul set to sweet tunes for the love of humanity, and that goes about seeking to do little daily acts of practical good to others—a soul that carries with it always the sweet spices of charity, and pity, and tenderness, will be the one which shall wear the brightest crown in the great "exhibition day" of eternity.

V. F. T.

A THOROUGHLY GOVERNED CITY.

New Orleans is at this time, according to the account of a private correspondent, in the condition of some country militia companies before the war, where all were officers and no privates. Our correspondent writes: "The military organization here is, I think, more extensive than that of the army of the Potomac, or even than the army headquarters at Washington.—We have at least four departments, all with their headquarters in this city, each with a General in command, and a numerous staff. There is, first, the Department of the Gulf, General Canby Commanding, with headquarters, staff and attendants. Second, the division of West Mississippi, General Hurlbut commanding, with headquarters here, and staff and numerous attendants. Third, the defences of New Orleans, General T. W. Sherman commanding, with headquarters, staff and numerous attendants. Fourth, General Andrews commanding colored troops, with a separate headquarters, staff, etc. If now you count up the corps, divisions and brigade staff, I think it might be shown that the Generals and their staffs who have at present their headquarters in this city numbers more than all the troops now here."

Our correspondent says nothing of Gen. Banks and his staff, who will, presently, it is said, be added to this army of officers. There is an old adage, "too many cooks spoil the broth," the truth of which is perhaps exemplified in the case of New Orleans, which, with so many Generals and departments and such a multitude of officers, is yet, if we can believe the accounts of persons residing there, neither clean nor healthful—the small pox raging there at present—nor moral.

N. Y. Post.

TO MAKE DRINKING GLASSES.—The following is a receipt for making cheap as well as good drinking glasses out of old bottles:

Take a claret bottle, or any kind of a glass bottle—bottles of thin white glass, with flat bottoms are the best—hold the bottle firmly by both ends; let another person, having a cup of water ready, pass a stout cotton cord twice round the bottle, and create a friction by pulling the ends of the cord to and fro rapidly for a minute or so; then let him jerk the cord off, dash the water on quick, and presto! you hold in one hand as serviceable a tumbler or goblet as you need wish, and in the other a neat but not gaudy glass candlestick!—The bottle should be held with a strap, piece of leather or other substance, with a hard straight edge, firmly around it at the intended point of severance, in order to keep the cord in one place during the friction, and to secure straight and smooth edges to the glassware. Old botties can be put to good use in this way.

PAINS AND PENALTIES.—Every soldier who has borne arms in this war against Lincoln, unless he will forswear his country and its cause and desert family and friends—as some few have basely done—is subject to "the pains and penalties" which Lincoln has pronounced against treason. They may be hanged; or despoiled of property; deprived of all their political rights and franchises; or banished from the country, to make room for the emigrants from the North, who desire to occupy this fair land. Are any of them prepared for this? If not, let them remember that Lincoln, in his interview with our Commissioners would give no assurance that these threatened pains and penalties should be remitted. They must accept his terms and surrender at discretion. "Unconditional submission" is what he exacts. Let this be remembered and every Southerner nerve himself for resistance.

Lynchburg Virginian.

Anson County has but twenty-four Justices of the Peace—seventeen of whom are between the ages of 50 and 75, and none of the remainder under 35. All of them were appointed previous to 1861. If she has any more they must have been appointed at the present session of the Legislature, and no return of them made to the County Court Clerk's office.

At the beginning of the war the voting population of the county was about 1,000. With so large a population we doubt if another county in the State can show a better record in regard to the number of its Magistrates.—*Argus.*

THE SUN.

IT SHINES FOR ALL

THIRTY-THIRD YEAR. NUMBER 10,177.

NEW YORK, WEDNESDAY, FEBRUARY 22, 1865.

PRICE ONE CENT—IN GOLD. TWO CENTS IN CURRENCY.

The Latest News

By Telegraph to the N. Y. Sun.

DOOM OF CHARLESTON!

The Federals in Full Occupation

RECAPTURE OF THE FORTS!

200 Guns Spiked!

REBELS FIRE THE CITY.

Great Destruction of Property.

A TERRIBLE EXPLOSION.

Several Hundred Lives Lost!

Rebel Iron-Clads Blown Up and Blockade Runners Captured.

REJOICING THROUGHOUT THE COUNTRY

A Glorious Washington's Birthday

A LITTLE "SET BACK" IN VIRGINIA.

Capture of Gens. Crook and Kelly

City and Miscellaneous News.

GREAT WORKINGMEN'S MEETING.

Friery to be Hung March 31st.

&c., &c., &c.

Charleston.

The City Occupied by Our Forces—Great Conflagration—Fearful Explosion—Loss of Several Hundred Lives, Etc.

By the arrival of the steamer Fulton at this port we have detailed accounts of the capture of Charleston. The Fulton entered the harbor gaily decorated with flags in honor of the event, and was greeted with rounds of hearty cheers by the crews of the various vessels which were passed.

The city was finally evacuated on Friday night, and the fact was discovered at Fort Moultrie at ten o'clock on Saturday morning. The fact was immediately signalled to the army, and the troops recently landed on James Island crossed over the Ashley River in boats and took possession of the city. There was no opposition experienced. It appears that the evacuation commenced three weeks ago. A rebel officer who deserted gave information which was not then believed, but which is now discovered to be accurate. The munitions and lighter stores have been removed, but the heavier articles were left behind for want of transportation and time. Our picket boats in the harbor saw the garrison retreating from Fort Sumter on Friday night. General Schemmelpfennig was the first military officer that entered the city. Admiral Dahlgren then ran up the harbor in a boat, and landed at two o'clock in the afternoon. He was joined by Gen. Gillmore soon after.

The rebels set fire to Charleston before they abandoned it, and exploded their magazines. The terrific explosions were heard before daylight on Saturday morning. The shock was felt on all our vessels. The air was filled with smoke, fire and burning fragments. Before and after daylight the city was fired in various places; the entire lower part was in flames, and it was feared that two-thirds of the city would be burned. Cotton to the amount of over two millions of dollars was destroyed.

The appearance of the streets as our troops entered was desolate in the extreme. The majority of the inhabitants, including all the middle and wealthy classes, had left, and the destitute and poor only remained behind. A few hundred rebel deserters, who had hidden in houses when the Confederates left the city, appeared, and begged to be taken prisoners, as they were weary of the war. The people who remain behind are in absolute poverty, and require necessaries more than the Savannah people. The only happy faces were the negroes. Crowds of colored men, women and children danced, sang, clapped their hands and manifested unmistakeable joy at the appearance of the Yankees. They all wanted food, and say that they would be glad to work. Some offered to take up arms against their masters.

The lower part of the city which was within range of our guns is a ruin. Some of the houses were knocked down. Bricks, broken chimnies and timber were lying everywhere in the streets, and fragments of shells were lying everywhere mid the ruins. The appearance of this portion of the city was extremely desolate and dreary.

The portion of the rebel army which remained in the city to the last were most of them thieves who plundered the inhabitants. They committed many shameful outrages, and most of them got off with their booty.

OFFICIAL DISPATCHES.

From Secretary Stanton.

WAR DEPARTMENT, Washington, Feb. 21, 8 P. M.

Major Gen. John A. Dix—The following special order has just been issued. You will see that it is executed in your Department.

E. M. STANTON, Secretary of War.

Ordered that a national salute be fired to-morrow noon, Feb. 22d, at West Point, and at every port, arsenal and army headquarters of the United States, in honor of the restoration of the flag of the Union upon Fort Sumter.

E. M. STANTON, Secretary of War.

From General Gillmore.

CHARLESTON, S. C., February 18, Via NEW YORK, February 21, 1865.

Major-General Halleck, Chief of Staff:

GENERAL,—The city of Charleston and all its defences came into our possession this morning with about two hundred pieces of good artillery and a supply of fine ammunition. The enemy commenced evacuating all the works last night, and Major Macbeth surrendered the city to the troops of General Schimmelfennig at 9 o'clock this morning, at which time it was occupied by our forces. Our advance on the Edisto from Bull's Bay hastened the retreat. The cotton warehouses, arsenals, quartermasters' stores, railroad bridges, and two iron-clads were burned by the enemy. Some vessels in the ship-yard were also burned. Nearly all the inhabitants remaining behind belong to the poorer class.

Very Respectfully,

Q. A. GILLMORE,
General Commanding.

Rejoicings.

Washington, Feb. 21.—The following official notice has been promulgated, dated Department of State, Washington, Feb. 21, 1865:

The Department building will be illuminated on the night of Washington's Birthday, in honor of the recent triumphs of the Union.

By order of the President.

(Signed) WILLIAM H. SEWARD, Secretary of State.

Washington, Feb. 21.—A salute of 100 guns was fired here to-day, in honor of the occupation of Charleston by our forces.

Troy, Feb. 21.—A salute of 100 guns was fired here this afternoon, in honor of the capture of Charleston.

Trenton, N. J., Feb. 21.—The Legislature is to meet in public to-morrow night, in honor of the Birthday of Washington and the fall of Charleston. Gov. Parker will preside, and C. C. Lathrop, of Burlington, is to deliver an address.

Philadelphia, Feb. 21.—The Twenty-second of February having been made a legal holiday by the Pennsylvania Legislature, it will be duly celebrated to-morrow. The Mayor of the city has ordered a national salute at sunrise, a salute of one hundred guns at noon, the ringing of the bells on the State House and churches, and preparations are making for the illumination of private houses in the evening. The Mayor in his proclamation refers to the abolishment of slavery, the capture of Charleston, etc, as cause for general rejoicing.

Boston, Feb. 21.—Governor Andrew has ordered a salute of 100 guns on the Common to-morrow, in honor of Sherman's triumphant march, and the fall of Charleston. One hundred guns will also be fired from Dorchester Heights.

From Western Virginia.

Capture of Generals Crook and Kelley.

Wheeling, Va., Feb. 21.—A party of rebel cavalry dashed into Cumberland before daylight this morning, surprised and captured the pickets, and carried off Generals Crook and Kelley. It seems to have been a very daring and well planned affair. Cavalry have been sent in pursuit.

The War in the Southwest.

Cairo, Feb. 21.—The Memphis BULLETIN learns from gentlemen who left Selma, Ala., on the 24th ult., and came through Meridian and Jackson, Miss., that Dick Taylor has a considerable force at Selma, and also at Meridian. At Selma, the rebels were manufacturing and turning out large quantities of munitions of war. Most of Hood's army had been sent to operate against Sherman. They were nearly naked and wholly dispirited, and had lost all hopes of successful resistance to the Federal troops. Large numbers were barefooted, and it is stated that 10,000 of Hood's men had their feet frost-bitten during their retreat from Nashville, in which they suffered more than during the previous three years of the war. Gen. Forrest was collecting a force at Jackson, Miss., for operations, it was said, against Vicksburg.

From Europe.

Four Days' Later News.

The China, from Queenstown 12th of February, has arrived.

A collection of official papers had been published concerning the state of affairs between the United States and Canada. A portion relates to the raid of Southerners to St. Albans.

The London TIMES, in its "City Article," insinuates that the Confederate armies in the West have derived abundant supplies from Federal traders, and says that it is therefore possible that instead of the South being crippled for want of material of war, the main result of blockade runners being more effectually shut out will be that the traffis and its gains will henceforth pass more largely into Federal hands.

The ARMY AND NAVY GAZETTE says, that Lee must not let the enemy occupy Wilmington if he intends to hold on to Richmond. Should he abandon it he may try a great *coup* to strike the North to the heart in its moment of elation. A sudden, well-conducted march into the District of Columbia, the capture of Washington, the invasion of Pennsylvania, even of New York itself, are possible.

In a debate in the House of Commons on the repeal of the commercial convention between England and the United States, Lord PALMERSTON stated that he did not think the House would be justified in regarding the course which had been taken by the United States as the indication of intended hostilities. We could not deny that things did take place on the lakes, of which the United States were justly entitled to complain. He entreated the House to abstain at present from entering into discussions which could only embarrass the Government, and not to assume gratuitously that the American people were animated by feelings of hostility towards England. The motion was then withdrawn.

A fire had occurred at Sandringham Hall, the residence of the Prince of Wales, but it was fortunately confined to a single room.

The DAILY NEWS accepts the official denial of the reported cession of certain Mexican provinces to France, but other journals, in view of similar official denials in the past, regard it with distrust.

The Paris MONITEUR publishes a decree referring the Bishops of Moulins and Besancon before the Council of State, for having committed an abuse of their ecclesiastical authority.

The intelligence from Japan is unsatisfactory. It is reported that the Mikado repudiates the late Convention. Prince Nagato had commenced rebuilding the batteries in the Straits de Simonosaki. The British forces were still in the Bay of Jeddo. Two French sailors had been murdered by the Japanese. Two Japanese had been executed for the recent assassination of two British officers.

A new Ministry had been formed at New Zealand, and it was said the seat of government was to be removed to Wellington. Government had announced that prompt steps would soon be taken to put down the rebellion.

Queenstown, Feb. 12.—The GLOBE's Paris correspondent says: No French minister to Washington will be appointed until the late Mr. Dayton's post is filled by the bearer of satisfactory instructions respecting the threats against Mexico.

The TIMES Paris correspondent says:

When the French Minister, Count Mercer, was recalled from Washington, the Americans were led to understand that no new agent would be accredited until President Lincoln should have recognized the Emperor of Mexico. This recognition has not been forthcoming, and there is no French Minister at Washington. The writer adds "It is believed that Mr. Bigelow will continue to act as United States Charge D'Affairs in Paris for some time.

The Spanish government is said to have resolved to prohibit the publication of the Pope's encyclical in Spain. Bishops who published it were not to be prosecuted.

Official instructions from the Russian government for the reorganization of Poland had reached Warsaw. The office of Governor of Poland is suppressed. The provincial governments are suspended, and the public administration will hendeforth be only through the departments of the respective ministers at St. Petersburg.

Satterthwaite's CIRCULAR says:

Since our last there has been a larger amount of business transacted in American Securities than during any week for a considerable period. Five-twenties improved at one time to 53, but later American news dispelling the peace rumors, and depressed the United States bonds about two per cent.

GRAVEYARD OF REBELLION.

Map Showing the Whole Field of Military Operations from Charleston on the South to Richmond on the North, together with the Cities and Railroads recently Captured by Sherman.

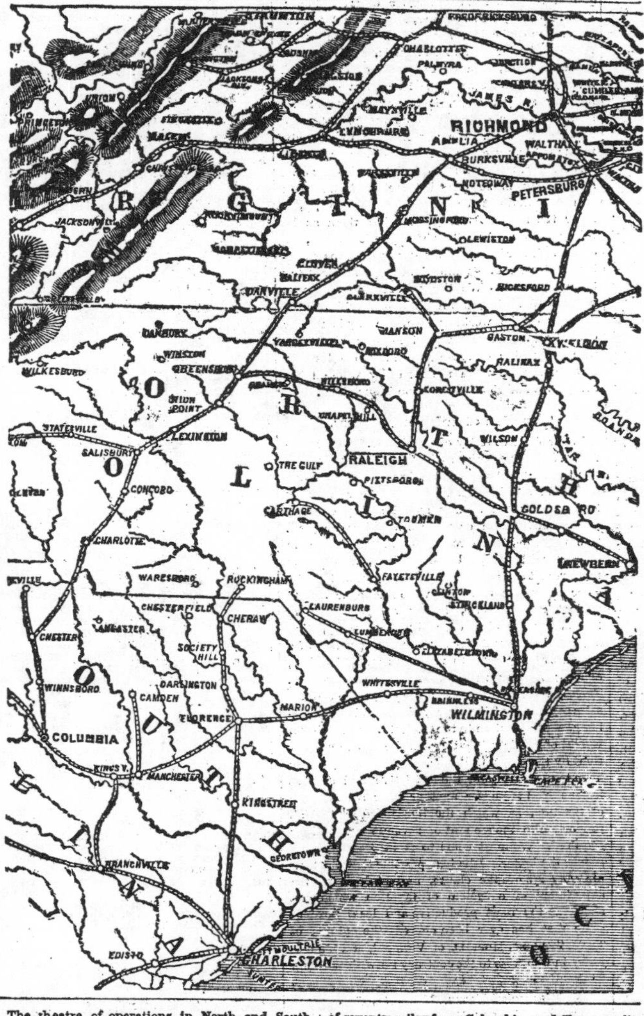

The theatre of operations in North and South Carolina, and Virginia are represented in the above map, together with the principal railroad lines, which form the centres of the combined movements. The reader will be enabled to comprehend at a glance the direct influence of General Sherman's strategy in compelling the evacuation of Charleston. With a large military force upon James Island, at a point two miles south of Charleston, and with Edisto and the various railroads to Branchville, Kingsville, Columbia and Florence in our possession, and an immense naval force at the mouth of Charleston harbor, it will be seen that the doomed city was cut off at all sides, and was enclosed with an extended ring of fire, which was gradually and surely contracting each day. The rebel garrison must therefore have experienced considerable difficulty in escaping. The distance from Charleston to Branchville is 62 miles. The capture of the latter place secured General Sherman the means of pushing forward his columns to these places in order to secure the desired end. From Branchville to Columbia is 70 miles, and from Branchville to Wilmington 216 miles. At last accounts General Sherman's advance had almost reached Charlotte, North Carolina, on the great railroad line to Richmond. This place is upwards of seventy miles from Columbia, and Sherman displayed unexampled activity in reaching his present position. He has already accomplished half the distance from Savannah to Petersburg. It will be seen that he now threatens Raleigh, the capital of North Carolina, and Wilmington. It is not probable that Sherman will be compelled to move in force against Wilmington in order to capture it. It has been already virtually flanked in the same manner as Charleston, and will probably be surrendered. But if not, the powerful Union force now moving from Newbern for Goldsboro will compel its evacuation. The force at Newbern, however, threatens Weldon as well as Goldsboro. Thus it will be seen that each step of Sherman's advance brings him nearer to powerful supports, and virtually threatens him. Beauregard's forces are said to be at Charlotte, or the vicinity, and a battle is regarded as imminent. But as Sherman occupies the inner lines, the Charleston garrison cannot participate in the impending contest, as it will be necessary for the rebels to make a wide circuit, in order to effect a junction with the main army. This is another triumph of Sherman's strategy, and illustrates his method of baffling and dividing his enemies, and neutralizing their forces so as to render them inoperative.

Congressional Proceedings.

XXXVIIIth CONGRESS—Second Session.

SENATE.

Washington, Feb. 21.—Mr. Johnson presented the memorial of the Maryland legislature remonstrating against the authorization of a news railroad between Washington city and Baltimore.

Mr. Morgan, from the Military Committee, reported a bill to extend the provisions of the Pension Law, as regards soldiers wounded in battle to those wounded while on picket duty.

A communication was received from the Secretary of War, in reply to a resolution of inquiry, stating that the names of persons held as political prisoners had been furnished, as required by law, to the Judges of the District and Circuit Courts of the United States, and of the District of Columbia. Ordered to be printed.—Recess.

An Evening Session was held, at which the Freedmen's Bureau Bill was debated, but no conclusion was arrived at.

HOUSE OF REPRESENTATIVES.

The Committee on Ways and Means reported that they have matured a bill authorizing the Secretary of the Treasury to borrow, from time to time, Six Hundred Millions of Dollars, to issue bonds for the same, payable forty years from date, or redeemable, at the pleasure of the Government, at the end of five years—the interest, if paid in coin, to be six per centum; if in currency, seven-thirty per centum.

Mr. Stevens offered a substitute—to borrow the same amount at eight per centum, and authorizing these bonds to be exchanged for others any time within two years, and to be exempt from taxation by State or Municipal authority. The bill will be considered next Thursday.

The House passed the bill to amend an act to aid in the construction of a railroad and telegraph line from Missouri to the Pacific Ocean.

The House also passed the Senate bill to facilitate the collection of debts of postmasters, and providing for the return to writers of letters in cases where there is a deficiency of postage, and also the bill establishing certain post routes.

The House resumed the consideration of the bill to provide a government for the insurrectionary States.

Mr. Ashley reported a substitute for the original bill, providing for the admission of Louisiana, Arkansas and Tennessee.

Mr. Davis, of Maryland, said that, from the present condition of affairs, by the 4th of July next armed rebellion will have failed to lift its brazen front. His object, as expressed in the bill, was to prevent the States now in rebellion from coming here next December and dictatorially clamoring for the admission of their representatives and 22 Senators. The President should treat those who hold power in the South as they deserve—strip them of their emblems of authority and expel them from the Executive Mansion, should they there intrude. He wished to prevent the rebels from sweeping in here next December and becoming the masters.

Mr. Mallory moved to lay the bill on the table, and this was agreed to.—yeas 91, nays 63.

The House took up the case of Mr. A P. Field for an assault upon Judge Kelly, a member of the House, and considered the resolution reported by the Select Committee providing that he be reprimanded.

Mr. Townsend and Mr. Nelson said a few words in extenuation of Mr. Field's offense and invoking charity.

Mr. Beamen dissented from the remarks of the preceding gentlemen and said Mr. Fields was not excusable for his conduct.

The resolution was agreed to by 82 against 49, the opposition members, with but few exceptions, voting in the negative.

The House proceeded to the consideration of the amendatory Enrollment bill.

The House, after amending and debating the 1st Section, struck it out by a vote of 66 against 49. This section made it the duty of every person who is or shall become liable to be enrolled, to report himself, the willful neglect of which was to be considered and punished as a misdemeanor.

Mr. Blair offered to the 2d Section an amendment that in future no credits be given, unless for men actually furnished. This would do away with paper credits.

This amendment was under consideration when the House adjourned.

News Items.

[*By Telegraph to the New York Sun.*]

SEVERAL paymasters, provided with funds left yesterday for the Army of the Potomac.

THE proposed Constitutional amendment to abolish slavery, was ratified by the Legislature of Wisconsin yesterday.

THE subscriptions to the 7-30 loan, received by Jay Cook & Co. yesterday, amounted to $4,088,100—the largest single Eastern subscription was one for $400,000 from New York.

THE Upper House of the Canadian Parliament, Monday night, finally voted, 45 yeas to 15 nays, to favor the Confederation scheme, and to present an address to the Queen, based on the resolutions of the Quebec Conference.

THE Senate in Executive session last night confirmed about five hundred nominations, a large number of them promotions in the regular army; the remainder assistant quarter masters, commissaries of subsistence, assistant adjutant Generals and other officers in the volunteer force.

THE St. Albans raid case was resumed at Montreal on Monday before Judge Smith. Mr. Kean for the prisoners spoke at length in opposition to the demand for extradition, and violently assailed the Upper Canada Judges for their decision in the Burley case. He was followed by Mr. Laflamme, and the court adjourned before he had finished his argument.

THE annual report of Thomas W. Conway, Superintendent of the Bureau of Free Labor, shows the following result: The number of freedmen now under Mr. Conway's charge supported by the Government is 1,400; expense to the Government for the year $113,000; number of freedmen on plantations in the Department, managed by the Bureau, 50,000; on plantations under culture by military order, 150,000. Amount of property transferred to Treasury, $1,000,240.

JOINT resolutions were offered in the New Jersey Senate yesterday, by Mr. Scovel, ratifying the anti-slavery amendment in the Constitution. Mr. Scovel moved to make them the special order for Friday. The President of the Senate decided that the motion of Senator Chandler, of Morris, to refer the resolutions to the Committee on Federal Relations, took precedence of Senator Scovel's motion. A large audience was present, and the discussion was the most interesting of the session.

IT is generally reported that all of the merchants in Washington and Baltimore, excepting the Wisenfeldts, who were convicted by Gen. Doubleday's military commission on the charge of selling goods to blockade runners, have been or will be released from confinement, the President having pardoned them. A number of these merchants had already been sent to the Albany penitentiary. Philip and Meyer Wallack, who were confined in the Old Capitol Prison, have been unconditionally pardoned and were released on Monday.

LOCAL NEWS.

NEW YORK AND THE VICINITY.

WASHINGTON'S BIRTHDAY—HOW IT WILL BE CELEBRATED—BUSINESS PLACES TO BE CLOSED—SALUTES—FIREWORKS, ETC.—The Common Council have at last favored the public with the programme adopted for the celebration of the anniversary of Washington's birthday, which occurs to-day. It appears that the observance will be more general than was at first supposed. Mayor Gunther has issued a proclamation recommending the people throughout the city to close all places of business and observe the anniversary as a holiday. All the departments and offices of the City and General Governments, the Stock Exchange, Produce Exchange, etc., will be closed, and the shipping in the harbor will display their colors during the day. The public buildings, hotels, and many of the stores and private residences will display the national emblem, and the sextons of the various churches will ring the church bells morning, noon and evening—Trinity Church ringing the chimes, as announced yesterday. The Common Council have very properly determined not to indulge in the usual dinner for the benefit of themselves and the favored few, and have concluded to expend all the money appropriated for the general celebration. They have provided for a salute of one hundred guns to be fired on the Battery at sunrise, and the same at Union Square. There will be no general turnout of the military, but the Seventh Regiment has received orders to parade at three o'clock P. M., and it may be that other regiments will join them. In the evening there will be a grand display of fireworks, and the pieces prepared for the occasion will doubtless be well worth seeing. The fireworks will be exhibited at City Hall, Union Square, Madison Square, Jackson Square, Tompkins Square, Mount Morris Square, Liberty Park, and the junction of East Broadway and Canal street. At the first-mentioned points the best pieces will be exhibited. The celebration to-day is designed as a jubilee over the capture of Charleston and Columbia, and the generally encouraging condition of the military situation, as well as the commemoration of Washington's birthday; and it will therefore be observed with greater *eclat* than it otherwise would. Aside from the general celebration, the day will be suitably observed by most of the public institutions in the city. The Institute for Reward of Orphans of Patriots will commemorate the day by concerts

Continued on the last page.

NEW YORK DAILY NEWS.

VOL. IX.....NO. 55. NEW YORK, MONDAY, MARCH 6, 1865. PRICE FOUR CENTS.

FROM THE SOUTH.

Sherman's Campaign Compared With that of Cornwallis.

"Rebel" Prospects in 1781 as Dark as in 1865.

The British Then and the Yankees Now Equally Confident.

ANCIENT EXAMPLES OF ARMING SLAVES

THE YANKEE CHARACTER ANALYZED.

VANITY ITS LEADING CHARACTERISTIC

Yankee Ambition to Possess the Continent.

Peace Between North and South the Signal of War With Europe.

Proceedings of the Confederate Congress.

Law for the Destruction of Property Liable to be Captured.

AMOUNT OF COTTON IN MOBILE.

A Historical Parallel—1781 and 1865—The Campaign Then and Now—Confident Predictions of the British—The "Rebels" Nearly Subdued—Sherman and Cornwallis—"One" Lee.

[From The Richmond Sentinel.]

Eighty-four years ago, this Spring, Virginia and the Carolinas were undergoing an ordeal far more trying even than that which is, once more, baptizing them in blood. Reduction of strongholds, evacuations of cities, defeats, retreats, desertions and panic alternating in every distressing and distracting form seemed to be the only fortune of the "rebels" of that day. Triumph led the despoiler forward, and went far to warrant the insolence with which he trod down all before him—all but the inextinguishable fire which lit the souls of the patriot braves, whom no disaster could dismay, and who, though little more than fighting ground was left them, could never be taught to utter the craven's watchword, "we surrender."

Let us recall some of the circumstances of that day, and note their analogy to what is passing around us. Eighty-four years ago, this Spring, the revolutionary struggle was on the eve of its successful close, but yet had never worn so disheartening an aspect. It had dwindled down to what the foe honestly regarded as its meanest dimensions. "The rebel power," wrote Lord Dunmore to his Government, "is wasted beyond any possible reinvigoration." And Lord Dunmore as truly believed what he thus penned, eighty-four years ago last January, as Sherman, writing from the same place, believes all he said a few days ago in the February which has just departed.

Eighty-four years ago, last January, Cornwallis felt confident of stamping out the dying spark by expelling Greene from his position in the Carolinas or crushing him there. The lordly rebel-crusher, therefore, undertook the expedition to Hickers' creek on the Pedee, telling Tarleton "to push Morgan to the wall" on the Pacolet. One fall of the Thorhammer was effectually to finish both, and loyalty to George Guelph was to be then universally re-established. He set out from his camp at Winnsborough on New Year's Day, 1781, to strike this final blow.

Retreat was so much the custom of the day with the "rebels" that Morgan changed his base the instant he found Tarleton crossing the river. Thereupon his situation became very perilous. The Broad River was not fordable in front of him, and there was a hostile army in his rear. His only escape was to the hills on his right, where he risked and won a battle at the famous Cowpens. Tarleton was fully confident of easy victory, and the earlier incidents of the battle sustained his hopes; but fortune shifted and he was defeated, and that part of Cornwallis's scheme spoiled.

Morgan's success, however, only gave him opportunity to make good the retreat from which he had turned to indulge Tarleton with battle. But it also afforded Greene the greatly desired opportunity of attempting a junction of his forces, and at once he hastened from the Pedee to embrace it. In this he was only partially successful, as the expeditious "flanking movements" of Cornwallis compelled the "rebels" to retreat. Greene hurriedly crossed the Yadkin, and, with the remainder of his forces under Huger, did not stop until he reached Guilford Court House. He had there but a brief respite, for Cornwallis was close on him with a new "flank movement."

The retreat and pursuit became a race, of which Virginia was the goal. If Cornwallis could only cut the "rebels" off from the Virginia recruits and supplies, he deemed them at his mercy. Greene outstripped him, however, and succeeded in putting the Dan river between them. Cornwallis, in despair, now abandoned the chase, and with his weary, over-marched troops, slowly retraced his steps. This was very pleasing to the exhausted "rebels," "for their long and hasty flight," says Hildreth, "was marked with their blood." Their last day's march was forty miles, and more than half the men who made it were shoeless, all were ill clad, and only half fed.

But Cornwallis having expelled Greene from the Carolinas, set about the re-establishment of the royal government. Marching upon Hillsborough, the State government fled to Newbern on his approach. At Hillsborough he planted the royal standard, and issued a "gracious proclamation;" a model for those who were to emulate his aims and efforts in our own time. He earnestly implored "loyalists"—the term then, as now, for submissionists and traitors—"to repair to his aid in restoring the constitutional government," almost the language of the enemy in the present day. Leaving his proclamation to do its work, he sent a force from Wilmington to expel the State authorities from their latest refuge at Newbern. The expedition was successful, and committed the same sort of depredations and enormities which signalize the course of their successors of this era, under like circumstances.

Exactly eighty-four years ago last Tuesday week, a body of submissionists responding to Cornwallis's proclamation, had assembled between the Haw and the Deep, to prove their grateful sense of the royal mercy, and to offer their services to the king. Suddenly they were pounced upon by one Lee, who led "rebel" cavalry, without respect to royal proclamations. Mistaking him for Tarleton they shouted, "Long live the King!" The delusion was short lived, and the cry was quickly exchanged for another: "Bless independence and spare us." Dashes like these were brilliant episodes of that time, and though indecisive, were auxiliary and encouraging. We have many such to brighten the pages of our own history.

Greene being in no position to cope with the overwhelming odds against him was confined to maneuvering. In this he was very successful. "Either from stupidity or design," wrote Cornwallis, that memorable Spring, "I can get no information, from any source, of what the rebels are doing." Toward the middle of March Greene unexpectedly appeared at Guilford, only twelve miles from the noble lord. Battle was joined, and "the rebels" once more defeated with the loss of all their artillery. Greene dreaded to cry halt until he had carried his disordered ranks twenty miles from the scene of conflict. Cornwallis, in no condition for pursuit, turned his victorious forces toward Fayetteville, and, as usual, issued a fresh proclamation to show the "loyalists" their duty and all others the hopelessness of further resistance.

Disappointed in the reception he met, he withdrew to Wilmington, that his men might find refreshment and rest. The routed and ragged rebels of Greene needed these far more; but they had also far more at stake, and must be "up and doing." South Carolina offered a promising field for their efforts, and thither they marched. Their route lay over a path, marked by the sufferings of Gates about a year before. Arriving at Hobkirk's Mills, near Camden, Lord Rawdon was met, and fought on the 25th of April. Again the enemy was victor, and the "ragged rebels" again retreated. Greene retreated to Ridgeley's Mills, twelve miles off, to recover and wait events.

The croaking critics of that day severely censured Greene for this battle. They insisted that he had no right to risk it, after detaching Lee, with his cavalry, to co-operate with Marion on the Santee. But the act which was alleged to have caused his particular defeat, secured a successful general campaign. Before battle was given at Hobkirk's Mills, Lee and Marion had captured Fort Watson, on the Santee, and secured the best line of communication between Camden and Charleston. This obliged re-enforcements for Rawdon to take a difficult and circuitous route. Rawdon, therefore, in vain looked for these re enforcements in time for battle.

They came, however, early enough to learn that Lee and Marion were in possession of Fort Motte, with all its supplies and stores, and that Rawdon would have, therefore, to surrender the fruits of his victory, and yield Camden up to the worsted Greene. Orangeburg and Fort Granby shared the fate of Motte, and multiplied the embarrassments of the seemingly victorious Rawdon. Worse than all, Lee threatened Augusta, and the commander at Charleston was fearful lest he, too, should swell "the rebel advantages." Thus Greene's defeat was, at all sides, producing victory and dread of victory. Rawdon crossed the Santee sick of his triumph, and the rebels, who were never again to frighten "the good loyalists," were terrifying them all over South Carolina.

Subsequent operations eventuated in the evacuation of Ninety-six by Rawdon. Greene had practically gained all he sought, and from pursued became pursuer. Thus ended the campaign, and with it Lord Rawd[illegible] efforts in Carolina, for he soon after sailed [illegible]gland.

No campaign was ever fuller [illegible]he vicissitudes of war than that of 1781. When it opened, victory appeared to be irremovably attached to the British banner. The Northern States were secure, and all the principal points and cities in the Carolinas and Virginia, and Georgia, were in the grasp of the foe—they seemed to be masters of the whole field. Yet, ere midsummer their power in the Carolinas was practically restricted to the region lying between the Santee and the Lower Savannah. In January, they had started out merely to extinguish the embers of "rebellion," and their efforts, all the Spring, bloomed with promise. Victory after victory, like those of Rawdon and Cornwallis in the Carolinas, gave strength to the presumption and lent apprehension to the most sanguine Revolutionist. But, a few months more, and their pretensions, with their power, were things of the past. Patriotic patience and valorous endeavor, blessed by an appeased Heaven, wrenched independence from the iron clutches of insatiate might and arrogant confidence. As it has been so it shall be—*dubit Deus his quoque finem.*

CONFEDERATE STATES CONGRESS.

Senate.

WEDNESDAY, March 1, 1865.

Prayer by the Rev. Mr. Dogget of the Methodist Church.

On motion, by Mr. Burnett of Ky., the Senate reconsidered the vote by which was passed the bill to provide for returned prisoners; and the further consideration of the bill was then postponed till to-day.

Mr. Simms of Ky. offered the following, which was agreed to:

Resolved, That the Select Committee on the Exchange of Prisoners be instructed to inquire into the treatment of returned prisoners, and that they also be instructed to inquire and report all neglect in transporting them to Richmond from the places of exchange, and who is responsible for such neglect.

Senate bill to authorize the Secretary of the Treasury to receive specie from the several States of the Confederate States, and use the same for the benefit of said States, was considered and passed.

Senate bill regulating the destruction of property under military necessity, as amended by the House, was taken up, and House amendments were concurred in and the bill passed.

The following is the bill, which awaits the approval of the President to become the law:

"*The Congress of the Confederate States of America do enact*, That hereafter, whenever cotton or tobacco, military or naval stores, or other property of any kind whatever, which may aid the enemy in the prosecution of the war, may be in an exposed position, where it would be liable to seizure and removal by the enemy, the general officer commanding the department or district where the property may be situated shall order the owners thereof to move the same to some place of safety, to be designated by him, if such removal, in the judgment of such general commanding, should be necessary to prevent the said property from falling into the hands of the enemy; and if the property is not removed within a reasonable time, to be fixed by the commanding general, by the owners thereof, it shall be lawful for the said general officer to have the same removed, at the expense of the owners, under general regulations to be prescribed by the Secretary of War, or to destroy the same, as now provided by law."

Mr. Semmes, from the Committee on Conference on the House bill to provide more effectually for the reduction and redemption of the currency, reported that the committee had not been able to agree, and asked to be discharged from the further consideration of the subject. The report was received, and the committee were discharged.

The Tax bill was then taken up, and Mr. Semmes of La. explained the amendments proposed by the majority of the Senate Finance Committee.

Mr. Oldham addressed the Senate on the minority report on the same bill.

The Senate then resolved into secret session.

House of Representatives.

The House met at the usual hour, and was opened with prayer by the Rev. Mr. Dickinson.

Mr. Staples of Virginia presented certain patriotic resolutions of the Twenty-fourth Virginia Regiment, which took the usual course.

Under the call of States for bills, resolutions, etc., the following were introduced:

By Mr. Fuller of North Carolina: Joint resolution of thanks to General Whiting, Colonel Lamb, and their officers and men, for their gallant defense of Fort Fisher against two attacks. Referred to Committee on Military Affairs.

By Mr. J. T. Leach of North Carolina: Joint resolutions approving the appointment of Gen. Lee as General-in-Chief, and recommending that he be vested with power to treat for peace. Referred to the same committee.

By Mr. Logan: A bill to facilitate the settlement of claims due deceased soldiers. Referred to the Judiciary Committee.

The House then resolved into secret session, and having spent some time therein, again resolved into open session and resumed the consideration of the unfinished business, viz: the bill to provide payment of cotton purchased in the Trans-Mississippi Department. Pending which, the House adjourned.

Resignation of Mr. Rives.

The whole country will regret to see the card of Mr. Rives, resigning his seat in the House of Representatives. Through the great events of the last four years he has been most of the time in the public service, and, though suffering from impaired health, has devoted himself to the cause with a fervor, courage and elation of spirit that nothing could abate or lower. His physical condition for the present unfits him for the labors of a Representative, but we will not permit ourselves to think that the lessons of his matured wisdom and the example of his sanguine courage are to be enjoyed no more in the public councils. We cordially wish for him a speedy restoration to health, and for the country his return to its service, in whatever capacity may be most agreeable to him.

Slavery in Ancient Times—An Element of Strength instead of Weakness.

[From The Richmond Dispatch.]

All history has shown that the nation with most slaves in ancient times was, *ceteris paribus*, the most powerful in war, and it is the remark of one of the best American students of antiquity that if there had been a State in Greece without slaves, the probability is, it would quickly have been overthrown by the neighboring slave States. We find, in the Jewish system, slavery formally established by a Divine decree. Long before the foundation of that system, we find the patriarch Abraham going to battle with a force of slaves, which the Scriptures inform us were "born in his house and bought with his money."

The Egyptians held slaves, as their monuments prove, and many of these slaves were negroes, as is clear from the representations on the royal sepulchers. The Greeks held vast numbers at the time of their greatest strength, and each nation in proportion to its power in war. Sparta had eight slaves to one freeman, and Athens nearly as many. The slaves of these nations greatly aided in their splendid conquests. At Platea five thousand Spartans were attended by thirty-five thousand Helots as light troops.

Slavery increased *pari passu* in Rome with the greatness of that country until the number of slaves in and around Rome exceeded the freemen in the proportion of twelve and fifteen to one. Industrial pursuits were almost entirely intrusted to slaves and freedmen, and as the country advanced these were enrolled as soldiers and trained as gladiators. It was only with the disappearance of slavery that domination of Rome over the rest of the world passed away; that her manners became corrupt, and she fell an easy prey to northern barbarians.

Cotton in Mobile—The Torch Ready to be applied—Hidden Cotton to be First Lighted.

[From The Mobile Register.]

An exaggerated statement has appeared in print respecting the amount of cotton in this city, which is represented as amounting to something between a hundred and twenty and a hundred and thirty thousand bales. The simple fact is that there is not one-sixth of the quantity stated, and what there is, is carefully noted, and its place of deposit known to the military authorities, who (should the emergency require) will effectually prevent its ever going into the hands of the Yankees; and we are able to state that the small lots which divers parties are understood to have surreptitiously removed from the warehouses to their own premises will have the precedence if it becomes necessary to apply the fire cure.

The Yankee Character—Vanity Stronger than Patriotism—The Yankees anxious to measure Swords with Europe—Peace between North and South would mean War between the United States and England and France.

[From The Richmond Whig.]

There is no point in the Yankee character more obtrusively apparent than its boastfulness. From Thyrsites to Munchausen the world has never seen such braggarts. There is nothing in which the Yankee does not believe himself to excel. There is nothing in which he does not believe himself to be superior to all the rest of the world. He carries philanthropy to fanaticism, and charlatanry to the utmost verge of imposture. His generosity is extravagance, and his economy is parsimony. He is quite as ready to deify Barnum as to worship Washington. He is proud of the country because it is big, and measures its relative importance by the number of its square miles. He boasts of everything that he has and everything that he is, and declares his unalterable conviction that the Yankee nation is destined at no very remote day to rule the nations, and to bring suppliant Europe to its feet. These qualities, sufficiently conspicuous before the war, have of late become remarkably aggravated.

Quite as much perhaps to this intense vanity as to any material interest are owing the passionate declarations of attachment to the Union, and the ferocious warfare urged against the South in order, if possible, to restore it. There are many influences, of course, and many motives, to be taken into account in estimating the strength of the Yankee sentiment which continues to support the war; but this one is undoubtedly among the most powerful. The restoration of the Union and the supremacy of the Constitution mean only the permanent domination of the Yankee nation, and the conquest of the South would prove far more a solace to Yankee vanity than a tribute to the quasi patriotism under which that feeling is valled. We repeat, that since the war this quality has exhibited itself more conspicuously than ever before.

The amazing resources developed by both of the parties to the contest, the vast extent of territory which has been the scene of military operations, the gigantic armies which have been called into the field, the tremendous armaments which have covered the seas, the number and magnitude of the battles which have been fought, have been so many incentives to self-laudation, and have raised the Yankees to an elevation, in their own esteem, quite beyond the reach of any present or historical competition. They fancy that the whole world is looking at them with astonishment—which is extremely gratifying to their vanity—and with alarm—which is even more gratifying. To be admired would be pleasant enough, but to be feared is surpassingly delightful.

It never indeed occurred to anybody to entertain admiration for the Yankees except in the sense of wonder at the unparalleled proficiency to which they have attained in all the arts of legalized plunder and organized robbery; but it is very natural that the comparatively pacific nations of Europe should feel some apprehension of a people who, in four years, can put into the field more than three millions of soldiers, and send to sea nearly a thousand armed ships. In the beginning of the war, the threats which were so freely uttered against England and France through the columns of Yankee newspapers, and on the floor of the Yankee Congress, were merely the outward manifestations of the natural boastfulness of the Yankee character. But as time passed on, and the military and naval power of the United States began to assume colossal proportions, what was first an empty menace was transformed into an earnest purpose.

We believe nothing to be surer than that at this moment the people of the Yankee States actually desire war with some European nation. They are madly anxious to measure strength with some one of the great historical nations of the world. They will not be satisfied until they make their way by the sword to the rank which they covet. At one time they boasted that a predominance in commerce, in industry and the pacific arts, would soon place them at the head of modern nations. Now they dream of asserting predominance by force of arms. While Europe has become pacific, they have grown bellicose. The spirit of aggression is in them. The lust of conquest has possessed itself of their souls. Not that they are now, more than before, a martial or a military people; but ambition, the passion for aggrandizement, and natural vanity, have asserted over them an uncontrollable supremacy. The South first, and then Canada, Mexico, Cuba, the whole continent, are to be conquered, annexed, Yankeeized.

He who does not see that the future history of the United States, should the South fall in this struggle, is to be a history of war until either Yankee ambition is crushed by defeat, or the American continent is subjugated by Yankees, is incapable of seeing anything. The only possible obstacle to this melancholy future of strife, in an age supposed to be consecrated to the arts of peace, is the independence of the Southern Confederacy. It is with the resources of these States that the Yankees expect to fight their battles with England for Canada, and with France for Mexico.

If there are any among us who dream that submission to the North would restore peace to us, they are, indeed, deceived. Instead of fighting the Yankees in defense of our homes and our rights, we should be forced to fight England in Canada, France in Mexico, and Spain in Cuba. We should endure the double misery of losing our honor and our independence, while forced to sacrifice ourselves on the altar of Yankee vanity and ambition. While the soldiers of Grant and Sherman return to peaceful homes, or settle upon the confiscated lands of the South, the soldiers of Lee and Beauregard would be fighting to plant the Yankee flag on the frozen waters of the St. Lawrence, or on the burning plains of Mexico. We should be in the armies of our Yankee masters precisely what the Irish are in the armies of England, and the Hungarians in the armies of Austria.

FROM MISSISSIPPI.

GEN. FORREST'S ADDRESS TO HIS TROOPS.

WHAT HE HAS ACCOMPLISHED.

MISCELLANEOUS REPORTS.

CAIRO, March 3, 1865.

The Jackson (Miss.) papers of the 18th ult. contain an address of the rebel General Forrest to his troops, recounting the result of his operations during the past year. He says they have fought fifty battles, killed and captured sixteen thousand of the enemy, captured two thousand horses and mules, sixty-seven pieces of artillery, fourteen transports, twenty barges, three hundred wagons, fifty ambulances, one hundred and five stand of arms, forty block houses, destroyed thirty-six railroad bridges, two thousand miles of railroad, six locomotives, and one hundred cars, amounting to fifteen millions of property. In accomplishing this he admits they were occasionally sustained by other troops, but says their regular number never exceeded five thousand. Two thousand had been killed or wounded, and two thousand taken prisoners. He tells them to prepare for renewed action, and warns them against being allured by syren songs of peace, for there can be no peace save upon their separate independent nationality.

General Imboden is in command of all the rebel military prisons in Georgia, Alabama and Mississippi.

Great scarcity of breadstuffs is said to exist. Roddy's Division has been breaking up distilleries, so that grain may be procured by suffering families and soldiers. Whisky is regarded as a worse enemy than the Yankees.

General Wirt Adams has ordered all gins and cotton on the Big Black River to be removed.

The river is still rapidly rising here. Much of the low land between Cairo, Mound City, and portions of the latter place, are submerged, interfering with operations on ships and navy yards.

The Hon. T. C. Callicot, Assistant Special Agent of the Transportation Department at Memphis, has been appointed Supervisor and Special Agent for the First Special Agency, comprising that part of the Mississippi Valley lying west of the Alleghany Mountains, east of the mouth of the Tennessee, and extending south to such parts of Alabama, Georgia, North Carolina and Virginia, are is or shall be occupied by the national forces operating from the North.

FROM NEW ORLEANS.

The Federal Consul of Matamoros at New Orleans—The Fleet to Attack Mobile—Markets—Matamoros Threatened—No Permits for Vessels to That Port to be Granted.

CAIRO, March 4, 1865.

The New Orleans Times of the 25th ult. says: The reported expulsion of the American Consul from Matamoros appears to be confirmed by his arrival at the Southwest Pass.

Permits to bring cotton within our lines have been issued at Memphis. For the week ending the 25th ult., over 26,000 bales of supplies were allowed to pass beyond our lines, valued at $220,000.

New Orleans dates of the 25th ult., say that the schooner Jane Laidlaw, reported lost off the mouth of the Rio Grande, had arrived safely.

A railroad has been constructed from the depot of the Jackson Road to the Mississippi River for military purposes, which will prove of great advantage in the transportation of troops and supplies.

Gen. Canby had returned to New Orleans from a visit of inspection to Mobile Bay and the adjacent points.

Commodore Palmer's fleet is in complete order and ready to commence the attack upon Mobile at any moment.

A garden for the cultivation of vegetables has been established at each post in General Canby's Department.

The health of the troops at the various posts is good.

The latest news from Matamoros is that the American flag had been hauled down by some unknown party.

Cotton at New Orleans ranged from 65 cents to 69 cents for good ordinary to strict middling. The business was limited owing to the unfavorable weather. Middling sugar ranged from 22 cents to 23 cents and 24 cents for fair to prime. Molasses, $1 25 to $1 27 per gallon.

Three cargoes of sugar and molasses had arrived from Cuba at New Orleans.

NEW ORLEANS, Feb. 25, 1865.

The Times says that it is reported that Gens. Cavajal and Cortina are marching on Matamoros, where General Mejia, with four thousand imperial troops, awaits their attack.

General Hurlbut has ordered that no permits for vessels or merchandise be granted for Matamoros until further orders.

OUR NEW ORLEANS CORRESPONDENCE.

The Draft—How it Works—What has been Done—The Interest in the Matter—Arrival of Gen. Thomas—Speculations on the Military Situation—The Army of the Tennessee—A New Military Railroad—Mobile Threatened—Arrival of Gen. Wallace and Staff—An Invasion of Texas Prophesied—Arrests of Military Men—Serious Charges.

NEW ORLEANS, Feb. 23, 1865.

The great and all-absorbing question of interest here at present is the draft. There were few who believed that it would be enforced, for the reason that Gen. Canby is not ignorant of the fact that a large majority of those subject to the draft have relatives, friends and neighbors in the Confederate armies; but they were undeceived on the 15th, when the drawing was commenced from the enrollment for the Fourth Municipal District. It was continued until the 18th, and then suspended until the 23d. In the meantime claims for exemption were to be heard and substitutes received. When the draft was suspended, eight hundred and one names had been drawn, from which the quota of that District (five hundred and five) is to be made up, selecting the names from the list in the order in which they were drawn.

Should the number drawn be reduced by exemptions below the number necessary to fill the quota, the draft will be resumed and continued until the quota is filled, or the enrollment exhausted. It it takes as long a time to make the draft in the other three districts, the people of this city will enjoy the sweets of misery long drawn out.

There are some few who will still hope that orders will come from Washington suspending this draft, which, if enforced to the extreme, will array father against son, brother against brother, and neighbor against neighbor, in deadly conflict. This hope, I fear, will not be realized. An Administration that approved the course of Gens. Butler and Banks is not likely to interfere with Gen. Canby's draft.

The draft has rendered the public almost wholly oblivious to other important events transpiring in this department. Scarcely anything else is talked about. The busy tongue of rumor has been nearly silenced by the all-absorbing question of the draft, and "grapevine intelligence" is but little inquired for. Even the newsboys have ceased their stereotyped cry of "Late Southern news," "Another new order," and substituted, "Full account of the draft." As a matter of course, the draft was a good thing for the journals, and they made the most of it, by issuing extra editions. It is an ill wind that blows nobody good, and as our journals are so seldom permitted to publish anything done by the military in this department, they are excusable for making the most out of this occasion, even if it is at the misery and cost of our citizens.

On the night of the 10th instant General Thomas and staff arrived in this city by way of the river. He brought the intelligence in reference to Peace Commissioners having been sent from Richmond. General Canby was waited upon to know if these facts could be published in the morning papers. He had no objections to the latter being published, but decidedly objected to having the arrival of General Thomas announced. Of course this was upon the plea that such announcement would be giving information to the enemy. If to prevent the Confederates being informed of this arrival was the general's object, he failed. Newspapers do not possess the powers of locomotion, consequently they could not have gone to the Confederates, unless they were carried there. If it was a matter of such importance to the Confederates, it was not necessary that it should be first announced in a city paper, before being conveyed to them. General Canby well knows that the Confederates have always been apprised in advance of any contemplated military movement in this Department, which is an evidence of the intense loyalty of the people, even some who are in confidence at headquarters. I will venture to assert that the Confederates were apprised of the fact that General Thomas and his army were en route for this city before he embarked at Cairo.

The Confederate General Forrest is well apprised of the movements of General Thomas's army, and is well aware that the Federal force at Florence is too small to venture on a raid toward Selma and Mobile.

It is now known that most of the Union army of the Tennessee is en route for this city, and it is believed by many that its destination is Mobile, from which point it will march through Alabama and Georgia to join Sherman, capturing Selma and Montgomery as it passes along. This may be successfully performed, but I doubt it. I am inclined to think that Mobile will be abandoned if threatened by a flank movement, as the city is of no military importance to the Confederacy, at least not enough to waste or endanger a force sufficient for its successful defense.

The fact that the military authorities here are building a railroad from the river to the lake, indicates a grand movement in the direction of Mobile. From the rear of the city there are two canals and one railroad running to the lake, neither of which is a mile from the river. And from the lower part of the city there is a railroad running from within a short distance of the river to the lake. These certainly could have supplied the transportation needed by the Government, unless a grand movement is intended in the direction indicated, in which event the transportation will be greatly facilitated by a railroad from the steamboat landing to the lake, as it will dispense with much handling of freight, which will be immense for an army of forty or fifty thousand.

This railroad was commenced on the 10th, and on the night of the 18th the cars passed over it, causing the death of a child. As it is made to traverse one of the most populous streets of the city, it is feared that many deaths will result therefrom.

General Wallace and staff, of the Army of the Tennessee, arrived here on the 19th. Of course his army is to follow him.

But little is said in reference to the invasion of Texas, but the concentration of troops here is said to be for that purpose; and, in order to insure success, that State is to be invaded at two distinct and distant points, with a view to dividing the army for its defense. Texas may be overrun in the absence of so large a number of her fighting men; but many persons doubt it. If all her sons were within her borders, to subjugate Texas would be found almost as difficult a task as subjugating the Confederacy.

There are rumors afloat that General Canby is to be superseded by General "Baldy" Smith; that General Hurlbut and several others have been suspended, and Colonel Robinson, Provost Marshal General, and a number of others have been arrested, it is said, for seizing the gold which the owners had been compelled to deposit with the agent of the Treasury Department. It is said they seized it for the purpose of confiscation—of course on private account. The journals are not permitted to discuss these matters or there might be some rich developments.

CRESCENT CITY.

FROM TENNESSEE.

Capture of the Federal Steamer Naugatuck—Arrival of Prisoners for Exchange—A Flood at Nashville.

MEMPHIS, March 3, 1865.

Guerrilla outrages, of a diabolical character, continue outside of our lines. The Government steamer Naugatuck is reported captured between here and Cairo by guerrillas, on Wednesday.

General McCook arrived here, en route to Helena, to relieve General Buford.

Two rebel steamers, with prisoners for exchange, arrived at the mouth of the Red River a few days ago, and others were on their way down that stream. Two or three of our upward bound steamers from New Orleans took the prisoners on board and conveyed them to that city.

NASHVILLE, March 4, 1865.

The heavy rains for the past three days have caused a great rise in the river, which is over its bank.

The city is entirely surrounded by water, and the lower part of it is completely submerged.

On the railroad running south much damage has been done by the washing away of bridges.

The trestle bridge over Stone River, near Murfreesboro, has been swept away; also, the one at Franklin.

There is no interruption as yet on the Louisville and Nashville Railroad.

The river rose seven feet yesterday and last night, and it is still rising.

Much damage has been done to property in the vicinity of the flood.

It is believed the flood will be the greates ever known.

Two soldiers of the Ninth Indiana were drowned yesterday in Edgefield.

Sailing of the Nova Scotian.

PORTLAND, Me., March 5, 1865.

The Nova Scotian, Captain Brown, sailed at 2 o'clock this morning for Londonderry and Liverpool.

THE FOURTH AT WASHINGTON.

MR. LINCOLN RE-INAUGURATED.

HIS SPEECH:

All About the Negro and Nothing About Mexico, John Bull or Louis Napoleon.

Remorseless War Declared Against the South.

ALL THEIR WEALTH TO BE SUNK.

MORE BLOOD DEMANDED.

THE VICE PRESIDENT INCOHERENT.

SCENES AT THE INAUGURAL.

THE HEAVENS WEEPING.

Miscegenation at the White House.

WASHINGTON, March 4, 1864.

The inauguration ceremonies are over. President Lincoln has for the second time formally entered upon the great responsibilities of his office. The following is an account of the ceremonies.

The morning was dark and gloomy. It rained in torrents. The streets were a sluice of mud. The procession formed on Sixteenth street, near Pennsylvania avenue, shortly before 11 o'clock, and notwithstanding the rain storm, the streets were thronged by the people. At about 11 o'clock, the procession commenced moving toward the Capitol from the corner of Sixteenth street and Pennsylvania avenue. The military escort consisted of several bands of music, two regiments of the Invalid Corps, a squadron of cavalry, a battery of artillery, and four companies of colored troops.

The ceremonies of the inauguration were somewhat delayed by the storm of the morning, and the detention of Mr. Lincoln in the Executive Chamber signing bills. They took place in the Senate Chamber.

A few minutes before twelve o'clock the official procession began to file into the chamber. First came the members of the Supreme Court, who were seated on the right of the Vice President's chair. Soon after Mr. Lincoln entered, escorted by Vice President Hamlin, and followed by the members of the Cabinet, the chiefs of the diplomatic corps, officers of the army and navy who have received the thanks of Congress, Governors, etc., in the order named in the programme of proceedings, all of whom were appropriately seated.

In a few minutes Vice President Hamlin briefly and feelingly bid farewell to the Senate as its presiding officer. He was followed by Mr. Johnson, Vice President elect, in a speech remarkable only for its incoherence, which brought a blush to the cheek of every Senator and official of the Government who was present. The oath of office as Vice President was then administered to Mr. Johnson, and the Senators elect to the Thirty-ninth Congress were sworn in, after which the official procession was formed and proceeded to the platform in front of the portico of the eastern front of the Capitol, where the ceremony of the inauguration of the President elect was concluded.

The appearance of Mr. Lincoln on the platform was the signal for a tremendous outburst of cheers. When the tumult subsided, the President stepped forward and delivered his inaugural address.

Mr. Lincoln's Speech.

Thr President said:

FELLOW COUNTRYMEN: At this second appearing to take the oath of the Presidential office, there is less occasion for an extended address than there was at the first. Then a statement somewhat in detail of a course to be pursued seemed very fitting and proper. Now, at the expiration of four years, during which public declarations have been constantly called forth on every point and phase of the great contest which still absorbs the attention and engrosses the energies of the nation, little that is new could be presented.

The progress of our arms—upon which all else chiefly depends—is as well known to the public as to myself; and it is, I trust, reasonably satisfactory and encouraging to all. With high hope for the future, no prediction in regard to it is ventured.

On the occasion corresponding to this four years ago all thoughts were anxiously directed to an impending civil war. All dreaded it; all sought to avoid it. While the inaugural address was being delivered from this place, devoted altogether to saving the Union without war, insurgent agents were in the city seeking to destroy it without war—seeking to dissolve the Union and divide the effects by negotiation.

Both paties deprecated war; but one of them would make war rather than let the nation survive, and the other would accept war rather than let it perish, and the war came.

One-eighth of the whole population were colored slaves, not distributed generally over the Union, but localized in the Southern part of it. These slaves constituted a pecular and powerful interest. All knew that this interest was somehow the cause of the war. To strengthen, perpetuate and extend this interest was the object for which the insurgents would rend the Union by war, while the government claimed no right to do more than to restrict the territorial enlargement of it.

Neither party expected for the war the magnitude or the duration which it has already attained. Neither anticipated that the cause of the conflict might cease, even before the conflict itself should cease. Each looked for an easier triumph and a result less fundamental and astounding.

Both read the same Bible and pray to the same God, and each invokes His aid against the other. It may seem strange that any men should dare to ask a just God's assistance in wringing their bread from the sweat of other men's faces; but let us judge not, that we be not judged. The prayers of both should not be answered. That of neither has been answered fully. The Almighty has His own purposes. Woe unto the world because of offenses, for it must needs be that offenses come; but woe to that man by whom the offense cometh. If we shall suppose that American slavery is one of these offenses—which, in the providence of God, must needs come, but which, having continued through His appointed time, He now wills to remove, and that He gives to both North and South this terrible war as the woe due to those by whom the offense came—shall we discern there is any departure from those Divine attributes which the believers in a living God always acribe to Him? Fondly do we

COLUMBIA PHŒNIX.

"Give each his due—both friends and foes;
And sketch the world just as it goes."

BY J. A. SELBY. COLUMBIA, S. C., TUESDAY, MARCH 21, 1865. VOL. 1.—NO. 1.

THE COLUMBIA PHŒNIX

IS PUBLISHED

Every Tuesday, Thursday and Saturday,

BY

JULIAN A. SELBY.

Single copies $. No subscriptions received. Advertisements inserted at $5 per square (ten lines) for each insertion.

CAPTURE, SACK and DESTRUCTION

OF THE

City of Columbia

I.

It has pleased God, in that Providence which is so inscrutable to man, to visit our beautiful city with the most cruel fate which can ever befall States or cities. He has permitted the cruel and malignant enemy to penetrate our country almost without impediment; to pollute our homes with his presence; to rob and ravage our dwellings, and to commit three-fifths of our city to the flames. Eighty-four squares, out of one hundred and twenty-four (?) which the city contains, have been destroyed, with scarcely the exception of a single house. The ancient capitol building of the State—that venerable structure which, for seventy years, has echoed with the eloquence and wisdom of the most famous statesmen—is laid in ashes; six temples of the Most High God have shared the same fate; eleven banking establishments; the schools of learning, the shops of art and trade, of invention and manufacture; shrines equally of religion, benevolence and industry; are all buried together in one congregated ruin. Humiliation spreads her ashes over our homes and garments, and the universal wreck exhibits only one common aspect of despair. It is for us, as succinctly but as fully as possible, and in the simplest language, to endeavor to make the melancholy record of our wretchedness, so that our sons may always remember, and the whole Christian world everywhere may read.

II.

When, by a crime, no less than blunder, Gen. Johnston was removed from the command of our armies in Georgia, which he had conducted with such signal ability, there were not a few of our citizens who felt the impending danger, and trembled at the disastrous consequences which they partly foresaw. The removal of a General so fully in the confidence of his troops, who had so long baffled the conquests, if he could not arrest the march, of the enemy, was of itself a proceeding to startle the thoughtful mind. The enemy loudly declared his satisfaction at the event, and on repeated occasions since has expressed himself to the same effect. He was emboldened by the change, and almost instantly after, his successes became rapid and of the most decided character.

Gen. Johnston was by nature, no less than training and education, the very best of our generals to be opposed to Gen. Sherman. To the nervo-sanguine temperament, eager and impetuous, of the latter, he opposed a moral and physical nature—calm, sedate, circumspect; cool, vigilant and wary—always patient and watchful of his moment—never rash or precipitate, but ever firm and decisive—his resources all regulated by a self-possessed will, and a mind in full possession of that military *coup d'œil* which, grasping the remotest relations of the field, is, probably, the very first essential to a general having the control of a large and various army.

The error which took Hood into the colder regions of Tennessee, at the beginning of winter, was one which the Yankee General was slow to imitate, especially as, in so moving, Hood necessarily left all the doors wide open which conducted to the seaboard. It required no effort of genius—nay, did not need even the suggestions of ordinary talent—to prompt the former to take the pathways which were thus laid open to him. Even had he not already conceived the propriety of forcing his way to the Atlantic coast, and to a junction with his shipping, the policy of then doing so would have been forced upon him by the proceeding of his rival, and by the patent fact that there were no impediments to such a progress. We had neither army nor general ready to impede his march. It suggested itself. The facility of such a progress, was clear enough, and, with that quickness of decision which distinguishes the temperament of Sherman, he at once rushed into the open pathway.

The hasty levies of regular troops, collected by Hardee, and the clans of scattered militia, gathered with great difficulty and unchained to service, were rather calculated to provoke his enterprise than to impede his march; and, laying waste as he went, after a series of small and unimportant skirmishes, he made his way to the coast, made himself master of Savannah, and, from the banks of that river, beheld, opened before him, all the avenues into and through South Carolina. It is understood that Hardee had in hand, to oppose this progress, something less than 10,000 men, while the force of Sherman was, in round numbers, something like 50,000, of which 33,000 consisted of infantry—the rest of artillery and cavalry.

III.

The destruction of Atlanta, the pillaging and burning of other towns of Georgia, and the subsequent devastation along the march of the enemy through Georgia, gave sufficient earnest of the treatment to be anticipated by South Carolina, should the same commander be permitted to make a like progress in our State. The Northern press furnished him with the *cri de guerre* to be sounded when he should cross our borders. "*Væ victis!*"—wo to the conquered!—woes unmitigated, unqualified, remorseless—in the case of a people which had been the first to sound the bugles of resistance to the encroachments of the Northern tyranny and usurpation! The howl of delight (such was the language of the Northern press) sent up by Sherman's legions, when they looked across the Savannah to the shores of Carolina, was the sure forerunner of the terrible fate which threatened our people, should the demonic furies be once let loose upon our lands. Our people felt all the danger. They felt that it required the first abilities, the most strenuous exertions, the most prompt and efficient reinforcements, to prevent the threatening catastrophe.

South Carolina had, for a long season, been made a sort of nursery for sick generals, and a sort of pasture ground for incompetence and imbecility. Hardee, though of acknowledged ability, and considered able as the leader of a corps, was not the man to grasp the business of a large army. All eyes looked to Gen. Johnston as the one man, next to Lee, to whom the duty should be confided and the trust. It was confidently hoped and believed that he would be restored to the command, and that adequate reinforcements would be furnished, to enable him, not only to meet the enemy, but to take the initiative in beating him from the [illegible]

Nashville Union.

EXTRA.

MONDAY, APRIL 3—1 O'CLOCK, P. M.

RICHMOND!

The Evacuation of Richmond and Petersburg.

Corroborated by Later Private Dispatches.

15,000 Prisoners and 50 Guns Captured.

We are indebted to a distinguished officer of the army for the following corroboration of the glorious news from Virginia:

NASHVILLE, April 3, 1865.

Editor of the Union:

WAR DEPARTMENT, April 3.—The enemy have evacuated Richmond and our troops under Gen. Wetzel marched into the city at half past eight o'clock this morning. Gen. Sheridan, by his flank movement, has compelled the enemy to evacuate city of Petersburg, and our flag is now floating over Richmond and Petersburg. We have up to the latest telegram, 1 P. M., had all corroborated, with the capture of 15,000 prisoners, and fifty pieces of artillery.

Gen. Lee said, prior to leaving the city of Richmond, that he could have stood Grant in his front for years, but the bold and successful march of Sherman to his rear completed the evacuation.

POST EXTRA

THE
Buffalo Post.
IS PUBLISHED
Every Day, Sundays Excepted,
At 190 Washington Street.
GEORGE J. BRYAN,
EDITOR AND PROPRIETOR.

TERMS—Delivered to Subscribers in the city at TWELVE CENTS PER WEEK, or $5 PER ANNUM when paid in advance.

Liberal discount to News Dealers and Newsboys.

Terms of Yearly Advertising made known at the office.

Marriages and Deaths, 25 Cents, limited to six lines.

Above rates will be rigidly adhered to, but will not interfere with anyexisting contracts.
GEORGE J. BRYAN,
Editor and Proprietor of Post.
Buffalo, August 9th, 1864.

Farm Wanted.

A party wishes to purchase a good farm of about 200 acres within 15 or 20 miles of Buffalo; it must be under good cultivation, with fruit and good buildings. Price location and description left or addressed to the subscriber at No. 3 Niagara st, will receive attention.

LEONARD WILSON,
Real Estate Agent.

Wanted.

A competent widow woman wishes a situation in some good family as housekeeper or nurse, can accept of a situation immediately as satisfactory reference given.

Address box 691 Buffalo Post office. mr23t

Daily Post.

OUR FLAG.

Union of Lakes, and a Union of Lands;
A Union, which none may sever;
A Union of hearts, and a Union of hands,
Round that Flag of our country Forever.

GLORIOUS NEWS.

Another Terrific BATTLE!

Richmond Taken!

VICTORY! VICTORY!

Petessburgh Evacuated!

A general Smash Up!

A Despatch from Gen. Grant from 8:30 this A. M. says Petersburg is evacuated.

He also thinks Richmond will soon be ours.

LATER.

He is rushing on to cut off Lee's retreat.

Secretary Stanton telegraphs Gen. Dix that Richmond was occupied by our troops this morning at 8 o'clock.

Frame Dwellings for Sale.

Fulton street No 104, 2 story, lot 58x161 barn and good well. Price $2500.

Louisiana street east side between Fulton and Elk street 2 story. Price $1450.

Miami street North side near Louisiana street 1½ story, 9 rooms, well and cistern, lot 34x100 Price $1600.

Exchange street north side first frame dwelling west of Louisiana. Price $3500.

South Division street No. 169, 1½ story. Price $1400.

South Division street No. 178, 2 story, 12 or 14 rooms in complete order. Price $3500.

Smith street west side first dwelling south of Carolina 1½ story. Price $800.

South Division street No. 2.., 2 story, good well and cistern will be sold very low.

North Division street No. 251 one story, 7 rooms Price $1800.

Carolina street south side first dwelling west of 9th street, 1 story, gas and good cistern. Price $1800.

Palmer street west side between Maryland and Hudson, 1 story flue lot with bearing fruit trees. Price $1600.

Ninth street No. 165, 2 story, lot 35x115. Price $2400.

Sixth street west side 1st dwelling north of Pennsylvania. Price $1000.

Sixth street west side fifth dwelling south of Pennsylvania, 1½ story, new in complete order. Price $1400.

Park street west side between Virginia and Allen, 1 story in fine order, fine lot to an Alley, bearing fruit trees and grape vines, good well and cistern. Price $1600.

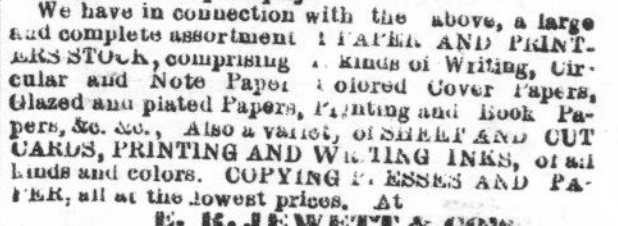

At No. 3 Niagara street,
mr10 LEONARD WILSON.

EVENING WHIG.

WM. IRA SMITH, Proprietor.

TUESDAY, APRIL 4, 1865.

SPECIAL NOTICE.

For the temporary accommodation of the citizens of Richmond who may wish the *Whig*, there will be tickets sold at the office in amounts from *two* to *five dollars* in Federal currency to responsible parties, and their obligation taken, payable in thirty days, so as to enable them to reach the latest news.

Call at the office, Whig Building.

THE publication of the *Whig* is resumed this afternoon, with the consent of the military authorities. The editor, and all who heretofore controlled its columns, have taken their departure. The proprietor and one *attache* of the recent editorial corps remain. The former has had a conference with General Shepley, the Military Governor, who has assented to the publication of the paper on conditions which will be cheerfully and faithfully complied with. The *Whig* will therefore be issued hereafter as a *Union paper*. The sentiments of attachment to our "whole country," which formerly characterized it as a journal, will again find expression in its columns, and whatever influence it may have for the restoration of the national authority will be exerted.

As soon as practicable a full and efficient editorial force will be organized. For the present we ask the indulgence of our readers. We will do the best we can under existing circumstances, promising a daily improvement in the variety and interest of the contents of the paper, until we shall make the *Whig* commend itself to the favor and support of all persons loyal to the Government of the United States.

The terms cannot, as yet, be definitely fixed. We shall commence with such charges, in Federal currency, as we conceive to be fair and seasonable. In a short time we will resume the issue of a double sheet.

POPULAR confidence in the National Government is conclusively demonstrated, says the New York *Times*, by the rapidity with which the new series of the 7-30 National Currency Loan is being absorbed. The first two days' subscriptions to the new series were about $5,500,000. At even this daily average rate, the whole series (of $300,000,000) will be marketed before the close of the coming month of July. From August 15, 1864, to February 1, 1865, (one hundred and sixty-nine days, all told,) the amount of the first series of the 7-30 loan marketed under the direct supervision of the Secretary of the Treasury was $133,000,000, or at the daily average rate of only about $771,000. From February 1 to March 27, 1865, (fifty-five days, all told,) under the immediate direction of Mr. Jay Cooke, General Subscription Agent, the sales of the loan reached $167,000,000, or a daily average rate of as much as $3,036,363.

THE *Herald* of Friday says: "The universal impression that we are fast approaching the closing scenes of the war, has been strengthened into a general conviction by our late important successes in North Carolina and in front of Petersburg. The general movements of the Union forces on both sides of the James, reported yesterday as having already commenced, has led to the opinion that within a few days we may expect to hear of the capture or evacuation of Richmond."

The people here were kept in the dark as to the true situation of affairs at the seats of war, and were deluded with fanciful accounts of defeats of portions of the Union forces. Their eyes have been opened by the events of Sunday and yesterday, and every person will concur in the opinion of the *Herald* that "we are fast approaching the closing scenes of the war."

SEVERAL days will elapse, we suppose, before business is actively resumed. Still there are stocks of goods in the city, and others will be rapidly introduced by loyal persons who may be authorized to carry on trade in Richmond. We suggest that parties having anything for sale in Richmond, especially the necessaries of life, will make the fact known through the advertising columns of the *Whig*.

THE *Whig* and *Sentinel* offices were the only newspaper establishments in Richmond spared by the conflagration yesterday. The *Enquirer* and *Dispatch* were totally destroyed. The press room and presses of the *Examiner* were destroyed, and the printing material removed. The *Whig* and *Sentinel* buildings were uninjured.

THE great fire in this city has necessitated the turning off of the gas at 21st street. Until the sidewalks are cleared of the *debris*, which prevents access to the "steps," a large portion of the community will be deprived of the use of gas. For the same reason we will only be able to publish an afternoon edition for the present. We are confident that the military authorities will soon cause the removal of the rubbish from the sidewalks. Candles are very scarce, and much inconvenience results from the absence of gas in the dwellings.

THE New York *Times* says that the following "sportive missive from Ex-Secretary of War Seddon," was captured during Gen. Sheridan's last expedition:

CONFEDERATE STATES OF AMERICA,
WAR DEPARTMENT,
RICHMOND, October 19, 1863.

Alex. Moseley, Esq:

Dear Sir—How do you stand the quiet of the country? I hope it palls in these stirring times. We miss your trenchant pen and would rather have you sowing tares for the enemy than wheat for ourselves. Are you too great a foe to impressments to allow yourself to be pressed again into harness? I wish you would at least lend a hand to drag us out of the dis-financial slough in which we are floundering worse and worse each day.

Very truly yours,
JAS. A. SEDDON.

SO far as we can learn everybody is highly gratified at the deportment of the troops who entered the city yesterday. There have been no acts of violence or disorder committed, as some persons apprehended; but, on the contrary, the soldiers conducted themselves with marked propriety and decorum.

WE learn that it is not improbable His Excellency, President Lincoln, will reach the city this afternoon.

THE OCCUPATION OF THE CITY.

We have been unable to obtain a full and connected account of the occupation of the city by the Union forces. The Mayor, we believe, proceeded in a carriage to the picket lines below Richmond, at 2 o'clock yesterday morning, for the purpose of surrendering the city, but we have had no opportunity to learn any particulars of the interview with the officer in command.

We subjoin the following, gathered from conversation with several officers this forenoon:

The picket line of the 2d Brigade of this Division, Col. M. T. Donohoe, 10th N. H. Vols., commanding, was advanced at day break the morning of the 3d instant.

Major J. C. Brooks, 9th Vt. Vols., A. A. Inspector General of the Division, and Capt. George A. Bruce, Judge Advocate, preceded the line with a few attendants, and were among the first that reached the city limits.

Lieut. Col. W. W. Barnberger, 5th Maryland Volunteers, Division officer of the day, directed the general movement of the picket line. Captain H. Q. Sargent, 12th New Hampshire Volunteers, and Captain A. E. Leavenworth, 9th Vermont Volunteers, senior officers of the advanced portion of this picket force, were among the first to reach the city, and on the arrival of Gen. Deven were immediately ordered to patrol the city and aid in quieting the alarm and confusion caused by the terrible conflagration then in progress.

THE SITUATION.

We have no particulars yet of the great battle of Sunday near Petersburg, which resulted in the complete triumph of the National forces. On Sunday night it was reported that the remnant of Gen. Lee's army had retreated to the Danville railroad, in the vicinity of Mattoax, 27 miles from Richmond. At what point, if any, it would make a stand, was wholly a matter of conjecture. We copy the following from the N. Y. *Herald* of Friday:

Nothing later regarding the new movement of the national armies before the rebel capital has been received, excepting the fact that it commenced on Wednesday last. All the sick and the wounded from the fighting of last Saturday and Monday were removed from the field hospitals of the Army of the Potomac on Tuesday, indicating preparations for active operations. The exchange of prisoners on James river is still continued, Col. Mulford, Union Exchange Commissioner, having recently exchanged as many as fourteen hundred in one day.

Regarding General Sherman's quiet but hasty trip from Goldsboro to City Point, and visit to General Grant, some interesting particulars are furnished by our Newbern and Fortress Monroe correspondents. Gen. Sherman, on the way, remarked to a friend that a talk of five minutes with General Grant would be sufficient for the mutual arrangement of their plans; but he spent nearly two days with the President, the Lieutenant General and the other distinguished official personage on James river. While General Sherman was in Newbern the rumor mongers circulated a story that proposals for a cessation of hostilities had been submitted to him by General Johnston, and that his visit to City Point was for the purpose of laying these before General Grant and General Lee. General Sherman returned to North Carolina in the same quiet way in which he came on from there, avoiding public demonstrations of respect for him which thousands were desirous of making.

[COMMUNICATED.

Once more, through the mercy and favor of Him, who is the giver of all good, we have the inexpressible joy and glorious privilege of greeting the Flag of the Union. For four years we have been a down-trodden, oppressed people. Volumes could not contain nor express the misery, suffering and sorrow which we have been subjected to. The darkest pages of the world's history, reveal nothing that can be compared to the terrible ordeal through which we have passed. We should be grateful indeed for this token of Divine favor in delivering us from the most tyrannical and despotic government which has existed since "darkness was changed into light." We shall now soon have that peace, prosperity and happiness which was once ours, and enjoy that freedom and liberty which was vouchsafed us by our sires of the Revolution.

H.

THE REBELLION "PLAYED OUT."

The following is from the Philadelphia *Inquirer* of 31st ultimo:

The readers of *The Inquirer* will remember the full report published in our issue on Friday last of the great mass meeting at the Academy of Music, for the purpose of extending our sympathies towards the Union men of the South who had been forced into the rebel ranks, and of pledging relief and employment to such of them as should desert the sinking ship of the rebellion and throw themselves upon the protection of the government. The article is beginning already to show its good effects. The great army edition of our paper having been, as usual, exchanged by our Union soldiers, after being read, served to leaven the rebel masses, and resulted as hereinafter stated.

Shortly after its circulation among the Georgia troops in Longstreet's corps of Lee's army, dissatisfaction began to work, and half of Bryan's brigade attempted to desert. This was prevented by force, but large numbers succeeded in making their escape, and some four hundred reached City Point a day or two since. Forty-three of these arrived in Philadelphia yesterday, and are now at the Volunteer Refreshment Saloon. Most of them are farmers, and their arrival affords an opportunity for putting into practical operation the sentiment of the great meeting of last week.

Several intelligent Georgians, who were among the party mentioned, visited the *Inquirer* office last evening. They seem to consider the Confederacy as pretty nearly "played out." They say that the desertions from Lee's army average over a hundred every day. The whole rebel force in front of Grant cannot, in their opinion, exceed forty thousand men, and if it should continue to be depleted at the rate mentioned, cannot long be available for evil. They say that Stephens left for the South immediately on his return from the late Peace Conference, and refuses to have anything more to do with the Confederacy. He has not since occupied his seat as presiding officer of the rebel Senate.

These deserters say that the whole South cannot muster a new regiment of recruits. Men and boys not in the army are rarities scarcely ever seen. Want of space prevents our detailing at any length the interesting accounts they give of affairs in Dixie. In conclusion, we again call the attention of those wishing to hire hands to the presence of these men, nearly all of whom are skilled workmen or farmers, and all ready and anxious for work.

NEWS FROM WASHINGTON.

We copy the following paragraphs from the Washington correspondence of the New York and Philadelphia papers of the 31st ult.:

From the N. Y. Times.

THE DISCHARGE OF THE ST. ALBANS RAIDERS.

The discharge of the St. Albans raiders has created a bad feeling here, and though the Government is inclined to reciprocate the kindly sentiments of many leading Canadians, sought to be carried out by acts of legislation, yet it is not to be presumed that a repetition of such farces can be taken as evidence of good faith or good intentions on the part of the Canadian authorities.

THE SAVANNAH COTTON.

Collector Draper, of New York, made a report to the Secretary of the Treasury to-day, with reference to the captured cotton at Savannah. The facts are substantially the same as has already appeared in the New York papers. The number of bales is reported at 38,500, nearly the whole of which, Mr. Draper says, belonged to the rebel Government.

ANOTHER PLEASURE TRIP.

Secretary Seward and a party of friends, consisting of the Spanish Minister, British Minister *ad interim* and several others, left last evening on an excursion down the Potomac to Fortress Monroe. This is, of course, another peace mission in the eyes of the speculators, but it will probably turn out that it is simply peace of mind.

From the New York Herald.

PRISONERS OF WAR DECLARED EXCHANGED.

Official notification has been received of the following exchanges of prisoners of war:—All United States officers and men, prisoners of war, not heretofore declared exchanged, who were delivered on parole at Savannah, Ga., and Charleston, S. C., during the months of November and December, 1864, and all not heretofore declared exchanged, delivered on parole on the James river, Va., from the 25th of November, 1864, to the 25th day of March, 1865, both days inclusive, and all navy prisoners delivered at any points up to March 10, 1865.

SHIPS OF WAR TO BE LAID UP.

It is under consideration by the Secretary of the Navy to retire about one-half of the vessels now in commission, and use the surplus seamen and landsmen employed on board for land service. This will add about twenty-five thousand to the effective land forces. The capture of all rebel ports will enable this important reduction to be made in the naval force and a large saving in expense of that branch of service.

THE TAX ON CIGARETTES.

Instructions will be sent to the internal revenue officers to-morrow to the effect that after the first of April cigarettes will be taxed as follows: Thirty-five cents per pound upon the smoking tobacco of which they are made, and the completed cigarettes five per centum advalorem. Cut tobacco may be inspected in boxes before packing at the place of its manufacture.

NATIONAL BANKS.

It has been ascertained at the Currency Bureau that the State banks of Massachusetts and New York are rapidly being converted into national banks. Those of Rhode Island have commenced availing themselves of the enabling act recently passed; and banks all over the country manifest a similar disposition. The law allows national banks to issue one-sixth of their circulation in notes of less denomination than five dollars.—The Currency Bureau has received some of such money, which will be issued to the banks in the order of their organization.

[From the Philadelphia Inquirer.]

MORE PEACE STORIES.

Parties here, who have been industriously engaged in circulating peace rumors for some time, insist that Mr. Seward has gone to City Point to confer with Mr. Lincoln upon peace, while others declare that the two foreign diplomatists were given to understand before leaving that they were to play the mediators. Mr. Lincoln's not having returned to-night, as was anticipated, gives some coloring to the latter statement.

But we have assurances from a responsible quarter that there are no peace negotiations in progress, and that the mission of Mr. Seward is to show his distinguished guests that we have within our means the power to make such a peace as will be permanent when it comes, which at the furthest will not be long.

THE TREASURY MURDER.

Miss Mary Harris, of Chicago, who shot the Treasury clerk, last winter, for failing to keep his promises of marriage, was to-day arraigned for murder, before Judge Olen. She was closely veiled, but was entirely self-possessed, and when pleading spoke out in a clear voice—not guilty. She is well provided with counsel, having four attorneys, and is exceedingly prepossessing in her appearance, her long black ringlets falling in profusion upon a close-fitting black coat. The court-room was crowded, although but few knew the trial was to come on.

[From the N. Y. Commercial Advertiser.]

In official circles the immediate downfall of the rebellion is considered certain. The most recent advices at the War department give assurance that neither Lee nor Johnston can either retreat or offer battle without the certain destruction of their armies.

It is understood on both sides that there must be a cessation of fighting for several days; and advices from Richmond state that every resort of diplomacy will be used for arranging a peace during the interim.

Yesterday morning Secretary Seward left the city, it is understood, for City Point.

Hon. Millard Fillmore had preceded him, at the suggestion, it is understood, of Jefferson Davis, on the ground of his friendly feeling toward the South; and it is generally believed here, in the best informed circles, that negotiations for an honorable peace are now in progress on board the River Queen.—Those best acquainted with the President's views consider it certain that his ultimatum will in no respect vary from that presented in Hampton Roads.

SUMMARY OF NEWS.

The negro Captain Ropert Small returned to Charleston a few days since, in the same vessel in which he escaped from the city in the Spring of 1862—the Planter. As it passed Fort Sumter it had all its three flags flying, and the Captain's face beamed with satisfaction as he saw the Stars and Stripes on its parapet once more. The Planter has been refitted since its flight from Charleston at an expense of $40,000.

The grave of Calhoun, in St. Philip's church yard, Charleston, is but a tomb made of brick, surmounted by a slab of marble, on which is the single word "Calhoun." Small bushes grow around, which had the appearance of being lately trimmed. Shells have struck all around it, and a fragment has taken off a portion from the marble slab which covers all that remains of the first secessionist.

A few days ago three families entered into a plot to invite Sheridan to a party and betray him into the hands of some of Mosby's guerrillas. But the wary Phil. Sheridan was not to be caught in such a trap. The plan was detected, and the conspirators arrested and sent forthwith beyond our lines to their friends at Richmond.

Two things are wholly different in nature and character. Political equality is a right. Social equality is a matter of taste and affinity. Fifth avenue and the Five Points are politically equal, but, in a social point of view, they are as far removed from each other as the poles. One is at the top, the other at the bottom of the scale.

Major General Palmer has published an order declaring that he will at once suppress all slave pens and other private establishments for the confinement of persons in the city of Louisville, and discharge the persons confined. This is a step in the right direction, and may prove an entering wedge to a great reform.

The Charleston *Courier* says:—"The recruiting officers in Charleston are head over heels in business. The colored men are flocking to the support of the United States flag by the dozen and the score. Companies are formed in a single day, and a full regiment comes out in a week.

An appeal is soon to be made to the Italians in this country to aid in contributing funds for the statue to be erected at Ravenna to the wife of Garibaldi, who died in the swamps on the Adriatic coast, preferring to share danger with her husband, rather than to enjoy luxury and comfort without him.

So great was the confusion during the last forty-eight hours of the session of the last Congress, that one resolution was engrossed, signed by the Vice-President and the Speaker of the House, and presented to the President for his signature, that had never been passed.

A mechanic of Milwaukie has manufactured two

wonderful pieces of cabinet work, intended as presents for the President and Mrs. Lincoln. One is an ordinary-sized centre table, of octagonal form, composed of twenty thousand different pieces of wood.

Five hundred Hungarian families want to emigrate to one of our Territories. An agent is at Washington trying to arrange for their transportation from Europe to Arizona.

General Roy Stone, of Pennsylvania, commandant of the military station at Alton, Illinois, has tendered his resignation to the War Office at Washington, and the same has been accepted.

John Overton, the Tennessee millionaire, who gave $5,000,000 to aid the rebellion, has deserted the cause, and is once more a peaceable citizen of Nashville.

One of Garibaldi's Generals has heen arrested in New Haven for keeping a barber shop open on Sunday, and was discharged because he did not talk English.

An Austrian Princess lately died in a debtor's prison in Vienna. Radzvill was her name.

The house of Rothschild has summoned all its agents abroad to a conference, which is about to take place in Paris.

Somebody calls the Confederates a nation of regicides. They burn their King—cotton.

Mr. Vallandigham refuses to be a candidate for Governor of Ohio. Sensible

Baron Rothschild has erected a church for the use of his servants.

THE LATEST NEWS.

Just before going to press, we have received a copy of the Philadelphia *Inquirer* of the 1st inst. We have only space for the following:

LATER PARTICULARS OF THE MOVEMENT OF THE ARMY OF THE POTOMAC.

WASHINGTON, March 31.—Information received from the Army of the Potomac to the evening of Wednesday is to the following effect:

The route taken by a portion of the army is the same one which it has traveled several times heretofore, namely, the Vaughn and Halifax roads, running south-west across Hatcher's Run.

The column started at three o'clock on the morning of the 29th inst. A large cavalry force, under General Sheridan, took the Halifax road, toward Dinwiddie Court House. The infantry colum crossed Hatcher's Run on the Vaughn road, but met no opposition until they reached within a short distance of the Boydtown plank road, where the enemy's pickets were found and driven back.

Griffin's division was sent up the Quaker road, and about 3 o'clock in the afternoon, a division of the enemy made its appearance, and not knowing the strength of our force, formed in line and charged, but the rebels were repulsed with heavy loss.

A number of prisoners were taken and brought in.

They said the move had been a complete surprise to them, as they had expected an attack in the vicinity of Fort Steadman, and that their troops had been massed there to meet it.

It is believed the rebels were hurrying men toward the Southside Railroad all the afternoon, in the hope of being able to prevent its destruction; but great confidence was felt that Sheridan would be a little ahead, and by the next night we would have news of its destruction at some point near Burkville. If this should be accomplished, it is claimed the evacuation of Petersburg and Richmond will quickly follow.

THE ADVANCE OF GRANT'S ARMY.

Information from the advance of Grant's army to Hatcher's Run, dated on Thursday morning, shows the locality of our army at that time to be in a line parallel with and east of the Boydtown plank road and west of Hatcher's Run. These important positions had been gained with but little resistance by the enemy.

The Fifth Corps had a sharp encounter with the rebels on the Quaker road on Wednesday, but lost in the affair less than three hundred men, and drove the rebels nearly a mile, with serious loss, capturing also a number of prisoners.

DISASTROUS FIRE AT PARKERSBURG.

A very disastrous fire occurred at Parkersburg, Virginia, about noon on the 28th ultimo, consuming an entire block in the heart of the city, including the Continental Hotel, Second National Bank, the first organized, the Parkersburg *Gazette* office, and many stores, dwellings, &c., with a large amount of goods. The total loss will probably amount to two hundred thousand dollars, and scarcely any insurance. Many persons lost all, and are rendered homeless. The fire is supposed to have been the work of an incendiary.

VIRGINIA, To Wit:—At Rules held in the Clerk's office of Westmoreland County Court, on the 1st Monday in February, 1865:

John Gutridge and Elizabeth his wife, Compl'ts,

against

William A. Gutridge and Frances his wife, who was Francis Adkins; William Peed and Louisa his wife, who was Louisa Adkins; William A. Wilkins, John Wilkins, Bushrod Wilkins, Jane Wilkins, James Wilkins, Richard Wilkins, Frederick Wilkins, Lucinda Wilkins and Joseph Wilkins, the last nine of whom are infants under the age of twenty-one years, heirs at law of Lucretia Wilkins, who was Lucretia Adkins; and Joseph Adkins, and William Antony, heir at law of Sarah Antony, who was Sarah Adkins, and Benjamin Adkins, Def'ts.

IN CHANCERY.

The object of this suit is to obtain a partition of the lands belonging to the estate of James Adkins, dec'd.

It appearing by satisfactory evidence that the defendants, William Antony and Benjamin Adkins, are non-residents of this Commonwealth, and they not having been served with a copy of the process in this cause: Therefore, it is ordered that they appear here within one month after the due publication of this order, and do what is necessary to protect their interests in the premises, and that a copy of this order be published once a week for four weeks successively in the Richmond Whig, a newspaper published in the city of Richmond, and that another copy thereof be posted at the front door of the Court House of this county on the first day of the next County Court.

Teste: J. WARREN HUTT, Clerk.

WALKER, P. Q.

A copy—Teste:

mh28—law4w J. WARREN HUTT, Clerk.

THE CITY.

THE EVACUATION OF RICHMOND BY THE CONFEDERATE ARMY—ITS OCCUPATION BY THE FEDERAL FORCES—GREAT FIRE—THE ENTIRE BUSINESS PORTION OF THE CITY DESTROYED—LIVES LOST, ETC., ETC.

The evacuation of Richmond commenced in earnest Sunday night, closed at daylight on Monday morning with a terrific conflagration, which was kindled by the Confederate authorities wantonly and recklessly applying the torch to Shockoe warehouse and other buildings in which was stored a large quantity of tobacco. The fire spread rapidly, and it was some time before the Fire Brigade could be gotten to work. A fresh breeze was blowing from the South, and the fire swept over great space in an incredible short space of time. By noon the flames had transformed into a desert waste that portion of the city bounded between 7th and 15th streets, from Main street to the river, comprising the main business portion. We can form no estimate at this moment of the number of houses destroyed, but public and private they will certainly number 600 or 800.

At present we cannot do more than enumerate some of the most prominent buildings destroyed.—These include the Bank of Richmond, Traders, Bank, Bank of the Commonwealth, Bank of Virginia, Farmers' Bank, all the banking houses, the American Hotel, the Columbian Hotel, the *Enquirer* Building on 12th street, the *Dispatch* office and job rooms, corner of 13th and Main streets; all that block of buildings known as Belvin's Block, the *Examiner* office engine and machinery rooms; the Confederate Post Office Department building, the State Court House, a fine old building situated on Capitol Square, at its Franklin street entrance; the Mechanic's Institute, vacated by the Confederate States War Department, and all the buildings on that Square up to 8th street, and back to Main street; the Confederate Arsenal and Laboratory, 7th streets.

At sunrise on Monday morning, Richmond presented a spectacle that we hope never to witness again. The last of the Confederate officials had gone; the air was lurid with the smoke and flame of hundreds of houses weltering in a sea of fire.

The streets were crowded with furniture, and every description of wares, dashed down to be trampled in the mud or burned up where it lay.—All the government store houses were thrown open, and what could not be gotten off by the government, was left to the people, who every where ahead of the flames, rushed in, and secured immense amounts of bacon, clothing, boots, &c.

Next to the river, the destruction of property has been fearfully complete. The Danville and Petersburg Railroad depots, and the buildings and shedding attached thereto. For the distance of half a mile from the north side of Main street to the river, and between 8th and 15th streets, embracing upwards of twenty blocks, presents one waste of smoking ruins, blackened walls and broken chimnies.

After the surrender of the city, and its occupation by Gen. Weitzel about 10 o'clock, vigorous efforts were set on foot to stop the progress of the flames. The soldiers reinforced the fire brigade, and labored nobly, and with great success. The flames east on Main street, were checked by the blowing up of the Traders' Bank about noon.

The flames gradually died out at various points as material failed for it to feed upon; but in particular localities the work of destruction went on until towards 3 or 4 o'clock, when the mastery of the flames was obtained, and Richmond was saved from utter desolation.

LOSS OF LIFE.

We regret to learn that a serious loss of life resulted from the blowing up of the powder magazine on the suburbs early on Monday morning. The shock was tremendous, jarring every house in the city, extinguishing the gas, and breaking a great quantity of glass in dwellings. It is said that thirty or forty persons, residents of the immediate neighborhood of the magazine, were either killed or wounded, but at this writing we have been unable to obtain particulars or names.

Mr. Isaac Davenport, an old citizen, was instantly killed by the falling of a portion of the wall of the American Hotel. The body was recovered. Mr. William Royster was seriously wounded by the explosion of a shell in one of the burning buildings.

It is believed that at least several other persons were buried under falling ruins, who are as yet unknown.

THE SALOONS.

The fire made sad havoc with the saloons, and none of any account remained. We enumerate Henry Smith's, Cary and Virginia street; Charles Hunt's, "Our House," Tom Griffin's, "Congress Hall," "The Place," "The Chicamauga," and a score of others. The burning of the saloons is very distressing, as hundreds of people rendered homeless by the fire will be unable to obtain food.

THE LOSS.

Of course, we cannot be expected at this time to enter into an estimate of the losses, but they are immense, and will amount to hundreds of millions of dollars.

DESTROYING THE LIQUOR.

When it was made known on Sunday morning that the evacuation of Richmond was a foregone conclusion, the City Council held a meeting, and in secret session passed an order for the destruction of all the liquor in the city. Accordingly, about the hour of midnight the work commenced under the direction of committees of citizens in all the Wards. Hundreds of barrels of liquor were rolled into the street, and the heads knocked in.—The gutters ran with a liquor freshet, and the fumes filled and impregnated the air. Fine cases of bottled liquors were tossed into the street from third story windows, and wrecked into a thousand pieces. As the work progressed some straggling Confederate soldiers, retreating through the city, managed to get hold of a quantity of liquor. From that moment law and order ceased to exist; chaos came, and a Pandemonium reigned.

PLUNDER AND PILLAGE.

Drunk with vile liquor, the soldiers—said to belong to Garey's cavalry—roamed from store to store on Main street, followed by a reckless crowd, drunk as they. With the butts of their muskets they dashed in the plate glass of the store doors, and entering, made a wreck of everything with the celerity of magic. Jewelry stores, clothing stores, boot and hat stores, and confectionary stores were objects of special attraction to these pillagers, who, be it remembered, were not Federal soldiers, but Confederate stragglers.

The following are some of the stores thus robbed: Jennet's jewelry store, Mitchell & Tyler's jewelry store, Semons' trimming store, Antoni's confectionary store, Pizzini's confectionary store, and nnmbers of others—all on Main street.

ANOTHER FIRE.

While the conflagration that originated in Shockoe warehouse was raging, the Dibrell warehouse, located on Cary street, between 21st and 22d, and stored with tobacco, was set on fire by Confederate order, and the fire swept over several squares. The Henrico county Court House was destroyed; the clerk's office and jail were saved. Smith's tobacco factory, on 21st, and Crew's factory, on Cary and 21st streets, were also burned, besides many dwellings.

BLOWING UP OF THE GUNBOATS—BURNING OF THE NAVY YARD AND BRIDGES.

About daylight on Monday morning the city was shaken to its foundations by the explosions proceeding from the blowing up of the Confederate iron clads in the river. The Patrick Henry was in flames at Rocketts, and the Navy Yard and all the public buildings therein situated were in process of destruction. Several of the smaller vessels were burned at the city wharves.

At 6 o'clock, the evacuation having been completed as far as the Confederate army was concerned, fire was set to Mayo's bridge and the Danville Railroad bridge, and these structures were soon in flames and fell into the river.

THE DESTRUCTION OF THE MILLS.

The most wanton and unnecessary part of the general burning was the destruction of the immense flouring mills of Messrs. Haxall & Crenshaw, on the basin Bank. The Haxall Mills were the largest and most extensive of any on this continent.

THE ORDER OF THE CITY.

has been excellent since the occupation by the Federal forces. We have not heard a single complaint on the part of citizens against the soldiers, and we are glad to record that the soldiers have found no reason to complain of the conduct of the citizens. We trust this gratifying state of affairs will continue.

NORTHERN MAIL.

We understand that mail communication with New York and other points North has been established from Richmond, and that a mail will be made up twice a day—morning and evening.

LOCATION OF HEADQUARTERS.

Major General Godfrey Wetzel, commanding the United States forces occupying Richmond, has taken the mansion of Jeff. Davis, corner of 12th and Marshall streets, for his residence and headquarters.

Brigadier General G. F. Shepley, Military Governor of Richmond, has his headquarters at the capitol.

Lieutenant Colonel Manning, Provost Marshal of the Army of the James, is acting Provost Marshal of Richmond, and has his headquarters in the City Hall.

Brigadier General Devens occupies the Governor's house.

BURNING OF A CHURCH.

Rev. Dr. Read's Presbyterian church, corner of Franklin and 8th streets, was set on fire by a shell exploding in Cook's foundry, and was burned to the ground. We believe some of the church furniture was saved. We will continue an account of the fire, with names of sufferers, and losses, from day to day, until we furnish something like a connected history of the great calamity.

OFFICIAL.

HEADQUARTERS DETACHMENT ARMY JAMES,
RICHMOND, VA., April 3d, 1865.

Major General GODFREY WEITZEL, commanding Detachment of the Army of the James, announces the occupation of the city of Richmond by the Armies of the United States, under command of Lieut. Gen. Grant.—The people of Richmond are assured that we come to restore to them the blessings of peace, prosperity and freedom, under the Flag of the Union.

The citizens of Richmond are requested to remain for the present quietly within their houses, and to avoid all public assemblages or meetings in the public streets.—An efficient Provost Guard will immediately re-establish order and tranquility within the city.

Martial law is, for the present, proclaimed.

Brigadier General George F. Shepley, United States Volunteers, is hereby appointed Military Governor of Richmond.

Lieutenant Colonel Fred. L. Manning, Provost Marshal General, Army of the James, will act as Provost Marshal of Richmond. Commanders of detachments doing guard duty in the city will report to him for instructions.

By command of Major General WEITZEL.

D. D. WHEELER, A. A. G.

HDQ'RS MILITARY GOVERNOR OF RICHMOND,
RICHMOND, VA., April 3, 1865.

I. The armies of the rebellion having abandoned their effort to ENSLAVE the people of Virginia, have endeavored to destroy by fire the Capitol which they could not longer occupy by their arms. Lieut. Col. Manning, Provost Marshal General of the Army of the James and Provost Marshal of Richmond, will immediately send a sufficient detachment of the Provost Guard to arrest, if possible, the progress of the flames. The Fire Department of the city of Richmond, and all the citizens interested in the preservation of their beautiful city, will immediately report to him for duty and render every possible assistance in staying the progress of the conflagration. The first duty of the Armies of the Union will be to save the city, doomed to destruction by the armies of the rebellion.

II. No person will leave the city of Richmond without a pass from the office of the Provost Marshal.

III. Any citizen, soldier, or any person whatever, who shall hereafter plunder, destroy or remove any public or private property, of any description whatever, will be arrested and summarily punished.

IV. The soldiers of the command will abstain from any offensive or insulting words or gestures towards the citizens.

V. No treasonable or offensive expressions insulting to the flag, the cause, or the armies of the Union, will hereafter be allowed.

VI. For an exposition of their rights, duties and privileges, the citizens of Richmond are respectfully referred to the proclamatious of the President of the United States in relation to the existing rebellion.

VII. All persons having in their possession, or under their control, any property whatever, of the so called Confederate States, or of any officer thereof, or the records or archives of any public officer whatever, will immediately report the same to Colonel Manning, Provost Marshal.

In conclusion, the citizens of Richmond are assured that, with the restoration of the Flag of the Union, they may expect the restoration of that peace, prosperity and happiness which they enjoyed under that Union, of which that flag is the glorious symbol.

G. F. SHEPLEY,
Brigadier General U. S. Volunteers, and
Military Governor of Richmond.

HDQ'RS MILITARY GOVERNOR OF RICHMOND,
RICHMOND, VA., April 3d, 1865.

GENERAL ORDER, No. 2.

No officer or soldier will enter or search any private dwelling, or remove any property therefrom, without a written order from the Headquarters of the Commanding General, the Military Governor, or the Provost Marshal General.

Any officer or soldier, with or without such order, entering any private dwelling, will give his name, rank and regiment.

Any officer or soldier entering a private dwelling without such authority, or failing to give his name, rank or regiment, or reporting the same incorrectly, will be liable to immediate and summary punishment.

G. F. SHEPLEY,
Brigadier General U. S. Volunteers, and
Military Governor of Richmond.

COMMISSIONER WATSON'S OFFICE,
RICHMOND, 2d March, 1865.

VIRGINIA.—In the Circuit Court of the City of Richmond, February 28th, 1865:

Elizabeth Selden Wickham, Maclurg Wickham, and John Wickham, administrators of James M. Wickham, dec'd, and in their own right, and other, Plt'ffs,

against

Julia Leigh, in her own right and as executrix of Benjamin Watkins Leigh, who was executor and trustee of John Wickham, deceased, and administrator de bonis non of James Maclurg, deceased, and other, Def'ts.

Maclurg Wickham and John Wickham, in their own right and as administrators of James M. Wickham, dec'd Plt'ffs,

against

Elizabeth S. Wickham, William Fanning Wickham and other, Def'ts.

and

Julia Leigh, Plt'ff,

and

William F. Wickham, in his own right and as executor of John Wickham, deceased, and as administrator de bonis non with the will annexed of James Maclurg, deceased, and of Walter Maclurg, deceased, and as administrator of Elizabeth Selden Wickham, deceased, and of Betsy Wickham, deceased, and other. Def'ts.

On the motion of Maclurg Wickham and John Wickham, administrators of James Maclurg Wickham, the Court doth order that William F. Watson do continue down their accounts as administrators as aforesaid, and report thereon to the Court, with such matters as he may deem pertinent or be required by any of the parties to these causes to state specially. And the Court doth direct that notice of the time and place of taking the accounts be published once a week for four successive weeks in the Richmond Whig, and that such publication be equivalent to personal service on the parties.

A copy—Teste,

BENJ. POLLARD, Clerk.

The parties to the said cases will please to take notice, that I have fixed upon Monday, the 3d day of April next, at the hour of 12 M. as the time, and this office as the place; when and where I shall proceed to discharge the duties required of me by the said decree. The parties interested can attend.

mh 3—w4w WM. F. WATSON, Comm'r.

The Philadelphia Inquirer.

PRICE TWO CENTS. PHILADELPHIA, TUESDAY, APRIL 4, 1865. PRICE TWO CENTS.

RICHMOND!

Babylon Is Fallen!!

GENERAL WEITZEL OCCUPIES THE CITY!

Philadelphia Colored Troops the First to Enter!

THE FLEEING REBELS FIRE THEIR CAPITAL.

Weitzel's Negroes Extinguish the Flames.

THE "INDOMITABLE ULYSSES" MARCHING ON.

Lee's Army In Full Retreat!

OUR FORCES CLOSE ON THEIR HEELS.

Enormous Losses of the Rebels!

OFFICIAL DESPATCHES FROM PRESIDENT LINCOLN.

The Whole Country in a Blaze of Enthusiasm!

JUBILEE AT THE NATIONAL CAPITAL.

Speeches by Stanton and Seward.

SPECIAL CORRESPONDENCE FROM THE FRONT.

OFFICIAL WAR GAZETTE.

FIRST BULLETIN.

WASHINGTON, April 3.—To Major-General Dix, New York:—The following telegram from the President, announcing the evacuation of Petersburg, and probably of Richmond, has just been received by the War Department,

E. M. STANTON, Secretary of War.

CITY POINT, Va., April 3.—Hon. E. M. Stanton, Secretary of War:—This morning General Grant reports Petersburg evacuated, and is confident Richmond also is. He is pushing forward to cut off, if possible, the retreating army.

A. LINCOLN.

SECOND BULLETIN.

Richmond is Ours.

WASHINGTON, April 3, 10·45 A. M.—Major-General Dix:—It appears from a despatch of General Weitzel, just received by this Department, that our forces under his command are in Richmond, having taken it at 8·15 this morning.

E. M. STANTON, Secretary of War.

THIRD BULLETIN.

Confirmation of the Capture of Richmond.

WASHINGTON, April 3, 12 M.—To Major-General Dix, New York:—The following official confirmation of the capture of Richmond, and announcing that the city is on fire, has just been received by this Department.

CITY POINT, Va., April 3, 11 A. M.—General Weitzel telegraphs as follows:—

"We took Richmond at 8.15 this morning. I captured many guns. The enemy left in great haste.

"The city is on fire in one place. We are making every effort to put it out.

"The people received us with enthusiastic expressions of joy.

"General Grant started early this morning, with the army, towards the Danville road, to cut off Lee's retreating army, if possible.

President Lincoln has gone to the front.

(Signed) T. S. BOWERS, Asst. Adjt.-Gen.

E. M. STANTON, Secretary of War.

FROM GRANT'S VICTORIOUS ARMY.

Special Correspondence of the Inquirer.

HEAD-QUARTERS ARMY OF THE POTOMAC, Saturday, April 1, 1865—Midnight.

From out of the "wilderness" of scrub oaks, dwarf pines, swamps, ravines and knolls, through and over which our lines stretch, some intelligible idea of our operations yesterday begin to be apparent. This State of Virginia is worth fighting for as embodying a political principle; but as so many acres of ground, it is not worth one single human life. We thought at the Wilderness that we had reached the acme of all that was horrible and miserable and perplexing in the aspect of nature, but then we had not seen the country sou hwest of Petersburg. A tangled mass of ravines and hillocks, of small streamlets running in all possible directions, of little by-roads shooting off to every point of the compass, seeming to come from nowhere, and to be leading nowhere, intersecting each other at every conceivable angle of dense forests of the meanest and most detestable kind of scrub oak and pine; picture this, and throw in here and there a worn-out open field, with an old dilapidated farm-house in the centre, and you have a faint picture of the difficulties of the country in which we are operating. Out of this knotted mass the "special" must pluck the salient points for the information of the public; must ride miles on miles even to see the front of one Corps, and visit its various head-quarters, and tired, at night must write out what he has seen, what heard, what opines from both; is it any wonder that under circumstances like these his accounts are sometimes vague, sometimes unsatisfactory. Give him a fight like Fort Steadman, where he knows the ground, and where the ground is open, he does well enough. Put him in the kind of country we are in now and he does as well as he can.

Premising that the day has been comparatively quiet on the right of our offensive line, composed of the Second and Twenty-fourth Corps, it is the intention first to give the public some idea of

The Relative Position of the Two Armies.

A battle, fierce, sanguinary and decisive, may come off any day on this very ground, and the people will take a natural interest in a section that has already become historic, and may become sacred in the nation's calendar.

First, it must be premised that our old line in front of Petersburg, from the Appomattox to the left of the Weldon Road, remains intact and held precisely as they were before our present movement was initiated, running, until yesterday, to Hatcher's Run, but changed from Fort Sampson to the left, by the advance of the Twenty-fourth Corps, consequent upon the capture of the enemy's intrenched picket line.

From Petersburg to Hatcher's Run, by the Vaughn Road is seven and a half miles, and by the Boydton Road seven miles. The Fifth Corps front is a prolongation of our line beyond the Boydton Road, with the cavalry beyond them again, the line facing generally northeast, the flank being towards the South Side Road, from the bend of the road to the southwest.

Thus much by way of necessary preface. It remains to sketch events to the present moment, and beginning on the right with

The Twenty-fourth Corps,

Two divisi[illegible] of which, those of Turner and Foster [illegible] ney's), all under the command of Major-General Gibbons, are operating here. Birney's Division has been held as a reserve thus far. Foster is on the right of the Twenty-fourth, then Turner, forming connection with Hayes, holding the right of the Second Corps. Along General Gibbons' front the day has been quiet. This morning just before daybreak the Rebels essayed an attack upon Turner's pickets, coming in the old yelling style, but they quickly came to grief. Turner's line did not budge an inch, except to gather in sixty of the adventurous Rebels as prisoners and to kill and maim some few more. The prisoners sent to the rear, Turner's line quietly composed itself again, and during the remainder of the day the Rebels behaving themselves well, and we not yet being ready to disturb the apparent peacefulness of the neighborhood, it has been quiet until about 9·30 P. M., when a brisk cannonading begun and yet continues (10·20 P. M.). What it means it is impossible to-night to say. It seems by the sound to be general, on the Sixth Corps front as well as the Twenty-fourth, and an occasional distant rumble from the right indicates that the Ninth Corps is also adding to the uproar.

Passing still to the left, and

The Second Corps,

The day has been as peaceful as on the right. Occasional picket skirmishing has been going on, but nothing more serious in the way of fighting. The men of the Corps have been busy, however, building roads to the rear, cutting timber to the front for the artillery to get range, and other work preliminary to action. While mentioning roads it is but justice to notice the labors of the Chiefs of pioneers of the several divisions; Captain G. W. Cook, Sixty-first New York, of the First, Captain H. Y. Russell, of the Second, and Captain Charles Bowers, Eighth New Jersey, of the Third, whose tasks, although herculean and apparently impossible, have been successfully accomplished. Energy will accomplish wonders, and the energy of these officers has already made passable the impassable country around Dabney's Mills and beyond, substantial corduroy roads now cutting the country in every direction, and rendering access to the various parts of the line easy and sure.

Just beyond night the Second Division line was advanced somewhat, being pushed close up to the Rebel fort at Hatcher Run, General Smythe covering it with his musketry so entirely that the Rebels cannot use its guns. Were it not for the very extensive slashing in front of this line, both before the Second and Twenty-fourth Corps, we could easily carry it by assault, but this slashing is so intricate that men can hardly crawl through it singly, and it would be impossible to maintain a line of battle through it under anything like a respectable fire.

General Mott still holds his position on the left of General Hayes, and presses as close upon the Rebel line as his confrere, but his line, like that of Hayes, has been quiet.

General Miles still stretches across the Boydton Road in the position occupied yesterday. His fight yesterday was a brilliant one, and answered fully the purpose for which it was begun, being a diversion in favor of the Fifth Corps. His onslaught upon their line near Burgess Mill induced the Rebels to hurry men to the threatened point, and thus gave Warren and Sheridan less to contend against.

General Humphries was heard of to-day, only on his skirmish line. He is determined to know exactly the position of the enemy on the front of his corps, and so he goes where he can see it.

Proceeding still to the left with the story of to-day, I take up

The Fifth Corps.

The operations of Gen. Warren yeste[r]day have already reached you. This morning early the Corps moved off on the Boydton Road. Griffin in advance, then Ayres next, Crawford north about two miles, and taking a road running nearly west, came in contact with the enemy near what the Rebels call Five Points, which, so near as it can be located with the assistance of imperfect maps, is from three to four miles northwest of Dinwiddie Court House.

In the afternoon General Warren got into line, with Griffin on the right, Ayres on the centre and Crawford on the left. It should be remembered here that this movement cut Sheridan and Warren off from all connection with the remainder of our army, and their fighting this afternoon has been an entirely independent affair. The distance at which the corps has been engaged, the difficulties of communication have been such that it is impossible to more than outline the affair, if even that can be done. Artillery was but little used, but the musketry was terrific along the whole line. The battle began at five in the afternoon, and by dark, when it ceased, the firing had receded far beyond the point of beginning, showing that our forces had driven the enemy from the field. The extent of our success, the relative losses of the contending forces, and other details necessary to a full knowledge of the history enacted to-day, it is impossible to send. The country in that section of Virginia corresponds to what surrounds us here, except that it is level. There are the same swamps, the same horrible pine forests, the same treacherous soil. Is this whole State of Virginia nothing but a wilderness of worn-out farms, swamps and pineries?

General Sheridan,

Moving this morning upon the left flank of Warren with the three cavalry divisions, has been, to-day at his old business of driving the Rebels before him. Custer, Devins and Davis have again proved themselves soldiers of mettle, but here, as with the Fifth Corps, we are without details. We know that Sheridan drove the enemy before him up the Boydton Road, and over the country to the neighborhood of Five Points; that he fought his infantry as well as cavalry in connection with the Fifth Corps, the battery attached to Custer's Division doing the most of the artillery work, and we are certain that the day has been a triumph for Sheridan and the Fifth Corps, but we know no more. The fighting has been an open field fight, and has occurred so near the South Side Railroad that a radical defeat there necessitates our occupancy of the road, and although no news of the event has reached us here, the probabilities are that the cavalry and the Fifth Corps are already engaged in the work of tearing it to flinders. The distance from Five Points to the South Side Road is only about a mile and a half, and a defeat there is fatal to the railroad.

General Grant

Still has his head-quarters at Dabney Mills. That impertubable face of his tells no tales whatever; things may be all right or all wrong, but not a line of his countenance betrays the knowledge to the observer, hence we get no news from looking at him.

General Meade

Was, this afternoon, at a point above a mile to the right of the Vaughn road, and the same distance to the left of Hatcher Run. This meeting of Generals Grant and Meade at so near the angle made by the Rebels at Hatcher Run indicates stirring work in its neighborhood tomorrow.

General Ord

Has established his head-quarters at Humphries' Station, and is in charge of our whole old line, from Hatcher Run to the Appomattox, as well as his own line on the Bermuda Hundred front and on the north of the James.

What of

The Enemy

During all these movements of ours? Longstreet's Corps, composed of the divisions of Pickett, Constant and Kershaw, have been transferred from the north of the James to our extreme left, and, together with Fitzhugh Lee's cavalry, seven thousand strong, has been fighting Sheridan and Warren to-day. Hill's Corps and Bushrod Johnson's division of Anderson's Corps are opposite the Second and Twenty-fourth Corps, and Gordon's Corps opposite the Sixth and Ninth. What they have got opposite Weitzel, north of the James, it is hard to say, as their whole army is already accounted for, except one division of Anderson's Corps.

The heavy cannonading spoken of in the early part of this letter still (midnight) continues unabated along the whole front of the Sixth and Ninth Corps, and news has just reached me that is preliminary to an assault in front of Petersburg, ordered to be made by the Sixth and Ninth Corps at daylight in the morning. I may possibly yet close this letter by the announcement of the capture of the long beleaguered city.

Later.

April 2, 6 A. M.—The news from Sheridan and Warren this morning is that the victory is overwhelming. The South Side Road in our possession, Longstreet's Corps utterly broken to pieces. We having more prisoners than we can take care of.

The tremendous cannonading, which began last night at 10½ o'clock, yet continues. No assault has yet been made.

E. CRAPSEY.

RICHMOND!

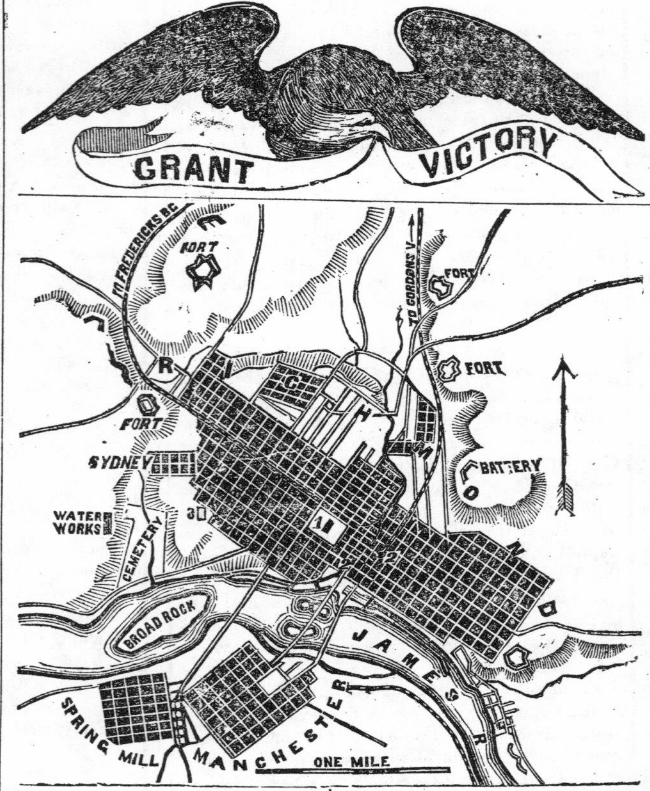

RICHMOND.

The Different Campaigns Against the Rebel Capital.

How Ulysses S. Gr[an]t (Unconditional Surrender Grant) [T]ook the Rebel Strong[h]old.

Richmond, the great hot-b[illegible] of Secession and months of anxious expectatio[n] through which we have passed, it is difficult to realize that the skillful plans and manœuvrings of "the indomitable Ulysses," have at length been crowned with success. And at this important stage of the war, with the capital of the enemy in our hands, and his main army broken and scattered, it may not be unprofitable to cast a cursory glance at the campaigns heretofore conducted against the Rebel capital.

At the first outbreak of the Rebellion, flushed with the cowardly firing on the national standard at Fort Sumter, and over-confident of success, the popular cry of "On to Richmond" was raised, and our legions were hurried into the disastrous battle of Bull Run, in July, 1861. With its dearly bought experience ended the first campaign against the beleaguered city which now lies at the mercy of our colored troops.

Then it was that McCLELLAN was placed in charge of our panic-stricken forces, and, after organizing and disciplining them, once more they were led "on to Richmond." The "Seven Days' Battles," the famous series of engagements presenting the strange military anomaly of seven distinct victories, combining to constitute a defeat, followed, ending in a second disastrous retreat in July, 1862. The enemy then assumed the offensive, and so continued a forward movement northward until his check at Antietam in September of that year. The campaign which was ended by that battle showed McCLELLAN to be so entirely outgeneraled by LEE that he was removed by the Government, and succeeded by General BURNSIDE.

On the 15th of December 1863, the new commander commenced the third movement against the Rebel capital. Defeated in the memorable battle of Fredericksburg on the 13th of December, BURNSIDE was replaced by HOOKER, who, after the terrible battle of Chancellorsville, May 2 and 3, 1863, was in turn superseded by General MEADE. When the latter, under the orders of the President, took command, on the 28th of June 1863, his army was mainly concentrated at Frederick, Md. The enemy we[illegible] advancing on Harrisburg, Pa., as obliged to assume the defensive, until by his brilliant victory at Gettysburg, the first of July, the enemy were sent "whirling" back from whence they came. It was not, however, until the 1st of December, that MEADE crossed the Rapidan and inaugurated the fifth campaign against Richmond.

Little was done, however, until early in March, 1864, when "Unconditional Surrender GRANT," who had just been commissioned as Lieutenant-General of the Army of the United States, assumed command of the Army of the Potomac. Activity at once became the order of the day, and on the 4th of May he moved against the enemy. Then it was that the great series of movements was inaugurated that have just culminated in a success whose magnitude has almost frenzied with joy the loyal people of the land. It is unnecessary to recapitulate the great events that have transpired in the working out of the Lieutenant-General's plan of advance. The great battles of the Wilderness, in May, satisfied the Federal Commander that it was by slow and gradual advances that his end was to be gained, and not by hasty or precipitate movements. His strategic operations were commenced, and now, after four long and weary years of conflict for the nation, he has the satisfaction of announcing to his Government the capture of the hitherto impregnable Rebel stronghold, Richmond. All honor to him and to his gallant band of heroes. Long will their deeds of patriotism and daring be remembered, and imperishable will be the record they have inscribed on the pages of the book of fame and national glory.

THE GREAT STRUGGLE

Army of the Potomac

SHERIDAN'S TERRIBLE FIGHT.

Fifth Corps Goes to His Aid!

LEE'S FORCES FALL RAPIDLY BACK!

His Dead and Wounded Left In Our Hands.

Sheridan Takes 4000 Prisoners

A NUMBER OF CANNON CAPTURED!

The Rebels on the Full Retreat!

SOUTH SIDE RAILROAD SEVERED

Lee Hemmed In On All Points!

Details of Saturday's Movements.

HEAD-QUARTERS OF THE ARMY OF THE POTOMAC, April 1.—The greater portion of this army has not been engaged with the enemy to-day, the time being occupied in erecting works on the new line, and repairing the roads connecting the different corps.

The late rains rendered it impossible to move the wagon trains as fast as the troops advanced, one train taking forty-eight hours to move five miles, one thousand men assisting. But through the untiring energy and perseverance of the officers in charge of the Quartermaster and Commissary Departments the army has been almost as well supplied as while in their old quarters.

When the news of Sheridan's repulse reached here last evening, a part of the Fifth Corps was at once despatched to his aid, and it is expected that to-night or in the morning we shall receive

It appears from that quar[ter] was moving on the road leading to a place called the Five Forks, which is about three miles from the South Side Railroad, when two brigades of Pickett's Division, which had been ordered in a great hurry, came down on a road which runs from Sutherland Station to the one on which we were.

Sheridan's cavalry having, for the most part, passed the junction, this movement of the enemy threatened to cut him off. He, however, discovered his danger in time to get to his command with only a slight loss, at the same time taking about one hundred prisoners.

Both of the Lees were present, but one of them at a respectful distance. On being reinforced this morning by the Fifth Corps, the enemy fell back so rapidly that their dead and many of their wounded fell into our hands, as well as those of our own unavoidably left behind yesterday afternoon.

The attack made on the enemy's line in front of the Twenty-fourth Corps was by Foster's Division, and about 200 prisoners were brought in, the One-hundred-and-forty-eighth New York taking the most of them.

Some three hundred or four hundred yards of ground was taken from them, and our picket line so much further advanced. At 4 A. M. this position was assaulted, and a few of our men captured, but in a very short time it was retaken with about sixty prisoners and a stand of colors.

Our loss up to the present time will not exceed 2500, while that of the enemy on some parts of the line at least was greater than our own, but of course the total cannot be given. Major Dickinson, of the Fifteenth New York Heavy Artillery, is wounded and a prisoner.

The sharp-shooters brought into the Fifth Corps head-quarters this morning sixteen cavalrymen, belonging to William Henry Lee's command. They had been on picket, and were cut off by the force which went to the assistance of Sheridan.

[SECOND DESPATCH.]

HEAD-QUARTERS ARMY OF THE POTOMAC, April 1, Midnight.—A courier from Sheridan has just arrived with the most cheering news. The combined forces of cavalry and Warren's infantry advanced against the enemy this afternoon, driving them several miles, and capturing about four thousand prisoners and a number of guns.

They retreated to Five Forks, where they were flanked by a part of the Fifth Corps, which had moved down the White Oak road. It was here the large number of prisoners were taken. The Rebels then retreated south, along the White Oak Road, and were vigorously pursued by General Sheridan, while McKensil's cavalry, from the Army of the James, advanced west on the Ford Road, toward the South Side Road, and after the messenger left was only about three miles from it, and would undoubtedly reach it before morning.

Thus the last great line of railroad the Rebels have to supply their capital and Lee's army is about to be severed, and it is firmly believed they will immediately leave their present positions at Petersburg and Richmond.

Sharp cannonading is now going on near the centre of the line held by the left of the Sixth Corps.

Ice Freshet on the St. Lawrence.

MONTREAL, April 3.—The river rose several feet on Saturday and was piled with ice to a great height. One of the shoves came near striking a tube of the Victoria Bridge. Yesterday morning the river rose much higher, flooding Williams, Wellington, and other streets. Between five and six o'clock in the evening the ice shoved again, and the water rushed over the revetment wall, flooding Commission street. At about 11 o'clock it again rose as high as St. Paul and St. Giles streets.

The Grand Trunk Railroad between Bonaventure and the Tanneries is inundated.

This morning the inundated points of the city are covered with rafts formed with scows and boats.

At present by far the greater part of the Western portion of the city is inaccessible, except by boats. The flood is causing the greatest suffering and distress.

LATER.—Four o'clock P. M.—The water is slowly falling.

St. Domingo.

NEW YORK, April 3.—Advices received to-day from San Domingo deny the rumors of a counter revolution there. The Republic is free from any tumult, and the new Government is quietly organizing.

General F. de Rojas has been elected President, and nine eminent Dominicans, seven of them Generals in the army, have been appointed as his Cabinet or advisers. Among them are Antonio Polonco, brother of the President. A sovereign Constitutional Congress consisting of nine representatives from each commune has been called, and was to have been convened at Santiago de Caller[illegible]

New-York Daily Tribune.

VOL. XXIV.....No. 7,486. NEW-YORK, TUESDAY, APRIL 4, 1865. PRICE FOUR CENTS.

VIRGINIA!

Richmond and Petersburg Taken!

Colored Troops the First to Enter the Slaveholders' Capital.

THE REBELS LEAVE IN HASTE.

Gen. Grant Attempting to Cut Off Lee's Escape.

A PORTION OF RICHMOND ON FIRE!

The Citizens Welcome the Union Troops.

Details of the Late Battles from Our Correspondents.

THE ENTHUSIASM OF THE NORTH.

Official Dispatches.

WAR DEPARTMENT, WASHINGTON, Monday April 3—10 a. m.

To Major-Gen. DIX: The following telegram from the President, announcing the EVACUATION OF PETERSBURG and probably of RICHMOND, has just been received by this Department.

EDWIN M. STANTON, Secretary of War.

CITY POINT, Va., Monday, April 3—9:30 a. m.

To the Hon. EDWIN M. STANTON, *Sec. of War.*

This morning Lieut.-Gen. Grant reports Petersburg evacuated, and he is confident that Richmond also is evacuated.

He is pushing forward to cut off, if possible, the retreating Rebel army. A. LINCOLN.

SECOND DISPATCH.

WAR DEPARTMENT, WASHINGTON, D. C., Monday, April 3—10 a. m.

To Major-Gen. DIX: It appears from a dispatch of Gen. Weitzel's, just received by this Department, that our forces under his command ARE IN RICHMOND, having taken it at 8:15 this morning. EDWIN M. STANTON, Secretary of War.

THIRD DISPATCH.

WAR DEPARTMENT, WASHINGTON, Monday, April 3—12 m.

To Major-Gen. DIX: The following official confirmation of the capture of Richmond, and the announcement that the city is on fire, has been received. E. M. STANTON, Secretary of War.

CITY POINT, Va., Monday, April 3—11 a. m.

To EDWIN M. STANTON, *Secretary of War.*

Gen. Weitzel telegraphs as follows:

"We took Richmond at 8:15 this morning. I captured many guns. The enemy left in great haste. The city is on fire in one place. Am making every effort to put it out.

"The people receive us with enthusiastic expressions of joy.

"Gen. Grant started early this morning with the army, toward the Danville road, to cut off Lee's retreating army, if possible.

"President Lincoln has gone to the front."

T. S. BOWERS, A. A. Gen.

FROM OUR SPECIAL CORRESPONDENTS.

Full Details of the Fighting.

Special Dispatch to The N. Y. Tribune.

WASHINGTON, Monday, April 3, 1865.

Capt. Ira M. Burritt, former staff officer in the Army of the Potomac, now chief special correspondent of *The Cincinnati Gazette* in that army, arrived at the front one day after the fighting began. His account of matters down to the 2d instant is, therefore, a little delayed, but it is so concise and clear as to still warrant transmission in full.

PREPARATORY OPERATIONS.

HDQRS. ARMY OF THE POTOMAC, April 1—10 p.m.

As you doubtless have accounts of the operations in progress here up to yesterday, I will confine myself to a brief synopsis.

The heaviest fighting has been done by the Fifth Corps and Sheridan's Cavalry.

THE FIFTH CORPS.

On Wednesday morning the Fifth Corps moved down the Halifax road and crossed Rowanty Creek, taking then a south-westerly course until it reached the Vaughan road. It moved up the Vaughan to the Quaker Road, turned to the right, keeping on this road until within a mile of the Boydtown Plank-road, when they met the enemy. Gen. Griffin, with the First Division attacked, and Gen. Crawford forming the Third Division on Griffin's left, met the enemy on the Butler farm, but pushed them back and reached the Boydtown road.

ON THURSDAY

morning the whole Fifth Corps line advanced across the Boydtown road with little opposition. In the afternoon Gen. Ayres, commanding the Second Division, moved one brigade across Gravelly Run and kept it there during the night.

FRIDAY.

The next morning Ayres's whole division crossed the Run, supported by Gen. Crawford's. After advancing a mile or more through a wooded country, broken occasionally into small clearings, the enemy was discovered in force. Gen. Ayres advanced Winthrop's Brigade, while the rest of his division and that of Gen. Crawfords were forming in the rear.

A REBEL ATTACK.

Before they had completed the deployment, however, and while the greater part of the Third Division was yet in mass, Johnson's Rebel Division charged Winthrop's single brigade, driving it back in some disorder, while at the same time Pickett's Division struck our two divisions in the left flank, attacking with more than its usual impetuosity.

FALLING BACK.

Both Ayres's and Crawford's men fought stubbornly, but at length fell back across the run, where the First Division and several batteries of artillery, which had been placed in position by Gen. Warren, covered the crossing, and drove back the enemy, who advanced incautiously with heavy loss.

A SECOND ADVANCE.

About two o'clock p. m. the whole Corps again advanced over the same ground, retaking all the positions from which they had been driven in the morning, and moved forward to White Oak Road, some two miles beyond Gravelly Run, capturing a battle-flag and a number of prisoners. In this position the troops rested during the night.

SATURDAY.

This (Saturday) morning at seven o'clock the Fifth Corps was again in motion, passing to the left, along the White Oak Road, to join Gen. Sheridan.

A DIFFICULT MOVEMENT.

They have executed the difficult movement of marching by a flank in the presence of the enemy, withdrawing the divisions in rear of each other, and marching them off successively from right to left, the left division (Crawford's) executing the same movement by brigade.

CONDUCT OF TROOPS.

The conduct of the troops has been above praise. Their loss has been severe in killed and wounded, the wounded being the heaviest in the Third Division, but was next to nothing in prisoners.

THE IRON BRIGADE.

The remnant of the old Iron Brigade of Crawford's Division, composed of the 6th and 7th Wisconsin with the 91st New-York, lately attached, commanded by Col. John A. Kellogg of the 6th, sustained their previous reputation.

BRAVE OFFICERS.

Brevet Lieut.-Col. D. B. Dailey of the 6th Wisconsin, commanded the 147th New-York in the Third Brigade, and together with Major H. A. Laycock of the veteran 56th Penn., was conspicuous for refusing to dismount and riding at the head of the brigade in the charge. Col. Dailey had his right hand shattered by a bullet early in the day, but insisted on leading his command in the afternoon.

SECOND CORPS.

While these events were taking place the Second Corps moved toward White Oak road by a more direct route from the left of our intrenchments than that taken by the Fifth, and established a connection with the right of the latter. It was sharply engaged yesterday, but lost less than the Fifth. Gen. Humphreys now occupies the line vacated by Warren's movement to the support of Sheridan, having extended to the left for that purpose.

GEN. SHERIDAN.

Meanwhile Sheridan, with four cavalry divisions, Custer's, Merritt's, Crooks and Kautz's, passing around the left of the whole army, went through Dinwiddie Court House, and toward the Southside road, with his usual rapidity.

THE REBELS WATCHING HIM.

The force which drove Crawford and Ayres across Gravelly Run, however, at once turned their attention to him, moving rapidly to the right, and after a desperate conflict he also was forced back within a mile of Dinwiddie Court-house.

AGAIN ON THE WAR PATH.

This morning he again took the initiative, however, having been joined by Gen. Warren, and has been driving in his turn. Heavy firing both of artillery and musketry could be heard away on the left at nightfall this evening showing that he and Warren are there at work, and at this late hour the booming of artillery in that direction is incessant. Some discharges of musketry have also taken place along the Second Corps to-night, as well as cannonading in the direction of the Appomattox. Everything is going well, and officers and men alike are hopeful of the result of the great crash which will come to-morrow.

PREPARATION FOR SUNDAY.

Gen. Wright is to attack with the whole Sixth Corps at 4 o'clock to-morrow.

LATER

April 2, 4 o'clock, a. m.

SUCCESS OF SHERIDAN.

The last heard from Sheridan was about midnight. He was then at Five Forks, the junction of the White Oak and Ford roads. He and Warren had taken about four thousand prisoners and several batteries of artillery. He was joined last evening by Miles's Division of the Second corps, and with the four corps of cavalry and four of infantry he pushed westward for the Southside road, which he is expected to reach at an early hour this forenoon.

CASUALTY.

Brevet Brig. Gen. Fred. Winthrop was killed during the fighting of the Fifth Corps yesterday.

THE REBELS ACTIVE.

Several attempts have been made during the early part of the night to break through the lines of the Second Corps on our left. Gen. Miles has retaliated with a demonstration which reached the abatis in front of the Rebel works along White Oak road. About 2 o'clock a. m. the Rebels made a prolonged and desperate assault upon the part of our line held by Gen. Ord on the right of the Second Corps.

LOSSES.

Our losses day before yesterday are reported at 1,500 killed and wounded, and a few prisoners. Owing to the lateness of the hour to which fighting was kept up last evening on the left, no accurate estimate of the casualties can be made as yet.

LEE'S ARMY.

Prisoners taken from all the corps of Lee's army show that it has not been weakened by sending a single division south.

SHORT OF CANNON.

As I write the opening volleys of Wright's charge in front of Fort Fisher are heard. The amount of artillery in use shows a scarcity of cannon on the Rebel side.

Whether Wright is successful or not, few fears are entertained that Sheridan will take the Southside Railroad.

Saturday's Fighting—Continued Success.

Special Dispatch to The N. Y. Tribune.

WASHINGTON, Monday, April 3, 1865.

One of our special correspondents (F. D.) in the Army of the Potomac, under date of April 2, a. m., writes as follows:

GRANT'S HEADQUARTERS.

Gen. Grant yesterday moved his headquarters to the Vaughan road, about half a mile west of Hatcher's Run.

SUCCESS OF SHERIDAN.

Glorious news has just arrived from Sheridan. He has struck the Southside Railroad, which he now holds. In the engagement yesterday afternoon he captured 4,000 prisoners and several batteries of artillery.

THE FIFTH CORPS.

The Fifth Corps, which was supporting the cavalry, have also taken 15 guns and about 2,000 prisoners, enabling Sheridan to drive back the force which in the latter part of yesterday checked his advance in the vicinity of Dinwiddie Court-House.

AN ATTACK ORDERED.

On receiving this news it was determined to give the enemy no time to send troops to their right, and at once a simultaneous attack was ordered all along the lines by the Ninth, Sixth, Twenty-fourth and Second Corps.

ITS SUCCESS.

The order was given about nine o'clock at night, and in less than an hour a furious assault began on the Rebel intrenchments in the fronts of their several commands, resulting in the enemy being driven in confusion from their first into their second line of works, with a loss of over 5,000 prisoners, several forts and about 20 pieces of artillery.

THE SECOND CORPS

was engaged all day with the enemy in their front, and in spite of the terrible fire of musketry poured into

See Eighth Page.

THE FIELD OF OPERATIONS IN VIRGINIA.

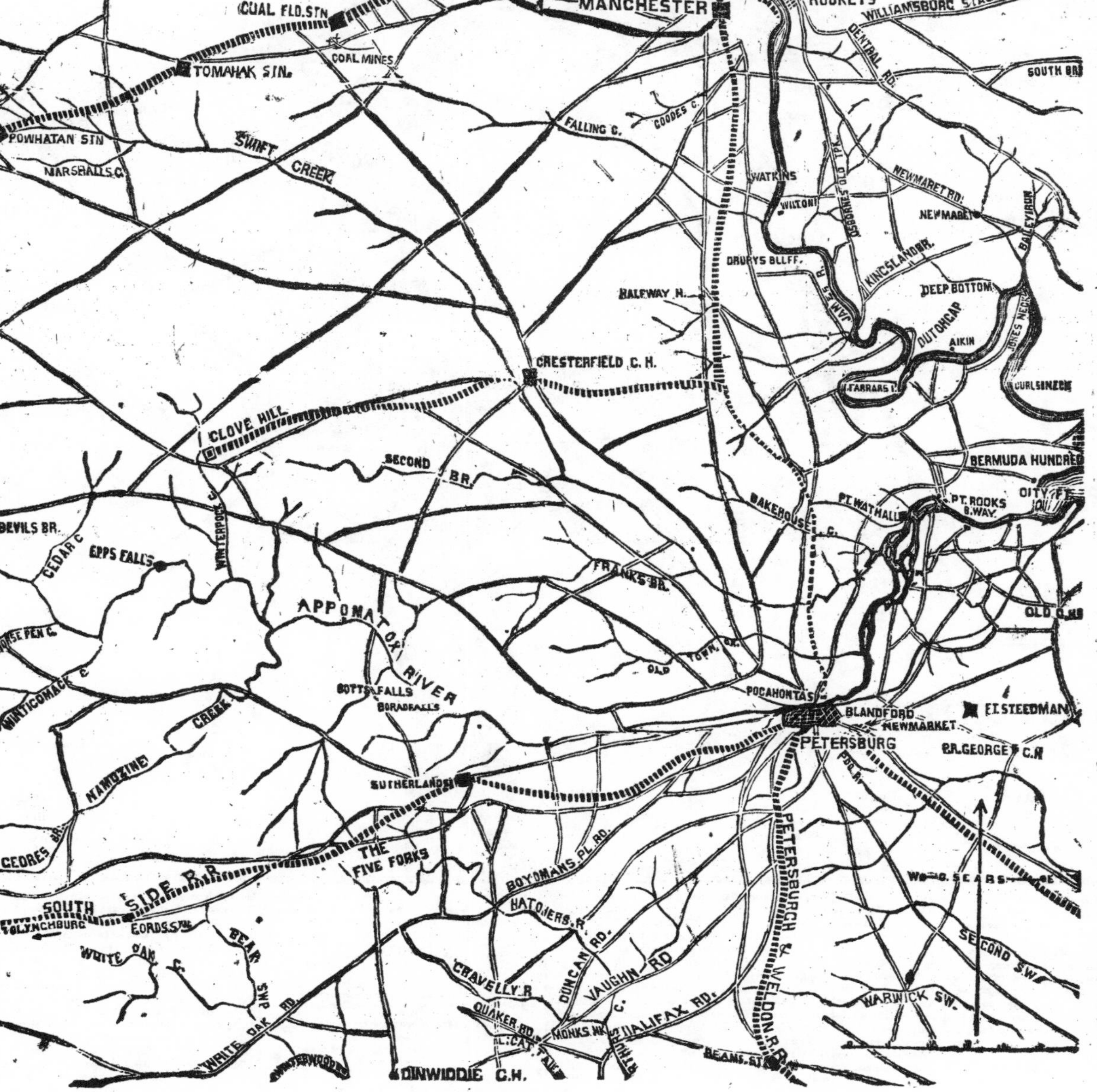

RICHMOND, AND THIRTY MILES AROUND IT.

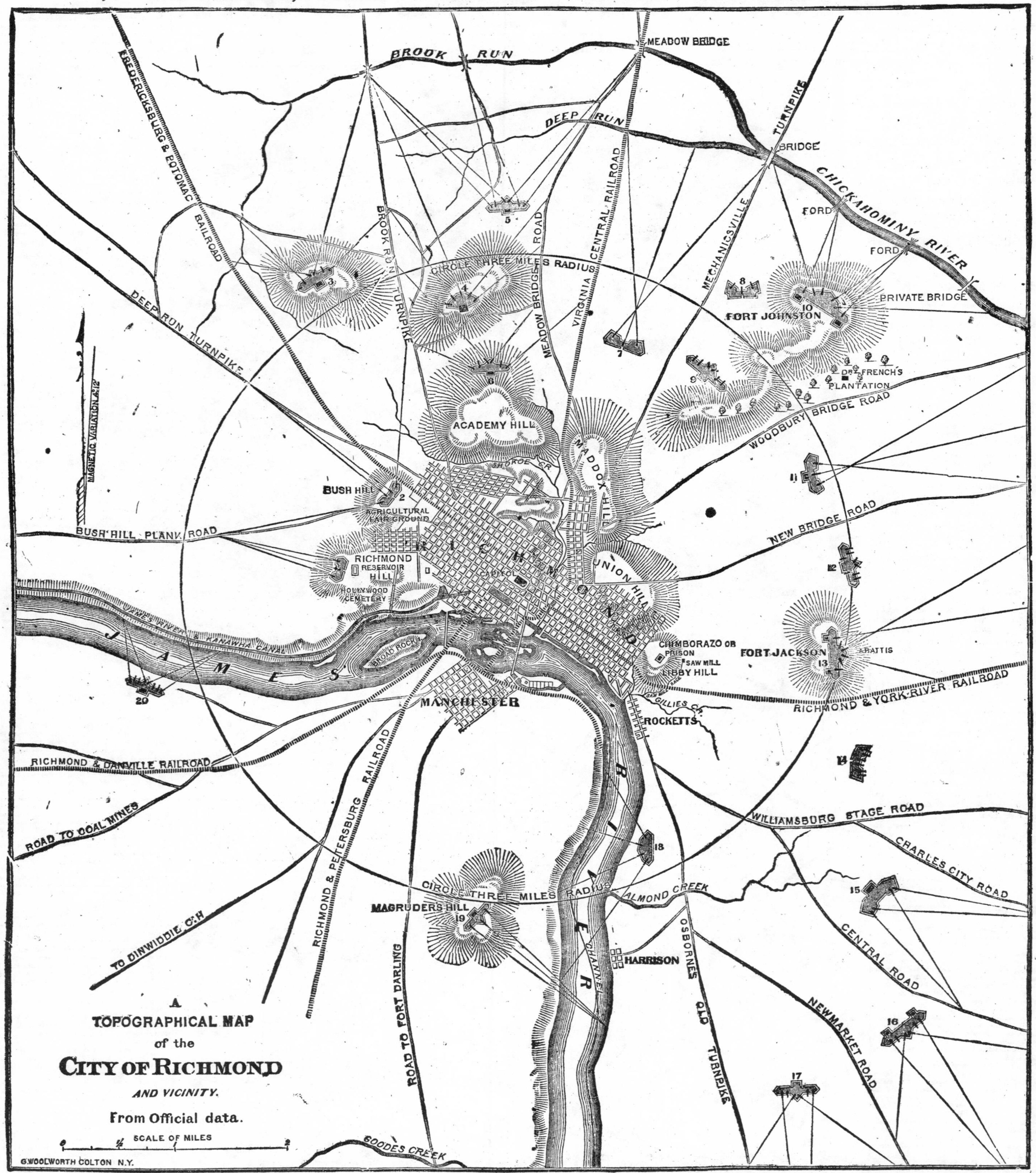

A
TOPOGRAPHICAL MAP
of the
CITY OF RICHMOND
AND VICINITY.
From Official data.

SCALE OF MILES
0 ½ 1 2

G. WOOLWORTH COLTON N.Y.

VIRGINIA.

Continued from First Page.

their ranks by the Rebels behind their works, succeeded in maintaining their new line several hundred yards in advance of the line they occupied in the morning. Two divisions of Hill's Corps held the Rebel line in front of the Second Corps, the other division being opposed to the Twenty-fourth Corps, which joins the Second on the right; the ground over which the Second Corps fought, was for the most part covered with pine forests, which, while affording good shelter to our men, were unfavorable for flank movements and the maintenance of our lines in close order.

TWENTY-FOURTH CORPS.

The Twenty-fourth Corps occupies the center of our line, holding the position previously occupied by the Second, its left connecting with the Second at Hatcher's Run, and its right joining the left of the Sixth Corps.

A FURIOUS CHARGE.

Before daylight this morning the Rebels made a furious assault on this position of our line, driving a portion of the Third Brigade from their breast-works, and capturing about eighty or a hundred prisoners. Their success however, did not last long, the 206th Pennsylvania, by a gallant charge compelling them to abandon their position and driving them back beyond their first battle line. A sharp fire was kept up all day by both sides. Owing to the hot fire by our sharpshooters, the enemy was unable to work his guns, and consequently very few casualties occurred on our side from shells. Our batteries however rained an incessant fire into their intrenchments, which must have caused them some loss.

SIXTH CORPS.

There was little fighting in front of the Sixth Corps until night, when considerable shelling occurred.

NINTH CORPS.

Quiet also reigned along the Ninth Corps front.

A GENERAL ENGAGEMENT.

So matters stood until 10 o'clock, when the Second Corps were started into sharper attention by a few shots on their front, soon swelling into battling volleys. The batteries joined their deep bass to the martial music and the pine woods rang with the clamor, and were fitfully illuminated by the glare. The firing spread rapidly to the front of the Twenty-fourth Corps, and on to the Sixth, then away to the right till it reached the Ninth Corps, about 11 o'clock, by which time the fighting was at its hight. Presently cheers broke out on the front of the Second, as the fire slackened. By 2½ the fire had nearly ceased along the whole line, but at 4 in the morning it suddenly broke out again, nearer than ever to the Second Corps, while sharp artillery practice was heard far to the right, and again the crash of battle sped from end to end of the line.

THE COLORS ADVANCING.

Close at 6, the battle is raging fiercely, and thank God the colors are advancing all along the line.

Details of Saturday's Operations.

From Our Special Correspondent.

HDQRS. ARMY OF POTOMAC,
MIDNIGHT, Saturday, April 1, 1865.

A SEVERE ENGAGEMENT ON THE LEFT.

In my last dispatch I announced the falling back of Sheridan's cavalry through Dinwiddie Court House yesterday afternoon and the consequent flanking of the Fifth Corps. I have now to announce the retirement of the enemy in that direction and the resumption of our line of yesterday beyond Dinwiddie Court House. My sphere at present being to record more specially the operations of the right of our new line, I am without full details of the action of this afternoon. Trustworthy reports from the troops engaged, however, give assurance that we have succeeded, after a furious engagement, in pushing back the enemy's lines and recovering the ground lost on yesterday.

WARREN AND SHERIDAN ENGAGED.

The retirement of Sheridan yesterday east of Dinwiddie Court-House, rendering a change of front on the part of the Fifth Corps imperative, the troops of Warren were consequently moved from their position across the White Oak road at midnight last night, down the Boydtown plank to the vicinity of the Butler House where they took a road leading west toward Ford Station on the Southside Railroad. Arriving at a place known as the Five Points, two and a half miles from the railroad, the command was halted, where it remained inactive until 3½ o'clock p. m.

In the meantime Sheridan, still further to the left was briskly engaging the enemy, and steadily driving him westward. At 3½ p. m. Warren again advanced his line north-westward, and after proceeding two miles, formed his corps in line of battle. At 5 o'clock the enemy, who had gradually given way before the advance of Warren, made a determined stand, and

See Fourth Page.

GRANT'S PETERSBURG PROGRESS.

VOL 1, PETERSBURG, VIRGINIA, APRIL 5, 1865 NO 2

"ETERNAL VIGILANCE IS THE PRICE OF LIBERTY" (AND TEN CENTS A COPY FOR OUR PAPER.)

GRANT'S PROGRESS

PUBLISHED BY

Eden & McCreery Proprietors.

MAJ: R. C. EDEN, CAPT. C. H. MCCREERY

PETERSBURG, VA.

Wednesday April 5th. 1865

ARMY OF THE POTOMAC.

Never has this veteran Army been in such splendid spirits as at the present time, The cheering news of great victories won by Sherman Sheridan and Thomas have made the men desirous to acquit themselves as brave soldiers should when again called to the conflict.—The Commanding General and all the officers and men have been impressed with the conviction, as never before, that the scenes of carnage in which they had so often been engaged were about to end. Listen to the men in their daily gatherings, and around their Camp fires at night and the almost unanimous opinion expressed is that they shall soon be released from warlike pursuits.. The contests thus far in this campaign show that thiey have fought with great gallantry. No army in the world has ever performed the hard fighting, that the Army of the Potomac has since its organization.—Always pitted against a large rebel army, led by their greatest General, it has won for itself a name that will be immortal.

The work left for it to do will be made short work. What stout hearts and willing hands *can* accomplish *will* be done by them. The thanks of a greateful country will be freely given them, and the pleasing reflection will be theirs through life that they aided in subduing the great rebellion.

Official Report of Bvt. Maj. Lonnsbery, A. A. A. G. 2nd Brig. 1st. Div. 9th. A. C.

COURT HOUSE, PETERSBURG, VA.
April 4th 1865.

BREVET COL. R. ELY,
Com'd'g 2nd Brigade,
Colonel—

In relation to the occupation of this city by two Regiments of your Brigade, temporarily under my command, I have the honor to report as follows:

At 2:30 A. M., you directed me to awaken the troops of the Command, and cause the 1st Mich. S. S. and the 2nd Mich. V. V., to form on the picket line, in front of, and on the right ot Fort McGilvery, for the purpose of occupying the rebel works in our front. I was instructed to send out scouts to reconnoitre the lines; to advance a heavy skirmish line supported by the 1st and 2nd Mich., and occupy the enemy's works if possible. Then, as soon as the balance of the Brigade should arrive in sight, to move forward cautiously, and rapidly as possible, and plant a flag on some public building in the City.

I awakened the Command as directed. Then directed Capt. Boughton, commanding 2nd Mich. V. V. and Capt. Evans, commanding 1st Mich. S. S. to form their Commands as quietly and as rapidly as possible, and report to me on the picket line in front of McGilvry for further orders. I then hastened to the picket line and ordered Lieut. Gore, com'd'g the pickets of the 1st Mich. to form his men as a company and deploy them as skirmishers in front of the abattis, lie down, and await further orders. In the mean time, I had Capts. Evans and Boughton arrived with their commands at about 3.10 A. M. I then reported to you, by orderly, that I would move at the end of twelve minutes unless I received orders to the contrary. The Command was rapidly formed, and both officers and men informed of the object of the movement, and properly instructed. At this time, the scouts reported that the rebels had left the picket line. I immediately moved forward, and reported to you, by orderly. So soon as I had reached the main works, I ordered the men to give three Yankee cheers, which were given with a "tiger," and then moved forward having first deployed thirty men of the 2nd Mich. as skirmishers, and threw them forward on the left of the skirmish line already advanced. On reaching the R. R. bridge, I was compelled to move some distance by the flank, but was careful to keep scouts well out. I again moved in line of battle so soon as the nature of the ground would permit. Upon reaching the city, I was again compelled to to move by the flank, but had scouts on both flanks. I directed Capt. Evans to detail Adjt. Buckbee, 1st Mich. S. S. with twelve men, to plant the flag on the Court House so soon as we should reach it. On striking Sycamore St. I met the first citizen, and pressed him to conduct us to the Court House. I formed the Command "on the right by file into line," and marched by the left flank until my center arrived in front of the Court House, when I halted, and caused the street to be picketed, and a Patrol to be sent forward with instructions to pick up Rebel stragglers &c. At this time, I was met by a deputation of citizens bearing a flag of truce, and desiring to surrender the city. I assured these Gentlemen that we came in the name of Liberty, and that we would protect both persons and property. After reassuring the gentlemen that all would be well with the citizens if they remained at home and conducted themselves in an orderly manner, I furnished an escoat to conduct them to their homes.

Capt. Boughton, commanding 2nd Mich. Vet. Vols. hoisted the flag of his Regiment over the Custom House at about 4:45 A. M.

During the advance, the men moved in a magnificent style. Not a man straggled, after arriving in the city, the men were most completely under the control of their officers.—Not a man left his place. The conduct of the officers and men of these Regiments was such as to reflect credit on our cause, and cast a lustre of glory over the Profession of Arms.

Respectfully Submitted.

I am, Colonel,
Your Obd't Serv't
C. A. LONESBERRY,
Capt. and A. A. A. Genl.
Bvt. Major U. S. V.

GENERAL ORDERS.

By General Orders, No. 1, Head Quarters Defenses of Petersburg, Va., April 4th, 1865, Maj. Gen'l G. K. Warren assumes command of the defences of Petersburg, in compliance with orders from H'd Qrs Army of the Potomac. His Head Quarters are with B'vt Maj. Gen'l O. B. Willcox, corner of Washington and Adams streets. His Aids are Maj. E. B. Cope and Capt. Jas. S. Wardsworth.

By orders of Maj. Gen'l Warren, Maj. Gen'l Benham is assigned to the command of defences of City Point. The Governor of Petersburg is directed to arrest all stragglers from other commands and send them direct to the front.

Richmond.

This nest of traitors is in Federal hands. The details of the occupation of the city, have not yet reached us. We learn it was taken possession of at 8 o'clock Monday morning, the 3d inst., by Maj Gen. Ord's forces. At 4½ o'clock in the morning of the same day the old flag floated from the Court House in this city, a few hours later, and Yankee Soldiers thronged the street of Richmond. We suppose the rebels will say the evacuation of these places—strongholds in the so called Confederacy—is another "blessing in disguise." They can now man their garrisons, fall back con[illegible] forces and fight till the bitter

TO OUR PATRONS.

Our paper of yesterday was not intended as a specimen of what we hope to make the *Progress* finally.—But the short space of time that we had, in which to get the matter up and struck off must be our excuse.—We got possession of the office at about noon, had to straighten up things generally among type, presses, &c. Then there were compositors to be hunted up who when found were, of course, out of practice and slow, and so it came about that it was fully six o'clock before we got to press. We shall continue to publish our paper in the form of the present number, Tri-weekly, every Monday, Wednesday, and Friday evening.

We shall endeavor to keep posted on all the latest news and for this purpose have established a telegraph line between our office and the Hospitals, Cook Shanties, Sutlers Store and all other places where true and reliable information may be had.

We shall have spies constantly on the watch to pick up items of interest including several contrabands of more than average stupidity.

We invite the assistance of our brother officers in the shape of letters on subjects connected with the profession and information on any topics of general interest that may come under their observation. In publishing anything anonymously, nor anything of a personal or abusive nature, nor reflecting on any acts or actions of the powers that be. This does not, of course, necessitate the publication of the writers name, which can be confided to us and not appear in public unless desired.

Our edition of yesterday sold so readily and rapidly that it taxed the resources of the office severely to keep the supply equal to the demand But with the aid of a power press lately discovered in the cellar of the establishment we hope to be able to keep pace with the call.

We beg to offer our thanks for the encouragement thus given us at the start and will endeavor to the best of our ability, to deserve such encouragement, in the future.

THE SITUATION.

The closing scenes of the rebellion are at hand. However strongly the rebels may heretofore have defended their bad cause, candid men, of either side can but see now that its days are numbered. The Union victories of the past few months have been brilliant ones. From all sides we have heard of the defeat of our enemies, of the deep dissatisfaction of very many of the Southern people, of the demorlization of the rebel troops and of the general gloom that hangs over the so called Confederacy. There have been no more brilliant achievments in the history of warfare than those of the Army of the Potomac, since the present campaign commenced. The Capitol of the Confederacy, against which have been hurled for four years large and well appointed Union armies, is at last in Federal hands. The Stars and Stripes proudly float over public buildings and where treason has been sustained, from which for many months, the ensign of our National existance has been banished and disgraced It is reported on good authority that in the recent operations about this City and Richmond 20,000 prisoners have been captured and that Gen'l Lee almost frantic with despair only succeeded in getting away with him 18,000 men.—Mean time Gen'l Sherman is not idle. We may soon expect to hear that his victorious legions are putting to rout the forces under Johnson. We are beginning to see the light of the morning, which is to bring peace to our distracted country.

It is well for all to throughly understand the object of the Govern-

cessful close. It is not to devastate, and destroy, or make sad homes. It is to enforce obedience to the constitution and the laws of the land. It is to maintain the government in its integrity, without which it would become a by word and reproach among the nations of the earth.—When this object shall have been gained lasting peace will be secure.

THEN AND NOW.

The following prophetic words are extracted from a speech made by a distinguished gentleman of the city of Petersburg, at the close of an election in the Court House in 1840 "[illegible] Union of States was a wonderful contrivance of human wisdom. The effort that made it could not have been uninspired by the Divine mind. It has, however, in its short career—short, as yet—been environed with serious dangers threatening its integrity in its territorial extent.—It has survived those dangers. It is destined to encounter still more serious dangers. It is not for me to look into the future. I can only indulge a hope and belief which I will express. Though the dangers do come to the Federal Union, which I apprehend will come—though the cloud of disunion may hang over the capital, and the sleeping thunderbolt be ready to leap from its stormy home and explode on its hearth-stones—though statesmen may be at fault and the wisest not see how to save that Union—yet, if alive, I will still indulge the hope and belief, and in case then I may be dead, I will now predict, however doubts and conflicts will arise and struggle how to save it, however States Rights may dispute its capacities to protect itself—after all that, from the lowering storm, some *United States Grant* of power, in the person of some great man, will spring forth, and, with an arm as powerful as Samson's, and a mind as philanthropic as Franklin's, extract the wrath from the cloud, until it shall dissolve in purple and gold and form the beautiful rainbow of peace to span again the star spangled banner spreading its ample folds to the fresh air of Heaven over the lands and the seas all around the whole earth."

DIRGE.

Farewell! to Secession! Its death knell is now tolling. Palsied, exhausted it stands trembling on the verge of an abyss of oblivion and turpitude.

It is dying, lingeringly and in agony, and from the devastated fields of Virginia, and its deserted homesteads, its death wail rings out with the fall of Petersburg. It was wisely said, "Be sure thy sin will find thee out," and the old heathen Horace has embodied the same idea in his *Raro antecedentem Scelestem deseruit pœna pede claudo.* And now on their sin has the punishment fallen. Petersburg and Richmond in our hands, Lee fleeing from the wrath to come, on every side men falling off from the cause like leaves in autumn, ignominy, ruin, misery behind and before, on the right hand and on the left. And on no state in the whole South has this weight of woe fallen heavier than on Virginia. She has fought bravely and obstinately, though in a bad cause and dearly has she paid the penalty. Her old title "Mother of Presidents," once proudly and rightfully her boast, will now be changed for the sad ignominious epithet "The Grave of Secession."

Exulting over a fallen foe adds no laurels to a victor's crown, and the bitter despondency that must now be felt by the most sanguine adherents of the Southern Confederacy inflicts a far graver punishment than bragging over a brave though misguided enemy. The Confederacy is dead—dead to all intents and purposes

may last yet a little longer; and now is the time to show magnanimity, for we can afford to do so. Let our intercourse as soldiers and gentleman be marked with courtesy towards those whom the fortune of war has placed under our control. "Bear and forbear" should now as ever be our motto. And when the blessing of peace restores us to our homes, we shall have a satisfaction in reflecting that we have not tarnished this, our crowning victory, by words or deeds which, after the first excitement of the moment is over, we should blush to acknowledge.

HOW ARE YOU JEFF?

His excellency (?) Jefferson Davis, must by this time, feel that he and his cause are *gone up* a great deal worse *straits* than if he had taken his projected yacht excursion the coming summer, and gone up the Straits of Gibraltar and the Mediterranean, and is, no doubt, a great deal sicker of the whole thing, than if he had merely suffered from *mal du mer* or sea sickness.—The extensive land Grant, U S. has taken up here, has encroached badly on his dominions and he will, probably, be soon reduced to the habitation of the fellow in the book, "a lodge in some vast wilderness" and oweing for that. Bankrupt in principle for several yaars, he will, probably, before long be bankrupt in pocket and become a Shakesperian nothing, "lacking a local habitation and a name." It is a pity he had not lived about the year A. D. 25, as Judas might no doubt have received some valuable hints from him with reference to the conduct of that little commercial transaction of his. But the comparison is hardly fair on the post mortem memory of Judas—*de mortuis nil nisi bonum,* and there is really nothing good about Jeff, unless it exist in infinitesimal Homœopathic doses invisible to the naked (mental) eye.

Farewell, Jeff, though we cannot, consistent with what little conscience we are [illegible] legally entitled to really wish you well—

So bad luck to him fairly, bad luck to him airly,
The devil admire him wherever he be—
May rattlesnaiks smite him and muskgeters bite him,
The traitor that brought these hard times upon me.

FAILURE OF GRANT'S CAMPAIGN!!!!

The above is the caption of an article in the Richmond *Whig*, and will take its place along with the unfulfilled prophecies of history. Though, in one sense, Grant's campaign has failed—in adding to the prospects of success to the rebel cause, unless the fall of Petersburg and Richmond is like the capture of Wilmington, Savannah, Charleston, &c, merely another blessing in disguise.

The Macon *Confederate* says that to match Yankee 200 pounder Parrotts the Confederates have 500-pounder Torpedoes attached to the nose of little canoes called *Davids.* Whenever one of these Torpedoes calls upon a Yankee vessel, there is nothing left of it but hair, blood, splinters, chimneys toppled over, a few swearing Yankees thrown into the river, ditto dead ones, and guns, ammunition, and all such useless plunder. These boats, or canoes, are great commissaries for cat fish.

NOTICE!

All persons DESTITUTE OF PROVISION will apply as follows:

In West Ward to W. L. Lancaster, Chairman.

In East Ward to H. W. Siggins, Chairman, at the old Express Office opposite the Ballingbroke Hotel.

In Central Ward to Robert P. Stainback Chairman No 45 Sycamore Street.

In South Ward to Col. Rowlett, Chairman at the South Ward Engine House.

AUCTION SALES.

To be sold very cheap (if not badly sold already) all that singularly, ineligible and worthless property known as

● THE SOUTHERN CONFEDERACY.

For particulars apply to Jefferson Davis Richmond, Va.

N. B. Liberal terms to agents of Maxilian, Louis Napoleon, or Victoria.

SALE OF NEGROES—I will sell to the highest bidder, for cash, at Nottoway Courthouse, on THURSDAY, the 6th day of April next, (court day) ten Negroes belonging to the estate of Uriah Lipscomb, deceased.

P. ● LIPSCOMB,
Com'r County Court, Nottoway.
mh 21, 28, 4th and 5th ap—4 ●

The above sale is postponed indefinitely, a different disposition of the property [illegible]

Local Depar[illegible]

Petersbu[illegible] ...ment.

[illegible] and its History.

The city of Petersburg was founded by the English in the earlier part of the seventeenth century, and so is one of the oldest on the continent. It was at first only a trading post, established by one Peter Jones for commerce with the Indians. This Peter, it appears, was considerable of a character, and by some means or other came into possession of most of the land on which the present city is built. The name of the city was at first "Peter's Point," from that celebrated Peter, but as it began to be builded up and the *Point* began to be covered over with *burghs*, the [illegible] common "judgment of mankind" declared the appellation of the town should b[illegible], and forever thereafter be, known as *Petersburg*. During the war with England, at the time of the Revolution, the town, after defending itself as best it could by a few American militia, was taken possession of by Gen. Phillips, accompanied by that first of our traitors, Benedict Arnold. The body of Gen. Phillips lies buried now in the grave-yard of the "old Blandford Church." It was a detachment of the army belonging to the gallant and ever to be remembered and beloved Lafayette, who, by cannonading these Britishers, had the effect to startle them; and so—as Gen. Grant did the other day to another set of intruders—speedily caused them to evacuate.

The town is noted for its manufacturing and exportation of tobacco. As long ago as 1810 there were fourteen ware houses in the city. The establishments for manufacturing consumable tobacco, before the out break of the present rebellion, were of a prolific variety "too numerous to be mentioned."

The manufacture of cotton has been also extensively engaged in and there are at present in the city five factories for the purpose. There [illegible] mills.

Among the public buildings of special note are the Court House, a moderate sized, rather pretty brick building on an eminence at the eastern part of the city, a Mechanic's Hall, an Exchange, a Masonic Hall, a Phœnix Hall, an Odd Fellows' Hall, including apartments for the Library Association, and a new granite building for a Custom House and a Post Office. There are four general banking establishments, ten churches—Baptist, Episcopalian, Methodist, Presbyterian, each two—and the colored people have several. There have been printed at one time in the city three daily newspapers—the *Intelligencer*, the *Express*, and the *Southern Democrat*, and one agricultural paper. An annual Agricultural Fair used to be held in the city. Petersburg is still lighted with gas and amply supplied with water by two aqueducts. The great Southern ærial line of rail-road passes through the city, and is intersected by the Southern Central road, which used to bring the town in communication with the west. A canal connects the city with the upper Appomattox, navigable for batteaux. Educational matters appear to have been pretty well attended to and there has been considerable of a degree of enterprise among the people. Population of the city, 22,000.

NOTORIETIES OF PETERSBURG.

In 1813, the Petersburg Volunteers, under command of Capt. Mc Rae, sent to the northern frontier, distinguished themselves at Fort Meigs and won from President Madison the epithet—"the Cockade of the Union" for the city. During the war with Mexico, two volunteer companies went out from Petersburg. Gen. Scott and the immortal John Randolph were both born in this vicinity.

EFFECTS OF THE SIEGE.

Not so much injury has been done to the place by our artillery as we (individually) expected to find. The upper and Western part of the town has been, indeed, but little affected. Strange to think of, nearly all branches of business in that part of the town has gone on apparently as usual, only with a necessarily diminished prosperity and even the [illegible] [illegible]

Our shells the citizens tell us, though, have been wont to strike in every part of the City, and some of them went clean over it. Nearly every church has been hit, and several of them more than once. Not many dwelling houses in that region have been touched and as far as we have been able to learn, in all the City, by all our shelling *only one white person has been killed*. In the lower and Eastern portion of the place, however, no little damage has been caused. On Ballingbrook, Lombard and Henry Streets especi[illegible] haps out of every [illegible], perhaps nineteen hav[illegible] twenty edifices, the [illegible] been struck, some of [illegible]umber quite destroyed, and the remainder badly honey-combed. We were in the old buildings once used for Theatrical purposes; from the stage where the players once split the ears of the groundlings or tore their own passion to tatters, we could see *tatters* enough sticking out in all the brick sides of the building and on the floor evidence sufficient, that the *ground* is sometimes *split* by a striking actor. Our canonading of the 4th of July last, we have been told, was the most destructive. The greatest real damage to the City, however, was done by the Confederate soldiers. They encamped round about and were continually passing through and stopping in it, and their boasted motto was "to lay hands on everything." The citizens tell us frankly they fear our army less than they did their own.

So much for Petersburg; the future of its history will no doubt be better than ever its past has been.

THE CONFEDERATE PRISONS.—Monday fornoon we visited the three localities one near the old market, another on High street and the third on Ettrick's Island where U. S. Soldiers, taken prisoners, have been wont to put up while sojourning in the city. The *hotel* first mentioned is a small, shabby—looking, old stone building, formerly used as a lock up for punishable Africans and containing three stories. The top one is an apartment close up against the rafters with a somewhat uncertain floor of loose boards and a ladder to climb up to it. The room below this is the stoutest of the three, has windows with iron bars before them and was in reality the main prison. The ground department is pretty much under the ground. Neither of the three ever could have been wonderfully comfortable. The prison on High Street is McCullough's tobacco factory—a three storied brick building, with its wings and a yard in the centre, the area of about an acre.—Only one wing of thir hotel, however, and its yard were open to the captive visitors and in this locality it was the Union Officers generally congregated. The Home to which our enlisted men resorted is the open space in close proximity with the river on Ettrick's Island. Here our home—debarred boys looked up day and night to the blue or spangled heavens above them and the only shelter they had was the dome of the firmament.

We found few evidences—only a few names on the walls and a little rubbish lying about—left behind by our soldiers of their having been in these localities. Probably the interpretation is, that their stay here was only temporary and, it may be, the confederate authorities were good policemen.

☞ Religious services were held in the Washington St. church, last evening. Addresses were made by Chaplain Hunting, of the First Division Hospital, 9th Army Corps, and by Rev. G. E. Hill, of the Christian Commission, from Massachusetts.

A full band from one of our regiments was present and added interest to the occasion. "America" was sung with great enthusiasm—the gallery was filled with colored folks.

DISGRACEFUL AFFAIR.—Last evening an attempt was made to violate a colored woman in the lower part of the city, by several negroes. They were fired on by the guard and one of the miscreants was secured and is safely lodged in the prison under the City Hall, in care of [illegible] [illegible] will [illegible]

[illegible]

Taken as a whole, the country people who send their produce to the Petersburg market, are the most liberal and warm hearted under the sun, and it affords us pleasure to hear the public testimony to their benevolent and philanthropic spirit. The evidences of this humanity [illegible] their part are so numerou[illegible] speak with fervor [illegible] we can hearts on [illegible] and with *bursting* [illegible] the encouraging subject. [illegible] Saturday we had Turkies pressed upon us at $75, $80 and $100 apiece, according to size and condition. Eggs were generously proffered at only $14 per dozen. Dressed chickens were kindly proffered at only $15 each, and geese could be had by simply exchanging $29 for one of the cackling creatures. Sweet potatoes were given away, provided the recipient would give in turn the trifling sum of $75 for every bushel received. We might go *on ad infinitum*, and enumerate the many marked evidences of kindness on the part of our dear, tender hearted country friends, but the above will suffice. Strange to tell, the towns people could not appreciate those acts of disinterested kindness, and many were heard to say, if they be our friends, God save us from all such.

☞ The enthusiastic welcome given to the *Yanks* by the negroes was shown by the exertions they made to save the bridge across the Appomattox, which had been fired by the retreating rebels. Great credit is due them for quenching the flames.

LADY VISITORS.—Our sanctum was yesterday graced by the presence of several ladies, and all of them loyal and of strong *Union* principle. The party composed Miss. H. P. Smith, Agent for N. Y. State, Mrs. Col. Logan, Miss. Semple, Del. Agt. and Mrs. Hurop, Ind. Agt. Their presence was very acceptable and did much to soothe [illegible] in our severe labors. They were under the escort of Messrs. Clark, Peak and Brown, of the San. Com.

CELEBRITIES.—Among the celebrated captures made on Monday morning may be reckoned Dr. Madison, Insp. Gen. Hosp of Va. C. S. A. The Dr. was, it appears, delayed during Sunday night analyzing a very choice article, Sp. Frum., and delayed his departure till the bridge across the Appomattox was in flames, and not being used to going under or over fire was unavoidably detained by circumstances, (Army of the Potomac) beyond his control. He probably abuses "the bridge that did'nt carry him safely over."

AND THE CRY IS STILL THEY COME.—Lieut. Hayson of the 3d. Penn. Cav. attached to General Meade's Head Quarters, arrived in town last night, with eleven prisoners of war, captured by Gen Sheridan's command on the road to Amelia Court House among whom was Brig. Gen. Baranger, Major Foote, Adj. Gen. to Bushrod Johnston, Major Ferguson, of Gen. Fitzhugh Lee's staff, Lieut. Ford of Gen. Beauregard's staff, and several non commissoned officers. The Lieut. leaves for City Point this A. M.

A GOOD MOVE.—We are informed that a petition has been signed by many of the leading citizens of Petersburg requesting that the 2nd Brig. 1st. Div 9th. A. C., be detailed to remain here as Provost Guard, and another petition for the appointment of Maj. Lonsberry as Prov. Mar. We are glad to see that the praiseworthy exertions of Col. Ely and Maj. L. to secure the comfort and well being of the citizens of Petersburg, have met with so signal a token of their approval.

A woman one hundred years old, residing on the banks of Salt river, in Bullitt county, Kentucy, gathered all her descendants at the old homestead, recently, to celebrate her centenary annaversary. She proposed a tost as follows: "[illegible] I have lived through Washington's war for independence, Jackson's war, the Mexican war, and [illegible] [illegible] coln and [illegible]

OATH OF PAROLE.

The following is the oath of parole for citizens, in order to pass without the limits of the city:

OFFICE OF PROVOST MARSHAL, Petersburg, Va., —— 1865.

I, ———, of ———, do solemnly and sincerely promise and swear that, so long as the forces of the United States hold possession of Petersburg, I will not, directly or indirectly, give aid, comfort, assistance or information to the military or civil authorities of the so called Confederate States of America; that I will not do anything, directly or indirectly, to the detriment or disparagement of the authority of the United States, and will, in good faith, conform to and obey the orders of said authorities.

———— ————

Sworn to and subscribed before me, } ——— ———

THE U. S. CHRISTIAN COMMISSION.—We are happy to learn that the U. S. Christian Commission have established a station in the City on Tabbs St., opposite to the Presbyterian Church (Dr. Hoges.')

This Commission is composed of clergymen of all denominations, who follow our army to do good to the souls and bodies of the soldier. We understand the Commission have obtained the use of the Presbyterian Church and last evening held religious services in the Lecture Room, which are to be continued every evening at 7½ o'clock.

These services have always been in other places highly interesting and profitable and, we are satisfied, will be so here. We need not add, all citizens and soldiers are cordialy invited to attend.

WOUNDED CONFEDERATES.—We are indebted to Dr. O. P. Chubb, Surgeon 20th Mich. Vol. Inf., for the following statement of the number of wounded rebels captured in this city and vicinity:

In the General Hospital, 150; Confederate States Hospital, 170, and 30 Federals; Dunlop Station Hospital 25. Total, 345.

These men were wounded too severely to allow of their removal, but are in good hands, and will meet with the kind and humane treatment their unfortunate condition demands. An Assistant Surgeon was left in charge of each hospital, which were nearly all destitute of proper and sufficient food; this has, however, been promptly supplied to them.

ENTERPRISE OF THE PROGRESS.—A creditable citizen of Petersburg said to us, "it was always reported the Yankees were a smart people, but on seeing them issue a paper in the evening, as they captured the city in the morning, that was evidence sufficient." Hereafter Grant's *Petersburg Progress* will not only be a convincing argument that "the world moves," but that the Lieut. General is the biggest mover in it.

ERRATTA.—The name of Private H. F. COPE, 2d Brig. 3d Div., in yesterdays paper, was inadvertently omitted. He is entitled to this correction, being one of the principal compositors.

PERSONAL.—We regret to learn that Bvt Maj General Potter of the 2nd. Div. 9 h., A. C. was severely wounded in the engagement of the 2nd, inst.

PRISONERS.—Upwards of 1300 prisoners were sent to City Point yesterday, in charge of Capt. E S Leadbeater. They were captured in and around the city on the morning of the 3d inst—the day the U. S. forces took possession of the city.

THE TWO MINNIES.

BY A REBEL SOLDIER.

[Suggested by reading a letter from MINNIE, saying—she prayed daily that the "*Minnie*" balls might spare me.]

There is a MINNIE that I love,
And a "*Minnie*" that I fear;
But the former is now absent—
The latter oft too near:
But one MINNIE prays for me each day,
That to "*Minnies*" I'll not fall a prey.

The voice of one is soft and sweet,
The other harsh and shrill—
One only speaks to bless mankind,
The *other* speaks to kill:
And, while MINNIE prays for me each day,
Yankee "*Minnies*" seek me for a *prey*

And when this sad war is over—
Our Independence *won*—
I'll bid adieu to [illegible]
And [illegible]

"ONLY ONE KILLED."

BY MAURICE BELL.

A brilliant dash was made, and we drove the enemy several miles, killing, wounding, and capturing many. Our loss only one killed.—Dispatch.

Hark, what means those deafening cheers?
Glorious news from the front, they say,
Joy to the country—to each who hears—
We've had a great success to-day.

We attacked at dawn; the enemy fled,
We following fast and pressing sore—
Leaving behind him many dead,
And wounded many, and prisoners more.

Well may each breast with rapture swell,
Each heart with patriot pride be thrilled
For best of all, and strange to tell,
We lost in the conflict, "only one killed."

"Only one killed!"—a loss how small,
Compared with the fruits of that brilliant dash.
Yet who shall say that it did not fall
With a force more dire than the lightning's crash?

Who was he—that single one—
Who, of all the conquering throng,
Lay all stark, when the fight was done,
Deaf to triumphal shout and song?

Ask of that old man, where he kneels,
While the tears down his face did roll,
And his withered frame to each heart appeals,
Shaken by agony, tearing his soul.

Ask of that fair form, prostrate near,
The roses dead on the tearless cheek,
Who has lain like a corpse since the people's cheer,
Was hushed by her wild, despairing shriek.

Ask those little ones, as they stand—
Their faces wild with a nameless pain—
Clinging in vain to the pulseless hand,
Craving their mother's smile—in vain!

Ask the sad friends clustering round—
The form of the husband, father, son,
What advantage HUMANITY found
In the fight where fell that "only one!"

Ask them—you need not seek them far—
Not once alone has the picture filled—
And you'll know the price at which heartless War
Buys its glory where "one" is "killed!"

A lady, who was in the habit of always leaving something or other behind her, whenever she went on a journey, was not long since promised by her husband the present of a handsome shawl, if, on the occasion of her leaving home the next day, she carried everything she wanted with her. The lady, of course, exerted herself to the utmost, and the pair set off to the place of their destination. They had not proceeded a mile, however, when the lady exhibited signs of fidgetiness, as usual, and on her husband inquiring as to the cause, she exclaimed, in a fright, "Goodness gracious! I forgot the baby!" So the shawl was lost for that time.

A witty young rascal, while passing through the town of ———, in Alabama, not long since, wanted some whiskey, and knowing it could be obtained only by a physician, wrote himself an order, signing it with his own name, to which a learned M. D. was attached. He presented it at the drug store of a gentleman, who though unrecognized by him, proved to be an old acquaintance. "Hallo, Frank!" said he, "when did you get to be a doctor?" "I'm not a doctor." Why, what's this M. D. to your name for, then?" Frank saw that he was caught, but determining to make the best of it, put on a very innocent look, and meekly answered: "Oh! that's for Mighty Dry!" Of course he got the whiskey.

A CURIOUS COINCIDENCE.—Read the article on the first page, entitled "Now and Then" It is an actual prophecy, having been delivered at the time. and on the occasion stated in the heading.

CHANGE OF FORCES.—Just as we are about going to press we learn that the forces under command of Brevet Major General Wilcox have been relieved by those under the command of Brvt. Maj. Gen. Ferrero. Col. George C. Kibbie, commanding Brigade, is to occupy the position held by Col. Ralph Ely. His Adj. Gen. is Capt. E. Donaldson. Capt. L. E. Carter is now Provost Marshall. The citizens of Petersburg had formed a good opinion of the forces that have been here; no doubt they will have equal cause to respect the conduct of those coming.

☞ A German newspaper contains the following advertisement: "A girl of good education of strict morals, being extremely handsome and of enticing manners, conversant with the keeping of hotel [illegible] [illegible]

EXTRA.

VIRGINIA!

GLORIOUS NEWS!

Sheridan Encounters the Retreating Rebels!

CAPTURE OF PRISONERS AND CANNON

Great Haul of Rebel General Officers

Lee will Probably be Forced to Surrender All that is Left of His Army.

[OFFICIAL.]

WAR DEPARTMENT,
WASHINGTON, Friday, April 7—10 a. m.

Maj.-Gen. DIX: Gen. Sheridan attacked and routed Lee's army, capturing Generals Ewell, Kershaw, Button, Corse, and many other general officers, several thousand prisoners, and a large number of cannon, and expects to force Lee to surrender all that is left of his army.

Details will be given as speedily as possible, but the telegraph is working badly.

EDWIN M. STANTON,
Secretary of War.

[For The Tribune.

"THE DAY WE CELEBRATE."

Bad luck to the man who is sober to-night!
He's a 'could-hearted *bodhagh*, or saycret Secesher,
Whose heart for the Ould Flag has niver been right,
An' who takes in the fame of his counthry no pleasure.
Och, murther! will none o' yez hould me, me dears!
Or it's out o' me shkin wid delight I'll be jumpin';
Wid me eyes swimmin' round in the happiest tears,
An' the heart in me breasht like a piston-rod thumpin'!

Musha, glory to God! for the news you have sint,
Wid your own purty fisth, Misther President Linkin!
An' may God be around both the bed an' the tint
Where our bully boy Grant does his atin' an' thinkin'!
Even Shtanton, to-night, we'll confiss he was right,
Whin he played the ould scratch wid our *have-you-his-carkiss*;
An' to gallant "Phil Sherry" we'll dhrink wid delight,
On whose bright plume o' fame not a spot o' the dark is!

Let the chapels be opened, the althars illumed,
An' the mad bells ring out from aich turret an' shteeple;
Let the chancels wid flowers be adorned an' perfumed,
While the *Sogarths*—God bless 'em!—give thanks for the people!
For the city is ours that "Mac" sought from the start,
An' our boys through its streets "Hail Columbia" are yellin';
An' there's Payce in the air, an' there's pride in the heart,
An' our Flag has a fame that no tongue can be tellin'!

To the *dioul* wid the shoddy-contractors, an' all
Them gold speculators, whose pie is now "humble"!
The cost o' beef, praties, an' whisky will fall,
An' what more could we ax—for the rints too will tumble?
On the boys who survive, fame an' pinsions we'll press,
Every orphan the war's med, a home we'll decree it;
An' aich soldier's young sweethart shall have a new dhress,
That will tickle her hayro, returnin' to see it!

Oh, land o' thrue freedom! oh, land of our love,
Wid your ginerous welcome to all who but seek it;—
May your stars shine as long as the twinklers above
An' your fame be so grand that no mortial can shpeak it!
All the winds o' the world as around it they blow,
No banner so glorious can wake into motion;
An' wid Payce in our *own* land, you know we may go,
Just to settle some thriflin' accounts o'er the ocean!

So come, me own Eileen! come Nora an' Kate,
Come Michael an' Pat, all your Sunday duds carry;
We'll give thanks in the chapel, an' do it in shtate,
An' we'll pray for the sowls o' poor Murtagh an' Larry.
Woe's me! in the black swamps before it they shleep,
But the good God to-night—whose thrue faith they have cherished—
His angels will send o'er the red fields a-shweep,
In aich cowld ear to breathe,—"Not in vain have you perished!"

So bad luck to the man who is sober to-night!
He's a cowld-hearted *bodhagh*, or saycret Secesher,
Whose heart for the Ould Flag has niver been right,
An' who takes in the fame of his counthry no pleasure!
Och, murther! will none o' yez hould me, me dears!
For its out o' me shkin, I'm afeard, I'll be jumpin';
Wid me eyes shwimmin' round in the happiest tears,
An' the heart in me breasht like a piston-rod thumpin'!

M. O'R.

New-York, April 3, 1865.

Evening Edition of the Tribune.

VOL. XXIV.....NO. 7,489. NEW-YORK, FRIDAY, APRIL 7, 1865. PRICE FOUR CENTS.

FROM SOUTH CAROLINA.

Monument to the Martyrs of the Race-Course—An Orphan-House to be Established—Life Among the Loyalists—Torpedoes and Guerrillas.

From Our Special Correspondent.

CHARLESTON, March 29, 1865.

Last Sunday morning a party of Northern men went out to the race-course to see where our brave soldiers were penned up, in an open field, without tents, without blankets and half naked, to be starved into the Rebel ranks, or an untimely grave, or turned over to the tomb-filling cruelties of a Confederate hospital. No fact in history is better attested than that fearful record of the slaveholders' crime. There is no doubt whatever that our soldiers were deliberately starved, almost to death, in order to compel them to replete the thinning ranks of the traitor, and that their steadfast loyalty under all temptations hurried hundreds of them into the World of Spirits. The annals of early Christianity, of the Catholic Church outside of Christendom, and of the various Protestant sects inside of it, have no grander heroisms to canonize than those of the men who were tempted by the evil ones in the pens of Andersonville, Salisbury, Belle Isle and Charleston, and who continued with their last feeble breath to act, if not say, to every effort to make them false to their country, Get thee behind me, Davis.

The colored people here tell fearful stories of the sufferings of our prisoners, while many of the oath-takers pretend to deny that any cruelties were practised. But their testimony is like their oath—false and for a purpose; and the terrible record will be made yet which will overwhelm many of them with confusion.

The race-course is one of the finest grounds of the kind in America. The prisoners were kept on it—just as it was when a race was to be run, excepting that around it there was a ditch dug to indicate the boundaries of the field of death. It seems incredible that men should become so fiendish as to inflict such cruelties on their brothers and countrymen. But inside of that ditch you see the grounds which formed the only bed of our brave men—little patches, six feet long, and wide enough for two or three, with petty ditches around them, to keep their earth-bed dry! They lay there with no covering but the sky; hot and cold, wet and dry, blistered by the sun, frozen by the sleet, drenched by every storm; heart-sick, home-sick, sick in body, sick of life, stung by vermin, bitten by insects, slowly turning into living skeletons by the agonizing agencies of hunger and disease, and the murderous malice of their guards. And yonder, over in the city, are some of the fiends who inflicted these cruelties by upholding the Rebellion which made them possible; and they already have the audacity to call themselves loyal, and to expect that they will be admitted into the Union—recognized as the rightful rulers of the only truly loyal population here! For they have "taken the oath," and expect that the glove of perjury will hide the "damned spot" on hands that are red with the blood of Northern men!

We went over to the headquarters of the race-course, or of the Jockey Club, and found a man there who had been its guardian spirit for forty years. He had not seen much of the prisoners, but allowed they were better fed than the Rebel soldiers themselves.

"Have you taken the oath?"

"O, yes, course, I have."

—Of course!

Now this loyal man had his complaint. He felt bad about one thing. He hated to see it. Why, "some niggers" had gone to Gen. Hatch and got permission to dig up the race-course for gardens!

"Nero fiddled when Rome was burning." Why should not the chivalry hereafter yell and shout and gamble and race over the field where our heroes were tortured to death? Why should not blacklegs and prostitutes and loafers have a glorious good time right near where our martyrs lie buried? These people don't see why!

We went over to the place where those who were found stiffened corpses in the morning on the race-course, or who dropped dead in their tracks, were buried without coffins and without any symbol of respect—all who died in one day in one hole, side by side, as closely as they could be packed together. No fence surrounds it, hogs run over it, the fouler feet of the traitor polute it. It is a patch 45 x 90 paces, and 253 heroes lie beneath its sods. Those who perished in the hospitals were buried in the Potter's field.

Our party were shocked at the disrespect shown to the resting place of the bodies of our martyrs, and before we left the race-course we all formed ourselves into a committee to raise funds to erect a fence and monument on the site. Little pieces of board, with a number only, are the only monuments our heroes have now.

Next morning the following address was issued:

To the Loyal People of South Carolina.

It is an established fact, that a large number of our soldiers died from exposure and want, in what is called the race-course, in the City of Charleston.

It therefore behooves us as loyal people that a fitting testimonial be made to the memory of these brave men, who died or were brutally murdered by being exposed without sufficient clothing or proper food, and with no other cover than the broad canopy of heaven, and then buried like dogs with nothing to mark their last resting place or to protect their remains.

A committee has been formed to raise funds to erect a suitable monument and fence to protect it, in honor of these brave soldiers who died in defense of their country; and we do hereby call upon every loyal man, woman and child in the State of South Carolina to aid us in the work, and respectfully ask ministers and their congregations to form committees to raise funds. The contribution has been limited to ten cents each, so that it will give every one the privilege, and debar none from aiding this noble work South Carolina alone should do the work, and raise $10,000 to complete it, and show the world that all her children have not degenerated or forgotten the duty they owe to the defenders of our starry flag.

All communications should be addressed to the Secretary of the Committee, at Charleston, S. C.

By order of the Committee.

CHARLES PAXSON, Secretary.

EXECUTIVE COMMITTEE.—James Redpath, Malden, Mass.; Charles Paxson, New-York; Timothy Hurley, Charlestown, Mass.; J. M. Smalley, Burlington, Vt.; M. C. Stagg, Stratford, Conn.; Charles H. Albee, Marlborough, Mass.; Dr. T. M. Hawkes, Manchester, N.H.; Rev. Mr. Corey, Christian Commission; Gilbert Pillsbury, N. E. Freedmen's Aid Society.

HONORARY MEMBERS.—Rev. Mr. Newcombe, Beaufort; Col. Beecher, Mount Pleasant; W. G. Tackaberry, Mitchelville; J. P. Blake, North Edisto; Reuben Tomlinson, St. Helena.

GRAND TREASURERS.—Brevet Major-Gen. Saxton, Admiral Dahlgren.

Before this letter is published the subscription will be opened.

Brig.-Gen. Hatch has agreed to give Rebel shot and shell enough, or other Rebel munitions of war, to melt for a fence.

An orphan house for the children of refugees will be opened here within a few days. It will be called "The Hatch Asylum."

The colored men are organizing into all sorts of literary and social societies, and are forming night schools, and otherwise working to qualify themselves to be the future rulers of South Carolina. On Monday there were 2,900 children at the seven public schools now open, and eighty teachers are engaged—nearly all of them natives of Charleston. Of the pupils between seven hundred and eight hundred are whites.

There is nothing doing here in a military way that is not contraband. It is sufficient to say that the guerrillas are being vigorously followed up. A torpedo exploded the other day in the harbor, but did little damage.

Astor-House Stetson is about to open the Charleston Hotel. The weather is heavenly—absolutely heavenly. This is too splendid a country to close up or give up. Let the policy of the North toward it be expressed in the negro sentiment: "We's a-guane to occupy de land!"

BERWICK.

THE FIRST ATTACK ON FORT FISHER.

Correspondence Between Gens. Butler and Whiting.

LOWELL, Mass., Feb. 22, 1865.

Major-Gen. W. H. C. WHITING, *Provisional Army of the Confederate States.*

SIR: I requested a short time ago, Lieut. Davenport, a young gentleman serving on my staff, to call upon you and obtain some particulars concerning the condition of Fort Fisher and its surrounding, at the time of the demonstration of the Union forces, under my command, against it, from the 16th to the 27th of December last.

From its subsequent capture, and other new dispositions of the forces on both sides, I ventured to conjecture that you would have no difficulty in furnishing me with the information I desired.

I had not heard before, of the severity of your wound, and the critical condition of your health, or I would not have troubled you at that time upon this subject, although of some importance and interest to myself.

I learn, however, from Lieut. Davenport, that you are intending soon to make your official report to you Government, and therefore I trust I am not intrusive or annoying in desiring your answers, as specifically as your memory and data will allow, to the questions hereto appended, which I have put in direct form partly to save you trouble, and still more especially in order to bring out the exact facts which at some time may be needed for the purposes of justice. This is also in accordance with your wish expressed to Lieut. Davenport "that any question which I desired to have you answer might be placed upon paper in some specific form."

Will you please state, therefore:

Question I.—What was the number of the garrison of Fort Fisher on the 16th, 17th and 18th of December last, designating the Regiments or Batallions?

Answer.—Five (5) Companies of the 36th Regiment, North Carolina Troops, and Adams's Light Battery, amounting to 667 aggregate, was the number of the garrison at Fort Fisher on the 16th, 17th and 18th of December last.

Question II.—What portion, if any, of the regular garrison of the Fort had been sent South?

Answer.—Five (5) Companies of the 36th Regiment North Carolina Troops (half of regiment) had been sent South.

Question III.—What reserves or coöperating forces were there, if any, and how near the Fort were they?

Answer.—About 800 reserves at Sugar Loaf, five (5) miles from the Fort.

Question IV.—What, if any, force was at Wilmington at that time?

Answer.—The advance of Hokes's Division arrived in Wilmington on the 22d of December last, were pushed to Sugar Loaf, and continued arriving until the close of the attack.

Question V.—Please give the day of the week or month when you first became aware of the presence of the Federal fleet, either of transports or of naval vessels, and what vessels did you observe first?

Answer.—On Tuesday, the 20th, twenty-five (25) vessels, including several frigates, were reported to me in the offing, all vessels of war.

Question VI.—At what time did any reënforcements, either from the Army of Northern Virginia, or elsewhere, reach Wilmington or its neighborhood?

Answer.—Answered in No. IV.

Question VII.—How near did the powder boat, which exploded, come to the fort?

Answer.—Between 1,200 and 1,500 yards—not nearer.

Question VIII.—Were you in the fort at that time?

Answer.—I was not.

Question IX.—Was the powder boat observed, and if so, what, if any, was the effect of the explosion?

Answer.—Powder Boat was observed, and reported at said night, aground and set on fire. Explosion reported at 12:45 a. m.; no effect at all on the fort. Explosion heard plainly in Wilmington, when I telegraphed Col. Lamb to know what it was. He replied, "Enemy's gun-boat blown up."

Question X.—At the time of the explosion of the powder-boat, how many men were there in the fort?

Answer.—Answer in No. I.

Question XI.—What was the effect of the naval fire of the first day upon the Fort?

Question XII.—How many and what guns did it dismount or disable?

Question XIII.—Please state whether any part, and if so how much of the damage to the Fort, by the fire of the Navy, was repaired during the night?

Answer to XI, XII, and XIII.—Casualties first day: Killed, none; wounded, one (1) mortally, three (3) severely, and nineteen (19) slightly; total, 23. Five (5) gun carriages disabled. Second day: Killed, three (3); wounded, nine (9) mortally, six (6) severely, and twenty-eight (28) slightly; total, 46. Damage but very slight. One (1) 10-inch, two (2) 32-pdrs., and one (1) 8-inch carriages disabled, and one (1) 10-inch gun disabled. Damages repaired at night. Enemy's fire formidable and sustained, but diffuse, unconcentrated. Apparent design of the fleet to silence the channel batteries, in order to force an entrance with his vessels, and not to attack by land. The garrison was in no instance driven from its guns, and fired in return according to orders, slowly and deliberately, 662 shot and shell.

Question XIV.—By reason of the cessation of the bombardment at night were you not able to rest and recruit your garrison?

Answer.—We were able to do both.

Question XV.—At the time of the landing, where was the supporting force, if any, to the Fort?

Answer.—Assembling at Sugar Loaf as fast as Hoke's people arrived.

Question XVI.—Were there any reënforcements brought into the fort between the time of the explosion of the powder boat and our landing. If so please state what and when.

Answer.—On the 23d, 110 men, Veteran Artillery of the 10th Regiment, N. C. T., 50 sailors, and the 7th Battalion jr. Reserves, about 250 strong, were thrown into the Fort.

Question XVII.—At the time our skirmish line was deployed before the Fort, what was the condition of the guns and defenses upon the land side, as to efficiency for defensive operations?

Answer.—The guns and defenses on the land front were in perfect order at the time referred to, except two (2) disabled guns on the left; 19 guns in position; palisade in perfect order, and mines the same, the wires not having been cut.

Question XVIII.—In view of the condition of the Fort and its garrison, would it have been possible, with either three (3) or six (6) thousand men to have taken the work by assault? [NOTE: In answering this question please give as many of the details, for the reason, you may give, as possible.]

Answer.—Possible, Yes. Probable, No. The work was very strong, the garrison in good spirits and ready, and the fire on the approaches (the assaulting column having no cover) would have been extraordinarily heavy. In addition to the heavy guns I had a battery of Napoleons on which I placed great reliance. The palisade alone would have been a most formidable obstacle.

Question XIX.—Please state whether, with a force holding the beach, from the nature of the ground, and from the configuration of the Cape Fear River, it would have been possible for the Confederates to have reënforced or provisioned the Fort to any extent?

Answer.—No difficulty at all by the river.

Question XX.—How did the strength of the garrison at the time of the first attack compare with the strength of the garrison at the time of the second attack?

Answer.—The garrison at the second attack was nearly doubly stronger, but not altogether of so good material.

Question XXI.—In view of the condition of the weather immediately following the demonstration of the 25th of December, and in view of the force that might have concentrated upon the Peninsular, as well above as below the place of landing, would it, in your judgment, have been possible for six thousand men, without artillery, to have held out there without being captured or overwhelmed from the 26th of December to the 15th of January?

Answer.—No; and it is a matter of grave charge against Gen. Bragg, that the whole force was not captured on the 26th of December. He had the force and the position.

Question XXII.—Please state as specifically as you may be able the differences in the condition of the Fort from the fire of the navy at the time of the first and second attack. Please state the effect of the fire.

Answer.—There was great difference in the position of the ships in the two attacks, and in the nature and effect of the fire. The first was a general bombardment, not calculated to effect particular damage. The second firing had for definite object the destruction of the land defenses, and the ships were placed accordingly to destroy them by enfilade and direct fire. On that front and the north-east salient the whole enormous fire was poured without intermission until the slope of the north-east salient was practicable for assault. Not a gun remained in position on the approaches, the whole palisade swept away, communication with the mines cut off, rendering them useless, and the men unable to stand to the parapets during the fire. There was all the difference in the world.

Question XXIII.—Please state whether or not the fire of the Navy, at the time of the second attack, was, unlike the time of the first attack continuous, and if so, for how long, and what number of guns were dismounted by it? Also, whether the garrison, at the time of the second attack, had any time to rest or recruit, or even to repair damages?

Answer.—In the second attack the fire was continuous during the night; not so heavy at night, but enough to prevent repairs, and to keep the garrison from rest and food; the land guns all disabled; field-pieces only left to depend on.

Question XXIV.—Would you have deemed it the part of wisdom on the part of the commander of the Federal forces to have exposed his troops in the situation referred to in question 21st?

Answer.—I do not. Neither attack was practicable in the presence of the supporting force, provided that had been under a competent officer. The first landing ought assuredly to have been captured entirely; and as for the second, although deriving much greater advantages from the different mode of attack by the fleet, and though pressed with great vigor, it is due to the supineness of the Confederate General that it was not destroyed in the act of assault.

W. H. C. WHITING,
Major-Gen. P. A. C. S., Prisoner of War.

HOSPITAL FORT COLUMBUS, Feb. 28, 1865.

Maj.-Gen. B. F. BUTLER, *U. S. A., Lowell, Mass.*

GENERAL: I have received your communication, addressing me certain questions relative to the two attacks on Fort Fisher.

As I find none which I can object to answer, I send you herewith the written answers, numbered according to the questions.

These are at your service for such use as you may desire to make of them. I have only to add that, in a similar manner, though less in detail, these questions are answered in my official report.

I am, General, very respectfully, your obedient servant,

W. H. C. WHITING,
Major-Gen. P. A. C. S., Prisoner of War.

P. S. Please acknowledge the receipt of this.

Tri Weekly Constitutionalist.

BY STOCKTON & CO   AUGUSTA GA. FRIDAY MORNING, APRIL 7, 1865.

From Evening Edition of Yesterday

No Speaking.—Mr Barnwell of the 2d Georgia having been called from the city, it will be impossible for him to address the citizens of Augusta this evening.

Great Swelling Words.—"That was a masterly performance," said Mr. Balloon to his friend Mr. Jones, as they emerged from the church where the Rev. Gassman had been discoursing on the Relation of the Infinite to the Impossible.

"Yes—no," replied Mr. Jones, "I suppose it was very fine, but it was out of my depth. I confess to being one of the sheep who 'looked up and were not fed.'"

"That's because you havn't a metaphysical mind," said Mr. Balloon, regarding his friend with pity; "you've got a certain faculty of mind, but I suspect you haven't the logical grasp necessary for the comprehension of such a sermon as that"

"I am afraid I haven't," said Mr. Jones.

"I tell you what it is, continued Mr. Balloon, Mr. Gassman has got a head. He is an intelligent man. I hardly know whether he is greater as a subjective preacher, or in the luminous objectivity of his *argumentum ad hominem*. As an inductive reasoner, who, he is perfectly great. With what synthetical power he refuted the Homoiousian theory! I tell you Homoiousianism will be nowhere after this."

"To tell the truth," said Mr. Jones, "I went to sleep at that long word, and didn't wake up until he was on theodicy."

"Ah, yes!" said Mr. Balloon, "that was a splendid specimen of ratiocinativice word painting. I was completely carried away when, in his singular terse and narrowy style, he took an analogical view of the antaropological."

But at this point Mr. Balloon "soared aloft" so high that he left the more terrestrial Mr. Jones.

[COMMUNICATED.]

Messrs. Editors:

I saw a recommendation to the ladies of the Confederacy a short time since, to cut off their hair, that it might be sent to Paris to be made up into braids, which were to be sold, to help liquidate the debt of our Government. Now those ladies whose hair, like my own, is silvered with age, will be denied the pleasure of helping in this matter, unless permitted to contribute in some other way. I propose, then, that those who wish to divest themselves of their tresses for the good of their country, and others who prefer it, can do their part by giving a piece of gold or silver. If such a call were made upon the ladies, I am certain there would be a general response. What will avail our gold and silver if we are subjugated? Whose will it be? not ours—of that we may be assured. Do, Mr Editor, give this matter your serious consideration, and if it is judged expedient, call upon our ladies at once. I hope all will respond to the call of our noble President, the men to swell the ranks of the army, and our women to make more sacrifices than they have already done. We all must feel the necessity of doing something to help our treasury. Thank God the resources of our noble State are not yet exhausted, and we have still men enough left to recruit our ranks to overflowing, who do not endorse Governor Brown's sentiment, nor have they been Yankeeized by the croaking of aliens.

An Old Woman.

Supplies for Lee's Army.—The Charlotte Bulletin contains an account of a meeting held at Iron station, Lincoln co, N C., for the purpose of raising supplies for Gen. Lee's army. The following contributions were made:

In corn, 87 bushels, wheat, 10 bushels, flour, 1800 pounds, meal 150 pounds and 5 bushels, bacon, 505 pounds, molasses 33 gallons.

The Last Blockade Runner.—A new blockade runner, named the Imogene, under the command of Captain Capper, late of the Will-o'-the-Wisp, has just made the passage from Cardiff to Madeira, *en route* to Bermuda, in four days and five hours—one of the fastest on on record.

[*Liverpool Courier.*

[From the New York Daily News, March 17.]

The Effects of Federal Victories.

Those who have faith in the doctrine of subjugation as an element of republican Government, profess to believe that the Southern Confederacy has been pushed to an extremity from which it can only be delivered by an extraordinary military achievement. We think, on the contrary, that the South is just about to develop its full power of resistance.—But, whatever the military situation may be, there are few who can be hopeful in regard to the prospective political condition of the republic. It is one of the peculiar attributes of this war, that Federal victories leave us as far as ever from a settlement of the question in dispute. In fact, the immediate effect of the successes of the Federal arms is to increase the financial disorder that oppresses the North. Even among the most earnest supporters of the administration, there is more uneasiness at this moment than there has been at any previous period, even of Federal disaster. The people of the North are begining to realize that the conquest of the South would be but the commencement of a new era of misfortunes—social, financial and political.

Although men may refuse to be guided by the promptings of justice and humanity, they cannot resist the sterner appeal that is made to their instincts of self preservation, when the shadow of calamity stretches across their path. It is no longer the lust of conquest that urges the North to prolong this struggle, for our people, in the midst of their rejoicing over recent Federal victories, are more conscious now than ever that Federal fleets and armies can subjugate neither the spirit nor the sympathies of the South. It is then possible that a foolish pride, a vindictiveness, or a craving for more Southern blood, more desolation to be visited Southern homes, prompts this persistence in unnatural strife long after its futility is apparent? With the courage of Northern soldiers and the abundance of Northern resources acknowledged by the world, are we ashamed to confess that we have undertaken a task that not courage, nor skill, nor resources can accomplish? We should rather rejoice that the design to subjugate an American people has failed. We should be proud to acknowledge that the South cannot be compelled to yield at the bayonet's point their political convictions; for by their prowess and their devotion to the cause that they hold sacred they have proved themselves worthy of the glorious ancestry that is our pride as well as theirs.

As it is, our gigantic efforts in the field baffled so far as they designed the enforcement of a political creed upon a people entitled to and deserving the privilge of self-government, the failure of the North is a blessing to the whole country. It attests that the spirit of our institutions is invulnerable to the sword, and that the only peril to our republicanism is in the cupidity or ambition of its guardians. The struggle has not been in vain, if, at its close the combatants shall realize that their inheritance is secure from the more influence of physical force; still better service will it have done, if it teaches us by an experience that comes not too late, how facile the advance of centralization in a condition of civil strife. That is our great peril. The conquest of the South would invite, would compel, perhaps, a military despotism over the whole country. That danger may be averted by the heroism and constancy of the Southern people; and in their vindication of the sovereignty of the States, our posterity will give them honor as the champions of a principle that is of no less value to the North than to the South.

But we have already paid too dear a price for this experience. Though we may pass the ordeal purified in spirit, in a material sense there will remain such wounds as centuries will not heal. With our financial system in irreparable disorder, we are standing at the threshold of a war with foreign powers. It is useless to shut our eyes to the lightning, and our ears to the thunder, and pretend that the storm is now about to burst upon us, when we are least prepared to meet its fury. The late Congress pledged this country to vindicate the republicanism of Mexico. It cannot recede from this position with out dishonor. If, in opposition to the action of the National Legislative bodies and to the sentiment of the people, the Executive should pay the tribute of fear and expediency to imperialism upon this continent event that base betrayed of republicanism would not save the Federal Government from a collision with Maximilian and his transatlantic sponsor. The intentions of the French Emperor, must be understood by this Administration. It is impossible that men trained to diplomacy, and constantly occupied in interpreting the manifestations of foreign sentiment, should be deceived as to the policy of the natural enemies of republicanism at this crisis.

We have already shown the numerous signs that demonstrate the purpose of France and her dependencies to propitiate the South by recognition, and, if neccessary, by armed intervention. Those who have followed, from the initiation of Napoleon's enterprise in Mexico, the development of this bold and prosperous intrigue, are conscious that the independence of the Confederacy is involved as an indispensable link in the well wrought chain of events by which the founders of the Mexican Empire hope to secure its stability

The interest, the honour, the political faith of the North demand that this conspiracy against republican institutions upon this continent be forbidden by our statesmanship and defeated by Federal fleets and armies. The Federal House, by a unanimous vote, devoted itself to the fulfilment of that mission, and the Senate, more recently, has accepted the obligation. Who among those representatives of the people will dare forsake that honorable and sacred cause?

Or in the Senate, what Senator will recall the words of defiance, the pledge of support to the Mexican Republic so lately uttered by that body? Or, throughout the length and breadth of the land, what American citizen will repudiate the action of his representatives, according sympathy and aid to a sister republic in its hour of extreme peril? This Government must redeem its pledge, and the obligation is none the less because it must be fulfilled at the sword's point.

Choose, then, whether we enter into the foreign war in alliance with the South leagued with a foreign foe against us. The election cannot be deferred for hesitation will cancel the priviledge of choise.

Let us suppose the South crushed into passive obedience to the Federal will, its allies whipped and humbled, and the Union reconstructed.—What then? The elements of discord would be [illegible]ork unceasingly to tumble this Union of [con]queror and conquered, of master and subject, [fro]m its unsure foundation. Eternal hatred, [b]itterness and jelousey would exist betw[een] the sections. The North boastful and arrog[ant] and the South, brooding in silence over [its h]umiliation, would present such a mocker[y of] republicanism that even patriotism would [find r]elief in accepting in its stead, an avowed [des]potism.

Every [dis]turbance with [illegible] Powers would be a sign[al f]or the pent [up vind]ictiveness of the subdu[ed] section to burst forth and at the period wh[en w]e most would be found lukewarm, at [the] best and, at the worst, arrayed in open ho[stil]ity, leagued with our foes, against us. Admit[ting] therefore, the ultimate supremacy of th[e F]ederal arms, triumph would prove, like P[an]dora, a "fascinating mischief," opening the [ca]sket of evils into the future of the Republic.

It is but the [gl]adiator's pride, the pride of muscle, of en[d]urance, of martial skill, that keeps up this [con]test so long after our better judgment has th[ro]wn the the warder down.—Better the presen[t s]acrifice of such a pride to the great sacrifice o[f in]terest, peace and happiness hereafter. There [is] but one way to secure friendship and [unity] of action in the common interest of repub[lican]ism between the sections.

From the [Co]lumbus Enquirer.

A Pra[ctica]ble Plan.

Many soldiers and [em]ployees of the Government have not been [pa]id for months. They or their families abso[lute]ly need the little pittance due them.

The pay officers ha[ve no] money. The machinery for its manu[fac]tories cannot now be worked.

The blockade is so [ne]arly effective as to make it hazardous, if [no]t impracticable, to export our hair or jewel[s] to a foreign market.

Wherever meetings have been held, the ladies have expressed an earnest desire to make every needed sacrifice.

We hail thers patriotic manifestations of their devotion to our cause, [a]s sure harbingers of success. The ladies [are co]nvinced of the fact that every earthly [illegible] is at stake; their hair, their jewels, the[ir ho]nor, their lives all depend upon the success [of] our brave heroes in the field.

All that makes life desirable or existence sufferable is involved in the momentous issue.

Let us make a united strenuou[s] to encourage and strengthen the hearts of our noble and veteran army now engaged in fru[str]ating the designs of our cruel and relentl[ess foe]; whose rapacity and diabolism can find no paralell in history.

THE PLAN.

Let all the jewels and hair in the Confederacy be regarded as pledged to re[lie]ve the Treasury from the present embarrass[ment].

Let every gentleman feel that his jewelry, too, is embraced in the pledge.

Let every paymaster and tax in kind agent be receivers of Confederate money to redeem the jewels and hair.

Let every one put his or her own valuation on the articles pledged and redeem them promptly, taking the receiver's receipt for the money. Let tax in kind agents forward the money to pay officers, and let these officers begin at once to pay off the soldiers with the means thus contributed.

THE CONSEQUENCE.

This plan is feasible, tangible, practicable and we think, unobjectionable It will enable every paymaster to respond promptly to the soldiers call for money. The "NO MONEY" card in all offices will be removed. Soldiers, who draw clothing and rations, will send their money to these families. Their families, with it, can buy provisions—and thus we can remove a strong Plea for desertion.

Value your hair and jewels and redeem them in Confederate Treasury notes.

My jewelry is worth but little, say $500; but my hair is valuable—my very limited means, exiled as I am from home and friends, will not justify me to redeeming it at above $1,000.

The sum I shall place in the paymaster's hand and take his receipt.

Let every patriotic lady in the South pursue this plan and the Treasury will be filled, the the gallant soldier paid, the farmers remunerated, and the whole community benefitted.

Some may not be able to redeem their hair.

Let patriotic men *volunteer* to redeem it with *cash*. Here's a chance for the old and phisically disabled and the soft place men to volenteer and serve their country successfully. What think you our houses and lands will be worth to us in the event our enemies are successful?—

See advertisement in Northern papers offering for sale "all the best lands in Alabama and Mississippi. Maps with topographical descriptions from the Public Land Office in Washington.—Title made in fee simple. Any Federal paper issues taken in payment."

If we fail to establish our independence, all our toil and trouble have been for naught.—

The precious lives, the valued blood of our farthers, brothers, sons and friends have poured out in vain.

But we must not fail. The vast expenditure of blood and treasure, the reccollection of the past, the hopes of the future forbid it. Let us erase the word from our vocabulary and resolve anew "never to give up the ship.

Let society refuse to recognize those who refuse or neglect to redeem their jewels, rather let us hope that all will cheerfully maintain their social position and that success will crown our efforts.

Nashville.

SPECIAL NOTICES.

TELEGRAPHIC.

Reports of the Press Association.

MESSAGE FROM THE PRESIDENT.

Danville, April 5th, 1865.

The President issued an address this morning to the people. He says that the General-in-Chief found it necessary to make such movements of troops as to uncover the Capitol. It would be unwise to conceal the moral and material injury to our cause resulting from the occupation of the capitol by the enemy, but it is equally unwise and unworthy of us to allow our energies to falter, or our efforts to become relaxed, under reverses however calamitous.

For many months the finest army of the Confederacy, under the command of a leader, whose presence inspires equal confidence in the troops and the people, has been greatly trammelled by the necessity of keeping constant watch over the approaches to the Capitol, and has been forced to forego more than one opportunity for promising enterprise.

It is for us, my countrymen to show by our bearing under reverses how wretched has been the self denial of those who have found us less able to endure misfortune with fortitude than to encounter danger with courage.

We have now entered upon a new phase of the struggle. Relieved from the necessity of guarding particular places, our army will be free to move from point to point and defeat the enemy in detail far from his base.

Let us but will it and we are free. Animated by that confidence in your spirit and fortitude which never yet failed me, I announce to you, fellow-countrymen, that it is my purpose to maintain your cause with my whole heart and soul; that I will never consent to abandon to the enemy one foot of the soil *of any one of the States* of the Confederacy.

That noble State whose ancient renown has been eclipsed by her still more glorious recent history; whose bosom has been bared to receive the main shocks of this war; whose sons and daughters have exhibited heroism so sublime as to render her illustrious in all coming time; that Virginia, with the help of the people, by the blessing of Providence, shall be still defended and no peace ever be made with the infamous invaders of her homes by the sacrifice of any of her rights or territory.

If by superiority of numbers we shall ever be compelled to withdraw from her lines, or those of any other border State, again and again shall we return until the baffled and exhausted enemy shall abandon in despair his endless and impossible task of making slaves of people resolved to be free.

Let us, then, not despond, my countrymen, relying on the never parting mercy and protection of our God, let us meet the foe with fresh defiance, with unconquered and unconquerable hearts.

Jefferson Davis.

Savannah Republican.

VOL. LXV. [NEW SERIES.] SAVANNAH, GEORGIA, SATURDAY MORNING, APRIL 8, 1865. [PRICE 5 CENTS.] NO. 99

THE REPUBLICAN

J. E. HAYES, Editor and Proprietor

SAVANNAH, GEORGIA.

SATURDAY MORNING, APRIL 8, 65

SHERMAN.

THE GREAT CONQUERING ARMY—DISTRIBUTION OF SUPPLIES—MORE ABOUT THE TRIUMPHAL MARCH THROUGH GEORGIA—THE LATE BATTLES—OUR LOSSES AND THOSE OF THE ENEMY—A CARGO OF THE "POOR WHITE TRASH"—THEIR DEGRADED CONDITION—PARTIAL LIST OF CASUALTIES.

RESTING AND REFITTING.

[Special Correspondence of the Inquirer.]

GOLDSBORO', March 26.

Round about this little Carolina town, stretching for miles away into the country, are the mighty hosts of Sherman. Here we behold the army of the war; the invincibles who have carved their way from the prairies of the West to where the Atlantic dashes in ceaseless surges against the eastern boundaries of Georgia. Thence from Georgia northward through the boasted natural stronghold, the swamps of the Carolinas, through the very heart of the mother of Secession and Treason, blustering, haughty South Carolina, now conquered, subjugated, humiliated, whichever expletive may suit them best. The South Carolinians boasted themselves Rebels, and through their State, as through the territory of a rebellious people, marched the conquering hosts of Sherman.

Distribution of Supplies.

Clothing is being issued to the men; never did soldiers need new clothing more. The regular army rations are also arriving in abundance. These might be dispensed with for some days yet, as far as the soldiers are concerned, having still on hand a few days' rations of forage. The commissary arrangements of this army seem wondrously strange to one who has only witnessed the regular supply department of our armies in Virginia. As the army came in here, our eyes were regaled with the novel sight of barouches filled with bacon. Natty buggies, containing disabled soldiers, and from the axles of these stylish little vehicles pendant hams dangled. Family carriages in tow of lumbering army wagons, and through the glass windows of these roomy and comfortable vehicles were visible piles of turkeys, chickens and geese. "Foraging in an enemy's country is not so bad a mode of subsisting after all," we remarked to ... at our side. "Ah!" said he, shaking his head deprecatingly, "this is nothing; you should have seen us in Georgia." For, to all our wondering exclamations, they reply that all we here behold is stale, flat and unprofitable, compared with the wonderful Georgia campaign. An irreverent wag of a Tennessee Sergeant was telling a group of his men, "that if they would all be good soldiers, and ever attentive to their Bibles in this life, in the hereafter celestial street ... would lead them in an eternal march ... interminable Georgia, praying for ..." This novel and startling the... grave approval of the group; a ... announced their determination to ... Sergeant's standard of rectitude ...

SAAC N... Late Exer... Office, and Ar... 2d Aud. Office. ISAAC ... Attorney

... ston's losses in the battles of the 19th and ... near Bentonville, will undoubtedly reach an aggregate of five thousand. The Fifteenth and Twentieth Corps buried of Rebel dead, and collected wounded, a total reaching two thousand five hundred. The small squads of prisoners taken by the Seventeenth and Fourteenth Corps, when put together, foot up a total of thirteen hundred. The entire number has been sent to Newbern; so there can be no doubt as the accuracy of the estimate. Among these prisoners is a scion of the house of Rhett. He was captured at Taylor's Hole Creek, inside of Kilpatrick's skirmish line. He drew his revolver on his captor when first summoned to surrender; the member of the house of Kilpatrick took cool aim with his "Spencer." The representative of the blood and chivalry of South Carolina dropped his revolver and gave himself up, to save his bacon, very like a common mortal. A. Huger, too, is among the motley group of prisoners, late a lieutenant in Joe Johnson's army.

The oath of allegiance was yesterday administered to A. C. Latham, High Sheriff of Craven county. The writs of Sheriff Latham have operated in but a limited bailiwick since March, 1862.

Refugees.

A new class of refugees have arrived here with Sherman's army. They are all, with rare exception, of the poorer class, representatives of the poor whites, women and children principally, whose husbands and fathers are in the Rebel army, or have died upholding the Rebel cause. Nearly all of them lived near the borders of the large plantations of the Carolinas, gaining a precarious subsistence and holding a rank not dissimilar from that of the *villiens* of feudal times. When fire and sword wasted mansion and plantation alike, these poor creatures knew not how to live. They received permission to follow the army, and trudged on after the soldiers. Questioning some of the women as to how they managed to carry their young children such long distances, they all replied, "We didn't carry them in; the Yankee sojers put all the wee ones in the wagons and carriages." All of them are cla... coarse homespun fabrics. Many of the female... their appearance give unmistakeable ... parentage higher than the pure corn- ... Women with hands, and eyes, and ... which an oil princess would ... piety of her fortune to possess, turned ... ds to take from their mouths cuds of ... of such size as to interfere with their ... ation. They all chew incessantly. Even ... girls of eight years of age chew.

... This seems like drawing the long bow, but seeing these little girls chewing and spirting forth the tobacco juice like old tars, I ventured to inquire their age of their mothers. Eight years was the response in many instances. They are utterly ignorant, have a confused idea of Christianity, and as to the war they know nothing, save that "the Yankees is gwine to free the niggers," the accomplishment of which laudable endeavor they have been taught to regard as the greatest calamity that could possibly befall the human family.

What is to be done with these people? The war is throwing light in upon the dark places of our country. The bony dwellers in the darkness are coming forth; the light of freedom glares their eyes. Will not some of the many Christian philanthropists of the North turn their attention to these new found heathens? They are our countrywomen, and these little ... chewing maidens may become the ... future Presidents. As it is they ... through the country ... their way to New- ... to provide for ... ms need- ed in their case. I am informed that numbers of them went from Fayetville to Wilmington.

The prisoners say their officers assured them of victory, telling them that Sherman's army was widely scattered, and that they had but to fall upon our left, attack, crush, then move on to our rear and capture the wagon trains. Comparing the statements of many different prisoners, it is made manifest that the possession of Sherman's trains was the object of Johnston's fierce and determined onset at Bentonville. To beat the entire army does not appear to have been any party of the Rebel leaders intention.

The entire mob of captive "Johnnies" are better supplied with abundant rations of pork and crackers, they not experiencing the treatment that our men receive at Rebel hands. The fastidiousness of these Rebs is amusing; some of them swore roundly at being compelled to ride from Goldsboro' to Newbern in flat open cars—These gentlemen in grey —— the Yankees for not having passenger cars at hand to convey them. Asking one of them if cushioned passenger cars were generally provided for them by their masters in Dixie, "No, sir," answered the Johnnie, "but our boys that's been took by you'uns deklar that you'uns use 'em fust rate, heap better nor our folks, an think if you'uns don't use we uns all like, ta'nt farr no how."

The prisoners, when questioned separately, declared it as their firm intention never to be exchanged, but to take oath of *religions*, as they call it. They distrust each other, and when together are sullen and uncommunicative.

A Rebel division Surgeon, left behind at Bentonville to look after his wounded, puts Johnston's loss at 500.

The Second Division of the Fourteenth Corps, buried 300 Rebel dead in their front.

Our Losses.

As the reports of brigade and division surgeons begin to come in, the first estimates of our losses prove to have been too high. The aggregate of our casualties will fall below 1500, not one-third of the Rebel loss. The Thirteenth Michigan loses the most heavily of any regiment, and behaved with distinguished gallantry. Of the Corps, the Fourteenth and Twentieth lost heaviest.

The First Brigade, First Division, of the Fourteenth Corps, lost in killed and wounded 120. The entire Division lost 308. The First Division of the Fifteenth Corps lost 90.

All our officers agree in saying that they never knew the Rebs to fight as well as they did at Bentonsville. Among our casualties are—

Major Eaton, 13th Mich., killed.
Lieut. Midgly, 21st Wis., killed.
Lt. Col. Miles, 79th Pa., wounded.
Capt. Swann, 38th Ind., wounded.
Lieut. Steele, 42d Ind., wounded, fatal.
Lieut. Rutledge, 42d Ind., wounded, fatal.

Our wounded are all in Goldsboro, and well cared for in houses. There are some few in tents, but all comfortable and doing well.

THE coasting trade of Chili will be opened to vessels of every nation on the first of May. The immediate effect of this will be to increase trade with San Francisco, and benefit our commerce there generally.—The imports of that country ... Valdivia, were $25,298,925 in 1855; $19,804,041 in 1856, and $31,800,209 in 1857. The exports were $19,110,589 in 1855; $18,159,522 in 1856, and $20,126,461 in 1857. The principal export is copper and copper ores.

A Good Boston Idea.

The most interesting feature of the week in Boston art circles was the exhibition of the nucleus of a national gallery of our Heroes of the present war. The founder has selected one thousand officers and two hundred and fifty privates, representing every loyal State, for the honors of the gallery, which is to be permanently located in this city, and will be a great feature to attract visitors from every part of the civilized world. Some seventy portraits are already completed, and many more are in progress. The gallery is to be limited, with some exceptions to those heroes who have been mustered out by the grim officer by whose agency we shall all, sooner or later, get our discharge. The friends of a deceased hero are expected to furnish his portrait for the gallery if they are able. In other cases the means have been raised by subscription, or furnished by the founder of his own liberal purse.—*Boston Herald.*

Every city, town and hamlet in our land should have its patriot gallery, where in future generations our children's children may gaze in sacred admiration at the loyal features of our nation's defenders.

Extension of Freedom in Kentucky.

LOUISVILLE, KY., March 14.—An order from Major General Palmer announced that by the act of Congress passed on the 3d of March, the wives and children of colored men who have enlisted or may enlist in the army are free. The order promised an enforcement of their rights by the military authorities if necessary, and urges the loyal men and women of Kentucky to encourage the enlistment of colored men in the army, and afterward to recognize them as upholders of the Government and defenders of their homes, and exhorts them to exercise Kentucky's accustomed benevolence and charity towards the helpless women and children thus made free.

Gen. James S. Brisbane has been appointed to superintend the organization of white and colored troops in Kentucky.

Increase of Rebel Deserters.

Deserters continue to arrive here at the rate of one hundred and fifty per diem. March foots up about three thousand, February was over twelve hundred, and April, from the present prospect, will run over five thousand. Rather a heavy drain this on Lee's army! There are three go the other way home where one comes North, is the assurance given by nearly all who come North.—*Philadelphia Enquirer.*

Another Delusion of the Rebel Mind.

[From the Richmond Whig, March 15.]

Napoleon and the Confederacy.

We see it stated that a reliable citizen of Augusta, Ga. reports that Mayor Macbeth, of Charleston, says the French Consul assured him that he had advices from the Emperor Napoleon to the effect that he would assert the independence of the Confederacy on the 4th of March, and, if necessary, support the declaration with armed intervention. French vessels are rendezvousing at convenient points on the Atlantic coast and Gulf of Mexico.

Kirby Smith not Expected to Do Any Fighting.

[From the Richmond Whig, March 15.]

A gentleman arrived here this morning direct from beyond the Mississippi. He reports everything quiet in the department of General Kirby Smith.—*Mobile Tribune.*

This has been the report for nearly ten months. We have ceased to look for war news from that quarter.

The mechanics of New York are engaged in a movement to secure higher wages. In the cases of masons, plasterers, stone-cutters and carpenters they have already succeeded.

A Chinese thief having stolen a missionary's watch, brought it back to him the next day for instructions how to wind it up!

New York has enlisted 400 negroes on her quota at Charleston.

NEWS FROM AUGUSTA.

Sights and Sensations—Extravagance and Extortion—Prices and Poverty—Our Congress and our Colors, etc., etc.

AUGUSTA, GA., March 21, 1865.

Yesterday was the usual time for the sensation reports, second edition of newspapers and the appearance of thousands of beautiful ladies and gilded soldiers to enliven the streets of this extravagant city, but the sensational was at a discount for once—not even a rumor disturbed the even atmosphere, though all the rest of the invoice occurred; however, the items happen daily at any rate. A brigade of handsome fellows, in beautiful new clothes, perambulate the streets, glittering and glistening in the sunshine, and a corps of lovely women exhibit their dry goods that cost a fortune per dress. But that is their business, and I don't have to pay for any of them, the blessed institutions that they enfold can justifiably request me to dry up on the subject.

Judging from the enormous extravagance and terrible prices that rule in this city, we do not wonder that the fate that overtook Sodom, a few years ago, should come over this place. Prices keep getting up, up, up, but I am ... they will not take the guilty parties, who caused it to ascend, to heaven with them. Notice for instance the prices that rule in the following extract

W. A. Ramsey & Co., at auction, on Friday last, obtained the following prices: Axes, $60; small pine tables, $28; wine glasses, $15; dishes, $37 a piece; mattresses, $115; faucets, $105; bureaus, $900; washstands, $400; carriages, $10,000; gold spectacles, $500; gold eyeglasses, $650; gold watches, $1,500; blankets, $175; wool hats, $600 per dozen; white hose $200 per dozen; carpets, $75 per yard; tea $100 per pound; candles, $20 per pound; sole leather, $18 per pound; Irish potatoes, $75 per bushel; English foolscap paper, $400 per ream; envelopes, $60 per thousand; piano, $5,000. These prices are but a part of the terrible crucifixion to which the people are being subjected to. A few successful persons managing to make enough to bear up under the pressure—But what becomes of the poor, who find much difficulty in getting money at all, and what they do get does not buy even decent homespun clothing.

Congress, before its adjournment, passed a bill changing the appearance of our national flag—For once Congress has done well, for the late flag was so much like a flag of truce, or a dirty shirt hung on a pole, that it never created any enthusiasm among our men, and always reminded us that we were too anxious entirely for peaceful symbols, even to the folly of flaunting them constantly in the face of a bloody enemy. The new flag is a composition between St. Andrew's and St. George's cross. There is as little blue and as much red as possible for effect, in it. There is no doubt that it will furnish more gratification than any of the former.

Sherman continues to threaten a flank movement, which, if successful, will cut the Danville road, by way of Raleigh or some other point in North Carolina. He is making a bold effort to carry out the programme announced before he left Savannah.

CANTIN.

The Wagon Train of the Army of Tennessee—Sherman's Position and Movements—The Tele... Charlotte to Columbia—Prices are Kept Up...

AUGUSTA, GA., March 24, 1865.

During the past two days the streets of this city have been very much enlivened by the passage of the wagon train of the Army of Tennessee. As the long train filed along the streets, the mules in pretty good condition and the drivers in good spirits, the procession attracted a large audience of army people and citizens. Thousands of jests, so common amongst soldiers, were bandied between the lazy, rollicking, indifferent, and almost good-for-nothing, drivers, and the dashing cavalry that have been occupying the streets during the past few days. Shouts and huzzas were given in all directions, especially when a lady, by any accident or intent, flaunted her handkerchief to the escorts that have attended the train through its transit from Tupelo, Miss., to this place. All necessary repairs and provisions for the trip will be made by Monday, when the long cavalcade will again resume the march for General Johnson's field of operations. Until then, the thousands of drivers, and details, and stragglers of all kinds, will remain in this vicinity, and we do not think it will be beneficial to them, for the very good reason, that they will have access to too much mean liquor, and will be certain to use it, to their great detriment.

The latest account from Sherman represents him in the vicinity of Cheraw and Wadesboro, threatening our forces at the latter place.—Rumors current that a battle was fought there a few days ago, but no official confirmation of it had been received up to a few hours ago.—There is a probability, however, that a collision may have occurred between Sherman's advance and a portion of our forces, that have been moving from Charleston to form a junction with Johnston's main army from Charlotte.

The telegraph line has been established between Charlotte and Columbia, putting the latter place in communication immediately with Richmond. The line by way of Branchville is being rapidly completed from Aiken to Columbia, and it is supposed will be finished in two weeks, when we will be again in immediate connection with the capital. I suppose a courier line will run between this place and Columbia to prevent unnecessary delay in the transmission of dispatches.

The fluctuations in trade and prices in this city are a source of amusement to those who do not have to purchase any of the articles offered for sale. The figures of one day are no index to the prices of the next. On the basis of such fluctuations, and to show you how the thing is done, you will go with me into the cosy resting place in the rear of a certain store. The proprietress has gone forward towards the door. We hear her voice:

"John, what are you selling those stockings for?"

"Ma'am! the lady said you offered them to her for two hundred dollars a dozen yesterday."

"Oh! dear me! There's fifty dollars a dozen lost. I forgot to tell you this morning to charge two fifty for them. Well! Mary, put fifty dollars more on the price of that eight hundred dollar handkerchief, and put—those stockings up to three hundred dollars a dozen, and that black spool cotton to twenty dollars a spool to-morrow, and don't sell more than two spools to one person."

"Ma'am—Customer wants to know how much this cheese is *now*. He got a half pound this morning at forty dollars."

(In a whisper)—"Aha! cheese is getting in demand, umha! (Aloud—Can't sell it for less than sixty dollars."

Customer disappears.

"How much did he take, Jenny?"

"Two pounds, ma'am, and said he would be in to-morrow for some more if it did not go over his pile."

"Two pounds? Don't sell more than a half pound to one person hereafter. Dear me; I'm afraid I've lost on that cheese.—Johnny, go and cut a half inch off of each of those wax candles, and add a pound of wheat flour to every ten pounds of that white sugar. (Coming back to the room chuckling and speaking to herself)—That's pretty good; wheat flour at three dollars a pound, and sell sugar at thirty—right good, um."

This fair storekeeper lives in much better style now than she did in peace times. We took a glass of wine and some sugar buns and left her in charming spirits over her prospect of three thousand dollars profit that day. No doubt she and the ten thousand speculators she represents, bless the good fortune that keeps the war going for their benefit.

CANTIN.

POETRY.

ORIGINAL AND SELECTED.

A GLEAM OF SUNSHINE.

This is the place. Stand still, my steed,
Let me review the scene,
And summon from the shadowy Past
The forms that once have been.

The Past and Present here unite,
Beneath Time's flowing tide,
Like footprints hidden by a brook,
But seen on either side.

Here runs the highway to the town;
There the green lane descends,
Through which I walked to church with thee,
O gentlest of our friends!

The shadow of the linden-trees
Lay moving on the grass;
Between them and the moving boughs,
A shadow, thou didst pass.

Thy dress was like the lilies,
And thy heart as pure as they;
One of God's holy messengers
Did walk with me that day.

I saw the branches of the trees
Bend down thy touch to meet,
The clover-blossoms in the grass
Rise up to kiss thy feet.

"Sleep, sleep to-day, tormenting cares,
Of earth and folly born!"
Solemnly sang the village choir
On that sweet Sabbath morn.

Thro' the closed blinds the golden sun
Poured in a dusty beam,
Like the celestial ladder seen
By Jacob in his dream.

And ever and anon, the wind,
Sweet scented with the hay,
Turned o'er the hymnbook's fluttering leaves
That on the window lay.

Long was the good man's sermon,
Yet it seemed not so to me;
For he spake of Ruth the beautiful,
And still I thought of thee.

Long was the prayer he uttered,
Yet it seemed not so to me;
For in my heart I prayed with him,
And still I thought of thee.

But now, alas! the place seems changed;
Thou art no longer here;
Part of the sunshine of the scene
With thee did disappear.

Though thoughts ... and breathe
A low and ceaseless sigh;

This memory brightens o'er the past,
As when the sun, concealed
Behind some cloud that near us hangs,
Shines on a distant field.

DANGEROUS EYES.

"Blue eyes melt; Dark eyes burn."
Cornish Saying.

The eyes that melt! The eyes that burn!
The lips that make a lover yearn!
These flashed on my bewildered sight,
Like meteors of the Northern Night!

Then said I, in my wild amaze,
What stars be they that greet my gaze?
Where shall my shivering rudder turn?
To eyes that melt, or eyes that burn!

Ah! safer far the darkling sea,
Than where such perilous signals be,—
To rock, and storm, and whirlwind, turn,
From eyes that melt, and eyes that burn!

All the Year Round.

AFFECTION.

There is in life no blessing like affection;
It soothes, it hallows, elevates, subdues,
And bringeth down to earth its native heaven;
It sits besides the cradle patient hours,
Whose sole contentment is to watch and love;
It bendeth o'er the death-bed, and conceals
Its own despair with words of faith and hope.
Life hath naught else that may supply its place;
Void is ambition, cold is vanity,
And with an empty glitter, without love.

Miss Landor.

Items.

Gen'l Hawley, in command at Wilmington, has issued an order for the delivering up to the Federal authorities of all rifles and muskets and their appertenances, swords, pistols, and military weapons and equipments that were formerly held by the ... Confederate authorities. It is known that a large quantity of small arms, of various descriptions, were hid in the city.

Alexander Milliner, a revolutionary soldier, died at Adams' Basin, thirteen miles from Rochester, N. Y., on Tuesday morning, at the age of one hundred and five years.

There was a fight between twenty of our troops and sixty guerrillas thirty miles from Paducah on Wednesday night. Twenty guerrillas were killed, including the notorious leader Capt. McDougal. Capt. McGregory was killed on our side.

Gen. Meredith has several expeditions out clearing West Kentucky of guerrillas.

Prof. Agassiz will take out with him a small flock of the finest American Spanish merino sheep, sent by Dr. George B. Loring, President of the Massachusetts Agricultural Society, to the Emperor of Brazil.

Gold coinage at the Philadelphia mint for January, $183,965; silver, $28,489; copper, $92,200. Total $304,654.

Austria and Prussia have agreed upon the flag for the mercantile marine of Schleswig-Holstein. It is composed of three horizontal bands, the upper one blue, that in the middle white, and the lower one red. The blue band is to have a yellow square by the side of the staff.

The expense of collecting internal revenue in this country is about two per cent., being one per cent. less than the expense of collecting revenue in England.

The Chicago Journal is treading on dangerous ground as will be seen by the following "notice to quit" which was served on it the other day: "Mr. Editor: Ef you doant stop a blown about the Fust Ward in ure paper, you may get inter trubul The First Ward are ol right. By trubul I mean gitten licked. Ures, First Ward."

The U. S. Navy Department claims the right to capture any merchant vessel returning from a blockade port after violating the blockade, such right to exist at any time during the return voyage.

A Catholic Orphan Asylum, to cost $40,000, is to be built the present year at Fort Wayne, Indiana.

Crossly & Sons' carpet manufactory at Halifax, England, is the largest in the world. It has a capital of $2,250,000, and employs 4,400 workmen.

CALENDAR FOR 1865.

1865.	SUNDAY	MONDAY	TUESDAY	WEDNESDAY	THURSDAY	FRIDAY	SATURDAY	1865.	SUNDAY	MONDAY	TUESDAY	WEDNESDAY	THURSDAY	FRIDAY	SATURDAY
JAN'Y	1	2	3	4	5	6	7	JULY	..	..	..	..	..	..	1
	8	9	10	11	12	13	14		2	3	4	5	6	7	8
	15	16	17	18	19	20	21		9	10	11	12	13	14	15
	22	23	24	25	26	27	28		16	17	18	19	20	21	22
	29	30	31	..	..	..	..		23	24	25	26	27	28	29
	..	..	..	..	..	..	..		30	31	..	..	..	..	..
FEB'Y	..	..	..	1	2	3	4	AUG'T	..	..	1	2	3	4	5
	5	6	7	8	9	10	11		6	7	8	9	10	11	12
	12	13	14	15	16	17	18		13	14	15	16	17	18	19
	19	20	21	22	23	24	25		20	21	22	23	24	25	26
	26	27	28	..	..	..	..		27	28	29	30	31	..	..
M'CH.	..	..	..	1	2	3	4	SEPT'R	..	..	..	..	..	1	2
	5	6	7	8	9	10	11		3	4	5	6	7	8	9
	12	13	14	15	16	17	18		10	11	12	13	14	15	16
	19	20	21	22	23	24	25		17	18	19	20	21	22	23
	26	27	28	29	30	31	..		24	25	26	27	28	29	30
APRIL	..	..	..	..	..	..	1		..	..	..	..	..	..	..
	2	3	4	5	6	7	8	OCT'R.	1	2	3	4	5	6	7
	9	10	11	12	13	14	15		8	9	10	11	12	13	14
	16	17	18	19	20	21	22		15	16	17	18	19	20	21
	23	24	25	26	27	28	29		22	23	24	25	26	27	28
	30	..	..	..	..	..	..		29	30	31	..	..	..	..
MAY..	..	1	2	3	4	5	6	NOV'R	..	..	..	1	2	3	4
	7	8	9	10	11	12	13		5	6	7	8	9	10	11
	14	15	16	17	18	19	20		12	13	14	15	16	17	18
	21	22	23	24	25	26	27		19	20	21	22	23	24	25
	28	29	30	31	..	..	..		26	27	28	29	30	..	..
JUNE.	..	..	..	..	1	2	3	DEC'R.	..	..	..	..	..	1	2
	4	5	6	7	8	9	10		3	4	5	6	7	8	9
	11	12	13	14	15	16	17		10	11	12	13	14	15	16
	18	19	20	21	22	23	24		17	18	19	20	21	22	23
	25	26	27	28	29	30	..		24	25	26	27	28	29	30
	..	..	..	..	..	..	..		31	..	..	..	..	..	..

Post Office Notice.

POST OFFICE, SAVANNAH, GA.,
April 1, 1865.

All key and open boxes must be re-assigned and paid for, one-quarter in advance, by April 1st, 1865, or mail matter for the same will be placed in the General Delivery.

Persons who paid for a full quarter during the months of February and March, and did not use their boxes previously, will be allowed a deduction for this quarter equal to the time the boxes were not used during the last quarter.

Persons having boxes will please furnish this office with lists of members of their families, or others, whose mail matter should be placed in their boxes; and would greatly facilitate distribution if they would request their correspondents to place the number of their box in the address of letters.

Persons having key boxes, who do not wish to retain the same, will please return the keys at once.

A. L. HARRIS,
Special Agent P. O. Dept.

apl1—5t

HEADQ'RS U. S. FORCES,
Savannah, Ga., March 28th, 1865.

GENERAL ORDER,
No. 25.

The City Market will be governed by the following regulations:

1. Sales may be made, by authorized persons, every day in the week, Sundays excepted, of butcher's meat, poultry, fruit, fish, vegetables, and all other kind ... subject to a scale of prices, which shall be fixed and posted in a conspicuous place in the Market.

2. From the 1st day of April until the 1st day of November, the Market shall be open, Sundays excepted, until 9 o'clock in the morning, and will close at the ringing of the Market bell.

3. Every person killing an ox or cow, or grown meat cattle, and exposing the same for sale within the city, shall take the hide and head of said animal slaughtered, attached to each other and not severed, to the Clerk of the Market, who shall record any marks about the same, and the day of the month it was brought to the market, and the book shall be subject to the inspection of any person during market hours. Any violation of the foregoing, or neglect on the part of the Clerk in not keeping the proper records will be punished by fine.

4. The Clerk of the Market will be responsible for the correctness of weights and measures used in the market, and will, from time to time, examine the same and destroy false weights and measures when found.

5. Any person exposing for sale in the market any articles of marketing at a higher price than that established for the same in the schedule of prices, will be subject to a fine and forfeiture of all right to make further sales in the market. The Clerk of the Market will report promptly to the Supervisor of Trade any violation of this paragraph.

6. The Clerk of the Market will act under the orders of the Supervisor of Trade. He will cause the market and adjacent grounds to be thoroughly policed each day, and the woodwork of the market ...

By command of
Brevet Maj. Gen. GROVER.
EDWARD G. DIKE, A. A. G.

mar 29 7

HEADQUARTERS U. S. FORCES,
SAVANNAH, GA., March 28th, 1865.

On and after this date articles in the Public Market of this City will be sold at prices as specified below. Persons violating this rule will be reported to this office and dealt with as the Military Law directs. All persons not having received permission to sell articles in the Market will at once make application to Lieut. Col. Neafie, Supervisor of Trade.

By command of Brev. Maj. Gen. C. GROVER.
ALFRED NEAFIE, Lieut. Col.
and Supervisor of Trade.

Ducks, per pair	$2 50
Geese, per pair	4 00
Turkeys, each	2 50 to 3 00
Fowls, per pair	1 50 to 2 00
Beef, fresh, best cut, per pound	40 cents.
Beef, fresh, second cut, per pound	25 "
Bacon	25 to 30 "
Mutton	30 "
Pork, fresh, per pound	25 to 30 cents
Eggs, per dozen	60 "
Mullets, per bunch (large size)	50 "
" " " (small size)	30 "
Sturgeon, per pound	7 "
Shad, each, large size	$1 00
Shad, each, small size	50 to 75 "
Trout, (salt water,) per bunch of 3.	50 "
" (fresh water,) per pound	30 "
Bass, large size, each, per pound	15 "
Bass, small size, each, per pound.	15 "
Whiting, per bunch of 5	50 "
Brim, per bunch of 5	50 "
Perch, per bunch of 5 (large size)	50 "
Jerked Beef, per pound	25 "
Suckers, per bunch of 5	50 "
Catfish, per bunch	50 "
Crabs, each	4 "
Prawns, per quart	50 "
Honey, per pound	25 "
Veal, per pound	30 "
Sausages, (fresh Pork,) per pound.	50 "
Sausages, (fresh Beef,) per pound	25 "
Shrimp, per quart	30 "
Oysters, per quart	40 "
Clams, per bushel	$2 00

CIRCULAR.

OFFICE PROVOST MARSHAL,
DISTRICT OF SAVANNAH, GA.,
March 23th, 1865.

The wives and families of Confederate officers who have not registered their names at this office *will do so at once.*

By Order of
BREVET MAJ.-GEN. C. GROVER. Com'd'g.
ROB'T P. YORK, Lt. Col. 75th N. Y. V. Vol., and Pro. Mar. Dist. of Savannah, Ga.

CIRCULAR.

SAVANNAH, March 10th, 1865.

All persons now engaged in trade of any nature whatsoever in this city, will report in writing to this office immediately:

1. By whose authority they are now doing business, date of permit, with locality.

2. Nature of business and the value of stock now on hand.

By command of Bvt. Maj. Gen. GROVER.
ALFRED NEAFIE,
Lt. Col. 156th N. Y. V.,
Supervisor of Trade for City of Sav'h.

HEADQUARTERS,
MIL. DIV. OF THE MISSISSIPPI,
In the Field, Savannah, Ga., Jan. 16, '65.

SPECIAL FIELD ORDERS,
No. 15.

I. The islands from Charleston South, the abandoned rice fields along the rivers for thirty miles back from the sea, and the country bordering the St. John's river, Florida, are reserved and set apart for the settlement of the negroes now made free by the acts of war and the Proclamation of the President of the United States.

II. At Beaufort, Hilton Head, Savannah, Fernandina, St. Augustine, and Jacksonville, the blacks may remain in their chosen or accustomed vocations; but on the islands, and in the settlements hereafter to be established, no white person whatever, unless military officers and soldiers detailed for duty, will be permitted to reside; and the sole and exclusive management of affairs will be left to the freed people themselves, subject only to the United States military authority and the acts of Congress. By the laws of war, and orders of the President of the United States, the negro is *free*, and must be dealt with as such. He cannot be subjected to conscription or forced military service, save by the written orders of the highest military authority of the Department, under such regulations as the President or Congress may prescribe. Domestic servants, blacksmiths, carpenters, and other mechanics will be free to select their own work and residence, but the young and able-bodied negroes must be encouraged to enlist as soldiers in the service of the United States, to contribute their share towards maintainig their own freedom and securing their rights as citizens of the United States. Negroes so enlisted will be organized into companies, battalions and regiments under the orders of the United States military authorities, and will be paid, fed and clothed according to law. The bounties paid on enlistment may, with the consent of the recruit, go to assist his family and settlement in procuring agricultural implements, seed, tools, boats, clothing and other articles necessary for their livelihood.

III. Whenever three respectable negroes, heads of families, shall desire to settle on land, and shall have selected for that purpose an island or a locality clearly defined, within the limits above designated, the Inspector of Settlements and Plantations will himself, or by such subordinate officer as he may appoint, give them a license to settle such island or district, and afford them such assistance as he can to enable them to establish a peaceable agricultural settlement. The three parties named will subdivide the land, under the supervision of the Inspector, among themselves, and such others as may choose to settle near them, so that each family shall have a plot of not more than (40) forty acres of tillable ground, and when it borders on some water channel, with not more than eight hundred feet front, in the possession of which land the military authorities will afford them protection until such time as they can protect themselves, or until Congress shall regulate their title. The Quartermaster may, on the requisition of the Inspector of Settlements and Plantations, place at the disposal of the Inspector one or more of the captured steamers, to ply between the settlements and one or more of the commercial poins heretofore named in orders, to afford the settlers the opportunity to supply their necessary wants and to sell the products of their land and labor.

IV. Whenever a negro has enlisted in the military service of the United States, he may locate his family in any one of the settlements at pleasure, and acquire ... privileges of a settler as though present in person. In like manner negroes may settle their families and engage on board the gunboats, or in fishing, or in the navigation of the island waters, without losing any claim to land or other advantages derived from this system. But no one, unless an actual settler as above defined, or unless absent on Government service, will be entitled to claim any right to land or property in any settlement, by virtue of those orders.

V. In order to carry out this system of settlement, a General Officer will be detailed as Inspector of Settlements, to regulate their police and general management, and who will furnish personally to each head of a family, subject to the approval of the President of the United States, a possessory title in writing, giving as near as possible the description of boundaries, and who shall adjust all claims or conflicts that may arise under the same, subject to the like approval, treating such titles altogether as possessory. The same General Officer will also be charged with the enlistment and organization of the negro recruits, and protecting their interests while so absent from their settlements; and will be governed by the Rules and Regulations prescribed by the War Department for such purpose.

VI. Brigadier General R. SAXTON is hereby appointed Inspector of Settlements and Plantations, and will at once enter on the performance of his duties. No change is intended or desired in the Settlement now on Beaufort Island, nor will any rights to property heretofore acquired be effected thereby.

By order of
MAJ. GEN. W. T. SHERMAN.
L. M. DAYTON,
Maj. and Ass't Adj't Gen'l.

SAVANNAH REPUBLICAN

SAVANNAH:

SATURDAY MORNING, APRIL 8, 1865.

REPORTED EVACUATION OF RICHMOND.

Our Forces Occupy the Confederate Capital.

GEN. LEE FALLING BACK TOWARDS BURKSVILLE JUNCTION.

We are indebted to Capt. John T. Baker, Inspector-General on Gen. Grover's staff, for files of the Augusta Constitutionalist of last Wednesday, from which we extract the following important paragraph:

EVACUATION OF RICHMOND.—A rumor has prevailed upon the streets the past few days, that our forces have successfully evacuated Richmond. No official information of this sort has been received, but we believe that it is generally understood that the Confederate Capital is in the hands of the enemy. The Yankees took possession on Monday afternoon, General Lee falling back towards Burksville Junction.

Return of Flag of Truce Boat.

Last evening the flag of truce boat Nelly Baker, Capt. Norris, returned from her trip to Sisters' Ferry, where she landed her lady passengers.—She left this city on Thursday afternoon last, and reached Sisters' Ferry at eight o'clock yesterday morning, and after landing her passengers returned, reaching her wharf about 7 o'clock.

We learn that the trip was a very pleasant one, and that all on board were in good spirits, particularly the ladies, who anticipated a joyful meeting in soon joining relatives and friends from whom they had been long separated. The Truce boat was met at Sisters' Ferry by Col. E. C. Anderson and quite a number of Confederate officers, who exchanged civilities with the Union officers on board of the steamer. The passengers and baggage were soon removed on shore and placed in conveyances, when a kind parting took place between the parties.

TO CORRESPONDENTS.—"Vagrant" has been unavoidably crowded out. He shall have a showing in our next.

First Provost Court—Judge Parsons, Presiding.

In this Court yesterday, Thomas H. Harden, executor of the estate of Mrs. Mary E. Demere was granted permission to collect the rents of said estate.

E. Mendell was given authority to collect his rents.

J. C. Pringle and Mrs. E. J. McIntyre, were granted permission to collect their rents.

In the case of G. R. Salisbury vs. Reading and Connell, the goods of the firm are to be kept in possession of the Provost Marshall until the case is settled. The case is to be heard on Monday, the 10th inst.

John Lewis was given authority to collect his rents.

Twenty two persons were allowed to take the oath of allegiance.

SECOND PROVOST COURT—CAPT. J. M. WALTON, JUDGE, PRESIDING.

Special Police vs. John Walver. The defendant was charged with selling ale to enlisted men in the U. S. army, and having liquor in his bar. He was fined in the sum of ten dollars.

Special Police vs. James Dobson, private in 14th N. H. Vols. The charge was forcibly taking a horse and wagon, the property of a negro man. The defendant was placed in confinement for five days.

Special Police vs. Joseph Weston, private 18th Ind. Vols. The defendant was charged with being drunk, and destroying private property belonging to a citizen in a saloon on Bull street. The defendant was ordered to replace the private property destroyed or its value in U. S. currency, and be placed in confinement six days.

Special Police vs. James L. Haupt. The defendant was charged with attempting to run off the Central Railroad track a train of cars containing Union prisoners, for the purpose of their destruction. It was ordered that the case be dismissed, and defendant released from arrest, he having taken the oath of allegiance to the U. S. Government, in accordance with the 1863, and subsequent General Orders No. 42, from the War Department.

Cyrus White vs. Thomas Manning, both colored. This was a claim for the recovery of a house in possession of defendant, rented by plaintiff from the proper owner. The defendant was ordered to give possession of the house in dispute to plaintiff within one week.

R. W. Campbell vs. Ann Armstrong, (colored.) The defendant was charged with the theft of a gold watch, the property of plaintiff, (a family relic.) It was ordered that in consequence of defendant living with plaintiff as his wife, defendant will turn over said watch to plaintiff on payment of fifty dollars for services rendered.

Mrs. Roselia Smith vs. J. K. Burch. This was a case for the recovery of the possession of a house, the property of defendant, and for the payment of a horse, alleged by plaintiff to have steathily carried away or destroyed by defendant. The further examination of this case was postponed for further evidence until the 8th inst.

EXHUMED.—The remains of Lt. A. W. Coe, of Battery I, 2d Illinois Artillery, who was killed during the siege of this city in December last, by an unexploded shell, which passed through his body, were on Thursday last exhumed by his brother, Mr. Corwell Woodworth, assisted by several officers of the army and navy, as also citizens. They had been interred on Dr. Cuyler's place in Effingham county, some fourteen miles from Savannah, on the Augusta and Savannah road. Mr. Woodworth desires to return thanks to all who contributed their assistance on the melancholy occasion.

BODY FOUND.—The body of an unknown man, (supposed to be white) in an advanced stage of decomposition, was found a short distance up the river on Thursday last, and, by Ensign Ross, with a detachment of the Pontiac's crew, taken ashore and decently interred.

From Florida.

The steamer Wyoming, Capt. Snow, arrived last evening. She left Jacksonville on the 27th, and Fernandina on the 28th ult., and has been detained on the passage by a break down.

The steamer Collins, previously reported as having been aground on St. Augustine bar, has five feet of water in her hold, and will be a total loss. The greater portion of her cargo has been saved.

It is reported that 4,000 prisoners are to be exchanged at Jacksonville.

On the passage the Wyoming met the U. S. gunboat Sayeroone at Doboy sound.

ARRIVAL OF ICE.—Last evening the bark Cecelian, from Boston, arrived with a cargo of ice, consigned to Messrs. Haywood, Gage & Co.

BEWARE OF COUNTERFEITS.—An immense number of counterfeit quarters and half-dollar currency notes are in circulation, and it will repay every one to exercise the strictest scrutiny in the reception of postal currency of these denominations. The counterfeits are generally upon this currency of the second issue, and a little care will in almost every instance insure the detection of the spurious. In the latter the "United States," on either upper corner of the face of the bill, appears very indistinct, as do also the steamboats and packages on the lower part of the note. The reverse also is wanting in distinctness and particularly the outline of the stars. In the counterfeits the straight line engraving is very inferior, and when the surface is not too much soiled for such examination, no better clue is afforded for their detection than the knowledge of that fact.

GEN. GRANT TAKES THE FIELD IN PERSON.—A correspondent of the Philadelphia Inquirer, dating his letter "Headquarters Army of the Potomac, in the Field, Gravelly Run, March 29, 9 P. M.," says: "General Grant has arrived with his staff. It is the first time the Lieutenant General has been personally with the army since October 27, and his presence bodes important events at hand. He came with all his little baggage that suffices him in the field. A half dozen wagons carry the houses and rations of himself and staff. The nation will be pleased to know that Grant is looking extremely well and takes to the field again as naturally as he did last spring."

BATTERY HUNTER, frequently called, after ten o'clock at night, "Hattery Bunter," is to be demolished says the Port Royal New South, and the ground between the Port Royal House and beach levelled off. During the first occupation of Port Royal it was doubtless very necessary as a part of our defences, but being now useless its demolition will be an improvement and add much to the appearance of our new city.

FROM REBELDOM.

By the truce boat Nelly Baker, which returned from Sisters' Ferry last evening, we are receip of the Augusta Constitutionalist of the 5th, from which we make the following extracts:

PRICES AT AUCTION.—Messrs. W. A. Ramsay & Co., at their auction sale in this city, on Friday last, obtained the annexed prices: Bedsteads, $230 to 500; Sofas 800 to 880; Bureaus 300 to 900; Chairs 50 to 200; Brocatelle furniture 2500 to 4,100 per sett; Matrasses 95 to 176; Child's Chair 140; Stoves 300 to 1200; Tables 80 to 150; Buggies 600 to 850; Harness 3000 to 3500 per set; Carriages 4000 to 6000; Negro boys 3000 to 3,500; Negro women 3,700 to 4,100; Woman and two children 4,500; Pianos 5,500 to 6,000; Plates 10 ... pagne glasses 350 to 360 per dozen; ... 1,200 to 1,800 per dozen; Knives and Forks 220 per doz; Trunks 800 to 1,200; Vests 50 to 80; Pants 74 to 150 per pair; Gold Watches 1500 to 2400; Cotton Cards 130 to 140 per pair; Sewing Machines 500 to 1500.

FLORIDA ITEMS.

EAST FLORIDA.—The Quincy Dispatch learns that on Friday, the 10th instant, Capt. Dickison, then at Waldo with his command, received information that a cavalry force of the enemy, numbering 200 men, had come out from St. Augustine, marched south to Volusia and there crossed the St. John's river. They took the precaution to burn the bridge over Oclawaha river, and proceeded to burn, destroy and plunder.—One large plantation near Ocala, was stripped of slaves, horses, mules cattle, &c., and then all the buildings were consigned to the flames.

Immediately upon the receipt of this intelligence, Capt. Dickison started with his command, and on reaching the Oclawaha river, found that the bridge had been burned. He could not reach the enemy in that direction, and was forced to turn eastward and strike the St. John's river at Horse Landing. Here it is supposed he crossed, but we have no further accounts from him. If the enemy has not moved very rapidly, Capt. D. has probably got between him and St. Augustine, and we may expect to hear of a brisk fight; as the Yankee cavaly is a body of new troops just sent down, and supposed to be about the best they have got.

DESERTERS SHOT.—Wm. Strickland, a deserter from Captain Griffin's cavalry company, and J. R. Brannon, a deserter from the 2d Florida Infantry, were shot to death with musketry by sentence of a court martial, in the vicinity of Tallahassee, on Saturday last. These men were members, or ringleaders of the gang that attempted to burn the trestle work of the P & Ga. Railroad over the Aucilla a short time since. They confess that they were sent by the Yankees to burn the trestle work, in order to prevent reinforcements being sent to General Miller when the enemy landed at St. Marks.

RAID IN EAST FLORIDA.—The raid into Marion county, says the Dispatch of the 22d, of which we gave some rumors last week, proves to have been made by a party of deserters and negroes, whose numbers are not known, ... Augustine, as was reported. They swept the extensive plantation of Mrs. Marshal, near Ocala, destroying fifty hogsheads of sugar and much other property, burning the buildings and carrying off slaves, mules, cattle, &c.—Brigadier-General Bullock made an effectual attempt to rally a sufficient force to attack them. They made good their retreat across the St. Johns river, but could not escape the ubiquitous, ever ready Captain Dickenson and his command, who captured and brought in twenty-four of them.

NEGRO SOLDIERS IN "OLE VIRGINNY."

RICHMOND, March 22.

Several thousand persons assembled in the Capitol Square this afternoon to witness the parade of a battalion of troops from Camps Jackson and Winder, including two companies of negroes.

The battalion marched through the principal streets headed by a brass band; and produced quite a sensation chiefly among the negro population. The interest of the occasion was lessened by a failure to uniform and equip the negro soldiers.

They were armed with muskets, and went through the manual as well as could be expected, for the short time they had been drilled. Several regiments of negroes are in the course of formation in different parts of Virginia.

REGULATIONS CONCERNING NEGRO TROOPS.

RICHMOND, March 25.

An order from the Adjutant General relative to recruiting colored troops in the Confederate States says an officer will be assigned in each State charged with the enrollment and disposition of all recruits. No slave will be accepted as a recruit unless with the owner's consent by written instrument, conforming as far as he may to the rights of freedmen.

Appointment of officers of companies will be made by the President. Officers employed in recruiting are enjoined to be provident and considerate—to bestow humane attention to whatever concerns the health, comfort and discipline of the troops—to a uniform observance of kindness and forbearance in the treatment of them, and especially to protect them from injustice and oppression.

Fortress Monroe.

[Special Correspondence of the Philadelphia Enquirer.]

Fortress Monroe, Va., March 20, 1865.

Gen. Sherman's Visit to Fortress Monroe.

Last Monday morning, at the hour of eleven o'clock, the despatch steamer *Russia* arrived here from Morehead City N. C., with Major-General Wm. Tecumseh Sherman on board, accompanied by several members of his staff, Brevet Brigadier-General Dodge, Chief Quartermaster of the Department of North Carolina, and a few other officers attached to his army, *en route* for the North, for the purpose of enjoying a short furlough. As the *Russia* with her distinguished passengers reached the shore, an immense crowd of civilians and officers assembled on the Baltimore wharf, to catch a glimpse of the able commander and great "Banker" of the West. Owing to the strong tide which was rendered by the prevalent westerly winds unusually swift, the steamer was a considerable length of time in making a landing at the wharf. During this incidental delay the General was walking up and down the hurricane deck of the steamer restlessly and impatiently, apparently anxious for the moment when he would be released from the inquisitive glance of the bystanders. At last, with the assistance of several tugs, the steamer was secured to the wharf, and after spending a few moments with the newly-made acquaintances, and bidding farewell to those of his officers bound North, the General embarked on the steamer *Blackbird*, and in a few moments was far out of sight, steaming rapidly up the James River, on his way to Lieutenant-General Grant's head-quarters. General Sherman appeared to be in the best of health and spirits, and seemingly has suffered but little from the fatiguing march of his forces through Georgia and the Carolinas.

In anticipation of the General's return from City Point, a number of officers attached to the Third Pennsylvania Artillery, with the post band, assembled in the commodious office of the Quartermaster's Department, to extend to him a serenade and the hospitalities of the Old Point. About 10 o'clock on the evening of Tuesday, the United States gun-boat *Bat* arrived from City Point and anchored in the stream, and General Sherman, a few moments afterward, quietly landed on the beach from a small boat, and proceeded into the fort, where he was met by his brother, Senator John Sherman, of Ohio, and a few friends. At midnight he re-embarked on board the *Bat*, which immediately got underweigh and steamed southwards.

The object of this unexpected visit by General Sherman was of course involved in deep mystery, especially at a time when his army was supposed to have been battling with Johnston's army in the vicinity of Goldsboro', and his whole attention occupied in directing its movements. His interview at the front with Lieutenant General Grant will doubtless be productive of the most important results, and combinatory movements of the two grand armies it is presumed will at once take place, with the view of the total defeat of the last remaining army of the Rebellion and the dismemberment of the Confederacy.

Already Grant's army is in motion, and ... on the war path to victory, as soon as its gallant Commander reaches it.

LOYAL MUSIC IN SOUTH CAROLINA.—A correspondent of the New-York Evening Post, with Sherman's army, writing from a South Carolina town, says:

As I am writing, I can hear the exquisite music of the Thirty-third Massachusetts band, who are serenading one of the general officers. This is the best band in the army, and the favorite of all of us.

They are playing operatic and national airs. There was a time when Massachusetts men were not permitted in this chivalric State. The wretches who insulted Judge Hoar and his daughter have not been consulted in this matter. Yes, there is that soul-stirring anthem, "John Brown," and "Rally round the flag," and the rest. When our troops marched into Columbia the other day the bands commenced and ended with "Hail Columbia."

RAID.—A detachment of the 3d and 35th U. S. C. T. left Jacksonville, Fla., on the 7th ult., on an expedition into Rebeldom.

They left the river at Fort Gates and struck out into the interior, returning by way of St. Augustine on the 12th, having marched over 300 miles, capturing 8 rebels, killing 26, burning 75 hogsheads of sugar, 350 bbls of syrup, 400 bbls. of whiskey, (too bad!) and a still and sugar works. They also brought in 80 contrabands, 6 prisoners, and about 25 horses and mules. The loss on our side was one killed and two wounded, in a fight with 32 of House's Cavalry at Lake Church Hill.

Port Royal New South.

LAND SALE.—The adjourned sale by the Tax Commissioners of the lots at "Land's End," which is to be the Brooklyn of New York, took place Wednesday. The purchasers and prices were as follows, viz:

A. C. Holmes, U. S. N.,	5 lots	$965.
Maj. Robt. Williams,	3 "	600.
Lt. Geo. A. Fisher,	2 "	200.
Geo. A. Springer,	2 "	800.
Miss Hill,	1 "	50.
Mrs. Gilmore,	4 "	1,000.
Maj. Thomas,	20 "	6,200.
Mr. Reed, (for a church)	1 "	10.
Mr. Moore,	1 "	10.

The lots running to the water on West side of Astor street brought about $ each; on east side $200; on Burmelia street, next block to Astor street $100, and $50 each. The total amount of sales was about $10,000.

Port Royal New South.

A NEW REGIMENT.—We learn that Maj. Henry Higgenson, formerly of Co. , 19th Illinois Vols.—a nephew to Col. T. W. Higginson, and who was a prisoner at Andersonville for many months, has applied to the War Department for permission to raise a regiment of Andersonville prisoners. The Major is now here and finds quite a number of his old comrades from that celebrated pest hole of Georgia.—*New South.*

CAPT. JOHN HAYS, A. Q. M. who has been in the Department for two years or more, and made a host of friends, who esteem him as a kind-hearted, courteous gentleman as well as a faithful officer, is to be relieved here as Quartermaster in charge of Marine Transportation and Forage. His successor is Captain Rockwell, A. Q. M.—*Port Royal New South.*

CAPT. JNO. H. MOORE, Chief Quartermaster of the District of Florida, and formerly stationed here as Chief Quartermaster of the Department, has been relieved and ordered to Charleston as Chief Quartermaster on Brig. Gen. Hatch's Staff.—*Port Royal New South.*

ONE of the wounded Rebel soldiers thought he was about to die, and feeling that he had many sins to answer for he requested that a minister should be sent to him. The Rev. Mr. H——, a Rebel parson, was called in. Sitting down beside the wounded man, and assuming all the sacerdotal airs, he gravely said:—My friend, in what state was your mind when you first felt that you would like to be baptized? Feebly and dolorously the feeble man replied, "Ar-kan-saw." The divine was instantly disgusted and rising from the sick bed in great indignation said, "Pshaw! that fellow don't know enough to go to heaven," and left the room.

FROM official returns just published, it appears that the population of Brussels on the 1st of January amounted to 148-932, of whom 80,371 were males, and 94,968 females.

BALTIMORE:

Disastrous Fire at Parkersburg—A Daring Rebel Outrage—A Railroad Passenger Train Attacked—The Passengers Robbed of over Two Hundred Thousand Dollars.

[Special Dispatch to the Phil. Enquirer.]

BALTIMORE, March 31.—A very disastrous fire occurred at Parkersburg, Va., about noon on the 28th inst., consuming an entire block in the heart of the city, including the Continental Hotel, Second National Bank, the first organized, the Parkersburg Gazette office, and many stores, dwellings, &c., with a large amount of goods. The total loss will probably amount to two hundred thousand dollars, and scarcely any insurance. Many persons lost all, and are rendered homeless. The fire is supposed to have been the work of an incendiary.

About seven o'clock yesterday evening a passenger train on the Baltimore and Ohio Railroad proceeding west, was attacked by a gang of forty or fifty guerillas about ten miles west of Cumberland. They signalled the conductor to stop. There were eight or ten passenger cars well filled, among whom were many ladies. The ruffians entered the cars with pistols and bowie knives in hand, presenting them at passengers indiscriminately, demanded their money, &c., and robbed them without distinction of sex, of all the money, watches, jewelry, &c., under threats of instant death.

The passengers delivered up their valuables, and were glad to escape unhurt. About two hundred thousand dollars in greenbacks alone were secured by these robbers. The cars were not injured and no prisoners taken. Many passengers returned to Cumberland. It is supposed that this is the same band who captured Generals Crook and Kelley some weeks ago.—The authorities are now on the alert.

Rebel Prisoners.

The rebel officers just released from imprisonment at Point Lookout, Maryland, have signed and published the following testimonial:

"Whereas, during the progress of this bloody war, now raging between the United States and the Confederate States governments, it has been customary for the contending parties to proclaim to the civilized world that the treatment extended to their men, when held as prisoners of war, was of the most barbarous and inhuman character. Without attempting to decide the truth or falsity of such charges, when coming from our enemies, or inquiring as to which party instituted the initiative in the abuses which have led to the cruel and rigorous system of retaliation at present existing in the treatment of prisoners of war, we most cheerfully bear witness to the fact that, during our short imprisonment at Point Lookout, Maryland, we were treated both by federal officers and soldiers in such a manner as to excite our surprise and demand our grateful acknowledgements therefor.

"Resolved, That we return to Major A. G. Brady provost marshal at this post, and his command, our sincere thanks for their uniformly kind and courteous attention to us while detained among them as prisoners of war.

"Resolved, That the Secretary of this meeting forward a copy of these proceedings to Major Brady."

"GEORGE S. HARRISON, Chairman.
"W. H. DAVIS, Secretary.

Five hundred rebel prisoners from the barracks at Rock Island passed through Cleveland last week on their way south to be exchanged. The Cleveland Leader describes their appearance:

"They were mostly youths, or very young men. Care, hardships and other agents had left lines on their faces, which gave them an oldish and stolid look, but the proportion of bearded men was very, very small. The large majority had apparently never shaved. A number of boys were in the ... who could not have been over fifteen or ... gent faces. ... were not more than ...

"They seemed to have the spirit of selfish competition keen as ever, and their digestive organs in prime condition. They seemed to have no antipathy to the Yankees. It was impossible to read ineradicable hate of the Yankee race on their faces or in their manners. They appeared quite like brethren, and one had the feeling and conviction in their presence, that the chasm between the North and the masses of the South is geographical only, as people's ideas, faiths, customs, virtues and vices usually are, and that the antagonism between the two sections is in reality not vital personal and sincere, but accidental and purely mechanical."

Sambo Unfaithful.

The free negro boatman who joined the black army of Jeff. Davis last week, over whose recruitment the Richmond papers indulged in ecstatic visions that all the free "niggers" in the Confederate States would at once "join the army of the South," has already dishonored the confidence which was placed in him. In other words, after three days of military glory, he has deserted, and worse than all, carried off twenty suits of clothing with him. The mournful story is told in the Richmond papers, and the case seems to be one of black ingratitude. This colored person had an opportunity to fight for the enslavement of his kindred and friends forever. He could have proved by his own bravery that "there are master races born to govern, and that there are slave races born to serve," and he might have sustained the "reaction against the mistaken civilization of the age." He chose not to do so. He deceived his "kind masters," and has run away with their clothing, at a time, too, when clothing is scarce. Should the Provost Marshal ever catch him, he will assuredly "catch it."

Investigation of Indian Affairs.

Senators Doolittle, Foster and Nesmith, and Representatives Windom, A. W. Hubbard, Higby and Ross, compose the Committee appointed under the joint resolution of Congress directing inquiry into the condition of the Indian tribes, and their treatment by the civil and military authorities. They are to hear the complaints of the Indian Chiefs, and examine fully into the conduct of Indian agents and superintendents, and also into the management of the Bureau of Indian Affairs.

SENTENCES CONFIRMED.—The finding and sentence in the Devlin and Cohill, New-York bounty broker cases, tried before General Bragg's Military Commission, of which Col. N. P. Chipman, of the War Department, is Judge Advocate, have been confirmed by the Secretary of War. John Devlin was sentenced to ten years in the penitentiary, and was fined ten thousand dollars. James Devlin, seven years imprisonment and five thousand dollars fine. John Cohill, five years imprisonment. They are to be sent to Clinton Prison. They are the first installment of a large batch of similar cases, and which bring to light the immense frauds practised on the Government. Steps are being taken to bring to justice these offenders in other parts of the country, and to prevent a recurrence of the frauds. The Commission is going forward rapidly in the examination.

THE Lynchburg Republican confirms the report that Mr. J. A. Sperry, editor of the Bristol Register, who was captured by the enemy in their late raid into Southwestern Virginia, has been turned over by the military to the civil authorities at Knoxville to be tried for treason. In what his treason consists we have not been advised. This is doubtless some of the arch-devil Brownlow's work.

[*Aug. Constitutionalist.*

GEN. BEAUREGARD'S OPINION.—It is rumored that Gen. Beauregard has stated that he feels confident in whipping Sherman, if he continues to advance. Also that he thinks everything now promises well for the future.—We hope the General has good grounds for his success, and that his brightest and most sanguine hopes will be realized.—*Aug. Constitutionalist.*

We "can't see it."

Summary of News.

A sister of Gen. Grant died, a few day ago, at her residence, in Covington, Ky.

An average of three hundred and fifty dollars a day is paid to rebel deserters for the muskets they bring in.

The Legislature of Illinois having laid a tax of one dollar for the first dog owned by any individual, two dollars for the second, and five dollars for each additional dog, an exchange says the State has "gone to the dogs."

The Moscow Gazette mentions an innovation introduced into the Nobles' Club at Odessa by the admission of ladies as members. They have to undergo the usual ballot, like members of the male sex.

The Postoffice route agent between Charleston and Branchville, South Carolina, has applied to the Postoffice Department for remuneration for services rendered after the secession of the State. This does not seem a modest step on the part of the route agent.

In Rhode Island the negroes are allowed to vote, and have put in nomination Edward Harris, of Cumberland, for Governor, and Rowland Hazard, of South Kingstown, for Lieutenant Governor, adopting the rest of the Union State ticket, and the Union candidates for representatives in Congress.

It seems a little curious that during General Couch's march from Wilmington, the army passed through three different lines of works, all of them facing northward, or in the direction in which Gen. Couch was moving. Had our troops encountered a largely superior force, the works might have proved very convenient for the Union army to have fallen back upon.

Rebel deserters, says the New York Tribune, say that General Early has taken a self-imposed pledge to not *drink* any more until he shall have whipped Sheridan. This is considered by Sheridan's officers as equivalent to the Rebel General's having taken the temperance pledge for life, to the no small damage of the Confederate distillers, and a corresponding fall in the price of corn.

The Richmond Examiner, in speaking of the recent colored military parade in that city, alludes with pride to Surgeon Turner's company, which "attracted most attention." The sensation they created might, however, have arisen from the fact afterwards stated by the Examiner. "They exhibited," it says, "all sizes, from three feet to six feet six, while the complexion ranged from black down to gingerbread and olive."

General John Frederick Hartranft, who recaptured Fort Steadman and turned defeat into victory, is a native of Montgomery County, Pa., and was born December 18, 1830. He was graduated at Union College, Schenectady, in 1853, and was in the practice of law till the commencement of the war. He has fought in North Carolina, Virginia, Pennsylvania, Tennessee and Mississippi, and always with marked distinction. The Telegraph at first confounded his name with that of Gen. Hartsuff.

The famous Seminole Chief, Osceola, was buried in Fort Moultrie, Charleston harbor. A press correspondent, who recently visited the place, writes:—"Inside of Fort Moultrie is Osceola's grave, a plain slab of marble with an iron rail fence. Everything round it has been knocked to pieces by our shells, but not one had touched it or even clipped the flowers around his grave. The inscription on it was this:—'To the memory of Osceola, Indian Chieftain, died in Fort Moultrie, 1839.'"

National Disgrace.

The inauguration balls at Washington have always been a disgrace, and that which took place last Monday evening seems to have been no better than its predecessors. We quote from the description of the supper given by the correspondents of the N. Y. Times and Herald:

Andy Johnson's plebeians outnumbered the aristocrats at least twenty to one. They threw shoddy and petroleum completely into the ... vellous. The men of these people was ... the spokes of a wheel; the women hopped, skipped and jumped about in a manner which would have made a French dancing master commit suicide. They introduced the figures of a quadrille into the Lancers, and a breakdown into a quadrille. They appeared to think every other dance was a waltz, and acted accordingly. The gallop, the schottische and varsovienne, the Danish and the redowa were all Greek to them. They understood nothing but a plain waltz and a plain quadrille, and appeared to think that they were exhibiting the greatest science when they were kicking up the most dust. Those of the plebeians who did not dance gathered around the doors of the supper rooms, and remained there from nine o'clock until the time that the supper room was opened.

Just before twelve o'clock the President was notified that supper was ready. The Presidential party then retired in the same order as they entered, and a rush was made to follow them.—Policemen kept back the crowd and the party got safely out of the ball room and were ushered in the supper room by a private entrance. Then the doors were thrown open to the guests, who dashed in pell mell in dreadful confusion, ladies being crushed against the walls, or dragged half fainting through the crush. Men tried to tear down the temporary doorway. The table was cleared almost in a moment, and after the first ten minutes the waiters would bring nothing except for a fee. In an hour there was nothing left to bring. At least half the people went away hungry.—There was no attempt to keep order. The committee men were not to be found, and the policemen were insolent and inefficient. It was impossible to get in or out of the supper room or near the table. No wines were furnished with the supper, and but little water. The coffee room was shrewdly located at the other end of the building, where nobody could get at it till the supper was over. The floor was covered with the *debris* of the supper. All the dresses which escaped spoilation below were spoiled here. The ladies were very angry—so were the men. Some bullied, some bribed the waiters, and ate the remains of other people's suppers. The mass surged to and fro like a sea. Plates were broken by dozens. There was a general mess. The President's party feasted at the upper end of the hall, and, having finished, attempted to pass out. But Andy Johnston's plebians were savage with hunger, and would not make way for anybody. The President's party were thus forced to enter an alcove between the cases of models, climb up stairs, and emerge upon a sort of balcony above the heads of the crowd, where they could look down upon the struggle for viands. Nobody cared to follow them now. The President and others of the party spoke in severe terms of the disorder.

The President's party now crowded along the narrow balcony, descended another flight of stairs, and passed out quietly, without being noticed. They at once proceeded to their dressing rooms without re-entering the ball room, and without being attended by a single outsider. In ten minutes they were dressed, and at precisely one o'clock they left the building by a side door. Their departure thus unceremoniously excited no comment among the ravenous throng inside.

THE Amendatory Enrollment bill, as it passed at the resent session of Congress, contains a provision that every person who, having been enlisted or drafted to serve in the national forces in the present struggle, has hitherto deserted, and shall not within sixty days present himself for duty, or who shall hereafter enlist or be drafted, and shall in like manner desert, will thereupon cease to be a citizen of the United States, and to be entitled as a citizen to vote.

NO MEAT.—In the Richmond Congress lately, Mr. Orr said that in his State he knew of hundreds and thousands of the wives of soldiers now in the trenches who had not had a mouthful of meat during the past six months. So far from there being a sufficiency of supplies, he said that if soldiers in front of Richmond were questioned, he ventured to affirm that the Senator would learn that these brave men had not meat rations issued to them for several days. Mr. Graham, of North Carolina, stated that there were also many families of soldiers in his State totally destitute of meat, who had been subsisting on bread alone for months past.

OPENING COMMUNICATIONS.—The correspondent of the New-York Tribune, who is with Sherman, gives the following account of the opening of communication between Schofield and Sherman:

"The day after Gen. Sherman's arrival at Fayettville, Captain Ainsworth reached that place from Wilmington on the tug Davidson, with despatches from Gen. Schofield. Capt. Ainsworth left Wilmington to come up the Cape Fear River, 120 miles, spite of the reports current that the river was filled with torpedoes and blocked up by trees, and by the rebel Chickamauga sunk across it, and that numerous rebel batteries were established at different points on the river. He made his trip up with entire safety, without losing a man, although continually fired into by the rebels along the shore. General Sherman complimented him most highly for his gallantry, and forthwith brevetted him 'Commodore.' His services in establishing communication were of great importance. On his return, his little vessel was well protected by cotton bales, given to the Commodore with the personal regards of General Sherman. Ainsworth, upon his arrival at Wilmington, turned over the cotton to the quartermaster, and keeps the regards of the General."

We suppose that the officer here spoken of is Captain Andrew Ainsworth, formerly of this city, and well and favorably known to many of our business men. He has been employed since the beginning of the war at Fortress Monroe as master of transportation and harbor master, but now appears to be rendering his usual efficient service in another quarter.—*Boston Adv.*

West Tennessee Thrown Open to Trade.

CAIRO, March 29, 1865.—General Washburne has thrown the entire district of West Tennessee open to trade. Citizens will be allowed to come freely to Memphis with the products of the country and take out a limited amount of family supplies. This will continue, however, only so long as people manifest a loyal, friendly feeling towards the government of the United States and do not abuse the privileges granted.

From California.

SAN FRANCISCO, March 22.—The mines of California are yielding heavily since the rains. The receipt of treasure for ten days is over $2,000,000. The deposits at the mint to-day were 1200 ounces of gold. Money is more in demand on account of speculative movements. Legal tenders are selling at 56 a 57, and there is an increased demand for the best mining stocks. Advices from Hong Kong to Jan. 25th say that the authorities at Canton have prohibited the exportation of rice. This news has caused that article to go up in San Francisco, where there are many Chinese consumers. Arrived, ship Hornet, from New York.

MARINE INETELLIGNCE.

SAVANNAH, APRIL 7th, 1865.

ARRIVED.

Steamer W W Coit, Crowell, Hilton Head
Steamer Wyoming, Snow, Jacksonville, Fla.
Steamer U S Grant, Dobbs, Hilton Head.
Flag of Truce steamer Nelly Baker, Norris, Sister's Ferry.
Bark Cecelian, from Boston, 12 days, with ice to Haywood, Gage & Co.

HEAD-QUARTERS U. S. FORCES,
Savannah, Ga., April 7th, 1865.

GENERAL ORDER,
No. 26.

Hereafter the purchase of Quartermaster's vouchers at a greater discount than five (5) per cent. is prohibited within the limits of this command.

By command of
Brevet Maj. Gen. C. GROVER.
EDWARD G. DIKE, A. A. G.

CIRCULAR.

OFFICE PROVOST MARSHAL,
DISTRICT OF SAVANNAH, GA.,
April 6, 1865.

Attention having been called to the fact that the Cemeteries of this City have been desecrated by visitors plucking flowers without authority, and injuring the trees and shrubbery in various ways, notice is hereby given, that any person hereafter found guilty of any such act, will be punished for the same.

The sticking up of handbills or posters in the streets of this City, is hereby prohibited, except upon Bulletin boards prepared for that purpose.

By order of
Brev.-Maj.-Gen. C. GROVER,
Commanding.
ROBERT P. YORK,
Lieut.-Col. 75th N. Y. V. V., and
Pro. Mar. Dist. of Savannah, Ga.

The Important Trade Order Issued by Gen. Grant.

H'D-QUARTERS OF THE U. S. A.
CITY POINT, VA., March 16, '65.

SPECIAL ORDERS,
No. 13.

First. The operations on all treasury trade permits and all other trade permits, and licenses to trade by whomsoever granted within the State of Virginia, (except that portion known as the Eastern shore,) and the States of North Carolina and South Carolina, and that portion of Georgia immediately bordering on the Atlantic, including the city of Savannah, are hereby suspended until further orders.

All contracts and agreements made under or by virtue of any trade permit or license, within any of said States or parts of States, during the existence of this order, will be deemed void, and the subject of such contracts or agreements will be seized by the military authorities for the benefit of the Government, whether the same is, at the time of such contracts or agreements, within their reach, or at any time thereafter comes within their reach, either by the operations of war or the act of the contracting parties or their agents.

The delivery of all goods contracted for and not delivered before the publication of this Order, prohibited. Supplies of all kinds are prohibited from passing into any of the St... parts of States, except such as necessary for the wants ... within the lines of actual ... pation, and under no circu... Military Commanders allow th... to pa... beyond the lines they actually hold.

By Command of
LT. GEN. GRANT.
P. S. BOWERS, A. A. Gen'l.
[OFFICIAL.]
F. S. PARKER, A. A. A. Gen'l.

The Philadelphia Inquirer.

PRICE TWO CENTS. PHILADELPHIA, SATURDAY, APRIL 8, 1865. PRICE TWO CENTS.

LEE'S LAST DEFEAT.

MAP SHOWING THE LINE OF HIS RETREAT, AND SHERIDAN'S VICTORIOUS PURSUIT.

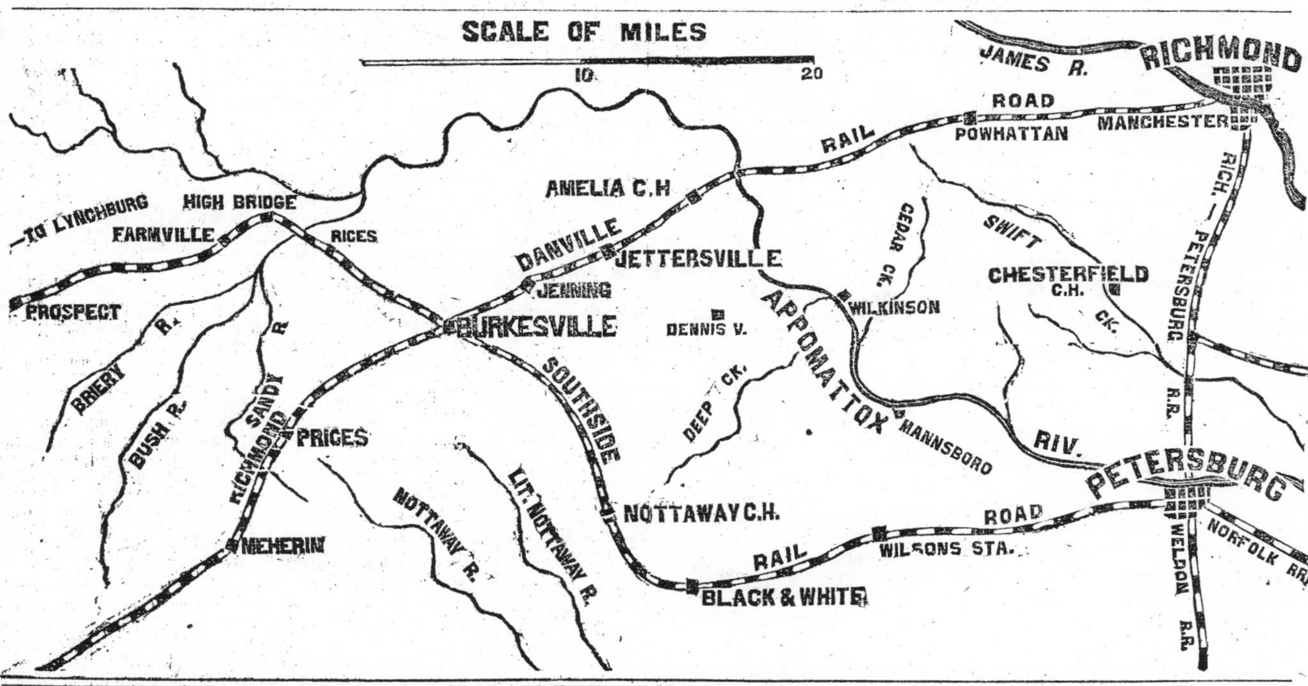

NEW VICTORIES!!

The Deeds of Our Modern Hero!

CAVALRY SHERIDAN AGAIN!

He Heads Off and Routs Lee!

THOUSANDS ON THOUSANDS OF PRISONERS!

Wholesale Capture of Knights-Errant

EWELL, THE REBEL HAYNAU, CAGED!

Curtis Lee, Kershaw, Corse, De Barre and Button Taken.

CAPTURE OF 14 CANNON!

Hundreds of Wagons, Caissons and Ambulances in Our Hands!

BATTLE AT BURKSVILLE!

Despatches From Our Generals.

GRANT, MEADE, SHERIDAN, WRIGHT AND HUMPHREYS.

Gen. Lee to Surrender or Be Annihilated!

GALLANTRY OF OUR TROOPS!

Glorious Old Second and Sixth Corps.

FIRST OFFICIAL GAZETTE.

WASHINGTON, April 7—10 A. M.—Major-General Dix:—General Sheridan attacked and routed General Lee's army yesterday, capturing Generals Ewell, Kershaw, Button, Corse, and many other general officers, several thousand prisoners and a large number of cannon, and expects to force Lee to surrender all that is left of his army.

Details will be given as speedily as possible, but the telegraph is working badly.

E. M. STANTON, Secretary of War.

SECOND OFFICIAL GAZETTE.

WASHINGTON, April 7.—Major-General Dix:—The following telegrams announcing the victory won yesterday, by Major-General Sheridan, over Lee's army, has just been received by this Department.

E. M. STANTON, Secretary of War.

CITY POINT, April 7—8 A. M.—Hon. Edwin M. Stanton, Secretary of War:—At 11·15 yesterday, at Burksville Station, General Grant sends the following from General Sheridan.

(Signed) A. LINCOLN.

April 6—11·15 P. M. — Lieutenant-General Grant:—I have the honor to report that the enemy made a stand at the inters[illegible] which Burkes Station Road [illegible] they were [illegible] divisions of the Sixth Army [illegible], and routed them handsomely, making a connection with the cavalry.

I am still pressing on with both cavalry and infantry.

Up to the present time we have captured Generals Ewell, Kershaw, Button, Corse, De Bare, Custis Lee, several thousand prisoners, fourteen pieces of artillery, with caissons, and a large number of wagons.

If the thing is pressed I think Lee will surrender.

(Signed) P. SHERIDAN, Major-General Commanding.

CITY POINT—9 A. M.—Hon. Secretary of War:—The following further just received:—

(Signed) A. LINCOLN.

BURKSVILLE, VA. — A. Lincoln:—The following telegrams are respectfully forwarded for your consideration.

(Signed) U. S. GRANT, Lieutenant-General.

SECOND ARMY CORPS, 7·30 P. M., April 6.—Major-General A. S. Webb:—Our last fight, just before dark, at Sailor's Creek, gave us two guns, three flags, considerable numbers of prisoners, two hundred wagons, seventy ambulances, with mules and horses to about one-half the wagons and ambulances.

There are between thirty and fifty wagons in addition abandoned and destroyed along the road, and some battery wagons, forges and limbers.

I have already reported to you the capture of one gun, two flags, and some prisoners; and the fact that the road for over two miles is strewed with tents, baggage, cooking utensils, some ammunition, and material of all kinds. The wagons are across the approach to the bridge, and it will take some time to clear it.

The enemy is in position on the heights beyond, with artillery; the bridge is partially destroyed, and the approaches on either side are of soft bottom land. We cannot advance to-morrow in the same manner as we have to-day.

As soon as I get my troops up a little nearer, I might push a column down the road and deploy it; but it is evident that I cannot follow rapidly during the night.

(Signed) A. A. HUMPHREYS, Maj.-Gen.

HEAD-QUARTERS, April 6—10 P. M.—Lieutenant-General Grant:—At daylight this morning I moved the Second, Fifth and Sixth Army Corps along the railroad in the direction of Amelia Court House. Soon after moving, reliable intelligence was received that the enemy was moving towards Farmville.

The direction of the Second and Fifth Army Corps was immediately changed from a northerly to a northwesterly direction, the directing corps, the Second, moving on to Deatonville, and the Fifth, heretofore in the centre, moving on the right of the Second, and the Sixth facing about, and moving by the left flank, taking position on the left of the Second.

It was understood that the cavalry would operate on the extreme left. The changes were promptly made; the Second Army Corps soon becoming engaged with the enemy near Deatonville, driving him by the right across Sailor's Creek, to the Appomattox.

The Fifth Army Corps made a long march, but its position prevented its striking the enemy's column before it had passed.

The Sixth Army Corps came up with the enemy about four P. M., and, in conjunction with the Second on its right and cavalry on its left, attacked and routed the enemy, capturing many prisoners, among them Lieutenant-General Ewell and General Custis Lee.

I transmit despatches from Generals Humphreys and Wright, which, in justice to the distinguished officers and the gallant corps they command, I send the War Department for immediate publication.

It is impossible at this moment to give any estimate of the casualties on either side, or of the number of prisoners taken, but it is evident to-day's work is going to be one of the most important of the recent brilliant operations.

The pursuit will be continued as soon as the men have a little rest. Griffin, with the Fifth Corps, will be moved by the left and right, and Humphreys continue the direct pursuit as long as it promises success.

(Signed) GEO. G. MEADE, Major-General.

HEAD-QUARTERS SIXTH CORPS, 10 P. M., April 6.—Major-General Wilde, Chief of Staff:—In pursuance of instructions, this morning, from Major-General Meade, I [illegible] to the left of by the short [illegible] the object of retaking posi[illegible] on the left of the Second Army Corps, striking the road running from Deatonville to Burk's station, at a point a little to the southward of the former place.

I found that the Second Army Corps was engaged to the front and right, and the cavalry heavily to my left. Moving down the road towards Burk's Station for perhaps a mile, and turning sharp to the right, I proceeded across towards a nearly parallel road, in which the enemy was moving, and along which he had thrown up a line of intrenchments.

As soon as the leading division, General Seymour's, could be formed, it was moved up on the road held by the enemy, which was carried. Then turning to the left, it was advanced down the road against a pretty strong resistance.

By this time Wheaton's Division was put in position as rapidly as possible on Seymour's left. The lines were again advanced, and we swept down the road for a distance of about two miles. Arriving at a deep and difficult creek we found the enemy had re-formed his line on the opposite side, where we attacked and drove him to a point a distance of half a mile further.

In the first attack a portion of the cavalry operated on our right flank; in its subsequent attack the mass of cavalry operated on our left and the right flank of the enemy.

The result has been a complete success.

The combined forces captured five general officers, among them Generals Ewell and Custis Lee, and large numbers of other prisoners.

I shall go in camp about two miles beyond this point and await instructions. The First and Third Divisions (Whiting's and Seymour's), and the artillery engaged to-day, behaved splendidly. A return of casualties will be forwarded as soon as possible. The corps has nobly sustained the reputation it earned on the 2d, as well as upon many previous hard fought battlefields.

(Signed) H. G. WRIGHT, Major-General.

FROM WESTERN LOUISIANA.

CAIRO, April 7.—Late Western Louisiana accounts represent a great scarcity of breadstuffs about Alexandria, and much suffering. The scarcity of forage has compelled the Rebel cavalry to depart for Texas, and their infantry has also been withdrawn from Alexandria, and are encamped at Natchitoches. The Confederate troops have been removed from Brownsville to Galveston, where they await the attack of the Federals. One of Jeff. Thompson's orders on assuming command of the Northern Sub-District directs the agents appointed in each county to exact one-third of all cotton offered for export, or collect one-third of the receipts.

Two hundred and twenty-nine bales of cotton passed up yesterday from Memphis for St. Louis.

OPERATIONS AGAINST MOBILE.

CINCINNATI, April 7.—Our special advices from Mobile are to April 1st. At that time our forces were closely investing Fort Branley. They have approached in parallel within three hundred yards, and are pushing up daily. The ground in the rear of these forts is sufficiently high to enable the troops to mine successfully. They will be so close in a few days that it will be necessary to make an assault, which must be decisive.

The Sixteenth Corps holds the right, the Thirteenth the left, inclosing the Rebels on three sides, while the gun-boats are endeavoring to close up the fourth side.

While trying to move up in front of the Spanish Fort, two gun-boats, the *Osage* and *Milwaukie*, were blown up by torpedoes and sunk. The water was shoal, not over eleven feet deep, and many of the crew escaped.

They were advancing without the usual torpedo-finder, which is a strong rope stretched in front of the boat, under water, and fastened on spars, so as to explode the torpedoes in advance. The Rebels have lined the bays and the land with torpedoes. General Granger narrowly escaped with his life.

General Steel's column has been heard from. He has reached Pollard's. He captured the Sixth Alabama Cavalry almost entire, including Gen. Clayton, the Major, Surgeon, four Captains and nine Lieutenants; also, two railroad trains and large droves of cattle.

FROM NORTH CAROLINA.

NEWBERN, N. C.—[illegible] preconcerted [illegible] was developed this morning, at half-past ten o'clock. Several large buildings, containing forage and ordnance, and commissary stores, were set on fire simultaneously, with the aid of phosphorus. The alarm was given and signaled at once throughout the city, and the fire department and the entire population promptly turned out, and the flames were extinguished in a short time without doing much damage. Seventy bales of hay and a few other articles were consumed. The extensive bridge over the Neuse River was fired at the same time in four places, but was also extinguished.

A Rebel officer has been discovered, and is now in confinement, and other suspicious parties are watched. The fire department has been on duty ever since, and is to be renewed this morning. A double guard has been stationed throughout the city to prevent like occurrences, and to arrest all suspicious persons. The excitement was very great yesterday and last night, but is now subsiding.

A rumor is afloat that the Rebel cavalry made a dash, yesterday, and struck the railroad this side of Goldsboro'. No such report has reached head-quarters, and as the telegraph line is in working order to Goldsboro', and the track is strongly guarded, the rumor is undoubtedly without foundation.

The Excursion to Fort Sumter.

TWO UNITED STATES VESSELS TO SAIL TO-DAY.

There is much excitement in regard to the excursion to Charleston Harbor, a very large number of persons desiring to witness the raising of the Federal flag on Fort Sumter, and the ceremonies on the occasion. The difficulty of procuring suitable transportation and permits to enter the fort will make the company of visitors from this port comparatively small.

Two United States vessels, the *Arago* and the *Suwo Nada*, are to start to-day from New York for Charleston, and will take persons who have been fortunate enough to receive passes from the Secretary of War. Mr. Beecher is expected to be one of the passengers of the *Arago*. Mr. Wm. Lloyd Garrison will also visit Charleston, in company with Mr. Beecher.

Another steamer is advertised to start to-day from New York if a sufficient number of passengers can be obtained early this afternoon at the rate of one hundred and fifty dollars each. The *Oceanus* will sail on Monday.

From California.

SAN FRANCISCO, April 4.—Advices from Japan, sixty days on the way, announced further reports of murders by natives of foreigners, and more complications with the foreign powers.

Arrivals in twenty days from Honolulu bring intelligence of liberal subscriptions to the Sanitary Commission and heavy earthquakes.

The fall of Richmond causes great rejoicing throughout this State.

Greenbacks have gone up to 60@65, and are rising.

SAN FRANCISCO, April 5.—Sailed, ship *Marmion* for Hong Kong, with $364,000 in treasure, consisting mostly of silver.

The St. Albans Raiders.

TORONTO, April 7.—The St. Albans robbers arrived here this morning, and were brought before the Recorder this afternoon, on a charge of misdemeanor, when they applied for a delay till Monday, in order to obtain counsel, which was granted. They were then remanded and the case adjourned until Monday.

WASHINGTON

Reopening of the Communications With Richmond.

LEAVING THE SINKING SHIP!

Recruiting of Negro Soldiers in Richmond.

OUR SPECIAL DESPATCHES

WASHINGTON, April 7, 1865.

Officers for Colored Troops.

The examination of officers for colored troops will be continued here, by the Board of which Brigadier-General Caldwell is President, in addition to the duty previously assigned to it of examining the cases of delinquent officers.

Squads of Rebel Deserters

And prisoners are on the streets, who have taken the oath of allegiance, and appear greatly pleased with the change in their affairs. Probably much of the business transacted here by the Departments supplying the army, will be transferred to Richmond, by the removal of some minor bureaus to that point, for greater convenience and closer proximity to active operations in the field.

Opening Communi[illegible] with Richmond.

Arrangements are already made to put in running order the Railroad from Aquia Creek to Richmond, and the construction corps left this morning to commence operations, and it is expected in ten days or two weeks this road will be open. The rebuilding of the bridge over the Rappahannock at Fredericksburg is the most serious obstacle, but great exertions will be used to have it built in the shortest possible time.

Leaving the Sinking Ship.

Persons arriving from Fredericksburg report that many families had arrived there from Richmond, having left before its evacuation.

Deserters from the Rebel Army

In large numbers are also wandering about in the vicinity, trying to reach the Union lines.

Brokers and the Seven-thirty Bonds.

The decision that brokers must pay a revenue tax on sales of Seven-thirty bonds will probably be virtually rescinded by declaring them fiscal agents of the Government for the disposal of these bonds, and consequently not subject to revenue taxation for such sales.

Interception of Lee.

Lee, it appears, was intercepted yesterday while attempting to strike across the country from Amelia Court House to Farmsville, a station on the Lynchburg Railroad, seventeen miles above Burkesville Junction, and fifty-six from Lynchburg.

Sheridan, by his rapidity of movement, having headed LEE off at Burkesville Junction, the latter, as a last resource, struck a cross angle between the Lynchburg and Danville Roads, in the desperate hope of reaching the Lynchburg Road in advance of his unrelenting pursuer. But Sheridan was again too rapid for the fleeing enemy, and he was overtaken near Deatonville, in Amelia county, and punished as detailed in the despatch.

With such an enterprising adversary on his track as Sheridan, Lee, even if he reaches Lynchburg, will scarcely carry with him a baker's dozen of his army.

Arrival of Rebel Officers.

The mail boat which arrived here this morning from City Point, brought up the Rebel Brigadier-General R. Barringer, commander of a division in Fitz Hugh Lee's Cavalry, and brother of Barringer, of North Carolina, formerly a member of Congress, Major J. D. Ferguson, on F. H. Lee's Staff; Major R. F. Foote, on the staff of Bushrod Johnson, and Lieutenant F. O. Ford, on General Barringer's Staff, all of whom were captured on Monday, about eight miles from Amelia Court House, by a party of General Sheridan's scouts, who, being dressed in Confederate uniforms, were enabled to advance close up to the officers and take them by surprise. Foote is a son of Senator H. S. Foote, having graduated at the Georgetown College. Barringer had but little say, and would simply reply in as few words as possible when a question was asked him.

[DESPATCHES TO THE ASSOCIATED PRESS.]

The Celebration at Fort Sumter.

It appears by an order from the War Department that the steamer *Red Jacket* will leave the wharf at the Arsenal, to convey to Old Point Comfort the persons invited to accompany General Anderson to Charleston, to be present at the hoisting of the United States flag over Fort Sumter. The *Arago* will touch at Old Point to receive them on board.

News from Richmond.

The mail boat brings no additional important details from City Point.

The fire in Richmond was not fully extinguished until Wednesday night.

A careful estimate showed that six hundred buildings were burned.

Boats have commenced to run regularly to Richmond.

Deserters and prisoners are hourly arriving from Richmond and the front, and the Rebel soldiers, with one accord, declare the cause of the Confederacy hopeless.

Capture of a Prize Schooner.

The Navy Department has also received information of the capture of the British schooner *Comus*, by the United States steamer *Iuka*, bound from St. Marks, Fla., to Havana, with a cargo of thirty-two bales of sea-island cotton.

The Steamer "Harriet Deford."

The Navy Department has received the following:—

POINT LOOKOUT, April 6.—*To Hon. Gideon Welles, Secretary of the Navy:* The *Harriet Deford* is in Indian creek, Virginia, blockaded by several of my gun-boats. As soon as the light draft gun-boats get up she will be recaptured or destroyed.

Respectfully, A. F. PARKER, Commanding Potomac Flotilla.

Information believed to be reliable reached Washington this afternoon, that the pirates who run the captured steamer *Harriet Deford* into Indian Creek, Va., destroyed the vessel, after removing sundry articles of the most value.

Secretary Seward.

Secretary Seward is rather more comfortable to-day than yesterday. His injuries are painful, but exhibit no unfavorable symptoms.

Refugees from Richmond.

Information [illegible] been received here that Frederic[illegible] [illegible] with families from Richmond, and that the country around the former place swarms with Rebel deserters on their way home.

Arrival of Rebel Prisoners at Washington

Brigadier-General Barringer, commander of a division of Fitzhugh Lee's cavalry, and several other Rebel officers of lower grades, were brought here to-day and committed to the Old Capitol.

Capture of Blockade Runners.

The Navy Department has been informed of the capture, off the coast of Florida, of the British schooners *Sort*, *Mary* and *Connes*. Their cargoes consisted of shoes, rum, cotton, percussion caps, etc. The vessels were sent to Key West for adjudication.

The President.

The President is not expected to return to Washington till the middle of next week.

From Texas.

CINCINNATI, April 7.—It is currently reported in New Orleans that we shall soon have news from Texas that will startle and gratify the whole country. It is known that a message has been received at Washington from the Trans-Mississippi Department, proposing that enough cotton should be shipped down the river to pay off the Rebel troops in Green Bay, and that they should then be discharged and allowed to take the oath of amnesty. A new Legislature is then to assemble, fresh from the people, to decide the question of independence or a return to the Union.

The Rebel chiefs are, in consideration of a special amnesty for themselves, to exercise their influence in electing a legislature favorable to reconstruction.

Great anxiety is felt to learn the result of General Lew Wallace's mission to Brownsville, and as to the purport of the late communications with Galveston.

From Cincinnati.

CINCINNATI, April 7.—General Hooker has returned to this city.

The markets exhibit more firmness than for some days past. Flour, $7; for superfine, $7·25. Wheat, choice red, 55@60c. Corn, 75c.; Cincinnati elevator, for shelled, same. Oats, 62@63c. Whisky, $2·10.

The river is falling, with twenty-six feet in the channel, ten feet on the rocks over the falls. The lower rivers are rising. The steamer *Onward* passed down yesterday for St. Louis, full of people and freight. The *Iron City* leaves for Pittsburg to-day. The *Pine Grove* is on her way up.

General Forrest and His Negroes.

CINCINNATI, April 7.—The Jackson *Free Trader*, of the 20th ult., says of General Forrest:—"We have just been informed that a few days since this truly noble man and distinguished officer called out twenty-six of his own negroes and said to them, all of you who are willing to become soldiers for the war, step forward and I will give to every one who does so, his free papers. Twenty-five of them immediately advanced, only one refusing, who was a peace man, but he would drive a wagon for his master during the year."

Enthusiasm in Maine.

BELFAST, Me., April 7.—The recent Federal successes have given a new impetus to recruiting in Maine.

Sixty men left here yesterday for the front, and the steamship *Rhode Island*, now lying in our harbor, has enlisted over a hundred seamen.

One thousand and fifty dollars, raised in this city by voluntary subscription, was sent to day by General Cony to aid the soldiers from Maine, wounded in the late engagements.

Evasion of the Tax on Whisky.

ST. LOUIS, April 7.—Extensive frauds by Illinois whisky distillers have been discovered, amounting to half a million of dollars, by evading the revenue tax. Fifteen hundred and four barrels, consigned to merchants in this city, have been seized, during the last week, by the authorities.

From New Orleans.

NEW YORK, April 7.—The steamer *Empire City* from New Orleans and Key West, brought one hundred and seventy bales of cotton, consigned to Captain Noyes, who will sell it immediately for the benefit of Rebel prisoners, it being the balance of that turned over by the Rebel General Maury for that purpose.

Fort Smith, Arkansas.

ST. LOUIS, April 7.—The report that the Rebels had captured Fort Smith, has been contradicted at head-quarters. The United States troops occupied [illegible] on the 17th ultimo.

Florida Union.

VOL. 1. JACKSONVILLE, FLORIDA, SATURDAY, APRIL 8, 1865. NO. 34.

THE FLORIDA UNION IS PUBLISHED EVERY SATURDAY MORNING BY W. C. MORRILL & J. K. STICKNEY.

TERMS:

Two Dollars per Annum in Advance.

No Subscriptions taken for less than Three months.

Single copies five cents.

ADVERTISEMENTS Twenty-five cents per line each insertion.

Advertisements not specifying time will be marked t f (till forbidden) and charged accordingly.

Book, Job and Card Printing of every variety neatly executed at the UNION office.

NEWS FROM THE NORTH.

Heavy Fighting by Gen. Grant, in front of Petersburg.

3000 REBELS CAPTURED.

Terrible Fighting by Sherma's Forces, With Decided Success.

GOLD FALLEN TO 1 51.

By the steamer Delaware, which arrived at this port on Wednesday last, we have received Northern papers to the 30th ult.

The rebels attacked our forces in front of Petersburg on the morning of the 25th ult., and succeeded in capturing Fort Steedman, having massed a large number of their troops in front of the 9th Corps, (a portion of which occupied the Fort,) and so sudden was the onset that nearly all the troops in it were captured; this part of the line was occupied by the Third Brigade of the First Division, 9th Corps. What in the morning appeared almost a disaster to the Union forces, proved to be a decided success, for the 9th Corps recaptured their lost Fort, driving the rebels from it before they could remove or destroy its guns. The rebels also succeeded in getting possession of Battery No. 11, immediately on the left of Fort Steedman, but were soon forced to relinquish it. The rebel loss in front of this Corps alone was nearly five thousand, losing nineteen hundred prisoners alone.

The Second and Sixth Corps, however, taking advantage of the attention the rebels were giving to the capture of Fort Steedman, pushed forward their forces and succeeded in not only capturing one of the main rebel lines in their front, but also captured some three thousand prisoners. The rebels made several attempts to retake their lines, but were repulsed with terrible slaughter; they again on the 27th made a desperate attempt to reposess their lost line, in front of the Sixth Corps, but our troops had had possession too long and know how to use the spade too well to allow them to retake it. It has now been made one of the Union main lines. To offset this the rebels have gained nothing.

A battle is reported to have taken place between Gen. Sherman's forces and Gens. Johnson, Bragg, and Hardee's forces, at Averysboro, situated on the Cape Fear River, about forty miles south of Raleigh, which resulted in a decided Union victory. Gen. Sherman with his army was at Goldsboro, resting and equiping, for further movements.

The Fight Before Petersburg.

At the point where the enemy charged, the main lines are one hundred and fifty yards apart, the ground between being level and free from obstructions, except the abatis in front of the works of each side. At this place firing between the pickets has been almost continuous, and scarcely a day passes without two or three being wounded on our side at least.

This part of the line has been occupied by the Third brigade of the First division of the Ninth corps, Gen. McLaughlin commanding. He has often expressed his ability to break through the enemy's lines here, and only yesterday he showed how it could be done to some visitors, who were inspecting tqe works.

This morning four divisions of the enemy were massed in the rear of their line, under the command of Gen. Terry, who was appointed to lead the charge. These troops consisted of Bushrod Johnson's, Walker's, Evans' and Gues' divisions, of Gen. Gordon's corps.

At five A. M. the charge was made, and the time occupied in crossing the space between the lines, cutting down the abattis and getting to the rear of the fort was the work of only a few minutes. Here they formed in line of battle, brigade front, and while one portion advanced on the fort the other swept the right in towards the Appomattox, expecting to flank and capture the whole line to the river. The latter party were met by the Seventeenth Michigan and driven back after some hard fighting.

The force that attacked the fort were repulsed by the garrison several times; but, their numbers being so superior to ours, they finally overpowered and took prisoners nearly all who were in it. They at once sent the captured over the works to their lines, and many succeeded in getting away and running back, the guard being very small that had charge of them.

Gen. Wixcox moved up part of his command from the right to the scene of action, and soon drove the enemy from the line on the right of the fort. Gen. Hartranft's division, lying partly in reserve and partly on the line, to the left, was quickly on the ground, with reinforcements, and at once assaulted the fort in turn from the rear, which the rebels seemed determined to hold at all hazards. These repeated charges were made, and after that the fighting here was over, the "Johnies" laying down their arms and surrendering.

To the left of Fort Steedman is located battery No. 11, which the enemy also managed to get possession of, but did not keep it long, and although they fought hard they were forced to relinquish it.

It was at first reported that the rebels had carried off three mortars; but this proves to have been a mistake. They took one over the side of the fort; but, in their haste to get back to their lines, they dropped it within a few yards of the breastworks, from which place it will be brought in to-night.

The loss of the enemy is much heavier than ours. Their dead and wounded number more than double ours, while we have over eighteen hundred prisoners, among them about forty officers.

The works on both sides were lined with soldiers watching the proceedings.

Grand Council of War at City Point.

[Washington Correspondent of the New York Herald.]

WASHINGTON, March 29, 1865.

The visit of Mr. Lincoln to Fortress Monroe and General Grant's headquarters is now believed here to have much more significance than was at first attached to it. It has been the occasion of a personal interview between him and General Sherman, and a council of war, in which the President and Gens. Grant, Sherman and Sheridan participated. The conference was evidently in regard to pending military operations, as immediately after the council broke up a general movement of the army of General Grant in front of Richmond was begun.

General Sherman came to this interview incognito. The fact of his coming was known to few in his own army, and to none at Fortress Monroe, except those who met him in the council. He returned last night to Goldsboro, via Wilmington, accompanied by Brevet Brigadier General Dodge, on the United States steamer Bat.

RUMORED PEACE NEGOTIATIONS.

The delay of the President at City Point has given a color of probability to the rumor in circulation in regard to the renewal of peace negotiations. An officer of the government, who arrived here to-day, brings the positive information that the rebel General Lee has, since the battle of Saturday last, renewed his request, preferred through Generals Longstreet and Ord, for a military convention to settle matters and agree upon terms of a cessation of hostilities and the establishment of peace. It is represented that General Lee has expressed the opinion that he cannot much longer remain in Richmond on account of the scarcity of supplies, caused by the destruction of the James River Canal; and in view of the tremendous combinations against him it would be madness to attempt any movement outside of his defences. He therefore deems a continuance of the contest a useless and criminal waste of life and blood.

It will be remembered that the request previously made for a military convention was declined by General Grant only because he was not then clothed with authority to treat on any other than purely military subjects. Now the President is at his side, and can confer upon him all the authority requisite for the convention proposed.

It is known that both the President and our leading military officers are anxious to secure the whole of the rebel armed forces in Virginia and North Carolina, for to scatter them into a multitude of guerilla bands in the mountain districts would greatly prolong the war. A proposition to surrender these forces will unquestionably elicit from Mr. Lincoln liberal concessions on the part of the government.

It is known that a movement has been initiated by General Sherman which will completely cut off the rebel army under Johnson from every available source of supply, and the movement on the part of General Grant will compel Lee either to starve his army in Richmond or to come out and risk an engagement in the open field, in which a disastrous defeat will be inevitable.

The facts induce the conviction here that before the return of the President to Washington the terms of peace will be agreed upon between Grant and Lee, and the armed rebellion be ended. The best informed officials here regard an immediate peace as almost beyond a doubt.

The rumor of another peace conference has received additional confirmation to-night from the fact that Mr. Seward has gone to the James river to-night to join Mr. Lincoln.

SHERMAN'S COMMUNICATIONS.

Advices from Wilmington are that railroad communication between that point and Goldsboro will be completed to-night. Duplicates of the bridges across the Northeast and Neuse rivers have been found all ready to be put up. There is now at Wilmington an abundance of rolling stock to supply all the requirements of the army at Goldsboro.

From the N. Y. Herald, March 30th.

More Peace Rumors.

It is now believed that the visit of the President to the armies on James river is of more importance than has heretofore been generally considered. Since he has been there a council of war has been held in which Mr. Lincoln, Generals Grant, Sherman, Meade, Ord, Sheridan and other military chiefs participated, and immediately after it broke up a general movement in front of Richmond was begun. Gen. Sherman came on quickly from Goldsboro, reaching City Point on last Monday, and leaving again for North Carolina on Tuesday.

We have the important report from Washington that General Lee, since the engagements of last Saturday, has renewed his request for a military convention to agree upon terms for a cessation of hostilities. It is said he has acknowledged that, on account of the cutting of his communications, the scarcity of supplies in Richmond, and the present formidable combinations against him, further military efforts on his part must be useless. It is understood that General Sherman's plans for cutting off General Johnston's rebel army from all available sources of supply are complete, and that General Grant's movement will compel Lee either to starve his troops in Richmond or come out and risk an engagement. In view of all these matters, many well informed people in Washington are sanguine that before President Lincoln's return from the James river peace will have been agreed upon between Generals Grant and Lee, and the rebellion be ended. Another matter of apparently some significance is the fact that Secretary Seward also left Washington for City Point last night.

Another engagement took place in the Army of the Potomac on last Monday morning, which, though confined to a small portion of the line, and of short duration, was of quite a serious character, at least for the rebels. A party of them, who pretended that they wished to desert, were allowed to approach the national lines, when they made a fierce attack on the front of one division of the Sixth corps, just before daybreak, for the purpose of recovering their advanced works, from which they were driven on Saturday. The assault was so sudden and furious that the Sixth corps troops were at first forced back; but they instantly rallied, repulsed the enemy on all points, and recovered and maintained their captured ground. The rebel loss during the short fight was heavy, while that of the Sixth corps was very slight. The entire first line of rebel works captured by the Second and Sixth corps on last Saturday is still held by them, and has been rendered so strong that any effort of the enemy for its recovery must prove futile.

The loss of the rebels on Saturday, in killed, wounded and prisoners, in their attack on the Ninth corps alone, is estimated at five thousand. Gen. Grant, in his official order, states that over nineteen hundred of them were capture at this point. To offset this they gained nothing. The Richmond papers only claim that five hundred Union soldiers were captured and admit that no guns were carried off. Gen. Grant says that in all the engagements of Saturday along the lines twenty-eight hundred rebel soldiers and ten rebel battle flags were captured. Both Gen. Lee's official despatch and the Richmond journals admit that the attack on the Ninth corps was a failure.

[From the New York Herald, March 29.]

The Fight of the 19th inst.

NEWBERN, N. C. March 24, 1865.

An attack was made upon the 20th corps on Sunday, the 19th, in the vicinity of Bentonsville, nearly thirty miles southwest of Goldsboro. It is represented by those who ought to be well advised, that Slocum's grand division, consisting of the Fourteenth and Twentieth corps, was making a feint movement or reconnoissance in the direction of Smithfield and Raleigh, the former place being about twenty-five miles west of Goldsboro, nearly on the line of railroad between Goldsboro and Raleigh. The attack of the enemy, like all their onsets, commenced impetuously; but they lacked the stubbornness and spirit to keep it up. On Sunday it cannot be denied that the Fourteenth and Twentieth corps had their hands full to sustain themselves against the attack made upon them. On the next day, however, the Fifteenth and Seventeenth corps came to the rescue, and the enemy were driven in confusion to and through Smithfield, in the direction of Raleigh. The chief command of the rebel army was held by General Johnston, although Gen. Robert E. Lee is said by some of the prisoners to have been present at Smithfield, giving general direction to movements. I greatly doubt this, however, but think that S. P. Lee, of Hood's old army, was present, and that he is confounded with the other Lee. There is no doubt about Hardee and Bragg having been present, and it is pretty certain that a portion of the rebel Army of Virginia was at or near the scene of conflict.

THE CASUALTIES

were pretty heavy the first day on both sides, and the hospitals in this place are being cleared as much as possible to make room for the wounded who can be removed so far. The next day the casualties were almost wholly upon the side of the rebels, and their killed and wounded were left in our hands.

THE REBELS PURSUED TO SMITHFIELD.

General Sherman pursued them no farther than Smithfield, and from there *has come to Goldsboro to refit his army*. A new outfit was needed throughout, and everything necessary for them has been sent forward to Kingston, and from there will be sent to Goldsboro as fast as possible.

THE ARMIES CONCENTRATED AT GOLDSBORO.

Generals Sherman, Schofield and Terry are now all at Goldsboro, although Terry's forces have advanced some distance beyond, and will exercise a vigilent watchfulness over the enemy. Terry met with no opposition in his advance, but made some valuable captures of locomotives and cars. Schofield received a hearty welcome from the citizens of Goldsboro, very few leaving the town.— The valiant editor of the Goldsboro *Journal* was among the first to depart. The ladies, particularly, gave our boys the best of cheer. The enemy burned about one thousand bales of cotton before leaving, having previously compelled owners in the country to bring it in and store it in the town.

Thirteenth and Sixteenth Army Corps.

GENERAL ORDERS—NO. 28.

WAR DEPARTMENT, ADJUTANT GENERAL'S OFFICE, WASHINGTON, Feb. 26, 1865.

The Thirteenth and Sixteenth army corps having been reorganized by Major General Canby, by direction of the President, Major General Gordon Granger is assigned to the command of the former, and Major General A. J. Smith to the latter, their assignments to date from February 18.

By order of

SECRETARY OF WAR.

E. D. TOWNSEND, Asst. Adjt. General.

From Mobile.

From the N. Orleans Independent, March 17.

A lady, in whom implicit confidence is placed, and who arrived here last week, direct from Mobile, states that when she left that city all appearances indicated that it was being evacuated by the rebel troops. Information has since been received here which would seem to justify the opinion. The report of its evacuation is also credited by the military authorities here. It matters very little whether Mobile be evacuated or not; whenever the federals want the city they'll march on it and take possession.

The heavy guns up the bay are still heard at all hours of the day, and a courier just in reports that the rebels have been driven from three batteries.

We are in almost hourly expectation of receiving the order to advance. Transportation has been cut down to the smallest limit possible.

Trade With Rebel States.

The bill to repeal the section of the act which provides for the appointment of agents to purchase cotton and other products of insurrectionary States was not vetoed by the President, but, it was said, failed to receive his signature, which amounts to about the same thing—namely, its failure to become a law.

The New-York Times.

VOL. XIV......NO. 4225. NEW-YORK, MONDAY, APRIL 10, 1865. PRICE FOUR CENTS

HANG OUT YOUR BANNERS

UNION

VICTORY!

PEACE!

Surrender of General Lee and His Whole Army.

THE WORK OF PALM SUNDAY.

Final Triumph of the Army of the Potomac.

The Strategy and Diplomacy of Lieut.-Gen. Grant.

Terms and Conditions of the Surrender.

The Rebel Arms, Artillery, and Public Property Surrendered.

Rebel Officers Retain Their Side Arms and Private Property.

Officers and Men Paroled and Allowed to Return to Their Homes.

The Correspondence Between Grant and Lee.

OFFICIAL.

WAR DEPARTMENT, WASHINGTON, April 9, 1865—9 o'clock P. M.

To Maj.-Gen. Dix:

This department has received the official report of the SURRENDER, THIS DAY, OF GEN. LEE AND HIS ARMY TO LIEUT.-GEN. GRANT, on the terms proposed by Gen. GRANT.

Details will be given as speedily as possible.

EDWIN M. STANTON, Secretary of War.

HEADQUARTERS ARMIES OF THE UNITED STATES, 4:30 P. M., April 9.

Hon. Edwin M. Stanton, Secretary of War:

GEN. LEE SURRENDERED THE ARMY OF NORTHERN VIRGINIA THIS AFTERNOON, upon the terms proposed by myself. The accompanying additional correspondence will show the conditions fully.

(Signed) U. S. GRANT, Lieut.-Gen'l.

SUNDAY, April 9, 1865.

GENERAL—I received your note of this morning, on the picket line, whither I had come to meet you and ascertain definitely what terms were embraced in your proposition of yesterday with reference to the surrender of this army.

I now request an interview in accordance with the offer contained in your letter of yesterday for that purpose.

Very respectfully, your obedient servant,

R. E. LEE, General.

To Lieut.-Gen. GRANT, Commanding United States Armies.

Sunday, April 9, 1865.

Gen. R. E. Lee, Commanding Confederate States Armies.

Your note of this date is but this moment, 11 50 A. M., received.

In consequence of my having passed from the Richmond and Lynchburgh road to the Farmville and Lynchburgh road, I am at this writing about four miles West of Walter's church, and will push forward to the front for the purpose of meeting you.

Notice sent to me, on this road, where you wish the interview to take place, will meet me.

Very respectfully, your ob'd't servant,

U. S. GRANT, Lieutenant-General.

APPOMATTOX COURT-HOUSE, April 9, 1865.

General R. E. Lee, Commanding C. S. A.:

In accordance with the substance of my letters to you of the 8th inst., I propose to receive the surrender of the Army of Northern Virginia on the following terms, to wit:

Rolls of all the officers and men to be made in duplicate, one copy to be given to an officer designated by me, the other to be retained by such officers as you may designate.

The officers to give their individual paroles not to take arms against the Government of the United States until properly exchanged, and each company or regimental commander sign a like parole for the men of their commands.

The arms, artillery and public property to be packed and stacked and turned over to the officers appointed by me to receive them.

This will not embrace the side-arms of the officers, nor their private horses or baggage.

This done, EACH OFFICER AND MAN WILL BE ALLOWED TO RETURN TO THEIR HOMES, not to be disturbed by United States authority so long as they observe their parole and the laws in force where they reside.

Very respectfully,

U. S. GRANT, Lieutenant-General.

HEADQUARTERS ARMY OF NORTHERN VIRGINIA, April 9, 1865.

Lieut.-Gen. U. S. Grant, Commanding U. S. A.:

GENERAL: I have received your letter of this date, CONTAINING THE TERMS OF SURRENDER OF THE ARMY OF NORTHERN VIRGINIA, as proposed by you. As they are substantially the same as those expressed in your letter of the 8th inst., THEY ARE ACCEPTED. I will proceed to designate the proper officers to carry the stipulations into effect.

Very respectfully,

Your obedient servant,

R. E. LEE, General.

THE PRELIMINARY CORRESPONDENCE.

The following is the previous correspondence between Lieut.-Gen. GRANT and Gen. LEE, referred to in the foregoing telegram to the Secretary of War:

CLIFTON HOUSE, VA., April 9, 1865.

Hon. Edwin M. Stanton, Secretary of War:

The following correspondence has taken place between Gen. LEE and myself. *There has been no relaxation in the pursuit during its pendency.*

U. S. GRANT, Lieutenant-General.

APRIL 7, 1865.

Gen. R. E. Lee, Commanding C. S. A.:

GENERAL: The result of the last week must convince you of the hopelessness of further resistance on the part of the Army of Northern Virginia in this struggle. I feel that it is so and regard it as my duty to shift from myself the responsibility of any further effusion of blood, by asking of you the surrender of that portion of the Confederate States Army, known as the Army of Northern Virginia.

Very Respectfully,

Your obedient servant,

U. S. GRANT,

Lieutenant-General,

Commanding Armies of the United States.

APRIL 7, 1865.

General: I have received your note of this date.

Though not entirely of the opinion you express of the hopelessness of further resistence on the part of the army of Northern Virginia, I reciprocate your desire to avoid useless effusion of blood, and therefore, before considering your proposition, *ask the terms you will offer, on condition of its surrender.*

R. E. LEE, General.

To Lieut.-Gen. U. S. GRANT, Commanding Armies of the United States.

APRIL 8, 1865.

To Gen. R. E. Lee, Commanding C. S. A.:

GENERAL: Your note of last evening in reply to mine of same date, asking the conditions on which I will accept the surrender of the Army of Northern Virginia, is just received.

In reply, I would say that *peace being my first desire, there is but one condition that I insist upon*, viz.:

That the men surrendered shall be disqualified for taking up arms again against the Government of the United States until properly exchanged.

I will meet you, or designate officers to meet any officers you may name, for the same purpose, at any point agreeable to you, for the purpose of arranging definitely the terms upon which the surrender of the Army of Northern Virginia will be received.

Very respectfully, your obedient servant,

U. S. GRANT, Lieut.-General,

Commanding armies of the United States.

April 8, 1865.

GENERAL: I received, at a late hour, your note of to-day, in answer to mine of yesterday.

I did not intend to propose the surrender of the Army of Northern Virginia, but *to ask the terms* of your proposition. To be frank, I do not think the emergency has arisen to call for the surrender.

But as *the restoration of peace should be the sole object of all*, I desire to know whether your proposals would tend to that end.

I cannot, therefore, meet you with a view to surrender the Army of Northern Virginia, but *as far as your proposition may affect the Confederate States forces under my command, and tend to the restaration of peace*, I should be pleased to meet you at 10 A. M., to-morrow, on the old stage road to Richmond, between the picket lines of the two armies.

Very respectfully, your obedient servant,

R. E. LEE,

General, C. S. A.

To Lieut.-Gen. GRANT, Commanding Armies of the United States.

APRIL 9, 1865.

General R. E. Lee, commanding C. S. A.:

GENERAL: Your note of yesterday is received. As I have no authority to treat on the subject of peace, the meeting proposed for 10 A. M. to-day could lead to no good. I will state, however, General, that *I am equally anxious for peace with yourself*; and the whole North entertain the same feeling. *The terms upon which peace can be had are well understood. By the South laying down their arms, they will hasten that most desirable event, save thousands of human lives. and hundreds of millions of property not yet destroyed.*

Sincerely hoping that all our difficulties may be settled *without the loss of another life*, I subscribe myself,

Very respectfully,

Your obedient servant,

U. S. GRANT,

Lieutenant-General United States Army.

REJOICINGS.

WILMINGTON, Del., Sunday, April 9.

Wilmington is in an uproar and blaze of glory, rejoicing over the greatest of victories yet achieved by our arms. Guns are firing, bells are ringing, and a large procession is proceeding through the streets. Such an excitement was never before witnessed in this city,

ALBANY, Monday, April 10—1 A. M.

There is great rejoicing here over the news of the surrender of Gen. LEE and his army.

The news was received at about 10 P. M., and about midnight State and Pearl streets were filled with people anxiously awaiting the particulars.

The bells are ringing, cannon firing, while the multitude are indulging in fireworks.

The Governor was called up and briefly addressed the throng around his residence.

The State House and many private residences are illuminated.

PHILADELPHIA, April 9.

The glorious announcement of LEE's surrender was received here about nine o'clock. It was telegraphed to all sections of the city, and was announced in the several churches. The *Ledger* office was illuminated in five minutes. The bell of Independence Hall was rung by the order of the Mayor. The firemen immediately assembled and blocked up the streets. Salutes were fired, and the whistles of the steam-engines and the cheers of the assembled multitudes made the whole city ring.

WORCESTER, Mass., Monday, April 9.

The news of the surrender of LEE and his army created an intense excitement here to-night. The bells were rung, guns were fired, bonfires kindled, the fire companies turned out, and many stores and buildings were illuminated.

PITTSBURGH, Pa., Sunday, April 9.

The news to-night brought nearly the entire population into the streets. The recruiting booths were turned into bonfires, salutes were fired, speeches were made, and bands played.

TRENTON, N. J., Sunday, April 9.

The glorious news was received here with cheering and ringing of bells. The people are turning out *en masse* to receive and rejoice over the glad tidings.

PROVIDENCE, R. I., Sunday, April 9—Midnight.

Bells are ringing, cannon are firing, and the citizens are out rejoicing over the news of LEE's surrender. A large bonefire is burning on Weybosset bridge.

FROM THE PACIFIC COAST.

Juarez said to be Coming to Washington by way of San Francisco—French Forces in Sinaloa—French War Steamers in California Ports—The Overland Mails.

SAN FRANCISCO, Friday, April 7.

The steamer *John L. Stephens*, from Mazatlan, brings $93,000 in treasure and a thousand bags of silver ore.

The Mazatlan *Times*, the Imperialist organ, give the report that JUAREZ was en route for Cape St. Lucas, whence he would sail for San Francisco on his way to Washington.

A French naval expedition had sailed, it was supposed, for Guaymas.

An Imperial force has moved to Sinaloa.

A correspondent of the San Francisco *Bulletin*, writing from Mazatlan, March 4, says that JUAREZ is still at Chihuahua with his ministers raising troops, though money, arms, and ammunition are scarce.

The French war steamer *Victoria* and transport *Du Rhine* was at Santa Barbara, on the coast of California. They hope to obtain supplies of coal at San Francisco.

The daily Overland Mail, hence to Salt Lake, resumed its trips yesterday. The first mail this way since the interruption arrived last night.

The recent meeting in behalf of the Christian Sanitary Commission, resulted in remittances, by telegraph, within the past few days, of $20,000 in gold.

The scarcity of flour and wheat continues. Extreme prices are obtained, and consequently trade does not improve much.

The Union Convention of Washington Territory have nominated A. A. DEWY as Congressional Delegate.

Military celebrations for the national victories were held throughout the State to-day.

A mass meeting in aid of the Soldiers' Relief Association was held here to-night.

THE VICTORY.

Thanks to God, the Giver of Victory.

Honors to Gen. Grant and His Gallant Army.

A NATIONAL SALUTE ORDERED.

Two Hundred Guns to be Fired at the Headquarters of Every Army, Department, Post and Arsenal.

[OFFICIAL.]

WAR DEPARTMENT, WASHINGTON, D. C., April 9, 1865—9:30 P. M.

Lieut.-Gen. Grant:

Thanks be to Almighty God for the great victory with which he has this day crowned you and the gallant armies under your command.

The thanks of this Department and of the Government, and of the People of the United States—their reverence and honor have been deserved—will be rendered to you and the brave and gallant officers and soldiers of your army for all time.

EDWIM M. STANTON, Secretary of War.

WAR DEPARTMENT, WASHINGTON, D. C., April 9, 1866—10 o'clock P. M.

Ordered: That a salute of two hundred guns be fired at the headquarters of every army and department, and at every post and arsenal in the United States, and at the Military Academy at West Point on the day of the receipt of this order, in commemoration of the surrender of Gen. ROBERT E. LEE and the Army of Northern Virginia to Lieut.-Gen. GRANT and the army under his command. Report of the receipt and execution of this order to be made to the Adjutant-General at Washington.

EDWIN M. STANTON, Secretary of War.

FROM RICHMOND.

Perils and Excitements of a Voyage Up the James—Scenes and Incidents Along the River.

From Our Own Correspondent.

RICHMOND, Va., Wednesday, April 5.

The inspiration of the scene and the scope of the theme before us are far beyond the feeble desscriptive powers of of the pen of your correspondent. No brilliant rhetoric, no vivid word-painting, no oratorical eloquence can portray the sublimity and immensity of the great victory. It is almost beyond the power of the human mind to comprehend its extent, and when you begin to descend to detail, the task is simply appalling in its magnitude. Think of a line of operations, held defensively and operated from offensively with such success, *thirty-nine miles long from flank to flank, thoroughly fortified throughout its entire length!* Think of the cities captured, of the fortificationss stormed and taken, with their hundreds of guns, great and small, of the material of war now in our hands, yet beyond the possibility of computation of the terrible battles, and the overwhelming defeat, and rout of the chief army of the rebellion of the prisoners captured. Counted by the tens of thousands; of the terrified flight of the arch-traitor and his few desperate minions; of the triumphant entry of ABRAHAM LINCOLN into treason's fallen capital. Let every lover of his country depict the vast scene in his own imagination for words to fitly discribe it falls altogether.

Through the courtesy of Provost-Marshal Gen. PATRICK, I enjoyed an exceedingly pleasant sail from City Point to the Richmond wharves this morning, on his fleet flag ship, the *Mattino*. Accompanying the General were Hon. C. H. DANA, Assistant Secretary of War, his wife and son, and Hon. ROSCOE CONKLING, member of Congress from New-York. The snake-like bends of the James between City Point and Varina Landing, were quickly passed, and at the latter place assurance was given that the river was clear for our vessel to the very docks of Richmond; but I can assure you that the navigation of the tortuous channel of the James thence to Richmond, thickly sown with obstructions and supposed torpedoes, was an exceedingly delicate task, and full of excitement. Our pilot knew the channel of old, but he knew not the warlike devices of the enemy.

We were, however, very fortunate, and the approach to the city, especially during the last eight miles from Drewry's Bluff, was full of the intensest interest, for over these waters the Union flag had never before floated during the war. When we leave Dutch Gap and that famous canal, which looks as though it might have been washed out by a billow, we at once enter upon the lines held by the enemy. Howlett House Battery, famous for its determined resistance to our engeneering operations on the north side of the river, stands abandoned and gloomy, with its twelve large guns still in the embrasures, but all silent as we steamed rapidly by. Another long and large earthwork appears on the left bank, mounting eight or ten guns, and bearing directly upon the mouth of the canal. This, too, like the rest, is abandoned, with its armament unimpaired. We next pass the wreck of the rebel gunboat, blown up by our batteries during the effort made to run through our fleet some months ago.

The next point of interest is Fort Brady, on the north bank of the river, and the left of the position of our Army of the James. What strikes one as very remarkable here is the fact that owing to the intricate windings of the James there are two rebel batteries, Howlett House and another, absolutely in the rear of this former position of our army. Fort Brady is the point where Gen. GIBBON opened on the retreating rebel rams. Had there been larger guns at his disposal, the range is so good that they would have stood a poor chance of escape.

We are now fairly in that part of the river held solely by the rebels, and a knowledge of the channel and obstructions is absolutely necessary to a safe voyage. The gunboat *Monticello* is therefore hailed, and on asking for information, a pilot who has been up and down is tendered with much politeness. The obstructions sunk by our own fleet are soon passed, likewise the fleet of monitors, and the next object which greets the vision is a gaily dressed tug, with a guard of marines, having in tow Admiral PORTER's barge with the President, on his return from Richmond, complacently seated in the stern sheets. It looks very much like a pic-nic. Following a short distance after is the President's handsome flag-ship, the *River Queen*. Not far behind is the beautiful steel gunboat *Bat*, ex-blockade runner, now general convoy to distinguished guests, and one of the fastest vessels in the navy. The *River Queen*, which took the President up the river, proceeded no farther than the obstructions at Drewry's Bluff. We are soon abreast of this historic fortification, and eager eyes scan closely its formidable walls and positions.

Here is the chief line of obstructions sunk by the rebels early in the war, and located as they are, directly under the guns of Fort Darling, subjecting every approaching thing to a terrible plunging fire, it is readily admitted that this was the impassable barrier to the naval advance on Richmond. The river here is very narrow, and the movement of large vessels attended with much danger. The obstructions were placed directly across the river, and filled it completely with the exception of a gap of fifty or sixty feet, left for the passage of the rebel fleet and flag-of-truce boats. They consist of the hulls of two or three old steamships, that formerly plyed between Richmond and New York. The wheel-houses, fast crumbling to decay, still rise above the water, and present the appearance of a melancholy ruin.

We pass so hurriedly under the guns of Fort Darling, that we have no good opportunity to observe its construction. We know it looks very strong, and on the north side it has one or two small outlying works on its flank. Our naval companions tell us that it is a casemated fortification, and with its surrounding field works, all parts of the fort itself, mounts not less than forty guns. All these, like hundreds more, are our trophies without blemish or injury.

Not far above Fort Darling lies the wreck of one of the famous rebel fleet in the James, the iron-clad *Virginia*. Whether she has been blown up or simply scuttled and sunk, cannot be ascertained from looking at her as she lies. She sank in deep water, and is careened over on her side, leaving a portion of her overhang visible above the water-line. Of the other iron-clad, the *Richmond*, we find no trace.

In the immediate vicinity of Fort Darling we pass through a very substantial bridge with a draw, used by LEE for the speedy transfer of troops from the north to the south side of the James. Ere reaching Richmond we pass two more of the same kind, though hardly so well built as the first; but all demonstrating that LEE had no pontoon briidges across the James anywhere—probably, because the rapid current rendered them unsafe, and probably, too, because he had not any pontoons to spare, when something else would answer just as well.

We have now steamed safely by all obstructions and chances of torpedoes, and the very pardonable trepidation which we felt in view of our possible danger, gives way to a feeling that just now is a moment in our lives, the significance, importance and sublimity of which cannot be justly appreciated. The City of Richmond is in view. The spires pointing heavenward; the smoke still rising from the conflagration's awful ruin, and the Stars and Stripes floating from a hundred house-tops and mastheads, all form a picture so sublimely grand and inspiring, that the human mind is simply lost in mute contemplation.

In a few moments we land at the Rockets, and a brisk walk of a mile and a half brings us to the Spotswood House, where we find dinner and a very comfortable room, amid hundreds of loyal guests.

L. L. CROUNSE.

First Impressions of Richmond—The Great Conflagration in the City—Who Was Responsible for it?—The Libby and Castle Thunder—Suffering for Food—Distribution of Supplies—Lee's Family.

From Our Own Correspondent.

RICHMOND, Thursday, April 6, 1865.

So many thousand facts are presented to the mind of the visitor here in such a very short space of time, that to record them systematically is almost impossible. The great features of the evacuation, the entrance of our troops, the conflagration, the President's visit and reception, have already been forwarded to you in detail by your correspondents who came in with the troops, and I will, therefore, allude to them only in a general way.

Let me say, though, at the outset, that the best part of the city is a ruin. That the awful fire kindled by the enemy, and which at first promised to consume but a few buildigns, was so fanned by the rising wind, that before it could be got under subjection, *thirty squares, comprising not less than eight hundred buildings in the very best and most valuable business part of Richmond were in ashes.* What the pecuniary loss is no one can estimate. Nearly all the principal mills, factories, warehouses, stores, banks and insurance offices were destroyed, and the losses being so heavy, the insurance companies, perhaps insolvent already from their countenance of the rebel currency, are now more than bankrupted, and thousands of property owners, computed wealthy in their actual possessions three days ago, are now reduced to beggary. It is among the things easily discernable, that this ruin, wrought by their own friends, to whom they have given all, and to whose tyranny they have submitted, with even cheerfulness, is the cause of far deeper gloom among many than that produced by the loss of the city or the defeat of their army. It is apparent indeed that the transfer of the city to the Union flag was not only *not distasteful to a very large portion of the people, many of them among the best classes, but even highly gratifying.* No captured city, not even Savannah nor Columbia, can present the ruin apparent here in Richmond. It will carry its painful evidences for half a score of years, and the only thing which will speedily alleviate the dire distress that must prevail, and give the city a chance for a speedy recovery from its present stagnation, is immediate peace. It is Richmond's only salvation. The origin of the fire and the incendiaries are so well and positively known that no extended investigation on these points is required. It seems that *Gen. Lee was not responsible for it, but that Jeff. Davis and his Secretary of War, Breckenridge, were.* The destruction of the supplies and the arsenal involved the destruction of the city, and it was so decided by the leading citizens. Gen. EWELL and Maj. CARRINGTON both protested against it in the most earnest manner, as did also a committee of citizens, but BRECKINRIDGE, in reply, exclaimed *that he didn't care a d—n if every house in Richmond was consumed, the warehouse must be burned.* Thus this wretched rebel, foisted into a powerful position with no constituents, is responsible for the dreadful ruin, and his master DAVIS is likewise responsible, because he silently countenanced it.

The fire was started in two places, among the supply warehouses near the wharves, and at the Danville Depot, where there were 1,500 hogsheads of tobacco belonging to the Confederate Government. This consumed the Danville Depot, also the Petersburgh Depot, and the bridge over the James to Manchester. The famous Libby Prison, and Castle Thunder, as I have already informed you, were not burned. They were reserved for a far more appropriate fate. I visited them yesterday, and found Castle Thunder used as a guard-house for factious and thieving negroes, caught in acts of plunder, while the Libby contained 700 rebel prisoners, officers and privates, temporarily shut up together. They looked through the iron gratings with gloomy countenances, while the Union guard outside seemed to richly enjoy the transition that the famous building had undergone, evidently having been there himself. The whirligig of time makes all things even, and the thousands of loyal officers and soldiers who have suffered the tortures and horrors of these dungeons may now contemplate their present uses with serene satisfaction, and yet without resentment.

A close inspection of Castle Thunder reveals one of the most hideous dungeons that can be conceived. We failed to see it, however, in all its filth and nastyness, for a strong force of men had been engaged two days in carrying out the accumulation of the past three years. The corporal of the guard who conducted us through, pointed out a spot on the floor on one of the main halls, not yet cleaned, where the dirt was three inches thick, and alive with vermin, *and yet on this floor, in this condition, prisoners were obliged to sleep either upon the dirt itself or upon palets of decaying straw.*

But I will not descant further upon this vile relic of the rebellion. Its career is too well known. The prisoners confined here, it will be recollected, were those against whom special vengeance was directed, prisoners of State, persons charged with harboring Union prisoners, Union officers charged with being spies, blockade-runners, &c. Well has it been said that a confinement in Castle Thunder is a foretaste of the tortures of the damned.

This building, together with the Libby belongs to the estate of JOHN ENDERS, and was leased by the rebel Government. They were originally built for stores, but subsequently turned into tabacco manufactories. But their base uses are now at an end.

This is the fourth day of the Union occupation, and the confusion in the city necessarily attendant upon such an evacuation, and such an occupation, is gradually subsiding. Could the ruins of the fire be removed from sight, Richmond would present an attractive appearance, for it is really a handsome city; but, after all, the saddest scenes are at the headquarters of the Provost-Martial, the Commissioners of Subsistence, and the office of Sanitary Commission, the latter being already established here. Gen. WEITZEL had no sooner established his headquarters here than thousands of citizens besieged him for rations. And as the city is now shut out from all supplies from the country, the crowd of applicants for subsistence is rapidly increasing. This morning there was nothing in the markets but a few small fish caught by negroes. The Capitol, the City Hall and the Capitol-square are filled with a great throng of all classes, condition, sexes and ages, with basket in hand and an appealing expression of face. What the regulations yet are in regard to the issue of rations to the citizens, I do not know, but a limited quantity is being supplied them at present.

In order to study this peculiar social feature of the rebellion, I mingled with these crowds this morning for a short time, to observe their temper, desires and condition. They were, of course, largely made up of what appeared to be the poorer classes, and many negroes were among them, some for subsistence for themselves and some as servants of families. I found many whose intelligent expression of countenance, fair features and attempted gentility of dress, indicated that they were of the higher classes, on whom the demands of want and hunger were as insatiable as upon those of less position. I noticed several ladies approach the officer in charge at the City Hall, genteelly attired, and with their faces so closely veiled as to defy the gaze of the keenest eye. They spoke in such tremulous tones when giving their names as to cause us to suspect their names were as foreign to them as the hunger they now sought to appease had been in days gone by. Many of the wealthiest families, however, who had the means, have far larger supplies of provisions on hand than was consistent with the repeated appeals of Confederate officials for such to spare from their bounty to feed the army.

The exodus of prominent citizens was confined mainly to those connected with the rebel government, and a few who had made themselves very conspicuous in rebel politics—all the rebel Cabinet and their chief assistants, though not much of their clerical force, got away. The preparations for the evacuation began very quietly among the officials. At noon of Sunday the important records of the departments were boxed up and carted to the depot; but very little suspicion was excited among the citizens as to the real state of the case. A strong guard was stationed at the Danville depot, and four trains were got ready, the first of which left, with DAVIS on board, at seven o'clock in the evening, and the last at midnight. DAVIS' family had gone into the country on the Friday preceeding, but not because of any apprehension that the city was to be given up. Very few families left the city, and there are very few vacant houses, the mansions of JEFF. DAVIS and GOV. BILLY SMITH being among those now in want of tenants. The family of Gen. LEE, consisting of his wife, who is an invalid, and three daughters, are among those who remain. They occupy a stylish house on Franklin-street, and for their protection a well disciplined guard is placed at the dwelling, and the family are scrupulously protected from annoyance of any character, the staring gaze of the passer-by hardly being allowed. This is the second time that Mrs. Gen. LEE has been in our hands. She was once captured by our cavalry near White House, in 1862, and sent through our lines to Richmond under flag of truce, by order of Gen. MCCLELLAN.

L. L. CROUNSE.

Union Sentiment in Richmond—Projects of Reconstruction—Distinguished Visitors—Recruiting Negro Troops—The Truth about Rebel Enlistment of Negroes.

From Our Own Correspondent.

RICHMOND, Friday, April 7, 1865.

I can give you news, to-day, which will gratify the heart of every loyal American. Virginia will return to the Union, and that right speedily. Desiring to ascertain the exact truth with reference to the alleged existence of a strong Union sentiment in the city, I availed myself of an opportunity to call upon certain gentlemen here whom I had heard alluded to by Secessionists as Union men, and I must say, that I spent two of the happiest hours of my life in full and free conversation with some of the most thorough and radical Union men in the country; men of wealth and position, whose faith has never wavered for an instant, and who, slaveholders, as they are, *demand that Virginia shall be taken back into the Union "under the Emancipation Proclamation;" that no vestige of the rebellion shall be tolerated; that the usurpation State, and Confederate, which has wrecked Virginia, shall not be recognized in a single respect;* that the State Government must be organized anew, by a convention of the people, as soon as that can be properly effected, and the State and its inhabitants thoroughly purged of treason in every shape.

Union sentiments, in this strong form exist here to a far greater extent than has yet been conceived; not alone among the poorer classes,—mechanics and laborers,—*but in wealthy and influential circles, where may be found men who have never lost faith in the Union;* who have confidently anticipated its triumph, and who greeted the old flag with tears of joy. They are men of the John Minor Botts school, and they are the leaven which shall leaven the whole lump here in this venerable old commonwealth of Virginia. They will delight to see the mass of the people treated with magnanimity, but they have felt too deeply the

Continued on Eighth Page.

The Philadelphia Inquirer.

PRICE TWO CENTS. PHILADELPHIA, MONDAY, APRIL 10, 1865. PRICE TWO CENTS.

VICTORY!! VICTORY!!

GEN. GRANT'S SUN OF AUSTERLITZ!

LEE FINDS HIS WATERLOO.

SURRENDER OF THE REBEL ARMY!!

GEN. GRANT'S TERMS ACCEPTED BY LEE.

THE REBELS WANT PEACE.

A GREAT AMOUNT OF WAR MATERIAL GIVEN UP!

REBEL ARMY PAROLED!!

THE NATION'S THANKS TO ITS GLORIOUS HEROES.

OFFICIAL WAR GAZETTE.

FIRST BULLETIN.

WAR DEPARTMENT, WASHINGTON, D. C., April 9, 1865—9 P.M.—Maj.-Gen. John A. Dix, New York:—This Department has just received an official report of the surrender, this day, of Gen, Lee and his army, to Lieutenant-General Grant, on the terms proposed by General Grant. The details will be given as speedily as possible.

EDWIN M. STANTON,
Secretary of War.

HEAD-QUARTERS ARMIES OF UNITED STATES, April 9th—4·30 P. M.—Hon. Edwin M. Stanton, Secretary of War:—General Lee surrendered the Army of Northern Virginia, this afternoon, upon terms proposed by myself. The accompanying additional correspondence will show the conditions fully.

(Signed) U. S. GRANT,
Lieutenant-General.

April 9, 1865.—General:—I received your note of this morning on the picket line, whither I had come to meet you and ascertain definitely what terms were embraced in your proposition of yesterday with reference to the surrender of this army.

I now request an interview in accordance with the offer contained in your letter of yesterday, for that purpose.

Very respectfully your obed't ser't,
R. E. LEE, General.

To Lieutenant-General U. S. Grant, Commanding United States Armies.

April 9th, 1865.—General R. E. Lee, Commanding Confederate States Armies:—Your note of this date is but this moment (11·50) eleven fifty A. M., received.

In consequence of my having passed from the Richmond and Lynchburg road to the Farmville and Lynchburg road, I am at this writing about four miles west of Waller's Church, and will push forward to the front for the purpose of meeting you. Notice sent to me on this road where you wish the interview to take place will meet me.

Very respectfully, your obd't serv't,
U. S. GRANT,
Lieutenant-General.

APPOMATTOX COURT HOUSE, April 9, 1865.—General R. E. Lee, commanding C. S. A.:—In accordance with the substance of my letter to you of the 8th inst., I propose to receive the surrender of the Army of Northern Virginia on the following terms, to wit:—

Rolls of all the officers and men to be made in duplicate. One copy to be given to an officer designated by me, the other to be retained by such officer or officers as you may designate. The officers to give their individual paroles not to take arms against the Government of the United States until properly exchanged, and each company or regimental commander sign a like parole for the men of their commands.

The arms, artillery and public property to be parked and stacked, and turned over to the officers appointed by me to receive them. This will not embrace the side-arms of the officers, nor their private horses or baggage.

This done, each officer and man will be allowed to return to their homes, not to be disturbed by United States authority so long as they observe their parole and the laws in force where they may reside.

Very respectfully,
U. S. GRANT, Lieutenant-General.

HEAD-QUARTERS, ARMY NORTHERN VIRGINIA, 9th April, 1865.—Lieut.-Gen. U. S. Grant, Commanding United States Army—General:—I have received your letter of this date containing the terms of surrender of the Army of Northern Virginia as proposed by you. As they are substantially the same as expressed in your letter of the 8th inst., they are accepted.

I will proceed to designate the proper officers to carry the stipulations into effect.

Very respectfully your obedient servant,
R. E. LEE, General.

The following is the previous correspondence between Lieutenant-General Grant and General Lee, referred to in the foregoing telegram to the Secretary of War:—

CLIFTON HOUSE, Va., April 9th, 1865.

Hon. Edwin M. Stanton, Secretary of War:—

The following correspondence has taken place between General Lee and myself. There has been no relaxation in the pursuit during its pendency:—

(Signed) U. S. GRANT, Lieut.-Gen.

April 7, 1865.—General R. E. LEE, Commanding C. S. A. General:—The result of the last week must convince you of the hopelessness of further resistance on the part of the Army of Northern Virginia in this struggle. I feel that it is so, and regard it as my duty to shift from myself the responsibility of any further effusion of blood by asking of you the surrender of that portion of the Confederate States Army known as the Army of Northern Virgina.

Very respectfully, your obedient servant,
U. S. GRANT,
Lieutenant-General Commanding Armies of the United States.

April 7th, 1865.—General:—I have received your note of this date. Though not entirely of the opinion you express of the hopelessness of further resistance on the part of the Army of Northern Virginia, I reciprocate your desire to avoid useless effusion of blood, and therefore, before considering your proposition, ask the terms you will offer on condition of its surrender.

(Signed) R. E. LEE, General.

To Lt.-Gen. Grant, Commanding Armies of the United States.

April 8th, 1865.—General R. E. Lee, Commanding C. S. A.:—General:—Your note of last evening, in reply to mine of same date, asking conditions on which I will accept the surrender of the Army of Northern Virginia is just received.

In reply, I would say, that peace being my first desire, there is but one condition I insist upon, viz: That the men surrendered shall be disqualified for taking up arms again against the Government of the United States until properly exchanged.

I will meet you, or designate officers to meet any officers you may name, for the same purpose, at any point agreeable to you, for the arranging definitely the terms upon which the surrender of the Army of Northern Virginia will be received.

Very respectfully, your obed't ser't,
U. S. GRANT, Lieut.-General,
Armies United States.

April 8th, 1865.—General:—I received at a late hour your note of to-day in answer to mine of yesterday. I did not intend to propose the surrender of the Army of Northern Virginia, but to ask the terms of your propositions.

To be frank with you, I do not think the emergency has arisen to call for the surrender of this army, but as the restoration of peace should be the sole object of all, I desire to know whether your proposals would tend to that end. I cannot, therefore, meet you with a view to surrender the Army of Northern Virginia, but as far as your proposition may affect the Confederate States forces under my command, and tend to the restoration of peace, I should be pleased to meet you at ten A. M. to-morrow, on the Old Stage road to Richmond, between the picket lines of the two armies.

Very respectfully, your obedient servant,
(Signed) R. E. LEE, General C. S. A.

April 9, 1865.—General R. E. Lee, Commanding C. S. A., General:—Your note of yesterday is rereceived. As I have no authority to treat on the subject of peace the meeting proposed for ten A. M. to-day could have no good effect.

I will state, however, General, that I am equally anxious for peace with yourself, and the whole North entertain the same feeling. The terms upon which peace can be had are well understood.

By the South laying down their arms, they will hasten that most desirable event, save thousands of human lives and hundreds of millions of dollars' worth of property not yet destroyed. Sincerely hoping that all our difficulties may be settled without the loss of another life, I subscribe myself,

Very respectfully, your obd't serv't,
(Signed) U. S. GRANT,
Lieutenant-General U. S. A.

SECOND OFFICIAL BULLETIN.

WAR DEPARTMENT, WASHINGTON, D. C., April 9th, 1865, 9·30 P. M.—Lieutenant-General Grant:—Thanks be to Almighty God for the great victory with which he has this day crowned you and the gallant army under your command. The thanks of this Department, and of the Government, and of the people of the United States, their reverence and honor, have been deserved and will be rendered to you and the brave and gallant officers and soldiers of your army, for all time.

(Signed) EDWIN M. STANTON,
Secretary of War.

THIRD BULLETIN.

WAR DEPARTMENT, WASHINGTON, D. C., April 9th, 10, P. M., 1865.—Ordered that a salute of two hundred (200) guns be fired at the Head-quarters of every Army and Department, and at every Post and Arsenal in the United States, and at the Military Academy at West Point, on the day of the receipt of this order, in commemoration of the surrender of General R. E. Lee and the Army of Northern Virginia to Lieutenant-General Grant and the army under his command. Report of the receipt and execution of this order to be made to the Adjutant-General, Washington.

EDWIN M. STANTON,
Secretary of War.

The above message was received at the American Telegraph Office by operators Heber C. Robinson and Joseph Bradley, who feel that this is the last opportunity they or any other operator in Philadelphia will ever have of receiving news that will awaken similar enthusiasm.

OUR RICHMOND LETTER.

Special Correspondence of the Inquirer.

RICHMOND, Va., Thursday, April 5.

Full accounts of the occupation of the city having already been sent by other of your specials, there is, comparatively, little new for me to say. Still, Richmond as it is to-day, and its surroundings, will furnish materials for letters for a long while to come.

The Libby Prison.

The first object of attraction to the soldiers and civilians is Libby Prison. Old Libby still stands, though all around it is a scene of ruins. A photographer is making a picture, and what a picture! If it was a heaven-ordained thing that colored troops should save the residences of the city from destruction, while the business part had been swept away by their own hands, it was but a poetic sequel that Libby should be filled with Rebels, and the glorious old blue mount guard at the doorways!

And how it looked! Rebels peering through the grated windows and swarming over the roof; longing eyes turned towards their homes, over which waved the old flag (what must have been their thoughts, if *they dare to think*)! in the distance the legions of loved ones murdered in that hell-hole. What can they *expect* at our hands? "*Ye who enter here leave all hope behind!*" That has been the fearful inscription stamped upon the minds of tens of thousands of patriots whom accidents of war threw into the hands of men whose malignant hate knew no bounds, and whose depraved hearts caused them to commit deeds for which there should be no forgiveness here, if hereafter—men like Davis and Lee, Stephens and Benjamin, men who attended church upon the Sabbath, who knew of the torture our men were undergoing but a few steps from their gilded mansions, whose word would have changed the treatment in an hour.

It has been stated and reiterated over and over again, by Secession sympathizers in the North, that they were treated as well as they had the means to do. The condition of things I have found here I can prove to have existed for the last four years, which show this to be false. Lumber and machine-shops are but a few yards distant; labor could have been had from the men themselves. The James River, but a few yards distant, and water at all times could have been had to keep the den clean. They had provision plenty stored in their immense warehouses close by; have always had plenty, and if their own army ever suffered it was because of the inefficiency of transportation from the canal and railroad here. At the base there should have been no want.

To pass through Libby and think of the sufferings that our men have been compelled to undergo, to see the loathsome corners where the sinks and water basins have emitted their foul vapors through the dark rooms, and to recall the names of the sick and faint murdered at the windows, where they had gone to get a few gasps of fresh air; to see samples of the food that was doled out, the wonder is that any men sustained life there for thirty days, summer or winter. That some epidemic never visited them, and swept all before it, is a marvel; and to-day I heard Rebel officers and privates whine, and even grow impudent, because they were put in such a place; and this too, when the privileges of sunning themselves on the roof and at the windows, and of receiving visits and food from their friends, were accorded them, which they denied to us. If there exists a man with the slightest desire to see the Rebel leaders and officers escape a single iota of the punishment they here earned, let him pay a visit to Libby, and if it does not vanish, then he is no friend of the soldier or of his country.

Captain Stewart

Who was selected to see to the forwarding and delivery of packages to our prisoners, is still here. For eight months he has stood by our boys, and like a ministering angel attended to their wants as best he could. He has still about five tons of boxes, &c., in his warehouse, which he has been unable to deliver for various causes. Last week there arrived about fifteen hundred of our prisoners from the South, taken from Sherman's army, in the most destitute condition. On Sunday last he was engaged clothing and shoeing them from 8 A. M. to 1 P. M., when an order came to put them on a boat at once, to go down and be exchanged. It was good news for the men, and he soon saw Libby empty, and its doors swing wide open. He suspected there was an intention of abandoning the city, but could not say or do anything. About midnight Major Turner came to him, and said, "Well, Captain, I am going to leave you Libby; we have concluded to evacuate the city." The Captain accepted it in the name of the United States.

At his request the warehouse adjoining Libby, in which our stores were, was not to be fired. Libby, adjoining, was spared for the same reason, and Pemberton, another jail the same as Libby, directly opposite, was also spared. On the opposite side from Pemberton was a tobacco warehouse filled with two million dollars' worth of French tobacco, which was fired in the morning. Captain Stewart and his clerk and two negroes got an axe, broke open Pemberton and tried to save it but failed; just as he would get the fire put out in one place it would catch in another, and his warehouse taking fire he was finally compelled to use his whole efforts to protect it, which he did.

Now, in the centre of two miles of charred ruins stands Libby, a monument to certify to the future the inhuman barbarity and degradation to which human slavery has sank the chivalry of Virginia. Let it remain, a satire upon the boasted civilization of the leaders of this Rebellion.

Among some letters that have fallen into our hands is one from the Rebel Adjutant-General, S. Cooper, addressed to his wife at Boydton, Mecklenburg county, Virginia. It is important as showing the utter despair of the Rebel cause. It shows that one week ago Jeff. Davis considered the capital lost and sent away his family. Mrs. Lee intended to have gone and Mrs. Mason could see no asylum nearer than Halifax:—

[No. 37.]

APRIL 1, 1865.

MY DEAR MARIA:—I received to-day your letter of March 24th, (No. 27). I find by it that you have received all my letters previous to the 21st of March. I have written you three since; that is, the 21st, 25th and 29th of March, and the one I am now writing is the 1st of April, so that there are but three letters from me besides this one, that are yet due you. I was pained on reading your letter that your mind is made up on coming to this city. You know not what you would have to encounter here, nor is it possible for you to know (unless you were here) of the privations which you would encounter here if you come. You say there is no place safer than where you are, except in Richmond, and that you expect to leave Clifton for this place in three weeks, by which time the roads will be passable.

Let me beg and urge you not to come here, and do not let your fancy picture comfort and safety to you here. Think of the distresses in Savannah and Columbia when Sherman's army took possession of those cities, and do not suppose that the same scenes may not be enacted here under like circumstances.

I met Mary Lee yesterday, and she told me her mother and sisters would not remain here, and also said the ladies in Savannah were selling their own clothing to buy themselves food. In all places the enemy have captured the Confederate money is considered by them as trash, and is not taken for the sale of any commodities. *So will it be here.* You know I have nothing but Confed. money, and how can you live upon that here under these circumstances? You will be reduced to starvation. That is lingering death to be sure, but it is not the less certain. You could not live upon your relations and friends here, as you seem to think, for a time, for they could no more live on the same means than yourself, and you would all be reduced to the same necessities and despair.

Call your mind to these facts, and do not let your apprehensions as to your present situation sway your judgment, and as you place *faith* in the protection of the Almighty, do not let that faith be shaken by the fear that He will fail you in the hour of need, which would only prove a *doubt* of His powers, or purpose to *save*.

Mrs. Davis and her children left here yesterday for the South, and other families are preparing to leave. Your sister Nannie, I understand, is much disturbed as to what to do, and inclines to leave the city. Grant is making every effort not to *fight* battles, but to starve the city and Lee's army by cutting off communications for supplies, and in that way gain an easy victory. His great purpose is to get possession of the Southside Railroad from Petersburg to Lynchburg, and if he accomplishes that, which he may possibly do, you will be prevented from reaching this city if you should start for it, and then you would be in a most helpless condition.

I give you these facts and suggestions for your consideration, and beg again that you will forgo your purpose to come here.

You tell me that Mr. Alexander seems most unwilling for you all to leave him; may God bless him for that; you could not be in better hands than in his. There is no necessity for you to leave him, and you could not be in better hands. Give my love to him and Miss Betty, and to his father. I must hurry Sam off to prevent you from coming: he has only been waiting the arrival of Cawood, who arrived two days since. He has brought all the things. * * *

Fondest love to Jennie and Sally.

Ever affectionately yours, S. C.

Mr. Ambler says your sister Eliza, Mrs. J. M. Mason, is going to Halifax for safety.

Castle Thunder Stands

On the upper side of the street, not very far from Libby. It is being cleaned out, and the lower part, formerly used for prisoners of State, will be taken for a guard-house for ordinary misdemeanors, while all Rebels will be consigned to Libby. Last Sunday the Rebels took out small numbers of prisoners, and started them under guards for Danville. Castle Thunder has its horrors, its untold tales of hope gone, stout hearts quailed, and maniacs come out, or the undertaker, a negro with a rude cart ended the case of "arbitrary arrests." About a dozen escaped from the guards, among whom are Captain S. Groonor, Lieutenant Church, and J. Hancock, of our army, charged with being spies.

The county jail was visited by Major Stevens, of the Fourth Massachusetts, and finding no provisions, and none having been had for twenty-four hours, he examined the books, and found from fifty to sixty men, women and children there, in the most squalid wretchedness. A little girl of about eight years of age attracted his attention, and he asked what she was in for. She replied, "she stole some bread to take home to her mother." The records proved her statements true, and as nearly all were in with the same charge—petty larcenies—the Major ordered the doors to be thrown wide open, and bid them "go and sin no more." A more grateful set could not have been found. Many thought they were there to die.

The "Examiner," "Dispatch," and "Enquirer"

Printiug offices were burned. The *Whig* and *Sentinel* remain. The *Whig*, anxious to keep on the paying side, has come out for the Union and has accordingly been furnished with considerable United States advertising, among which we find the advertisement for the new Seven-thirty loan of Jay Cooke. Its editors and reporters remain, but have not all taken the oath of allegiance. The *Sentinel*, Jeff.'s organ, refuses to turn around, and is accordingly silent. The *Whig* comes out in the afternoon in a little sheet about the size of a sheet of foolscap. There is an excellent field for a loyal paper here.

President Lincoln and Lady in Richmond.

Mrs. Lincoln, accompanied by Senators Sumner and Harlan, and a dozen friends, arrived this morning, and spent the day in looking around the city, and will leave to-night on the *River Queen*.

Mr. Lincoln was here yesterday, and left last night, going down to City Point; he sent his own boat ahead, and got into the small yawl of Commodore Porter, and with a half dozen sailors he rode in it, in tow of a tug; part of the time he steered and seemed to enjoy the trip. He was very enthusiastically received wherever he went.

Major-General Devens

Has located himself in Governor Letcher's house. General Weitzel had his head-quarters in Jeff Davis' mansion, but has given it up for General Grant, Mrs. Grant having come up from City Point to-day. Assistant Secretary of War Dana and Mrs. Dana left to-night for City Point; he has been here two days looking after the interests of the Government.

Union Prisoners in the South.

Generals Hoffman and Mulford are here. There are no more prisoners of ours now in the enemy's lines, except such as are in Southern Georgia and in the Southwest. Those in the region of the Mississippi are to be exchanged at Vicksburg. No definite arrangements have been made yet for those in Georgia, but there will be soon.

The Markets were Very Thin

To-day. Shad at fifty cents (nothing but greenbacks and specie now recognized here); eggs, 60 butter, 75; beef, 25; some asparagus, I believe was also offered. Ample facilities will be given to get in produce.

Mail Boats to Washington.

To-morrow we are to have a regular line of mail boats, leaving here at six A. M., arriving about half-past six P. M., and about twenty-eight hours from Washington.

The railroad to Petersburg will probably be completed to-morrow. It will take some time to rebuild the railroad bridge at this point, and in the meantime two pontoon bridges have been laid down.

Rebel Bonds "on the Street."

Among the papers and documents thrown to the winds on the exit of the Confederacy was about a million or two of Rebel bonds, some of them coupons. They are very cheap now, but as there is no designated place at which said coupons are to be paid they are not in very great demand.

Begging Papers and Food.

The people are nearly all out to-day on the streets, and are all either begging passes or food. White and black are all now on an equality; or the colored are rather the surest of favors, as no one questions their loyalty, and but few white folks have very comfortable records to dwell upon. No food or passes, without first taking the oath, is a bitter pill for some, but it is generally taken, with a gentle squirm. Nearly every one has an idea that Uncle Sam is an immense cornucopia, who has only to be squeezed and out comes an unlimited quantity of stores of all kinds, and as they are not to be expected to starve, *sequitur*, they are to be dealt out regular rations.

Richmond a Second New Orleans.

We have here a second New Orleans; perhaps not quite so bad, but bad enough, anyhow. The poorer classes of whites wont work if they can get along without by any make-shift. The seedy bankrupt F. F. V.'s don't expect to work. Their families want their servants to dress, feed and clothe them, but have no money to hire them, and the colored population have an idea that they must be paid in "Yankee money," "No Confeds." There is an absolute necessity for a social revolution, Confederate money is worthless; the State banks are no better, and the people have little else.

Richmond has great natural facilities for being a great commercial city, but unless she is *regenerated*, she *must die out*. No one looks for much of a change in the old Secesh here; they are ignorant, prejudiced and stupid; they will never learn, and cannot and do not want to forget their Secesh; they cling to the delusion with a strange fanaticism. They seem to admit that their cause is hopeless, and that it has not paid, but they go on and prate about being let alone, and being independent, won't reason, and cannot argue, and *never think*.

The merchants who have not been burned out, and whose hands are stained with treason—men who have aided and abetted, and many of whom have participated, have quit only because it *did not pay*.

Advent of the Sutlers.

The sutlers have come in the last three days like an avalanche! They are seizing the best stores and opening out their stocks marked at prices that sound like Confederate currency, but mean greenbacks. The popular dodge seems to be for a sutler to go to a Secesher and get him to take him in in order to throw around his house the mask of loyalty, and divert from his attention the Provost Marshal and the officers of the law. Some of these bargains should be looked into.

The Northern Papers in Richmond.

THE PHILADELPHIA INQUIRER and the New York papers made their appearance this morning, and were eagerly bought up at ten cents a piece. But few, if any of the citizens buy them.

This afternoon the

Sequel to "the Great Mass Meeting

To fire the Southern heart," was held in the African Church. At an early hour the building was crowded to excess by the colored population and the services in honor of the *entree* of the Union army were held in the presence of about two thousand five hundred persons. The exercises were purely religious, but conducted in their own way. They are Baptists, but sing with with a native fernor that one seldom hears. They sang a hymn commencing with—

"Jesus, mine all, to Heaven is gone,
He whom I fix my hopes upon;"

And after each two lines the whole congregation would sing a chorus, repeating the same line four to six times.

"I am going to join this army of the Lord."

Half a dozen of the Christian Commission delegates being present, one of their number made a prayer. During his appeals for divine strength and guidance, the audience continued to exclaim, at intervals:—"Glory to God!" "Amen," "Bress God," "Bress de Lord," "Thank God," "Lord Jesus."

Rev. Prof. Burrows, of Andover, Massachusetts, preached a sermon for them, and a more attentive and sincere congregation never were assembled before. Two front rows of seats were reserved for the colored soldiers, who, in their neat blue uniforms and shining buttons, made quite a display. Three or four of them were formerly slaves, and were recognized by some of their old acquaintances, who greeted them as though they had entered the city as conquerors.

They look upon our army as having been sent to avenge their many wrongs. They are wild with enthusiasm, and over fifty joined one of our regiments here doing guard duty. With a little exertion ten thousand can be had here in three weeks. A thorough investigation satisfies me that the Rebels did not get fifty men the whole month they tried to "fire the colored heart" to fasten tighter their own chains, but *Sambo* and *Cuffee* said they did not see it! The assurance that the Yanks would work them to death, and perpetrate all enormities that could be conceived of upon them did not answer. Major Turner had charge of the service; he drilled his men in a warehouse near Libby; he had about forty-five boys and idiots, who had no uniforms and no vim. He told Capt. Stewart that "nigger is gone up." The battalion we read of were the servants at the hospital, who refused to enlist into the regnlar service; and thus their frantic appeals of "help me or I sink," to a race they have robbed and degraded for over two centuries.

Davis' Next Base of Opertions.

Opinion differs as to the next base of Davis; some say Danville, others Lynchburg. One thing is certain, a month ago he commenced his preparations to move to the latter place; at the time the canal was destroyed by Sheridan, he had commenced, and five boat loads were in transit and were returned and finally burned. The loss of their canal, which really was the main feeder of the city and army, was a very severe blow to him, his appeals to the farmers were mocked at; they were appalled at the magnitude of the destruction and merely said it was "no use to try;" he lost the South Side road; he had left but one railroad, it worthless, and despair seized him.

Lee's Confessions.

It is well known from official documents that were found that Lee, over two months ago, notified the Rebel Senate that he could not hold Richmond with his present army, but Davis insisted that it must be done. When the time come to retreat he had but the one road practicable, and that was to Danville. He set out for that point, and we now have a rumor that he subsequently turned toward Richmond. His private property was all got away, or sold, except his carriage, built in New Orleans. It has been a very fine affair, and was on the cars to go, but the train did not get off in time, and our cavalry coming in the train was fired, but some

Continued on the Eighth Page.

OUR RICHMOND LETTER.

Continued from the First Page.

negroes pulled the carriage out, and it is only a little scorched on one side. It is now held by the Quartermaster's Department.

John C. Makes his Exit.

Among the very last to leave was Breckenridge, the Secretary of War. He went out at about seven on Monday morning, and if our cavalry had been an hour sooner he would have been caught. He was opposed to burning private property, but could not control his crew. He sat on his horse on the Manchester side for half an hour looking at the flames lapping up the accumulated wealth of half a century. Twenty millions will not repair the damage done on Monday. Twenty-four squares destroyed, factories, machine shops, stores, &c., all gone.

Destruction of Rebel Records.

The records of the War, Navy, Treasury, Post Office, Congress, Virginia Legislature are all lost! Lost forever! For there were few if any duplicates of portions or parts. What were not burned, are now scattered by the winds beyond recovery. So the Rebel Government is really dissolved; their Capital sacked by their own men; their army a fleeing mob; no place to go; no friends to meet them. Davis can truly say, "Which way I go am hell; myself am hell!" None ever expect to see him in Richmond again.

Contrabands at Work.

To-day the Provost has a number of contrabands endeavoring to get the gas and water pipes running into the burned district closed, so we can have the gas works put in order and the city lit up at night. At present we are without lights except such as is had from a few stray candles brought in by our troops and in the possession of the citizens! A few days will answer to complete the work, as the gas works are not injured, and there is coal on hand enough for the present.

The water works are still in operation.

Colonel Howard, Chief Quartermaster

Of the Army of the James, arrived here last, and is opening a large depot of supplies below the city proper, at the wharves known as the Rocketts.

Our Fleet up to the City.

A small fleet has already arrived, and a dozen gun-boats lie with their large muzzles frowning upon the city. The monitor fleet has not come up, and lies below about ten miles. The channel is being marked out, and so far we have had no trouble with torpedoes, many of which are known to be in and near the channel, and the torpedo-boats belonging to the navy are now engaged in dragging for them. Half a dozen were found this morning and exploded without doing any damage.

None have been put down lately, as when the enemy concluded to evacuate Richmond, time was not left. In fact, most of the obstructions were left with the marks put upon them for their own pilots, and consequently were no trouble at all to us.

Wouldn't Follow Jefferson Davis,

In a conversation with the old captain of the Rebel flag-of-truce boat, (who declined to follow the retreating Confederacy, and saved his boat to put in our service), we learn that the torpedoes put down are of several kinds, and were sunk at different times by various persons and finally they got so confused, no one knew where they were. He being so thoroughly acquainted with the channel, and having an excellent pilot, never had any trouble.

A few months ago he had been down to Cox's wharf with prisoners, and in company with another boat they started to return without any load, and the other boat, which had not run the channel quite so often, concluded to make a quick trip to Richmond. The captain of the *Allison* cautioned the pilot against torpedoes, but he said he knew where they all were, and in less than an hour his boat was blown to pieces.

U. H. PAINTER.

THE REBEL TRANS-MISSISSIPPI ARMY.

Affairs in Texas—Feeling of the People.

CINCINNATI, April 8.—S. M., an old resident of Mobile, left that city on the 1st of last December, crossed the Mississippi, on the 14th, at Bruinsburg, Miss., and thence traveled by way of Alexandria and Waco, Austin, San Antonio, Texas, and returned by way of Shreveport and Monroe La. On the 19th of February he left San Antonio, and on the 19th of March left Shreveport, and arrived at Natchez on the 25th. From this source we gather the following:—

Major-General Walker is in command of the Rebels in the Department of Texas, Buckner has the Department of Louisiana, and Magruder that of Arkansas. The head-quarters of the Department of Louisiana are still at Shreveport.

There are under Walker about 8000 infantry, at Galveston, Texas, and nearly all the cavalry of that Department are foraging on the Brazos and Trinity rivers.

General Polignac is at Grand Ecore, with about seven thousand men. There are also some unattached brigades in that vicinity. Forney's Division is at Kechi, twenty-one miles from Shreveport, on the road to Mansfield. Churchill's Division is thirty miles east of Shreveport, at Minden, Mo. General Parsons has a small division of about four thousand infantry between Camden and Homer, in Arkansas, in winter quarters.

Magruder is at Camden with one brigade of infantry and one of cavalry, numbering together about five thousand. Swamp Harrison's Brigade is between Minas and Oak Hills. General Lee's guerrillas have crossed to the west of the Mississippi, in consequence of his refusal to obey the orders of his superior, Buckner. He was operating in the neighborhood of Deer Creek at last accounts.

The effective force of the Trans-Mississippi Department is fifty-three thousand, which is the actual number as taken from the estimates of Smith's Adjutant-General.

The army is in fine condition in everything except discipline, having plenty of clothing, provisions and ordnance stores. It is, however, becoming badly demoralized on account of the continued bad news from the East Mississippi Department.

Nearly everybody is wild with the cotton mania. About 5000 wagons are employed in hauling cotton from Louisiana, Texas, and the Indian Territory to Matamoros.

Specie is more plenty in Texas than ever before, and yet goods are very high. Confederate currency is not used to any extent in Texas.

A large majority of the people are in favor of a reconstruction of the Union, and would move in that direction were they not prevented by the military authorities from collecting any organization. The people are generally tired, dispirited, and worn out with the war, and would be willing to settle on almost any terms, had they the power.

It is generally understood that Kirby Smith is doing a big thing in the cotton business, and he is regarded as inefficient in military affairs.

There was an order at Shreveport from Richmond for 40,000 troops to cross the Mississippi; but as the troops refused to cross last summer, it was generally thought that force would not be employed to compel them.

A system of volunteering and new organization had, however, been adopted, under which many were volunteering to cross, though it was impossible to estimate the number. Our informant saw this order at the Adjutant-General's office at Shreveport.

Mr. S. M. owns a plantation in Alabama, and also a ranche in Texas, and he was enabled to travel under the supposition that he was going from place to place on business.

Governor Watts, of Alabama, had passes from Dick Taylor to cross the Mississippi into Texas, and from the chief of secret service of the Trans-Mississippi Department, and from Swamp Harrison to recross on his return to Alabama.

From New Orleans, via Cairo.

NEW ORLEANS, April 2—via CAIRO, April 8—The *Times* says the monitors *Osage* and *Milwaukie* were sunk by torpedoes in Mobile Bay while attempting to get in range of the Spanish Fort. They were not very materially damaged, and can easily be raised and repaired.

The *True Delta* says it was the *Essex* and *Milwaukie*.

The *True Delta* says, Forrest's army is breaking up, large numbers of men daily deserting and going home, mostly Texans. One hundred and fifty deserted in one day.

The steamship *Liberty* sailed April 2d for New York, via Havana, with a full load of cotton.

Baton Rouge advices of April 3d represent the river as rising. The crevasse six miles above that place, on the west side, is one mile wide, very deep, and is still widening. The country back of it is overflowed to the depth of six feet. The troops at Morganzia have been placed on steamboats, and fears are entertained for the fort. General Herron has a large working party on the levee at work.

Arrival of Rebel Prisoners.

NEW YORK, April 9.—The steamship *Matanzas* arrived this morning from City Point with nine hundred Rebel prisoners, part of those captured at Bentonsville, Goldsboro' and Columbia. They are in charge of Captain N. W. Perkins, of the Thirteenth Connecticut. Among the prisoners is Colonel Rhett, of Fort Sumter notoriety.

LATEST NEWS FROM THE SEAT OF WAR.

E. M. Stanton, Secretary of War:—General Lee has made an unconditional surrender of the Army of Northern Virginia. U. S. GRANT.

Send a large stock of Medicines to City Point at once. You can get them at KROMER'S, No. 403 CHESNUT Street, Philadelphia.

LATEST NEWS FROM THE SEAT OF WAR.

E. M. Stanton, Secretary of War:—General Lee has made an unconditional surrender of the Army of Northern Virginia. U. S. GRANT.

Send a large stock of Medicines to City Point at once. You can get them at KROMER'S, No. 403 CHESNUT Street, Philadelphia.

FINANCIAL.

BOARDING.

OIL COMPANIES.

GOODS FOR THE LADIES.

MISCELLANEOUS.

NEW PUBLICATIONS.

LATEST NEWS FROM THE SEAT OF WAR.

E. M. Stanton, Secretary of War:—General Lee has made an unconditional surrender of the Army of Northern Virginia. U. S. GRANT.

Send a large stock of Medicines to City Point at once. You can get them at KROMER'S, No. 403 CHESNUT Street, Philadelphia.

COAL COMPANIES.

TAILORS & TAILORS' GOODS.

MINING COMPANIES.

THE NEW YORK HERALD

WHOLE NO. 10,451. NEW YORK, MONDAY, APRIL 10, 1865. PRICE FOUR CENTS.

THE END.

SURRENDER OF LEE AND HIS WHOLE ARMY TO GRANT.

TERMS OF SURRENDER.

All Honor to Grant, Meade, Sheridan, Ord, Humphreys, Wright, Griffin, Parke, and their Brave Troops.

Highly Interesting Details of the Fighting Before the Surrender.

Ord Makes a Forced March of Thirty Miles a Day South of Lee's Line of Retreat.

Our Main Columns Follow Closely in the Enemy's Rear.

The Woods Filled with Rebel Stragglers and the Roads Strewn with Cannon, Caissons, Wagons, Ambulances, Muskets, Sabres, Knapsacks and Cartridge Boxes.

Announcement of the Capture of Richmond to the Troops.

INTENSE ENTHUSIASM.

Our Men Clamor to be Led Forward.

Stoneman, with a Force of Union Cavalry, Reported Destroying the Railroad Between Danville and Greensboro.

JEFF. DAVIS AT DANVILLE, &c., &c., &c.

THE SURRENDER.

Secretary Stanton to General Dix.

WAR DEPARTMENT, WASHINGTON, April 9—9 o'clock P. M.

To Major General DIX, New York:—

This department has received the official report of the surrender, this day, of General Lee and his army to Lieutenant General Grant *on the terms proposed by General Grant.*

EDWIN M. STANTON, Secretary of War.

General Grant to Secretary Stanton.

HEADQUARTERS, ARMIES OF THE UNITED STATES, April 9—4:30 P. M.

Hon. EDWIN M. STANTON, Secretary of War:—

General Lee surrendered the Army of Northern Virginia this afternoon, *upon the terms proposed by myself.* The accompanying additional correspondence will show the conditions fully.

U. S. GRANT, Lieutenant General.

The Preliminary Correspondence.

CLIFTON HOUSE, VA., April 9, 1865.

Hon. EDWIN M. STANTON, Secretary of War:—

The following correspondence has taken place between General Lee and myself. *There has been no relaxation in the pursuit during its pendency.*

U. S. GRANT, Lieutenant General.

GENERAL GRANT TO GENERAL LEE.

APRIL 7, 1865.

General R. E. LEE, Commanding Confederate States Army:—

GENERAL—The result of the last week must convince you of the hopelessness of further resistance on the part of the Army of Northern Virginia in this struggle. I feel that it is so, and regard it as my duty to shift from myself the responsibility of any further effusion of blood, by asking of you the surrender of that portion of the Confederate States army, known as the Army of Northern Virginia.

Very respectfully, your obedient servant,

U. S. GRANT, Lieutenant General, Commanding Armies of the United States.

GENERAL LEE TO GENERAL GRANT.

APRIL 7, 1865.

GENERAL—I have received your note of this date.

Though not entirely of the opinion you express of the hoplessness of further resistance on the part of the Army of Northern Virginia, I reciprocate your desire to avoid useless effusion of blood, and therefore, before considering your proposition, ask the terms you will offer on condition of its surrender.

R. E. LEE, General.

To Lieutenant General U. S. GRANT, Commanding Armies of the United States.

GENERAL GRANT TO GENERAL LEE.

APRIL 8, 1865.

To General R. E. LEE, Commanding Confederate States Army:—

GENERAL—Your note of last evening, in reply to mine of same date, asking the conditions on which I will accept the surrender of the Army of Northern Virginia is just received.

In reply, I would say that, peace being my first desire, there is but one condition that I insist upon, viz:—

That the men surrendered shall be disqualified for taking up arms again against the government of the United States until properly exchanged.

I will meet you or designate officers to meet any officers you may name for the same purpose at any point agreeable to you, for the purpose of arranging definitely the terms upon which the surrender of the army of Northern Virginia will received.

Very respectfully, your obedient servant,

U. S. GRANT, Lieutenant General, Commanding Armies of the United States.

GENERAL LEE TO GENERAL GRANT.

APRIL 8, 1865.

GENERAL—I received at a late hour your note of to-day in answer to mine of yesterday.

I did not intend to propose the surrender of the Army of Northern Virginia, but to ask the terms of your proposition. To be frank, I do not think the emergency has arisen to call for the surrender.

But as the restoration of peace should be the sole object of all, I desire to know whether your proposals would tend to that end.

I cannot, therefore, meet you with a view to surrender the army of Northern Virginia; but as far as your proposition may affect the Confederate States forces under my command and tend to the restoration of peace, I should be pleased to meet you at ten A. M. to-morrow, on the old stage road to Richmond, between the picket lines of the two armies.

Very respectfully, your obedient servant,

R. E. LEE, General C. S. A.

To Lieutenant General GRANT, Commanding Armies of the United States.

GENERAL GRANT TO GENERAL LEE.

APRIL 9, 1865.

General R. E. LEE, Commanding Confederate States Army:—

GENERAL—Your note of yesterday is received. As I have no authority to treat on the subject of peace, the meeting proposed for ten A. M., to-day, could lead to no good. I will state, however, General, that I am equally anxious for peace with yourself; and the whole North entertain the same feeling. The terms upon which peace can be had are well understood. By the South laying down their arms they will hasten that most desirable event, save thousands of human lives and hundreds of millions of property not yet destroyed.

Sincerely hoping that all our difficulties may be settled without the loss of another life, I subscribe myself,

Very respectfully, your obedient servant,

U. S. GRANT, Lieutenant General, U. S. A.

THE TERMS.

GENERAL LEE TO GENERAL GRANT.

APRIL 9, 1865.

GENERAL:—I received your note of this morning on the picket line, whither I had come to meet you and ascertain definitely what terms were embraced in your proposition of yesterday with reference to the surrender of this army.

I now request an interview in accordance with the offer contained in your letter of yesterday for that purpose,

Very respectfully, your obedient servant,

R. E. LEE, General.

To Lieutenant General GRANT, commanding United States Armies.

GENERAL GRANT TO GENERAL LEE.

APRIL 9, 1865.

General R. E. LEE, Commanding Confederate States Armies:—

Your note of this date is but this moment (fifty minutes past eleven A. M.) received.

In consequence of my having passed from the Richmond and Lynchburg road to the Farmville and Lynchburg road, I am, at this writing, about four miles west of Walter's Church, and will push forward to the front for the purpose of meeting you.

Notice sent to me on this road where you wish the interview to take place will meet me.

Very respectfully, your obedient servant,

U. S. GRANT, Lieutenant General.

GENERAL GRANT TO GENERAL LEE.

APPOMATTOX COURT HOUSE, April 9, 1865.

General R. E. LEE, Commanding Confederate States Army:—

In accordance with the substance of my letter to you of the 8th instant, I propose to receive the surrender of the Army of Northern Virginia on the following terms, to wit:—

Rolls of all the officers and men to be made in duplicate; one copy to be given to an officer designated by me, the other to be retained by such officers as you may designate.

The officers to give their individual paroles not to take arms against the government of the United States until properly exchanged, and each company or regimental commander sign a like parole for the men of his command.

The arms, artillery and public property to be parked and stacked and turned over to the officers appointed by me to receive them.

This will not embrace the side arms of the officers, nor their private horses or baggage.

This done, each officer and man will be allowed to return to their homes, not to be disturbed by United States authority so long as they observe their parole and the laws in force where they may reside.

Very respectfully,

U. S. GRANT, Lieutenant General.

GENERAL LEE TO GENERAL GRANT.

HEADQUARTERS, ARMY OF NORTHERN VIRGINIA, April 9, 1865.

Lieutenant General U. S. GRANT, Commanding United States Armies:—

GENERAL—I have received your letter of this date, containing the terms of surrender of the Army of Northern Virginia as proposed by you. As they are substantially the same as those expressed in your letter of the 8th inst., they are accepted. I will proceed to designate the proper officers to carry the stipulations into effect.

Very respectfully, your obedient servant,

R. E. LEE, General.

THANKS TO GRANT AND HIS ARMY.

WAR DEPARTMENT, WASHINGTON, D. C., April 9—9:30 P. M.

Lieutenant General GRANT:—

Thanks be to Almighty God for the great victory with which he has this day crowned you and the gallant armies under your command.

The thanks of this Department, and of the government, and of the people of the United States their reverence and honor have been deserved—will be rendered to you and the brave and gallant officers and soldiers of your army for all time.

EDWIN M. STANTON, Secretary of War.

NATIONAL SALUTE.

WAR DEPARTMENT, WASHINGTON, D. C., April 9—10 P. M.

Ordered:—That a salute of two hundred guns be fired at the headquarters of every army and department, and at every post and arsenal in the United States, and at the Military Academy at West Point, on the day of the receipt of this order, in commemoration of the surrender of General R. E. Lee and the Army of Northern Virginia to Lieutenant General Grant and the army under his command; report of the receipt and execution of this order to be made to the Adjutant General, Washington.

EDWIN M. STANTON, Secretary of War.

THE PREVIOUS FIGHTING.

CITY POINT.

Mr. J. R. Trembly's Despatch.

CITY POINT, April 8—8 A. M.

THE LATEST FROM THE FRONT.

I have just arrived from General Grant's camp at Burkesville. As I left yesterday morning heavy firing of artillery was heard in the direction of High Bridge or Farmville, some fifteen miles north of Burkesville, and a little above the scene of the important captures of Friday evening. It was kept up vigorously for an hour, when it slackened off to a scattering fire, which was kept up with more or less frequency of reports until after twelve o'clock, when I passed out of hearing distance.

SUPPLIES GOING FORWARD.

Supplies were taken by rail yesterday as far as Sutherland station, ten miles from Petersburg. The different corps trains were all taking on loads last evening, and will reach the army to-morrow.

THE RAILROAD BEING RAPIDLY RECONSTRUCTED.

A large force is pushing the work on the track, and expect to reach Wellville to-day and Burkesville in two days more. A slight change of the gauge required retards the work; but all is going on finely, and everybody is happy.

THE PURSUIT.

Mr. S. Cadwallader's Despatches.

NEAR BLACK AND WHITES, April 5—10 A. M.

THE CORPS MOVEMENTS IN THE PURSUIT.

The Twenty-forth corps encamped near Wilson's station last night, and moved this far this morning along the line of railroad to Burkesville Junction. Generals Grant and Ord are with this column. The Fifth corps and cavalry pushed on to Jettersville, on the Richmond and Danville Railroad, about ten miles north of Burkesville Junction, and arrived there without any fighting till last night. The Second, Sixth and Ninth corps are following closely in their rear on the roads between this and the Appomattox, and are already within supporting distance of Sheridan's advance. By to-night the latter corps will all undoubtedly be on the Danville road, and the Twenty-fourth corps very near, if not quite, to the junction.

LEE'S APPARENT FORCE.

Sheridan reports Lee to apparently not have more than twenty thousand men, and these nothing more than a disordered, disorganized mob. It is, probably, being daily swelled in numerical force by the arrival of stragglers and small organized detachments, but its *morale* will scarcely be improved by these, and no successful opposition can be offered us at any point for days or weeks.

PROSPECTS OF SPEEDILY FINISHING LEE AND JOHNSTON.

If our plans work as proposed Lee will be irretrievably separated from Johnston, and the two rebel armies speedily driven out of Virginia and North Carolina. By supreme efforts they may escape to the interior with armies the size of respectable body guards, and thence make their way westward to the Mississippi and Texas during the present season and cross into Mexico for an asylum. It may be considered a maxim in war that a retreating army can outmarch a pursuing one. This favors their escape. Lee's and Johnston's armies must henceforth be the objective points of ours and Sherman's operations. Where they retreat we must follow.

LEE'S PROBABLE EFFORTS TO JOIN JOHNSTON.

Lee will attempt to pass down towards Danville, through Scottville, Cumberland Court House and Farmville, on the macadamized road. The railroad trains loaded with subsistence for the rebel troops at Petersburg were ordered to the latter place when Petersburg was taken, and are reported to be there yet, awaiting the expected arrival of Lee's army. Jeff. Davis and Cabinet remained in Richmond until three o'clock A. M. on Monday morning, and then took their final departure for Danville in a box car attached to a train transporting wounded men.

GENERAL GRANT AND THE REBEL GENERALS.

It should not be forgotten that by discomfiting General Lee General Grant has added the last rebel general to his list of those he has signally defeated during the war. Beginning with the galaxy of rebel commanders of greater or lesser magnitude at Fort Donelson, he defeated Beauregard badly at Shiloh, and history will so record it; Johnston and Pemberton at Vicksburg; almost annihilated Bragg at Chattanooga, and has now scattered and routed the army of the hitherto invincible Robert E. Lee to an extent that surpasses belief. The gallant men composing the flower of Sherman's army are Grant's old soldiers of the Army of the Tennessee. Educated by him and trained to victory under his leadership, they not only never suffered a defeat, but they were everywhere and at all times overwhelmingly victorious. The present commanders of that army imbibed their present prospect and determination to a large extent from the example and discipline of the Lieutenant General. Even Sherman himself—invincible soldier and accomplished statesman that he is—caught the fire of his brilliant career from the quiet Grant. To many this may seem strange; but at the outset of the war General Sherman was a theoretic soldier, General Grant a practical one; the former adhered closely to military rule, the latter often acted at the suggestion of common sense; the former was opposed to cutting loose from the base above Vicksburg and starting off into the enemy's country, the latter followed the bent of his own inclinations, and set the world the example of raiding with an entire army. To the future historian must be left the task of recording the impress made by one man upon the military minds of his time.

ARRIVAL AT BLACK AND WHITES STATION.

The head of the column reached this place at two o'clock, and has been passing briskly ever since. Rebel infantry passed here in small detachments on Sunday, going westwardly.

LEE'S MOVEMENTS.

Since then, by the statements of the citizens, it is a somewhat noticeable fact that although Lee's intentions, as reported, were to fall back on Danville, he ordered that portion of his troops cut off from his main command, by our piercing the centre on Sunday, to cross the Appomattox and join him between Amelia Court House and Richmond. It proves that he feared to trust his army to fall back directly toward Danville by Burkesville Junction, and felt that his only hope of reaching and even concentrating them was to have them rejoin him as soon as possible.

FINE ROADS AND GOOD MARCHING.

The march to-day has been over good roads, through a beautiful, undulating country, and through one of the richest counties of the Old Dominion. The wealthy inhabitants have generally abandoned their homes. The middle and poorer classes receive us sensibly in all cases, and joyously in some.

THE NEGROES ANXIOUS TO SEE GENERAL GRANT.

The negroes are everywhere delighted, and crowd up in large numbers to see General Grant. An old man said he "had heard right smart about General Grant, and never heard no good of him. He did never think he should live to see him here." Yah, yah, yah.

NOTTOWAY COURT HOUSE.

The village of Nottoway Court House, as it is usually called, is an old, dilapidated looking concern, composed of a few dozens of old unpainted frame houses, and two or three brick ones. The court house and surrounding offices are substantial brick edifices, and stand in a pleasantly shaded square, about two hundred yards to the left of the main road going westward. Streets or street Nottoway has not. The road through it is rather more sinuous and cut up by gullies than elsewhere in the neighborhood. A few empty box cars were captured and a few dollars worth of saddlery trimmings. Nearly all else of value had been removed.

A REBEL BANNER.

A rebel banner was found in the place, entirely new, of heavy blue silk, elegantly trimmed with gold lace and fringe and surmounted with the Roman spear head and lictor's axe. On one side of the banner the following inscription surrounded a laurel wreath:—"Presented to the Nottoway corps by the ladies of Nottoway. *Primi potest non potest opprimi*" The other side bore the Virginia coat of arms.

In the clerk's office was found a large collection of records, dating back to 1787, embracing court proceedings, a book of wills, election returns, deeds and other legal papers, which would offer interesting material for months of investigation. But the march of an army makes too much history daily for the correspondent to devote much time to that of the past.

AGAIN IN THE SADDLE.

Two hours found us in the saddle again, pushing on for the head of the column.

GENERAL SHERIDAN ENGAGES THE ENEMY.

As the Lieutenant General was viewing Nottoway Court House a staff officer arrived, with despatches from General Sheridan, stating that he had encountered the enemy in small force near Jettersville, ten miles north of Burkesville Junction, had driven him back with heavy loss, and had captured a large number of prisoners, animals, some artillery, and part of a wagon train. General Sheridan was of opinion that Lee had not more than twenty thousand to thirty thousand men, and that they were almost without organization.

ANXIETY OF THE TROOPS TO INTERCEPT LEE.

Our column had intended going into camp for the night a short distance beyond Nottoway Court House, but this news convinced the General that Lee's only hope of escape was by making forced marches to the southwest line, where he could cross the Lynchburg road beyond us. He at once ordered the march. He intended to reach Burkesville Junction, nine miles distant. The men had already tramped over twenty miles, of road, but on being informed of the stirring news from Sheridan and the necessity for interrupting Lee's flight southward, the men clamored to march all night, and started off briskly, cheering and yelling, and kept it up for miles. Whenever General Grant was recognized as he rode past the marching column, the entire line broke out into the most noisy and boisterous expressions of delight. Sometimes one division would resume the cheering as another had exhausted itself, and the shouting would be perpetual along miles of the road.

JETTERSVILLE, April 6—11 A. M.

GENERAL GRANT JOINS THE ADVANCE.

Soon after receiving the first despatch two trusty scouts arrived from General Sheridan with a second. Its contents were of a character to determine General Grant to ride across the country to the former's headquarters. The headquarters train was ordered to proceed to the Junction and await him there, and taking four staff officers and a small escort of cavalry he followed the lead of the scouts and arrived at this place about eleven o'clock P. M.

IN LINE OF BATTLE.

Last night the army lay in line of battle, stretching across three or four miles of country, and facing substantially northward. Custer's division of cavalry lay on the right flank and McKenzie's on the left. The infantry line was formed with the Sixth corps on the right, the Fifth in the centre and the Second on the left.

LEE REFUSES TO FIGHT.

During the night Lee moved off many of his trains, and, it is now feared, will be able to elude this column. Ord will march on this morning in the direction of Lynchburg, and cut off his retreat to any point south of that. Unless Lee abandons all his trains throws away baggage, clothing and everything that encumbers rapid marching, he cannot escape.

AGAIN MOVING.

The Sixth corps is being transferred from the right to the left. The whole army has marched about five miles this morning, on the road to Deatonsville, six miles, a little north of west, and on a parallel and only a short distance south of it.

JETTERSVILLE.

Jettersville, like many other southern places first introduced to Northern readers, is but an insignificant station on the railroad, numbers but a half dozen buildings all told, and has nothing to boast of excepting an old revolutionary church, built at some remote period in the settlement of the State. It stood the ravages of time unaltered, until two seasons ago, when the old roof and weather boarding gave place to new. The aristocratic bethel of early days is now an obscure and unfrequented free church to such itinerating ministers as have no churches or congregations elsewhere. The old inhabitants of Jettersville absconded on the approach of the Yankee army, and no one was left familiar with its traditions.

LEE'S REAR GUARD ENCOUNTERED.

In the forenoon the Second and Fifth Corps succeeded in falling upon Gordon's corps, which acted as rear guard to Lee's retreating army, in the vicinity of Deatensville, and succeeded in stampeding portions of it, and capturing large numbers of prisoners, and a portion of the wagon train. Gordon took up one position after another on the hill tops, covering the rebel line of march and succeeding in retarding our pursuit to a limited extent.

THE REBEL ARMY FALLING TO PIECES.

Refugees, deserters and prisoners state that the rebel army is forsaking its ranks by thousands and scattering to their homes in every direction. If these accounts are true, we shall never have another respectable battle with our old adversaries.

JEFF. DAVIS ESTABLISHES HIMSELF AT DANVILLE.

A refugee from Danville says that trains were arriving there all day Monday from Richmond loaded with fugitives and stores. Jeff. Davis and Cabinet reached there in the afternoon, and that Jeff. was conveyed to the residence of a Mr. Sutherland, in the latter's private carriage, which had been awaiting his arrival some hours. The last train out of Richmond, he asserts, was filled with stragglers, who found a locomotive and some cars left behind, and furnished the engineers and firemen from their own number.

STONEMAN REPORTED BETWEEN DANVILLE AND GREENSBORO.

He brings the information that Beauregard telegraphed Jeff. Davis on Tuesday that Stoneman was on the railroad, tearing it up at High Point, between Danville and Greenboro. A glance at the map will show the importance of this to Lee and Johnston. He also says the people are hoping Lee will surrender what is left of his army, and thus end the contest and save the lives of his remaining soldiers.

BURKESVILLE JUNCTION, April 7—8 P. M.

SHERIDAN'S SPLENDID SUCCESS NEAR BURKESVILLE.

General Grant and staff left Jettersville soon after five o'clock P. M. yesterday, and rode to this place where his headquarters trains had been ordered to await him during the night. A staff officer arrived from General Sheridan's headquarters with the glorious news that Sheridan, aided by Wright's and Humphrey's corps, succeeded late in the evening in capturing thirteen thousand prisoners, several hundred wagons, fourteen pieces of artillery and the following general officers:—Lieutenant General Ewell and Major Generals Kershaw, Barton, Corse, De Bose, Custis Lee, Hunton and Dick Anderson. The rebel army is thought to be practically disintegrated.

LEE'S CHANCES GETTING WORSE.

It is not believed that Lee can escape with troops enough to justify any further attempts to prolong the war. He is falling back somewhat towards Lynchburg in the endeavor to pass around our columns and get to Danville. Ord is going out south of the Lynchburg road from here by forced marches to cut him off. All works to our advantage.

THE WEATHER.

The weather and roads are excellent. The troops wild with enthusiasm. Cars running to Wilson's station. Will be here in a few days.

THE SECOND CORPS.

Mr. Wm. J. Starks' Despatches.

HEADQUARTERS, SECOND CORPS, April 4, 1865.

HEADQUARTERS ON THE NAMOZINE.

Headquarters of the corps are established this evening upon the Namozine road, six miles from the point left this morning.

FINE WEATHER, BUT TERRIBLE ROADS.

Although the day in itself has not been particularly eventful, it has been a laborious one for the troops, who have been hard at work in repairing the roads for the passage of the artillery trains.

The rations of the troops expire this evening, and supplies have been working their way to the front over the most horrible roads. Fortunately the weather has continued pleasant, or they would have been impassable.

THE MORALE OF THE REBEL ARMY.

A large number of prisoners, stagglers and deserters from the rebel army have been brought in during the day, and it is stated that the woods on the flanks of our column are filled with them. Forty-eight surrendered themselves to an orderly riding along the road. They appeared with a flag of truce, and, sitting down under a tree, à la Grant and Pemberton, discussed the terms of surrender. They were guaranteed the possession of their private property, with the exception of gold watches. As they had none of these no difficulty was found in arranging terms.

ARRIVAL OF CAVALRY FROM DINWIDDIE.

Two divisions of the cavalry corps—the First and Third—marched up from the vicinity of Dinwiddie, striking the Namozine road at eleven o'clock this morning. They report a sharp fight with the enemy yesterday afternoon, in which though greatly outnumbered, they held their own for three hours, when they fell back. Their loss, particularly in officers, was heavy.

MOVEMENTS OF THE OTHER COLUMNS.

The Sixth corps are in our rear, marching by the same road. The Twenty-fourth, with a negro division, under General Ord, marched down the Cox road, leaving the other column at Southerland station, its objective point is supposed to be Burkesville station or vicinity, where it will form a junction with the Army of the Potomac.

THE ARMY LIVING PARTLY ON THE COUNTRY.

The scarcity of rations for the last twenty-four hours has caused a deal of foraging, and large numbers of chickens, pigs, legs of mutton, &c., may be seen hanging on the persons of the men as they march along; with this exception the inhabitants are well treated.

THE MEN IN GOOD SPIRITS.

The troops are in exuberant spirits and confident of an early termination of the war.

We move at an early hour for Burkesville station, the that object being to cut off Lee's retreat, as he is moving in direction, with a view of reaching Lynchburg. The Fifth corps, which, with the cavalry, is in the advance, will doubtless reach that point to-night.

HEADQUARTERS, SECOND CORPS, JETTERSVILLE, VA., April 5, 1865.

General Sheridan, with the Fifth corps and the cavalry, reached this point, two miles and a half from Burkesville station, last evening, and found the enemy in his front. He immediately telegraphed to General Meade that he was between the rebels and Lynchburg, and requested that the troops move forward immediately.

FORWARD.

At twelve, midnight, we were again in the saddle; but the roads were so obstructed by the trains that it was nearly daylight before the column was well on the road. In the meantime rations were issued to the men, and the cry of hard tack, which had greeted the approach of every commissary for the last twenty-four hours, ceased.

EXPECTATIONS OF A BATTLE.

We reached this point about two o'clock, where we found the Fifth corps, which had intrenched itself in anticipation of an attack. The Second division of cavalry, under General Crook, has been fighting the enemy since morning.

GENERAL CROOK STRIKES THE ENEMY'S TRAIN.

General Crook struck the enemy's train, destroying three miles of wagons and the contents. The officers report that with another brigade they could have capture the entired train.

LARGE CAPTURES.

Two thousand prisoners, a battery of Armstrong guns and six flags were captured. During the day the prisoners were marched past the troops, on the way to the rear, with our flags swung at their head. Tremendous cheers went up from our men as they filed through the works.

THE SECOND CORPS TAKES POSITION.

The Second corps was placed in position, under the direction of General Sheridan, immediately on its arrival, as he was in momentary anticipation of an attack. The Second and Third divisions are on the left of the Fifth; the Sixth corps is rapidly moving up and will soon be in position. General Ord's command will form a junction before morning; the works of the Fifth corps are being extended. Though anticipated for some hours, no attack has taken place up to this hour, five o'clock P. M.

LEE'S OPPORTUNITY PASSED.

Lee has been outmarched and outgeneralled, and his golden opportunity has passed. Had he been able to bring up his troops so as to attack the Fifth corps yesterday evening, or at an early hour this morning, he might, by a bold push, have broken through and escaped. As it is his retreat is cut off. What course the rebel chieftain will pursue cannot be surmised. It is not improbable that he will risk everything on the chances of a great battle, failing in which his surrender or the dissolution of his army will be a matter of necessity.

THE FIFTH CORPS.

Mr. L. A. Hendrick's Despatches.

HEADQUARTERS, FIFTH ARMY CORPS, NEAR SWEATHOUSE CREEK, April 3—8 P. M.

THE FIRST DAY'S PURSUIT OF THE ENEMY.

My despatch of two P. M. announced us near the banks of the Appomattox. We were then within sight of the river. Instead of crossing the river at that point we turned our course to the left. The day's march was sixteen miles. We probably should have made a longer march, were it not for separating the troops too far from the trains, which, on account of the bad roads, are still dragging their slow length along with a compulsory dilatoriness inseparable from army movements at this time of the year.

GENERAL SHERIDAN IN THE FIFTH CORPS.

During several miles of to-day's march General Sheridan was with General Griffin at the head of the corps column. As he passed by the troops he was recognized by every officer and soldier and cheered with the liveliest enthusiasm. Our men believe in Sheridan. Under his leadership the word defeat has been blotted from their vocabulary. I need not describe Sheridan. Everybody knows the man. His richly bronzed complexion and full face are the picture of health. His square, compact physique reveal his wonderful powers of endurance. His eyes sparkle with confidence, command, victory. He rode a magnificent black horse. In striking contrast to him is General Griffin. The latter is taller, slightly built and of sallow complexion; but there is a nervous energy in every movement, nervous power glowing in his eyes, and the massive breadth and formation of his chin show an invulnerable pertinacity of will that brooks no opposition and inevitably leads him in time of action where the battle rages the fiercest.

CAPTURE OF THE TWO REBEL ASSISTANT ADJUTANT GENERALS.

Halting at three P. M. news reached us of the capture by the cavalry of Major Foot, General Bushrod Johnson's Assistant Adjutant General, and Major Ferguson, Assistant Adjutant General of General Fitzhugh Lee. General Johnson was with them when captured and narrowly escaped being taken prisoner. His having the swiftest horse saved him. Several attempts were made to bring him to a halt by carbine cartridges, but he was contemptuously regardless of these flying invitations to accept Union hospitalities. I saw the prisoners. Both are comparatively young men, well dressed, and treat their capture with seeming quiet indifference.

OUR ROUTE OF MARCH.

Principally along the Namozine road has been to-day's march. We crossed three streams, Sweathouse creek, Deep run and Namozine river. The last, though called a river, having as little claim to this pretentious designation as the other streams of more modest nomenclature. Amelia county which we have been traversing, and within the limits of which we still are, is a rich and beautiful section of the State. The ground is gently undulating, and in places the view is highly picturesque. At intervals are large plantations with fields of growing wheat, and others already plowed and waiting the seed of the husbandmen, who fled their homes in advance of our coming.

DAY OF JUBILEE TO CONTRABANDS.

The bulk of the negroes managed to stay behind and join our marching column. The contrabands exhibit the usual characteristics of this class—motley in dress, representing all the Shakspere ages, and with every grade of intelligence, from the dull unconscious gaze to eyes in fine frenzy rolling. Our incoming has brought joy to many Ethiopian breasts, and caused their bosom's load to sit lightly on their throne.

SCENES ALONG THE ROUTE.

The haste of the enemy's retreat has been indicated all along the route. In my last despatch I alluded to abandoned cannon and stragglers filling the woods. To-day we found more prisoners, dismantled caissons, large quantities of artillery ammunition thrown away, stalled wagons and ambulances—most of the former having the mark "U. S." on them, and other designations bringing back painful memory of Pope's campaign—and horses, saddles, muskets, sabres and all the usual evidences of an active retrograde movement. A hunter after rebel relics would have had no difficulty in gratifying his propensity in this regard to the fullest extent.

BIVOUAC ON THE NIGHT OF THE 3D.

To-night the troops are bivouacked in a fine piece of woods, and headquarters are under a tree in a field near by. We expect a long march to-morrow. The troops have stood the march well.

THE FALL OF RICHMOND.

I make the subject of my closing paragraph what ought to have been the opening. This afternoon the fact was made known to the troops while marching, by an officer said to have come from Lieutenant General Grant. I have seen enthusiastic soldiers before. I will not attempt to describe the enthusiastic outburst caused by this intelligence. Caps and muskets were thrown into the air, and many a heart was lifted with joy to the clouds. Who will not believe now that the backbone of the rebellion is broken, and the vertebral column unmistakably fractured. And this reminds me to say that after our victory gained at Five Forks, captured officers said:—"You have won Petersburg now, and the fall of Richmond follows." And so it was. And thus it will be seen, although the Sixth and Ninth corps first marched into Petersburg, and the army of the James was the first to enter Richmond, that, after all, the grand victory was gained by the cavalry and Fifth corps in that ever memorable battle and more memorable victory at Five Forks.

HEADQUARTERS, FIFTH ARMY CORPS, NEAR JETTERSVILLE, ON DANVILLE RAILROAD, April 4—4 P. M.

HANDSOME MARCHING.

A march of twenty miles, which, notwithstanding its length and the heat of the middle of the day, has been attended with very little straggling, brought us to our present position.

THE ENEMY REPORTED IN THE VICINITY.

Rumors that the enemy was in large force in the vicinity induced extra caution at the last end of the march. The corps was massed in an open field. It was an hour after sundown. The dim moon gave a misty light. An order was issued prohibiting the lighting of any fires.

ADVANCE IN LINE OF BATTLE.

The corps was formed in line of battle. There was something grand in that moving battle line. War is full of horror, mixed with grand and stirring scenes. In this simple scene of advance, and the hazy moon and stillness of the hour and dim shadows of the open woods and consciousness of possible speedy bloody strife and hot conflict of cannon and musketry, there was a serious and solemn sublimity surpassed by few spectacles of war.

"What means this?" I asked General Griffin, seeing the battle line forming.

"It means a possible fight. The whole of Lee's army is said to be in our front."

But there has been no fight up to this hour. Our battle line is in position. Not a gun has been fired.

THE DIRECTION OF THE LINES.

The line crosses the Danville Railroad, the First division, now commanded by Brevet Major General Bartlett, being on the west side of the road. Earthworks are being thrown up along the entire line. Our headquarters are only about fifty rods in the rear of our works.

JEFF. DAVIS AND FAMILY.

Day before yesterday Jeff. Davis and family passed over the railroad which we now hold, in his exodus from the rebel capital. Thirty-six hours delay in this journey of Jeff. might have compelled the fulfilment of that poetic allusion to the probable fate of Mr. Davis wherein he is referred to so tenderly in connection with a sour apple tree.

TWO REBEL OFFICERS CAPTURED IN A HAND CAR.

Scarcely had General Bartlett's brigade got across the railroad when two rebel lieutenants came shooting down the road in a hand car. Their journey was cut short. From their story they started to enter Petersburg, and, finding that in possession of our troops, started for Richmond, when, finding the latter place occupied also by our forces, they made their way in this direction.

THE MARCH ON THE FOURTH INSTANT.

The march of to-day was merely a repetition of yesterday—captures of more stragglers and flocking to the Union standard of more contrabands, besides picking up a large number of cattle and sheep and the confiscation of

[CONTINUED ON EIGHTH PAGE.]

THE END.

CONTINUED FROM FIRST PAGE.

forage. The general appearance of the country is about the same. Tobacco, pigs and adult chickens were largely levied upon. We passed through two so-called villages—Maunsboro and Dennisville—the former consisting of two houses and a blacksmith shop, and the latter having the advantage of an additional house and a mill close by—a mill whose age suggests that it might be the one about which Mr. Bolt is called upon to refresh his memory.

GENERAL BARRENGER AND STAFF PRISONERS.

Through the adroitness of one of Gen. Sheridan's scouts General Barrenger, who commanded a brigade in Wade Hampton's cavalry, was captured to-day, along with his staff. The scout offered to put the General and his aids on the way to avoid our troops, but instead brought them within our lines. General Barrenger, I understand, has talked very savagely since about Yankee tricks.

ASSIGNMENT OF BRIGADIER GENERAL JOSEPH HAYES.

This gallant officer has been given his old command—First brigade, Second division—which brigade he commanded when captured in the Weldon Railroad fight. Officers and men are exceedingly gratified at his return.

LIEUTENANT COLONEL DUNN.

To-day Lieutenant Colonel Dunn, formerly Chief of Ambulance corps, joined the corps in his new capacity, as Lieutenant Colonel, commanding Fifth New York. He is a tried, efficient and popular officer.

CAPTORS OF REBEL COLORS.

The following are the names, as far as reported, of the captors of rebel colors in our recent fights:—Captain J. N. Scott, Company B, 157th Pennsylvania, of the 16th North Carolina infantry; private G. J. Shapp, Company E, 191st Pennsylvania; Sergeant Hiram A. Delvie, Company I, 11th Pennsylvania, of the 32d Virginia infantry; Sergeant Robert F. Shipley, Company A, 140th New York, of the 9th Virginia; private David Edwards, Company H, 146th New York, of the 24th North Carolina; private D. Everson, Company D, 153d New York, of the 14th Virginia; Sergeant Thomas Murphy, Company G, 146th New York; Corporal August Kause, Company H, 15th New York heavy artillery; Captain A. E. Fernald, 20th Maine; private C. M. Gardner, Company E, 32d Massachusetts; Lieutenant David Koogle, Company F, 7th Maryland.

A furlough of twenty-five days will at once be granted to the above officers and men. Names of regiments to which the flags belonged do not appear on all of them. There are still several flags and their captors to be reported.

HEADQUARTERS, FIFTH ARMY CORPS,
NEAR JETTERSVILLE, ON THE DANVILLE RAILROAD,
April 5—7:30 P. M.

THE ENEMY NOT DISPOSED TO SHOW FIGHT.

The expected battle has not been fought to-day. It was supposed from information reaching us, or the indications, that the enemy would venture an attack. The active preparations made in such anticipation have made the day, notwithstanding the absence of a general engagement, a busy and exciting one. There have been marching and countermarching of infantry, the moving to and fro of artillery, and rapid marching back and forth of cavalry.

CONCENTRATION OF THE ARMY.

The Second corps joined us during the day. The Ninth corps is in our vicinity. General Meade has his headquarters close by. Everything is in readiness to-night for accepting or renewing battle.

THE CAVALRY ENGAGED—CAPTURES.

All the fighting to-day has been by the cavalry. They captured a portion of General Longstreet's wagon train, five cannons and several hundred prisoners. The wagons were burned, and the prisoners and cannon were marched by our headquarters. The cannon were marked "Sir W. G. Armstrong, 1864," and have never been used in battle. The captain who was taken with them bought them in Europe, and says that he has spent four plantations in aid of the confederacy.

PRISONERS.

Among the prisoners are two colonels, five captains, three lieutenants and one surgeon. Colonel Clark, one of the prisoners, is said to have been chief of artillery of General Bragg. Colonel Terrell, the other colonel, was formerly in the United States service. The latter is said to report Johnston's forces at Strong creek, and also that Lee has a force of one hundred thousand men in our front. I give these reported statements for what they are worth.

OUR LOSSES IN THE CAVALRY.

In the cavalry engagement we lost quite heavily. Colonel Janney, First New Jersey, was killed, and General Gregg wounded and taken prisoner.

LADIES GOING SOUTH.

On the train captured to-day was Captain Somers, his wife and two children. Mrs. Somers begged that her husband be allowed his parole to see her and her children at a safe distance from the army. General Devens got him a parole of twenty-four hours. Captain Somers states that a large number of women and children were on the train that escaped capture, trying to work their way south.

DESIGNS OF THE ENEMY.

It is supposed that if the enemy does not attack us here he will make an effort to cross the Appomattox at Stony Point, and then, striking the Richmond and Lynchburg turnpike, make tracks in the direction of the latter place. The probability is that Generals Meade and Sheridan may insist on having a voice in the carrying out of the enemy's programme.

SPIRITS OF THE ARMY.

The army was never in more jubilant spirits. Four days rations were issued to-day.

MAIL COMMUNICATION OPEN.

Among all the sources of congratulation there is none more gratifying than the announcement of mail communication being opened again. For three days we have been moving, lost from the outer world. Our mail and supplies for the present will reach us at Sutherland station, on the Southside Railroad.

THE NINTH CORPS.

Mr. J. Walton Fitch's Despatches.

HEADQUARTERS NINTH ARMY CORPS,
WELLESVILLE, Va., April 5—9 P. M.

CAMP AT WELLESVILLE.

The Ninth corps resumed its march this morning from Ford's station, about twenty miles from Petersburg, and again moved by the Cox road, as before. We halt to-night at Wellesville, distant from Burkesville twenty-one miles. The two divisions of this corps now together are the only troops moving on the Cox road, and the entire trains of the army are under their immediate guardianship, our main force having advanced upon the Namozine road, running nearly parallel with the route traversed by us, and at this point is about fourteen miles to the north. A large proportion of the army supply trains are far in our advance to-night, making good time.

THE NINTH CORPS SHARES THE GENERAL ENTHUSIASM.

The men have manifested throughout the march of to-day the same unflagging vigor and spirit that has characterized their movements since the advance of Monday, and, though laden heavily, they give promise of moving with continued alacrity and promptitude.

ORDER ON THE MARCH.

Strict orders have been issued for the prevention of house burning, and thus far very few have been consigned to the flames, and none, I believe, in which the original occupants were still remaining. Neither is the destruction of other property indulged in to any considerable extent, though we find as we advance that the inhabitants are nearly destitute of provisions, and in some instances solicit the protection of a guard about their premises, and in their extremity, beg for subsistence from our passing trains.

THE CONDITION OF THE SOUTHSIDE RAILROAD.

This road, as far as our present advance from Petersburg, is apparently in need of very slight repair to make it available for transportation, unless some large bridge has been destroyed. It is more than probable that the road will be in use within the next week.

The Commander-in-Chief is reported to have stopped for a short time this morning at a house about a mile above Corps headquarters, and to-night occupied as headquarters of the Second division.

CONGRATULATORY ADDRESS FROM GENERAL GRIFFIN.

The following congratulatory order was issued on the 3d inst. to the Second brigade of the Second division, by General Griffin, its commander, who is now, in the absence of General Potter, in command of the Second division:—

HEADQUARTERS, SECOND BRIG., SECOND DIV.,
NINTH ARMY CORPS, NEAR HANCOCK'S STATION, Va.,
April 2, 1865.

The General commanding desires to express, so far as he has language to do so, his heartfelt pride and satisfaction at the brave and gallant conduct of the officers and soldiers of his brigade in carrying at the point of the bayonet the almost impregnable lines of Petersburg. Never was greater valor displayed. Never were more heroic deeds performed. The daring deeds of this day need not be recounted here. They will live in history and in the hearts of your countrymen while time shall last.

The 2d of April will never be forgotten while your country has a name. This glorious achievement is doubtless the deathblow of the rebellion—the finishing stroke of the war. Proudly and joyfully will we return to our homes to enjoy the blessings of that peace which you by your perseverance and gallantry have so nobly conquered.

By command of Brigadier General S. G. GRIFFIN.
IRA G. WILKINS, Lieutenant and A. A. A. G.
Official—T. CHILD, Lieutenant and A. A. A. G.

HEADQUARTERS, NINTH CORPS,
NEAR BURKESVILLE JUNCTION,
SOUTHSIDE RAILROAD, April 6—Midnight.

The headquarters of this corps are located to-night near the Southside Railroad, about ten miles from the Burkesville Junction of that road, with one brigade of the Second division advanced to that point.

Major General Parke has been in telegraphic communication with the headquarters of the army for some hours, and his advices, so far as known, indicate that our troops have been pushed forward with great celerity, and have, by the energy of their disposition, succeeded in foiling General Lee's design of leading us a long and wearisome stern chase. Of course but little definite information is afforded on this point; but I deem it not inexpedient to state that the grand combinations of the opening campaign are progressing right speedily toward the desuction of Lee's retreating army.

PROGRESS OF THE TRAINS.

The immense trains that are moving under convoy of this corps are getting over ground amazingly well, and, aside from the deep indentures of their own wheels, they find the roads tolerably smooth and dry.

HOW THE TROOPS FEEL.

I have before alluded to the general jollity and good feeling manifested by the troops of the Ninth corps since their advance from Petersburg; and I have no occasion on this, the fourth day of their march, to record any other than the same agreeable intelligence to-night. As the night before they came into camp singing "When Johnnie comes marching home again," nearly a whole brigade having caught the refrain and rendering it with a zest that made it appreciable for miles about.

AT BAY.

Commencing about ten o'clock this morning and continuing at intervals throughout the day and evening, we have heard the booming of a heavy cannonade to the west and southwest, which has gradually worked around slightly to our left. That it is the whole rebel army brought to a stand under the harassment of Sheridan's pursuing cavalrymen, closely attended by the advance of our infantry, is the general speculation.

LEE'S BAGGAGE AND HEADQUARTERS FLAG REPORTED CAPTURED.

We had a report about noon to-day that Lee's headquarters flag and baggage had been captured by us, and that General Gregg was captured by the rebels, and subsequently wrested from them and restored to his command.

FIRE AND THE SWORD.

The perfect subordination and good conduct of our troops, not only in the capture of Petersburg, but during the present march, has been a matter of frequent comment by the inhabitants whom we encountered; but, unfortunately, the considerable number of stragglers and followers of our wagon trains have, as we advanced, taken occasion to make a number of diversions from the main line of travel, to indulge their destructive propensities upon such property as was without the observation of our officers.

FRIDAY MORNING, April 6, 1865.

VICTORY.

The splendid successes of yesterday's fight have just been reported here, and are provoking the enthusiastic comment of all save the original occupants of the sacred soil, who overhear the story of their reverses quite aghast at the great defeat which it foreshadows. There is a possibility that our headquarters will not be moved to-day.

THE SURRENDER OF LEE.

Scene of Grant's Operations Against Lee in Virginia; of Sherman's Operations Against Johnston in North Carolina; of Stoneman's Operations on the Danville and Greensboro Railroad, and of Hancock's Movement from Staunton.

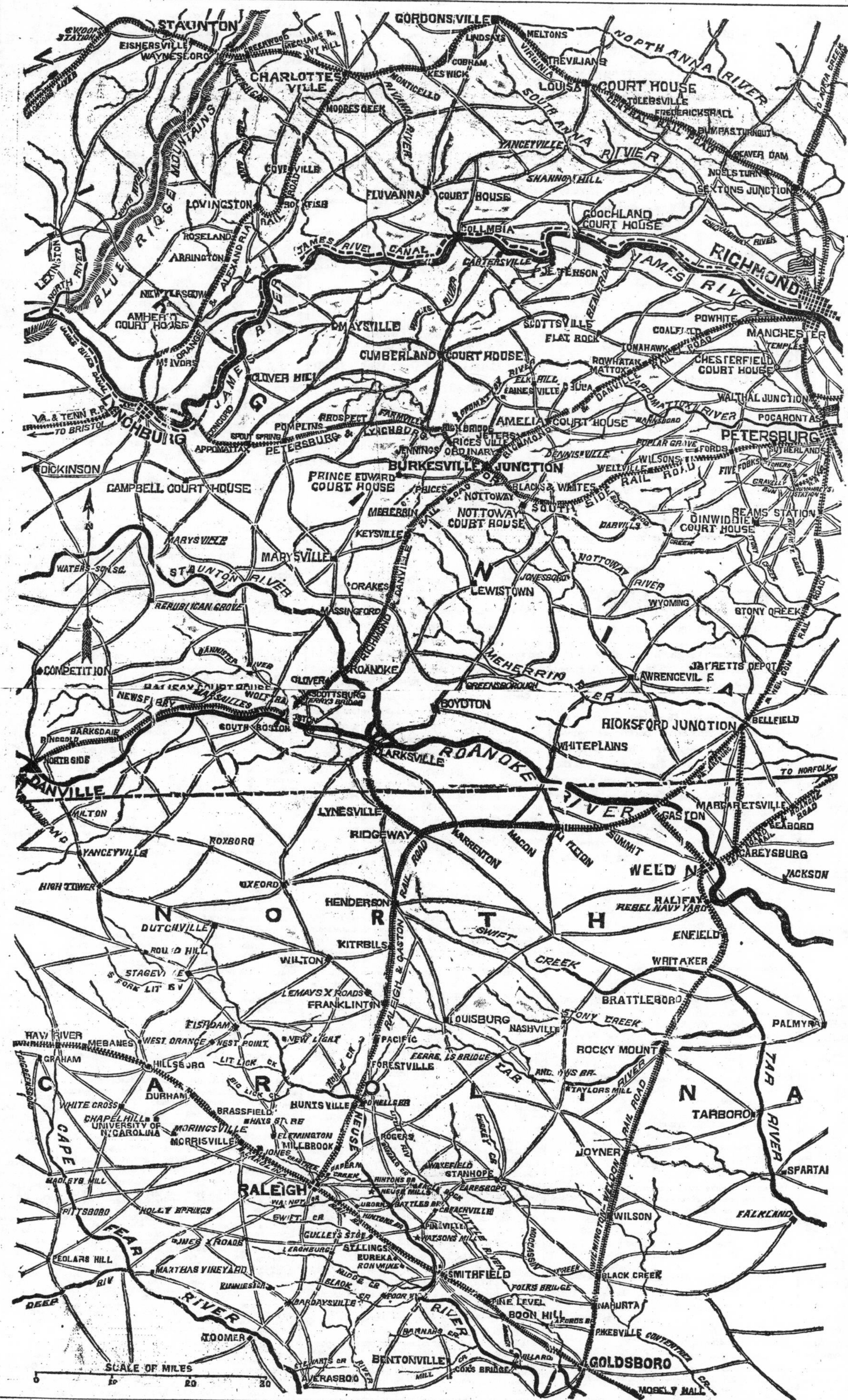

THE TWENTY-FOURTH CORPS.

Mr. John A. Brady's Despatch.

HEADQUARTERS, TWENTY-FOURTH ARMY CORPS,
BURKESVILLE JUNCTION, April 5, 1865.

FORCED MARCHING.

At eleven o'clock to-night the troops of this command reached this point, after a forced march from Wilson's station of nearly thirty miles. The march was commenced morning, at six o'clock, with Turner's Western Virginia division in the advance.

Immediately in rear of the troops of this corps, Birney followed with his division of the Twenty-fifth corps.

NOTTOWAY COURT HOUSE.

The column reached Nottaway Court House about two P. M., and found everything there in almost its peace condition. The few rebel stragglers who passed through here in rapid flight had no time to burn any of the few cars lying on the road. A car full of hay, belonging to the rebel government was found on the road in front of the station master's, and proved an acceptable addition to the stock of forage for the horses.

CONFEDERATE MONEY.

Confederate money has here reached its proper level, and is actually considered only in the light of waste paper. The citizens of Nottoway tell us that as soon as the negroes heard of our advance they refused to take the money at any price for the game and fish they are accustomed in this section of the country to peddle around. Before the capture of Richmond they had a large supply of gold on hand in the rebel Treasury, and were redeeming every one of their notes that was offered at the rate of one dollar in specie, half gold, half silver, for sixty dollars in paper money. Many, however, hoping that the paper would rise in value had neglected to get their notes cashed until too late.

NEWS FROM SHERIDAN.

It was at first intended to halt the column for the night after passing the Court House. A despatch, however, was received from Sheridan announcing the fact that he had captured six pieces of artillery and two hundred supply wagons at Painsville, and requesting Grant to push as large a force as possible on to Burkesville Junction, when he hoped to have Lee, who is short of everything, so completely hemmed in as to force him to surrender.

This despatch was read to the troops amid great cheering, and the wearied men resumed their knapsacks and moved on. It was eleven o'clock to-night before the column reached the Junction, and hardly waiting to build fires or cook supper the troops threw themselves on the ground, and were almost instantly in deep slumber.

GRANT JOINS SHERIDAN.

The greater number of the mounted orderlies accompanying Generals Ord and Gibson were seized by General Grant to escort him in a dash across the country to join General Sheridan.

SHERIDAN INTERCEPTS A TELEGRAM.

It is reported that General Sheridan tapped a telegraph wire and intercepted a message to General Lee, announcing that the commissary had two million rations on hand, and wished instructions as to forwarding them. General Sheridan immediately sent instructions to forward the rations in the name of General Lee, and has every hope that he will be able to intercept them. Lee's army is said to be in line of battle at Amelia Court House, about ten miles from here.

THE CAVALRY.

Mr. J. B. Wardell's Despatches.

HEADQUARTERS, CAVALRY DIVISION,
FARM HILL, April 3, 1865.

THE ENEMY IN POSITION.

The Second brigade, Colonel Wells commanding, moved out on the advance after the retreating rebels this morning, and met their rear guard about two miles from the position occupied last night, strongly intrenched across Namozine creek, having destroyed the bridge after crossing and felled large trees across the ford to impede our further rapid progress. Just before coming up to them a caisson filled with ammunition, both canister and shell, was found near the road, with all the lids open, left by the rebels.

THE ENEMY ENGAGED.

On advancing up to the creek, the enemy opened fire upon the advanced skirmishers, but with little effect, our line coming up and returning it with vigor. It being found impossible to charge them from the obstructions in the way, a section of United States Battery A was brought up, and in a few minutes shelled them from their position, obliging them to fall back out of range in great confusion. A number of men were at once dismounted, and in half an hour succeeded in removing all the obstructions and allowing the command to cross the creek, which, at the deepest point, was not over four feet.

EVIDENCE OF THE ENEMY'S DEMORALIZATION.

Immediately upon crossing a rapid march was ordered and in a short time the most complete evidence of utter and fearful demoralization of the rebels was apparent on every side. The road was strewn with wagons, ambulances, dead and wounded, horses and mules, caissons filled with ammunition, dozens of boxes of ammunition thrown out to lighten the load, mess utensils, arms, &c.—all speaking of defeat and fears of capture.

OUR FLANKERS DISCOVER CANNON AND AMMUNITION SECRETED IN THE WOODS.

I omitted to mention in its proper place that before crossing the creek flankers were sent out who discovered four pieces of artillery, two wagons loaded down with ammunition, and two ambulances, left by the rebels hid away in the woods.

In several places along the road large quantities of all kinds of ammunition were discovered strewn along the fences and the fences set on fire, with the evident diabolical intention of causing an explosion to retard and destroy our column as far as possible. In some spots the dry wood burned fiercely; but, fortunately, through the precautions taken, no injury resulted from their scheme.

ARRIVAL AT NAMOZINE CHURCH.

Passing on rapidly, several miles we came to Namozine church, or, as it is sometimes called, Poplar Grove church, at the intersection of two roads. The road to the left leading direct to Lynchburg, the one to the right of the church to Bevil's bridge across the Appomattox on to Amelia Court House.

BARRENGER'S REBEL BRIGADE ENCOUNTERED.

The Second brigade, taking the road to the left, soon encountered the enemy's cavalry of Barrenger's brigade, who, although they made desperate efforts to escape, were nearly worn out with fighting and running. A portion of them turned and fired upon the advance; but our men, without in the least halting, charged in upon them, scattering them like sheep, many abandoning their horses and arms and taking to the woods, where they were picked up and brought in prisoners. So eager were they in getting away that in many places the road was completely blocked up, those in the rear urging their horses upon those in front.

CASUALTIES.

In this charge Captain Goodrich, of the Eighth New York cavalry, was shot through the head, a ball entering the inside corner of the right eye and coming out at the top of his head. He was carried back to the church in an unconscious condition, the ball having passed through the brain. He expired in a short time. Capt. Farlee, of the Third New Jersey, was wounded in four places—through the right shoulder, the left hand, the right thigh and the scrotum. A ball remains in the latter wound.

GALLANTRY OF LIEUTENANT CUSTER.

Lieutenant Custer, a brother of the general and aid-de-camp on his staff, in this same charge and rout of the rebels, showed that he possessed some of the characteristics which have rendered the general so famous and popular, both with the army and the public. Advancing at the head of the charging column, he became separated from the rest of the command in his impetuosity, and, alone and unaided, captured a rebel battle flag and fourteen Johnnies, bringing them all successfully into our lines.

CAPHART OVERTAKES THE REBELS.

The Third brigade, Colonel Caphart, taking the road to the right of Namozine church, pushed on rapidly towards Dennisville, crossing Deep creek at the lower ford, the bridge having been destroyed. Immediately upon crossing the brigade started after the rebels on the run, and soon overtook them. Spreading on each side of the road, our men went in under the wildest excitement, and soon the crack, crack of the deadly carbine, growing fainter in the distance, told of our success in the chase—for it could be called nothing else—and occasionally a wounded Union soldier, lying by the roadside, told us that, like the closely pressed and wounded stag, some poor rebel had turned at bay and delivered his fire before receiving ours in turn, or being taken prisoner.

COLONEL PENNINGTON ORDERED FORWARD.

General Custer, who continually kept in the advance, seeing that unless we had more men up to the front, to spread out over the country, many of the enemy would escape him by hiding in the woods, sent back to hurry up the First brigade (Colonel Pennington's), which was advancing up the same road. On receiving the order Colonel Pennington rushed up his brigade as fast as possible passed the General, and to the inspiring music of the band dashed in with the greatest impetuosity, the men screaming with delight.

RUNNING DOWN THE REBELS.

Two or three miles were thus rapidly passed over, every few rods a squad of our men emerging from the woods, having in charge from two to twenty rebels who were completely blowed, and had been captured after a long run. Both brigades kept up the chase, driving, killing, wounding and capturing the rebels to Bevil's ford where they expected to cross the river, but finding the bridge down, the enemy were obliged to take a road to the left, leading a distance of seven miles to a crossing on the upper Appomattox. The First brigade was halted near to the ford for the purpose of gathering together the scattered men, while the Third continued on up the road the rebels had taken.

THE REBEL OFFICERS DESERTING THEIR MEN.

Prisoners taken at this time reported that they had no organized command, their commander, General Cook, having left them. They were not desirous of fighting or making a stand, but simply were doing all in their power to escape and get away, they knew not where; and the sentiment among them, as they expressed it, was every

CONTINUED ON FIFTH PAGE.

THE SUN.

IT SHINES FOR ALL

THIRTY-THIRD YEAR. NUMBER 10,216.

NEW YORK, MONDAY, APRIL 10, 1865.

PRICE ONE CENT—IN GOLD
TWO CENTS IN CURRENCY.

OUR NATION REDEEMED

SURRENDER OF LEE AND HIS WHOLE ARMY.

THE TERMS.

Officers and Men Paroled and Told to go Home.

THE COUNTRY WILD WITH JOY.

&c., &c., &c.

OFFICIAL.

WAR DEPARTMENT,
WASHINGTON, April 9th, 1865,
9 o'clock, P. M.

To Major-General Dix,

New York:

This Department has received the official report of the surrender, this day, of General Lee and his army to Lieutenant-General Grant on the terms proposed by General Grant.

Details will be given as speedily as possible.

EDWIN M. STANTON,
Secretary of War.

GEN. GRANT TO SEC. STANTON.

Headquarters Armies of the United States,
4.30 P. M., April 9th.

Hon. EDWIN M. STANTON,
Secretary of War:

General Lee surrendered the Army of Northern Virginia this afternoon upon the terms proposed by myself. The accompanying additional correspondence will show the conditions fully.

Signed, U. S. GRANT,
Lieut.-Gen.

GENERAL LEE TO GENERAL GRANT.

April 9, 1865.

General:—I received your note of this morning on the picket line, whither I had come to meet you and ascertain definitely what terms were embraced in your proposition of yesterday with reference to the surrender of this army.

I now request an interview in accordance with the offer contained in your letter of yesterday for that purpose.

Very Respectfully,
Your Obedient Servant,
R. E. LEE, General.

To Lieut. General Grant, Commanding U. S. Armies.

GENERAL GRANT TO GENERAL LEE.

April 9, 1865.

General R. E. LEE, Commanding Confederate States Armies:

Your note of this date is but this moment, 11:50 A. M., received.

In consequence of my having passed from the Richmond and Lynchburg road to the Farmville and Lynchburg road, I am at this writing, about four miles west of Walker's church, and will push forward to the front for the purpose of meeting you.

Notice sent to me on this road where you wish the interview to take place will meet me.

Very Respectfully,
Your Obedient Servant,
U. S. GRANT,
Lieutenant General.

The Terms of Surrender Offered by General Grant.

Appomattox Court House,
April 9, 1865.

General R. E. LEE, Commanding C. S. A.:

In accordance with the substance of my letter to you of the 8th inst. I propose to receive the surrender of the Army of Northern Virginia, on the following terms, to wit:

Rolls of all the officers and men to be made in duplicate, one copy to be given to an officer designated by me, the other to be retained by such officers as you may designate.

The officers to give their individual paroles not to take arms against the Government of the United States until properly exchanged, and each company or regimental commander sign a like parole for the men of their commands.

The arms, artillery and public property to be packed and stacked and turned over to the officers appointed by me to receive them.

This will not embrace the side-arms of the officers, nor their private horses or baggage.

This done—each officer and man will be allowed to return to their homes, not to be disturbed by United States authority so long as they observe their parole and the laws in force where they may reside.

Very Respectfully,
U. S. GRANT,
Lieutenant General.

THE SURRENDER.

GENERAL LEE TO GENERAL GRANT.

Headquarters Army of
Northern Virginia, April 9, 1865.

Lieutenant General U. S. GRANT, Commanding U. S. A.

General:—I have received your letter of this date containing the terms of surrender of the Army of Northern Virginia as proposed by you. As they are substantially the same as those expressed in your letter of the 8th inst., they are accepted. I will proceed to designate the proper officers to carry the stipulations into effect.

Very Respectfully,
Your Obedient Servant,
R. E. LEE, General.

THE PREVIOUS CORRESPONDENCE.

The following is the previous correspondence between Lieutenant-General Grant and General Lee referred to in the foregoing telegram to the Secretary of War. There has been no relaxation in the pursuit during its pendency:

GRANT TO LEE.

APRIL 7th, 1865.

General R. E. Lee,
Commanding C. S. A.:

GENERAL—The result of the last week must convince you of the hopelessness of further resistance on the part of the Army of Northern Virginia in this struggle. I feel that it is so, and regard it as my duty to shift from myself the responsibility of any further effusion of blood, by asking of you the surrender of that portion of the Confederate States army, known as the Army of Northern Virginia.

Very respectfully, your obt. servant,
U. S. GRANT, Lieutenant-General,
Commanding Armies of the United States.

LEE TO GRANT.

APRIL 7, 1865.

General:—I have received your note of this date. Though not entirely of the opinion you express of the hopelessness of further resistance on the part of the army of Northern Virginia, I reciprocate your desire to avoid useless effusion of blood, and therefore before considering your proposition, ask the terms you will offer, on condition of its surrender?

R. E. LEE, General.

To Lieut.-Gen. U. S. Grant, commanding armies of the United States.

GRANT TO LEE.

APRIL 8, 1865.

To Gen. R. E. Lee,
Commanding C. S. A.:

GENERAL:—Your note of last evening in reply to mine of same date, asking the conditions on which I will accept the surrender of the Army of Northern Virginia, is just received.

In reply, I would say, that peace being my first desire, there is but one condition that I must insist upon, viz:

That the men surrendered shall be disqualified from taking up arms again against the Government of the United States until properly exchanged.

I will meet you, or designate officers to meet any officers you may name for the same purpose, at any point agreeable to you, for the purpose of arranging definitely the terms upon which the surrender of the Army of Northern Virginia will be received.

Very respectfully, Your Obedient Servant,
U. S. GRANT, Lieut.-Genl. Commanding
Armies of the United States.

LEE TO GRANT.

APRIL 8, 1865.

GENERAL:—I received at a late hour your note of to-day in answer to mine of yesterday.

I did not intend to propose the surrender of the Army of Northern Virginia, but to ask the terms of your proposition. To be frank, I do not think the emergency has arisen to call for the surrender. But as the restoration of peace should be the sole object of all, I desire to know whether your proposals would tend to that end.

I cannot, therefore, meet you with a view to surrender the Army of Northern Virginia, but as far as your proposition may affect the C. S. forces under my command and tend to the restoration of peace, I should be pleased to meet you at ten a. m. to-morrow on the old stage road to Richmond, between the picket lines of the two armies.

Very respectfully,
Your obedient servant,
R. E. LEE,
General C. S. A.

To Lieut. Gen. GRANT,
Commanding Armies of the United States.

GRANT TO LEE.

APRIL 9th, 1865.

General R. E. Lee, Commanding C. S. A.:

GENERAL—Your note of yesterday is received. As I have no authority to treat on the subject of peace, the meeting proposed for ten A. M. to-day could lead to no good. I will state, however, General, that I am equally anxious for peace with yourself; and the whole North entertain the same feeling. The terms on which peace can be had are well understood, By the South laying down their arms they will hasten that most desirable event, save thousands of human lives and hundreds of millions of property not yet destroyed.

Sincerely hoping that all our difficulties may be settled without the loss of another life, I subscribe myself,

Very Respectfully,
Your obedient servant,
U. S. GRANT, Lieut. General U. S. A.

Congratulatory Dispatch from Secretary Stanton.

WASHINGTON, D. C.—9:30 P. M.,
APRIL 9th, 1865.

Lieut.-Gen. Grant:

Thanks be to Almighty God for the great victory with which he has this day crowned you and the gallant armies under your command. The thanks of this Department, and of the Government, and of the United States—their reverence and honor have been deserved—will be rendered to you and the brave and gallant officers and soldiers of your army for all time.

EDWIN M. STANTON, Secretary of War.

A GRAND SALUTE ORDERED.

WAR DEPARTMENT,
WASHINGTON, D. C., 10 o'clock P. M.,
April 9th, 1865.

Ordered, That a salute of two hundred guns be fired at the headquarters of every army and department, and at every post and arsenal in the United States, and at the Military Academy at West Point, on the day of the receipt of this order, in commemoration of the surrender of General R. E. Lee and the Army of Northern Virginia to Lieutenant General Grant and the army under his command; report of the receipt and execution of this order to be made to the Adjutant General, Washington.

EDWIN M. STANTON, Secretary of War.

REJOICINGS.

Wilmington, Del., April 9.—Wilmington is in an uproar and blaze of glory, rejoicing over the greatest of victories yet achieved by our arms. Guns are firing, bells are ringing, and a large procession is proceeding through the streets. Such an excitement was never before witnessed in this city.

Worcester, Mass., April 9.—The news of the surrender of Lee and his army created an intense excitement here to night. The bells were rnng, guns were fired, bonfires kindled, the fire companies turned out, and many stores and buildings were illuminated.

Pittsburg, Pa., April 9.—The news to-night brought nearly the entire population into the streets. *The recruiting booths were turned into bonfires*, salutes were fired, speeches were made, and bands played.

Trenton, N. J., April 9.—The glorious news was received here with cheering and ringing of bells. The people are turning out *en masse* to receive and rejoice over the glad tidings.

Philadelphia, April 9.—The glorious announcement of Lee's surrender was received here about nine o'clock. It was telegraphed to all sections of the city, and was announced in the several churches. The bell of Independence Hall was rung by the order of the Mayor. The firemen immediately assembled and blocked up the streets. Salutes were fired, and the whistles of the steam engines, and the cheers of the assembled multitudes made the whole city ring.

Providence, R. I., April 9—*Midnight.*—Bells are ringing, cannon are firing, and the citizens are out rejoicing over the news of Lee's surrender.

Albany, April 10.—1 *A. M.*—There is great rejoicing here over the news of the surrender of General Lee and his army. About midnight State and Pearl streets were filled with people anxiously inquiring the particulars. The bells are ringing, cannon firing, while the multitude are indulging in fireworks. Tho Governor was called and briefly addressed the throng gathered around his residences. The State House and many private residences are illuminated.

General Lee and his Family.

The following interesting article, embodying reminiscences of the rebel GENERAL LEE and his family, together with a description ot his magnificent ancestral homestead on the Potomac, in which he resided before the war, we extract from the NATIONAL INTELLIGENCER of the 6th inst.:

A visit to the Arlington mansion and surrounding estate, a few days since, filled us with oppressive and melancholy reflection. Four years ago, Robert E. Lee, then a lieutenant-colonel of cavalry in the Union army, and now Commander-in-Chief of the rebel army, was with his family in the happy possession of that magnificent inheritance. More than one-half of the estate, consisting of a thousand acres, was covered with a splendid forest of oak and other timber, and the rich and productive fields adorned with the hand of culture. To-day what a change! The venerable ancestral mansion, erected by the honored son by adoption of the Father of his Country, and for half a century his cultivated and delightful home, is now in the centre of a vast cemetery of those who have fallen in the service of their country. Two hundred and fifty acres of this estate, surrounding the mansion have been permanently appropriated for burial purposes by the Government, and enclosed by a substantial and handsome fence. Nearly five thousand soldiers have already been there buried, and the number is daily growing larger. In 1853, Mrs. Curtis the mother of Mrs. General Lee, died in the Arlington mansion and was buried in a sequestered and delightful grove near the mansion; and in 1857 Mr. Custis died, and his remains were deposited by her side, a vast concourse of persons of every rank testifying their reverance for the departed by their presence at the obsequies. That sequestered grove, thus selected by its owner as the last resting place for himself and his, has been in the tempest of the times invaded, the forest has been transformed into a field of the dead, and the two marble columns marking the remains of George Washington Parke Custis and Mary Lee Fitzhugh, his wife, now rise in the midst of more than four thousand patriot soldiers' graves. Nearly the whole of the timber and wood has been swept from the entire estate and used for war purposes. The Freedman's Village is established upon one portion of the land thus cleared, and it is all being put under cultivation by contraband negro labor.

Mr. Custis inherited this estate from his father, who was the son of Mrs. General Washington by a former husband. Soon after his mother died, in 1802, he, then about twenty-five years of age, came here from Mount Vernon, and with his young and accomplished wife took up their residence in the Arlington mansion, which he had then just erected, and which evermore was their beautiful and cultivated home. The fruits of this Union were four daughters, all of whom died in infancy, except Mary Custis, the wife of Gen. Robert E. Lee. * * *

The mansion is now occupied by the officer in command of the post and his subordinates. The dining-hall is used as an office. In this room are three old-fashioned book-cases, containing some four hundred volumes, principally old books—broken sets, and of very small value. The parlor adjoining the hall is not occupied, the only article in it being a mahogany sideboard, which came from Mount Vernon. In the parlor beyond are two sofas and six stuffed mahogany chairs, covered with scarlet velvet; two marble-top tables, a sideboard, and a piano stool, matching the chairs. On the walls are several coarse large portraits, and one or two fine oil paintings. There are also two old engravings, of a classical mythological character, hanging with the rest. The room in the southerly wing, used by Gen. Lee for his office, is now used as a bed-room; and all the upper part of the mansion is used for a like purpose. The building is not injured. The flower garden has been enclosed by a new fence, and was laid out and tastefully adorned this spring.

The grave of each soldier is neatly marked by a wooden slab at the head and the foot, painted white, inscribed with the name of the soldier and his company and regiment, and at a little distance these slabs have the appearance of marble. The mounds are to be neatly covered with sod.

General Robert Edmund Lee is the son of General Henry Lee, of Revolutionary memory, and known as "Light Horse Harry," whose mother was the beautiful Miss Grimes, General Washington's first love, and whom he celebrated as "the lowland beauty." General Henry Lee was twice married. By the first marriage he had two children, Henry (an officer in the war of 1812) and Lucy. By the second wife—a Miss Carter, of Shirly—he had five children, two daughters, Anne and Mildred, and three sons. The sons were Charles Carter, Robert Edmund, (the General,) and Sidney Smith, the last-named an officer in our navy, aud now in the rebel navy.

General Robert E. Lee was born in 1808, and is; consequently, fifty-seven years of age. He graduated second in his class, in 1829, (Judge Charles Mason, of this city, and formerly Commissioner of Patents, standing first in that class,) and was assigned to the Engineer Corps, as second lieutenant in 1835 Assistant Astronomer, fixing the boundary between Ohio and Michigan; in 1836 promoted first lieutenant; captain in 1838; chief engineer under Scott, in Mexico, and greatly distinguished, being promoted successively, by merit, major, lieutenant colonel, and colonel, for his gallantry; in 1852 superintendent Military Academy; in 1855 transferred as lieutenant colonel of the new regiment of cavalry; March 18th, 1861, promoted colonel of the 1st cavalry, resigned April 25th, following, and reluctantly embarked in the rebellion.

The following are the children of General Lee: George Washington Custis Lee, about thirty-three years of age; Mary Custis Lee, about thirty; William Henry Fitzhugh Lee, about twenty-seven; Annie Lee died at Berkeley Springs, in 1863, and would have been now about twenty-five; Agnes Lee, about twenty-three; Robert E. Lee, about twenty; Mildred Lee, about eighteen. None of them have married except William Henry Fitzhugh, whose wife, Miss Charlotte Wickham, died at Richmond in 1863. The eldest son, George, graduated at the head of his class, at West Point, in 1854, and was a first lieutenant in the corps of engineers when he followed his father into the Southern service. William Henry was farming upon the White House estate, which belonged to the Custis inheritance, when the war opened. He was commissioned second lieutenant in the 6th infantry in 1857, but resigned in 1859. Robert was at a military school in Virginia. The sons, it is well known, are all officers in the rebellion. The three surviving daughters are with their mother, who, it is believed, has latterly been at Lynchburg.

Mr. Custis, at the time of his death, owned some two hundred slaves, who, by his will, were to be free at the termination of five years from his death, which period expired October 10th, 1862. The most of these slaves were kept on the White House estate, and all the valuable portion were carried South; some twenty or more old men and women and young children were left at Arlington. Mr. Custis's mother owned the White House estate, and resided there, when she became the wife of General Washington.

From Richmond.

Interesting Items from the Whig of the 6th.

The Richmond WHIG, of the 6th inst., (published under Union auspices), contains much interesting matter relative to the evacuation of Richmond, together with scenes and incidents preceding that event. It appears that the necessity of evacuating Richmond had been manifest to Lee for a month previous to its actual occurrence, and a vast amount of material belonging to the rebel government had already been removed. The citizens of Richmond, however. were kept blissfully in ignorance upon this point, and until the very last they felt confident that the city would be successfully defended. Matters continued thus until the Sundhy morning preceding the evacuation, when Lee telegraphed to Davis that his lines had been penetrated in a number of places by our troops, and that unless he could regain the lost ground, Richmond must be evacuated the following night. He also added that his men were not "coming up to their work." A few hours afterward Lee sent another dispatch to Richmond, to the effect that all efforts to re-establish his lines had proven fruitless, and that Richmond must be given up.

On the receipt of this news the rebel officials hurriedly began their preparations for departure. Still the people were kept in the dark regarding the true condition of affairs, and although the shrewd ones began to discover the actual nature of the situation, the greater part of the population remained in ignorance of the facts until evening. The gold and silver coin belonging to the Louisiana banks, which had been "appropriated" by the rebel government, was hurried to the railroad and started for Danville, together with the specie of the Richmond banks. The next thing the officials did was to take care of themselves and their most valuable effects. Several trains were made up on the Danville road. Davis left at 7 o'clock, and Breckinridge, who seems to have been the pluckiest of the lot, waited until the following morning, when, at an early hour, he started out on horseback, intending to follow the fortunes of the army.

On Sunday evening, when the facts became generally known, the Richmond Council held a meeting and determined to destroy all the liquor in the city as a precaution against outrages from drunken stragglers and soldiers, when there was no longer a force to restrain them. Accordingly, a committee was appointed for each ward, and all the liquor that could be found was emptied into the street. Soldiers and vagabonds, however, did get enough to insure drunkenness, and during Sunday Richmond must have presented a scene akin to Pandemonium—fires burning in many parts of the city, the streets lighted up by the flames of their burning buildings, and in that light hundreds of drunken men shone forth, committing all manner of excesses. The Government storehouses and private stores were broken into, and their contents thrown into the street.

The WHIG, in concluding the article from which this is a condensation, says: Truly, the ways of Providence are inscrutable. This burning of our goodly city would seem at first glance an unmitigated evil. But there is another view to be taken of it. It has one certain good effect. If there lingered in the hearts of any of our people one spark of affection for the Davis dynasty, this ruthless, useless, wanton handing over to the flames their fair city, their homes and affairs, has extinguished it forever.

ADDITIONAL ITEMS.

The transition from enormous prices and a depreciated currency to reasonable rates and real money has come so suddenly upon the citizens that it will be some time before they can properly realize the change. Butter, that was scarce at twenty-five a pound, is now plentiful at fifty and sixty cents a pound. Eggs that were hidden away at twenty-five dollars per dozen, come out readily at the beck of thirty cents. Other commodities are at an equal ratio.

Monday morning, pending the excitement and confusion growing out of the evacuation of the city by the evacuation of the city by the Confederate government the three hundred and fifty odd convicts confined in the State Penitentiary managed to effect a grand jail delivery of themselves, but on Thursday over one hundred of them were recaptured and returned to the institution.

Sutlers' stores are springing up like a pleasant oasis all over the business part of the city left unscathed by the fire, and old times are being revived by a sight of the substantials and luxuries enjoyed before the war put them beyond the reach of the cuisines of Richmond. People will live, breathe and move and have their being once more.

A mail is made up daily at the Capitol, closing at [illegible] o'clock in the morning, and going by steamer, by way of City Point, Fortress Monroe and Annapolis. The northern return mail will arrive in the evening.

Four of the detective officers of the Confederate government, who resigned and remained behind when the government changed its base, have been arrested, together with Wiley, the turnkey of Castle Thunder under Confederate *regime*, and Frederick Shaffer, the Confederate bread commissary for the Union prisoners, and all committed to the Libby Prison.

An immense number of Confederate coupon bonds with the coupons all registered and signed, were thrown into the streets of Richmond during the recent evacuation. They were picked up by everybody who had any inclination to subject themselves to that trouble, and can be purchased from the boys for a very insignificant sum.

The functions of the Mayor and Police have been suspended for the present, and military law governs the city. In the present unsettled state of affairs this is, perhaps, proper and highly necessary. In time we may look for the restoration of our municipal government upon a Union foundation, and the resumption of legislation in all its departments.

BY TELEGRAPH.

Washington, April 9.—The Richmond WHIG of Friday, the 7th inst., says that Mrs. Lincoln and Mrs. Grant arrived there on Thursday, and, accompanied by several prominent Government officials, rode through the city in carriages with an escort of cavalry, and returned to City Point in the evening, whither the President had already gone. Among other prominent persons in Richmond, are Vice-President Johnson, Senator Harlan, Ex-Senator Preston King, and Assistant Secretary of War Dana.

The river obstructions are being removed as expeditiously as possible, and forty-eight hours will not elapse, we opine, before we hear of steamers at Rockets direct from New York, Philadelphia and Baltimore. The river at City Point is filled with a Sutler's fleet awaiting permits to enable them to bring their supplies up to Richmond. Improvement renovation and reconstruction must assuredly follow in the wake of the Union armies in things political as well as things material.

A strong force of laborers is to be at once put at work on the broken points of the Richmond, Fredericksburg, Acquia Creek & Potomac Railroad, and its completion, which will occur within the next few weeks, will put Richmond in railroad communication with the capital of the United States again. The iron bands broken by the ruthless hand of war, welded again, will once more re-unite a divided people in bonds too strong to be put asunder.

A great many men whom the tyrannical rebel conscription has for three years driven from the face of day, and forced to hide and skulk like felons, assured by the presence of the Union forces and the Star Spangled Banner, have ventured once more to show themselves among their fellows. For the first time during the war, the city may truly be said to be quiet, and life and property safe. Not a noise more uncouth than the sound of military bands and army wagons disturbs the ear of day or night. The garroters and burglars that infested the rebel capital have either knocked the dust of the city from their feet and followed the Confederate flag, or they have prudence enough to forego the practice of their nefarious arts.

The Petersburg railroad is unbroken, in both track and bed, except in one or two places, all the distance from that city to Richmond. Trains are now running on the road, and the welcome whistle of the locomotive is heard again.

The WHIG also contains the following:

RECONSTRUCTION.

MEETING OF THE VIRGINIA LEGISLATURE.

An informal meeting of the members of the Virginia Legislature remaining in the city was held in the law building, Franklin street, this morning, for consideration of the propositions of President Lincoln to re-assemble the Legislature for the purpose of authorizing a convention to take Virginia back into the bonds of the Union. The propositions of President Lincoln were laid before the meeting. A formal meeting was appointed to take place at four o'clock this afternoon, to which time the meeting adjourned.

The Virginia Legislature adjourned on the 18th of March, to meet on the 29th of that month. They met on the 29th without a quorum. According to the Constitution they could, under such circumstances, only adjourn from day to day. This they did until Sunday last, the day of the evacuation, when they held a meeting in the evening, and dispersed without resolution, some going off with the Governor, and some leaving on a canal boat chartered for the purpose, according to law. The members now in the city are the only remaining legal representatives of the State of Virginia. It is important to state that the Legislature of 1865 is authorized by the Constitution to call a Convention for the purpose of settling and adjusting the basis of representation. This question is settled—but a Convention called for any purpose is omnipotent.

Effect of Mr. Lincoln's Proposition to the Virginia Legislature.

Washington, April 9.—The proposition of President Lincoln, as stated in the WHIG, to reassemble the Virginia Legislature at Richmond, for the purpose of authorizing a Convention to take back the State into the bonds of the Union, interferes with the government claiming to represent that State, with Pierpont as Governor, and its capital at Alexandria. The legislature at the latter place several months ago, having received from the Secretary of State a certified copy of the proposed constitutional amendment to abolish slavery, ratified the same by a nearly unanimous vote; and among other acts conferred a franchise for constructing a railroad from Washington to Fredericksburg. The Pierpont government contemplate an early removal to Richmond; but the event to which reference is above made, does not encourage the consummation of that design.

From Mobile.

The Operations Well Under Way—Important Successes.

The news from Mobile has assumed a more explicit form. The combined land and naval forces are now fairly at work, and the siege is progressing in a manner that warrants the hope of early success. Mobile being the last city left to the rebels, the progress of operations there will naturally be looked upon with marked interest. It is a strong position, having good natural advantages for defense, and these have been well improved by the

Continued on the last page.

(Continued from the First page.)

rebels. No Southern city, however, has yet successfully withstood a land and naval attack, and since the garrison of Mobile is known to be weak, we may expect to learn in a few days that the Gulf City has succumbed to the Union pressure, and added the last to the list of recaptured cities.

The investment of Spanish Fort—a formidable earthwork on the east side of Mobile Bay—was commenced by Gen. Granger's corps on the 26th ult. On the 27th, our forces were formed in line of battle, and lively skirmishing was kept up during the whole day, the rebels being driven back and forced to take refuge in their rifle-pits. On the same day our skirmishers and workers advanced to within 80 yards of the fort, while three or four of our batteries were planted from 300 to 400 yards away. Large numbers of torpedoes were discovered planted in roads and ways leading to the fort, and several serious accidents occurred through the explosion of some of them—in several instances our men being either killed or dangerously wounded.

About 2 o'clock on the morning of the 30th, a portion of the Ninety-first Illinois and the Fiftieth Indiana were sent out to relieve a portion of our advanced line of skirmishers. In the darkness they lost their way, and encountered the enemy's pickets, by whom they were fired upon. The volley being returned by our men, a brisk musketry fire was soon opened along the entire line. Our skirmishers were at first driven back, but General Veach advancing with his entire division, the rebels were speedily forced to seek the cover of their works, having been repulsed along the whole line. They are supposed to have suffered heavily. An artillery duel was then commenced, and continued until nearly daylight.

The forces under General Steele, which left Pensacola on the 20th March, encountered no other opposition than bad roads for several days. On the 26th, however, they were confronted by a cavalry brigade under the rebel General Clauson. After a short, sharp fight, the command of the rebel brigadier was either killed, captured or put to flight. The captures amounted to twenty-three officers, including General Clauson, four hundred men and four hundred and fifty horses. At another point on their march they succeeded in cutting the Mobile and Montgomery Railroad, and capturing two wagon trains. A brigade of cavalry, under Lieutenant Colonel Spurling, also captured one hundred prisoners.

While these movements were going forward on the land side of the fort, the navy was preparing to cooperate on the water front.

On the 28th the monitors Winnebago, Kickapoo, Chickasaw, Milwaukie and Osage, with the "double-ender" Octorara, crossed Black River for the purpose of investing the fort and cutting off all communication with Mobile, and thereby eventually compelling the entire garrison to surrender. Unfortunately the Milwaukee, a double turreted ship, while backing into line of battle struck a torpedo and sunk in ten feet of water. One man only was injured by the explosion. On the following day the Osage, in changing her position, encountered a similar engine of destruction, which exploded, damaging her so seriously that she almost immediately went to the bottom. Four men were killed and eight wounded—two of the latter died on the following day. An attempt was to be made to raise the sunken vessels, and submarine armors for the purpose had been sent for from Pensacola.

The Milwaukee is known to have been one of the finest vessels of the class ever built. She was nearly twice the size of the original Monitor, and had two turrets, one of which was worked by steam. She was built at Cincinnati. The Osage was also a very formidable vessel. She was a single turreted Monitor and carried an eleven inch gun. She was built up the Mississippi.

Spanish Fort, the immediate object of attack, was built by the early Spanish settlers, and is more than 300 years old. It is the principal land defence of Mobile, remaining in possession of the rebels, and when it succombs, the evacuation or surrender of the city must speedily follow.

From the Pacific Coast.

San Francisco, April 7.—The Mazatlan TIMES, the Imperialist organ, gives the report that Juarez was *en route* for Cape St. Lucas, whence he would sail for San Francisco on his way to Washington. A correspondent of the San Francisco BULLETIN, however, writing from Mazatlan, March 4, says that Juarez is still at Chihuahua with his ministers, raising troops, though money, arms and ammunition are scarce. A French naval expedition has sailed, it was supposed, for Guaymas. An Imperial force has moved to Sinaloa.

New York State Legislature.

Senate.

Albany, April 8.—BILLS REPORTED.—For the protection of the New York Fire Department Fund. Incorporating the Subaqueous Metallic Dock and Pier Company. Repealing the act forbidding Supervisors from being Commissioners of Deeds. To provide for the payment of certain extraordinary expenses in Brooklyn.

BILLS PASSED.—The New York Riot Bonds Bill. The Poughkeepsie Bounty Bill. For the Protection of planted oysters in Queens County. Relative to the State Lunatic Asylum and Insane Female Convicts. Incorporating the Workingmen's Co-operative Association of Troy. To incorporate the New York and Brooklyn Turkish Bath Company. The Gettysburgh National Monument Bill. It appropriates $25,000.

The Third Avenue Railroad Extension Bill came up on its third reading, and was amended by providing that the company comply with the restrictions and regulations in force, and pay car license to the Corporation of New York, and was then laid aside.

A resolution was adopted requesting the return from the Assembly of the Second Avenue Railroad Extension Bill.

The New York and Brooklyn Storage Company Bill was lost, and a motion to reconsider the vote by which this was done was laid on the table.

Assembly.

BILLS PASSED.—Relative to the Howard Home for Little Wanderers in New York. Granting the consent of the State to the sale of certain lands in New York to the United States for a Custom-house.

The New York and Brooklyn Ferry Railroad Bill was then passed by—yeas, 78; nays, 31.

Relative to the Pacific Mail Steamship Company, to authorize an increase of capital stock; which was lost, 53 against 41. A motion to reconsider was laid on the table. Relative to criminal offences in the Metropolitan Police District, which prohibits carrying of concealed weapons without license from the Police Commissioners.

On motion of Mr. J. L. Smith, the bill relative to the fund of the Fire Department was referred to the Judiciary Committee, with power to report: complete.

REPORTS.—To authorize the establishment of a New York institution for the Blind; to amend the act to increase the capital stock of the Manhattan Gas Company. To enable the New York City Inspector more effectually to discharge his duties; complete. To incorporate the Elective Medical Society; complete. Also complete, relative to the fund of the New York Fire Department. To exempt the New York Ophalmic Society from taxation: complete.

PROCLAMATION BY GOV. FENTON.

Thursday, April 20th, named a Day of Thanksgiving for our Victories.

Albany, April 8.—Upon conferring with many prominent citizens of this State, Friday, the 14th inst., the day appointed by the President for the National ceremonies in raising the United States flag at Fort Sumter, was deemed a most appropriate occasion for thanksgiving, prayer and praise to Almighty God for our national successes and the bright prospects of returning peace and fraternal harmony. In deference, however, to the wishes now made known to me of many patriotic persons, representing some of our religious denominations, that the designated day be solely devoted to the solemn observance of Church service, I, Reuben E. Fenton, Governor of the State of New York, do therefore amend my proclamation, and set apart Thursday, the 20th inst., for the purposes recommended.

(Dated) April 8. (Signed) R. E. FENTON.

General Intelligence.

[By Mail to the New York Sun.]

OVER five hundred rebel officers, of all grades, are now in the Old Capitol Prison.

THE body of General Winthrop, killed in front of Petersburg, was brought to Washington on Saturday.

IT is a mistake to suppose Wilmington was left bare. Large quantities of cotton are being found in private houses, and both British and American gold abound there, and silver is not scarce.

THE Government has received notice that five thousand Union prisoners are at Darien, Ga., ready for exchange. This delivery will release very nearly all the Union prisoners in the far South.

IN Harwich, Mass., Saturday evening, while some citizens were loading a cannon, to fire a salute in honor of our recent victories, the gun went off prematurely, killing J. H. Robbins and J. M. Baker, and wounding Franklin Robbins.

THE Waterbury (Conn.) Machine Company's Works, and the Union Spectacle Factory, were destroyed by fire on Saturday morning. Loss about $50,000.

THE Navy Department is informed of the capture of the British schooner R. H. Vermilyea, by the steamer Quaker City. Cargo—Coffee, clothes, rum, tobacco, shoes, etc.

ABOUT twenty pilots, charged with having formerly been employed on blockade steamers running between the West Indies and Wilmington, N. C., have been arrested at the latter city.

ONE hundred Canadians passed through Worcester on Thursday, on their way to the mills at Wauregan, Connecticut. One couple, says the SPY, were blessed with a brood of twenty-three children, enough to run a small factory without other help.

THE Missouri REPUBLICAN, of the 6th inst., says: a letter has been received from a member of the Ninety-fifth Illinois infantry, stationed at New Orleans, stating that all but one hundred and seventy of that regiment perished in a storm, on the 28th ult., while on board a transport in the bay of Mobile.

LOCAL NEWS.

NEW YORK AND THE VICINITY.

THE SURRENDER OF LEE.

About half-past ten o'clock last evening, telegraphic dispatches were received at the SUN OFFICE announcing the surrender of General Lee and his whole army. Immediately the office was illuminatd, and a large placard announced the glad tidings. A crowd of people assembled in and around the office, who manifested their joy by repeated cheering and other demonstrations. Notwithstanding the lateness of the hour, the news was disseminated through the city, and wherever people were assembled in the hotels and other places, the liveliest expressions of joy were immediately exhibited.

PALM SUNDAY was celebrated yesterday in all the Catholic churches. At St. Patrick's Cathedral, Archbishop McCloskey was solemnly invested with the sacred "Pallium," a badge of authority conferred by the Pope of Rome. The ceremony was performed by Bishop Loughlin, of Brooklyn, who ascended the altar dressed in full canonicals. The Archbishop having descended from his throne and knelt before the Bishop, while he repeated in Latin the oath of fidelity to the Church, and his duties, the Pallium, which was carried on a cushion, was then handed to Bishop Loughlin, who placed it round the neck of the Archbishop. It is a kind of band, made of pure lambs' wool, about three inches in width, and portions hang down behind and before; it is white, and has black crosses on it. While investing the Archbishop, appropriate prayers were recited and the responses sung by the choir. Having performed the investiture, the Bishop descended from the altar, and the Archbishop took his place and pronounced the Apostolic benediction.

On Easter Sunday the Archbishop will give the Papal benediction by special authority, that being the only occasion on which he can give it.

THE FORT SUMTER CELEBRATION.—On Saturday the Government transport Arago sailed from the foot of Beach street, N. R., for Fort Sumter, where the old flag, which was lowered four years ago, will be raised once more amid the general rejoicing of the loyal people of the United States. The old flag, which has been for the last four years preserved in the vaults under the Bank of Commerce, was borne to the pier on a Post-office van, which was handsomely decorated with flags; it was enclosed in a box, and was given in charge of Sergeant Peter Hart, who, it will be remembered nailed the flag to the staff, but subsequently lowered it by command of General (then Major) Anderson, when the fort was about to be evacuated, and on him the honor will devolve of raising it again by the same order on Friday next, and by command of the same officer. On the same van was the original Fort Sumter mail-bag, addressed "Major Anderson, U. S. A., Fort Sumter, April 14, 1865." General Anderson, with his lady and four children, were early on board, as were General Dix and his daughter. As the Commandant of the Department of of the East appeared, several of the crowd took up his memorable words, "If any man attempt to haul down the American flag, shoot him on the spot," and he and General Anderson, were cheered lustily. The next notable persons who appeared were the Rev. Henry Ward Beecher, Wm. Lloyd Garrison, Senator Wilson, Theodore Tilton, George Thompson, and a number of other invited guests, among whom were Major Generals Crawford and Doubleday, who were also officers in the fort when it surrendered. Among the invited guests are found the names of Lieut.-General Scott, the Governors of all the loyal States and Territories, the President, Vice President, and Cabinet; the U. S. Supreme Court Judges, the Military Committee of the Senate, and a large number of ladies. The number of invitations altogether were two hundred, out of which number only thirty-one sent excuses. The remainder, including the members of the Cabinet, will go on board at Fortress Monroe. The Arago moved off at 12 o'clock precisely, amid the cheers of the multitude. God speed her on her mission. The following is a list of the officers who garrisoned the fort in 1861, with their rank then and now:

Major Robert Anderson	now	Major General.
Surgeon S. W. Crawford	"	do.
Capt. A. Doubleday	"	do.
Capt. T. Seymour	"	do.
1st Lieut. Jeff. C. Davis	"	do.
2d Lieut. J. N. Hall	"	1st Lieutenant.
Capt J. G. Foster	"	Major General.
1st Lieut. T. Talbot	"	1st Lieutenant.
1st Lieut. G. W. Snyder	"	do.
2d Lieut. R. K. Meade	"	do.

NAVAL.—The following steamers have arrived at this port:

United States steamer Vicksburg, from Hampton Roads. The Vicksburg has been actively engaged in blockade duty off Wilmington, and played a prominent part in the capture of that city.

Steam transport Merrimack, from New Orleans 22d inst., with 200 sick and wounded soldiers. A. Beach, Co. G, 9th N. Y. Cavalry; Simeon Walker, 21st N.Y. Battery; and E. Winnell, Co. C, 34th N. Y., died on the passage and were buried at sea.

Steamship Matanzas, from City Point, bringing 900 rebel prisoners, among whom are the following rebel officers; Col, Alfred Rhett, of Fort Sumter notoriety; Lieut. E. Mathews, 1st Reg. S. C.; Lieut. V. P. Mellard, aid-de-camp to Col. Rhett, and Alfred H. Dunkin, War Tax Collector, Confederate States. She reports that Admiral Porter arrived at City Point on the flag ship Malvern, on the 6th inst. from Richmond. The River Queen, (President Lincoln's boat) was at City Point when the Matanzas left.

A NEW RAILROAD LINE started running on Saturday evening, as follows: From foot of 14th st., N. R., to Hudson, through Hudson to Bleecker, and across Broadway to Crosby; through Crosby to Grand, and through Grand to Elm; thence through Elm to Reade, through Reade to Centre, and down through Park Row to Beekman; down Beekman to South, and through South to Fulton; up Fulton to William, through William to Ann, and thence through Park Row back. The tracks through Beekman, William and Ann streets are single; the others are double.

THE YEAR OF JUBILEE.—The colored folks of this city will celebrate on the 18th inst., in honor of the abolition of slavery in the District of Columbia and the bright prospects of emancipation generally. They propose to have a military parade, and an entertainment at Cooper Institute. They have invited General Butler, and several other laudators of their race, to be present.

THE SPECIAL COMMITTEE of the Common Council met on Saturday, and determined to test the legality of the Fire Department Act lately passed by the Legislature.

THE METHODIST EPISCOPAL CONFERENCE which has been in session for some days, adjourned on Saturday, after making a most important amendment to their articles of discipline, by which lay delegates will in future be admitted to the Conference and have a voice therein. Hitherto this was the only religious body in which the laws governing it were made entirely by the clergy.

RECRUITING.—The Volunteer Committee recruited about forty men on Saturday, and a considerable number were recruited by the provost marshals. To-day the Committee will cease mustering in men, and will send all applicants to the provost marshals, in accordance with a resolution already published.

CENTRAL PARK.—On Saturday, three buffaloes, a bull, cow and calf arrived here on board the steamer Hudson, from Morehead City, N. C. They were captured near Columbia, S. C., by the foragers of Gen. Wood's division, 14th Army Corps, during the recent grand march of Gen. Sherman northward, and sent to Gen. Meigs, who presented them to our Central Park Commissioners, and the animals are now located in the Park, and make a valuable addition to the zoological collection there.

THE BRITISH AMBASSADOR.—Sir Frederick Bruce, the new British Ambassador, who arrived here a few days ago, left for Washington at midnight on Saturday,

THE JEWISH PASSOVER.—This memorable feast of the Jews will commence this evening, and continue till sunset on Tuesday, the 18th inst.

SIMON STERN, Esq., will deliver the third of a series of lectures for the advancement of science and art, at the Cooper Union this evening. The subject for this evening is: "Strikes, Trade Unions and Friendly Societies."

A GIRL THAT WAS NOT A GIRL.—On Saturdey morning, an effeminate looking Canadian named James Day *alias* Jennie Lamont, who is only 18 years of age, was arrested by officer Barbalet, of the 15th Precinct, on a charge of disorderly conduct. Since January last the accused has been employed as a waiter girl, at No. 654 Broadway, and so discreet was his deportment that no suspicion of his sex was awakened until Friday night, when it is supposed that one of his female associates devulged his secret. For a year past the prisoner has been employed in other saloons on Broadway, during all of which time he has maintained his disguise so guardedly that he was not detected. In fact, it is stated that many of the patrons of the various dens were duped to such a degree, and infatuated to such an extent, that they took the festive youth out to supper, and riding through Central Park, besides paying him other flattering and seductive attentions. Justice Dodge committed the young scapegrace to prison, in default of $1,000 bail, but late on Saturday afternoon released him on his own reconnoisance, with an admonition not to repeat the offence.

FIRE.—About one o'clock yesterday morning a fire occurred among some old rags in the basement of the rear building 70 Thompson street, occupied by John Puster, rag and paper dealer. Damage to stock $25; to building $50; no insurance; cause unknown.

At 9½ o'clock last evening a fire broke out in a wooden shed used as a kitchen, in the rear of the two story house 176 William street. The first floor, occupied by L. Perrenot as a confectionery, was damaged by water to the amount of about $50. Damage to building about $50. The fire originated from the partition catching fire from a stove, which was placed against it.

BROOKLYN.

THE FURMAN STREET DISASTER—INVESTIGATION BEFORE THE CORONER.—The investigation into the circumstances connected with the recent disaster in Furman street, whereby four persons lost their lives, was commenced before the Coroner and a jury on Saturday afternoon. Several witnesses were examined.

James S. Smith, residing in Portland avenue, near Dekalb, testified that he was on the roof of the burning building, with others, and while there, was cautioned to step back. Some 20 or 30 men were on the roof at the time. Mr. George Harland cautioned them to leave. The firemen remained. They were playing on the fire. A minute or two after the warning the roof fell in. There was some one who directed the movements of the firemen, but heard no orders given.

Wm. Wessels, of 158 York street, Jersey City, testified that he was upon the roof of the burning building, 93 Furman street; told the Chief Engineer that it was useless to throw any water there, and was told to mind his own business. Some one cautioned him that the roof was in danger of falling any minute. The caution was loud enough to be heard by all. The firemen were apparently doing no good there, as they were throwing the water into the street. After the caution, most of the citizens left. Was just in the rear when the roof went in. Labored under the impression that the Chief Engineer went down with the rest.

E. D. Herbert, of No. 90 Hicks street, heard the Chief give an order, and supposed it to be an order to vacate the roof, some 10 or 15 minutes before the accident.

Robert Barr, Assistant Engineer, testified that he was present at the fire, but heard no orders given for the people to get off the roof. Had been at the fire about half an hour when the roof fell in, and assisted several men out of the ruins. The question of the security of these buildings had never been raised among the firemen to his knowledge. Had no conversation with the Chief Engineer that night, and did not consider that there was any danger. Did not know the Chief was there at the time the roof fell in. Did not think it safe to have a covering of earth on these buildings.

George Golgan, of No. 7 Engine, testified that the Chief Engineer ordered the men on the roof to cease playing, as they were throwing the water on those below. As the order was not obeyed, he went on the roof himself. The fire had been burning about half an hour at the time. In a few minutes thereafter the Chief Engineer gave the order to stop playing the roof fell in.

The inquisition will be resumed this afternoon at one o'clock.

THE DRAFT.—The draft was resumed in the 3d district on Saturday, and the names of those enrolled in the Second Ward were put in the wheel and drawn out. Among those drawn are C. Jerome Hopkins, the artist, and Mr. James Farley, sergeant, of the 14th regiment.

MARINE NEWS.

April 10—S. Rises, 5 29—S. Sets, 6 34—M'n sets..05 04.

ARRIVED.

STEAMSHIPS—United States, Morehead City; Merrimack, New Orleans; Star of the South, Beaufort, via Fortress Monroe; Zodiac, Beaufort; Granada, Norfolk, Va: Hudson, Beaufort, N C, via Fortress Monroe; Meteor, Fortress Monroe; Ben Deford, Hatteras Inlet; John Gibson, Alexandria; Vicksburg, [U. S. gunboat] Hampton Roads; Ellen S Terry, Newbern, NC, via Fortress Monroe: Matanzas, City Point, via Fortress Monroe.

SHIP—Southampton, Whitney, London, with mds.

BARKS—Sea Gem, Cardiff, via Boston; Rechabite, Trinidad, Cuba.

BRIGS—D B Doane, Trinidad, Cuba; T H A Pitt, Bermuda: Onda, Para; Maple Valley, Cienfuegos; Water Lily, Rio Grande del Sud; Grace Worthington, Belize; Tasso, Castellamare; Angostura, Cindad Bol.

SCHOONERS—Hendrick Fish, Virginia; Hope, Mayaguez, P R; Bessie, Arroyo, P R; H W Godfrey, Norfolk; America, Virginia; Washington, do; Elias Dudley, Providence; United Brothers, New Haven; Fawnee; Newburg for Providence; John R McFeo, Albany for Bridgeport; O E Jones, New Haven; Higgins, Providence; Henrietta, Hartford; J H Hine, N Haven; J S Swan, Wellfleet; M C Town, New Haven; Geddes, Newport; James Parker, New London; Minnesota, Providence; Annie J Purcell, Northport for Baltimore; Petrel, New Haven for Elizabethport; Helen P, Hartford; Ruth Halsey, New London for Albany; Roxanna Burley, New Haven; John H Bell, Westerly for Newburg; Farmer, Northport; Chase, Providence for Elizabethport.

BELOW—Bark Rechabite, of New Glasgow; S B Doane, of Bangor, from Trinidad.

Too Late for Classification.

BOUNTIES PAID FIREMEN AND SEAmen for U. S. Navy; $600 for a substitute for one year. Apply to T. NEWTON, 6 Wall st. 375

TO BAKERS—WANTED A FIRST RATE man on bread and cake. Apply 128 Fulton ave, Brooklyn. 377

WANTED—OPERATORS ON SHOP AND infantry pants, a girl to learn the trade, and a girl for housework. Call all this week at 101 East 15th st, bet. 2d and 3d aves. 378

WANTED—AN OPERATOR ON HOWE'S or Singer's machine; a young man preferred. Call at 217 South First st, Williamsburgh.
374 JAMES O'BRIEN.

WANTED—2 GOOD CARRIAGE SMITHS. Apply to A. WILKEY, 32 Boerum st, Brooklyn. 376

FOR SALE AND TO LET.

FOR SALE OR TO LET, 320 NINTH AVE, 4 story brick house and store, bet. 30th and 31st sts. Apply to J. & W. DENHAM, 8th ave, cor 16th st, from 8 in the morning to 9 in the evening. 256

A FARM OF 23 ACRES FOR $460, NEAR the L. I. R. R., 40 miles from N. Y., land level and fertile, produces good crops, is well adapted to raising market truck, fruit, &c.; more land if wanted, at $20 an acre. E. A. BUNCE, 7 Chambers st. 13

A GOOD SIZED STORE AND BACK-rooms to let, at 115 Baxter st. One of the best stands for a grocery or other business in the 14th Ward. 90

FOR SALE AT A BARGAIN—4 Substantial brick houses in Williamsburgh; rents monthly in advance. Inquire at 23 Concord st, Brooklyn, at 6 o'clock P. M. Terms easy—title good. 302

FOR SALE VERY LOW, WITH OR Without furniture, the splendid residence No. 66 Columbia st, Brooklyn Heights, overlooking the Bay of New York, and commanding a magnificent view in every direction. Brown stone front and modern improvements. Lot 29 by 150, extending from Columbia to Furman st. The front on Furman st consists of a solid stone arched fire-proof building. Apply in Brooklyn to S. HONDLOW, Montague and Court st, or to A. E. BEACH, care of MUNN & CO., 37 Park Row, N. Y. 448

FOR SALE—A FARM OF 80 ACRES, 60 improved, 20 miles from Newburgh, 12 miles from Middletown, ½ mile from village, stores, school, church, postoffice, &c. $1000 cash required. Immediate possession. J. E. HATCH, 375 9th ave. 110

FOR SALE—THE 3-STORY, HIGH STOOP, brick house and lot, No. 355 East 10th st. House 20 ft. 10 in. by 40. Lot half the block. $3,500 can remain on bond and mortage. Title perfect. Possession May 1st, 1865. Apply as per bill on the premises. 410

FOR SALE—A TWO STORY HOUSE AND lot for $1,000; one for $1,550; also a new two story and basement, 7 rooms with grates, marble mantles, folding doors; terms to suit the purchaser. P. McCABE, 18th st, Seventh ave, Brooklyn. 301

FOR SALE CHEAP—A NEAT 2-STORY and attic frame house, with extension, a good cellar, gas, water, marble mantels, &c. complete. Terms easy. Inquire of G. DITMARS, Builder, 62 Eleventh st, Williamsburgh, L. I. 357

FOR SALE CHEAP—IN WILLIAMSburgh, a new two-story basement and attic frame house, with ten rooms. Enquire of H. BRUNDAGE, 21 Devoe st. 255

TO LET—THE 2D FLOOR OF A 2-STORY house, in Bowden ave, South Bergen, N J.; 4 nice rooms, with a large attic, suitable for a small family, 3d house from cor. of Monticello ave, on South side; horse R. R. cars pass within 50 yards, every 10 minutes during the day, to and from Jersey City. Rent, $9 per month. Inquire there or at 50 Rose st, N. Y. 446

TO LET OR LEASE—147 AND 149 WEST 35th st, between Broadway and 7th ave, suitable for manufacturing or stable purposes. For further particulars apply to WM. D. ANDREWS & BRO., 414 Water st. 348

THE DRAFT—THE SUBSCRIBER OFFERS his farm, situated in the pleasant village of Selden, L. I., 2 miles from depot, and 45 miles from the city, consisting of a new house, 22x26, extension 12x12, 1½ story high, 30 acres cleared land, good growth locust, no incumbrance on it; price $1,600; terms easy; possession immediately. For further particulars address E. EDWARDS, Patchogue, Long Island. Good barn, new, 22x22. 428

TO LET CHEAP, IN VIEW OF CENTRAL Park, apartments for small families without children; from $4 to $5 a month. Inquire cor. 9th ave and 100th st, in the store. 325

TO LET—THE TWO UPPER STORIES OF LYON & ISAAC'S Drilling Machine Factory, No. 9 Jane st, suitable for a segar maker, chair seater and other business, or for storage. Apply on the premises. 19

TO LET—THE UPPER PART OF A 2-story cottage on Broadway, near Central Park, suitable for a gentleman and wife. 190

$500 THOUSAND WORTH OF REAL Estate for sale on the lines of the New Jersey R. R., Perth Amboy and Woodbridge and New Jersey Central R. R., embracing some 40 farms and as many houses and lots, in towns. The greater number of these pleasant and healthy homes are within one hour of the foot of Cortlandt st, New York. J. A. MARTIN, Real Estate Agent, Rahway, N. J. 104

$1100 WILL BUY A NICE, SMALL farm of 19 acres, with house and barn, in Jersey, 20 miles from the city. Apply to PAYTEN, 95 Division st. 278

$4400 WILL BUY A 4-STORY BRICK house and lot in the 13th Ward; $2,000 cash. $3,500 will buy a nice 3-story brick house and lot in Yorkville; $1,500 cash. Possession May 1st. Apply to PAYTEN, 95 Division st. 277

$2100 WILL BUY A TWO STORY house and lot, near depot and horse cars in Morrissania. Apply quickly to depot master, Melrose. Take steam cars from 26th st. Not at home on Sundays. 429

SEWING MACHINES.

SEWING MACHINE DEPOT, NO. 939 BROADWAY,
Corner Twenty-second-st,
(up-stairs,)
where may be found a complete assortment of Wheeler & Wilson's
SEWING MACHINES,
SILKS,
COTTON,
NEEDLES, &c.
Operators with Machines by the day or week (competent to do family sewing).
Machines to rent by the month.
Machines repaired, and instruction given in their use.
ESPECIAL ATTENTION is called to the completeness of the adjusting and repairing department.
The complete success of the Subscriber in accommodating all up-town residents during the past year, has only been measured by an ability to give entire publicity of the conveniences of such an establishment. With greater facilities for the coming year, any increase of patronage will receive the same prompt attention as formerly.
N. B.—The Manufacturers' Depot for the sale of BROWN'S celebrated Patent BABY-TENDER.
443 J. T. ELLIS.

SEWING MACHINES, ALL FIRST CLASS machines, new and 2d hand, for sale, to rent or exchange. Machines sold on part payment. Machines bought and repaired, at 335 Broadway, up stairs, room 3, over book store. 419

SEWING MACHINES FOR SALE AND TO Let.—Singer's and Wheeler & Wilson's, always on hand, also cash paid for second hand machines. Sewing machine trimmings at 186 Rivington st. 402

SEWING MACHINES—2 WHEELER AND Wilson's machine in perfect order; also 1 Singer machine, No. 2, for sale cheap at 165 West 39th st. 164

BOARD AND ROOMS.

HOTEL GARNI—ON THE EUROPEAN plan, for gentlemen only. Nice furnished bedrooms, each a separate room, from $1 25 to $1 75 per week; double bedrooms from $2 to $6 per week, 135 East 38th st, near 3d avenue. 429

FURNISHED FRONT ROOMS, WITH every convenience for housekeeping for gentleman and wife. No children taken, Americans preferred. Apply at 366 Grand st., private entrance. 147

TO LET—A NEATLY FURNISHED 3D story front room, with closet attached, in a private family. Satisfactory references required. Apply 229 West 28th st. 3

DENTISTRY.

A MOST WONDERFUL DISCOVERY—Teeth extracted without pain, or no charge. Beautiful teeth inserted, $1 each. Teeth inserted with or without extracting the roots. All operations warranted. J. JAY VILLERS, 155 Grand st., 2 blocks from Broadway. 342

BEAUTIFUL AND USEFUL—TEETH ON silver or gold, $1 to $2 each tooth; rubber, full sets, $15 to $20. Teeth extracted without pain, or filled with gold or other fillings, 50 cents upwards. All cases warranted. By Dr. H. VILLERS, 43 Bowery, opposite the old Theatre. 343

AMUSEMENTS.

BARNUM'S AMERICAN MUSEUM,
AFTERNOON AT 3. EVENING AT 7½.
MAREMMA OF MADRID;
Or, THE MAN, SPIRIT, AND MORTAL.
Splendid Scenery, Costumes and Music.
Great Dancing Giraffe..............TONY DENIER.
MORNING AT 11.—PUNCH and JUDY.
Clog Dance, Fancy Dances, Songs.
80 LIFE SIZE MOVING WAX FIGURES.
Wax figure from life of the Rebel Spy,
ROBERT C. KENNEDY.
PETROLEUMANIA. PETROLEUMANIA.
A working model of a pumping well.
Prof. HUTCHINGS, LIGHTNING CALCULATOR.
WOODROFFE'S BOHEMIAN GLASS BLOWERS
TWO GLASS STEAM ENGINES in motion.
Fat Woman, Giantess, Circassian Girl, Dwarf, Living Otters, Grand Aquaria, a million curiosities. Admission 30 cents. Children under ten 15 cents. 118
GRAND NATIONAL POULTRY, PIGEON AND RABBIT SHOW, April 24th, $500 PREMIUMS. Send for circulars.

COOPER UNION FOR THE ADVANCEment of Science and Art. The third lecture of the free course, given under the supervision of the Board of Trustees, by SIMON STERN, Esq., will be delivered at the large Hall of the Institute, on Monday evening, April 10th, at 8 o'clock, P. M. Subject—"Strikes, Trades' Unions, and Friendly Societies." Working men are cordially invited to attend. Admittance free to all.
107 ABRAM S. HEWITT, Secretary.

GRAND BILLIARD EXPOSITION.—
FOR TWO NIGHTS ONLY,
TUESDAY AND WEDNESDAY,
APRIL 11 AND 12,
at the
HALL OF THE UNION,
COOPER INSTITUTE.
The wonderful
M. CARME,
from Paris and Versailles, assisted by
M. PHELAN
and
W. GOLDTHWAITE,
will give two Seances, as above, demonstrating the Science of Billiards, including the remarkable power of the "masse" and other difficult shots.
Seats will be reserved for gentlemen accompanied by ladies. Commencing at Eight o'clock P.M. precisely.
TICKETS ONE DOLLAR EACH. 270

THE HIPPOTHEATRON—HAVE YOU BEEN TO THE CIRCUS?
14th Street, opposite the Academy of Music,
IF NOT, GO!
Matinees every Wednesday and Saturday. 338

VARIETIES THEATRE, 37 & 39 BOWERY.
Grand double company, first week of the great Thompson & Kenna. First week of Master Winter Ravel of the Ravel Troupe. Donnelly's half hour of Fun, Doctor O'Toole. The Meddlesome Monkey. Fifty new acts. Matinee Wednesday and Saturday. 132

INSTRUCTION.

A—BOOKKEEPING, WRITING, ARITHmetic, spelling and grammar. Course of instruction costs $10 to $20. Apply at PAINE'S Old Established Academy, 62 Bowery. Open every day and evening throughout the year. 266

TOWNSEND'S ACADEMY, 260 BOWERY, below Houston st. Open day and evening. Students thoroughly drilled in Bookkeeping, Arithmetic, Algebra, Writing, Spelling, Grammar, &c. Those whose early education has been neglected receive private instruction. Ladies' Department. 331

GENERAL BUSINESS.

CARPETS, OILCLOTHS, MATTINGS, &c., selling off low for cash, at 452 Canal st.—Tapestry, 3-plys, ingrain, stair matting, fine oilcloth, rugs, door mats, stair druggets, &c. Old carpets taken in exchange. 414

CARPETS, CARPETS, OILCLOTHS AND Furniture.—$200,000 worth at an immense sacrifice, at the large establishment of H. O'FARRELL, 267, 269 and 271 West 35th st, cor. 8th ave. 351

ENFEEBLED AND DELICATE CONSTITUtions, of both sexes, use HELMBOLD'S Extract Buchu. It will give brisk and energetic feelings and enable you to sleep well. 386

FOR NON-RETENTION OR INCONTINence, irritation, inflammation or ulceration of the bladder, or kidneys, diseases of the prostrate glands, stone in the bladder, calculus, gravel or brick-dust deposit, and all diseases of the bladder, kidneys an dropsical swellings,
USE HELMBOLD'S FLUID EXTRACT BUCHU.

LEAKY ROOFS CURED WITH RUBBE paint, 1 to 1½ cents per foot, according to co dition, and warranted. No. 596 Grand st, No. 5 Beeman st, No. 153 Bowery, No. 375 Ninth ave, No. 5 Sixth ave, No. 48 Eighth ave, No. 25 Pine st, room No. 11 South 7th st, Williamsburgh, and cor. Oxfo st. and Fulton ave, Brooklyn. 404

PAWNBROKERS' TICKETS PURCHASE of clothing, dry goods, &c. A large lot of rea made clothing on hand. Business coats, $3 to $ black frocks, $5 to $20; cassimere pants, $3 to $ vests, $1 to $6. GEO. LEVIE, 427 Broome st.

THE HIGHEST CASH PRICE PAID F old newspapers, pamphlets, books and wa paper of every description. STOCKWELL & F ERSON, 25 Ann st, 1 door west of Nassau. 327

THE YOUNG LADIES MARRIAGE P tion Association, office 247 Broadway, room This association is formed to promote and encou early and happy marriages by presenting each m ber with an elegant set of Furniture, valued at on her wedding day. N. B. Circulars sent by giving full explanations and information free. P send for circulars.

WHITEWASHING, KALSOMINING, pet-shaking and house-cleaning done by TURNER, 96 West 30th st. All orders prompt tended to. 40

SHIPPING.

BILLS £1 AND UPWARDS,
Union Bank of London, and
Royal Bank of Ireland,
For sale by
365 WELLS, FARGO & C

EMIGRATION FROM ENGLAND, LAND, &c, by STEAMSHIPS AND SA PACKETS,
At reduced rates.
TAPSCOTT, BROS. & CO.'S CELEBRATED OF LONDON AND LIVERPOOL PACKE
Sailing every five days.
Drafts, payable throughout England, Ireland land and Wales, at the lowest possible rates.
TAPSCOTT, BROS. & CO.,
319 86 South st, New Yo

FOR LIVERPOOL—TAPSCOTT'S L The favorite clipper ship ATMOSPHER Thursday, April 13. For passage, apply to
TAPSCOTT, BROS. & CO., 86 So
FOR LONDON—X LINE.
Ship VILLA FRANCA sails April 11.

PASSAGE FROM AND TO LIVER and London—By the Old Black Star Lin Liverpool, the CONSTITUTION sails on Apr For London, The CON. GRINNELL, Apri For passage apply to WILLIAM & GUION, st.

PASSAGE CERTIFICATES AT RE rates to and from Liverpool, Glasgow, Der fast, Dublin, Cork, Galway, &c, by Mail S and first class Packet Ships. Also drafts sol est rates payable in Great Britain and Ire ELEAZER JONES & CO, Agents, 23 Broad

STEAM TO QUEENSTOWN AND POOL.—VIRGINIA, sails Saturday, A HELVETIA sails April 22d. Cabin passage age $25, gold or equivalent in currency. WILLIAMS & GUION, 29 Broadway.

PERSONAL NOTICE

BRIDGET COSTELLO — INFOR wanted of her by her sister, ANN, 24 st, N. Y.

BALM OF WHITE LILLIES—T cellent preparation for skin diseases, su ples, Blotches, Tan, &c., can always be obta South Second st, Williamsburgh, and at ave, New York. Price 35 cents per bottle.

INFORMATION WANTED OF FARAHER, who lately resided at 8 F Any information of her will be thankful by her farther, PATRICK FARAHER, at ton st, N. Y.

LEFT HIS HOME, SATURDAY, 25th, a boy 13 years of age, named MIDMER; had on grey clothes, cloth cap left cheek near his ear. Any informat thankfully received by his afflicted pare address R. MIDMER, 371 Carleton ave, B

REUBEN PLASS, ESQ., PLEAS your address to J. M., box 903 Sun off

GROCERIES.

GO TO THOMAS R AGNEW, 260 Greenwich st, cor. of Murry st, and wil find teas, coffees, fish, flour and ever cheaper than any store in New York house.

THE RICHMOND WHIG.

VOL. 1---NO. 6. RICHMOND, VA., APRIL 10, 1865. PRICE: FIVE CENTS.

Another Great Battle Fought.

VICTORY FOR GENERAL SHERIDAN.

Defeat of General Lee's Army.

[illegible] GENERALS PRISONERS.

[illegible] KERSHAW AMONG THEM.

Thousands of Prisoners Taken.

LARGE CAPTURES OF ARTILLERY.

SHERIDAN'S ACCOUNT OF THE FIGHT.

HE "ROUTED THEM HANDSOMELY."

THINKS "LEE WILL SURRENDER."

Continued Retreat of the Enemy.

SHERIDAN STILL PURSUING.

WAR DEPARTMENT,
WASHINGTON, April 7, 10 A. M.

Major General Dix, New York:

General Sheridan attacked and routed Lee's army yesterday, capturing Generals Ewell, Kershaw, Button, Corse, and many general officers, several thousand prisoners, and a large number of cannon, and expects to force Lee to surrender all that is now left of his army. Details will be given as speedily as possible, but the telegraph is working badly.

(Signed) EDWIN M. STANTON.

[SECOND DESPATCH.]

WAR DEPARTMENT,
WASHINGTON, April 7—11 A. M.

Major-General Dix, New York:

The following telegrams, announcing the victory won yesterday by Major-General Sheridan over Lee's army, have just been received.

EDWIN M. STANTON,
Secretary of War.

FROM THE PRESIDENT.

CITY POINT, 8.35 A. M., April 7.

To the Honorable Secretary of War:

At 11.15 P. M. yesterday, at Burkesville Station, General Grant sends me the following from General Sheridan.

[Signed] A. LINCOLN.

SHERIDAN'S DESPATCH.

April 6—11.15 P. M.

Lieutenant-General Grant:

I have the honor to report that the enemy made a stand at the intersection of the Burk's Station road with the road upon which they were retreating. I attacked them with two divisions of the Sixth Army Corps and routed them handsomely.

Making a connection with the cavalry, I am still pressing on with both cavalry and infantry.

Up to the present time we have captured Generals Ewell, Kershaw, Button, Corse, De Bare and Custis Lee; several thousand prisoners, fourteen pieces of artillery, with caissons, and a large number of wagons.

If the thing is pressed I think Lee will surrender.

(Signed) P. H. SHERIDAN,
Major General Commanding.

[THIRD DESPATCH.]

CITY POINT, 9 A. M., April 7.

Hon. Secretary of War:

The following further particulars is just received.

(Signed) A. LINCOLN.

BURKESVILLE, VA., April 3.

To His Excellency A. Lincoln,
President of the United States:

The following despatches are respectfully forwarded for your information.

(Signed) U. S. GRANT,
Lieutenant General.

DETAILS.

SECOND ARMY CORPS, April 6—7:30 P. M.

Major-General A. S. Webb:

Our last fight, just before dark, at Sailors' Creek, gave us two guns and three flags, a considerable number of prisoners, two hundred wagons and seventy ambulances, with mules and horses to the number of about one-half the wagons and ambulances.

There are between thirty and fifty wagons in addition abandoned or destroyed along the road, some battery wagons, forges and limbers.

I have already reported to you the capture of one gun, two flags and some prisoners, and the fact that the road for over ten miles is strewed with tents, baggage, cooking utensils, some ammunition and material of all kinds.

The wagons are across the approach to the bridges, and it will take some time to clear it.

The enemy is in position on the heights beyond with artillery. The bridge is partially destroyed, and the approaches on the other side are of soft bottom land.

We cannot advance to-morrow in the same manner as we have to-day. As soon as I get my troops up a little (we are considerably mixed), I might push a column down the road and deploy it; but it is evident that I cannot follow rapidly during the night. (Signed) A. A. HUMPHREYS,
Major General.

FROM GENERAL MEADE.

HEADQUARTERS OF GENERAL MEADE,
10 P. M., April 6.

Lieutenant General Grant:

At daylight this morning I moved the Second, Fifth and Sixth Army Corps above the railroad in the direction of Amelia Court House.

It was understood that the cavalry would operate on the extreme left. The changes were promptly made.

Soon after morning reliable intelligence was received that the enemy was moving towards Farmville. The direction of the Second and Fifth Army Corps was immediately changed from a northerly to a northwesterly direction, and the directing Corps, the Second, moving on Deatonville, and the Fifth, heretofore in the centre, moved on the right of Second, and the Sixth facing about and moving by the left flank, taking position on the left of the Second.

The Second Army Corps soon becoming engaged with the enemy near Deatonville, driving him by the right across Sailor's Creek to the Appomattox.

The Fifth Army Corps made a long march, but the position prevented it striking the enemy's column before it had passed.

The Sixth Army Corps came up with the enemy about 4 P. M., and, in conjunction with the Second on its right and the cavalry on its left, attacked and routed the enemy, capturing many prisoners. Among them Lieut. Gen. Ewell and Gen. Custis Lee.

I transmit a despatch from Gens. Humphreys and Wright, which, in justice to these distinguished officers and the gallant corps they commanded, I beg may be sent to the War Department for immediate publication.

It is impossible at this moment to give any estimate of the casualties on either side, or of the number of prisoners taken, but it is evident that to-days work is going to be one of the most important of the recent brilliant operations.

The pursuit will be continued so soon as the men have a little rest. General Griffin, with the Fifth Army Corps, will be moved by the left, and Wright and Humphreys continue the direct pursuit as long as it promises success.

(Signed) GEO. G. MEADE,
Major General.

DESPATCH OF GEN. WRIGHT.

HEADQ'RS SIXTH ARMY CORPS,
April 6, 10, P. M.

Maj. Gen. Webb, Chief of Staff, Army of Potomac:

In pursuance with instructions of this morning from Maj. Gen. Meade, I moved by way of Jetersville, by the shortest practicable road to the left of Deatonville, with the object of there taking position on the left of the Second Army Corps, striking the road running from Deatonville to Burke's Station.

At a point little to the southward of the former place, I found that the Second Army Corps was engaged to front and right, and the cavalry heavily to my left. Moving down the road towards Burke's Station, perhaps a mile, and turning sharp to the right, I proceeded across toward a nearly parallel road, on which the enemy was moving, and along which he had thrown up a line of intrenchments. As soon as the leading division (Gen. Seymour's) could be formed, it was moved up on the road held by the enemy, which was carried. Then turning to the left it was advanced down the road against a pretty strong resistance. By this time Wheeton's Division was put in position as rapidly as possible on Seymour's left. The lines were again advanced, and we swept down the road for a distance of about two miles, arriving at a deep and difficult creek. We found the enemy had reformed his line on the opposite side, where we attacked and drove them to a point a distance of half a mile further.

In the first attack a portion of the cavalry operated on our right flank. In its subsequent attacks the mass of cavalry operated on our left and the right flank of the enemy.

The result has been a complete success. The combined forces captured five general officers, among them Generals Ewell and Custis Lee, and large numbers of other prisoners.

I shall go into camp about two miles beyond this point and await instructions.

The First and Third divisions—Wheaton's and Seymour's—engaged to-day, behaved splendidly.—A return of casualties will be forwarded as soon as possible. The corps has nobly sustained the reputation it earned on the 2d inst., as well as upon many previous hard-fought battle-fields.

H. S. WRIGHT,
Major-General Commanding.

From the New York Herald.

NEWS FROM WASHINGTON.

WASHINGTON, April 6, 1865.

THE HEALTH OF SECRETARY SEWARD.

Secretary Seward's condition is much improved to-day from what it was last night, and he is now as comfortable as can be expected. In addition to the other injuries sustained by Secretary Seward, it was discovered to-day that his right jaw had been fractured. He was comparatively easy this afternoon.

AFFAIRS IN THE SHENANDOAH VALLEY.

A letter from Winchester, dated yesterday, states that the cavalry, under the command of Gen. Torbert, which started up the valley on the 3d inst., had not returned. As far as heard from they had met with no considerable body of rebels. The report that a large body of rebel infantry and cavalry had been seen in the vicinity of Strasburg was believed to be without foundation. Every precaution is being taken, however, to prevent a surprise or repel any attack that might be attempted. The roads are in good condition, and the Army of the Middle Military Division is ready for a move in any direction where their services may be required.—The One Hundred and Sixty-fifth regiment, New York Volunteers, or Second Zouaves, as they are more generally known, which has been doing duty as provost guard at Winchester for the last four months, has been relieved by the Fifth New York artillery. Their departure was much regretted by the citizens, the officers and men, by their gentlemanly behavior and soldier-like conduct, having won the respect of every citizen.

PURSUIT OF THE CAPTURED STEAMER HARRIET DE FORD.

Three hours after information (yesterday) reached the Navy Department of the capture of the steamboat Harriet Deford, eight or ten vessels had started in pursuit of the pirates.

PAYMENT OF SHERMAN'S TROOPS.

All the funds required to pay Gen. Sherman's army in full will be ready by the middle of next week. It will require eleven millions of dollars for this purpose.

SERENADE BY A REBEL BAND.

Among the arrivals of deserters to-day was a full band, which delivered themselves up with their instruments at Petersburg. It is composed principally of musicians from the bands of the 12th Virginia and 45th North Carolina rebel regiments. They had secreted themselves for ten days in Petersburg, awaiting an opportunity to desert, which was afforded them upon the occupation of that city by the Union troops. This afternoon, after taking the oath of allegiance, the band proceeded, in their rebel uniforms, to serenade Maj. Gen. Augur, commanding this department, and afterwards to the War Department, to compliment Secretary Stanton. The earnestness with which they gave the tune, "Ain't you glad you are out of the wilderness?" attracted much attention.

THE TOBACCO SPECULATORS.

The War Department has been literally besieged to-day by a whole brigade of tobacco speculators, anxious to obtain passes to Richmond to buy tobacco. It is asserted that some special trade permits were granted, but the most of the applicants were advised to wait until the wounded soldiers in the recent battles had been properly cared for.

FRENCH CLAIM ON SLIDELL'S PROPERTY.

Some time ago Slidell, the Rebel representative at Paris, gave a mortgage to a French banker for sixty thousand dollars upon his property in New Orleans. The banker now claims the property under the laws of Louisiana, and suit is to be instituted in the United States Court, and it will be made a test case. Interesting and important legal points will be raised under the Confiscation act, the decision of which will govern similar cases hereafter.

HEALTH OF SECRETARY SEWARD.

WASHINGTON, April 7.—Secretary Seward is rather more comfortable to-day than yesterday.—His injuries are painful, but exhibit no unfavorable symptoms.

[illegible]

Grafton D. Hanson has been appointed chief clerk of the Paymaster General's office. He is represented to be a gentleman of courteous manners and well qualified for that position of trust and responsibility.

Another despatch to the *Herald*, dated 6th inst., says:

The railroad from Aquia Creek via Fredericksburg to Richmond is to be immediately rebuilt. It is expected that one thousand laborers will go to Aquia Creek to-morrow to relay the track from that place to Fredericksburg. The grading of the road has not been materially injured, and the old and most direct route will be reopened in a short time.

A number of capitalists here and in New York have already filed an application to establish a national bank at Richmond, and it will probably be done in a short time.

A refugee who arrived here to-day from Fredericksburg states that the conscripting officers in that section are more active than ever, in conscripting citizens and arresting deserters, since the evacuation of Richmond. Every house in Fredericksburg is crowded with people from Richmond, who fled from there on the evacuation of the place.

Colonel D. H. Strother, "Porte Crayon," having resigned his commission in the army, is preparing his recollections of the campaigns in which he has taken part in the present war, which will be accompanied by illustrations from the artist's own pencil. Colonel Strother's experience includes the first seizure of Harper's Ferry, Ball's Bluff, Cedar Mountain, the second Bull Run campaign, South Mountain, Antietam, the Port Hudson and Red River campaigns of General Banks in Louisiana General Sigel's march up the Shenandoah Valley to New market, and General Hunter's foray to Lynchburg.

Begging is in China a sacred trade; in many cities the beggar-king gains as much as 100,000 taels yearly. At festivals, and especially at wedding ceremonies, which last for three days, he sends a deputation to the house of the bride and bridegroom, who are obliged to pay them the stipulated ransom. If they refuse the extortion, they have their dwellings invaded by several scores of dirty rascals, whom they are presently willing to pay any price to get rid of.

The Maryland Legislature has repealed nearly all of the old acts of that State oppressive to the colored population, which used to be so cruelly enforced in this district. Among them were the laws "prohibiting meetings of negroes for religious purposes, unless conducted by a white person;" "prohibiting trade with free negroes." "prohibiting the navigation of vessels by negroes;" and "prohibiting negroes to keep a dog or gun without license."

A Springfield physician was called upon to attend a soldier's widow through a long and severe attack of pneumonia. He rode six miles for every visit during some of the severest weather of the past winter, and on her recovery presented her with his bill of nearly $50, receipted in full, "In consideration of services rendered him and his country by her lamented husband."

Large quantities of pure white alabaster, of the finest quality, are taken from the Mammoth Cave, and manufactured into ornaments of various kinds, such as necklaces, breastpins, ear-rings, crosses, charms, etc. This substance is susceptible of the highest polish, and the ornaments into which it is converted are greatly admired for their brilliancy and beauty.

The postoffice at Hampton, Elizabeth county, has been opened by order of the Postoffice Department, and Kennon Whiting is appointed postmaster.

The War Department has ordered the Examining Board, of which Major-General Casey is President, to immediately adjourn to Richmond, Va.

FROM PETERSBURG AND THE ARMY.

A letter in the New York *Herald* from Dinwiddie C. H., 3d inst., (Mr. C. H. Hannam,) says that the deputation from Petersburg to surrender the city were met by General Edwards and Colonel Nagle, corps and division officers of the day, and also by Major M. L. Butterfield, of General Wheaton's staff. The Mayor handed them a letter for transmission to General Grant or any other general officer, stating that the city had been abandoned by Lee's army and would be surrendered to our troops. The letter was forwarded to Major-General Wright, who returned an answer stating that General Parke had already entered the city from the other side, and any further proceedings were unnecessary.—The Mayor then returned, and was accompanied to his house by Major Butterfield, where Roger A. Pryor was met, who stated that he had abandoned the Southern Confederacy, as he believed the cause was a complete failure.

The same correspondent says:

ENTHUSIASTIC RECOGNITION OF MAJOR GENERAL MEADE.

During a temporary halt this afternoon Major General George B. Meade passed the Sixth corps on his way to the front. He was recognized by the men and greeted with loud and enthusiastic cheers. For a short time the scene was one which can be better imagined than described, so great was the enthusiasm inspired by the presence of the Commander of the Army of the Potomac. Caps were waved and lusty cheers given in a manner which is only seen and heard when thousands of soldiers are greeting a commander who has won their confidence and respect. General Meade returned the greeting of the Sixth corps by repeated bows, although compelled to bestow considerable attention on the management of the spirited horse he was riding. On reaching the spot where Gen. Wheaton was standing he reined in his horse, and said to him, laughingly, "The Sixth corps men are in such good spirits that they seem determined to break my neck," to which General Wheaton replied that he imagined they were proud of their success; when Gen. Meade, with much feeling, said;—"Yes, we all know, and the country shall know, that the Sixth corps did the business. To them we owe our success, and we feel very grateful to them for it."

RECOGNITION OF GEN. WRIGHT'S SERVICES.

The valuable services which Gen. Wright rendered to the country yesterday are to be recognized [illegible] to be a Brigadier General in the regular army. This prompt action on the part of the government is as gratifying to the corps as the promotion is well deserved by Gen. Wright.

GENERAL LEE SUPERINTENDS THE FIRE OF ONE OF HIS BATTERIES.

The rebel Generals, like our own, exposed themselves to the hottest fire yesterday. General Lee commanded a battery of three light pieces in person. They were in a fort captured by Gen. Edwards' brigade of Gen. Wheaton's division, and if Gen. Lee had but delayed his departure for a few minutes longer he would have been captured.—Gen. Hill's headquarter flag—a blue ground with a white cross in the centre—is now at these headquarters, in the possession of Gen. Wright.

Mr. Cadwallader, of the *Herald*, under date of 4th instant, says:

ANOTHER STATEMENT HOW THE REBEL GENERAL HILL WAS KILLED.

Mrs. Wallace, of Petersburg, and cousin to General A. P. Hill, states that the latter desired to obtain a nearer view of a portion of our line during the attack of the 2d inst., and, leaving his staff behind in a place of safety, rode forward, accompanied by a single orderly, and soon came upon a squad of our men who had advanced along [illegible] far beyond our lines. He immediately ordered them to surrender, which they were on the point of doing, under the supposition that a column of troops were at his heels. They soon discovered he was nearly unattended, and shot Hill through the heart and wounded the orderly dangerously.

THE REBEL GEN. LEE LEADS A BRIGADE IN PERSON.

When Wright had cut his way through the rebel lines Lee saw he must be promptly repulsed, or all was lost. So vital was this considered that he led a brigade in person, and narrowly escaped death from the explosion of a shell, which stunned him for an instant and killed several in his vicinity.—But even his presence failed to inspire his troops. A feeble assault was made and so easily repulsed that Gen. Wright never thought it worth reporting.

HENRY A. WISE REPORTED KILLED.

It is reported that Henry A. Wise was killed, but I could trace it to no positive foundation.

THE REBEL GENERAL PICKETT NOT IN COMMAND OF HIS DIVISION.

An intelligent resident of Petersburg states that Pickett was not in command of his division in front of Sheridan, in consequence of a quarrel with Longstreet, which caused his suspension.

THE LOSSES SUSTAINED BY LEE.

Lee is believed to have lost twenty thousand men this week which we can account for, and nearly an equal number will probably be lost in addition by desertions and straggling.

OUR OWN LOSSES.

Our losses in killed and wounded and prisoners will certainly not exceed five or six thousand for the past week.

CAPTURES BEFORE THE EVACUATION OF PETERSBURG.

We had captured fifty guns and ten thousand prisoners before the evacuation of Petersburg.

Liebig, the celebrated German chemist, has gone to London to superintend the application of the sewerage of that city to the purposes of agriculture. Millions of dollars' worth of manure are annually wasted in this and other large cities by neglecting to secure the drainings from the large and populous places for manure.

THE GRAND FINALE!

SURRENDER OF GENERAL LEE With the Remnant of his Army!

THE WAR VIRTUALLY ENDED!

Since the defeat of Gen. Lee's army near Petersburg, on Sunday last, and the vigorous pursuit of his demoralized and fugitive forces by the Union troops under the command of Lieutenant General Grant, no event of the war has been anticipated with more certainty than the ultimate surrender of the "Army of Northern Virginia."

The anticipation has been *realized*, and the people, North and South, who have longed for the restoration of Peace may now rejoice at the prospect of an early fruition of their heart's desire.

The surrender of General Lee and his army is tantamount to an end of the Rebellion and the termination of the war.

We are indebted to Hon. C. A. Dana, Assistan Secretary of War, for the subjoined official statement of the surrender:

Some correspondence with regard to the surrender of Gen. Lee's army took place on the 8th instant, and on Sunday a letter was addressed by Gen. Grant to Gen. Lee, as follows:

"General—In accordance with the substance of my letter to you of the 8th instant, I propose to receive the surrender of the Army of Northern Virginia on the following terms, to wit:

Rolls of the officers and men to be made in duplicate, one copy to be given to an officer designated by me, and the other to be retained by such officer or officers as you may designate.—The officers to give their individual parole not to take up arms against the Government of the United States until properly exchanged, and each company or regimental commander sign a like parole for the men of their commands, the arms, artillery and public property to be parked and stationed, and turned over to the officers appointed by me to receive them. This will not embrace the side arms of the officers nor their private horses nor baggage. This done, each officer and man will be allowed to return to his home, not to be disturbed by United States authority so long as he observes his parole, and the laws in force where he may reside."

General Lee says, in reply:

"I have received your letter of this date containing the terms of surrender of the Army of Northern Virginia, as proposed by you. As they are substantially the same as those expressed in your letter of the 8th instant, they are accepted. I will proceed to designate the proper officers to carry the stipulation into effect."

FROM MOBILE

The naval attack on the defences of Mobile was commenced on the 28th ult., when seven of the national gunboats moved in towards the shore of the bay and opened on the rebel forts. After sending one hundred and eighty shells into Spanish Fort and other works, without eliciting a return from the enemy, they withdrew. The iron-clad Milwaukee was blown up in the bay on the 29th by a rebel torpedo. There was no firing on the forts by the fleet on the 29th; but on the 30th it again resumed the attack, with what results we have not learned.—New Orleans papers of the 6th inst. stated that information had been received at army headquarters in that city that General Canby's army was within five miles of Mobile; that he had siege guns in positions from which shells could be thrown into the suburbs, and that the attack on Fort Blakely, the main defence, had already began. General Dick Taylor is said to be in command at Spanish Fort, while General Maury commands in the city.

FROM BRITISH HONDURAS.

The *Herald's* special advices from British Honduras, dated at Belize on the 24th of March, convey the important intelligence that the English war steamer Cordelia arrived there from Jamaica on the 20th ultimo with troops to reinforce the colonial garrison, and that the whole of the regular army stationed in Jamaica were under orders to be ready to embark for Belize at any moment, so that Queen Victoria should have there a force sufficient to oppose the carrying into effect of Maximilian's decree annexing the possession to the crown of Mexico. The writer expresses his opinion that Great Britain will not give up the colony without a fight, in which the newly-made Emperor will have a poor chance. A local trouble had been produced by an attempt of the English Government to extend the northern boundaries of the colony so that the Queen's authority may be carried one hundred and twenty miles further into Yucatan.

THE LATE FIRE.

LIST OF THE OWNERS OF THE BUILDINGS DESTROYED.

We subjoin a list of the owners of the real estate destroyed during the late conflagration in this city, and the value of the property respectively owned by them. We do not claim entire accuracy for the list, although it has been compiled with much care. It is impossible to prepare a perfectly correct list.

As railroad property is not taxed by the State, the valuation of this class of property does not appear upon the books of the Commissioners of the Revenue. It is therefore not included in this enumeration. For the same reason, the State Armory, Henrico Court House and Jail, are also omitted.

It is proper to remark that the annexed figures represent the assessed valuation of 1860, which is always below the market value. In a few days we will endeavor to publish a full list of the merchants who were sufferers by this great calamity:

Allen, Jos estate	$95,000
Allison, Ann, estate	7,000
Ayres, Jas and wife	3,000
Anderson, Richard estate	7,250
Allan, Louisa G	25,000
Allan, John and Wm, and Wm Galt's est.	12,000
Alvey and Lipscomb	18,500
Atkinson, John W	5,000
Ayres, Samuel	7,300
Ainslie, Geo A	1,350
Alvey, Richard T	8,000
Andrews, John G	400
Beers, Wm	1,650
Bargamin, Paul	8,000
Barksdale, Wm J est.	1,500
Browne, Jas D	3,500
Bank of Richmond	3,000
Breant, Germain	3,500
Bargamin G & A	8,000
Farmers' Bank of Virginia	13,000
Bank of Virginia	9,000
Bulloch, Ann	5,000
Bulloch, Rebeca	5,000
Bowen, Henry	3,800
Bargamin, A estate	6,500
Bulloch, Catherine W estate	3,000
Brooks, Jas G	15,500
Bowe, N F	4,250
Belvidere Manuf. Co. (paper mill)	20,000
Bacon, Baskerville & James	16,000
Belvin, J A	21,000
Blair, Sarah A E	4,000
Bruggermer, Henry	1,250
Bradley, M M trustee	6,000
Burnett, Septemia (free)	9,200
Bruer, Bernhard	7,000
Breesee, O F	17,000
Botto, Catherine	1,500
Cannon, Henry and J A Belvin trustees	17,500
Crenshaw, Wm G, Jos H, J R and Jas H Grant (each one-quarter)	37,300
Cohen, Joshua	5,000
Cullen, Eliza T and Pat	15,000
Crenshaw, N C	6,000
Cabell, H C	725
Cottrell, Samuel	33,000
Crenshaw, L D	68,000
Chalkley, O H	12,000
Crane & Exall, trustees	4,000
Crenshaw, Jas H	20,000
Cooper, M S est.	2,500
Carpenter, Walter	6,500
Crew, Cornelius	15,000
Curotti, Jos A	2,700
Cowles, Thos est	1,000
Crane, J C trustee	2,000
Campbell, C	6,000
Davenport, Isaac	18,000
Devereux, N	5,500
Duval, A and others, trustees	14,000
De Voss, E W and F W Hannewinkle	2,500
Dunton, Sarah L	5,000
Dunlop, Moncure & Co	14,000
Dunnavant, Wm W est	4,000
Damotte, Claude	500
Dickman, Eliza	1,000
Daniel, Walter R	400
Exchange Bank,	20,000
Exall, Henry	45,000
Edmond & Davenport,	7,000
Faris, John A	1,500
Fulcher, Wm W	12,500
Foster, J B	1,500
Frank, George	2,000
Fahr, P J Williams & Jos Reuter,	1,600
Gary, R O	1,200
Griffin, Fendall	9,000
Gray, Wm	3,500
Gray, Wm F	14,000
Galt, Jas	19,000
Græme, John	25,000
Grant, Jas H	28,000
Gordon, John N	2,500
Goddin, W	18,000
Gude, Anton	4,700
Gooch, Chas W (estate,)	5,500
Glinn, Wm R	1,000
Hendren, Sarah E	4,000
Harvie, Edw'd, est.	2,000
Hunt, Daniel & T J Barnes, trustees,	1,000
Hammond, Wm	3,500
Hyman, Lewis	5,000
Hubbard & Gardner,	2,500
Hastings, Sam'l est.	2,000
Haxall, R B	14,000
Hill, Alex'r est.	5,000
Hudson, R N	11,500
Harris, A T	5,000
Haxall, Wm H	3,100
Haxall, R B	400
Haxall, R B & B W	2,000
Haxall, R B & W H & Co,	1,200
Harwood, Samuel W,	6,500
Hix, Jos K	3,000
Haxall, B W	12,000
Habliston & Bro	6,000
Hitchcock, Jno H	6,000
Harrison, P est. E W H Gordon & Julian Harrison, trustees for Henningham C Harrison,	55,000
Johnston, Ro est. Sophia & Olivia Johnston,	7,500
Johnston, Henry est.	800
Jacobs, Hetta est.	5,500
Johnson, Daniel	75
Jarvis, Wm est.	6,000
Johnston, Richard	1,250
James River and Kanawha Canal Co,	2,500
Johnston, Peyton	1,000
Johnson, Olivia and Sophia, and Andrew, trustee,	2,500
Kinnaird, Jas est.	5,000
Kent, Paine & Co	52,000
Labouris, Bertrand est.	2,100
Levy, Dan'l and Abram	3,750
Lipscomb, Jas E	60
Lowe, George F	1,500
Lintz, George	3,000
Lintz & Brimmer, trustees,	500
Lyon, Eliza	2,500
Morriss, Richard G	19,000
Miller, Samuel	30,000
Menders, John	2,000
Mitchell, Wm Jr est. and Julia A	39,000
Macfarland, Wm H and M Robinson	5,500
Miles, G Z	9,500
Montague, L L and J Sizer, trustees,	4,000
Mangum, Micajah	3,000
Masonic Temple Association of Virginia	2,000
Moses, Alfred	9,000
Milhiser, Jos	6,000
Mahoney, John, trustee,	9,000
McCann, M, trustee,	500
Nott, Alexander,	3,950
Nesbit, Daniel, Mary Bigelow,	2,950
Nott, John C,	2,200
Nott, Robt, est, and Robt and John Harrold, trustees,	8,500
Notting, E O,	2,750
Osborne, John J,	6,000
Price, Thos R,	32,000
Putzel, Adam L,	800
Petty, Hannah W,	9,000
Purcell, John, Charles and others,	10,500
Quarles, John D, estate,	4,000
Renter, Jos,	1,000
Reynolds, Ann,	1,000
Reinhart, John, trustee,	2,500
Rutherfoord, John,	12,000
Rutherfoord, Wm,	9.500
Rahm, Philip, estate,	11,500
Rosser, George, estate,	9,000
Robinson, Samuel C,	22,500
Robinson, John A,	200
Ritter, Wm,	18,500
Randolph, Wm B,	13,500
Richmond Fire Association,	6,000
Robinson, Wyndham,	5,000
Ryan, Wm,	3,000
Ross, Henry,	800
Schmidt, John M	800
Sullivan, D O	1,750
Stephenson, Thomas, est.	10,000
Standard, Ro C, and Jas Lyons, Trustees,	8,500
Southall, George W	6,000
Sutton, Ann	3,750
Shaffer, John C	8,000
Schuman, Charles	500
Stewart, D K and heirs,	10,350
Stewart, Brice and heirs,	5,200
Smith, Wm Ira	14,000
Samanni, Thos est.	3,500
Snyder, Asa	20,000
Stanard, Martha	8,200
Sullivan, Florence	800
Seddon Jas A and others	12,000
Scott, H L Gould and others	6,500
Scott, Mrs Gracie	15,230
Sampson & Pae,	10,500
Steel, Alex Trustee	1,400
Shinault, H	1,000
Tolka, Jas	1,000
Thomas, James Jr.,	13,000
Taylor, Susan B	2,000
Thomas, A & Son,	15,000
Thomas, A est.	30,000
Totty, B W	1,750
Triplett, Nannie J	4,000
Taylor, Wm Trustee,	2,500
Tinsley, Wm N	700
Thompson, P M	900
Traders' Bank,	6,500
Vial, S P, estate,	27,000
Von Groning, D	6,500
Virginia Mechanics Institute,	20,000
Virginia Fire & Marine Ins. Co.,	15,000
Whitlock, Chas E	1,500
Wickham, Wm F, trustees,	2,500
Wight, Ann E	12,500
Whitfield, Richard	4,000
Whitfield, John F	4,500
Warwick, Jas	13,000
Warwick, Abraham	24,000
Wallace, Wm, estate,	7,000
Winter, B	800
Womble, Jno, estate, & Jas H Poindexter,	10,000
Warwick & Barksdale,	202,000
Wickham, Wm, & F McClurg,	1,800
Wickham, John	13,000
Wallace, Catherine & Sons,	5,000
Wortham, C & E, trustees,	12,000
Williams, Jessee	300
Watkins, Claiborne, trustee,	6,500
Winston, Jos P	14,000
Wortham, C & E, trustees,	6,100

The aggregate value of the property destroyed, and above enumerated, foots up two million one hundred and forty-six thousand two hundred and forty dollars.

Imposing as these figures appear, they are far short of the truth, for the reason already stated, that real estate was, before the war, invariably assessed much below the value which it would have commanded in the market. Our list covers no more than the value of the bricks and mortar destroyed.

THE TWO CURRENCIES.

A grave financial question is bothering the business men of Richmond, who heretofore have had dealings exclusively in Confederate currency. Those who owe, on commission or otherwise, refuse to pay except in the funds current previous to the evacuation, while those to whom debts are due refuse to receive any funds except the Federal currency now in vogue, with the premium at which gold, silver, and Federal currency was rated on Saturday, April 1st. There is a grand embroglio in a financial way, and we have no idea how it will end; but we think those who have had the use of Confederate money should pay for it in the regular proportion established by premium.

THE WHIG.

Circumstances, over which we have in vain endeavored to have control, have obliged us heretofore to issue an evening edition on a reduced scale. Hereafter we shall issue a full-sized sheet, and have taken the necessary steps to secure a more perfect printing of the same. Our paper, also, will be improved in quality; the print will be more legible; the edition will include all the important Northern news, besides all local items of interest; in short, hereafter we shall have a live newspaper.

THE RICHMOND POSTOFFICE.

Mr. D. B. Parker, Special Agent of the United States Postoffice Department, is, as we have previously stated, in charge of the Richmond postoffice. Mr. Parker has shown most commendable zeal in putting the office to rights and preparing a the way for a speedy resumption of mail communication. Letters addressed to parties at any point in the United States will be received at the postoffice and forwarded to their destinations.

It is expected that a mail will be received from the North and delivered during the current week.

THE LATEST NEWS.

We received, last night, Baltimore, Philadelphia and New York papers of Saturday. Owing to the absence of gas, we are unable to quote extensively from them in this issue. They contain, however, very little news of importance. The following is a summary of the latest European advices:

The steamship China arrived at New York yesterday, bringing later foreign news. Sir Frederick Bruce, the newly appointed British minister to Washington, is a passenger by the China. The Rebel ram Stonewall left Ferrol on the 21st, and was accompanied to sea by a Spanish frigate. The United States frigates Niagara and Sacramento immediately followed, and the Rebel ram finding escape impossible returned to port. A debate took place in the House of Lords on American affairs, in which Lord John Russell admitted that our Government was justified in the measures it had adopted towards Canada. The House of Commons had voted in favor of the Quebec fortification bill.

NAVAL ARMAMENTS IN AMERICA.

In the House of Commons, on the 2d of March, Mr. H. Baillie moved that a select committee be appointed to inquire whether her Majesty's ships were at present armed in a manner suited to the necessities and requirements of modern warfare.

The Marquis of Hartington, Under Secretary of the Navy, in reply, said: The honorable member said that the ships of several other nations were much better off than ours. The Americans had undoubtedly got bigger guns than we had, but be doubted whether they were much better. The rifled guns of the Americans, which were held up to our admiration last year, had proved perhaps the greatest failure on record. It came from the Americans themselves, from their bureau of naval ordnance and from other official reports, that the Parrott was the only rifled naval gun they had in their service, and that in their opinion was the simplest and best gun that had been constructed. They had it, however, on the authority of Admiral Porter, that almost every one of those guns employed at Wilmington the other day, burst, that they were utterly discredited, and that he thought it probable they would be entirely withdrawn from the American navy. He was justified, therefore, in saying that the Americans had not, at this moment, a rifled gun at all with which to arm their Navy. What would honorable members on the other side of the house say if it could be said at this moment that we had not got a rifled gun for our navy? (Hear, hear) Did the honorable member wish us to follow the example of the Americans, and arm our ships with Parrott guns, which did not burst, as our Armstrong guns, with a slight chink or opening, but in such a manner as to endanger, if not to destroy the lives of a great part of the crew? As to the enormous smooth bore guns which the Americans were now arming their Navy with, he thought it a mistake to say that they were superior to anything we had got. We had got wrought iron guns of ten and a half inches calibre and twelve tons weight, such as the guns on board the Royal Sovereign, which he believed were equal to anything the Americans possessed. They were certainly not so large a calibre as some of the American guns, but they were guns of wrought iron instead of cast iron; they were guns whose charge was about one-fifth the weight of the projectile, and he did not believe that any American gun would fire a charge of over one eighth or one-tenth the weight of the projectile.

The navy were becoming aware that a rifled gun of the same weight of metal was much more advantageous than a smooth bore gun for the purpose of battering iron-plated ships; but the weight of the gun and the charge of powder fired by these smooth-bore guns were such as to justify the assertion that they must be at least equal in power to the 10 inch and 11-inch guns with which the Americans were at present arming their Navy. He mentioned these facts to show that even at the present moment we were not so hopelessly behind the Americans as the honorable member wished the House to believe. It must be remembered that the Americans were not in a state of repose as we were at present; they were not in a state of preparation; they were not in a state in which they were able to consider calmly what was the best gun and to arm their Navy accordingly. But for the last three or four years they had been employing their Navy to a great extent, and it would be most unfair to compare the condition of our naval ordnance with theirs.

THE RICHMOND WHIG.

VOL. 1--NO. 7. RICHMOND, VA., APRIL 11, 1865. PRICE: FIVE CENTS.

[From the New York Herald, April 8.]

BIOGRAPHICAL SKETCHES.

Among the rebel Generals killed at Petersburg are Lieut. Gen. Hill, and Brigadier Generals W, H. F. Lee and Pegram; while among those whose surrender to Sheridan as already announced are Lieut. Gen. Ewell, Major General Kershaw and Brigadier Generals Corse, De Bose and Custis Lee. Virginia, as usual, has suffered the most.—The three Generals killed were all from Virginia, while of the six captured four were from the same State.

SKETCH OF LIEUT. GEN. AMBROSE POWELL HILL, JR., OF VIRGINIA.

Ambrose P. Hill was one of the giants of Lee's army, and disputed with Longstreet and Ewell for the place in the affections of the rebel people which "Stonewall" Jackson once held. Hill was a native of Culpeper county, Va. He was born, we believe, in 1826, and at the time of his death was only 39 years of age. He entered West Point in 1843, with O. B. Willcox, James B. Fry, A. E. Burnside, E. G. Viele, of the United States army, and Henry Heth, of the rebel forces, and graduated in 1857, number fifteen in his class. He was commissioned second lieutenant by brevet of the First Artillery, July 1, 1847, and second lieutenant in full in the August following. He was subsequently promoted first lieutenant, First Artillery, but resigned March 1st, 1861, and was appointed Colonel of the 13th Va. infantry, which he commanded at Manassas. He was engaged as brigade commander at the battle of Williamsburg, in May, 1862, and was promoted Brigadier on that field, and immediately afterwards a Major General. As such he commanded the extreme left of the rebel army in the seven days' battles before Richmond, June, 1862, and divided with Stonewall Jackson the rebel honors of those conflicts. In command of this division he made the campaign under Lee against Pope into Maryland, was engaged at Antietam fighting Burnside, and covered the retreat of the rebel army from that disastrous field. On the reorganization of Lee's army after the battle of Fredericksburg, Hill was promoted and placed in command of the Third corps of the army, which position he held at the time of his death. At Chancellorsville and Gettysburg he again distinguished himself. During the battles of the Wilderness, May, 1864, he was disabled by disease, and his command was placed temporarily under General Jubal Early. August 25, 1864, Hill, having resumed command, fought the battle of Ream's Station, and since then has been posted on the left of the rebel position before Petersburg. During the battle on the 1st instant his command was separated from the rest of the rebel army, and in endeavoring to restore communication he was killed. His body was interred at Petersburg on Sunday, April 2.

BRIGADIER GENERAL WILLIAM H. FITZHUGH LEE, OF VIRGINIA.

This officer, killed at Petersburg, was the second son of Robert E. Lee, and was born at Arlington House, Virginia, about the year 1832. He did not receive an appointment to West Point, but was educated at William and Mary's College, Virginia. He received, however, the appointment of second lieutenant in the United States Army, June 30, 1855, and was assigned to the Second infantry. He held this rank until the breaking out of the rebellion, when he hastened to follow the example of his father, and resigned April 30, 1861, to accept a captaincy of cavalry in the rebel army. He was attached to J. E. B. Stuart's cavalry command. His first expedition of any importance was in June, 1862, when, under Stuart, he made the circuit of McClellan's army, on the Pamunkey river. At this time he was a colonel commanding a brigade, but was soon after rewarded with a brigadier general's commission. He was engaged in the famous cavalry battle at Beverly Ford, Va., June 9, 1863. He here received a painful wound in the thigh, and was removed to the house of Col. W. H. Wickham, in Hanover county. Here he was captured a few days subsequently by Gen. Spear, in his raid on the Pamunkey, and carried to the White House. He was sent North and confined, being for a time held as hostage for Captain Sawyer. On his release he was assigned to duty in command of a division of Stuart's cavalry corps. This command was subsequently given, on Stuart's death, to Fitzhugh Lee, a cousin of W. H. F. Lee, and the latter remained in command of his division until his death, on the 2d inst., before Petersburg.

BRIGADIER GENERAL WILLIAM JOHNSON PEGRAM, OF VIRGINIA.

This young officer, who was killed in the battle of the 2d inst., was in the twenty-fourth year of his age, and a native of Petersburg, Va. He was one of the three sons of General James W. Pegram, who perished in the steamer Lucy Long, on the Ohio river, in 1844, and brother of the Rebel General John Pegram, who was lately killed at the battle of Hatcher's Run. One of young Pegram's uncles was the late Captain George Pegram, of Elizabethtown, N. J., who was an aid-de-camp to General Scott. Another uncle is Colonel William Pegram, of Kentucky.

At the breaking out of the war William Johnson Pegram was a student of law at the University of Virginia, at Charlottesville; but left his studies to volunteer in the ranks of the "Richmond Howitzers,"—the first artillery company raised in Richmond at the beginning of the war—under the command of the then Captain George W. Randolph, late Secretary of War of "the Confederacy." As a private in the ranks he fought in the first battle of Manassas, and was noted on the field for gallantry by General Joseph E. Johnston. During the engagements around Richmond in 1862 he celebrated his twenty-first birthday amid the carnage of battle. At Cedar Run he was again noted on the battle-field for gallant action. At the battle of Chancellorsville Gen. Lee, noticing the ability with which Pegram handled his guns, ordered an additional number of batteries to be placed under his command. At the battle of Gettysburg he displayed signal ability, and was promoted a colonel of artillery on the subsequent reorganization of the army. He was lately made a brigadier general and placed in command of a brigade in Hill's corps. In appearance he was a beardless boy, of delicate stature, tall and slim, with blue eyes and light hair.

LIEUT. GEN. ROBERT STODDARD EWELL, OF VIRGINIA.

General Sheridan captured General Ewell on the 8th inst., while endeavoring to escape from Richmond. His capture is an important event of the campaign, as Ewell was one of the first men in the rebel army—next in importance, indeed, to Lee himself.

Ewell was born in the District of Columbia, in 1820. He is a brother of Benjamin S. Ewell, who graduated third in his class, and who, after being an instructor for years at West Point, and President of the Williamsburg (Virginia) William and Mary College, went into the rebel army, to be contented with the rank of Colonel and Adjutant General to Gen. Johnston. Richard S. Ewell, without being so studious, was a more practical man than his brother, and graduated thirteenth in his class, next to George H. Thomas, lower down than W. T. Sherman, Stewart Van Vliet, and ahead of Bushrod R. Johnson, Col. Oliver L. Shepperd and Gen. Thomas Jordan.

Ewell entered the United States Army July 1, 1840, as brevet Second Lieutenant; was promoted to Second Lieutenant November 1, 1840; First Lieutenant, September 18, 1845; brevet Captain, August 20, 1847, for gallantry at Contreras and Cherubusco, Mexico. In June, 1857, he was engaged with the Indians in New Mexico. In 1858, he was in charge of the United States troops at Fort Buchanan, New Mexico. He resigned May 1, 1861, his position as Captain of Dragoons, to which he had been promoted, and joined the Rebel Army of Virginia in time to participate as a Brigadier General in the battle of Bull Run, July 21, 1861. During the inactivity which followed this engagement, Ewell was promoted major general and assigned to a division of the Second, or Stonewall Jackson's, corps. In this capacity he fought in the battles of Front Royal and Cedar Mountain during the valley campaign in 1862. During the battle of Chancellorsville, in May, 1863, he succeeded Jackson, who was wounded, in command of the Second corps, and, on the death of Jackson, was appointed, on the latter's earnest recommendation, a lieutenant general, and permanently assigned to the Second corps. With this command he fought at Winchester, Gettysburg, and during the first day of the battle of the Wilderness, May 1864. He was here wounded and his corps was given to Jubal Early. Ewell retired to Richmond and assumed command of the Department of Henrico. It was during his flight from this department that he was captured by Sheridan.

MAJOR GENERAL J. B. KERSHAW, OF SOUTH CAROLINA.

Gen. Kershaw, reported captured by Sheridan, commanded a division of Longstreet corps (First.) He is a native of South Carolina. He was not a graduate of West Point; and his first military service was as Colonel of the Second South Carolina infantry, which he raised, at Bull Run, July 21, 1861, and in which battle he distinguished himself by coming "in at the death." During the long inactivity which followed the battle of Bull Run, Kershaw was transferred to the Peninsula, under Magruder. His brigade (Third, Fourth, Fifth and Eighth South Carolina) was in Lafayette McLaws' division, of Magruder's forces, and was engaged in all the battles fought during McClellan's investment of Yorktown and the retreat to Richmond. He was engaged as a Brigadier General in the same division during the subsequent battles before Richmond, at Manassas, and during the first Maryland invasion, particularly at Antietam, Fredericksburg, Chancellorsville and Gettysburg. In September, 1863, he was sent with the remainder of Longstreet's corps to Georgia, and was engaged at Chickamauga September 19 and 20, and subsequently, in November of the same year, in an attack on Knoxville (Fort Saunders.) McLaws was suspended from command for his action on this occasion, and Kershaw succeeded him. He returned to Virginia from East Tennessee in April, 1864, in time to engage in the battles of the Wilderness and Spottsylvania. He has since been actively engaged in the campaign and defence of Richmond, and has met his fate at the hands of General Sheridan's forces.

BRIGADIER GENERAL CORSE, of VIRGINIA,

Who is also reported captured by General Sheridan, is a native of Virginia. When the rebellion began he raised a regiment of infantry (the Seventeenth Virginia), and was commissioned its colonel. While in command of the regiment he was engaged at Bull Run. In September, 1863, he was in command of Pickett's old brigade, of Longstreet's corps, Pickett having been promoted to be a major general. In May, 1864, he was detached from this division and sent to the vicinity of Newbern, N. C., but returned under Beauregard, in June, 1864, to the defence of Petersburg. He was here promoted brigadier general, and regularly assigned to Pickett's old brigade.

BRIGADIER GENERAL DE BOSF.

General De Rose, also captured, is a native of Georgia, and has been actively engaged in various capacities in the war since its beginning. He lately succeeded General W. P. Wofford in command of the Georgia brigade, of Kershaw's division, Longstreet's corps, composed of the Twelfth, Sixteenth and Twenty-fourth Georgia regiments, Third Georgia sharpshooters and Phillip's and Cobb's legions. It is not improbable, from the fact of the capture of Kershaw, Barton and De Bose, all of whom belong to Longstreet's corps, that that organization has been very materially interfered with.

BRIGADIER GENERAL SETH M. BARTON, OF VIRGINIA.

General Barton is a native of Fredericksburg, Va., where he was born in 1829. He entered West Point in 1845 and graduated in 1849, standing number twenty-eight in the class of which Q. A. Gillmore ranked first, J. G. Parke second, J. K. Duncan (rebel) fifth, Absalom Baird ninth, Rufus Saxton eighteenth, and R. W. Johnston thirtieth. He entered the United States Army as brevet second lieutenant, Third infantry, on July 1, 1849. October 31, 1857, he was promoted captain in the First infantry, but resigned June 11, 1861, to take position in the rebel army. He was sent to the West and assigned to the command of a brigade under Gen. Stevenson, then in Bragg's command in Tennessee. When Sherman made his advance on Vicksburg, Stevenson's division was sent to Gen. S. D. Lee's assistance, and arrived at the City of the Hills in time to assist in the repulse of Sherman's forces.—He was captured at Vicksburg. On his exchange he was assigned to the command of a brigade of Kershaw's division, of Longstreet's corps, of Lee's army, and was captured while endeavoring to escape with his command.

BRIGADIER GENERAL GEORGE WILLIAM CUSTIS LEE, OF VIRGINIA.

This officer, who is reported captured by General Sheridan, is the first son of General Robert E. Lee. He was born at Arlington Heights, in 1831, entered West Point in 1850, graduating July 1, 1854, and entered the United States Army as brevet second lieutenant. October 20, 1859, he was commissioned first lieutenant in the Engineer corps, but resigned May 2, 1861, and, following his father's example, entered the Rebel army. After the failure of his father in Western Virginia, and his retirement to the shades of the War Department at Richmond, young Custis Lee was made a colonel and placed on the staff of Jeff. Davis. When his father was called to the field, in 1862, Custis Lee remained on with the Rebel President, and his name appears on the Rebel Army Register for 1864 as "Colonel and aid to the President." During the spring session of the rebel Congress in 1864 Lee was nominated and confirmed a brigadier general, and was shortly afterwards assigned to duty with Ewell. During the siege of Richmond he commanded a large brigade of regular and militia troops, including the former Lieutenant General Pemberton's artillery, on the north side of the James river, his headquarters being on the famous Chapin farm. In January last it was reported that Lee had been nominated a major general, but if so he was never confirmed.

A TOUCHING SCENE.—The last *adieux* between Napoleon and Eugenie and the Duke de Morny were extremely touching. It is said that the Duke, feeling himself growing weaker, said to the Emperor, who was weeping by the side of the Empress, "Come, sire, we must part." At these words the Empress, bursting into tears, threw herself at the foot of the bed, and the Emperor could not repress his sobs. The Archbishop of Paris and M. Rouher had some difficulty in withdrawing him from the spot and supporting him till he reached his carriage. It is affirmed that the Duke has left to his heirs a fortune of fifteen millions. A *post mortem* examination of the body of the Duke was effected; M. Robini, professor at the Paris Academy of Medicine, being the principal person engaged in the proceedings. The result arrived at was that the patient had succumbed to an exceedingly grave anemic state, occasioned by an organic lesion of the pan-creatic gland and a diseased liver. The brain weighed one thousand five hundred and thirty-two grammes, or two hundred and thirty-two above the average.

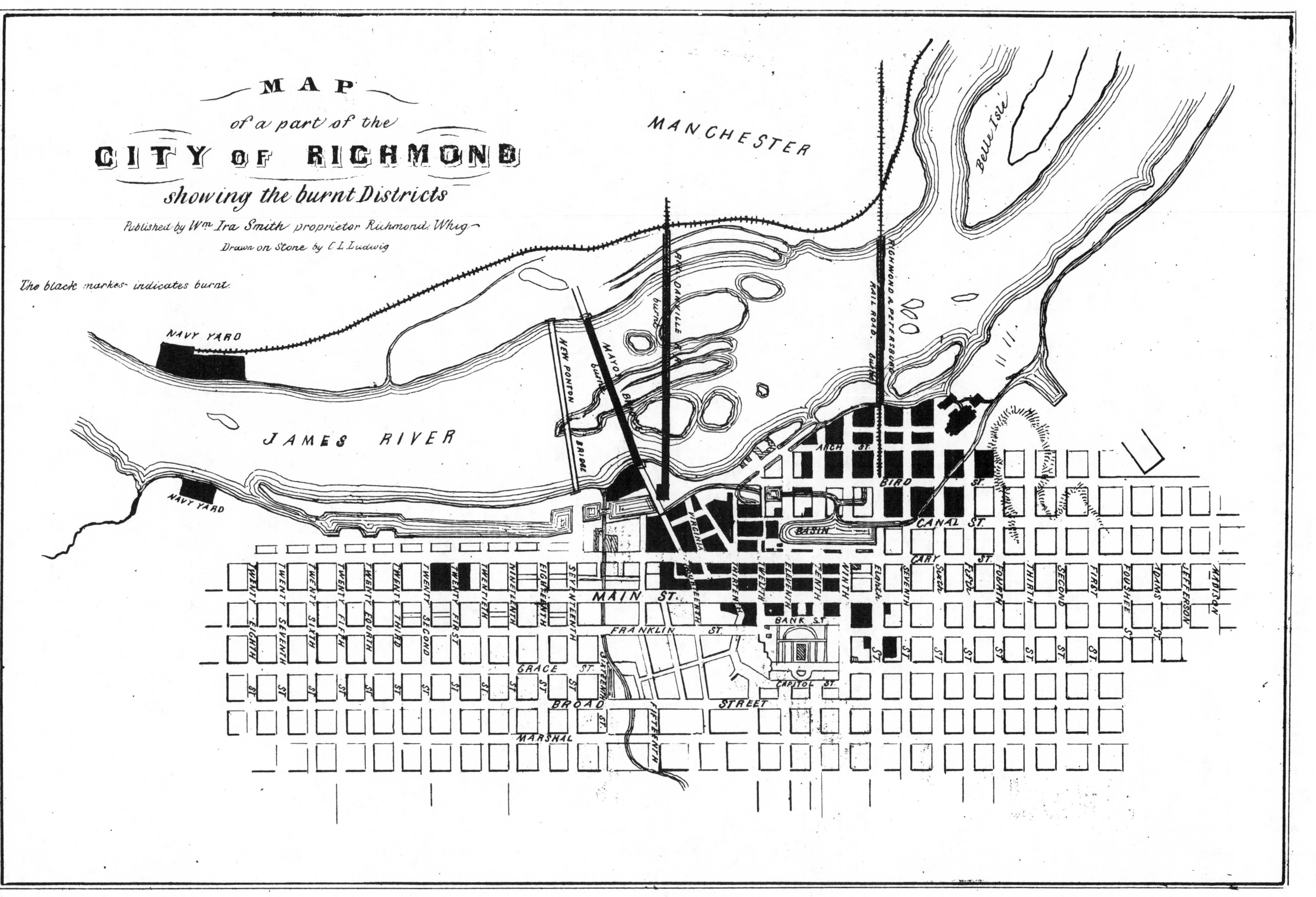
MAP
of a part of the
CITY OF RICHMOND
showing the burnt Districts
Published by Wm Ira Smith proprietor Richmond Whig
Drawn on Stone by C.L. Ludwig
The black markes indicates burnt.
MANCHESTER
Belle Isle
JAMES RIVER
NAVY YARD
NAVY YARD
RICHMOND & PETERSBURG
RAIL ROAD. burnt
R.R. DANVILLE R.R.
burnt
MAYO'S BRIDGE
burnt
NEW PONTON BRIDGE
ARCH ST.
BIRD ST.
CANAL ST.
CARY ST.
BASIN
VIRGINIA
MAIN ST.
BANK ST.
FRANKLIN ST.
GRACE ST.
CAPITOL ST.
BROAD STREET
MARSHAL
MADISON
JEFFERSON
ADAMS ST.
FOUSHEE ST.
FIRST ST.
SECOND ST.
THIRTH ST.
FOURTH ST.
Fifth ST.
Sixth ST.
SEVENTH ST.
Eighth ST.
NINTH
TENTH
ELEVENTH
TWELFTH
THIRTEENTH
FOURTEENTH
FIFTEENTH
SIXTEENTH ST.
SEVENTEENTH ST.
EIGHTEENTH ST.
NINETEENTH ST.
TWENTIETH ST.
TWENTY FIRST ST.
TWENTY SECOND ST.
TWENTY THIRD ST.
TWENTY FOURTH ST.
TWENTY FIFTH ST.
TWENTY SIXTH ST.
TWENTY SEVENTH ST.
TWENTY EIGHTH ST.

Daily Journal and Messenger.

By S. ROSE & Co. | Macon, Ga., Tuesday Morning, April 11, 1865. | Vol. XLIII—No. 35.

MORNING EDITION.

BY TELEGRAPH.

TELEGRAPHIC REPORTS OF THE PRESS ASSOCIATION

Latest from the Front.

Lee and Grant Fighting Daily.

Heavy Fighting Thursday.

Enemy's Loss very Heavy.

Yankee Rumor of Napoleon's Recognition of the Southern Confederacy.

Movements of the Enemy.

Burning of Richmond and Harsh Treatment of the Blacks.

DANVILLE, March 9.—Gen. Lee has moved to the vicinity of Farmville, followed by Grant, fighting daily. Heavy fighting Thursday—no particulars.

The enemy have established hospitals at the Junction, where a large number of their wounded are. Their loss was very heavy in the late fights. They are not approaching this way on the line of the Richmond and Danville railroad, communication being still open to Kingsville.

Our wounded soldiers, who escaped from the enemy, say they are uneasy about foreign war. It is reported that a courier from the enemy brings news that the New York Herald says the Emperor Napoleon recognized this Government on the 5th of March.

DANVILLE, April 9.—A column of cavalry is reported at Perry Courthouse, thirty-eight miles from Danville, probably Stoneman's.

A skirmish took place near there Saturday, without result. Also a column of the enemy is reported near Lynchburg.

Persons coming from Richmond confirm the burning and say the enemy treated the blacks harshly.

MONSIEUR TONSON COME AGAIN.

Our telegrams bring fresh reports of the Recognition. Wall street, we presume, is at the bottom of this fresh sensation. Napoleon "recognized the Confederacy on the 5th of March!" Crash goes stocks, up goes gold, and a fine time generally have Bulls and Bears over this admirable little piece of financial strategy. Well, it is a matter with which we of the South need not trouble ourselves. Gens. Lee and Johnston are taking care of our interests, and we think the question of recognition will be satisfactorily settled when they get through.

GLORIOUS NEWS FROM GEN. JOHNSTON.—If street reports be true, says the South Carolinian of the 22d, we have achieved a third and, this time, a decisive victory. The rumor repeated is, that on Monday Gen. Johnston again attacked Sherman in front and on his flank, and after a severe battle, drove him in confusion from the field, capturing a large number of prisoners, and utterly demoralizing the Federal army.

Gens. Johnston and Hoke are both reported to have had their horses shot under them.

The word we have from Sherman is, that he was "double quicking for a new base without ammunition, and with the loss of seventy pieces of artillery." It seems to have been another Bull Run affair.

These being only rumors, says the Columbus Times, our people should receive them "*cum grano salis*," but where there is so much smoke, there must be some fire.

Orders have been received at Salisbury to prepare the prisons for five thousand prisoners. This is direct from a reliable source.

The Alabama Situation.

The Columbus *Times* of Sunday has the following:

FROM MOBILE.—From a gentleman who left Mobile just a week ago yesterday we learn that the Yankee force had made no impression upon our defences at Blakely and Spanish Fort, and that the authorities were confident of our ability to hold the city. If Forrest will only attend to the raiders from above, Maury will certainly manage the mob from Pensacola. The retention of Mobile is simply a question of meat and bread, and we have strong hope that Forrest will compel its decision in our favor.

LATEST REPORTS FROM SELMA.—We are informed says the Montgemery Mail of the 8th inst., that an officer of Gen. Adam's staff went down to Selma under flag of truce on Wednesday to request permisssion of the Federal authorities for Mrs. General Adams, the wife of our distinguished commander to pass terough their lines. Mrs. A. was a sojourner in Selma during the battle and it was impossible for her to leave the city during the evacuation. The officer in charge of the escort and flag of truce, has returned to Montgomery. They were not permitted to cross the river, and the interview was on the river bank opposite the city. The Federals seemed anxious to learn the whereabouts of Forrest. They claim 2,600 prisoners as the result of the engagements at Plantersville and Selma. They also intimate that their losses were heavy. It appears that only one square, including the postoffice building, was destroyed. The Federals burned the navy works, and the firing of the other buildings, was un authorized. The flag of truce party make no men of the reported attack of Forrest on the city, Monday and Tuesday.

WEST POINT, GA.—The West Point Bulletin tells the following story:

A soldier, who is more than usually concerned upon the subject of religion, reported a few days since to Dr. Heard, in charge of the hospitals of this place. The Dr. asked him to what command he belonged.

"To —— company, —— regiment, Hood's old division, Hardee's corps."

"Well sir," said the Doctor, "You are a long ways from your command."

"But there is a command, Doctor, far higher than that, which I am trying to reach."

Dr.—"What command is that?"

Soldier.—"The command of Heaven, sir."

A brother soldier close by spoke up as follows:

"Well, sir, you are the worst lost man in all the world. West Point isn't on the road to Heaven, sir."

FROM TEXAS.—The United States papers contain an official dispatch from Gen. Magruder, which gives the particulars of the fight at Dardanelle, and the subsequent capture of one steamer, the firing of another, and the sinking of another.

Our forces captured eighty-two prisoners, killed and wounded twenty-seven, besides a number drowned. Our loss was one killed and fifteen wounded.

POINTS DECIDED BY THE SUPREME COURT OF GEORGIA, AT MACON, MARCH TERM, 1865.

These decisions we have published before, but republish them consolidated, at the especial request of some of our friends:

Jones vs. Billingslea—Jones vs. Cutliff: Habeas Corpus—Persons exempted from Confederate service as managers of their own farms, are nevertheless, liable to serve in the State militia.

Thornton vs. Towns: Application for Injunction.—On a rule to show cause why an injunction should not be granted, the answer of the defendant to the allegations of the bill, and affidavits supporting the answer, were held sufficient to warrant a refusal of the injunction.

Leonard vs. Acee: Habeas Corpus—A tax assessor of the Confederate States is exempt from military service in the militia.

Brook vs. McClusky—McLane vs. Collins: Habeas Corpus—Soldiers belonging to the Confederate States Reserves, who are arrested for felony, by the civil authorities of the State, and admitted to bail, are liable to be ordered back to their command while going at large, and to be put again on duty. Those cases are controlled in principle by the case of Alfred vs. Irwin, decided at Milledgeville, in November last.

White and Rowland vs. Sellers: Habeas Corpus.—A soldier cannot obtain his discharge from the army by habeas corpus because he has been elected and has qualified as a constable since he entered his service.

Smith vs. Harris—Morgan vs. Bonham.: Habeas Corpus. Under the Act of Congress of Feb. 17, 1864, men between the ages of 17 and 50 years, and none others, are liable to military service; and a conscript in the reserve forces, who, since the passage of that act, has attained to the age of 50 years, may, if still held for service, he discharged by habeas corpus.

The Governor, for the use of Rutherford, vs. Raley and others: Action on Sheriff's Bond. An attorney who, by negligently suffering the money of his client to lie in the hands of the Sheriff, makes himself liable for it, and then without the compulsion of a suit pays up the debt, has a right of action on the Sheriff's bond for his reinbursement. It is the Sheriff's duty to pay over the money without demand; and if the omission of that duty work an injury to the attorney, he, by the express words of the statute, may support an action on the bond. The statute itself creates whatever privity is necessary to the maintenance of such action

Cobb vs. Black: Habeas Corpus.—In an equity case, the Judge having, under the code, appointed a Receiver in vacation, and ordered the defendant to turn over to him the assets in dispute, may also in vacation enforce obedience to the order by attachment for contempt.

2. Such attachment is not punitive merely, but remedial, and therefore the imprisonment of the party under it may endure so long as the party continues disobedient. The limitations fixed by the code to the term of imprisonment for contempt generally, are not applicable.

Hall vs. The State: Simple Larceny.—1. Where the prisoner owned a cow similar to the one which the indictment charged him with stealing, and the question was whether he had not by mistake and in good faith taken and disposed of the latter, believing it to have been the former, evidence is admissible to show that some time after the transaction he went to the other owner and said that if the cow taken was his, he, the prisoner, had made a mistake, and then offered to pay and did pay the other for it.

2. The verdict in this case was contrary to the evidence.

Smith vs. Green and Postell: Cetiorari—1. Garnishment founded on a void action or on a void judgment is itself void.

2. A distress warrent for rent cannot be the foundation for a garnishment.

Alderman vs. Chester: In Equity:—The distributees of an estate clear of all encumbrance, may agree among themselves that one of them shall have and enjoy during her life such part of the property as she may select, and that after her death the entire estate shall belong to the other distributees; and though such agreement be made orally, and never reduced to writing, it will be enforced by a Court of Equity, after the life interest contemplated has been fully enjoyed. The contract is not void under the statute of frauds; nor does it contravene the rule of law against creat-

Parker vs. Kaughmann—Clark vs. Brady: Habeas Corpus.—1. The power of Congress to raise armies by conscription is not restricted to men able for active service in the field, but extends to such also as, though unable for that service, are capable of performing the duties of "provost or hospital guard, or clerks, or clerks' guards, agents, employees or laborers in the commissary, quartermaster or ordinance departments, or of clerks or employees of navy agents, of the duties requisite in the execution of the enrollment Acts, or other similar duties." The 6th section of the Act of Feb. 17, 1864, entitled "An Act to Organize Forces to Serve During the War," is therefore constitutional.

2. In executing that section of the Act, it is necessary that the report of the Board of Surgeons should specify the particular duty for which each man is capable. A report in general terms, that the conscript is fit for light duty, is not sufficient. In administering the military statutes of the country, a strict conformity to their provisions is requisite.

Cowart vs. Williams—*Ejectment.*

A judgment establishing a copy of a lost deed, rendered on notice to the heirs at law of the grantor, but without notice to our claiming the land as devisee under his last will, is not conclusive upon such devisee, or upon those claiming under him.

Amos vs. the State, McBryde vs. the State, } *Indictment for Gambling.*

Though the indictment in charging the offense, lay it on a day subsequent to the time when the new code went into effect, the defendant may, nevertheless, be convicted on evidence of having played and betted on a day prior to that time.

DESTRUCTION OF CHERAW, S. C.—Chancellor Inglis, of Cheraw, communicates to the South Carolinian some particulars of the destruction of that place, derived from a surgeon who was present during the occupation and departure of Sherman's army. He says:

"The entire business portion of the town—that is, front street—is burned to the ground, except one house, which from his discription of the locality, I suppose to be the only building on the street which was occupied by a private family.—That fact demonstrates that the burning of the stores and warehouses was not accidental, but that, on the contrary, the enemy could and did control the extent of the conflagration according to their pleasure. There was not sufficient other force there to resrain the flames. No dwelling in the body of the town was burned. Several places, just outside of the corporation limits, or within a mile or two of them was burned, including my own and brother-in-law, Gen. Prince's and others, whose owners' name he did not remember. He did not hear of any acts of personal violence or outrage. But every house, large and small, of whatever class of tenant, black or white, slave or free, was pillaged and stripped of all valuables that could be carried away. The people are almost entirely without provisions or clothing. But one horse or mule was left in the town and neighborhood.

"Gen. Blair's corps first entered the town. He made his headquarters in the residence of one of our wealthiest citizens, and appropriated the best he could find in it. When appealed to by the lady of the house to interfere with the plundering of the common soldiers, who, in the basement, were breaking trunks. &c., he repaired to the scene, but only to share in the spoil. Sherman himself came into Cheraw on the second day.—He was not at Society Hill, as reported, nor was any portion of his infantry or artillery marched in that direction. A cavalry raiding party of 2,500 went down that way, and on to Florence, whence they were repulsed by 120 of our men left there in charge of the prisoners who were too sick to be removed. What this party accomplished on their route, so long as they encountered no resistance, he did not state.

"The condition of the people of Cheraw must be most deplorable. The population of the town being 7,500, is composed in large part of refugee families. Before our own army reached the neighborhood, it was extremely difficult to get fire wood and almost impossible to buy corn or meat. In ordinary times, the wants of the town in these particulars, are largely supplied from North Carolina. The destruction of the bridge on the Pee Dee and Thompson's Creek has almost isolated the town. Even if the adjoining country had a supply, it would be almost impossible, owing to these obstructions, and their deprivation of all means of transportation for themselves, to procure it. The whole of the adjacent country has, doubtless, been ravaged by the foe, and not only the means of present subsistence taken away, but all power to create future means destroyed.

A FREE WILL OFFERING.

If we are an imperial race, a race born to command and be the heirs of freedom, we should hesitate at nothing in the way of self abnegation that knits us in the band of brotherhood and fortifies the case beyond a peradventure. Our blood has flowed like water; from Gettysburg to the Rio Grande the land is strewn with our slain brethren and their gore cries to God for vengeance. This offering, the most precious of all, we have sent to the altar of immolation without stint, almost without murmur.

Of our property we have been lavish. That is, in the beginning, when every heart was a glow and the sun shone brightly. But when the dark day came and the thunder rolled and the demon of gain made his foul den in our souls, we hugged the ingot and the bale, saying in action if not in speech: My sons and brothers may go, but spare my negroes, spare my pigs, my cows, my chickens and eggs! This monstrous paradox had obtained such force that it needed the insatiable hand of the plundering foeman to clutch it from our thoughts. In a moment, the property that men had begrudged their country melted away like snow before the burning march of that country's ravager.

Now that it has become necessary to choose one of two alternatives, we hope to see no backsliding and no halting between.

If our country was worth the sacrifice of blood, it is now doubly worth the sacrifice of property, when that property is already forfeited to the filthy Yankee whenever he win by our defection; And by our defection alone can he make us his retainers and his bondmen.

Nations which have obtained their liberty have secured it not only by the sacrament of blood but the price of property. The Dutch cheerfully yielded their plate and jewels to the coming, and the Prussians exchanged their gold for iron crosses which became more precious than lucre, since they glittered on the breast of honor as the insignia of manhood and liberty.

Are we less generous than the Dutch or less constant than the Prussian?

An opportunity is afforded us to test that interrogatory.

If we decline to support our country with a free will offering of the useless plate and jewelry which not only encumbers our strong boxes but is a mill stone round our souls—then we deserve extinction as a nation, for liberty is not given by God as a child's rattle, but a prize to be won like heaven.

Columbia became the reservoir of hidden treasures. Where is Columbia and the treasures thereof? And so it will be universally, if we have not worth and virtue. The spoiler will come like a thief in the night and wrest our gilded idols away.

Let the Government appoint proper agents, and we hope for a generous answer from the people. Let the people combine, and each State contribute to the liquidation of the debt due its soldiers.

We regard this proposition of Mr. Trenholm's as a crucial test of patriotism to its appeal. [illegible] we be redeemed among the worthy, or be weighed in the balance and found wanting, as those who mocked and feasted at the banquet of Belshazzar.

[*Constitutionalist.*

Why the Battle was Lost.

"History," says Lord Bolingbroke, "is philosophy teaching by example." One great fault in historians is that they frequently do not trace events to their hidden causes, and another is that they ignore the decrees of overruling Providence.

We have one history of a great war that is free from these defects. We allude to the war by Joshua for the conquest of Palestine, and a lesson most appropriate to our own times and circumstances may be drawn from a defeat suffered by the great Captain of Israel in the battle of Ai.

Flushed with the capture of Jericho, Joshua sent forth a corps of his army to capture the little army. Never marched forth a body of troops more confident of victory. But a sudden panic struck them and they fled. The contagion spread through the whole host, and affected the great heart of Joshua himself.

The matter would be altogether unintelligible but that the historian who records it lifts the veil and unfolds the secret actions of men and the deep designs of Providence. We learn at a word why the battle was lost;

"Israel hath sinned; therefore they could not stand before their enemies, because they were accursed."—Josh. vii., 11, 12.

But what was the sin? Was it committed by the whole people? Was it a national sin? Not at all. It was the sin of one man, and he a private citizen, and not even in the army that was defeated. What, then, was this so great sin which caused the curse of God to rest on the whole people? Hear his own confession: "When I saw among the spoils (at the capture of Jericho) a goodly Babylonish garment, and two hundred shekels of silver, and a wedge of gold of fifty shekels weight, then I coveted them and took them."

Covetousness, covetousness, covetousness brought the curse upon Israel and lost the battle. Is there any wonder that we lose battles?

There is no evidence that Achan was in the army that was defeated at Ai; there is no evidence that any one in that army knew what he had committed; yet in consequence ot that unknown sin a panic seized them and they were defeated.

The value of the spoil *impressed* by Achan (to use the poraseology of this day) was small. A hundred dollars in silver, perhaps four hundred dollars in gold, and a fine mantle—this was the prize for which Achan brought defeat on his countrymen and death on himself and his family. But the amount hid away by many of our covetous men now would count up by the ten thousands.

The battle of Ai was lost in consequence of *one* sin of *one* man. Is it any wonder we lose battles when our sinners are numbered by the thousand, and our transgressions by the ten thousand? Yet any one sin of any one man may be the cause of the disasters. Reader, is it *your* sin that lost the last battle?

The battle of Jonesboro', followed by the destruction of Atlanta and the desolation of the State, may have been lost by the covetousness of one single Georgian. Are you the guilty man?

It is said that the great battle of Missionary Ridge was lost by a panic prevailing in an Alabama brigade. It may have been caused by the covetousness of a single Alabama planter or speculator. Are you the Achan?

It is said that the battle of Nashville was lost by a panic in Bate's division, and thus all Tennessee is lost to us. Was it the covetousness of some Tennessee speculator that lost the battle and brought the curse of God on his State? For what greater curse than to be governed by Brownlow?

Joshua could gain the victory only by removing the cause of the sin. If we must suffer defeat until covetousness and the consequent curse of God are removed from us, how long, oh Lord! must we suffer? How long?—*Baptist Banner.*

GOOD TESTIMONY.—It has been intimated by the supporters of Gov. Brown, that no evidence could be adduced of the demoralizing influence of his opposition to the Confederate authorities upon our own troops, and its incouragement of the enemy. We think the following, from the Columbus *Times* is pretty good evidence:

If any one has a doubt that the captious and factious course of Gov. Brown has been prolific of injury to our cause, he has but to converse with one of our recently returned prisoners in order to have the matter cleared up. We heard yesterday from the lips of one of these men, that he and his unfortunate comrades, while in prison, were constantly taunted by the Yankees with the statemt that the Confederacy had gone up, that Gov. Brown intended to carry Georgia back into the Union, etc. He further remarked that numbers of our men were induced to remain in Yankeeland, after their release, by the conviction that the Confederate army and Government could not long withstand the persistent attack of the enemy in the front and the no less relentless and much more dreaded assault *in the rear*, and, thus despairing of success, they did not care to throw away their lives in the vain effort to sustain a doomed cause. If Gov. Brown could hear the deep and earnest imprecations which these battle-scarred heroes are heaping upon his name, he would hang his head in shame, and would pray God to wipe out the very thoughts of him from their memory.

SOUTH CAROLINIA LEGISLATURE.—An extra session of the South Carolina Legislature has been convened to meet at Greenville, on the 25th of April.

STRUCK BY LIGHTNING.—A terrific thunder-storm passed over this place about one or two o'clock on Thursday morning last, and we regret to state the house of S. B. Stephens, Esq., was struck by lightning and greatly injured. The escape of Mr. Stephens and his family sems to those who have visited his residence since the occurrence and seen the 'wreck of matter' there, almost miraculous. The joists and sills of the house were torn up or shattered, the clapboards ripped off and the pillars splintered. Inside, the cornices, moulding and plastering were torn off, and windows broken. The furniture was scattered about and some of it broken, and the crockery and glassware smashed to pieces. A loaded gun was fired off and its position reversed. A flask of powder had been suspended from the muzzle of the gun by a cord, and after the discharge, the flask was found suspended by the cord from the butt of the gun. A jug of honey was broken, but a jug of turpentine, standing by it, was untouched. Had the turpentine been fired, the building and its contents would have been consumed. A heavy piece of a window-frame was thrown against the opposite wall with great force, very nearly hitting Mr. S. The freaks of the electric fluid were so numerous that we cannot relate all of them; but the most curious circumstance of all is that, although there were two lightning-rods attached to the house, they availed nothing to protect the building.

The loss of Mr. Stephens will reach several thousand dollars; though it is not to be estimated in money now, as it is impossible for him to replace the many valuable and necessary household articles so instantaneously destroyed.—*Quincy Dispatch.*

DR. MARSHALL AND THE POPE.—I am deemed a Methodist. Most people so regard me. I do not think there can be any mistake on this point, but it becomes me, as it does every citizen of the South, to give expression to my gratitude to the venerable Pope of Rome for his generous appreto have us recognized, at least as a people struggling bravely for the inalienable rights of man. At least once in the history of the Catholic Church, the "successor of St. Peter" follows worthily in the footsteps of his great Master. When the Savior of mankind stood upon the surging waves of the Sea of Galilee and beheld the ship on which his followers were embarked almost famished in the midst of the tempest, He exclaimed, "Peace, be still." Thus the great and good man, Pio Nino, whose virtues accumulate with his years, would check the storm of war. He prays that the ship of our fortunes may soon be moored in the haven of peace. I bless his name and shall revere his memory.

Catholic Europe sympathizes with the head of its church, while Greek Europe lends itself to the purpose of our foes. Let this and the temporal interests of the Old World take what shape and direction they may, we may confidently rely upon our own resources.

IMPORTANT ARREST.—That energetic officer, Detective Reece, recently succeeded in arresting a soldier named John A. Newton, of the 34th North Carolina regiment, upon the charge of forging and selling soldiers' discharges, furloughs and retired papers. Accused is a one legged soldier, and is supposed to belong to a regularly organized gang, the members of which for some months past have been roaming about the States of North Carolina, Georgia and Tennessee, selling the soldiers furloughs, discharges and retired papers. A large lot of blanks were found in his possession, and he confessed that he has furloughed, discharged and retired over 4,000 soldiers. The prices charged for these papers were as follows:

Discharges, $800; retired papers, 1,000; furloughs for sixty days, $400; for a less time than sixty days, $300. He confesses that the blanks found in his possession were printed in Augusta, Ga. Newton is a printer by profession, and had in his possession a quartermaster's stamp and inking apparatus. Detective Reece has been on the track of Newton for about five weeks, watching his every movement, and having fully posted himself, pounced upon him in his room, No. 25, South Carolina Soldiers' Home. He was immediately carried before the provost marshal, who, after a partial examination of the case, committed Newton to the Castle.—*Richmond Examiner.*

HON. ALLEN F. OWEN.—We regret to learn of the death of this gentleman, in this county, near Upatoie P. O., a few days ago. He will be remembered as the American Consul at Havana during a portion of the administration of Millard Fillmore, and who zealously labored to prevent the execution of the Lopez filibusters after capture.—He was a man of sterling integrity and stood high in the community where he lived and was best known.—*Columbus Enquirer 9th.*

"Now, gentlemen," said Sheridan to his guests, as the ladies left the room, "let us understand each other. Are we to drink like men or beasts?"—Somewhat indignant, the guests exclaimed, "Like men of course," "Then," he replied, "we are going to get wholly drunk, for brutes never drink more than they want."

NOTICE,

TO ALL WHOM IT MAY CONCERN.—The following Certificates of Deposit, having been stolen from me, or destroyed by the enemy, the public are hereby cautioned not to trade for the same, as I shall proceed to establish them according to law: Certificate, No. 3,410, for $1,100, dated March 16th, 1864, and one dated March 28th, 1864, No. 151, for $100, signed W. B. Johnston, Depositary, and issued to Thomas Gibson.

mar8-4w THOS. GIBSON.

LEGAL ADVERTISEMENTS.

Brought to Jail.

IN Bibb county, in September last, a Negro Boy named BILL, who says that he belongs to a Mrs. Susan Williams, a refugee from Tennessee to Marietta, Ga.

Also, brought to Jail, in October last, a Negro Boy named ED, who says he belongs to Thomas Cleveland, who went to the war from Canton, Ga., and met his company in Calhoun, Ga., where he went with him.

Also, brought to Jail, in October last, a Boy named JOHN, who says he belongs to Angus Morris, of Atlanta, Ga.

Also, brought to Jail, in November last, a Negro Boy named DANIEL, property of J. Cameron, of Tennessee.

Also, brought to Jail, in December last, a Negro Boy named GEORGE, property of George Willett, of Savannah, Ga.

The owners of said negroes are requested to come forward, prove property, pay charges and take them away, or they will be sold to pay expenses. Apply to

LEM CHERRY, Sheriff,
Or J. JOSEPH HODGES,
Macon, Ga., March 27th, 1865. Dept. Sheriff.
mar28-wtf.

NOTICE.—All persons indebted to MATHEW H. SANDWICH, late of Upson county, deceased, are hereby required to make immediate payment. And all persons having demands against the said deceased are requested to present them to the undersigned properly proven, within the time prescribed by law.

AMOS WORRILL,
mar28-1m Administrator.

GEORGIA, Crawford County.—Whereas, James N. Matthews applies to me for letters of Administration on the estate of Williaam Sloan, late of said county, deceased.

These are therefore to cite and admonish all an singular the kindred and creditors of said dec'd, to be and appear at my office within the time prescribed by law, and show cause—if any—why said letters should not be granted.

Given under my hand and official signature at office, Feby. 23d, 1865. JAMES J. RAY,
mar1 -30d* Ordinary

Bibb Sheriff's Sale.

WILL be sold before the Court House Door, in the city of Macon, Bibb county, within the legal hours of sale, on the First TUESDAY in June, the following NEGROES, to-wit: A Negro Woman named MARY ANN, about twenty-years of age, and her four children—ANN, FENTON, and two girl children, EMMA and OLIVIA, and a Negro Man named JOHN 24 years of age. Levied on as the property of Britton S. Ware, under mortgage fi fa, issued from Bibb Superior Court, in favor of M. S. Thomson, against the said Britton S. Ware, property pointed out in said mortgage fi fa.

Also, levied on boy TOM as the property of Britton S. Ware, to satisfy a Tax Execution from Twiggs county, against said Britton S. Ware.

J. JOSEPH HODGES,
March 28th 1865. Dept. Sheriff.
mar28-w[illegible]

Strayed or Stolen,

A Large Red COW. Her horns have been bored, and a piece of the horn is split off at one of the holes. She is marked in the ears, but mark not recollected. She has been missing since Thursday last. Any information of her whereabouts will be thankfully received at the

mar21-tf JOURNAL & MESSENGER OFFICE.

Certificate Lost.

NOTICE is hereby given, that the subscriber has lost the CERTIFICATE, herein described, given by Wm. B. Johnston, Depository, at Macon, and that I shall proceed to establish it in terms of the law. Certificate No. 1,504. Value in old currency, three hundred and eighty-five dollars; new currency, two hundred and fifty-six dollars and sixty-six cents. PAT. PAYTON.

apr9-w4t*

Administrator's Sale.

BY virtue of an order of the Ordinary of Crawford county, will be sold, before the Court House door, in the town of Knoxville, on the First Tuesday in May next, the following NEGROES: Charles, a man, about 28 years old; Lucy, a woman, about 23 years old, and her Five Children—Harrison, a boy, 8 years old, Hampton, a boy, 6 years old, Epsey, a girl, 4 years old, Edwa, a girl, 2 years old, and her infant child, 6 months old. Sold as the property of Raymond R. Parham, deceased, for the benefit of the heirs and creditors, this March 10th, 1865.

LEONIDAS BLUSTER,
JAMES T. PARHAM.
Administrators.

GEORGIA, Dooly County.—Whereas, Larkin Joiner applies to me for Letters of Administration on the estate of Garret Linsey, late of said county, deceased.

This is therefore to cite and admonish all persons concerned to be and appear at my office on or before the first Monday in April next, and show cause—if any they have—why Letters of Administration should not be issued to said applicant.

Given under my hand and official signature, this February 28th, 1865. WM. H. DAVIES,
mar4-30d Ordinary.

NOTICE.—All persons indebted to Mathew Smith late of Lee county, Georgia, deceased, are hereby required to make immediate payment. And all persons having demands against the said deceased, are requested to present them properly authenticated, within the time prescribed by law. This February 22, 1865.

Address me at Millwood, Dooly county, Ga.
mar4-40d* JOHN HENRY, Executor.

ESTRAY NOTICE.

GEORGIA, Macon County.—We the undersigned freeholders, residing in the 1070th District G. M., in said county, have this day examined an estray cow and calf exhibited to us by William B. Jones, of Said District and county, taken up of the same, do certify that said estrays are of the following description, to wit: cow black with white feet, marked with a swollow fork in each ear, and about three or four years old—calf red and white, five or six months old, unmarked, and appraised by us at one hundred dollars. This Feby. 20th, 1865.

J. B. GRIFFIN,
G. A. HOLSONBAKE, } Frs.
A true extract from the estray book book of said county.
mar 1—2m A. H. GREER, Clk.

Notice to Debtors and Creditors.

ALL persons indebted to the Estate of Benjamin H. Stroud, late of Crawford county, deceased, are requested to make immediate payment; and those having demands against said estate will present them in terms of the law. This March 31st, 1865.

S. F. STROUD, Administrator,
apr2-w40d With Will Annexed.

GEORGIA, Houston County.—Sixty days after date, I will apply to the Court of Ordinary of said county, for leave to sell a lot of land, near 1½ Station, S. W. Railroad, containing 202½ acres, belonging to the estate of James M. Hammock, deceased.

MARTHA HAMMOCK,
apr7-w2m Adm'x.

GEORGIA, Houston County.—ORDINARY'S OFFICE FOR SAID COUNTY.—Whereas, Wm. P. Lemmons, Administrator, de bonis not, of Abner P. Stubbs, late of said county deceased, petitions the undersigned for Letters of Dismission from his said trust.

These are therefore to cite all persons interested, to be and appear at my office, on or before the first Monday in November next, to show cause, if any they have, why said letters should not be granted.

Given under my official signature, this April 5th, 1865.
apr7-w6m W. T. SWIFT, Ordinary.

GEORGIA, Houston County.—ORDINARY'S OFFICE FOR SAID COUNTY.—Whereas, Jas. R. Burnam, petitions the undersigned for Letters of Administration upon the estate of Lorenzo D. Law, late of said county, deceased.

This is therefore to cite and admonish all persons concerned to be and appear at my office on or before the first Monday in May next, and show cause, if any they have, why said letters should not be granted.

Given under my official signature, this March 28th, 1865.
mar31-w1m WM. T. SWIFT, Ordinary.

Notice,

IS hereby given to all persons, against trading for TWO (2) certain Promissory NOTES, for Five Thousand Six Hundred and Twenty-five dollars each, made by me, and payable to E. W. Hughes, or bearer; due January 1st, 1865, and January 1st, 1866. Having complied with the terms of contract, by tendering payment for said notes in the Confederate treasury notes of the new issue, I am determined to let the law take its course.

Twiggs county, Ga., March 27th, 1865.
apr5-eod15t DR. U. A. RICE.

TWO MONTHS after date application will be made to the Court of Ordinary of Dooly county, for leave to sell all the lands belonging to the estate of Gordon W. Hamilton, late of Dooly county, dec'd.

feb 1 47-2m* SIMON ROYAL, Adm'r.

GEORGIA, Dooly County.—Whereas, James Holt applies to me for the Administratorship of J. T. Warren, minor child of John Warren, deceased.

This is therefore to cite and admonish all persons concerned to be and appear at my office on or before the first Monday in April next ane show cause—if any they have—why the Guardianship of said minor should not be entrusted to said applicant.

Given under my hand and official signature, February 28th, 1865. WM. H. DAVIES,
mar4-30d Ordinary.

Journal & Messenger.

S. Rose & S. B. Burr,
PROPRIETORS.

THE DAILY JOURNAL & MESSENGER.

Daily per month....	$ 8 00
" 2 "	16 00
" 3 "	24 00

No subscription taken for longer than three months.
ADVERTISING.—Three dollars per square of ten lines for each insertion.
A discount to contract advertisers and county officers.
Obituaries and Marriage notices to be paid for at advertising rates.
CASH IN ADVANCE will be invariably exacted.

MACON, GEORGIA:

Tuesday, April 11th, 1865.

To Our Subscribers.

Those of our subscribers who only subscribed for one month are notified that without they order their paper continued, we shall stop it. No paper will be continued after the time expires for which it was paid; this is an invariable rule and will be strictly adhered to. S. ROSE & CO.

☞ Remember that we take none but Confederate money (not ragged), city of Macon, and State of Georgia money. Parties sending us any other will loose it, as we cannot be troubled to return it, and hold it worthless.

PERRY HOUSE, COLUMBUS.—We are indebted to mine host of the Perry House, in Columbus, for many courtesies while in his city, and by the way, we would recommend the traveling public to give him a call. His house is pleasantly situated, is turnished as well as the market will afford, and his servants are attentive.

DEATH OF LIEUT. E. P. HOLSTEAD.

We regret to learn that Lieut. E. P. HOLSTEAD, of the Bartow Artillery, was killed in one of the recent battles in North Carolina. The writer of this knew him intimately as an apprentice in his establisement, and a more faithful, honorable and intelligent boy it has never been his good fortune to have under him. Responding promptly to the call of country Mr. Holstead joined the Bartow Artillery, and so deported himself as a soldier and a gentleman, that his companions in arms elected him from the ranks to the office of Lieutenant.—The service has lost no truer or better man since this war commenced. We pray God that these sacrifices may not be without good fruts. In this instance, we feel as if we had lost a near and dear relative, for next to our own sons, we esteemed this brave and noble young man. He fills a patriots grave, and we trust now rests in peace with the faithful of the Lord.

HAS HE SUSTAINED THE CAUSE OF COUNTRY?

The organs of Gov. Brown, copying after himself, are much in the habit of seeking, by the multiplicity of their words and a noisy assumption of superior regard for State and popular rights, to persuade the people that they have, in Governor Brown, a more reliable friend and champion—that he, of all others, is the man most to be trusted in these perilous times, and that, but for him, Georgia would have been crushed under the heels of "enemies from abroad" and "usurpers" at home. Now all such pretentions as these are rediculous, vain-glorious and without warrant of fact. Unfortunately for the interests of country, the people are too ready to adopt the special pleadings of such third-rate lawyers and pobiticians as Governor Brown and his [illegible] They do not take the time and trouble to winnow the grain of truth from the bushel of falsehood in which these demagogues envelope their wordy pretentions. Men should be judged by their acts, not their professions—by the good which results prove from their practices, rather than by the speciousness of their theories.

Has the policy of Gov. Brown advanced the interest of our common cause? This is the question that every true patriot should ask himself, before deciding upon the Governor's merits. Has his course promoted the success of the Southern Confederacy in her struggle against the ruthless invader of our soil and rights? Has he inspired confidence, encouraged the hopes of our people, infused spirit and energy into our troops? Has he given a cordial support and rendered prompt aid to the measures of the Confederate authorities? Has he instructed his people to hold up the hands of the Administration, that it might be encouraged to persevere in its efforts to secure our independence?

If Gov. Brown has done these things, he deserves the approbation of the people, not only of his own, but of the Confederate States. On the contrary, if his policy has been adverse to the great end and aim of the struggle in which we are engaged; if he has weakened the popular confidence in the integrity, and capacity of the President and his co-ordinate departments of Government, if he has dispirited our troops in the field by exciting dissentions at home; if he has arrayed himself in captious opposition to the Confederate authorities; if he has given aid and comfort to traitors at home and enemies abroad by his persistent assaults upon the President, the laws and the constituted authorities of the Confederacy, then he merits condemnation.

We ask, then, the direct and plain question—Has the policy of Gov. Brown been calculated to aid the success of the Confederate cause? We desire the people to reject all extranious issues, dispel from their minds the clouds of sophistry which obscure the sun-light of truth, and answer honestly—do they believe that the course of Gov. Brown, in warring upon the President and Congress, has advanced the interests of our great strugle for independence? Has it been such an one as was calculated to harmonise all interests, inspire populer confidence in those having direction of the war, and tending to stimulate unity of action, redoubled energy and unfaultering resolve to conquer? In short, has Gov. Brown acted like a man whose heart and soul were wedded to the one grand idea of saving his country at all hazards and at every sacrifice? As the people in their own consciences may answer these questions, will Gov. Brown stand approved or condemned by them.

HURRAH FOR THE LITTLE GIRLS.—The Charlotte Bulletin says:

We are informed that the patriotic little Misses of Charlotte, between the ages of twelve and fifteen, have organized themselves into a society for the purpose of knitting socks for our soldiers. This is a laudable undertaking, and should be encouraged and sustained by older citizens. We have a list of the names of the officers elect, which we may take occasion to publish at some future day.

WAR AMENDMENTS OF OTHER TIMES.—A writer in Blackewood some years ago remarked, let your proceedings towards an enemy in battle be as sharp but as polished as your sword. In battle it is the duty of each party to kill, capture and disable as many of the enemy as possible. When a man is disabled the object is gained as well as if he were killed, and no liberal minded soldier would wish to do more. At the battle of Fontenoy it is related the British Royal Guards politely called out "Tires Messisurs les Gardes Francaises." The other corps replied "the French Guard never fire first!" upon which their opponents, having given them the option, put an end to the chivalrous contest by opening their fire and annihillating their adversaries. During the protracted campaigns in the Peninsular, the exasperated citizens of Oporta threatened an attack on the garrison of Almeida, which, by the convention of Cintra was to be embarked at Oporta and sent to France. The Captain commanding the British detachment declared that in the event of a raising of the citizens he would stand by the French to the last. The Portugese then permitted the embarkation to go on without interruption.

At Lisbon, where complaints of French stealing were laid before the English, a conscientious French General in leaving, observed to his host, "I think you will bear me witness that when I entered your house I had two portmanteaus." This being admitted he said to the English officer, "You will now bear me witness, General, that I am retiring with but one."

At the battle of Palavira, the French Marshal, Mortier, took the greatest care of the English sick and wounded, and supplied some officers with money. He gave one officer credentials to return home through Paris, where he was present at the fetes for the marriage of Napoleon I.

After the close of the battle of Busaco, a French out-post remained nearer the English lines than was warranted by relative positions. Crawford sent the French a message to remove it. The officer commanding said he had to obey superior authority and remain until forced away. A few shots from the English satisfied the honor of the Frenchman, and he withdrew from a position where he could easily have been annihilated.

Near Corrunat, a French patrol advanced too far. "Will I shoot him?" asked the English sentinel? "By no means, replied the officer, and the dragoon speedily withdrew. A Frenchman found on the Corunna field a British officer almost dead. He was well cared for and finally recovered and proved to be a Napier.

After the engagement of Fuentes d'Onor, the village lay between the armies. Men from both sides got scattered over the place, and to prevent confusion a line of demarkation was drawn along a street. At Lisbon the English frequently supplied the French with cigars, coffee and other luxuries.

In one of these Peninsular engagements, a French dragoon came across an English cavalier who had lost an arm: as they approched each other, the Englishman raised the bloody stump to endeavor to save his head from the coming blow. The Frenchman perceiving his condition, instead of killing him, dropped his sword to the salute and galloped on. Favorite officers were always exchanged when a request was made to have them back for others of equal rank. At the first assault on Sebastopol, a young officer was found wounded far forward on the beach. A French [illegible] who had witnessed his gallantry, ran up and kissed him.

Wellington went out one day with his escort to reconnoitre the Adour river. In passing round the Bayonne fortress a lot of unarmed soldiers, then the garrison rushed out to see him. The English could have swept them all away but would not do it, seeing they were unable to make any defense.

THE TOBACCO SPECULATION.—We have obtained the main facts of the great Tobacco Speculation, in reference to which there were so many rumors last week. It appears that an agent of a New York mercantile house, whose name it is inexpedient to publish at this time, proposed to certain parties in this city to contract with him for the delivery of a specified quantity of manufactured tobacco, at Fredericksburg, he undertaking for his principals to remove the tobacco from that goint, with the implied consent of the United States authorities, provided the Confederate authorities would indicate their consent in writing, to the proposed transaction. The tobacco was to be paid for on its delivery at Fredericksburg. The New York house was vouched for by an influential member of Congress, who had intimate business relations with the concern. One of the Confederate bureaux became indentified with the scheme, by reasons of the representations which had been made to its officers, and by the prospect proposed agreement by the parties on the other side.

The contract was accordingly entered into, "sealed, signed and delivered," with a satisfactory endorsement from the predecessor of the present Secretary of War, who was, no doubt, induced to believe that it was "all right." Nothing was said in the contract about bacon. The *quid pro quo* was money.

In execution of the contract on this side, about 4,000 boxes of fine to extra manufactured tobacco were purchased here at rates varying from $4 to $7 per pound, Confederate currency. Of this amount, 1,237 boxes weighing 132,578 pounds, and valued at $700,000, were forwarded to Fredericksburg, in charge of Doctor Rose, who was induced by assurances from Richmond, which he could not discredit, to act as consignee and custodian of the tobacco until delivered according to agreement.

He was not, in any sense, as we understand, a party to the contract. What became of the tobacco is known to our readers. Dr. Rose was carried off by the Yankees to be tried for engaging in contraband traffic.

The name of Gen. Singleton has been connected with this transaction. We state, on authority of an officer of the bureau referred to, that he had no lot or part in it, directly or indirectly. The loss of the tobacco will fall upon the contractors here, unless the New York parties to the contract will fulfill their obligation by indemnifying the bureau with which they contracted.—[*Richmond Whig.*

SHERIDAN.—A certain wealthy nobleman invited the dramatist to visit him during the hunting season at his country seat. Sheridan went, but being no sportsman, found it rather dull work.—At length, one day finding himself left alone, he concluded to take a gun and fixings and trying his luck. An attendant gamepeeper proffered his services, which were promptly declined, determined that his want of skill should not be made the subject of remark in the servants' hall. The result of his tramp might be anticipated, and he found himself returning homeward without even a feather for his trophy, convinced of one of two things, to wit: either that his gun was a poor one, or that he did not understand its use.

Crossing the field, in the centre of which was a pond, around which was gathered a large flock of geese, ducks, hens, &c., he noticed a farmer leaning upon the fence, watching their gambols, and was seized with an irresistible desire to try his skill upon the feathered objects of his attention. Accordingly, he went up to the farmer, who seemed quite indifferent to his approach and thus accosted him:

"My friend, what shall I give you for permission to discharge both barrels in the midst of the flock?"

"Wull," answered the North countryman, "ai dun know; are thou much iver shot?"

"Much of a shot? Oh!" (slightly embarrassed,) "middling—only middling."

"Wull, how far wilt thou stan' off?"

"How far? Oh, say about twenty yards."

"Wull, ar shood think thou might's give a harf a ginny."

"Half a guinea! Pretty good price; however, I'll do it."

Accordingly the ground was measured, Sheridan took his stand, and, with a deliberate aim discharged both barrels, killing and wounding more than he anticipated.

"Ha! ha?" he laughed, picking up the spoils and approaching the old farmer, who seemed quite undisturbed by the result, "you didn't expect I should kill so many of them, did you?"

"Wull, no. I carnt say I did; but still yer know *its nothing to Iyer know, decos they don't belong to I.*"

After the correspondence which has been published between Gen. Lee and Gen. Grant, relative to the establishment of peace, he must be a very silly or a very obstinate individual who believes that the Yankee Government contemplates peace upon any other terms than those of absolute submission. We have always believed this to be the case. It is perfectly consistent with everything that has come from Lincoln himself, either directly or through third parties. Thus far, at least, we have nothing to complain of. We have been plainly told, from the beginning, what we had to expect. Like the propagator of the Mahomedan doctrine, the Yankees have, from the first, presented us with his creed in one hand and a sword in the other. We are required to swallow the oath or the sword, and no other alternative has been presented to us.

Surely, then, it is time for all men who do not think of submission to stop talking about peace. There is *no* peace, and there will be none, as long as the Yankees believe it is within their power to subjugate us. Convinced of the impracticability of *that*, they will be eager enough to make peace. For our own part, we are convinced that this will be the last grand effort they will ever make to effect our subjugation. We already see how their armaments have fallen off in magnitude, nor do we believe they will ever be able to raise them to their old standard. What they hope is, that we will give way first. They know they are not able to go much further themselves, and they hope to finish us before they yield to complete exhaustion.

That our people will not do this, we should think nothing more would be needed to convince us than the knowledge that they are fully aware of the only terms on which the Yankees will design to let us have peace. It would be the most terrible peace that the world ever beheld. The Caledonian warrior is made by Tacitus to say of the Romans: "They make a desert and call it peace." But this would not be a mere material desert—that we might stand. It would create a *moral* desert. It would make us a nation of slaves, and the Yankees our masters.—*Richmond Whig.*

THE CAVALRY FIGHT WITH HAMPTON.—The Herald's correspondent, describing the cavalry engagement in which Gen. Hampton routed Kilpatrick, an official account of which has been published, says:

Our cavalry had not all come up, owing to the bad state of the roads. Col. Spencer's brigade and Col Way's command were at once placed in position and waited the attack of the rebel cavalry. Just before daybreak on the morning of the 10th instant, and before the brigades of Gen. Atkins and Col. Jordan had arrived, Hampton came in front of Kilpatrick's position and massed his troops, consisting of three divisions, under Hume, Allen and Butler. The attack was made in three columns. Wheeler led the right, Hampton the centre, and Butler the left, and was perfectly irresistible. Kilpatrick's first line, under Lieut. Col. Way, was actually ridden over; headquarters and artillery captured, and at one time the entire camp, including the entire staff, and Col. Spencer, commanding the 3d brigade, were in the enemy's possession. But Gen. Kilpatrick made his escape, joined the brigade of Col. Spencer, which was falling back on foot, stubbornly disputing every inch of ground.

[The writer goes on to claim that the fortunes of the day shifted, and ended in a victory to Kilpatrick, whose loss, he says, was not over a hundred, etc. We have no room for a falsehood so palpably contradicted by the Confederate official report.—*Richmond Sentinel.*]

Eight Hundred Wagons and Veterans INNUMERABLE.

At the very moment when the horrid nightmare of ennui was about to settle down upon the so lately excited masses of our town and district, began the passage through said town and district, of a part of the wagon train of the army of Tennessee. These wagons, amounting to five or six hundred, had been congregating in Augusta for many weeks previous, and during the last ten days have been passing steadily through Edgefield to Ninety-six or Campbell's en route for North Carolina, to join the army. They have been accompanied by various bodies of cavalry; sometimes single companies; once or twice large and splendid regiments. All this time our town has been more or less filled with soldiers. Hundreds of bushels of corn and mountains of fodder have been hauled from the plantations near at hand, and deposited in the park, which ornaments our public square, for the feeding of the horses composing these wagon teams. The wagons have [illegible] lage. Our beautiful [illegible] park now looks like a cow pen. Not that we intend to complain; God forbid! For the park is by no means injured, neither trees nor railing having been damaged. A good raking and sweeping will soon set it in order again.

In consequence of all this passing of men and wagons, our people have been considerably excited. And on Sunday last, this excitement reached its hight. General Stephen D. Lee, that young South Carolinian of such prominent military ability and such exalted personal worth and integrity, had been in Augusta for some weeks before, gathering around him all furloughed men and absentees of the army of Virginia as happened to be south and west of Augusta. Gen. R. E. Lee's amnesty proclamation, and above all, the reinstatement of Gen. Johnston, has caused absent soldiers to flock to their commands by regiments; and on Sunday afternoon last, Gen. S. D. Lee led nearby Edgefield between eight and ten thousand as noble veterans as ever wielded their right arm for liberty. These troops did not pass directly through the town, but encamped some ten miles to the right. Almost the entire population went out to see and receive them. Every equipage of every sort, and every horse that had four legs, was in requisition. "Young men and maidens, old men, women, children," were there. The ladies were in full force, full beauty, and brimfull of enthusiasm. They smiled and wept, waved and cheered, and spread boquets broadcast. No less than one thousand million jonquils and daffodils have been sacrificed (and nobly) in the cause.

The troops seemed to be divided into five brigades, commanded respectively by Brig. Gens. Featheaston, Sharp, Brantly, Maney and Anderson. Each brigade was followed by its wagon train. Besides the infantry, there were two batteries of artillery: thirteen twelve pounder Napoleon guns. Among these regiments were glorious banners that have waved from Shiloah to Franklin, and from Manassas to Hatcher's Run.

These soldiers have been (lately, at all events) well fed and cared for, they looked comfortably clad, and their general physique was very fine. The soldiery bearing too, was as fine as their physical development. Each of them appeared to be every inch a soldier. They march with a firm tread and erect bearing of men inured to arms, to hardships and dangers, and equal to all the exigencies of war. Intelligence, patriotism and courage were visibly stamped upon their brows. Their conduct (as of all that have passed through Edgefield) was unexceptionable, exhibiting thorough discipline, gentle refinement and manly dignity.

Lt. Gen. Lee and staff, while in Edgefield, were partakers of the never failing hospitalities of ex-Gov. Pickens.

And now they are all gone; gone where they will doubtless surpass their former achievements, glorious and memorable as these have been. The roll of the drum is no more heard in our environs; the shrill shriek of the ear piercing fife has ceased to wake the echoes; the clangor of the martial trumpet has died away like the last expiring sounds of the Æolian harp, and quiet has once more settled down upon our monotonous village.—*Edgefield Advertiser*, 22d.

RESPONDING NOBLY.—We are gratified to see that the people of our State are responding to the call of Governor Vance for contributions for the support of our armie. Meetings are being held in all portions of the State not within the Yankee lines, and liberal donations made.

North Carolina has done her duty in sending men to the field, and she will not be outdone by any other State in supporting the men in the field. Her soldiers are doing their duty, and her people are doing theirs.—*Raleigh Progress*, *March* 21.

BY TELEGRAPH.

TELEGRAPHIC REPORTS OF THE PRESS ASSOCIATION.

AUGUSTA, April 10.—Stoneman burned the Eagle Factory in Cridell County, Va., on Thursday, March 30th.

Five thousand Yankees occupied Salem, April 1st. Their supposed design was to reach Danville, Greensboro', or lodge on the Railroad between the two places.

There is one Yankee regiment in the Kernstown Valley, Va.

Northern papers say that the expedition which failed at the Natural Bridge, Fla., was intended to release three thousand prisoners at Thomasville, Ga.

Gen. Thomas's official report states that from Sept. 7th to Jan 20th, the last five and a half months, amount captured was thirteen thousand one hundred and eighty-nine, including seven Generals, one thousand officers, seventy-two pieces of artillery, and that he received over two thousand deserters, a large amount of valuable ammunition and other war material. The Yankee loss was under two thousand.

Brownlow, the Governor elect for Tennessee, lately recovered $25,000 from two secessionists of Knoxsville, for malicious treatment in 1860. Commenting on the verdict, his paper says: "Impoverish the villains, take all. They have given their effects to Union men whom they have crippled and impoverished; let them be slain, and after slain, let them be drowned," with other savage anathemas.

The New York Times of the 22d denounces the above language with scathing comments.

On March 7th the House of Commons met in London. Sir Packington said, in appointing Mr. Reed in his present experience and efficiency as chief constructioner, they were trifling with the interests of England, when they allowed men of great skill and experience to leave the service at a time when war might break out any moment; and they might be compelled to send a fleet across the Atlantic, possibly upon the shortest notice.

Right Rev. Alonzo Spotter, bishop and president of the Episcopal church, diocese of Pennsylvania, has gone to California on account of ill health.

A regular post office is established with the army. Persons writing will address properly, name, company, regiment, and brigade, Johnston's army.

Letters and paper mail has arrived from Richmond and points of North Carolina—old dates.

The Southern Express arrived from points north of here yesterday, (9th) and brought Richmond dates and papers of 29th of March, from Raleigh April 1st, and Charlotte April 4th.

IN WHOSE SERVICE.—There are those among us, many of them, too, controlling public sentiment through the agency of the press, whose every utterance is one of complaint at the management of our national affairs, or of venomous abuse against those who are entrusted with the management and control of the government. If a law is passed, they discover nothing in it except flaws; if a battle is fought, they see nothing in it except blunders; and in their eyes, want of sagacity in devising and imbecility in executing, are the most prominent characteristics of our public servants. In the political sky they discern no ray of hope; to them it is ever lurid with impending wrath. They draw no augury of good from the present, past or future.

They have no words of cheer or commendation: they can only utter the language of desponding cowards, or of hopeful traitors. Miserable comforters, contemptible grumblers and vile croakers are they all, They are enemies of our cause, battling with might and main to defeat our whole purpose to be free. Too narrow-minded to be generous; too factious to be patriotic, such purblind fault finders suppose the public mind too obtuse to discern between carping, malicious, vindictive, and just, liberal and proper criticism.

And do such insidious sneerers and grumblers aid our cause by their unceasing, unqualified censure; their indiscriminate abuse of everything and everybody connected with the government? Is it their object to do so? Are they, by these never-ending croakings and complaints, aiming to encourage the hearts of our people; to keep them steadfast in the great work of achieving our independence? or do they design the contrary? Are they not aiming at distraction, dissension, undermine the government and ensure its ultimate failure? Under whose banner are they enlisted? In whose behalf are they battling? On which side are they fighting? Are they striving to build up or pull down the Confederacy? to uphold the hands of our rulers and sustain the hearts of our people, or to weigh down and crush them? Was ever a cause, great or small, prospered by such means? And are such creatures too ignorant to know, or too wicked to regard, the evil that results from their course. Are men who weaken, distract, demoralize and corrupt public sentiment by their vicious counsels, patriots? What are they? Specious dissemblers, whom "winged vengeance" will yet overtake and by preserving the "perishable infamy" of their names, render it immortal. [*Eufaula Spirit.*

FROM CAROLINAS.—The Yankees have established a negro recruiting office at Summerville, twenty-five miles above Charleston, and a negro brigade garrisons the town. The citizens it is understood, asked for a guard of protection, and the negroes were sent to afford it.

At Fayettville, N. C., the enemy destroyed the arsenal buildings, the market house, the court house, the printing offices, all the mills, cotton factories, oil works and a large number of dwellings. A letter from that place states that the citizens are in a starving condition.

A few days since a squad of thirty-five Yankee cavalry dashed into the village of Monroe, Union county, N. C., remained about an hour and left, carrying off all the horses and mules they could gather up. A train of wagons, ten in number, belonging to a party of refugees from Chester District, had just reached the village and were standing in the street when the Yankees appeared. Of course the train was seized, and horses, mules and wagons, with their contents, and nineteen negro men, were carried off. Thirteen of the negroes escaped from the enemy and returned to Monroe the same night. The loss is a heavy one to the unfortunate refugees. The women and children that accompanied the wagons were left standing in the streets of Monroe.

AUCTION PRICES.—At the auction sale of Messrs. W. A. Ramsey & Co., at the late residence of Mr. Thomas Gardner, on Wednesday last, the following prices were obtained: one china dinner sett, three hundred and eighty-one pieces, $5,100; one green china sett, eighty pieces, $2,550; one white china sett, ninety-five pieces, $5,000; celery glasses, $18 to 22 each; punch glasses, $19 each; champagne glasses, $12 to 12,50 each; wine glasses, $20 to 22,50 each; cordial glasses, $25 each; decanters, $120 to 150 each; celery stands, $105 each; glass pitchers, $62 to 255 each; ice cream bowls, $300 each; finger bowls, $8 to 18 each; vases, $190 to 475 each; gas fixtures, $60 to 300 each; tumblers, $25 to 50 each; jelly glasses, $18 each; bed room sets, crockery, $425 to 850 each; china egg cups, $4 to 7 each; doll heads, $100 each; one baby house furnished, $1500; one tapestry carpet, $7000; one medallion carpet, $10,500; one brocatelle sett parlor furniture, $15,000; one rosewood sett bed room furniture, $17,000; one rosewood piano, $28,000.—*Chronicle & Sentinel.*

PRACTICING WHAT HE PREACHES.—In Governor Vance's appeal the reader will notice, says the Winston Sentinel, that his excellency has tendered one-half of his year's supply of provisions for the soldiers of Gen. Lee's army, and that he further intends to put his family upon the limited rations allowed to our soldiers. This is the true spirit of patriotism, and it has frequently been manifested by Governor Vance, not only in the private walks of life, but in unnumbered public and official efforts to further the welfare of our defenders in every way that promised to promote their comfort and ability to withstand the hardships of a soldier's life. Go thou and do likewise. What a marked contrast such patriotic action presents to the mean practice of so many who are hoarding and refusing to part with but a portion of what they can well spare.

The Telegraph

THURSDAY MORNING, APRIL 13

PUBLISHED BY

FREDERICK EGRY,

At $2.00 per Year

J. T. LANGSTROTH, - - EDITOR.

LIBERTY AND UNION, NOW AND FOREVER, ONE AND INSEPERABLE.

The glorious news of the surrender of Lee, with his whole army, to the invincible Grant has already been flashed over the wires and borne by rushing car or hurrying stage to every hamlet of the North. Already have cannon thundered, bonfires blazed, and the old flag, God bless it, waved triumphantly in every section of the loyal States and with cheer and huzza the people have made the welkin ring for our brave soldiers and their gallant leaders. Hardly had we realized that Richmond was "ours and fairly won" when the telegraph informed us of the capture of Lee's Field Marshals and the successful cornering of the entire rebel army, and before we had fairly grasped this news the culminating point was reached by the tidings that Lee and the remnant of his forces had surrendered to Gen. Grant on his own terms.

Thus ends, in a blaze of glory, the four years war for the preservation of the nation's life. With the rebel capital in our posession, with the General in chief and the Army of Northern Virginia prisoners, with every fort along the whole sea-board in our hands, with every important City of the rebels ours, the gigantic slave holders rebellion, with its corner stone of slavery knocked out and ground into fragments, is prostrated: Without an available army, without money and without credit, with neither arms, rations, pay or leaders for its few remaining troops, the rebel Government can make further resistance only in the imagination of northern traitors. Lee a prisoner on parole, Davis and his fellow conspirators fugitives and vagabonds, Slavery forever gone and Gen. Anderson raising the old flag over Fort Sumpter while Henry Ward Beecher delivers an oration, these are the sights on which the sun will shine on the 14th of April 1865, four years from the day when the exultant rebels beheld our flag lowered for the first time, at the attack of domestic foes.

In the great dome of the Capital, illuminated for the first time since its completion in honor of the capture of Richmond, was emblazoned in letters of fire these words "it is the Lords doing and it is marvelous in our eyes." The nation to day recognizes the hand of the Almighty in these great events. The whole land is ablaze with rejoicing and the cannon thunders, the cheers vocalize, the illuminations blaze and the banners trace on the air the great voice of the American people *"Liberty and Union now and Forever, One and Inseparable."*

The war is virtually at an end. Resistance, if yet attempted, will avail nothing. The rebels know this and a few days will witness State after State knocking again at the door of the Union. We shall welcome them back in kindness and with mercy, extending to the deluded masses the protection and privileges found no where else, as they have learned to their cost, while denying to the leaders and chief criminals the rights and immunities they have so fully sacrificed. They left us as Slave States, they will return as FreeCommon-wealths, swelling the number and adding to the luster of these United States, no longer the supporter of Slavery, but now in reality and truth "the land of the *Free* and the home of the brave.

And what of our heroes, to whose strong right arms under God, we owe this victory, Many alas have fallen, yet a grateful nation will honor their memories, will deck with garlands of imortality their humble graves, and will tenderly care for their bereaved families. For those who come back, from whatever fields of duty, the people have the same welcome, the nation the same thanks.—Undismayed by danger, unshaken by hardship and suffering, confronted by implacable foes in front, and assailed by insidious traitors in the rear, they have stood firm, never faltering, never wavering, ready alike to fight, to suffer and to vote, and to day the nation hails them its heroes, its saviors. All honor to them, the bravest of the brave, returned at last from war to the firesides preserved by their valor long and happy be their lives, as they add dignity to our communities and show to admiring descendants "how fields were won" by their indomitable courage.

A large Union caucus was held at Columbus on the 5th. It was decided to hold the Convention on the 21st of June. Speeches were made by General Schenck, Hon. J. A. Bingham, and others.

The Democratic city of Peoria, Ill., went Union at the late municipal election by majorities ranging from 43 to 259.

According to the latest returns, the majority for the Union ticket in Connecticut is 11,066.

The Maryland Legislature has repealed nearly all the old acts of oppression to the colored population.

Secretary Seward was thrown from a carriage in Washington on the 5th inst, the horses having ran away, and so badly injured that but faint hopes of his recovery are entertained.

The Subscriptions to the 7-30 loan last week footed up $14,805,800.

Jeff. Davis and a part of the rebel Congress are reported to have left Danville for Charlotte. N. C., on Monday.

Victory Again!

LATEST FROM THE ANANCONDA!

Surrender of Lee!

HIS WHOLE ARMY OURS!

THEY ARE PAROLED!

GRANT STRIKES ILE

LEE TAKES STOCK IN THE UNION!

HE CANT SEE IT AT FIRST!

BUT IS UNDER CONVICTION!

IS ON THE ANXIOUS SEAT!

GRANT CONVERTS HIM!

Davis "Sloped for Texas."

Official Correspondence!

BRING OUT THE CANNON!

RALLY ROUND THE FLAG!

How are you Peace Party!

How about "Four years failure."

HOW ABOUT AN ARMISTICE?

Welcome Peace through war.

Exit Peace Democracy!

Grand Official Bulletin.

SURRENDER OF LEE'S ARMY.

WAR DEPARTMENT, WASHINGTON,
April 9—9 P. M.

Major General Dix, New York:

This Department has received the official report of the surrender this day of General Lee and his army, to Lieut.-General Grant, on the terms proposed by General Grant.

[Signed,] E. M. STANTON,
Secretary of War.

HEADQUARTERS ARMIES OF THE U. S.,
April 9—4:30 P. M.

To Hon. E. M. Stanton, Sec. of War:

General Lee surrendered the Army of Northern Virginia this afternoon, upon the terms proposed by myself.

The accompanying additional correspondence will show the condition fully.

[Signed,] U. S. GRANT, Lieut.-Gen.

THE PRELIMINARY CORRESPONDENCE.

The following is the previous correspondence between Lieutenant-General Grant and General Lee, referred to in the foregoing telegram to the Secretary of War.

GENERAL GRANT TO THE SECRETARY OF WAR.

CLIFTON HOUSE, VA., April 9.

Hon. E. M. Stanton Sec. of War;

The following correspondence has taken place between General Lee and myself. There has been no relaxation in the pursuit during its pendency.

[Signed,] U. S. GRANT, Lieut.-Gen.

GRANT PROPOSES THAT LEE SURRENDER.

April 7, 1865.

Gen R. E. Lee, Commanding C. S. A.

GENERAL: The result of the last week must convince you of the hopelessness of further resistance on the part of the Army of Northern Virginia in this struggle. I feel that it is so, and regard it as my duty to shift from myself the responsibility of any further effusion of blood, by asking of you the surrender of that portion of the Confederate States Army known as the Army of Northern Virginia.

Very respectfully, your ob't serv't,
U. S. GRANT,
Commanding Armies of the U. S.

LEE ASKS THE CONDITIONS.

April 7, 1865.

GENERAL: I have received your note of this date. Though not entirely of the opinion you express of the hopelessness of further resistance on the part of the Army of Northern Virginia, I reciprocate your desire to avoid useless effusion of blood, and, therefore, before considering your proposition, ask the terms you will offer, on condition of its surrender.

[Signed] R. E. LEE General.

To Lieut.-Gen. U. S. Grant, commanding Armies of the U. S.

GRANT'S ONE CONDITION.

April 8. 1865

General R. E. Lee, commanding C. S. A.:

GENERAL: Your note of last evening in reply to mine of the same date, asking the conditions on which I will accept the surrender of the Army of Northern Virginia, is just received. In reply, I will say that peace being my first desire, there is but one condition I insist upon, viz: that the men surrendered shall be disqualified for taking up arms again against the Government of the United States until properly exchanged. I will meet you, or designate officers to meet any officers you may name, for the purpose of arranging definitely the terms upon which the surrender of the Army of Northern Virginia will be received.

Very respectfully, your obedient servant,
U. S. GRANT,
Lieutenant-General com'd'g A. U. S.

LEE WANTS TO TREAT ON PEACE.

April 8, 1865

GENERAL: I received at a late hour your note of to-day in answer to mine of yesterday. I did not intend to propose the surrender of the Army of Northern Virginia, but to ask the terms of your proposition. To be frank I do not think the emergency has arisen to call for the surrender of this army; but as the restoration of peace should be the sole object of all, I desire to know whether your proposals would tend to that end. I would not, therefore, meet you with a view to surrender the Army of Northern Virginia; but as far as your proposition may effect the C. S. forces under my command, and tend to the restoration of peace, I should be pleased to meet you at 10 A. M. to-morrow, on the old stage road to Richmond, between the picket lines of the two armies.

Very respectfully, your obedient servant,
R. E. LEE, General C. S. A.

To Lieut.-Gen. Grant, Commanding Armies of U. S.

GRANT DECLINES PEACE NEGOTIATIONS.

April 9, 1865.

Gen. R. E. Lee, Commanding C. S. A.:

Your note of yesterday is received. As I have no authority to treat on the subject of peace, the meeting proposed for 10 A. M. to-day could not lead to any good. I will state however, General, that I am equally anxious for peace with yourself, and the whole North entertain the same feeling. The terms upon which peace can be had are well understood. By the South laying down their arms, they will hasten that most desirable event, save thousands of human lives, and hundreds of millions of property not yet dedestroyed. Sincerely hoping that our difficulties may be settled without the loss of another life, I subscribe myself

Very respectfully your obedient servant,
U. S. GRANT, Lieut.-Gen. U. S. A.

GENERAL LEE TO GENERAL GRANT.

April 9th, 1865,

GENERAL: I received your note of this morning on the picket line, whither I had come to meet you, and ascertain definitely what terms were embraced in your proposition of yesterday with reference to the surrender of this army. I now request an interview in accordance with the offer contained in your letter of yesterday, for that purpose,

Very respectfully, your obedient servant,
R. E. LEE, General,

Lieut.-Gen. Grant, Comm'g U. S. Armies

GEN. GRANT TO GEN LEE.

April 9, 1865.

Gen. R. E. Lee, Commanding the Confederate States Armies:

Your note of this date is but this moment (11:50 A. M.) received, in consequence of my having passed from the Richmond & Lynchburg to the Farmville & Lynchburg road. I am at this writing about 4 miles west of Walter's Church and will push forward to the front for the purpose of meeting you. Notice sent to me on this road where you wish the interview to take place, will meet me.

Very respectfully your obedient servant,
U. S. GRANT, Lieut.-General

GRANT'S TERMS OF SURRENDER.

APPOMATTOX COURT HOUSE, April 9.

Gen. R. E. Lee, Commanding C. S. A:

In accordance with the substance of my letter to you of the 8th inst., I propose to receive the surrender of the Army of Northern Virginia on the following terms to wit: Rolls of all the officers and men to be made in duplicate, one copy to be given to an officer designated by me, the other to be retained by such officers as you may designate. The officers to give their individual paroles not to take up arms against the Government of the United States until properly exchanged; each company or regimental commander sign a like parole for the men of their commands.

The arms, artillery and public property to be packed and stacked and turned over to the officers appointed by me to receive them. This will not embrace the side-arms of the officers nor their private horses or baggage. This done, each officer and man will be allowed to return to their homes, not to be disturbed by the United States authorities so long as they observe their parole, and the laws in force where they may reside.

Very respectfully, U. S. GRANT,
Lieutenant-General.

LEE ACCEPTS GRANT'S TERMS.

HEADQUARTERS ARMY OF NORTHERN VA.,
April 9.

Lieut.-Gen. U. S. Grant, com'd'g U. S. A:

GENERAL: I have received your letter of this date, containing the terms of surrender of the Army of Northern Virginia as proposed by you. As they are substantially the same as those expressed in your letter of the 8th inst., they are accepted. I will proceed to designate the proper officers to carry the stipulations into effect.

Very respectfully, your ob't servant,
R. E. LEE, General.

THANKSGIVING FROM THE WAR DEPARTMENT.

WAR DEPARTMENT, D. C.,
9:30 P. M., April 9, 1865.

To Lieutenant General Grant:

Thanks be to Almighty God for the great victory with which He has this day crowned you and the gallant army under your command. The thanks of this Department of the Government and of the people of the United States, their reverence and honor have been deserved and will be given to you and the brave and gallant officers and soldiers of your army for all time.

[Signed] E. M. STANTON,
Secretary of War.

HARK FROM THE TOMBS!

The dead have come to life again, the lost are found. That great martyr to Democratic principle, the exiled Valandigham, currently supposed to have been buried last November, has at last turned up alive and kicking and in as good a state of preservation as could be looked for under the circumstances. The magnates of the Democracy, who had deemed him politically dead, may not welcome his re-entree and his once devoted followers may not hail his second advent, but regardless of this, at the potent summons of a military Commission assembled to try his brother conspirators of Chicago, he bounds into the ring at Cincinnati and Merry-Andrew-like exclaims, here I am! The Democracy have long been afflicted by visions of military Commissions going about like roaring lions seeking whom they might devour, but this puts them in the light of ghouls resurrecting the dead for the purposes of mastication.

And yet the operation so unfortunate for the party in this case may easily be turned to a good use in the future. Why not resurrect Andrew Jackson, formerly one of their shining lights, or Douglass, or even Long and Cox. Let us have a vision of Calhoun, let us renew acquaintance with Jefferson.

Like the ghost in Hamlet, Val. discloses some troublesome secrets. It seems that he was pregnant with a letter to the faithful Democracy of the North, but for want of a mid-wife was obliged to delay delivery.—How long shall this thing continue? Cannot the great Apostle be induced, even at this late day, to give us his counsel. He says in his testimony:

There was an informal meeting of members held in Windsor about the 15th of April, Mr. McMaster was present; also Dodd, Judd and others. At that meetting the entire business transacted related to the Chicago Convention, and the condition of the Democratic party. It was agreed that I should write a letter addressed to the Democrats of the United States, defining what I believe to be the duty of the Democratic party in the appreaching Presidential election. This was the only meeting of the organization at which I was present, except an informal meeting of members during the Chicago Convention, at which I presided as chairman, the question before us being that of a platform and nomination. The reason no letter ever was written is the failure of some one in not sending me a letter that that was to call mine out.

The election unhappily took place without the ventilation of Val's views in the manner proposed. For the benefit of the future historian we trust that some one of the faithful will even yet send him a letter to call his out. Come to the rescue of the Apostle; he being risen from the dead the still-born letter should also be reanimated.

We commend this subject to the consideration of the "chosen" of Hamilton. We trust that some one of them may be possessed of nerve enough to address the dead-restored-to-life martyr, and should they be at a loss where to direct their letter we refer them to the opening residence of Vallandigham's testimony. "I reside in Dayton, and am now practicing Law." With a sigh for the victories of his practice, and hoping they may not suffer from it as did the Democratic party, we await that letter.

NEWS OF THE WEEK.

An official dispatch from General Weitzel reports the capture at Richmond of 4,000 prisoners, 3,000 of whom were wounded, five hundred pieces of artillery, and five thousand stand of arms. Lee telegraphed Davis on Sunday afternoon that he would be compelled to evacuate. The announcement was read in churches. All the leading men got off that evening. Ewell fired the city, and the greater part of the business portion of the town was burned.

It is proposed, in New York, to celebrate the recent victories about the 20th inst, by appropriate thanksgiving service in all the churches. Committees of arrangements have been appointed.

The Louisville Press says unusual activity is prevailing among colored troops in Kentucky, during the last few days, and recruiting is very lively. The 125th Colored Infantry, Colonel Armstrong, has obtained two hundred recruits within the last few days.

The Tennessee Legislature, on the 5th, commenced business by unanimously ratifying the Constitutional amendment abolishing slavery. General Thomas, General Rousseau and other distinguished military gentlemen were present at the inauguration of Governor Brownlow.

The report that the rebel Major-General Ambrose Powell Hill was killed in the recent battles near Petersburg is confirmed.—He was buried in that city on Sunday, the day of his death.

The New Orleans Independent publishes a letter purporting to have been written on the 3d of January last, by Major C. S. West, Judge Advocate of General Kirby Smith, to Governor Murrah, of Texas. It is claimed that the letter was inspired by Gen Smith. The letter says, in substance, that as it is evident the rebel army and Government east of the Mississippi are rapidly getting demolished, and that the same power which is vanquishing everything at the East can conquer the West also, it is time to be preparing for the inevitable future. It is suggested that in view of existing facts, it would be well for the Governor to either call a Convention or convene the Legislature. It claims that there are 52,000 rebel troops west of the Mississippi, which the Independent says is a great exaggeration; that these troops would probably refuse a call from the Richmond authorities to cross the river, and suggests that instead of embarking in a useless struggle at the East, and abandoning Texas to her fate, it would be better to go to Mexico, and there, by fighting seccessfully to maintain a republic against an empire, to earn the right to return home, with the blot of treason effaced from their escutcheon. The letter has been the subject of much comment in the Texas papers, and, if genuine, may be regarded as a feeler thrown out by Kirby Smith.

The Governor of New York has designated Friday, the 14th inst., the day of the flag-raising on Fort Sumpter, as a thanksgiving day, and the Governor of Pennsylvania has requested special thanks for the late victories to be made in all the churches in that State on next Sunday.

Gen. Saxton and other officials indulged the freedmen of Charleston in a grand demonstration on the 21st ult. About 4,200 colored persons of both sexes, marched in procession through the streets, carrying banners and mottoes. The various trades were represented—the ship carpenters carrying their adzes; the blacksmiths their hammers, etc.; the firemen wearing their red shirts; while on a cart was a group portraying an occupation now happily extinct in the city. On the vehicle an auctioneer stood over two women seated on a block with their children standing about them. A boy was also in the cart, whose office was to ring a bell with all the energy he possessed. The cart bore the announcement; "A number of negroes for sale;" and as it moved along the auctioner would appeal to the crowd for a bid, making use of the phrases which are usually heard in a negro auction room. Attached to the cart was a long rope, tied to which was a number of men and woman. Next was a hearse, bearing a coffin, and having the inscriptions:—"Slavery is dead;" "Who owns him?" "No one;" "Sumpter dug his grave on the 13th of April, 1861," The hearse was followed by mourners dressed in deep black. There were 1,800 school-children in the possession. The utmost good order prevailed throughout the day, and so great was the enthusiasm that no less than 300 colored recruits enlisted.

Henry S. Foote returned to New York as a steerage passenger, and was arrested soon after his arrival and lodged in jail.

It is announced that Garibaldi's daughter Teresita has given birth at Caprera to a boy who, by his grandfather's desire, has been christened Lincoln, in honor of the "American President who has abolished slavery."

Organizations are already in progress for the establishment of four National Banks in Richmond.

The sales of 730s Tuesday were the largest reported for some time amounting to $3,132,400.

The total damage by the fire at Richmond is estimated at $3,000,000. Eight hundred hogsheads of tobacco owned by France were destroyed.

Joe Johnson is reported retreating northward, to form a junction with Lee. We think he will succeed, and end his marches in the same manner as his superior officer.

Gold closed in New York Tuesday at 145. Stocks were weak, and some of them lower. Government securities, however were active and higher.

The President announces to foreign powers that if they do not give our war vessels all the port privileges allowed by the comity of nations, they may expect similar treatment from us.

Charleston Courier.

NEW SERIES..No. 42 CHARLESTON, S. C., UNITED STATES OF AMERICA, FRIDAY MORNING, APRIL 14, 1865 VOL. I.

THE
CHARLESTON COURIER
IS PUBLISHED EVERY MORNING
BY WHITTEMORE & JOHNSON,
(GEO. WHITTEMORE.........G. W. JOHNSON.)
No. 43 HAYNE-STREET,
SECOND DOOR EAST OF MEETING-ST.

TERMS—INVARIABLY IN ADVANCE:
ONE YEAR......$20
SIX MONTHS......10
THREE MONTHS......5

No subscription will be received for a less period than three months.

SINGLE COPIES TEN CENTS, to be had at the Office.

News Boys served at a discount.

ADVERTISING.

Per square of TEN LINES Nonpareil type or space occupied by the same number of lines, TWO DOLLARS for the first insertion; ONE DOLLAR for each continuation.

Half square—ONE DOLLAR for each insertion; FIFTY CENTS for each subsequent insertion.

When an advertisement makes less than a half square, the charge will be TWENTY CENTS per line for the first, and TEN CENTS for every subsequent insertion.

All advertisements must be paid for at the Counting Room, previous to insertion.

Special contracts will be made with parties who desire to advertise for any term exceeding three months.

THE END OF THE REBELLION!

LAUS DEO!

Surrender of Gen. Robert E. Lee and the Entire Army of Northern Virginia.

TWO SOLDIERS IN COUNCIL.

A GREAT CAPTAIN PERFORMS A HUMANE ACTION.

GLORY TO GRANT!

FULL DETAILS OF THE TERMS OF THE CAPITULATION.

CORRESPONDENCE BETWEEN THE TWO GENERALS.

WILD ENTHUSIASM OVER THE NEWS.

The glorious news of the surrender of General R. E. LEE and the entire Army of Northern Virginia to Lieutenant General GRANT is contained in the New York papers of the 10th, for copies of which we are indebted to Purser E H. ROCKWELL, of the steamer "Oceanus." The following are the official orders and correspondence as published:

WAR DEPARTMENT,
Washington, April 9—9 o'clock P. M.

To Major General DIX, New York:

This Department has received the official report of the surrender, this day, of General LEE and his army to Lieutenant General GRANT, on the terms proposed by Gen. GRANT.

Details will be given as speedily as possible.

EDWIN M STANTON,
Secretary of War.

HEADQ'RS ARMIES OF THE UNITED STATES,
April 9—4:30 P. M.

Hon. EDWIN M. STANTON, Secretary of War:

General LEE surrendered the Army of Northern Virginia this afternoon, upon the terms proposed by myself. The accompanying additional correspondence will show the conditions fully.

(Signed) U. S. GRANT,
Lieutenant General.

THANKS TO GEN. GRANT AND THE ARMY.

WAR DEPARTMENT,
Washington, D. C., 9:30 P. M., April 9.

Lieutenant General GRANT:

Thanks be to Almighty God for the great victory with which He has this day crowned you and the gallant armies under your command.

The thanks of this department, and of the Government, and of the people of the United States—their reverence and honor have been deserved—will be rendered to you and the brave and gallant officers and soldiers of your army for all time.

EDWIN M STANTON,
Secretary of War.

LET THE CANNON SPEAK.

WAR DEPARTMENT, WASHINGTON D. C.,
April 9—10 o'clock, P. M.

ORDERED: That a salute of two hundred guns be fired at the headquarters of every army and department, and at every post and arsenal in the United States, and at the Military Academy at West Point, on the day of the receipt of this order, in commemoration of the surrender of General R. E. LEE and the army of Northern Virginia to Lieutenant-General GRANT, and the army under his command; report of the receipt and execution of this order to be made to the Adjutant-General, Washington.

EDWIN M. STANTON,
Secretary of War.

THE CORRESPONDENCE.

CLIFFTON HOUSE, VA., April 9.

Hon. EDWIN M. STANTON, Secretary of War:

The following correspondence has taken place between General LEE and myself. There has been no relaxation in the pursuit during its pendency.

U. S. GRANT,
Lieutenant General.

I.

GENERAL GRANT TO GENERAL LEE.

APRIL 7.

General R. E. LEE, Commander C. S. A.:

GENERAL: The result of the last week must convince you of the hopelessness of further resistance on the part of the Army of Northern Virginia in this struggle. I feel that it is so, and regard it as my duty to shift from myself the responsibility of any furher effusion of blood, by asking of you the surrender of that portion of the C. S. Army, known as the Army of Northern Virginia.

Very respectfully, your obedient servant,
U. S. GRANT,
Lieutenant General Commanding Armies of the United States.

II.

GENERAL LEE TO GENERAL GRANT.

APRIL 7.

GENERAL: I have received your note of this date. Though not entirely of the opinion you express of the hopelessness of further resistance on the part of the Army of Northern Virginia, I reciprocate your desire to avoid useless effusion of blood, and therefore, before considering your proposition, ask the terms you will offer, on condition of its surrender. R. E. LEE, General.

To Lieutenant General U. S. GRANT, Commanding Armies of the United States.

III.

GENERAL GRANT TO GENERAL LEE.

APRIL 8

To General R. E. LEE, Commanding Confederate States:

GENERAL: Your note of last evening, in reply to mine of same date, asking the conditions on which I will accept the surrender of the Army of Northern Virginia, is just received.

In reply, I would say that peace being my first desire, there is but one condition that I insist upon, viz:

That the men surrendered shall be disqualified for taking up arms again against the Government of the United States until properly exchanged.

I will meet you, or designate officers to meet any officers you may name for the same purpose, at any point agreeable to you, for the purpose of arranging definitely the terms upon which the surrender of the Army of Northern Virginia will be received.

Very respectfully,
Your obedient servant,
U. S. GRANT,
Lieutenant General Commanding Armies of the United States.

IV.

GENERAL LEE TO GENERAL GRANT.

APRIL 8.

GENERAL: I received at a late hour your note of to-day in answer to mine of yesterday.

I did not intend to propose the surrender of the Army of Northern Virginia, but to ask the terms of your proposition. To be frank, I do not think the emergency has arisen to call for the surrender. But as the restoration of peace should be the sole object of all, I desire to know whether your proposals would tend to that end.

I cannot, therefore, meet you with a view to surrender the Army of Northern Virginia, but as far as your proposition may effect the Confederate States forces under my command, and lead to the restoration of peace. I should be pleased to meet you at 10 A. M. to-morrow, on the old stage road to Richmond, between the picket lines of the two armies.

Very respectfully, your obedient servant,
R. E. LEE,
General Confederate States Armies.

To Lieutenant General GRANT, Commanding Armies of the United States.

V.

GENERAL GRANT TO GENERAL LEE.

General R. E. LEE, Commanding C. S. A.:

GENERAL: Your note of yesterday is received. As I have no authority to treat on the subject of peace, the meeting proposed for ten A. M. to-day could lead to no good. I will state, however, General, that I am equally anxious for peace with yourself, and the whole North entertain the same feeling. The terms upon which peace can be had are well understood. By the South laying down their arms they will hasten that most desirable event, save thousands of human lives, and hundreds of millions of property not yet destroyed.

Sincerely hoping that all our difficulties may be settled without the loss of another life, I subscribe myself,

Very respectfully, your obedient servant,
U. S. GRANT,
Lieutenant-General U. S. A.

VI.

GENERAL LEE TO GENERAL GRANT.

APRIL 9, 1865.

GENERAL: I received your note of this morning on the picket line, whither I had come to meet you and ascertain definitely what terms were embraced in your proposition of yesterday with reference to the surrender of this army.

I now request an interview in accordance with the offer contained in your letter of yesterday for that purpose.

Very respectfully,
Your obedient servant,
R. E. LEE, General.

To Lieutenant General GRANT, Commanding United States Armies.

VII.

GEN. GRANT TO GEN. LEE.

APRIL 9

General R. E. LEE, Commanding Confederate States Armies:

Your note of this date is but this moment (11:50 A. M.) received.

In consequence of my having passed from the Richmond and Lynchburg road to the Farmville and Lynchburg road, I am at this writing about four miles West of Walter's Church, and will push forward to the front for the purpose of meeting you.

Notice sent [illegible] the interview to take place will meet me.

Very respectfully,
Your obedient servant,
U. S. GRANT,
Lieutenant General.

THE TERMS.

APPOMATTOX COURT HOUSE, April 9, 1865.

General R. E. LEE, Commanding C. S. A.:

In accordance with the substance of my letter to you, of the 8th instant, I propose to receive the surrender of the Army of Northern Virginia on the following terms, to wit:

Rolls of all the officers and men to be made in duplicate, one copy to be given to an officer designated by me, the other to be retained by such officers as you may designate.

The officers to give their individual paroles not to take up arms against the United States until properly exchanged, and each company or regimental commander sign a like parole for the men of their commands.

The arms, artillery and public property to be packed and stacked, and turned over to the officers appointed by me to receive them. This will not embrace the side-arms of the officers, nor their private horses or baggage.

This done, each officer and man will be allowed to return to their homes, not to be disturbed by United States authority so long as they observe their parole and the laws in force where they may reside.

Very respectfully,
U. S. GRANT, Lieutenant General.

VIII

THE SURRENDER.

HEADQ'RS ARMY OF NORTHERN VIRGINIA,
April 9, 1865.

Lieutenant-General U. S. GRANT, Commanding U. S. A.:

GENERAL: I have received your letter of this date containing the terms of surrender of the Army of Northern Virginia, as proposed by you. As they are substantially the same as those expressed in your letter of the 8th instant, they are accepted. I will proceed to designate the proper officers to carry the stipulations into effect.

Very respectfully, your obedient servant,
R. E. LEE, General.

THE REBEL MONITOR TEXAS.—The rebels, previous to evacuating Richmond, sank their new single turreted monitor "Texas" across the channel of the river. The "Texas" has only been launched a little upwards of a month.

A Successful Expedition.

General HARTWELL, who started on an expedition several days ago, returned yesterday, having successfully scoured the country for about sixty miles along the Santee river and both sides of the South Carolina Rail Road as far as Vances' Ferry. Small bodies of FERGUSON's rebel cavalry were met and dispersed, but could not be overtaken, being mounted on fleet horses and General HARTWELL's forces consisting altogether of infantry. The country had been devastated by the bushwhackers. Many of the old planters had been stripped of everything. Negroes flocked to Gen. HARTWELL from all directions, and about fifteen hundred were brought in.

The General had an interview with Lieutenant PETTUS, commanding FERGUSON's scouts, and through him forwarded a communication to Gen. FERGUSON in reference to the depredations and outrages committed by the rebel bushwhackers upon unarmed citizens and planters. The parties professed to be acting under the orders of Gen. FERGUSON, and were particularly violent towards any white person manifesting a favorable disposition to the Union troops or who had taken the oath of allegiance. All negroes found off their owner's plantation by these parties were immediately shot down in their tracks.

General HARTWELL suggested to General FERGUSON the propriety of withdrawing all armed scouts from the country which his (General FERGUSON's) forces did not occupy, as their presence would require the sending out of armed parties to protect the negroes, which would cause much devastation and trouble through the country. Gen. FERGUSON's headquarters were at Aiken, and the rebel Major General YOUNG's at Ninety-six. Lieut. PETTUS, who held the interview with Gen. HARTWELL, is a son of ex-Governor PETTUS, of Mississippi.

The wealthy planters in the section visited by our troops expressed the bitterest animosity toward the Yankees, and their determination to fight it out. General HARTWELL placed a guard over the mansion of Mr. N. MAZYCK PORCHER to preserve it from destruction. After our troops left, however, the house was stripped of all its contents, elegant furniture, fine paintings, library, &c, and afterwards burned to the ground.

The expedition returned without the loss of a single man. It is believed, however, that a number of the rebel [illegible] of their parties.

Lieutenant PETTUS, by some mistake, was detained a prisoner for a short time, it being supposed that he was acting without authority. Several orders of General FERGUSON's were produced, of which the following are copies:

HEADQUARTERS CAVALRY BRIGADE,
March 19, 1865.

I send Lieutenant Pettus with a scouting party to ascertain and report the movement of the enemy; also, to protect citizens as much as possible from marauding parties, and recommend him to the attention of all citizens.

S. W. FERGUSON, Brigadier General.

HEADQUARTERS CAVALRY BRIGADE,
[Order No. —] March 19, 1865.

Lieut. Pettus will proceed with his scouts in the vicinity of the enemy's lines around Charleston, between the Edisto and Cooper Rivers, ascertain the strength, position, &c, of their different parties, and report to me at Aiken. He will at the same time send me information how a communication can reach him, and will operate against the enemy until further orders.

S. W. FERGUSON, Brig. Gen.

HEADQUARTERS CAVALRY BRIGADE,
NINETY SIX, S C., March 29, 1865.

LIEUTENANT—The Brigadier General Commanding directs that you continue with your party under the orders you first received until further orders, reporting any movement of importance to General Young, at Aiken. Our brigade starts to-day for North Carolina. The General wishes the scouts to keep the negroes in order and protect the country.

Very respectfully, your obedient servant,
T. K. JONES, A. A. A. G.

Mass Meeting.

By request of Brevet Major General SAXTON, the Colored People will assemble at Zion's Church on Saturday morning, April 15th, at ten o'clock A. M., when the Hon. HENRY WILSON, of Massachusetts, will address them.

The children of the Public Schools are requested to meet at the Morris-street School House nine o'clock Saturday morning.

MARINE NEWS.

HARBOR MASTER'S OFFICE,
CHARLESTON, S. C., April 13, 1865.

ARRIVALS.

Schooner C. W. Hynson, Shaw, from Hilton Head. Coal for Navy.

Schooner S. D. Wilder, Darrah, from Hilton Head. Coal for Army.

Steamer Golden Gate, Fitzgerald, from Hilton Head, 2½ A. M.

Steamer Blackstone, Berry, from Hilton Head.

DEPARTURES.

Bark Deney, Smith, for Philadelphia.

Brig C. H. Frost, Small, for Philadelphia.

Steamer Hudson, Evans, for Beaufort, 11½ A. M.

CHARLESTON.

FRIDAY MORNING. APRIL 14. 1865.

NOTICE.

HEADQUARTERS, CITY OF CHARLESTON, }
CHARLESTON, S. C. April 14, 1865. }

ON ACCOUNT OF THE CEREMONIES TO TAKE place at Fort Sumter *This Day*, the office hours at these Headquarters will be from 8 to 9 o'clock, A. M.

The Postoffice will be closed at 10 A. M.

By order of WM. GURNEY, Colonel 127th N. Y. Volunteers, Commanding Post. H. A. BATTERSON, Second Lieutenant 127th N. Y. Volunteers, and Assistant Adjutant General. April 14

The War News.

The latest intelligence we have of military operations is contained in the New York dailies of the 9th. Elsewhere will be found important extracts.

GRANT expresses his confidence in being able to capture the remaining portion of the rebel army, including LEE himself. At last accounts LEE's army was being pursued in the direction of Lynchburg. GRANT was at Farmville, from which place the rebels had been driven. GRANT was determined to push the enemy with all the vigor that a victorious army possesses. LEE was aiming to concentrate his forces at Lynchburg, but it was thought positive that the movements of our army would prevent LEE from carrying out his design.

On the night of the 5th LEE attempted to quietly slip his troops out of Amelia Court House. The movement became known to GRANT, who ordered a portion of his forces to advance in three columns. Two of these columns came up with the rear of the retreating enemy, and, after a brief engagement, captured nearly an entire corps. The remaining rebels pushed in very bad order toward the Appomattox River. It was believed that Gen. ORD, with two corps, would place himself between Lynchburg and LEE.

Among the captures on the 6th are Generals EWELL, KERSHAW, BARTON, CORSE, DEBOSE and CUSTIS LEE. The rebels also lost several thousand men as prisoners, fourteen pieces of artillery, and an immense quantity of wagons and ambulances.

The army of LEE is completely routed, and, we have little doubt, destroyed. The brilliant success which has attended GRANT in his recent operations before Richmond has served to thrill the hearts of the Union people with the wildest enthusiasm and delight. We confidently believe that the next news from the North will inform us of the total downfall and destruction of the rebellion.

JEFF. DAVIS left Richmond the night before the evacuation. It was not definitely known where he had gone. It was believed by many that he would forsake the rebel cause and endeavor to reach Mexico.

The enemy made an effort [illegible] Petersburg and Richmond, but the fires were extinguished by our troops.

The destruction of property by the rebels is immense. Their losses in men during the five days' operations are put down at fully twenty-five thousand. The Union loss is estimated at eight thousand.

The line of the rebel retreat is marked with abandoned cannon, and small arms, and army property of every description.

News of SHERMAN was contained in the Richmond "Whig," published on the day preceding that of the evacuation. The impression prevailed that he had left Goldsboro' and was making his way toward Weldon. Arriving at Weldon, he would doubtless proceed with all possible despatch to join his columns with the Army of the Potomac. This movement would compel JOHNSTON to take up the line of march, and he would probably attempt to connect his forces with LEE's. The position of affairs on the 8th, however, favors the belief that JOHNSTON is completely isolated from the other rebel forces.

President LINCOLN had visited Richmond and was received by the inhabitants with manifestations of great joy. He had given receptions to army and navy officers in the mansion formerly occupied by JEFF. DAVIS. Judge CAMPBELL and Mr. MYERS, the former one of the rebel Peace Commissioners who met Mr. LINCOLN and Mr. SEWARD in Hampton Roads some weeks since, remained in Richmond, and were admitted to audiences by the President. The object of Judge CAMPBELL and Mr. MYERS was supposed to be the offering of propositions for the submission of the rebel leaders. The result of the conferences had not been made known.

Richmond has daily mail communication with the North *via* Fortress Monroe.

The following brief summary of the operations at Mobile is taken from the New York "Herald" of the 9th: "The investment of the strong rebel position of the old Spanish Fort, one of the principal defences of the city, on the East side of Mobile bay, by the Thirteenth and Sixteenth army corps, took place on the 27th ult., and on that and the four succeeding days heavy skirmishing and artillery firing between besiegers and besieged was kept up. The National troops were gradually approaching the work, and on the 29th were intrenched within seventy yards of the enemy's rifle pits. The Union killed and wounded in the two corps up to the 31st were estimated at about eight hundred. Two National iron-clads, the Monitors "Milwaukee" and "Osage," were blown up in Mobile bay on the 28th and 29th ult., by rebel torpedoes, killing four men and wounding seven. As the vessels sunk in shallow water, it is thought they can be raised. As at every other point where the rebels establish themselves, both water and land for miles around Mobile are thickly planted with these infernal contrivances. On shore several casualties from them had occurred, and the troops had dug up a large number. The navy was actively co-operating with the army, and kept up a vigorous shelling of both sides of the bay. A fleet of rebel vessels, some of them no mean antagonists, was lying on Blakely river, below the city, and a battle between them and the National gunboats was hourly looked for. In fact it was believed at Dauphin Island on the 31st ult., the date of our latest accounts, that it had taken place, as very heavy firing in the direction of Spanish Fort was heard during the whole of that day."

General STEELE had arrived in front of Mobile and opened communication with General CANBY's force. On his march from Pensacola, Fla, he met with but slight opposition. The enemy either fled or surrendered. Many threw down their arms and begged for mercy. General STEELE had captured one Brigadier General, twenty-two other officers, four hundred men, and four hundred and fifty horses. He had also captured two wagon trains, and cut the Mobile and Montgomery Rail Road. Everything in Alabama was looking well for the Union cause.

It seems that a party of rebel emissaries made an attempt to destroy Newbern, N. C., on the 21 inst., but failed in this design. A number of Government buildings and the bridge over the Neuse River were fired simultaneously, but the prompt action of the Union soldiers speedily extinguished the flames. Prisoners captured by SHERMAN's men were arriving at Fortress Monroe daily. A force of rebel cavalry were reported to be making dashes in SHERMAN's rear, but they did not receive credit for accomplishing anything of importance.

The rebel ram "Stonewall," which had been lying for some time in the harbor of Ferrol, Spain, proceeded seaward on the 21st ult., and was followed by the Spanish frigate "Concepcion" and the United States steamers "Niagara" and "Sacramento." It was the purpose of the United States steamers to attack the ram, but when they came within range the ram suddenly turned and put back to her anchorage. The rebel officers say they did not fight because of the heavy sea prevailing, while it is stated by others that the French Government interfered.

The steamer "Harriet Deford," which was seized in the Patuxent River, Maryland, by a gang of rebels, and converted into a pirate, proved to be of little service to them. The gunboats [illegible] stroy the captured vessel.

A large quantity of secreted cotton had been dicsovered at Wilmington, N. C., and it is stated that gold and silver, the fruits of the blockade running business, was plentiful.

The premium on gold in New York was down to 48½ on the 8th inst.

A DESERVED PROMOTION.—We take special delight in announcing the promotion of Capt. W. L. M. BURGER, Assistant Adjutant General to the Commanding General, to the rank of Major in his special department. Major BURGER has been long identified with the Department of the South, where he has served with more than ordinary ability. He was with the original Expeditionary Corps at the time of the taking of Port Royal, filling the office of Adjutant in the New York Volunteer Regiment, and was subsequently appointed to the position of Assistant Adjutant General to General GILLMORE. He has performed duty at nearly all the principal engagements which have occurred in this Department, and has also been through a number of the Western campaigns. Major BURGER has the reputation of being one of the most efficient and valuable Assistant Adjutant Generals in the service, and we are confident that his recent promotion is well and justly merited.

SECRETARY STANTON COMING TO CHARLESTON.—It is now positively asserted that the Secretary of War is on his way to this city. In expectation of his coming, Admiral DAHLGREN has ordered that, whenever he is known to be in any vessel, the United States vessels present will show an ensign at each mast-head, and man yards as he passes; if they have no yards then they will man the rigging. The "Pawnee" will fire a salute at Charleston, and the vessel carrying the largest number of guns will salute at other places as the vessel of the Secretary passes.

NAVAL SALUTE.—In honor of the capture of Richmond and Petersburg, by order of Admiral DAHLGREN, a salute of twenty-one guns was fired in this harbor at one o'clock, P. M., on Monday, by the flag steamer "Philadelphia," the steam sloops "Tuscarora" and "Pawnee," and the steamers "Mary Sanford" and "Acacia."

We had the pleasure of a visit last evening from Mr. ELIAS LONGLEY, of the Cincinnati "Gazette."

FORT SUMTER.

Departure of the Arago with General Anderson and other Officials.

THE OLD FLAG AND THE FORT SUMTER MAIL BAG ON BOARD,

&c., &c., &c.

The Government Transport "Arago," Captain GADSDEN, sailed from the foot of Beach-street, New York, at noon on Saturday, 8th instant, for Fort Sumter, to raise the old flag once more over that historical fort. The vessel selected is a magnificent paddle wheel steamer of large dimensions. At ten o'clock those invited to assist in the celebration began to come on board, and sixty-one were on deck when the anchor was weighed. A postoffice van, decorated with flags, drove down to the pier between eleven and twelve o'clock, amidst the cheers of the crowd. On the van was the original Fort Sumter mail bag, addressed "Major ANDERSON, Fort Sumter, April 14, 1865," and also the old Fort Sumter flag, enclosed in a box and placed in charge of Sergt. HART, whose name is indelibly associated with the defence of the fort. HART was the man who lowered the flag when the fort was evacuated, and he is to raise it again at a given signal on Good Friday next. For the last four years the flag has been in the vaults under the Bank of Commerce. Mr. KNAPP, Superintendent of the Postoffice, and Messrs. PARCELLS and YEOMAN, clerks, were in charge of the van and its valuable relics.

General Anderson, the hero of Sumter, with his lady, son and three daughters, went early on board, and was the cynosure of all eyes on the crowded wharf as he chatted a few moments with friends near him. "There goes General Anderson," was uttered all around as the General proceeded up the gangway to the deck. General Dix and Miss Dix followed immediately after. As soon as the General appeared more than one in the crowd repeated the patriotic words of the veteran: "If any man attempts to haul down the American flag shoot him on the spot."

The carriages now rolled rapidly up, and in a short time there were congregated on the wharf Henry Ward Beecher, Geo. Thompson, Lloyd Garrison, Theodore Tilton, Senator Wilson and many other notables.

Brigadier General Van Vliet, Chief Quartermaster, was early on board the Arago, and remained till a few moments before the lines were cast loose and the vessel steamed from her moorings. The duty of locating the passengers devolved upon him; and in the face of the usual difficulties, where each had some personal preferences to advance for special consideration, it must be said that the General displayed inexhaustable urbanity, and finally discharged his delicate duties to the satisfaction of all on board. Nearly two hundred invitations were issued, and thirty-one refusals were received. The remainder of the guests, with the members of the Cabinet, are expected to come on board at Fortress Monroe. Punctually at twelve o'clock the steamer moved off, the glowing sunshine giving promise of a glorious trip. There is no doubt that, with [illegible] the most courteous and gentlemanly treatment at the hands of Captain Gadsden, and the comforts of a splendidly supplied ship, will have a pleasant voyage to the end.

We subjoin a list of the

INVITED GUESTS.

Gen Anderson, wife, son and three daughters.

Officers of Fort Sumter, viz: Major General S W Crawford, Major General Abner Doubleday, Brigadier General T Seymour, Major General Jeff C Davis, Captain Norman J Hall, Major General John G Foster, Rev Mathias Harris, Sergeant Peter Hart.

Lieutenant General Scott.

The Governors of Maine, New Hampshire, Vermont, Massachusetts, Rhode Island, Connecticut, New York, New Jersey, Pennsylvania, Maryland, West Virginia, Virginia (Governor Pierrepont), Tennessee, Kentucky, Ohio, Michigan, Indiana, Illinois, Iowa, Wisconsin, Minnesota, Kansas, California, Oregon, Missouri, Nevada.

Vice President Andrew Johnson.

The members of the Cabinet, viz: Hon Wm H Seward, Hon J R Usher, Hon Wm Dennison, Hon Hugh McCulloch, Hon Gideon Welles, Hon Jas Speed.

The Supreme Court of the United States, viz: Chief Justice Chase, Mr Justice Catron, Mr Justice Grier, Mr Justice Swayne, Mr Justice Davies, Mr Justice Wayne, Mr Justice Nelson, Mr Justice Clifford, Mr Justice Millar, Mr Justice Field.

The Military Committee of the Senate, viz: Hon H Wilson, Hon J M Howard, Hon E D Morgan, Hon B Gratz Brown, Hon Henry S Lane, Hon J W Nesmith, Hon Daniel Clark.

Governor David Todd, Commodore C Ryan, F W Ballard, Hon W Strong, Wm R W Hooper, Hon James Thompson, Rev Henry Ward Beecher, wife and son; Rev Samuel Scoville, Hon Wm H Kelly, Hon Henry Wilson, Mr Daniel Dougherty, John T Howard, Courtlandt Parker, Hon John M Brodhead and wife, Hon Thomas N Stillwell, Theodore Tilton, L J Ellenwood, Wm Lloyd Garrison, Phylda Daydon, Hon W L Kellogg, Andrew Benedict, Wm M Beach and son, James Frieland, Miss Ellen A Low, Dr Storrs, Miss Mary Storrs, Sergeant Peter Hart, Mr Lasker Howard, Hon Geo Thompson, Mr Justice Swayne, A B Hogg and wife, Col F Jordan and wife, Hon Louis W Hall, Geo R Shoenburger, Wm Watts, Hon Judge Davies, E D Morgan, Jr, Cambridge Livingston, A A Low and wife, Captain Norman, J Hall, Hon Chas Anderson, M C McCulloch, Joseph Hoxie, General Dix and daughter, H W Smith, Professor D H Mahan, Professor Chas Davies, H J Winser, William Welch, Hon Geo W Woodward, Hon John M Reed, Hon David Agnew, Admiral Farragut and wife, Captain R Lincoln, Dr John T Metcalf and daughter, Major General David Hunter, Hon John H Clifford, Hon Chas Sumner, C Dewey, Esq, Hon Moses Hampton, Hon Henry W Williams, Hon Ira Harris, Hon William M Meredith, Hon William Wilkins, Hon William Robinson, Hon L M Howe, James L Hutchinson, Esq, John McDonald Crossan, Esq, Hon David Richie, Dr R W Hooper, L Anderson, Esq, John Tucker, Jr, Hon Schuyler Colfax, Bishop M Simpson, Major General Halleck, Major General Hitchcock, Brigadier General Delafield, Brigadier General Fry and wife, Brigadier General E D Townsend and two sons, Lieutenant Colonel Samuel Breck, Hon G V Fox, Assistant Secretary of the Navy; Rev Daniel Curry, D D, Rev G R Crooks, Hon M F Odell, Mr Frank Moore, Hon B Howard, A Augustus Low, Chas Beach, Oscar G Sawyer, G Griswold Gray.

SCENES AT THE CHARLESTON HOTEL.—The official correspondence announcing the glorious news of the surrender of LEE's army, was read to a dense crowd assembled at the Charleston Hotel, and received with wild shouts of enthusiasm. The splendid bands of the 127th New York Volunteers and the 14th Maine, were in attendance and played alternately National and patriotic tunes, receiving the unbounded applause of the admiring crowds.

The drawing rooms and private parlors of the Hotel were thrown open by the generous host, STETSON, and refreshments liberally furnished.

Senator WILSON and General WASHBURNE were called out and made brief but eloquent speeches and were heartily cheered. We regret that the demands on our space prevents us from giving even a synopsis of these patriotic addresses. Major General ANDERSON was expected but did not arrive till a late hour.

THE FALL OF FORT PULASKI.—The members of the Department Staff gave a magnificent ball at Hilton Head on Wednesday night last, in commemoration of the fall of Fort Pulaski. Among the guests present were Major General GILLMORE, Major General DIX, wife and daughter, General WASHBURNE and a large number of other officers and ladies, residents of Hilton Head, and who came from the North on the steamer "Arago" to participate in the Sumter celebration. The building in which the ball was given was put up expressly for the occasion on the Green between the Department Headquarters and the office of the Assistant Adjutant General. The decorations were of a splendid order. The roof was hung with festoons of flags and streamers, and on the floor was painted the American flag, eagle and shield, with a brief motto appropriate to the event. The festivities were continued till early morn to the satisfaction and enjoyment of the participants.

WELL MERITED.—It gives us pleasure to notice the fact of the promotion of Lieutenant LEONARD B. PERRY, Acting Assistant Adjutant General to General HATCH, to the rank of Captain in the Adjutant General's Department. Captain PERRY has been with General HATCH for some months, and in the Department of the South for a long term. He has always performed his duties in a highly creditable and satisfactory manner, and we are truly rejoiced to see that his efforts have not escaped the notice of his superior officers.

[illegible]—A white lad named ORAN H. BASSETT, about thirteen years of age, saved a little colored boy from drowning, at the risk of his own life, on Wednesday afternoon. The colored boy was fishing for crabs on the wharf near WALKER & SALTUS' Sash Factory, West of Lynch-street, when he fell in the water and would have drowned, having sunk twice but was saved by young BASSETT, who jumped overboard after him, encumbered with his clothes, and succeeded in bringing him near the wharf, holding his head above water until assistance was rendered him by a colored man, when they were both drawn out together.

PERSONAL.—Hon. HENRY WILSON, U. S. Senator from Massachusetts, arrived in the city yesterday.

Mr. J. ADRIAN SUYDAM, Mr. J. CORLIES WHITE and D. C. MOREHEAD, M. D., arrived from New York on the steamer "Oceanus," and are guests at the Charleston Hotel. We are favored by these gentlemen with Northern papers of the 10th.

THANKS.—We are indebted to Mr. PHILLIP CALLANANE, Steward of the steamer "Blackstone," for a list of arrivals by that steamer.

ARRIVAL OF ASSISTANT SECRETARY FOX.—The steamer "Santiago de Cuba," from Havana, and having on board Assistant Secretary of the Navy Fox, arrived at this port last evening.

NAVAL COURTS.—Our Port Royal correspondent states that there have been several trials by Naval General Court Martial, on board the steamer "James Adger," in that harbor. One of the cases was that of a boy named ROBERT CLARK, on board the schooner-gunboat "Sophronia," who was tried for striking an officer. The testimony put in for the defence, however, was such as to "turn the tables" completely on the officer, who was immediately brought up for trial for striking and maltreating the boy.

THEATRE.—There was another good attendance at the Theatre last evening, and the play of the "Little Treasure" performed with excellent effect. The comidetta of "Bamboozling" extorted peals of laughter. The double dance of the Langley Sisters also elicited great enthusiasm.

SALT WATER BATHING.—We are glad to learn that the White Point Bathing House is undergoing repair, under the superintendence of its former proprietor, Mr. M. MCMANMON, and will shortly be re-opened to the public.

THE COURIER.

GEO. WHITTEMORE, G. W. JOHNSON, } EDITORS.

TERMS—INVARIABLY IN ADVANCE:
ONE YEAR..$20
SIX MONTHS..10
THREE MONTHS..5

☞ Single Copies TEN CENTS—News Boys supplied at a discount.
☞ No subscription will be received for a less period than three months.

OFFICE No. 43 HAYNE-STREET, SECOND DOOR EAST OF MEETING-STREET.

GRANT---LEE.

PROGRESS OF THE ROUT OF LEE'S ARMY.

ANOTHER BRILLIANT VICTORY.

DESPERATE AND SANGUINARY BATTLE NEAR BURKESVILLE.

SHERIDAN ATTACKS THE ENEMY AND ROUTS THEM.

CAPTURE OF SIX REBEL GENERALS.

Generals Ewell, Custis Lee, Corse, Kershaw, Button, and De Barre, Taken Prisoners.

LARGE CAPTURES OF PRISONERS, GUNS, WAGONS AND MUNITIONS.

LEE'S ARMY BROKEN UP.

SHERIDAN STILL PRESSING ON WITH CAVALRY AND INFANTRY.

FULL DETAILS OF THE VICTORY.

OFFICIAL REPORTS FROM PRESIDENT LINCOLN SECRETARY STANTON, GENS. GRANT, SHERIDAN, WRIGHT AND HUMPHREYS.

FIRST DISPATCH.

[Official.]

WAR DEPARTMENT, WASHINGTON, April 7—10 A. M.

Major General Dix New York:

General Sheridan attacked and routed Lee's army, capturing Gens Ewell, Kershaw, Button, Corse and many other general Officers, several thousand prisoners and a large number of cannon, and expects to force Lee to surrender all that is left of his army.

Details wi l be given as speedily as possible, but the telegraph is working badly.

EDWIN M. STANTON,
Secretary of War.

SECOND DISPATCH.

[Official.]

WAR DEPARTMENT, WASHINGTON, April 7—11 A. M.

Major General Dix:

The following telegrams announcing the victory won yesterday by Major General Sheridan over Lee's army, have just been received by this department.

EDWIN M STANTON,
Secretary of War.

CITY POINT, April 7—8 35 A. M.

Hon. Secretary of War:

At 11.15 P. M, yesterday, at Burkesville Station, Gen. Grant sends me the following from Gen. Sheridan.

A. LINCOLN.

DISPATCH FROM GEN. SHERIDAN

Thursday, April 6—11:15 P. M.

Lieut. Gen. GRANT:

I have the honor to report that the enemy made a stand at the intersection of the Burkes Station Road with the road upon which they were retreating.

I attacked them with two divisions of the Sixth Army Corps, and rou ed them handsomely, making a connection with the cavalry. I am still pressing on with the cavalry and infantry. Up to the present time we have captured Generals Ewell, Kershaw, Button, Corse, DeBare and Custis Lee, several thousand prisoners, fourteen pieces of artillery, with caissons, and a large number of wagons. If the thing is pressed I think Lee will surrender

P. H. SHERIDAN,
Major General Commanding.

CITY POINT, Friday, April 7—9 A. M.

Hon. Secretary of War:

The following further intelligence is just received.

A. LINCOLN.
BURKESVILLE, Va.

To A LINCOLN:

The following telegram is respectfully forwarded for your information.

U. S GRANT,
Lieutenant General.

DISPATCH FROM GEN. MEADE.

MEADE'S HEADQUARTERS, April 6—10 P. M.

To Lieut. Gen. GRANT:

At daylight this morning I moved the Second, Fifth and Sixth Army Corps along the rail road, in the direction of Amelia Court House. Soon after moving reliable information was received that the enemy was moving toward Farmville. The direction of the Second and Fifth Army Corps immediately changed from a Northerly to a Northwesterly direction, and the directing corps, the Second, moving on Deatonville, and the Fifth, heretofore in the centre, moved on the right of the Second, and the Sixth facing about and moving by the left flank, taking position on the left of the Second. It was understood the cavalry would operate on the extreme left. The changes were promptly made. The Second Army Corps soon becoming engaged with the enemy, near Deatonville, driving him by right across Sailor Creek to the Appomattox. The Fifth Army Corps made a long march, but its position prevented its striking the enemy's column before it had passed. The Sixth Army Corps came up with the enemy about 4 P M., and, in conjunction with the Second on its right and cavalry on its left, attacked and routed the enemy, capturing many prisoners, among them Lieutenant General Ewell and General Custis Lee I transmit dispatches both from Generals Humphreys and Wright, which, in justice to these distinguished officers and the gallant corps they command, I beg may be sent to the War Department for immediate publication It is impossible at this moment to give any estimate in the casualties on either side, or of the number of prisoners taken, but it is evident to-day's work is going to be one of the most important of the recent brilliant operations.

The pursuit will be continued as soon as the men have a little rest. Griffin, with the Fifth Army Corps, will be moved by the left, and Wright and Humphreys continue the direct pursuit as long as it promises success.

GEO. G. MEADE, Maj Gen.

DISPATCH FROM GEN HUMPHREYS.

SECOND ARMY CORPS, Thursday, April 6—7 30 P. M.

Major General A. S. WEBB:

Our last fight, just before dark, at Sailor's Creek, gave us two guns, three flags and a considerable number of prisoners, two hundred wagons, seventy ambulances, with mules and horses to about one-half of the wagons and ambulances. There are between thirty and fifty wagons in addition abandoned and destroyed along the road, some battery wagons, forges and limbers. I have already reported to you the capture of one gun, two flags and some prisoners, and the fact that the road for over two miles is strewed with tents, baggage, cooking utensils, some ammunition, and materials of all kinds.

The wagons are across the approach to the bridges, and it will take some time to clear it The enemy is in position on the heights beyond with artillery. The bridge is partially destroyed, and the approaches on the other side are of soft bottom land We cannot advance to morrow in the same manner we have to-day. As soon as I get my troops up a little (we are considerably mixed) I might push a column down the road to deploy it, but it is evident I canno follow rapidly during the night.

A. A. HUMPHREYS,
Major General.

DISPATCH FROM GEN. WRIGHT.

HEADQUARTERS SIXTH ARMY CORPS, Thursday, April 6—10 P. M.

Maj Gen WEBB, Chief of Staff, Army of Potomac;

In pursuance of instructions of this morning from Maj Gen. Meade, I moved from Jeffersville by the shortest practicable road to the left of the Deatonville, with the object of there taking position on the left of the Second Army Corps, striking the road running from Deatonville to Burke's Station, at a point a little to the Southward of the former place. I found that the Second Army Corps was engaged to the front and right, and the cavalry heavily to my left. Moving down the road towards Burke's Station, perhaps a mile, and turning sharp to the right, I proceeded across toward a nearly parallel road, on which the enemy was moving, and along which he had thrown up a line of intrenchments.

As soon as the leading division, Gen. Seymour's, could be formed, it was moved up on the road held by the enemy, which was carried. Then turning the left, it was advanced down the road against a pretty strong resistance. By this time, Wheaton's division was put in position, as rapidly as possible, on Seymour's left.

The lines were again advanced, and we swept down the road for a distance of about two miles Arriving at a deep and difficult creek we found the enemy had reformed his line on the opposite side, where we attacked and drove him to a point, a distance of half a mile further.

In the first attack a portion of the cavalry operated on our right flank. In its subsequent attack the mass or cavalry operated on our left and right flank of the enemy.

The result has been a complete success. The combined forces captured five general officers; among them Generals Ewell and Custis Lee and large numbers of other prisoners.

I shall go in camp about two miles beyond this point, and await instructions. The First and Third Divisions, Wheaton's and Seymour's, and the artillery engaged to-day, behaved splendidly.

A return of casualties will be forwarded as soon as possible.

The corps has nobly sustained the reputation it earned on the 2d inst., as well as upon its many previous hard fought battle fields.

H. G. WRIGHT,
Major General Commanding

SECRETARY STANTON TO GEN. DIX

WAR DEPARTMENT, Washington, April 8, 1865

Major General Dix, New York:

A telegram from General Grant, dated this day at twelve o'clock noon, at Farmville, sixteen miles West of Burkesville Station, says that the enemy have been pushed from the road towards Danville, and are now pursued towards Lynchburg, and that he is very confident of receiving the surrender of Lee and what remains of his army.

EDWIN M. STANTON,
Secretary of War.

Hartford Daily Courant.

VOL. XXIX--NO. 88. HARTFORD, CONNECTICUT, SATURDAY MORNING, APRIL 15, 1865. WHOLE NO. 8210.

EXTRA.

4 1-2 O'CLOCK, A. M.

AWFUL CALAMITY

TERRIBLE LOSS TO THE NATION!

PRESIDENT LINCOLN ASSASSINATED!

ATTEMPT TO ASSASSINATE SECRETARY SEWARD!

He Still Lives.

THE ASSASSINS ESCAPE!

FULL PARTICULARS.

WASHINGTON, April 14.—President Lincoln and wife, with other friends, this evening visited Ford's Theatre for the purpose of witnessing the performance of the "American Cousin." It was announced in the papers that General Grant would also be present, but that gentleman took the late train of cars for New Jersey.

The theatre was densely crowded, and everybody seemed delighted with the scene before them. During the third act, and while there was a temporary pause for one of the actors to enter, a sharp report of a pistol was heard, which merely attracted attention, but suggesting nothing serious, until a man rushed to the front of the President's box, waving a long dagger in his right hand, and exclaiming: "*Sic Semper Tyrrannes,*" and immediately leaped from the box, which was in the second tier, to the stage beneath and ran across to the opposite side, making his escape amid the bewilderment of the audience from the rear of the theatre, and mounting a horse fled.

The screams of Mrs. Lincoln first disclosed the fact to the audience that the President had been shot, when all present rose to their feet, rushing toward the stage, many exclaiming: "Hang him! hang him!" The excitement was of the wildest possible description, and of course there was an abrupt termination of the theatrical performance.

There was a rush toward the President's box, when cries were heard, "Stand back and give him air." "Has any one stimulants?"

On a hasty examination its was found that the President had been shot through the head, above and back of the temple, and some of the brain was oozing out. He was removed to a private house opposite to the theatre. The surgeon general of the army and other surgeons, were sent for to attend to his condition. On examining the private box, blood was discovered on the back of the cushioned rocking chair on which the President had been sitting, also on the partition and on the floor. A common single barrelled pocket pistol was found on the carpet. A military guard was placed in front of the private residence, to which the President had been conveyed, and an immense crowd was in front of it, all deeply anxious to learn the condition of the President. It had been previously announced that the wound was mortal, but all hoped otherwise. The shock to the community was terrible. At midnight the cabinet, whither Messrs. Sumner, Colfax and Farnsworth, Judge Curtiss, Governor Oglesby, General Meigs, Colonel Hay, and a few personal friends, with Surgeon General Barnes, and his immediate assistants, were around his bedside. The President was in a state of syncope, totally insensible, and breathing slowly. The blood oozed from the wound at the back of his head. The surgeons exhausted every possible effort of medical skill, but all hope was gone.

The parting of his family with the dying President, is too sad for description. The President and Mrs Lincoln did not start for the theatre until fifteen minutes after eight o'clock. Speaker Colfax was at the White House at the time, and the President stated to him that he was going, although Mrs. Lincoln had not been well, because the papers had announced that General Grant and they were to be present, and as General Grant had gone North he did not wish the audience to be disappointed.

He went with apparent reluctance, and urged Mr. Colfax to go with him, but that gentleman had made other engagements, and, with Mr. Ashman of Massachusetts, bid him good bye.

When the excitement at the theatre was at its height, reports were circulated that Secretary Seward had also been assassinated. On reaching this gentleman's residence, a crowd and a military guard were found at the door, and on entering it was found that the reports were based on truth. Everybody there was so excited that scarcely an intelligible word could be gathered, but the facts are substantially as follows:—About ten o'clock, a man rang the bell, and the call having been answered by a colored servant, he said he had come from Dr. Verdi, Secretary Seward's family physician, with a prescription, at the same time holding in his hand a small piece of folded paper and saying in answer to a refusal, that he must see the Secretary, as he was intrusted with particular directions concerning the medicine. He still insisted on going up, although repeatedly informed that no one could enter the chamber. The man pushed the servant aside and walked heavily toward the Secretary's room, and was there met by Mr. Frederick Seward, of whom he demanded to see the Secretary, making the same representation which he did to the servant. What further passed in the way of colloquy is not known, but the man struck him on the head with a billy, severely injuring the skull and felling him almost senseless. The assassin then rushed into the chamber and attacked Major Seward, paymaster U. S. A., and Mr. Hansell, a messenger of the State Department, and two male nurses, disabling them all. He then rushed upon the Secretary, who was lying in a bed in the same room, and inflicted three stabs in the neck, but severing, it is thought and hoped, no arteries, though he bled profusely.

The assassin then rushed down stairs, mounted his horse at the door, and rode off before an alarm bell could be sounded, and in the same manner as the assassin of the President.

It is believed that the injuries of the Secretary are not fatal, nor those of either of the others, although both the Secretary and the Assistant Secretary are very seriously injured.

Secretaries Stanton and Welles, and other prominent officers of the government, called at Secretary Seward's house to inquire into his condition and there heard of the assassination of the President. They then proceded to the house where he was lying, exhibiting, of course, intense anxiety and solicitude. An immense crowd was gathered in front of the President's house, and a strong guard was also stationed there, many persons evidently supposing he would be brought home. The entire city to-night presents a scene of wild excitement, accompanied by violent expression of indignation and the profoundest sorrow; many shed tears. The military authorities have despatched mounted patrols in every direction, in order, if possible, to arrest the assassins. The whole metropolitan police are likewise vigilant for the same purpose.

The attacks, both at the theatre and at Secretary Seward's house, took place at about the same hour, (ten o'clock), thus showing a preconcerted plan to assassinate those gentlemen. Some evidence of the guilt of the party who attacked the President, are in possession of the police.

Vice President Johnson is in the city, and his headquarters are guarded by troops.

The President is still alive, but his case is absolutely hopeless.

OFFICIAL DISPATCH.

WAR DEPARTMENT,
WASHINGTON, April 15—1:30 a. m.

Maj.-Gen. Dix:—This evening, at about 9½ o'clock, at Ford's Theatre, the President, while sitting in his private box, with Mrs. Lincoln, Mrs. Harris, and Major Rathbun, was shot by an assassin, who suddenly entered the box and approached behind the President. The assassin then leaped upon the stage, brandishing a large dagger or knife, and made his escape in the rear of the theatre. The pistol ball entered the back of the President's head and penetrated nearly through the head. The wound is mortal. The President has been insensible ever since it was inflicted, and is now dying.

About the same hour, an assassin, whether the same or not, entered Mr. Seward's apartments, and under pretense of having a prescription, was shown to the Secretary's sick chamber. The assassin immediately rushed to the bed and inflicted two or three stabs on the throat and two on the face. It is hoped the wounds may not be mortal. My apprehension is that they will prove fatal. The nurse alarmed Mr. Frederick Seward, who was in an adjoining room, and hastened to the door of his father's room, where he met the assassin, who inflicted upon him one or more dangerous wounds. The recovery of Frederick Seward is doubtful. It is not probable that the President will live through the night.

General Grant and wife were advertised to be at the theatre this evening, but he started to Burlington, N.J., at 6 o'clock this evening. A cabinet meeting, at which General Grant was present, the subject of the state of the country and the prospect of a speedy peace, was discussed. The President was very cheerful and hopeful, and spoke very kindly of General Lee and others of the confederacy, and of the establishment of a government in Virginia. All the members of the cabinet, except Mr. Seward, are now in attendance upon the President. I have seen Mr. Seward, but he and Frederick were both unconscious.

(Signed) EDWIN M. STANTON,
Secretary of War.

THE NATION MOURNS.

We are called upon to write the most heart-rending news that has been written since this nation was born—news that will carry sadness and gloom all over the land; that will cause a wail of anguish to gush forth from all the people. Shall we, must we say it, that our beloved President Lincoln, who has thus far been so providentially spared, has been assassinated in cold blood by a murderer—a rebel—who, not satisfied with attempts to destroy the life-blood of the nation, has stricken down, with a cowardly hand, the very head of the nation?

We would that this great calamity might have been spared to us, and especially at this hour of the Nation's triumph. May God in his wisdom overrule the event, to the confusion of our enemies, and to the good of the Nation; may we be enabled to say, "We are cast down, but we are not forsaken, for the Lord is on our side."

The duties of the President now devolve upon Vice President Johnson. That he may be endowed with wisdom for the great responsibilities which lay before him, let all Christians unite in earnest prayer to God.

We refer to the telegraphic dispatches for full particulars of the cruel murder. At 2½ o'clock this morning the President was alive, but could not possibly live but a few hours.

We also have the sad news that about the same hour that the President was murdered another assassin entered the residence of Secretary Seward, and with a dagger inflicted wounds which it is believed will prove mortal; and also, it is feared, fatally stabbed Assistant Secretary Frederick Seward. Does not this murderous deed call for sterner justice against traitors and enemies of our government? We defer further comments to another hour.

As soon as the sad intelligence of the assassination of the President was received from a source which entitled it to full credit, a message was sent from this office to Senator Dixon and Postmas Cleveland. he latter procured a carriage and at once notified Mayor Stillman, Councilman Strong, and others. The Mayor took measures to have the bells tolled as soon as the news is received of the death of the President.

Senator Dixon will at once proceed to Washington.

Incendiary Fires.

There were five incendiary fires in New Haven yesterday, and one in Meriden. Citizens, be on your guard! The rebel emissaries are at work! In Hartford, Trinity College chapel was set on fire about 3 o'clock yesterday afternoon, but was providentially discovered and extinguished. The flames, however, broke through the roof, before the fire was discovered. It is the duty of every good citizen to exercise the utmost vigilance in this hour of our country's peril. Prowling bands of midnight assassins and incendiaries are roaming about, and they are undoubtedly here in our own midst. Again we say, Be on your guard!

The Philadelphia Inquirer.

PRICE TWO CENTS. PHILADELPHIA, SATURDAY, APRIL 15, 1865. PRICE TWO CENTS.

MURDER

OF

PRESIDENT LINCOLN!

His Assassination Last Night, While at Ford's Theatre, in Washington!

J. WILKES BOOTH THE SUPPOSED MURDERER.

THE PISTOL BALL ENTERS HIS BRAIN!

THE ASSASSIN IN HIS PRIVATE BOX.

The Murderer Leaps Upon the Stage and Escapes.

A HORSE IS WAITING FOR HIM.

Mr. Lincoln Dying at Midnight

The Farewell of His Family.

SAD AND SOLEMN SCENES

ATTEMPT TO KILL SEC'Y SEWARD!

His Bedchamber Entered by the Villain.

HIS WOUNDS THOUGHT TO BE MORTAL

Assistant Secretary Seward also Fatally Stabbed.

TERRIBLE EXCITEMENT IN WASHINGTON

OFFICIAL GAZETTE.

WASHINGTON, April 15—1·30 A. M.—Major-General Dix:—This evening, about 9·30 P. M., at Ford's Theatre, the President, while sitting in his private box with Mrs. Lincoln, Miss Harris and Major Rathburn, was shot by an assassin, who suddenly entered the box and approached behind the President.

The assassin then leaped upon the stage, brandishing a large dagger or knife, and made his escape in the rear of the theatre.

The pistol ball entered the back of the President's head, and penetrated nearly through the head. The wound was mortal.

The President has been insensible ever since it was inflicted and is now dying.

About the same hour an assassin, whether the same or another, entered Mr. Seward's house, and, under pretense of having a prescription, was shown to the Secretary's sick chamber. The Secretary was in bed, a nurse and Miss Seward with him.

The assassin immediately rushed to the bed, inflicted one or two stabs in the throat and two in the face. It is hoped the wounds may not be mortal. My apprehension is that they will prove fatal.

The noise alarmed Mr. Frederick Seward, who was in an adjoining room, and he hastened to the door of his father's room, where he met the assassin, who inflicted upon him one or more dangerous wounds. The recovery of Frederick Seward is doubtful.

It is not probable that the President will live through the night.

General Grant and wife were advertised to be at the theatre this evening, but he started to Burlington at six o'clock this evening. At a Cabinet meeting, at which General Grant was present to-day, the subject of the state of the country and the prospects of a speedy peace were discussed.

The President was very cheerful and hopeful. He spoke very kindly of General Lee and others of the Confederacy, and the establishment of the Government in Virginia.

All the members of the Cabinet, except Mr. Seward, are now in attendance upon the President. I have seen Mr. Seward, but he and Frederick were both unconscious.

EDWIN M. STANTON,
Secretary of War.

SECOND BULLETIN.
The Latest—The Supposed Assassin.

WASHINGTON, April 15—3 A. M.—Major-General Dix, New York:—The President still breathes but is quite insensible as he has been ever since he was shot.

He evidently did not see the person who shot him, but was looking on the stage, as he was approached behind.

Mr. Seward has rallied, and it is hoped he may live. Frederick Seward's condition is very critical. The attendant who was present was stabbed through the lungs, and is not expected to live. The wounds of Major Seward are not serious.

Investigation strongly indicates J. Wilkes Booth as the assassin of the President. Whether it was the same or a different person that attempted to murder Mr. Seward remains in doubt.

Chief Justice Carter is engaged in taking the evidence. Every exertion has been made to prevent the escape of the murderer. His horse has been found on the road near Washington.

EDWIN M. STANTON,
Secretary of War.

THE PARTICULARS.

WASHINGTON, April 14.—President Lincoln and his wife, together with other friends, this evening, visited Ford's Theatre for the purpose of witnessing the performance of the American Cousin.

It was announced in the papers that General Grant would also be present, but that gentleman instead took the late train of cars for New Jersey.

The theatre was densely crowded, and everybody seemed delighted with the scene before them.

During the third act, and while there was a temporary pause for one of the actors to enter, the sharp report of a pistol was heard, which merely attracted attention, but suggested nothing serious, until a man rushed to the front of the President's box, waving a long dagger in his right hand, and exclaiming "*Sic semper tyrannis!*" and immediately leaped from the box, which was of the second tier, to the stage beneath, and ran across to the opposite side, thus making his escape, amid the bewilderment of the audience, from the rear of the theatre, and, mounting a horse, fled.

The screams of Mrs. Lincoln first disclosed the fact to the audience that the President had been shot, when all present rose to their feet rushing toward the stage, many exclaiming "Hang him! hang him!"

The excitement was of the wildest possible description, and, of course, there was an abrupt termination of the theatrical performance.

There was a rush towards the Presidential box, when cries were heard, "Stand back! Give him air! Has any one stimulants?"

On a hasty examination it was found that the President had been shot through the head, above and back of the temporal bone, and that some of the brain was oozing out.

He was removed to a private house opposite to the theatre, and the Surgeon-General of the army and other surgeons were sent for to attend to his condition.

On an examination of the private box blood was discovered on the back of the cushioned rocking-chair on which the President had been sitting, also on the partition and on the floor. A common single-barreled pocket pistol was found on the carpet.

A military guard was placed in front of the private residence to which the President had been conveyed. An immense crowd gathered in front of it, all deeply anxious to learn the condition of the President. It had been previously announced that the wound was mortal, but all hoped otherwise.

The shock to the community was terrible.

At midnight the Cabinet, with Messrs. Sumner, Colfax and Farnsworth, Judge Carter, Governor Oglesby, General Meigs, Colonel Hay, and a few personal friends, with Surgeon-General Barnes, and his medical associates, were around his bed-side.

THE PRESIDENT IN A DYING CONDITION AT MIDNIGHT.

The President was in a state of *syncope*, totally insensible, and breathing slowly, the blood oozing from the wound at the back of his head. The surgeons were exhausting every possible effort of medical skill, but all hope was gone.

The parting of his family with the dying President is too sad for description.

The President and Mrs. Lincoln did not start to the theatre till fifteen minutes after eight o'clock. Speaker Colfax was at the White House at the time, and the President stated to him that he was going, although Mrs. Lincoln had not been well, because the papers had advertised that General Grant and they were to be present, and as General Grant had gone North, he did not wish the audience to be disappointed.

He went with apparent reluctance and urged Mr. Colfax to go with him, but that gentleman had made other engagements, and with Mr. Ashman, of Massachusetts, bid him good-bye.

THE LATEST—THE CONDITION OF THE PRESIDENT.

WASHINGTON, April 15—2·30 A. M.—The President is still alive, but is growing weaker. The ball is lodged in his brain, three inches from where it entered the skull. He remains insensible and his condition is utterly hopeless.

The Vice President has been to see him, but all company except the Cabinet, his family, and a few friends, are rigidly excluded.

Large crowds still continue in the street, as near to the house as the line of guard will allow.

ATTEMPTED ASSASSINATION OF SECRETARY SEWARD.

When the excitement at the theatre was at its wildest height, reports were circulated that Secretary Seward had also been assassinated.

On reaching this gentleman's residence, a crowd and a military guard were found at the door, and on entering it was ascertained that the reports were based upon truth. Everybody there was so excited that scarcely an intelligible account could be gathered, but the facts are substantially as follows:—

About ten o'clock a man rang the bell, and the call having been answered by a colored servant, he said he had come from Dr. Verdi, Secretary Seward's family physician, with a prescription, at the same time holding in his hand a small piece of folded paper and saying, in answer to a refusal, that he must see the Secretary, as he was intrusted with a particular direction concerning the medicine.

He still insisted on going up, although repeatedly informed that no one could enter the chamber. The man pushed the servant aside and walked quickly to the Secretary's room, and was there met by Mr. Frederick W. Seward of whom he demanded to see the Secretary, making the same representation which he did to the servant.

What further passed in the way of colloquy is not known, but the man struck him on the head with a billy, severely injuring the skull, and felling him almost senseless. The assassin then rushed into the chamber [illegible] Army, and Mr. Hansell, a messenger of the State Department, and two male nurses, disabling them all. He then rushed upon the Secretary, who was lying in bed in the same room, and inflicted three stabs in the neck, but severing, it is thought, and hoped, no arteries.

The assassin then rushed down stairs, mounted his horse at the door and rode off before an alarm could be sounded, and in the same manner of the assassin of the President. It is believed the injuries of the Secretary are not fatal, nor those of the others, although both the Secretary and the Assistant Secretary are very seriously injured.

Secretaries Stanton and Welles, and other prominent officers of the Government, called at Secretary Seward's house to inquire into his condition, and there heard of the assassination of the President. They proceeded to the house where he was lying, exhibiting, of course, intense anxiety and solicitude.

An immense crowd was gathered in front of the President's House, and a strong guard also stationed there, many persons evidently supposing that he would be brought to his home.

The entire city to-night presents a scene of wild excitement, accompanied by violent expressions of indignation, and the profoundest sorrow. Many shed tears.

The military authorities have despatched mounted patrols in every direction, in order, if possible to arrest the assassin, while the Metropolitan police are alike vigilant for the same purpose.

The attack, both at the theatre and at Secretary Seward's house, took place at about the same hour (ten o'clock), thus showing a preconcerted plan to assassinate these gentlemen. Some evidences of the guilt of the party who attacked the President are in possession of the police.

Vice President Johnson is in the city, and his hotel quarters are guarded by troops.

General Grant Receives the News.

We learn that General Grant received intelligence of this sad calamity soon after midnight, when at Walnut street wharf, on his way to Burlington, New Jersey.

SHERMAN.

Reorganization of Sherman's Army—General Items of Interest.

Special Correspondence of the Inquirer.

GOLDSBORO, N. C., April 8, 1865.

A Reconstruction.

A nominal reorganization of General Sherman's army has been ordered, and the additional troops, under Schofield and Terry, have been formed into an integral part of the grand army now under his leadership.

The Army of Georgia.

The Fourteenth and Twentieth Corps, hitherto known as the left wing, will in future be designated "the Army of Georgia," and will be commanded by Major-General Slocum.

The Army of the Tennessee.

The Fifteenth and Seventeenth Corps, heretofore known as the right wing, will now be distinguished by the title of "The Army of the Tennessee," under the command of Major-General Oliver O. Howard. The "Army of the Ohio," consisting of the Twenty-third and Tenth Corps, will constitute the centre, under Major-General John M. Schofield.

Major-General Joseph A. Mower, lately commanding the First Division of the Seventeenth Corps, assumed the command of the Twentieth Corps, vice Williams.

Prisoners.

Two prisoners were taken on picket line yesterday, members of the Fiftieth North Carolina infantry. They are sullen and morose dogs, not at all communicative. From their admissions and assertions we gather that Johnston is working like a beaver in the vicinity of Smithfield. Whether concentrating an army there, hurrying an evacuating one, or supplying one at a distance with Smithfield for an important intermediate post, we are at a loss to determine.

FROM RICHMOND!

WEITZEL RELIEVED FROM COMMAND.

Gen. E. O. C. Ord His Successor.

A BUNCOMBE PROCLAMATION FROM JEFF. DAVIS.

He Hasn't Heard of Lee's Surrender.

HE THINKS EVERYTHING LOOKS WELL!

"Gen. Lee Will Never Give Up."

REBEL PROSPECTS PROMISING!

Usual Lying Braggadocia

GEN. LEE IN RICHMOND.

He Advises Johnston to Surrender!

GRANT ORDERS SHERMAN TO GIVE HIM A CHANCE.

OUR RICHMOND CORRESPONDENCE.

Special Correspondence of the Inquirer.

RICHMOND, Va.,
Wednesday Night, April 12, 1865.

The Great Event

Of the day has been the arrival of Major-General E. O. C. Ord, the commander of the Department of Virginia. General Ord, through his whole career, has shown remarkable administrative qualifications, and brings to the discharge of the duties of his enlarged command a perfect acquaintance with its requirements, and a large experience in its details. Probably no officer could have been selected by General Grant who would better fill the difficult *role* General Ord will be called upon to perform. Nor is his capacity in council his only claim on the regard of his country. His services in the field have been arduous and brilliant, showing him one of our first soldiers. Twice wounded since the war began, his scars are honorable witnesses of his service and his bravery.

That the conflicting interests, the jealousies, the perplexities already arising around him will be fairly and fearlessly dealt with, none who know the man can doubt.

A Grand Salute

Of two hundred guns was fired to-day in honor as the salute was in accordance with a General Order of the War Department.

The City

Is quiet and orderly, and fast becoming as respectable in appearance as circumstances will permit. Large gangs of negroes are kept constantly at work clearing the streets of the *debris* of the evacuation, but their progress in the burned district is very slow. There the ghastly monuments of Rebel barbarism will remain for weeks and months, silent but effective witnesses to the vindictive malignity of the despotism that attempted to destroy a city it could no longer hold. Outside of the burned district, however, Richmond is fast becoming again the beautiful city it was in its better days, and but for the ruin wrought by Breckinridge and Ewell the tourist would find little to remind him of its recent terrible history. One important adjunct of a city, viz., gas, was wanting during the first days of our occupation, but that has been remedied, and to-night all the houses are lighted with a very superior article.

Everybody's impression of Richmond, so long beleagured, so long defended, so long the centre of all that was false in American politics, will be interesting after the nation has recovered from the wild delirium of joy under which it is now laboring, and when that time comes mine shall be forthcoming.

A Trip to Burkesville

Was attempted yesterday, but resulted in a miserable failure. Leaving City Point at three A. M., the train which was going out specially to bring in General Grant, pounded and twisted and tortured along that miserable apology of a railroad called the South Side, until four miles beyond Wilson's Station, when a capsized locomotive barred further progress, and after hours of waiting a return train to City Point was taken. This episode of personal experience is mentioned only to anathematize that Southside Railroad. A more wretched affair it is impossible to conceive of, and it is hardly stretching truth to say that there is not a decent rail or sound tie in its whole length. How the Rebels managed to get the amount of work out of it they did it is hard to say. Want of repairs is its ailment. For four years it has not been ditched; rails have only been replaced when utterly worn out; new ties put down when the old absolutely refused to longer hold a spike. The force working the road was meagre in numbers; those employed in repairing it were more so. To a section of nine miles and a half east from Wilson's, five men were the allowance, and railroad men can easily imagine in what repair they would keep a road originally none of the best, and constantly worked beyond its capacity.

The road can hardly be called serviceable, and if the military situation shall demand its use for any time, we shall be obliged practically to rebuild it.

The Richmond and Petersburg Road

Is said to be in far better condition, and to be in reality a railroad. Our great interest, however, is centring in the Richmond, Fredericksburg and Potomac Road, and from it we have as yet no reliable advices. This whole community is anxious for speedier communication with the North than by the present out of the way route, via Fortress Monroe, and is waiting impatiently for the opening of the road to Aquia Creek. That it will soon be done everybody believes, but exactly when, nobody appears to know.

General Grant

Will in a few days proceed to Washington, and it is not now generally expected that he will visit the city he has captured. He announced to his staff to-day that he should give them immediately fifteen days leave of absence, and the military family that has been together so long will for that time be broken up. No staff in the army has been worked harder than that of the Lieutenant-General, and they have nobly earned a short respite from labor.

General Grant himself was to-day at City Point, giving no outward sign of the glorious history he created during the few days he was absent. He is the same imperturbable Grant. Looming to-day far above all compeers, or more correctly, having no compeer in all history, he seems himself to be the only man who is unconscious of the fact, and is the same man outwardly that he was during the earliest days of the war, when newspapers called him "the blunderer of the Mississippi." There is no exultation in his manner; not a change in his demeanor. This man who issues no congratulatory orders, who refuses to visit the city he has conquered, only because he has no business there, is great even in his unconsciousness of his greatness.

Exactly where General Grant will go next it is not proper to state, even were it definitely known; but there are faint remains of organized Rebellion in distant parts of the land, and his tireless energy will soon be at work on some of them.

An Incident

Of the late surrender exhibits Fitz Hugh Lee and Rosser in no enviable light. After General Lee had formally surrendered his army, these two men stole away, and were not to be found to give their parole. Neither of them were ever possessed of either talents or influence, and their defection is of no consequence to anybody but themselves. There is every probability that sooner or later they will fall into our hands, and then even their impudence can claim no immunity.

Impudence,

By the way, seems to be the great staple of nearly every man wearing the Rebel uniform. No organized force of the Rebellion remaining in Virginia, the officers on parole in Richmond still flaunt their grey before our eyes on the street, as if it were the badge of honorable service instead of what it is, the livery of a defeated, crushed, wiped-out Rebellion. Some of them seem to act as though they expected to wear it during their natural lives, and to glory in it forever. But even Southern chivalry may on this point be taught a lesson in good manners before long.

EDWARD CRAPSEY.

WASHINGTON.

[SPECIAL DESPATCHES TO THE INQUIRER.]

WASHINGTON, April 14.

Jeff. Davis, on his Arrival

At Danville, issued a proclamation to the people of the South. He had not heard of the surrender of Lee. It contains nothing new. The same old story. Full of "sound and fury, signifying nothing."

Arrival of Rebel Officers.

A batch of four hundred and forty Rebel officers arrived here this afternoon from City Point. They comprise the officers captured by General Sheridan in the battle at Amelia Court House. Among them was Lieutenant-General Ewell, Major-General's Kershaw, Defose, Barton, Corse, Hunter, and Simms, also Commodores Hunter and Tucker of the Rebel navy. They were taken before Colonel Ingraham, Provost Marshal. It is understood that the latter officers are to be sent to Fort Warren, the others will be distributed among the other forts. They attracted considerable attention marching down Pennsylvania Avenue.

Guerrillas to be Exterminated.

Now that the largest part of Virginia is within the lines of our army, it is the intention of the Government to clear the country between Washington and Richmond of the scoundrelly set of robbers and thieves, in the shape of guerrillas infesting this region.

Retrenchment of Expenses.

It is estimated that the retrenchment of Government expenses to take place immediately will amount to upwards of one million dollars per day. Both the Secretary of War and the Secretary of the Navy have gone vigorously at work in this direction. The pruning hook will [illegible] the diseased and rotten material in

[DESPATCHES TO THE ASSOCIATED PRESS.]

Sherman's Movements—Johnston Retreating South.

Intelligence has been received that General Sherman's army moved from Goldsboro on Monday.

General Johnston is reported to have retreated southward toward South Carolina, on learning of the surrender of General Lee's army.

It is supposed that the Rebels intend to make a stand in Georgia and the trans-Mississippi States, more with a view of obtaining favorable terms, than from any hope of establishing any independent Government.

If Johnston intends to fight or prolong the war, Sherman has the means and ability to crush him.

Secretary Seward's health does not yet cease to inspire some alarm, but it is believed that he will recover.

The political excitement on the great questions opening upon the nation is intense, and is apparently increasing.

The Pirate "Shenandoah."

The Government has received information that at the latest date the pirate *Shenandoah* was at Melbourne, for the purpose of removing her spar deck, cabin and houses, and to alter her ports so as to fit the ship for working four more 8-inch guns, which she had in her hold. Her officers hoped to enlist a hundred more men.

The Treasury Department has received three books, the entry in one of them being March 18, 1861, at Montgomery, Ala., containing the names of the agents appointed by the Confederate Government to raise funds for the benefit of that concern. It also gives information on the subject of subscriptions to bonds, including letters of instructions.

Rebel Prisoners in Washington.

About 440 Rebel officers arrived here to-night from City Point, including Generals Ewell, Corse, Hunter, Barton, Kershaw, Du Bose and Simons, and Major Campbell Bowen, Assistant Adjutant to General Ewell, together with Commodore Hunter and J. B. Tucker, of the Rebel Navy.

The officers above named will at once be sent to Fort Warren in charge of Captain Forehand, Ninth Veteran Reserve Corps, and Captain Russell, Assistant Provost Marshal. The remaining four hundred and forty have been committed to the Old Capitol. While in the Provost Marshal's office, General Ewell declared that he did not order the burning of Richmond, but that it was done by the mob.

A gentleman from City Point says that Ewell yesterday sent a card to Richmond for publication, to the same effect. The indignation against him in that city is intense. Ewell and the other General officers claim that, although captured previous to Lee's surrender, they are entitled to the benefit of the terms between the latter and General Grant.

No Possibility of an Extra Session.

According to information from intimate friends of the President, who have recently conversed with him, he does not think there will be any necessity for an extra session of Congress; nor has he yet come to any determination as to issuing a proclamation addressed to the people of the South.

From Richmond.

THE CITIZENS RETURNING TO THEIR ALLEGIANCE—ARRIVAL OF GENERAL LEE.

BALTIMORE, April 14.—The Richmond *Whig*, of yesterday, contains little news of importance. It announces the arrival of General Lee on the night previously.

The *Whig* publishes the oath of allegiance, to which it says citizens will be required to swear and subscribe. The Provost Marshal's office is crowded with people anxious to take it, and the only question among the citizens seems to be who shall be the first to renew their citizenship.

The Alleged Charges Against General Carrington.

CINCINNATI, April 14.—General Carrington publishes a card, saying the charges against him are all infamous attempts to obliterate the credit of his services in Indiana. His friends say the matter grows out of a misunderstanding with the paymasters, and all money for which he is responsible is deposited in bank ready to be turned over.

The Funeral of General Smyth.

WILMINGTON, Del., April 14.—The remains of Brigadier-General Thomas A. Smyth arrived here to-day at 1 o'clock, and will be interred on Monday afternoon at 2 o'clock, with appropriate ceremonies.

THE EVENING TELEGRAPH

DOUBLE SHEET—THREE CENTS.] PHILADELPHIA, SATURDAY, APRIL 15, 1865. [DOUBLE SHEET—THREE CENTS.

DEATH OF THE PRESIDENT.

THE NATIONAL HORROR.

OFFICIAL GAZETTE.

ASSASSINATION OF THE PRESIDENT.

[illegible] Accomplice the Murderers.

THE TRAGEDY PLANNED FOR THE FOURTH OF MARCH.

It is Delayed Until Richmond Should be Heard From.

ONE OF THE TWO ESCAPED TO BALTIMORE.

WASHINGTON, April 15, 4·10 A. M.—Major-General Dix, New York.—The President continues insensible, and is sinking.

Secretary Seward remains without change.

Frederick Seward's skull is fractured in two places, besides a severe cut upon the head. The attendant is still alive, but hopeless. Major Seward's wound is not dangerous.

It is now ascertained with reasonable certainty that two assassins were engaged in the horrible crime, J. Wilkes Booth being the one that shot the President. The other is a companion of his, whose name is not known. The description is so clear that he can hardly escape.

It appears from a letter found in Booth's trunk, that the murder was planned before the 4th of March, but fell through then, because the accomplice backed [illegible] until Richmond [illegible]. Booth and his accomplice were at the livery stable at 6 o'clock last evening, and left there about 10 o'clock, or shortly before that hour.

It would seem that for several days they have been seeking their chance, but for some unknown reason it was not carried into effect until last night.

One of them has evidently made his way to Baltimore. The other has not yet been traced.

EDWIN M. STANTON, Secretary of War.

DEATH OF THE PRESIDENT.

WASHINGTON, April 15.—Major-General Dix:—Abraham Lincoln died this morning at twenty-two minutes after 7 o'clock.

E. M. STANTON, Secretary of War.

FURTHER PARTICULARS.

The Assassination Last Night While at Ford's Theatre in Washington.

PISTOL BALL PENETRATES THE BRAIN

Mr. Lincoln Dying at Midnight.

FAREWELL OF PRESIDENT'S FAMILY

SAD AND SOLEMN SCENES.

THE ASSASSIN IN HIS PRIVATE BOX.

The Murderer Leaps Upon the Stage and Escapes.

WASHINGTON, April 14.—The President of the United States was shot while attending at Ford's Theatre to-night. It is feared that the wounds are mortal.

President Lincoln and his wife, together with other friends, this evening visited Ford's Theatre for the purpose of witnessing the performance of *The American Cousin*.

It was announced in the papers that General Grant would also be present, but that gentleman instead took the late train of cars for New Jersey.

The theatre was densely crowded, and everybody seemed delighted with the scene before them.

During the third act, and while there was a temporary pause for one of the actors to enter, the sharp report of a pistol was heard, which merely attracted attention, but suggested nothing serious, until a man rushed to the front of the President's box, waving a long dagger in his right hand, and exclaiming, *Sic semper tyrannis!* and immediately leaped from the box, which was of the second tier, to the stage beneath, and ran across to the opposite side, thus making his escape, amid the bewilderment of the audience, from the rear of the theatre, and mounting a horse, fled.

The screams of Mrs. Lincoln first disclosed the fact to the audience that the President had been shot, when all present rose to their feet, rushing towards the stage, many exclaiming, "Hang him! hang him!"

The excitement was of the wildest possible description, and, of course, there was an abrupt termination of the theatrical performance.

There was a rush towards the Presidential box, when cries were heard, "Stand back! Give him air! Has any one stimulants?"

On a hasty examination it was found that the President had been shot through the head, above and back of the temporal bone, and that some of the brain was oozing out.

He was removed to a private house opposite to the theatre, and the Surgeon-General of the army and other surgeons were sent for to attend to his condition.

On an examination of the private box blood was discovered on the back of the cushioned rocking-chair on which the President had been sitting, also on the partition and on the floor. A common single-barrelled pocket pistol was found on the carpet.

A military guard was placed in front of the private residence to which the President had been conveyed. An immense crowd gathered in front of it, all deeply anxious to learn the condition of the President. It had been previously announced that the wound was mortal, but all hoped otherwise.

The shock to the community was terrible.

At midnight the Cabinet, with Messrs. Sumner, Colfax, and Farnsworth, Judge Carter, Governor Oglesby, General Meigs, Colonel Hay, and a few personal friends, with Surgeon-General Barnes, and his medical associates, were around his bedside.

The President in a Dying Condition at Midnight.

The President was in a state of *syncope*, totally insensible, and breathing slowly, the blood oozing from the wound at the back of his head. The surgeons were exhausting every possible effort of medical skill, but all hope was gone.

The parting of his family with the dying President is too sad for description.

The President and Mrs. Lincoln did not start to the theatre till fifteen minutes after 8 o'clock. Speaker Colfax was at the White House at the time, and the President stated to him that he was going, although Mrs. Lincoln had not been well, because the papers had advertised that General Grant and they were to be present, and as General Grant had gone North, he did not wish the audience to be disappointed.

He went with apparent reluctance, and urged Mr. Colfax to go with him; but that gentleman

An Attempt to Kill Secretary Seward.

HIS BEDCHAMBER ENTERED BY THE VILLAIN.

Frederick W. and Major Seward Knocked Senseless.

SECRETARY SEWARD STABBED THREE TIMES IN THE NECK.

Terrible Excitement in Washington.

When the excitement at the theatre was at its wildest height, reports were circulated that Secretary Seward had also been assassinated.

On reaching this gentleman's residence, a crowd and a military guard were found at the door, and on entering, it was ascertained that the reports were based upon truth. Everybody there was so excited that scarcely an intelligible account could be gathered, but the facts are substantially as follows:—

About 10 o'clock a man rang the bell, and the call having been answered by a colored servant, he said he had come from Dr. Verdi, Secretary Seward's family physician, with a prescription, at the same time holding in his hand a small piece of folded paper, and saying, in answer to a refusal, that he must see the Secretary, as he was intrusted with a particular direction concerning the medicine.

He still insisted on going up, although repeatedly informed that no one could enter the chamber. The man pushed the servant aside and walked quickly to the Secretary's room, and was there met by Mr. Frederick W. Seward, of whom he demanded to see the Secretary, making the same representation which he did to the servant.

What further passed in the way of colloquy is not known, but the man struck him on the head with a billy, severely injuring the skull, and felling him almost senseless. The assassin then rushed into the chamber and attacked Major Seward, Paymaster in the United States Army, and Mr. Hansell, a messenger of the State Department, and two male nurses, disabling them all. He then rushed upon the Secretary, who was lying in bed in the same room, and inflicted three stabs in the neck, but severing, it is thought and hoped, no arteries.

The assassin then rushed down stairs, mounted his horse at the door, and rode off before an alarm could be sounded, and in the same manner of the assassin of the President. It is believed the injuries of the Secretary are not fatal, nor those of the others, although both the Secretary and the Assistant Secretary are very seriously injured.

Secretaries Stanton and Welles, and other prominent officers of the Government, called at Secretary Seward's house to inquire into his condition, and there heard of the assassination of the President. They proceeded to the house where he was lying, exhibiting, of course, intense anxiety and solicitude.

An immense crowd was gathered in front of the President's House, and a strong guard also stationed there, many persons evidently supposing that he would be brought to his home.

The entire city to-night presents a scene of wild excitement, accompanied by violent expressions of indignation, and the profoundest sorrow. Many shed tears.

The military authorities have despatched mounted patrols in every direction, in order, if possible, to arrest the assassin, while the Metropolitan police are alike vigilant for the same purpose.

The attack, both at the theatre and at Secretary Seward's house, took place at about the same hour (10 o'clock), thus showing a preconcerted plan to assassinate these gentlemen. Some evidences of the guilt of the party who attacked the President are in possession of the police.

Vice-President Johnson is in the city, and his hotel quarters are guarded by troops.

CONDITION OF SECRETARY SEWARD.

Assistant Secretary Seward in a Critical Condition.

WASHINGTON, April 15, 10·30 A. M.—Secretary Seward is in a more comfortable condition at this hour.

Assistant Secretary Seward is in a critical condition.

THE ASSASSINATION.

Further Particulars of the Sad Event.

THE SCHEME AND ITS EXTENT.

The Design to Kill Secretary Stanton Frustrated.

SPUR AND HAT OF THE MURDERER FOUND.

The Excitement in Washington.

[illegible] conversation. The following additional particulars have been obtained:—

The assassin of the President left behind him his hat and a spur. The hat was picked up in the President's box, and has been identified by parties to whom it has been shown, and accurately described as the one belonging to the suspected man by other parties not allowed to see it before describing it.

The spur was dropped on the stage, and that also has been identified as the one procured at a stable where the same man hired a horse in the evening.

Two gentlemen who went to apprise the Secretary of War of the attack on Mr. Lincoln, met at the residence of the former a man muffled in a cloak, who, when accosted by them, hastened away without a word.

It had been the Secretary's intention to accompany Mr. Lincoln, and occupy the same box, but a press of business prevented. It therefore seems evident that the aim of the plotters was to paralyze the country by at once striking down the head and the arm of the country.

As soon as the dreadful event was announced in the streets, Superintendent Richards and his assistants were at work to discover the assassin. In a few moments the telegraph had aroused the whole police force of the city. Mayor Wallach and several members of the city government were soon on the spot. Every measure of precaution was taken to preserve order in the city, and every street was patrolled.

At the request of Mr Richards, General Augur sent horses to mount the police. Every road out of Washington was picketed, and every possible avenue of escape thoroughly guarded. The steamboats about to depart down the Potomac were stopped.

The *Daily Chronicle* says:—As it is suspected that the conspiracy originated in Maryland, the telegraph flashed the mournful news to Baltimore, and all the cavalry was immediately put upon active duty.

Every road was picketed, and every precaution taken to prevent the escape of the assassins. A preliminary examination was made by Mr Richards and his assistants.

Several persons were called to testify, and the evidence, as elicited before an informal tribunal, and not under oath, was conclusive to this point, that the murderer of the President was John Wilkes Booth.

His hat was found in the private box and identified by several persons who had seen him within the last two days, and the spur which he dropped by accident after he jumped to the stage was identified as one of those which he had obtained from the stable where hired his horse.

This man Booth has played more than once at Ford's Theatre, and is of course acquainted with its exits and entrances, and the facility with which he escaped behind the scenes is easily understood. The person who wounded Secretary Seward left behind him a slouched hat and an old rusty navy revolver.

The chambers were broken loose, as if done by striking. The loads were drawn from the chambers, one being but a rough piece of lead, and the other balls smaller than the chambers, wrapped in paper, as if to keep them from falling out.

THE DYING SCENES.

WASHINGTON, April 15, 11 A. M.—The *Star* extra says:—At twenty minutes past 7 o'clock the President breathed his last, closing his eyes as if falling to sleep, and his countenance assuming an expression of perfect serenity.

There was no indications of pain, and it was not known that he was dead until the gradually decreasing respiration ceased altogether.

The Rev. Dr. Gurley, of the New York Avenue Presbyterian Church, immediately on its being ascertained that life was extinct, knelt at the bedside and offered an impressive prayer, which was responded to by all present.

Dr. Gurley then proceeded to the front parlor where Mrs. Lincoln, Captain Robert Lincoln, Mr. John Hay, the private Secretary, and others were waiting, where he again offered prayer for the consolation of the family.

The following minutes, taken by Dr. Abbott, show the condition of the President throughout the night:—[illegible] pulse 44; 11·05 P. M., pulse 45, and growing weaker; 11·10 P. M., pulse 45; 11·15 P. M., pulse 42; 11·20 P. M., pulse 45; respiration 27 to 29; 11·25 P. M., pulse 42; 11·32 P. M., pulse 48 and full; 11·40 P. M., pulse 45; 11·45 P. M., pulse 45, respiration 22; 12·08 P. M., respiration 22; 12·15 P. M., respiration, 21 echmose of both eyes; 12·30 P. M., pulse 54; 12·32 P. M., pulse 60; 12·35 P. M., Pulse 66; 12·40 P. M., pulse 69, right eye much swollen; and echemose; 12·45 P. M., pulse 70, respiration 27; 12·55 P. M., pulse 80, struggling motion of arms; 1 A. M., pulse 86, respiration 30; 1·30 A. M., pulse 95, appearing easier; 1·45 A. M., pulse 86, very quiet, respiration irregular.

Mrs. Lincoln present. 2·10 A. M., Mrs. Lincoln retired with Robert Lincoln to an adjoining room; 2·30 A. M., the President is very quiet, pulse 54, respiration 28.

2·30 A. M., the President very quiet; pulse 54, respiration 28; 2·52 A. M., pulse 48, respiration 30; 3 A. M., visited again by Mrs. Lincoln; 3·25 A. M., respiration 24, and regular; 3·35, P. M., prayer by the Rev. Dr. Gurley; 4 A. M., respiration 26 and regular; 4·15 A. M., pulse 60, respiration 25; 5·50 A. M., respiration 28 and regular sleeping; 6 A. M., pulse failing, respiration 28; 6·30 A. M., still failing and labored breathing; 7 A. M., symptoms of immediate dissolution; 7·22 A. M., death.

Surrounding the death-bed of the President were Secretaries Stanton, Welles, Usher, Attorney-General Speed, Postmaster-General Dennison, M. T. Field, Assistant Secretary of the Treasury; Judge Otto, Assistant Secretary of Interior; General Halleck, General Meigs, Senator Sumner, F. R. Andrews, of New York; Gen. Todd, of Dacotah; John Hay, Private Secretary; Governor Oglesby, of Illinois, General Farnsworth, Mr. and Miss Kenny, Miss Harris, Captain Robert Lincoln, son of the President, and Dr. E. W. Abbott, R. K. Stone, C. D. Gatch, Neal Hall, and Leiberman. Secretary McCulloch remained with the President until about 5 A. M., and Chief Justice Chase, after several hours attendance [illegible] diately after the President's death [illegible] Stanton, and held in the room in which the corpse lay. Secretaries Stanton, Welles, and Usher, Postmaster-General Dennison, and Attorney-General Speed, were present.

AFTER THE DECEASE.

The President's body was removed from the private residence, opposite Ford's Theatre, to the Executive mansion, this morning at half-past 9 o'clock, in a hearse, and wrapped in the American flag.

It was escorted by a small guard of cavalry, General Augur and other military officers following on foot.

A dense crowd accompanied the remains to the White House, where a military guard excluded the crowd, allowing none but persons of the household and personal friends of the deceased to enter the premises. Senator Yates and Representative Farnsworth being among the number admitted.

The body is being embalmed, with a view to its removal to Illinois.

Owing to the melancholy event, the Superintendent of Police has caused all places where liquor is sold to be closed during this day and night.

The flags over the departments and throughout the city are at half-mast. Scarcely any business is being transacted anywhere, either on private or public account.

Our citizens, without any preconcerted action whatever, are draping their premises with festoons of mourning.

The bells are tolling. All is sadness. Strong men weep in the streets. The grief is widespread, and deep—a strange contrast to the joy so lately manifested over our recent military victories.

This is indeed a day of gloom. Reports prevail that Mr. Frederick W. Seward is dead, but this is not true. Information was, however, obtained by direct inquiry at half-past 10 o'clock that his condition is considered critical. His head is horribly injured.

Secretary Seward suffers intense pain. The gashes made upon his cheek and throat are frightful, but still he is not believed to be in immediate danger, nor in a worse state than his son Frederick.

Major A. H. Seward received two wounds, one in the arm, but no fears are entertained as to his recovery.

Mr. Hansell, an employe of the State Department, who was kindly assisting in nursing Mr. Seward, received a stab in the back. His shoulder-blade prevented the knife or dagger from penetrating far into his body. The prospects are that he will recover.

A report is circulated, and repeated by almost everybody, that Booth was captured fifteen miles this side of Baltimore. If it be true, as asserted, that the War Department has received such information, it will doubtless be officially promulgated.

The Government Departments are closed by order and will be draped with the usual emblems of mourning. The roads leading to and from the city are guarded by military, and the utmost circumspection is observed as to all attempting to enter or leave the city.

JOHN WILKES BOOTH.

SKETCH OF THE MURDERER.

John Wilkes Booth was born in Harford county, and not in Baltimore city. He is much addicted to drink, and having lost heavily recently in oil speculations, was supposed to be laboring under temporary insanity. The madness of the act would seem to justify this. He was for some time business agent for his brother Edwin in the West.

He made his first appearance on the stage at the Arch Street Theatre, in this city, some years ago, under the name of John Wilkes, and was considerably liked.

Some time after he made his first appearance as a star at Columbus, Ga., and while there was accidently shot by the manager.

He has been in Washington for some months past, ostensibly for the purpose of organizing an oil company, but really for the purpose of consummating his scheme of wholesale assassination, under the direction of Mosby. There is no doubt that Booth contemplated the act long ago, and only delayed its execution because of some private instructions from Moseby.

Only a month ago he obtained a pass to go to Virginia, ostensibly to buy some land, but really to consult with Moseby and other leaders relative to the murder of Mr. Lincoln and his Cabinet.

He was well acquainted with all the exits and internal arrangements of Ford's Theatre, and kept a horse at livery in a stable immediately in the rear of the theatre.

Booth is a brother of Mrs. John S. Clarke, wife of the celebrated comedian.

Mr. Booth worked hard to have Mr. Ford engage a Mr. C., a Baltimorean engaged at his theatre some time since, and the latter is probably one of his accomplices.

Booth is a very fine-looking man, with black hair and eyes, stately form, and easy carriage.

EFFECT OF THE NEWS

[illegible] ble events that occurred [illegible] night, and the grief of all good men is apparent everywhere at the demise of the President.

No flags were hoisted in this city this morning until the state of the President was known, when they were all placed at half-mast. The people appear perfectly horrified, and the utmost rage is undoubtedly felt towards all known secessionists and Rebel sympathizers.

Easton.

EASTON, April 15.—The announcement of the assassination of President Lincoln has caused the most profound regret. All business is suspended. A man who expressed traitorous sentiments was almost killed by the citizens, and with difficulty was saved from hanging.

Washington.

TEN THOUSAND DOLLARS REWARD FOR THE MURDERERS.

WASHINGTON, April 15.—President Lincoln died this morning at half-past seven o'clock.

Major-General Augur, commanding the Department of Washington, has offered a reward of ten thousand dollars to the party or parties arresting the murderer of the President, and the assassin of the Secretary of State and his son.

This morning at 6 o'clock there was no change in the condition of Secretary Seward. The *Chronicle* says a letter found in J. Wilkes Booth's trunk identifies him as the murderer.

Harrisburg.

HARRISBURG, April 15.—The news of the assassination of the President and the attempted assassination of the Secretary of State was received here with feelings of the most profound regret by all classes of the community.

A mass meeting of the citizens was held at the Court House, and the celebration of the victories, which was to have come off to-day, is ordered to be postponed. All the flags and other decorations intended for the festive display are being draped in the emblems of mourning. The church and other bells of the city are to be tolled at noon, and the citizens have been invited to meet at the Methodist Church at 4 o'clock, to unite with the ministry in religious services proper for the occasion.

Baltimore.

BALTIMORE, April 15.—The feeling here at the horrible crime which has deprived the country of its beloved President is too deep for utterance. Sorrow profound, and rage intense, pervades all loyal hearts. All kindly feelings towards Rebels and Rebel sympathizers has, as it were, been obliterated, and one intense feeling of detestation and abhorrence for all connected with the Rebellion takes its place.

All the flags are at half-mast, and, draped in mourning, denote the public grief, while the bells are tolling mournfully.

NEW YORK, April 15, Noon.—All the places of business are rapidly closing, and the streets are assuming a sombre hue. The various hotels, the New England Rooms, Post Office, Custom House, and other public places are being draped.

The Corn Exchange met, passed suitable resolutions, ordering the building draped, and adjourned.

THIRD EDITION

INAUGURATION OF PRESIDENT JOHNSON.

His Inaugural Address.

WASHINGTON, April 15, Noon.—Andrew Johnson was sworn into office as President by Chief Justice Chase to-day at 11 o'clock. Secretary McCulloch, Att[illegible]

President Johnson remarked:—

"The duties are mine—I will perform them, trusting in God."

Installation of Vice-President Johnson.

WASHINGTON, April 15.—At an early hour this morning the Hon. Edwin M. Stanton, Secretary of War, sent an official communication to the Hon. Andrew Johnson, Vice-President, that in consequence of the sudden and unexpected death of the Chief Magistrate, his inauguration should take place as soon as possible, and requesting him to state the place and hour at which the ceremony should be performed.

Mr. Johnson immediately replied that it would be agreeable to him to have the proceedings take place at his rooms in the Kirkwood House, as soon as the arrangements could be perfected.

Chief Justice Chase was informed of the fact, and repaired to the appointed place in company with Secretary McCulloch of Treasury Department, Attorney-General Speed, F. P. Blair, Sr., Hon. M. Blair, Senators Foot of Vermont, Ramsey of Minnesota, Yates of Illinois, Stewart of Nevada, Hall of New Hampshire, and General Farnsworth of Illinois.

At 11 o'clock the oath of office was administered by the Chief Justice of the United States, in his usual solemn and impressive manner.

Mr. Johnson received the kind expressions of the gentlemen by whom he was surrounded in a manner which showed his earnest sense of the great responsibility so suddenly devolved upon him, and made a brief speech, in which he said:—

"The duties of the office are mine; I will perform them. The consequences are with God. Gentlemen, I shall lean upon you. I feel that I shall need your support. I am deeply impressed with the solemnity of the occasion, and the responsibility of the duties of the office I am assuming."

Mr. Johnson appeared to be in remarkably good health, and has a high and realizing sense of the hopes that are centred upon him. His manner was solemn and dignified, and his whole

WASHINGTON, April 15.—It is ascertained on the best authority, that Booth, the murderer of the President, has been arrested.

GRANT RETURNS TO WASHINGTON.

LIEUTENANT-GENERAL U. S. GRANT, upon hearing the sad news of the assassination of President LINCOLN, determined to return to Washington as soon as possible. He remained up all last night, suffering great mental agony, and departed for Washington in a special train at 8·15 this morning.

For The Evening Telegraph.

DIRGE.

BY RICHARD COE.

Toll! toll! toll!
On every hand,
Ye bells throughout the land;
Washington's great compeer now lies,
With death-sealed eyes,
And pallid face upturned towards the skies!
Toll! toll! toll!
On every hand,
Ye bells throughout the land!
Toll! toll! toll!
Weep! weep! weep!
On every hand
Ye patriots in the land
Brave Lincoln dead! Great God! and can it be?
"Henceforth there 's nothing in mortality
That 's serious!" Help us to look to Thee!
Weep! weep! weep!
On every hand,
Ye patriots in the land,
Weep! weep! weep!
Pray! pray! pray!
On every hand,
Ye Christians in the land.
No more his honest face will greet the sun—
His day is finished, and his labor done;
A crown of glory rests his brow upon!
Pray! pray! pray!
On every hand,
Ye Christians in the land;
Pray! pray! pray!

PHILADELPHIA TRADE REPORT.

SATURDAY, April 15.—The "Corn Exchange Association" met this morning, but transacted no business, and adjourned after the adoption of the preamble and resolutions to be found in another column. Business throughout the city was suspended.

—Two Smiths and one Smyth "govern" the New England States. Rhode Island and Vermont have the Smiths, and New Hampshire the Smyth.

BY J. L. PENNINGTON & CO.

THE DAILY PROGRESS.

VOL. VI. RALEIGH, SATURDAY, APRIL 15, 1865. NO. 130.

FROM THE NORTH.

We have been placed in possession of a N. Y. "Herald" of the 7th, from which we make copious extracts. Under the head of "The Situation," the "Herald" says:

The battles before Petersburg and the defeat and pursuit of Lee are the most remarkable operations of this war, and the complete success, which we may now reasonably hope for, will mark them as among the most brilliant examples of modern warfare.—From the moment of taking the offensive General Grant has forced upon the enemy every strategical and tactical movement which he has made. It may be said with truth that Grant has commanded both his own and Lee's army. His great object in massing his forces on his left, it is now apparent, was to force Lee to take position or to retreat by the routes on the north side of the Appomattox river. By the success of Sheridan's battle on the 2d inst., Grant became possessed of the interior or shorter lines to Burkesville, and with his usual promptitude he moved in pursuit. The advance of his left reached Burkesville on the 5th inst. at nightfall, the rear bringing up at Black and White station, on the Southside Railroad, while his right was concentrated by noon of the same day at Jetersville, on the Danville Railroad, ten miles northeast of Burkesville. In the meantime Lee was moving by the longer routes, and, being delayed by the necessity of crossing the Appomattox river, was only able to form in line of battle at Amelia Court House on the same evening, being actually ten [illegible] rapid [illegible] General Grant has not only succeeded in interposing himself as an impassable barrier to the junction of the rebel armies of Lee and Johnston, but is actually marching to attack Lee from the very point upon the possession of which Lee's safety depended.—Grant has the rebel army in a position from which, if defeated, it has no line of retreat. Lee has been "headed off" and forced to make a stand in a position in which defeat results either in unconditional surrender or equally disastrous retreat.

Some further intelligence regarding the rebel ram Stonewall and the two United States vessels watching her movements—the steamships Niagra and Sacramento—is given by our Corunna Spain correspondent, under date of the 16th ult. The Niagra and Sacramento were still at Corunna, keeping steam up all the time, so as to be ready to instantly move out and attack the rebel ram should she go to sea from Ferrol, where she was still lying, and which is only about nine miles from Corrunna. On the 13th ult. the Niagara went in search of a vessel which it was understood was to leave Calais on the 10th with men and supplies for the Stonewall, but returned to Corunna on the 14th without finding her. It was rumored that the Stonewall would be shortly seized by the Spanish government and transferred to the French.

A body of national cavalry, under Gen. Torbert, started up the Shenandoah valley on last Monday.—As far as heard from they have met with little opposition.

The naval attack on the defences of Mobile was commenced on the 28th ult., when seven of the national gunboats moved in towards the shore of the bay and opened on the rebel forts. After sending one hundred and eighty shells into Spanish Fort and other works, without eliciting a return from the enemy, they withdrew. Rebel accounts state that there was also heavy skirmishing at Spanish Fort on that and the succeeding day with the national troops, and that a regular siege by the latter appeared propbable as no general attack had been made. A rebel despatch of the 29th from Mobile says there were then forty-seven national vessels of all classes in sight. The iron-clad Milwaukee was blown up in the bay on the 29th by a rebel torpedo. There was no firing on the forts by the fleet on the 29th; but on the 30th it again resumed the attack, with what results we have not learned. New Orleans papers of the 6th inst., stated that information had been received at army headquarters in that city that General Canby's army was within five miles of Mobile; that he had siege guns in position from which shells could be thrown into the suburbs, and that the attack on Fort Blakely, the main defence, had already began. General Dick Taylor is said to be in command at Spanish Fort, while General Maury commands in the city. We give this morning a map of Mobile city and bay.

Governor Fenton, of this State, has issued a proclamation appointing Friday next, the 14th inst., to be observed as a day of thanksgiving for the recent glorious national triumphs.

The whole North is still stirred with rejoicings over the late grand successes of our armies. From innumerable cities, towns and villages we have accounts of illuminations, ringing of bells, firing of cannon and all manner of joyful demonstrations.

HIGHLY IMPORTANT FROM RICHMOND—PEACE NEGOTIATIONS RESUMED.

We have the information direct from Richmond that President Lincoln is there actually engaged upon the business of peace, that on Tuesday evening last he had a private conference with Judge Campbell, one of the three rebel commissioners in the famous Hampton Road conference. Judge Campbell, it is understood, by and with the advice and consent of Jeff. Davis, with the rebel evacuation of Richmond, remained behind to see what could be done in behalf of his despairing rebel associates and followers in a treaty of peace. We are further informed that Wednesday last had been appointed as the day for a more formal meeting between the President, General Weitzel and one or two others on the Union side, and some other prominent rebel leaders on their side, and that high expectations were entertained that peace would speedily follow.

We attach the highest importance to this intelligence; for we accept it as substantially true. It is altogether probable that Davis may have come to the conclusion that if he desires, in behalf of himself and his ruling confederates, any abatement or commutation of the pains and penalties of treason, now is his only time, while yet he maintains something like a respectable show of resistance in the field. That Judge Campbell is hopeful of some liberal concessions from Mr. Lincoln, for the sake of immediate peace, we are fully disposed to believe. But what can the President do, with the laws of Congress restricting him to a fixed line of action? Sworn to see the laws faithfully executed, can he go beyond them? He cannot; but he can promise some modifications, so far as they may be attainable through a message to Congress, with the meeting of an extra session upon the subject. He may go still further in the exercise of his military discretion, which in such a war as this cannot be regulated by Congressional enactments.

We know nothing of the purposes or views of President Lincoln in connection with his visit to Richmond; but we do know something of his humane disposition, and shall be somewhat disappointed if we do not receive before his departure from Richmond the announcement of a proclamation which will finish the disarming of the rebellion, and win back the masses of the Southern people to the blessings of the Union and of peace.

AFFAIRS IN RICHMOND.

MAJOR-GENERAL WEITZEL'S HEADQUARTERS, Richmond, Va., April 4, 1865.

The constant recurrence of enlivening scenes in Richmond since the Union accession, is so much in contrast with the sober realities of a life in camp, to which I have been so largely accustomed of late, that I have not as yet addressed myself to the writing up of those many scenes marking rebel life and manners which will go to history, when written as remembrances of our occupation of the rebel capital.

PRESIDENT LINCOLN IN RICHMOND.

Perhaps, however, it may be said, no one incident of all this drama will so attract and fix the attention of the American people and the civilized world as the appearance to-day in the city of Richmond—erased capital of infernal traitors—of Abraham Lincoln, President of the United States.

HIS ARRIVAL AND GREETING.

[illegible] President would enter Richmond, and held counsel with all who might be desirous of lending a helping hand to the restoration of the Union.—Mr. Lincoln left City Point in the flagship Admiral Porter, accompanied by the Bat, and, ascending the James, arrived at Rockett's Landing early in the day. He was accompanied in the way of a guard, by one company of marines and one company of armed sailors (a distinction without a difference). As the President approached the headquarters of Major General Weitzel the salutes were opened, and he was found to be accompanied by Admiral Porter and an immense crowd of the people, who accorded to their liberator the cordial acclamations of a race owing him so much. It was truly a cheering sight to see Abraham Lincoln walking, rather than riding in pageant, the streets of Richmond—proud, but fallen city of the South—followed by an admiring crowd, where, but a few hours before, he would have been the subject of rebel jest and ribaldry, which his own patience has overcome, even to the approaching point of rebel reconsideration of folly.

Mr. Lincoln in Jeff. Davis' late Residence.

The President, upon his arrival in the city, was immediately escorted, by his own choice, upon foot, to the headquarters of Major Gen. Weitzel, commanding department, which are in the house of Jefferson Davis, and the threshold of which that arch-rebel crossed for the last time on Sunday evening, to take the cars for Danville, followed by his broken army. The President of the United States receiving the congratufations of an admiring auditory in the city of Richmond, and within the (late) domestic precints of Jefferson Davis, needs no comment to cause the American people to believe that the atrocious struggle is quite at its end

A Recepton.

Major Gen Weitzel, upon the sudden appearance of Mr. Lincoln, held extemporized drawing room receptions in the Executive mansion of the confederacy, to which the President loaned, in his presence, the chiefest attraction. He was introduced to the leading general and staff officers of the department of Virginia and the Army of the James now present in Richmond, among whom were Generals Shepley, Kautz, Devens, Roberts, Col. Ed. W. Smith, Assistant Adjutant General; Col. F. S. Manning, Provost Marshal General Army of the James; Col. Coughlin, Provost of the Department of Virginia; Col. Placidus Ord, Assistant Adjutant General; Colonel Donnohoe, commanding brigade; Col. W. V. Hutchings, Majs A. H. Stevens, D. D. Wheeler, E. E. Graves, Captains Fred Martin, Lewis Weitzel, Fitch, Graves, Howard, Lieut. H. S. Merrell, United States Army, and Lieutenant Struble.

The President rides through the City.

Just subsequent to the reception there was a private conference, after which the President rode out to see the city of Richmond—object of all his Presidential affections.

Return to his Steamer in the James.

The ride over, the President proceeded to his ship, leaving us to the kindly realm of future developments. The President's condition of body and mind is best understood by the presentation of the fact, that physical inability, confessed to those with him in his carriage, alone prevented him from hoisting the flag of his country over the ancient Capitol building of Virginia—several hundred years of age in respect of patriotism, only four years old in treason.

The present Contents of Libby.

The late prison of Union patriots—Libby Prison—rejoices to-day in a crowded complement of rebel officers and soldiers. They are there for the express purpose of being permitted to libbyize just as our men suffered.

Honors to General Weitzel.

The following telegraphic dispatch was received this evening by Maj. Gen. Weitzel, the first of the Union Generals to enter Richmond. The dispatch is signed by the Mayor and other prominent citizens:

CINCINNATI, April 4, 1865.

Major General Weitzel:—

The Queen City of the West sends greeting to her native son. He has deserved well of the republic.

This gratifying dispatch found Gen. Weitzel surrounded by a number of friends, all of whom shared in the glorious enterprise of the occupancy of Richmond.

Sobriety—An Order.

The following order indicates that nobody shall keep grocery in or about Richmond.

OFFICE PROVOST MARSHAL, Richmond April 3, 1865.

All places in the city of Richmond where intoxicating liquors are sold are hereby ordered to be immediately closed. Any person whatever, who shall sell or give to any enlisted man of the armies of the United States any intoxicating liquor, will be immediately arrested and summarily punished.

By direction of
Brig. Gen. GEO. F. SHEPLEY,
Military Governor of Richmond.
FRED. L. MANNING, Lieut. Col. and Provost Marshal of Richmond.

THE ARMY IN PURSUIT.

Sutherland Station, Va., April 4, 1865.

The Magnificence of Grant's Operations against Richmond and Petersburg.

The more the military movements of this week by the armies operating against Richmond are considered and studied, the more the attentive reader of history will find them unlike, but superior to, the most brilliant achievements of the ablest generals of the world. But few seiges of modern days have been so prolonged as this of Petersburg and Richmond. On [illegible] ing skill been expended. [illegible] affords no parallel to this in the length of the lines constructed and held by us. No finer strategy has ever been recorded of any general than has been displayed by General Grant in deceiving Lee as to his real point of attack; a more audacious assault was never made on an enemy's works than the successful one of the Sixth corps, by command of Lieutenant General Grant; and at such trifling expense of men and material.

But the striking difference between this and the decided achievements of other chieftains is, that it was directed against the enemy's line of communication at such an immense distance. No pitched battles have been fought this week for the possession of Richmond; a comparatively small portion of our forces have been in actual battle for the possession of Petersburg; yet the strategy of General Grant has been such as to give us the former at small cost, and to compel the evacuation of the other without a shot, though so many miles away.

The real battles for Richmond were fought by Sheridan and Wright, on separate days. The former compelled Lee to weaken his line, and the latter took advantage of its weakness. Lee made the gravest mistake imaginable in sending Pickett's division so far from the defences of Petersburg. While he strengthened his flank we penetrated his centre. His army was completely cut in two. Its separate parts can never be wholly reunited. The fatal error will cost him one half of his army.

General Grant's confidence in the success of his Plans.

So confident was General Grant of the success of his plans, as soon as he discovered the position of Pickett, that the moment that an assault was determined upon on the centre Sheriden's cavalry and the Fifth army corps were ordered to push out directly westward, in order to be nearer the line of retreat which the enemy must take up. And when the assault was successful, and Petersburg ours, the entire army was immediately put in motion for the same purpose, and in the same direction. Petersburg was taken yesterday morning. General Grant's headquarters were ten miles west of that city last evening. Such celerity of movement is novel in war, and bewildering to an adversary.

The Situation on the Night of the 4th Inst.

The military situation to-night is substantially as follows:

General Grant's headquarters are at Sutherland station; General Meade's are a half mile distant, and nearly in the rear; General Ord's are not much further away, but more to the northward; those of General Sheridan and the Fifth corps are more than thirty miles west of Petersburg, beyond the Namozine creek; those of the Second corps north of the Appomattox, and five miles northwesterly from here those of the Sixth corps two miles in our rear, with the Ninth immediately behind it. The grand army is evidently headed for Burkesville or the nearest point on the Danville Railroad. General Grant long ago expressed the sentiment that Lee's army, instead of the city of Richmond, was his objective point.

Nothing Positive Known of Lee.

Nothing positive is known of Lee's whereabouts. He is supposed to be on his way to Lynchburg via Burkesville Juncton.

The President has an Interview with General Grant.

The President rode out to Petersburg yesterday forenoon for the purpose of seeing the famous city, and had in the meantime a short interview with General Grant. He was overjoyed at the success of our arms, and can now return to Washington in renewed spirits.

Curiosity to see the President.

Much pardonable curiosity was manifested by all classes to see the President and the Lieutenant General. One old German seized the President's hand, pressed it to his lips and thanked God." he was now released from his yoke."

The Citizens of Petersburg Remain.

The citizens generally remained behind. In fact, but few had warning of its intended evacuation in time to escape the Yankees. But little bitterness was manifested by them, and quite a respectable proportion seemed rather satisfied than otherwise at the final termination and our occupancy. One remarkable thing was that the children of Petersburg speak frequently in a very commonplace manner of "the demoralization" of the rebel army. They say, "Oh, yes, you Yankees whipped us at last; you got in; our soldiers were so demoralized they wouldn't fight." Such remarks were common among the masters and misses of the most respectable families. Such childish remarks may at first seem unimportant; but they are the small, unerring indications of the prevailing belief of Southern parents. The children do but repeat the oft-heard remark.

Another Statement how the Rebel General Hill was Killed.

Mrs. Wallace, of Petersburg, and cousin to General A. P. Hill, states that the latter desired to obtain a nearer view of a portion of our line during the attack of the 2d inst., and, leaving his staff behind in a place of safety, rode forward, accompanied by a single orderly, and soon came upon a squad of our men who had advanced along ravines far beyond our lines. He immediately ordered them to surrender, which they were on the point of doing, under the supposition that a column of troops were at his heels. They soon discovered he was nearly unattended, and shot Hill through the heart and wounded the orderly dangerously.

The Rebel General Lee leads a Brigade in Person.

When Wright had cut his way through the rebel lines Lee saw he must be promptly repulsed or all was lost. So vital was this considered that he led a brigade in person, and narrowly escaped death from the explosion of a shell, which stunned him for an instant and killed several in his vicinity. But even his presence failed to inspire his troops. A feeble assault was made and so easily repulsed that General Wright never thought it worth reporting.

Henry A. Wise reported killed.

It is reported that Henry A. Wise was killed, but I could trace it to no positive foundation.

The Rebel General Pickett not in command of his Division.

An intelligent resident of Petersburg states that Pickett was not in command of his division in front of Sheridan, in consequence of a quarrel with Longstreet, which caused his suspension.

The Lossess sustained by Lee.

Lee is believed to have lost twenty thousand men this week which we can account for, and nearly an equal number he lost in addition by desertions and straggling.

Our own losses.

Our losses in killed [illegible] past week.

Captures before the Evacuation of Petersburg.

We had captured fifty guns and ten thousand prisoners before the evacuation of Petersburg.

Sheridan captures more Prisoners.

General Sheridan reports the capture of one thousand three hundred prisoners yesterday.

NEWS FROM WASHINGTON.

Washington, April 6, 1865.

The Health of Secretary Seward.

Secretary Seward's condition is much improved to-day from what it was last night, and he is now as comfortable as can be expected. In addition to the other injuries sustained by Secretary Seward, it was discovered to-day that his right jaw had been fractured. He was comparatively easy this afternoon.

Affairs in the Shenandoah Valley

A letter from Winchester, dated yesterday, states that the cavalry, under the command of General Torbert, which started up the valley on the 3d inst., and not returned. As far as heard from they had met with no considerable body of rebels. The report that a large body of rebel infantry and cavalry had been seen in the vicinity of Strasburg was believed to be without foundation. Every precaution is being taken, however, to prevent a surprise or repel any attack that might be attempted. The roads are in good condition, and the Army of the Middle Military Division is ready for a move in any direction where their services may be required. The One Hundred and Sixty-fifth regiment, New York Volunteers, or Second Zouaves, as they are more generally known, which has been doing duty as provost guard at Winchester for the last four months, has been relieved by the Fifth New York artillery. Their departure was much regretted by the citizens, the officers and men, by their gentlemanly behavior and soldier-like conduct, having won the respect of every citizen.

Pursuit of the Captured Steamer Harriet Deford.

Three hours after information (yesterday) reached the Navy Department of the capture of the steamboat Harriet Deford eight or ten vessels had started in pursuit of the pirates.

Paymet of Sherman's Troops.

All the funds required to pay General Sherman's army in full will be ready by the middle of next week. It will require eleven millions of dollars for this purpose.

Serenade by a Rebel Band.

Among the arrivals of deserters to-day was a full band, which delivered themselves up with their instruments at Petersburg. It is composed principally of musicians from the bands of the Twelfth Virginia and Forty-fifth North Carolina rebel regiments. They had secreted themselves for ten days in Petersburg, awaiting an opportunity to desert, which was afforded them upon the occupation of that city by the Union troops. This afternoon, after taking the oath of allegiance, the band proceeded, in their rebel uniforms, to serenade Mrjor General Augur, commanding this department, and afterwards to the War Department, to compliment Secretary Stanton. The earnestness with which they gave to the tune, "Ain't you glad you are out of the wilderness?" attracted much attention.

The Tobacco Speculators.

The War Department has been literally besieged to-day by a whole brigade of tobacco speculators, anxious to obtain passes to Richmond to buy tobacco. It is asserted that some special trade permits were granted, but the most of the applicants were advised to wait until the wounded soldiers in the recent battles had been properly cared for.

French Claims on Slidell's Property.

Some time ago Slidell, the rebel representative a Paris, gave a mortgage to a French banker for sixty thousand dollars upon his property in New Orleans. The banker now claims the property under the laws of Louisiana, and suit is to be instituted in the United States Court, and it will be made a test case. Interesting and important legal points will be raised under the Confiscation act, the decision of which will govern similar cases hereafter.

LOVE YOUR ENEMIES.

Angry looks can do no good,
And blows are dealt in blindness;
Words are better understood,
If spoken but in kindness.

Simple love far more hath wrought,
Although by childhood muttered,
Than all the battles ever fought,
Or oaths that men have uttered.

Friendship oft would longer last,
And quarrel be prevented,
If little words were let go past—
Forgiven, not resented.

Foolish things are frowns and sneers,
For angry thoughts reveal them;
Rather drown them all in tears,
Than let another feel them.

1865. Counting-House 1865

CALENDAR.

	Sunday	Monday	Tuesday	Wed'day	Thu'day	Friday	Sat'day
JAN	1	2	3	4	5	6	7
	8	9	10	11	12	13	14
	15	16	17	18	19	20	21
	22	23	24	25	26	27	28
	29	30	31				
FEB				1	2	3	4
	5	6	7	8	9	10	11
	12	13	14	15	16	17	18
	19	20	21	22	23	24	25
	26	27	28				
MAR.				1	2	3	4
	5	6	7	8	9	10	11
	12	13	14	15	16	17	18
	19	20	21	22	23	24	25
	26	27	28	29	30	31	
APRL							1
	2	3	4	5	6	7	8
	9	10	11	12	13	14	15
	16	17	18	19	20	21	22
	23	24	25	26	27	28	29
	30						
MAY		1	2	3	4	5	6
	7	8	9	10	11	12	13
	14	15	16	17	18	19	20
	21	22	23	24	25	26	27
	28	29	30	31			
JUNE					1	2	3
	4	5	6	7	8	9	10
	11	12	13	14	15	16	17
	18	19	20	21	22	23	24
	25	26	27	28	29	30	

	Sunday	Monday	Tuesday	Wed'day	Thu'day	Friday	Sat'day
JULY							1
	2	3	4	5	6	7	8
	9	10	11	12	13	14	15
	16	17	18	19	20	21	22
	23	24	25	26	27	28	29
	30	31					
AUG'T			1	2	3	4	5
	6	7	8	9	10	11	12
	13	14	15	16	17	18	19
	20	21	22	23	24	25	26
	27	28	29	30	31		
SEPT						1	2
	3	4	5	6	7	8	9
	10	11	12	13	14	15	16
	17	18	19	20	21	22	23
	24	25	26	27	28	29	30
OCT'R	1	2	3	4	5	6	7
	8	9	10	11	12	13	14
	15	16	17	18	19	20	21
	22	23	24	25	26	27	28
	29	30	31				
NOV				1	2	3	4
	5	6	7	8	9	10	11
	12	13	14	15	16	17	18
	19	20	21	22	23	24	25
	26	27	28	29	30		
DEC'R						1	2
	3	4	5	6	7	8	9
	10	11	12	13	14	15	16
	17	18	19	20	21	22	23
	24	25	26	27	28	29	30
	31						

At the present time, when the railroads of North Carolina and Virginia are the highways of the hostile armies, the following tables of distances will be found convenient for reference by the students of the situation:

WILMIGNTON AND WELDON.

From Wilmington to	Miles.	From Wilmington to	Miles.
Northeast,	10	Magnolia,	49
Marlboro',	12	Warsaw,	50
Rocky Point,	15	Bowden,	60
Burgaw,	23	Faison,	64
South Washington,	30	Mount Olive,	7[illegible]
Leesburg,	34	Dudley,	7[illegible]
Teachy,	39	Everettsville,	79
Rose Hill,	42	Goldsboro',	85

ATLANTIC AND NORTH CAROLINA.

From Newbern to	Miles	From Newbern to	Miles.
Bachelor's Creek,	8	Kinston,	38
Tuscarora,	11	Falling Creek,	40
Core Creek,	17	Mosely Hall,	45
Dover,	23	Bests,	50
Southwest,	29	Goldsboro',	59

NORTH CAROLINA ROAD.

From Goldsboro' to	Miles.	From Goldsboro' to	Miles.
Boon Hill,	12	Mebane's,	98
Smithfield,	22	Haw River,	104
Stallings,	34	Graham,	106
Raleigh,	48	Comp's Shops,	108
Morrisville,	61	Gibsonville,	115
Durham,	74	McLean's,	122
Hillsboro',	88	Greensboro',	130

RALEIGH AND GASTON.

From Raleigh to	Miles.	From Raleigh to	Miles.
Huntsville,	10	Warrenton,	58
Forrestville,	16	Macon,	62
Franklinton,	25	Littleton,	73
Kitrell's	35	Summit,	79
Henderson,	42	Gaston,	82
Ridgeway Junctoin,	55	Weldon,	94

ROANOKE VALLEY.

From Ridg'y Junc. to	Miles.	From Ridg'y Junc. to	Miles.
Townesville,	10	Clarksville,	22

RICHMOND AND DANVILLE.

From Richmond to	Miles.	From Richmond to	Miles.
Manchester,	1	Merherrin,	65
Powhite,	8	Keysville,	73
Coalfied,	11	Drake's Branch,	81
Tomahawk,	18	Mossingford,	84
Powhatan,	22	Roanoke,	90
Mattoax,	27	Clover,	94
Chula,	30	Scottsburg,	100
Amelia Courthouse,	36	Boston,	109
Jetersville,	43	New's Ferry,	117
Jennings Ordinary,	50	Barksdale,	127
Burksville,	55	Ringgold,	135
Price's,	61	Danville,	140

SOUTHSIDE RAILROAD.

From Petersburg to	Miles.	From Petersburg to	Miles.
Southerland's,	10	Farmville,	69
Ford's,	20	Prospect,	79
Wilson's,	27	Pamplin's,	87
Wellville,	31	Appomattox,	99
Blacks and Whites,	37	Spout Spring,	105
Nottoway C. H.	43	Concord,	110
Burksville,	52	Lynchburg,	123
Rice's	61		

M. de Montholon, the new French Ambassador to Washington, was for many years a citizen of Richmond. He is a son of the famous General Montholon, who accompanied Napoleon to St. Helena, and remained with him until his death, and who, while on that island, wrote voluminous memoirs, of great historical value, under the dictation of his chief. Afterwards, as is well known, General Montholon, always a decided Bonapartist, joined the present Emperor of the French, in that rash expedition which resulted in the capture of both, and their confinement in the fortress of Ham. While the father was still in prison, the Prince de Joinville made a tour through the United States, and, in passing through this city, fell in with the son, with whom he become so much pleased that he carried him with him on his travels. Shortly after he was appointed French Consul at New York, it is believed, through the interposition of the Prince. Since the rise of Napoleon, Montholon has been a great favorite, as he ought to be, if for nothing else, yet for the fidelity and sufferings of his father in the cause of the Bonapartes. He spent all the earlier years of his life in the United States, [illegible] married an American lady, the daughter of [illegible]. He is a man of talents and of very prepossessing address. He was a great favorite in society while he lived here.—*Rich. Dispatch.*

THE RIGHT WAY TO READ.—When the late Jeremiah Evarts was in the fifth year of his age, he came to his father and asked him for a new book. His father asked him if the last book he had given him was worn out. "Oh, no sir," said Jeremiah, "but I have read all of the sense out of it." He meant to say that he had read it thoroughly, and had made himself master of all the ideas it contained.

DAILY PROGRESS.

RALEIGH, N. C.

SATURDAY, APRIL 15, 1865.

General Sherman Occupies Raleigh —The War Nearly Over.

On Tuesday last the Confederate army commenced passing through Raleigh, retreating Westward, and on Thursday morning the rear guard disappeared; and as it was lost sight of at the head of Hillsboro street, the head of Gen. Kilpatrick's column appeared at the foot of Fayetteville street. The city had been surrendered by the local authorities, who had received a promise of protection for persons and property from the Federal General, and the entrance of the advancing column was as quiet as a gala day parade. When nearing the Capitol, however, the advance was fired on by some of the Confederate cavalry who had [illegible] was injured. One of these men who thus violated the rules of civilized warfare was summarily disposed of by order of Gen. Kilpatrick.

The old flag was at once suspended from the Capitol flag staff, and its appearance was hailed with demonstrations of joy by the troops and most of the citizens who were present. The morning was very inclement, however, rain was falling, and but few persons were out.

Mayor Harrison and the board of commissioners, and Hon. K. Rayner who accompanied them to confer with General Sherman, deserve much credit for the manner in which they surrendered the town and procured protection for the citizens.

General Kilpatrick's cavalry passed rapidly but orderly through town, but the General had guards stationed and protection extended to all citizens until the 14th army corps arrived, when the cavalry guards were relieved by General Hobart's brigade, and guards were placed at the house of every citizen who requested it, and throughout the day and night the most perfect order was maintained, and so far this community has but little, if anything, to complain of.

And now a word to the people of North Carolina. We have been pleading for peace for the last two years, but the State and Confederate authorities insisted on fighting it out, and as it has been evidently fought out, we now appeal to the people of the State to submit to the laws and authority of the United States, and stop the worse than useless shedding of blood. Gen. Sherman has positive knowledge of the capitulation of General Lee's whole army, and as the only hope of the cause was in that army, there can be no reasonable excuse for continuing the struggle. The army of Gen. Johnston consists of only some 35,000 men of all arms—the men are jaded, worn out, dispirited and despondent, and unless he capitulates now, he will be destroyed before he can get out of the State.

And now that the Federal authorities are victorious they can afford to be generous, and we learn that President Lincoln, who entered Richmond with Grant's army, has proclaimed the willingness of the Government to grant amnesty and full pardon to all who have made war against it, this amnesty even to include the leaders of the rebellion.

Taking, then, all these facts into consideration, there is no course left the people of North Carolina, and of the South, but to ground their arms and return to their allegiance. We learn that Mr. Davis and other leaders were in consultation at Greensboro' on Wednesday, and we do most devoutly trust that they will yield to the inexorable logic of events, and tender to the United States authorities a full and final surrender of all armed opposition to its authority. There is no peace, no prosperity, no safety for the people of North Carolina but in the old Government and under the old flag, and we advise them to cease to war upon the one and refuse to receive the protection of the other.

Stoneman was said to be fighting a Confederate force at the Yadkin bridge, six miles this side of Salisbury, on Thursday evening, and we have but little doubt but that he burnt the bridge at that place, thus cutting the communication between Salisbury and Greensboro. Sheridan is also said to be coming down that way, all in Johnston's front.

The Capitulation of Lee's Army.

The following correspondence, kindly furnished us by Gen. Sherman, will remove all doubt as to the surrender of Gen. Lee's whole army. The fact is, he was terribly whipped at Petersburg on the 1st and 2nd of April, and had but little to surrender:

[U. S. MILITARY TELEGRAPH.]

By telegraph from Headquarters Armies U. S., April 9th, 1865.

To Maj. Gen. Sherman: Gen. Grant directs me to forward the following correspondence for your information:

(Signed,) T. S. Bowers, A. A. G.

Appomattox C. H., April 9th, 1865.

Gen. R. E Lee, Commanding C. S. A.:

General:—In accordance with the substance of my letter to you, of the 8th inst., I propose to receive the surrender of the Army of Northern Virginia on the following terms, to-wit:

Rolls of all the officers and men to be made in duplicate, one copy to be given to an officer [illegible] to be retained by such officer or officers as you may designate; the officers to give their individual paroles not to take up arms against the government of the United States until properly exchanged. Each company or regimental commander sign a like parole for the men of their command. The arms, artillery and public property to be parked and stacked and turned over to the officer appointed by me to receive them. This will not embrace the side arms of the officers nor their private horses or baggage. This done, each officer and man will be allowed to return to their homes, not to be disturbed by U. S. authorities so long as they observe their parole and the laws in force where they may reside.

Very respectfully,

(Signed,) U. S. Grant, Lieut. Gen.

Headquarters Army No. Va., April 9th, 1865

Lt. Gen. U. S. Grant, Commanding Armies of U. S.:

General:—I have received your letter of this date containing the terms of surrender of the Army of Northern Virginia as proposed by you. As they are substantially the same as those expressed in your letter of the 8th inst they are accepted. I will proceed to designate the proper officers to carry the stipulation into effect.

Very respectfully,

Your obedient servant,

(Signed,) R. E. Lee, General.

We are gratified to be able, through the courtesy of General Slocum, to lay the following General Order before our readers:

Headquarters Army of Georgia, Near Sneedsboro', N. C., March 7, 1865

General Orders. No. 8.

All officers and soldiers of this command are reminded that the State of North Carolina was one of the last States that passed the Ordinance of Secession and that from the commencement of the war, there has been in the State a strong Union party. Her action on the question of Secession was undoubtedly brought about by the traitorous acts of other States, and by intrigue and dishonesty on the part of a few of her own citizens. The act never even met the approval of the great mass of her people.

It should not be assumed that the inhabitants are enemies to our government and it is to be hoped that every effort will be made to prevent any wanton destruction of property or any unkind treatment of citizens.

By command of

Maj. Gen H. W. SLOCUM,

Rob't Dechert, Capt. and A. A. G.

Pressman Wanted.

Any one capable of running a Northrop Power press can get a good situation with good pay at the Progress office. Apply immediately.

On arriving in the city on Thursday morning, Gen. Sherman established his headquarters at the Palace, the house previously occupied by the Governor of the State, and from which he fled the day previous to Gen. Sherman's arrival. A number of gentlemen, citizens, have called to pay their respects to the great chieftain, and all came away well pleased with his frankness of manner and agreeable bearing. He is a gentleman of excellent figure, tall and as straight as an arrow, and of commanding presence.

The grand review which came off here on yesterday was by far the greatest display of the kind that has ever been seen in North Carolina, and was witnessed with great satisfaction, not only by the officers and men of the Federal army present, but also by a large number of citizens.

In Favor of Peace.

We hear a report that Ex-Governors Swain, Morehead and Graham and other prominent gentlemen are urging a cessation of hostilities and submission to the laws and authority of the United States government. If this be true, as we hope it is, we appeal to these distinguished gentlemen to make the fact known to the public at once, and they will find that the great mass of the people, at home and in the army, will rally to them.—The contest now being, according to all human calculation, a hopeless one, a further sacrifice of life by Mr. Davis and the leaders will be nothing but deliberate murder. We know that the great mass of the people of North Carolina are devoted to the old government, and that they prefer returning to it to continued resistance, and as they now have the protection of Federal bayonets and a chance to express their devotion to the old order of things, let them be heard. [illegible] present di[illegible]ties but in peace, and there can be no peace but in a restoration of the government.

We call upon our leading men, in the name of good government and for the sake of humanity, to exert themselves and use their influence to put a stop to this carnival of death.

Lee's Army Gone.

Let none of our people for a moment doubt the truth of the rumor of the surrender of General Lee's army. True to the system of frauds and deceptions that have been passed upon us for three years the leaders refused to let the Southern people know the great disaster that had overtaken Lee's army, but as Gen. Sherman has been furnished with the correspondence preceeding the surrender, there can be no doubt of the fact. Gen. Lee's army is gone, and unless Johnston's be surrendered, it will be captured or destroyed within the next thirty days.—Sherman is in vigorous pursuit of Johnston, and he must either capitulate or surrender before he gets out of the State, for the disparity of numbers is such that he cannot risk a battle.

We trust that Mr. Davis and his friends will determine to abandon the cause and thus relieve those few of our people who still cling to them, of the disagreeable necessity of abandoning them.

The correspondence surrendering Gen. Lee's army will be found in another column.

Price of the Progress.

For the present we shall take no mail subscribers, but as soon as the mails are restored and we have a post office, and a post master, we shall resume business in the old way. For the present we can only furnish the paper at the counter, and at the following rates: Single copies 10 cents, and to newsboys and agents at the rate of $5 a hundred.

Fort Sumter.

On the 12th day of April, 1861, the first gun of the war was fired upon Fort Sumter, and on the 14th the flag was lowered and the Fort surrendered. On yesterday, just four years from the surrender, it was announced that the same old flag that was lowered was again to be hoisted by the same hands to its old place. Rev. Henry Ward Beecher was to deliver an address. No doubt yesterday was a grand day at Sumter.

General Slocum.—This gentleman, the right bower of Gen. Sherman and one of the most successful of the Generals in the Federal army, commands the 14th and 20th corps. He is a gentleman of most agreeable and easy manners, of fine conversational powers and fascinating address. There is none of the appearance of the savage about him, and we would as soon have taken him for a poet, painter, or searcher after abstract theories as the great warrior that he is.—No one can spend a half hour in his company without being most favorably impressed.

The 5th Ohio Cavalry was the first troops that showed the stars and stripes on the streets of this city and to hoist the old flag from the State house. This regiment also protected the town until it was turned over to Gen. Hobart, whose brigade has since been doing guard duty. The deportment of all these troops has been excellent, and the bearing of Gen. Hobart has made a most favorable impression on all who have come in contact with him.

THE LOCAL'S COLUMN.

Philosophy.—The Local does not pretend to be a philosopher, but he has found great advantage at times in calling philosophy to his aid.—Such was the case on last Wednesday night.—Squads of Confederate cavalry were dashing about our streets, and it was known that the Federals would enter the next morning. Our better half and *another* widow who lived next door were nervous and restless—in fact they were frightened. They would meet at the fence running between the two houses, not to allay, but to increase each other's fears. The cavalry that night would rob and burn, and the Federals the next morning would have all the babies fried up for breakfast and the women roasted for dinner. The Local tried to ridicule them out of their fears, for there is no use to try to reason women out of them. But ridicule failed. They consulted together about burying things—but where? Finally they agreed upon a place, and just then recollected they had nothing to bury. The Local called philosophy to his aid and at his usual time went to bed. This provoked the *widows*. They did not call him a "brute," but it is evident they thought him one. But we [illegible] *widow* would endeavor to rouse him: "Just listen at the cavalry—they are drunk, and whooping and shouting about the streets. How can you lie there and snore so?" The Local would reply that he *did* hear them, and then he would turn over and snore on the other side, which the *widows* declared was "provoking."—He only replied that they would be still more provoked the next morning when they found out their babies were not to be fried nor themselves roasted. Thus passed off the night, the Local having philosophically slept pretty well, considering, and the *widows* having scarcely slept at all. Early on Thursday morning the Federal cavalry entered, and the first thing done was to leave a guard at every house for the protection of it and its inmates. The widows all became sunshine at once, notwithstanding there was a drizzling rain. They forgot all about being cooked, and betook themselves to cooking. The Local felt relieved. The day passed quietly away, and on Friday morning, after a good night's rest, we all awoke, feeling that we had slept in the United States—very agreeable to widows.

Surrender of our City.—Early on Thursday morning our Mayor, Wm. H. Harrison, Esq., accompanied by Commissioners Creech, Farriss, Poole and Richardson, and also by Hon. Kenneth Rayner, Dr. McKee and other citizens, went out with a flag of truce to meet Gen. Kilpatrick, in command of the advance of the Federal army. They met him but a short distance from the city. No correspondence was held, but Hon. K. Rayner, we learn, made a very handsome little speech to Gen. Kilpatrick, on behalf of the delegation and the people of Raleigh, surrendering the City, in their name, to him. Gen. Kilpatrick replied that he intended to occupy the City and plant the old flag there: that he was in close pursuit of the retreating Confederate army, and intended to overtake and crush it; but that the lives and the property of the citizens should be protected. So far, his word has been kept to the utmost ability of the officers.

Outrages.—The rear guard of the Confederate cavalry broke open several stores and other houses during Wednesday night, carrying off what little they could find, and then wantonly breaking up show cases, tearing down shelves and doing other damage.

On Thursday night the store of Mr. L. H. Adams was opened and his iron safe carried off and broken into. We learn it contained several thousand dollars in Confederate money. One or two other stores were also entered, but we presume they contained but little. On the whole we have had as few such outrages as could have been expected. The city is well guarded, and comparative quiet prevails. There is a guard posted at every private residence, store—in fact everywere where desired.

Burning of the N. C. Depot.—The depot building of the N. C. Railroad at this place was set on fire and it and its contents entirely consumed, early last Thursday morning. It is said it was done by orders of the Confederate authorities. Large quantities of meat, meal, flour, &c., were burned. The building also contained bomb shells and cartridge boxes which exploded, sometimes at intervals and sometimes in rapid succession, hurling the deadly missiles in all directions. We learn that two or three persons were more or less injured, and it is almost miraculous that so little damage was done by the flying bullets and fragments of shells.

The State commissary was not burned.

Provisions.—The poor and others of our city have procured considerable supplies from the Confederate and State commissaries, both of which were thrown open to the people. Streams of men, women and children, white and black lined the streets, going to and coming from the depot. It was a timely offering to the necessities of our citizens. And yet thousands of bushels of corn, salt and other commodities have been burned. Even at the time of this writing (Friday) a large pile of corn is slowly smoldering, and people are grabbling it out and bearing it off.

Then and Now.—For four years this country has been deluged in blood, a useless sacrifice upon the altar of unhallowed ambition. The dark wing of war overshadowed the land and we rushed under the cover of its baleful shadow, and blindly followed the originators of our troubles to the verge of the precipice of worse than Turkish despotism. Our property has been seized; our personal rights and privileges wrested from us; taxes have been piled mountain high upon us, and then Pelion placed upon Ossa; our children and our sons have been torn from us to bare their breasts to the "leaden hail and iron rain;" and in the sacred name of Liberty we have been led step by step, to surrender almost the last vestidge of liberty into the hands of one who knew power only to abuse it, and whose grasping ambition made him reckless of means in the prosecution of his aims. From thrift and prosperity we have been reduced to poverty; from plenty to the brink of starvation; and from happiness to abject misery. We had never been sick, and knew not how to appreciate health; we had never known want or oppression, and knew not how to appreciate plenty and freedom. We plunged into war and weeping and wailing have filled the land and blood has stained the earth.

And all for what? Not even for an abstraction We can now realize the fact that we were duped, as a people, by the wicked designs of bad men who perverted the [illegible] accomplishment of their own base ends.

But the scene changes. The white dove of peace is hovering over us. If we entered upon the war with pleasure, we hail the prospect of peace with rapture. We sowed the wind and we have reaped the whirlwind. Would that the past four years could be blotted from the record of time! Vain wish! The dead cannot be recalled—the past cannot be undone. We can only look to the future and hope trusting in an all-wise and merciful God. War stirred the bitter fountains of the soul, but its sweet waters swell up at the welcome sound of peace. Our recuperative energies will astonish even ourselves and in a few years we shall see the desolate places blooming again.

Fire.—The Machine Shop, with a grist mill attached, in the South-eastern portion of the city, and which belonged to Mr. P. Theim, was set on fire and burned down at an early hour on Thursday night. It was the unauthorized work of some soldiers, we learn. A fine engine, a large quantity of machinery, tools, &c., were consumed. The grist mill was a great convenience to our people, and its loss will be severely felt.

An Astonished Boy.—We met with a little boy yesterday that was considerably astonished. Said he "I've been looking at a heap of these Yankees, and I haven't seen any of them with horns yet." We told him we saw a few of them the night before that had had *horns*.

Post Commandant.

The 23d Army Corps arrived yesterday and Gen. Sterls, of the 1st Division, was placed in command of the Post, office at the Capitol. The City was at once divided into districts and guards posted so as to protect the persons and property of citizens.

JOB PRINTING.

PRINTING FOR ARMY AND CITIZENS

Will be executed at the office of the Daily Progress with dispatch. Orders solicited.

City Subscribers

Will have to call or send to the Counting room for their papers for the present.

Food for Weak Stomachs.—In the "Memoirs of Count Segur," vol 1, page 168, there is the following anecdote: "My mother, (the Countess de Segur) being asked by Voltaire respecting her health, told him that the most painful feeling she had arose from the decay of her stomach and the difficulty of finding any kind of aliment that it could bear. Voltaire, by way of consolation, assured her that he was once for nearly a year in the same state, and believed to be incurable; but that, nevertheless, a very simple remedy had restored him. It consisted in taking no other nourishment than yolks of egg, beaten up with the flour of potatoes and water." Though this circumstance took place as far back as fifty years ago, and respected so extraordinary a personage as Voltaire, it is astonishing how little it is known, and how rarely the remedy has been practiced. Its efficacy, however, in case of debility, cannot be questioned, and the following is the mode of preparing this valuable article of food, as recommended by Sir John Sinclair: Receipt—Beat up an egg in a bowl, and then add six tablespoonfuls of cold water, mixing the whole well together: then add two tablespoonsfuls of the farina of potatoes, to be mixed thoroughly with the liquor in the bowl. Then pour in as much boiling water as will convert the whole into jelly, and mix it well. It may be taken either alone with the addition of a little milk, and moist or best sugar, not only for breakfast, but in cases of great stomachic debility, or in consumptive disorders, at the other meals. The dish is light, easily digested, extremely wholesome and nourishing. Bread or biscuit may be taken with it as the stomach gets stronger.

The Last of the Rebel Rams.—The bed of the Mississippi river, from Cairo to the Gulf, over a thousand miles, is pretty thickly strewn with the relics of rebel rams and gunboats; the remains of a whole fleet lie scattered along the bottom of the Yazoo, the fragments of several flotillas rest in the mud of the bayous of Louisiana and in the Red river; and in almost every river and harbor, from Mobile around the coast to Richmond, the changing tides roll over the broken skeletons of rebel iron-clads, built only to be blown up. Perhaps the only one now remaining above water carrying the rebel ensign is that one at Halifax, on the Roanoke, which ought to be caught alive, if possible, and preserved as last of the rebel rams.

The New-York Times.

VOL. XIV......NO. 4230. NEW-YORK, SATURDAY, APRIL 15, 1865. PRICE FOUR CENTS

AWFUL EVENT.

President Lincoln Shot by an Assassin.

The Deed Done at Ford's Theatre Last Night.

THE ACT OF A DESPERATE REBEL

The President Still Alive at Last Accounts.

No Hopes Entertained of His Recovery.

Attempted Assassination of Secretary Seward.

DETAILS OF THE DREADFUL TRAGEDY.

[OFFICIAL.]

WAR DEPARTMENT, WASHINGTON, April 15—1:30 A. M.

Maj.-Gen. Dix:

This evening at about 9:30 P. M., at Ford's Theatre, the President, while sitting in his private box with Mrs. LINCOLN, Mrs. HARRIS, and Major RATHBURN, was shot by an assassin, who suddenly entered the box and approached behind the President.

The assassin then leaped upon the stage, brandishing a large dagger or knife, and made his escape in the rear of the theatre.

The pistol ball entered the back of the President's head and penetrated nearly through the head. The wound is mortal. The President has been insensible ever since it was inflicted, and is now dying.

About the same hour an assassin, whether the same or not, entered Mr. SEWARD's apartments, and under the pretence of having a prescription, was shown to the Secretary's sick chamber. The assassin immediately rushed to the bed, and inflicted two or three stabs on the throat and two on the face. It is hoped the wounds may not be mortal. My apprehension is that they will prove fatal.

The nurse alarmed Mr. FREDERICK SEWARD, who was in an adjoining room, and hastened to the door of his father's room, when he met the assasin, who inflicted upon him one or more dangerous wounds. The recovery of FREDERICK SEWARD is doubtful.

It is not probable that the President will live throughout the night.

Gen. GRANT and wife were advertised to be at the theatre this evening, but he started to Burlington at 6 o'clock this evening.

At a Cabinet meeting at which Gen. GRANT was present, the subject of the state of the country and the prospect of a speedy peace was discussed. The President was very cheerful and hopeful, and spoke very kindly of Gen. LEE and others of the Confederacy, and of the establishment of government in Virginia.

All the members of the Cabinet except Mr. SEWARD, are now in attendance upon the President.

I have seen Mr. SEWRRD, but he and FREDERICK were both unconscious.

EDWIN M. STANTON,
Secretary of War.

DETAIL OF THE OCCURRENCE.

WASHINGTON, Friday, April 14—12:30 A. M.

The President was shot in a theatre tonight, and is, perhaps, mortally wounded.

Secretary SEWARD was also assassinated.

SECOND DISPATCH.

WASHINGTON, Friday, April14.

President LINCOLN and wife, with other friends, this evening visited Ford's Theatre for the purpose of witnessing the performance of the "American Cousin."

It was announced in the papers that Gen. GRANT would also be present, but he took the late train of cars for New-Jersey.

The theatre was densely crowded, and everybody seemed delighted with the scene before them. During the third act, and while there was a temporary pause for one of the actors to enter, a sharp report of a pistol was heard, which merely attracted attention, but suggesting nothing serious, until a man rushed to the front of the President's box, waving a long dagger in his right hand, and exclaiming "*Sic semper tyrannis,*" and immediately leaped from the box, which was in the second tier, to the stage beneath, and ran across to the opposite side, making his escape amid the bewilderment of the audience from the rear of the theatre, and, mounting a horse, fled.

The screams of Mrs. LINCOLN first disclosed the fact to the audience that the President had been shot, when all present rose to their feet, rushing toward the stage, many exclaiming "Hang him! hang him!"

The excitement was of the wildest possible description, and of course there was an abrupt termination of the theatrical performance.

There was a rush toward the President's box, when cries were heard: "Stand back and give him air." "Has any one stimulants." On a hasty examination, it was found that the President had been shot through the head, above and back of the temporal bone, and that some of the brain was oozing out. He was removed to a private house opposite to the theatre, and the Surgeon-General of the army, and other surgeons sent for to attend to his condition.

On an examination of the private box blood was discovered on the back of the cushioned rocking chair on which the President had been sitting, also on the partition and on the floor. A common single-barreled pocket pistol was found on the carpet.

A military guard was placed in front of the private residence to which the President had been conveyed. An immense crowd was in front of it, all deeply anxious to learn the condition of the President. It had been previously announced that the wound was mortal; but all hoped otherwise. The shock to the community was terrible.

The President was in a state of syncope, totally insensible, and breathing slowly. The blood oozed from the wound at the back of his head. The surgeons exhausted every effort of medical skill, but all hope was gone. The parting of his family with the dying President is too sad for description.

At midnight, the Cabinet, with Messrs. SUMNER, COLFAX and FARNSWORTH, Judge CURTIS, Gov. OGLESBY, Gen. MEIGS, Col. HAY, and a few personal friends, with Surgeon-General BARNES and his immediate assistants, were around his bedside.

The President and Mrs. LINCOLN did not start for the theatre until fifteen minutes after eight o'clock. Speaker COLFAX was at the White House at the time, and the President stated to him that he was going, although Mrs. LINCOLN had not been well, because the papers had announced that Gen. GRANT and they were to be present, and, as Gen. GRANT had gone North, he did not wish the audience to be disappointed.

He went with apparent reluctance and urged Mr. COLFAX to go with him; but that gentleman had made other engagements, and with Mr. ASHMAN, of Massachusetts, bid him good bye.

When the excitement at the theatre was at its wildest height, reports were circulated that Secretary SEWARD had also been assassinated.

On reaching this gentleman's residence a crowd and a military guard were found at the door, and on entering it was ascertained that the reports were based on truth.

Everybody there was so excited that scarcely an intelligible word could be gathered, but the facts are substantially as follows:

About 10 o'clock a man rang the bell, and the call having been answered by a colored servant, he said he had come from Dr. VERDI, Secretary SEWARD's family physician, with a prescription, at the same time holding in his hand a small piece of folded paper, and saying in answer to a refusal that he must see the Secretary, as he was entrusted with particular directions concerning the medicine.

He still insisted on going up, although repeatedly informed that no one could enter the chamber. The man pushed the servant aside, and walked heavily toward the Secretary's room, and was then met by Mr. FREDERICK SEWARD, of whom he demanded to see the Secretary, making the same representation which he did to the servant. What further passed in the way of colloquy is not known, but the man struck him on the head with a "billy," severely injuring the skull and felling him almost senseless. The assassin then rushed into the chamber and attacked Major SEWARD, Paymaster of the United States army and Mr. HANSELL, a messenger of the State Department and two male nurses, disabling them all, he then rushed upon the Secretary, who was lying in bed in the same room, and inflicted three stabs in the neck, but severing, it is thought and hoped, no arteries, though he bled profusely.

The assassin then rushed down stairs, mounted his horse at the door, and rode off before an alarm could be sounded, and in the same manner as the assassin of the President.

It is believed that the injuries of the Secretary are not fatal, nor those of either of the others, although both the Secretary and the Assistant Secretary are very seriously injured.

Secretaries STANTON and WELLES, and other prominent officers of the government, called at Secretary SEWARD's house to inquire into his condition, and there heard of the assassination of the President.

They then proceeded to the house where he was lying, exhibiting of course intense anxiety and solicitude. An immense crowd was gathered in front of the President's house, and a strong guard was also stationed there, many persons evidently supposing he would be brought to his home.

The entire city to-night presents a scene of wild excitement, accompanied by violent expressions of indignation, and the profoundest sorrow—many shed tears. The military authorities have dispatched mounted patrols in every direction, in order, if possible, to arrest the assassins. The whole metropolitan police are likewise vigilant for the same purpose.

The attacks both at the theatre and at Secretary SEWARD's house, took place at about the same hour—10 o'clock—thus showing a preconcerted plan to assassinate those gentlemen. Some evidence of the guilt of the party who attacked the President are in the possession of the police.

Vice-President JOHNSON is in the city, and his headquarters are guarded by troops.

ANOTHER ACCOUNT.

Special Dispatch to the New-York Times.

WASHINGTON, Friday, April 14, 11:15 P. M.

A stroke from Heaven laying the whole of the city in instant ruins could not have startled us as did the word that broke from Ford's Theatre a half hour ago that the President had been shot. It flew everywhere in five minutes, and set five thousand people in swift and excited motion on the instant.

It is impossible to get at the full facts of the case, but it appears that a young man entered the President's box from the theatre, during the last act of the play of "Our American Cousin," with pistol in hand. He shot the President in the head and instantly jumped from the box upon the stage, and immediately disappeared through the side scenes and rear of the theatre, brandishing a dirk knife and dropping a kid glove on the stage.

The audience heard the shot, but supposing it fired in the regular course of the play, did not heed it till Mrs. LINCOLN's screams drew their attention. The whole affair occupied scarcely half a minute, and then the assassin was gone. As yet he has not been found.

The President's wound is reported mortal. He was at once taken into the house opposite the theatre.

As if this horror was not enough, almost the same moment the story ran through the city that Mr. SEWARD had been murdered in his bed.

Inquiry showed this to be so far true also. It appears a man wearing a light coat, dark pants, slouch hat, called and asked to see Mr. SEWARD, and was shown to his room. He delivered to Major SEWARD, who sat near his father, what purported to be a physician's prescription, turned, and with one stroke cut Mr. SEWARD's throat as he lay on his bed, inflicting a horrible wound, but not severing the jugular vein, and not producing a mortal wound.

In the struggle that followed, Major SEWARD was also badly, but not seriously, wounded in several places. The assassin rushed down stairs, mounted the fleet horse on which he came, drove his spurs into him, and dashed away before any one could stop him.

Reports have prevailed that an attempt was also made on the life of Mr. STANTON.

MIDNIGHT.

The President is reported dead. Cavalry and infantry are scouring the city in every direction for the murderous assassins, and the city is overwhelmed with excitement. Who the assassins were no one knows, though every body supposes them to have been rebels.

SATURDAY MORNING -1 O'CLOCK.

The person who shot the President is represented as about 30 years of age, five feet nine inches in height, sparely built, of light complexion, dressed in dark clothing, and having a genteel appearance. He entered the box, which is known as the State box, being the upper box on the right hand side from the dress-circle in the regular manner, and shot the President from behind, the ball entering the skull about in the middle, behind, and going in the direction of the left eye; it did not pass through, but apparently broke the frontal bone and forced out the brain to some extent. The President is not yet dead, but is wholly insensible, and the Surgeon-General says he cannot live till day-break. The assassin was followed across the stage by a gentleman, who sprang out from an orchestra chair. He rushed through the side door into an alley, thence to the avenue and mounted a dark bay horse, which he apparently received from the hand of an accomplice, dashed up F, toward the back part of the city. The escape was so sudden that he effectually eluded pursuit. The assassin cried "*sic sempre*" in a sharp, clear voice, as he jumped to the stage, and dropped his hat and a glove.

Two or three officers were in the box with the President and Mrs. LINCOLN, who made efforts to stop the assassin, but were unsuccessful, and received some bruises. The whole affar, from his entrance into the box to his escape from the theatre, occupied scarcely a minute, and the strongest of the action found everybody wholy unprepared. The assault upon Mr. SEWARD appeares to have been made almost at the same moment as that upon the President. Mr. SEWARDS wound is not dangerous in itself, but may prove so in connection with his recent injuries. The two assassins have both endeavored to leave the city to the northwest, apparently not expecting to strike the river. Even so low down as Chain Bridge, cavalry have been sent in every direction to intercept them.

SATURDAY, 1:30 o'clock A. M.

The President still lies insensible. Messrs. STANTON, WELLS, MCCULLOCH, SPEED and USHER are with him, as also the Vice-President, the Surgeon-General, and other Surgeons.

There is a great throng about the house, even at this hour.

2 o'clock A. M.

The President still lives, but lies insensible, as he has since the first moment, and no hopes are entertained that he can survive.

The most extravagant stories prevail, among which one is to effect, that Gen. GRANT was shot while on his was to Philaphia, of course this is not true.

Another is, that every member of Mr. SEWARD's family was wounded in the struggle with the assassin there. This also is untrue. Mr. FRED. SEWARD, the Assistant Secretary, and Major CLARENCE SEWARD, of the army, were wounded, neither of them dangerously.

THE CONDITION OF THE PRESIDENT.

WASHINGTON, April 15—2:12 A. M.

The President is still alive; but he is growing weaker. The ball is lodged in his brain, three inches from where it entered the skull. He remains insensible, and his condition is utterly hopeless.

The Vice-President has been to see him; but all company, except the members of the Cabinet and of the family, is rigidly excluded.

Large crowds still continue in the street, as near to the house as the line of guards allows.

THE SIEGE OF MOBILE.

Fierce Bombardment of the Spanish Fort—Mobile Papers Announce the Capture of Selma.

NEW-ORLEANS, Saturday, April 8, via CAIRO, Friday, April 14.

A special dispatch to the New-Orleans *Times*, from the Spanish Fort, dated April 5, says:

"A furious fire was opened on the rebel forts last night from our entire line. During the bombardment a small magazine in the Spanish Fort exploded. The damage is unknown. Quiet prevailed on the 5th. Deserters report from 18,000 to 20,000 troops in and about Mobile, including all the State Reserves, and about 2,000 in the Spanish Fort. The loss outside the Spanish Fort up to the 4th instant amounted to about 500 killed and wounded. The rebel loss exceeds ours."

Adjt.-Gen. THOMAS arrived at New-Orleans on the morning of the 7th.

Mobile papers of the 4th inst. announce the capture of Selma, Alabama, with 23 pieces of artillery, and a large amount of Government property.

Fort Sumter Celebration in Bangor.

BANGOR, Me., Friday, April 14.

The restoration of the Old Flag to Fort Sumter was celebrated here to-day by a national salute at noon, by a display of all the flags on public and private buildings, and by the raising of the Stars and Strips one thousand feet above the city by means of a monster kite bearing the name of U. S. GRANT.

The Madrid *Bolsa* says if the Pope should leave Rome, Spain would confer upon him the Balearic Isles.

The *Politica* says the Pope would rather inhabit the Montpensier Palace at Seville.

EUROPEAN NEWS.

TWO DAYS LATER BY THE EUROPA.

The Insult to Our Cruisers by Portugal.

The American Minister at Lisbon Demands Satisfaction.

Dismissal of the Commander of Fort Belan Requested.

Further Advance in Five-Twenties.

FINANCIAL AND COMMERCIAL.

HALIFAX, Friday, April 14.

The steamship *Europa*, from Liverpool on the 1st, via Queenstown on the 2d inst., arrived here at 2 o'clock this morning. She has 43 passengers for this port, and 30 for Boston. Her dates are two days later than those already received.

The steamship *Cuba*, from New-York, arrived at Liverpool at noon on the 1st inst.

THE STONEWALL AFFAIR.

A Lisbon dispatch, of the 31st of March, says that the American Minister at Lisbon has demanded satisfaction of the Portuguese Government for the firing upon the *Niagara* and *Sacramento* by the Portuguese forts. He also requests the dismissal of the Commander of Fort Belan, and a salute of twenty-one guns to the American flag.

Nothing as yet has been decided in regard to the matter.

A PROPHECY FROM RICHMOND.

The correspondent of the London *Times*, writing from Richmond on the 4th of March, says:

"I am daily more convinced that if Richmond falls and LEE and JOHNSTON are driven from the field, it is but the first stage of this colossal revolution which will then be completed. There will ensue a time when every important town of the South will require to be held by a Yankee garrison, when exultation in New-York will be exchanged for soberness and right reason, and when it will be realized that the closing scenes of this mightiest revolutionary drama will not be played out, save in the times of our children's children."

GREAT BRITAIN.

Parliamentary proceedings on the 30th ult. were unimportant.

In the House of Commons, on the 31st, Lord C. PAGET said that the Admiralty had received no proposal for sanctioning or supporting any fresh attempt to reach the North Pole. He was, therefore, unable to say what course the government would take if such a proposal were made.

Mr. NEWDEGATE put some questions as to the idea of the Pope taking up his residence in England, as indicated in some foreign journals.

Lord PALMERSTON replied that the government respected the Pope personally very much, but for him to come to England would be both an anachronism and a solecism.

The revenue returns for the financial year, ending March 31, show a net increase of over £104,000 on the year. Notwithstanding the great reductions in taxation, the revenue exceeds by nearly half a million sterling the estimates of Mr. GLADSTONE.

Messrs. BARING's circular says that large business has been done in 5-20 bonds, and that prices advanced early in the week to 57⅞@58, but have since relapsed to 56⅝@57—the demand being chiefly from the continent.

On Friday, the telegrams per the steamship *Cuba* were received, and 5 20s again advanced to 57¾@58¼. Erie and Illinois Central Shares have also attracted attention, and have again advanced.

The Bank of England on the 30th ult. reduced its rate of discount to 4 per cent., at which there is a fair demand for money. This movement strengthened the English funds, and Consols are buoyant and advancing.

KELSON, TRITTON & Co., East India and general merchants, have suspended payment. Their liabilities are estimated at £900,000 sterling.

Another provincial bank has suspended, the Portsmouth and South Hants Banking Company. Their liabilities are about £170,000 sterling.

The Birmingham and Joint Stock Banking Company had agreed to take up the business of Atwood & Spooner's Bank, which lately suspended at Birmingham, and to pay the creditors 11s. 3d. on the pound.

The West India Mail steamer had arrived, with over two and a quarter millions of dollars in specie. She also brought several Captains of blockade-runners, whose occupations were gone.

THE ATLANTIC TELEGRAPH.

The French Government will probably send one or two steamers to accompany the two that are sent by the English Government with the *Great Eastern* across the Atlantic, at the time of laying the Atlantic cable, and it is hoped that the United States Government will do the same.

FRANCE.

Weekly returns from the Bank of France show an increase of cash on hand of over ten and a half millions francs.

In the French Chambers of the 30th, M. JULES FAVRE spoke upon the necessity for political liberty, but was interrupted by the President and declined to finish his speech. The amendment was rejected.

The amendment in favor of the liberty of the press was debated, but rejected by a large majority.

It is stated that NAPOLEON will leave Paris early in May, not returning until November. His physicians have recommended seven months' absence in the country air.

The Bourse is firm, 67.45.

SPAIN.

The *Epoca* states that the Minister of War tendered his resignation, and that Gen. LEORSUNDI refused to place him.

A later dispatch says the Minister of War resigned from ill health.

Gen. RIVERA succeeded to the office.

DENMARK.

The King relieved M. HELLEEN, Minister of Justice, of his functions. HELLEEN represented the alliance between the Reactionary and extreme Democratic parties. It is supposed that all members of the late Cabinet will return to their posts.

ITALY.

In the allocutions delivered at the last consistory the Pope expressed surprise and sorrow at the sad events which have recently taken place in Mexico. His Holiness hoped MAXIMILIAN would abandon the course upon which he had entered, and satisfy the just desires of the Holy See. The Pope further thanked the Bishops of the Catholic world, especially those of Italy, for defending the religion and liberties of the Church, despite the decrees of the secular authorities.

PRUSSIA.

In the Military Committee of Chambers, the Deputies amendment was introduced with the object of effecting a reconciliation between the government and chamber, and proposing a maximum strength of the army at 180,000 men, which was rejected by 11 to 8. The committee also rejected the general military estimates and navy estimates and amendments, thus refusing the whole military and naval proposals of the government.

AUSTRIA.

Count MENSDORFF had made some ministerial explanation in the Lower House Reichsrath. He said the views of the government on the question of the Duchies would be communicated in the Federal Diet on the 6th of April.

As regards relations with Italy, he said the government desired to promote the material interests of the two countries, but that Italy maintained a hostile attitude to the government. He desired to economize, but must maintain the position of Austria as a great Power.

INDIA.

A private Calcutta telegram of March 27 reports commercial affairs in much the same state as on the 25th, when slight improvement had taken place.

BRAZIL.

LONDON, Sunday, April 2.

The Brazilian mail has reached Lisbon, bringing the following dates:

RIO DE JANEIRO, Saturday, March 11.

Exchange 25⅝@26¼.

COFFEE.—Sales of good firsts at 65Ⅱ06. Shipments 100,000 bags. Stock, 100.000 bags. Freights 50Ⅱ62½.

BAHIA, Saturday, March 11.

Exchange 26¼.

Cotton nominal.

PERNAMBUCO, Saturday, March 11.

Exchange 26⅜@27.

Montivedeo has surrendered to Gen. FLORES. The Brazilians now occupy the city.

LATEST VIA LIVERPOOL.

LIVERPOOL, Saturday Evening, April 1, 1865.

The *Times* to-day has an editorial on the amended tariff law of the United States. It says: "It is impossible to find an excuse for it. Tried by the light of reason or by the results of experience it is alike condemned."

It ironically credits the framers of the scheme with peculiar wisdom in selecting the 1st of April for its inauguration.

The *Army & Navy Gazette* says: "The work of the United States Navy has now been accomplished, and it must be confessed that in the hands of FARRAGUT and PORTER the high reputation which the officers and seamen of that Power established soon after the national existence of itself, has been greatly enhanced."

LATEST VIA QUEENSTOWN.

LONDON, Saturday, April 1.

There is no news of importance this morning.

PARIS, Friday, March 31—P. M.

The Bourse is steady. The Rentes closed at 67f. 30c.

COMMERCIAL.

LIVERPOOL MARKET.

LIVERPOOL, April 31.—Evening.

The Market report was received per *Moravian*.

COTTON—The stock of Cotton in port is 580.000 bales by actual count, being 13,000 bales below the estimates, of which amount 49,000 bales are American.

TRADE REPORT.

The Manchester market was firmer with an upward tendency.

BREADSTUFFS—The market is easier. Messrs. RICHARDSON, SPENCE & Co., and others, report: Flour dull and easier. Wheat quiet and quotations are barely maintained; red Western 8s.@8s. 8d. Corn inactive; mixed 27s. 6d.

PROVISIONS—The market is downward. WAKEFIELD, NASH & Co., and others, report: Beef has a downward tendency. Pork heavy and declined 2s. 6d. Bacon firmer and holders demand an advance. Lard dull and easier at 58s.@61s. Butter flat and declining. Tallow downward.

PRODUCE.—Ashes easier at 28s. 6d. for Pots, and 30s. for Pearls. Sugar, flat. Coffee, quiet and steady. Rice, quiet and steady. Clover Seed, firmer. Jute, 10s.@30s. lower. Cod Oil, quiet at 57s. Sperm Oil, no sales. Linseed Oil, steady. Resin, very dull. Spirits Turpentine, quiet at 65s.@66s.

PETROLEUM—BOULT, ENGLISH & BRANDON report: Petroleum firm, at 1s. 11d.@2s. for refined; no crude in market.

LONDON MARKETS.

FLOUR firm; WHEAT steady. IRON advancing; bars and rails, £6 10s.@£6 15s.; Scotch pig, 52s. 3d. SUGAR inactive. COFFEE active at a decline of 1s.@2s. TEA steady at 10½d. for common Congou. RICE steady. SPIRITS TURPENTINE firm at 67s. PETROLEUM steady at £18 for crude, 2s. for refined SPERM OIL nominal at £82. TALLOW downward, at 40s @43s. LINSEED OIL flat.

LATEST COMMERCIAL.

LIVERPOOL, Saturday, April 1—Evening.

COTTON—Sales to-day 6,000 bales, including 2,000 bales to speculators and exporters. The market is less firm but quiet and unchanged.

BREADSTUFFS—The market is quiet and steady.

PROVISIONS—The market is dull.

PRODUCE—The market is quiet and steady. Petroleum firm at 2s.@2s. 0½d. for refined.

LONDON, Saturday, April 1—Evening.

CONSOLS closed at 89¾@90. for money.

AMERICAN STOCKS—Illinois Central Railroad 61¾@62¼; Erie Railroad 36¼@36¾; United States Five-twenties 57⅝@58¼.

Gen. Lee in Richmond—The Oath of Allegiance.

BALTIMORE, Friday, April 14.

The Richmond *Whig* of yesterday contains little of importance. It announces the arrival of Gen. LEE on the night previous.

The *Whig* publishes the oath of allegiance, which it says citizens will be required to swear and subscribe to. The Provost-Marshal's office is crowded with people anxious to take it, and the only question among citizens seems to be who shall be first to renew their citizenship.

Rejoicings at Cincinnati.

CINCINNATI, Friday, April 14.

Business was entirely suspended to-day. The city was universally decorated with flags, and great enthusiasm prevailed. The procession was an immense affair, comprising the entire police force, Gens. HOOKER and WALLICH, with their staffs, four regiments of National Guards, discharged veterans, ward organizations, the Fenian Brotherhood, the Fire Department, and a large number of colored citizens. All the bells in the city were rung, and salutes were fired at 6 o,clock this evening. To-night the city is brilliantly illuminated, and there is generally a display of fireworks.

Fire.

ROCHESTER, N. Y., Friday, April 14.

The cabinet warehouse of JAMES E. HAYDON, of this city, was partially destroyed by fire this morning. The stocks of HUMPHREY REEDY & Co., stove dealers, HASTINGS & MCVEAN, paper dealers, S. B. ROBY, saddlery and hardware dealers, and the agency of the American Tract Society, were damaged. Total loss, $30,000; insurance, $20,000. The origin of the fire is unknown.

The Funeral of Gen. T. A. Smyth.

WILMINGTON, Del., Friday, April 14.

The remains of Brig.-Gen. T. A. SMYTH arrived here to-day at 1 o'clock, and will be interred on Monday afternoon with appropriate ceremonies.

An Unseaworthy War Steamer.

To the Editor of the New-York Times:

UNITED STATES STEAMER MUSCOOTA, HAMPTON ROADS, Va., Wednesday, April 12, 1865.

This vessel has returned to this port, having made her fourth attempt to make a cruise to the Pacific. On each occasion she has proved herself to be an unsafe sea boat. On her last trial she narrowly escaped being lost in the Gulf Stream. Inclosed you will find a list of her officers; please publish. Respectfully, &c.,

ARTHUR BURTIS, Jr., Paymaster.

List of officers attached to the U. S. steamer *Muscoota*, one thousand tons, 10 guns:

Commander GEO. M. RANSOM, Lieut. Thos. S. Spencer, Ass't Paymaster Arthur Burtis, Jr., Ass't Surgeon Danl. McMurtrie, Act'g Master Geo. R. Durand, Act'g Ensigns Robt. M. Clark, Jas. Courtney, John D. Thomas, Chas. A. Stewart, Second Ass't Engineers Robert H. Gunnell, Jas. H. Grasmer, Henry Snyder, Act'g Third Ass't Engineers Robt. L. Case, Geo. Taylor, Geo. Westinghouse, Jr., Masters Fred'k. A. Beatie, A. L. Spinney, Wm. Merrill, Captain's Clerk Geo. S. Dana, Paymasters Clerk P. B. Hathaway.

Arrivals in the City.

Gov. Jos. A. Gilmore, Concord, N. H., is stopping at the Fifth-avenue Hotel.

Hon. O. N. Shannon, Cincinnati; Gen. B. F. Stringfellow, Atchison; Dr. N. Greene, Louisville, and Wm. D. Griswold, Terre Haute, are stopping at the Metropolitan Hotel.

COLLISION.—The steamship *La Favorete*, while returning from a trial trip and passing up the East River, collided with the Catharine Ferry-boat *Manhassett*, as she was entering her slip on the Brooklyn side, doing considerable damage to the *Manhassett*, by tearing away a portion of the gentlemen's cabin, and somewhat injuring the hull. Fortunately nobody was hurt.

The New-York Times.

VOL. XIV......NO. 4230. NEW-YORK, SATURDAY, APRIL 15, 1865. PRICE FOUR CENTS

AWFUL EVENT.

President Lincoln Shot by an Assassin.

The Deed Done at Ford's Theatre Last Night.

THE ACT OF A DESPERATE REBEL

Attempted Assassination of Secretary Seward.

Rumored Attempt on the Life of Mr. Stanton.

DETAILS OF THE DREADFUL TRAGEDY.

WASHINGTON, Friday, April 14—12:30 A. M.

The President was shot in a theatre to-night, and is, perhaps, mortally wounded.

Secretary SEWARD was also assassinated.

SECOND DISPATCH.

WASHINGTON, Friday, April 14.

President LINCOLN and wife, with other friends, this evening visited Ford's Theatre for the purpose of witnessing the performance of the "American Cousin."

It was announced in the papers that Gen. GRANT would also be present, but he took the late train of cars for New-Jersey.

The theatre was densely crowded, and everybody seemed delighted with the scene before them. During the third act, and while there was a temporary pause for one of the actors to enter, a sharp report of a pistol was heard, which merely attracted attention, but suggesting nothing serious, until a man rushed to the front of the President's box, waving a long dagger in his right hand, and exclaiming "*Sic semper tyrannis.*" and immediately leaped from the box, which was in the second tier, to the stage beneath, and ran across to the opposite side, making his escape amid the bewilderment of the audience from the rear of the theatre, and, mounting a horse, fled.

The screams of Mrs. LINCOLN first disclosed the fact to the audience that the President had been shot, when all present rose to their feet, rushing toward the stage, many exclaiming "Hang him! hang him!"

The excitement was of the wildest possible description, and of course there was an abrupt termination of the theatrical performance.

There was a rush toward the President's box, when cries were heard: "Stand back and give him air." "Has any one stimulants." On a hasty examination, it was found that the President had been shot through the head, above and back of the temporal bone, and that some of the brain was oozing out. He was removed to a private house opposite to the theatre, and the Surgeon-General of the army, and other surgeons sent for to attend to his condition.

On an examination of the private box blood was discovered on the back of the cushioned rocking chair on which the President had been sitting, also on the partition and on the floor. A common single-barreled pocket pistol was found on the carpet.

A military guard was placed in front of the private residence to which the President had been conveyed. An immense crowd was in front of it, all deeply anxious to learn the condition of the President. It had been previously announced that the wound was mortal; but all hoped otherwise. The shock to the community was terrible.

The President was in a state of syncope, totally insensible, and breathing slowly. The blood oozed from the wound at the back of his head. The surgeons exhausted every effort of medical skill, but all hope was gone. The parting of his family with the dying President is too sad for description.

At midnight, the Cabinet, with Messrs. SUMNER, COLFAX and FARNSWORTH, Judge CURTIS, Gov. OGLESBY, Gen. MEIGS, Col. HAY, and a few personal friends, with Surgeon-General BARNES and his immediate assistants, were around his bedside.

The President and Mrs. LINCOLN did not start for the theatre until fifteen minutes after eight o'clock. Speaker COLFAX was at the White House at the time, and the President stated to him that he was going, although Mrs. LINCOLN had not been well, because the papers had announced that Gen. GRANT and they were to be present, and, as Gen. GRANT had gone North, he did not wish the audience to be disappointed.

He went with apparent reluctance and urged Mr. COLFAX to go with him; but that gentleman had made other engagements, and with Mr. ASHMAN, of Massachusetts, bid him good bye.

When the excitement at the theatre was at its wildest height, reports were circulated that Secretary SEWARD had also been assassinated.

On reaching this gentleman's residence a crowd and a military guard were found at the door, and on entering it was ascertained that the reports were based on truth.

Everybody there was so excited that scarcely an intelligible word could be gathered, but the facts are substantially as follows:

About 10 o'clock a man rang the bell, and the call having been answered by a colored servant, he said he had come from Dr. VERDI, Secretary SEWARD's family physician, with a prescription, at the same time holding in his hand a small piece of folded paper, and saying in answer to a refusal that he must see the Secretary, as he was entrusted with particular directions concerning the medicine.

He still insisted on going up, although repeatedly informed that no one could enter the chamber. The man pushed the servant aside, and walked heavily toward the Secretary's room, and was then met by Mr. FREDERICK SEWARD, of whom he demanded to see the Secretary, making the same representation which he did to the servant. What further passed in the way of colloquy is not known, but the man struck him on the head with a "billy," severely injuring the skull and felling him almost senseless. The assassin then rushed into the chamber and attacked Major SEWARD, Paymaster of the United States army and Mr. HANSELL, a messenger of the State Department and two male nurses, disabling them all, he then rushed upon the Secretary, who was lying in bed in the same room, and inflicted three stabs in the neck, but severing, it is thought and hoped, no arteries, though he bled profusely.

ANOTHER ACCOUNT.

Special Dispatch to the New-York Times.

WASHINGTON, Friday, April 14, 11:15 P. M.

A stroke from Heaven laying the whole of the city in instant ruins could not have startled us as did the word that broke from Ford's Theatre a half hour ago that the President had been shot. It flew everywhere in five minutes, and set five thousand people in swift and excited motion on the instant.

It is impossible to get at the full facts of the case, but it appears that a young man entered the President's box from the theatre, during the last act of the play of "Our American Cousin," with pistol in hand. He shot the President in the head and instantly jumped from the box upon the stage, and immediately disappeared through the side scenes and rear of the theatre, brandishing a dirk knife and dropping a kid glove on the stage.

The audience heard the shot, but supposing it fired in the regular course of the play, did not heed it till Mrs. LINCOLN's screams drew their attention. The whole affair occupied scarcely half a minute, and then the assassin was gone. As yet he has not been found.

The President's wound is reported mortal. He was at once taken into the house opposite the theatre.

As if this horror was not enough, almost the same moment the story ran through the city that Mr. SEWARD had been murdered in his bed.

Inquiry showed this to be so far true also. It appears a man wearing a light coat, dark pants, slouch hat, called and asked to see Mr. SEWARD, and was shown to his room. He delivered to Major SEWARD, who sat near his father, what purported to be a physician's prescription, turned, and with one stroke cut Mr. SEWARD's throat as he lay on his bed, inflicting a horrible wound, but not severing the jugular vein, and not producing a mortal wound.

In the struggle that followed, Major SEWARD was also badly, but not seriously, wounded in several places. The assassin rushed down stairs, mounted the fleet horse on which he came, drove his spurs into him, and dashed away before any one could stop him.

Reports have prevailed that an attempt was also made on the life of Mr. STANTON.

MIDNIGHT.

The President is reported dead. Cavalry and infantry are scouring the city in every direction for the murderous assassins, and the city is overwhelmed with excitement. Who the assassins were no one knows, though every body supposes them to have been rebels.

FROM RICHMOND.

Present Feeling in Richmond—Call to the People of Virginia to Inaugurate a State Legislature—Chances of Its Failure—Administration of Gens. Weitzel and Shepley—Gen. Ord in Command—Revival of Business and Improvements—Condition of the People—Mrs. Gen. Lee.

From Our Own Correspondent.

RICHMOND, Va., Thursday, April 13, 1865.

The stunning effect experienced by all who found themselves mixed up in the tornado of wondrous events which have just swept over this part of the world, has nearly subsided. People are gradually regaining their senses, becoming convinced that all they have seen and heard was not a wild dream, but sober reality, and the frenzy of joy over past and passing events is succeeded by calm and deliberate calculation for the future. The malady of rebellion reached its crisis when the electrifying news was spread over the land, that LEE's remnant of an army had surrendered to GRANT, and, henceforth, those who have so long been chronicling the exciting details of daily conflicts in the field, will be engaged in the far less brilliant and stirring, but more joyous, pursuit of telling you how the patient is progressing to new and more vigorous health. It is true that we have not yet heard of the actual surrender of JOHNSTON's army, of the taking of Mobile, of what the wandering hordes of Trans-Mississippi rebels may have done, or are going to do, &c. But the whole thing is already so far a foregone conclusion in the minds of all men here—both Union and rebel—that I really don't believe that anything which these helpless fragments of the dead Confederacy could now attempt will affect the calculations of any man of business more than the war upon BILLY BOWLEGS in Florida disarranged the mercantile transactions of New-York or Boston.

Things are marching rapidly, as you will see by the published address "to the people of Virginia," in the *Whig* of to-day, inviting the Governor, Lieutenant-Governor, members of the Legislature, and various prominent citizens of Virginia, to assemble in Richmond on the 25th inst., for the purpose of discussing "the restoration of peace to the State of Virginia, and the adjustment of questions involving life, liberty and property, that have arisen in the State, as a consequence of the war."

Although it is well for the people of Virginia to lose no time in ventilating, among themselves, all questions respecting the dreary position in which this iniquitous rebellion has placed them, I must confess that I have but little faith in their *immediately* coming to anything like good and practical results. The minds of the people are still in too keen a state of fermentation, bewilderment and conflicting passions, for anything like calm and solid reasoning. In spite of the highly respectable and gifted names coupled with that invitation, I venture to say that many will come to that gathering without the remotest idea of practically adapting themselves to the circumstances actually surrounding them. Instead of realized how thoroughly this whole fabric of secession has crumbled into dust,—that slavery is as if it had never been,—that the whole doctrine of States' Rights, as opposed to national authority has been proved a gigantic humbug by *thousands*,—that it is the majesty of the "people of the United States" which now reigns supreme in Richmond and Virginia—many, I have no doubt, will go to work as if there were still some vestige of "State Sovereignty" about them; and, instead of approaching the outraged dignity and peace of the nation, as penitents and suppliants, will come with their pockets full of absurd "compromises" and "provisors;" haughtily supposing that the country will go to ruin, unless Uncle Sam comes, hat in hand, to beg the much-injured and much-offended Mrs. Virginia to come and help him make his laws and conduct his affairs. Few of them, I venture to assert, really feel that matters are the very reverse; that Virginia is in the position of a spoiled child who has just received a sound whipping for her naughtiness, that she is now ignominiously set in the corner for wholesome punishment, and that it matters very little to Uncle Sam whether she takes months or years to stop sobbing and sulking before she comes penitently to beg pardon for her transgression, to receive the paternal kiss and join her joyous sisters; for, to that complexion she *must* come at last. I may be wrong in my suspicions about this effort to reorganize the State just now—I sincerely hope it may prove to be so—but I must confess that, after considerable interchange of opinions with the people, and a peep into quite a number of good families, I am driven to this conclusion. Of course this will all change—*must* change—with time; but it is unnaturally soon to expect it yet. In the meantime while there is but one care for us—martial law—administered with as much lenity as the altered condition of affairs can warrant. What, for instance, was manifestly wise and indispensable, in controlling rampant, defiant New-Orleans, would be utterly cruel and unnecessary for downfallen, mourning and resigned, but still proud Richmond.

No one understood this better than the two distinguished officers who have had the control of this city since its occupation by our forces—Maj.-Gen. GODFREY WEITZEL and Brig.-Gen. G. F. SHEPLEY—for both had ample experience in governing in New-Orleans and elsewhere, and thoroughly understood both the faults and the merits of Southern character. Maj.-Gen. ORD, having arrived yesterday and assumed the reins of government, both these officers leave this morning for other fields of usefulness—much to the regret of the whole population. It is not that the latter are not sure of receiving equally kind and generous treatment from one of Gen. ORD's well-known character, but both WEITZEL and SHEPLEY had, in this brief time, won the respect and confidence of all who had not known them previously. Gen. WEITZEL goes, I believe, to Petersburgh; Gen. SHEPLEY's destination I have not yet heard.

Business is already reviving—stores are being opened one after another—and I doubt not that a month or two from now, people who saw Richmond in the first days of our occupation will, on revisiting it, be astonished at the change. *Free* negroes are already at work, by the hundreds, cleaning the streets of the bricks and rubbish caused by the conflagration, and working at it with a will and pleasure that I question if an overseer ever got out of them with his lash. Beside the cleaning of the streets, those lofty weird-looking remnants of shattered walls, which loomed up in every direction, are being pulled down; so that pedestrians can now walk along unobstructed streets, without the dread of being crushed to pieces at every footstep. We also reveled in the luxury of gas for the first time last night at the Spottswood House, and altogether things are improving rapidly.

As to trade, there is every likelihood of this market being speedily glutted, to overflowing, with all kind of necessaries, though we cannot boast of much yet—judging, at least, by the food at the Spotswood House, the only hotel yet in full blast, and where, it is to be presumed, the proprietors are giving the best they can. The army sutlers and traders, as a matter of course, are swarming among us like bees; but I fear they will soon find they have more than enough to supply the population, if they continue pouring in as they have done during the last few days.

The condition of such a city as Richmond is extremely painful and anomalous. The only people, as a class, who can really be said to have money are the floating population from the North, who have come here on speculation or from curiosity, and who will, doubtless, continue to pour in and out for some time to come. Of the actual residents, hundreds hitherto lapped in luxury and, till yesterday, accounted wealthy, are to-day on a level with absolute beggars. Money they have, but in Confederate paper, $1,000 of which is not worth the price of a good dinner, except to some curiosity-monger in search of these rebel rags. These people are living in fine houses, but, literally, many of them without any manifest means of sustaining life. "Let them work," says the industrious and self-dependent Northerner. True, but work at what? and where is the employer? The males, from old age to boyhood, are mostly killed off by the war, or are to be seen hobbling on crutches along the streets, hopeless cripples for life. The sufferers are mainly widows, with their helpless and dependent daughters. How is the suffering of all such people to be met? let them swallow their pride as they may, and God knows they have plenty of it yet remaining. I have myself been a personal witness of much of it here among these hapless ladies, and while I pitied and condemned them inwardly for their self-inflicted suffering, I found my heart unconsciously yielding an extorted homage to what would be more than Spartan bravery, if not devoted to so wicked and unreasonable a cause. If there be a Northern man with one particle of malignity in his heart, let him come here; let him dive into the secret recesses of domestic suffering among those who have so long been considered his enemies, and if he does not feel (however foolish they may yet be in their lingering pride) that he has had vengeance enough, I, for one, envy him not his manhood.

Mrs. LEE is still here upon a bed of suffering, and receiving all proper care and attention from our authorities. The stories of her death are all false. I met a gentleman yesterday, well acquainted with the family, who had just seen her, and informed me that she was no better nor worse than she had been for months past. Gen. LEE is daily expected here to see her.

The poorer classes of the community are being constantly relieved by the government; and among these are stealthily included many who, before the war, were reckoned among the independent and upper ranks. Some idea of the extent of this charity may be gleaned from the fact, since Sunday last, over 60,0000 rations have been issued by our Commissary Department, thereby assisting more than 2,500 families; and this quite independent of the great labors of the Sanitary and Christian Commissions, and the private magnificence of benevolent individuals who cannot see misery go unaided.

J. R. HAMILTON.

FROM WILMINGTON.

Accident on the Railroad—An Appeal for the Refugees and Freedmen.

From Our Own Correspondent.

WILMINGTON, N. C., Friday, April 7, 1865.

The down train from Goldsboro, last night, met with an accident near Magnolia, resulting in the death of two discharged soldiers, and serious injury to several others. The engineer is said to have been intoxicated, and was running the train at the rate of twenty miles an hour, when an axle broke, throwing several of the cars off the track, and entirely demolishing several others.

Two soldiers of the First United States Colored Infantry were killed by bushwhackers yesterday, while doing safeguard duty at a house near Magnolia.

The organization and progress of the freedmen's schools here, under the supervision of the American Missionary Association, has been remarkably successful, and reflects great credit on the agents and missionaries who have been in charge. Fifteen days after the occupation of this place by the Union army, Mr. W. L. COAN, one of the agents, arrived here, and, with the aid of Gen. HAWLEY, commanding the district, in less than forty-eight hours a night school was established. Subsequently, a day-school was also organized. The blacks were overjoyed, and their profuse demonstrations were extremely ludicrous. Gen. HAWLEY addressed them at the first organization. In five days, the schools, day and night, included about one thousand pupils, and they are now in a prosperous condition, under the superintendence of Mr. J. G. LANGLEY, of Massachusetts. The arrival of several teachers from the North this week has added a new impulse to the cause, and everything is working finely. Rev. S. S. ASHLEY, and the efficient and energetic superintendent of negro affairs in this State, Capt. H. JAMES, A. Q. M., and Misses MARY BROWNSON, H. L. TRUE, S. L. DAFFIN and Mrs. C. L. MORSE, and E. L. PIPER, teachers, are domiciled in the mansion and former residence of HENRY NUTT, Esq., a prominent rebel. It is one of the finest residences in the city, and being the earnings of slaves—none of whom remain on the premises—it could not be devoted to a better purpose.

Rev. Mr. ASHLEY will become the superintendent of Freedmen's affairs, as Capt. JAMES' assistant, and will have a general oversight of the educational as well as physical interests of the negroes.

A new school mission will be established at Smithville next week. The blacks, generally, are desirous of learning, and after a little time devoted to discipline make attentive and apt scholars.

The following letter from Gen. HAWLEY explains itself. It is to be hoped that the generous people of the North will respond promptly thereto:

HEADQUARTERS DISTRICT OF WILMINGTON, WILMINGTON, N. C., April 5, 1865.

Capt. Horace James, A. Q. M., Superintendent of Negro Affairs, Department of North Carolina:

SIR: This district was suddenly constituted, and in addition to the freedmen found within its limits and those who naturally came in from the surrounding country, six or seven thousand of them came down—most of them in one body—from the army of Major-Gen. SHERMAN. In supervising all these and providing for their immediate necessities, the energies of the few officers and soldiers upon whom the burden fell were exerted to the utmost. Add to this nine thousand paroled prisoners were most unexpectedly delivered here, totally destitute, thousands of them going into hospitals immediately, and that several thousand white persons had to be fed, and you will see that generous as the government is, in all such matters, there must be embarrassment and suffering. We are utterly unable to furnish many of the necessities of life.

I wish that you would appeal to the benevolent and liberal people of the North, who have already done so much. We need clothing for destitute whites and blacks. In endeavoring to put the freed population upon the large plantations on the Cape Fear River, we are greatly embarrassed by the want of axes, shovels, hoes—light and heavy—hammers, saws, nails and a few plows. I think that if you estimate for the wants of fifteen thousand laboring people, you will not get more than can be judiciously used. Your own experience will guide you in this better than any suggestion. What we need, we need this very day, for the planting season is upon us, and we have many people houseless, or improperly crowded.

Very respectfully, your obedient servant,
(Signed) JOSEPH R. HAWLEY,
Brigadier-General Commanding.

Five hundred colored laborers are being employed here to serve as a construction corps for Gen. SCHOFIELD's army. They will be paid from $10 to $25 a month. The employment of the contrabands in this manner materially increases the effective strength of our army.

E. P. BROOKS.

THE SIEGE OF MOBILE.

Fierce Bombardment of the Spanish Fort—Mobile Papers Announce the Capture of Selma.

NEW-ORLEANS, Saturday, April 8, via CAIRO, Friday, April 14.

A special dispatch to the New-Orleans *Times*, from the Spanish Fort, dated April 5, says:

"A furious fire was opened on the rebel forts last night from our entire line. During the bombardment a small magazine in the Spanish Fort exploded. The damage is unknown. Quiet prevailed on the 5th. Deserters report from 18,000 to 20,000 troops in and about Mobile, including all the State Reserves, and about 2,000 in the Spanish Fort. The loss outside the Spanish Fort up to the 4th instant amounted to about 500 killed and wounded. The rebel loss exceeds ours."

Adjt.-Gen. THOMAS arrived at New-Orleans on the morning of the 7th.

Mobile papers of the 4th inst. announce the capture of Selma, Alabama, with 23 pieces of artillery, and a large amount of Government property.

Fort Sumter Celebration in Bangor.

BANGOR, Me., Friday, April 14.

The restoration of the Old Flag to Fort Sumter was celebrated here to-day by a national salute at noon, by a display of all the flags on public and private buildings, and by the raising of the Stars and Strips one thousand feet above the city by means of a monster kite bearing the name of U. S. GRANT.

EUROPEAN NEWS.

TWO DAYS LATER BY THE EUROPA.

The Insult to Our Cruisers by Portugal.

The American Minister at Lisbon Demands Satisfaction.

Dismissal of the Commander of Fort Belan Requested.

Further Advance in Five-Twenties.

FINANCIAL AND COMMERCIAL.

HALIFAX, Friday, April 14.

The steamship *Europa*, from Liverpool on the 1st, via Queenstown on the 2d inst., arrived here at 2 o'clock this morning. She has 43 passengers for this port, and 30 for Boston. Her dates are two days later than those already received.

The steamship *Cuba*, from New-York, arrived at Liverpool at noon on the 1st inst.

THE STONEWALL AFFAIR.

A Lisbon dispatch, of the 31st of March, says that the American Minister at Lisbon has demanded satisfaction of the Portuguese Government for the firing upon the *Niagara* and *Sacramento* by the Portuguese forts. He also requests the dismissal of the Commander of Fort Belan, and a salute of twenty-one guns to the American flag.

Nothing as yet has been decided in regard to the matter.

A PROPHECY FROM RICHMOND.

The correspondent of the London *Times*, writing from Richmond on the 4th of March, says:

"I am daily more convinced that if Richmond falls and LEE and JOHNSTON are driven from the field, it is but the first stage of this colossal revolution which will then be completed. There will ensue a time when every important town of the South will require to be held by a Yankee garrison, when exultation in New-York will be exchanged for soberness and right reason, and when it will be realized that the closing scenes of this mightiest revolutionary drama will not be played out, save in the times of our children's children."

GREAT BRITAIN.

Parliamentary proceedings on the 30th ult. were unimportant.

In the House of Commons, on the 31st, Lord C. PAGET said that the Admiralty had received no proposal for sanctioning or supporting any fresh attempt to reach the North Pole. He was, therefore, unable to say what course the government would take if such a proposal were made.

Mr. NEWDEGATE put some questions as to the idea of the Pope taking up his residence in England, as indicated in some foreign journals.

Lord PALMERSTON replied that the government respected the Pope personally very much, but for him to come to England would be both an anachronism and a solecism.

The revenue returns for the financial year, ending March 31, show a net increase of over £104,000 on the year. Notwithstanding the great reductions in taxation, the revenue exceeds by nearly half a million sterling the estimates of Mr. GLADSTONE.

Messrs. BARING's circular says that large business has been done in 5-20 bonds, and that prices advanced early in the week to 57¾@58, but have since relapsed to 56½@57—the demand being chiefly from the continent.

On Friday, the telegrams per the steamship *Cuba* were received, and 5 20s again advanced to 57¾@58¼. Erie and Illinois Central Shares have also attracted attention, and have again advanced.

The Bank of England on the 30th ult. reduced its rate of discount to 4 per cent., at which there is a fair demand for money. This movement strengthened the English funds, and Consols are buoyant and advancing.

KELSON, TRITTON & Co., East India and general merchants, have suspended payment. Their liabilities are estimated at £900,000 sterling.

Another provincial bank has suspended, the Portsmouth and South Hants Banking Company. Their liabilities are about £170,000 sterling.

The Birmingham and Joint Stock Banking Company had agreed to take up the business of Atwood & Spooner's Bank, which lately suspended at Birmingham, and to pay the creditors 11s 3d. on the pound.

The West India Mail steamer had arrived, with over two and a quarter millions of dollars in specie. She also brought several Captains of blockade-runners, whose occupations were gone.

THE ATLANTIC TELEGRAPH.

The French Government will probably send one or two steamers to accompany the two that are sent by the English Government with the *Great Eastern* across the Atlantic, at the time of laying the Atlantic cable, and it is hoped that the United States Government will do the same.

FRANCE.

Weekly returns from the Bank of France show an increase of cash on hand of over ten and a half millions francs.

In the French Chambers of the 30th, M. JULES FAVRE spoke upon the necessity for political liberty, but was interrupted by the President and declined to finish his speech. The amendment was rejected.

The amendment in favor of the liberty of the press was debated, but rejected by a large majority.

It is stated that NAPOLEON will leave Paris early in May, not returning until November. His physicians have recommended seven months' absence in the country air.

The Bourse is firm, 67.45.

SPAIN.

The *Epoca* states that the Minister of War tendered his resignation, and that Gen. LERSUNDI refused to place him.

A later dispatch says the Minister of War resigned from ill health.

Gen. RIVERA succeeded to the office.

DENMARK.

The King relieved M. HELLEEN, Minister of Justice, of his functions. HELLEEN represented the alliance between the Reactionary and extreme Democratic parties. It is supposed that all members of the late Cabinet will return to their posts.

ITALY

In the allocutions delivered at the last consistory the Pope expressed surprise and sorrow at the sad events which have recently taken place in Mexico. His Holiness hoped MAXIMILIAN would abandon the course upon which he had entered, and satisfy the just desires of the Holy See. The Pope further thanked the Bishops of the Catholic world, especially those of Italy, for defending the religion and liberties of the Church, despite the decrees of the secular authorities.

PRUSSIA.

In the Military Committee of Chambers, the Deputies amendment was introduced with the object of effecting a reconciliation between the government and chamber, and proposing a maximum strength of the army at 180,000 men, which was rejected by 11 to 8. The committee also rejected the general military estimates and navy estimates and amendments, thus refusing the whole military and naval proposals of the government.

AUSTRIA.

Count MENSDORFF had made some ministerial explanation in the Lower House Reichsrath. He said the views of the government on the question of the Duchies would be communicated in the Federal Diet on the 6th of April.

As regards relations with Italy, he said the government desired to promote the material interests of the two countries, but that Italy maintained a hostile attitude to the government. He desired to economize, but must maintain the position of Austria as a great Power.

INDIA.

A private Calcutta telegram of March 27 reports commercial affairs in much the same state as on the 25th, when slight improvement had taken place.

BRAZIL.

LONDON, Sunday, April 2.

The Brazilian mail has reached Lisbon, bringing the following dates:

RIO DE JANEIRO, Saturday, March 11.

Exchange 25⅝@26¼.

COFFEE.—Sales of good firsts at 65||06. Shipments 100,000 bags. Stock, 100,000 bags. Freights 50||62½.

BAHIA, Saturday, March 11.

Exchange 26¼.

Cotton nominal.

PERNAMBUCO, Saturday, March 11.

Exchange 26⅜@27.

Montivedeo has surrendered to Gen. FLORES. The Brazilians now occupy the city.

LATEST VIA LIVERPOOL.

LIVERPOOL, Saturday Evening, April 1, 1865.

The *Times* to-day has an editorial on the amended tariff law of the United States. It says: "It is impossible to find an excuse for it. Tried by the light of reason or by the results of experience it is alike condemned."

It ironically credits the framers of the scheme with peculiar wisdom in selecting the 1st of April for its inauguration.

The *Army & Navy Gazette* says: "The work of the United States Navy has now been accomplished, and it must be confessed that in the hands of FARRAGUT and PORTER the high reputation which the officers and seamen of that Power established soon after the national existence of itself, has been greatly enhanced."

LATEST VIA QUEENSTOWN.

LONDON, Saturday, April 1.

There is no news of importance this morning.

PARIS, Friday, March 31—P. M.

The Bourse is steady. The Rentes closed at 67f. 30c.

COMMERCIAL.

LIVERPOOL MARKET.

LIVERPOOL, April 31.—Evening.

The Market report was received per *Moravian*.

COTTON—The stock of Cotton in port is 580,000 bales by actual count, being 13,000 bales below the estimates, of which amount 49,000 bales are American.

TRADE REPORT.

The Manchester market was firmer with an upward tendency.

BREADSTUFFS—The market is easier. Messrs. RICHARDSON, SPENCE & Co., and others, report: Flour dull and easier. Wheat quiet and quotations are barely maintained; red Western 8s.@8s. 8d. Corn inactive; mixed 27s. 6d.

PROVISIONS—The market is downward. WAKEFIELD, NASH & Co., and others, report: Beef has a downward tendency. Pork heavy and declined 2s. 6d. Bacon firmer and holders demand an advance. Lard dull and easier at 58s.@61s. Butter flat and declining. Tallow downward.

PRODUCE—Ashes easier at 28s. 6d. for Pots, and 30s. for Pearls. Sugar, flat. Coffee, quiet and steady. Rice, quiet and steady. Clover Seed, firmer. Jute, 10s.@30s. lower. Cod Oil, quiet at 57s. Sperm Oil, no sales. Linseed Oil, steady. Resin, very dull. Spirits Turpentine, quiet at 65s.@66s.

PETROLEUM—BOULT, ENGLISH & BRANDON report: Petroleum firm, at 1s. 11d.@2s. for refined; no crude in market.

LONDON MARKETS.

FLOUR firm; WHEAT steady. IRON advancing; bars and rails, £6 10s @£6 15s; Scotch pig, 52s. 3d. SUGAR inactive. COFFEE active at a decline of 1s.@2s. TEA steady at 10½d. for common Congou. RICE steady. SPIRITS TURPENTINE firm at 67s. PETROLEUM steady at £18 for crude, 2s. for refined. SPERM OIL nominal at £82. TALLOW downward, at 40s.@43s. LINSEED OIL flat.

LATEST COMMERCIAL.

LIVERPOOL, Saturday, April 1—Evening.

COTTON—Sales to-day 6,000 bales, including 2,000 bales to speculators and exporters. The market is less firm but quiet and unchanged.

BREADSTUFFS—The market is quiet and steady.

PROVISIONS—The market [illegible]

PRODUCE—The market is quiet and steady. Petroleum firm at 2s.@2s. 0½d for refined.

LONDON, Saturday, April 1—Evening.

CONSOLS closed at 89¾@90 for money.

AMERICAN STOCKS—Illinois Central Railroad 61⅝@62¼; Erie Railroad 35¼@35½; United States Five-twenties 57⅜@58¼.

Gen. Lee in Richmond—The Oath of Allegiance.

BALTIMORE, Friday, April 14.

The Richmond *Whig* of yesterday contains little of importance. It announces the arrival of Gen. LEE on the night previous.

The *Whig* publishes the oath of allegiance, which it says citizens will be required to swear and subscribe to. The Provost-Marshal's office is crowded with people anxious to take it, and the only question among citizens seems to be who shall be first to renew their citizenship.

Rejoicings at Cincinnati.

CINCINNATI, Friday, April 14.

Business was entirely suspended to-day. The city was universally decorated with flags, and great enthusiasm prevailed. The procession was an immense affair, comprising the entire police force, Gens. HOOKER and WALLICH, with their staffs, four regiments of National Guards, discharged veterans, ward organizations, the Fenian Brotherhood, the Fire Department, and a large number of colored citizens. All the bells in the city were rung, and salutes were fired at 6 o,clock this evening. To-night the city is brilliantly illuminated, and there is generally a display of fireworks.

Fire.

ROCHESTER, N. Y., Friday, April 14.

The cabinet warehouse of JAMES E. HAYDON, of this city, was partially destroyed by fire this morning. The stocks of HUMPHREY REEDY & Co., stove dealers, HASTINGS & MCVEAN, paper dealers, S. B. ROBY, saddlery and hardware dealers, and the agency of the American Tract Society, were damaged. Total loss, $30,000; insurance, $20,000. The origin of the fire is unknown.

The Funeral of Gen. T. A. Smyth.

WILMINGTON, Del., Friday, April 14.

The remains of Brig.-Gen. T. A. SMYTH arrived here to day at 1 o'clock, and will be interred on Monday afternoon with appropriate ceremonies.

An Unseaworthy War Steamer.

To the Editor of the New-York Times:

UNITED STATES STEAMER MUSCOOTA, HAMPTON ROADS, Va., Wednesday, April 12, 1865.

This vessel has returned to this port, having made her fourth attempt to make a cruise to the Pacific. On each occasion she has proved herself to be an unsafe sea boat. On her last trial she narrowly escaped being lost in the Gulf Stream. Inclosed you will find a list of her officers; please publish.

Respectfully, &c.,

ARTHUR BURTIS, Jr., Paymaster.

List of officers attached to the U. S. steamer *Muscoota*, one thousand tons, 10 guns:

Commander GEO. M. RANSOM, Lieut. Thos. S. Spencer, Ass't Paymaster Arthur Burtis, Jr., Ass't Surgeon Danl. McMurtrie, Act'g Master Geo. R. Durand, Act'g Ensigns Robt. M. Clark, Jas. Courtney, John D. Thomas, Chas. A. Stewart, Second Ass't Engineers Robert H. Gunnell, Jas. H. Grasmer, Henry Snyder, Act'g Third Ass't Engineers Robt. L. Case, Geo. Taylor, Geo. Westinghouse, Jr., Masters Fred'k. A. Beatie, A. L. Spinney, Wm. Merrill, Captain's Clerk Geo. S. Dana, Paymaster's Clerk P. B. Hathaway.

Arrivals in the City.

Gov. Jos. A. Gilmore, Concord, N. H., is stopping at the Fifth avenue Hotel.

Hon. O. N. Shannon, Cincinnati; Gen. B. F. Stringfellow, Atchison; Dr. N. Greene, Louisville, and Wm. D. Griswold, Terre Haute, are stopping at the Metropolitan Hotel.

COLLISION.—The steamship *La Favorete*, while returning from a trial trip and passing up the F[illegible] River, collided with the Catharine Ferry-boat [illegible]*hasset*, as she was entering her slip on the P[illegible] side, doing considerable damage to the M[illegible] by tearing away a portion of the gentlem[illegible] and somewhat injuring the hull. Fortu[illegible] was hurt.

THE NEW YORK HERALD.

WHOLE NO. 10,456. NEW YORK, SATURDAY, APRIL 15, 1865. PRICE FOUR CENTS.

IMPORTANT.

ASSASSINATION OF PRESIDENT LINCOLN.

The President Shot at the Theatre Last Evening.

SECRETARY SEWARD DAGGERED IN HIS BED, BUT NOT MORTALLY WOUNDED.

Clarence and Frederick Seward Badly Hurt.

ESCAPE OF THE ASSASSINS.

Intense Excitement in Washington.

Scene at the Deathbed of Mr. Lincoln.

J. Wilkes Booth, the Actor, the Alleged Assassin of the President, &c., &c., &c.

THE OFFICIAL DESPATCH.

WAR DEPARTMENT, WASHINGTON, April 15—1:30 A. M.

Major General Dix, New York:—

This evening at about 9:30 P. M., at Ford's Theatre, the President, while sitting in his private box with Mrs. Lincoln, Mrs. Harris and Major Rathburn, was shot by an assassin, who suddenly entered the box and approached behind the President.

The assassin then leaped upon the stage, brandishing a large dagger or knife, and made his escape in the rear of the theatre.

The pistol ball entered the back of the President's head and penetrated nearly through the head. The wound is mortal.

The President has been insensible ever since it was inflicted, and is now dying.

About the same hour an assassin, whether the same or not, entered Mr. Seward's apartments, and under pretence of having a prescription was shown to the Secretary's sick chamber. The assassin immediately rushed to the bed and inflicted two or three stabs on the throat and two on the face.

It is hoped the wounds may no tbe mortal. My apprehension is that they will prove fatal.

The nurse alarmed Mr. Frederick Seward, who was in an adjoining room, and he hastened to the door of his father's room, when he met the assassin, who inflicted upon him one or more dangerous wounds. The recovery of Frederick Seward is doubtful.

It is not probable that the President will live through the night.

General Grant and wife were advertised to be at the theatre this evening, but he started to Burlington at six o'clock this evening.

At a Cabinet meeting, at which General Grant was present, the subject of the state of the country and the prospect of a speedy peace were discussed. The President was very cheerful and hopeful, and spoke very kindly of General Lee and others of the confederacy, and of the establishment of government in Virginia.

All the members of the Cabinet except Mr. Seward, are now in attendance upon the President.

I have seen Mr. Seward, but he and Frederick were both unconscious.

EDWIN M. STANTON,
Secretary of War.

THE HERALD DESPATCHES.

WASHINGTON, April 14, 1865.

Assassination has been inaugurated in Washington. The bowie knife and pistol have been applied to President Lincoln and Secretary Seward. The former was shot in the throat, while at Ford's theatre to-night. Mr. Seward was badly cut about the neck, while in his bed at his residence.

SECOND DESPATCH.

WASHINGTON, April 14, 1865.

An attempt was made about ten o'clock this evening to assassinate the President and Secretary Seward. The President was shot at Ford's Theatre. Result not yet known. Mr. Seward's throat was cut, and his son badly wounded.

There is intense excitement here.

Details of the Assassination.

WASHINGTON, April 14, 1865.

Washington was thrown into an intense excitement a few minutes before eleven o'clock this evening, by the announcement that the President and Secretary Seward had been assassinated and were dead.

The wildest excitement prevailed in all parts of the city. Men, women and children, old and young, rushed to and fro, and the rumors were magnified until we had nearly every member of the Cabinet killed. Some time elapsed before authentic data could be ascertained in regard to the affair.

The President and Mrs. Lincoln were at Ford's theatre, listening to the performance of the American Cousin, occupying a box in the second tier. At the close of the third act a person entered the box occupied by the President, and shot Mr. Lincoln in the head. The shot entered the back of his head, and came out above the temple.

The assassin then jumped from the box upon the stage and ran across to the other side, exhibiting a dagger in his hand, flourishing it in s tragical manner, shouting the same words repeated by the desperado at Mr. Seward's house, adding to it, "The South is avenged," and then escaped from the back entrance to the stage, but in his passage dropped his pistol and his hat.

Mr. Lincoln fell forward from his seat, and Mrs. Lincoln fainted.

The moment the astonished audience could realize what had happened, the President was taken and carried to Mr. Petersen's house, in Tenth street, opposite to the theatre. Medical aid was immediately sent for, and the wound was at first supposed to be fatal, and it was announced that he could not live; but at half-past twelve he is still alive, though in a precarious condition.

As the assassin ran across the stage, Colonel J. B. Stewart, of this city, who was occupying one of the front seats in the orchestra, on the same side of the house as the box occupied by Mr. Lincoln, sprang to the stage and followed him; but he was obstructed in his passage across the stage by the fright of the actors, and reached the back door about three seconds after the assassin had passed out. Colonel Stewart got to the street just in time to see him mount his horse and ride away.

This operation shows that the whole thing was a preconcerted plan. The person who fired the pistol was a man about thirty years of age, about five feet nine, spare built, fair skin, dark hair, apparently bushy, with a large mustache. Laura Keene and the leader of the orchestra declare that they recognized him as J. Wilkes Booth the actor, and a rabid secessionist. Whoever he was, ir is plainly evident that he thoroughly understood the theatre and all the approaches and modes of escape to the stage. A person not familiar with the theatre could not have possibly made his escape so well and quickly.

The alarm was sounded in every quarter. Mr. Stanton was notified, and immediately left his house.

All the other members of the Cabinet escaped attack.

Cavalrymen were sent out in all directions, and dispatches sent to all the fortifications, and it is thought they will be captured.

About half-past ten o'clock this evening a tall, well dressed man made his appearance at Secretary Seward's residence, and applied for admission. He was refused admission by the servant, when the desperado stated that he had a prescription from the Surgeon General, and that he was ordered to deliver it in person. He was still refused, except upon the written order of the physician. This he pretended to show, and pushed by the servant and rushed up stairs to Mr. Seward's room. He was met at the door by Mr. Fred Seward, who notified him that he was master of the house, and would take charge of the medicine. After a few words had passed between them he dodged by Fred Seward and rushed to the Secretary's bed, and struck him in the neck with a dagger, and also in the breast.

It was supposed at first that Mr. Seward was killed instantly, but it was found afterwards that the wound was not mortal.

Major Wm. H. Seward, Jr., paymaster, was in the room, and rushed to the defence of his father, and was badly cut in the *mele* with the assassin, but not fatally.

The desperado managed to escape from the house, and was prepared for escape by having a horse at the door. He immediately mounted his horse, and sung out the motto of the State of Virginia, "*Sic Semper Tyrannis!*" and rode off.

Surgeon General Barnes was immediately sent for, and he *examined Mr. Seward and pronounced him safe.* His wounds were not fatal. The jugular vein was not cut, nor the wound in the breast deep enough to be fatal.

WASHINGTON, April 15—1A. M.

The streets in the vicinity of Ford's Theatre are densely crowded by an anxious and excited crowd. A guard has been placed across Tenth street and F and E streets, and only official persons and particular friends of the President aro allowed to pass.

The popular heart is deeply stirred, and the deepest indignation against leading rebels is freely expressed.

The scene at the house where the President lies *in extremis* is very affecting. Even Secrétary Stanton is affected to tears.

When the news spread through the city that the President had been shot, the people, with pale faces and compressed lips, crowded every place where there was the slightest chance of obtaining information in regard to the affair.

After the President was shot, Lieutenant Rathbun, caught the assassin by the arm, who immediately struck him with a knife, and jumped from the box, as before stated.

The popular affection for Mr. Lincoln has been shown by this diabolical assassination, which will bring eternal infamy, not only upon its authors, but upon the hellish cause which they desire to avenge.

Vice President Johnson arrived at the White House, where the President lies, about one o'clock, and will remain with him to the last.

The President's family are in attendance upon him also.

As soon as intelligence could be got to the War Department, the electric telegraph and the Signal corps were put in requisition to endeavor to prevent the escape of the assassins, and all the troops around Washington are under arms.

Popular report points to a somewhat celebrated actor of known secession proclivities as the assassin; but it would be unjust to name him until some further evidence of his guilt is obtained. It is rumored that the person alluded to is in custody.

The latest advices from Secretary Seward reveals more desperate work there than at first supposed. Seward's wounds are not in themselves fatal; but, in connection with his recent injuries, and the great loss of blood he has sustained, his recovery is questionable.

It was Clarence A. Seward, instead of Wm. H. Seward, Jr., who was wounded. Fred. Seward was also badly cut, as were also three nurses, who were in attendance upon the Secretary, showing that a desperate struggle took place there. The wounds of the whole party were dressed.

ONE O'CLOCK A. M.

The President is perfectly senseless, and there is not the slightest hope of his surviving. Physicians believe that he will die before morning. All of his Cabinet, except Secretary Seward, are with him. Speaker Colfax, Senator Farwell, of Maine, and many other gentlemen, are also at the house awaiting the termination.

The scene at the President's bedside is described by one who witnessed it as most affecting. It was surrounded by his Cabinet ministers, all of whom were bathed in tears, not even excepting Mr. Stanton, who, when informed by Surgeon General Barnes, that the President could not live until morning, exclaimed, "Oh, no, General; no—no;" and with an impulse, natural as it was unaffected, immediately sat down on a chair near his bedside and wept like a child.

Senator Sumner was seated on the right of the President's couch, near the head, holding the right hand of the President in his own. He was sobbing like a woman, with his head bowed down almost on the pillow of the bed on which the President was lying.

TWO O'CLOCK A. M.

The President is still alive, but there is no improvement in his condition.

THE PRESS DESPATCHES.

WASHINGTON, April 15—12:30 A. M.

The President was shot in a theatre to-night, and is perhaps mortally wounded.

SECOND DESPATCH.

WASHINGTON, April 15—1 A. M.

The President is not expected to live through the night. He was shot at a theatre.

Secretary Seward was also assassinated. No arteries were cut.

Additional Details of the Assassination.

WASHINGTON, April 15—1:30 A. M.

President Lincoln and wife, with other friends, this evening visited Ford's theatre, for the purpose of witnessing the performance of the American Cousin.

It was announced in the papers that General Grant would also be present; but that gentleman took the late train of cars for New Jersey.

The theatre was densely crowded, and all seemed delighted with the scene before them. During the third act, and while there was a temporary pause for one of the actors to enter, a sharp report of a pistol was heard, which merely attracted attention, but suggested nothing serious, until a man rushed to the front of the President's box, waving a long dagger in his right hand, and exclaiming "*Sic semper tyrannis!*" and immediately leaped from the box, which was in the second tier, to the stage beneath, and ran across to the opposite side, making his escape, amid the bewilderment of the audience, from the rear of the theatre, and, mounting a horse, fled.

The screams of Mrs. Lincoln first disclosed the fact to the audience that the President had been shot, when all present rose to their feet, rushing towards the stage, many exclaiming "Hang him! Hang him!"

The excitement was of the wildest possible description, and of course there was an abrupt termination of the theatrical performance.

There was a rush toward the President's box, when cries were heard:—"Stand back and give him air." "Has any one stimulants?"

On a hasty examination it was found that the President had been shot through the head, above and back of the temporal bone, and that some of the brain was oozing out.

He was removed to a private house opposite to the theatre, and the Surgeon General of the army and other surgeons sent for to attend to his condition.

On an examination of the private box blood was discovered on the back of the cushioned rocking chair on which the President had been sitting, also on the partition and on the floor. A common single barreled pocket pistol was found on the carpet.

A military guard was placed in front of the private residence to which the President had been conveyed. An immense crowd was in front of it, all deeply anxious to learn the condition of the President. It had been previously announced that the wound was mortal, but all hoped otherwise. The shock to the community was terrible.

At midnight the Cabinet, with Messrs. Sumner, Colfax and Farnsworth, Judge Curtis, Governor Oglesby, General Meigs, Colonel Hay, and a few personal friends, with Surgeon General Barnes and his immediate assistants, were around his bedside.

The President was in a state of syncope, totally insensible, and breathing slowly. The blood oozed from the wound at the back of his head.

The surgeons exhausted every possible effort of medicinal skill; but all hope was gone.

The parting of his family with the dying President is too sad for description.

The President and Mrs. Lincoln did not start for the theatre until fifteen minutes after eight o'clock. Speaker Colfax was at the White House at the time, and the President stated to him that he was going. Mrs. Lincoln had not been well, because the papers had announced that General Grant and they were to be present, and, as General Grant had gone North, he did not wish the audience to be disappointed.

He went with apparent reluctance, and urged Mr. Colfax to go with him; but that gentleman had made other engagements, and, with Mr. Ashmun, of Massachusetts, bid him goodby.

When the excitement at the theatre was at its wildest height reports were circulated that Secretary Seward had also been assassinated.

On reaching this gentleman's residence a crowd and a military guard were found at the door, and on entering it was ascertained that the reports were based on truth.

Everybody there was so excited that scarcely an intelligible word could be gathered. But the facts are substantially as follows:—

About ten o'clock a man rang the bell, and the call having been answered by a colored servant, he said he had come from Dr. Verdi, Secretary Seward's family physician, with a prescription, at the same time holding in his hand a small piece of folded paper, and saying, in answer to a refusal, that he must see the Secretary, as he was entrusted with particular directions concerning the medicine.

He still insisted on going up, although repeatedly informed that no one could enter the chamber. The man pushed the servant aside, and walked hastily towards the Secretary's room, and was then met by Mr. Frederick Seward, of whom he demanded to see the Secretary, making the same representation which he did to the servant.

What further passed in the way of colloquy is not known; but the man struck him on the head with a billy, severely injuring the skull and felling him almost senseless.

The assassin then rushed into the chamber and attacked Major Seward, Paymaster United States Army, and Mr. Hansell, a messenger of the State Department, and two male nurses, disabling them all.

He then rushed upon the Secretary, who was lying in bed in the same room, and inflicted three stabs in the neck, but severing, it is thought and hoped, no arteries, though he bled profusely.

The assassin then rushed down stairs, mounted his horse at the door, and rode off before an alarm could be sounded, and in the same manner as the assassin of the President.

It is believed that the injuries of the Secretary are not fatal, nor those of either of the others, although both the Secretary and the Assistand Secretary are very seriously injured.

Secretaries Stanton and Welles, and other prominent officers of the Government, called at Secretary Seward's house to inquire into his condition, and there heard of the assassination of the President.

They then proceeded to the house where he was lying, exhibiting of course intense anxiety and solicitude.

An immense crowd was gathered in front of the President's house, and a strong guard was also stationed there. Many persons evidently supposing he would be brought to his home.

The entire city to-night presents a scene of wild excitement, accompanied by violent expression of indignation and the profoundest sorrow; many shed tears.

The military authorities have despatched mounted patrols in every direction, in order, if possible, to arrest the assassins. The whole metropolitan police are likewise vigilant for the same purpose.

The attacks, both at the theatre and at Secretary Seward's house, took place at about the same hour—ten o'clock—thus showing a preconcerted plan to assassinate those gentlemen. Some evidences of the guilt of the party who attacked the President are in the possession of the police.

Vice President Johnson is in the city, and his headquarters are guarded by troops.

THE STATE CAPITAL.

Rejection of the New York Fire Commissioners—Passage of the Central Railroad Fare Bill—Great Excitement Over the Health Bill, &c.

ALBANY, April 14—11:40 P. M.

Legislation each day is now so rapid here that a detail or analysis of its progress is out of the question. To-day the long pending Central Railroad bill passed the Senate, and is virtually a law if the Governor does not veto it. But the result may be foreshadowed in the veto sent in to-day of the Dry Dock and Battery Railroad.

The Health bill, which two days since was bound by caucus rules to have a sure passage, was to-night defeated by republican votes. The Collector of the port of New York, who has had an elaborate organization up for his retention in the office of Commissioner of Charities, was thrown overboard and the power of all his patronage disregarded in the strife to secure this position, which has been his pet desire and speciality for many years. All these occurrences have a political significancy which it would take too much time and space to develop. The excitement of the day has been the Health bill, and that excitement has been so incoherent as to be indescribable. The attempt made last night to kill off the bill was renewed to-day at an early hour. It has been lost for want of a sufficient vote, and laid on the table for reconsideration. A motion was made to call it up for a final vote, a short time after the reading of the journal, by its opponents. The tactics against the measure were led by Weed, of Clinton, in whose fresh abilities the democrats [illegible]. He gained their ablest accession in upon that the previous question. The vote of fifty-three to sixty-one disclosed the fact that the friends of the bill were in the minority, and a panic at once was created among them. An adroit suggestion was sent to the Speaker—understood—to be from Henry J. Raymond, who was on the floor—to rule that this vote did not carry the bill, and another must be taken, as for the third reading of the bill. Hereupon Mr. Van Buren, of New York, moved to adjourn, which the Speaker entertained amidst the greatest uproar, Weed and others insisting that such action was out of order.

While the vote was being taken a few more republicans were drummed up, and the motion carried by one or two votes. Hereupon the wildest scenes of confusion took place, all the members gathered in a crowd before the Speaker's desk in the most excited condition, shouting, disputing and threatening each other and the Speaker. One member from New York got upon a desk, and in the midst of a clamor for bets, offered at a thousand dollars, shouted and taunted the republicans, daring any man to bet. He shook his two fists with handsfull of greenbacks. Others clamored in like manner, and the scene resembled the most exciting days at the gold room in New York. In the midst of all this were heard the clapping of hands and the triumphant imitations of the mock chanticleer of the republicans, while the democrats uttered the most violent denunciations of the Speaker to his face for his rulings.

This scene was disposed of only to be reproduced for the evening session. Mr. Weed renewed his assaults upon the bill to bring it to a final vote, while its diminished friends sought to postpone this action. Messrs. Van Buren, Stuart, Reed, Brandreth, Wood and Parker sought alternately to postpone or to kill time by fillibustering, after prolonged, excited and most disorderly proceedings.

A final vote was forced upon the friends of the bill at a late hour. Sixty-one voted for the bill and fifty-one against it. Sixty-five votes being necessary to its passage, it was lost. Mr. Salmon, of New York, who had made himself obnoxious by the vehemency of his opposition to the bill, was sought to be involved in proceedings before the bar of the House; but the Speaker was evidently discouraged from any such attempts. The management for the bill on the floor of the House was understood to be in the hands of the radicals, under the lead of Fields. Boole was in the lobby in person. Mayor Gunther, Carr and others of his opponents were here yesterday to urge on the passage of the bill. It is alleged that the republican interest was sold out by the radicals.

The Fire Commissioners encountered a decided capsize in executive session. The defeat of the Health bill was pending on their consideration, and the Assembly had adjourned in the extraordinary manner of the morning. The names were at first confirmed, Senator Laimbier, who had made the chief opposition, moving the confirmation. This action was, however, reconsidered on motion of Senator Andrews, on the ground of the promises made in the Assembly to the democrats, who passed it, that the board would comprise two democrats. The names were accordingly sent back to the Governor.

The continuation of Boole in office by the defeat of the Health bill is accompanied by the passage of a resolution continuing the Senate investigating committee, to sit during the summer and examine the other departments. The feeling here is that Boole was treated as an invidious exception, and the thing will be made even all round.

The action determined on in caucus yesterday in regard to Draper and the Board of Charities, was desked by resolution to-day, and is coupled with the defeat of Rufus F. Andrews as candidate for United States District Attorney at New York, as a satisfactory manifestation of Thurlow Weed's power.

The passage of the Central Railroad Fare bill was conducted through the form of third reading with no excitement, and with the limit of seven per cent dividends. The increase of half a cent per mile for three years is thought only reasonable.

IMPORTANT FROM SOUTH AMERICA.

Surrender of Montevideo to Gen. Flores—Brazil in Possession of the City, &c.

The Brazilian mail arrived at Lisbon April 2, bringing the following advices:—

Montevideo has surrendered to General Flores.

The Brazilians now (March 11) occupy the city.

RIO JANEIRO, March 11, 1865.

Exchange 25⅝ a 26¼.

Coffee—Sales of good firsts at 65.66. Shipments, 100,000 bags. Stock, 100,000 bags. Freights, 50.62½.

BAHIA, March 11, 1865.

Exchange 26¼. Cotton nominal.

PERNAMBUCO, March 11, 1865.

Exchange 26½ a 27.

News from San Francisco.

SAN FRANCISCO, April 12, 1865.

The exports of treasure for the quarter just ended show a falling off of about six and a half millions as compared with the same period last year.

SAN FRANCISCO, April 14, 1865.

The Pacific mail steamship Sacramento sailed to-day, with a large number of passengers, for New York, and $1,153,000 in treasure, of which nearly $700,000 go to New York.

The steamship Moses Taylor sailed for San Juan del Sur, with numerous passengers.

The market continues variable and unsettled, and traders pursue a continuous policy. Prices of Eastern goods are slowly falling.

Sailed, ship Flying Eagle, for Boston.

New Orleans Markets.

NEW ORLEANS, April 8, Via CAIRO, April 14, 1865.

The New Orleans markets are at a stand still. Low middling cotton is quoted at 42c. per pound, and good superfine flour at $9 per barrel.

THE REBELS.

JEFF. DAVIS AT DANVILLE.

His Latest Appeal to His Deluded Followers.

He Thinks the Fall of Richmond a Blessing in Disguise, as it Leaves the Rebel Armies Free to Move from Point to Point.

He Vainly Promises to Hold Virginia at All Hazards.

Lee and His Army Supposed to be Safe.

Breckinridge and the Rest of Davis' Cabinet Reach Danville Safely.

The Organ of Governor Vance, of North Carolina, Advises the Submission of the Rebels to President Lincoln's Terms, &c., &c., &c.

Jeff. Davis' Last Proclamation.

VIRGINIA TO BE HELD BY THE REBELS AT ALL HAZARDS.

DANVILLE, Va., April 5, 1865.

The General-in-Chief found it necessary to make such movements of his troops as to uncover the capital. It would be unwise to conceal the *moral and material injury to our cause resulting from the occupation of our capital* by the enemy. It is equally unwise and unworthy of us to allow our own energies to falter and our efforts to become relaxed under adverses, however calamitous they may be. For many months *the largest and finest army* of the confederacy, under command of a leader whose presence inspires equal confidence in the troops and the people, has been greatly trammelled by the necessity of keeping constant watch over the approaches to the capital, and has thus been forced to forego more than one opportunity for promising enterprise. It is for us, my countrymen, to show by our bearing under reverses how wretched has been the self-deception of those who have believed us less able to endure misfortune with fortitude than to encounter dangers upon a new phase of the struggle. Relieved from the necessity of guarding particular points, *our army will be free to move from point to point* to strike the enemy in detail far from his base. *Let us but will it and we are free.*

Animated by that confidence in spirit and fortitude which never yet failed me, I announce to you, fellow countrymen, that it is my purpose to maintain your cause with my whole heart and soul; that I will never consent to abandon to the enemy one foot of the soil of any one of the States of the confederacy. That Virginia—noble State—whose ancient renown has been eclipsed by her still more glorious recent history; whose bosom has been bared to receive the main shock of this war; whose sons and daughters have exhibited heroism so sublime as to render her illustrious in all time to come—that Virginia, with the help of the people and by the blessing of Providence, *shall be held and defended*, and no peace ever be be made with the infamous invaders of her territory.

If by the stress of numbers we should ever be compelled to a temporary withdrawal from her limits, or those of any other border State, again and again will we return, until the baffled and exhausted enemy shall abandon in despair his endless and impossible task of making slaves of a people resolved to be free.

Let us, then, not despond, my countrymen; but, relying on God, meet the foe with fresh defiance and with unconquered and unconquerable hearts.

JEFFERSON DAVIS.

The Evacuation of the Rebel Capital.

THE FIRST REBEL ACCOUNT OF HOW THE CITY WAS ABANDONED.

[From the Danville (Va.) Register, April 5.]

Persons who left the capital Sunday night and Monday morning represent that the scene which followed the evacuation of the city by our troops beggars description. To preserve order and protect the property of the citizens who unavoidably remained there, as far as could be done, the Nineteenth Virginia militia, under Colonel Evans, was placed on police duty in the city, to await the coming of the enemy; but accounts state that they failed to render any aid or protection to the people whatever. On Sunday night a mob of the lower classes of the city, composed, it is said, mostly of the foreign element, visited a number of the largest storehouses of the city and robbed them of their contents. It is affirmed that Main street was pillaged, and then burned, and that some of the milling establishments were also committed to the flames. We have no doubt that a considerable portion of that brave city has been laid in ashes, and a number of its people insulted, outraged, robbed and massacred. How painful the thought that the place should be given over to rapine and plunder, even before the public enemy entered its limits. But the fact only proves that the people of Richmond have had secret enemies in their own midst scarcely less savage and even more treacherous and vindictive than the open foe.

We are told that the people banded together during the violent proceeding of the mob and resisted them with force, a street fight ensuing, in which several persons were killed.

No intelligence has reached us of the enemy's troops occupying the city. The last trains on the Danville railroad which came out of the place left Monday morning, and passengers upon them had heard nothing from the enemy. The greater portion of Grant's army was transferred to the south side of James river some days ago, only the command of General Ord, which is composed mostly, if not entirely, of negro troops, being left on the north side. This command will enter and occupy the city. Some of our people who are acquainted with the character of General Ord think they have reason to hope that his treatment of the unfortunate people of Richmond will not be so hard, and cruel and inhuman as that which has fallen upon the heads of our fellow citizens in some other captured cities.

The newspapers of Richmond, we suppose, all fell into the hands of the enemy. The evacuation of the city was so sudden and unexpected—scarcely any one being prepared for it—that no time was left for the removal of so cumbrous an establishment as a city newspaper office. In a few days we may expect to hear that the *Enquirer* or the *Whig* or the *Examiner* is issued as a Yankee paper.

All the rolling stock of the Richmond and Danville Railroad in running order was saved on the retreat from Richmond. A few old cars, not in a movable condition, were left at Manchester. No train was captured by the enemy near the junction, as was at one time reported; and, indeed, we do not believe that any body of Yankees had struck the road at any point up to yesterday evening.

The Secretary of War, the Quartermaster General, Commissary General and a number of other officers of the government, left Richmond on horseback, and will probably arrive at this place to-morrow.

Should General Lee establish his lines east of the junction, we suppose the State Legislature will be convened at Lynchburg.

All the specie and other valuables belonging to the banks in Richmond were removed from the city on Sunday, and have been carried to places of safety.

A considerable amount of goods purchased by the State for distribution to the people, we regret to learn, had to be left behind. Also the State archives remained in the city; but we perceive no motive the enemy can have in destroying them, as they will, no doubt, endeavor to occupy the city permanently, and establish a State government at Richmond under the federal Union.

Lee's Army Supposed to be in a Safe Position.

[From the Raleigh Confederate, April 7.]

This is the time for rumor manufacturers who are engaged in a wholesale business. Sometimes they have it that whole brigades deserted in the last great battle; among others, Cook's brigade is selected as the bearer of this stigma. We are assured that such a statement has no foundation whatever; that no treachery induced the disaster at Petersburg; that our forces fought splendidly, and the enemy only succeeded by overwhelming numbers. We are convinced, too, from facts which we cannot mention, that *Lee's army is in a safe position*, and that *his future movements will be directed with the skill and energy which distinguish this great captain.*

Having anticipated the probable loss of Richmond, and fully recognizing the importance of the disaster, we are, nevertheless, not of the number of those who give up the cause. In the Southern confederacy this day there is military strength of men, material and supplies to make independence certain. It is with the *people themselves* whether they secure or lose their liberties.

Rebel Particulars of the Battle at Petersburg.

[From the Raleigh Confederate, April 7.]

An officer who left Richmond at nine o'clock on Monday morning last informs us that at the time he left the city was in flames from Cary to Canal streets. The Shockoe warehouse and other entrepots of supplies were burning. The bridges also had been fired.

No mob or violence of any kind had occurred up to the period when he left, so that the reports of a destructive mob on Sunday night are untrue. The enemy's cavalry entered the city as the train moved off that he came out in. The story of the mob, therefore, we hope, is entirely erroneous.

This officer describes the fighting on Saturday as terrific beyond description. The enemy forced column after column on our works, lapping our lines on the extreme right. They came nine columns deep. Eight lines faltered and were broken by the obstinacy of our defences; but the ninth broke over our forces like a whirlwind. He says the destruction of the enemy was immense. Our loss, we think, consisted mainly in the prisoners taken by the enemy. All the prisoners whom we captured were drunk, having been prepared according to Yankee tactics for this dreadful ordeal. Lieutenant General A. P. Hill was certainly killed. General Fitz. Lee was not killed, as reported, nor General W. H. F. Lee. No general officer from North Carolina was killed, as far as he heard. On Monday Sheridan attacked Fitz. Lee and was handsomely repulsed.

The Organ of Governor Vance, of North Carolina, Advising General Lee to Submit on Mr. Lincoln's Terms.

[From the Raleigh Confederate, April 7.]

The *Conservative* occasionally seems to fall into very mysterious hands, and to come under the control of an incomprehensible influence. On the day before yesterday that paper availed itself of a period of extreme reverse and disaster to renew the attempt to cast odium on a portion of our own citizens which ever since the reverses began, and after it was no longer politic to claim that they "made the revolution." Yesterday it sends to the public a leader of still more extraordinary import. From what we comprehend of it, it seems to be *a distinct proposition to submit and surrender upon the terms proposed by Lincoln.* This has never yet, that we recollect of, been more distinctly proposed, even by journals whose loyalty has been called in question. The *Conservative* says:—"It is nonsense to propose to treat with the North with any expectation of the concession that the confederacy is a government," and hence, says the *Conservative*, "if our authorities are determined to force this condition upon the North, as a basis of negotiation, then the North will never negotiate." What is this but surrender? Not only surrender, but an assertion to the world that the defence of the last four years has been of a position which is one of sheer nonsense—one which the North "never could admit!" We have not seen in this controversy so bold and unconditional a justification of the Northern invasion; for, if we sought to force a claim inconsistent with reason, and to demand an "admission" which "is an absurdity in anything like government," and the North only resisted such claim and refused such admission, then we are in the wrong and the Yankee government is right, and the writer of the article to which we are replying does well when he *advises General Lee not to* "*block up his way, at the threshold, by presenting a basis to which he knows the enemy will not yield,*" but "to meet him on his own ground," as "the only way to open the negotiation." When we remember what "his own ground" is, upon which the *Conservative* proposes to meet the enemy, we may readily understand how much it is prepared to concede. "His own ground" measured the length of three propositions; submission to the laws and constitution of the United States, the laying down of our arms, and acquiescence in Lincoln's proclamations. This is the ground on which the author of the editorial desires General Lee to meet Lincoln and "secure a talk about peace." We have no idea that Governor Vance will support this idea; but it is very unfortunate that now, in the very moment when everything should be said to uphold the hopes and confidence of the army and people, such sentiments should obtain publication in the organ of the Governor.

High Prices in an Overstocked Market.

[From the Raleigh Confederate, April 7.]

Our market, on the arrival of the Weldon train, on yesterday, *became overstocked* with shad; *they went off slowly at $50 per pair.*

Exchange of the Rebel General Vance.

[From the Ashville (N. C.) News.]

The exchange of prisoners seems to go steadily on. We have seen a large number of our mountain boys, who have reached home after a protracted imprisonment. Among others we were gratified to meet Brigadier General R. B. Vance, who reached home some days since. He looks rather worsted by his long confinement, but, as usual with him, is full of life, cheerful and buoyant. The General is a great favorite of the people of this section, and everybody was glad to see him.

City Intelligence.

EASTER SUNDAY AT ST. ANN'S CHURCH.—The admirers of sacred music, made truly effective by a well trained choir, have an opportunity of indulging their taste by repairing to St. Ann's church on Easter Sunday evening, the doors opening at seven, the concert begining at eight. Three of the pieces are from Gordigiani, three from Rossini and one from each of the composers Verdi, Donizetti, Verrimst, Dachauer and Gounod. We need only mention the names of Signor Remi and Messrs. Schmitz, Schubert and Dachauer to insure confidence in the vocal results. The ladies are quite distinguished for contralto and soprano execution, and no exertion will be spared to make the musical feast worthy of the day.

A NEW CHURCH.—An advertisement among our religious notices announces the opening of the new Church of the Holy Trinity, Madison avenue, corner of Forty-second street, on Sunday. Sermons will be preached at the three sessions by Rev. Dr. Tyng, of St. George's; Rev. Dr. Dyer, and the Rev. Stephen H. Tyng, Jr., the pastor of the church. It promises to be an occasion of great interest to residents on Murray Hill.

CROTON AQUEDUCT CONTRACTS.—The following contracts have been issued by this department:—Laying crosswalks from southeast corner of Fifty-ninth street and Broadway to the junction of Broadway and Eighth avenue, Matthew Murray, $625. Cobble stone pavement in Hammond street, west of Thirteenth avenue, Christy Dowd, $1,896 80. Sewer in Forty-third street, from Lexington avenue to Fourth avenue, John Duffy, Jr., $1,913 50. Sewer in Forty-sixth street, from Eleventh avenue to seventy-five feet west of Tenth avenue, John Rourke, $5,223 50. Fifty-second street, sewer from Sixth to Seventh avenues, Joseph Moore, $4,880. Sewer in 125th street, from Fifth avenue through Manhattan street to Tenth avenue, James Cunningham, $22,941 35.

MISS EMMA HARDINGE delivers her able lecture on "Politics in the Pulpit" this evening, at Dodworth Hall. To test the lady's ability, any questions the audience desire to ask will be answered.

MAN DROWNED.—On the morning of the 13th instant a journeyman housepainter, whose name is believed to be Barnard Burns, was accidentally drowned at Guntherville, Long Island. His body has not yet been claimed by his friends. Mr. J. B. Acker, of No. 9 Macdougal street, will give facilities to any one who can identify the corpse.

THE NEW YORK HERALD.

WHOLE NO. 10,456. NEW YORK, SATURDAY, APRIL 15, 1865. PRICE FOUR CENTS.

IMPORTANT.

ASSASSINATION OF PRESIDENT LINCOLN.

The President Shot at the Theatre Last Evening.

SECRETARY SEWARD DAGGERED IN HIS BED, BUT NOT MORTALLY WOUNDED.

Clarence and Frederick Seward Badly Hurt.

ESCAPE OF THE ASSASSINS.

Intense Excitement in Washington.

Scene at the Deathbed of Mr. Lincoln.

J. Wilkes Booth, the Actor, the Alleged Assassin of the President, &c., &c., &c.

THE OFFICIAL DESPATCH.

WAR DEPARTMENT, WASHINGTON, April 15—1:30 A. M.

Major General DIX, New York:—

This evening at about 9:30 P. M., at Ford's Theatre, the President, while sitting in his private box with Mrs. Lincoln, Mrs. Harris and Major Rathburn, was shot by an assassin, who suddenly entered the box and approached behind the President.

The assassin then leaped upon the stage, brandishing a large dagger or knife, and made his escape in the rear of the theatre.

The pistol ball entered the back of the President's head and penetrated nearly through the head. The wound is mortal.

The President has been insensible ever since it was inflicted, and is now dying.

About the same hour an assassin, whether the same or not, entered Mr. Seward's apartments, and under pretence of having a prescription was shown to the Secretary's sick chamber. The assassin immediately rushed to the bed and inflicted two or three stabs on the throat and two on the face.

It is hoped the wounds may not be mortal. My apprehension is that they will prove fatal.

The nurse alarmed Mr. Frederick Seward, who was in an adjoining room, and he hastened to the door of his father's room, when he met the assassin, who inflicted upon him one or more dangerous wounds. The recovery of Frederick Seward is doubtful.

It is not probable that the President will live through the night.

General Grant and wife were advertised to be at the theatre this evening, but he started to Burlington at six o'clock this evening.

At a Cabinet meeting, at which General Grant was present, the subject of the state of the country and the prospect of a speedy peace were discussed. The President was very cheerful and hopeful, and spoke very kindly of General Lee and others of the confederacy, and of the establishment of government in Virginia.

All the members of the Cabinet except Mr. Seward, are now in attendance upon the President.

I have seen Mr. Seward, but he and Frederick were both unconscious.

EDWIN M. STANTON,
Secretary of War.

THE HERALD DESPATCHES.

WASHINGTON, April 14, 1865.

Assassination has been inaugurated in Washington. The bowie knife and pistol have been applied to President Lincoln and Secretary Seward. The former was shot in the throat, while at Ford's theatre to-night. Mr. Seward was badly cut about the neck, while in his bed at his residence.

SECOND DESPATCH.

WASHINGTON, April 14, 1865.

An attempt was made about ten o'clock this evening to assassinate the President and Secretary Seward. The President was shot at Ford's Theatre. Result not yet known. Mr. Seward's throat was cut, and his son badly wounded.

There is intense excitement here.

Details of the Assassination.

WASHINGTON, April 14, 1865.

Washington was thrown into an intense excitement a few minutes before eleven o'clock this evening, by the announcement that the President and Secretary Seward had been assassinated and were dead.

The wildest excitement prevailed in all parts of the city. Men, women and children, old and young, rushed to and fro, and the rumors were magnified until we had nearly every member of the Cabinet killed. Some time elapsed before authentic data could be ascertained in regard to the affair.

About half-past ten o'clock this evening a tall, well dressed man made his appearance at Secretary Seward's residence, and applied for admission. He was refused admission by the servant, when the desperado stated that he had a prescription from the Surgeon General, and that he was ordered to deliver it in person. He was still refused, except upon the written order of the physician. This he pretended to show, and pushed by the servant and rushed up stairs to Mr. Seward's room. He was met at the door by Mr. Fred Seward, who notified him that he was master of the house, and would take charge of the medicine. After a few words had passed between them he dodged by Fred Seward and rushed to the Secretary's bed, and struck him in the neck with a dagger, and also in the breast.

It was supposed at first that Mr. Seward was killed instantly, but it was found afterwards that the wound was not mortal.

Major Wm. H. Seward, Jr., paymaster, was in the room, and rushed to the defence of his father, and was badly cut in the *melé* with the assassin, but not fatally.

The desperado managed to escape from the house, and was prepared for escape by having a horse at the door. He immediately mounted his horse, and sung out the motto of the State of Virginia, "*Sic Semper Tyrannis!*" and rode off.

Surgeon General Barnes was immediately sent for, and he *examined Mr. Seward and pronounced him safe*. His wounds were not fatal. The jugular vein was not cut, nor the wound in the breast deep enough to be fatal.

The President and Mrs. Lincoln were at Ford's theatre, listening to the performance of the American Cousin, occupying a box in the second tier. At the close of the third act a person entered the box occupied by the President, and shot Mr. Lincoln in the head. The shot entered the back of his head, and came out above the temple.

The assassin then jumped from the box upon the stage and ran across to the other side, exhibiting a dagger in his hand, flourishing it in a tragical manner, shouting the same words repeated by the desperado at Mr. Seward's house, adding to it, "The South is avenged," and then escaped from the back entrance to the stage, but in his passage dropped his pistol and his hat.

Mr. Lincoln fell forward from his seat, and Mrs. Lincoln fainted.

The moment the astonished audience could realize what had happened, the President was taken and carried to Mr. Petersen's house, in Tenth street, opposite to the theatre. Medical aid was immediately sent for, and the wound was at first supposed to be fatal, and it was announced that he could not live; but at half-past twelve he is still alive, though in a precarious condition.

As the assassin ran across the stage, Colonel J. B. Stewart, of this city, who was occupying one of the front seats in the orchestra, on the same side of the house as the box occupied by Mr. Lincoln, sprang to the stage and followed him; but he was obstructed in his passage across the stage by the fright of the actors, and reached the back door about three seconds after the assassin had passed out. Colonel Stewart got to the street just in time to see him mount his horse and ride away.

This operation shows that the whole thing was a preconcerted plan. The person who fired the pistol was a man about thirty years of age, about five feet nine, spare built, fair skin, dark hair, apparently bushy, with a large mustache. Laura Keene and the leader of the orchestra declare that they recognized him as J. Wilkes Booth the actor, and a rabid secessionist. Whoever he was, it is plainly evident that he thoroughly understood the theatre and all the approaches and modes of escape to the stage. A person not familiar with the theatre could not have possibly made his escape so well and quickly.

The alarm was sounded in every quarter. Mr. Stanton was notified, and immediately left his house.

All the other members of the Cabinet escaped attack.

Cavalrymen were sent out in all directions, and dispatches sent to all the fortifications, and it is thought they will be captured.

WASHINGTON, April 15—1 A. M.

The streets in the vicinity of Ford's Theatre are densely crowded by an anxious and excited crowd. A guard has been placed across Tenth street and F and E streets, and only official persons and particular friends of the President are allowed to pass.

The popular heart is deeply stirred, and the deepest indignation against leading rebels is freely expressed.

The scene at the house where the President lies *in extremis* is very affecting. Even Secretary Stanton is affected to tears.

When the news spread through the city that the President had been shot, the people, with pale faces and compressed lips, crowded every place where there was the slightest chance of obtaining information in regard to the affair.

After the President was shot, Lieutenant Rathbun, caught the assassin by the arm, who immediately struck him with a knife, and jumped from the box, as before stated.

The popular affection for Mr. Lincoln has been shown by this diabolical assassination, which will bring eternal infamy, not only upon its authors, but upon the hellish cause which they desire to avenge.

Vice President Johnson arrived at the White House, where the President lies, about one o'clock, and will remain with him to the last.

The President's family are in attendance upon him also.

As soon as intelligence could be got to the War Department, the electric telegraph and the Signal corps were put in requisition to endeavor to prevent the escape of the assassins, and all the troops around Washington are under arms.

Popular report points to a somewhat celebrated actor of known secession proclivities as the assassin; but it would be unjust to name him until some further evidence of his guilt is obtained. It is rumored that the person alluded to is in custody.

The latest advices from Secretary Seward reveals more desperate work there than at first supposed. Seward's wounds are not in themselves fatal; but, in connection with his recent injuries, and the great loss of blood he has sustained, his recovery is questionable.

It was Clarence A. Seward, instead of Wm. H. Seward, Jr., who was wounded. Fred. Seward was also badly cut, as were also three nurses, who were in attendance upon the Secretary, showing that a desperate struggle took place there. The wounds of the whole party were dressed.

ONE O'CLOCK A. M.

The President is perfectly senseless, and there is not the slightest hope of his surviving. Physicians believe that he will die before morning. All of his Cabinet, except Secretary Seward, are with him. Speaker Colfax, Senator Farwell, of Maine, and many other gentlemen, are also at the house awaiting the termination.

The scene at the President's bedside is described by one who witnessed it as most affecting. It was surrounded by his Cabinet ministers, all of whom were bathed in tears, not even excepting Mr. Stanton, who, when informed by Surgeon General Barnes, that the President could not live until morning, exclaimed, "Oh, no, General; no—no;" and with an impulse, natural as it was unaffected, immediately sat down on a chair near his bedside and wept like a child.

Senator Sumner was seated on the right of the President's couch, near the head, holding the right hand of the President in his own. He was sobbing like a woman, with his head bowed down almost on the pillow of the bed on which the President was lying.

TWO O'CLOCK A. M.

The President is still alive, but there is no improvement in his condition.

THE PRESS DESPATCHES.

WASHINGTON, April 15—12:30 A. M.

The President was shot in a theatre to-night, and is perhaps mortally wounded.

SECOND DESPATCH.

WASHINGTON, April 15—1 A. M.

The President is not expected to live through the night. He was shot at a theatre.

Secretary Seward was also assassinated. No arteries were cut.

Additional Details of the Assassination.

WASHINGTON, April 15—1:30 A. M.

President Lincoln and wife, with other friends, this evening visited Ford's theatre, for the purpose of witnessing the performance of the American Cousin.

It was announced in the papers that General Grant would also be present; but that gentleman took the late train of cars for New Jersey.

The theatre was densely crowded, and all seemed delighted with the scene before them. During the third act, and while there was a temporary pause for one of the actors to enter, a sharp report of a pistol was heard, which merely attracted attention, but suggested nothing serious, until a man rushed to the front of the President's box, waving a long dagger in his right hand, and exclaiming "*Sic semper tyrannis!*" and immediately leaped from the box, which was in the second tier, to the stage beneath, and ran across to the opposite side, making his escape, amid the bewilderment of the audience, from the rear of the theatre, and, mounting a horse, fled.

The screams of Mrs. Lincoln first disclosed the fact to the audience that the President had been shot, when all present rose to their feet, rushing towards the stage, many exclaiming "Hang him! Hang him!"

The excitement was of the wildest possible description, and of course there was an abrupt termination of the theatrical performance.

There was a rush toward the President's box, when cries were heard:—"Stand back and give him air." "Has any one stimulants?"

On a hasty examination it was found that the President had been shot through the head, above and back of the temporal bone, and that some of the brain was oozing out.

He was removed to a private house opposite to the theatre, and the Surgeon General of the army and other surgeons sent for to attend to his condition.

On an examination of the private box blood was discovered on the back of the cushioned rocking chair on which the President had been sitting, also on the partition and on the floor. A common single barreled pocket pistol was found on the carpet.

A military guard was placed in front of the private residence to which the President had been conveyed. An immense crowd was in front of it, all deeply anxious to learn the condition of the President. It had been previously announced that the wound was mortal, but all hoped otherwise. The shock to the community was terrible.

At midnight the Cabinet, with Messrs. Sumner, Colfax and Farnsworth, Judge Curtis, Governor Oglesby, General Meigs, Colonel Hay, and a few personal friends, with Surgeon General Barnes and his immediate assistants, were around his bedside.

The President was in a state of syncope, totally insensible, and breathing slowly. The blood oozed from the wound at the back of his head.

The surgeons exhausted every possible effort of medicinal skill; but all hope was gone.

The parting of his family with the dying President is too sad for description.

The President and Mrs. Lincoln did not start for the theatre until fifteen minutes after eight o'clock. Speaker Colfax was at the White House at the time, and the President stated to him that he was going. Mrs. Lincoln had not been well, because the papers had announced that General Grant and they were to be present, and, as General Grant had gone North, he did not wish the audience to be disappointed.

He went with apparent reluctance, and urged Mr. Colfax to go with him; but that gentleman had made other engagements, and, with Mr. Ashmun, of Massachusetts, bid him goodby.

When the excitement at the theatre was at its wildest height reports were circulated that Secretary Seward had also been assassinated.

On reaching this gentleman's residence a crowd and a military guard were found at the door, and on entering it was ascertained that the reports were based on truth.

Everybody there was so excited that scarcely an intelligible word could be gathered. But the facts are substantially as follows:—

About ten o'clock a man rang the bell, and the call having been answered by a colored servant, he said he had come from Dr. Verdi, Secretary Seward's family physician, with a prescription, at the same time holding in his hand a small piece of folded paper, and saying, in answer to a refusal, that he must see the Secretary, as he was entrusted with particular directions concerning the medicine.

He still insisted on going up, although repeatedly informed that no one could enter the chamber. The man pushed the servant aside, and walked hastily towards the Secretary's room, and was then met by Mr. Frederick Seward, of whom he demanded to see the Secretary, making the same representation which he did to the servant.

What further passed in the way of colloquy is not known; but the man struck him on the head with a billy, severely injuring the skull and felling him almost senseless.

The assassin then rushed into the chamber and attacked Major Seward, Paymaster United States Army, and Mr. Hansell, a messenger of the State Department, and two male nurses, disabling them all.

He then rushed upon the Secretary, who was lying in bed in the same room, and inflicted three stabs in the neck, but severing, it is thought and hoped, no arteries, though he bled profusely.

The assassin then rushed down stairs, mounted his horse at the door, and rode off before an alarm could be sounded, and in the same manner as the assassin of the President.

It is believed that the injuries of the Secretary are not fatal, nor those of either of the others, although both the Secretary and the Assistand Secretary are very seriously injured.

Secretaries Stanton and Welles, and other prominent officers of the Government, called at Secretary Seward's house to inquire into his condition, and there heard of the assassination of the President.

They then proceeded to the house where he was lying, exhibiting of course intense anxiety and solicitude.

An immense crowd was gathered in front of the President's house, and a strong guard was also stationed there. Many persons evidently supposing he would be brought to his home.

The entire city to-night presents a scene of wild excitement, accompanied by violent expression of indignation and the profoundest sorrow; many shed tears.

The military authorities have despatched mounted patrols in every direction, in order, if possible, to arrest the assassins. The whole metropolitan police are likewise vigilant for the same purpose.

The attacks, both at the theatre and at Secretary Seward's house, took place at about the same hour—ten o'clock—thus showing a preconcerted plan to assassinate those gentlemen. Some evidences of the guilt of the party who attacked the President are in the possession of the police.

Vice President Johnson is in the city, and his headquarters are guarded by troops.

THE LATEST NEWS.

Secretary Stanton to General Dix.

WAR DEPARTMENT, WASHINGTON, April 15—3 A. M.

Major General DIX, New York:—

The President still breathes, but is quite insensible, as he has been ever since he was shot. He evidently did not see the person who shot him, but was looking on the stage, as he was approached from behind.

Mr. Seward has rallied, and it is hoped he may live.

Frederick Seward's condition is very critical.

The attendant who was present was shot through the lungs, and is not expected to live.

The wounds of Major Seward are not serious.

Investigation strongly indicates J. Wilkes Booth as the assassin of the President. Whether it was the same or a different person that attempted to murder Mr. Seward remains in doubt.

Chief Justice Cariter is engaged in taking the evidence.

Every exertion has been made to prevent the escape of the murderer. His horse has been found on the road near Washington.

EDWIN M. STANTON, Secretary of War.

Our Special Washington Despatch.

WASHINGTON, April 15, 1865.

When the fatal shot was fired, Mrs. Lincoln, who was alongside of her husband, exclaimed, "Oh! why didn't they shoot me—why didn't they shoot me?"

There is evidence that Secretary Stanton was also marked for assassination. On receipt of intelligence at the War Department of the attack on the President, two employes of the department were sent to summon the Secretary. Just as they approached his house, a man jumped out from behind a tree box in front of the house and ran away. It is well known to be the custom of the Secretary to go from the department to his house between nine and twelve P. M., and usually unattended. It is supposed that the assassin intended to shoot him as he entered the house, but failed from the fact that Mr. Stanton remained at home during the evening.

The circumstantial evidence is very strong that J. Wilkes Booth is the person who shot the President. Several parties who are well acquainted with him, and saw the assassin when he jumped from the box, are positive that he is the man. It is also reported that Booth's horse was saddled at the side door of the theatre, and was rode off by the assassin. If he is the man, it is impossible for him to escape. The horse of the man who made the attack on Secretary Seward has been found near the Lincoln Hospital, bathed in sweat, and with blood upon the saddle cloths.

THREE O'CLOCK A. M.

There is up to this time no material change in the President's condition.

The Press Despatch.

WASHINGTON, April 15—[illegible]

The President is still alive, but he is growing weaker. The ball is lodged in his brain, three inches from where it entered the skull. He remains insensible, and his condition is utterly helpless.

The Vice President has been to see him; but all company except the members of the Cabinet and of the family is rigidly excluded.

Large crowds still continue in the street, as near the house as the line of guards allow.

IMPORTANT FROM SOUTH AMERICA.

Surrender of Montevideo to Gen. Flores—Brazil in Possession of the City, &c.

The Brazilian mail arrived at Lisbon April 2, bringing the following advices:—

Montevideo has surrendered to General Flores.

The Brazilians now (March 11) occupy the city.

RIO JANEIRO, March 11, 1865.

Exchange 25⅝ a 26¼.

Coffee—Sales of good firsts at 65.66. Shipments, 100,000 bags. Stock, 100,000 bags. Freights, 50.62½.

BAHIA, March 11, 1865.

Exchange 26¼. Cotton nominal.

News from San Francisco.

SAN FRANCISCO, April 12, 1865.

The exports of treasure for the quarter just ended show a falling off of about six and a half millions as compared with the same period last year.

City Intelligence.

EASTER SUNDAY AT ST. ANN'S CHURCH.—The admirers of sacred music, made truly effective by a well trained choir, have an opportunity of indulging their taste by repairing to St. Ann's church on Easter Sunday evening, the doors opening at seven, the concert begining at eight. Three of the pieces are from Gordigiani, three from Rossini and one from each of the composers Verdi, Donizetti, Verrimst, Dachauer and Gounod. We need only mention the names of Signor Remi and Messrs. Schmitz, Schubert and Dachauer to insure confidence in the vocal results. The ladies are quite distinguished for contralto and soprano execution, and no exertion will be spared to make the musical feast worthy of the day.

A NEW CHURCH.—An advertisement among our religious notices announces the opening of the new Church of the Holy Trinity, Madison avenue, corner of Forty-second street, on Sunday. Sermons will be preached at the three sessions by Rev. Dr. Tyng, of St. George's; Rev. Dr. Dyer, and the Rev. Stephen H. Tyng, Jr., the pastor of the church. It promises to be an occasion of great interest to residents on Murray Hill.

MISS EMMA HARDINGE delivers her able lecture on "Politics in the Pulpit" this evening, at Dodworth Hall. To test the lady's ability, any questions the audience desire to ask will be answered.

MAN DROWNED.—On the morning of the 13th instant a journeyman housepainter, whose name is believed to be Barnard Burns, was accidentally drowned at Guntherville, Long Island. His body has not yet been claimed by his friends. Mr. J. B. Acker, of No. 9 Macdougal street, will give facilities to any one who can identify the corpse.

THE REBELS.

JEFF. DAVIS AT DANVILLE.

His Latest Appeal to His Deluded Followers.

He Thinks the Fall of Richmond a Blessing in Disguise, as it Leaves the Rebel Armies Free to Move from Point to Point.

He Vainly Promises to Hold Virginia at All Hazards.

Lee and His Army Supposed to be Safe.

Breckinridge and the Rest of Davis' Cabinet Reach Danville Safely.

The Organ of Governor Vance, of North Carolina, Advises the Submission of the Rebels to President Lincoln's Terms, &c., &c., &c.

Jeff. Davis' Last Proclamation.

VIRGINIA TO BE HELD BY THE REBELS AT ALL HAZARDS.

DANVILLE, Va., April 5, 1865.

The General-in-Chief found it necessary to make such movements of his troops as to uncover the capital. It would be unwise to conceal the *moral and material injury to our cause resulting from the occupation of our capital* by the enemy. It is equally unwise and unworthy of us to allow our own energies to falter and our efforts to become relaxed under adverses, however calamitous they may be. For many months *the largest and finest army* of the confederacy, under command of a leader whose presence inspires equal confidence in the troops and the people, has been greatly trammelled by the necessity of keeping constant watch over the approaches to the capital, and has thus been forced to forego more than one opportunity for promising enterprise. It is for us, my countrymen, to show by our bearing under reverses how wretched has been the self-deception of those who have believed us less able to endure misfortune with fortitude than to encounter dangers with courage.

We have now entered upon a new phase of the struggle. Relieved from the necessity of guarding particular points, *our army will be free to move from point to point* to strike the enemy in detail far from his base. *Let us but will it and we are free.*

Animated by that confidence in spirit and fortitude which never yet failed me, I announce to you, fellow countrymen, that it is my purpose to maintain your cause with my whole heart and soul; that I will never consent to abandon to the enemy one foot of the soil of any one of the States of the confederacy. That Virginia—noble State—whose ancient renown has been eclipsed by her still more glorious recent history; whose bosom has been bared to receive the main shock of this war; whose sons and daughters have exhibited heroism so sublime as to render her illustrious in all time to come—that Virginia, with the help of the people and by the blessing of Providence, *shall be held and defended*, and no peace ever be be made with the infamous invaders of her territory.

If by the stress of numbers we should ever be compelled to a temporary withdrawal from her limits, or those of any other border State, again and again will we return, until the baffled and exhausted enemy shall abandon in despair his endless and impossible task of making slaves of a people resolved to be free.

Let us, then, not despond, my countrymen; but, relying on God, meet the foe with fresh defiance and with unconquered and unconquerable hearts.

JEFFERSON DAVIS.

The Evacution of the Rebel Capital.

THE FIRST REBEL ACCOUNT OF HOW THE CITY WAS ABANDONED.

[From the Danville (Va.) Register, April 5.]

Persons who left the capital Sunday night and Monday morning represent that the scene which followed the evacuation of the city by our troops beggars description. To preserve order and protect the property of the citizens who unavoidably remained there, as far as could be done, the Nineteenth Virginia militia, under Colonel Evans, was placed on police duty in the city, to await the coming of the enemy; but accounts state that they failed to render any aid or protection to the people whatever. On Sunday night a mob of the lower classes of the city, composed, it is said, mostly of the foreign element, visited a number of the largest storehouses of the city and robbed them of their contents. It is affirmed that Main street was pillaged, and then burned, and that some of the milling establishments were also committed to the flames. We have no doubt that a considerable portion of that brave city has been laid in ashes, and a number of its people insulted, outraged, robbed and massacred. How painful the thought that the place should be given over to rapine and plunder, even before the public enemy entered its limits. But the fact only proves that the people of Richmond have had secret enemies in their own midst scarcely less savage and even more treacherous and vindictive than the open foe.

We are told that the people banded together during the violent proceeding of the mob and resisted them with force, a street fight ensuing, in which several persons were killed.

No intelligence has reached us of the enemy's troops occupying the city. The last trains on the Danville railroad which came out of the place left Monday morning, and passengers upon them had heard nothing from the enemy. The greater portion of Grant's army was transferred to the south side of James river some days ago, only the command of General Ord, which is composed mostly, if not entirely, of negro troops, being left on the north side. This command will enter and occupy the city. Some of our people who are acquainted with the character of General Ord think they have reason to hope that his treatment of the unfortunate people of Richmond will not be so hard, and cruel and inhuman as that which has fallen upon the heads of our fellow citizens in some other captured cities.

The newspapers of Richmond, we suppose, all fell into the hands of the enemy. The evacuation of the city was so sudden and unexpected—scarcely any one being prepared for it—that no time was left for the removal of so cumbrous an establishment as a city newspaper office. In a few days we may expect to hear that the *Enquirer* or the *Whig* or the *Examiner* is issued as a Yankee paper.

All the rolling stock of the Richmond and Danville Railroad in running order was saved on the retreat from Richmond. A few old cars, not in a movable condition, were left at Manchester. No train was captured by the enemy near the junction, as was at one time reported; and, indeed, we do not believe that any body of Yankees had struck the road at any point up to yesterday evening.

The Secretary of War, the Quartermaster General, Commissary General and a number of other officers of the government, left Richmond on horseback, and will probably arrive at this place to-morrow.

Should General Lee establish his lines east of the junction, we suppose the State Legislature will be convened at Lynchburg.

All the specie and other valuables belonging to the banks in Richmond were removed from the city on Sunday, and have been carried to places of safety.

A considerable amount of goods purchased by the State for distribution to the people, we regret to learn, had to be left behind. Also the State archives remained in the city; but we perceive no motive the enemy can have in destroying them, as they will, no doubt, endeavor to occupy the city permanently, and establish a State government at Richmond under the federal Union.

Lee's Army Supposed to be in a Safe Position.

[From the Raleigh Confederate, April 7.]

This is the time for rumor manufacturers who are engaged in a wholesale business. Sometimes they have it that whole brigades deserted in the last great battle; among others, Cook's brigade is selected as the bearer of this stigma. We are assured that such a statement has no foundation whatever; that no treachery induced the disaster at Petersburg; that our forces fought splendidly, and the enemy only succeeded by overwhelming numbers. We are convinced, too, from facts which we cannot mention, that *Lee's army is in a safe position*, and that *his future movements will be directed with the skill and energy which distinguish this great captain.*

Having anticipated the probable loss of Richmond, and fully recognizing the importance of the disaster, we are, nevertheless, not of the number of those who give up the cause. In the Southern confederacy this day there is military strength of men, material and supplies to make independence certain. It is with the *people themselves* whether they secure or lose their liberties.

Rebel Particulars of the Battle at Petersburg.

[From the Raleigh Confederate, April 7.]

An officer who left Richmond at nine o'clock on Monday morning last informs us that at the time he left the city was in flames from Cary to Canal streets. The Shockoe warehouse and other entrepots of supplies were burning. The bridges also had been fired.

No mob or violence of any kind had occurred up to the period when he left, so that the reports of a destructive mob on Sunday night are untrue. The enemy's cavalry entered the city as the train moved off that he came out in. The story of the mob, therefore, we hope, is entirely erroneous.

This officer describes the fighting on Saturday as terrific beyond description. The enemy forced column after column on our works, lapping our lines on the extreme right. They came nine columns deep. Eight lines faltered and were broken by the obstinacy of our defences; but the ninth broke over our forces like a whirlwind. He says the destruction of the enemy was immense. Our loss, we think, consisted mainly in the prisoners taken by the enemy. All the prisoners whom we captured were drunk, having been prepared according to Yankee tactics for this dreadful ordeal. Lieutenant General A. P. Hill was certainly killed. General Fitz. Lee was not killed, as reported, nor General W. H. F. Lee. No general officer from North Carolina was killed, as far as he heard. On Monday Sheridan attacked Fitz. Lee and was handsomely repulsed.

The Organ of Governor Vance, of North Carolina, Advising General Lee to Submit on Mr. Lincoln's Terms.

[From the Raleigh Confederate, April 7.]

The *Conservative* occasionally seems to fall into very mysterious hands, and to come under the control of an incomprehensible influence. On the day before yesterday that paper availed itself of a period of extreme reverse and disaster to renew the attempt to cast odium on a portion of our own citizens, which has been a favorite policy with its political leaders ever since the reverses began, and after it was no longer politic to claim that they "made the revolution." Yesterday it sends to the public a leader of still more extraordinary import. From what we comprehend of it, it seems to be *a distinct proposition to submit and surrender upon the terms proposed by Lincoln*. This has never yet, that we recollect of, been more distinctly proposed, even by journals whose loyalty has been called in question. The *Conservative* says:—"It is nonsense to propose to treat with the North with any expectation of the concession that the confederacy is a government," and hence, says the *Conservative*, "if our authorities are determined to force this condition upon the North, as a basis of negotiation, then the North will never negotiate." What is this but surrender? Not only surrender, but an assertion to the world that the defence of the last four years has been of a position which is one of sheer nonsense—one which the North "never could admit?" We have not seen in this controversy so bold and unconditional a justification of the Northern invasion; for, if we sought to force a claim inconsistent with reason, and to demand an "admission" which "is an absurdity in anything like government," and the North only resisted such claim and refused such admission, then we are in the wrong and the Yankee government is right, and the writer of the article to which we are replying does well when he *advises General Lee not to "block up his way, at the threshold, by presenting a basis to which he knows the enemy will not yield,"* but "to meet him on his own ground," as "the only way to open the negotiation." When we remember what "his own ground" is, upon which the *Conservative* proposes to meet the enemy, we may readily understand how much it is prepared to concede. "His own ground" measured the length of three propositions; submission to the laws and constitution of the United States, the laying down of our arms, and acquiescence in Lincoln's proclamations. This is the ground on which the author of the editorial desires General Lee to meet Lincoln and "secure a talk about peace." We have no idea that Governor Vance will support this idea; but it is very unfortunate that now, in the very moment when everything should be said to uphold the hopes and confidence of the army and people, such sentiments should obtain publication in the organ of the Governor.

High Prices in an Overstocked Market.

[From the Raleigh Confederate, April 7.]

Our market, on the arrival of the Weldon train, on yesterday, *became overstocked* with shad; *they went off slowly at $50 per pair.*

THE STATE CAPITAL.

Rejection of the New York Fire Commissioners—Passage of the Central Railroad Fare Bill—Great Excitement Over the Health Bill, &c.

ALBANY, April 14—11:40 P. M.

Legislation each day is now so rapid here that a detail or analysis of its progress is out of the question. To-day the long pending Central Railroad bill passed the Senate, and is virtually a law if the Governor does not veto it. But the result may be foreshadowed in the veto sent in to-day of the Dry Dock and Battery Railroad.

The Health bill, which two days since was bound by caucus rules to have a sure passage, was to-night defeated by republican votes. The Collector of the port of New York, who has had an elaborate organization up for his retention in the office of Commissioner of Charities, was thrown overboard and the power of all his patronage disregarded in the strife to secure this position, which has been his pet desire and speciality for many years.

A final vote was forced upon the friends of the bill at a late hour. Sixty-one voted for the bill and fifty-one against it. Sixty-five votes being necessary to its passage, it was lost. Mr. Salmon, of New York, who had made himself obnoxious by the vehemency of his opposition to the bill, was sought to be involved in proceedings before the bar of the House; but the Speaker was evidently discouraged from any such attempts. The management for the bill on the floor of the House was understood to be in the hands of the radicals, under the lead of Fields. Boole was in the lobby in person. Mayor Gunther, Carr and others of his opponents were here yesterday to urge on the passage of the bill. It is alleged that the republican interest was sold out by the radicals.

The Fire Commissioners encountered a decided capsize in executive session. The defeat of the Health bill was pending on their consideration, and the Assembly had adjourned in the extraordinary manner of the morning. The names were at first confirmed, Senator Laimbier, who had made the chief opposition, moving the confirmation. This action was, however, reconsidered on motion of Senator Andrews, on the ground of the promises made in the Assembly to the democrats, who passed it, that the board would comprise two democrats. The names were accordingly sent back to the Governor.

The continuation of Boole in office by the defeat of the Health bill is accompanied by the passage of a resolution continuing the Senate investigating committee, to sit during the summer and examine the other departments. The feeling here is that Boole was treated as an invidious exception, and the thing will be made even all round.

The action determined on in caucus yesterday in regard to Draper and the Board of Charities, was desked by resolution to-day, and is coupled with the defeat of Rufus F. Andrews as candidate for United States District Attorney at New York, as a satisfactory manifestation of Thurlow Weed's [illegible]

THE NEW YORK HERALD.

WHOLE NO. 10,456. NEW YORK, SATURDAY, APRIL 15, 1865. PRICE FOUR CENTS.

IMPORTANT.

ASSASSINATION OF PRESIDENT LINCOLN.

The President Shot at the Theatre Last Evening.

SECRETARY SEWARD DAGGERED IN HIS BED, BUT NOT MORTALLY WOUNDED.

Clarence and Frederick Seward Badly Hurt.

ESCAPE OF THE ASSASSINS.

Intense Excitement in Washington.

Scene at the Deathbed of Mr. Lincoln.

J. Wilkes Booth, the Actor, the Alleged Assassin of the President,

&c., &c., &c.

THE OFFICIAL DESPATCH.

WAR DEPARTMENT, WASHINGTON, April 15—1:30 A. M.

Major General DIX, New York:—

This evening at abo t 9:30 P. M., at Ford's Theatre, the President, while sitting in his private box with Mrs. Lincoln, Mrs. Harris and Major Rathburn, was shot by an assassin, who suddeny entered the box and approached behind the President.

The assassin then laped upon the stage, brandishing a large dagger or knife and made his escape in the rear of the theatre.

The pistol ball entred the back of the President's head and penetrated early through the head. The wound is mortal.

The President has ben insensible ever since it was inflicted, and is now dyng.

About the same hor an assassin, whether the same or not, entered Mr. Sewrd's apartments, and under pretence of having a preeription was shown to the Secretary's sick chamber. The assassin immediately rushed to the bed and inflicted two r three stabs on the throat and two on the face.

It is hoped the wound may not be mortal. My apprehension is that they v prove fatal.

The nurse alarmed Mr. Frederick Seward, who was in an adjoining room, and hastened to the door of his father's room, when he et the assassin, who inflicted upon him one or more gerous wounds. The recovery of Frederick Seward ioubtful.

It is not probable thse President will live through the night.

General Grant and v were advertised to be at the theatre this evening, he started to Burlington at six o'clock this evening.

At a Cabinet meeti at which General Grant was present, the subject of state of the country and the prospect of a speedy pe were discussed. The President was very cheerful a opeful, and spoke very kindly of General Lee and ot of the confederacy, and of the establishment of go ment in Virginia.

All the members e Cabinet except Mr. Seward, are now in attendance the President.

I have seen M ward, but he and Frederick were both unconscious

EDWIN M. STANTON,
Secretary of War.

THE H ALD DESPATCHES.

WASHINGTON, April 14, 1865.

Assassinatio s been inaugurated in Washington. The bowie kn d pistol have been applied to President Lincoln and ary Seward. The former was shot in the throat, t Ford's theatre to-night. Mr. Seward was badly c ut the neck, while in his bed at his residence.

SECOND DESPATCH.

WASHINGTON, April 14, 1865.

An atten s made about ten o'clock this evening to assassinat President and Secretary Seward. The President hot at Ford's Theatre. Result not yet known. ward's throat was cut, and his son badly wounded.

There se excitement here.

ils of the Assassination.

WASHINGTON, April 14, 1865.

Wash was thrown into an intense excitement a ew mi efore eleven o'clock this evening, by the announ that the President and Secretary eward inated and were dead.

city. Men, women and children, old and young, rushed to and fro, and the rumors were magnified until we had nearly every member of the Cabinet killed. Some time elapsed before authentic data could be ascertained in regard to the affair.

About half-past ten o'clock this evening a tall, well dressed man made his appearance at Secretary Seward's residence, and applied for admission. He was refused admission by the servant, when the desperado stated that he had a prescription from the Surgeon General, and that he was ordered to deliver it in person. He was still refused, except upon the written order of the physician. This he pretended to show, and pushed by the servant and rushed up stairs to Mr. Seward's room. He was met at the door by Mr. Fred Seward, who notified him that he was master of the house, and would take charge of the medicine. After a few words had passed between them he dodged by Fred Seward and rushed to the Secretary's bed, and struck him in the neck with a dagger, and also in the breast.

It was supposed at first that Mr. Seward was killed instantly, but it was found afterwards that the wound was not mortal.

Major Wm. H. Seward, Jr., paymaster, was in the room, and rushed to the defence of his father, and was badly cut in the *mele* with the assassin, but not fatally.

The desperado managed to escape from the house, and was prepared for escape by having a horse at the door. He immediately mounted his horse, and sung out the motto of the State of Virginia, "*Sic Semper Tyrannis!*" and rode off.

Surgeon General Barnes was immediately sent for, and he *examined Mr. Seward and pronounced him safe.* His wounds were not fatal. The jugular vein was not cut, nor the wound in the breast deep enough to be fatal.

The President and Mrs. Lincoln were at Ford's theatre, listening to the performance of the American Cousin, occupying a box in the second tier. At the close of the third act a person entered the box occupied by the President, and shot Mr. Lincoln in the head. The shot entered the back of his head, and came out above the temple.

The assassin then jumped from the box upon the stage and ran across to the other side, exhibiting a dagger in his hand, flourishing it in a tragical manner, shouting the same words repeated by the desperado at Mr. Seward's house, adding to it, "The South is avenged," and then escaped from the back entrance to the stage, but in his passage dropped his pistol and his hat.

Mr. Lincoln fell forward from his seat, and Mrs. Lincoln fainted.

The moment the astonished audience could realize what had happened, the President was taken and carried to Mr. Petersen's house, in Tenth street, opposite to the theatre. Medical aid was immediately sent for, and the wound was at first supposed to be fatal, and it was announced that he could not live; but at half-past twelve he is still alive, though in a precarious condition.

As the assassin ran across the stage, Colonel J. B. Stewart, of this city, who was occupying one of the front seats in the orchestra, on the same side of the house as the box occupied by Mr. Lincoln, sprang to the stage and followed him; but he was obstructed in his passage across the stage by the fright of the actors, and reached the back door about three seconds after the assassin had passed out. Colonel Stewart got to the street just in time to see him mount his horse and ride away.

This operation shows that the whole thing was a preconcerted plan. The person who fired the pistol was a man about thirty years of age, about five feet nine, spare built, fair skin, dark hair, apparently bushy, with a large mustache. Laura Keene and the leader of the orchestra declare that they recognized him as J. Wilkes Booth the actor, and a rabid secessionist. Whoever he was, it is plainly evident that he thoroughly understood the theatre and all the approaches and modes of escape to the stage. A person not familiar with the theatre could not have possibly made his escape so well and quickly.

The alarm was sounded in every quarter. Mr. Stanton was notified, and immediately left his house.

All the other members of the Cabinet escaped attack.

Cavalrymen were sent out in all directions, and despatches sent to all the fortifications, and it is thought they will be captured.

WASHINGTON, April 15—1 A. M.

The streets in the vicinity of Ford's Theatre are densely crowded by an anxious and excited crowd. A guard has been placed across Tenth street and F and E streets, and only official persons and particular friends of the President are allowed to pass.

The popular heart is deeply stirred, and the deepest indignation against leading rebels is freely expressed.

The scene at the house where the President lies *in extremis* is very affecting. Even Secretary Stanton is affected to tears.

When the news spread through the city that the President had been shot, the people, with pale faces and compressed lips, crowded every place where there was the slightest chance of obtaining information in regard to the affair.

After the President was shot, Lieutenant Rathbun, caught the assassin by the arm, who immediately struck him with a knife, and jumped from the box, as before stated.

The popular affection for Mr. Lincoln has been shown by this diabolical assassination, which will bring eternal infamy, not only upon its authors, but upon the hellish cause which they desire to avenge.

Vice President Johnson arrived at the White House, where the President lies, about one o'clock, and will remain with him to the last.

The President's family are in attendance upon him also.

As soon as intelligence could be got to the War Department, the electric telegraph and the Signal corps were put in requisition to endeavor to prevent the escape of the assassins, and all the troops around Washington are under arms.

Popular report points to a somewhat celebrated actor of known secession proclivities as the assassin; but it would be unjust to name him until some further evidence of his guilt is obtained. It is rumored that the person alluded to is in custody.

The latest advices from Secretary Seward reveals more desperate work there than at first supposed. Seward's wounds are not in themselves fatal; but, in connection with his recent injuries, and the great loss of blood he has sustained, his recovery is questionable.

It was Clarence A. Seward, instead of Wm. H. Seward, Jr., who was wounded. Fred. Seward was also badly cut, as were also three nurses, who were in attendance upon the Secretary, showing that a desperate struggle took place there. The wounds of the whole party were dressed.

ONE O'CLOCK A. M.

The President is perfectly senseless, and there is not the slightest hope of his surviving. Physicians believe he will die before morning. All of his Cabinet, except Secretary Seward, are with him. Speaker Colfax, Senator Farwell, of Maine, and many other gentlemen, are also at the house awaiting the termination.

The scene at the President's bedside is described by one who witnessed it as most affecting. It was surrounded by his Cabinet ministers, all of whom were bathed in tears, not even excepting Mr. Stanton, who, when informed by Surgeon General Barnes, that the President could not live until morning, exclaimed, "Oh, no, General; no—no;" and with an impulse, natural as it was unaffected, immediately sat down on a chair near his bedside and wept like a child.

Senator Sumner was seated on the right of the President's couch, near the head, holding the right hand of the President in his own. He was sobbing like a woman, with his head bowed down almost on the pillow of the bed on which the President was lying.

TWO O'CLOCK A. M.

The President is still alive, but there is no improvement in his condition.

THE PRESS DESPATCHES.

WASHINGTON, April 15—12:30 A. M.

The President was shot in a theatre to-night, and is perhaps mortally wounded.

SECOND DESPATCH.

WASHINGTON, April 15—1 A. M.

The President is not expected to live through the night. He was shot at a theatre.

Secretary Seward was also assassinated. No arteries were cut.

Additional Details of the Assassination.

WASHINGTON, April 15—1:30 A. M.

President Lincoln and wife, with other friends, this evening visited Ford's theatre, for the purpose of witnessing the performance of the American Cousin.

It was announced in the papers that General Grant would also be present; but that gentleman took the late train of cars for New Jersey.

The theatre was densely crowded, and all seemed delighted with the scene before them. During the third act, and while there was a temporary pause for one of the actors to enter, a sharp report of a pistol was heard, which merely attracted attention, but suggested nothing serious, until a man rushed to the front of the President's box, waving a long dagger in his right hand, and exclaiming "*Sic semper tyrannis!*" and immediately leaped from the box, which was in the second tier, to the stage beneath, and ran across to the opposite side, making his escape, amid the bewilderment of the audience, from the rear of the theatre, and, mounting a horse, fled.

The screams of Mrs. Lincoln first disclosed the fact to the audience that the President had been shot, when all present rose to their feet, rushing towards the stage, many exclaiming "Hang him! Hang him!"

The excitement was of the wildest possible description, and of course there was an abrupt termination of the theatrical performance.

There was a rush toward the President's box, when cries were heard:—"Stand back and give him air." "Has any one stimulants?"

On a hasty examination it was found that the President had been shot through the head, above and back of the temporal bone, and that some of the brain was oozing out.

He was removed to a private house opposite to the theatre, and the Surgeon General of the army and other surgeons sent for to attend to his condition.

On an examination of the private box blood was discovered on the back of the cushioned rocking chair on which the President had been sitting, also on the partition and on the floor. A common single barreled pocket pistol was found on the carpet.

A military guard was placed in front of the private residence to which the President had been conveyed. An immense crowd was in front of it, all deeply anxious to learn the condition of the President. It had been previously announced that the wound was mortal, but all hoped otherwise. The shock to the community was terrible.

At midnight the Cabinet, with Messrs. Sumner, Colfax and Farnsworth, Judge Curtis, Governor Oglesby, General Meigs, Colonel Hay, and a few personal friends, with Surgeon General Barnes and his immediate assistants, were around his bedside.

The President was in a state of syncope, totally insensible, and breathing slowly. The blood oozed from the wound at the back of his head.

The surgeons exhausted every possible effort of medicinal skill; but all hope was gone.

The parting of his family with the dying President is too sad for description.

The President and Mrs. Lincoln did not start for the theatre until fifteen minutes after eight o'clock. Speaker Colfax was at the White House at the time, and the President stated to him that he was going. Mrs. Lincoln had not been well, because the papers had announced that General Grant and they were to be present, and, as General Grant had gone North, he did not wish the audience to be disappointed.

He went with apparent reluctance, and urged Mr. Colfax to go with him; but that gentleman had made other engagements, and, with Mr. Ashmun, of Massachusetts, bid him goodby.

When the excitement at the theatre was at its wildest height reports were circulated that Secretary Seward had also been assassinated.

On reaching this gentleman's residence a crowd and a military guard were found at the door, and on entering it was ascertained that the reports were based on truth.

Everybody there was so excited that scarcely an intelligible word could be gathered. But the facts are substantially as follows:—

About ten o'clock a man rang the bell, and the call having been answered by a colored servant, he said he had come from Dr. Verdi, Secretary Seward's family physician, with a prescription, at the same time holding in his hand a small piece of folded paper, and saying, in answer to a refusal, that he must see the Secretary, as he was entrusted with particular directions concerning the medicine.

He still insisted on going up, although repeatedly informed that no one could enter the chamber. The man pushed the servant aside, and walked hastily towards the Secretary's room, and was then met by Mr. Frederick Seward, of whom he demanded to see the Secretary, making the same representation which he did to the servant.

What further passed in the way of colloquy is not known; but the man struck him on the head with a billy, severely injuring the skull and felling him almost senseless.

The assassin then rushed into the chamber and attacked Major Seward, Paymaster United States Army, and Mr. Hansell, a messenger of the State Department, and two male nurses, disabling them all. He then rushed upon the Secretary, who was lying in bed in the same room, and inflicted three stabs in the neck, but severing, it is thought and hoped, no arteries, though he bled profusely.

The assassin then rushed down stairs, mounted his horse at the door, and rode off before an alarm could be sounded, and in the same manner as the assassin of the President.

It is believed that the injuries of the Secretary are not fatal, nor those of either of the others, although both the Secretary and the Assistand Secretary are very seriously injured.

Secretaries Stanton and Welles, and other prominent officers of the Government, called at Secretary Seward's house to inquire into his condition, and there heard of the assassination of the President.

They then proceeded to the house where he was lying, exhibiting of course intense anxiety and solicitude.

An immense crowd was gathered in front of the President's house, and a strong guard was also stationed there, many persons evidently supposing he would be brought to his home.

The entire city to-night presents a scene of wild excitement, accompanied by violent expression of indignation and the profoundest sorrow; many shed tears.

The military authorities have despatched mounted patrols in every direction, in order, if possible, to arrest the assassin. The whole metropolitan police are likewise vigilant for the same purpose.

The attacks, both at the theatre and at Secretary Seward's house, took place at about the same hour—ten o'clock—thus showing a preconcerted plan to assassinate those gentlemen. Some evidences of the guilt of the party who attacked the President are in the possession of the police.

Vice President Johnson is in the city, and his headquarters are guarded by troops.

THE LATEST NEWS.

Secretary Stanton to General Dix.

WAR DEPARTMENT, WASHINGTON, April 15—3 A. M.

Major General DIX, New York:—

The President still breathes, but is quite insensible, as he has been ever since he was shot. He evidently did not see the person who shot him, but was looking on the stage, as he was approached from behind.

Mr. Seward has rallied, and it is hoped he may live.

Frederick Seward's condition is very critical.

The attendant who was present was shot through the lungs and is not expected to live.

The wounds of Major Seward are not serious.

Investigation strongly indicates J. Wilkes Booth as the assassin of the President. Whether it was the same or a different person that attempted to murder Mr. Seward remain in doubt.

Chief Justice Carter is engaged in taking the evidence. Every exertion has been made to prevent the escape of the murderer. His horse has been found on the road near Washington.

EDWIN M. STANTON, Secretary of War.

Our Special Washington Despatch.

WASHINGTON, April 15, 1865.

When the fatal shot was fired, Mrs. Lincoln, who was alongside of her husband, exclaimed, "Oh! why didn't they shoot me—why didn't they shoot me?"

There is evidence that Secretary Stanton was also marked for assassination. On receipt of intelligence at the War Department of the attack on the President, two employes of the department were sent to summon the Secretary. Just as they approached his house, a man jumped out from behind a tree box in front of the house and ran away. It is well known to be the custom of the Secretary to go from the department to his house between nine and twelve P. M., and usually unattended. It is supposed that the assassin intended to shoot him as he entered the house, but failed from the fact that Mr. Stanton remained at home during the evening.

The circumstantial evidence is very strong that J. Wilkes Booth is the person who shot the President. Several parties who are well acquainted with him, and saw the assassin when he jumped from the box, are positive that he is the man. It is also reported that Booth's horse was saddled at the side door of the theatre, and was rode off by the assassin. If he is the man, it is impossible for him to escape. The horse of the man who made the attack on Secretary Seward has been found near the Lincoln Hospital bathed in sweat, and with blood upon the saddle cloths.

THREE O'CLOCK A. M.

There is up to this time no material change in the President's condition.

The Press Despatch.

WASHINGTON, April 15—2:12.

The President is still alive, but he is growing weaker. The ball is lodged in his brain, three inches from where it entered the skull. He remains insensible, and his condition is utterly helpless.

The Vice President has been to see him; but all company except the members of the Cabinet and of the family is rigidly excluded.

Large crowds still continue in the street, as near the house as the line of guards allow.

IMPORTANT FROM SOUTH AMERICA.

Surrender of Montevideo to Gen. Flores—Brazil in Possession of the City, &c.

The Brazilian mail arrived at Lisbon April 2, bringing the following advices:—

Montevideo has surrendered to General Flores.

The Brazilians now (March 11) occupy the city.

RIO JANEIRO, March 11, 1865.

Exchange 25⅝ a 26¼.

Coffee—Sales of good firsts at 65.66. Shipments, 100,000 bags. Stock, 100,000 bags. Freights, 50.62½.

BAHIA, March 11, 1865.

Exchange 26¼. Cotton nominal.

News from San Francisco.

SAN FRANCISCO, April 12, 1865.

The exports of treasure for the quarter just ended show a falling off of about six and a half millions as compared with the same period last year.

City Intelligence.

EASTER SUNDAY AT ST. ANN'S CHURCH.—The admirers of sacred music, made truly effective by a well trained choir, have an opportunity of indulging their taste by repairing to St. Ann's church on Easter Sunday evening, the doors opening at seven, the concert begining at eight. Three of the pieces are from Gordigiani, three from Rossini and one from each of the composers Verdi, Donizetti, Verrimst, Dachauer and Gounod. We need only mention the names of Signor Romi and Messrs. Schmitz, Schubert and Dachauer to insure confidence in the vocal results. The ladies are quite distinguished for contralto and soprano execution, and no exertion will be spared to make the musical feast worthy of the day.

A NEW CHURCH.—An advertisement among our religious notices announces the opening of the new Church of the Holy Trinity, Madison avenue, corner of Forty-second street, on Sunday. Sermons will be preached at the three sessions by Rev. Dr. Tyng, of St. George's; Rev. Dr. Dyer, and the Rev. Stephen H. Tyng, Jr., the pastor of the church. It promises to be an occasion of great interest to residents on Murray Hill.

MISS EMMA HARDINGE delivers her able lecture on "Politics in the Pulpit" this evening, at Dodworth Hall. To test the lady's ability, any questions the audience desire to ask will be answered.

EXTRA.

Saturday, April 15, 8:45 o'Clock A. M.

DEATH OF THE PRESIDENT!!

Secretary Stanton to General Dix.

WAR DEPARTMENT, WASHINGTON, April 15, 1865.

To Major General DIX, New York:—

Abraham Lincoln died this morning at twenty-two minutes after seven o'clock.

EDWIN M. STANTON,
Secretary of War.

THE REBELS.

JEFF. DAVIS AT DANVILLE.

His Latest Appeal to His Deluded Followers.

He Thinks the Fall of Richmond a Blessing in Disguise, as it Leaves the Rebel Armies Free to Move from Point to Point.

He Vainly Promises to Hold Virginia at All Hazards.

Lee and His Army Supposed to be Safe.

Breckinridge and the Rest of Davis' Cabinet Reach Danville Safely.

The Organ of Governor Vance, of North Carolina, Advises the Submission of the Rebels to President Lincoln's Terms,

&c., &c., &c.

Jeff. Davis' Last Proclamation.

VIRGINIA TO BE HELD BY THE REBELS AT ALL HAZARDS.

DANVILLE, Va., April 5, 1865.

The General-in-Chief found it necessary to make such movements of his troops as to uncover the capital. It would be unwise to conceal the *moral and material injury to our cause resulting from the occupation of our capital* by the enemy. It is equally unwise and unworthy of us to allow our own energies to falter and our efforts to become relaxed under adverses, however calamitous they may be. For many months *the largest and finest army* of the confederacy, under command of a leader whose presence inspires equal confidence in the troops and the people, has been greatly trammelled by the necessity of keeping constant watch over the approaches to the capital, and has thus been forced to forego more than one opportunity for promising enterprise. It is for us, my countrymen, to show by our bearing under reverses how wretched has been the self-deception of those who have believed us less able to endure misfortune with fortitude than to encounter dangers with courage.

We have now entered upon a new phase of the struggle. Relieved from the necessity of guarding particular points, *our army will be free to move from point to point* to strike the enemy in detail far from his base. *Let us but will it and we are free.*

Animated by that confidence in spirit and fortitude which never yet failed me, I announce to you, fellow countrymen, that it is my purpose to maintain your cause with my whole heart and soul; that I will never consent to abandon to the enemy one foot of the soil of any one of the States of the confederacy. That Virginia—noble State—whose ancient renown has been eclipsed by her still more glorious recent history; whose bosom has been bared to receive the main shock of this war; whose sons and daughters have exhibited heroism so sublime as to render her illustrious in all time to come—that Virginia, with the help of the people and by the blessing of Providence, *shall be held and defended*, and no peace ever be be made with the infamous invaders of her territory.

If by the stress of numbers we should ever be compelled to a temporary withdrawal from her limits, or those of any other border State, again and again will we return, until the baffled and exhausted enemy shall abandon in despair his endless and impossible task of making slaves of a people resolved to be free.

Let us, then, not despond, my countrymen; but, relying on God, meet the foe with fresh defiance and with unconquered and unconquerable hearts.

JEFFERSON DAVIS.

The Evacution of the Rebel Capital.

THE FIRST REBEL ACCOUNT OF HOW THE CITY WAS ABANDONED.

[From the Danville (Va.) Register, April 5.]

Persons who left the capital Sunday night and Monday morning represent that the scene which followed the evacuation of the city by our troops beggars description. To preserve order and protect the property of the citizens who unavoidably remained there, as far as could be done, the Nineteenth Virginia militia, under Colonel Evans, was placed on police duty in the city, to await the coming of the enemy; but accounts state that they failed to render any aid or protection to the people whatever. On Sunday night a mob of the lower classes of the city, composed, it is said, mostly of the foreign element, visited a number of the largest storehouses of the city and robbed them of their contents. It is affirmed that Main street was pillaged, and then burned, and that some of the milling establishments were also committed to the flames. We have no doubt that a considerable portion of that brave city has been laid in ashes, and a number of its people insulted, outraged, robbed and massacred. How painful the thought that the place should be given over to rapine and plunder, even before the public enemy entered its limits. But the fact only proves that the people of Richmond have had secret enemies in their own midst scarcely less savage and even more treacherous and vindictive than the open foe.

We are told that the people banded together during the violent proceding of the mob and resisted them with force, a street fight ensuing, in which several persons were killed.

No intelligence has reached us of the enemy's troops occupying the city. The last trains on the Danville railroad which came out of the place left Monday morning, and passengers upon them had heard nothing from the enemy. The greater portion of Grant's army was transferred to the south side of James river some days ago, only the command of General Ord, which is composed mostly, if not entirely, of negro troops, being left on the north side. This command will enter and occupy the city. Some of our people who are acquainted with the character of General Ord think they have reason to hope that his treatment of the unfortunate people of Richmond will not be so hard, and cruel and inhuman as that which has fallen upon the heads of our fellow citizens in some other captured cities.

The newspapers of Richmond, we suppose, all fell into the hands of the enemy. The evacuation of the city was so sudden and unexpected—scarcely any one being prepared for it—that no time was left for the removal of so cumbrous an establishment as a city newspaper office. In a few days we may expect to hear that the *Enquirer* or the *Whig* or the *Examiner* is issued as a Yankee paper.

All the rolling stock of the Richmond and Danville Railroad in running order was saved on the retreat from Richmond. A few old cars, not in a movable condition, were left at Manchester. No train was captured by the enemy near the junction, as was at one time reported; and, indeed, we do not believe that any body of Yankees had struck the road at any point up to yesterday evening.

The Secretary of War, the Quartermaster General, Commissary General and a number of other officers of the government, left Richmond on horseback, and will probably arrive at this place to-morrow.

Should General Lee establish his lines east of the junction, we suppose the State Legislature will be convened at Lynchburg.

All the specie and other valuables belonging to the banks in Richmond were removed from the city on Sunday, and have been carried to places of safety.

A considerable amount of goods purchased by the State for distribution to the people, we regret to learn, had to be left behind. Also the State archives remained in the city; but we perceive no motive the enemy can have in destroying them, as they will, no doubt, endeavor to occupy the city permanently, and establish a State government at Richmond under the federal Union.

Lee's Army Supposed to be in a Safe Position.

[From the Raleigh Confederate, April 7.]

This is the time for rumor manufacturers who are engaged in a wholesale business. Sometimes they have it that whole brigades deserted in the last great battle; among others, Cook's brigade is selected as the bearer of this stigma. We are assured that such a statement has no foundation whatever; that no treachery induced the disaster at Petersburg; that our forces fought splendidly, and the enemy only succeeded by overwhelming numbers. We are convinced, too, from facts which we cannot mention, that *Lee's army is in a safe position*, and that *his future movements will be directed with the skill and energy which distinguish this great captain.*

Having anticipated the probable loss of Richmond, and fully recognizing the importance of the disaster, we are, nevertheless, not of the number of those who give up the cause. In the Southern confederacy this day there is military strength of men, material and supplies to make independence certain. It is with the *people themselves* whether they secure or lose their liberties.

Rebel Particulars of the Battle at Petersburg.

[From the Raleigh Confederate, April 7.]

An officer who left Richmond at nine o'clock on Monday morning last informs us that at the time he left the city was in flames from Cary to Canal streets. The Shockoe warehouse and other entrepots of supplies were burning. The bridges also had been fired.

No mob or violence of any kind had occurred up to the period when he left, so that the reports of a destructive mob on Sunday night are untrue. The enemy's cavalry entered the city as the train moved off that he came out in. The story of the mob, therefore, we hope, is entirely erroneous.

This officer describes the fighting on Saturday as terrific beyond description. The enemy forced column after column on our works, lapping our lines on the extreme right. They came nine columns deep. Eight lines faltered and were broken by the obstinacy of our defences; but the ninth broke over our forces like a whirlwind. He says the destruction of the enemy was immense. Our loss, we think, consisted mainly in the prisoners taken by the enemy. All the prisoners whom we captured were drunk, having been prepared according to Yankee tactics for this dreadful ordeal. Lieutenant General A. P. Hill was certainly killed. General Fitz. Lee was not killed, as reported, nor General W. H. F. Lee. No general officer from North Carolina was killed, as far as he heard. On Monday Sheridan attacked Fitz. Lee and was handsomely repulsed.

The Organ of Governor Vance, of North Carolina, Advising General Lee to Submit on Mr. Lincoln's Terms.

[From the Raleigh Confederate, April 7.]

The *Conservative* occasionally seems to fall into very mysterious hands, and to come under the control of an incomprehensible influence. On the day before yesterday that paper availed itself of a period of extreme reverse and disaster to renew the attempt to cast odium on a portion of our own citizens, which has been a favorite policy with its political leaders ever since the reverses began, and after it was no longer politic to claim that they "made the revolution." Yesterday it sends to the public a leader of still more extraordinary import. From what we comprehend of it, it seems to be *a distinct proposition to submit and surrender upon the terms proposed by Lincoln.* This has never yet, that we recollect of, been more distinctly proposed, even by journals whose loyalty has been called in question. The *Conservative* says:—"It is nonsense to propose to treat with the North with any expectation of the concession that the confederacy is a government," and hence, says the *Conservative*, "if our authorities are determined to force this condition upon the North, as a basis of negotiation, then the North will never negotiate." What is this but surrender? Not only surrender, but an assertion to the world that the defence of the last four years has been of a position which is one of sheer nonsense—one which the North "never could admit?" We have not seen in this controversy so bold and unconditional a justification of the Northern invasion; for, if we sought to force a claim inconsistent with reason, and to demand an "admission" which "is an absurdity in anything like government," and the North only resisted such claim and refused such admission, then we are in the wrong and the Yankee government is right, and the writer of the article to which we are replying does well when he *advises General Lee not to "block up his way, at the threshold, by presenting a basis to which he knows the enemy will not yield,"* but "to meet him on his own ground," as "the only way to open the negotiation." When we remember what "his own ground" is, upon which the *Conservative* proposes to meet the enemy, we may readily understand how much it is prepared to concede. "His own ground" measured the length of three propositions; submission to the laws and constitution of the United States, the laying down of our arms, and acquiescence in Lincoln's proclamations. This is the ground on which the author of the editorial desires General Lee to meet Lincoln and "secure a talk about peace." We have no idea that Governor Vance will support this idea; but it is very unfortunate that now, in the very moment when everything should be said to uphold the hopes and confidence of the army and people, such sentiments should obtain publication in the organ of the Governor.

High Prices in an Overstocked Market.

[From the Raleigh Confederate, April 7.]

Our market, on the arrival of the Weldon train, on yesterday, *became overstocked with shad; they went off slowly at $50 per pair.*

THE NEW YORK HERALD.

WHOLE NO. 10,456. NEW YORK, SATURDAY, APRIL 15, 1865. PRICE FOUR CENTS.

IMPORTANT.

ASSASSINATION OF PRESIDENT LINCOLN.

The President Shot at the Theatre Last Evening.

SECRETARY SEWARD DAGGERED IN HIS BED, BUT NOT MORTALLY WOUNDED.

Clarence and Frederick Seward Badly Hurt.

ESCAPE OF THE ASSASSINS.

Intense Excitement in Washington.

Scene at the Deathbed of Mr. Lincoln.

J. Wilkes Booth, the Actor, the Alleged Assassin of the President,

&c., &c., &c.

THE OFFICIAL DESPATCH.

War Department, Washington, April 15—1:30 A. M.

Major General Dix, New York:—

This evening at about 9:30 P. M., at Ford's Theatre, the President, while sitting in his private box with Mrs. Lincoln, Mrs. Harris and Major Rathburn, was shot by an assassin, who suddenly entered the box and approached behind the President.

The assassin then leaped upon the stage, brandishing a large dagger or knife, and made his escape in the rear of the theatre.

The pistol ball entered the back of the President's head and penetrated nearly through the head. The wound is mortal.

The President has been insensible ever since it was inflicted, and is now dying.

About the same hour an assassin, whether the same or not, entered Mr. Seward's apartments, and under pretence of having a prescription was shown to the Secretary's sick chamber. The assassin immediately rushed to the bed and inflicted two or three stabs on the throat and two on the face.

It is hoped the wounds may not be mortal. My apprehension is that they will prove fatal.

The nurse alarmed Mr. Frederick Seward, who was in an adjoining room, and he hastened to the door of his father's room, when he met the assassin, who inflicted upon him one or more dangerous wounds. The recovery of Frederick Seward is doubtful.

It is not probable that the President will live through the night.

General Grant and wife were advertised to be at the theatre this evening, but he started to Burlington at six o'clock this evening.

At a Cabinet meeting, at which General Grant was present, the subject of the state of the country and the prospect of a speedy peace were discussed. The President was very cheerful and hopeful, and spoke very kindly of General Lee and others of the confederacy, and of the establishment of government in Virginia.

All the members of the Cabinet except Mr. Seward, are now in attendance upon the President.

I have seen Mr. Seward, but he and Frederick were both unconscious.

EDWIN M. STANTON,
Secretary of War.

THE HERALD DESPATCHES.

Washington, April 14, 1865.

Assassination has been inaugurated in Washington. The bowie knife and pistol have been applied to President Lincoln and Secretary Seward. The former was shot in the throat, while at Ford's theatre to-night. Mr. Seward was badly cut about the neck, while in his bed at his residence.

SECOND DESPATCH.

Washington, April 14, 1865.

An attempt was made about ten o'clock this evening to assassinate the President and Secretary Seward. The President was shot at Ford's Theatre. Result not yet known. Mr. Seward's throat was cut, and his son badly wounded.

There is intense excitement here.

Details of the Assassination.

Washington, April 14, 1865.

Washington was thrown into an intense excitement a few minutes before eleven o'clock this evening, by the announcement that the President and Secretary Seward had been assassinated and were dead.

The wildest excitement prevailed in all parts of the city. Men, women and children, old and young, rushed to and fro, and the rumors were magnified until we had nearly every member of the Cabinet killed. Some time elapsed before authentic data could be ascertained in regard to the affair.

About half-past ten o'clock this evening a tall, well dressed man made his appearance at Secretary Seward's residence, and applied for admission. He was refused admission by the servant, when the desperado stated that he had a prescription from the Surgeon General, and that he was ordered to deliver it in person. He was still refused, except upon the written order of the physician. This he pretended to show, and pushed by the servant and rushed up stairs to Mr. Seward's room. He was met at the door by Mr. Fred Seward, who notified him that he was master of the house, and would take charge of the medicine. After a few words had passed between them he dodged by Fred Seward and rushed to the Secretary's bed, and struck him in the neck with a dagger, and also in the breast.

It was supposed at first that Mr. Seward was killed instantly, but it was found afterwards that the wound was not mortal.

Major Wm. H. Seward, Jr., paymaster, was in the room, and rushed to the defence of his father, and was badly cut in the *mele* with the assassin, but not fatally.

The desperado managed to escape from the house, and was prepared for escape by having a horse at the door. He immediately mounted his horse, and sung out the motto of the State of Virginia, "*Sic Semper Tyrannis!*" and rode off.

Surgeon General Barnes was immediately sent for, and he *examined Mr. Seward and pronounced him safe.* His wounds were not fatal. The jugular vein was not cut, nor the wound in the breast deep enough to be fatal.

The President and Mrs. Lincoln were at Ford's theatre, listening to the performance of the American Cousin, occupying a box in the second tier. At the close of the third act a person entered the box occupied by the President, and shot Mr. Lincoln in the head. The shot entered the back of his head, and came out above the temple.

The assassin then jumped from the box upon the stage and ran across to the other side, exhibiting a dagger in his hand, flourishing it in a tragical manner, shouting the same words repeated by the desperado at Mr. Seward's house, adding to it, "The South is avenged," and then escaped from the back entrance to the stage, but in his passage dropped his pistol and his hat.

Mr. Lincoln fell forward from his seat, and Mrs. Lincoln fainted.

The moment the astonished audience could realize what had happened, the President was taken and carried to Mr. Petersen's house, in Tenth street, opposite to the theatre. Medical aid was immediately sent for, and the wound was at first supposed to be fatal, and it was announced that he could not live; but at half-past twelve he is still alive, though in a precarious condition.

As the assassin ran across the stage, Colonel J. B. Stewart, of this city, who was occupying one of the front seats in the orchestra, on the same side of the house as the box occupied by Mr. Lincoln, sprang to the stage and followed him; but he was obstructed in his passage across the stage by the fright of the actors, and reached the back door about three seconds after the assassin had passed out. Colonel Stewart got to the street just in time to see him mount his horse and ride away.

This operation shows that the whole thing was a preconcerted plan. The person who fired the pistol was a man about thirty years of age, about five feet nine, spare built, fair skin, dark hair, apparently bushy, with a large mustache. Laura Keene and the leader of the orchestra declare that they recognized him as J. Wilkes Booth the actor, and a rabid secessionist. Whoever he was, it is plainly evident that he thoroughly understood the theatre and all the approaches and modes of escape to the stage. A person not familiar with the theatre could not have possibly made his escape so well and quickly.

The alarm was sounded in every quarter. Mr. Stanton was notified, and immediately left his house.

All the other members of the Cabinet escaped attack.

Cavalrymen were sent out in all directions, and despatches sent to all the fortifications, and it is thought they will be captured.

Washington, April 15—1 A. M.

The streets in the vicinity of Ford's Theatre are densely crowded by an anxious and excited crowd. A guard has been placed across Tenth street and F and E streets, and only official persons and particular friends of the President are allowed to pass.

The popular heart is deeply stirred, and the deepest indignation against leading rebels is freely expressed.

The scene at the house where the President lies *in extremis* is very affecting. Secretary Stanton is affected to tears.

When the news spread through the city that the President had been shot, the people, with pale faces and compressed lips, crowded every place where there was the slightest chance of obtaining information in regard to the affair.

After the President was shot, Lieutenant Rathbun, caught the assassin by the arm, who immediately struck him with a knife, and jumped from the box, as before stated.

The popular affection for Mr. Lincoln has been shown by this diabolical assassination, which will bring eternal infamy, not only upon its authors, but upon the hellish cause which they desire to avenge.

Vice President Johnson arrived at the White House, where the President lies, about one o'clock, and will remain with him to the last.

The President's family are in attendance upon him also.

As soon as intelligence could be got to the War Department, the electric telegraph and the Signal corps were put in requisition to endeavor to prevent the escape of the assassins, and all the troops around Washington are under arms.

Popular report points to a somewhat celebrated actor of known secession proclivities as the assassin; but it would be unjust to name him until some further evidence of his guilt is obtained. It is rumored that the person alluded to is in custody.

The latest advices from Secretary Seward reveals more desperate werk there than at first supposed. Seward's wounds are not in themselves fatal; but, in connection with his recent injuries, and the great loss of blood he has sustained, his recovery is questionable.

Fred. Seward was also badly cut, as were also three nurses, who were in attendance upon the Secretary, showing that a desperate struggle took place there. The wounds of the whole party were dressed.

One o'Clock A. M.

The President is perfectly senseless, and there is not the slightest hope of his surviving. Physicians believe that he will die before morning. All of his Cabinet, except Secretary Seward, are with him. Speaker Colfax, Senator Farwell, of Maine, and many other gentlemen, are also at the house awaiting the termination.

The scene at the President's bedside is described by one who witnessed it as most affecting. It was surrounded by his Cabinet ministers, all of whom were bathed in tears, not even excepting Mr. Stanton, who, when informed by Surgeon General Barnes, that the President could not live until morning, exclaimed, "Oh, no, General; no—no;" and with an impulse, natural as it was unaffected, immediately sat down on a chair near his bedside and wept like a child.

Senator Sumner was seated on the right of the President's couch, near the head, holding the right hand of the President in his own. He was sobbing like a woman, with his head bowed down almost on the pillow of the bed on which the President was lying.

Two o'Clock A. M.

The President is still alive, but there is no improvement in his condition.

THE PRESS DESPATCHES.

Washington, April 15—12:30 A. M.

The President was shot in a theatre to-night, and is perhaps mortally wounded.

SECOND DESPATCH.

Washington, April 15—1 A. M.

The President is not expected to live through the night. He was shot at a theatre.

Secretary Seward was also assassinated. No arteries were cut.

Additional Details of the Assassination.

Washington, April 15—1:30 A. M.

President Lincoln and wife, with other friends, this evening visited Ford's theatre, for the purpose of witnessing the performance of the American Cousin.

It was announced in the papers that General Grant would also be present; but that gentleman took the late train of cars for New Jersey.

The theatre was densely crowded, and all seemed delighted with the scene before them. During the third act, and while there was a temporary pause for one of the actors to enter, a sharp report of a pistol was heard, which merely attracted attention, but suggested nothing serious, until a man rushed to the front of the President's box, waving a long dagger in his right hand, and exclaiming "*Sic semper tyrannis!*" and immediately leaped from the box, which was in the second tier, to the stage beneath, and ran across to the opposite side, making his escape, amid the bewilderment of the audience, from the rear of the theatre, and, mounting a horse, fled.

The screams of Mrs. Lincoln first disclosed the fact to the audience that the President had been shot, when all present rose to their feet, rushing towards the stage, many exclaiming "Hang him! Hang him!"

The excitement was of the wildest possible description, and of course there was an abrupt termination of the theatrical performance.

There was a rush toward the President's box, when cries were heard:—"Stand back and give him air." "Has any one stimulants?"

On a hasty examination it was found that the President had been shot through the head, above and back of the temporal bone, and that some of the brain was oozing out.

He was removed to a private house opposite to the theatre, and the Surgeon General of the army and other surgeons sent for to attend to his condition.

On an examination of the private box blood was discovered on the back of the cushioned rocking chair on which the President had been sitting, also on the partition and on the floor. A common single barreled pocket pistol was found on the carpet.

A military guard was placed in front of the private residence to which the President had been conveyed. An immense crowd was in front of it, all deeply anxious to learn the condition of the President. It had been previously announced that the wound was mortal, but all hoped otherwise. The shock to the community was terrible.

At midnight the Cabinet, with Messrs. Sumner, Colfax and Farnsworth, Judge Curtis, Governor Oglesby, General Meigs, Colonel Hay, and a few personal friends, with Surgeon General Barnes and his immediate assistants, were around his bedside.

The President was in a state of syncope, totally insensible, and breathing slowly. The blood oozed from the wound at the back of his head.

The surgeons exhausted every possible effort of medicinal skill; but all hope was gone.

The parting of his family with the dying President is too sad for description.

The President and Mrs. Lincoln did not start for the theatre until fifteen minutes after eight o'clock. Speaker Colfax was at the White House at the time, and the President stated to him that he was going. Mrs. Lincoln had not been well, because the papers had announced that General Grant and they were to be present, and, as General Grant had gone North, he did not wish the audience to be disappointed.

He went with apparent reluctance, and urged Mr. Colfax to go with him; but that gentleman had made other engagements, and, with Mr. Ashmun, of Massachusetts, bid him goodby.

When the excitement at the theatre was at its wildest height reports were circulated that Secretary Seward had also been assassinated.

On reaching this gentleman's residence a crowd and a military guard were found at the door, and on entering it was ascertained that the reports were based on truth.

Everybody there was so excited that scarcely an intelligible word could be gathered. But the facts are substantially as follows:—

About ten o'clock a man rang the bell, and the call having been answered by a colored servant, he said he had come from Dr. Verdi, Secretary Seward's family physician, with a prescription, at the same time holding in his hand a small piece of folded paper, and saying, in answer to a refusal, that he must see the Secretary, as he was entrusted with particular directions concerning the medicine.

He still insisted on going up, although repeatedly informed that no one could enter the chamber. The man pushed the servant aside, and walked hastily towards the Secretary's room, and was then met by Mr. Frederick Seward, of whom he demanded to see the Secretary, making the same representation which he did to the servant.

What further passed in the way of colloquy is not known; but the man struck him on the head with a billy, severely injuring the skull and felling him almost senseless.

The assassin then rushed into the chamber and attacked Major Seward, Paymaster United States Army, and Mr. Hansell, a messenger of the State Department, and two male nurses, disabling them all.

He then rushed upon the Secretary, who was lying in bed in the same room, and inflicted three stabs in the neck, but severing, it is thought and hoped, no arteries, though he bled profusely.

The assassin then rushed down stairs, mounted his horse at the door, and rode off before an alarm could be sounded, and in the same manner as the assassin of the President.

It is believed that the injuries of the Secretary are not fatal, nor those of either of the others, although both the Secretary and the Assistand Secretary are very seriously injured.

Secretaries Stanton and Welles, and other prominent officers of the Government, called at Secretary Seward's house to inquire into his condition, and there heard of the assassination of the President.

They then proceeded to the house where he was lying, exhibiting of course intense anxiety and solicitude.

An immense crowd was gathered in front of the President's house, and a strong guard was also stationed there. Many persons evidently supposing he would be brought to his home.

The entire city to-night presents a scene of wild excitement, accompanied by violent expression of indignation and the profoundest sorrow; many shed tears.

The military authorities have despatched mounted patrols in every direction, in order, if possible, to arrest the assassins. The whole metropolitan police are likewise vigilant for the same purpose.

The attacks, both at the theatre and at Secretary Seward's house, took place at about the same hour—ten o'clock—thus showing a preconcerted plan to assassinate those gentlemen. Some evidences of the guilt of the party who attacked the President are in the possession of the police.

Vice President Johnson is in the city, and his headquarters are guarded by troops.

THE LATEST NEWS.

Secretary Stanton to General Dix.

War Department, Washington, April 15—3 A. M.

Major General Dix, New York:—

The President still breathes, but is quite insensible, as he has been ever since he was shot. He evidently did not see the person who shot him, but was looking on the stage, as he was approached from behind.

Mr. Seward has rallied, and it is hoped he may live.

Frederick Seward's condition is very critical.

The attendant who was present was shot through the lungs, and is not expected to live.

The wounds of Major Seward are not serious.

Investigation strongly indicates J. Wilkes Booth as the assassin of the President. Whether it was the same or a different person that attempted to murder Mr. Seward remains in doubt.

Chief Justice Cartter is engaged in taking the evidence.

Every exertion has been made to prevent the escape of the murderer. His horse has been found on the road near Washington.

EDWIN M. STANTON, Secretary of War.

Our Special Washington Despatch.

Washington, April 15, 1865.

When the fatal shot was fired, Mrs. Lincoln, who was alongside of her husband, exclaimed, "Oh! why didn't they shoot me—why didn't they shoot me?"

There is evidence that Secretary Stanton was also marked for assassination. On receipt of intelligence at the War Department of the attack on the President, two employes of the department were sent to summon the Secretary. Just as they approached his house, a man jumped out from behind a tree box in front of the house and ran away. It is well known to be the custom of the Secretary to go from the department to his house between nine and twelve P. M., and usually unattended. It is supposed that the assassin intended to shoot him as he entered the house, but failed from the fact that Mr. Stanton remained at home during the evening.

The circumstantial evidence is very strong that J. Wilkes Booth is the person who shot the President. Several parties who are well acquainted with him, and saw the assassin when he jumped from the box, are positive that he is the man. It is also reported that Booth's horse was saddled at the side door of the theatre, and was rode off by the assassin. If he is the man, it is impossible for him to escape. The horse of the man who made the attack on Secretary Seward has been found near the Lincoln Hospital, bathed in sweat, and with blood upon the saddle cloths.

Three o'Clock A. M.

There is up to this time no material change in the President's condition.

The Press Despatch.

Washington, April 15—2:12.

The President is still alive, but he is growing weaker. The ball is lodged in his brain, three inches from where it entered the skull. He remains insensible, and his condition is utterly helpless.

The Vice President has been to see him; but all company except the members of the Cabinet and of the family is rigidly excluded.

Large crowds still continue in the street, as near the house as the line of guards allow.

IMPORTANT FROM SOUTH AMERICA.

Surrender of Montevideo to Gen. Flores—Brazil in Possession of the City, &c.

The Brazilian mail arrived at Lisbon April 2, bringing the following advices:—

Montevideo has surrendered to General Flores.

The Brazilians now (March 11) occupy the city.

Rio Janeiro, March 11, 1865.

Exchange 25⅝ a 26¼.

Coffee—Sales of good firsts at 65.66. Shipments, 100,000 bags. Stock, 100,000 bags. Freights, 50.62½.

Bahia, March 11, 1865.

Exchange 26¼. Cotton nominal.

News from San Francisco.

San Francisco, April 12, 1865.

The exports of treasure for the quarter just ended show a falling off of about six and a half millions as compared with the same period last year.

City Intelligence.

Easter Sunday at St. Ann's Church.—The admirers of sacred music, made truly effective by a well trained choir, have an opportunity of indulging their taste by repairing to St. Ann's church on Easter Sunday evening, the doors opening at seven, the concert begining at eight. Three of the pieces are from Gordigiani, three from Rossini and one from each of the composers Verdi, Donizetti, Verrimst, Dachauer and Gounod. We need only mention the names of Signor Remi and Messrs. Schmitz, Schubert and Dachauer to insure confidence in the vocal results. The ladies are quite distinguished for contralto and soprano execution, and no exertion will be spared to make the musical feast worthy of the day.

A New Church.—An advertisement among our religious notices announces the opening of the new Church of the Holy Trinity, Madison avenue, corner of Forty-second street, on Sunday. Sermons will be preached at the three sessions by Rev. Dr. Tyng, of St. George's; Rev. Dr. Dyer, and the Rev. Stephen H. Tyng, Jr., the pastor of the church. It promises to be an occasion of great interest to residents on Murray Hill.

Miss Emma Hardinge delivers her able lecture on "Politics in the Pulpit" this evening, at Dodworth Hall. To test the lady's ability, any questions the audience desire to ask will be answered.

Man Drowned.—On the morning of the 13th instant a journeyman housepainter, whose name is believed to be Barnard Burns, was accidentally drowned at Guntherville, Long Island. His body has not yet been claimed by his friends. Mr. J. B. Acker, of No. 9 Macdougal street, will give facilities to any one who can identify the corpse.

POSTSCRIPT.

Saturday, April 15—10 A. M.

DEATH OF THE PRESIDENT!!

Condition of Secretary Seward.

Ten Thousand Dollars Reward Offered for the Arrest of the Assassins.

J. Wilkes Booth Identified as the Murderer of the President,

&c., &c., &c.

Secretary Stanton to General Dix.

War Department, Washington, April 15—4:10 A. M.

To Major General Dix:—

The President continues insensible and is sinking.

Secretary Seward remains without change.

Frederick Seward's skull is fractured in two places, besides a severe cut upon the head. The attendant is still alive but hopeless. Major Seward's wounds not dangerous.

It is now ascertained with reasonable certainty that two assassins were engaged in the horrible crime, Wilkes Booth being the one that shot the President, and the other a companion of his whose name is not known, but whose description is so clear that he can hardly escape.

It appears from a letter found in Booth's trunk that the murder was planned before the 4th of March, but fell through then because the accomplice backed out until "Richmond could be heard from."

Booth and his accomplice were at the livery stable at six o'clock last evening, and left there with their horses about ten o'clock, or shortly before that hour.

It would appear that they had for several days been seeking their chance, but for some unknown reason it was not carried into effect until last night.

One of them has evidently made his way to Baltimore—the other has not yet been traced.

EDWIN M. STANTON,
Secretary of War.

War Department, Washington, April 15, 1865.

To Major General Dix, New York:—

Abraham Lincoln died this morning at twenty-two minutes after seven o'clock.

EDWIN M. STANTON,
Secretary of War.

Our Special Washington Despatch.

Washington, April 15—8 A. M.

The President died at half-past seven o'clock this morning.

The bells throughout the city are tolling. The public departments and most of the places of business are closed.

Secretary Seward is pretty comfortable this morning, the wounds inflicted upon him not being dangerous in themselves, but serious for his advanced age and previously weak condition.

Mr. Frederick Seward is very dangerously wounded, his skull having been fractured by a blow from the butt of a pistol in the hand of the assassin.

The most profound sensation prevails here, and the deepest realization of the irreparable loss which the nation has sustained pervades the minds of the people.

The Press Despatch.

Washington, April 15—8:40 A. M.

President Lincoln died this morning at half-past seven o'clock.

Major General Augur, commanding the Department of Washington, has offered a reward of ten thousand dollars to the party or parties arresting the murderer of the President, and the assassin of the Secretary of State and his son.

This morning, at six o'clock, there was no change in the condition of Secretary Seward.

The *Chronicle* says a letter found in J. Wilkes Booth's trunk identifies him as the murderer of the President.

THE REBELS.

JEFF. DAVIS AT DANVILLE.

His Latest Appeal to His Deluded Followers.

He Thinks the Fall of Richmond a Blessing in Disguise, as it Leaves the Rebel Armies Free to Move from Point to Point.

He Vainly Promises to Hold Virginia at All Hazards.

&c., &c., &c.

Jeff. Davis' Last Proclamation.

VIRGINIA TO BE HELD BY THE REBELS AT ALL HAZARDS.

Danville, Va., April 5, 1865.

The General-in-Chief found it necessary to make such movements of his troops as to uncover the capital. It would be unwise to conceal the *moral and material injury to our cause resulting from the occupation of our capital* by the enemy. It is equally unwise and unworthy of us to allow our own energies to falter and our efforts to become relaxed under adverses, however calamitous they may be. For many months *the largest and finest army* of the confederacy, under command of a leader whose presence inspires equal confidence in the troops and the people, has been greatly trammelled by the necessity of keeping constant watch over the approaches to the capital, and has thus been forced to forego more than one opportunity for promising enterprise. It is for us, my countrymen, to show by our bearing under reverses how wretched has been the self-deception of those who have believed us less able to endure misfortune with fortitude than to encounter dangers with courage.

We have now entered upon a new phase of the struggle. Relieved from the necessity of guarding particular points, *our army will be free to move from point to point* to strike the enemy in detail far from his base. *Let us but will it and we are free.*

Animated by that confidence in spirit and fortitude which never yet failed me, I announce to you, fellow countrymen, that it is my purpose to maintain your cause with my whole heart and soul; that I will never consent to abandon to the enemy one *foot of* the soil of any one of the States of the confederacy. That Virginia—noble State—whose ancient renown has been eclipsed by her still more glorious recent history; whose bosom has been bared to receive the main shock of this war; whose sons and daughters have exhibited heroism so sublime as to render her illustrious in all time to come—that Virginia, with the help of the people and by the blessing of Providence, *shall be held and defended*, and no peace ever be be made with the infamous invaders of her territory.

If by the stress of numbers we should ever be compelled to a temporary withdrawal from her limits, or those of any other border State, again and again will we return, until the baffled and exhausted enemy shall abandon in despair his endless and impossible task of making slaves of a people resolved to be free.

Let us, then, not despond, my countrymen; but, relying on God, meet the foe with fresh defiance and with unconquered and unconquerable hearts.

JEFFERSON DAVIS.

The Evacution of the Rebel Capital.

THE FIRST REBEL ACCOUNT OF HOW THE CITY WAS ABANDONED.

[From the Danville (Va.) Register, April 5.]

Persons who left the capital Sunday night and Monday morning represent that the scene which followed the evacuation of the city by our troops beggars description. To preserve order and protect the property of the citizens who unavoidably remained there, as far as could be done, the Nineteenth Virginia militia, under Colonel Evans, was placed on police duty in the city, to await the coming of the enemy; but accounts state that they failed to render any aid or protection to the people whatever. On Sunday night a mob of the lower classes of the city, composed, it is said, mostly of the foreign element, visited a number of the largest storehouses of the city and robbed them of their contents. It is affirmed that Main street was pillaged, and then burned, and that some of the milling establishments were also committed to the flames. We have no doubt that a considerable portion of that brave city has been laid in ashes, and a number of its people insulted, outraged, robbed and massacred. How painful the thought that the place should be given over to rapine and plunder, even before the public enemy entered its limits. But the fact only proves that the people of Richmond have had secret enemies in their own midst scarcely less savage and even more treacherous and vindictive than the open foe.

We are told that the people banded together during the violent proceeding of the mob and resisted them with force, a street fight ensuing, in which several persons were killed.

No [illegible] of the enemy's troops occupying the city. The last trains on the Danville railroad which came out of the place left Monday morning, and passengers upon them had heard nothing from the enemy. The greater portion of Grant's army was transferred to the south side of James river some days ago, only the command of General Ord, which is composed mostly, if not entirely, of negro troops, being left on the north side. This command will enter and occupy the city. Some of our people who are acquainted with the character of General Ord think they have reason to hope that his treatment of the unfortunate people of Richmond will not be so hard, and cruel and inhuman as that which has fallen upon the heads of our fellow citizens in some other captured cities.

The newspapers of Richmond, we suppose, all fell into the hands of the enemy. The evacuation of the city was so sudden and unexpected—scarcely any one being prepared for it—that no time was left for the removal of so cumbrous an establishment as a city newspaper office. In a few days we may expect to hear that the *Enquirer* or the *Whig* or the *Examiner* is issued as a Yankee paper.

All the rolling stock of the Richmond and Danville Railroad in running order was saved on the retreat from Richmond. A few old cars, not in a movable condition, were left at Manchester. No train was captured by the enemy near the junction, as was at one time reported; and, indeed, we do not believe that any body of Yankees had struck the road at any point up to yesterday evening.

The Secretary of War, the Quartermaster General, Commissary General and a number of other officers of the government, left Richmond on horseback, and will probably arrive at this place to-morrow.

Should General Lee establish his lines east of the junction, we suppose the State Legislature will be convened at Lynchburg.

All the specie and other valuables belonging to the banks in Richmond were removed from the city on Sunday, and have been carried to places of safety.

A considerable amount of goods purchased by the State for distribution to the people, we regret to learn, had to be left behind. Also the State archives remained in the city; but we perceive no motive the enemy can have in destroying them, as they will, no doubt, endeavor to occupy the city permanently, and establish a State government at Richmond under the federal Union

THE NEW YORK HERALD.

WHOLE NO. 10,456. NEW YORK, SATURDAY, APRIL 15, 1865. PRICE FOUR CENTS.

IMPORTANT.

ASSASSINATION OF PRESIDENT LINCOLN.

The President Shot at the Theatre Last Evening.

SECRETARY SEWARD DAGGERED IN HIS BED, BUT NOT MORTALLY WOUNDED.

Clarence and Frederick Seward Badly Hurt.

ESCAPE OF THE ASSASSINS.

Intense Excitement in Washington.

Scene at the Deathbed of Mr. Lincoln.

J. Wilkes Booth, the Actor, the Alleged Assassin of the President,

&c., &c., &c.

THE OFFICIAL DESPATCH.

War Department,
Washington, April 15—1:30 A. M.

Major General Dix, New York:—

This evening at about 9:30 P. M., at Ford's Theatre, the President, while sitting in his private box with Mrs. Lincoln, Mrs. Harris and Major Rathburn, was shot by an assassin, who suddenly entered the box and approached behind the President.

The assassin then leaped upon the stage, brandishing a large dagger or knife, and made his escape in the rear of the theatre.

The pistol ball entered the back of the President's head and penetrated nearly through the head. The wound is mortal.

The President has been insensible ever since it was inflicted, and is now dying.

About the same hour an assassin, whether the same or not, entered Mr. Seward's apartments, and under pretence of having a prescription was shown to the Secretary's sick chamber. The assassin immediately rushed to the bed and inflicted two or three stabs on the throat and two on the face.

It is hoped the wounds may not be mortal. My apprehension is that they will prove fatal.

The nurse alarmed Mr. Frederick Seward, who was in an adjoining room, and he hastened to the door of his father's room, when he met the assassin, who inflicted upon him one or more dangerous wounds. The recovery of Frederick Seward is doubtful.

It is not probable that the President will live through the night.

General Grant and wife were advertised to be at the theatre this evening, but he started to Burlington at six o'clock this evening.

At a Cabinet meeting, at which General Grant was present, the subject of the state of the country and the prospect of a speedy peace were discussed. The President was very cheerful and hopeful, and spoke very kindly of General Lee and others of the confederacy, and of the establishment of government in Virginia.

All the members of the Cabinet except Mr. Seward, are now in attendance upon the President.

I have seen Mr. Seward, but he and Frederick were both unconscious.

EDWIN M. STANTON,
Secretary of War.

THE HERALD DESPATCHES.

Washington, April 14, 1865.

Assassination has been inaugurated in Washington. The bowie knife and pistol have been applied to President Lincoln and Secretary Seward. The former was shot in the throat, while at Ford's theatre to-night. Mr. Seward was badly cut about the neck, while in his bed at his residence.

SECOND DESPATCH.

Washington, April 14, 1865.

An attempt was made about ten o'clock this evening to assassinate the President and Secretary Seward. The President was shot at Ford's Theatre. Result not yet known. Mr. Seward's throat was cut, and his son badly wounded.

There is intense excitement here.

Details of the Assassination.

Washington, April 14, 1865.

Washington was thrown into an intense excitement a few minutes before eleven o'clock this evening, by the announcement that the President and Secretary Seward had been assassinated and were dead.

The wildest excitement prevailed in all parts of the city. Men, women and children, old and young, rushed to and fro, and the rumors were magnified until we had nearly every member of the Cabinet killed. Some time elapsed before authentic data could be ascertained in regard to the affair.

About half-past ten o'clock this evening a tall, well dressed man made his appearance at Secretary Seward's residence, and applied for admission. He was refused admission by the servant, when the desperado stated that he had a prescription from the Surgeon General, and that he was ordered to deliver it in person. He was still refused, except upon the written order of the physician. This he pretended to show, and pushed by the servant and rushed up stairs to Mr. Seward's room. He was met at the door by Mr. Fred Seward, who notified him that he was master of the house, and would take charge of the medicine. After a few words had passed between them he dodged by Fred Seward and rushed to the Secretary's bed, and struck him in the neck with a dagger, and also in the breast.

It was supposed at first that Mr. Seward was killed instantly, but it was found afterwards that the wound was not mortal.

Major Wm. H. Seward, Jr., paymaster, was in the room, and rushed to the defence of his father, and was badly cut in the *melee* with the assassin, but not fatally.

The desperado managed to escape from the house, and was prepared for escape by having a horse at the door. He immediately mounted his horse, and sung out the motto of the State of Virginia, "*Sic Semper Tyrannis!*" and rode off.

Surgeon General Barnes was immediately sent for, and he *examined Mr. Seward and pronounced him safe.* His wounds were not fatal. The jugular vein was not cut, nor the wound in the breast deep enough to be fatal.

The President and Mrs. Lincoln were at Ford's theatre, listening to the performance of the American Cousin, occupying a box in the second tier. At the close of the third act a person entered the box occupied by the President, and shot Mr. Lincoln in the head. The shot entered the back of his head, and came out above the temple.

The assassin then jumped from the box upon the stage and ran across to the other side, exhibiting a dagger in his hand, flourishing it in a tragical manner, shouting the same words repeated by the desperado at Mr. Seward's house, adding to it, "The South is avenged," and then escaped from the back entrance to the stage, but in his passage dropped his pistol and his hat.

Mr. Lincoln fell forward from his seat, and Mrs. Lincoln fainted.

The moment the astonished audience could realize what had happened, the President was taken and carried to Mr. Petersen's house, in Tenth street, opposite to the theatre. Medical aid was immediately sent for, and the wound was at first supposed to be fatal, and it was announced that he could not live; but at half-past twelve he is still alive, though in a precarious condition.

As the assassin ran across the stage, Colonel J. B. Stewart, of this city, who was occupying one of the front seats in the orchestra, on the same side of the house as the box occupied by Mr. Lincoln, sprang to the stage and followed him; but he was obstructed in his passage across the stage by the fright of the actors, and reached the back door about three seconds after the assassin had passed out. Colonel Stewart got to the street just in time to see him mount his horse and ride away.

This operation shows that the whole thing was a preconcerted plan. The person who fired the pistol was a man about thirty years of age, about five feet nine, spare built, fair skin, dark hair, apparently bushy, with a large mustache. Laura Keene and the leader of the orchestra declare that they recognized him as J. Wilkes Booth the actor, and a rabid secessionist. Whoever he was, it is plainly evident that he thoroughly understood the theatre and all the approaches and modes of escape to the stage. A person not familiar with the theatre could not have possibly made his escape so well and quickly.

The alarm was sounded in every quarter. Mr. Stanton was notified, and immediately left his house.

All the other members of the Cabinet escaped attack. Cavalrymen were sent out in all directions, and despatches sent to all the fortifications, and it is thought they will be captured.

Washington, April 15—1 A. M.

The streets in the vicinity of Ford's Theatre are densely crowded by an anxious and excited crowd. A guard has been placed across Tenth street and F and E streets, and only official persons and particular friends of the President are allowed to pass.

The popular heart is deeply stirred, and the deepest indignation against leading rebels is freely expressed.

The scene at the house where the President lies *in extremis* is very affecting. Even Secretary Stanton is affected to tears.

When the news spread through the city that the President had been shot, the people, with pale faces and compressed lips, crowded every place where there was the slightest chance of obtaining information in regard to the affair.

After the President was shot, Lieutenant Rathbun, caught the assassin by the arm, who immediately struck him with a knife, and jumped from the box, as before stated.

The popular affection for Mr. Lincoln has been shown by this diabolical assassination, which will bring eternal infamy, not only upon its authors, but upon the hellish cause which they desire to avenge.

Vice President Johnson arrived at the White House, where the President lies, about one o'clock, and will remain with him to the last.

The President's family are in attendance upon him also.

As soon as intelligence could be got to the War Department, the electric telegraph and the Signal corps were put in requisition to endeavor to prevent the escape of the assassins, and all the troops around Washington are under arms.

Popular report points to a somewhat celebrated actor of known secession proclivities as the assassin; but it would be unjust to name him until some further evidence of his guilt is obtained. It is rumored that the person alluded to is in custody.

The latest advices from Secretary Seward reveals more desperate work there than at first supposed. Seward's wounds are not in themselves fatal; but, in connection with his recent injuries, and the great loss of blood he has sustained, his recovery is questionable.

It was Clarence A. Seward, instead of Wm. H. Seward, Jr., who was wounded. Fred. Seward was also badly cut, as were also three nurses, who were in attendance upon the Secretary, showing that a desperate struggle took place there. The wounds of the whole party were dressed.

One o'Clock A. M.

The President is perfectly senseless, and there is not the slightest hope of his surviving. Physicians believe that he will die before morning. All of his Cabinet, except Secretary Seward, are with him. Speaker Colfax, Senator Farwell, of Maine, and many other gentlemen, are also at the house awaiting the termination.

The scene at the President's bedside is described by one who witnessed it as most affecting. It was surrounded by his Cabinet ministers, all of whom were bathed in tears, not even excepting Mr. Stanton, who, when informed by Surgeon General Barnes, that the President could not live until morning, exclaimed, "Oh, no, General; no—no;" and with an impulse, natural as it was unaffected, immediately sat down on a chair near his bedside and wept like a child.

Senator Sumner was seated on the right of the President's couch, near the head, holding the right hand of the President in his own. He was sobbing like a woman, with his head bowed down almost on the pillow of the bed on which the President was lying.

Two o'Clock A. M.

The President is still alive, but there is no improvement in his condition.

THE PRESS DESPATCHES.

Washington, April 15—12:30 A. M.

The President was shot in a theatre to-night, and is perhaps mortally wounded.

SECOND DESPATCH.

Washington, April 15—1 A. M.

The President is not expected to live through the night. He was shot at a theatre.

Secretary Seward was also assassinated. No arteries were cut.

Additional Details of the Assassination.

Washington, April 15—1:30 A. M.

President Lincoln and wife, with other friends, this evening visited Ford's theatre, for the purpose of witnessing the performance of the American Cousin.

It was announced in the papers that General Grant would also be present; but that gentleman took the late train of cars for New Jersey.

The theatre was densely crowded, and all seemed delighted with the scene before them. During the third act, and while there was a temporary pause for one of the actors to enter, a sharp report of a pistol was heard, which merely attracted attention, but suggested nothing serious, until a man rushed to the front of the President's box, waving a long dagger in his right hand, and exclaiming "*Sic semper tyrannis!*" and immediately leaped from the box, which was in the second tier, to the stage beneath, and ran across to the opposite side, making his escape, amid the bewilderment of the audience, from the rear of the theatre, and, mounting a horse, fled.

The screams of Mrs. Lincoln first disclosed the fact to the audience that the President had been shot, when all present rose to their feet, rushing towards the stage, many exclaiming "Hang him! Hang him!"

The excitement was of the wildest possible description, and of course there was an abrupt termination of the theatrical performance.

There was a rush toward the President's box, when cries were heard:—"Stand back and give him air." "Has any one stimulants?"

On a hasty examination it was found that the President had been shot through the head, above and back of the temporal bone, and that some of the brain was oozing out.

He was removed to a private house opposite to the theatre, and the Surgeon General of the army and other surgeons sent for to attend to his condition.

On an examination of the private box blood was discovered on the back of the cushioned rocking chair on which the President had been sitting, also on the partition and on the floor. A common single barreled pocket pistol was found on the carpet.

A military guard was placed in front of the private residence to which the President had been conveyed. An immense crowd was in front of it, all deeply anxious to learn the condition of the President. It had been previously announced that the wound was mortal, but all hoped otherwise. The shock to the community was terrible.

At midnight the Cabinet, with Messrs. Sumner, Colfax and Farnsworth, Judge Curtis, Governor Oglesby, General Meigs, Colonel Hay, and a few personal friends, with Surgeon General Barnes and his immediate assistants, were around his bedside.

The President was in a state of syncope, totally insensible, and breathing slowly. The blood oozed from the wound at the back of his head.

The surgeons exhausted every possible effort of medicinal skill; but all hope was gone.

The parting of his family with the dying President is too sad for description.

The President and Mrs. Lincoln did not start for the theatre until fifteen minutes after eight o'clock. Speaker Colfax was at the White House at the time, and the President stated to him that he was going. Mrs. Lincoln had not been well, because the papers had announced that General Grant and they were to be present, and, as General Grant had gone North, he did not wish the audience to be disappointed.

He went with apparent reluctance, and urged Mr. Colfax to go with him; but that gentleman had made other engagements, and, with Mr. Ashmun, of Massachusetts, bid him goodby.

When the excitement at the theatre was at its wildest height reports were circulated that Secretary Seward had also been assassinated.

On reaching this gentleman's residence a crowd and a military guard were found at the door, and on entering it was ascertained that the reports were based on truth.

Everybody there was so excited that scarcely an intelligible word could be gathered. But the facts are substantially as follows:—

About ten o'clock a man rang the bell, and the call having been answered by a colored servant, he said he had come from Dr. Verdi, Secretary Seward's family physician, with a prescription, at the same time holding in his hand a small piece of folded paper, and saying, in answer to a refusal, that he must see the Secretary, as he was entrusted with particular directions concerning the medicine.

He still insisted on going up, although repeatedly informed that no one could enter the chamber. The man pushed the servant aside, and walked hastily towards the Secretary's room, and was then met by Mr. Frederick Seward, of whom he demanded to see the Secretary, making the same representation which he did to the servant.

What further passed in the way of colloquy is not known; but the man struck him on the head with a billy, severely injuring the skull and felling him almost senseless.

The assassin then rushed into the chamber and attacked Major Seward, Paymaster United States Army, and Mr. Hansell, a messenger of the State Department, and two male nurses, disabling them all.

He then rushed upon the Secretary, who was lying in bed in the same room, and inflicted three stabs in the neck, but severing, it is thought and hoped, no arteries, though he bled profusely.

The assassin then rushed down stairs, mounted his horse at the door, and rode off before an alarm could be sounded, and in the same manner as the assassin of the President.

It is believed that the injuries of the Secretary are not fatal, nor those of either of the others, although both the Secretary and the Assistant Secretary are very seriously injured.

Secretaries Stanton and Welles, and other prominent officers of the Government, called at Secretary Seward's house to inquire into his condition, and there heard of the assassination of the President.

They then proceeded to the house where he was lying, exhibiting of course intense anxiety and solicitude.

An immense crowd was gathered in front of the President's house, and a strong guard was also stationed there. Many persons evidently supposing he would be brought to his home.

The entire city to-night presents a scene of wild excitement, accompanied by violent expression of indignation and the profoundest sorrow; many shed tears.

The military authorities have despatched mounted patrols in every direction, in order, if possible, to arrest the assassins. The whole metropolitan police are likewise vigilant for the same purpose.

The attacks, both at the theatre and at Secretary Seward's house, took place at about the same hour—ten o'clock—thus showing a preconcerted plan to assassinate those gentlemen. Some evidences of the guilt of the party who attacked the President are in the possession of the police.

Vice President Johnson is in the city, and his head quarters are guarded by troops.

THE LATEST NEWS.

Secretary Stanton to General Dix.

War Department,
Washington, April 15—3 A. M.

Major General Dix, New York:—

The President still breathes, but is quite insensible, as he has been ever since he was shot. He evidently did not see the person who shot him, but was looking on the stage, as he was approached from behind.

Mr. Seward has rallied, and it is hoped he may live.

Frederick Seward's condition is very critical.

The attendant who was present was shot through the lungs, and is not expected to live.

The wounds of Major Seward are not serious.

Investigation strongly indicates J. Wilkes Booth as the assassin of the President. Whether it was the same or a different person that attempted to murder Mr. Seward remains in doubt.

Chief Justice Carlter is engaged in taking the evidence.

Every exertion has been made to prevent the escape of the murderer. His horse has been found on the road near Washington.

EDWIN M. STANTON, Secretary of War.

Our Special Washington Despatch.

Washington, April 15, 1865.

When the fatal shot was fired, Mrs. Lincoln, who was [illegible] exclaimed, "Oh, why didn't they shoot me—why didn't they shoot me!"

There is evidence that Secretary Stanton was also marked for assassination. On receipt of intelligence at the War Department of the attack on the President, two employes of the department were sent to summon the Secretary. Just as they approached his house, a man jumped out from behind a tree box in front of the house and ran away. It is well known to be the custom of the Secretary to go from the department to his house between nine and twelve P. M., and usually unattended. It is supposed that the assassin intended to shoot him as he entered the house, but failed from the fact that Mr. Stanton remained at home during the evening.

The circumstantial evidence is very strong that J. Wilkes Booth is the person who shot the President. Several parties who are well acquainted with him, and saw the assassin when he jumped from the box, are positive that he is the man. It is also reported that Booth's horse was saddled at the side door of the theatre, and was rode off by the assassin. If he is the man, it is impossible for him to escape. The horse of the man who made the attack on Secretary Seward has been found near the Lincoln Hospital, bathed in sweat, and with blood upon the saddle cloths.

Three o'Clock A. M.

There is up to this time no material change in the President's condition.

The Press Despatch.

Washington, April 15—2:12.

The President is still alive, but he is growing weaker. The ball is lodged in his brain, three inches from where it entered the skull. He remains insensible, and his condition is utterly helpless.

The Vice President has been to see him; but all company except the members of the Cabinet and of the family is rigidly excluded.

Large crowds still continue in the street, as near the house as the line of guards allow.

IMPORTANT FROM SOUTH AMERICA.

Surrender of Montevideo to Gen. Flores—Brazil in Possession of the City, &c.

The Brazilian mail arrived at Lisbon April 2, bringing the following advices:—

Montevideo has surrendered to General Flores.

The Brazilians now (March 11) occupy the city.

Rio Janeiro, March 11, 1865.

Exchange 25⅝ a 26¼.

Coffee—Sales of good firsts at 65.66. Shipments, 100,000 bags. Stock, 100,000 bags. Freights, 50.62½.

Bahia, March 11, 1865.

Exchange 26¼. Cotton nominal.

News from San Francisco.

San Francisco, April 12, 1865.

The exports of treasure for the quarter just ended show a falling off of about six and a half millions as compared with the same period last year.

City Intelligence.

Easter Sunday at St. Ann's Church.—The admirers of sacred music, made truly effective by a well trained choir, have an opportunity of indulging their taste by repairing to St. Ann's church on Easter Sunday evening, the doors opening at seven, the concert begining at eight. Three of the pieces are from Gordigiani, three from Rossini and one from each of the composers Verdi, Donizetti, Verrimst, Dachauer and Gounod. We need only mention the names of Signor Remi and Messrs. Schmitz, Schubert and Dachauer to insure confidence in the vocal results. The ladies are quite distinguished for contralto and soprano execution, and no exertion will be spared to make the musical feast worthy of the day.

A New Church.—An advertisement among our religious notices announces the opening of the new Church of the Holy Trinity, Madison avenue, corner of Forty-second street, on Sunday. Sermons will be preached at the three sessions by Rev. Dr. Tyng, of St. George's, Rev. Dr. Dyer, and the Rev. Stephen H. Tyng, Jr., the pastor of the church. It promises to be an occasion of great interest to residents on Murray Hill.

Mrs Emma Hardinge delivers her able lecture on "Politics in the Pulpit" this evening, at Dodworth Hall. To test the lady's ability, any questions the audience desire to ask will be answered.

Man Drowned.—On the morning of the 13th instant a journeyman housepainter, whose name is believed to be Barnard Burns, was accidentally drowned at Gunther's, Long Island. His body has not yet been claimed by his friends. Mr. J. R. Acker, of No. 9 Macdougal street, will give facilities to any one who can identify the corpse.

POSTSCRIPT

Saturday, April 15—10 A. M.

DEATH OF THE PRESIDENT!!

Secretary Stanton to General Dix.

War Department,
Washington, April 15—4:10 A. M.

To Major General Dix:—

The President continues insensible and is sinking.

Secretary Seward remains without change.

Frederick Seward's skull is fractured in two places, besides a severe cut upon the head. The attendant is still alive but hopeless. Major Seward's wounds not dangerous.

It is now ascertained with reasonable certainty that two assassins were engaged in the horrible crime, Wilkes Booth being the one that shot the President, and the other a companion of his whose name is not known, but whose description is so clear that he can hardly escape.

It appears from a letter found in Booth's trunk that the murder was planned before the 4th of March, but fell through then because the accomplice backed out until "Richmond could be heard from."

Booth and his accomplice were at the livery stable at six o'clock last evening, and left there with their horses about ten o'clock, or shortly before that hour.

It would appear that they had for several days been seeking their chance, but for some unknown reason it was not carried into effect until last night.

One of them has evidently made his way to Baltimore—the other has not yet been traced.

EDWIN M. STANTON,
Secretary of War.

War Department,
Washington, April 15, 1865.

To Major General Dix, New York:—

Abraham Lincoln died this morning at twenty-two minutes after seven o'clock.

EDWIN M. STANTON,
Secretary of War.

THE REBELS.

JEFF. DAVIS AT DANVILLE.

His Latest Appeal to His Deluded Followers.

He Thinks the Fall of Richmond a Blessing in Disguise, as it Leaves the Rebel Armies Free to Move from Point to Point.

He Vainly Promises to Hold Virginia at All Hazards.

Lee and His Army Supposed to be Safe.

Breckinridge and the Rest of Davis' Cabinet Reach Danville Safely.

The Organ of Governor Vance, of North Carolina, Advises the Submission of the Rebels to President Lincoln's Terms,

&c., &c., &c.

Jeff. Davis' Last Proclamation.

VIRGINIA TO BE HELD BY THE REBELS AT ALL HAZARDS.

Danville, Va., April 5, 1865.

The General-in-Chief found it necessary to make such movements of his troops as to uncover the capital. It would be unwise to conceal the *moral and material injury to our cause resulting from the occupation of our capital* by the enemy. It is equally unwise and unworthy of us to allow our own energies to falter and our efforts to become relaxed under adverses, however calamitous they may be. For many months *the largest and finest army of* the confederacy, under command of a leader whose presence inspires equal confidence in the troops and the people, has been greatly trammelled by the necessity of keeping constant watch over the approaches to the capital, and has thus been forced to forego more than one opportunity for promising enterprise. It is for us, my countrymen, to show by our bearing under reverses how wretched has been the self-deception of those who have believed us less able to endure misfortune with fortitude than to encounter dangers with courage.

We have now entered upon a new phase of the struggle. Relieved from the necessity of guarding particular points, *our army will be free to move from point to point*, strike the enemy in detail far from his base. *Let us but will it and we are free.*

Animated by that confidence in spirit and fortitude which never yet failed me, I announce to you, fellow countrymen, that it is my purpose to maintain your cause with my whole heart and soul; that I will never consent to abandon to the enemy one foot of the soil of any one of the States of the confederacy. That Virginia—noble State—whose ancient renown has been eclipsed by her still more glorious recent history; whose bosom has been bared to receive the main shock of this war; whose sons and daughters have exhibited heroism so sublime as to render her illustrious in all time to come—that Virginia, with the help of the people and by the blessing of Providence, *shall be held and defended*, and no peace ever be made with the infamous invaders of her territory.

If by the stress of numbers we should ever be compelled to a temporary withdrawal from her limits, or those of any other border State, again and again will we return, until the baffled and exhausted enemy shall abandon in despair his endless and impossible task of making slaves of a people resolved to be free.

Let us, then, not despond, my countrymen; but, relying on God, meet the foe with fresh defiance and with unconquered and unconquerable hearts.

JEFFERSON DAVIS.

The Evacuation of the Rebel Capital.

THE FIRST REBEL ACCOUNT OF HOW THE CITY WAS ABANDONED.

[From the Danville (Va.) Register, April 5.]

Persons who left the capital Sunday night and Monday morning represent that the scene which followed the evacuation of the city by our troops beggars description. To preserve order and protect the property of the citizens who unavoidably remained there, as far as could be done, the Nineteenth Virginia militia, under Colonel Evans, was placed on police duty in the city, to await the coming of the enemy; but accounts state that they failed to render any aid or protection to the people whatever. On Sunday night a mob of the lower classes of the city, composed, it is said, mostly of the foreign element, visited a number of the largest storehouses of the city and robbed them of their contents. It is affirmed that Main street was pillaged, and then burned, and that some of the milling establishments were also committed to the flames. We have no doubt that a considerable portion of that brave city has been laid in ashes, and a number of its people insulted, outraged, robbed and massacred. How painful the thought that the place should be given over to rapine and plunder, even before the public enemy entered its limits. But the fact only proves that the people of Richmond have had secret enemies in their own midst scarcely less savage and even more treacherous and vindictive than the open foe.

We are told that the people banded together during the violent proceeding of the mob and resisted them with force, a street fight ensuing, in which several persons were killed.

No intelligence has reached us of the enemy's troops occupying the city. The last trains on the Danville railroad which came out of the place left Monday morning, and passengers upon them had heard nothing from the enemy. The greater portion of Grant's army was transferred to the south side of James river some days ago, only the command of General Ord, which is composed mostly, if not entirely, of negro troops, being left on the north side. This command will enter and occupy the city. Some of our people who are acquainted with the character of General Ord think they have reason to hope that his treatment of the unfortunate people of Richmond will not be so hard, and cruel and inhuman as that which has fallen upon the heads of our fellow citizens in some other captured cities.

The newspapers of Richmond, we suppose, all fell into the hands of the enemy. The evacuation of the city was so sudden and unexpected—scarcely any one being prepared for it—that no time was left for the removal of so cumbrous an establishment as a city newspaper office. In a few days we may expect to hear that the *Enquirer* or the *Whig* or the *Examiner* is issued as a Yankee paper.

All the rolling stock of the Richmond and Danville Railroad in running order was saved on the retreat from Richmond. A few old cars, not in a movable condition, were left at Manchester. No train was captured by the enemy near the junction, as was at one time reported; and, indeed, we do not believe that any body of Yankees had struck the road at any point up to yesterday evening.

The Secretary of War, the Quartermaster General, Commissary General and a number of other officers of the government, left Richmond on horseback, and will probably arrive at this place to-morrow.

Should General Lee establish his lines east of the junction, we suppose the State Legislature will be convened at Lynchburg.

All the specie and other valuables belonging to the banks in Richmond were removed from the city on Sunday, and have been carried to places of safety.

A considerable amount of goods purchased by the State for distribution to the people, we regret to learn, had to be left behind. Also the State archives remained in the city; but we perceive no motive the enemy can have in destroying them, as they will, no doubt, endeavor to occupy the city permanently, and establish a State government at Richmond under the federal Union.

The Organ of Governor Vance, of North Carolina, Advising General Lee to Submit on Mr. Lincoln's Terms.

[From the Raleigh Confederate, April 7.]

The *Conservative* occasionally seems to fall into very mysterious hands, and to come under the control of an incomprehensible influence. On the day before yesterday that paper availed itself of a period of extreme reverse and disaster to renew the attempt to cast odium on a portion of our own citizens, which has been a favorite policy with its political leaders ever since the reverses began, and after it was no longer politic to claim that they "made the revolution." Yesterday it sends to the public a leader of still more extraordinary import. From what we comprehend of it, it seems to be *a distinct proposition to submit and surrender upon the terms proposed by Lincoln.* This has never yet, that we recollect of, been more distinctly proposed, even by journals whose loyalty has been called in question. The *Conservative* says:—"It is nonsense to propose to treat with the North with any expectation of the concession that the confederacy is a government," and hence, says the *Conservative*, "if our authorities are determined to force this condition upon the North, as a basis of negotiation, then the North will never negotiate." What is this but surrender? Not only surrender, but an assertion to the world that the defence of the last four years has been of a position which is one of sheer nonsense—one which the North "never could admit?" We have not seen in this controversy so bold and unconditional a justification of the Northern invasion; for, if we sought to force a claim inconsistent with reason, and to demand an "admission" which "is an absurdity in anything like government," and the North only resisted such claim and refused such admission, then we are in the wrong and the Yankee government is right, and the writer of the article to which we are replying does well when he *advises General Lee not to "block up his way, at the threshold, by presenting a basis to which he knows the enemy will not yield,"* but "to meet him on his own ground," as "the only way to open the negotiation." When we remember what "his own ground" is, upon which the *Conservative* proposes to meet the enemy, we may readily understand how much it is prepared to concede. "His own ground" measured the length of three propositions; submission to the laws and constitution of the United States, the laying down of our arms, and acquiescence in Lincoln's proclamations. This is the ground on which the author of the editorial desires General Lee to meet Lincoln and "secure a talk about peace." We have no idea that Governor Vance will support this idea; but it is very unfortunate that, at the very moment when everything should be said to uphold the hopes and confidence of the army and people, such sentiments should obtain publication in the organ of the Governor.

Exchange of the Rebel General Vance.

[From the Ashville (N. C.) News.]

The exchange of prisoners seems to go steadily on. We have seen a large number of our mountain boys, who have reached home after a protracted imprisonment. Among others we were gratified to meet Brigadier General R. B. Vance, who reached home some days since. He looks rather worsted by his long confinement, but, as usual with him, is full of life, cheerful and buoyant. The General is a great favorite of the people of this section, and everybody was glad to see him.

THE NEW YORK HERALD.

WHOLE NO. 10,456. NEW YORK, SATURDAY, APRIL 15, 1865. PRICE FOUR CENTS.

IMPORTANT.

ASSASSINATION OF PRESIDENT LINCOLN.

The President Shot at the Theatre Last Evening.

SECRETARY SEWARD DAGGERED IN HIS BED, BUT NOT MORTALLY WOUNDED.

Clarence and Frederick Seward Badly Hurt.

ESCAPE OF THE ASSASSINS.

Intense Excitement in Washington.

Scene at the Deathbed of Mr. Lincoln.

J. Wilkes Booth, the Actor, the Alleged Assassin of the President,

&c., &c., &c.

THE OFFICIAL DESPATCH.

WAR DEPARTMENT, WASHINGTON, April [illegible] A. M.

Major General Dix, New York:—

This evening at about 9:30 P. M., at Ford's Theatre, the President, while sitting in his private box with Mrs. Lincoln, Mrs. Harris and Major Rathburn, was shot by an assassin, who suddenly entered the box and approached behind the President.

The assassin then leaped upon the stage, brandishing a large dagger or knife, and made his escape in the rear of the theatre.

The pistol ball entered the back of the President's head and penetrated nearly through the head. The wound is mortal.

The President has been insensible ever since it was inflicted, and is now dying.

About the same hour an assassin, whether the same or not, entered Mr. Seward's apartments, and under pretence of having a prescription was shown to the Secretary's sick chamber. The assassin immediately rushed to the bed and inflicted two or three stabs on the throat and two on the face.

It is hoped the wounds may not be mortal. My apprehension is that they will prove fatal.

The nurse alarmed Mr. Frederick Seward, who was in an adjoining room, and he hastened to the door of his father's room, when he met the assassin, who inflicted upon him one or more dangerous wounds. The recovery of Frederick Seward is doubtful.

It is not probable that the President will live through the night.

General Grant and wife were advertised to be at the theatre this evening, but he started to Burlington at six o'clock this evening.

At a Cabinet meeting, at which General Grant was present, the subject of the state of the country and the prospect of a speedy peace were discussed. The President was very cheerful and hopeful, and spoke very kindly of General Lee and others of the confederacy, and of the establishment of government in Virginia.

All the members of the Cabinet except Mr. Seward, are now in attendance upon the President.

I have seen Mr. Seward, but he and Frederick were both unconscious.

EDWIN M. STANTON,
Secretary of War.

THE HERALD DESPATCHES.

WASHINGTON, April 14, 1865.

Assassination has been inaugurated in Washington. The bowie knife and pistol have been applied to President Lincoln and Secretary Seward. The former was shot in the throat, while at Ford's theatre to-night. Mr. Seward was badly cut about the neck, while in his bed at his residence.

SECOND DESPATCH.

WASHINGTON, April 14, 1865.

An attempt was made about ten o'clock this evening to assassinate the President and Secretary Seward. The President was shot at Ford's Theatre. Result not yet known. Mr. Seward's throat was cut, and his son badly wounded.

There is intense excitement here.

Details of the Assassination.

WASHINGTON, April 14, 1865.

Washington was thrown into an intense excitement a few minutes before eleven o'clock this evening, by the announcement that the President and Secretary Seward had been assassinated and were dead.

The wildest excitement prevailed in all parts of the city. Men, women and children, old and young, rushed to and fro, and the rumors were magnified until we had nearly every member of the Cabinet killed. Some time elapsed before authentic data could be ascertained in regard to the affair.

About half-past ten o'clock this evening a tall, well dressed man made his appearance at Secretary Seward's residence, and applied for admission. He was refused admission by the servant, when the desperado stated that he had a prescription from the Surgeon General, and that he was ordered to deliver it in person. He was still refused, except upon the written order of the physician. This he pretended to show, and pushed by the servant and rushed up stairs to Mr. Seward's room. He was met at the door by Mr. Fred Seward, who notified him that he was master of the house, and would take charge of the medicine. After a few words had passed between them he dodged by Fred Seward and rushed to the Secretary's bed, and struck him in the neck with a dagger, and also in the breast.

It was supposed at first that Mr. Seward was killed instantly, but it was found afterwards that the wound was not mortal.

Major Wm. H. Seward, Jr., paymaster, was in the room, and rushed to the defence of his father, and was badly cut in the mêlée with the assassin, but not fatally.

The desperado managed to escape from the house, and was prepared for escape by having a horse at the door. He immediately mounted his horse, and sung out the motto of the State of Virginia, *"Sic Semper Tyrannis!"* and rode off.

Surgeon General Barnes was immediately sent for, and he *examined Mr. Seward and pronounced him safe.* His wounds were not fatal. The jugular vein was not cut, nor the wound in the breast deep enough to be fatal.

The President and Mrs. Lincoln were at Ford's theatre, listening to the performance of the American Cousin, occupying a box in the second tier. At the close of the third act a person entered the box occupied by the President, and shot Mr. Lincoln in the head. The shot entered the back of his head, and came out above the temple.

The assassin then jumped from the box upon the stage, and ran across to the other side, exhibiting a dagger in his hand, flourishing it in a tragical manner, shouting the same words repeated by the desperado at Mr. Seward's house, adding to it, "The South is avenged," and then escaped from the back entrance to the stage, but in his passage dropped his pistol and his hat.

Mr. Lincoln fell forward from his seat, and Mrs. Lincoln fainted.

The moment the astonished audience could realize what had happened, the President was taken and carried to Mr. Petersen's house, in Tenth street, opposite to the theatre. Medical aid was immediately sent for, and the wound was at first supposed to be fatal, and it was announced that he could not live; but at half-past twelve he is still alive, though in a precarious condition.

As the assassin ran across the stage, Colonel J. B. Stewart, of this city, who was occupying one of the front seats in the orchestra, on the same side of the house as the box occupied by Mr. Lincoln, sprang to the stage and followed him; but he was obstructed in his passage across the stage by the fright of the actors, and reached the back door about three seconds after the assassin had passed out. Colonel Stewart got to the street just in time to see him mount his horse and ride away.

This operation shows that the whole thing was a [illegible] [illegible]stol was a man about thirty years of age, about five feet nine, spare built, fair skin, dark hair, apparently bushy, with a large mustache. Laura Keene and the leader of the orchestra declare that they recognized him as J. Wilkes Booth the actor, and a rabid secessionist. Whoever he was, it is plainly evident that he thoroughly understood the theatre and all the approaches and modes of escape to the stage. A person not familiar with the theatre could not have possibly made his escape so well and quickly.

The alarm was sounded in every quarter. Mr. Stanton was notified, and immediately left his house.

All the other members of the Cabinet escaped attack.

Cavalrymen were sent out in all directions, and despatches sent to all the fortifications, and it is thought they will be captured.

WASHINGTON, April 15—1 A. M.

The streets in the vicinity of Ford's Theatre are densely crowded by an anxious and excited crowd. A guard has been placed across Tenth street and F and E streets, and only official persons and particular friends of the President are allowed to pass.

The popular heart is deeply stirred, and the deepest indignation against leading rebels is freely expressed.

The scene at the house where the President lies *in extremis* is very affecting. Secretary Stanton is affected to tears.

When the news spread through the city that the President had been shot, the people, with pale faces and compressed lips, crowded every place where there was the slightest chance of obtaining information in regard to the affair.

After the President was shot, Lieutenant Rathbun, caught the assassin by the arm, who immediately struck him with a knife, and jumped from the box, as before stated.

The popular affection for Mr. Lincoln has been shown by this diabolical assassination, which will bring eternal infamy, not only upon its authors, but upon the hellish cause which they desire to avenge.

Vice President Johnson arrived at the White House, where the President lies, about one o'clock, and will remain with him to the last.

The President's family are in attendance upon him also.

As soon as intelligence could be got to the War Department, the electric telegraph and the Signal corps were put in requisition to endeavor to prevent the escape of the assassins, and all the troops around Washington are under arms.

Popular report points to a somewhat celebrated actor of known secession proclivities as the assassin; but it would be unjust to name him until some further evidence of his guilt is obtained. It is rumored that the person alluded to is in custody.

The latest advices from Secretary Seward reveals more desperate work there than at first supposed. Seward's wounds are not in themselves fatal; but, in connection with his recent injuries, and the great loss of blood he has sustained, his recovery is questionable.

Fred. Seward was also badly cut, as were also three nurses, who were in attendance upon the Secretary, showing that a desperate struggle took place there. The wounds of the whole party were dressed.

ONE O'CLOCK A. M.

The President is perfectly senseless, and there is not the slightest hope of his surviving. Physicians believe that he will die before morning. All of his Cabinet, except Secretary Seward, are with him. Speaker Colfax, Senator Farwell, of Maine, and many other gentlemen, are also at the house awaiting the termination.

The scene at the President's bedside is described by one who witnessed it as most affecting. It was surrounded by his Cabinet ministers, all of whom were bathed in tears, not even excepting Mr. Stanton, who, when informed by Surgeon General Barnes, that the President could not live until morning, exclaimed, "Oh, no, General; no—no;" and with an impulse, natural as it was unaffected, immediately sat down on a chair near his bedside and wept like a child.

Senator Sumner was seated on the right of the President's couch, near the head, holding the right hand of the President in his own. He was sobbing like a woman, with his head bowed down almost on the pillow of the bed on which the President was lying.

TWO O'CLOCK A. M.

The President is still alive, but there is no improvement in his condition.

THE PRESS DESPATCHES.

WASHINGTON, April 15—12:30 A. M.

The President was shot in a theatre to-night, and is perhaps mortally wounded.

SECOND DESPATCH.

WASHINGTON, April 15—1 A. M.

The President is not expected to live through the night. He was shot at a theatre.

Secretary Seward was also assassinated. No arteries were cut.

Additional Details of the Assassination.

WASHINGTON, April 15—1:30 A. M.

President Lincoln and wife, with other friends, this evening visited Ford's theatre, for the purpose of witnessing the performance of the American Cousin.

It was announced in the papers that General Grant would also be present; but that gentleman took the late train of cars for New Jersey.

The theatre was densely crowded, and all seemed delighted with the scene before them. During the third act, and while there was a temporary pause for one of the actors to enter, a sharp report of a pistol was heard, which merely attracted attention, but suggested nothing serious, until a man rushed to the front of the President's box, waving a long dagger in his right hand, and exclaiming *"Sic semper tyrannis!"* and immediately leaped from the box, which was in the second tier, to the stage beneath, and ran across to the opposite side, making his escape, amid the bewilderment of the audience, from the rear of the theatre, and, mounting a horse, fled.

The screams of Mrs. Lincoln first disclosed the fact to the audience that the President had been shot, when all present rose to their feet, rushing towards the stage, many exclaiming "Hang him! Hang him!"

The excitement was of the wildest possible description, and of course there was an abrupt termination of the theatrical performance.

There was a rush toward the President's box, when cries were heard:—"Stand back and give him air." "Has any one stimulants?"

On a hasty examination it was found that the President had been shot through the head, above and back of the temporal bone, and that some of the brain was oozing out.

He was removed to a private house opposite to the theatre, and the Surgeon General of the army and other surgeons sent for to attend to his condition. [illegible] covered on the back of the cushioned rocking chair on which the President had been sitting, also on the partition and on the floor. A common single barreled pocket pistol was found on the carpet.

A military guard was placed in front of the private residence to which the President had been conveyed. An immense crowd was in front of it, all deeply anxious to learn the condition of the President. It had been previously announced that the wound was mortal, but all hoped otherwise. The shock to the community was terrible.

At midnight the Cabinet, with Messrs. Sumner, Colfax and Farnsworth, Judge Curtis, Governor Oglesby, General Meigs, Colonel Hay, and a few personal friends, with Surgeon General Barnes and his immediate assistants, were around his bedside.

The President was in a state of syncope, totally insensible, and breathing slowly. The blood oozed from the wound at the back of his head.

The surgeons exhausted every possible effort of medicinal skill; but all hope was gone.

The parting of his family with the dying President is too sad for description.

The President and Mrs. Lincoln did not start for the theatre until fifteen minutes after eight o'clock. Speaker Colfax was at the White House at the time, and the President stated to him that he was going. Mrs. Lincoln had not been well, because the papers had announced that General Grant and they were to be present, and, as General Grant had gone North, he did not wish the audience to be disappointed.

He went with apparent reluctance, and urged Mr. Colfax to go with him; but that gentleman had made other engagements, and, with Mr. Ashmun, of Massachusetts, bid him goodby.

When the excitement at the theatre was at its wildest height reports were circulated that Secretary Seward had also been assassinated.

On reaching this gentleman's residence a crowd and a military guard were found at the door, and on entering it was ascertained that the reports were based on truth.

Everybody there was so excited that scarcely an intelligible word could be gathered. But the facts are substantially as follows:—

About ten o'clock a man rang the bell, and the call having been answered by a colored servant, he said he had come from Dr. Verdi, Secretary Seward's family physician, with a prescription, at the same time holding in his hand a small piece of folded paper, and saying, in answer to a refusal, that he must see the Secretary, as he was entrusted with particular directions concerning the medicine.

He still insisted on going up, although repeatedly informed that no one could enter the chamber. The man pushed the servant aside, and walked hastily towards the Secretary's room, and was then met by Mr. Frederick Seward, of whom he demanded to see the Secretary, making the same representation which he did to the servant.

What further passed in the way of colloquy is not known; but the man struck him on the head with a billy, severely injuring the skull and felling him almost senseless.

The assassin then rushed into the chamber and attacked Major Seward, Paymaster United States Army, and Mr. Hansell, a messenger of the State Department, and two male nurses, disabling them all.

He then rushed upon the Secretary, who was lying in bed in the same room, and inflicted three stabs in the neck, but severing, it is thought and hoped, no arteries, though he bled profusely.

The assassin then rushed down stairs, mounted his horse at the door, and rode off before an alarm could be sounded, and in the same manner as the assassin of the President.

It is believed that the injuries of the Secretary are not fatal, nor those of either of the others, although both the Secretary and the Assistand Secretary are very seriously injured.

Secretaries Stanton and Welles, and other prominent officers of the Government, called at Secretary Seward's house to inquire into his condition, and there heard of the assassination of the President.

They then proceeded to the house where he was lying, exhibiting of course intense anxiety and solicitude.

An immense crowd was gathered in front of the President's house, and a strong guard was also stationed there. Many persons evidently supposing he would be brought to his home.

The entire city to-night presents a scene of wild excitement, accompanied by violent expression of indignation and the profoundest sorrow; many shed tears.

The military authorities have despatched mounted patrols in every direction, in order, if possible, to arrest the assassins. The whole metropolitan police are likewise vigilant for the same purpose.

The attacks, both at the theatre and at Secretary Seward's house, took place at about the same hour—ten o'clock—thus showing a preconcerted plan to assassinate those gentlemen. Some evidences of the guilt of the party who attacked the President are in the possession of the police.

Vice President Johnson is in the city, and his head-quarters are guarded by troops.

THE LATEST NEWS.

Secretary Stanton to General Dix.

WAR DEPARTMENT,
WASHINGTON, April 15—3 A. M.

Major General Dix, New York:—

The President still breathes, but is quite insensible, as he has been ever since he was shot. He evidently did not see the person who shot him, but was looking on the stage, as he was approached from behind.

Mr. Seward has rallied, and it is hoped he may live.

Frederick Seward's condition is very critical.

The attendant who was present was shot through the lungs, and is not expected to live.

The wounds of Major Seward are not serious.

Investigation strongly indicates J. Wilkes Booth as the assassin of the President. Whether it was the same or a different person that attempted to murder Mr. Seward remains in doubt.

Chief Justice Carlter is engaged in taking the evidence.

Every exertion has been made to prevent the escape of the murderer. His horse has been found on the road near Washington.

EDWIN M. STANTON, Secretary of War.

Our Special Washington Despatch.

WASHINGTON, April 15, 1865.

When the fatal shot was fired, Mrs. Lincoln, who was alongside of her husband, exclaimed, "Oh! why didn't they shoot me—why didn't they shoot me?"

There is evidence that Secretary Stanton was also marked for assassination. [illegible] receipt of intelligence at the War Department of the attack on the President, [illegible] Secretary. Just as they approached his house, a man jumped out from behind a tree box in front of the house and ran away. It is well known to be the custom of the Secretary to go from the department to his house between nine and twelve P. M., and usually unattended. It is supposed that the assassin intended to shoot him as he entered the house, but failed from the fact that Mr. Stanton remained at home during the evening.

The circumstantial evidence is very strong that J. Wilkes Booth is the person who shot the President. Several parties who are well acquainted with him, and saw the assassin when he jumped from the box, are positive that he is the man. It is also reported that Booth's horse was saddled at the side door of the theatre, and was rode off by the assassin. If he is the man, it is impossible for him to escape. The horse of the man who made the attack on Secretary Seward has been found near the Lincoln Hospital, bathed in sweat, and with blood upon the saddle cloths.

THREE O'CLOCK A. M.

There is up to this time no material change in the President's condition.

The Press Despatch.

WASHINGTON, April 15—2:12.

The President is still alive, but he is growing weaker. The ball is lodged in his brain, three inches from where it entered the skull. He remains insensible, and his condition is utterly helpless.

The Vice President has been to see him; but all company except the members of the Cabinet and of the family is rigidly excluded.

Large crowds still continue in the street, as near the house as the line of guards allow.

IMPORTANT FROM SOUTH AMERICA.

Surrender of Montevideo to Gen. Flores—Brazil in Possession of the City, &c.

The Brazilian mail arrived at Lisbon April 2, bringing the following advices:—

Montevideo has surrendered to General Flores.

The Brazilians now (March 11) occupy the city.

RIO JANEIRO, March 11, 1865.

Exchange 25⅝ a 26¼.

Coffee—Sales of good firsts at 65.66. Shipments, 100,000 bags. Stock, 100,000 bags. Freights, 50.62½.

BAHIA, March 11, 1865.

Exchange 26¼. Cotton nominal.

News from San Francisco.

SAN FRANCISCO, April 12, 1865.

The exports of treasure for the quarter just ended show a falling off of about six and a half millions as compared with the same period last year.

City Intelligence.

EASTER SUNDAY AT ST. ANN'S CHURCH.—The admirers of sacred music, made truly effective by a well trained choir, have an opportunity of indulging their taste by repairing to St. Ann's church on Easter Sunday evening, the doors opening at seven, the concert begining at eight. Three of the pieces are from Gordigiani, three from Rossini and one from each of the composers Verdi, Donizetti, Verrimst, Dachauer and Gounod. We need only mention the names of Signor Remi and Messrs. Schmitz, Schubert and Dachauer to insure confidence in the vocal results. The ladies are quite distinguished for contralto and soprano execution, and no exertion will be spared to make the musical feast worthy of the day.

A NEW CHURCH.—An advertisement among our religious notices announces the opening of the new Church of the Holy Trinity, Madison avenue, corner of Forty-second street, on Sunday. Sermons will be preached at the three sessions by Rev. Dr. Tyng, of St. George's; Rev. Dr. Dyer, and the Rev. Stephen H. Tyng, Jr., the pastor of the church. It promises to be an occasion of great interest to residents on Murray Hill.

MISS EMMA HARDINGE delivers her able lecture on "Politics in the Pulpit" this evening, at Dodworth Hall. To test the lady's ability, any questions the audience desire to ask will be answered.

MAN DROWNED.—On the morning of the 13th instant a journeyman housepainter, whose name is believed to be Barrard Burns, was accidentally drowned at Guntherville, Long Island. His body has not yet been claimed by his friends. Mr. J. B. Acker, of No. 9 Macdougal street, will give facilities to any one who can identify the corpse.

POSTSCRIPT.

Saturday, April 15—10 A. M.

DEATH OF THE PRESIDENT!!

Condition of Secretary Seward.

Ten Thousand Dollars Reward Offered for the Arrest of the Assassins.

J. Wilkes Booth Identified as the Murderer of the President,

&c., &c., &c.

Secretary Stanton to General Dix.

WAR DEPARTMENT,
WASHINGTON, April 15—4:10 A. M.

To Major General Dix:—

The President continues insensible and is sinking.

Secretary Seward remains without change.

Frederick Seward's skull is fractured in two places, besides a severe cut upon the head. The attendant is still alive but hopeless. Major Seward's wounds not dangerous.

It is now ascertained with reasonable cer[illegible] horrible crime, Wilkes Booth being the one that shot the President, and the other a companion of his whose name is not known, but whose description is so clear that he can hardly escape.

It appears from a letter found in Booth's trunk that the murder was planned before the 4th of March, but fell through then because the accomplice backed out until "Richmond could be heard from."

Booth and his accomplice were at the livery stable at six o'clock last evening, and left there with their horses about ten o'clock, or shortly before that hour.

It would appear that they had for several days been seeking their chance, but for some unknown reason it was not carried into effect until last night.

One of them has evidently made his way to Baltimore—the other has not yet been traced.

EDWIN M. STANTON,
Secretary of War.

WAR DEPARTMENT,
WASHINGTON, April 15, 1865.

To Major General Dix, New York:—

Abraham Lincoln died this morning at twenty-two minutes after seven o'clock.

EDWIN M. STANTON,
Secretary of War.

Our Special Washington Despatch.

WASHINGTON, April 15—8 A. M.

The President died at half-past seven o'clock this morning.

The bells throughout the city are tolling. The public departments and most of the places of business are closed.

Secretary Seward is pretty comfortable this morning, the wounds inflicted upon him not being dangerous in themselves, but serious for his advanced age and previously weak condition.

Mr. Frederick Seward is very dangerously wounded, his skull having been fractured by a blow from the butt of a pistol in the hand of the assassin.

The most profound sensation prevails here, and the deepest realization of the irreparable loss which the nation has sustained pervades the minds of the people.

The Press Despatch.

WASHINGTON, April 15—8:40 A. M.

President Lincoln died this morning at half-past seven o'clock.

Major General Augur, commanding the Department of Washington, has offered a reward of ten thousand dollars to the party or parties arresting the murderer of the President, and the assassin of the Secretary of State and his son.

This morning, at six o'clock, there was no change in the condition of Secretary Seward.

The *Chronicle* says a letter found in J. Wilkes Booth's trunk identifies him as the murderer of the President.

THE REBELS.

JEFF. DAVIS AT DANVILLE.

His Latest Appeal to His Deluded Followers.

He Thinks the Fall of Richmond a Blessing in Disguise, as it Leaves the Rebel Armies Free to Move from Point to Point.

He Vainly Promises to Hold Virginia at All Hazards.

&c., &c., &c.

Jeff. Davis' Last Proclamation.

VIRGINIA TO BE HELD BY THE REBELS AT ALL HAZARDS.

DANVILLE, Va., April 5, 1865.

The General-in-Chief found it necessary to make such movements of his troops as to uncover the capital. It would be unwise to conceal the *moral and material injury to our cause resulting from the occupation of our capital* by the enemy. It is equally unwise and unworthy of us to allow our own energies to falter and our efforts to become relaxed under adverses, however calamitous they may be. For many months *the largest and finest army* of the confederacy, under command of a leader whose presence inspires equal confidence in the troops and the people, has been greatly trammelled by the necessity of keeping constant watch over the approaches to the capital, and has thus been forced to forego more than one opportunity for promising enterprise. It is for us, my countrymen, to show by our bearing under reverses how wretched has been the self deception of those who have believed us less able to endure misfortune with fortitude than to encounter dangers with courage.

We have now entered upon a new phase of the struggle. Relieved from the necessity of guarding particular points, *our army will be free to move from point to point* to strike the enemy in detail far from his base. *Let us but will it and we are free.*

Animated by that confidence in spirit and fortitude which never yet failed me, I announce to you, fellow-countrymen, that it is my purpose to maintain your cause with my whole heart and soul; that I will never consent to abandon to the enemy one foot of the soil of any one of the States of the confederacy. That Virginia—noble State—whose ancient renown has been eclipsed by her still more glorious recent history; whose bosom has been bared to receive the main shock of this war; whose sons and daughters have exhibited heroism so sublime as [illegible] with the help of the people and by the blessing of Providence, *shall be held and defended*, and no peace ever be be made with the infamous invaders of her territory.

If by the stress of numbers we should ever be compelled to a temporary withdrawal from her limits, or those of any other border State, again and again will we return, until the baffled and exhausted enemy shall abandon in despair his endless and impossible task of making slaves of a people resolved to be free.

Let us, then, not despond, my countrymen; but, relying on God, meet the foe with fresh defiance and with unconquered and unconquerable hearts.

JEFFERSON DAVIS.

The Evacution of the Rebel Capital.

THE FIRST REBEL ACCOUNT OF HOW THE CITY WAS ABANDONED.

[From the Danville (Va.) Register, April 5.]

Persons who left the capital Sunday night and Monday morning represent that the scene which followed the evacuation of the city by our troops beggars description. To preserve order and protect the property of the citizens who unavoidably remained there, as far as could be done, the Nineteenth Virginia militia, under Colonel Evans, was placed on police duty in the city, to await the coming of the enemy; but accounts state that they failed to render any aid or protection to the people whatever. On Sunday night a mob of the lower classes of the city, composed, it is said, mostly of the foreign element, visited a number of the largest storehouses of the city and robbed them of their contents. It is affirmed that Main street was pillaged, and then burned, and that some of the milling establishments were also committed to the flames. We have no doubt that a considerable portion of that brave city has been laid in ashes, and a number of its people insulted, outraged, robbed and massacred. How painful the thought that the place should be given over to rapine and plunder, even before the public enemy entered its limits. But the fact only proves that the people of Richmond have had secret enemies in their own midst scarcely less savage and even more treacherous and vindictive than the open foe.

We are told that the people banded together during the violent proceeding of the mob and resisted them with force, a street fight ensuing, in which several persons were killed.

No intelligence has reached us of the enemy's troops occupying the city. The last trains on the Danville railroad which came out of the place left Monday morning, and passengers upon them had heard nothing from the enemy. The greater portion of Grant's army was transferred to the south side of James river some days ago, only the command of General Ord, which is composed mostly, if not entirely, of negro troops, being left on the north side. This command will enter and occupy the city. Some of our people who are acquainted with the character of General Ord think they have reason to hope that his treatment of the unfortunate people of Richmond will not be so hard, and cruel and inhuman as that which has fallen upon the heads of our fellow citizens in some other captured cities.

The newspapers of Richmond, we suppose, all fell into the hands of the enemy. The evacuation of the city was so sudden and unexpected—scarcely any one being prepared for it—that no time was left for the removal of so cumbrous an establishment as a city newspaper office. In a few days we may expect to hear that the *Enquirer* or the *Whig* or the *Examiner* is issued as a Yankee paper.

All the rolling stock of the Richmond and Danville Railroad in running order was saved on the retreat from Richmond. A few old cars, not in a movable condition, were left at Manchester. No train was captured by the enemy near the junction, as was at one time reported; and, indeed, we do not believe that any body of Yankees had struck the road at any point up to yesterday evening.

The Secretary of War, the Quartermaster General, Commissary General and a number of other officers of the government, left Richmond on horseback, and will probably arrive at this place to-morrow.

Should General Lee establish his lines east of the junction, we suppose the State Legislature will be convened at Lynchburg.

All the specie and other valuables belonging to the banks in Richmond were removed from the city on Sunday, and have been carried to places of safety.

A considerable amount of goods purchased by the State for distribution to the people, we regret to learn, had to be left behind. Also the State archives remained in the city; but we perceive no motive the enemy can have in destroying them, as they will, no doubt, endeavor to occupy the city permanently, and establish a State government at Richmond under the federal Union.

GRANT.

The Execution of the Details of the Surrender.

The Army Taking Position Along the Southside Railroad.

LEE IN RICHMOND.

Rosser and Fitzhugh Lee Refuse to be Surrendered by General Lee.

Names of Some of the Captured Rebel Army and Navy Officers,

&c., &c., &c.

Mr. S. Cadwallader's Despatch.

APPOMATTOX, C. H., April 10, 1865.

My despatch of yesterday was hurriedly closed by the departure of a HERALD messenger for City Point. My despatch of to-day shall be confined to some additional details of the great culminating events of the rebellion, as they presented themselves to me, without much regard to importance or order.

CARRYING OUT THE TERMS OF THE SURRENDER.

The appointment of officers to carry out the terms of surrender were made by both parties during the night, and a conference between Generals Grant and Lee was held on the brow of the hill, one-fourth of a mile north of the Court House, at ten o'clock A. M. General Grant and staff had hardly arrived when General Lee, accompanied by an orderly, galloped up the hill and rode to the side of the Lieutenant General. General Grant's staff, General Ord and staff, General Griffin and staff, General Gibbon and staff, General Sheridan and staff, were all on the ground, grouped in a semi-circular position. The country to the northward was open, cultivated land. The Court House stands on a ridge, or continuation of small hills, extending east and west.

THE REBEL ARMY.

Lee's army lay on a parallel ridge, with a ravine and little rivulet between, nearly north of our forces. The head of his column was mainly composed of trains and artillery. The infantry and cavalry brought up the rear. Consequently but a small portion of the rebel army was visible from the Court House.

A CONVERSATION.

As Lee rode up the hillside on a gallop, General Grant stopped his horse forward two or three rods to meet him. Lee rode squarely up, saluted in military form, and wheeled his horse side by side to the left of General Grant. The two chieftains then entered into a conversation that lasted nearly two hours, until the officers appointed on both sides to carry out the terms of surrender had reported for duty. The tableau at this time was the finest ever witnessed. The two distinguished leaders of the mightiest hosts of the world sat quietly in their saddles discussing the past, present and future in free and easy offhand conversational style.

During the conference General Lee stated that if General Grant had acceded to his proposal for a personal interview some weeks ago peace would have undoubtedly resulted therefrom. Much of the conversation was, of course, private and unheard. But enough was gleaned to know that Lee acknowledged himself completely beaten, the power of the Southern confederacy utterly destroyed, and any further prolongation of the war a useless effusion of blood. The opinion was universal among rebel officers that Johnston would surrender to Sherman without a battle on hearing that the Army of Northern Virginia had done so to General Grant.

THE CONVERSATION ENDED.

Shortly before eleven o'clock the interview between the generals was ended by Lee saluting and riding slowly down the slope, across the hollow and into his camp on the hill beyond. General Grant turned the head of his thoroughbred Cincinnatus towards the Court House, followed by his staff and a large retinue of general officers.

MEETING OLD FRIENDS.

Within half an hour thereafter the officers designated by General Lee to carry out the stipulations of surrender arrived, and were accompanied by a large number of noted rebel officers. The large veranda and yard in front was soon filled with groups of Union and rebel officers in earnest conversation. Half the "regulars" on either side found some old acquaintance or West Point classmate among the others, and in many instances the greetings were warm and unaffected. The men who but the day before were seeking each other's destruction now chatted quietly [illegible] the incidents of the past, and [illegible]spect. Almost the first questions from rebel officers were—"Well, what are you going to do with—what are you going to do with us?"

THE EFFECT OF GENERAL GRANT'S TERMS.

The belief seemed widespread among intelligent officers that the United States government had pledged itself to grant no amnesties for the offence of treason, and that they must "all hang together or hang separately." On learning that General Grant had taken no advantage of their necessities and desperate situation, but had voluntarily extended to them the same magnanimous terms offered two days before and refused by General Lee, they expressed themselves exceedingly gratified. Discussion of the matter among themselves seemed to greatly strengthen this feeling. All admitted that their army had no further power of resistance, and that it was compelled to surrender on our own terms. They appeared surprised to find no exhibition of vindictiveness on our part. Judging from their hearty confessions of generous and liberal treatment by us one would conclude they expected to have been chained together as felons to grace the triumphal march of our victorious general.

At first some may be inclined to think General Grant not sufficiently exacting. But no one who witnessed the behavior of the rebel officers and listened to their conversation on the subject could long doubt the wisdom of his policy.

LEE'S ARMY DELIGHTED.

Lee's whole army goes home delighted that they are out of the service, and grateful to General Grant for sparing them all unnecessary humiliation. The moral effect of this on the mass of the Southern people cannot be over estimated.

ISSUING RATIONS.

On Sunday evening Colonel Morgan, Chief Commissary of Subsistence for the armies operating against Richmond, issued twenty thousand rations of bread and meat to the rebel army, and on Monday was able to add the rations of sugar, coffee and salt.

Mr. J. Walton Fitch's Despatch.

HEADQUARTERS, NINTH CORPS, ARMY OF THE POTOMAC, BURKESVILLE JUNCTION, April 11, 1865.

There is no change in the situation of this corps since the date of my last despatch. The line of the Southside Railroad from here to Petersburg is still under the guardianship of our troops, and the immense wagon trains of the army are safely convoyed through their midst to the victorious force beyond. Our advance guard consists of Curtin's brigade, located at Farmville—a village about eighteen miles from these headquarters, and containing nearly two thousand inhabitants, nearly all of whom still occupy their homes.

WHAT NEXT?

Speculations are rife, not alone in the camps, but among officers of every grade, as to what disposition will be made of this army, now that the finishing stroke has been administered to the enemy that confronted it. Already the probability of a Mexican campaign is being discussed, and at least three-fourths of the officers that express an opinion regarding the imminence of a rupture with the would-be empire, are anxious to join the crusade against the Power endeavoring to establish itself in our midst, and restore the wearer of the crown to his "native heath" and retirement.

AN ARMY OF OCCUPATION.

I hear it stated as probable that Burkesville junction—the present location of these headquarters—may be constituted a military post for some months to come owing to its important railroad communications and centrality. It is evident that some extensive system of provost guards or police will require to be inaugurated in the event of the withdrawal of our forces from this vicinity, as the country will remain in an extreme state of unrest and disquietude for months thereafter. No more unfortunate event could happen to the interests of the inhabitants hereabouts than the immediate and total withdrawal of our troops, as stragglers and deserters from both armies, now roaming through the forests contiguous, would immediately organize into extensive bands of highwaymen, and subject the people to all the terrors and apprehension attending the receipts of the visits of the redoubtable Dick Turpin "in ye olden time." The amount of private property in this vicinity and along the whole line of the road now receiving the attention and protection of picket guards furnished by this corps is immense, and covers a large area of country. It is this magnanimous and generous attendance to the interests of the inhabitants that is winning them over to the fealty they forsook, and which will, as soon as the brief sting of pride attending their subjection wears off, cause them to look upon the old government and its administers as the source of all success and well being.

It would be a cowed and spiritless race that took kindly and indifferently the dispensation that has been vouchsafed this unfortunate rebellion; and that there exists a sensitiveness and petulance from the effect of the just though cruel blow which has wounded the pride of its participators is but natural, and cannot be satisfied save by kindly approach and gentle treatment.

That the great body of the people we find here in the interior experience heartfelt satisfaction at the end of the war I am positive, and that ultimately they will be brought to the grace from which, in an evil hour and amid unfortunate counsels, they fell, I am equally sanguine.

CAPTURED GUNS.

A considerable portion of the guns captured by us in the late pursuit are now being daily received here. Many of them are of very superior make and are of the Armstrong pattern.

GENERAL GRANT'S BODY GUARD—"FOURTH REGULARS."

This veteran regiment, from whose ranks have sprung upwards of twenty generals, in commands in the service of the government and the rebellion, and among whom were numbered Grant and Sheridan, arrived here this evening from the front, upon their way to join the Lieutenant General—whose body guard they are—having marched from Prospect Hill since eight o'clock in the morning—a distance of thirty-three miles. They will probably take the train from this locality to City Point. The regiment is in command of Major Collins.

Prominent among the rumors of a movement of the Ninth corps is the report that it will be sent to Danville, about seventy miles from its present locality. Nothing has yet transpired to corroborate this supposition. Go where it may, the old Ninth corps will never refuse the "wager of battle" with any antagonist courageous enough to confront it.

EXTRA.

Saturday, April 15, 2 o'Clock P. M.

THE NATIONAL CALAMITY.

The Condition of Secretary Seward and His Sons.

Frederick Seward Not Expected to Recover.

Additional Particulars of the Assassination of President Lincoln,

&c., &c., &c.

Telegram.—Saturday, 10-15 A. M.

WASHINGTON, April 15, 1865.

The trunks of J. Wilkes Booth were seized last night. An examination of his papers by Attorney General Speed has discovered a letter to him in regard to the plot. From this letter it appears that the plot was to have been executed before the 4th of March, but for some reason not stated it was delayed until last night.

Further disclosures in regard to the evidence obtained is withheld for the present. A Cabinet meeting takes place at noon to-day, to take such action as the immediate exigencies necessitate.

Frederick Seward is very low and but little hope is entertained of his surviving his wound.

Secretary Seward is more comfortable than could reasonably be expected under the circumstances.

Telegram—Saturday, 1:20 P. M.

WASHINGTON, Saturday—1:20 P. M.

There is no material alteration in the condition of either Secretary Seward or Fred. Seward. Major Seward was not dangerously wounded.

The President died very quietly at twenty-two minutes past seven o'clock; so quietly that it was hardly known when he ceased to breathe. Mrs. Lincoln, Captain Robert Lincoln and others were in an adjoining room at the time. Around the deathbed of the President were all the members of the Cabinet, except Messrs. Seward and McCulloch—the latter having left a short time before the end.

A Cabinet meeting was held in the room in which the corpse lay, immediately after the President died, of the members of the Cabinet present. Another Cabinet meeting is to be held at twelve o'clock, at which time Vice-President Johnson will take the oath and be inaugurated as President.

The remains were placed in a temporary coffin and removed to the White House soon after nine o'clock this morning.

An escort of cavalry—Union Light Guard—under the command of Lieutenant Jamison, accompanied the remains, which were followed by General Augur, commanding Department of Washington; General Rucker, depot quartermaster; Colonel Pelouze, of the War Department; Captain Finley Anderson, Acting Adjutant General Hancock's corps; Captain D. G. Thomas, Clothing Depot; Captains J. H. Crowell and C. Baker. The solemn procession moved slowly up Tenth street to G, and thence to the White House, the large crowd present along the route standing uncovered. Immediately on the guard being removed a rush was made towards the house occupied during the night by the President, remaining about the entrance for some time.

The report that the assassin had been captured has not been confirmed. It is hardly possible that he can escape, and we are momentarily in expectation of hearing of his arrest.

Further Particulars of the Assassination of President Lincoln.

WASHINGTON, April 15, 1865.

The assassin of President Lincoln left behind him his hat and a spur.

The hat was picked up in the President's box, and has been identified by parties to whom it has been shown as the one belonging to the suspected man, and accurately described as the one belonging to the suspected man by other parties not allowed to see it before describing it.

The spur was dropped upon the stage, and that also has been identified as the one procured at a stable where the same man hired a horse in the evening.

Two gentlemen who went to the Secretary of War to apprize him of the attack on Mr. Lincoln met at the residence of the former a man muffled in a cloak, who, when accosted by them, hastened away

It had been Mr. Stanton's intention to accompany Mr. Lincoln to the theatre and occupy the same box, but the press of business prevented.

It therefore seems evident that the aim of the plotters was to paralyze the country by at once striking down the head, the heart and the arm of the country.

As soon as the dreadful events were announced in the streets, Superintendent Richards and his assistants were at work to discover the assassin.

In a few moments the telegraph had aroused the whole police force of the city.

Mayor Wallach and several members of the city government were soon on the spot, and every precaution was taken to preserve order and quiet in the city.

Every street in Washington was patrolled at the request of Mr. Richards.

General Augur sent horses to mount the police.

Every road leading out of Washington was strongly picketed, and every possible avenue of escape was thoroughly guarded.

Steamboats about to depart down the Potomac were stopped.

The *Daily Chronicle* says:—

As it is suspected that this conspiracy originated in Maryland, the telegraph flashed the mournful news to Baltimore, and all the cavalry was immediately put upon active duty. Every road was picketed, and every precaution taken to prevent the escape of the assassin. A preliminary examination was made by Mr. Richards and his assistants. Several persons were called to testify and the evidence, as elicited before an informal tribunal, and not under oath, was conclusive to this point—the murderer of President Lincoln was *John Wilkes Booth*. His hat was found in the private box and identified by several persons who had seen him within the last two days, and the spur which he dropped by accident, after he jumped to the stage, was identified as one of those which he had obtained from the stable where he hired his horse.

This man Booth has played more than once at Ford's theatre, and is of course acquainted with its exits and entrances, and the facility with which he escaped behind the scenes is easily understood.

The person who assassinated Secretary Seward left behind him a slouched hat and an old rusty navy revolver. The chambers were broken loose from the barrel, as if done by striking.

Loads were drawn from the chambers, one being but a rough piece of lead and the other balls, smaller than the chambers, wrapped in paper, as if to keep them from falling out.

WASHINGTON, April 15—Eleven o'Clock A. M.

The *Star* extra says:—

At twenty minutes past seven o'clock the President breathed his last, closing his eyes as if falling to sleep, and his countenance assuming an expression of perfect serenity. There were no indications of pain, and it was not known that he was dead until the gradually decreasing respiration ceased altogether.

The Rev. Dr. Gurley, of the New York avenue Presbyterian church, immediately, on its being ascertained that life was extinct, knelt at the bedside and offered an impressive prayer, which was responded to by all present.

Dr. Gurley then proceeded to the front parlor where Mrs. Lincoln, Captain Robert Lincoln, Mrs. John Hay, the private secretary and others were waiting, where he again offered a prayer for the consolation of the family.

The following minutes taken by Dr. Abbott, show the condition of the late President throughout the night:—

Eleven o'clock—Pulse 44.

Five minutes past eleven—Pulse 45 and growing weaker.

Ten minutes past eleven—Pulse 45.

Quarter past eleven—Pulse 42.

Twenty minutes past eleven—Pulse 45, respiration, 27 to 29.

Twenty-five minutes past eleven—Pulse 42.

Thirty-two minutes past eleven—Pulse 48 and full.

Forty minutes past eleven—Pulse 45.

Quarter to twelve—Pulse 45, respiration 22.

Twelve o'clock—Pulse 48, respiration 22.

Quarter-past twelve—Pulse 48, respiration 21.

Echmos both eyes.

Half-past twelve—Pulse 45.

Thirty-two minutes past twelve—Pulse 60.

Thirty-five minutes past twelve—Pulse 66.

Forty minutes past twelve—Pulse 69, right eye much swollen and [illegible].

Forty-five minutes past twelve—Pulse 70.

Fifty-five minutes past twelve—Pulse 80, struggling motion of arms.

One o'clock—Pulse 86, respiration 30.

Half-past one—Pulse 95, appearing easier.

Forty-five minutes past one—Pulse 86; very quiet; respiration irregular. Mrs. Lincoln present.

Ten minutes past two—Mrs. Lincoln retired with Robert Lincoln to an adjoining room.

Half-past two—President very quiet; pulse 54; respiration 28.

Fifty-two minutes past two—Pulse 48; respiration 30.

Three o'clock—Visited again by Mrs. Lincoln.

Twenty-five minutes past three—Respiration 24, and regular.

Thirty-five minutes past three—Prayer by the Rev. Dr. Gurley.

Four o'clock—Respiration hard; regular.

Quarter past four—Pulse sixty; respiration twenty-five.

Fifty minutes past five—Respiration twenty-eight, regular; sleeping.

Six o'clock—Pulse failing; respiration twenty-eight.

Half-past six—Still failing and labored breathing.

Seven o'clock—Symptoms of immediate dissolution.

Surrounding the deathbed of the President were Secretaries Stanton, Wells, Usher, Attorney General Speed, Postmaster General Dennison, M. R. Field, Assistant Secretary of the Treasury, Judge Otto, Assistant Secretary of the Interior, General Halleck, General Meigs, Senator Sumner, R. F. Andrews, of New York, General Todd, of Dacotah, John May, Private Secretary, Governor Oglesby, of Illinois, General Farnsworth, Mrs. and Miss Kenney, Miss Harris, Captain Robert Lincoln, son of the President, and Doctors E. W. Abbott, R. K. Stone, C. D. Gatch, Neal Hall and Mr. Lieberman. Secretary McCulloch remained with the President until about five o'clock, and Chief Justice Chase, after several hours attendance during the night, retired early this morning.

Immediately after the President's death a Cabinet meeting was called by Secretary Stanton, and held in the house in which the corpse lay. Secretaries Stanton, Welles and Usher, Postmaster General Dennison and Attorney General Speed were present. The results of the conference are as yet unknown.

The above particulars concerning the President's death are from the extra *Evening Star*.

SINCE THE DEATH.

WASHINGTON, April 15, 1865.

The President's body was removed from the private residence opposite Ford's theatre to the Executive Mansion this morning at half-past nine o'clock, in a hearse, and wrapped in the American flag. It was escorted by a small guard of cavalry, General Augur and other military officers following on foot.

A dense crowd accompanied the remains to the White House, where a military guard excluded the crowd, allowing none but persons of the household and personal friends of the deceased to enter the premises, Senator Yates and Representative Farnsworth being among the number admitted.

The body is being embalmed, with a view to its removal to Illinois.

Flags over the Departments and throughout the city are at half-mast. Scarcely any business is being transacted anywhere, either on private or public account.

Our citizens, without any preconcert whatever, are draping their premises with festoons of mourning.

The bells are tolling mournfully. All is the deepest gloom and sadness. Strong men weep in the streets. The grief is widespread and deep, and in strange contrast to the joy so lately manifested over our recent military victories.

This is indeed a day of gloom.

Reports prevail that Mr. Frederick W. Seward, who was kindly assisting the nursing of Secretary Seward, received a stab in the back.

His shoulderblade prevented the knife or dagger from penetrating into his body.

The prospects are that he will recover.

A report is circulated, repeated by almost everybody, that Booth was captured fifteen miles this side of Baltimore. If it be true, as asserted, that the War Department has received such information, it will doubtless be officially promulgated.

The government Departments are closed by order, and will be draped with the usual emblems of mourning.

The roads leading to and from the city are guarded by the military, and the utmost circumspection is observed as to all attempting to enter or leave the city.

THE PUBLIC GRIEF.

Washington.

WASHINGTON, April 15, 1865.

The excitement throughout Washington is intense, and the horrible proceedings of last night the only theme of conversation.

Philadelphia.

PHILADELPHIA, April 15, 1865.

The most intense horror is excited by the lamentable fate of President Lincoln. The city was decorated with flags and streamers, and every house gave evidence of preparations for the illumination fixed for Monday evening. The public joy gives place to mourning, and there is a deep feeling of rage.

Saratoga.

SARATOGA, April 15, 1865.

The news of the assassination of President Lincoln was received with profound regret by all the leading men here. They have no faith in Johnson's ability to carry the country safely through the present crisis.

Newark.

NEWARK, N. J., April 15, 1865.

Profound grief prevails here over the mournful tragedy at Washington. Flags are at half mast and places of business are closed. The streets are filled with crowds of people discussing the sad event. The *Daily Advertiser* office is heavily draped with mourning.

The Wall Street Resolutions.

Whereas, it has pleased Almighty God to take from us Abraham Lincoln, the President of the United States, by a sudden and awful visitation; and by this great calamity befalling us in the hour of our national triumph, we are warned by the uncertainty of all human affairs and our absolute dependence for our safety and protection as a nation upon the mercy and wisdom of Divine Providence; therefore

Resolved, That in this hour of our deep affliction we humbly implore that the Divine protection and support vouchsafed to us as a nation hitherto, which has borne us through years of bitter trial and brought us safely through the storms of war to victory and the prospect of peace, will not now be withdrawn from us, but that having taken from us the chosen and beloved chief magistrate who has so earnestly and faithfully and wisely labored and toiled in the behalf of this people, God will in his mercy enlighten, guide and strengthen his servants upon whom devolves the authority of the Government, so that they may wisely and justly administer the power confided to them.

Resolved, That while we bow in submission to the mysterious dispensation which thus afflicts us, as men and citizens, we must express the anguish and grief which fills our hearts, that the death of Abraham Lincoln is a calamity not to this nation alone, but to the civilized world.

Resolved, That while in his personal character exhibiting the kindliest and most generous nature, he in his public career manifested and illustrated in the highest degree the capacity of free institutions to inspire and develope true greatness of character. That his services to the nation through all the years of trial and danger, his unwavering devotion, his high courage and enduring hope have endeared him forever to the hearts of the people, and in their memories as in history, he will be recorded as the first patriot of the age. Alas! that he should be also the most distinguished martyr in the sacred cause of liberty!

Resolved, That as by the last acts of his life the President proved that kindness, charity and a spirit of conciliation toward the enemies of the republic animated him and dictated his policy, so we believe that we best honor his memory by emulating his spirit and example and continuing to labor for the restoration of peace and harmony in the land.

Resolved, That to the bereaved wife and children of the lamented dead we tender our deep and heartfelt sympathies, but can offer no better consolation than the assurance that the whole people weep with them and feel the loss to be irreparable.

Resolved, That we tender to the officer upon whom, by this sad calamity, the Executive authority devolves, our sympathy in the trying position in which he is placed, and the assurance of our cordial and unwavering support in the measures which, guided by Divine wisdom, he may adopt for the speedy accomplishment of the great objects for which his lamented predecessor labored and died.

Resolved, That it be recommended to the citizens to close all places of business to-day as early as practicable, and that they remain closed until after the burial of the deceased President.

Resolved, That it be requested that all places of public amusement be closed for this evening, and that the question of the further closing of all such sources of pleasure be referred to the sympathy, loyalty and reverence of the managers.

Resolved, That a committee of thirteen citizens of New York be sent to Washington to attend the funeral of the President, and to tender such aid and sympathy to the government as may be needful and proper, and that said committee consist of the following gentlemen:—Moses Taylor, Jonathan Sturges, William E. Dodge, Hamilton Fish, Moses H. Grinnell, William M. Evarts, Charles H. Russell, Edwards Pierrepont, Samuel Sloan, John J. Astor, Jr., F. B. Cutting, R. M. Blatchford, Charles H. Marshall.

PROCLAMATION

By the Mayor of New York.

MAYOR'S OFFICE, NEW YORK, April 15, 1865.

CITIZENS OF NEW YORK—The death of the President of the United States may well excite your profound grief and amazement. I respectfully recommend that business be suspended, and that a public mourning for the departed Chief Magistrate be observed throughout the city.

C. GODFREY GUNTHER, Mayor.

THE THEATRES.

It is understood that none of the theatres will be open to-night. Several of the managers have already notified us that their houses will be closed.

Circular from the Provost Marshal General.

WAR DEPARTMENT, WASHINGTON, D. C., April 15—9:40 A. M.

It is believed that the assassins of the President and Secretary Seward are attempting to escape to Canada. You will make a careful and thorough examination of all persons attempting to cross from the United States into Canada, and will arrest of suspicious persons. The most vigilant scrutiny on your part and the force at your disposal is demanded. A description of the parties supposed to be implicated in the murder will be telegraphed you to-day; but in the meantime be active in preventing the crossing of any suspicious persons.

By order of the SECRETARY OF WAR.

N. L. JEFFERS, Brevet Brigadier General, Acting Provost Marshal General.

INAUGURATION OF VICE PRESIDENT JOHNSON AS PRESIDENT OF THE UNITED STATES.

WASHINGTON, April 15—12 o'clock.

Andrew Johnson was sworn into office as President of the United States by Chief Justice Chase to-day at eleven o'clock.

Secretary McCulloch and Attorney General Speed and others were present.

PRESIDENT JOHNSON'S SPEECH.

He remarked:—

"THE DUTIES ARE MINE. I WILL PERFORM THEM, TRUSTING IN GOD."

Movements of General Grant.

PHILADELPHIA, April 15, 1865.

General Grant arrived in this city late last night, on his way to Jersey, but was intercepted on his way to Walnut street wharf by a despatch from the office of the Associated Press, and it is supposed he returned to Washington immediately.

BURLINGTON, N. J., April 15, 1865.

Lieutenant General Grant left Burlington for Washington at six o'clock this morning.

NEWS FROM SAN FRANCISCO.

SAN FRANCISCO, Cal., April 14, 1865.

A movement has been started in California for a subscription to purchase a homestead for the family of John Brown, who are residing at Red Bluff.

Northern despatches announce the return of Colonel Bulkley, of the Russian Overland Telegraph line. His expedition through the interior of British Columbia is well under way.

Governor Loine will not issue his anticipated call for two more regiments of volunteers from this State.

The United States District Court have sentenced the captain and mates of the ship Great Republic to various terms of imprisonment for extreme cruelty to seamen on the late voyage of the ship to this port. The case created a deal of feeling against them.

A letter from Guaymas, Mexico, to the *Bulletin* of this city, says that Governor Pesquiera has made ample preparations to defeat any force the imperialists can send against Sonora. He had ordered the illumination of Guaymas whenever Richmond was taken by the United States troops, and native bands had been taught to play our national airs.

SHERMAN.

HIS ARMY MOVING.

The March Begun on the 9th Instant.

SHERMAN'S FIRST SPEECH.

JOHNSTON'S ARMY WEST OF RALEIGH.

Only His Cavalry Holding the Capital of the State.

He is Reported Endeavoring to Form a Junction with Lee.

The Ram Albemarle Raised in Good Condition.

Occupation of Murfreesboro, N. C., by Our Fleet,

&c., &c., &c.

Our Special Washington Despatch.

WASHINGTON, April 14, 1865.

Reliable information has been received here from Goldsboro to the 10th instant. General Sherman started from Goldsboro early on the morning of the 10th, moving on Raleigh. There was no fighting except the usual skirmishing. It was General Sherman's expectation that he would reach Raleigh in four days.

Daily communication will be kept up with the army and the railroad will be repaired at once.

Mr. D. P. Conyngham's Despatch.

NEWBERN, N. C., April 11, 1865.

THE NEWS OF THE FALL OF RICHMOND IN SHERMAN'S ARMY.

Sherman's veterans testified their rejoicings at the fall of Richmond in the most noisy and phrenzied manner. At night the men took it into their heads to improvise a general salute by putting powder into hollow logs and blowing them up. This, accompanied by the cheers of the men, the capering of dancing negroes, who appeared to be bit by tarantulas, and the music of several bands, made the scene enlivening enough.

SHERMAN MAKES A SPEECH.

A crowd of soldiers and citizens, accompanied by a band, made a favorable demonstration in front of General Sherman's headquarters. They loudly and vociferously called for the General. He had to make his appearance, and, after thanking the men, said:—

We have glorious news, soldiers. Richmond is ours, and the rebel army is broken up and demoralized. I have a letter from General Grant, in which he says that he is pursuing Lee, and wishes to have us press Johnston, which I think we'll do. (Cries of "We will; we will.") We don't mean to let him rest, so be prepared for the march in a few days.

Loud cheers were given for Sherman, for Grant and his army, and the men returned to their quarters congratulating one another.

THE ARMY ON THE MARCH.

On the afternoon of the 9th a part of Schofield's column took up their line of march, and yesterday morning the whole army broke camp and debouched from the different encampments around Goldsboro into column along the different lines of march.

ORGANIZATION OF THE ARMY.

The army is divided into three different columns—one under General Slocum, another under General Schofield, and the third under General Howard. The men are in excellent condition and spirits, eager to meet the enemy and wind up "the darned affair."

JOHNSTON'S POSITION.

Johnston's army has occupied a line of intrenchments along the Neuse river, some twenty miles from Goldsboro, but has fallen back within a few days *west of Raleigh*. Colonel Spencer, Third brigade, Kilpatrick's cavalry, sent some orderlies towards Raleigh. They got to the rear of Hampton's cavalry and ascertained that Johnston had evacuated the town, and that it was occupied by four or five thousand cavalry. Hampton had his headquarters eight miles east of Raleigh, on the Smithfield and Raleigh road. Johnston is reported gone to Greensborough, on the junction of the Danville and Charlotte road. It is evident that he is trying to form a junction with Lee, and will then fall back to Western Georgia and Alabama. They have important arsenals at Macon, Columbus and Augusta. They cannot strike for Eastern Tennessee, as Thomas is heading them off there, so their route will be through North and South Carolina and Georgia.

I do not expect immediate fighting, except what the cavalry will make.

STATE OF THE CONFEDERACY.

I have just laid hands on a Raleigh *Confederate* of April 7, in which was Jeff. Davis' last proclamation from his new capital, which I have telegraphed. Though he admits that the fall of Richmond will have a serious moral effect, still he thinks it is in reality no great loss, as it leaves Lee's army free for active operations anywhere. He states that "our army will be free to move from point to point." That is true, for they are now rapidly moving each on his own hook, and giving up the confederacy as a "gone coon."

The *Confederate* goes it strong on the *Conservative*, Governor Vance's organ, for suggesting that overtures for peace should be made to the Union government. There is a civil war in the camp, and it is fast becoming a Kilkenny catawauling affair.

INCIDENTS OF SHERMAN'S MARCH.

Towards the evening of the 10th Major General Howard, staff, escort and some mounted infantry were in advance, when they struck some rebel cavalry, who opened on them, killing a horse of one of the General's staff and wounding some men. The General himself had a narrow escape. His men charged on the rebels, and captured about one hundred, and two pieces of artillery.

A PAYMASTER NEARLY CAPTURED.

On the 9th Major Pulsifer was passing from Wilmington to Goldsboro, when he stopped to pay the troops at Burgan, some twenty miles from Wilmington. The troops had moved forward that morning, except a squad of nineteen men, under Lieutenant Colonel Parker. The Major followed up the troops, and towards evening a troop of rebel cavalry swept into the town, gobbling up the little force there and the telegraph operator. They stopped the latter and made him cut the wires. They partially injured the bridge.

THE CONDITION OF SHERMAN'S ARMY.

When Sherman struck Goldsboro the army was shoeless and ragged, but they are now thoroughly clad and refitted. Brigadier General Easton, who is chief quartermaster to the army, was busily engaged hurrying forward supplies, while Sherman was making his sweeping march from Savannah. He had established depots at Beaufort, Morehead City and other points, and as soon as Sherman reached Goldsboro supplies were rapidly forwarded to him. Several hundred cars were plying backward and forward, and when the army started it had thirty day's rations on hand, and such a surplus of clothes that some had to be returned.

As supplies are the sustaining power of an army, too much praise cannot be bestowed on General Easton for his indefatigible and successful administration.

COLONEL WRIGHT,

Chief Engineer of Railroads, has done much in assisting the Quartermaster's Department by the rapid manner in which he put the railroad in order. The railroad from here to Goldsboro is as safe for travelling purposes as any of the New York lines.

Tracks were laid, bridges built and communication opened with wonderful celerity, under the management of Colonel Wright.

As we are going to keep a base open, it is of the utmost importance to have such men at the head of affairs.

There have been some changes made in commanders. Colonel Patrick Jones has returned from New York, with the well merited rank of brigadier, to his brigade, Second brigade, Second division, Twentieth corps. Few officers have done more to merit a star than General Jones.

Colonel Mendel, Thirty-third New Jersey, has been appointed chief of General Slocum's staff, ranking as brigadier.

Colonel Schofield, brother to General Schofield, has been appointed brigadier general and chief of his brother's staff.

Brigadier General C. C. Wolcott has been promoted from the command of a brigade to the command of the First division, Fourteenth army corps.

Captain John L. Hover has been promoted to a majority.

Captain Hovey and two men captured seventy-eight men and officers near Goldsboro. He struck on them, persuaded them that they were surrounded, and actually frightened them into a surrender.

Lieutenant L. B. Mitchel, ordnance officer, Fifteenth army corps, promoted to be captain and aid on General Ayres' staff.

Major Max Woodhull, Adjutant General, Fifteenth army corps, has been promoted to a lieutenant coloneicy.

Lieutenant W. H. Barlow, Quartermaster, promoted to a captaincy and assistant quartermaster.

Captain Montgomery Rochester, Assistant Adjutant General on General Sherman's staff, has been assigned to duty as assistant adjutant general of the army of Georgia, General Slocum commanding. This will give Captain Rochester the silver leaf. Captain Rochester is an old and distinguished officer, having been all through the war from the first Bull run fight. The Captain well deserves his promotion.

Brigadier General Webster has just returned to Newbern from the front. General Webster, as Chief of General Sherman's staff, is about establishing his headquarters at Newbern. The General's reputation and executive abilities are too well known to need any comment. During Sherman's imporant Atlanta campaign he ably managed the bureau at Nashville.

Captain W. R. Tuttle accompanied the General. He is chief of conductors on the military railroads. His efficient services in Tennessee are sufficient guarantee that the military management of the railroads in North Carolina will be ably conducted.

General Charles Crufts and staff have returned from his command of the detachments of the army of the Cumberland which had been left in Tennessee, and which he brought out to the command of his division.

THE REBEL RAM ALBEMARLE.

The celebrated rebel ram Albemarle has been raised by Messrs. Underwood & Co., and is now lying in North river, at the mouth of the canal, waiting to be towed into Norfolk. They have been nearly one month in getting her up. It will be recollected that this monster was blown up by a torpedo, on the 27th of October, 1864, by Lieutenant Cushing and eleven men.

She is not seriously injured. Much of her plating had to be removed to lighten her. Her guns, which were two one hundred-pounder Brook rifle guns, English manufacture, had been taken off by Captain Macomb, in charge of the fleet, and sent to Washington. Her boilers and machinery are uninjured, and she is at present under steam. The Albemarle was one of the most formidable rams of the confederacy, and was built at Halifax, N. C. She has several indentations in her sides from the different shots and shells fired into her, and an unexploded shell was found buried under her iron plating. She had twenty-eight inches of timber and four inches of plating. She is a regular leviathan, and can be put in full repair at a very small cost. In her were found officers' clothing, arms and twenty-eight cans of powder uninjured. She had Liverpool coal on board, which must have run the blockade.

THE LAST OF THE REBEL RAMS.

The new rebel ram, which had been building at Halifax, and was anxiously expected to commence operations, was discovered on the 8th instant, near Plymouth, a regular shell, having been burned to the water's edge. The pickets near Plymouth saw her coming down the river and gave the alarm. Colonel Frankle turned out a squadron of cavalry and two sections of artillery to charge on her, but they found her helplessly lying against the obstructions, where they placed guards over her, where she now remains. Thus died the last of the rebel rams.

AN EXPEDITION TO MURFREESBORO, N. C.

The Shamrock flagship, Commander Macomb; the Wychusing, Valley City and Hunchback went up the Chowan river to Winton, with the intention of covering the crossing of a body of cavalry at Winton, which was to operate towards the Weldon railroad. The cavalry advance guard found the enemy in position at Winton, but the fleet opened on them, soon scattering them. The fleet then ferried over the troops to the south side of the river, and then proceeded to Murfreesboro, on the Meherrin river, about eighteen miles from Weldon. The sailors took possession of the town, the Mayor formally surrendering it to Commander Macomb.

Next day the cavalry charged about twenty-five rebel cavalry into the town and captured them.

Murfreesboro is a good sized town, and is taken possession of now for the first time by the Yanks. The fleet returned to Winton and Plymouth, where it is now lying.

Our Newbern Correspondence.

NEWBERN, N. C., April 10, 1865.

THE ARMY UNDER ORDERS TO MOVE.

Some portions of Sherman's army received orders three or four days ago to be in readiness for marching orders, and it was the original intention that the army should move on the 7th. Grant's successes, however, have somewhat changed the programme, and, although the time of moving is delayed a day or two, yet there will not be much difference in the results. Some of the army, the Seventeenth corps particularly, were to have commenced moving this morning, and as Johnston is now said to be making off in the direction of Danville and Hillsboro, and Grant is pushing in the direction of Lynchburg or Danville (at this writing), of course Sherman will also take a step in that direction.

Since the burning of the vessels on the Neuse river a few mornings since, no further demonstrations have been made on our communications. That was an insignificant affair, comparatively, and a small guard could easily have prevented it. The raiders also burned the upper works of the steamer Mystic, which was sunk in the river a fortnight since. All but her upper works was under water, and her damage, therefore, is light. It is also reported that the small steamer, General Shepley was burned at the same time, but I have not heard this confirmed as yet. These interruptions do not interfere at all with the sending forward of supplies.

I mentioned in my last that General Howard had established his business headquarters here, although the General himself has returned to the front. Since then General Easton, Chief Quartermaster Military Division of the Mississippi, has also removed his headquarters to this place, and General Beckwith, Chief Commissary of Sherman's army, has also done the same. General Sherman's business headquarters (aside from his field headquarters at Goldsboro,) are also to be established here, having arrived yesterday. These straws, together with the fact that other prominent officers connected with Sherman's army are establishing themselves here, are taken by many as indications that this is to be continued as a base for some time yet, with perhaps Raleigh as the extreme inland base after it is taken, if Sherman chooses to move on that line.

TRAINS TO GOLDSBORO.

Two regular trains are running daily now to Goldsboro, and generally one or more extra trains additionally. The road is open also direct to Wilmington from Goldsboro, and trains are making those trips every day. Some very good passenger cars that were captured by General Terry at Faison's depot, when he was on the march to join Schofield and Sherman, are now being used by us between here and Goldsboro, and between the latter place and Wilmington.

THE OLD STEAMER LONG ISLAND REBUILT.

Lieutenant Bradley, to whom Captain Wing, Chief Quartermaster of this post, has assigned a good portion of the duties that formerly devolved upon Captain Kimball, promoted to the position of depot quartermaster for Sherman's army at this point, relaunched the old Long Island last Saturday. She was a side-wheel steamer that was partially burned a year or so ago, and has been rebuilt in the government yard here. The launch was a successful one, and the boat is, or will be, a credit to the workmen whom Lieutenant Bradley keeps employed in the boat building department.

THE WHITE AND BLACK NORTH CAROLINA REFUGEES.

The number of white and black refugees that are coming in here now by the railroad, from the country surrounding Goldsboro and this side of there, is immense. The whites are generally of a class who have evidently seen better days. Some of them bring along a few articles of furniture, and perhaps a poverty stricken cow or horse, but no contrabands. The latter have learned to look out for themselves, and from the number of old beds, chairs, cooking utensils, and rubbish of every description that they bring in with them, one naturally infers that they have also learned to look out for something else besides themselves. The negroes have had a new camp established for them, a little way outside of the fortifications surrounding the town. They are given land to work and materials to work with, and they generally manage to support themselves pretty comfortably. When the males are able-bodied they are given work on the railroads, or by the quartermasters in some of their departments. The whites are mostly taken care of, when they desire it, by Dr. Page, superintendent of white refugees, and also chief agent here of the Sanitary Commission. The doctor rations them and secures employment for them when it is possible. The town is filling up with these whites, some of whom have lived here before, but who return to find Uncle Samuel in possession of their property, and no rent coming from it, of course. Others, who have lost their all, have come hither to get nearer the sea coast, in the hopes of finding the staff of life plentier, or of discovering some more quiet spot than they have been living in under the despotism of Jeff. Davis. Poor creatures, with all the past against them they are to be pitied beyond anything I could say for them. Of the blacks there must be fully fifteen thousand in the city and adjoining it in the outskirts. They reconcile themselves to their new situation more readily, and attribute all their troubles to the goodness of "Father Abraham" and their Maker, both of whom they devoutly believe to be working out the problem of their deliverance.

A CURIOUS ARMY MAIL.

Mr. Chas. Hibbard, our assistant postmaster in this city, informs me that a few days since they sent off a mail from Sherman's army which numbered two hundred and thirty thousand letters and packages. The "bummers" evidently know how to read and write. The mail from that army averages about sixty thousand at every departure. It is a curiosity to look at some of the packages, which are certain to be sent to the dead letter office, they being contraband of the mail.

Fifteen hundred of Wheeler's cavalry came into Goldsboro yesterday, it is said, and surrendered themselves prisoners of war.

Our Goldsboro Correspondence.

GOLDSBORO, N. C., April 7, 1865.

A report has just been received from Raleigh, stating that Governor Vance will call the Legislature together for the purpose of repealing the act of secession, and restoring North Carolina to the Union.

The Charge Against Gen. Carrington.

CINCINNATI, April 14, 1865.

Gen. Carrington has published a card, saying that the charges against him are all infamous attempts to obliterate the credit of his services in Indiana. His friends say the matter grew out of a misunderstanding with paymasters, and that all the money for which he is responsible is deposited in bank, ready to be handed over.

Died.

CARTER.—On Friday evening, April 14, ELIZABETH, relict of Samuel Carter, in the 83d year of her age.

The relatives and friends of the family are respectfully invited to attend the funeral, from her late residence, No. 701 Second avenue, near Thirty-eighth street, on Monday afternoon, at one o'clock.

Philadelphia papers please copy.

KEARNEY.—At Nashville, Tenn., on Saturday, April 8, SUSAN, wife of the late Edward Kearney, of Carndonagh, county Donegal, Ireland.

Notice of the funeral hereafter.

[For other Deaths see Second Page.

EXTRA.

DEATH

OF THE

PRESIDENT.

WAR DEPARTMENT,
WASHINGTON, April 15, 1865.

Major-General DIX: ABRAHAM LINCOLN died this morning at twenty-two minutes after 7 o'clock.

EDWIN M. STANTON,
Secretary of War.

SECOND DISPATCH.

SECRETARY SEWARD'S CONDITION.

Further Particulars Respecting the Bloody Transaction.

The Deed Deliberately Planned.

Two Assassians Engaged in the Work

IDENTIFICATION OF ONE OF THE MURDERERS.

The Escape of one of them to Baltimore.

WAR DEPARTMENT,
WASHINGTON, April 15, 1865—4:10 a. m.

To Major-Gen. DIX: Secretary Seward remains without change. Frederick Seward's skull is fractured in two places, beside a severe cut upon the head. The attendant is still alive, but hopeless. Major Seward's wounds not dangerous.

It is now ascertained with reasonable certainty that two assassins were engaged in the horrible crime, Wilkes Booth being the one that shot the President, and the other a companion of his whose name is not known, but whose description is so clear that he can hardly escape. It appears from a letter found in Booth's trunk that the murder was planned before the 4th of March, but fell through then because the accomplice backed out until "Richmond could be heard from."

Booth and his accomplice were at the Livery Stable at six o'clock last evening, and left there with their horses about ten o'clock or shortly before that hour.

It would seem that they had for several days been seeking their chance, but for some unknown reason it was not carried into effect until last night.

One of them has evidently made his way to Baltimore—the other has not yet been traced.

EDWIN M. STANTON, Sec. of War.

See the Fourth and Eighth pages of this sheet for the particulars of the attempted Assassination of the President and Secretary Seward.

VETERAN TEMPERANCE CORPS.—A meeting of persons who have abstained from the use of intoxicating drinks during the third of a century and upward has been called for Tuesday evening next, at Room No. 24 Cooper Institute, for the purpose of organizing a Veteran Temperance Corps.

The Union League Club on the Victories.

At a full meeting of the Club Thursday evening, the following resolutions, reported by Mr. Jay from the Executive Committee, were unanimously adopted. The last resolution, referring to the reciprocal treatment to be henceforth accorded to foreign vessels, was received with warm applause:

Resolved, 1. That in view of the recent memorable exploits of the Army of the Potomac, compelling the evacuation of Petersburg and Richmond and the surrender by the Rebel Lee of the insurgent forces of Northern Virginia, this Club, in common with all Christian men and loyal citizens, are impressed with a feeling of deep thankfulness to Almighty God for having graciously preserved us from the plottings of traitors at home and their abettors abroad: and for having vindicated, by His all-powerful arm, the permanence of our constitution, the unity of our country, the supremacy of our Government, and the honor of our flag.

2. That we welcome these victories, not simply as terminating a long, bloody and costly strife, and establishing the American republic in her proper preëminence among the great powers of the world, but we hail them as restoring the southern section of our land to freedom, civilization and peace, and that we entertain none but feelings of compassion and good will toward those masses of our southern countrymen who have been deluded and coerced into Rebellion by wicked men at the North and at the South, who, false to their oaths and their honor, have sought in vain to destroy their country.

3. That we cordially recognize the fact that the steadfast loyalty of the colored population of the South has materially assisted to rescue our land from the treachery of Rebels in arms, and that the debt of gratitude due to them by loyal Americans can in no way be better repaid than in earnest and united efforts for their elevation and education in all that befits their new position as citizens of the republic they have helped to save.

4. That remembering the glorious page in our history which has been illumined by the heroic deeds of our army and navy during the last four years, and of which we were sadly reminded yesterday by the funeral obsequies of our own brave and lamented Winthrop, no time should be lost in organizing suitable homes and modes of employment for our wounded and disabled heroes soon to return to us from the field of war.

5. That we tender to the President of the United States our heartiest congratulations on this bright dawning of his second administration after the clouds and gloom that encompassed the first, and we cordially thank him for his two recent proclamations—the one closing certain of our seaports in the exercise of the sovereign power of the American people; and the other notifying foreign nations that henceforth their ships in our ports will be excluded from all privileges which, under whatever pretext, are denied in their harbors to the vessels of the United States.

Evening Edition of the Tribune.

VOL. XXV.....NO. 7,496. NEW-YORK, SATURDAY, APRIL 15, 1865. PRICE FOUR CENTS.

FROM THE ARMY OF THE POTOMAC.

The Surrender of Gen. Lee's Army—Details and Incidents Antecedent and Subsequent.

From Our Special Correspondent.

HDQRS. GEN. SHERIDAN'S CAVALRY CORPS, APPOMATTOX COURT-HOUSE, VA., Sunday Night, April 9, 1865.

BEFORE THE SURRENDER.

The position of affairs just before the surrender was as follows: Sheridan's Cavalry had struck the Rebel column on the main Lynchburg Road and cut it in two, west of the Appomattox Court-House, and, together with his infantry support, was now facing east and driving the rear portion of the column (which was the main portion) back the way it had come, while the Second and Sixth Corps, which had been following it up on the same road, now lay as a lion in the path of retreat. In other words, the main portion of the Rebel column, with Gen. Lee in the midst of it, was completely cut off, surrounded and hemmed in. There was no chance of escape. The column had been driven from the Danville to the Lynchburg Road, and now its course on the latter was stopped. There was no other road for it to take. Twenty-five thousand men—nearly one half of whom had already thrown away their arms in their demoralization—were at the mercy of twice or three times as many victorious muskets and sabers!

DRIVEN TO THE WALL.

While the Second and Sixth Corps were pounding the column forward with their artillery, and Sheridan's Cavalry and the Twenty-fourth and Fifth Corps were driving it back with all arms, like sheep in a slaughter pen, the Rebel Gen. Gordon, who was in the beleaguered column, sent forward to Gen. Sheridan's lines a flag of truce, proposing a surrender of the entire command and asking an armistice until the terms of capitulation could be agreed upon. The order was immediately passed along Gen. Sheridan's lines to cease firing, which was promptly obeyed, followed by the cheers of the troops who understood the reason for the order.

A FLAG OF TRUCE.

Our skirmish line going east had now been advanced to within a quarter of a mile of the Court-House, and the armies were within full view of each other, Gen. Sheridan's forces resting on a circle of cleared hills immediately west of the Court-House, and the head of the Rebel column, well closed up, lying in a valley about a mile to the eastward. Orders were issued to both sides for the troops to remain in the same position as they were, when the flag-of-truce was sent forward and the firing ceased. On the reception of the flag-of-truce and accompanying message by Gen. Sheridan, he sent an aid to accompany Gen. Gordon, at his request, to the Court-House, to talk over the matter of a surrender. Soon Gen. Gordon arrived, accompanied by the Rebel Gen. Wilcox, and they were met in the village by Gens. Sheridan and Ord; these were also joined by Gen. Longstreet, who soon afterward came up.

ITS RESULT.

The result of this inter[illegible] matter of a surrender to Generals Grant and Lee, both of whom, it was understood, were within reaching distance, consequently a messenger was sent by Gen. Sheridan down the Lynchburg road to the rear of the Rebel column, near which Gen. Grant had his Headquarters, (in the saddle) and in the course of an hour or so the general arrived, in response to the message, at Gen. Sheridan's Headquarters in a dooryard in the west end of the village. Lieut.-Col. Price, of Gen. Sheridan's staff, was then dispatched into the Rebel lines to escort Gen. Lee to the village, to be met on intermediate or neutral ground by Gen. Grant. In a short time Gen. Lee, accompanied by Col. Price and two or three of his own aids rode up to the residence of Major McLean, alighted and went in. To make sure of his identity I asked an aid of Gen. Long, who was on a visit to Gen. Sheridan at the time, what officer that was.

LEE AND GRANT.

"That," said he, "is the greatest man the country ever produced, Gen. Robt. E. Lee."

That General was soon joined by Gen. Grant, with two or three of his staff, at Major McLean's, the two being introduced by Col. Price. After an exchange of the usual civilities, Gen. Lee opened the negotiation by saying:

"Well, General, you have got us in a tight place, and to save the useless effusion of blood, I propose to surrender this command on such honorable conditions as you, as a magnanimous General, may prescribe."

"You are right General," replied Gen. Grant, "in expecting magnanimous terms, magnanimity and liberality I am happy to say, is the policy of the Government I represent. As you ask nothing, I take the more pleasure in tendering the most liberal terms in my power, I therefore propose the surrender of all officers and men as prisoners of war, subject to exchange or parole, and, of course an unconditional surrender of all public property, such as trains, supplies, arms, ordnance, and other munitions of war. If I could have the assurance of Gen. Lee that it would be safe for us, I would gladly parole every officer and man on the spot and allow him to go to his home."

Gen. Lee—"I think I can safely promise that no officer or private of the army of Northern Virginia would knowingly and wilfully violate his parole of honor."

"Gen. Grant—"To what forces does this surrender extend?"

Gen. Lee—"I can only surrender that portion of the Confederate forces now in your power, I cannot speak for the remainder at present."

Gen. Grant—"Well, that is all we can ask at this time. I understand the surrender to embrace all the men and material of the army of Northern Virginia now in transit in this column?"

Gen. Lee—"You are right. I will recall the advance of the column, which I consider in your power."

Gen. Grant—"Well, I propose to take immediate possession of all the public property, and parole all the officers and men on the spot, the officers to retain their side arms and private horses."

Gen. Lee—"That is all we can ask!"

THE TERMS.

The terms of capitulation were accordingly drawn up on this basis, at the dictation of Gen. Grant, by one of his aides, and, after some further exchange of social civilities, the interview terminated, Gen. Lee, with his white hair and beard flowing in the soft April wind, mounting his fine grey horse and riding back to camp, and Gen. Grant repairing to his new headquarters on the west side of the town.

HOW LEE LOOKS.

Gen. Lee looks well, though somewhat anxious and careworn, and a good deal whiter about the head and face, they say, than he was four years ago. It is understood that on being paroled he will immediately start for Richmond, where his family is.

After the surrender Gen. Gordon addressed his troops, intimating to them that the war was about over, and advising them on being paroled to repair to their homes and become good citizens again of the old Union. This advice was received with the most vociferous cheering by the Rebel soldiers. They even went so far as to fire a salute in honor of the surrender and no more fighting.

OUR CAPTURES.

The Rebel arms and trains, and various munitions of war, have been taken possession of this afternoon, by infantry detachments from the Fifth and Twenty-fourth Corps, and the paroling will be attended to to-morrow. The number of prisoners is estimated at about 25,000, with 2,000 supply wagons, 200 artillery guns and 12,000 stand of small arms, a great many of these having been thrown away, ILLINOIAN.

From Our Special Correspondent.

HDQRS. ARMY OF THE POTOMAC, FOUR MILES EAST OF APPOMATTOX COURT-HOUSE, April 11.

The remains of the Rebel army are to be marched from Burkesville, under escort of the Fifth Corps.

Last night about 600 of the cavalry under Hampton left and dispersed. Not more than 12,000 men now remain with Gen. Lee, and the army is melting away. If left a few days longer where it is, there would be nearly nothing left of it.

The *materiel* of the army is trifling, there not being more than 30 guns, and these are of light caliber—the guns selected for the attempt to be made to cut through our cavalry.

THE REBEL ARMY AS PRISONERS OF WAR.

The army is lying quietly about its fires. The men to-day look as cleanly and healthy as our own. The rank and file appear to be in very good spirits, glad, no doubt, to get home. As to the officers, they affect to be cheerful, but must feel mortified at the result of the efforts of the great Rebel army.

Food must be scarce among them, for they drew only three days' rations on the 3d, so that they have been living on the country for six days. In spite of this, and the rapid marches they have made, with the want of rest, etc., the men are not meager.

OULD AND HATCH.

These two officers have been at these headquarters most of to-day. Col. Hatch is a man of good size, and an easy, prepossessing manner. In his grey uniform he was an object of no little interest at these headquarters.

THE NEXT STEP

by this army will be to return to Burke's Station, there to be at its new depot of supplies, and draw rations for fresh operations which are not known now. The roads are now in a broken state, and it is necessary to draw supplies by rail. Last night and to-day rain fell; and the weather is lowering. In view of this, it is necessary to get back to the line of railroad, and happily it is not now desirable to go on any farther in this direction.

GEN. LEE.

All of us have been very curious to see this great officer—the Hannibal of the day—but no one being allowed to pass the line of sentries, only a few staff officers got a look at him. From one of these I learn that Gen. Lee wore a look of cheerful ease, and sat with his staff as he was wont to do in the days of his success, when his name was on the lips of every one. Of his great officers few now remain with him, Hill being dead, Ewell in our hands, and others of lesser note being also absent, dead, or in our hands.

Gen. Lee may be said to have lost everything but honor, his army being reduced to the strength of a mere corps, his guns mostly gone, and his trains totally lost. He can, however, bear his disaster with good grace, for he made a very good fight, and may ascribe his defeat to the want of a cavalry force equal to that of this army.

GUNS BURIED.

[illegible] carriages with the limbers and caissons having been first burned. This was a last effort of the enemy to prevent their guns from falling into our hands. The number of guns hidden in this way is not known. Only a few have been dug up.

THE NEXT WAR.

Men begin already to talk of the next war, and Mexico is mentioned by all as the theater of the next contest in which our arms will be engaged. The spirit of fight has not yet been sated with the younger men of this army.

There is a report that Gen. Lee is to see the President. If this be so, it is to be hoped that the General will again be made a friend of the Government. F. D.

Coming Back.

From Our Special Correspondent.

BURKSVILLE, VA., Tuesday, April 11, 1865.

Our troops are all coming back to this point, to be ready for any new movement that may be ordered.

SHERIDAN.

Sheridan's cavalry left Appomattox Court House early on Monday morning. The rebel prisoners were all being paroled, and were starting for their homes in squads, companies and regiments. There is a general feeling throughout the country here that the war is over, and everybody is rejoicing accordingly. More anon. ILLINOIAN.

Music.

THE GERMAN OPERA.

There is already much excitement in regard to the performances of the Grand German Opera Company, under the management of Mr. Leonard Grover. The strength of the company is commented on, and confidence is felt that the large and varied *reportoire* will be carried out in perfect faith. The works to be performed are of the highest character—those which we do not hear from the Italian singers, and the change from the perpetual Verdi or Donizetti, will be welcomed by a large majority of our musical people. Report speaks highly of the performance of Beethoven's wonderful Opera, "Fidelio," by this company and much pleasure is anticipated in hearing it. It is a work with which the public should be more familiar. The sale of reserved seats at the usual places, goes on briskly and the general impression seems to be that the brief season of the German Opera will be highly successful. The season commences on Monday evening next with the popular opera of Faust.

MLLE. DE KATOW AND MR. JAMES M. WEHLI'S CONCERT.

Last night these artists gave their farewell evening concert at Irving Hall. Considering that it is Holy Week, the attendance was very large. After Mr. Wehli had played his first selections, and received the usual honor of an encore, there was a pause in the programme. After much delay, Mr. Wehli came forward and announced that Mlle. De Katow had just received information that her father had died suddenly, and that it would be impossible for her to appear; at the same time saying that he would play an extra piece to supply her place. Mr. Wehli played superbly on this occasion. He seemed to feel that the burden of the entertainment had fallen upon him, and exerted himself accordingly. His fingers were in admirable order, so that in delicacy and brilliancy of execution he excelled most of his previous performances. His selections were all of the most pleasing character, and were individually calculated to exhibit the various phases of his superb technique—that wonderful equality which enables him to execute passages of great force, with no more apparent exertion than he exerts for the most delicate and pianissimo *fioriture*—and scales in thirds, sixths, and octaves as easily as the simple scales. Mr. Wehli is unquestionably one of the most eminent; as he is the purest exponent of the true school of pianoforte playing, and it is this perfection of style which exerts so potent a spell over his audience, that they do not tire of listening to him, but, on the contrary, strain a privilege of the public by encoring him so unmercifully that he has almost always to play double the number of pieces set down in the programme. This is a crowning evidence of the delight which he affords and of the extraordinary popularity he has achieved, without clap-trap and without puffing. The piano, one of Chickering's Grands, was altogether the finest instrument he has yet played upon. In exquisite purity and liquid beauty of tone of the entire upper registers; in full and singing qualities of the midde tones, and in sonorous power of the bass, it certainly is unequaled as far as we know. Such an instrument is an additional power vouchsafed to a skilful executant.

This morning Mr. Wehli will appear at a matineé at Irving Hall, which will be his last appearance in New-York for many months, as he leaves the city on Monday for an extended tour through the West. We advise all our lady amateur pianists to attend, for his playing is a lesson in taste and style worth many times the price of admission.

CONCERT AT IRVING HALL.

This evening, Miss Stella Bonheur, a young aspirant for public approbation, gives a concert at Irving Hall. She has been studying very assiduously, and report speaks of her voice as very fine, and of her progress as remarkable. In addition to which she is said to have a fine personal appearance. She will be assisted by several eminent artists, among them Mr. S. B. Mills and Mr. Eben.

CONCERT AT NIBLO'S SALOON.

Miss Teresa McKenna will give her second grand concert at Niblo's Saloon on Monday evening next, 17th inst., when she will be assisted by several distinguished artists, among whom are George W. Morgan, esq., of Grace Church, Senor Gonzalez, Madame Coletti, George Simpson, and several others. We understand Miss McKenna will sing several of Moore's charming melodies. For further particulars we refer to our advertising columns.

NEW-JERSEY ITEMS.

THE FUNERAL OF COL. JANEWAY.—The funeral of the late Col. Hugh H. Janeway, 1st New-Jersey Cavalry killed in battle near Jettersville, will take place this (Saturday) afternoon, at 2 o'clock, in the First Presbyterian Church, Washington-st., Jersey City. The special committee appointed by the Common Council to make arrangements for the obsequies request of the citizens to close their places of business during the funeral ceremonies, and that the flags on the shipping and on all private residences be displayed during the day at half mast. The remains will be conveyed to New-Brunswick for interment.

Naval Movements.

THE NAVY YARD STRIKES—THE WORKMEN STILL HOLD OUT.

The following table shows the diminution in wages prescribed by the recent order issued to the Navy Yard operatives:

Ship Carpenters, 50c. per diem; Joiners, 50c.; Riggers, 50c.; Caulkers, 50c.; Blacksmiths, 25c.; Spar Makers, 50c.; Gun-Carriage Makers, 50c.

Of the above classes of workmen there are nearly 3,000 employed in the yard, all of whom have struck. The founderymen, machinists, masons, block-makers, sawyers, laborers and several minor branches still continue work, and they number all told about 3,500 men.

THE COMMITTEE AT WASHINGTON.

A committee empowered to lay the grievances of the strikers before the head of the Navy Department at Washington left this city on Wednesday night. A telegram is expected every moment which will show whether the order reducing the pay of mechanics emanated from Secretary Welles, and if so whether it will be still persisted in, or what course will be pursued by the Department. The strikers say that the obnoxious order reducing the wages emanated not from the head of the Navy Department, but from one of its bureaus, which is represented by an economical [illegible] compelling from 1,500 to 2,000 men—blacksmiths, fasteners, teamsters, sawyers, laborers, and the remaining portion of the joiners—to stop work; so that the yard instead of being partially will be almost entirely deserted. All the out-door workmen have ceased labor, and the yard already presents the quiet air of repose usually seen on Sundays.

THE SHIP CARPENTERS AND CAULKERS.

These two branches of labor represent the most effective and important in the yard. Our reporter, upon inquiry from these branches, learned that these trades had not had their wages reduced outside of the yard, except in a few instances, in what is called "new work." The caulkers assert that the rate of wages shall be controlled the same as it is outside. The hours of labor of caulkers outside is nine hours per diem at $4 50; heretofore in the yard it has been 10 hours at the same rate; they now labor outside 10 hours, and get $5 10, and they demand for their 10 hours of labor in the yard $5. The demand for the labor of caulkers outside is greater than that of the other branches of ship-building. The demand for ship carpenters is, however, pretty extensive outside, as is attested by the fact that a large number of ship-carpenters yesterday took their tools away from the yard, as they had secured occupation at their original wages elsewhere. The ship-carpenters complain against the invidious distinction drawn in the reduction of their wages, viz.: whatever is done on the outside or bottom of a vessel, which is called "old work," the workmen gets one half-dollar less per diem than for new work, which constitutes work done on all other parts of the vessel. The common distinction outside the yard is that old work constitutes work done on a vessel, either outside or inside, after she leaves the yard where she was built, or when she is put in commission, and new work all other labor.

THE PRESENT DEMAND FOR LABOR.

The demand for mechanical labor is so great at the Yard now that the United States steamer Monongahela, which came here recently to be thoroughly overhauled, will have to go elsewhere, and preparations are being made to send her to Philadelphia. The expense of sending that vessel to that port will be fifty times as much as would pay the extra wages of the Navy Yard operatives. It is anticipated that the other vessels which are at the Yard for an overhauling will be sent to Boston. The Colorado, 52 guns; the Hartford, 28 guns, and the Brooklyn, 26 guns, are but partially overhauled, when these vessels are in great demand by the officers who are to command them.

THE MEDITERRANEAN FLEET.

The Colorado, 52 guns, which is one of the vessels being hurried up, but now put back by the strike, will be the flag-ship of the Mediterranean Squadron, consisting of 30 vessels of war under the command of Rear-Admiral Goldsborough. Capt. Case, Executive Officer of the Navy-Yard, will be the Fleet Captain, and it is expected the whole fleet will be in the Mediterranean this Summer. Admiral Goldsborough is particularly anxious to be at his station in those waters since the daring insult offered by the Portuguese Government toward our Navy in firing upon the United States men-of-war Sacramento and Niagara at Lisbon.

Meeting of the Workingmen's Union.

Last evening a special meeting of the Workingmen's Union, representing the different Trades' Societies of New-York City was convened at the Hall of the Association, No. 267 Bowery. The meeting was called to order by the President of the Association, Mr. WM. HARDING, who explained its nature. The object they had in view was to express their sympathy with and send material aid to the Iron Puddlers of North Staffordshire, England, who had struck for an advance of wages. In South Staffordshire they had received "a fair day's pay for a fair day's work," but the employers in North Staffordshire contended that the workingmen there enjoyed advantages which were unknown in any other part of England, and still further that owing to the cheapness of iron and high price of coal they were unable to compete with the manufacturers in Belgium and France.

In consequence of this, it was said that all the employers in England and Wales agreed to "look out" all the men in South Stafford who were on the strike. It was now believed that the difficulty was settled, and that the great principle for which labor had been so long contending was finally established, namely: that "labor can stand on the same platform as capital." For at the meeting convened at Stoke-upon-Trent, the English puddler sat side by side with the nobleman.

The different societies represented at the meeting were the Shade Painters, Mr. Quinn; Amalgamated Engineers, Mr. McLeod; Tailors, Mr. Cashman; Plumbers, Mr. Beatty; Dry Goods, Mr. Neville; Coachmakers, Mr. Harding; Dry Dock Painters, Mr. Beatty; Bricklayers and Iron Molders.

It was finally moved and carried that a committee of five be appointed to draft a series of resolutions expressing the sympathy of the workingmen of New-York with the workingmen of Great Britain, and tendering them material aid in case they needed it. The members of the committee are Messrs. Neville, McLeod, Bailey, Beatty and Lucker. They are to notify the different trades belonging to the Union, and see that the matter receives due publicity.

THE SUSPENSION OF THE DRAFT.—It is understood the suspension of the draft affects all men who have been drafted, and who have not actually been mustered into the service. Drafted men who have been notified to appear will probably not be called upon to report, and it is expected that an order will be issued immediately by Gen. Fry making this fact public.

THE DRAFT.

Ninth Ward.

The gentlemen of the Ninth Ward who have suddenly recovered from a recent severe attack of the draft, assembled last evening at Bleecker Buildings to condole with one another at the loss of incentives to active patriotism. Ex-Alderman Chas. J. Chipp resumed the Chair from the last adjournment, and the Treasurer, Mr. John Wilson, read his report, to the effect that 147 individuals had contributed about $7 500, of which $6,130 have been collected, and $750 now remain unused in the Treasury. A committee of three, Judge Dodge and Messrs. John W. Thorne and F. LaBaugh, were appointed to audit the accounts, and see to the public advertisement of the same to the satisfaction of all concerned.

A resolution was then presented by Sinclair Tonsey, esq., which was unanimously carried, and read as follows:

Resolved, That the funds remaining on hand, after all expenses have been paid, shall be donated to the managers of the Soldiers' Orphan Home at Flushing, L. I.

A resolution, presented by J. W. Thorne, esq., expressing the thanks of the citizens of the Ninth Ward to the officers and committees of the Association for their arduous labors was unanimously adopted, as also the following, presented by J. W. Farr, esq.

Resolved, That a vote of thanks be, and they hereby are, tendered to Capt. Charles R. Coster, Provost Marshal of the Sixth Congressional District, of New-York, for the able, dignified and gentlemanly courtesy extended to the Committee appointed by this meeting.

With three rousing cheers for Gen. Grant and the noble armies which have aided in the extinction of the Rebellion, the Association of the Ninth Ward in aid of Drafted Men adjourned *sine die*.

Sixteenth Ward.

There was a call made upon the citizens of the Sixteenth Ward to assemble last evening at the Court-Room, corner of Twenty-second-st. and Seventh-ave., for the purpose of aiding in filling the quota without the enforcement of a draft. The meeting was advertised to take place at 8 o'clock, but when that time arrived, and no one came with it, we reasonably supposed that the proclamation received by Major Dodge yesterday morning put a damper upon the proceedings and that the meeting would not be held.

This Ward has certainly done its utmost to comply with the demand of the President and furnish the required number of men as recruits. Both the ladies and gentlemen have been canvassing the district for money to help pay for substitutes for those drafted and held, but whose presence in the city is indispensable to their families.

They have worked arduously, and can now rest from their toils.

BROOKLYN ITEMS.

THE RETURN OF PEACE.—The city was ornamented with flags yesterday, in honor of the return of Peace. Every public building and many private residences had banners flying. The Kings County Supervisors Bounty Committee held a meeting yesterday morning and adopted the following resolutions:

Resolved, That this county pay no more bounty for recruits or volunteers.

Resolved, That in case of drafted men held to service, the Provost-Marshals are requested to give time to ascertain whether such drafted men cannot be discharged; and in case such drafted men cannot be discharged, or given time, then this county will pay such drafted men for one year's substitutes or their bounty.

THE DRAFT.—There is very little business doing at the Provost-Marshal's office of the Third District. The following will show the quota required and the deficiency under the last call: First Ward, quota, 29; deficiency, 12. Second Ward, quota, 133; deficiency, 64. Third Ward, full. Fourth Ward, quota, 78; deficiency, 21. Fifth Ward, quota, 221; deficiency, 120. Seventh Ward, quota, 164; deficiency, 80. Eleventh Ward, quota, 189; deficiency, 105. Thirteenth Ward, quota, 224; deficiency, 91. Nineteenth Ward, quota [illegible] Twentieth Ward [illegible] required, but the result has not yet been officially declared.

THE STRIKE IN THE NAVY-YARD.—A number of the Navy-Yard strikers still hold out. Hundreds were standing outside of the gates yesterday waiting for something to turn up. Hon. Messrs. Raymond, Humphrey and Darling are expected to intercede in their behalf. Some have gone to work at the prices dictated by the Government, but many stand out in the expectation of better terms. A committee sent to Washington have not yet returned.

FORT SUMTER.—100 guns were fired last evening from the City Hall Park, Brooklyn, in honor of the raising of the old Flag over Fort Sumter. A band of music added to the interest of the occasion, all of which was gotten up at the expense of the Hon. Moses F. Odell.

THE COST OF THE WAR.—The total amount of money appropriated by Kings County for the relief of volunteers' families and paying bounties, since 1862, is $5,271,185 83. The number of men furnished to the army and navy was about 30,000.

KINGS COUNTY CIRCUIT COURT, Monday, April 17.—Nos. 73, 74, 3, 19, 2, 20, 25, 34, 35, 39, 43, 47, 52, 79.

The First California-built Ocean Steamship.

From The San Francisco Bulletin, March 15.

There now lies at the foot of Steuart-st. something which must be looked upon with pride by all Californians. It is the steamship Del Norte, built by Henry Owens of this city for the Ben. Holladay line, and destined to run between San Francisco and Humboldt and Crescent City, for the transportation of passengers and freight. This is the first ocean steamship ever built entire on the Pacific coast, and it is not only a credit to its builder, but demonstrates the fact that such things can be made here as well as at the East. The following are her dimensions: Length of keel, 187 feet; breadth of beam, 30 feet; depth of hold, 17 feet 3 inches; length over all, 200 feet. She was launched Dec. 14. Since that time she has been lying at her present berth, receiving her machinery and finishing touches, and is expected to be ready for service about the 6th of April. She has a large oscillating engine, taken from the Republic, of 105 nominal horse power, and capable of being worked to 400 horse power. Her cylinder is 54 inches, with 6 feet stroke. The paddle-wheels are 25¼ feet in diameter; buckets 6¼ feet long, and 1½ feet wide. The air pump, for steam condensation, raises 900 tuns three times per minute. The steam condenser is an ingenious contrivance, and great results are expected from it. There are two fresh-water tanks of a capacity of about 750 gallons each, and two boilers, which were made by Coffey & Risdon, and are what are denominated low-pressure drop flue boilers. Each boiler is 23 feet long by 9 feet 2 inches in diameter. The amount of heating surface in them is 2,000 feet. They are made very strong, being thoroughly braced inside, and have perforated doors for the admission of air to consume the gas and smoke. The rivets underneath are covered with a flange to prevent the bilge water from rusting them, as it would otherwise be very apt to, for it has almost the eating qualities of vitriol. Iron stays keep the boilers in position instead of the old-fashioned saddles. The machinery and boilers are about midships. This gives a large space forward for freight. On the main deck forward is also much room for freight and steerage passengers, with portholes for sliding the freight through. The main saloon is aft, and will be fitted up in a tasteful manner. There are 18 staterooms, capable of accommodating 50 cabin passengers. The officers' quarters will be on the upper deck, and, of course, very roomy and pleasant. The Del Norte is about 800 tuns register, and is rigged with two masts. Her machinery is being put in under the direction of John Bermingham, Superintendent of the California and Oregon steamship line. As before remarked, she will be ready for her trial trip in about three weeks.

THE PRESBYTERIAN GENERAL ASSEMBLY AND THE SECEDERS.—*The Presbyterian* in an article upon the General Assembly to convene at Pittsburgh next month, says:

But a matter of great moment is the settlement of the *status* of the Southern ministers and churches that may desire to unite with us. This subject will be one of no inconsiderable perplexity. A small portion—very small, indeed—of our Church, composed of adherents of Dr. Stuart Robinson, would like to see the Assembly rescind all its various deliverances on the subjects of the country and Slavery—and especially of the latter—from the Spring of 1861 until the present. Another party larger than the one we have mentioned, but still small, would be willing to receive back the southern ministers and churches that separated themselves from us, simply upon their application, without asking any questions or making any inquiry concerning their ecclesiastical connection. But the great body of the ministers and members of our church will demand, that before these erring ones can be restored to full fellowship as before, they must confess their sin in separating from us—in committing treason against both Church and State—and must also pledge themselves to fidelity in the future. Nor will our Church ever again tolerate such teachings with regard to Slavery as prevailed in times past in some parts of our ecclesiastical connection.

COMPANY K, 7TH REGIMENT, N. Y. S. N. G.—In compliance with regimental orders, this Company, now under command of Capt. E. P. Rogers, will assemble at their armory, on Wednesday evening, 19th inst., at 7½ o'clock, and fire one hundred guns in honor of the glorious victories achieved by our armies, and also in commemoration of the prompt marching of the Regiment on the 19th of April, 1861, in response to the call for military aid to defend the National Capital. Officers who were formerly members of the company, and honorary members, are invited to be present and participate in the proceedings. The services of this Company in furnishing officers to the armies of the Union during the war now closing have been highly important and valuable, and the sanguinary fields of Gettysburg, Camden, Manassas, Antietam, and the Wilderness, bear proud yet sorrowful testimony to the courage, patriotism, and gallantry of their comrades. Out of 104 members, 57 returned to the war, 19 entering the Regular and 38 the Volunteer army, of whom 7 were killed in action, and 1 died in the service. They filled the following positions: 1 brigadier-general, 2 colonels, 2 lieutenant-colonels, 4 majors, 20 captains, 25 lieutenants, 1 surgeon, and 2 naval officers. To the 1st Regiment New-York Volunteers the Company furnished nine officers, as follows: 2 colonels, 1 lieutenant-colonel, 1 adjutant, 3 captains, and 2 lieutenants.

Various Items.

The congregation under the pastoral care of the Rev. G. W. Hosmer, D. D., at Buffalo, have presented him with $1,000 raised by subscription, with the request that he will expend the same in a six months' journey for the benefit of his health.

The Wilmington (N. C.) *Herald* of April 5 reports the arrival there on the previous day of the first through train from the army at Goldsborough. A benevolent society has been organized in the town, with daily meetings, for the purpose of preparing linen, bandages, bed-clothes and other articles for the use of those in hospital.

At the municipal election in Sacramento, Cal., March 14, the regular Union ticket was elected by an average majority of 900 votes.

Mr. Potter Palmer of Chicago reports an income last year of $338,483, which will probably enable Potter to keep clear of public support for the present.

Capt. S. A. Emerson has been appointed Harbor Master at Wilmington, N. C., relieving Capt. Fitch.

Mr. John W. Thompson of Farmington, Conn., was caught in a belt at a grist-mill in West Hartford last Wednesday, and received injuries from which he died in a short time.

It is believed that West Pawlet, Vt., produces more potatoes than any town of its size in the country. Last year there was sent from the railway station there 160,000 bushels.

Hon. John Cradlebaugh, formerly delegate from Nevada, has been appointed Adjutant-General of that State by the Governor, and the Senate has confirmed the appointment.

It is said that the French Minister at Richmond has gone to Washington to submit a claim for the French tobacco destroyed last week.

At Mobile, a Mrs. Smith, representing herself to be an agent of the Sanitary Commission, was proved to be an impostor, and guilty of smuggling goods and selling the same to the soldiers, and was sent out of the Department with the earliest dispatch.

Mrs. Deborah Allen Belcher, who recently died at Belfast, Me., at the age of 82, was the last survivor of the ten children of the Rev. Timothy Fuller, among whom was the Hon. Timothy Fuller, the father of Madame Ossoli (Margaret Fuller) and Chaplain Fuller.

John F. Bailey has been appointed Collector of Internal Revenue for the Fourth Collection District of this State, in place of John Mack removed.

John Terry, engineer in Way's tannery at Shandaken, Ulster County, was instantly killed last Friday, by becoming entangled in machinery.

Memphis News.

The Memphis Argus of April 7 gives full particulars of the loss of the steamer M. R. Cheek and her cargo of 120 bales of cotton, which disaster took place March 21, on the Ouachita River, on the passage from Bayou Bartholomew to Monroe City, La. The following account was furnished by an eye witness:

"When about 15 miles below Ouachita City—the boat being under full headway, and a very strong headwind blowing—the alarm of fire was given. All hands immediately rushed on deck, and found that the cotton had caught fire from a spark from the furnace of the boat. The flames spread with the rapidity of lightning, and although every exertion was made by the officers and crew to subdue them, their efforts were of no avail; and in less time than it takes to write this, the boat was burned to the water's edge and sunk. The crew saved only what clothes they had on at the time, and were very fortunate to escape in that way. Several of the deck crew jumped overboard; but only two were lost, and the ot[illegible] One of them was seen [illegible] drown, in the flames, as he was confined to his bed at the time, and has not been seen since the fire first broke out. Two other negroes were injured—one of them badly burned, but not dangerously.

At the time the accident occurred we were in a part of the river where the banks were overflowed, which made it almost impossible to reach dry land with the boat. In fact, nothing short of a special interposition of Divine Providence could have saved the crew. When the engineer was forced by the heat to leave his post, he left both engines working full stroke; and before the tiller rope was burned, the pilot had her started for the timber. The boat went through brush and trees, breaking down and running over trees fully three feet through, as though they were simply willows, when about twenty yards from the bank we ran against a very large tree, which bent over and the boat lodged upon it. The crew then had to wade to the shore in water about waist deep. On reaching Monroe we found the Zephyr lying there, and our crew took passage on her; otherwise they would have foun[illegible]ifficult to get transportation to the Mississippi River.

"The Cheek was owned by Captains B. J. B. Weaver and Ben Johnson of St. Louis, and commanded by W. C. Pomeroy, who, it is needless to say, did everything in his power to extinguish the flames, and, when finding further exertions useless, to save the lives of his crew. The boat was insured in the following offices: Washington, Phenix, Metropolitan, Manhattan and Home, of New-Haven, the agent of whom, Mr. B. T. Tomlinson, so soon as the legal and required proof had been handed in, gave the owners a check for the full amount of her insurance."

The same paper states that on April the steamer Liberty No. 2 brought from Louisville two of Adams & Co.'s safes, one of which, containing $100,000, was lost overboard in fifteen feet water. *The Argus* says:

"The Company at once offered a reward of $1,000 for its recovery, whereupon Mr. Apperly, mate of the Liberty, sounded for it with a long pole, and succeeded in finding it, when one of the deck hands took hold of the pole and went down to it, attached a rope, with which he was provided, to one of the handles, when it was easily hoisted to the surface, and replaced in the wagon. The reward was at once paid Mr. Apperly, who divided it with his fellow mate, and those of the deck hands who assisted him in its recovery. The job took but half an hour, and Mr. A. says, as it paid so well, that he has no objection to taking a few more contracts of a similar nature."

LEE AND EWELL.—The Washington dispatch of *The Philadelphia Press* gives the following facts respecting Gens. Lee and Ewell:

Lee has found something better to do than journeying to New York to be gaped at by a curious populace. Since his capture he has expressed himself as penitent for his share in the Rebellion, of which he has undoubtedly been the ablest supporter. Its weakness he saw long ago, but hoped by the genius that was in him and some fortunate contingency to succeed. But the battles of Fame Cross Roads, Deatonsville, and the concluding skirmishes near the Appomattox (an account of which has been furnished) proved to him the cause was hopeless, and he surrendered. He has already given proof of his penitence. He is about to go to Raleigh, or to whatever place Johnston may now be, to endeavor to induce him to surrender his army and stay further bloodshed. That he will be successful, both through his own great example and influence, and the present weakness of Johnston, there is scarcely room to doubt.

EWELL AT THE METROPOLITAN.

Of the three Lieutenant-Generals with whom Lee began the war, there is but one remaining, and he is Ewell, the one-legged General, who is now at the Metropolitan on parole. Your readers know him well. It was he who led the invasion which roused your people and sent them in thousands—

"Militiamen untrain'd to war,
To fight upon the border."

Stonewall Jackson fell at Chancellorsville; A. P. Hill at Sutherlands. These were his trusty lieutenants—brave and dashing—but the Union they in their treason despised has punished them with the quick retribution of the whistling bullet. He looks well, and seems to take his capture and the downfall of his cherished "Confederacy" with a good deal of philosophy.

AN EXPLANATION.—Mr. A. A. Latham, the party who was treated with considerable violence at Portland, Me., last Tuesday, for alleged indignity offered by him toward the American flag, has published a card as follows:

Having been charged with offering disrespect to our national flag by having removed a small one from one of the cars on a train about to leave this city yesterday, I beg to say that in so doing I considered I was carrying out an old established rule that no flag but those used for signals should be exhibited on any train; and I had no intention of offering any slight to our flag or interfering in any way with manifestations of joy, in which I was disposed to join most cordially.

A. A. LATHAM.

COMMITTED SUICIDE.—Last evening Frederick Hughes jumped from the attic window of his boarding-house, No. 51 Oak-st., and falling on the pavement, fractured his skull, causing instant death. He had been ill for the previous four days. The body was taken to the Fourth Precinct Station-house, and a coroner notified to hold an inquest.

GAZETTE EXTRA.

Chattanooga, Saturday, April 15, 6 P. M.

Death of President Lincoln!

SEWARD BADLY WOUNDED!

WASHINGTON, 12:30 A. M. April 15.

The President was shot in the theatre to-night. He is perhaps mortally wounded.

SECOND DISPATCH.

The President is not expected to live through the night. He was shot at the theatre.

Secretary Seward was also assassinated, but no arteries were cut.

WASHINGTON, April 15.

President Lincoln and wife, with their friends, last evening visited Ford's Theatre for the purpose of witnessing the performance of "Our American Cousin." It was announced in the papers that General Grant would also be present, but that gentleman took the late train of cars for New Jersey. The theatre was immensely crowded, and everybody seemed delighted with the scene before them. During the third act, and while there was a temporary pause for one of the actors to enter, the sharp report of a pistol was heard, which momentarily attracted the attention, but suggested nothing serious, until a man rushed to the front of the President's box, waving a long dagger in his right hand, and exclaiming "*Sic Semper Tyrannis*" and immediately leaped from the box which was in the second tier, to the stage beneath and ran across to the opposite side of the stage, making his escape amid the bewilderment of the audience, in the rear of the theatre and mounting a horse fled.

The screams of Mrs. Lincoln first discovered the facts to the audience, that the President was shot, when all present rose their feet, rushing to the stage, many exclaiming "hang him."

The excitement was of the wildest possible description, and of course, there was an abrupt intermission of the theatrical performance. There was a rush towards the President's box, when cries were heard, "Stand back; give him air; has any one stimulants."

After a hasty examination it was found that the President had been shot through the head, above and back of the femoral bone, and that some of the brain was oozing out. He was removed to a private house opposite the Theatre and the Surgeon General of the army and the other Surgeons called, to attend to his condition.

On an examination of the private box, blood was discovered on the back of the cushioned rocking chair upon which the President had been sitting; also on the partition and floor. A common, single-barreled pocket pistol was found upon the carpet. A military guard was placed in front of the residence to which the President had been carried. An immense concourse of people was in front of it, all deeply anxious to learn the condition of the President. It had been previously, announced that the wound was mortal, but all hoped otherwise.—The shock to the community was terrible. At midnight, the Cabinet, Messrs. Sumner, Farnsworth, Judge Bates, Gov. Oglesby, Gen. Meigs, Col. Hays, and a few personal friends, with Surgeon-General Barnes and his immediate assistants, were at his bedside.

The President was in a state of syncope, totally insensible and breathing slowly. The blood oozed from the wound at the back of his head. The Surgeons used every possible effort in medical skill, but all hope was gone. The parting of his family with the dying President, is too sad for description.

The President and Mrs. Lincoln did not go to the threatre until fifteen minutes after eight o'clock.

Speaker Colfax was at the White House at the time, and the President stated to him that he was going, although Mrs. Lincoln had not been well, because the papers had announced that Gen. Grant was to be present, and as Gen. Grant had gone north, he did not wish the audience to be disappointed. He went with apparent reluctance and urged Speaker Colfax to go with him, but that gentleman had made other engagements, and with Mr. Ashman, of Mass., bid him good bye.

WAR DEPARTMENT, WASH., April 15.

To Major General Dix:

Abraham Lincoln died this morning at twenty-two minutes after seven o'clock.

E. M. STANTON.

Major General JAMES B. STEEDMAN directs that all places of business be closed

[EDITOR GAZETTE.]

SECOND DISPATCH.

WAR DEPARTMENT, 4 A. M, Apr. 15.

Major General Dix:

The President continues insensible and is sinking. Secretary Seward remains without change. Fred. K. Seward's skull is fractured in two places, besides a severe cut on the head, the *attendant* is still alive but hopeless. Major Seward's wounds are not dangerous. It is now ascertained with reasonable certainty that two associates were engaged in the horrible affair. Wilkes Booth being the one that shot the President and the other, a companion of his whose name is not known, but whose description is so clear that he can hardly escape. It appears from letters found in Booth's trunk that the murder was planned before the fourth of March, but fell through then because the accomplice backed out until Richmond could be heard from.

Booth and his accomplice were at the Livery Stable at 6 o'clock last evening and left there with their horses about 10 o'clock, or shortly before that hour. It would seem that they had for several days been seeking their chances, but for some unknown reason, it was not carried into effect until last night. One of them has evidently made his way to Baltimore, the other has not yet been traced.

(Signed) E. M. STANTON.

WASHINGTON, April 15.

When the excitement at the theatre was at its wildest height, reports were circulated that Secretary Seward had also been killed. On reaching this gentleman's residence, a crowd and a military guard were found around his door, and upon entering the mansion, it was ascertained that the reports were based on truth; everybody there was so excited that scarcely an intelligible word could be gathered, but the facts are substantially as follows:

About ten o'clock a man rang the bell, and the call was answered by a colored servant; he said he had come from Dr. Veridier, Secretary Seward's family physician, with a prescription, at the same time holding in his hand a small piece of folded paper, and saying in answer to a refusal, that he must see the Secretary, as he was intrusted with particular directions concerning the medicines. He still insisted on going up, although repeatedly informed that no one could enter the chamber. He pushed the servant aside and walked boldly towards the Secretary's room. He was then met by Mr. Fred Seward, of whom he demanded to see the Secretary, making the same representation which he did to the servant. What further passed in the way of colloquy is unknown, but the man struck him on the head with a billiett, injuring the skull and felling him almost senseless.

The assassin then rushed into the chamber and attacked Mr. Seward, the paymaster of the United States, a Mr. Hansel, a messenger of the State Department, and two male nurses, disabling them. He then rushed upon the Secretary, who was lying in bed in the same room, and inflicted three stabs in his neck, but severing, it is thought and hoped, no arteries, though he bled profusely. The assassin then rushed down stairs, mounted his horse and rode off before an alarm could be given.

NASHVILLE, April 15.

The most intense feeling exists throughout the country regarding the terrible events which occurred at Washington. The day of rejoicing has been turned into one of heartfelt mourning. Business has been entirely suspended throughout the land.

NEW YORK, April 15.

The Herald's Goldsboro correspondence says that Sherman's army commenced its advance on the 9th, moving in three columns, under Howard, Slocum and Schofield. During the rejoicings over the news of Richmond, Sherman was called out by his troops, and he addressed a few words to them, saying that he was informed that Richmond had been captured, and that Lee was flying in dismay. He said that Grant wrote to him that he was pursuing Lee, and hoped that he would press Johnston, which, said Sherman I think we will do. The soldiers cried we will! we will! Sherman then told his soldiers that he did not intend to let Johnston have any rest.

Johnston has evacuated Raleigh, moving west, and leaving the town in possession of Hampton's Cavalry.

On the evening of the 10th, a small force of Howard's mounted Infantry were attacked by some rebel cavalry, who however, were soon dispersed with a loss of one hundred men and two pieces of artillery.

WASHINGTON, April 15, 2 P. M.

Vice President Andrew Johnson was sworn in as President of the United States at 11 o'clock this morning.

Charleston Courier.

NEW SERIES..No. 43 — CHARLESTON, S. C. UNITED STATES OF AMERICA, SATURDAY MORNING, APRIL 15 1865. — VOL. I.

THE
CHARLESTON COURIER
IS PUBLISHED EVERY MORNING
BY WHITTEMORE & JOHNSON,
(GEO. WHITTEMORE.........G. W. JOHNSON.)
NO. 43 HAYNE-STREET,
SECOND DOOR EAST OF MEETING-ST.

FORT SUMTER.

The Raising of the "Old Flag" by Maj. Gen. Anderson.

Salutes by the Army and Navy.

AN ADDRESS BY REV. HENRY WARD BEECHER.

A Crowd of Visitors from the North.

A Grand Gala Day in Charleston.

THE MAGNIFICENT APPEARANCE OF THE VESSELS.

A Reception by General Gillmore.

The Staff Officers of Gen. Hatch Give a Ball in the Evening.

The historic old flag was yesterday replanted on Fort Sumter. The day, the occasion, and the event marks a new era for South Carolina, and hereafter will be among the most memorable in her annals.

At an early hour in the morning our streets were made lively by crowds of citizens wending their way along the principal streets to the wharves. National flags were to be seen waving from numerous private as well as the public buildings. Vehicles of every description were in great demand. Crowds of army and navy officers as well as citizens were at the hotel in waiting for carriages to convey them to the different steamers upon which they had been invited to take passage to the fort. A band of music in front of the hotel discoursed most charming music, and made that rendezvous doubly attractive.

About six o'clock the arrival of the steamer "Diamond," General GILLMORE's flagship, with that officer and his staff, together with a number of the distinguished visitors on board, was announced by a salute. Long before ten o'clock the wharves and streets leading to them, along which it was supposed the visitors would pass, were thronged by the crowd, anxious to see the distinguished strangers. All the vessels in the harbor were decorated with colors, and made a gay appearance.

The following order of Major General GILLMORE, for the carrying out of the President's intentions, was issued:

HEADQUARTERS, DEPARTMENT OF THE SOUTH,
Hilton Head, S. C., April 10, 1865.
[*General Orders, No 41.*]

Friday next, the 14th inst., will be the fourth anniversary of the capture of Fort Sumter by the rebels. A befitting celebration on that day, in honor of its reoccupation by the National forces, has been ordered by the President, in pursuance of which Brevet Major General Robert Anderson, United States Army, will restore to its original place on the fort, the identical flag which, after an honorable and gallant defence, he was compelled to lower to the insurgents in South Carolina, in April, 1861.

The ceremonies for the occasion will commence with prayer, at thirty minutes past 11 o'clock, A. M.

At noon precisely the flag will be raised, and saluted with one hundred guns from Fort Sumter, and with a National salute from Fort Moultrie and Battery Bee on Sullivan's Island, Fort Putnam on Morris Island, and Fort Johnson on James island; it being eminently appropriate that the places which were so conspicuous in the inauguration of the rebellion, should take a part not less prominent, in this national rejoicing over the restoration of the national authority.

After the salutes, the Reverend Henry Ward Beecher will deliver an address.

The ceremonies will close with prayer and a benediction.

Colonel Stewart L Woodford, Chief of Staff, under such verbal instructions as he may receive, is hereby charged with the details of the celebration, comprising all the arrangements that it may be necessary to make for the accommodation of the orator of the day, and the comfort and safety of the invited guests from the army and navy, and from civil life.

By command of Major General Q A. GILLMORE.
W. L. M. BURGER,
Assistant Adjutant General.

Admiral DAHLGREN issued the following order:

FLAGSHIP PHILADELPHIA,
Charleston Harbor, S. C., April 13, 1865.
[*General Order, No. 36.*]
(Third Yearly Series.)

The public prints announce the surrender of the rebel army under General Lee, to the Commanding General of the United States Army.

As the ceremony ordered for the formal restoration of the Union flag to Sumter will occupy the greater part of to-morrow, it only remains to give the rest of the day to some appropriate recognition of an event which seems to leave no further power of effective resistance to the rebellion.

The vessels of the Squadron will therefore dress ship, in full colors, to-morrow at 8 o'clock A. M, and at the same time every vessel will fire a National salute of twenty-one guns.

Twenty-one guns will also be fired at sunset, when the flags are hauled down.

JOHN A. DAHLGREN,
Rear Admiral, Commanding
South Atlantic Blockading Squadron.

The steamer "Canonicus," lying at South Atlantic Wharf, had been kindly assigned by Gen. HATCH and Col. GURNEY for the accommodation of a large number of visiting officers and invited civilians, with their families. On board of her was the splendid post band of the 127th New York Volunteers. Gen. HATCH and staff and Col. GURNEY and staff made their appearance a little before ten o'clock. As they stepped on board the band struck up "Hail Columbia."

The following is a list of Gen. GILLMORE's Staff present:

Colonel S. L. Woodford, Chief of Staff
Major W. L. M. Burger, Assistant Adjutant General.
Major Goureaud, Inspector General.
Dr. Clymer, Medical Director.
Major Thompson, Provost Marshal General.
Captain Bragg, A. D. C
Lieutenant James, A. D. C.
Lieutenant Frank Geise, Assistant Provost Marshal General.
Capt Merrill, Chief Signal Officer.
Major Elliott Chief Paymaster.
Major Thomas, Chief Quartermaster.
Colonel Ames, Chief of Artillery.
Captain Pratt, Ordnance Officer.

The following is a list of General HATCH's Staff present:

Captain E B Van Winkle, Chief of Staff.
Captain Leonard B Perry, Assistant Adjutant General.
Captain John H Moore, A Q M.
Lieutenant Henry Hagens, Depot Quartermaster.
Captain D R Hunt, A Q M.
Captain J T Pratt, Assistant Provost Marshal.
Captain W W Sampson, Acting Assistant Inspector General.
Captain Emil Marthell, Chief Commissary.
Captain F K Smith, Assistant Quartermaster.
Lieutenant F A Wilcoxson, Acting Chief Quartermaster.
Lieutenant Paul, Assistant Provost Marshal.
Lieutenant Ladd, Assistant Provost Marshal.
Lieutenant T C Videl, Chief Signal Officer.
Captain Gardner, A D C.
Lieutenant McMartin, A D C.
Captain James Grace, Ordnance Officer.
Lieutenant S M Edwards, Chief Engineer in charge of works and repairs at Fort Sumter.
Surgeon Brownson.
Lieutenant Jewitt, Assistant Adjutant General.
Captain Caldwell, Chief of Artillery.
Assistant Surgeon Rector, Health Officer.

List of Colonel GURNEY's Staff on board steamer "Canonicus":

Lieutenant Henry A Batterson, Acting Assistant Adjutant General.
Hon D C Coddington, Volunteer Aid.
Lieutenant James F Haviland, Inspector General.
Lieutenant George N Little, A D C.
Captain John L Poppe, A D C.
Captain H H Jenks, Commissary.
Captain E S Henry.
Dr George R Cutter, Chief Medical Officer.
Dr Theodore Artaud, Assistant Surgeon.
Captain Henry J Weston, A D C.
Lieutenant P J Weidensaur, A A Q M.
Lieutenant George S Sammis, Assistant Post Treasurer.

In addition to the above were General HARTWELL and Staff, Major WM WEST, 55th Massachusetts, Dr. GEO. H. FOSSARD, and others.

STARTING OF THE STEAMERS.

About ten o'clock the various steamers, with flags flying, music playing, and amid the enthusiastic cheers of the spectators, cast loose from their moorings and steamed towards Fort Sumter, the "Canonicus" taking the lead. Following in her wake were the steamers "Blackstone," "Oceanus," "Delaware," "W. W. Coit," "Nelly Baker," "Golden Gate," "Anna Maria," and the renowned steamer "Planter," all crowded with passengers.

General GILLMORE's flag-ship, the steamer "Diamond," had already landed a large party from Hilton Head at the fort, previous to the arrivals from the city.

THE FORT.

On their arrival at the fort the visitors passed from the boat to the wharf recently erected on the West angle. A flight of steps leading to the parapet had been erected, and another to the centre of the parade ground. Detachments of marines and sailors from the different vessels, under the command of Lieutenant Commander WILLIAMS, the 127th New York and 35th Massachusetts Volunteers, were drawn up in line on either side, and presented a fine appearance. A platform, surrounded with evergreens, was erected in the centre of the parade ground, with an arched canopy overhead covered with national flowers, made by six Union ladies of Charleston, and intermingled with beautiful wreaths of evergreen and flowers.

In front of the platform were the seats capable of accommodating between three and four thousand visitors. On the stage beside the speaker's stand was a golden eagle holding a handsome wreath of flowers and evergreen. The flag staff had been erected immediately in the centre of the parade ground, and the halyards adjusted by three of the crew of the "Juniata," who took part in the assault on Fort Sumter, ordered by Admiral DAHLGREN, September 9th, 1863.

The arrangements made under the superintendence of Major WEISS, were excellent, and were a complete success.

The number of persons in attendance is variously estimated at about three thousand, including between four and five hundred citizens. Among the latter we observed Charleston's Union representative, Dr. A. G. MACKEY, and his family.

About eleven o'clock Rear Admiral DAHLGREN arrived and was enthusiastically cheered. He was followed by Fleet Captain BRADFORD and from two to three hundred naval officers of the Squadron and visitors. The following is a list of naval visitors who participated in the celebration:

Commander Stephen C Rowan, formerly of the New Ironsides, and Commander William Reynolds, of the New Hampshire.
A A Paymaster William Ives, James Adger.
A A Surgeon George C Reynolds, Chenango.
A A Paymaster A D Bache, Chenango.
A A Master Joseph Martin, Chenango.
A A Paymaster George W Allen, Nantucket.
A Surgeon E M Corson, Nantucket.
A A Paymaster R W Allen, Houghton.
A A Paymaster C A Cabbo, Mingoe.
[illegible] Engineer Joshua Follansbee, Juniata.
Assistant Paymaster Robert P Lisle, Canonicus.
Chief Engineer —— Macomb, Canonicus.
Surgeon H N Beaumont, Canonicus.
Ensign —— Centre, Canonicus.
A V Lieut T E Baldwin, New Hampshire.
A A Paymaster L Brigham, New Hampshire.
A 3d Assistant Engineer Carleton, New Hampshire.
A 2d Assistant Engineer L T Safford, Nahant.
A 2d Assistant Engineer G W Sooley, Adger.
A 2d Assistant Engineer J W Saville Canonicus.
Lieuts Alfred T Mahan, John S McGleassy and John De Haven Mauley.
Acting 3d Assistant Engineer Richard Morgan.
Acting Masters G W Wood, S E Chapin, C C Ricker.
A A Surgeon H C Vaughan.
A A Paymaster G De F Barton.
Fleet Captain Bradford, Fleet Paymaster Watmough, Fleet Judge Cowley, Fleet Engineer Danby, and Lieutenant Commander E O Matthews, of the Staff, officers of all the vessels in the harbor.

Previous to the arrival of Major General ANDERSON, a song entitled "Victory at Last," composed by WM. B. BRADBURY, was sung by the composer, the audience joining in the chorus.

ARRIVAL OF MAJOR GENERAL ROBERT ANDERSON.

At half-past eleven, the sound of music followed by the continued cheering of the crowd on the parapets was the signal of the arrival of Major General ROBERT ANDERSON and the distinguished personages accompanying him.

Major General GILLMORE entered the parade ground with Major General ANDERSON on the right, and Miss ANDERSON on the left. Their entrance was hailed with enthusiastic shouts of delight. After them came the following distinguished visitors:

Rev Henry Ward Beecher and family; Col Charles Anderson, brother of Major General Anderson, arm in arm with Mr Theodore Tilton, editor of the New York Independent; Wm Lloyd Garrison and George Thompson; Prof Davies, of West Point; Major General Doubleday; Gen E D Townsend, Adjutant General U S A; General John A Dix, Provost Marshal General Fry, Col Stewart L Woodford and lady, Judge Holt, Gen Saxton and Staff, Medical Director Clymer, Provost Marshal General Thompson, Col Bogart, Major W L M Burger, Captain Bragg, Captain Merrill, Rev Matthias Harris, Rev R S Storrs, Jr, D.D, Joseph Hoxie, Sergeant Hart, with the old flag and Fort Sumter mail bag.

Among others on the stage were G. V. FOX, Assistant Secretary of the Navy, Commodore GILLIS, Commodore ROWAN, and others, whose names we were unable to obtain.

THE CEREMONIES.

The ceremonies were opened with the recitation of the Te Deum, as follows:

TE DEUM LAUDAMUS.

We praise thee, O God; we acknowledge thee to be the lord.
All the earth doth worship thee, the Father everlasting.
To thee all Angels cry aloud; the Heavens, and all the Powers therein.
To thee Cherubim, and Seraphim continually do cry,
Holy, Holy, Holy, Lord God of Sabaoth;
Heaven and earth are full of the Majesty of thy Glory.
The glorious company of the Apostles praise thee.
The goodly fellowship of the Prophets praise thee.
The noble army of Martyrs praise thee.
The holy Church throughout all the world doth acknowledge thee;
The Father, of an infinite Majesty;
Thine adorable, true, and only Son;
Also the Holy Ghost, the Comforter.
Thou art the King of Glory, O Christ.
Thou art the everlasting Son of the Father.
When thou tookest upon thee to deliver man, thou didst humble thyself to be born of a Virgin.
When thou hadst overcome the sharpness of death, thou didst open the Kingdom of Heaven to all believers
Thou sittest at the right hand of God, in the Glory the Father.
We believe that thou shalt come to be our Judge.
We therefore pray thee, help thy servants, whom thou hast redeemed with thy precious blood.
Make them to be numbered with thy Saints, in glory everlasting.
O Lord, save thy people and bless thine heritage.
Govern them, and lift them up for ever.
Day by day we magnify thee;
And we worship thy Name ever, world without end.
Vouchsafe, O Lord, to keep us this day without sin.
O Lord, have mercy upon us, have mercy upon us.
O Lord, let thy mercy be upon us, as our trust is in thee
O Lord, in thee have I trusted; let me never be confounded.

Prayer was then offered up by the Rev. MATTHIAS HARRIS, Chaplain U S. Army, who made the prayer at the raising of the flag, when Major ANDERSON removed his command from Fort Moultrie to Fort Sumter, December 27, 1860.

PRAYER

Almighty and Everlasting God, the Supreme Governor of the Universe, who art and ever hast been a strong tower of defence unto Thy servants, the people of the United States, against the face of their enemies, especially in the great struggle in which they have engaged for the maintenance of that Constitution and Union—with those rights and liberties bequeathed to us by our patriotic fathers—we yield Thee praise and thanksgiving for our deliverance from those great dangers wherewith we have been encompassed; for the many victories achieved by the skill and courage of our gallant army and navy; for the glad tidings we have heard this day, and for the cheering prospects of a speedy and honorable peace. But with shame and confusion of face we acknowledge that we are not worthy of the least of Thy mercies. We confess that in time past, when we were safe and all things were quiet about us, we were forgetful of Thee our God, and refused to hearken to the voice of Thy word and to obey Thy commandments. Yet, from the dangers which the craft and prowess of our foes have wrought against us, not our own merit but Thy mercy—not our foresight but Thy Providence—not our own arm but Thy right hand and Thine arm—did rescue and deliver us. Not unto us, O Lord, but unto Thy name be ascribed all honor and praise. And we humbly beseech Thee make us truly sensible of Thy goodness towards us, and give us hearts always ready to express our thankfulness, not only by words, but in our lives; that we may henceforth obediently walk in Thy holy commandments; and leading a quiet and peaceable life in all godliness and honesty, may continually offer unto Thee our sacrifice of praise and thanksgiving for all Thy mercies towards us. [illegible] O most glorious and gracious Lord God, without whose enlightening wisdom and sustaining grace human wisdom and human might can accomplish no good thing—we humbly beseech Thee, as for the people of the United States in general, so especially for all in authority, who are set over us by Thy grace and providence to govern us; that Thou wouldst be pleased to endue them with grace, wisdom and understanding, requisite for so high a trust in this hopeful yet perilous crisis of our country. Direct and prosper all their consultations and efforts—to the suppression of all rebellious resistance against the Constitution and Government—to the advancement of Thy glory—to the lasting good, safety and welfare of Thy people—that all things may be so ordered and settled by their endeavors, upon the best and surest foundations, that unity and concord, peace and happiness, religion and piety may be established among us for all generations—that, as in time past, we may be a united, prosperous and happy people. These and all other necessaries for them, for us and for the whole nation, we humbly beg in the name and mediation of Jesus Christ, our most blessed Lord and Saviour. And oh God bless the good old flag of our Union, and grant by Thy grace and by the influences of Thy Holy Spirit that our erring sisters may return in peace, and enjoy protection and repose under her folds. Amen.

This was followed by the reading by the Rev. R S. STORRS, Jr., D. D., and the audience alternately, of Psalms 126, 47, 98 and 20.

Major ANDERSON's dispatch to the Government, dated steam ship "Baltic," off Sandy Hook, April 18th, 1861, announcing the fall of Fort Sumter, was read by Brevet Brigadier General E. D. TOWNSEND, Adjutant General United States Army.

RAISING THE FLAG.

Major General ANDERSON and Sergeant HART then stepped forward on the platform and unfurled the glorious old banner amid the deafening cheers of the assemblage. General ANDERSON and Sergeant HART then raised the flag, with an evergreen wreath attached, the occupants on the stage all joining in taking hold of the halyards. The scene of rejoicing that followed as the flag reached the top of the staff was indescribable. The enthusiasm was unbounded. There was a simultaneous rising, cheering and waving of hats and handkerchiefs for fully fifteen minutes.

As the starry emblem floated out gracefully to the strong breeze, the joyful demonstrations were repeated, which were responded to by music from the bands and the thundering salutes from the forts and the fleet. A salute of two hundred guns was fired by battery M, Captain BARKER, and Company B, Captain CALDWELL, of of 3d the Rhode Island Artillery, stationed in the fort.

SPEECH OF GENERAL ANDERSON.

When the cheering had subsided, General ANDERSON, on being introduced by JOSEPH HOXIE, Esq., addressed the assemblage and said:

My friends, and fellow-citizens, and brother-soldiers—By the considerate appointment of the Honora-

[Continued on Second Page.]

THE NEW YORK HERALD.

WHOLE NO. 10,457. NEW YORK, SUNDAY, APRIL 16, 1865. PRICE FIVE CENTS.

OUR LOSS.

The Great National Calamity.

DEATH OF THE PRESIDENT.

Sad Details of the Terrible Event.

The Last Moments of the President.

SCENE AT THE DEATH BED.

The Life and Services of Mr. Lincoln.

IDENTIFICATION OF THE MURDERER.

John Wilkes Booth the Assassin.

Secretary Seward Thought to be Out of Danger.

FREDERICK SEWARD NO BETTER.

THE METROPOLIS IN MOURNING.

THE EXCITEMENT.

MEETING IN WALL STREET.

Speeches of Generals Butler and Burnside, Daniel S. Dickinson and Others.

ALL THEATRES CLOSED.

THE GRIEF OF THE NATION.

Business Suspended Throughout the Country.

THE NEW GOVERNMENT.

Inauguration of Andrew Johnson as President.

The Policy of Mr. Lincoln to be the Policy of Mr. Johnson.

THE CABINET UNCHANGED.

SKETCH OF MR. JOHNSON.

HIS LAST SPEECH.

The Return of General Grant to Washington,

&c., &c., &c.

THE OFFICIAL DESPATCHES.

THE PLOT OF THE ASSASSIN.

Secretary Stanton to General Dix.

WAR DEPARTMENT,
WASHINGTON, April 15—4:10 A. M.

To Major General Dix:—

The President continues insensible, and is sinking.

Secretary Seward remains without change.

Frederick Seward's skull is fractured in two places, besides a severe cut upon the head. The attendant is still alive, but hopeless. Major Seward's wounds are not dangerous.

It is now ascertained with reasonable certainty that two assassins were engaged in the horrible crime—Wilkes Booth being the one that shot the President, and the other a companion of his, whose name is not known, but whose description is so clear that he can hardly escape.

It appears, from a letter found in Booth's trunk, that the murder was planned before the 4th of March, but fell through then because the accomplice backed out until "Richmond could be heard from."

Booth and his accomplice were at the livery stable at six o'clock last evening, and left there with their horses about ten o'clock, or shortly before that hour.

It would appear that they had for several days been seeking their chance, but for some unknown reason it was not carried into effect until last night.

One of them has evidently made his way to Baltimore; the other has not yet been traced

EDWIN M. STANTON,
Secretary of War.

DEATH OF THE PRESIDENT.

Secretary Stanton's Second Despatch.

WAR DEPARTMENT,
WASHINGTON, April 15, 1865.

To Major General Dix, New York:—

Abraham Lincoln died this morning at twenty-two minutes after seven o'clock.

EDWIN M. STANTON,
Secretary of War.

THE NEW GOVERNMENT.

Secretary Stanton's Third Despatch.

WAR DEPARTMENT,
WASHINGTON, April 15—3 P. M.

Major General Dix, New York:—

Official notice of the death of the late President, Abraham Lincoln, was given by the heads of departments this morning, to Andrew Johnson, Vice President, upon whom the constitution devolved the office of President. Mr. Johnson, upon receiving this notice, appeared before the Hon. Salmon P. Chase, Chief Justice of the United States, and took the oath of office as President of the United States, and assumed its duties and functions. At twelve o'clock the President met the heads of departments in Cabinet meeting at the Treasury building, and among other business the following was transacted:—

First—The arrangements for the funeral of the late President were referred to the several secretaries, as far as relates to their respective departments.

Second—William Hunter, Esq., was appointed Acting Secretary of State during the disability of Mr. Seward and his son, Frederick Seward, the Assistant Secretary.

Third—The President formally announced that he desired to retain the present secretaries of departments of his Cabinet, and they would go on and discharge their respective duties in the same manner as before the deplorable event that had changed the head of the government.

All business in the departments was suspended during the day.

The surgeons report that the condition of Mr. Seward remains unchanged. He is doing well.

No improvement in Mr. Frederick Seward.

The murderers have not yet been apprehended.

EDWIN M. STANTON,
Secretary of War.

ANNOUNCEMENT TO MINISTER ADAMS.

Acting Secretary Hunter to Mr. Derby.

WASHINGTON, April 15, 1865.

To J. C. DERBY, United States Despatch Agent, New York:—

Send a copy of the following to Mr. Adams at London by the steamer of to-day, if in time:—

CHARLES FRANCIS ADAMS, &c., &c.:—

The sad duty devolves upon me to announce the assassination of the President at Ford's theatre last night by a pistol shot from a person who entered his box for the purpose. The assassin escaped, but it is supposed has since been arrested.

The President died at half-past seven o'clock this morning.

Vice President Johnson has assumed the functions of President, having been sworn in by the Chief Justice.

About the same time an attempt was made by, it is believed, a different person to assassinate Mr. Seward; but the murderer only succeeded in inflicting painful and severe wounds, principally upon his face.

Mr. F. W. Seward was beaten over the head with a heavy weapon in the hands of the person who attacked his father, and is grievously hurt. His brother was also wounded by the dagger of the assassin, as was Mr. Hansell, a messenger of the department, who was with the Secretary, and the male nurse in attendance.

WILLIAM HUNTER,
Acting Secretary of State.

[The above despatch was sent off by the Portland steamer at three P. M. yesterday.]

MR. SEWARD'S WOUND NOT MORTAL.

Despatch to Mr. Clarence A. Seward, From a Member of the Family.

WASHINGTON, April 15, 1865.

I have just left Mr. Seward's house. His wounds are bad, but not mortal. He is composed. He has lost much blood, but no arteries were cut.

Frederick's skull is fractured badly in two places above the temples. He is insensible, and I fear will die. His brother's wounds are very slight.

The Governor's throat would have been cut if he had not rolled out of bed.

LATER.

Governor Seward has been informed of the murder of Mr. Lincoln. He is composed and no worse. Frederick remains unconscious. The doctor says his condition is highly critical, but not hopeless.

SEARCH FOR THE ASSASSINS.

Circular from the Provost Marshal General.

WAR DEPARTMENT,
PROVOST MARSHAL GENERAL'S BUREAU,
WASHINGTON, D. C., April 15—9:40 A. M.

It is believed that the assassins of the President and Secretary Seward are attempting to escape to Canada. You will make a careful and thorough examination of all persons attempting to cross from the United States into Canada, and will arrest suspicious persons. The most vigilant scrutiny on your part and the force at your disposal is demanded. A description of the parties supposed to be implicated in the murder will be telegraphed you to-day; but in the meantime be active in preventing the crossing of any suspicious persons.

By order of the SECRETARY OF WAR.
N. L. JEFFERS, Brevet Brigadier General, Acting Provost Marshal General.

DETAILS OF THE CALAMITY.

THE HERALD DESPATCHES.

WASHINGTON, April 15—4:40 P. M.

THE DARK DAY OF THE NATION.

The sun set last night upon a jubilant and rejoicing people. The whole nation was exhilarated with the success which had attended our armies in the field and the final overthrow of the rebellion. But it rose this morning upon a sorrow-stricken people. The flags which had waved from almost every housetop were lowered to half-mast, the sunshine of yesterday was changed to mourning and weeping, and the day at Washington was heralded by the tolling of bells announcing to a sorrowing people the departure of the spirit of him who but yesterday was the Chief Magistrate of the nation. The Presidential mansion, which had been decorated and festooned with flags and evergreens, was changed to the sad and solemn drapery of mourning. The several departments, which but yesterday were the scene of joyous life and activity, to-day presented the stillness of the grave. During the night the hand of the assasin had deprived the nation of its Chief Magistrate, and the dagger had been applied to the prostrate form of the chief member of the Cabinet and those of his immediate household. For the first time in the annals of this democratic republican government the tragic scenes of the Roman empire and the French revolution had been enacted in our midst, and almost in sight of the place where repose the ashes of the Father of this free country. The ship of state for a brief space of time was without a pilot or helmsman. New hands were called upon to guide her in the storm, and we can only hope and pray that the Ruler of all things may grant that she may safely outride the storm and escape the rock upon which other nations have been wrecked, and make her onward voyage upon a calm and peaceful sea. The scenes inaugurated were so new, unexpected and startling to this country that the public were appalled at the shocking tragedy. We have read accounts of similar scenes in the history of other nations, but they were before never brought home to our doors. It is not, therefore, at all to be wondered at that the people were almost dumbfounded as the startling intelligence spread over the city that the assassin had carried out his hellish plot upon the person of the President of the United States.

THE PRESIDENTIAL PARTY FOR THE THEATRE FORMED.

It was announced in the afternoon papers here yesterday that the President and Mrs. Lincoln and General Grant would attend Ford's theatre in the evening, to witness the representation of the American Cousin. When the public saw this announcement they had no idea of the result that was to follow. General Grant left in the evening train, with his wife, for Burlington, New Jersey. Both the President and Mrs. Lincoln were reluctant to attend the theatre, but the former thought they had better go, for the reason that General Grant would not be there, and the public would be disappointed (it having been so prominently announced) if they did not attend. It was the intention of Secretary Stanton to join them at the theatre, but pressing business prevented his going.

THE LAST WORDS FROM MR. LINCOLN'S PEN.

At about half-past seven P. M. Hon. George Ashmun called at the White House, and was ushered into the parlor, where Schuyler Colfax was seated, waiting for a short interview with the President on business which had a bearing upon his proposed overland trip. A few moments elapsed, when President Lincoln entered the room, and a short conversation took place, touching upon various matters. The President was in a happy and jovial frame of mind. Mr. Ashmun desiring to see him on special business, and there being no time to attend to it then the President took out a card, and, placing it on his knee, wrote on it as follows:—

Allow Mr. Ashmun and friend to come to me at nine A. M. to-morrow. A. LINCOLN.
April 14, '65.

These were the last words that he penned. It was the last time that he signed his name to any order, document or message. The last words written by him were thus making an engagement for the morrow—an engagement which he was not allowed to meet. Before the hour had arrived he was no more.

THE DEPARTURE FOR THE THEATRE.

Mr. Lincoln finally stated that he must go to the theatre, and warmly pressed Speaker Colfax and Mr. Ashmun to accompany him; but they excused themselves on the score of previous engagements. At about eight P. M. Mr. and Mrs. Lincoln started for the carriage, the latter taking the arm of Mr. Ashmun and the President and Mr. Colfax walking together. As soon as the President and Mrs. Lincoln were seated in the carriage the latter gave orders to the coachman to drive around to Senator Harris' residence for Mrs. Harris. As the carriage rolled away they both said "Goodby, goodby," to Messrs. Ashmun and Colfax, and the carriage had in a moment more disappeared from the ground in front of the White House. A few moments later the Presidential party of four persons—namely, the President and Mrs. Lincoln, Miss Harris and Mr. Rathbon, of Albany, step-son of Senator Harris, arrived at the theatre and entered the front and left hand upper private box.

THE QUIET OF NIGHT RUDELY BROKEN.

The tranquil but joyous scenes which had characterized the national capital for several days past were everywhere manifest in the streets. Bands of music were performing pleasant airs in all directions, and there was nothing in the appearance of the city which indicated that any unusual scene was to transpire, much less that the tragic events which followed would take place. The city was fast settling down into the quiet of repose. Most of the citizens had sought the quiet of their residences. The theatres were the only places which presented any life, when the quiet was broken by the report flying like magic all over the city that the President and Secretary Seward had been assassinated. The reports were so contradictory, and the numerous opposite statements of men who claimed to be eye witnesses, rendered it impossible to get at the real facts for many hours. The following, however, are the most authentic accounts, and in the main are substantially correct, at least as near as can be obtained up to the present moment of writing:—

THE ASSASSINATION.

But a moment before the attack was made, the President was leaning forward, resting his head on his hand in his accustomed careless way, his eyes bent upon the stage, and enjoying a hearty laugh. A noise was heard, and the form of a person descended from the box occupied by the President. With one leap he planted himself upon the stage and assumed a tragical posture, flourished a dagger, turned and faced the audience, shouting "*Sic semper tyrannis!*" also "The South is avenged!" in a tone sufficiently distinct to be heard in all parts of the theatre. The audience, of course, were shocked and dumbfounded. The suddenness of the affair and the melodramatic manner in which the desperado went through his performance gave to the whole thing the appearance of being part of the play. As quick as a flash he disappeared at the rear of the stage, followed by J. B. Stewart, a lawyer of this city, who only missed him by about four feet, as the door was closed by the assassin in Stewart's face. The delay in getting it open again gave him a few seconds' start, and he made his escape.

STATEMENT OF MISS HARRIS.

Miss Harris, who was in the box with the President, makes the following statement:—

Nearly one hour before the commission of the deed the assassin came to the door of the box, and, looked in to take a survey of the position of its occupants. It was supposed at the time that it was either a mistake or the exercise of an impertinent curiosity. The circumstance attracted no particular attention at the time. Upon his entering the box again Major Rathbon arose and asked the intruder his business. He rushed past the Major without making a reply, and placing his pistol close to the back of the President's head, actually in contact with it, fired, and instantly sprang upon the cushioned baluster of the box, when he made a backward plunge with his knife, aimed at the face or breast of Mr. Lincoln. Major Rathbon, springing forward to protect the President, received the stab in his arm. The murderer then jumped upon the stage and effected his escape.

MRS. LINCOLN'S STATEMENT.

The rapidity with which the fiendish act was committed upon the President was astounding. Mrs. Lincoln saw the form of a person go down from the box and thought that Mr. Lincoln had fallen out, and looked to see if she could see him on the floor, and barely saw the culprit jump to the stage when all was over; she turned her eyes to the box and saw that Mr. Lincoln's head had dropped forward upon his breast, and at once realized what had transpired. Thus it is that in an unexpected hour a great calamity has fallen upon the nation. All feel the affliction, from the highest to the lowest, and bow with grief at the sad and lamentable event.

CONFUSION IN THE THEATRE.

The most intense excitement ensued in the theatre. Every effort was made to quiet, but to no avail. A rush was made for the door, and the theatre was soon empty.

J. W. BOOTH IDENTIFIED AS THE ASSASSIN.

The circumstances of the murder, the air, manner and movements of the man were such that almost every person who had known J. Wilkes Booth declared at once that it was him. Some of the actors on the stage and members of the orchestra declared that they would bet their life upon its being Booth. In making his escape he lost his hat, which was identified as Booth's. A spur was recognized as one obtained by Booth at a stable on that day. In fact the evidence momentarily accumulating fixes beyond a doubt the author of the bloody tragedy.

THE PRESIDENT REMOVED FROM THE THEATRE.

A guard of soldiers rushed to the box occupied by the President as soon as it was known that he was shot, and he was immediately taken out to the house of Mr. Peterson, on the opposite side of Tenth street.

THE MURDER OF THE PRESIDENT ANNOUNCED TO HIS SON.

The murder of the President was at once announced at Grover's theatre. Little Tad Lincoln was in attendance there, and the moment that he heard the statement he seemed to go almost crazy, shrieked and sobbed in a heartrending manner. The poor boy was taken to the White House, and was soon quieted when it was ascertained that his father was still alive.

THE ASSASSINATION OF MR. SEWARD.

Simultaneously with the tragic events at Ford's theatre, and, as near as can be ascertained, at the precise moment another fiend entered the house of Secretary Seward, after some parleying with the servants, and it seems there dealt out his blows in all directions. Some six or seven persons who were in attendance upon the family during the night have made their positive statements of the manner in which the assault was made here, but no two of them agree. It is well established that he applied at Seward's residence as the pretended bearer of a prescription of medicine. Having succeeded in evading the servant at the door he rushed to Seward's chamber, but was confronted by Fred. Seward, when he had quite a parley for a moment about the medicine which he had been directed to deliver in person. Finding that he could not succeed in that way he made an attack upon Fred. Seward. The desperado was a large and powerful man. He was determined to enter the bedchamber, and drew his pistol and snapped it twice, but did not succeed in discharging it. He struck Seward twice upon the head with such force that it not only felled him to the floor and crushed the skull in two or three places, but also breaking the pistol, separating the chamber from the barrel. He then immediately rushed into the room and applied his knife to Secretary Seward, who was lying prostrate in bed. It is evident, from the wounds, that he tried to cut the Secretary's throat. He succeeded in inflicting severe gashes upon his face, laying open both cheeks; but his blows were partially warded off by the bedclothes about the Secretary's neck and by the additional fact that Mr. Seward rolled out upon the floor. A soldier by this time had entered the room and sprung upon the assassin's back. He stabbed the soldier in the side and succeeded in breaking away, and, after wounding Major Seward, another son of the Secretary, and an attendant, succeeded in making his escape from the house, mounted his horse and rode away, shouting "*Sic semper tyrannis!*" as he sprang into the saddle.

THE ASSASSIN'S WEAPONS.

The pistol was a large navy revolver, and was broken in pieces by the force of the blows, and was one of Whitney's (of Connecticut) make. The knife was some ten or twelve inches in length, and was also left in the house. The only dangerous wounds inflicted there were those upon Frederick Seward.

THE CABINET INFORMED OF THE TRAGIC OCCURRENCE.

Word was immediately sent to the War Department to give the alarm. Two of the *attaches* of the department started for Stanton's residence. As they arrived in front of his house a man with a cloak about him ran from behind the box of a tree and left. Stanton, upon receiving notice, immediately hastened to Seward's residence, where he met most of the other members of the Cabinet. It was there that he received the intelligence of the assault upon Lincoln.

"SEWARD IS SAFE."

Surgeon General Barnes, who was at Willard's Hotel at the time, was sent for, and but a few moments elapsed before half a dozen physicians arrived at Seward's residence. A report started that Seward was dead. A messenger came for Dr. Barnes, summoning him into the presence of the President. He had barely time to make an examination of Secretary Seward's wounds, when he left. As he passed out of the house he whispered to a friend "Seward is safe."

THE PRESIDENT'S WOUNDS MORTAL.

This furnished relief and tended to centre the anxiety upon Mr. Lincoln. Mr. Stanton and other members of the Cabinet hastened to the side of Mr. Lincoln. Medical and surgical aid was obtained and everything done that could be to relieve, and, if possible, restore the President to life; but it was soon ascertained that it was impossible for Mr. Lincoln to survive, the only question being how many hours he would linger.

THE EXCITEMENT AT WASHINGTON.

Guards were stationed at the corners of the streets leading to the house where the President's body lay. The excitement in the locality was intense. Loud cries of vengeance were uttered, and at one time it was feared that an attack would be made upon the Old Capitol prison, where were confined a large number of rebel prisoners; but under the precautionary measures of some of the more considerate all such demonstrations were prevented.

THE TELEGRAPH WIRES CUT.

The telegraph at the same time with the attack upon the President and Secretary Seward was interrupted. This necessitated the despatch of couriers in all directions. The wires were soon restored and communication with the fortifications in all directions secured.

GENERAL GRANT REPORTED KILLED.

About this time a rumor was started that General Grant had been killed, but there was no foundation whatever for the statement. Colonel Bowers telegraphed to General Grant, which reached him just as he arrived at the depot in Philadelphia. He replied that he was safe and would immediately return.

CIRCUMSTANTIAL EVIDENCE AGAINST THE MURDERERS.

Thus passed the slow hours. Rumors, vague, contradictory, marvellous and startling, were floating about the city. Every few moments strong circumstantial evidence was turned up pointing directly to the parties who performed the atrocious deeds. Long before the President expired the authorities were perfectly satisfied as to who committed both the deeds. The city and military authorities commenced investigations. While the Cabinet ministers and other dignitaries, with the surgeons, were watching over the President every effort was made to capture the murderers. Couriers mounted on fleet horses rushed to and fro; the sound of the hoofs of the horses was heard in all directions. This sound mingled with that of the voices of the riders made the effect somewhat tragic. The city and military authorities deserve a great deal of credit for their energy and vigilance. The tidings at last came that one of the horses had been captured, nearly exhausted, at the outskirts of the city—the bridle bloody. This was identified as the horse ridden off by the assassin from Seward's residence. This gave some hope that the authors of the horrible crime might be captured. On this point speculations became numerous.

SCENES AT THE PRESIDENT'S DEATHBED.

As night had nearly passed away and the streaks of morn were discovered in the east the statement was made that the President might live a day yet. The excited crowds dispersed, leaving comparatively few in the streets. From the moment that the President was shot up to his death he was insensible, and exhibited no signs of pain, recognized no person, and, in fact, I believe did not open his eyes. The blood troubled his breathing, often making it exceedingly difficult. He was watched with tender care, and all that could be was done for him; but his fate had been ruled. For some cause Providence had willed that he should be taken away from us. Vice President Johnson visited the President during the night, but remained only about an hour. In fact, many of those who had rushed to assist in taking care of the President, found that their presence obstructed rather than gave assistance, and therefore left. Among these were many members of Congress and Western men. The number present was reduced to but few before he breathed his last.

LAST MOMENTS OF THE PRESIDENT.

At about five o'clock this morning I reached the house of Mr. Peterson, where the President lay in his dying agonies. He was lying upon the bed, apparently breathing with great difficulty. He was entirely unconscious, as he had been ever since his assassination. His eyes were protruding from their sockets and suffused with blood. In other respects his countenance was unchanged. At his bedside were the Secretary of War, Secretary of the Navy, Secretary of the Interior, Postmaster General and the Attorney General; Senator Sumner, General Farnsworth, General Todd, cousin to Mrs. Lincoln; Major Hay, M. B. Field, General Halleck, Major General Meigs, Rev. Dr. Gurley, Geo. Oglesby, of Illinois; Drs. E. N. Abbott, R. K. Stone, C. D. Hatch, Neal, Hall and Lieberman. In the adjoining room were Mrs. Lincoln, her son, Captain Robert Lincoln; Miss Harris, who was with Mrs. Lincoln at the time of the assassination of the President; Rufus F. Andrews and two lady friends of Mrs. Lincoln, whose names I did not ascertain. Mrs. Lincoln was under great excitement and agony, wringing her hands and exclaiming, "Why did he not shoot me instead of my husband? I have tried to be so careful of him, fearing something would happen, and his life seemed to be more precious now than ever. I must go with him," and other expressions of like character. She was constantly going back and forth to the bedside of the President, exclaiming, in great agony, "How can it be so!" The scene was heartrending, and it is impossible to portray it in its living light. It beggars description, and can better be imagined than described. Captain Robert Lincoln bore himself with great firmness, and constantly endeavored to assuage the grief of his mother by telling her to put her trust in God and all would be well. Occasionally, being entirely overcome, he would retire into the hall and give vent to most heartrending lamentations. He would recover himself and return to his mother, and, with remarkable self-possession, try to cheer her broken spirits and lighten her load of sorrow. His conduct was the most remarkable exhibition of calmness in a trying hour that I have ever seen. About a quarter of an hour before the President died his breathing became very difficult, and in many instances seemed to have entirely ceased, so that the surgeons who were holding his pulse supposed him to be dead. He would again rally and breathe with so great difficulty as to be heard in almost every part of the house. Mrs. Lincoln took her last leave of him about twenty minutes before he expired, and was sitting in the adjoining room when it was announced to her that he was dead. When the announcement was made she exclaimed, "Oh, why did you not tell me that he was dying." The surgeons and the members of the Cabinet, Senator Sumner, Captain Robert Lincoln, General Todd, Mr. Field and Mr. Andrews were standing at his bedside when he breathed his last. Senator Sumner, General Todd, Robert Lincoln and Rufus Andrews stood leaning over the headboard of the bed watching every motion of the beating breast of the dying President. Robert Lincoln was resting himself upon the arm of Senator Sumner. The members of the Cabinet were standing by the side of the bed—Secretary Stanton at the left of Mr. Andrews, Mr. Andrews near Mr. Lincoln's head. Next to him was Mr. Dennison, and the others arranged along at his left, and the surgeons were sitting upon the side and foot of the bed, holding the President's hands, and with their watches observing the slow declension of the pulse, and watching the ebbing out of the vital spirit. Such was the solemn stillness for the space of five minutes that the ticking of the watches could be heard in the room. At twenty-two minutes past seven A. M. his muscles relaxed and the spirit of Abraham Lincoln fled from its earthly tabernacle "to that bourne from which no traveller returns." As he drew his last breath the Rev. Dr. Gurley addressed the Throne of Grace with a fervent prayer for his heartbroken family and his mourning country. The countenance of the President was beaming with that characteristic smile which only those who have seen him in his happiest moments can appreciate; and except the blackness of his eyes his face appeared perfectly natural. He died without a struggle, and without even a perceptible motion of a limb. Calmly and silently the great and good man passed away. The morning was calm, and the rain was dropping gently upon the roof of the humble apartment where they laid him down to die. Guards had been stationed to keep the people from the house, and no noise could be heard in the streets save the footsteps of the sentry passing to and fro, as he guarded all that remained of Abraham Lincoln. The body servant of the President entered the room just before he died, and as the breath left the body of Mr. Lincoln this servant manifested the deepest sorrow. All present felt the awful solemnity of the occasion, and no man could have witnessed the touching scenes without melting to tears. Even stoical Stanton, whose coolness and self-possession were remarkable, could not keep back the silent monitors of the inward sorrow which rolled out from his eyes upon his cheeks. Mrs. Lincoln remained but a short time, when she was assisted into her carriage, and with her son Robert and other friends she was driven to the house where but last evening she left for the last time with her honored husband, who never again was to enter that home alive.

The following minutes, taken by Dr. Abbott, show the condition of the late President throughout the night:—

Eleven o'clock—Pulse 44.

Five minutes past eleven—Pulse 45 and growing weaker.

Ten minutes past eleven—Pulse 45.

Quarter past eleven—Pulse 42.

Twenty minutes past eleven—Pulse 45, respiration 27 to 29.

Twenty-five minutes past eleven—Pulse 42.

Thirty-two minutes past eleven—Pulse 48 and full.

Forty minutes past eleven—Pulse 45.

Quarter to twelve—Pulse 45, respiration 22.

Twelve o'clock—Pulse 48, respiration 22.

Quarter-past twelve—Pulse 48, respiration 21. Ecchymosis both eyes.

Half-past twelve—Pulse 45.

Thirty-two minutes past twelve—Pulse 60.

Thirty-five minutes past twelve—Pulse 66.

Forty minutes past twelve—Pulse 69, right eye much swollen and ecchymosis.

Forty-five minutes past twelve—Pulse 70.

Fifty-five minutes past twelve—Pulse 80, struggling motion of arms.

One o'clock—Pulse 86, respiration 30.

Half-past one—Pulse 95, appearing easier.

Forty-five minutes past one—Pulse 86; very quiet; respiration irregular. Mrs. Lincoln present.

Ten minutes past two—Mrs. Lincoln retired with Robert Lincoln to an adjoining room.

Half-past two—President very quiet; pulse 54; respiration 28.

Fifty-two minutes past two—Pulse 48; respiration 30.

Three o'clock—Visited again by Mrs. Lincoln.

Twenty-five minutes past three—Respiration 21, and regular.

Thirty-five minutes past three—Prayer by the Rev. Dr. Gurley.

Four o'clock—Respiration hard; regular.

Quarter past four—Pulse 60; respiration 25.

Fifty minutes past five—Respiration 28, regular; sleeping.

Six o'clock—Pulse failing; respiration 28.

Half-past six—Still failing and labored breathing.

Seven o'clock—Symptoms of immediate dissolution.

Twenty-two minutes past seven—Death.

POST-MORTEM EXAMINATION OF THE BODY.

A post-mortem examination was immediately held, and the ball extracted from the front lobe of the brain. The body was then taken to the Presidential mansion, and will there be embalmed preparatory to its conveyance to its final resting place.

A few locks of hair were removed from the President's head for the family previous to the remains being placed in the coffin.

THE CABINET CONVENED IN AN ADJOINING ROOM.

Immediately after the President expired Secretary Stanton convened the Cabinet in an adjoining room. What there took place I am, of course, unable to say.

A few moments after the death of the President Secretary Stanton despatched one of his couriers to have the bells throughout the city rung. The order was executed without delay. The first notification that the public had here of the death of the President was through the tolling of the bells. It was generally, and in fact universally, known that it was impossible for Mr. Lincoln to live; but still the intelligence that he had actually breathed his last greatly increased the gloom, and the whole city seemed to be bowed down with grief. Sorrow, sadness and woe were depicted upon every countenance on account of our great national calamity. Arrangements were at once made for the removal of the body to the White House.

The remains of the late President were placed in a temporary coffin and removed to the White House soon after nine o'clock this morning.

An escort of cavalry—Union Light Guard—under the command of Lieutenant Jamison, accompanied the remains, which were followed by General Augur, commanding Department of Washington; General Rucker, depot quartermaster; Colonel Pelouze, of the War Department; Captain Finley Anderson, Acting Adjutant General Hancock's corps; Captain D. G. Thomas, clothing depot; Captains J. H. Crowell and C. Baker. The solemn procession moved slowly up Tenth street to G, and thence to the White House, the large crowd present along the route standing uncovered. Immediately on the guard being removed a rush was made towards the house occupied during the night by the President, and the crowd remained about the entrance for some time.

THE CONDITION OF THE SEWARD FAMILY.

The death of the President again turned the attention of the public to the family of Seward. I doubt if there ever was so great subdued and pent up rage as that which existed here. Every scrap of news relative to the wounds of Seward, and those of his household, was seized with great avidity.

HOW SECRETARY SEWARD RECEIVED THE NEWS OF THE PRESIDENT'S DEATH.

Secretary Stanton called upon Seward just before twelve o'clock. Mr. Seward, recognizing him at once, asked him why the President had not called upon him. Seward up to this had no knowledge or had the remotest idea that the assassin had attacked any person outside of his house. Upon Stanton, therefore, devolved the unpleasant duty of informing him of the fate of the President. Considering it best not to keep him longer in ignorance of the sad event, Stanton gave him a short and succinct statement of what had transpired, and he at once appeared to comprehend the great events of the past night. Instead of having the effect to depress him it seemed to nerve him to meet his own afflictions, and his symptoms have been encouraging and hopeful all day. The other members of his household and attendants who were wounded appear to have been more injured than supposed last night. Frederick Seward and one of the attendants are in a more precarious condition than Secretary Seward. The symptoms of the former are hopeful, but he is in a critical condition. Two pieces of skull have been taken out, and it is probable that the next twenty-four hours will decide the question whether he will recover or not.

WASHINGTON IN MOURNING.

The entire city is draped in mourning. It seemed that all were engaged in draping their buildings with crape. The department buildings were all tastefully draped. The War Department was literally covered. The pillars were thickly draped, and the entire front was richly festooned with black. The other buildings were arranged with good taste, but not so extensively as the War Department. The hotels, private residences and places of business were also appropriately dressed in black. In short, a mantle of gloom was thrown over the entire national capital.

The day of the funeral had not, up to this evening, been fixed, the family not having yet been consulted about it. It may take place on Monday, or at an earlier day than Thursday, as had been suggested by friends. The remains will be removed to Springfield, Illinois.

The city councils met this evening to take such action as will be expressive of their regret for the death of the President.

The clergy of the city have also called a meeting for a similar purpose.

Nothing has been talked of or thought about here today except the atrocious assassination and attempt at assassination made last evening by secession sympathizers and desperadoes. Hundreds of absurd rumors have been circulated all day. There has been no disturbance, and no attempts at disturbance, save a few individual collisions with parties who were wicked and foolish enough to give utterance to disloyal or atrocious sentiments. In every case of this kind the parties were promptly arrested and committed to the guard house. In the present temper of the public no tolerance exists towards those who are disposed to manifest sympathy with assassins, or the cause which they are attempting to avenge. These diabolical outrages have, for the time at least, caused a great revulsion of public feeling, and there is little disposition to conciliate or temper justice with mercy. This feeling of resentment against the mass of the rebels will doubtless be moderated when a full investigation shall have shown that these acts have been committed by a few fanatical zealots, crazed by the ruin which has overtaken the cause of treason, and the destruction and extinction of their bogus confederacy.

To-night the streets are more quiet, and the excitement is gradually subsiding. Everything possible is being done to secure the assassins.

The church of Dr. Gurley, where Mr. Lincoln usually attended service, has been very beautifully draped with mourning both inside and out. The pew usually occupied by the President and his family has been appropriately decorated with the habiliments of woe, and will to-morrow be closed. To-morrow is Communion Sabbath, and, under the afflicting circumstances, the services will be peculiarly impressive and affecting.

WASHINGTON, April 15—11:45 A. M.

An autopsy of the corpse of Mr. Lincoln is now being made at the White House. The coffin has been prepared, and the body will be placed in it as soon as the embalming process is completed. The embalming of the body has been entrusted to Dr. Brown, of the firm of Brown & Alexander, embalmers, of this city. The coffin is of handsome mahogany, covered with black cloth and lined with lead, with an interior lining of white silk. Upon a silver plate is the inscription:—

ABRAHAM LINCOLN,
SIXTEENTH PRESIDENT OF THE UNITED STATES,
BORN FEBRUARY 12, 1809,
DIED APRIL 15, 1865.

The body will be embalmed by three o'clock, and preparations will be made for the body of the President to lie in state at the White House on Monday.

A dense crowd accompanied the remains to the White House, where a military guard excluded the crowd, allowing none but persons of the household and personal friends of the deceased to enter the premises, Senator Yates and Representative Farnsworth being among the number admitted.

The body is being embalmed, with a view to its removal to Illinois.

Flags over the departments and throughout the city are at half mast. Scarcely any business is being transacted anywhere, either in private or public account.

Our citizens, without any preconcert whatever, are draping their premises with festoons of mourning.

The bells are tolling mournfully. All is the deepest gloom and sadness. Strong men weep in the streets. The grief is widespread and deep, and in strange contrast to the joy so lately manifested over our recent military victories.

This is indeed a day of gloom.

The government departments are closed by order, and will be draped with the usual emblems of mourning.

Immediately after the President's death a Cabinet meeting was called by Secretary Stanton, and held in the house in which the corpse lay. Secretaries Stanton, Welles and Usher; Postmaster General Dennison and Attorney General Speed were present. The results of the conference are as yet unknown.

CONDITION OF THE SECRETARY AND ASSISTANT SECRETARY.

Mr. Fred. Seward's skull has been trepanned, and he is as comfortable as could be expected. There are no additional unfavorable symptoms and but slight hopes of his recovery. Secretary Seward remains about the same as through the day.

At the Cabinet meeting yesterday, which lasted over two hours, the future policy of the government towards Virginia was discussed, the best feeling prevailing. It is stated that it was determined to adopt a very liberal policy,

CONTINUED ON FOURTH PAGE.

THE NATION MOURNS ITS LOSS.

The Philadelphia Inquirer.

PRICE TWO CENTS. PHILADELPHIA, MONDAY, APRIL 17, 1865. PRICE TWO CENTS.

THE GREAT TRAGEDY!

A Nation Mourns Its Honored President!

JOY CHANGED TO MOURNING!

The Great Martyr to Liberty!

MURDER OF THE PRESIDENT.

Full Details of the Assassination.

ACCOUNT OF A DISTINGUISHED EYE-WITNESS.

Mr. Lincoln's Death-bed Scenes

A NOBLE PATRIOT GONE TO REST!

Escape of the Dastard Assassin.

MR. SEWARD STILL ALIVE.

His Condition Is Favorable.

Andrew Johnson Inaugurated as President!

HIS INAUGURAL ADDRESS.

Views of the New President.

HE RETAINS THE OLD CABINET!

Official Gazette from Sec'y Stanton.

OUR SPECIAL DESPATCHES

THE GREAT NATIONAL TRAGEDY.

Special Despatch to the Inquirer.

WASHINGTON, April 16.

The monstrous crime of Friday night shocked this city with an agony unutterable. Yesterday morning men walked the streets, and looked into each other's eyes, and found no words willing to leave their lips. Their hearts were surcharged with grief and a wrath inexpressible.

That any Rebel even could be so base as to assassinate the man who within the past ten days has held out the olive branch of peace, and exhibited so great a desire to forgive, was a crime for which Washington, as well as the nation, was unprepared. But the deed was consummated, and Washington, lowering her flags of joy, clothed them in habiliments of mourning. The transition from jubilance to grief and woe was a shock more sudden than ever before befel a community or people. The glorious banner which went up in the morning in honor of its restoration to Fort Sumter, in the short space of twenty-four hours came down to half-mast.

The rejoicing of Friday was turned to mourning, and the light of joy which illumed all faces but a few hours previous, gave way to tears and gloom. When the news of President Lincoln's death was announced, universal silence and grief pervaded the city. Everybody was impressed with the solemn and awful event. Funeral weeds were hung from every window, and the sables of mourning were draped on fronts and about the marble columns of all the public buildings.

THE ASSASSINATION.

From a distinguished officer of the army, who was sitting near the President's box at the time of the assassination, we have received the following interesting statement:—

Account of a Distinguished Eye-witness.

On the night of Friday, April 14th, 1865, in company with a friend, I went to Ford's Theatre, arriving there just after the entrance of President Lincoln and the party accompanying him. My friend and I, after viewing the Presidential party from the opposite side of the dress circle, went to the right side and took seats in the passage above the seats of the dress circle and about five feet from the door of the box. During the performance the attendant of the President came out and took the chair nearest the door.

I sat, and had been so sitting, about four feet to his left and rear for some time. A man, whose face I do not distinctly remember, passed me, and inquired of one sitting near me where the President's messenger was, and learning his identity, exhibited to him an envelope, apparently official, having a printed heading, and superscribed in a bold hand. I could not read the address, and did not try. I think now it was meant for Lieutenant-General Grant. The man went away. Some time after I was disturbed in my seat by the approach of a man, who desired to pass upon the aisle in which I was sitting.

Giving him room by bending my chair forward, he passed me, and stepped one step down upon the level below me. Standing there he was almost in the line of sight, and I saw him while watching the play. He stood, as I remember, one level above the messenger, and remained there perhaps one minute, apparently looking at the stage, and the orchestra below. Then he drew a number of visiting cards from his pocket, from which, with some attention, he drew or selected one. These things I saw distinctly. I saw him stoop, and I think descend upon the level with the messenger, and by his right side. He showed the card to the messenger.

My attention was then more closely fixed upon the scene, and I do not know whether the card was carried in by the messenger, or his assent given to the entrance of the man who presented it. I saw, a few moments after, the man entering the door of the lobby leading to the box, and the door closing behind him. This was seen because I could not avoid observing it, the door side of the proscenium box and the stage being all within the direct and right oblique lines of sight. How long I watched the play after this entering, I do not know. It was, perhaps, two or three minutes, possibly four.

The house was still, the large audience listening to the dialogue between "Florence Trenchard" and "May Meredith," when the sharp report of a pistol rang through the house. It was apparently fired behind the scenes upon the right of the stage and behind the President's box. While it startled every one, yet it was evidently accepted by every one as an introduction to some new passage, several of which had been introduced in the early part of the play. A moment after a man leaped from off the box directly down, nine feet, on the stage, and ran rapidly across, bareheaded, and holding an unsheathed dagger in his right hand, the blade of which flashed brightly as he came within ten feet of the opposite exit.

In the gaslight I did not see his face as he leaped or ran, but I am confident that he was the man I saw enter. As he leaped he cried distinctly and aloud the motto of the State of Virginia—"*Sic semper tyrannis.*" The hearing of this and the sight of the dagger explained fully to me the nature of the deed he had committed. In a second more he had disappeared behind the side scene; consternation seemed for a moment or two to rivet every one to the seat. The next moment confusion reigned supreme. I saw the features of the man distinctly before he entered the box, having surveyed him contemptuously before he entered, supposing he was an ill-bred fellow who was pressing a selfish matter upon the President in his hours of leisure.

The Appearance of the Assassin.

The assassin of the President is about five feet nine-and-a-half inches in height, black hair, and I suppose, black eyes. He did not turn his face more than quarter front, as artists term it. His face was smooth, as I remember, with the exception of a moustache of moderate size. Of this I am not positive. He was clad in a black coat, approximating to a dress frock coat, dark pantaloons and wore a stiff-rimmed, flat-topped, round-cornered black hat of felt. He was a gentlemanly looking person, having no decided or obtrusive marks. He seemed for a moment or two to survey the house with the deliberation of a habitue of the theatre.

PARTICULARS OF THE DEATH OF MR. LINCOLN.

WASHINGTON, April 16.—Through the kindness of Hon. Maunsell B. Field, Assistant Secretary of the Treasury, who was present during the last hours of President Lincoln, we are furnished with the following interesting details:—

Account of Secretary Field,

Last Friday evening, at about half-past ten o'clock, I was sitting in the reading room at Willard's Hotel, engaged with a newspaper, when a person hurriedly entered the hotel and passed up the hall, announcing in a loud tone of voice that the President had just been shot at Ford's Theatre. I started to my feet and had hardly reached the office when two other persons came in and confirmed the report, which at first I was hardly able to credit. I had parted about fifteen minutes previously with Mr. Mellen, of the Treasury Department, who had retired to his room for the night, and I at once went to him and communicated what had occurred, and we started together for the scene of the tragedy.

We found the streets already crowded with excited masses of people, and when we reached the theatre there was a very large assemblage in front of it, as well as of the opposite house, belonging to Mr. Peterson, into which the President had been conveyed. The people around the theatre related to us substantially the general facts connected with the assassination, which have since been communicated to the public. The impression was prevalent, however, at that time, that the President had been shot in the breast, about the region of the heart, and that the wound might not prove fatal. After a few minutes we crossed the street, and endeavored to gain admission into the house where Mr. Lincoln lay. This I effected with some little difficulty.

The first person whom I met in the hall was Miss Harris, daughter of United States Senator Ira Harris, of New York, who had been at the theatre with the Presidential party. She informed me that the President was dying, but desired me not to communicate the fact to Mrs. Lincoln, who was in the front parlor. Several other persons who were there confirmed the statement as to Mr. Lincoln's condition. I then entered the front parlor, where I found Mrs. Lincoln in a state of indescribable agitation. She repeated over and over again, "Why didn't he kill me? why didn't he kill me?"

I asked her if there was any service I could render her, and she requested me to go for Dr. Stone or some other eminent physician. Both Dr. Stone and Surgeon-General Barnes had been already sent for, but neither had yet arrived. On my way out, I met Major T. T. Eckert, of the War Department, who told me that he was himself going for Dr. Stone. I then went for Dr. Hall one of the most distinguished surgeons in the district. I found him at home and he at once accompanied me. When we again reached the neighborhood of the house, access had become very difficult, guards having been stationed on every side.

After much effort I was enabled to obtain admission for Dr. Hall, but was not at that time permitted to enter myself; accordingly, I returned to Willard's. The whole population of the city was by this time out, and all kinds of conflicting stories were being circulated. At three or four o'clock I again started for Peterson's house. This time I was admitted without difficulty. I proceeded at once to the room in which the President was dying. It was a small chamber, in an extension or back building, on the level with the first or parlor floor. The President was lying on his back, diagonally across a low double bedstead, his head supported by two pillows on the outer side of the bed.

The persons in the room were the Secretaries McCulloch, Stanton, Welles and Harlan; Postmaster-General Dennison, the Attorney-General, the Assistant Secretary of the Interior, Senator Sumner, of Massachusetts; General Halleck, General Augur, General Meigs, General J. F. Farnsworth, of Illinois; General Todd, of Dacotah; the President's Assistant Private Secretary, Major Hay, the medical gentlemen, and perhaps two or three others. Dr. Stone was sitting on the foot of the bed. An army surgeon was sitting opposite the President's

See Last Column.

J. WILKES BOOTH, THE ASSASSIN.

THE SCENE OF THE GREAT TRAGEDY.

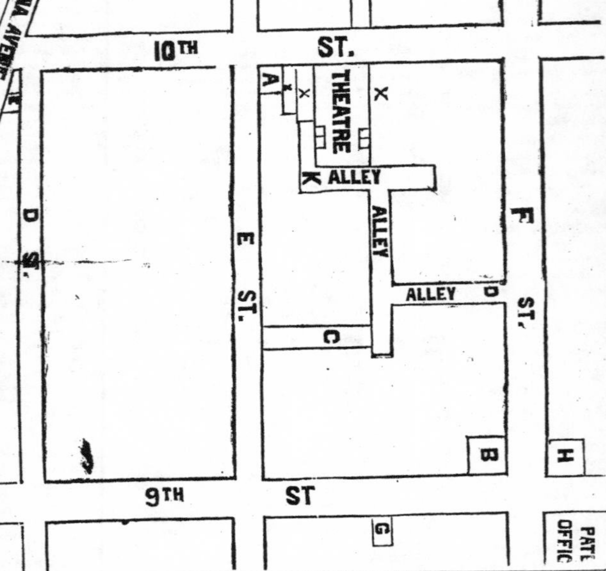

Ford's Theatre has no side entrance from the front.

A—Public School.

B—Herndon House (Hotel).

C—The only vacant lot communicating with the alley.

D—The only alley outlet to F street.

E—Bank (formerly Savings Bank).

I—Restaurants.

G—Newspaper Office.

H—Model House.

Most of the lots go back to the alleys.

I—House taken to after the act.

K—The alley by which the murderer escaped.

FORD'S THEATRE.

The Locality and Description of the Edifice.

Ford's Theatre, the scene of the late terrible disaster, is situated on Tenth street, just above E street, in Washington. It is a large edifice, constructed of brick, and of plain appearance. Its internal arrangements are somewhat novel, differing from those in our own city. There are eight private boxes instead of six, as is the case in the Philadelphia theatres. The four lower boxes, two on each side of the stage, are scarcely more than loopholes, and are very excellent points from which those who wish to see and remain unseen may take inspection. The apertures which appear above the stage are about three feet square. Consequently the boxes immediately above them are elevated but a short distance above the stage, a distance which any one could easily leap, even were his nerves not freshly braced from the commission of a murder.

The four upper boxes are *the* boxes of the theatre, and are very elegant and spacious. They give a tone of elegance to the auditorium, and are sumptuously appointed. It is in them that the most magnificent displays of toilette are made upon nights of opera, and that at once command the whole house, and are central points of inspection from it. Each accommodates quite a party, and the *locale* is so arranged that the greater portion of the occupants, except those in the back of the box, are in full view of the audience.

The box which the President occupied, and which was known as THE PRESIDENT'S BOX, consisted of the two upper boxes on the right hand side of the house as you face the stage, thrown into one. Mr. Lincoln was always accompanied by a party, which, although limited to personal friends and foreign officials, to whom courtesy required the extension of an invitation, was always sufficiently large to render more than one box necessary for comfort.

The proprietor of the theatre had, therefore, at the commencement of the present season, made arrangements by which these two boxes could at any time be thrown into one. They are fitted up with great elegance and taste. The curtains are of fine lace and buff satin, the paper dark and figured, the carpet Turkey, the seats velvet, and the exterior ornamentations are lit up with a chaste chandelier suspended from the outside. A winding staircase leads up to the lobbies which conduct to the box, and unless the arrangements are more stringent than they used to be, no decently dressed person would find much difficulty, probably, in entering one of those boxes after they had once been opened for the ingress of the party using them.

The Rest of the House.

The parquet consists of cane-seat chairs, rising in very gradual elevation, so that even the most distant observers obtain a fair view of the stage, and the entire parquette on an opera night, viewed from the stage or private boxes, resembles an exquisitely variegated parterre. The first tier or balcony is very commodious, and opens into a retiring-saloon elegantly illuminated and appointed. A second tier, corresponding to the family circle, completed the portion of the house dedicated to the accommodation of the audience. The house would hold probably between two and three thousand people.

The Murderer's Way of Exit.

There are two alleys at Ford's Theatre. One leads from the stage, along the east side of the theatre, between the theatre and a refreshment saloon, and so out to Tenth street. The alley is neatly paved, and is boarded and papered on both sides. The entry to it from the stage is through a glass door, and the exit from it on to Tenth street through a wooden one.

The other passage-way leads from the back of the theatre to a small alley which communicates with Ninth and other streets, and conducts to a livery stable locality. It was in this alley that the horse of the murderer was kept waiting.

The Tenth street door would have been too public, and escape, even temporary, a matter of impossibility. But the escape by the alley leading from the back of the stage was comparatively safe.

There are two doors there, one used for the egress and ingress of the actors, and the other devoted to the accommodation of scenery and machinery. It was through the smaller one that the assassin made his exit.

Circumstances have by this time settled the crime upon J. Wilkes Booth, who, from his engagements at this theatre, was perfectly familiar with all its minutiæ. He also kept a horse at the livery stable at the back of the theatre.

head, occasionally feeling his pulse, and applying his fingers to the arteries of the neck and the heart.

Mr. Lincoln seemed to be divested of all clothing except the bed coverings. His eyes were closed, and the lids and surrounding parts so injected with blood as to present the appearance of having been bruised. He was evidently totally unconscious, and was breathing regularly but heavily, and with an occasional sigh escaping with the breath; there was scarcely a dry eye in the room, and the scene was the most solemn and impressive one I ever witnessed. After a while Captain Robert Lincoln, of General Grant's staff, and eldest son of the President, entered the chamber and stood at the head-board, leaning over his father.

For a time his grief completely overpowered him, but he soon recovered himself and behaved in the most manly manner until the closing of the scene. As the morning wore on the condition of the President remained [illegible] about seven o'clock. In the meantime, it came on to rain heavily, and the scene from the windows was in dreary sympathy with that which was going on within. Just before this Mrs. Lincoln had been supported into the chamber and had thrown herself moaning upon her husband's body. She was permitted to remain but a few minutes, when she was carried out in an almost insensible condition.

At about seven o'clock the President's breathing changed in a manner to indicate that death was rapidly approaching. It became low and fitful, with frequent interruptions. Several times I thought that all was over, until the feeble respiration was resumed. At last, at just twenty-two minutes past seven o'clock, without a struggle, without a convulsive movement, without a tremor, he ceased breathing, and was no more. Thus died this great, pure, kind-hearted man, who never willingly injured a human being; the greatest martyr to liberty the world has ever seen.

Shortly after his death, finding that his eyes were not entirely closed, I placed my hands upon them. One of the attendant surgeons first put nickel cents upon them, and then substituted silver half dollars. It was twenty minutes or half an hour before the body commenced to grow cold. The lower jaw began to fall slightly, and the lower teeth were exposed. One of the medical gentlemen bound up the jaw with a pocket handkerchief. Mr. Stanton threw down the window shades, and I left the chamber of death. Immediately after the decease the Rev. Dr. Gurley had offered up a fervent and affecting prayer in the room, interrupted only by the sobs of those present.

When I left the room he was again praying in the front parlor. Poor Mrs. Lincoln's moans were distressing to listen to. After the prayer was over I entered the parlor and found Mrs. Lincoln supported in the arms of her son Robert. She was soon taken to her carriage. As she reached the front door she glanced at the theatre, opposite, and exclaimed several times, "Oh! that dreadful house!" "That dreadful house!" Immediately thereafter guards were stationed at the door of the room in which the President's body lay. In a few minutes I left myself. It is hoped that some historical painter will be found capable of portraying that momentous death scene.

Autopsy of the Late President.

The ball entered the skull midway between the left ear and the centre of the back of the head, and passed nearly to the right eye. The ball and two loose fragments of lead were found in the brain. Singularly enough, both orbital roofs were fractured inwardly, properly from contre coup. The tenacity of life was specially noticed by every surgeon in attendance. The brain was taken out, and will probably be weighed, although it may be difficult to arrive at its true weight, as a considerable portion escaped from the wound.

The autopsy of the President was made in the presence of Surgeon-General Barnes, Dr. Crane and Dr. Stone, of this city, by Drs. Woodward, Notson and Curtis, of the regular army.

The Corpse of Mr. Lincoln.

The corpse of the late President has been laid out in the room known as the guests' room, in the northwest wing of the White House. He is dressed in the suit of black clothes worn by him at his last inauguration.

A placid smile rests upon the features, and the deceased seems to be in a calm sleep, while flowers have been placed upon the pillow and over the breast above the kindest heart that ever throbbed. The corpse of the late President will be laid out in state, in the East Room, on Tuesday, in order to give the public an opportunity to see once more the features of him they loved so well. The preparations are being made to that end under the supervision of Mr. John Alexander, upholsterer. The catafalque upon which the body will rest is to be placed in the south part of the East Room, and is somewhat similar in style to that used on the occasion of the death of President Harrison.

Steps will be placed at the side to enable the public to mount to a position to get a perfect view of the face. The catafalque will be lined with fluted white satin, and on the outside it will be covered with black cloth and black velvet. Rev. Dr. Gurley, of the New York Avenue Presbyterian Church, where the President and family have been accustomed to worship, will doubtless be the officiating clergyman. The remains will be temporarily deposited in the vault of the Congressional Cemetery, and hereafter taken to Mr. Lincoln's home, at Springfield, Illinois. The remains of little Willie Lincoln are deposited in a vault at Oak Hill Cemetery, we believe.

The Funeral of President Lincoln.

Wednesday, it is understood, was determined upon to-day as the day for the funeral of our late President, Abraham Lincoln.

The Funeral Car.

The funeral car, which is being prepared for the occasion, is to be a magnificent affair. It is to be built on a hearse body, the extreme length fourteen feet. The body of the car will be covered with black cloth, from which will hang large festoons of cloth on the side and end, gathered and fastened by large rosettes of white and black satin over bows of white and black velvet. The bed of the car, on which the coffin will rest, will be eight feet from the ground, in order to give a full view of the coffin; and over this will rise th ecanopy, the supports of which will be draped with black cloth and velvet.

The top of the car will be decorated with plumes. The car will be drawn by six or eight horses, probably white, with black trappings, each led by a groom.

Voice of the Clergy.

The American Methodist Episcopal Conference also reported resolutions, which were unanimously adopted, lamenting the premature death of President Lincoln, as being irreparable to the nation. Rev. Doctors Gurley, Gillette, Hall, Regan, Butler and Channing, representing six Christian denominations,

Continued on the Eighth Page.

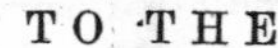

TO THE

MEMORY

OF

ABRAHAM LINCOLN,

PRESIDENT OF THE UNITED STATES OF AMERICA,

Who died a Martyr to his Country,
Falling under the hands of a Traitor Assassin,
On the night of the 14th Day of Apr. 1865,
The Fourth Anniversary of the beginning of the great
WAR OF REBELLION,
Through which he had led the Nation to a Glorious Triumph,
Just completed, when the Dastardly Revenge of
Vanquished Treason was wrought in his monstrous murder.

The Great Republic loved him
As its Father,
And reverenced him as the Preserver of its National Life.
The oppressed People of all Lands looked up to him
As the Anointed of Liberty, and hailed in him the Consecrated
Leader of her Cause.
He struck the chains of Slavery from Four Millions
Of a despised Race, and, with a Noble Faith in Humanity,
Raised them to the admitted dignity of Manhood.

By his Wisdom, his Prudence, his Calm Temper, his Steadfast Patience,
His lofty Courage and his loftier Faith,
He Saved the Republic from Dissolution;
By his Simple Integrity he illustrated the neglected Principles
Of its Constitution, and Restored them to their just Ascendancy;
By all the Results of his Administration of its Government,
He Inaugurated a New Era
In the History of Mankind.
The Wisdom of his Statesmanship was excelled
Only by its Virtuousness.
Exercising a Power which surpassed that of Kings,
He bore himself always as
The Servant of the People,
And never as its Master.

Too sincere in the Simplicity of his Nature to be affected by an elevation
The Proudest among Human Dignities,
He stands in the ranks of the Illustrious of all Time as
The Purest Exemplar of Democracy.
While Goodness is beloved,
And Great Deeds are Remembered,
The World will never cease to Revere
The Name and Memory
OF

ABRAHAM LINCOLN.

RICHMOND WHIG.

WM. IRA SMITH, Proprietor.

OUR TERMS

TO REGULAR SUBSCRIBERS.

Persons desiring to become regular subscribers to the Richmond Whig can now do so, by mail or otherwise.

OUR TERMS

for the present, until we can more definitely ascertain the regulations of the United States governing such matters, will be as follows:

For One Year, $10.
Six Months, 6.
Three Months 3.

to which will be added $6, per year (or its proportion for a shorter period, for the prepayment of postage, which is now required.

Should any change be made that will benefit either the subscribers or Publisher, a satisfactory adjustment will be made.

TO AGENTS.

As some inducement to parties to interest themselves in raising "clubs" for the Whig in any city or town in the United States, we will furnish (20) twenty copies or over at $9 per copy, the postage for the term of subscription of each paper to be added.

☞We will adhere strictly to the CASH SYSTEM!

and shall endeavor to make our prices compare favorably with those of any paper published in the Union.

The price of the Whig is Five Cents per copy.

News Agents and Boys will be charged $3 50 per 100 copies.

Advertisements will be charged at the rate of 75 cents per square, of 8 lines or less.

Larger advertisements upon contract.

News Boys are instructed that they shall receive the tickets marked W. I. S. A. C. Cole, E. H. R. and I. R. A in payment for the Whig from the purchasers on the streets, and they will be received from the boys at the office as five cents, in payment of their purchases.

FIVE CENTS is all the boys are allowed to charge for the papers.

SPECIAL NOTICE.

The undersigned proprietor of the Richmond Whig will be in New York on the 17th, 18th, 19th and 20th of this month. Persons desiring to subscribe to or advertise in the Whig, can leave their names and post office, together with their advertisements, with James Wilde, Jr., & Co., 55 and 57 White street, and they will be received.

Persons wishing to become Agents can have the opportunity by calling upon me there.

WM. IRA SMITH.

New York Herald, Times, Tribune, News and Commercial Advertiser insert the above, and send bill to James Wilde, Jr., & Co., for payment.

WM. IRA SMITH.

SPECIAL NOTICES.

☞For the temporary accommodation of the citizens of Richmond who may wish the *Whig*, there will be tickets sold at the office to the amount of ONE DOLLAR in Federal currency to responsible parties, and their obligation taken, payable in thirty days, so as to enable them to reach the latest news. Call at the office, Whig Building.

☞Citizens will be visited this week, by authorized agents, for the purpose of receiving subscribers to the Whig.

☞Persons at the North, or elsewhere, desiring to subscribe regularly to the Whig, for six or twelve months, will please notify us through the mail; and about the 1st of May we will be able to regulate the terms, and will then forward the bills for the amount of subscription. In the meantime the paper will go forward.

Send on your names, and give us the proper support.

☞All communications sent to this office must be accompanied by the name and address of the writer. We will not undertake to return rejected communications.

OFFICIAL DIRECTORY.

Major Gen. Godfrey Weitzel and Brig. Gen. G. F. Shepley have their headquarters at the mansion formerly occupied by Jeff. Davis, corner of Clay and Twelfth streets—continuation of Governor street.

Brig. Gen. Chas. Devens has his quarters at the late residence of Dr. Pleasants, in Morson's row, Governor street.

Brevet Brig. Gen. E. H. Ripley has his headquarters at the City Hall.

Brevet Brig. Gen. John E. Mulford, Agent for the Exchange of Prisoners, has an office at the "Female Institute," corner of Clay and 10th streets—(first floor.)

Major General A. V. Kautz, First Division, Twenty-fifth Army Corps, headquarters at Richmond House.

Major General Casey's headquarters are at the corner of Sixth and Main streets.

Captain Wm. Vondoehn, Adjutant General.

Major Atherton H. Stevens, Jr., Provost Marshal, has his residence at the French Consul's house and his office at Major Carrington's late place. Persons requiring permits, passes, etc., can get them at the latter place.

A Military Commission, of which Major J. L. Stackpole, Judge Advocate, is President, is in daily session in the Hall of Congress for the examination of cases of persons confined by the Rebel authorities.

Major J. L. Stackpole, Judge Advocate of Department of Virginia, office in Female Institute, on Tenth street.

Lieutenant Colonel W. A. Conover, U. S. V., Acting Medical Director of Department of Virginia, office in Custom House.

Surgeon A. C. Benedict, U. S. V., Surgeon-in-Chief Third Division Twenty-fourth Army Corps and Troops attached, office in Clifton House.

Acting Staff Surgeon Wm. H. Palmer, U. S. A., Post Surgeon, at Stuart Hospital.

Acting Assistant Surgeon Sanders, U. S. A., in charge U. S. Dispensary, corner Broad and Eighth streets.

Surgeon E. P. Morong, U. S. V., Medical Director of Twenty-fifth Army Corps, office on Tenth street, near Capitol.

Lieutenant Colonel John Coughlin, Provost Marshal General of the Department of Virginia, office in the Custom House, on Bank street.

Captain Abel E. Leavenworth, Ninth Vermont Vols., Assistant Provost Marshal, Custom House Building.

Assassination of President Lincoln!

The heaviest blow which has ever fallen upon the people of the South has descended. Abraham Lincoln, the President of the United States, has been assassinated! The decease of the Chief Magistrate of the nation, at any period, is an event which profoundly affects the public mind, but the time, manner, and circumstances of President Lincoln's death render it the most momentous, the most appalling, the most deplorable calamity which has ever befallen the people of the United States.

The thoughtless and the vicious may affect to derive satisfaction from the sudden and tragic close of the President's career, but every reflecting person will deplore the awful event. Just as everything was happily conspiring to a restoration of tranquility, under the benignant and magnanimous policy of Mr. Lincoln, comes this terrible blow. God grant that it may not rekindle excitement or inflame passion again.

That a state of war, almost fratricidal, should give rise to bitter feelings and bloody deeds in the field was to be expected, but that the assassin's knife and bullet should follow the great and best loved of the nation in their daily walks and reach them when surrounded by their friends, is an atrocity which will shock and appals every honorable man and woman in the land.

The secrecy with which the assassin or assassins pursued their victim's indicates that there were but few accomplices in this inhuman crime. The abhorrence with which it is regarded on all sides, will, it is hoped, deter insane and malignant men from the emulation of the infamy which attaches to this infernal deed.

We cannot pursue the subject further. We contemplate too deeply and painfully the terrible aspects of this calamity to comment upon it further.

The facts, as we have officially ascertained them, are subjoined: The President visited Ford's Theatre Friday night, and about thirty minutes past ten o'clock, whilst leaving the Theatre, was wounded in the head by a pistol shot fired by John Wilkes Booth. He died at twenty-two minutes past seven yesterday morning.

Mr. Seward was also wounded in his own house. He is in a fair way to recover.

The people of Petersburg had this afflicting news yesterday before it was made public here. Judge W. T. Joynes, Roger A. Pryor, John Lyon, and other prominent citizens, united in a call for a public meeting to express, if words could do so, their grief for so sad an event, their abhorrence of the deed, and their sympathy for the bereaved. We know that the citizens of Richmond will take similar action.

IF any arguments were now needed to convince the people of the South that the effort to destroy the Union was an act of folly rather than of wisdom, such arguments would be found in the utter overthrow of the false philosophy on which the disunion leaders based their movement. The institution of slavery is only one of the many public interests which were involved in the questions at issue; but as it is one, of paramount importance, we will briefly show how little the disunionists understood its true position, and how unfounded have been their hopes concerning it.

The great and patriotic men of the South, in the days of Washington and Jefferson, saw the radical evils of slavery, and sought to avert them by inaugurating a system of gradual emancipation, and from that day forward the wisest and most thoughtful of our Southern citizens—men holding broad lands and working them with their own slaves—have felt and known that the sentiment of the civilized world was against the institution, and that the only hope of retaining it was by retaining the protection which the Federal system afforded it *in the States where it existed.*

But a favorite dream of the disunionist was the establishment of an independent slaveholding Republic. The apostles of the Secession creed taught that a dissolution of the Union would confirm and permanently establish slavery in the South; that the institution, instead of being weakened and destroyed, would be vindicated in the eyes of the world as a Divine appointment of labor, intended to endure as long as man inhabited the earth.

The immediate object with which the Northern people entered upon the war was not the destruction of slavery. Their design was to preserve the Union, to uphold the just authority of the Nation, to defend the right of a people to protect themselves from ruin and disorganization by the acts of those who had no substantial cause of complaint against their Government.

In the early months of the war, Southern leaders claimed that slavery was an element of military strength to the South; that the slaves would work the farms, raise corn, wheat and bacon, while the white men fought in the armies. For some time this delusion continued. But in proportion as the advance of the United States armies occurred, the inevitable result, foreseen by the wisest of Southern statesmen, followed. The solution of the question of slavery has been purely the result of the laws of war. When the South invited war, she abandoned slavery. To suppose that invading armies would fail to weaken their adversaries by calling to their aid such of the male population of the invaded country as would join them, was a delusion which only madness could have cherished.

The Southern slave owners have discovered by the revelations of the war that, however faithful and personally attached to them their negroes may have been, they desire freedom. They must now admit that slavery has received its death blow. The last and most fatal wound was inflicted by the South herself. When slaves were invited to volunteer for military service, the tacit admission was made that they were *persons* privileged to enter into the military elements of the struggle between the North and the South, and that, therefore, the military measures and policy which freed them were legitimate results of the state of war.

The change which has thus been effected is of momentous import. To change the *status* of the whole laboring class of a country as wide as the Southern States is a work which cannot go on without extensive embarrassment and dislocation. To substitute for the involuntary servitude formerly prevailing the voluntary servitude in which contracts are made, wages are allowed, time is computed and all the relations of the free labor system are recognized, will require time and patience. But the work has been commenced, and the wise among our people will soon be satisfied that their condition will not be the worse for the change. The emancipated negroes will also learn that if they will eat they must work, and that industry and good temper are their best policy.

AMERICAN VESSELS FIRED UPON BY A PORTUGUESE FORT.

The United States frigates Niagara and Sacramento have for some time been engaged in chasing the rebel ram Stonewall. The latter has at length succeeded in escaping from the port of Ferrol. On March 27th her arrival in Lisbon, the capital of Portugal, is announced. The Portuguese authorities ordered her to leave the harbor. The Niagara and Sacramento arrived immediately after, and were ordered by the Portuguese Government not to sail before the expiration of twenty-four hours after the departure of the Stonewall. The commanders of the frigates are charged by the Portuguese with having disregarded this order, and, while attempting to sail before the proper time, were fired upon by the Portuguese fort. The commanders of our steamers are, on the other hand, reported to have had no intention to sail, but merely to have shifted their anchorage. Diplomatic notes, it is further reported, have already been exchanged in regard to this matter. The rebel organ of London, *The Index*, volunteers the further announcement that the great Powers would protect Portugal if the United States should attempt to impose upon her.

It would be useless to offer any comment upon this affair until the facts have been established.—If the statements of the commanders of our steamers are correct, our Government will know how to vindicate the honor of the national flag. At all events, the relations of the foreign Governments to Rebel vessels are now on the point of undergoing a revision, which will make the renewal of such events impossible.—*New York Tribune.*

Washington, April 13.—It is believed that no official information has yet been received in regard to the firing by the Lisbon forts on the United States vessels Niagara and Sacramento. This event may be regarded as a fresh illustration of the complication almost inevitable in case of the continuance of the policy of foreign Powers in regard to our ships of war, against which the proclamation of yesterday so emphatically protests. There is reason to anticipate that the effect of that proclamation will be to restore our vessels hereafter to the enjoyment of customary rights and hospitalities in foreign ports, and in the meantime this occurrence is not likely to pass without such action on the part of our Government as the facts when ascertained shall be found to demand.

SINGLE COMBAT.

The correspondent of the New York *Times* says:

One of the most singular and lamentable events of the war, carrying one back to the days of the chivalric Knights, when each foeman challenged his adversary to hand-to-hand conflict, with the attendant hosts as spectators, occurred on Friday last, on the left of the line, during a skirmish between a portion of the Twenty-fourth corps and a brigade of Rebel cavalry. Gen. Reed, Chief of Staff to Gen. Ord, being up at the front, suddenly recognized an old acquaintance in the person of Gen. St. Clair Deering, commanding a brigade of South Carolina cavalry. Whether they had been in former times friends or foes I cannot say; but they met now as foes, and, in full view of the opposing forces present, they held a tournament of death, fighting with pistols, until, almost simultaneously, Reed fell dead, and Deering mortally wounded.

The French Embassy at Washington is reported to have received intelligence of the dangerous illness of the Emperor Napoleon.

Atlanta, or what remains of it, is occupied by a rebel force under Howell Cobb, and he has his headquarters there. The railroad has been repaired, and is now running regularly between Atlanta and Macon.

Lieutenant General Grant, accompanied by Chief of Staff, arrived at Washington Thursday from City Point. It is reported that General Grant will visit his home in Philadelphia before returning to the army.

MORE VICTORIES.

LYNCHBURG SURRENDERED TO A SCOUTING PARTY.

SELMA AND MONTGOMERY CAPTURED.

[OFFICIAL WAR BULLETIN.]

War Department, April 12,

Major General Dix, New York:

The capture of Selma by our forces is reported by Major General Geo. H. Thomas.

The surrender of Lynchburg is also officially reported.

Edwin M. Stanton, Secretary of War.

Headquarters Department Cumberland, Nashville, Tenn., April 11, 1865.

Major General H. W. Halleck, Chief of Staff:

I send the following, just received from Huntsville, Ala., for the information of the Secretary of War. I am inclined to believe it, although, as yet, I have received no report direct from General Wilson:

Huntsville, Ala., 4 A. M., April 11.

Major General G. H. Thomas:

The following is just received from Col. Hoover, at Somerville:

"Men directly through from Selma report that place captured by Gen. Wilson's forces on the 2d inst. Forrest and Roddy, with their entire commands, were captured. Our men dismounted and charged the intrenchments and carried all before them. They also report Montgomery captured."

(Signed) R. S. Granger.

Geo. H. Thomas, Major General.

City Point, Va., April 12, 1865.

Hon. Edwin M. Stanton, Secretary of War:

Lynchburg surrendered yesterday to a Lieutenant of Griffin's forces, at the head of a scouting party. General Grant has ordered Mackenzie's brigade of cavalry to occupy the town and take care of public property.

C. A. Dana, Assistant Secretary of War.

THE ERA OF PEACE.

HIGHLY IMPORTANT ORDER FROM THE WAR DEPARTMENT.

THE CLOSING UP OF THE WAR.

All Drafting and Recruiting to be Stopped.

THE MILITARY ESTABLISHMENT TO BE REDUCED.

MILITARY RESTRICTIONS UPON TRADE AND COMMERCE REMOVED.

War Department, Washington, April 13, 1865—6 P. M.

To Maj. Gen. Dix, New York:

This department, after mature consideration and consultation with the Lieutenant General upon the results of the recent campaigns, has come to the following determinations, which will be carried into effect by appropriate orders, to be immediately issued:

First.—To stop all drafting and recruiting in the loyal States.

Second.—To curtail purchases for arms, ammunition, Quartermaster and Commissary supplies, and reduce the expenses of the military establishment in its several branches.

Third.—To reduce the number of general and staff officers to the actual necessities of the service.

Fourth.—To remove all military restrictions upon trade and commerce, so far as may be consistent with public safety.

As soon as these measures can be put in operation, it will be made known by public orders.

Edwin M. Stanton, Secretary of War.

THE ORDER SUSPENDING TRADE OPERATIONS IN CERTAIN STATES REVOKED.

Hdqrs Armies of the United States, In the Field, Virginia, April 11, 1865.

Special Order, No. 74.—Second paragraph of Special Orders, No. 48, of the date of March 10, 1865, from these headquarters, suspending trade operations within the State of Virginia, except that portion known as the Eastern shore, and the States of North Carolina and South Carolina and that portion of the State of Georgia immediately bordering on the Atlantic, including the city of Savannah, until further orders is hereby revoked.

By command of Lieut. Gen. Grant.

T. S. Bowers, Assistant Adjutant General.

FROM EUROPE.

THE FIRING ON THE NIAGARA.

OUR CONSUL DEMANDS REDRESS.

Halifax, April 13.—The steamship Europa, from Liverpool on the 1st, via Queenstown on the 2d, arrived here at two o'clock this morning.

The American Minister has demanded satisfaction of the Portuguese Government for firing into the Niagara. He demands that the American flag shall be saluted by the forts which fired into our vessels, and the dismissal of the Governor of the port. The American commanders deny any intention of sailing when fired at.

Other European political news is unimportant.

The surrender of Montevideo to Flores, and its occupation by the Brazilians, is confirmed.

COMMERCIAL INTELLIGENCE.

Liverpool, April 1.—Cotton less firm, but quiet, and prices unchanged. Breadstuffs quiet and steady. Provisions dull. Produce quiet.

London, April 1, P. M.—Consols 89 7-8a90 for money. Illinois Central 61 3-4a62 1-4; Erie 36 1-4. United States Five-Twenties 57 1-5a58 1-4.

Spiritual.—Mr. John H. Addison, a London broker, who has recently been praised by the Spiritualist journals in England as "one of the strongest mediums who has yet appeared," has amused himself, first by performing before select circles of friends all the tricks of the Davenport Brothers, and secondly by writing to the London *Star* to say that he is no "medium" at all, but did it for fun. The *Spiritual Times* and the *Spiritual Magazine*, which took up Mr. Addison as a remarkable being, now drop him in great disgust.

THE MORNING BULLETIN.

BY JAMES B. BINGHAM.

MEMPHIS:

MONDAY - - - APRIL 17

CROWDED OUT.

At the moment of going to press, we are compelled to leave out an editorial on the "Terrible Calamity," which has made us a nation of mourners, in order to make room for full particulars of the transaction, the proceedings of yesterday's meeting, &c.

PRESIDENT LINCOLN ASSASSINATED.

SECRETARY SEWARDS' THROAT CUT

THE MURDERER ARRESTED.

[OFFICIAL.]

WASHINGTON, April 15.

President Lincoln was assassinated last night at Ford's Theatre. He was shot through the head, and died this morning. Secretary Seward was also assassinated—his throat cut by a desperado, who cut down Fred. Seward, his son, a nephew and two nurses before reaching the secretary's bed. At last accounts he was still alive.

WAR DEPARTMENT, WASHINGTON April 15.—To Major General Dix:

Abraham Lincoln died this morning at twenty-two minutes after 7 o'clock.

E. M. STANTON,
Sec'y of War.

DETAILS!

WAR DEPARTMENT, 4:10 A. M.

To Major Gen. Dix:

The President continues insensible and is sinking. Secretary Seward remains without change.

Frederick Seward's skull is fractured in two places besides a severe cut on the head.

The attendant is still alive but hopeless.

Major Seward's wounds are not dangerous.

It is now ascertained, with reasonable certainty, that two assassins were engaged in the horrible crime, J. WILKES BOOTH being the one who shot the President, and the other a companion of his whose name is not known, but whose description is so clear that he can hardly escape.

It appears from a letter found in Booth's trunk that the murder was planned before the 4th of March, but fell through then, because the accomplice backed out until Richmond could be heard from. Booth and his accomplice were at the livery stable at 6 o'clock last evening, and left there with their horses about 10 o'clock, or shortly before that hour.

It would seem that they had been seeking their chance, but for some unknown reason it was not carried into effect until last night. One of them has evidently made his way to Baltimore, the other has not yet been traced.

[Signed.] E. M. STANTON.

LATER!

Secretary Seward is dead.

STILL LATER!

Booth is arrested.

[Signed] RANKIN.

NEW YORK, April 15—9 A.M.—Intense sorrow is depicted on all countenances at the events that occurred in Washington last night.

The grief of all good men is apparent everywhere at the demise of the President.

No flags were hoisted in this city this morning, until the state of the President was known, when they were all placed at half mast.

People appear perfectly horrified and the utmost rage is undoubtedly felt towards all known secessionists and rebel sympathizers.

CAIRO, April 15, 11:30 P. M.—The mournful intelligence of the death of the President of the the U. S. and Secretary Seward has thrown the whole north into a state of excitement and rage unequalled in the annals of history. Dispatches from the Northern cities state that buildings are draped with mourning, places of buildings closed, funeral knel's tolling, flags at half mast, clad in black. At Cairo an immense crowd of people assembled in front of Headquarters at 12 M. to listen to an address from Maj. Gen. N. P. Banks, who is on the Pauline Carroll en route for New Orleans.

His speech was short but affecting, during which the tears were seen trickling down his face, as also down the features of many others. During his remarks he deplored the sad event, eulogized the President and Secretary, and said that the President had been brought by the people from obscurity, had piloted the country through trials never before endured by any nation, and as the bright star of peace was seen appearing in the dim horizon of the future, he sank to rest.

An Illinois copperhead, for rejoicing at the death of the President, was immediately shot. He died instantly, fifteen balls entering his body.

VERY LATEST BY TELEGRAPH.

Up to Saturday Night.

THE ASSASSINATION CONCOCTED IN MARYLAND.

ANDREW JOHNSON INAUGURATED PRESIDENT.

HE MAKES A SPEECH.

NARROW ESCAPE OF SECRETARY STANTON.

SECRET'Y SEWARD NOT DEAD.

BOOTH NOT CAPTURED.

J. WILKES BOOTH THE ASSASSIN.

Great Excitement in the North.

Revelations of the Conspiracy.

Booth's Supposed Accomplice.

[*Official*]—*War Dep't*—To Maj. Gen. Dix.

WASHINGTON, April 15.

Official notice of the death of the late President, Abraham Lincoln, was given by the head of the departments this morning, to Andrew Johnston, Vice President, upon whom the Constitution devolved the office of President. Mr. Johnston, upon receiving the notice, appeared before the Hon. Salmon P. Chase, Chief Justice of the United States, and took the oath of office as President of the United States and assumed the duties and functions at 12 o'clock. The President met the Heads of the Department in Cabinet meeting at the Treasury building, and among other business, the following was transacted:

First, The arrangements for the funeral of the late President were ordered to the several Secretaries, as far as relates to their respective departments. Second, William Hunter, Esq., was appointed acting Secretary of the State during the disability of Mr. Seward and his son Frederick Seward, the Assistant Secretary. Third, The President formally announced that he desired to retain the present Secretaries of Departments of his Cabinet, and they would go on and discharge their respective duties in the same manner as before the deplorable event that had changed the head of the government.

All business in the Departments was suspended during the day.

The surgeons report that the condition of Mr. Seward remains unchanged. He is doing well.

No improvement in Mr. Fred. Seward.

The murderers have not yet been apprehended.

(Signed) E. M. STANTON.

WAR DEPARTMENT, PROV. MAR. GEN'S BUREAU, WASHINGTON, April 15, 9:40 A M.—*Circular*.—It is believed that the assassins of the President and Secretary Seward are attempting to cross from the United States into Canada. You will make a thorough and careful examination of all persons attempting to cross into Canada, and will arrest all suspicious persons. The most vigilant scrutiny on your part, and the force at your disposal, is demanded. A description of the parties supposed to be implicated in the murder will be telegraphed to you to-day, but in the mean time be active in preventing the crossing of any suspicious person.

By order of the Secretary of War.

[Signed] N. L. JEFFERS,
Brevet Brig. Gen., Acting Provost Marshal General.

WASHINGTON, Apr 15, 11 A.M.—Andrew Johnson was sworn into office as President of the United States by Chief Justice Chase to-day at 11 o'clock.

Secretary McCulloch and Attorney General Speed and others were present.

He remarked, "The duties I will perform, trusting in God."

WASHINGTON, April 15.—There is no confirmation of the report that the murderer of the President had been arrested.

Among the circumstances tending to fix a participation in the crime on Booth, were letters found in his trunk, one of which, apparently from a lady, supplicated him to desist from the perilous undertaking in which he was about to embark, as the time was inauspicious, the mine not yet being ready to be sprung.

The extra *Intelligencer* says, from the evidence obtained, it is rendered highly probable that the man who stabbed Mr. Seward and his son is John Surratt, of Prince George county, Maryland.

The horse he rode was hired at Naylor's stable, on 14th street.

Surratt is a young man with light hair and goatee; his father is said to have been Postmaster of Prince Gerge's county.

About 12 o'clock last night, two men crossed Annacosta bridge, one of whom gave his name as Booth, and the other as Smith. The latter is believed to be John Surratt.

Last night a riderless horse was found which has been identified by the proprietor of one of the stables, previously mentioned, as having been hired from his establishment.

Accounts are conflicting as to whether Booth crossed the bridge on horseback or on foot, but as it is believed that he rode across, it is presumed that he had exchanged his horse.

NEW YORK, April 15, 12:30 P. M.—A dispatch from Washington says Frederick Seward is not dead, but in a critical condition.

BURLINGTON, N. J., April 15.—Lt. Gen. Grant left here for Washington at 6 o'clock this morning. Signed

MRS. U. S. GRANT.

WASHINGTON, April 15, 11 A. M. The Star Extra says: At 7:30 o'clock the President breathed his last, closing his eyes as if falling to sleep in perfect serenity. There was no indications of pain, and it was known that he was unconscious until the gradually decreasing respiration had ceased altogether.

The Rev. Dr. Gurley, of the New York Avenue Presbyterian church, immediately on its being ascertained that life was extinct, [illegible] impressive prayer, which was responded to by all present. Dr. Gurley then proceeded to the front parlor where Mrs. Lincoln, Capt. Robt. Lincoln, Mr. John Hay, the private secretary, and others were waiting, where he again offered a prayer for the consolation of the family. Immediately after the President's death a Cabinet meeting was held in the room in which the corpse lay. Secretary Stanton, Wells and Usher, Postmaster General Dennison and Attorney General Speed were present.

From information in the possession of the authorities, it is evident that the scope of the plot was intended to be much more comprehensive.

The Vice President and other prominent members of the administration were particularly inquired for by the suspected parties, and their precise localities accurately obtained, but providentially, in their cases, the scheme miscarried.

A boat was at once sent down the Potomac to notify the gunboats on the river of the awful crime, in order that all possible means should be taken for the arrest of the perpetrators. The most ample precautions have been taken and it is not believed the culprits will long succeed in evading the overtaking arm of justice.

NEW YORK, April 15.—The Post's Washington special says that Mr. Hansell, the messenger of the State Department, who was in attendance upon Mr. Seward, is dead.

Secretary Seward is in a very precarious condition.

It is reported that Booth was captured this morning. The story is that his horse threw him and injured him so severely that he was obliged to seek relief in a house on the Seventh street road.

The Post also publishes a dispatch to Clarence A. Seward, which says Mr. Seward's wounds are [illegible] He is composed. [illegible] but not mortal. [illegible] He has lost much blood, [illegible] are cut.

[illegible] Governor's throat would have been cut if he had not rolled out of bed.

The doctor says Frederick's condition is highly critical, but not entirely hopeless.

WASHINGTON, April 15.—The President's body was removed from the private residence, opposite Ford's theatre, to the Executive mansion, this morning at 9:30, in a hearse, and wrapped in the American flag. It was escorted by a small guard of cavalry. Gen. Augur and other military officers moved in front. A dense crowd accompanied the remains to the White House, where a guard excluded the crowd, allowing none but persons of the household and personal friends of the deceased to enter the premises. Stanton, Yates, and Representative Farnsworth, were among the number. The body is being embalmed with a view to its removal to Illinois.

WASHINGTON, April 15.—The assassin of President Lincoln left behind him his hat and spur. The hat was picked up in the President's box, and has been identified by parties to whom it has been shown, as the one belonging to the suspected [illegible] accurately described by other parties—those who are not allowed to see it before describing it.

The spur was dropped upon the stage, and that also has been identified as the one procured at a stable where the same man hired a horse for the evening.

Two gentlemen who went to the Secretary of War to apprise him of the attack on Mr. Lincoln, met, at the residence of the former, a man muffled in a cloak, who, when accosted by them, hastened away.

It had been Mr. Stanton's intention to accompany President Lincoln to the theater, and occupy the same box, but the press of business prevented his going.

It therefore seems evident that the aim of the plotter was to paralyze the country by at once striking down the head, the heart and the arm of the country.

As soon as the dreadful events were announced in the streets, Superintendent Richards and his assistants were at work to discover the assassin.

In a few moments, the telegraph had aroused the whole police force of the city.

Mayor Wallach and several members of the city government were soon on the spot and every precaution was taken to preserve order and quiet in the city.

Every street in the city was patrolled at the request of Mr. Richards.

General Augur sent his horses to mount the police. Every road leading out of Washington was strongly picketed, and every avenue of escape strongly guarded. Steamboats about to depart down the Potomac were stopped.

The Daily Chronicle says it is suspected that this conspiracy orignated in Maryland.

By telegraph flashed the mournful news to Baltimore, and all the cavalry was immediately put upon active duty. Every road was picketed, and every precaution taken to prevent the escape of the assassin.

A preliminary examination was made by Mr. Richards and his assistants.

Several persons were called to testify, and the evidence, as elicited before an informal tribunal, and not under oath, was conclusive, and to the point.

The murderer of President Lincoln was John Wilkes Booth. His hat was found in the private box and identified by several persons who had seen him within the last two days; and the spur, which he dropped by accident after he jumped to the stage, was identified as one of those which he had obtained from the stable where he hired his horse.

This man Booth has played more than once at Ford's theatre, and is, of course, acquainted with its exit and entrances, and the facility with which he escaped is easily understood.

The person who attacked Secretary Seward left behind him a slouched hat and an old rusty navy revolver. The chambers were broken loose from the barrel, as if done by striking. The loads were drawn from the chamber, one being but a rough piece of lead, and the other balls, smaller than the chambers, wrapped in paper as if to keep them from falling out.

WASHINGTON, April 15.—At an early hour this morning, Hon. E. M. Stanton sent an official communication to Hon. Andrew Johnson, Vice President of the United States, stating that in consequence of the sudden and unexpected death of the Chief Magistrate, his inauguration should take place as soon as possible, and requesting him to state the place and hour at which the ceremony should be performed.

Mr. Jonnson at once replied that it would be agreeable to him to have the proceedings take place at his rooms, in the Kirkwood House, as soon as the arrangements could be perfected.

Chief Justice Chase was informed of the fact and repaired to the appointed place in company with Secretary McCulloch of the Treasury department, Attorney General Speed, Hon. F. P. Blair, Hon. Montgomery Blair, Senators Foote of Vermont, Ramsey of Minnesota, Yates of Illinois, Stuart of Nevada, Hale of New Hampshire, and Representative Farnsworth of Illinois.

At 11 o'clock the oath of office was administered by the Chief Justice of the United States, in the usual solemn and impressive manner.

Mr. Johnson received the kind expressions of the gentlemen in a manner which showed his earnest sense of the great responsibility so suddenly devolved upon him and made a brief speech, in which he said the duties of the office are mine. I will perform them. The consequences are with God. Gentlemen, I will lean upon you. I feel that I shall need your support. I am deeply impressed with the solemnity of the occasion, and the responsibility of the duties of the office I am assuming.

Mr. Johnson appeared to be in remarkably good health, and has a high and realizing sense of the hopes that are centered upon him.

His manner was solemn and dignified, and his whole bearing produced a most gratifying impression upon those who participated in the ceremonies.

It is probable that during the day President Johnson will issue his first proclamation to the American people.

It is expected, though nothing has been definitely determined upon, that the funeral of the late President Lincoln will take place on or about Thursday next.

It is supposed that his remains will be temporarily deposited in the Congressional cemetery.

The results of the conference are as yet unknown.

Reports prevail that Mr. Frederick Seward, who was was kindly assisting the nursing of Secretary Seward, received a stab in the back. His shoulder blade prevented the knife or dagger from penetrating into his body.

The prospects are that he will recover.

A report was circulated, and repeated by most everybody, that Booth was captured 15 miles this side of Baltimore. If it be true, as asserted, that the War Department has received such information, it will doubtless be officially promulgated.

Government offices are closed by order, and will be draped with emblems of mourning.

The roads leading to and from the city are guarded by the military and the utmost circumspection is observed [illegible] attempting to enter or leave [illegible] as to all

NEW YORK, April 1[illegible] the city, business are rapidly c[illegible]. All places of are assuming a som[illegible] closing and the streets

The various [illegible] sombre hue, rooms, the P[illegible] hotels, the New England other pu[illegible] Post Office, Custom House and mourn[illegible] public places, are being draped in

[illegible]

The Corn Exchange met and passed suitable resolutions and ordered the building [illegible] to be draped in mourning and then adjourned.

The Commission Merchants have resolved to close their places of business.

The Gold room is closed.

The regular board of brokers adjourned after passing appropriate resolutions.

All the banks in the city are closed.

An immense meeting of merchants and citizens is being held in Wall street, presided over by Mr. Draper.

Speeches were made by Messrs. Benter, Dickinson, and others.

The crowd there was immense.

Appropriate resolutions were submitted to the meeting and adopted, and a company of thirteen eminent merchants and citizens appointed to go to Washington to attend the funeral of the President.

BUFFALO, April 15.—The Governor of New York has issued a proclamation revoking the proposed thanksgiving for recent victories, on April 20th, and changing it to prayer and humiliation, for our great affliction.

WASHINGTON, April 15.

A most terrible assassination, unparalelled in the history of our country, occurred a few moments before 11 P. M. to-night, at Ford's Theater. President Lincoln and Mrs. Lincoln were seated in a private box on the right hand of the stage, witnessing the last act of "Our American Cousin." At a moment when it was unusually quiet, the sharp, quick report of a pistol was heard, and a man sprang out of the box to the stage, some ten feet down, and, with knife gleaming in hand, ran across the stage, out into the side alley, mounted a [illegible] like lightning up Tenth street. The audience, for a moment, seemed paralyzed, for glancing at the box, the President was observed to have fallen back, as if killed or badly wounded.

In one moment the terrible reality burst upon the audience, as they rushed towards the stage and saw the fainting form of the President brought down the narrow stair way, when it was discovered that he had been shot through the head, and badly, if not mortally, wounded. Accompanied by Mrs. Lincoln, he was taken across the street into a private residence, and there immediately cared for. Pen fails to describe the scene of excitement. The fact of assassination was realized, together with the fact that the assassin had escaped. The streets all around the theatre are blocked up with people, and all along the avenue it has sped like wildfire.

Immediate steps were taken to ferret out the assassin. Police stations were notified, and everybody aided, all to no purpose.

At midnight, at an examination, people who noticed the assassin (a man with black hair, whiskers and moustaches) say that he entered the dress circle and passed around the entrance of the private box, when without waiting a moment, he fired at the back of the President, through the closed door. He then rushed into the same box, through another open door (two boxes being thrown into one), and jumped upon the stage as described. The pistol hole in the door shows the fact of firing through the closed door, while the pistol found dropped on the stage shows that it was a deringer.

The diabolical plot seemed carefully arranged, for few men knew well enough the crooked way behind scenes of theaters to get out. He escaped the observation of those on the stage. Everybody who knows the man say that J. Wilkes Booth, the actor, is the assassin. The evidence is concurrent, at this late and excited hour, to that effect. I visited the stage five minutes after the scene occurred. It was covered with people. The actors say the assassin cried as he jumped down, "I AM REVENGED—*Sic Semper Tyrannis.*"

SECOND DISPATCH.

WASHINGTON, April 14—12 P. M.—It is just ascertained that the assasination has extended further Secretary Seward's throat has been cut by another assassin, who entered his house, passed up to his bedroom and committed the terrible deed. Maj. Seward met the assassin who was coming down stairs and was stabbed in the face.

Thousands are puring into the street, but the people are cooler than one would imagine in view of the terrible scene just enacted.

One man was arrested on the stage at Ford's theatre, and is in a cell at the police headquarters. The crowd is so great around Seward's reidence that nothing can be ascertained. Reports, of course, say that he cannot live.

It is not believed that Stanton, Welles or Dennison is harmed. In fact, it is known the latter is not.

THIRD DISPATCH.

WASHINGTON, April 15—12:15 A. M.—President Lincoln is alive, though reports of his death widely prevail, and cause deep grief.

Secretary Sewards wound is not pronounced fatal. Major Seward is only badly cut—not killed.

General Grant was expected to be at the theatre, and would have been another mark for the assassin, but luckily he left for Philadelphia at P. M.

J. Wilkes Booth cannot be found; his horse is also gone fom his stable.

FOURTH DISPATCH.

WASHINGTON, April 15—1:30 A.M.—The President is still alive, but is sinking rapidly. He is unconscious. There have been no arrests except of witnesses.

FIFTH DISPATCH.

WASHINGTON, April 15—2:30 A. M.—All the Secretaries, save Seward, have arrived at the house where the President is lying, under an armed escort. Surgeon General Barnes says the President cannot live till daylight. Miss Laura Keene testifies that J. Wilks Booth was the assassin.

SIXTH DISPATCH.

WASHINGTON, April 15—3 A. M.—The President is still alive at this hour, but entirely unconscious No hope seems to be felt of his recovery

Another Account.

WASHINGTON, April 15.—President Lincoln and wife with other friends, this evening visited Ford's theatre, for the purpose of witnessing the performance of Our American Cousin.

It was announced in the papers that General Grant would also be present, but that gentleman took the late train of cars for New Jersey.

The theatre was densely crowded and all seemed delighted with the scene before them. During the third act, and while there was a temporary pause for one of the actors to enter, sharp report of a pistol was heard, which merely attracted attention, but suggested nothing serious, until a man rushed to the front of the President's box waving a long dagger in his right hand, and exclaiming "SIC SEMPER TYRANNIS," immediately escaped from the box, which was in the second tier to the stage, beneath, and ran across to the opposite side of the stage, making his escape amid the bewilderment of the audience, from the rear of the theatre, where he mounted a horse and fled.

The screams of Mrs. Lincoln first disclosed the fact to the audience that the President had been shot, when all present rose to their feet rushing to the stage, many exclaiming, "hang him."

The excitement was one of the wildest possible description and of course there was an abrupt intermission of theatrical performance. There was a rush towards the President box, when cries were heard, "stand back, give him air—has any one stimulants?"

On a hasty examination it was found that the President had been shot through the head, above at back of the temporal bone, and that some of the brain was oozing out.

He was removed to a private house opposite the theater, and the Surgeon General of the army and other surgeons sent for to attend to his condition.

On examination of the private box, blood was discovered on the back of the cushion rocking chair on which the President had been sitting also on the partition and on the floor. A common single barrelled pistol was found on the carpet.

A military guard was placed in front of the private residence to which the President has been conveyed.

At midnight the Cabinet, Messrs. Sumner, "Biplay," and Farnsworth, Judge Bates, Gen. Oglesby with Surgeon Gen. Barnes and his immediate assistants, were around his bedside.

The President was in a state of syncope, totally insensible, and breathing slowly; the blood oozed from the wound in the back of his head.

The surgeons exhausted every possible effort of medical skill, but all hopes was gone.

The partings of the family with the dying President, is too sad for description.

Proclamation by the Lieut. Governor of Illinois.

CHICAGO, April 15.

To the People of Illinois:

Abraham Lincoln has fallen by the hand of the assassin. He upon whom the nation has relied through all the dark hours of the rebellion, the exalted patriot, the wise, the vigilant, the incorruptible statesman, has been stricken down while joy filled every heart that the constitution and the laws had been maintained triumphantly. In the hour of victory, Illinois mourns the loss of her noblest son, and the nation weeps that her second Washington is no more. The slaveholders' most accursed rebellion has gone to its doom while perpetrating the most infamous crime in the history of the world.

It becomes us, therefore, to bow before Almighty God, humbly to confess and repent of the sins which have brought this great calamity upon us, to implore Him to look in mercy upon the nation, and to bring it out of all its troubles, that He will give strength and wisdom to him who is now the Executive and to all who are in authority, that He will give entire success to our arms, and that He will speedily restore to the nation the blessings of unity and peace.

Therefore in the absence of his excellency, Governor Oglesby I, William Bross, Lieutenant Governor of Illinois, do issue this, my proclamation, and request the people of the State, either on to-morrow or upon the Sabbath next succeeding thereto, to engage in such special religious services as they shall deem appropriate, and specially that they devoutedly implore Almighty God to have mercy upon us, that He will restrain the wrath of man, and cause the remainder of His wrath to praise him.

Done at the City of Chicago, this 15th day of April, in the year of our Lord one thousand eight hundred and sixty five.

WM. BROSS, Lieut. Gov. of Ill.

The re equipment of SHERMAN's army had been completed on the 8th, and it was then prepared for a new campaign to extinguish JOHNSTON's force.

It is understood that WILLIAM PITT SHERMAN, of New York, will succeed JOHN WILSON as Third Auditor of the Treasury, WILSON succeeding FIELDS as Assistant Secretary.

GENERAL LEE IN RICHMOND.

Interesting and Exciting Details.

GRANT AND LEE'S INTERVIEW.

General Ord Assumes Command at Richond.

Lee Promises to Induce Johnson's Army to Give Up.

Gen. Grant's Rebuff of Davis.

Sherman's Movements.

MOVEMENTS OF GEN. WILSON,

Alabama Overrun by his Cavalry.

ADVANCE UPON MOBILE.

Important from North Carolina

Call by Governor Vance for a Meeting of the Legislature.

The Secession Ordinance to be Repealed.

MOB RULE IN RALEIGH.

The City Sacked and Burned.

Great Excitement in New York.

NEW YORK, April 14.—The World's special says it is reported that as soon as Lee decided he would have to surrender, he set to work to devise some plan by which action on his part would result in peace.—What passed at the interview between him and Grant is not publicly known, but from subsequent occurrences it may be safely inferred that the terms of surrender were but a minor portion of the questions discussed. It is quite probable he proposed to Grant, if generous terms were granted him to surrender, he would go himself to General Johnston and urge him to surrender likewise. In furtherance of this plan Grant was to go to Washington and urge a stoppage of recruiting and the issue of an amnesty proclamation, while General Lee would go to Raleigh and urge Johnston to surrender.

The Times' special says that General Grant will remain in Washington several days.

E. L. Spink, of Illinois, has been appointed Secretary of Dacotah Territory.

Official information has been received that Sherman marched from Goldsboro, for Raleigh last Monday.

The Tribune's special says that General Grant made the announcement, on his way to Washington, that he would demonstrate to the Government that our military expense may now be reduced one million per day without infringing on the efficiency of the army.

General Weitzel has been sent with his colored troops to Petersburg.

General Ord takes command in Richmond.

General Lee is expected to be present at the convocation of the Virginia Legislature.

The Herald's Washington special says that General Grant represents Lee as zealous in his efforts to stop the further effusion of blood, and instead of coming North, is urging all the commanders of Southern armies to surrender without further resistance. Lee considers his work as important as Grant did his in coming to Washington to reduce the expenses of the Government.

It appears that Jeff. Davis sent a messenger to General Grant to inquire whether the Government would allow him to leave the country never more to return.

Grant's reply was that it was his business to fight down the rebellion, and not to answer such questions.

It also appears that Jeff. Davis and other rebel officials, were interested personally in the blockade running business, and made handsome fortunes.

The Herald's advices from Goldsboro', of the 10th, says it was believed there that Johnston's army had left Raleigh, in the in the direction of Charlotte, leaving a small cavalry force to cover its rear.

The Herald's Washington special says that besides the reduction in army expenses, those of the navy are also to be cut down.

The Herald's Corrunna correspondent says the ram Stonewall hoisted the rebel flag before she was out of French hands, and that a deep responsibility rests upon the French and Spanish cabinets on her account, as well as with the United States Government for not sending over a sufficient force to destroy her at once.

The Herald's Richmond dispatch says it is known that Lee's Virginia troops deserted by thousands, and so weakened the the fallen chieftain that he was obliged to surrender.

The Times' correspondent says that Gen. Lee asked Grant to explain what was meant by personal effects, and said many of his cavalry owned their horses.

Grant said the horses must be turned over to the United States, which Lee admitted was entirely correct; but Grant said he would instruct his officers to allow those men who owned horses to retain them, as they would be needed to till their farms.

Lee expressed great gratification for such generous consideration, and said it would have a very good effect.

Lee could not tell how many he had to surrender, so many had been killed and deserted.

Lee informed Grant that his men were short of provisions, whereupon the latter ordered 25,000 rations served to them.

When Lee announced the liberal terms he had secured to his officers, they expressed their satisfaction.

The troops received the announcement with cheers.

Afterward an hour of friendly intercourse took place between the officers of the two armies.

The *Times'* correspondent says in a skirmish General Reed on our side, and General Deering on the rebel side, met in full view of the forces, and held a tournament of death, fighting with pistols until, almost simultaneously, Reed fell dead and Deering mortally wounded.

COLUMBUS, O., April 14.—To-night, in honor of recent victories, there is the greatest demonstration and display ever witnessed in the capital city. The whole city is illuminated and decorated; flags, transparencies, mottoes, torch light processions over a mile long. Speaking in Capitol square afternoon and evening by distinguished orators. The people are out in their might.

NEW YORK, April 14.—The *World* has graphic accounts of the pursuit and surrender of Lee. It appears the 2d and 5th corps came first upon Lee's rear from the east, just west of Amelia Court House. The army of the James at the same time pressed forward from the southeast. The 6th corps came in between and struck Ewell's corps, and with Sheridan's cavalry captured that commander with most of his command.

A moment before Ewell sent a note to Lee, urging him to surrender. Our line now forming three-fourths of a circle northeast and south around the rebel force pressed on until Saturday evening, when Custer's and Merritt's cavalry reached Appomattox Court House, on the Heaps Clover Hill, the county seat of Appomattox county, west of the rebel army and completing the circle.

During Saturday night Lee thought he could cut his way through, and reach Danville, directly south. Having encountered cavalry only at the point he had selected for his enterprise, on Sunday morning he made the attempt, but in the meantime the 5th corps came up, and the rebels received a shock which told them at last all was over. Negotiations for surrender then followed.

WASHINGTON, April 14th.—It is believed here in certain quarters that the movement for the return of Virginia to the Union covers an effort of the State Rights politicians of that State to obtain possession of the State government.

The order of reduction of the army has spread consternation among political Generals, who, it is understood, are to be the first thrown overboard.

Gen. Grant keeps himself secluded since his arrival in the city. He has had several interviews with the President and head of the War department.

Most comprehensive measures for the pacification of the South are known to be in contemplation.

NEW YORK, April 14th.—The Post's Washington special says:

Gen. Weitzel has been superseded in command at Richmond. Rumors were afloat this morning that he had been removed because the Government disapproved his action in granting safe conduct to the rebel Virginia Legislature, but the report is now contradicted.

Gen. Ord having made Richmond the headquarters of the Army of the James, takes command, out ranking Weitzel.

Advices just received from Goldsboro report that Sherman's army moved on the 10th inst.

Gen. Lee arrived in Richmond on Thursday and at once proceeded to his home.

In the selection of the 1st of April for its inauguration, the Army and Navy Gazette says that the work of the U. S. Navy has now been accomplished, and it must be confessed that in the hands of Farragut and Porter, the high reputation which the officers and seamen of that power are held have been greatly enhanced.

NEW YORK, April 14.—The Commercial says it is reported that Johnston has retreated South, and it is supposed the rebels intend to make a stand in Georgia and the Trans-Mississippi, more with a view to securing better terms than from any hope of establishing an independent government.

NEW YORK, April 14.—A vessel, which arrived at Nassau on the 30th, reported that Galveston was garrisoned by 1,200 troops. Twelve Federal vessels were off the bar.

NEW YORK, April 14.—There was no stock board to-day. Gold has ranged from 145½ to 146.

WASHINGTON, April 14.—Some of the foreign journals have reported that it is the intention of our Government to acknowledge the Mexican Empire. A recent assertion of the President, however, does not support that opinion, for he has recognized Jose A. Godery, as Consul to the Mexican Republic, at San Francisco.

CINCINNATI, April 14.—Gen. Carrington publishes a card saying that the charges against him are infamous attempts to obliterate the credit of his services in Indiana, His friends say the matter grew out of a misunderstanding with the Paymasters, and all money for which he is responsible is deposited in bank ready to be turned over.

BALTIMORE, April 14.—The Richmond Whig of yesterday contains little of importance. It announces the arrival of General Lee on the night previous.

The Whig publishes the oath of allegiance, which it says the citizens will be required to swear and subscribe to.

The Provost Marshal's office is crowded with people anxious to take it, and the only question among the citizens seems to be who shall be first to renew their citizenship.

The New York Expres has information from one of its editors from Richmond, stating that Jeff Davis on the 5th penned a proclamation at Danvill saying that Virginia had been reoccupied by the federal forces and that the war would be continued.

Sherman was at Raleigh, and Johnston, it is believed, was retreating it was thought for Augusta, where the rebels were trying to make a nucleus of another army.

The Express says it knows for a certainty that Stoneman with 6,000 cavalry has reached Yadkin River Valley, Yadkin county, North Carolina. He was moving to the rail road between Greensboro and Danville, and as Johnston is north of this his retreat by this time is cut off.

PHILADELPHIA, April 14.—Jay Cooke reports the subscriptions to the 7-30 loan to-day at $3,642,000, including a single subscription of nearly $500,000 from New York, and two large western subscriptions one from Pittsburg of $160,000 and one from Chicago of $100,000. The number of individual subscriptions for the amounts of $50 and $150 was 2,500.

CINCINNATI, April 14—Business is entirely suspended here to day, the city is universally decorated with flags, and great enthusiasm prevails. The procession was a grand affair, comprising the entire police force, Generals Hooker and Willich with their staffs, four regiments of National Guards, discharged veterans, ward organizations, fenian brotherhood, fire department, and a large number of colored citizens. All the bells in the city were rung, salutes were fired at six o'clock in the morning, at noon, and at six in the evening. To-night the city is brilliantly illuminated and there is a general display of fire-works.

NEW YORK, April 15.—A rebel despatch dated Augusta, April 5, indicates that Alabama is overrun by Union cavalry under Wilson and other commanders toward Mobile. General Cook's force is reported to have burned Red Mountain Iron Works, and the village of Elaton, and tapped the telegraph at several places, sending dispatches to rebel officers. Two columns of Yankees are also reported advancing upon Columbus, Mississippi. The same dispatch says that Secretary Seward is dead.

The rebel steamer Gertrude, with a cargo valued at $200,000, was sunk in Spanish river, near Mobile, on the 31st, by collision with the Natchez.

The Herald's Washington special says that President Lincoln yesterday revoked the passes to Hunter, Letcher and other leading rebels to visit Richmond. The President was willing to have a Convention held, but did not want it controlled by those men.

NEW YORK, April 16.—The Danville Register, of the 6th, says that Breckinridge, the rebel Quartermaster and Commissary General, and other officers were expected to reach that city on horseback on the 16th.

The Herald's correspondent says that an expedition lately went up the Chowan river North Carolina, and captured Winston and Murfreesboro'.

The ram which the rebels had been building at Halifax has been destroyed. The ram Albemarle has been raised by our men and found to be not seriously injured.

The Herald's Goldsboro' correspondent has a report from Raleigh, saying that Governor Vance will call the North Carolina Legislature together, to repeal the secession ordinance.

The World's Goldsboro' dispatches to the 10th says the Raleigh Confederate of the 9th says the city was sacked and fired by a mob of the lower classes on the 16th. The Virginia Reserves were left to protect the people, but were unable to do so. The mob took possession of some of the large warehouses and stores, and robbed them.

LOUISVILLE, April 14.—The Fire Department, with the City Council, made an imposing appearance to day, in honor of the restoration of the stars and stripes over Fort Sumter. Business generally was suspended. One hundred guns were fired. The public buildings, newspaper offices, express, telegraph offices, and many private residences were splendidly illuminated in the evening. We noticed that Generals Palmer and Oriskine, with their staffs and a portion of the 30th Ohio, were in the civic procession.

NEW YORK, April 15.—The following is the substance of Jeff. Davis' late proclamation, dated Danville, April 5th:

The General-in-chief found it necessary to make such movements of his troops as to uncover the capital. It would be unwise to conceal the moral and material injury to our cause resulting from the occupation of our Capital by the enemy. It is equally unwise and unworthy of us to allow our efforts to become relaxed under reverses, however calamitous they may be. For many months, the largest and finest army of the Confederacy, under command of a leader whose presence inspired equal confidence in the troops and the people, has been greatly trammeled by the necessity of keeping constant watch over the enemy's approach to our Capital, and has been forced to forego more than one opportunity for promising enterprises.

ABRAHAM LINCOLN, PRESIDENT OF THE UNITED STATES, AND W. H. SEWARD SECRETARY OF STATE, ASSASINATED IN COLD BLOOD

The Feeling in Memphis.

Its Effects upon the Country.

Editor Bulletin:

Language fails to describe the deep seated and patriotic indignation which pervaded the loyal heart throughout the city, after the news yesterday, of the above startling and extraordinary intelligence. That such fiendish and diabolical malignity should have developed itself a few weeks ago, no one who is familiar with the spirit of secession would have been at all surprised. If the councils which inspired the devilish deeds which set in fearful peril the lives of a hundred thousand innocents a few months ago in the city of New York, had succeeded in effecting at an *earlier* date, this damning deed of infamy and disgrace, even then the great people who are fighting for the perpetuity of free government, would have felt no wonder; but *now*, when the great rebellion after four years of bitter warfare has been fairly whipped; now when their leading General has surrendered all show of resistance to terms, the magnanimity of which finds no precedent; now when their wily chief has abandoned his followers to their fate, and is seeking to hide and skulk away from the government which fed, clothed, educated and supported him—all these facts, I say, lend an enormity to the crime compared with which the world furnishes no counterpart. Forever be execrated, either he who performed the deed, or he that lent it sympathy. May all earth's people curse him. May he be buried with his face downward, and may no ministering spirit visit his black abode forever. But turning from the *Immortal Dead*, what is to be the effect upon the living. I believe it will be grand and salutary. God has ever raised up great men to fill great emergencies. I have never been one of those to endorse each individual political act of him who is now the President of this great nation—Andrew Johnson. I have never been one to lavish indiscriminate praises upon any man, but I rejoice now in the fact that the nerve which directs the strong arm of this nation is a steady nerve; I am glad that there is an iron Jockson at the head of the government which will not temporize or play with treason; and I rejoice, because *we of the South* are directly interested in maintaining the results which have been won through the patient and persevering patriotism—through the wise councils of him and them who have been stricken down by hellish hands just as they were ready to reach *the true greatness* which immortality itself will be swift to accord them.

If there had been wanting *one* act to cement the nation's patriotic purpose, the act of the assassin when he fell upon that nation's servant in almost death's defenseless chamber, would give it the crowning glory. If it had been necessary to re-inspire with love of country the millions who boast of its institutions, the damning spirit which directed the fatal shot into the person of that country's chiefest idol, would thrill with fervent valor all his lordly subjects. Yes, the glory of the United States is not dimmed. Her star shines brighter to-day than at any time before. The lustre of her escutcheon is more and more brilliant in this her hour of grief. The heart of the million beats now with only one desire,—to wipe out from the land the foul and filthy spirit of dishonor. ERNEST.

NEW ADVERTISEMENTS

GENERAL ORDERS NO. 44.

Headquarters District of West Tenn.,
Memphis, Tenn., April 17, 1865.

The nation mourns the untimely and violent deaths of the President of the United States, Abraham Lincoln, and the late Secretary of State, William H. Seward.

All officers of this command will wear the usual badge of mourning upon the left arm for thirty days from the date of this order.

As a mark of respect to the illustrious dead, the public buildings of the city, and all places of military business, will be closed this day from sunrise to sunset.

The funeral gun will be fired at every half hour, beginning at sunrise and ending at sunset of this day.

By order of Major General C. C. Washburn.

W. H. MORGAN,
apl7-1w Major & Assistant Adjutant General.

PROCLAMATION OF THE MAYOR.

Mayor's Office,
Memphis, 17th April, 1865.

In obedience to the desire as indicated by the universal demonstrations of mourning and sorrow by our citizens on the announcement of the assassination of the President and Secretary of State of the Republic, as well as in compliance with the wishes as expressed at the meeting at Odd Fellows' Hall yesterday evening, all business houses will be closed all of this day, and business of all kinds will be suspended.

The fire bells and church bells will be tolled at intervals of thirty minutes from 8 o'clock A. M. to 6 P. M.

No public hacks or cabs will be allowed on the streets before 6 o'clock P. M.

Maj. J. P. Foster, Chief of Police, will see that this latter clause is enforced; and J. E. Randle, Chief of Fire Department, will direct the tolling of the bells.

W. O. LOFLAND,
apl7-1t Acting Mayor.

SPECIAL ORDERS, NO. 94.

Headquarters, Post and Defenses of Memphis,
Memphis, Tenn., April 16, 1865.

PARAGRAPH III.

* * * * * *

In consequence of the death of His Excellency, President Lincoln, paragraph V. of Special Orders No. 92 from these headquarters, dated April 14, 1865, is hereby revoked.

The review of the Enrolled Militia ordered therein, will be postponed until a more suitable occasion.

By order of Brigadier General A. L. Chetlain.

JOHN G. WOODRUFF,
apl7-1t Captain and A. A. A. G.

GENERAL ORDERS, NO. 23.

Headquarters, Enrolled Militia,
District West Tennessee,
Memphis, Tenn., April 16, 1865.

Out of respect to the memory of our late Chief Magistrate, Abraham Lincoln, General Orders No. 27, from these headquarters are hereby revoked, and all militia exercises of the day dispensed with.

By order of Brig. Gen. M. T. Williamson.

D. V. B. HALLAM,
apl7-1t Lieutenant and A. A. A. G.

PLEASURE POSTPONED.

The Ball of the German Cassino that was to have taken place on to-morrow (TUESDAY) evening is postponed until further notice, in consequence of the death of President Lincoln.

apl7-2t J. ALEXANDER, President.

MASONIC NOTICE.—THE regular Assembly of Eureka Council No. 6, of Royal and Select Masters, will be held in their Council Chamber, Odd Fellows' Building, this MONDAY evening, 17th inst., at 8 o'clock. A prompt attendance of all the members is desired, as business of importance will come before the Council—degrees conferred, etc. Royal and Select Masters are fraternally invited. By order of

D. C. TRADER, T. I. G. M.

N. J. WIGGIN, Recorder. apl7-1t

THE MEMBERS OF MEMPHIS GROVE No. 2, U. A. O. D., are hereby notified to attend a Degree meeting, TUESDAY evening, April 18, 1865, at 7½ o'clock, for work in the Crimson Degree. Members of Tennessee Grove No. 1, and transient brethren in good standing, are fraternally invited. By order of the N. A.

ap.7-2t L. MARKS Secretary.

COW LOST.—A GRISLEY COW with a small piece of rope about her horns. A liberal reward will be paid for her delivery at Washington Hospital, to C. B. HARL.

apl7-1t*

LOCAL NEWS

NOTICE TO DEALERS AND CARRIERS.—Orders for morning papers MUST come in before 5 o'clock the previous evening, or they cannot be received. Newspaper dealers and carriers please notice.

THE DAILY BULLETIN

Is regularly served, by trusty carriers, in every neighborhood in and around Memphis, for TWENTY FIVE CENTS PER WEEK. We have now made arrangements to supply all orders for the paper, and with punctuality. Orders for the paper may be left with the carriers or at the office.

THE NEWS.

The news of the assassination of President Lincoln and Secretary Seward was received by all classes of our citizens with the most profound feeling of sorrow, mingled with dismay; no excitement was manifested, but in the faces of all it could be seen that the great national calamity was felt deeply. It was the silent grief that will be terrible in the reaction, and is more poignant than grief violently demonstrated.

The city was immediately decked with emblems of mourning, tastefully arranged, and many devices and inscriptions singularly appropriate and beautiful are to be seen over the stores on our principal thoroughfares, among which the following on the store of Mr. W. R. MOORE, which was one of the first draped, was the most striking:

THE GREAT NATIONAL HEART BLEEDS WITH GRIEF, AND ALL CIVILIZATION MOURNS THE LAMENTED DEAD.

Several secessionists who could not repress their satisfaction over the news, but on the contrary, gave loud and joyful utterance to it, were arrested yesterday morning, and are now in military confinement. Among these were the bar keeper of the Worsham House, and a man named Reeves said to reside in South Memphis. We learn that they are to be tried immediately by Court Martial.

ORDER OF THE DAY.—By order of Gen. Washburn, all public and private business is to be suspended to-day from sunrise to sunset, in consequences of the great national calamity. The funeral gun will be fired every half hour.

NO MILITIA EXERCISES.—All militia exercises will be dispensed with to-day, in consequence of the death of President Lincoln.

IN LIMBO.—The parties arrested yester day and confined in Irving Prison, on charges of giving utterance to gratification over the horrible news from Washington, viz: the assassination of President Lincoln and Mr Seward, were as follows: Charles Burton, Burdeshau, R. B. Rivers, C. B. Randal, Mr. and Mrs. D. T. Desmond, F. S. Latham, J. B. McNees, James O. Day, Jas. Braniff, and William S. Scales. All firmly protest against the charges, and plead unswerving loyalty.

William F. Landreth and William Dunnin, guerrillas, captured near the lines, were also imprisoned.

THEATRE.—There will be no performance at the Memphis Theatre to-night.

HARRY WEATHERBEE'S saloon 91 Jefferson street, will be closed to-day.

The new saloan of Weatherbee & Cornell, corner of Second and Jefferson streets, will also be closed.

THE NATIONAL CALAMITY.

MEETING OF OLD CITIZENS.

ASSASSINATION DENOUNCED.

The news of the assassination of President Lincoln and Secretary Seward was received yesterday morning, and caused the most profound sensation. The tremendous consequences that may ensue—the disasters that may result, were fully realized, and none were more prompt to denounce the atrocious deed than many who have been active sympathizers with the Southern Confederacy. The following was circulated in a handbill at the different churches ann on the streets:

"PUBLIC MEETING OF OLD CITIZENS."

"MEMPHIS, Sunday, April 16, 1865. The undersigned, old resident citizens of Memphis being desirous of giving public expression to their sentiments of heartfelt sorrow for the great public calamity which has befallen the country, in the assassination of Abraham Lincoln, the late President of the United States, and of Wm. H. Seward, the late Secretary of State, do respectfully request all old citizens who sympathize with us, to meet us at Odd Fellows' Hall, at 4 o'clock, this afternoon, to give proper publicity to our sentiments of grief and sorrow.

Miles Owen, D M Leatherman, Jno A Nooe, James Elder, Wm P Mitchel, W T Irwin, S Venable, W F Hardin, I Hill, S H Gates, G T Irwin, Geo Winchester, Mr T J Sale, C L Wilcox, F R Farnsworth, N B Hill, Jas Mynis, Wm Park, S H Dunscomb, Nixon, Wood & Co, E Ensley, jr, E M Apperson, Galbraith & Stewart, Jno Martin J J Rawlings, P Miller, George B Grant, J B Bingham, D Cockrell, Sam'l P Walker, H G Smith, P P Frame, A K Taylor, W B Miller, B B Nabers, J W Leftwich, S B Williamson, John L Taylor, A K Taylor, T P Aylett, H Owen, J S Drake, J W Smith, W H Wood, Jno Kirk, Eugene Magiveny, E McDavitt, J T Stratton, R C Malone, Frank Mahan, J P Bowles, Fletcher Lane, Dr R C Creighton, J M McCombs, William H Fitch, jr, S Fred Hailman, R F Brown, J N Barnett, R C Brinckley T S Ayres, A Herron, Jno Farrington, E W M King, J P C Hammond, W K Poston, John F Sale, Wm T Taylor, C S Fenner, Jno Pitman, R M Drake, W B Greenlaw, Dr J R Frazier, J C Jones, Machael Magivney, Dr S Gilbert, B Bayliss, H F Farnsworth, J S Toof, Wm Bowles, R Topp, Garland Ware, C C Cleaves, Jno C Grierson.

At the appointed hour the meeting in Odd Fellows Hall, and was convened by calling James Elder, Esq, to the Chair and appointing Samuel P. Walker, Secretary.

A committee appointed to report resolutions expressive of the sense of the meeting, consisted of Messrs. H. G. Smith, D. Leatherman, E. McDavis, R. F. Brown M. [illegible] Ferguson, I. M. Hill, B. Hill, A. W. L[illegible], F. H. Latham, D. Cockrell, P. Bur[illegible] —— Menken, F. W. Smith, Miles Owen, [illegible] and B. T. Turian. Dr. Hammond [illegible] [committee] were out the room

While the Com[illegible] Among the prom became densely packe[d] [illegible] we observed inent old citizens pres[ent] [illegible] Lofland, Dr. Messrs. D. Cockrell, W. C. [illegible] Dickinson, Creighton, Dr. Irwin, Dr. [illegible] Dr. G. D. Dr. Pittman, J. W. McKinny, [illegible] Johnson, Emmet Mix, A. Seesel, Dr. Bayliss, John F. Sale and August Hitzfield.

The entry of Maj. Gen. Washburne, Maj. Gen. Banks and Brig. Gen. Chetlain, who took seats upon the stage, drew forth loud applause.

The committee having returned with the preamble and resolutions that had been prepared, Mr. H. G. Smith addressing the Chairman and the meeting, said that the committee had committed to him the charge of presenting the resolutions that he held in his hand, and asking the citizens of Memphis to adopt them, as the expression of their sentiments and feelings.

The following resolutions were then read by Mr. Smith:

The dreadful intelligence has just been announced to the people of Memphis of the assassination of the President and of the Secretary of State, of the United States. Spontaneously, universally, they assemble on this holy day set apart to the service of Almighty God, to testify their abhorence of the atrocious crime, and to declare their grief at the death of Mr. Lincoln and Mr. Seward.

And this they do, as men, native and bred in the States of the South, apart from and forgetting their sympathies, past and present, in regard to the rebellion, and speaking the common sentiments which inspire them, and which ought to inspire all men who possess the common instincts of humanity.

And further, because of our conviction, that more than to any other, to the wisdom, prudence and humanity of Mr. Lincoln and Mr. Seward at the head of the power of the United States, the people of the South had begun to rely, for the ability and disposition to restore peace to our bleeding land, unity to the government, harmony to the people North and South, the equality of the States, and an end to the carnage and desolation that afflict our beloved land of the South.

And further, because of our further conviction, that in the present most trying exigency of the country, while the death of those eminent men is a great loss to the whole country, it is especially a calamity to the South—

Therefore, Resolved, That the citizens of Memphis, without distinction of party, deplore the death of Mr. Lincoln and Mr. Seward—

And denounce in terms of utmost abhorrence, their assassination—

And that the people of the South will receive the intelligence of their assassination with indignation and horror—

Open and fair warfare is manly and honorable, and often grand and glorious—assassination is always cowardly and brutal.

Mr. Smith moved the adoption of the resolutions. This was seconded by W. P. Hammond, who amended it with the proposition that the vote should be taken standing and in silence. The resolutions were then put to vote, and the whole audience rose to their feet, and thus in silence endorsed the resolutions.

MASS MEETING IN COURT SQUARE

Memphis Brands as Atrocious the Assassination of President Lincoln.

An immense and spontaneous meeting was held in Court square yesterday afternoon to express the profound grief of our citizens, without distinction of party, at the death of President Lincoln, and the detestation felt by our whole people at the atrociousness of an act that places the South on a vastly worse condition than she would have been in, if this had not occurred.

Never have we seen a meeting where there was deeper feeling and where there was more entire accord of sentiment.

There was no formal organization, but Major General Banks was introduced to the audience by Maj. Gen. Washburn and was loudly applauded.

General Banks seemed weary and worn, and his voice had not its usual ringing, tone but his brief remarks were most appropriate and touching. He said: "Fellow citizens, I could not well refuse the invitation of the General, whom I have known in the field, who has introduced me to you and whom I have also known in the council halls of the nation, and the request of the Committee of your own citizens that I should mingle an expression of my sympathy with yours upon the sad occurrence and great calamity which to-day overshadows with sadness the hearts of the American people.

You will see that I am not in voice to make an address, since I am way worn and weary with travel. I have scarcely strength of voice for any occasion, much less such a one as calls you together. It was such a man, so dull, so dead of care that drew old Priam's curtains in dead of night and would have told him that his Troy was burned, but here before steam could bear me the news was told. The President is dead.

Gen. Banks then expressed his hopes that Secretary Seward would survive. Last evening at 6 o'clock he had received a dispatch from Washington, which informed him that the Secretary of State was still living.

Of the President and Secretary he said they did not end nature's great career by natures act. They fell by an act of assassination, more atrocious than any in history, which had, in a moment, bereft the nation of its honest, its tried and its trusted leader. I am glad to know that the people of Memphis, that a portion of the people of the State of the patriot Jackson, have no sympathy with or would suggest such crimes as that which has been perpetrated. It is enough for us to know that assassination never yet attained its purpose. It has been tried often in different countries but never yet did assassination attain the end it had in view, by crime. It is condemned by man—and condemned and punished by God, [loud applause.] The President and Secretary of State had no enemies, but there were many who misunderstood them.—There were many who misinterpreted their views and believed that they were hostile to themselves—but the time will come—it had come when the whole country will acknowledge that these men were inspired by feelings of patriotism, and love of the whole country and love of the whole people. They labored for, and desired nothing, so much as to see the whole American people restored to the labor and happiness, they enjoyed before the outbreak of this treasonable rebellion.

They have not died because of their individual acts or individual opinions. It was because they represented the government of the American people, which was established and sanctioned by our patriotic fathers, and redeemed by the blood of our brothers in this day. It was because they represented this, that they were stricken down in the full strength of manhood. I rejoice that the united voice of the people of Memphis will give to the country assurance of their sympathy with the whole country, and with the expression that will rise up from every village and every place in the country, giving their opinion of the act. We will not, therefore, mingle with the sentiment of this day, any other expression than that of grief. We will make no determination except it be that the act of a private assassin shall not be consummated by the destruction of the government. We will here declare that with more tenacity, more energy than ever before, we will maintain the institutions and government of our fathers. We will now be tried as a nation has never been tried before. True nations have been tried before—nations have had to vindicate fancied or real rights by victories. Heroes have been created, governments have been overthrown, but it is only through great calamities like murdering our trusted leaders and throwing us into anarchy that is the greatest trial of a nation. Every nation of Europe and of Asia has suffered such calamities, and have been overthrown or destroyed by them. It is for the American people to know that they can rise above the greatest calamities that have befallen any people, and sustain under them American institutions and liberties. Fellow-citizens of the South, you have sustained a greater loss than the people of the North. You have lost a protector who was unwilling that a hair of the head of any individual in any part of the country should be injured more than was necessary. No man has been so filled with love in life, and at the moment when he was stricken down by death, before God, I believe there was not a feeling in his heart that was not for your welfare and prosperity. (Applause) An unknown man who had forced his way into the confidence of the people, until in rebel papers and rebel council they expressed the opinion that he was superior to their own chieftains.

The great object of Mr. Lincoln's life and Mr. Seward's life was carried out. The object of their labors and their lives was accomplished. The rebellion was overthrown, and the Union of the States, was as far as arms are concerned, was effected and irrevocable. You have read in the declarations of Mr. Lincoln before his death, his views upon reconstruction, and having been the most part of the time since the rebellion broke out in the South, and much of it in the very trough of the rebellion, I believe the only path to the restoration of the Union lies in the course and in the channels indicated by him a few days before his death. Let us imitate his love for all the people of the continent, and like him even in the hour of death, let us sustain those men upon whom by constitutional provision the legislature of the country depend—not holding man responsible for calamities that devolve upon our nation, but accepting the great struggle has heaped upon us, and only asking that all shall be true to constitutional rights and liberty.

GEN. WASHBURN said: Fellow citizens: I know myself too well to be willing to trust myself to address you now, nor would I mar the effect of the eloquent remarks of my friend, Gen. Banks. It is no time for me at least to talk. I have no power to address you—so overpowered are my feelings by the events that have been announced that I must ask you to excuse me. Gen. Washburn made a brief reference to his hopes that as the war was closed and law and order being fast restored, he could resign without the least injury to the public interest, and his profound grief at the event which had cast a cloud over our national horizon. He had confidence that the people of the South would not tolerate assassination. The people of Memphis, at least, said he, will not sanction a dishonorable warfare. Thanking the people for promptly expressing their profound grief at the death of President Lincoln and their horror of the atrocious crime that caused his death, Gen. Washburn retired.

GEN. CHETLAIN was called, and said: *Fellow citizens*: It is impossible for me to address you upon this occasion. I have lost, with you, in the death of President Lincoln, a wise ruler and an able statesman, and I have lost more—I have lost a personal and a warm friend, and you will excuse my speaking on this occasion. I know how the people of Memphis feel, and know that you will excuse me.

There were cries for Mr. Cameron, who was introduced to the assemblage, and made a very fine speech, eulogistic of Mr. Lincoln, and deploring the event that had cast a gloom over the whole country.

The meeting, at the conclusion of Mr. Cameron's remarks, dispersed to their several homes.

The suddenness with which the merchants on Main street, and many other citizens draped their houses in mourning, showed how general and profound was the regrets of our people. Court square was very finely draped by our municipal authorities.

DRUIDS.—There is to be a degree meeting of Memphis Grove No. 2, U. A. O. D., on Tuesday night.

City Items.

NOTICE.—Purchasers of Real Estate at the City Tax Sales, will please come forward and settle. F. L. WARNER, City Tax Collector. ap15-3t

E. F. RISK, 322½ Main street, requests all persons who wish a good Stove, to call and examine his stock of the best make. He has also a large assortment of Tinware of his own manufacture, to which he calls attention of planters, merchants and the public generally. mh19-1m

NEW ADVERTISEMENTS

FOR RENT—A LARGE Store House on Main street. Also—three desirable Residences, one of which is in the suburbs. Apply to BOOTH & BURTON, 22 Madison street. ap16-3t*

MILLINERY—MRS. SHUTTLEWORTH having returned from England, wishes to inform her friends and the ladies of Memphis, that having opened in the above business, is prepared to furnish anything in the millinery line. Also, Straw Goods cleaned and pressed; Ostrich Feathers renovated, on Union street, one door from Desoto street. ap16-1w

NOTICE TO DEALERS IN COIN OR BULLION.

Treasury Department, Second Agency, Memphis, Tenn., April 15, 1865.

The military restrictions concerning the purchase and sale of coin or bullion in this city, having been removed by General Orders No. 43, C. S., Headquarters District of West Tennessee, the attention of dealers is directed to the following regulation prescribed by the Hon. Secretary of the Treasury, series 29th July, 1864.

"XXXII. All transportation of coin or bullion to any State or section heretofore declared to be in insurrection, it absolutely prohibited, except for military purposes, and under military orders, or under the especial license of the President."

Any violation of the foregoing regulation, will involve the seizure of any coin or bullion so transported. WM. W. ORME, Supervising Special Agent, &c., Second Agency. B. BOWLING, Chief Clerk. ap16-1w

NOTICE—THE PUBLIC are hereby cautioned against buying or negotiating three promissory notes, dated Memphis, April 11th, 1865, at 30, 60, and 90 days respectively, for three thousand dollars ($3000) each, drawn by me in favor of Kirtland & Co., the same having been obtained by false pretenses. GEO. R. RODGERS. Memphis, April 14, 1865. ap15-2t

R. HERRON. L. LEHMAN.
HERRON & LEHMAN,
ATTORNEYS AT LAW,
ROOM NO. 5, SECOND FLOOR, AYERS' BUILDING,
No. 274 Second street, Opposite Court Square, MEMPHIS, TENN. ap15-3mo*

THE CO-PARTNERSHIP heretofore existing under the name of VAN BEEK, CLARK & CO., is this day dissolved by the withdrawal of S. P. C. Clark.

The business will be continued under the name and style of VAN BEEK, WEAR & CO. All business connected with the late firm, must be settled with Van Beek, Wear & Co.

GEO. W. VAN BEEK.
S. P. C. CLARK.
W. G. WEAR.
Memphis, April 4, 1865. C. A. NORTON.
ap15-1w

H. H. METTE,
RECTIFYER OF WHISKY,
—AND—
Manufacturer of Cider Vinegar,
NO. 8 EXCHANGE BUILDING,
(NEW NUMBER 164 FRONT ST.,)
MEMPHIS, TENN.

TO THE MERCHANTS OF MEMPHIS,
I call particular attention to my favorite brands of
WHISKY,
And to my superior
CIDER VINEGAR,
Which I can sell to the trade at eastern prices.
All orders will be promptly attended to. ap15-2

DURBIN WARD, Late Col. 17th O. V. I. JNO. C. FEBLES, Late Major 7th Ind. V. C.
CHARLES H. ROBINSON.
WARD, FEBLES & CO.,
ATTORNEYS AT LAW,
AND
CLAIM AGENTS,
No. 44 NORTH COURT Street, Memphis, Tenn.

In addition to the regular business, in all the Federal, State and county Courts, this firm is enabled, by the residence of one of its members in Washington City, to prosecute and speedily collect all claims against the United States government for Quartermaster and Subsistence stores, taken by, or furnished to the U. S. Army and Navy, claims of officers for horses and equipments, lost in the service of the United States, bounty, back pay, pensions, &c. The firm will also attend promptly to the adjustment and settlement of all causes brought before the Court of Claims, and the Supreme Court of the United States, which may be entrusted to them. ap14-3mo.

ATTENTION, SOLDIERS AND CITIZENS.—U. S. Government Leg Depot, where Government furnishes the army and navy leg to soldiers gratis, or its value applied on the anatomical leg, which has lateral motion at the ankle like the natural one. Also, citizens furnished on private account.

At 32 Union street, Memphis, Tennessee;
73 Pine street, St. Louis, Missouri;
Cincinnati, Ohio;
Chicago, Illinois;
Rochester, New York;
658 Broadway, New York;

For prices and particulars, call at office, or address DOUGLAS BLY, M. D., U. S. Government Commissioner, or LOUIS LOCKWOOD, Agent. ap14-1w*

BUCHANAN & CO.,
WHOLESALE DEALERS IN
PURE BOURBON,
—AND—
RECTIFIED WHISKIES,
[illegible] Landing, Cincinnati, Ohio.
ap14 3mo

RIVER NEWS

MEMPHIS, April 16.

BOATS LEAVING THIS DAY.—For St. Louis: Belle Memphis, captain Muselman; Mollie Able, captain Greenleaf. For Evansville: Superior, captain Dexter. For New Orleans: Lady Gay, captain ——; Elnora Correl, captain Correl.

The weather continues pleasant and genial. Business at the landing is fair, but will be suspended to-day. The river is very slowly falling, with abundance of water in every direction for largest size boats.

ARRIVALS.—Peytona from New Orleans; Sultana, J. T. McCombs, Pauline Carroll, Platte Valley, and Belle Memphis from St. Louis; Golden Eagle from Cincinnati; Superior from Louisville.

DEPARTURES.—Peytona for Louisville; G. W. Graham for St. Louis; Sultana, J. T. McCombs, and Pauline Carroll for New Orleans; Platte Valley for White River.

BOATS DUE.—Mollie Able, Rebecca, M. E. Forsyth, St. Patrick.

MISCELLANEOUS.—By order of the commanding General, all business will be suspended to-day, from sunrise to sunset, as a mark of repect to the memory of Mr. Lincoln. The Sultana was the first to bring the news of his assassination. She came in with flags at half mast, and decked in mourning. Major General Banks was a passenger on the Pauline Carroll, for New Orleans. Everybody is in the greatest excitement over the horrible news from Washington.

We are under obligations to the officers of the Sultana, Golden Eagle, J. T. McCombs, Pauline Carroll, and Belle Memphis for news, favors, etc.

FINANCIAL AND COMMERCIAL.

SATURDAY EVENING, April 15.

The money market is gradually getting closer, and business at the banks is light. There is a material falling off in deposits. No exchange making except from shipments of currency, and no discounts except to dealers strictly gilt edged. Transactions in gold and uncurrent money are limited, and quotations are unchanged:

	BUYING.	SELLING.
Gold,	140	145@150
Exchange on the North,	—	½ prem
Union bank of Tennessee,	55	60
Planters do of do	60	70
Bank of do	30	40
Other Southern banks nominal.		

In provisions and groceries there seems to have been very little change during the week, and in the face of the depression in Northern markets prices have generally ruled firm. The market is quiet, transactions being limited almost exclusively to the immediate wants of purchasers.

Feed is dull and drooping, with supply in excess of demand. There has been a material decline in prices during the week. We quote from wholesale prices at the landing.

Coal is steady at $1 50.

Lumber is unchanged from our last report, the demand being light. A speedy decline in prices is anticipated.

Cotton is dull and nominal. There was some inquiry to day at 20c, but we learned of no sales.

There has been some marking down in dry goods during the week, as an inducement to purchase, but transactions are nevertheless light, and rates nominal.

In our advertising columns will be seen a notice from Gen. Orme in reference to traffic in coin and bullion.

Memphis Wholesale Markets.

APPLES—Green $[illegible].
BACON—Sides, 24@[illegible]c ℔.
BUTTER—30@40c ℔.
BEANS—$2 75@3 00 ℔ bushel.
BAGGING—25.
CORN MEAL—$[illegible] ℔ bbl.
COFFEE—Rio, 38@42c.
COAL—Pittsburg, $1 50.
CANDLES—Star, ℔ ℔, 32@33.
CHEESE—24@26c.
EGGS—30@35c ℔ doz.
FEED—[illegible] none; Hay timothy, ℔ ton $45; Corn ℔ bushel $1@1 10; Oats, 90c.
FLOUR—Superfine, ℔ bbl, $9 40@ $10; Extra $10 50@12 00; Extra, $13 00@13 75.
FISH—White, No. 1, half barrel, $12 00@13 00; White No. 2, half barrel $11 00; Mackerel, No. 1, half barrel, $12 00@12½; Mackerel No. 2, half bbl, $11 00@11 00; Mackerel, No. 2, in kits, $3 50; Dry Cod, ℔ ℔, 12½c.
HAMS—New, 24@25c.
HIDES—Dry Beef, flint 10c.; do do salt, 8c.; Green Beef, 4c.; do do salt, [illegible]; Deerskins, 30c.
LIME—℔ bbl, $2 50@3 00.
LIQUORS—Rectified whky, $2 25@2 50; Domestic Brandy, $3 00@4 00; Imported Brandy, $12@20; Ale and Beer, $11 per bbl.
LEATHER—White oak per pound, 60c.; Hemlock per pound, 55c.
LUMBER—Dressed floors, $70@80; rough, $50@60 ℔ 1000 feet; laths, none; rough Boards, $40@50 ℔ 1000 feet.
MOLASSES—N. O., per gallon, $1 30@1 40.
ONIONS—$ — ℔ bushel.
POTATOES—$5 50@6 00 ℔ barrel.
RICE—West India, 16@18c ℔.
SALT—$5 50@7 00 ℔ bbl.
SOAP—Palm, 16@18c.; German, 16@18c.
SUGAR—Common to fair Louisiana, ℔ ℔, 20@28c.; Powdered and Crushed, 28c.
TOBACCO—Plug, 75@$1; ay Apple and Twist, $1@1 25.
TEA—Imperial, ℔ ℔, $2@2½; Black, $1 25@2 00.

New York Market.

NEW YORK, April 12.—There was a slight rising at the stock exchange on railroads. The market was up at ½ per cent., with very little pressure to sell. There was a sudden advance in Illinois Central to-day, which was the feature of the market. The stock had been heavily oversold on seller's option, with a prospect of covering contracts in the London stock exchange at a handsome profit. The market was bold up on the other side without obtaining any considerable number of shares, hence there was an awkward corner. Border state bonds in demand, with an upward tendency. Governments lower: 5-20s sold as low as 107. The Bremen steamer brought a number of orders to sell without limit.

The gold market keeps firm and better towards the close. The gold room was quiet. The supply of money still exceeds the demand. Dry goods trade quite active this week. Domestic fabrics, especially prints, firmly held. Buyers from a distance have been holding back and now are compelled to purchase to supply themselves with goods, hence the demand is very good. Foreign goods of a desirable style were plenty, and were bought quite freely by jobbers and retailers, at full prices. There is every prospect of active trade for the balance of the season. Many merchants from the interior are here for a second time, and report business very good. A meeting of tobacco merchants was held yesterday, at which a memorial to the Secretary of the Treasury, setting forth the views and wishes of the assemblage, was adopted and transmitted to Washington.

FOR SALE.

FOR SALE OR CHARTER, a good COTTON BOAT. Will carry 246 bales. Apply at GALBRATH & STEWART, Front street, between Monroe and Union. ap14-3t*

FOR SALE OR LEASE—A large Two Story Brick Building, suitable for a manufacturing establishment, or a double tenement. Apply immediately at No. 6 Court street. ap12-1w

FOR SALE—A BARGAIN A fine RESIDENCE on Court street extended 15 minutes walk from Court Square, containing 11 Rooms, fine cellar, kitchen and servants rooms, a good cistern lot 50x150 feet. Also, a nice Cottage Residence on Dunlap street, containing four rooms and kitchen, a fine cement cistern lot 50x200 feet. The title to all of which is guaranteed. Enquire of W. D. WYLIE, 56 Jefferson street. ap11-1w

FOR SALE.

Owing to the unusual opportunities for speculation, and use of money in commercial pursuits, I am authorized to sell for CASH,

A VERY VALUABLE BUSINESS PROPERTY, ON THE NORTH SIDE OF COURT SQUARE, Embracing TWO STORES and a number of well regulated offices, bringing in a revenue of 10 per cent. on $48,000.

ALSO,

A most Magnificent and Superb Residence in Chelsea, one mile from Court Square.

The residence is in complete order; is of brick, with frame attached wing, covering an area of about 75 by 50 feet; large halls and promenading verandas; two suits of parlors, dining room, with attached pantry; six large, beautiful, and dry sleeping or family rooms, with complete bathing arrangements; a well arranged kitchen, wash house, and four servants' rooms. Also—a commodious barn, carriage house, &c.; two large cisterns, and a fine assortment of Fruit, Evergreens and flowers. THIS VILLA contains ten acres of ground; is situated on Seventh street extended, with a front of 500 feet on said street, and convenient to churches, schools, market houses, and good walks to any portion of the city.

ALSO—300 feet on the west side of Main street, between Huling and Tremont streets.

ALSO—A comfortable residence with twenty acres of ground, on the corner of Hernando and Walker streets, 1½ miles from Court Square.

The Papers and Deeds to all of said property, are COMPLETE, and immediate possession given to all, or any of it. Apply, for one week, to

J. M. WOODWARD, Agent,
ap12-1w at Frieman Bros. 295 Main st.

S. C. McCLURE & CO.
Have Removed their Bank to
—CORNER OF—
FRONT AND JEFFERSON STREETS.
ap4-1m

ROBERT MOORE & CO.,
COTTON FACTORS
—AND—
COMMISSION MERCHANTS,
No. 49 Walnut street,
CINCINNATI,
—AND—
No. 281 Front street,
MEMPHIS.

Liberal cash advances made on consignment of Cotton made to their house in Cincinnati, or New York. ap1-2m

MISCELLANEOUS

NOTICE IS HEREBY GIVEN, that the copartnership heretofore existing between Jacob Gottlieb, H. C. Ezekiel, John H. O'Shaughnessy, and R. M. Kirtland, under the name and style of

KIRTLAND & CO.,

Doing the business of Retail Dry Goods Merchants in the city of Memphis, Tennessee, is, this day, dissolved, by the consent of a majority of the partners, as, by the articles of copartnership is authorized.

And the public is hereby notified, not to trust said R. M. Kirtland, or to recognize his acts as a member of the above named firm, he having retired from the firm.

The business of the firm will hereafter be conducted at the old stand by the remaining members of the firm. JACOB GOTTLIEB, per J. H. O'SHAUGHNESSY. H. C. EZEKIEL, Agent. JOHN H. O'SHAUGHNESSY.

Memphis, Tenn., April 11, 1865. ap13-1w

T. DEMMONS,
HOUSE,
SIGN AND STEAMBOAT
PAINTER,
GRAINER, GLAZER,
—AND—
PAPER HANGER,
NO. 14 WASHINGTON STREET
Under the Old Theater.

CEILINGS AND SIDE-WALLS KELSEMINED OR COLORED.

Particular Attention Paid to Country Work.

Orders solicited, and prompt attention given. ap13-3mo

NOTICE—IF R. W. HILL, son of G. W. Hill, is in the city, he can find his WIFE by calling at J. H. LOWENSTINE & BRO., No. 2[illegible] Main street. ap13-1w*

JUST RECEIVED,
—AND—
FOR SALE LOW.

FLOUR, BACON;
SHOULDERS, HAMS AND SIDES;
CHOICE LEAF LARD;
BROWN SUGAR;
CO REFINED WHITE;
CRUSHED,
POWDERED SUGAR;
COFFEE;
MOLASSES;
SYRUPS,

Mackerel, Candles, Soap, Rice, Tobacco, Whisky, Brandies, Wines, etc., etc., all of which we will sell at the

LOWEST CASH PRICE.

Be sure to call at No. 176 Front street, before purchasing elsewhere.

Liberal cash advances made on Cotton.

NEVILS, GLISSON & CO.
ap14-1mo

LOW PRICES AT 246 FRONT ROW. Best Sugar-cured hams, 25c. only; best Rio Coffee, 45c.; Sugar, 25c.; Flour, $8 50 to $10; Meal $7 00; Calico, 25c.; Domestic, 30c. to 50c; Shoes, 50c. to $4; Hats, Boots, Clothing and all kinds of Family and Plantation supplies very low. Come and buy what you want and get what you buy. J. M. D. MILLER & CO. fe13-ap11-3mo

J. T. BLAIR, Marshall co., Miss.
J. T. BLAIR & CO.,
COTTON
—AND—
COMMISSION MERCHANTS,
No. 233 Main street,
(CLAY BUILDING.)

We constantly pay the highest prices for Cotton. ap1-1m

DR. CHARLES THORNTON
OFFICE,
Southwest corner Main and Gayoso street
mh21-8m MEMPHIS.

JUST RECEIVED AND
LOW FOR SALE,

Flour from $8 to $14. Bacon from 20c to 25c per ℔.
SHOULDERS, HAMS AND SIDES.
Choice Leaf Lard 25c per ℔.
CO Refined White, 25c per ℔.
Powdered Sugar from 26c to 28c.
Molasses from $1 30 to $1 50.
Brown Sugar from 20c to 25c.
Crush from 26c to 28c.
Coffee from 38c to 40c.
Syrup from $1 50 to 1 65.

Mackerel, Candles, Soap, Rice, Tobaccos, Whisky, Brandies, Wines, Teas, &c., &c., &c., all of which I will sell at the

Lowest Cash Price.

Be sure to call at the sign of the

BIG HAM,
NO. 211 MAIN STREET,
Before purchasing elsewhere.
LIBERAL ADVANCES MADE ON COTTON.
R. H. GLISSON,
ap8-2w No. 211 Main street.

VALUABLE
COTTON PLANTATION FOR SALE.

The most valuable Cotton Plantation (for its size) in the State, is for sale. It contains 300 acres of choice land, 110 in high cultivation, all subject to culture. The timber on the unimproved land, will pay for all of it. Good wood yard landing at all stages of the water. Good improvements. Fine gin and mill. Cistern water, and a place remarkable for health. Located on an Island near the city, and above high water. Hands on the place sufficient to make 100 bales cotton. Stock, farming utensils, corn, all on the place, and every thing in excellent order. To a good purchaser, it will be sold on

VERY LOW TERMS,

And on time, if desired. The purchaser can more than pay for it with one crop. Apply to

McDonald & Johnson,
ap7-8w No. 278 Front Row.

DENTISTRY.

DR. J. B. & WM. WASSON,
PRACTICAL DENTISTS,

Office 297 Main street, west side, between Madison and Monroe, over Elson & Bro.'s and Friedman & Co.'s stores.

All operations in the profession performed in the most skillful manner. Special attention is called to the manner in which we extract teeth, by means of an Anaesthesia applied externally to the gums, preventing all severe pain or suffering, incurring no risks or liabilities so frequent from the use of other Anaesthetic agents. By the application of a preparation, the severest aching of the teeth can be allayed instantly, thus avoiding the necessity of the extraction of an aching tooth. We solicit the patronage of all those who can appreciate a skillful and scientific operation.

PROPRIETORS OF THE MEMPHIS DENTAL DEPOT, No. 297 Main street, west side. ap7-1m

BATES & CO.,
COTTON AND TOBACCO FACTORS,
—AND—
General Commission Merchants,
NO. 270 FRONT STREET,
MEMPHIS, TENNESSEE.
ap8[illegible]

STORAGE! STORAGE
STORAGE!!!
310 Main st., and 34 Monroe st.,
WILL STORE AND SELL
COTTON, CORN, HAY,
And all kinds of Merchandise.
Have ample room for all purposes.
SMITH & DENIE,
Cotton Factors and Commission Merchants
mh19-3mo

NOTICE.

U. S. Assessor's Office, 1st District State of Tennessee, Memphis, April 14, 1865.

The citizens of Memphis and Shelby county, are hereby notified that I have commenced the annual assessment for 1865, said assessment embracing the income for 1864, licenses from May 1865 to May 1866, and the tax on gold and silver plate, carriages, pianos, gold watches, &c.

The law requires that the above returns be made at the office of the Assistant Assessors, within ten days from the time of receiving proper blanks. Failures to make returns within the time specified subjects the party to twenty-five per cent. penalty.

The attention of all is directed to the instruction contained in the blanks upon which returns are to be made.

The office of the Assistant Assessor, 4½ Madison street, will be open from 9 A. M., to 5 P. M., until the annual assessment is completed.

ap15-tf H. F. COOPER, Assessor

AUCTION SALES,

AUCTION SALE OF
FINE FURNITURE,
No. 33 JEFFERSON ST.,
BY A. S. LEVY & CO.,

We will sell on WEDNESDAY morning, the 19th inst., at 10 o'clock, the entire Furniture of the Senate, No. 33 Jefferson street, without reserve, consisting of

Fine Parlor Setts,
Medalion Carpets,
Brussels Carpets.
Rosewood Sideboards,
Fine Tables, Looking Glasses,
Wash-stands, Bedsteads,
Bed room Setts,
Spring, Hair and Excelsior Mattresses,
Pictures, Vases, Shades, &c. &c.

Sale without reserve.
ap17-3t A. S. LEVY, Auctioneer.

GOVERNMENT SALE, AT AUCTION, OF CONDEMNED MEDICAL PROPERTY,

No. 56 Jefferson Street,
ON TUESDAY MORNING, APRIL 18TH,
AT 10 O'CLOCK A. M.
CONSISTING OF

100 Blankets;
15 Leather Buckets;
5 Medicine Chests;
4 Mess Chests; 18 Coffee Mills;
19 Hospital Knapsacks;
200 Knives and Forks;
21 Butcher and Bread knives; 67 Lanterns.

By order of Capt. H. Stevens, Medical Purveyor U. S. A. W. D. WYLIE & CO., Auctioneers. ap16-3t

NOTICE!

THE SALE OF
ELEGANT FUNRITURE,
DIAMONDS, &c.,

Announced for Tuesday last, having been postponed, will positively take place on TUESDAY, the 18th inst., at the Salesrooms of

W. H. PASSMORE & CO.,
37 UNION STREET.
THE FURNITURE COMPRISES

Parlor Setts,
Carpets, Pier Glasses,
Fire Boards, Engraving,
Chamber Set's, Pianos,
Melodeons, Sofas,
Oil Paintings.

THE DIAMONDS CONSIST OF
BREASTPIN AND EAR-RINGS.

Mattresses,
Extension Tables,
Crockeryware,
Cane Seat Chairs,
One Fine Chandelier,
Pillows, Bolsters, &c., &c.

W. H. PASSMORE & CO.,
ap16-3t Auctioneers.

MISCELLANEOUS.

STEAMBOAT FOR SALE—The entire new and well-built sternwheel steamer G. A. THOMSON. Has good power. Can be run cheap, and will carry 500 tons on 5½ feet water. Draws 22 inches forward, and 26 inches aft. Is 10 feet between decks. Apply to JAS. B. BULL, ap11-10t No. 2 Olive street, St. Louis, Mo.

$25 REWARD—LOST, EITHER on Main or Front streets, between Adams and Madison street, a roll of money containing from $125 to $150. The finder will receive the above reward by leaving the same at 284 Front Row. ap14-1w.* W. W. BIRGE.

ADMINISTRATOR'S NOTICE.—All persons indebted to the estate of James Adams, deceased, are hereby notified to make payment of the same; and all persons having claims against the said estate, are hereby notified to present the same for payment as the law directs. Mr. GEO. WINCHESTER, at the Custom House, is my agent. A. G. ADAMS, Administrator of James Adams, deceased. Memphis, Tenn., April 5, 1865. ap7-2w*

NOTICE TO THE LADIES
NEW STYLE HAIR BRAIDS,
New Cascade Waterfalls,
NEW BOWS FRISE,
Hair Braids, Natural Curls,
WIGS AND TOUPETS,
Millinery and Fancy Notions,
And all BRAIDS changed in New Style, at
MRS. L. GUILMARD,
No. 62½ Jefferson street, near Postoffice.
mh28-1m

DR. J. P. DROMGOOLE

Respectfully informs his numerous friends that he has returned, and tenders his

Professional Services

to the citizens of Memphis in the various branches of the Medical Profession.

Having practiced medicine Seventeen Years, he has ceased to practice for glory, and is now working for money, and money he must have. His regular patrons must expect to make MONTHLY settlements if not, he prefers to remain in his office and weep over past losses. He is willing to do a LIBERAL share of CHARITY practice. His charges same as those established by the profession.

OFFICE HOURS—9 to 10 and 3 to 4.

OFFICE—120 1-2 Beal street
(OVER WILKERSON'S DRUG STORE,)
Residence, Corner Hernando and Linden streets, Op. Methodist Church
MEMPHIS March 29, 1865. mh29-3m

MARLAND L. PERKINS,
ATTORNEY AT LAW
—OFFICE IN—
WALKER'S BLOCK.
ap8-3m

NOTICE—L. D. BOND, ONE of the partners of the firm of BOND & JONES having recently died, his interest in the House will be represented by MRS. M. C. BOND, his mother, and the business will continue as heretofore. The House feels thankful for past patronage, and solicits a continuance of the same. J. N. JONES. MRS. M. C. BOND. ap12-1w

BELLEFONTAINE
COTTON EXPRESS.
Only Ten (10) Days to New York
from Evansville, Ind.
TIME GUARANTEED.

We are Agents of the above well known

Lightning Express Line.

For the transportation of Cotton to all the

EASTERN CITIES.

TIME BILLS LADING WILL BE GIVEN.
ALL REBATES PAID PROMPTLY AT OUR OFFICE.
FOSTER, GWYN & CO.,
ap4-3mo Agents, 280 Front street.

BOOTS AND SHOES.

FRIEDMAN BROTHERS,
295 Main street.

We are daily receiving large additions to our complete and well selected stock of

BOOTS AND SHOES,
Hats, Trunks, Valises, Bags, &c,
DIRECT FROM MANUFACTURERS.

Our buyer being constantly in the market, we are enabled to offer

Great Inducements to Dealers

Who will find it to their interest to give us a call.

Our Retail Departments

Are furnished, as usual, with the best CUSTOM MADE WORK of the most celebrated makers. Constantly adding, fresh and fashionable goods.

FRIEDMAN & BROS,
ap2-2mo 295 Main street.

FOR RENT.

FOR RENT—ROOMS AND an OFFICE, suitable for a doctor or lawyer, or any other man. Inquire at 34½ Union street, between Main and Second. apr7 3w*

STEAMBOATS

MERCHANTS' AND PEOPLE'S LINE.
For Vicksburg, Natchez and New Orleans.

SOUTHWESTER .... JONES, master.

This elegant passenger packet will leave as above on THIS DAY, the 17th inst., at 10 A. M. For freight or passage apply on board, or to JOS. ELLIOTT, Agent, ap17-1t No. 13 Madison street.

MEMPHIS AND ST. LOUIS PACKET COMPANY.
Daily United States Mail Line,
For Cairo and St. Louis.

BELLE MEMPHIS .... MUSSELMAN, Master.

This splendid passenger packet will leave as above on THIS DAY, the 17th inst., at 5 P. M. For freight or passage apply on board, or to W. C. POSTAL, Sup't, St. Louis Packet Co., on Wharfboat, ap17-1t Foot of Jefferson street.

REGULAR WEDNESDAY PACKET
For Helena, White River and DeValls Bluff.

REBECCA .... BANFIL, Master.

This splendid passenger packet will leave as above on WEDNESDAY, the 19th inst., at 4 P. M. For freight or passage apply on board, or to LARRY HARMSTAD, Agent, ap16-4t 14 Jefferson street.

For Cairo, Evansville and Louisville

SUPERIOR .... H. T. DEXTER, Master.

This splendid passenger packet will leave as above MONDAY, 17th inst., at 4 P. M. For freight or passage apply on board or to JOS. ELLIOTT, Agent, ap16-2t No. 13 Madison street.

For Pine Bluff and Little Rock.

[illegible] .... [illegible]

Will leave for above and intermediate points TUESDAY, 18th inst., at 5 P. M. For freight or passage apply on board or to F. M. VINSON, Agent, ap17-2t No. 276 Front Row.

For Evansville and Louisville.

SUPERIOR .... DEXTER, Master.

This splendid passenger packet will leave as above on TUESDAY, the 18th inst., at 5 P. M. For freight or passage, apply on board, or to F. M. VINSON, Agent, ap17-2t 276 Front Row.

MEMPHIS AND CINCINNATI PACKET COMPANY.
For Cairo, Louisville and Cincinnati.

GOLDEN EAGLE .... KATES, Master.

This spendid passenger packet will leave as above on TUESDAY, the 18th inst., at 4 P. M.

For freight or passage apply on board, or to LARRY HARMSTAD, Agent, No. 14 Jefferson street. ENOCH TAYLOR, Agent, ap16 3t No. 278 Front Row.

FOR NASHVILLE.
Regular Semi-Weekly Passenger Packet.

The splendid passenger steamer M. S. MEPHAM H. G. McCOMAS, master, will leave Cairo for Nashville on every SATURDAY, at 12 M. Passengers leaving Memphis on THURSDAY EVENING Boat will make sure connection with M. S. MEPHAM at Cairo.

The splendid passenger steamer IMPERIAL, BEN HOWARD, master, will leave Cairo for Nashville on every WEDNESDAY at 12 M. Passengers by MONDAY EVENING Boat will make sure connection with Imperial at Cairo. For further information apply to JOS. ELLIOTT, Agent, ap1-3mo No. 13 Madison street.

REGULAR MEMPHIS AND HELENA
For Helena,

GOLDEN ERA .... JOHNSON, Master.

This splendid passenger packet having entered the Memphis and Helena trade as a regular mail and despatch boat, will leave Memphis for Helena, every TUESDAY, THURSDAY and SATURDAY throughout the season. For freight or passage, apply on board, or to HARRY HARMSTAD, Agent, mar4-3m 14 Jefferson Street.

SIDE-WHEEL STEAMBOAT FOR SALE.—I have for sale a steamboat suitable for the cotton trade, will carry 1,200 bales cotton. Said steamboat is in good running order, and will be sold at a reasonable price, apply to LARRY HARMSTAD, Agent, ap14-3t No. 14 Jefferson street.

MILITARY ORDERS

GENERAL ORDERS, NO. 43.

Headquarters, District of West Tennessee, Memphis, Tenn., April 14, 1865.

Any military restrictions heretofore existing in this District in regard to dealing in gold, are hereby removed, and the same is subject solely to the orders and regulations of the Treasury Department.

By order of Major General C. C. Washburn. W. H. MORGAN, ap15-3t Major and Assistant Adjutant General.

SPECIAL ORDERS, NO. 92.

Headquarters Post and Defences of Memphis, Memphis, Tenn., April 14, 1865.

PARAGRAPH V.

The Enrolled Militia of this command, Brig. Gen. T. Williamson, commanding, will be reviewed by the Major General commanding District of West Tennessee at the Fair Grounds, on Monday, the 17th instant, at 3 o'clock, P. M.

By order of Brig. Gen'l A. L. Chetlain. JNO. G. WOODRUFF, ap15-3t Captain and A. A. A. Gen.

GENERAL ORDERS, NO. 22.

Headquarters Enrolled Militia, District of West Tennessee, Memphis, Tenn., April 14, 1865.

In pursuance of Special Orders No. 92, Headquarters Post and Defences of Memphis, the several regiments and detachments of this command will parade for review and inspection on Monday the 17th instant.

The signal gun will be fired at 12 M. precisely, at which hour all business throughout the city will be suspended. Roll call, and the distribution of the monthly passes, are ordered promptly at 1-30 P. M., and all members not present at that time will be reported absent without authority.

All members unable to parade will report to their respective Surgeons at 1 P. M., for examination.

Major Gen. C. C. Washburne, commanding district will be the reviewing officer.

By order of Brigadier General M. T. Williamson. D. W. HALLAM, Lieut. and Adj't. Asst. Adj't. Gen.

GENERAL ORDERS, NO. 42.

Headquarters District of West Tennessee, Memphis, Tenn., April — 1865.

The following specified General Orders issued from these headquarters being no longer consistent with that policy, which more recent events have rendered proper for the Commanding General to adopt, and being also inconsistent with more recent orders, are hereby revoked:

Of the series of 1864, General Orders No. 74, District of West Tennessee, defining the lines of actual military occupation, establishing conditions of trade, &c., and so much of General Orders No. 85 as impose the payment of $2 by parties obtaining permits to carry arms; of the series of 1865, General Orders No. 10, regulating the taking out of supplies, and imposing certain requirements upon persons arriving at the picket lines, and upon strangers arriving at the city of Memphis by river; No. 12, requiring the registration of ownership of real estate, and the filing a statement of moneys and effects belonging to persons absent within the enemy's territory; No. 13, with regard to the validity of oaths of allegiance; No. 14, explanatory of said order No. 10; No. 3, (circular) preventing the return during the war of persons arriving at and going beyond the picket lines; No. 13, with regard to certain persons therein named deemed to have elected to register themselves as enemies of the United States; No. 26, defining the conditions of trade in cotton. All other general orders issued from the headquarters District of West Tennessee, prior to March 4, 1865, inconsistent with orders since issued, are also revoked.

By order of Maj. Gen. C. C. Washburn. W. H. MORGAN, ap15-3t Major & Assistant Adjutant General.

SEALED PROPOSALS

SEALED PROPOSALS.

Office City Engineer, Memphis, April 7, 1865.

Will be received at this office until the SEVENTEENTH of the present month, at 12 o'clock M., for making additions and repairs at the Engine House, on the corner of Adams and Second streets.

Plans and specifications of the work may be seen at this office. FRANCIS FOSTER, ap8-td City Engineer.

SEALED PROPOSALS.

Office City Engineer, Memphis, March 25, 1865.

Will be received at this office until the SEVENTEENTH OF APRIL next, at 12 o'clock M., for furnishing the materials and constructing Brick Wings at the Auction street Bridge. Details of the work and the blank form of the proposals, can be obtained at this office. Bids must be endorsed as follows, viz: "Proposals for work on Auction street Bridge." The Improvement Committee reserve the right to reject any or all of the proposals. mh26-24t FRANCIS FOSTER, City Engineer.

MISCELLANEOUS.

JOHN B. GRAY,
(LATE ADJUTANT GENERAL OF MISSOURI.)
No. 51 Third street,
ST. LOUIS, MO.
AGENT
FOR
Claimants Against the U. S.
OR
STATE GOVERNMENT.
ap6-3mo

A. T. SHAW, M. D.,
PHYSICIAN AND SURGEON,
—OFFICE—
AYERS' BUILDINGS, SECOND STREET.
Residence: 601 Front (formerly Shelby street.
mh17-3m*

INTELLIGENCE OFFICE.
C. W. POOL
HAVING OPENED A
General Intelligence Office,
No. 40 Jefferson street.

(North side,) between Main and Second, takes pleasure in announcing to the citizens of Memphis that he is now prepared to furnish help of all kinds, white or black.

N. B.—Special attention given to the letting of Houses and Rooms. mh30-2w

THE DAILY STANDARD.

VOL. I. RALEIGH, N. C., WEDNESDAY, APRIL 19, 1865. NO. 3.

Gen. Sherman's Rule in North Carolina.

Gen. Sherman came into North Carolina to save, not to destroy, and from the order of Gen. Slocum, published yesterday, our people can see that the army is commanded to respect persons and property in this State. We have heard of excesses and outrages, however, but we know that those in authority are doing all they can to suppress them and restore order. These outrages are committed by stragglers and not by foragers or organized troops, and when reported and the guilty parties can be identified they are punished. Gen. Sherman looks upon North Carolina as part and parcel of the American Union, and has already, we are informed, issued an order that those of her people who are within his lines be respected and treated as citizens of the United States.

The rule in the city has been not only mild but kind, and we were assured, yesterday, that patrols were being organized to preserve order and prevent marauding by stragglers in the surrounding country.

But war is terrible and the presence of large armies distressing, under the most favorable circumstances, and hence our only relief is in that peace which can only be restored by the restoration of the National authority and the observance of the laws of the United States by all the people of all the States; and to secure this it is only necessary to lay down our arms and demand that protection and security that the government cannot refuse to American citizens. When Gen. Johnston's army shall have stacked arms and the men shall have dispersed, we suppose that neither Davis or Vance, or any of their adherents will urge the scattered fragments of armies in the Cotton States to make further resistance; and so the prospect that all armed resistance to the government will cease very soon, amounts almost to a certainty. And we can assert further that no one desires this more ardently than Gen. Sherman. He is not cruel, nor vindictive: he will war upon all men in arms against the government whose officer he is, but as soon as a man lays down his arms and expresses a willingness to submit to the national authority, Gen. Sherman becomes his friend. While stragglers who hang upon the army may rob and plunder persons in the country, a thing which no one regrets more than Gen. Sherman, we know that by his order the destitute are being fed from his stores, and many, left in an almost starving condition by the Confederate authorities, will be saved thereby.

But Gen. Sherman has the chief command of an immense army, and of course cannot look after every man's house or farm, or see all who have complaints to make, but Gen. Schofield, who commands the department of North Carolina, and Gen. Stiles, who commands in this city, will see and hear all who have been wronged, and do all in their power to relieve them; and to those gentlemen we refer all who may be annoyed by stragglers or in want of protection.

Gen. Sherman is anxious for the return of peace and quiet, and is doing all he can to secure them and we hope to be able to announce, in a few days, that the rebellion has ceased, that all our people have returned to their allegiance, and that the Union soldiers are on their way to their homes where loved ones anxiously await them. We have conversed with no officer, or man, in the Union army that does not express an ardent desire for an early peace upon the basis of a restored Union, with the equality of the people of the two sections and a return of friendship and social and commercial intercourse.

We bid our people be of good cheer, for the day of our deliverance is at hand.—*Progress.*

Daniel Webster on the Union

I profess, sir, in my career, hitherto, to have kept steadily in view the prosperity and honor of the whole country, and the preservation of our federal union. It is to that union we owe our safety at home, and our consideration and dignity abroad. It is to that union that we are chiefly indebted for whatever makes us most proud of our country. That union we reached only by the discipline of our virtues in the severe school of adversity. It had its origin in the necessities of disordered finance, prostrate commerce, and ruined credit.—Under its benign influences, these great interests immediately awoke, as from the dead, and sprang forth with newness of life. Every year of its duration has teemed with fresh proofs of its utility and its blessings; and, although our territory has stretched out wider and wider, and our population spread farther and farther, they have not outrun its protection or its benefits. It has been to us all a copious fountain of national, social, and personal happiness. I have not allowed myself, sir, to look beyond the union, to see what might lie hidden in the dark recess behind. I have not coolly weighed the chances of preserving liberty when the bonds that unite us together shall be broken asunder. I have not accustomed myself to hang over the precipice of disunion, to see whether, with my short sight, I can fathom the depth of the abyss below; nor could I regard him as a safe counsellor in the affairs of this government, whose thoughts should be mainly bent on considering, not how the union should be best preserved, but how tolerable might be the condition of the people when it shall be broken up and destroyed. While the union lasts, we have high, exciting, gratifying prospects spread out before us, for us and our children. Beyond that I seek not to penetrate the veil. God grant that, in my day, at least, that curtain may not rise. God grant, that on my vision never may be opened what lies behind. When my eyes shall be turned to behold, for the last time, the sun in heaven, may I not see him shining on the broken and dishonored fragments of a once glorious union; on states dissevered, discordant, belligerent; on a land rent with civil feuds, or drenched, it may be, in fraternal blood! Let their last feeble and lingering glance, rather behold the gorgeous ensign of the republic, now known and honored throughout the earth, still full high advanced, its arms and trophies streaming in their original lustre, not a stripe erased or polluted, nor a single star obscured—bearing for its motto, no such miserable interrogatory, as *What is all this worth?* Nor those other words of delusion and folly, *Liberty first, and Union afterwards*—but everywhere, spread all over in characters of living light, blazing on all its ample folds, as they float over the sea, and over the land, and in every wind under the whole heavens, that other sentiment, dear to every true American heart—Liberty *and* Union, now and forever, one and inseparable!—*Daniel Webster.*

The Nobility of Labor.

Extract from an Address delivered by W. W. Holden, at Fayetteville, N. C., November 3d, 1859.

I have said, fellow citizens, that agriculture is the chief pursuit of man; yet it is dependent on, and indissolubly connected with the mechanic arts. They exist together, they flourish together, or they languish and decline together. Slight, neglect, injure one, and you injure the other. If the farmer feeds us, the mechanic clothes us. If the farmer looks to the soil for support, and for sustenance for others, he looks to it and labors in it with the implements which the mechanic has placed in his hands. Every ship that sails; every fortification that towers along the deep; every improvement upon our rivers, lakes and seas; every town and city that adorns the surface of the world; every temple dedicated to law, art, science, and religion; every telegraph wire, annihilating space; every steam-car, uniting the interests and sympathies of distant communities; every telescope, sweeping the heavens and bringing other worlds largely before our vision; every microscope, revealing the hidden wonders of the world around us; every printed book, which informs, instructs, delights and elevates the mind; every fabric and contrivance which contributes to our convenience and comfort, or which protects us from the heat of summer and the cold of winter, is the direct result of mechanical ingenuity, industry and skill.

Let no man be ashamed of mechanical labor. Some of the greatest and best men that ever graced the earth with their presence, were mechanics. The hard hand of toil is infinitely more honorable than the soft hand of sloth and luxury. Rather let the mechanic be proud of his skill, of his industry, and of his usefulness to society. Let him honor his vocation, and his vocation will honor him. The true test of merit is in the performance of duty in whatsoever situation we may be placed. Tried by this test, the mechanics and working men of North Carolina are the equals of any and all others. Be true, gentlemen mechanics, to yourselves, to your country, and to your God. Be loyal to your State and to its interests, as you always have been, and as your brother mechanics were before you, who followed WASHINGTON, the farmer, and Greene, the blacksmith, and Morgan, the wagoner, and Sherman, the shoemaker, and Franklin, the printer, in the war of independence. Remember that you are now a power in the State; and that common Schools and internal improvements are constantly increasing your intelligence, your influence and your power. Remember that labor of all kinds, rightly appreciated and justly protected and rewarded, is the happiest temporal inheritance of man. Its fruits are seen every where, benefitting, gladdening and blessing the earth. Labor, of whatsoever kind, is the life of the State. When it prospers, all interests flourish; when it languishes, all interests decline. Let us, then, cherish, encourage and honor it; and let the mechanics, whose interests and destinies are inseparably associated with those of the farmers, resolve to do their full part in advancing the prosperity and augmenting the glory of our good old State.

"Toil swings the axe, and forests bow;
The seeds break out in radiant bloom;
Rich harvests smile behind the plow,
And cities cluster round the loom:
Where tottering domes and tapering spires
Adorn the vale and crown the hill,
Stout Labor lights its beacon fires,
And plumes with smoke the forge and mill.

The monarch oak, the woodland's pride,
Whose trunk is seamed with lightning scars,
Toil launches on the restless tide,
And there unrolls the flag of stars;
The engine with its lungs of flame,
And ribs of brass and joints of steel,
From Labor's plastic fingers came,
With sobbing valve and whirling wheel.

'Tis Labor works the magic press,
And turns the crank in hives of toil,
And beckons angels down to bless
Industrious hands on sea and soil.
Here sun-browned Toil, with shining spade,
Links lake to lake with silver ties,
Strung thick with palaces of trade,
And temples towering to the skies."

HEADQUARTERS.—Gen. Sherman's headquarters are at the Governor's Mansion.

Gen. Slocumb's headquarters are at the Saunder's house, Hillsboro' street, just west of the railroad crossing.

Gen. Howard's headquarters are at St. Mary's, Hillsboro' street.

Gen. Schofield's headquarters are at the residence of Mr. Grimes, two squares north of the Capitol.—Gen. Schofield commands the Department of North Carolina.

Gen. Stiles, in command of the City, has his headquarters in the Capitol Square.

Col. Warner, Provost Marshal, occupies the Governor's room at the Capitol.—*Progress.*

THE SOLDIER'S DREAM.

Our bugles sang truce—for the night cloud had lowered,
And the sentinel stars set their watch in the sky;
And thousands had sunk on the ground overpowered,
The weary to sleep, and the wounded to die.

When reposing that night on my pallet of straw,
By the wolf-scaring fagot that guarded the slain;
At the dead of the night a sweet vision I saw,
And thrice ere the morning I dreamt it again.

Methought from the battle field's dreadful array,
Far, far I had roamed on a desolate track;
'Twas autumn—and sunshine arose on the way
To the home of my fathers, that welcomed me back.

I flew to the pleasant fields traversed so oft
In life's morning march, when my bosom was young;
I heard my own mountain-goats bleating aloft,
And knew the sweet strain that the corn-reapers sung.

Then pledged we the wine cup, and fondly I swore
From my home and my weeping friends never to part;
My little ones kissed me a thousand times o'er,
And my wife sobbed aloud in her fullness of heart.

Stay, stay with us—rest, thou art weary and worn:
And fain was their war-broken soldier to stay;
But sorrow returned with the dawning of morn,
And the voice in my dreaming ear melted away.

Campbell.

Anecdote of General Sherman.

The extraordinary success with which Gen. Sherman has conducted his campaign during the last nine months has secured for him the affections of the American people beyond that of any other military officer. He has become as popular as a military officer, as Vice Admiral Farragut has as a naval commander. Anything relating to him is therefore interesting. Through an officer in his command, recently arrived, I have obtained the circumstances of an amusing scene said to have taken place between General Sherman and the British Consul at Savannah, which, to say the least, is characteristic of that Officer, as well as the self-sufficient style of her Majesty's officials in the South.

On the arrival of General Sherman at Savannah, he saw a large number of British flags displayed from buildings, and had a curiosity to know how many British Consuls there were there. He soon ascertained that these flags were on buildings where cotton had been stored away, and at once ordered it to be seized. Soon after that, while the General was busily engaged at the headquarters, a pompous gentleman walked in, apparently in great haste, and enquired if he was Gen. Sherman?—Having received an affirmative reply, the pompous gentleman remarked, 'That when he left his residence United States troops were engaged in removing his cotton from it when it was protected by the British flag.'

'Stop, sir,' said General Sherman, 'not your cotton, sir, but my cotton; in the name of the United States government, sir. I have noticed,' continued General Sherman, 'a great many British flags all here, protecting cotton; I have seized it all in the name of my government.'

'But, sir,' said the Consul, indignantly, 'there is scarcely any cotton in Savannah that does not belong to me.'

'There is not a pound of cotton here, sir, that does not belong to me, for the United States,' responded Sherman.

'Well, sir,' said the Consul, swelling himself up with the dignity of his office and reddening in the face, 'my government shall hear of this. I shall report your conduct to my government, sir.'

'Ah! pray, who are you, sir?' said the General.

"Consul to her British Majesty, sir?"

"Oh! indeed!" responded the General. "I hope you will report me to your government.—You will please say to your government, for me, that I have been fighting the English government all the way from the Ohio river to Vicksburg, and thence to this point. At every step I have encountered British arms, British munitions of war, and British goods of every description, at every step, sir. I have met them, sir, in all shapes; and now sir, I find you claiming all the cotton, sir. I intend to call upon my government to order me to Nassau at once."

"What do you propose to do there?" asked the Consul, somewhat taken aback.

"I would," replied the General, "take with me a quantity of picks and shovels, and throw that cursed sand-hill into the sea, sir; and then I would pay for it, sir—if necessary. Good day, sir."

It is needless to add that Gen. Sherman was not again troubled with the officious representative of her Majesty's government.

"John, can you tell me the difference between attraction of gravitation and attraction of cohesion?"

"Yes, sir. Attraction of gravitation pulls a drunken man to the ground, and the attraction of cohesion prevents his getting up again."

A gentleman hearing a lady praise the eyes of a certain prominent clergyman, wrote the following:

I cannot praise the doctor's eyes,
I never saw his glance divine,
For when he *prays* he shuts his eyes,
And when he *preaches* he shuts mine.

Every vote cast in Tarboro' and Wilson was "for Convention." We understand that *three groans* were given in each of those towns for *Abe Lincoln and W. W. Holden*, and for other leading submissionists in Raleigh! Well!!—*Goldsboro' Rough Notes.*

We feel complimented when blackguards groan at us because we are for the Union. We shall not take the trouble even to grunt at them.

Let them groan. That is about all they can do. If war should come these very fellows would be found calling on the pine thickets and hollow logs to save them from the wrath of the invading army. The greatest cowards are those who groan most at enemies who are miles away. They will never groan over wounds received in defending their country.

The oligarchs who instruct their minions when and at whom to groan, hate Lincoln, not only because he is a Republican, but because he split rails for his daily bread when a young man; they hate Douglas because he worked at the cabinet-maker's trade for his daily bread when a young man; they hate Andrew Johnson because he worked at the tailor's trade for his daily bread when a young man; and they hate Holden because, being only a printer, he dared to aspire to be Governor of North Carolina. Holden will not belittle himself by hating these creatures in return. *They* know that he is as true to the South as they are, but they seek to ruin him by associating him with a Republican.

In reply to all this Holden only asks leave to add to his record the following: The said Holden appeared before the people of Wake for a seat in the Convention. He was assailed, catechized, misrepresented, pursued, maligned, but he spoke for himself, and then the people voted. *He was endorsed by* 1,937 *of the freemen of Wake.* He is therewith content. "Groan sinners, groan."—*Standard, March* 20, 1861.

KENTUCKY RIFLEMEN.—The renown which Kentucky riflemen have obtained for precision and skill in handling the rifle has become world-wide, and excited the attention and wonder of the warriors of other nations. In battle they have stood as cool and collected, although the first time in action, as the oldest veterans in Europe; pouring in their deadly fire with unerring aim.

"I shot that officer," exclaimed a rifleman, as he saw an officer fall at New Orleans.

"I shot him in the right eye," replied the other rifleman.

"And I shot him in the left eye," was the response.

After the battle, it was found that an officer had been shot in both eyes. This unerring precision can only be obtained by long practice and thorough drilling.

At the first settlement of the State, they were compelled to be constantly under arms, as it were, to guard against the wild Indian and murderous tomahawk. As the father, so the child grew up, taught in earliest infancy possible, to poise the rifle and direct its aim. As ammunition was not always convenient to be had, the father would dole out to his son a certain number of cartridges for his rifle, for each of which he must bring home some sort of game, or get a taste of hickory for every missing shot.

Many years ago I was conversing with my father on the wonderful skill of the Kentuckians, when he related the following anecdote:

"I was out in the wilds of Kentucky, some years before the war, on a surveying expedition, and had an opportunity of studying the character of the earlier setlers for a considerable length of time.—It became necessary for me to stop a few days at a log tavern, and to while away the time I took my rifle and explored the woods for game, of which there was an abundance. The landlord had a little son, about ten years of age, who accompanied me with his rifle, and always had extremely good luck. On one occasion the fates seemed averse to him, for perceiving a squirrel on a very high branch of a tree, he up with his rifle and blazed away, and down came the squirrel. The look of dismay with which he viewed the game, I shall never forget. Dropping the butt of his rifle on the ground, he burst into tears. In the utmost surprise, I inquired what the matter was. He answered—

"Daddy'll lick me."

"Lick you! what for?"

"Because I didn't hit him in the head."

I soothed him all I could, but the day's pleasure was over. On returning to the tavern I interceded for him all in my power to save him from the hickory, but it was of no use; the application must be made, if only for example.

"No, no, stranger; if I let him off I break a standing rule of our State. I was never let off and what was good for me is good for him. He must shoot right, or put up with what he gets."

The hickory was applied, but no bones were broken. Such training as that, which was universal in those parts, tells the secret of Kentucky rifle shooting.

"What does cleave mean, papa?" "It means to stick together." "Does John stick wood together when he cleaves it?" "Hem! means to separate." "Well, then, pa, does a man separate from his wife when he cleaves to her?" "Hem! don't ask foolish questions, child."

The Daily Standard.

WILLIAM W. HOLDEN,
EDITOR AND PROPRIETOR.

Liberty and Union, now and forever, one and inseparable.---DANIEL WEBSTER.

RALEIGH: WEDNESDAY, APRIL 19, 1865.

The Daily Standard.

We begin to-day the publication of the *Daily Standard*, and for the present will issue neither a Weekly or Semi-Weekly edition of the *Standard*. When communication is fully resumed, the Weekly and Semi-Weekly *Standard* will be revived.

Our City subscribers will be supplied with the Daily for the present.

Price of Daily *Standard*, single copy, 10 cents; newsboys, $5 per hundred copies—federal currency.

Advertisements: one square, first insertion, $1; each subsequent insertion, 50 cents.

Death of Mr. Lincoln--Public Meeting in Raleigh.

One of the largest meetings ever held by our citizens assembled at the Courthouse yesterday evening, at four o'clock, at short notice, to express the profound regret felt by all our people at the announcement of the death of Mr. Lincoln. The proceedings will be found below. There was but one feeling of abhorrence for the deed and its cowardly perpetrators. The Mayor of the City presided, and the resolutions were unanimously adopted by the meeting.

We have placed our columns in mourning to-day, as some evidence of the feeling which pervades our people at the death by a felon hand of one illustrious by his position, and who, had his life been spared, would doubtless have shown himself a kind and generous friend to our people. The death of Mr. Lincoln is a national misfortune, and will be deeply deplored in every portion of the country.

For the Standard.

The meeting was called to order by Mayor Harrison, at 4 o'clock, who, in a few pertinent remarks, stated its object to be for the purpose of expressing the feelings and sentiments of our citizens of every party, in relation to the melancholy intelligence of the death of President Lincoln, in the manner announced in this morning's papers.

Quent. Busbee, Esq., was requested to act as Secretary; and, on motion of R. C. Badger, Esq., the Mayor appointed a committee of five to draw Resolutions expressive of the feelings of the meeting.

Messrs. Richard C. Badger, B. F Moore, W. W. Holden, Kenneth Rayner and J. L. Pennington, were appointed a committee, who retired and soon reported the following resolutions, which were adopted unanimously:

WHEREAS, It has been officially announced that Abraham Lincoln, President of the United States, has been assassinated, and that at the same time an attempt was made to assassinate William H. Seward, Secretary of State of the United States:

Resolved, That we, the citizens of Raleigh, avail ourselves of the earliest opportunity to express our utmost abhorrence of the atrocious deed.

Resolved, That while such a deed at any time would deserve the indignation of civilized men, we regard it as peculiarly unfortunate and calamitous, that it should be destined to mark the close of a long continued struggle in arms just at the moment when the prospects of a speedy peace were cheering a land which had been so long drenched with fraternal blood; and that for ourselves, as a community, we repudiate and protest against any affiliation or sympathy with such outrages and atrocities as in violation of our moral sentiments as a Christian and civilized people, and destructive of the order and well being of all society.

Resolved, That a copy of these resolutions be presented to Gen. Sherman, Chief-in-Command, and to Gen. Schofield, commander of this department, and be published in the city papers.

On motion of Dr. McKee the meeting adjourned.

W. H. HARRISON, Mayor,
Chairman,

Q. BUSBEE, Secretary.

It is proper that we should say that in speaking of Gov. Vance and the State government, we do not mean to include such officials as the State Treasurer, the Secretary of State, the Comptroller of State, and the Surgeon General. These are good and true men. All of them remained here with the exception of Mr. Worth, who left under circumstances over which he had no control. And in making these exceptions, which occur to us as we write, it is not our purpose to cast reflections on other officials who remained in Raleigh.

We are requested to state that Hon. R. S. Donnell, Speaker of the House of Commons, and Surgeon General E. Warren, would have attended the meeting of the citizens held yesterday, had they been apprised of it. They cordially endorse the action of the meeting.

SLAVERY.—We do not propose now to discuss this question, but we desire to say that slavery is the prime cause of secession and of all the unutterable horrors of this war; and that if the institution stands in any respect in the way of a speedy adjustment of our difficulties, let it be swept away. Every thing must yield to the greatest good of the greatest number of our people, and to the restoration of harmony under one common flag. We think more of peace and the Union than we do of slavery. The slavery propagandists went to war on an abstraction about the institution in the Territories, and the result is they have lost it in the States.

Thanks to Grant and his Army.

WAR DEPARTMENT,
WASHINGTON, D. C., April 9--9:30 P. M.

Lieutenant General GRANT:—

Thanks be to Almighty God for the great victory with which he has this day crowned you and the gallant armies under your command.

The thanks of this Department, and of the government, and of the people of the United States their reverence and honor have been deserved—will be rendered to you and the brave and gallant officers and soldiers of your army for all time.

EDWIN M. STANTON,
Secretary of War.

NATIONAL SALUTE.

WAR DEPARTMENT,
WASHINGTON, D. C., April 9—10 P. M.

Ordered:—That a salute of two hundred guns be fired at the headquarters of every army and department, and at every port and arsenal in the United States, and at the Military Academy at West Point, on the day of the receipt of this order, in commemoration of the surrender of General R. E. Lee and the Army of Northern Virginia to Lieutenant General Grant and the army under his command; report of the receipt and execution of this order to be made to the Adjutant General, Washington.

EDWIN M. STANTON,
Secretary of War.

[From the Richmond Whig, April 6.]

The Potent Power of Greenbacks.

The transition from enormous prices and a depreciated currency to reasonable rates and real money has come so suddenly upon the citizens that it will be some time before they can properly realize the change. Butter that was scarce at twenty five dollars a pound is now plentiful at fifty and sixty cents a pound. Eggs that were hidden away at twenty-five dollars per dozen came out readily at the beck of thirty cents. Other commodities are at an equal ratio. Sutlers' stores are springing up like pleasant oases all over the business part of the city left unscathed by the fire, and old times are being revived by a sight of the substantials and luxuries enjoyed before the war put them beyond the reach of the cuisines of Richmond. People will live, breathe and move and have their being once more.

[From the Richmond Whig, April 7.]

Distinguished Visitors at Richmond.

Mrs. President Lincoln and Mrs. General Grant arrived in the city on yesterday afternoon. The party, accompanied by several prominent government officials, rode through the city in carriages, with an escort of cavalry, and returned to City Point in the evening, whither the President had already gone.

Vice President Andrew Johnston, Hon. Mr. Harlan, Secretary of the Interior, and Hon. Preston King are also here.

Assistant Secretary of War Dana is in Richmond.

Secretaries Wm. H. Seward and E. M. Stanton are expected during the present week.

Adams' Express Company are about to establish a branch house of the company in Richmond from City Point.

Improvement, renovation and reconstruction must assuredly follow in the wake of the Union armies. In things political, as well as things material, a strong force of laborers is to be at once put at work on the broken points of the Richmond, Fredericksburg, Aquia Creek and Potomac Railroad, and its completion, which will occur within the next few weeks, will put Richmond in rail communication with the Capital of the United States. Again the iron bands, broken by the ruthless hand of war, welded again, will once more re-unite a divided people in bands too strong to be put asunder. The river obstructions are, we believe, being removed as expeditiously as possible, and forty-eight hours will not elapse, we opine, before we hear of steamers at Rocketts, direct from New York, Philadelphia and Baltimore. The river at City Point is filled with a sutler's fleet awaiting permits to enable them to bring their supplies up to Richmond.

[From the Richmond Whig, April 7.]

The Richmond Unionists Venturing out of their Hiding Places.

A great many men whom the tyrannical rebel conscription has for three years driven from the face of day, and forced to hide and skulk like felons, assured by the presence of the Union forces and the "Star Spangled Banner," have ventured once more to show themselves among their fellows. We saw yesterday a gentleman of this class. It had been more than three years since we saw him before. On that occasion, he was distributing copies of the speech made in the Virginia Convention by the Hon. Sherrard Clemans; he was an out and out Botts's man, and very soon had to hide himself from the Davis minions. What this poor man and such as he have suffered during this war none but themselves can ever know.—They have lived in poverty and constant dread and apprehension. Again they taste the blessings of liberty and walk the earth as freemen. The joys of their recovered freedom go far to compensate them for all their sufferings.

THE TRUE GENTLEMAN.—He is courteous and affable to his neighbors. As the sword of the best tempered metal is most flexible, so the truly generous are most pliant and courteous in their behavior to their inferiors.

MAKING IT PLAIN.—Two Dutchmen had occasion to go to a blacksmith's on business, and finding the smith absent from the shop, they concluded to go to the house. Having reached the door, said one to the other:

"Come, Hans, you ax about de smit?"

"Nein, nein," said the other, "but you can tell better as I can, so den I knocks."

The mistress of the house came to the door.—Here was a dilemma. At length Hans spoke.

"Is de smit mitin?"

"Sir?" said the woman.

"Is de smit mitin?"

"I don't understand you," said the woman.—Hans then blowed out, "Vot, de debil, I say is de smit mitin?"

The other Dutchman, perceiving that the woman could not understand Hans, stepped up, and pushing him aside, said:

"Led me come up what can say somedings. Is de blacksmit shop in the house?"

A Rebel Commission.

The ex Rebels had another meeting on Saturday, and appointed Judge Campbell, General J. R. Anderson (he of the Tredegar Works), N. P. Tyler (of the *Enquirer*), D. Burr (of the City Council), and H. W. Thor[...]ley, to visit Extra Billy Smith and endeavor to get him to make terms with Mr. Lincoln, and co[...]me back to Richmond. These representatives [...] sent the men who have tried to destroy the Union for four years; men who led the people and instigated the many damnable deeds that it makes one sick to recall to memory! They clung to the idea until all hope was gone, and they found themselves in our possession, and now they want to preserve the money they have made off the Rebellion, and secure for political power. They are still our enemies; still deem slavery a Christian institution; still look upon us as their hated conquerors, and upon themselves as innocent victims; but the love of wealth comes in, and they perjure themselves by taking the oath of allegiance. Talk to one of them five minutes, and he will betray himself every other sentence.

ANOTHER CLASS OF CITIZENS.

Then there is another set of Union men, we have been r[...]cked and persecuted for four years. They are not so forward to make a display, but are none the less earnest and loyal. They have held several meetings, and to-morrow will hold another. Ex Solicitor Whiting, of the War Department, is here counselling with them, and will meet them to-morrow morning.—*Richmond Correspondent Philadelphia Enquirer.*

For the Standard.

On President Lincoln's Death.

BY R. M.

Lincoln, our noble President, is dead!
Dead—let the nation mourn.
Eternal glories cluster round his head,
For him 'tis glory's morn.

Our glorious President is gone, for aye,
Killed by a murderer's hand;
His blessed spirit shines in heaven's bright day,
While sorrow fills the land.

Oh! doubly cruel was the traitorous lead,
And doubly bright the blood,
That left his heart while his pure spirit fled
To its final rest with God.

What honored title shall his memory crown?
What monument be built
To tell to other worlds his great renown,
And his assassin's guilt?

His monumental stone is in our souls,
His memory's sacred shrine,
Shall last while the eternal ocean rolls
Mingling with the divine.

PAGE'S STATION, N. C., April 17, 1865.

Lamartine on the Religion of Revolutionary Men.

I know—I sigh when I think of it—that hither to the French people have been the least religious of all the nations of Europe. Is it because the idea of God—which arises from all the evidences of nature, and from the depth of reflection—being the profoundest and weightiest idea of which human intelligence is capable, and the French mind being the most rapid, but the most superficial, the lightest, the most unreflective of all European races, this mind has not the force and severity necessary to carry far and long the greatest conception of the human understanding?

Is it because our governments have always taken upon themselves to think for us? Is it because we are and have been a military people, a soldier nation, led by kings, heroes, and ambitious men, from battle field to battle-field, making conquests and never keeping them, ravaging, dazzling, charming, and corrupting Europe; and bringing home the manners, vices, bravery, lightness, and impiety of the camp to the fireside of the people?

I know not, but certain it is that the nation has an immense progress to make in serious thought if she wishes to be free. If we look at the characters, compared as regards religious sentiments, of the great nations of Europe, America, even Asia, the advantage is not for us. The great men of our country live and die, forgetting completely the only idea for which it is worth living and dying; they live and die looking at the spectator, or at most at posterity.

Open the history of America, the history of England, and the history of France; read the great lives, the great deaths, the martyrdoms, the great words at the hour when the ruling thought of life reveals itself in the last words of dying—and compare.

Washington and Franklin fought, spoke, suffered, always in the name of God, for whom they acted; and the Liberator of America died confiding to God the liberty of the people and his own soul.

Sydney, the young martyr of patriotism, guilty of nothing but impatience, and who died to expatiate his country's dream of liberty, said to his jailor: "I rejoice that I die innocent towards the king, but a victim resigned to the King on High, to whom all life is due."

The republicans of Cromwell only sought the way of God even in the field of battle. Their politics were their faith their reign a prayer, their death a psalm. One hears, sees, feels that God was in all the movements of these great people.

But cross the sea, traverse La Mancha, come to our times, open our annals, and listen to the last words of the great political actors of the drama of our liberty. One would think that God was eclipsed from the soul, that his name was unknown in the language. History will have the air of an atheist when she recounts to posterity these annihilations, rather than deaths of celebrated men in the greatest year of France! The victims only have a God; the tribune and lictors have none.

Look at Mirabeau on the bed of death. "Crown me with flowers," said he, "intoxicate me with perfumes, let me die to the sound of 'delicious music!" Not a word of God or of his soul. Sensual philosopher, he desired only supreme sensualism, a last voluptuousness in his agony.

Contemplate Madam Roland, the strong-hearted woman of the Revolution, on the cart that conveyed her to death. She looked contemptuously on the besotted people who killed their prophets and sybils. Not a glance towards heaven! Only one word for the earth she was quitting—"O Liberty!"

Approach the dungeon door of the Girondins. Their last night is a banquet; the only hymn, the Marseillaise!

Follow Camille Desmoulins to his execution. A cool and indecent pleasantry at the trial, and a long imprecation on the road to the guillotine, were the two last thoughts of this dying man on his way to the last tribunal.

Hear Danton on the platform of the scaffold, at a distance of a line from God and eternity. "I have had a good time of it; let me go to sleep." Then to the executioner, "you will show my head to the people—it is worth the trouble!" His faith, annihilation; his last sigh vanity. Behold the Frenchman of this latter age!

What must one think of the religious sentiments of a free people whose great figures seem thus to march in procession to annihilation, and to whom that terrible minister, death itself recalls neither the threatenings nor promises of God!

The republic of these men without a God has quickly been stranded. The liberty won by so much heroism and so much genius has not found in France a conscience to shelter it, a God to avenge it, a people to defend it against the atheism which has been called glory. All ended in a soldier and some apostate republicans travestied into courtiers. An atheistic republicanism cannot be heretic. When you terrify it, it bends; when you would buy it, it sells itself. Who would take any heed? The people ungrateful and God non-existent! So finish atheist revolutions.

Rejoicings over the Recent Victories.

ALBANY.

Special Despatch to the Inquirer:

ALBANY, April 11.—An immense meeting in behalf of the United States Christian Commission was held last evening, in Tweddle Hall. His Excellency, Governor Fenton, presided. Prayer was offered by the venerable William B. Sprague, D. D. Addresses were delivered by Governor Fenton, Ex-Governor Pollock, of Pennsylvania, the gallant Major General Robinson, who lost a leg at Spottsylvania Court House, Hon. Ira Harris, United States Senator from New York, and George H Stuart, of Philadelphia. The wildest enthusiasm prevailed, and frequent references were made to the late glorious victories. A collection, amounting to several thousand dollars, was taken up. Messrs. Pollock and Stuart, of Philadelphia, also addressed the State Legislature, by invitation, in congratulation over the late great victories.

NASHVILLE.

NASHVILLE, April 10.—The surrender of Lee's army was received with great demonstrations of joy. The Senate and House adjourned, and business was generally suspended, and there are displays of flags, banners and transparencies, and illuminations throughout the city.

LOUISVILLE.

LOUISVILLE, April 10.—The city is decorated with flags to day in honor of Lee's surrender. A salute of 200 guns was fired.

A Fighting Turk.

"Pierce Pungent," in the New York *News*, tells the following good story: "During the operations of the allies in the Crimea, it was resolved to carry the water in from a beautiful spring of the finest Croton to the camp. Leather pipes or hose were employed: while the water was being supplied, the minaret sounded to prayer, and one of the Turkish soldiers immediately went flop on his knees to praise Allah! Unfortunately he went down right upon the hose, and his weight consequently stopped the current of that 'first of elements,' as Pindar calls water in his Olympaid.

'Get up,' cried an English soldier. '*Voulez vous avoir la bonte, mon cher, Monsier le Turque*,' cried a Frenchman, with native politeness, to 'git up.'

'That ain't the way to make a Turk move,' cried another; 'this is the dodge.' So saying, he knocked his turban off. Still the pious Mussulman went on with his devotions.

'I'll make him stir his trumps,' said another Englishman, giving him a remarkably smart kick. To the wonder of all, still, the unturbaned, well kicked follower of the prophet went praying on as though he was a forty horse parson.

'Hoot way, mon—I'll show you how we serve obstinate folk at auld Reekie,' quietly observed a Scotchman; he was, however, prevented for the Turk, having finished his '*Allah vis en allah*,' rose and began to take off his coat, then to roll up his sleeves, and then to bedew his palms with saliva, and then to put himself in the most approved boxing attitude, *a la* Yankee Sullivan.

He then advanced in true Tom Hyer style to the Englishman who had kicked him on the lumbar region. 'A ring! a ring!' shouted the soldiers and sailors, perfectly astonished to see a Turk such an adept in the fistic art.

The Englishman, nothing loth to have a bit of fun with a Turk of such a truly John Bull state of mind, set to work, but found he had met his master—in five minutes he had received his *quantum suff.* As the Turk coolly replaced his coat and turban, he turned round and said to the admiring bystanders, in the pure brogue "Bad luck to ye, ye spalpeens; when ye're afther kicking a Turk, I'd advise ye the next time to jist be sure he's not an Irishman.'

The mystery was solved—our Turk was a Tipperary man!

THE NATION MOURNS ITS LOSS.

The Philadelphia Inquirer.

PRICE TWO CENTS. PHILADELPHIA, THURSDAY, APRIL 20, 1865. PRICE TWO CENTS.

FUNERAL OF ABRAHAM LINCOLN!

Our National Grief!

SOLEMN SCENES AT WASHINGTON

Capital Draped in Mourning!

FUNERAL SERVICES AT THE WHITE HOUSE.

Mournful and Impressive Ceremonies

BISHOP SIMPSON'S OPENING PRAYER.

Eulogy by Rev. Dr. Gurley.

NOBLE TRIBUTE TO OUR LATE PRESIDENT.

Solemn March to the Capitol!

AN IMPOSING SCENE!

Military and Civic Procession.

PRESIDENT JOHNSON AND CABINET.

Diplomatique Corps in Attendance.

Philadelphia Firemen Present.

THE DELEGATIONS FROM THE NORTHERN STATES.

Arrival of the Cortege at the Capitol.

THE REMAINS IN STATE IN THE ROTUNDA.

[SPECIAL DESPATCHES TO THE INQUIRER.]

WASHINGTON, April 19.

Our National Grief.

To-day Washington, the heart of the nation, bows in sorrow. The broad, bright April sun moves upward to the zenith and pours his genial beams down upon a stricken capital and a weeping nation. Nature wears a smiling face, but how marked the contrast between the outward sunshine and the great gloom which enshrouds every loyal heart throughout the land.

Abraham Lincoln dead! Abraham Lincoln, the beloved President, the noble ruler, the man whose heart was large enough to take in the sufferings of the whole human family, the man whose sympathies were ever extended to all in distress, from the most exalted to the humblest. Abraham Lincoln, the patriot, who through four years of war has borne aloft the glorious Stars and Stripes, and vowed that they should never be lowered, that they should again float over a reunited people, *is dead! dead by an assassin's hand*, and, to-day, as one man, one heart, at this hour his weeping countrymen assemble to do reverence to his remains as they pass from the Presidential mansion to the rotunda of the shrouded capitol. Oh! how the bosom swells with grief unutterable! How words find no lips to speak them! How the tears are choked in their channels, and how unforgiving is the indignation, the wrath, that sleeps in every breast and burns in every eye! Our country has never known such a day as this. When Sumter was attacked, and our fathers' flag was lowered before treason, men wept; but their tears were the rain drops preceding the storm-flood which was to sweep Rebellion ultimately from existence.

This day another feeling prevails, a feeling of grief for the departed nobleman who brought us through scenes of tribulation to the borders of the promised land, with our standard unsullied and resplendent with victory. Is it a wonder that Washington mourns to-day; that every hamlet, village, town and city in the land, at this hour puts on the emblems of sorrow, and bows down in the dust before the terrible dispensation which an All-wise Providence has permitted to visit us in the moment of triumph?

On every hand are evidences of the mighty shadow which has stalked in between our joys and our hopes, and darkened them with the veil of night. It is hard to realize the fearful fact that Mr. LINCOLN—Father ABRAHAM, as we delighted to call him—has been ruthlessly snatched from us and consigned to the grave. But the sound of the drum, the minute guns, the sad faces of men, women and children, gathered along Pennsylvania avenue, all tell us the harrowing truth.

At 11 o'clock those invited to attend the funeral ceremonies in the White House began to assemble, while all the avenues leading to it were crowded with the military forming for procession, and the sidewalks were blockaded with an anxious and orderly multitude of spectators.

The Scenes at the White House.

Long before 10 A. M. the avenue from the

See Last Column.

THE FUNERAL CAR OF PRESIDENT LINCOLN.

THE COFFIN.

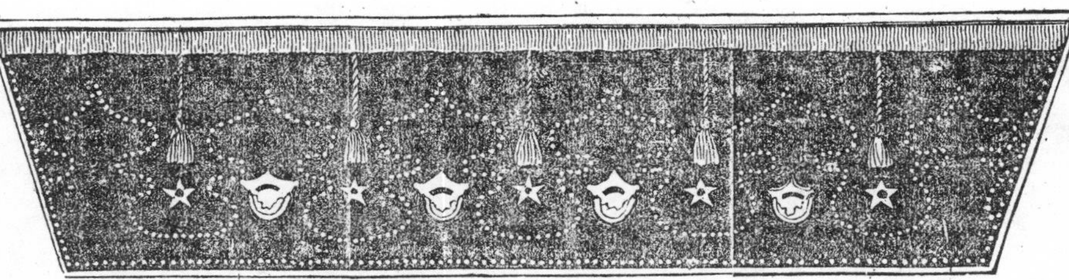

The Coffin.

The coffin used to convey to their last resting place the mortal remains of our late beloved Chief Magistrate, is of the most magnificent description. Its cost was between one thousand and two thousand dollars, and it is probably the handsomest ever constructed in this country. It is of mahogany, lined with lead, and covered with black cloth, of the richest and most expensive quality, heavily fringed with silver, with four silver medallions on each side, in which are set the handles. The outside of the coffin is festooned with massive silver tacks, representing drapery, in each fold of which there is a silver star, and the outer edges are adorned with silver braid, with five tassels, five inches in length, each side having upon it four massive handles, and at the head and foot there are stars. Upon the top there is a row of silver tacks, extending the entire length on both sides, about two inches from the edge. Upon the centre is a silver plate, encircled by a shield, formed also of silver tacks, and the face lid and top are united with five silver stars. The inside of the face lid is raised with white satin, the centre piece being trimmed with black and white silk braid, fastened at each corner with four silver stars. The remainder of the inside of the coffin is lined with box-plaited satin, the pillow and lower surface being of fine white silk, and the whole being encircled with chenille as in fringe. The upper third of the coffin, lined with rich white satin, was thrown back, so as to reveal the head and bust. Upon the foot of the coffin was placed a magnificent anchor, composed of flowers, which was forwarded from New York. Upon the middle was a bouquet of evergreens and leaves, upon which rested a single white japonica, the contribution of a delegation from California. Upon the floor of the bier around the coffin was a heavy wreath of white japonicas and roses.

The Funeral Car.

The funeral car was also a magnificent affair. It was built on a hearse body, the extreme length of which was fourteen feet. The body was covered with black cloth of the richest quality, from which hung large festoons of cloth on the sides and ends, gathered and fastened by large rosettes of black and white satin, over bows of black and white velvet. The bed of the car on which rested the coffin, was eight feet from the ground, in order to enable the vast crowds to have a full view of the coffin. Over this rose the canopy, the supports of which were draped with black cloth and velvet. The top of the car was very handsomely decorated with plumes, and was drawn by eight splendid horses, each led by a groom.

The Catafalque.

The catafalque upon which the coffin containing the remains of the late President was placed, was eleven feet high, sixteen feet long and ten feet wide, the coffin resting on a surface about three feet from the floor, surrounded with a wreath of evergreens and japonicas. From the four corners of the surface upon which the coffin rests, rose firm posts, some six feet in height, which were surmounted by a curved canopy, extending one foot over either end. The inside, or ceiling of this canopy, was composed of white fluted silk or satin. The top was covered with the finest quality of black alpaca, and graceful festoons of the same rich material bordered it, while heavy curtains, also formed of black alpaca, were looped back to the posts. The surface of the dais or platform was covered with black broad-cloth, and was bordered with a heavy black silk fringe and festoons of alpaca, confined with rosettes of the same fabric.

PROCLAMATION BY GOVERNOR CURTIN.

HARRISBURG, April 19.—The following highly important despatch was received by Governor Curtin this morning:—

WASHINGTON, April 19.—To his Excellency, Governor A. G. Curtin:—The remains of the late President, Abraham Lincoln, will leave Washington on Friday morning at eight o'clock, to go by way of Baltimore to Harrisburg, and thence to Philadelphia and New York by the time table, as arranged. The remains will reach Harrisburg at eight P. M. (Friday), and leave at twelve noon, on Saturday, for Philadelphia, where they will remain until four o'clock on Monday morning, and then be conveyed to New York.

A copy of the time table and programme will be forwarded to you to-morrow. You are respectfully invited to meet the remains with your staff, at such point as you may designate to this Department, and accompany them so far as you may be pleased to go. You will please signify to this Department by telegraph where you will join the remains; whether you will take charge of them at Harrisburg; where you will have them placed while they remain at the capital of your State, and what honors you desire to pay while there. By order of the Secretary of War. E. D. TOWNSEND, Brigadier-General A. A. G.

In reply to the above intelligence, His Excellency immediately despatched as follows:—

HARRISBURG, April 19, 1865.—To Brigadier-General Townsend, War Department:—I propose to take charge of the remains at the line of the State, and to accompany them till they leave the State. I will meet them at the border, at Harrisburg. They will be placed in the Capitol. All the military and civil honors that can be arranged will be shown. Measures are being taken for that purpose. I will send another despatch. A. G. CURTIN.

In the name of and by the authority of the Commonwealth of Pennsylvania, ANDREW G. CURTIN, Governor of the said Commonwealth,

A Proclamation.

The remains of the murdered patriot, Abraham Lincoln, President of the United States, will arrive in the State on Friday evening next, on their way to the place of interment in Illinois. They will come from Baltimore to Harrisburg; thence they will, on Saturday, be conveyed to Philadelphia, and thence, on Monday morning, to New York. I shall meet them at the State line, and take charge of them while in the Commonwealth. I recommend that all business be suspended during their passage through the State. Local authorities and people everywhere join the State authorities heartily in paying honor to the memory of the martyred statesman who has fallen a victim to the savage treason of assassins. By the Governor, A. G. CURTIN.

ELY SLIFER, Sec'y of the Commonwealth.

The President's Body Coming to Philadelphia.

Special Despatch to the Inquirer.

WASHINGTON, April 19.—It has been definitely settled that the remains of our late Chief Magistrate will pass through Philadelphia *en route* for Springfield. This we have on the best authority. It is also stated that the idea of passing through New York has been abandoned.

Capitol to the White House commenced to fill up with people, and by 10·30 it was almost impossible to wend one's way to the White House. The soldiers kept an open space in the avenue, and through it we passed to the White House, to which a few newspaper men were admitted, THE INQUIRER being the only Philadelphia paper having a correspondent.

None were admitted except by these cards, which were inscribed as follows:—

GREEN ROOM.
ADMIT THE BEARER TO THE
THE 19TH OF APRIL, 1865.

Upon entering we found the pall bearers in the reception room awaiting the arrival of those who were to participate in the sad rites. In the centre of the east room was the catafalque.

Around the coffin was a large wreath of white camelias, orange blossoms and evergreens. At the feet was a beautiful anchor, of choicest flowers, sent by Hon. Mrs. Sperry, of Connecticut; at the head a cross of white camelias, and the delicate white exotics which, with a basket of flowers, was the present of Mrs. J. H. Orne, of Philadelphia. A number of wreaths were scattered around in profusion.

Around the room steps had been raised gradually in height from the centre, so that one standing upon the outside could see over the heads of those in front.

Upon the centre, east side of the catafalque, was the

President and Cabinet.

Upon their right was the

Diplomatic Corps,
The Assistant Secretaries,
Governors of States and Territories,
The Judiciary,
The Army and Navy,
The New York Delegation.
Pall Bearers.

Upon the left of the President were the

Supreme Court, then
The Senate,
Members of the House of Representatives,
Illinois and Kentucky Delegation,
The Clergy,
City Authorities.

Upon the west side were the Press; upon the south side, and at the foot of the catafalque were the family of Mr. Lincoln.

The guard of honor, consisting of Major-Gen. Hunter and Brigadier-General Dyer, marched in silence to and fro. The lilies, the orange blossoms and the choicest of flowers that decked the corpse filled the room with the sweetest fragrance. The windows shrouded with crape kept out the light, and made the gloom that all felt seem like being in a living tomb!

The echoes of the funeral dirges in the distance seemed like the terrible murmur of the avenging God's wrath at the impiety of the damning crime that brought us all here as mourners. As the various delegations came in they quietly took the places assigned them. Not a word was spoken loudly. Whispers faint, as though the loved one was sleeping after his weary troubles and all feared to wake him, were the only noises that marred the death-like stillness of the room, which had been the scene of two similar services. First, over the body of William Henry Harrison, then over the gallant General Zachary Taylor, now over Mr. Lincoln, loved more than any man since the days of Washington.

The exceeding great grief of Mrs. Lincoln was such that she was unable to be present at the services, and the chairs for herself and her sons were vacant.

The mourners present were:—

Hon. J. G. Nicolay, the President's Confidential Secretary, and his colleague, Major John Hay.

Mr. N. W. Edwards and Mr. C. M. Smith, brothers-in-law of Mrs. Lincoln.

Dr. L. Beecher Todd, of Lexington, Ky.

General J. B. S. Todd, of Dacotah, cousins of Mrs. Lincoln.

Upon the left of President Johnson was Ex-Senator P. King, of New York; and upon his right Hannibal Hamlin, Ex-Vice President.

Behind Mr. King was Mr. Stanton.

Behind the President was Secretary McCulloch.

Behind Mr. Hamlin were Chief Justice Chase and Secretaries Welles, Dennison, Speed and Usher.

At twelve o'clock the room was filled, the President and Cabinet having entered last. The profound silence was broken by the President and Hon. Hannibal Hamlin stepping to the coffin, and with a pale and solemn look gazed for a few moments upon the corpse and then turned and again occupied their places in front.

Rev. Mr. Gurley then announced the order of exercises, which were opened by Rev. Dr. Hall reading the funeral service of the Episcopal Church, commencing "I am the resurrection and the life, saith the Lord."

Bishop Simpson's Prayer.

The opening prayer was made by Bishop Matthew Simpson, D. D., Methodist Episcopal, who in the course of it said that in the hands of God were the issues of life and death. Our sins had called for his wrath to descend upon us as individuals and as a community. For the sake of our blessed Redeemer forgiveness was asked for all our transgressions, and that all our iniquities may be washed away, while we bow under this sad bereavement which has caused a wide-spread gloom not only in this circle but over the entire land. An invocation was made that we might all submit to God's holy will. Thanks were returned for the gift of such a man as our Heavenly Father had just taken from us, and for the many virtues which distinguished all his transactions; for the integrity, honesty and transparency of character bestowed upon him, and for having given him counsellors to guide our nation through perils of unprecedented sorrow.

He was permitted to live to behold the breaking of the clouds which overhung our national sky, and the disintegration of the Rebellion. Going up the mount he beheld the land of promise, with its beauty and happiness, and the glorious destiny reserved for us as a nation. Thanks were also returned that his arm was strengthened, and wisdom and firmness given to his heart to pen a declaration of emancipation, by which were broken the chains of millions of the human race. God be thanked, the assassin who struck down the Chief Magistrate had not the hand to again bind the suffering and oppressed. The name of the beloved dead would ever be identified with all that is great and glorious with humanity on earth. God grant that all who stand here intrusted with the administration of public affairs may have the power, strength and wisdom to complete the work of his servant so gloriously begun, and may the successor of the deceased President not bear the sword in vain.

God grant that strength may be given to him, and to our military, to perfect victory, and to complete the contest now nearly closed. May the spirit of rebellion soon pass away. May the last vestige of slavery, which caused the Rebel-

Continued on the Eighth Page.

THE NATION MOURNS ITS LOSS.

THE DAILY MORNING CHRONICLE.

Office—CHRONICLE BUILDING.
406 Ninth Street west, between E and F.

TERMS OF SUBSCRIPTION.
Thirty Cents per week, payable to the carriers.
Mailed to subscribers out of the city, Ten Dollars per annum, and in proportion for a shorter period.
Payment to be invariably in advance.
No mail subscriptions received for a shorter period than Three Months.
RATES OF ADVERTISING.—One square, one insertion, $1 00; for all subsequent insertions, half price. Six lines, Nonpareil measure, or less, constitute a square.
City Items, 25 cents a line.
Special Notices, 20 cents a line for the first insertion; for all subsequent insertions, half price.

Daily Morning Chronicle.

VOLUME III. WASHINGTON, THURSDAY MORNING, APRIL 20, 1865. NUMBER 144.

THE SUNDAY MORNING CHRONICLE.
A Literary and Political Journal.
TERMS OF SUBSCRIPTION.
THREE DOLLARS A YEAR, invariably in advance and in proportion for any shorter period of not less than THREE MONTHS. Single copies FIVE CENTS.

THE WEEKLY CHRONICLE,
ISSUED EVERY SATURDAY.
THREE DOLLARS PER ANNUM. Two DOLLARS for SIX MONTHS. No subscription received for less than SIX MONTHS, except from soldiers, for whom the WEEKLY CHRONICLE will be sent to any address for THREE MONTHS, for ONE DOLLAR.

THE OBSEQUIES

THE CEREMONIES IN THE PRESIDENTIAL MANSION.

THE DISTINGUISHED CROWD IN ATTENDANCE.

THE ORATION AND PRAYERS

AN IMMENSE PROCESSION.

SPLENDID MILITARY DISPLAY.

DELEGATIONS FROM A DISTANCE.

SERVICES AT THE CAPITOL.

A GUARD OF HONOR.

THE REMAINS LYING IN STATE.

THE PUBLIC ADMITTED TO THE CAPITOL TO-DAY.

Of all the memorable days in the annals of the United States, none will be remembered by the present generation, or read of in history by those who come after us with stronger feelings of regret and pride, than yesterday; regret at the distressing manner of the death of so great and good a benefactor of his country, and pride in the ample demonstrations of respect and gratitude for his services.

The brief time which had elapsed since the dire calamity bereft the nation of its chosen head, all classes of a benefactor, and the misguided people of the South of their most merciful friend, prevented the extended preparations and the universal attendance from all sections of the country, which would otherwise have been certain. All that could be present upon such short notice were here to manifest their grief and participate in paying the last sad tribute of respect to him whom the people, without distinction of party, so much loved.

At an early hour yesterday morning, every street and avenue leading from the Capitol to the President's Mansion, was alive with people. The associations which had made arrangements to join in the procession were formed between nine and ten o'clock. The clerks of the several departments also gathered together at about the same hour. Before noon, Pennsylvania avenue was crowded as it had never been. Nearly every house in the city was closed, and all the inmates—proprietors, servants, and lodgers—went forth to pay their tribute of respect and veneration to Abraham Lincoln, the best friend of the people, and the latest and greatest President of the United States. By the time the procession was formed—at two o'clock—the crowd of spectators had gathered upon the sidewalks three or four deep, and another line was formed upon the street.

Ceremonies at the East Room.

The Treasury Department was besieged at nine o'clock, by applicants for entry, and long before ten, Lafayette Square and that portion of the avenue which faces the Executive Mansion presented a mass of faces which it passed the powers of reportorial arithmetic to estimate or number.

At ten o'clock we entered the East Room, where lay Abraham Lincoln, on the same catafalco, and in the same coffin we have already described. This room, the same in which Harrison and Taylor lay in state, was far more artistically prepared for the coming ceremonies. The plates of its four large mirrors were covered with white crape, while their frames were hidden by the falling folds of a black drapery similar to that which covered the blood-red damascene and white lace curtains of the windows. The Venetian shutters being partly closed, the rich red of the walls stained the partially admitted light already toned down by the heavy masses of black, and through the dark shadows of the catafalco the light seemed to struggle in dim religious rays that stole rather than leaped back from the silver ornaments of the coffin and the shrouded surfaces of the polished mirrors.

Silent as statues of grim barons shrined in Gothic cathedral, were the three watchers with the great dead President—Major General Hunter, Brigadier General Dyer, and Captains Nesmith and Dewsen, of General Hardin's staff. They stirred but little, except General Hunter, who occasionally strode backward and forward by the head of the coffin. Sometimes halting and resting his gauntleted hand on a corner of the catafalco, he would stand in thought for a few minutes, and again resume his slow and silent strides.

The peculiar light, the severe bearing of the armed officers, the oppressive colors and the awful structure in the middle of the room, created a feeling of indescribable awe. There was something strange, too, in finding the body of Abraham Lincoln, the very apostle of peace, the dispenser of mercy, guarded by men of war, with a solemn severity that forced upon the mind the recollection of the vast power of armed men he wielded to effect his beneficent purposes.

What added greatly to the awing effect of the room, was a series of seats or steps which were covered with black, and partitioned off, as it were, with thin white lines, descended from the northern, eastern, and southern side of the room, to about five feet of the base of the black temple of death placed in the centre of the room. Along the western side of these were placed fifteen chairs, covered with black, and ranged along the wall for the use of the members of the Press.

The series of seats or steps partitioned off by lines of white, were reserved for the various groups expected, by a card being laid on each with writing, stating the use for which it was intended.

The northwestern corner was reserved for the pall bearers; next, to the eastward, was the partition ticketed for the New York delegation; next came that of the Army and Navy, then that of the Judiciary, and behind these, officers of the Sanitary and Christian Commissions; next were stationed Governors of various States and Territories, Heads of Bureaus, Assistant Secretaries, then the Diplomatic Corps, beside which were the President and Cabinet, and alongside of these stood the Senators, beyond which were members of the House of Representatives, clergymen from all parts of the United States, and the city authorities.

The first to enter the room were the ministers of religion, among which were clergymen of all denominations, and from every State in the Union.

New York Delegation.

The New York delegation next entered. It was composed of

Simeon Draper,	Moses H. Grinnell,
General Strong,	Jonathan Sturges,
Moses Taylor,	Charles P. Daley,
James Brown,	Edwards Pierpont,
John Jacob Astor,	William M. Evarts,
Samuel Sloane,	Denning Duer,
William E. Dodge,	Charles H. Russell,
S. Blatchford.	

It must certainly be admitted that New York could scarce do more than send her first citizens. Added to those already named, the following gentlemen appeared as a peculiar delegation from the New York Chamber of Commerce:

Carl H. Waller,	Hon. A. M. Bradford,
William Barton,	William Vermilye,
F. S. Winston,	Hiram Walbridge,
William Borden,	William Orton,
James M. Green,	Alderman Bryce,
Alderman Norton,	Councillor Lent,
Councillor Cost,	Councillor Peterson,
Councillor Brady,	Thomas Levy,
General Strong.	

Among the Governors of States, we could see in the allotted partition—

Fenton, New York,	Andrew, Massachusetts,
Oglesby, Illinois,	Brough, Ohio,
Stone, Iowa,	Buckingham, Ky.,
Parker, New Jersey,	Pierpoint, Virginia.

Lieutenant Governor Cox, of Maryland, was also present, Governor Bradford being absent on account of illness.

There were many Senators present, but the position in which we were placed did not allow us to see more than a few. These were Senators Foster, Ramsey, Harris, Chandler, Cowan, Sumner, McDougal, Saulsbury, Wade, Johnson, Creswell, Williams, Norton, Stewart, Nye, Conness, and Collamer.

Among the members of the lower House, we noticed Speaker Colfax. There were so many present that our crowded columns cannot find space for them all.

Beside President Johnston stood the Hon. Preston King and ex-Vice President Hamlin.

The members and executive officers of the United States Sanitary Commission attended the ceremonies at the Executive Mansion in a body, the following named gentlemen being present:

Rev. H. W. Bellows, D. D.; C. R. Agnew, M. D.; Professor Wolcott Gibbs; Elisha Harris, M. D.; Rev. Dr. Hill, President Harvard College; E. B. Elliott, Esq.; John Y. Culyer, Esq.; J. B. Abbott, Esq.; M. P. Barry, Esq.; George J. Sicard, Esq.; George T. Strong, Esq.; Horace Binney, Esq.; C. J. Stille, Esq.; J. Foster Jenkins, M. D.; J. S. Newberry, M. D.; F. N. Knapp, Esq.; John S. Blatchford, Esq.; John Bowne, Esq.; Darius Forbes, Esq.; Dr. J. Nichols.

The Cabinet.

All these various groups were nearly placed in their appointed sections, when the Cabinet and the Chief Justice of the United States entered with the new President. As the various secretaries filed in, all eyes were turned upon them, and when the last had entered, a slight but perceptible stir ran through the audience, showing that the very absence of him who had been selected as the fellow victim of the dead man in the room, brought him the more vividly back to the memory of those present; and as the courtly Corps Diplomatique entered and looked at the assembly, one could see that they felt there was nothing wanting but himself alone.

The Metropolitan Police, under Superintendent A. C. Richards, were arranged along each side of the procession, and rendered efficient service in keeping the avenue clear of the great crowds who had congregated to witness the passage of the funeral procession.

General Officers.

Lieutenant General Grant sat about five feet from the base of the catafalco; near him were Admirals Farragut and Goldsborough, and at the other end of the room we noticed Major General Hitchcok.

Who Were Not Present.

The expected delegation from Springfield did not arrive in time to take part in the ceremonies, and as with them were expected many of Mr. Lincoln's immediate relatives, their failure to arrive caused much disappointment. As it was, there were present of Mr. Lincoln's family two of his brothers-in-law, R. M. W. Edwards and C. M. Smith; also, two cousins, Dr. L. Beecher Todd, of Lexington, Kentucky, and General B. S. Todd, of Dacotah.

Mr. Lincoln's Family.

Mrs. Lincoln did not enter the East Room, being too ill from nervous prostration and an incipient fever, brought on by the awful excitement and sorrow to which she has been subjected. She never leaves her room, in which she has the medical attendance of Dr. Stone, as well as that of Dr. Todd.

The two sons of Mr. Lincoln, Master Thaddeus and Robert Lincoln, Esq., both attended; but it was easy to see that it required all the resolution the latter could summon to master the grief that agitated him.

Ladies Present.

There were but seven ladies present in the East Room—Mrs. Sprague, Mrs. Usher, Mrs. Stanton, Mrs. Welles, Miss Hattie Chase, and Mrs. Denison and daughter.

Officiating Clergy.

The officiating clergy were Dr. Hall, of the Episcopal Church of the Epiphany, who read the burial service of his Church; Bishop Simpson, of the Methodist Episcopal Church; Dr. Gurley, who pronounced the funeral address, and Dr. Gray, Chaplain of the Senate, who closed the services in the East Room with a short, fervent, and eloquent prayer.

The Corps Diplomatique.

All the representatives of foreign governments, ambassadors, secretaries, and *attachés* were present, in full court costume, and their high collared and heavy gilt coats, their vests decorated with various orders, rendered them a glittering group in an assemblage dressed in sombre black.

The Assemblage.

Having described in detail the various groups that successively entered the room, it only remains, ere detailing the ceremonies, to convey some idea of the effect produced by the room when filled with such an assemblage, as contrasted with its solemn loneliness when we first entered it.

There were in all about six hundred persons in the room. Of these six hundred hardly fifty but were known as leading men of the country either in commerce, laws, ethics, literature, statesmanship, or in practical generalship on sanguinary fields. One half of them will certainly leave names likely to linger long on the pages of American history. Diplomacy, arts, arms, science, all of to-day, all of living interest, a part of the breathing, throbbing age, were there; and as these men stood up, and the ambassadors leaned forth to scan the scene, no eye that dropped upon the stilled face in the coffin but was moistened.

One of the most touching tributes of love and affection, so generally paid by many of the citizens of Washington to the mortal remains of the noblest of our Chief Magistrates since the days of Washington, was that by Mrs. A. Jardin, corner of Eighteenth and M streets, who yesterday morning brought a most beautiful wreath of white rosebuds and other choice flowers and evergreens to the White House, and placed it on the coffin of the deceased at the Presidential Mansion.

The Ceremonies.

When all who were priveleged to enter had taken their assigned positions, the Rev. Dr. Hall read the following;

Lord, let me know my end, and the number of my days; that I may be certified how long I have to live.

Behold, thou hast made my days as it were a span long, and mine age is even as nothing in respect of Thee; and verily every man living is altogether vanity.

For man walketh in a vain shadow and disquieth himself in vain; he heapeth up riches and cannot tell who shall gather them.

And now, Lord, what is my hope? Truly my hope is even in Thee.

Deliver me from all my offences; and make me not a rebuke unto the foolish.

When thou with rebukes dost chasten man for sin, thou makest his beauty to consume away, like as it were a moth fretting a garment: every man is therefore but vanity.

Hear my prayer, O Lord, and with thine ears consider my calling; hold not thy peace at my tears:

For I am a stranger with thee, and a sojourner, as all my fathers were.

O spare me a little, that I may recover my strength, before I go hence, and be no more seen.

Lord, thou hast been our refuge, from one generation to another.

Before the mountains were brought forth, or ever the earth and the world were made, thou art God from everlasting, and world without end.

Thou turnest man to destruction; again Thou sayest, Come again, ye children of men.

For a thousand years in Thy sight are but as yesterday; seeing that it is past as a watch in the night.

As soon as Thou scatterest them they are even as asleep, and fade away suddenly like the grass.

In the morning it is green, and groweth up; but in the evening it is cut down, dried up, and withered.

For we consume away in Thy displeasure; and are afraid at Thy wrathful indignation.

Thou has set our misdeeds before Thee; and our secret sins in the light of Thy countenance.

For when thou art angry, all our days are gone; we bring our years to an end, as it were a tale that is told.

The days of our age are threescore years and ten; and though men be so strong that they come to fourscore years, yet is their strength but labor and sorrow; so soon passeth it away and we are gone.

So teach us to number our days, that we may apply our hearts unto wisdom.

Glory be to the Father, and to the Son, and to the Holy Ghost!

As it was in the beginning, is now, and ever shall be, world without end. Amen.

At the conclusion of the Psalm, Bishop Simpson offered the following

Prayer.

Almighty God, our Heavenly Father, as with smitten and suffering hearts we come into Thy presence, we pray, in the name of our blessed Redeemer, that Thou wouldst pour upon us Thy Holy Spirit, that all our thoughts and acts may be acceptable in Thy sight. We adore Thee for all Thy glorious perfections. We praise Thee for the revelation which Thou hast given us in Thy works and in Thy Word. By Thee all worlds exist. All beings live through Thee. Thou raisest up kingdoms and empires, and castest them down. By Thee kings reign and princes decree righteousness. In Thy hand are the issues of life and death. We confess before Thee the magnitude of our sins and transgressions, both as individuals and as a nation. We implore Thy mercy for the sake of our Redeemer. Forgive us all our iniquities. If it please Thee, remove Thy chastening hand from us, and, though we be unworthy, turn away from us Thine anger, and let the light of Thy countenance again shine upon us.

At this solemn hour, as we mourn for the death of our President, who was stricken down by the hand of an assassin, grant us also the grace to bow in submission to thy holy will. May we recognize thy hand high above all human agencies, and thy power as controlling all events, so that the wrath of man shall praise Thee, and that the remainder of wrath thou wilt restrain. Humbled under the suffering we have endured and the great afflictions through which we have passed, may we not be called upon to offer other sacrifices. May the lives of all our officers, both civil and military, be guarded by Thee; and let no violent hand fall upon any of them. Mourning as we do for the mighty dead by whose remains we stand, we would yet lift our hearts unto Thee in grateful acknowledgment for Thy kindness in giving us so great and noble a commander. Thou art glorified in good men, and we praise Thee that Thou didst give him unto us so pure, so honest, so sincere, and so transparent in character. We praise Thee for that kind, affectionate heart, which always swelled with feelings of enlarged benevolence. We bless Thee for what Thou didst enable him to do; that Thou didst give him wisdom to select for his advisers and for his officers, military and naval, those men through whom our country has been carried through an unprecedented conflict.

We bless Thee for the success which has attended all their efforts, and victories which have crowned our armies; and that Thou didst spare Thy servant until he could behold the dawning of that glorious morning of peace and prosperity which is about to shine upon our land; that he was enabled to go up as Thy servant of old upon Mount Pisgah, and catch a glimpse of the promised land. Though his lips are silent and his arm is powerless, we thank Thee that Thou didst strengthen him, to speak words that cheer the hearts of the suffering and the oppressed; and to write that declaration of emancipation which has given him an immortal reward; that though the hand of the assassin has struck him to the ground, it could not destroy the work which he has done, nor forge again the chains which he has broken. And while we mourn that he has passed away, we are grateful that his work was so fully accomplished, and that the acts which he has performed will forever remain.

We implore Thy blessing upon his bereaved family, Thou husband of the widow. Bless her who, broken-hearted and sorrowing, feels oppressed with unutterable anguish. Cheer the loneliness of the pathway which lies before her, and grant to her such consolations of Thy spirit and such hopes, through the resurrection, that she shall feel that "Earth hath no sorrows which Heaven cannot heal."

Let Thy blessing rest upon his sons, pour upon them the spirit of wisdom, be Thou the guide of their youth, prepare them for usefulness in society, for happiness in all their relations. May the remembrance of their father's counsels, and their father's noble acts, ever stimulate them to glorious deeds, and at last may they be heirs of everlasting life.

Command thy rich blessings to descend upon the successor of our lamented President. Grant unto him wisdom, energy, and firmness for the responsible duties to which he has been called; and may he, his cabinet, officers and generals who shall lead his armies, and the brave soldiers in the field, be so guided by thy counsels that they shall speedily complete the great work which he had so successfully carried forward.

Let thy blessing rest upon our country. Grant unto us all a fixed and strong determination never to cease our efforts until our glorious Union shall be fully re-established.

Around the remains of our loved President may we covenant together by every possible means to give ourselves to our country's service until every vestige of this rebellion shall have been wiped out, and until slavery, its cause, shall be forever eradicated.

Preserve us, we pray Thee, from all complications with foreign nations. Give us hearts to act justly toward all nations, and grant unto them hearts to act justly toward us, that universal peace and happiness may fill our earth. We rejoice, then, in this inflicting dispensation Thou hast given, as additional evidence of the strength of our nation. We bless Thee that no tumult has arisen, and in peace and harmony our Government moves onward; and that Thou hast shown that our Republican Government is the strongest upon the face of the earth. In this solemn presence, may we feel that we too are immortal! May the sense of our responsibility to God rest upon us; may we repent of every sin; and may we consecrate anew unto Thee all the time and all the talents which Thou hast given us; and may we so fulfil our allotted duties that finally we may have a resting-place with the good, and wise, and the great, who now surround that glorious throne! Hear us while we unite in praying with Thy Church in all lands and in all ages, even as Thou hast taught us, saying——

The Bishop here closed with the Lord's Prayer.

A portion of the distinguished audience then seated themselves upon their sable seats to hear Dr. Gurley deliver the following:

Funeral Address.

As we stand here to-day, mourners around this coffin and around the lifeless remains of our beloved Chief Magistrate, we recognize and we adore the sovereignty of God. His throne is in the Heavens, and his kingdom ruleth over all. He hath done, and He hath permitted to be done, whatsoever He pleased. "Clouds and darkness are round about him; righteousness and judgment are the habitation of his throne." His way is in the sea, and his path in the great waters, and his footsteps are not known. "Canst thou by searching find out God? Canst thou find out the Almighty unto perfection? It is as high as heaven; what canst thou do? Deeper than hell; what canst thou know! The measure thereof is longer than the earth, and broader than the sea. If he cut off, and shut up, or gather together, then who can hinder him? For he knoweth vain men; he seeth wickedness also; will he not then consider it?" We bow before his infinite majesty. We bow, we weep, we worship.

"Where reason fails, with all her powers,
There faith prevails, and love adores."

It was a cruel, cruel hand, that dark hand of the assassin, which smote our honored, wise, and noble President, and filled the land with sorrow. But above and beyond that hand there is another which we must see and acknowledge. It is the chastening hand of a wise and a faithful Father. He gives us this bitter cup. And the cup that our Father has given us, shall we not drink it?

"God of the just, thou gavest us the cup:
We yield to thy behest, and drink it up."

"Whom the Lord loveth he chasteneth." O how these blessed words have cheered and strengthened and sustained us through all these long and weary years of civil strife, while our friends and brothers on so many ensanguined fields were falling and dying for the cause of liberty and union! Let them cheer, and strengthen, and sustain us to-day. True, this new sorrow and chastening has come in such an hour and in such a way as we thought not, and it bears the impress of a rod that is very heavy, and of a mystery that is very deep. That such a life should be sacrificed, at such a time, by such a foul and diabolical agency; that the man at the head of the nation, whom the people had learned to trust with a confiding and a loving confidence, and upon whom more than upon any other were centred, under God, our best hope for the true and speedy pacification of the country, the restoration of the Union, and the return of harmony and love; that he should be taken from us, and taken just as the prospect of peace was brightly opening upon our torn and bleeding country, and just as he was beginning to be animated and gladdened with the hope of ere long enjoying with the people the blessed fruit and reward of his and their toil, and care, and patience, and self-sacrificing devotion to the interests of liberty and the Union. O it is a mysterious and a most afflicting visitation. But it is our Father in heaven, the God of our fathers, and our God, who permits us to be so suddenly and sorely smitten; and we know that His judgments are right, and that in faithfulness He has afflicted us. In the midst of our rejoicings we needed this stroke, this dealing, this discipline; and therefore He has sent it. Let us remember, our affliction has not come forth of the dust, and our trouble has not sprung out of the ground. Through and beyond all second causes let us look, and see the sovereign permissive agency of the great First Cause. It is His prerogative to bring light out of darkness and good out of evil. Surely the wrath of man shall praise Him, and the remainder of wrath He will restrain. In the light of a clearer day we may yet see that the wrath which planned and perpetrated the death of the President, was overruled by Him whose judgments are unsearchable, and his ways past finding out, for the highest welfare of all those interests which are so dear to the Christian patriot and philanthropist, and for which a loyal people have made such an unexampled sacrifice of treasure and of blood. Let us not be faithless, but believing.

"Blind unbelief is prone to err,
And scan his work in vain;
God is his own interpreter,
And He will make it plain."

We will wait for his interpretation, and we will wait in faith, nothing doubting. He who has led me so well, and defended and prospered us so wonderfully during the last four years of toil, and struggle, and sorrow, will not forsake us now. He may chasten, but He will not destroy. He may purify us more and more in the furnace of trial, but He will not consume us. No, no! He has chosen us as He did his people of old in the furnace of affliction, and He has said of us as he said of them. "This people have I formed for myself; they shall show forth my praise." Let our principal anxiety now be that this new sorrow may be a sanctified sorrow; that it may lead us to deeper repentance, to a more humbling sense of our dependence upon God, and to the more unreserved consecration of ourselves and all that we have to the cause of truth and justice, of law and order, of liberty and good government, of pure and undefiled religion. Then, though weeping may endure for a night, joy will come in the morning. Blessed be God! despite of this great and sudden and temporary darkness, the morning has begun to dawn—the morning of a bright and glorious day, such as our country has never seen. That day will come and not tarry, and the death of a hundred Presidents and their Cabinets can never, never prevent it. While we are thus hopeful, however, let us also be humble. The occasion calls us to prayerful and tearful humiliation. It demands of us that we live low, very low, before Him who has smitten us for our sins. O that all our rulers and all our people may bow in the dust to-day beneath the chastening hand of God! and may their voices go up to Him as one voice, and their hearts go up to Him as one heart, pleading with Him for mercy, for grace to sanctify our great and sore bereavement, and for wisdom to guide us in this our time of need. Such a united cry and pleading will not be in vain. It will enter into the ear and heart of Him who sits upon the throne, and he will say to us, as to his ancient Israel, "In a little wrath I hid my face from thee for a moment; but with everlasting kindness will I have mercy upon thee, saith the Lord, thy Redeemer."

I have said that the people confided in the late lamented President with a full and a loving confidence. Probably no man since the days of Washington was ever so deeply and firmly embedded and enshrined in the very hearts of the people as Abraham Lincoln. Nor was it a mistaken confidence and love. He deserved it—deserved it well—deserved it all. He merited it by his character, by his acts, and by the whole tenor, and tone, and spirit of his life. He was simple and sincere, plain and honest, truthful and just, benevolent and kind. His perceptions were quick and clear, his judgment were calm and accurate, and his purposes were good and pure beyond a question. Always and everywhere he aimed and endeavored to *be* right and to *do* right. His integrity was thorough, all-pervading, all-controlling, and incorruptible. It was the same in every place and relation, in the consideration and the control of matters great or small, the same firm and steady principle of power and beauty that shed a clear and crowning lustre upon all his other excellences of mind and heart, and recommended him to his fellow-citizens as *the* man, who, in a time of unexampled peril, when the very life of the nation was at stake, should be chosen to occupy, in the country and for the country, its highest post of power and responsibility. How wisely and well, how purely and faithfully, how firmly and steadily, how justly and successfully he did occupy that post and meet its grave demands in circumstances of surpassing trial and difficulty, is known to you all, known to the country and the world. He comprehended from the first the perils to which treason had exposed the freest and best Government on the earth, the vast interests of liberty and humanity that were to be saved or lost forever in the urgent impending conflict; he rose to the dignity and momentousness of the occasion, saw his duty as the Chief Magistrate of a great and imperilled people, and he determined to do his duty, and his whole duty, seeking the guidance and leaning upon the arm of Him of whom it is written, "He giveth power to the faint, and to them that have no might he increaseth strength." Yes, he leaned upon His arm. He recognized and received the truth that "the kingdom is the Lord's, and He is the governor among the nations." He remembered that "God is in history," and he felt that nowhere had his hand and his mercy been so marvellously conspicuous as in the history of this nation. He hoped and he prayed that that same hand would continue to guide us, and that same mercy continue to abound to us in the time of our greatest need. I speak what I know, and testify what I have often heard him say, when I affirm that that guidance and mercy were the prop on which he humbly and habitually leaned; they were the best hope he had for himself and for his country. Hence, when he was leaving his home in Illinois, and coming to this city to take his seat in the executive chair of a disturbed and troubled nation, he said to the old and tried friends who gathered tearfully around him and bade him farewell, "I leave you with this request: *pray for me.*" They did pray for him; and millions of others prayed for him; nor did they pray in vain. Their prayer was heard, and the answer appears in all his subsequent history; it shines forth with a heavenly radiance in the whole course and tenor of his administration, from its commencement to its close. God raised him up for a great and glorious mission, furnished him for his work, and aided him in its accomplishment. Nor was it merely by strength of mind, and honesty of heart, and purity and pertinacity of purpose, that He furnished him; in addition to these things He gave him a calm and abiding confidence in the overruling providence of God and in the ultimate triumph of truth and righteousness through the power and the blessing of God. This confidence strengthened him in all his hours of anxiety and toil, and inspired him with calm and cheering hope when others were inclining to despondency and gloom. Never shall I forget the emphasis and the deep emotion with which he said, in this very room, to a company of clergymen and others, who called to pay him their respects in the darkest days of our civil conflict: "Gentlemen, my hope of success in this great and terrible struggle rests on that immutable foundation, the justice and goodness of God. And when events are very threatening, and prospects very dark, I still hope that in some way which man cannot see all will be well in the end, because our cause is just, and God is on our side." Such was his sublime and holy faith, and it was an anchor to his soul, both sure and steadfast. It made him firm and strong. It emboldened him in the pathway of duty, however rugged and perilous it might be. It made him valiant for the right; for the cause of God and humanity, and it held him in steady, patient, and unswerving adherence to a policy of administration which he thought, and which all now think, both God and humanity required him to adopt. We admired and loved him on many accounts—for strong and various reasons; we admired his childlike simplicity, his freedom from guile and deceit, his staunch and sterling integrity, his kind and forgiving temper, his industry and patience, his persistent, self-sacrificing devotion to all the duties of his eminent position, from the least to the greatest; his readiness to hear and consider the cause of the poor and humble, the suffering and the oppressed; his charity toward those who questioned the correctness of his opinions and the wisdom of his policy; his wonderful skill in reconciling differences among the friends of the Union, leading them away from abstractions, and inducing them to work together and harmoniously for the common weal; his true and enlarged philanthropy that knew no distinction of color and race, but regarded all men as brethren, and endowed alike by their Creator "with certain inalienable rights, among which are life, liberty, and the pursuit of happiness;" his inflexible purpose, that what freedom had gained in our terrible civil strife should never be lost, and that the end of the war should be the end of slavery, and, as a consequence, of rebellion; his readiness to spend and be spent for the attainment of such a triumph—a triumph the blessed fruits of which shall be as wide-spreading as the earth, and as enduring as the sun. All these things commanded and fixed our admiration, and the admiration of the world, and stamped upon his character and life the unmistakable impress of *greatness.* But more sublime than any or all of these, more holy and influential, more beautiful, and strong, and sustaining, *was his abiding confidence in God and in the final triumph of truth and righteousness through Him and for His sake.* This was his noblest virtue, his grandest principle, the secret alike of his strength, his patience, and his success. And this, it seems to me, after being near him steadily, and with him often, for more than four years, is the principle by which, more than by any other, "he, being dead, yet speaketh." Yes; by his steady enduring confidence in God, and in the complete ultimate success of the cause of God, which is the cause of humanity, more than in any other way, does he now speak to us and to the nation he loved and served so well. By this he speaks to his successor in office, and charges him to have faith in God. By this he speaks to the members of his cabinet, the men with whom he counseled so often and was associated so long, and he charges them to have faith in God. By this he speaks to all who occupy positions of influence and authority in these sad and troublous times, and he charges them all to have faith in God. By this he speaks to this great people as they sit in sackcloth to-day, and weep for him with a bitter wailing, and refuse to be comforted, and he charges them to have faith in God. And by this he *will* speak through the ages and to all rulers and peoples in every land, and his message to them will be, "Cling to liberty and right; battle for them; bleed for them; die for them, if need be; and have confidence in God." O that the voice of this testimony may sink down into our hearts to-day and every day, and into the heart of the nation, and exert its appropriate influence upon our feelings, our faith, our patience, and our devotion to the cause now dearer to us than ever before, because consecrated by the blood of its most conspicuous defender, its wisest and most fondly-trusted friend. He is dead; but the God in whom he trusted lives, and He can guide and strengthen his successor, as He guided and strengthened him. He is dead; but the memory of his virtues, of his wise and patriotic counsels and labors, of his calm and steady faith in God, lives, is precious, and will be a power for good in the country quite down to the end of time. He is dead; but the cause he so ardently loved, so ably, patiently, faithfully represented and defended—not for himself only, not for us only, but for all people in all their coming generations, till time shall be no more—that cause survives his fall, and will survive it. The light of its brightening prospects flashes cheeringly to-day athwart the gloom occasioned by his death, and the language of God's united providences is telling us that, though the friends of liberty die, liberty itself is immortal. There is no assassin strong enough and no weapon deadly enough to quench its inextinguishable life, or arrest its onward march to the conquest and empire of the world. This is our confidence, and this is our consolation, as we weep and mourn to-day. Though our beloved President is slain, our beloved country is saved. And so we sing of mercy as well as of judgment. Tears of gratitude mingle with those of sorrow. While there is darkness there is also the dawning of a brighter, happier day upon our stricken and weary land. God be praised that our fallen chief lived long enough to see the day dawn and the daystar of joy and peace arise upon the nation. He saw it, and he was glad. Alas! alas! He only saw the *dawn.* When the *sun* has risen, full-orbed and glorious, and a happy reunited people are rejoicing in its light, it will shine upon his grave. But that grave will be a precious and a consecrated spot. The friends of liberty and of the Union will repair to it in years and ages to come, to pronounce the memory of its occupant blessed, and, gathering from his very ashes, and from the rehearsal of his deeds and virtues, fresh incentives to patriotism, they will there renew their vows of fidelity to their country and their God.

And now I know not that I can more appropriately conclude this discourse, which is but a sincere and simple utterance of the heart, than by addressing to our departed President, with some slight modification, the language which Tacitus, in his life of Agricola, addresses to his venerable and departed father-in-law: "With you we may now congratulate; you are blessed, not only because your life was a career of glory, but because you were released, when, your country safe, it was happiness to die. We have lost a parent, and, in our distress, it is now an addition to our heartfelt sorrow that we had it not in our power to commune with you on the bed of languishing, and receive your last embrace. Your dying words would have been ever dear to us; your commands we should have treasured up, and graved them on our hearts. This sad comfort we have lost, and the wound for that reason pierces deeper. From the world of spirits behold your disconsolate family and people; exalt our minds from fond regret and unavailing grief to the contemplation of your virtues. Those we must not lament; it were impiety to sully them with a tear. To cherish their memory, to embalm them with our praises, and, so far as we can, to emulate your bright example, will be the truest mark of our respect, the best tribute we can offer. Your wife will thus preserve the memory of the best of husbands, and thus your children will prove their filial piety. By dwelling constantly on your words and actions, they will have an illustrious character before their eyes, and, not content with the bare image of your mortal frame, they will have what is more valuable—the form and features of your mind. Busts and statues, like their originals, are frail and perishable. The soul is formed of finer elements, and its inward form is not to be expressed by the hand of an artist with unconscious matter—our manners and our morals may in some degree trace the resemblance. All of you that gained our love and raised our admiration still subsists, and will ever subsist, preserved in the minds of men, the register of ages, and the records of fame. Others, who have figured on the stage of life and were the worthies of a former day, will sink, for want of a faithful historian, into the common lot of oblivion, inglorious and unremembered; but you, our lamented friend and head, delineated with truth, and fairly consigned to posterity, will survive yourself, and triumph over the injuries of time."

When the speaker closed there was a moment of silence, followed by a general movement; and ere they had stilled again, Dr. Grey, the chaplain of the United States Senate, had taken the place of Dr. Gurley, where he offered the following

Closing Prayer.

O Lord God of Hosts, behold a nation prostrate before Thy throne, clothed in sackcloth, who stand around all that now remains of our illustrious and beloved chief. We thank Thee that Thou hast given to us such a patriot, and to the country such a ruler, and to the world such a noble specimen of manhood. We bless Thee that thou hast raised him to the highest position of trust and power in the nation; and that Thou hast spared him so long to guide and direct the affairs of the Government in its hour of peril and conflict. We trusted it would be he who should deliver Israel, that he would have been retained to us while the nation was passing through its baptism of blood; but in an evil hour, in an unexpected moment, when joy and rejoicing filled our souls, and was thrilling the heart of the nation, he fell. O God, give grace to sustain us under this dark and mysterious providence! Help us to look up unto Thee and say, Not our will but Thine, O God, be done. We commend to Thy merciful regard and tender compassion the afflicted family of the deceased. Thou seest how their hearts are stricken with sorrow and wrung with agony. O help them, as they are now passing through the dark valley and shadow of death, to fear no evil, but to lean upon Thy rod and staff for support. O help them to cast their burden upon the Great Burden-bearer, and find relief. Help them to look beyond human agencies and human means, and recognize thy hand, O, God, in this providence, and say: It is the Lord; let him do what seemeth good in his sight; and as they proceed slowly and sadly on their way with the remains of a husband and father, to consign them to their last resting place, may they look beyond the grave to the morning of Resurrection, when that which they now sow in weakness shall be raised in strength; what they now sow a mortal body shall be raised a spiritual body; that they now sow in corruption shall be raised in incorruption, and shall be fashioned like unto Christ's most glorious body. O God of the bereaved, comfort and sustain this mourning family. Bless the new Chief Magistrate. Let the mantle of his predecessor fall upon him. Bless the Secretary of State and his family. O God, if possible according to thy will, spare their lives, that they may render still important service to the country. Bless all the members of the Cabinet. Endow them with wisdom from above. Bless the commanders of our army and navy, and all the brave defenders of the country, and give them continued success. Bless the ambassadors from foreign courts, and give us peace with the nations of the earth. O God, let treason, that has deluged our land with blood, and devastated our country, and bereaved our homes, and filled them with widows and orphans, and has at length culminated in the assassination of the nation's chosen ruler—God of justice, and avenger of the nation's wrong, let the work of treason cease, and let the guilty author of this horrible crime be arrested and brought to justice. O hear the cry and the prayer and the tears now arising from a nation's crushed and smitten heart, and deliver us from the power of all our enemies, and send speedy peace unto all of our borders, through Jesus Christ, our Lord. Amen.

Removal of the Body.

The prayer being ended, a detailed detachment of the veteran reserve corps entered the room, and, the coffin having been closed, conveyed it from the catafalco to the funeral car awaiting it at the main entrance to the mansion. As soon as it was placed upon the car, the gentlemen in the east room passed out in their appointed order, fell into their assigned places, and the funeral cortege passed on in the broad sunlight to Pennsylvania avenue.

At three o'clock the crowd was as densely packed as possible, throughout the entire length of the procession, from the Presidential Mansion to the Capitol, a distance of a mile. Every roof, window, doorway, balcony, and step, as well as the pavements and the portion of the street between the curbs, upon which the eager spectators could not be prevented from somewhat infringing, was overwhelmingly crowded. The spectacle was grand beyond description, and the demonstrations of the people, as the funeral cortege passed, were most touching. The colored people formed a large portion of the crowd, and their tearful eyes and sorrowful countenances, as the hearse which contained the remains of their friend and liberator passed, only expressed the mourning of the nation over the death of its best defender.

Order of Procession.

The procession, as it left the Presidential Mansion, was formed and marched in the following order:

Tenth Veteran Reserve Corps, with regimental band.
Ninth Veteran Reserve Corps, Colonel Gile, with regimental band.
Battalion of Marine Corps, and band.
Two Batteries 84th United States Artillery.
16th New York Cavalry, Colonel Sweitzer.
8th Illinois Cavalry, Colonel Clendenin.
13th New York Mounted Band.
General Ketchum, and Staff.
General Slough, and Staff.
Commander of Escort and Staff, mounted.
Navy Officers, on foot.
Army Officers, on foot.
Surgeons and Assistant Surgeons, on foot.
Cavalry and Infantry Officers, mounted.
Clergy.
General Grant and Officers, in carriage.
CATAFALCO, CONTAINING CORPSE,
and guarded by 1st Virginia Artillery, on foot.
President's Horse, gray, with boots of President in stirrups.
President's Guard.
Six Carriages, single file, containing the Relatives of Deceased.
The Delegations of the States of Illinois and Kentucky, as mourners.
The President.
The Cabinet Ministers.
Foreign Legations.
Senators and Congressmen.
The Chief Justice and Associate Justices of the Supreme Court and City Courts.
The Assistant Secretaries of the different Departments.
Knights Templar and Band.
Philadelphia City Councils.
Presidents of the Christian and Sanitary Commissions.
Satterlee's Band, of Philadelphia.
Perseverance Hose Company, No. 5, of Philadelphia.
Washington City Councils.
Citizens of Washington.
Fourth United States Battery and Band.
Delegations representing Ohio, New Jersey, and California.
Clerks of the Treasury Department.
Clerks of the Ordnance Department.
Clerks of the Post Office Department.
Clerks of the War Department.
Clerks of the Interior Department.
Army Surgeons, mounted.
Battalion of the Quartermaster General's office, and band.
Baltimore City Councils, and Custom House officers.
Quartermaster's Band.
Fenian Brotherhood.
First Regiment Meigs Home Guard.
Second Regiment Meigs Home Guard.
Employés Quartermaster General's Office.
Eighth Illinois Cavalry Band.
United States Military Railroad Employés.
National Republican Union Association, of the Seventh Ward.
Citizens of Alexandria with band; also Friendship No. 1, and Sun No. 2, fire companies of same city.
Potomac Hose Company, Georgetown.
Mount Vernon Association, of Alexandria, Va.
Lincoln Hospital Soldiers.
Mechanics and Workingmen from Mt. Clare, Baltimore.
Baltimore and Ohio Railroad Employés.
Finley Hospital Band and Soldiers of Hospital.
Arsenal Employés.
Roman Catholic Schools, led by Father Wiget.
Gonzaga and Georgetown Colleges.
Merrith's Band.
East Baltimore Union League.
Hebrew Congregation.
Turners.
Baltimore City Cornet Band.
Order of Ancient Good Fellows.
Federal City Division No. 2, Sons of Temperance, followed by
Carver Hospital Band.
Good Samaritan, No. 1.
Aurora Division, No. 9; Equal Division, No. 4;
Lincoln Division, No. 17; Central Division, No. 12; Empire Division,
No. 19; Hope Division, No. 18;
Everett Division, No. 25;
Mount Vernon Division;
Grand Division; 1,500
in all
Mount Pleasant Band.
Columbia Typographical Society.
Emory Hospital Band, and soldiers of Hospital.
Washington United Benevolent Association (colored.)
Harmony Lodge, No. 18, G. U. O. of O. F. (colored).
King Hezekiah's Pasture, No. 3, F. A. A. M. (colored).
Union Grand Lodge, F. A. A. M. (colored).
Citizens and strangers.

The 22d Pennsylvania colored infantry, Colonel Terry commanding, direct from Petersburg, arrived in town yesterday noon, and took a position on the Avenue, near Sixth street. (This regiment was recently under General Weitzel, and was the second to enter Richmond.) As the head of the column approached where the 22d was standing "at rest," the band struck up a dirge, and the regiment immediately moved forward, thereby becoming the head of the procession.

The Funeral March.

The grand and beautiful funeral march, performed for the first time by the United States Marine Band, in the obsequies of our deceased and beloved Chief Magistrate, was composed and dedicated to the occasion by Brevet Major General J. G. Barnard.

Paroled Officers.

Some four hundred and fifty paroled officers, of every grade and arm of the service, arrived from Camp Parole, Annapolis, early yesterday morning. They were under the command of Brigadier General Chamberlin, and having met in front of the Executive Mansion at noon, joined in the funeral procession.

Municipal and Other Visitors.

A joint committee of the Aldermen and Common Council of New York arrived in Washington yesterday morning, and stopped at the Seaton House. They were received by a committee of the Common Council of the District, and formed in procession with the Common Council of Washington. Alderman Brice was chairman of the committee, and Owen Cavenaugh secretary. The badge worn by the committee was handsomely draped, the device being the coat of arms of the city, having engraved thereon the respective names of the members of the body. The badge was about two inches in circumference, and remarkably neat and appropriate in its appearance. The members of this company constitute a fine-looking body of men.

The Philadelphia City Councils, the Committee of the Union League Club of New York city, and the committee of Merchants and citizens of New York, appeared in the funeral procession.

The New York Chamber of Commerce, headed by Simeon Draper, Esq., called upon President Johnson. The President was appropriately addressed by Mr. Draper, and responded in a very patriotic and impressive manner. They also joined in the procession.

When the procession started, minute guns were fired from batteries stationed near St. John's church, City Hall, and on East Capitol street. The bells of all the churches and of the fire engine houses also continually tolled.

The sight from the Capitol probably presented the most imposing view of the procession that could be attained at any point. Those who were privileged to entrance in the Capitol were universal in their declarations that it was the grandest and most imposing demonstration they had ever seen. It appeared to us like a grand panorama, in which the figures were statuesque, and gradually presented to the view. The crowd was too immense to bring within the scope and comprehension of ordinary vision, even with the aid of a glass.

At the Capitol.

As it approached the Capitol, every arrangement practicable to secure order and resist the pressure of the crowd was made. The vacant space on the east front of the Capitol was completely cleared. A cordon of infantry, and a line of cavalry, including many officers of high rank, as well as the many paroled officers mentioned elsewhere, formed an effectual barrier to the crowd, and with the aid of the police, well ordered by Superintendent Richards, kept the space which had been cleared wholly unobstructed.

There was also placed in front of the old portico and steps of the Capitol, in the centre, a stand, upon which the coffin might be placed when removed from the funeral car, the latter being too high to be reached from the ground. The steps and the entrance were also cleared of all persons save the members of the Capitol, under the excellent direction of Captain Newman, who lined each side of the steps, and who, having had charge of the entire building, had excluded from the building all persons but a few representatives of the press, who had duly authorized passes.

The Rotunda.

On entering the rotunda, we found the grand paintings and statues, which represent the discovery of America and of the Mississippi, the settlement of the country, the foundation of the Government, the struggles of the colonists with the Indians, the Revolutionary War, &c., all familiar to our fellow-citizens of all sections of the Union, and of the most important historic interest, draped with mourning.

Among those draped were: The Discovery of the Mississippi by De Soto, 1541; The Baptism of Pocahontas, Jamestown, Va., 1613; The Landing of Columbus, October, 1492; Embarkation of the Pilgrims from Delfthaven, in Holland, July 21, 1620; The Declaration of Independence, July 4, 1776; The Surrender of General Burgoyne, Saratoga, N. Y., October, 1777; The Surrender of Cornwallis, Yorktown, Va., October, 1781; and General Washington Resigning his Commission to Congress, at Annapolis, Maryland, December 23, 1783.

The rotunda was otherwise neatly draped. The most noticeable feature of the tasteful and appropriate arrangements for the decorations was the absence of all drapery upon the statue of Washington, save a black sash, draping the bust after the style of military mourning.

The Catafalco

prepared for the purpose of laying the President's remains in state, was deposited in the centre of the rotunda, and was a neat and appropriately simple structure. Its dimensions are as follows: The base is eight feet six inches long, four feet wide, and one foot high; the dais is seven feet long, two feet six inches wide, and two feet high. It is covered with fine black cloth, with union columns, representing bundles of *fasces* at the corners, and trimmed with silver lace, encircling the entire edge. Upon the sides of the dais were entwined guns, swords, and bayonets, representing every branch of the army. This structure was the work of Mr. Job Angus.

Arrival of the Remains.

At half past three o'clock, Hon. B. B. French, Superintendent of the Public Buildings, accompanied by Jas. O. Clephane, one of the civic marshals, entered the rotunda, followed by the clergy and the physicians who were in attendance upon the late President's last hours. They took their several positions at the head of the catafalco, and twelve sergeants of the Veteran Reserve Corps, each from a different company, then entered, bearing the coffin, which they deposited upon the catafalco. Lieutenant-General Grant, Major-General Halleck, Assistant Adjutant General Nichols, Admirals Farragut, Goldsborough, and Stringham entered next, and after them the new President and the Cabinet, followed in turn by the remaining pall bearers. Messrs. Nicolay and Hay, the secretaries of Mr. Lincoln, followed.

The pall-bearers arranged themselves in a circle around the catafalco. Generals Grant and Halleck, and the Admirals, the President, and the Cabinet, took positions at the foot of the coffin, some ten feet from it—the two secretaries standing on the left side in front of the pall-bearers. A few prominent gentlemen, among whom were the Hon. Simon Cameron, Generals Hunter and Meigs, also entered the rotunda and approached the coffin, after which the services were proceeded with by Dr. Gurley, as follows:

Burial Service.

It is appointed unto men once to die. The dust returns to the earth as it was, and the spirit to God who gave it. All flesh is as grass, and all the glory of man as the flower of grass; the grass withereth, and the flower thereof falleth away. We know that we must die and go to the house appointed for all living. For what is our life? It is even a vapor that appeareth for a little time and then vanisheth away. Therefore be ye also ready, for in such an hour as ye think not the Son of Man cometh. Let us pray.

Lord, so teach us to number our days that we may apply our hearts unto wisdom. Wean us from this transitory world. Turn away our eyes from beholding vanity. Lift up our affections to the things which are above, where Christ sitteth on the right hand of God. There may our treasure be, and there may our hearts be also. Wash us in the blood of Christ; clothe us in the righteousness of Christ; renew and sanctify us by his word and spirit; lead us in the paths of piety for his name's sake; gently, Lord, O gently lead us through all the duties, and changes, and trials of our earthly pilgrimage; dispose us to pass the time of our sojourning here in fear, denying ungodliness and wordly lusts, and living soberly, righteously, and godly in this present world; and when at the last our turn shall come to die, may we be gathered to our fathers having the testimony of a good conscience; in the communion of the Christian church; in the confidence of a certain faith; in the comfort of a reasonable religious and holy hope; in favor with thee our God; and in perfect charity with the world; all which we ask through Jesus Christ, our Blessed Lord and Redeemer. Amen.

Forasmuch as it hath pleased Almighty God, in his wise providence, to take out of this clay tabernacle, the soul that inhabited it, we commit its decaying remains to their kindred element, earth to earth, ashes to ashes, dust to dust; looking for the general resurrection through our Lord Jesus Christ, at whose coming to judge the world, earth and sea shall give up their dead, and the corruptible bodies of them that sleep in Him shall be fashioned like unto his glorious body according to the working whereby he is able even to subdue all things unto himself. Wherefore, let us comfort one another with these words.

And now may the God of peace that brought again from the dead our Lord Jesus, that great Shepherd of the sheep, through the blood of the everlasting covenant make you perfect in every good work to do his will, working in you that which is well pleasing in his sight, through Jesus Christ, the Resurrection and the Life, our Redeemer and our Hope, to whose care we now commit these precious remains, and to whose name be glory forever and ever. Amen.

The late President's body-guard and a company of the Veteran Reserve Corps then formed a cordon around the coffin. The building was cleared, by order of Secretary Stanton, and the body-guard of the President, and a guard of honor composed of several officers remained in charge, with the Capitol police, under charge of Captain Newman, to remain there all night.

The Last Opportunity to View the Remains.

The Capitol will be open to-day, and the public will be admitted to the rotunda from eight o'clock A. M. until six o'clock P. M., to enter at the west door, and pass out at the east door.

LATER FROM EUROPE.

SANDY HOOK, April 19.—The steamship Persia, from Liverpool April 8 and Queenstown the 9th, is now passing this point, with dates two days later.

Consols for money, 90⅜@90⅝.

Five-twenties, 57¼@83.

Arrived from Baltimore, ship Johan Wilhelming at Bremen.

IN ONE of the processes of steel-pen making, done by females, at Birmingham, a quick worker will cut in one day of ten working hours two hundred and fifty gross, or thirty-six thousand pens, which involves seventy-two thousand distinct motions of the arm—two in every second.

SHERMAN.

HIS OCCUPATION OF RALEIGH.

CELEBRATION OF LATE VICTORIES.

GOLDSBOROUGH, April 9, 1865.

This morning the busy preparations for an immediate advance are observable in the streets of this town and the camps around it. All last night wagons thronged the roads and horsemen rushed to and fro with orders and replies. A portion of the left wing, General Slocum commanding, has already started, and the rest will be under way ere the day closes. The centre and right wing are expected to leave to-morrow.

The destination of the march is evidently Raleigh, or wherever else the redoubtable Johnston may choose to court defeat by making a stand. The only strategic points being the rebel armies, and those being on wheels at present, it is not unlikely that the Western army has another long march before it.

Last night occurred almost the only public demonstrations which have been made in celebrating the capture of Richmond and Petersburg, and this was generally a spontaneous affair. As the shades of evening began to render earthly matters rather gloomy, a rocket was seen to course its whizzing way toward the sky. This was followed by another and another, and the soldiers soon began to greet each fiery messenger with cheers and musket salutes. Until a late hour of the night the 4th of July revelry was continued. The band of the 33d Massachusetts, said to be the best in the army, discoursed some delightful music at General Sherman's headquarters, where quite a crowd collected in the expectation of hearing a speech from the old hero.

Being repeatedly called upon, Sherman at last made his appeance with a lantern in his hand, and walking down to the gate of the yard, said to the soldiers outside: "I'll tell you what I'll do, boys. I will read you the last despatch, just an hour old," and with this characteristic speech, he gave way to Major Strong, of his staff, who read a telegram from the Lieutenant General, dated near Burksville, saying that he had Lee's army pressed hard; Lee's men were scattering and going to their homes by thousands, and that he was retreating upon Danville, and directing Sherman to press Johnston, and we will finish the affair at once.

After hearing this despatch, three cheers were given for General Shermam, and most of the crowd wended their way to their quarters, satisfied with having once again seen their commander.

THE OCCUPATION OF RALEIGH.

GOLDSBOROUGH, N. C., April 14.—Our forces entered and occupied Raleigh yesterday. Very little opposition was made. The advance of General Sherman to the city was attended with but slight skirmishing.

Johnston has fallen back, it is conjectured, in the direction of Greensboro. Even if there is no intention on his part to surrender at present, his capture is but a matter of a few days. It is believed here, however, that he intends to surrender, and the delay in doing so is inexplicable to the people hereabouts.

The railroad is now running twelve miles beyond this place, and communication will be had with Raleigh in a few days.

BOOTH.

HE IS SPOKEN TO ON A RAILROAD TRAIN.

An Extra Train Sent After Him.

READING, April 19.—Booth, the assassin, it is supposed, was on the passenger train that left here at six o'clock for Pottsville. A gentleman noticed him on the train before it reached Pottsville, spoke to him, and shook hands with him. During the conversation, Booth colored up several times, and appeared annoyed, and desirous of avoiding observation. The gentleman is positive it is Booth, he having known him several years. Why he did not give the alarm at once, or before the train left, I do not know; but just as the train left, he notified several of the officers of the road, and an extra train was immediately sent in pursuit of the train. Telegrams were sent to all points upon the line of the railroad. The result is unknown, as yet.

SECOND DESPATCH.

READING, April 19.—The extra train did not overtake the regular train, but arrived at Pottsville after it.

The conductor informed the party that the suspected man got off at Port Clinton. The train returned, but the man had gone, which way, or how, no one appeared to know.

MORE ABOUT BOOTH.

[From the Buffalo Courier, April 17.]

We are assured by a gentleman who claims to have positive knowledge on the subject that Booth is an own cousin of the rebel Captain Beall, who was executed a few weeks since on Governor's Island. A very strong effort, it will be remembered, was made to induce the President to pardon Beall, but without avail. It would be eminently consistent with the known character of Booth, if, in consequence of this fact, he had bound himself to be the avenger of his relative, and had pursued his hellish purpose to its consummation mainly from motives of personal revenge.

HIS IDEA OF IMMORTAL FAME.

[From the Cleveland Leader, April 17.]

We learn on the best authority that when Wilkes Booth was in this city a year and a half ago, he remarked to a prominent citizen that "the man who killed Abraham Lincoln would occupy a higher niche of fame than George Washington." This demonstrates that his infamous deed was long premeditated.

LONG CONTEMPLATION OF THE CRIME.

[From the Chicago Journal.]

A theatrical gentleman of this city informs us that in the early part of 1863, during an engagement of J. Wilkes Booth at McVicker's theatre, he made the remark one day, "What a glorious opportunity there is for a man to immortalize himself by killing Lincoln!"

"What good would that do?" he was asked.

He then quoted these lines:

"The ambitious youth who fired the Ephesian dome
Outlives in fame the pious fool who reared it."

"Well, who was that ambitious youth—what was his name?" was then asked.

"That I don't know," Booth replied.

"Then where's the fame you speak of?"

This, our informant tells us, nonplussed him.

From this it would seem that the assassin has had the commission of this horrid crime in his mind for at least two or three years.

General Wallace Resumes Command.

By the following order, issued yesterday, it will be seen that Major General Lew. Wallace resumes command of the Middle Department. Brevet Brigadier General Morris, who has so satisfactorily administered the affairs of the Department during the absence of General Wallace, takes command of Fort McHenry and the other defences of the city:

HEADQUARTERS MIDDLE DEPARTMENT,
EIGHTH ARMY CORPS,
BALTIMORE, MD., April 19, 1865.

General Orders, No. 85.

The undersigned respectfully announces his resumption of command of the Department, lately so well conducted by Brevet Brigadier General W. W. Morris. LEW. WALLACE,
Major General Commanding.

Official: D. P. THRUSTON, Capt. and A. D. C.

SPECIAL ORDER.

HEADQUARTERS MIDDLE DEPARTMENT,
EIGHTH ARMY CORPS,
BALTIMORE, MD., April 19, 1865.

General Orders No. 86.

The gray uniform worn by certain young men, said to be students, has become so offensive to loyal soldiers and citizens that it is prohibited in this Department.

This order will take effect from and after the 25th of the present month. By command of
MAJOR GENERAL WALLACE.
GEORGE H. HOOKER, Assistant Adj. Gen.
Official: D. P. THRUSTON, Capt. and A. D. C.

IT IS REPORTED that the Bishop of Oxford will introduce in Parliament a bill to enable existing bishops to nominate two suffragan bishops, from whom the crown is to choose one as a successor to the bishop of the diocese. If carried, some of the premier's perquisites will be gone.

THE vote of the New Hampshire soldiers adds 706 to the plurality of General Marston, 548 to that of Mr. Rollins, and 593 to that of Mr. Patterson, for Congress.

THE RICHMOND TIMES.

VOL. I.—NO. 1. FRIDAY MORNING, APRIL 21, 1865. PRICE FIVE CENTS.

The Richmond Times

IS PUBLISHED DAILY (EXCEPT SUNDAY) BY

CHAS. H. WYNNE.

Office N. W. corner Main and Fourteenth Streets.

The TIMES will give all the military, naval, political and foreign intelligence of the day.

The price of the TIMES will be five cents per copy. It will be served to subscribers in the city for thirty cents a week—payable to the carrier. Carriers and News Dealers will be furnished at the rate of three dollars per hundred copies.

TERMS OF ADVERTISING.

Advertisements will be inserted at the rate of seventy-five cents per square for each insertion. Eight lines, or an equivalent space, constitute a square.

No notice can be taken of anonymous correspondence. Whatever is intended for publication must be authenticated by the name and address of the writer—not necessarily for publication, but as a guaranty for his good faith.

We will, under no circumstances, return unsolicited communications.

The Evacuation of Richmond.

A COMPLETE HISTORY.

[In view of the almost universal desire among our citizens for papers containing accounts of the particulars of the evacuation of Richmond and its occupation by the United States forces, we have taken the pains to compile, from files of Northern papers, a full and complete history of the event—giving all the particulars of the surrender of the city, the entry of the troops, the great conflagration, the burning of the tobacco and bridges, the scenes of pillaging and plundering, with full description of the city and its prominent points of interest, the feeling of the people, &c. This account should be preserved, as it will be valuable hereafter as a historical document, and this may be the last opportunity our citizens may have of securing what in fact forms one of the most important pages in the history of this war. We have endeavored to compile this account from the most reliable and authentic sources, and we preface it with the following official despatches announcing the evacuation of the city and its occupation by the United States authorities on the morning of the third day of April, 1865.]

The Official Despatches.

The following are the official despatches announcing the evacuation and occupation of Richmond by the Federal forces:

Despatch from Secretary Stanton.

War Department,
Washington, April 3—10 A. M.

Major General Dix, New York:

It appears from a despatch of General Weitzel, just received by this department, that our forces under his command *are in Richmond*, having taken it at fifteen minutes past eight this morning. EDWIN M. STANTON, Secretary of War.

Second despatch from Secretary Stanton.

War Department,
Washington, April 3—12 M.

Major-General Dix, New York:

The following official confirmation of the capture of Richmond, and the announcement that the city is on fire, has been received.

EDWIN M. STANTON,
Secretary of War.

City Point, April 3—11 A. M.

Hon. Edwin M. Stanton, Sec'y of War:

General Weitzel telegraphs as follows:

We took Richmond at a quarter past eight this morning. I captured many guns.

The enemy left in great haste.

The city is on fire in one place. Am making every effort to put it out.

The people received us with enthusiastic expressions of joy.

General Grant started early this morning with the army towards the Danville road, to cut off Lee's retreating army if possible.

President Lincoln has gone to the front.

T. S. BOWERS,
Acting Adjutant General.

What was Captured in Richmond.

Washington, D. C.,
April 4, 1865, 11:15 A. M.

Major General John A. Dix, New York:

The following particulars, dated at City Point, April 4, 8 A. M., give the latest information received from Richmond:

General Weitzel telegraphs from Richmond that of railroad stock he found there twenty-eight locomotives, forty-four passenger and baggage cars, and one hundred and six freight cars.

EDWIN M. STANTON,
Secretary of War.

War Department,
Washington, April 5—10 P. M.

Major General John A. Dix, New York:

A telegram, just received by this department from Richmond, states that General Weitzel captured in Richmond one thousand, well prisoners and five thousand rebel wounded, found in the hospitals; five hundred pieces of artillery and five thousand stand of arms were captured.

The President went to Richmond yesterday, and returned to City Point to-day.

EDWIN M. STANTON,
Secretary of War.

Further Particulars.

War Department,
Washington, April 5—10:20 P. M.

Major-General John A. Dix, New York:

The following details respecting the capture of Richmond and its occupation by the Union forces have been telegraphed to this department from that city:

EDWIN M. STANTON, Secretary of War.

General Weitzel learned, at 3 o'clock on the morning of Monday, that Richmond was being evacuated, and at daylight moved forward, first taking care to give his men breakfast, in the expectation that they might have to fight. He met no opposition, and on entering the city was greeted with hearty welcome from the mass of the people. The Mayor went out to meet him and to surrender the city, but missed him on the road.

General Weitzel finds much suffering and poverty among the population. The rich as well as the poor are destitute of food. He is absut to issue supplies to all who take the oath. The inhabitants now number about twenty thousand, half of them of African descent.

It is not true that Jeff. Davis sold his furniture before leaving. It is all in his house, where I am now writing. He left at 7 P. M. by the Danville railroad.

All the members of Congress escaped. Hunter has gone home. Judge Campbell remains here.

General Weitzel took here one thousand prisoners, besides the wounded. These number five thousand, in nine hospitals. He captured cannon to the number of at least five hundred pieces. Five thousand muskets have been found in one lot. Thirty locomotives and three hundred cars are found here.

The Petersburg railroad bridge is totally destroyed; that of the Danville road partially, so that connection with Petersburg can easily be made.

All the rebel vessels are destroyed, except an unfinished ram, which has the machinery in her perfect.

The Tredegar Works are unharmed, and the machinery here to-day, under General Weitzel's orders.

Libby Prison and Castle Thunder have also escaped the fire, and are filled with rebel prisoners of war.

The theatre opens here to-night.

General Weitzel describes the reception of the President yesterday as enthusiastic in the extreme.

Despatch from the Assistant Secretary of War.

Aiken's Landing, Virginia,
April 5—11:30 A. M.

Hon. E. M. Stanton, Secretary of War:

The Rebel iron-clads were exploded. The Virginia lies sunk in the James river above the obstructions.

Ewell set the city on fire. All the business portion of Main street to the river was destroyed. The bridges across the river were also destroyed.

Many of the families remain. Mrs. Lee remains.

At Petersburg the public stores were burned and a few houses caught fire, but not much damage was done to the city. The bridges there were also destroyed.

I will report fully from Richmond. I cannot get a clear idea of our loss. The only General killed is Winthrop. Potter is dangerously wounded in the groin.

General Grant has commanded the armies in person since the beginning of the operations.

C. A. DANA,
Assistant Secretary of War.

INTERESTING DETAILS.

The Lines before Richmond on the night of the Evacuation.

[From the Philadelphia Inquirer.]

When General Ord withdrew to the lines investing Petersburg he carried with him exactly one-half of his army, being Turner's and Foster's Divisions, of the Twenty-fourth Corps, and Birney's Division, of the Twenty-fifth (colored) Corps. On the north side, occupying his entire line, he left Weitzel, with Kautz's Division of the Twenty-fourth Corps, and Ashborne's and Thomas' Divisions, of the Twenty-fifth Corps.

Saturday, while the greatest scenes of history were enacting around Petersburg, Weitzel's entire line was perfectly quiet, not a shot anywhere. The enemy made a great show; every man on the line doubtless had orders to make himself appear as much as possible like six.—Weitzel's command certainly had such orders; both sides were playing the same game, and one was probably as little deceived as the other. When night came on the Rebel bands played vociferously and persistently in various parts of their lines; probably half the bands in the Rebel camps had been called into requisition in the game of attempted deception. Weitzel followed the example set him; he set all his bands to work upon our National airs, and the night was filled with melodious strains, conflicting somewhat, however, in their political significance.

Towards midnight, however, this musical contest ceased, and a silence, complete and absolute, brooded over the contending lines. At the hour specified the camps were startled into life again by the explosions already detailed.—To Weitzel's clear brain the full meaning of the event came home at once, and he did not need the confirmatory lurid light he saw hanging over the Rebel capital to tell him that the hour had almost come. His orders were to push on whenever satisfied of his ability to enter the city, and summoning what patience he could he waited the short interval until daylight, when he sent out the Fifth Massachusetts cavalry to reconnoitre. Its report soon came in, no enemy to be found; his camps deserted, whatever force had been there, and it is difficult yet to designate the particular organization, gone in the darkness of the night. The way to Richmond was open. Southwest of Petersburg had been found the key that had unlocked its stubborn gates, and Weitzel was instantly on the road.

Osborne's Division took, by a singular coincidence, the river road known as the Osborne old turnpike, and Kautz and Thomas moved on the Darbytown and Newmarket road, and began their march into the city.

Additional Particulars of the Evacuation—Preparations for the Evacuation.

Sunday morning, April 2, broke upon Richmond calmly and pleasantly. There were rumors of evacuation, but very few supposed the event was at hand. General Lee telegraphed to Davis giving an account of the general attack upon his lines, stating that his lines had been pierced in many places, and that unless he could re-establish them Richmond must be given up that night. His tone was, for the first time since the war, despondent; he said his men were not coming up to their work. Subsequently, he telegraphed that all efforts to re-establish his lines had been utterly unsuccessful. Immediately began among the officials in Richmond a panic. Wagons on the streets, boxes and trunks were being hastily loaded at the departments, and driven to the Danville Depot. Those who had determined to evacuate with the fugitive Government looked on with amazement; then, convinced of the fact, rushed to follow the Government's example. Vehicles with two horses, one horse, or even no horse at all, suddenly rose to a premium value that was astounding, and ten, fifteen, and even a hundred dollars in gold or Federal currency was offered for a conveyance. Suddenly, as if by magic, the streets became filled with men, walking as though for a wager, and behind them excited negroes with trunks, bundles and luggage of every description. All over the city it was the same—wagons, trunks, bandboxes and their owners, a mass of hurrying fugitives, filling the streets. The banks were all open, and depositors were as busy as bees removing their specie deposits; and the directors were equally active in getting off their bullion. Hundreds of thousands of dollars of paper money was destroyed, both State and Confederate. Night came, and with it came confusion worse confounded.—There was no sleep for human eyes in Richmond Sunday night.

Meeting of the City Council to Prepare for the Evacuation.

At the request of the Mayor, a meeting of the Council was held on the evening before the evacuation, to consult as to what was best to be done under the circumstances. The Council, after much discussion, passed a resolution appointing committees for each of the three wards to destroy all liquor. The object of this step was to prevent disorder resulting from the intoxication of the troops of either army.

The Council held another conference, and this time, being assured by the Secretary of War that the Confederate pickets would be withdrawn from the Richmond front at three o'clock Monday morning, and that it was calculated that the city would be evacuated about night, it was determined that a committee of prominent citizens should attend the Mayor with a flag of truce to the intermediate line of fortifications, and that there he might hand over the city to the United States authorities.

Destroying the Liquor.

About the hour of midnight the work commenced, under the direction of committees of citizens in all the wards. Hundreds of barrels of liquor were rolled into the street and the heads knocked in. The gutters ran with a liquor freshet, and the fumes filled and impregnated the air. Fine cases of bottled liquors were tossed into the street from third story windows, and wrecked into a thousand pieces. As the work progressed some straggling soldiers, retreating through the city, managed to get hold of a quantity of the liquor. From that moment law and order ceased to exist: chaos came and a Pandemonium reigned.

The Order to Fire the City.

About midnight the Mayor received positive information that an order had been issued from Ewell's headquarters to fire the four principal tobacco warehouses of the city, namely: Public Warehouse, situated at the head of the basin, near the Petersburg railroad depot; Shockoe Warehouse, situated near the centre of the city, side by side with the Gallego flour mills; Mayo's Warehouse, and Dibrell's Warehouse, on Cary street, a square below the Libby prison. Knowing that the burning of these immense buildings, situated as they were, involved the destruction of at least the business portion of the city, the Mayor forthwith despatched a committee of gentlemen to remonstrate with the Confederate authorities against the execution of the order. The committee, consisting of Mr. James A. Scott and others, were referred to Major Melton, one of a large number of Adjutant and Inspector-Generals of the War Department, to whom, it appeared, had been entrusted the work. Melton would hear nothing on the subject, and characterized the statement that burning the warehouses would destroy the city as "a cowardly pretext on the part of the citizens, trumped up to endeavor to save their property for the Yankees." There was nothing left for the citizens but to submit. Resistance was thought of, but the Confederate authorities had guarded against such an event by holding in the city, to execute the work, two large battalions of Southern troops.

Sudden Exit of the Treasure and Officials.

On Sunday morning the gold and silver coin belonging to the Louisiana banks was run down to the Danville train with hot haste, so also was the specie of the Richmond banks. Then the programme for the departure of the officials was arranged. A number of trains were to leave during the evening, still there was not room for all who thought it desirable to get away. Davis left the city at night at eight o'clock by rail for Danville, his family having been sent out five days before. On the train he had horses and carriages embarked, in case the road was interrupted, in order to easily make his way by these means. In spirits he was very much depressed, and bore the appearance of an exceedingly haggard and careworn man, his countenance clearly betraying the loss of his cause. He expressed himself as being yet determined not to give up, but to put forth another effort to redeem his hopeless and sunken fortunes. I think it may be relied upon that he has not yet altogether abandoned his cause, though it is positively known he has but little hope left. His residence was desolate indeed, and everything betokened the extraordinary haste with which he abandoned his capital and home.

Billy Smith, Governor of Virginia, did not evacuate the gubernatorial mansion until one o'clock this morning, when he fled, leaving Mrs. Smith behind, and all the furniture in his house, which he had heretofore threatened to burn. The residence of the Governor was occupied as the headquarters of General Charles Devens, commanding a division in the Twenty-fourth corps.

John Cabell Breckinridge, ex-Vice President of the United States and Secretary of War, fled the city so late as half-past six Monday morning.

The Virginia Legislature were in session so late as nine o'clock Saturday night, when they took a series of canal boats and started for Columbia by way of the James River and Kanawha Canal.

Blowing up the Rams—Burning the Bridges, &c.

The rebel rams in the James river were blown up on Sunday morning just a few hours before our troops entered the city. The Richmond, Virginia, and another one, were all blown to the four winds of heaven, and now lie at the bottom of the James. The Patrick Henry, a receiving ship, was scuttled. Such shipping, very little in amount, as was lying at the Richmond wharves, was also fired, save, perhaps, the flag of truce steamer Allison.

The bridges leading out of the city—namely, the Danville Railroad bridge, the Petersburg Railroad bridge, Mayo's bridge, leading to Manchester and the opposite side of the James—were severally burned.

Scenes at the Commissary Storehouse.

At daybreak Monday morning the scene at the Commissary Depot, at the head of the dock, beggared description. Hundreds of Government wagons were loaded with bacon, flour and whiskey, and driven off in hot haste to join the retreating army. Thronged about the depot were hundreds of men, women and children, black and white, provided with capacious bags, baskets, tubs, buckets, tin pans and aprons, cursing, pushing and crowding, awaiting the throwing open of the doors, and the order for each to help himself. When the Government wagons had gotten off all the stores possible, it was found that several hundred barrels of whiskey remained in the upper story.

One after another, in hasty procession, the barrels were rolled to the hatchway, the heads knocked out, and the whiskey poured continuously into the dock in a current almost strong enough to have swept a man off his feet. Between two hundred and three hundred barrels were thus poured out.

About sunrise the doors were opened to the populace, and a rush that almost seemed to carry the building off its foundation was made, and hundreds of thousands of pounds of bacon, flour, &c., were soon swept away by a clamorous crowd.

(*To be continued to-morrow*)

The Richmond Times

FRIDAY, APRIL 21, 1865.

Office: Corner Main and Fourteenth Streets.

OUR PAPER.

We present this morning to the public the first number of the Richmond *Times*. It has been usual on such occasions to inflict the reader with a "salutatory," but we think that one of those customs which, as Shakspeare would say, is "more honored in its breach than in its observance."

But we may be pardoned for a word in regard to our paper. Owing to the confusion and pressure always attendant upon the publication of a *new* paper, we have not been able to present it this morning as we would desire. In a few days the disadvantages under which we have labored will have been removed, and we hope to be able then, or very soon thereafter, to give to our patrons a *double sheet*. Until then, we shall endeavor, by condensation in our selections, and the introduction of small type, to present daily to our readers all the news of the day. The papers at the present time are verbose, and it is often the information of a whole article can be conveyed in a single paragraph. The best newspaper, like the best writer, is that one which gives to the reader the most information and at the same time takes from him the least time.

It is the aim of the proprietor to make the *Times* a first-class paper, and no pains or expense shall be spared for this purpose. One promise we can safely make to its patrons: IT SHALL ALWAYS GIVE THE LATEST NEWS FROM ALL PARTS OF THE COUNTRY. Arrangements are now under way to secure correspondents in the principal cities of the North; and as soon as it is practicable we shall lay before our readers every morning the latest news in *special telegraphic despatches from Washington*. Under the present facilities of communication we shall continue to give unexcelled compilations of Northern and foreign news, with a full record of local events—having secured for our city department the services of a gentleman who has been connected with the Richmond press for a number of years.

We promise to introduce several features of improvement in our paper, and in a few days our readers shall have evidence of it.

Parties wishing to take the *Times* can leave or send their names to the office, corner of Main and Fourteenth streets. Our terms will be found on the first page.

THE DEPARTMENT OF VIRGINIA.

It being generally understood, although not officially announced, that Major General Edward O. C. Ord has been succeeded in the command of the Department of Virginia by Major-General Halleck, a brief sketch of the military career of General Ord, who enjoys great distinction as a soldier, will be read with interest.

General E. O. C. Ord is a native of Maryland, and about forty five years of age. He is a man of fine appearance, and pleasant and genial in his manners. He graduated at West Point when he was a class-fellow with Generals Sherman, Halleck and other distinguished officers in 1842 and '43, and went to California in 1846 as First Lieutenant in the Fourth United States Infantry, and was engaged for some years in the coast survey.

When the war broke out Major Ord was appointed Brigadier-General of Volunteers and ordered East, and assigned to the command of a brigade in the Army of the Potomac. He was first engaged at the battle of Drainsville, and was promoted to Major-General of Volunteers in May, 1862, and ordered West. In September, 1862, he moved with three divisions to Iuka, and after the battle at that point returned to Corinth with the principal army, and was assigned to the command of the District of Jackson, Tennessee.

General Ord was severely wounded at the crossing of Hatcher's Run. When sufficiently recovered he was appointed a member of the Buel Commission, but was relieved before the Commission completed its labors, and was assigned to a command under General Dix, Department of Virginia.

In May, 1863, General Ord was ordered to report to General Grant at Vicksburg, and was assigned to the command of the Thirteenth Army Corps. After the fall of Vicksburg he accompanied General Sherman in the pursuit of Johnston to Jackson, Mississippi.

In August, 1863, the Thirteenth Corps was ordered to the Department of the Gulf, and the General remained in that Department in command of the Corps until March, 1864, when he was relieved and ordered to West Virginia.—He remained here until assigned to the command of the Eighth Corps and Middle Department in July. He was, at his own request, relieved from this command and ordered to report to General Grant at Petersburg. General Ord was then assigned to the command of the Eighteenth Corps.

When the Army of the James moved to the north side on the 29th September, a detachment of the Eighteenth Corps, under command of General Ord, carried Fort Harrison by assault, and the General was again wounded. Upon the consolidation of the Tenth and Eighteenth Corps, forming the Twenty-fourth, General Ord was assigned to that command, and eventually, upon General Butler being removed, was placed in command of the Department of Virginia.

Upon the retirement of General Ord from the command of this department, it is but just to say that his administration has been marked by a high sense of justice, and has challenged the universal approbation of the people of Richmond. His duties have been discharged in a most acceptable manner.

It is understood that General Ord has been given a more important and extended command, having been assigned the Department of the South, embracing the States of Florida, Georgia and South Carolina. It is supposed his headquarters will be at Charleston.

We propose continuing these sketches of the United States officers in command of the Department of Richmond, which cannot fail to be interesting at this time—many of them being strangers to the people of Virginia. As soon as it can be prepared, we shall give a sketch of Major-General Halleck, who assumes the command of this department. To-morrow we shall give a very full and interesting sketch of General Devens in command of the United States forces in and about the city of Richmond.

THE WAR NEWS.

[Compiled from the Evening Edition of the Baltimore American 18th.]

Expected Surrender of Johnston.

Washington, April 17.—Information has been received by the Government from General Sherman that he was in communication with General Johnston, with a view to the surrender of the latter.

General Sherman would offer the same terms that General Grant did to Lee, and it was supposed they would be accepted.

Mosby Wants to Surrender.

Washington, April 16.—General Augur has received information of the desire on the part of Mosby to surrender his band at Fairfax Court House to-morrow morning. Our forces will receive the surrender. Mosby claims to belong to the Army of Northern Virginia, commanded by Lee, and expects the same terms given to the latter by Lieutenant-General Grant.

A Surrender in the Valley.

Imboden, one of the leaders in the Valley, a Winchester dispatch says, with his command of two regiments, has sent a flag-of-truce to the Union commander in that vicinity, proposing to surrender on the same terms as those granted to Lee's army. It is not stated whether he was allowed to do so or not.

THE LATEST FROM THE NORTH.

Arrest of the Perpetrator of the Assault on Mr. Seward.

The Northern papers did not arrive last night—the latest date in the city being the Baltimore *American* of last Tuesday, evening edition. We get from it the following:

Washington, April 18.—Late last night a man disguised as a laborer, and carrying a pick on his shoulder, approached the house occupied by the family of Surratt, in this city, and was seen to enter, when he was arrested, and upon washing the dirt from his face, proved to be quite a different looking person from what his appearance at first indicated.

The colored servant of Secretary Seward was sent for, when he immediately exclaimed: "*That's the man; I know him by his general appearance and his mouth!*" The servant said there could be no mistake. He is believed to be Surratt, who perpetrated the dreadful crime at Secretary Seward's house.

Probable Capture of the Assassin.

A gentleman who passed Point Lookout yesterday morning was informed by an officer from one of our gunboats that Booth and the other conspirators, about thirty in number, were in St. Mary's county, heavily armed, and endeavouring to make their way across the Potomac, which was strongly picketed and no one allowed to pass. He also stated that on Sunday evening a small squad of our cavalry had a collision with them and had been repulsed, but succeeded in capturing one of them. The cavalry in the meantime had been reinforced, and the next morning were understood to have them completely surrounded and their escape was deemed impossible.

Condition of Mr. Seward.

The latest intelligence from Secretary Seward, we are happy to state, represents him as much better, in possession of all his faculties, and but little doubt is entertained of his recovery. His son Frederick has also improved, and, although in a critical condition, the symptoms are favorable.

Reception by President Johnson.

Washington, April 18.—President Johnson this morning received a large delegation of citizens of Illinois, and afterwards about fifty clergymen and others connected with the Christian Commission. He expressed his high appreciation of their confidence in him, and made to each party a speech indicative of his public course in the future.

THE GREAT TRAGEDY!

Particulars of the Assassination!

The President's Death-Bed Scene!

FUNERAL CEREMONIES!

Statement of an Eye-Witness.

Mr. James P. Ferguson, who was present at the theatre on the night of the assassination, makes the following statement:

When the second scene of the third act of the play was reached, Mr. Ferguson saw (and recognized) John Wilkes Booth making his way along the dress circle to the President's box. Mr. Ferguson and Booth had met in the afternoon and conversed, and were well acquainted with each other, so that the former immediately recognized him. Booth stopping two steps from the door, took off his hat, and holding it in his left hand, leaned against the wall behind him. In this attitude he remained for half a minute; then he stepped down one step, put his hands on the door of the little corridor leading to the box, bent his knee against it, the door opened, Booth entered, and was for the time hidden from Mr. Ferguson's sight.

The shot was the next thing Mr. F. remembers. He saw the smoke, then perceived Booth standing upright, with both hands raised, but at that moment saw no weapon or anything else in either. Booth then sprang to the front of the box, laid his left haud on the railing in front, was checked an instant evidently, by his coat or pants being caught in something or held back by somebody. (It was by Major Rathburn.)

A post in front obstructed the view of Mr. Ferguson, but Booth soon changed his position and again was clearly seen by Mr. F. He now had a knife in his right hand, which he also laid upon the railing, as he had already his left, and vaulted out. As his legs passed between the folds of the flag decorating the box his spur, which he wore on the right heel, caught the drapery and brought it down, tearing a strip with it. When he let go the railing he still clutched the shining knife. He crouched as he fell, falling on one knee and putting forth bends to help himself to recover an erect position, which he did with the rapidity and agility of an athlete.

Having recovered his equilibrium, Booth strode across the stage to the first entrance, passing behind the actor on the stage (Harry Hawk). When he reached the other side of the stage, just ere he became invisible by passing into the entrance, he looked up, and Mr. Ferguson said he heard him say, "I have done it," and then he lost sight of him.

The Murderer's Preparations.

The Washington *Star* gives the following particulars:

During the day Booth had evidently visited the box, as is shown by the preparations made for the assassination. Behind the door of the passage a hole had been made in the wall, in which at night Booth inserted the end of a board as a brace against the door, thereby precluding any one from following him from the dress circle. The screws were next removed from the lock of the farther door opening into the double box, the thread of the screw holes broken, and the lock and screws replaced, so that, should the inmates of the box fasten the door by which they entered, the other door might be easily pushed open.

Judge Olin and others, on a visit to the theatre, satisfied themselves by actual experiment that the door ostensibly locked could thus be pushed in with the greatest ease. The aperture in the panel of the door, which was thought to have been a bullet hole, and thus formed a contradictory feature in the chain of evidence, it now appears was made with a knife, and was designed to enable the assassin to survey the position of the occupants of the box previous to entering himself. The large arm chair always used by the President at the theatre had been removed from its usual position, enabling the murderer to carry out his design more readily as he passed through the box. A pocket knife, the one probably with which the hole was cut in the door, was found lying on the cushion of the balustrade when Mr. Lincoln's party entered the box.

The Assassin's Coat Found.

Yesterday a light-colored sack coat, fully answering to the description of that worn by the attempted assassin of the Messrs. Seward, was found near Fort Saratoga, which is situated on the north of the city, not far from the Soldiers' Home. The coat was stained with blood. In one of the pockets were found a false moustache and a small brush.

The coat and the articles found in it were delivered at the Provost Marshal's office. It is believed that this discovery will furnish an additional clue to the route of the criminal.

The Laying in State.

[From the Washington Star.]

The preparations for laying out in state the corpse of the late President will be completed this evening, and to-morrow an opportunity will be afforded the public to view the features of the deceased for the last time. We have been requested to state that no one will be allowed to loiter about the White House through curiosity; but all will be required to pass out of the building after having viewed the corpse. This measure is requisite that a jam may be avoided and order preserved.

The Coffin

In which the late President is to be buried is a magnificent affair indeed, costing above one thousand dollars. It is of mahogany, lined with lead, and covered with the finest black cloth.

The outside of the coffin is festooned with massive silver tacks, representing drapery, in each fold of which is a silver star. There are eight massive handles to the coffin, four being placed on each side. The outer edges of the coffin are tastefully scalloped with silver braid to which are attached five tassels of five inches in length.

A row of silver tacks encircles the entire top of the coffin, being placed two inches from the outer edge, while a silver plate, encircled by a shield formed of tacks of the same material, occupies a central position on the top lid, with stars at the head and foot of the coffin on the outside.

The inside of the face lid is raised with white satin, the centre piece being trimmed with black and white silk braid, fastened down with sixteen silver stars, four to each corner. The face lid and the top of the coffin is fastened together with five silver stars.

The inside of the coffin is superbly lined with box-plaited satin, the bottom and pillow being of the finest white silk, while rich three-inch cheniel satin fringe encircles the entire inside.

Preparations for the Funeral.

Washington, April 17.—At a meeting of the members of the Senate and House of Representatives, convened at the Capitol on Monday, April 17, 1865, at noon, Hon. Lafayette S. Foster, of Connecticut, President *pro tem.* of the Senate, was called to the chair, and Schuyler Colfax, of Indiana, was chosen as Secretary.

Senator Foot, of Vermont, stated the object of the meeting to be to make arrangements relative to the funeral of the deceased President of the United States.

On motion of Senator Sumner, of Massachusetts, a committee of five members from each House was ordered to report at 4 P. M. to-day what action it is fitting for this meeting to take.

The Chairman appointed Senators Sumner of Massachusetts, Harris of New York, Johnson of Maryland, Ramsay of Minnesota, and Conness of California, and Representatives Washburne of Illinois, Smith of Kentucky, Schenck of Ohio, Pike of Maine, and Coffroth of Pennsylvania.

At 4 P. M. the meeting convened pursuant to adjournment. Mr. Sumner, from the committee heretofore appointed, reported that they had settled to appoint as pall-bearers on the part of the Senate Mr. Foster, of Connecticut, Mr. Morgan, of New York, Mr. Johnson, of Maryland, Mr. Yates, of Illinois, Mr. Wade, of Ohio, and Mr. Conness, of California. On the port of the House: Mr. Dawes, of Massachusetts, Mr. Coffroth, of Pennsylvania, Mr. Smith, of Kentucky, Mr. Colfax, of Indiana, Mr. Worthington, of Nevada, Mr. Washburne, of Illinois.

They also recommend the appointment of one Member of Congress from each State and Territory to act as a Congressional Committee to accompany the remains of the late President to Illinois, and present the following names as such committee.

Maine, Mr. Pike; New Hampshire, Mr. E. H. Rollins; Vermont, Mr. Foot; Massachusetts, Mr. Sumner; Rhode Island, Mr. Anthony; Connecticut, Mr. Dixon; New York, Mr. Harris; New Jersey, not appointed; Pennsylvania, Mr. Cowan; Delaware, not appointed; Maryland, not appointed; Ohio, Mr. Schenck; Kentucky, Mr. Smith; Indiana, Mr. Julian; Illinois, not appointed. The delegation for Missouri is not yet appointed. Michigan, Mr. Chandler; Iowa, not yet appointed; Wisconsin, not appointed; California, Mr. Shannon; Minnesota, Mr. Ramsey; Oregon, Mr. Williams; Kansas, Mr. S. Clarke; Western Virginia, Mr. Whaley; Nevada, Mr. Nye; New Mexico, not yet appointed; Utah, not appointed; Washington Territory, not appointed; Nebraska, Mr. Hitchcock; Colorado, Mr. Bradford; Dakotah, Mr. Nadd; Arizona, not appointed; Idaho, Mr. Wallace; Montana, not appointed.

They also recommend the adoption of the following resolution:

Resolved, That the Sergeants-at-Arms of the Senate and House of Representatives, with their necessary assistants, be requested to attend the committee accompanying the remains of the late President, and to make all the necessary arrangements.

All of which was concurred in unanimously.

Mr. Sumner, from the same committee, also reported the following, which was unanimously agreed to:

"The members of the Senate and House of Representatives now assembled in Washington, humbly confessing their dependence upon Almighty God, who rules all that is done for human good, make haste, at this informal meeting, to express the emotions with which they have been filled by the appalling tragedy which has deprived the nation of its head and covered the land with mourning, and in further declaration of their sentiments unanimously

1. *Resolve*, That in testimony of veneration and affection for the illustrious dead, who has been permitted, under Providence, to do so much for his country and for liberty, they will unite in the funeral services, and by an appropriate committee, will accompany his remains to their place of burial in the State from which he was taken for the national service.

2. That in the life of Abraham Lincoln, who, by the benignant favor of republican institutions, rose from humble beginnings to the height of power and fame, they recognize an example of purity, simplicity and virtue which should be a lesson to mankind, while in his death they recognize a martyr whose memory will become more precious as men learn to prize those principles of constitutional order and those rights, civil, political and human, for which he was made a sacrifice.

3. That they invite the President of the United States, by solemn proclamation, to recommend to the people of the United States to assemble on a day to be appointed by him, publicly to testify their grief and to dwell on the good which has been done on earth by him whom we now mourn.

THE RICHMOND TIMES.

4. That a copy of these resolutions be communicated to the President of the United States, and also that a copy be communicated to the afflicted widow of the late President, as an expression of sympathy in her great bereavement.

The meeting then adjourned.

L. F. S. Foster, Chairman.

Schuyler Colfax, Secretary.

Action of the Diplomatic Corps.

It is understood that the members of the diplomatic body yesterday held a meeting at the Russian Legation, and appointed a committee of three, Baron Gerolt, the Minister from Prussia, M. Molino, the Minister from Costa Rico, and Colonel Raasloff, the Minister from Denmark, to represent the body and to convey, on behalf of their colleagues, the expressions of their deeply felt sympathy with the family of the late President and the Government and the people of the United States on the occasion of the recent sad events. The committee waited upon the acting Secretary of State, and through him sought an interview with Captain Robert Lincoln, which the latter, for obvious reasons, felt obliged to decline, while expressing his thanks for the sympathy tendered. The diplomatic body have also decided to join in all outward demonstration of sorrow which have been determined upon by the authorities and the citizens.

The Remains to be Taken to Illinois.

It is probable that the remains, after lying at the Capitol during Wednesday night, will be removed on Thursday morning in charge of the committee to Illinois by the way of Baltimore, Philadelphia, New York, Albany, Buffalo, Cleveland and Toledo. The time at which the corpse will reach these different cities has not yet been arranged. The subject is now under advisement. At least a week will be occupied in reaching Illinois, as there will be stoppages on the way.

Many Philadelphians at present in Washington are anxious that the committee from Springfield, Illinois, should pass through Philadelphia on their way West with the remains.—*Washington Chronicle.*

Mrs. Lincoln.

Mrs. Lincoln bears up under her terrible bereavement with becoming fortitude. The families of the members of the Cabinet have paid her every attention, and many of our citizens have tendered her their sincerest sympathies and striven to alleviate the fearful agonies of mind which she has endured for three days past. Mrs. Welles, wife of the Secretary of the Navy, has been with her most of the time since the terrible tragedy occurred.

The Address to the Armies.

War Department, Adj't Gen'ls Office,
Washington, April 16, 1865.

General Orders No. 66:

The following order of the Secretary of War announces to the armies of the United States the untimely and lamentable death of the illustrious Abraham Lincoln, late President of the United States:

War Department,
Washington, April 16, 1865.

The distressing duty has devolved upon the Secretary of War to announce to the armies of the United States that at twenty-two minutes after seven o'clock, on the morning of Saturday, the 15th day of April, 1865, Abraham Lincoln, President of the United States, died of a mortal wound inflicted upon him by an assassin.

The armies of the United States will share with their fellow-citizens the feelings of grief and horror inspired by this most atrocious murder of their great and beloved President and Commander-in-Chief, and with profound sorrow will mourn his death as a national calamity.

The headquarters of every department, post, station, fort and arsenal will be draped in mourning for thirty days, and appropriate funeral honors will be paid by every army, and in every Department, and every military post, and at the Military Academy at West Point, to the memory of the late illustrious Chief Magistrate of the nation and Commander in Chief of its armies.

Lieutenant-General Grant will give the necessary instructions for carrying this order into effect.

Edwin M. Stanton,
Secretary of War.

On the day after the receipt of this order at the headquarters of any military division, department, army, post, station, fort and arsenal, and at the Military Academy at West Point, the troops and cadets will be paraded at ten o'clock A. M., and the orders read to them, after which all labors and operations for the day will cease, and be suspended, as far as practicable in a state of war.

The National flag will be displayed at half-staff.

At dawn of day thirteen guns will be fired, and afterwards, at intervals of thirty minutes between the rising and setting sun, a single gun, and at the closing of the day a National salute of thirty-five guns.

The officers of the armies of the United States will wear the badge of mourning on the left arm and on their swords, and the colors of their commands and regiments will be put in mourning for the period of six months.

By command of

Lieutenant-General Grant,

W. A. Nichols, Assistant Adjutant-General.

Intense Excitement in the North.

New York, April 17.—Three parties were to-day each sentenced to six months' imprisonment in the Penitentiary for uttering treasonable sentiments.

Last evening a squad of young men visited the house of Mrs. John Tyler, the widow of the Ex-President, on Staten Island, and demanded and obtained a rebel flag, which has long been hanging prominently in her parlor. The parlor of Mrs. Tyler is where Secessionists have often gone during the war; and was the headquarters of a rebel sewing society. The flag was sent to General Dix.

Several Secessionists are reported to have been beaten by infuriated Unionists, on hearing their comments made on the assassination.

A man was thrown from the Brooklyn ferry boat into the river to-day for using disloyal language. His life was saved by a passing boat.

Baltimore, April 17.—Westminster, Md., was the scene of quite an excitement on Saturday when the news of the murder of the President became known. A public meeting was held, when resolutions were adopted declaring that no person who had ever left Carroll county to take up arms in the interest of the rebellion should be permitted to return to it, no matter whether he be paroled or not. The office of the *Democrat,* a paper notorious for its abuse of Mr. Lincoln, was visited by the citizens, its proprietor ordered to leave, and the contents of the establishment destroyed.

Washington, April 17.—This morning several prisoners from Prince George's county were brought in. As they were being taken to the Old Capitol prison a large crowd followed, increasing in numbers at every corner, although, as a precautionary measure, the route taken was down the back streets.

The crowd was a motley one, all ages and colors being represented, and the report that the parties were Booth and Surratt gaining credit, as they reached the vicinity of the Baltimore depot the cry was raised, "Hang them!" "kill them!" and at the same the prisoners were attacked with stones; they were struck several times, as were also the guard.

After the guard had been struck a number of times, reaching a street, faced about and made ready to defend themselves with their muskets. The prisoners were delivered to the superintendent of the prison, each of them having been somewhat bruised by the flying missiles. Among other arrests to-day were, it is said, several men in female apparel.

LOCAL DEPARTMENT.

The Richmond Markets—Tariff of Prices. The change from night to day was never more sudden or great than the change of prices growing out of the occupation of Richmond by the United States authorities. This change permeates every department of trade and has affected the price of everything, from a pound of beef to a box of matches. It is reasonable to suppose that great interest is felt by our people to know the new tariff of prices, and we have therefore compiled, with considerable pains, the subjoined statement of the condition of the markets, which may be relied on as correct for the present, though it cannot be considered as any criterion for permanent reference. The existing uncertainty of affairs and scarcity of goods, together with the limited facilities for doing business, cause figures to rule very high; but doubtless matters will change for the better in a short while. When business is resumed prices will come down, and the condition of the community be vastly improved.

Provisions and Groceries.—Flour, $16@18 ℔ barrel; corn meal, $3 ℔ bushel; bacon, 30@35c. ℔ ℔; coffee, 45@50c. ℔ ℔; tea—black, $1 50; green, $2 50; sugar, 25@30c. ℔ ℔; sorghum, $1 ℔ gallon; washing soap, 25c. ℔ ℔; cheese, 40c. ℔ ℔; salt fish—herrings, 50@60c. ℔ dozen; mackerel (No. 2), $2 ℔ dozen; codfish (weighing about 18 ounces), 10c. a piece; Scotch herrings, 20c. ℔ dozen; candles—adamantine, 50c; tallow, 30c, ℔ ℔.

Sutler's Stores.—As most every article enumerated above is kept for sale in these establishments, the ruling prices being the same, it is only necessary to mention such as has not been noted down. Mason's blacking, a commodity much needed, retails for 10c. per box. Toilet soap—Low's Brown Windsor (genuine) 20c. per cake; Imitation (Webb's Manchester) 10c. per cake.

The above quotations are for sales made at retail. Below will be found the wholesale prices, as obtained from Messrs. Kimberly Brothers, of Baltimore and Fortress Monroe, a branch of whose house has been established on Fifteenth street, between Main and Cary, No. 12:

Cheese, 25@30c. ℔ ℔; adamantine candles, 35c. ℔ ℔.; flour, $12 50@$16 ℔ bbl; coffee, 40@42c. ℔ ℔; tea, (green) $2 10 ℔ ℔; bacon—hams, (best sugar cured) 26@28c. ℔ ℔; shoulders, 22c. ℔ ℔; sides, 25c. ℔ ℔; dried beef, 25c. ℔ ℔, by the piece; Bologna sausage, 20@25c. ℔ ℔, by retail; tripe, per half barrel, $13—choice article; beef tongues, $7@7 50 per dozen; fresh peaches, tomatoes, &c., in cans, $10 per case of two dozen cans; washing soap, 12½c. ℔ block or 10 ounces; onions, $6 per barrel.

We shall continue our quotations from time to time, as the change in prices may demand.

Family Marketing.—Fresh meat—beef, veal and shoat, 20@25c. ℔ ℔, supply limited and quality inferior; corned beef, 12½@20c. ℔ ℔; fowls—chickens, 30@40c. a piece; live geese, $1 50@1 75 a piece. Fresh fish—shad, 75c.@$1 50 ℔ pair, some sales of small size at 25c. a piece; herrings, $1 ℔ bunch; perch, 75c. ℔ bunch. Butter, 50c. ℔ ℔; lard, 35@40c. ℔ ℔. Vegetables—Irish potatoes, 75c. ℔ peck; asparagus, 20c. ℔ bunch; lettuce, 25c. ℔ dozen; turnip salad, 40c. ℔ peck; kale, 25@30c. ℔ peck; pie plant, 25c. ℔ bunch; onions, 5@10c. ℔ bunch. Eggs, 50c. ℔ dozen; brooms—country made, 15c.; staff made, with wire lashings, 75c. a piece; hominy, 10c. ℔ quart; peas, 10c. ℔ quart.

Dry Goods and Shoes.—In dry goods scarcely any has been received in Richmond since the evacuation, and therefore no established prices can be obtained. Parties having them on hand generally fix their own prices, according to the patterns called for. Calicos can now be bought for 35c. per yard; unbleached cottons, 40 and 45c. per yard. We were informed yesterday by a merchant that advices received by him from the North represented a heavy decline in all classes of dry goods, which, if so, will produce a similar decline in this market. The sutlers have on hand small lots of gentlemen's shoes, (high quarters) which they are retailing at $4@$4 50 per pair.

Northern Papers.—A limited number of news depots, for the sale of periodicals, newspapers, cheap publications, stationery, &c., have been established, all of whom seem to do a good business. The New York *Herald, Times, News* and *Tribune,* and Philadelphia *Inquirer,* most prominent before the public as secular newspapers, command ten cents a piece. *Harper's Weekly* and *Frank Leslie's Illustrated,* 20c. each; New York *Ledger, Saturday Evening Courier,* &c., ten cents each. Stationary, envelopes, &c., according to quality.

Rebuilding.—We learn that active preparations are being made by the Government to rebuild at an early day the Danville railroad and Mayo's bridges across James river, and probably the Petersburg railroad bridge, all of which were destroyed by fire during the recent terrible conflagration. Already a neat and substantial bridge has been erected across the canal leading to Hunter's Steel Works, and workmen are now engaged in clearing away the rubbish preparatory to putting up new buildings there.

It is also encouraging to notice that private enterprise is awake and contracts have already been made for the erection of business stands on several portions of Main street. At the corner of Main and Eighth streets Captain Martin M. Lipscombe, master brick-layer, is busily engaged in erecting a spacious building, which he has contracted to put up for Mr. Brent, to be used as a store underneath and an art gallery above, while on the corner below, Messrs. Regnault, Maule & Beville propose erecting a large auction and commission house.

Let the work go on, and in a few months the city will prosper, and a large number of our worthy citizens, who have experienced great suffering in consequence of being thrown out of employment, will find plenty to do, whereby they can furnish food to their families and add gladness to their hearts.

The Post Office.—No appointment of postmaster has yet been made for this city, but the mails are received and distributed here with considerable regularity. For the convenience of our readers we will state that a mail leaves Richmond for Norfolk, Portsmouth and all the Northern cities every morning, closing at 4½ o'clock A. M. The time of its arrival daily in this city is between 6 and 8 o'clock in the afternoon. Daily mail communication also exists between Petersburg and Richmond. As yet no regular mails are transmitted to and from interior points in the State, but it is contemplated to make arrangements for doing so as early as possible.

To Advertisers.—Advertising is the great secret of success. The most successful men are those who advertise most liberally. There are men now worth their hundreds of thousands of dollars who would this day be comparatively poor but for the business built up by advertising.

The present—when all the old dealers are burnt out, and the old landmarks of the city are obliterated—is a most desirable time of advertising for dealers who have goods and wares to sell. The trade of the city has been so suddenly diverted from its usual channel and stocks of goods swept away by the fire that the people know not where to buy. The merchant who now advertises is the man who will get the trade. The people look to the papers as a directory.

It will be the aim of the proprietor to make the *Times* the great advertising medium of the city, and the patronage of all classes of merchants and dealers is respectfully solicited. The most particular attention will be given to the insertion and classification of advertisements, and notice will be made calling the attention of the public to each one.

Parties wishing to advertise will not wait to be called on for their advertisements, but will send them to the office, corner of Main and Fourteenth streets.

Important Notice.—Passes to persons *not* belonging to the Army of the James are given by Captain C. E. Scoville, A. D. C., Capitol building. Applications for permits to transact business in the city or its vicinity should be addressed to Captain W. W. Beckwith, office in the Governor's room, Capitol Building.

Amusements.—The performances at the Richmond Theatre are highly entertaining, and nightly attract large and appreciative audiences. Manager Ogden leaves nothing undone to merit public favor, and has the gratification to know that his efforts are rewarded with success.

At the "Varieties," on Franklin street, the performances of Messrs. Buckley and Budd's United Minstrels and Brass Band are greeted nightly with great applause by large audiences. Their bill for to-night is an excellent one.

Stabbing Affray.—A very serious stabbing affray, which will probably result in the death of the injured party, occurred yesterday morning, at an early hour, in the upper end of Sidney, near Camp Winder. It appears that a youth named Thomas McCarrack, residing near by, had an altercation with Robert Jasper, another youth, during which the latter drew a knife and stabbed his antagonist in the lower abdomen, inflicting a wound which it is thought by his physician may result fatally. The wounded party was removed to his mother's residence.

Sentries Shot.—Within the past few nights two sentries—one on guard at the Libby prison and the other at the reservoir, near Hollywood cemetery—have been shot by persons unknown. The guard at the Libby was instantly killed; but, fortunately, the wound inflicted upon the one at the reservoir was in the leg and not very serious in its character. It is not known whether the circumstances were the results of accidents or by design; but every effort will doubtless be made to ferret out the guilty parties.

Outrage Upon a Citizen.—A few nights since, the residence of Mr. Nathan Hardgrove, in Sidney, was forcibly entered by two men, believed to be escaped Penitentiary convicts, who proceeded to his chamber, and, with drawn pistols, demanded his money or his life. Finding no money upon his person, the outlaws took from him a gold watch, and then commanded other members of Mr. Hardgrove's family to show them where his money was kept, as they felt satisfied he must have some. All protestations proved fruitless; they would not be satisfied, and swore they would kill every one of the family unless they found the money. This conduct so much alarmed a little daughter of Mr. Hardgrove that she went to her drawer and took from it a few dollars in specie, which she had received from time to time as presents, and gave it to them, after which they went off, promising to return again.

Robbery by Negroes.—We learn that on Tuesday night last a party of negroes, armed with clubs and knives, proceeded to the house of a gentleman living on the outskirts of the city, and robbed him of everything to eat he had on hand, besides a large lot of his best furniture. Suspected parties have been arrested, who will be severely dealt with if the guilt is fastened upon them.

Commendable Liberality.—On Saturday morning last the firm of Kimberly Brothers, of Baltimore, distributed to the poor of Richmond, from their branch house on Fifteenth street, between Main and Cary, three thousand pounds of fresh beef, of fine quality. Such liberality should act as an incentive for others who are able to do likewise.

To Persons Out of Employment.—There are hundreds of persons in the city out of employment. Most of this unfortunate class are ready and anxious to work, but the great difficulty is to find it. We can give employment to some active and enterprising men in canvassing the city for the *Times*—a business that will be light and at the same time very profitable. Here is a chance for persons who wish to get work.

Notice to Advertisers.—For want of room and the pressure of business attendant upon the publication of the first number of the *Times,* we have been compelled to defer our notice with reference to the advertisements which appear in our columns. It will be published to-morrow morning.

THE RICHMOND TIMES.

Special Notices.

☞ NOTICE.—The friends and customers of the subscriber are informed that he may be found at the store of Messrs. J. W. Gentry & Co., nearly opposite to his old stand, who have kindly permitted him to offer for sale the small remnant of his stock which was rescued from the flames. JOHN C. PAGE, JR.
apr21

☞ TO BUILDERS.—I am prepared to remove and clean the Bricks, &c., from foundations, cut new foundations, or any work in that line. Have had many years experience in such work. Give me a call at J. B. GALLAGHER'S Drug Store, on Main street, between Seventh and Eighth. JOHN A. FOSTER.
apr21—1w

☞ CORNS, BUNIONS, CALLOSITIES, DISEASED Nails, &c., and all diseases of the FEET, treated without pain to the patient, by Dr. SCHULTZ, the Physician and Chiropodist.
Office Wall street Hotel, Wall street, near Franklin. (See sign of Foot.) Ladies and Children attended as usual.
"If you value health, keep Corns from your feet."
apr21—1w

☞ R. H. DIBRELL for the present can be found at ANDERSON'S WAREHOUSE, corner of Canal and Eighth streets, ready to attend to consignments with which his former patrons and the public generally may intrust him. apr21—2w

CHAS. H. WYNNE,

STEAM-PRINTING PRESSES

CORNER MAIN & 14th STS.

RICHMOND, VIRGINIA.

Having resumed operations, I am prepared to fill orders with despatch, in a workmanlike manner.
CARDS, CIRCULARS,
BILL-HEADS, DRAFTS,
BLANKS, HAND-BILLS,
PROGRAMMES, &c.
And every description of

JOB PRINTING

Executed at moderate rates, at short notice, and with accuracy. apr21

AMUSEMENTS.

NEW RICHMOND THEATRE,
Corner Seventh and Broad Streets.
Mrs. E. MAGILL, - - - MANAGERESS
R. DORSAY OGDEN, ACTING & STAGE MANAGER

FRIDAY EVENING, APRIL 21st, 1865,
The performance will commence with the beautiful Overture,
CROWN DIAMONDS, - - - ORCHESTRA
When, by request, will be presented this evening the great French play of the

MYSTERIOUS STRANGER,

OR THE

DEVIL IN PARIS!

Count Henri Beaushill, J. Harrison
Count Vanille, W. C. Talbot
Captain Gasconade, R. J. Brown
Crequet, J. Wells
Chicore, H. Allen
The Mysterious Stranger, The Princess, Fan-Fan, a Gamin de Paris, Captain Du Marc, Clarisse Delville, } Miss SALLIE PARTINGTON in six characters.
Mad de Luceval, Mrs. C. DeDar

During the piece,

A GRAND BAL MASQUE!

OVERTURE, - - - - ORCHESTRA
BALLAD, - - - Miss B. MIDDLETON
GRAND PAS SEUL, - Miss JESSIE WARNER

To conclude with the amusing Comedietta, in two acts, of

ANDY BLAKE,

THE IRISH DIAMOND!
ANDY BLAKE, - Miss SALLIE PARTINGTON

Will soon be produced, with grand effect, a grand Historical Play, in five acts, by R. D. Ogden, entitled

ROBESPIERRE,

OR THE

FATE OF REVOLUTIONS!

apr21—1t

BUCKLEY & BUDD'S OPERA HOUSE,
Franklin street, one door below Exchange Hotel.

BUCKLEY & BUDD'S

Celebrated Minstrels and Brass Band

Received nightly with the most unbounded delight by audiences composed of the elite of the city, both civic and military, to witness their chaste parlor entertainments.
GRAND COMPLIMENTARY BENEFIT
TO
PROFESSOR KELP,
The renowned Violinist,
Assisted by all the Stars of this Mammoth Troupe.
NEW SONGS, DANCES AND BURLESQUES.
Miss INEZ FLOYD, the acknowledged favorite of Richmond, has kindly volunteered, and will sing some of her most charming ballads.
HARRY BUDD and BILLY LEWIS in their mirth-provoking eccentricities. Miss CARRIE BENTLY, the favorite Danseuse of the South, will also appear, assisted by Mr. JOHNSON, the well known Actor and Delineator. BILLY PELL, late of the New Orleans Theatre, will sing some of his inimitable comic songs. If you wish to pass a pleasant evening and enjoy a hearty laugh don't fail to be on hand to-night.
LA PETITE ALICE, the prodigy of the world (only six years old), will appear in her celebrated Atakapas Jig.
Combining in the whole the greatest concentration of talent ever witnessed in this city.
Seats may be secured at the Hall from 11 to 1 A. M., and from 3 to 5 P. M.
GRAND TABLEAU!
Sic Semper Tyrannis
OF THE
FALL OF THE REBELLION!
In which will be presented a grand terrific combat between Miss CARRIE BENTLY and Mr. JOHNSON.
The whole to conclude with the laughable farce, in white faces, entitled
THE GAL THAT WANTS A HUSBAND!
Admission 50 cents. No extra charge for reserved seats. Private boxes, $3.
Strict order will be rigidly enforced. No improper character will be admitted.
Doors open at 7¼; commence at 8¼ precisely.
To-morrow,
GRAND COMPLIMENTARY BENEFIT
TO
HARRY BUDD AND BILLY LEWIS!
(See advertisement.) apr21—1t*

Sales at Auction.

By Hanes & Co., Auctioneers, 54 Main street.

WE will sell, at the Horse Lot, on SATURDAY next, the 22d instant, several
HORSES,
MULES,
VEHICLES, &c.
apr21—2t HANES & CO., 54 Main street.

AUCTIONEERS.

NOTICE.—The subscribers have taken the store formerly occupied by Messrs. Redwood & Phillips, No. 54 Main street, for the purpose of conducting a
General Auction and Commission Business,
Under the name and style of
HANES & CO.
They will sell by auction or at private sale all kinds of GOODS, WARES AND MERCHANDISE.
They solicit from their friends and the public generally consignments, with the assurance that their interest will always be cared for.
They will also sell at the Horse Lot, every Saturday, HORSES, MULES, VEHICLES, &c.
Sales made of Real Estate or of persons declining house keeping on reasonable terms.
Being extensively known, they refer to the citizens generally. HANES & CO.
CHARLES C. HANES, of the firm of Redwood, Phillips & Co.
D. H. ATKINSON and W. H. GILLESPIE, of the firm of D. H. Atkinson & Co.
apr21—eod3t

REGNAULT & CO.,
Auctioneers and Commission Merchants,
OFFICE CORNER MAIN AND NINTH STREETS,
(Opposite Adams' Express Company,)

BY PERMISSION of the Provost Marshal General, have resumed their business as General Auctioneers and Commission Merchants, and respectfully offer their services to their friends and the public generally for the sale of all kinds of
MERCHANDISE,
GROCERIES,
COUNTRY PRODUCE,
FURNITURE, &c.
Their storehouse was destroyed by fire on the 3d of April last. A larger and more commodious one will be at once erected opposite the Spotswood Hotel, and, for a few weeks, our office will be on the corner of Main and Ninth streets, opposite the office of Adams' Express Company.
We promise a strict attention to all business, with prompt sales and quick returns.
JOHN F. REGNAULT,
WM. L. MAULE,
apr21—6t WM. J. BEVILL.

D. F. BOOTH, AUCTIONEER, having a long experience in the
AUCTION BUSINESS,
Begs leave to tender his services to the public generally. Will attend to sales of families declining housekeeping, merchants and others.
Also, will receive on consignment, to be sold at store,
MERCHANDISE,
GROCERIES,
FURNITURE, &c.
Also, will sell every Saturday, at 10 o'clock, on Council Chamber Hill, HORSES, MULES, VEHICLES, &c.
Office first door above Main Street, on Fourteenth, east side, and any Goods left with Messrs. TOLLESON & CATLETT, 193 Broad Street, will meet with prompt attention. apr21—6t

E. B. COOK, AUCTIONEER, No. 70 Main Street,
Respectfully informs his friends and the public generally, that he has resumed business at his old stand for the sale of
Merchandise, Groceries,
Dry Goods, Furniture, &c.
Will also give personal attention to all sales at private residences, and Live Stock, &c., at the Horse Lot.
apr21—1w

Tobacco and Cigars.

TOBACCO AND VARIETY STORE,
Ninth Street, opposite the Capitol Square,
Richmond, Va.
THOMAS C. C. DREWRY
Respectfully announces to his friends and customers, and the public generally, that he has taken the small store on the west side of Ninth street, between Franklin and Grace streets, and immediately opposite the Capitol Square, where he has a fine stock of
MANUFACTURED and
SMOKING TOBACCO,
PIPES, PENS,
PAPER, ENVELOPES, &c.,
Which he will be happy to dispose of on accommodating terms, FOR CASH.
COMMISSION BUSINESS.
He would also state to his friends that he has rented an office in the same building, for the purpose of carrying on
A General Commission Business,
And would be happy to receive consignments from his friends in the city or from any part of Virginia or North Carolina.
apr21—1m THOMAS C. C. DREWRY.

JOHN BOUCHER,
181 Broad street, between Fifth and Sixth,
CIGAR MANUFACTURER,
Keeps constantly on hand the best CIGARS, TOBACCO, &c., which he offers to the public upon as reasonable terms as they can be purchased elsewhere in the city.
apr21—1m

Watches, Jewelry, &c.

C. C. WALTER, dealer in
Watches, Clocks, Jewelry, &c.,
131 Broad street, (*Opposite R. F. & P. R. R. Depot,*)
RICHMOND, VA.
☞ Watches, Clocks and Jewelry repaired and warranted. apr21—1w

C. SCHUMANN & BROTHER,
CLOCK, WATCHMAKERS AND JEWELERS,
Broad, between Second and Third Streets, Richmond, Va.
apr21—1m

MR. MARK WALTER,
PRACTICAL WATCHMAKER.
Watches and Jewelry
Repaired with neatness and dispatch.
Broad Street, (west side,) second door below Brook Avenue.
apr21—3m

Photographic Art.

VANNERSON & JONES,
NEW ART GALLERY,
No. 77 Main street,
Between 14th and 15th, (formerly Whitehurst's,)
RICHMOND, VA.
Ambrotypes Photographs,
and Cartes de Visite.
(*Plain and Colored, from Locket to Life Size.*) apr21—tf

JACKSON & HARRIS,
PHOTOGRAPH GALLERY,
No. 163 Broad Street, Richmond.
apr 21—1w

Business Chances.

FOR SALE—
KING'S NEW DYE WORKS,
Near the city Gas Works and Steamship wharf, suitable for a Sutler or Grocery store. Apply to
E. KING,
apr21—tf Dyer, Main street, near the Spotswood.

FOR SALE—The KEY of one of the best stores in Richmond, near the Spotswood Hotel.
E. KING,
apr21—tf Dyer, &c.

Hotels, Restaurants, &c.

RICHMOND SALOON,
225 Franklin street, four doors above Exchange Hotel.
PETER MATTHEWS, Proprietor.
(Formerly of the Planters' House, on Tenth Street, which was destroyed during the recent conflagration.)
Having re-opened at this eligibly situated stand, he can promise his friends and customers, and the public generally, always a fresh supply of everything usually kept in a first-class Restaurant.
FRESH FISH, VEGETABLES, &c.
Procured every day.
Strangers visiting Richmond, who prefer not to stop at a hotel, will find it advantageous to take their meals at this Saloon.
Private dining rooms for parties desiring them.
apr21—3t

NEW MARKET HOTEL,
Corner Sixth and Marshall Streets.
R. EMERSON, Proprietor.
Comfortable accommodations can always be had at this Hotel. Being eligibly located in a retired, and at the same time central, part of the city, it affords peculiarly advantageous inducements for strangers visiting the city to put up at.
Attached to this Hotel, is a spacious and well-arranged
BALL ROOM,
Which will be rented to parties desiring to give entertainments of that description. apr21—3t*

"GENERAL GRANT RESTAURANT."
No. 259 Main Street, above the Spotswood Hotel.
MEALS AT ALL HOURS
May be had, and everything usually found in a first-class establishments in the North.
Persons visiting Richmond will find it to their advantage by paying a visit to the
"General Grant Restaurant."
C. BAUMHARD,
apr21—1w Proprietor.

PARK HOUSE,
Broad Street, between Eighth and Ninth.
W. BURNS, Proprietor.
Meals furnished at all hours, upon the most reasonable terms.
Everything which the markets can afford will always be on hand. apr21—3m

OLD BROAD STREET HOTEL SALOON,
J. B. SMITH, Proprietor.
North side Broad, between Eighth and Ninth Streets.
Richmond, Va.
N. B.—Parties desiring the services of SMITH'S BRASS BAND, can leave their orders at the Saloon. apr21—1m

EXCHANGE RESTAURANT,
No. 2 Exchange Building, Fourteenth street.
MEALS furnished at all times of the best the market affords.
C. G. HUNTER,
apr21—tf Proprietor.

H. NEUROHR,
323 Broad street.
LAGER BEER SALOON.
TOBACCO,
CIGARS,
PIPES,
apr21—2w MATCHES, &c.

Boarding and Lodging.

MR. COURTNEY, corner of Main and Eighth streets, (just above the Spotswood Hotel,) is prepared to accommodate BOARDERS, either permanent or transient, on the most reasonable terms. Every effort will be made to give satisfaction. apr21

PERMANENT OR TRANSIENT BOARDERS (gentlemen only) can be accommodated at
Mrs. BOWMAN'S,
Franklin street, between 15th and 17th streets.
apr21—1w

Boots and Shoes.

JAMES BOLTON,
No. 172 Broad street, between Sixth and Seventh,
Boot and Shoe Manufacturer,
Keeps constantly on hand the best assortment of Ladies and Gentlemen's BOOTS AND SHOES of his own manufacture, made from the best material and by the most competent workmen.
Repairing of all kinds done in the neatest manner, upon reasonable terms. apr21—1w

LAWYERS.

A. JUDSON CRANE,
ATTORNEY AND COUNSELLOR.
☞ Office, for present, Canal, between Fourth and Fifth.
apr21—3m

Gunsmiths and Locksmiths.

NOTICE.—SPORTSMEN can have their GUNS, RIFLES and PISTOLS, repaired at L. C. BELL'S, No. 221, Broad street, between Third and Fourth. Housekeepers can have their LOCKS repaired, KEYS fitted, BELL HANGING or repairing done at BELL'S. Always on hand and for sale, GUNS, RIFLES, PISTOLS, and all kinds of SPORTING AMMUNITION. On hand and for sale, LOCKS of every description. apr21—1m

J. L. HARDWICKE,
No. 254 Main Street.
LOCKSMITH AND BELL-HANGER.
All kinds of Locks made to order, and Bell-Hanging attended to at the shortest notice. Orders will receive prompt attention. apr21

Plumbing and Gas-Fitting.

PLUMBING, GAS FITTING AND TINNING
Promptly done by
BARRETT & SHAWLEY,
Franklin Street, opposite Metropolitan Hall.
apr21—2w

Merchant Tailors.

R. HARDESTY,
Franklin street, 3 doors west of Shockoe Creek,
MERCHANT TAILOR,
Does all kinds of work in his line, cheap for cash.
apr21—3t

WILLIAM BOWLES,
Corner of Governor and Franklin,
MERCHANT TAILOR.
Cutting, Repairing, Making, &c., done to order at the shortest possible notice. apr21—2w

Military Trimmings.

JOHN HARTZ,
No. 215 Broad Street, between Fourth and Fifth,
Dealer in all kinds of
Trimming and Furnishing Goods.
A well selected assortment of MILITARY TRIMMINGS on hand and for sale. apr21—1w

BADGES.—All Officers wanting BADGES made, can have them made to order at
Mrs. LEWIS',
apr21—2w 98 Main street.

ZIMMER & CO.,
Wholesale and retail
Confectioners and Candy Manufacturers,
At their old stand, No. 17 Main street. apr21—1w.

Commission Merchants.

J. H. MARTIN. E. M. CARDOZO.

Martin & Cardozo,

COMMISSION MERCHANTS

FOR THE SALE OF
MANUFACTURED AND LEAF TOBACCO,
WHEAT, FLOUR, CORN,
BACON, HAY, LUMBER, WOOD,
AND OTHER PRODUCE,
RICHMOND, VIRGINIA.
☞ Warehouse on Basin Bank. apr21—1w

JOHN W. GENTRY & CO.,
No. 78 Main street, Richmond, Va.,
COMMISSION MERCHANTS.
Having one of the largest and most commodious business houses in the central portion of the city, we respectfully solicit consignments from our friends and the public generally, feeling assured that entire satisfaction will be given.
☞ Attention invited to our large assortment of superior SMOKING and CHEWING TOBACCO, CIGARS, PIPES, FANCY ARTICLES, &c., &c. apr21—2w

DRUGGISTS.

R. W. POWERS,
Corner Main and Fifteenth Streets.
Druggist and Apothecary,
Keeps on hand always a well selected stock of FRESH DRUGS, MEDICINES and TOILET ARTICLES. Is prepared to put up PRESCRIPTIONS at all hours, both day and night, on the most reasonable terms. apr21

POWER & McPHAIL,
(Successors to E. J. Picot.)
DRUGGISTS AND PHARMACEUTISTS,
Corner Seventeenth and Main Streets,
RICHMOND, VA.,
Keep always on hand a large and well selected stock of DRUGS and MEDICINES, and are prepared to fill all orders in their line of business.
Prescriptions carefully compounded. apr213taw1m

JAMES B. GALLAGHER,
No. 255 Main street, between Seventh and Eighth,
DRUGGIST AND APOTHECARY.
He will always keep a fresh and general supply of DRUGS and MEDICINES. Also a supply of PERFUMERIES, FANCY ARTICLES, &c.
Prescriptions carefully put up at all hours, both day and night. apr21—1w

LIGHT! LIGHT! LIGHT!
KEROSENE OIL
KEROSENE OIL.
A supply received and for sale by
CHARLES JOHNSTON, Druggist,
apr21—2t 18th and Main streets.

GROCERIES, &c.

WE WOULD respectfully invite the attention of the citizens of Richmond to our complete assortment of

Family Groceries,

Consisting of
JAVA AND LAGUAYRA COFFEE,
BROWN, WHITE AND CRUSHED SUGARS,
SYRUPS AND HONEY,
PICKLES AND CANNED FRUIT,
TOBACCO, CIGARS, &c.
CHEESE, BUTTER AND LARD,
MACKEREL AND HERRINGS,
FLOUR AND MEAL,
CRACKERS, CAKES, &c. Also

Fancy Articles.

LUBIN'S EXTRACTS and PERFUMES of all kind,
HAIR BRUSHES, COMBS, &c.
And a general variety of all articles usually found in a
First Class Grocery and Notion House.
Prices will be found to be at least fifteen per cent. less than any other establishment in the city.
BAUMHARD & LAWSON,
Nos. 257 and 259 Main Street,
apr21—1w Between Seventh and Eighth.

THOMAS PHILLIPS & CO.,
Corner of Seventh and Broad Streets,
Have always on hand a choice assortment of
FAMILY GROCERIES, PRODUCE, &c.
☞ Cheap for CASH ONLY. apr21—1m

CHARLES L. TODD,
Sixth Street, between Marshall and Clay,
Grocer and Commission Merchant,
Keeps constantly on hand a choice assortment of FAMILY GROCERIES, which will be sold as reasonable as they can be bought at any other store in the city. apr21—1w

FAMILY GROCERIES,
At reduced rates, at
E. F. Griffin & Co's.,
At the store formerly occupied by A. A. Hughes, 202 Broad Street, between First and Foushee Streets.
Prices reasonable, and at prices to suit the times.
apr21—1w

CARTER & MONTEIRO,
No. 229 Main Street.
Having resumed our business, we request our friends to call and examine our stock of
Groceries, Tobacco and Fancy Goods.
apr21

PAINTING.

HOUSE AND SIGN PAINTING
DONE IN THE BEST STYLE,
At No. 6 Wall street, between Main and Franklin.
ALSO,
Glazing Done at Moderate Rates.
Orders thankfully received and punctually attended to.
apr21—1w P. McKEON.

RUSSELL W. ALLEN,
SIGN AND ORNAMENTAL PAINTER,
WILLIAM S. WOODSON,
SIGN PAINTER, GRAINER, &c.,
R. G. ALLEN,
THE YOUNG ARTIST,
Are all to be found at No. 195 Broad street, corner of Fifth, prepared to do all kinds of work at short notice, and PLAIN PAINTING in the best manner.
We return our thanks to our old customers, and hope they will call on us when they want anything in our line. Strangers will be assured of our doing the fair thing.
apr21—3t

HOUSE AND SIGN PAINTING.
JOHN W. LEE & S. Y. LANDRUM
Beg to inform their friends and the public that they continue as heretofore to execute all orders in the above business, and solicit calls from their friends. Office on Grace Street, corner of Eighth.
LEWIS L. MONTAGUE also has his office at the same place, where he will be pleased to receive orders for SIGN WORK of all kinds from his old patrons and the public.
apr21—1w

Dry Goods.

JULIUS MEYER,
No. 175 Broad street, between Sixth and Seventh.
DRY GOODS AND FANCY STORE.
Sales made upon reasonable terms, and polite attention given his customers.
A fair stock of CROCKERY WARE on hand, which it is desirable to close up. apr21—2t

The Daily Telegraph

EXTRA.

HOUSTON, APRIL 21, 1865.

BY TELEGRAPH.

SHREVEAORT, April 21.—Gen. Lee with the army of Virginia has surrendered to Gen. Grant. Headquarters Armies of the United States, April 9, 4-30 P. M. To Hon. E. M. Stanton, Secretary of War. Gen. Lee surrendered the army of Northern Virginia this afternoon upon the terms proposed by myself. The accompanying additional correspondence will show the conditions more fully. U. S. GRANT,
Lt. Gen'l.

April 9th, 1865.—General. I received your note of this morning on the picket line, whither I had come to meet you and ascertain definitely what terms were embraced in your propositions of yesterday with reference to the surrender of this army. I now request an interview in accordance with the offer contained in yours of yesterday for that purpose.

Very respectfully, your obd't serv't,
R. E. LEE.

CAMP U. S. A., April 9.—To Gen. R. E. Lee Commanding Confederate States Armies:—Your note of this date is but this moment 11:15 A. M., received in consequence of my having passed from the Richmond and Lynchburg railroad to the Danville and Lynchburg railroad. I am at this writing about four miles west of Walter's Church, and will push forward to the front for the purpose of meeting you.

Notice sent to me on this road where you wish the interview to take place will meet me. Very respectfully,
U. S. GRANT, Lt. Gen.

APPOMATOX C. H., April 8.—Gen. R. E. Lee, etc.:—In accordance with the substance of my letter to you of the 8th inst., I propose to receive the surrender of the army of Northern Virginia, on the following terms, to-wit: Rolls of all the officers and men to be made on duplicate, one copy to be given to any officer designated by me, the other to be retained by such officers as you may designate.

The officers to give their individual paroles not to take up arms against the Government of the United States, until properly exchanged, and each company or regiment commanders sign a like parole for the men of their commands. The arms, artillery and public property to be picked, selected and turned over to the officers appointed by me to receive them. This done each officer and man will be allowed to return to their homes, not to be disturbed by the U. S. authorities so long as they observe their parole and the laws in force where they may reside. Respectfully,
U. S. GBANT, Lieut. Gen.

Headq'rs, Army Northern Virginia,
April 9th, 1865.

To Lieut. Gen. Grant.

I have received your letter of this date, containing terms of surrender of the Army of Northern Virginia, as proposed by you, and as they are the same expressed by you in your letter of the 8th inst., they are accepted. I will proceed to designate the proper officers to carry the stipulations into effect. Very respectfully,
(Signed) R. E. LEE, Gen'l.

CLIFTON HOUSE, Va., April 9th.
Hon. E. M. Stanton, Sec'y of War

The following correspondence has taken place between Gen. Lee and myself. There has been no relaxation in pursuit during its pendence. U. S. GRANT, Lt Gen.

APRIL 7, 1865.—Gen. R. E. Lee—The result of the last week must convince you of the hopelessness of further resistance on the part of the Army of Northern Virginia in this struggle. I feel that it is so, and regard it as my duty to shift from myself the responsibility of any further effusion of blood, by asking of you the surrender of that portion of the Confederate States Army, known as the Army of Northern Virginia. Very respectfully,
U. S. GRANT,
Lieut. Gen.

April 7.—General: I have received your note of this date, though not of the opinion you express of the hopelessness of further resistance on the part of the army of Northern Va. I respect your desire to evade the useless effusion of blood, and therefore, before considering your proposition, I ask the terms you will offer of conditions of surrender.
(Signed,) R. E. LEE.

April 8, 1865.—Your note of last evening, in reply to mine of the same date, asking on what conditions I will accept the surrender of the army of Northern Virginia, is received, in reply I would say that peace being my first desire, there is but one condition that I insist on, that the men surrendered shall be disqualified from taking up arms against the government of the United States, until properly exchanged

I will meet you or designate officers to meet any officer you may name, for the same purpose, at any point agreeable to you, for the purpose of arranging definitely the terms on which the surrender of the army of Northern Virginia, will be received. Very respectfully,
U. S. GRANT,
Lieut. Gen.

HD. QRS. ARMIES OF THE
C. S. '65.

General: I received at a late hour your note in answer to mine yesterday. I did not intend to propose the surrender of the army of Northern Virginia, but to ask the terms of your proposition. To be frank, I do not think the emergency has arrived to call for a surrender, but as a restoration of peace, should be the sole object of all I desire to know whether your proposals tend to that end.

I cannot therefore meet you with a view to surrender the army of Northern Virginia, but as far as your proposition may affect the Confederate States' army forces under my command and tend to the restoration of peace, I should be pleased to meet you at 10 A. M., to-morrow, at the old stage road to Richmond, between the picket stations of both armies.
R. E. LEE.

April 9, 1865.—Your note of yesterday is received I have no authority to treat on the subject of peace The meeting proposed for 10, a. m., to-day could lead to no good I am equally anxions for peace with yourself, and the whole North entertains the same feelings. Terms upon which peace can be had are well understood by the South.

By laying down their arms they will hasten that most desirable event, save thousands of human lives, and hundreds of millions of property, not yet destroyed. Sincerely hoping that all our difficulties may be settled without the loss of another life, I subscribe myself very respectfully,
U. S. GRANT, Lt. Gen'l.

Headq'rs, Trans-Mississippi Dep't,
Shreveport, La., April 21, '65.

Soldiers of the Trans-Mississippi Army, the crisis of our revolution is at hand, great disasters have overtaken us. The Army of Northern Virginia, and our commander-in-chief are prisoners of war. With you rests the hopes of our nation, upon your action depends the fate of our people.

I appeal to you in the name of the cause you have so heroically maintained, in the name of your firesides and families so dear to you, in the name of your bleeding country whose future is in your hands, show that you are worthy of your position in history, prove to the world that your hearts have not failed in the hour of disas- and that to the last moment you will siu tho holy cause which has been so iously battled for by your brethren East of the Mississippi.

You possess the means of long resisting invasion. You have hopes of succor from abroad. Protract the struggle, and you will surely receive the aid of nations, who already deeply sympathize with you. Stand by your colors, maintain your discipline, the great resources of this department, its vast extent, the numbers the discipline and the efficiency of the army, will secure to our country terms that a proud people can with honor accept, and may under the providence of God be the means of checking the triumph of our enemy, and of securing the final success of our cause.
E. KIRBY SMITH.

SHREVEPORT, April 21.—The New Orleans Times of the 15th, says that Mobile is now in possession of the Union forces, and that Forrest has met with disaster near Eastport. CONSCRIPT.

The Montana Post.

D. W. TILTON & CO., Proprietors.

VIRGINIA CITY, M. T.

Saturday, - - - - April 22d, 1865.

COME AT LAST.

By the last mail, we have received the confirmation of the surrender of General Lee and his army. Practically speaking, this is the end of the rebellion. For this crowning victory to our arms let the thanks of a grateful nation ascend to the Great Disposer of Events, and may the future career of the Republic be as prosperous as Liberty and Peace can make it.

THE FLOUR DIFFICULTY.

One of the most sacred duties of a journalist, as well as one of his most honorable privileges, in a free country, is the thorough discussion of all questions affecting the public weal, and the relentless exposure and refutation of all those sophistical arguments and subterfuges by which men seek to justify crimes against their fellows, committed with a view to the self aggrandizement of the few, at the expense of the suffering of the many. With this feeling uppermost in our mind we address ourself to the consideration of the events of the last few days.

The history of the acts of the Flour Committee and their supporters is given in another place; our present business is the examination of the causes that led to the action of the people.

A few weeks back, flour was selling at about $23 per sack, in this market, when the efforts of a few short sighted men were directed to raising the price. Overshooting the mark, they imprudently commenced a combination, with a view to a monopoly of the article, and succeeded in buying up the stock in hand, to such an extent as practically insured them the control of the market. From the prices above named the staple article of subsistence in these mountains rose suddenly till it reached $45.

Now no law (did such an one exist) can make right out of that which is morally wrong, and in view of the severity of the winter and the impossibility of a miner's earning money for the support of his family, the raising of the price of flour at such a time, by combination and speculative purchase, is a wrong that should insure lasting ignominy to the perpetrators. A further increase was a still greater and more inexcusable iniquity than the former. It has been stated that the speculators had lost money previously, and wanted to make themselves square. If this is a justification of their acts, we might as well repeal all laws against road agents, for though their method of operating is bolder, yet the principle (that a loss or a want is to be supplied by the pillage of another) is the same; and all the acts of depredation committed in this Territory, were nothing, in comparison with the devastion and slaughter that any accidental scuffle would have brought about, during Tuesday.

One man has no right to be enriched at the expense of a community. One man is as good, in the eyes of American law, as another, and it is ridiculous to say that a man may starve a population to benefit himself. Instinct says NO. Let men make what they can in a barter of superfluities or by a trade in anything but necessary food, clothing, medicine or the like, and we have nothing to say; but it is absurd to think that Anglo-Saxon Mountaineers will stand like a trained dog, and, as a test of submission, *point* at food, while starving, without daring to touch it. This will do for Austrians or Russians but in the mines, men act on the square or suffer the penalty. Monopoly is odious and must not be even mentioned as tolerable to free men. One life is too much pay for all the flour in St. Louis.

The attempt at monopoly is a public wrong, indictable at common law, which is the law of this Territory. Such offences are so commonly winked at—or at any rate so often tolerated—that men of the stripe of our extortionists often think they have a legal right to forestall the market and enhance the prices of articles of necessity. The reverse is however the case, and we trust that our officials will prove themselves worthy of their trust by an honest endeavor to enforce the penalties of the law against the offenders who have by their acts incited the intervention of armed force on the part of the people, to prevent the starvation of those whose means were inadequate to meet the outrageous demands of all-grasping speculators. We saw, but a few days back, indications of the temper of the people, enough to satisfy any reasoning man of the danger of attempting to defy the inhabitants of a mining district; but it did not operate as a warning to these greedy of gain. They were careless of the misery their conduct must entail upon many an honest laborer and his family as well as upon others far less used to hardship, and with as scanty means to meet the attack on their purses. Buoyed up to a sense of security, by the prompt action of the authorities in quelling the last disturbance—these worthy representatives of Gripe and Holdfast determined to make catspaws of the officials and the citizens, and while under the shelter of their protection, they ran up flour, in a day, to $100 per sack and openly boasted that they had a right to sell for what they pleased; intimating their intention to raise prices still higher. Quickly on the heels of their jubilation came their downfall, with none to pity them.

All resorts to violence or even enforcement of *rights* by other than judicial authority, where such exists with due power to back its decrees is unquestionably illegal and in the end injurious; but the responsibility rests with the men who provoked the popular demonstration we have witnessed this week. In the attempt to fill their own purses, what have these traders done? They have given a bad name to the rest of the many honest merchants of this community, who would scorn such an act as battening on the necessities of the people. They have substituted for the equitable sway of our civic authority, the tyranny of mob law; they have raised an evil report and created a false impression of the character of our people; they have worked for the diversion of capital from our Territory, and they have done their best to bring about such a state of things as would inevitably prevent a supply of provisions from being brought into market, for fear of seizure by excited and hungry men. They have done all this in the face of the law of the land, and in defiance of that higher law whose epitome is to be found in the precept: "Whatsoever therefore ye would that men should do unto you, do ye also so unto them." And for what is all this brought about? Why, that two or three should make a fortune on the ruin of the social happiness and at the peril of the best interests of thousands. Now, there are none living who more detest the exercise of judicial functions by crowds of men than we do; but *necessity knows no law*, and it has ere now been the mother of a sort of half sister to the present offspring of popular justice highly beneficial, for a time in this community, and although we cannot but believe that this action of the masses, will, in the end prove injurious to themselves, yet we cannot withhold a tribute of praise due to those who restrained excesses which have been hitherto thought inseparable from such a multitudinous executive. Those people also deserve credit for their ready compliance with all suggestions on the part of reliable men, for the prevention of the evils likely to accrue from a resort to physical force on so large a scale. We hope that we shall never again witness a similar scene, and that steps will be taken to prevent a recurrence of the opportunity to do wrong, which might have caused such misery and ruin as has been providentially averted. A positive pledge has been given that no interference will be made with the property of the packers and freighters who shall bring provisions to this city for the future. Before closing this article we feel bound to cite as an instance, among many, of the harm done to the character of innocent men by the conduct we have deprecated. The store and warehouse of a merchant near us was four or five times searched, and a belief entertained manifestly to his prejudice as a business man, that some 200 sacks were still secreted—the fact being that the last of his stock was sold for the relief of the needy, at $40 per sack less than he could have obtained from twenty applicants.

To sum up the matter shortly, we ask whether the citizens could acquit a few greedy individuals of blame—much less, defend them—if, as was but too likely, the place had been fired and some of our worthiest residents killed? And again, when seeking to fix the responsibility on the right shoulders, let it be enquired whether these things would have happened, if the speculators had been satisfied with even $50 per sack? The answers to these queries must settle the question we are debating, and the rule by which to judge fairly of these transactions is the "good of the many before the interest of the few."

Missouri Navigation---Ophir.

Since we last called the attention of the public to this subject, there has been considerable interest taken by long-headed people, about the town of Ophir, and any number of lots could be disposed of if the company were willing so to do; but they take a much more generous and comprehensive view of the matter, and one which, while it will subserve the best interests of every merchant in the Territory, will, at the same time conduce to the prosperity of the town. The building of a large city is quite out of the range of speculation; it is a necessity, and will soon be demonstrated to be a certainty. The American Fur Company's steamer will perhaps go up to the the Fort; but no man in his senses will risk forty miles of difficult and shallow navigation, to get to a place where there is neither fuel nor feed, while both are to be had in abundance, at Ophir. The truth is that all the trains going thither have to move down to this neighborhood, in order to be fed. The climate is excellent, there being little snow, and horses now in this town, wintered at large, without a pound of hay or feed of any kind, working all the time. Blacksmiths, a baker, merchants, mechanics and several others have gone and are going over to settle permanently and to erect substantial buildings; liberal inducements having been offered by the Company to such people. Oxen have been purchased, which will leave in a few days, to assist the operation of the Lumber Company, whose affairs will be managed by Capt. F. W. Moore (the only white man who has navigated all the Missouri) J. Kiskadden and A. S. Smith. Plenty of fine pine lies contiguous to the Marias, and this will be felled and floated to Ophir, where a steam saw mill will be erected, for the purpose of converting it for building uses. In order that the public may have some guarantee of the soundness of the whole scheme we append a list of the names of the leading men of the Ophir town company:

President.—W. F. Moore.
Secretary.—Moses Clark.
Treasurer.—N. W. Burris.

E. P. Lewis, Capt. W. F. Davidson, G. B. Parker, George Hill.

W. F. Davidson is President of the Milwaukie and St. Paul Packet Company, and also president of the Idaho Steam Packet Company. E. P. Lewis is the well known Recorder of Deer Lodge county, and Geo. B. Parker is a well to do and energetic citizen here. The remainder of the gentlemen have the reputation of being good business men, and there can be no doubt that the great desideratum of a good town at the head waters of the Missouri is at length in a fair way of attainment. A first rate hotel will be erected next fall, which will be a great inducement to business men wintering there. A solid and substantial fortune awaits any man of energy, who plants his stake at Ophir, and no more important service can be rendered to the community than the erection of a town at a point whither heavy goods can be brought by water, avoiding the weary journey and many casualties of a pilgrimage across the plains.

THE BEST NEWS YET!

SURRENDER OF LEE AND HIS WHOLE FORCE TO GEN. GRANT!

Jeff.'s whereabouts uncertain!!

THE CONFEDERACY "GONE UP!"

Gen. Anderson plants the same Flag on Sumpter that he hauled down!

200 guns fired at each head-quarters in honor of the victory!

Washington, April 8.

The Richmond Whig of Thursday evening says, the transition from enormous prices and depreciated currency to reasonable rates and real money has come so suddenly upon the citizens, that it will be some time before they can properly appreciate the change. Butter, which was scarce at $25 a pound, is now plenty at fifty and sixty cents. Eggs that were hid away at $200 per dozen, are now selling at 30 cents, and other commodities have declined in equal ratio.

Pending the excitement and confusion consequent upon the evacuation on Sunday, 350 convicts in the State Penitentiary managed to escape, but on Tuesday over 100 were recaptured and returned to prison.

Military Governor Shipley has authorized a detail of colored troops to clear away the ruins of the great fire so as to expose the broken gas pipes. Sutlers' stores are springing up all over the business part of the city left by the fire, and old times are being revived by the sight of substantials and luxuries which were enjoyed before the war. Mails are made up daily for the North. Four Confederate detectives, who resigned and remained behind when their goverment changed its base, have been arrested, together with Wiley, Turnkey of Castle Thunder, and Frederick Shaffer, bread commissary of the Union prisoners, and all committed to Libby. The functions of the Mayor and the police are suspended for the present and military law governs in the city.

The Whig gives additional particulars of the evacuation, which had been going on for months, but the people were blinded and they refused to believe that removal meant evacuation, as they all declared that the measures were only precautionary.

On Sunday morning the gold and silver coin belonging to the Louisiana banks and recently appropriated by the Confederate Congress was sent down to Danville by train, also the specie of the Richmond banks. Then the programme for the departure of the officials was arranged. A number of officers were to leave during the evening. Still there was not room for all who thought it desirable to get away. Davis left at 7 p. m. Breckinridge went on horseback with the last of the army on Monday morning. Gov. Smith ran off during the night.

New York, April 8.

A meeting of prominent citizens in the Custom House to-day, adopted an address to President Lincoln, requesting a day to be designated when the people may assemble to offer thanks and praise for the brilliant successes which, under Divine Providence, have been secured by the persistent energy, sagacity and fidelity of the government, and by the skill, intrepidity and self-sacrificing devotion of the army and navy.

Washington, April 8.

No Dix:—A telegram from Grant, dated 12 noon to-day, at Farmville, 46 miles west of Burks' Station, says the enemy have been pushed from the road toward Danville, and are now being pursued toward Lynchburg, and that he is very confident of receiving the surrender of Lee and what remains of his army.

(Signed,) STANTON.

The Post's special says, there is no doubt that Hunter and Campbell remained in Richmond to see what could be done about peace. The President will probably soon issue another amnesty proclamation.

The Richmond Whig says, Gov. Smith made a speech on Sunday, saying, the rebel troops were victorious and Richmond would not be evacuated. He then left on horseback.

A large number of rebel prisoners arrived in Washington this morning. They are desirous of taking the oath of allegiance.

A Richmond letter of the 6th says, the new state of affairs in this city gives general satisfaction to the rebels who, to show their gratitude, tender every attention and information to our soldiers, and on the soldiers' part they are kind and courteous, thus giving the lie to the false reports in the rebel papers.

New York, April 8.

The steamer Arago, with Gen. Anderson and some 300 other distinguished persons, sailed for Charleston this afternoon. Four other steamers for the same destination also sailed, crowded with passengers.

The Herald's correspondent who ascended the James River from City Point to Richmond says, just below Chapin's Farm, was the new iron-clad unfinished ram Texas. She had a plain flush deck, but no armament and engines, and was very light in the water. The river was found lined with formidable works on both sides, with the guns all remaining. Such had been the haste to evacuate, that some guns were spiked only with wrought iron and nails.

The Commercial's special says, it is believed that Lee has succeeded in reaching the Appomattox, where it intersects the Lynchburg railroad five miles west of Burkesville and is pushing for the former place. Grant's superior cavalry will enable him to overhaul the fugitives. It is hinted that there was a want of harmony and cooperation between some subordinate commanders during the advance on Burkesville Junction. Had not this been so, it is said that Lee could not have reached further than Amelia.

Advices from Richmond on Thursday evening say, several rebel civil officers retreated along with Lee, not having previously left the city. The railroad from Richmond to Burkesville Junction will be opened immediately and used as a line of supply. An attempt to raise some of the vessels sunk in the James river is to be made. The guns at Fort Darling were not destroyed as previously reported. Many of the prisoners arriving here are taking the oath of allegiance.

War Department, Washington, April 9.

This Department has just received the official report of the surrender this day by Gen. Lee of his army to Lieut. Gen. Grant on the terms proposed by Lieut. Gen. Grant. The details will be given as speedily as possible.

(Signed,) EDWIN M. STANTON.

H. Qs. Armies of the U. S., 4:35 p. m. }
April 9, 1865. }

Hon. Edwin M. Stanton, Secretary of War:—Gen. Lee surrendered the army of Northern Virginia this p. m. upon terms proposed by myself. The accompanying additional correspondence will show the conditions fully.

(Signed,) U. S. GRANT, Lieut. Gen.

April 9, 1865.

Gen. I received your note of this morning on the picket line, whither I had come to meet you and ascertain definitely what terms were embraced in your proposition of yesterday, with reference to the surrender of this army. I now request an interview, in accordance with the offer contained in your letter of yesterday, for that purpose. Very respectfully your obedient servant.

(Signed,) R. E. LEE, Gen.

To Lieut. Gen. U. S. Grant, commanding U. S. Armies.

April 9, 1865.

Gen. R. E. Lee, commanding C. S. A:—Your note of this day is but this moment, 11 50 a m., received, in consequence of my having passed from the Richmond and Lynchburg road to the Farmville and Lynchburg road. I am at this writing about four miles west of Walter's Church, and will push forward to the front for the purpose of meeting you. A notice sent to me on this road where you wish the interview to take place, will meet me.

Very respectfully, your obedient servant.

(Signed,) U. S. GRANT, Lt. Gen.

Appomatox C. H., April 9, 1865.

Gen. R. E. Lee, commanding C. S. A:—In accordance with the substance of my letter to you of the 5th inst., I propose to receive the surrender of the army of Northern Virginia on the following terms, to-wit: rolls of all the officers and men to be made in duplicate, one copy to be given to an officer designated by me, the other to be retained by such officer or officers as you may designate. The officers to give their individual parole not to take up arms against the Government of the United States until properly exchanged, and each company or regiment commander to sign a like parole for the men of his command. The arms, artillery, and public property to be parked and stacked and turned over to officers appointed by me to receive them. This will not embrace the side arms of the officers, nor their private horses or baggage. This done, each officer and man will be allowed to return to his home, not to be disturbed by the United States authority, so long as they observe their parole and the laws in force where they may reside.

Very respectfully,

(Signed,) U. S. GRANT, Lt. Gen.

Headquarters, army Northern Va., }
April 9th, 1865. }

Lt. Gen. U. S. Grant, commanding U. S. A:—General:—I have received your letter of this date, containing the terms of surrender of the army of Northern Virginia as proposed by you. As they are substantially the same as those expressed in your letter of the 8th inst., they are accepted. I will proceed to designate the proper officers to carry the stipulations into effect. Very respectfully, your obedient servant.

(Signed,) R. E. LEE, Gen.

The following is the previous correspondence between Lt. Gen. Grant and Gen. Lee, referred to in the foregoing:

To the Secretary of War, Clifton House, Va., April 9, 1865.

Hon. E. M. Stanton, Secretary of War: The following correspondence has taken place between Gen. Lee and myself. There has been no relaxation in the pursuit during its pendency.

(Signed,) U. S. GRANT, Gen.

April 7, 1865.

Gen. R. E. Lee, commanding C. S. A. Gen:—The results of last week must convince you of the hopelessness of further resistance on the part of the army of Northern Virginia. In this struggle I feel that it is so, and regard it as my duty to shift from myself the responsibility of any further effusion of blood, by asking of you the surrender of that portion of the C. S. A., known as the army of Northern Virginia. Very respectfully, your obedient servant.

(Signed,) U. S. GRANT, Lt. Gen.

April 7, 1865.

Lieut. Gen. Grant: Gen:—I have received your note of this date. Though not entirely of the opinion you express of the hopelessness of further resistance on the part of the army of Northern Virginia, I reciprocate your desire to avoid useless effusion of blood, and therefore, before considering your proposition, ask the terms you will offer on condition of its surrender.

(Signed,) R. E. LEE, Gen.

April 8.

Gen. R. E. Lee, commanding C. S. A. Gen.—Your note of last evening, in reply to mine of the same date, asking the conditions on which I will accept the surrender of the army of Northern Virginia, is just received. In reply, I would say that peace being my first desire, there is but one condition I insist upon, viz., that the men surrendered shall be disqualified from taking up arms again, against the Government of the United States until properly exchanged. I will meet you or designate officers to meet officers you may name, for the same purpose, at any point agreeable to you, for the purpose of arranging definitely the terms upon which the surrender of the army of Northern Virginia will be received. Very respectfully your obedient servant.

(Signed) U. S. GRANT, Lt. Gen.

April 8.

Gen.—I received at a late hour your note of to-day, in answer to mine of yesterday. I did not intend to propose the surrender of the army of Northern Virginia, but to ask the terms of your proposition. To be frank with you, I do not think the emergency has arisen to call for the surrender of this army, but as the restoration of peace should be the sole object of all, I desire to know whether your proposals would tend to that end. I cannot meet you with a view to surrender the army of Northern Virginia, but as far as your proposition may affect the C. S. forces under my command, and tend to the restoration of peace, I should be glad to meet you at 10 a. m. tomorrow, on the old stage road to Richmond between the picket lines of the two armies. Very respectfully, &c.,

(Signed) R. E. LEE, Gen.

April 8, 1865.

Gen. R. E. Lee, commanding C. S. A. Your note of yesterday is received. As I have no authority to treat on the subject of peace, the meeting proposed for 10 a. m. to-day, could lead to no good. I will state, however, General, that I am equally anxious for peace, with yourself, and the whole North entertain the same feeling. The terms upon which peace can be had are well understood. By the South laying down their arms, they will hasten that most desirable event and save thousands of human lives, and hundreds of millions of property not yet destroyed. Sincerely hoping that all our difficulties may be settled without the loss of another life, I subscribe myself very respectfully, your obedient servant.

(Signed) U. S. GRANT, Lt. Gen.

War Department, Washington, }
April 9, 9:30 p. m., }

Lieut.-General Grant:—Thanks be to Almighty God, for the great victory with which He has this day crowned you and the gallant army under your command. The thanks of this Department of the Government, and of the people of the United States and their reverence and honor have been deserved, and will be rendered to you and the brave and gallant officers and soldiers of your command for all time.

(Signed) EDWIN M. STANTON, Secretary of War.

War Department, Washington, }
April 9, 10 p. m. }

It is ordered that a salute of 200 guns be fired at the headquarters of departments, and at every post and arsenal in the United States, and at the military academy at West Point, on the day of the reception of this order, in commemoration of the surrender of Gen. R. E. Lee and the army of Northern Virginia to Lieut. Gen. Grant and the army under his command. The report of the receipt and execution of this order is to be made to the Adjutant General in Washington.

(Signed) EDWIN M. STANTON, Secretary of War.

New York, April 9.

The Herald's Richmond correspondent referring to the interview of the rebel commissioners at Richmond, says, the first conference lasted but a short time and was adjourned to the flag-ship Malvern. The result of these conferences cannot be made public at present.

The Herald's Mobile Bay correspondent of the 31st says, it appears that Granger's and Smith's corps marched from Danby's Mills on the 25th, for Blakely, meeting with but slight opposition only on the first day. On the 26th the 13th corps moved towards Spanish Fort, a strong earthwork, encountering and driving in the rebel cavalry. In the evening, Granger encamped on the left of that fort. The 6th corps continued on towards Blakely, encamping at Sibley's Mills, five miles from that town on the 26th. In the morning of the 27th our forces advanced on Spanish Fort, driving in the rebels, capturing their rifle pits and establishing our batteries within 400 yards of the Fort. On the 29th our forces were entrenched within 70 yards of the Fort. Several lives have been lost by the torpedoes strewn around. Our loss averages 150 per day. Three hundred of the enemy had been cut off by a portion of our force, but not yet captured, owing to their taking refuge in the swamps. Early on the morning of the 30th the rebels made an attack and were handsomely repulsed, with heavy loss. The rebel fleet and gunboats are on the right within musket shot of our troops. Earthworks are being constructed to mount siege guns. Our losses up to the first are about 800. Five of our gunboats and the gunboat Octorara have crossed Blakely Bar, and others are arriving. On the 31st siege guns and mortars were being placed in position. Heavy cannonading was opened on Spanish Fort and continued all day. The result is not known.

Steele's column left Pensacola on the 19th. He captured a train of cars at Greenwood. At Pollard, Alabama, two rebel cavalry regiments were routed, and Brig. Gen. Clausen, 22 officers, 400 men, and 450 horses were captured. On the 27th, Col. Spurling, with a detachment of the 2d Maine and the 1st Florida cavalry, cut the Mobile and Montgomery railroad, and captured two wagon trains and 100 prisoners. General Steele and force had arrived at Blakely, six miles from Spanish Fort and would soon unite with Canby.

A naval letter to the Herald states that the monitor Milwaukie was blown up by a torpedo on the 28th, and the Osage on the 29th, both while operating on Spanish Fort. Four sailors were killed on the Osage, and six seriously injured. Only one was injured on the Milwaukie. One of the turrets of the Milwaukie is still out of water and is in working order and is used. The Osage is submerged too deep to be used. They will probably be raised. The rebels are busy sending down torpedoes and fire rafts. The force in Spanish Fort is estimated at between 6,000 and 7,000, it having been reinforced from Mobile, by water, on the night of the 29th.

It is rumored that Forrest and his whole force had reached Blakely. The rebel ram Nashville, and the gunboats Tuscaloosa, Morgan and Natchez, are in Blakely river, evidently intending to give battle to our monitors. On the west of the bay, our gunboats have had several skirmishes with the water batteries, driving the rebels from their guns. The rebel troops in Spanish Fort are commanded by Maury.

New York, April 10.

The Herald's correspondent's account of the pursuit of Lee's army says, the 24th corps reached near Black's and White's station, on the south side of the railroad on the morning of the 5th, with Gens. Grant and Ord. The 5th corps and cavalry pushed on to Jettesville, on the Danville rail road, and arrived without any fighting till the night of the 4th. The 2d, 6th and 9th were following close in their rear, and by night of the 5th they were all up on the Danville road, and on the 24th up to the Burkesville junction. It appears that Lee ordered that portion of his army, cut off by our piercing the enemy's line on Sunday, to join him at Amelia Court House, fearing to have them attempt to reach Burkesville junction, and so on to Danville. When Gen. Grant reached Nottaway Court House, the staff officers arrived, stating that Sheridan had encountered the enemy in small force at Jettesville, driving him, and making important captures. Our column had intended to go to camp, but Grant thought that Lee's only hope was in forced marches and he therefore ordered the advance continued. The men, who had already tramped twenty miles, on being informed of the stirring news from Sheridan, clamored to march all night, and started off with cheers.

Soon after a dispatch was received from Sheridan and its contents were such as to cause Grant to leave the road and cut across the country to Sheridan's headquarters.

On the night of the 5th the army lay in line of battle, stretching across three or four miles of country, and facing Jettesville. Custar's division of cavalry lay on the right flank, and McKenzie's on the left. The infantry was formed with the 6th corps on the right, the 5th in the centre, and the 2d on the left. During the night, Lee moved off many of his trains, and it was feared that he would elude this column. Ord was to march in the morning towards Lynchburg, and cut off his retreat to any point south of that.

Memphis, April 8—via Cairo, 9.

The Bulletin of this evening says a report prevails, which is well authenticated, that Selma, Alabama, was captured and burned a few days ago, by the cavalry force of General Thomas' command.

Payment of the Water Rate.

A copy of sections 9 and 11 of the charter of the Virginia Water Company, is published in this paper. We presume that it is necessary or it would not appear. In our opinion, none but a person mean enough to be universally despised would ever wilfully avoid the payment of a debt so just as the water bill, in this city especially. When we reflect upon the liquid horror—a solution of copper flavored with miscellaneous abominations—which used to form the staple beverage of the sober inhabitants of Virginia City, our gratitude to those who have so successfully labored to remove this evil, should prevent us from any attempt to defraud persons whose works have made them public benefactors.

Fire, Cisterns and Alarm Bells.

In a wooden city like ours every precaution should be taken to prevent fire, by seeing that stove pipes are so fixed as to prevent the possibility of fire communicating from them, if they accidentally become red hot, and, also, that they be regularly cleaned out when foul. The neglect of these matters is the fruitful cause of fires. The next thing to be attended to is the providing of ample facilities for giving the alarm and extinguishing the flames. The city authorities would merit the gratitude of every householder, if they were to provide a good fire alarm, either a bell or, what is at least as efficient, a large triangle of bar steel. Cisterns should also be sunk in the central parts of each ward, at least. At the fire on Sunday, the hydrant gave out, and were it not for a conjunction of favorable circumstances in the shape of season and weather, we might have had little to boast of to-day, notwithstanding all the efforts of the fire companies and the efficient aid of the citizens. Nothing so much reconciles people to taxation as the knowledge that some at least of the money collected is expended for the protection of life and property. Fire is our greatest enemy, and no man will grudge the outlay necessary to place our means of controling it on an efficient footing.

Virginia City Water Company.

Sections 9 and 11 of the charter of Virginia City water Company are here published as notice to all the citizens of Virginia City, that are using water from the hydrants.

SEC. 9.—If any person or persons shall knowingly and designedly use the water aforesaid, with intent to use the same without a permit first obtained for that purpose, he shall, on conviction thereof, be subject to a fine of not less than five dollars nor more than fifty dollars, for each offence, to be recovered before any court having jurisdiction thereof, in the name of and for the use of said company.

SEC. 11.—If any person or persons, shall neglect or refuse to pay any sum or sums of money due to said company on account of the use of the water of said company, the same may be collected by suit in the name of said company, and said company shall also have the right to stop the supply of water to such person or persons.

NOTICE TO ALL.—If any person using water from the hydrants shall neglect to pay for the water when the money is due, he shall pay twenty-five per cent extra, per month, and if such person fails to pay in one month from the time the money is due, he shall be prohibited from the use of the water.

NEW ADVERTISEMENTS.

NATIONAL POLICE GAZETTE.

GEORGE W. MATSELL & CO. EDITORS AND PROPRIETORS | NEW YORK: FOR THE WEEK ENDING APRIL 22, 1865 | VOL. XX. NO. 1025.—[PRICE TEN CENTS.

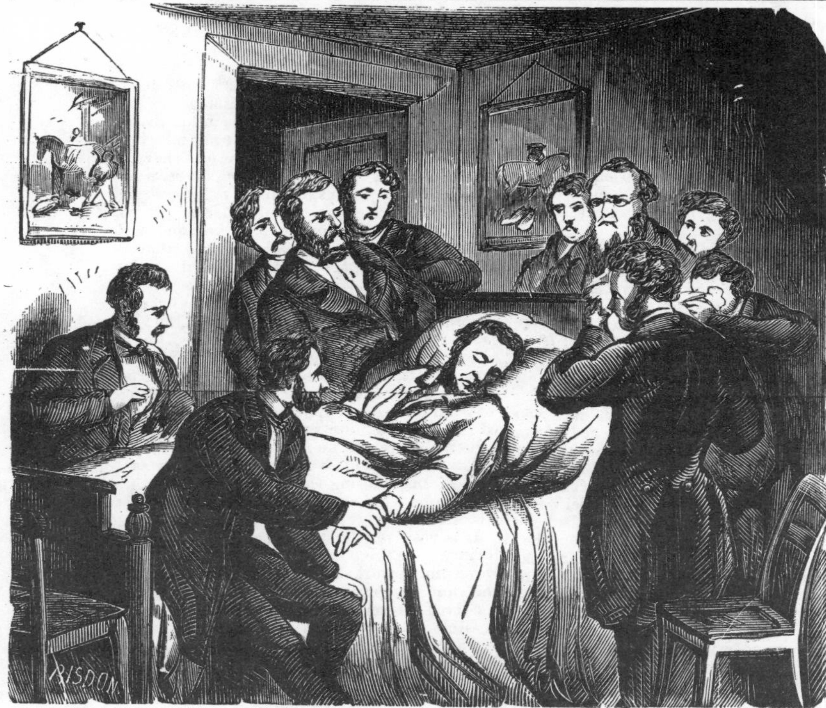

Scene at the Death-bed of the President.

Assassination of Abraham Lincoln, President of the United States.

Fight with the Assassin in Secretary Seward's Room.

Frederick Seward's Encounter with the Assassin.

The Assassination of Wm. H. Seward, Secretary of State.

John Wilkes Booth, the Assassin.

THE

ASSASSIN'S

CARNIVAL.

THE RICHMOND TIMES.

VOL. I.—NO. 2. SATURDAY MORNING, APRIL 22, 1865. PRICE FIVE CENTS.

The Richmond Times

IS PUBLISHED DAILY (EXCEPT SUNDAY) BY

CHAS. H. WYNNE.

Office N. W. corner Main and Fourteenth Streets.

The TIMES will give all the military, naval, political and foreign intelligence of the day.

The price of the TIMES will be five cents per copy. It will be served to subscribers in the city for thirty cents a week—payable to the carrier. Carriers and News Dealers will be furnished at the rate of three dollars per hundred copies.

TERMS OF ADVERTISING.

Advertisements will be inserted at the rate of seventy-five cents per square for each insertion. Eight lines, or an equivalent space, constitute a square.

No notice can be taken of anonymous correspondence. Whatever is intended for publication must be authenticated by the name and address of the writer—not necessarily for publication, but as a guaranty for his good faith.

We will, under no circumstances, return unsolicited communications.

The Evacuation of Richmond.

A COMPLETE HISTORY.

[CONTINUED.]

Pillaging and Plundering—Stores Broken Into and Sacked, &c.

During the night of evacuation a saturnalia begun in the city. About dusk the government commissaries begun the destruction of their immense quantities of stores. Several hundred soldiers and citizens gathered in front of the building, and contrived to catch much of the liquor in pitchers, bottles and basins, that was poured out. This liquor was not slow in manifesting itself. The crowd became a mob, and began to howl. Soon other crowds had collected in front of other government warehouses. At some, attempts were made to distribute supplies, but so frenzied had the mob become, that the officers in charge, in many cases, had to flee for their lives.

All through the night, crowds of men, women and children traversed the streets, rushing from one store-house to another, loading themselves with all kinds of supplies, to be thrown away immediately on something more tempting offering itself. Men could be met rolling hogsheads of bacon, molasses, sugar, barrels of liquor, bushels of tea and coffee; others had wheelbarrows loaded with all manner of goods, while others again had gone into the plundering business in a large way, and were operating with bags, furniture wagons and drays. This work went on fast and furious until after midnight, about which time large numbers of straggling soldiers made their appearance on the streets, and immediately set about robbing the principal stores on Main street. Drunk with vile liquor, the soldiers roamed from store to store, followed by a reckless crowd, drunk as they. With the buts of their muskets they dashed in the plate glass of the store doors, and entering, made a wreck of everything with the celerity of magic. Jewelry stores, clothing stores, boot and hat stores, and confectionery stores, were objects of special attraction to these pillagers.

An inspection of the burnt district on the morning after the evacuation showed that we did not over-estimate the extent of the area burned over, or the number of houses destroyed. The fire commencing at the Shockoe Warehouse, radiated front and rear, and on two wings, burning down to, but not destroying, the store No. 77 Main street, south side, half way between Fourteenth and fifteenth streets, and back to the river, through Cary and all the intermediate streets. Westward, on Main, the fire was stayed at Ninth street, sweeping back to the river. On the north side of Main the flames were stayed between Thirteenth and Fourteenth streets. From this point the flames raged on the north side of Main up to Eighth street, and back to Bank street. The familiar aspect and face of Main street is changed so completely that those best acquainted with the buildings cannot point them out with certainty. The busy street of a few days ago is but an amphitheatre of crumbling walls and tottering chimneys. Old boundaries and landmarks are so entirely obliterated that it is with the greatest difficulty that the sites of particular stores can be pointed out, the debris of brick and granite and iron destroying any trace of the cross streets; they can be distinguished only by the openings in the ruins.

The Custom House, late Confederate Treasury, passed through the ordeal of fire unscathed, from the fact that the edifice is of granite and fire-proof. The Bank of the Commonwealth presents a granite front, but is a mere shell, as also is the Bank of Virginia. At one time during Monday morning the Spotswood Hotel was in great danger, the flames leaping towards its location with great rapidity; but a merciful Providence caused a lull in the breeze, and blew the flames out of their track.

The aggregate value of the property destroyed, and above enumerated, foots up several millions. Imposing as these figures appear they are far short of the truth, for the reason already stated, that real estate was, before the war, invariably assessed much below the value which it would have commanded in the market.

Explosion of Shells.

While the city was burning, about 9 o'clock on Monday morning, terrific shell explosions, rapid and continuous, added to the terror of the scene, and led to the impression that the city was being shelled by the retreating Confederate army from the Southside, but the explosions were soon ascertained to proceed from the Government arsenal and laboratory, then in flames.

The Burning of the Tobacco—The Spread of the Conflagration.

The evacuation of Richmond closed with a terrific conflagration, which was kindled by the Confederate authorities applying the torch to Shockoe warehouse and other buildings, in which were stored a large quantity of tobacco. The fire spread rapidly, and it was some time before the fire brigade could be gotten to work. A fresh breeze was blowing from the south, and the fire swept over great space in an incredible short space of time. By noon the flames had transformed into a desert waste that portion of the city bounded between Seventh and Fifteenth streets, from Main street to the river, comprising the main business portion. We can form no estimate of the number of houses destroyed, but public and private, they will certainly number six or eight hundred. Among some of the most prominent buildings destroyed were the Bank of Richmond, Traders' Bank, Bank of the Commonwealth, Bank of Virginia, Farmers' Bank, all the banking houses, the American Hotel, the Columbian Hotel, the *Enquirer* building on Twelfth street, the *Dispatch* office and job rooms, corner of Thirteenth and Main streets; all that block of buildings known as Belvin's Block; the *Examiner* office, engine and machinery rooms; the Confederate Postoffice Department building; the State Court House, a fine old building situated on Capitol Square, at its Franklin street entrance; the Mechanics' Institute, vacated by the Confederate War Department, and all the buildings on that square up to Eighth street and back to Main street; the Confederate arsenal and laboratory, Seventh street.

The streets were crowded with furniture and every description of wares, dashed down to be trampled in the mud or burned up where it lay. All the Government storehouses were thrown open, and what could not be gotten off by the Government was left to the people, who, everywhere ahead of the flames, rushed in and secured immense amounts of bacon, clothing, boots, &c.

Next to the river the destruction of property was fearfully complete. The Danville and Petersburg railroad depots, and the buildings and shedding attached, for the distance of half a mile from the north side of Main street to the river, and between Eighth and Fifteenth streets, embracing upwards of twenty blocks, presents one waste of smoking ruins, blackened walls and smoking chimneys.

Scenes During the Fire—Stores Broken into and Sacked.

[From the Washington Chronicle.]

Sunday night was very noisy. People were running to and fro; the troops shouting and screaming. Towards morning the laboratory was fired with a tremendous explosion; Fort Darling was blown up with a terrific report, and the rams were blown up somewhat later.

It was near eight when our troops entered the city. They had seen black dense columns of smoke ascending from the city, but had no idea of the extent of the conflagration. It required some effort to tame down the riotous crowd, and more to induce them to take part in the struggle to put it out. The firemen were slow in coming to the rescue until the arrival of our troops, for fear that they would be interfered with by the rebel soldiery, and so the flames were under full headway. Unfortunately, the wind was from the south. The great flouring mills caught from the tobacco warehouse, and communicated the fire to the blocks on Cary and thence to Main street, and in spite of the most desperate exertions, block after block took fire, and now from Eighth to Fifteenth is one mass of ruins. Every bank in the city is destroyed—the Bank of Virginia, of Richmond, of the Commonwealth, the Farmers' Bank, the Traders', and the Exchange Bank.—The War Department, on Ninth, near Main, is a mass of ruins. The *Enquirer* and the *Dispatch* offices were burned to the ground. The county court-house, the American hotel, and a host of the finest and largest stores in the city, some of them with heavy stocks, have fallen in order to prevent the Yankees from getting a few pounds of tobacco and bacon. Libby prison escaped. The Spotswood house was saved by the most indefatigable exertions, though the fire raged almost entirely around it, destroying the square in front, and a short distance up the hill, the church of the Rev. Dr. Read, Presbyterian, on Franklin street, near Ninth.

During the fire, a reign of terror and pillage was inaugurated, and scenes of the most disgraceful pillage ensued. Stores were emptied in no time of tobacco, jewelry, boots and shoes, and clothing. Jewelry, clothing, and liquor stores, and private houses were sacked. To make bad worse, despite the precautions of the authorities, who had ordered the destruction of all the liquor in the groggeries, a considerable quantity of liquor was obtained, and the mob grew both noisy and violent, yelling and howling, and swearing, as they bore off great plugs and packages of tobacco, pieces of clothing, articles of jewelry, &c. The fire revealed immense amounts of provisions—whether the accumulations of the Government or of speculators, does not appear, although citizens say the latter. Thousands immediately engaged in the scarcely reprehensible work of removing to their houses family supplies. "The niggers got it all," said a leading citizen, with a wrath he made little attempt to conceal. I do not doubt they "toated off" largely.

Not a few families are beggared by this destruction of private property by the fire. Men who counted their wealth by thousands are now reduced to poverty, and one of the most pitiable sights I have ever seen was presented in the Capitol grounds last evening, where, in groups fearfully numerous, dismayed and weeping, families were gathered around the remains of their household goods that had been snatched from destruction. Some of them, houseless and homeless, remained all night under the open sky.

The Surrender of the City.

[From the New York Herald.]

General Weitzel's command, which is composed exclusively of colored troops, had been for a considerable time located on the north side of James river, within a few miles of Richmond, and he had therefore but to march in and take possession immediately on its early abandonment by the rebels.

On the instant General Weitzel, so clear was his mind upon this subject, despatched Major A. H. Stevens, of the Fourth Massachusetts cavalry, and Major E. E. Graves, of his staff, with forty cavalry, to investigate the condition of affairs on the roads leading to the rebel works and thence to Richmond. This party had not proceeded far within the rebel lines when they espied a shabby carriage approaching, the driver waving a white flag. The flag-of-truce party was met at the line of fortifications just beyond the junction of the Osborne turnpike and Newmarket road, but a few miles from the city. The surrender was formally made, and in the following manner:

Approaching the vehicle, it was found to contain Mayor Mayo, the head of the Richmond city government; Judge Meredith, of the Superior Court of Richmond; Judge Lyons, and several other worthies, who announced that they had come out to surrender the city to the competent authority. This took place within a distance of two miles from the city, after the Union majors had found their way through several lines of torpedoes, and was marked by the following conversation:

Major Stevens—Who is in command of this flag-of-truce?

Judge Meredith—It is Mr. Mayo, Mayor of the city of Richmond.

The Judge at the same time introduced the Mayor and all of his associates to Major Stevens and Major Graves.

Mayor Mayo then handed Major Stevens a small slip of paper, upon which was written the following:

"It is proposed to formally surrender to the Federal authorities the city of Richmond, hitherto capital of the Confederate States of America, and the defences protecting it up to this time."

The document was approved of, and, Major Stevens accepting its terms in behalf of his commanding general, it was at once transmitted to Major General Weitzel, who had already sent out his skirmish line, and upon the receipt of Mayor Mayo's surrender, instantly moved his column upon the evacuated city and took possession.

The gallant Majors then took charge of the rebel flag of truce party and advanced upon the city.

[This account does not describe the manner and incidents of the surrender *correctly*. Some of the party who made the surrender on the part of the city have promised to prepare for publication a full and complete narrative of the affair, which we hope to present in our next chapter (in Monday's paper.) It is our object to make this compilation as truthful as possible, and it is proposed by the parties concerned to have such a narrative prepared that the public may have a full and authentic version of the event. All of the committee who were charged with the surrender testify to the courteous manner and bearing of Major Stevens, and the rare fidelity with which he kept his promise of protecting the private property of citizens.—TIMES.]

The Flag Raised Over the Capitol.

With a thought and a flash they immediately proceeded to the Capitol, and creeping to its summit, planted the stars and stripes. The national symbols thus hoisted by the halyards consisted of two bright and tasteful guidons from companies E and H of the Fourth Massachusetts cavalry, of which Stevens is one of the field officers. The colors of the Union were greeted by prolonged cheers and other popular demonstrations of applause on the part of civilians and contrabands.

The City on Fire—Efforts to Put it Out.

All the commercial part of the city was found to be in flames, General Ewell having ordered the destruction of the public buildings, which order General Breckinridge, Secretary of War, strove earnestly to have countermanded, but without avail.

Major Stevens directed the alarm bells to be sounded, and at once assumed direction of the Fire Department of the city, consisting of a few men, two steam fire engines and four worthless hand engines, and a large amount of hose ruined by the retreating rebels.

The following is Major Stevens' order upon the subject:

City of Richmond, Va., April 3, 1865.

General Order No. 1.

This city now being occupied by Federal forces, the officers of the Fire Department and police of the city will immediately report to the Mayor's room for instructions, for the purpose of preserving property and order in the city.

By command of

Major-General GODFREY WEITZEL.

ATHERTON H. STEVENS, Jr., Major and Provost Marshal, Twenty-fifth Army Corps.

The efforts to subdue the flames were arduous but finally successful. The damage by the conflagration caused by Ewell can hardly be estimated. In greenbacks it will not fall short of from twenty to thirty millions of dollars.—Tobacco, cotton goods, machinery, stores, warehouses, banks, shops, stalls, dwellings, and even hovels of mechanics and laborers, did not escape the terrible fury of the fire, and rich and poor, loyal and disloyal, suffered alike.—Main street, from the landing up to the Spotswood Hotel, on both sides of the street, is one heap of smouldering ruins. The walls, as a general thing, have been pulled down, and the greater portion of the street is blocked up by bricks from the ruins, which are fast being ground into fine powder by the many army wagons passing up and down, giving the pedestrian more of an appearance of having walked through the State of New Jersey than the principal street of the rebel capital.

The entire business portion of the city is a heap of smouldering ruins, and nothing but the absence of wind saved the entire city from destruction.

It is positively asserted that General Breckinridge gave the order that the tobacco and the Government workshops should be set fire to, and the close proximity of other valuable property rendered its escape from destruction almost impossible.

The greater portion of the tobacco destroyed is said to have belonged to France and England.

The Appearance of the City while the Troops were Entering.

As we entered, the scene was grand in the extreme. The entire commercial portion of the city was in flames, and through the dense lurid smoke would frequently be heard the terrific noises arising from the wholesale explosions of powder, shell and cartridges, which had doubtless been stored for the express purpose of exploding to harass our forces and impede our entrance to the city. The effect was wholly the reverse, and I do not hear that a single life was lost by these awful outbursts of powder.

(*To be continued to-morrow*)

The Richmond Times

SATURDAY, APRIL 22, 1865.

Office: Corner Main and Fourteenth Streets.

ENLARGEMENT OF OUR PAPER.

Our paper is no longer an experiment; it is a success. We have been so much encouraged by the handsome and liberal support accorded us by the people of Richmond, that we have decided to issue *on and after Monday* A DOUBLE SHEET. By this means we shall be able to largely increase the amount of reading matter, and to make the *Times* what we contemplated, a NEWS and BUSINESS paper.

Of the success of our paper we have never had a doubt. We felt assured that an intelligent and discriminating public would sustain us in the enterprise, and we are glad to say that our most sanguine anticipations have been more than realized. The demand for our paper yesterday was so great that we were not able to supply it.

With the enlargement of our sheet we shall be able to initiate many improvements, among which will be the insertion of financial and commercial articles, the publication of literary articles, so indispensable to society, "Spirit of the Press," which portrays the opinions of leading journals upon grave matters of political policy, and the presentation daily of a very full record of local events, together with full compilations of Northern, Foreign, and Home news.

We shall print the *Times* on the very best white paper and in clear, beautiful type.—Without intending to be invidious, we would invite our readers to observe the mechanical execution of our paper, and say if they ever saw it excelled in Richmond. In fact, we have one of the most complete establishments in all the South, and besides our facilities for printing a paper, we are prepared to execute all kinds of job printing.

We would again remind advertisers that we intend to make the *Times* the great advertising medium of the city. We have already received a large patronage in this line, but the enlargement of our sheet on next Monday will give us *sixteen* more columns of room. We will then be enabled to better accommodate them, and at the same time enhance the interest of the paper for the general reader, by increasing the amount of reading matter. By a close arrangement and classification of advertisements we are making our paper, as it were, a business directory—a thing just needed now, when the locations of the stores have been turned topsy-turvy by the recent change of affairs, and the business portion of the city blotted out. Dealers who wish patronage must let the public know *where* they are to be found.

NO CHANGE.

We are glad to be able to announce that General Ord has not been relieved of command by General Halleck, as was reported yesterday. General Halleck comes here to take charge of *civil* matters—General Ord retaining his position as the military commander of this department. It is supposed that the ordering of General Halleck here is simply to relieve General Ord of some of the arduous duties of his office by disconnecting the *civil* affairs from the military.

We feel assured this announcement will give great satisfaction to the people of Richmond. General Ord has won the regard of all classes by the courteous and considerate discharge of his duties, and they would regret any change that might be made. We feel no hesitation in saying that it is the universal wish of the people of Richmond that General Ord be retained in his present position.

DEPARTMENT OF RICHMOND.

General DEVINS, in command of all the United States forces in and about the city of Richmond, was, at the outbreak of the war, a lawyer in the city of Worcester, Massachusetts. Animated by the patriotism which the necessities of the occasion demanded, he accepted the commission of Major in command of a battalion of rifles of the Massachusetts volunteer militia. These were among the first troops that reached Annapolis under General Butler in 1861.—While serving with these troops at Fort McHenry, General Devins was appointed by the Governor of Massachusetts Colonel of the Fifteenth Massachusetts regiment, one of the regiments raised for three years, and at once took the command of it.

This regiment was at first heavily engaged at the unfortunate affair of Ball's Bluff or Leesburg, where it led the advance and covered the retreat of the Federal forces, losing nearly one-half of the number it had engaged. Colonel Devins was slightly wounded, but after nightfall swam the Potomac to avoid falling into the hands of the enemy, the route being complete and all means of retreat being cut off.

While in front of Yorktown, in 1862, with his regiment, Colonel Devins was appointed Brigadier-General for gallantry at Ball's Bluff, and took command of a brigade in the Fourth Corps, which he commanded during the whole campaign of that year, with the exception of six weeks after the battle of Fair Oaks, in which he was seriously wounded.

In the spring of 1863 General Devins was ordered to the command of a division of the Eleventh Corps, and was again badly wounded at the battle of Chancellorsville. Upon his partial recovery, he was ordered to the command of the draft rendezvous in Massachusetts, and subsequently appointed inspector of the various recruiting stations and draft rendezvous in the North.

In the spring of 1864 General Devins returned to the field, and was placed by Major-General W. F. Smith in command of a division of the Eighteenth Corps, which distinguished itself at Cold Harbor in June, 1864—breaking the enemy's lines, and taking a large number of prisoners.

On the breaking up of the Eighteenth Corps, General Devins was assigned to the command of the Third Division of the Twenty-fourth Corps. This division was left to hold the defences on the north of the James, in conjunction with a division of the Twenty-fifth; and to it must be accorded the honor of being the first to take possession of the enemy's defences, and the first to enter the city of Richmond on the morning of April 3d.

This is a sufficiently fair record, but it must in justice be added that General Devins is a man of intelligence and most courteous manners, and that he enjoys the entire confidence of his troops.

THE WAR NEWS!

Sherman's Occupation of Raleigh!

Reported Capture of Gov. Vance!

THE FALL OF MOBILE!

Newbern, April 15.—The superintendent of the railroad arrived here from Goldsboro' yesterday.

He states that Governor Vance was captured by our cavalry between Hillsboro' and Raleigh, on the 13th. A report states that he, Vance, had been sent to Sherman by General Johnston, who was at Hillsboro', with instructions to surrender the State of North Carolina to General Sherman, but these instructions were afterward countermanded, and Vance was returning to General Johnston without seeing Sherman, when he was captured.

He is now a prisoner of war, not having carried out his mission. The report also states that Jeff. Davis and family had joined General Johnston at Hillsboro', which is about thirty miles west of Raleigh. Sherman's forces entered Raleigh a few days since, and are moving beyond that place after Johnston, who continues to fall back without fighting.

Capture of Salisbury, N. C., with many Prisoners and Immense Quantities of Supplies.

Lenoir, Caldwell county, N. C., April 6.—The expedition under Major-General Stoneman, which left Knoxville, Tennessee, on the 10th ultimo, struck the East Tennessee railroad on the 14th ultimo at Wytheville, Christiansburg and Salem. Between these points thirty-three bridges were burned, and twenty-five miles of track totally destroyed, and besides many prisoners were taken, and considerable quantities of corn and other stores destroyed.

On the 6th instant General Stoneman arrived in front of the rebel line for the defence of the town of Salisbury, N. C., at 6 A. M. on the 12th instant.

This line, defended by artillery and infantry, was now forced, and our forces entered Salisbury at 10 A. M., capturing 8 stands of colors, 19 guns, 1164 prisoners, 1000 stand of arms and accoutrements, 1,000,000 rounds of small ammunition and 1000 rounds of fixed ammunition and shells, 60,000 pounds of powder, 75,000 complete suits of clothing, 350,000 army blankets, and 20,000 pounds of bacon, 100,000 pounds of salt, 20,000 pounds of sugar, 27,000 pounds of rice, 10,000 pounds of saltpetre, 50,000 bushels of wheat, $10,000 worth of medical supplies, 7,000 bales of cotton.

Thirteen pieces of artillery were brought away, and all other stores not needed for our immediate command were destroyed. The greater part of these supplies had just been received from Raleigh. One large arsenal, machinery complete, with depots, two engines and trains, several bridges between Greensboro' and Danville, with several miles of railroad track, were destroyed. Our loss was very few in killed and wounded. Among the latter Captain R. Morrow, Assistant Adjutant General of Stoneman's staff.

The Capture of Mobile.

Cairo, Ill., April 18.—Letters dated at Spanish Fort, April 9th, say the left lunette of the Spanish fort having been previously taken by General Smith, the enemy evacuated the other parts of the fort at daylight on the 9th, and Colonel Bertam's Brigade immediately occupied the fort, and found two brass howitzers, one 20 and one 30-pounder parrot gun; 64 Napoleons, two 6-pounders, one 8-inch mortar, one 8-inch columbiad, a large quantity of ammunition, a number of horses and mules, but few rations.

All the guns were spiked with nails.—The prisoners taken were 25 officers and 527 men.

The capture of Spanish Fort gives us Forts Alexis, Eugene and Bleakely.

New Orleans, April 13.—The *Times* has the following special:

Lakeport, April 13.—I have just arrived from Mobile. The Stars and Stripes were hoisted on Batteries Porter and Mackintosh at 10.30 A. M. yesterday, and on Big Church steeple, in Mobile, at 2.30 P. M. General Granger's forces occupy the city. The rebels commenced evacuating on the 10th, and continued until yesterday, when all left. The tug-boat Allen was blown up by a torpedo yesterday.

THE PRESIDENT'S REMAINS.

Their Removal to Illinois.

CONDITION OF MR. SEWARD.

Address of President Johnson.

[Compiled from Northern Papers.]

The Removal of the Remains.

War Department,
Washington, April 19—1 P. M.

Major-General Dix, New York:

The arrangements for conveying the President's remains from Washington to Springfield, Illinois, has been changed this morning, and they will go direct from Washington to Philadelphia, Harrisburg, Pittsburg, Fort Wayne, and thence to Springfield.

EDWIN M. STANTON,
Secretary of War.

The Body Lying in State.

[From the Washington Star.]

Long before the hour announced for opening the gates to allow the public to view the features of the deceased for the last time, an immense crowd of persons had assembled.

The East Room, in which the remains were laid, was tastefully decorated in mourning.—The windows at either end of the room were draped with black berege.

The catafalque, upon which the coffin containing the remains was placed, is eleven feet high, sixteen feet long and ten feet wide, the coffin resting on a surface about three feet from the floor, surrounded with a wreath of evergreens and japonicas.

The corpse, as it lay in state in the East Room, was in charge of the following officers, representing both the army and the navy: On the part of the army, General Hitchcock, General Eaton, Captain Penrose, Captain Van Lear and Lieutenant-Colonel W. Sinclair. On the part of the navy, Commander E. Stone, of the Monitor Montauk; Lieutenant McNair, Lieutenant A. B. Young and Lieutenant N. H. Farquhar.

It was a sad and solemn sight indeed to witness the large crowd of persons slowly and mournfully wending their way into the room and pass the corpse, some of the number actually sobbing aloud with grief as they took a final look at the revered remains.

The Last Marks of Respect.

Washington, April 18, 10 *P. M.*—There arrived here this evening two committees from New York, to be present at the obsequies to-morrow. One committee represents the great meeting in Wall street last Saturday. They called on the President this evening. Subsequently the Union League Committee were also presented to the President.

A committee of the Common Council of New York are expected here to-morrow morning.

Among the most beautiful tributes to the memory of the late President is a beautiful floral design. It is in the shape of an anchor, and composed of Japonicas and other exotics, most beautifully arranged. It has been placed on the centre of the President's coffin.

[From the New York Herald.]

As this is the day on which the funeral of our late lamented President takes place in Washington, there will be a solemn observance of it and a general suspension of business throughout the loyal States. Several of the Governors have issued proclamations recommending to the people of their respective Commonwealths abstention from their ordinary secular pursuits and the tolling of the church bells from noon till 1 o'clock in the afternoon.

The Funeral.

Washington, April 19.—The Avenue is crowded with people to witness the funeral procession. Civil and military bodies are passing to the appointed place of rendezvous. All business is entirely suspended, and the citizens have turned out *en masse* to pay the last sad tribute of respect to the memory of the late President. Every window, house top and available spot are filled with people, and it is thought it will be an hour or two before the funeral cortege passes.

The following is the order of procession:

Funeral Escort in column of March.
One Regiment of Cavalry.
Two Batteries of Artillery.
Battalion of Marines.
Two Regiments of Infantry.
Commander of Escort and Staff.
Dismounted Officers of Marine Corps.
Navy and Army in the order named.
Mounted Officers of Marine Corps.
Navy and Army in the order named.
All Military Officers to be in uniform with side arms.

Then followed the civic procession, consisting of Congressmen, heads of departments, &c.

The President's Family.

The New York *Commercial* proposes that subscriptions be opened and a sum made up sufficiently large to enable the members of the late President's family to live in ease and comfort for the rest of their lives. It also suggests that a colossal monument to the memory of Mr. Lincoln be erected in Central Park or some other portion of the city of New York.

The City Council of Baltimore have sent Mrs. Lincoln a letter of condolence.

Secretary Seward and Son Improving.

Washington, April 18.—Secretary Seward is much better to-day, as is also Mr. Frederick Seward, who is gradually regaining full consciousness. It is now confidently hoped and expected that both the Secretary and Assistant Secretary will speedily recover.

Washington, April 18, 10.45 *A. M.*—The Secretary continues to improve. He slept better last night than he has since his first injury.

Frederick is gradually regaining consciousness.

Both decidedly better.

GEORGE E. BAKER,
Agent Department of State.

Speech of President Johnson.

Washington, April 18.—In accordance with resolutions passed at a meeting of the citizens of Illinois, the citizens of that State waited upon his Excellency, Andrew Johnson, President of the United States, to pay their respects to him. Speeches were made on the occasion.

President Johnson, after expressing his thanks for the mark of respect, and his deep grief at the lamented death of President Lincoln, said:

Here, gentlemen, you perhaps expect me to present some indication of my future policy. I shall enter upon the discharge of my great duty firmly and steadfastly. [Applause.] The American people must be taught, if they do not already feel, that treason is a crime, and must be punished. [Applause.] That the Government will not always bear with its enemies. That it is strong not only to protect, but to punish. [Applause.] The people must understand that it is the blackest of crimes, and will be surely punished. [Applause.] I make this allusion, not to excite the already exasperated feelings of the public, but to point out the principles of public justice which should guide our action at this particular juncture, and which accord with sound public morals. Let it be engraven upon every heart that treason is crime, and traitors should suffer its penalty. [Applause.]

I speak in no spirit of unkindness. I leave the events of the future to be disposed of as they arise. I do not harbor bitter or revengeful feelings towards any. In general terms, I would say that public morals should be established upon the sure and infallible principle of justice. [Applause.]

When the question of exercising mercy comes before me, it will be considered calmly and judicially, remembering that I am the Executive of the Nation. I know that men love to have their names spoken of in connection with acts of mercy, and how easy it is to yield to this impulse. But we must not forget that what may be mercy to the individual is cruelty to the State. [Applause.]

In regard to my future course I will now make no professions—no pledges. I have been connected somewhat actively with public affairs, and to the history of my past public acts, which is familiar to you, I refer for those principles which have governed me heretofore and will guide me hereafter.

My past life, and especially my course during the present unholy rebellion, is before you.—I have no principles to retract. I have no professions to offer. Professions and promises would be worth nothing at this time. I shall not attempt to anticipate the future. As events occur and it becomes necessary for me to act I shall dispose of each as it arises, deferring any declaration or message until it can be written paragraph by paragraph in the height of events as they transpire.

MOVEMENTS OF GENERAL GRANT.—General Grant is to leave here on Friday for Burlington, New Jersey. He will probably go next week to Richmond, which he has not yet visited.—The President and Cabinet are anxious he should remain as much as possible in Washington, in order that they may have his advice in Cabinet meetings at this important crisis of national affairs.—*New York Herald, 19th.*

Tri-Weekly Constitutionalist.

STOCKTON & CO — AUGUSTA GA. SUNDAY MORNING, APRIL 23. 1865.

DAILY CONSTITUTIONALIST.

CHAN E OF RATES.

Until further notice, the subscription price for our paper will be as follows:

Daily..$10 per month.
Tri-Weekly.....................................7 for 1 month.
" " ....20 " 3 "
Weekly..10 " 3 "
" ....4 " 1 "

No subscription received for a longer period than three months.

ADVERTISING RATES.

First week, $5 per square each insertion.
Second " 4 " " " "
Third " 3 " " " "
Fourth " 2 " " " "
One square first month, $80 00.
" " second " 60 00.
" " third " 40 00.

April 7, 1865.

From Evening Edition of Yesterday

COL. C. A. L. LAMAR.—We understand that this gentleman was killed on the bridge over the Chattahoochee river, while engaged in the defence of Columbus.

FIGHT AT COLUMBUS.—Col. C. A. L. Lamar was killed at Columbus, Ga.

A report was in circulation that Hon. Robert Toombs was also killed at the same place, but we are assured that Mr. Toombs was on his way home yesterday; therefore the report is untrue.

ROBBERY.—Capt. Moffit, who was robbed on the street last night, would be thankful to the party if they would put in the postoffice his orders and papers.

Gen. Hampton, in his dash on Kilpatrick, captured the wagon train and a portion of their artillery, and R. E. Young, A. G. Goodwin, P. F. Frazee, Wm. Morris and wife, who went off with the Yankees from Columbia, S. C., in their late raid through that State, were killed.

UNCALLED FOR TELEGRAPHIC MESSAGES.—The following messages remain at the telegraph office and cannot be delivered for want of proper address:

Mrs M C Frost, M B Massey, J D Ramsey.

The Enemy in Georgia.

Whatever, says the Atlanta Intelligencer, may have been the success of the enemy who are now in heavy force raiding over Georgia, we have the consolation of knowing that upon the their approach on West Point and on Columbus, they were gallantly met, and every inch of their advance to occupy those places disputed with heroic valor by the comparatively few who were to defend them.

At West Point, all we know in regard to its defence is, that our forces were commanded by Gen. Tyler, and that the enemy was gallantly repulsed in his charges upon our breastworks several times with considerable loss to him in both killed and wounded; and but for his great superiority in numbers, and the fact, as stated, that the ammunition of Gen. Tyler's command was exhausted, we have no doubt that the enemy would have been driven back, and West Point retained by its brave defenders. Report says our losses were small in the fight, but no names of the wounded or killed have been reported. Two or three trains of cars were captured by the enemy.

In endeavoring to make his escape from one of these trains that had run off the track, a Mr W C Thrower, a highly respectable citizen of Atlanta, who had charge of it—an Engineer by profession was shot through the lungs and fell into the hands of the enemy. It is feared that he died from the effects of the terrible wound. In the capture of West Point, the enemy got into his possession much plunder, public and private. How he demeaned himself towards its helpless citizens and private property we have yet to learn; we fear as usual.

At Columbus, we learn, the contest was fierce and terrible, resulting on both sides, we are advised, with heavy losses in killed and wounded. The fight, it is said, was a hand to hand one on the bridge, in which great personal bravery was manifested by the heroic few who were straining every nerve to hold the city; but "the power of numbers" prevailed, and Columbus, like West Point, fell; and thus over the Chattahoochee, whose waters were blood stained in the contest, the enemy has again entered Georgia.

THE SIMPLE SECRET.—Twenty clerks in a store. Twenty "hands" in a printing office. Twenty apprentices in a ship-yard. Twenty young men about a village. All want to get on in the world, and all expect to do so. *One* of the clerks will rise to be partner, and make a fortune. *One* of the compositors will own a newspaper and become an influential and prosperous citizen. *One* of the apprentices will come to be a master builder. *One* of the young villagers will get a handsome farm and live like a patriarch. But which is destined to be the lucky individual? Luck? There is no luck about it. The thing is almost as certain as the rule of three. The young fellow who will distance his competitors is he who masters his business, who preserves his integrity, who lives cleanly and purely, who never gets into debt, and who gains friends by deserving them. There are some ways to fortune that *look* shorter than this old, dusty highway. But the staunch men of the community, the men who achieve something really worth having, good fortune, good name, and serene old age, all go this road.

CAPITULATION OF LEE'S ARMY.

General Lee a Prisoner of War.

Sad Details.

From the Carolinian we make a summary of the sad intelligence below. Prior to the eventful Sunday of capitulation, and from the evacuation of Richmond and Petersburg, our army suffered from retreat and disasters, and was sorely pressed from overwhelming odds, but still fought bravely, until completely surrounded:

Sunday, April 10th—A bright, clear, beautiful day, but it opened gloomily. Our army had reached Appomatox Court House, on the road to Lynchburg. Thomas, with his army, had arrived before us and effected a junction with Grant; cavalry, infantry and artillery completely surrounded our little command. We had from five to eight thousand prisoners, and only eight thousand effective men with muskets, all told. The supply of ammunition was nearly exhausted. In this emergency General Lee determined to cut his way through. Orders were given fo a grand charge, and our troops massed accordingly.

General Grimes' division led the charge, followed successively by two others. The engagement commenced shortly after sunrise, and was continued until our men had broke through the Federal lines, driven them nearly a mile and a half and captured several pieces of artillery, and some hundreds of prisoners. The old spirit of fight was unsubdued. Meanwhile a heavy force of cavalry threatened our flanks. For some reason General Lee issued orders to the troops to cease firing and withdraw.

Subsequently an officer, said to be Gen. Custar of the Yankee cavalry, entered our lines with a flag of truce. Whether his appearance was in response to a request from General Lee, or he was the bearer of a formal demand for the surrender initiated by Gen'l Grant, we are not informed. At this time, our army was in line of battle on or near the Appomatox road, the skirmishers thrown out, while 250 yards from these, on an eminence, was a large body of Federal cavalry.

Soon after the return of Gen. Custar to his lines, Gen. Grant, accompanied by his staff, rode to the headquarters of Gen. Lee, which were under an apple tree near the road. The interview is described as exceedingly impressive. After the salutatory formalities, which were doubtless brief and business-like, General Lee tendered his sword to Grant in token of surrender. That officer, however, with a courtesy for which we must accord him due respect, declined to receive it, or receiving it declined to retain it, and accompanied its return with substantially the following remarks:

"General Lee keep that sword. You have won it by your gallantry. You have not been whipped, but overpowered, and I cannot receive it as a token of surrender from so brave a man."

The reply of Gen. Lee we do not know. But Grant and himself are said to have been deeply affected by the occasion and to have shed tears. The scene occurred between ten and eleven o'clock A. M., when the sad event became known to the army, officers and men gave way to their emotions and some among the veterans wept like children. A considerable number swore that they never would surrender and made their way to the woods. Generals Gary of South Carolina and Rosser of Virginia, with a few followers, cut their way out and escaped. But the bulk of the army, the men who for four years have done battle so nobly for the cause, together with leaders like Longstreet, Gordon, Kershaw and others whose names are forever distinguished, were obliged to accept the proffered terms.

These were—capitulation with all the honors of war—officers to retain their side arms and personal property and the men their baggage. Each one was thereupon paroled and allowed to go his way.

During Sunday and Monday a large number of Federal soldiers and officers visited our camps and looked curiously on our commands, but there was nothing like exultation, no shouting for joy and no word uttered that could add to the mortification already sustained. On the contrary every symptom of respect was manifested, and the Southern army was praised for the noble and brave manner in which it had defended our cause.

The force of the Yankee army is estimated at 200,000 men. Our own, at the time of surrender, embraced not more than 8,000 effective infantry and 2,000 cavalry, but it is said that the total number paroled was about 23,000 of all arms and conditions.

All the Federals spoke of General Lee in unbounded praise. The remark was frequently made "he would receive as many cheers in going down our lines as Gen. Grant himself."

It is understood that Gens. Lee, Longtreet and other officers are now on parole in the city of Richmond.

The following is a true copy of General Lee's Address to his army, issued after the surrender to General Grant at Appomatox C. H., on Sunday. April 9th, 1865

HEADQUARTERS ARMY NORTHERN VA. }
April 10, 1865. }

GENERAL ORDERS, }
No. 9 }

After four years of arduous service, marked by unsurpassed courage and fortitude, the Army of Northern Virginia has been compelled to yield to overwhelming numbers and resources.

I need not tell the brave survivors of so many hard fought battles who have remained steadfast to the last, that I have consented to this result from no distrust of them. But feeling that valor and devotion could accomplish nothing that could compensate for the loss that would have attended the continuance of the contest I determined to avoid the useless sacrifice of those whose past services have endeared them to their countrymen.

By the terms of the agreement officers and men can return to their homes and remain until exchanged. You will take with you the satisfaction that proceeds from the consciousness of duty faithfully performed, and I earnestly pray that a merciful God will extend to you his blessing and protection.

With unceasing admiration of your constancy and devotion to your country and a grateful remembrance of your kind and generous consideration for myself, I bid you an affectionate farewell.

R. E. LEE, General.

Below is a special order embracing Gen. Grant's order for the passage of paroled soldiers to their homes and also the form of pass given them.

HEADQ'RS ARMY OF N. V. }
April 10, 1865. }

Special Order }
No. —. }

All officers and men of the Confederate service paroled at Appomatox C. H. Va., who, to reach their homes are compelled to pass through the lines of the Union armies, will be allowed to do so, and to pass free on all Government transports and military railroads.

By command of Lt. Gen. GRANT,
E. S PARKER,
Lt. Col. A. A. G.

By command of
R. E. LEE,
C. L. VENABLE, A. A. G.

[FORM OF PASS.]

APPOMATTOX, C. H. VA., }
April 10th, 1865. }

The bearer —— of Co —— right —— of ——, a paroled prisoner of the Army of Northern Virginia, has permission to go to his home and there remain undisturbed.

Lastly is the form of the parole of honor signed by commanding officers of divisions &c., in behalf of the men in their command. This is taken from a copy of one signed by General Fitz Hugh Lee.

I, the undersigned, commanding officer of —— do for the within named prisoners of war belonging to the army of Northern Virginia, who have been this day surrendered by Gen. R. E. Lee, C. S. A., commanding said army, to Lieut. Gen. U. S. Grant, commanding the armies of the United States, hereby give my solemn parole of honor that the within named shall not hereafter serve in the armies of the Confederate States or in any military capacity whatever against the United States of America, or render aid to the enemies of the latter, until properly exchanged in such manner as shall be mutually approved by the respective authorities.

Done at the Appomattox Court House, Va., this 9th day of April 1865.

Albert Pike.

The hyacinthine curls waved recently in Savannah; the brow of Jove towered there; "the greatest poet, the greatest orator," and the most superhuman Know-Nothing of his age, was at his post; in a word, Albert Pike attended the commercial convention. At his nod Olympus shook, and we presume his audience slept.—Honey may have dropped from his tongue, as in the case of Homer's Ulysses, but the true Southern men assembled in Savannah, believed it to be molasses of an inferior brand. The bees may have gathered round his lips, as they buzzed round the lips of Plato in his cradle, but shrewed people suspected them to be drones.

Albert is a remarkable man. We were under the impression that he was defunct long ago—indeed, we regarded him as "one of our dead," Byron was right when he declared it strange that

"The mind, that very fiery particle,
Should let itself be snuffed out by an article;"

but the Delta assuredly went as close to snuffing out Albert Pike, or the narrow mind which goes by that name, as could be accomplished without a fatal and melancholy result. It caused the public to laugh at him—a process which is equivalent to a sort of moral thugging—and, accordingly, he was silent for two years and a half.

It appears, however, that either his ghost or himself—the ghost in all likelihood—turned up at the Savannah convention, and did a very characteristic thing, viz: made a speech. A ghost with a "splendid head of hair," with huge whiskers, a rubicund face, a deal of unpublished poetry flashing from its eyes, and such a beard! A peripatetic ghost; here, to-day, like Corporal Trim's mortal, and gone to-morrow. In Charleston, in Memphis, in New Orleans, everywhere, appearing to the astonished inhabitants, and talking as hugely as Hamlet's progenitor—sometimes arising in such a questionable shape that we might be pardoned for asking him, like Giles Scroggins in the story—"are you a ghost, or only an undigested piece of meat?"

Of course the apparition delivered an oration, and joking aside, it deserves an exorcism for its pains. Albert, or his *simulacrum*, assailed the Southern party, denounced the revival of the slave trade—hinted at gradual emancipation—laughed at the idea of Southern literature and art—presented himself, or itself, as a specimen of Massachusetts education, and altogether, was extremely absurd. Albert undertakes to defeat the party of chivalry—he, the Albert of the party of Sala! Poor troubled ghost? It is only muttering, perhaps, in its uneasy sleep. The South must submit to every Northern theory; Albert says so. The extension of slavery is undesirable; Albert says so. The formation of a purely Southern party is impossible; Albert says sa. A local literature can never be achieved; Albert says so. And to all this we say, in reply, —*Apage Satanus*—depart, poor ghost, into brimstone and sulphur, for we see something of Satan in your cut. You are one of the prating humbugs who have kept the South in her present position; your time is up; go!—*New Orleans Delta, about* 1854.

The Art of Fighting the French Army.

"Prince Frederick Charles, of Prussia, in a pamphlet, printed some years ago, gave, as the first principle of the French army, that the French soldier always marches forward; the second, he says is, that the moral is superior to to the physical force. So Marshall Canrobert, when he had a *coup de main* on his hands, in the Crimea, always asked his soldiers 'Do you feel equal to it? They never answered 'No;' and the promise, which they themselves had given to their general, was the guarantee of their success. The third principle of the French, according to the prince, is to hold themselves in a serried column, against an enemy which is badly disciplined, and unaccustomed to military manœuvres; and, on the contrary, to fight with disordered ranks, and like skirmishers, when they have to do with regular and well disciplined troops. The fourth French principle is, never to defend themselves passively. Of this, the prince says: 'If it happens that the French are attacked by a close column, they proceed in this way, and it is especially excellent, when the attack is not supported by a *corps de reserve*. The French riflemen give way, at the point of attack; the attacking column, imagining that this is the commencement of a retreat, pushes on, but soon the riflemen present a new front; one or two columns advance; the sharpshooters surround the enemy, on all sides; he hesitates, he losses time; he cannot turn back; there he is compelled to fight, and is abandoned to his fate. The French soldiers are ordered in this case, not to kill any more, but to make prisoners; because a soldier can take five or six prisoners in the time required to kill one man.

'It is a principle,' says the prince, 'in the French army, that an attack, when once resolved upon, can never be executed too soon, or too rapidly. In Italy, fire seldom lasted over a quarter of an hour before they came to the bayonet; oftentimes, they did not burn a cartridge during the attack. It appears, now, that the French attacked at a full run, to which they are exercised during peace, so that, when they reach the enemy, they are 'not out of breath.' The prince claims many of these principles as of Prussian origin. He believes that they are not even the product of the French national character, and that the temparament of the Prussian soldiers is admirably adapted to their adoption. In conclusion, he proposes, first, to employ riflemen by columns of one company each; second, to dispose the armed in depth, rather than in breadth, which increases the power of resistance on the flanks, and prevents a rapid loss of men; and thirdly, the disposition of an army as much as possible like the squares on a chess-board, which is the best means of sustaining the impetuous attack of such men as the Zouaves, and Turcos, made on a full run, and with the bayonet. Perhaps it would be well for some of our own authorities to study these principles.'

SPECIAL NOTICES

CONSIGNEES PER AUGUSTA & SAVANNAH RAIL ROAD. April 22, 1865.—Merchandise—Mrs C M Davies, R F Connally, N & M Bureau, S Miller.

OFFICE POST Q. M. TAX IN KIND, }
Thomson, Ga., April 18, 1865. }

Planters of this District take notice and pay al Tithes due by you, by the 1st day of June. A failurl will subject you to the five fold penalty.

Your ob't serv't,
J. M. ELLIOTT,
Capt. and A. Q. M. 5th C. D.

apr5 1m

HEADQUARTERS. }
AUGUSTA, GA., April 6th, 1865 }

GENERAL ORDERS, }
No. 15. }

I. Major J. B. Derman, A. A. G., having, in accordance with Special Orders, No. 49, A. & I. G. O., reported this day at these Head Quarters, is hereby assigned to duty as Assistant Adjutant General, and will be obeyed and respected accordingly.

B. D. FRY,
ap 18 6t Brig. Gen. Comd'g Dist.

OFFICE MEDICAL DIRECTOR, }
DEPARTMENT SO. CA., GA, & FLA. }
NEWBERRY, April 12, 1865.

CIRCULAR.

All Medical Officers in the Field Department, who were prevented from joining their commands during the evacuation of the city of Charleston and the coast, or who are now on duty in this Department, will report forthwith by letter to these Headquarters, stating, if not on duty, the cause of their absence, and if on duty, will state on what duty, to whom reporting, and by whom assigned. Surgeon T. L. Ogier, Medical Director, having by order, dated March 28 h, returned to the Department of South Carolina, Georgia and Florida, and resumed his duties.

T. L. OGIER,
Medical Director F'ld Dep'mt.
ap18 d1w

TO ABSENTEES—OFFICIAL.

BOONE HILL, April 6th, 1865.

SPECIAL ORDER.

All men belonging to the cavalry service in this my are ordered to report at Raleigh forthwith. Dismounted men will come by train. I earnestly call on my men to repair to the front.

ap15 12 WADE HAMPTON, Lt. Gen.

JUST RECEIVED AT 313 BROAD STREET—
840 yards superfine Linen Shirting,
300 " Colored Calico;
50,000 Needles, 200 to 10;
500 yards Red Flannel;
20 doz Misses Hose;
And a general assortment of other goods, which will be sold cheap, by
T. PHIBBS,
ap22 3 At the old store of S. Dickey.

TO HIRE—A first rate Cook, Washer, &c. Apply to W. H. SMITH,
ay22 3* E. Tenn. & Ga R. R. Shop.

SUGAR—2 hhds good quality New Orleans Sugar, just received on consignment and for sale by D. L. ADAMS & SONS.
ap22 2*

FOR SALE!

50 BOXES Bar Soap;
5 casks Lime.
ap22 2 McCORD & WALTON.

PAPER AND NEEDLES—35,000 Needles, assorted;
40 reams Note and Letter Paper.
On consignment and for sale by
ap21 12 NEAL & WHITLOCK.

WANTED TO RENT—A four or five room house, with usual outbuildings and garden, in or within three miles of Augusta.
J. RICKMAN,
ap21 3* 267 Broad street.

WANTED IMMEDIATELY A small Camera Lucida. Apply at
ap19 5* THIS OFFICE.

FOR SALE—1 fine Rockaway, (new);
1 fine Carriage.
C D McCOY,
No. 45, cor. Centre and Ellis streets
ap21 eod 1w

TO HIRE—A good house servant and cook. Apply at 351 Broad Street.
ap20 4*

TO RENT—A commodious dwelling in Summerville, near the Arsenal, opposite the residence of M. Wilkinson. For terms apply to Mrs. E. Moore, or
W. A. WALTON,
ap20 6* No 122 Greene street.

A LADIES WATCH—An extra fine 18 K Gold Lady's Watch of Superior quality and fine time keeper left with me for sale, Also, a large Store for rent.
Apply at 336 Broad Street.
ap19 4

J. C. MILLNER,

AUCTION AND GENERAL

COMMISSION MERCHANT,

NO. 274 BROAD STREET, AUGUSTA, GA

W. B. GRIFFIN,

AUCTIONEER.

WILL give his prompt and personal attention to all business entrusted to him. Such as Merchandize, Bonds, Stocks, Negroes, Real Estate, Tobacco, &c., &c. Liberal advances made on consignments in Store.

REFERENCES.

Robt H May, Mayor,	Ross & Seymour, Macon,
J A Ansley & Co.,	J Walker, Mayor, Danville, Va.
Churchill & Johnson,	W W Keen, Danville.
Dr M E Swinney,	W T Sutherland, Danville.
Hickman & Co.	

ap19 1m

TO RENT UNTIL 1st OCTOBER.

H. F. Russell & Co,

AUCTIONEERS,

Will rent a house containing five rooms with closets and all necessary out buildings, all in good order.

Pleasantly situated on the Sand Hills.

Apply immediately. ap19 tf

Exchange Restaurant.

THE EXCHANGE RESTAURANT, corner of Ellis and McIntosh streets, is open to the eating public, and will serve meals at all hours of the day, at the shortest notice and in the best style. Everything the market affords can be had. All orders for meals to be sent out promptly attended to.

ap13 1m H. RAWLS.

Wanted to Hire,

A GOOD COOK.

Apply to F. CORRA,
ap18 tf 202 Broad Street.

FIFTY SHARES

Georgia Railroad and Banking Company Stock,

For sale by SOLOMON COHEN.
ap 11 tf

TO RENT—Until the 1st of October next, a very handsome and comfortable Country Residence, two and a half miles from the Augusta Bridge, on the Carolina side, containing fourteen rooms, most of which are furnished.—All necessary outbuildings, stables, &c., are in fine order; a well of never failing, delightful water in the yard, with plenty of wood convenient; a peach orchard of about 1,500 trees, now in prime bearing condition; also a grape vineyard. The fruit crop, if properly managed, will avail an income near equal to the rent, which must be payable in advance.

Apply to JAMES T. GARDINER,
ap15 tf McIntosh Street.

"SELLING OFF."

BLOCKADE GOODS

At Reduced Prices.

10 KEGS Bi Carb Soda;
5 bbls Borax;
5 cases English Mustard, (Colman's) 1 and ½ lb cans;
20 cases French White Red Wine Vinegar;
3 Eighth casks French Brandy;
5 bbls Linseed Oil;
1500 pairs English Cotton Cards, No. 10;
200 " Wool Cards;
400 setts Knives and Forks;
100 gross Pearl Buttons;
50 doz Shoe Knives;
200 lbs Black and Drab Flax Thread;
50 doz assorted Razors;
20 doz Undershirts;
25 doz Drawers;
25 doz Children's Round Combs;
100 reams Note Paper;
200 gross Pens and Pen Holders;
100 gross Hooks and Eyes;
500,000 Gun Caps;
20 gross Tumblers;
300 cases Smoking Tobacco;
20 doz Ladies Belts;
300 yds Melton Cloth;
50 kegs English White Lead;
10,000 lbs Hoop Iron;
Large lot of HARDWARE and other goods.

Apply to M. HYAMS,
ap1[illegible] Corner Broad & McIntosh.

MRS. M. E. DAVIS would respectfully inform her customers and the public generally, that she is located at No. 9 McIntosh street, 3d door below Reynolds.

Bonnets and Hats Pressed. Dyed and Altered in the latest styles. Bonnets and Hats for sale. and made to order. Children's Hats, Caps and Turbans made. Also, Gentlemen's Panama and Leghorn Hats cleaned or dyed.

Wanted immediately, two good Hat Pressers; those who understand straw sewing; none others need apply.

ap21 4*

SUNDRIES.

Sugar,
Coffee,
Quinine,
Morphine,
Pepper,
Whiskey,
Brandy,
Cards,
Sheetings,
Shirtings, &c.

For sale by E. B. LONG & CO.
ap20 eod 6t

Notice.

APPLICATION will be made to the Confederate Depositary at Augusta, Ga., for duplicates of the following 4 per cent. Certificate, No. 5681, dated March 25, 1864, for one thousand dollars, the same having been lost.

ap14 law6w* J. J. BROWN.

RAISE YOUR OWN MULES.—A fine Jack will stand at Byrd & Crim's old stables, in rear of Southern States Hotel, from this date until 1st July.

Terms ten (10) bushels of corn or its equivalent in money. ap15 11t*

J. R. KEEN. C. R. KEEN. T. COLEMAN.

J. R. KEEN & CO.

COMMISSION MERCHANTS,

AUGUSTA, GA.

WILL give their individual attention to the Sale or Purchase of all kinds of Produce or Merchandize. Commissions 5 per cent. and Taxes. Storage at Reasonable Rates. Insurance effected when requested. Motto—Quick Sales and Prompt Returns.

REFERS TO

J. A Ansley & Co.	J. B. Ross.
G. R. Crump & Co.	E. Bond,
	Geo. T. Rogers & Son.
	Dunn & Manghum.
Augusta, Ga.	Macon, Ga.

ap 18 tf

MULE STOLEN—A medium sized mouse colored Horse Mule, galled on the shoulders, otherwise in good order, was stolen near the Market yesterday (Saturday,) morning. It may be offered for sale or trade, in, or near the city. Also, with it an old Saddle and Curb-bit Bridle. A liberal reward will be paid for the return of the Mule, or for information that will lead to its recovery at the Constitutionalist Office.

ap 16 tf

To Rent.

A WORK SHOP, 80 by 80 feet, with or without water power near the Augusta Factory.

H. T. NELSON.

march 31—tf

DAILY CONSTITUTIONALIST

PUBLISHED BY

STOCKTON & CO.

AUGUSTA, GA.,

SUNDAY MORNING, APRIL 23, 1865.

"To exhort to sacrifices—to stimulate to exertion—to shame despondency—to divert from untimely concessions—are stern but needful duties to be dischaged in gloomy times."—*Burke*.

Particulars of the Killing of Lincoln and Seward.

The latest Nashville and Chattanooga papers received through the lines contain full and interesting particulars of "the tragedy in high life," which recently occurred in Washington City, resulting in the death of the two archfiends of the revolution.

It appears that on the evening of the 11th, Lincoln, much against his will, was persuaded to visit the theatre in the Federal capital, where was to be represented a popular piece, entitled "Our American Cousin." He occupied as usual on such occasions a private box, accompanied by his wife. The representation of the drama had hardly begun when a pistol shot was heard, but this noise created no stir in the large assemblage, and no excitement was manifest until far above the buz and hum of the many-voiced multitude, came the screams and cries of Mrs. Lincoln.

Immediately a man jumped from the box in front of the foot lights, brandishing a dagger, and exclaiming, "*Sic semper tyrannis! Virginia is avenged!*" The crowd, as if stricken with paralysis, offered no obstacle to the egress of the author of this doughty deed, and he escaped.

Great excitement prevailed when the nature of the catastrophe was understood. Lincoln was shot through the head, and survived until next day.

About the same hour this little dramatic spectacle, not announced in the bill, was being presented at the theatre, a gentleman called at the residence of Mr. Seward, and called for that right honorable Secretary. The servant responding to the bell, stated that his master was sick, and had refused company. The gentleman persisted, stating that he had a prescription from an eminent physician of Washington, and must see him.

At this juncture Mr. F. W. Seward appeared upon the scene, and denied the visitor admission. Some little parleying ensued when the unwelcome guest struck young Seward over the head with a bludgeon, fracturing his skull and doing away with that portion of the Seward family. He immediately rushed through the hall and entered the room of Secretary Seward. In this apartment there were collected five gentlemen, including the Paymaster General of the Army. The visitor did not stop to explain his business, but approaching the bed upon which Seward was ren[illegible] [illegible] his throat. A general melee then took place, and it was found necessary to dispatch a Mr. Hansall.

Whereupon 'Brutus' disappears from the scene, and all Yankeedom mourns and howls over the discomfiture of its two leading tyrants.

Yankee Account of the Occupation of Richmond.

ARKANSAS LANDING, VA., April 5—11:30 A. M.
Hon. E. M. Stanton, Secretary of War:

Little is known at City Point. There are but few officers left, and these are overwhelmed with work.

Lee telegraphed to Davis at 3:30, Sunday that he was driven back and must evacuate. This was announced in church. Davis had sold his furniture previously, at auction, and was ready to leave. All the leading men got away that evening.

The rib iron-clads were exploded.

The Virginia lies sunk in the James River, above the obstructions.

General Ewell set the city on fire. All the business portion, from Main Street to the river, was destroyed. The bridges across the river, were also destroyed. Many of the families remain. Mrs. Lee remains. At Petersburg all the public stores were burned and a few houses caught fire, but not much damage was done the city. The bridges there were also destroyed I will report more fully from Richmond. I can not now get a clear idea of our loss. The only General killed was Wintrop. Potter is dangerously wounded in the groin. General Grant has commanded the armies in person since the beginning of operations.

[Signed] C. A. DANA,
Assistant Secretary of War.

A SINGULAR MURDER.—The Winston Sentinel contains an account of a singular murder recently committed in Stokes county, N. C., at the house of W. P. Kallum, Esq. It seems that two persons, calling themselves respectively Capt. Wm. C. Williams and Lieut. John W. Moore, and representing themselves to be Kentuckians, belonging to Morgan's cavalry, have been in that section for some time past, deporting themselves as gentlemen.

On the night of the murder, they went to bed as usual. A little before day the family was aroused by the report of firearms in the room in which they slept, and presently the Captain ran out of the house, still firing, and shouting that deserters were attacking the house, and had shot the Lieutenant. During the day it was rendered certain that Williams himself was the murderer. The Sentinel says:

"Now what induced the Captain to commit the deed is a mystery; they were not known to have had any hard feeling toward each other, though they were somewhat reserved, and talked but little to each other in company. It might have been for money, as the Captain had said a few days before that the Lieutenant had eleven or twelve thousand dollars with him, all of which, together with the Lieutenont's horse and saddle, the Captain carried off—again, it might have been that the Captain was spying out the condition of [illegible] aying some plans for plun- [illegible] eared the Lieutenant might, [illegible] gence in the glass, reveal, [illegible] im. It is well enough for [illegible] alarmed and to be on the

The Capture of Richmond.

Yankee Accounts!

We have been kindly placed in possession of the Cincinnati Enquirer, of the 6th of April, from which we cull the following telegraphic summary of events in Virginia:

THE TERRIBLE FIGHT.

NEW YORK, April 5.—The Herald's correspondence has the following account of operations on Sunday:

At midnight of Saturday, General Wilcox had orders to demonstrate on the right of his line, so as to draw the rebels from the left preparatory to operations in that quarter. The next morning, Admiral Porter and all the artillery in the works on the right were also set to work. Wilcox's skirmish lines were advanced, the rebels were aroused, and soon sharp volleys of musketry were heard, indicating that they were at work. Amid the noise and smoke the skirmishers pushed on until reaching the outskirts of Petersburg, when they met a heavy body of rebels advancing upon them.

A brisk engagement followed, but our numbers were so small that we were compelled to withdraw. Wilcox then got orders to attack Fort Malone, on the left. He massed a column for the purpose. While this was being done, similar dispositions were making further on the left, and a system of cannon signals had been agreed upon to fix the moment of starting, that all might assault simultaneously. Owing to a mist which hung over the field, the preparations had been concealed from the enemy. At 4 o'clock the signal was given. The men advanced quickly and in perfect order, with fixed bayonets. That they went to stay was indicated by being accompanied by a detachment of heavy artillery, prepared to turn and work the enemy's guns.

Presently musketry was heard, and the rebel picket line was reached, now a hearty cheer, followed by the roar of musketry. The cheering and musketry firing is taken up and rung along to the left, until it is lost in the distance. Instantly the artillery on both sides is at work, and two hundred big guns belch forth their thunder. But the work is quickly done. Harriman, of the 37th Wisconsin, Acting Brigadier General, gave the order to charge up, and away the noble fellows went, over the breastworks, rifle-pits, abattis, chevaux-de-frise, the parapet of the fort, into the main works, and the deed was accomplished.

For one moment the thunderstruck rebels looked, and then took to flight; but our fellows were too quick for all of them, and captured 250. Nine guns were found in this fort, and quickly trained, were set at work annoying the rebel batteries. This, with the simultaneous operations further to the left, cut the rebel line in two, took from them commanding positions, and a large amount of valuable artillery. Scarcely were we in quiet possession of the fort, when the rebels having reorganized their forces and picked up some reinforcements, came up with a determined effort to retake the fort.

They made a most desperate effort—assaulting up against terrific discharges of grape and canister, and withering volley of musketry, but it was to no purpose. Four times during the day did they attempt to retake this important position, but were each time sent reeling back in disorder, losing heavy each time. It was in one of these assaults that the rebel General A. P. Hill lost his life, seeking in person to lead his men up to the works. Meantime the Sixth and Twenty-fourth Corps, having broken through the rebel lines in their front, were swung around to the rear, and coming down both upon their rear and flank, it was evident that Petersburg was lost to the rebellion. The movements of the Sixth Corps were so rapid that Gen. Lee himself narrowly escaped capture. As it was, his headquarters fell into our hands.

The Tribune's correspondent recounts the operations on our left. At 4:30 Sunday morning the Sixth Corps left its lines to attack the enemy's left centre. It moved in echelon, so as to enable the Corps to throw forward its left, and flank the works of the enemy, one after another. Soon a battery of four guns opened upon the First Division, but, by a rapid change of the Twelfth Brigade, it was immediately captured.—The batteries of the enemy now opened from every point, but on went our gallant braves. The left soon reached some works in their front, and one by one they fell into our hands. At 10:30 a grand picture of war presented itself.

The line of corps, with its left in advance; was sweeping on toward two heavy forts. The rebels plied their guns vigorously, and shells burst thickly over our lines. On pushed the left division until it struck the Southside Railroad. Against the two forts swept the Second Division, our artillery playing upon the forts from commanding positions incessantly, until our men were close up to them. Then a dash was made upon the works, but it was repulsed. Again it was tried, and this time it met with success; but so resolute were the rebels inside, that some of them used the bayonet for a short time, as these works fell into our hands.

A loud cheer rent the air, and the enemy were seen hastily retiring to their second line, which opened sharply in an effort to stay our advance. About this time Sheridan appeared on the field, and was received with loud cheers by the Sixth Corps, who look up to him with great respect. At this moment, too, our entire line was changing its long front to the right, and slowly before it the broken line of the enemy was falling back upon their rear defenses.

Against the line to which they fell back, a heavy force was now pitted, composed of parts of the Twenty-fourth, Sixth and Twenty-fifth Corps, and nearly all fresh troops. A lull took place, and when the force was ready to move it was plain that a distinct action was to be fought. Dusk stole over the scene, and the attack was deferred for the next day.

While the above fighting was taken place, the Sixth Corps and cavalry, under Sheridan, turned the right wing of the rebel army, taking from 4,000 to 5,000 prisoners.

The Second Corps, connecting with the Fifth, was also victorious, notwithstanding they had, perhaps, the roughest ground to fight over, and a brave, determined foe in the rebel Third Corps.

The line of defenses in front of the Ninth Corps was stronger than those at any other point. It delivered many assaults during the day, and suffered severely. At night it found itself close up to the main line of the defenses, but unable to go farther. The First Division of the Tenth Corps aided the Ninth greatly.

WASHINGTON, April 5.—The War Department has just received the following order:—

The Examining Board, of which Major General Casey is President, will immediately adjourn to Richmond, Va., at which place he will resume its present duties.

Major General Casey will, in addition take general superintendence of recruiting and mustering colored troops in Richmond, Va., and the adjacent country.

WASHINGTON, April 5.—Hon G W McLellen, Second Assistant Postmaster General, to-day received the following dispatch:

RICHMOND, April 4.—I have taken possession of the Richmond Postoffice in the name of the Postoffice Department of the United States. I found a large quantity of United States property; pouches, locks, safes, &c. Mails that should have left the city to-day are all here pouched and filed. I have not yet had an opportunity of conferring with the military authority, but the Provost Marshal has kindly placed a guard over the buildings and effects.

D. B. PARKER, Special Agent.

A KISS IN THE DARK.—Holcroft, the well-known dramatist, supped one evening at Opie's. After the cloth had been removed, numerous stories were told, among which was one of a gentleman, who having put out his candle on going to bed, read in phosphorescent characters on the wall, "Confess thy sins." The gentleman fell on his knees, and as expected, began to confess his sins aloud, not from terror, however, for, aware it was a trick to terrify him, devised by a certain waggish young lady in the house, and hearing a little bustle on the stairhead, he guessed rightly that she and her comrades were there to enjoy his discomfiture He confessed, as the last and greatest of his sins, that "he had kissed Miss —— frequently in the dark," and so turned the tables on his tormentor with a vengeance, a lesson she never forgot.

From the Camden Journal and Confederate.

A Villainous Yankee Letter.

We publish the following letter from a Yankee to his wife in Boston, which was found near this place after the Yankees had left. It is undoubtedly genuine, and will serve greatly to dispel the last lingering belief still remaining in some deluded minds, that the plundering and thieving of the Yankee army was, if winked at, certainly not shared in by those in authority. We see from this letter that from Sherman himself down to the lowest drummer in his army, the plundering is conducted on system, and the booty shared upon established principles. We do not think that anything is necessary to produce a correct conviction of the Yankee character in this community, where it is everywhere written in characters so plain, that he who runs may read, but as one of the curiosities of the times, we thought it not unworthy of insertion:

CAMP NEAR CAMDEN, S. C.,
February 26th, 1865.

My Dear Wife: I have no time for particulars. We have had a glorious time in this State. Unrestricted license to burn and plunder was the order of the day. The chivalry have been stript of most of their valuables. Gold watches, silver pitchers, cups, spoons, forks, &c., are as common in camp as blackberries. The terms of plunder are as follows: The valuables procured are estimated by companies. Each company is required to exhibit the results of its operations at any given place—one-fifth and first choice falls to the share of the Commander-in-Chief and Staff; one-fifth of the corps commanders and staff; one-fifth to field officers of regiment, and two-fifths to the company. Officers are not allowed to join in these expeditions without disguising themselves as privates. One of our corps commanders borrowed a suit of rough clothes from one of our men and was very successful at this place. He got a large quantity of silver (among other things an old time silver milk pitcher) and a very fine gold watch from a Mr. DeSaussure at this place. DeSaussure is one of the F. F. V.'s of South Carolina, and was made to fork out liberally.

Officers over the rank of captain are not made to put their plunder in the estimate for general distribution. This is very unfair, and for that reason, in order to protect themselves, subordinate officers and privates keep back everything that they can carry about their persons—such as rings, earrings, breastpins, &c., &c., of which, if I live to get home, I have about a quart. I am not joking—I have at least a quart of jewelry for you and all the girls—and some No. 1 diamond rings and pins among them. Gen. Sherman has silver and gold enough to start a bank. His share in gold watches and chains alone at Columbia, was two hundred and seventy-five (275.)

But I said I could not go into particulars. All the general officers, and many besides, have valuables of every description [illegible] embroidered ladies pocket handkerchiefs. (I have my share of them too.) We took gold and silver enough from the d—n rebels to have redeemed their infernal currency twice over. This (the currency) wherever we came across it, we burned, as we considered it utterly worthless.

I wish all the jewelry this army has could be carried to the "Old Bay State." It would deck her out in glorious style; but alas, it will be scattered all over the North and middle States. The damned niggers, as a general rule, preferred to stay at home—particularly after they found out that we only wanted the able-bodied men (and to tell you the truth, the youngest and best looking women.) Sometimes we took off whole families and plantations of niggers, by way of repaying some influential secessionist. But the useless part of these we soon managed to loose—sometimes in crossing rivers, sometimes in other ways.

I shall write to you again from Wilmington, Goldsboro or some other place in North Carolina. The order to march has arrived and I must close hurriedly. Love to grandmother and to aunt Charlotte. Take care of yourself and the children. Don't show this letter out of the family.

Your affectionate husbands,
THOS. J. MYERS, Lieut. &c.

P. S.—I will send this by the first flag of truce to be mailed; unless I have an opportunity of sending it to Hilton Head. Tell Sally I am saving a pearl bracelet and ear rings for her. Bob Lambert got the necklace and breastpin of the same set. I am trying to trade him out of them. These were taken from the Miss Jamisons, daughters of the president of the S. C. secession convention. We found these ladies on our trip through Georgia.

Situation at Goldsboro'.

We learn from an entirely reliable party who left Goldsboro' on Wednesday last, that Sherman and Schofield are quietly resting at that place. They claim to have 130 000 men, but intelligent persons who have come out think they have about 100 000. As soon as the Federals entered Goldsboro', guards were stationed and order maintained; and up to Wednesday last the citizens had not been molested in person or property. No property had been burnt in the town, and only one citizen, Mr Richard Washington, had been requested to give up his residence. Mr. W's house was used as headquarters and both hotels as Hospitals.

The poor had been furnished with rations and some of the better classes had been furnished with coffee, sugar, tea, etc. But few persons had left the town and those who remained were quietly attending to their business. One man, a secessionist, had gone forward to take the oath of allegiance, but they would not let him do it. The oath had not been required of any one.

Within a very short time after entering Goldsboro', the Federals had erected three lines of works around the town and now the place is strongly fortified. They are running cars to Newbern and Wilmington and getting supplies in immense quantities.

The people of the county of Wayne, outside of Goldsboro', have fared badly at the hand of the Federals and in many instances are in a very destitute condition. The houses of J W Collier and W K Lane are said to have been burnt.

We learn from other sources that Sherman is supplying all who apply with food, and that many persons who live ten and twelve miles this side of Goldsboro go there for rations.

Sherman is recruiting and reorganizing his army and it is thought he will move, most probably in the direction of Raleigh, very soon.—*Raleigh Progress, 8th.*

THE MEXICAN EMPIRE AND THE CONFEDERACY.—The Houston Telegraph of February 8th prints the correspondence which lately passed between Col. Pryon, commanding at San Antonio, and Gen. Florentine Lopez, commanding Maximilians troops on the border of the Rio Grande. The former assures Gen. Lopez that it is the desire of his Government to cherish the most amicable relations with the imperial Government of Mexico, and further, that the entende cordiale existing shall not be disturbed. The Colonel also thanks the General for protecting the interest of the Confederates. The reply of General Lopez is subjoined:

MESIA DIA, MEXICAN EMPIRE.
Lopez Brigade, Com-in-Chief.

Colonel: I feel gratified at the high consideration you extend to me, and guided always by sentiments of heartfelt justice, I confess my sympathy for the noble cause of the South and frankly extend my sincere friendship.

Being placed in command of this military line under his majesty Emperor Maximilian, the sons of the Confederacy can rely on full security of their persons and interests and the hospitalities which this land affords.

The Confederacy may rest assured that the representatives of Mexico along the "Bravo" frankly offer their friendship, as also a full security that no raid will be permitted to organize on Mexican soil for the invasion of your territory.—With the assurance that our relations will continue friendly, I have the honor to offer you my distinguished considerations. God and order.

FLORENTINO LOPEZ,
Brig. Gen.

Piedras Negras, Jan. 10, 1865.

YANKEE FAITHLESSNESS.—Some months ago an arrangement was perfected whereby cotton was to be sent to the North from Mobile, entrusted to the care of General Beall, a Confederate prisoner, who was released from Johnson's Island on parole for the purpose. By him it was to be sold and the proceeds to be invested in blankets and clothing for our prisoners. We are informed by an officer, who has just returned from Northern prisons, that with its characteristic meanness, the Yankee Government has, for several weeks, withheld the supply, and some of our men are consequently again in want. Goods shipped to Elmira, only three days' distant from New York City, had not been received in a month, and at Johnson's Island the supply was even more tardy. Meanwhile effort is made to induce our soldiers to take the oath, and when persuasions fail, starvation is resorted to as the next effective expedient. The result is that those who proved true to the cause have returned home swearing vengeance, and will neither take prisoners nor be taken themselves.—*South Carolinian*.

From the Sentinel.

England's Responsibility for African Slavery in America.

Lord John Russell having thought proper in a speech recently made in Parliament, to denounce the institution of slavery, as it exists in this country, as disgraceful to the Confederate States, it would be well, if the following historical facts could be brought to his attention; proving that whatever of criminality and infamy may be attached to slavery as it exists here rests upon the British Government and people, by whom it was forced upon us:

Four companies were chartered by the British Government, to carry on the African slave trade. See Brit. Encyclop, under the head of companies, vol. 5, page 226. Of one of these companies Queen Elizabeth, and probably all her ministers, were members, and derived heavy profits from the traffic.

The Royal African Trading company erected a large building in Thread Needle street, London, then called the "South Sea House," for the pur- [illegible]
le to the South Sea, and
[illegible] with negroes. See
[illegible] 250, in account of the
[illegible] on.
[illegible] was sent from England
[illegible] d the Island of Gone, in
[illegible] ure to England the traf-
[illegible] from that part of Africa,
[illegible] of England, by Hume,
[illegible] boasted in a speech to
[illegible] by the treaty of Utrecht,
[illegible] the assiento or contract
[illegible] ish West India Islands
[illegible] had been enjoyed by the
[illegible] e 230 Hume's England.)
[illegible] stipulated that from the
[illegible] 1st May, 1743, the com-
[illegible] to the West Indies 144,-
[illegible] of 4,000 negroes a year,
[illegible] re thirty-three pieces of
[illegible] all for all royal duties."
[illegible] ume's England.
[illegible] revolution broke out, 3,-
[illegible] n had been engaged in
[illegible] de, were, by that event,
[illegible] nt, at the single port of
[illegible] ol. 15, History of Eng-
[illegible] Richmond stated in Par-
[illegible] r of ships that had been
[illegible] African trade, previous
[illegible] ras 200, of the value of
[illegible] umber had been educed
[illegible] d loss to Britain of £1,-
[illegible] , of the 15th vol. of the
[illegible] Treaty of Peace, made
[illegible] ebruary, 1763, between
[illegible] s objected to in England
[illegible] of its provisions would
[illegible] enjoying the whole pro-
[illegible] an slaves. See 14 vol.,
[illegible] and.
[illegible] revolution, acts were
[illegible] egislatures of New York,
[illegible] tias, and no less than 23
[illegible] uppress the slave trade;
[illegible] by the British Govern-
[illegible] they would diminish
[illegible] ets from this traffic.
[illegible] of the misdeeds of the
[illegible] he Constitution of Vir-
[illegible] vention of Virginia in
[illegible] words. "By prompting
[illegible] us among us, those very
[illegible] uman use of hi negative,
[illegible] sion to exclude by law."
[illegible] Government are there-
[illegible] God and man for the ex-
[illegible] and whatever odium may
[illegible] st on them. M.

[illegible] ERS.—A large number
who are cut off from
[illegible] ee, Kentucky, and oth-
[illegible] dering about over the
[illegible] l we fear, some of them
[illegible] mperative duty of the
[illegible] citizens to take these
[illegible] nes, and, by adminis-
[illegible] ndeavor to recruit their
[illegible] gies, and prepare them
[illegible] he hardships of camp
[illegible] ble men have been ab-
[illegible] nearly four years, and
[illegible] States have been over-
[illegible] the enemy, and upon
[illegible] sent adrift upon the
[illegible] Those of us who have
[illegible] any of the horrors of
[illegible] for an appeal to be
[illegible] for the wants of these
[illegible] rne for so long a time
[illegible] mp life. Numbers of
[illegible] vledge, are arriving at
[illegible] d from there they are
[illegible] country, seeking some
[illegible] epose in quiet for the
[illegible] allowed to remain at
[illegible] mostly from Tennessee
[illegible] ny of them have not
[illegible] anywhere in the Con-
[illegible] es have been left with-
[illegible] nd they are unable to
[illegible] *ambers Tribune.*

[illegible] T.—"Many years since
[illegible] man—Dr. Turnbull—
[illegible] h the value, and pro-
[illegible] mp lands of Florida,
[illegible] and brought out, from
[illegible] colony of about seven
[illegible] inorcans, as laborers,
[illegible] aking of sugar, and
[illegible] people were engaged
[illegible] ar to that which the
[illegible] ing the coolies in Ja-
[illegible] system. They were
[illegible] because of their being
[illegible] leem, by their labor,
[illegible] age, and the cost of
[illegible] ry to the support of
[illegible]. At the end of the
[illegible] to receive stipulated
[illegible] n prosperously, for a
[illegible] ere erected, extensive
[illegible] e dug, and the lands
[illegible] ought under cultiva-
[illegible] energies of the labor-
ers began to flag; their employer became impatient; their task-masters became more urgent; blows and stripes were resorted to, with a view of inducing them to more active work, till, at length, the Minorcans took to running away. Three of these fugitives arrived at St. Augustine, where their tale of suffering, and wrong excited the sympathy of the Spaniards, who, pursuing their old game towards the English, urged them to return, and raise a general insurrection. This advice they followed, and, in a short time, there was a complete *emeute*. The whole body of laborers dropped their tools, refused to work, and marched off, in a body towards St. Augustine.

Thus ended Dr. Turnbull's scheme for raising sugar with free white labor—another proof to the British, by one of their own countrymen, that for the tropical products of agriculture, on anything like an extensive scale, no other than negro slave labor can, with certainty, be depended upon. Dr. Turnbull displayed much judgment in the selection of his lands, being those in the vicinity of New Smyrna. It is stated to be a fact well known, that on the plantation of Mr. Dummitt, near that place, land of the description above mentioned, has produced four hogsheads of sugar per acre—the greatest yield of sugar ever produced in Florida."

Particulars of the Killing of Lincoln and Seward.

The latest Nashville and Chattanooga papers received through the lines contain full and interesting particulars of "the tragedy in high life," which recently occurred in Washington City, resulting in the death of the two archfiends of the revolution.

It appears that on the evening of the 11th, Lincoln, much against his will, was persuaded to visit the theatre in the Federal capital, where was to be represented a popular piece, entitled "Our American Cousin." He occupied as usual on such occasions a private box, accompanied by his wife. The representation of the drama had hardly begun when a pistol shot was heard, but this noise created no stir in the large assemblage, and no excitement was manifest until far above the buz and hum of the many-voiced multitude, came the screams and cries of Mrs. Lincoln.

Immediately a man jumped from the box in front of the foot lights, brandishing a dagger, and exclaiming, "*Sic semper tyrannis! Virginia is avenged!*" The crowd, as if stricken with paralysis, offered no obstacle to the egress of the author of this doughty deed, and he escaped.

Great excitement prevailed when the nature of the catastrophe was understood. Lincoln was shot through the head, and survived until next day.

About the same hour this little dramatic spectacle, not announced in the bill, was being presented at the theatre, a gentleman called at the residence of Mr. Seward, and called for that right honorable Secretary. The servant responding to the bell, stated that his master was sick, and had refused company. The gentleman persisted, stating that he had a prescription from an eminent physician of Washington, and must see him.

At this juncture Mr. F. W. Seward appeared upon the scene, and denied the visitor admission. Some little parleying ensued when the unwelcome guest struck young Seward over the head with a bludgeon, fracturing his skull and doing away with that portion of the Seward family. He immediately rushed through the hall and entered the room of Secretary Seward. In this apartment there were collected five gentlemen, including the Paymaster General of the Army. The visitor did not stop to explain his business, but approaching the bed upon which Seward was ren[illegible] [illegible] his throat. A general melee then took place, and it was found necessary to dispatch a Mr. Hansall.

Whereupon 'Brutus' disappears from the scene, and all Yankeedom mourns and howls over the discomfiture of its two leading tyrants.

EXECUTIVE DEPARTMENT,
Macon, April 17, 1865.

Maj. Gen. G. W. Smith:

As it is reported that Columbus has fallen into the hands of the enemy, you will change the place of rendezvous of the Militia. All east of the Oconee will rendezvous at Augusta and report to Brig. Gen. Fry until further orders. All others at Macon.

All Aids de Camp, and the Reserve Militia over fifty years of age are required to see that they respond with the least possible delay.

JOS. E. BROWN.

HEADQ'RS FIRST DIV. GA MILITIA,
Macon, April 17, 1865.

General Order No. 2.

In obedience to the above directions from His Excellency, the Governor, General Orders No. 1, April 15, 1865, from these Headquarters, are hereby modified and changed as to the place of rendezvous of the Georgia Militia.

All that portion af the Militia lying east of the Oconee river will rendezvous immediately at Augusta Ga., and the ranking officer present will report to Brig Gen. Fry. The remainder will report, without delay, at Macon.

By order of
G. W. SMITH, Maj. Gen.

THOS. HARDEMAN, JR., A. A. G.
ap22

CONSTITUTIONALIST

SUNDAY MORNING, APRIL 23, 1865.

Tri-Weekly.

One month $7 00
Three months 20 00

THE KILLING OF LINCOLN.

The Chattanooga Gazette of a late date has been received at Atlanta. The reported death of Lincoln is confirmed. The Gazette is draped in mourning. We learn that a Marylander named Smith shot Lincoln at the Theatre, and, escaping in the hurly burly that ensued, made his way to Seward's apartment. The Secretary's son attempted to defend his father but was mortally wounded. Smith then attacked Seward and stabbed him in several places. It is thought that the Secretary may recover although his injuries are of a serious character. The Gazette does not mention any dramatic ejaculation by the modern Brutus. He seemed to be satisfied with deeds without words.

From Middle Georgia.

Rumors, says the Macon Confederate, are plentiful, and so diverse that it is impossible to arrive at the truth.

The outward train on the Macon and Western Railroad returned last evening, it being reported that the enemy was at Thomaston, or within some twelve miles of the road.

The party of the enemy reported to have been near LaGrange on Monday, it is said, turned back before reaching that place.

We are informed that an engineer and conductor went, on yesterday, to within eighteen miles of Columbus, where they learned that there was heavy fighting going on, stating they could hear the reports of the cannonading.

It was also stated that it was thought Forrest was there, and that he was driving the enemy. It is too late for us to investigate these statements and ascertain their credibility.

Daring Assault.

About 11 o'clock last night, says the Atlanta Register, some one came up to Col. G. W. Lee's gate and called to know if he was in. The Colonel went to the door and wished to know who desired to see him. The man gave his name as Lieut. Suttle, and wanted to see the Colonel on some private business. The Colonel not recognizing the name or voice, told the man if he wished to see him he must come in. The man objected to coming in, as his business was of a strictly private nature; but the Colonel assuring him that he could not see him outside the house he came in. After the Colonel had viewed him, he said, "now you have seen me, I would like for you to step out with me for what I want to say to you is private."

The Colonel then followed him out towards the gate, and when they reached it, the Lieutenant said to a companion, "tell the lieutenant to bring up that posse of men and we will show him how to disobey orders." Col. Lee. being armed, defied them and their posse, whereupon one of the men made a strike at him with a slung shot, and struck him in the back. The Colonel was stunned somewhat by the blow but not sufficient to lose his presence of mind. The two assassins attempted to run off as soon as the blow was made, but the Colonel commenced firing on them and succeeded in striking one of them in the region of the spine. The other made his escape. The Colonel then procured a posse of men and made a search for the assassins. The wounded one was found where he had crawled up to the Colonel's gate and was begging to be taken in. The Colonel had him carried in the house and Dr. D'Alvigny was called in. The Doctor thinks he will die to-day.

Nothing yet has transpired to throw light upon the motive that prompted the assassination.

It would be well for people who are called upon late at night to imitate the Colonel's example of cautiousness.

A Remarkable Woman.—We wish it distinctly understood that in publishing we do not vouch for the veracity of the following remarkable incident. An exchange paper gives this account of an eccentric lady still at large in the city in which the incident is said to have occurred:

"A lady entered one of the cars yesterday, and found every seat taken. A gentleman rose and invited her to accept the seat he had vacated. She did so, politely thanking him for his kindness. The lady wore a dark delaine dress, plain shawl, and an ordinary tan colored straw hat. She had a fair complexion, smiling countenance, keen black eyes, and an expression that indicated a good degree of intelligence. Her appearance was neat and tidy, her face was free from dirt and paint, her hair was smoothly combed, without curls or frizzles, or beau catchers. There was nothing in the appearance or deportment of this individual, that would attract special attention, or lead any one to suspect that she was not in sound mind, save the fact that she bowed politely and thanked the gentleman who gave her his seat. This eccentricity is sufficient to show that the lady is not in sound mind, and she ought not to be at large."

The Right Point.—From the Caddo Gazette, published at Shreveport, La., (and for which we are indebted to a friend,) we take the following sentence, which concludes an editorial reviewing the campaign of General Hood. It breathes the true spirit, and we are pleased to give it a place in our colums:

"When our forces are concentrated, and we have fewer fortified cities to defend, the tide of battle will turn in our favor. The Yankees can never subjugate the Southern people, for we will fight them more successfully when we have lost all our property, and have nothing left but the right to be freemen, and the unconquerable determination to maintain that right."

"A lady, being so unfortunate as to have her husband hang himself on an apple tree, the wife of a neighbor immediately came to beg a branch of the tree, for grafting. "For who knows," said she, "but it may bear the same kind of fruit!"

St. Domingo has apparently settled down for a long rest from tumult and trouble. The "colored citizens of African descent" are reorganizing their civil government and repairing their constitution. They propose to confer the privileges of citizenship on such well behaved white men as may render service to the republic; but their candidates for office must be "to the manor born." The distress occasioned by the great fire in Port au Prince, is being relieved by extensive voluntary contributions.

From the Caddo Gazette.

The Trans-Mississippi and Gen. Kirby Smith.

(Concluded.)

Let us examine the reason which determined him.

It is very natural that the people both of Louisiana and Arkansas should think that their respective States were the most important. History teaches us also, that subordinate commanders of armies and districts, with their eyes fixed upon their own localities and the enemy opposed to them, and with the natural desire of distinction and success, are prone to magnify the importance of their position, and to think that they should be especially reinforced. But the General commanding a department, dependent upon itself for its means of defence and offence, must take a survey of the whole field of action, and must decide upon his own responsibility what is best for the whole cause. He is not to look to the winning of a battle alone; he must win campaigns. The subordinate officer is given an army and directed to operate with it for specific objects. If it is lost, the higher authority is expected to supply its place. A commander in Gen. Smith's position, charged with the defence of an immense territory, with insufficient means and isolated from all support, cannot lightly jeopardize an army whose loss he cannot repair; nor allow one column of an enemy to seize upon arsenals, depots, workshops, etc., although by permitting it he might win renown, or possibly inflict great loss upon him in another quarter.

On the other hand, Banks with a force, double the strength of ours, was entrenched at Grand Ecore, supported by gunboats. He had two pontoon bridges established, so that if he desire to avoid, or was worsted in an engagement, he could cross the river, and by marching down its left bank or over the country to the Ouachita at Harrisonburg—relieve himself from molestation by our army.

The country being destitute of supplies, it was impossible to dislodge him by undertaking a sustained operation upon his communications. It would have been simple madness to march up and assault it in its then position the army which we had failed to whip in a fair field at Pleasant Hill. Finally, had Banks been driven to the Atchafalaya, the campaign would have terminated, as the gunboats controlled that stream.

On the other hand, Steele with a force not larger than Gen. Smith could bring against him, had come out of his fortifications, and was now distant from them over one hundred miles. If he could be reached and his infantry disordered—his army would become the prey of our cavalry, with his army, would fall the fortifications of Little Rock, Pine Bluff and Duval's Bluff giving us control of Northern Arkansas, where it was known that we could obtain ten thousand recruits. The political organizations which the enemy were industriously establishing, would be broken up, and the way would be opened to Missouri for our infantry.

Again, with Banks at Grand Ecore—stunned it is true, but not seriously hurt—a renewal of the advance was not improbable, either upon the original plan, or upon the north side of the Red river; looking to a junction with Steele in the neighborhood of Minden. This would have made their combined armies irresistable. In this position of affairs, Gen. Smith did not feel himself at liberty to allow Steele either to advance upon his depots, or to establish himself in the valley of the Ouchita. It was known that the President had almost demanded that an effort to re-occupy the valley of the Arkansas should be made.—Finally, the Arkansas troops had marched without hesitation or a murmur to relieve Louisiana, and both they and the citizens confidently relied on the commanding General for succor as soon as it was in his power to afford it.

The Arkansas and Missouri troops, and Walker's division of Texans, were brought back to Shreveport, with Gen. Taylor in command; Gen. Polignac being left to observe Banks.

When they reached Shreveport Steele who had hesitated at Prairie D'An, moved by his left upon Camden.

Then Gen. Smith remained to send Gen. Taylor back to his army while he would command in person the column against Steele.

Churchill was to move by the upper road upon Camden, Walker was to move to Minden and halt. Gen. Smith hurried to Gen. Price's headquarters near Camden, now occupied by the enemy, who were in strong works constructed by our engineers.

If Steele attempted a junction with Banks, Walker would be in a position to oppose it, and could be quickly joined by Churchill.

If Steele crossed the Ouachita so as not to be overtaken, Gen. Walker followed by Churchill would move down on the left side of Red river and join Gen. Thayer in his operations against Banks.

If Steele stopped at Camden, Walker would move up and assist in his capture.

The day after General Smith reached General Price, the cavalry, (Gen. Maxey commanding) surprised a foraging brigade of the enemy at Poison Springs—dispersed it, capturing its train and battery.

Gen. Smith, learning that Steele had received two hundred wagons loaded with provisions from Pine Bluff, despatched General Fagan across the Ouachita, who captured at Mark's Mill a brigade with four hundred wagons and a battery, all on their way to Pine Bluff.

This determined the retreat of Steele, who crossed the Ouachita and fled towards Little Rock.

Gen. Smith made an extraordinary effort to overtake him, sending instructions to General Fagan (who after the battle of Mark's Mill had gone towards Little Rock) to watch the crossings of the Saline, and to oppose to the last extremity the passage of the enemy.

He was delayed some hours in crossing the river, but by forced marches caught up with Steele on the Saline. Fortune now favored the enemy. It had rained incessantly, which impeded the progress and wearied the energy of troops.

The river bottom where the enemy were attacked, was filled with water; in places up to the hips and waists of the men. The battle raged furiously for six or eight hours with musketry alone, when it was found that the enemy, abandoning his dead and wounded, had crossed the river, destroyed his pontoons, and retreated rapidly. The river now overflowed its banks, our men were entirely exhausted by a march of fifty-five miles and a battle, and could not pursue.—Their supplies had also given out. The dispatches which were sent to Gen. Fagan had failed to reach him. To prevent his horses from starving, instead of being in position to complete the ruin of Steele's army; attracted by the firing, he arrived upon the field at the close of the battle, in such a state of exhaustion as to be incapable of following up the enemy had it otherwise been practicable.

Gen. Smith had failed to accomplish what he had hoped for, but he had captured from Steele ten pieces of artillery—compelling him to throw as many more into the river, near one thousand wagons, and killed and captured four thousand of his men. He had ejected him from the valley of the Ouachita and rendered him incapable of moving again for weeks or months to come. He was now free to use his whole force against Banks.—He confidently hoped that the low stage of water in Red river would not admit of the passage of the fleet over the falls at Alexandria, and that he would have time to reach there and engage him in decisive operations. The troops were moved immediately in that direction, and Gen. Walker's division reached Alexandria one week after the enemy evacuated the place. This division had marched since the enemy landed at Simsport seven hundred miles and had fought in three pitched battles.

In the mean time Gen Taylor, with great audacity, had annoyed the enemy's army and fleet as they fell back towards Alexandria, and after they reached there, had thrown a part of his little force upon the river below that place where the enemy had been reinforced by some 8 00 men from Texas, including two divisions of the 8th army corps. There he captured transports and gunboats until they ceased to attempt to pass.—The enemy had now accomplished a work deemed impossible, viz: dammed the river so as to throw the water into the channel, thereby enabling them to float over even their iron clads. As soon as this was done, the fleet and army moved down the river to Fort De Russey, where they separated.

Gen. Taylor was not s[...]
the march, but he attack[...]
Bayou, where a very seve[...]
—occurred. This ended [...]

It was necessarily d[...]
and when the conceptio[...]
in which each part of it [...]
whom it was assigned; t[...]
ry upon which the conce[...]
be effected; the absenc[...]
transportation for either [...]
the disparity of force; th[...]
enemy in effecting his o[...]
upon him; and the mora[...]
is considered, it must be [...]
most brilliant of the war.

Gen. Smith had before [...]
depressed, won the admi[...]
his offensive movement i[...]

In the Trans-Mississip[...]
equally capable of condu[...]
tions. That while by a[...]
can dissolve an enemy's [...]
chance is denied him, he [...]
tiently before overpowe[...]
has gathered all his ene[...]
army before two converg[...]
the mass of his force to b[...]
then the other, defeating [...]

As to there being an [...]
New Orleans, I am sure t[...]
examine the subject, you [...]
have been as easy for Ge[...]
Monroe.

As to sending reinforc[...]
detaining the enemy u[...]
might be said if it was proper to publish it. Certain it is, that when Hood's movement into Tennessee was being made, Price's advance into Missouri, and Magruder's attitude in Arkansas, occupied for six weeks or two months thirty-five thousand of the enemy.

For many reasons, nothing permanent was expected from this northern advance. It was intended is a diversion—the only aid in the circumstances, which Gen. Smith could render the Cis Mississippi. Its duration, from its nature, had certain limits, and Gen. Smith had every reason to believe that it would correspond with Hood's movement, so as materially to diminish the resistance which he had to encounter.

In conclusion, Mr. Editor, may it not, with all respect be doubted that your course in relation to Gen Smith has been dictated by an entire spirit of fairness?

May it not be fairly believed that you have acted hastily upon the statements of persons who designedly, and from interested purpose, sought to make your paper an engine to injure him?

Is it in the proper spirit to be grumbling at the Trans-Mississippi Department, and to be attributing to its commanding officer the failures of the Cis-Mississippi service?

Did we receive any aid from you in our hour of utmost need?

Did we complain because you failed to seize New Orleans, which is on your side of the Mississippi, when Bank's whole army and Porter's fleet were detained so long, far involved in the interior of this department?

Have we complained that you failed to make a diversion in our favor, in the supreme crisis of the campaign? We did not, because we knew you would have done so, were it in your power.

This department has sent east of the Mississippi largely over 100,000 men, since the beginning of the war; not one have we received in return, except officers, which you either sought to promote or get rid of. For two years we have not received any aid from the Cis-Mississippi in men, supplies or arms. We have not even been furnished with Treasury notes to pay off our soldiers, who have been marching and fighting all this while without pay.

In that time General Smith had succeeded in bringing some order out of the chaos which he found existing here. He has powder mills, arsenals, workshops, where before there were none. The shot which repelled the enemy last year was made of iron extracted from its ore, although no mine had ever before been worked within the limits of his command.

The army has been clad, shod, subsisted and furnished with munitions and transportation without any aid or direct support of the Government.

Should not these facts make you pause in your denunciation.

Instead of crying to this weak department for relief, should you not admire the administration which has shown it to be capable of self-sustentation.

Should you not, as we have done, bring out your men and resolve to hold your portion of the common lines, resting satisfied that your countrymen on this side of the Mississippi will spare no effort to aid you, by reinforcement or diversion, when it is practicable to do so?

TRANS-MISSISSIPPI.

From the New York Herald, March 22d.

Particulars of Gen. Newton's Expedition.

KEY WEST, March 15, 1865.

In my letter of the 12th inst, I gave some details of a fight that took place by the Natural Bridge, eight miles above Newport, Fla. The information, furnished as it was by persons who could see but portions of the affair, was necessarily imperfect. By the arrival of General Newton and other officers yesterday, however, I have received such statements as to enable me to correct any inaccuracies that may have crept into my former report.

At the outset it is but to say that his object was not to reach Thomasville but to occupy St. Marks, with the view of making that place a base for future operations, and that, consequently, so far the expedition was not a failure; and though he did not capture St. Marks, and was compelled to retreat before a superior force about two thousand five hundred, and not six thousand, as first stated—he did so in good order, with a piece of cannon captured from the enemy, and after the destruction of extensive salt works and a shot and shell factory.

Let it be understood also that considerable delay took place in landing, consequent on a dense fog, in the midst of which several of the gunboats went ashore, thus giving warning to the enemy and enabling him to prepare a warm reception for our troops. Had the gunboats been able to ascend the St. Marks river and shell the town, St. Marks would have been easily captured. The General acquits the commanders of the gunboats of all blame in the matter, and cheerfully acknowledges the readiness to co-operate with him in the affair.

Previous to landing the troops an expedition was sent to cut the railroad bridge and two turnpike bridges over the Ocklockonee river, and to destroy the trestle work over the Aucilla river. Another expedition was sent to cut the railroad between St Marks and Tallahasse. These operations, if successful, would have isolated the two places.

On debarking at the lighthouse, on the 4th inst., the command was moved forward about two miles and a half, where it was encamped to await the landing of the artillery, ammunition and ambulances. On the following morning an advance was made along the road towards the bridge over the East river, where it was found that the planking had been torn up by the enemy, who was posted on the opposite side, with one piece of artillery, prepared to dispute the passage.

Fire was first opened by two campanies of the 2d colored regiment, commanded by Major Lincoln. They made a gallant charge toward the bridge over the open space intervening before which the enemy fled with great rapidity. They were followed by the two companies, which acted as skirmishers capturing the piece of artillery, which was immediately turned on the flying rebels. The gun taken was without limbar or caisson, which had been taken away by the enemy.

The bridge was promptly repaired by the soldiers of the 99th colored regiment, and crossing, the line of march was commenced towards Newport, a few of the enemy's cavalry being discerned now and then. On reaching Newport a dense column of smoke seemed to indicate that the bridge, which it was necessary to cross, was being destroyed. Accordingly Major Weeks and his 2d Florida were sent on in advance to endeavor to save the bridge. He arrived too late, however, as the fire had made too much headway, in their way, a wide and deep ditch, impassable to troops, and were compelled to return.

Finding that the enemy were too strong in number and position, while the Union troops were posted in a low, marshy position, it was determined to withdraw about three hundred yards in the rear, in an open pine barren, which had been previously selected. This was done in good order, the enemy not making any opposition to the movement.

The rebels, now supposing that our forces were in full retreat, advanced in force, with artillery and infantry; but to their surprise, they were received by a perfect line of infantry, supported by artillery. Two desperate charges were made by the enemy, but they were repulsed with heavy loss on the part of the assailants, and the Union troops remained masters of the field. This was the last seen of the rebel troops. Some of their cavalry were occasionally seen on the return march.

Officers and men behaved splendidly. The blacks are highly spoken of for their conduct in charging, which seems to be their *forte*. Among the officers honorably mentioned is Maj. Weeks, of the Florida cavalry, who fought desperately. Capts. Rigney and Harding, of the Ninety-ninth, also particularly distinguished themselves. It was the latter gentlemen who brought off the captured guns.

In the absence of the official returns the exact number of casualities cannot be ascertained, but they are estimated at one hundred and fifty, in killed, wounded and missing. Of these it is supposed that thirty are prisoners.

Lieutenant Wilson, with twenty-five men of the Ninety-ninth, (colored) who were on outpost duty, were captured by the rebels.

The following is a list of the officers killed and wounded, as far as is known here:—

Killed:

Lieut Sanfield, 99 th colored.
Lieut Carrington, Gen Newton's Staff.

Wounded:

Col Townsend, 2d colored, slightly.
Major Lincoln, 2nd colored, mortally, (since dead.)
Capt Tracey, Gen Newton's staff, severely.
Capt Grant, 2d colored, slightly.
Lieut Seymour, 2d colored, severely.
Lieut Woodworth, 2d colored, severely.
Lieut Murphy, 2d colored, mortally, (since dead.)
Col Piersoll, 99th colored, slightly.
Col Brown, 2d colored, slightly.
Hospital Steward, U S A, slightly.

I ought to mention the conduct of Capt. Fontane, late of the Marine corps, who volunteered to serve on the expedition, and behaved well in the fight. He was slightly injured by the recoil of a gun. Captain Fontane is the grandson of Colonel Alexander Patterson, the veteran ex-Mayor of this city. He was on board the Mississippi when she was burned, opposite Port Hudson, on the memorable 14th and 15th of March, 1863, when Admiral Farragut forced the passage of the batteries. The Captain was taken prisoner by the rebels on that occasion.

Major General Sam Jones commanded the rebels in the late fight. Brigadier General Miller also took part.

The funeral of Maj. Lincoln and Lieutenants Carrington and Murphy, took place yesterday, from the United States barracks. During the day, all the flags of the public offices, vessels-of-war and private individuals were displayed at half mast. At three o'clock, P M, by order of Mayor Gwynn, all places of business were closed; and at 4 o'clock, the funeral procession moved off. There was the usual military escort, followed by a hearse, with the body of Maj. Lincoln, in a mahogony coffin, on which was laid his cap, sword and other equipments. His riderless horse was led in the rear. Behind came another hearse, containing the remains of the two Lieutenants, their coffins bearing similar insignia to those of the Major. Lieut Carrington's horse followed. There were present a very large number of navy officers, in pursuance of a special order from Admiral Stribling. The citizens also mustered in force, and among them was a large attendance of the members of the Key West Literary Association, according to notice from the President, Mr. Locke, in reference to Maj Lincoln, the immediate ex-President. Thus to the music of the Portuguese Hymn, played by the drum and fife, the funeral *cortege* proceeded to the cemetery, where the solemn rites of the Church were celebrated by the Rev O E Herrick, rector and post chaplain, who delivered an impressive address on the occasion.

Home.—The following beautiful passage is from the pen of Dr. Guthrie:

Home! To be home is the wish of the seamen on stormy seas, and lonely watch. Home is the wish of the soldier, and tender visions mingle with the troubled dreams of trench, and field. Where the palm-tree waves its graceful plumes, and birds of jeweled lustre flash, and flicker from among gorgeous flowers; the exile sits staring upon vacancy; a far away home lies on his heart; and borne, on the wings of fancy, over intervening seas, and lands, he has swept away to home, and hears the lark sing the above his father's fields, and sees his fair-haired boy brother, with light foot, and childhood's glee, chasing the butterfly by his native stream. And in his best hours, home, his own sinless home—a home with Father above that starry sky—will be the wish of every Christian man. He looks around him—the world is full of suffering: he is distressed by its sorrows, and vexed with its sins. He looks within him—he finds much in his own corruptions to grieve for. In the language of a heart repelled, grieved, vexed, he often turns his eye upwards, saying, "I would not live always." No; not for all the gold of the world's mines—not for all the pearls of her seas—not for all the pleasures of flashing, frothy cup—nor for all the crowns of her kingdoms, would I live always. Like a bird about to migrate to those sunny lands where no winter sheds her snows, or stripts the grove, or binds the streams, he will often, in spirit, be pluming his wing for the hour of his flight to glory."

Cure for Hog Cholera.—Mr. John F. Foster of this county, informs us that he has discovered a sovereign remedy for hog cholera, which is as follows:

Take corn and the leaves of poison ivy, boil it in a pot till the strength of the ivy has been extracted, and then feed the hogs plentifully with the corn. It will make them stagger as if drunk, but it will do them no harm. No danger from fowls eating the corn. Mr. F. informs us that this remedy has never failed. If the hog is past eating, drench him three times a day with half a pint of the liquor.

Athens Watchman.

THE KILLING OF LINCOLN.

The Chattanooga Gazette of a late date has been received at Atlanta. The reported death of Lincoln is confirmed. The Gazette is draped in mourning. We learn that a Marylander named Smith shot Lincoln at the Theatre, and, escaping in the hurly burly that ensued, made his way to Seward's apartment. The Secretary's son attempted to defend his father but was mortally wounded. Smith then attacked Seward and stabbed him in several places. It is thought that the Secretary may recover although his injuries are of a serious character. The Gazette does not mention any dramatic ejaculation by the modern Brutus. He seemed to be satisfied with deeds without words.

TELEGRAPHIC.

Reports of the Press Association.

OCCUPATION OF MACON BY THE ENEMY.

(PRESS AGENTS DISPATCH.)

AUGUSTA, April 21, 1865.

The enemy entered Macon at 7 o'clock, on the evening of April 20th.

An armed guard only occupies the city today.

A Yankee operator is in the telegraph office.

The enemy is respecting the armistice, but no private business was permitted to pass over the lines.

The enemy are awaiting instructions from Gen. Sherman before anything further is permitted.

They hold the city as a captured place.

LINCOLN ASSASSINATED.

SEWARD MORTALLY WOUNDED.

We publish the following dispatch, which purports to come through Mr. Barr, the telegraphic superintendent of Gen. Johnston's army. It bears upon its face many evidences of the sensational, and we advise our readers to take it, for the present, with a grain of salt:

WASHINGTON, April 12, 1865.

To Maj. Gen. Sherman:

Lincoln was murdered about ten o'clock last night in this city by an assassin who shot him in the head with a pistol ball,

About the same hour Mr. Seward's house was entered by another assassin who stabbed the Secretary in several places but it is thought he may recover. His son Frederick may possibly die of wounds received from the assassin.

The assassin of the President leaped from the box, brandishing a dagger, exclaiming, "*Sic Semper tyrannis! Virginia is avenged!*" Mr. Lincoln fell senseless from his seat, and continued in that condition until twenty-two minutes after 10 o'clock this morning, at which time he breathed his last.

Vice-President Johnson now becomes President and will take the oath of office and assume the duties to-day.

[Signed] E. M. STANTON,
Secretary of War.

A VICTORY IN SOUTH CAROLINA

GEN. YOUNG DEFEATS THE ENEMY.

STATESBORO, April 20, 1865.

To Brig. Gen. Fry:

We have had hard fighting for three days, killing and wounding many of the enemy.

He is now retreating rapidly.

Some rolling stock fell into his hands, but not much.

My loss is not heavy.

We are still fighting.

(Signed) P. M. B. YOUNG.

THE ARMISTICE.

GREENSBORO', April 20, 1865.

Brig. Gen. Fry:—

General Order No. 14 reads thus: It is announced to the army that a suspension of hostilities has been agreed upon, pending negotiations between the two Governments.

During its continuance the two armies are to occupy their present position.

By command of

GENERAL J. E. JOHNSTON,

ARCHER ANDERSON, A. A. G.

The armistice above disclosed applies to your command and the forces opposing you. Publish and communicate it to the army.

Realities of Insanity.—Dr. Winslow gives us to understand that madness is, for the most part, a condition of awful suffering. I used to think that though there might be dreadful misery on the way to madness, yet once reason was fairly overthrown, the sufferings was over. This appears not to be so. All the miserable depression of spirits, all the incapacity to banish distressing fears and suspicions, which paved the way to real insanity, exist in an intensified degree when insanity has actually been reached. The poor maniac fancies he is surrounded by burning fires, that he is encircled by wreathing snakes, that he is in hell, tormented by devils; and we must remember that the misery caused by firmly believing a thing which does not exist is precisely the same as that which would be occasioned to a sane person if the things imagined were facts. It seems, too, that many insane people are quite aware that they are insane, which of course, aggravates what they endure. It must be a dreadful thing when the mind passes the point up to which it is still useful and serviceable, though unsound, and enters upon the stage of recognized insanity. It must be dreadful to feel that you are not quite yourself; that something is wrong; that you cannot discard suspicions and fears which are foolish and groundless. This is a melancholy stage, and if it lasts long, a very perilous one. Great anxiety, if continued for any length of time, is almost certain to lead to some measure of insanity. The man who, night and day, is never far from the thought of how he is to pay his way to maintain his children, is going mad. It is thoroughly evil when one single thought comes to take entire possession of the mind. It shows the brain is going. It is no wonder, my friendly reader, that so many men are, mentally, screws. There is something perfectly awful in reading what are the prominent symptoms of insanity.—*Frazer's Magazine.*

Delicacy.—Among the features that adorn the female character, delicacy stands foremost within the province of good taste. Not that delicacy always in quest of something to be ashamed of, which makes merit of a blush, and simpers at the constrction which its own ingenuity has put upon an innocent remark: this spurious kind of delicacy which maintains its pure and undeviating walk among women in the society of men which shrinks from no necessary duty, and can speak, when required with seriousness and kindness, of things at which it would be ashamed to smile or blush—the delicacy which knows how to confer a benefit without wounding the feelings of another, which can give alms without assumtion and which pains not the most sensative being in creation.

The great thing for which we should seek and pray, is, that whatever be our lot it may be a sanctified one.

The skin of a boiled egg appled to a boil, will draw off the matter and relieve the soreness in a few hours.

The Philadelphia Inquirer.

PRICE TWO CENTS. PHILADELPHIA, TUESDAY, APRIL 25, 1865. PRICE TWO CENTS.

PRESIDENT LINCOLN'S REMAINS IN INDEPENDENCE HALL.

OUR DEAD PRESIDENT

Departure of the Remains from Philadelphia.

PASSAGE OF THE CORTEGE THRO' NEW JERSEY.

Thousands of Mourners Along the Route.

ARRIVAL AT NEW YORK.

The Corpse Lying in State at the City Hall.

METROPOLIS DRAPED IN MOURNING.

New York's Tribute to the Martyr.

THE SOLEMNITIES IN THE CITY.

PROGRESS OF THE FUNERAL TRAIN.

NEW YORK, April 24, 10 A. M.—The funeral party started from the Continental Hotel, at Philadelphia, at two o'clock this morning, and halted before the State House until the coffin was conveyed to the funeral car. The transparency which adorned the front of the building, the portrait of the President, with a dark border representing a coffin, afforded a relief to the surrounding gloom of the morning, the words "Rest in Peace" still blazing from the gas jets above it. The Invincibles, and other city organizations, with torches, composed a part of the procession and the City Troop acted as the escort. A band of music played dirges on the march.

AN INTERIOR VIEW OF THE RAILROAD CAR CONVEYING THE REMAINS OF PRESIDENT LINCOLN.

The procession reached the Kensington Depot at four o'clock. Thousands of men, women and children were still in the streets, and not a few half-dressed residents in that neighborhood, who apparently had just risen from their beds, ran forward to join the large crowd in waiting at the depot.

The funeral party with difficulty pressed their way to the cars. Mr. W. H. Gatzmer, General Agent, and Messrs. A. W. Markley, Joseph P. Bradley and John L. McKnight, Directors of the Camden and Amboy Railroad Company, and F. Walcott Jackson, General Superintendent, were among the civilians.

The running of the road was under the direction of Mr. R. S. Van Rensselaer.

At a few minutes after four o'clock the train started. A locomotive preceded it by ten minutes. The engine is trimmed with the national flag, draped with mourning, and there is a telegrapher and two signal men accompanying it to guard against accidents.

The train consisted of nine elegant cars, provided by the Camden and Amboy Railroad, all tastefully trimmed. The funeral car last night was additionally decorated; heavy silver fringe being placed at the end of the black covering of the several panels, and the festoons being fastened with stars and tassels of similar material.

First Lieutenant J. A. Durkee and Lieutenant Murphy spent the entire of last night in thus improving the exterior of the car and clothing the interior with additional drapery. The materials were contributed by Philadelphians.

There was on board the cars a committee from Newark, consisting of the Mayor of that city, Joseph P. Bradley, Esq., and the President and other members of Councils, together with eight additional citizens. These and the Mayor of Washington and other civilians occupied seats in the front car.

Next in order were the Senators and members of the House of Representatives, with their respective officers. Then followed the Iowa and Illinois delegations and representatives of the several States and Territories. The guard of honor occupied the next car, and after this was that containing the remains of the late President and his little son Willie. The last car was occupied by Rear-Admiral Davis, Major-Generals Dix and Hunter, Brigadier-General Townsend, Assistant Adjutant-General of the United States Army (Adjutant-General Thomas is detained at home by sickness), Brevet Brigadier-General Barnard, Generals Caldwell, Eaton, Ramsey, Major Field, of the Marine Corps, Captain Taylor and Captain Penrose, and other army and navy officers.

At a few minutes past four o'clock the train left the Kensington station and soon reached Bristol, where several hundred persons had assembled. The sun was now rising in its full glory, beautifully illuminating the rural scene.

Governor Parker came on board at the State line at Morrisville with his staff, consisting of Adjutant-General R. F. Stockton, Quartermaster-General Perrin, and others of his staff. They were accompanied by U. S. Senator John P. Stockton, Rev. Henry Miller, and Colonel Murphy, and were received by Governor Curtin, of Pennsylvania, who had joined the funeral party at Harrisburg.

The Delaware River was crossed at 5½ o'clock. As the train passed through Trenton the bells were tolled. Immense throngs of spectators had gathered on every hill-top, and the line of road, and other advantageous points were occupied. The train proceeded onward until it reached the station, where it stopped for thirty minutes.

The population were assembled in much larger numbers, for this was a much more attractive point. The station was elaborately festooned, and the national banner deeply draped.

A detachment of the Veteran Corps was drawn up in line on the platform, showing that the people of Trenton, like all other true patriots, were not unmindful of the great loss which has befallen the nation in the violent death of a beloved and honored President.

Through New Jersey.

TRENTON, April 24.—The funeral train reached here at 5:30 this morning. Governor Parker and staff, of New Jersey, were taken on board at the

Continued on the Eighth Page.

LYNCHBURG VIRGINIAN EXTRA.

LYNCHBURG, VA., TUESDAY MORNING, APRIL 25, 1865.

[From the Herald of the 17th.]

DITIONAL ACCOUNTS OF THE ASSASSINATION.

Several accounts have been given of the cumstances attending the murder of President Lincoln. The following thrilling and ailed accounts have been obtained from se who were immediately in attendance on him just before, at the time of the murt and just after the fatal shot was fired.—ey may differ in some minor details from ne of those hitherto given, but in the in agree with them, and the differences y be accounted for by the various impresns received in a moment of so much in se excitement.

MAJ. RATHBUN'S STATEMENT.

The President's box at Ford's theatre is a able one, or what ordinarily constitutes o boxes, in the second tier, at the left of stage When occupied by the Presiden l party the separating partition is remov and the two are thus thrown into one.—is box is entered from a narrow, dark lway, which in turn is separated from the ss circle by a small door. The examina of the premises discloses the fact that assassin had fully and deliberately pre red and arranged them for his diabolical rpose previous to the assembling of the dience. A piece of board one inch thick, inches wide and about three feet in length ved for a bar, one end being placed in an lentation excavated in the wall for the rpose about four feet from the floor, and other against the molding of the door nel a few inches higher than the end in wall, so that it would be impossible to it out of place by knocking on the door the outside. The demon having thus arded against intrusion by any of the au nce, next proceeded to prepare a means of serving the position of the parties inside box. With a gimlet or small bit he red a hole in the door panel, which he af-wards reamed out with his knife so as to ve it litte larger than a buckshot on the side, while it was sufficiently large on the tside on the dark entry for him to place his e against with convenience, and see the sition occupied by the President and his ends. Both box doors were perforated in e manner. But there were spring locks each of these doors, and it was barely ssible that they might be fastened. To ovide against such an emergency the ew which fasten the bolt hasps to the d had been partially withdrawn, and left that while they would hold the hasps to wood they would afford little or no re-tance to a firm pressure upon the door the outside.

LIBERATE PREPARATIONS FOR THE MURDER.

Having thus provided for a sure and easy trance to the box, the next business was insure a clear and unobstructed passage to locality of the victim by such an arrange nt of the chairs and sofas as would place e other occupants at considerable distance m him. The rocking or easy chair occu ed by Mr. Lincoln was found in the front rner of the box farthest from the stage.—nother, for Mrs. Lincoln, a little more re-ote from the front, while the other chairs d sofa were all placed ... near the stage, leaving the ... of the ... ous box clear for the ... e actor. These preparations ... nceived by a maddened brain, designed by fool, nor executed by a drunkard. They ar most unmistakable evidence of genius, dustry and perseverance in the perfect ac-mplishment of a deliberate murder.

At a few minutes past eight in the evening the President and Mrs. Lincoln called at e residence of Senator Harris, corner of fteenth and H streets, where they took iss Clara Harris and Maj. Henry R, Rath n, United States Army, into their carri e, and proceeded to the theatre. Shortly ter they entered the fatal box the Presi nt seated himself in the chair designed for m by the assassin. Mrs. Lincoln took one ar him, Miss Harris the one at the oppo te corner, fronting the audience, and Maj. athbun seated himself upon the sofa, a few et behind Miss Harris. There were no ther persons in the box, and no one entered left it until about the time of the assassi ation. Charles Forbes, the personal atten ant of the President, had been told by Mrs. incoln to remain near the box, as he might e wanted. The President seemed well, ough somewhat sad, and spoke very little. e arose once during the performance, went the door of the box, put on his overcoat nd then returned to his chair and sat down.

The deed was perpetrated during the second scene of the third act of the piece, by ome man who must have approached stealthily and unseen through the dark passage the back of the box. Major Rathbun was ot aware of his presence till hearing the eport of a pistol, and, looking round, saw he flash, and dimly through the smoke the orm of a man in the box, not more than six eet from the President. As the Major sprang owards him he heard him shriek some word ike "freedom." He then seized him. The ssassin shook loose from the officer's grasp, nd at the same time made a violent thrust t his left breast with the knife which he eld in his hand. Major Rathbun caught he blow on his left arm near the shoulder, nd at once sprang for him again, but only ucceeded in grasping his clothing, which he artly tore from him as he leaped from the ox to the stage. The Major then cried out "Stop that man," and, supposing it impossible for him to escape through the crowd elow, rushed back to the President and to he aid of Mrs. Lincoln, who, for the first ime realizing what had occurred, was shrieking for help. The President had not changed his position, except that his eyes were losed and his head slightly bent forward.—Major Rathbun saw at a glance that he was mortally wounded. He went to the door of the box for the purpose of procuring medical aid, and to his astonishment found the outer door at the end of the dark hall from which the boxes are entered firmly barred on the inside with a piece of wood wedged across about four feet from the floor; so that those outside who were knocking for admission could not get in. Tearing away the fastenings and passing in ... persons who

body from the theatre, and accordingly the whole party, including Major Rathbun, who had charge of Mrs Lincoln, proceeded to a house opposite. It was now found that the Major was seriously wounded, and becoming quite faint from loss of blood He was sent home by his surgeon

THE RAPIDITY OF THE ASSASSIN'S MOVEMENT.

The whole time occupied from the firing of the pistol in the box to the leaping upon the stage was not over thirty seconds The President never spoke or unclosed his eyes from this time until his death. The clothing of Major Rathbun and the dress of Miss Harris were bespattered with blood from the wound of the Major. The wound of the President did not bleed at all

PREPARATIONS FOR THE FUNERAL

Washington, April 17.—At a meeting of the members of the Senate and House of Representa ives, convened at the Capitol on Monday, April 17, 1865, at noon. Hon. Lafayette S Foster, of Connecticut, President *pro tem.* of the Senate, was called to the chair, and Schuyler Colfax, of Indiana, was chosen as Secretary.

Senator Foot, of Vermont, stated the object of the meeting to be to make arrangements relative to the funeral of the deceased President of the the United States

On motion of Senator Sumner, of Massachusetts, a committee of five members from each House was ordered to report at 4 P. M. to-day what action it is fitting for this meeting to take.

The Chairman appointed Senators Sumner of Massachusetts, Harris of New York; Johnson of Maryland, Ramsey of Minnesota, and Conness of California, and Representatives Washburne of Illinois, Smith of Kentucky, Schenck of Ohio, Pike of Maine, and Coffroth of Pennsylvania.

At 4 P. M, the meeting convened pursuant to adjournment. Mr. Sumner, from the committee heretofore appointed, reported that they had settled to appoint as pall-bearers on the part of the Senate Mr Foster, of Connecticut, Mr Morgan, of New York, Mr. Johnson, of Maryland, Mr. Yates, of Illinois, Mr. Wade, of Ohio, and Mr. Conness, of California. On the part of the House; Mr. Dawes, of Massachusetts Mr. Coffroth, of Pennsylvania, Mr. Smith, of Kentucky, Mr. Colfax of Indiana, Mr Worthington, of Nevada, Mr. Washburne, of Illinois

LETTER FROM GEN. LONGSTREET.

LYNCHBURG, VA.,
April 24th, 1865.

As much apprehension seems to exist as regards *whom* were included in the surrender of the Army of Northern Virginia, and as many applications are daily made to me for explanation, I deem it proper to state for the information of all concerned that the Army was surrendered because it was surrounded, and it was thought that it could not make its escape without a great and useless sacrifice of human life. It was never intended to give up the *Confederate cause* with the Army of Northern Virginia, hence *only* those were intended to be included in the surrender who were actually within the enemy's lines, near Appomattox Court House, at the *time* of the surrender, and such Artillery belonging to the Army of Northern Virginia as was cut off by the movement of the enemy at Appomattox Court House, and still remained within twenty miles of the Court House at the time of the surrender.

No one was intended to be included except the Artillery above mentioned, who was outside the enemy's lines at the time of the surrender. No furloughed or detailed man, nor any man absent with or without leave, belonging to the Army of Northern Virginia, was intended to be included in the surrender.

J. LONGSTREET,
Lieut. Gen. and Sr. Comd'r
for Army Northern Virginia.

IMPORTANT EUROPEAN ITEMS.

"TOO LATE" FOR INTERVENTION.

[London (March 30) correspondence of Manchester Guardian.]

I have reason to know that the Emperor Napoleon has more than once disclaimed recently any intention of renewing his offer of interposition either separately or conjointly with us, in America. "I would have done it," he said to an Englishman to whom he was talking the other day, "two years ago, or even one year ago; but it is now too late."

Richard Cobden, M. P., died in England April 2, aged sixty-one years.

The London Times, commenting on the prospects of the Jeff Davis rebellion, says:—

The organized resistance of the South is now almost confined to the vicinity of Richmond, and the continuance of the war in its present form depends upon the genius of General Lee alone.

The French Embassy at Washington is reported to have received intelligence of the dangerous illness of the Emperor Napoleon.

No Passage for Paroled Prisoners.—By order of Gen. Patrick, Provost Marshal General, no passports to go North will be given, at present, to paroled officers or soldiers of the Confederate army. We are not officially informed of the causes that prompted this restriction, but we are satisfied that the order is a judicious one, in view of the present state of affairs ...

THE NEW GOVERNMENT.

OFFICIAL ACCOUNT OF THE INAUGURATION OF ANDREW JOHNSON. —HIS ADDRESS IN FULL—WHAT HIS POLICY IS TO BE, &C.

WASHINGTON, April 16, 1865.

Attorney General Speed yesterday morning waited upon Hon. Andrew Johnson, Vice President of the United States, and informed him of the sudden and unexpected decease of President Lincoln, and requested that an early hour might be appointed for the inauguration of his successor. The following is a copy of the communication referred to:—

WASHINGTON CITY, April 15.

SIR,—Abraham Lincoln, President of the United States, was shot by an assassin last evening at Ford's theatre, in this city, and died at the hour of twenty two minutes after seven o'clock. About the same time at which the President was shot an assassin entered the sick chamber of the Hon. Wm. H. Seward, Secretary of State, and stabbed him in several places in the throat, neck and face, severely if not mortally wounding him.—Other members of the Secretary's family were dangerously wounded by the assassin while making his escape. By the death of President Lincoln the office of President has devolved upon you. The emergency of the government demands that you should immediately qualify, according to the requirements of the constitution, and enter upon the duties of President of the United States. If you will please make known your pleasure, such arrangements as you deem proper will be made.

Your obedient servants,
HUGH McCULLUCH,
Secretary of the Treasury.
EDWIN M. STANTON,
Secretary of War.
GIDEON WELLES,
Secretary of the Navy.
WM. DENNISON,
Postmaster General.
J. P. USHER,
Secretary of the Interior.
JAS. SPEED,
Attorney General.

To Andrew Johnson, Vice President of the

A special meeting of the Cabinet was held ... at ten o'clock

CONFEDERATE OFFICERS CAPTURED ON THE 6TH.

The New York "Herald" publishes the following list of Confederate officers captured on the 6th, who were in Washington on their way to New York.—This list is interesting and it would be well to preserve it as most of those officers are Virginians, and many of them from this portion of the State:

Lieut Gen Ewell, Gen Corse, Gen Barton, Gen Hunton, Gen J P Simons, Gen J T DeBose, Gen Custis Lee, Gen Kershaw and staff, Col C C Sanders, 24th Ga; Lieut Col J C Timberlake, 53d Va; Lieut N S Hutchens, 3d Ga; Lieut Col Hamilton Phil, Georgia Legion; Major J M Goggen, Maj E L Caston, Capt J M Davis, Capt Carwall, Capt J W Walker, A. A. G., Capt C S Dwight, Capt. McRae Cane, 16th Ga; Col Armstrong, 18th Ga; Capt L Bass, 25th Va battery. Lieut Col E P False, 22d Va. battery; Maj F C Smith, 24th Ga; Capt J. F Tompkins, 22d Va; Lieut H C Thompkins, 22d Va; Capt W C Winn, 22d Va; Adj S D Davies, 47th Va; H W O Gatewood, 37th Va; Adj Williams, 3d Ga. sharpshooters; Lieut J L Buford, Capt. J L Jarrett, 69th Va; Lieut J T Fanneyhaugh, 20th Va battery; Capt J A Haynes, 55th Va: Capt A Reynolds, 55th Va; Capt J H Fleet, 55th Va; Capt V H Faulteroy, 55th Va; Lieut W C Robinson, 55th Va; Lieut Thomas Faulteroy, 55th Va; Capt R T Bland, 55th Va; Adj R L Williams, 55th Va; Lieut J R P Humphries, 55th Va; Lt. E J Ragland, 53d Va; Lieut A B Willingham, 53d Va; Lieut Col T G Barbour, 24th Va; Capt W F Harrison, 24th Va; Lieut Col Jas Howard, 18th and 20th Va battery; Capt A Austin Smith, Ordnance Officer; Capt McHenry Howard, Gen Custis Lee's staff; Lt. J F Porteous, Ordnance Officer; Maj J.

... them do not more than pay ... and are a source of no profit to the publisher. Let the office for the ...

LETTER FROM GEN. LONGSTREET.

LYNCHBURG, VA.,
April 24th, 1865.

As much apprehension seems to exist as regards *whom* were included in the surrender of the Army of Northern Virginia, and as many applications are daily made to me for explanation, I deem it proper to state for the information of all concerned that the Army was surrendered because it was surrounded, and it was thought that it could not make its escape without a great and useless sacrifice of human life. It was never intended to give up the *Confederate cause* with the Army of Northern Virginia, hence *only* those were intended to be included in the surrender who were actually within the enemy's lines, near Appomattox Court House, at the *time* of the surrender, and such Artillery belonging to the Army of Northern Virginia as was cut off by the movement of the enemy at Appomattox Court House, and still remained within twenty miles of the Court House at the time of the surrender.

No one was intended to be included except the Artillery above mentioned, who was outside the enemy's lines at the time of the surrender. No furloughed or detailed man, nor any man absent with or without leave, belonging to the Army of Northern Virginia, was intended to be included in the surrender.

J. LONGSTREET,
Lieut. Gen. and Sr. Comd'r
for Army Northern Virginia.

THE ERA OF PEACE

HIGHLY IMPORTANT ORDER FROM THE WAR DEPARTMENT.

THE CLOSING UP OF THE WAR.

ALL DRAFTING AND RECRUITING TO BE STOPPED.

THE MILITARY ESTABLISHMENT TO BE REDUCED.

MILITARY RESTRICTIONS UPON TRADE AND COMMERCE REMOVED

WAR DEPARTMENT, WASHINGTON
April 13, 1865—6 P. M.

To Maj Gen. Dix New York:

This department, after mature consideration and consultation with the Lieutenant General upon the results of the recent campaigns, has come to the following determinations, which will be carried into effect by appropriate orders, to be immediately issued:

First.—To stop all drafting and recruiting in the loyal States.

Second.—To curtail purchases for arms, ammunition, Quartermaster and Commissary supplies, and reduce the expenses of the military establishment in its several branches.

Third.—To reduce the number of general and staff officers to the actual necessities of the service

Fourth.—To remove all military restrictions upon trade and commerce, so far as may be consistent with public safety.

As soon as these measures can be put in operation, it will be made known by public orders

EDWIN M. STANTON, Secretary of War.

THE ORDER SUSPENDING TRADE OPERATIONS IN CERTAIN STATES REVOKED

HDQRS ARMIES OF THE U. S
IN THE FIELD, VA., April 11, 1865.

Special Order, No. 74.—Second paragraph of Special Orders, No 48, of the date of March 10, 1865, from these headquarters, suspending trade operations within the State of Virginia, except that portion known as the Eastern shore, and the States of North Carolina and South Carolina and that portion of the State of Georgia immediately bordering on the Atlantic, including the city of Savannah until further orders is hereby revoked.

By command of Lieut. Gen. GRANT.
T. S. BOWERS, Assistant Adjutant General.

THE ADDRESS TO THE ARMIES.

War Department, Adj't. Gen'ls Office,
Washington, April 16, 1865.

General Orders No. 66:

The following order of the Secretary of War announces to the armies of the United States, the untimely and lamentable death of the illustrious Abraham Lincoln, late President of the United States:

WAR DEPARTMENT,
Washington, April 15, 1865

The distressing duty has devolved upon the Secretary of War to announce to the armies of the United States that at twenty two minutes after seven o'clock, on the morning of Saturday, the 15th day of April, 1865, Abraham Lincoln, President of the United States, died of a mortal wound inflicted upon him by an assassin.

The armies of the United States will share with their fellow-citizens the feeling of grief and horror inspired by the most atrocious murder of their great and beloved President and Commander-in-Chief, and with profound sorrow will mourn his death as a national calamity.

The headquarters of every department, post, station, fort and arsenal will be draped in mourning for thirty days, and appropriate funeral honors will be paid by every army, and in every Department, and every military post, and at the Military Academy at West Point, to the memory of the late illustrious Chief Magistrate of the nation and Commander-in-Chief of its armies.

Lieut.-Gen. Grant will give the necessary instructions for carrying this order into effect.

EDWIN M. STANTON,
Secretary of War.

On the day after the receipt of this order at the headquarters of any military division, department, army, post, station, fort and arsenal, and at the Military Academy at West Point, the troops and cadets will be paraded at ten o'clock, A. M., and the orders read to them, after which all labors and operations for the day will cease, and be suspended, as far as practicable in a state of war.

The National flag will be displayed at half-staff

At dawn of day thirteen guns will be fired, and afterwards, at intervals of thirty minutes between the rising and setting sun, a single gun, and at the closing of the day a National salute of thirty-five guns.

The officers of the armies of the United States will wear the bade of mourning on the left arm and on thier swords, and the colors of their commands and regiments will be put in mourning for the period of six months.

By command of
Lieutenant-General GRANT,
W. A. NICHOLS, Assistant Adjt. Gen.

ITEMS.

A soldier who was in this city yesterday, just from that command, said that Johnston surrendered his army last Wednesday. We did not see him, or we would have obtained more particulars.

A gentleman arrived in this city yesterday from Richmond, who conversed with a citizen of that city, well-known here, who stated positively that ...

The Philadelphia Inquirer.

PRICE TWO CENTS. PHILADELPHIA, WEDNESDAY, APRIL 26, 1865. PRICE TWO CENTS.

THE FUNERAL!

President Lincoln's Remains In New York.

120,000 MOURNERS VIEW THE BODY.

An Immense Throng in the Streets.

A GRAND CIVIC AND MILITARY PROCESSION.

Three Hours Passing a Given Point.

MONSTER MEETING IN UNION SQUARE

George Bancroft, the Historian.

HIS ORATION ON MR. LINCOLN'S LIFE AND DEATH.

A Glorious Tribute to the Martyr.

THE REMAINS DEPART FOR ALBANY.

Gathering of People Along the Route

THE GREAT NATIONAL FUNERAL.

VIEW OF THE CITY HALL, NEW YORK, AND THE HEARSE BEARING THE REMAINS OF PRESIDENT LINCOLN.

THE FUNERAL PROCESSION IN NEW YORK.

NEW YORK, April 25.—A constant stream of people have been passing through the room in the City Hall, where the remains of the late President have been exposed to view, ever since yesterday afternoon. They pass at the rate of eighty per minute.

At midnight the German singers, numbering about one thousand voices, chaunted dirges. Throughout the night the long line of citizens, anxious to view the remains, was kept moving.

Early this morning it seemed diminished very little, and soon after daylight was lengthened greatly, extending from Warren to John streets on the west side of the City Hall, while there was another line of greater length running through the streets on the east side of the hall.

Broadway and all the adjoining streets in the vicinity were thronged by people anxious to secure a place in the line, or, failing in that, to catch a glimpse of the hearse when it passed.

All places of business are closed, while the upper stories of every building along the route of the procession are occupied by anxious spectators.

The preparations for the funeral procession of the President are on an immense scale, including nearly every military and civic organization of New York, Brooklyn, and other neighboring towns. By a special order to General Dix the Secretary of War requests that colored societies shall be assigned a place in the line, and directions have been issued accordingly. The streets over which the procession is to pass are already being crowded with eager spectators, and the whole demonstration promises to be of the most imposing character.

As the schedule of the War Department directs the departure of the funeral train at 4 P. M., we shall probably be spared the delay usual on such occasions.

The religious ceremonies at Union Square will be conducted by clergymen of several denominations, including Archbishop McCloskey, Dr. Tyng, Dr. Osgood, Dr. Thompson and Rabbi Isaacs. An oration will be delivered by Hon. George Bancroft.

The scenes at the City Hall yesterday were similar to those reported from Philadelphia on Sunday. The arrangements for viewing the body were as bad as possible, and neither police nor military were able to preserve order in the mass of people struggling for admittance. The disorder increased after nightfall, and was very discreditable both to the people and the authorities.

The military display is very large, including more than twenty regiments, besides several batteries and troops of cavalry, all State troops.

The day is fine, and the streets are swarming with citizens and people from the surrounding country. It is believed that about forty thousand persons visited the remains yesterday.

NEW YORK, April 25, 1 o'clock.—The procession is now moving with the remains to the Hudson River Railroad Depot. It is one of the most imposing and impressive spectacles ever witnessed in New York. Indeed, perhaps, it was never equaled.

There are no vehicles in the line of procession, and it moves with an inspiring solemnity to the mournful music of the various military bands. The military are out in full force, as also a very large number of civic societies, trades unions, officials and civilians in general.

One of the festoons in front of the City Hall took fire this morning, causing great excitement as the cry of fire was made. The presence of mind of an officer, who promptly tore down the burning drapery, saved a rush in the crowd, which, in all probability, would have caused the loss of life.

The crowd on Broadway was so great that it was found necessary to run chains around the space through which the procession was to pass in the park. The number who viewed the remains is estimated at one hundred and twenty thousand and as many more were deprived of the privilege by the expiration of the allotted time.

The funeral car upon which the remains were carried in the procession is a superb piece of mechanism. The main platform is fourteen feet long, eight wide, and fifteen in height. On the platform, which is five feet from the ground, is a dais, six inches in height, on which the coffin rests.

Above the dais is an elegant canopy, supported by four columns, curving upward at the centre and surmounted by a minature temple of liberty. The platform is covered with black cloth, which falls at the sides nearly to the ground, and is edged with silver bullion fringe.

Festoons of black cloth also hang from the sides, festooned with silver stars and also edged with silver bullion. The canopy is trimmed in like manner, in black cloth, festooned and spangled with silver bullion, the corners surmounted by a rich plume of black and white feathers. At the base of each column are three American flags slightly inclined, festooned and covered with crape.

The temple of Liberty is represented as deserted, having no emblems of any kind in or around it, except a small flag on the top at half-mast. The inside of the car is lined with white satin, fluted; from the centre of the roof is suspended a large eagle with outspread wings, having in its talons a laurel-wreath. The platform around the coffin was strewn with flowers.

The car was drawn by sixteen grey horses, covered with black cloth trimming, each led by a groom.

New York has amply paid her last tribute of respect to the remains of Abraham Lincoln. They were escorted to the Hudson River Railroad depot by a funeral procession never equaled in this country, and perhaps in the world. Leading the line were two divisions of State militia, including infantry, cavalry and artillery, besides a battalion of marines. Immediately following, was the Seventh regiment, State militia, which has done guard duty since the arrival of the funeral cortege in this city. The regiment looked magnificently, some two-thirds of it doing the immediate escort duty, while the balance were formed in a hollow square around the hearse. Inside this square was still another guard of honor of military and naval officers.

Next followed carriages, three abreast, and stretching for a long distance, containing the City Government, delegations from Washington and other places, and including many military and naval officers, and representatives of different nations resident here, Governor Fenton, Ex-Governors of the State, members and ex-members of the Legislature, and others. Next were the employees in the Custom House, Sub Treasury and Post Office, in themselves a large body of men, and following them the officers of the Brooklyn Navy Yard and officers and ex-officers of the army and volunteer service. The navy contributed several hundred of its officers to the procession.

The various clubs were next represented, the Loyal Leaguers appearing in great numbers, and the Tammany Society and the Democratic General Committees making effective displays.

The citizens of the Pacific Coast were largely represented, a striking feature being Seth Hinman, who presented an elk horn chair to the late President, and who was dressed in a curious looking buffalo suit. The Sons of Temperance also turned out very effectively, but the most remarkable feature of the procession was the immense number of Masons, who were next in the line, each man wearing on his coat a sprig of evergreen. Perhaps ten thousand of the Order were in the procession.

The Irish societies followed in nearly as great numbers as on St. Patrick's Day. Many other associations were fully represented, the procession closing with large delegations from all kinds of societies from Brooklyn, and finally several thousand respectably dressed negroes.

It was three hours in passing a given point, and as the end of it reached the depot the corpse of our martyred President was many miles away from the city.

Take the procession together it was one of the largest if not the very largest ever seen in New York, and the utmost feeling was manifested everywhere. The passing of the coffin was the signal for all to uncover their heads.

Over the floor of the hearse in which the coffin rested were strewed the most beautiful flowers. The hearse itself was a theme of praise from all as the most appropriate for the occasion. All along the route an immense concourse of people lined the streets, filled the windows, stoops and house tops, all of whom seemed of one accord in respect to the memory of the departed.

At the depot the hearse was drawn through the line of military with all due ceremony. Everything, in fact, went off well, and no accident occurred during the day. Minute guns were fired all day, and bells were tolled during the time of removal of the remains to the depot. After the procession passed an immense meeting was held in Union Square, at which a funeral oration was delivered by the Hon. George Bancroft, of which the following is a summary.

Mr. Bancroft's Address.

Mr. Bancroft said—Our grief and horror at the crime which has clothed the continent in mourning, find no adequate expression in words and no relief in tears. Neither the office with which Mr. Lincoln was invested by the approved choice of a mighty people, nor the most simple-hearted kindness of nature could save him from the fiendish passions of relentless fanaticism. The wailings of the millions attend his remains as they are borne in solemn procession over our great rivers, along the seaside, beyond the mountains, across the prairie to their final resting place in the valley of the Mississippi.

The echoes of his funeral knell vibrate through the world, and the friends of freedom of every tongue and in every clime are his mourners. The members of the Government which preceded his administration opened the gates to treason, and he closed them. When he went to Washington the ground on which he trod shook under his feet, and he left the republic on a solid foundation.

Traitors had seized the public forts and arsenals, and he recovered them for the United States. The Capitol, which he found the abode of slaves, is now only the abode of the free. The boundless public domain, which was grasped at, and, in a great measure, held for the diffusion of slavery, is now irrevocably devoted to freedom. Then men talked a jargon of the balance of power in a Republic between slave States and free States, and now the foolish words are blown away forever by the breath of Maryland, Missouri and Tennessee. The atmosphere is now purer than ever before, and insurrection is vanishing away. The country is cast into another mould, and the gigantic system of wrong which had been the work of more than two centuries, is dashed down, we hope, forever.

As for himself personally, he was then scoffed at by the proud as unfit for his station; and now, against the usage of later years, and in spite of numerous competors, he was the unbiased and undoubted choice of the American people for a second term of service. Through all the mad baseness of treason he retained the sweetness of a most peaceful disposition, and the slaughter of myriads of the best on the battle-field and the more terrible destruction of our men in captivity by the slow torture of exposure and starvation, had never been able to provoke him into harboring one vengeful feeling or one purpose of cruelty.

How shall the nation most completely show its sorrow at Mr. Lincoln's death? How shall it best honor his memory? There can be but one answer. Grief must take the character of action, and breathe itself forth in the assertion of the policy to which he fell a sacrifice. The standard which he held in his hand must be unfurled again, higher and more firmly than before, and must be carried on to triumph above everything else. His emancipation proclamation must be affirmed and maintained. Events have removed every doubt of its legality and binding force.

Mr. Bancroft incidentally alluded to the usurpation of the power of the Executive by General Sherman, saying, "from this bad act, which the people with one united voice condemn, no great evil will follow save the shadow on his own fame."

He referred in familiar terms to President Johnson, to whom it remained to consummate the vindication of the Union, and to that Union Abraham Lincoln has fallen a martyr. His death, which was meant to sever it beyond repair, binds it more closely and more firmly than ever. From Maine to the northwest boundary on the Pacific it makes us one.

The country may have needed an imperishable grief to touch its inmost feeling. The grave that receives the remains of Lincoln receives the martyr to the Union. The monument which will rise over his body will bear witness to the Union. His enduring memory will assist, during countless ages, to bind the States together, and to unite to the love of our one indivisible country. Peace to the ashes of our departed friend, the friend of his country, and of his race. Happy was his life, for he was the restorer of the Republic. He was happy in his death, for the manner of his end will plead forever for the Union of the States and the freedom of man.

Since the departure of his remains the city has become quiet.

THE PROGRESS TO ALBANY.

Special Despatch to the Inquirer.

ALBANY, April 25.—Our train arrived on the opposite side of the river at 11·30, and at 11·50 we arrived at Albany. Our run from New York has been one continued ovation of mourning. When we passed along the same route, four years ago, on the triumphal tour of Mr. Lincoln to Washington, the display was great, but this far eclipses that in numbers and feeling.

General Dix and others accustomed to judge of such demonstrations estimate that near a million and a half of people witnessed the passing of the funeral cortege in New York city, and sixty thousand participated in the ceremonies. An actual count of those viewing the corpse in the city puts it at one hundred and ten thousand.

On reaching the Hudson River Railroad depot, General Winfield Scott got out and walked into the depot to see the departure of the train, which consisted of eight fine new cars of the Hudson Company, and the United States funeral car, and the car of the Philadelphia and Baltimore Company for the Guard of Honor, which had been brought over from Jersey City on the boat.

General Dix and staff and Governor Fenton and staff joined us on the train. Senator Cowan and Hon. Leonard Myers left us, and Hon. F. Bailey remained to represent Pennsylvania in the Congressional delegation. Admiral Farragut came on board to go out to Hastings and join his family. A church close by the railroad depot, which four years ago was one of the few that exhibited the flag on our passing, has the following motto: "He left us, upheld by our prayers. He returns embalmed in our tears," in large white letters on a black ground over the church door.

Out of the suburbs not so many people were visible, until we had run out some distance, as they had all gone into the city to see the procession. Whole rows of houses were closed, and no signs of any one in the vicinity; but about three miles out we passed a steamboat with a large load of passengers, all of whom uncovered their heads, and the bell of the boat was tolled.

At Carmersville about a thousand persons were assembled, with draped flags. All stood with uncovered heads. At Fort Washington, Linwood, Riverdale and at Mount Vincent similar exhibitions were seen. At the latter place about two hundred ladies were in line, with the flag covered with black crape.

At Yonkers two pieces of artillery from different locations fired minute guns, and several thousand persons were grouped upon both sides of the track, and stood uncovered until we were out of sight. At the station we found a large arch over the road, with "we mourn a nation's loss." On the base, "He died for truth."

At Peekskill a very large display of bunting took place, and thousands were in attendance. At half-past six we reached West Point. Minute guns were fired from the fort across the river. A company of regular cavalry and two companies of cadets from the United States Institute were in line. The train halted with the hearse, just opposite them.

The whole staff of the Academy were present, and many of the military and civilians got off and paid their respects. A band from the Academy played some mournful airs. Mrs. French and one or two others were invited into the car to see the coffin. The cadets presented a very fine appearance, standing like statues, though many of them recognized their friends and relatives. Senator Harris had a son there.

At Tarrytown twenty-four young ladies were grouped together, in white dresses and black rosettes. A very large number of people were here. At Sing Sing a number of convicts were out in their striped dress, and lifted their hats.

At Cold Springs and Fishkill there were about one thousand people at each, with all the emblems of grief displayed, and numbers of wagons, showing that here, as in other places, the surrounding conntry had been drained of its population.

At Poughkeepsie we stopped twenty minutes for supper, and left at 7·50. About twenty thousand persons were around the station at Eastman's.

A band played funeral dirges, and minute guns were fired. The goddess of liberty, represented by a little girl in white and black mourning, stood upon the platform.

It was now grown so dark that we could no longer see the crowds at the stations as we rushed by, but thousands were scattered along the road, and occasionally bonfires would be kindled or bells tolled to mark the sadness of the hour.

Arriving at East Albany we were soon transferred to the ferry boat and were escorted by a company of infantry, and a fire company, with torches. The corpse was taken to the Capitol, through thousands of people, who filled the streets, though it was midnight.

The body is being prepared for public view, and large numbers are waiting in the street to insure a glance when it is thrown open at half-past one o'clock A. M.

Funeral Services in Detroit.

DETROIT, Mich., April 25.—The obsequies of President Lincoln, to-day, were the most imposing ever witnessed here. The procession was over four miles long, headed by detachments of military, followed by a magnificent funeral car, officers of the army and navy, officers of the British army, officers of the State and City Government, Canadian civil officers, public schools, Masons, Odd Fellows, various benevolent societies, trades unions, etc. The ceremonies concluded with an oration by Senator Howard.

The Obsequies of President Lincoln at Columbus.

COLUMBUS, Ohio, April 25.—The remains of President Lincoln will arrive at Columbus on Saturday, April 29th, at 7·30 A. M. The City Council, city officials, and a large number of citizens of Cincinnati will come up from that place to participate in the ceremonies. Orders were received yesterday to forward immediately to the front all the troops now in camp in Ohio and Indiana.

An Incident in Booth's Life.

PITTSBURG, April 25.—Mr. Duncan, a reliable citizen of Pittsburg, has just returned from Meadeville, and mentions a singular circumstance in connection with the assassin Booth. While stopping at the McHenry House, in Meadeville, on the fourth of June last, Booth wrote on a pane of glass with his diamond ring the following words:—"Abe. Lincoln departed this life August 13th, 1864, by the effects of poison."

Booth's name was written on the hotel register in the same handwriting. Several of his friends, at different times, occupied the same room. A complete register has been kept of all the names of the occupants of that room since June last.

THE LATEST NEWS

OFFICIAL WAR GAZETTE.

GENERAL GRANT AT RALEIGH

He Delivers His Message to Sherman.

JOHNSTON IS NOTIFIED OF ITS CONTENTS.

The Truce Suddenly Terminated

Civil Matters to be Left Entirely to Government Action.

IMPORTANT MILITARY ORDER

Richmond Declared Open to Domestic Commerce.

GEN. HANCOCK'S APPEAL.

Colored People Called On to Ferret Out the Assassins.

OFFICIAL WAR GAZETTE.

Important from General Grant—The Truce with Johnson Suspended.

WAR DEPARTMENT, WASHINGTON, April 4—10 P. M.—Major-General Dix, New York:—A despatch has just been received by the Department from General Grant, dated Raleigh, 9 A. M., April 24th. He says:—"I reached here this morning, and delivered to General Sherman the reply to his negotiation with Johnston. Word was immediately sent to Johnston, terminating the truce, and informed that civil matters could not be entertained in any convention between army commanders."

EDWIN M. STANTON,
Secretary of War.

IMPORTANT MILITARY ORDER.

Richmond Opened to Domestic Commerce.

HEAD-QUARTERS MILITARY DIVISION OF THE JAMES, RICHMOND, Va., April 25, 1864.—General Orders No. 2.—First. All restrictions upon domestic commerce and trade, except as to articles contraband of war, in the State of Virginia, as insurgent territory, are, by the authority of the President, revoked in respect to all ports and counties of this State which have duly submitted to the authority and are in military possession of the United States.

Second. Arms, ammunition; all articles from which ammunition is manufactured; all locomotives, cars and railroad stock; all telegraph wires and apparatus; all Rebel uniforms and grey cloth for manufacturing them, and all spirituous liquors are to be deemed contraband of war.

Third. The Commanding General of the Military Division has authority to make such exceptions to the trade hereby authorized as in his opinion circumstances may require.

By order of Major-General Halleck.

Approved by order of the Secretary of War.

JAMES A. HARDIE,
Brevet Brigadier-General, Inspector-General
United States Army.

DEVELOPMENTS AT RICHMOND.

JEFF. DAVIS AND THE REBEL SECRET SERVICE FUND—HE MAKES HEAVY DRAFTS UPON THE TREASURY—HOW HE HAS BEEN FEATHERING HIS NEST.

Special Correspondence of the Inquirer.

RICHMOND, Va., April 22, 1865.

In Rumaging Yesterday

Among some waste papers, which were scattered profusely over the floor of one of the rooms of the Custom House, which building was used as the Executive Department of the Rebel Government, the originals of the following documents were discovered, which will give some idea of the manner in which Jeff. Davis expended the funds of the Confederacy for "secret service" and "necessities and exigencies," which, of course, will cover any and every purpose for which he might see proper to expend the money, which was at his command in unlimited amounts.

These warrants show that fully a year ago, the shrewd Davis was quietly accumulating funds in Europe, in gold, with the view of making himself comfortable in the event of the failure of the Rebellion, or, it may be, that these sums were swallowed up by the rapacious sympathising agents abroad, who were thus enabled to mould public opinion in Europe into the belief that the resources of the Confederacy were ample, for who would suppose the Rebels to be poor, when their paid agents were so extravagant in their display of means. But to the documents:—

2615—APRIL 26, 1864.

No. 32—[Department mark].

EXECUTIVE OFFICE,
RICHMOND, April 25, 1864.

To the Secretary of the Treasury—Sir:—Please cause a warrant for the sum of ONE MILLION DOLLARS, payable out of the appropriation for "Secret Service," act of 15th February, 1864, to be issued in favor of Hon. J. P. Benjamin, Secretary of State.

Payable in foreign countries.

£206,185, 11s. 4d.

Exchange on England requested.

JEFFERSON DAVIS,
President C. S. A.

Appropriation for Secret Service, $1,000,000.

The Appropriation for "Necessities and Exigencies."

There appears to have been also an appropriation under this head, which Davis frequently resorted to and expended as he pleased. In this case, as in the previous one, the money was sent abroad in conformity with the following warrant:—

2572—APRIL 14, 1864.

No. 31.

EXECUTIVE OFFICE,
RICHMOND, April, 14, 1864.

To the Secretary of the Treasury—Sir:—Please cause a warrant for the sum of fourteen thousand five hundred and fifty dollars, payable out of the appropriation for "necessities and exigencies under laws already passed or which may be passed," &c., &c., to be issued in favor of Hon. J. P. Benjamin, Secretary of State.

Two bills of exchange on England requested, each for £500.

£1000—$4850
3
———
$14,550

JEFFERSON DAVIS,
President C. S. A.

Appropriation for "necessities and exigencies"..$14,550

In explanation of the above, it should be stated that the Rebel currency had depreciated to 33½ per cent., which caused the warrant to be

Continued on the Eighth Page.

The Philadelphia Inquirer.

PRICE TWO CENTS. | PHILADELPHIA, FRIDAY, APRIL 28, 1865. | PRICE TWO CENTS.

BOOTH THE ASSASSIN

He is Traced to his Hiding Place

HE REFUSES TO SURRENDER HIMSELF

The Capture of Harold.

BOOTH SHOWS FIGHT

THE BARN SET ON FIRE.

Death of the Murderer of Lincoln!

HOW BOOTH WAS DISCOVERED.

Loyal Negroes Guide His Pursuers.

HIS BODY AT WASHINGTON.

Full Particulars of the Pursuit and Capture.

OFFICIAL GAZETTE.

WASHINGTON, April 27, 9·30 A. M.—Major-General Dix, New York:—J. Wilkes Booth and Harold were chased from the swamp in St. Mary's county, Maryland, to Garrett's farm, near Port Royal, on the Rappahannock, by Colonel Baker's force.

The rear of the barn in which they took refuge was fired. Booth, in making his escape, was shot through the head and killed, lingering about three hours, and Harold was captured.

Booth's body and Harold are now here.

(Signed) EDWIN M. STANTON,
Secretary of War.

[Port Royal, Va., near which Booth and Harold were taken, is on the south side of the Rappahannock, about twenty miles below Fredericksburg. The belief heretofore entertained that Booth, after committing his crime, took refuge in the southern counties of Maryland, with a view to crossing the Potomac into Virginia, is confirmed.]

THE PURSUIT AND DEATH OF BOOTH.

[SPECIAL DESPATCHES TO THE INQUIRER.]

WASHINGTON, April 27.

Booth, after assassinating President Lincoln and making a tragic exit from the stage of the theatre, mounted his horse and rode off, accompanied by an accomplice, named Harold, a young Marylander. To avoid suspicion, they separated, meeting at a place called Marlboro.

Booth in jumping from the box, had fractured one of the small bones of his left leg, just above the ankle, and the limb had swollen during the ride, causing much pain. Harold took him to the house of a Dr. Mudge, where the boot was cut off and the limb bandaged.

The two fugitives remained some days in Maryland, and Harold states that he saw the cavalry and detectives very near their place of concealment several times.

They were harbored by sympathizers with the Rebel cause, and the only persons who have given any information about them are those loyal Southerners who are easily distinguished by their dark skins.

Col. Baker on the Track of the Assassins.

Meanwhile, Colonel L. C. Baker, Provost Marshal of the War Department, had taken no part in the search made in Maryland for Booth by a large military force, aided by Colonel Olcott and the New York detectives, as he was waiting for some definite information of his whereabouts.

On Monday afternoon he received intelligence that Booth and Harold had probably crossed the Potomac at Swan's Point. Those engaged in searching for them did not know that they had crossed. Having consulted maps of Virginia, which he obtained from the office of the Coast Survey, Colonel Baker made up his mind that Booth and Harold must have gone to the vicinity of Port Royal, a quiet village below Fredericksburg, on the Rappahannock.

He accordingly wrote to General Hancock, requesting him to detail a commissioned officer and twenty-five cavalrymen to report to any one he might designate. He then gave instructions to two of his detective force, Lieutenant Luther B. Baker and E. J. Conger, formerly Lieutenant-Colonel of the cavalry regiment which Colonel Baker commanded.

The Escort,

Which subsequently reported and started off under the orders of Detectives Casker and Conger, belonged to the Sixteenth New York Cavalry, which has for some months been looking after Moseby's guerrillas over in Virginia.

The Commander of the Escort.

Lieutenant Edward P. Dougherty, who commanded the escort, was at one time a resident in Boston. When the Rebellion broke out he came here as a private in the New York Seventy-first, in which regiment he fought at the first Bull Run. He afterwards enlisted in the Berdan Sharp-shooters, and was then transferred into the Sixteenth New York cavalry, where he has so distinguished himself as to secure promotion.

He was especially commended last fall when, on making a reconnoissance near Culpeper Court House with a small force, he encountered Kershaw's Rebel cavalry Division, but gallantly cut his way out.

Booth's Executioner.

Sergeant Boston Corbett, who shot Booth, is a religious enthusiast, who has made the character of Cromwell his study. He was born in England, is about thirty-three years old, and is by trade a hat finisher.

About seven years since, while in Boston, he experienced religion, and when baptised, assumed the name of the city where he became converted, and since then he has always prayed for Divine instruction before taking any step in life, and he says that he has always been prompted what to do.

He was at one time a prisoner at Andersonville, Georgia, and was one of a party of sixteen who escaped. They were hunted down with blo[illegible]hounds, and only himself and one of his compan[illegible]s were brought back alive.

On the Sun[illegible] after President Lincoln was assassinated Serg[illegible] Corbett obtained leave to attend services at [illegible]tree Chapel here, and there prayed fervently that the assassins might be punished.

How the Assassins were Discovered.

The detectives and their escort went down on a steamboat to Belleplain, where they landed before day on Monday morning, and struck across for the Rappahannock.

There is a ferry above Port Royal and the ferryman denies having ferried over any men answering to the descriptions of Booth and Harold. But a colored man looking over Lieutenant Baker's shoulder at a photograph of Booth, which he was showing the ferryman, exclaimed:—"I saw that man across the river—he was in a wagon with three other men." The loyal although sable Virginian was right. It appears that Booth and Harold had crossed the Potomac in a canoe, for which they paid three hundred dollars, and were met on the Virginia shore by two Confederate officers with a two-horse wagon. Booth wore a grey suit without any military insignia of rank.

At Port Royal the detectives learned that one of the Confederate officers had a sweetheart at Bowling Green, and had probably gone there. So the party started in pursuit, passing on their way a farm where resided two brothers, named William and John Garrett, who have been in the Rebel army, their house being about a quarter of a mile from the road.

After having gone about three miles from the Garretts' house the party met a loyal Virginian, of dark skin, of course, and from him learned that Booth and Harold were at the Garretts'. "Right about!" was the word, and about three o'clock in the morning the pursuers arrived there.

Statement of the Garretts.

Here let us state what the Garretts say about their visitors who came to their house on Friday or Saturday of last week.

The fugitives were brought in a wagon by two Confederate officers, who spoke of Booth as a wounded Marylander on his way home, and that they wished to leave him there a short time, and would take him away by the 26th.

Booth limped somewhat, and walked on crutches about the place, complaining of his ankle. He and Harold regularly took their meals at the house, and Booth kept up appearances well.

One day, at the dinner table, the conversation turned on the assassination of the President, when Booth denounced the assassination in the severest terms, saying that there was no punishment severe enough for the perpetrator. At another time some one said, in Booth's presence, that rewards, amounting to $200,000, had been offered for Booth, and that he would like to catch him, when Booth replied, "Yes, it would be a good haul, but the amount would doubtless soon be increased to $500,000.

After our cavalry passed towards Bowling Green, Booth and Harold applied to one of the Garretts for two horses, that they might ride to Louisa Court House, but he fearing that the horses would not be returned refused to let them go. Some words of recrimination passed between Booth and Harold, and the Garretts becoming suspicious that all was not right urged them to leave. This they refused to do unless they could be supplied with horses; and the Garretts then said that if they remained they must sleep in the barn. One of the Garretts went to sleep in the corn crib, fearing, as he says, that the strangers would steal their horses.

Preparations for the Capture.

On returning to the Garrett's House, Lieutenant Baker halted his force and going in obtained a reluctant confession from the brother there where the criminals were. Going out again, Lieutenant Baker aroused his escort, who had nearly all gone to sleep, and took them to the barn, around which he stationed then. He then advanced to the door and knocking with the butt of his revolver said, "Booth we want you." "Here I am," replied the assassin, "who are you, Confederate or Yankee?" Lieutenant Baker informed him who he was and summoned him to surrender, but met with a defiant refusal.

Quite a parley ensued, Harold at one time expressing a desire to surrender, which Booth rebuked, denouncing him as a coward. Booth could see the party outside through the cracks of the barn, but they could not see him. He swore that he would never be taken alive, and declared that he could kill at least five men and then kill himself, should they attempt to break into the barn.

The Barn Fired.

At last, Lieutenant Baker, fearing that the guerrillas and the paroled Rebel soldiers, with whom the country swarmed, would come to the rescue, posted the calvarymen around the barn, and going to one end of it, which was filled with hay, pulled some through a crack and lighted it. The flames ran up the crack to the top of the haymow, over which they spread. The inside of the barn was now lighted up.

When Booth first saw the fire he clambered up on the mow, and vainly attempted to extinguish it. He then returned to his position on the floor between the two doors, with his back against the hay-mow, a revolver in each hand, and a Spencer carbine between his legs.

Harold Surrenders.

Meanwhile, the soldiers had approached the barn, and Harold, dropping his pistol, gave himself up, receiving Booth's malediction as he left the burning barn.

Death of Booth.

Just afterwards the roof over the hay-mow began to crack as if it was falling in, and Booth made a movement. Some of those who were watching him say that he was about to kill himself, while others declare that he was intending to break out and escape. Be this as it may, Sergeant Corbett had a sight at him through a wide crack with his cavalry six-shooter, and pulled trigger. The ball entered about where the President was shot, but passed entirely through Booth's head. The murder has been avenged. "It's all up now," shrieked Booth, "I'm gone," and he staggered towards the door of the barn. Lieutenant Baker received him, and taking him from the blazing barn, laid him on the ground, then sat down and took his head in his lap.

Booth did not deny his crime, and showed no signs of repentance or of humanity, except to ask Lieutenant Doherty to give a message to his mother. His death was not easy, but at three minutes after seven his spirit passed away into the presence of an avenging God.

Return of the Escort.

Nothing remained for the party to do but to regain their steamboat at Belle Plain.

How Harold Was Taught to Walk.

They had to bring Booth's body in a cart, and at first Harold had to walk, to which he, as a Maryland gentleman, objected; but after a rope was placed around his neck with a slip noose, and the other end of it was fastened to a cavalryman's saddle he started off, taking good care that the rope should not tighten.

The Remains of Booth.

From Belle Plain Lieutenant-Colonel Conger rode overland to Alexandria, and reported to Colonel Baker yesterday afternoon, at half-past five.

When he left there were some hopes that Booth's wound was not mortal.

Colonel Baker went to Alexandria to meet the steamer, and since then the body of Booth, by direction of the Secretary of War, has remained in his custody.

Surgeon-General Barnes, with an assistant, made an autopsy on the remains this afternoon. Their final disposition is unknown to the public as yet.

Such are the leading events of the escape, pursuit and arrest of the assassin of President Lincoln, obtained from unquestionable sources.

Of course, every member of the expedition, civil or military, regards himself as the principal agent, and some wonderful stories are told; but what I have stated may be relied upon as correct.

This is, however, but the second act in the great conspiracy, the first act of which cost us our President. Other arrests have been made. Other arrests are to be made, and in due time the public will learn the extent and the deliberate wickedness of the whole crime. They will also see that much of what has been published about arrests of the party who attacked Secretary Seward and other matters are bosh. Colonel Baker has detected the criminal, and the Secretary of War, who knows the facts better than any one else, gives him the credit.

Appearance of the Body.

Booth's moustache had been cut off apparently with scissors, and his beard allowed to grow, changing his appearance considerably. His hair had been cut somewhat shorter than he usually wore it.

Booth's body, which we have before described, was at once laid out on a bench and a guard placed over it. The lips of the corpse are tightly compressed, and the blood has settled in the lower part of the face and neck. Otherwise the face is pale and wears a wild, haggard look, indicating exposure to the elements and a rough time generally in his skulking flight. His hair is disarranged and dirty, and apparently had not been combed since he took his flight. The head and breast is alone exposed to view, the lower portion of his body, including the hands and feet, being covered with a tarpaulin thrown over it. The shot which terminated his accursed life entered on the left side at the back of the neck, a point, curiously enough, not far distant from that in which his victim, our lamented President, was shot.

A Spencer carbine, which Booth had with him in the barn at the time he was shot by Sergeant Corbett, and a large knife, with blood on it, supposed to be the one which Booth cut Major Rathbone with in the theatre box on the night of the murder of President Lincoln, and which was found on Booth's body, have been brought to the city. The carbine and knife are now in the possession of Colonel Baker, at his office.

Booth had upon his person some bills of exchange, but only about $175 in Treasury notes.

The bills of exchange, which are for a considerable amount, found on Booth's person, were drawn on banks in Canada in October last. About that time Booth was known to have been in Canada.

It is now thought that Booth's leg was fractured in jumping from the box in Ford's Theatre upon the stage, and not by the falling of his horse while endeavoring to make his escape, as was at first supposed.

The Captured Assassins.

The greatest curiosity is manifested to view the body of the murderer Booth, which yet remains on the gun-boat in the stream off the Navy Yard. Thousands of persons visited the yard to-day in hopes of getting a glimpse at the murderer's remains, but none were allowed to enter who were not connected with the yard. The wildest excitement has existed here all day, and regrets are expressed that Booth was not taken alive.

Sergeant Corbett.

It is said that in pulling the trigger upon Booth, he sent up an audible petition for the soul of the criminal,

The pistol used by Corbett was the regular large-sized cavalry pistol. He was offered a thousand dollars this morning for the weapon with its five undischarged loads.

An Autopsy.

This afternoon, Surgeon-General Barnes, with an assistant, held an autopsy on the body of Booth.

Booth not in Rebel Uniform.

It now appears that Booth an Harold had on clothing which was originally of some other color than the Confederate grey, but being faded and dusty, presented that appearance.

Booth's Mistress.

The news of Booth's death reached the ears of his mistress while she was in a street car, which caused her to weep bitterly, and drawing a photograph likeness of the murderer from her pocket, kissed it fondly several times.

The Demeanor of Harold.

Harold, thus far, has evaded every effort to be drawn into conversation by those who have necessarily come in contact with him since his capture, but his outward appearance indicates that he begins to realize the position in which he is placed, and that there is no hope for his escape from the awful doom that certainly awaits him. His relations and friends, in this city, are in the greatest distress over the disgrace that he has brought upon himself.

Bowling Green.

Bowling Green, near which place Booth was killed, is a post village, the capital of Caroline county, Virginia, on the road from Richmond to Fredericksburg, forty-five miles north of the former, and is situated in a fertile and healthy region. It contains two churches, three stores, two mills and about three hundred inhabitants.

DEATH SCENE OF THE ASSASSIN.

Map Showing the Place where Booth was Killed and Harold Captured.

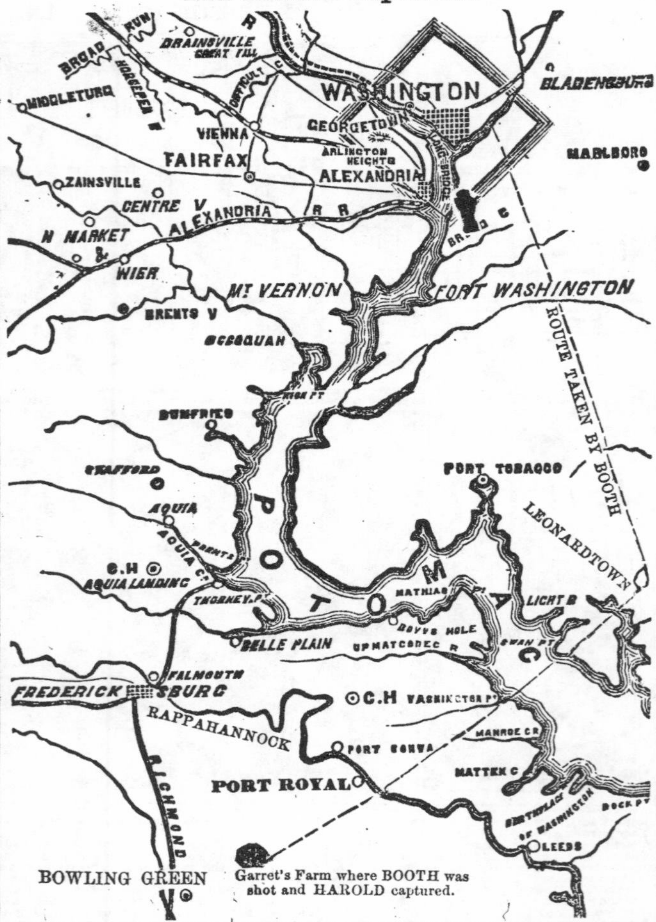

Garret's Farm where BOOTH was shot and HAROLD captured.

STONEMAN'S MOVEMENTS IN NORTH CAROLINA

KNOXVILLE, April 27.—Since the last intelligence from General Stoneman's command, the following is a summary of what it has accomplished:—

One portion of the command, under Colonel Palmer, moved down the Catawba River, dispersing parties going southwest from Johnston's army. He captured upwards of two thousand prisoners, and two pieces of artillery, and amongst other things destroyed, was the immense railroad bridge over the Catawba River, eleven hundred and twenty-five feet long, and sixty feet high. Then learning that a general armistice had been entered into between Sherman and Johnston, Colonel Palmer ceased operations.

The other portion of the command, under General Gillem, attacked and routed a Rebel force under Major-General McCowan, at Morgantown, taking one piece of artillery, and afterwards forcing the pass through the Blue Ridge held by the Rebel forces under General Martin, taking six guns, and could have captured or destroyed the whole force, had General Gillem not been met by General Martin, with a flag-of-truce, and bearing a letter from General Sherman, countersigned by General Johnston, and directed to General Stoneman, ordering a general suspension of hostilities, and a withdrawal of the forces under General Stoneman.

THE PRESIDENTIAL OBSEQUIES.

The Remains at Buffalo.

BUFFALO, N. Y., April 17.—The train was met at the depot in this city by a large concourse of people, and the funeral party were entertained at Bloomer's dining rooms by the city authorities.

The procession formed between seven and eight o'clock, and marched to St. James Hall, the coffin being prominently in view on the funeral car. The body was taken from the car and deposited on a dais in the hall.

In the gallery, outside the canopy, was the St. Cecilia Society, an amateur musical association, who, as the remains were brought in, sang with deep pathos, "Rest, spirit, rest."

The society then placed a heart composed of white flowers at the head of the coffin, and the public were then admitted.

BUFFALO, April 27.—As erroneous statements have been made in the press, it is necessary to say, on the authority of the embalmer and undertaker, that no perceptible change has taken place in the body of the late President since we left Washington. In that city the physicians removed a part of the brain only for the autopsy, but this was replaced so that no part of the body whatever is now deficient.

The remains were visited throughout the day, from 9·30 A. M. until 8 P. M., by an immense number of persons. The arrangements generally are pronounced better than elsewhere on the route. During the morning an anchor, made of camelias, was presented by a party of ladies from the Unitarian Church of Buffalo, and was laid on the coffin.

A cross of white flowers was also laid upon his coffin at the request of Major-General Dix. The procession, with the remains, left St. James' Hall at 8·45 P. M., escorted to the depot by military, followed by a large crowd. The depot was surrounded by persons anxious to get a last view of the coffin as the train left about 11 P. M. for Cleveland.

Treatment of a Traitor at Harrisburg.

Special Despatch to the Inquirer.

HARRISBURG, April 27.—On last Saturday week, when the news reached here of the assassination of the President, a man on the street gloried in the fact, and made a most obscene remark in regard to the corpse. The people desired to treat the man in a summary manner, but a guard of soldiers took possession of him. This afternoon he was marched through the principal streets to the tune of the Rogue's March, holding in his hand a board, with this inscription:—"William Young, a traitor too cowardly to fight for the Rebels, ejects his vulgar venom by insulting the remains of our dead President."

The soldiers desired to ride him on a rail, but the officers would not allow it.

On being released he was followed by a large crowd yelling and hooting at him, treating him rather roughly.

NORTH CAROLINA.

Sherman-Johnston Conference.

DETAILS OF THE INTERVIEW.

A Stormy Scene Between Kilpatrick and Wade Hampton.

THE REBEL STAFF COLD AND SUPERCILIOUS.

Torpedo Left on the Railroad by the Rebs.

GRAND REVIEWS OF THE TROOPS

OLD TECUMSEH AS A REVIEWING OFFICER.

A Description of Some of His Bright Particular Stars.

SHERMAN DESTROYING REBEL POWDER MILLS

Railway Travel Under the Rebel Rule.

Special Correspondence of the Inquirer.

RALEIGH, April 22.

The Conference

Between Sherman and Johnston, with its attendant incidents, was kept private. Now that the main features of the conditions agreed upon have been promulgated to the army, and the results of the carefully guarded interviews made known to the entire community, a brief *resume* of the circumstances and preliminaries incident to the meeting of the two great chieftains may be made public. A historic interest will ever surround this meeting of Sherman and Johnston.

Preparatory

To treating for terms our forces explored the railroad as far as within our lines. This act was performed under the direction of Colonel E. K. Kirby. On Saturday night, the 15th inst, the locomotive Walter Raleigh was slowly backing up the track of the North Carolina Railroad. The engine was manipulated by an engineer who, two days before, was in the service of the Rebels.

To prevent him rushing his engine into ambuscades or into unpleasant proximity to Rebel pickets, Colonel Kirby kept his revolver, loaded, capped and cocked, close to the head of the engineer. Ten miles from Morrisville Station, the tender of the engine, which was in advance, as the locomotive was backing, struck a torpedo, which exploded with a report loud as a six-pounder. The force of the explosion threw the tender from the track, and caused the occupants of the tender to throw impromptu somersaults through the air. No one, fortunately, was severely injured. A negro fireman, who sat on the front edge of the tender, was most severely injured of the party, sustaining the fracture of a leg. The tender was bent out of straight into curved lines. It was, however, replaced upon the track; and the engine run back to Gage's Station.

During Sunday, the 16th, the track was more successfully explored. The telegraph was repaired and put in working order to Durham Station.

The Interview.

Early on Monday morning, the 17th instant, General Sherman, attended by his staff and Colonel Kirby, of General Blair's staff, proceeded up the road to Durham Station. On reaching our cavalry line, they were joined by General Kilpatrick and his staff. The engine then proceeded to Durham. At this point General Kilpatrick had saddle-horses in waiting for the party. They rode five miles from Durham, and pulled up at an unpretending one-story frame house. The only attraction about this diminutive cot was, that it was embowered in umbrageous trees.

Generals Joseph E. Johnston and Wade Hampton, accompanied by a bevy of staff officers, were already on the ground. Generals Sherman and Johnston, alone and unattended, at once entered the cottage. They remained in conference for two hours. What passed between the Generals they alone can make known.

Outside the Cottage

Remained Generals Kilpatrick, Wade Hampton, and the staff officers. General Kilpatrick approached General Hampton and greeted him cordially. General Hampton replied coldly and superciliously. He told General Kilpatrick, "that for himself he was not disposed to give up the war, that he would never fraternize with us, but would retaliate with torch and sword, for the war that we had waged. He found a great deal of fault with our method of carrying on war. For a time General Kilpatrick was disposed to be conciliatory. But the supercilious taunts of Hampton, at last roused "Kill," and he retorted in more fitting terms to the groundless reproaches of the persistent Rebel. Hampton boasted of the surprise he carried out against General Kilpatrick's camp near Fayetteville. Though he did not allude to the champion captured in Georgia. The cavalry chiefs parted in no very amicable mood.

The Staff Officers

Of Wade Hampton imitated the boorish and senseless conduct of their sulky leader. General Sherman's officers were disposed to be sociable and friendly, but all their overtures were haughtily refused. They answered in monosyllables to direct questions, kept themselves together, and repelled all courteous intercourse. The Adjutant-General of Hampton, Captain McClellan, said to be a relative of George B. McClellan, delivered himself of some bitter remarks against the Union and its defenders. Two officers of General Johnston's *suite* proved an honorable exception in this ungentlemanly conduct of the Rebel staff officers. These two gentlemen, whose names we suppress from motives of delicacy, conducted themselves as officers and gentlemen, which is far more than can be said for their companions. The parting between the officers of the respective staffs was consequently very cool and distant.

Wade Hampton

Is a man of fine physique. He stands full six feet in height, and is symmetrically proportioned for strength and manly grace. He is of a decided dark complexion, has regular features, wears a full beard and moustache of glossy black. His black hair is, contrary to the prevailing Southern custom, cropped short. His dark eyes have a deep penetrating glance. From his appearance we would judge him to be forty

Continued on the Eighth Page.

No. 500—Vol. XX.] NEW YORK, APRIL 29, 1865. [Price 10 Cents. $4 00 Yearly. 13 Weeks $1 00.

ABRAHAM LINCOLN.

Assassinated Good Friday, 1865.

BY EDMUND C. STEDMAN.

"Forgive them, for they know not what they do!"
He said, and so went shriven to his fate—
Unknowing went, that generous heart and true.
Even while he spoke the slayer lay in wait,
And when the morning opened Heaven's gate
There passed the whitest soul a nation knew.
Henceforth all thoughts of pardon are too late;
They, in whose cause that arm its weapon drew,
Have murdered Mercy. Now alone shall stand
Blind Justice, with the sword unsheathed she wore.
Hark, from the eastern to the western strand,
The swelling thunder of the people's roar:
What words they murmur—Fetter not her hand!
So let it smite, such deeds shall be no more!

N. Y. Tribune.

The Martyr President.

On the 14th of April, 1861, the flag of the United States went down on the beleaguered walls of Fort Sumter. Its little garrison of seventy men succumbed to the thousands of traitors who had been permitted to pile up, unmolested, battery on battery around it, and the treason nursed so long in South Carolina had there its first triumph. The rebellion, then commenced in cowardice, ended on the fourth anniversary of that eventful day in assassination. Every step in its progress had been marked by some crime more heinous than the last. Persecution and murder of men and women for their adhesion to the flag of their fathers; Fort Pillow massacres; systematic starvation of Union prisoners; plots to burn crowded cities, and to dash railway trains down precipices, to say nothing of wholesale incendiarism on the high seas, have been among the common incidents of the war on the part of the South, and have passed into history as the characteristics of the rebellion. But one thing was necessary to complete the deep damnation of the monster treason of the 19th century. That hideous culmination was achieved on the night of April 14th, 1865, when Abraham Lincoln, the loved and honored head of the nation, was slain by a rebel assassin! Slain while unarmed and unsuspicious, slain from behind, with every incident that could lend a darker hue to the atrocity of the act. Almost at the same moment, a maimed and wasted statesman, helpless on a couch of suffering in a dimly-lighted sick chamber, was assaulted and stabbed by another foul emissary of the monster crime! Nor was there a single accessory of cowardice and brutality wanting here. Nothing indeed was wanting in the design, scope and execution of both acts, to invest them with a character more horrid and repulsive than attaches to any similar events in the wide annals of murder! The commencement, the progress, and the close of the rebellion—treason, wanton barbarity, assassination! Unrelieved by a single trait, lightened up by no single act of generosity, it stands in history one black, hideous blotch on civilization and mankind! Posterity will regard it, even through the haze of time, with a shudder, and parallels for its atrocities will only be found in the records of the darker days of the French Revolution, or in the bloody traditions of Dahomey!

Abraham Lincoln has joined the noble army of Freedom's Martyrs. "Christ died to make men holy; he died to make men free!" When that great, kind, expansive heart ceased to beat, humanity lost not alone its first representative man, but mankind lost its truest and best friend. Even the red-handed, dismayed and skulking traitors of the South found room in his broad sympathies, and a mercy there which perhaps encroached on God's first attribute of justice. Passing strange that the two men highest in position in the nation, and most disposed to leniency and forgiveness, were these that this hell-born treason selected for its last and most distinguished victims! Did Heaven order that its ultimate act should be to shut fast and bar for ever the half-opened door of national sympathy? Did Providence frown on the possible weakness that would condone treason and betray the cause for which five hundred thousand of our brothers have died and still fester in uncoffined graves!

Far be it from us to attempt lightly to interpret the inscrutable ways of the Almighty, but

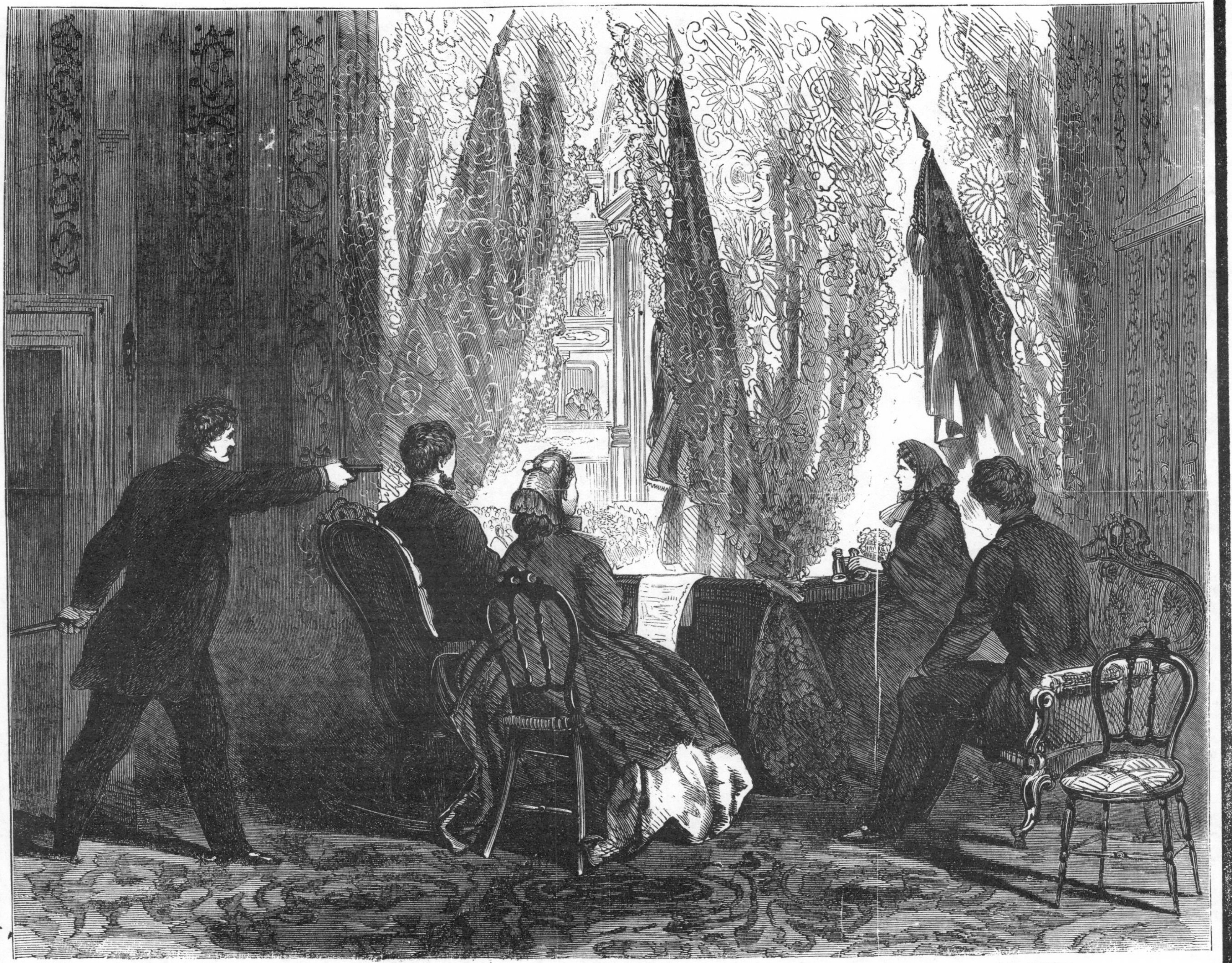

Booth. Mr. Lincoln. Mrs. Lincoln. Miss Harris. Major Rathbun.

ASSASSINATION O PRESIDENT LINCOLN IN HIS PRIVATE BOX AT FORD'S THEATRE, WASHINGTON, APRIL 14.

HARPER'S WEEKLY.
A JOURNAL OF CIVILIZATION.

Vol. IX.—No. 435.] NEW YORK, SATURDAY, APRIL 29, 1865. [SINGLE COPIES TEN CENTS. $4,00 PER YEAR IN ADVANCE.

THE MURDER OF THE PRESIDENT.

The Fourteenth of April is a dark day in our country's calendar. On that day four years ago the national flag was for the first time lowered at the bidding of traitors. Upon that day, after a desperate conflict with treason for four long, weary years—a conflict in which the nation had so far triumphed that she breathed again in the joyous prospect of coming peace—her chosen leader was stricken down by the foul hand of the cowardly assassin. Exultation that had known no bounds was exchanged for boundless grief. The record upon which had been inscribed all sorts of violence possible to the most malignant treason that ever sought to poison a nation's heart had been almost written full. But not quite full. Murder had run out its category of possible degrees against helpless loyalists in the South, against women and children whose houses had been burned down over their heads, and against our unfortunate prisoners, who had been tortured and literally starved to death. But there still remained one victim for its last rude stroke—one victim for whom, it was whispered in rebel journals South and North, there was still reserved the dagger of a Brutus. Beaten on every field of recognized warfare, treason outdid its very self, and killed our President.

The man who lent himself to traitors for this vile purpose was John Wilkes Booth, who sold himself, it may be, partly for the pieces of silver, but chiefly for the infamous notoriety attaching to such an act. There was an ancient villain who deliberately purposed to perpetuate the memory of his name among men by an act of awful sacrilege—a sacrilege so striking as never to be forgotten—and he burned the temple of the Ephesian Diana. Erostratus gained his end, and has been remembered accordingly. A memory far more detestable is in store for John Wilkes Booth, who dared, by the commission of an infinitely greater sacrilege, to bring a whole people to tears.

He was the third son born in America of the eminent English tragedian Junius Brutus Booth. There were three brothers, Junius Brutus, Jun., Edwin, and John Wilkes, all of whom inherited a predilection for the stage. Edwin, however, is the only one of these who has attained a very eminent position as an actor, and he is probably surpassed by no living man. In justice to him it is proper here to state that he is true and loyal, and exacts our sincerest sympathy. The elder Booth, father of these three actors, died thirteen years ago. He passed the quieter portion of his life upon his farm, in Harford County, some thirty miles from Baltimore. John Wilkes Booth, the murderer, was born in 1839, and is now only twenty-six years of age. He went upon the stage at the early age of seventeen, simply as John Wilkes. As stock actor he gained a fair reputation, and afterward assuming his full name, he began a more ambitious career. But, partly on account of his dissolute habits, he never achieved a marked success. He performed chiefly in the South and West. He has appeared but few times before a New York audience. In person he bears considerable resemblance to his father. His eyes are dark and large; his hair of the same color, inclined to curl; his features finely moulded; his form tall, and his address pleasing. He abandoned his profession recently on account of a bronchial affection. It is said that he has frequently threatened to kill President Lincoln. His companions have been violent Secessionists, and there are doubtless many others involved to a greater or less degree in his crime. The attempt to assassinate Secretary Seward was made probably by an accomplice. It is supposed that Secretary Stanton and Andrew Johnson were to have been added to the list of victims. The latter, at least, received on Friday a card from Booth, but was not at home.

Those who were acquainted with Booth's movements on the fatal Friday say that his manner was restless. He knew that the President and his party intended to be present at Ford's Theatre in the evening. He asked an acquaintance if he should attend the performance, remarking that if he did he would see some unusually fine acting. It was the general expectation that General Grant would form one of the President's party, and there are many who suppose that a blow was intended for him as well as the President. The latter had passed the day in the usual manner. In the morning his son, Capt. Robert Lincoln, breakfasted with him.—The Captain had just returned from the capitulation of Lee, and the President listened with great interest to his narration of the detailed circumstances. After breakfast he conversed for an hour with Speaker Colfax about his future policy as to the rebellion which he was about to submit to his Cabinet. At 11 o'clock the Cabinet met. Both the President and General Grant were present. Having spent the afternoon with Governor Oglesby, Senator Yates, and other leading citizens of his State, he went to the theatre in the evening with Mrs. Lincoln, in order to unite in the general expression of popular joy for our late victories. The party consisted of Mrs. Senator Harris and daughter, and Major Henry Rathbone, of Albany. They arrived at ten minutes before nine o'clock, and occupied a private box overlooking the stage. The play for the evening was *The American Cousin*.

Booth came upon his errand at about 10 o'clock. He left his horse in charge at the rear of the theatre, and made his way to the President's box. This box is a double one, in the second tier at the left of the stage. When occupied by the Presidential party the separating partition is removed, and the two boxes are thus thrown into one. We give an accurate plan of the box on page 259.—According to Major Rathbone's statement, the assassin must have made his preparations in the most deliberate manner beforehand. Of this fact there are at least four proofs, as we shall see: Stealthily approaching the dark passage-way leading to the box, Booth, after having effected an entrance, closed the hall-door, and then, taking a piece of board which he had prepared for the occasion, placed one end of it in an indentation excavated in the wall, about four feet from the floor, and the other against the moulding of the door-panel a few inches higher. He thus made it impossible for any one to enter from without; and securing himself against intrusion in that direction, he proceeded to the doors of the box. There were two of these. Here also the villain had carefully provided beforehand the means by which he might, unnoticed himself, observe the position of the parties inside. With a gimlet, or small bit, he had bored a hole in the door-panel, which he afterward reamed out with his knife, so as to leave it a little larger than a buck-shot on the inside, while on the other side it was sufficiently large to give his eye a wide range. To secure against the doors being locked (they both had spring-locks), he had loosened the screws with

RICHMOND WHIG.

SATURDAY MORNING.........APRIL 29, 1865

OUR TERMS

TO REGULAR SUBSCRIBERS.

Persons desiring to become regular subscribers to the RICHMOND WHIG can now do so, by mail or otherwise.

OUR TERMS

for the present, until we can more definitely ascertain the regulations of the UNITED STATES governing such matters, will be as follows

For One Year,	$10.
" Six Months,	6.
" Three Months	3.

to which will be added $6, per year (or its proportion for a shorter period, for the prepayment of POSTAGE, which is now required.

Should any change be made that will benefit either THE SUBSCRIBERS or Publisher, a satisfactory adjustment will be made.

TO AGENTS.

As some inducement to parties to interest themselves in raising "clubs" for the WHIG in any city or town in the United States, we will furnish (20) twenty copies or over at $9 per copy, the postage for the term of subscription of each paper to be added.

☞ We will adhere strictly to the

CASH SYSTEM!

and shall endeavor to make our prices compare favorably with those of any paper published in the Union.

The price of the Whig is FIVE CENTS per copy.

News Agents and Boys will be charged $3 50 per 100 copies.

Advertisements will be charged at the rate of 75 cents per square, of 8 lines or less.

Larger advertisements upon contract.

SPECIAL NOTICES.

☞ All letters on business, sent to this office, should be addressed to the *Proprietor* of the *Whig*. All other communications should be addressed to the *Editor*.

☞ For the temporary accommodation of the citizens of Richmond who may wish the *Whig*, there will be tickets sold at the office to the amount of *ONE DOLLAR* in Federal currency to responsible parties, and their obligation taken, payable in thirty days, so as to enable them to reach the latest news. Call at the office, Whig Building.

News Boys are instructed that they SHALL RECEIVE the tickets marked W. I. S., A. C. COLE, E. H. R. and I. R. A in payment for the Whig from the purchasers on the streets, and they will be received from the boys at the office as five cents, in payment of their purchases.

FIVE CENTS is all the boys are allowed to charge for the papers.

☞ Citizens will be visited this week, by AUTHORIZED AGENTS, for the purpose of receiving subscribers to the Whig.

☞ Persons at the North, or elsewhere, desiring to subscribe regularly to the Whig, for six or twelve months, will please notify us through the mail; and about the 1st of May we will be able to regulate the terms, and will then forward the bills for the amount of subscription. In the meantime the paper will go forward.

Send on your names, and give us the proper support.

☞ All communications sent to this office must be accompanied by the name and address of the writer. We will not undertake to return rejected communications.

PEACE!

SURRENDER OF GEN. JOHNSTON

CESSATION OF HOSTILITIES IN THE CAROLINAS AND GEORGIA!

The following highly important despatch from North Carolina was received yesterday by General Halleck:

RALEIGH, N. C., April 26, 1865.

Major General Halleck, Richmond:

Johnston surrendered the forces in his command, embracing all from here to the Chattahoochee, to Sherman, on the basis agreed upon between Lee and myself for the Army of Northern Virginia.

U. S. GRANT,
Lieutenant General.

A previous bulletin from the War Department was as follows:

WAR DEPARTMENT,
WASHINGTON, April 25, 10:10 P. M.

Major General Dix, New York:

A despatch has just been received by this Department from General Grant, dated Raleigh, 9 A. M., April 24th. He says:

"I reached here this morning and delivered to General Sherman the reply to his negotiations with Johnston. Word was immediately sent to Johnston, terminating the truce, and information that civil matters could not be entertained in any convention between army commanders."

(Signed) EDWIN M. STANTON,
Secretary of War.

A special Washington despatch to the New York Times, dated 25th, says:

We have information from Sherman's army, to-day, of an important character. It appears Johnston's first letter to Gen. Sherman proposed a surrender of his army on the same terms Lee surrendered. A meeting was arranged, at which Wade Hampton was present; he protested against the terms of surrender, and declared he would not surrender his cavalry force, supposed to be only about three thousand strong. Thereupon Sherman consented to delay, for the purpose of giving Johnston and Hampton an opportunity to consult Jeff. Davis.—Another meeting was arranged for the next day. On that day the parties again met and at the first sitting the remarkable memorandum or basis of agreement was presented and at once signed. It is further shown that before Sherman signed the memorandum he had received news of the assassination of President Lincoln.

The Herald's Washington correspondent says:

A letter of the Richmond correspondent of the London Times, dated March 4, foreshadows Gen. Sherman's recent policy, and has given rise to much comment and discussion in official circles here to-day. It is regarded as significant in view of what has occurred recently in North Carolina, and shows that the rebel leaders have relied upon working on Gen. Sherman's character and his antecedents to aid them in an extremity like that which has begun.

JOHNSTON'S SURRENDER.

The surrender of Gen. Joseph Johnston officially announced by Lieut. General Grant will be hailed with satisfaction by all persons who desire that Peace shall be restored to our distracted country. It will surely extinguish the last substantial hope of the infatuated devotees of Disunion. What additional proof can they require of the futility of further resistance to the national authority? There is now no formidable body of Confederate troops East of the Mississippi, and we should not be surprised to hear at any moment, that Kirby Smith had surrendered or disbanded his demoralized forces. With the dissolution of the Trans-Mississippi army all organized opposition to the Government of the United States will cease, and the Constitution and laws will be again enforced throughout the length and breadth of the Union.

The Chattahoochee river, referred to in Lieutenant-General Grant's despatch, separates Georgia from Alabama. All the Rebel troops now in North Carolina, South Carolina and Georgia are, therefore, embraced in the terms of capitulation agreed upon by Generals Sherman and Johnston.

THE ARMY OF THE POTOMAC.

This glorious army, after four years of such warfare as the world has never before seen, is being broken up, its old adversary, the Army of Northern Virginia, having been vanquished and dispersed. The Sixth corps has marched to Danville, which place, it is believed, it will hold for the present.

The Fifth corps is posted along the Southside Railroad, guarding that important line; and the Ninth corps, which until lately has been performing that duty, is now on its way to Washington, if it has not arrived there, whence, rumor has it, it is to be transferred to a distant point in the rebellious States.

The Second corps is awaiting orders, while the Twenty-fourth corps is near this city.

THE DANVILLE RAILROAD.

Mr. Lewis E. Harvie, President of the Richmond and Danville Railway, has, we learn, made an offer to General Grant to put the road in running order on certain terms. These terms were not accepted at first, but subsequently General Grant directed the General commanding to accept the offer if Mr. Harvie took the oath of allegiance. At last accounts the latter had not conformed to this requirement. It is very necessary to have this road in running order for the supply of the troops at Danville, and it is to be hoped the Directory of the road will speedily comply with the conditions named by General Grant.

THE RELATIONS BETWEEN THE UNITED STATES AND PORTUGAL—WHY THE GOVERNOR OF BELEM WAS DISMISSED.

A despatch from Lisbon, on the 11th inst., on the subject of the relations existing between the United States and Portugal, states that the Governor of Belem was dismissed, not for having fired on the United States ships Niagara and Sacramento when the were approaching the bar, but for continuing to fire upon them when they had struck their flags and turned towards Lisbon. At a public demonstration in honor of the continuation of amicable relations between the two nations a reciprocal salute was fired in honor of the respective flags.

AFFAIRS IN KENTUCKY—THE CONSTITUTIONAL AMENDMENT.

The settlement of the Slavery question by the final abolition of the Institution, is engaging the attention of the authorities in Kentucky. General Brisbane, Superintendent of organization of colored troops in that State, has written a letter to Governor Bramlette, calling attention to the disturbed condition of labor in that State, and urging him to call the Legislature together and pass the Constitutional Amendment. The General says the slaves are nominally free and the masters can no longer depend on their labor, and points out the evils that must arise from the present half slave and half free condition of the State.

He claims that the passage of the amendment would quiet the minds of the negroes, and cause them to remain at home and till the soil now so much in need of their labor. More than twenty thousand of the most valuable slaves have already gone into the army; so that Kentucky must choose either to have her slave population abscond and freed by the army, or to save her labor to the soil by granting unconditional freedom to the slaves at home.

The Governor replies, concurring in the opinion that slavery can no longer be retained in Kentucky, that labor must be reorganized on a free basis.

THE RUSSIAN EPIDEMIC.

The latest news from St. Petersburg fortunately allays the fears which already began to be felt throughout the world in consequence of the epidemic disease in that city. The highest medical authorities now agree that the epidemic is not the plague, but only a somewhat more violent kind of fever well known in other countries. The hygienic condition of St. Petersburg is less satisfactory than that of the other larger cities of Europe, and is believed to be the direct cause of the increased rate of mortality. The correctness of the first statistical reports of the cases of sickness and deaths is denied, and the most recent returns are not calculated to cause any alarm.

THE CAPTURE OF BOOTH!

HIS REFUSAL TO BE TAKEN ALIVE

DEFIANT BRAVADO OF THE ASSASSIN.

HE IS KILLED BY SERGEANT CORBETT, OF THE 16TH NEW YORK CAVALRY.

Through the courtesy of Mr. D. F. Webster, of the Adams' Express, we received last night a copy of the Washington *Republican* of Thursday evening, containing interesting particulars of the capture of John Wilkes Booth, the assassin of President Lincoln, and one of his accomplices in the murder, David C. Harold.

It had been ascertained that Booth and Harold crossed the Potomac river at or near Aquia Creek. Early Wednesday morning a squad of men belonging to the 16th New York cavalry discovered the fugitives in a barn on the road leading from Port Royal to Bowling Green, in Caroline county, Va.—What ensued is described by the *Republican* as follows;

"We have had an interview with two of the cavalrymen engaged in the capture of the assassins.—From them we learn that the whole party consisted of twenty-eight, including two detectives.

The first information respecting Booth's crossing the river, and his probable whereabouts, was obtained from disbanded rebel soldiers, who were met with in all directions in that part of the country.

From one and another of these the clue to Booth's movements was gathered and held, until just at daybreak they came upon the barn where he and Harold were secreted.

A parley was held, and Booth manifesting the most desperate determination not to be taken alive, and to take as many of the lives of the party as possible, Lieut. Edward P. Doherty, who commanded the scouting party, determined to make short work of him.

When Harold saw the preparations for firing the barn, he declared his willingness to surrender, and said he wouldn't fight if they would let him out.

Booth, on the contrary, was impudently defiant, offering, at first, to fight the whole squad at one hundred yards, and subsequently at fifty yards.—He was hobbling on crutches, apparently very lame. He swore he would die like a man, etc.

Harold having been secured, as soon as the burning hay lighted the interior of the barn sufficiently to render the scowling face of Booth, the assassin, visible, Sergeant Boston Corbett fired upon him, and he fell.

The ball passed through his neck. He was pulled out of the barn, and one of his crutches and carbine and revolvers secured.

The wretch lived about two hours, whispering blasphemies against the Government and messages to his mother, desiring her to be informed that he died for his country.

At the time Booth was shot he was leaning upon one crutch and preparing to shoot his captors.—Only one shot was fired in the entire affair, that which killed the assassin.

Lieut. Doherty is one of the bravest fellows in the cavalry service, having distinguished himself in a sharp affair at Culpeper Court House and on other occasions.

The 16th New York cavalry is commanded by Col. Nelson Sweitzer, and has been doing duty in Fairfax county. This regiment formed part of the cavalry escort on the day of the President's obsequies in Washington.

The body of Booth, and the assassin's accomplice, Harold, were placed on board the Ida and sent to Washington, arriving here about 1 o'clock this morning.

The Atlanta papers have received information of Mr. Lincoln's assassination, but make no comments upon it. They also deny the surrender of Lee, and affirm that Gen. Grant lost 6,000 men in the battle of Amelia Court-House.

Religious Notice.—Elder JAMES B. TAYLOR will preach in Sycamore Meeting-house to-morrow (SUNDAY) morning, at 11 o'clock. The public are invited to attend.

Washington  Chronicle.

VOL. I.—NO. 51.] WASHINGTON, SATURDAY, APRIL 29, 1865. [THREE DOLLARS PER ANNUM.

J. D. EHLERS ENGR.

BOOTH, THE ASSASSIN.

EXTRA CHRONICLE

APRIL 27, 1865.

BOOTH KILLED!

HARROLD CAPTURED!

BOOTH'S BODY IN WASHINGTON!

HARROLD IN SAFE QUARTERS!

BOOTH secretes himself in a Barn, which is fired. He tries to escape, is SHOT through the Head, lingers three hours, and Dies.

[OFFICIAL WAR BULLETIN.]

WAR DEPARTMENT, WASHINGTON, April 27—9.30 A. M.

Major General Dix, New York:

J. WILKES BOOTH and HARROLD were chased from the swamps in St. Mary's county, Md., pursued yesterday morning to Garrett's farm near Port Royal, on the Rappahannock, by Colonel Baker's force. The barn in which they took refuge was fired, Booth was shot and killed, and Harrold captured.

Booth's body and Harrold are now here.

EDWIN M. STANTON, Secretary of War.

"Booth, in making his escape, was shot through the head and killed, lingering about three hours, and Harold captured.

"THOS. T. ECKERT,
"Commanding, &c,"

BOOTH.

Nothing has gone so far to confirm us in the idea that the cowardly assassination of President Lincoln would abolish parties in the North and unite all loyal men, whatever may have been their differences of opinion, on the great question whether the American people shall be one nation or many, than the subjoined article from the Cincinnati *Times*. The very forcible and able editorial which we copy below will give a fair indication of the revolution of feeling which has taken place in the west.

Conjectures are very plentiful as to the motive which inspired the assassination of Abraham Lincoln. Despite the horrible nature of the crime, the completeness of the conspiracy which brought it about, the dexterity with which it was executed, the skill by which the murderer made his escape, the concert of action between two or more confederates, and the successful progress of a well-devised scheme of concealment against the power of large rewards and a network of military and civil police, there are those who believe, or affect to believe, that Booth was the victim of a monomania, that he conscientiously thought he had a mission to kill the President, that he cherished these wicked but honest delusions until he was inspire[d] by a frenzy beyond control, and, like Guy Fawkes and Charlotte Corday, was finally buoyed up for the desperate enterprise of ridding the world of a tyrant, by convictions of duty and destiny. The theorists who put forward a plea of this kind are often persons whose loyalty cannot be disputed, but whose judgment we venture to dispute upon every feature of the petty abstraction set up in favor of the assassin. They will pardon us, and will not, we feel assured, accuse us of an overheated or exaggerative temper, if we are unable to find a single extenuation for the most deliberate, the most unprovoked, the most cruel, the most cowardly murder which ever darkened the long black-letter list of crime.

1.—*Its Deliberation.*—Booth hovered about Washington through the winter. Letters found in his trunk indicate that the time originally fixed was the 4th of March. The delay occasioned by the shortcoming of an accomplice deferred the plan for ten days. During those ten days events transpired which demonstrated that the rebellion was fairly crushed, and that that there was no hope for it in the future. They also illustrate the kind heart and the conservative policy of Mr. Lincoln, and had begun to endear him even to his enemies; so that if there was a plea for his taking off in the mind of a monomaniac on the 4th of March, it must have been weakened materially by the 14th; and if the murder was not resolved upon coolly and resolutely, there was full time for the operations of the better instincts of humanity and conscience.

II.—*Its cruelty.*—There was to be no mistake or miscarriage about the matter. The murderer understood the various exits and entrances of the place which he had selected for his crime, but lest there should be any mistake, he [illegible] careful reconnoissance. When he first op[ened] the door of the private box, and looked in on the President's party, his heart would have so[ftened], had its functions been alive, and he would [have] shrunk away from his purpose with ho[rror]. There was genial, honest Old Abe, seeking a little respite from the cares of State, and full of the happy spirit of an amusing drama. There was his wife by his side. There was a young girl, too, and a gallant officer, a mutual friend of all, and the quartette were as unconscious of danger, and as innocent as the babes in the wood. Who could assail them with a brutal purpose but a man lost to all the accusations of conscience, without humanity or compassion?

III.—*Its Cowardice.*—When Guy Fawkes, who was a real monomaniac, and inspired by [illegible] of the attributes of heroism, undertook [illegible] commons, he prepared [illegible] himself. He attested his sincerity [illegible] the sacrifice of his own person. The mine [illegible] was to send the State to its last account [illegible] also to carry Guy Fawkes before his heavenly master to receive the reward of his martyrdom. When Charlotte Corday killed Robespierre, she had no thought of preserving her life, and with the inspiration of the fanatic submitted without a murmur to her fate. Now, Guy Fawkes and Charlotte Corday were undoubtedly deliberate assassins. We may applaud or condemn the cause in which they embarked, according to our own opinions, yet they were murderers, and only elicit our tolerance because of the universal belief in their sincerity. Booth is a murderer of a very different pattern. His deed was planned with the craft of a madman, but also with the caution of a man whose love of life is greater than his love for any cause. He had no [idea] of becoming a martyr. His plan was to commit a brutal assassination, and then to get away, and in the accomplishment of this purpose [he has] been singularly successful. Had he been a monomaniac, zealous in a certain faith and passion, his desires would have been satisfied with the death of his victim, and, instead of [leaping] upon the stage, brandishing his dagger for a vainglorious effect, and disappearing, according to the most approved rules of dramatic art, in the background, he would have hurled himself like a hero into the arms of the infuriated mob, or plunged his weapon into his own heart.

Booth, therefore, can neither claim the admiration or compassion of posterity as a bigot or a hero. His cruelty, cowardice, and deliberation imply that his motive was worldly, and that a false idea of notoriety, *or the more vulgar, but more probable, inducement of pecuniary gain, set him on.* The evidence in support of this mercenary consideration is strong. For many months he has not appeared in his profession, and has lived in the most expensive style, without any visible resources. The plausible assertion that he had "struck oil" will hardly pass current with those who are familiar with the purposes of the rebel leaders, as illustrated in the following advertisement, which appeared in the Selma (Ala.) *Dispatch*, last December:

ONE MILLION DOLLARS WANTED to have peace by the first of March. If the citizens of the Southern Confederacy will furnish me with the cash, or good securities for the sum of one million dollars, I will cause the lives of Abraham Lincoln, William H. Seward, and Andrew Johnson to be taken by the first of March next. This will give us peace, and satisfy ourselves that cruel tyrants cannot live in a "land of liberty." If this is not accomplished, nothing will be claimed beyond the sum of fifty thousand dollars, in advance, which is supposed to be necessary to reach and slaughter the three villains. I will give myself $1,000 towards this patriotic purpose. Every one wishing to contribute will address box X, Cahaba, Alabama.

December 1, 1864.

This barefaced and cold-blooded proposition affords a key to the motive of Booth. A money-mania indeed held possession of his brain. Gold was his inspiration, his zeal, his heroism. The brutal lust for the wages of blood was the fanaticism which thrilled him and made a cowardly murderer, not a pitiable madman of him.

But the red mark is on him, and he will walk among men a doomed outcast. [illegible] disclose himself to his fellow-crea[tures] [illegible] cannot hide himself from the eye [illegible]

ARREST OF JUNIUS BRUTUS BOOTH.

HE IS CONFINED IN THE OLD CAPITOL.

ALLEGED CAUSE OF HIS ARREST.

PHILADELPHIA, April 26.—Junius Brutus Booth was arrested in this city at 8 o'clock this morning, and taken to Washington, where he is now confined in the Old Capitol prison. It is understood his arrest was caused on suspicion of his knowledge of the intention of his brother, to assassinate President Lincoln, based upon his letter to Wilkes, published in yesterday morning's papers, regarding Richmond and oil.

[The letter referred to is said to have been addressed to J. Wilkes Booth by his brother at Ford's Theatre. It states in substance that as Richmond had fallen, and Lee had surrendered, it was advisable to abandon the oil business. A postscript was added, signed "Alice," to the same effect.]

PHILADELPHIA, April 26.—The *Ledger* reports[?] [illegible]y that the rumor that Junius Brutus Booth was arrested here on Tuesday is not a fact. It is ascertained from a relative of his that he visited the vicinity of New York, where his mother is represented as suffering from her son's conduct. He was arrested at New York and taken to Washington.

PHILADELPHIA, April 26.—The reporters of Forney's *Press* furnish the following regarding the arrest of Junius Brutus Booth: He was arrested at a private residence of a friend in this city. The detectives had been on the *qui vive* for several days past. He was placed in a close carriage and driven to the Baltimore depot, and taken in the first train to Washington. He was arrested, it is stated, upon evidence in certain documents in possession of the United States authorities, an extract of which was published on Monday.

This extract literally alludes to the oil business, as not likely to be profitable, because Richmond had been captured and Lee had surrendered. Those who are well acquainted with the chirography of the prisoner, believe it to have been written by him.

Alice, who also concurs in the recommendation to the assassin to abandon the oil business—is said to be a woman who is intimately ac[quainted] with the assassin.

IMPORTANT REPORT.

[illegible] Rebels to be Indicted.

HARRISBURG, April 26.—It is reported in official circles that the district attorney of Franklin county will bring before the grand jury of the court, soon to convene in that county, bills of indictment against General McCausland, Harry Gilmore, and other leading rebels, for levying war upon the inhabitants of Franklin county, for pillage, arson, and murder. There can be no doubt that true bills will be found, when G[overnor] [illegible] will immediately demand the wretches thus indicted from the governor of Virginia for trial in Pennsylvania. Before the proposed action of the district attorney of Franklin county was known, it was contemplated by the executive of Pennsylvania to make a formal demand for McCausland and Gilmore. This action is now postponed to await the result of the proceedings before a Franklin county grand jury.

Order by General Hancock.

HDQRS. MIDDLE MIL. DIVISION,
WASHINGTON, D. C., April 24.

To the colored people of the District of Columbia and of Maryland, of Alexandria and the border counties of Virginia:

Your President has been murdered! He has fallen by the assassin and without a moment's warning, simply and solely because he was your friend and the friend of our country. Had he been unfaithful to you and to the great cause of human freedom he might have lived. The pistol from which he met his death, though held by Booth, was fired by the hands of treason and slavery. Think of this and remember how long and how anxiously this good man labored to break your chains and to make you happy. I now appeal to you, by every consideration which can move loyal and grateful hearts, to aid in discovering and arresting his murderer. Concealed by traitors, he is believed to be lurking somewhere within the limits of the District of Columbia, of the State of Maryland, or Virginia. Go forth, then, and watch, and listen, and inquire, and search, and pray, by day and by night, until you shall have succeeded in dragging this monstrous and bloody criminal from his hiding-place. You can do much; even the humblest and feeblest among you, by patience and unwearied vigilance, may render the most important assistance. Large rewards have been offered by the Government, and by municipal authorities, and they will be paid for the apprehension of this murderer, or for any information which will aid in his arrest. But I feel that you need no such stimulus as this. You will hunt down this cowardly assassin of your best friend, as you would the murderer of your own father. Do this, and God, whose servant has been slain, and the country which has given you freedom, will bless you for this noble act of duty.

All information which will lead to the arrest of Booth, or Suratt, or Harold, should be communicated to these headquarters, or to General Holt, Judge Advocate General, at Washington, or, if immediate action is required, then to the nearest military authorities.

All officers and soldiers in this command, and all loyal people, are enjoined to increased vigilance.

[W.] S. HANCOCK,

SHERMAN.

OFFICIAL WAR BULLETIN.

WAR DEPARTMENT,
WASHINGTON, D. C., April 22—10 P. M.

Major General J. A. Dix, New York:

Yesterday evening a bearer of despatches arrived from General Sherman. An agreement for a suspension of hostilities, and a memorandum of what is called a basis for peace, had been entered into on the 18th instant by General Sherman with the rebel General Johnston, the rebel General Breckinridge being present at the conference. A Cabinet meeting was held at 8 o'clock in the evening, at which the action of General Sherman was disapproved by the President, by the Secretary of War, by General Grant, and by every member of the Cabinet. General Sherman was ordered to resume hostilities immediately, and he was directed that the instructions given by the late President, in the following telegram, which was penned by Mr. Lincoln himself at the Capitol, on the night of the 3d of March, were approved by President Andrew Johnson, and were reiterated to govern the action of military commanders.

On the night of the 3d of March, while President Lincoln and his Cabinet were at the Capitol, a telegram from General Grant was brought to the Secretary of War, informing him that General Lee had requested an interview or conference, to make an arrangement for terms of peace. The letter of General Lee was published in a message of Davis to the rebel Congress. General Grant's telegram was submitted to Mr. Lincoln, who, after pondering a few minutes, took up his pen and wrote with his own hand the following reply, which he submitted to the Secretary of State and Secretary of War. It was then dated, addressed, and signed by the Secretary of War, and telegraphed to General Grant:

PRESIDENT LINCOLN'S INSTRUCTIONS.

"WASHINGTON, March 3, 1865, 12 P. M.

"*Lieutenant General Grant:*

"The President directs me to say to you that he wishes you to have no conference with General Lee, unless it be for the capitulation of General Lee's army, or on some minor and purely military matter. He instructs me to say that you are not to [decide, discuss, or confer upon any politi]cal question. Such questions [the President] holds in his own hands, and will submit them to no military conferences or conventions. Meantime you are to press to the utmost your military advantages.

"EDWIN M. STANTON,
"Secretary of War."

The orders of General Sherman to General Stoneman, to withdraw from Salisbury and join him, will probably open the way for Davis to escape to Mexico or Europe with his plunder, which is reported to be very large, including not only the plunder of the Richmond banks, but previous accumulations. A despatch received by this Department says:

"It is stated here by respectable parties, that the amount of specie taken south by Jeff. Davis and his partisans is very large, including not only the plunder of the Richmond banks, but previous accumulations. They hope, it is said, to make terms with General Sherman or some other southern commander, by which they will be permitted, with their effects, including the gold plunder, to go to Mexico or Europe. Johnston's negotiations look to that end."

After the Cabinet meeting last night, General Grant started for North Carolina, to direct operations against Johnston's army.

EDWIN M. STANTON,
Secretary of War.

Memorandum, or Basis of Agreement, made this eighteenth day of April, A. D. 1865, near Durham Station, in the State of North Carolina, by and between General Joseph E. Johnston, commanding Confederate Army, and Major General W. T. Sherman, commanding Army of the United States, in the State of North Carolina, both being present:

1. The contending armies now in the field to maintain the *status quo*, until notice is given by the commanding general of any one to its opponent, and reasonable time, say forty-eight hours, allowed.

2. The Confederate armies now in existence to be disbanded, and conducted to their several State capitals, therein to deposit their arms and public property in the State arsenal, and each officer and man to execute and file an agreement to cease from acts of war, and to abide the action of both State and Federal authorities. The number of arms and munitions of war to be reported to the Chief of Ordnance at Washington City, subject to the future action of the Congress of the United States, and in the meantime to be used solely to maintain peace and order within the borders of the States respectively.

3. The recognition by the Executive of the United States of the several State governments, on their officers and legislatures taking the oath prescribed by the Constitution of the United States; and where conflicting State governments have resulted from the war, the legitimacy of all shall be submitted to the Supreme Court of the United States.

4. The re-establishment of all Federal courts in the several States, with powers as defined by the Constitution and laws of Congress.

5. The people and inhabitants of all these States to be guaranteed, so far as the Executive can, their political rights and franchises, as well [as their rights of person and property, as defined] by the Constitution of the United States, and of the States respectively.

6. The Executive authority of the Government of the United States not to disturb any of the people by reason of the late war, so long as they live in peace and quiet and abstain from acts of armed hostility, and obey the laws in existence at the place of their residence.

7. In general terms, the war to cease, a general amnesty, so far as the Executive of the United States can command, on the condition of the disbandment of the Confederate armies, distribution of the arms, and the resumption of peaceable pursuits by the officers and men hitherto composing said armies.

Not being duly empowered by our respective principals to fulfil these terms, we individually and officially pledge ourselves to promptly obtain an answer thereto, and to carry out the above programme.

W. T. SHERMAN,
Major General, comdg. army U. S., in N. C.
J. E. JOHNSTON,
General, commanding C. S. A., in N. C.

DISAPPROVAL, AND REASONS THEREFOR.

It is reported that this proceeding of General Sherman was disapproved for the following among other reasons.

1. It was an exercise of authority not vested in General Sherman; and on its face shows that both he and Johnston knew that General Sherman had no authority to enter into any such arrangement.

2. It was a practical acknowledgment of the rebel Government.

3. It undertook to re-establish the rebel State governments that had been overthrown at the sacrifice of many thousand loyal lives and immense treasure, and placed the arms and munitions of war in the hands of the rebels at their respective capitals, which might be used as soon as the armies of the United States were disbanded, and used to conquer and subdue the loyal States.

4. By the restoration of the rebel authority in their respective States, they would be enabled to re-establish slavery.

5. It might furnish a ground of responsibility by the Federal Government to pay the rebel debt, and certainly subjects the loyal citizens of rebel States to the debt contracted by rebels in the State.

6. It would put in dispute the existence of loyal State governments, and the new State of West Virginia, which has been recognized by every department of the United States Government.

7. It practically abolished the confiscation laws, and relieved the rebels, of every degree who had slaughtered our people, from all pains and penalties for their crimes.

8. It gave terms that had been deliberately, repeatedly, and solemnly, rejected by President Lincoln, and better terms than the rebels had ever asked in their most prosperous condition.

[9. It formed no basis of true and lasting peace, but relieved the rebels from the pressure of our] victories, and left them in condition [to renew] their efforts to overthrow the United States Government and subdue the loyal States whenever their strength was recruited and any opportunity should offer.

CANBY—HANCOCK.

OFFICIAL WAR BULLETIN.

WAR DEPARTMENT,
WASHINGTON, April 22, 1865.

Major General Dix, New York:

In a despatch dated at Mobile, 5 P. M., April 14th, Major General Canby reports as follows:

"We find in Mobile, and its defences, on the west side of the bay, over one hundred and fifty guns, and a very large amount of ammunition and supplies of all kinds, and about one thousand prisoners. Inventories are now being taken and a detailed report will be forwarded as soon as they are completed. The quantity of cotton will probably reach thirty thousand bales, and there is a large amount of provisions and forage."

Major General Hancock reports that nearly all of Mosby's command have surrendered, including nearly or quite all of the officers, except Mosby himself. Some of Mosby's own men are hunting him for a reward of $2,000 offered for him by Gen. Hancock, who has been directed to establish his headquarters at Washington. The counties of Prince George, Charles, and St. Mary's, have, during the whole war, been noted for hostility to the Government, and its protection to rebel blockade-runners, rebel spies, and every species of public enemy. The murderers of the President harbored there before the murder, and Booth fled in that direction. If he escapes, it will be owing to rebel accomplices in that region. The military commander of the department will speedily take measures to bring the rebel sympathizers and accomplices in murder to a sense of their criminal conduct.

EDWIN M STANTON,
Secretary of War.

The Seven-Thirties.

PHILADELPHIA, April 26.—Subscriptions to the seven-thirty loan yesterday, from all parts of the Union, as telegraphed to Jay Cooke, amount to $4,162,000. The largest single subscriptions were: $100,000 from Cincinnati, $200,000 from Washington, $500,000 from New York, and $250,000 from Boston. The number of individual subscriptions of less than $100, by wo[rkingmen] [illegible]

THE SIXTH CORPS.

VOLUME I. DANVILLE, VA., MONDAY, MAY 1, 1865. NUMBER 4.

ODE
TO THE Q. M. DEPARTMENT.

—o—

In glorious rhyme I fain would chime
 The praises of the kingly mule,
Whose silvery laugh exceeds by half
 The sweetness taught in music's school.

At break of day he takes his way,
 The "right of road" the troops must yield,
His tearful eyes to Heaven uprise
 To see them plod thro' swamp and field.

And when afar the sounds of war
 Grate harshly on his tender ear,
He knows his place—'tis no disgrace
 For any mule to keep the rear.

But if perchance with ambulance
 His orders came to seek the front,
He falters not—his toils forgot,
 He succors those who've borne the brunt.

And when at night the camp-fire light
 Bespeaks the wearied soldier's rest,
With hurried tramp he seeks the camp
 And feels his presence will be blest.

"Mules of the Pack" upon your back
 What treasures in abundance lie,
You stand supreme, no mule in team
 For stately pomp with thee can vie.

And happy they, these mules obey,
 We humbly bow to worship them,
No tongue can tell, nor organ swell—
 The glories of an "A. Q. M."

Would I were one, from sun to sun
 I'd gambol with the playful mule,
I'd call them birds and gentle words,
 Nor care who called me simpering fool.

I'd scorn the throng, my merry song
 Should echo through each wood and dale,
I'd kick and bite, and howl all night,
 And know my strength could never fail.

But vain desire, my thoughts aspire
 Too high, too high for one so low,
I can but gaze, and tell their praise,
 And mark them as they proudly go.

MILITARY DIRECTORY.

Roster of Staff Officers at Head Quarters of the Sixth Army Corps, commanded by Major Gen'l H. G. Wright:

Major C. H. Whittelsey, Ass't Adjutant General.

Lieut. Col. Walter S. Franklin, Inspector General.

Capt. Lay, Commissary of Musters.

Major Arthur McClellan, A. D. C.

Major R. F. Halsted, A. D. C.

Major Thos. L. Haydn, A. D. C.

Major Henry W. Farrar, A. D. C.

Major Stephen H. Manning, Acting Chief Quarter Master.

Major James K. Scofield, Acting Chief Commissary.

Lieut. Col. S. A. Holman, Medical Director.

Acting Staff Surgeon, S. J. Allen, Medical Inspector.

Major D. J. Miln, Provost Marshal.

Capt. George E. Wood, Chief Ambulance Officer.

Major E. K. Russell, Acting Commissary of Subsistence.

Lieut. Thos. H. Fearey, Signal Officer.

Lieut. Jas. W. Dixon, Acting A. D. C.

Lieut. Alex. Samuels, Acting Asss't Quarter Master.

FIRST DIVISION DIRECTORY.

Staff Officers at Head Quarters of First Division, 6th Corps, commanded by Brevet Major General Frank Wheaton.

Lieut Col George Clendenin, jr, A A General.

Lieut Col R P Lincoln, A A I General.

Major A M Tyler, Ass't Commissary Musters.

Major C D Cleveland, Ordnance Officer.

Major M L Butterfield, Division Engineer.

Major John Snodgrass, Ass't A D C.

Capt. George A Bernard, A D C.

Lieut William J Cooke, A D C.

Dr. Redford Sharpe, Surgeon in Chief.

Capt Sol W Russell, jr, Provost Marshal.

Capt Vanderweed, Assistant Provost Marshal.

Capt Chas G Finney, Assistant Quarter Master.

Capt Jas G Fitts, Assistant Commissary of Subsistence.

Lieut H E Hindmarsh, Judge Advocate.

Lieut Charles F. Kennedy, Quarter Master 3d Brigade, 2d Division, 6th Corps, Main street, one door below Masonic Hall.

HEAD QUARTERS' DIRECTORY.

Maj. Gen. H. G. WRIGHT, Commanding 6th A. Corps, Main street, opposite Maj. Sutherlin's.

Col. T. W. HYDE, Military Governor, Mr. Walker's, Main st.

Major D. J. MILN, Provost Marshal Sixth Army Corps, at Mr. Watkin's, on Main street. Office hours from 9 a. m. to 4 p. m., when all Provost Marshal business immediately connected with the Corps is transacted. No business done on Sunday.

Lt. Col. FLETCHER, Provost Marshal of Danville, at the Virginia Bank Building, on Main street, where all Provost Marshal business connected with the town is transacted.

Special Orders.

Medical Director of the Post.

H'D Q'RS 6TH ARMY CORPS,
Danville, April 29, 1865.

Special Order
No. 90.

Lieut. Col. S. A. Holman, Medical Director, will at once assume control of the hospitals at this place, and will direct the Confederate Surgeons now here to report to him for service in their hospitals.

He will issue from the trains such temporary supplies for the hospitals as may be necessary.

By command of Major Gen. Wright.
C. H. WHITTELSEY,
Ass't Adj't Gen.

Assistant Provost Marshall.

HDQRS. POST OF DANVILLE,
April 28th, 1865.

Special Orders.

Capt. James M. Gere, 122nd New York Volunteers is hereby detailed as Assistant Provost Marshal of Danville; and will report to Lieut.-Col. Fletcher for duty. By command
COL. T. W. HYDE.
WM. H. LONG, A. A. G.

GENERAL ORDERS.

REGULATIONS IN REGARD TO PASSES

H'D QR'S 6TH ARMY CORPS,
Danville, Va., April 30, 1865.

GENERAL ORDERS
No. 2.

I. In order to remove a misapprehension in the minds of some relative to the passes required in and about this place, the following regulations are promulgated for the information and guidance of all concerned.

I. No officers or men will be permitted to visit the town without a written pass from either Division or Brigade Commanders. This, however, will not apply to General or Staff Officers, or mounted Orderlies when on duty.

II. Passes will not be granted to more than one-fifth (1-5) of the officers in each organization, nor to more than two (2) enlisted men from each Company. Those granted to the men will expire at or before 6 P. M. daily.

III. Neither Officers nor men will be permitted to pass through the picket line without special authority from these head Quarters—General Officers and Staff Officers, when on duty, alone excepted.

IV. Citizens will be permitted to pass the picket line, in the day time, into and out of the town, without being required to have passes.

V. Paroled prisoners of war are entitled to the same privileges as citizens, excepting that they may be required to show their parole passes.

VI. Officers and soldiers of the Confederate States Army not paroled, will be arrested and sent to the office of the Provost Marshal.

By Command of Major Gen. Wright.
C. H. WHITTELSEY,
Ass't Adj't Gen.

May 1

GEN. WRIGHT'S CONGRATULATORY ORDER.

HEADQ'RS 6TH ARMY CORPS,
Danville, Va., April 27th, 1865.

General Orders, No. 9.

The Major General Commanding desires to express his great gratification at the accomplishment of the late march of the Corps from Burkesville Junction. In four days and four hours not less than one hundred miles have been traversed; a march almost unprecedented in this or any other war, even under the most favorable auspices.

Without the incitement of anticipated victory; without the hope of even meeting an enemy, or of adding aught of glory or of renown to the already brilliant career of the Corps, it is by the exhibition of such qualities as have been shown during the past few days, patience, endurance, fidelity, that the true soldier creates and sustains his own reputation, and the pride and admiration of his Commanders.

While endeavoring to bestow all merited praise upon the command at large, the General commanding cannot conceal his regret and mortification at the conduct of those men, few as they may be, who, as regardless of orders as of decency, have, by their ruthless plundering and marauding among peaceful citizens, shown themselves utterly unworthy the name of soldiers. The disgraceful acts of these few men have made them the sole exception to the general commendation.

Let these men remember that they have but to follow the noble example of their comrades to enable them to bear their share hereafter in the good name which history will not fail to award this Corps.

By command of
MAJ. GEN. WRIGHT.
C. H. WHITTELSEY,
Ass't Adj't General.

TO THE CITIZENS OF DANVILLE.

H'D QR'S POST OF DANVILLE,
April 29th, 1865.

General Orders
No. 3.

The military power of the so-called Confederate States being at an end, and its Government removed from the State of Virginia, it is enjoined upon all good citizens to become reconciled to the old Government, to heal past grievances, to consider the military authority as temporarily here for their protection, and to go on in their daily avocations and duties, with confidence that they will be unmolested therein. All cases where citizens come in collision with, and all complaints against the military forces must be immediately referred to these Head Quarters, or to the Provost Marshal of the city.

No citizen or soldier will be allowed to take redress of grievances in his own hands.

Religious services may be held, public and private schools be continued, business carried on subject to regulations already promulgated by the War Department. No obstructions will be placed by the military upon citizens coming and going at will, or upon free speech, so long as nothing is said or done prejudicial to the Government of the United States.

All citizens desiring to take the oath of allegiance to the United States, can do so at the office of the Provost Marshal.

By command of Col. T. W. HYDE,
Commanding Post,
WM. H. LONG,
Major and A. A. General.

PASSES FOR OFFICERS & SOLDIERS.

HEADQ'RS 3RD BRIG., 2D DIV.,
6th Corps, April 29th, 1865.

General Orders No. 20.

No officers or soldiers of this command, except Commanding Officers of Regiments, will be allowed to enter town without a pass, unless it be in obedience to orders from these Headquarters. An Orderly from each Regiment will be provided with a permanent pass.

By order of Col. T. W. Hyde.
WM. H. LONG,
Major and A. A. Gen.

TO PAROLED OFFICERS.

H'D Q'RS POST OF DANVILLE,
April 29th, 1865.

General Orders
No. 2.

I. All paroled officers of the late Confederate States service residing in Danville and vicinity, and wearing uniform, will report to the Provost Marshal.

II. Paroled officers will not be permitted to wear their side arms, or to carry weapons.

By command of Col. T. W. HYDE,
Commanding Post.
WM. H. LONG,
Major and A. A. Gen.

POSTAL ARRANGEMENTS FOR THE CITIZENS OF DANVILLE.

H'D Q'RS POST OF DANVILLE,
April 29th, 1865.

General Orders
No. 4.

All mail matter to be sent to established Post Offices in the United States by citizens of Danville and vicinity will be left sealed, at the Office of the Provost Marshal.

By command of Col. T. W. HYDE.
WM. H. LONG,
Major and A. A. Gen.

WARNING TO MARAUDERS.

H'D Q'RS 6TH ARMY CORPS,
Halifax Court House,
April 26th, 1865.

General Orders
No. 8.

The attention of officers and soldiers is called to the many orders heretofore issued relative to straggling and marauding. These orders must in future be strictly observed, and the Major General commanding explicitly enjoins upon all officers to use their utmost endeavors to suppress this evil, which appears to be daily increasing.

The taking of property, public or private, by officers or soldiers, without proper authority, is theft, and is so regarded, not only by the laws of war in all civilized nations, but also by the orders of our Government. It is a disgrace to the Army and Corps to which we belong, and the aid of every officer and man who calls himself a soldier is invoked for its suppression.

Hereafter, no property of any description will be taken without written orders from these Head Quarters, and under the supervision of an officer; and for this receipts will be given, by such officer, according to the form prescribed in existing orders.

The command is, and will be, fully supplied with rations, and there is no possible excuse for individuals taking any article of provisions from the people of the country through which we pass.

If officers of every grade will do their duty in this matter, the evil referred to will speedily cease.

This order will be read at the head of every Regiment and Battery in this command.

By command of Major Gen. Wright.
C. H. WHITTELSEY,
Ass't Adj't General.

EXTENSION OF THE MILITARY LINES OF THE UNITED STATES.

H'D Q'RS 6TH ARMY CORPS,
Danville, Va., April 28, 1865.

General Orders
No. 10.

[EXTRACT.]

II. The following order from the War Department is promulgated for the information and guidance of all concerned.

By command of Maj. Gen. Wright.
C. H. WHITTELSEY,
Ass't Adj't Gen'l.

—

WAR DEPARTMENT,
Adjutant General's Office,
Washington, April 26th 1865.

General Orders
No. 74.

Extension of the Military lines of the United States, General Orders No. 70, War Department, Adjutant General's Office, April 17th, 1865, is amended to read as follows: "Ordered that the military lines of the United States be extended to include within them the States of Virginia and Tennessee, and that all military restrictions upon internal trade within said lines are annulled, except in arms, ammunition, gray cloths, and all articles from which ammunition is manufactured; locomotives, cars, railroad iron and machinery for operating railroads, telegraph wires, insulators and instruments for operating telegraphic lines, which articles are contraband of war, and all trade in and importation thereof within the limits aforesaid is absolutely prohibited.

By order of the Secretary of War.
(Signed) W. A. NICHOLS,
Ass't Adj't General.

—

H'D Q'RS 6TH CORPS,
April 28th, 1865.

Official:
C. H. WHITTELSEY,
Ass't Adj't General.

H. Q. 3D BRIG., 2D DIV., 6TH CORPS.,
Danville, Va., April 29th, 1865.

[CIRCULAR.]

Citizens will be allowed to leave and enter town without a pass. Officers and soldiers of the late Rebel Army must have a pass or parole to leave town, but none will be required to enter it.

Officers and soldiers, and all other persons must leave and enter town on one of the main roads.

By order of Col. T. W. Hyde.
WM. H. LONG,
Major and A. A. General.

THE SURRENDER OF JOHNSTON'S ARMY.

H'D Q'RS 6TH ARMY CORPS,
Danville, Va., April 28th, 1865.

General Orders
No. 10.

I. The Major General commanding announces to the command that Johnston's army has surrendered upon the same terms as those granted to Lee's army.

H. G. WRIGHT,
Maj. Gen. Commanding.

Official:
C. H. WHITTELSEY,
Ass't Adjutant General.

DAILY CORPS.

DANVILLE:

MONDAY MORNING,..... MAY 1. 1865.

Around the Altar.

After years of turmoil and strife North and South knelt together round God's Altar yesterday. From Western Lakes and Southern swamps, from Eastern rivers and sluggish bayous the "Union of States" was fully represented. It was a solemn and impressive scene. Over fields red with blood strewn with the dead and dying, and enveloped in the smoke of battle had all those prayerful men fought their way to the throne of the Almighty. Hearts were full with thoughts too great for utterance, as the mind travelled back over the events of the last four years; and then when the hymn of praise and prayer arose from brothers reunited, each one acknowledged that though "His ways are not as our ways," yet "He doeth all things well."

This reunion of North and South in the House of God, where hearts are softened and minds are opened, will in the immediate present and the fast coming future bear good fruit. Its benefits are incalculable, for there in the immediate presence of the Great Ruler of the Universe, and in the house dedicated to His service, was guidance for the future, and forgiveness for the past, asked by earnest men who had often looked the "King of Terrors" in the face on many a battlefield.

Let us all hope, and all pray that as a merciful God has spared us to see the end of the great Rebellion, and made us all once again citizens of this earthly Union, that he will, after death, make us one in the great Union of Angels and Saints above.

The Situation.

By the surrender of Gen. Johnston's army in North Carolina, the authority of the National Government is virtually restored in all the States east of the Mississippi River. There is now no organized force in resistance to the Government save that in the Trans-Mississippi Department, and we may safely say that that is of no consequence in the present condition of affairs; for nothing is easier than for such a force of Federals to be thrown across the river in a short time as will compel these men to lay down their arms, as those of Lee and Johnston have done. Indeed we shall be surprised if they do not act sensibly in the matter, and go home of their own accord without farther ceremony. They will have very little inducement to attempt the protraction of a hopeless struggle, now that the two main pillars of the rebel structure have broken and fallen to the ground.

We hope it may be thus. There should be no more of this fratricidal war, but peace and reconciliation throughout the broad limits of the Republic.

We very much regret to hear that the old and efficient Commissary of the 3rd Brigade, 2nd Division, 6th A. C., Capt George T. Burroughs, has tendered his resignation. Capt. Burroughs entered the service at the very first of the war and having served out his time received an honorable discharge—since which time he has been connected with the above named Brigade, and all have recognized in him a good officer.—Prompt and attentive to his duties he has always had at heart the best interests of his Department, and having a fine business tact it has always been well up to the standard.

Our best wishes go with him. He will be succeeded by Lieut. J. T. Cornue, of the 122 N. Y.

A Picture of Cæsar.

The following graphic description of this renowned warrior is taken from the new work, by the French Emperor, on "The life of Cæsar":

To these natural gifts, developed by a brilliant education, were joined physical advantages. His lofty stature, and his finely moulded and well proportioned limbs, imparted to his person a grace which distinguished him from all others. His eyes were dark, his glance penetrating, his complexion colorless, and his nose straight and somewhat thick. His mouth was small and regular, and the lips, rather full, gave to the lower part of his face an expression of kindliness, while his breadth of forehead indicated the development of the intellectual faculties. His face was full, at least in his youth; but in the busts which were made toward the close of his life, his features are thinner, and bear the traces of fatigue.

His voice was sonorous and vibrating; his gestures noble, and an air of dignity pervaded his whole person. His constitution, which at first was delicate, grew robust by sober living and by his habit of exposing himself to the inclemency of the seasons. Accustomed from his youth to manly exercise, he was a bold horseman, and he supported with ease privations and fatigues. Habitually abstemious, his health was not weakened by excess of labor nor by excess of pleasure. Nevertheless, on two occasions, once at Cordova and then at Thapsus, he had a nervous attack, which was erroneously thought to be epilepsy. He paid particular attention to his person, shaved with care or had the hairs plucked out; he brought forward artistically his hair to the front of his head, and this, in his more advanced age, served to conceal his baldness.

He was reproached with the affectation of scratching his head with only one finger for fear of deranging his hair. His dress was arranged with exquisite taste. His gown was generally bordered with the laticlam, ornamented with fringes to the hands, and was bound round the loins by a sash loosely knotted—a fashion which distinguished the elegant and effeminate youth of the period. But Scylla was not to be deceived by this show of frivolity, and he was wont to recommend that people should have an eye on that young man with the flowing sash. He had a taste for pictures, statues and gems; and he always wore on his finger, in memory of his origin, a ring on which was engraved the figure of an armed Venus.

To sum up, there were found in Cæsar, physically and morally, two natures which are rarely combined in the same person. He joined aristocratic fastidiousness of person to the vigorous temperament of the soldier; the graces of mind to the profundity of thought; the love of luxury and of the arts to a passion for military life in all its simplicity and rudeness. In a word, he joined the elegance of manner which seduces to the energy of character which commands. Such was Cæsar at the age of eighteen, when Scylla possessed himself of the dictatorship. He had already attracted the attention of the Romans by his name, his wit, his engaging manners, which were so pleasing to men, and still more so, perhaps, to women. (Liv. II., cap. i.)

[Communicated.]

To Virginians.

It is clearly the duty of every good citizen to resume his usual avocation, pursuing the even tenor of his way, and obeying implicitly the rules and regulations laid down for his government by those in authority. Now that the United States has asserted her authority over the land which has, by rebel combinations, been led astray from her fostering care, she—judging from the experience of the past month—is willing that the past shall be buried in oblivion, and will only require, even from those who have broken faith with her, to return to their allegiance, and say or do naught calculated to defeat the object in view—the restoration of the Union.

VIRGINIUS.

Dahlias are like the most beautiful women without intellectuality. They strike you with astonishment by their exterior splendor, but are miserably destitute of those properties which distinguish and render agreeable less imposing flowers. Had nature given the fragrance of the rose or the lily to the dahlia, it would have been the most magnificent gem of the garden; but, wanting scent, it is like a fine woman without mind.

IMPORTANT From GREENSBORO'.

Gen. Wright's Veterans the First Federal Soldiers to Enter the Town.

THEY ARE WELCOMED BY THE INHABITANTS.

EVERYBODY DELIGHTED, &c., &c., &c.

The town of Greensboro', N. C., has been occupied by the Sixth Corps. Before mid-night on Saturday General Wright received a despatch from Lieut. Col. Franklin, Inspector General of the Sixth Corps, dated Greensboro', N. C., April 29th, 10.30 p. m., stating that the town had been occupied by an advance guard of the Sixth Corps.

No Federal soldiers were found there.

The inhabitants received our men with every sign of satisfaction, and there is no doubt but that many of them have always been loyal to the Government of the United States.

On Sunday (yesterday) morning Lt. Col. S. A. Holman, Medical Director of this Post, started for Greensboro' to look after the condition of hospitals at that place. He was accompanied by Major S. H. Manning, Major Russell and Captain Lay, of General Wright's staff.

Notice to Correspondents.

RACING CALENDAR.—You ask us what course you should take to get up some races? We answer, emphatically, the Danville *course*. Send in your order and we will print "Correct Cards of the Races" with despatch, and on reasonable terms.

ELECTRICITY.—Your paper on "Where lightning comes from, and where it goes to," was received per mail this morning, and immediately submitted to the notice of the lightning conductor of our establishment. His comments on it were very vivid, and, in accordance with his loudly expressed desire, we beg respectfully to decline publishing it at this time, as the light thrown by the subject you treat of is much too fleeting.

PETROLEUM.—We have not yet heard that the Sixth Corps have struck oil. We know they have, as you say made one regular ten stroke, however, in reaching Danville ahead of Gen. Sheridan's cavalry.

ANXIOUS ONE.—We take considerable pleasure in relieving your anxiety, by informing you that baking powder is a rising article in the market. Nothing goes up so fast, (unless it may be balloons,) or sells so rapidly. We have a friend who privately informed us his brightest anticipations would be realized by receiving a car load from the North.

P. S.—LATER.—He has just sent a note telling us his spirits have been raised by receiving, per telegraph, the following message:

"The goods have started, B—gs."

INDIGNATION.—We must apologise for not inserting your article on "The social condition of Ancient Peruvians." We have no doubt they were a very interesting people, but at the present time our readers are busily engaged enjoying the hospitalities of the modern Danvillians.

Notice to Contributors.

Correspondents will please not send in their favors so plentiful, as the mail is unable (or has been thus far) to bring any of them to us.

We found Amanda R's article on the sidewalk so far defaced that we could only make out "my dearest." But, soberly, we would like to have the people interest themselves in the paper, and send in items. A paper needs assistance outside of its own limits, and we trust our request will be granted.

The debt of Vermont amounts to $1,648,845, or $5,21 for each person in the State. The debt is principally funded, and is payable in 1861, 1874 and 1897.

LOCAL MATTERS, &c.

YESTERDAY was a quiet day in town. Religious exercises were held at the different churches, and the best order prevailed.

"For the President of the United States, and all in Authority under him."

As this prayer ascended from our pulpits yesterday an involuntarily responsive "Amen" burst from the lips of all assembled. May it ever be uttered as fervently and responded to as earnestly.

OUR PAPER.—In a few days the publishers of the "Sixth Corps" will make arrangements to come in possession of the latest papers from the Northern cities and from Richmond, and will then be enabled to make their pet sheet more interesting to all classes of readers, by giving daily a full resume of all the more important news from abroad. At present they labor under the disadvantages of receiving no mails what ever.

SPRING is putting down her green carpet in the Square, over the fields, in the country lanes, cutting and fitting it to accommodate all the branching highways and meandering streams as a careful upholsterer cuts and fits his tapestry. Over the fields and meadows, over the mountains, hillocks and valleys, over the great battle plains, over the graves of the slain and buried, creeping up between the bones of the unburied, the grassy carpet springs. With this putting down of nature's carpeting does not end the work of nature's upholstry. Dame nature hangs a green curtain against the distant woods, and the eye, on a day of clear, warm sunlight like yesterday, looks out upon a green cloud rising like an impalpable mist. Spring is with us once again.

Of the twelve revolutionary patriots living on the 1st of January, 1863, but five survived to welcome the last new year. Lemuel Cook resides at Clarendon, N. Y., and does not know his age; Samuel Downing resides at Edinburg, Saratoga county, N. Y., and is ninety-eight years old; William Hutchins resides at Penobscot, Me., and is one hundred years old; Alexander Maroney resides at Yates, Orleans county, N. Y., and is ninety-four years old; James Burham lives in Missouri, and is one hundred years of age.

DOG LOST.—Strayed, or was stolen from the lot of the Exchange Hotel, five or six days ago, a small black puppy, of the feminine gender, with white spots about the head. A liberal reward will be paid for her return. apl 29-1t

Notice.

THERE is at the Mayor's office, one gold watch, one black cloth cloak, bunch cotton, candles and other articles, taken from negroes, supposed to have been stolen. Persons having lost such articles will please call and examine them; otherwise they will be disposed of as the law directs.

W. L. ROBINSON, Chief Police.
Danville, Va., March 15, 1865—dtf

Order of Gen. Johnston.

TERMS OF SURRENEER.

ARMY OF TENNESSEE,
Greensboro, N. C., April 27.

Special Order No. 18.

By the terms of a military convention made on the 26th by Gen. W. T. Sherman, of the U. S. A., and Gen. J. E. Johnston, C. S. A., the officers and men of this army are to bind themselves not to take up arms against the U. S. until properly relieved from that obligation, and shall receive guarantees from the U. S. officers against molestation by the U. S. authorities so long as they observe that obligation and the laws in force where they reside; for these objects duplicate muster rolls will be made immediately, and after the distribution of the necessary papers, the troops will march under their officers to their respective States, and there be disbanded; all retaining their personal property. The object of this convention is pacification to the extent of the authority of the commanders, who made it. Events in Virginia, which broke every hope of success by war, imposed on its General the duty of sparing the blood of this gallant army, and saving the country from further devastation and our country from ruin.

J. E. JOHNSTON,
General Commanding:
Official: Archer Anderson,
A. A. G.

The Philadelphia Inquirer.

PRICE TWO CENTS. | PHILADELPHIA, FRIDAY, MAY 5, 1865. | PRICE TWO CENTS.

THE LATEST NEWS

Latest from Richmond.

PROMINENT CITIZENS TAKING THE OATH

Virginia Resuming Her Allegiance.

JEFF. DAVIS' PHYSICIAN AMONG THE CONVERTS

Deserts His Old Patron.

END OF MOSEBY, THE GUERRILLA.

HE FINDS HIS LAST DITCH.

FUNERAL OF PRESIDENT LINCOLN.

Closing Scenes at Springfield.

SOLEMN AND IMPOSING CEREMONIES.

AFFAIRS IN PETERSBURG.

Resumption of Trade and Its Results.

CONDITION OF SECRETARY SEWARD AND SON.

They Continue to Improve.

Interesting from Washington.

OUR RICHMOND CORRESPONDENCE.

OATH TAKING—CITIZENS GENERALLY RESUMING THEIR ALLEGIANCE—JEFF. DAVIS' FAMILY PHYSICIAN TAKES THE OATH—NEWS FROM MOSEBY—A REMINISCENCE OF MERCIER—"THE WILD HUNT FOR OFFICE" UNDER THE REBEL REGIME—DESERTERS IN THE MOUNTAINS—GENERAL ORDERS—THEATRICALS—THE STANDARD OF VALUE.

Special Correspondence of the Inquirer.

RICHMOND, Monday, May 1.

A month to-day since the battle of Five Forks, and not only is the Rebellion dead, but its most ardent supporters, men who day and night [illegible] for it, wrote for it, talked for it, fought for it, not only admit it to be dead, but are coming up in crowds to resume their allegiance to the United States. Who a month ago would have predicted events which have since become history. Who would have said that the Southern people would have shown the good sense that has characterized their conduct since Lee's capitulation. It is immaterial whether they express contrition for the past or not. What the country desires is security for the future, and that Virginia is guaranteeing more and more every day.

It was thought by some when General Order No. 4 was issued, on Saturday, that there would be considerable agitation observable in the circles of late Secessionists; that men would talk loweringly of proscriptive rule, of test oaths, of tyranny and subjugation. Nothing of the kind has been heard. Whatever they may think, these people say very little. General Order No. 4 has gone into operation in Richmond with as little display of feeling as it would have created in New York or Philadelphia.

Some prominent men took the oath before the Order was issued, and of these those connected with the *Whig* were, William Iva Smith, proprietor; John Graline, Jr., editor; P. H. Gibson, assistant editor; J. M. Hanna, local editor; W. A. R. Nye, foreman, and twenty-three others connected with the establishment in various capacities.

Among those who on Saturday and to-day have resumed their allegiance by solemn oath, are Joseph Mayo, the Mayor; J. E. Meredith, Judge of the Circuit Court; W. H. Lyons, Judge of the Hustings Court; T. U. Dudley, City Sergeant; Thomas H. Ellis, President of the James River Canal Company; W. P. Munford, Secretary of same Company; P. H. Aylett (long a prominent man of the State); J. Caskie, President of the Bank of Virginia; W. H. Macfarland, President of the Farmers' Bank; C. E. Wortham, W. H. Christian, J. Davenport, C. F. M. Garnet, L. D. Crenshaw, B. Conyers, S. A. Glover, J. Mayo, J. Beale, J. Lyons, E. H. Rhoads, J. R. Allen, J. R. Broocks, J. Rutherford. Nor are citizens anxious to resume their avocations the only ones coming in and taking the oath.

At Colonel Evans' office twelve hundred and twenty-seven men of Lee's army are registered as having taken it, and to-day was signalized by the appearance of four Surgeons as applicants for the renewed citizenship. Two of them to whom the oath was administered were Major J. B. Cullem, of Longstreet's staff, and Major A. Y. P. Garnet, Jeff. Davis' physician, who went away in the fugitive Rebel's retinue, but deserted his fortunes at Danville, and returned, reaching this city yesterday. Dr. Garnet is the individual Daniel used to anathematize as the court physician.

The Oath

Being administered is what is known as the Amnesty Oath, and is as follows:—

I, ——, do solemnly swear, in the presence of Almighty God, that I will henceforth faithfully support, protect and defend the Constitution of the United States, and the Union of the States thereunder; and that I will in like manner abide by and faithfully support all Acts of Congress passed during the existing Rebellion with reference to slaves, so long and so far as not repealed, modified or held void by Congress, or by decision of the Supreme Court; and that I will in like manner abide by and faithfully support all Proclamations of the President made during the existing Rebellion, having reference to slaves, so long and so far as not modified or declared void by decision of the Supreme Court—So help me God.

Throwing aside all abstractions as to ethical questions, omitting all inquiries into whether these men are taking this oath freely and willingly, and it is a cheering omen of coming tranquillity that they are taking it at all, there can be no doubt of the fact that they are taking it with a conscientious determination to fulfill its obligations, which, after all, is the only practical question. That they will mourn in the dismantled temple of State Rights for their idols that have been cast down, is but natural, and the mantle of charity will hide the lingering sin for the mass of the worshippers.

The names I have embraced in this letter will show that the wealth, the intellect, the social and political power of Richmond is resuming its allegiance, as well as its labor. I will frankly own that I did not expect this result from Order No. 4. Remembering events in Nashville, Memphis, Vicksburg, New Orleans and other cities, remembering the earnestness, not to say vindictiveness, of Virginia in the war while the war lasted, it will readily be acknowledged that none but the most sanguine could have anticipated the results we now see. It is proverbial that men live fast in revolutions, but there is no parallel in history to the events in Virginia for the past month. No people ever abided the result of an appeal to arms more faithfully than this. For four years they waged a relentless war upon the Union, gave their best blood freely, put into the contest, as with the earnestness of one man, their treasure and talent.

When Lee's surrender convinced them of the hopelessness of further contest, recognizing truly what was at stake in the war, they surrendered the dogma of Secession and the institution of slavery. All they ask now is peace. Purged of the heresies that brought on the war, they look forward to coming years of returning prosperity. As to the fall of the men who led them into the valley of the shadow of death, they care nothing. The President can hang the political leaders, "the conscious and intelligent traitors," and hear no protest from Virginia.

The Tidings From Moseby,

Brought in this morning by a late member of his gang, is equally significant of the revolution in public sentiment, going on all over the State. His story is, that on Friday last eight hundred of the band were assembled at Salem, in Roanoke county. Moseby made them a speech, saying the war was over, and all was lost, and advising them to return to their farms and bear themselves as peaceable citizens. As for himself, he said there could be no peace; he must fly the country, and should depart immediately for Texas and Mexico.

The men took his advice, the band separated, and the guerrilla chief, attended by only about a dozen of his freebooters, left the scene after a formal leave-taking. If this story be true, and it probably is, thus exit Moseby; the places that knew him, and where was he not, shall know him no more.

A Reminiscence of Mercier

And his visit to Richmond fell in my way yesterday. The public will remember that the pilgrimage of the French Minister to the Rebel capital excited much public curiosity at the time, and that he was very reticent on the subject always. The object of his visit here was purely commercial, but some of the leading Rebels could not resist the temptation of sounding him on the all-absorbing topic of intervention. Mercier, considering his position as he should, evaded replies to the hints cast at him. At last, one day, in conversation with Wigfall, the fiery but boorish Texan, after various surmises as to what England and France ought to do, put a direct question as to why they did not interfere and put an end to the war. Mercier was roused at last, and Wigfall got the satisfactory answer that England and France were afraid to interfere; that the power and energy and resources displayed by the North had alarmed all Europe. The Texan said "h—ll," and having said it was silent.

This anecdote being undoubtedly authentic, it is pleasant to have such positive proof of the wholesome respect entertained for us by the European powers.

"The Wild Hunt for Office,"

So commences a letter to Extra Billy Smith dated June 4, 1864, "In this county, at the recent election, fully demonstrates that we have hosts of 'good citizens' who are willing to serve their country in some capacity or other, preferring, however, the civil to the military; any thing but the army or the bullets of the enemy for them.

"The conduct of some in this county on election day, cannot be called creditable, if it might not be termed disgraceful; as many as twenty-five candidates running in one district for justice of the peace, with corresponding numbers for commissioner of revenue, &c. So great was the competition for positions affording an asylum for substitute men and conscript men generally, there seemed to be a wild rush for every office. Whisky flowed freely, and it is reported with much truthfulness, I have no doubt, that some men seeking high position carried liquor into the mountains, electioneering with deserters, and of course inviting them to the polls; and I learn that the votes of about one hundred of this class of men were polled for sheriff in this county."

Thus, and much more, wrote one Dunn to Billy Smith, Governor of Virginia, and the particular revelation he makes is, not that there was a wild hunt for office, for that was natural enough, but that there were deserters in the mountains of Virginia in sufficient numbers to attract the attention of office seekers.

General Orders

Nos. 48 and 49, although not of recent date, are part of official history, and are appended:—

HEAD-QUARTERS DEPARTMENT OF VIRGINIA, ARMY OF THE JAMES, RICHMOND, Va., April 26, 1865.—General Orders No. 48.—The following named commissioned officers of colored troops having been found guilty by a military commission of the offenses set opposite their names, are hereby dismissed the service, subject to the approval of the President:—

Lieutenant-Colonel Dexter E. Clapp, Thirty-eighth United States Colored Troops, for borrowing money from enlisted men and suppressing the order prohibiting the same.

Second Lieutenant S. B. Bancroft, Thirty-eighth United States Colored Troops, for peddling candy, tobacco and trinkets to the enlisted men. He also repaired watches for enlisted men of his regiment while an officer in it.

Second Lieutenant John E. White, Thirty-eighth United States Colored Troops, for peddling tobacco to enlisted men, while recruiting.

By command of Major-General Ord.

ED. W. SMITH,
Assistant Adjutant-General.

HEAD-QUARTERS DEPARTMENT OF VIRGINIA, ARMY OF THE JAMES, RICHMOND, Va., April 27, 1865.—General Orders No. 49.—General Orders No. 38, current series from these head-quarters, is hereby modified to read as follows:—The Sub-District of the Peninsula is hereby constituted and will embrace the country bordered on the north by the York and Pamunkey Rivers, including Gloucester and Mathews counties; on the east by the Chesapeake Bay; on the south by the James River, and on the west by the Fredericksburg Railroad; exclusive of the city of Richmond, and Fort Pocahontas and Fortress Monroe. Brevet Brigadier-General B. C. Ludlow, United States Volunteers, is assigned to the command of the Sub-District of the Peninsula, and in relation to all military matters will report to Brigadier-General George H. Gordon, commanding District of Eastern Virginia. In all matters pertaining to negro affairs he will report direct to these headquarters. Gen. Ludlow will establish his head-quarters at Williamsburg.

By command of Major-General Ord.

ED. W. SMITH, Asst. Adjt.-Gen.

The Theatre

Here has already experienced the regeneration that invariably keeps pace with the advance of our armies and our civilization, and opened to-night with a first-class company, secured North by Mr. Ogden since the occupation. Thus in all things, even to the mimic life of the stage, is Northern abundance called on to repair the waste and desolation worked upon the South by the war she inaugurated. While noticing that the prices of the theatre were to-night reduced to a just figure, it is well to note that

Prices

Generally are altogether too high here. The standard of value seems to be the Rebel currency at the rate of fifteen for one in greenbacks. As the trash was never in reality worth anything at all, and even before the occupation was sold in Richmond at thirty for one in gold, it is hardly proper that we should now be obliged to submit to these extortions, or that we should allow Secessionists to make a distinction against United States currency that does not exist now, whatever may have been the case at former periods. This is a case that might probably be safely left to regulate itself were it not for the fact that extortioners but rarely let go their prey after they have once fastened upon it.

EDWARD CRAPSEY.

CORBETT, THE EXECUTIONER OF BOOTH.

SKETCH OF BOSTON CORBETT.

Singular Incidents of his Life.

The friends of Sergeant Boston Corbett, the soldier who shot the assassin Booth, have furnished some interesting incidents of his life, which are not mentioned in any of the accounts already printed.

It appears that Corbett, who is a man of eccentric habits and disposition, and in some respects of remarkable character, was born in England in 1832, that he came to this country when he was seven years of age and resided in this city till about ten years ago, working at his trade as a hatter. He worked also in Boston, Troy, Albany, Richmond, Va., and in other cities. In Virginia he was obnoxious, on account of his anti-slavery opinion, and was compelled to leave the State. He had married, but his wife died, and he is still a widower.

Why Corbett Changed His Name.

Corbett, whose name was originally Thomas H., made a profession of religion in Boston, and joined the Methodist Church, having been baptized under the name of "Boston" Corbett. He became exceedingly enthusiastic, and devoted himself entirely to the faith he had accepted. He was at the same time impulsive, doing without hesitation what he thought was right, and acting without much regard to the opinions of others. When asked why he changed his name to Boston, he replied that when converted he was born anew, and thought it proper to distinguish his second birth by taking a new name. He had, he added, the happiness to obtain religion in the chief city of Massachusetts, and in recognition of that fact, had called himself Boston.

Corbett at His Trade.

Just before the beginning of the war Corbett worked at his trade in this city, but had much difficulty in getting along and paying his way. He was exceedingly liberal, believed it to be his duty to divide his means with the poor, and often left himself without the means of living comfortably. Faithful and skillful in his occupation, he nevertheless failed to find constant employment, because he was unwilling to work for any man who did wrong, and as nearly all his employers conducted themselves in some manner contrary to his ideas of right, Corbett lost much for conscience sake.

Quarrel with a Broadway Hatter.

Corbett once worked for a hatter in Broadway, but disagreed with him, and finally declined to work in his shop longer for the following reasons:—It appears the hatter was in the habit of purchasing old hats, dressing them neatly, and selling them as new articles. Corbett objected to this proceeding, and remonstrated with his employer, telling him that he had no right to dispose of hats worth only three dollars and fifty cents for five dollars. The hatter persisted, and Corbett left.

Corbett's Patriotism—A Church Trouble.

In the earlier stages of the Rebellion Corbett took strong ground in favor of maintaining the national authority. He thought it right to shoot traitors wherever they could be found. Some female members of the church with whom he associated differed from him as to the propriety of such language; besides, they did not think it right to kill under any circumstances, and a charge was made against him, though in an indefinite form, of having done that which was "inconsistent" with Christianity. When he inquired for particulars, he was aswered that he had announced his willingness to "shoot men like dogs." He rejoined that the Rebels deserved just that; he would first say to them:—"God have mercy on your souls," and then "pop them off." Corbett has since declared that when shooting at a Rebel, he always makes such a prayer; and the accounts are to the effect that he repeated it before he killed Booth.

He Enters the Army and Re-enlists Without Bounty.

Corbett served with the Twelfth Regiment of this city when it took the field in 1861, and when it was captured he declined to give up his musket, saying that the Rebels should never have any of the Government property if he could prevent it. He hid his piece under a rock, and it was not found. Corbett afterwards enlisted in a three months' regiment, and finally entered the Sixteenth Cavalry. His friends say he refused to take the bounty, preferring to serve his country without any remuneration of that kind. It is unnecessary to recapitulate his military history. He conducted himself with singular bravery throughout. One incident will illustrate his character.

Corbett Rebukes his Colonel and is put in the Guard-house.

While Corbett was in the Twelfth regiment and was a private, his Colonel used profane language when on parade. Corbett stepped out of the ranks and reproved him, saying that he had violated military regulations and the laws of God, and he considered it his duty to reprimand him. Corbett then took a Bible out of his pocket and read the commandment, "Thou shalt not swear," &c. The result was that Corbett was ordered into the guard-house for punishment. He went cheerfully, declaring on the way that he had done only what was right, and that he was willing to accept what should come of it.

In the guard-house he sung psalms, disturbing the other prisoners. He was then directed by the officer in charge not to sing any more, but he would not obey, and did as he pleased. But it seems the Colonel was not willing to punish Corbett, and sent word to him by a captain that he should be liberated if he would say he was sorry. Corbett replied that he would do no such thing. He told the captain, however, to say he had only offended the colonel, and the colonel had offended God; and he would never ask the colonel's pardon till that officer should himself ask pardon for his sin. Corbett was soon after released unconditionally.

From Baltimore.

Special Despatch to the Inquirer.

BALTIMORE, May 4.—Minute guns were fired to-day, from noon until sunset, commemorating the late President Lincoln's final interment at Springfield. The booming cannon and the sad occasion caused a general gloom which seemed to impress all hearts.

The Eleventh Indiana, General Wallace's celebrated old regiment, was reviewed to-day in front of his head-quarters, by the General, and it was an imposing occasion.

It is supposed now, since the final burial of the late President, all draperies will be removed from the buildings this week. No one seems disposed to be the first to move in the matter.

From Canada.

MONTREAL, May 4.—Beverly Tucker, for whom a reward of twenty-five thousand dollars has been offered by the United States Government, publishes a letter, saying that whoever asserts that he had anything to do with the assassination or knowledge of the plot to capture Lincoln or Seward, blackens his soul with perjury. He never heard of Booth or any of the others arrested, before the examination, and he was not here when Booth was. He has sent for a copy of the evidence so as to disprove it.

Sanders is still residing here.

Surrender of Another Rebel Force.

MEMPHIS, May 3, via CAIRO, May 4.—Jeff. Thompson surrendered his entire army yesterday to Captain Mitchell.

The Constitutional Amendment Passed in Connecticut.

HARTFORD, Conn., May 4.—The Constitutional Amendment was unanimously passed by both branches of the Connecticut Legislature this evening.

THE INTERMENT OF PRESIDENT LINCOLN.

SPRINGFIELD, Ill., May 8, 1865.—About noon the remains of President Lincoln were brought from the State House, and placed in the hearse. The funeral procession was under Major-General Hooker, Marshal-in-Chief, and Brigadier-Generals Cook and Oaks. The military and firemen appeared finely, and the guard of honor was the same as during the entire route. The procession, including the Governors of seven States, members of Congress, State and municipal authorities, delegations from adjoining States, Free Masons, Odd Fellows and citizens, including colored persons arrived at Oak Ridge Cemetery at one o'clock. On the left of the vault in which the remains were deposited immediately on their arrival was a platform, on which singers and an instrumental band performed appropriate music. On the right was the speaker's stand.

The vault is at the foot of a knoll, in a beautiful part of the ground, which contains forest trees of all kinds. It has a doric gable resting on pilasters, the main wall being rustic in style. The vault is fifteen feet high, and about the same in width, with semicircular wings of brick projecting from the hill side. The material is limestone, procured at Joliet, Illinois. Directly inside of the ponderous doors is an iron grating. The interior walls are covered with black velvet, dotted with evergreens. In the centre of the velvet is a foundation of brick-work, capped with a marble slab, on which the coffin rests. The front of the vault is trimmed with evergreens.

The dead march in Saul was sung, accompanied by the band, as the remains were deposited.

Thousands of persons assembled at the cemetery before the arrival of the procession, and the scene was one of most intense solemnity. The religious exercises were commenced by the singing of a dirge. Then followed the reading of appropriate portions of Scripture and a prayer. After a hymn sung by the choir, the Rev. Mr. Hebbans read the last inaugural of President Lincoln. Another dirge was sung by the choir, when Bishop Simpson delivered a funeral address, which was in the highest degree solemn and patriotic, and portions of it were applauded. Another dirge and a hymn followed, when the benediction was pronounced by the Rev. Dr. Gurley. The procession then reformed and returned to the city.

Our mournful duty of escorting the mortal remains of Abraham Lincoln hither is performed. We have seen them deposited in the tomb. Bereaved friends, with subdued and grief-stricken hearts, have taken their adieu, and now turn their faces homeward, ever to remember the affecting and impressive scenes which they have witnessed. The injunction, so often repeated on the way, "Bear him gently to his rest," has been obeyed, and the great heart of the nation throbs heavily at the portals of the tomb.

WASHINGTON.

[SPECIAL DESPATCHES TO THE INQUIRER.]

WASHINGTON, May 4.

Respect for the Memory of the Late President.

The closing of all the Departments to-day at noon, in respect to the memory of the late President, gives the city the appearance of Sabbath. At sunset salutes were fired from all the fortifications around the city, and bells were tolled.

The Conspirators

And accomplices of Booth are now confined in what was formerly the old Penitentiary Building, situated at the junction of the Eastern Branch of the Potomac or Anacosta and the Potomac, and adjoining the Arsenal. At the commencement of the Rebellion those convicts in prison were sent to Albany, and those convicted of serious offenses were also sent there, while the Baltimore House of Correction was used for juvenile offenders. Mrs. Surratt and sixteen leading male conspirators are now confined there, hand-cuffed, closely guarded and forbidden intercourse with one another, or with outsiders.

The confession of Harold, and the documentary evidence found on Booth's body, fastens, beyond cavil, the plot and its full sanction upon Jeff. Davis and his Canada commissioners. A building is now being fitted up at the arsenal for their trial. The whole point of land known as the Washington Arsenal is under a strong military guard. The Board for the trial will be completed to-night or to-morrow and announced. It has been determined to push the trial rapidly through. The Court will sit early and late.

Six stenographers will be on hand to take down testimony and write it out the same day. It has not yet been determined whether it will be open or not, but the present probability is that it will.

It is a rather noteworthy fact that no lawyer has yet been found degraded enough to offer his services in behalf of these criminals.

An Evil to be Remedied.

Remonstrances against making the whole North a botany bay for Southern criminals in the guise of paroled and repentant traitors, have been pouring in for some time. Washington is becoming so infested with them that measures are being taken by the loyal citizens here to remedy the evil. A mass meeting is called for by a hundred of the leading Unionists here, the call setting forth:—"The armed forces of the Rebellion have been almost entirely overthrown. The enmity of many of its leaders and adherents is, however, undiminished. Not a few of them were, at its commencement, residents of the District and immediately adjacent parts of Maryland and Virginia. It has been ascertained that a considerable number of them will attempt to return or have returned to their former residences and claim the rights and privileges of loyal citizens. This should be prevented. The Government has so determined. It is in the power of those who have been faithful to that Government during its four years of peril and convulsion to greatly aid in the carrying out of this determination. The best plan of doing so should be a matter of consultation and deliberation.

"Many loyal citizens are of opinion that the former residents of the District who have participated in the Rebellion should not be permitted to return, or remain within its limits or in its vicinity, and that those who have approved of their treasonable acts and desire future association with them should be rewarded as partakers of their guilt. The hours for both words and deeds have arrived. A public mass meeting will be held in front of the City Hall on Tuesday evening, 9th instant, at 8 o'clock, at which resolutions will be presented, able speeches will be delivered and committees appointed.

"Citizens of the District of Columbia! appear at the appointed meeting and proclaim, as others have done, that men who have willingly endeavored to destroy the Government can have no home in the Capital of the nation. Patriotism, as well as our own safety and peace, call for the proposed action."

The recent meeting held in Philadelphia to tender work and homes to these outcast felons was taken advantage of by them to lay a plot to burn the entire city. It was fortunately discovered in time. But people here and in Baltimore have determined that if Philadelphia will court the favor of such men, they shall not rest here. The Secretary of War has forbid the giving of free transportation to these men by army officers.

Arrival of Colored Troops from the Front.

The Twenty-fourth United States Colored Troops arrived here to-day, from the front, and marched along the avenue and attracted general admiration for their soldierly bearing.

Bids for Flour.

Bids were opened to-day for flour, amounting to about 25,000 barrels, offered at rates ranging from $8·50 to $9·50 per barrel.

While the troops are in this vicinity they will be furnished with fresh bread.

Reducing the Number of Naval Officers.

The process of reducing the number of Naval officers is going on rapidly. Those asking for furloughs are given discharges.

[DESPATCHES TO THE ASSOCIATED PRESS.]

The Funeral Ceremonies.

By order of the President all the public buildings were closed after 12 o'clock to-day, out of respect to the late President, whose final funeral obsequies were in progress at Springfield. The Courts also adjourned and all the municipal offices were closed. Many of our citizens closed their stores a portion of the day. Half hour guns were fired during the latter portion of the day, closing with a national salute at sundown.

By order of the Secretary of War, the War Department and all its Bureaus was closed at twelve o'clock, and will continue so throughout the remainder of the day, in respect to the memory of President Lincoln. Minute guns are to be fired every half hour at the Arsenal, closing at sundown with a national salute.

The Condition of Secretary Seward and His Son.

WASHINGTON, May 4, 1865—9 A. M.—Hon. E. M. Stanton, Secretary of War—Sir:—I have the honor to report that the Secretary of State passed a restless night, but his strength has not been affected by it.

Mr. F. Seward continues to gain slowly, and pronounces himself much better.

Very respectfully, J. K. BARNES,
Surgeon-General.

WASHINGTON, May 4, 9 P. M.—Hon. E. M. Stanton, Secretary of War—Sir:—I have the honor to report that the condition of the Secretary of State and of Mr. F. Seward is quite as favorable as at the last report.

Very respectfully, J. K. BARNES,
Surgeon-General.

Sherman on His Way to Washington.

General Sherman was at Point Lookout yesterday, on his way to Washington.

Return of the Army of the Potomac.

The principal portion of the Army of the Potomac is already on the march here.

Contract for Flour.

Bids were opened here yesterday for furnishing the Subsistence Department with flour. 24,800 barrels were offered at prices ranging from $8·50 to $9·50 per barrel. All the flour offered was

Continued on the Eighth Page.

BE CAREFUL TO OPEN THIS PAPER BEFORE CUTTING IT.

FRANK LESLIE'S ILLUSTRATED NEWSPAPER

Entered according to the Act of Congress in the year 1864, by Frank Leslie, in the Clerk's Office of the District Court for the Southern District of New York.

No. 501—Vol. XX.] NEW YORK, MAY 6, 1865. [Price 10 Cents. $4 00 Yearly. 13 Weeks $1 00.

Alas, Sherman!

Among the men whom the nation delighted (and still delights) to honor was and is Gen. Sherman, the brilliant Marshal of the calm, inflexible and trenchant Grant—whose wide generosity has always overflowed towards his subordinates, and is as grand as his own subordination to the lawful authorities of the country is conspicuous. As Lieutenant-General of the armies of the United States, he held parliamentary intercourse with the General commanding the forces of the rebellion, but he did so in the purest military sense. He never undertook to compromise the nation. He frankly told the chief in arms of the most gigantic Treason the world ever saw, that he had no office beyond that of soldier in the field. He undertook no adjustment of questions outside of the soldier's province. He said in words that will live among the most memorable in History, when proposing terms of capitulation to Lee, "I regard it as my duty to shift from myself the responsibility of any further effusion of blood, by asking you to surrender." He revolved within his own sphere. He did precisely what was within his duty and authority to do. He did not undertake to dictate, even by implication, the policy of the country, but told the subtle rebel commander, who vainly sought to entrap his liberal and generous spirit, by making the surrender of his army the condition of amnesty to traitors, that "the terms upon which peace could be had were well understood," and these were "by laying down their arms" and submitting to the authority of the nation. Mark: the first General of the United States was then dealing with the first General of the rebellion; in a military sense these were the two pre-eminent men in this terrible conflict. Grant acted purely within his line of duty and scope of power.

But what happens now? A Lieutenant subordinate, a brilliant and justly succe ful General within his range of duty, but who had nothing more to do with the planning of the great campaign that has terminated successfully than dozens of others, has undertaken to settle all the great questions to which that struggle has given rise. Neither Heaven or earth ever witnessed a presumption equal to this! What authority or right had Johnston, the wretched, hundred-times beaten Johnston, who had not a single soldier ready or willing to use arms in support of a fallen cause, and who himself could not count upon a dozen followers to help save him from a well-earned

ASSASSINATION OF PRESIDENT LINCOLN—THE MURDERER LEAPING UPON THE STAGE, AND CATCHING HIS SPUR IN THE FLAG WHICH HUNG BEFORE THE PRESIDENT'S BOX.—FROM A SKETCH BY OUR SPECIAL ARTIST, ALBERT BERGHAUS.

The Philadelphia Inquirer.

PRICE TWO CENTS. PHILADELPHIA, WEDNESDAY, MAY 10, 1865. PRICE TWO CENTS.

PEACE!

HIGHLY IMPORTANT PROCLAMATION OF THE PRESIDENT.

HOSTILITIES DECLARED AT AN END!

Restoration of the Federal Authority Throughout the Land.

THE DEPARTMENTS TO RESUME THEIR FUNCTIONS.

OUTLAWRY OF THE REBEL CRUISERS.

THEY ARE TO BE TRIED AND HUNG AS PIRATES.

SUBMISSION OR DEATH THE ALTERNATIVES.

TRIAL OF THE ASSASSINS!

THE SESSIONS TO BE SECRET.

OFFICIAL ORDER OF THE PRESIDENT.

ORGANIZATION OF THE MILITARY COURT.

The Last Rebel Chief Caves In.

DICK TAYLOR SURRENDERS HIS ENTIRE ARMY!

OFFICIAL DESPATCHES FROM GEN. WILSON.

JEFF. DAVIS' ESCAPE IMPOSSIBLE.

IMPORTANT PROCLAMATION BY THE PRESIDENT

WASHINGTON, May 9.—President Johnson has issued a proclamation declaring that

Whereas, Armed resistance to the authority of this Government in certain States heretofore declared to be in insurrection *may be regarded as virtually at an end*, and the persons by whom that resistance, as well as the operations of insurgent cruisers were directed, are fugitives or captives;

And whereas, it is understood that some of these cruisers are still infesting the high seas, and others are preparing to capture, burn and destroy vessels of the United States;

The President enjoins all naval, military and civil officers of the United States diligently to endeavor by all lawful means to arrest the said cruisers and to bring them into a port of the United States, in order that they may be prevented from committing further depredations on commerce, and that the persons on board of them may no longer enjoy impunity for their crimes.

And he further proclaims and declares that if, after a reasonable time shall have elapsed for this proclamation to become known in the ports of nations claiming to have been neutrals, the said insurgent cruisers and the persons on board of them, shall continue to receive hospitality in the said port, the Government will deem itself justified in refusing hospitality to the public vessels of such nations in the ports of the United States, and in adopting such measures as may be deemed advisable towards vindicating the national sovereignty.

Virginia.

The President has also issued an Executive order to re-establish the authority of the United States, and execute the laws within the geographical limits known as the State of Virginia.

It is ordered that all acts and proceedings of the political, military, and civil organizations which have been in a state of insurrection and Rebellion within the State of Virginia against the authority and laws of the United States, and of which Jefferson Davis, John Letcher, and William Smith were late the respective chiefs, are declared null and void.

All persons who shall exercise, claim, pretend or attempt to exercise any political, military or civil power, authority, jurisdiction or right by, through or under Jefferson Davis, late of the city of Richmond, and his confederates, or under John Letcher or William Smith and their confederates, or under any pretended political, military or civil commission or authority issued by them or of them since the 17th day of April, 1861, shall be deemed and taken as in rebellion against the United States, and shall be dealt with accordingly.

The Secretaries of the State, War, Treasury, Navy and the Interior Departments, and the Postmaster-General are ordered to proceed to put in force all the laws of the United States pertaining to their several departments, and the District Judge of such district to proceed to hold courts within the said State, in accordance with the provisions of the acts of Congress.

The Attorney-General will instruct the proper officers to libel and bring to judgment, confiscation and sale, the property subject to confiscation, and enforce the administration of justice within said State, in all matters, civil and criminal, within the cognizance of the Federal Courts; to carry into effect the guaranty of the Federal Constitution, of a Republican form of State Government, and afford the advantage and security of domestic laws, as well as to complete the re-establishment of the authority of the laws of the United States, and the full and complete restoration of peace within the limits aforesaid.

Francis A. Pierepoint, Governor of the State of Virginia, will be aided by the Federal Government, so far as may be necessary, in the lawful measures which he may take for the extension and administration of the State Government throughout the geographical limits of the said State.

FROM WASHINGTON.

[SPECIAL DESPATCHES TO THE "INQUIRER."]

WASHINGTON, May 8, 1865.

Trial of the Conspirators.

The Court for the trial of the conspirators again assembled this morning in the Penitentiary. The Court was full, and after some customary preliminary formalities, adjourned. To-morrow the arraignment of one or more of the prisoners will take place and witnesses will at once be called.

All the rooms formerly occupied by the Warden are now fitted up for the convenience of the Court and official reporters. Bedding has been furnished, and they will remain there, night and day, until the case is completed. Major-General Hartranft, of Pennsylvania, is in command of the jail, and not Hartsuff, as the telegraph made me say to-day.

The Proceedings to be Secret.

The statement made in several papers that the Court would sit with open doors, is incorrect. It has been the intention for several days to have nothing divulged as the trial progresses.

Official Opinion of the Attorney-General

While the subject of the trial was under discussion at the Cabinet meeting, Attorney-General Speed presented a written opinion upon the subject of military and civil trials. He considers that the President was *de facto* as well as *de jure* Commander-in-chief of the Army and Navy in time of war; the crime was committed at a military post, garrisoned and under the command of a military governor.

He also thought that the Court should not be open to spectators, as there is a very large number of witnesses to be examined, and none should know what the others have testified to, which could not be prevented if the papers published the entire testimony. The examination of all the witnesses is far from being as thorough as it will be in Court where much additional light is expected to be thrown upon the conspiracy as it progresses.

More Arrests.

Additional arrests continue to be made. Captain S. D. Franklin arrested S. Donaldson, who is involved in both the conspiracy and the plot to burn Philadelphia. He has been committed to the Old Capitol.

Mrs. Surratt.

Mrs. Surratt, who is in irons, bears up better than most of the men.

She, it will be remembered, was the leading spirit next to Booth, and when the determination was arrived at to murder the late President Lincoln that particular night, she went around to inform the others, and passed down into Maryland to see that the stopping places were all in order for Booth and Harold, in their flight. Her husband is dead.

Her son, John Surratt, was to have murdered the Secretary of War, but left before the hour, and passed North *en route* to Canada, going via Springfield, Mass. Her two daughters were not put in prison, and one of them, Annie, is said to be very sick. Rumor says dying. It does not seem possible for Mrs. Surratt to escape the gallows at an early day.

She is about fifty to fifty-five years old, though she does not appear to be over forty-five. She is large in form; very stout; has a keen grey eye; a resolute look; rather ugly; has light hair, and any man would set her down at once for a perfect virago. Her two daughters are not believed to have been cognizant of the conspiracy, and will be put upon the witness stand.

Arnold's Story.

Sam Arnold (who was arrested at Fortress Monroe) as well as other witnesses state that one plan was to capture Mr. Lincoln some night between the War Department and White House, where he was accustomed to go alone late at night. He was then to be hurried down through the garden of the White House, thence to what is known as the old Van Ness house on Seventeenth street, near the confluence of Tyber and Potomac Rivers.

This house is built near the old homestead of David Burns, a Scotchman, whose plantation embraced about one-third of Washington City. He grew rich from the sales of land. About the year 1820 General Van Ness built a house on the old homestead. It is a large brick commodious house, two stories and a half high. The partition walls all run to the same depth as cellar walls. At some subsequent period the cellars made by these walls were dug out, and one of them has a trap door going down through the floor, and was formerly used for a wine cellar. Another was used for a slave prison, and still another for an ice house.

On the death of Vanness, fifteen years ago, it was sold to one Thomas Green, who owned the Warrenton Springs in Virginia. Green's sons are all in the Rebel army, and he has of late years used his house as a rendezvous for these conspirators.

A Diabolical Plan.

Had they been able to have gotten Mr. Lincoln across the Potomac and into Moseby's hands, all well. But if not then he could have been secreted in this house.

There is about two acres around the house filled with high trees and close shrubbery, with a high brick wall along the street, shutting the house from the street, and any cries from it would be effectually drowned long before reaching the street. Both Green and his wife are now in the Old Capitol, and the Veteran Reserves now stand guard around the building, and no one can enter the inclosure without a pass from the Secretary of War.

Several times since the war broke out has this house been an object of suspicion, and several arrests have been made there, but not until the late murder were the secret vaults and passages found and the infernal character of the den ascertained.

Davis & Co. Photographed and Advertised.

Colonel L. C. Baker has had photographs of Davis, Tucker, Clay, Sanders, Cleary and Thompson, with full descriptions of their stature, hair, eyes, &c., prepared on large handbills, stating the price set upon the heads of each one, and their crime, of being accessories to the assassination.

These handbills, similar to the rewards offered for horse thieves, will be posted through Canada and Europe, so that these criminals, should they be allowed to escape via Halifax, will be tracked wherever they go and marked forever. There is no sequestered spot for them. No rest for them in this world.

The Harris Court-martial.

The Court-martial, of which Major-General John S. Foster is President, and Major Winthrop is Judge Advocate, resumed the case of Benjamin G. Harris this morning, upon the charge of violating the fifty-sixth article of war in harboring two Rebel soldiers, Chapman and Read, on the night of the 26th of April.

Aloysius Fenwick was sworn for the defense, and testified that he lives about a mile and a-half from Leonardtown, and that the accused resides half way between his place and the town; on the night of the 26th two men applied for accommodations, which he declined to give; they told him they were paroled prisoners from Lee's army, and one showed his parole; the other Read, stating that he had lost his in crossing the Potomac.

Witness told them they might stay in his barn. He did not receive any money from them. The men left his door and went out into the road through the gate about seventy-five yards distant. As it was dark he did not see which direction they took after reaching the road. He thought they staid all night in his barn, which was on the road towards Leonardtown, but did not know. He could not tell where the men went after they left him; he had known the accused about fifteen years; was one of his constituents, and voted for him in the last Congressional election; he had taken the oath of allegiance prescribed by the constitution of Maryland.

He was then cross-examined by the Judge-Advocate—He had known Harris for some years; is an old friend of Harris.

Question—Did you vote for Harris at the last election?

Objected to by Harris on the ground that it had nothing to do with the case.

The Judge Advocate stated he had a perfect right to show that the witness was friendly to Harris and biased towards him. The Court overruled the objection of Harris and allowed the question to be asked. Witness answered he did vote for Harris at the last election. Witness did not keep a hotel; did not furnish the men with lodgings or accommodations whatever.

Give the entire conversation that occurred between you and the two men on the subject of lodging.

The men asked me if I could accommodate them; I told them I could not. I asked them where they were from, and how long they had been in Virginia.

Question—Where did the men go when they left your house?

Answer—I cannot say, sir.

Question—That is not an answer.

Answer—I don't know where they went; of my own knowledge I can say where I think they went.

Objected to by Harris on the ground that witness could not tell anything only what he knew.

Question—Did you not tell the men they might stay on some part of your premises?

Answer—I told them they might go in my barn; they did not pay me any money.

Question by Mr. Harris—Did you not when you voted for me take the oath prescribed by the constitution of Maryland?

Answer—I did, sir.

Question by the Court—State to the best of your knowledge and belief where the men went when they left your house.

Answer—I think they went in my barn.

The accused said he had no other witness, and asked the Court to adjourn until Thursday morning, to allow him time to prepare his defense.

The Judge Advocate introduced as testimony the order of Lieutenant-General Grant to Major-General Ord, commanding the Department of Virginia, dated April 18th, 19th and 20th, directing that paroled prisoners should not be given transportation, that those at Fortress Monroe should be returned to Richmond, and that none should be permitted to enter our lines except they surrender their parole and become prisoners of war, or become citizens by conforming to the terms of amnesty.

The accused presented a formal objection to the introduction of the orders, and upon being asked his grounds for the objection, stated he had no specific reasons, but objected upon general grounds. The Judge Advocate declined to entertain the objection, for the reason that it was evidently intended only for outside effect.

A member of the Court regarded it as trifling with the Court, and the accused finally explained that he would make the objection upon general grounds, subject to other objections. At the request of the accused, in order to afford time for the preparation of the argument for the defense, the Court adjourned till Thursday morning, at eleven o'clock.

Communication with the Southern States.

Since it has been already published, it may no longer be deemed improper to state that for some time the War Department have been in communication by telegraph with the Southern States down into the heart of Georgia, via Raleigh down to Macon.

Another Big Reward for Davis.

From the latter point General Wilson telegraphs that previous to getting the official despatch offering a reward of a hundred thousand dollars for Jeff. Davis, he had put a price of one hundred thousand dollars in gold on him, to be taken from the gold carried by these fugitives. This makes nearly a *quarter of million in green-backs upon him.*

Jeff.'s Movements.

On May 3d, or the evening of the 4th, he passed through Washington, accompanied by only six men, said to be John C. Breckinridge, James H. Reagan, G. A. Trenholm, J. P. Benjamin and two others unknown. His plunder was twelve hours in his rear, and the cavalry who set out with him had nearly one-half deserted. He was pushing for the Mississippi, and feared capture at every moment. Wilson says he had his scouts upon every road, and *felt pretty certain of capturing him.*

He found the people remarkably willing to aid him in the pursuit. He had no more trouble than if he were passing through our own territory. Hourly intelligence from that region is expected. It is hardly possible that he can escape.

The Pennsylvania Troops.

The War Department have concluded that the Pennsylvania regiments shall be sent home to be mustered out. They will not be paid off here. Governor Curtin and General Reynolds left here to-night.

They secured an order for the One-hundred-and-eighty-sixth and One-hundred-and-eighty-seventh Regiments to be placed on duty along the border, and as many more troops as are needed will be added. They will be stationed along the border at Bedford, Hancock, Greencastle, &c. This precaution is taken to prevent guerrillas from burning barns and plundering the farmers, &c.

Reduction of Naval Expenses.

In order that the expenses of the Government may be reduced as much as possible, and the necessity for keeping so many vessels employed on the Potomoc flotillas, the vessels of which have for some months patrolled. Commander Parker has, in compliance with an order of the Department, reduced the number of vessels to be hereafter employed in the flotilla to about one half.

Those not yet ordered to go out of commission are, it is said, the following:—*Don*, flag-ship, *Delaware, Banshee, Stepping Stone, Commodore Read, Curritue, Wyandank*, store-ship, *Adelia, Ella*, despatch boat, *Heliotrope, Primrose, Perriwinkle, Little Ada, Moccasin, Nansemond, Picket Launch, No. 4, Rescue, Verbena, and Picket Launch, No. 6*, numbering twenty in all. It is expected that the vessels to go out of commission will commence to arrive at the yard shortly, and probably the most of them will be sold there.

[DESPATCHES TO THE ASSOCIATED PRESS.]

The Trial of the Assassins—The Counsel for the Accused.

The Court for the trial of the conspirators concerned in the assassination of President Lincoln, and the attempted assassination of Secretary Seward, convened to-day *pro forma*, to arrange the rules and mode of proceeding in said court. It is not yet determined whether the proceedings shall be made public as the trial progresses.

The prisoners, David E. Harold, George A. Atzeroth, Lewis Payne, Samuel B. Arnold, Michael McLaughlin, Samuel Mudd and Mrs. M. S. Surratt, on being brought before the Military Commission, to-day, were asked whom they desired to select as counsel, when they named the following gentlemen:—

Harold—Messrs. Fred. Stone, Jos. H. Bradley and Jas. M. Carlisle. Payne—Mr. Mason Campbell, of Baltimore. Mrs. Surratt—Hon. Reverdy Johnson and Mr. Wm. Wallace Kirby. Dr. Mudd—Mr. Robert James Brent, of Baltimore. The other prisoners did not name counsel.

The following order was read:—

EXECUTIVE CHAMBER, WASHINGTON CITY, May 1st, 1865.—*Whereas*, The Attorney-General of the United States hath given his opinion that the persons implicated in the murder of the late President, Abraham Lincoln, and the attempted assassination of the Honorable William H. Seward, Secretary of State, and in an alleged conspiracy to assassinate other officers of the Federal Government at Washington City, and their aiders and abettors, are subject to the jurisdiction of and legally liable before a Military Commission,

It is ordered:—

First. That the Assistant Adjutant-General detail nine competent military officers to serve as a Commission for the trial of said parties, and that the Judge Advocate-General proceed to prefer charges against the said parties for their alleged offenses, and bring them to trial before the said Military Commission.

That the said trial or trials be conducted by the said Judge Advocate-General, and, as recorded thereof, in person, aided by such Assistant or Special Judge Advocates, as he may designate; and that the said trials be conducted with all diligence consistent with the ends of justice, and said Commission to sit without regard to hours.

Second. That Brevet Major-General Hartranft be assigned to duty as special Provost Marshal-General, for the purposes of said trial, and attendance upon the said commission, and the execution of its mandates.

Third. That the said Commission establish such order or rules of proceeding as may avoid unnecessary delay, and conduce to the ends of public justice. ANDREW JOHNSON,

Adjutant-General's office, Washington, D. C., May 6th, 1865.

(Official copy) W. A. NICHOLS,
Assistant Adjutant-General.

John A. Bingham, of Ohio, and Brevet Colonel Burnett, were then introduced to the Court as Assistant Judge Advocates, for the trial of the case designated under the order of the President.

The Court then adjourned until ten o'clock to-morrow, to allow the prisoners an opportunity of retaining counsel, and of conferring with them.

Indignation Meeting in Washington.

A public meeting of about fifteen hundred persons was held in front of the City Hall to-night, at which speeches were made and resolutions passed having in view the prevention of the returning or remaining within the limits of the District of Columbia of its former residents who have participated in the Rebellion. The ground is taken that the men who have wilfully endeavored to destroy the Government can have no home in the Capital of the Nation.

Reduction of Army Officers.

An order has been issued from the Adjutant-General's office for reducing the number of company and staff officers of volunteer regiments. It says:—"By direction of the President all company and staff officers of volunteer regiments absent from their commands on account of physical disability, or by virtue of leaves of absence granted them on their return to loyal States as prisoners of war, will be honorably mustered out of the service of the United States on the 15th inst. Said officers will immediately apply by letter to the Adjutant-General of the army for their muster out and discharge papers.

"In case of physical disability from disease or wounds, the letter must be accompanied by a medical certificate of the usual form. The post office address of the officer must be given with care in all cases."

Resignations of Officers.

Many officers are sending in their resignations to the War Department, and all are promptly accepted. The number of Generals whose resignations have been accepted up to this morning amount to thirteen. Orders have been issued from the War Department directing the dismissal of a large number of the citizen clerks in the Quartermaster's Department, and the substitution of enlisted men.

Extension of the Goodyear Rubber Patent.

On the application of Henry B. Goodyear, Administrator of the estate of Nelson Goodyear, the Commissioner of Patents has extended the patent for seven years of Nelson Goodyear, for the invention of hard rubber, the reissue being in two divisions. The invention in this case consists in preparing from the gum commonly known as India rubber, a new material to be used in the place of horn, whalebone, wood, ivory or similar substances. It is called hard rubber. The extension was opposed by Horace G. Day, but it was granted on the ground of the novelty and utility of the invention, its value and importance to the public, and because the inventor was not adequately remunerated, for no want of diligence on his part.

An extension was also granted, to-day, to Edward Hamilton, of Chicago, for his car ventilator and duster.

Rebels Not Allowed to Return to Washington.

A resolution was introduced in the City Councils last night, admonishing and warning those men who left their homes in this city at the commencement of the Rebellion, and openly defied the National Government, and engaged in their horrid work of treason, that their return at this time would be exceedingly repugnant to the loyal citizens of Washington, and would be regarded as an act unproductive of good, but fraught with much harm. This resolution caused an exciting debate of a personal character.

A public meeting is called for to-night, to prevent Rebels from returning to Washington. Quite a large number are already here.

Internal Revenue Decision.

The Commissioner of Internal Revenue has decided that losses in merchandise can be deducted only from gains on merchandise, but in this case particular brands of merchandise need not be repeated. So in speculations; the loss or gain from stocks may affect the loss or gain from produce speculated in.

Rejoicings in Bremen.

The State Department has received the following translation of an extract from the proceedings of the Legislative Body of the free city of Bremen:—

"SESSION OF THE LEGISLATIVE BODY, Wednesday, April 19, 1865.—At the opening of the session, the President Judge, F. A. Meyer, addressed the assembly as follows:—

"Before we begin to transact our regular business, let us remember the joyful and most important news which has arrived in these last days from the other side of the Atlantic ocean. Let us remember and enjoy the great victory won by the armies of the Union over the Rebellion of the slaveholders. Bremen is, and has always been, in the most intimate connection with the United States. Many of our sons are fighting in the ranks of the Federal army, and the men of freedom and the Germans have shown that persistency and valor must finally conquer victory, even over the infuriated struggling elements of the enemy. Gentlemen, let us show our sympathy with the American Union by rising from our seats."

The entire assembly arose and gave enthusiastic cheers for the American Union and for the victory of the just cause.

From Nashville.

NASHVILLE, May 8.—Brokers and bankers are cautioned against buying vouchers audited here by Captain Charles F. Wing, A. Q. M., as large amounts were captured by guerrillas in the recent raid on the Ohio and Mississippi Railroad, on the 6th inst.

Captain James F. Rusling, Chief Quartermaster of the Department of Cumberland, has been promoted to the rank of Colonel and Inspector of Quartermasters of this Department.

THE UNION ARMIES HOMEWARD BOUND.

Special Despatch to the Inquirer.

PETERSBURG, May 6, by Telegraph, via Washington, May 9th.

The Fifteenth Corps.

The Fifteenth Corps will encamp around Petersburg to-night.

Sherman's Army.

General Sherman's army left Neuse River near Raleigh, on Monday, May 1st.

Army of the Tennessee.

The Army of the Tennessee, Major-General O. O. Howard, commanding, passed northward through Louisburg, Warrenton, Lawrenceville, and Dinwiddie Court House.

Slocum's Army.

The Army of Georgia, Major-General Slocum commanding, passed far to the left, moving direct to Richmond via Appomattox Court House.

Orders respecting the conduct of troops toward the citizens were issued by both army and corps commanders. They were very strict and were faithfully observed. The flanks of the column were vigilantly patrolled; and all stragglers were arrested and reported to their superior officer for punishment. Foraging was conducted by commissioned officers, who were instructed to pay the highest market price for all supplies. A correspondent who came in the rear says:—

I traveled on the same road thirty miles in rear of the Fifteenth and Seventeenth Corps, whose "bumming" propensities were so notoriously developed in South Carolina, and found the citizens everywhere speaking in the most flattering terms of the conduct of the troops. The people generally are almost destitute of the plainest necessaries of life, and look forward with considerable anxiety to an early opportunity of exchanging the coveted greenbacks for food and raiment.

As I have found it in the past two-and-a-half years of experience in the South the poorer classes, the white laborers and the blacks, are in ecstacies over our success. The wealthy slave owners, the aristocrats, harbor still a bitter and undying hostility towards us. A great many of the prominent landholders on our line of march are anxious to sell their plantations at a sacrifice and quit the country.

A Good Speculation.

Colonel Ross, of General Logan's staff, purchased a fine plantation at a nominal price, of an aristocratic North Carolinian, who is preparing to expatriate himself. This class of people talk very hopefully of an early embroilment of our Government with foreign Powers, and declare that when that comes the subjugated malcontents of the South will rally again under the standards of our foes and thus realize their wild dream of a Southern Confederacy.

At Warrenton, and in Brunswick county, Va., we found the most inveterate and intolerable Rebels. The roads are lined with Rebel officers and soldiers, returning their homes. They are invariably more courteous than the stay-at-home aristocrats, who are sullen, and often insolent. The country we came through shows no marks of war's ravages, by which the soldiers account for the untamed pride and arrogance that characterizes the people.

Major-General John A. Logan's Fifteenth Corps has made the most remarkable march on record. Since leaving Raleigh the Corps marched one hundred and fifty-five miles in five and a half days, bridging three large streams, the Neuse, the Roanoke and the Nottoway.

CANBY.

HIGHLY IMPORTANT FROM NEW ORLEANS—SURRENDER OF DICK TAYLOR'S ARMY—ALL THE REBEL FORCES EAST OF THE MISSISSIPPI INCLUDED.

NEW ORLEANS, May 3, via Cairo, May 8.—General A. J. Smith, with his command, occupied Montgomery, Ala., on the 25th ult., and General Steel occupied Selma on the 27th.

On Sunday last General Canby met Dick Taylor fifteen miles from Mobile, and opened negotiations for the surrender of the Rebel forces. Nothing decisive was determined upon, but Taylor was allowed several days to consider the proposition. It is believed he has acceded to the terms before this, as he must have been influenced to that end by the surrender of Johnston.

An extensive land-slide, on the banks of the river at Algiers, took place last night, heavily damaging the shipyard of Vail & Connery, also that belonging to the Government.

Low middling cotton is quoted at 36c.; strictly ditto is held at 40c.

The cotton market is buoyant, with a reported advance.

The Surrender of Dick Taylor.

NEW YORK, May 9.—The *Times* has a Washington despatch, which says:—

Information was received at army head-quarters to-day, of the final and complete surrender of Dick Taylor's forces in Alabama and Mississippi to General Canby.

It is a remarkable fact that this news and other despatches from General Wilson were received by telegraph direct from Macon, Ga., to this city. General Wilson is still in Macon, and the telegraph lines through North and South Carolina and Georgia are intact. The escape of Davis is therefore next to impossible.

FROM NORTH CAROLINA.

DEMORALIZATION OF JOHNSTON'S ARMY—VINDICTIVENESS TOWARDS THEIR LEADERS—HATRED OF JEFF. DAVIS.

BALTIMORE, May 9.—A gentleman who has just arrived here from North Carolina reports that the Rebel troops surrendered by Johnston are greatly demoralized, and nearly beyond the control of their officers, who are striving to march them to their respective States. The officers have become the objects of intense hate, and it is as much as their lives are worth to venture away from the lines. Quite a number have been murdered by their soldiers, who seem to be tempted to murder them to get possession of the small sums of specie which the officers are understood to possess. The Rebel soldiers express intense feeling against Jeff. Davis and various members of his Cabinet, and there is no doubt that if he or any of the leaders of the Rebellion fall into their hands they will fare badly. At last accounts our cavalry were in vigorous pursuit of Jeff. Davis.

Missouri.

THE REBELS COMING IN—SURRENDER OF MORE OF THEIR TROOPS.

ST. LOUIS, May 8.—Major Cooper, with a Rebel battalion one hundred and fifty strong, surrendered to General Sandtown, at Springfield, Mo., on Saturday, and took the oath of allegiance.

Thirty of Price's men took the oath at Cassville yesterday, and considerable numbers are arriving from other points.

From Cairo.

CAIRO, Ill., May 8.—The steamer *Atlantic* brought nine hundred and eighty-five Rebel prisoners from New Orleans to Vicksburg.

Wm. Murphy, the notorious Rebel boat-burner, captured at New Orleans, was also brought up and taken to St. Louis, in charge of United States Detective Dunford.

FEDERAL UNION.

"The Federal Union—IT MUST AND SHALL BE PRESERVED!"—Jackson

SELMA, ALABAMA, WEDNESDAY, MAY 10, 1865.

PUBLISHED BY
NEELD & CANTLEY.

THE WAR OVER.—It has never fell to our lot as a journalist, says the Mobile News of the 6th inst., to publish more cheering and glorious news than is contained in our columns to-day. The war is over—theoretically, practically, literally. Four years of bitterness, darkness and bloodshed have dragged their slow length along, but at last the glorious, blessed sun of peace shines out, more bright, more blessed still, that it has so long been behind the gloom and darkness. Oh how the heart swells up and the utterance is almost choked for joy that the great, glad day has come at last when "men who last week were foes are talking in groups," mysteriously, affectionately, and the wife and the prattling child are once more clasped to the bosom of their husband and father, who shall henceforth take up the ploughshare for the sword, and "shall not learn war any more!"

Let no one who is a discreet friend to his country fail to attend the meeting of the citizens of Dallas county appointed for this day. The hour is a critical one, and the emergency great. Let passion and prejudice give way to wisdom, and all will be well.

The review of the troops which came off on Monday evening and reported to us as embracing the whole of the United States forces at this post, was merely that of a brigade. We understand that Gen. Andrews will review the 3d Brigade, Col. Moore commanding, at 5½ o'clock P. M. It will be an opportunity for our people to see some of the best infantry troops in the army.

By an awkward mischance items of news of too old a date crept into our issue of yesterday contradictory of the fact that Johnston had surrendered or that peace had been made east of the Chattahoochie or in this department. Intelligent readers who have watched the succession of events as officially reported, were not misled, we trust, while unobservants will rejoice none the less that peace, is now upon us without the slightest peradventure.

Cully of the 3d Brigade

Surrender of Gen. Dick Taylor and Com. Farrand.

Maj. Gen. Canby, accompanied by Gen. Osterhaus, his Chief of Staff, Brig. Gen. Andrews, Provost Marshal General, Col. Christensen, A. A. G., and Capts. Garrett and Perkins, A. D. C., left the city yesterday morning at 8.30 for Citronelle, for the purpose of completing the negotiation of the surrender of all the Confederate troops in the (late rebel) Department of East Louisiana, West Mississippi, Alabama and East Florida, under Lieut. Gen. R. Taylor, C. S. A.

Admiral Thacher, U. S. N., by invitation of Gen. Canby, was one of the party.

The steam train which had conveyed the parties to Whistler had to be left there, and the remainder of the route went over in a hand car, owing to a bridge having been destroyed over a stream near Eight Mile.

The hand-car was met some two miles from Citronelle by a train in charge of Capt. Bullock, of Gen. Taylor's staff, when a transfer of its passengers to the steam train was effected, which soon arrived at Citronelle.

In the house of Dr. Borden, where the conference was held, were found Gen. Taylor and staff, Commodore Farrand and Lieut. Commander Myers, of the navy, and a large concourse of other officers in the rebel service.

The utmost good feeling was manifested by the rebel officers towards the representatives of our Government, and Commodore Farrand and Lieut. Commander Myers seemed particularly pleased to meet again, after the lapse of so many years, their old friends of the navy.

The Confederate officers frankly expressed themselves fairly beaten, but no bitterness seemed to remain with them.

The most favorable opinion of the magnanimity of the United States Government pervaded the minds of all.

The opinion was freely expressed that should the United States become involved in a war with a foreign nation, she would find a large number of her late enemies side by side with her in the defence of the principles of our common country.

Gen. Taylor surrendered his army on the same terms as did Gen. Lee.

[Mobile News, 6th inst.

General News Items.

It is said that Johnston endeavored to have the pardon of Davis included in the terms of surrender, but the Lieutenant General declined.

Fifty thousand men are about to be dismissed from the service of the United States.

Edwin Booth has asked for the body of his brother, but has been refused. Its resting place is to remain a secret.

In a late interview with Gen. Lee, including his views upon State rights, he questioned the justice of holding the political leaders only to a strict accountability for the rebellion, saying that the acts of Davis were the acts of the whole people, and that he (Davis) was one of the last to give in his adhesion to secession.

Secretary Seward was so much better that he was able to ride on the 26th ult. His son also continues to improve.

A deplorable act of popular frenzy was the recent outrage upon the beautiful residence of ex-President Fillmore at Buffalo. He had neglected to drape his house in mourning weeds for the death of the President. The rabble smeared the face of the mansion with black ink. Mr. Fillmore is a Northern man and confessedly the purest of patriots.

The Government has forbid the arrival of any more paroled prisoners in Washington until the present excitement is allayed.

A speech of the new President, on accepting the nomination of the Vice-President, has been reproduced, in which appears the declaration that when peace is made Louis Napoleon's Mexican Empire would be taken in hand and driven back to the shores of Europe.

There is a rumor that Mr. Adams has demanded of the British Government the closing up of all her Majesty's ports to the further entrance of Confederate vessels.

Hon. F. N. Kellogg, of Michigan, has been appointed special Treasury Agent for the State of Alabama.

TELEGRAPHIC.

Interesting from the North.

NEW YORK, May 2, via MERIDIAN, May 9.

In view of the fact that the Confederate ram Stonewall is afloat and supposed to be making her way to this coast, the Government has made preparations for her reception by placing iron clads in our harbors. The Roanoke and other iron clads, besides a torpedo boat, are in readiness in this harbor.

The Herald's Washington special says Gen. Grant, on his return to Washington, set about making an arrangement for the contemplated heavy decrease of our military force and consequent reduction of Government expenses. It is thought the army will soon be reduced four hundred thousand men.

The Herald's correspondent says the Second Army Corps has exclusive charge of affairs in the vicinity of Burksville Junction, protecting the inhabitants from marauding bands of Lee's discharged men.

The Tribune's special says that Harrold has made a voluntary confession.

Gen. Grant is reported to have said that when he informed Sherman of the disapproval of the terms he had forwarded to Washington, the latter frankly admitted that he had made a mistake in not having it put in writing that slavery was dead, but that it was an understanding between them as to permitting the rebel Legislatures to assemble. He agreed to that because he had just learned that the Virginia Legislature was permitted to assemble by authority of the President, and in the absence of official instructions he interpreted the President's desire to be that the rebel civil governments should be retained for the preservation of order and to avoid maintaining a military force in those States, as well as to do away with the irritation likely to grow out of a military government. As to the amnesty it was only to cover officers and soldiers. When his attention was called to the wording, he replied with much spirit "that does not express the understanding between us."

We have been favored by Rev. Mr. Chittenden, Chaplain of the 24th Indiana, for papers of a late date, for which he has our heartfelt thanks.

We are under lasting obligations to Mr. Wm. Stitt, mail agent of the 2d Division, 13th Army Corps, for late New Orleans and Mobile papers.

Mr. P. Marchand, clerk of the steamer Tarascon, will also accept our thanks for similar favors.

Paroled men from Johnston's army are passing in squads through Selma almost daily. They are toilworn but glad enough that the war is over.

There are many "darkies" who have the opinion that their freedom, as vouchsafed by the United States, will justify them in kicking up their heels and sleeping in the sunshine, just as the humor may prompt them. Poor creatures they have revelled in this delusion until yesterday. They are now at work upon the streets.

The Boston papers publish a letter from Edwin Booth (brother to the assassin) to the manager of the Boston theatre relative to the suspension of his engagement. The letter closed as follows: "While mourning in common with all other loyal hearts the death of the President, I am oppressed by private woe not to be expressed in words. But whatever calamity may befall me or mine, my country, one and indivisible, has my warmest devotion."

The Rev. Dr. Dix, of Trinity, says Booth may live in the South for years without being detected, but justice will find him sooner or later. The Doctor does not believe the crime was instigated by the Southern people. Southern civilisation, he thinks, has a higher tone and better spirit than to countenance such an act of infamy.

The grand jury at Toronto, Canada, have found bills of indictment against J. Thompson, C. C. Clay, Wm. Lawrence, W. H. Cleany, McDonald and Bennet Young, for breach of neutrality laws.

Selma Alabama
May the 10th /65

Brother Ruben,

Your interesting Sheet of April 10th was received yesterday and perused with A great deal of interest;
Glad to hear that you are getting along so fine. But feel sorry to learn of the death of little Jacob Hess. I was in hopes that he would recover. I suppose David and Mary will take it very hard. But such are the ways of this world.
Myself and all the friends in the Regiment are enjoying the best of health.
The boys are all Speculating on the prospects of returning home soon. By the present appearance of things I think you can count on me as A harvest hand this summer.
You state that Dalton got drunk when they heard of the fall of Richmond. Now this will do very well for once but they should not make A fassion of it or else some more of them might get into the same fix that Underwood got into.
It is rumored that we will leave this place this week but I cannot vouch for the truth of it.
I have not got time to write much this evening because I will have to get ready for review which is to come of at half past five.
If there is not enough news on this side just turn over and you will find the rest in print.

From your brother

D Buchwalter
Co. H" 114th O.V.I
2nd Div 13, A. C
Selma Ala

THE LOUISVILLE DAILY JOURNAL.

VOLUME XXXV. LOUISVILLE, KENTUCKY, SUNDAY, MAY 14, 1865. NUMBER 171.

TELEGRAPHIC NEWS.

Sherman Remains with his Army.

Confederate Documents Secured.

Condition of the Richmond Roads.

Inauguration of the Loyal Gov'ment.

Further in Regard to the Stonewall.

Important Intelligence from Mexico.

The Republican Cause Strengthened.

Effect of the Great Federal Successes

President Jaurez with a Large Force

The News from Raleigh, N. C.

Rebels Unsubdued in North Carolina.

Feud between Sherman and Halleck.

☞ Quantrell, the notorious Kansas guerilla, arrived in this city yesterday morning about 11 o'clock. He was conveyed in a country wagon on a bed of straw, and a few pillows, and guarded by Terrill's men, disguised as guerillas. He is wounded through the left breast, and it is thought he will die. All the honor for his capture is due to Captain Terrill and his company of "decoy-guerrillas."

On Wednesday Terrill and his men surprised and charged on Quantrell's gang, five miles beyond Taylorsville, killing three of the outlaws and dispersing the remainder. They were also on the scent of Berry's guerillas, and only one hour behind them, when they received an order to report to the General Commanding. Quantrell has been sailing under the name of Clark, and it is supposed by many that i is not the veritable Kansas outlaw, but we understand that Terrill and part of his company are intimately acquainted with him. One fact that will strongly corroborate their assertions is that a picture of a young lady was found in his possession which one of the parties recognized as being the likeness of Miss Hickman, who resides within five miles of the Kansas line. Quantrell also stated that the three followers of his who were killed were from Missouri.

The news of his capture will cause great joy throughout the Union. The inhuman outrages that he committed years ago, such as burning the town of Lawrence, &c., are still fresh in the memory of our people.

The Philadelphia Inquirer.

PRICE TWO CENTS. | PHILADELPHIA, TUESDAY, MAY 16, 1865. | PRICE TWO CENTS.

THE CONSPIRACY!

The Charges and Specifications Against the Assassins.

JEFF. DAVIS AND BOOTH CONSPIRE TOGETHER.

Sanders, Tucker, Thompson and Clay!

THE MURDERERS INCITED BY DAVIS & COMPANY.

Extent and Character of the Plot.

DESIGN AND INTENTION OF THE CONSPIRATORS.

Aid to the Rebellion the Grand Object.

Intended Murder of Johnson, Seward and General Grant.

Parties Implicated Who Are Not Yet Arrested.

Progress of the Trial on Monday

INTERESTING AND IMPORTANT TESTIMONY!

ARNOLD SETS UP A PLEA.

THE TRIAL OF THE ASSASSINS.

WASHINGTON, May 15.—The witnesses examined this afternoon showed the intimacy of [illegible]

Mr. Cox, for the defense, objected to the whole of his evidence, on the ground that the mere fact of intimacy was not evidence of conspiracy.

Judge Advocate Holt said they had fully established the intimacy of the party in Washington, and simply proposed to show the intimacy which existed in Baltimore.

The Court overruled the objection; but ordered it to be put on record.

It appeared from the testimony of David Stanton that on the night of the illumination, the 13th of April, O'Laughlin was prowling in the house of the Secretary of War; but having no business there, he was ordered out. General Grant was in the parlor at that time.

The Court remained in session until 7 o'clock.

A number of witnesses were examined as to the occurrences at the theatre on the night of the assassination.

The Charges and Specifications.

The following is a copy of the charges and specifications against David E. Harold, Geo. A. Atzeroth, Lewis Payne, Michael O'Laughlin, John H. Surratt, Edward Spangler, Samuel Arnold, Mary E. Surratt, and Samuel A. Mudd:—

Charge 1. For maliciously, unlawfully, and traitorously, and in aid of the existing armed Rebellion against the United States of America, on or before the 4th day of March, A. D. 1865, and on divers other days between that day and the 15th day of April, A. D. 1865, combining, confederating, and conspiring together with one John H. Surratt, John Wilkes Booth, Jefferson Davis, George N. Sanders, Beverley Tucker, Jacob Thompson, William C. Cleary, Clement C. Clay, George Harper, George Young, and others unknown, within the Military Department of Washington, and within the fortified and intrenched lines thereof, Abraham Lincoln, late, and at the time of said combining, confederating and conspiring, President of the United States of America, and Commander-in-Chief of the Army and Navy thereof; Andrew Johnson, then Vice President of the United States aforesaid; William H. Seward, Secretary of State of the United States aforesaid, and Ulysses S. Grant, Lieutenant-General of the Army of the States aforesaid, then in command of the Armies of the United States, under the direction of the said Abraham Lincoln, and in pursuance of, and in prosecuting said malicious, unlawful, and traitorous conspiracy aforesaid, and in aid of said Rebellion, afterwards, to-wit:—On the 14th day of April, A. D., 1865, within the Military Department of Washington aforesaid, and within the fortified and intrenched lines of said Military Department, together with the said John Wilkes Booth, and John H. Surratt, maliciously, unlawfully, and traitorously murdering the said Abraham Lincoln, then President of the United States and Commander-in-Chief of the Army and Navy of the United States as aforesaid, and maliciously, unlawfully, and traitorously assaulting with intent to kill and murder the said William H. Seward, then Secretary of State of the United States as aforesaid; and lying in wait with intent maliciously, unlawfully, and traitorously to kill and murder the said Andrew Johnson, then being Vice-President of the United States, and the said Ulysses S. Grant, then being Lieutenant-General and in command of the armies of the United States as aforesaid.

Specification 1. In this, that they, the said David E. Harold, Edward Spangler, Lewis Payne, John H. Surratt, Michael O'Laughlin, Samuel Arnold, Mary E. Surratt, George A. Atzeroth and Samuel A. Mudd, incited and encouraged thereunto by Jefferson Davis, George N. Sanders, Beverley Tucker, Jacob Thompson, William C. Cleary, Clement C. Clay, George Harper, George Young, and others unknown, citizens of the United States aforesaid, and who were then engaged in armed Rebellion against the United States of America, within the limits thereof, did, in aid of said armed Rebellion, on or before the 6th day of March, A. D. 1865, and on divers other day and time between that day and the 15th day of April, A. D. 1865, combine, confederate and conspire together at Washington city, within the Military Department, and within the intrenched fortifications and military lines of the said United States, there being unlawfully, maliciously, and traitorously to kill and murder Abraham Lincoln, then President of the United States aforesaid and Commander-in-Chief of the Army and Navy thereof, and unlawfully, maliciously, and traitorously to kill and murder Andrew Johnson, then Vice-President of the United States, upon whom on the death of said Abraham Lincoln, after the 4th day of March, A. D. 1865, the office of President of the said United States, and Commander-in-Chief of the Army and Navy thereof, would devolve, and to unlawfully, maliciously, and traitorously kill and murder Ulysses S. Grant, then Lieutenant-General under the direction of the said Abraham Lincoln in command of the Armies of the United States aforesaid; and unlawfully, maliciously, and traitorously to kill and murder William H. Seward, the Secretary of State of the United States aforesaid, whose duty it was by law upon the death of said President and Vice President of the United States aforesaid, to cause an election to be held for electors of President of the United States, the conspirators aforesaid designing and intending by the killing and murder of the said Abraham Lincoln and Andrew Johnson, Ulysses S. Grant and William H. Seward aforesaid, to deprive the army and navy of the said United States of a constitutional commander-in-chief, and to deprive the armies of the United States of their lawful commander, and to prevent a lawful election of President and Vice President of the United States aforesaid, and by the means aforesaid to aid and comfort the insurgents engaged in armed rebellion against the said United States as aforesaid, and thereby to aid in the subversion and overthrow of the said United States

And being so combined, confederated, and conspiring together in the prosecution of such unlawful and traitorous conspiracy, on the night of the 14th day of April A. D., 1865, at the hour of about 10 o'clock and 15 minutes P. M., at Ford's Theatre on Tenth Street, in the city of Washington, and within the Military Department and military lines aforesaid, John Wilkes Booth, one of the conspirators aforesaid, in pursuance of said unlawful and traitorous conspiracy, did then and there unlawfully, maliciously, traitorously and with intent to kill and murder the said Abraham Lincoln, discharge a pistol, held in the hands of him, the said Booth, the same being then loaded with powder and a leaden ball, against and upon the left and posterior side of the head of Abraham Lincoln, and did thereby then and there inflict upon him, the said Abraham Lincoln, then President of the said United States and Commander-in-Chief of the Army and Navy thereof, a mortal wound, whereof afterwards, to wit, on the 15th day of April, A. D. 1865, at Washington City aforesaid, the said Abraham Lincoln died, and thereby then and there, in pursuance of said conspiracy, the said defendants, and the said John Wilkes Booth, did unlawfully, traitorously, and maliciously, and with the intent to aid the Rebellion as aforesaid, murder the President of the United States as aforesaid.

In further prosecution of the unlawful, traitorous conspiracy aforesaid, and of the murderous and traitorous intent of said conspiracy, the said Edward Spangler, on the said 14th day of April, A. D. 1865, at about the same hour of that day as aforesaid, within said military department and the military lines aforesaid, did aid and assist the said John Wilkes Booth to obtain entrance to the box in said theatre in which said Abraham Lincoln was sitting at the time he was assaulted and shot as aforesaid by John Wilkes Booth, and also did then and there aid said Booth in barring and obstructing the door of the box of said theatre so as to hinder and prevent any assistance to or rescue of the said Abraham Lincoln against the murderous assault of the said John Wilkes Booth, and did aid and abet him in making his escape after the said Abraham Lincoln had been murdered in manner aforesaid.

And in further prosecution of said unlawful, murderous and traitorous conspiracy, and in pursuance thereof, and with the intent as aforesaid, the said David E. Harold, on the night of the 14th of April, A. D. 1865, within the Military Department and military lines aforesaid, abet and assist the said John Wilkes Booth in the killing and murder of the said Abraham Lincoln, and did then and there aid, and abet and assist him, the said John Wilkes Booth, in attempting to escape through the military lines aforesaid, and accompany and assist the said John Wilkes Booth in attempting to conceal himself and escape from justice after killing and murdering the said Abraham Lincoln as aforesaid.

And in further prosecution of said unlawful and traitorous conspiracy, and of the intent thereof as aforesaid, the said Lewis Payne did, on the same night of the 14th day of April, A. D. 1865, about the same hour of 10 o'clock 15 minutes P. M., at the city of Washington, and within the military department and military lines aforesaid, unlawfully and maliciously make an assault upon the said William H. Seward, Secretary of State as aforesaid, in the dwelling house and bed-chamber of him, the said William H. Seward; and there, with a large knife held in his hand, unlawfully, traitorously, and in pursuance of the said conspiracy, strike, stab, cut, and attempt to kill and murder the said William H. Seward, and did thereby, then and there, and with the intent aforesaid, with said knife inflict upon the face and throat of the said William H. Seward divers grievous wounds; and the said Lewis Payne, in further prosecution of the said conspiracy, at the same time and place last aforesaid, did attempt, with the knife aforesaid, and a pistol held in his hand, to kill and murder Frederick W. Seward, Augustus W. Seward, Emerick W. Hansell, and George F. Robinson, who were then striving to protect and rescue the said William H. Seward from murder by the said Lewis Payne, and did then and there, with the said knife and pistol held in his hand, inflict divers wounds upon the head of the said Frederick W. Seward, and upon the persons of the said Augustus W. Seward, Emerick W. Hansell, and George F. Robinson.

And in the further prosecution of the said conspiracy and its traitorous and murderous designs, the said Geo. A. Atzeroth did, on the night of the 14th of April, A. D. 1865, and about the same hour of the night aforesaid, within the military department, and the military lines aforesaid, lie in wait for Andrew Johnson, then Vice President of the United States aforesaid, with the intent unlawfully and maliciously to kill and murder him, the said Andrew Johnson.

And in the further prosecution of the conspiracy aforesaid, and of its murderous and treasonable purposes aforesaid, on the night of the 13th and 14th of April, 1865, at Washington City, and within the military lines aforesaid, the said Michael O'Laughlin did then and there lie in wait for [illegible] the said Samuel Arnold did, within the military department and military lines aforesaid, on or about the 6th day of March, A. D. 1865, and on divers other days and times between that day and the 15th day of April, A. D. 1865, combine, conspire with and aid, counsel and abet, comfort and support the said John Wilkes Booth, Lewis Payne, George A. Atzeroth, Michael O'Laughlin, and their confederates in the said unlawful, murderous and traitorous conspiracy, and in the execution thereof as aforesaid.

And in the further prosecution of the said conspiracy, Mary E. Surratt did, at Washington City, and within the military department and military lines aforesaid, on or before the 6th day of March, A. D. 1865, and at divers other days and times between that day and the 20th day of April, A. D. 1865, receive, entertain, harbor and conceal, aid and assist, the said John Wilkes Booth, David E. Harold, Lewis Payne, John H. Surratt, Michael O'Laughlin, George A. Atzeroth, Samuel Arnold, and their confederates, with a knowledge of the murderous and traitorous conspiracy aforesaid, and with intent to aid, abet and assist them in the execution thereof, and in escaping from justice after the murder of the said Abraham Lincoln, as aforesaid, with intent to aid, abet and assist them in the execution thereof, and in escaping from justice after the murder of the said Abraham Lincoln, in pursuance of the said conspiracy, in the manner aforesaid.

By order of the President of the United States.

J. HOLT, Judge Advocate-General.

Proceedings of Monday, May 15.

On Saturday it was moved that if the record created no objection on the part of the Judges Advocate, or of the counsel for any or all of the accused, the presence of the several witnesses need not be considered of material necessity.

Mr. Aiken, assistant counsel for Mrs. Surratt, expressed his willingness to accede to such an arrangement, except in the case of Weichman, whom he desired present not, however, that the witness might hear the record of his testimony read, but that he might re-examine him on new ground, which, as he alleged, had been brought forth in the examination of the subsequent witnesses.

It was decided by the Court that the reason so stated did not justify the delay that the finding and recalling of Weichman would occasion, and the reading of the record was proceeded with.

After a time Mr. Weichman entered and heard the reading of the portion of his cross-examination conducted by Mr. Ewing, and several corrections made.

Mr. Johnson, the senior counsel of Mrs. Surratt, when the whole of the testimony rendered by Mr. Weichman had been read from the record, applied to be permitted to ask of him some question before he retired. This was objected to by Major-General Wallace. The President then remarked that the witness had been already examined by the counsel, and a fair opportunity afforded. The Judge Advocate General then asked whether it was to be a cross-examation, and being told by the counsel that it was, the Court, under the Advocate's suggestion, determined that as he could call up the witness hereafter of the defense, it would be an economy of time. General Wallace withdrew his objection, adding, however, that he did so only for this time. He said:—"I placed my objection on the ground that these objections would prove interminable, unless stopped by some rule, after counsel have once had a full opportunity for cross-examination.

Examination by Hon. Reverdy Johnson—Q. I understood you to say on Saturday that you went with Mrs. Surratt the first time, on Tuesday before the assassination, in a buggy. Do you recollect whether you stopped on the way to Surrattsville? A. Yes sir.

Q. Where? A. We stopped on two or three occasions.

Q. Did you stop at Uniontown! A. I do not know the particular point, whether it was at Uniontown or not.

Q. Did you stop at a village? A. We stopped on the road at no particular village that I remember.

Q. How do you know Mr. Floyd? A. I have met him three times.

Q. Did you know him as the keeper of the hotel? A. I knew him as the man who had rented Mrs. Surratt's house from her, because I copied off the instrument.

Q. Do you recollect seeing him buy a buggy on the way from Washington to Surrattsville, on Tuesday? A. Yes. sir; we met his carriage; it drove past us; Mrs. Surratt called to Mr. Floyd; Mr. Floyd got out and approached the buggy; Mrs. Surratt put her head out and had a conversation with him.

Q. Did you hear it? A. No sir.

Q. Did you hear anything about shooting-irons?

Question objected to by Assistant Judge Advocate Bingham. The question was then withdrawn.

Witness—I heard nothing mentioned about shooting irons; Mrs. Surratt spoke to Mrs. Offatt about having this man, Howell, take the oath of allegiance and get released, and said she was going to apply to General Augur or Judge Turner for that purpose.

Q. How long was that interview between Mr. Floyd and Mrs. Surratt on that occasion? A. That I couldn't say exactly; I don't think it was more than five or eight minutes; I don't carry a watch myself, and I have no precise means of knowing.

By Judge Holt—Q. I understood you to say you did not hear the whole of this conversation? A. I did not hear the conversation between Mr. Floyd and Mrs. Surratt; Mrs. Surratt spoke to Mr. Floyd at some distance from the buggy, and I couldn't hear it.

By Mr. Johnson—Q. Do you recollect whether it was raining at that time? A. I don't think it was raining at that particular time; it was a cloudy, murky day; I cannot say whether it was raining or not; I don't remember.

The reading of the record was resumed, and being finished by half-past one, the Court took a recess.

After the recess, John M. Lloyd was recalled, and asked if he could identify the carbines shown to him as the ones referred to in his previous testimony?

Witness—The one with the cover on I do not recognize; I do not think the cover looks like the same; it was a kind of grey cloth; the other looks like the one I saw; I recognize the fixture for breech-loading, which attracted my attention, and which I examined; if the Court will allow me I wish to make a statement. When I was examined before I stated that it was on Monday when I met Mrs. Surratt at Uniontown. I was confused by my being summoned to Court on two successive Mondays. The first Monday I was summoned to Court I did not go. I met Mrs. Surratt at Uniontown; the next day after I went to Court, and consequently it must have been on the Tuesday after the second Monday I was summoned. I also wish to make another statement. I testified in my last examination that I was not certain whether I carried the bundle given me by Mrs. Surratt up stairs or not. I cannot now recollect distinctly, but I think it likely I laid it on the sofa in the dining room.

By Judge-Advocate Holt.—Q. You are sure it was the same bundle you examined here? A. Yes, sir, I am sure it was the same bundle.

By Mr. Aiken.—Q. Did I understand you to say you were in liquor at the time you had this conversation with Mrs. Surratt? A. I was somewhat in liquor, as I think I told you on Saturday.

Q. And on that account is it that you are at fault in your testimony, and wish to make this explanation? A. I was not positive whether I carried the bundle up stairs or not. The question was unexpected. If I had expected it, I might have recollected more distinctly in my former examination.

Testimony of Mary Vantine.

Examined by Judge Holt.—Q. Do you reside in the city of Washington? A. I do; at No. 420 G street.

Q. Do you keep rooms for rent? A. I do.

Q. Will you look at the prisoners at the bar and state whether, in the month of February last, you saw any of them; and if so, which? A. Two of those gentlemen had rooms at my house, Arnold and O'Laughlin.

Q. What time in February did they take rooms in your house? A. As near as I can recollect it was on the 10th. I cannot state positively the date.

Q. Did you know J. Wilkes Booth in his lifetime? A. I knew him by his coming to my house to see gentlemen who had rooms there.

Q. Did he or not come very often to see the prisoners, O'Laughlin and Arnold? A. Yes, frequently.

Q. Would he remain for a good while in conversation with them? A. As a general thing he would go into their rooms and I could see nothing further of them.

Q. Did these prisoners leave the city and return several times? A. They left on Saturday to go to their homes, as I understood, in Baltimore.

Q. Do you know whether Booth accompanied them or not? A. I think not.

Q. Were these interviews between Booth and them alone or was Booth accompanied by other persons? A. I never saw any one with him.

Q. They told you his name was J. Wilkes Booth, did they? A. Yes. Arnold did; I inquired who he was and he said J. Wilkes Booth.

Q. Did he call for them frequently and not find them in? A. Yes; sometimes.

Q. Did he manifest much anxiety to see them on these occasions? A. Frequently; when they were away he would call three or four times before they would return; he would appear very anxious to see them.

Q. Would he on such occasions leave messages for them? A. Sometimes he would request, if they came in before he called again, to say that they would find him at the stable; sometimes he would go into their room and write a note.

Q. Look at the photograph now shown you, and say if you recognize it as the man you call Booth? A. I cannot see without my glasses (glasses brought in and handed to witness); I should not call it a good likeness; I recognize it as Booth, but like a very poor likeness.

Q. Do you remember the last time Booth played in this city, about the 18th or 20th of March. A. Yes.

Q. Did these prisoners present you with complimentary tickets for the play that night? A. Yes. I expressed a wish to see him, and O'Laughlin gave me the tickets.

Q. Did there seem to be any difference in the intimacy of his association with these two men, and if so, with which was he the most intimate? A. I can't say. He would sometimes inquire for one, and sometimes for the other, though I think he more frequently inquired for O'Laughlin.

Q. Did you ever see any arms in their room? A. I saw a pistol once, and but once.

Q. Do you remember at any time seeing a man call A very rough looking person—a laboring man or mechanic? A. Not a laboring man. There was a man who used to come sometimes. I think he passed one night with them, from his coming out very early in the morning.

Q. Do you know his name? A. I would know him if I saw him; he was what would be called a respectable-looking mechanic, not what *you* would call a gentleman.

Q. Could you describe him at all? A. Not very minutely; his skin was hard, as if it had been exposed to the weather.

Q. Do you recognize him as among the prisoners at the bar? A. No.

Q. Did these prisoners seem to have any business transactions with Booth, and if so, of what character? A. They said they were in the oil trade.

Q. Did they seem to have an extensive correspondence? Did many letters come to them? A. Not a great many.

Q. Where did they generally come from? A. I never noticed; they were brought in and laid down.

Q. They were addressed to the names of O'Laughlin and Arnold, were they? A. Yes; sometimes to one and sometimes to the other.

Q. You say Booth came sometimes by day and sometimes at night? A. Not frequently at night; I do not know as ever I saw him at night; he might have come there without my seeing him; I slept in the back part of the house and persons might come out the front part of the house without my seeing them.

Q. You do not know whether, when they went out and stayed late at night, they were with Booth or not? A. No.

Q. You have not seen them since the time they left your house? A. No.

Q. Which was about the 20th of March? A. I think so; it was the Monday after the Saturday on which Booth played.

Q. Did you ever see Booth ride out in the evenings with these men? A. No, I do not think I ever did. I could not positively say whether I did or not. He frequently came to my house in a carriage and inquired for them. I never saw them, that I recollect, ride out together.

Cross-examined by Mr. Coxe.—Q. Did these prisoners say they were or had been in the oil business? A. They said that they were in.

Q. Was that during the first or latter part of the time they occupied a room at your house? A. I think they had been there two or three weeks.

Q. Did they say anything when they went away from your house, where they were going? A. To Pennsylvania.

Q. Did they say anything about having abandoned the oil business? A. No; not that I recollect.

Q. Were they much in their rooms, or were they moving about? A. They were not in their room a great deal.

Q. Did they occupy it regularly at night? A. They were out sometimes.

Q. Do you fix the 20th of March as the day they left? A. If you can ascertain what night Booth played I can tell you; it was the Monday following.

Q. Was *Pescara* the play? A. Yes.

Q. You cannot speak with certainty of anybody being with them besides Booth? A. No, not anybody that I know; others may have gone into their room, I could not say in regard to that.

Q. I ask you whether Booth's visits were most frequent in February, or the latter part of the time they were there in March? A. I think they were pretty much the same all through the time they were there; he was a pretty constant visitor.

Q. Were you present at any conversations between them? A. No, I was not.

Q. You never heard any of their conversations? A. No.

Q. Did they room up stairs? A. No, in the back parlor.

Testimony of Henry Williams (Colored).

Q. State to the Court whether you are acquainted with the prisoners O'Laughlin and Arnold; look and see if you remember to have seen them before? A. I know Mr. O'Laughlin, but not Mr. Arnold.

Q. Did you ever meet Mr. O'Laughlin, and where? A. In Baltimore.

Q. When was that? A. In March last; I carried a letter to him.

Q. From whom did you carry the letter to him? A. From Mr. Booth.

Q. John Wilkes Booth, the actor? A. Yes sir.

Q. Did you carry the letter to him alone, or to him and Arnold? A. I carried one to Arnold and gave it to a lady, and she said she would give it to him.

Mr. Coxe here said that unless this question was to be followed up he would object to it.

The objection of the counsel was overruled, and the examination proceeded.

Q. So you delivered it at the boarding house of O'Laughlin? Did he tell you where O'Laughlin lived? A. He said on Exeter street.

Q. But did you carry a letter to Arnold? A. No, sir, I carried one up there to the house; I did not know who it was for, myself.

Q. Who from? A. Mr. Booth gave it to me; he first called me and asked me if I would take a letter down there: I didn't know for whom it was; he first told me to carry it to the number that was on the letter.

Q. You carried more than one? A. Two.

Q. To whom did you deliver the second? A. To Mr. O'Laughlin.

Q. Do you know for whom it was? A. He told me it was for Mr. O'Laughlin; I knew Mr. O'Laughlin, and was glad when I saw him in the theatre, because it saved me night walking.

Q. For whom did O'Laughlin say the letter was. A. Well, I said here is a letter Mr. Booth gave me for you, and that was all.

Q. Booth told you then this letter was for O'Laughlin?

Mr. Cox here remarked again, I must object to this evidence, as it is not followed up as to what he did after the receipt.

The Judge Advocate-General remarked that the object was simply to show the intimacy of those men by their correspondence.

Mr. Cox said he objected to any evidence of Booth's sending a letter to any individual. It was simply an act of Booth's own, to which the defendant was not privy.

The Judge Advocate-General then said that they did not offer the letter in evidence at all, but simply their correspondence with each other. The objection was finally entered upon the record, but was overruled by the Court.

Q. When did I understand you to say this letter was carried? A. It was in March.

Q. Are you sure? A. Yes sir, in March last.

Q. Late or early in March? A. About the middle of the month; I was coming along there near the mineral water store, and he said, couldn't I take a note for him; I said I could; I had to go in front; he said for me to take the note and he would pay me; I asked him where, and he said to Fayette street.

Q. You said something about the theatre; what theatre? A. The Holliday Street Theatre.

Q. You say you found O'Laughlin in the theatre; what part of the theatre? A. In the dress circle, in the afternoon.

Q. How did you find him? A. I went up with Pitch, and found him there.

Q. All you know about it is that you just gave the note to him and came away? A. Yes, sir.

Q. When Booth gave you the other letter, that was not for O'Laughlin? A. No, sir; that was for a house in in Fayette Street. He just gave me the number of the house.

Q. He did not tell you who it was addressed to? A. No, sir.

Testimony of J. P. Early.

J. P. Early sworn.

Q. Do you know the prisoners, O'Laughlin and Arnold? A. I know O'Laughlin.

Q. Have you been on the cars with them coming from Baltimore to this city? A. Yes, with O'Laughlin, on the Thursday previous to the assassination.

Q. Was Arnold on the cars? A. No sir, not to my knowledge at least.

Q. That was the day previous to the assassination? A. Yes, Thursday, the night of the illumination.

Q. Do you know where he went to stay after you arrived? A. There were four of us, and when we stopped to get shaved between Third and Four-and-a-half streets, he asked me to walk down as far as the National Hotel with him.

Q. Did he take a room there? A. No sir, he did not.

Q. Did you see him associate with Booth? A. No sir, I never saw Booth but once, and that was upon the stage.

Q. Did he make any inquiry for Booth? A. I did not hear him.

Q. Did you see O'Laughlin during that day? A. I was with him the greater part of that day.

Q. Where? A. We slept at the Metropolitan that night, and then went to Welch's and had breakfast for four of us; as we were passing the National Hotel, I stopped to go to the water-closet; when I came out I met Mr. Henderson, who said he was waiting for Mr. O'Laughlin, who had gone up stairs to see Booth; we waited three-quarters of an hour, and he not coming down, we went out.

Q. When did you see him again? A. About four o'clock.

Q. What time did he go to see Booth? A. I should say it was about noon, perhaps.

Q. What was the latest hour at which you saw him on Friday? A. I don't recollect exactly; I had been been drinking considerably, but I distinctly recollect I saw him come out of a restaurant pretty late; I can't say whether it was after the assassination.

Q. Can you give the name of the restaurant? A. I believe the name, at present, is "Lee Shore."

Q. Did you see him at the time or immediately after you heard of the assassination of the President? A. I can't say I did; I went to bed shortly after that; I think I distinctly recollect his coming out with Fowler.

Q. Who is Fowler? A. I don't know exactly; he used to be employed by O'Laughlin's brother once.

Q. Did O'Laughlin go to Baltimore the next day? A. Yes, on the three or half-past three o'clock train; I forget which it is.

Q. Where did he go to in Baltimore? A. Well, after we arrived we went down Baltimore street, as far as High, down to Fayette, and from there we went and asked to see a gentleman's wife who was lying here sick in Washington; and then we came down and went to O'Laughlin's; going down, we met h's brother on the way, who told O'Laughlin that there had been parties looking for him; he asked me if I would wait, and then he asked me in; he then went up, and said he was not going to stay home that night.

Q. Did he show much excitement about the assassination? A. I can't say he did, but his brother said he would be after him on account of his intimacy with Booth.

Cross-examination by Mr. Cox.—Q. Who was with O'Laughlin besides yourself? A. There was Henderson, Edward Murphy and myself.

Q. What was your purpose in coming down? A. We came to have a little good time, and to see the illumination.

Q. Did he join you in Baltimore? A. He came with Henderson.

Q. Where did you stay on Thursday night? A. At the National Hotel. Henderson, me and Smith stopped in one room, and as O'Laughlin signed the register last they gave him a room to himself.

Q. Who arranged to sleep [illegible] night? A. It was about 2 o'clock on Friday morning.

Q. Was it you who woke him in the morning? A. Yes, sir, and then we went down and got breakfast.

Q. Where? A. At Welch's, on the avenue, near Tenth street, and after breakfast we went back, about 10 o'clock, to the National Hotel.

Q. Did you hear him state what he was going to see Booth for, or that he was going to see Booth at all? A. No sir, not at that time.

Q. Did Booth come down? A. He did not.

Q. You don't know whether he actually saw Booth or not? A. I do not, sir; we remained in the hotel three-quarters of an hour waiting for him, and he not coming down, Henderson concluded to go, but as we went out he had some cards written by the card-writer there; we walked down the avenue, I think, as far as the "Lee Shore," and he not being there we went back and got the cards that the writer had written for Henderson; he wrote my name on a samplecard; we then proposed to send cards to Booth's room as a hint to O'Laughlin to come down; the cards were returned, as there was nobody in the room.

Q. How long during that day was O'Laughlin in your company? A. We took a stroll around the city, in different parts of it, and had dinner again at Welch's.

Q. Did you stroll around together? A. Yes sir.

Q. You dined at Welch's? A. Yes sir.

Q. At what hour? A. Between twelve and two.

Q. Do you know Stern's clothing store? A. Yes sir.

Q. Was it over that? A. No sir. I think it was further up the avenue.

Q. What time did you get through dinner? A. It took us over an hour.

Q. Where did you go after dinner? A. Around town again, and we went on a visit.

Q. Was O'Laughlin with you all the time? A. I can't say he was after dinner, but I recollect that between four and five o'clock he went with me to a friend's house.

Q. To pay a visit? A. Yes sir; and we had dinner a second time.

Q. That was on Friday? A. Yes sir.

Q. How soon did you leave there? A. We left there about 6 o'clock.

Q. You are not certain that O'Laughlin was with you all the afternoon? You don't suppose he was with you between the first and second dinners? A. I am not positive; I think we separated, O'Laughlin and Henderson going one way, and Michael and myself another.

Q. You are not certain? A. No sir.

Q. After 6 o'clock where did you go? A. After we came up from the place near the Baltimore depot, where we had paid the visit, we returned to the Lee Shore House, and were then joined by the other two.

Q. How late was that? A. I don't exactly recollect. We stayed around there until between 7 and 8 o'clock, and then went back to Welch's and had supper. We were there at the time the procession passed up the avenue to the Navy Yard.

Q. What time was that? A. Between eight and nine o'clock.

Q. How late did you stay there? A. Until our supper was ready: we then went to the Lee Shore House.

Q. Did you stay there till you went to bed? A. I did, sir.

Q. Do I understand you to say you were there after the assassination? A. Yes sir.

Q. Where is the house? A. Between Third and Four-and-a-half streets, near the *Globe* office; the second door I believe from the *Globe* office.

Q. Did you speak to O'Laughlin when he was in company with Fowler? A. Yes sir.

Q. Was not that after you received the news of the assassination? A. I am not certain.

Q. Were you all there? A. Yes sir.

Q. Where did you stay that night? A. I staid at that house.

Q. Did O'Laughlin? A. Not that I know of.

Q. Had you been drinking? A. Yes sir.

Q. Now charge your memory whether it was after the news of the assassination reached you or not? A. I should judge it was about 10 o'clock.

Q. Where was Murphy? A. He had left us in the avenue.

Q. He was not with you at that time? A. No sir.

Q. Where was Henderson? A. In the bar-room, I believe.

Q. Now I will ask you when you came down on Thursday, whether the whole party had not arranged to go back on Friday? A. Yes, that was the intention; at least I understood so.

Q. During this visit did you see anything in O'Laughlin—anything desperate, which would lead you to suppose—

Objected to by the Assistant Judge Advocate Brigham.

Q. How was his conduct? A. The same as I ever saw; he was rather jovial.

Q. Was he in good spirits? A. Very much so, coming down to the cars.

Q. Any nervousness? A. No sir.

Q. I will ask you whether you were near Willard's Hotel during Friday, or Friday evening? A. We were not as far up as Willard's, I think; I don't recollect passing there.

Q. What induced you to stay later than you intended? A. Well, it was the liquor.

Q. Didn't Lieutenant Henderson press you to stay?

The question was objected to by Assistant Judge Advocate Bingham, on the ground that it was a cross-examination as to Henderson, whose name was not on the record yet.

Major-General Lew Wallace remarked that Mr. Henderson himself could be brought into Court.

The Court asked Mr. Cox if the question was withdrawn, to which Mr. Cox replied—No, sir.

The objection, however, was sustained by the Court.

Q. You stated that probably the liquor kept you there. Now I will ask you if anything else did? A. I cannot say.

Q. State what time you went up to the depot in the morning? A. We did start to go at eleven on Saturday morning, and went as far as the depot, and Hende

Continued on the Eighth Page.

JEFF. DAVIS

AS "THE STERN STATESMAN"—(Last Act.)

J. D. (*Wolsey*).—Farewell, a long farewell to all my greatness!
This is the state of man; To-day he puts forth
The tender leaves of hope, to-morrow blossoms,
And bears his [illegible] honors [illegible]
And, when he thinks, good easy man, full surely
His greatness is a ripening, nips his root,
And then he falls as I do. I have ventured,
Like little wanton boys that swim on bladders,
This many summers in a sea of glory;
But far beyond my depth; my high-blown pride
At length broke under me; and now has left me,
Weary, and old with service, to the mercy
Of a rude stream, that must for ever hide me.
Is that poor man that hangs on princes' favors!
There is, betwixt that smile we would aspire to,
That sweet aspect of princes, and their ruin,
More pangs and fears than wars or women have;
And when he falls, he falls like Lucifer,
Never to hope again!—*Henry VIII, Act 3, sc. 2.*

The Philadelphia Inquirer.

PRICE TWO CENTS. PHILADELPHIA, THURSDAY, MAY 18, 1865. PRICE TWO CENTS.

THE GREAT TRIAL

Proceedings of Wednesday.

THE PURSUIT OF THE ASSASSINS!

Dr. Mudd's Participation in the Great Plot!

HIS EFFORTS TO HIDE THE FELONS!

He Endeavors to Put Pursuers Off Their Track!

REBEL OFFICER'S EVIDENCE

Harold Boasts, "We Are the Assassinators!"

BOOTH OPPOSES OPEN CONFESSION!

Important Testimony of Colonel Congers!

THE CAPTURE OF HAROLD AND DEATH OF BOOTH.

Interesting Details of the Murderer's Last Moments.

BOOTH'S WEAPONS SHOWN IN COURT

Sergeant Boston Corbett on the Witness Stand!

HIS REASON FOR KILLING BOOTH

Suspicious Movements of Assassins Previous to the Murder.

ATZEROTH SUPPLIES THE HORSES!

THE TRIAL OF THE CONSPIRATORS.

WASHINGTON, May 17.—General Harris said that on Saturday, for what he deemed justifiable reasons, he had objected to Hon. Reverdy Johnson appearing here as counsel. He now asked to have read a letter from Reverdy Johnson, dated Baltimore, October 7, 1864, addressed to William D. Bowie, C. C. Magruder, John D. Bowling, Prince George's county, in which he takes the ground that the oath prescribed by the Constitutional Convention was illegal, and concludes as follows:—"It is indeed the only way in which the people can protect themselves, and no moral injunction will be violated by such a course, because the exaction of the oath was beyond the authority of the Convention, and as a law therefore void."

Testimony of William Williams.

William Williams was called as a witness, and testified as follows:—

Q. Will you state to the Court whether, after the assassination, you were ever engaged in the pursuit of the assassins? A. Yes sir: I started on April 17th, with Major O'Beirne, and pursued to Surrattsville.

Q. State whether, in the course of that pursuit, you went to the residence of the prisoner, Dr. Mudd? A. Yes sir: we went there on Tuesday, the 18th; when we arrived there Dr. Mudd was not at home, but we saw his wife, and she told us she would send for him, that he was in the neighborhood; when he came I asked him whether any strangers had been that way; he said not; we questioned him about two men having been at his house, one with a broken leg, and he denied that they had; he spoke to some other officers.

Q. Did you mention the time when you supposed these men had been there? A. Not on our first visit; I did not.

Q. Did you have any further consultation with him upon that? A. No sir, not on our first visit.

Q. He denied altogether that there had been any strangers there, you say. A. Yes.

Q. Who made the remark about the man with the broken leg having been there? A. One of the other officers.

Q. Did you hear his reply? A. I am not positive what it was, but he made a reply.

Q. Did he on that occasion state to you when he heard for the first time of the assassination of the President? A. Yes sir; he said it was in church Sunday morning.

Q. Did he converse freely with you; was his manner frank or evasive? A. He seemed to be a little uneasy, and not willing to give us the information without being asked for everything.

Q. When did you see him the second time? A. On Friday, the 21st.

Q. What occurred then? A. We went there for the purpose of arresting him; he was not at home, but Mrs. Mudd sent for him; when he arrived at the house Lieutenant Lovett asked him a question or two, and then I asked him about the two men being at his house, and whether he had seen them, and then he said that he had: I asked him, also, if they were Booth and Harold; he said they were not; that he was introduced to Booth last fall, and knew him; he had been introduced to Booth by Mr. Thompson; after we arrested him we showed him this picture, and after looking at it a little while he said at first he did not recollect the features, but that it looked like Booth across the eyes; I informed Mrs. Mudd that we would have to search the house, and then she said that one of the men had left a boot up stairs in bed, and she went for and brought the boot: it was a long riding boot, with the New York maker's name and the name of J. Wilkes written inside: the boot was cut about two inches up from the instep.

Q. Did she say that the doctor had set the leg of the man? A. Yes sir.

Q. How long did he say they remained at the house? A. He stated to me they left between three and four in the afternoon on Saturday.

Q. Did he state to you at what hour they came? A. About daybreak.

Q. Did they leave on horseback or on foot? A. He said they left on horseback; Mrs. Mudd said they left on foot.

Q. Did you understand her to be speaking of one or both of them when she said they went on foot? A. I understood her to say Booth, and I believe it was Dr. Mudd who said the injured man went away on crutches, which he said had been made for him by one of his men.

Cross-examination by Mr. Stone—Q. Was Lieut. Lovett present? A. Yes sir.

Q. On both Tuesday and Friday? A. Yes sir.

Q. Was Mrs. Mudd in the parlor when she made this declaration about the boot? A. She was standing at the door.

Q. Where was Dr. Mudd? A. He was in the parlor.

Q. Could he hear what Mrs. Mudd said? A. I judge he could; he was no further than where you are sitting there.

Q. [illegible] the first one who mentioned about Booth to you? A. [illegible] search the house, and then she said that the men had left the boot there, and went up and brought it down.

Q. Was it on Tuesday or Friday that he told you the first knowledge he had of the death of the President was derived at church the Sunday before? A. On Friday, I think.

Q. Do you remember that any one asked him in your presence, A. I do not.

Q. You were all together in one room? A. Yes sir.

Q. Did you or Lieutenant Lovett ask him about two strangers who had been at his house any time previous? A. We both asked him.

Q. Which asked him first? A. I don't remember.

Q. Did he give the same reply to both? A. I think he did, sir.

Q. Do you feel confident of that? A. His reply to me on Tuesday, was that they had not been there; I think it was the same he said to Lieutenant Lovett.

Q. Do you remember on the Friday of the examination who asked him first? A. I think it was Lovett.

Q. Do you remember whether he asked about two strangers, or about Booth and Harold? A. About strangers, I think.

Q. What answer did he make on Friday? A. The question was whether two strangers had been there; one with a broken leg; and then he said he had set the man's leg; that one of them was, apparently, about seventeen or eighteen years of age; that they had knocked at the door, and he had looked out at the window and asked who they were; they replied that they were friends, and wanted to get in: and Dr. Mudd came down stairs, and with the assistance of the young man, helped the injured man from his horse and took him to his parlor and placed him on the sofa.

Q. Did he describe the strangers? A. He said one was about seventeen or eighteen; that the other had a moustache and long thin whiskers; I asked him if they were natural whiskers? he said he could not tell.

Q. Did he tell you the color of the other man's hair? A. No; not that I remember.

Q. Did he tell you his height? A. I am not positive.

Q. Did he give any description of his dress? A. I think he said the injured man had a shawl; I am not certain.

Q. Did he describe the dress of the younger man? A. I don't remember his saying anything about it.

Q. Did he describe his height and general appearance? A. He said he was a smooth-faced young man, about seventeen or eighteen.

Q. Did he tell you the direction they took, and did you search for tracks in the direction indicated, and if so, did you find any? A. Yes, we found tracks, but other teams were constantly passing, and the road is not much traveled.

Q. Did you go on Tuesday across the swamp? A. Yes; we went all through the swamp on Tuesday and Friday, after we came back.

Q. Were you one of the party who went to see Mr. Wilmer's house? A. Yes sir.

Q. What time did you get there? A. Thursday or Tuesday night; I think it was late in the evening when we got there.

Q. What time did you say you got to Wilmer's? A. I think it was Wednesday evening.

Q. Did you hear anything of them on the road? A. I did not.

Q. This was before the doctor was carried to Bryantown? A. Yes sir.

Q. Were you and Mr. Lloyd under Lieutenant Lovett's orders? A. I was acting under Major O'Beirne's orders, but in his absence was under Lieutenant Lovett, who had charge of the squad, I suppose.

Q. Was Mr. Lloyd with you? A. Yes sir.

Q. Were you in the Court when his testimony was read? A. I was not.

The Court here took a recess.

On the Court reassembling the testimony was continued.

Testimony of Simon Gavasan.

Q. Will you state whether you are acquainted with Dr. Mudd? A. Yes sir.

Q. Were you not at his house the Tuesday following the assassination? A. Yes sir, I was.

Q. State what inquiries you made of him there to aid you in the pursuit of the murderers, and what replies he made? A. We went there on the forenoon of that Tuesday, the 18th; we went to his house, and we made inquiries whether any two men had passed there on the morning of Saturday, after the assassination; he said "no," and then, when we asked more particularly whether two men came, one of them having his leg fractured, he said "yes;" we asked him what time, and he said, "at four or half-past four in the morning they rapped at his door, and he being alarmed at the noise came down and let them in; he said another man assisted the injured man into the house; he said he attended to the fracture as well as he could, but that he had not much fracture; the person with the fractured leg stayed in the parlor at first, but after that was taken up to one of the rooms up stairs, and remained there till between three and five o'clock in the afternoon on Saturday: he said they then left there, and he went part of the way with them, but that previous to that he [illegible] have the wounded man taken away, but that he could not find one; he said he went part of the way on the road with them, but they first inquired the way to Allen's Fresh, and that they also inquired the way to Dr. Wilmer's, and he said he showed them the roads.

Q. Did you ask him whether he knew these persons? A. He said at first "No, not at all."

Q. On the subsequent days did you have any interview with him, and if so when? A. On Friday, the 21st.

Q. State what occurred then? A. We went there to arrest him and search his house. He was not in, but his wife sent for him; when he came we informed him that we would have to search his house; his wife then went up stairs and brought a boot down; we examined the boot and found "J. Wilkes" marked on the leg of the boot. She also brought a razor down, which one of the party took in charge.

Q. Did you repeat your inquiry as to who they were? A. We asked him if it was not Booth? he said he thought not.

Q. Did you get any reason for his so thinking? A. He said he had whiskers on, and also had his moustache shaved off; probably he shaved it off up stairs.

Q. Did he speak of having known him before? A. Yes; when we made inquiries he said he was introduced last fall by a man named Thompson.

Cross-examination by Mr. Ewing.—Q. Who was the chief of the party who were with you? A. We had no chief.

Q. Who was in charge of the party? A. Lieutenant Lovett came in charge of a cavalry detachment, but we went under the orders of Major O'Beirne.

Q. In the absence of Major O'Beirne, were you not under the order of Lieutenant Lovett?. A. Yes sir, partly.

Q. Who commenced the conversation with Mudd on Tuesday? A. That I am not able to say.

Q. How long did the conversation last? A. Probably one hour.

Q. In your presence? A. Yes sir.

Q. Did not Lieutenant Lovett conduct the inquiries chiefly? A. No sir; the doctor was asked questions by all of us.

Q. Did not Dr. Mudd himself bring the boot down to you? A. No sir; his wife brought it down.

Q. Who was it given to? A. The one nearest the door.

Q. Did you, in point of fact, make a search of the house? A. We did not go up stairs; when we found the boot and razor we considered it satisfactory evidence that Booth and Harold had been in the house.

Q. Did you go to meet Mudd on Friday as he was going to the house? A. No sir.

Q. Did Lieutenant Lovett? A. There might have been one or two other officers; I am not sure.

Q. Did you ask him on Tuesday for a description of the party? A. No sir; I believe the photograph of Booth was shown to him and that he did not recognize it as one of the parties that was at his house, but that there was something about the forehead and eyes that resembled one of them.

Q. Did he point out to you the road they went across the swamp? A. No sir, he said he had made inquiries how they would get to the Rev. Dr. Wilmer's.

Q. He mentioned that on Tuesday? A. Yes sir.

Q. Did he tell you how to get to Dr. Wilmer's? A. Yes sir.

Testimony of Mrs. Emma Offutt.

Q. State whether or not you are the sister-in-law of John Floyd? A. Yes sir.

Q. State whether or not, on the Tuesday, the 11th of April, you were at his house? A. Yes sir.

Q. You saw Mr. Floyd on that day? A. Yes sir, I was in the carriage with Mr. Floyd.

Q. On that occasion did you happen to meet Mrs. Surratt? A. Yes sir.

Q. State to the Court where the meeting took place? A. Somewhere near Uniontown.

Q. State whether or not a conversation took place between Mr. Floyd and Mrs. Surratt on that day? A. Yes, they talked together.

Q. Did you hear any of the conversation? A. Yes sir, some of it.

Q. Under what circumstances did the conversation take place? A. Our carriages passed each other before we recognized who it was, and Mr. Floyd went out to her carriage, and they had a conversation which took place at her carriage, and not at ours.

Q. Were you at Mr. Floyd's again on Friday, the 14th of April? A. Yes sir.

Q. State whether you saw the prisoner, Mrs. Surratt, there? A. Yes sir.

Q. Did you observe any conversation between her and Mr. Floyd on that day? A. Yes; I saw them talking together, but I did not hear them at all; I had occasion to go to the back part of the house.

Q. Did the conversation take place in the back part of the house or in the yard? A. In the yard, sir.

Q. Had Mr. Floyd been to town that day? A. No sir, he had been to Marlborough, attending court.

Q. What did he bring with him when he came back? A. Some oysters and fish, and that is how he came to drive into the back part of the yard.

Q. Was any one else in the yard at the time of this conversation? A. No sir.

Cross-examination by Mr. Aiken.—Q. How far apart were the two carriages when you went past each other? A. Two or three yards; I think they talked but a very few minutes together.

Q. Did Mr. Floyd state what the conversation was? A. No sir.

Q. Nor what the conversation on the 14th was about? A. No; he did not.

Q. Have you been acquainted with Mrs. Surratt for some time? A. Ever since last summer, I believe.

Q. What time did she arrive at Mr. Floyd's on the 14th? A. At about 4 o'clock, I think

TRIAL OF THE CONSPIRATORS.

Interior View of the Court Room Occupied by the Military Commission.

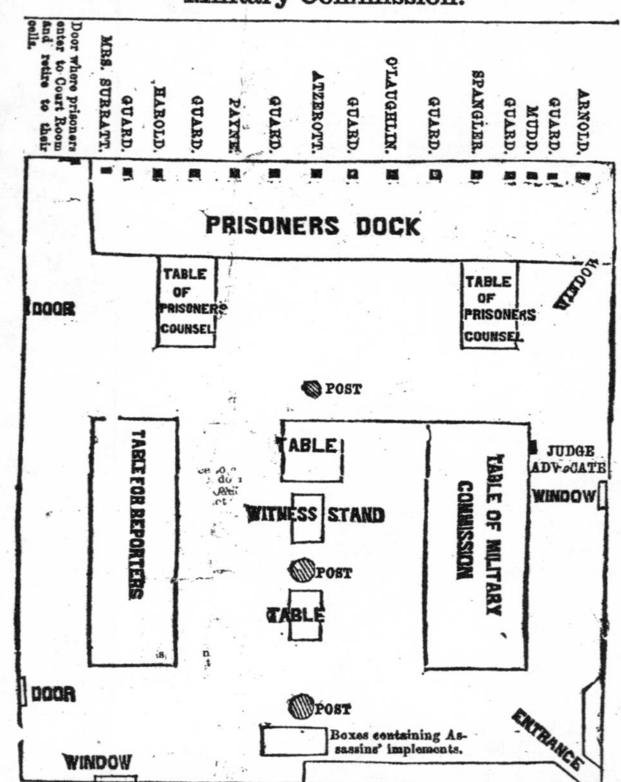

Q. Did you hear any conversation with her previous to Mr. Floyd's coming home? A. Yes sir; in the parlor.

Q. Did you learn what the conversation was on that day?

Question objected to and waived.

Q. Did Floyd make any statement in reference to his business with Mrs. Surratt? A. No sir.

Q. Did Mrs. Surratt have any business with you on that day? A. No sir.

Q. Did Mrs. Surratt place in your hands any package? A. No sir.

Q. During your visit to Mr. Floyd's did you hear anything about shooting irons?

Assistant Judge Advocate Bingham objected, and the objection was sustained by the Court.

Testimony of William P. Jebb.

Q. Look at the prisoners and see if you recognize any or all of them? A. [illegible]

Q. State when you first saw [illegible] A. Since the 25th of last October I have been in Caroline county, Maryland, as commissary agent in the Confederate service: I was in the cavalry service, but was wounded on the 9th of January, and after that was appointed commissary agent; when I was on my way, in April, to Fauquier county I got down to Port Conway and saw a wagon on the wharf.

Q. When was that? A. On the 18th of April.

Q. The Monday after the assassination? A. No sir: the Monday week after the murder; there were three of us together, we saw the wagon and rode down on the wharf, and before we reached the wagon we saw a man get out of it and it seemed to us as if he put his hand into his bosom; I don't remember whether we hailed the ferry or not; this one man got out of the wagon and came where we were and said:—"What command do you belong to?" Ruggles said Moseby's command; then he said, "Where are you going?" I said, "It is a secret; where are you going?"

Q. Did you ask him what command he belonged to? A. He said he belonged to A. P. Hill's Corps. He said his brother was wounded below Petersburg, and asked if we would take him down to the lines. Harold asked us then to take a drink, but none of us drank, and we declined. I got down and carried out three horses and tied them up, and Harold came and touched me, and said he wanted to speak to me, and said, "I suppose you are raising a command to go South;" and then said he would like to go with us. I said that I could go with no man that I didn't know anything about, and then he made this remark:—"*We are the assassinators of the President.*" I was so shocked that I did not know what to say, and I made no reply. Lieutenant Ruggles was near by, watering his horse, and I called to him; he came there, and then Booth came up and Harold introduced him; after introducing himself Booth had a mark upon his hand, I remember, J. W. B.; we went across the river, Booth riding on Ruggles' horse, and he said he wanted to pass under the name of Boyd; we went to a lady's house, and I asked her if she could take in a wounded soldier; she at first consented, and then said she could not; we then went up to Mr. Garrett's, where we left Booth; Harold and the rest of us went on within a few miles of Bowling Green; the next day Harold returned towards Garrett's, and that was the last I saw of him till after he was captured.

Q. Did I understand you that Booth went alone to Garrett's? A. No sir; Ruggles, Booth, Bainbridge and I rode up to Garrett's and we left Booth there and Harold came on with us to Bowling Green and had dinner.

Q. Do you know where Harold went to from Bowling Green? A. No sir; he left us the next day at two or three o'clock.

Q. Now when you saw him on Wednesday morning he was in custody then? A. Yes sir.

Q. Before he said to you "we are the assassinators of the President," had you told him you were in the Confederate service? A. Why he could see that, because we were in Confederate uniform.

Cross-examined by Mr. Stone.—Harold wanted you to aid him in going further South? A. Yes; but we had no facilities to aid him.

Q. Did he seem disappointed? A. Yes sir.

Q. Was Booth present when you were talking with Harold about their being the assassinators of the President? A. Not when he first told me; he and Bainbridge came up after.

Q. Did he seem to be much agitated? A. Yes sir.

Q. What did Booth say? A. He said "I didn't intend telling that."

Q. But Harold did tell? A. Yes, he had told before Booth came up.

Q. Can you recollect whether he said that he had killed the President? A. No; he said, "We are the assassinators of the President;" then a few moments afterwards he said, "Yes, he is the man, J. Wilkes Booth, who killed the President."

By Mr. Aiken.—Q. Have you ever taken the oath of allegiance? A. No, sir; but I am perfectly willing to do so.

Testimony Lieut.-Colonel C. J. Congers,

By Judge Holt—Q. State to the Court whether you and others were engaged in the pursuit of the murderers of the President. If so, please take up the narrative at the point where you met the Confederate soldier Jebb, who has given his evidence, and state what occurred afterwards. A. I found him in a room in the hotel in Bowling Green, in bed: I expected to find somebody else; as I went in he began to get out of bed; I said, "Is that you, Jebb?" he said, "Yes;" I said, "Get up, I want you;" he got up, and I told him to put on his clothes, and come into the part of the room where I was: I said to him, "Where are the two men who came with you across the river at Port Royal?" there were two men in the room with me; Jebb said to me, "can I see you alone;" I said yes, and Lieuts. Baker and Doherty went out of the room. He reached out his hand to me and said, "I know who you want, and I can tell you where they are now; they are on the road to Port Royal, about three miles from here, at the house of Mr. Garrett, and if I show you where they are now you can get them; I said "have you a horse?" he replied he had; I told him I had just come from there, and he seemed for a moment to be considerably embarrassed; he said he thought we came from Richmond, but if we had passed by Garrett's he could not tell me whether the men were there or not; I told him it did not make any difference, we could go back and see: he got out his horse and we started; just before we got to the house Jebb, who was riding with me, said "we are near where we go through a gate, let us stop here and look round;" I rode, in the first place, alone, to find the gate, about as far as I understood him to say it was, but did not see any opening; there was a hedge, or rather a bushy fence, that side of the road. I turned round and went back, and told him I did not see any gate in that direction; we then rode on some three hundred yards further and stopped again; Jebb went with Lieutenant Baker and myself to find the gate; I sent Lieutenant Baker on to the gate while I went back myself for the cavalry; we returned rapidly, and a guard was stationed round the building; when I went to the house Lieutenant Baker was telling some one to strike a light and come out; I think the door was open when I got there; the first individual I saw when I got there, whose name was said to have been Garrett; I said to him, "Where are the men who stopped at your house?" "They have gone." "Gone where?" "Gone to the woods." "Whereabouts in the woods have they gone?" he then commenced to tell me that they came there without his consent, and that he did not want them to stay: I said, "I don't want any long stories from you, I just want to know where those men have gone?" he [illegible] turned to one of the men and told him to bring me a lariat, and threatened to hang the man to a locust tree [illegible] knew; one of his sons then came in [illegible] don't hurt the old man, he is scared; I will tell you where these men are; I said that is what I want; he said they are in the barn, and as soon as I got there I heard somebody walking about on the hay; I stationed men around the barn, and Lieutenant Baker said to one of the young Garretts (there had two of them appeared by this time) "you must go in the barn and get the arms from that man;" I think he made some objection to going in, and Baker said, "They know you, and you must go in;" Baker then said to the men inside that one of the men with whom they had been stopping was coming in to get their arms and they must deliver them up: Garrett went in, but came out very soon and said, "This man says, '—— you, you have betrayed me,' and threatened to shoot me;" I asked him how he knew the man was going to shoot him; he said, "He reached down in the hay and got the revolvers;" I directed Baker then to tell the men inside that they were to come out and deliver themselves up, and that if they did not in five minutes we would set the barn on fire; Booth said, "Who are you? what do you want?" Lieutenant Baker answered, "We want you; we know who you are; give up your arms and come out; Booth replied, "Give us a little time to consider;" Baker said, "Very well," and some ten or fifteen minutes elapsed, probably, before anything further was said, when Booth again asked, "Who are you? what do you want?" I said, to Baker, do not by any possible intimation or remark let him know who we are; if he chooses to take us for Rebels or friends we will take advantage of it; we will not lie to him about it, but we will not answer any questions on that subject; simply insist on his coming out if he will; Baker replied to Booth, "It don't make any difference who we are, we know who you are and we want you:" Booth said, "This is hard, because it may be I am to be taken by my friends;" some time during the conversation Booth said, "Captain, I know you to be a brave man, and I believe you to be honorable; I have got but one leg; I am a cripple; if you will withdraw your men 100 yards from the door I will come out and fight you:" Lieutenant Baker replied, "we did not come here to fight, we simply come to make you prisoners;" once after that he said, "if you will take your men 50 yards from the door I will come out and fight; give me a chance for my life;" there was the same reply, and with a singularly theatrical voice, Booth called out, "well, my brave boys, you may prepare a stretcher for me;" I requested one of the Garretts to pile some pine boughs against the barn; he soon came to me and said, "this man says if I put any more brush up there he will put a ball through me;" said I, "very well, you need not go there anymore:" After a while Booth said;—"There is a man here who wants to come out;" Lieutenant Baker said "Very well; let him take his arms and come out;" some talk passed between them in the barn; one of the expressions I heard Booth use to Harold was, "You —— coward, will you leave me now? but go, go, I would not have you stay with me:" further words ensued between them, which I supposed had reference to bringing out the arms, which was one of the conditions on which Harold was directed to come out; what the words were was not heard; he came to the door and said, "Get me out;" Lieutenant Baker says to him, "Hand out your arms;" the reply was, "I have none;" Baker said, "You carried the carbine; you must hand it out;" Booth replied, "The arms are mine, I have got them;" Baker said, "This man carried the carbine, and must bring it out;" Booth said, "Upon the word and honor of a gentleman the arms are mine; I have got them;" I told Baker to never mind the arms, but let this man out; Harold put out his hands, and Lieut. Baker took hold of him and brought him out, and passed him to the rear; I then went around the barn, pulled some straw out and twisted a little rope, as big as your finger, and fired it and stuck it back; it seemed to be loose, broken hay, that had been taken up from the barn floor; it blazed very rapidly, and lit up the barn at once: I looked through one of the cracks, and just then heard something drop on the floor, which I supposed to be Booth's crutch.

When I first noticed him his back was towards me; he was looking towards the front door; he then came back within five feet of the corner of the barn; the only thing I noticed he had in his hand when he came was a carbine; he raised the carbine to his breast and looked along the cracks rapidly; he then looked at the fire and from the expression of his face I am satisfied he looked to see if he could put it out, but he could not, it was burning too rapidly; I started to go round to the front of the barn again, and when I was about half around I heard the report of a pistol; I went on around to the door, went in and found Lieutenant Baker looking at him, and rather holding or raising him up; I said he had shot himself: Baker said he had not; I asked where he was shot; we raised him up and the blood ran out of his wound; I then said "Yes, he has shot himself."

Lieutenant Baker replied very earnestly he had not. I said that we must carry him out or this will soon be burning us; we took him up and carried him out on the grass, a little way from the door beneath a locust tree; I went back into the barn to see if the fire could be put out and returned to where he was lying; before this I supposed him to be dead; he had all the appearances of a dead man, but when I came back his eyes and mouth were moving; I called immediately for water, and put some on his face: he seemed to revive and attempted to speak; I put my ear down to his mouth and heard him say, "Tell my mother I died for my country;" I repeated the words to him and said, "Is that what you would say?" he said "Yes;" they carried him to the porch of Garrett's house and laid him on a straw bed or tick; at that time he had revived considerably, and could talk in a whisper so as to be intelligibly understood.

He could not speak above a whisper; he wanted water; I gave it to him: he wanted to turn on his face; I said he could not lie on his face; he wanted to be turned on his side; we turned him on his side three times, but he could not lie with any comfort and asked immediately to be turned back: he asked me to put my hand on his throat and press down, which I did; he said "harder;" I pressed as hard as I thought necessary: he made a very strong exertion to cough, but was unable to do so; I supposed he thought there was blood in his throat; I asked him to put out his tongue, which he did; I said, there is no blood in your throat; he repeated several times, two or three times at least, "Kill me, kill me;" I replied, "I do not want to kill you; I want you to get well;" I then took what things he had in his pocket and tied them up in a paper; I had previously sent for a physician, who came there to see him; he was not then quite dead; he would once, perhaps, in five minutes gasp; his pulse would almost die out, and then there would be a slight motion again; I left him, with the prisoner Harold, in charge of Lieutenant Baker, saying that if Booth revived again to wait an hour, and if likely to recover to send over to Belle Plain for a surgeon from one of the gun ships; if not, to get the best conveyance he could and bring him over, dead or alive.

Q. You left before he died. A. No; I stayed there some ten minutes; after that the doctor who was there said he was dead.

Q. You have seen the dead body since? A. Yes.

At this point the knife, belt, cartridge-box, pistols, pocket compass, and carbine, in possession of Booth when he was killed, were produced in Court, and identified by the witness.

Q. Is that what is called a Spencer rifle? A. Yes. It is a Spencer rifle or carbine. It is a cavalry weapon. It has that mark on the breech of it.

Q. Were these arms loaded? A. Yes, the pistols were loaded when brought into Secretary Stanton's office; I unloaded this carbine myself; I did not count the number of balls in it; there was one in the barrel and the chamber was full; the chamber was bent; some one had tried to unload it previously, and I was called to get it out.

A spur and file was also exhibited to the witness, and he was asked if he could identify them?

Witness.—That file was taken out of Booth's pocket; the spur is like the one he had on, but I could not identify it as the same spur.

Witness then examined [illegible] the bill of exchange found on the person of Booth.

Q. In what State and county did this occur? A. I think it is in Caroline county, State of Virginia, three miles south of Port Royal, on the road to Bowling Green.

Q. Do you recognize the prisoner Harold as the one you took out of the barn? A. I do.

Q. What articles did you take from Harold, if any? A. I took a little piece of a map of the State of Virginia, including a part of Chesapeake Bay.

Q. Do you remember whether the map embraced the part of Virginia where they were? A. It did; it covered that portion of Virginia known as the Northern Neck.

Q. Was it a map prepared in pencil? A. No; it was part of an old school map that had been originally sixteen inches square (portion of a map shown to witness); yes, that is it; that is the only property found on him.

Cross-examined by Mr. Stone.—Q. Did you find any arms on Harold? A. No.

Q. You stated that Booth had some conversation in the barn before he came out; did you observe whether in that conversation Harold seemed willing to surrender himself? A. I do not know anything about it, except from the remark I have stated that Booth made; I did not hear any part of the conversation.

Q. In that remark Booth spoke harshly to Harold, and called him a coward, did he not? A. Yes.

Q. How long were you at the barn? A. I think I looked as soon as I conveniently could after we got to the barn, and it was about two o'clock in the morning; Booth was shot and carried on the grass about fifteen minutes past three, so that we must have remained there about an hour and a quarter.

Q. Was he carried almost immediately on to the grass after he was shot? A. Yes.

Q. Did you hear Booth say anything else in relation to Harold than you have stated? A. No.

Q. Do you remember hearing him say that Harold was not to blame? A. I have an indistinct recollection of something of that kind; I will tell you as near as I can what it was; he said, "Here is a man who wants to come out," and I think he added, "who had nothing to do with it;" that is as near as I can remember what he said; after that Harold came out.

By Judge Holt.—Q. Had you seen Booth previously, so that you could recognize the man who was killed as the same person? A. I thought I could recognize him from his resemblance to his brother; I had often seen his brother, Edwin Booth, and was satisfied this was the man, from his resemblance to him.

Testimony of Sergeant Boston Corbett.

Examined by Judge Holt.—Q. You may state what part you took in the pursuit, capture and killing of Booth, beginning the narration at the point when you arrived at the house. A. When I arrived at the house my superior officer, Lieutenant Dougherty, told me that Booth was there and directed me to deploy men at the house and it was ascertained that Booth was not in the house, but in the barn; the greater part of the guard were then withdrawn from the house and placed around the barn and orders were given to allow no one to escape; we had been previously cautioned to see that our arms were in readiness for use; after being ordered to surrender and told that the barn would be fired if they did not, we remained there for some minutes; Booth inquired who we took him for; he said his leg was broken, and what did we want with him; he was told that it made no difference who we were: that we knew who they were, and that they must surrender themselves as prisoners; he wanted to know where they would be taken to if they gave themselves up; no reply was given; the parley lasted much longer than the time first stated, probably, I should think, fully half an hour, more or less in the course of that time many words passed, and Booth positively declared he would not surrender; at one time he said, "Well, my boys, you may get a stretcher for me;" at another time he said, "Well, Captain, make quick work; shoot me through the heart," or words to that effect, so that I knew he was perfectly desperate, and would not surrender; after a while I heard whispering there: Booth had previously declared there was no other person in there; the other person, who proved to be Harold, seemed to be trying to persuade Booth to surrender; we could not hear the words; after a while, Booth sung out, "Captain, there is a man in here who wants to surrender;" words followed; I could not hear what they were; Booth said, "Oh, go out, and save your life;" he then called out, "I declare before my Maker, this man is innocent of any crime whatever," or words to that effect; further words followed, in which Harold seemed to tell Booth that he would not surrender; he was told to take his arms and come out; Harold declared he had no arms; Booth also declared that this other man was unarmed; that the arms belonged to him; immediately after this, Harold having been taken out with arms, detective Lieutenant-Colonel Conger came over to the side where I was, and directed the barn to be fired; I had been previously standing before a crack in the boards, large enough to put in your hand; I knew that Booth could see us and could have picked us off, and he, in fact, once made the remark, "I could have picked three or four of your men off," "just draw your men off fifty yards and I will come out;" he used such words many times; when the fire was lighted, which was almost immediately after Harold had been taken out of the barn, I could then see him distinctly in about the middle of the barn; he started at first towards me, and I had a full front dress view of him; I could have shot him much easier than at the time I did, but as long as he made no demonstration I did not shoot him; I kept my eye on him steadily: he turned towards the other side; he brought his piece up to an aim and I supposed was going to fight his way out; I thought the time had come, and I took a steady aim upon him and shot him; the ball entered his head a little back of the ear and came out a little higher on the other side of the head; he lived, I think, until about seven o'clock that morning, perhaps two or three hours after he was shot; I did not hear him speak after he was shot, except to cry out when he was shot; others stated that he did utter words after that, but I did not hear any after I shot him.

Q. State whether you recognize the prisoner Harold as the man you took out of the barn? A. Yes, that is the man.

Q. Did you know Booth before? A. No; but I was perfectly satisfied from the first, when Booth said his leg was broken, and also from his desperate replies that he would not be taken alive, that he was the man; I knew no other man would act in such a way.

Cross-examined by Mr. Stone.—Q. You say that you judged from the conversation between Booth and Harold in the barn that Booth was anxious to surrender? A. I rather thought so.

Q. But that after Booth refused to surrender, Harold seemed to speak as if he desired to stay with him? A. Yes.

Q. And it was after that that Booth made his declaration? A. Yes; he declared before his Maker that the man with him was innocent of any crime; I also wish to state, with permission of the Court, as improper motives have been attributed to me, that I offered twice to Lieutenant-Colonel Conger and Lieutenant Baker to go into the barn and take these men, telling them that I had rather go in than stand there before the crack exposed to his fire; I thought it was less dangerous, for while I could not see them they could see us; I did not fire the ball from fear, but because I was under the impression at the time that he had started to the door to fight his way through and that I thought he would harm some of our men if I did not.

Testimony of John Fletcher.

Examined by Judge Holt.—Q. State your business? A. I am the foreman of Naylor's livery stable.

Q. Do you know the prisoner Atzeroth? A. Yes.

Q. State whether or not you seen him about the third of April last? A. Yes; he came to the stable at that time, between six and seven o'clock, with another gentleman and two horses; they said they wanted to put up their horses there; I ordered their horses down into the stable; the other gentleman who was with Atzeroth, told me he was going to Philadelphia, and that he would leave these horses in Atzeroth's care [illegible] I have never seen that man since we kept the horses at the stable and sold one of them to a Mr. Thompson, a stage contractor. We kept the brown horse at the stable until

Continued on the Eighth Page.

The Philadelphia Inquirer.

PRICE TWO CENTS. PHILADELPHIA, FRIDAY, MAY 19, 1865. PRICE TWO CENTS.

THE ASSASSINS!

Trial of Booth's Accomplices!

YESTERDAY'S TESTIMONY.

Unraveling of the Mystery!

EVIDENCE AGAINST J. H. SURRATT.

His Hopes Gone and Prospects Blighted!

JUDGE OLIN'S EXAMINATION OF FORD'S THEATRE.

Plan to Capture Mr. Lincoln!

"SAM" ARNOLD'S LETTER TO "JOHN."

He Wants "John" to Go to Richmond.

DAVIS TO BE CONSULTED BEFORE ATTEMPTING MURDER!

The Plot to Burn Northern Cities and Steamers.

OFFICIAL REBEL EVIDENCE SHOWN!

Prof. McCullogh's Infernal Scheme

GENERAL HARRIS, OF MISSOURI, IMPLICATED!

J. D. Endorses the Diabolical Design!

EVIDENCE OF IMPORTANT WITNESSES

The Assassins Begin to Realize Their Proximity to the Gallows.

THE TRIAL OF THE CONSPIRATORS.

WASHINGTON, May 18.—The Court, after the evidence taken on Wednesday had been read, proceeded to the examination of witnesses.

Testimony of A. R. Reeve.

By the Judge Advocate.—Q. State where you reside. A. At Brooklyn, New York.

Q. In what business were you engaged in March last? A. In the telegraph business.

Q. Look at this despatch, and state what you know in regard to it. A. It was handed to me at the St. Nicholas Hotel by J. Wilkes Booth, to be sent to Washington.

Q. Will you read it? The witness read as follows:—"New York, March 23, 1865.—To —— Weischman, Esq., No. 541 H street, Washington, D. C.—Tell John to telegraph the number and street at once. J. Booth."

Q. That was J. Wilkes Booth? A. It was.

Q. Was it sent on the day of its date? A. It was sent on the 23d of March to this city.

Cross-examined by Mr. Aiken.—Q. How do you identify that telegram? A. I remember that he signed the name of "J. Booth," instead of J. Wilkes Booth, which was his full name.

Q. Were any remarks made to you by the man who gave you that despatch at the time of his giving it to you? A. No sir; I was busy at the time, but in sending it I noticed that the middle name was left out.

Q. Are you in the habit of keeping all despatches sent? A. Yes sir.

By Judge Holt.—Q. Is this the original despatch? A. Yes sir.

By Mr. Aiken.—Q. What sort of a looking person gave you that despatch? A. If I saw his likeness I could tell.

Re-Examination of Lewis Weischman.

By Judge Holt.—Q. Look at that telegram and state whether you received it on the day of its date. A. I cannot say that I received it on the 23d of March, but I received a telegram of the exact nature of this one.

Q. Who is the person referred to there as John? A. John Surratt was frequently called John.

Q. Did you not deliver the message to him? A. I delivered the message to him the same day.

Q. What did he say? A. I questioned him as to what was meant by the number and street; he replied to me Don't be so—— inquisitive.

Q. See whether this is the telegram you delivered? A. It is.

The witness, by request of the Judge Advocate, then read the telegram, which was a copy of the one given above.

Q. Did you know the handwriting of Booth? A. I have seen his handwriting, and could recognize his autograph.

The witness was here shown the original telegram, purporting to have been written by Booth, and said, that is his handwriting.

Q. State whether, on or about the 4th of March last, you had an interview in your room with John Wilkes Booth, John Surratt and Payne, the prisoner at the bar? A. I will state that as near as I can recollect it was after the 4th of March, and the second time that Payne visited the house; when I returned from my office one day at half-past four o'clock and went to my room, I rang the bell for Dan, the negro servant, and in reply to an inquiry which I addressed to him he told me that John had ridden out at about half-past two o'clock in the afternoon, with six others, on horseback; on going down stairs I found Mrs. Surratt weeping bitterly and asked her what was the matter: she said to me, "go down and make the best of your dinner, John has gone away;" about half-past six o'clock John Surratt came home and was very much intoxicated; in fact he rushed frantically into the room; he had one of Sharp's small six-barrel revolvers in his hand; I said "John, why are you so much excited?" he replied, "I will shoot any man who comes into this room; my hopes are gone and my prospects blighted; I want something to do; can you get me a clerkship?" The prisoner, Payne, came into the room, and about fifteen minutes afterwards Booth came into the room, and was so much excited that he walked frantically around the room several times without noticing me; he had a whip in his hand; the three then went up stairs into the second story, and they must have remained there together about twenty minutes; subsequently I asked Surratt where he had left Payne; he said Payne had gone to Baltimore; I asked him where Booth had gone; he said to New York; some two weeks afterwards Surratt, when passing the post office, inquired for a letter under the name of James Sturdy, and I asked him why a letter was sent to him under a false name; he said he had particular reasons for it; this must have been two weeks after this affair, before the 20th of March; the letter was signed Wood, and the writer stated that he was at the Revere House in New York; that he was looking for something to do, but would probably go to some boarding-house in Grand street; I think West Grand street; this was the whole substance of the letter.

Q. Are you familiar with Booth's handwriting or simply with his autograph? A. I have seen his autograph at the hotel and have also seen his autograph at the house.

Q. Here is a note signed R. E. Watson—will you look at it and see whether that is Booth's handwriting? A. No sir, I would not recognize that as Booth's handwriting.

Q. Was there any remark made in their excited conversation on the occasion of which you have spoken as to where they had all been riding? A. No sir, they were very guarded; Payne made no remark at all; the only remarks made were those excited remarks by Surratt.

Q. Surratt had been riding, you say, and Booth had a whip in his hand? A. Yes sir.

Q. He appeared to have been with them also? A. Yes sir, he was much excited.

Cross-examined by Mr. Aiken.—Q. What time in the day did you meet Mr. Floyd on his way to Washington? A. It must have been about ten o'clock in the morning.

Q. Did you hear any of the conversation that passed between him and Mrs. Surratt at that time? A. No sir; I leaned back in my buggy, and Mrs. Surratt leaned sideways and whispered some words in Mr. Floyd's ear.

Q. Did she afterwards say anything to you as to what the conversation was about? A. No sir; the only conversation that I heard at that time was between her and Mrs. Ott; she was talking about Mr. Howell.

By Mr. Johnson.—Q. Was that at the same time? A. No sir; it was after the conversation between Floyd and herself.

Q. Was it on the same spot? A. No sir.

By Mr. Ewing.—Q. Do you recollect when it was that Booth played "Pescara," in the *Apostate*? A. Yes sir; he played it that night; that must have been about the 24th of March.

Q. Was it not the day before or the day after their return from the ride that he played in the "Apostate?" A. That I cannot say; it must have been after the 4th of March; this man Payne was stopping at the house at the time, and when he came to the house he made some excuse to Mrs. Surratt, saying he would like to have been there before the 4th of March, but could not get there; by that circumstance I recollect that it was after the 4th of March; whether it was before or after the day that Booth played "Pescara" I can't say.

Q. Did you go to see that play? A. Yes sir; Booth sent complimentary tickets, at least gave a pass to Surratt for two, and he asked Surratt whether he thought I would go; Surratt said he thought not; when Surratt asked me I did go: the pass was a written one, and the door-keeper at first refused us admission.

Q. State whether the affair of the ride was before or after Booth played in the *Apostate*? A. To the best of my recollection it was before.

Q. How long before? A. Well, as near as I can recollect, about two weeks before.

Q. You cannot state [illegible] whether it was before or after the play in the *Apostate*? A. [illegible] would not like to state positively.

By Mr. Eakin—Q. How did you learn anything with reference to the antecedents of Mrs. Slater? A. Through Mrs. Surratt herself.

Q. What did Mrs. Surratt tell you? A. Mrs. Surratt stated to me that she came to the house in company with this man Howe; that she was a North Carolinian, I believe; that she spoke French, and that she was a blockade runner or bearer of despatches.

Q. Where were you at the time Mrs. Surratt told you this? A. I was in the house, in the kitchen, or at least in the dining-room.

Q. Are you certain beyond all doubt that Mrs. Surratt ever told you that Mrs. Slater was a blockade runner? A. Yes sir.

Q. Had you before that time ever seen Mrs. Slater at the house of Mrs. Surratt? A. I myself saw her only once; I learned she had been to the house twice.

Q. Never mind what you learned; you saw her only once? A. Only once.

Q. How long was she there? A. Only one night.

Q. Did you have any conversation with her yourself? A. She drove us to the door in a buggy, the bell rang, and Mrs. Surratt told me to go out and take her trunk; there was a young man in the buggy with her; that was all the conversation I had with her; she had her mask down, one of those short masks that ladies wear.

On being interrogated by the Court as to the meaning of the word mask, the witness said that he intended to signify a veil of the ordinary description.

Q. Was any one besides yourself present on the occasion of this conversation? A. Not that I remember.

Q. On what day was that? A. It was some time in February; I do not remember the precise day.

Q. Did you hear anything said about Mrs. Slater afterwards? A. No sir.

Q. What was Mrs. Surratt's exact language in giving you this information? A. She said that this woman was from North Carolina, and that if she got North, there would be no danger for her, because, being French, she could immediately apply to the French Consul: that was about the only language I can remember.

By Mr. Doster.—Q. When John Surratt returned to the house in a state of excitement did he tell you the occasion of his excitement? A. No sir; he showed me his pistol and said that he would shoot any man who came into the room; I said, "John, why are you so excited, why don't you settle down like a sensible young man?" He said, "my hopes are gone, my prospects blighted, can you get me a clerkship?" Those were his precise words; I looked at him and thought he was foolish.

Q. You remarked that Mrs. Surratt was weeping bitterly; did she state the cause of her grief? A. She merely said go down and make the best you can of your dinner; that John had gone away; John, when he returned, said to me that he had on three pairs of drawers; I thought from that he was going to take a long ride.

By Mr. Eakin.—Q. By whom were you called upon first to give your testimony in this case? A. I was called by the War Department.

Q. By what member of the War Department? A. I was called on by Judge Burnett.

Q. Were you arrested? A. I surrendered myself up on Saturday morning, at eight o'clock, to Superintendent Richards, of the Metropolitan Police force; I stated to him what I knew of these men, Payne, Harold and Booth, visiting Mrs. Surratt's; I stated also what I knew of John Surratt.

Q. What was your object in doing this? A. My object was to assist the Government.

Q. Were any threats ever made to you by any officer of the Government, if you did not give this information? A. Not at all.

Q. Were any inducements held out to you by any officer of the Government? A. Not at all; I read in the papers that morning a description of the assassin of Secretary Seward; he was described as a man who wore a long grey coat; I had seen Atzeroth wearing a long grey coat; I went down to Tenth street, and met a gentleman, to whom I communicated my suspicions, and then went and delivered myself up to Superintendent Richards, of the Metropolitan Police force, and told him where this man Payne had been stopping, and also Atzeroth and Harold; I was then sent to General Augur's office; after leaving that place, I met a man who kept a stable at Thirteenth and E streets, who stated that a man had been to his place to hire a horse; he described the man as being of small stature, having black eyebrows and a kind of a smile on his face; he said the name was Harold; I then went with officer McDevitt to Harold's house, and procured photographs of himself and Booth; officer McDevitt procured a photograph of Surratt; I related what I knew of Harold's habit of riding through Maryland, and that he had many acquaintances there, and that the assassins would probably take their course through Maryland.

Q. Did you ever say previous to your surrendering yourself and going to the office of Colonel Burnett, that you were fearful of an arrest? A. I myself had a great deal of fear; being in this house where these people were. I knew that I would be brought into public notice.

Q. I am not asking what you had to fear; but what you said?

Judge Bingham—You had better allow him to answer in his own way. A. As far as concerned my cognizance of anything wrong, I had no fears at all; when I surrendered myself to the Government I surrendered myself because I thought it to be my duty; it was hard for me to do so, situated as I was with respect to Mrs. Surratt and family; but it was my duty, and as such I have since regarded it.

Q. Did you at any time during the year 1863 board at a hotel called the Reynolds House? A. I did sir.

Q. Did you become acquainted there with a gentleman who went by the name of St. Marienn? A. I will state that in 1863 I met this St. Marienn in Maryland at a village called Ellangowan; he was introduced to me by a clergyman and was at that time teaching school; he spoke French, English and Italian fluently and his manners were very fascinating; he said then he had come from Montreal, and that he had been unfortunate in this country, having lost some five or six thousand dollars, the proceeds of a farm formerly owned by him in Canada; he stated also that he came to New York, embarked in a vessel to go to South America, and that the vessel was captured and he was thrown into Fort McHenry, from which place he was released through the agency of the French Consul; the witness added that the person to whom he referred, becoming destitute of means, took a situation on a farm; that he (the witness) subsequently met him, and finally promised to do all he could for him; two weeks after returning to Washington he was called upon by St. Marienn.

Judge Bingham then stated that there was no necessity for any further explanation.

Q. Did you pay his board at the Reynolds House, or become responsible for it?

Judge Bingham—I object to the question as being a matter of no consequence whether the witness did or did not.

Q. Did he state to you at any time that there was no aristocracy at the North, and he wished to go South?

Judge Bingham—I object to that also, as it is no matter whether he did or did not.

Q. Did he state to you that if he could not get to the South in any other way he would join a Federal regiment and desert?

Judge Bingham—I object to that, too, he is not a witness here.

Q. Do you know whether Mr. Reynolds reported any of his "St. Marienn's" treasonable talk or language at that time to the War Department?

Judge Bingham—I object to that, too; I would like to know what that is introduced for.

Mr. Eakin—It is introduced for the purpose of showing that the witness on the stand was a sympathizer with the Confederates and Rebels, and that he assisted this man to get away to the South. I will have something else to prove afterwards.

The President of the Court—The time for our usual recess has arrived; the Court will now take a recess until two o'clock.

A recess was accordingly taken.

Upon the reassembling of the Court, the question propounded by Mr. Eakin was again put, and Judge Bingham said that he objected to the question on the ground that it was on immaterial matters that were not in evidence, and should not be admitted in this manner. Of what concern was it what Reynolds reported. If the gentleman proposed to ask the witness whether he himself was guilty of any treasonable practices, nobody would object to it. The objection was then sustained.

Mr. Eakin—In as much as the Judge Advocate has informed us that he will not object to any questions that may be asked the witness with respect to his own conduct, I will address a few interrogatories to that effect.

Q. Did you give notice to St. Marienn that he would probably be arrested by the Government? A. No sir; I had no time to give such notice; St. Marienn rose one morning early and left; he afterwards enlisted in a Delaware regiment, and was taken prisoner and lodged in Castle Thunder.

Q. Are you a Clerk in the War Department? A. I have been.

Q. Did you, while a Clerk in the War Department, agree to communicate to any of the prisoners at the bar any information you might obtain from that Department? A. No sir.

Q. Are you acquainted with Mr. Howell? A. I have.

Q. What was Howell's first name? A. When he was at the house he gave the name of Spencer; he refused to give me his right name at the house; I afterwards learned from John Surratt that his name was Augustus Howell.

Q. Were you intimate with him? A. I was introduced to him; I never had any conversation with him; on the contrary, I said to Captain Gleason, of the War Department, "Captain, there is a blockade-runner at our house, shall I give him up?" I agitated the question for three days, but I thought it might be the only time that the man might be there, and I let him go.

Q. Did you ever have any conversation with Howell in relation to going South yourself? A. I told him that I would like to go South; that I had been a student of divinity, and would like to be in Richmond for the purpose of continuing my studies.

Q. Did he offer to make any arrangements in Richmond with a view to getting you a place there? A. No sir.

By Mr. Clampitt.—Q. Was it your desire to go to Richmond for the purpose of continuing your theological studies? A. Yes sir.

Q. For what reason? (Objected to.)

By Mr. Eakin.—Q. While you were in the War Department did this man, Howell, teach you a cipher? A. Yes sir; he showed me an alphabet.

Q. What was the purpose of his teaching you the cipher? A. He stated no particular purpose.

Q. Was it not for the purpose of corresponding with you from Richmond? A. No sir; he made no arrangement for corresponding: the cipher alphabet was in my box, and no doubt was found there; I once wrote a poem of Longfellow's in this cipher, and that is the only use I made of it; I showed the poem written in that cipher to Mr. Cruikshank, of the War Department.

Q. Is that all the use you ever made of the cipher? A. Yes sir: I never had a word of correspondence with Howell, and never saw him the second time until I saw him in prison.

Q. Was any objections ever made by any of these prisoners at the bar to your being present at their conversations? A. Not any that I heard, but they always withdrew themselves; when Surratt was in the parlor he would converse with me for about five minutes on general topics, and he would then give Booth a nudge, or Booth would give him a nudge, and they would go and sit up stairs for two or three hours; I never had a word of private conversation with them which I would not like the world to hear.

Q. Did Howell give you the key to that cipher? A. He showed me the cipher or alphabet and how to use it.

Q. He taught you it, did he not? A. I made no use of it whatever, except on that particular occasion, when I showed it to Mr. Cruikshank.

Q. That was not an answer to my question; he taught you the cipher, did he not? A. Well, yes, sir.

Q. Now, according to the best of your recollection, how soon was that after his return from Richmond? A. He had returned from New York, and he did not tell me when he had returned from Richmond, because it was the first and only time I ever saw the man in my life; he was well acquainted with Mrs. Surratt, and his nickname around the house was Spencer; he had been at the house a day or day and a half before I met him.

Q. Did he tell you that that was the cipher used in Richmond? A. No sir.

Q. You stated that the prisoners were free and unreserved in their conversation while in your presence? A. They spoke in my presence on general topics, and so on; they never spoke to me of their private business.

Q. Do we understand you as stating to the Court that in all your conversations with them you never learned of any intended treasonable act or conspiracy of theirs? A. I never did: I would have been the last man in the world to have suspected John Surratt, my schoolmate and companion, of the murder of the President of the United States.

Q. You state that your suspicions were aroused at one time by something you saw at Mrs. Surratt's? A. My suspicions were aroused by John Surratt, and by this man Payne and Booth coming to the house; my suspicions were again aroused by their frequent private conversations, by seeing Payne and Surratt with bowie-knives, and by finding a moustache in my room.

Q. Your suspicions were not aroused, then, by the fact of Surratt having on three pair of drawers? A. I thought he was going to take a long ride in the country, and perhaps he was going South.

Q. Then, as your suspicions were aroused on all these different occasions, and you had reason to believe that there was something in the wind that was improper, did you communicate your suspicions to the War Department? A. My suspicions were not of a fixed or definite character; I did not know what they intended to do. I made a confidante of Captain Gleason, of the War Department, and told him that Booth was a secret sympathizer; I mentioned snatches of conversation I had heard, and said to him, "Captain, what do you think of this all?" we even talked over what they might possibly be at; whether they could be bearers of despatches or blockade-runners; at one time I saw in the papers the capture of President Lincoln freely discussed, and I said to him, "Captain, do you think any party would attempt to capture the President?" He laughed and hooted at the idea.

Q. You did, then, hear of a proposition of that kind? A. I did not hear, but it was freely discussed in the papers; if you will refer to the *Tribune* of March 19th, you will see it mentioned; it was merely a casual remark that I made; these suspicions arose in my mind after this horseback ride: I remarked to Captain Gleason that Surratt had come back, and told him that what they had been after had failed.

Q. How came you to connect the matter of the capture of the President, of which you read in the newspaper, with any of these parties?

The question was objected to by Judge Bingham as being wholly immaterial or irrelevant. The objection was sustained.

Q. Were you on intimate personal relations with the prisoners at the bar? A. Not intimate relations; I met them merely because they boarded at Mrs. Surratt's house; I met Atzeroth and went to the theatre with him; I looked upon him, as did every one in the house, as a good-hearted countryman.

Q. But you were a schoolmate with John Surratt? A. John had been my companion for seven years.

Q. Did you still profess to be a friend of his when you gave the information that you did to the War Department? A. I was his friend, but when my suspicions as to the danger of the Government were aroused, I preferred the Government to John Surratt; I did not know what he was contemplating; he said he was going to engage in cotton speculations and in the oil business.

Q. You did not know what he was contemplating; why then did you forfeit your friendship to him? A. I never forfeited my friendship; he forfeited his friendship to me.

Q. How so; by engaging in cotton speculations? A. No sir; by placing me in the position in which I am now; I think of the two I was more a friend to him than he was to me.

By Mr. Ewing.—Q. You spoke of reading a publication in the *Tribune*, of March 19th, referring to a plot to capture the President? A. Yes sir.

Q. Can you not, by connecting that circumstance with the ride which these parties had in the country, fix more definitely the time of that ride—whether before or after the date of that publication? A. I think it was after it; I would also state that I saw in the Washington *Republican* a statement concerning a contemplated assassination of President Lincoln, and Surratt once made a remark to me that if he succeeded in [illegible] cotton spec[illegible]tion his country would [illegible] forever and his name would go down [illegible] country, [illegible] You [illegible] appeared [illegible] was after March 19th? A. Yes sir.

Q. Was your remark to Captain Gleason, respecting [illegible] capture of the President, made after the ride? A. Yes sir; I said to Capt. Gleason that Surratt's mysterious, incomprehensible business had failed, and I added, "Let us think over what it could have been;" we mentioned a variety of things, even the breaking open of the Old Capitol Prison: I would mention that after that ride, my suspicions were not so much aroused as before it, because neither Payne nor Atzeroth had been at the house since; the only one of them who visited was the man Booth.

Q. Have you ever seen the prisoner, Arnold? A. No sir.

Q. Did you first meet the prisoner, Dr. Samuel Mudd, on Seventh street, opposite the Odd Fellows' Hall? A. I did.

The witness further testified that Mrs. Surratt lived in the house on H street, next to the corner of Sixth, and that the point on Seventh street at which he met Dr. Mudd, was not on a direct route from the Pennsylvania House or the National Hotel to Mrs. Surratt's.

Re-Examination of John Greenawalt.

By the Judge Advocate.—Q. In describing the poorly dressed man who called at your house with Atzeroth on the morning of the 15th of April, you said that his hair was black, but omitted to state the color of his beard and moustache; state it now? A. Their color was dark.

Testimony of James Walker (Colored.)

By the Judge Advocate.—Q. State whether or not on the 14th of April last you were living at the Pennsylvania House in this city and your business there. A. I was living there; I was twelve months there on the 4th of April last; my business was to make fires, carry water, &c.

Q. State whether or not you ever saw the prisoner Atzeroth at that house, and under what circumstances? A. He came there about 2 o'clock on the morning of the 15th of April, and left between 5 and 6 o'clock in the morning.

Q. Did he come there on foot, or on horseback? A. The first time he came on horseback, and I held the horse for him at the door.

Q. What hour was that? A. It was between 12 and 1 o'clock, I believe.

Q. What did he do while you were holding his horse? A. He went into the bar; I do not know what he done there; he came out again, and asked me to get him a piece of switch, which I did, when he rode off.

Q. Did you notice whether he had arms with him? A. I did not notice what he had; I did not see anything.

Q. When he came back at two o'clock was he on foot or on horseback? A. On foot; I was laying down and rose and let him in.

Q. Did he have a room? A. He desired to go to No. 52, I told him it was taken up; he stopped at No. 53.

Q. At what hour did he leave on that morning? A. Between five and six o'clock.

Q. Where did you see him at that hour? A. I went for a hack for a lady who was going in the 6·15 train, and when I was returning I overtook him as he was walking along slowly; he made no remark to me.

Q. Did you see another man who stopped there that night? A. He left in the morning about four or five minutes before Atzeroth, having stopped in the same room; he had no baggage.

Q. Do you remember his appearance? A. When he came in it was dark, the gas being pretty low; he seemed to have on dark clothes, and wore a slouched hat; he went to his room immediately, having paid for it in advance.

Q. Will you look at the prisoners at the bar and see if any of them resemble this man? A. I cannot say sir.

The cross-examination of this witness elicited no new points of interest. He testified that the horse used by Atzeroth on the night in question, was apparently a small light bay horse; he had seen Atzeroth have a belt containing a pistol and knife some four or five days before the assassination, but could not identify the weapons. He did not see any weapons on Atzeroth on the night of the 14th, or the morning of the 15th. Atzeroth had no conversation with the man by whom he was accompanied at the time.

Testimony of William Clendenin.

By Judge Holt.—Q. Look at that knife (the knife supposed to have been thrown away by Atzeroth on the night of the assassination) and say if you ever had it in your hand before? A. Yes. On passing down F street on the morning after the assassination on the south side of the street, between Eighth and Ninth, I saw a colored man pick up something from the gutter about ten feet from me; as I came up I asked him what it was and he gave the knife to me; a lady spoke to me from the third story window, and she saw the knife in the gutter and sent the colored man down to get it; I took it and gave it to the Chief of Police; this was on the Saturday morning of the assassination.

Cross-examined by Mr. Doster—Q. What time in the morning? About 6 o'clock.

Q. Whereabouts precisely on F street was it? A. In front of Creaser's house; it lay as if it had been thrown under the carriage step.

Testimony of J. S. McPhail.

By Judge Holt.—Q. State whether or not you had a conversation with Atzeroth in prison in which he said that on the night of the assassination of the President, he had thrown his knife away in the streets of Washington.

Question objected to by Mr. Doster, on the ground that the confession of the witness was under duress.

Q. Under what circumstances was the statement made to you? A. I received information that he desired to see me, and I went to see him accordingly; I found him in a cell in prison in irons.

Mr. Doster argued that the condition of the prisoner was such as to intimidate him, and to make his confession under such circumstances was improper to be given as evidence, and cited many authorities to sustain his objections.

The witness stated that he was Provost Marshal-General of the State of Maryland, which fact Atzeroth knew. Witness further stated that a brother-in-law of Atzeroth was on his force and a brother was temporarily on his force also.

Both of them repeatedly desired the witness to see Atzeroth, and he went there with the permission of the Secretary of War simply at their instance. The prisoner was in irons, but had no cover over his face or head. The objection of the Counsel was sustained by the Court.

Witness then answered the question asked him in the affirmative.

Cross examined by Mr. Doster—Q. That was all he said? A. I did not say that. I answered the question, Yes.

Q. Did he describe the knife, or name the place where he threw it away? A. He said he threw it away just above the Hearndon House, which is on the corner of Ninth and F streets.

Q. Did he also say where his pistol was? A. He stated that it was at Matthews & Co.'s, Georgetown, in possession of a young man named Caldwell.

Q. Did he state how he got it there? A. He said he went there and borrowed $10 on the pistol, on Saturday morning, April 15th.

Q. Did the prisoner mention to you a certain coat containing a pistol and bowie knife, and exchanging it in the Kirkwood House, and if so did he state who it belonged to? A. He stated that the coat at the hotel belonged to Harold.

Mr. C. Stone, counsel for Harold, in a very loud voice exclaimed, "I object to that testimony." (Laughter.)

Testimony of Lieutenant W. R. Keen.

By Judge Holt.—Q. Did you pass the night of the 14th of April at the Pennsylvania House, in this city? A. I did.

Q. Did you see Atzeroth at the house that night? A. I did.

Q. Under what circumstances did you see him? A. I came into the hotel about 4 o'clock on Saturday morning; he was in bed when I arrived in my room; I asked him whether he had heard of the murder of the President, he said yes, and remarked what an awful thing it was; after that I went to bed, and when I awoke, about 7 o'clock, he was gone.

Q. Did you see his arms? A. Not there; when he occupied room No. 51, I saw him have a knife and a revolver.

Q. How long before the assassination? A. I think it was the Sunday before, or the Sunday a week; I would not be positive: the bowie knife had a sheath. (A knife was shown to witness.) I could not swear that was the knife; but it was a knife about that size.

Q. State under what circumstances you saw the arms? A. He went out and left the knife on the bed; I took it and put it under my pillow; when he came in he asked, "Luke, did you see my knife;" he said he wanted that, and remarked, "if one fails I will have the other;" I handed it to him and he went out.

Q. Did he have a pistol? A. Yes, he always carried that around his waist.

Cross-examined by Mr. Doster.—Q. Did you know the prisoner, Atzeroth, before you met him at the Pennsylvania House? A. Yes sir.

Q. Did you speak about the assassination of the President immediately on going into the room that morning? A. No: he was in bed when I came right opposite, and it was five or ten minutes before I spoke to him.

Q. Did he say anything more than that it was an awful thing? A. I believe that is all.

Q. Was he undressed? A. He was in bed; I do not know whether he was undressed or not.

Q. You mention the prisoner calling you Luke, were you on intimate terms with him? A. Yes; that was the only name I ever heard him call me.

Q. Did you see him after this affair? A. No sir.

Q. When he said that if this failed the other would not, what else did he say? A. I do not know; this was a week or ten days before the assassination.

Q. At the time you heard the words had you been drinking with the prisoner? A. Yes, we had two or three drinks while we were lying in bed.

Q. Were these remarks made after these drinks? A. Yes.

Q. What kinds of drinks were these? A. Whisky cocktails, I believe.

Q. Do you remember anything else that was said in that interview? A. No; that was about all.

Testimony of Washington Briscoe.

By Judge Holt.—Q. On the night of the 14th April did you see the prisoner, Atzeroth, and if so, at what time? A. I did see him; he got into the car at Sixth street, and rode towards the Navy Yard; it was between half-past eleven and twelve o'clock.

Q. What did he say? [illegible] asked me to let him sleep [illegible] heard of the [illegible] at the store with me.

Q. Where was your store? A. Down [illegible] Yard; I told him I could not let him sleep there.

[illegible] his manner? A. He seemed to be excited.

Q. Did he urge you, or seem to be very anxious to sleep with you? A. Yes: he asked me three times.

Q. What became of him? A. He rode down as far as I did; got out when I did, and asked me again; the gentleman with me did not invite him to stop, and of course I had no right to do so.

Q. How long had you known him? A. Some seven or eight years.

Q. Did he then express his determination to go anywhere else? A. He said he was going back to what was formerly the "Kimmel" House, now the "Pennsylvania" House, in C street.

Cross-examined by Mr. Doster.—Q. Did you notice the precise time when you met Atzeroth that evening? A. No, but I think it was about half-past eleven or twelve o'clock.

Q. What time was it when he left you that evening, as near as you can tell? A. Near twelve o'clock; he stopped at the corner of J and Garrison streets, near the Navy Yard to wait until a car came back.

Q. What was his manner; did he appear [illegible] disturbed? A. I judged from his manner that he was a little excited.

Q. Had he been drinking? A. I hardly know; I did not notice particularly.

Testimony of Rev. Dr. W. H. Ryder.

Examined by Judge Holt.—Q. State your residence and profession. A. I reside in Chicago, and am a clergyman.

Q. State whether you recently made a visit into Richmond, and at what time? A. I left Chicago on the 9th of April, and arrived in Richmond on the 14th, where I remained till the 21st.

Q. While there did you find in the Capitol the archives of the so-called Confederate States, and if so, in what condition? A. I did; they were pretty generally confused, and scattered about on the floor.

Q. Did you, in common with others, pick up papers from the floor? A. Yes.

Q. State whether the paper you now hold in your hand was picked up in the Capitol at Richmond under the circumstances you mention? A. Yes; I picked it up either in the building or immediately about the building, or it was handed to me by some one who picked it up in the rubbish about the room; there were one or two persons with me; they were stooping down, and when they found anything of importance they would pick it up and preserve it; in some instances the orderly who was in attendance would hand me something, and I would put it in my pocket; having thus collected quite a number of things, they were thrown into a common receptacle and put into a box and forwarded to Chicago: this was one of the papers found.

The paper referred to was read by the Judge Advocate, as follows:—

"RICHMOND, February 11, 1865.—His Excellency Jefferson Davis, President C. S. A:—When Senator Johnson, of Missouri, and myself waited upon you, some days since, in relation to the project of annoying and harrassing the enemy by means of burning their shipping, towns, etc., etc., there were several remarks made by you upon the subject that I was not fully prepared to answer, but which, upon subsequent conference with parties proposing the enterprise, I find cannot apply as objections to the scheme. First, the combustible material consists of several preparations, and not one alone, and can be used without exposing the party using them to the least danger of detection whatever. The preparations are not in the hands of Mr. Daniel, but are in the hands of Professor McCullogh, and are known but to him and one other party, as I understand.

"Second. There is no necessity for sending persons in the military service into the enemy's country, but the work may be done by agents, and in most cases by persons ignorant of the facts, and, therefore, innocent agents. I have seen enough of the effects that can be produced to satisfy me that in most cases without any danger to the parties engaged, and in others but very slight, that:—First. We can first burn every vessel that leaves a foreign port for the United States. Second. We can burn every transport that leaves the harbor of New York, or other Northern ports, with supplies for the armies of the enemy in the South. Third. Burn every transport and gun-boat on the Mississippi River, as well as devastate the country of the enemy and fill his people with terror and consternation.

"I am not alone of this opinion, but many other gentlemen are as fully and thoroughly impressed with the conviction as I am. I believe we have the means at our command, if promptly appropriated and energetically applied to demoralize the Northern people in a very short time. For the purpose of satisfying your mind upon the subject I respectfully but earnestly request that you will have an interview with General Harris, formerly a member of Congress from Missouri, who, I think, is able, by conclusive proofs, to convince you that what I have suggested is perfectly feasible and practicable.

"The deep interest I feel for the success of our cause in this struggle, and the conviction of the importance of availing ourselves of every element of defense, must be my excuse for writing you and requesting you to invite General Harris to see you. If you should see proper to do so, please signify to me the time when it will be convenient for you to see him.

"I am, respectfully, your obedient servant,

"W. S. O'LAHM."

On the back of the letter are two indorsements, the first being "Hon. W. S. O'Lahm, Richmond, February 12, 1865 In relation to plans and means of burning the enemy's shipping, &c. Preparations are in the hands of Professor McCullogh, and are known to only one party. He asks the President to have an interview with General Harris, formerly M. C. from Missouri, on the subject." The other is "The Secretary of State, at his convenience, will please see General Harris, and learn what plan he has for overcoming the difficulty heretofore experienced. J. D. 20th February, 1865. Received February 17, 1865."

Testimony of John Potts.

Examined by Judge Holt.—Q. State your occupation. A. I am Chief Clerk of the War Department, and have been so for twenty years.

Continued on the Eighth Page.

DAVID C. HAROLD,

The Accomplice of Booth in the Murder of President Lincoln.

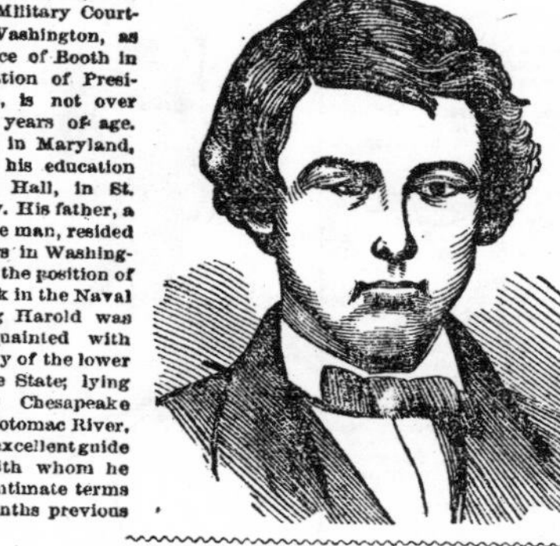

David C. Harold, now on trial by the Military Court-martial at Washington, as the accomplice of Booth in the assassination of President Lincoln, is not over twenty-three years of age. He was born in Maryland, and received his education at Charlotte Hall, in St. Mary's county. His father, a most estimable man, resided for many years in Washington, and held the position of principal clerk in the Naval Store. Young Harold was perfectly acquainted with the topography of the lower portion of the State; lying between the Chesapeake Bay and the Potomac River, and made an excellent guide for Booth, with whom he was on most intimate terms for several months previous to the assassination. Harold led a very dissipated life and was notoriously indolent, while it was a matter of general surprise how he obtained means to live. It is probable now that money was furnished him from the secret service fund of the Rebel Government, as well as to Booth, Payne and the other conspirators.

Harold is an inveterate talker, and a great coward, as his anxiety to surrender when in Garrett's barn sufficiently proves. Since his capture he has been talkative and reticent by turns, and although wearing generally an indifferent air while in court, when in his cell he frequently gives way to fits of weeping. The portrait above is from his photograph, taken since his confinement in the prison.

THE PRISONERS' MANACLES.

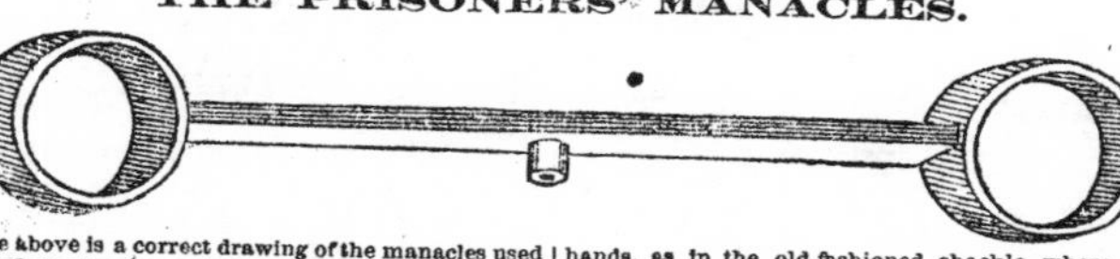

The above is a correct drawing of the manacles used in confining the arms of the prisoners. The wristlets are attached to an iron bar, about twelve inches in length, which prevents the wearer from joining his hands, as in the old-fashioned shackle, where the clasps are connected by chain links, thus effectually preventing the culprit from unfastening or breaking them.

The Philadelphia Inquirer.

PRICE TWO CENTS. PHILADELPHIA, SATURDAY, MAY 20, 1865. PRICE TWO CENTS.

THE TRIAL

Yesterday's Proceedings

FURTHER DEVELOPMENTS OF THE FIENDISH PLOT.

Some New Links in the Chain of Evidence.

THE ASSAULT ON SEC'Y SEWARD.

Interesting Details of the Deed.

PAYNE IS IDENTIFIED AS THE ASSAILANT!

Major Seward Swears to His Identity!

NURSE AND SERVANT ON THE STAND.

Demoniacal Gaiety of Payne.

HE LAUGHS AT THE RECITAL OF HIS OWN DEPRAVITY.

The Gallows His Certain Doom.

HIS ACCOMPLICES TO SHARE HIS FATE

Outraged Justice to be Vindicated!

ADDITIONAL PROOF OF REBEL COMPLICITY!

Discovery of Some of Booth's Private Papers.

THEY ARE IN CONFEDERATE CIPHER.

THE TRIAL OF THE CONSPIRATORS.

WASHINGTON, May 19.—The witnesses for the defense were to-day dismissed until Monday. About twenty have thus far been summoned. The United States have probably thirty more witnesses to examine, and as the effort will be made to conclude the testimony for the prosecution to-morrow, the trial will probably be closed next week.

Testimony of Colonel J. H. Taylor.

By Judge Holt.—Q. State whether you are connected with the Provost Marshal's office at Washington? A. No sir; I am on duty at the head-quarters of the Department at Washington.

Q. Look at that paper, marked No. 7, and state whether you ever before had it in your hands, and from whom you received it? (The paper referred to was one taken from the trunk of J. Wilkes Booth, and in regard to which the witness, Lieutenant Tyrrell, testified that it was written in the cipher of the Confederate States.) A. I have had it in my hands; I received it from Lieutenant Tyrrell, an officer on duty in the Provost Marshal's office, on the night of the 14th of April; I gave it to Colonel Wells on the 15th.

Q. You received it from Lieutenant Tyrrell as one of the papers found in the trunk of J. Wilkes Booth? A. Yes sir; for which I had sent him.

Testimony of Charles Rosch.

By Judge Advocate Holt.—Q. Do you recognize the prisoner, Edward Spangler? A. I do not know him personally; I was not present at his arrest.

Q. Did you go to his house after his arrest? A. Yes sir.

Q. What did you find there? A. A carpet bag, in which was a piece of rope, which I measured afterwards and found to be eighty-one feet in length; the twist appeared to have been taken out of it; there was nothing else in the carpet bag except some blank paper and a dirty shirt collar.

Q. Where was that carpet bag with the rope left? A. At the house where Spangler took his meals, on the N. W. corner of Seventh and H streets.

Q. When was it left? A. That I do not know.

Q. Who were with you when you took the rope? A. Two of the military of the Provost Marshal's force; I do not know their names.

Q. You did not see Spangler himself there? A. I did not; I was to go with the other officers to secure the papers, and we missed him; consequently I was not there when he was arrested.

Q. Had the carpet bag been opened? A. No sir; we made out to open it with some keys we found.

Cross-examined by Mr. Ewing.—Q. Where is the house at which you found the carpet bag? A. It is situated on the northwest corner of Seventh street and H street.

Q. Who gave it to you? A. We took it when we found it belonged to Spangler.

Q. Who was there? A. A man who was commonly called "Jake," who worked at the theatre in company with Spangler; this man told me that was Spangler's carpet bag, and that was all that Spangler had at the house.

Q. What persons were living or staying in the house. Did you see? A. There were a couple of persons, boarders, I presume, I did not know any of the parties.

Q. In what room did you find the carpet bag? A. In a bed room up stairs.

Q. In what part of the house? A. As near as I can judge, it was on the south side of the house; that is, the room faced the south.

Q. Describe the room? A. It was right near where Jake kept his trunk.

The Commission reassembled at two o'clock, after the usual recess.

Testimony of Chas. H. Rosch, Continued.

Q. Look at that coil of rope and state whether or not it is the same which you found in Spangler's carpet-bag? A. (Looking at the rope.) I believe and am satisfied that it is.

Q. What did you do with the monkey wrench? A. I found no monkey wrench; I would here beg leave of the Court to correct so much of the testimony as refers to the locality which I stated; upon reflection I am convinced that the house was on the northeast corner of Seventh and H streets; the room was on the second floor.

Q. What was the number of the room. A. There was no number.

Testimony of Wm. Eaton, (Continued.)

Q. State to the Court whether you arrested the prisoner, Edward Spangler, and on what day? A. I arrested him; I do not recollect the day; it was the week after the assassination.

Q. Where did you arrest him? A. In a house on Seventh street, near the Patent Office; it must have been on the southeast corner of Seventh street and H.

Q. Do you know whose house it was? A. I do not.

Q. Did you find any weapons in his possession? A. No sir, I did not search him.

Q. Was it his boarding-house? A. I think it was.

Q. Who was with him? A. There were some ladies in the house.

Testimony of William Wallace.

By the Judge Advocate.—Q. State whether or not some time after the assassination of the President you arrested the prisoner, O'Laughlin? A. I did; on the 17th of April.

Q. Where? A. At the house of a family named Bailey, in High street, Baltimore.

Q. Was that his boarding house? A. I think not; I think his boarding house, or the house where he stopped, was that of his brother-in-law, No. 57 Exeter street.

Q. Did you ask him why he was there instead of his boarding house? A. I did; he said that when he arrived in town on Saturday he was told that the officers had been looking for him; and that he went away to the house of a friend of his, where he stopped on Saturday or Sunday night.

Q. Did he ask you what you had arrested him for? A. He seemed to understand what it was for.

Q. Did he ask you at all in regard to the cause? A. Nothing that occurs to my mind at present.

Q. Did he speak of the assassination of the President at all? A. He spoke of it as being a very bad affair.

Q. Did you find any arms in his possession? A. No sir; we searched him and found none whatever.

Cross-examined by Mr. Fox.—Q. Did the brother-in-law of the prisoner send for the prisoner or go with you to arrest him?

Judge Bingham objected to the question.

Mr. Cox stated that the object was to show that the brother-in-law of the prisoner went after him voluntarily.

Judge Bingham replied that the question was not properly a portion of the cross-examination, but was altogether new matter. What the prisoner said to his brother-in-law had not been offered in evidence, and, in addition to that, it had been shown that the prisoner had resolved not to be taken at home, and was going to change his boarding-house.

Mr. Cox.—The object of the prosecution, I presume, is to show that the purpose of the prisoner in changing his lodgings was to avoid arrest, the witness having testified that the prisoner was found elsewhere. I desire to ask him whether he found the prisoner at the instance of his (the prisoner's) brother-in-law.

The objection was overruled, the Commission deciding that the question should be answered.

A. The prisoner's brother-in-law, Mr. Mallsby, I am well acquainted with; he was recommended to me on Sunday evening as being a good Union man, as one in whom I could place confidence; he knew I was looking for Mr. O'Laughlin; I told him I wished him to assist me; he said that anything he could do to assist me he would do; that if he could get any information concerning the prisoner he would impart it to me; that on Sunday evening or Monday morning he came to me and told me that he thought if I went with him we could find O'Laughlin; I then went with him and arrested the prisoner.

Q. Did the prisoner say anything about having received any information as to whether the detectives had been at his house? A. I think he said that when he got to his house on Saturday afternoon he heard that they had been there.

Q. Did he protest his innocence of the crime? A. He said he knew nothing whatever about it.

Q. Did he say he could show his innocence by the persons with whom he had been in company? A. He said he could account for his whereabouts all the time that he was in Washington, through parties who were there with him.

Q. Did he say he left home after being advised that detectives were there after him? A. I do not remember that he said so.

Testimony of James Gifford.

By the Judge Advocate.—Q. State whether you have been connected with Ford's Theatre in this city, and in what capacity? A. I have been in the capacity of builder.

Q. You were the carpenter of the building? A. Yes sir.

Q. Did you occupy that position on the 14th and 15th of April last? A. Yes sir.

Q. Did you observe the President's box on that day? A. No sir; I was not in it.

Q. Do you recollect having seen any one in it? A. Well, I saw Mr. Harry Clay Ford in it at one time, and Mr. Reybold.

Q. Any one else? A. No sir.

Q. Did you observe a large rocking chair which was in the President's box on the day of the 14th? A. I did not notice it on the 14th.

Q. When did you see it? A. I saw it on the following Sunday in the box.

Q. Do you know when it was placed in the box, and by whom? A. I do not.

Q. Do you know whether it was ever there before? A. I do not think it has been there before during this season; I saw it last season.

Q. Do you know who took it away? A. No sir.

Q. Do you know whether the stage scenes remain now as they were on the morning of the assassination

The witness' reply was somewhat inaudible at the reporter's desk, but he was understood to say that with the exception of a slight disarrangement which had been made by order of the Secretary of War in order to secure a view of the stage, the scenes were in the same position as on the morning of the assassination.

Q. Have you examined the wall in the President's box? A. Yes sir.

Q. When did you examine it? A. I think it was on Monday morning after the assassination when I first saw it.

Q. You had not seen it before? A. No sir.

Q. When had you been in the box last? A. I cannot state positively; I judge it was within a week.

Q. Do you think that if the mortice had been there, you would have observed it? A. Yes sir, I should think so.

Q. Had it the appearance of having been very recently made? A. It looked so to me.

Q. By what instrument would you suppose it to have been made? A. I should think it was made by a knife.

Q. Would it not require a good while to make it with a knife? It is quite a large mortice? A. It would require a man some fifteen minutes, I should judge.

Q. If the three doors of the place were all closed it would have been entirely dark there, would it not? A. Yes sir.

Q. Do you not think that one or more of those doors must have been opened when this mortice was made? A. It might have been so; some light would have been required, I should think.

Q. Would not such an operation, made with an open door, be likely to attract the attention of persons connected with the theatre? A. If a knife were used it would not; if a chisel or hammer were used, they would create sounds.

Q. What were the duties of the prisoner, Spangler? A. He worked on the stage, made scenery, fixed up the stage, &c.

Q. Was the decoration of this box within the line of his duties? A. No sir; there was a gentleman there by the name of Reybold, who was an upholsterer, whose duty it was to decorate the box, but he had a stiff neck, so he told me afterwards; when I asked him if I did not see him in the box he said, yes, but I did not decorate it.

Q. Where were you at the moment of the assassination of the President? A. I was standing about ten feet from the centre of the big lamp, just at the edge of the platform.

Q. On the stage? A. No sir; in front of the house, outside; I came out to the front of the house after having been in three or four minutes.

Q. You allude to the front part of the theatre? A. Yes sir.

Q. Had you been behind the scenes? A. Yes sir.

Q. How long before? A. About twenty minutes before.

Q. While there did you see the prisoner, Spangler? A. Yes sir.

Q. What was he doing? A. He was on the left hand side; I came out before the curtain and went up; he was waiting to transact his business, which was scene shifting.

Q. Was it not usual for the passage way which leads to the back door to be kept entirely free of obstructions while a piece was being played? A. The outside passage was always kept free; the entrances were more or less filled with chairs and tables, though that depended on what was being played; sometimes, as in pieces where a large number of seats were used, the passages became jammed up.

Q. Do you know who made the mortice on the bar which was found there? A. I do not.

Cross-examined by Mr. Ewing.—A paper, which purported to be a plan of the interior of the theatre, was shown to the witness, with the request that he should state whether it was correctly drawn. The witness pointed out that it was deficient in several particulars.

Q. State whether the passage-way across the stage to the outer door was ordinarily obstructed during the play? A. Only by people when there was a large company on the stage; there were never any chairs, tables or scenery in the way.

Q. Was it not necessary to keep the passage-way clear in order to allow the actors and actresses to pass without obstruction from the dressing room to the stage? A. Yes sir.

Q. How is the back door, the small one, usually left? A. It is usually left open after the performance is over.

Q. Do you mean that it is swinging open, or merely unlocked? A. Left unlocked; the only door that is left open is the door leading to the side of the house.

Q. State what position Mr. Spangler occupied during the performance. A. His business was on the left hand side of the stage, the right hand from the audience.

Q. Was that on the side of the President's box? A. Yes.

Q. State at what times during the performance you were on the stage that night? A. I was on the stage until the curtain went up; when it was lowered I came around on the stage to see that everything was right.

Q. State at what times during the evening when you came on the stage between the acts you saw Mr Spangler? A. I could not state the time exactly; I judge that the last time I saw him was about half-past nine o'clock.

Q. State whether you saw him each time? A. Yes sir, each time.

Q. He was your subordinate, was he not? A. Yes sir.

Q. State where you were during that play when you were not on the stage? A. I was in the front of the house; I walked down to D street and Tenth to look at a big lamp which I had put up there; during the performance of the first act I walked up to the corner of Tenth street and F, and took a glass of ale; during the second act and during the third act I did not leave the house at all.

Q. You were then in front of the theatre part of the time between the second and third act? A. I was on the stage between the acts.

Q. Where were you during the performance of the second act? A. To the best of my knowledge I was then in the front.

Q. All the time? A. Not all the time.

Q. How much of the time? A. Well I do not know; I walked in and stayed, may be, five or ten minutes and walked out.

Q. State whether or not you saw the prisoner, Spangler, at any time during that play in front of the theatre? A. I did not; I do not think he could have been in front of the theatre without my knowing it, because the scene would have gone wrong if he had left the stage.

PORTRAITS OF THE CONSPIRATORS.

LEWIS C. PAYNE.

SAMUEL C. ARNOLD.

Q. Did you ever see Spangler wear a moustache? A. No sir; he never wore one since I knew him.

Q. Do you know how he was dressed that evening? A. No sir; I did not take any notice of him.

Q. How was he dressed ordinarily? A. About the same as he is now.

Q. Was not the *American Cousin* a play in which the scenes were shifted a good deal? A. They were what we call plain scenes; there was not much shifting; I believe there were some five or six scenes in each act.

Q. Then Spangler's presence there would have been indispensable to the performance? A. Yes sir; if he had not been there the scenes would not have gone on.

Q. Did you hear Booth call Spangler that night? A. No sir.

Q. What had Spangler to do with Booth? A. Nothing, that I know of; Booth was rather friendly, and everybody about the house was friendly with him; he had a winning way about him that would make every person like him; he was a good natured, jovial kind of man.

Q. Was he not very much in the habit of frequenting the theatre? A. I would see him there [illegible] week, then he would go off and I would no[illegible] for a couple of weeks.

Q. Did he not have access to the thea[illegible] of the employees would have? A. Yes sir.

Q. He had access by the back entrance at any time? A. Yes sir, at any time when the employees might go in.

Q. Day and night? A. At any time when the house was not locked up.

Q. Was not Spangler a sort of a drudge for Booth? A. He appeared so; he used to go down and help fix Booth's horses; I have seen him myself once or twice fixing up the horse.

Q. Was that hole in the wall cut into the brick? A. No sir, I believe not; to the best of my knowledge it was cut in only an inch.

Q. And it could have been done with a pen-knife? A. Yes sir; I think it might have been done with a pen-knife.

The witness was here shown the stick or bar found in the President's box, which, however, he failed to identify in any manner.

Q. How long would it have taken with an ordinary pocket knife to cut the hole in the wall of which you have spoken? A. I suppose that a man, intent upon mischief, would have done it in ten or fifteen minutes; after the face of the plaster was once broken it could be accomplished very easily.

Q. I believe you stated that you did not know how the lock in the door of the President's box came to be loose? A. I do not know.

Q. When did you first hear that the President was coming to the theatre? A. I heard it between 11 and 12 o'clock on that day.

Q. Do you know whether he was invited to the theatre? A. I do not.

Testimony of Mrs. Martha Murray.

By Judge Holt.—Q. Look at the prisoners at the bar and see if you can recognize any of them? A. I have not seen any of them, unless it is that gentleman (pointing to Payne, who was directed to stand up); he has the same appearance of a man I saw.

Q. Was the person of whom you speak a boarder at your house? A. Yes sir.

Q. Under what name did he pass? A. I did not hear any name; when Mr. McDevitt came to the house afterwards I showed him the name on the book which I thought was entered when he came there, and Mr. McDevitt cut the name out of the book; I cannot remember what the name was.

Q. How long did he remain there? A. He came on Friday and left on Friday, two weeks afterwards.

Q. You keep the Herndon House, do you not? A. My husband does.

Q. Was the Friday on which he left the 14th of April last? A. Yes; the day the President was killed.

Q. What time in the day did he leave? A. About 4 o'clock; we had dinner at half-past 4; this gentleman said he was going away, and wanted to settle his bill, and wished dinner before the regular dinner hour; I gave orders to have an early dinner given him; I never saw anything further concerning him.

Q. Did he come to your house as an invalid? A. No; he said he came from the cars about 11 or 12 o'clock.

Q. Did he come alone, or with others? A. He came alone.

Q. Was he visited by others while there? A. I expect he was.

Q. Would you be able to recognize any person who visited him? Look at the prisoners. A. I do not see any one I could recognize; I never noticed any one, but one evening when at the supper table this gentleman came in; I had finished my supper, and got up, and did not pay any further attention; I left them sitting at the table.

Q. Had any one spoken to you for a room for this man before he came? A. No, not to my knowledge; some gentlemen have spoken to me for rooms, but I do not recollect any one speaking for this man.

Q. Do you remember whether John H. Surratt called at your house? A. I do not know him; I never heard of him till this circumstance.

Cross-examined by Mr. Doster.—Q. State to the Court the location of the Herndon House. A. It is on the corner opposite the Patent Office.

Testimony of Wm. R. Wells (Colored.)

By Judge Holt.—Q. State whether or not on the 14th of April last you were living in the house of Mr. Seward, Secretary of State, and if so in what capacity? A. I was in the capacity of a waiter.

Q. Look at the prisoners at the bar, and see if you recognize either of them. A. *Yes, I recognize that man* (pointing to Paine.)

Q. Did he attempt to come into the house of Mr. Seward on the night of the 14th of April? A. He did.

Q. State the circumstances connected with his entrance into the house. A. When he came he rang the bell and I went to the door, and this man came in: he had a little package in his hand, and said it was medicine from Dr. Verdi; he said he was sent by Dr. Verdi with particular directions how he was to take the medicine, and he said he must go up; I told him he could not go up; he then repeated the words over a good while, telling me he must go up, "must see him, must see him." I told him he could not go up, that it was against my orders; that if he would give me the medicine I would tell him how to take it if he would leave me the directions; he said that would not do, and I started to go up, and finding he would go up I started past him and went up the stairs before him; I asked him to excuse me; I thought perhaps he would say that I refused to let him come up; I thought perhaps he might be sent by Dr. Verdi, and that he would tell Mr. Seward that I tried to stop him; he said, "All right;" I noticed that his step was very heavy, and I asked him not to walk so heavy, he would disturb Mr. Seward; he met Mr. Frederick Seward on the steps outside the door, and had some conversation with him in the hall.

Q. If you heard that conversation state it? A. He said to Mr. Fred. Seward that he wanted to see Mr. Seward; Mr. Fred. Seward told him that he could not see him; he said that his father was asleep at that time, to give him the medicine and he would take it to his father; that would not do; he said he must see him, he must see him; Mr. Fred. said, "you cannot see him, you cannot see him;" he kept on saying he must see him; Mr. Fred. says, "I am the proprietor here; I am Mr. Seward's son; if you cannot leave it with me you cannot leave it all;" he had a little more talk, and still holding the little package in his hand; Mr. Fred. would not let him see him any way; he started towards the steps as if to go down, and I started to go down before him; I had gone about three steps, and turned around, saying "do not walk so heavy;" by the time I had turned round he jumped back and struck Mr. Frederick Seward, and by the time I had turned clear around, Mr. Frederick Seward had fallen, and thrown up his hands, then I ran down stairs and called "murder;" I went to the front door and cried murder; I then ran down to General Augur's head-quarters at the corner; I saw no guard there, and ran back; by that time three soldiers had come out of the building and followed me; I had got about half way back to the house when I saw the man run out and get on his horse; he had on a light overcoat, and no hat, but he had on a hat when he came into the house; I had not seen the horse at all before I halloed to the soldiers "there he is getting on his horse;" he got on his horse and started off, and I followed him as far as the corner of I and Fifteen-and-a-half streets; he turned up Vermont avenue, and I lost sight of him there.

Q. Did you see with what he struck Mr. Fred. Seward? A. I did not exactly see whatever it was; it appeared to be round and wound with velvet; I took it to be a knife afterwards.

Q. How many times did he strike him? A. I saw him raise his hand twice; I did not wait to see how many times he hit him; he hit him twice, and then I ran down stairs.

Q. Did this man say anything as he struck him? A. When he jumped back again he just said to him, "You," and hit him over the head; that is all I heard him say

Q. Was Dr. Verdi Mr. Seward's family physician? A. He was.

Q. Did Payne advise you in talking to you? A. No, he did not say much to me; he only kept saying "Must see him," and walking very slowly forward all the time.

Q. Had you ever seen this man before, that you know of? A. No; never that I know of.

Q. When you came out did you observe any person about the door or pavement? A. No sir; no one at all.

Q. You did not observe his horse? A. I did not see any horse at all.

Q. How far from him were you at any time after he mounted his horse? A. I might have been as far as from here to that door, about twenty feet.

Q. Did you see the color of the horse? A. He appeared a bay horse, very stout; he did not appear to be a very hardy horse, and did not appear to be going very fast till he got to I street, and then he got away from me altogether.

Cross-examined by Mr. Doster.—Q. How old are you? A. I don't know exactly; I reckon between nineteen and twenty.

Q. How long had you been at Mr. Seward's? A. Three months.

Q. Have you ever been to school? A. Yes, four or five years.

Q. Where precisely was this man standing when you had this conversation with him? A. He was just inside the door; I had closed the door.

Q. Did he give you the package of medicine at any time? Q. No he did not hand it to me.

Q. You say he talked rough to you? A. He did not talk rough; he had a very fine voice when he came in.

Q. You say you recognize that man as the prisoner at the bar; state what there is about the man that resembles the man you saw that night? A. I noticed his hair, his pantaloons and his boots; that night he was talking to Mr. Fred. Seward nearly five minutes; he had on very heavy boots, black pants, light overcoat and a brown hat; his face was very red at the time he came in; he had very coarse black hair.

Q. Have you seen the same boots on this man? A. Yes, the night they captured him.

Q. Have you seen the same clothes on him? A. I have seen the same pantaloons; he had on black pantaloons.

Q. And would you infer from the fact that he wore black pants that it was the same man? A. No, I know his face.

Q. What points about his face besides his hair did you notice? A. I noticed when he talked he kind of raised the corner of his lip and showed a wrinkle in his jaw, as though his teeth were very tight; I knew him the moment I saw him.

Q. Did he talk when you recognized him the first time? A. He did not talk then, but I noticed the raising of his lip that I had seen when he was talking with me.

Q. When have you seen the prisoner before since the night of the assassination? A. I saw him on the 17th at General Augur's head-quarters.

Q. How did you happen to go there to see him? A. They sent for me to the house; Mr. Webster and another gentleman came for me.

Q. What did they say to you? A. He sent a man up to the room where I was, and asked me to get up; I asked him what they wanted; it was in the night, about two or three o'clock; he said Mr. Webster wanted me; I had been getting up every night since the thing happened, and I asked him to ask Mr. Webster to come up to my room; I was tired of getting up at night; when I got up and saw Mr. Webster, he told me he wanted me to go down to General Augur's; I went down there; there was a light, very bright, in the hall at the time; they asked me how light it was at Mr. Seward's that night; I told them it was not light in our hall, that the burner did not give but very little light; they asked me what kind of a looking man the one was who came to see Mr. Seward; I told them he had black hair, thin lips, a fine voice, very tall and broad across the shoulders; there were about twenty or thirty gentlemen in there; they brought in one man and asked me if he was the one, and then brought in another; neither looked like him, and I told them no; they then opened the middle door, and this man came walking in; at the door the light was turned up very bright; as soon as I saw him, I put my finger right on his face, and said, "I know him, that was the man."

Q. Did either of the two men they showed you before look like the man? A. No, one had moustaches, the other whiskers.

Q. Were they as tall as this man? A. No, they were short; they did'nt look at all like this man.

Q. Had you at that time heard of any reward for the apprehension of the supposed assassin of Mr. Seward? A. Yes, I had heard of a reward for the different ones, but I had not heard of a reward offered for this one, and have not yet; I saw a bill posted up the next morning from General Augur's head-quarters, offering a reward, but not for this man.

Q. Did any one offer you money before for this man's apprehension? A. No sir.

Q. Did anybody threaten you? A. No sir.

Q. When the prisoner struck Mr. Seward and you went down stairs, did you find any soldiers there? A. No; the passage was free; the door was closed; I went down, opened the door, and kept on down to the corner.

Q. What kind of a pace had the horse when he rode away? A. It seemed as if he went very slow at first, for I kept up with him till he got to I street; then he went off at a rapid rate.

Testimony of Sergt. George F. Robinson.

By Judge Holt.—Q. State whether or not, on the night of the 14th of April last, you were at the residence of Wm. H. Seward, Secretary of State? A. I was.

Q. In what capacity there? A. In attendance as nurse upon Mr. Seward.

Q. Look at the prisoners here and see if you recognize either of them as having been at that house that evening? A. I see one of them who looks like him; the one in his shirt (pointing to Payne).

Q. State the circumstances attending the encounter between the person of whom you speak and Mr. Seward? A. The first I saw of him I heard a scuffling in the hall; I opened the door to see what the trouble was; as I opened the door he stood close up to it; as soon as it was opened wide enough he struck me and knocked me partially down and then rushed up to the bed of Mr. Seward, struck him and maimed him; as soon as I could get on my feet I endeavored to haul him off the bed and he turned on me; in the scuffle there was a man come into the room who clutched him; between the two of us we got him to the door, or by the door, when he clinched his hand around my neck, knocked me down, broke away from the other man and rushed down stairs.

Q. What did he strike you with? A. He struck me with his fist the last time; the first time with a knife.

Q. Did he stab you, and if so, where? A. Yes, here (pointing to about the centre of his forehead).

Q. Did he say anything when he struck you? A. He did not that I heard.

Q. Did he pass immediately to the bed of Mr. Seward when he first knocked you down? A. He did.

Q. Did you see him strike Mr. Seward? A. *I did.*

Q. With the same weapon he struck you with? A. Yes.

Q. How often? A. I saw him cut twice.

Q. Did he seem to be cutting at his head or where? A. He struck beyond the head and neck the first time; then he struck him in the neck.

Q. Describe how he held the knife? A. He held it in this way (raising the hand which held the knife, pointing downwards).

Q. Did it seem to be a large knife? A. It did.

Q. Did he say anything at all after stabbing him? A. Not that I heard.

Q. Did you observe the wound that had been inflicted? A. I did.

Q. Look at this knife and see if it is the same one held in his hand? A. It was about the length of that. It looked as though it might not be as wide as that, but I only saw it in motion.

Q. Describe the character of the wounds inflicted on Mr. Seward? A. There was one cutting his face down on the left side, and another one cutting his neck below. I think they were both made by the same blow. He was sitting partially up in bed at the time, his head reclining so that the same blow might have made both. The other cut was on the opposite side of the neck. There were three wounds in all. It was all bloody when I saw it. I do not know but there may have been more.

Q. Was Mr. Seward in his bed at the time? A. He was.

Q. From what cause? A. He had been thrown from his carriage.

Q. Were his limbs broken? A. I was told that one of his arms was broken and his jaw fractured.

Q. While striking him did Mr. Seward get out of his bed or remain in bed? A. He remained and received the stabs in bed.

Q. Did he during the struggle roll from the bed or remain in bed? A. He rolled out after we had left the bed; when I came back I found he was lying on the floor.

Q. You say that this man, during the whole of this bloody work, made no remark at all; that he said nothing? A. I did not hear him make any remark.

Q. When he came out of the room had Frederick Seward risen from the floor, or was he still lying? A. I did not see Mr. Frederick Seward around at all.

Q. Where was he when this man came out? A. The first I saw of Mr. Frederick he was in the room standing up; he had come inside the door.

Q. You say he knocked you down when he came into the room; what did he strike you with? A. I suppose with a knife; he struck me the last time with his fist; he had his arm around my neck and let go and struck me.

Q. Did he immediately go down stairs? A. He did.

Q. Did you see his encounter with Major Seward? A. I did not see that.

Q. After he left was any thing picked up which he left behind? A. There was, a revolver and his hat.

Q. Look at this revolver and see if you recognize it as the one he left? A. I should judge it was; I did not notice this in it (pointing to the rammer.)

Q. I understand the Mr. Seward you speak of to be the Secretary of State, and the house you speak of to be in Washington city? A. Yes sir.

Q. Do you recognize this as the hat that was picked up?

A light-brown felt slouch hat was shown. General Wallace requested that the hat produced might be tried on Payne. It was handed to Payne's guard, who placed it on his head to the evident amusement of Payne himself.

General Wallace said, "Does it fit loosely?" The guard replied, "No, it fits tight."

Mr. Doster, (Payne's counsel), "It is too small for him, I should say," (laughter.)

Testimony of Major A. H. Seward.

Examined by Judge Holt.—Q. State whether you are the son of Wm. H. Seward, Secretary of State? A. I am his son.

Q. Were you or not at his house on the night of the 14th of April last? A. I was.

Q. Will you state whether or not that night any one of the prisoners at the bar made his appearance at that house? A. *Yes, I saw this large man who has no coat on* (Payne.)

Q. State the circumstances attending your meeting with him that evening? A. I retired to bed about 7 o'clock on the night of the 14th, with the understanding that I would be called at 11 o'clock, to set up with my father; I very shortly fell asleep, and so remained until wakened by the screams of my sister; I jumped out of bed and ran into my father's room in my shirt and drawers; the gas in the room had been shut down rather low, and I saw what appeared to be two men, one trying to hold the other; my first impression was that my father had become delirious, and that the nurse was trying to hold him. I went up and took hold of him, but saw at once from his size and the struggle that it was not my father; it then struck me that the nurse had become delirious and was striking about the room at random; knowing the delicate state of my father's health, I endeavored to shove the person I had hold of to the door, with the intention of putting him out of his room; while I was pushing him he struck me five or six times over the head with whatever he had in his left hand; I supposed it at the time to be a bottle or a decanter he had seized from the table; during this time he repeated with an intensely strong voice—"I am mad, I am mad;" on reaching the hall he gave a sudden turn and breaking away from me, disappeared down stairs; while in the vicinity of the door of my father's room, as I was pushing him out, when he came opposite the light in the hall it shone on him, and I saw him distinctly; I saw that he was a very large man, with dark straight hair, smooth face and no beard; I noticed the expression of his countenance; I then went into my room and got my pistol which had to be taken out from the bottom of my carpet bag; I then went down stairs, intending to shoot the person if he attempted to return; while standing at the door the servant boy came back and said the man had ridden off on horseback; I then realized for the first time that the man was an assassin who had entered the house for the purpose of murdering my father?

Q. Did you then return to your father's room? A. I suppose it was five minutes before I got back; there was quite a crowd collected at the door; I sent for a doctor, and made arrangements to keep the crowd out; it may not have been three minutes.

Q. State whether you examined the number and character of the wounds given your father and brother, Mr. Fred. W. Seward? A. No, I did not examine them that night; I was beaten very badly myself. I found when I got up stairs again; after my father's wounds had been dressed and after my arm had been bandaged, I went in and saw my father; he had one very large gash on his right cheek, besides a cut on his throat, on the right side, and one under his left arm; I did not examine my brother's wounds; I did not know that night how badly he was hurt; the next day he was insensible and so remained, and it was four or five days before I saw what his wounds were.

Q. What did you then discover? A. There were two wounds about here (pointing to the left side of the head, over the ear); after the piece of the skull had been taken out it left the brain exposed.

Q. Had he received any stab at all from the knife? A. I never saw anything of my brother during the whole time.

Q. Did the wound indicate that a knife had been used? A. I thought myself it was done by a knife, but the surgeon seemed to think it was done by the hammer of the pistol; it was such a wound as I would have supposed might have been done with a knife.

Q. Did you see a pistol picked up in that room? A. I did not; I know there was one picked up.

Q. Did you see any article of clothing? A. Yes; a hat.

Q. Would you recognize it? (producing a hat). A. Yes, I am quite certain that is the hat; I saw the hat after it had been picked up and put in a bureau drawer; it was taken out and shown to me the next day; I did not see it that night.

Q. And you say you supposed it to have been the nurse? A. Yes; I had no idea who the man was until he was out of the house.

Q. You say that you were struck with a knife? A. The surgeons think it was with a knife I was struck; I supposed at the time it was with a bottle or a decanter; that the nurse had become delirious and was striking at random.

Q. *Do you feel entirely satisfied that the person at the bar is the same man?* A. *I do.*

Cross-examined by Mr. Doster.—Q. Be good enough to state whether this is the first time you have seen the prisoner since he was taken? A. No; I saw him on board the monitor the day after he was taken.

Q. Did you identify him then? A. Yes.

Q. Please state the circumstances. A. He was brought up on the monitor; I took hold of him the same way I did in the room, and looked up in his face; he had the same features, with his size, his proportions, his swarthy face, and no beard that I noticed, and when he was made to repeat the words, "I am mad, I am mad," I recognized the same voice, varying only in intensity.

Testimony of Richard C. Morgan.

Examined by Judge Holt.—Q. State whether or not on the 17th or 18th of April last, you were in the service of the Government, and if so, in what capacity? A. I am in the service of the War Department, acting under the orders of Colonel Olcutt.

Q. State whether on one or both of these days, you had possession of the house of the prisoner, Mrs. Surratt? A. Yes.

Q. State where that house is? A. No. 548 H street, city of Washington.

Q. State whether or not you took possession of the house, and what occurred there? A. About twenty minutes past 11 o'clock on the evening of the 17th of April, in company with other officers, I went to the house of Mrs. Surratt for the purpose of seizing the papers that might be found, and of arresting the inmates of the house; after we had been at the house about ten minutes, and Major Smith, Captain Weunerskerch, and some other officers, had arrested the inmates of the house, who were in the parlor all ready to come out, I had sent an officer for a carriage to take them away, when I heard a knock and a ring at the door at the same time; Captain Weunerskerch and myself went to the door and opened it, the prisoner, Payne, came in; he had a pickaxe in his hand; he had on a grey coat and black pants, a hat made out of the sleeves of a shirt, I judged; as soon as he came in and immediately closed the door, he said, "I guess I am mistaken," said I, "who do you want to see?" He replied, "Mrs. Surratt;" said I, "you are right, walk in." He took a seat. I said, "what did you come here for, this time of night?" he said he came to dig a gutter; that Mrs. Surratt had sent for him; I asked him when and, he said in the morning; I asked him where he last worked, and he said somewhere on Ninth street; I asked him where he boarded, he said he had no boarding house, that he was a poor man, and earned his living with the pickaxe in his hand; I asked him how much he made a day, he said, nothing at all sometimes, sometimes one dollar, and sometimes one dollar and fifty cents; "have you any money?" "Not a cent." I asked him why he came at this time of night? he said he came to see where it was to be dug, so that he could commence early in the morning; I said, have you had no previous acquaintance with Mrs. Surratt? he said, No; I said, why did she select you for this work? he replied, that she knew he was working in that neighborhood; that he was a poor man, and she came to him; I asked him how old he was, and he said about twenty; I asked him where he was from; he said from Fauquier county, Va.; previous to this he had pulled out an oath of allegiance, handed it to me and said, that will show you who I am; it contained the name of Louis Payne, Fauquier county, Va.; I asked him if he was from the South; he said he was; I asked him when he left there; he said two months ago, in February; I asked him why he left; he said that he had to leave or go into the army; that he preferred to earn his living with the pick-axe; I asked him if he

Continued on the Eighth Page.

Entered according to the Act of Congress in the year 1864, by FRANK LESLIE, in the Clerk's Office of the District Court for the Southern District of New York.

No. 503—Vol. XX.] NEW YORK, MAY 20, 1865. [Price 10 Cents. $4 00 Yearly. 13 Weeks $1 00.

The sketch below was furnished by one of the two officers employed in the duty of sinking the body of Booth in the middle of the Potomac. Although not authorised to divulge his name, I am able to vouch for the truth of the representation.

New York, May 10th, 1865. F. LESLIE.

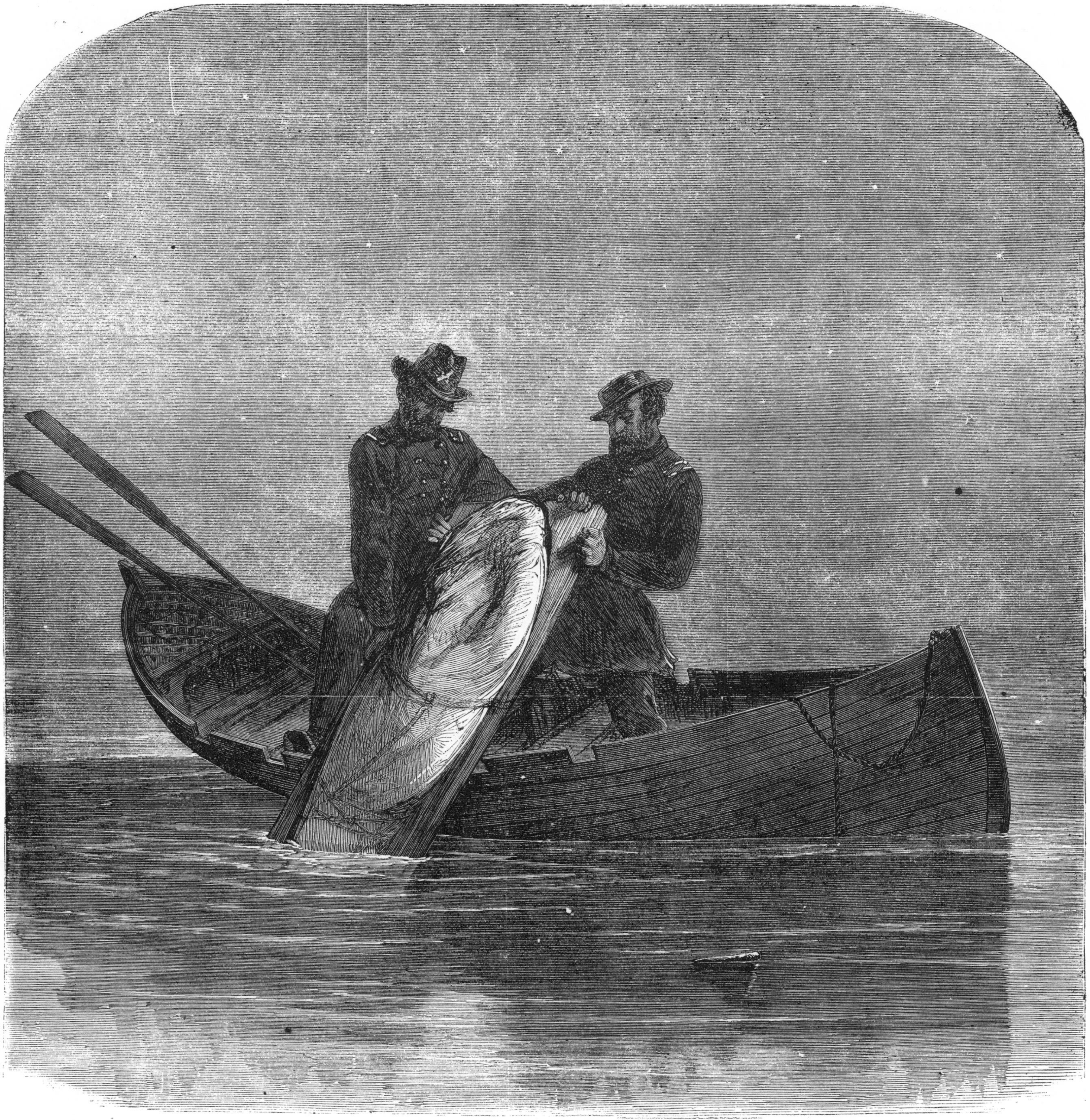

THE ASSASSIN'S END—FINAL DISPOSITION OF THE BODY OF JOHN WILKES BOOTH.—AN AUTHENTIC SKETCH.

The Philadelphia Inquirer.

PRICE TWO CENTS. | PHILADELPHIA, MONDAY, MAY 22, 1865. | PRICE TWO CENTS.

THE CONSPIRACY!

TRIAL AT WASHINGTON!

Saturday's Proceedings.

TESTIMONY OF SECRETARY DANA.

Identification of Booth's Cipher.

IT IS THE SAME AS THAT USED BY JEFF. DAVIS!

MOST IMPORTANT DEVELOPMENTS.

Correspondence Between Richmond and Canada!

HOW MR. LINCOLN WAS TO BE DEFEATED.

THE COLONIZATION OF VOTERS.

Longstreet to Attack Sheridan and March North!

The Plot to Burn Our Towns, Cities and Shipping!

MUDD STILL DEEPER IN THE MUD!

Booth's Financial Matters in Canada!

THE COURT ROOM CLEARED

An Important But Mysterious Witness!

THE TRIAL OF THE ASSASSINS AND CONSPIRATORS!

Sitting of the Court-Martial at Washington. Interior View of the Court Chamber.

TRIAL OF THE CONSPIRATORS.

WASHINGTNN, May 20.

The first witness examined to-day was Assistant Secretary of War Dana, as follows:—

Testimony of Mr. C. A. Dana.

Q. State what position you occupy in the Government? A. I am Assistant Secretary of War.

Q. Look at the instrument before you, and state if you have ever seen it before? A. I took it out of the office of Mr. Benjamin, the Rebel Secretary of State, in Richmond; I arrived in Richmond on Wednesday, the 6th, and went into his office, where this was found, and brought it away with me, or rather, I sent it to Major Eckert, of the War Department; I saw it was the key to an official cipher; there were many papers and things lying around there, and as this seemed to be interesting, I took it away.

Q. Did you find it in a trunk? A. No sir; Benjamin's office consisted of a series of three or four rooms (I think four), Benjamin's personal office being the innermost of all; this was in the room next to his, occupied by his confidential secretary or assistant; most of the articles had been taken away; the record had been taken away, but I found several interesting documents—this amongst them.

By the Court.—Q. I should like to know the object of the instrument? A. It is a key to a cipher, by which certain letters of the alphabet can be used for other letters, and by using these pointers such a cipher can be translated or plain writing turned into cipher by interpretation.

Note.—The machine is about a foot long and eight inches high, and consists of a cylinder of wood, which has a paper envelope encircled with letters. This cylinder revolves in pivot holes at each end, and a bar across the top contains wooden indices pointing down to the letters.

Testimony of Major Eckert.

Q. Look at that cipher, and state if it was found in the trunk of J. Wilkes Booth; compare it with this other cipher of which Assistant Secretary Dana has just spoken, and state whether or not they are the same? A. They are the same, sir.

Q. You are somewhat familiar, are you not, with these things? A. Yes sir.

Q. You have no doubt as to these being the same? A. None at all, sir.

Q. State whether or not cipher despatches have from time to time fallen into the hands of the War Department, and been referred to you for examination? A. They have, sir.

Q. State whether they were the same cipher as this? A. Some of them were, sir; they were worked on the same principle.

Q. I speak now of the despatches of the 13th and 19th of October last; have you them now in your possession? A. I have, sir.

Q. These are the translations? A. Yes sir.

Q. Have you the originals? A. No sir; I have copies.

Q. State whether they are written in the same cipher of which you have spoken? A. I think they are; they may be different in the key word, but the principle is the same.

Q. Have you translated them? A. The clerks have.

Q. Were they worked out without any knowledge of this instrument at the time? A. Yes sir.

Q. Are these translations of those despatches? A. Yes sir.

The following were then read:—

OCTOBER 13.—We again urge the immense necessity of our gaining immediate advantages; strain every nerve for victory. We now look upon the re-election of Lincoln in November as almost certain, and we need to whip his hirelings to prevent it. Besides, with Lincoln re-elected, and his armies victorious, we need not hope even for recognition, much less the help mentioned in our last. Holcombe will explain this. Those figures of the Yankee armies are correct to a unit. Our friend shall be immediately set to work as you direct.

OCTOBER 19, 1864.—Your letter of the 18th instant is at hand. There is yet time enough to colonize many voters before November. A blow will shortly be stricken here; it is not quite time. General Longstreet is to attack Sheridan without delay, and then move North as far as practicable towards unprotected points. This will be made instead of the movement before mentioned. He will endeavor to assist the Republicans in collecting their ballots. Be watchful and assist him.

Q. State whether the original was sent to its address? A. Yes sir.

Q. From what direction did the cipher of the 13th come? A. It came from Canada, and went to Richmond.

Q. From what direction did the cipher of the 19th come? A. It came from Richmond and went to Canada.

Testimony of General Hamilton.

Q. State whether you are familiar with the handwriting of H. S. Oldham? A. Yes sir; as familiar as I am with that of any man living.

Q. State whether that (handing him a paper) is in his handwriting or not? A. Yes sir.

The following is the paper handed to the witness:—

RICHMOND, Feb. 11, 1865.—His Excellency Jefferson Davis, President Confederate States of America:—When Senator Johnson and myself waited upon you, some days since, in relation to the project of annoying and harrassing the enemy by means of burning their shipping, towns, etc., etc., there were several remarks made by you upon the subject that I was not fully prepared to answer, but which, upon subsequent conference with the parties proposing the enterprise, I find cannot apply as objections to the scheme.

First. The combustible material consists of several preparations, and not one alone, and can be used without exposing the party using them to the least danger of detection whatever. The preparations are not in the hands of Mr. Daniel, but are in the hands of Professor McCullough, and are known but to him and one other party, as I understand it.

Second. There is no necessity for sending persons in the military service into the enemy's country; but the work may be done by agents, and in most cases by persons ignorant of the facts, and therefore innocent agents.

I have seen enough of the effects that can be produced to satisfy me that in most cases, without any danger to the parties engaged, and in others but very slight, we can:—1. Burn every vessel that leaves a foreign port for the United States. 2. We can burn every transport that leaves the harbor of New York [illegible] Northern ports with supplies for the armies of the enemy in the South. 3. Burn every transport and gun-boat on the Mississippi River, as well as devastate the country and fill his people with terror and consternation.

I am not alone in this opinion, but many other gentlemen are as fully and thoroughly impressed with the conviction as I am. I believe we have the means at our command, if promptly appropriated and energetically applied, to demoralize the Northern people in a very short time. For the purpose of satisfying your mind on the subject, I respectfully but earnestly request that you will have an interview with General Harris, formerly a member of Congress from Missouri, who, I think, is able, by conclusive proofs, to convince you that what I have suggested is perfectly feasible and practicable.

The deep interest I feel for the success of our cause in this struggle, with the conviction of the importance of availing ourselves of every element of defense, must be my excuse for writing you and requesting you to invite General Harris to see you. If you should see proper to do so, please signify the time when it will be convenient for you to see him.

I am, respectfully, your obedient servant,

W. S. OLDHAM.

On the back of the letter are the two indorsements, the first being "Hon. W. S. Oldham, Richmond, February 12, 1865."

Q. State whether or not at the time of writing it he was a member of the Senate of the so-called Confederate States from Texas? A. I was present when he was elected by the Rebel Legislature of Texas to a seat in the Senate of the so-called Confederacy; since then I know it as a matter of public history; I have seen many speeches, resolutions, and bills introduced by him into that Senate, and published in the public prints.

Q. You are a citizen of Texas, formerly a member of Congress from there? A. Yes sir.

Q. Do you know the McCullogh mentioned in that letter? A. No sir.

Testimony of Surgeon-General Barnes.

Q. State to the Court whether or not you made an examination of the body of Booth after his death? A. Yes sir.

Q. Describe to the Court the scar which is alleged to have been on the neck and the general appearance of the body? A. On the left side of the neck there was a scar, occasioned by an operation performed by Dr. May for the removal of a tumor; it looked like the scar from a burn rather than an incision.

Q. How near the ear was it? A. Three inches below the ear.

Testimony of Frank Bloice.

Q. Where do you live? A. In Charles county.

Q. In the town or country? A. In the country, sir.

Q. How far from Bryantown? A. About half a mile.

Q. Were you there on the Saturday after the murder? A. I was there on Saturday evening, about four o'clock: as near as I can come to the time it was between three and four.

Q. Did you see Dr. Mudd there? A. Yes sir.

Q. What time do you think that was? A. Between three and four, sir.

Q. Where did you see him? A. He came into a store while I was there.

Q. State whether the soldiers had arrived from Washington then? A. I don't know, sir, whether they had or not.

Q. Were you around about the town? A. I was in the store when he came in; I did not take much notice.

Q. What time did you leave the store? A. About just before night.

Q. When did he start? A. I didn't see him when he started; I did'nt take much notice of him.

By the Court.—Was the report of the President's assassination in Bryantown at that time? A. I don't know sir.

Q. Did you hear it? A. No sir, I didn't hear until the roads were guarded; that was a little before night.

Q. You heard it before you left Bryantown? A. Oh, yes sir.

Testimony of J. H. Ward.

Q. State where you live? A. Near Bryantown, Charles county.

Q. State whether you were there on the afternoon of the day following the murder of the President? A. I was; I live in the suburbs of the village; I went so soon as I finished my dinner, and arrived there about one o'clock; and so soon as I arrived I observed the military were in town with Lieutenant Murray, and perceived a great excitement, not only with the military, but with the people, and I imagined they were going to search the houses; as my wife was alone I went home lest she should be alarmed; a nigger came soon afterwards and said—

Objected to.

Witness.—I must explain the facts because I know but little; I left him and went to the village; Lieutenant Dana had put the village under martial law, and the people were excited about getting home.

Q. Did you see Dr. Mudd? A. I can't say, the excitement was so great; I can't say I saw the Dr.

Q. What is your opinion, to the best of your recollection, about your having seen Dr. Mudd? A. I would not like to say positively, but it occurs to me from faint memory that he was there; the excitement has been so great ever since that time that I cannot say positively.

Q. You say the military were there and the people were much excited, and you returned home; how long did you remain at home? A. About three-quarters of an hour.

Q. Did you then hear of the assassination of the President? A. Yes sir.

Q. Did you hear who the assassin was? A. Yes sir, Booth; some gave him the name of Boose.

Q. Did you hear it everywhere spoken of? A. Yes sir, at Bryantown I did.

Q. What time do you suppose you heard it? A. It was, I think, between one and two o'clock; it was a cloudy day, and I never paid any particular attention but I think it was one and two o'clock.

Q. What time did you leave Bryantown? A. I could not give you the precise time; it was between two and three o'clock that I left the second time; it was then I found the military, and in a few minutes they told me that the President had been assassinated, and I came back.

Q. You say some said it was Booth and some said it was Boose that was spoken by some soldiers with whom the English language was not conversant? A. They would call him Borth, Booths and Boose; those who could speak audibly said it was Booth; those who had an amalgamation of the languages said it was Booths.

Q. Where were you when you first heard the President was assassinated? A. At home; I wanted to tell you it was through the authority of the darkey.

Q. Who was the darkey? A. Charles Bloice, the brother of the fellow whose testimony has just been taken.

Q. Did you ask him who assassinated the President? A. I have no knowledge of asking him, and I think he never told me.

Q. In what direction from the centre of the town do you live? A. I live in the eastern direction, principally in the suburbs.

Q. On the road between Pine Town and Dr. Mudd? A. I live close to the road leading to Bryantown.

Q. My question is do you live near or on the road between Bryantown and Dr. Mudd's? A. No sir.

Q. Is it your impression that you saw Dr. Mudd in the town? A. My impression is if it be Dr. Mudd that I saw—I saw him get on his horse; but I could not swear that it was Dr. Mudd.

Q. Did you see the face of this person? A. No sir not that I know of; but I could tell him by a side or a back view.

Q. How close were you to him? A. About ten or twenty yards, standing on the porch of the store.

Q. You are only able to swear to a faint impression? A. Yes, sir.

Q. What was the color of the horse this man was going to? A. I don't know.

Q. Do you know the horse Dr. Mudd usually rides? A. I have seen him on a great many horses, and there was a great many horses connected there; I have seen him ride a bay horse.

Q. Did you see Dr. Mudd when you first went into town? A. I think not.

Q. Was it immediately on your arrival on the second time? A. Yes, sir.

Q. Were you personally acquainted with Dr. Mudd? A. I have been for two years and five months, before that I had no personal acquaintance with him.

Testimony of Lieutenant Dana.

Q. State whether or not, on the day following the President's assassination, you were in pursuit of the assassins at Bryantown? A. Yes sir.

Q. State what hour you arrived there on that day? A. I sent an advance guard of four men, they arrived there twenty minutes or half an hour before I did; I arrived there very near one o'clock that afternoon, Saturday afternoon.

Q. State whether, on your arrival, the news of the assassination was spread all around there? A. Yes sir.

Q. Was there any person mentioned as the assassin? was J. Wilkes Booth? A. Yes sir, and some of the citizens asked me if I knew for certain it was he; as early as a quarter past — o'clock it was known that the President was assassinated and who the assassin was.

Q. Are you acquainted at all with the prisoner at the bar, Dr. Mudd? A. No sir.

Q. Have you any knowledge whether you met him on that occasion? A. No sir.

Testimony of Robert Nelson (Colored).

Q. Do you live in Washington? A. Yes sir; I did live in Virginia.

Q. Look at that knife, and state whether you found it in the street, and if so, when and where? A. It looks like the one I found opposite to Secretary Seward's.

Q. When did you find it there? A. The Saturday morning after the Secretary was stabbed.

Q. Did you find it on the pavement or in the middle of the street? A. In the middle of the street.

Q. Who did you give it to? A. Dr. Wilson.

Cross-examination.—Q. You say it was the same one? A. I said it was one like it.

Q. It was not in a sheath? A. No, it was not in a sheath at all.

Q. Was it in the street or the gutter? A. It was in the middle of the street.

Q. Right in front of the door? A. Yes sir.

Q. What time of day was it? A. Early in the morning; I was going to market; it was about five or six, I think.

Testimony of Dr. Wilson.

Q. Doctor, look at that knife and state whether or not it is the knife you received from any one? A. This is the knife I received from the colored boy, just come from the stand, on Saturday, about ten o'clock in the day.

Q. On the 15th of April? A. Yes sir.

Q. Where did he give it to you? A. In the library of Mr. Seward; in the Seward library; he brought it in the door and handed it to me.

Testimony of Colonel J. B. Stewart.

Q. State to the Court whether or not you were at Ford's Theatre on the night of the assassination. A. Yes sir, I was.

Q. Did you see the assassin jump from the box? A. I did, at about 10½ o'clock; I was sitting in the front chair near the orchestra, on the right hand side; there are two aisles to the orchestra, and my side was on the corner, on the left hand, right under and bringing me immediately next to the music stand; at the report of the pistol I was startled; I was speaking to my sister, my head being turned to the left; I glanced back to the stage; an exclamation was made and a man leaped from the President's box, lighting on the stage. He came down with his back slightly towards the audience, but as he was rising his face came fully in view; I rose and attempted to leap on the stage; I made two or three steps on the railing to the right after alighting from where I sat and keeping my attention on the man who had alighted upon the stage and who had jumped from the President's box; when I reached the stage, on looking to the left I perceived he had disappeared on the left hand egress; I exclaimed "stop that man," and then went past the length of the stage, and turning to the right, was at a distance of twenty feet from the door; but the door was slammed to. I ran and got to the door very quick, but on coming to the door I swung it the wrong way, but I remedied that and passed out; as I approached the door after I had last said, stop that man, some one said he has gone on a horse, and I heard the tramping of a horse; when I got out the door, I perceived a man mounting a horse; he was at that instant barely mounted; the moon was just beginning to rise, and I could see him better; the horse was moving as though prematurely spurred in mounting; I ran in the direction to which the horse was heading, at about eight or ten feet from the head of the horse, and the rider brought him around to the right again; the horse's feet were rattling violently on the stones; I crossed in the same direction, and was now on the right hand side of the horse, but he was gaining on me; when about two-thirds of the way out of the alley he brought the horse forward and swept to the left of F street; I commanded him to stop; it all occupied but two seconds.

Q. You found the door closed; did you see anybody about the door? A. I did.

Q. One or more persons? A. I passed several in the passage, one or two men, perhaps five persons altogether; but near the door, on the right hand side, I passed a person standing, who seemed in the act of turning; I noticed everything; my mind is impressed with all that occurred, and I saw a person there who didn't seem to be moving about.

Q. Look at the prisoners and see if you recognize the man. A. I see but one face that would recall him to my mind.

Q. Which one? A. That one.

By the Court.—Stand up, Spangler. Witness.—That one looks more like the man than any other there.

Q. Describe his appearance.

Mr. Stewart here placed himself in an attitude, in order to show the Court the position in which he had seen the man, which was a three-fourths view.

Witness.—I didn't observe so far as to have a clear impression of his visage; he was turning from the door towards me.

Cross-examination.—Q. Was it the passage way between the scene and the green-room, about two and a half feet in width, through which Booth ran? A. I don't know where the green-room is; I never was there, but if I had a plan of the building I could point it out.

Assistant Judge Advocate Burnett then handed to Mr. Stewart a plan of the theatre by which he explained the route taken by Booth and by himself, and on which he marked the spot where he had seen the man alluded to in the latter part of his examination in chief.

Q. When you got out of the door the person was just rising into his saddle? A. He was in his saddle leaning forward; his left foot apparently was in the stirrup; he was leaning to the left; the horse was leaving the walk in a sort of motion making apparently a circle; he was sufficiently mounted to go with the horse without being unbalanced; he was getting the horse under control for a forward movement.

Q. You could not say then that he had just got into the saddle? A. He was balancing himself in the saddle; I would form an opinion from his position and the motion of his horse that the moment he got his foot into one stirrup he started the horse, who having the rein drawn on one side more than the other did not at once make a straightforward movement.

By Judge Holt.—Q. I understood you to say that all the persons you met with in the passage as you approached exhibited great excitement, except this particular man? A. Every person that came under my notice in the brief space of not over two or three seconds as I ran through the stage toward the door were greatly agitated, and seemed literally bewildered, except the person near the door, who did not seem to be under the same excitement.

By Mr. Ewing.—Q. How long did it take you after entering that passage to get to the door? A. I can hardly time myself; I was running as hard as I could, and was only obstructed by passing these persons; it seemed to me about as quick as you would count one, two, three, four, five, from the report of the pistol until I reached the door; I knew the discharge of the pistol was either by accident or design, and that it was by design was solved by the man jumping on the stage; my impression was when he came from the President's box that the President had been assassinated; I was so much under that impression that though I had not heard a word after the person on the horse had gone off, I informed the people in the alley there that the person who went off on that horse had shot the President.

Q. You say you saw only the profile of this person in the passage? A. The profile and full face as he passed round.

By Judge Holt.—Q. Did you recognize Booth when you saw him on the Stage? A. Oh, yes; after I went out and returned I took my family home, and immediately ran down the street towards the house of Secretary Stanton, but finding persons had been there, I turned and went rapidly back to the police station; found Captain Richards, Superintendent of Police; gave him my name and what information I had, and said to him I thought I knew who it was; I had known Booth before by sight; some two years before; I was introduced to him one evening at the Metropolitan Hotel; then I had seen him on the stage, but I noticed him more during the past winter at the hotel; I was two evenings with some ladies at a hop at the National Hotel, and noticed this gentleman leisurely moving about the parlor; every person except the one I have mentioned, seemed to be perfectly bewildered on the stage; I felt very much vexed at his getting away.

By the Court.—How long was it after you heard the door slam until you saw this man balancing himself in the saddle? A. Not more than while I was making two steps.

Q. Are you satisfied that the door was closed by some other person than the one who went out of the door? A. I could not possibly be satisfied of that; there was nothing to preclude the possibility that the door was closed by Booth himself.

Q. Are you satisfied that the person you saw inside the door was in a position, had he been so disposed, to have interrupted the exit of Booth? A. Beyond a doubt he was.

Q. From his manner, he was cool enough to have done it? A. He showed no agitation like the other people did.

By Mr. Ewing.—Q. Were not the other persons you have spoken of also in a position to have interrupted the exit of Booth? A. O yes, at least at the moment I saw them every person I met could have obstructed my motion, except one person, who was three or five feet off to the right; that was the person I described who seemed to be passing off.

Q. Then the person you speak of nearest the door was in no better position to have obstructed the passage of Booth than any of the others, so far as you know? A. None whatever.

By the Court.—Q. Could this man nearest the door have opened it and gone out before you went out? A. Yes, the door was immediately within the control of the person who stood there.

By Mr. Ewing.—Q. Do you know whether any person on the stage, or in the passage as you went out, knew that the assassination had been committed? A. I cannot say that; they acted very much like people astounded at something that had just occurred.

Testimony of Robert A. Campbell.

Examined by Judge Holt.—Q. State where you reside? A. Montreal, Canada.

Q. Are you or not connected with the Ontario Bank of that city? A. I am, as first teller.

Q. Look upon that account, and state whether or not it is a correct abstract from the books of that bank? A. It is; I examined it before I came away.

Q. What is it? A. It is the account of Jacob Thompson with the Ontario Bank, Montreal.

Q. State on what day the account commences? A. The account commences May 30th, 1864; prior to that however, he left sterling exchange, drawn on the Rebel agents at Liverpool or London for collection; as soon as agents advised us of the bills being paid, the proceeds were placed to his credit; the first advices we had was May 30, and two thousand pounds sterling was the amount.

Q. State when the account closed? A. The account closed April 11, 1865.

Q. State the aggregate amount of credit and the aggregate amount drawn? A. The aggregate amount of credit was $64,987,323; there is now a balance due him of about $176·30.

Q. Has he drawn lately to any considerable extent? A. He has drawn $300,000 very nearly since March 1; he bought at one time $100,000 in sterling exchange.

Q. State the amount drawn out between the 1st and 10th of April? A. The first entry in April is on the 4th, a very small check of $100; there is a deposit receipt under date of 6th of April. of $180,000 which was to be paid when presented; on the 8th of April he purchased 440 pounds sterling exchange, and also 4000 pounds sterling on the same date; on the 24th of March he purchased $100,000 sterling.

Q. You know Jacob Thompson personally? A. Yes, I know him.

Q. State whether or not since the 14th of April last he has left Montreal? A. He has; I heard him say myself he was going away, and I know he has not been seen in the bank lately; one of the last transactions was a check given to a hotel keeper for, as I supposed, board; he said he was going overland to Halifax, *en route* to Europe.

Q. Can you fix the date of that? A. I could not; since then he has disappeared from Montreal.

Q. How long was this before navigation opened? A. I think about two weeks; I know I thought it strange he was going overland, when by waiting two weeks he could have taken a steamer.

Q. He was known and recognized as the agent of the Confederate States? A. His account was simply with Jacob Thompson; we did not know what he was; by newspaper report he was the financial agent of the Rebels; we knew that he bought Southern sterling exchange bills on their agents in the old country; a part of the time he resided in Upper Canada, and a part of the time in Montreal.

Q. Have you known him to be connected with other money transactions with other banks in Canada? A. Oh, yes; I knew of one transaction of fifty thousand with Niagara District Bank, at St. Catharines; that was a check drawn to the order of Mr. C. C. Clay, and deposited by him in Niagara District Bank; that bank sent it to us, and we put it to their credit; the date of that was August 16th, 1864.

Q. Did you know J. Wilkes Booth, the actor? A. I did; I had one or two transactions with him.

Q. How often did you see him in Canada? A. I could not say, I may have seen him a dozen times; I remember distinctly seeing him there.

Q. Did he have a small account at your bank? A. Yes he has still to his credit four hundred and odd dollars.

Q. Have you any knowledge how that credit arose? A. It was from a deposit that did not go through my hands, but through the hands of another receiving teller. The memorandum says check drawn on Merchants' Bank by Davis, 225 and ten twenty-dollar bills

Q. Who was Davis, the person referred to as drawing the check? A. He was a broker in Montreal, and I am not sure whether he was introduced by Davis, or by T. C. Martin from the States, somewhere from Richmond or Baltimore; when Booth came into the bank he purchased a bill of exchange for sixty-one pounds and some odd shillings; he said he was going to run the blockade; he asked whether in case he should be captured his captors could make use of the exchange; I said no, not unless he indorsed the bill; he then said he would take three hundred dollars' worth, for which I think he paid American gold; these are the only two transactions he had with us.

Q. Look at these bills of exchange taken from the body of Booth and say whether these are the ones you refer to. A. They are Ontario Bank bills; there is no doubt about that.

Q. State whether or not these drafts were intended for use in the States or for general disbursement? A. We can never tell that; we never ask our customers any questions; checks are generally made payable to bearer, but in certain instances the word "bearer" is scored out and "order" put over; Mr. Thompson, besides these sterling exchange transactions, has bought from us several times United States currency (greenbacks).

Q. In large sums? A. He bought on August 25th fifteen thousand dollars in greenbacks; July 14th, thirteen thousand one hundred and twenty-four dollars; that was the amount in gold; I could not say what was the amount in greenbacks; at that time I think exchange was about fifty-five.

Q. Did any of these transactions occur during the past spring? A. On the 14th of March he bought one thousand dollars at 44¾, for which he paid five hundred and fifty-three dollars in gold; he bought several drafts in New York.

The Judge Advocate-General stated that there was only one other witness he desired to examine to-day. He was a very important witness; but for the same reasons stated in another instance, it was not desirable that his examination should be public.

The Court was thereupon cleared, and the remainder of its deliberations for the day were in secret session.

FROM NEW ORLEANS, HAVANA AND MEXICO.

NEW YORK, May 20.—The steamer *Evening Star*, from New Orleans on the 13th, arrived at this port this morning. Her advices have been anticipated by the telegraph from Cairo.

The papers contain some Mexican news. When Colonel Towiskisky went out to attack the Liberals, at Nava, the greater part of his cavalry deserted when ordered to charge. He fired upon them with his infantry, and commenced retreating, but he fell into an ambush and was killed. The remainder of his troops surrendered immediately.

The Liberals had marched within eight miles of Piedras Negras.

Maximilian's native troops cannot be trusted. A letter from Rio Grande city says:—A new revolution is breaking out on the frontier. Both the Cortinas have joined their forces with Leon at Camargo, and are expected to attack Matamoros.

The steamer *Constitution* has arrived at New Orleans, from Annapolis, with five hundred paroled Rebel soldiers.

NEW YORK, May 20.—The steamer *Mississippi*, from Mew Orleans on the 12th, and Key West on the 15th, has arrived. The Sand Key and Key West lights were not lighted, in consequence of the ram *Stonewall* being at Havana and taking in ammunition, and being expected to come into Key West. The *Powhatan* was sent over to Havana, also the *Ariel* and *Dale*, to keep the *Stonewall* from coming out. Great excitement prevailed at Key West in regard to the matter.

The New Orleans *True Delta*, of the 13th inst., has the following:—A gentleman who has recently arrived in this city from Havana, informs us that he met ex-Senator Gwin, of California, and was shown indubitable evidence that Sonora had been ceded to France by Maximilian. Mr. Gwin also showed our informant, whose veracity is beyond question, his patent of nobility, as Duke of the French Province of Sonora, signed by Napoleon, and bearing the seal of France.

DAILY PROGRESS.

RALEIGH, N. C.

THURSDAY, MAY 25, 1865.

See Fourth Page for Latest News.

Who are the Union Men?

The Vance and Davis secessionists, here and elsewhere, are now endeavoring to make Union officers and soldiers believe that they have been the truest and most consistent Union men in North Carolina, and that those of us who have been hunted down, persecuted and threatened with mob violence on account of our opposition to the despotism of the twoarch-traitors, are the worst of secessionists. They even go farther and have the impudence to begin to work the wires to secure the offices of State. They have become so fat on the forage of Vance and Davis, and so sleek on the luxuries of the blockade, that they are confirmed in the idea that they have a divine right to office and all the patronage and plunder that accompanies the most corrupt administrations. Men who have been mobbed and hunted down for devotion to the Union, these Janus-faced *patriots* call secessionists, while they are preparing to parcel out the offices the people will soon be called on to fill, among men that have been active in their efforts to destroy the Union, or those whose Unionism has been of a passive and silent character. Mr. Holden, they say, will not do for Governor, and they propose the names of gentlemen who still cling to the idea that we must have a lease of ten or twenty years on slavery—men whose lips were sealed during the reign of terror that swept over this State last summer—men who neither spoke for, wrote for, or voted for the Union candidate for Governor.

What claims have such men upon the loyal masses of the State? Who dare bring forward a man for position, now, whose moral cowardice closed his lips when it cost something to oppose the Davis tyranny and plead for a restoration of the Union? We know there are a number of prominent gentlemen throughout the State who profess to have been for the Union all the time—(and they now urge their claims for favors and for office as such)—who stumped for Vance and voted for Vance last summer, notwithstanding "his Excellency" was for fighting "until hell froze over and then fight on the ice." Others there are who took no part for Vance and the war party, but they took very good care to take no part against them; and though they may have felt intense affection for the Union in their hearts, they did nothing to strengthen the bands of those that were engaged in fighting its battles. Strange indeed that persons who profess to be Union men should urge for the high position of Governor, a man who was not known to be with us even to the extent of voting for our candidates, last summer. As well for the Union men to bring Vance back and elect him Governor, as to elect a man who took no active part against him last summer.

But the minions of Vance and Davis, the oligarchs, say that we must have some new man, some man who has no record and is not a politician, to secure harmony! Harmony, indeed. It was such harmony that gave us Jeff Davis, secession, war, blood, carnage and ruin! For the sake of harmony we must embrace, first, secession, war and ruin; and then to return to the Union we must embrace and elevate to office the very authors of our ruin to perpetuate the harmony they have inaugurated. Mr. Holden, they say, will not do for Governor, they want a new man. Of course they do; anybody but the fearless, bold, outspoken friends of the Union who have denounced them and their corruptions through the trying scenes of the last three years. And then they want one who can keep the head of the defunct, *effete* aristocracy above water. Mr. Holden sprang from the people, his wealth was not inherited but was acquired by honest toil—he is the friend of the laboring masses and is idolized by them, and for all this these toadies and "stall-federate" admirers of Vance, who are now in search of a new man, would procure the assassination of Mr. Holden, could they find a Booth to do the work, rather than see him elevated to the Gubernatorial chair by that overwhelming majority which they know awaits him whenever the people are allowed to have a free and fair ballot. Money was unsparingly used by these men, here, last summer, to defeat Mr. Holden, because he was the friend of the people, the enemy of the slaveocracy and devoted to the Union: and now they have the impudence to talk of getting out another man to oppose him.—Once for all, we tell these men that their political influence has departed with their niggers; that they have no longer the bayonets of Davis and Vance to back their insolent demands: and that Mr. Holden is the first, last and only choice of the people of the State for Governor when the time to elect comes, and that they mean to elect him. He will be the candidate of the loyal Union men of the State, and any opposition that may be gotten up against him will be the joint work of the partizans of Davis and Vance, and the slaveocracy who have hitherto considered themselves a privileged class; and they will be considered the enemies of the government and treated as such.

We say to the tried and true Union men throughout the State that an effort is being made in this city, by the "stall-federate" minions of the late reigning powers, to bring about a fusion between the Davis and Vance war men to carry the elections and fill the offices by secessionists and the enemies of the Government, and the first move will probably be, to introduce the name of some *quasi* Union man as a candidate for Governor under the plea of harmony. We know the leaders, the prime movers and the manœuverers in this plot to defeat the wishes of the loyal masses, and we mean to unfrock and expose them and their tools when the proper time arrives. No friend of the Union, no man who is loyal to the Government will be thus used by these instruments of the defunct aristocracy, and we caution all good Union men against their spurious wares. They got possession of Vance, a man whose election in 1862 was a Union triumph of thirty odd thousand in North Carolina, and he fell; and whoever now consents to play the figure-head for them must follow Vance and Davis, for their blight is more deadly than the Upas, more fatal than the simoon of the desert. They may prostitute the word Union, as they prostituted that of Conservative last summer, and enter their man as a full-blooded Union man, but as they have not the bayonets of the cold-blooded murderer, Davis, to control the ballot box, they will not be able to get for him more than 15,000 votes in the State, about the real secession strength; and we shall probably vote an aggregate of 80,000.

When the people go to the polls to vote for Governor and other State officers, these representatives of the defunct aristocracy will find out who the real Union men of the State are.

Who Shall be our Military Governor?

Anxious as we all are for the restoration of civil law and civil rule in North Carolina, we are aware that a military reign must precede the restoration of civil authority. We can have no elections until the loyal voters of the State are enrolled, nor do the people know how or when to proceed without some one to look to—some one possessed with authority and vested with power to issue proclamations and prescribe the mode and manner of proceeding. It being the determination of the government to ignore and declare void all acts of the Legislature passed since the beginning of the rebellion, the people of North Carolina find themselves exactly in the condition of those of a territory that have no government: and hence we must begin at the beginning—first determine who are entitled to the rights of citizenship, then lay the ground work of the edifice, and then proceed with the building.

Every man we meet desires to know when we are to have an election for delegates to a Convention, when elect members to the Legislature, Congress, a Governor, &c. We can only answer in general terms. In the first place we must have a Military Governor, under whose supervision the loyal men of the State may be enrolled and the *status* of voters determined: then we must have judges or poll holders appointed for all the counties throughout the State; and then, we must have a proclamation ordering an election for delegates to a Convention, which Convention when it assembles, will be clothed with full power to change, alter or abolish the Constitution, and to do any and everything that a free people of a Sovereign State may do. This Convention may prescribe the mode and manner of proceeding in the election of a Governor, members to the Legislature and members to the National Congress. It may also settle all questions which are likely to arise between the free white man and the free colored man relative to labor, the rights of citizenship, &c., and so alter the Constitution and so frame our statute laws as to secure protection and justice to all, the greatest good to the greatest number.

To be plain, then, we can do nothing without a Convention, and we can have no Convention without a military Governor, or some one clothed with power to issue proclamations ordering elections: and as the President will hardly undertake to order elections in North Carolina, directly, we take it for granted that a military Governor will be appointed, and that very soon.—And who shall be appointed?—a military man or a civilian? Gen. Schofield, Gen. Palmer, Gen. Terry, Mr. Holden or somebody else?—We have no objection whatever to giving utterance to our individual impressions and individual preferences. Some weeks ago we expressed the opinion that some competent military man should be appointed, and gave our reasons therefor, and further observation and research has only tended to strengthen and confirm our conviction. The appointment of a military man will hush all party clamor, for it is to be supposed that an army officer will know no party, faction or clique, but that he will be governed in all matters pertaining to the position by motives of duty. If a civilian be appointed military Governor he would have necessarily to be subordinate to the Commander of the Department, and of course there would be clashing and confusion. And as the Commandant of the Department has control of the troops now doing duty, and who are to remain here until civil rule is restored, we are clearly of the opinion that it would be better for the General Government, better for us, for him and all concerned that he be appointed military Governor, and thus combine the character of Governor and Department Commander in one person. Gen. Schofield feels a deep interest in the future of the State, as he does of the whole country; he is anxious to see us fully restored to the Union and left to ourselves, and we trust that the President will take the same view of it that many of our people do, and appoint him. If he be appointed military Governor we think we can promise the people of the State that within a few months they will have all the machinery of a State government in full operation, the civil law will be restored, and we shall have peace, protection and quiet throughout all our borders.

We do not pretend to say that the other gentlemen named are not fully competent to the duties of the office of military Governor—and as far as Mr. Holden is concerned we know he is the choice of the loyal people of the State at the polls, and we feel confident they will elect him when the time comes—but for the reasons stated, reasons that are entirely conclusive to our mind, we prefer Gen. Schofield to any other man for military Governor.

Union Meetings in Wake.

From our advertising columns it will be seen that there are to be Union Meetings at Rolesville, New Hill and Wiley Lynn's, in this county, within the next few days: At Rolesville on Saturday, May 27th, at Lynn's Thursday, June 1st, and at New Hill Saturday, June 3rd. Prominent gentlemen are expected to be present at each of these places to address the people, and we hope the people will turn out and hear them. The Union sentiment in Wake is overwhelming, and though smothered by trickery and fraud to some extent last summer, now that the tyranny of rebel bayonets is withdrawn, it is speaking out; and when again the people of Wake are permitted to approach the ballot box it will be seen that the opponents of the Union ticket, should such monstrosities dare present themselves, will not poll a corporal's guard.

As it is certain that an order for an election of delegates to a State Convention will soon be issued, we would respectfully suggest that it might be well for the loyal men of the county to express their preferences at these district meetings for the men they would like to represent them in that body. We have any number of good and true men in the county, but the coolest, most discreet and ablest that we have should be sent to the Convention; for some of the most important questions ever brought before the people of North Carolina are to be discussed and acted upon by the men that shall be selected to compose the next State Convention. We caution the loyal people of the county not to be deceived or betrayed by packed Conventions, or court-house cliques, but to express themselves freely and fully in their district and neighborhood meetings, and contend for and support those men whom they deem best competent and most worthy to represent them.

We shall attend all the meetings referred to, if possible, for we desire to see and mingle with the people in the country, so that we may be able to reflect their true sentiments. And we hope that all, whatever may have been their antecedents or former political sympathies, will turn out and attend these meetings, and assist by their presence and votes in restoring law and order within the State, and the State to the Union around which all our affections should cluster.

The Last Scene.

There is something very ridiculous in the fact that the great leader of the rebellion should at last attempt to escape pursuit by assuming the apparel of a woman, and those of his followers who have given us such nauseating doses concerning his *moral courage*, must feel deeply humiliated at this last act in the thrilling drama. Of the last scene the Philadelphia *Inquirer* says:

Perhaps there was something needed to put the people of the United States in a good humor after their recent calamities which affected every mind. Nothing could, therefore, have come to them more comical in its suggestions than the ideas of "the man of destiny," "the stern statesman," the intensely admired head of the disloyal sympathizers with Rebellion, ending his tragic career with the ludicrous exit of a low comedian in a farce. This great "Bombastes," who, at the beginning of the war declared that it was necessary to make the North "smell Southern powder and feel Southern steel," after desperate endeavors to carry out his threat, after being "the rose and expectancy of the fair State, the glass of fashion and the mould of form," after "swimming in a sea of glory," ends his career of lofty pretensions by donning his wife's petticoats, and attempting to run from the soldiers who pursued him. The exordium was sublime, the peroration was ridiculous. The incident shows that this monster, who had the fierceness of Robespierre, and the malignity of Marat, was at heart a coward, who, instead of meeting his fate bravely, endeavored to evade it by the device of a *Jerry Sneak*.

The *finale* was necessary to the condemnation of the play. Had this man died "fighting in the last ditch;" had he stood before his enemies with the bravery of a soldier who may die, but will never be disgraced, poetry might have hereafter lamented his heroic fate in its choicest strophes. He would have cast a gleam of respectability over his cause, even in its ruin; but, instead of the courage which would have led him to meet his fate like a hero, his innate cowardice urged him to adopt a course which compels his exit from the scene in the furtive disguise of a thief. What a preposterous ending to a "noble career;" what a rebuke to those disloyal praters, who for four years have been representing this individual to be the model of a statesman and gentleman—a gentleman, forsooth!—a gentleman meets his accountabilities boldly. An imposter puts on disguises, and endeavors to cheat the fate which he has not strength of soul to meet.

THE EMANCIPATION AND FREE LABOR QUESTIONS IN THE SOUTH.

One of our war correspondents in North Carolina furnishes us, from a learned gentleman of the late Southern slaveholding aristocracy, a very gloomy view of their prospects under the new system about to be introduced among them of universal emancipation and free labor. This philosopher of the exploded *regime* of "the peculiar institution" is clearly of the opinion that the poor Southern whites are too lazy to work, and that the negroes can only be made to work under a master. He concludes, therefore, that the Southern planters will have to look to the North for thier laborers, and he is about to come North himself on this mission, by way of a beginning.

But this North Carolinia philosopher takes only a superficial view of his subject. It is true that under the Southern slavery system, the blacks, as a rule, have done as little work as possible, and have required the constant vigilance of an overseer, whip in hand, to keep them at it. But the reason for this is very obvious. The slave had so much, from day to day and year to year, in food and clothing, whether his day's work was more or less than the average of an able-bodied field hand. Besides, the constant danger menacing him of being sold and moved off from "the old place" without a moment's warning, took away from him almost every inducement, beyond the present day, to add to the comforts of his cabin. Nor had he any rights of property upon which he could rely with any feeling of security.—Hence the lazy habits and pilfering propensities of the Southern blacks under the slavery system; for why should he labor when he could avoid it, when the result to him was all the same? And why, with the reputation of a rogue, should he hesitate to steal a chicken, a pig or a bag of corn, if "none of the white folks could spot him?"

The poor whites of the South have also fallen into their lazy, shiftless habits from this institution of slavery. Why should they be degraded to the level of "niggers" by working, if they can contrive, by fair means or by foul, to vegetate from day to day? They are a degraded caste; but, taking their cue from the lordly slaveholder, they can still boast that in the right to work just when they choose they are "a step above the niggers." Hence the laziness and degradation of the Southern poor whites. Slavery has had its compensations to the negro; but to the Southern poor white it has been an unmittigated curse, though, in his stupidity, he has been a stickler for the institution because "it keeps down the niggers."

Now, with this institution of slavery removed, the Southern blacks will be encouraged to labor with the reward of its profits before them as their own, and with the knowledge that there is no master to support them if they neglect their work. The degradation, too, being removed from labor, and dignity and honor being imparted to it, as a test of individual merit, to whites and blacks, the poor whites of the South will no longer be ashamed to work for a living. The lordly planters themselves will cease to be ashamed of it; and for active work they have had a good training from the necessities of labor imposed upon them by this terrible war. We dare say that the planters of the rebellious States and their families—especially their high-spirited, self-sacrificing, but strangely infatuated women—have done more hard work during the last four years than in all their lives before. It shows that where there is a will there is a way; and under this great revolution of Southern emancipation the way will be found for engaging Southern whites and blacks in active industry, from the will which the removal of slavery will inspire. The war, moreover, has made room for a large infusion of Northern industry, and thus emigration will pour in, and will soon leaven the whole lump of Southern society under the new system of free labor.—*Herald.*

A dispatch was received in this city on Tuesday announcing that Messrs. Holden, Dick and others who accompanied them had arrived in Washington City. We suppose they will be back in four or five days.

Treasury Department,
SIXTH SPECIAL AGENCY,
Raleigh, N. C., May 25th, 1865.

THE FOLLOWING ARTICLE OF U. S. TREASURY Regulations, issued May 9th, 1865, is hereby published for the benefit of persons desiring to carry on business in Raleigh and vicinity:

"ARTICLE VII.

Persons desiring to keep a supply store at any place within an insurrectionary State, shall make application therefor to the nearest officer of the Treasury Department, which application shall set forth that the applicant is loyal to the government of the United States; and upon filing evidence of such loyalty a license for such Supply Store shall forthwith be granted, and the person to whom the license is given shall be authorized to purchase goods at any other Supply Store within the insurrectionary States, or at such other point in the United States as he may select.

The party receiving such license shall pay therefor the license fee prescribed by the Internal Revenue Law."

All parties engaged or about to engage in business, are respectfully notified to comply with the above regulations.

CHAS. H. WOODS,
Local Special Ag't U. S. Treasury.

Office on second floor corner of Fayetteville and Hargett Street, in the Smith building. May 25-tf

UNION MEETING IN CRABTREE DISTRICT.

THERE WILL BE A MEETING OF THE FRIENDS of the Union at Wiley Lynn's on **Thursday, June 1st, 1865,** and all loyal men of the county are invited to attend. Several prominent gentlemen are expected to be present to address the meeting.

Rally for the old flag and the Union of our fathers.

May 25-td MANY UNION MEN.

THE DAILY PROGRESS.

A Union Paper at the Capital of North Carolina.

Having determined to remain in Raleigh and make the PROGRESS one of the permanent fixtures of the Capitol of the State, we appeal to our friends throughout the State to exert themselves to extend its circulation.

Bastiles, prisons and courts of star chamber having been abolished by the Union armies, and the old flag having again been unfurled on the capitol of our good old State, never again to be lowered by the hand of treason, the people can read those papers that advocate their principles and express their own sentiments, without the fear of the rack or the stake; and it is our determination to make THE PROGRESS worthy the confidence of the intelligent masses.

We have associated with us in the editorial management of the paper gentlemen of experience and of acknowledged talent and ability, and we shall spare neither labor or expense to render the paper worthy of the capitol of the State and a welcome visitor in every loyal family.

Though it is our determination to make the PROGRESS a live newspaper, we shall not ignore those great questions that so deeply affect our immediate future and which must be speedily acted upon and settlod. We shall give to the administration of PRESIDENT JOHNSON an active and zealous support, and will exert whatever of power or influence we may possess to restore harmony, peace and prosperity to our native State. We love the Union and we love North Carolina, and all our energies and whatever of talents we may possess, or shall be able to command in the management of the paper, shall be employed for the preservation of the one and to increase the prosperity of the other.

In the management of our publications we shall know no North, no South, no East, no West, but will labor earnestly and continually for the welfare of our whole country.

THE WEEKLY PROGRESS,

The publication of which has been interrupted by the derangement of the mails, will be resumed immediately, and we make an earnest appeal to our friends to exert themselves in extending its circulation.

May 4th, 1865. J. L. PENNINGTON & CO.

MILITARY GOVERNMENT OF THE CITY.

Col G F Granger, commanding 3d Brig 2d Div 10th A C, Post Commander.
Lt H S Sanford, 115th N Y Vols. A A A General, and Post Adjutant.
Capt S C F Smith, 9th Me Vols, A A I Gen.
Major George B Dyer, 9th Me. Vols, Pro Marshal.
Lt Wm K Norton, 4th N H Vols, Assistant Pro Marshal.
Lt George S Dailey, 9th Maine Vols, Assistant Pro Marshal.
Capt Chas F Weeks, 9th Me Vols, A A Q M.
Capt Geo C Almy, C S.
Surgeon Jno Knowlson, 169th N Y Vols, Chief Med Officer.
Capt E R Mosher, 169th N Y Vols, A D C.
Lt Ed Vanderzee, 169th N Y Vols, A D C.

OFFICERS OF 115TH REG'T N Y VOLUNTEERS.

N J Johnson, Lt Col Commanding.
E L Walrath, Major.
Nicholas De Graff, Act Adjutant.
Martin McMartin, Qr Master.
Lieut A C Slocum, Commanding Co A.
Lieut A Collier, do do B.
Lieut C L Clark, do do C.
Capt Wm H Shaw, do do E.
Capt E B Savage, do do G.
Lieut M McIntosh, do do I.
Lieut J M Hill, do do K.

OFFICERS OF 9TH MAINE VOLUNTEERS.

Joseph Noble, Lieut Col Commanding.
George B Dyer, Major.
Henry H Wadsworth, Adjutant.
Geo S Hay, Qr Master.
Otis P Rice, As Surgeon.
Lieut Wm A Babcock, Commanding Co A.
Capt L F McKenney, do do B.
" Geo W Brown, do do C.
" Benj J Hill, do do D.
" J C Beal, do do E.
Lieut W F Denning, do do F.
" S A Doten, do do G.
" A H Chase, do do H.
Capt Geo S Colbath, do do I.
Capt S S Mann, do do K.

OFFICERS 4TH N. H. VOLS.

Lt. Col. F. W. Parker, Commanding.
" Geo W Huckins, A R Q M.
1st Lt Alfred Marland, Acting Adjutant.
" Joseph Wingate, commanding Co. A.
" Leonard A Gay, do do B.
Capt Louis McD Bussey, do do C.
1st Lt Sam'l H Prescott, do do D.
Capt Wm T Barker, do do E.
" Clarence L. Chapman, do do F.
2d Lt Patrick Dowd, do do G.
1st Lt Edwin Whitford, do do H.
Capt Geo F Quimby, do do I.
" Geo W Huckins, do do K.

OFFICERS 13TH IND. VOLS.

J H Lawrence, Major, commanding.
Saxey Ryan, Lt and Adjutant.
A H Baily, Lt and R Q M.
N A Chamberlain, Ass't Surgeon.
Silas Clark, Capt commanding co A.
C Cary, 1st Lt.
M Gonser, 2d Lt.
Wm H Lowe, Capt commanding co B.
J H Kinnear, 1st Lt.
R H Jones, 2d Lt.
T Riefle, Capt commanding co C.
S Morrison, 1st Lt.
A O Mitchell, 2d Lt.
R J Graham, Capt commanding co D.
J J Gurley, 1st Lt.
J Sherrow, 2d Lt.
W T Stepp, Capt commanding co E.
J C Boyd, 1st Lt.
Wm A Ketchum, 2d Lt.
Companies F, G, H, I and K are commanded by officers whose names have been mentioned.

OFFICERS OF 169TH REG'T N Y VOLS.

J A Colvin, Lieut Col commanding.
Joseph H Allen, Major.
John Knowlson, Surgeon.
E W Church, Acting Adj't and Q M.
Lieut Ed Jacques, commanding co A.
Lieut J B Foot, commanding co B.
Capt J H Warren, commanding co C.
Lieut B McGuire, commanding co D.
Capt H Mulhall, comd'g co E.
Capt E R Smith, comd'g co F.
Lieut E Van Santword, comd'g co G.
Lieut C G Francisco, comd'g co H.
Capt J H Dunn, comd'g co I.
Lieut J H Straight, comd'g co K.

DAILY PROGRESS.

THURSDAY, MAY 25, 1865.

Important Order.

The following order assigning Capt. J. C. Beal to the superintendence of Freedmen for the district composed of the counties composing Gen. Ames' command, is one of great importance to all who are interested; and we respectfully refer all in search of information on that head to Capt. Beal:

HEADQUARTERS TENTH ARMY CORPS, (*In the field, Raleigh N. C.*) May 24, 1865

SPECIAL ORDERS, No. 48.

III. In compliance with the Provisions of Par. IX. of General Orders No. 46 C. S from Headquarters Department of North Carolina, Capt. J. C. Beal, 9th, Maine Volunteers, is hereby appointed Superintendent of Freedmen of the District, composed within the limits of this command, and will be obeyed and respected accordingly.

By command of Brevet Maj Gen. Ames,
CHAL A. CARLTON,
Maj. & A. A. G.

The Counties of District comprised within the command of the 10th Army Corps—are Person, Orange, Chatham, Wake, Granville, Wayne, Sampson, Johnson, Wilson, Green, Moore, Richmond, Cumberland, Robinson, Harnett, Northampton, Halifax, Edgecomb, Warren, Duplin and Franklin.

DRUNKENNESS.—From the amount of drunkenness visible for the last day or two, it is evident that some person or persons have violated existing orders, and sold liquor without authority. It is the duty of all good citizens who are knowing to the sale of liquor by unauthorized persons to report it to the Provost Marshal's office, and we hope it will be done. It is bread, and not grog-shops that this people now want. We suspect that most of the liquor is dealt out clandestinely by the venders of beer, by eating house keepers, &c., but they will have to be sharp to elude the vigilance of Col. Granger and Major Dyer.

AN EXCURSION.—Capt. Garoutte, Chief of Transportion for the Post we believe, took the pupils of the Deaf and Dumb Institution on an excursion to Neuse river yesterday, and we doubt not but the day was most pleasantly passed by those who composed the party. The Captain kindly invited us to accompany the gay throng, but business prevented our doing so. We trust that Mr. Palmer, the worthy Principal of the Institution, or some one else capable of doing so, will give us a detailed account of the day's festivities.

NORTHERN PAPERS.—Officers, soldiers and citizens who may receive Northern papers in advance of the mail will greatly oblige us by sending them to this office. Until we can get regular mails and receive the press reports, we shall be under lasting obligations for such favors,

HORRIBLE MURDER AND WHOLESALE ROBBERY.—On Monday night a horrible case of murder and robbery was committed on the Washington road a few miles from town upon the family of a Mr. Grace. The particulars, as we got them are as follows:

Two white men, recognised by Mrs. Grace as a man, (a citizen) by the name of Wise, and one of the construction corps who has recently bought land and settled out in that neighborhood, by the name of John Dorton, accompanied by two darkies, went to the house of Grace after night and on knocking at the door, it was opened by Grace's son aged about 10 years, when they shot him through the head killing him instantly. They then proceeded to rob indiscrimnately, money and everything else upon which they could lay their hands.

The white men left in the direction of Washington and the negroes for Newbern. Detectives are in pursuit and they may yet be brought to town.—*Newbern Times.*

The Kentucky Legislature assembled on the 16th, but no quorum was present. Chief Justice Bullitt is to be tried on the charge of conspiracy against the Government.

LATEST NEWS.

Bank's Removed—He is Succeeded by Canby.

Davis to Arrive at Washington and be Put on Trial with the other Criminals.

PROGRESS OF THE TRIAL.

PAYNE IDENTIFIED AS THE MAN THAT ATTEMPTED TO ASSASSINATE MR. SEWARD.

THE GRAND REVIEW—MEXICAN EMIGRATION.

A copy of the *Herald* of the 20th, received too late to afford time to make extended extracts, contains some important items of news, which we give, in place of extended details.

General Banks has been relieved from the command of the Department of the Gulf, and Gen'l. Canby appointed in his stead. The change has been made by President Johnson, as alleged, upon investigations, and reports recently made by a special commission appointed to look into the affairs connected with the administration of Gen'ls. Butler and Banks.

The report that Jeff. Davis would pass through Nashville, and Louisville *en route* to Washington, is contradicted. He passed from Macon to Augusta, and thence to Savannah, where he was put on board a steamer, and proceeded *via*. Fortress Monroe to Washington. A Government armed vessel convoyed the steamer, which was expected to land the rebel President and party in Washington yesterday.—It was currently reported that he would be immediately put on trial, with the other criminals, charged with conspiracy to assassinate the President.

The trial was progressing. Among other witnesses examined on the 19th were the younger Seward who fully identified the prisoner Paine as the man who attempted to assassinate his father, and who wounded himself and the assistant secretary of State. The colored boy who admitted the assassin also identified him. The parties connected with the theater were closely examined, and developed important facts touching that portion of the conspiracy.

There was a large rush of visitors to Washington from all parts of the country to witness the coming great review of the army.

The Mexican Emigration Movement is still progressing, though without any visible authorization or responsible head. It meets the reprobation of all respectable parties.

WASHINGTON, May 18.

The clouds are gathering in ominous aspect around the ill starred empire af the fated Montezuma and the heroic Guatemozin. Mexico, periled even now in her wisest policy, seems to be blindly, foolishly rushing upon the inevitable destiny which has marked her down upon the world's map as but a province, an added state if you please, of the great America republic. We need hardly look with covetous eyes upon her beautiful valleys and noble plateaus, for they are already, to the prescient eye of no uncommon wisdom, clothed in the golden colors of actual possession.

Very long ago was said, indeed, that whom the gods would destroy they first make mad. Maximilian came to his new empire on these western shores as the proud heir of an ancient house, tracing their lineage to the Cæsars—can it be that the fatal madness has thus quickly overtaken the representative of the Hapsburgs in the new found halls of Aztecs? More than a shadow for these intimations, striking as they appear, may be found in the advices recently received from the Southwest. There is now a plausibility and consistency in what at first seemed the contumacy and rashness of Kirby Smith. No longer is the whilom rebel leader the last defender of the "stars and the bars," ignominious as has been their end; but it is as the ally and supporter of the young Emperor of Mexico that he defies the power and dares the vengeance of the United States.

That the last of the rebel generals, his cause utterly defeated, his comrades mostly disgraced and in exile, himself in no way insured against a traitor's doom—should, in such a dilemma, gladly accept the proffer of an alliance with and service under so distinguished a chief as Maximilian, is in no way to be wondered at; the wonder would rather be if he did not with avidity avail himself of any such fortunate opportunity. But that the cautious, conservative, dignified supporter of the ancient privileges of royalty should, as is to-day reported on high authority, have negotiated with Kirby Smith, the rebel commander in Texas, thereby involving himself inevitably in the destruction which has already come upon the utterly ruined cause of secession, if as if some mysterious faculty had taken possession of his faculties, leaving us no choice of alternatives, forcing upon us that action which it would be exceedingly difficult, if not possible to avoid.

There is more than a color of probability to the announcement that Kirby Smith will not surrender without further fighting. The rear guard of the Confederacy, thus enfolding within itself the last remnants of that *virus* of secession, which had been so effectually eradicated elsewhere, will retreat toward its old, but never before open friends, and do its last fighing as a two-fold work in support of its new ally and against the old authority of the government they would have destroyed.

Maximilian wants a bulwark, a break-water against the strong tide of emigration which is everywhere organizing for Mexico, the sovereignty of which he is conscious of holding by so poor a title. Kirby Smith also wants anything but submission to the authority which he has so recklessly defied; and numerous advices received here from various sources confirm the impression that they are thus seeking, each by the help of the other, to attain their ends.—In no other way can the accounts of so many and so frequent interviews with the envoys of the Emperor at the out post or the camp of the rebel general be accounted for. In the light of these advices the refusal of Kirby Smith to surrender is plain as day, and his probable future policy at once explained.

It is needless to add that our emigration societies will have to make far better progress than they have thus far, in order to find any relic of this little arrangement by which whilom King Max and the last rebel general are intending to keep "armed emigrants" out of Mexico. The government is fully up to the duplicity which has all along marked this sympathy with the rebel cause, and, beside the swift punishment with which it will pursue rebels everywhere, states fully committed to a broad and comprehensive policy embracing the future of the whole continent. This will be but a convenient—a providentially appointed occasion for carrying it into execution.

PRICE LIST.

Proceedings of a Post Council of Administration which re-convened at Headquarters Post of Raleigh, N. C., May 8th, 1865, in accordance with the following orders:

HD'QRS POST OF RALEIGH, N. C., April 24th, 1865.

SPECIAL ORDER, No. 1.

I. A Post Council of Administration to consist of the following named officers, is hereby appointed to meet at the Capitol Building at 10 o'clock, A. M., to-morrow, the 25th inst., or as soon thereafter as practicable, for the purpose of establishing a Price List for the sale of goods by Purveyors, and other authorized Traders at this Post, and such other business as may be brought before it:
Maj. J. H. Allen, 169th N. Y. Vols.
Maj. J. H. Lawrence, 13th Ind. Vols.
Capt. S. C. F. Smith, A. A. I. G., 9th Me. Vols.
1st Lieut. Ed. P. Jaques, 169th N. Y. Vols.

By order of
Col. G. F. GRANGER,
Com'd'g Post.

H. S. SANFORD,
Post Adjutant.

HD'QRS POST OF RALEIGH, N. C., May 8th, 1865.

SPECIAL ORDER, No. 5.

The Post Council of Administration appointed by Special Order No. 1, Headquarters Post of Raleigh, N. C., April 24th, 1865, will re-convene at these Headquarters at 10 o'clock, A. M., this day or as soon thereafter as practicable.

By order of
Col. G. F. GRANGER,
Com'd'g Post.

H. S. SANFORD,
Post Adjutant.

The Post Council of Administatration re-convened at Headquarters, Post of Raleigh, N. C., pursuant to the above orders, all the members being present, and proceeded to revise the Price List established by them April 24th, 1865.

After due consultation they would respectfully recommend that the following Price List be established:
J. H. Allen, Maj. 169th N. Y. Vols.
J. H. Lawrence, Maj. 13th Ind. Vols.
S. C. F. Smith, Capt. 9th Maine Vols., and A. A. I. G.
Ed. P. Jaques, 1st Lieut. 169th N. Y. Vols.

Apples each,	5 to 10
Butter, per lb.,	65
Brooms each,	40 to 60
Boots per pr.,	$10 to 20
Buttons—shirt per doz.,	10
" —horn per doz.,	10
Blacking per box,	10 to 15
Brushes—blacking each,	40 to $1
" —clothes "	75
" —hair "	50 to $1
" —tooth "	25 to 75
" —shaving "	25
Beef dried per lb.,	50
Bologna Sausage per lb.,	50
Cakes—Ginger per lb.,	30
" —Tea per lb.,	50
Crackers per lb.,	30
Cheese per lb.,	50
Candles,	10 each
Cigars each,	10 to 20
Combs, coarse and fine, each	15 to 50
Codfish per lb.,	20
Cups—tin (qts.)	25
Cups—tin with bails and covers,	40
Collars—paper per box,	50
Caps—officer,	$2 to 4
Drawers per pr.,	$1 to 3
Emery paper per sheet,	5
Eggs per doz.,	60
Envelopes per bunch,	20 to 40
Fruit—2 lb. cans,	$1
" —1 lb. cans,	75
Flour per lb.,	10
Figs per lb.,	60
Gloves—Cott. per pr.,	25 to 40
" —Buckskin per pr.,	$1 to 2
" —Gauntlets per pr.,	$3 to 5
Handkerchiefs—Linen,	50 to $1
" —Cotton,	35 to 60
" —Silk,	$1 to 2
Hats,	$5 to 6
Ham per lb.,	40
Ice per ton,	$40
" lb.,	5
Ink per bottle,	15
Knives—Pocket,	$1 to 2.50
Knives and Forks,	50 to $1
Looking Glasses—Pocket,	10 to 25
Lemons each,	10
Milk—Borden's per can,	75
Other Brands,	60
Milk per qt.,	20
Meats—2 lb. cans,	$1
" —1 lb. cans,	75
Mustard per bottle,	50
Mackerel each,	15 to 20
Matches per bunch,	5 to 10
Newspapers—Daily,	10
Needles per paper,	10
Oranges each,	10
Oil—Armor, per bottle,	10
Oil—Sweet " " (Small)	10 to 20
(Large	25
Oysters—Small cans,	75
" —Large,	$1
Onions per lb.,	10
Poultry—2 lb. cans,	$1.25
Pickles per jar,	50 to 75
Paper—Note per qr.,	40
"Letter and Cap per qr,	50
Potatoes per lb.,	10
Pepper per paper,	10
Pepper per ¼ lb. paper,	25
Ploughs large,	$14
Plougs small,	$7
Ploughshares,	35 to $1
Pipes—Common,	10
" —Wood,	25 to $1
" —Rubber,	50 to $1.50
Pencils—Lead,	10 to 25
Pans—Sauce,	75 to $1 25
" Frying,	50 to $1
Pots—Tin (Coffee)	75 to $1
Plates—Tin,	20
Pins, per paper,	15
Raisins per lb.,	60
Razors each,	$1 to 2
Razor Strops each,	50 to 75
Syrup—Golden per bottle,	50
Soap—Shaving per cake,	15 to 20
" —Castile per 1-4 lb. cake,	25
Suspenders per pr.,	$1 to 2
Scissiors per pr.,	50 to $1
Shoe Strings per pr.,	5
Sardines per box,	60
Spoons—Table each,	15
" —Tea each,	10
Socks—Cotton per pr.,	40 to $1
" —Woolen per pr.,	35 to 75
Shoes per pr.,	$4 to 7
Shirts—Wool each,	$3 to 7
" —Linen,	$2 to 4
Tobacco—Smoking,	
"Killickinick" per 1 lb. bale,	$1.25
"Big Lick" per 1 lb. bale,	$1.25
Per paper,	15 to 25
Tobacco—Fine Cut Chewing,	
"Solace" per paper,	15
All other brands per paper,	10
Tobacco—Plug per lb.,	$1
" —Navy Plug,	$1.50
Thread per bunch,	10
Tongues—Smoked per lb.,	50
Vegetables—Small cans,	50
" —Large "	75
Wallets—Calfskin,	75 to $1.50
" —Morocco,	50 to $1.50
Wash Basins—Tin,	75
Worcestershire Sauce—Large size,	75
Small size,	50
Yeast Powder per box,	20

PRICE LIST FOR BARBERS.

Shaving,	10
Hair Cutting,	15
Champooning,	25

All articles not enumerated on the above Price List shall be sold at a *nett profit* of not more than 40 per cent.

On all purchases made at wholesale a discount of not less than 30 per cent. shall be made from the prices established and published in the above List.

HD'RS POST OF RALEIGH, N. C., May 8th, 1865.

The proceedings of the Post Council of Administration which re-convened in accordance with Special Order No. 5, from these Headquarters are approved and the above Price List by them established will be strictly adhered to in their sales by all Sutlers and Purveyors authorized to transact business at this Post. Any complaints by any person of a violation of the requirements of the above list will be at once investigated and if found authentic the place of business of the party so offending will be immediately closed by the Provost Marshal. The places of business of every person engaged in the sale of goods will be visited daily by the provost guard and if any store or other place of business is found without a copy of this Price List posted in a conspicuous place it will be closed by Provost Marshal.

By order of
G. F. GRANGER,
Col. 9th Maine Vols.
Comd'g Post.

H. S. SANFORD
Post Adjutant.

California is jubilant over the capture of the ex-Rebel President. The people of Sacramento hung him in effigy.

OFFICIAL ORDERS.

Headq'rs Department of N. C., ARMY OF THE OHIO, Raleigh, N. C., May 15, 1865.

GENERAL ORDERS, No. 52.

THE FOLLOWING ORDERS FROM HEADQTARTERS Military Division of the James are published for the information and guidance of all in the Department of North Carolina, which now forms part of that Military Division.

HEADQ'RS MIL. DIVISION OF THE JAMES, Richmond, Va., April 28, 1864.

GENERAL ORDERS, No. 4.

I. Clerks of courts of records in Richmond and Petersburg will be permitted to resume their functions on taking the oath of allegiance.

II. All attorneys, counsellors, advocates and proctors and others licensed to practice a particular profession, trade or business; the presidents, directors and officers of all corporations, and all persons availing themselves of the benefit of General Order No. 2, in regard to trade will be required to take the oath of allegiance to the United States. Any person in the above mentioned order, who, without taking the oath, shall, after the first of May next, attempt to practice any licensed profession, or engage in any licensed trade or business, or shall exercise the functions of a president, director, or officer of any corporation, will be arrested. The foregoing provisions will be enforced in other parts of the State as early as practicable.

III. All persons making claims for restoration of private property, before a Provost Martial, or any other military officer, court, or commission, will be required to take the oath of allegiance to the United States, and until the claimant takes the prescribed oath, his claim will neither be granted nor considered.

IV. All officers of customs in this Military Division are requested to give no clearances or permits to ship or land goods or other articles of trade, to any person or for the benefit of any person who has not taken the oath of allegiance to the United States.

V. No marriage license will be issued until the parties desiring to be married take the oath of allegiance to the United States, and no clergyman, magistrate, or other person authorized by State laws to perform the marriage ceremony, will officiate in such capacity until he himself and the parties contracting matrimony have taken the prescribed oath of allegiance.

VI. Any person acting in violation of these orders will be arrested, and a full account of the case reported to these Headquarters.

By order of Major General HALLECK:
J. C. KELTON,
Asst. Adj't Gen'l.

By command of Major General SCHOFIELD:
J. A. CAMPBELL,
Asst. Adj't Gen'l.

OFFICIAL:
FRED'K ANDERSON,
H. & Act. Asst. Adj't Gen'l.

OFFICE PROV. MARSHAL,

POST OF RALEIGH, N. C., May 22nd, 1865.

GENERAL ORDER No 2.

IN COMPLIANCE WITH GENERAL ORDER NO. 52, dated Headquarters Deqartment, N. C., Army of the Ohio, Raleigh N. C. May 15th 1865. All parties who practice their professions or engaged in any business will immediately report to this office and take the prescribed oath of allegiance All failing to comply with this order will be arrested and reported to Headquarters of this Department.

By order of
GEO. B. DYER,
Maj. & Provost Marshal.

May 23-1w.

Headq'rs Department of N. C., (ARMY OF THE OHIO,) Raleigh, N. C., April 27th, 1865.

GENERAL ORDERS, No. 31.

THE COMMANDING GENERAL HAS THE GREAT satisfaction of announcing to the Army and to the People of North Carolina that hostilities within this State have definitely ceased; that for us the war is ended, and it is hoped that peace will soon be restored throughout our country.

It is now the duty of all to cultivate friendly relations with the same zeal which has characterized our conduct of the war, that the blessings of union, peace and material prosperity may be speedily restored to the entire country. It is confidently believed and expected that the troops of this army and the people of North Carolina will cordially unite in honest endeavors to accomplish this great end.

All good and peaceable citizens will be protected and treated with kindness, while those who disturb the peace, or violate the laws, will be punished with the severity of martial law.

The troops will be distributed so as best to secure the interests of the United States Government and protect the people, until a civil goverument can be established in harmony with the Constitution and laws of the United States. The most perfect discipline and good conduct are enjoined upon all officers and soldiers, and cordial support upon all good citizens.

All who are peaceably disposed are invited to return to their homes, and resume their industrial pursuits. Such as have been deprived of their animals and wagons by the hostile armies will be temporarily supplied, as far as practicable, upon application to the nearest Provost Marshal, by loans of the captured property in possession of the Quartermaster's Department. The needy will also be supplied, for the time being, with subsistence stores from the Commissary Department.

It will be left to the Judicial Department of the Government to punish those political leaders who are responsible for secession, rebellion and civil war, with all its horrors. Between the Government of the United States and the people of North Carolina there is peace.

By command of Major-General Schofield:
J. A. CAMPBELL,
Assistant Adjutant General.

May 20-1w

OFFICIAL ORDERS.

Headq'rs Department of N. C., (ARMY OF THE OHIO,) Raleigh, N. C., April 27th, 1865.

GENERAL ORDERS, No. 32.

TO REMOVE A DOUBT WHICH SEEMS TO EXIST in the minds of some of the people of North Carolina, it is hereby declared that by virtue of the Proclamation of the President of the United States, dated January 1st, 1863, all persons in this State heretofore held as slaves are now free; and that it is the duty of the Army to maintain the freedom of such persons.

It is recommended to the former owners of the freedmen to employ them as hired servants at reasonable wages. And it is recommended to the freedmen that when allowed te do so, they remain with their former masters, and labor faithfully so long as they shall be treated kindly and paid reasonable wages, or that they immediately seek employment elsewhere in the kind of work to which they are accustomed. It is not well for them to congregate about towns or Military Camps.—They will not be supported in idleness.

By command of Major General Schofield:
J. A. CAMPBELL,
Assistant Adjutant General.

May 20-1w

Headq'rs Department of N. C., (ARMY OF THE OHIO,) Raleigh, N. C., May 4, 1865.

GENERAL ORDERS, No. 35.

MAJOR-GENERAL J. D. COX, WITH HIS CORPS, and two Brigades of Gen. Kilpatrick's Cavalry, will occupy Greensboro', Salisbury, Charlotte and such other points as he may deem necessary, and take care of the Western portion of the State.

Major-General A. H. Terry, with his Corps, and one Brigade of General Kilpatrick's Cavalry, will occupy Raleigh, Goldsboro', Fayetteville and such other points as he may deem necessary, and take care of the Central portion of the State.

Brigadier-Generals Palmer and Hawley will command the Coast Districts as heretofore.

The troops will visit all parts of the State, disperse or capture all bands of guerrillas and marauders, and collect all military arms (other than the side arms of paroled officers) which may be found in the State

The Corps and District Commanders will, as soon as practicable, send to each county under their jurisdiction a discreet officer, with a sufficient force to organize a small Company of the most responsible loyal citizens to serve as a local police force until further orders. As far as necessary the Companies so organized will be furnished with captured arms and ammunition, but will receive no compensation for their services.

All the members will be required to take the oath of allegiance to the Government of the United States, and an oath to preserve the peace, prevent crime and arrest criminals, as far as practicable, within their county, and to obey all lawful orders of the United States Military authorities.

Criminals arrested by the police companies will be sent to the nearest Military Post for trial, by Military Commission. A full statement of the crimes and the names of witnesses, must be sent with the prisoners in each case.

By command of Major-General Schofield:
J. A. CAMPBELL,
Assistant Adjutant General.

May 20-1w

Headq'rs Department of N. C., (ARMY OF THE OHIO,) Raleigh, N. C., May 12, 1865.

GENERAL ORDERS, No. 45.

I. HEREAFTER COMMERCIAL INTERCOURSE IN the State of North Carolina, in articles not contraband of war, will be restricted only by the regulations of the Treasury Department.

The following articles are contraband of war, to-wit: arms, ammunition, and all articles from which ammunition is manufactured, gray uniforms and cloth, locomotives, cars, railroad iron and machinery for operating railroads, telegraph wires, insulators, and instruments for operating telegraph lines.

All *military* restrictions upon trade in articles other than those above enumerated are removed.

II. Hereafter no military tax will be imposed upon citizens for passes or permits of any kind, nor for any other reason whatever, and all orders from whatever source authorizing such taxes are hereby revoked.

By command of Maj. Gen. Schofield:
J. A. CAMPBELL,
Assist. Adj't Gen'l.

May 20-1w

Headq'rs Department of N. C., (ARMY OF THE OHIO,) Raleigh, N. C., May 15, 1865.

GENERAL ORDERS, No. 46.

THE FOLLOWING RULES ARE PUBLISHED FOR the government of Freedmen in North Carolina, until the restoration of civil government in the State:

I. The common laws governing the domestic relations, such as those giving parents authority and control over their children, and guardians control over their wards, are in force. The parent's or guardian's authority and obligations take the place of those of the former master.

II. The former masters are constituted the guardians of minors and of the aged and infirm, in the absence of parents or other near relatives capable of supporting them.

III. Young men and women, under twenty-one years of age, remain under the control of their parents or guardians until they become of age, thus aiding to support their parents, and younger brothers and sisters.

IV. The former masters of freedmen may not turn away the young or the infirm, nor refuse to give them food and shelter; nor may the able bodied men or women go away from their homes, or live in idleness, and leave their parents, children, or young brothers and sisters to be supported by others.

V. Persons of age, who are free from any of the obligations referred to above, are at liberty to find new homes wherever they can obtain proper employment; but they will not be supported by the government, nor by their former masters, unless they work.

VI. It will be left to the employer and servant to agree upon the wages to be paid; but freedmen are advised that for the present season they ought to expect only moderate wages, and where their employers cannot pay them money, they ought to be contented with a fair share in the crops to be raised. They have gained their personal freedom. By industry and good conduct they may rise to independence and even wealth.

VII. All officers, soldiers and citizens are requested to give publicity to these rules, and to instruct the freed people as to their new rights and obligations.

VIII. All officers of the Army, and of the county police companies, are authorized and required to correct any violation of the above rules within their jurisdiction.

IX. Each District commander will appoint a superintendent of freedmen, (a commissioned officer,) with such number of assistants (officers and non-commissioned officers) as may be necessary, whose duty it will be to take charge of all the freed people in his District, who are without homes or proper employment. The superintendents will send back to their homes all who have left them in violation of the above rules, and will endeavor to find homes and suitable employment for all others. They will provide suitable camps or quarters for such as cannot be otherwise provided for, and attend to their discipline, police, subsistence, &c.

X. The superintendents will hear all complaints of guardians or wards, and report the facts to their District commanders, who are authorized to dissolve the existing relations of guardian and ward in any case which may seem to require it, and to direct the superintendent to otherwise provide for the wards, in accordance with the above rules.

By command of Major General Schofield:
J. A. CAMPBELL,
Assistant Adjutant General.

May 20-1w

Headq'rs Department of N. C., (ARMY OF THE OHIO,) Raleigh, N. C., May 17, 1865.

GENERAL ORDERS, No. 56.

Gratuitous issues of rations to citizens will cease on and after the 31st of May instant.

The surplus Commissary Stores in this Department will be sold to citizens at the various military posts, in small quantities for family use.

Sales will be made by any Post Commissary upon the order of the Post Commander, which order will be based upon an oath of the person desiring to purchase, that the supplies purchased shall not be re-sold, but shall be used for his or her own family, or be given to the poor. All persons must take the oath of allegiance before being permitted to purchase.

The prices will be fixed by the Chief Commissary, and will be such as to cover the actual cost to the government, including the cost of transportation.

By command of Major General Schofield,
J. A. CAMPBELL,
Assistant Adjutant General.

May 20-1w

UNION MEETING IN ROLESVILLE.

THERE WILL BE A UNION MEETING AT ROLESVILLE Saturday the 27th inst. Speaking to commence at 11 o'clock. All Union men in favor of restoring civil law and order are invited to attend.

MANY CITIZENS.

May 20-td

The Philadelphia Inquirer.

PRICE TWO CENTS. PHILADELPHIA, WEDNESDAY, MAY 31, 1865. PRICE TWO CENTS.

INFAMY!

Jeff. Davis Gloats Over Mr. Lincoln's Murder.

VILLANY OF THE REBEL CHIEFTAIN!

He Wishes the Assassination Plot Extended!

PRESIDENT JOHNSON ONE OF HIS WOULD-BE VICTIMS!

He Wants Sec'y Stanton Slain!

INFAMOUS SPEECH AT CHARLOTTE.

Yesterday's Proceedings

INTERESTING SCENES!

The Rebel General Johnston On the Stand!

HOWE OBJECTS TO HIS TESTIMONY.

The Rebel Officer Denounced as a Perjured Traitor!

HIS EJECTION FROM THE COURT ROOM PROPOSED!

MORE TESTIMONY FOR THE DEFENSE

Attempts to Impeach the Veracity of the Witnesses!

INTRODUCTION OF SEVERAL REBEL OFFICERS.

THE TRIAL OF THE CONSPIRATORS.

WASHINGTON, May 30.—Visitors of both sexes continue to crowd the court room almost to suffocation. At the trial Messrs. B. Hubbard, John E. Roberts and Charles E. Follows, of Col. Baker's Detective Force, are in attendance, enforcing order and courteously attending to their appropriate duties.

The record of the previous day having been read, the prosecution proceeded to call three witnesses, the remaining being for the defense. Their testimony was as follows:—

Testimony of Lewis F. Bates.

By Judge Advocate Holt.—Q. State where you reside. A. In Charlotte, N. C.

Q. How long have you resided there? A. Little over four years.

Q. In what business have you been engaged there during the past year? A. I have been engaged as Superintendent of the Southern Express Company for the State of North Carolina.

Q. State whether or not you saw Jefferson Davis recently at Charlotte, N. C., and under what circumstances. A. He stopped at my house on the 19th of April last.

Q. Did he make an address to the people on that occasion? A. He did, on the steps of my house.

Q. State whether or not, in the course of that address, or towards the close of it, a telegram was received by him announcing the assassination of the President of the United States. A. It was.

Q. From whom? A. From John C. Breckinridge.

Q. Did he or did he not read that telegram to the crowd? A. He did.

Q. Look at this (exhibiting to witness a telegram), and see whether it is the same despatch? A. I should say that it was.

The despatch was then read, as follows:—

GREENSBORO., April 19, 1865.—His Excellency President Davis:—President Lincoln was assassinated in the theatre in Washington, on the night of the 14th inst. Seward's house was entered on the same night and he was repeatedly stabbed, and is probably mortally wounded.

(Signed) JOHN C. BRECKINRIDGE.

Q. State what Jefferson Davis said after reading this despatch to the crowd. Endeavor to recollect his precise language. A. At the conclusion of his speech to the people he read this despatch aloud and made this remark:—"*If it were to be done it were better that it were done well.*"

Q. You are sure these are the words? A. These are the words.

Q. State whether or not, in a day or two afterwards, Jefferson Davis, John C. Breckinridge and others, were present in your house at Charlotte? A. They were.

Q. And the assassination of the President was the subject of conversation? A. A day or two afterwards that was the subject of their conversation.

Q. Can you remember what John C. Breckenridge said? A. In speaking of the assassination of President Lincoln he remarked to Davis that he regretted it very much; that it was unfortunate for the people of the South at that time; Davis replied, "*Well, General, I don't know; if it were to be done at all, it were better it were well done; and if the same were done to Andrew Johnson, the beast, and to Secretary Stanton, the job would then be complete.*"

Q. You feel confident that you recollect the words? A. These are the words used.

Q. State whether or not the regret which John C. Breckenridge expressed at the assassination was because of its criminality, or simply because it was unfortunate for the people of the South at that time? A. I drew that conclusion.

Q. Was there any remark made as to the criminality of the act? A. No sir; he simply remarked that he regretted it as being unfortunate for the South.

Q. Of what State are you a native? A. Of Massachusetts.

Testimony of J. C. Courtney.

Q. Where do you reside? A. At Charlotte, N. C.

Q. In what business were you engaged there? A. In the telegraph business in connection with the Southern Express Company.

Q. Look at the telegraph despatch of which Mr. Bates has just spoken, and state whether or not it passed over the wires at the date indicated? A. Yes sir; that is a true copy. (A copy of the message telegraphed on the 19th of April last, to Jefferson Davis, was shown to witness.)

Q. From what point? A. From Greensboro', signed by John C. Breckinridge.

Q. This despatch was sent from the office to Jefferson Davis at Charlotte? A. When the message was received he was *en route* to Charlotte; it was delivered to him at Mr. Bates' house, in Charlotte.

Judge Advocate Holt then stated that, inasmuch as the counsel for the prisoner, Spangler, had not as yet opened the case for the defense, he desired to call another witness for the prosecution in regard to that prisoner.

No objections being made, the following witness was called:—

Testimony of Jacob Ritterspach.

By Assistant Judge Advocate Bingham.—Q. State whether you were a carpenter at Ford's theatre down the 14th of April last? A. I was.

Q. Were you present on the night of the 14th when the President was shot? A. I was.

Q. Which box in the theatre did the President occupy that night? A. It was on the left hand side of the stage, the right hand side as you come in from the front.

Q. When the shot was fired did you hear anybody cry "Stop that man?" A. I did.

Q. State where you were and what you did when you heard the cry "Stop that man?" A. I was standing on the stage, about the centre, behind the scenes, when somebody cried out, "The President is shot!" Then I saw a man running across the stage towards the back-door; he had a knife in his hand; I ran to the last entrance, and as I came up to him he grabbed for me, and struck at me with his knife; I jumped back; he then ran out and slammed the door shut; then I went to open the door, and I thought it was kind of fast; I could not get it open very readily; at that time somebody cried out, "Which way?" and I answered "This way." Then I got out, but the man had got on his horse and gone down the alley; I then came in and met Spangler.

Q. What Spangler? A. Edward Spangler, the prisoner, and he kind of slapped me on the mouth with his open hand, and said, "*Don't say which way he went;*" I asked him what he meant by slapping me in the mouth, and he said, "For God's sake, shut up!" that was all he said.

Q. When you went out that door had anybody else besides the man with the knife gone out before you? A. I did not see anybody.

Q. Did anybody go out after you? A. Yes, but I do not know who it was.

Q. Did you leave the door open when you ran out? A. Yes sir.

Q. What was your business on the stage? A. My business was to shove the wings.

Q. State what sort of a man, if any, went out after you. A. I thought he was a tall, pretty stout man.

Q. Do you know him? A. No sir, I did not notice him particularly.

Q. When you came back into the theatre was the door open or shut? A. It was open.

Cross-examined by Mr. Ewing.—Q. State where you were standing when you heard the pistol fired. A. In the centre of the stage.

Q. Where was Spangler then? A. He was about in the same place, just about where we shoved off the scenes; he was standing there, and seemed to look pale.

Q. You are certain you both stood there when the pistol was fired? A. Yes sir.

Q. Did you know that the pistol had been fired immediately after it happened? A. Not right away; I did not know what had happened until I heard somebody halloo "Stop that man; the President is shot."

Q. When you came back whereabouts was Spangler? A. In the same place where I left him.

Q. Was there a crowd there? A. The actors were there and some strangers; there were some women standing there belonging to the theatre; I do not know their names?

Q. Do you not know one of them? A. I do not know any of their names, not having been acquainted with them; I had been there only four weeks.

Q. Did any one of them take any part in that play that night? A. Yes sir, some of them did.

Q. What parts did they take? A. I do not know what parts, but one they used to call Jenaie.

Q. How close was she to you when Spangler struck you? A. About three or four feet.

Q. She heard Spangler state the words you have given? A. I do not know.

Q. He said it loud enough for her to hear? A. Not so very loud.

Q. He said it in the usual tone? A. Yes sir, he looked scared and kind of crying.

Q. Did you hear the people crying "burn the theatre?" A. No sir; I just heard them hallooing "hang him, shoot him," that was all I heard.

Q. You mentioned what Spangler did and said to you to several persons since then? A. Yes sir; I do not know, I think I told some detectives that came there.

Q. Did you tell either of the Messrs. Ford? A. No sir; I told Gifford.

Q. What did you tell Gifford that Spangler said? A. I told him Spangler said I should not say which way he ran.

Q. When did you tell Gifford? A. The same week. I think that I was released from Carrol prison, the week before last.

Q. Do you not know what they called the detective whom you told? A. No sir; he had black whiskers and a very heavy moustache, and weighed about 140 pounds.

Q. Can you recollect anybody else to whom you told it? A. I might have said something about it at the table in the house where I boarded.

Q. Did you see Booth open the door? A. Yes sir.

Q. Did you see him shut it? A. No sir.

Q. How close to you was this big man who run out after you? A. He might have been five or six yards from me when I heard him or somebody else halloo out "which way;" I have not seen that man since.

Q. How long was it before you came back to where Spangler was standing? A. It might have been two or three minutes.

Q. And he was crying? A. He looked so; he seemed scared.

Q. What did you say to him before he spoke to you as you have stated? A. I did not say anything.

Q. Were you at supper with Spangler on the night before the assassination? A. Yes sir; we boarded together.

Robert Martin, a witness for the defense, being called, stated that he was mistaken in that portion of his testimony of yesterday referring to the visit of the prisoner, Dr. Samuel A. Mudd, to his house on the 4th of April. It was Jerret Mudd, not the prisoner, who visited him, and the date was 11th instead of 4th of April. The witness further stated that the prisoner, in company with Jerrett Mudd, called on him while he was in market in Washington on the 24th of December last, and that he saw the prisoner again on the 23d of March, in company with Mr. Lewellyn, the occasion of these gentlemen stopping over night at his house, and that he did not recollect seeing him on any other occasion.

Jerry Dyer, a witness for the defense, being recalled, stated that he had never gone into Virginia. He intended to say that he had not crossed the Potomac since 1861, but did get to Richmond, Virginia, at that time with the party who had been sleeping in the pines.

By Assistant Judge Advocate Bingham—Q. Who were the parties whom you accompanied to Richmond at the time of which you speak? A. Ben. Gwynn and Andrew Gwynn.

Q. That was after the Rebellion commenced? A. Yes sir.

Q. Did you see Jefferson Davis while you were in Richmond? A. I did, but I never spoke to him in my life; I remained in Richmond only about a week, and did not meet with any of the officers of the Rebel organization there except Taylor, to whom I went to get a pass.

Q. What business took you to Richmond? A. I went there to avoid arrest.

Q. You preferred to fall into the hands of the enemy? A. I regretted very much the necessity of going there.

Q. To what pines do you refer in your testimony? A. To the pines about Dr. Mudd's house.

Q. Did you sleep in the pines at night? A. Yes sir.

Q. Who fed you? A. Dr. Samuel A. Mudd.

Mr. Ewing objected to a further examination of this witness, as all these facts had already been stated by him in his examination in chief.

General Hunter inquired whether the witness had not sworn that he was a loyal man and had been such from the beginning of the Rebellion?

Judge Bingham replied that he so understood.

Q. Did you not belong to an association hostile to the Government of the United States? A. I belonged to a cavalry company.

Q. Was it not the purpose of that organization to stand by the State of Maryland in any position she might take, loyal or disloyal? A. That I do not know.

Q. Did you not publicly proclaim yourself in favor of the secession of Maryland? A. Not that I am aware of; I may have done it.

By Mr. Ewing.—Q. State whether when you went to Virginia you entered into the Confederate service. A. I did not; I did not go for that purpose.

Q. State whether when you returned you took the oath of allegiance. A. I did.

Q. State whether you have done any act to aid or encourage the Rebellion since taking the oath? A. I have not, that I am aware of.

By Mr. Bingham.—Q. When did you take this oath of allegiance? A. In 1861; I am not positive as to that; I know it was a short time after I returned.

Q. Who administered the oath of allegiance? A. One of the lieutenants or captains; I think, down at General Hooker's camp.

Testimony of Marcellus Gardner.

By Mr. Ewing.—Q. State whether you know the prisoner, Dr. Samuel A. Mudd. A. I do.

Q. State whether he has ever said anything to you about offering his land for sale, and, if so, when? A. I have heard him, on several occasions, during the past two years, state that he wanted to sell out.

Q. Were you at the church in the neighborhood on the Sunday after the assassination? A. Yes sir.

Q. Was the fact of the assassination of the President then known and talked about at the church? A. Yes sir; I think it was generally known.

Q. State whether the name of the assassin was generally known. A. I think not.

Q. Did you see Dr. Mudd there? A. Yes sir.

Q. State whether you heard Dr. Mudd say anything as to how he regarded the assassination.

Assistant Judge Advocate Bingham objected to the question.

Mr. Ewing said that he had again brought this question before the Court for the purpose of calling their attension specially to the character of the declaration which he expected to prove, that Dr. Mudd spoke of the assassination as an atrocious and revolting crime, and a terrible calamity to the country; and that he spoke of it generally among his neighbors at the church in that way. The prisoner was charged with a concealment of the fact of those two men being at his house, which was a concealment extending over Sunday, and his declarations showing his feelings with reference to the crime during the time he was alleged to have been acting accessory to it were admissable.

The objection of the Judge Advocate was sustained, and the question was not put.

Mr. Ewing then stated that he had no further examination of the witness to make.

Testimony of Jos. N. Saylor.

By Mr. Stone.—Q. Where do you reside? A. In the Eighth Election District of Prince Georges county, Maryland.

Q. State whether you know the general reputation of Daniel G. Thomas for truth and veracity. A. I know his general reputation in that respect pretty well, both from report and observation; it is bad.

Q. From his general character for truth and veracity would you believe him on his oath? A. From my own knowledge of him I would not.

Q. How long have you known Thomas? A. Since he was a small boy.

Q. Did you know his general character for truth and veracity before this war? A. I have known him all the time; I never heard him spoken of well at any time; his reputation is that he never tells the truth when a lie will answer his purpose.

Cross-examined by Judge Holt.—Q. Did you ever know of Mr. Thomas speaking falsely when under oath? A. I never knew him to be sworn.

Q. Did you ever hear it charged upon him that he swore falsely? A. I do not know that I ever did.

Q. The reputation of which you speak is, that he talks idly, extravagantly and unreliably, but that reputation does not extend to any statements which he would make while under oath. A. I never heard that he had been charged with swearing falsely.

Q. Is he not reported to be an honest and loyal man in his neighborhood? A. Well, he is sometimes one thing, and sometimes another, just as the prospects of either side vary.

Q. Have you been loyal yourself since the Rebellion? A. I have.

Q. Have you constantly desired that the Government should succeed in suppressing the Rebellion? A. Always.

In reply to some further questions, the witness said that his ground for suspecting the loyalty of Mr. Thomas at particular times, were based upon what that person had told others; that personally he was very friendly with Mr. Thomas, their residences being near each other; that he had never had any private or political differences with that gentleman, and that the reputation of Dr. George Mudd, as a loyal man and a supporter of the Government, was universal in that neighborhood.

Testimony of Wm. A. Mudd.

By Mr. Stone.—Q. Do you know Dr. S. A. Mudd? A. I do.

Q. How far do you live from him? A. About a mile and a half.

Q. State whether at any time last year you saw a Captain White, from Tennessee, or a Lieutenant Perry, at or about Dr. Samuel Mudd's premises. A. I never did.

Q. Did you see Andrew or Ben Gywnn or George Gwynn about his premises at any time last year? A. No sir; I have not seen Andrew Gwynn since he left for the South; Mr. George Gwynn I have seen at our church several times since he returned.

Q. Did you see any person staying out in the woods, about Dr. Mudd's, during last year? A. I did not; I never saw a man there that I had heard of as having been South, except one; I recollect seeing Mr. Ben Gwynn at the Doctor's; I rode up, and ascertained from him that he was scouting, or something of that kind; that has been quite three years ago; it may have been in the first year of the war; it was the time I understood they were after him.

Testimony of Francis S. Walsh.

By Mr. Stone—Q. Where do you reside? A. I have lived in this city since 1837. I am a druggist.

Q. Do you know the prisoner Harold? A. Yes, I have known him ever since he was a boy. I have known him intimately since October, 1863.

Q. Has he been in your employ. A. He was for nine months, as a clerk.

Q. State as near as you can his character? A. He lived in my house; I knew nothing objectionable in his character. He was like most young men light and trifling in some things, but in his moral character I saw nothing to find fault with. He was temperate in his habits and regular in his hours.

Q. State whether he was or was not in his general character more of a boy than a man? A. I think so.

Q. State whether or not he was easily influenced or persuaded by any one around him? A. I should think he was: more easily than boys or young men of his age; he was boyish in many respects.

By Judge Holt.—Q. What do you suppose to be his age? A. About twenty-two years.

Testimony of James Nokes.

By Mr. Stone.—Q. Where do you reside? A. I have lived at the Navy Yard in this city since 1827.

Q. Do you know the prisoner Harold? A. I have known him from his birth, about twenty-two years, I believe.

Q. Have you seen a good deal of him? A. I have been intimate in his family for about eighteen or nineteen years.

Q. How large a family? A. Seven or eight; he was the only son.

Q. State what is his general character for boyishness; whether he was easily persuaded or led away. A. I have always looked upon him as a light, trifling boy, of very little reliability.

Q. Is he or is he not easily persuaded by any one around him? A. I should think he was.

Q. More so than the generality of young men of his age? A. Yes sir, I am certain of that.

Q. Would he be especially liable to be led away by any one of fascinating address? A. I have never heard him enter into any argument with any one; all his conversation that I have heard has been of a light and trifling character.

Testimony of William H. Kiellotts.

By Mr. Stone.—Q. Where do you reside? A. I have lived in this city for fifteen years.

Q. State whether you know the prisoner, Harold, well? A. I do.

Q. Have you known him all the time? A. Yes; for nearly thirteen years.

Q. State whether you saw him during the month of February last? A. I think I did.

Q. How often? A. I could not say how often; I was at home; I live next door to his father's, and have occasionally seen him in the yard, morning and afternoon; I suppose I saw him nearly every day.

Q. State whether or not he is of a trifling character, and easily persuaded. A. I believe he is; I saw him very often in boys' company; I should think he was more of a boy than a man; he never associated with men at all.

Testimony of Emma Harold.

By Mr. Stone.—Q. State whether you are the sister of the prisoner, David E. Harold. A. I am.

Q. State whether he was at home on the 15th of February last? A. Yes; I remember it from the fact of sending a valentine to him, which he received on the 15th.

Q. Had you any talk with him in relation to that valentine on the 15th? A. No; but my sister had.

Q. State what was the next date you can fix on which he was at home? A. The 19th; I remember that date by the fact that I brought a pitcher of water up stairs; he met me in the hall, and wanted I should give it to him; he tried to take it away from me; I held on to it, and it spilled over; that was the Sunday morning after St. Valentine's day.

Q. And you do not remember his being at home between these times? A. He was at home, but I cannot fix the day.

Testimony of Gen. Edward Johnston.

The Rebel Major-General Edward Johnston was here called to the stand.

Gen. Howe.—Before this witness is sworn I wish to submit a motion to the Court. I will state the facts upon which I base the motion. It is well known, as it is to a great many officers of the army, that the person now on the stand, Edward Johnston, was educated at the National Military Academy, at Government expense, and that since that time, for years, he has held a commission in the army of the United States. It is well known in the army that it is a condition precedent to resigning a commission that an officer should take an oath of allegiance and fidelity to the Government. In 1861 it became my duty as an officer to fire upon a Rebel party of which this man was a member. That party struck down and killed loyal men who were in the service of the Government; since that time it is notorious to all the officers of the army that the man now here introduced as a witness has openly borne arms against the United States, except when he has been a prisoner in the hands of the Government; I understand that it is proposed he shall testify before this Court; he comes here as a witness, with his hands red with the blood of his loyal countrymen, shot by him or by his assistants, in violation of his solemn oath as a man and as an officer; I submit, therefore, to this Court whether he does not stand in the eye of the law as an incompetent witness; I regard the offering as a witness of a man standing in open violation of the obligations of an oath administered to him as an officer as an insult to the Court, and an outrage upon the administration of justice; I move that this man, Edward Johnston, be ejected from the Court as an incompetent witness.

General Ekin—I rose to second the motion. I am glad that this question has now been presented to the Court. I regard this man as clearly incompetent as a witness. In my judgment, of all the men in this country, for those who have been educated by the Government, nourished by the Government, protected by the Government, and who have joined the enemies of the Government, to come into a Court of justice, and especially before a military commission of a character such as that here assembled, is the height of impertinence, and I trust the resolution which has been presented will be adopted by this commission without hesitation.

Mr. Aiken—Before the Commission decides upon the motion of Gen. Howe it is proper for me to say that I was not aware of the fact that because a person had borne arms against the Government it would disqualify and render him incompetent as a witness. Therefore, I could not, of course, have intended any insult in introducing Gen. Johnston as a witness. It will also be recollected that at least one witness who has borne arms against the Government was introduced here by the Judge Advocate without objection of any member of the Court.

General Kautz—Q. Does this person appear here as a volunteer witness?

Mr. Aiken—He does not.

The Judge Advocate-General—I feel bound to say, that as a rule of law, before a witness be rendered so infamous as to become absolutely incompetent to testify he must be convicted by judicial proceeding, and the record of that proceeding must be produced as the basis of his incompetency; without that condition any evidence of his guilt only applies to his credibility.

This Court can discredit him as far as they please upon that ground, but I do not think the law would authorize the Court to declare this witness incompetent, however unworthy he may be of credibility.

General Lew Wallace—I hope, for the sake of the character of this investigation, and for the sake of public justice, not for that of the person introduced as a witness, but for that of the prisoners at the bar, now on trial, the officer making the motion will withdraw it.

General Howe—Upon the statement of the Judge Advocate-General that this person is not technically an incompetent witness, I withdraw the motion.

By Mr. Aiken.—Q. What is your present status as a prisoner of war? A. I am a United States prisoner of war, captured at Nashville, now confined at Fort Warren, in Boston harbor.

Q. Were you or were you not an officer in the so-called Confederate service, and, if so, of what rank? A. I was a Brigadier-General in the Confederate States army from the year 1863 up to the date of my capture.

Q. Did you have a higher rank than that? A. I did.

Q. Are you acquainted with Henry Steinacker? A. I am acquainted with a man who went by that name and who represented himself to me as Henry Von Steinecker.

Q. Was he a member of your staff? A. He was not.

Q. Did he rank as an engineer officer, and receive pay as such? A. He did not rank as an officer, neither as an engineer, staff, or line officer; he was a private.

Q. To what regiment and company did he belong? A. He belonged to the Stonewall Brigade, Second Virginia Infantry, I think; I am not positive on that point; I do not remember the company.

Q. Was the Second Virginia Infantry attached to your division? A. It was part of the Stonewall Brigade, and that was one of the brigades of my division.

Q. State to the Court how, when, and under what circumstances Von Steinacker presented himself to you. A. In the month of May, 1863, a man accosted me in Richmond, in Capitol Square, by my name and the rank I bore in the United States Army, as Major Johnson; he told me he had served under me—

Judge Bingham—What has that to do with it? there has been no inquiry made as to his services under you—

Witness—Well, he met me in Richmond and applied for a position in the Engineer Corps, stating that he had served under me previously; that he was a Prussian by birth, and an engineer by education, and he would like to get in the Engineer Corps in our service.

Judge Bingham—You need not tell what he said

Witness—He applied to get into our service; I had no such position to give, and declined giving it, and he left me; he called again and made a second application for the position; I told him I could not give it to him; I was then ordered off to Fredericksburg, and in about a week this man appeared there again, and made application for a position either in the Engineer Corps or on my Staff; I told him I could not give him a position in either, but that if he would enlist as a private, from his representations of himself as an engineer and a draughtsman, I would put him on duty in the Engineer Corps as a private; on these conditions he enlisted as a private in the Stonewall Brigade, Second Virginia Infantry, and I assigned him to special duty at headquarters; he was to act as draughtsman and assist my engineer officer, and he so continued to act till I was told he had left.

Q. Was he subjected to court-martial at that time?

Question objected to by Judge Bingham, on the ground that records of courts-martial must be produced, and he did not think there were any courts down in Virginia in these days that could try at all.

Mr. Aiken stated that, as under the circumstances the records of the court could not be produced, parole evidence could be admitted, and he presumed the question was not seriously objected to.

The objection was sustained by the Court.

Q. Where in Virginia was your encampment after the battle of Gettysburg? A. Near Orange Court House.

Q. Do you know or not of a meeting of the officers of that Brigade at the camp of the Second Virginia Regiment? A. I know nothing of it, and never heard anything of the kind.

Q. Did you ever learn the fact that a secret meeting was held there at that time? A. I never heard of any such secret meeting.

Q. Did you ever at any meeting of the officers of your division hear plans discussed for the assassination of the President of the United States? A. I never heard any plans discussed in any meeting of the officers, nor did I ever hear the assassination of the President alluded to by any individuals in my division.

Q. Are you acquainted with J. Wilkes Booth, the actor? A. I am not; I never saw him.

Q. Look at that picture (Booth's) and see if you ever saw the man? A. Never, to my knowledge; I did not know, in fact, there was such a man until after the assassination of President Lincoln.

Q. Have you a personal knowledge of the fact of Lieutenant David Cockerill losing a horse?

Judge Bingham—I object. We do not propose the question of horse stealing here, it is not in the issue.

Mr. Aiken—The charge was made in the paper presented that Von Steinecker had been guilty of horse stealing, and I understood we were to be permitted to prove any allegations in that paper.

Colonel Burnett—Anything that is legitimate and competent to be proved. We did not go further.

The objection was sustained by the Court.

Q. Did you ever learn anything while at the South of a secret association by the name of "The Knights of the Golden Circle," or "Sons of Liberty?" A. I never belonged to any such association myself, and never knew any one who was reported to belong to them, and never knew anything of them.

Q. While in Richmond have you heard it freely spoken of in the street and among your acquaintances that the assassination of the President of the United States was a desirable result to be accomplished? A. I never heard it spoken of as a desirable object to be accomplished; in fact, as I said before, I never heard any officer or person allude to the assassination of the President as desirable, to the best of my recollection.

Q. Was Von Steinecker a member of Gen. Blenker's staff? A. Not that I know of; he told me that he was.

Q. Did he state to you that he was a deserter from our service? A. He stated to me that he had deserted or attempted to desert, and was apprehended.

Cross-examined by Judge Bingham.—Q. Have you ever been in the service of the United States? A. I have.

Q. Were you educated at the United States Military Academy? A. Yes sir.

Q. How long had you been in the army of the United States? A. I graduated in 1838.

Q. And had been in our army down to the breaking out of the Rebellion? A. Yes sir.

Q. What was your rank in the army at that time? A. Captain and Brevet Major of the Sixth United States Infantry.

Q. State how you got out of the service of the United States. A. I tendered my resignation, which was accepted.

Q. Tendered it to whom? A. To the Adjutant General of the United States; I tendered it in May, 1861; it was not accepted for three or four weeks; I received the acceptance of my resignation in June following.

Q. Did you then enter into the Rebel service. A. I went to my home in Virginia, where I remained a few weeks; I then entered the Confederate States' service, and have been in it ever since.

Q. What was the final rank held by you in that army? A. Major-General.

Q. Were you a Major-General in 1863? A. I was for a part of 1863; I think my rank as Major-General commenced in February of that year.

Testimony of Mrs. Mary E. Jenkins.

Examined by Mr. Stone.—Q. State whether you know David E. Harold. A. Yes, I know him.

Q. Can you state whether he was or was not in Washington on the 18th of last February? A. He was at my house on the 18th and received my rent; I have his receipt to show.

Testimony of Mrs. Potts.

Examined by Mr. Stone.—Q. State whether you know one of the accused, David E. Harold. A. Yes.

Q. State to the Court whether he was or was not in Washington on the 20th of February last. A. I cannot state whether he was or was not; he came to my house on the 19th, and I told him I would send the money to the house, which I did; I did not see him the next day; he used to come to my house, and when I would not be prepared to see him I would tell him I would send the money to his house; his receipt was dated the 20th of February.

Testimony of the Rebel Major H. K. Douglass.

Examined by Mr. Aiken.—Q. State to the Court whether you ever held a commission in the so-called Confederate service? A. I have, several; my last commission was that of Major and A. A. G.; I served as such on the staff of six general officers, and among others on that of Major-General Edward Johnston.

Q. Are you acquainted with Henry Von Steinacker? A. I know a man by the name of Von Steinacker; I do not know what his first name is.

Q. Was he or not a private in your service; and if so, in what regiment? A. He was in the Second Virginia Infantry, Stonewall Brigade.

Q. Did he receive the pay, bounty and allowances of a private? A. I don't know.

Q. Do you recollect, after the return of your army from Gettysburg, where it was encamped. A. I was wounded at Gettysburg, and left in the hands of the enemy; I was a prisoner for nine months.

Q. When you returned to camp did you meet Von Steinacer again? A. I do not remember seeing him again. I got a letter from him immediately after I returned to camp.

Q. Do you know of any secret meetings ever being held in your camp, at which the assassination of President Lincoln was discussed? A. No I do not.

Q. Were you acquainted with J. Wilkes Booth, the actor? A. No.

By the Court.—Q. Were you ever in the United States service? A. I was not; with the permission of the Court I would like to make a statement. General Howe, "I object to the *prisoner* making any statement." General Foster, "I hope the witness will be allowed to make his statement." The President, "If no further objection is made the witness will proceed with his statement.

Witness, "I just wish to say to the Court, understanding that evidence has been given by which implication has been cast on the "Stonewall Brigade," that as a man who has held positions in that brigade as private, and line and staff officer, I think their integrity as men, equal to their reputation for gallantry as soldiers, would forbid them to be employed as night assassins of President Lincoln. In their behalf I only wish to say that I do not believe they knew anything about or in the least sympathized in any such unrighteous or unsoldierly action."

Testimony of Oscar Henricks.

Examined by Mr. Aiken—Q. Have you been in the service of the so-called Confederate States. A. I have as engineer officer at one time on the staff of General Edward Johnston, and at others that of different General officers.

Q. State whether you are acquainted with Henry Von Steinacker? A. I am.

Q. When and under what circumstances did that commence? A. He was detailed by me as draughtsman immediately after General Johnston took command.

Q. Was he employed as such? A. I employed him as such.

Q. Did he ever have the rank or pay of an Engineer officer? A. He did not.

Q. Are you acquainted with J. Wilkes Booth, the actor? A. I am not.

Q. Did you ever see a person calling himself by that name in camp? A. No sir.

Q. Do you know of any secret meetings of officers ever taking place in your camp, at which the assassination of President Lincoln was discussed? A. None ever did take place.

Q. Did you ever learn the fact that Von Steinacke was a member of General Blenker's Staff?

Question objected to by Judge Bingham, and withdrawn.

Q. Did you ever learn the fact of his deserting the service of the United States?

Question objected to by Judge Bingham, and withdrawn.

Q. Do you know that fact? A. I do not, only from his statements and acknowledgments on several occasions to me.

Q. Have you ever heard of or been cognizant of a secret treasonable society, for the purpose of the assassination of the President of the United States? A. I am not cognizant of any, nor have I ever heard of any.

Q. Were any members of your staff or yourself members of an organization known as Knights of the Golden Circle or Sons of Liberty. A. So far as I am concerned I never have been, nor do I know of any of the others having been.

Q. Have you heard declarations made in Richmond to the effect that President Lincoln ought to be assassinated? A. I have not.

Testimony of Thomas C. Nott.

Examined by Mr. Aiken—Q. Where do you reside and what is your occupation? A. I reside in Prince George county, and have been tending bar at Mrs. Surratt's place for Mr. Floyd.

Q. Did you see Mr. Floyd on the 14th of last April? A. Yes sir, I saw him in the morning of that day, and also just before sunset.

Q. What was his condition at that time? A. He was pretty tight when I saw him; he was going around to the kitchen in a buggy; he had been to Marlboro', and was carrying round there some fish and oysters; I did not see him when he came back, and the next I saw of him he was fixing a buggy Mrs. Surratt was in.

Q. Had he been for weeks before drinking a good deal? A. Yes, he had been tight pretty nearly every day and night too.

Q. Did he really have the appearance of an insane man? A. He did at times

Cross-examined by Judge Bingham.—Q. Did you see him tie the buggy of Mrs. Surratt? A. With assistance he did; I do not know whether Mr. Floyd, Mr. Weichman or Captain Gwynn tied it; they were all there; I was not present at the buggy; I saw them fixing it, and that is all I saw; I was across the street, returning from the stable.

Q. And do you know how tight a man is by looking across the street? A. No; I was with him after that, nearly all night.

By Mr. Clampitt —Q. Do or do you not know whether Mr. Floyd attended Court at Marlboro' that day? A. He did.

Q. Where did you first see him that afternoon? A. Driving around the kitchen; he came round to the front of the house while Mrs. Surratt was there.

Q. Did you hear any conversation that took place between Mr. Floyd and Mrs. Surratt? A. I did not.

Q. How close were you to the buggy? A. Probably fifteen or twenty yards off.

By Judge Bingham.—Q. What Captain Gwynn was that who was at Mrs. Surratt's buggy? A. Captain Ben. Gwynn.

Q. Upon reflection do you not recollect that he had gone before Mrs. Surratt came? A. I do not recollect anything of the kind.

Testimony of J. Z. Jenkins.

Examined by Mr. Aiken.—Q. Where do you reside? A. In Prince George county.

Q. Were you or were you not at Surrattsville on the 14th of April last? A. I was.

Q. Are you acquainted with Lewis J. Weichman? A. Yes.

Q. Were you at Surrattsville at the time he drove up to the house with Mrs. Surratt? A. Yes.

Q. Did Mrs. Surratt or not at that time show you a letter? A. She did, from George Calvert.

Q. Did she show you any other papers? A. She showed two judgments obtained by Charles B. Calvert in the Circuit Court of our county, against Mr. Surratt.

Q. Do you know, of your own knowledge, whether that business brought Mrs. Surratt to Surrattsville that day? A. I only know she showed me this letter and judgments.

Q. Did you transact any business for Mrs. Surratt that afternoon? A. I made the interest out on the judgments.

Q. Did she express to you during her entire stay at Surrattsville that day any wish or desire to see John M. Floyd? A. She did not.

Q. Were you at the place when Mr. Floyd drove up? A. Yes.

Q. What was his condition at that time? A. He was very much intoxicated.

Q. Was Mrs. Surratt upon the point of going away when Floyd drove up? A. Yes: she had been ready to start for some time before Floyd drove up; she had business with Captain Gwynn, and when he came she went back and stopped.

Q. At what time did you leave? A. About sundown, I judge.

Q. Have you, during the last year or two, been on terms of intimacy with Mrs. Surratt? A. Yes sir.

Q. Have you, in all your intercourse with her, heard her breathe a word of disloyalty to the Government? A. Not to my knowledge.

Q. Have you at any time ever heard her make any remark or remarks showing her to have a knowledge of any plan or conspiracy to assassinate the President, or any member of the Government? A. No sir.

Q. Have you ever heard her mention at any time any plan for the capture of the President? A. I have not.

Q. Have you been frequently at the house of Mrs. Surratt when Union troops were passing? A. Yes sir.

Q. From your personal knowledge of the transactions that occurred then and there, can you state whether or not she was in the habit of giving them milk, tea, and such other nourishment as she had in the house? A. Yes, frequently.

Q. Was she in the habit of receiving pay for it? A. Sometimes she did and sometimes she did not.

Q. Do you recollect on or about the time of a large number of horses escaping from Giesboro' whether or not any of them were taken up and kept on her premises? A. Some of them, I disremember how many.

Q. Were these horses fed and kept by her or not? A. Yes.

Q. Were they all given up? A. Every one.

Q. Do you know whether she took a receipt for them? A. She received a receipt, but never got any pay.

Q. Can you state whether you ever knew Mrs. Surratt to commit any overt act of any description against the Government? A. I never did.

Q. Was it not Mrs. Surratt's constant habit to express warm sympathy for the sick and wounded of our army? A. I do not remember ever hearing her say anything about that.

Q. Do you know of a defective eyesight on her part? A. I have been present when she would be unable to read or sew by gas light; this has been the fact for several years.

Q. Do you recollect on any occasion of her failing to recognize immediately friends who were near her? A. I do not recollect any.

Q. Do you not recollect that on one occasion Mrs. Surratt gave the last ham she had to Union soldiers? A. I do not.

Q. Do you know of a person by the name of A. S. Howell? A. Yes, I have seen him; he stopped at the hotel, I think twice.

By Mr. Clampit.—Q. Did you or not, meet Mrs. Surratt on the Tuesday preceding the assassination? A. I can't say on Tuesday; it was a few days before.

Q. When you met her did not you ask for the news, and did not she state in reply that our army had captured General Lee's army?

The question was objected to by Colonel Burnett, as irrelevant.

Mr. Clampit said he desired to show that the prisoner at that time, exhibited a loyal feeling in the matter.

Colonel Burnett replied that the only legitimate means of proving loyalty were to prove her reputation for and acts of loyalty; these could not be proved by her declarations.

Mr. Clampit replied that as the Government had endeavored to prove the disloyalty of the accused, he thought it was competent to prove her loyalty, but he would nevertheless vary his question, and ask the witness what was the reputation of Mrs. Surratt for loyalty? A. Very good.

Q. You have never heard her express any disloyal sentiment? A. No sir.

Cross-examined by Colonel Burnett.

Q. What relation are you to the prisoner, Mrs. Surratt? A. She is my sister.

Q. Where did you reside while she was living at Surrattville? A. About a mile and a half this side, and I have been residing there since.

Q. Are you now under arrest? A. I am. I was arrested and brought here last Thursday week.

Q. Where were you on the evening of the day previous to your arrest? A. At Lloyd's Hotel.

Q. Did you meet at that place Mr. Coltenback? A. Yes.

Q. Did you have any conversation with him at that time in reference to this trial? A. Yes, sir, we were talking about the trial.

Q. Did you meet a man by the name of Cottingham there? A. Yes, I went there with him.

Q. At the time you met Coltenback, what was said about the trial in reference to the witnesses summoned against Mrs. Surratt? A. I think I told him I would look at the paper and see.

Q. Anything else? A. Not that I know of; I might have told him that my sister found his family.

Q. What relevancy had that to the conversation? A. I disremember how the conversation commenced.

Q. Did you at that time and place say to Mr. Coltenback that if he, or any one like him, undertook to testify against your sister, you would see that they were got out of the way? A. I did not say anything of the kind.

Q. Did you say you would send any man to hell who testified against your sister? A. I did not.

Q. Did you use any threats against him if he appeared as a witness against your sister? A. No, nothing like that.

Q. State what you did say on that subject? A. I told

Continued on the Eighth Page.

New Series, Vol. 14, No. 6.} HONOLULU, JUNE 1, 1865. {Old Series, Vol. 22.

CONTENTS
For June, 1865.

THE FRIEND.

JUNE 1, 1865.

☞ It affords us gratification to record the fact that every possible effort has been made by loyal Americans and others in Honolulu to honor the memory and becomingly notice the death of President Lincoln. The sad intelligence was received May 8th, and on the following day at 12 o'clock M. there was convened at Fort street Church the largest gathering of foreigners, for religious purposes, we have ever seen in Honolulu. Mr. McBride, our Minister Resident, appropriately stated the object for which the assembly had been called together. The choir followed with appropriate music. Select portions of Scripture were read, and a prayer offered by the Rev. S. C. Damon. His Honor, Chief Justice Allen, then addressed the audience, and was followed by the Rev. E. Corwin. Their addresses have already been published. All the exercises were most solemn and impressive.

Religious exercises becoming the occasion were also held in the Roman Catholic and Reformed Catholic Churches.

The Hawaiian Government ordered the National Flag lowered, and all officers to wear crape for fourteen days. We cannot imagine any observance, omitted, the performance of which could have added a deeper solemnity to the day, or been the occasion of showing additional respect to the Illustrious Dead.

Events of such momentous magnitude as the closing of the civil war in America, and the death of President Lincoln, occur but seldom in the slow progress of centuries. The Great Rebellion had most marvelously disturbed the elements of society and trade throughout the world, and now to have, from the receding thunder clouds of war, an angry flash prostrates the noble man at the head of the great Republic, makes the civilized world stand aghast. We hope the waves of political strife and civil war will soon subside, and when the elements do become tranquil and calm, may it be in obedience to Him who said to the troubled waters of the Galilean Lake, eighteen hundred years ago, "Peace, be still."

May 24th, Queen Victoria's Birthday. Mr. Green, H. B. M's Acting Commissioner and Consul General, gave a lunch at the Town Hall on this occasion. It was an exceedingly pleasant gathering of the citizens and subjects of various nationalities. Mr. Green merits the thanks of the community for thus observing this event. It is well to pour a little oil upon the troubled waters. Americans are always happy to honor Queen Victoria. Not only is she a good Queen, but a good mother, and a good Christian. We respect and love her. Her influence has been good in all circles and walks of life. Her Court has been one of the purest that ever existed on earth, and the world has felt its influence. "*Long live Queen Victoria.*"

☞ We have received letters from Rev. L. Smith, H. M. Whitney, Esq., and John H. Cole, Esq., in all of which there are references to the profound impression made upon the people of San Francisco, by the announcement of President Lincoln's death.

God Putteth down One, and Setteth Up Another.

A SERMON

On the Death of Abraham Lincoln ;

Preached in the Seamen's Chapel, Honolulu, May 14, the First Sabbath after receiving the sad Intelligence of his Assassination by J. W. Booth :

By Rev. S. C. Damon.

[Published by Request.]

Psalm lxxv:7—"But God is the Judge; He putteth down one, and setteth up another."

John xiii:7—"What I do, thou knowest not now; but thou shalt know hereafter."

In the administration of the affairs of this world God is ever doing and permitting things to be done, the reasons for which cannot be seen by short-sighted mortals. Such is God's method of proceeding, that we are continually compelled to take many things on trust. Faith in Him is the great lesson which He is ever teaching mankind. He has drawn an impenetrable veil before our eyes, shutting out the future from our view. "Ye know not what shall be on the morrow," or "what a day may bring forth." How impressively these scriptural declarations and those of my text are illustrated by events which have recently transpired on the other side of the globe. All the loyal people of that great country, stretching from the shores of the Atlantic to the Pacific, and from the Gulf to the Lakes, were preparing for such a day of thanksgiving and jubilee as never had been witnessed on the Western Continent. The national feeling which, during four years of civil war had been repressed, was rising, and about to burst forth in such scenes and shouts of rejoicing as would have made the "welkin ring." The dove of peace which had, during those four long years, been confined to the ark, rocked and tossed upon the troubled waters of civil strife, political contentions and cruel war, had now been released, and with the olive branch in her mouth, was winging her flight over mountains and valleys, broad savannahs and boundless prairies. The good news was flashed with lightning speed over the land and the world. The dark clouds were rolling away, and the sun of the nation's glory was beginning to shine, and the rainbow of peace was distinctly seen spanning a continent, as in days of yore, when lo! from the receding black clouds of secession, treachery and slavery, there darted forth a fiendish

FRANK LESLIE'S ILLUSTRATED NEWSPAPER

Entered according to the Act of Congress in the year 1864, by FRANK LESLIE, in the Clerk's Office of the District Court for the Southern District of New York.

No. 505—VOL. XX.] NEW YORK, JUNE 3, 1865. [PRICE 10 CENTS. $4 00 YEARLY. 13 WEEKS $1 00.

The Assassination—Complicity of Davis.

THE evidence elicited in the great trial of the persons arrested for complicity in the murder of the President, and in the attempt on the life of Mr. Seward, establishes the fact that there existed a deeply-laid and wide-spread conspiracy, more than a year in maturing: first, for the abduction or assassination of the President; and secondly, for wholesale piracy on the Lakes and incendiarism in our Northern cities. The agents in this conspiracy had their headquarters in Washington, and the leaders revolved between Richmond and Canada. It is proved that both Booth and Surratt went often within the rebel lines, and had communication with the rebel authorities. It is proved that Booth and Beale, who was hung, for, among other things, the attempt to burn New York, not only met in conference in the Shenandoah Valley, but that the latter was sent, with the Lake pirates and St. Albans raiders into Canada, by authority of the rebel government, on what was called "detached service." The connection between the gang in Canada, for whom, it will be remembered, Mr. Davis claimed the rights of "belligerents," on the ground that they were commissioned by him and assigned by him on special service—we say the connection between these robbers, incendiaries, and murderers, and the gang assigned to the "detached service" of abducting or murdering the President is complete. That Mr. Davis knew about the scheme of burning our cities, and of "carrying alarm and consternation throughout the North," is shown by documents under his own hand. The testimony is not yet all in, and there is some which has not yet been made public, which may prove direct complicity on the part of Mr. Davis in the plot to assassinate Mr. Lincoln and his Cabinet. Be that as it may, it is established by evidence and logical deduction that he was fully acquainted with and approved that part of the conspiracy, which Beale and Kennedy and their associates failed to accomplish in New York, but in which Burley and the St. Albans robbers and murderers were more successful. Cognizant of one part of the plot, he could not be ignorant of the other. Viewed as a crime, the heinousness of attempting to burn crowded

CAPTURE OF JEFFERSON DAVIS, AT IRWINSVILLE, GA., AT DAYBREAK OF MAY 10TH, BY COL. PRITCHARD AND MEN, OF WILSON'S CORPS.

THE COLUMBIA DAILY PHŒNIX.

$1 a Month, in Advance. "Let our just Censure attend the true Event."—*Shakspeare.* Single Copies Five Cents.

By J. A. SELBY. COLUMBIA, S. C., SATURDAY MORNING, JUNE 3, 1865. VOL. 1.—NO. 56.

THE COLUMBIA PHŒNIX,

PUBLISHED DAILY, EXCEPT SUNDAY,

BY JULIAN A. SELBY.

TERMS—IN ADVANCE.

SUBSCRIPTION.

Six months, - - - - - - - $5
One month, - - - - - - - 1

ADVERTISING.

One square, (ten lines,) one time, 50 cts
Subsequent insertions, - - 35 cts
Special notices ten cents per line.

The Dangers of the Union.

Secession, in actual practice, was not in itself necessarily dangerous to the Union. The only supposable evils of that act to the continuance of the Union began in the determination of the Federal Government to meet it by force of arms. A policy of compromise and mutual concession had characterized the workings of the Constitutional compact up to that moment; but having been thenceforth spurned for a policy of compulsion and mutual slaughter, that change in the modes of Federal Government withdrew the Union from the citadel of its real strength—the popular sense of its sanctity.

Bloody battle has crushed the States that asserted, by their secession, rights independent of the Union. And Federal power, as it stands brandishing its reeking sword over those prostrate sovereignties, is flushed with the pride of complete triumph. Brawling faction sees only the physical fact, and cries out, in the blindness of its passions, for ruin and revenge, now that it proclaims the Union perpetual! Brainless counsellor! The conqueror that you worship, with the instinct of a slave raised to authority, with the venom of a cur yelping at a chained lion, has, as he stands over his fallen foe, not only a front of brass, but, mark you, has feet of clay. The rights conceived by the sword, all history declares to be, so surely as great political consequences follow general laws, destined to die by the sword. The Union remains still exposed to the fatal consequences of the blunder of armed coercion, and can be saved but by restoring it to the only fountain of its healthy life, popular love and reverence.

In the North, the Union has been associated with a grinding despotism. Conscription has stamped it in many a desolate household with the mark of Cain. Arbitrary power has torn it from the Penates of private life to be crushed under the heels of the men whose hearts and brains it has fired with hate in the cells of Federal dungeons. Ferocious 'loyalty' has degraded it to the basest uses of a political utensil; and, as a consequence, has thrust it upon hundreds of thousands of men by whom it had been held in life-long love and reverence as a type of insults and of factious passions.

At the South, the Union assumed the attributes of a fiend let loose in war. A fierce invader, it fell, as Satan fell from Heaven, from the empyrean of popular love into the depth of flaming hate. Like the destroying angel, it slew the first born in all that land. The women and little ones, and the aged men of those regions, it sent out upon the highways to proclaim it a curse. The habitations of the land it destroyed with fire, until the wolves, hiding in their blackened ruins, declared the Union, in their midnight howls, to be a crime against humanity. The corn and the honey, and the grass of the field, and the seed and the plows, the horses and the cattle, and every living thing—except the women and little ones, and old men, whom its mercy had cast out to starve—the Union utterly destroyed, until millions of people by whom it had once been worshipped throughout the borders of that country, shrank from it with execration as from a thing of hell.

North and South the Union has ceased to be a holy thing. The sanctity by which it had been hedged round has been broken down; and hates which have emerged through the breach await but a shift of the political storm to sweep it forever from the sight of men. Must the true friend of the Union add one more drop to the volume of those raging memories?

The political history of Mississippi foreshadows the dangers of the Union now, even while flushed with the triumph of its first trial. Mr. Jefferson Davis and Mr. Henry S. Foote canvassed that State about fifteen years ago on a question of conditional secession. The side of the Union was successful; but from the day on which it had been made there a question of party, it continued to fall from the position of a popular idol. 'Disunionists *per se*,' as they called themselves, appeared in the State in surprising numbers after that contest on contingent disunion; and, finally, notwithstanding the triumph of the Union in the person of Mr. Foote, became so numerous that the storm of secession, in 1860, swept through the State like a fire through a prairie. With the wounds of despotic power, and of savage belligerency still festering in its moral life, of this passage of its history in a Southern State, declares to-day, while the Union leans upon its bloody sword, in review of victorious thousands of armed agents of its will, that it carries in its bosom the seeds of death.

Strong, physically, as it is to-day, the Union was never weaker, morally. Like many a gallant soldier, it has escaped the casualties of battle with fever in its blood and canker in its bosom. For all its stalwart looks it still moves on, into the shadows of inevitable dissolution.

The war of the sections was one of, we hope, worthier objects than a mere assertion of brute force. Patriotism, however short-sighted, looked to that bloody struggle for a healing of the wounds which its inception had opened in the body of the Union. How much nearer that result are we to-day than we were when McClellan's army was hurled back from Richmond? Good faith to the memories of the soldiers who have been led to slaughter for that purpose, solemn duty to the civilians who, in a mistaken patriotism, have sustained the war, demand that the Union be as soon and as effectually as possible given back to the only keeping in which it can ever be held safe, that of universal popular affection.

The union of these States cannot exist by brute force. The blunder that removed it from the strong defence of popular love, repeats itself when it attempts to maintain it by a system of brutal terrorism. That very terrorism will, if carried out, prove its destruction. Popular dread but removes it still farther from the only conditions of its maintenance—popular love. Cutting Booth's head off, or giving his dismembered body a dishonored burial, has served but to weaken the Government, by degrading it to the level of those grim despotisms that every man in the country names with clenched teeth. Every page of history shows that terror is a rope of sand on the limbs of political conviction.

Treason cannot possibly be placed, in popular acceptation, side by side with private crimes. An attempt to accomplish that result is an attempt to undo all the theories of free political education. The right of asylum in universal justice, separates treason from offences against humanity. The murderer is made, by public treaties, a subject of extradition, but no country would consent to surrender to his sovereign the unsuccessful rebel. The right of revolution takes the offence of the 'traitor' out of the category of social crimes; and makes an attempt to place him among malefactors, a mere struggle against all the principles of society.

The terrible wounds in the body of the Union can be healed but by the most tender conciliation. The 'justice' of which men speak in reference to the policy of reconstruction is but another name for a revenge which can be appeased but at the cost of the Union. The capture of Mr. Davis is one of the most unfortunate things that could have occurred to the people of both sections; for it brings up the real difficulties of the hour in a form most dangerous to the only policy which can save the country—that calculated to erase all bloody memories. Mr. Davis falls into the hands of the Government as a man whom the civilized world refuses to regard a criminal. His purity of private life, his singleness of purpose, his splendid powers of administration are acknowledged, outside the miserable curs that now bark at his heels, by all Christendom. The elected representative of millions of free born men, and men too who have placed their conviction of right in making that election under the guaranty of their lives, he stands before mankind the chosen chief of sovereign States, borne down, like Poland, by the weight of crushing columns. Treason, rebellion and even allegations of 'conspiracy,' may or may not be proven against him; but the Administration, if it have any respect for its own character, for the character of this Republic, may make up its mind that it can offer no wanton indignity, lay no violent hands on the person of Mr. Davis, without an outrage against the feelings and the conscience of both hemispheres. Harmless that unhappy gentleman now is and if sent quietly back to his plantation in Mississippi ever will be; but if a brainless purpose or a bloody passion should take his life, he will have become a martyr, around whom, as around the subjects of the judicial murders of the Irish rebellion, the memory of his countrymen will utter for evermore a nucleus of all the enmities of the future, the curses that now rise to their throats with choking passion against what they hold the fiend of their recent experience, the Union.

Terrorism, as a policy of the present, is the suggestion of a brutal incapacity. If war has been necessary for a restoration of the Union, then, of a verity, must it have been made but with the aim of bringing the sections together within the operations of their old system of mutual conciliation. The Union, if it is to be in reality saved, must be plucked from the burning passions that crackle and flame around it, North and South; and planted in a place of safety, not within the fears but the loves of the people, by an act of amnesty that, giving hates no individual memory to rally around, will win their hearts back in a unanimous burst of admiration for its sublime beneficence.—*New York News.*

The Appreciation of Greenbacks.

The necessity of large expenditures caused the issual of greenbacks; the continuance of that necessity brought about their depreciation, and its determination will restore them to their face value. An outlay of three millions per day, it is evident, could not be met in specie; nor could it be continued, as it has been, in paper money, without that money sinking below par. When the issual stopped, it is equally evident that—presupposing the stoppage to be permanent, and the existing issues not too great for the requirements of the country—the process of depreciation must cease, and that of appreciation begin. Now this is the precise condition of the currency to-day. The rapid pacification of the country, and the little danger of a rupture with France, make it almost a foregone conclusion that there will be no more greenbacks issued, and the only question is whether the present volume of currency be too great for the requirements of the country. We think not.

Even previous to the evacuation of Richmond, and when, to all appearances, General Lee was holding his own there, United States Treasury notes, that had fallen to two hundred and forty, rose to one hundred and fifty. At this time, it must be remembered that these notes circulated only in the North, and within the lines of the Federal armies in the South, and, on every principle of political economy, had they been largely in excess there of the demand for them, they could no more have risen in value than the *assignats* of France could have bought the guineas of England.

Since the surrender of Lee, and the downfall of the Confederacy, this process of appreciation has gone on with astounding celerity. Every fresh indication of returning order in the South, has given Wall street a joyful thrill, and when an entire resumption of coasting and inland trade shall have opened up the whole of this country to the reception of Federal currency, it is not too much to say that the equalization of financial demand and supply, will make greenbacks equal to gold. No doubt there are many who will hoot at this declaration, and point in derision to the bills of Law's Bank, and the *assignats* of the Revolution, to wild-cat issues and shinplaster dollars, to Continental money and Confederate notes. To some extent we can understand this contemptuous incredulity; for, truth to tell, it would be hard to find a sadder botch than was made of our poor Confederate money. From the hour of its birth till *in extremis* it was tinkered with an assiduity that gave great scope to invention, but left little ground for hope. Its nostrums were legion, but one idea pervaded them all—the currency was to be repudiated into solvency, as Sangrado bled men into sickness that they might enjoy health. This ingenious scheme failed, but its brilliancy is a theme on which we could love to dwell. Robbing Peter to pay Paul is a stale device, but to rob both and pay neither is a most rare inspiration—half Captain Macheath and half Jeremy Diddler. Unfortunately our people never appreciated this style of genius. They were narrow-minded enough to think no law could dignify swindling and no argument justify; they came thus to hate and to fear paper money, to believe that gold and silver alone are really representatives of value, and the results of this opinion, and of the shiftless, unprincipled financiering that led to its formation, are to be seen in the distrust wherewith greenbacks are regarded. To one who does not know our people, and has not shared with them the ups and downs of the war—to a Northern or English banker, for instance—it would be difficult to convey an idea of their unwillingness to believe that any paper money whatsoever can maintain its face valuation. Legal tender laws, price schedules, penalties for non-reception, and the whole spawn of coercive legislation, would be ineffectual to change this estimate, for just legislation has heretofore been associated in the popular mind with fresh tinkering and a further depreciation. An exposition of well settled principles, and a statement of undeniable facts will alone work any change for the better. In another part of this article we have set forth those maxims of finance that regulate the value of currency, and shall now mention certain facts to show that it is not mere newspaper theorizing to say greenbacks are approximating gold. These are facts, then. The war is over, and with it any necessity for an increase of the currency is obviated. Six hundred thousand soldiers are to be speedily discharged, and expenditures at the rate of four hundred millions per annum have ceased to be necessary. With the resumption of trade, the currency now for the most part pent up in the North, will diffuse itself over the South. With the issual of bonds by the Government, like the consols of England, large amounts will be retired from circulation, and the payment of taxes and Government dues will still further reduce the volume of currency.

Then the problem of currency will be put in a shape the plainest man can understand, and the formula to express it will be this—if constant issue and confined circulation depreciate a paper money, cessation of issual, universality of reception, and legal absorption will force that money to par.

[*Augusta Constitutionalist.*

When Dr. Johnson asked the widow Porter to be his wife, he told her candidly that he was of mean extraction, he had no money, and that he had an uncle hanged. The widow replied that she cared nothing for his parentage, that she had no money herself, though she had fifty relations that deserved hanging. So they made a match of it.

Papa, why do they plant guns; do they grow and have leaves? No, my son, but like plants, they shoot, and then others do the leaving.

Headq'rs Department of the South,

HILTON HEAD, S. C., MAY 15, 1865.

GENERAL ORDERS NO. 63.

I. THE proclamation of A. G. Magrath, styling himself Governor of South Carolina, dated at Headquarters, Columbia, South Carolina, May 2, 1865, declaring that all subsistence stores and the property of the Confederate States within the limits of the State should be turned over and accounted for by the Agents of the State, appointed for that purpose, and directing that the subsistence stores so turned over shall be used for the relief of the people of the State; and the proclamation of Joseph E. Brown, styling himself Governor of Georgia, dated at the capital of that State, on the 3d day of May, 1865, requiring the officers and members of the General Assembly to meet in extraordinary session at the Capitol, in Milledgeville, on Monday, the 22d day of May, 1865; and the proclamation of A. K. Allison, styling himself Acting Governor of Florida, dated at Tallahassee, on the 8th day of April, 1865, giving notice and direction that an election will be held on Wednesday, the 7th day of June, 1865 for Governor of the State of Florida; are, each and all of them, declared null and void; it having become known to me, from trustworthy information, that the aforesaid A. G. Magrath, Joseph E. Brown and A. K. Allison, are disloyal to the United States, having committed sundry and divers acts of treason against the same, in adhering to their enemies, giving them aid and comfort.

The persons and peoples, to whom the proclamations hereinabove referred to have been respectively addressed, are therefore enjoined and commanded to give no heed whatever thereto, or to any orders, proclamations, commissions or commands, emanating from persons claiming the right to exercise the functions and authority of Governor in either of the States of South Carolina, Georgia or Florida, unless the same shall have been promulgated by the advice or consent of the United States authorities.

II. The policy and wishes of the General Government toward the people of these States, and the method which should be pursued by them in resuming or assuming the exercise of their political rights, will doubtless be made known at an early day.

It is deemed sufficient, meanwhile, to announce that the people of the black race are free citizens of the United States, that it is the fixed intention of a wise and beneficent Government to protect them in the enjoyment of their freedom and the fruits of their industry, and that it is the manifest and binding duty of all citizens, whites as well as blacks, to make such arrangements and agreements among themselves, for compensated labor, as shall be mutually advantageous to all parties. Neither idleness nor vagrancy will be tolerated, and the Government will not extend pecuniary aid to any persons, whether white or black, who are unwilling to help themselves.

III. District and Post Commanders throughout this Department will at once cause this order to be circulated far and wide, by special couriers or otherwise, and will take such steps to secure its enforcement as may by them be deemed necessary.

Q. A. GILLMORE,
may 26 Major General Commanding.

COLUMBIA.

Saturday Morning, June 3, 1865.

Labor—Its Value.

The workingman is the only substantial citizen, all other things being equal. Everything which goes to diminish the amount of positive performance among a people—which goes to lessen the grand results of human labor—is of necessity evil. There is unhappily, in our country, a very universal distaste to labor. Our labor is but too much imported from abroad. We loathe and despise the severer tasks of that industry which removes mountains and fills the deserts with fruits and blossoms. Our people, afflicted with certain childish vanities, prefer to fill the ranks of the professions with useless recruits, who add nothing to their dignity or character, and lessen, by just their own strength, the number of the legitimate producers of the country. This is to multiply unnecessary consumers of the capital they were intended to produce. Society is very much like a bee-hive; if the drones are allowed to remain, even where they do not propagate, the contents of the hive will very soon be exhausted. That society which dares not grapple heartily with the essential tasks of field and highway, must forbear, only with daily loss of its most wholesome characteristics. With us the cry seems evermore for money. The want of money is the one want which we everywhere unite to deplore. The proper subject of complaint is want of industry. Money is one of the most dangerous of all social possessions. It is a wondrous power, the very use of which requires a previous training of head and heart, which cannot be too careful or too strict. Few people know properly how to use it, keeping moral standards before their eyes. Most persons not accustomed to its employment, not trained to the use of power, become gamblers with wealth, and the fancies and the appetites take the control of that which can be used with safety only by a justly judging morality and a sage experience. The Americans, a young and consequently a poor people, were, of all others, the least prepared to use it judiciously. In many respects, at one period in the history of the world, the Spaniards were the richest people in the world. But they were previously among the poorest, and their riches, after a brief career of recklessness, pride, lust and other passions, engendered by this very sudden excess of wealth, brought them to something worse than their original condition. The Spaniards are now not only the poorest and feeblest, but the most degraded of all the powers of Christendom. The present is a fruit of their immediately previous condition. It was the discovery of Spanish America and its rich possessions to which their poverty is due. They were not prepared to use judiciously their own resources, and squandered wastefully what they had unexpectedly acquired, but not till it had taught them wants, habits and indulgences which they are no longer able to supply. As the descendants of the expelled Moors of Granada still keep the keys of the ancient homestead, still dreaming to get back; so the Spaniard still waits, dreaming that the Providence which brought him Mexico and Peru will again restore them to his possession. The case of a nation is not improperly illustrated by individual example. Take the instance of the youthful heir of the old miser—one whom the sordid passion of the sire has, while he lived, kept within the most contracted limits of a base and slavish economy. Let him, while still young, be admitted freely among the hoards of which he has only dreamed before, and note with what pains-taking earnestness he dissipates them! It is his boast, indeed, that he does so, even as expensive frivolities and meretricious life are become a boast with us. "It's gone at last!" was the only half-desponding exclamation of one of these profligates a few years ago, as he acknowledged his ruin; but, suddenly looking up, with a sort of exultation in his manner, as if there had been some degree of merit in the very recklessness of his waste: "But may be I didn't *hum it* while it lasted." Was there ever a more perfect boy? That his *top hummed* while it was going, was a great consolation for its loss. A whole people become thus profligate at seasons, sharing the vices of the individual, for such excesses are epidemical. The Southerners have presented for a number of years the melancholy spectacle of a people *humming* it, just like the silly boy; with the simple difference that their *humming* is no longer a subject of congratulatory chuckle. For some ten years longer, we shall be prudent enough to forbear to *hum it;* but there are periodical returns for all such maladies, and a return of seeming prosperity for a longer period than usual, unless we learn to respect money less and industry more, will be sure to bring us to our sack-cloth again. Seriously, our levity of character is a great evil in our constitution. It can, scarcely be otherwise until we honor labor more. She methodizes all the faculties, and makes all the securities of virtue as well as fortune. Mere sleight of hand will not answer. We must go back to the deserted fields, making our own corn and cabbages, and gathering in the harvest with our own hands.

Youth.

The loss of youth is one of the most touching of all subjects in the thought of him who has past the meridian. There is an impressive anecdote given by the historian of one of the monarchs of France—the Superb Louis, perhaps, but we really forget which—who was heard to say, while gazing upon the beauties of his palace and grounds: "And I must leave all these!" Could anything be more mournful? His thoughts and feelings had prepared him for no better world. There were no equivalents for what he lost! Here is a passage on a like topic, which we have paraphrased from the "Faust" of Goethe:

"Oh! give me back the days when I, myself,
Was growing still; when, ever freshly springing,
Life was a fountain of perpetual music,
That knew not break or discord; when the world
Was veiled in sacred mists—in mists made glorious
By the endowing fancy; when the bud
Still bore miraculous sweetness; when I gathered
From every sterile dale a wealth of flowers,
Which never glad me now! How rich my stores
When I had nothing—and how ample all
The nothing I possessed. Oh! give me back
The instinctive passion for the hidden truth—
The joy that brought delusion, yet denied
That I should doubt its treasure. Give me back
All those wild impulses—those matchless passions,
Now swollen with fullest energy of hatred,
Now with the glory and the might of love;
Oh! give me back my youth."

The New York papers are filled with accounts of the review of Sherman's troops in Washington by the President and Cabinet. The display was continued several days, and it is stated that over 200,000 troops were in line. The *Herald* thinks that neither Napoleon or Wellington ever saw so many veterans in one army at a time. The city was crowded with strangers from all parts of the Union.

To be infirm of purpose, is to be evil of purpose. A strong will, if not absolutely virtue itself, is yet absolutely necessary to all the virtues. He who does not resolve well, will perform ill. Weakness of resolve is mostly wickedness. Indecision of character is laxity of principle. It leaves the mind at the mercy of the passion; and impulse, which is seldom found associated with a rigid will, is quite as unsteady in principle as in performance. Such a character works precipitately and rashly, with the purpose of concealing the deficiency of which he is himself conscious. He thus frequently precipitates himself in action, which he dare not subject to argument. He may tremble at the danger which impends, but he dreads still more lest you should suspect the true nature of his fears.

In addition to the gold snuff book mentioned as having been presented by the Free Masons of this State to brother Albert G. Mackey, of Charleston, S. C., on Saturday night, he was also presented with a handsome volume, illustrative of the principles of masonry, and a check for $1,500. It is understood that a much larger sum has been subscribed by the brethren, to mark their appreciation of Mr. Mackey's loyalty as a man and fidelity as a mason.

[*New York Herald.*

A Frenchman was tried in Richmond the other day by a drum-head court martial, for striking a woman in one of the markets with a cane. He was convicted, and in punishment was paraded through the streets to the tune of the "Rogue's March," with a placard, labelled, "This for striking a woman." The populace enjoyed the affair more than the Frenchman.

A Fund for Gen. Lee.—The New York *Express* says a fund is being raised in Baltimore for presentation to Gen. Lee; $40,000 has been already secured, with the promise of $60,000 additional.

At a recent Sabbath school celebration in Brooklyn, it is estimated that 20,000 children participated.

Proclamation by the President.

Whereas, by the proclamation of the President, of the 11th day of April last, certain ports of the United States therein specified, which had previously been subject to blockade, were, for objects of public safety, declared, in conformity with previous special legislation of Congress, to be closed against foreign commerce during the national will, to be thereafter expressed and made known by the President;

And whereas events and circumstances have since occurred which, in my judgment, render it expedient to remove that restriction, except as to the ports of Galveston, La Salle, Brazos de Santiago, Point Isabel and Brownsville, in the State of Texas;

Now, therefore, be it known, that I, Andrew Johnson, President of the United States, do hereby declare that the ports aforesaid, not excepted as above, shall be open to foreign commerce from the first day of July next; that commercial intercourse with the said ports may from that time be carried on subject to the laws of the United States, and in pursuance of such regulations as may be prescribed by the Secretary of the Treasury. If, however, any vessel from a foreign port shall enter any of the before named excepted ports in the State of Texas, she will continue to be held liable to the penalties prescribed by the Act of Congress, approved on the 13th day of July, 1861, and the persons on board of her to such penalties as may be incurred pursuant to the laws of war for trading or attempting to trade with an enemy.

And I, Andrew Johnson, President of the United States of America, do hereby declare and make known that the United States of America do henceforth disavow to all persons trading or attempting to trade in any of the United States in violation of the laws thereof, all pretence of belligerent right and privileges; and I give notice, from the date of this proclamation, all such offenders will be held and dealt with as pirates.

It is also ordered that all restrictions upon trade heretofore imposed in the territory of the United States East of the Mississippi River, save those relating to contraband of war, to the reservation of the rights of the United States, to property purchased in the territory of an enemy, and to the twenty-five per cent. upon purchases of cotton, are removed. All provisions of the internal revenue law will be carried into effect under the proper officer. In witness whereof, I have hereunto set my hand and caused the seal of the United States to be affixed.

Done at the city of Washington this twenty-second day of May, in the year of our Lord one thousand eight hundred and sixty five, and of the independence of the United States of America, the eighty-ninth.

ANDREW JOHNSON.

By the President:
W. Hunter, Acting Secretary of State.

The total police force of London last year was 7,490, and its expense two millions eight hundred thousand dollars. There were 29 superintendents, 211 inspectors, 725 sergeants and 6,172 constables.

The Shenandoah was reported to be at Hong Kong at latest advices, and some alarm was felt that she might capture American vessels at sea.

Land is in demand in London, and has been sold at the high price of one million dollars per acre.

The new sewerage system of London is going to cost four millions sterling.

Local Items.

The office of the *Columbia Phœnix* is on Gates street, second door from Plain.

General Gillmore arrived in Charleston yesterday morning. It is believed that he will pay Columbia a visit.

If any of our readers are desirous of renewing their acquaintance with old friends—Messrs. Codfish, Mackerel, Herring and Cheese—they have only to glance over the advertisements in the *Phœnix* for the past few days, to find their whereabouts.

☞ Personal.—All subscribers to the *Phœnix* whose subscriptions have expired, will please come forward and renew, in specie or provisions; otherwise their papers will be stopped.

☞ We wish it distinctly understood that our terms are *cash*. No advertisements will, therefore, be inserted unless paid for in advance.

We present the following schedule of rates, in the case of the most obvious commodities. For one month's subscription to the *Phœnix*, we will receive either of the following, viz:

1 bushel corn. 1½ bush. peas or potatoes
5 pounds butter. 25 lbs. flour.
7 " lard. 4 lbs. candles.
7 " bacon. 9 qts. rice.
8 dozen eggs. 4 head of chickens.

Wood, vegetables and provisions generally received at fair market rates approaching the specie standards.

Something of the Place of Davis' Confinement.

Fortress Monroe, within whose sturdy walls Jeff. Davis is now studiously guarded by United States soldiers, is situated on the extreme end of the peninsula formed by the James and York Rivers, and is the lower extremity of the section of country whereon McClellan fought his campaign of 1862. By reason of Hampton Creek being on the one side and the Chesapeake Bay on the other, a promontory within a promontory is formed. It is nearly insulated by Hampton, leaving a narrow strip of land on the side nearest to Chesapeake Bay, which connects it with the main land.

To escape from Fortress Monroe, if it is earnestly desired to keep one there, is simply a pure impossibility. To its Eastward is the whole width of Chesapeake Bay at its junction with the Atlantic Ocean, a distance of perhaps more than twenty miles intervening between it and Cape Cod. To the South, it is separated from the nearest point of land by the Hampton Roads. To the Westward is Hampton Creek, broadening as its comes Southward into an ample bay separating the fortress from the nearest point of land to the West and Northward, except on the North, where is the strip of beach previously referred to.

The fort itself is a regular polygon, and is surrounded by a wet ditch thirty yards wide. It is the most extensive and massive of the permanent fortifications of the United States, its enormous area being fully capable of holding several Fort Sumters. It has a water battery towards the sea, which is of itself a formidable work.

The immediate place of confinement of Jeff. Davis will be in the casemates, several of which have been thoroughly prepared for this purpose within the past few days. These casemates are rock ribbed and arched mansions within the fort, each well nigh constituting a fort within itself. Within a few days, they have been made doubly secure; the embrasures looking to the wet ditch, as well as the windows looking to the interior of the work, having been most heavily barred with iron, in the form of gratings.

On the parches of these casemates are mounted 15 inch Rodman guns. As an evidence of the capability of these casemates and arches to withstand resistance, it may be stated that they are fully competent to sustain the shock of the explosions of the monsters of modern warfare.

The only connections from the fort with the mainland are, by the main sallyport and a small postern in one of the bastions; the wet ditch being spanned at each of these points by a draw bridge, which can be raised at pleasure, thus cutting off all communication.

The other State prisoners accompanying Davis will be provided for in a manner similar to himself. At all events, they will be secure against escape. A pleasant assurance for the country to have.

[*New York Herald.*

Headq'rs United States Forces,
CITY OF COLUMBIA, S. C.,
May 27, 1865.

GENERAL ORDERS NO. 3.

ALL citizens having in their possession any property that rightfully belongs to the United States Government, according to the terms of surrender of Gen. Jos. E. Johnston, C. S. A., to Gen. W. T. Sherman, U. S. A., will immediately report the same to these headquarters.

Persons having mules, horses and wagons, will, for the present, be permitted to retain the same for the purpose of carrying on their work. Any person failing to comply with this order within a reasonable time, will not only be deprived of any farther use of said property, but will also subject themselves to punishment by military authority. By command of

N. HAUGHTON,
Lieut. Col. 25th O. V. V.,
Com'dg City of Columbia, S. C.

W. J. Kyle, Lieut. 25th O. V. V. I. and Post Adjutant. may 29

Headq'rs United States Forces,
CITY OF COLUMBIA, S. C.,
May 27, 1865.

GENERAL ORDERS NO 4.

IN order to prevent any disturbance which may arise from the improper use of intoxicating liquors, it is hereby ordered that, for the present, no intoxicating liquors will be sold or given away to any citizen or soldier, unless permission is granted from these headquarters. Any one found guilty of disobeying this order, will not only have his goods confiscated, but will be subject to punishment by military law. By command of

Lieut. Col. N. HAUGHTON,
Commanding Post.

W. J. Kyle, Lieut. 25th O. V. V. I. and Post Adjutant. may 29

Headquarters, Northern District,
DEPARTMENT OF THE SOUTH,
Charleston, S. C., April 25, 1865.

Circular to Planters, etc.

NUMEROUS applications have been made to me for information as to the policy to be adopted on the subject of labor.

All can understand the importance of making a crop the present season, and foresee the misery and suffering consequent upon its failure.

In the present unsettled state of the country, and in the absence of any recognized State authorities, I find it my duty to assume control of the plantations near the military lines, and order as follows:

1st. The planters, after taking the oath of allegiance, will assemble the freedmen (lately their slaves) and inform them that they are free, and that henceforth they must depend upon their own exertions for their support.

2d. Equitable contracts in writing will be made by the owners of the land with the freedmen for the cultivation of the land during the present year.

Payment will be made in kind, and the allowance of one half the crop is recommended as fair compensation for the labor, the landlord furnishing subsistence until the crop is gathered.

These contracts will be submitted to the nearest military or naval commander for approval and endorsement.

When the above requirements are complied with, protection will be granted as far as military necessity will allow; but where no contract is made, the crop raised will be considered forfeited for the use of the laborers. Should the owners refuse to cultivate it, they will be considered as endeavoring to embarrass the Government, and the land will be used for colonies of the freedmen from the interior.

JOHN P. HATCH,
June 1 Brig. Gen. Commanding.

Headq'rs United States Forces,
CITY OF COLUMBIA, S. C.,
May 27, 1865.

GENERAL ORDERS NO. 2.

INFORMATION having been received at these headquarters of the existence of armed bands of marauders infesting the country and committing depredations on the property of peaceful citizens, it is hereby ordered that all persons composing such will be considered and treated as outlaws, and if caught, will receive the severest punishment of military law.

The United States Government is desirous of protecting all peaceful and law-abiding citizens, and they will confer a favor on these headquarters, and do justice to themselves, by giving any information they may have in their possession respecting the names and movements of such bands, and, if possible, aiding in their capture.

The time has arrived when it behooves every citizen to do all in his power to assist the military forces of the United States to restore peace and harmony throughout the land. By order of

Lieut. Col. N. HAUGHTON,
25th O. V. V. I., Com'dg U. S. Forces,
City of Columbia.

W. J. Kyle, 2d Lieut. 25th O. V. V. I. and Post Adjutant. may 29

THE REVEILLE.

VOL. I. CARVER U. S. GENERAL HOSPITAL, WASHINGTON, D. C., JUNE 10, 1865. No. 32.

For the Reveille.

THE STRAWBERRY GIRL.

One summer day, and many such there are,
When nature, in her robes of purity,
Like some fair creature lovely and serene,
Her face with health all glowing as the morn,
Her dress most comely, and a well shaped form,
A model true of grace and beauty rare,
Wild flowers and violets nestling at her feet
That gently press them so they fragrance breathe,
And in her hands holds out the early fruit,
The first the season yields, of ruddy hue,
That creeps on humble vines along the ground,
So tempts the palate and delights the taste.
In quest of these the earths prime offerings,
A maiden by a novel fancy moved,
Betook her to the verdant rural fields
That lay beyond the city, where her home
O'erlooks the blue Penobscot, calm and deep,
That bears the commerce of a noble State.
Though young, her eye beheld the beautiful,
And saw the charms that captivate the mind;
Wild blossoms seemed to welcome her with smiles,
The bee hummed o'er the flowery mead the while,
In neighboring woods the thrush and oriole sang,
The sweet aroma of the luscious fruit
Regaled her senses, while she gathered full
Her basket with strawberries large and ripe.
A certain pleasure filled her youthful heart
At her departure from that fruitful field,
And many a vine lay bleeding on the ground,
Which light feet wounded as they pressed them down,
Green leaves she gathered from the bending boughs,
Of oak and maple, which with careful hand,
Laid on the fruit, preserved it nice and fresh.
Then with elastic step she homeward turned,
While thought was busy with an artifice,
A pretty trick, by which to sell her stock
As some poor girl pursuing thus her craft;
For in the lap of ease and plenty reared,
She knew no harder toil than study gives,
Or the diversion of a pleasant task.
The sun was low and twilight falling fast,
That o'er the city crept with solemn shades,
When at a friendly door alone appeared
A fair young stranger all in neat attire.
Her cheeks like lilies of the valley looked,
Which sometime wore the blooming rose of health.
A costume short arranged with care and taste,
With snow white collar that adorned her neck,
Her modest mien, soft voice and down cast eye,
At once deceived an unsuspicious friend
Nor look nor tone her inward glee betrayed,
As with mild speech the maiden offered thus:
'Do you some nice strawberries wish to buy?"
To whom the lady, "We are well supplied."
"But they are choice, I picked them all to-day,
And I'm so weary now, for it is late,
And I have far to walk to reach my home;
To-night I hope to sell them; will you buy?"
A touch of nature lay in this appeal
That gives to eloquence a vital charm.
Fatigued and pale and amiable withal,
To eyes that saw but seeing were deceived,
She sold her berries and the lady too.

H. C. D.

ONE OF PRESIDENT LINCOLN'S STORIES AS TOLD BY CARPENTER.—Shortly afterward, he told us this story of "Andy Johnson" as he was familiarly in the habit of calling him. It was a few weeks prior to the Baltimore convention, before it was known that Gov. Johnson would be the nominee for the Vice-Presidency. Said he, "I had a visit last night from Colonel Moody the fighting Methodist parson' as he is called in Tennessee. He is on his way to the Philadelphia conference, and, being in Washington over night, came up to see me. He told me," he continued, "this story of Andy Johnson and Gen. Buel, which interested me intensely. Col. Moody was in Nashville the day that it was reported that Buel had decided to evacuate the city. The rebels strongly re-inforced were said to be within two days' march of the capital. Of course the city was greatly excited. Said Moody, 'I went in search of Johnson at the edge of the evening, and found him at his office, closeted with two gentlemen, who were walking the floor with him, one on each side. As I entered they retired, leaving me alone with Johnson, who came up to me manifesting intense feeling and said, 'Moody, we are sold out! Buel is a traitor! He is going to evacuate the city, and in forty-eight hours we shall all be in the hands of the rebels.' Then he commenced pacing the floor again, twisting his hands, and chafing, like a caged tiger, utterly insensible to his friend's entreaties to become calm. Suddenly he turned and said, 'Moody, can you pray?' 'That is my business, sir, as a minister of the Gospel,' returned the Colonel. 'Well, Moody, I wish you would pray,' said Johnson; and instantly both went down upon their knees at opposite sides of the room. As the prayer became fervent, Johnson began to respond in true Methodist style. Presently he crawled over on his hands and knees to Moody's side, and put his arm over him, manifesting the deepest emotion. Closing the prayer with a hearty 'Amen!' from each, they arose. Johnson took a long breath, and said, with emphasis, 'Moody, I feel better!' Shortly afterward he asked, 'Will you stand by me?' 'Certainly, I will,' was the answer. 'Well, Moody, I can depend upon you; you are one in a hundred thousand!' He then commenced pacing the floor again. Suddenly he wheeled, the current of his thought having changed, and said, 'Oh! Moody, I don't want you to think I have become a religious man because I asked you to pray. I am sorry to say it, but I am not, and have never pretended to be, religious. No one knows this better than you; but, Moody, there is one thing about it—I DO believe in ALMIGHTY GOD! And I believe also in the BIBLE, and I say I'll be *damned* if Nashville shall be surrendered!'"

And Nashville was not surrendered!

HOW TO OPEN OYSTERS.—"Talking of opening oysters," said old Hurricane, "why, nothing's easier, if you only know how."

"And how's how?" inquired Straight.

"Scotch snuff," answered old Hurricane, very sententiously. "Scotch snuff. Bring a little of it ever so near their noses, and they'll sneeze their lids off."

"I know a genius," observed Mr. Karl, who has a better plan. He spreads the bivalves in a circle, seats himself in the centre, and begins spinning a yarn. Sometimes, it's an adventure in Mexico; sometimes it's a legend of his love; sometimes a marvelous stock transaction. As he proceeds, the 'natives' get interested; one by one they gape, my friend whips 'em out, peppers 'em, and swallows 'em."

"That'll do," said Straight, with a deep sigh. "I wish we had a dozen of the bivalves here—they'd open easy."

ONE of our Western villages passed an ordinance forbidding taverns to sell liquor on the Sabbath to any persons except travelers. The next Sunday every man in town who wanted a "nip" was seen walking around with a valise in one hand and two carpet bags in the other!

A COOK may not have as many boils as Job, but then they are as big as kettles.

The Philadelphia Inquirer.

PRICE TWO CENTS. PHILADELPHIA, WEDNESDAY, JUNE 14, 1865. PRICE TWO CENTS.

RECONSTRUCTION!

Important Proclamations by the President!

REORGANIZATION IN MISSISSIPPI!

WM. L. SHARKEY PROVISIONAL GOVERNOR.

The Functions of the Various Government Departments to be Resumed.

THE BLOCKADE RAISED!

Trade Restrictions With Rebeldom Are Removed!

THINGS CONTRABAND OF WAR

No Recognition of Slavery!

BONDMEN FOREVER FREE

IMPORTANT FROM EUROPE.

Opposing Governments of Mexico.

PRESIDENT JOHNSON PROCLAIMS STRICT NEUTRALITY!

Our Fortress Monroe Correspondence

GENERAL ORD RELIEVED FROM COMMAND.

General A. H. Terry His Successor.

PROCLAMATIONS BY PRESIDENT JOHNSON.

By the President of the United States.

A PROCLAMATION.

Whereas the Fourth Section of the Fourth Article of the Constitution of the United States declares that the United States shall guarantee to every State in the Union a republican form of government, and shall protect each of them against invasion and domestic violence; and whereas the President of the United States is by the Constitution, made Commander-in-chief of the Army and Navy, as well as chief Executive Officer of the United States, and is bound by solemn oath faithfully to execute the office of President of the United States, and to take care that the laws be faithfully executed; and whereas, the Rebellion which has been waged by a portion of the people of the United States against the properly constituted authorities of the Government thereof, in the most violent and revolting form, but whose organized and armed forces have now been almost entirely overcome, has in its revolutionary progress deprived the people of the State of Mississippi of all civil government; and whereas, it becomes necessary and proper to carry out and enforce the obligations of the United States to the people of Mississippi in securing them in the enjoyment of a republican form of Government;

Now, therefore, in obedience to the high and solemn duties imposed upon me by the Constitution of the United States, and for the purpose of enabling the loyal people of said State to organize a State Government whereby justice may be established, domestic tranquility ensured and loyal citizens protected in all their rights of life, liberty and property, I, Andrew Johnson, President of the United States and Commander-in-chief of the Army and Navy of the United States, do hereby appoint William L. Sharkey, of Mississippi, Provisional Governor of the State of Mississippi, whose duty it shall be, at the earliest practicable period, to prescribe such rules and regulations as may be necessary and proper for convening a convention, composed of delegates to be chosen by that portion of the people of said State who are loyal to the United States, and no others, for the purpose of altering or amending the Constitution thereof, and with authority to exercise within the limits of said State all the powers necessary and proper to enable such loyal people of the State of Mississippi to restore said State to its constitutional relations to the Federal Government, and to present such a republican form of State government as will entitle the State to the guarantee of the United States therefor, and its people to protection by the United States against invasion, insurrection and domestic violence.

Provided that in any election that may be hereafter held for choosing delegates to any State Convention, as aforesaid, no person shall be qualified as an elector, or shall be eligible as a member of such convention unless he shall have previously taken and subscribed the oath of amnesty as set forth in the President's proclamation of May 29th, A. D. 1865, and is a voter qualified as prescribed by the constitution and laws of the State of Mississippi in force immediately before the 9th of January, A. D. 1861, the date of the so-called Ordinance of Secession; and the said Convention when convened, or the Legislature that may be thereafter assembled, will prescribe the qualifications of electors and the eligibility of persons to hold office under the constitution and laws of the State, a power the people of the several States composing the Federal Union have rightfully exercised from the origin of the Government to the present time.

And I do hereby direct, first, that the military commander of the Department and all officers and persons in the military and naval service aid and assist the said Provisional Governor in carrying into effect this proclamation, and they are enjoined to abstain from in any way hindering, impeding or discouraging the loyal people from the organization of a State Government as herein authorized.

Second. That the Secretary of State proceed to put in force all laws of the United States, the administration whereof belongs to the State Department, applicable to geographical limits aforesaid.

Third. That the Secretary of the Treasury proceed to nominate for appointment, assessors of taxes and collectors of customs and internal revenue, and such other officers of the Treasury Department as are authorized by law, and put in execution the revenue laws of the United States within the geographical limits aforesaid. In making appointments the preference shall be given to qualified loyal persons residing within the districts where their respective duties are to be performed. But if suitable residents of the district shall not be found, then persons residing in other States or districts shall be appointed.

Fourth. That the Postmaster-General proceed to establish post offices and post routes, and put into execution the postal laws of the United States within the said State, giving to loyal residents the preference of appointment; but if suitable residents are not found, then to appoint agents, &c., from other States.

Fifth. The District Judge of the Judicial District in which Mississippi is included shall proceed to hold courts within said State in accordance with the provisions of the act of Congress. The Attorney-General will instruct the proper officers to libel and bring to judgment, confiscation and sale property subject to confiscation and enforce the administration of justice within said State in all matters within the cognizance and jurisdiction of the Federal Courts.

Sixth. That the Secretary of the Navy take possession of all public property belonging to the Navy Department within said geographical limits, and put in operation all acts of Congress in relation to naval affairs having application to said State.

Seventh. That the Secretary of the Interior put in force the laws relating to the interior department, applicable to the geographical limits aforesaid.

In testimony whereof, I have hereunto set my hand, and caused the seal of the United States to be affixed.

Done at the City of Washington, the 13th day of June, in the year of our Lord one thousand eight hundred and sixty-five, and of the independence of the United States, the eighty-ninth.

[L. S.] ANDREW JOHNSON.

By the President:—

WILLIAM H. SEWARD, Secretary of State.

ANOTHER PROCLAMATION.

By the President of the United States:—

A PROCLAMATION.

Whereas, By my proclamation of the 29th of April, 1865, all restrictions upon internal, domestic and commercial intercourse, with certain exceptions therein specified and set forth, were removed in such parts of the States of Tennessee, Virginia, North Carolina, South Carolina, Georgia, Florida, Alabama, Mississippi, and so much of Louisiana as lies east of the Mississippi River as shall be embraced within the lines of the national military occupation;

And, whereas, By my proclamation of the 22d of May, 1865, for reasons therein given, it was declared that certain ports of the United States which had been previously closed against foreign commerce, should, with certain specified exceptions, be reopened to such commerce on and after the first day of July next, subject to the laws of the United States, and in pursuance of such regulations as might be prescribed by the Secretary of the Treasury;

And whereas, I am satisfactorily informed that dangerous combinations against the laws of the United States no longer exists within the State of Tennessee; that the insurrection heretofore existing within the said State has been suppressed; that within the boundaries thereof the authority of the United States is undisputed, and that such officers of the United States as have been duly commissioned, are in the undisputed exercise of their official functions;

Now, therefore, be it known that I, Andrew Johnson, President of the United States, do hereby declare that all restrictions upon internal, domestic and coastwise intercourse and trade, and upon the removal of products of States heretofore declared in insurrection, reserving and excepting only those relating to contraband of war as hereinafter recited, and also those which relate to the reservation of the rights of the United States to property purchased in the territory of an enemy heretofore imposed in the territory of the United States, of the Mississippi River, are annulled: and I do hereby direct that they be forthwith removed, and that on and after the first day of July next, all restrictions upon foreign commerce with said ports, with the exception and reservation aforesaid, be likewise removed, and that the commerce of said States shall be conducted under the supervision of the regularly appointed officers of the Customs, provided by law, and such officers of the Customs shall receive any captured and abandoned property that may be turned over to them under the law of the military and naval forces of the United States, and dispose of such property as shall be directed by the Secretary of the Treasury.

The following articles, contraband of war, are excepted from the effect of this proclamation:—Arms, ammunition, all articles from which ammunition is made, and grey uniforms and cloths; and I hereby also proclaim and declare, that the insurrection, so far as it relates to, and within the State of Tennessee, and the inhabitants of the said State of Tennessee, as reorganized and constituted under the recently adopted constitution and reorganization, and accepted by them is suppressed, and, therefore, also all the disabilities and disqualifications attached to said State and the inhabitants thereof, consequent upon any proclamations issued by virtue of the fifth section of the act entitled, "An act further to provide for the collection of duties on imports and for other purposes," approved the 13th day of July, 1861, are removed, but nothing herein contained shall be considered or construed as in any wise changing or impairing the penalties and forfeitures for treason heretofore incurred under the laws of the United States, or any of the provisions, restrictions or disabilities set forth in my proclamation bearing date the 29th day of May, 1865, or as impairing the existing regulations for the suspension of the habeas corpus, or the exercise of military law in cases where it shall be necessary for the general public safety and welfare during the existing insurrection; nor shall this proclamation affect or in any way impair any laws heretofore passed by Congress and duly approved by the President, or any proclamation or order issued by him during the aforesaid insurrection, abolishing slavery, or in any way affecting the relations of slavery, whether of persons or property; but, on the contrary, all such laws and proclamations heretofore made or issued, are expressly saved and declared to be in full force and virtue.

In witness whereof I have hereunto set my hand and caused the seal of the United States to be affixed.

Done at the city of Washington, the 13th day of June, in the year of our Lord 1865, and of the independence of the United States of America the eighty-ninth. ANDREW JOHNSON.

By the President. WILLIAM H. SEWARD, Secretary of State.

From Charleston and Savannah.

NEW YORK, June 13.—The steamer *Fulton* brings Savannah dates of June 9, via Charleston and Port Royal, S. C., on the 10th. Among the passengers are Major-General Grover and staff.

The Savannah *Herald* says the Twenty-eighth Massachusetts Volunteers and Thirty-seventh Pennsylvania Volunteers arrived on the 8th.

The Charleston *Courier* gives gratifying accounts of the revival of business there. Every day at least half a dozen new stores are opened. It says the burned district will be rebuilt.

A correspondent of the Port Royal *New South* clams that the deep water of its harbor, its readiness of access, the salubrious climate and fertility of soil, render it the place of all others indicated by nature for a great commercial city. All that it needs is a short piece of railroad to connect it with the main land.

WASHINGTON

AN UNFORTUNATE RAILROAD ACCIDENT.

Two Soldiers Killed and Twenty-nine Wounded!

SUFFERERS TAKEN TO DOUGLAS HOSPITAL.

Progress of the Trial of the Assassins

RETURN OF IRON-CLADS FROM HAVANA.

A Letter from Commander Maury.

[SPECIAL DESPATCHES TO THE "INQUIRER."

WASHINGTON, June 13, 1865.

An Unfortunate Accident

Occurred this afternoon between five and six o'clock, on the Baltimore and Ohio Railroad, at Kendall Green, about a mile and a half out from the depot, by which two soldiers were killed instantly and twenty-nine wounded. A troop train, with soldiers going home, met the Northern passenger train, due here at 5·20 P. M.

The troop train was switching off upon a siding to allow the passenger train to pass. The engineer of the passenger train, instead of waiting until the troop train had got upon the siding, kept on, without reversing his engine, and struck the middle of the troop train, demolishing two cars containing discharged soldiers of Battery A, First New Jersey Artillery. No person on the passenger train was injured.

The engineer jumped from his engine and escaped. The engine was considerably injured by the collision, but none of the cars were damaged. The wounded and dead soldiers were brought to the depot on the passenger train, and the wounded were removed to the Douglas Hospital, where they were professionally treated by Dr. Wm. F. Norris, Surgeon in charge. The two men killed were named Henry Sachs and Grocer. The bodies were taken to the Soldiers' Rest, at the Depot.

The following is a list of the wounded who were conveyed to Douglas Hospital:—

John Smith, Jacob Galenbeck, Ferdinand Coyle, Daniel McGeeher, Corp. William Freedmen, Anthony Jutz, George Kessler, Hagan Christian, Wm. H. Casey, Jacob Wolloff, Fred. Brehmire, Peter Luben, William Stüewe, Henry Eisenberry, Lewis Fabian, John Schereibel, Dennis Brown, Frank Grace, John Fallon, Wm. Quincke, Joseph Miller, Robert Snow, Gottleib Ringwald, Joseph Bleiler, Wm. Menges, Charles Hohoocler, Charles Sorger, George Casler.

Dennis Brown is severely wounded in the hip and head, which may result fatally. He has a family at Newark, and desired that they be informed of his situation. The wounds of the others are painful, but not dangerous, being mostly bruises. The wounded and dead all belong to the same battery, which was raised at Newark, N. J., and they were on their way to that city. They are nearly all Germans, with one or two Irish among them.

The officers of the railroad were untiring in their exertions to mitigate the sufferings of the wounded men. A working party was immediately despatched by Superintendent Koontz, to clear away the wreck, which was speedily accomplished. The six and seven-thirty P. M. trains for Philadelphia were detained a short time, but no detention to any other trains occurred.

The Trial of the Conspirators.

At the trial of the conspirators to-day, Dr. Jas. C. Hall, one of the medical gentlemen selected to examine Payne as to his alleged insanity, gave his testimony. His opinion was such as to justify a reasonable suspicion as to the insanity of Payne. The earnest manner of the Doctor and his evident reliability produced a deep impression upon the Court, and as he desired to make another examination, to more fully satisfy himself upon the matter, the Commission decided to have a more thorough examination made, and selected Dr. Stevens, Assistant Physician at the Government Insane Asylum, Surgeon-General Barnes and Surgeon Norris, to make another examination to-morrow, of the prisoner. All the evidence for the defense is now closed. The Government has one or two more witnesses to examine, which, with the testimony of the medical gentlemen in Payne's case, will probably occupy to-morrow's session.

It is expected that the Commission will adjourn over one or two days to allow the counsel an opportunity to prepare their arguments, which will be presented in writing.

Reverdy Johnson

Has prepared an argument in defense of Mrs. Surratt, which is understood to object to the jurisdiction of the Commission in trying the case, and he cites numerous authorities in support of his position. It is expected that Mr. Johnson will deliver his argument in person, but should he be absent it will be read by one of the other counsel for the prisoner.

Convicted.

T. M. Delaney, a citizen of Maine, who was arrested at Augusta, Me., by Col. L. C. Baker, for forging soldiers' enlistments and various other frauds, has been convicted, and to-day started for Concord, N. H., being sentenced to be imprisoned for the period of ten years, to pay a fine of forty-five thousand dollars, and to be imprisoned until the fine is paid.

Before the officer took him away he offered to pay the fine, if he was pardoned, but as he made an enormous fortune by his swindling in this connection his offer was not entertained.

The Cabinet

To-day had a very protracted session, lasting over three hours. They were down stairs in the Blue room. Very important matters were under discussion.

The Brazilian Mail Line.

The project of a Brazilian line of mail steamships has fallen through, owing to the parties in New York, who received the contract, failing to comply with their agreement. There is not now sufficient time to advertise for other lettings and matters will be postponed until after another session of Congress.

[DESPATCHES TO THE ASSOCIATED PRESS.]

Return of the Iron-clads from Havana.

The Navy Department has received a communication from Admiral S. W. Godon, dated on board the United States flag-ship *Susquehanna*, Hampton Roads, June 12, in which he says:—

"I have the honor to inform the Department of my arrival here to-day in company with the *Monadnock*, *Chippewa* and *Monticello*. The *Canonicus*, in tow of the *Fahkee*, was sent into Port Royal on the 9th inst., when abreast of that place, for coal, as she had less than one day's supply.

"In my letter of the 2d instant I informed the Department of the intended visit of the Captain-General of Cuba to the Monitors, on the following day. He was accompanied by a number of barges and a large staff, comprising several of the dignitaries of the place, and as he passed ahead of the flag-ship on the way, the iron-clad was saluted by the former vessel. With very little urging the Captain-General was induced to go on board the *Monadnock*, and after having thoroughly examined her, the *Canonicus* was visited, and the party finally came on board this ship.

"I accompanied the Captain-General to his barge, and he remarked to me that in making these visits he was acting contrary to usage, if not to the Spanish law, but he evidently wished me to understand that in doing so it was his wish to be marked in his attention. By my request we also visited the *Stonewall*, and the unfavorable light in which that vessel appeared when contrasted with our own iron-clads, could not fail in making an impression.

"The squadron left Havana on the 6th. The houses and wharves were crowded to witness the departure of the monitors, whose movements created the greatest surprise and interest. The *Monadnock* I consider a perfect success. She has steamed along with this ship, has given no trouble, and has caused me no anxiety.

"I will not be guilty here of the bad taste of expressing regrets at not falling in with the *Stonewall* at sea in the midst of her destructive career, in order to prove with what ease she could have been taken. I think it better that her end should have been the insignificant one it is. One-half the force at my command could have captured her and yet be entitled to no special praise. The *Monadnock* alone, I have already said, is her superior in every way. I am happy to say we are without sickness in the command.

"I inclose a characteristic letter from M. F. Maury, formerly of our navy, received the day before I left Havana. The Rebellion could hardly have well ended without a special parole to that gentleman."

LETTER OF COMMANDER MAURY.

AT SEA, May 25.—Sir:—In peace, as in war, I follow the fortunes of my native State, Virginia. I read in the public prints that she has practically confessed defeat and laid down her arms. I am here, without command, officially alone, and bound on matters of public concern, abroad. Nevertheless, as I consider further resistance worse than useless, I deem it proper formally so to confess it, and to pledge you in the words of honor that should I find myself before the final inauguration of peace within the jurisdiction of the United States, to consider myself a prisoner of war, bound by the terms and conditions which have been or may be granted to General Lee and his officers.

Be pleased to send your answer through my son, Colonel R. L. Maury, a paroled prisoner of war in Richmond.

In the meantime, and until I hear to the contrary, I shall act as though my surrender had been formally accepted on the above named terms and conditions. Respectfully, &c.,

M. F. MAURY,

Commander, Confederate States Navy.

To Commander United States Naval Forces in Gulf of Mexico.

The Proclamation.

The proclamation just issued appointing Judge Sharkey Provisional Governor of Mississippi is precisely the same as that appointing W. W. Holden Governor of North Carolina, with the exception of the names of the persons and the States. Judge Sharkey is represented to have been a Union man throughout the Rebellion, and from his honesty and purity of character, will doubtless be acceptable to the people of Mississippi.

Suffering in North Carolina.

An arrival from North Carolina represents great suffering among the people there, especially the freedmen.

The President.

The President to-day adopted a new rule of refusing to see visitors on Tuesdays and Fridays. A Cabinet session was held to-day.

Returning Soldiers.

Nearly all the soldiers have left here for their homes. The forts still remain garrisoned, and no discharges have been made from the Veteran Reserve Corps.

Prisoners of War.

The Secretary of War has ordered all prisoners of war, and other persons sentenced during the war, to be released from Fort McHenry.

United States Marshal.

Daniel R. Goodloe was to-day appointed United States Marshal here.

Treaty with Honduras.

The treaty between the United States and the Republic of Honduras is officially proclaimed. It provides for perpetual amity and reciprocal freedom of commerce and navigation with the various Governments with which it may have relation; for separate recognition of perpetual neutrality, and for the protection of the contemplated Honduras Interoceanic Railway from the Atlantic to the Pacific.

Honduras agrees that the right of way or transit over such route shall at all times be open and free to the Government and citizens of the United States, for all lawful purposes whatever. In consideration of these concessions, the United States engages, in conjunction with Honduras, to protect the same from interruption, seizure or unjust confiscation, from whatever quarter the attempt may proceed, so long as the spirit and intention of this article on this subject shall be preserved.

The Acting Assistant Secretary of State

In consequence of the continued indisposition of Mr. Fred. W. Seward, Clarence A. Seward, Esq., of New York, has been appointed by the President Acting Assistant Secretary of State.

Appointments for San Francisco.

Noah Books, Washington correspondent of the Sacramento *Union*, has been appointed Naval Officer, and Ex-Congressman Thomas B. Shannon, Surveyor of the port of San Francisco.

The Assassination Trial.

The prosecution in the conspiracy trial has three or four more witnesses to examine. The defense has closed, and only awaits the report of the medical survey as to the alleged insanity of Payne. Arnold's father was permitted an interview with his son to day, the former freely shedding tears.

The Old Capitol Jail.

The Old Capitol Jail has been nearly cleared of prisoners, there being less than one hundred there at the present time, of which number the majority are sick and wounded Rebels.

Military Assignments.

Major-General Terry has been assigned to the military command of Virginia, and Major-General Ord to the command of Oregon.

Visit to the President.

The Mayor of Savannah, accompanied by two other members of the city government, arrived here to-day, to confer with the President.

From California.

SAN FRANCISCO, June 7.—The arguments in the Salvador piracy case were concluded to-day. The commission will probably not allow its finding to be publicly known until the President has been advised. The parties charged with the attempt to seize the steamer *Colon* have been held to answer before the county Court on the charge of grand larceny.

The evidence does not clearly show what was the purpose of the intended seizure. Efforts are still quietly making to induce parties to enlist in the emigration association for Mexico.

Arrived, steamer *Brother Jonathan*, from the Southern Coast, with $155,000 in gold, from Victoria, and $192,000 from Portland, Oregon. The northern mines are reopening to trade, and begin to yield largely again.

SAN FRANCISCO, June 8.—The overland mail has arrived with New York dates of May 13. Preparations are making here for the grandest celebration of the Fourth of July ever known on the Pacific coast. Arrived, steamer *Constitution*.

From Buffalo.

BUFFALO, June 13.—We learn from an entirely responsible authority that a man calling himself F. A. St. Lawrence, and claiming to have been a Colonel in the Rebel army, is acting as an agent of George N. Sanders, Tucker, Cleary & Co., in Canada, endeavoring, by the offer of large sums of money, to induce persons to go to Washington to rebut the testimony of the witnesses against the assassination conspirators.

EUROPE.

Interesting News from the Continent.

THE FRENCH SUBSCRIPTION FOR MRS. LINCOLN.

The Government Forbid It and Seize the Money.

PRESIDENT JOHNSON ON THE EMPEROR MAXIMILIAN.

Our Government "Strictly Neutral."

NEW YORK, April 13.—The steamer *Scotia* arrived this afternoon, from Liverpool, with dates to the 3d inst.

The Princess of Wales was safely delivered of a son on the 3d inst., and was doing well.

Parliament adjourned on the 2d inst., for the holidays.

The reported success of the Canadian delegation does not prove to be true. Mr. Cardwell had stated in the House of Commons that the Conference was not concluded, but hoped that a report would shortly be made. It was reported that England was expected to bear the brunt of the large expenditure.

La Patrie denies authoritatively the statement that France is about to send 10,000 men to reinforce Maximilian.

The *Globe* denies that M. Eloin, whose business it was to inform the sovereigns of France, Belgium and Austria as to the real state of Mexico, had an interview with President Johnson, as reported by the French papers, and says that he was unable to open even informal relations with either of the Presidents or any member of the Cabinet.

The French Government had prohibited the two sous subscription to present to Mrs. Lincoln a medal. The police in the provinces had seized the subscriptions.

Napoleon is expected to return about the 6th inst.

The *Presse* says that Prince Napoleon has no intention to leave France.

The Financial Committee of the Austrian Reichsrath had reduced the war budget by fifteen millions.

Bombay telegrams of the 31st ult. make no allusion to the reported bank failures, or any further mercantile embarrassment.

Rio de Janeiro advices of the 10th state that an alliance has been signed between Brazil, Uruguay and the Argentine Confederacy.

The forces are marching against Paraguay.

It is reported that Buenos Ayres has declared war.

The London *Times* thinks there need be no apprehension that the war will be either serious or prolonged.

The demand for discount at the Bank of England was moderate. The funds remained uninfluenced by the influx of gold.

Fulaber & Cooper, East India merchants of Liverpool, have failed with liabilities amounting to £140,000.

The demand for United States Five-Twenties continued.

Latest via Liverpool.

It is stated, from Paris, that Mr. Bigelow, the United States Minister, has given the French Government the most positive assurances that the Washington Cabinet is firmly resolved to respect, and cause to be respected, the strictest neutrality with regard to Mexico, now placed under the protection of France.

Martial law has been abolished in Hungary.

In the Prussian Chamber of Deputies the bill for the increase of the Prussian navy was discussed, and rejected by a large majority. In the debate Herr Von Bismarch repelled the assertion that the Prussian Government had entered into negotiations with Denmark for the surrender of North Schleswig. He said the non-settlement of the question of the Duchies was attributed to the dilatory declarations of the Duke of Augustenburg. If the Duchies agreed to the Prussian condition it was indifferent what construction they gave to themselves.

Consols closed at 90¼@90⅜ for money; United States Five-Twenties, 67@67½; Erie, 50@50½; Illinois Central, 76¼@76¾.

Latest Commercial Intelligence.

By Telegraph to Queenstown.

LIVERPOOL, Saturday Night, June 3.—Cotton.—Sales to-day, 8000 bales. The market was dull and declined ⅛d. Sales to speculators and importers, 2000 bales. Breadstuffs dull. Provisions quiet. Produce quiet and steady.

LONDON, June 3, Evening.—Consols closed at 89¾, ex dividend. United States Five-twenties, 65¼@66; Illinois Central, 75@75½; Erie Railroad, 48¾@49½.

PARIS, June 4.—The Bourse closed quiet at 67·32 for Rentes.

LATE AND INTERESTING NEWS FROM MEXICO.

THE LIBERALS GAINING GROUND.

There is Not an Imperialist in Some of the States.

THE FRENCH DESPAIR OF PACIFYING THE COUNTRY.

50,000 MORE FRENCH TROOPS ARE NEEDED.

French Admiral Wants Max. to Buy the "Stonewall"

DR. GWIN AND HIS SONORA PROJECT.

NEW YORK, June 13.—The *Post's* Vera Cruz correspondence of June 1 says the Emperor is still on his pleasure tour through the country, while everything is at a stand-still in the capital awaiting his return.

The Liberals have gained more ground during the last month than they have lost during the last year.

General Negrete still holds Monterey, Saltillo, and all the country between those cities and the coast.

The attack on Matamoros failed owing to the threatening position taken by the Rebels at Brownsville when the Liberals approached Matamoros.

The whole State of Tamaulipas, with the exception of Tampico and Matamoros, is in the hands of the Liberals.

In the State of Michoacan the Count de Portier has been badly beaten by the Liberal troops, under General Regulus, and in the States of Tobasco and Chiapas not a Frenchman nor Imperialist is to be found. The veteran General Alvarez still holds his position as Governor of the State of Guerrero. The whole coast south of Vera Cruz, except Campeachy, remains in the undisputed possession of the Juarists. The French despair of pacifying the country unless fifty thousand more French troops are sent there.

Dr. Gwin has arranged his Sonora project. It only awaits Maximilian's signature. He goes as Director-General of Emigration to the States of Sonora, Chihuahua, Durango and Tamaulipas. Eight thousand French troops go with him to protect the emigrants and fortify the frontier against the excursions of the dreaded Yankees. Dr. Gwin's son is to get all the railroads of Sonora. Of course no emigrants are to be admitted except picked Confederates, and all Northerners are excluded. The French Admiral has gone to persuade Maxamilian to purchase the *Stonewall* at Havana, with which he is confident he can defend the coast against the whole American fleet.

From Maracaibo.

NEW YORK, June 13.—Arrived, barque Teresa, from Maracaibo. She reports that a raid took place on the night of May 20th, under General Pullager, with 200 followers.

The death of President Lincoln caused great grief. The flags were placed at half-mast, and other demonstrations of sorrow and respect made.

Robbery.

PORTSMOUTH, Ohio, June 13.—The law office of William H. Rollin was robbed yesterday of four $1000 bonds on the Marysville, Kentucky, Railroad.

LEWIS PAYNE.

J. W. ATZEROTT.

SAMUEL ARNOLD.

THE CONSPIRATORS AND THE CONSPIRACY.

WE omitted in our last number any account of the Conspiracy trial going on at Washington, because we did not deem the proceedings of sufficient importance. We recur to the subject this week, and give portraits—drawn from photographs taken by GARDNER, of Washington—of six of the conspirators, viz.: of PAYNE, ATZEROTT, HAROLD, SPANGLER, O'LAUGHLIN, and ARNOLD. We also give on page 408 portraits of the members composing the military court engaged in the trial.

There has been further evidence offered to prove the connection of the rebel authorities with the burning of steamboats on the Western rivers. But as these efforts were directed against Government vessels, the evidence in its relation to the assassination of President LINCOLN does not have any especial importance. The same may be said of the evidence proving that the City Point explosion was due to rebel agency.

On Friday, June 17, a curious bit of evidence was offered, going to prove that the *Daily News*, the rebel organ in New York city, has been supported during the war in a great measure by the Richmond authorities. This was no surprise when it was considered that recently, upon the close of the war, JOHN MITCHELL, the editor of the Richmond *Enquirer*, had been invited to take the editorial charge of the *News* and had accepted. The evidence is perfectly reliable, coming from the assistant manager of the Montreal bank, and proves that a check for $25,000 was last August drawn from rebel deposits and in favor of BENJAMIN WOOD, the proprietor of the *News*.

In connection with the events relating to the assassination, the portrait which we give on page 412 of Mr. FREDERICK SEWARD will be of unusual interest to our readers.

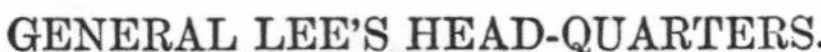

GENERAL LEE'S HEAD-QUARTERS.

GENERAL LEE'S Head-quarters at Petersburg, the ruins of which are illustrated on page 404, were at the house of Mr. TURNBULL, grandson of PETER JONES, founder of Petersburg, and chief magistrate of the county. LEE so little expected the results of the attack upon his lines that he had scarcely time to get away. A good deal of fighting took place in the vicinity of the house, but whether it was burned by the troops or the shells is not certain. Our men advanced beyond it, threw up a line of rifle-pits, and held the ground till the evacuation.

PRINCE NAPOLEON'S SPEECH AT AJACCIO.

THE recent speech of Prince NAPOLEON at Ajaccio, in Corsica, the birth-place of the first NAPOLEON, is the momentous event of the day. The occasion upon which this speech was made was in itself an interesting epoch to Frenchmen. A monumental statue of the great NAPOLEON was to be uncovered. For two generations NAPOLEON had been the French idol—as WASHINGTON is the idol of Americans. For an idea to gain absolute control over Frenchmen it had only been necessary to pronounce it Napoleonic. Within a few years the prestige of that omnipotent name had raised LOUIS NAPOLEON first to the Presidency and thence to the throne. With the assumption of the crown LOUIS had become an ardent advocate of Imperialism. Chiefly because Imperialism was peculiarly adapted to his purposes. Only recently he had brought from the commencement of the Christian era a type for the reconstruction of the political systems of the nineteenth century. That type was Cæsarism. To render Imperialism and Cæsarism more palatable to Frenchmen he had sought to invest them with Napoleonic sanctity.

Just here, and at the most opportune occasion, he was encountered by Prince JEROME, also a scion of NAPOLEON, though not wielding the imperial sceptre nor wearing the purple. It was a matter of common remark that the Prince bore a striking resemblance to the elder NAPOLEON, while the Emperor had not the least trace of any such likeness in his features. Prince JEROME ventured much, it might seem, in daring to confront the Emperor upon topics which were so vital. So much the more heroic then was the act. If the Prince had made his utmost endeavor he could scarcely have put himself in an attitude of greater antagonism with his imperial cousin than he did in this remarkable speech.

But what did Prince NAPOLEON say at Ajaccio that the world should so much wonder at? In the first place, he dared to pronounce the Napoleonic Idea to be essentially Democratic. But whatever he may have thought of NAPOLEON he certainly left no possible room for doubt as to his own leanings. He spoke of Democracy as of something certain to be ultimately successful the world over. He even ventured to point with triumph to the war which the American Republic had for four years waged against aristocracy, and the glorious result of that war as a token of the times. He opposed LOUIS'S Mexican policy, and spoke with favor of the MONROE doctrine. Is it any wonder that the expression of such ideas by a Prince of the blood startled the imperial court? Why, here was treason by the wholesale—a pregnant fountain of treason and perhaps of revolution!

This speech, though its effect has been so startling, was no sudden outburst on the Prince's part. He expressed only what he was already known to believe and feel. If he spoke with more than his wonted boldness, it was because the course which events had taken on the American continent had so completely vindicated his political creed. Yet his speech was a surprise—and to no one more so than to the Emperor. LOUIS had thought to bridle the Prince's tongue, and to insure his subordination by making him Vice-President of the Council of State. JEROME did not feel the obligation, and when his best opportunity offered he made the best use of it.

The Emperor's reception of the speech was just

DAVID C. HAROLD.

EDWARD SPANGLER.

MICHAEL O'LAUGHLIN.

No. 512—VOL. XX.) NEW YORK. JULY 22, 1865. (PRICE 10 CENTS. $4 00 YEARLY. 13 WEEKS $1 00.

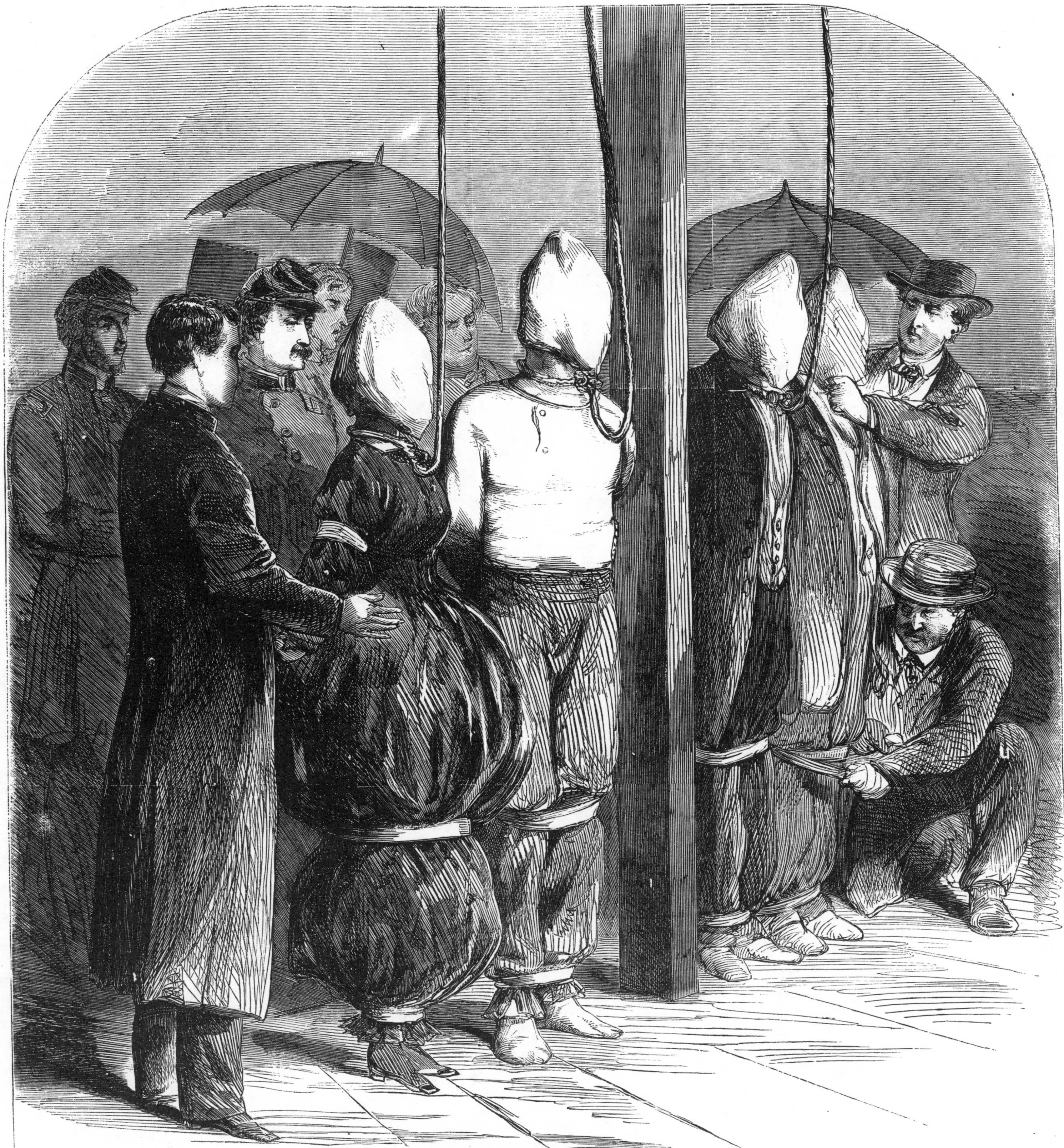

EXECUTION OF THE CONSPIRATORS IN WASHINGTON, D. C.—THE FINAL PREPARATIONS—APPEARANCE OF THE CRIMINALS ON THE SCAFFOLD.—FROM A SKETCH BY OUR SPECIAL ARTIST, D. B. GULICK.

ANDERSONVILLE PRISON SCENES, ILLUS

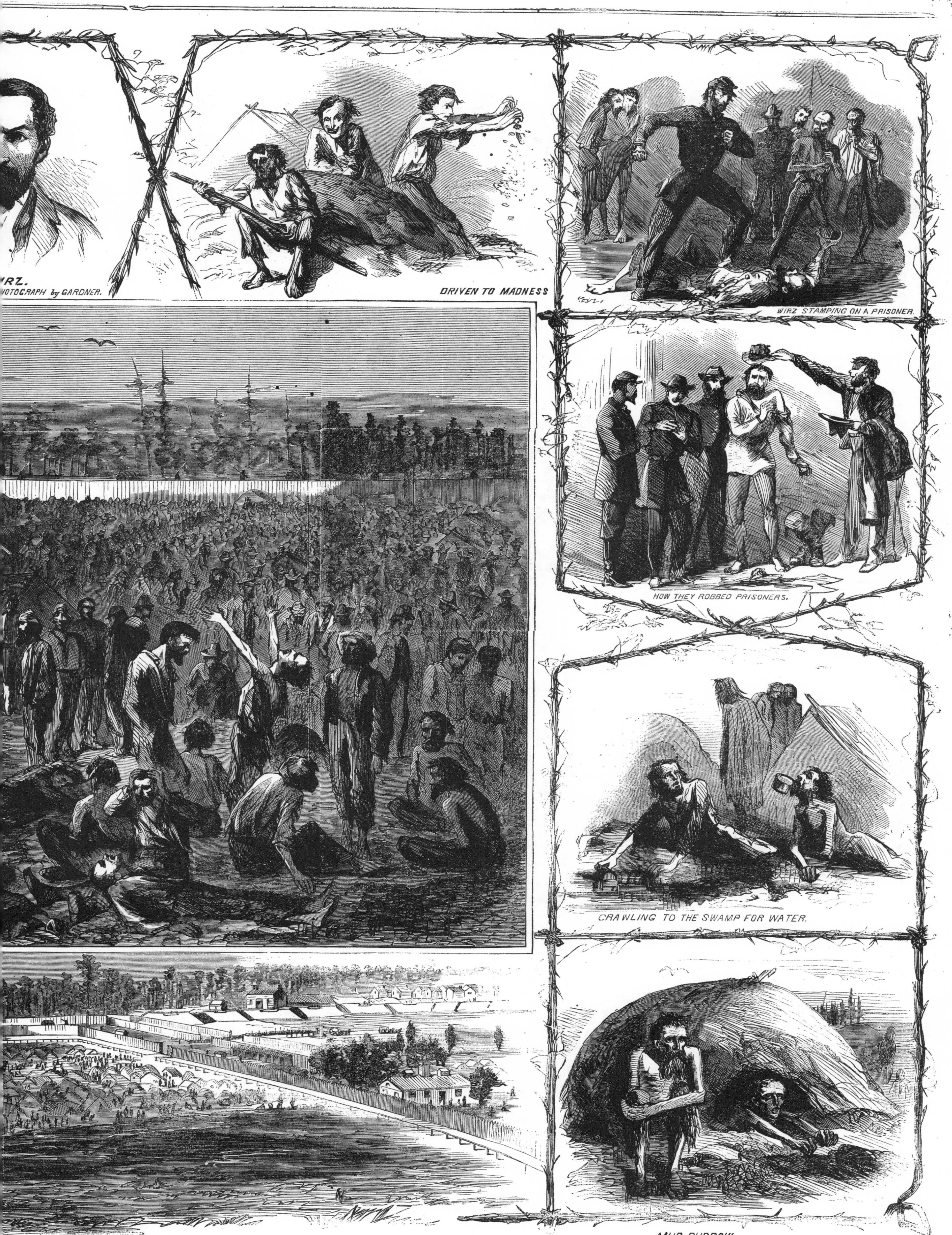

...NG CAPTAIN WIRZ'S TRIAL.—[See Page 582.]

THE SUN.

IT SHINES FOR ALL

Number 10,396. NEW YORK, SATURDAY, NOVEMBER 11, 1865. Thirty-Third Year.

The Latest News

By Telegraph to the N. Y. Sun.

EXECUTION OF WIRZ.

HIS DYING WORDS.

SCENES ON THE SCAFFOLD.

General Washington Dispatches

Reorganization.

North and South Carolina Going Wrong.

THE PRESIDENT SETS HIS FOOT DOWN.

Holden and Perry Not to Vacate.

Important from South America.

SPAIN DECLARES WAR AGAINST CHILI

A Blockade Proclaimed.

News From Hayti.

THE REBELS AND THE ENGLISH.

A British Ship Blown Up.

&c., &c., &c.

EXECUTION OF WIRZ.

Scenes at the Scaffold.

Washington, Nov. 10.—This morning Father Boyle administered the sacrament to Capt. Wirz. and Father Wigget, also of the Roman Catholic Church, then placed upon the prisoner the black robe, remarking as he did so, "I hope this will be turned into a white one in the other world.' "At 20 minutes past 10 o'clock Captain Wirz came from his cell in the Old Capital Prison, accompanied by Provost Marshal Russel and other officers, and by Fathers Boyle and Wigget, and passing between the military guard they ascended the scaffold. The prisoner was then seated. The scaffold was twelve feet square and twenty-two feet to the top beam with a trap twelve feet from the ground. The guard consisted of the 195th Pennsylvania Volunteers and three detachments of the Veteran Reserve Corps, under the command of Captain Walbridge, the Military Superintendent of the Old Capitol Prison. There were several hundred spectators present, besides the military, civilians having been admitted on special passes. Amid profound silence, Provost Marshal Russel proceeded to read the order of the War Department, founded on the verdict of the court-martial which tried the prisoner.

The prisoner was charged and convicted of combining, con ederating and conspiring with Jefferson Davis, J. A. Seddon, Howell Cobb, John H. Winder, Richard B. Winder, Isaiah White, W. S. Winder, W. Shelby Reed, R. R. Stevenson, S. P. Moore, —— Kerr, late Hospital Steward at Andersonville, James Duncan, Wesley W. Turner, Benjamin Harris, and others, whose names are unknown, and who were then engaged in armed rebellion against the United States, maliciously and traitorously, and in violating the laws of war, to impair and injure the health and destroy the lives by subjecting torture and great suffering, by confining in unhealthy and unwholesome quarters, by exposing to the inclemency of winter and to the dews and burning sun of Summer, by compelling the use of impure water, and by furnishing insufficient and unwholesome food, of large numbers of Federal prisoners, to wit: The number of about 45,000 held as prisoners of war at Andersonville, within the lines of the so-called Confederate States, on or before the 27th of March, 1865, and at divers times between that day and the 10th day of April, 1865, to the end that the armies of the United States might be weakened and impaired, and that the insurgents engaged in armed rebellion against the United States might be aided and comforted, etc. The order states that the prisoner was found guilty of the second charge, namely: Murder, in violation of the laws and customs of war, and guilty of all the specifications, excepting the 4th, 10th, and 13th, which three set forth that he killed a prisoner by shooting him with a revolver, that he ordered a sentinel to fire upon another with a revolver, and that he shot another with a revolver, so that he died. The order concludes as follows: Sentence—And the Court do therefore sentence him, Henry Wirz, to be hanged by the neck until he be dead, at such time and place as the President of the United States may direct, two-thirds of the members of the Court concurring therein. And the Court also find the prisoner, Henry Wirz, guilty of having caused the death in the manner as alleged in specification 11, charge 2, by means of dogs, of three prisoners of war, in his custody, and soldiers of the United States, one occurring on or about the 15th day of May, 1864, another occurring on or about the 11th day of July, 1864; another occurring on or about the 1st day of September, 1864; but which finding, as here expressed, has not and did not enter into the sentence of the Court as before given.

Second, The proceedings, finding and sentence in the foregoing case having been submitted to the President of the United States, the following are his orders:

"EXECUTIVE MANSION, Nov. 3, 1865.

The proceedings, finding and sentence of the Court in the within case, are approved, and it is ordered that the sentence be carried into execution by the officer commanding the Department of Washington, on Friday, the tenth day of November, 1865, between the hours of six o'clock in the morning and 12 o'clock noon.

ANDREW JOHNSON,
President of the United States.

Third, Major General C. C. Augur, Commanding the Department of Washington, is commanded to cause the foregoing sentence, in the case of Henry Wirz, to be duly executed in accordance with the President's order.

Fourth, The Military Commission, of which Major General Lewis Wallace, U. S. Vols., is President, is hereby dissolved, by command of the President of the United States.

(Signed) E. D. TOWNSEND, A. A. G.

Wirz conversed with those on the platform with seeming calmness and self-possession, and it was remarked that he had a smiling countenance. To his spiritual adviser he said: "I am innocent. I have to die, but I can die like a man. I have hope in the future. I have nothing more to say." His legs and hands were tied, the noose passed around his neck, and the black cap placed over his face. He stood erect without faltering, evidently having nerved himself for the solemn event. Those on the platform retired to the railing, leaving the doomed man in the centre of the structure. After a few moments of profound quiet, the drop, at a preconcerted signal, fell. The sounds thus occasioned, having reached the ears of the promiscuous crowd outside of the Old Capitol grounds, but who were not privileged to view the execution, was responded to by repeated shouts of approbation. The convict, directly after falling, was considerably convulsed in his legs, but the agony was soon over. He hung about fifteen minutes, and then was cut down. His body was laid upon a stretcher and conveyed to the prison, where it was placed in a coffin and transferred to Father Boyle for interment. His neck was broken by the fall. All the proceedings occupied about three-fourths of an hour.

SECOND DISPATCH.

Washington, Nov. 10 P. M.—Mr. Schade again waited upon the President this morning, to make a final effort to save Capt. Wirz from the death penalty, but at that time, unknown to him, the prisoner had been hanged. The President, however, could see no reason for changing the sentence, and stated that Mr. Schade was the only one who made an earnest appeal in behalf of the prisoner. When between 8 and 9 A. M. Mr. Schade took leave of Captain Wirz, the latter expressed his thanks for what he had done for him, and regretted that it was not in his power to reward him. Mr. Schade said he believed he would die like a man, to which Captain Wirz replied, "It is hardly necessary to tell me that I intend to die like a man." Mr. Schade says he was called upon by several persons last night, as was also Father Boyle, who communicated information purporting to come from a member of the Cabinet, to the effect that if Wirz would acknowledge that Jeff. Davis was connected with the atrocities at Andersonville his sentence should be commuted. Although Mr. Schade did not place full confidence in the reports, he considered it to be his duty to relate the rumor to the prisoner at his last conference with him. Capt. Wirz, in reply said: "Mr. Schade you know I have always told you that I did not know anything about Jeff. Davis. He had no connection with me as to what was done at Andersonville, and if I knew he had I would not become a traitor against him or any one else to save my life." Among his last acts Capt. Wirz addressed a letter to Mr. O. S. Baker, one of his counsel, in which he remarked he had not said a word that could be construed into a reflection upon him. He merely stated that he had not solicited him as his counsel at first, but accepted of his services cheerfully. He concluded as follows: "I will say again, as I said before that I believe you have done all you could for me, and therefore accept my thanks—the thanks of a dying man." The following letter was written by Wirz before mounting the gallows:

OLD CAPITOL PRISON, Nov. 10th, 1865.

"MR. SCHADE, Dear Sir:—It is no doubt for the last time I address myself to you what I have said to you often and often I repeat; accept my thanks, my sincere heartfelt thanks for all you have done for me. May God reward you; I cannot, still I have something more to ask of you and I am confident that you will not refuse to receive my dying request. Please help my poor family; my dear wife and children. War, cruel war has swept everything from me and to-day my wife, my children are beggars. My life is demanded as an atonement. I am willing to give it; and I hope that after a while I will be judged differently from what I am now. If any one ought to come to the relief of my family it is the people of the South, for whose sake I have sacrificed all. I know you will excuse me for troubling you again—Farewell, dear sir. May God bless you! Your thankful."

H. WIRZ.

Past Life of Capt. Wirz.

Of the personal history of this notorious criminal, or so much of it as relates to his career since his arrival in this country, in 1849, the following is a correct summary, condensed from the detailed narrative of Wirz himself:

Henry Wirz was born in Zurich, Switzerland, in November, 1823, in which city his father and brother still reside—the father holding office in the Custom House, the brother being blind. Early apprenticed to a profession for which he had no esteem, he soon left his employer, and shortly afterwards, finding all efforts to induce his father to allow him the choice of his favorite profession in vain, he left his home and is next heard of in Italy, through which country he travelled extensively until 1849, when he sailed for the United States. Arriving at New York, he endeavored to obtain a situation in this city as assistant physician, but being unable to speak the English language, the effort proved unavailing. From New York, Wirz next proceeded to Connecticut, where he remained nearly six months, when he quit that State, and proceeded to Lawrence, Mass., where he worked as a weaver. From thence he went to Northampton, in the same State, where he found employment as superintendent of a water-cure establishment. While acting in that capacity, Wirz formed the acquaintance of one Dr. Webber, from Kentucky, in whose employ he was soon engaged, and with whom he went to Hopkinsville, Kentucky. His roving disposition still predominating, he soon quit the Doctor's service, and proceeded from thence to Louisville, Ky., where he remained until the fall of 1855, when he received and accepted the offer of overseer on a plantation in Natches, Miss., where he remained until the breaking out of the rebellion. When, in 1861, the demon of rebellion sounded the alarm for the army of its worshipers, Wirz was one of the earliest to enlist against his adopted country, joining an independent company of Louisiana troops as a private. This company was soon marched to Richmond where it was detailed for guard duty at Howard's Factory prison. A few days after its arrival here, Wirz still acting in the capacity of private, was promoted to the rank of orderly, to the officer then in command of that post. One day, while at leisure, Wirz, in glancing over the books of the prison, discovered that no roll of the prisoners had as yet been attempted, an omission which he immediately assumed the responsibility of supplying. While engaged in this self-imposed task, Gen. Winder, then in command of the prisons in Richmond, happened into the room occupied by Wirz, and observing the newly installed clerk, inquired his name and employment. Winder appeared much pleased at the effort, remarking, "Just the thing we want, my man," at the same time inquiring particularly of the rank of the subaltern, and promising an immediate consideration of his case with regard to a promotion. Two days after this Wirz was promoted to the rank of sergeant, and ordered on detached service. In December, 1861, Wirz was ordered to prepare for the removal of several hundred of the prisoners then under his command at Howard's factory prison, to a military prison in Tuscaloosa, Ala., and who, in company with an officer from the last named post, he was to accompany to their new quarters. Here he remained as a minor officer of the prison until May, 1862, when the institution was broken up, and the prisoners removed to Montgomery. From this point Wirz immediately returns to Richmond, when he is again promoted, at the instigation of his friend Winder, to the rank of Captain, and immediately detailed as Aid-de-Camp to Gen. Joe Johnston, in which capacity he served during the memoriable Fair Oaks battle, and during which he received a severe wound in the arm, which was a source of annoyance to him up to the time of his death. Incapacitated for field service, he was next appointed Assistant Provost Marshal at Manchester, Va., in which capacity he served nearly two weeks, when, tiring of the office, he was relieved on his own solicitation. This occurred at a time when the subject of a general exchange of prisoners was being first agitated. While in Richmond, soliciting his discharge from the duties of Provost Marshal, circumstances forced him into an acquaintance with Commissioner Ould, who suggested to him the task of proceeding throughout the South to ascertain the whereabouts and number of Federal prisoners. This offer was acceptable to Wirz, and after some delay, occasioned by the refusal of Winder to grant the necessary leave of absence, permission was obtained from the War Department. From Richmond Wirz proceeded to Petersburgh, and from thence successively to Macon, Ga., Shreveport, Vicksburgh, and Austin, Texas, visiting the various depots for prisoners for the requisite lists. This task accomplished, Wirz is next heard of in Richmond, and acting in the capacity of Chief of "Secret Police" of that city. This office, however, also proved distasteful to Wirz, who, finding all attempts to be relieved from the position unavailing, tried the "sick" dodge, which proved successful, when he obtained a 30 days' furlough, for the purpose of visiting his family in Tuscaloosa. At the expiration of this term he was again ordered to report to Richmond, where he soon received orders from the Secretary of the Navy to accompany a large quantity of guns and ammunition, destined for General Kirby Smith, then in command of the trans-Mississippi Department. With these he proceeded as far as Port Hudson, La., beyond which point they could not be transported, owing to the strict blockade of the Red River by a portion of our navy, under Farragut. Seeing the guns at this point, Wirz again returns to Richmond. His wounds now again becoming troublesome, incapacitating him from further service, he applied for and received a furlough of four months, receiving permission to visit Europe in the interval, where he proposed to have a surgical operation performed upon his arm. To accomplish this voyage, he secured passage (after borrowing some $16,000 in Confederate money, which he converted into rebel bonds) on one of the blockade-runners plying between Wilmington and Liverpool, paying for the passage $100 in gold. Serious reverses—such as the fall of Port Hudson, and the defeat of Lee at Gettysburg—occurring during the interval between his departure from home and arrival in England, he discovered, upon his arrival at Liverpool, that Confederate securities had depreciated in value to a fearful extent—being then quoted at about ten cents on the dollar. In this unenviable condition, with barely sufficient funds to pay for a return passage, Wirz was forced to beg the loan of a few hundred pounds from a secession sympathizer in London, with which he was enable to complete his contemplated tour through England, including a visit to his father, in Switzerland. Returning to Richmond in February, 1864, Wirz was next ordered to Augusta, where he was to attend to the Federal prisoners passing through that city on their way to Andersonville. Here he remained for two weeks, when he was ordered to Andersonville to relieve W. S. Winder, then in command of that military prison. It is there that the fiendish disposition of the inhuman monster first reveals itself. Merciless and cruel, wreaking his vengeance in torture and starvation, on the helpless prisoners placed under his charge, his subsequent history is a ghastly record of blood, with which the world is already too familiar. Wirz leaves a wife and child, a daughter of ten years, who reside at Cadiz, Kentucky.

Reorganization.

A Tight Rein to be Kept upon the Ex-Rebel States.

Washington, Nov. 10.—It is ascertained from an official source that the army of the United States has not been reduced so low as seems to have been supposed. Its full and available strength exceeds 180,000 men, of which about half is on each side of the Mississippi River.

To-day members of the late North Carolina Convention and other gentlemen of that State, visited the President, when Hon. Mr. Reade, on behalf of the Convention over which he had the honor to preside, presented for his favorable consideration, certain of its proceedings, saying, among other things, that the first act of the Convention was to declare her uninterrupted connexion with the Union, and that the ordinance of May, 1861, by which she was attempted to be severed, was null and void. This was done by a vote very nearly approaching unanimity; and thus the first issue in the late war was yielded. The next thing done was to prohibit slavery, and this was done by an unanimous vote; and a committee of able lawyers was provided to prepare wholesome laws for the consideration of the Legislature; and thus the second issue in the late war was yielded. The Convention having yielded what was involved in the war, and being of the opinion that the State was, and always had been, in the Union, and that our relations had only been disturbed and not destroyed, respectfully asks your excellency to declare, on the part of the authorities of the United States, as the State has done on her part, that our Government relations have been reconciled. The Convention instructed the Legislature to provide for the payment of the debts of the State; declared all debts contracted in aid of the rebellion to be illegal, and prohibited the payment of the same. Mr. Read said, "We have heard that notwithstanding the State might yield, and as he understands it, has yielded all that was involved in the war, and notwithstanding our people were submissive, well disposed, and anxious for fraternal relations, her delegation in Congress would not be admitted unless they had qualifications not prescribed by the Constitution; that they would be required to take an oath which few men in the State can take, affirming not merely that they are right now, but that they have never done wrong. The exclusion of her delegation upon any such test as is suggested, would be felt by our people universally as such a deep wrong, that it would put their strong devotion to the Government and their lively hope of perfect reconciliation to the severest trial. They can understand the bitterness of strife and the aversion to treason, but they will be confounded at the repulsion of offered friendship and avowed loyalty. The Convention, therefore, respectfully asks Congress to repeal the test oath. I have thought it respectful both to you and to Congress, that this request should pass through your hands, with the hope that your Excellency's magnanimity would add to it some reflection which would avail that body."

After further remarks by Mr. Reid, in which he spoke of the confidence reposed in him by North Carolina, the President responded as follows:

HON. MR. REID—I received from you, with pleasure, a copy of the proceedings of the Convention of North Carolina. I reciprocate cordially the conciliatory spirit in which you have addressed me. The Convention of North Carolina has done much and well towards restoring that State to her proper national relations, but something yet remains to be done to render that restoration immediately practicable. An acceptation of the Congressional amendment abolishing slavery throughout the United States, by the Legislature of the State of North Carolina, is in my judgment practically important to the successful restoration which is so much desired by all. Without answering specifically the questions you have proposed to me, it will be sufficient to say that my action must depend upon events, and that Mr. Holden will be again instructed to continue the exercise of his functions as Provisional Governor until he shall have been expressly relieved by orders to that effect.

The following is a copy of the telegram addressed to his Excellency B. F. Perry, Provisional Governor of South Carolina:

Your letter of the 4th is just now received. While much has been done in South Carolina that is conducive to peace and restoration, the President still thinks that it is impossible to anticipate events. He expects, therefore, that you will continue to exercise the duties heretofore devolved upon you as Provisional Governor of South Carolina, until you shall be relieved by his order. He observes with regret that neither the Convention nor the State Legislature has pronounced the debts and obligations contracted in the name of the State for unconstitutional, and even rebellious purposes, to be void. He equally regrets that the State seems to decline the Congressional amendment of the Constitution of the United States, abolishing slavery. I telegraphed to you yesterday as follows:—"The President directs me to write to you that an early adoption of the Congressional amendment of the Constitution of the United States, abolishing slavery by the South Carolina Legislature, is deemed peculiarly important, and especially desirable with reference to the general situation of the Union." I have now only to say the President's opinions, before expressed, remain unchanged.

W. H. SEWARD.

Death of the Only Brother of President Johnson.

Washington, Nov. 10.—A dispatch was received this morning, by the Secretary of the Treasury, from E. W. Shelton, Special Agent, dated Galveston, 4th, via New Orleans, 6th instant, announcing the death of William Johnson, Esq., the only brother of the President of the United States, and the Collector at Velasco. He died from the effects of an accidental gunshot wound.

Death of Hon. Jacob Collamer.

Montpelier, Vt., Nov. 10.—Hon. Jacob Collamer, United States Senator from Vermont, died at his residence in Woodstock last evening at ten o'clock. The Vermont Legislature adjourned *sine die* at eight o'clock this morning.

[Hon. Jacob Collamer was born in Troy, New York, but removed, when a child, to Burlington, Vermont. He graduated at the College there in 1810. He served in the army in the war of 1812; studied law and was admitted to practice in 1813. From 1833 to 1841 he was Judge of the Supreme Court. In 1843 he was elected to Congress, where he served for six years. In 1849 he was made Postmaster General by President Taylor. In 1850 he resigned, and was made a Judge in Vermont, which place he held until 1854. He was then elected United States Senator, and in 1861 was again elected to the same place. His term would expire in 1867. Judge Collamer was much respected by all who knew him, and his judgment in political matters was always governed by the principles of integrity which controlled his whole life.]

POLITICAL INTELLIGENCE:

North Carolina.

Raleigh, N. C., Nov. 10.—Nine Counties heard from officially, give Holden, Governor, 3,878, and Worth, 5,489. Worth friends claim his election, though Holden's do not give it up.

Maryland.

Baltimore, Nov. 10.—Latest returns from the 12th Judicial District indicate the election of Spence, Union candidate, provided certain illegal votes, taken in disregard of the Registry Law, shall be thrown out. Union men claim that the law was openly disregarded in some districts.

Nevada.

San Francisco, Nov. 9.—The State election in Nevada for local officers, members of the Legislature and Congressmen, took place on the 7th inst. D. R Ashley, Republican, for Congress, has about 1,000 majority.

Alabama.

Mobile, Nov. 9.—Langdon is undeniably elected to Congress. Mr. Langdon was an Old Line Whig in other days. He was recently Mayor of Mobile,—where he has long been known as a steady going, clear headed conservatiae.

Important from South America:

Spain Declares War Against Chili—A Blockade Proclaimed—Arrogant Conduct of the Spanish Admiral—Panic in Valparaiso—Run on the Banks, Etc.

The steamship Ocean Queen, from Aspinwall Nov. 1st, arrived at this port yesterday morning. By this arrival we have important intelligence from South America. *Spain has formally declared war against Chili.* The Panama STAR of Oct. 31st says:

On the 18th of September—the 56th anniversary of the country's liberation from Spanish rule—the Spanish Admiral Pareja sent to the Government, demanding immediate satisfaction from Chili for insults said to have been offered to Spain, and that if in four days the reparation he demanded was not given, he would proceed to extreme measures. It will be remembered that the Spanish Minister, Senor Tavira, months ago, acting with full powers from his Government, accepted as satisfactory the declarations of the Chilian Ministers on the question that had been at issue; and the anxiety which had at that time prevailed, gave place to feelings of assurance that friendly relations were to continue with Spain. But now Senor Tavira is summarily recalled, and Pareja, invested with full powers, proceeds, on the moment of his reaching Chilian waters, to demand, not the reopening of the questions, nor to state why his Government overturns what their accredited minister had done in their name, but peremptorily to demand that Chili shall humble herself to salute the Spanish flag in token of submission, and thereby admit that Spain was in the right, after which he would be prepared to state what satisfaction his Government might accept.

The Government replied on the 22d, that Chili would not accede to Pareja's demands, upon receiving which the Amiral immediately forwarded an "ultimatum" that hostile measures the next day would be adopted, and on the 24th, declared the Chilian ports blockaded. The Congress refused the "ultimatum," declared war, and authorized a loan of twenty million dollars for that purpose. Admiral Pareja had issued a circular allowing ten days to neutral vessels to continue discharging, or loading for a neutral port.

The affair created quite a panic in the city, and a run was immediately made upon the banks, who were compelled to suspend cash payments.

The latest advices state that Chili was preparing, with great energy, to resist the demands of the Admiral. The conduct of Pareja, it is expected, will involve him in difficulties with the foreign powers. With England a collision had already arisen out of the capture of the steamer Mattas Cousino, which sailed under the English flag. The Admiral when he saw that he had made a "mistake," not only immediately released the vessel, but offered an apology for the insult to the flag. The Italian counsel at Valapariso had also protested against the arbitrary measures adopted by the Admiral. Considerable correspondence has passed between the foreign consuls, who "consider it their duty" to ask the Commander in Chief of H. C. M. Squadron in the Pacific, that he be good enough to indicate to them those ports of the coasts of Chile where the blockade has been established.

Pareja replies, by stating that his government have ordered the blockade of all the ports, which he will endeavor to accomplish. The President has given an order, dated October 7th, which cannot fail to offer a splendid opportunity for blockade running. Said order allows the importation and exportation of goods by foreign vessels, free of custom house duties of any kind, in all of the more considerable of the smaller harbors and inlets along the coast, 38 in number.

Haytia.

Trouble Between the Rebels and the English—A British Ship Blown Up.

Captain Potter, of the brig Henry and Louise, from Port au Prince, arrived to-day, reports as follows: News had reached that city that the British war ship Bulldog, of twelve guns, was blown up by her commander on the 25th at Cape Haytien. It appears the British Consul had some Haytians under his protection, and Salnave, the rebel leader, made a demand for them, which the Consul refused, and he then broke in the doors and took the Haytians out and shot them. The British ship Bulldog was lying in port and her commander asked for satisfaction and receiving no answer, began firing on Fort Peckelet; and the fort replied, and by some mismanagement of the commander he got his ship on a reef, and after getting his men into the boats he set fire to the ship and she blew up. It was reported that the commander got on board one of President Geffrard's boats and left for Jamaica. The affairs of the country are in a very unsettled state.

From Europe.

Funeral of Lord Palmerston.

The Steamships Etna and Cuba brings files containing full accounts of the funeral of Lord Palmerston, which took place Oct. 27th, The London STAR of the 28th inst. says:

While crowds were gathering in front of Cambridge House and along the line of route, the City of London presented a very peculiar appearance, as in almost every direction there were indications of the sincere desire entertained by the inhabitants to exhibit respect to the memory of the deceased statesman. The Royal Exchange, the Stock Exchange, and the Guildhall were entirely closed, as were nearly all houses of business throughout the country. Vast numbers of people were early astir, taking up positions in those thoroughfares through which it had been announced that the procession would pass. Of course the chief centre of attraction was in Piccadilly, near Cambridge House, the town residence of the late noble lord. The route taken by the procession was thronged by an immense concourse of people, and the balconies of houses were crowded with ladies and gentlemen. The procession reached Westminster Abbey exactly at one o'clock. It was remarked that along the entire route, when the hearse passed, people not only in the balconies of the houses, but many of those in the crowd respectfully raised their hats. At some few minutes after twelve o'clock the gates of Marlborough House were thrown open, and soon after the blind of one of the bay windows was raised, and some ladies were observed to take up their position there. To the evident delight of all who were fortunate enough to be located at the opposite side of Pall Mall, the centre lady was soon recognized as the Princess of Wales. At twenty minutes past twelve o'clock precisely the head of the funeral procession turned the corner of St. James's street and entered Pall Mall. As if to escape notice as much as possible, just as the procession turned into Pall Mall, which caused nearly all eyes to be turned in that direction, a closed private carriage and pair, with two footmen, came out from Marlborough House and drove round into the park. This quiet looking carriage contained the Prince of Wales. His Royal Highness went by the park to Westminster Abbey, where he was received by the Very Rev. the Dean of Westminster, and conducted to the Royal stall. In singular contrast to the bustle and stir which was everywhere prevalent in the streets, those within the Abbey sat or stood expectant in a cold and decorous silence. A sombre crowd of persons filled the long avenues of the nave, but the spaces immediately adjoining the grave were kept vacant for future use. In the south transept a large gallery, draped in black cloth, was erected, whereon were ranged a considerable number of the late statesman's colleagues, among whom we recognized many of the men best known in England. At a few moments before one, the coffin arrived at the west door of the Abbey, were it was met by the Archdeacon of Westminster, Lord Thyne, Archdean Wadsworth, and a host of others. The opening sentences of the burial service was then chaunted by the choir. Meanwhile, there came up the nave and through the sacrarium a procession of boys dressed in white, followed by certain funereal figures, bearing before them the nodding plumes of the hearse. Then followed the coronet of Lord Palmerston, borne upon a crimson velvet cushion, and immediately behind came the coffin itself, to which all eyes were at once directed. The Prince of Wales, who had followed the coffin thus far, left the procession to take his seat next the Dean's stall; while the coffin was placed under the lantern, the late lord's coronet being placed upon its top, the 90th psalm, "Lord, thou hast been our refuge, &c.," was sung by the choir, followed by the reading of the 15th chapter of St. Paul's Epistle to the Corinthians. Those who had formed the procession now came up through the choir and followed the corse—Dean Stanley being in front, accompanied by the Prince of Wales and the Duke of Cambridge. The coffin, stripped of its covering, was then placed by the side of the grave, while the procession gradually poured in and surrounded the small black incision in the floor, which seemed so petty a thing in that great space. At the foot of the grave stood the chief mourners; at the head stood the bearer of the coronet; the Prince of Wales and the Duke of Cambridge occupied a raised platform to the left of the Dean's stall; by the side of the grave were the pall bearers, while further out was the semicircle of people formed by those who had come up from the choir. The choristers were ranged on the east side of the transept, opposite the Dean; and when the coffin had been thus deposited they proceeded to sing "Man that is born of a woman hath but a short time to live, and is full of misery;" and as the last notes died down in a deep bass the coffin, at a quarter to two o'clock, was lowered into the grave. Dean Stanley then read the next lesson, followed by the reading of the prayer and collect. The voice of the Dean was then heard, midst the thundering of the organ, pronouncing the Benediction, and we knew the ceremony was over

News Items.

[By Telegraph to the New York Sun.]

GOV. BUCKINGHAM, of Connecticut, has also postponed Thanksgiving Day until the 7th of December.

GOVERNOR BRADFORD, of Maryland, has issued a proclamation for Thanksgiving, appointing the day named by the President.

THE amount of money stolen from the American Express at Chicago, on Sunday morning, was only $40,000. The robbers were arrested on Thursday night, and all the money was recovered.

THERE was a destructive fire on Thursday night at Philadelphia, at Bancroft's Mills, between Media and Chester streets. One of the largest factories, with contents, was destroyed. Loss $50,000.

THE Governor of Maryland has offered a reward of $500 for the arrest of the incendiaries who destroyed the colored Methodist Church at Midlington, Kent county. The motive was that the building was used as a day school for colored children.

A DISPATCH from Lawrence, Kansas, says the Indians are becoming troublesome again on the plains. On Monday last they attacked the whites at Pole Creek, and captured the mail, ambulance, mules and some Government horses. Gen. Heath is reported to have recently had a battle with them and killed twenty nine redskins.

A RENCONTRE took place yesterday at Alexandria, Va., between Dr. Maddox, of Fauquier County, and Major Dixon, Paymaster in the United States army. Major Dixon received a ball in the side, penetrating the bowels. His speedy death is pronounced certain. Dr. Maddox has surrendered himself up to the civil authorities.

TREATIES have been concluded with nine powerful Indian tribes, including the Winneconjoes, Blackfeet, Sioux and Two Kettle Sioux—numbering about 6,200 souls, and portions of the Yanctons, Sans Arics and Onppapahs, representing about 6,400 souls. The latest telegram from Major General Curtis states that information had been received from other powerful tribes of their desire to meet the Commissioners and treat for peace. The Department is also advised of treaties with the Cheyennes, Arrapoes, Osages, Apaches, Camanches and Kiowas—numbering some 12,000 or 15,000 souls.

General Intelligence.

[By Mail to the New York Sun.]

DURING December and January next there is to be an exhibition of Italian grown cotton at Naples.

A MONUMENT, seventy-four feet high, to O'Connell, was lately inaugurated at Ennis, Ireland.

A HOSPITAL for cancer and skin diseases has been added to the benevolent institutions of Liverpool.

THE war claims against the National Governments of the States of Illinois, Ohio, Wisconsin, New York, Delaware and Minnesota have been settled by the Treasury Department.

RUFUS M. WRIGHT's outbuildings at Worthington, Mass., were burned on Tuesday evening, with thirty tons of hay, ten cattle and thirty sheep. The house was saved with great exertion. No insurance.

THERE is talk in St. Petersburg, Russia, of a further reduction in the Russian army. Sixty thousand soldiers, it is said, will be sent to their homes. Moreover, the term of military service, which is at present fifteen years, is to be reduced to seven. A few years ago it was twenty-eight.

A GREAT land slide occurred at Race Bond, Tenn., forty miles above Memphis, recently. A portion of the bank, about 300 feet in length, and 75 in depth, fell down like an avalanche on the barges near the shore, containing 2,400 bales of hay, crushing them to atoms.

AN appeal to the women of Ireland has been published by the wives of some of the Fenian prisoners in Dublin. It sets forth the state of destitution into which they have been plunged, attributing it to the acts of the British Government. The address avows sympathy with the prisoners, and yet appeals to the women of Ireland of all creeds and politics to contribute to their support.

ON the 28th ult., the following dispatch from Liverpool appeared in the London papers: "The steamer Mexican, from Colon, which has arrived here, reports having passed in latitude 42 north, longitude 40 west, a large bright barrel, with a pole attached. It appeared to be stationary, as if buoyed, and it was supposed to be one of the Atlantic telegraph buoys."

THE election of the Hon. N. P. Banks to Congress from the sixth district of Massachusetts, was one of the greatest triumphs of his life. He had four-fifths of all the votes cast. He was in Boston, in the evening, where he was congratulated upon his success by Anson Burlingame, Senator Wilson, Gov. Andrew, A. H. Bullock, Gov. elect, Charles Sumner, Gov. Parsons, of Alabama, and Henry Ward Beecher.

THE Jamaica Colonial STANDARD, of Oct. 16th, publishes the official report of the British General Nelson, in command at Morant Bay, in which he asserts that every Jamaica insurrectionist is being summarily hung as soon as captured. Also that Her Majesty's gunboat opened fire upon a collection of about 800 women and children: that after three shells from her 32-pounders were exploded among them they were dispersed. The howl of the English press over this brutality is impatiently awaited.

GEORGE ARNOLD, better known to the public under the signature of "McArone," died at his home, Strawberry Farms, New Jersey, Thursday morning, in the thirty-second year of his age. Though young in years, he was old in intellectual culture and polish, having written many and excellent poetical and prose contributions for the periodicals of the day. He was a constant writer for, among other publications, the ATLANTIC MONTHLY, HARPER'S MAGAZINE, the LEADER and WEEKLY REVIEW. He wrote, as a cotemporary remarks, "with surprising facility, stories, poems, essays, reviews, editorials and witticisms," and his demise will be mourned by a large circle of friends and acquaintances. His various writings will probably be collected and published in book form. He died from the effects of a stroke of paralysis.

(Continued on the Last Page.)

THE SUN.

IT SHINES FOR ALL

Number 10,428. NEW YORK, TUESDAY, DECEMBER 19, 1865. Thirty-Third Year.

The Latest News

By Telegraph to the N. Y. Sun.

SAFE AT LAST!

Slavery Legally Abolished!!

Notification by Secretary Seward.

IMPORTANT FROM ALABAMA.

The State Fully Reconstructed.

Provisional Governor Parsons Relieved.

Explosion at the Capitol.

THE WHOLE CITY SHAKEN.

Several Persons Killed.

PROCEEDINGS OF CONGRESS.

Important Business Transacted.

SPEECH OF MR. STEVENS.

THE EX-REBEL STATES.

Extreme Radical Views.

LATER EUROPEAN NEWS.

The Fenian Trials.

TWO MORE VICTIMS.

Mexican Affairs.

10,000 AUSTRIANS FOR MAX.

Death of the King of Belgium.

&c., &c., &c.

SLAVERY LEGALLY DEAD.

Notification by Secretary Seward.

Washington, Dec. 18.—The following notification has been issued:

William H. Seward, Secretary of State of the United States.

To all to whom these Presents may come, Greeting:

Know ye that, whereas the Congress of the United States, on the first of February last passed a resolution, which is in the words following, namely:

"A resolution submitting to the Legislatures of the several States a proposition to amend the Constitution of the United States.

"*Resolved*, by the Senate and House of Representatives of the United States of America in Congress assembled, two-thirds of both Houses concurring, than the following Article be proposed to the Legislatures of the several States as an amendment to the Constitution of the United States, which, when ratified by three-fourths of said Legislatures, shall be valid to all intents and purposes as a part of said Constitution, namely:

"ARTICLE XIII.—Section 1.—Neither slavery nor involuntary servitude, except as a punishment for crime whereof the party shall have been duly convicted, shall exist within the United States or any place subject to their jurisdiction.

"Section 2.—Congress shall have power to enforce this article by appropriate legislation."

And, whereas, it appears from official documents on file in this Department that the amendment to the Constitution of the United States, proposed as aforesaid, has been ratified by the Legislatures of the States of Illinois, Rhode Island, Michigan, Maryland, New York, West Virginia, Maine, Kansas, Massachusetts, Pennsylvania, Virginia, Ohio, Missouri, Nevada, Indiana, Louisiana, Minnesota, Wisconsin, Vermont, Tennessee, Arkansas, Connecticut, New Hampshire, South Carolina, Alabama, North Carolina and Georgia, in all twenty-seven States;

And, whereas, the whole number of States in the United States is thirty-six,

And whereas, the before specially named States, whose Legislatures have ratified the said proposed amendment, constitute three fourths of the whole number of States in the United States;

Now, therefore, be it known that I, William H. Seward, Secretary of State of the United States, by virtue and in pursuance of the second section of the Act of Congress, approved the 20th of April, 1818, entitled "An Act to provide for the publication of the Laws of the United States and for other purposes," do hereby certify that the amendment aforesaid has become valid to all intents and purposes as a part of the Constitution of the United States.

In testimony whereof I have hereunto set my hand and caused the seal of the Department of State to be affixed. Done at the City of Washington, this 18th day of December, in the year of our Lord 1865, and of the Independence of the United States of America the 90th.

WM. H. SEWARD,
Secretary of State.

Alabama.

Provisional Governor Parsons Relieved.

Washington, Dec. 18.—The following has been addressed by Mr. Seward to Mr. Parsons:

DEPARTMENT OF STATE,
WASHINGTON, Dec. 18. 1865.

To His Excellency Lewis E. Parsons, Provisional Governor of the State of Alabama, Montgomery, Ala.:—*Sir*,—The time has arrived, in the judgment of the President of the United States, when the care and conduct of the proper affairs of the State of Alabama may be remitted to the constitutional authorities chosen by the people thereof, without danger to the peace and safety of the United States. By direction of the President of the United States, therefore, you are relieved from the trust which was heretofore reposed in you as Provisional Governor of the State of Alabama. Whenever the Governor elect shall have accepted and become qualified to discharge the duties of the executive office, you will transfer the papers and property of the State now in your custody to His Excellency the Governor elect. It gives me especial pleasure to convey to you the President's acknowledgment of the fidelity, the loyalty and the discretion which have marked your administration. You will please give me a reply specifying the day on which this communication is received.

(Signed,) WM. H. SEWARD.

TERRIBLE EXPLOSION.

Washington Shaken To Its Foundations—Several Persons Killed.

Washington, Dec. 18.—An explosion took place this afternoon, about 2 o'clock, in a small building situated at the Arsenal, and in which workmen were engaged in sorting ammunition, removing cartridges, etc., which was most terrible and disastrous in its effects. The force of the explosion was felt at remote distances in the city. Several persons are reported killed and several others are so badly hurt that their recovery is deemed impossible. They are all employes, who have formerly been in the army, and who have been given work at the arsenal. The house in which the explosion took place was demolished and soon became a mass of flames. The exertions of the firemen, who were soon at the scene of the disaster, extinguished the flames of the ruined building, and thus prevented a conflagration which would have proved very calamitous, as other buildings near by were stored with ammunition. The following parties are known to be killed: Jeremiah Mahony, Patrick Riordan, James Moran, Michael McDermott, John Teely, Marshall Whiteley, John Mohan and Peter Garichey. The 214th Pennsylvania Regiment was on duty at that post, and rendered valuable assistance. The bodies of some those injured are torn in a horrible manner.

SAD NEWS.

Death of Governor Corwin.

Washington, Dec. 18.—Governor Corwin died at half-past two o'clock this afternoon. Present in the chamber at the time of his death were, Senators Davis and Guthrie, of Kentucky, and Lane, of Indiana, and J. C. Wetmore, Esq., and others.

Thomas Corwin was born in Kentucky, on the 29th of July, 1794. His father, who soon after the birth of Thomas removed to Ohio, was a farmer, and the first twenty years of Corwin's life was passed in tilling the soil, and obtaining enough schooling to enable him, in the Winter of 1816, to abandon farming and enter upon the study of law. In 1818 he was admitted to practice, and a few years later was a rising man in this profession. In 1822 he was a member of the State Legislature, and in 1831 was sent to Congress by his constituents. He represented the Warren [Ohio] district until 1840, when he was elected Governor of the State. In 1845 the Whigs in the Legislature of Ohio elected Mr. Corwin United States Senator, and during the Mexican war, Senator Corwin "led the opposition," denouncing the war in unmeasured terms. In 1850 Mr. Fillmore appointed Governor Corwin "Secretary of the Treasury." In 1858 Mr. Corwin was again elected to Congress. In 1860 Mr. Lincoln apointed him U. S. Minister to Mexico, a position that he held until quite recently, when he returned home to resign his office, and as it appears to end a somewhat brilliant career.

POLITICAL INTELLIGENCE.

North Carolina.

Raleigh, N. C., Dec. 18.—The Legislature of this State adjourned this morning, to meet again on the first of February next. No law was passed or bill presented for the government and protection of the freedmen.

California.

Sacramento, Dec. 16.—The Legislature to-day elected Cornelius Cole U. S. Senator, to succeed Mr. McDougall.

CONGRESSIONAL PROCEEDINGS.

Thirty-ninth Session.

SENATE.

Washington, Dec. 18.—Mr. Grimes presented the petition of Vice Admiral Farragut and eleven hundred other naval officers, asking for an increase of pay, which was referred to the Committee on Naval Affairs.

A resolution was passed instructing the Secretary of the Senate to pay out of the Contingent Fund to Mrs. Mary Collamer the amount due to Hon. Jacob Collamer at the time of his death.

Mr. Doolittle, from the Committee on Indian Affairs, reported a resolution, which was adopted, for the expenditure of five hundred thousand dollars for the support of destitute Indians in the Southern dependencies, and the purchase of agricultural implements for said Indians, the money to be taken from a fund of twelve hundred thousand dollars now in the possession of the Secretary of the Interior for such purpose.

Mr. Wilson offered a resolution providing for the appointment of an examining board to relieve officers of the regular army who have not rendered meritorious service in the late war, and to fill their places by appointments from the regular army Veteran Reserve Corps and the volunteer force; which was referred to the Military Committee.

Mr. Wilson explained the object of the above resolution. He said there were men in the regular army who had rendered no service, comparatively, during the war; while many, who had commanded corps and divisions, would have to return to subordinate positions in the regular army. It was the object of the resolution to enable the country to take advantage of the experience which many officers in the regular and volunteer service had obtained in the past four years.

Mr. Fessenden called up the House bill for the refurnishing and repairing of the President's House, which was passed.

Mr. Wilson offered the following, which was adopted:

Resolved, That the Committee on Commerce be instructed to inquire into and report upon the manner in which American vessels transferred during the rebellion to British owners, are now being refurnished with American registers, and, if the same be not in accordance with law, what legislation, if any, is necessary to prevent such transaction.

Mr. Doolittle introduced a bill in relation to the qualifications of jurors, and to writs of error in certain cases, which provides that no person shall be held incompetent to act as a grand juror by reason of having formed or expressed an opinion upon the matter in question, founded upon public rumor, statements of the public journals, or the common history of the times; provided he be otherwise competent, and it appear to the satisfaction of the Court that notwithstanding such opinion he can and will act impartially and true presentment make according to the evidence. It further provides that in trials for public offences against the United States no person shall be held incompetent to act as a juror on account of having formed an opinion as above, founded upon like information, if otherwise competent and impartial.

Mr. Foot presented the following, which was adopted:

The Joint Committee appointed to consider and report by what token of respect and affection it may be proper to express the deep sensibility of the nation to the event of the decease of their late President, Abraham Lincoln, have, according to order, had the same under consideration, and, as the result of their deliberations, report the following resolutions, and recommend their adoption:

Resolved, That the melancholy event of the violent and tragic death of Abraham Lincoln, late President of the United States, having occurred during the recess of Congress, and, the two Houses sharing in the general grief, and desiring to manifest their sensibility upon the occasion of that public bereavement; therefore be it

Resolved, By the Senate, the House of Representatives concurring, That the two Houses of Congress will assemble in the Hose of Representatives on Monday, the 12th of February next—that being his anniversary birth-day—at the hour of 12, meridian, and that in the presence of the two Houses there assembled, an address upon the life and character of Abraham Lincoln, late President of the United States, be pronounced by the Hon. E. M. Stanton, and that the President of the Senate *pro tem.* and the Speaker of the House of Representatives be requested to invite the President of the United States, the heads of the several Departments, the Judges of the Supreme Court, the representatives of foreign Governments near this Government, and such officers of the army and navy as have received the thanks of Congress, who may then be at the seat of Government, to be present on the occasion; and be it further

Resolved, That the President of the United States be requested to transmit a copy of these resolutions to Mrs. Lincoln, and to assure her of the profound sympathy of the two Houses of Congress for her deep personal affliction, and of their sincere condolence for the late National bereavement.

Mr Morgan introduced a bill to amend the laws relative to certain officers at New York, which provide for the appointment of appraisers by the President, with the advice and consent of the Senate, and assistant appraisers by the Secretary of the Treasury, one of whom, with special reference to his duties, shall be an examiner of drugs and chemicals. It also provides that instead of the clerks now employed for the examination and appraisement of goods, examiners shall be appointed, who shall receive their appointments from the Secretary of the Treasury. It further provides that it shall be unlawful for any employes of the Custom House to be employed in any mercantile or commercial business. The compensation of the Appraiser is fixed at $5,000, and the Assistant Appraiser at $3,000 per annum, payable monthly.

The bill was referred to the Committee on Commerce.—Adjourned.

HOUSE OF REPRESENTATIVE[S].

Mr. Benjamin G. Harris, of Maryland; Sam. McLean, Delegate from Montana, and Wm. H. H[illegible]er, Delegate from Utah, respectively, appeared and qualified by taking the required oath.

Mr. Smith also offered a resolution and demanded the "previous question," that James M. Johnson, elected to the Thirty-ninth Congress from the Third Congressional District of Arkansas, be admitted to the privileges of the floor during the pendency of his claim as a representative.

Mr. Stevens, of Pennsylvania, and Mr. Ashley, of Ohio, objected to the introduction of the resolution, and Mr. Smith withdrew the question for the present.

Mr. Price, of Iowa, offered a resolution, which was referred to the Committee on Reconstruction, That no State recently in the rebellion ought to be entitled to representation until such State shall, by its Legislature, or the properly constituted authorities, adopt the amendments to the Constitution, securing the payment of National debts and repudiating the rebel debt.

Mr. Washburne, of Illinois, introduced a bill repealing all laws providing for fishing bounties. Referred to the Committee on Commerce.

Mr. Grinnell introduced a bill providing that no commission shall hereafter be issued to any civil or military officer of the Government resident in Utah until he has filed in the office where such commission issues a disavowal of the doctrine and practice of polygamy, and that no compensation shall be allowed to any such officers in that Territory without such disavowal. The bill was referred to the Committee on the Judiciary.

On motion of Mr. Loan, it was resolved that the Select Committee on Freedmen be instructed to inquire into the expediency of some immediate legislation securing to the freedmen and colored citizens of the States recently in rebellion the political and civil rights of other citizens of the United States, and that they report by bill or otherwise.

Mr. Baker offered the following:

Whereas, Class rule and aristocratic principles of government have burthened well nigh all Europe with an enormous public debt and a standing army, which press as a prodigious incubus on the people, absorbing their substance, impeding their culture, and impairing their business; and, whereas, the class rule as an aristocratic element of slaveholding which found a place in our Republic, has proved itself in a like manner hurtful to our people by degrading labor and prohibiting popular education in a large section of our country, by striving to rend our Union into fragments, by causing the blood of hundreds of thousands of patriots to flow, and by compelling the people to impose on themselves a debt of European magnitude in defence of liberty, nationality and civilization on this Continent; therefore

Be it resolved, As the sense of this House that once for all we should have done with class rule and aristocracy as a privileged power before the law in this Nation, no matter where or in what form they may appear, and that in restoring the normal relations of the States lately in rebellion, it is the high and sacred duty of the representatives of a free people to proceed upon the true as distinguished from the false democratic principle, and to realize and secure the largest attainable liberty to the whole people of the Republic, irrespective of class or race.

On motion of Mr. Conkling, the above was referred to the Committee on Reconstruction.

Mr. Moulton asked leave to offer a resolution that, if not incompatible with the public interests, the President be requested to communicate to this House the reasons why Jefferson Davis, said to be confined at Fortress Monroe, has not been tried for treason against the Government; and if any, what obstacles are in the way of his trial as a State criminal.

Objection being made, the resolution went over under the rule.

Mr. Thornton, of Illinois, offered a resolution declaring that questions relative to the elective franchise should be referred to the several States. Tabled.

Mr. Orth, of Indiana, moved that the President be called on to inform the House, or furnish the House with any information as to the application of the so called Mexican Empire to obtain a recognition from the United States.

Mr. Stillwell, of Indiana, offered a resolution to the effect that the people who have been in rebellion against the Government, and who have submitted to the laws of the United States, and adopted a republican form of government, repealed the ordinances of secession, passed the constitutional amendment forever abolishing slavery, repudiated the rebel debt, and passed laws protecting the freedman in his liberty, the representatives of the people elected to Congress having received their certificates of election from their respective Governors should be received as members of the Thirty-ninth Congress when they shall take the test oath.

The above was referred to the Committee on Reconstruction.

Mr. Hill, of Indiana, introduced the following resolution:

Resolved, That the act of July 2, 1862, prescribing an oath to be taken and subscribed to by persons elected or appointed to office under the Government of the United States, before entering upon the duties of such offices, is of binding force and effect in all the departments of the public service, and should in no instance be dispensed with.

A motion was made to lay the resolution on the table, which was disagreed to by yeas, 22; nays, 126. The resolution was then passed.

A message was received from the Senate accompanied by a report from that body proposing appropriate action consequent upon the death of President Lincoln. The report was unanimously concurred in.

Mr. Washburne, of Illinois, from the Select Committee appointed to take action on the bill for the relief of Mrs. Lincoln, etc., reported the same with a substitute, namely, that the Secretary of the Treasury pay to Mrs. Mary Lincoln, widow of Abraham Lincoln, twenty-five thousand dollars.

Mr. Wentworth moved that the sum of one hundred thousand, instead of twenty-five thousand dollars, be appropriated.

This was disagreed to, and the bill pppropriating twenty-five thousand dollars, as above reported, was passed.

Mr. Wilson of Iowa, reported a bill from the Judiciary Committee, extending the right of suffrage in the District of Columbia.

On motion of Mr. Wilson, the House suspended the rules for that purpose, and the bill was made the special order for the 10th of January next.

Mr. Alley, of Massachusetts, offered the following:

Resolved, That this House cordially concurs in the views of the Secretary of the Treasury in relation to the necessity of the contraction of the currency, with a view to an early resumption of specie payments, as the business interests of the country will permit, and we hereby pledge co-operation to that end as speedily as possible.

The resolution was agreed to by yeas, 144; nays, 6.

On motion of Mr. Stevens, of Pennsylvania, the House went into Committee of the Whole on the State of the Union, on the President's annual Message. Mr. Stevens, of Pennsylvania, said:

A candid examination of the power and proper principles of reconstruction can be offensive to no one, and may possibly be profitable by exciting inquiry. The President assumes that no one doubts, that the late rebel states have lost their constitutional relations to the Union, and are incapable of representation in Congress, except by permission of the Government. It matters but little with this admission, whether you call them States out of the Union, and now conquered territories, or assert that because the Constitution forbid them to do what they did do, that they are only dead as to all national and political action, and will remain so until the Government shall breathe into them the breath of life anew, and permit them to occupy their former position—in other words, that they are not out of the Union, but only dead carcasses lying within the Union. In either case, it is very plain that it requires the action of Congress to enable them to form a State Government, and send Representatives to Congress. Nobody, I believe, pretends that with their old constitutions and frames of government, they can be permitted to claim their old rights under the Constitution. They have torn their constitutions into atoms, and built on their foundations fabrics of a totally different character. Dead men cannot raise themselves; dead States cannot restore their own existence as it was. Whose especial duty is it to do it? In whom does the Constitution place the power? Not in the judicial branch of the Government, for it only adjudicates and does not prescribe laws. Not in the Executive, for he only executes and cannot make laws. Not in the commander-in-chief of the armies, for he can only hold them under military rule until the sovereign legislative power of the conqueror shall give them law. There is, fortunately, no difficulty in solving the question. There are two provisions in the Constitution under one of which the case must fall. The fourth article says: "New States may be admitted by the Congress into this Union." In my judgment this is the controlling provision in this case. Unless the law of nations is a dead letter, the late war between two acknowledged belligerents, severed their original compacts and broke all ties that bound them together. The future condition of the conquered power depends on the will of the conqueror. They must come in as new States, or remain as conquered provinces. Congress; the Senate and House of Representatives; with the concurrence of the President, is the only power that can act on the matter. But suppose, as some dreaming theorists imagine that these States have never been out of the Union, but have only destroyed their State governments, so as to be incapable of political action, then the fourth section of the fourth article applies, which says, "The United States shall guarantee to every State in the Union a Republican form of government." Who is the United States? Not the judiciary, not the President, but the sovereign power of the people exercised through their representatives in Congress, with the concurrence of the Executive. It means the political government, the concurrent action of both branches of Congress and the Executive. The separate action of each amounts to nothing either in admitting new States or guaranteeing Republican Governments to lapsed or outlawed States. Whence springs the preposterous idea that either the President or the Senate, or the House of Representatives, acting separately, can determine the right of States to send members or Senators to the Congress of the Union? To prove that they are and have been out of the Union for all legal purposes, and are now conquered subjects to the absolute disposal of Congress, I will suggest a few ideas and adduce a few authorities. If the so-called Confederate States of America were an independent belligerent, and were so acknowledged by the United States and by Europe, or had assumed and maintained an attitude which entitled them to be considered and treated as a belligerent, then during such time they were precisely in the condition of a foreign nation with whom we were at war, nor need their independence as a nation to be acknowledged by us to produce that effect. Mr. Stevens then quoted from Mr. Justice Grier, in the prize cases, all the law on these points. After such clear and repeated decisions, he said, it is something worse than ridiculous to hear men of respectable standing attempting to nullify the law of nations and declare the Supreme Court of the United States in error, because, as the Constitution forbids it, the States could not go out of the Union *de facto*. After proceeding further in his argument, he remarked, it is obvious that the first duty of Congress is to pass a law declaring the condition of these outside or defunct States, and providing proper civil government for them. Since the conquest they have been governed by martial law. Military rule is necessarily despotic, and ought not to exist longer than is absolutely necessary. As there are no symptoms that the people of these provinces will be prepared to participate in a Constitutional Government for some years, I know of no arrangement so proper for them as Territorial Governments. There they can learn the principles of freedom, and eat the fruit of foul rebellion under such Governments.

Mr. Stevens continued his remarks in this spirit at considerable length, after which the House adjourned.

From Europe.

Five Days Later News.

Portland, Dec. 18.—The steamship Peruvian, from Londonderry the 8th instant, has arrived here.

The Shenandoah put back to Liverpool on the 6th instant, with loss of sails and short of coals. She experienced heavy gales, and only reached Longitude 25° on the 1st of December, when she was put about.

THE FENIANS.

The trial of O'Leary, the Fenian, terminated on the 6th instant, with a verdict of "guilty." The prisoner addressed the Court, and denied that he was a traitor. He said that he owed no allegiance to the Queen of England, nor obedience to British laws. He was not, he said, surprised at the verdict, for a government which had safely packed the bench had no difficulty in obtaining a verdict from a jury. When he had been convicted on such slight evidence, there would be no difficulty found in convicting all the rest who were to come. He declared that he had been morally assassinated, and pointing to one of the crown counsel, designated him as "that miserable man." Dante had placed traitors in the ninth circle of his Inferno, but Dante had defined a traitor to be a man who betrayed his king, his country, his friends and his benefactors. As for him, England was not his country, and he was no traitor. With respect to the shedding of blood and the destruction of property, that was the necessary consequence of all revolutions, and so it was of wars; but the persons who disturbed the country were not rebels, but agitators. Hampden and Elliott were traitors, and Jeffreys and Norbury were loyal men.

The Judge sentenced the prisoner to 20 years penal servitude.

London, Dec. 8.—The third Fenian trial, that of Michael Moore, the pike maker, has been concluded. He was convicted of treason, and sentenced to ten years penal servitude.

All the Fenian prisoners were removed on the night of the 2d instant from the jail whence Stephens, the Head Centre of Ireland, escaped, to Kilmainham Jail, owing to alleged disaffection among the officials at the Richmond Bridewell. Among the latest arrests of members of the Fenian Brotherhood is the clerk of an important Government functionary in Tipperary.

The London TIMES congratulates the Irish Government on being able to secure successive convictions of leading Fenians, with so little difficulty in spite of everything that can be done for their defense. It says: "It would appear that a fresh jury is empannelled for each case, so that every conviction represents the result of independent judgment by a distinct body of men."

GENERAL ENGLISH NEWS.

The London TIMES, in announcing an official investigation into the affairs of Jamaica says: That it is due to Governor Eyre, no less than to public opinion in England, that a full and searching inquiry should be made into the history of the Jamaica rebellion, and we learn with the utmost satisfaction that such an inquiry is to be instituted forthwith.

A numerous deputation from the Baptist Missionary Society had an interview with Mr. Cardwell, the Colonial Secretary, to present a memorial praying for an inquiry into the proceedings in Jamaica.

It is stated that there is to be a new ceremonial in the opening of Parliament. The Queen, instead of using a "State carriage," will occupy what is called a "dress carriage," and the robes of State, instead of being worn by the Queen, will be laid upon the throne. The speech itself, instead of being read by the Queen, will be read by the Lord Chancellor.

The case of Mrs. Yelverton vs. the SATURDAY REVIEW, for libel at Edinburgh, resulted in a verdict for the defendants, the jury standing nine for them and three against them. The verdict was received with "hissing" in the Court. The jury were absent six hours.

FRANCE.

General Schofield's visit to Paris continued to attract attention.

The Paris PRESSE believes that whatever the tenor of General Schofield's instructions may be, the evacuation of Mexico is likely to be the result.

The Paris correspondent of the London GLOBE says that General Schofield is stated to have arrived on a political mission from Washington, and had called on Drouyn de L'Huys, and adds: "It is supposed that the object of his visit is for the purpose of soothing down some passage in the impending message of President Johnson, meant rather for home service than for France." General Schofield is also expected to explain the appointment of General Logan as Minister to Mexico, accredited to Juaraz, General Logan is to start in search of a Mexican President or Republican Court, and is to report progress in that voyage of discovery.

The TIMES Paris correspondent mentions the arrival of Gen. Schofield and says that it is rumored that he is charged to treat for the evacuation of Mexico by the French troops. The writer says that he has reason to believe, on very fair authority, that the French Government has not received any communication of the kind alluded to from the American Government, and that there is as yet no fact to show or expect that it will be made.

A Paris telegram of the 6th inst., states that Gen. Scofield is not entrusted with any political mission, and that he visits Europe for the benefit of his health with the intention of making a lengthened stay on the continent.

The cattle plague, in the shape of contagious "typhus fever," is said to have been imported into the Jardin d'Acclimation, Paris, by two gazelles received from England. An order has consequently been issued prohibiting the importation of all animals into France, except horses, mules, asses and dogs.

SPAIN.

A Madrid letter, of the 3d inst., says that the rejection of mediation by the Spanish Government in the Chilian difficulty is again announced in the semi-official Correspondencia de Espana.

The Madrid EPOCA publishes a note from Admiral Pareja to the English Minister at Valparaiso. The Minister had written the Admiral stating that he could not believe that Valparaiso would be blockaded, in view of the large amount of property owned by foreigners in the city. The Admiral curtly replied that if proper warning was given to neutrals to remove their effects, it was the incontestable right of belligerents to resort to bombardment. We therefore gave due warning.

AUSTRIA.

The Hamburg papers state that a portion of the Heligoland Rock, having been long undermined by the sea, had fallen, and was engulphed in the waves. Out of five hundred inhabitants on the Island seventy are said to have perished.

TWO DAYS LATER.

Arrival of the Cuba.

Halifax, Dec. 18.—The steamship Cuba, from Queenstown the 10th inst., has arrived at this port.

THE FENIANS.

The special commission for the trial of the Fenian prisoners would adjourn in Dublin on the 13th inst., until the 6th of January, the interim being devoted to the trial of Cork prisoners.

The trial of Halligan, an employe in the IRISH PEOPLE's newspaper office, is progressing.

The channel fleet is ordered to winter in Ireland, and the officers are not to be allowed the usual leave of absence. The ARMY AND NAVY GAZETTE says there are between nineteen and twenty thousand of the regular army in Ireland.

GENERAL ENGLISH ITEMS.

The affairs of Jamaica continued to absorb great attention. The Peace Society had addressed a memorial to Earl Russell on the subject. A deputation from the Anti-Slavery Society was to wait on Mr. Cardwell, the Colonial Secretary, on the same subject on the day the Cuba left Liverpool. Sir Henry Storks, Governor of Malta, has been summoned to England. Reports say he will be sent to Jamaica, with a Commission of Inquiry, which will be composed of Sir H. Storks, Sir E. Head, late Governor of Canada, and a legal gentleman.

The weekly return of the cattle disease in England shows a continued increase. An official letter from the Consul General at Odessa states that the cattle plague exists permanently on the Steppes of Kherson and is cured by sudorifics. The Royal Agricultural Society have resolved that its usual annual meeting shall not take place until next year on account of the cattle diseases.

Captain Waddell, of the Shenandoah, remained in Liverpool, and will continue to do so until the extradition claim of the United States Government is adjusted.

FRANCE.

The PALL MALL GAZETTE says that the message of President Johnson is looked for in Paris with unusual interest, owing to the belief that it contains paragraphs commenting on the action of France in Mexico, which will require explanation.

The PATRIE says that negotiations are progressing between Austria and Mexico for the more speedy enrollment of the ten thousand Austrians, who, under the original arrangement, were to be recruited in Austria in five years, at the rate of two thousand men a year.

SPAIN AND CHILI.

The Paris PATRIE says that President Johnson has ordered the American Minister at Chili to offer his good offices for the settlement of the Hispano-Chilian affair. It adds that the friendly intervention of England and France also affords ground to expect that the difficulty will be amicably adjusted.

SWEDEN.

In the House of Nobles, the Government bill for reform in the Constitution was adopted by 361 against 294. The Chamber of the Clergy unanimously passed the bill, which has thus gone through all the four Chambers. There was great rejoicing throughout the country over the event, and a great public festivity and illumination at Stockholm was preparing in honor of it.

Verg Latest per the Cuba.

Liverpool, Dec. 10.—It is said that Austria and Mexico are negotiating for the more speedy enrollment of the ten thousand Austrians, which were to be furnished Mexico during five years.

The King of the Belgians died on the 9th inst.

At an American Banquet, given at Paris, Mr. Bigelow, the United States Minister, expressed very pacific sentiments, and Gen. Schofield proposed as a toast: "Friendship between France and the United States."

The PATRIE says that Gen. Schofield is about to proceed to England on a confidential mission from President Johnson to prevent any difficulties arising between Great Britain and America.

Mr. Cardwell, the Colonial Secretary, has promised the Anti-Slavery Society that a searching inquiry should be made into the late proceedings in Jamaica.

The three mates and boatswain of the ship Antarctic, lying in the Mersey, bound for New York, have been lodged in jail, charged with killing the cook and steward.

BELL'S LIFE publishes an account of a complimentary dinner given John C. Heenan by the Victoria Club of London, prior to his visiting America.

The assent of Queen Victoria to the betrothal of

(Continued on the Last Page.)

THE SUN.

IT SHINES FOR ALL

Number 10,429. NEW YORK, WEDNESDAY, DECEMBER 20, 1865. Thirty-Third Year.

The Latest News

By Telegraph to the N. Y. Sun.

The Ex-Rebel States.

GEORGIA LEFT TO HERSELF

Provisional Gov. Johnson Relieved.

Message of the President.

General Condition of the Southern States.

THE PRESIDENT HOPEFUL.

Opinions of General Grant.

EXCITEMENT IN THE SENATE.

Mr. Sumner Attacks the President.

OTHER CONGRESSIONAL PROCEEDINGS

The Rebel Debt.

A Constitutional Amendment to Prevent its Payment.

City and Miscellaneous News.

Horrible Scene in Ann Street.

A MAN IN FLAMES.

Fire Parade To-Day

The Strong Divorce Case.

&c., &c., &c.

RECONSTRUCTION.

Georgia Delivered Over to the Elected State Authorities.

Washington, Dec. 19.—The following has been addressed by Mr. Seward to Gov. Johnson:

DEPARTMENT OF STATE, WASHINGTON, Dec. 19, 1865.

To His Excellency James Johnson, Provisional Governor of the State of Georgia, Milledgeville, Ga.:

SIR:—The time has arrived when, in the judgment of the President of the United States, the care and conduct of the proper affairs of the State of Georgia may be re-united to the Constitutional authorities chosen by the people thereof, without danger to the peace and safety of the United States. By direction of the President, therefore, you are relieved from the trust which was heretofore reposed in you as Provisional Governor of the State of Georgia, whenever the Governor elect shall have accepted and become qualified to discharge the duties of the Executive office. You will transfer the papers and property of the State now in your custody to his Excellency the Governor elect. It gives me especial pleasure to convey to you the President's acknowledgment of the fidelity, the loyalty and the discretion which have marked your administration. You will please give me a reply specifying the day on which this communication is received. I have the honor to be your Excellency obedient servant. WM. H. SEWARD.

Mr. Seward has also addressed a similar communication to the elected Governor of Georgia, concluding as follows:

"I have the honor to tender you the co-operation of the Government of the United States, whenever it may be found necessary, in effecting the early restoration and the permanent prosperity and welfare of the State over which you have been called to preside." [Signed] WM. H. SEWARD.

THE EX-REBEL STATES.

Message from the President to the Senate.

To the Senate of the United States:

In reply to the resolution adopted by the Senate, on the 12th, I have the honor to state that the rebellion waged by a portion of the people against the properly constituted authorities of the Government of the United States has been suppressed; that the United States are in possession of every State in which the insurrection existed; and that, as far as could be done, the courts of the United States have been restored, post offices re-established, and steps taken to put into effective operation the revenue laws of the country. As the result of the measures instituted by the Executive, with the view of inducing a resumption of the functions of the State comprehended in the inquiry of the Senate, the people in North Carolina, South Carolina, Georgia, Alabama, Mississippi, Louisiana, Arkansas and Tennessee have recognized their respective State Governments, and are yielding obedience to the laws and Government of the United States with more willingness and greater promptitude than under the circumstances could reasonably have been anticipated. The proposed amendment to the Constitution, providing for the abolition of slavery forever within the limits of the country, has been ratified by each one of these States, with the exception of Mississippi, from which no official information has been received; and in nearly all of them measures have been adopted, or are now pending, to confer upon the freedmen the privileges which are essential to their comfort, protection and security. In Florida and Texas the people are making commendable progress in restoring their State governments, and no doubt is entertained that they will, at an early period, be in a condition to resume all of their practical relations with the Federal Government. In that portion of the Union lately in rebellion the aspect of affairs is more promising than, in view of all the circumstances, could well have been expected. The people throughout the entire South evince an audible desire to renew their allegiance to the Government, and to repair the devastations of war by a prompt and cheerful return to peaceful pursuits. An abiding faith is entertained that their actions will conform to their professions, and that in acknowledging the supremacy of the Constitution and the laws of the United States, their loyalty will be unreservedly given to the government whose leniency they cannot fail to appreciate, and whose fostering care will soon restore them to a condition of prosperity. It is true that in some of the States the demoralizing effects of the war are to be seen in occasional disorders, but these are local in character, not frequent in occurrence, and are rapidly disappearing as the authority of the civil power is extended and sustained. Perplexing questions were naturally to be expected from the great and sudden change in the relations between the two races; but systems are gradually developing themselves under which the freedman will receive the protection to which he is justly entitled, and by means of his labor make himself a useful and independent member of the community in which he has his home. From all the information in my possession, and from that which I have recently derived from the most reliable authority, I am induced to cherish the belief that sectional animosity is surely and rapidly merging itself into a spirit of nationality, and that representation connected with a properly adjusted system of taxation, will result in a harmonious restoration of the relations of the States to the National Union.

The report of Carl Schurz is herewith transmitted as requested by the Senate. No report from the Hon. John Covode has been received by the President. The attention of the Senate is invited to the accompanying report of Lieut.-Gen. Grant, who recently made a tour of inspection through several of the States whose inhabitants participated in the rebellion. ANDREW JOHNSON.

Washington, D. C., Dec. 18, 1865.

General Grant's Report.

HEADQUARTERS ARMY OF THE UNITED STATES, Dec. 18, 1865.

His Excellency, A. Johnson, President of the United States:

Sir.—I reply to your note of the 16th inst., requesting a report from me giving such information as I may be possessed of, coming within the scope of the inquiries made by the Senate of the United States, in their resolution of the 12th inst. I have the honor to submit the following, with your approval, and also that of the Honorable Secretary of War:

I left Washington City on the 27th of last month, for the purpose of making a tour of inspection throughout some of the Southern States lately in rebellion and to see what changes were necessary in the disposition of the military forces of the country, how these forces could be reduced, and expenses curtailed, &c.; and to learn as far as possible the feelings and intentions of the citizens of these States towards the general government. The State of Virginia being so accessible to Washington City and information from this quarter therefore being readily obtained, I hastened through the State without conversing or meeting with any of its citizens. In Raleigh, N. C., I spent one day; in Charleston, S. C., two days; and in Savannah and Augusta, Ga., each one day. Both in travelling and whilst stopping I saw much and conversed freely with the citizens of those States as well as with officers of the Army who have been stationed among them.

The following are the conclusions come to by me. I am satisfied the mass of thinking men of the South accept the present situation of affairs in good faith. The questions which have hitherto divided the sentiments of the people of the two sections—Slavery and State Rights, or the right of a State to secede from the Union—they regard as having been settled forever by the highest tribunal—arms—that man can resort to. I was pleased to learn from the leading men I met that they not only accepted the decision arrived at as final, but now the smoke of battle has cleared away, and time has been given for reflection, that this decision has been a fortunate one for the whole country, they receiving the like benefits from it with those who opposed them in the field and in the council. Four years of war, during which law was executed only at the point of the bayonet throughout the States in rebellion, have left the people possibly in a condition not to yield that ready obedience to civil authority the American people have generally been in the habit of yielding. This would render the presence of small garrisons throughout those States necessary until such time as labor returns to its proper channel, and civil authority is fully established. I did not meet any one, either those holding places under the government, or citizens of the Southern States, who thought it practicable to withdraw the military from the South at present. The white and the black mutually require the protection of the General Government. There is such universal acquiescence in the authority of the General Government throughout the portions of the country visited by me, that the mere presence of a military force, without regard to numbers, is sufficient to maintain order. The good of the country requires that the force kept in the interior, where there are many freedmen [elswhere in the Southern States than at forts upon the sea coast no force is necessary], should all be white troops. The reasons for this are obvious, without mentioning many of them. The presence of black troops lately slaves demoralizes labor, both by their advice and furnishing in their camp a resort for the freedmen for long distances around. White troops generally excite no opposition, and therefore a small number of them can maintain order in a given district. Colored troops must be kept in bodies sufficient to defend themselves. It is not the thinking men who would do violence towards any class of troops sent among them by the General Government; but the ignorant in some places might; and the late slave, too, who might be imbued with the idea that the property of his late master should belong to him, at least should have no protection from the colored soldier. There is danger of collision being brought on by such causes. My observations lead me to the conclusion that the citizens of the Southern States are anxious to return to self-government within the Union as soon as possible; that whilst reconstructing they want and require protection from the Government; that, they think is required by the Government, and is not humiliating to them as citizens; and that if such a course was pointed out, they would pursue it in good faith. It is to be regretted that there cannot be a greater commingling at this time between the citizens of the two sections, and particularly of those entrusted with the law making power.

I did not give the operations of the Freedmen's Bureau that attention I would have done if more time had been at my disposal. Conversations, however, on the subject with officers connected with the Bureau, led me to think that in some of the States its affairs have not been conducted with good judgment or economy, and that the belief widely spread among the freedmen of the Southern States that the lands of their former owners will, at least in part, be divided among them, has come from the agents of this Bureau. This belief is seriously interfering with the willingness of the freedmen to make contracts for the coming year. In some form the Freedmen's Bureau is an absolute necessity, until civil law is established and enforced, securing to the freedmen their rights, and full protection. At present, however, it is independent of the military establishment of the country, and seems to be operated by the different agents of the Bureau according to their individuals notions. Everywhere General Howard, the able head of the Bureau, made friends by the just and fair instructions and advice he gave. But the complaint in South Carolina was that when he left things went on as before. Many, perhaps the majority of the agents of the Freedmen's Bureau, advise the freedmen that by their own industry they must expect to live. To this end they endeavor to secure employment for them, and to see that both contracting parties comply with their engagements. In some cases, I am sorry to say, the freedmans' mind does not seem to be disabused of the idea that the freedman has the right to live without care or provision for the future. The effect of the belief in the division of lands is idleness and accumulation in camps, towns and cities. In such cases I think it will be found that vice and disease will tend to the extermination or great destruction of the colored race. It cannot be expected that the opinions held by men at the South for years can be changed in a day; and therefore the freedmen require for a few years, not only laws to protect them, but the fostering care of those who will give them good council and on whom they can rely. The Freedmen's Bureau being separated from the military establishment of the country, requires all the expense of a separate organization. One does not necessarily know what the other is doing, or what orders they are acting under. It seems to me this could be corrected by regarding every officer on duty with *troops* in the Southern States as agents of the Freedmen's Bureau, and then have all orders from the head of the Bureau sent through the Department commanders. This would create a responsibility that would create uniformity of action throughout the South; would insure the orders and instructions from the head of the Bureau being carried out, and would relieve from duty and pay a large number of employes of the Government.

I have the honor to be, very respectfully, your obedient servant. U. S. GRANT, Lieutenant General.

POLITICAL INTELLIGENCE.

California.

Sacramento, Cal., Dec. 18.—Resolutions ratifying the Constitutional amendment abolishing Slavery favorably passed the State Legislature to-day.

Colorado.

Denver City, Dec. 18.—The Legislature elected to-day John Evans and Jerome B. Chaffee, [Republicans] United States Senators.

The Death of Gov. Corwin.

A Washington correspondent writes:

No premonition of illness had been observed in Gov. Corwin at any time in the evening up to his sudden attack, and it is stated that he never appeared in better spirits, and was unusually prolific of amusing and entertaining anecdotes. Throughout the evening he was surrounded by various circles, composed of Senators and Representatives, Judges and distinguished personages, whom he kept in an almost continual roar of laughter, with stories of his adventures in Mexico. At 10 o'clock Gov. Corwin entered the supper-room and took a seat upon a sofa, but did not partake of refreshment of any kind. Here he was surrounded by friends, and at about 10½ o'clock, when he had just concluded one of his Mexican stories, and when the ring of laughter from his auditors had scarcely ceased, he suddenly turned to the gentleman at his side, and said in a feeble voice, "It's too warm here," accompanying the words with a convulsive movement of his hand, as if trying to catch hold of something for support. He was raised upon his feet, but had taken but two or three steps when his strength gave way, and he was carried into a bed-chamber by Hon. J. A. Garfield and Gen. Durbin Ward and other friends. He never spoke again, and was unconscious until he died, except for a few minutes after he became ill.

Alabama.

Arrest of Captain Semmes, Etc.

Montgomery, Ala., Dec. 16.—Judge Busteed, of the United States District Court, has decided that the Congressional oath for attorneys and civil officers is constitutional.

Raphael J. Semmes (of the pirate Alabama) was arrested last evening, by order from Washington, and is now en route to the North under guard.

CONGRESSIONAL PROCEEDINGS.

Thirty-Ninth Session.

SENATE.

Washington, Dec. 19.—Mr. Wilson introduced a bill the more effectually to provide for the national defence by establishing a uniform militia throughout the United States. It is his bill of February last, organizing the general militia system, and providing a Military Bureau of the Government. The bill was referred to the Committee on Military Affairs.

Mr. Doolittle introduced a bill in relation to the Freedmen's Bureau, which authorizes the President to extend and maintain a branch of that Bureau in any State in which slaves have been emancipated by the operations of the war, or amendments of the constitution, and also authorizes him to suspend its operation in or withdraw the military forces from the States in which he is satisfied that hostilities have ceased, the insurrection been suppressed, peace and order restored, and the civil authority established, and the laws so modified as to procure equal protection to all persons in all their civil rights without distinction of race or color, including the right to make contracts, sue and be sued, appear as witnesses, buy or sell real or personal estate, and all the rights of property and personal liberty.

The bill was referred to the Committee on Military Affairs.

Mr. Conness introduced a bill to amend an act for the disposal of coal lands and town property, which allows the right to enter 160 acres of coal lands to any person actually engaged in coal mining upon the premises at the passage of that act, and fixes the price at $20 per acre.

The bill was referred to the Committee on Public Lands.

Mr. Wilson offered a resolution, calling upon the Secretary of War for a detailed statement of the numerical strength of the Regular army, the number of officers and men, where stationed and how employed, etc. The resolution was adopted.

Mr. Lane, of Indiana, from the Committee on Pensions, reported a bill to amend a pension law of last winter, so as to include those who have lost both feet in the naval service among those entitled to $20 per month, as already provided for those who have suffered a similar loss in the military service, which was passed.

Mr. Anthony introduced a joint resolution, which was passed, to increase the bonds of the Superintendent of Public Printing from $40,000 to $80,000.

Mr. Anthony called up the House resolution for adjournment of Congress from Wednesday next to January 9, 1866, and moved to amend it by striking out January 9th and inserting January 3d, 1866. The resolution was passed as amended by Mr. Anthony.

Mr. Trumbull gave notice of a bill to enlarge the powers of the Freedman's Bureau, so as to secure freedom to all persons within the United States, and protect every individual in the full enjoyment of the rights of person and property, and furnish him the means of their vindication.

Mr. Trumbull—In giving this notice, I desire to say it is given in view of the adoption of the Constitutional Amendment abolishing slavery. Whatever diversity of opinion there may be as to the actual adoption of the amendment at this time, in consequence of the abnormal condition of some of the Legislatures which have ratified it, there can be no doubt that it will soon, and, probably, before action could be had in Congress, have the sanction of a sufficient number of States to put its adoption beyond cavil. I have never doubted that under the second section of the amendment it would be competent for Congress to protect every person within the United States in all the rights of person and property belonging to a free citizen; and to secure those rights is the objects of the bill I propose to introduce. I think it important that action should be taken on this subject at an early day, both for the purpose of quieting apprehension in the minds of the many friends of freedom, lest by local legislation or a prevailing public sentiment in some of the States, persons of the African race should continue to be oppressed, and, in fact, deprived of true freedom; and for the purpose of showing to those among whom slavery has heretofore existed, that unless they by local legislation provide for the real freedom of their former slaves, the Federal Government will, by virtue of its own authority, see that they are fully protected.

Mr. Anthony moved that the chair appoint a special committee on reconstruction, provided for by a recent resolution; which was adopted.

Mr. Anthony offered a resolution that until otherwise ordered, all papers relating to the question of representation of the States lately in rebellion, be referred to the Special Committee of Fifteen.—Passed over under the rules.

Mr. Cowan said a message had just been received from the President in response to a resolution calling for information as to the condition of the States lately in rebellion. He called for the reading of that Message. The Message of the President was read.

[This Message is published elsewhere in the columns of the SUN.]

Mr. Cowan then called for the reading of a report made to the President by General Grant, concerning his late visit in the South. General Grant's report was then read.

[This report is published elsewhere in the columns of the SUN.]

Mr. Sumner—I wish to make one remark with reference to the business before the Senate. I wish to know whether the report of Major-General Carl Schurz is annexed to the Message of the President.

Mr. Foster (in the chair)—The the Chair understands that it is.

Mr. Sumner—Then I think it had better be read.

Several Senators—It is too long.

Mr. Sumner—At any rate we can begin it; it is a very important document. The Senate will remember that when the report was made out on the condition of affairs in Kansas, every word was read at that desk. Now the question involved is much more important. We have a message from the President, which is like the whitewashing message of Franklin Pierce with regard to the atrocities in Kansas. I think the Senate had better listen to the report of Gen. Schurz on this important subject.

Mr. Johnson said he was surprised to hear the Senator from Massachusetts characterize the message as an attempt to whitewash. There was no whitewashing about it. It was a fair and clear statement of facts, called for by the Senate. He thought the report of Gen. Schurz had better be printed, together with the other documents.

The reading of Gen. Schurz's report was commenced, but the Clerk had not proceeded far when

Mr. Sherman moved that the further reading be dispensed with, and that the report be printed.

Mr. Sumner—I shall not object to that if the Senator from Ohio thinks that it is proper we should on this important occasion dispense with the reading. I think the Senate could not listen to anything of more importance than that accurate and authentic report regarding the actual condition of things in these States. Here is an eminent citizen, lately a Major General in the army of the United States, sent on a special mission by the President to visit these States, and report upon their condition. He has made his visit, not hasty, like General Grant, for instance, or some other officers or citizens, but a visit occupying time, and extending through the different States, and he has recorded the results in an elaborate document. Now, sir, if the question were a trivial one; if it were a transitory question, I would think with the Senator from Ohio, that it had better not be read. If the Senator insists upon his motion, I shall not object.

Mr. Sherman had no doubt that the report of Gen. Schurz was elaborate, able and interesting. He would much prefer to read it, however, than hear it read, where there was confusion and noise, as in the Senate.

Mr. Doolittle.—The Senator from Massachusetts gave expression to one remark which brought, it seems to me, injustice to himself, and which he ought to qualify, if not altogether to retract. Speaking of the message just received from the President, he said it was like the whitewashing message of Franklin Pierce to cover up the transactions in Kansas; and that the affairs in these States sought to be covered up and whitewashed by the message of the President, were much worse than those affairs in Kansas. Now, Mr. President, I think the Senator from Massachusetts must have let fall that expression without giving it sufficient thought.

Mr. Sumner—I have nothing to qualify, nothing to modify, nothing to retract. In former days, there was but one Kansas to suffer under illegal power; now there are eleven Kanseses suffering only as one suffered. Therefore, sir, as eleven are more than one, so is the enormity of the present time more than the enormity of the days of Franklin Peirce.

Mr. Dixon—The charge has been directly made in the Senate that the President of the United States has sent in a whitewashed report—a report intended to cover up, by falsehood and misstatements, certain facts. Now, sir, as a friend of the President, I cannot sit quietly and listen in silence to such charges. I sustain the policy of the President as I understand it. If he has specially displayed any character in this struggle, it is that uncompromising love of truth, love of country, and love of Union.

Mr. Doolittle—Whether the President's policy be right or not, the Senator charges upon the President of the United States falsehood in substance, by saying his message is a whitewashing report. I was not pained because the honorable Senator differed from the President on this question; but I was very much chagrined to hear that Senator question the integrity of the President.

Mr. Sumner—I am sorry that I have given pain to my honorable friends. I certainly did not intend to do so. They suggest that the question has been raised as to the policy of the President. I have raised no such question, and have expressed no opinion in regard to it. My honorable friends rose, one after another, and, like two lexicographers, proceeded to give a definition of the word "whitewash." I do not accept their definition. I intended no such meaning as either the Senator from Connecticut or the Senator from Wisconsin has attempted to give. I have no reflection to make on the patriotism or truth of the President of the United States. When I spoke, I spoke of a document that had been read at the desk, and I characterized it as I thought it ought to be characterized. I simply undertook, to-day, after hearing the document read at the desk, to characterize it as the patriotic party of 1856 characterized the message of Franklin Pierce.

Mr. Dixon.—I am glad to hear the disclaimer now made by the Senator from Massachusetts, although he declared he had no explanation to make—nothing to retract. He now says he did not use the word in the sense in which it is always understood. Very well; if he thinks the word "whitewashing" a proper term to apply to the message of the President, and means nothing by it, I am content to allow him to give his own definition.

The question was then stated by the Chair to be on the motion of Mr. Sherman to print the report of Gen. Schurz with the other documents, and it was carried.

Mr. Wade presented a resolution, calling for the report of Gen. Howard on the condition of the freedmen, which was accepted, and the Senate soon after adjourned.

HOUSE OF REPRESENTATIVES.

Mr. Farnsworth, of Illinois, offered a resolution reciting the allegation that Mr. Harris, member from Maryland, had been convicted by a Court-martial of disloyalty, expressing sympathy with Jefferson Davis, and saying that the assassination of Mr. Lincoln came too late, &c., therefore, that the Committee on elections be instructed to inquire into the facts and report such action as may be proper, and, to aid in such investigation, have power to send for persons and papers. The resolution was passed—137 against 21.

Mr. Washburn, of Illinois, from the Committee on Commerce, reported a bill to facilitate postal, commercial and military communication between the States. Every railroad company is authorized to carry passengers, freight and Government supplies and mails from one State to another, and receive compensation therefor.

Messrs. Washburn and Garfield advocated its passage. Messrs. O'Neil, of Pennsylvania; John L. Thomas, of Maryland, and Rogers, of New Jersey, opposed its passage—the last two arguing that the bill was a blow at their States.

Mr. Washburne said the bill was general, and applicable to all the States.

The bill was ordered to be engrossed, 92 to 52.

The House now concurred in the Senate's amendment to the holiday amendment resolution, and asked a Committee of Conference.

Mr. Wilson, of Iowa, from the Committee on the Judiciary, reported a joint resolution proposing an amendment to the Constitution forbidding the payment of the rebel debt. After debate the proposition passed, 149 against 11.—Adjourned.

News Items.

By Telegraph to the New York Sun.]

THE first forty miles of the Union Pacific Railway to Omaha West, was finished on Monday.

HON. M. HALL MCALLISTER, late Judge of the United States Circuit Court at San Francisco, died there yesterday morning.

THE first executive session confirmed Herman Kriesmann, formerly Secretary of Legation at Berlin, to be Consul at Berlin.

THE announcement that General Gillmore had resigned his position in the regular army is untrue. He still retains his rank in the Engineer Corps and his brevet rank of Major-General in the regular service.

A FIRE at Owensboro, Kentucky, on Friday, consumed the block of buildings on the corner of 2d and St. Ann streets, occupied as business houses by Messrs. Morris, Blair, Rosenfield, Rothschild, and others. Loss $230,000.

THE Russian-American telegraph expedition was near Talla Lake on the 13th of November—all well. The line has been completed four hundred and forty miles above New Westminster, and the wire for four hundred miles more was on the ground.

THE Fenians in St. Louis, Miss., on Saturday night voted to sustain General Sweeney, the Fenian Secretary of War, and resolved to take no further action in the present difficulties of the Brotherhood, until the arrival in the country of Stephens, the Head Centre of Ireland.

THE loss to steamboat property on Saturday by the moving of the ice gorge at St. Louis, Miss., including their cargoes, is about $250,000, of which about $16,000 is insured. The ice gorged again on Saturday night and has not moved since. Another crash is looked for at any moment.

SECRETARY STANTON has applied to Congress for an appropriation of one hundred thousand dollars to purchase Ford's Theatre, to be fitted up for the custody of papers relating to sick or wounded soldiers during the rebellion, and to hospitals, and the operations of the medical and surgical departments of the army.

Two negro men, John Walker and Robert McKey, convicted of larceny by the New Hanover County (N. C.) Court, have been sentenced to be sold into servitude for a period not exceeding five years. The sentence is agreeable to the laws of the State of North Carolina, in relation to freedmen before the war.

A LITTLE girl in Pennsylvania was lately reproved for playing out of doors with boys, and informed that being seven years old, she was "too big for that now." But with all imaginable innocence she replied: "Why, grandma, the bigger we grow, the better we like 'em." Grandma took time to think.

General Intelligence.

[By Mail to the New York Sun.]

A NEGRO in Natchez recently shot another for the offence of calling him a d—d abolitionist.

HORACE MAYNARD says: "Thad. Stevens has the Southern Confederacy in his breeches pocket, and means to keep it there for a good while."

The English army is to be supplied with linen shirts on account of the scarcity of cotton. The Irish linen men are jubilant.

JOE and Bill Benton went to New Orleans with a flat boat of corn. Joe writes to his father thus—"Nu Orleens, Gune 5—Dear Dad markets is dull and corn mighty lo and Bills dead. J. B."

THE Washington STAR says: The small-pox is prevailing to a considerable extent among the colored population, and a number of deaths have occurred. Several have been picked up in the streets in an advanced stage of the disease.

ONE of the largest farmers in the United States is Mr. Bidwell, of California, the Chairman of the Committee on Agriculture in the House of Representatives. He owns 25,000 acres of land, and last year his wheat crop was 38,000 bushels.

THE Farmers' Bank, of Kentucky, having lost $60,000 by the Morgan raid in June, 1864, sued J. W. Witherspoon, a returned Morgan officer, attached his land and got judgment from a Circuit for the whole sum. He appeals the case.

THE number of men paid at the Boston Navy Yard for the month of November was 3 522, receiving $216,226. The number of men discharged during the month was 1,500, leaving 2,022 men now at work in the Yard.

As a specimen of what can be accomplished by the employment of freedmen, Col. J. J. Williams, a planter of Florida, states that with a force of about one hundred colored hands he raised during this year from 200 to 250 bales of cotton, each bale weighing 500 pounds.

MARY HASKELL, a New Bedford, Mass., girl of 15, has been bound over for trial on a charge of bigamy with her sister's husband. Mary was married when she was 13, but her husband was sent to State Prison, and so she took up with her brother-in-law.

A MAN named Francis Rourke, while in an intoxicated condition, attempted to jump on the platform of a train while in motion, at Wallingford, Ct., on Saturday. He missed his footing, however, fell upon the track, and one of the cars passed over his body, cutting off both his legs and one arm. He died in a few hours.

A LETTER from Pit Hole City, Pa., speaks of crime as still rampant there. The quietly disposed inhabitants generally stay at home after dark, as it is dangerous to travel the streets at night. A few days since the Post-office was broken open, and the letters therein robbed of money, drafts, &c., of the estimated value of $250,000.

ON Thanksgiving Day, a young lady at Westboro, Mass., after a short acquaintance, married a returned soldier. On the following morning the young bride donned her cloak and bonnet, and evading her husband's questions as to where she was going, left the house, and took the next train of cars out of town. She has not since been heard from.

IN the U. S. District Court at Philadelphia, Judge Cadwallader, on Saturday, sentenced Isaiah Pascoe, late master plumber at the Navy Yard there, to an imprisonment in the penitentiary for eighteen months. Pascoe, it will be remembered, was one of the parties implicated in the wholesale stealings that were so prevalent at the Navy Yard during the year 1864.

SOME miners in Nevada County, California, were recently working a quartz vein, when they struck a cave in their ledge. No opening has been found in the cave save that one found by the miners. Close to the edge of this subterranean vault was found a cannon ball inclosed in solid quartz, as if it had grown with the quartz, and buried 75 feet beneath the earth's surface. The ball was perfect in shape, and when the dirt was taken off was found to be as smooth as if it had just come from the mould.

ALL kinds of manufacturing are unusually active at Providence, R. I., and the various business establishments are now overrun with orders, while new enterprises are being started. The Union Horseshoe Company employs three hundred men, and turns out daily twelve tons of horseshoes and a ton and a half of toe-calks. The Perkins Sheet Iron Foundery has just finished a rolling mill and other buildings at a cost of $150,000; the Phenix Iron Foundery has lately put up $30,000 worth of new buildings, and the Silver Spring Bleachery has spent $40,000 in the same direction. The Nicholson File Company are expending $40,000 on buildings, and will commence the manufacture of files in February.

THE Petersburgh, Va. EXPRESS says: A venerable freedman, passing through Bank street at an early hour the other morning, just in front of the writer of this, planted his foot on a five-dollar bill, and there held it, fearing to stoop and pick it up, lest some one should see him and claim it. We saw the adroit trick, but not having owned as much as a five-dollar bill for many months, passed the old darkey unmolested. Hour after hour elapsed, and there the unfortunate finder stood, firm as a rock, with the enormous brogan entirely covering the five-dollar greenback. At no moment could he see the surging crowd so abate as to afford him an opportunity to recure his prize without a contest with some disputant. Finally darkness came, to the great relief of the sable gentleman, and he quietly transferred the V. from its lowly place, and exalted it to a position in the folds of his capacious pocket.

LOCAL NEWS.

NEW YORK AND THE VICINITY.

PARADE OF THE FIRE DEPARTMENT.—The Metropolitan Fire Department will have its first public parade to-day. The line will be formed at a quarter to 2 o'clock precisely in 14th street, right resting on 8th avenue, and extending towards Broadway. Dodworth's Band of twenty-five pieces will precede the companies which will be divided into eight divisions, under Chief Engineer Kingsland, aided by Assistant-Engineer Joseph L. Perley, and Engineer Gilberts J. Orr and Eli Bates as Special Aids. The procession will also comprise thirty Engine and ten Hook and Ladder Companies.

The following regulations are to be observed:

Line will be formed at 1:45 P. M., precisely. Officers and men will appear in full uniform.

Foremen of companies are instructed to take the most direct route, and so arrange as to have their apparatus on the ground fifteen minutes prior to the time for formation of line, and immediately on arrival report to the Marshal of the Division to which they are assigned.

Companies will form in the following order, horses' heads towards Broadway:

Engines Companies.
Foreman, Assistant Foreman.
Six Privates, in one section.
Steamer—(Engineer and Stoker on Engine.)
Hook and Ladder Companies.
Foreman, Assistant Foreman.
Eight Privates in one section.
Truck.

After line is formed no smoking will be allowed nor will any officer or member be permitted to leave the line until dismissed.

Line of march will be up Fourteenth street to Broadway, down Broadway, passing the Fire Commissioners and guests in review at the Metropolitan Hotel; continuing down Broadway to the Park, passing in review in front of the City Hall, His Honor the Mayor, the Boards of Supervisors, Aldermen, and Councilmen, Heads of Departments, &c.

On passing out of the east gate of the Park, the

(Continued on the Last Page.)

VOL. III. NO. 6.] PUBLISHED BY THE AMERICAN TRACT SOCIETY, BOSTON. [JUNE, 1866.

THE YANKEE KITCHEN.

This is the picture of a New-England kitchen nearly a hundred years ago. It was war time; and the father of the family was away in the army; and the mother, no matter how smart she was, had hard work to keep her household fed and clothed, and her home and little farm in order. Provisions and cloth were scarce and high; and poor people like these had to weave their own cloth, and raise their own provisions. They had to get along on very small supplies in those days. These children have brought in some stalks of Indian corn; and what do you think they are going to do with them? They will wring and bruise them so that the sap will more readily come out; and then the mother will boil them till the sap becomes sirup, or sugar, — a very great luxury to boys and girls then. If it was only sugar-cane, now, instead of corn-stalks, what a good supply of sweet juice they would have had! But sugar-cane does not grow in New England: the climate there is too cold for it.

GRAND ARMY SCOUT AND SOLDIERS' MAIL

THEN NOW

WE DRANK FROM THE SAME CANTEEN

A Weekly Paper Devoted to the Interest of the Grand Army of the Republic.

VOL. III.—No. 43. PHILADELPHIA, PA., SATURDAY, OCTOBER 4, 1884. PRICE—FOUR CENTS

CONTENTS.

DRIVING HOME THE COWS.

Out of the clover and blue-eyed grass
He turned them into the river lane;
One after another he let them pass,
Then fastened the meadow bars again.

Under the willows and over the hill,
He patiently followed their sober pace;
The merry whistle for once was still,
And something shadowed the sunny face.

Only a boy! and his father had said
He never could let his youngest go;
Two already were lying dead
Under the feet of the trampling foe.

But after the evening work was done,
And the frogs were loud in the meadow swamp,
Over his shoulder he slung his gun
And stealthily followed the foot-path damp.

Across the clover and through the wheat
With resolute heart and purpose grim.
Though cold was the dew on his hurrying feet,
And the blind bats flitting startled him.

Thrice since then had the lanes been white,
And the orchards sweet with apple bloom;
And now when the cows came back at night,
The feeble father drove them home.

For news had come to the lonely farm
That three were lying where two had lain,
And the old man's tremulous, palsied arm
Could never lean on a son's again.

The summer day grew cold and late,
He went for the cows when the work was done;
But down the lane, as he opened the gate,
He saw them coming one by one;

Brindle, Ebony, Speckle and Bess,
Shaking their horns in the evening wind;
Cropping the butter-cups out of the grass—
But who was it followed close behind?

Loosely swung in the idle air
The empty sleeve of army blue;
And worn and pale, from the crisping hair,
Looked out a face that the father knew.

For Southern prisons will sometimes yawn
And yield their dead unto life again;
And the day that comes with a cloudy dawn
In gold glory at last may wane.

The great tears sprang to their melting eyes;
For the heart must speak when the lips are dumb,
And under the silent evening skies
Together they followed the cattle home.

South Mountain

AND

Antietam.

The Part Borne by Each Regiment

(CONCLUDED.)

As we have seen, about noon of September 17th, after the 1st, 12th and 2d Corps on the Union right had been fighting so bravely since early morning with the troops of Jackson, Hood, McLaws, Walker, D. H. Hill and R. H. Anderson, in the vicinity of the Dunker Church, the Roulette and Piper Houses and the "sunken road," Franklin had arrived with Slocum's and Smith's Divisons of the 6th Corps and formed them in readiness to vigorously attack the exhausted and disordered troops on the Confederate left. On the Union left, Burnside, by the charge of the 51st Pennsylvania and 51st New York had carried the stone bridge on the Rohrersville Road, and Rodman's Division of his corps had crossed the Antietam at a ford a little below the bridge, and there was nothing to prevent the crossing of the balance of his four divisions. In the centre was Porter with two fresh divisions of the 5th Corps, Morrell's and Sykes', the latter of which had already crossed the stone bridge on the Keedysville or Boonsboro Pike. A vigorous and united attack by the eight fresh divisions of Burnside, Porter and Franklin, it is now known, would have resulted in the defeat and ruin of Lee's Army, and its surrender would have occurred there and then, instead of at Appomattox, after two years and a half more of sacrifice and suffering on both sides. But such was not to be the destiny of our country.

On the right, Sumner believing that the enemy was themselves about to attack, countermanded the attack Franklin was about to make with the divisions of Slocum and Smith. In the centre, McClellan, deceived by the false reports of deserters and spies as to the strength and position of the enemy, insisted upon holding the 5th Corps under Porter in reserve. On the left, Burnside halted to reform his line and to wait until his whole corps had crossed, which consumed two hours, during which A. P. Hill had arrived from Harper's Ferry to the reinforcement of Lee, with his large division of twenty-eight regiments of splendid troops.

It was now three o'clock and the 9th Corps led by Burnside and Cox, both of whom were exposed at times to great personal risk, had taken a position on the hills between the Antietam and Sharpsburg. Wilcox's Division was on the right of the road, Rodman's on the left, Cox's in support of them, and Sturgis' near the bridge in reserve. The batteries of Durell, Clark, Cook and Simmons. had also crossed the creek and gone into position.

Portions of Burnside's command were fast driving before them Longstreet's small force, and had almost reached the town of Sharpsburg. On the right of the pike, the 45th and 100th Pennsylvania, and 46th New York, of Wilcox's Division, supported by the 30th Ohio, of Cox's Division, charged forward and seized a strong position around a stone mill on the edge of the town, while on the left, the 9th New York, (Hawkins' Zouaves), of Rodman's Division, had charged and captured one of the enemy's batteries, when A. P. Hill fell upon the left flank of Rodman's Division, composed of Fairchild's Brigade, the 9th, 89th and 103d New York, and Harland's Brigade, the 4th Rhode Island, 8th, 11th and 16th Connecticut. To meet this sudden and impetuous attack Rodman was compelled to face his division to the left, thus leaving an opening between his division and that of Wilcox, on his right. Into this open space Archer's Brigade, the 5th Alabama, 19th Georgia, and 1st, 7th and 14th Tennessee, at once advanced, quickly followed by Branch's Brigade, the 7th, 18th, 28th, 33d and 37th North Carolina, and Pender's Brigade, the 16th, 22d, 34th and 38th North Carolina. These troops fiercely attacked the right of Rodman's Division, while the front was attacked by others of Hill's troops, supported by Toombs' Georgia Brigade, of Longstreet's Corps. Thus attacked in front and flank the division suffered terribly, and after Gen. Rodman fell mortally wounded, it yielded its ground in some disorder, which was checked by the arrival of Scammon's Brigade, of Cox's Division, the 12th, 23d and 30th Ohio, which, making a change of front to left, stopped the advance of Hill's troops. But the Confederates returned to the attack, which now extended along the right of the corps, held by Wilcox's Division, composed of Christ's Brigade, the 28th Massachusetts, 17th Michigan, 79th New York and 50th Pennsylvania, and Welsh's Brigade, the 8th Michigan, 46th New York, 45th and 100th Pennsylvania.

For a time the battle was confined to the front and left flank, but the right of the corps soon became exposed, when Warren's Brigade, the 5th and 10th New York, of Morrell's Division, of the 5th Corps, was sent to its support. Sturgis' Division, composed of Nagle's Brigade, the 2d Maryland, 6th and 9th New Hampshire, and 48th Pennsylvania, and Ferrero's Brigade, the 51st Pennsylvania, 51st New York, 21st and 35th Massachusetts, which had been held in reserve, was now brought up and the battle was continued between the 9th Corps and A. P. Hill's Division with great fury, but as it was getting dark the corps, which was in an isolated and exposed position, and was closely pressed, fell back upon the hills along the Antietam, and the battle of Antietam was ended.

It was the bloodiest battle of the war up to that time. Twenty thousand killed or wounded men lay on the narrow battlefield. The Union losses amounted to "two thousand and ten killed, and nine thousand four hundred and sixteen wounded and one thousand prisoners." Generals Mansfield, Richardson and Rodman had been killed, and Hooker, Meade and several other general officers had been wounded. The Confederate losses in proportion to the number of troops engaged were still heavier, their killed being sixteen hundred, and their wounded seven thousand, not including the wounded captured, and more than three thousand prisoners.

The battle had been a serious defeat for the Confederate army, but it might have been an overwhelming one had the several attacks by the Union troops been made at the same time. The 1st, 12th, 2d and 9th Corps had all gone into action separately, at different times, and while they fought with the greatest courage and tenacity, they did not accomplish what they would have accomplished by a general and combined attack upon the enemy.

The 18th was spent in burying the dead and preparing for a renewal of the battle. There was, however, a division of opinion among the Union generals, some urging an immediate movement against the enemy, and others opposing it.

During the day Couch's Division, of the 4th Corps (assigned to the 6th Corps September 26), and Humphrey's Division (composed of new troops from Pennsylvania), of the 5th Corps, joined the army. Thus reinforced, McClellan ordered an attack to be made on the morning of the 19th on the enemy in the position they held since the battle. But during the night, Lee taking advantage of the low water in the Potomac, crossed his army into Virginia.

The next morning (September 19) portions of the 5th Corps, under Porter, crossed the river in pursuit, driving before it Lawton's Georgia Brigade, which disputed the passage of the river at Shepherdstown. After the reconnoissance the Union forces recrossed to the Maryland side. The Confederate army retired to Martinsburg, Jackson protecting the rear, and on the 20th, with A. P. Hill's and Early's Division, he surprised Porter, all of whose corps had not crossed the river. Forming his division in two lines, Hill attacked Porter in front, while Early's Division was in ambush near the heights along the river. A charge by Hill and Early at the same time, routed Porter's troops. The force of this attack fell upon the Corn Exchange

(Continued on page 2.)

PERSONAL RECOLLECTIONS

AND

EXPERIENCES

OF AN

Obscure Soldier.

BY T. F. WALTER,

Company A, 91st P. V. V., Post 8, Phila.

(CONTINUED.)

The orders issued by the War Department was, that all men who had served two years or longer of a three years' enlistment, who would volunteer for three years more, unless sooner discharged, could begin the new term at once, and would receive a bounty of four hundred and two dollars from the Government, together with a furlough and transportation to visit home for thirty days.

Regiments that re-enlisted, three-fourths of their men could return home in a body, taking their arms and colors, and have a chance to recruit. Commissioned officers, however, could not re-enlist. Here was a temptation, especially for us in the ranks.

Dreary winter was upon us, and a desolate country was around us, while—

"In happy homes we saw the light
Of household fires, gleam warm and bright,"

when we thought of being in Philadelphia during and after the holidays, with plenty of money in our pockets. But we did not fail to remember Antietam, Fredericksburg, Chancellorsville and Gettysburg, as well as the campaign that had just ended; and I believe there was a good many like myself, who had concluded that money could not compensate men for enduring the terrors and risks of battle. We knew the South was yet very powerful, as well as far from being subdued, so that if we enlisted for three years more, the hardships of the past might be as almost nothing in comparison with what the future might bring us ere the war would end.

The officers immediately busied themselves to secure the enlistment of the regiment, for, by succeeding in that, they would have a chance to accompany the organization home on a veteran furlough. We were in no hurry either to accept the Government offer or to gratify the officers, with whom the men scarcely deigned to discuss the matter, though it was much canvassed among themselves.

In thinking it over, finally, I decided that it was foolishness for me to talk of quitting soldiering so long as I could do a soldier's duty, or the war lasted. I decided that it was better to see the conflict through in our good company that I knew and

(Continued on page 6.)

Gettysburg Compiler

95TH YEAR GETTYSBURG, PA., WEDNESDAY, JULY 2, 1913 NO. 46

CHAMBERSBURG ST —1863

50TH ANNIVERSARY IS HERE

THE BLUE AND GRAY IN POSSESSION OF GETTYSBURG

The Most Unique Camp Ever Held Sends a Message of Peace to The World.

The Fiftieth Anniversary of the Battle of Gettysburg toward which the eyes of the nation have been turned for several years is here, the hosts of Blue and Gray have for a second time invaded the town, and there is but one commander.

President Woodrow Wilson, Commander-in-Chief of the Army and Navy, will be in Gettysburg on Friday, July 4th.

Meanwhile the great anniversary opens with the War Department in charge, the work under the general supervision of Maj. Gen. James B. Aleshire, Chief Quartermaster, U. S. A., at Washington, with Major James E. Normoyle in personal charge at Gettysburg.

Major Normoyle is ably assisted by Major A. R. Grove, Captains Humphreys, Dalton, Sergeant Grey, and a host of army men, regular details from the infantry, cavalry and artillery, and again there is a small army of Boy Scouts who are carrying the orders and making themselves generally useful.

On Saturday, the first and second cooks and kitchenmen arrived, an army of 1800. There were experienced cooks from the Regular Army, and exprienced cooks from New York, Philadelphia and other cities. This advance guard was a sight to see, for they came in no formation, but that of a mob, and a crowd of nearly two thousand can make confusion when dropped into a community. These men were quickly sorted out by those in authority and as quickly as they were registered were taken in hand by a large medical corps and stripping naked were examined to see whether free from diseases that would interfere with the discharge of their duties. According to report about ten were not accepted. There are 600 first cooks at $4.00 a day, 600 second cooks at $3.00 a day, and 1200 kitchenmen helpers, at $1.50 a day, and several hundred tents have been required for their accommodation.

The first Blue and Gray coats in the great camp city of over 5,000 tents arrived on Saturday, and although the camp was not officially opened until Saturday evening, every one was taken care of as they arrived and a number slept in camp Saturday night. A few inaccuracies have been noted in the press of the country, that the visitors were to be under military discipline, but such is not the case. The veterans of Blue and Gray will be cared for, their every want attended to under military discipline but the camp is as free as air to them to enjoy to their hearts' content. In every tent there are cots, lanterns, basins and buckets. Breakfast will be served each day from 6.30 to 8 a. m., dinner from 12 to 1.30 p. m., and supper from 5.30 to 7.00 p. m. Everything is for the hosts of Blue and Gray to take possession of according to their wishes and to go and come as they please over the great battlefield.

There has never been such a camp as the present one in the history of our country and it is not likely to ever happen again. The preparations have been on a gigantic scale. There are miles and miles of streets, all conspicuously numbered and named. Every tent is numbered and it is going to be as easy for every Yankee and Johnnie to find his own tent as for him to find his own residence at home, and whether he comes home before dark or after dark there will be no trouble to find the latch key for the camp at night is almost as light as day from 500 electric lights. A more beautiful sight can not be imagined and worth the miles to come here to see is this great wigwam city with its hundreds of sparkling lights under the quiet stars at night.

The camp has been well supplied with the best water. Not only has the town supply been used to some extent but the four artesian wells resulted in four streams of fine water, analyzed and 'pronounced pure and wholesome by the government chemist at Washington. Four reservoir tanks have been erected to distribute this water and pipes carry it to points throughout the camp. Along the streets are numerous sanitary bubbling fountains, the water being conveyed through ice chests sunk in the ground and when lips are placed to the bubbling fountain, ice cold water is enjoyed. Every want of the veteran is sought to be supplied. The signal corps of the army strung over 200 miles of wire last week and rigged up nearly one hundred telephones and any need of the veteran can be called from these phones or if he desires he can communicate with any portion of the country that can be reached by telephone.

Should the veteran fall ill, a complete hospital service has been provided, regular army hospitals have been scattered through the camp, there is a large Red Cross hospital, there are doctors and nurses for an emergency. The town enjoys the protection of a fine field hospital that could not be better located for quietness, along the Brick Yard Lane under State Health Commissioner Dixon and this hospital is not only for the veteran, but the general public and the people of the town. Any call of distress will bring one of the ambulances with physician and nurse and all that medical science and careful nursing can do will be done for those who fall ill in crowded Gettysburg and done as thoroughly and well as in the home city of any one unfortunately taken ill.

All through the camp there are squads of Boy Scouts to wait upon the veteran, to direct him, to carry water to his tent and run errands for him.

It is difficult to give an adequate picture of the preparations for this great anniversary of the Battle of Gettysburg. As the hosts of Blue and Gray descended upon the camp from the trains that poured in from the Reading and Western Maryland railroads, as this host takes possesion of the camp, and as they begin to enjoy what has been provided for them, there will sink into their hearts and souls the significance of the anniversary, the celebration of the half century of peace between brothers, and when the great camp is over this significance will be scattered among millions and the blessings of peace will be told to children and grandchildren, and the million dollars spent for this anniversary, and the millions of dollars that have been spent in the marking of this battlefield will only have been worth while as they bear the message of peace not only to this country but to all the world. Such an anniversary as this convinces that the day is not far off when wars shall have ceased and when nations at home and abroad will arbitrate. Such an anniversary of peace, with such a message to the Union and the world should as quickly as it can be done be memorialized in some permanent way. This unique gathering of the hosts of Blue and Gray deserves as enduring a memorial as any at Gettysburg marking the spot of an engagement between brothers.

Surgeon General Weaver of the National Guard of Pennsylvania has prepared a set of health rules and by the observance of the same he believes the veteran can add greatly to his enjoyment of the occasion. They are as follows:

Get as much sleep as possible and be regular about it.

Adhere in your diet to the rations furnished by the regular army, which are ample in quantity and sufficiently varied to gratify and satisfy all tastes.

Don't indulge in intoxicating drinks. They disturb digestion and make you more susceptible to fatigue and disease.

Don't try to meet all the old comrades at once. The camp is a big one but you have a week of it before you. Take it easy.

While the hosts of Blue and Gray come to Gettysburg in 1913 over two ribbons of steel the old routs of down the Chambersburg pike, the Fairfield road, the York pike, the Harrisburg and Carlisle roads, Emmitsburg road, and the Baltimore pike were not deserted. They were almost as much infested with the human as fifty years ago, but this time they came in automobiles. Gettysburg never saw such a throng of autos as on Sunday, June 29, 1913, and it at once demonstrated the great service of the State Constabulary in charge of Superintendent of State Police John C. Groome. The main streets were as thickly crowded as Broadway, New York or Market street, Philadelphia, and with the State police in Square and at the street corners, the procession in the street and on the pavement moved with safety.

What the size of the host of Blue and Gray will be can only be told when they are all here. On Saturday night advice was received that ten thousand more veterans were in sight than expected. Good weather is adding to the numbers with the arrival of every train. Pennsylvania is over-running the figures of last week. Departures all over New York it is estimated on Saturday would reach 12,500 instead of ten thousand, the 1800 reported from Virginia ten days ago has increased to 3000, and not all of them of the Gray, for among the first met was one of the Blue from Richmond. So they come, every State contributing both of the Blue and Gray, illustrating how this great nation has mixed, mingled, and intermingled until the most of us are native to the Stars and Stripes instead of to any one particular spot.

Major Normoyle and his assistants will be ready for any number that will come. It is believed that the total number of veterans will run over 60,000 before the last one arrives, and the guess of the old chairman looks fearfully foolish in the light of the present facts, and Gettysburg sounded warnings all the time that guessing at numbers would not solve that problem. The Pennsylvania Legislature before it adjourned appropriated an additional $35,000 and as soon as the news was sent to Secretary of War Garrison he ordered additional trains to be sent here with more tents, supplies and rations and the work of taking care of the veteran went ahead and will go ahead until all have been cared for.

Gettysburg was more beautifully decorated with the National colors and bunting than ever before in its history. The Public Square presents a beautiful sight with its many flags flying and the constant throng of people. Over the big camp at headquarters flies the Stars and Stripes, but in the camp there are battle flags, State flags and Confederate flags. At one point in camp can be found a flag with the Stars and Stripes on one side, on the other a replica of the Confederate battle flag and beneath these words:

"Let us have peace.—Grant."

"Duty is the sublimest word in any language.—Lee."

Pennsylvania, half the host with Uncle Sam, is represented here in the person of Governor John K. Tener, who has his headquarters on the college campus. He arrived with his staff on Sunday. The members of the 50th Anniversary of the Battle of Gettysburg Commission are also here, Col. John M. Schoonmaker, the chairman, and all the members, veterans of many battlefields, and many of them carrying scars, two of them with reminders of the battle of Gettysburg, Generals R. B. Rickets and W. D. Dixon.

In the language of members of the Commission, the Duke of Gettysburg is also here, otherwise the Secretary of the Commission, Col. Lewis E. Beitler.

One of the first things found to be overlooked was a distinctive badge for the occasion. The secretary was too busy bluffing even to attend to so simple a matter. Either Pennsylvania or Congress should be asked to strike off a distinctive peace medal and get it into the hands of every veteran who was present at the Gettysburg jubilee. It was a disappointment to many that something of the kind had not been provided but it is not too late to make good the oversight.

It is most gratifying to the hosts of Blue and Gray that Comander-in-Chief President Wilson will be at Gettysburg on Friday, and the announcement on Sunday to this effect was received with expressions of delight. It is dollars to doughnuts that if Senator Penrose's candidate for president, had been in the White House, that Senator Penrose's Governor of Pennsylvania would have seen to it that Senator Penrose's President would have been officially invited months ago. It was only one month ago that those in authority in Pennsylvania told President Wilson that he was expected to be present at Gettysburg and no one could have justly complained if the engagements of the President made months ahead had prevented his attendance.

It was Congressman A. Mitchell Palmer of Pennsylvania, who brought about a different condition of affairs. He had a conference with the President on last Saturday and pointed out the importance of the Gettysburg celebration, that did not appear in the late invitation; its nation-wide significance and particularly the spirit of sectional sympathy that would result from a speech by a Southern-born President at the reunion of the North and South.

When the President realized the situation as made clear by Congressman Palmer he immediately altered his plans. Governor Tener was telegraphed that President Wilson would be here and Secretary Tumulty gave out this statement from the President.

'The President has felt constrained to forego his chance for a few days of much needed rest in New Hampshire next week because he feels it his duty to attend the celebration at Gettysburg on Friday, the Fourth of July."

Veterans' Verdict of Camp.

The Blue and Gray had but words of one meaning to say about the great peace camp. It was "all right," "fine," "splendid," "A little cool and made good use of blanket." Dozens have answered the questions put to them that it was more than expected and they were satisfied and surely this verdict must be gratifying to Major Normoyle and his host of workers as well as to everyone interested in Gettysburg.

Reunions.

Reunions by the score, yea hundreds have been planned, of Company, Regiment, Brigade and larger organizations. The big tent is being partitioned off to provide for as many of these reunions as can be held there. They will be held all over the battlefield, at the monuments of the various regiments. They will be held in Gettysburg, in the Post Room and other points.

G. A. R. Encampment.

The opening of the State encampment of the Grand Army of the Republic last week was marked by two very interesting events. The first was the camp fire in the Court House on last Thursday evening.

Hon. Wm. T. Ziegler, commander of Corporal Skelly Post No. 9, presided and the address of welcome was made by Prof. Charles F. Sanders. Past Commander Powell was then given charge of the meeting and there was singing and talking that delighted the large audience of several hundred that crowded the room. The old war songs "We're Tenting To-Night on the Old Camp Ground," "Rally Round the Flag, Boys," and other patriotic songs were sung. Among the speakers were Commander-in-Chief Alfred Beers who spoke of events of the coming week and suggested that a permanent memorial be erected to the memory of the women of the Civil War, who made the greatest sacrifices of the war. Thomas H. Cole, of Erie, department commander, made a short address and other veterans gave short talks, everyone being delighted with the evening.

The other event was the marching of the boys of 1863 to the opening session of the encampment held in Xavier Hall on last Friday morning. They were escorted to the hall by Colonel Stewart and five squads of the Sons of Veterans preceded by the Allentown Band.

It was the Grand Army boys who caught the eye. They looked like the veterans they were, nearly every one gray of hair, but they carried themselves like boys of years ago, marching with precision. There were between four and five hundred in the parade and at many points they received ovations from the people on the sidewalk.

Little business was done at the meeting except the election of officers for the ensuing year, William J. Wells of Norristown, being chosen for Department Commander, Hendrick E. Paine, Scranton, Senior Vice Commander, J. W. McClure, Lancaster, Junior Vice Commander, Rev. M. L. Ganoe, a former pastor of the Methodist Church of this place, now of Altoona, Chaplain, Dr. James E. Sillman of Erie, Medical Director. The reports showed a membership of 17,826 in Pennsylvania Posts. Indiana was chosen over Lancaster for the winter meeting.

The encampment as a distinctive organization meeting was overshadowed by the great preparations for the big anniversary with arrivals coming in for same in every train.

Toll Free to Gettysburg.

As indicated several weeks ago Gettysburg would likely be toll free by time of the Anniversary. When the matter was placed in the hands of the courts orders were to be held up until the Supreme Court had spoken in the Fulton County case as to whether the Sproul Roads Act was constitutional or not. The Supreme Court handed down a decision on last Friday declaring the Sprouls Act to be constitutional. On Saturday the State acted and the Gettysburg and Chambersburg and the Gettysburg and Petersburg turnpikes were ordered to be taken over and about ten o'clock Saturday night, June 28 the word was received at the gates near Gettysburg that the March to Gettysburg on the pike was to be tollless and remain so ever afterwards.

Auto Car Service.

The auto car service from Gettysburg to Caledonia began last week. The car makes three trips daily arriving at Gettysburg at 7.25 a. m., 12.25 and 4.45 p. m. and arriving at 10.35 a. m., 2.35 and 7.35 p. m. At Caledonia connection is made with the Chambersburg and Gettysburg Electric Railway for Chambersburg.

THE GRAY AND BLUE HANDSHAKE

THEY WERE THERE.

(By Samuel Ellsworth Kiser.)

"The fastest work I ever done
Was chasin' Yankees at Bull Run;
I seem to see them goin' yet;
My! How they did get up and get!
They made the blue streak, gettin' out,
That you have often heard about;
We showed them up in that affair—
Was you among the Yankees there?

"Yes, I was there, and I admit
That mebby I'd be runnin' yit
If Meade had not—excuse my smile—
Took charge at Gettysburg awhile;
Says he: 'Let's kind of stick around,
Since we've got back on our own ground.'
Was you among the Johnnies who
Got mixed up with that streak of blue?"

"Say, Yank, old friend, when Grant cut loose
You boys sure raised the very duce;
'Twas no disgrace to have to yield,
With such a captain in the field."
"You're right, friend Johnny Reb, you're right,
And, Moses, how you boys did fight!
Each man a hero, yes, siree—
'Twas no disgrace to lose with Lee."

—By permission of Henry Barrett Chamberlin and the "Chicago Record-Herald."

OFFICIAL PROGRAM OF FIFTIETH ANNIVERSARY OF THE BATTLE OF GETTYSBURG

1863 **1913**

TUESDAY—JULY 1.—Veterans' Day, 2 to 4 P. M.

Col. J. M. Schoonmaker, chairman of commission, presiding.

Meeting called to order by presiding officer.

Opening prayer by Rev. George Edwards Lovejoy, chaplain-in-chief Grand Army of the Republic.

Address by Lindley M. Garrison, Secretary of War.

Address of welcome by Governor John K. Tener, of Pennsylvania.

Address by Hon. Alfred B. Beers, commander-in-chief Grand Army of the Republic.

Address by General Bennett H. Young, commander-in-chief United Confederate Veterans.

Closing prayer by Rev. H. M. Hamill, chaplain-general United Confederate Veterans.

WEDNESDAY—JULY 2.—Military Day, 2 to 4 P. M.

Col. Andrew Cowan, Louisville, Ky., presiding.

Music.

Meeting called to order by presiding officer.

Prayer.

Address by Major-General John R. Brooke, of Pennsylvania, representative of Northern forces in the battle.

Address by Sergt. John C. Scarborough, of North Carolina, representative of Southern forces in battle.

Reading of Lincoln's Gettysburg cemetery dedication speech, by Barry Bulkley.

Address by Gen. John C. Black.

Music.

THURSDAY—JULY 3.—Governors' Day, 2 to 4 P. M.

Governor John K. Tener, of Pennsylvania, presiding.

Music.

Meeting called to order by presiding officer.

Prayer.

Address by Governor Tener.

Address by Gov. James B. McCreary, of Kentucky.

4.30 P. M. New York Veterans will hold meeting in Big Tent, Gov. Sultzer presiding.

Reunion of Philadelphia Brigade and Pickett's division at the "bloody angle."

Fireworks display at 8 P. M.

FRIDAY, JULY 4.—Peace Day, President Wilson presiding.